HALLIWELL'S
FILMGOER'S
&
VIDEO VIEWER'S
COMPANION

By the same author

Halliwell's Film Guide
Halliwell's Guide to the Best Comedies
Halliwell's Guide to the Best Children's Films

HALLIWELL'S FILMGOER'S & VIDEO VIEWER'S COMPANION

LESLIE HALLIWELL

IITH EDITION

EDITED BY JOHN WALKER

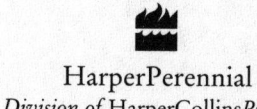

HarperPerennial

A Division of HarperCollinsPublishers

This book is published in Great Britain by
HarperCollins*Publishers*

First HarperPerennial edition published 1995

ISSN 1066-2912
ISBN 0-06-273338-9

CONTENTS

FOREWORD TO
THE FIRST EDITION (1965)
by Alfred Hitchcock

Thirty or forty years ago, when the idea of the cinema as an art form was new, people started to write highbrow treatises about it. Unfortunately, few of the books seemed to have much connection with what one saw at the local picture-house. Even earlier began the still-continuing deluge of fan magazines and annuals, full of exotic photographs but short on solid information. We film-makers had our own reference books, but these were often incomprehensible to the layman and gave him more undigested facts than he needed. Nobody wrote for the sensible middlebrow picturegoer who was keenly interested in the craft of the cinema without wanting to make a religion of it.

The volume you hold in your hand aims to be the first comprehensive reference book in English for that numerous but neglected audience. I feel sure it will be welcome, for audiences are taking an increasingly serious interest in their films these days — even in the flippant ones.

A concise guide to film matters past and present is obviously a good thing to have on a handy shelf, especially when the best of the old films are constantly cropping up on TV. I hope it will prove possible to bring out revised and corrected editions on a regular basis. Not that many glaring errors will be discovered: the author has done his homework rather better than the villains in my films, who always seem to get found out sooner or later.

Speaking personally, I don't know whether it is more flattering or disturbing to find oneself pinned down like a butterfly in a book which recounts all the macabre details of one's career. But being a stickler for detail myself, I must, and do, submit; and I wish the enterprise well.

PREFACE TO
THE FIRST EDITION

This book is for people who like movies. Especially, it's for those who enjoyed the golden ages of the 30s and 40s, now revisiting us on television, when the big studios of Hollywood turned out highly efficient and varied entertainment without being too pretentious about it. Nowadays, independent producers aim higher, which sometimes only means that they have further to fall; and most films are half as long again as they should be. But the good ones keep turning up, and Jeanne Moreau and Elvis Presley and Peter O'Toole have fans just as enthusiastic as those of Bette Davis and George Formby and Rudolph Valentino.

Everyone who watches films, whether on TV or on the big screens, frequently thinks of something he'd like to check: a star's age, a director's name, what else that funny little fellow with the moustache has been in. To find out the answer to this sort of question it's sometimes been necessary to consult upwards of a dozen fairly inaccessible volumes. This book aims to bring all the available sources together while at the same time excluding inessential or dated information. A fully comprehensive work on these lines would be almost the size of the *Encyclopaedia Britannica*; but this 'potted' one should satisfy most requirements.

The arrangement is completely alphabetical, and you won't find an index at the end because the whole book is one vast index. Most of the entries refer to actors, including not only stars but several hundred familiar names from the supporting cast, people whose valiant service has seldom been recorded. Then there are directors, producers, musicians, writers and photographers – the principal ones at least. The more important the person, the longer the entry, that's a rough general rule: routine contributors get a couple of lines, Edward G. Robinson spreads over half a page. All told, however, you'll find very few of your favourites missing: if they've stuck in your memory, they're probably here. As to the list of credits, the aim has been to give the first important picture, the most recent, and a sampling of the more significant titles in-between: the peak period is usually when the dates are most closely crowded. Stage work has not normally been detailed, nor has TV.

There are also notes on well-known film series, on films which have been frequently remade, on films with similar titles; on technical terms, on organizations, on general subjects like censorship and screen ratios.

The emphasis is firmly on Britain and Hollywood: the book is aimed at the general filmgoer, not at the egghead student of film culture who shuns commercial entertainments in favour of middle-European or Oriental masterpieces which never get further than the National Film Theatre or a very few art-houses. However, references to important foreign films and personalities are fairly numerous and, even admitting its selectiveness in this field, the book still ranges more widely than anything else published in English.

No one has been omitted simply because he is dead: the entries have been selected from the whole history of the cinema. But the silent period is covered in less detail than the talkies, and probably few readers will quarrel with that.

This is a collection of facts rather than opinions; if a few of the latter *have* crept in, they are usually the ones most generally held.

London, July 1965
L.H.

PREFACE TO
THE ELEVENTH EDITION

The year 1995 is a time for celebration, both of the thirtieth anniversary of *Halliwell's Filmgoer's Companion* and, more importantly, of the 100th anniversary of cinema. So this eleventh edition makes the most of the occasions by adding new sections to its coverage, including a concise year-by-year history of cinema from its beginnings (and from a British perspective), as well as details of the winners of the American Academy Awards, of its British and European equivalents, and of the main prizes at the leading film festivals of Cannes, Berlin, and Venice. There are also more than 1,400 new entries, as well as an updating of existing information. In all, some 200,000 words have been added in order to make the *Companion* ever more comprehensive in its coverage.

While films as such are not covered in this volume (for them, refer to the annual updates of *Halliwell's Film Guide*), note is taken of significant remakes, sequels, and series. One reviewer of the last edition seemed daunted by the number of entries relating to the past. The truth is that, through television and video, we have such easy access to films of all decades that long-dead actors and directors remain our contemporaries. The poet Roy Fuller understood this when, in his *Movies on TV* (1982), he writes of looking up in *Halliwell* the actress Lucille Bremer, discovering that she was retired, and asking 'How can that be?' when she could still melt his heart. But today's personalities and developments are to be found within in abundance.

The history of cinema is an odd one. Although film has grown into a complex industry as well as an art, it has remained fairly conservative. In roughly the same span of time, jazz has gone through several revolutions, so that much of today's music would not be recognizable to the originators. Yet the difference between movies such as *The Lost World* of 1926 and *Jurassic Park* of 1993 is relatively small, one of technical, rather than artistic, advance. Film is a curious form, for it has always offered compensations beyond art and entertainment. Even bad movies can tell an audience much about the everyday realities of living at a particular time. It has also preserved many other forms of entertainment. If film was kept alive in the early days by music-hall and vaudeville showings, it returned the compliment by preserving for future generations the art of popular entertainers, from Little Titch to the Big Yin. And it offered the most talented, such as Charlie Chaplin and Buster Keaton, an opportunity to extend their abilities beyond a stage sketch. If, so far, the future of film has seemed much like its past, then that is about to change as, like every other form of recorded entertainment, it goes digital. Indeed, film is likely to cease to exist as film, something recorded on acetate, as technology becomes computerized. Already, it is possible to have films piped down telephone lines direct to a television set and, in much the same way, there are plans to distribute films to cinemas by cable, thus ensuring that audiences never again have to watch worn and scratched prints. The film *The Crow* was saved, following Brandon Lee's tragic and untimely death, by using computer techniques to put him in scenes in which he never actually appeared. Just as some of the dinosaurs in *Jurassic Park* owed their existence to computer graphics, so there are continuing experiments to create computerized human actors.

All forms of recorded entertainment, reduced as they are to streams of numbers, are beginning to coalesce. In the future, we may all be film-makers, manipulating computer-created actors, or being manipulated by them. Certainly, the next hundred years for cinema should be even more exciting and entertaining than the delights of the past and present.

For expert advice in preparing this edition, I owe particular thanks to William C. Clogston, and to David Hattenstone, Howard Thomas, Bob Mastrangelo, Jordan R. Young, Don Minifie, William J. Slattery, Russell Green, R. C. Buckland and, indeed, the many who have written to me with suggestions and criticisms. I am grateful to Peter Preston, editor of the *Guardian*, for permission to reprint the results of its readers' poll of contemporary films. I am also appreciative of the support I've received from Valerie Hudson of HarperCollins, Ian Paten, my editor, Gloria Ferris and Rivers Scott, my agents, and, above all, from my wife Barbara, the ideal companion for this particular filmgoer.

John Walker

EXPLANATORY NOTES

Alphabetical order All entries are in alphabetical order, on normal dictionary lines, but fictional characters are listed under the complete name, so that Antoine Doinel is under 'A' and Sherlock Holmes under 'S'. Mac and Mc are treated as one, although the spelling is of course kept distinct. Names such as Von Stroheim come under 'V' and Cecil B. De Mille under 'D'. All names, whatever their nationality, are treated as if the last name were the surname, e.g. Zhang Yimou will be found under Yimou, Zhang.

Personal dates The birth year of an actor or actress is often obscured beyond the powers of a crystal ball, and in some cases is impossible to discover in an industry that is averse to ageing. In general, the earliest date in print is the one preferred as most likely to be accurate.

Doubtful dates are prefaced by 'c.' (*circa*).

(*) indicates that the person has died, but the date of death is uncertain.

Film titles The title by which the film is known in its English-speaking country of origin is given. Foreign-language titles are generally translated when the film has been released in English-speaking countries, with the original title following in brackets.

Film dates It can be as difficult to ascertain the correct date of a film as it is to determine the personal dates of its stars. Some films sit on the shelf for several years before being released, while frequently more than 12 months can pass between an American film's release in its home country and in Britain. There is an undoubted area of confusion: *Casablanca*, for instance, was given a 50th-anniversary re-release in 1992, yet the film was not officially released until 1943, and also bears a 1943 copyright date. But it was shown to critics in November 1942, so it can also qualify as a movie from the earlier year. The aim here is to give wherever possible the date when the film was first publicly shown in its country of origin.

Filmographies Complete filmographies are indicated by the symbol ■. A complete entry should not necessarily be taken as a sign of eminence or as a seal of approval. Some people simply made very few films or had compact typical careers which are worth detailing as instances of what goes on in the film industry: the gradual climb, the good cameo role, the star period, the two or three 'dogs' in a row, the gradual decline, the cheap exploitation movie. Filmographies cannot be completed for several major directors and stars because not all of their earlier films can be traced.

Incomplete lists normally end with 'etc.', which means that there may be up to as many films again as have been listed, while 'many others' indicates that the list has only scratched the surface. These lists usually include either the first film or the most significant role of the subject, and end up with his or her most recent work, with dates coming closest together over the most prolific and significant period.

A subject's most significant films are indicated by italics. The reader may interpret 'significant' as meaning commercial, artistic, critical or personal success.

Short films (less than 50 minutes or so) are not normally accounted for unless the subject worked chiefly in this field.

Almost every performer and director now works in TV as well as films, and many make their reputations these days on the small screen. For this reason, significant appearances in television series are also listed after the filmographies. The main lists also include some, but not all, of a subject's TV movies, made for any of its forms from cable to satellite, and are indicated by '(TV)' after the title. The majority of the TV movies listed have also been released on video-cassette.

Quotes These are introduced by the symbol ¶. Quotes by the subject are indicated by his or her initials; from other sources by ther person's name.

Rosettes (☉) These are bestowed for significant work in a particular field over a sizeable period of film history, upon people with remarkable talents which are not easily duplicated. For rosette winners, one film is singled out in which the person concerned was at his or her peak.

Abbreviations The main ones used are:

a	actor	fx	special effects
ed	editor	m	musical score
AA	Academy Award, indicating	md	musical director
	the winning of a Hollywood	oa	original author
	Oscar, awarded annually by	orig sp	original screenplay
	the Academy of Motion	p	producer, which covers all
	Picture Arts and Sciences		the many varieties of the
AAN	indicates a nomination for an		breed, from executive
	Academy Award		producer to associate
BFA	ng of a British Film Academy		producer, co-producer, etc.
	award, awarded by the	pd	production designer
	British Academy of Film and	ph	cinematographer
	Television Arts	s	song(s)
ch	choreographer	w	screenwriter
d	director	wd	writer and director

When more than one person is involved in an activity, it is indicated by co-, so that co-w means that at least two writers wrote a particular film.

The symbol '&' means that the function abbreviated is in addition to that normally expected of the subject. In an actor's list, '& wd' would mean that he or she also wrote and directed.

A

'A' picture.
A term used to indicate the most important film in the days of double-feature programmes, one that used the talents of a studio's top actors, directors and technicians. The distinction between 'A' pictures and supporting films, or 'B' pictures, disappeared with the demise of double features in the 1950s.

Aaker, Lee (1943–).
Child actor whose career faded in his early teens, when he quit the profession.

The Atomic City 52. Desperate Search 52. No Room for the Groom 52. My Son John 52. Jeopardy 53. Take Me to Town 53. Arena 53. Hondo 53. Rin Tin Tin, Hero of the West 55, etc.

TV series: Adventures of Rin Tin Tin 54–59.

Aames, Willie (1960–) (William Upton).
American leading actor, who began as a clean-cut teenager on television, but has found worthwhile adult roles harder to find.

Frankenstein (TV) 73. Scavenger Hunt 79. Paradise 82. Zapped! 82. Cut and Run (It.) 85. Killing Machine (Sp.) 86. Eight Is Enough: A Family Reunion (TV) 87. Eight Is Enough: Wedding (TV) 89, etc.

TV series: We'll Get By 75. Swiss Family Robinson 75–76. Eight Is Enough 77–81. We're Movin' 82. Charles in Charge 84–85.

Aaron, Caroline (1954–).
American actress.

Heartburn 86. Crimes and Misdemeanors 89. Edward Scissorhands 90. Alice 90. This Is My Life 92, etc.

Aaron, Sidney.
Pseudonym used by Paddy Chayevsky for his last film script, *Altered States*.

Abady, Temple (1903–1970).
British composer, from the theatre.

The Woman in the Hall 47. Miranda 48. All over the Town 49. Folly to Be Wise 52. Kill Me Tomorrow 58, etc.

Abbott, Bud (1895–1974) (William Abbott).
American comedian, the brusque and slightly shifty 'straight man' half of Abbott and Costello, cross-talking vaudevillians of long standing who became Universal's top stars of the early 40s. Bud, seldom seen without his hat, was the bully who left the dirty work for his partner, never believed his tall but true stories of crooks and monsters, and usually avoided the pie in the face.

■ One Night in the Tropics (their only supporting roles) 39. *Buck Privates* 40. In The Navy 41. *Hold That Ghost* 41. Keep 'Em Flying 41. Ride 'Em Cowboy 41. Rio Rita 42. Pardon My Sarong 42. Who Done It? 42. It Ain't Hay 43. Hit the Ice 43. Lost In A Harem 44. *In Society* 44. Here Come the Co-Eds 45. *The Naughty Nineties* (featuring their famous 'Who's On First' routine) 45. Abbott and Costello in Hollywood 45. The Little Giant (a doomed attempt to work separately within the same film) 46. The Time of Their Lives (an interesting failure) 46. Buck Privates Come Home 47. The Wistful Widow of Wagon Gap 47. The Noose Hangs High 48. *Abbott and Costello Meet Frankenstein* 48. Mexican Hayride 48. Africa Screams 49. Abbott and Costello Meet the Killer 49. Abbott and Costello in the Foreign Legion 50. Abbott and Costello Meet the Invisible Man 51. Comin' Round the Mountain 51. Jack and the Beanstalk 52. Abbott and Costello Lost in Alaska 52. Abbott and Costello Meet Captain Kidd 52. Abbott and Costello Go to Mars 53. *Abbott and Costello Meet Dr Jekyll and Mr Hyde* 53. Abbott and Costello Meet the Keystone Kops 55. Abbott and Costello Meet the Mummy 55. Dance with Me Henry 56.

After a TV series (1953) using up all their old routines, the team split and Abbott retired. See *Costello, Lou*. In 1975 there was published *Who's On First*, a selection of frame-by-frame routines, by Richard J. Anobile. Bob Thomas's biography, *Bud and Lou*, was published in 1977, and appeared in 1978 as a TV movie, with Harvey Korman and Buddy Hackett.

~All Abbott and Costello movies depended for their effectiveness on the number of old vaudeville routines included, such as the following: 'All Because You Don't Like Mustard' and 'Jonah and the Whale' (*One Night in the Tropics*); 'Drill' (*Buck Privates*); 'Bussing the Bee' and 'Seven Times Thirteen Is Twenty-Eight' (*In the Navy*); 'The Moving Candle' (*Hold That Ghost, Meet Frankenstein*); 'Don't Order Anything' (*Keep 'Em Flying*, borrowed from Laurel and Hardy's *Man o' War*); 'Poker Game' (*Ride 'Em Cowboy*); 'Ten Dollars You're Not There' (*Rio Rita*); 'The Poisoned Drink' (*Pardon My Sarong*); 'The Telephone Call' (*Who Done It*); 'Bagel Street' (*In Society*); 'The Magic Act' and 'Slowly I Turned' (*Lost in a Harem*); 'The Mirror' and 'Who's on First' (*The Naughty Nineties*); 'Hole in the Wall' (*The Noose Hangs High*); 'Identification' and 'Silver Ore' (*Mexican Hayride*); 'The Gorilla' (*Africa Screams*); 'The Shovel Is My Pick' (*Meet the Mummy*).

✪ For bringing authentic vaudeville to Hollywood in a few imperishable routines; and for cheering up a generation at war. *Abbott and Costello Meet Frankenstein.*

¶ Abbott and Costello's comedy depended on caricature and contrast: the fat and the thin, the nervous and the foolhardy, the stupid and the stupider. Their work falls into well-remembered routines and reactions. There is chubby, terrified Costello calling after his partner:
Ch-ch-ch-ch-i-ck!
There is his shy admission:
I'm a ba-a-a-ad boy!
There is the old pantomime gag of his seeing something alarming and running to tell his partner; by the time the latter returns the thing has naturally disappeared. There are repetitive routines such as the 'Slowly I Turned' scene from *Lost in a Harem*, with its Laurel and Hardy-like inevitability. Most memorably there is skilful nightclub cross-talk, seen at its best in the 'Who's On First' sketch which first brought them to fame. Here is part of it:
A: You know, these days they give ballplayers very peculiar names. Take the St Louis team: Who's on first, What's on second, I Don't Know is on third . . .
C: That's what I want to find out. I want you to tell me the names of the fellows on the St Louis team.
I'm telling you. Who's on first. What's on second, I Don't Know is on third.
– Who's playing first?
Yes.
– I mean, the fellow's name on first base.
Who.
– The fellow playing first base.
Who.
– The guy on first base.
Who is on first.
– Well, what are you asking me for?
I'm not asking you, I'm telling you. Who is on first.
– I'm asking you – who is on first?
That's the man's name.
– That's who's name?
Yes.
– Well, go ahead, tell me.
Who!
– All I'm trying to find out is, what's the guy's name on first base.
Oh no, What is on second.
– I'm not asking you who's on second.
Who's on first.
– That's what I'm trying to find out!
What's the guy's name on first base?
What's the guy's name on second base.
– I'm not asking who's on second.
Who's on first.
– I Don't Know.
He's on third . . .
And so on, for another five minutes.

Abbott, George (1887–1995).
American playwright and producer of lively commercial properties. He sporadically invaded Hollywood to supervise their filming, and stayed briefly to perform other services.

Autobiography: 1963, *Mister Abbott*.

AS ORIGINAL AUTHOR: Four Walls 28. Coquette 28. *Broadway* 29 (and 42). Three Men on a Horse 36. On Your Toes 39. The Boys from Syracuse 40. *The Pajama Game* (& co-d) 57. *Damn Yankees* (& co-d) 58, etc.

AS PRODUCER: *Boy Meets Girl* 38. Room Service 38. The Primrose Path 40. *The Pajama Game* 57. *Damn Yankees* 58, etc.

AS DIRECTOR: Why Bring That Up? 29. The Sea God 30. Stolen Heaven 31. Secrets of a Secretary 31. My Sin 31. Too Many Girls 40, etc.

¶ I must confess that one of my main defects as a director has always been an incurable impatience. – *G.A.*

Many great minds have made a botch of matters because their emotions fettered their thinking. – *G.A.*

Abbott, John (1905–).
British-born character actor with staring eyes, specializing in eccentric parts; in Hollywood from 1941.

Mademoiselle Docteur 37. The Return of the Scarlet Pimpernel 37. The Saint in London 39. The Shanghai Gesture 41. Mrs Miniver 42. They Got Me Covered 42. Jane Eyre 43. The London Blackout Murders (lead) 43. The Vampire's Ghost 45. Deception 46. *The Woman in White* 48 (a memorable performance, as the grotesque invalid Frederick Fairlie). The Merry Widow 52. Public Pigeon Number One 57. Gigi 58. Who's Minding the Store? 63. Gambit 66. The Store 66. 2000 Years Later 69. The Black Bird 75. Slapstick 84, many others.

Abbott, Philip (1923–).
American 'second lead' of the 50s.

Bachelor Party 57. *Sweet Bird of Youth* 62. The Spiral Road 62. Miracle of the White Stallions 63. Those Calloways 65. Tail Gunner Joe (TV) 77, etc.

TV series: *The F.B.I.* 65–73. Rich Man, Poor Man – Book II 76–77.

Abel, Alfred (1880–1937).
German character actor of weighty personality, in films from 1913.

Dr Mabuse 22. Phantom 22. Metropolis 26. Gold 28. Narkose (& d) 29. Congress Dances 31. Salon Dora Greene 33. Das Hofkonzert 36. Kater Lampe 36. Frau Sylvelin 38, etc.

Abel, Walter (1898–1987).
American character actor with stage experience. Made his Hollywood debut as D'Artagnan, but later settled enjoyably into variations on a single performance of harassment and nervousness, whether as father, friend of the family or professional man.

■ *The Three Musketeers* 35. The Lady Consents 36. Two in the Dark 36. The Witness Chair 36. Fury 36. We Went to College 36. Second Wife 36. Portia on Trial 37. Wise Girl 37. Law of the Underworld 38. Racket Busters 38. Men with Wings 38. King of the Turf 39. Miracle on Main Street 40. Dance Girl Dance 40. *Arise My Love* (which provided him with a key line: 'I'm not happy. I'm not happy at all') 40. Michael Shayne Private Detective 40. Who Killed Aunt Maggie? 40. *Hold Back the Dawn* 41. Skylark 41. Glamour Boy 41. *Beyond the Blue Horizon* 42. *Star Spangled Rhythm* 42. Holiday Inn 42. Wake Island 42. So Proudly We Hail 43. Fired Wife 43. Follow the Boys 44. *Mr Skeffington* 44. An American Romance 44. *The Affairs of Susan* 45. Duffy's Tavern 45. *Kiss and Tell* 45. The Kid from Brooklyn 46. 13 Rue Madeleine 46. The Fabulous Joe 47. *Dream Girl* 48. That Lady in Ermine 48. So This is Love 53. Night People 54. The Indian Fighter 55. The Steel Jungle 56. *Bernardine* 57. Raintree County 57. Handle with Care 58. Mirage 65. Quick Let's Get Married 66. Zora 71. The Man without a Country (TV) 74. Silent Night, Bloody Night 74. The Ultimate Solution of Grace Quigley 84.

Famous line *Arise My Love*: 'I'm not happy. I'm not happy at all!'

Abie's Irish Rose.
Anne Nichols' long-running Broadway comedy of 1927, about a Catholic girl marrying into a Jewish family, has twice been filmed: by Victor Fleming in 1928 and by Edward Sutherland in 1946. The theme has frequently been borrowed, as in the 1973 TV series *Bridget Loves Bernie*.

abortion,
unmentionable on the screen for many years save in Continental dramas like *Carnet de Bal* 37, and officially ostracized exploitation pictures like *Amok* 34, was first permitted as a Hollywood plot point in *Detective Story* 51. Six years later, *Blue Denim* concerned an abortion that was prevented; and the later abortion scenes in *The Best of Everything* 59, *Sweet Bird of Youth* 62, *The Interns* 62, and *Love with the Proper Stranger* 64 scarcely displayed an obsession with the subject. Meanwhile however the British gave it full rein in *Saturday Night and Sunday Morning* 60, *The L-Shaped Room* 62, *Alfie* 66, and *Up the Junction* 68; by which time it had certainly lost its shock value. By 1969 Hollywood felt confident enough to use it as the plot point of a commercial thriller, *Daddy's Gone A-Hunting*, and in 1972 it became the specific subject of *To Find A Man*.

above the title.
Credits that appear on posters or the screen before the title of a film. At one time, such billing was an indication of star status, though that no longer necessarily holds; these days it is more to do with deal-making and the massaging of egos than with the ability to draw an audience to a film. Only a few producers and directors, such as Cecil B. De Mille, Alfred Hitchcock and Steven Spielberg, have achieved above the title billing, and even fewer writers have managed it, of whom the most prominent is Stephen King.

Abraham, F. Murray (1939–).
American character actor.

■ They Might Be Giants 71. Serpico 73. The Sunshine Boys 75. All the President's Men 76. The Ritz 76. The Big Fix 78. Scarface 83. *Amadeus* (AA) 84. The Name of the Rose 86. Personal Choice 88. An Innocent Man 89. La Nuit du Serail 89. Russicum 89. Slipstream 89. La Batalla de los Tres Reyes 90. Bonfire of the Vanities 90. Cadence 90. Mobsters 91. National Lampoon's Loaded Weapon 1 93. Sweet Killing 93. The Last Action Hero 93. Surviving the Game 94. Jamila 94. L'Affaire (Fr.) 94. Nostradamus 94.

Abrahams, Jim (1944–).
American director, screenwriter and actor, usually in collaboration with Jerry and David Zucker (qqv).

The Kentucky Fried Movie (a, co-w) 77. Airplane! (a, co-wd) 80. Top Secret! (co-wd) 84. Ruthless People (co-d) 86. The Naked Gun: From the Files of Police Squad (co-w) 88. Big Business (d) 88. Welcome Home Roxy Carmichael (d) 91. Hot Shots! (co-w, d) 91. Hot Shots! Part Deux (co-w, d) 93, etc.

Abril, Victoria (1959–).
Spanish leading actress, who moved to France in the early 80s.

Mother, Dearly Loved (Mater Amatisima) 79. The Beehive (La Colmena) 81. The Moon in the Gutter (La Lune dans le Caniveau) 81. On the Line (Rio Abajo) 84. Our Father (Padre Nuestro) 84. The Witching Hour (La Hora Bruja) 85. Max, Mon Amour 85. Time of Silence (Tiempo de Silencio) 86. Baton Rouge 88. Tie Me Up! Tie Me Down! (¡Atame!) 90. Lovers (Amantes) 91. High Heels (Tacones Lejanos) 91. Wonderful Times (Une Epoque Formidable) 91. Too Much Heart (Demasiado Corazón) 92. Kika 93. Intruso 93. Jimmy Hollywood 94, etc.

abstract film.
One in which the images are not representational but fall into visually interesting or significant

patterns: e.g. Disney's *Fantasia*, Norman McLaren's hand-drawn sound films, etc.

Academy Awards.
Merit prizes given annually since 1927 by the American Academy of Motion Picture Arts and Sciences. The award is in the form of a statuette known in the trade – for reasons variously explained – as Oscar, and each April the ABC network televises the award ceremonies as an increasingly pretentious spectacular: Johnny Carson in 1979 called it 'two hours of sparkling entertainment spread out over a four-hour show'. See Appendix for full list of awards.

Books: *The Academy Awards* by Paul Michael (1968), *Inside Oscar* by Mason Wiley and Damien Bolo (1985), *60 Years of the Oscar* by Robert Osborne (1989), *The Oscars: The Secret History of Hollywood's Academy Awards* by Anthony Holden (1993), *The Academy Awards Handbook* by John Harkness (1994).

¶ The Oscar means one thing – an added million-dollar gross for the picture. It's a big publicity contest. Oh, the voting is legitimate, but there's the sentimentality. One year when I was a candidate, when Elizabeth Taylor got a hole in her throat, I cancelled my plane. – *Shirley Maclaine*

In the myth of the cinema, Oscar is the supreme prize. – *Federico Fellini*

As you danced, you saw the most important people in Hollywood whirling past you. – *Joan Crawford at first Oscar ceremony*

The statuette is a perfect symbol of the picture business – a powerful athletic body clutching a gleaming sword, with half of his head, the part that holds his brains, completely sliced off. – *Frances Marion, 1928*

Academy Frame.
The standard film frame in a ratio of 4 to 3, more usually referred to as 1.33 to 1.

Academy Leader.
Regulation length of film attached to the front of a reel about to be projected, bearing a 'countdown' and various standard images to facilitate focusing.

accelerated motion.
An effect obtained by running the camera more slowly than usual: when the resulting film is projected at normal speed, the movements seem faster because they occupy fewer frames than would normally be the case. The opposite of *slow motion* (qv).

Accent on Youth.
Samuel Raphaelson's successful Broadway play about a lazy playwright spurred to success by his young secretary has been filmed three times. In 1935 Herbert Marshall and Sylvia Sidney were directed by Wesley Ruggles. In 1950 it turned up as *Mr Music*, with Bing Crosby and Nancy Olson, directed by Richard Haydn; and in 1959 it emerged again as *But Not for Me*, with Clark Gable and Carroll Baker, directed by Walter Lang.

ACE.
Initials that indicate membership of the American Cinema Editors, a professional society for film and TV editors.

acetate.
Another word for safety base, which replaced nitrate stock in the 50s and is much slower to burn.

Achard, Marcel (1899–1974).
French writer.

The Merry Widow 34. Mayerling 36. Alibi (oa) 37. The Strange Monsieur Victor 38. Untel Père et Fils 40. Monsieur la Souris 43. The Paris Waltz (d only) 50. Madame De 52. La Garçonne 57. A Woman Like Satan 59. A Shot in the Dark (oa) 64.

Acheson, James.
English costume designer, now in international films.
Time Bandits 81. Water 84. Brazil 85. Highlander 86. The Last Emperor (AA) 87. Dangerous Liaisons (AA) 88. The Sheltering Sky 90, etc.

Acker, Jean (1893–1978).
American screen and stage actress, the first wife of Rudolph Valentino (1919–21).
Are You a Mason? 15. Arabian Knight 20. Brewster's Millions 21. The Woman in Chains 23. The Girl Habit 31. No More Ladies 35. My Favorite Wife 40. The Thin Man Goes Home 44. Spellbound 45. Something to Live For 52, etc.

Acker, Sharon (1935–).
Anglo-American leading lady.
Lucky Jim (GB) 57. Waiting For Caroline (Can.) 67. Point Blank 67. The First Time 69. Act of the Heart 70. A Clear and Present Danger (TV) 70. Hec Ramsey (TV) 72. The Stranger (TV) 73. The Hanged Man (TV) 74. Our Man Flint: Dead On Target (TV) 76. The Hostage Heart (TV) 77. The Murder That Wouldn't Die (TV) 79. Happy Birthday to Me 81.
TV series: The Senator 70. Perry Mason 73. Executive Suite 76.

Ackermann, Bettye (1928–).
American general purpose actress.
Face of Fire 59. Companions in Nightmare (TV) 68. Rascal 69. M*A*S*H. 70, etc.
TV series: Ben Casey 60–64.

Ackland, Joss (1928–).
British actor of larger-than-life personality; much on TV.
Seven Days to Noon 49. The Ghost Ship 53. Rasputin the Mad Monk 65. Crescendo 69. Mr Forbush and the Penguins 71. The House That Dripped Blood 71. Villain 71. England Made Me 72. The Happiness Cage (US) 72. Hitler: The Last Ten Days 73. Penny Gold 73. The Three Musketeers 73. The Black Windmill 74. S.P.Y.S. 74. Great Expectations 75. Royal Flash 75. Operation Daybreak 76. Silver Bears 78. Who is Killing the Great Chefs of Europe? 78. Saint Jack 79. The Apple 80. Rough Cut 80. Dangerous Davies (TV) 81. Lady Jane 85. A Zed and Two Noughts 85. White Mischief 88. It Couldn't Happen Here 88. Popielusko 88. Lethal Weapon 2 89. To Forget Palermo (Dimenticare Palermo) 89. The Bridge 90. The Hunt for Red October 90. Tre Colonne in Cronaca 90. The Object of Beauty 91. Bill & Ted's Bogus Journey 91. Once Upon a Crime 92. The Mighty Ducks 92. The Princess and the Goblin (voice) 92. Nowhere to Run 93. Mad Dogs and Englishmen 95, etc.

Ackland, Rodney (1908–1991).
British writer, sporadically in films from 1930, usually in association with other scenarists.
Autobiography: 1954, The Celluloid Mistress.
Shadows 31. Number Seventeen 32. The Case of Gabriel Perry (a only) 35. Bank Holiday 38. Young Man's Fancy 39. 49th Parallel (co-w, AAN) 41. Dangerous Moonlight 41. Hatter's Castle 41. Thursday's Child (& d) 43. Wanted for Murder 46. Temptation Harbour 47. Queen of Spades 48, etc.

Acord, Art (1890–1931).
American star of silent westerns. Sound ended his career and he committed suicide.
The Squaw Man 13. A Man Afraid of His Wardrobe 15. The Moon Riders 20. In the Days of Buffalo Bill 21. The Oregon Trail 23. The Call of Courage 25. Rustler's Ranch 26. Sky High Corral 26. Hard Fists 27. Loco Luck 27. Two Gun O'Brien 28. Bullets and Justice 29. Wyoming Tornado 29, etc.

Acosta, Rodolfo (1920–1974).
Cold-eyed Mexican-American character actor, a frequent western villain or henchman.
The Fugitive 48. One Way Street 50. Yankee Buccaneer 52. Hondo 54. Bandido 56. The Tijuana Story (leading role) 57. Flaming Star 60. How the West Was Won 62. Rio Conchos 64. Return of the Seven 66. Flap 70. The Great White Hope 70, many others.
TV series: High Chaparral 67.

Acres, Birt (1854–1918).
British cinematograph pioneer, American born, later projector manufacturer. Claimed to be the first producer of cinema films in Britain.
Haycart Crossing, Hadley 94. The Derby 95. Boxing Kangaroo 96. A Visit to the Zoo 96. Princess Maud's Wedding 96. An Unfriendly Call 97, etc.

acting
¶ A short selection of attitudes.

Acting is like roller-skating. Once you know how to do it, it is neither stimulating nor exciting. – George Sanders
In Europe an actor is an artist. In Hollywood, if he isn't working, he's a bum. – Anthony Quinn
The secret of my success? I speak in a loud clear voice and try not to bump into the furniture. – Alfred Lunt
We who play, who entertain for a few years, what can we leave that will last? – Ethel Barrymore
Actors are cattle. – Alfred Hitchcock (NB. When attacked for this remark Hitch claimed he had been misquoted: what he really said was: 'Actors should be treated like cattle.')
Film acting is unquestionably a director's medium. – Charles Chaplin (NB. Chaplin used to advise his silent actors: 'Don't sell it. Remember they're peeking at you.')
Scratch an actor – and you'll find an actress. – Dorothy Parker
Acting is a question of absorbing other people's personalities and adding some of your own experience. – Paul Newman
Don't act – think! – F.W. Marnau
Actors and burglars work better at night. – Cedric Hardwicke
I always had one ear offstage, listening for the call from the bookie. – Walter Matthau
The only thing you owe the public is a good performance. – Humphrey Bogart
Joan Crawford is the only actress to read the whole script. Most actresses just read their own lines to find out what clothes they're going to wear. – Anita Loos
You spend all your life trying to do something they put people in asylums for. – Jane Fonda
The best actors in the world are those who feel the most and show the least. – Jean-Louis Trintignant
I'm afraid to look, because I'm probably awful. – George Raft
There are lots of methods. Mine involves a lot of talent, a glass, and some cracked ice. – John Barrymore
The main problem of the actor is not to let the

audience go to sleep, then wake up and go home feeling they've wasted their money. – Laurence Olivier
Acting is a way to overcome your own inhibitions and shyness. The writer creates a strong, confident personality, and that's what you become – unfortunately, only for the moment. – Shirley Booth
The movies are the only business where you can go out front and applaud yourself. – Will Rogers
I learn the lines and pray to God. – Claude Rains
Talk low, talk slow, and don't say too much. – John Wayne
First wipe your nose and check your flies. – Alec Guinness

action still.
A photograph of a scene as it actually appears in the film as opposed to one specially posed for publicity purposes. Sometimes called a frame blow-up. In TV, an 'action stills' programme has come to mean one consisting of still photographs given a semblance of life by camera movement.

actor-directors
were rare until around 1950 but are becoming increasingly common. Those who have dared to direct themselves include Woody Allen, Alan Arkin, Sergei Bondarchuk, Marlon Brando, Mel Brooks, Richard Burton, Richard Carlson, John Cassavetes, Charles Chaplin (always), John Clements, Jean Cocteau, William Conrad, Noël Coward, Jules Dassin, John Derek, Clint Eastwood, Pierre Etaix, José Ferrer, Mel Ferrer, Albert Finney, Peter Fonda, Jodie Foster, Al Freeman Jnr, Mel Gibson, Hugo Haas, Laurence Harvey, David Hemmings, Paul Henreid, Charlton Heston, Dennis Hopper, Robert Hossein, Leslie Howard, Robert Hutton, Buster Keaton, Gene Kelly, Burt Lancaster, Stan Laurel, Jerry Lewis, Peter Lorne, Ida Lupino, Burgess Meredith, Ray Milland, George Montgomery, Robert Montgomery, Anthony Newley, Paul Newman, Edmond O'Brien, Dennis O'Keefe, Laurence Olivier, Nigel Patrick, Carl Reiner, Ralph Richardson, Peter Sellers, Frank Sinatra, Mark Stevens, Barbra Streisand, Jacques Tati, Peter Ustinov, Erich von Stroheim, Tom Walls, John Wayne, Orson Welles, Cornel Wilde.
Many of these gave up after one attempt, and might well have had more sustained directorial careers if, like the following, they had stuck to directing other actors: Richard Attenborough, Lionel Barrymore, James Cagney, Ricardo Cortez, Helmut Dantine, Richard Haydn, Lionel Jeffries, Alf Kjellin, Charles Laughton, Jack Lemmon, Roddy McDowall, Karl Malden, Walter Matthau, Elaine May, John Mills, Gene Nelson, Jack Nicholson, Sean Penn, Dick Powell, Anthony Quinn, Cliff Robertson, Mickey Rooney, Don Taylor, Marshall Thompson, Mai Zetterling.
On the whole, however, perhaps the lesson of the lists is that actors should stick to acting.

actors
have seldom been the subject of biopics. Anna Neagle appeared as Peg Woffington, with Cedric Hardwicke as David Garrick, in Peg of Old Drury 35, and Garrick was played by Brian Aherne in The Great Garrick 37. Miriam Hopkins was Mrs Leslie Carter in Lady with Red Hair 41. Charlie Ruggles (of all people) played Otis Skinner in Our Hearts Were Young and Gay 44, Richard Burton was Edwin Booth in Prince of Players 54, and Kim Novak was Jeanne Eagels 56. The 60s brought Julie Andrews and Daniel Massey as Gertie Lawrence and Noël Coward in Star! Of the idols of its own creation, Hollywood has so far given us biographies of

Valentino, Jean Harlow, Lon Chaney, Diana and John Barrymore, Lillian Roth, Buster Keaton, Pearl White, W.C. Fields and Gable and Lombard.

The Actors' Studio.
Lee Strasberg's drama school in New York was well publicized during the 50s as the source of 'method' acting, which was practised by Marlon Brando among others. It corresponded closely with the Stanislavsky system: actors underwent curious mental exercises to assimilate themselves into their characters. Originally founded in 1947 by Elia Kazan and Cheryl Crawford, it now seems to have been more fashionable than influential, and after Strasberg's death in 1982 its mention was greeted by many people with a faint smile.

ACTT.
The Association of Cinematograph, Television and Allied Technicians, a British trade union.

Acuff, Eddie (1908–1956).
American supporting comedian, remembered as the postman in the 'Blondie' series.
    Shipmates Forever 35. The Petrified Forest 36. The Boys from Syracuse 40. Hellzapoppin 41. Guadalcanal Diary 43. It Happened Tomorrow 44. The Flying Serpent 46. Blondie's Big Moment 47, many others.

Adair, Jean (1873–1953).
American stage actress best remembered by film fans as one of the sweetly murderous aunts in *Arsenic and Old Lace*.
■ In the Name of the Law 22. Advice to the Lovelorn 33. *Arsenic and Old Lace* 44. Something in the Wind 46. Living in a Big Way 47.

Adair, Robert (1900–1954).
English character actor, from the American stage. Born in San Francisco, he was educated at Harrow, made his screen debut as Captain Hardy in *Journey's End*, and spent his mid-career in Hollywood.
    Journey's End 30. Raffles 32. King of the Jungle 33. Limehouse Blues 35. The Prince and the Pauper 37. Brilliant Marriage 38. Jamaica Inn 39. Man on the Run 49. The Gambler and the Lady 52. Meet Mr Callaghan 54, etc.

Adam, Alfred (1909–1982).
French character actor, usually of weak or villainous roles.
    La Kermesse Héroïque 35. Carnet de Bal 37. Boule de Suif 45. La Ferme du Pendu 48. The Witches of Salem 56. Maigret Sets a Trap 61. Le Président 61. Vivre sa Vie 62. La Vie Conjugale 63. Les Fêtes Galantes 65. Que la Fête Commence 74, etc.

Adam, Ken (1921–) (Klaus Adam).
German-born art director, in films from 1947. Born in Berlin, he was in Britain from the mid-30s. The 60s were for him a period of spectacular inventiveness.
    Queen of Spades 48. Around the World in Eighty Days (AAN) 56. The Trials of Oscar Wilde 60. *Dr Strangelove* 63. Goldfinger 64. The Ipcress File 65. Thunderball 65. Funeral in Berlin 66. *You Only Live Twice* 67. Chitty Chitty Bang Bang 68. Goodbye Mr Chips 69. The Owl and the Pussycat 70. Sleuth 72. Live and Let Die 73. Barry Lyndon (AA) 75. The Seven Per Cent Solution 76. The Spy Who Loved Me (AAN) 77. Moonraker 79. Pennies from Heaven 80. King David 84. Agnes of God 85. Crimes of the Heart 86. The Deceivers 88. Dead-Bang 89. The Freshman 90. The Doctor 91.

Undercover Blues 93. Addams Family Values (AAN) 93. The Madness of King George 95, etc.

Adam, Ronald (1896–1979).
British character actor specializing in well-bred but stuffy professional men.
    The Drum 38. Escape to Danger 43. Green for Danger 46. Bonnie Prince Charlie 48. Angels One Five 51. Private's Progress 55. Reach for the Sky 56. Cleopatra 62. The Tomb of Ligeia 64. Who Killed the Cat? 66. Zeppelin 71, many others.
~Adam was also a busy writer, his best-remembered work being the play *An English Summer*, about the Battle of Britain.

Adams, Beverly (1945–).
Canadian-born leading lady in Hollywood films.
    Winter a GoGo 63. The New Interns 64. *The Silencers* 66. Birds Do It 66. Murderers' Row 66. The Torture Garden (GB) 67. The Ambushers 67, etc.

Adams, Brooke (1949–).
American leading lady of the *jolie laide* type; showed more promise than performance.
    Shock Waves 77. Invasion of the Body Snatchers 78. *Days of Heaven* 78. The First Great Train Robbery 79. A Man, a Woman and a Bank 79. Cuba 79. Tell Me a Riddle 80. The Dead Zone 83. Almost You 84. Key Exchange 84. The Stuff 85. Man on Fire 87. The Unborn 91. Stephen King's Sometimes They Come Back 91. Gas Food Lodging 92. The Last Hit (TV) 93, etc.
    TV series: O.K. Crackerby 65–66.

Adams, Casey (1917–).
See under *Max Showalter* (his real name, which he has recently used).

Adams, Claire (1900–1978).
Canadian-born leading lady of silent films. She retired early and in 1938 moved to Australia following her second marriage.
    Riders of the Dawn 20. The Penalty 20. The Killer 21. Just Tony 22. Stepping Fast 23. Where the North Begins 23. Oh, You Tony! 24. The Fast Set 24. The Big Parade 25. The Sea Wolf 26. Married Alive 27, etc.

Adams, Don (1926–).
American comedian, from night-clubs and television, best known for his Emmy-winning performance as Maxwell Smart in the spy spoof *Get Smart*.
    The Nude Bomb 80. Jimmy the Kid 82. Back to the Beach 87, etc.
    TV series: Get Smart 65–70. The Partners 71–72. Don Adams' Screen Test 75. Check It Out 85–88.

Adams, Dorothy (1900–1988).
American character actress, usually of timorous or sullen ladies.
    Broadway Musketeers 38. The Flame of New Orleans 41. Laura 44. The Best Years of Our Lives 46. The Foxes of Harrow 48. Carrie 52. Three for Jamie Dawn 56. The Big Country 58. From the Terrace 60. Peeper 76, etc.

Adams, Edie (1927–) (Elizabeth Edith Enke).
Pert American singer-comedienne, widow of Ernie Kovacs.
■ The Apartment 60. Lover Come Back 62. Call Me Bwana 63. It's a Mad Mad Mad Mad World 63. Under the Yum Yum Tree 63. *Love with the Proper Stranger* 64. The Best Man 64. Made in Paris 66. The Oscar 66. *The Honey Pot* 67. Box Office 82. The

Haunting of Harrington House 82. Shooting Stars 85. Adventures Beyond Belief 87.
    TV work includes: Evil Roy Slade 71. The Return of Joe Forrester 75. Word Games (Mrs Columbo) 79.

Adams, Ernie (1885–1947).
Short American character actor, from the stage, most often in westerns.
    A Regular Girl 19. The Pony Express 25. The Main Event 27. The Tip-Off 31. Breed of the Border 33. Gun Lords of Stirrup Basin 37. Ridin' the Lone Trail 37. The Man Who Came to Dinner 41. The Perils of Pauline 47. Return of the Bad Men 48, etc.

Adams, Gerald Drayson (1904–).
Canadian screenwriter, former literary agent.
    Dead Reckoning 47. The Big Steal 49. The Golden Horde 51. Flaming Feather 51. The Black Sleep 56. Kissing Cousins 64. Harum Scarum 65, many others.

Adams, Jane (1921–).
American actress of the 40s.
    House of Dracula 45. Gunman's Code 46. The Brute Man 46. Batman and Robin 49. Rising Son (TV) 90. Vital Signs 90. Light Sleeper 92, etc.

Adams, Jill (1930–).
Pert British leading lady, former model, who decorated a number of lightweight films in the 50s.
    The Young Lovers 54. Doctor at Sea 55. Private's Progress 55. The Green Man 56. Brothers in Law 57. Carry On Constable 60. Doctor in Distress 63. Promise Her Anything 66, etc.

Adams, Julie (formerly Julia) (1926–) (Betty May Adams).
American leading lady in Hollywood from 1947. Her essentially soft and sympathetic nature made the slight change of first name seem especially apt.
    Hollywood Story 51. Bright Victory 51. Bend of the River 52. Mississippi Gambler 53. The Creature from the Black Lagoon 54. One Desire 55. Away All Boats 56. Slaughter on Tenth Avenue 57. Raymie 60. Tickle Me 65. Valley of Mystery 67. The Last Movie 71. McQ 72. The McCullochs 75. Killer Force 76. The Killer Inside Me 76. Black Roses 88. Catchfire (US: Backtrack) 89, etc.
    TV series: Yancey Derringer 58–59. The Jimmy Stewart Show 71. Code Red 81.

Adams, Maud (Maude) (1945–) (Maud Wikstrom).
Persistently promising Swedish-American leading lady of the 70s.
    The Boys in the Band 70. The Christian Licorice Store 71. Rollerball 74. The Man with the Golden Gun 74. Killer Force 76. Tattoo 81. Octopussy 83. Playing for Time (TV) 80. Nairobi Affair (TV) 85. Hell Hunters 86. Jane and the Lost City 87. The Women's Club 87. Deadly Intent 88. Ski School 89. Soda Cracker 89. The Kill Reflex 90. Initiation: Silent Night, Deadly Night 4 91, etc.
    TV series: Chicago Story 82. Emerald Point N.A.S. 83–84.

Adams, Nick (1931–1968) (Nicholas Adamschock).
American leading man who usually played neurotic or aggressive types; never quite made the big time. Died of a drug overdose.
    Somebody Loves Me (debut) 52. Mister Roberts 55. *No Time for Sergeants* 58. Pillow Talk 59. Hell is for Heroes 62. The Hook 63. Twilight of Honor (AAN) 63. Monster of Terror (GB) 66. Young

Dillinger 66. Frankenstein Conquers the World
(Jap.) 66. Fever Heat 67, etc.
TV series: The Rebel 59–60.

Adams, Richard (1920–).
British best-selling novelist who sees the world
from the animals' point of view. His *Watership
Down* and *The Plague Dogs* were somewhat
unsatisfactorily turned into cartoon features.

Adams, Robert (1906–).
West Indian actor, former teacher, prominent in
British films of the 40s.
    Sanders of the River (debut) 35. King Solomon's
Mines 37. Caesar and Cleopatra 45. Men of Two
Worlds (leading role) 47. Old Mother Riley's
Jungle Treasure 52. Man of Africa 52. Sapphire 59,
etc.

Adams, Stanley (1915–1977).
American character actor. Committed suicide.
    The Atomic Kid 54. Hell on Frisco Bay 56.
Breakfast at Tiffany's 61. Nevada Smith 66. The
Clones 74, etc.

Adams, Tom (1938–).
Burly British leading man whose career might
have flourished better in the 50s.
    The Great Escape 63. Licensed to Kill 65. Where
the Bullets Fly 66. The Fighting Prince of Donegal
66. Fathom 67. Subterfuge 69. The Fast Kill 72.
The Onedin Line (TV) 79. Mask of the Devil (TV)
84.
    TV series: Spy Trap 75.

Adamson, Harold (1906–1980).
American lyricist, usually with Jimmy McHugh.
    Dancing Lady 33. Kid Millions 34. Suzy 36. That
Certain Age 38. Nob Hill 45. If You Knew Susie 48.
Gentlemen Prefer Blondes 52. An Affair to
Remember 57, many others.

Adamson, Joy (1910–1980).
Austrian-born wild-life expert who wrote *Born
Free* and *Living Free*. A long-time resident of Kenya,
she was mysteriously murdered.

adaptations.
A high proportion of feature films have been
adapted from other media. A poem was the basis
of *The Set-Up*, but mostly the studios have raided
novels and plays for their material. The cost of
such rights used to be minimal, but can now run
into millions of dollars, the rights to *Annie* having
allegedly cost a quarter of the film's $35m budget.
A bonus however has appeared in the form of
television mini-series, which thirty or forty years
after the film version, when the original material
would be unfashionable with film audiences, have
started the money flowing again for such items as
My Cousin Rachel, *The Citadel* and *How Green Was
My Valley*.
    At one time Hollywood had the reputation of
using only the title of the items it bought. Certainly
the Bulldog Drummond and Sherlock Holmes
series bore little relation to the stories on which
they were allegedly based: it seemed to be a point
of honour with screenwriters to do better (if they
could). *The Grapes of Wrath* was given an upbeat
ending. *Pride and Prejudice* had its period advanced
fifty years to a time when the fashions were more
alluring. *Wuthering Heights* lost its second half.
Rebecca reduced its hero from a murderer to an
accessory after the fact. *Foreign Correspondent* took
not a single incident from its alleged basis, *Personal
History* by Vincent Sheean. *Forever Amber's* heroine
became far more sinned against than sinning. *These
Three* was adapted by Lillian Hellman from her

own play *The Children's Hour*, but she had to
change the central relationship from lesbian to
heterosexual. *The Killers* wore out Hemingway's
short story in the first ten minutes, and filled out
the next ninety with new material. *Forbidden Planet*
placed the plot of Shakespeare's *The Tempest* in outer
space. Graham Greene's *The Quiet American* saw its
point exactly reversed. Bernard Shaw was
persuaded to add a happy ending (now the
accepted one) to his anti-romantic *Pygmalion*. And
Noël Coward's *Design for Living* saw the light of day
in Hollywood with only one line intact, allegedly
'Kippers on toast'.
    It has to be admitted that some excellent films
have resulted from this tampering, and
'rearrangement' may seem in many cases
preferable to the too-literal transcriptions in recent
years of such properties as *Sleuth*, *The Best
Whorehouse in Texas*, the Neil Simon comedies,
and *Death Trap*, in which last case a new twist
ending was added, but so lamely that the
audience failed to grasp it.
    Among the most skilled adapters from the
'golden age' are Dudley Nichols, Ben Hecht, Jules
Furthman, Lamar Trotti, Philip Dunne, Casey
Robinson, Samson Raphaelson, R. C. Sherriff,
John Balderston and Donald Ogden Stewart.

Addams, Charles (1912–1988).
American cartoonist of ghoulish humour, much in
the *New Yorker* from 1940. TV in 1964–65 ran
The Addams Family, about creepy characters in a
cobwebby house, which became the basis of a
successful feature film in 1991. With regard to
films he is best remembered for his remark on
attending the premiere of *Cleopatra*: 'I only came
to see the asp.'

Addams, Dawn (1930–1985).
Smart and glamorous British leading lady in
international films. Films mainly unremarkable.
    Night into Morning 51. Plymouth Adventure 52.
The Robe 53. The Moon Is Blue 53. Khyber Patrol
54. A King in New York 57. The Silent Enemy 58.
The Two Faces of Dr Jekyll 60. The Black Tulip
64. Ballad in Blue 65. Where the Bullets Fly 66.
Vampire Lovers 70. Sappho 70. Vault of Horror 73,
etc.
    TV series: Star Maidens 77.

Addinsell, Richard (1904–1977).
British composer.
    The Amateur Gentleman 36. Fire over England
37. Goodbye Mr Chips 39. Gaslight 40. *Dangerous
Moonlight* (including 'Warsaw Concerto') 40. Love
on the Dole 41. Blithe Spirit 45. Scrooge 51. Beau
Brummell 54. The Prince and the Showgirl 57. The
Admirable Crichton 57. The Waltz of the Toreadors
62, etc.

Addison, John (1920–).
British composer, in films from 1948. From the
mid-80s he scored TV movies.
    The Guinea Pig 49. Seven Days to Noon 50. The
Man Between 53. Private's Progress 55. *Reach for
the Sky* 56. Lucky Jim 57. I Was Monty's Double
58. Look Back in Anger 59. The Entertainer 60.
A Taste of Honey 61. The Loneliness of the Long
Distance Runner 62. *Tom Jones* (AA) 63. Guns at
Batasi 64. Moll Flanders 65. Torn Curtain 66. A
Fine Madness 66. The Honey Pot 67. Smashing
Time 67. Country Dance 70. Mr Forbush and the
Penguins 71. Sleuth 72. Dead Cert 74. A Bridge
Too Far 77. The Seven Per Cent Solution 77.
Centennial (TV) 78. Pearl (TV) 80. Strange
Invaders 83. The Ultimate Solution of Grace
Quigley 84. Code Name: Emerald 85. Phantom
of the Opera (TV) 90, etc.

addresses
which have formed film titles include *13 West
Street*, *13 Rue Madeleine*, *13 East Street*, *13 Demon Street*
(TV), *Ten North Frederick*, *10 Rillington Place*, *15
Maiden Lane*, *26 Acacia Avenue*, *99 River Street* and
711 Ocean Drive. Then there were *42nd Street*, *52nd
Street* and *The House on 92nd Street*, not to mention
Flamingo Road, *Stallion Road*, *Madison Avenue*, *Rue
de l'Estrapade*, *Montparnasse 19*, *Quai des Orfèvres*,
Piccadilly, *Bond Street*, *St Martin's Lane*, etc. Nor
should one forget Anna Neagle's London series:
Piccadilly Incident, *The Courtneys of Curzon Street*,
Spring in Park Lane, *I Live in Grosvenor Square* and
Maytime in Mayfair. A clever scheme for disposing
of an enemy was worked out in *Address Unknown*.

Addy, Wesley (1913–).
Thin American character actor, usually of
humourless or sinister appearance. He married
actress Celeste Holm in 1966.
    The First Legion 51. My Six Convicts 52. Kiss
Me Deadly 55. The Big Knife 55. Timetable 57. The
Garment Jungle 58. Ten Seconds to Hell 59.
Whatever Happened to Baby Jane? 62. *Seconds* 66.
Mister Buddwing 66. The Grissom Gang 71.
Network 76. The Europeans 79. The Verdict 82. The
Bostonians 84, many others.

Adjani, Isabelle (1955–).
Franco-German leading lady of international films.
    Faustine 71. The Slap 74. *The Story of Adèle H*
(AAN) 75. The Tenant 76. Barocco 77. The Driver
78. Nosferatu 78. The Brontë Sisters 79. Clara et
les Chics Types 80. Possession 80. Quartet 81. One
Deadly Summer 83. Subway 85. Maladie d'Amour
86. Ishtar 87. Camille Claudel (AAN) 88. La Reine
Margot 94, etc.

Adler, Buddy (1906–1960) (Maurice Adler).
American producer, with Columbia from 1948,
Fox from 1954 (head of studio from 1956).
    The Dark Past 48. No Sad Songs for Me 50.
Salome 53. *From Here to Eternity* (AA) 53. Violent
Saturday 55. *Love is a Many Splendored Thing* 55.
The Left Hand of God 55. Bus Stop 56. Anastasia
56. A Hatful of Rain 57. South Pacific 58. *The Inn
of the Sixth Happiness* 58, etc.

Adler, Jay (1896–1978).
American character actor, brother of Luther Adler;
usually played hoboes, small-time gangsters, etc.
    No Time to Marry 38. My Six Convicts 52. 99
River Street 54. The Big Combo 55. Sweet Smell of
Success 57. The Brothers Karamazov 58. Seven
Guns to Mesa 60. The Family Jewels 65, many
others.

Adler, Larry (1914–).
American harmonica virtuoso whose chief
contribution to films is the score of *Genevieve* 53;
also composed for *The Hellions* 61. *The Hook* 63.
King and Country 63. *High Wind in Jamaica* 64; and
appeared in *St Martin's Lane* 38. *Music for Millions*
44.

Adler, Luther (1903–1984) (Lutha Adler).
Heavy-featured American character actor,
member of well-known theatrical family (brother
Jay, sister Stella).
    ■ Lancer Spy 37. Cornered 45. Saigon 48. The
Loves of Carmen 48. *Wake of the Red Witch* 48.
House of Strangers 49. D.O.A. 50. South Sea
Sinner 50. Under My Skin 50. Kiss Tomorrow
Goodbye 50. M 51. The Magic Face (as Hitler) 51.
The Desert Fox 51. Hoodlum Empire 52. The Tall
Texan 53. The Miami Story 54. Crashout 55. The
Girl in the Red Velvet Swing 55. Hot Blood 56. The
Last Angry Man 59. Cast a Giant Shadow 66. *The*

Brotherhood 68. Crazy Joe 74. Murph the Surf 74. The Man in the Glass Booth 75. Mean Johnny Barrows 75. Voyage of the Damned 76. Absence of Malice 81.

TV series: The Psychiatrist 71. Also many guest appearances, especially in Naked City.

Adler, Richard (1921–).
American composer and lyricist who with his partner Jerry Ross (1926–55) (Jerold Rosenberg) wrote *The Pajama Game* and *Damn Yankees*.

Adler, Stella (1902–1992).
American stage actress, sister of Luther and Jay Adler. Known at one time as Stella Ardler.

Love on Toast 38. Shadow of the Thin Man 41. My Girl Tisa 48, etc.

Adlon, Percy (1935–).
German producer-director and screenwriter. A former actor, broadcaster and documentary film-maker, he founded his own production company in 1978. His international success came in 1987 with *Bagdad Café*, which made a star of Marianne Sägebrecht and subsequently became the basis for a TV series starring Whoopi Goldberg.

Celeste 81. Five Last Days (Letz Funf Tage) 82. The Swing (Die Schaukel) 83. Sugar Baby (Zuckerbaby) 86. Bagdad Café 87. Rosalie Goes Shopping 89. Salmonberries 91. Younger and Younger 93, etc.

The Admirable Crichton.
J. M. Barrie's comedy, about master and man reversing roles after being shipwrecked on a desert island, has long fascinated film-makers. (Goldwyn is said to have lost interest after discovering that it was not what it sounded, a naval drama.) De Mille filmed it in 1919 as *Male and Female*, with Thomas Meighan and Gloria Swanson; a musical version, *We're Not Dressing*, turned up in 1934 with Bing Crosby and Carole Lombard; a further variation, *Our Girl Friday*, was filmed by Noel Langley in 1953 starring Kenneth More and Joan Collins; and in 1957 Kenneth More and Diane Cilento appeared in a more or less straight version of the play, under its original title, directed by Lewis Gilbert. More also appeared on the stage in a musical adaptation, *Our Man Crichton*.

Adolfi, John G. (1888–1933).
American director at his peak in the transitional period between silent and sound. Began as an actor, but quickly turned to directing and found steady work. Three years before his death he formed an association with George Arliss and filmed the star's stage successes.

A Man and His Mate 15. The Sphinx 16. A Modern Cinderella 17. A Child of the Wild 17. Queen of the Sea 18. Who's Your Brother? 19. The Darling of the Rich 22. The Little Red Schoolhouse 23. Chalk Marks 24. The Phantom Express 25. The Checkered Flag 26. Husband Hunters 27. The Little Snob 28. Fancy Baggage 29. The Show of Shows 29. Dumbbells in Ermine 30. Sinner's Holiday 30. College Lovers 30. The Millionaire 31. Alexandra Hamilton 31. Compromised 31. The Man Who Played God 32. A Successful Calamity 32. Central Park 32. The King's Vacation 33. The Working Man 33. Voltaire 33, many others.

Adoree, Renee (1898–1933) (Jeanne de la Fonté).
French leading lady, former circus bareback rider, who became an exotic star of Hollywood films in the 20s but could not transfer to sound and died of tuberculosis.

The Strongest 20. Made in Heaven 21. Monte Cristo 22. The Eternal Struggle 23. Women Who Give 24. The Bandolero 24. Man and Maid 25. Exchange of Wives 25. *The Big Parade* 25. La Bohème 26. The Exquisite Sinner 26. Tin Gods 26. The Flaming Forest 26. Heaven on Earth 27. Mr Wu 27. On ze Boulevard 27. Back to God's Country 27. The Cossacks 28. The Michigan Kid 28. The Mating Call 28. The Pagan 29. Tide of Empire 29. Redemption 30. Call of the Flesh 30.

Adorf, Mario (1930–).
Swiss actor in European films.

The Girl Rosemarie 59. Station Six Sahara 63. Major Dundee (US) 65. Ten Little Indians 66. The Red Tent 71. Journey to Vienna 73. Fedora 78. The Tin Drum 79. L'Empreinte des Greantes 80. Lola 81. Smiley's People (TV) 80. Marco Polo (TV) 81. The Holcroft Covenant 85, etc.

Adreon, Franklin (1902–).
American second feature director.

Canadian Mounties vs Atomic Invaders (serial) 53. No Man's Woman 55. This Man Is Armed 56. Hell's Crossroads 57. The Steel Whip 58. The Nun and the Sergeant 62. Cyborg 2087 66. Dimension Five 66, etc.

Adrian (1903–1959) (Adrian Adolph Greenberg).
American costume designer, with MGM 1927–42 and credited with the authentic images of Garbo, Shearer, Harlow, etc. Married Janet Gaynor; quit films after being forced to create ordinary clothes for Garbo in *Two-Faced Woman*, a film that also ended Garbo's career. He opened his own successful fashion house and then retired to a ranch in Brazil, returning only to design the costumes for the stage version of *Camelot*. Committed suicide.

¶ If I'm copied, it's because of my clothes and Adrian does those. – *Joan Crawford*

Adrian, Iris (1912–1994) (I. A. Hostetter).
American character actress, former Ziegfeld Follies dancer, familiar from the early 30s as wisecracking or tawdry blonde.

Paramount on Parade 30. Rumba 35. Our Relations 37. Professional Bride 41. The G-String Murders 42. Spotlight Scandals 44. I'm from Arkansas 45. Road to Alcatraz 46. The Paleface 48. G.I. Jane 51. Highway Dragnet 54. The Buccaneer 59. That Darn Cat 65. The Odd Couple 68. Scandalous John 71. The Shaggy D.A. 76. Murder Can Hurt You (TV) 78. Herbie Goes Bananas 80, many others.

TV series: The Ted Knight Show 78.

Adrian, Max (1903–1973) (Max Bor).
Irish stage actor of high camp personality; latterly a star of mischievous revue and an impersonator of Bernard Shaw. Too richly flavoured to star in films, but made occasional character appearances.

■ The Primrose Path 34. Eight Cylinder Love 34. A Touch of the Moon 36. To Catch a Thief 36. Nothing Like Publicity 36. The Happy Family 37. When the Devil Was Well 37. Why Pick on Me? 37. Macushla 38. Merely Mr Hawkins 38. *Kipps* 41. Penn of Pennsylvania 41. *The Young Mr Pitt* 42. Talk About Jacqueline 42. Henry V 45. Her Favorite Husband 50. Pool of London 51. The Pickwick Papers 52. *Dr Terror's House of Horrors* 65. *The Deadly Affair* 66. Funeral in Berlin 66. Julius Caesar 70. The Music Lovers 70. The Devils 71. *The Boy Friend* 71.

advertising
appears seldom as a background to movies, but when it does, satire is usually in the air, as in *Christmas in July, The Hucksters, Mr Blandings Builds His Dream House, It Should Happen To You, Lover Come Back, Good Neighbor Sam, How to Succeed in Business without Really Trying, Putney Swope, How to Get Ahead in Advertising, Every Home Should Have One* (aka *Think Dirty*) and *Crazy People*. It was played fairly straight in *Madison Avenue* and *The Narrowing Circle*.

aeroplanes:
see *airplanes*

Agar, John (1921–).
American leading man, once married to Shirley Temple; mainly in low-budgeters.

Fort Apache 48. Sands of Iwo Jima 49. The Magic Carpet 52. The Golden Mistress 53. Bait 54. Joe Butterfly 56. Daughter of Dr Jekyll 57. The Brain from Planet Arous 58. Journey to the Seventh Planet 61. Of Love and Desire 63. Cavalry Command 65. Waco 66. The St Valentine's Day Massacre 67. The Curse of the Swamp Creature 67. The Undefeated 69. Big Jake 71. King Kong 76. How's Your Love Life? 77. The Amazing Mr No-Legs 78. Perfect Victims 88. Miracle Mile 89. Fear 89. The Perfect Bride 91, etc.

Agate, James (1877–1947).
British drama critic with a passion for Sarah Bernhardt. He performed some reluctant stints of film reviewing, and the results are compiled in two volumes of *Around Cinema*. They show him as a highbrow waffler rather than a wit, and no real appreciation of the art of film comes through.

Agee, James (1909–1955).
One of America's most respected film critics, he also wrote novels and screenplays (e.g. The African Queen 51). A posthumous collection of his reviews was published under the title *Agee on Film*, and the screenplays followed. His novel *A Death in the Family* was filmed in 1963 as *All the Way Home*. ✪ For his brief, witty, incisive reviews which perfectly encapsulate hundreds of 40s films.

agent.
An intermediary who acts on behalf of talent and takes ten per cent (rising to fifteen) of the rewards. Agents were partly blamed for the decline of Hollywood because many were too concerned to increase their client's income, and therefore their own, at the expense of sound economic film-making. Some also became producers, though few succeeded.

~When agent Leland Hayward married his client Margaret Sullavan, a friend cabled him: 'Congratulations on getting the other ninety per cent.'

¶ An agent is a guy who is sore because an actor gets ninety per cent of what he makes. – *Alva Johnston*

Ager, Cecelia (1898–1981).
American critic for various New York magazines in the 30s. Wrote a book of essays, *Let's Go to the Pictures*.

Ager, Milton (1893–1979).
American composer and former vaudeville accompanist who, with lyricist Jack Yellen, wrote the score for Sophie Tucker's first movie, *Honky Tonk* 29. The partnership's biggest hit was that movie's 'Happy Days Are Here Again', which has also turned up in *Beau James* 57, *This Earth Is Mine* 59, and *The Night of the Iguana* 64.

Chasing Rainbows (s) 30. King of Jazz (s) 30. They Learned about Women (s) 30, etc.

Agfacolor.
German multilayer colour process, widely used in Europe and basically the same as Russian Sovcolor and American Anscocolor (which became Metrocolor). Noted for softness and often lack of sharpness.

Aghayan, Ray (1934–).
Iranian-born costume designer, in America.
Father Goose 64. Do Not Disturb 65. The Glass Bottom Boat 66. Caprice 67. Doctor Dolittle 67. Gaily, Gaily (AAN) 69. Hannie Calder 72. Lady Sings the Blues (AAN) 72. Funny Lady (AAN) 75, etc.

Agnew, Robert (1899–1983).
American leading juvenile of silent pictures. Born in Louisville, Kentucky, he began on the stage and retired soon after the coming of sound to work at Warner Brothers as an assistant director.
The Valley of Doubt 20. The Passion Flower 21. Without Fear 22. The Spanish Dancer 23. Wine of Youth 24. The Great Love 25. She's My Baby 26. The Heart of Salome 27. The Heart of Broadway 28. Extravagance 30. The Naughty Flirt 31. Gold Diggers of 1933 33, etc.

Agostini, Philippe (1910–).
French director. Born in Paris, he was formerly a leading cinematographer of the 40s, who worked with such directors as Bresson, Carné and Ophuls.
AS CINEMATOGRAPHER: Carnet de Bal (co-ph) 37. Les Anges du Pêche 43. Les Dames du Bois de Boulogne 44. Les Portes de la Nuit 46. Pattes Blanches 48. Le Plaisir (co-ph) 49. Rififi 55, etc.
AS DIRECTOR: Le Naif aux 40 Enfants 57. Tu es Pierre 58. Le Dialogue de Carmélites 59. La Soupe aux Poulets 63. La Petite Fille Qui Cherche le Printemps 71, etc.

Agresti, Alejandro (1961–).
Argentinian director and screenwriter, a former cameraman, now based in Holland.
El Hombre que Ganó la Razón 86. Love is a Fat Woman (El Amor es una Mujer Gorda) 88. Secret Wedding (Boda Secreta) 89. City Life (co-d) 89. The Night of the Wild Donkeys (De Nacht de Wilde Ezels) (a, p) 89. Luba 91. How to Survive a Broken Heart (a) 91. Modern Crimes (& a) 92. Just Good Friends 92. Pieces of Love 93. El Acto en Cuestión 93, etc.

Agutter, Jenny (1952–).
British actress who came to leading roles as a teenager.
■ East of Sudan 64. Gates to Paradise 67. Star! 68. ◀ Start Counting 69. *The Railway Children* 70. Walkabout 70. The Snow Goose (TV) 71. A War of Children (TV) 72. Logan's Run 76. The Eagle Has Landed 77. Equus 77. Dominique 78. China Nine Liberty Thirty Seven 78. The Riddle of the Sands 79. Sweet William 79. The Survivor 80. Amy 81. An American Werewolf in London 81. Secret Places 84. Silas Marner (TV) 85. Dark Tower 87. King of the Wind 89. Child's Play 2 90. Darkman 90. Freddie as FR07 (voice) 92.

Ah, Wilderness!
Eugene O'Neill's gentle comedy of growing up in a small American town was produced on Broadway in 1933. In 1935 it was filmed by Clarence Brown, with Eric Linden, Lionel Barrymore, Wallace Beery and Mickey Rooney. In 1947 Rouben Mamoulian remade it as a semi-musical, *Summer Holiday*: in the same roles were Mickey Rooney, Walter Huston, Frank Morgan and Jackie Jenkins.

Aherne, Brian (1902–1986).
Gentle-mannered British leading man of stage and screen; resident from 1933 in Hollywood and New York, where he became the American ideal of the charming Britisher. A child actor who trained under Italia Conti, he was on stage from the age of nine. His first wife was Joan Fontaine.
Autobiography: 1969, *A Proper Job*. Also published a memoir of George Sanders: 1979, *A Dreadful Man*.
■ The Eleventh Commandment 24. King of the Castle 25. The Squire of Long Hadley 26. Safety First 26. A Woman Redeemed 27. *Shooting Stars* 28. Underground 29. The W Plan 30. Madame Guillotine 31. *I Was A Spy* 33. *Song of Songs* 33. What Every Woman Knows 34. The Fountain 34. *The Constant Nymph* 34. Sylvia Scarlett 35. I Live My Life 35. *Beloved Enemy* 36. *The Great Garrick* 37. Merrily We Live 38. Captain Fury 39. *Juarez* (as Emperor Maximilian) (AAN) 39. Vigil in the Night 40. *The Lady In Question* 40. Hired Wife 40. *My Son My Son* 40. The Man Who Lost Himself 41. Skylark 41. Smilin' Through 41. My Sister Eileen 42. Forever and a Day 43. A Night to Remember 43. First Comes Courage 43. What a Woman! 43. The Locket 46. Smart Woman 48. Angel on the Amazon 48. *I Confess* 53. Titanic 53. Prince Valiant 54. A Bullet is Waiting 54. *The Swan* (first comic character role) 56. The Best of Everything 59. Susan Slade 61. *Lancelot and Guinevere* (as King Arthur) 63. The Waltz King 64. The Cavern 65. Rosie 67.

Aherne, Patrick (1901–1970).
Irish light actor, brother of Brian Aherne; in America from 1936. He was married to Renee Houston.
A Daughter in Revolt 25. Huntingtower 27. The Game Chicken 31. Trouble Ahead 36. Green Dolphin Street 47. The Paradine Case 48. Bwana Devil 52. The Court Jester 56, etc.

Ahlberg, Mac (1931–).
Swedish director.
I a Woman 67. The Swedish Fanny Hill 68. The Voyeur 69. I a Woman Part Two 70. Nana 70, etc.

Ahn, Philip (1911–1978).
American actor of Korean parentage, seen in Hollywood films as an assortment of Asiatic types.
The General Died at Dawn 36. Thank You Mr Moto 38. Charlie Chan in Honolulu 38. They Got Me Covered 42. China Sky 45. Rogues' Regiment 48. I was an American Spy 51. Love is a Many Splendored Thing 55. Never So Few 59. Diamond Head 63. Thoroughly Modern Millie 67. The World's Greatest Athlete 73. Voodoo Heartbeat 75, many others.
TV series: Kung Fu 71–73.

Aidman, Charles (1925–1993).
American character actor, mostly on TV. He was narrator of the TV series *The Twilight Zone* 85–87.
The Hour of the Gun 67. Countdown 67. Kotch 72. Dirty Little Billy 72. Amelia Earhart (TV) 76. Twilight's Last Gleaming 77. Zoot Suit 81. Prime Suspect (TV) 81. Uncommon Valor 83, etc.

AIDS,
a deficiency of the immune system caused by infection with HIV (human immunodeficiency virus), became headline news in July 1985 when Rock Hudson, seriously ill in a Paris clinic, issued a statement to the press to the effect that he had 'acquired immune deficiency syndrome'. He died later that year. Since that time many more performers and others involved in showbusiness have died from AIDS – the American magazine

Premiere reported in its February 92 issue that AIDS deaths in Hollywood were 'climbing into the thousands' – and Hollywood personalities have been involved in fund-raising to combat the disease. That concern has so far not resulted in many films on the subject, though Larry Kramer, producer and screenwriter of *Women in Love* and other films, has written a play, *The Normal Heart*, and a book about it, and Oscar Moore, editor of the trade paper *Screen International*, published a novel, *A Matter of Life and Sex*, in which the central character dies of AIDS. The first was a low-budget film, *Parting Glances* 86, directed by Bill Sherwood, who died of AIDS four years later aged 37; it was followed by a mainstream movie, *Longtime Companion* 90; an Oscar-winning documentary, *Common Threads: Stories from the Quilt* 89; a Spanish comedy, *Love in the Time of Hysteria* (*Solo con Tu Pareja*) 92, directed by Alfonso Cuaron, and Israeli director Amos Guttman's *Amazing Grace* 92. Since then, it was been dealt with in *Savage Nights* (*Les Nuits Fauves*) 92, written and directed by its star Cyril Collard, who died of AIDS shortly after completing it; Derek Jarman's *Blue* 93, made shortly before he died of AIDS; *Philadelphia* 93, which won an Oscar for its star, Tom Hanks, but annoyed many activists with its timid treatment of homosexuality; and in the TV film *And the Band Played On* 94. Independent film-makers have treated the subject with greater irreverence, notably in Gregg Araki's *The Living End* 92, and John Greyson's *Zero Patience* 94, the first AIDS musical.

Aiello, Danny (1935–).
American actor.
The Front 76. Fingers 77. Bloodbrothers 78. Fort Apache, the Bronx 81. Once Upon a Time in America 84. The Purple Rose of Cairo 84. The Stuff 85. Man on Fire 87. Moonstruck 87. The Pick-Up Artist 87. Radio Days 87. The January Man 88. White Hot 88. Do the Right Thing (AAN) 89. Harlem Nights 89. Russicum 89. Jacob's Ladder 90. Once Around 90. Hudson Hawk 91. The Closer 91. The Pickle 92. Ruby 92. 29th Street 92. Mistress 92. The Cemetery Club 93. The Pickle 93. Me and the Kid 93. Leon (US: The Professional) (Fr.) 94, etc.

Aimée, Anouk (1932–)
(Françoise Sorya Dreyfus).
Svelte French leading lady who captured many hearts in the days when she was known simply as 'Anouk'. She has subsequently lent her poise to many routine features.
La Maison sous la Mer 47. *Les Amants de Verone* 49. The Golden Salamander (GB) 49. Le Rideau Cramoisi 51. The Man Who Watched Trains Go By (GB) 52. Les Mauvaises Rencontres 55. Contraband Spain (GB) 55. Pot Bouille 56. Montparnasse 19 58. La Tête Contre les Murs 58. Les Dragueurs 59. The Journey (US) 59. La Dolce Vita 60. *Lola* 61. Sodom and Gomorrah 61. Eight and a Half 63. La Fuga 65. *Un Homme et une Femme* (AAN) 66. Justine (US) 69. The Model Shop (US) 69. The Appointment (US) 69. Si C'était à Refaire 76. Mon Premier Amour 78. The Tragedy of a Ridiculous Man 81. General of the Dead Army 83. Success is the Best Revenge 84. Long Live Life 84. A Man and a Woman: 20 Years Later 86. Arrivederci e Grazie 88. La Table Tourante 88. Bethune: The Making of a Hero 90. Il y a des Jours . . . et des Lunes 90. Ruptures 92. Les Marmottes 93. Prêt-à-Porter 94, etc.

Aimos, Raymond (1889–1944).
French general-purpose actor of the 30s; died from war injuries.

Vingt Ans Après 22. Le Quatorze Juillet 32. Le Dernier Millardaire 34. Mayerling 36. Le Golem 36. La Belle Equipe 36. Quai des Brumes 38. De Mayerling à Sarajevo 40. Lumière d'Eté 42. Les Petites du Quai aux Fleurs 43, etc.

Ainley, Henry (1879–1945).
British stage actor in occasional films, a former accountant.

She Stoops to Conquer 14. The Prisoner of Zenda 15. Rupert of Hentzau 15. The Great Adventure 15. The Manxman 16. Quinneys 19. The Prince and the Beggarmaid 21. Sweet Lavender 23. The Good Companions 32. The First Mrs Fraser 32. As You Like It 36, etc.

Ainley, Richard (1910–1967).
British-born actor, son of Henry Ainley.

As You Like It 36. The Frog 37. A Stolen Life 39. Lady with Red Hair 40. The Smiling Ghost 41. White Cargo 42. Above Suspicion 43. Passage to Hong Kong 49, etc.

air balloons,
of the spherical type with a hanging basket, have provided picturesque climaxes in films as diverse as Trottie True, The Wizard of Oz and Charlie Bubbles, while the initial part of the journey in Around the World in Eighty Days was accomplished in a splendidly ornate example of the species, and a dramatically styled version was used in Five Weeks in a Balloon. Balloons were popular for comic gags in silent films, notably Buster Keaton's Balloonatic. The most charming adaptation of the idea was in The Red Balloon, at the end of which a group of toy balloons carried the boy hero off into the sky; and the director of that film next made Stowaway in the Sky, which was about an air balloon over France. Balloons also featured in Those Magnificent Men in Their Flying Machines, Mysterious Island, The Great Bank Robbery, Chitty Chitty Bang Bang, The Great Race, Black Sunday.

Barrage balloons, a familiar sight in the Britain of World War II, seldom featured in films apart from the Crazy Gang's Gasbags; but zeppelins or dirigibles were featured in Dirigible itself, Hell's Angels, Madame Satan, The Assassination Bureau, The Red Tent, Zeppelin, and of course in The Hindenburg.

airplane deaths
among film actors are few, considering the millions of airplane miles travelled annually since the majority of films began in the 50s to be made on location. Grace Moore was killed when a public plane crashed at Copenhagen Airport, and Leslie Howard was lost at sea on a semi-official flight in 1943. (Some say the Nazis shot down his plane in the belief that Churchill was aboard.) Deaths which have resulted from crashes of small private aircraft include those of Carole Lombard, Audie Murphy, Will Rogers and Robert Francis; while Vernon Castle and Phillips Holmes died in planes on active service.

airplanes,
one of the most exciting inventions of the twentieth century, have naturally been a popular source of cinematic thrills. Films about aviation itself began with the newsreel shots of attempts by early birdmen, some of them with tragic results: these have been well preserved in a Robert Youngson one-reeler of the early 50s, This Mechanical Age. In the 20s began the long series of spectacular aerial dramas: Wings, Hell's Angels, Dawn Patrol, Lucky Devils, Devil Dogs of the Air, F.P.I, Wings of the Navy, Men with Wings, Test Pilot, Only Angels Have Wings. British films on aviation

were rare, exceptions being the exciting Q Planes and Korda's ill-fated documentary Conquest of the Air; but 1939 brought a need to show the nation's strength, and this was done superbly in such films as The Lion Has Wings, Squadron Leader X, Target for Tonight, The First of the Few, Coastal Command, Flying Fortress, Journey Together and The Way to the Stars. When America entered the war we were deluged with aerial melodramas, mostly with high-sounding titles and high propagandist content: Eagle Squadron, International Squadron, I Wanted Wings, Winged Victory, A Wing and a Prayer, The Wild Blue Yonder, Bombardier, God Is My Co-Pilot, Flying Tigers, Captains of the Clouds, Dive Bomber, Air Force, Flight Command, Thirty Seconds over Tokyo, and many others. Even Disney weighed in with the instructional Victory Through Air Power.

During the 40s began the still-continuing stream of biographies of aviation pioneers and air aces: They Flew Alone (Amy Johnson), Gallant Journey (John Montgomery), Flight for Freedom (Amelia Earhart), Captain Eddie (Eddie Rickenbacker), The McConnell Story, Reach for the Sky (Douglas Bader), The Dam Busters (Dr Barnes Wallis and Guy Gibson), The Spirit of St Louis (Lindbergh), The One That Got Away (Franz von Werra), Wings of the Eagle (Spig Wead), Von Richthofen and Brown, etc. Fictional additions to this cycle include Ace Eli and Rodger of the Skies and The Great Waldo Pepper.

Post-war air dramas from Hollywood showed a considerable increase in thoughtfulness. The responsibility of power was examined in Command Decision, Twelve O'Clock High, The Beginning or the End, Strategic Air Command and others, while the future of aviation was the subject of such films as On the Threshold of Space, Towards the Unknown and X-15. But there has also been room for spectaculars like Lafayette Escadrille, Bombers B-52, The Longest Day and The Blue Max, for such romantic dramas as Blaze of Noon, Chain Lightning, Tarnished Angels and The Bridges at Toko-Ri, and even for the more routine melodramatics of Sky Commando, Battle Taxi, 633 Squadron, Sky Tiger, Jet Pilot, Flight from Ashiya and The Flight of the Phoenix. Britain too has turned out routine recruiting thrillers like The Red Beret and High Flight, with a nod to civil aviation in Out of the Clouds; against these can be set the earnest probing of The Sound Barrier and The Man in the Sky, the affectionate nostalgia of Angels One Five and Conflict of Wings. Airport and its all-star sequels are in a category of their own, that of aerial multi-drama, inspired by The High and the Mighty, Jet Over the Atlantic and Jetstorm and continuing into the 70s with Skyjacked.

In films where aviation itself is not the main subject, planes can be used for a wide variety of dramatic purposes. In Triumph of the Will Hitler's arrival at Nuremberg was made to seem godlike by clever photography of his plane descending through the clouds. A very different effect was given in The Best Years of Our Lives which began with three war veterans being given a lift home in the nose of a bomber; and the same film, in the scene when Dana Andrews walks through a scrapyard full of the planes he has so recently been flying in the war, produced a ruefully moving sense of waste and futility. Godlike again was Raymond Massey's fleet of futuristic planes in Things to Come; and impeccable trick photography gave memorable punch to a musical, Flying Down to Rio, in which chorus girls apparently performed on the wings of planes in mid-air.

Any list of the most spectacular plane sequences should include Cary Grant being chased through the cornfield in North by Northwest; Claudette Colbert and Ray Milland escaping from Spain in Arise My Love; King Kong being cornered on the

Empire State Building; the plane crashing into the sea in Foreign Correspondent; the climax of Murphy's War, and, of course, the climactic sequences of films already mentioned, such as Hell's Angels, The Blue Max, The Sound Barrier and Dawn Patrol. Comedy flying sequences can be equally thrilling, as shown by George Formby in It's in the Air, Abbott and Costello in Keep 'Em Flying, the Marx Brothers in A Night in Casablanca, Laurel and Hardy in The Flying Deuces, Duggie Wakefield in Spy for a Day, Buddy Hackett and Mickey Rooney in It's a Mad Mad Mad Mad World, Jimmy Edwards in Nearly a Nasty Accident, Pat Boone in Never Put It In Writing, W. C. Fields in Never Give a Sucker an Even Break, Spencer Tracy in State of the Union, Jack Lemmon in The Great Race, Fred MacMurray (flying a Model T) in The Absent-minded Professor, James Stewart in You Gotta Stay Happy, and practically the whole cast of Those Magnificent Men in Their Flying Machines. Air hostesses were featured in Come Fly With Me and Boeing-Boeing.

Plane crashes have been the dramatic starting point of many films including Lost Horizon, Five Came Back, Back from Eternity, Fate Is the Hunter, The Night My Number Came Up, Broken Journey, SOS Pacific, The Flight of the Phoenix, Sands of the Kalahari, Survive!, Hey I'm Alive (TV) and Family Flight (TV). The fear that a plane will crash has also been a potent source of screen melodrama, especially in such films as No Highway, The High and the Mighty, Julie, Zero Hour, Jet Storm, Jet over the Atlantic, The Night My Number Came Up, the Airport series, and Skyjacked, which focus on the emotional reactions of passengers. The proximity of planes to heaven has been useful in fantasies like Here Comes Mr Jordan, A Guy Named Joe, A Matter of Life and Death and The Flight That Disappeared. Finally, plane-building was used as a symbol of power in The Carpetbaggers; and symbols of a more fearsome kind are the atomic bombers which figured so largely in Dr Strangelove and Fail Safe.

In 1980 the airplane crash or near-crash genre, which had been done to death in such TV movies as SST: Disaster in the Sky and Murder on Flight 502, was effectively parodied in Airplane!, which took its thread of plot from Zero Hour and hung on to it every airplane joke that anybody could think of. 1983's Airplane II: The Sequel was far less funny, and just to show that parody doesn't harm the chances of the jut-jawed stuff, along on TV soon after came Starflight: The Plane That Couldn't Land. Firefox dealt with Soviet state-of-the-art fighter planes, with Clint Eastwood having to 'think Russian' in order to fly the one he steals; Top Gun gave us Tom Cruise as an élite naval aviator and was followed by the lower-budget Iron Eagle series of derring-do in the skies, a genre that was mercilessly mocked by Hot Shots!

See also: documentaries; helicopters.

airships
were historically short-lived, and being expensive to reconstruct appeared in few films and never very good ones. Some of the atmosphere can however be gained from Madame Satan, Hell's Angels, The Assassination Bureau, Zeppelin and The Hindenburg.

Aitken, Maria (1945–).
Lanky British comedy actress, popular on TV.

Some Girls Do 69. Mary, Queen of Scots 71. Half Moon Street 87. A Fish Called Wanda 88, etc.

Aitken, Spottiswoode (1869–1933) (Frank Aitken).
Scottish-born character actor, usually as benign old men, in silent films in Hollywood, from the stage. He appeared in several of D. W. Griffith's

films, including the role of Dr Cameron in *The Birth of a Nation*.

The Battle 11. The Avenging Conscience 14. The Birth of a Nation 14. Intolerance 15. Stage Struck 17. Her Kingdom of Dreams 19. Nomads of the North 20. The Unknown Wife 21. Manslaughter 22. The Young Rajah 22. Six Days 23. The Eagle 25. The Goose Woman 25. Roaring Fires 27, many others.

aka.
A 70s abbreviation for 'also known as'.

Aked, Muriel (1887–1955).
British character actress usually seen as comedy spinster or gossip.

A Sister to Assist 'Er 22 and 47. The Mayor's Nest 32. *Rome Express* 32. Friday the Thirteenth 33. Cottage to Let 41. Two Thousand Women 44. The Wicked Lady 45. *The Happiest Days of Your Life* 50. The Story of Gilbert and Sullivan 53, etc.

Akeley, Carl E. (1864–1926).
American taxidermist and photographer, inventor in the early 20s of a tripod camera which first made steady panning possible.

Akerman, Chantal (1950–).
Belgian director and screenwriter who learned her craft in New York in the early 70s.

Saute Ma Ville 68. La Chambre 72. News from Home 76. Dis Moi 80. L'Homme à la Valise 83. The Golden Eighties 86. Seven Women, Seven Sins (co-d) 87. Histoires d'Amérique 89. Night and Day (Nuit et Jour) 91. Window Shopping 92. D'Est 93, etc.

Akins, Claude (1918–1994).
Solidly built American character actor who was usually cast as a western villain until it was realized that he could just as well play a burly middle-aged hero, Wallace Beery-style. In the late 70s he was much in demand as a TV star.

■ From Here to Eternity 53. Bitter Creek 54. The Caine Mutiny 54. The Raid 54. The Human Jungle 54. Down Three Dark Streets 54. Shield for Murder 54. The Sea Chase 55. Battle Stations 56. The Proud and Profane 56. Johnny Concho 56. The Burning Hills 56. The Sharkfighters 56. Hot Summer Night 57. The Kettles on Old Macdonald's Farm 57. The Lonely Man 57. Joe Dakota 57. The Defiant Ones 58. Onionhead 58. Rio Bravo 59. Don't Give Up the Ship 59. *Porgy and Bess* 59. Yellowstone Kelly 59. The Hound Dog Man 59. Comanche Station 60. Inherit the Wind 60. Claudelle Inglish 61. Merrill's Marauders 62. How the West Was Won 62. Black Gold 63. A Distant Trumpet 64. The Killers 64. Ride Beyond Vengeance 64. Return of the Seven 66. Incident at Phantom Hill 66. First to Fight 67. Waterhole Three 67. The Devil's Brigade 68. The Great Bank Robbery 69. Flap 70. A Man Called Sledge 71. The Night Stalker (TV) 71. Skyjacked 72. Battle for the Planet of the Apes 73. In Tandem (TV) 73. Timber Tramps 75. Tentacles 77. Tarantulas: The Deadly Cargo 77. Monster in the Closet 86. Sherlock Holmes: The Incident at Victoria Falls (TV) 91. Falling from Grace 92.

TV series as star: *Movin' On* 74–75. B.J. and the Bear 79. The Misadventures of Sheriff Lobo 79–81. Legmen 84.

Akins, Zoë (1886–1958).
American playwright whose *The Greeks Had a Word for It* was filmed as *Gold Diggers*; *The Old Maid* was later filmed with Bette Davis.

Screenplays include: Eve's Secret 25. Morning Glory 32. Camille 37. Desire Me 47.

Akkad, Moustapha.
Syrian producer and director.

Mohammad, Messenger of God (p, d) 77. Lion of the Desert (p, d) 81. Appointment with Fear 85 (p). Free Ride 86. Halloween 5 (p) 89, etc.

Akst, Albert (c. 1890–1958).
American editor, long at MGM.

The Raven 35. Johnny Eager 42. Meet Me in St Louis 44. Ziegfeld Follies 46. Easter Parade 48. Annie Get Your Gun 50. Royal Wedding 52. The Band Wagon 53. Moonfleet 55. Somebody Up There Likes Me 56, many others.

The Alamo,
originally a cottonwood tree, gave its name to a Franciscan mission in San Antonio, where in 1836 180 Americans were overpowered and slaughtered by 4,000 Mexicans. As those who died included such legendary figures as Jim Bowie and Davy Crockett, the siege of the Alamo has figured in many a film, notably *Man of Conquest* 39, *The Last Command* 55 and *The Alamo* 60; while in *San Antonio* 45, Errol Flynn and Paul Kelly had a non-historic fight in the mission ruins.

Alazraki, Benito (1923–).
Mexican director best known abroad for his 1955 film of Indian life, *Roots*.

Alba, Maria (1905–) (Maria Casajuana).
Spanish actress and dancer, born in Barcelona, who was in American films of the late 20s and 30s.

Girl in Every Port 28. Hell's Heroes 30. Mr Robinson Crusoe 32. Chandu on the Magic Island 34. Return of Chandu 34, etc.

Albee, Edward (1928–).
American playwright whose only significant contribution to cinema was *Who's Afraid of Virginia Woolf?* 66. *A Delicate Balance* however was filmed in 1973.

¶ 'I have a fine sense of the ridiculous but no sense of humour.' – *Quote from Who's Afraid of Virginia Woolf?*

Alberghetti, Anna Maria (1936–).
Italian-American operatic singer who came to films as a teenager and has made occasional appearances.

Here Comes the Groom 51. The Stars Are Singing 53. The Medium 54. The Last Command 55. Ten Thousand Bedrooms 57. Cinderfella 60, etc.

Alberni, Luis (1887–1962).
Spanish-American character actor who played countless small film roles, usually featuring his mangled English.

Santa Fe Trail 30. Svengali 31. The Kid from Spain 32. Topaze 33. Flying Down to Rio 33. Roberta 35. Anthony Adverse 36. The Housekeeper's Daughter 39. That Hamilton Woman 42. Captain Carey USA 49. What Price Glory 52. The Ten Commandments 57, etc.

Albers, Hans (1892–1960).
Leading German actor with broad experience.

Irene d'Or 23. A Midsummer Night's Dream 25. Rasputin 29. The Blue Angel 30. Drei Tage Liebe 31. FP 1 32. Gold 33. Peer Gynt 35. Casanova 36. Baron Munchausen 43. The White Hell of Pitz Palu 53. Der Greifer 58. Kein Engel ist so Rein 60, etc.

Albert, Eddie (1908–) (Eddie Albert Heimberger).
American character actor with radio and stage experience: for nearly forty years he has been playing honest Joes, nice guys and best friends, seldom winning the girl but allowing himself an occasional meaty role out of character.

■ Brother Rat 38. On Your Toes 39. *Four Wives* 39. Brother Rat and a Baby 40. An Angel from Texas 40. My Love Came Back 40. A Dispatch from Reuters 40. Four Mothers 41. The Wagons Roll at Night 41. Out of the Fog 41. Thieves Fall Out 41. The Great Mr Nobody 41. Treat 'Em Rough 42. Eagle Squadron 42. Ladies' Day 43. Lady Bodyguard 43. Bombardier 43. Strange Voyage 45. Rendezvous with Annie 46. The Perfect Marriage 46. *Smash Up* 47. Time out of Mind 47. Hit Parade of 1947 47. The Dude Goes West 48. You Gotta Stay Happy 48. The Fuller Brush Girl 50. Meet Me After the Show 51. You're in the Navy Now 51. Actors and Sin 52. *Carrie* 52. *Roman Holiday* (AAN) 53. The Girl Rush 55. *Oklahoma!* 55. I'll Cry Tomorrow 55. *Attack!* (his most serious role) 56. *The Teahouse of the August Moon* 56. The Sun Also Rises 57. The Joker is Wild 57. The Gun Runners 58. *The Roots of Heaven* 58. *Orders to Kill* (GB) 58. Beloved Infidel 59. The Young Doctors 61. The Two Little Bears 61. Madison Avenue 62. The Longest Day 62. Who's Got the Action? 62. The Party's Over (GB) 63. Miracle of the White Stallions 65. Captain Newman MD 63. Seven Women 65. See the Man Run (TV) 71. Fireball Forward (TV) 72. McQ 72. The Take 72. The Heartbreak Kid (AAN) 72. *The Longest Yard* 74. Escape to Witch Mountain 75. The Devil's Rain 75. Promise Him Anything (TV) 75. Hustle 76. Whiffs 76. Birch Interval 76. Moving Violation 76. The Word (TV) 78. Airport 80 The Concorde 79. Foolin' Around 80. How to Beat the High Cost of Living 80. Take This Job and Shove It 81. Yes Giorgio 82. Yesterday 80. This Time Forever 81. The Act 84. Dreamscape 84. Goliath Awaits (TV) 84. Head Office 85. Stitches 85. In Like Flynn (TV) 85. Turnaround 86. Head Office 86. The Big Picture 88. Brenda Starr 89. Return to Green Acres (TV) 90. The Girl from Mars 91. Brenda Starr 92.

TV series: *Leave It to Larry* 52. *Green Acres* 65–71. *Switch* 75–78. Falcon Crest 86. Beauty and The Beast 89–90.

Albert, Edward (1951–).
American light actor, son of Eddie Albert; his career to date has been somewhat disappointing.

■ The Fool Killer 65. Butterflies Are Free 72. Forty Carats 73. Midway 76. The Domino Principle 77. The Purple Taxi 77. The Greek Tycoon 78. The Word (TV) 78. Silent Victory (TV) 79. The Last Convertible (TV) 79. When Time Ran Out 80. Galaxy of Terror 81. Butterfly 81. The Squeeze 81. Blood Feud (TV) 81. The House Where Evil Dwells 82. Ellie 84. Getting Even 86. Distortions 87. Terminal Entry 87. The Underachievers 88. Fist Fighter 88. The Rescue 88. Mindgames 89. Wild Zone 89. Exiled in America 90. Body Language 92. Shootfighter: Fight to the Death 93. The Ice Runner 93. Guarding Tess 94.

TV series: The Last Convertible 79. The Yellow Rose 83–84. Falcon Crest 86.

Albert, Marvin H.
American screenwriter.

Duel at Diablo 66. Rough Night in Jericho (co-w) 67. Lady in Cement (co-w) 68. A Twist of Sand 68, etc.

Albertson, Frank (1909–1964).
American light leading man, later character actor, in films since 1922 when he began as extra and prop boy.

Prep and Pep 28. Just Imagine 31. A Connecticut Yankee 31. Dangerous Crossroad 33. Alice Adams 35. Fury 36. The Plainsman 37. *Room Service* 38.

Bachelor Mother 39. The Man from Headquarters 40. Man Made Monster 41. Mystery Broadcast 43. Arson Squad 45. The Hucksters 47. The Last Hurrah 58. Bye Bye Birdie 63, many others.

Albertson, Jack (1907–1981).
American character actor who started as a straight man in burlesque.

Miracle on 34th Street 47. Top Banana 54. The Harder They Fall 56. Man of a Thousand Faces 57. The Shaggy Dog 59. Period of Adjustment 62. A Tiger Walks 64. How to Murder Your Wife 65. *The Subject Was Roses* (AA) 68. Justine 69. Rabbit Run 70. *Willy Wonka and the Chocolate Factory* 71. The Poseidon Adventure 72. Pick Up on 101 72. Charlie's Balloon (TV) 78. Dead and Buried 81, etc.

TV series: Ensign O'Toole 62–64. Dr Simon Locke 72. *Chico and the Man* 74–77. Grandpa Goes to Washington 78.

Albertson, Mabel (1901–1982).
American character comedienne, typically cast as nosy neighbour or wise and witty grandma.

Mutiny on the Blackhawk 39. She's Back on Broadway 53. Ransom 56. Forever Darling 56. *The Long Hot Summer* 58. Home Before Dark 58. *The Gazebo* 60. Period of Adjustment 62. *Barefoot in the Park* 67. On a Clear Day You Can See Forever 70. What's Up Doc? 72, etc.

Albicocco, Jean-Gabriel (1936–).
French director with a pictorial eye.
■ The Girl with the Golden Eyes 61. Le Rat d'Amérique 62. *Le Grand Meaulnes* 67. L'Amour au Feminin (part) 68. Le Coeur Fou 70. Le Petit Matin 71.

Albright, Hardie (1903–1975) (Hardy Albrecht).
Underused American leading man of the 30s, of Scottish and Jewish parentage.
■ Young Sinners 31. Hush Money 31. Skyline 31. Heartbreak 31. A Successful Calamity 32. So Big 32. The Purchase Price 32. Jewel Robbery 32. The Crash 32. Three on a Match 32. Cabin in the Cotton 32. This Sporting Age 32. The Match King 32. The Working Man 32. Song of Songs 33. *Three Cornered Moon* 33. The House on 56th Street 33. Nana 34. Crimson Romance 34. The Ninth Guest 34. White Heat 34. Beggar's Holiday 34. The Scarlet Letter 34. Two Heads on a Pillow 34. The Silver Streak 34. Sing Sing Nights 34. Women Must Dress 35. Ladies Love Danger 35. Calm Yourself 35. Champagne for Breakfast 35. Red Salute 35. Granny Get Your Gun 40. Ski Patrol 40. Carolina Moon 40. Flight from Destiny 41. Men of the Timberland 41. Bachelor Daddy 41. Marry the Boss's Daughter 41. The Loves of Edgar Allan Poe 42. Lady in a Jam 42. Pride of the Yankees 42. Army Wives 44. Captain Tugboat Annie 45. The Jade Mask 45. Sunset in Eldorado 45. Angel on My Shoulder 46. Mom and Dad 57.

Albright, Lola (1925–).
Stylish, tough-talking American leading lady; roles for her Stanwyck-like personality were hard to find.

Champion 49. The Good Humour Man 50. Arctic Flight 52. The Tender Trap 56. The Monolith Monsters 57. Seven Guns to Mesa 60. *A Cold Wind in August* 61. Kid Galahad 62. The Love Cage 65. Lord Love a Duck 66. The Way West 67. Where Were You When the Lights Went Out? 68. The Impossible Years 68, etc.

TV series: *Peter Gunn* 58–60.

Albright, Wally (1925–).
Curly-haired American juvenile actor, in films from the age of one, who appeared in Our Gang shorts and quit in 1954 to follow business interests.

Thunder 29. East Lynne 31. The Prodigal 31. Zoo in Budapest 33. The Count of Monte Cristo 34. Black Fury 35. The Woman I Love 37. What Price Vengeance 37. The Wild One 54, etc.

alcoholics
have been familiar screen figures since movies began: Jack Norton and Arthur Housman made a living playing little else, and other comic inebriates include James Stewart in *Harvey*, William Powell in *The Thin Man* and its successors, Wallace Beery in *Ah Wilderness* (followed by Frank Morgan in *Summer Holiday*), Dean Martin in *Rio Bravo* (followed by Robert Mitchum in *El Dorado*), Jackie Gleason in *Papa's Delicate Condition*, and Dudley Moore in *Arthur*.

More serious studies of alcoholism include Fredric March (followed by James Mason) in *A Star is Born*, Bing Crosby in *The Country Girl*, James Cagney and Gig Young in *Come Fill The Cup*, Spencer Tracy in *The People Against O'Hara*, Michael Redgrave in *Time Without Pity*, Claude Rains in *The White Tower*, Ingrid Bergman in *Under Capricorn*, Chester Morris in *Blind Spot*, Ray Milland in *The Lost Weekend* and *Night into Morning*, Jack Lemmon and Lee Remick in *Days of Wine and Roses*, Julie London in *The Great Man*, Van Johnson in *The Bottom of the Bottle*, Henry Fonda in *The Fugitive*, Lars Hanson in *The Atonement of Gosta Berling*, Susan Hayward in *Smash Up* and *I'll Cry Tomorrow*, Burt Lancaster in *Come Back Little Sheba*, Thomas Mitchell (followed by Bing Crosby) in *Stagecoach*, David Farrar in *The Small Back Room*, Bette Davis in *Dangerous*, Jason Robards in *Long Day's Journey Into Night*, Gregory Peck in *Beloved Infidel*, Donald O'Connor in *The Buster Keaton Story*, George Murphy in *Show Business*, Charles Laughton (followed by Robert Newton) in *Vessel of Wrath* (US, *The Beachcomber*), James Dunn in *A Tree Grows in Brooklyn*, Joan Fontaine in *Something to Live For*, Myrna Loy in *From the Terrace*, Maurice Ronet in *Le Feu Follet*, Kenneth More in *Dark Of The Sun*, Frank Sinatra in *The Joker is Wild*, Claire Bloom in *Red Sky At Morning*, Chester Morris in *Blind Spot*, Dick Van Dyke in *The Morning After* (TV), and Meg Ryan in *When a Man Loves a Woman*.

See also: *drunk scenes*.

Alcott, John (1931–1986).
British cinematographer.

A Clockwork Orange 71. Barry Lyndon (AA) 75. March or Die 77. Someone Is Killing the Great Chefs of Europe 78. The Shining 79. Terror Train 80. Fort Apache, the Bronx 81. Greystoke: The Legend of Tarzan, Lord of the Apes 84. Baby 85. No Way Out 87. White Water Summer 87, etc.

Alcott, Louisa M. (1832–1888).
American novelist whose cosy family tales *Little Women* (qv) and *Little Men* have been frequently plundered by movie-makers.

Alda, Alan (1936–).
American leading actor and director, son of Robert Alda.
■ Gone Are the Days 63. The Extraordinary Seaman 68. Paper Lion 68. Catch 22 70. Jenny 70. The Mephisto Waltz 71. To Kill A Clown 72. The Glass House (TV) 72. The Moonshine War 74. Kill Me if You Can (as Caryl Chessman) (TV) 77. *Same Time Next Year* 78. California Suite 78. The Seduction of Joe Tynan (& w) 79. *The Four Seasons* (& w, d) 81. Sweet Liberty (& w, d) 86. A New Life (& w, d) 88. Crimes and Misdemeanors 89. Betsy's Wedding (& w, d) 90. Whispers in the Dark 92. Manhattan Murder Mystery 93. And the Band Played On (TV) 94. White Mile (TV) 94. Canadian Bacon 94.

TV series: *M*A*S*H* 72–82.

¶ I wouldn't live in California. All that sun makes you sterile. – *A.A.*

Alda, Robert (1914–1986) (Alphonso d'Abruzzo).
American actor with radio and stage experience.
Rhapsody in Blue (as George Gershwin) 45. Cloak and Dagger 46. The Beast with Five Fingers 47. Nora Prentiss 47. April Showers 48. Tarzan and the Slave Girl 50. Two Gals and a Guy 51. Beautiful but Dangerous (Italian) 55. Imitation of Life 59. Cleopatra's Daughter 63. The Girl Who Knew Too Much 68. I Will, I Will, for Now 76. Bittersweet Love 76, etc.

TV series: Supertrain 79.

Alden, Mary (1883–1946).
American actress, from the stage, best known for her work with D. W. Griffith.

The Battle of the Sexes 14. The Old Maid 14. Home, Sweet Home 14. Birth of a Nation 15. The Good-Bad Man 16. The Unpardonable Sin 19. Milestone 20. Trust Your Wife 21. Man with Two Mothers 22. Pleasure Mad 23. Babbit 24. Soiled 24. The Plastic Age 25. Brown of Harvard 26. Twin Flappers 27. Ladies of the Mob 28. Sawdust Paradise 28. Girl Overboard 29. Hell's House 32. Strange Interlude 32, etc.

Alden, Norman (1924–).
American character actor.

Operation Bottleneck 60. Man's Favorite Sport 63. The Devil's Brigade 68. Tora Tora Tora 70. Kansas City Bomber 72. Semi-Tough 77, etc.

TV series: Fay 75.

Alderton, John (1940–).
British light leading man, a popular figure in several long-running TV series including *Emergency Ward Ten*, *Please Sir*, *Upstairs Downstairs*, *Thomas and Sarah*, *My Wife Next Door* and *Father's Day*. Married to actress Pauline Collins.

The System 64. Duffy 68. Hannibal Brooks 69. Please Sir 71. Zardoz 74. It Shouldn't Happen to a Vet 76.

Aldo, G. R. (1902–1953) (Aldo Graziati).
Italian cinematographer. He was killed in a car crash while working on *Senso*.

La Chartreuse de Parme 47. La Terra Trema 48. The Last Days of Pompeii 49. *Miracle in Milan* 51. Othello 51. Umberto D 52. Indiscretion 53. La Provinciale 53. Senso 54.

Aldon, Mari (1930–).
American leading lady of the 50s; former ballet dancer.

Distant Drums 51. This Woman Is Dangerous 52. The Barefoot Contessa 54. Summertime 55. The Mad Trapper 72, etc.

Aldredge, Theoni V. (1932–).
Greek costume designer, in America, from the stage.

Girl of the Night 60. No Way to Treat a Lady 68. The Great Gatsby (AA) 74. Eyes of Laura Mars 78. Can't Stop the Music 80. Rich and Famous 81. Annie 82. Ghostbusters 84. Moonstruck 87. We're No Angels 89. Stanley & Iris 90. Other People's Money 91. Milk Money 94, etc.

Aldrich, Robert (1918–1983).
American director who declined from gritty realism to inflated melodrama. His own producer from 1962.
■ Big Leaguer 53. World for Ransom 53. *Apache* 54. *Vera Cruz* 54. *Kiss Me Deadly* (& p) 55. The Big

Knife (& p) 55. Autumn Leaves 56. *Attack!* (& p) 57. Ten Seconds to Hell 59. The Angry Hills 59. The Last Sunset 60. Sodom and Gomorrah (co-d) 63. *Whatever Happened to Baby Jane?* 62. Four For Texas 63. Hush Hush Sweet Charlotte 64. The Flight of the Phoenix 65. *The Dirty Dozen* 66. The Killing of Sister George 68. The Legend of Lylah Clare 69. Too Late the Hero 69. The Grissom Gang 71. Ulzana's Raid 72. Emperor of the North Pole 73. The Longest Yard 75. Hustle 76. Twilight's Last Gleaming 77. The Choirboys 77. The Frisco Kid 79. All the Marbles 81.

¶ A director is a ringmaster, a psychiatrist and a referee. – *R.A.*
His films are invariably troubled by intimations of decadence and disorder. – *Andrew Sarris, 1968*

Aldridge, Michael (1920–1994).
English character actor, with a nice line in suave comedy and aristocratic vagueness.
Bank Holiday Luck 47. Murder in the Cathedral 51. Mouse on the Moon 63. Chimes at Midnight 66. Follow Me (aka The Public Eye) 71. Tinker, Tailor, Soldier, Spy (TV) 80. The Barchester Chronicles (TV) 82. Bullshot 83. Turtle Diary 85. Mussolini – The Untold Story (TV) 85. Shanghai Surprise 86. Clockwise 86, etc.
TV series: The Man in Room 17 65–66. Love for Lydia 77. Charlie 84. Charters and Caldicott 85. Last of the Summer Wine 85–89.

Alea, Tomás Gutiérrez (1928–).
Leading Cuban film director and screenwriter. Born in Havana, he studied law and then went to Rome to study cinema before returning to Cuba where he was one of the founders of ICAIC, the country's film institute set up to create a national cinema following Castro's revolution.
Stories of the Revolution (Historias de la Revolución) 60. Cumbite 64. Death of a Bureaucrat (La Muerte de un Burocrata) 66. Memories of Underdevelopment (Memorias del Subdesarrollo) 68. El Arte del Tobaco 74. The Last Supper (La Última Cena) 76. The Survivors (Los Sobrevivientes) 79. Up to a Point (Hasta Cierto Punto) 83. Letters from the Park (Cartas de la Parque) 88. Strawberry and Chocolate (Fresa y Chocolate) 94, etc.

Aleandro, Norma (1936–).
Argentinian leading actress, now in international films, from the stage and television. She won the best actress award at the Cannes Film Festival for her role in *The Official Story.*
La Muerte en las Calles 52. La Fiaca 68. Guemes, the Land in Arms 71. The Truce (La Tregua) 74. Don't Touch the Girl 76. The Official Story (La Historia Oficial) 85. Gaby – A True Story (US) (AAN) 87. Cousins (US) 89. Dark Holiday (US) (TV) 89. Vital Signs (US) 90. One Man's War (GB) 91. The Tombs (Sp.) 91, etc.

Aleichem, Sholem (1859–1916) (Solomon Rabinovitch).
Russian/Jewish storyteller whose *Tevye the Milkman* was much filmed in Yiddish and finally emerged as *Fiddler on the Roof.*

Alekan, Henri (1909–).
French cinematographer.
Mademoiselle Docteur 37. Bataille du Rail 44. *La Belle et la Bête* 46. Les Maudits 47. *Une Si Jolie Petite Plage* 48. Anna Karenina 48. Juliette ou la Clef des Songes 50. Austerlitz 60. Topkapi 64. Lady L 65. Triple Cross 66. Mayerling 68. Red Sun 71. The Territory 81. La Belle Captive 83. Esther 86.

Wings of Desire (Der Mimmel über Berlin) 87. Jerusalem 89. Bilitis, My Love 91, etc.

Alexander, Ben (1911–1969) (Nicholas Benton Alexander).
American boy actor of silent days; later character man.
The Little Americans 17. Little Orphan Annie 18. Hearts of the World 18. Tangled Threads 19. Family Honor 20. Boy of Mine 23. Penrod and Sam 23. Pampered Youth 25. Scotty of the Scouts 26. All Quiet on the Western Front 30. Are These Our Children? 31. Tom Brown of Culver 33. Stage Mother 33. Flirtation 34. Annapolis Farewell 35. Born to Gamble 35. Splendor 35. Red Lights Ahead 37. Shall We Dance? 37. Western Gold 37. The Leather Pushers 40. Criminals Within 41. Dragnet 54. Man in the Shadow 57, many others.
TV series: *Dragnet* 51–58. The Felony Squad 66–68.

Alexander, Jane (1939–) (Jane Quigley).
American stage actress in occasional films.
■ The Great White Hope (AAN) 70. A Gunfight 71. Welcome Home Johnny Bristol (TV) 71. The New Centurions 72. Miracle on 34th Street (TV) 73. This Is the West That Was (TV) 74. Death Be Not Proud (TV) 75. *All the President's Men* (AAN) 76. *Eleanor and Franklin* (TV) (as Eleanor Roosevelt) 76. The Betsy 78. Kramer versus Kramer (AAN) 79. Brubaker 80. Playing for Time (TV) 80. Night Crossing 82. Testament (AAN) 83. City Heat 84. Malice in Wonderland (TV) (as Hedda Hopper) 85. Sweet Country 86, Blood and Orchids (TV) 86. Square Dance 86. Building Bombs 89. Glory 89. An American Place 89. Stay the Night 92.

¶ I never thought of myself as pretty as a child, and I have tried to bring that awareness to my roles. – *J.A.*
Things come up suddenly these days, but that's all right because I work better under pressure. – *J.A.*

Alexander, Jason (1959–) (Jay Greenspan).
American actor, from juvenile roles on television.
Pretty Woman 89. White Palace 90. I Don't Buy Kisses Anymore 92. Coneheads 93. The Paper 94. North 94. Blankman 94, etc.
TV series: E/R 84–85.

Alexander, Jeff (1910–1989).
American composer.
Westward the Women 51. Escape from Fort Bravo 53. The Tender Trap 55. Gun Glory 57. Ask Any Girl 59. Kid Galahad 61. The Rounders 65. Speedway 68. Dirty Dingus Magee 70. The Sex Symbol (TV) 74. Kate Bliss and the Tickertape Kid (TV) 78. The Sea Gypsies 78, many others.

Alexander, John (1897–1982).
Portly American stage actor with amiable personality.
The Petrified Forest 36. Flowing Gold 41. A Tree Grows in Brooklyn 44. *Arsenic and Old Lace* (as Uncle Teddy) 44. Mr Skeffington 45. The Jolson Story 46. Summer Holiday 48. Fancy Pants (as Theodore Roosevelt) 50. The Marrying Kind 52. The Man in the Net 59. One Foot in Hell 60, etc.

Alexander, Katherine (1901–1981).
American actress specializing in sympathetic second leads.
The Barretts of Wimpole Street 34. The Painted Veil 34. The Dark Angel 36. Double Wedding 37. The Great Man Votes 39. The Hunchback of Notre Dame 39. The Vanishing Virginian 42. The Human

Comedy 42. Kiss and Tell 45. John Loves Mary 49, etc.

Alexander, Richard (1903–1989).
Massive character actor who played villains in many serials and westerns and was also Prince Barin, rightful ruler of Mongo, in the serials *Flash Gordon* 36 and *Flash Gordon's Trip to Mars* 38.

Alexander, Ross (1907–1937).
Budding American leading man of the early 30s: shot himself. He was married to Ann Nagel.
■ The Wiser Sex 32. Flirtation Walk 34. Gentlemen Are Born 34. Loudspeaker Lowdown 34. Social Register 34. Shipmates Forever 35. A Midsummer Night's Dream 35. Captain Blood 35. We're in the Money 35. Going Highbrow 35. Maybe It's Love 35. Brides Are Like That 36. I Married a Doctor 36. Hot Money 36. Here Comes Carter 36. Boulder Dam 36. China Clipper 36. Ready Willing and Able 37.

Alexander, Terence (1923–).
British light leading man of the 50s, often in ineffectual roles; by the 80s he was a popular character support in the TV series *Bergerac.*
The Woman with No Name 51. The Gentle Gunman 52. The Runaway Bus 54. Portrait of Alison 55. The One That Got Away 57. Danger Within 59. The League of Gentlemen 60. The Fast Lady 62. The Long Duel 67. Waterloo 70. Vault of Horror 73. The Internecine Project 74. Ike (TV) 79. That Englishwoman 90, many others.

Alexander the Great (356–322 BC).
A mighty warrior who became king of Macedonia at the age of 20 and quickly overran most of the Mediterranean before he died of fever at the age of 33. He was played by Richard Burton in Robert Rossen's rather stolid 1956 biopic; William Shatner took over in a failed TV pilot of 1963; and 1980 brought forth a mini-series.

Alexandrov, Grigori (1903–1983) (G. Mormonenko).
Distinguished Russian director, former assistant to Eisenstein.
Internationale 32. *Jazz Comedy* 34. *Circus* 36. *Volga-Volga* 38. The Bright Road 40. Spring 47. Glinka 52. From Man to Man 58. Lenin in Poland 61. Before October 65.

Alexieff, Alexandre (1901–1982).
Franco-Russian animator who devised a method of illuminating pins stuck through a screen at various levels to produce a picture. Chief examples are *A Night on a Bare Mountain* 33, and the titles for *The Trial* 62.

Algar, James (1912–).
American writer-director of Disney's *True Life Adventures* and associated productions.
The Living Desert 53. *The Vanishing Prairie* 54. The African Lion 55. White Wilderness 58. Jungle Cat 60. The Legend of Lobo 63. *The Incredible Journey* 63. The Gnome-Mobile 67, etc.

Algonquin Round Table.
A meeting-place in the dining-room of the Algonquin Hotel of New York journalists, columnists, writers and actors during the 20s. They included Franklin P. Adams, Heywood Broun, Robert Benchley, George S. Kaufman, Marc Connelly, Alexander Woollcott, Robert E. Sherwood, Ring Lardner, Dorothy Parker, Ben Hecht, Deems Taylor, Charles MacArthur, Harpo Marx and Tallulah Bankhead. Noted for its wit, reported in newspaper and magazine columns by

many of the participants, it was commemorated in Alan Rudolph's film *Mrs Parker and the Vicious Circle* 94, as well as in two books – *The Vicious Circle* by Margaret Case Harriman (1951) and *The Algonquin Wits* (1968), edited by Robert E. Drennen – and a novel, Grace Atherton's *Black Oxen*, published in 1932.

Among its witticisms:

What is so rare as a Woollcott first edition? asked Alexander Woollcott as he autographed one of his books.

A Woollcott second edition, said Franklin P. Adams. Woollcott also complained:

Everything I like is either illegal, immoral, or fattening.

Robert Benchley remarked:

Let's get out of these wet clothes and into a dry martini.

Dorothy Parker said:

That woman speaks eighteen languages and can't say 'No' in any of them

and, when a guest boasted of the longevity of her marriage by saying 'I've kept him for seven years', replied:

Keep him long enough and he'll come back in style.

After listening to the recitation of a work by a dead poet, Ring Lardner asked:

Did he write that before or after he died?

¶ The Round Table was made up of a motley and nondescript group of people who wanted to eat lunch, and that's about it. – *George S. Kaufman*

The Round Table was also a kind of obstetrics ward and testing and development laboratory for some of the best humor and best humorists the United States has ever produced. – *Scott Meredith*

Algren, Nelson (1909–1981).

American novelist who wrote of life's seamy side. He served as a model for the novelist Lewis Brogan in Simone de Beauvoir's *The Mandarins*.

Books included *The Man with the Golden Arm* and *A Walk on the Wild Side*.

Ali Baba.

The *Arabian Nights* story, of a poor camel-driver who outwits 40 thieves by trailing them to their magic cave which opens to a password, has been a favourite with film-makers. Edison made a version in 1902, William Fox in 1919. In 1944 Jon Hall starred in *Ali Baba and the Forty Thieves*, while in 1952 Tony Curtis was *Son of Ali Baba*. (The 1944 film was remade, with much use of footage from the original, in 1964 as *Sword of Ali Baba*, starring Peter Mann.) Meanwhile in 1954 Fernandel appeared in a French comedy version under Jacques Becker's direction. Eddie Cantor dreamed he was Ali Baba in *Ali Baba Goes to Town* 37, and the character has appeared in many other *Arabian Nights* films. A superior spelling was adopted for *The Adventures of Hajji Baba* 56, in which John Derek played the role.

Ali, Muhammed (1942–) (Cassius Clay).

Black American heavyweight boxing champion, internationally known for his cheerfully boastful manner, for staying too long at the top, and for converting to Islam. Tried playing himself in *The Greatest* 77; also starred in a TV mini-series, *Freedom Road*.

¶ When you're as great as I am, it's hard to be humble. – *M.A.*

Alice in Wonderland.

This Victorian nonsense classic was written by Lewis Carroll (C. L. Dodgson) and published in 1865. Most film versions – and there have been several silent ones – have included material from *Through the Looking Glass*, published in 1871. Since sound there have been two American productions using actors (in 1931 with little-known players and in 1933 with Charlotte Henry and an all-star Paramount cast); a 1950 French version with Carol Marsh and Bunin's puppets; a rather stiff and unimaginative Disney cartoon in 1951; a stolid British live-action version in 1972; and a disturbingly surreal production, using live-action and stop-motion animation, by Jan Svankmajer in 1988. In 1985 EMI brought out Dennis Potter's *Dreamchild*, in which the aged Alice Liddell, played by Coral Browne, goes to New York and is questioned about her relationship with Lewis Carroll.

Alison, Dorothy (1925–1992).

Australian actress resident in Britain.

Mandy 52. Turn the Key Softly 53. The Maggie 54. Reach for the Sky 56. The Long Arm 56. The Scamp 57. Life in Emergency Ward Ten 59. Georgy Girl 66. Pretty Polly 68. Blind Terror 71. The Amazing Mr Blunden 72. A Town Like Alice (TV) 80. A Cry in the Dark 88, etc.

all-star films.

The phrase usually connotes giant musicals of the kind which started in the early days of talkies, when each studio put on an extravaganza displaying the talents of all its contract artistes, often to little effect.

Titles included *Movietone Follies, Paramount on Parade, The Hollywood Revue of 1929* (MGM), *Show of Shows* (Warner), *King of Jazz* (Universal) and *Elstree Calling*. The practice was revived during World War II: *Star Spangled Rhythm* (Paramount), *Thank Your Lucky Stars* (Warner), *Follow the Boys* (Universal), *Hollywood Canteen* (Warner) and *Stage Door Canteen* helped to cheer up the armed forces. Paramount continued into the later 40s with *Variety Girl* and *Duffy's Tavern*, and Warner came up with *It's a Great Feeling* and *Starlift*. *Carnegie Hall* applied the technique to classical music.

Meanwhile dramatic films had found the value of an occasional all-star cast. *Grand Hotel, If I Had a Million, Dinner at Eight* in the early 30s were followed ten years later by *Tales of Manhattan, Forever and a Day* and *Flesh and Fantasy*, while the adoption of particular authors later in the 40s produced all-star episodic films such as Somerset Maugham's *Quartet* and O'Henry's *Full House*. From the 50s, an occasional grand-screen epic would pack itself with stars: *Around the World in Eighty Days, How the West Was Won, The Greatest Story Ever Told, The Longest Day* and *A Bridge Too Far* were perhaps the most significant of these. Robert Altman's film about Hollywood, *The Player*, featured 69 stars, mainly playing themselves.

Allan, Elizabeth (1910–1990).

British leading lady with stage experience; adept at delicate or aristocratic heroines.

Alibi 31. Black Coffee 31. Michael and Mary 32. Nine Till Six 32. The Lodger 33. Java Head 34. *David Copperfield* (US) 34. Mark of the Vampire (US) 35. *A Tale of Two Cities* (US) 36. Camille (US) 36. Michael Strogoff (US) 37. Inquest 38. Saloon Bar 40. The Great Mr Handel 42. Went the Day Well? 42. He Stoops to Conquer 44. No Highway 51. The Heart of the Matter 54. The Brain Machine 55. Grip of the Strangler 58, etc.

Allan, Ted (1916–).

Canadian playwright and screenwriter.

Lies My Father Told Me (AAN) 75. Falling in Love Again (co-w) 80. Love Streams (oa, co-w) 84. Bethune – The Making of a Hero 90, etc.

Alland, William (1916–).

American actor, originally with Orson Welles' Mercury Theatre: played the enquiring reporter in *Citizen Kane* 41. Later became staff producer for Universal-International: *It Came from Outer Space* 53. *This Island Earth* 56. *The Lady Takes a Flyer* 58. *The Rare Breed* 65, etc. Independently produced and directed *Look in Any Window* 61.

Allbritton, Louise (1920–1979).

American leading lady of the 40s, mainly in light comedy.

■ Danger in the Pacific 42. Parachute Nurse 42. Pittsburgh 42. Who Done It? 42. Fired Wife 43. Good Morning Judge 43. It Comes Up Love 43. *Son of Dracula* 43. Bowery to Broadway 44. Follow the Boys 44. Her Primitive Man 44. San Diego I Love You 44. This is the Life 44. Men in Her Diary 45. That Night with You 45. Tangier 46. The Egg and I 47. Don't Trust Your Husband 48. Sitting Pretty 48. Walk a Crooked Mile 48. The Doolins of Oklahoma 49. Felicia (Puerto Rico) 64.

Allégret, Marc (1900–1973).

French director of superior commercial films. Born in Switzerland, he began as a documentary film-maker.

Mam'zelle Nitouche 31. Fanny 32. Lac Aux Dames 34. Les Beaux Yeux 35. Gribouille 37. Orage 38. Entrée des Artistes 38. L'Arlésienne 42. Petrus 46. Blanche Fury (GB) 47. Maria Chapdelaine 50. Blackmailed (GB) 51. Futures Vedettes 55. Lady Chatterley's Lover 55. En Effeuillant La Marguerite 56. Un Drôle de Dimanche 58. L'Abominable Homme des Douanes 62. Le Bal du Comte d'Orgel 69, etc.

Allégret, Yves (1907–1987).

French director, brother of Marc Allégret. He began as an assistant to Jean Renoir and came to notice in the late 40s with thrillers in the *film noir* tradition.

Les Deux Timides 41. Dédée 47. Une Si Jolie Petite Plage 48. Manèges 49. Les Orgueilleux 53. Oasis 54. Germinal 62. Don't Bite, We Love You 76, etc.

Allen, Adrianne (1907–).

British light actress, mostly on stage. Mother of Daniel Massey, ex-wife of Raymond.

Loose Ends 31. Black Coffee 31. The Morals of Marcus 35. The October Man 47. Vote for Huggett 49. The Final Test 53. Meet Mr Malcolm 54, etc.

Allen, Barbara Jo (1905–1974) (also known as Vera Vague).

American comedy actress, well known on radio with Bob Hope.

Village Barn Dance 40. Ice Capades 41. Mrs Wiggs of the Cabbage Patch 42. In Rosie's Room 44. Snafu 45. Square Dance Katy 50. The Opposite Sex 56, etc.

Allen, Chesney (1894–1982).

British light comedian, for many years teamed with Bud Flanagan and the Crazy Gang, from whose more violent antics he stood somewhat aloof. He retired in the 40s for health reasons, but long outlived the other gang members, and in 1982 was still singing and reminiscing on radio.

■ A Fire Has Been Arranged 35. Underneath the Arches 37. Okay for Sound 37. Alf's Button Afloat 38. The Frozen Limits 39. Gasbags 40. We'll Smile Again 42. Theatre Royal 43. Here Comes the Sun 44. Dreaming 44. Life Is a Circus 58. Dunkirk 58.

Allen, Chet (1940–1984).
Child star who sang the title role in the first performance of Menotti's television opera *Amahl and the Night Vistors* 51, and made one film before lapsing into obscurity. Committed suicide.
Meet Me at the Fair 52.

Allen, Corey (1934–).
American supporting actor, specializing in depraved adolescents, who turned director in the 70s, mainly of TV films.
The Mad Magician 54. Night of the Hunter 55. Rebel without a Cause 55. The Shadow on the Window 57. Party Girl 58. Private Property (lead) 60. Sweet Bird of Youth 62. The Chapman Report 62. Thunder and Lightning (d only) 77. Avalanche (d, co-w) 78. Stone (TV) 79. Brass (TV) 85. The Last Fling (TV) 87. Star Trek: The Next Generation (TV) 87. The Ann Jillian Story (TV) 88, etc.

Allen, Dede (1925–).
American editor.
Odds Against Tomorrow 59. The Hustler 61. America America 63. *Bonnie and Clyde* 67. Little Big Man 70. Serpico 73. Dog Day Afternoon (AAN) 75. The Missouri Breaks 76. Slapshot 77. The Wiz 78. Reds (& co-p, AAN) 81. The Breakfast Club 85. The Milagro Beanfield War 88. Let It Ride 89. Henry and June 90. The Addams Family 91, etc.

Allen, Elizabeth (1934–) (Elizabeth Gillease).
American leading lady with stage experience.
From the Terrace 60. Diamond Head 63. Donovan's Reef 63. Cheyenne Autumn 64. Star spangled Girl 71. The Carey Treatment 72, etc.
TV series: Bracken's World 69. The Paul Lynde Show 72.

Allen, Fred (1894–1956) (John F. Sullivan).
Baggy-eyed American radio comedian: very occasional films.
Autobiography: 1954, *Treadmill to Oblivion*.
■ Thanks a Million 35. Sally, Irene and Mary 38. Love Thy Neighbour 41. *It's in the Bag* 45. We're Not Married 52. Full House 53.

¶ My eyes look as though they are peeping over two dirty ping pong balls. – *F.A.*
California's a great place . . . if you happen to be an orange. – *F.A.*
You can count on the thumb of one hand the American who is at once a comedian, a humourist, a wit and a satirist, and his name is Fred Allen. – *James Thurber*

Allen, Gracie (1902/6–1964).
American comedienne who projected a scatterbrained image for 30 years on radio, TV and films, usually with her husband George Burns.
The Big Broadcast 32. College Humor 33. International House 33. Six of a Kind 34. *We're Not Dressing* 34. The Big Broadcast of 1936 35. Here Comes Cookie 35. Love in Bloom 35. The Big Broadcast of 1937 36. College Holiday 36. *A Damsel in Distress* 37. College Swing 38. *The Gracie Allen Murder Case* 39. Honolulu 39. Mr and Mrs North 41. Two Girls and a Sailor 44.

Allen, Henry Wilson 'Heck' (1912–1991).
Prolific writer, under the pseudonyms of Will Henry and Clay Fisher, of western novels, seven of which were filmed. Previously, from 1943–55, he worked for MGM's cartoon unit and wrote the stories for many of Tex Avery's cartoons.
The Tall Men (oa) 55. Santa Fe Passage (oa) 55. Pillars of the Sky (oa) 56. Yellowstone Kelly (oa) 59. Journey to Shiloh (oa) 68. Young Billy Young (oa) 69. Mackenna's Gold (oa) 69.

¶ Being an intellectual is a helluva handicap, in almost anything. It's always been a handicap to me. – *H.A.*

Allen, Hervey (1888–1949).
Popular American novelist whose mammoth *Anthony Adverse*, published in 1933, was filmed three years later.

Allen, Irving (1905–1987).
Polish-American producer. Hollywood experience from 1929.
Avalanche (d) 47. Sixteen Fathoms Deep (d) 50. New Mexico (p) 51. Slaughter Trail (d, p) 51. In Britain from early 50s as co-founder of Warwick Films (Cockleshell Heroes, Zarak, etc.). The Trials of Oscar Wilde 60. The Hellions 61. The Long Ships 64. Genghis Khan 65. The Silencers 66. The Ambushers 67. Hammerhead 68. Cromwell 70, etc.
TV series: Matt Helm 75.

Allen, Irwin (1916–1991).
American writer-producer who began with semi-instructional entertainments and then switched to fantasy and disaster movies.
The Sea Around Us (AAN) 50. The Animal World 56. The Story of Mankind (& d) 57. The Big Circus 59. The Lost World (& d) 61. A Voyage to the Bottom of the Sea (& d) 62. Five Weeks in a Balloon (& d) 63. The Poseidon Adventure 72. The Towering Inferno (& co-d) 74. The Time Travelers (TV) 76. Swarm 78. Hanging by a Thread (TV) 79. Beyond the Poseidon Adventure 79. When Time Ran Out 80, etc.
TV series in similar vein: Voyage to the Bottom of the Sea 64–68. Lost in Space 65–68. Time Tunnel 66–67. Land of the Giants 68–70. The Swiss Family Robinson 75–75, etc.

¶ If I can't blow up the world in the first ten seconds, then the show is a flop. – *I.A.*

Allen, Jay Presson (1922–).
American screenwriter with literary aspirations.
The Prime of Miss Jean Brodie (AAN) 69. Cabaret (AAN) 72. Travels with My Aunt 72. Just Tell Me What You Want 79. Prince of the City (AAN) 81. Deathtrap 82. Lord of the Flies 90, etc.

Allen, Jim (1926–).
English television playwright and screenwriter of working-class life, often for director Ken Loach. A former building worker and miner, he began as a scriptwriter for the television soap opera *Coronation Street*.
The Lump (TV) 67. Days of Hope (TV) 76. The Spongers (TV) 78. United Kingdom (TV) 81. The Gathering Seed (TV) 83. Raining Stones 93. Land and Freedom 95, etc.

Allen, Joan (1956–).
American actress.
All My Sons (TV) 86. Fat Guy Goes Nutzoid 86. Manhunter 86. Peggy Sue Got Married 86. Tucker: The Man and His Dream 88. In Country 89. Without Warning: The James Brady Story (TV) 89, etc.

Allen, Karen (1951–).
American leading lady.
Animal House 78. Manhattan 79. The Wanderers 79. Raiders of the Lost Ark 81. Shoot the Moon 82. Split Image 82. Starman 85. Backfire 87. The Glass Menagerie 87. Scrooged 88. Secret Places of the Heart 89. Exile 89. Sweet Talker 91. King of the Hill 93. Ghost in the Machine 94, etc.

Allen, Lewis (1905–1986).
British director in Hollywood; his career started well but spluttered out.
■ Our Hearts were Young and Gay 44. *The Uninvited* 44. The Unseen 45. Those Endearing Young Charms 46. The Perfect Marriage 46. The Imperfect Lady 46. Desert Fury 47. So Evil My Love 48. Sealed Verdict 48. Chicago Deadline 49. Valentino 51. Appointment with Danger 51. At Sword's Point 52. Suddenly 54. A Bullet For Joey 55. Illegal 56. Another Time Another Place 58. Whirlpool (GB) 59. Decision at Midnight (MRA film) 63.

Allen, Lewis M. (1922–).
American producer with theatrical experience. He is married to screenwriter Jay Presson Allen (qv).
■ The Connection 60. The Balcony 63. Lord of the Flies 64. Fahrenheit 451 66. The Queen 68. Fortune and Men's Eyes 71. Never Cry Wolf 83. On Valentine's Day 86. End of the Line 87. O.C. and Stiggs 87. Swimming to Cambodia 87. Miss Firecracker 89. Lord of the Flies 90.

Allen, Nancy (1950–).
American leading lady, former wife of Brian de Palma.
The Last Detail 73. Carrie 76. 1941 79. Home Movies 79. Dressed to Kill 80. Blowout 81. Strange Invaders 83. The Buddy System 84. Not for Publication 84. The Philadelphia Experiment 84. Robocop 87. Sweet Revenge 87. Poltergeist III 88. Limit Up 89. Robocop 2 90. Robocop 3 93. Acting on Impulse 93. Les Patriotes (Fr.) 94, etc.

Allen, Patrick (1927–).
Lantern-jawed British leading man who after playing assorted villains and heroes in routine films established himself as TV's *Crane*.
1984 55. High Tide at Noon 57. The Long Haul 57–8. Dunkirk 58. Tread Softly Stranger 58. I Was Monty's Double 58. Never Take Sweets from a Stranger 60. The Traitors 62. Captain Clegg 62. The Night of the Generals 66. Night of the Big Heat 67. When Dinosaurs Ruled the Earth 69. Puppet On a Chain 71. Diamonds on Wheels 73. Persecution 74. Hard Times (TV) 78. The Wild Geese 78. The Sea Wolves 80. Who Dares Wins 82. The Thirteenth Day of Christmas (TV) 85, etc.
TV series: Body and Soul 93.

Allen, Rex (1922–).
American singing cowboy, popular on radio, in vaudeville and in second features.
Arizona Cowboy 50. Under Mexicali Stars 50. The Old Overland Trail 53. The Phantom Stallion 53, etc.
TV series: Frontier Doctor 52.

Allen, Sian Barbara (1946–).
American actress of the 70s.
You'll Like My Mother 72. The Family Rico (TV) 72. Scream Pretty Peggy (TV) 73. Billy Two Hats 73. Eric (TV) 75. Smash-Up On Interstate 5 (TV) 76. The Lindbergh Kidnapping Case (TV) 76, etc.

Allen, Steve (1921–).
American radio and TV personality, in occasional films.
Autobiography: 1992, *Hi-Ho Steverino! My Adventures in the Wonderful Wacky World of TV.*
■ Down Memory Lane 49. I'll Get By 51. *The Benny Goodman Story* 56. The Big Circus 59. College Confidential 60. Don't Worry, We'll Think of a Title 66. A Man Called Dagger 67. Warning Shot 67. Now You See It, Now You Don't (TV) 67. Where were You When the Lights Went Out? 68.

The Comic 69. The Sunshine Boys 75. Heartbeat 79. The Ratings Game (TV) 84.

¶ When I can't sleep, I read a book by Steve Allen. – *Oscar Levant*

I'm fond of Steve Allen, but not so much as he is. – *Jack Paar*

Allen, Woody (1935–) (Allen Stewart Konigsberg).

Bespectacled American actor, director and screenwriter, a former night-club comedian of smart one-liners and neurotic imaginings. His second wife was actress Louise Lasser (1966–71), and he has a son by actress Mia Farrow.

Biography: 1991, *Woody Allen* by Eric Lax.

■ What's New Pussycat (& w) 65. *Casino Royale* (& co-w) 67. What's Up Tiger Lily? (& w) 67. Take the Money and Run (& w, d) 69. Don't Drink the Water (w only) 69. *Bananas* (& co-w, d) 71. Everything You Always Wanted to Know About Sex (& w) 72. *Play It Again Sam* (& w) 72. Sleeper (& co-w, d) 73. *Love and Death* (co-w, d) 76. The Front 76. *Annie Hall* (& co-w, d) (AAwd, best picture, AANa) 77. *Interiors* (w, d only) (AANw, d) 78. *Manhattan* (& w, d) (AANw, BFA) 79. Stardust Memories (& w, d) 80. A Midsummer Night's Sex Comedy (& w, d) 82. Zelig (& w, d) 83. Broadway Danny Rose (& w, d) (AAw, AANd) 84. The Purple Rose of Cairo (w, d only) (AAw, BFAw) 85. *Hannah and Her Sisters* (& w, AANd) 86. Radio Days (w, d only) 87. September (w, d only) 87. Another Woman (w, d only) 88. Crimes and Misdemeanors (& w, d) (AANw, d) 89. New York Stories (& w, d) 89. Alice (w, d only) 90. Scenes from a Mall 91. Shadows and Fog (& w, d) 92. Manhattan Murder Mystery (& co-w, d) 93. Bullets over Broadway (wd) 94.

✪ For creating the most individual body of work in American cinema and capturing the stressful pleasures of modern urban living. *Manhattan.*

¶ With me, it's just a genetic dissatisfaction with everything. – *W.A.*

To me, American serious pictures always have one foot in entertainment, and I like more personal drama, though there may not be a market for it. – *W.A.*

I don't want to achieve immortality through my work. I want to achieve it through not dying. – *W.A.*

Most of the time I don't have much fun. The rest of the time I don't have any fun at all. – *W.A.*

I don't believe in an afterlife, but I'm bringing along a change of underwear. – *W.A.*

It's not that I'm afraid to die. I just don't want to be there when it happens. – *W.A.*

If only God would give me a sign. Such as making a large deposit in my name in a Swiss bank. – *W.A.*

Love is the answer, but while you're waiting for the answer, sex raises some pretty good questions. – *W.A.*

Life is divided into the horrible and the miserable. – *W.A.*

Don't knock masturbation: it's sex with someone you love. – *W.A.*

I was suicidal, and would have killed myself, but I was in analysis with a strict Freudian, and if you kill yourself they make you pay for the lessons you miss. – *W.A.*

He has a face that convinces you that God is a cartoonist. – *Jack Kroll*

The only thing Woody Allen has in common with Ingmar Bergman is Sven Nykvist. – *Joe Queenan*

Alley, Kirstie (1955–).
American actress.

Star Trek II 82. Blind Date 83. Champions 83. Runaway 84. North and South (TV) 85. Summer School 87. Shoot to Kill (aka Deadly Pursuit) 87. Look Who's Talking 89. Loverboy 89. Madhouse 90. Sibling Rivalry 90. Look Who's Talking Too 90. Look Who's Talking Now 93. David's Mother (TV) 94, etc.

TV series: Masquerade 83–84. North and South 85. Cheers 87–92.

Allgeier, Sepp (1890–1968).
German cinematographer.

Best-known films include: *Diary of a Lost Girl* 29. *The White Hell of Pitz Palu* 29. *William Tell* 33.

Allgood, Sara (1883–1950).
Irish character actress, long with the Abbey Theatre and from 1940 in Hollywood.

■ *Blackmail* 29. *Juno and the Paycock* 30. The World, the Flesh and the Devil 32. The Fortunate Fool 33. Irish Hearts 34. Lily of Killarney 34. The Passing of the Third Floor Back 35. Riders to the Sea 35. Lazybones 35. Peg of Old Drury 35. It's Love Again 36. Pot Luck 36. Southern Roses 36. *Storm in a Teacup* 37. The Sky's the Limit 37. The Londonderry Air 38. Kathleen Mavourneen 38. *That Hamilton Woman* 41. *How Green Was My Valley* (AAN) 41. Dr Jekyll and Mr Hyde 41. Lydia 41. The War Against Mrs Hadley 42. Roxie Hart 42. This Above All 42. It Happened in Flatbush 42. Life Begins at 8.30 42. City without Men 43. Jane Eyre 44. *The Lodger* 44. *Between Two Worlds* 44. The Keys of the Kingdom 44. The Strange Affair of Uncle Harry 45. Cluny Brown 46. Kitty 46. The Spiral Staircase 46. Mother Wore Tights 47. The Fabulous Dorseys 47. Ivy 47. Mourning Becomes Electra 47. My Wild Irish Rose 47. One Touch of Venus 48. The Man from Texas 48. The Girl from Manhattan 48. The Accused 48. Challenge to Lassie 49. Sierra 50. Cheaper by the Dozen 50.

Allied Artists Corporation.
An American production company, more recently involved in TV, which flourished throughout the 30s and 40s as a purveyor of routine crime and comedy second features. Its policy was to put out the poorer product under the banner of its subsidiary, *Monogram Pictures Corporation*; the 'quality' AA product was little in evidence until the 50s, when films like *Love in the Afternoon*, *Friendly Persuasion* and *Al Capone* came from this stable. Meanwhile the Monogram films, boasting such attractions as Frankie Darro, the East Side Kids, the Bowery Boys, Bela Lugosi and Charlie Chan, had their faithful following, and in France attracted highbrow cinéastes to such an extent that Jean-Luc Godard dedicated his film *A Bout de Souffle* to Monogram.

Allio, René (1924–).
Thoughtful French director and screenwriter with sparse output, from the theatre, a former artist and set designer.

■ Les Armes Mortes 60. La Meule 63. *The Shameless Old Lady* 65. L'Une et l'Autre (& w) 67. Pierre et Paul 69. Les Camisards 72. Rude Journée pour la Reine 73. Moi, Pierre Rivière, Ayant Égorgé Ma Mère, Ma soeur, Mon frère 76. Retour à Marseille 80. L'Heure Exquise 81. Le Matelot 512 84.

Allison, May (1895–1989).
Blonde American leading lady in silent pictures, often as a romantic lead opposite Harold Lockwood (qv). In two years, they appeared together in more than 20 films. She retired in the 20s.

A Fool There Was 15. The Masked Rider 16. The River of Romance 16. Big Tremaine 16. The Promise 17. The Hidden Children 17. Peggy Does Her Darndest 19. In for Thirty Days 19. Extravagance 21. Flapper Wives 24. The City 26. The Telephone Girl 27, etc.

Allister, Claud (1891–1970) (Claud Palmer).
British character actor associated with monocled silly-ass roles.

Bulldog Drummond (US) 29. The Private Life of Henry VIII 32. The Private Life of Don Juan 34. Dracula's Daughter (US) 36. Captain Fury (US) 39. Charley's Aunt (US) 41. Kiss the Bride Goodbye 44. Gaiety George 46. Quartet 48. Kiss Me Kate (US) 53, etc.

Allman, Greg (1947–).
American rock musician and actor. He formed The Allman Brothers band in the late 60s and was briefly married to Cher in 1975 – she filed for divorce nine days after the wedding.

Rush Week 91. Rush 91.

Allwyn, Astrid (1909–1978).
Swedish-American leading lady of minor movies in the 30s.

Reputation 32. Only Yesterday 33. Follow the Fleet 36. Dimples 37. Love Affair 39. Mr Smith Goes to Washington 39. Unexpected Uncle 41. No Hands on the Clock 41. Hit Parade of 1943 43, etc.

Allyson, June (1917–) (Ella Geisman).
Husky-voiced American leading lady who could play a tomboy or a tease, and was equally ready with a smile or a tear. Started in 1937 two-reelers, then spent five years as a Broadway chorus dancer before making her Hollywood screen debut. Her cute sexiness kept her popular for fifteen years. Married to Dick Powell 1945–63.

Autobiography: 1982, *June Allyson.*

■ Best Foot Forward 43. Girl Crazy 43. Thousands Cheer 43. Meet the People 44. *Two Girls and a Sailor* 44. *Music For Millions* 44. Her Highness and the Bellboy 45. The Sailor Takes a Wife 45. Two Sisters from Boston 45. Till the Clouds Roll By 46. The Secret Heart 46. High Barbaree 47. Good News 47. The Bride Goes Wild 48. The Three Musketeers (singing 'Thou Swell') 48. *Little Women* (as Jo) 49. The Stratton Story 49. The Reformer and the Redhead 50. Right Cross 50. Too Young to Kiss 51. The Girl in White 52. Battle Circus 53. Remains to be Seen 53. *The Glenn Miller Story* 54. Executive Suite 54. Woman's World 54. Strategic Air Command 55. *The Shrike* (her most dramatic role) 55. The McConnell Story 56. The Opposite Sex 56. You Can't Run Away from It 56. Interlude 57. My Man Godfrey 57. Stranger in My Arms 59. They Only Kill Their Masters 72. See the Man Run (TV) 72. Letters from Three Lovers (TV) 73. Blackout 77. Vegas (TV pilot) 78. The Kid with the Broken Halo (TV) 82.

TV series: *The June Allyson Show* 59–61.

¶ MGM was my mother and father, mentor and guide, my all-powerful and benevolent crutch. When I left them, it was like walking into space. – *J.A.*

In real life I'm a poor dressmaker and a terrible cook – anything in fact but the perfect wife. – *J.A.*

Almendros, Nestor (1930–1992).
Spanish-American cinematographer.

Autobiography: 1984, *A Man with a Camera.*

La Collectioneuse 66. Ma Nuit Chez Maud 68. Claire's Knee 70. L'Enfant Sauvage 69. Two English Girls 71. Love in the Afternoon 72. Cockfighter 74. The Story of Adèle H 75. Madame Rosa 77. Days *of Heaven* (AA) 78. Going South 78. Love on the Run 79. Kramer vs Kramer 79. The Blue Lagoon 80. The Last Metro 81. Still of the Night 82. Sophie's Choice 82. Vivement Dimanche 83. Pauline at the Beach 83. Places in the Heart 84. Heartburn 86. Nadine 87. New York Stories 89. Billy Bathgate 91, etc.

Almereyda, Michael (1960–).
American experimental film-maker. His *Another Girl Another Planet* was shot using a Fisher-Price Pixel toy video camera.

A Hero of Our Time 85. Twister 89. Another Girl Another Planet 92.

See also: *Pixelvision.*

Almodóvar, Pedro (1951–).
Spanish producer and director of camp comedies. He began as a cartoonist and stage actor with an experimental group.

Laberinto de Pasiones (Labyrinth of Passions) 82. Dark Habits (Entre Tinieblas) 84. What Have I Done to Deserve This? 85. Matador 86. Law of Desire (La Ley del Deseo) 87. *Women on the Verge of a Nervous Breakdown* (Mujeres al Borde de un Ataque de Nervios) 88. Tie Me Up! Tie Me Down! (¡Atame!) 90. High Heels (Tacones Lejanos) 91. Kika 93. Acción Mutante (p) 93, etc.

¶ Absolutely all of my life is in my films. The way in which I do my autobiography is never direct. I am behind, in the shadow, of everything. – *P.A.*

I am a good confessor. I think you need to be, to be a good director. – *P.A.*

I am very worried about what's happening on Spanish television, with so much reality-based programming. There's so much interest in rapists and murderers that soon they'll have to get agents. – *P.A.*

Almond, Paul (1931–).
Canadian director, from TV.
■ Isabel 68. Act of the Heart 70. The Journey 72. Final Assignment 81. Up and Down 83. Captive Hearts 87. The Dance Goes On 92.

Alonso, Maria Conchita (1956–).
Cuban-born leading actress, in America from the mid-80s.

Moscow on the Hudson 84. Fear City 85. A Fine Mess 86. Touch and Go 86. Blood Ties 87. Extreme Prejudice 87. The Running Man 87. Colors 88. Vampire's Kiss 88. Predator 2 90. McBain 91, etc.

Alonzo, John A. (1934–).
Mexican-American cinematographer.
Bloody Mama 70. *Vanishing Point* 71. Sounder 72. Lady Sings the Blues 72. Hit! 73. The Naked Ape 73. Conrack 74. Chinatown 74. Once Is Not Enough 75. The Fortune 75. *Farewell My Lovely* 75. The Bad News Bears 76. Black Sunday 77. Close Encounters of the Third Kind (co-ph) 77. F.M. (d) 78. Norma Rae 79. Tom Horn 80. Black Roads 81. Zorro the Gay Blade 81. Blue Thunder 83. Cross Creek 83. Scarface 83. Runaway 84. Out of Control 85. Nothing in Common 86. Overboard 87. Real Men 87. Steel Magnolias 89. The Guardian 90. Internal Affairs 90. Navy SEALS 90. Housesitter 92. The Meteor Man 93. Clifford 94, etc.

Alper, Murray (1904–).
American small-part character actor often seen as cab driver, soldier, etc.

The Royal Family of Broadway 30. The Girl Habit 31. Seven Keys to Baldpate 35. Winterset 36. Cocoanut Grove 38. The Roaring Twenties 39. Black Friday 40. The Maltese Falcon 41. The Big

Shot 42. Mug Town 43. Wing and a Prayer 44. Angel on My shoulder 46. Sleep My Love 48. Lost Continent 51. Devil's Canyon 53. Tanganyika 54. Calypso Joe 57. The Leech Woman 60. The Nutty Professor 63. The Outlaws is Coming 65, many others.

Alperson, Edward L. (1896–1969).
American independent producer, mainly of hokum pictures; former film salesman.

Black Beauty 47. Dakota Lil 50. Invaders from Mars 53. New Faces 54. The Magnificient Matador 56. I Mobster 59. September Storm 60, many others.

Alpert, Hollis (1916–).
American critic.
Books include *The Dreams and the Dreamers* 62; *The Barrymores* 64.

'also known as':
see *aka*.

Alt, Carol (1960–).
American actress and model.
Portfolio 88. Bye Bye Baby (It.) 89. My First Forty Years (It.) 89. My Wonderful Life 90. A Family Matter (aka Vendetta) (TV) 91. Ring of Steel 93, etc.

Altman, Robert (1925–).
American director who had a big commercial success with *M*A*S*H.* He followed with some successful large-scale ensemble works, but dwindling commercial success led him to small-scale films, often adaptations of stage plays. He made a triumphant return to critical and some commercial success in 92 with *The Player,* a satire on Hollywood.

■ The Delinquents (& wp) 55. The James Dean Story (co-d & p) 57. Nightmare in Chicago 64. Countdown 68. That Cold Day in the Park 68. *M*A*S*H* (AAN) 70. Brewster McCloud 71. McCabe and Mrs Miller 71. Images 72. The Long Goodbye 72. Thieves Like Us 73. California Split 74. *Nashville* (AAN) 75. Buffalo Bill and the Indians 76. The Late Show (p only) 77. Welcome to L.A. (p only) 78. 3 Women (& wp) 78. *A Wedding* (& co-w, p) 78. Remember My Name (p only) 78. Quintet (& co-w, p) 78. A Perfect Couple (& co-w, p) 79. Rich Kids (p only) 79. Health (& co-w, p) 79. Popeye 80. Come Back to the Five and Dime, Jimmy Dean, Jimmy Dean 82. Streamers 83. Secret Honor 84. Fool for Love 85. Beyond Therapy 87. O.C. and Stiggs 87. Aria (co-d) 87. Vincent and Theo 90. *The Player* 92. *Short Cuts* (AAN) 93. Mrs Parker and the Vicious Circle (p) 94. Prêt-à-Porter (aka Ready-to-Wear) (co-w, d) 94.

¶ Film-making is a chance to live many lifetimes. – *R.A.*

What is a cult? It just means not enough people to make a minority. – *R.A.*

The majors don't want to make the same pictures I do, and I'm too old to change. – *R.A. 1986*

It's very hard to find anyone with any decency in the business. They all hide behind the corporate structure. They're like landlords who kick people out of tenement buildings. There's no compassion, and there's certainly no interest in the arts. – *R.A.*

Alton, John (1901–).
Hungarian-born cinematographer, in Hollywood from 1924. Noted for the quickness of his work and a distinctive, dramatic chiaroscuro approach, influenced by Rembrandt, that helped define *film*

noir, he retired at the peak of his career. He won an Oscar for his colour work, shooting the ballet sequence in *An American in Paris* 51. He wrote the first text-book on cinematography, *Painting with Light.*

Courageous Dr Christian 40. Atlantic City 44. T-Men 47. He Walked by Night 48. The Black Book 49. Father of the Bride 50. *An American in Paris* (AA) 51. The People Against O'Hara 51. Battle Circus 53. The Big Combo 55. Tea and Sympathy 56. The Teahouse of the August Moon 56. The Brothers Karamazov 58. Elmer Gantry 60, etc.

¶ I stopped because I wanted to live. That was no life, to work at the studio, get up at six every morning and fight the producers. I had enough. I looked at my bank book and I said, 'That's it!' – *J.A.*

He gave you quality and suggestions like no other cameraman that I ever worked with, and I've worked with the best of them. – *Joseph H. Lewis*

He recognised that shadows were just as important as the light. – *Bernard Vorhaus*

Alton was not afraid of the dark. – *Todd McCarthy*

Alton, Robert (1897–1957) (Robert Alton Hart).
American director, mainly of musical sequences:
Strike Me Pink 36. Showboat 51. There's No Business Like Show Business 55, many others. Directed features: Merton of the Movies 47. Pagan Love Song 50.

Alvarado, Don (1900–1967) (José Paige).
American 'Latin lover' of the 20s; later appeared in character roles.

The Loves of Carmen 26. Drums of Love 27. The Battle of the Sexes 28. The Bridge of San Luis Rey 29. Rio Rita 29. Morning Glory 33. The Devil Is a Woman 35. The Big Steal 49, etc.

Alvarado, Trini (1967–).
American actress.
Times Square 80. Sweet Lorraine 87. Satisfaction 88. The Chair (aka The Hot Seat) 89. Stella 90. American Blue Note 90. American Friends 91. The Babe 92. Little Women 94, etc.

Alves, Joe (1938–).
American production designer.
■ Winning 69. Pufnstuf 70. Sugarland Express 74. Jaws 75. Close Encounters of the Third Kind (AAN) 77. Jaws II 78. Escape from New York 81. Jaws 3-D (& d) 83. Starman 84. Everybody's All-American 88. Freejack 92. Geronimo: An American Legend 93.

Alwyn, William (1905–1985).
Prolific British composer who progressed from documentary scoring to fictional narrative.

Fires Were Started 42. World of Plenty 43. The Way Ahead 44. *The True Glory* 45. The Rake's Progress 45. Odd Man Out 46. Captain Boycott 47. *The Fallen Idol* 48. The History of Mr Polly 49. The Magic Box 51. The Card 52. The Crimson Pirate 53. The Million Pound Note 54. The Ship That Died of Shame 55. Geordie 55. Manuela 57. Carve Her Name With Pride 58. A Night to Remember 58. The Swiss Family Robinson 60. The Running Man 63, etc.

Alyn, Kirk (1910–).
American leading man, chiefly remembered for playing Superman in the 1948 serial version. Other roles in Lucky Jordan 42. Sweet Genevieve 47. Radar Patrol vs Spy King (serial) 50. Scalps 82, etc.

Amadori, Luis Cesar (1903–1977).
Prolific Argentinian director, dramatist and
composer, a former journalist and music critic. Born
in Italy, he moved to Argentina as a child and was
also a theatrical producer before beginning to direct
films in his mid-30s. He made more than 60 and
worked in Spain for a decade from 1958,
following the overthrow of Perón.

Puerto Nuevo (co-d) 36. Napoleon 41. Carmen
43. Mosquita Muerta 46. Albéniz 47. Don Juan
Tenorio 49. Nacha Regules 50. El Gritto Sagrado
54. Amor Prohibido 58. Mi Último Tango 60.
Como Dos Gotas de Agua 63. Cristina Guzmán 68.
Amor en el Aire 68, etc.

Amann, Betty (1907–1990).
Leading actress, born in Bavaria of American
parents, who trained for the stage in America,
began her career in German films, and worked in
England in the 30s before going to Hollywood in
1939 to appear in a few minor films.

Temptation 29. The Perfect Lady 31. Rich and
Strange 31. Strictly Business 32. Pyjamas
Preferred 32. Daughter of Today 33. McGlusky the
Sea Rover 35. In Old Mexico 39. Nancy Drew –
Reporter 39. Isle of Forgotten Sins 44, etc.

Amaral, Suzana (1933–).
Brazilian director, from television.
Hour of the Star (A Hora dele Estrela) 85.

Amateau, Rod (1923–).
American radio writer who in the early 50s briefly
became a film director and then turned his attention
to half-hour comedy TV films, of which he has
since made many hundreds.

The Rebel 51. Monsoon 52. Pussycat Pussycat I
Love You 70. The Statue 70. Where Does It Hurt?
(& co-p, co-w) 72. Drive in 76. Loveliness 84. The
Garbage Pail Kids Movie 87, etc.

Amato, Giuseppe (1899–1964) (Giuseppe
Vasaturo).
Italian producer.
Four Steps in the Clouds (& w) 42. Open City
45. Shoe Shine 46. Bicycle Thieves 49. Umberto
D 52. Don Camillo 52. La Dolce Vita 59, many
others.

Ambler, Eric (1909–).
Popular British novelist (works filmed include The
Mask of Dimitrios, Journey into Fear, Background to
Danger, Hotel Reserve, The Light of Day).
Also screenwriter: The Way Ahead 44. The
October Man 47. The Magic Box 51. The Card 52.
The Cruel Sea (AAN) 54. A Night to Remember
57. The Wreck of the Mary Deare 59, etc.

Ambler, Joss (1900–1959).
British character actor, often seen as heavy father
or police inspector.
Captain's Orders 37. Meet Mr Penny 38. Come
On George 39. Contraband 40. Penn of
Pennsylvania 41. The Big Blockade 42. The Next
of Kin 42. The Silver Fleet 43. Candles at Nine 44.
The Agitator 45. The Years Between 46. Mine Own
Executioner 47. Who Goes There 52. Miss Tulip
Stays the Night 55. The Long Arm 56. Soho
Incident 56, many others.

Ambrose (1896–1971).
British bandleader of the 30s and later.
■ Soft Lights and Sweet Music 36. Kicking the
Moon Around 38.

Ameche, Don (1908–1993) (Dominic Felix Amici).
American leading man with stage and radio
experience. A pleasant light hero of mainly trivial

films, he returned to Broadway in the 60s and
became popular on TV as a circus ringmaster. His
film career revived with Trading Places.
■ Sins of Man 36. Romona 36. Ladies in Love 36.
One in a Million 37. Love is News 37. Fifty Roads
to Town 37. You Can't Have Everything 37. Love
Under Fire 37. In Old Chicago 38. Happy Landing
38. Josette 38. Alexander's Ragtime Band 38.
Gateway 38. The Three Musketeers (musical
version; as D'Artagnan) 39. Midnight 39. The Story
of Alexander Graham Bell (which started a long-
standing joke about Ameche inventing the
telephone) 39. Hollywood Cavalcade 39. Swanee
River (as Stephen Foster) 39. Lillian Russell 40.
Four Sons 40. Down Argentine Way 40. That Night
in Rio (dual role) 41. Moon Over Miami 41. Kiss
the Boys Goodbye 41. The Feminine Touch 41.
Confirm or Deny 41. The Magnificent Dope 42.
Girl Trouble 43. Heaven Can Wait (under Lubitsch,
his best acting performance) 43. Happy Land 43.
Something to Shout About 43. Wing and a Prayer
44. Greenwich Village 44. It's In the Bag 45. Guest
Wife 45. So Goes My Love 46. That's My Man
47. Sleep My Love 48. Slightly French 49.
Phantom Caravan 54. Fire One 55. A Fever in the
Blood 61. Rings Around the World 66. Picture
Mommy Dead 66. Shadow Over Elveron (TV) 68.
Suppose They Gave a War and Nobody Came 70.
The Boatniks 70. Gidget Gets Married (TV) 71.
Trading Places 83. Cocoon (AA) 84. A Masterpiece
of Murder (TV) 85. Bigfoot and the Hendersons
87. Cocoon: The Return 88. Coming to America
88. Things Change 88. Oscar 91. Folks! 92. Sunstroke
92. Corrina, Corrina 94.

Amelio, Gianni (1945–).
Italian director.
La Fine del Gioco (TV) 70. Colpire al Cuore 82.
I Ragazzi di Via Panisperna 88. Open Doors 90.
Stolen Children (Il Ladro di Bambini) 92. Lamerica
94, etc.

The American Cinema,
by Andrew Sarris. An influential book, first
published 1968 (in paperback). Sarris lists every
American director he can think of, and ranks him
and his films in one of eleven categories: Pantheon
Directors; The Far Side of Paradise; Expressive
Esoterica; Fringe Benefits; Less Than Meets the
Eye; Lightly Likeable; Strained Seriousness;
Oddities, One-Shots and Newcomers; Subjects for
Further Research; Make Way for the Clowns; and
Miscellany.

The American Civil War,
despite the peaks of The Birth of a Nation and Gone
with the Wind, was long thought to be an
uncommercial subject for film-makers, and
certainly this was confirmed by the cool reception
of The General, So Red the Rose, and The Red Badge
of Courage, among others: the cry 'Fort Sumter has
been fired upon' became a guaranteed laugh with
any audience. Many westerns considered the
after-effects of the war, but the conflict itself was
dealt with only occasionally, perhaps because of
budget problems. Drums in the Deep South, Alvarez
Kelly, Prince of Players, Prisoner of Shark Island, Escape
from Fort Bravo, The Outlaw Josey Wales and The Good
the Bad and the Ugly were among those to touch
on the subject, while Shenandoah dealt thoroughly
with the resulting problems for one family. In the
80s, television took up the subject with vigour but
no style, in such mini-series as Beulah Land, The
Blue and the Gray, and North and South, the story
having been previously told in such longer serials
as The Americans and Centennial. In 89, the Oscar-
winning Glory dealt with the first black soldiers
recruited to fight under a young white officer.

Gettysburg, 94, dealt with the war's decisive battle
in a film originally made for television which ran
for 4½ hours.

American Film Institute.
Government-sponsored body rather belatedly
founded in 1967. Based in Washington, its
comprehensive catalogue will provide full detail
on every American film ever made. Its first director
was George Stevens Jnr.

American International Pictures.
Independent production company founded in
1955 by Samuel Z. Arkoff and James H. Nicholson
(both qv). After a profitable splurge of Z pictures
churned out mainly by Roger Corman the
company began to set its sights on the big time. In
1980 the ailing company was taken over by
Filmways, which in 1982 was in its turn taken
over by Orion.

The American Revolution.
Because the subject means no sale in several
international markets, this has not been a popular
subject with film-makers. D. W. Griffith's America
in 1924 was the most thoroughgoing
reconstruction. A year later, Janice Meredith
covered some of the same ground. Alexander
Hamilton (31) starred George Arliss and had Alan
Mowbray as George Washington. Walt Disney's
Johnny Tremain showed revolutionary figures
through the eyes of an apprentice silversmith. John
Paul Jones, the sailor patriot, was played in 1959
by Robert Stack in the film of the same name. In
1959 Bernard Shaw's The Devil's Disciple was filmed
with Burt Lancaster, Kirk Douglas and Laurence
Olivier. Lafayette (1962) showed the war from the
viewpoint of the French soldiers sent to assist. 1776
(72) is a musical version from the Broadway stage
with Howard da Silva as Ben Franklin. In the mid-
70s public broadcasting viewed the revolutionary
years through a serial drama, The Adams Chronicles.
1984 brought an 8-hour mini-series with Barry
Bostwick as George Washington.

Ames, Adrienne (1909–1947) (Adrienne Ruth
McClure).
American light leading lady of the 30s.
Girls About Town 31. Husband's Holiday 32. A
Bedtime Story 33. You're Telling Me 34. Woman
Wanted 35. City Girl 38. Panama Patrol 39, etc.

Ames, Leon (1903–1993) (Leon Wycoff).
American character actor, a specialist in harassed
or kindly fathers and suave professional men.
Murders in the Rue Morgue 32. 13 Women 32.
Parachute Jumper 33. The Count of Monte Cristo
34. Reckless 35. Stowaway 36. Charlie Chan on
Broadway 37. Mysterious Mr Moto 38. Code of
the Streets 39. Ellery Queen and the Murder Ring
41. Crime Doctor 43. Meet Me In St Louis 44. Thirty
Seconds Over Tokyo 44. Son of Lassie 45.
Weekend at the Waldorf 45. Yolanda and the Thief
45. Song of the Thin Man 47. A Date with Judy
48. Little Women 49. Battleground 49. Crisis 50.
On Moonlight Bay 51. Let's Do It Again 53. Peyton
Place 57. From the Terrace 60. The Absent-minded
Professor 61. The Monkey's Uncle 65. On a Clear
Day You Can See Forever 70. Hammersmith is Out
72. Just You and Me, Kid 79. Testament 83. Jake
Speed 86. Peggy Sue Got Married 86, many others.
TV series: Life With Father 54. Father of the Bride
61. Mister Ed 60–65.

Ames, Preston (1905–1983).
American production designer, who won
Academy Awards for An American in Paris 51 and
Gigi 58.

Brewster McCloud 70. Lost Horizon 73. Beyond ▪e Poseidon Adventure 79. Oh God Book Two ▪. The Pursuit of D. B. Cooper 81, etc.

▪mes, Ramsay (1924–   ) (Ramsay Philips).
▪nerican leading lady who started as a Universal ▪arlet but didn't make much of a mark.
Ali Baba and the Forty Thieves 44. The ▪ummy's Tomb 44. Calling Dr Death 44. A ▪ave, a WAC and a Marine 44. Alexander the ▪eat 56. The Running Man 63, etc.

▪mfitheatrof, Daniele (1901–1983).
▪ussian composer and arranger, in Hollywood ▪om 1938.
I'll Be Seeing You 43. Letter from an Unknown ▪oman 48. The Lost Moment 48. The Desert Fox ▪. The Naked Jungle 54. The Trial 55. Heller in ▪nk Tights 60. Major Dundee 65, many others.

▪mick, Mädchen (1970–   ).
▪nerican leading actress who gained fame as ▪elly in the TV series Twin Peaks.
Don't Tell Her It's Me 90. Sleepwalkers 92. Twin ▪aks: Fire Walk with Me 92. Dream Lover 94. ▪ve, Cheat & Steal 94.
TV series: Twin Peaks 90.

▪midei, Sergei (1904–   ).
▪alian scriptwriter, associated with neo-realism.
Pietro Micca 38. Rome, Open City (AAN) 45. ▪isa 47. Domenica d'Agosto 50. The Bed (Il ▪tto) 54. General Della Rovere (Il Generale Della ▪vere) 59. La Fuga 64. Fumo di Londri 66. Maigret ▪ Pigalle 67. Why? (Detenuto in Attesa di Giudizio) ▪. Tales of Ordinary Madness (Storie di ▪rdinaria Follia) 81. La Nuit de Varennes 82, etc.

▪miel, Jon (1948–   ).
▪itish director from television.
The Singing Detective (TV) 87. Queen of Hearts ▪. Tune in Tomorrow (aka Aunt Julia and the ▪riptwriter) 90. Sommersby 93, etc.

▪mis, Sir Kingsley (1922–   ).
▪itish light novelist. Films of his books include:
▪cky Jim 57. Only Two Can Play (That Uncertain ▪eling) 62. Take a Girl Like You 70.

▪mis, Martin (1949–   ).
▪iglish novelist, journalist and screenwriter who ▪as briefly a child actor. He is the son of novelist ▪ Kingsley Amis.
A High Wind in Jamaica (a) 65. Saturn 3 (w) ▪. The Rachel Papers (oa) 89.

▪mis, Suzy (1958–   ).
▪merican leading actress.
Fandango 85. Big Town 87. Plain Clothes 88. ▪cket Gibraltar 88. Twister 89. Where the Heart ▪ 90. Rich in Love 92. Watch It 93. The Ballad of ▪ttle Joe 93. Two Small Bodies 93. Blown Away ▪, etc.

▪nnesia
▪s been a favourite theme of the movies, and the ▪e 'Who am I?' long since became immortal. ▪roes and heroines who have suffered ▪emorably from the affliction include Ronald ▪lman in Random Harvest, John Hodiak in ▪mewhere in the Night, Greta Garbo in As You ▪sire Me, George Peppard in The Third Day, Cornell ▪rchers in Istanbul, Gregory Peck in Spellbound ▪d Mirage, Phyllis Calvert in The Woman With No ▪ame, Genevieve Page in The Private Life of Sherlock ▪lmes, Jennifer Jones in Love Letters, Laird Cregar ▪ Hangover Square, William Powell in I Love You ▪ain and Crossroads, Joan Fontaine in The Witches

and James Garner in Mister Buddwing. In While I Live Carol Raye was the archetypal film amnesiac, emerging out of the mist complete with theme tune. In Portrait of Jennie Jennifer Jones played a ghost who forgot she was dead, and the same might be said of the passengers in Outward Bound (remade as Between Two Worlds) and Thunder Rock. The prize for audacity was won by the scriptwriters of The Mummy's Curse, with its dainty modern maiden who managed to forget that she was really a 3000-year-old mummy! Perhaps the cutest twist of all was suffered by Dan Duryea in Black Angel and Boris Karloff in Grip of the Strangler: having spent the film's running time tracking down a murderer, each discovered himself to be the culprit. The theme was taken probably as far as it can go in Clean Slate 94, in which Dana Carvey wakes up each morning unable to remember anything from the day before.
See: psychology.

Amos, John (1940–   ).
American actor.
Sweet Sweetback's Baadasssss Song 71. World's Greatest Athlete 73. Let's Do It Again 75. Future Cop 76. Willa (TV) 79. To Elvis, with Love (aka Touched by Love) 80. Beastmaster 82. American Flyers 85. Coming to America 88. Lock Up 89. Die Hard 2 90, etc.
TV series: The Mary Tyler Moore Show 70–73. Maude 73–74. Good Times 74–76. Roots 77. Hunter 84–85.

Amos 'n' Andy.
The original blackface double act, immensely popular for many years on American radio, consisted of Freeman F. Gosden (1899–1982) and Charles Correll (1890–1972). They made one film in 1932, Check and Double Check.

Amram, David (1933–   ).
American composer.
Pull My Daisy 57. The Young Savages 60. Splendor in the Grass 61. The Manchurian Candidate 62. The Arrangement 69, etc.

Amy, George J. (1903–1986).
American editor.
The Gorilla 30. Underworld 31. Doctor X 32. Footlight Parade 33. The Mystery of the Wax Museum 33. Dames 34. Lady Killer 34. Captain Blood 35. The Charge of the Light Brigade 36. Green Pastures 36. Dodge City 39. The Letter 40. The Sea Hawk 40. The Sea Wolf 41. Yankee Doodle Dandy 42. Air Force 43. Confidential Agent 45. Three Strangers 46. Life with Father 47. The Sound of Fury 50. Clash by Night 52. A Lion is in the Streets 53, many others.

Amyes, Julian (1917–1992).
British director who became a TV executive.
A Hill in Korea 56. Miracle in Soho 56, etc.

anachronisms
are fun to spot, but the ones involving language are easy to defend: ancient Romans may not have used modern slang phrases such as 'nuts to you', but nor did they speak in English anyway. Rarely indeed do the studios let through such gaffes as the extra who wore a wristwatch in The Viking Queen, or the TV aerials in 'Victorian' London in The Wrong Box. Mistakes we did enjoy include the use of dynamite in Tap Roots, which was set in 1860 (dynamite was not invented until 1867); the death of Laird Cregar by Tower Bridge in The Lodger, set several years before Tower

Bridge was built; and the modern lounge suits sported by Colin Clive in James Whale's Frankenstein films, otherwise apparently set in nineteenth-century Europe. Even TV movies are not immune: The Triangle Factory Fire Scandal includes a Chaplin movie visit but is set in 1909 before Chaplin made a film. But then, even Shakespeare put a striking clock in Julius Caesar.
See: boo-boos.

anaglyph.
A simple system for making three-dimensional films. The two slightly differing images are printed in different colours, usually red and green, and viewed through similarly coloured lenses to sort them out into a single image. (The alternative is to use polaroid, which distinguishes the two images through lenses invisibly stripped in different directions.)

anamorphic lens.
One which, in a camera, 'squeezes' a wide picture on to standard film; in a projector, 'unsqueezes' the image to fill a wide screen (usually of a 2.45:1 aspect ratio); e.g. CinemaScope, Panavision, TohoScope, HammerScope, WarnerScope, DyaliScope, which are not essentially different from each other.
See also: aspect ratio.

Anchia, Juan Ruiz:
see Ruiz-Anchia, Juan.

ancient Egypt
has not been a popular stopping place for movie-makers. Several films based on the Bible (qv), notably The Ten Commandments, have stayed awhile, and there were detailed reconstructions in The Egyptian, Land of the Pharaohs, and Kawalerowicz's Pharaoh. Otherwise it has been most frequently seen in flashbacks in The Mummy and its sequels.

Anders, Allison (1954–   ).
American director.
Border Radio (co-d) 88. Gas Food Lodging 92. Mi Vida Loca 93.

Anders, Glenn (1889–1981)
American stage actor who made occasional film appearances, usually sinister.
Laughter 30. By Your Leave 35. Nothing but the Truth 41. The Lady from Shanghai 48. M 51. Behave Yourself 51, etc.

Anders, Luana (1940–   ).
American leading lady of minor movies of the 60s.
Life Begins at Seventeen 58. The Pit and the Pendulum 61. The Young Racers 63. Dementia 13 63. That Cold Day in the Park 68. B.J. Presents 71. When the Legends Die 72. Shampoo 75. The Missouri Breaks 76. Goin' South 78. Personal Best 81. Movers and Shakers 84, etc.

Anders, Merry (1932–   ).
American light leading lady.
Les Misérables 52. Phffft 54. The Dalton Girls 57. Violent Road 58. The Hypnotic Eye 60. 20,000 Eyes 61. House of the Damned 63. Tickle Me 65. Legacy of Blood 71, etc.
TV series: The Stu Erwin Show 54. It's Always Jan 55. How to Marry a Millionaire 58. The Time Travellers 64, etc.

Anders, Rudolph (1895–1987).
German-born character actor who also acted under the names Rudolph Amendt and Robert O.

Davis (1939–44). In Hollywood from the 30s, and often cast as a German agent.

The Fountain 34. I Met Him in Paris 37. Confessions of a Nazi Spy 39. The Great Dictator 40. To Be or Not to Be 42. Watch on the Rhine 43. Escape in the Desert 45. Under Nevada Skies 46. Actors and Sin 51. Phantom from Space 53. She Demons 58. On the Double 61. The Pigeon that Took Rome 62. The Prize 63, etc.

Andersen, Hans Christian (1805–1875).
Danish writer of fairy tales, impersonated by Danny Kaye in Goldwyn's 1952 biopic. Many of his tales were filmed by Disney as *Silly Symphonies*, and one of them was the basis of *The Red Shoes* 48.

Anderson, Barbara (1945–).
American leading lady, chiefly remembered as Ironside's pretty assistant in the TV series.

Visions (TV) 72. Don't Be Afraid of the Dark (TV) 73. Strange Honeymoon (TV) 74. You Lie So Deep My Love (TV) 75. Doctors' Private Lives (TV) 79, etc.

TV series: A Man Called Ironside 67–75.

Anderson, Daphne (1922–) (Daphne Scrutton).
British light actress chiefly associated with the stage.

Trottie True 49. The Beggar's Opera 52. Hobson's Choice 54. A Kid for Two Farthings 55. The Prince and the Showgirl 57. Snowball 60. Captain Clegg 62. The Scarlet Pimpernel (TV) 82.

Anderson, Donna (1938–).
American leading lady.

On the Beach 59. Inherit the Wind 60.

Anderson, Eddie 'Rochester' (1905–1977).
Comedian long associated with Jack Benny on radio and TV. His gravel voice and rolling eyes were familiar in the 30s and 40s, but his amiable stereotype became unpopular in a race-conscious age. As he said in a 1970 TV appearance, when invited to resume his old role of butler, 'Massah Benny, we don' do dat no mo' . . .'

What Price Hollywood 30. Three Men on a Horse 35. *Green Pastures* 36. Jezebel 38. *You Can't Take It With You* 38. *Gone With the Wind* 39. *Topper Returns* 41. Tales of Manhattan 42. The Meanest Man in the World 42. *Cabin In The Sky* (leading role) 43. Broadway Rhythm 44. The Show-Off 46. It's a Mad Mad Mad Mad World 63, many others.

TV series: *The Jack Benny Show* 53–65.

Anderson, Ernest
American character actor.

In This Our Life 42. Three for Bedroom C 52. The Well 52. Whatever Happened to Baby Jane? 62, etc.

Anderson, G. M. ('Bronco Billy') (1882–1971) (Max Aronson).
American silent actor, an unsuccessful vaudeville performer who drifted into films in *The Great Train Robbery* 03. Later co-founded the Essanay company and made nearly four hundred one-reel westerns starring himself. Retired in 1920; reappeared in 1965 in *The Bounty Killer*. Special Academy Award 1957 'for his contribution to the development of motion pictures'.

Anderson, Gerry (1929–).
British puppeteer who via his Century 21 productions made TV series such as *Four Feather Falls, Supercar, Fireball XL5, Captain Scarlet, Joe 90, Thunderbirds*. Less successfully he moved into gimmicky live-action with *UFO* and *Space 1999*,

and into feature films with *Journey to the Far Side of the Sun*.

Anderson, Herbert (1917–1994).
Mild-mannered American actor.

Till We Meet Again 40. The Body Disappears 41. The Male Animal 58. I Bury the Living 68. Sunrise at Campobello 60. Rascal 69, etc.

TV series: *Dennis the Menace* 59–63.

Anderson, James (1921–1969).
American general-purpose supporting actor.

Sergeant York 41. The Great Sinner 49. Donovan's Brain 53. I Married a Monster from Outer Space 57. The Ballad of Cable Hogue 70, many others.

Anderson, Jean (1908–).
British stage and screen actress often cast as sympathetic nurse, tired mother, or spinster aunt.

The Mark of Cain 47. Elizabeth of Ladymead 49. White Corridors 51. The Franchise Affair 51. A Town Like Alice 56. Heart of a Child 57. Robbery Under Arms 57. Solomon and Sheba 59. Half a Sixpence 67. The Night Digger 71. The Lady Vanishes 79. Screamtime 83, many others.

TV series: *The Brothers* 71–76.

Anderson, John (1922–1992).
Tall, thin, pale-eyed American character actor.

The True Story of Lynn Stuart 58. Psycho 60. Ride the High Country 62. The Satan Bug 65. Welcome to Hard Times 69. Soldier Blue 70. The Hancocks (TV) 76. The Lincoln Conspiracy (as Lincoln) 78. The Deerslayer 78. Donner Pass – the Road to Survival (TV) 84. Firehouse 87, etc.

Anderson, John Murray (1886–1954).
Canadian-born director, producer, writer, lyricist and choreographer, mainly for stage revues, a former ballroom dancer and art dealer. Educated at Edinburgh Academy and Lausanne University, he studied at RADA under Sir Herbert Beerbohm-Tree and began writing and staging his own productions in New York from 1919, as well as directing Ziegfeld Follies and musicals in New York and London. In the cinema, his main achievement was devising, co-writing and directing the innovative musical revue *The King of Jazz* 30.

Autobiography: 1954, *On without My Rubbers*.

Lilies of Broadway 31. Bathing Beauty (water ballet) 44. New Faces (deviser) 54, etc.

Anderson, Dame Judith (1898–1992) (Frances Margaret Anderson).
Australian stage actress whose splendidly icy presence made her a hit on Broadway and gave her a long career there. Her occasional movies were seldom notable, but she will be remembered for her inimitable Mrs Danvers in *Rebecca*.

■ Blood Money 33. *Rebecca* (AAN) 40. Forty Little Mothers 40. Kings Row 41. Free and Easy 41. Lady Scarface 41. All Through the Night 42. Edge of Darkness 43. Stage Door Canteen 43. Laura 44. And Then There Were None 45. The Diary of a Chambermaid 46. The Strange Love of Martha Ivers 46. The Specter of the Rose 46. Tycoon 47. The Red House 47. Pursued 47. The Furies 50. Salome 53. The Ten Commandments 56. Cat on a Hot Tin Roof 58. Cinderfella 60. Macbeth (TV) 60. Don't Bother to Knock 61. A Man Called Horse 70. Inn of the Damned 74. Star Trek III: The Search for Spock 84.

~In 1984, at the age of 86, she made her TV soap opera debut as the grand dame in Santa Barbara (which happens to be her home town).

¶ I have not myself a very serene temperamen – J.A.

Famous line (*And Then There Were None*): 'Very stupid to kill the servants: now we don't even kno where to find the marmalade.'

Anderson, Kevin (1960–).
American leading actor, from the stage. He was member of Chicago's Steppenwolf Theater.

Risky Business 83. Pink Nights 87. Orphans 8' Miles from Home 88. In Country 89. Orpheus Descending (TV) 91. Liebestraum 91. Sleeping with the Enemy 91. Hoffa 92. The Night We Nev Met 93. Rising Sun 93. The Wrong Man 93, etc.

Anderson, Lindsay (1923–1994).
Maverick British director of stage and screen, a former critic. Born in Bangalore, India, he was educated at Oxford University and co-founded t film magazine *Sequence*. Beginning as a documentary film-maker and a member of the Free Cinema group (qv), he worked as a theatre director before making features. His closest collaboration was with writer David Storey, directing 12 of his plays and his screenplays *This Sporting Life* and *In Celebration* (from Storey's play). He was the author of a book on the work of John Ford.

O Dreamland 53. Thursday's Children 54. Eve Day Except Christmas 57. *This Sporting Life* 63. T White Bus 67. *If* 68. *O Lucky Man* 72. In Celebratii 74. The Old Crowd (TV) 79. Chariots of Fire (as actor) 81. Britannia Hospital 82. The Whales of August 87. Blame It on the Bellboy (as actor) 9. Is That All There Is (TV doc) 92, etc.

¶ He's a prime example of somebody who, one he has created something, tries to support it with a scaffolding of theory. But it's all rubbish: either it's worked or it hasn't. – Tony Richardson

To make a film is to create a world. – L.A.

I suppose I'm the boy who stood on the burni deck whence all but he had fled. The trouble is don't know whether the boy was a hero or a bloody idiot. – L.A.

He was a loner. There was an absoluteness of stance about him, an uncompromising quality which gave him many disciples, but also hundre of enemies. – Karel Reisz

One of the most remarkable creative personalities of our time and, in some respects, possibly the most remarkable. – David Storey

Anderson, Loni (1946–).
Blonde American leading lady.

The Magnificent Magical Magnet of Santa Me (TV) 77. The Jayne Mansfield Story (title role) 80. Sizzle (TV) 81. Stroker Ace 83. All Dogs Go Heaven (voice) 89. Sorry, Wrong Number (TV) 8 Blown Away 90. White Hot: Mysterious Murder of Thelma Todd (TV) 91. Munchie 92, etc.

TV series: WKRP in Cincinatti 78–82. Partner in Crime 84. Easy Street 86–87.

Anderson, Mary (1920–).
American supporting actress.

Gone with the Wind 39. Cheers for Miss Bishop 41. Lifeboat 43. *The Song of Bernadette* 44. Wilson 44. To Each His Own 46. Underworld Story 50. The Jury 53. Dangerous Crossing 53, etc.

Anderson, Max (1914–1959).
British documentary director, with the GPO Film Unit from 1936, later Crown Film Unit. Best known for *The Harvest Shall Come* 41. *Daybreak ii Udi* 48.

Anderson, Maxwell (1888–1959).
American middlebrow playwright, many of whose plays were filmed.

What Price Glory? 27 & 52. *All Quiet on the Western Front* (screenplay) 30. Mary of Scotland 36. Winterset 37. Elizabeth and Essex (Elizabeth the Queen) 39. The Eve of St Mark 44. Key Largo 48. Joan of Arc (Joan of Lorraine) 48. The Wrong Man (orig sp) 56. The Bad Seed 56. Anne of the Thousand Days 70.

Anderson, Michael (1920–).
British director who graduated to the international scene.

■ Waterfront 50. Hell Is Sold Out 51. Night Was Our Friend 52. Will Any Gentleman? 53. House of the Arrow 54. *The Dam Busters* 55. *1984* 55. *Around the World in Eighty Days* (AAN) 56. Yangtse Incident 56. Chase a Crooked Shadow 57. Shake Hands with the Devil 59. The Wreck of the Mary Deare 59. All the Fine Young Cannibals 60. The Naked Edge 61. Flight from Ashiya 62. Wild and Wonderful 63. Operation Crossbow 65. *The Quiller Memorandum* 66. *The Shoes of the Fisherman* 68. Pope Joan 72. Doc Savage 75. Conduct Unbecoming 75. Logan's Run 76. Orca 77. Dominique 78. The Martian Chronicles (TV) 79. Bells 79. Murder by Phone 82. Second Time Lucky 83. Separate Vacations 86. Sword of Gideon (TV) 86. The Jeweller's Shop 88. Millennium 89. Young Catherine (TV) 91. The Sea Wolf (TV) 93.

Anderson, Michael, Jnr (1943–).
British juvenile lead, former child actor, son of director Michael Anderson.

The Moonraker 57. The Sundowners 60. In Search of the Castaways 61. Play It Cool 62. The Greatest Story Ever Told 65. Major Dundee 65. The Sons of Katie Elder 65. The Glory Guys 65. WUSA 69. The Last Movie 71. Sunset Grill 92, etc.

TV series: The Monroes 66.

Anderson, Philip W. (1915–1980).
American editor.

Sayonara 57. Cash McCall 59. The FBI Story 59. Ocean's Eleven 60. The Parent Trap 61. Gypsy 62. A Man Called Horse 70, many others.

Anderson, Richard (1926–).
Thoughtful-looking American supporting actor.

The People Against O'Hara 51. The Story of Three Lovers 53. Escape from Fort Bravo 54. Forbidden Planet 56. Paths of Glory 57. *The Long Hot Summer* 58. Compulsion 59. Seven Days in May 64. Seconds 66. Macho Callahan 70. Doctors' Wives 71. The Honkers 72, etc.

TV series: Mama Rosa 50. Bus Stop 61. Perry Mason 65–66. Dan August 70. Six Million Dollar Man 73–78. Bionic Woman 76–77. Cover Up 84. Dynasty 86–87.

Anderson, Robert (1917–).
American playwright who became an occasional Hollywood scriptwriter.

Tea and Sympathy (from his play) 56. Until They Sail 57. The Nun's Story 59. The Sand Pebbles 66. I Never Sang for My Father (from his play) (AAN) 70.

Anderson, Rona (1926–).
Scottish actress whose film career has been desultory.

Sleeping Car to Trieste 48. Poet's Pub 49. Home to Danger 51. Black Thirteen 54. The Flaw 55. Stock Car 55. Man with a Gun 58. Devils of Darkness 65. The Prime of Miss Jean Brodie 69, etc.

Anderson, Warner (1911–1976).
American supporting actor of solid presence but no outstanding personality.

This Is the Army 43. Destination Tokyo 43. Objective Burma 45. Abbott and Costello in Hollywood 45. Weekend at the Waldorf 45. Bad Bascomb 46. Dark Delusion 47. Song of the Thin Man 47. Command Decision 48. The Doctor and the Girl 49. *Destination Moon* (leading role) 50. The Blue Veil 51. *Detective Story* 51. Only the Valiant 51. A Lion is in the Streets 53. The Caine Mutiny 54. Drum Beat 54. The Blackboard Jungle 55. The Line-Up 58. Armored Command 61. Rio Conchos 64, many others.

TV series: The Doctors 52. The Line-Up 59. *Peyton Place* (as the newspaper editor) 64–68.

Anderson, William M.
Australian editor, in Hollywood.

Don's Party 76. The Getting of Wisdom 77. Money Movers 78. Breaker Morant 80. The Club 80. Gallipoli 81. Puberty Blues 83. The Year of Living Dangerously 83. Tender Mercies 83. Stanley 84. Razorback 84. King David 85. Big Shots 87. 1969 88. Signs of Life 89. Dead Poets Society 89. Old Gringo 89. Robocop 2 90. Green Card 90. At Play in the Fields of the Lord 91. 1492: Conquest of Paradise 92, etc.

Andersson, Bibi (1935–).
Swedish actress who has ventured into international films.

Smiles of a Summer Night 55. *The Seventh Seal* 56. *Wild Strawberries* 57. The Face 58. So Close to Life 60. The Devil's Eye 61. Square of Violence 63. Now About These Women 64. My Sister My Love 66. Duel at Diablo 66. *Persona* 66. A Question of Rape 67. The Story of a Woman 69. *The Kremlin Letter* 69. A Passion 70. The Touch 71. *Cries and Whispers* 72. My Husband, His Mistress and I 76. I Never Promised You a Rose Garden 77. An Enemy of the People 78. Quintet 79. Airport 79 — the Concorde 79. Exposed 83. The Last Summer 84. Poor Butterfly 86. Babette's Feast 87. Fordringsagare 89. The Butterfly's Dream (Il Sogno della Farfalla) (It.) 94. Dreamplay (Dromspel) 94, etc.

Andersson, Harriet (1932–).
Swedish actress, a member of Ingmar Bergman's company.

Summer with Monika 52. *Sawdust and Tinsel* 53. A Lesson in Love 54. *Smiles of a Summer Night* 55. Through a Glass Darkly 62. To Love 64. Now About These Women 64. The Deadly Affair (GB) 66. *Cries and Whispers* 72. The White Wall (Den Vita Väggen) 75. The Sabina 79. Fanny and Alexander 82. Summer Nights (Sommarkvaller Pa Jorden) 87. Blankt Vapen 90, etc.

Andes, Keith (1920–).
American light actor, usually in secondary roles.

The Farmer's Daughter 47. Clash by Night 52. Blackbeard the Pirate 52. Back from Eternity 56. The Girl Most Likely 58. Tora! Tora! Tora! 70. The Ultimate Impostor (TV) 79, etc.

TV series: This Man Dawson 59. Glynis 63. Search 73.

Andresen, Bjorn (1955–).
Swedish actor, best known for playing the beautiful boy in *Death in Venice* 71.

Andress, Ursula (1936–).
Swiss-born glamour star, in international films.

The Loves of Casanova (It.) 54. *Dr No* 62. Four for Texas 63. Fun in Acapulco 64. She 64. Nightmare in the Sun 64. *What's New Pussycat?* 65. Up to His Ears 65. The Tenth Victim 65. Once Before

I Die 66. The Blue Max 66. Casino Royale 67. The Southern Star 69. Perfect Friday 70. Red Sun 71. Five Against Capricorn 72. The Life and Times of Scaramouche 76. Loaded Guns 76. The Fifth Musketeer 77. The Clash of the Titans 81. Mexico in Flames 82. Big Man 88. The Chinatown Murders (TV) 89, etc.

Andrews, Anthony (1948–).
British leading actor who graduated through TV.

QB VII (TV) 74. A War of Children (TV) 74. Take Me High 74. David Copperfield (TV) 74. Percy's Progress 75. Operation Daybreak 76. Les Adolescentes 76. The Scarlet Pimpernel (title role) (TV) 82. Ivanhoe (TV) 82. Sparkling Cyanide (TV) 83. Under the Volcano 84. The Holcroft Covenant 85. The Second Victory 86. Suspicion (TV) 87. The Lighthorsemen 87. Hanna's War 88. The Strange Case of Dr Jekyll and Mr Hyde (TV) 89. Lost in Siberia 91, etc.

TV series: *Danger UXB* 78. *Brideshead Revisited* 81.

Andrews, Dana (1909–1992) (Carver Daniel Andrews).
American leading man who showed promise in a wide variety of 40s roles, but whose somewhat hard and immobile features limited him in middle age.

■ The Westerner 40. Lucky Cisco Kid 40. Sailor's Lady 40. Kit Carson 40. Tobacco Road 41. Belle Starr 41. Swamp Water 41. Ball of Fire 41. Berlin Correspondent 42. Crash Dive 43. *The Ox Bow Incident* 43. North Star 43. *The Purple Heart* 44. Wing and a Prayer 44. Up in Arms 44. Laura 44. State Fair 45. Fallen Angel 45. *A Walk in the Sun* 45. Canyon Passage 46. *The Best Years of Our Lives* 46. Boomerang 47. Night Song 47. Daisy Kenyon 47. The Iron Curtain 48. Deep Waters 48. No Minor Vices 48. Britannia Mews 48. Sword in the Desert 49. *My Foolish Heart* 50. Where the Sidewalk Ends 50. Edge of Doom 50. The Frogmen 50. Sealed Cargo 51. I Want You 51. Assignment Paris 52. Elephant Walk 53. Duel in the Jungle 54. Three Hours to Kill 54. Smoke Signal 55. Strange Lady in Town 55. Comanche 56. While the City Sleeps 56. Beyond a Reasonable Doubt 56. Night of the Demon 57. Spring Reunion 57. Zero Hour 57. The Fearmakers 58. Enchanted Island 58. The Crowded Sky 60. Madison Avenue 62. Crack in the World 65. The Satan Bug 65. In Harm's Way 65. Brainstorm 65. Town Tamer 65. The Loved One 65. Battle of the Bulge 65. Johnny Reno 66. Spy in Your Eye 66. Hot Rods to Hell 67. The Frozen Dead 67. Cobra 67. Ten Million-Dollar Grab 68. The Devil's Brigade 68. The Failing of Raymond (TV) 71. Innocent Bystanders 72. The First 36 Hours of Dr Durrant (TV) 75. Airport 75 75. Take a Hard Ride 75. Shadow in the Streets (TV) 76. The Last Tycoon 76. Ike (TV) 79. Good Guys Wear Black 79. Born Again 79. The Pilot 79. Prince Jack 84.

TV series: Bright Promise (daily soap opera) 71. The American Girls 78. Falcon Crest 82.

Andrews, Edward (1914–1985).
Beaming, bespectacled American character actor who could effortlessly become hearty, hen-pecked or sinister.

■ *The Phenix City Story* 55. The Harder They Fall 56. Tea and Sympathy 56. These Wilder Years 56. *The Unguarded Moment* 56. Tension at Table Rock 56. Three Brave Men 57. Hot Summer Night 57. The Tattered Dress 57. Trooper Hook 57. The Fiend That Walked the West 58. Night of the Quarter Moon 59. *Elmer Gantry* 60. The Absent-Minded Professor 61. The Young Savages 61. Love in a Goldfish Bowl 61. The Young Doctors 61. Advise and Consent 62. Forty Pounds of Trouble 62. Son of Flubber 62. The Thrill of It All 63. A Tiger Walks 64. The Brass Bottle 64. Good Neighbor Sam 64.

Kisses for My President 64. Youngblood Hawke 64. Send Me No Flowers 64. The Man from Galveston 64. Fluffy 65. The Glass Bottom Boat 66. Birds Do It 66. Tora! Tora! Tora! 70. The Trouble with Girls 70. The Million Dollar Duck 71. How to Frame a Figg 71. Now You See Him Now You Don't 72. Avanti 72. Charley and the Angel 73. The Photographer 75. Gremlins 84. Sixteen Candles 84.
TV series: Broadside 64. Supertrain 79.

Andrews, Harry (1911–1989).
Tough-looking British stage and screen actor. Often played sergeant-majors or other no-nonsense characters.

The Red Beret (debut) 52. The Black Knight 54. Helen of Troy 55. *A Hill in Korea* 56. Alexander the Great 56. Moby Dick 56. Saint Joan 57. *Ice Cold in Alex* 58. The Devil's Disciple 59. Solomon and Sheba 59. Circle of Deception 60. The Best of Enemies 62. Lisa 62. 55 Days at Peking 62. Barabbas 62. The Informers 63. The System 64. *The Hill* 65. Sands of the Kalahari 65. The Agony and the Ecstasy 65. Modesty Blaise 66. *The Deadly Affair* 66. The Jokers 67. Danger Route 67. The Charge of the Light Brigade 68. The Night They Raided Minsky's (US) 68. The Seagull 68. A Nice Girl Like Me 69. The Battle of Britain 69. Country Dance 70. Entertaining Mr Sloane 70. Wuthering Heights 70. Burke and Hare 71. Nicholas and Alexandra 71. I Want What I Want 71. The Ruling Class 72. Man of La Mancha 72. Theatre of Blood 73. The Mackintosh Man 74. Man at the Top 74. The Bluebird 76. Equus 77. The Four Feathers (TV) 78. Death on the Nile 78. The Big Sleep 78. Superman 78. SOS Titanic (TV) 80. The Curse of King Tut's Tomb (TV) 80. Hawk the Slayer 80. The Seven Dials Mystery (TV) 83, etc.

Andrews, Julie (1935–) (Julia Wells).
British star of Hollywood films. A singing stage performer from childhood who became the original stage Eliza of *My Fair Lady* but failed to get the film role. She zoomed to international stardom the same year but her refreshingly old-fashioned image seemed to pall rather quickly. She is married to director Blake Edwards.
■ *Mary Poppins* (AA) 64. *The Americanization of Emily* 64. *The Sound of Music* (AAN) 65. Torn Curtain 66. Hawaii 66. *Thoroughly Modern Millie* 67. *Star!* 68. Darling Lili 69. The Tamarind Seed 74. '10' 79. Little Miss Marker 80. S.O.B. 81. Victor/ Victoria (AAN) 82. The Man Who Loved Women 83. Duet for One 86. That's Life 86. Tchin-Tchin 91.

¶ One senses that she is realistic enough to have enjoyed the good times while they lasted, and to fall from grace gracefully. But she may fight. After *The Sound of Music*, Christopher Plummer said that:
Working with her is like being hit over the head with a Valentine's card.
And some anonymous gentleman described her as:
Like a nun with a switchblade.
Moss Hart said:
She has that wonderful British strength that makes you wonder why they lost India.
Miss Andrews does seem to merit the suggestion of steel beneath the velvet. When she accepted her Oscar, which many thought went to her out of sympathy because Warners refused her the film of *My Fair Lady*, her little speech ran:
I'd like to thank all those who made this possible – especially Jack Warner.
Having got to the top by being sweet and old-fashioned, she quickly showed signs of disliking her own image.
I don't want to be thought of as wholesome,

she said in 1966, and promptly proved it by accepting a sexy role. She was also seen wearing a badge which read:
Mary Poppins is a junkie.
But her serene self-confidence may be something of a sham. She once said:
Films are much more my level. On stage I never feel quite enough . . .
One way or another, she achieved, briefly, a worldwide image best expressed by a *Time* magazine interviewer:
She's everybody's tomboy tennis partner and their daughter, their sister, their mum . . . She is Christmas carols in the snow, a companion by the fire, a laughing clown at charades, a girl to read poetry to on a cold winter's night . . .

Andrews, Lois (1924–1968).
American light leading lady.
Dixie Dugan 43. Roger Touhy Gangster 44. The Desert Hawk 50. Meet Me After the Show 51, etc.

Andrews, Robert Hardy (1903–1976).
American screenwriter.
If I Had a Million (oa) 32. Bataan 44. The Cross of Lorraine 44. The Hairy Ape 44. Tarzan Goes to India 62, etc.

The Andrews Sisters: Patty (1920–1992), Maxine (1918–), Laverne (1915–1967).
American close harmony singing group, popular in light musicals of the 40s.
■ Argentine Nights 40. In The Navy 41. Buck Privates 41. Hold That Ghost 41. Give Out Sisters 42. Private Buckaroo 42. What's Cookin'? 42. Always a Bridesmaid 43. How's About It? 43. Follow the Boys 44. Hollywood Canteen 44. Moonlight and Cactus 44. Swingtime Johnny 44. Her Lucky Night 45. Make Mine Music (voices) 46. Road to Rio 47. Melody Time (voices) 48.

Andrews, Stanley (1892–1969).
American character actor, often seen as grizzled western veteran. He more or less ended his career as the 'old ranger' host of TV's *Death Valley Days*.
Evelyn Prentice 34. Mississippi 35. Murder Man 35. Pennies from Heaven 36. Desire 36. Madame X 37. Nancy Steele Is Missing 37. Hold That Co-Ed 38. Alexander's Ragtime Band 38. Kentucky 38. Beau Geste 39. Union Pacific 39. The Blue Bird 40. Meet John Doe 41. My Gal Sal 42. Murder My Sweet 44. Adventure 45. It's a Wonderful Life 46. Robin Hood of Texas 47. Northwest Stampede 48. The Last Bandit 49. Arizona Cowboy 50. Vengeance Valley 51. Woman of the North Country 52. Ride Vaquero 52. Dawn at Socorro 54. The Treasure of Ruby Hills 55. Frontier Gambler 56. Cry Terror 58, many others.

Andrews, Tige (1924–) (Tiger Androwaous).
Lebanese-American supporting actor, usually an amiable tough.
Mr Roberts 55. The Wings of Eagles 57. Imitation General 58. China Doll 58. A Private Affair 59. The Last Tycoon 76, etc.
TV series: *The Detectives* 59–62. *The Mod Squad* 68–73.

Andrews, Tod (1920–1972).
Burly American leading man of minor action films; previously known as Michael Ames.
Now Voyager 42. Action in the North Atlantic 43. From Hell It Came 60. In Harm's Way 64, etc.
TV series: The Gray Ghost 57.

Andreyev, Boris (1915–).
Russian leading actor.
Tractor Drivers 39. Two Soldiers 43. The

Last Hill 44. Song of Siberia 47. The Fall of Berlin 49. Ilya Muromets 56. The Gordeyev Family 59. The Cossacks 61. Aladdin 67, many others.

Andrien, Jean-Jacques (1944–).
Belgian producer, director and screenwriter.
La Pierre Qui Flotte (w) 71. Le Fils d'Amour Es Mort (co-w, d) 75. Le Grand Paysage d'Alexis Droeven (co-w, d) 81. Mémoires (co-w, d) 84. Australia (co-w, d) 89, etc.

Andriot, Lucien (1897–1979).
French American cinematographer long in Hollywood.
Two Lives 15. Oh Boy 19. Why Trust Your Husband 21. Hell's Hole 23. Gigolo 26. White Gol 27. The Valiant 28. Hallelujah I'm a Bum 33. Ann of Green Gables 34. The Gay Desperado 36. The Lady in Question 40. The Hairy Ape 44. The Southerner 45. And Then There Were None 45. Dishonored Lady 47. Outpost in Morocco 49. Borderline 50. Home Town Story 51, many other Later in television.

anecdotes

¶ The more scintillating luminaries of Hollywood's golden age were the subjects of many stories which may or may not have been true; most of us will wish to think they were. Here's a selection, interspersed with a few bits of pure fiction.

The waspish New York wit Dorothy Parker sper some years in Hollywood as a scriptwriter. For th first few weeks in the studio no one ever came into her office: whether from awe or from jealous she was ignored. She soon fixed things by taking her name off the door and putting in its place a sig reading: MEN.

The same Miss Parker had periods of indolence and when asked for the third time why she had not delivered a script as agreed, snapped:
Because I've been too fucking busy – and vice versa.
Miss Parker had many a battle of wits with Clare Boothe Luce, author of *The Women*. On one occasion they almost collided in a doorway. 'Age before beauty,' cooed Miss Luce, standing back. Miss Parker sailed through. 'Pearls before swine,' she remarked.

Drink was often the downfall of the acting classes: it was certainly the reason why a film called *The Captain Hates the Sea* went way over budget on its Catalina Island location; the actors were having too much liquid fun. The producer wired from Hollywood in desperation: RETURN AT ONCE; THE COST IS STAGGERING. The answer came: SO IS THE CAST.

One famous drinker, W.C. Fields, had a guilty conscience about his success. 'During my years o poverty,' he once told an interviewer, 'I swore tha if I ever got to the top I'll start a foundation to he' underprivileged children. For years I could do nothing about it. Then came Hollywood and riches.' 'And did you start the foundation?' asked the interviewer, pencil poised. 'Naw,' drawled Fields. 'I didn't. I said to myself, the hell with them.'

For all their wealth, the Hollywood stars were an unhappy lot. Nick Schenk once walked round the MGM Studio, which he virtually owned, and commented: 'I've never seen so many miserable people making a hundred thousand dollars a year.'

The loss of youth's freshness concerned most of the star actresses. Marlene Dietrich once berated her photographer for unacceptable close-ups. 'What's the matter with you?' she stormed. 'Eigh

ars ago you used to take marvellous pictures of
e.' 'Ah,' he said tactfully; 'but I was much
ounger then.'

Cinema owners too have always bemoaned their
t. They say a couple of them once met on the
reet. 'How's business?' said one.

'Terrible. Two years ago I lost ten thousand
ollars, last year it was twenty-five, and this
ear I look like being forty thousand dollars
own.'

'But Ike, if things are so bad, why do you stay
show business?'

His friend shrugged. 'A fellow's got to live.'
Movies sometimes lose a lot of money; they also
st a lot to make. The famous story about Cecil B.
e Mille suggests why. De Mille, they say, was
eparing to shoot an elaborate and expensive scene
hich had to be got right the first time. Five
ousand extras were on hand, not to mention
mels, elephants, stunt men and a flock of birds
be released at the critical moment. Four
meras were at strategic points to accomplish the
at of recording this event, the key shot being from
umber four in a helicopter hovering overhead.
fter a day of preparation the master director called
ction!' The many and varied performers were
leashed; fire raged; rain poured down;
uildings collapsed. The master sighed and spoke
the cinematographers through his mike. 'O.K.,
umber one?' 'Fine, chief.' 'Number two?' 'Just
eat, Mr De Mille.' 'Number three?' 'Perfect.'
umber four?' No answer. 'Number four?' The
tercom crackled into life: 'Ready when you are,
r De Mille.'

De Mille was often accused of buying up books
d using nothing but the title. They say that he
nce invited a famous author to a première and
ked him afterwards what he thought of the
m. 'Why, excellent,' said the distinguished guest.
Vho wrote it?' De Mille was nonplussed: 'You
d. We bought it from you.' 'I would never have
own,' said the author. 'In fact, I'd like to use one
your variations for a new novel.' 'That's all
ght,' said De Mille, 'but you'll have to give us an
tion on the film rights.'

Another première. Otto Preminger invited
wish comedian Mort Sahl to be his personal guest
the first showing of the four-hour Preminger
ic about the beginnings of the state of Israel,
xodus. After three and a half hours had passed,
ahl got to his feet wearily, turned to his host,
d said: 'Otto – let my people go!'

Hollywood is the place which popularized
vorce. They say that when Elizabeth Taylor took
er sixth husband, and the justice of the peace
anted details of her previous marriages, she
id: 'What is this, a memory test?'

Then there were the two moppets playing on a
everly Hills lawn. One said to the other: 'That
an coming through the door is my daddy.' Her
um looked and sighed. 'Oh, him. We had him
st year.'

And three Hollywood kids were playing games.
et's play marriages,' said one, 'and I'll be
ama.'

– 'And I'll be Papa.'

– 'And I'll be the judge.'

The much-married Zsa Zsa Gabor met a new
an who offered her diamonds.

'Darling,' she said, 'I never take gifts from a
rfect stranger. But who's perfect?'

Finally, the moguls. The autocratic David O.
lznick was overfond of writing memos. A
ember of his staff did something wrong, was
arful of the worst, and thought he might as well
t it over with. So he sent Selznick a note
eginning: 'In reply to your memo of
morrow . . .'

When he was making *Gone with the Wind*
Selznick was desperate for the services of Clark
Gable as Rhett Butler. But Gable was under
contract to Louis B. Mayer. So Selznick rang Mayer,
and the conversation is reported as follows:

'Louis, we're both in terrible trouble about Clark
Gable.'

'Why?'

'Well, you've got him and I want him.'

It was not always safe to offer even the right advice
to the moguls. When Goldwyn planned to star
Anna Sten in *Nana*, one of his favourite directors
warned him against it. Goldwyn persisted, and the
movie was a disaster. From that day forth Goldwyn
never hired the director again, and when
someone asked him why, he averred: 'That man
was associated with one of my greatest flops.'

For obvious reasons Goldwyn's staff tended to
agree with whatever the boss said. Even this nettled
him, and on one occasion he burst out: 'I don't
want yes-men around me. I want you to disagree
once in a while – even if it costs you your job!'

Goldwyn ran rough cuts of his movies at home
on a Sunday night, trying them out on the family.
One such evening as soon as the end title came
up he pitched into the director and editor, saying
it was a lousy film and he couldn't understand it.
'Oh, come now,' said the daring director, 'surely
you exaggerate. I'll bet your son here understood
every word and every scene.' Goldwyn turned to
the ten-year-old boy, who said: 'Why, yes, Pop: it
was fine, I had no problem.' The director's triumph
was short-lived, for Goldwyn turned on him with:
'What business do you think I'm in? Making
pictures for children?'

Angel, Danny (Daniel M.) (1911–).
British producer, in films from 1945.

Mr Drake's Duck 50. Albert R.N. 53. The Sea
Shall Not Have Them 54. Reach for the Sky 56.
Carve Her Name with Pride 57. The Sheriff of
Fractured Jaw 58. West Eleven 63, etc.

Angel, Heather (1909–1986).
British-born leading lady of the 30s; in Hollywood
from 1933.

City of Song 30. *Berkeley Square* 33. The Informer
35. The Mystery of Edwin Drood 35. Last of the
Mohicans 36. Army Girl 38. Pride and Prejudice
40. Time to Kill 42. Lifeboat 43. In the Meantime,
Darling 44. The Saxon Charm 48. The Premature
Burial 62.

TV series: Peyton Place 64–69.

Angeli, Pier (1932–1971) (Anna Maria Pierangeli).
Sensitive-looking Italian actress who after some
stage experience at home moved to Hollywood
but found only occasional worthy roles. Twin sister
of Marisa Pavan, she was married to singer Vic
Damone. Committed suicide.

■ Tomorrow Is Too Late (It.) 50. Tomorrow Is
Another Day (It.) 51. *Teresa* 51. The Light Touch
51. The Devil Makes Three 52. The Story of Three
Loves 52. Sombrero 53. The Flame and the Flesh
54. The Silver Chalice 54. Santerella (It.) 54.
Somebody Up There Likes Me 56. Port Afrique
56. The Vintage 57. Merry Andrew 58. SOS Pacific
60. The Angry Silence 60. Musketeers of the Sea
(It.) 62. White Slave Ship 62. Sodom and
Gomorrah 63. Battle of the Bulge 65. Spy in Your
Eye 66. Missione Morte (It.) 66. Per Mille Dollari
al Giorno (It.) 66. Shadow of Evil 67. Red Roses for
the Fuehrer (It.) 67. One Step to Hell 68. Vive
America (Sp.) 68. Les Enemoniades (Sp.) 70.
Every Bastard a King 70. Adio Alexandra (It.) 71.
Nelle Pieghe Della Carne 71. Octaman 72.

Angelopoulos, Theodoros (1936–).
Greek director whose *The Travelling Players* was
widely praised in 1975.

The Broadcast (Ekpombi) 68. Reconstruction
(Anaparastassi) 70. The Hunters (I Kynighi) 77.
Alexander the Great (O Megalexandros) 80.
Athens 1982 82. Voyage to Cythera (Taxidi Sta
Kythera) 84. The Beekeeper (O Melissokomos) 86.
Landscape in the Mist (Topio Stin Omichli) 88.
The Suspended Step of the Stork (To Meteoro
Vima To Pelargou) 91. Le Regard d'Ulysse 94, etc.

angels
made appearances in many silent films: *Intolerance*,
The Four Horsemen of the Apocalypse, *The Sorrows of
Satan*, and the many versions of *Uncle Tom's Cabin*
and *Faust* were among them. Since sound, they
have remained a favourite Hollywood device, but
have naturally tended to lose their wings and
become more whimsical, less awesome and often
of somewhat ambiguous reality, to be explained
away in the last reel as a result of the hero's bump
on the head. The last completely serious angels
were probably those in the all-Negro *Green Pastures*
37; since then they have been played by Claude
Rains in *Here Comes Mr Jordan*, Jeanette
MacDonald in *I Married an Angel*, Kenneth Spencer
(and others) in *Cabin in the Sky*, Jack Benny (and
others) in *The Horn Blows at Midnight*, Clifton Webb
and Edmund Gwenn in *For Heaven's Sake*, Henry
Travers in *It's a Wonderful Life*, Leon Ames in
Yolanda and the Thief, Kathleen Byron and a great
many extras in *A Matter of Life and Death*, Robert
Cummings in *Heaven Only Knows*, Cary Grant in
The Bishop's Wife, several actors in *Angels in the
Outfield*, James Mason in *Forever Darling*, Diane
Cilento in *The Angel Who Pawned Her Harp*, John
Philip Law in *Barbarella*, and Harry Belafonte in
The Angel Levine. In 1978 Warren Beatty remade
Here Comes Mr Jordan as *Heaven Can Wait* and
spawned several ineffective TV imitations including
Ray Bolger in *Heaven Only Knows*.

Used in a figurative sense, the word 'angel' has
continued to be a favourite title component: *I'm
No Angel*, *Angel*, *The Dark Angel*, *Angels with Dirty
Faces*, *Angels Wash Their Faces*, *Angel and the Badman*,
Angel Face, *Angel Baby*, *Angels in Disguise*, *The Angel
Wore Red*, *Angels One Five*, *Angels in Exile*, etc.

See also: *fantasy*.

Angelus, Muriel (1909–) (M.A. Findlay).
British leading lady of the 30s who had a brief
Hollywood career before retiring in 1940.

The Ringer 30. Hindle Wakes 31. The Light That
Failed 39. The Great McGinty 40. The Way of All
Flesh 40, etc.

Anger, Kenneth (1932–).
American independent film-maker who grew up
in Hollywood and also wrote *Hollywood Babylon*,
scurrilous exposés of the private lives of its stars.
His films are mainly short, inscrutable and
Freudian.

Fireworks 47. Eaux d'Artifice 53. Inauguration
of the Pleasure Dome 54. Scorpio Rising 64.
Kustom Kar Kommandos 65. Invocation of My
Demon Brother 69. Lucifer Rising 80, etc.

Angers, Avril (1922–).
British character comedienne whose film
appearances have been infrequent.

Skimpy in the Navy 50. Lucky Mascot 51. The
Green Man 56. Devils of Darkness 65. The Family
Way 66. Two a Penny 68, etc.

Anglade, Jean-Hugues (1965–).
French leading actor, on stage from 1978.

L'Indiscrétion 82. Subway 85. Betty Blue 90.

Nikita (US: La Femme Nikita) 90. Jona Che Visse nella Balena 93. Les Marmottes 93. Queen Margot (La Reine Margot) 94. Killing Zoe 94, etc.

Anhalt, Edward (1914–).

American middlebrow scriptwriter.

With his wife *Edna Anhalt* (1914–):

Bulldog Drummond Strikes Back 48. Panic in the Streets 50. The Sniper (AAN) 52. Not as a Stranger 54. The Pride and the Passion 56. The Young Lions 58, etc.

Alone: A Girl Named Tamiko 63. Becket (AA) 64. Hour of the Gun 67. The Boston Strangler 68. The Mad Woman of Chaillot 69. Jeremiah Johnson (co-w) 72. Luther 74. The Man in the Glass Booth 76. Escape to Athena 79. The Holcroft Covenant 85. The Take 90. Alexander the Great (TV) 91, etc.

animals,

as Walt Disney knew, are a sure way to success at the box office, with dogs well established as number-one providers. Dog stars of the movies have included Rin Tin Tin, Strongheart (his closest rival), Ben (Mack Sennett's comedy dog), Pete (of 'Our Gang'), Asta (of the 'Thin Man' series), Daisy (so popular in the 'Blondie' films that he starred in his own movies), and of course the immortal Lassie. Less publicized canines have successfully taken on dramatic roles in such films as *The Voice of Bugle Ann, Oliver Twist, Umberto D, Greyfriars Bobby, Owd Bob, Old Yeller, Savage Sam, The Ugly Dachshund* and *The Spy with a Cold Nose;* while Dick Powell was reincarnated as a very handsome Alsatian in *You Never Can Tell.* Rhubarb has been the only 'starred' cat, though felines have played important roles in *The Cat and the Canary, The Cat Creeps, Cat Girl, Shadow of the Cat, Breakfast at Tiffany's, The Incredible Journey, A Walk on the Wild Side, The Three Lives of Thomasina, That Darn Cat, The Torture Garden* (with its diabolical pussy), *The Wrong Box, The Goldwyn Follies* (in which the Ritz Brothers were memorably assisted by hundreds of cats to sing 'Hey Pussy Pussy'), *The Bluebird* (in which a sleek black feline was humanized very satisfyingly into Gale Sondergaard), *The Tomb of Ligeia, Eye of the Cat,* and several versions of *The Black Cat.*

Other animals to achieve something like stardom have included Balthasar the donkey, Flipper the dolphin, Gentle Ben the bear, Cheta the chimp (in the Tarzan films), Slicker the seal (in *Spawn of the North*), the chimp in *The Barefoot Executive,* Clarence the Cross-eyed Lion (not to mention Fluffy), the *Zebra in the Kitchen,* and a great many horses including Rex (*King of the Wild Horses*), Tarzan (with Ken Maynard), Fritz (with William S. Hart), Tony (with Tom Mix), Silver (with Buck Jones), Champion (with Gene Autry) and Trigger (with Roy Rogers). *Born Free* and its sequels made stars of lions; *Ring of Bright Water* and *Tarka the Otter* did the same for otters, and *Benji* for a little dog; then there was *The Belstone Fox;* the deer in *The Yearling;* the dolphins in *The Day of the Dolphin;* the bear in *Grizzly;* the host of assorted animals in *Doctor Dolittle;* the bear cub in *The Bear;* the kitten and puppy in *Milo and Otis;* and the killer whale in *Free Willy.* Perhaps one shouldn't count the anthropoids in *Planet of the Apes.*

animation.

The filming of static drawings, puppets or other objects in sequence so that they give an illusion of movement. Sometimes called 'stop-frame animation' because only one frame of film is exposed at a time.

Leading figures in the history of animation include Winsor McKay (qv) who in 1909 introduced Gertie the Dinosaur, Emile Cohl

(qv), Len Lye (qv), Max Fleischer (qv), Walt Disney (qv), the UPA Group (qv), Norman McLaren (qv), William Hanna and Joe Barbera (qv), Halas and Batchelor (qv), Ralph Bakshi (qv) and Richard Williams (qv).

Best books on the subject are *The Technique of Film Animation* by John Halas and Roger Manvell; *The Art of Walt Disney* by Christopher Finch; *The Animated Film* by Ralph Stephenson.

Anime.

A Japanese term for animated films, applied particularly to its own tradition, which differs from the American style, as exemplified in the work of the Walt Disney studios. Japanese animation is often based on comic books and features more adult fantasies, often marked by an excess of sex and violence and drawing on local legends and myths. The graphic techniques are often stylized: the heroes and heroines tend to cuteness, with large round eyes. The best film so far is Otomo Katsuhiro's *Akira* 87, though many others are gaining a cult following in the West owing to their release on video and there are several magazines devoted to Anime. The Anime style has influenced some action films, such as *Gunhed,* and other live-action films are being based on animated originals, such as the gangster epic *Crying Freeman.* The process is likely to quicken with the trend for computer games inspiring movies, since these also are influenced by Japanese comic-book styles.

Book: 1993, *Anime! A Beginner's Guide to Japanese Animation* by Helen McCarthy.

See also: *Manga.*

Anka, Paul (1941–).

Canadian pop singer of the 60s, subject of documentary *Lonely Boy* 62. Also acted the same year in *The Longest Day,* and composed the theme song.

Captain Ron 92.

Ankers, Evelyn (1918–1985).

British leading lady who did not so much act as react. She also looked decorative, and after going to Hollywood in 1940 she appeared as the well-bred heroine of innumerable co-features. Married Richard Denning.

The Villiers Diamond 33. Rembrandt 36. Knight without Armour 37. Over the Moon 39. Hold that Ghost 41. Bachelor Daddy 41. *The Wolf Man* 41. The Ghost of Frankenstein 42. The Great Impersonation 42. The Mad Ghoul 43. Hers to Hold 43. His Butler's Sister 43. Ladies Courageous 44. Weird Woman 44. The Frozen Ghost 45. The French Key 46. The Lone Wolf in London 47. The Texan Meets Calamity Jane 50. No Greater Love 60, etc.

Ankrum, Morris (1896–1964) (Morris Nussbaum).

American stage actor seen in innumerable films as lawyer, judge or western villain.

Buck Benny Rides Again 40. Light of the Western Stars 40. Tales of Manhattan 42. *Tennessee Johnson* 42. Let's Face It 43. Barbary Coast Gent 44. The Hidden Eye 45. The Harvey Girls 46. Joan of Arc 48. Rocketship XM 50. My Favourite Spy 51. Son of Ali Baba 52. Apache 54. Earth Versus the Flying Saucers 56. Badman's Country 59. The Most Dangerous Man Alive 61, many others.

Annabella (1909–) (Suzanne Charpentier).

French leading lady of the 30s, in international films; once married to Tyrone Power.

Napoleon 26. Le Million 32. Le Quatorze Juillet 33. Under the Red Robe 36. Dinner at the Ritz 37. Wings of the Morning 37. Suez 38, Hôtel du Nord

38. Bridal Suite 39. Bomber's Moon 42. Tonight W Raid Calais 43. 13 Rue Madeleine 46. Don Juan (sp) 50, etc.

Annakin, Ken (1914–).

British director of very variable output. Formerly a journalist.

■ Holiday Camp 47. Here Come the Huggetts 4 Broken Journey 48. Miranda 48. Quartet (part) 4 Vote for Huggett 49. Landfall 49. Double Confession 50. Trio (part) 50. The Huggetts Abro 51. Hotel Sahara 51. Robin Hood 52. The Plante Wife 52. The Seekers 53. The Sword and the Ro 53. You Know What Sailors Are 53. Value for Money 55. Three Men in a Boat 56. Loser Takes All 56. Across the Bridge 57. Nor the Moon by Night 58. *The Swiss Family Robinson* 60. Third Ma on the Mountain 61. *Very Important Person* 61. Tl Longest Day 62. The Hellions 62. Crooks Anonymous 62. The Informers 63. *The Fast Lady* 63. *Those Magnificent Men in Their Flying Machines* 6 Battle of the Bulge 65. The Biggest Bundle of The All 66. The Long Duel 67. Monte Carlo or Bust 6 Call of the Wild 72. Paper Tiger 75. The Fifth Musketeer 78. The Pirate (TV) 79. Cheaper to Ke Her 80. The Pirate Movie 82. Pippi Longstocking 88.

Annaud, Jean-Jacques (1943–).

French director and screenwriter who began his career with educational films for the army, and commercials.

Black and White in Color (La Victoire en Chantant) (AA) 78. Hot Head (Coup de Tête) 8C Quest for Fire 82. The Name of the Rose 86. Th Bear (L'Ours) 88. The Lover (L'Amant) 92, etc.

Annis, Francesca (1945–).

British leading lady, former juvenile player.

The Cat Gang 58. Cleopatra 62. The Eyes of Annie Jones 63. Flipper and the Pirates (US) 64 The Pleasure Girls 65. Run with the Wind 66. Tl Walking Stick 69. Macbeth 71. Krull 83. Coming Out of the Ice (TV) 83. The Secret Adversary (T 83. Dune 86. I'll Take Manhattan (TV) 86. Unde the Cherry Moon 86. Doomsday Gun (TV) 94, e

TV series: *Lillie* (title role) 78. Partners in Crim 83.

Ann-Margret (1941–) (Ann-Margret Olsson).

Swedish-American sex symbol and formidable cabaret performer; a hard worker who gradually became a good actress.

Autobiography: 1994, *Ann-Margret: My Story* (with Todd Gold).

■ Pocketful of Miracles 61. State Fair 62. *Bye By Birdie* 62. Viva Las Vegas 64. Kitten with a Whip 64. Bus Riley's Back in Town 65. The Pleasure Seekers 65. Once a Thief 65. *The Cincinnati Kid* 65. Made in Paris 66. The Swinger 66. Stagecoa 66. Murderers' Row 66. The Tiger and the Pussyc 67. Mr Kinky 68. Rebus (It.) 68. Seven Men and One Brain (It.) 69. C.C. and Co. 70. *Carnal Knowledge* (AAN) 71. R.P.M. 71. The Train Robbe 73. The Outside Man 73. Tommy (AAN) 75. The Twist 76. Joseph Andrews 76. The Last Remake Beau Geste 77. The Cheap Detective 78. Magic 78. The Villain 79. Middle Age Crazy 80. I Ough to Be in Pictures 82. Lookin' to Get Out 82. The Return of the Soldier 82. Who Will Love My Children? (TV) 83. Twice in a Lifetime 85. The Tv Mrs Grevilles (TV) 86. 52 Pick-Up 86. A Tiger's Tale 87. A New Life 88. Newsies (GB: Newsboys 92. Queen (TV) 93. Grumpy Old Men 93. Nobod Children 94.

Anouilh, Jean (1910–1987).

Skilful and versatile French playwright who

orked in the cinema as a screenwriter and
rector. Several of his plays have also been filmed.
Les Dégourdis de la Onzième (w) 36. Le
oyageur sans Bagage (d, oa) 43. Monsieur
incent (w) 47. Anna Karenina (GB) (w) 47.
ttes Blanches (w) 48. Caroline Chérie (w) 50.
ux Sous de Violette (d) 51. Le Chevalier de la
uit (w) 53. Waltz of the Toreadors (oa) 62. La
onde (w) 64. Becket (oa) 64, etc.

sara, Michael (1922–).
merican actor with stage experience, specializing
 Indian roles.
Action in Arabia 44. Only the Valiant 51. The
obe 53. The Egyptian 54. Sign of the Pagan 54.
ane 55. Jupiter's Darling 55. Pillars of the Sky
. The Ten Commandments 56. The Tall Stranger
. The Lone Ranger 58. The Comancheros 62.
nd Now Miguel 66. Guns of the Magnificent
even 69. Stand Up and be Counted 72. The Bears
d I 74. Dear Dead Delilah 75. The Day of the
nimals 76. The Manitou 77. Lethal 84. Knights
 the City 86, etc.
TV series: *Broken Arrow* 56–8. Law of the
ainsman 59.

nschutz, Ottomar (1846–1907).
lish inventor who devised a motion-picture
mera and patented his Elektrotachyscope, a
evice for showing his pictures, in 1887.

nscocolor.
merican process derived from Agfacolor (qv).

nspach, Susan (1945–).
merican leading lady, from the stage.
 The Landlord 70. Five Easy Pieces 70. Play It
gain Sam 72. Blume in Love 72. Nashville 75. The
g Fix 78. Running 79. The Devil and Max Devlin
. Gas 81. Montenegro 82. Misunderstood 84.
ue Monkey 87. Into the Fire 87. Blood Red 89.
ack to Back 90. The Rutanga Tapes 90. Killer
stinct 90.
TV series: The Yellow Rose 83.

nstey, Edgar (1907–1987).
ritish documentary producer (Housing Problems
. Enough to Eat 36, etc.). Long-time Chief Films
fficer for British Transport.

nstey, F. (1856–1934) (Thomas Anstey Guthrie).
ritish humorous novelist. Works filmed: *Vice
ersa* 48 and 88. The Brass Bottle 64.

nswer print.
he first complete combined print supplied by the
boratory, usually with no very careful attempt
 grade colour or contrast.

nt, Adam (1954–) (Stuart Leslie Goddard).
ritish rock singer of the 80s who became an actor
 his popularity waned at the end of the decade.
Jubilee 78. Nomads 86. Slamdance 87. Cold
eel 87. Spellcaster 88. World Gone Wild 88. Trust
e 89. Midnight Heat 91. Acting on Impulse 93,
c.

ntheil, George (1900–1959).
merican composer, former concert pianist.
The Plainsman 37. The Buccaneer 38. Angels
ver Broadway 40. Specter of the Rose 46. Knock
 Any Door 49. The Fighting Kentuckian 49. In
Lonely Place 50. The Sniper 51. Actors and Sin
2. The Juggler 53. Not as a Stranger 55. The Pride
nd the Passion 57, etc.

Anthony, Joseph (1912–1993) (J. A. Deuster).
American director from stage and TV; former small
part actor and dancer.
■ The Rainmaker 56. The Matchmaker 58. Career
59. All in a Night's Work 61. The Captive City 63.
Tomorrow 72.

Anthony, Lysette (1963–).
English leading actress.
Ivanhoe (TV) 82. Oliver Twist (TV) 82. Krull 83.
The House on Kirov Street 87. Looking for Eileen
87. Without a Clue 88. Switch 91. Husbands and
Wives 92. The Hour of the Pig 93. Look Who's
Talking Now 93. A Brilliant Disguise 94. The Hard
Truth 94, etc.
TV series: Dark Shadows 91.

Anthony, Tony (1937–).
American leading man who had some success in
tough Italian westerns.
A Stranger in Town 67. The Stranger Returns
68. Samurai on a Horse 69. Blindman 71. Comin'
at Ya 81. Treasure of the Four Crowns 82, etc.

Antin, Manuel (1926–).
Argentinian director, producer, screenwriter,
novelist, poet and playwright.
La Cifra Impar 62. Los Venerables Todos (& oa)
62. Circe 64. Don Segundo Sombre 69. Juan
Manuel de Rosas 78. Far Away and Long Ago (Allá
Lejos y Hace Tiempo) 78. La Invitación 82, etc.

anti-Semitism
was understandably not a popular subject with
film-makers when the function of movies was
simply to entertain. Amiable comic Jews were
permitted, in Abie's Irish Rose, Potash and Perlmutter,
and the Cohen and Kelly series; and it was readily
acknowledged that Jewry provided a flow of star
talent without which show business could not
continue. But thoughtful movies on the Jewish
plight were almost non-existent, unless one counts
such epics as The Wandering Jew 33 and Jew Süss
34. Occasionally came a cry from Europe, as in
Professor Mamlock 36, but it was not really until The
Great Dictator 40 that the film-going public was
made aware of what was happening to the Jews
in Germany. For propaganda purposes the Nazis
put out a number of anti-Semitic films such as
Der Ewige Jude and another version of Jew Süss; the
only real reply during World War II was a gentle
British movie called Mr Emmanuel. In Tomorrow the
World 44, from the play about an ex-Nazi youth
in America, the subject was touched on; but not
till the reconstruction days of 1947 could a spade
really be called a spade. In a taut murder thriller
called Crossfire, the victim was changed from a
homosexual to a Jew; then came Gentleman's
Agreement, in which a gentile reporter posed as a
Jew to expose anti-Semitism in America. Perhaps
this interest was stimulated by the immense
popularity of The Jolson Story, with its sympathetic
portrait of a Jewish home; but the confusion in
American minds is demonstrated by the fact that
David Lean's Oliver Twist was banned in 1948
because of Alec Guinness's 'caricature' of Fagin!
During the last decade or so there seems to have
been sporadic interest in the subject. The birth of
Israel generated such movies as Sword in the Desert,
Exodus, Judith and Cast a Giant Shadow, and
Christopher Isherwood's Berlin stories of the early
30s became first a play and film called I Am a
Camera and later a musical and film called Cabaret.
Poignant recollections of World War II by a girl
who died in Auschwitz produced a book, play and
film called The Diary of Anne Frank, and a little
British film called Reach for Glory, which took a
swipe at the consequences of intolerance. In 1971

the world's most successful stage musical, Fiddler
on the Roof, was filmed; dealing with the Russian
pogroms, the story has been filmed many times
before in Yiddish, usually under the title Tevye the
Milkman. The 70s saw the pendulum swinging to
the extent that we were almost swamped by films
and actors proclaiming their Jewishness: Barbra
Streisand, Bette Midler, Woody Allen, Elliott
Gould, George Segal. The plight of the Jews under
Hitler was again explored in a dozen television
epics including Inside the Third Reich, Blood and
Honour, The Winds of War, The Wall and The House
on Garibaldi Street and in the cinema in Steven
Spielberg's Schindler's List; while feature films on
the subject of Jewishness were The Pawnbroker and
The Chosen.

Antoine Doinel.
A character who served as an alter ego for
director François Truffaut in a series of semi-
autobiographical films, each starring over a period
of 20 years Jean-Pierre Léaud, who was 13 when
he was picked to play the role in The 400 Blows (Les
Quatre Cent Coups) 59, the first of the sequence. It
was followed by Antoine et Colette, part of the
compilation film Love at Twenty (L'Amour à 20 Ans)
62, Stolen Kisses (Baisers Volés) 68, Bed and Board
(Domicile Conjugal) 70, and Love on the Run (Amour
en Fuite) 79, a series which follows Doinel from
his unhappy adolescence and dead-end jobs to his
becoming a writer, a lover, an unhappy husband
and a father. Truffaut once wrote, 'The character
of Antoine Doinel is always on the run, always
late, a young man in a hurry.'

Anton, Susan (1950–).
American actress.
Goldengirl 79. Spring Fever 81. Cannonball Run
II 84. Options 88. Lena's Holiday 91, etc.
TV series: Presenting Susan Anton 79. Stop
Susan Williams 79.

Antonelli, Laura (1941–).
Sultry Italian leading actress.
A Man Called Sledge 70. Divine Nymph 71. High
Heels (Docteur Popaul) 72. How Funny Can Sex
Be? (Sessomatto) 73. Malicious (Malizia) 73. Till
Marriage Do Us Part 77. The Innocent
(L'Innocente) 77. Tigers in Lipstick (aka Wild
Beds) 78. Passion of Love (Passione d'Amore) 82.
Rimini, Rimini 87, etc.

Antonio, Lou (1934–).
Tough-looking American character actor who has
dabbled successfully in TV direction.
America America 63. Hawaii 66. Cool Hand
Luke 67. Sole Survivor (TV) 69. The Phynx 70.
Partners in Crime (TV) 73. Someone I Touched
(TV) 75. The Gypsy Warriors (TV) 78. Breaking Up
Is Hard to Do (TV) 79. Between Friends (TV) 83.
Mayflower Madam (TV) 87, etc.
TV series: The Snoop Sisters 73. Dog and Cat 77.

Antonioni, Michelangelo (1912–).
Italian director whose reputation was boosted in
the 50s by the ardent support of highbrow film
magazines. Co-scripts all his own films, which
largely jettison narrative in favour of vague
incident and relentless character study.
Cronaca di un Amore 50. Le Amiche 55. Il Grido
57. L'Avventura 59. La Notte 60. L'Eclisse 62. The
Red Desert 64. Blow-Up (GB) (AAN) 67. Zabriskie
Point (US) 69. The Passenger 74. The Oberwald
Mystery 81. Identification of a Woman 82, etc.

¶ I feel like a father towards my old films. You
bring children into the world, then they grow
up and go off on their own. From time to time

you get together, and it's always a pleasure to see them again. – M.A.

Antonutti, Omero.
Italian leading actor.
Padre Padrone 77. Night of the Shooting Stars 82. Basileus Quartet 82. Good Morning Babylon 87. *The Fencing Master* 92. Whistle Stop (Una Estación de Paso) 92. The Greek Labyrinth 92. Genesis: The Creation and the Flood (Genesi: La Creazione e il Diluvio) 94, etc.

Antony, Scott (1950–).
British leading juvenile of the early 70s.
Baxter 72. Savage Messiah 73. Dead Cert 73. The Mutations 74.

Anwar, Gabrielle (1969–).
English leading actress.
Manifesto 88. If Looks Could Kill 91. Wild Hearts Can't Be Broken 91. Scent of a Woman 92. Body Snatchers 93. The Three Musketeers 93, etc.

Apfel, Oscar (1874–1938).
American character actor.
Ten Nights in a Bar Room 22. The Social Code 23. Perils of the Coastguard 26. Code of the Cow Country 27. Not Quite Decent 29. Five Star Final 31. Wicked 31. The Maltese Falcon 31. High Pressure 32. Make Me a Star 32. Before Dawn 33. The House of Rothschild 34. Bordertown 35. The Plot Thickens 36. The Toast of New York 37, many others.

Applebaum, Louis (1918–).
Canadian composer who spent time in Hollywood.
Tomorrow the World 44. The Story of GI Joe (AA) 45. Lost Boundaries 48. Teresa 51. The Whistle at Eaton Falls 51. Walk East on Beacon 52. The Mask 61, etc.

Applegate, Christina (1972–).
American actress, on-screen as a teenager.
Jaws of Satan (aka King Cobra) 85. Streets 90. Don't Tell Mom the Babysitter's Dead 91. Wild Bill 95, etc.
TV series: Heart of the City 86–87. Married . . . with Children 87–89.

Apted, Michael (1941–).
British director, from TV.
■ Triple Echo 72. Stardust 74. The Squeeze 77. Agatha 79. Coal Miner's Daughter 80. Continental Divide 81. P'tang Yang Kipperbang (TV) 82. Gorky Park 83. First Born 84. 28 Up 84. Bring on the Night 85. Critical Condition 87. Gorillas in the Mist 88. The Long Way Home 89. Class Action 91. Thunderheart 92. Incident at Oglala (doc) 92. Crossroads (TV) 92. Blink 94. Nell 94.

Aquanetta (1920–) (Burnu Davenport).
Exotic American leading lady of easterns and horrors in the early 40s.
Arabian Nights 42. Jungle Captive 43. Jungle Woman 44. Dead Man's Eyes 44. Tarzan and the Leopard Woman 46, etc.

Araki, Gregg.
American director of movies on homosexual themes.
The Long Weekend 89. The Living End 92. Totally F***ed Up 93, etc.

Aranda, Vicente (1926–).
Spanish director and screenwriter. Born in Barcelona, he spent most of the 50s in Venezuela before returning to the city to form his own production company in the mid-60s.
Brilliant Future (Brillante Porvenir) 64. Fata Morgana 66. The Cruel Women (Las Crueles) 69. The Bloody Bride (La Novia Ensangrentada) 72. Clara Is the Price (Clara Es el Precio) 74. Sex Change (Cambio de Sexo) 77. The Girl in the Golden Panties (La Muchacha de las Bragas de Oro) 80. Murder in the Central Committee (Asesinato en el Comité Central) 82. Fanny Pelopaja 84. Time of Silence (Tiempo de Silencio) 86. El Lute 87. El Lute II 88. Si Te Dicen Que Cai 89. *Lovers* (Amantes) 91. Intruder (Intruso) 93. Turkish Passion (Pasiones Turcas) 94, etc.

Arau, Alfonso (1932–).
Mexican actor, director and producer. Best known internationally as an actor as the bandit El Guapo in *Three Amigos!*, in the 50s he performed in the song-and-dance act Arau and Corona, and spent the early 60s in Cuba. He is married to the Mexican screenwriter and novelist Laura Esquivel (qv). *Like Water for Chocolate*, from his wife's novel and screenplay, was one of the few Mexican films of recent years to find a worldwide audience.
The Barefoot Eagle (d) 67. The Wild Bunch (a) 69. Scandalous John (a) 71. El Rincón de las Virgenes (a) 72. Calzonzin Inspector (a, d) 74. Tivoli (a) 74. Posse (a) 75. Mojado Power (d) 80. Used Cars (a) 80. Chido Guan (d) 84. Romancing the Stone (a) 84. Three Amigos! (a) 86. Walker (a) 87. Stones for Ibarra (a) (TV) 88. Dynamite and Gold (aka Where the Hell's the Gold?) (a) (TV) 88. *Like Water for Chocolate* (Como Agua para Chocolate) (p, d) 92. Estrellita Marinera (d) 94. A Walk in the Clouds (d) 95, etc.

Arbeid, Ben (1924–).
British producer.
The Barber of Stamford Hill 62. *Private Potter* 63. Children of the Damned 64. Murder Most Foul 65. The Jokers 67. Assignment K 68. Hoffman 70. The Hireling 71. The Water Babies 76. Eagle's Wing 79.

Arbuckle, Roscoe 'Fatty' (1887–1933).
Grown-up fat boy of American silent cinema. His highly successful career, mainly in two-reelers, came to grief after a sensational murder trial in 1921, and his only subsequent films were a few two-reelers in the early 30s; he also directed a few films as William Goodrich.
Biographies: 1976, *The Day the Laughter Stopped* by David A. Yallop. 1990, *Frame-Up! The Untold Story of Roscoe 'Fatty' Arbuckle* by Andy Edmonds.
In the Clutches of the Gang (as a Keystone Kop) 13. Fatty and Mabel's Simple Life 15. Mabel and Fatty's Married Life 16. Fatty's Flirtation 16. Fickle Fatty's Fall 17. His Wedding Night 17. Out West 17. The Bell Boy 17. The Round Up 20. The Life of the Party (feature) 20. The Travelling Salesman (feature) 21. Gasoline Gus (feature) 21, many others.

¶ Roscoe always said, I'll make it, darling, and you spend it. – *Minta Durfee (wife)*
He could throw two pies at once in different directions, but he was not precise in this feat. – *Mack Sennett*

arc.
A high-powered lamp used in projectors and studio lighting, its illumination consisting of an electrical discharge between two carbon rods.

Arcand, Denys (1941–).
French-Canadian director. He began as a director of commercials and documentaries.
La Maudite Galette 72. Réjeanne Padovani 73. Gina 74. Le Crime d'Ovide Plouffe (TV) 83. The Decline of the American Empire (AAN) 86. Jesus of Montreal 89. Montreal Sextet (co-d) 91. Love and Human Remains 93, etc.

Archaeology of the Cinema
by C.W. Ceram. A well-received study of the technical development of the cinema up to 1897 published by Thames & Hudson in 1965.

Archainbaud, George (1890–1959).
American director, mainly of routine westerns.
Fool's Gold 19. The Shadow of Rosalie Byrnes 20. Single Wives 24. Men of Steel 26. College Coquette 29. The Lost Squadron 32. The Return of Sophie Lang 36. Her Jungle Love 38. Thanks for the Memory 38. Untamed 40. The Kansan 43. Woman of the Town 44. King of the Wild Horse 47. Hunt the Man Down 51. Last of the Pony Riders 53, many others.

Archard, Bernard (1916–).
Lean, incisive British actor with repertory experience; became famous on TV as *Spycatcher*.
Village of the Damned 60. The List of Adrian Messenger 63. Face of a Stranger 66. Song of Norway 70. The Horror of Frankenstein 70. The Purple Twilight (TV) 79. The Sea Wolves 80. Krull 83. King Solomon's Mines 85. Hidden Agenda 9. etc.

Archer, Anne (1947–).
American leading lady, the daughter of John Archer and Marjorie Lord.
The All-American Boy 70. The Honkers 72. Cancel My Reservation 72. Trackdown 76. Paradi Alley 78. Green Ice 80. Waltz Across Texas 82. Th Naked Face 84. The Check is in the Mail 85. Fat Attraction (AAN) 87. Love at Large 90. Narrow Margin 90. Eminent Domain 91. Nails 92. Patrio Games 92. Family Prayers 93. Body of Evidence 93. Short Cuts 93. Clear and Present Danger 94.
TV series: Bob and Carol and Ted and Alice 7 Seventh Avenue 77. The Family Tree 83. Falcon Crest 85.

Archer, John (1915–) (Ralph Bowman).
American leading man of routine second feature
Flaming Frontier 38. Gangs Inc. 41. Crash Div 43. The Last Moment 47. White Heat 49. Destination Moon 50. A Yank in Indo-China 52. Rodeo 53. The Stars Are Singing 53. No Man's Woman 55. Emergency Hospital 59. Blue Hawai 62. Apache Rifles 64. I Saw What You Did 65. H to Frame a Figg 71, etc.

Archibugi, Francesca (1961–).
Italian director.
Mignon Has Left (Mignon è Partita) 87. Towar Evening (Verso Sera) 90. The Great Pumpkin (I Grande Cocomero) 92.

archive.
A vault, usually government-sponsored, containing a selection of films to be preserved fo research and for posterity.

Ardant, Fanny (1949–).
French leading lady.
Les Chiens 79. Les Uns et les Autres 80. The Woman Next Door 81. *Vivement Dimanche* 82. Benvenuta 83. Sun and Moon 84. Swann in Lov 84. Desiderio 84. Family Business (Conseil de Famille) 86. Australia 89. Three Sisters (Paura e amore) 90. La Femme du Déserteur 91. Nothing but Lies (Rien que des Mensonges) 91. The Deserter's Wife 92. Afraid of the Dark 92. Amok 93. Le Colonel Chabert 94, etc.

Arden, Eve (1908–1990) (Eunice Quedens).
American comedy actress, a tall, cool lady who spent a generation as the wisecracking friend of the heroine. Originally a Ziegfeld girl.

Song of Love 29. Dancing Lady 33. Oh Doctor 37. *Stage Door* 37. Having Wonderful Time 38. At the Circus 39. Comrade X 40. Ziegfeld Girl 41. That Uncertain Feeling 41. Whistling in the Dark 41. Let's Face It 43. *Cover Girl* 44. *The Doughgirls* 44. *Mildred Pierce* (AAN) 45. Night and Day 46. The Unfaithful 47. *The Voice of the Turtle* 47. The Lady Takes a Sailor 49. *Paid in Full* 50. Curtain Call at Cactus Creek 50. *Tea for Two* 50. *Three Husbands* 50. *We're Not Married* 52. The Lady Wants Mink 53. Our Miss Brooks 56. *Anatomy of a Murder* 59. *The Dark at the Top of the Stairs* 60. Sergeant Deadhead 65. A Very Missing Person (TV) 71. All My Darling Daughters (TV) 72. *Grease* 78. Under the Rainbow 81. Grease II 82, etc.

TV series: *Our Miss Brooks* 52–56. The Eve Arden Show 59. Mothers-in-Law 67–69.

¶ For patenting the comic image of the cool, sophisticated but usually manless career woman.
Mildred Pierce.

Arden, Robert (1921–).
Anglo-American actor resident in Britain; former vocalist.

Two Thousand Women 44. No Orchids for Miss Blandish 48. *Confidential Report* 56, etc.

TV series: Saber of London 58–60.

Ardolino, Emile. (1953–1993).
American director from TV and dance theatre, a former actor. Died of AIDS.

He Makes Me Feel Like Dancin' (doc) (AA) 83. Dirty Dancing 87. Chances Are 89. Three Men and a Little Lady 90. Sister Act 92. George Balanchine's The Nutcracker 93. Gypsy (TV) 93, etc.

Ardrey, Robert (1907–1980).
American screenwriter, novelist and playwright.

They Knew What They Wanted 40. *Thunder Rock* (& oa) 43. The Green Years 46. The Three Musketeers 48. Madame Bovary 49. Quentin Durward 56. The Wonderful Country 58. The Four Horsemen of the Apocalypse 62. Khartoum (AAN) 66, etc.

Argentina
has been making films since the turn of the century, many having claim to sophistication, but the only ones to receive world distribution and acclaim were those of Leopoldo Torre-Nilsson (qv) in the 50s.

Argento, Asia (1975–).
Italian leading actress, the daughter of director Dario Argento and actress Daria Nicolodi.

Dreams and Needs (Sogni e Bisogni) 85. Demons 86. The Zoo 88. The Church 89. Palombella Rossa 89. Close Friends (L'Amiche del Cuore) 92. Trauma 93. Perdiamoci di Vista 94. Queen Margot (La Reine Margot) 94, etc.

Argento, Dario (1940–).
Italian thriller director and screenwriter. He is the father of actress Asia Argento.

Book: *Broken Mirrors/Broken Minds: The Dark Dreams of Dario Argento* by Maitland McDonagh (1991).

The Bird with Crystal Plumage (& w) 70. One Night at Dinner (& w) 70. Cat O'Nine Tails (& w) 71. Four Flies on Grey Velvet 71. Le Cinque Giornate 73. Deep Red (& w) 77. Suspiria (& w) 77. Inferno 80. Unsane (Tenebrae) (& m, w) 82. Creepers (& w) 85. Demons (Demoni) (w) 85. Demons 2

(Demoni 2) (w) 86. Opera (& w) 87. Two Evil Eyes (Due Occhi Diabolici) (co-w, co-d) 89. The Sect (La Setta) (w) 91. Trauma (& co-w) 93, etc.

Argyle, John F. (1911–).
British director.

Paradise Alley 31. Smiling Along 31. Mutiny on the Elsinore (p only) 36. Tower of Terror (p only) 41. Send for Paul Temple (& p) 46. Once a Sinner (p only) 50, etc.

Aristaráin, Adolfo (1943–).
Argentinian director, screenwriter and producer, a former film actor. Born in Buenos Aires, he went to Spain in the late 60s and spent six years there, working as an assistant director on films by Sergio Leone, Melvin Frank, Lewis Gilbert, Peter Collinson and others before returning home. His output includes political thrillers and musicals.

The Lion's Share (La Parte del León) 78. La Playa del Amor 79. La Discoteca del Amor 80. Time for Revenge (Tiempo de Revancha) 81. The Last Days of the Victim (Los Últimos Días de la Víctima) 82. The Stranger (US) (d only) 87. A Place in the World (Un Lugar en el mundo) 92.

Arkin, Alan (1934–).
American leading character actor, from Broadway.

Autobiography: 1979, *Halfway through the Door: An Actor's Journey toward the Self.*

■ The Russians Are Coming, The Russians Are Coming (AAN) 66. Woman Times Seven 67. *Wait Until Dark* 67. Inspector Clouseau 68. *The Heart Is a Lonely Hunter* (AAN) 68. Popi 69. The Monitors 69. *Catch 22* 70. *Little Murders* (& d) 71. Deadhead Miles 72. Last of the Red Hot Lovers 72. Freebie and the Bean 74. Rafferty and the Gold Dust Twins 75. Hearts of the West 75. The Seven Per Cent Solution (as Freud) 76. *The Other Side of Hell* (TV) 77. Fire Sale (& d) 77. The In-Laws 79. The Magician of Lublin 79. Simon 79. Improper Channels 80. Chu Chi and the Philly Flash 81. Full Moon High 81. Deadhead Miles 82. The Return of Captain Invincible 83. Big Trouble 84. Joshua Then and Now 85. Bad Medicine 85. Coupe de Ville 90. Edward Scissorhands 90. Havana 90. The Rocketeer 91. Glengarry Glen Ross 92. Cooperstown (TV) 93. Indian Summer 93. North 94.

Arkoff, Samuel Z. (1918–).
American executive producer, co-founder with James H. Nicholson of American International Pictures.

Autobiography: 1992, *Flying Through Hollywood by the Seat of My Pants* (with Richard Trubo).

Arlen, Alice.
American screenwriter.

Silkwood (co-w, AAN) 83. Alamo Bay 85. Cookie (co-w) 89, etc.

Arlen, Harold (1905–1986) (Hyman Arluck).
American song composer ('Happiness Is Just a Thing Called Joe', 'That Old Black Magic', 'Blues in the Night', 'Stormy Weather', 'Accentuate the Positive', many others).

Film scores include: Strike Me Pink 36. Love Affair 39. The Wizard of Oz (AA for 'Over the Rainbow') 39. Cabin in the Sky 43. A Star Is Born 54. I Could Go On Singing 63, etc.

Arlen, Michael (1895–1956) (Dikran Kuyumjian).
Armenian novelist, educated in England. In the 20s his *The Green Hat* was the basis for Garbo's *A Woman of Affairs*, and in 1948 his short story 'A Gentleman from America' became The Fatal Night.

¶ My forebears were successful crooks living on the slopes of Mount Ararat. – *M.A.*

For all his reputation. Arlen is not a bounder. He is every other inch a gentleman. – *Alexander Woollcott*

Arlen, Richard (1898–1976) (Cornelius van Mattemore).
Rugged American leading man who rose from extra to star in the 20s, became the durable hero of scores of 'B' pictures, and later played bits.

In the Name of Love 25. Rolled Stockings 27. *Wings* 27. *The Four Feathers* 28. Thunderbolt 29. *The Virginian* 29. The Sea God 30. Touchdown 31. College Humor 33. Three-Cornered Moon 33. She Made Her Bed 34. Heldorado 35. Secret Valley 36. Murder in Greenwich Village 37. Call of the Yukon 38. Mutiny on the Blackhawk 39. Legion of Lost Flyers 39. Hot Steel 40. Men of the Timberland 41. Torpedo Boat 42. Alaska Highway 43. Minesweeper 43. The Lady and the Monster 44. Storm over Lisbon 44. The Phantom Speaks 45. Accomplice 46. Speed to Spare 48. Grand Canyon 49. Kansas Raiders 50. Flaming Feather 52. Sabre Jet 53. Devil's Harbour 54. The Mountain 56. Raymie 60. Cavalry Command 63. Law of the Lawless 64. The Human Duplicators 65. Apache Uprising 66. Red Tomahawk 67. Buckskin 68. Won Ton Ton 76, many others.

Arletty (1898–1992) (Leonie Bathiat).
Celebrated French actress of stage and screen adept at the portrayal of world-weary, sophisticated women.

■ Un Chien Qui Rapporte 31. Don't Walk About in the Nude 32. Enlevez Moi 32. Un Fil à la Patte 33. Feue la Mère de Madame 33. La Belle Aventure 33. Une Idée Folle 33. Un Soir de Réveillon 34. Je Te Confie Ma Femme 34. Le Voyage de Monsieur Perrichon 34. La Guerre des Valses 35. Pension Mimosas 35. La Fille de Madame Angot 35. L'Ecole des Cocottes 36. Amants et Voleurs 36. La Garçonne 36. Un Mari Rêve 36. Aventure à Paris 36. Faisons un Rêve 36. Messieurs des Ronds-de-Cuir 36. Les Perles de la Couronne 37. Aloha 37. Mirages 37. Desire 37. Le Petit Chose 38. La Chaleur du Sein 38. *Hôtel du Nord* 38. *Le Jour Se Lève* 39. Fric Frac 39. Circonstances Attenuantes 39. Tempête 40. Madame Sans Gêne 41. The Woman I Loved the Most 42. Bolero 42. L'Amant de Borneo 42. *Les Visiteurs du Soir* 43. *Les Enfants du Paradis* 44. Portrait d'un Assassin 49. L'Amour, Madame 52. Gibier de Potence 52. Le Père de Mademoiselle 53. Le Grand Jeu 54. L'Air de Paris 55. Huis Clos 55. Mon Curé Chez les Pauvres 56. Vacances Explosives 57. Le Passager Clandestin 58. Et Ta Soeur? 59. Maxime 59. Drôle de Dimanche 60. La Gamberge 61. Les Petits Matins 61. La Loi des Hommes 61. The Longest Day 62. Tempo di Roma 63. Le Voyage à Biarritz 63.

Arling, Arthur E. (1906–).
American cinematographer.

Gone with the Wind (co-ph) 39. The Yearling (AA) 46. The Homestretch 47. You're My Everything 49. Wabash Avenue 50. Red Garters 54. I'll Cry Tomorrow 55. Pay the Devil 57. The Story of Ruth 60. Notorious Landlady 62. My Six Loves 63. Straitjacket 63. The Secret Invasion 64, many others.

Arliss, Florence (1871–1950).
British character actress who appeared in a few of the films of her husband George Arliss, from *The Devil* to *The House of Rothschild.*

Arliss, George (1868–1946) (George Augustus Andrews).
Distinguished British stage actor of the old school

who in middle age was persuaded to face the cameras and unexpectedly became a star both in Britain and America, presenting a gallery of kings, statesmen, rajahs, eccentric millionaires and rather unconvincing hoboes.

Autobiographies: 1926, *On The Stage*. 1927, *Up the Years from Bloomsbury*. 1940, *My Ten Years in the Studios*.

■ The Devil 21. *Disraeli* 21. *The Green Goddess* 23. The Ruling Passion 23. *Disraeli* (AA) 29. *The Green Goddess* (sound) (AAN) 30. Old English 30. Millionaire 31. Alexander Hamilton 31. The Man Who Played God 32. Successful Calamity 32. The King's Vacation 33. The Working Man 33. Voltaire 33. *The House of Rothschild* 34. The Tunnel 34. The Last Gentleman 34. Cardinal Richelieu 35. The Iron Duke 35. The Guvnor 35. East Meets West 36. His Lordship 37. Dr Syn 37.

✪ For the sheer autocratic determination which made him a world star despite his very limited and inflexible talent. *The House of Rothschild*.

¶ His small dark eyes held an ancient sadness; but his taut triangular mouth seemed always to be repressing an irrepressible mirth. – *Bette Davis*

The talking picture is like a dress rehearsal in the theatre. It never gets those moments of inspiration when an audience lifts an actor out of himself. So I say that no player in pictures can ever be seen at his best. – *G.A.*

Arliss, Leslie (1901–1987).
British writer who worked on Orders Is Orders 32. Jack Ahoy 34. Rhodes of Africa 36. Pastor Hall 39. The Foreman Went to France 42. Then turned director and made some of the popular Gainsborough costume melodramas of the 40s.

The Night Has Eyes 42. The Man in Grey 43. Love Story 44. The Wicked Lady 45. A Man about the House 47. Idol of Paris 48. The Woman's Angle 52. Miss Tulip Stays the Night 55. See How They Run 55, etc.

Armendariz, Pedro (1912–1963).
Massive Mexican actor with expansive personality; became a star in his own country, then moved on to Hollywood and Europe. Committed suicide.

Rosario 36. Isle of Passion 41. *Maria Candelaria* 43. The Pearl 46. The Fugitive 47. Maclovia 48. Fort Apache 48. Three Godfathers 48. Tulsa 48. We Were Strangers 49. The Torch 50. *El Bruto* 52. Lucretia Borgia 52. Border River 54. The Conqueror 56. Manuela 57. The Wonderful Country 59. Francis of Assisi 61. Captain Sinbad 63. *From Russia with Love* 63, etc.

Armendariz, Pedro, Jnr (1930–).
Mexican-American character actor.

The Magnificent Seven Ride 72. The Deadly Trackers 73. Earthquake 74. La Chevre 81. Treasure Island 90. Tombstone 94, etc.

Armetta, Henry (1888–1945).
Italian-born character actor, long in US, where he was on stage before going to Hollywood. Typecast as excitable, gesticulating foreigner.

My Cousin 18. The Silent Command 23. Street Angel 28. Romance 30. Strangers May Kiss 31. The Unholy Garden 31. Prosperity 32. What! No Beer? 33. The Man Who Reclaimed His Head 34. After Office Hours 35. Poor Little Rich Girl 36. Make a Wish 37. Everybody Sing 38. Dust be my Destiny 39. *The Big Store* 41. Anchors Aweigh 45. Colonel Effingham's Raid 46, many others.

Armida (1913–) (Armida Vendrell).
Mexican actress, performing as a singer and a

dancer as a child, who went on to appear in many westerns.

The International Revue 29. Border Romance 30. Gaiety 43. Fiesta 47. Jungle Goddess 49, etc.

Armitage, George B.
American director and screenwriter.

Gas-s-s-! Or It Became Necessary to Destroy the World in Order to Save It! (w) 70. Vigilante Force (wd) 76. The Last of the Finest (co-w) 90. Miami Blues (wd) 90, etc.

Armstrong, Alun (1946–).
British Shakespearean character actor, occasionally in films.

The Duellists 77. A Bridge Too Far 77. Krull 83. The French Lieutenant's Woman 83. Billy the Kid and the Green Baize Vampire 85. White Hunter, Black Heart 90. London Kills Me 91. Split Second 92. Blue Ice 92. Goodbye Cruel World (TV) 92. Patriot Games 92. Black Beauty 94. Braveheart 95, etc.

Armstrong, Bess (1953–).
American leading lady.

Jekyll and Hyde Together Again 82. High Road to China 83. Jaws 3-D 83. Nothing in Common 86. Second Sight 89. The Skateboard Kid 93. Dream Lover 94. My So-Called Life (TV) 94, etc.

TV series: On Our Own 77–78. All Is Forgiven 86. Married People 90–91.

Armstrong, Gillian (1950–).
Australian director.

My Brilliant Career 80. Starstruck 82. Mrs Soffel (US) 84. High Tide 87. The Last Days of Chez Nous 91. Fires Within 91. Little Women 94, etc.

Armstrong, Louis (1900–1971).
Gravel-voiced American jazz trumpeter and singer, affectionately known as 'Satchmo' (satchel mouth). Sporadic screen appearances, chiefly in guest spots.

■ Pennies from Heaven 36. Every Day's a Holiday 37. Dr Rhythm 38. Artists and Models 38. Going Places 39. *The Birth of the Blues* 41. Cabin in the Sky 43. Jam Session 44. Atlantic City 44. Hollywood Canteen 44. *New Orleans* 47. A Song Is Born 48. The Strip 51. *Here Comes The Groom* 51. Glory Alley 51. *The Glenn Miller Story* 54. *High Society* 56. *Satchmo The Great* 57. The Beat Generation 59. *The Five Pennies* 59. *Paris Blues* 61. *Jazz On A Summer's Day* 61. When the Boys Meet the Girls 62. A Man Called Adam 66. Hello Dolly 69.

Armstrong, R. G. (1917–).
Tough, serious-looking American supporting actor.

Never Love a Stranger 58. *Ride The High Country* 62. Major Dundee 66. El Dorado 66. The Great White Hope 71. Stay Hungry 76. Heaven Can Wait 78. Reds 81. Hammett 82. Evilspeak 82. Angels Die Hard 84. Children of the Corn 84. The Best of Times 86. Bulletproof 88. Dick Tracy 90, etc.

TV series: T.H.E. Cat 66–67.

Armstrong, Robert (1896–1973) (Donald Robert Smith).
Tough American character actor often seen as cop, sheriff, trail boss or shady investigator.

The Main Event 27. Big Money 30. The Tip-Off 31. The Most Dangerous Game 32. *King Kong* (his best role, as foolhardy film producer Carl Denham) 33. Son of Kong 33. G-Men 35. Mystery Man 37. Sky Raiders 41. Outside the Law 41. Dive Bomber 41. The Mad Ghoul 43. Gangs of the Waterfront 45. *Mighty Joe Young* (a continuation of his Kong

role) 49. Las Vegas Shakedown 55. For Those Who Think Young 63, many others.

Famous line (*King Kong*): 'Oh no, it wasn't the airplanes. It was beauty killed the beast.'

Armstrong, Todd (1939–).
Stalwart American leading man of the 60s.

Walk on the Wild Side 62. Jason and the Argonauts 63. King Rat 65. A Time for Killing etc.

TV series: Manhunt 60–61.

army comedies
have always been popular, and most well-know comedians have at least one to their credit. Lau and Hardy were in *Pack Up Your Troubles* and *Blockheads and Great Guns*; Abbott and Costello i *Buck Privates*; Wheeler and Woolsey in *Half Sho Sunrise*; Buster Keaton in *The Dough Boys*; Char Chaplin in *Shoulder Arms*; Harry Langdon in *A Soldier's Plaything*; Larry Semon in *Spuds*; Georg Jessel in *Private Izzy Murray*; Joe E. Brown in *So of Guns*; Jimmy Durante and Phil Silvers in *You in the Army Now*; The Ritz Brothers in *We're in Army Now*; Norman Wisdom in *The Square Peg*; Jerry Lewis in *The Sad Sack*; Martin and Lewis i *At War With The Army*; Bob Hope in *Caught In t Draft*; Frank Randle in *Somewhere In England*; Arthur Lucan in *Old Mother Riley Joins Up*; Geor K. Arthur and Karl Dane in *Rookies*; Wallace Be and Raymond Hatton in *Behind The Front*; Alan Carney and Wally Brown in *Adventures of A Roo and Rookies In Burma*; Joe Sawyer and William Tracy in several comedies including *Tanks a Mill About Face* and *Fall In*; Tom Wilson and Heimie Conklin in *Ham And Eggs At The Front*; George Sidney and Charlie Murray in *Lost At The Front.*

Other American successes in the genre includ *What Did You Do In The War, Daddy?*; *Two Arabi Knights*; *What Price Glory?*; *The Cockeyed World*; *T Sergeant Mulligan*; *The Teahouse of The August Mo The Wackiest Ship In the Army*; *Operation Mad Ba* and above all *M*A*S*H*. Britain has provided *Carry On Sergeant*; *Private's Progress*; *On The Fidd I Only Asked*; *Idol On Parade* and *Reluctant Heroe*

Outstanding TV series: Britain's *The Army Gar* and Hollywood's *Bilko* series with Phil Silvers; *Hogan's Heroes*; *McHale's Navy*; *Gomer Pyle U.S.M. M*A*S*H*.

Arnall, Julia (1931–).
Austrian-born actress resident in Britain.

Man of the Moment 54. I Am a Camera 55. L 56. House of Secrets 56. Man without a Body 5 Mark of the Phoenix 59. The Quiller Memorandum 66. The Double Man 67, etc.

Arnatt, John (1917–).
Solid, pipe-smoking British character actor, mos on TV.

Only Two Can Play 62. Dr Crippen 63. Licens to Kill 66. The Breaking of Bumbo 70. Crucible Terror 71. Bluebell (TV) 85. House of Cards (TV 90, many others.

TV series: Robin Hood (as the hero's perpetua adversary) 55–59.

Arnaud, Léon (1904–).
French composer (and conductor) in Hollywood

Babes in Arms 39. The Big Store 41. Dubarry Was a Lady 43. Easter Parade 48. Three Little Wo 50. Sombrero 53. Seven Brides for Seven Broth 54. Blue 68, etc.

Arnaud, Yvonne (1892–1958).
French actress and pianist, long popular on the British stage.

■ Desire 20. The Temptress 20. Canaries Sometimes Sing 30. Tons of Money 31. On Approval 31. *A Cuckoo in the Nest* 33. Princess Charming 34. Lady in Danger 34. Widow's Might 36. The Gay Adventure 36. The Improper Duchess 36. Stormy Weather 36. Neutral Port 40. Tomorrow We Live 42. Woman to Woman 46. The Ghosts of Berkeley Square 47. Mon Oncle 58.

Arnaz, Desi (1915–1986) (Desiderio Alberto Arnaz y de Acha).
Diminutive but explosive Cuban who began his career as a singer and later formed his own Latin-American band. Performed in minor film musicals during 40s, then married Lucille Ball, founded Desilu Studios, and appeared in the long-running TV series *I Love Lucy* 50–61. Later films include *The Long Long Trailer* 54. *Forever Darling* 56. *The Escape Artist* 82. Produced TV series *The Mothers-in-Law* 57–58.

Arnaz, Desi, Jnr (1953–).
American juvenile lead of the 70s, son of Desi Arnaz and Lucille Ball. Had years of training on his mother's TV series.
  Red Sky at Morning 70. Marco 73. Billy Two Hats 74. She Lives (TV) 74. Joyride 77. How to Pick Up Girls (TV) 78. A Wedding 79. The Night the Bridge Fell Down (TV) 80. The House of Long Shadows 83. The Mambo Kings (playing his father) 92, etc.

Arnaz, Lucie (1951–).
American leading lady, daughter of Lucille Ball and Desi Arnaz.
  Who Is the Black Dahlia? (TV) 75. Billy Jack Goes to Washington 77. Death Scream (TV) 78. The Mating Season 80. Second Thoughts 83.

Arne, Peter (1920–1983) (Peter Arne Albrecht).
Unsmiling Anglo-American actor in British films, usually as dastardly villain. He was murdered, clubbed to death in his London flat.
  Time Slip 55. The Purple Plain 55. *The Moonraker* 57. Ice Cold in Alex 57. *Danger Within* 58. *The Hellfire Club* 61. The Black Torment 64. Khartoum 66. Battle Beneath the Earth 68. Murders in the Rue Morgue 71. Straw Dogs 71. Antony and Cleopatra 72. Providence 77. Victor/Victoria 82, etc.

Arnell, Richard (1917–).
British composer. The Land 40. The Third Secret 63. The Visit 64. The Man Outside 67. The Black Panther 77, etc.

Arness, James (1923–) (James Aurness).
Giant-size American leading man who found his greatest fame on TV. Brother of Peter Graves.
  The Farmer's Daughter 47. Battleground 49. Wagonmaster 51. The Thing (title role) 52. Big Jim McLain 53. Them 54. The Sea Chase 55. The First Traveling Saleslady 56. The Alamo: Thirteen Days to Glory (TV) 87. Gunsmoke: Return to Dodge (TV) 87. Gunsmoke: The Long Ride (TV) 93, many others.
  TV series: Gunsmoke (as Marshal Dillon) 55–75. How the West Was Won 76–79. McLain's Law 81–82.

  I just wanted to see California. I wasn't thinking of acting. – *J.A.*
  The greatest spirtual cleansing I can imagine is a dive into a big surf. – *J.A.*

Arnheim, Rudolf (1904–).
German–American critic whose published writings include *Film as Art* 32 and *Art and Visual Perception* 58.

Arno, Sig (1895–1975) (Siegfried Aron).
German comedy actor in US from early 30s; latterly typecast as funny foreigner.
  Manon Lescaut 26. Pandora's Box 28. The Loves of Jeanne Ney 28. Diary of a Lost Girl 29. The Star Maker 38. The Great Dictator 40. The Palm Beach Story 42. Up In Arms 44. The Great Lover 48. On Moonlight Bay 51. The Great Diamond Robbery 53, many others.

Arnold, Edward (1890–1956) (Guenther Schneider).
Rotund but dynamic American actor who played go-getter leading roles in the 30s. Although he later became typed as kindly father/apoplectic business man, he never lost his popularity.
  Autobiography: 1940, *Lorenzo Goes To Hollywood.*
■ When the Man Speaks 16. The Wrong Way 17. Rasputin and the Empress 32. Okay, America 32. Afraid to Talk 32. Three on a Match 32. Whistling in the Dark 33. The White Sister 33. The Barbarian 33. Jennie Gerhardt 33. Her Bodyguard 33. The Secret of the Blue Room 33. *I'm No Angel* 33. *Roman Scandals* 33. Madame Spy 34. Sadie McKee 34. Thirty Day Princess 34. Unknown Blonde 34. Hideout 34. Million Dollar Ransom 34. The President Vanishes 34. Wednesday's Child 34. Biography of a Bachelor Girl 35. Cardinal Richelieu 35. *The Glass Key* 35. *Diamond Jim* 35. *Crime and Punishment* 35. Remember Last Night? 35. Sutter's Gold 36. *Meet Nero Wolfe* 36. *Come and Get It* 36. John Meade's Woman 37. *The Toast of New York* 37. Easy Living 37. Blossoms on Broadway 37. The Crowd Roars 38. *You Can't Take It With You* 38. Let Freedom Ring 39. Idiot's Delight 39. Man About Town 39. *Mr Smith Goes To Washington* 39. Slightly Honourable 40. The Earl of Chicago 40. Johnny Apollo 40. Lillian Russell 40. The Penalty 41. The Lady from Cheyenne 41. Meet John Doe 41. Nothing But the Truth 41. Unholy Partners 41. Design for Scandal 41. Johnny Eager 41. *All That Money Can Buy* (as Daniel Webster) 41. The War Against Mrs Hadley 42. *Eyes in The Night* 42. The Youngest Profession 42. Standing Room Only 44. Janie 44. *Kismet* 44. Mrs Parkington 44. Main Street After Dark 44. Weekend at the Waldorf 45. The Hidden Eye 45. Ziegfeld Follies 46. Janie Gets Married 46. *Three Wise Fools* 46. No Leave No Love 46. The Mighty McGurk 46. My Brother Talks to Horses 46. *Dear Ruth* 47. *The Hucksters* 47. Three Daring Daughters 48. Big City 48. Wallflower 48. Command Decision 48. John Loves Mary 49. Take Me Out to the Ball Game 49. Big Jack 49. Dear Wife 49. The Yellow Cab Man 50. Annie Get Your Gun 50. The Skipper Surprised His Wife 50. Dear Brat 51. Belles on Their Toes 52. City That Never Sleeps 53. Man of Conflict 53. Living It Up 54. The Houston Story 56. The Ambassador's Daughter 56. Miami Exposé 56.
◎ For maintaining an ebullient star personality through two decades of talkies, despite his unromantic physique. *Diamond Jim.*

Arnold, Jack (1916–1992).
American director.
  It Came from Outer Space 53. The Glass Web 53. Girls in the Night 53. The Creature from the Black Lagoon 54. Tarantula 55. Red Sundown 56. The Tattered Dress 57. *The Incredible Shrinking Man* 57. Pay the Devil 57. The Lady Takes a Flyer 58. High School Confidential 58. The Mouse That Roared (GB) 59. No Name on the Bullet 59. Bachelor in Paradise 61. A Global Affair 63. Hello Down There 68. Black Eye 73. The Swiss Conspiracy 76, etc.

Arnold, Malcolm (1921–).
British composer.

The Sound Barrier 52. Island in the Sun 56. *The Bridge on the River Kwai* (AA) 57. Inn of the Sixth Happiness 58. Tunes of Glory 60. The Chalk Garden 64. The Heroes of Telemark 65. Africa – Texas Style! 67. The Reckoning 68. Battle of Britain 69. David Copperfield (TV) 70, etc.

Arnold, Roseanne (1952–) (Roseanne Barr).
Outspoken plump American actress, a former stand-up comic, who is a star on TV but not, so far, on film. Formerly married to actor Tom Arnold.
  Autobiography: 1990, *My Life as a Woman.*
  She-Devil 89. The Woman Who Loved Elvis (TV) 93.
  TV series: Roseanne 88– .

Arnold, Tom.
American actor and producer. Formerly married to Roseanne Arnold.
  Backfield in Motion (TV) 91. Hero (GB: Accidental Hero) 92. The Woman Who Loved Elvis (TV) 93. Undercover Blues 93. True Lies 94, etc.
  TV series: Roseanne 89– .

Arnoul, Françoise (1931–) (Françoise Gautsch).
Sultry French leading lady of sex melodramas in the 50s.
  Quai de Grenelle 50. Forbidden Fruit 52. Companions of the Night 53. La Rage au Corps 53. The Sheep Has Five Legs 54. French Can-Can 55. The Face of the Cat 57. The Devil and the Ten Commandments 61. Le Dimanche de la Vie 66. The Little Theatre of Jean Renoir 69, etc.

Arnt, Charles (1908–1990).
American character actor often seen as snoop, suspicious character, or just plain ordinary fellow.
  Ladies Should Listen 34. The Witness Chair 36. Remember the Night 40. Blossoms in the Dust 41. Twin Beds 42. Up in Arms 44. Cinderella Jones 46. *Dangerous Intruder* 46. That Brennan Girl 47. Wabash Avenue 50. Veils of Baghdad 53. Miracle of the Hills 59. Sweet Bird of Youth 62, many others.

Aromarama.
A process that linked smells to sequences in a movie, the perfume being pumped through the air-conditioning system into the auditorium. It was first used for the screening of a documentary, *The Great Wall of China* 59, but, like the similar Smell-O-Vision (qv), was never more than a short-lived gimmick.

Arquette, Alexis (1970–).
American actor, the brother of Rosanna and Patricia Arquette.
  Last Exit to Brooklyn 89. Jumpin' at the Boneyard 92. Miracle Beach 92. Jack Be Nimble 93. Threesome 94. Don't Do It 94. Pulp Fiction 94, etc.

Arquette, Cliff (1906–1974).
American comedy actor familiar on radio and TV as hillbilly Charlie Weaver. Appeared with Abbott and Costello in *Comin' Round the Mountain.*

Arquette, Lewis.
American character actor, the son of Cliff Arquette and father of Rosanna, Patricia and Alexis.
  Loose Shoes 80. Nobody's Fool 80. The Horror Show 89. Syngenor 90. Book of Love 91. The Linguini Incident 92. Sleep with Me 94, etc.
  TV series: The Waltons 78–81.

Arquette, Patricia (1968–).
American leading actress, in routine movies until

True Romance. She is the sister of Rosanna Arquette.

A Nightmare on Elm Street Part Three: Dream Warriors 87. Pretty Smart 87. Far North 88. Indian Runner 91. Prayer of the Rollerboys 91. Trouble Bound 93. Ethan Frome 93. *True Romance* 94. Holy Matrimony 94. Ed Wood 94. Infinity. 95, etc.

¶ I never had a huge need to be a big movie star or a billionaire. – *P.A.*

I think raising my baby is the most artistic thing you can do. – *P.A.*

Arquette, Rosanna (1959–   ).
American leading lady of the 80s, usually in sultry roles.

Harvest Home (TV) 78. More American Graffiti 79. Gorp 80. S.O.B. 81. *Johnny Belinda* (TV) 82. *The Executioner's Song* (TV) 83. Baby It's You 83. Off the Wall 84. Desperately Seeking Susan (BFA) 85. 8 Million Ways to Die 85. The Aviator 85. Silverado 85. After Hours 85. Nobody's Fool 86. Amazon Women on the Moon 87. The Big Blue 88. Black Rainbow 89. New York Stories 89. Wendy Cracked a Walnut 90. Flight of the Intruder 91. Son of the Morning Star (TV) 91. Sweet Revenge 91. The Linguini Incident 92. The Wrong Man 93. Nowhere to Run 93, etc.

TV series: Shirley 79–80.

Arrighi, Luciana.
Australian production designer.

My Brilliant Career 80. Privates on Parade 84. The Ploughman's Lunch 84. Mrs Soffel 84. The Return of the Soldier 85. Madame Sousatzka 88. The Rainbow 89. Close My Eyes 91. Howards End (AA) 92. The Remains of the Day (AAN) 93. Only You 94, etc.

Arrighi, Nike (1946–   ).
Italian-Australian leading lady.

Don't Raise the Bridge, Lower the River 67. The Devil Rides Out 68. One Plus One 68. Women in Love 69. Countess Dracula 70. Day for Night 73, etc.

Arsène Lupin.
The gallant French jewel thief and part-time detective, created at the beginning of the century by Maurice Leblanc, has been the subject of many films, the first being a Vitagraph 1917 version starring Earle Williams. In 1932 the Barrymore brothers were in *Arsène Lupin*, John taking the title role; in 1938 Melvyn Douglas was in *Arsène Lupin Returns;* Charles Korvin took over in 1944 for *Enter Arsène Lupin;* in 1957 there was Robert Lamoureux in *The Adventures of Arsène Lupin;* and in 1962 Jean-Claude Brialy starred in *Arsène Lupin Contre Arsène Lupin.* A French TV series ran during the 70s.

art director.
Technician responsible for designing sets, sometimes also costumes and graphics. 'Production designer' is a more pretentious way of saying much the same thing. The importance of this work to the finished product first became noticeable in *Intolerance* and the German expressionist films of the 20s, then in such diverse talking films as *The Old Dark House, Things to Come, The Cat and the Canary* (both versions), *Citizen Kane, Trouble in Paradise, The Mystery of the Wax Museum, A Matter of Life and Death, Les Enfants du Paradis,* and *Kings Row.* Important figures (all qv) include William Cameron Menzies, Anton Grot, Cedric Gibbons, Ken Adam, Vincent Korda, Hans Dreier, Alfred Junge, Carmen Dillon.

art house.
American term (now displacing 'specialized hall' in GB) for cinema showing classic revivals and highbrow or off-beat new films of limited commercial appeal.

The Art of the Film,
by Ernest Lindgren. A useful primer by a longtime curator of the National Film Archive; first published 1948 and revised in 1963.

Artaud, Antonin (1896–1948).
French drama critic and writer who dabbled in films.

Napoleon (a) 26. The Passion of Joan of Arc (a) 28. *The Seashell and the Clergyman* (w) 28.

Artemyev, Eduard.
Russian composer.

Solaris 72. At Home among Strangers 74. A Slave of Love 76. Platanov 77. Stalker 79, etc.

Arthur.
The legendary British king of the 5th or 6th century, central figure of the courtly love tradition and alleged creator not only of the democratic Round Table but of the idyllic city and palace of Camelot, has figured in several movies, especially in recent years when we seem to have had need to cherish our legends. There have been three annual versions, to begin with, of *A Connecticut Yankee at King Arthur's Court;* in the 1949 version Cedric Hardwicke played the King as having a perpetual cold. In 1942, Arthur Askey dreamed he was a member of the Round Table in *King Arthur Was a Gentleman.* In 1964 Disney presented in cartoon form the childhood of Arthur in *The Sword in the Stone.* In slightly more serious vein, Mel Ferrer was Arthur in *Knights of the Round Table* 54, with Robert Taylor as Lancelot and Ava Gardner as Guinevere. Anthony Bushell had the role in *The Black Knight* 54 and Mark Dignam took over in *Siege of the Saxons* 64. In the 1963 *Lancelot and Guinevere,* the three roles were taken respectively by Brian Aherne, Cornel Wilde and Jean Wallace; in the 1967 musical *Camelot,* by Richard Harris, Franco Nero, and Vanessa Redgrave. In the 70s there came Bresson's *Lancelot du Lac* and Rohmer's *Perceval.* In 1980 John Boorman gave us a noisy, violent version of the legend, *Excalibur.*

TV series on the subject have included *Sir Lancelot,* an Australian cartoon series called *Arthur!,* and a Welsh serial called *Arthur of The Britons.* There is also a TV movie, *Arthur the King.*

Arthur, Beatrice (1923–   ) (Bernice Frankel).
Dominant American comedy actress, a big TV hit 1972–76 as 'Maude'.

That Kind of Woman 58. Lovers and Other Strangers 69. Mame 73. History of the World: Part I 81, etc.

TV series: Maude 72–76 (after occasional stints as the character in All in the Family). Amanda's 83. *The Golden Girls* 85–92.

¶ All this time I've just wanted to be blonde, beautiful, and 5 feet 2 inches tall. (She's 5 feet 11 inches). – *B.A.*

Famous line (*Auntie Mame*): 'Oh my God – somebody's been sleeping in my dress!'

Arthur, George K. (1899–1985) (G. K. A. Brest).
Small but gamy hero of the British silent screen, popular in such films as *Kipps* 21. *A Dear Fool* 22. Went to Hollywood and was popular for a while. Became a financier and distributor of art shorts.

Madness of Youth 23. Lights of Old Broadway 25. The Salvation Hunters 25. Irene 26. The Boy Friend 26. Rookies (first of a series of comedies with Karl Dane) 27. Baby Mine 28. The Last of Mrs Cheyney 29. Chasing Rainbows 30. Oliver Twist 33. Riptide 34. Vanessa (last to date) 35.

Arthur, Jean (1905–1991) (Gladys Greene).
Petite, squeaky-voiced American leading actress who after a long and dreary apprenticeship was especially notable as the determined feminist heroine of social comedies in the 30s and 40s.

■ Cameo Kirby 23. The Temple of Venus 24. Fast and Fearless 24. Seven Chances 25. The Drug Store Cowboy 25. A Man of Nerve 25. Tearing Loose 25. Thundering Through 26. Born to Battle 26. The Hurricane Horseman 26. The Fighting Cheat 26. The Cowboy Cop 26. Twisted Triggers 26. The College Boob 26. The Block Signal 26. Husband Hunters 27. The Broken Gate 27. Horseshoes 27. The Poor Nut 27. Flying Luck 27. The Masked Menace 27. Wallflowers 28. Easy Come Easy Go 28. Warming Up 28. Brotherly Love 28. Sins of the Fathers 29. The Canary Murder Case 29. Stairs of Sand 29. The Mysterious Dr Fu Manchu 29. *The Greene Murder Case* 29. The Saturday Night Kid 29. Halfway to Heaven 29. Street of Chance 30. Young Eagles 30. Paramount on Parade 30. The Return of Dr Fu Manchu 30. Danger Lights 30. The Silver Horde 30. The Gang Buster 31. Virtuous Husband 31. The Lawyer's Secret 31. Ex-Bad Boy 31. Get That Venus 33. The Past of Mary Holmes 33. Whirlpool 34. The Defense Rests 34. The Most Precious Thing in Life 34. *The Whole Town's Talking* 35. Public Hero Number One 35. Party Wife 35. Diamond Jim 35. The Public Menace 35. *If You Could Only Cook* 35. *Mr Deeds Goes to Town* 36. The Ex Mrs Bradford 36. Adventure in Manhattan 36. *The Plainsman* (a) Calamity Jane) 36. More Than a Secretary 36. *History is Made at Night* 37. *Easy Living* 37. *You Can't Take It With You* 38. Only Angels Have Wings 39. *Mr Smith Goes to Washington* 39. Too Many Husbands 40. Arizona 40. *The Devil and Miss Jones* 41. *The Talk of the Town* 42. *The More the Merrier* (AAN) 43. A Lady Takes a Chance 43. The Impatient Years 44. A Foreign Affair 48. Shane 53.

TV series: The Jean Arthur Show 66.

Arthur, Johnny (1883–1951) (John Williams).
American character actor, mainly in comedies, including Our Gang shorts, and often as a downtrodden little man. His best, and least characteristic, role was as the villain Sakima in the serial *The Masked Marvel* 43.

The Unknown Purple 23. The Desert Song 29. It's a Wise Child 31. Traveling Saleslady 35. Crime and Punishment 35. The King Steps Out 36. Danger on the Air 38. Road to Singapore 40. Henry Aldrich Gets Glamour 43, etc.

Arthur, Robert (1909–1986) (R.A. Feder).
American producer, mainly with Universal.

Buck Privates Come Home 46. Abbott and Costello Meet Frankenstein 48. The Big Heat 53. Man of a Thousand Faces 57. The Great Impostor 60. Lover Come Back 60. That Touch of Mink 62. Father Goose 64. Shenandoah 65. Blindfold 66. Hellfighters 68. Sweet Charity 69. One More Train to Rob 73, many others.

Arthur, Robert (1925–   ) (Robert Arthaud).
American actor, former radio announcer, in general supporting roles since 1945.

Roughly Speaking 45. Twelve O'Clock High 49. Ace in the Hole 51. Young Bess 54. Top of the World 55. Hellcats 57. Young and Wild 58, many others.

rundell, Denis (1898–1988).
itish character actor (radio's Dr Morelle).
The Show Goes On 35. The Return of Carol
eane 38. Pimpernel Smith 41. Colonel Blimp 43.
rnival 46. The History of Mr Polly 49. Something
oney Can't Buy 52, etc.

rvanitis, Georgos (1941–).
eek cinematographer, associated with the films
director Theodoros Angelopoulos (qv).
Reconstruction (Anaparastassi) 70. Days of 36
meres Tou 36) 72. The Travelling Players (O
iassos) 75. Assault to Agathon 75. Iphigenia 76.
e Huntsman (aka The Hunters) (I Kynighi) 77.
exander the Great (O Megalexandros) 80.
oyage to Cythera (Taxidi Sta Kithira) 84. *The
ekeeper* (O Melissokomos) 86. Komitas 87.
ndscape in the Mist (Topio Stin Omichli) 88.
ustralia 89. The Suspended Step of the Stork (To
eteoro Vima To Pelargou) 91. The Butterfly's
ream (Il Sogno della Farfalla) 94, etc.

rvidson, Linda (1884–1949).
merican silent actress, first wife of D. W. Griffith;
e played leads in a few of his early shorts, then
tired.

rzner, Dorothy (1900–1979).
former editor who became Hollywood's only
oman director of the 30s.
Fashions for Women 27. Get Your Man 27. Ten
odern Commandments 27. Manhattan Cocktail
. The Wild Party 29. Sarah and Son 30.
aramount on Parade (part) 30. Anybody's Woman
. Honour Among Lovers 31. Working Girls 31.
errily We Go to Hell 32. Christopher Strong 33.
ana 34. *Craig's Wife* 36. The Bride Wore Red 37.
ance Girl Dance 40. First Comes Courage 43.

.S.C.
ften seen on credit titles after the names of
nematographers, these initials stand for the
merican Society of Cinematographers, a
rofessional association, membership of which is
y invitation only. Its aims since its foundation in
918 have been 'to advance the art and science of
inematography'.

asche, Oscar (1871–1936).
eavily built, powerful Australian-born actor-
anager and playwright, of Scandinavian
escent. Author of the libretto for the musical *Chu
hin Chow*, which ran for 2,238 performances in
ondon and has been filmed twice, as a silent and
1934. He was on the London stage from 1893,
ften in Shakespeare, and appeared in a few
ritish films of the 30s.
Don Quixote 33. My Lucky Star 33. Two Hearts
Waltz Time 34. Scrooge 35. Eliza Comes to Stay
. Robber Symphony 36, etc.

How I would like that fellow to play
Desdemona to my Othello, because I should
njoy strangling the life out of his carcase. – O.A.
n a fellow actor

ashbrook, Dana (1967–).
merican actor.
Waxwork 88. Return of the Living Dead Part II
8. Girlfriend from Hell 89. Ghost Dad 90. Twin
eaks: Firewalk with Me 92, etc.

Ashby, Hal (1929–1988).
merican director who tended to smother his
ndoubted talent under layers of oblique
pproaches, and often outstayed his welcome.
s EDITOR: The Russians Are Coming, The Russians

Are Coming 66. In the Heat of the Night (AA) 67.
The Thomas Crown Affair 68, etc.
AS DIRECTOR: The Landlord 70. Harold and Maude
71. The Last Detail 73. Shampoo 75. Bound for
Glory 76. *Coming Home* (AAN) 78. Being There 79.
Second Hand Hearts 80. Lookin' to Get Out 82. Let's
Spend the Night Together 83. The Slugger's Wife
85. Eight Million Ways to Die 85.

Ashcroft, Dame Peggy (1907–1991).
Distinguished British stage actress who appeared
in films only occasionally.
The Wandering Jew 33. *The Thirty-Nine Steps* 35.
Rhodes of Africa 36. *Quiet Wedding* 40. The Nun's
Story 58. Secret Ceremony 68. Sunday Bloody
Sunday 71. Joseph Andrews 77. Hullaballoo over
Bonnie and George's Pictures 78. *A Passage to India*
(AA, BFA) 84, etc.
TV series: Edward and Mrs Simpson (as Queen
Mary) 78. *The Jewel in the Crown* 84.

Asher, Jack (1916–).
British cinematographer, brother of director
Robert Asher.
Lili Marlene 42. Jassy 47. The Good Die Young
53. The Young Lovers 54. Reach for the Sky 56.
Dracula 58. She'll Have to Go (& co-p) 61. The
Intelligence Men 65. The Early Bird 65. That
Riviera Touch 66, many others.

Asher, Jane (1946–).
British leading lady, former child performer in
films from 1951.
Mandy 52. The Greengage Summer 60. The Girl
in the Headlines 63. The Masque of the Red Death
64. Alfie 66. *Deep End* 71. Henry VIII and His Six
Wives 72. Runners 83. Success is the Best Revenge
84. Dreamchild 85. Paris by Night 88, etc.
TV series: Wish Me Luck 89–90. Eats for Treats
91. The Choir 95.

Asher, Max (1880–1957).
American silent film comedian, from vaudeville.
He was known as 'the funniest Dutch comedian
in pictures', starring in dozens of shorts, and also
played Mike in the popular Mike and Jake series of
comedy shorts. He played character parts in the
late 20s and early 30s before retiring to become
a make-up man.
Mike and Jake at the Beach 13. Mike and Jake
in Mexico 13. Mike and Jake at College 13. In
the Year 2014 14. Pete's Awful Crime 15. When
Hiram Went to the City 15. Hiram's Inheritance
15. Suds of Love 17. Rip Van Winkle 21. The
Courtship of Miles Standish 23. The Shooting of
Dan McGrew 24. The Carnival Girl 26. Painting
the Town 27. Show Boat 29. Sweethearts on
Parade 30. The Perils of Pauline (serial) 33. Little
Man, What Now? 34, many others.

Asher, Robert (1915–).
British director.
Follow a Star 59. Make Mine Mink 60. The
Bulldog Breed 60. She'll Have to Go (co-p, co-w,
co-d) 61. On the Beat 62. A Stitch in Time 63. The
Intelligence Men 65. The Early Bird 65. Press for
Time 66.

Asher, William (1919–).
American 'B' director.
■ Leather Gloves (co-d) 48. The Shadow on the
Window 57. The Twenty-Seventh Day 57. *Beach
Party* 63. Johnny Cool 63. Muscle Beach Party 64.
Bikini Beach 64. Beach Blanket Bingo 65. How
to Stuff a Wild Bikini 65. Fireball 500 66. Night
Warning 83. Movers and Shakers 84.

Asherson, Renée (1920–).
British stage actress in occasional films.
Henry V 44. The Way Ahead 44. The Way to the
Stars 44. The Small Back Room 49. The Cure for
Love 50. The Day the Earth Caught Fire 62.
Rasputin the Mad Monk 65. The Smashing Bird I
Used to Know 68. Memento Mori (TV) 92.
Harnessing Peacocks (TV) 93, etc.

Ashley, Edward (1904–) (E. A. Cooper).
British leading man who went to Hollywood but
never did better than third leads.
Men of Steel 33. Underneath the Arches 37.
Spies of the Air 39. *Pride and Prejudice* 40. Bitter
Sweet 41. The Black Swan 42. Nocturne 46. The
Other Love 47. Tarzan and the Mermaids 48.
Macao 52. The Court Jester (as the Fox) 56. Herbie
Rides Again 73. Won Ton Ton 76. Beyond the Next
Mountain 87, etc.

Ashley, Elizabeth (1939–) (Elizabeth Cole).
Cool American leading lady who makes sporadic
appearances.
Autobiography: 1978, *Actress: Postcards from the
Road*.
■ *The Carpetbaggers* 64. Ship of Fools 65. The Third
Day 65. Harpy (TV) 70. Marriage of a Young
Stockbroker 71. When Michael Calls (TV) 71. The
Face of Fear (TV) 71. Second Chance (TV) 71.
Your Money or Your Wife (TV) 72. The Heist (TV)
73. The Magician (TV) 73. Golden Needles 74.
Paperback Hero 75. Rancho de Luxe 75. 92 in the
Shade 75. One of my Wives is Missing 76. The
Great Scout and Cathouse Thursday 76. Fire in the
Sky (TV) 77. Coma 78. Windows 80. Split Image
82. Svengali (TV) 82. Dragnet 87. Dangerous
Curves 88.

Ashman, Howard (1951–1991).
American lyricist, in collaboration with composer
Alan Menken (qv for list of films). Died of AIDS.

Ashton, John.
American character actor.
Breaking Away 79. Borderline 80. Beverly Hills
Cop 84. King Kong Lives 86. Some Kind of
Wonderful 87. Beverly Hills Cop II 87. Midnight
Run 88. She's Having a Baby 88. L.A. Gangs
Rising 89. Curly Sue 91. The Tommyknockers (TV)
93, etc.
TV series: Dallas 78–79. Breaking Away 80–81.
Hardball 89–90.

Ashton, Roy (1918–).
British make-up artist.
Curse of Frankenstein 57. Dracula 58. The
Mummy 59. Curse of the Werewolf 61. The Reptile
66. Vault of Horror 73. The Monster Club 81, etc.

Askew, Luke (1937–).
American character actor, usually in westerns.
Cool Hand Luke 67. The Green Berets 68. Easy
Rider 69. The Great Northfield Minnesota Raid
72. The Culpepper Cattle Company 72. Posse 75.
Rolling Thunder 77. Wanda Nevada 79. The
Warrior and the Sorceress 84. Back to Back 90.
Dune Warriors 91, etc.

Askey, Arthur (1900–1982).
Diminutive (5'2") British comedian with music-
hall experience; gained fame as 'Big Hearted
Arthur' in radio shows.
Autobiography: 1975, *Before Your Very Eyes*.
■ Calling All Stars 37. Band Wagon 39. Charley's
Big-Hearted Aunt 40. *The Ghost Train* 41. I Thank
You 41. Back Room Boy 42. King Arthur Was a
Gentleman 42. Miss London Ltd 43. Bees in
Paradise 44. The Love Match 54. Ramsbottom

Rides Again 56. Make Mine a Million 58. Friends and Neighbours 59. The Alf Garnett Saga 72.

Askin, Leon (1907–).
Rotund American supporting actor who often plays sinister or comic Russians.
  Autobiography: 1990, *Quietude and Quest*.
  Road to Bali 52. Knock on Wood 54. Son of Sinbad 55. My Gun Is Quick 58. One Two Three 61. Do Not Disturb 65. The Maltese Bippy 69. Dr Death 73, many others.

Askwith, Robin (1950–).
British leading man of 70s low comedy, most recently on stage in London, New Zealand and Australia.
  If 68. Bartleby 70. Nicholas and Alexandra 71. The Four Dimensions of Greta 71. Bless this House 73. Confessions of a Window Cleaner 74. Confessions of a Pop Performer 75. Confessions of a Driving Instructor 76. Stand Up Virgin Soldiers 77. Let's Get Laid 78, etc.
  TV series: Bottle Boys 83–86.

Aslan, Grégoire (1908–1982) (Kridor Aslanian).
Armenian character actor, usually in comic or villainous roles.
  Sleeping Car to Trieste 48. Occupe-Toi d'Amélie 49. Last Holiday 50. Cage of Gold 50. Confidential Report 53. He Who Must Die 56. Roots of Heaven 56. The Criminal 60. Cleopatra 62. Paris When It Sizzles 64. The High Bright Sun 65. Moment to Moment 65. Our Man in Marrakesh 66. Lost Command 66. A Flea in Her Ear 68. You Can't Win Them All 70. Sinbad's Golden Voyage 73, many others.

Asner, Edward (1929–).
Chubby American character actor who usually plays tough guys, sometimes with a heart of gold. He was a provocative union leader in a long-running actors' strike, and his successful series *Lou Grant* was cancelled allegedly because of his political views.
  The Satan Bug 65. The Slender Thread 65. El Dorado 66. The Venetian Affair 67. Gunn 67. The Todd Killings 70. The Skin Game 71. Rich Man Poor Man (TV) 76. Hey I'm Alive (TV) 76. Gus 76. The Life and Assassination of the Kingfish (as Huey Long) (TV) 77. Roots (TV) 77. The Gathering (TV) 78. Fort Apache, the Bronx 82. O'Hara's Wife 82. Anatomy of an Illness (TV) 83. Daniel 83. The Christmas Star (TV) 86. Bronx Zoo (TV) 87. JFK 91. Heads (TV) 94, etc.
  TV series: Slattery's People 64. *The Mary Tyler Moore Show* 70–74. *Lou Grant* 77–82. Off the Rack 85. Thunder Alley 94.

¶ I really wanted to be an adventurer, to lay
‖ pipeline in South America or be a cabin boy . . . but I didn't have the guts. – *E.A.*
  I don't know him well, but he seems an extremely angry and short-tempered man. He's enormously sensitive to criticism. – *Charlton Heston*

Asp, Anna (1946–).
Swedish production designer, noted for her work with Ingmar Bergman.
  Face to Face 76. Autumn Sonata 78. Fanny and Alexander (AA) 82. After the Rehearsal 84. The Sacrifice 86. Pelle the Conqueror 87. Katinka 88. The Best Intentions 92. The House of the Spirits 94, etc.

aspect ratio.
Relative breadth and height of screen. Before 1953 this was 4:3 or 1.33:1. 'Standard' wide screen varies from 1.66:1 to 1.85:1. Anamorphic processes are wider: SuperScope 2:1, CinemaScope and most others 2.35:1 (or 2.55:1 with magnetic stereophonic sound). Vista-Vision, a printing process, was shot in 1.33:1 but recommended for screening at up to 2:1, i.e. with top and bottom cut off and the rest magnified. The TV screen is fixed at 1.33:1, therefore all wide-screen films lose something when played on it.

Asquith, Anthony (1902–1968).
British director, son of Lord Oxford and Asquith, nicknamed 'Puffin'. His films were always civilized and usually entertaining but both the early experiments in technique and the later upper-class comedies and dramas suffered from the same lack of warmth and humanity.
  Biography: 1973, *'Puffin' Asquith* by R. J. Minney.
  ■ *Shooting Stars* (co-d) 28. *Underground* 30. A Cottage on Dartmoor 30. The Runaway Princess 30. Tell England 31. Dance Pretty Lady 31. Marry Me 32. The Window Cleaner 32. Lucky Number 33. Unfinished Symphony 34. Moscow Nights 35. Forever England 35. *Pygmalion* (co-d) 37. *French Without Tears* 39. Freedom Radio 40. *Quiet Wedding* 40. Cottage to Let 41. Uncensored 42. We Dive at Dawn 43. *The Demi-Paradise* 43. Welcome to Britain (doc) 43. Two Fathers 44. *Fanny by Gaslight* 44. *The Way to the Stars* 45. While the Sun Shines 46. *The Winslow Boy* 48. The Woman in Question 50. *The Browning Version* 50. *The Importance of Being Earnest* 51. The Net 53. The Final Test 53. The Young Lovers 54. Carrington VC 55. On Such a Night (doc) 55. *Orders to Kill* 58. The Doctors' Dilemma 59. Libel 60. The Millionairess 61. Guns of Darkness 62. Two Living One Dead 62. *The VIPS* 63. The Yellow Rolls-Royce 64.

Assante, Armand (1949–).
American leading man.
  The Lords of Flatbush 74. Paradise Alley 78. Prophecy 79. Lady of the House (TV) 79. Private Benjamin 80. Love and Money 82. I the Jury 83. Unfaithfully Yours 84. Belizaire the Cajun 85. The Penitent 88. Animal Behavior 89. Eternity 90. Q & A 90. The Marrying Man (aka Too Hot to Handle) 91. Hoffa 92. The Mambo Kings 92. 1492 92. Triple Indemnity 93. Fatal Instinct 93. Trial by Jury 94. Judge Dredd 95, etc.

assassination
has not been a favourite film subject, though historical incidents have been examined in *Julius Caesar, Sarajevo, Nicholas and Alexandra, Nine Hours to Rama, The Assassination of Trotsky, Gandhi, The Parallax View* and *JFK*. Assassination attempts have figured in *Suddenly, The Man Who Knew Too Much, Foreign Correspondent, The Manchurian Candidate* and *The Day of the Jackal*.

assistant director.
More properly 'assistant to the director', being concerned with details of administration rather than creation.

associate producer.
Usually the actual producer or supervisor of the film, the title of 'executive producer' having been taken by the head of the studio.

Associated British
was the only British complex of companies which had power comparable to that of the Rank Organization (qv). Its history is tied up with Elstree Studios, originally owned by British International Pictures, which after many mergers emerged as Associated British in 1933. The men involved in the story are producer Herbert Wilcox, John Maxwell, a lawyer who turned film distributor and later founded the ABC cinema chain, and J. Williams, a wealthy exhibitor. Distribution was arranged through Pathé Pictures, which became powerful partner. Elstree was the first British studio to wire for sound (*Blackmail*) and the first to produce a bilingual talkie (*Atlantic*). Throughout the thirties it turned out fifteen films a year, usually unambitious but competent; and unmistakably British. In 1940 a great number of shares were sold to Warner Brothers, and in 19 the distribution arm became known as Warner-Pathé. Other associated companies include Pathé News, Pathé Laboratories, Pathé Equipment, and ABC Television. In 1969, after several years of comparative inactivity, the complex was taken over by EMI. In the 80s Cannon took over all the companies, but promptly sold the library to Jerry Weintraub.

Association of Cinematograph, Television and Allied Technicians.
ACTT: the British film-makers' union. Founded 1931.

Asta.
A wire-haired fox-terrier who appeared (impersonated by several dogs) in *The Thin Man* and other films between 1934 and 1947.

Astaire, Fred (1899–1987) (Frederick Austerlitz).
American dancing star whose inimitable finesse and good humour delighted two generations. His half-spoken singing was almost equally delightful and the films in which he was teamed with Ginger Rogers(*) have a magic all their own. Academy Award 1949 'for his unique artistry and his unique contribution to the techniques of motion pictures'.
  Autobiography: 1959, *Steps in Time*.
  ■ Dancing Lady 33. *Flying Down to Rio 33. *The Gay Divorcee 34. *Roberta 35. *Top Hat 35. *Follow the Fleet 36. *Swing Time 36. *Shall We Dance? 37. A Damsel in Distress 37. *Carefree 38. *The Story of Vernon and Irene Castle 39. Broadway Melody of Second Chorus 40. You'll Never Get Rich 41. Holiday Inn 42. You Were Never Lovelier 42. The Sky's the Limit 43. Yolanda and the Thief 45. Ziegfeld Follies 46. Blue Skies 46. Easter Parade 48. *The Barkleys of Broadway 48. Three Little Words 50. Let's Dance 50. Royal Wedding 51. The Belle of New York 52. The Band Wagon 53. Daddy Long Legs 55. Funny Face 57. Silk Stockings 57. On the Beach (dramatic role) 59. The Pleasure of His Company (dr) 61. Notorious Landlady (dr) 62. Finian's Rainbow 68. The Midas Run (dr) 69. The Over The Hill Gang Rides Again (dr: TV film) 71 That's Entertainment, Part Two 74. The Towering Inferno (AAN) 75. The Amazing Dobermans (dr) 76. The Purple Taxi (dr) 77. A Family Upside Down (dr) (TV) 78. The Man in the Santa Claus Suit (dr) (TV) 80. Ghost Story (dr) 81.
  TV series: It Takes a Thief 65–69.
  ☼ For his apparently lighter-than-air constitution, his brilliantly inventive dancing, his breezy elegance, his unlikely but effective voice, and his pleasing longevity. Top Hat.

¶ The most famous quote about the screen's
‖ nimblest dancer is the report of the studio talent scout on his first screen test:
  Can't act. Can't sing. Slightly bald. Can dance little.
In later years, when he was a household name around the world, he tried to match that for humility:
  I have no desire to prove anything by dancing

have never used it as an outlet or as a means of expressing myself. I just dance.
d:
just put my feet in the air and move them around.
t in another mood, he did once confess:
suppose I made it look easy, but gee whiz, did work and worry.
ne Kelly summed up his appeal:
He can give the audience pleasure just by walking across the floor.
d Mr Kelly graciously added:
f I'm the Marlon Brando of dancing, he's Cary Grant.
aham Greene put it another way:
The nearest we are ever likely to get to a human Mickey Mouse.
A. Lejeune produced this analysis:
I have never met anyone who did not like Fred Astaire. Somewhere in his sad monkey-sad face, his loose legs, his shy grin, or perhaps the anxious diffidence of his manner, he has found the secret of persuading the world.
dré Sennwald, in a review of *The Gay Divorcee*, as equally percipient:
The audience meets Mr Astaire and the film at their best when he is adjusting his cravat or saying delicious things with his flashing feet that a lyricist would have difficulty putting into words.
hile Fred Astaire said in his 80s:
When they review my shows, they don't say whether they're good or bad – they just write about how old I am.

sterix.
inning, diminutive, moustachioed Gaul, the ro of strip cartoons created by Alberto Uderzo d René Goscinny. The stories, about a village of auls that the invading Romans are unable to feat, satirize many aspects of contemporary life. ss successful are the series of animated films sed on the books.
Asterix the Gaul 67. Asterix and Cleopatra 70. e Twelve Labours of Asterix 75. Asterix in itain 86. Asterix and the Big Fight 89, etc.

sther, Nils (1897–1981).
ave, exotic Swedish leading man in Hollywood om the mid-20s. He was married to Vivian uncan (qv).
Topsy and Eva 27. Sorrell and Son 27. The Blue anube 28. Laugh Clown Laugh 28. The Cossacks 8. Loves of an Actress 28. The Cardboard Lover 8. Our Dancing Daughters 28. Dream of Love 28. /ild Orchids 29. *The Single Standard* 29. The Wrath f the Seas 29. Letty Lynton 32. The Washington lasquerade 32. *The Bitter Tea of General Yen* 32. torm at Daybreak 33. The Right to Romance 33. v Candlelight 34. Madame Spy 34. The Crime octor 34. The Love Captive 34. *Abdul the Damned* GB) 35. Make Up (GB) 37. Dr Kildare's Wedding ay 41. The Night Before the Divorce 41. The Night f January 16th 41. Sweater Girl 42. Night lonster 42. The Hour Before Dawn 44. *The Man in alf Moon Street* 44. Son of Lassie 45. Jealousy 45. he Feathered Serpent 49. That Man from Tangier 0. Vita Frun 62. Gudrun 63.

stin, John (1930–).
merican comic actor with stage experience. He as formerly married to actress Patty Duke.
West Side Story 61. That Touch of Mink 62. andy 68. Viva Max 68. Evil Roy Slade (TV) 72. et to Know Your Rabbit 72. The Brothers O'Toole 3. Freaky Friday 77. Body Slam 87. Gremlins 2: he New Batch 90. The Silence of the Hams (It) 4, etc.

TV series: I'm Dickens He's Fenster 63. The Addams Family 64. Operation Petticoat 77. Mary 85–86.

Astin, MacKenzie (1973–).
American actor, the son of John Astin and Patty Duke and brother of Sean Astin.
The Garbage Pail Kids Movie 87. Iron Will 94.
TV series: The Facts of Life 85–88.

Astin, Sean (1971–).
American adolescent actor, the son of John Astin and Patty Duke.
The Goonies 85. Like Father Like Son 87. White Water Summer 87. Staying Together 89. The War of the Roses 89. Memphis Belle 90. Toy Soldiers 91. Encino Man (GB: California Man) 92. Where the Day Takes You 92. Rudy 93, etc.

Astor, Gertrude (1887–1977).
American silent screen actress, on stage from the age of 13.
Uncle Tom's Cabin 27. The Cat and the Canary 28. Camille 36. How Green Was My Valley 40. The Man Who Shot Liberty Valance 62, many others.

Astor, Mary (1906–1987) (Lucille Langehanke).
American leading lady who despite a stormy and well-publicized private life remained a star from the mid-20s to the mid-40s and remained in demand for character roles.
Autobiographies: 1959, *My Story*. 1971, *A Life on Film*. Novels include: *Image of Kate* 1966. *A Place Called Saturday* 1969.
SILENT FILMS: The Beggar Maid 21. The Bright Shawl 23. Puritan Passions 23. *Beau Brummell* 24. Inez from Hollywood 25. *Don Q Son of Zorro* 25. *Don Juan* 26. Rose of the Golden West 27. Two Arabian Knights 27. Heart to Heart 28. Romance of the Underworld 29, etc.
■ SOUND: Ladies Love Brutes 30. The Runaway Bride 30. Holiday 30. The Lash 30. The Sin Ship 30. The Royal Bed 30. Other Men's Women 31. Behind Office Doors 31. White Shoulders 31. Smart Woman 31. Men of Chance 31. The Lost Squadron 32. A Successful Calamity 32. Those We Love 32. *Red Dust* 32. The Little Giant 33. Jennie Gerhardt 33. The Kennel Murder Case 33. Convention City 33. The World Changes 33. Easy to Love 34. The Man with Two Faces 34. Return of the Terror 34. Upper World 34. The Case of the Howling Dog 34. I am a Thief 34. Man of Iron 35. Red Hot Tires 35. Straight from the Heart 35. Dinky 35. Page Miss Glory 35. The Murder of Dr Harrigan 35. The Lady from Nowhere 36. And So They Were Married 36. *Dodsworth* 36. Trapped by Television 36. *The Prisoner of Zenda* 37. *The Hurricane* 37. Paradise for Three 38. No Time to Marry 38. There's Always a Woman 38. Woman against Woman 38. Listen Darling 39. *Midnight* 39. Turnabout 40. Brigham Young 40. *The Great Lie* (AA) (her most splendid bitchy performance) 41. *The Maltese Falcon* 41. *Across the Pacific* 42. *The Palm Beach Story* 42. Young Ideas 43. Thousands Cheer 43. *Meet Me in St Louis* 44. Blonde Fever 44. Claudia and David 46. Desert Fury 47. Cynthia 47. Fiesta 47. *Act of Violence* 49. Cass Timberlane 49. *Little Women* (as Marmee) 49. Any Number Can Play 49. A Kiss Before Dying 56. The Power and the Prize 56. The Devil's Hairpin 56. This Happy Feeling 58. Stranger in my Arms 59. *Return to Peyton Place* 61. *Youngblood Hawke* 64. Hush Hush Sweet Charlotte 64.
✪ For amiably sending herself up in half a dozen portraits of mature but fallible women between 1936 and 1942; and for sheer durability. *The Great Lie*.

¶ I was never totally involved in movies. I was making my father's dream come true. – M.A.

Famous line (*The Great Lie*): 'If I didn't think you meant so well, I'd feel like slapping your face.'

Astruc, Alexandre (1923–).
French director, former film critic.
The Crimson Curtain 51. Les Mauvaises Rencontres 54. Une Vie 56. La Proie Pour l'Ombre 61. L'Education Sentimentale 61. La Longue Marche 65. Flammes sur L'Adriatique 67, etc.

¶ The fundamental problem of the cinema is how to express thought. – A.A.

Atchley, Hooper (1887–1943).
American character actor, from the stage. Committed suicide.
Love at First Sight 29. The Santa Fe Trail 30. Arizona Terror 31. Trouble in Paradise 32. Gun Justice 33. The Three Musketeers (serial) 34. Mystery Mountain (serial) 34. Law beyond the Range 35. Ace Drummond (serial) 36. A Day at the Races 37. Mr Wong, Detective 38. Pirates of the Skies 39. The Gay Caballero 40. Adventures of Red Ryder (serial) 40. Dick Tracy vs Crime, Inc (serial) 41. The Little Foxes 41. Gentleman Jim 42. Mission to Moscow 43. G-Men versus the Black Dragon (serial) 43. The Song of Bernadette 43, etc.

Ates, Roscoe (1892–1962).
Short, stuttering American character actor, on stage from 1915 and films from 1929. A former violinist and vaudeville performer, he played Eddie Dean's sidekick in many second-feature westerns.
South Sea Rose 29. Billy the Kid 30. Cimarron 31. Renegades of the West 33. Alice in Wonderland 33. Riders of the Black Hills 38. Gone with the Wind 39. Chad Hannah 40. Bad Men of Missouri 41. Sullivan's Travels 42. Stars over Texas 46. West to Glory 47. Black Hills 48. Thunder in the Pines 49. The Blazing Forest 52. The Stranger Wore a Gun 53. Abbott and Costello Meet the Keystone Cops 53. Meet Me in Las Vegas 56. The Birds and the Bees 57. The Ladies' Man 61, etc.
TV series: The Marshall of Gunsight Pass 50.

Atherton, William (1947–).
American actor of the 70s, with stage background.
The New Centurions 72. Class of '44 73. The Sugarland Express 74. The Day of the Locust 74. The Hindenburg 76. Looking for Mr Goodbar 77. Malibu (TV) 83. Ghostbusters 84. Real Genius 85. No Mercy 86. Intrigue 90. Die Hard 2 90. Oscar 91. Chrome Soldiers 92. The Pelican Brief 93, etc.

Atkins, Christopher (1961–).
American actor who began by starring opposite Brooke Shields in *The Blue Lagoon*.
The Blue Lagoon 80. The Pirate Movie 82. A Night in Heaven 83. Mortuary Academy 88. Listen to Me 89. Shakma 90. Exchange Lifeguards 93, etc.
TV series: Dallas 83–84.

Atkins, Eileen (1934–).
British character actress, highly regarded on stage. She was co-creator of the TV series Upstairs, Downstairs and The House of Elliott. Formerly married to actor Julian Glover.
■ *Inadmissible Evidence* 68. I Don't Want to Be Born 75. Equus 77. She Fell Among Thieves (TV) 78. The Dresser 83. Let Him Have It 91. The Lost Language of Cranes (TV) 91. Wolf 94. Cold Comfort Farm (TV) 95.

Atkinson, Rowan (1955–).
English actor and comedian, best known as the
hapless Mr Bean, which from 1990 revived silent
slapstick comedy on television. He studied
electrical engineering at Newcastle University and
then went to Oxford University, where he
appeared in the Oxford Revue and then performed
a one-man show before teaming with Mel Smith
and Griff Rhys Jones in the TV series *Not the Nine
O'Clock News*.

Never Say Never Again 83. The Tall Guy 89. The
Appointments of Dennis Jennings (short) 89. The
Witches 90. Hot Shots! Part Deux 93. Four
Weddings and a Funeral 94, etc.

TV series: Not the Nine O'Clock News 81–82.
Blackadder 83–84. Blackadder II 85. Blackadder III
87–88. Blackadder Goes Forth 89–90.

Attenborough, Richard (1923–) (Lord
Attenborough).
British character actor who escaped from early
typecasting as a young coward, revealed an
ambitious range of characterizations, and went on
to produce and direct. He became a life peer in
1993. Married to actress Sheila Sim in 1945.
■ *In Which We Serve* 42. Schweik's New
Adventures 42. The Hundred Pound Window 43.
Journey Together 43. A Matter of Life and Death
46. School for Secrets 46. The Man Within 47.
Dancing with Crime 47. *Brighton Rock* 47. London
Belongs to Me 48. *The Guinea Pig* (as a 13-year-old)
49. The Lost People 50. Boys in Brown 50.
Morning Departure 50. Hell is Sold Out 51. The
Magic Box 51. The Gift Horse 52. Father's Doing
Fine 53. Eight O'Clock Walk 54. The Ship that
Died of Shame 54. *Private's Progress* 55. The Baby
and the Battleship 56. Brothers in Law 56. The
Scamp 58. Dunkirk 58. *The Man Upstairs* 58.
Danger Within 58. I'm All Right Jack 58. Sea of
Sand 58. Jetstorm 59. SOS Pacific 59. *The Angry
Silence* (& co-p) 59. *The League of Gentlemen* (& co-
p) 59. Only Two Can Play 62. *Whistle Down the
Wind* (p only) 62. The Dock Brief 62. All Night Long
62. *The Great Escape* (US) 63. *Seance on a Wet
Afternoon* (& p) 64. The Third Secret 64. *Guns at
Batasi* (BFA) 64. The Flight of the Phoenix (US)
65. The Sand Pebbles (US) 66. Doctor Dolittle 67.
The Bliss of Mrs Blossom 68. The Last Grenade 68.
Only When I Larf 68. *Oh What a Lovely War* (co-
p and d only) 69. David Copperfield 69. The Magic
Christian 70. A Severed Head 70. *Loot* 71. 10
Rillington Place 71. Young Winston (d only) 72.
Conduct Unbecoming 75. Rosebud 75. Brannigan
75. And Then There Were None 75. A Bridge Too
Far (d only) 77. The Chess Players (India) 78.
Magic (d only) 78. The Human Factor 79. *Gandhi*
(p, d only) (AA) 82. A Chorus Line (d only) 85.
Cry Freedom (d only) 87. Chaplin (d) 92. Jurassic
Park (a) 93. *Shadowlands* (p, d) 93. Miracle on
34th Street (a) 94.
✪ For being a prime mover in most aspects of
British entertainment for half a century and
demonstrating in an age of hyperbole and bluster
the effectiveness of understatement. *Shadowlands*.

Atterbury, Malcolm (1907–1992).
American character actor.
Dragnet 54. I Was a Teenage Werewolf 57. Blood
of Dracula 57. Rio Bravo 59. The Birds 63. Seven
Days in May 64, etc.
TV series: Thicker than Water 73. Apple's Way
74–75.

Atwater, Barry (1918–1978).
American character actor.
Nightmare 56. Pork Chop Hill 59. Sweet Bird of
Youth 62. Return of the Gunfighter (TV) 66. The
Night Stalker (TV) 72, etc.

Atwill, Lionel (1885–1946).
Incisive but rather stolid British actor who went
to Hollywood in 1932 and stayed to play teutonic
villians, mad doctors and burgomasters.
■ Eve's Daughter 18. For Sale 18. The Marriage
Price 19. The Highest Bidder 21. Indiscretion 21.
The Silent Witness 32. *Doctor X* 32. The Vampire
Bat 33. The Secret of Madame Blanche 33. *The
Mystery of the Wax Museum* 33. Murders in the Zoo
33. The Sphinx 33. Song of Songs 33. The Secret
of the Blue Room 33. The Solitaire Man 33. *Nana*
34. Beggars in Ermine 34. Stamboul Quest 34. One
More River 34. The Age of Innocence 34. The
Firebird 34. The Man Who Reclaimed His Head
35. Mark of the Vampire 35. *The Devil is a Woman*
35. The Murder Man 35. Rendezvous 35. Captain
Blood 35. Lady of Secrets 36. Absolute Quiet 36.
Till We Meet Again 36. *The Road Back* 37. The High
Command 37. Last Train from Madrid 37. The
Great Garrick 37. Lancer Spy 37. Three Comrades
38. The Great Waltz 38. *Son of Frankenstein*
(memorable as the one-armed police chief) 39. *The
Three Musketeers* 39. *The Hound of the Baskervilles* 39.
The Gorilla 39. The Sun Never Sets 39. Mr Moto
Takes a Vacation 39. The Secret of Dr Kildare 39.
Balalaika 39. Charlie Chan in Panama 39. The
Mad Empress 40. Johnny Apollo 40. Charlie
Chan's Murder Cruise 40. The Girl in 313 40.
Boom Town 40. The Great Profile 40. *Man Made
Monster* 41. The Mad Doctor of Market Street 42.
To Be Or Not To Be 42. The Strange Case of Dr RX
42. The Ghost of Frankenstein 42. Pardon My
Sarong 42. Cairo 42. Night Monster 42. Junior G-
Men of the Air (serial) 42. *Sherlock Holmes and the
Secret Weapon* (as Moriarty) 42. Frankenstein Meets
the Wolf Man 43. House of Frankenstein 44.
Captain America (serial) 44. Raiders of Ghost City
(serial) 44. Lady in the Death House 44. Secrets of
Scotland Yard 44. Fog Island 45. Genius at Work
45. Crime Incorporated 45. *House of Dracula* 45.
Lost City of the Jungle (serial) 46.

❡ See, one side of my face is gentle and kind,
incapable of anything but love of my fellow
man. The other profile is cruel and predatory and
evil, incapable of anything but lusts and dark
passions. It all depends which side of my face is
turned towards you – or the camera. – *L.A.*
One doesn't easily forget, Herr Baron, an arm
torn out by the roots. – *L.A. in Son of Frankenstein*
My dear, why are you so pitifully afraid?
Immortality has been the dream, the inspiration of
mankind through the ages. And I am going to give
you immortality! – *L.A. in The Mystery of the Wax
Museum*

Auberjonois, René (1940–).
American character actor.
M*A*S*H 70. Brewster McCloud 71. McCabe
and Mrs Miller 71. Images 72. Pete 'n Tillie 72.
Panache (TV) 76. The Hindenberg 76. King Kong
76. Eyes of Laura Mars 78. Where the Buffalo
Roam 80. The Christmas Star (TV) 86. Walker 87.
Police Academy 5: Assignment Miami Beach 88.
The Little Mermaid (voice) 89. The Feud 90. The
Lost Language of Cranes (TV) 91. The Player 92.
The Ballad of Little Joe 93, etc.
TV series: Benson 80–85. Star Trek: Deep Space
Nine 93– .

Aubert, Lenore (1913–).
Yugoslavian actress in Hollywood from the late
30s, usually in sinister roles.
Bluebeard's Eighth Wife 38. They Got Me
Covered 43. Action in Arabia 44. *Wife of Monte Cristo*
46. The Other Love 47. Return of the Whistler 48.
Abbott and Costello Meet Frankenstein 48. Abbott and
Costello Meet the Killer 49. Une Fille sur la Rou
52, etc.

Aubrey, Anne (1937–).
British leading lady of a few comedies and
adventures in the late 50s.
No Time To Die 58. The Man Inside 58. The
Secret Man 58. The Bandit of Zhobe 59. Idle on
Parade 59. Killers of Kilimanjaro 59. Jazzboat 60
In the Nick 60. Let's Get Married 60. The Hellio
61. Assignment Munich (TV) 72. The Carey
Treatment 73.

Aubrey, James T. (1918–1994).
Production executive, nicknamed 'The Smiling
Cobra'. He was president of CBS-TV at the heigh
of its success (1959–65), and, from 1969–73, in
charge of MGM, during which period he cut cos
by cancelling movies and selling many of the
studio's assets, including its wardrobe and props
from its classic films. Then became an independe
producer, mainly of TV movies. Married actress
Phyllis Thaxter (1944–63).
Futureworld 76. The Hunger 83, etc.

❡ I don't want to hear any more bullshit about
the old MGM. The old MGM is gone. – *J.T.A*
Jim Aubrey doesn't know as much about film
as a first-year cinema student. – *Blake Edwards*
No man in history ever had such a lock on su
an enormous audience. – *Life magazine on Aubrey,
at CBS*

Aubrey, Jimmy (1887–1984).
English music-hall comedian and actor. Born in
Liverpool, he was a member of Fred Karno's
troupe that toured America and also included
Charlie Chaplin and Stan Laurel. He starred in sile
comedy shorts, with Oliver Hardy as the heavy,
and had bit parts in a few Laurel and Hardy
comedies before becoming a character actor in
early talkies.
Footlights and Fakers 17. She Laughs Last 20.
Their Purple Moment 28. That's My Wife 29.
Courage in the North 35. Aces and Eights 36,
etc.

Aubrey, Skye (1945–).
American leading lady of a few 70s films: daught
of James Aubrey, TV executive.
Vanished (TV) 71. The Carey Treatment 72. Th
Longest Night (TV) 72. The Phantom of Hollywoo
(TV) 73, etc.

Aubry, Cecile (1929–) (Anne-José Benard).
Petite French leading lady of the early 50s. Now
children's author.
Manon 49. The Black Rose 50. Bluebeard 51. L
Ironia 54, etc.

Auclair, Michel (1922–1988) (Vladimir Vujovic).
French leading man.
La Belle et la Bête 46. Les Maudits 47. Manon
49. Justice Est Faite 50. Henriette 52. Funny Fac
(US) 56. The Fanatics 57. Rendezvous de Minuit
61. Symphony for a Massacre 64. The Day of the
Jackal 73, etc.

Audiard, Michel (1920–1985).
French writer-director.
Mr Peek-a-Boo (w) 51. Gas Oil (w) 55. Les
Misérables (w) 57. Babette Goes to War (w) 60.
Monkey in Winter (w) 62. Mélodie en Sous-Sol
(w) 63. Tendre Voyou (w) 66. Opération Léontir
(wd) 68. Le Drapeau Noir (wd) 71. Tendre Poule
(wd) 78. Le Cavalcur (wd) 79, many others.

Audley, Maxine (1923–1992).
British stage actress who made occasional film appearances.

The Sleeping Tiger 54. The Barretts of Wimpole Street 57. The Vikings 58. Our Man in Havana 59. The Trials of Oscar Wilde 60. Hell Is a City 60. A Jolly Bad Fellow 64. Here We Go Round the Mulberry Bush 67. Frankenstein Must Be Destroyed 69, etc.

Audran, Stéphane (1933–).
Cool French leading actress, in international films. Married Jean-Louis Trintignant and Claude Chabrol.

La Bonne Tisane 58. Les Cousins 59. Les Bonnes Femmes 60. Les Godelureaux 61. La Signe du Lion 62. Landru 63. Le Tigre Aime la Chair Fraiche 64. Paris vu Par 65. The Champagne Murders 67. Les Biches 68. La Femme Infidèle 69. The Lady in the Car with Glasses and a Gun 70. Just Before Nightfall 71. Without Apparent Motive 71. The Discreet Charm of the Bourgeoisie 72. Les Noces Rouges 73. Dead Pigeon on Beethoven Street 73. And Then There Were None 74. The Black Bird 75. Vincent, Paul, François and the Others 76. Folies Bourgeoises 76. Silver Bears 77. Violette Nozière 78. The Prisoner of Zenda 79. Eagle's Wing 79. Le Coeur a l'Envers 80. The Big Red One 80. Brideshead Revisited (TV) 80. Blood Relatives 81. Coup de Torchon 82. The Blood of Others 84. Cop au Vin 84. Mistral's Daughter (TV) 84. Les Plouffe 85. The Gypsy 85. Babette's Feast 87. Quiet Days in Clichy 90. Betty 92, etc.

Audry, Jacqueline (1908–1977).
French director whose films were usually written by her husband, Pierre Laroche.

Gigi 49. L'Ingénue Libertine 50. Olivia 51. Huis Clos 54. In Six Easy Lessons 57. Mitsou 57. Les Petits Matins 62. Soledad 66. Le Lis de Mer 70, etc.

Audsley, Mick.
British editor.

The Hit 85. Dance with a Stranger 85. My Beautiful Laundrette 86. Prick Up Your Ears 87. Sammy and Rosie Get Laid 87. Dangerous Liaisons 88. Soursweet 88. We're No Angels 89. The Grifters 90. Hero (GB: Accidental Hero) 92, etc.

Auer, John H. (1909–1975).
Hungarian-born American director, turning out 'B' films since the 30s.

■ Frankie and Johnnie 35. The Crime of Dr Crespi 35. Rhythm in the Clouds 37. Circus Girl 37. Outside of Paradise 38. Invisible Enemy 38. I Stand Accused 38. A Desperate Adventure 38. Orphans of the Street 38. Forged Passport 39. SOS Tidal Wave 39. Smuggled Cargo 39. Calling All Marines 39. Thou Shalt Not Kill 40. Women in War 40. Hit Parade of 1941 40. A Man Betrayed 41. The Devil Pays Off 41. Pardon My Stripes 42. Moonlight Masquerade 42. Johnny Doughboy 42. Tahiti Honey 43. Gangway for Tomorrow 43. Seven Days Ashore 44. Moonlight in Manhattan 44. Pan Americana 45. Beat the Band 47. The Flame 48. I Jane Doe 48. Angel on the Amazon 48. The Avengers 50. Hit Parade of 1951 50. Thunderbirds 52. City that Never Sleeps (& p) 53. Hell's Half Acre (& p) 54. The Eternal Sea (& p) 55. Johnny Trouble (& p) 57.

Then to TV.

Auer, Mischa (1905–1967) (Mischa Ounskowsky).
Lanky Russian comedy actor with prominent eyes and wild gestures. Went to Broadway after the revolution, and in 1928 arrived in Hollywood; after several false starts found himself much in demand for noble idiot roles in broken English.

■ Something Always Happens 28. Marquis Preferred 28. The Benson Murder Case 30. Inside the Lines 30. Just Imagine 30. Women Love Once 30. The Unholy Garden 31. The Yellow Ticket 31. Delicious 31. The Midnight Patrol 32. No Greater Love 32. Mata Hari 32. Scarlet Dawn 32. The Monster Walks 32. Dangerously Yours 33. Sucker Money 33. Infernal Machine 33. Corruption 33. After Tonight 33. Cradle Song 33. Girl Without a Room 33. Wharf Angel 34. Bulldog Drummond Strikes Back 34. Stamboul Quest 34. I Dream too Much 34. The Crusades 35. Mystery Woman 35. Lives of a Bengal Lancer 35. Clive of India 35. Sons of Guns 36. Murder in the Fleet 36. The House of a Thousand Candles 36. One Rainy Afternoon 36. The Princess Comes Across 36. My Man Godfrey (in which his gorilla impersonation really put him on the map) (AAN) 36. The Gay Desperado 36. Winterset 36. That Girl from Paris 37. Three Smart Girls 37. Top of the Town 37. We Have Our Moments 37. Pick a Star 37. Marry the Girl 37. Vogues of 1938 37. 100 Men and a Girl 37. Merry Go Round 37. It's All Yours 38. Rage of Paris 38. You Can't Take It With You 38. Service de Luxe 38. Little Tough Guys in Society 38. Sweethearts 38. East Side of Heaven 39. Unexpected Father 39. Destry Rides Again 39. Alias the Deacon 40. Sandy is a Lady 40. Public Deb Number One 40. Spring Parade 40. Seven Sinners 40. Trail of the Vigilantes 40. The Flame of New Orleans 41. Hold That Ghost 41. Moonlight in Hawaii 41. Hellzapoppin 41. Cracked Nuts 41. Twin Beds 42. Around the World 43. Lady in the Dark 44. Up in Mabel's Room 44. A Royal Scandal 45. Brewster's Millions 45. And Then There Were None 45. Sentimental Journey 46. She Wrote the Book 46. Sofia 48. The Sky is Red 52. Song of Paris 52. Confidential Report 55. Futures Vedettes 55. The Monte Carlo Story 58. Mam'zelle Pigalle 58. The Foxiest Girl in Paris 58. A Dog a Mouse and a Sputnik 60. We Joined the Navy 62. Ladies First 63. The Christmas that Almost Wasn't 66. Drop Dead Darling 66.
☻ For assuring the world that Russians could be fun. Twin Beds.

Famous line (Lady in the Dark): 'This is the end! The absolute end!'

Auger, Claudine (1942–).
French leading lady, in occasional films abroad.

In the French Style 63. Thunderball 65. Triple Cross 66. Jeu de Massacre 67. The Devil in Love 67. The Bastard 68. The Crimebuster 77. Travels with Anita 79. Fantastica 80. Lovers and Liars 81. The Associate 82. Secret Places 84, etc.

August, Bille (1948–).
Danish director and screenwriter, a former cinematographer. He has won the Palme d'Or at the Cannes Film Festival with Pelle the Conqueror and The Best Intentions.

■ In My Life 78. Zappa (wd) 83. Twist and Shout (wd) 84. Buster's World (TV) 85. Pelle the Conqueror (Pelle Erobreren) (wd) 88. The Best Intentions (Den Goda Viljan) (d) 92. The House of the Spirits (wd) 93.

August, Joseph (1890–1947).
Distinguished American cinematographer.
SELECTED SILENTS: The Narrow Trail 17. Tiger Man 18. Square Deal Sanderson 19. Sand 20. O'Melley of the Mounted 21. Travellin' On 22. Madness of Youth 23. Dante's Inferno 24. Tumbleweeds 25. The Road to Glory 26. The Beloved Rogue 26. Fig Leaves 26. Two Arabian Knights 27. Honor Bound 28. The Black Watch 29.
■ SOUND FILMS: Men Without Women 30. Double Crossroads 30. On Your Back 30. Up the River 30.

Seas Beneath 31. Mr Lemon of Orange 31. Quick Millions 31. The Brat 31. Heartbreak 31. Charlie Chan's Chance 31. Silent Witness 32. Mystery Ranch 32. Vanity Street 32. No More Orchids 32. That's My Boy 32. Man's Castle 33. Master of Men 33. As the Devil Commands 33. Cocktail Hour 33. Circus Queen Murder 33. The Captain Hates the Sea 34. Among the Missing 34. The Defense Rests 34. Black Moon 34. Twentieth Century 34. No Greater Glory 34. Sylvia Scarlett 35. After the Dance 35. The Informer 35. I'll Love You Always 35. The Whole Town's Talking 35. The Plough and the Stars 36. Mary of Scotland 36. Every Saturday Night 36. A Damsel in Distress 37. Music for Madame 37. Super Sleuth 37. Fifty Roads to Town 37. Michael Strogoff 37. Sea Devils 37. Gun Law 37. This Marriage Business 38. The Saint in New York 38. The Hunchback of Notre Dame 39. Gunga Din 39. Nurse Edith Cavell 40. Man of Conquest 40. Melody Ranch 40. Primrose Path 40. All that Money Can Buy 41. They Were Expendable 45. Portrait of Jennie 48.
☻ For the imperishable visuals of his half-dozen melodramatic masterpieces. Portrait of Jennie.

Auld, Georgie (1919–1990) (John Altwerger).
Jazz tenor saxophonist and occasional actor. Best known for his recordings with Benny Goodman in the 40s, he played a bandleader and dubbed Robert De Niro's saxophone playing in Martin Scorsese's New York, New York 77. He also dubbed fellow saxophonist Dexter Gordon's playing in Unchained 55.

Aulin, Ewa (1949–).
Scandinavian leading lady in international films.
Candy 68. Start the Revolution without Me 69. This Kind of Love 72, etc.

Ault, Marie (1870–1951) (Mary Cragg).
British character actress of stage and screen, usually in dialect comedy roles.

Woman to Woman 24. The Lodger 26. Hobson's Choice 31. Major Barbara 41. Love on the Dole 41. We Dive at Dawn 43. I See a Dark Stranger 46. Madness of the Heart 49, many others.

Aumont, Jean-Pierre (1909–) (J.-P. Salomons).
French leading man, in films from 1931, Hollywood from 1941.
Autobiography: 1977, Sun and Shadow.
Jean de la Lunc 32. Maria Chapdelaine 35. Drôle de Drame 36. Hôtel du Nord 38. The Cross of Lorraine 42. Assignment in Brittany 43. Heartbeat 46. Song of Scheherazade 48. The First Gentleman (GB) 48. Charge of the Lancers 53. Lili 53. Hilda Crane 56. The Seventh Sin 57. The Devil at Four O'Clock 61. Five Miles to Midnight 63. Castle Keep 69. La Nuit Américaine 73. The Happy Hooker 75. Catherine and Company 75. Seven Suspects for Murder 77. Nana 83. Shadow Dance 83. The Blood of Others 84. Sweet Country 86. Johnny Monroe 87. A Nôtre Regrettable Epoux 88. Becoming Colette 92, etc.

Aurel, Jean (1925–).
French writer-director, originally of documentary shorts.

14–18 (d) 63. La Bataille de France (d) 64. De l'Amour (wd) 65. Manon 70 (wd) 68. Les Femmes (wd) 69. Comme un Pot de Fraises (wd) 74. The Woman Next Door 81. Vivement Dimanche (w) 83. Confidentially Yours (w) 84, etc.

Aurenche, Jean (1904–1992).
French writer who with Pierre Bost (1901–1975) wrote many well-known films.

Hôtel du Nord 38. Sylvie et le Fantôme 45. La Symphonie Pastorale 46. *Le Diable au Corps* 46. Occupe-Toi d'Amélie 49. Dieu A Besoin des Hommes 50. *The Red Inn* 51. *Les Jeux Interdits* 51. Ripening Seed 53. Gervaise 56. En Cas de Malheur 57. L'Affaire d'Une Nuit 60. The Clockmaker 76. De Guerre Lasse 87. Fucking Fernand 87. Les Palanquins des Larmes 88, etc. Aurenche worked alone on the screenplay of *Woman in White* 65.

Auric, Georges (1899–1983).
French composer who became director of the Paris Opéra.
   Autobiography: 1974, *Quand J'étais Là*.
   Le Sang d'un Poète 30. *À Nous la Liberté* 31. Lac aux Dames 34. L'Alibi 37. Orage 38. L'Eternel Retour 43. Dead of Night 45. Caesar and Cleopatra 45. La Belle et la Bête 46. It Always Rains on Sunday 47. Corridor of Mirrors 48. Passport to Pimlico 49. *Orphée* 49. *Belles de Nuit* 52. Roman Holiday 53. The Wages of Fear 53. Father Brown 54. Rififi 55. The Witches of Salem 56. Gervaise 56. The Picasso Mystery 56. Bonjour Tristesse 57. La Chambre Ardente 62. The Mind Benders 63. Thomas the Impostor 65. Therese and Isabelle 68. The Christmas Tree 69, many others.

Aurthur, Robert Alan (1922–1978).
American novelist and screenwriter.
   Edge of the City 56. Warlock 59. For Love of Ivy 68. The Lost Man 70, etc.

Austen, Jane (1775–1817).
The most delightful of English novelists has been oddly neglected by the screen, but the 1940 version of *Pride and Prejudice* is a distinguished and amusing one.

Austin, Albert (1855–1953).
English actor and director in Hollywood, from music hall. Born in Birmingham, he became a member of Fred Karno's group, touring America before making his film debut, working with Chaplin on his two-reel comedies for Mutual.
   The Floorwalker 16. The Fireman 16. The Vagabond 16. One A.M. 16. The Count 16. The Pawnshop 16. Behind the Screen 16. The Rink 16. Easy Street 17. The Cure 17. The Immigrant 17. The Adventurer 17. A Dog's Life 18. Shoulder Arms 18. A Day's Pleasure 19. The Kid 21. Pay Day 22. Trouble (d) 22. A Prince of a King (d) 23. The Gold Rush 25. City Lights 31, etc.

Austin, Charles (1878–1944).
English music-hall comedian who made a few films. He was on the halls from 1896, notably as cockney policeman Parker P.C.
   Parker's Weekend 16. The Exploits of Parker 18. Hot Heir 31. It's a Cop (co-w) 34. School for Stars (story) 35, etc.

Austin, Charlotte (1933–).
American leading lady who moved from musicals to monsters in the 50s.
   Sunny Side of the Street 51. The Farmer Takes a Wife 53. How to Marry a Millionaire 53. Gorilla at Large 54. Desirée 54. Daddy Long Legs 55. How to Be Very Very Popular 55. Bride of the Beast 58, etc.

Austin, Jerry (1892–1976).
Dwarf American actor.
   Saratoga Trunk 43. Adventures of Don Juan 47, etc.

Austin, Ray (1932–).
British director, mostly of TV episodes, in America from the early 50s.

House of the Living Dead 73. Sword of Justice (TV) 79. Salvage I (TV) 79. Tales of the Gold Monkey (TV) 82. The Zany Adventures of Robin Hood (TV) 84. Return of the Six Million Dollar Man and the Bionic Woman (TV) 87. The New Zorro (TV) 92, etc.

Austin, Ron
American screenwriter.
   The Happening 67. Harry in Your Pocket 73, etc.

Austin, William (1891–1975).
English character actor, mainly in Hollywood. Born in Georgetown, British Guiana, he trained in London but made his stage debut in Los Angeles in 1919.
   Ruggles of Red Gap 21. Silk Stockings 24. Mysterious Dr Fu Manchu 29. Return of Dr Fu Manchu 31. High Society 32. Three Men in a Boat 33. Alice in Wonderland (as the Gryphon) 33. The Private Life of Henry VIII 33. The Gay Divorcee 35. Dr Rhythm 38. Sherlock Holmes 40. Charley's Aunt 41. Return of Monte Cristo 46. The Ghost & Mrs Muir 47. Batman 50, etc.

Australia
has long had a vigorous cinema movement, but it did not suit the rest of the world to take much note of it until the 70s. Now many of its outstanding directors, actors and cinematographers have migrated to Hollywood. In the 30s and 40s, producer and director Ken G. Hall at the Cinesound Studios turned out popular local films, but J. Arthur Rank's investment in the company after the Second World War ended its involvement in production. The continent's best-known director until the 50s was Charles Chauvel, but even his films have travelled remarkably little. The archetypal Australian actor was Chips Rafferty, a tough, no-nonsense performer surviving hazardous adventures. In the 50s and 60s, many films with an Australian theme were made by the British, particularly Ealing Studios (including *The Overlanders*, *The Shiralee*, and *Eureka Stockade*), and the Americans, with such films as *On the Beach* and *Summer of the Seventeenth Doll* (with Ernest Borgnine and John Mills cast as Australian cane-cutters). That trend reached its nadir in 1970 with Tony Richardson's *Ned Kelly*, starring Mick Jagger as the legendary outlaw, and its apogee in 1971 with Nicolas Roeg's *Walkabout*. In the early 70s Australia's traditional rough-edged action adventures gave way on the one hand to Barry Mackenzie-style smut and on the other to macabre, stylish curiosities such as *The Cars That Ate Paris* and *Picnic At Hanging Rock*; there developed from these a new, serious Australian school including such internationally well-regarded general movies as *Newsfront* and *The Chant of Jimmie Blacksmith*. Peter Weir and Fred Schepisi became OK directorial names; such films as *Breaker Morant* and *Gallipoli* were given international fanfares; *The Man from Snowy River* broke all records in Australia; Helen Morse, Mel Gibson, Bryan Brown and Judy Davis showed that Australia had skilled actors; *Mad Max* showed that Australia could dispense stylish violence with the best of them. In 1982, however, the bubble seemed about to burst. Hollywood began to steal the best talents, and the Australian unions became greedy for the kind of salaries that only Hollywood could afford to pay, while at home a valuable tax concession was withdrawn, making finance for home-grown movies more difficult. In the mid-80s, the affable comedian Paul Hogan scored an international success with his comedy *Crocodile Dundee*, but has so far failed to repeat it with his later films. By that time, much Australian talent was working in America. Directors George

Miller, Peter Weir, Fred Schepisi, Bruce Beresford, Phillip Noyce, Russell Mulcahy and Simon Wincer were busy in international films, along with cinematographers Ian Baker and Dean Semler. Jane Campion, who although born in New Zealand regards herself as an Australian director, scored with *The Piano* 93. Directors John Duigan and the Dutch-born Paul Cox kept alive Australia's reputation for intelligent, thoughtful movies, while Geoffrey Wright, with *Romper Stomper* and *Metal Skin*, and Rolf de Heer, with *Bad Boy Bubby*, showed that there was still plenty of high-tension talent around.
   Meanwhile Australian television doggedly aped Hollywood, grinding out soap operas such as *The Sullivans*, *Cop Shop*, *Country Practice* and *Sons and Daughters*, with occasional mini-series ranging from the poverty-stricken *Sara Dane* to the more smoothly ambitious *A Town Like Alice* and *For the Term of His Natural Life*. The main problem turned out to be the lack of native subject matter, once producers had exhausted World War I, Botany Bay and sheep shearing.

Autant-Lara, Claude (1903–).
French director, usually of stylish romantic dramas; former assistant to René Clair.
   Ciboulette 33. L'Affaire du Courier de Lyons 37. *Fric Frac* 39. Lettres de l'Amour 42. Douce 43. Sylvie et le Fantôme 45. *Le Diable au Corps* 46. *Occupe-Toi d'Amélie* 49. *The Red Inn* 51. Ripening Seed 53. Le Rouge et le Noir 54. Marguerite de la Nuit 55. La Traversée de Paris 56. *En Cas de Malheur* 57. The Green Marc's Nest 59. Le Bois des Amants 60. The Count of Monte Cristo 61. Le Meurtrier 62. Thou Shalt Not Kill 62. The Woman in White 65. Les Patates 69. Le Rouge et le Blanc 70. Gloria 77, etc.

¶ The director must consider himself surrounded by enemies; what I mean is that, in a business where the taste of one man must prevail, he is surrounded by people who want to do nothing but impose their own tastes. – *C.A.-L.*

Auteuil, Daniel (1950–).
French leading actor, from the stage, where he played with the Théâtre National Populaire. His early parts tended to be comic, although since *Jean de Florette* brought him to international attention he has played more varied roles.
   Le Sex Shop 73. Jean de Florette 87. *Manon des Sources* 87. Romuald et Juliette 89. *A Heart in Winter* (Un Coeur en Hiver) 91. The Elegant Criminal (Lacenaire) 92. My Favourite Season (Ma Saison Préférée) 93, etc.

auteur.
A term used in the 60s and 70s by egghead critics to denote directors whom they judge to have a discernible message or attitude which runs throughout their work. Oddly enough the term is not applied to authors.

authenticator.
Studio researcher responsible for establishing accuracy of all script details, ensuring use of 'clear' telephone numbers, etc.

authors as actors
are few. Alexander Woollcott once had fun playing opposite Noël Coward in *The Scoundrel*; Irvin S. Cobb tried to take over the mantle of Will Rogers on the latter's death; Mickey Spillane played his own hero Mike Hammer in *The Girl Hunters* and also appeared in *Ring of Fear*. Otherwise literary lions have aspired only to bit parts, such as Compton Mackenzie in *Whisky Galore* and Hugh

Walpole in *David Copperfield*. Somerset Maugham did contribute lengthy introductions to three compendiums of his short stories, but they were virtually eliminated from the release prints. Jacqueline Susann and Peter Benchley appeared as interviewers in *Valley of the Dolls* and *Jaws* respectively. Writer-director Bryan Forbes did become a popular juvenile in the 50s, and John Osborne turned villain in *Get Carter*, while Truman Capote was the sinister host of *Murder by Death*. Actors who became authors include David Niven, Dirk Bogarde, Ruth Chatterton, Mary Astor, Elissa Landi, Errol Flynn and Corinne Griffith; and many others wrote autobiographies, more or less unaided.

automobiles

with personality enough to become movie titles include *Genevieve*, *The Fast Lady*, *La Belle Américaine*, *The Solid Gold Cadillac*, *The Yellow Rolls-Royce*, *Chitty Chitty Bang Bang*, *The Gnome-Mobile* and *The Love Bug*. Other cars with individuality were James Bond's tricksy Aston Martin in *Goldfinger* and the one that ran on two wheels in *Diamonds are Forever*; the Flying Wombat in *The Young at Heart*; the gadget-filled limousine in *Only Two Can Play*; the airborne Model T in *The Absent-minded Professor*. The Model T was also Laurel and Hardy's favourite car, and they wrecked a great many in their time; other old cars were featured in *The Reivers* and TV's *The Beverly Hillbillies*. Multitudes of old and strange cars were featured in *The Great Race*, *It's a Mad Mad Mad Mad World*, *Monte Carlo or Bust*.

Comic car chases have been featured by Mack Sennett, Abbott and Costello, W. C. Fields and countless other comedians, and a new car was splendidly wrecked in *Tobacco Road*. Realistic chases became more and more violent in the 70s. *Bullitt* and *The French Connection* were box-office hits almost for this reason alone, and imitations included *Robbery*, *Vanishing Point*, *Freebie and the Bean*, *The Car*, *The Driver*, *The Blues Brothers*, *Smokey and the Bandit*, *Every Which Way But Loose*, *The Gauntlet* and *The Hunter*. The best television film of the genre was undoubtedly *Duel*, but series from *The Dukes of Hazzard* to *T. J. Hooker* based their appeal on the number of cars crashed each week. The ultimate spoof was probably *Knight Rider*, in which the car became a secondary hero, talking back to its master and making most of his decisions.

See: *motor racing*.

Autry, Gene (1907–).

Easy-going Texan who made innumerable minor westerns 1934–54 as singing cowboy, usually with his horse Champion. Beginning as a singer on radio, billed as 'Oklahoma's Yodeling Cowboy', he presented a clean-living image: he refused to hit anyone smaller than himself and would not smoke or drink on-screen. He made 58 features for Republic, often with his sidekick from radio, Lester 'Smiley' Burnette, or his later partner Pat Buttram. From 1937–42, he was the top western star, turning to TV in the 50s and retiring in 1960. Spin-offs he produced from his own TV series included *The Adventures of Champion* 55–56, and *Annie Oakley* 54–56, featuring his frequent movie co-star Gail Davis.

Boots and Saddles 37. Under Western Stars 38. Carolina Moon 40. Back in the Saddle 41. Sunset in Wyoming 42. Range War 46. Sioux City Sue 47. Guns and Saddles 49. Gold Town Ghost Riders 53. Alias Jesse James 59, many others.

TV series: The Gene Autry Show 50–56.

¶ In my day, most people thought dance hall girls actually danced. – G.A.

Autry used to ride off into the sunset. Now he owns it. – *Anon*

Avakian, Aram (1926–1987).
American director.
■ Lad – a Dog 62. The End of the Road 69. Cops and Robbers 73. 11 Harrowhouse 74.

Avalon, Frankie (1939–) (Francis Avallone).
American light leading man and pop singer, former trumpeter.
Guns of the Timberland 60. The Alamo 60. Voyage to the Bottom of the Sea 62. Beach Blanket Bingo 65. I'll Take Sweden 65. Sergeant Deadhead 66. Fireball 500 66. Pajama Party in a Haunted House 66. How to Stuff a Wild Bikini 66. Skidoo 68. The Take 74. Grease 78. Back to the Beach 87, etc.

avant-garde.
An adjective generally used to describe artists 'in advance of their time'; especially used of French surrealists in the 20s, e.g. Kirsanoff, Buñuel, Germaine Dulac.

Avary, Roger (1965–).
American screenwriter and director.
Pulp Fiction (co-w) 94. Killing Zoe (wd) 94.

Avati, Pupi (1938–) (Giuseppe Avati).
Italian director. He is a former jazz musician and factory worker who decided to work in films after seeing Fellini's 8½.
Balsamus l'Uomo di Satana 68. Thomas the Possessed (Thomas . . . gli Indemoniati) 69. La Mazurka del Barone 74. Bordella 75. Le Strelle nel Fosso 78. Zeder 83. Us Three (Noi Tre) 84. Fiesta di Laurea 85. The Last Minute 87. Boys and Girls (Storia di Ragazzi e Ragazze) 89. Bix 91. Brothers and Sisters 92. Magnificat 93. Declarations of Love 94, etc.

Avedon, Doe (1928–).
American leading lady who had a very short career before retiring to marry. She is the former wife of the director Don Siegel.
■ The High and the Mighty 54. Deep in My Heart 55. The Boss 56.
TV series: Big Town 55.

Averback, Hy (1925–).
American director with much TV experience, especially in comedy series.
Chamber of Horrors 66. Where Were You When the Lights Went Out? 68. *I Love You Alice B. Toklas* 68. The Great Bank Robbery 69. Suppose They Gave a War and Nobody Came 70. Where the Boys Are 84, etc.

Avery, Margaret
American character actress.
Magnum Force 73. Which Way Is Up? 77. The Fish that Saved Pittsburg 79. The Lathe of Heaven 80. The Color Purple (AAN) 85. Blueberry Hill 88. Riverbend 89, etc.

Avery, Tex (1907–1980) (Fred Avery).
American animator, best known for MGM cartoons which combined savagery with hilarity. He created Droopy.

Avery, Val
American character actor.
King Creole 58. Too Late Blues 61. Hud 63. The Hallelujah Trail 65. The Pink Jungle 68. The Travelling Executioner 70. The Laughing Policeman 73. Let's Do It Again 75. Heroes 77.

The Wanderers 79. Choices 81. Courage (TV) 86, etc.

Avildsen, John G. (1936–).
American director and screenwriter.
■ Turn on to Love 67. OK Bill 68. Guess What We Learned at School Today 69. *Joe* 70. Cry Uncle 71. Roger the Stoolie 72. Save the Tiger 73. WW and the Dixie Dance Kings 75. Foreplay (co-d) 75. *Rocky* (AA) 76. Slow Dancing in the Big City 78. The Formula 80. The President's Women 81. Neighbors 81. A Night in Heaven 83. The Karate Kid 84. The Karate Kid II 86. Happy New Year 87. For Keeps 88. The Karate Kid Part III 89. Lean on Me 89. Rocky V 90. The Power of One 92. Lane Frost 93. 8 Seconds 94.

Avnet, Jon (1949–).
American director, producer and screenwriter.
Outlaw Blues (p) 77. Risky Business (p) 83. Between Two Women (co-w, d) (TV) 86. Less than Zero (p) 87. Men Don't Leave (p, d) 90. Fried Green Tomatoes (p, co-w, d) 91. The Mighty Ducks (p) 92, etc.

Axel, Gabriel (1918–).
French-born director and screenwriter who makes movies in Denmark. He mainly works as a stage actor and director in Denmark and France.
Guld Og Gronne Skove 59. Den Rode Kappe 67. Med Kaerlig Hilsen 71. Familien Gyldenkaal 75. Babette's Feast (AA) 87. Christian 89. Prince of Denmark (& co-w) 93, etc.

Axelrod, George (1922–).
American comedy writer.
■ Phffft 54. The Seven Year Itch (oa) 55. Bus Stop 56. Will Success Spoil Rock Hunter? (oa) 57. Breakfast at Tiffany's 61. The Manchurian Candidate 62. Paris When It Sizzles 64. Goodbye Charlie 64. How to Murder Your Wife (& p) 65. Lord Love a Duck (& pd) 66. The Secret Life of an American Wife (& pd) 68. The Lady Vanishes 79. The Holcroft Covenant 85. The Fourth Protocol 87, etc.

Axt, Dr William (1888–1959).
American composer, almost entirely for MGM in the 30s.
Don Juan 26. Ben Hur 26. White Shadows of the South Seas 28. Smilin' Through 32. Dinner at Eight 33. The Thin Man 34. David Copperfield 35. Piccadilly Jim 36. Parnell 37. Yellow Jack 38. Stand Up and Fight 39, many others.

Axton, Hoyt (1938–).
American character actor.
The Black Stallion 79. Cloud Dancer 79. Endangered Species 82. Heart Like a Wheel 82. Liar's Moon 84. Gremlins 84. Dixie Lanes 88. Retribution 88. We're No Angels 89. Disorganised Crime 89. The Rousters (TV) 90. Season of Change 94, etc.

Ayala, Fernando (1920–).
Argentinian producer, director and screenwriter. In the late 50s, together with Hector Olivera, he founded Aries, the country's most successful and longest-surviving production company. His early films dealt with social problems; his later ones concentrate more on entertainment.
Ayer Fue Primavera 55. El Jefe 58. El Candidato 59. Paula Cautiva 63. Primero Yo 64. Las Locas del Conventillo 65. La Fiaca 68. El Profesor Hippie 69. Argentisima (co-d) 71. Argentisima II (co-d) 72. Los Médicos 78. Plata Dulce 82. Sobredosis 86. Dios los Cria 91, etc.

Aykroyd, Dan (1952–).
Canadian revue comedian who made his name on *Saturday Night Live*.
■ 1941 79. Mr Mike's Mondo Video 79. The Blues Brothers 80. Neighbours 81. Dr Detroit 82. Nothing Lasts Forever 82. Twilight Zone 83. Trading Places 83. Ghostbusters 84. Into the Night 84. Spies Like Us 85. Dragnet 87. Caddyshack II 88. The Couch Trip 88. The Great Outdoors 88. My Stepmother Is an Alien 88. Driving Miss Daisy (AAN) 89. Ghostbusters II (& w) 89. Loose Cannons 90. Nothing But Trouble (& wd) 91. My Girl 91. This Is My Life 92. Charlie 92. Sneakers 92. This Is My Life 92. Coneheads (& co-w) 93. My Girl 2 94. North 94. Exit to Eden 94.

¶ I have this kind of mild nice-guy exterior, but inside, my heart is like a steel trap. I'm really quite robotic. – *D.A.*
   The entertainment business is not the be-all and end-all for me. – *D.A.*

Aylmer, Sir Felix (1889–1979) (Felix Edward Aylmer Jones).
Distinguished British stage character actor, a respected industry figure who from 1950 was president of Equity, the actors' trade union. In films he mainly played schoolmasters, bankers, bishops, etc.
   The Wandering Jew 33. The Iron Duke 35. Tudor Rose 36. As You Like It 36. *Victoria the Great* 37. The Citadel 38. Saloon Bar 40. *The Ghost of St Michael's* 41. Mr Emmanuel 44. Henry V 44. The Ghost of Berkeley Square 47. *Hamlet* (as Polonius) 48. Edward My Son 49. Quo Vadis 51. Ivanhoe 52. The Master of Ballantrae 53. Knights of the Round Table 54. The Angel Who Pawned Her Harp 54. Saint Joan 57. *Separate Tables* 58. *Never Take Sweets from a Stranger* 60. Exodus 60. The Chalk Garden 64. Becket 64. Decline and Fall 68. Hostile Witness 68, many others.

Aylward, Gladys (1901–1970).
British missionary whose exploits in China were fictionalized in *Inn of the Sixth Happiness*, in which she was played by Ingrid Bergman.

Ayres, Agnes (1898–1940) (Agnes Hinkle).
American leading lady of the silent screen.
   Forbidden Fruit 19. The Affairs of Anatol 20. *The Sheik* 21. Racing Hearts 23. When a Girl Loves 24. Morals for Men 25. Her Market Value 26. Son of the Sheik 26. Eve's Love Letters 29, many others.

Ayres, Lew (1908–) (Lewis Ayer).
Boyish American leading man of the 30s; he occasionally got a chance to prove himself a comfortable and friendly actor, but his career suffered during World War II when he declared himself a conscientious objector.
■ *The Kiss* 29. The Sophomore 29. Many a Slip 30. *All Quiet on the Western Front* 30. Common Clay 30. East is West 30. Doorway to Hell 30. Iron Man 31. Up for Murder 31. The Spirit of Notre Dame 31. Heaven on Earth 31. The Impatient Maiden 32. Night World 32. Okay America 32. *State Fair* 33. Don't Bet On Love 33. My Weakness 33. Cross Country Cruise 34. She Learned About Sailors 34. Servants' Entrance 34. Let's Be Ritzy 34. Lottery Lover 35. The Silk Hat Kid 35. The Leathernecks have Landed 36. Panic on the Air 36. Shakedown 36. Lady be Careful 36. Murder with Pictures 36. The Crime Nobody Saw 36. *Last Train from Madrid* 37. Hold 'Em Navy 37. Scandal Street 38. King of the Newsboys 38. *Holiday* (a key performance as Katharine Hepburn's drunken brother) 38. Rich Man Poor Girl 38. *Young Dr Kildare* 38. Spring Madness 38. Ice Follies 39. Broadway Serenade 39. Calling Dr Kildare 39. These Glamour Girls 39. The Secret of Dr Kildare 39. Remember? 39. Dr Kildare's Strange Case 40. Dr Kildare Goes Home 40. The Golden Fleecing 40. Dr Kildare's Crisis 40. Maisie Was a Lady 41. The People vs Dr Kildare 41. Dr Kildare's Wedding Day 41. Fingers at the Window 42. Dr Kildare's Victory 42. *The Dark Mirror* 46. The Unfaithful 47. *Johnny Belinda* (AAN) 48. The Capture 50. New Mexico 51. No Escape 53. Donovan's Brain 54. *Advise and Consent* 61. *The Carpetbaggers* 64. Hawaii Five-O (TV pilot) 68. Marcus Welby MD (TV pilot) 68. Earth II (TV) 71. She Waits (TV) 72. The Man (TV) 72. The Biscuit Eater 72. The Stranger (TV) 72. The Questor Tapes (TV) 73. Battle For Planet of the Apes 73. Heatwave (TV) 74. Francis Gary Powers (TV) 76. End of the World 77. Greatest Heroes of the Bible (TV) (as Noah) 78. Damien-Omen II 78. Of Mice and Men (TV) 81. Cast the First Stone (TV) 89.
   TV series: Hawkins 74. Lime Street 85.

Ayres, Robert (1914–1968).
Canadian actor of strong silent types, long resident in Britain.
   They Were Not Divided 49. Cosh Boy 52. Contraband Spain 55. It's Never Too Late 55. A Night to Remember 57. The Sicilians 63. Battle Beneath the Earth 68, many others.

Ayrton, Randle (1869–1940).
British character actor.
   My Sweetheart 18. The Wonderful Year 21. Chu Chin Chow 23. Southern Love 24. Nell Gwynne 26. Passion Island 26. Glorious Youth 28. Comets 30. Dreyfus 31. Jew Süss 34. Me and Marlborough 35. Talk of the Devil 36, etc.

Aznavour, Charles (1924–) (Shahnour Aznavurjan).
Armenian leading man of the small but rugged school.
   Autobiography: 1972, *Aznavour by Aznavour*.
   La Tête Contre les Murs 58. *Shoot the Pianist* 60. Passage du Rhin 61. Cloportes 65. Candy 68. The Adventures 70. The Games 70. Un Beau Monstre 70. And Then There Were None 75. Sky Riders 76. Folies Bourgeoises 76. The Tin Drum 79. Les Fantômes du Chapelier 82. Der Zauberberg 82. Yiddish Connection (& w) 86. Migrations 88. Il Maestro 89. Les Années Campagne 91, etc.

¶ Love now. Tomorrow, who knows? – *C.A.*

B

'B' picture.
A low-budget production usually designed as part of a double bill or to support a more important feature. There are four excellent books on the subject: *B Movies* by Don Miller, *The Wonderful World of B Films* by Alan G. Barbour, *Kings of the Bs* by Todd McCarthy and Charles Flynn and *The Big Book of B Movies* by Robin Cross.

Babbitt, Art (1907–1992).
Leading animator, whose career began in the 20s. He worked for Disney, animating the Wicked Queen in *Snow White* and the dance of the mushrooms in *Fantasia*, for Warner's Looney Tunes, UPA and Hanna-Barbera.
Snow White and the Seven Dwarfs 37. Pinocchio 40. Fantasia 40. The Thief and the Cobbler 93, etc.

Babcock, Barbara (1937–).
American character actress.
Heaven with a Gun 68. The Last Child (TV) 71. Bang the Drum Slowly 73. Chosen Survivors (TV) 74. Salem's Lot (TV) 79. The Lords of Discipline 83. Heart of Dixie 89. Happy Together 90. Far and Away 92, etc.
TV series: Dallas 78–82. Hill Street Blues 81–85. The Four Seasons 84. Mr Sunshine 86.

Babenco, Hector (1946–).
Argentinian-born director who worked in Brazil and then, declaring that Brazilian cinema was dead, moved to Hollywood.
Lucio Flavio 78. Pixote 81. Kiss of the Spider Woman (AAN) 85. Ironweed 87. At Play in the Fields of the Lord 91, etc.

babies
who have achieved screen stardom include Baby Parsons and Baby Peggy in silent days, Baby Le Roy in the early 30s and Baby Sandy in the early 40s. Shirley Temple and the Our Gang cast were scarcely weaned when they hit the big time. Other films about particular babies include *Bachelor Mother*, *Bobbikins*, and *A Diary for Timothy*.
There was a shortlived TV series about a talking baby called *Happy*, a trend that reached the cinema with *Look Who's Talking* 89, *Look Who's Talking Too* 90, and *Look Who's Talking Now* 93, and Lucille Ball worked her own confinement into her weekly half-hour. More recently there has been a lamentable fashion for diabolical infants: *Rosemary's Baby*, *It's Alive*, *I Don't Want to be Born* and *The Devil within Her*.

Baby Le Roy (1931–) (Le Roy Overacker).
American toddler who appeared to general delight in comedies of the early 30s. The story goes that W. C. Fields once spiked his orange juice with gin . . .
A Bedtime Story 33. Tillie and Gus 33. Miss Fane's Baby is Stolen 33. The Old Fashioned Way 34. The Lemon Drop Kid 34. It's a Gift 35. etc.

Baby Peggy (1917–) (Peggy Montgomery).
American child star of the 20s. Later appeared under her own name, and in the 70s published two books, *The Hollywood Posse* and *Hollywood Children*.
Peggy Behave 22. Captain January 23. The Law Forbids 24. The Speed Demon 25. April Fool 26. The Sonora Kid 27, etc.

Baby Sandy (1938–) (Sandra Henville).
American infant performer who made money for Universal in the early 40s.
■ East Side of Heaven 39. Unexpected Father 39. Little Accident 39. Sandy Is a Lady 40. Sandy Gets Her Man 40. Sandy Steps Out 41. Bachelor Daddy 41. Melody Lane 41. Johnny Doughboy 42.

Bacall, Lauren (1924–) (Betty Jean Perske).
Sultry American leading actress who after stage experience made her film debut opposite Humphrey Bogart ('If you want anything, just whistle . . .') and subsequently married him. Her image gradually changed to that of an astringent and resourceful woman of the world, and in 1970 she made a triumphant return to the Broadway stage in *Applause*.
Autobiography: 1978, *Lauren Bacall*.
■ To Have and Have Not 44. Confidential Agent 45. The Big Sleep 46. Dark Passage 47. Key Largo 48. Young Man with a Horn 50. Bright Leaf 50. How to Marry a Millionaire 53. Woman's World 54. The Cobweb 55. Blood Alley 55. Written on the Wind 57. Designing Woman 57. The Gift of Love 58. Northwest Frontier (GB) 59. Shock Treatment 64. Sex and the Single Girl 64. Harper 66. Murder on the Orient Express 74. The Shootist 76. Health 79. The Fan 81. Appointment with Death 88. Mr North 88. Misery 90. Dinner at Eight (TV) 90. Innocent Victim 90. Star for Two 91. All I Want For Christmas 91. The Portrait (TV) 93. A Foreign Field (TV) 93. Prêt-à-Porter 94.
~She made an uncredited cameo appearance in *Two Guys from Milwaukee* 46.

¶ Slinky! Sultry! Sensational! – *1944 promotion for L.B.*

I used to tremble from nerves so badly that the only way I could hold my head steady was to lower my chin practically to my chest and look up at Bogie. That was the beginning of The Look. – *L.B.*
I was not a woman of the world. I'd lived with Mother all my life. – *L.B.*
What I learned from Mr Bogart I learned from a master, and that, God knows, has stood me in very good stead. – *L.B.*

Bacalov, Luis Enrique.
Prolific Spanish-born composer, working in Italy.
La Banda del Buco 60. The Gospel According to St Matthew (AAN) 65. Django 66. A Bullet for the General (Quién Sabe?) 66. L'Amica 69. Roma Bene 71. La Rosa Rossa 73. Le Maestro 79. City of Women 80. Entre Nous (Coupe de Foudre) 83. Le Juge 83. Le Transfuge 85. The Postman (Il Postino) 94, many others.

Baccaloni, Salvatore (1900–1969).
Italian opera singer who played some comedy roles in American films.

■ Full of Life 56. Merry Andrew 58. Rock a Bye Baby 59. Fanny 61. The Pigeon That Took Rome 62.

Bach, Barbara (1951–) (Barbara Goldbach).
American leading lady, first in Italian films, who played the female lead in *The Spy Who Loved Me* 77. Married former Beatle Ringo Starr.
Force Ten from Navarone 78. The Humanoid 79. Up the Academy 80. Caveman 81. The Unseen 81. Give My Regards to Broad Street 83.

Bacharach, Burt (1929–).
American composer.
Lizzie (s) 57. What's New Pussycat? (m) 65. Casino Royale (m) 67. Butch Cassidy and the Sundance Kid (AAs, m) 69. The April Fools (m) 69. Lost Horizon (s) 73. Together? 79. Arthur (AAs) 81. Night Shift 82. Best Defence 84. Arthur 2: On the Rocks 88, etc.

¶ The groovy thing about pop music is that it's wide open. Anything can happen. – *B.B.*

Bachelor, Stephanie (1924–).
American leading lady of 40s 'B' pictures.
Lady of Burlesque 43. Her Primitive Man 44. Lake Placid Serenade 44. Scotland Yard Investigator 45. I've Always Loved You 46. Blackmail 47. King of the Gamblers 48, etc.

back projection.
A method of producing 'location' sequences in the studio: the players act in front of a translucent screen on which the scenic background is projected.

backstage
is a term suggesting musicals about putting on a show. But other types of film have taken place mainly or climactically in this area. Thrillers: *The Velvet Touch*, *Stage Fright*, *The Phantom of the Opera*, *Charlie Chan at the Opera*, *Cover Girl Killer*, *Murder at the Vanities*, *The G-String Murders*, *Theatre of Death*. Dramas: *A Double Life*, *Applause*, *The Blue Angel*, *Limelight*, *Les Enfants du Paradis*, *Act One*. Comedies: *A Night at the Opera*, *Hellzapoppin*, *The Guardsman*, *The Royal Family of Broadway*, *Curtain Up*, etc. Musicals themselves got off to a pretty good start in the early 30s, best and most typical of them being *42nd Street*, which was amiably spoofed in *Movie Movie* 78.

Backus, Jim (1913–1989).
Burly American character comedian, perhaps most famous as the voice of Mr Magoo in UPA cartoons of the 50s. Stock, vaudeville and radio experience.
Autobiography: 1958, *Rocks on the Roof*.
The Great Lover 49. Hollywood Story 51. His Kind of Woman 51. I Want You 51. Pat and Mike 52. Androcles and the Lion 53. Rebel Without a Cause 55. The Great Man 56. Man of a Thousand Faces 57. Macabre 58. Ice Palace 60. Boys' Night Out 62. It's A Mad Mad Mad Mad World 63. Advance to the Rear 64. Billie 65. Where Were You When the Lights Went Out? 68. Now You See Him Now

You Don't 72. Pete's Dragon 77. There Goes the Bride 80, etc.

TV series: *I Married Joan* 52–56. Hot off the Wire 60. *Gilligan's Island* 64–66. Blondie 68.

Baclanova, Olga (1899–1974).
Russian actress who played leads in a few American films.

Street of Sin 27. Docks of New York 28. *Freaks* 32. Billion Dollar Scandal 33. Claudia 43, etc.

Bacon, Irving (1893–1965).
American character actor in films from 1920, often as not-so-dumb country type or perplexed official.
Street of Chance 30. Million Dollar Legs 32. Private Worlds 35. Sing You Sinners 38. Meet John Doe 41. Pin Up Girl 44. Monsieur Verdoux 47. Room for One More 52. A Star is Born 54. Fort Massacre 58, many others.

Bacon, Kevin (1958–).
American actor.
National Lampoon's Animal House 78. Starting Over 79. Friday the 13th 80. Hero at Large 80. Only When I Laugh 81. Diner 82. Forty Deuce 82. Enormous Changes at the Last Minute 83. Footloose 84. Quicksilver 86. Planes, Trains and Automobiles 87. She's Having a Baby 88. Criminal Law 89. The Big Picture 89. Tremors 90. Flatliners 90. JFK 91. A Few Good Men 92. The Air Up There 94. The River Wild 94. Murder in the First 94, etc.

¶ I've been a film star so long that I don't know what it would feel like not to be one. – K.B.

Bacon, Lloyd (1890–1955).
American director, long under contract to Warner; former actor in Chaplin silents. Competent rather than brilliant, he nevertheless handled several memorable films among the mass of routine.
■ Private Izzy Murphy 26. Fingerprints 26. Broken Hearts of Hollywood 26. The Heart of Maryland 26. White Flannels 27. A Sailor's Sweetheart 27. Brass Knuckles 27. Pay As You Enter 28. The Lion and the Mouse 28. Women They Talk About 28. *The Singing Fool* 28. Stark Mad 29. Honky Tonk 29. No Defense 29. Say It with Songs 29. So Long Lefty 30. She Couldn't Say No 30. A Notorious Affair 30. The Other Tomorrow 30. Moby Dick 30. The Office Wife 30. Kept Husbands 31. Sit Tight 31. Fifty Million Frenchmen 31. Gold Dust Gertie 31. Honor of the Family 31. Manhattan Parade 32. Fireman Save my Child 32. Alias the Doctor 32. The Famous Ferguson Case 32. *Miss Pinkerton* 32. Crooner 32. Footlight Parade 32. You Said a Mouthful 32. *42nd Street* 33. *Picture Snatcher* 33. Mary Stevens MD 33. Son of a Sailor 33. *Wonder Bar* 34. A Very Honorable Guy 34. He Was Her Man 34. Six Day Bike Rider 34. *Here Comes the Navy* 34. Devil Dogs of the Air 35. In Caliente 35. Broadway Gondolier 35. The Irish In Us 35. Frisco Kid 35. Sons of Guns 36. Cain and Mabel 36. Gold Diggers of 1937 36. *Marked Woman* 37. Ever Since Eve 37. San Quentin 37. Submarine D1 37. *A Slight Case of Murder* 38. Cowboy from Brooklyn 38. *Boy Meets Girl* 38. Racket Busters 38. Wings of the Navy 39. *The Oklahoma Kid* 39. Indianapolis Speedway 39. Espionage Agent 39. A Child Is Born 40. Invisible Stripes 40. Three Cheers for the Irish 40. *Brother Orchid* 40. Knute Rockne, All American 40. Honeymoon for Three 41. Footsteps in the Dark 41. Navy Blues 41. Affectionately Yours 41. Honeymoon for Three 41. Larceny Inc 42. Wings for the Eagle 42. Silver Queen 42. Action in the North Atlantic 43. The Sullivans 44. *Sunday Dinner for a Soldier* 44. Captain Eddie 45. Home Sweet Homicide 45. Wake Up and Dream 46. I Wonder Who's Kissing Her Now 47. You were Meant for Me 48. Give My Regards to Broadway 48. Don't Trust Your Husband 48. Mother Is a Freshman 49. It Happens Every Spring 49. Miss Grant Takes Richmond 49. Kill The Umpire 50. The Good Humor Man 50. The Fuller Brush Girl 50. Call Me Mister 51. Golden Girl 51. The Frogmen 52. The I Don't Care Girl 53. The Great Sioux Uprising 53. Walking My Baby Back Home 53. The French Line 54. She Couldn't Say No 54.

Bacon, Max (1904–1969).
Plump English character actor, usually in cockney roles. He was a former drummer and singer with Ambrose's Orchestra.
Soft Lights and Sweet Music 36. Calling All Stars 37. Kicking the Moon Around 38. King Arthur Was a Gentleman 42. Bees in Paradise 44. Pool of London 51. The Gambler and the Lady 52. Espresso Bongo 59. The Entertainer 60. Crooks in Cloisters 63. The Sandwich Man 66. Privilege 67. Chitty Chitty Bang Bang 68, etc.

The Bad Guys,
by William K. Everson. A well-researched pictorial history of screen villains, published in 1964.

bad language.
It now seems impossible that in 1938 the phrase 'not bloody likely' in Shaw's *Pygmalion* could have caused a minor sensation; or that in 1942 the seamen in *In Which We Serve* could not say 'Hell' or 'damn' in front of American audiences. But these things happened. Perhaps it was in 1953 that the rot really set in, when Otto Preminger accepted a Legion of Decency 'C' rating and the loss of a production seal for his film of *The Moon Is Blue* rather than rob it of the words 'virgin' and 'mistress'. Three years later, Mickey Shaughnessy in *Don't Go Near the Water* was allowed to mouth obscenities while the soundtrack amusingly bleeped them out. By the time *Pygmalion* was remade in 1964 as *My Fair Lady* the phrase originally so shocking would have had no dramatic effect; it was replaced by 'Move your bloomin' arse'. In 1967–68 the floodgates really opened. *Poor Cow* and *Who's Afraid of Virginia Woolf?* were the first to allow 'bugger'. In *Here We Go Round the Mulberry Bush* Maxine Audley reproaches her husband as follows: 'Darling, you've got him pissed again.' And in *A Flea in Her Ear* Rex Harrison unchivalrously instructs Rosemary Harris to 'piss off'. That still-notorious four-letter word beginning with F was first uttered by Marianne Faithfull in *I'll Never Forget Whatshisname*, and then by Elizabeth Taylor in *Boom*. And the slang word for defecation was first uttered in *In Cold Blood*, *Boom*, *Rosemary's Baby* and *Secret Ceremony*. In general, the effect of such words on the big screen has merely been to show how meaningless, harmless and stupid they are; but over-use of them is worse than pretending they don't exist, and one wonders whether films of the mid-70s such as *Lenny*, *Serpico*, *The Last Detail*, *Shampoo* and *Dog Day Afternoon* would have been any poorer without them. By the 80s, it was rare to find even an 'A' or 'PG' film without bad language.

Badalamenti, Angelo.
American composer.
Gordon's War 73. Law and Disorder 74. Across the Great Divide 76. Blue Velvet 86. Nightmare on Elm Street III 87. Tough Guys Don't Dance 87. Weeds 87. Cousins 89. Twin Peaks (TV) 90. The Comfort of Strangers 90. Wild at Heart 90. Wait Until Spring, Bandini 90. Shattered 91. Other People's Money 91. Twin Peaks: Fire Walk with Me 92. Hotel Room (TV) 93. Naked in New York 93, etc.

Baddeley, Angela (1904–1976).
British stage character actress, sister of Hermione Baddeley. Popular on TV as Mrs Bridges in *Upstairs Downstairs* 70–75.
■ The Speckled Band 31. Arms and the Man 32. The Ghost Train 32. The Safe 32. Those Were the Days 34. The Citadel 38. Quartet 48. Zoo Baby 5 Tom Jones 63.

Baddeley, Hermione (1906–1986).
British character comedienne, adept at blowsy roles; long stage experience. Born in Shropshire, she was performing from the age of 14 and at 16 was a star in the play *The Likes of 'Er*, going on to work in Cochran's revues in London's West End.
Autobiography: 1984, *The Unsinkable Hermione Baddeley*.
■ A Daughter in Revolt 27. The Guns of Loos 28 Caste 30. Love Life and Laughter 34. Royal Cavalcade 35. Kipps 41. It Always Rains on Sunda 47. *Brighton Rock* 47. No Room at the Inn 48. Quartet 48. *Passport to Pimlico* 49. Dear Mr Prohac 49. The Woman in Question 50. There is Anothe Sun 51. Tom Brown's Schooldays 51. Hell is Sold Out 51. Scrooge 51. Song of Paris 52. Time Gentlemen Please 52. *The Pickwick Papers* 52. Cos Boy 53. Counterspy 53. The Belles of St Trinian's 54. Women without Men 54. *Room at the Top* (AAN) 59. Jetstorm 59. Espresso Bongo 59. Let's Get Married 60. Midnight Lace 60. Information Received 61. Rag Doll 61. Mary Poppins 64. The Unsinkable Molly Brown 64. Do Not Disturb 65. Harlow 65. Marriage on the Rocks 65. Bullwhip Griffin 67. The Happiest Millionaire 67. Up the Front 72. The Black Windmill 74. Chomps 79. There Goes the Bride 80. The Secret of Nimh (voice) 80.
TV series: Camp Runamuck 65–66. The Good Life (US) 71. Maude 74–77.

¶ I have spent most of my life working in the theatre – which is always my greatest love, but the films and television were the providers of the little luxuries of life. – H.B.

Badel, Alan (1923–1982).
British stage and screen actor of considerable sensitivity, not easy to cast in leading roles.
The Stranger Left No Card 53. Salome 53. *Three Cases of Murder* 55. Magic Fire 56. This Sporting Life 63. Children of the Damned 64. *Arabesque* 66 Otley 69. Where's Jack? 69. *The Adventurers* 70. Th Day of the Jackal 73. Luther 73. Telefon 77. Forc Ten From Navarone 78. The Riddle of the Sands 79 Nijinsky 80. Shogun (TV) 82, etc.

Baden-Semper, Nina (1945–).
West Indian leading lady, popular on British TV.
Kongi's Harvest 73. Love Thy Neighbour 74.

Badger, Clarence (1880–1964).
American director at his peak in the 20s.
Jubilo 19. Doubling for Romeo 21. Miss Brewster's Millions 26. It 27. Hot News 28. Three Weekends 28. No No Nanette 31. The Bad Man 32. Rangle River 39, etc.

Badham, John (1939–).
American director with a sharp visual style.
The Impatient Heart (TV) 71. Isn't It Shocking? (TV) 73. The Godchild (TV) 74. *The Law* (TV) 74. The Gun (TV) 74. Reflections of Murder (TV) 74. The Keegans (TV) 76. The Bingo Long All Stars and Travelling Motor Kings 76. *Saturday Night Feve* 77. Dracula 79. Whose Life Is It Anyway? 81. Wa Games 83. Blue Thunder 83. American Flyers 84. Short Circuit 85. Stakeout 87. Bird on a Wire 90.

e Hard Way 91. Point of No Return 93. Another
akeout 93. Drop Zone 94, etc.

adham, Mary (1952–).
merican teenage actress.
   To Kill a Mockingbird (AAN) 63. This Property
Condemned 66. Let's Kill Uncle 66.

adiyi, Reza S. (1936–).
anian-born director in America, from TV, where
e came to fame by devising the title sequence
or Hawaii Five-O.
   The Eyes of Charles Sand (TV) 72. Trader Horn
3. Of Mice and Men (TV) 81. Blade in Hong Kong
TV) 85, etc.

aer, Buddy (1915–1986) (Jacob Henry Baer).
merican heavyweight prizefighter, brother of
ax.
   Africa Screams 49. Quo Vadis 51. Jack and the
eanstalk 52. Slightly Scarlet 56. Snow White and
e Three Stooges 61, etc.

aer, Max (1909–1959).
ormer American world heavyweight champion
ho made several films.
   The Prizefighter and the Lady 33. Riding High
0. The Iron Road 55. The Harder They Fall 56.
ver She Goes 58, etc.

aer, Max, Jnr (1937–).
merican actor who spent nine years playing
ethro in TV's The Beverly Hillbillies, then
ecame an independent producer.
   Macon County Line 74. The McCulloughs (& a,
y 75. Ode to Billy Joe (d only) 76. Hometown,
SA (d only) 79, etc.

aer, Parley
merican character actor, usually as professional
ype.
   Comanche Territory 50. Deadline USA 52. D-
ay Sixth of June 56. Cash McCall 60. Gypsy 62.
luffy 65. The Amazing Dobermans 66.
ounterpoint 67. Young Billy Young 69. Punch and
ody (TV) 74. Rodeo Girl 80. White Dog 82, etc.
   TV series: The Adventures of Ozzie and Harriet
5–61. The Andy Griffiths Show 62–63. Double
ife of Henry Phyfe 66.

agdadi, Maroun (1950–).
ebanese director who studied film in Paris in the
id-70s.
   Little Wars 82. L'Homme Voilé 87. Hors la Vie
1. La Fille de l'Air 92, etc.

aggott, King (1874–1948).
all, powerful American leading man of silent
dventure dramas. Made a few early talkies, then
etired.
   Lady Audley's Secret 12. Ivanhoe 12. Dr Jekyll
nd Mr Hyde 13. The Corsican Brothers 15.
loonlight Follies 21. Going Straight 22.
umbleweeds (d only) 25. Notorious Lady 27. The
zar of Broadway 30. Once a Gentleman 30.
careheads 32. Romance in the Rain 34.
lississippi 35. Come Live with Me 41. Abbott and
ostello in Hollywood 45, many others.

ailey, John (1942–).
merican cinematographer.
   Welcome to L.A. 77. Boulevard Nights 79.
merican Gigolo 80. Ordinary People 80. Honky
onk Freeway 81. Racing with the Moon 84.
ilverado 85. Brighton Beach Memoirs 86.
rossroads 86. Swimming to Cambodia 87. The
ccidental Tourist 88. My Blue Heaven 90. In the

Line of Fire 93. Groundhog Day 93. China Moon
(d) 94, etc.

Bailey, Pearl (1918–1990).
American entertainer and Broadway star.
   Autobiography: 1968, The Raw Pearl.
   Variety Girl 47. Isn't It Romantic? 48. Carmen
Jones 54. That Certain Feeling 55. St Louis Blues
57. Porgy and Bess 59. All the Fine Young
Cannibals 60. The Landlord 69. Norman, Is That
You? 76, etc.

Bailey, Raymond (1904–1980).
American small part actor, often a crook or lawyer.
   Secret Service of the Air 39. Tidal Wave 40. I
Want to Live 55. Picnic 56. The Incredible
Shrinking Man 57. Al Capone 59. From the
Terrace 60, many others.
   TV series: My Sister Eileen 59. The Many Loves
of Dobie Gillis 61–62. The Beverly Hillbillies (as
Drysdale) 62–70.

Bailey, Robin (1919–).
British comedy character actor with a penchant for
dialects as well as the extremes of 'Oxford English'.
A television star in such series as I Didn't Know You
Cared, Sorry I'm a Stranger Here Myself, Potter.
   School for Secrets 46. Private Angelo 49. Glory
at Sea 52. Just My Luck 57. Hell Drivers 58. The
Spy with the Cold Nose 66. You Only Live Twice
67. The Four Feathers (TV) 78. Screamtime 83. Jane
and the Lost City 87, etc.
   TV series: I Didn't Know You Cared 75–79.
Sorry I'm a Stranger Here Myself 81–82. Potter 83.
Charters and Caldicot 85.

Bain, Barbara (1931–).
American leading lady, once married to Martin
Landau. Best known on TV in series Mission
Impossible (66–72). Space 1999 (75–76).
   Murder Once Removed (TV) 71. Goodnight My
Love 72. A Summer Without Boys (TV) 73.
Destination Moonbase Alpha 75. Skinheads 88.
Trust Me 89, etc.

Bainter, Fay (1892–1968).
American character actress who came to films from
the stage in 1934 and specialized in stalwart but
sympathetic matrons.
■ This Side of Heaven 34. Quality Street 37. The
Soldier and the Lady 37. Make Way for Tomorrow
37. Jezebel (AA) 38. White Banners (AAN) 38.
Mother Carey's Chickens 38. The Arkansas
Traveller 38. The Shining Hour 39. Yes My Darling
Daughter 39. The Lady and the Mob 39.
Daughters Courageous 39. Our Neighbours the
Carters 39. Young Tom Edison 40. Our Town 40.
A Bill of Divorcement 40. Maryland 40. Babes on
Broadway 42. Woman of the Year 42. The War
Against Mrs Hadley 42. Mrs Wiggs of the Cabbage Patch
42. Journey for Margaret 43. The Human Comedy
43. Presenting Lily Mars 43. Salute to the Marines
43. Cry Havoc 43. The Heavenly Body 43. Dark
Waters (rare villainous role) 44. Three is a Family
44. State Fair 45. The Virginian 46. The Kid from
Brooklyn 46. The Secret Life of Walter Mitty 47. Deep
Valley 47. Give My Regards to Broadway 48. June
Bride 48. Close to My Heart 51. The President's
Lady 53. The Children's Hour (AAN) 62. Bon Voyage
62.

Baio, Scott (1961–).
American teenage actor of the early 80s.
   Bugsy Malone 76. Foxes 81. The Boy Who
Drank Too Much (TV) 81. Something for Joey
(TV) 81. Zapped! 82. Evil Laugh 88, etc.
   TV series: Happy Days 77–84. Joanie Loves
Chaci 82–83. Charles in Charge 84–85.

Baird, Stuart. (1948–).
Leading British editor, now working in Hollywood.
He was a creative consultant at Warner 1989–92
after being called in to rescue Tango and Cash. He
also worked uncredited on the final cuts of
Predator, New Jack City, Scrooged and Robin Hood:
Prince of Thieves.
   Tommy 75. Lisztomania 75. The Omen 76.
Valentino 77. Superman (AAN) 78. Superman II
80. Altered States 80. Outland 81. Five Days One
Summer 82. Revolution 85. Ladyhawke 85. Lethal
Weapon 87. Gorillas in the Mist (AAN) 88. Lethal
Weapon II 89. Tango & Cash 89. Die Hard 2 90.
Radio Flyer 92. Demolition Man 93. Maverick 94,
etc.

¶ If your megapic doesn't click, call Baird.
– Variety

Baird, Teddy (c. 1900–).
British producer, in films since 1928 after
journalistic experience.
   The Browning Version 51. The Importance of
Being Earnest 52. Carrington V.C. 56. Two Living
One Dead 62, etc.

Bakaleinikoff, Constantin (1898–1966).
Russian music director, long in US. With RKO
1941–52.
   Own scores include Notorious 46. Mourning
Becomes Electra 47. Mr Blandings Builds His Dream
House 48. The Conqueror 56, many others.

Bakalyan, Richard
American character actor, usually as villain.
   The Brothers Rico 57. Up Periscope 59. Panic in
Year Zero 62. Von Ryan's Express 65. The
St Valentine's Day Massacre 67. Chinatown 74.
Return from Witch Mountain 78, etc.

Baker, Art (1898–1966) (Arthur Shank).
American general-purpose actor.
   Once Upon a Time 44. Spellbound 45. The
Farmer's Daughter 47. Cover Up 48. Take One False
Step 49. Cause for Alarm 51. Living It Up 54.
Twelve Hours to Kill 60. Young Dillinger 65. The
Wild Angels 66, etc.

Baker, Blanche (1956–).
American actress, the daughter of Carroll Baker.
   The Seduction of Joe Tynan 79. French Postcards
79. Mary and Joseph: A Story of Faith (TV) 79. The
Awakening of Candra (TV) 81. Cold Feet 84.
Sixteen Candles 84. Raw Deal 86. Shakedown 88.
The Handmaid's Tale 90, etc.

Baker, Buddy (1918–).
American composer for Walt Disney films.
   Summer Magic 63. A Tiger Walks 64. The
Gnome-Mobile 67. Napoleon and Samantha
(AAN) 72. The Apple Dumpling Gang 75. The
Shaggy D.A. 76. Hot Lead and Cold Feet 78. The
Apple Dumpling Gang Rides Again 79. The Devil
and Max Devlin 81. The Fox and the Hound 81,
etc.

Baker, Carroll (1931–).
American leading lady who tried to vary her sex-
symbol status via roles of melodramatic intensity.
After her Hollywood career fizzled she made many
exploitation pictures in Italy.
   Easy to Love 53. Giant 56. Baby Doll (AAN) 56.
The Big Country 58. The Miracle 59. But Not for
Me 59. Something Wild 61. Bridge to the Sun 61.
How the West Was Won 63. The Carpetbaggers 64.
Station Six Sahara 64. Cheyenne Autumn 64. The
Greatest Story Ever Told 65. Sylvia 65. Mr Moses
65. Harlow 65. Jack of Diamonds 67. The Sweet

Body of Deborah 68. Paranoia 68. The Harem 68. The Spider 70. The Fourth Mrs Anderson 71. Captain Apache 71. Bloody Mary 72. Baba Yaga Devil Witch 74. Andy Warhol's Bad 77. The Devil Has Seven Faces 77. The World Is Full of Married Men 79. The Watcher in the Woods 80. Star 80 83. The Secret Diary of Sigmund Freud 84. Native Son 86. Ironweed 87. Blonde Fist 91. Cybereden (It.) 93, etc.

¶ More bomb than bombshell. – *Judith Crist*

Baker, Chet (1929–88) (Chesney H. Baker). Cool American jazz trumpeter and singer who made his name playing with the Gerry Mulligan Quartet in the early 50s. His later career was hampered by his drug addiction and he moved to Europe in the 60s, dying after a fall from a hotel window in Amsterdam. He was the subject of a documentary, *Let's Get Lost* 89.

Baker, Diane (1938–). Demure-looking American leading actress who can also handle unsympathetic roles. Many TV guest appearances.

■ *The Diary of Anne Frank* 59. The Best of Everything 59. Journey to the Centre of the Earth 59. The Wizard of Baghdad 61. Tess of the Storm Country 61. Hemingway's Adventures of a Young Man 62. The 300 Spartans 62. Nine Hours to Rama 63. Stolen Hours 63. *Strait Jacket* 63. *The Prize* 63. Della (TV) 64. *Marnie* 64. *Mirage* 65. Sands of Beersheba 66. The Dangerous Days of Kiowa Jones 66. The Horse in the Grey Flannel Suit 68. Krakatoa, East of Java 68. Murder One (TV) 69. The Badge or the Cross (TV) 70. Do You Take This Stranger? (TV) 70. Wheeler and Murdoch (TV) 70. The Old Man Who Cried Wolf (TV) 70. A Little Game (TV) 71. Killer By Night (TV) 71. Congratulations, It's A Boy (TV) 71. A Tree Grows in Brooklyn (TV) 74. The Dream Makers (TV) 75. The Last Survivors (TV) 75. Baker's Hawk 76. The Summer of Sixty-Nine (TV) 77. Danger in the Skies 79. The Pilot 82.

TV series: *Here We Go Again* 73. The Blue and the Grey 82.

Baker, Eddie (1897–1968) (Edward King). American comic actor, one of the original Keystone Kops.

Hold Your Breath 24. All at Sea 29. City Lights 31. Monkey Business 31. Babes in Toyland 34. Land of Fury 55, etc.

Baker, George (1929–). British leading man, also on stage and TV.

The Intruder 52. The Dam Busters 55. A Hill in Korea 56. The Woman for Joe 56. *The Moonraker* 57. Tread Softly Stranger 58. No Time for Tears 59. Lancelot and Guinevere 63. Curse of the Fly 65. Mr Ten Per Cent 67. Justine 69. On Her Majesty's Secret Service 69. The Spy Who Loved Me 77. Print Out (TV) 79. Hopscotch 80. North Sea Hijack 80. The Secret Adversary (TV) 82. Goodbye Mr Chips (TV) 84. A Woman of Substance (TV) 84. For Queen and Country 88, etc.

TV series: I, Claudius 77.

Baker, Graham American director.

The Final Conflict 81. Impulse 84. Alien Nation 88. Born to Ride 91, etc.

Baker, Hylda (1908–1986). British comedienne in northern music-hall tradition.

■ Saturday Night and Sunday Morning 60. She Knows You Know 61. Up the Junction 68. Oliver! 68. Nearest and Dearest 73.

Baker, Ian. Australian cinematographer, associated with the films of Fred Schepisi.

Libido 73. The Devil's Playground 76. The Chant of Jimmy Blacksmith 78. Barbarosa 81. The Clinic 82. Iceman 84. Plenty 85. Roxanne 87. A Cry in the Dark 88. The Punisher 89. Everybody Wins 90. The Russia House 90. Six Degrees of Separation 93, etc.

Baker, Joe Don (1943–). Tough American leading man.

Cool Hand Luke 67. Guns of the Magnificent Seven 69. Adam at Six a.m. 70. Wild Rovers 71. Mongo's Back in Town (TV) 71. Welcome Home Soldier Boys 72. Junior Bonner 72. *Charley Varrick* 72. *Walking Tall* 72. The Outfit 73. Golden Needles 74. Mitchell 74. Framed 75. Crash 76. The Pack 77. To Kill a Cop (TV) 77. Power (TV) 79. Joysticks 83. The Natural 84. Fletch 84. Getting Even 85. The Killing Time 87. The Living Daylights 87. Criminal Law 88. The Children 90. Cape Fear 91. The Distinguished Gentleman 92. Ring of Steel 93. Reality Bites 94, etc.

TV series: Eischied (GB: Chief of Detectives) 79.

Baker, Kathy (1950–). American leading actress who began as a child and then spent time in France, studying Cordon Bleu cookery.

The Right Stuff 83. The Killing Affair 86. My Sister's Keeper 86. Street Smart (AAN) 87. Clean and Sober 88. Permanent Record 88. Dad 89. Jacknife 89. Edward Scissorhands 90. Article 99 92. Mad Dog and Glory 93. Lush Life 93, etc.

TV series: Picket Fences 92.

Baker, Kenny (1912–1985). American crooner, popular in the late 30s but subsequently little heard of.

King of Burlesque 36. The Goldwyn Follies 38. The Mikado (GB: as Nanki Poo) 39. 52nd Street 39. At the Circus 39. Hit Parade of 1941. 40. Silver Skates 43. Doughboys in Ireland 43. The Harvey Girls 46, etc.

Baker, Lenny (1945–1982). American actor of stage and screen. He died of cancer.

The Hospital 71. The Paper Chase 73. *Next Stop, Greenwich Village* 76, etc.

Baker, Phil (1896–1963). American radio personality who appeared in a few films.

Gift of Gab 34. The Goldwyn Follies 38. The Gang's All Here 43. *Take It or Leave It* 44, etc.

Baker, Rick (1950–). American make-up and special effects artist.

Octaman 71. Schlock 72. The Thing with Two Heads 72. It's Alive 74. King Kong 76. *Star Wars* 77. The Incredible Melting Man 77. *An American Werewolf in London* (AA) 81. Greystoke (AAN) 84. Teen Wolf 85. Harry and the Hendersons (AA) 87. Gorillas in the Mist 88. Gremlins 2: The New Batch 90, etc.

Baker, Robert S. (1916–). British producer: co-founder with Monty Berman of Tempean Films, which since 1948 has produced many co-features, also *The Saint* and other TV series.

■ AS DIRECTOR: Blackout 50. 13 East Street 52. The Steel Key 53. Passport to Treason 56. Jack the Ripper 59. The Siege of Sidney Street 60. The Hellfire Club 60. The Treasure of Monte Cristo 61.

Baker, Roy Ward (1916–). Notable British director whose career declined in the 60s. Served apprenticeship at Gainsborough 1934–39, then war service.

The October Man 47. The Weaker Sex 48. *Morning Departure* 50. I'll Never Forget You (US) 51. *Inferno* (US) 52. Don't Bother to Knock (US) 52. Passage Home 54. Jacqueline 56. Tiger in the Smoke 56. *The One That Got Away* 57. *A Night to Remember* 58. The Singer Not the Song (& p) 60. Flame in the Streets (& p) 61. The Valiant 61. Two Left Feet 63. Quatermass and the Pit 67. The Anniversary 68. Moon Zero Two 69. The Vampire Lovers 70. Scars of Dracula 70. Dr Jekyll and Sister Hyde 71. Asylum 72. And Now the Screaming Starts 73. Vault of Horror 73. The Legend of the Seven Golden Vampires 74. The Monster Club 80. The Flame Trees of Thika (TV) 81, etc.

Baker, Sir Stanley (1927–1976). Virile Welsh actor who rose from character roles to stardom, projecting honesty or villainy with equal ease.

Biography: 1977, *Portrait of an Actor* by Anthony Storey.

■ Undercover 41. All Over the Town 48. Obsession 49. Your Witness 50. The Rossiter Case 51. Cloudburst 51. Captain Horatio Hornblower 51. Home to Danger 51. Whispering Smith Hits London 52. Lili Marlene 52. *The Cruel Sea* 53. The Red Beret 53. Hell Below Zero 54. Knights of the Round Table 54. The Good Die Young 54. Beautiful Stranger 54. Helen of Troy 55. Alexander the Great 55. A Hill in Korea 56. *Richard III* (as Henry Tudor) 56. Child in the House 56. Checkpoint 57. *Campbell's Kingdom* 57. Violent Playground 57. Hell Drivers 57. Sea Fury 58. The Angry Hills 59. Blind Date 60. Jet Storm 60. Yesterday's Enemy 60. Hell is a City 60. *The Criminal* 60. The Guns of Navarone 61. Sodom and Gomorrah 62. A Prize of Arms 62. The Man Who Finally Died 62. Eva 62. In the French Style 63. *Zulu* (& co-p) 63. Dingaka 65. Sands of the Kalahari (& co-p) 65. Accident 67. Robbery (& co-p) 67. Code Name: Heraclitus (TV) 67. Where's Jack? 68. Girl with Pistol 68. The Games 69. The Last Grenade 69. Perfect Friday 71. Popsy Pop 71. Schizoid 71. Who Killed Lamb? (TV) 72. Innocent Bystanders 72. Graceless Go I (TV) 74. Zorro 75.

TV series: How Green Was My Valley 76.

Baker, Tom (1936–). British character actor with a larger-than-life air. On TV as Doctor Who 74–82. The second of his three wives was actress Lalla Ward.

Nicholas and Alexandra (as Rasputin) 71. Luther 73. Vault of Horror 73. The Mutations 74. Sinbad's Golden Voyage 75. Angels Die Hard 84. The Zany Adventures of Robin Hood 84, etc.

TV series: Medics 91–94.

¶ Doctor Who was the most wonderful part – I was a madman to give it up. They wouldn't give me the film, would they? They won't know how to do it. Popular films are tawdry, about images and not about thinking. – *T.B.*

The Doctor Who Society in America have conventions and I go among them and lay on hands. Middle-aged ladies stick their tongues in my ear under the pretext of listening. The odd thing is that after the age of 47 chunky little females have tongues like shrapnel. It makes me slightly deaf. A blessing in disguise in our business. – *T.B.*

I like the dead. They're so uncritical. – *T.B.*

Bakewell, William (1908–1993).
American general-purpose actor.
The Heart Thief 27. All Quiet on the Western Front 30. Spirit of Notre Dame 31. Three Cornered Moon 33. Cheers for Miss Bishop 41. Davy Crockett 54, many others.
TV series: The Pinky Lee Show 50.

Bakshi, Ralph (1938–).
American director of animated features. Born in Palestine, he became a director of Terrytoons cartoons from 1964, including creating the *Sad Cat* series 65–68, directing a series of 17 James Hound cartoons 66–67, spoofing James Bond, and a series of 10 *The Mighty Heroes* 69–71, with such characters as Diaper Man and Cuckoo Man. He also directed for Famous Studios two of the *Go-Go Toons* series 67, and three of the *Fractured Fables* series 68. His first animated features featured sex and drugs, his later ones concentrated on sword and sorcery, while *Cool World* mixed animation and live action.
Book: 1989, *The Animated Art of Ralph Bakshi*.
Fritz the Cat (wd) 72. Heavy Traffic (wd) 73. Coonskin (aka Streetfight) (wd) 75. Hey, Good Lookin' (p, wd) 75 (released 82). Wizards (d) 77. Lord of the Rings (d) 78. American Pop (d) 81. Fire and Ice (d) 83. Cool World 92, etc.

Bakula, Scott (1954–).
American leading actor, best known for his role as Dr Sam Beckett in the 90s TV series *Quantum Leap*.
The Last Fling (TV) 86. Sibling Rivalry 90. Necessary Roughness 91. Color of Night 94, etc.
TV series: Gung Ho 86–87. Eisenhower & Lutz 88.

Balaban, Barney (1888–1971).
American executive, former exhibitor, president of Paramount 1936–64.

Balaban, Burt (1922–1965).
American director, son of Barney Balaban.
Stranger from Venus (GB) 54. Lady of Vengeance 57. High Hell 58. Murder Inc. 60. Mad Dog Coll 61. The Gentle Rain 66, etc.

Balaban, Robert (Bob) (1945–).
American character actor turned director.
Midnight Cowboy 69. Me Natalie 69. Close Encounters of the Third Kind 78. Altered States 80. Prince of the City 81. Absence of Malice 81. Whose Life Is It Anyway? 82. End of the Line 88. Dead Bang 89. Parents (d) 89. Bob Roberts 92. For Love or Money 93. Amos & Andrew 93. My Boyfriend's Back (d) 93. The Last Good Time (d) 94, etc.

Balanchine, George (1904–1983).
Distinguished Russian-born American choreographer who worked occasionally in Hollywood.
Dark Red Roses 29. The Goldwyn Follies 38. I Was an Adventuress 40. George Balanchine's The Nutcracker 93.

Balazs, Bela (1884–1949) (Hubert Bauer).
Hungarian writer. Wrote book, *Theory of the Film*.
Die Dreigroschenoper 31. *The Blue Light* 31.

Balchin, Nigel (1908–1970).
British novelist: books filmed include: *Mine Own Executioner, The Small Black Room, Suspect* ('A Sort of Traitors'). Has also adapted other people's work for the screen: *The Barbarian and the Geisha, The Blue Angel* (remake), etc.

Balcon, Jill (1925–).
British actress, daughter of Sir Michael Balcon. She is the mother of Daniel Day-Lewis.
Nicholas Nickleby 47. Good Time Girl 48. Highly Dangerous 50. Edward II 91, etc.

Balcon, Sir Michael (1896–1977).
British executive producer. During a long and distinguished career he headed Gainsborough, Gaumont-British, MGM-British, Ealing, Bryanston and independent production companies, and was directly responsible for the planning and production of many famous films. He served as a model for the character of the mill-owner, played by Cecil Parker, in *The Man in the White Suit*.
Autobiography: 1969, *A Lifetime of Films*.
His more personal projects include: Woman to Woman 23. The Pleasure Garden 25. The Lodger 26. Easy Virtue 27. Man of Aran 33. The Man Who Knew Too Much 34. The 39 Steps 35. Sabotage 37. A Yank at Oxford 38. The Citadel 38. Goodbye Mr Chips 39. Convoy 40. The Next of Kin 42. The Bells Go Down 42. Champagne Charlie 44. Dead of Night 45. The Captive Heart 46. Hue and Cry 46. Nicholas Nickleby 47. It Always Rains on Sunday 48. Scott of the Antarctic 48. Kind Hearts and Coronets 49. Whisky Galore 49. Passport to Pimlico 49. The Blue Lamp 50. The Man in the White Suit 51. The Lavender Hill Mob 51. The Cruel Sea 53. The Ladykillers 55. Dunkirk 58. Saturday Night and Sunday Morning 60. Tom Jones 63.
✪ For steering his part of the British film industry in very much the right way, and for refusing to lower his standards. *Dead of Night*.

¶ I always look for people whose ideas coincide with mine, and then I'm ready to give them a chance to make a name for themselves. – *M.B.*
We made films at Ealing that were good, bad and indifferent, but they were indisputably British. They were rooted in the soil of the country. – *M.B.*

Balderston, John (1889–1954).
Anglo-American screenwriter, usually in collaboration, with a penchant for romantic and fantastic themes.
Frankenstein 31. *The Mummy* 32. Smilin' Through 32 and 41. *Berkeley Square* (oa) 33. The Mystery of Edwin Drood 35. *Mad Love* 35. Lives of a Bengal Lancer (AAN) 35. *Bride of Frankenstein* 35. Beloved Enemy 36. *The Prisoner of Zenda* 37. Victory 40. Tennesse Johnson 42. Gaslight (AAN) 44. Red Planet Mars 52, many others.

Baldi, Ferdinando
Italian director.
David and Goliath (co-d) 59. Duel of the Champions 71. Blindman 71. Get Mean 76. My Name Is Trinity 76. The Sicilian Connection 77. Comin' at Ya 81. Treasure of the Four Crowns 83, etc.

baldness
has proved an attraction for a number of actors, including Yul Brynner, Telly Savalas, Edgar Kennedy and Leon Errol. Many others have been at pains to conceal it.

Baldwin, Adam (1962–).
American actor, the brother of Alec Baldwin.
My Bodyguard 80. Ordinary People 80. D.C. Cab 84. Reckless 84. Hadley's Rebellion 84. Love on the Run (TV) 85. Bad Guys 86. Full Metal Jacket 87. Cohen and Tate 88. Next of Kin 89. Internal Affairs 90. Predator 2 90. Radio Flyer 91. Bitter

Harvest 93. Eight Hundred Leagues down the Amazon 93, etc.

Baldwin, Alec (1958–).
American leading actor. He is the brother of actor William Baldwin. Married Kim Basinger.
Forever, Lulu 86. Beetlejuice 88. Married to the Mob 88. She's Having a Baby 88. Talk Radio 88. Working Girl 88. Great Balls of Fire 89. Alice 90. The Hunt for Red October 90. Miami Blues 90. The Marrying Man (aka Hot To Handle) 91. Prelude to a Kiss 92. Glengarry Glen Ross 92. Malice 93. The Getaway 94. The Shadow 94. Heaven's Prisoners 95, etc.
TV series: Knots Landing 84–85.

Baldwin, Daniel (1961–).
American actor, the brother of Alec Baldwin.
The Heroes of Desert Storm 91. Nothing but Trouble 91. Harley Davidson and the Marlboro Man 91. Car 54, Where Are You? 91. Dead on Sight 94, etc.
TV series: Homicide: Life on the Street 93.

Baldwin, Faith (1893–1978).
American novelist.
Scenario credits include: The Moon's Our Home 36. Men Are Such Fools 37. Apartment for Peggy 50. Queen for a Day 51.

Baldwin, Stephen (1966–).
American leading actor, the brother of Alec Baldwin.
The Beast 88. Born on the Fourth of July 89. Bitter Harvest 93. Posse 93. Threesome 94. 8 Seconds 94. A Simple Twist of Fate 94, etc.
TV series: The Young Riders 89–92.

¶ If there's one thing I learned in the business, it's at least have your package looking good. – *S.B.*

Baldwin, Walter (1887–1977).
American character actor, often in owlish or countrified roles.
Angels Over Broadway 40. All That Money Can Buy 41. Kings Row 42. Happy Land 43. I'll Be Seeing You 44. The Lost Weekend 45. The Best Years of Our Lives 46. Mourning Becomes Electra 47. The Man from Colorado 48. Cheaper by the Dozen 50. Carrie 52. Scandal at Scourie 53. Glory 55. Cheyenne Autumn 64. Rosemary's Baby 68, many others.

Baldwin, William (1963–).
American actor, the brother of actor Alec Baldwin.
Born on the Fourth of July 89. Internal Affairs 90. Flatliners 90. Backdraft 91. Three of Hearts 93. Sliver 93, etc.

Bale, Christian (1974–).
Welsh teenage actor who made his screen debut in the leading role in *Empire of the Sun*.
Empire of the Sun 87. Land of Faraway 88. Henry V 89. Treasure Island (TV) 90. Newsies (GB: News Boys) 92. Swing Kids 93. Little Women 94, etc.

Balfour, Betty (1903–1978).
British comedienne of silent days, a popular favourite of the 20s as pert heroine of *Cinders, Love Life and Laughter* and the *Squibs* series.
The Brat 30. The Vagabond Queen 30. Paddy the Next Best Thing 33. Evergreen 35. Squibs (remake) 36. 29 Acacia Avenue 45, etc.

Balfour, Michael (1918–).
American character actor in British films who usually plays dumb gangsters, cabbies, etc.

No Orchids for Miss Blandish 48. Obsession 50. Venetian Bird 53. The Steel Key 55. Breakaway 56. Fiend without a Face 58. Make Mine Mink 60. Fahrenheit 451 66. The Fixer 68. The Private Life of Sherlock Holmes 70. Joseph Andrews 77. Candleshoe 78. The Holcroft Covenant 85, many others.

TV series: Mark Saber 55.

Balin, Ina (1937–1990) (Ina Rosenberg).
American leading lady, with stage experience.

Compulsion 58. The Black Orchid 59. The Comancheros 62. The Patsy 64. The Greatest Story Ever Told 65. Run Like a Thief 68. Charro 69. The Projectionist 71. The Don is Dead 73, etc.

Balin, Mireille (1909–1968).
French leading lady.

Don Quixote 33. Pepe le Moko 36. Gueule d'Amour 37, etc.

Ball, Lucille (1911–1989).
American comedienne, a former Goldwyn girl who after a generally unrewarding youth in the movies, turned in middle age to TV and became known as one of the world's great female clowns and a highly competent production executive. She was formerly married to actor Desi Arnaz.

■ Broadway Thru a Keyhole 33. Blood Money 33. Roman Scandals 33. Moulin Rouge 33. Nana 34. Bottoms Up 34. Hold that Girl 34. Bulldog Drummond Strikes Back 34. The Affairs of Cellini 34. Kid Millions 34. Broadway Bill 34. Jealousy 34. Men of the Night 34. Fugitive Lady 34. Carnival (first billed role) 35. Roberta 35. Old Man Rhythm 35. Top Hat 35. The Three Musketeers 35. I Dream Too Much 35. Chatterbox 36. Follow the Fleet 36. The Farmer in the Dell 36. Bunker Bean 36. That Girl from Paris 36. Don't Tell the Wife 37. *Stage Door* 37. Joy of Living 38. Go Chase Yourself 38. Having A Wonderful Time 38. *The Affairs of Annabel* 38. Room Service 38. The Next Time I Marry 38. Annabel Takes a Tour 38. Beauty for the Asking 39. Twelve Crowded Hours 39. Panama Lady 39. *Five Came Back* 39. That's Right You're Wrong 39. The Marines Fly High 40. You Can't Fool Your Wife 40. Dance Girl Dance 40. Too Many Girls 40. A Guy, a Girl and Gob 40. Look Who's Laughing 41. Valley of the Sun 42. *The Big Street* (serious role) 42. Seven Days Leave 42. *Du Barry was a Lady* 43. Best Foot Forward 43. Thousands Cheer 43. Meet the People 44. *Without Love* 45. Abbott and Costello in Hollywood 45. Ziegfeld Follies 46. The Dark Corner 46. *Easy to Wed* 46. Two Smart People 46. Lover Come Back 46. Lured 47. *Her Husband's Affairs* 47. *Sorrowful Jones* 49. Easy Living 49. Miss Grant Takes Richmond 49. *Fancy Pants* 50. The Fuller Brush Girl 50. The Magic Carpet 50. *The Long Long Trailer* 54. Forever Darling 56. *The Facts of Life* 60. Critic's Choice 63. A Guide for the Married Man 67. *Yours Mine and Ours* 68. Mame 73. Stone Pillow (TV) 85.

TV series: *I Love Lucy* 51–55. *The Lucy Show* 62– 68. *Here's Lucy* 68–73. Life with Lucy 86.

Ball, Suzan (1933–1955).
American leading lady of the early 50s.

Untamed Frontier 52. East of Sumatra 53. City Beneath the Sea 53. War Arrow 54. Chief Crazy Horse 55, etc.

Ball, Vincent (1924–).
Australian actor, in England for a time.

A Town Like Alice 56. Robbery under Arms 57. Danger Within 58. Identity Unknown 60. Where

Eagles Dare 68. Oh What a Lovely War 69. Deadline (Aus) 81. Phar Lap (Aus) 83. The Year My Voice Broke (Aus) 87, etc.

Ballard, Carroll (1937–).
American director with a flair for wild life.

The Black Stallion 80. Never Cry Wolf 83. Nutcracker: The Motion Picture 86. Wind 92, etc.

Ballard, Kay(e) (1926–) (Catherine Balotta).
American comedienne with stage experience.

The Girl Most Likely 56. A House is Not a Home 64. Freaky Friday 77. Falling in Love Again 80. Tiger Warshaw 87. Modern Love 90. Eternity 90, etc.

TV series: The Mothers-in-Law 67–68. The Doris Day Show 70–71.

Ballard, Lucien (1908–1988).
Distinguished American cinematographer. He was married to actress Merle Oberon (1945–49).

Crime and Punishment 35. The King Steps Out 36. Craig's Wife 36. The Shadow 37. Penitentiary 38. *Blind Alley* 39. The Villain Still Pursued Her 40. Wild Geese Calling 41. The Undying Monster 42. Orchestra Wives 42. Holy Matrimony 43. *The Lodger* 44. *Laura* (co-ph) 44. This Love of Ours 45. Temptation 46. Night Song 47. Berlin Express 48. The House on Telegraph Hill 51. O. Henry's Full House 52. *Inferno* (3-D) 53. New Faces 54. White Feather 55. The Proud Ones 56. *The Killing* 56. Band of Angels 57. Murder by Contract 58. Al Capone 59. Pay or Die 60. The Parent Trap 61. Ride the High Country 62. *The Caretakers* (AAN) 63. The New Interns 64. Boeing Boeing 65. Nevada Smith 66. *Hour of the Gun* 67. Will Penny 68. *The Wild Bunch* 69. True Grit 69. The Ballad of Cable Hogue 70. The Hawaiians 70. What's the Matter with Helen? 71. Junior Bonner 72. The Getaway 72. Breakout 75. Breakheart Pass 76. St Ives 76, etc.

ballet

sequences have been a boon to many indifferent films, permitting a brief glimpse into a world that is strange, alarming, but graceful and glamorous. From the time of *The Goldwyn Follies* 38, any Hollywood musical with aspirations had to have a ballet sequence, some of the most memorable being in *The Pirate*, *On the Town*, *An American in Paris*, *Singin' in the Rain*, and *The Band Wagon*. The custom died out in the 50s, since when there has been an over-abundance of unimaginatively presented full-length stage ballets with famous dancing stars. These, filmed at low cost, have found a market, but expensive film ballets like *Tales of Hoffman*, *Invitation to the Dance* and *Black Tights* had tougher going. Dramatic films set in the ballet world have included *La Mort du Cygne* (remade in Hollywood as *The Unfinished Dance*), *The Red Shoes* and *The Spectre of the Rose*; lighter stories in which the heroine is a ballerina (usually a novice) include *Waterloo Bridge*, *Carnival*, *Dance Little Lady*, *On Your Toes* and *St Martin's Lane*. Several comedians have found themselves pursued by plot complications on to a stage and forced to take part clumsily in the ballet in progress: Jack Buchanan in *That's a Good Girl*, Danny Kaye in *Knock on Wood*, Morecambe and Wise in *The Intelligence Men*; even Laurel and Hardy donned tutus in *The Dancing Masters*.

By the 70s, ballet had lost its general popularity. *Nijinsky* accentuated the homosexual element. Rudolf Nureyev, on film in several straight ballets, turned actor as *Valentino*. Following him came fellow Russian Mikhail Baryshnikov who, in *The Turning Point* 77, not only danced but was nominated for an Oscar as best supporting actor. With the same director, Herbert Ross, he tried for something similar ten years later in *Dancers*, but

without the same impact. Perhaps the boldest attempt to bring ballet to the big screen so far has been Carroll Ballard's *Nutcracker: The Motion Picture* in 86.

Ballhaus, Michael (1935–).
German cinematographer who worked on many of Fassbinder's films before moving to Hollywood in the 80s.

Whity 70. Adele Spitzeder 72. The Bitter Tears of Petra von Kant (Die Bitteren Tränen der Petra von Kant) 72. Adolf und Marlene 77. Despair 78. The Marriage of Maria Braun (Die Ehe der Maria Braun) 79. Malou 81. Reckless 84. Heartbreakers 84. After Hours 85. The Color of Money 86. Under the Cherry Moon 86. Broadcast News (AAN) 87. The House on Carroll Street 88. Dirty Rotten Scoundrels 88. The Last Temptation of Christ 88. Working Girl 88. The Fabulous Baker Boys (AAN) 89. GoodFellas 90. Postcards from the Edge 90. Guilty by Suspicion 90. What about Bob? 91. The Mambo Kings 92. Bram Stoker's Dracula 92. The Age of Innocence 93. I'll Do Anything 94. Quiz Show 94. Outbreak 95, etc.

balloons:
see *air balloons*.

ballyhoo.
An expressive term, allegedly Irish in origin, used in show business to denote the kind of publicity that has nothing to do with the merits, or indeed the actual contents, of the film in question.

Balsam, Martin (1919–).
American character actor of quiet and comfortable presence: range varies from executive to stagecoach driver.

■ On the Waterfront 54. *Twelve Angry Men* 57. *Time Limit* 57. Marjorie Morningstar 58. Al Capone 59. Middle of the Night 59. Everybody Go Home (It.) 60. *Psycho* (as the ill-fated private detective) 60. Ada 61. Breakfast at Tiffany's 61. The Captive City 62. Cape Fear 63. Who's Been Sleeping in My Bed? 63. *The Carpetbaggers* (as the Louis B. Mayer type studio chief) 64. Youngblood Hawke 64. *Seven Days in May* 64. Harlow 65. The Bedford Incident 65. *A Thousand Clowns* (AA) 65. After the Fox 66. Hombre 67. Me Natalie 69. Trilogy (TV) 69. *The Good Guys and the Bad Guys* 69. Tora! Tora! Tora! 70. Catch 22 70. Little Big Man 70. The Old Man Who Cried Wolf (TV) 70. Hunters Are for Killing (TV) 70. *The Anderson Tapes* 71. Confessions of a Police Commissioner (It.) 71. The Man (TV) 72. Night of Terror (TV) 72. *Summer Wishes Winter Dreams* 73. The Stone Killer 73. Six Million Dollar Man (TV) 73. Money to Burn (TV) 74. Trapped Beneath the Sea (TV) 74. The Taking of Pelham 123 74. Murder on the Orient Express 74. Miles to Go Before I Sleep (TV) 75. Corruption in the Halls of Justice (It.) 75. Mitchell 75. Death Among Friends (TV) 75. All the President's Men 76. Two Minute Warning 76. Raid on Entebbe (TV) 77. The Sentinel 77. Silver Bears 77. Rainbow (TV) 78. The Seeding of Sarah Burns (TV) 79. The House on Garibaldi Street (TV) 79. Aunt Mary (TV) 79. The Love Tapes (TV) 79. Cuba 79. There Goes the Bride 80. The Salamander 80. Little Gloria . . . Happy at Last (TV) 82. The Goodbye People 84. St Elmo's Fire 85. Death Wish 3 85. Delta Force 85. Space (TV) 87. Queenie (TV) 87. Private Investigations 87. Two Evil Eyes (Due Occhi Diabolici) 89. Cape Fear 91. Innocent Prey 92. The Silence of the Hams (It.) 94.

TV series: Archie Bunker's Place 81–82.

Balser, Ewald (1898–1978).
Austrian character actor in German films.

Rembrandt (title role) 42. The Last Act 48. Eroica
as Beethoven) 49. William Tell 56. Jedermann
62, many others.

Bancroft, Anne (1931–) (Anna Maria Italiano).
Warm, ambitious and effective American leading
actress who after TV experience went to Hollywood
in 1952 and made inferior routine films; fled to
Broadway stage and after triumph in *The Miracle
Worker* returned to films as a star. She married Mel
Brooks in 1964.

◼ Don't Bother to Knock 52. Tonight We Sing 53.
Treasure of the Golden Condor 53. The Kid from
Left Field 53. Demetrius and the Gladiators 54. The
Raid 54. Gorilla at Large 54. A Life in the Balance
55. New York Confidential 55. The Naked Street
55. The Last Frontier 55. Walk the Proud Land 56.
Nightfall 56. The Restless Breed 57. The Girl in
Black Stockings 57. So Soon to Die (TV) 57. *The
Miracle Worker* (AA, BFA) 62. *The Pumpkin Eater*
(AAN, BFA) 64. *The Slender Thread* 65. Seven
Women 65. *The Graduate* (AAN) 68. *Young Winston*
72. The Prisoner of Second Avenue 75. The
Hindenburg 76. Lipstick 76. Silent Movie 76. Jesus
of Nazareth (TV) 77. *The Turning Point* (AAN) 77.
The Elephant Man 80. Fatso (also directed) 80.
Marco Polo (TV) 81. To Be or Not to Be 83. Garbo
Talks 84. Agnes of God (AAN) 85. Night Mother
86. *84 Charing Cross Road* 87. Torch Song Trilogy
88. Bert Rigby, You're a Fool 89. Honeymoon in
Vegas 92. Broadway Bound (TV) 92. Malice 93.
Point of No Return 93. Mr Jones 93. Oldest Living
Confederate Widow Tells All (TV) 94.

Bancroft, George (1882–1956).
Burly American actor who after a period in the
Navy became popular in Broadway musicals and
straight plays. Went to Hollywood in the 20s and
found his strong masculine personality much in
demand for tough or villainous roles, almost
always in run-of-the-mill films.

The Journey's End 21. *Driven* 21. *Pony Express* 25.
Code of the West 25. *Old Ironsides* 26. *Underworld* 27.
White Gold 27. Docks of New York 28.
Thunderbolt (AAN) 29. Derelict 30. Ladies Love
Brutes 30. Scandal Sheet 31. Lady and Gent 33.
Blood Money 34. Mr Deeds Goes to Town 36. John
Meade's Woman 37. Angels with Dirty Faces 38.
Stagecoach 39. Each Dawn I Die 39. Young Tom
Edison 40. Texas 41. Syncopation 41. Whistling in
Dixie 42, many others.

❡ When words roll from his tongue, you expect
them to be punctuated by lightning. – *N.Y.
Times, 1929*

Band, Albert (1924–) (Alfredo Antonini).
Italian-born director and producer, in Hollywood
since the 40s.

The Young Guns 56. I Bury the Living (& p) 58.
Face of Fire 59. I Pascali Rossi 63. The Tramplers
(& p) 66. A Minute to Pray, a Second to Die (p,
co-w only) 68. Dracula's Dog 78. She Came to
the Valley 79. Ghoulies II 88. Honey, I Blew Up
the Kid (p) 92. Prehysteria (co-d) 93. Dragon
World (co-p) 93, etc.

Band, Charles (1952–).
American producer and director of low-budget
horror movies, many of them released direct to
video. The son of Albert Band, he is founder of the
production company Full Moon Entertainment.
AS PRODUCER: Ghoulies 85. Re-Animator 85.
Crawlspace (ex p) 86. Troll (ex p) 86. Eliminators
86. Catacombs 87. Puppetmaster 89. Puppetmaster
II 90. Puppetmaster III 91. Netherworld 91. Bad
Channels 91. Demonic Toys 91. Arcade 92. Dragon
World 93. Oblivion (& story) 94, etc.

AS DIRECTOR: Crash! 77. Parasite 81. Metalstorm:
The Destruction of Jared-Syn 83. The
Dungeonmaster (co-d) 85. Future Cop 85.
Trancers 85. Pulsepounders 88. Meridian: Kiss of
the Beast 90. Trancers II 91. Doctor Modrid (co-
d) 91. Trancers III 92. Prehysteria (co-d) 93, etc.

Band, Richard H. (1953–).
American composer, the son of Albert Band.
Laserblast 78. The Day Time Ended 79. Dr
Heckle and Mr Hype 80. Parasite 82. Time Walker
83. Ghoulies 85. Re-Animator 85. Eliminators 86.
Terrorvision 86. Troll 86. Dolls 87. Prison 88.
Puppet Master 89. Bride of Re-Animator 90, etc.

Banderas, Antonio (1960–).
Spanish leading actor, associated with the films of
Pedro Almodóvar.

Labyrinth of Passion (Laberinto de Pasiones) 82.
The Stilts (Los Zancos) 84. Matador 86. The Law
of Desire (La Ley del Deseo) 87. Baton Rouge 88.
Women on the Verge of a Nervous Breakdown
(Mujeres al Borde de un Ataque de Nervios) 88.
Baton Rouge 88. Tie Me Up! Tie Me Down!
(¡Atame!) 90. Cuentos de Borges I 91. The Mambo
Kings 92. A Woman in a Rain (Una Mujer bajo
la Lluvia) 92. Il Giovane Mussolini (as Mussolini)
93. ¡Dispara! 93. Philadelphia 93. Of Love and
Shadows 94. Interview with the Vampire 94, etc.

Banerjee, Victor (1946–).
Indian leading actor, occasionally in international
films.

The Chess Players (Shatranj Ke Khilari) 77. The
Home and the World (Ghare Baire) 84. Hullabaloo
over Georgie and Bonnie's Pictures 78. A Passage
to India 84. Foreign Body 86. World Within, World
Without (Mahaprithivi) 91. Bitter Moon 92, etc.

Bankhead, Tallulah (1902–1968).
Gravel-voiced, highly theatrical leading lady of
American stage and screen. The daughter of an
eminent politician, she titillated Broadway and
London in the 20s by her extravagant
performance on stage and off, and later tended to
fritter away her considerable talents by living too
dangerously. Films never managed to contain her.
Autobiography: 1952, *Tallulah*.

◼ When Men Betray 18. Thirty a Week 18. A
Woman's Law 28. His House in Order 28. *Tarnished
Lady* 31. My Sin 31. The Cheat 31. Thunder Below
32. The Devil and the Deep 32. Faithless 32. Stage
Door Canteen 43. *Lifeboat* 43. *A Royal Scandal* 45.
Main Street to Broadway 53. *Fanatic* (GB) 65.

❡ She said of herself:
I'm as pure as the driven slush.
What one remembers about Miss Bankhead is not
her merit as a performer, which in her heyday was
considerable, but rather her well-publicized
lifestyle, which kept her in the headlines
throughout the 20s and 30s. As Mrs Patrick
Campbell said:
Tallulah is always skating on thin ice. Everyone
wants to be there when it breaks.
The lady herself issued such statements as:
Cocaine isn't habit-forming. I should know –
I've been using it for years.
As a result, in her later years:
They used to photograph Shirley Temple
through gauze. They should photograph me
through linoleum.
But it was more sad than funny when someone
asked:
Are you really the famous Tallulah?
and got the answer:
What's left of her.
She concluded:

The only thing I regret about my past is the
length of it. If I had it to live over again I'd
make the same mistakes, only sooner.
Sooner or later she alienated most of her friends.
Howard Dietz was the one who said:
A day away from Tallulah is like a month in the
country.

Banks, Don (1923–1980).
Australian composer in Britain.
Captain Clegg 62. Hysteria 65. Die Monster Die
65. The Reptile 66. The Mummy's Shroud 67. The
Torture Garden 68, etc.

Banks, Leslie (1890–1952).
Distinguished British stage actor who after
unsuccessful experiments in home-grown silent
films started his film career in Hollywood. His
sophistication seemed to be enhanced by his war-
scarred profile.

◼ *The Most Dangerous Game* 32. Strange Evidence
33. The Fire-Raisers 33. I am Suzanne 33. Night
of the Party 33. The Red Ensign 34. *The Man Who
Knew Too Much* 34. The Tunnel 35. *Sanders of the
River* 35. Debt of Honour 36. The Three Maxims
36. Fire Over England 36. Farewell Again 37. Wings
of the Morning 37. *Twenty-one Days* 39. Jamaica
Inn 39. Dead Man's Shoes 39. The Arsenal Stadium
39. Sons of the Sea 40. Busman's Honeymoon 40.
The Door with Seven Locks 40. Neutral Port 40.
Ships with Wings 41. Cottage to Let 41. The Big
Blockade 42. Went the Day Well? 42. *Henry V* (as
Chorus) 44. Mrs Fitzherbert 47. The Small Back
Room 48. Madeleine 49. Your Witness 50.

Banks, Monty (1897–1950) (Mario Bianchi).
Italian comic dancer who appeared in many silent
two-reel comedies of the 20s then moved to Britain
and later turned director. He was married to Gracie
Fields.

Atlantic 30. Weekend Wives 31. Almost a
Honeymoon (d) 31. Tonight's the Night (d) 32. No
Limit (d) 35. We're Going to be Rich (d) 38. Great
Guns (US) (d) 41, etc.

Banky, Vilma (1898–1991) (Vilma Lonchit).
Austro-Hungarian star of American silents,
discovered by Sam Goldwyn during a European
holiday. Popular in the 20s but could not make
the transition to sound. Married Rod la Rocque.

◼ Im Letzen Augenblick (Hung.) 20. Galathea
(Hung.) 21. Tavaszi Szerelem (Hung.) 21.
Veszlyeben a Pokol (Hung.) 21. Kauft Mariett-
Aktien (Ger.) 22. Das Auge des Toten (Ger.) 22.
Schattenkinder des Glucks (Ger.) 22. Die Letzte
Stinde (Ger.) 23. The Forbidden Land (Aust.) 24.
Clown aus Liebe (Aust.) 24. The Lady from Paris
(Ger.) 24. Das Bildnis (Aust.) 25. Sollman
Heiraten (Ger.) 25. *The Dark Angel* 25. The Eagle
25. Son of the Sheik 26. The Winning of Barbara
Worth 26. The Night of Love 27. The Magic Flame
27. Two Lovers 28. The Awakening 28. This Is
Heaven 29. A Lady to Love 30. De Sehnsucht Jeder
Frau (Ger.) 30. The Rebel (Ger.) 33.

❡ She spoke no English at all: for their love scenes
in *The Dark Angel*, she spoke in her own
language while co-star Ronald Colman chatted
away about cricket. – *John Baxter, The Hollywood
Exiles*

Bannen, Ian (1928–).
British stage and TV actor who has been effective
in several films.

Private's Progress 55. The Birthday Present 57.
Carlton Browne of the F.O. 58. Macbeth 59. *A
French Mistress* 60. *Suspect* 60. On Friday at Eleven
61. Station Six Sahara 63. Rotten to the Core 65.

The Hill 65. The Flight of the Phoenix (AAN) 65. Sailor from Gibraltar 66. Penelope 67. Lock Up Your Daughters 69. Too Late the Hero 69. Fright 71. Doomwatch 72. The Offence 72. The Mackintosh Man 73. Bite the Bullet 75. The Sweeney 77. Bastards Without Glory (It.) 78. The Watcher in the Woods 80. Eye of the Needle 81. Gandhi 82. Night Crossing 82. Gorky Park 83. Defence of the Realm 85. Lamb 85. Hope and Glory 87. The Courier 88. George's Island 89. Ghost Dad 90. The Big Man 90. Damage 92. A Pin for the Butterfly 94, etc.

TV series: Doctor Finlay 92.

Banner, John (1910–1973).
American character actor of Polish origin; usually played explosive Europeans.

Once Upon a Honeymoon 42. The Fallen Sparrow 44. Black Angel 47. My Girl Tisa 48. The Juggler 53. The Rains of Ranchipur 56. The Story of Ruth 60. Hitler 63. Thirty-six Hours 64, etc.

TV series: Hogan's Heroes 65–70. Chicago Teddy Bears 71.

Bannon, Jim (1911–).
American actor with radio experience: played second feature leads in the 40s and starred in a western series as 'Red Ryder' in the 50s.

The Missing Juror 44. I Love a Mystery 45. The Thirteenth Hour 47. Daughter of the Jungle 49. The Man from Colorado 49. Rodeo 53. Chicago Confidential 58. Madame X 65, many others.

TV series: Adventures of Champion 55–56.

Banton, Travis (1894–1958).
American costume designer, long at Paramount, noted for dressing Mae West and Marlene Dietrich.

The Wild Party 29. Morocco 29. The Vagabond King 30. Dishonored 31. Shanghai Express 32. *The Scarlet Empress* 34. *The Devil Is a Woman* 35. The Crusades 35. Maid of Salem 37. Angel 37. Letter from an Unknown Woman 48, etc.

Bar, Jacques (1921–).
French producer, often in association with American companies.

Where the Hot Wind Blows 60. Vie Privée 61. A Monkey in Winter 62. Joy House 64. Once a Thief 65. The Guns of San Sebastian 67. The Mysterious Island of Captain Nemo 73, etc.

Bara, Nina (1925–1990).
Argentinian actress, best remembered for her role as Tonga in TV's children's series *Space Patrol* 51–52.

Missile to the Moon 58, etc.

Bara, Theda (1890–1955) (Theodosia Goodman).
American actress, the first to be called a 'vamp' (because of her absurdly vampirish, man-hungry screen personality). An extra in 1915, she was whisked to stardom on some highly imaginary publicity statistics (she was the daughter of an Eastern potentate, her name was an anagram of 'Arab death', etc.). *A Fool There Was* 16 is remembered for its classic sub-title, 'Kiss Me, My Fool!'; in 1919, her popularity waning, she forsook Hollywood for the Broadway stage, and when she returned in 1925 was forced to accept parts burlesquing her former glories, e.g. *Madame Mystery* 26. Wisely, she soon retired.
■ The Two Orphans 15. The Clemenceau Case 15. The Stain 15. Lady Audley's Secret 15. The Vixen 16. *A Fool There Was* 16. Sin 16. Carmen 16. Romeo and Juliet 16. The Light 16. Destruction 16. Gold and the Woman 16. The Serpent 16. Eternal Sappho 16. East Lynne 16. Her Double Life 16.

Cleopatra 17. Madame Du Barry 17. Under Two Flags 17. Camille 17. Heart and Soul 17. The Tiger Woman 17. Salome 18. When a Woman Sins 18. The Forbidden Path 18. The She Devil 18. Rose of the Blood 18. Kathleen Mavourneen 19. La Belle Russe 19. When Men Desire 19. The Siren's Song 19. A Woman There Was 20. The Price of Silence 21. Her Greatest Love 21. The Hunchback of Notre Dame 23. The Unchastened Woman 25. Madame Mystery 26. The Dancer of Paris 26.

¶ She was divinely, hysterically, insanely
  malevolent. – *Bette Davis*
  She made voluptuousness a common American commodity, as accessible as chewing gum. – *Lloyd Morris*

Baratier, Jacques (1918–).
French director of shorts and occasional features, a former theatre critic.

Paris la Nuit 55. Goha 57. La Poupée 62. Dragées au Poivre 63. L'Or du Duc 65. Le Désordre à Vingt Ans 67. La Décharge 70, etc.

Barbeau, Adrienne (1945–).
American leading lady, mostly on TV.

Red Alert (TV) 77. Someone's Watching Me (TV) 78. The Disappearance of Flight 401 (TV) 79. The Fog 80. Escape from New York 81. Swamp Thing 82. Creep Show 82. The Next One 84. Seduced 85. Back to School 86. Two Evil Eyes (Due Occhi Diabolici) 89. Cannibal Women in the Avocado Jungle of Death 89. Doublecrossed (TV) 91, etc.

TV series: Maude 72–78.

Barber, Glynis (1955–).
South African leading lady in Britain. Became popular on TV in Dempsey and Makepeace 85.

The Wicked Lady 83. Edge of Sanity 89, etc.

Barbera, Joe (1910–).
American animator who with William Hanna (qv) created Tom and Jerry at MGM in 1937 and controlled the output until 1957: 'the cinema's purest representation of pure energy'. Later formed an independent company which produced dozens of 'semi-animated' cartoon series for TV, including the adventures of Yogi Bear, Huckleberry Hound, the Jetsons, the Flintstones, Magilla Gorilla, Scooby Doo and Snagglepuss.

Barbier, George (1865–1945).
American character actor remembered in talkies as a blustery but essentially kindly old man.

Monsieur Beaucaire 24. The Big Pond 30. The Sap from Syracuse 30. The Smiling Lieutenant 31. No Man of her Own 32. One Hour with You 32. Million Dollar Legs 32. The Big Broadcast 32. Mama Loves Papa 33. Tillie and Gus 34. Ladies Should Listen 34. *The Merry Widow* 34. The Crusades 35. The Cat's Paw 35. The Milky Way 36. The Princess Comes Across 36. *On the Avenue* 37. Hotel Haywire 37. Tarzan's Revenge 38. Little Miss Broadway 38. Sweethearts 38. News is Made at Night 39. The Return of Frank James 40. *The Man Who Came to Dinner* 41. Weekend in Havana 41. The Magnificent Dope 42. Song of the Islands 42. Hello Frisco Hello 43. Weekend Pass 44. Her Lucky Night 45, many others.

Barbieri, Gato (1934–) (Leandro Barbieri).
Argentinian jazz saxophonist and composer.

Before the Revolution (It) 64. Last Tango in Paris (&a) (It) 73. The Pig's War 75. Firepower (GB) 79. Stranger's Kiss (US) 83. Diario di un Vizio (It.) 93, etc.

Barclay, Don (1892–1975).
Chubby American character actor, on screen from 1914.

Frisco Kid 35. Man Hunt 36. I Cover the War 37. Outlaw Express 38. The Oklahoma Kid 39. The Falcon's Brother 42. Frankenstein Meets the Wolf Man 43. Shine On Harvest Moon 44. My Darling Clementine 46. Mr Perrine and Mr Traill 48. The Long Gray Line 55. A Hundred and One Dalmatians (voice) 61. Mary Poppins 64. Half a Sixpence 68, etc.

Barcroft, Roy (1902–1969) (Howard H. Ravenscroft).
Beefy American character actor, usually seen as a western heavy. In hundreds of films and serials including:

Mata Hari 31. A Woman Commands 32. Night Key 37. Flaming Frontiers 38. Mexicali Rose 39. The Phantom Creeps 39. Bad Man from Red Butte 40. Flash Gordon Conquers the Universe 40. Wide Open Town 41. Riders of Death Valley 41. Romance on the Range 42. Hoppy Serves a Writ 43. Hidden Valley Outlaws 44. The Vampire's Ghost 45. My Pal Trigger 46. Rustlers of Devil's Canyon 47. Train to Alcatraz 48. Secret Service Investigator 48. Law of the Golden West 49. Radar Patrol vs Spy King 50. Night Riders of Montana 51. Ride the Man Down 52. El Paso Stampede 53. Rogue Cop 54. Oklahoma! 55. The Last Hunt 56. Band of Angels 57. Escort West 59. When the Clock Strikes 61. Six Black Horses 62. He Rides Tall 64. Billy the Kid vs Dracula 66. Rosemary's Baby 68. The Reivers 69. Monte Walsh 70.

Bardem, Juan-Antonio (1922–).
Spanish director and screenwriter, jailed in the 70s for political activities as a member of the Communist party; until the mid-80s he was unable to find work in Spain.

Welcome Mr Marshall (w) 52. *Death of a Cyclist* 54. Calle Mayor 56. Vengeance 57. Sonatas 59. Los Inocentes 62. Los Pianos Mecanicos 64. The Uninhibited 68. Variétés 71. Behind the Shutters 74. The Dog 77. Lorca, la Muerta de un Poeta 87, etc.

Bardette, Trevor (1902–1977).
American character actor, usually seen as western villain.

They Won't Forget 37. The Oklahoma Kid 39. Dark Command 40. The Moon Is Down 43. The Whistler 44. The Big Sleep 46. Song of India 49. The Texas Rangers 51. Lone Star 52. The Desert Song 53. Destry 54. The Man from Bitter Ridge 55. The Hard Man 57. The Mating Game 59. Papa's Delicate Condition 63. Mackenna's Gold 69, many others.

Bardot, Brigitte (1934–).
Pulchritudinous French pin-up girl who, given world publicity as a 'sex kitten', used her small but significant talents to make some routine movies very profitable. Her four husbands include director Roger Vadim (her first) and actor Jacques Charrier. In 1986 she set up a foundation to care for the welfare of animals.

Biography: 1994, *Bardot: Two Lives* by Jeffrey Robinson.

Act of Love 54. Doctor at Sea (GB) 55. *The Light Across the Street* 55. Helen of Troy 55. *And God Created Woman* 56. Heaven Fell That Night 57. Une Parisienne 57. *En Cas de Malheur* 57. Please Mr Balzac 57. The Devil is a Woman 58. Mam'zelle Pigalle 58. Babette Goes to War 59. Please Not Now 61. *The Truth* 61. *Vie Privée* 61. *Love on a Pillow* 62. *Contempt* 64. Dear Brigitte 65. *Viva Maria* 65.

Two Weeks in September 67. Shalako 68. *The Novices* 70. The Legend of Frenchy King 72. Don Juan 73, etc.

¶ For twenty years I was cornered and hounded like an animal. I didn't throw myself off my balcony only because I knew people would photograph me lying dead. – *B.B.*

I started out as a lousy actress and have remained one. – *B.B.*

France's most ogled export. – *Time 1956*

It was the first time on the screen that a woman was shown as really free on a sexual level, with none of the guilt attached to nudity or carnal pleasure. – *Roger Vadim*

The cinema means nothing to me. I cannot remember it. – *BB in 1994*

Bare, Richard (1909–).
American director who moved into TV.
Smart Girls Don't Talk 48. Flaxy Martin 48. The House Across the Street 49. This Side of the Law 51. Return of the Frontiersman 51. Prisoners of the Casbah 53. Shoot-Out at Medicine Bend 57. This Rebel Breed 60. I Sailed to Tahiti with an All-Girl Crew 67. Wicked, Wicked 73, etc.

Bari, Lynn (1915–1989) (Marjorie Fisher; aka Marjorie Bitzer).
Pert American 'second lead', often in 'other woman' roles. A chorus graduate, she was given plenty of work in the 30s and 40s but almost all of it was routine.
Dancing Lady 33. Stand Up and Cheer 34. Thanks a Million 35. Sing Baby Sing 36. Wee Willie Winkie 37. Josette 38. Return of the Cisco Kid 39. Hollywood Cavalcade 39. Earthbound 40. *Sun Valley Serenade* 41. Moon Over Her Shoulder 41. *The Magnificent Dope* 42. Orchestra Wives 42. Hello Frisco Hello 43. *The Bridge of San Luis Rey* 44. Tampico 44. Captain Eddie 45. Shock 45. *Margie* 46. The Man from Texas 48. On the Loose 51. Has Anybody Seen My Gal? 52. Francis Joins the WACS 54. Women of Pitcairn Island 56. Damn Citizen 58. Trauma 64. The Young Runaways 68, many others.
TV series: Boss Lady 52.

Baring, Norah (1907–) (Norah Baker).
British leading lady.
Underground 28. Cottage on Dartmoor 29. At the Villa Rose 30. Murder 30. The Lyons Mail 31. The House of Trent 33, etc.

Barker, Bradley (1883–1951).
American actor in silent films and animal impersonator who first supplied the roars for Leo, the MGM's trademark lion.
Erstwhile Susan 19. Adam and Eva 23. Into the Net (serial) 24. The Early Bird 25. The Brown Derby 26. The Potters 27. The Ape 28, etc.

Barker, Clive (1952–).
British horror author, screenwriter and director.
Rawhead Rex (oa) 87. Hellraiser (wd) 87. Transmutations (w) 88. Nightbreed (wd) 89. Sleepwalkers (a) 92. Candy Man (oa) 92. Hellraiser III: Hell on Earth (p) 92.

¶ True horror is seeing my stories turned into poor films. – *C.B.*

Barker, Eric (1912–1990).
British character comedian long popular on radio with his wife Pearl Hackney.
Autobiography: 1956, *Steady Barker*.
Carry On London 37. Concert Party 37. On Velvet 38. *Brothers in Law* 57. Happy Is the Bride

58. Blue Murder at St Trinian's 58. Carry On Sergeant 58. Left, Right and Centre 59. Carry On Constable 60. Heavens Above 63. The Bargee 65. The Great St Trinian's Train Robbery 66. Maroc 7 67. There's a Girl in My Soup 70, etc.

Barker, Jess (1914–).
Lightweight American leading man of minor 40s films. He was formerly married to Susan Hayward.
Cover Girl 44. Keep Your Powder Dry 44. This Love of Ours 45. Take One False Step 49. Shack Out on 101 56. The Night Walker 65, etc.

Barker, Lex (1919–1973).
Blond, virile-looking American actor who in 1948 was signed to play Tarzan. After five films the role passed to another actor and Barker's stock slumped, but he continued to make routine action adventures.
Battles of Chief Pontiac 52. The Price of Fear 56. Jungle Heat 57. The Girl in the Kremlin 57. Terror of the Red Mask 59. La Dolce Vita 60. Robin Hood and the Pirates 60. Winnetou I 63. Victim Five 63. Old Shatterhand 64. Winnetou II 64. Kali-Yug, Goddess of Vengeance 64. Winnetou III 65. Dynamite Morgan 67. Woman Times Seven 67. Winnetou and Shatterhand 68, etc.

Barker, Ma (1880–1935) (Kate Barker).
Notorious American outlaw of the 30s, who with her four sons terrorized the central states before being shot in Florida. She was played by Jean Harvey in *Guns Don't Argue* 55, Lurene Tuttle in *Ma Barker's Killer Brood* 60, Shelley Winters in *Bloody Mama* 70, and Claire Trevor in an episode of *The Untouchables*. So-called fictional variants were played by Blanche Yurka in *Queen of the Mob* 40, Irene Dailey in *The Grissom Gang* 71 and Angie Dickinson in *Big Bad Mama* 74.

Barker, Ronnie (1929–).
Portly but versatile British TV comedian, rarely seen in films; immensely popular in *The Two Ronnies* and *Porridge*. He retired in 1988.
Doctor in Distress 63. The Bargee 64. The Man Outside 67. *Futtock's End* 70. Robin and Marian 76. Porridge 79, etc.

Barker, Sir Will G. (1867–1951).
Pioneer British producer of the cinema's fairground days. A former salesman and cameraman, he founded the original Ealing studio.
Henry VIII 11. Jim the Fireman 12. Sixty Years a Queen 13. Greater Love Hath No Man 13. The Fighting Parson 14. Jane Shore 15, many others.

Barkin, Ellen (1954–).
American leading actress, usually in sexy roles. She married actor Gabriel Byrne in 1988.
Diner 82. Tender Mercies 82. Daniel 83. Eddie and the Cruisers 83. Enormous Changes at the Last Minute 83. The Adventures of Buckaroo Banzai Across the Eighth Dimension 84. Harry & Son 84. Terminal Choice 85. The Big Easy 86. Desert Bloom 86. Down by Law 86. Made in Heaven 87. Siesta 87. Clinton and Nadine (aka Blood Money) (TV) 88. Johnny Handsome 89. Sea of Love 89. Switch 91. Man Trouble 92. This Boy's Life 93. Bad Company 94. Wild Bill 95, etc.

Barkworth, Peter (1929–).
Smooth British comedy actor, mostly on TV; very popular in diffident roles.
A Touch of Larceny 61. Tiara Tahiti 62. No Love for Johnnie 63. Where Eagles Dare 69. Escape from the Dark 76. Champions 84, etc.
TV series: *Telford's Change* 78.

Barnard, Ivor (1887–1953).
British character actor of stage and screen, often of henpecked or nosey parker types, on stage from 1908.
Waltz Time 33. The Wandering Jew 34. Storm in a Teacup 37. Pygmalion 38. The Saint's Vacation 41. Hotel Reserve 44. The Wicked Lady 45. Great Expectations 46. Oliver Twist 48. *Beat the Devil* (his last and best role, as a vicious killer) 53, many others.

Barnes, Barry K. (1906–1965) (Nelson Barnes).
Stylish British stage actor, in occasional films. He was married to Diana Churchill.
The Return of the Scarlet Pimpernel 38. *This Man is News* 38. The Ware Case 38. Prison without Bars 39. The Midas Touch 40. Spies of the Air 40. The Girl in the News 41. Dancing with Crime 46. Bédelia 46, etc.

Barnes, Binnie (1905–) (Gitelle Barnes).
Self-confident British light actress who, after varied experience, made a few early British talkies, then went to Hollywood in 1934 and played mainly smart, wise-cracking ladies. Married Mike Frankovich.
Love Lies 31. Murder at Covent Garden 31. Heads We Go 33. *The Private Life of Henry VIII* (as Katherine Howard) 33. The Private Life of Don Juan 34. Diamond Jim 35. The Last of the Mohicans 35. The Magnificent Brute 36. *Three Smart Girls* 37. The Adventures of Marco Polo 38. Three Blind Mice 38. The Divorce of Lady X 38. *The Three Musketeers* 39. Till We Meet Again 40. Tight Shoes 41. Skylark 41. *Three Girls About Town* 41. The Man from Down Under 43. Barbary Coast Gent 44. *Up in Mabel's Room* 44. It's in the Bag 45. The Spanish Main 45. If Winter Comes 47. My Own True Love 48. Shadow of the Eagle 50. Fugitive Lady 51. Decameron Nights 53. *The Trouble with Angels* 66. Where Angels Go, Trouble Follows 68. Forty Carats 72, many others.

Barnes, George (c. 1880–1949).
American actor whose claim to fame was playing the outlaw who, in close-up, fired his revolver directly at the audience at the end (or, in some versions, the beginning) of *The Great Train Robbery* 03.

Barnes, George (1893–1953).
Distinguished American cinematographer.
The Haunted Bedroom 19. Silk Hosiery 21. Hairpins 22. Dusk to Dawn 24. *The Eagle* 25. *Son of the Sheik* 26. Janice Meredith 27. Sadie Thompson 28. Our Dancing Daughters 28. *Bulldog Drummond* 29. The Trespasser 29. *Condemned* 29. Raffles 30. Five and Ten 31. The Unholy Garden 31. Street Scene 31. The Wet Parade 32. Sherlock Holmes 32. Peg O' My Heart 33. *Footlight Parade* 33. Massacre 34. *Dames* 34. Flirtation Walk 34. In Caliente 35. The Singing Kid 36. Black Legion 36. *Marked Woman* 37. Hollywood Hotel 37. Gold Diggers in Paris 38. *Jesse James* 39. *Rebecca* (AA) 40. Devil's Island 40. Hudson's Bay 40. *Meet John Doe* 41. *Ladies in Retirement* 41. Rings on Her Fingers 42. Once Upon a Honeymoon 42. Mr Lucky 43. *Frenchman's Creek* 44. *Jane Eyre* 44. None But the Lonely Heart 44. *Spellbound* 45. The Spanish Main 45. The Bells of St Mary's 45. *From This Day Forward* 46. Sinbad the Sailor 47. Mourning Becomes Electra 47. The Emperor Waltz 48. The Boy with Green Hair 48. *Force of Evil* 49. Let's Dance 50. Mr Music 50. Riding High 50. Here Comes the Groom 51. Something to Live For 52. *The War of the Worlds* 53. Little Boy Lost 53, etc.

Barnes, Joanna (1934–).
American actress occasionally seen in cool supporting roles. Also a novelist.
Home Before Dark 58. Spartacus 60. The Parent Trap 61. Goodbye Charlie 64. The War Wagon 67. B.S. I Love You 70. I Wonder Who's Killing Her Now? 76, etc.

Barnes, Peter (1931–).
British dramatist and screenwriter, a former film critic and story editor.
Offbeat 60. Ring of Spies (aka Ring of Treason) 63. The Ruling Class 72. Enchanted April 91, etc.

Barnes, T. Roy (1880–1937).
English-born actor who went to America as a child. He spent 12 years in vaudeville in a comedy act with his wife, Bessie Crawford, and was on stage from 1914.
Scratch My Back 20. Adam and Eva 23. The Great White Way 24. Seven Chances 25. Body and Soul 27. Chicago 27. Dangerous Curves 29. Kansas City Princess 34. It's a Gift 34. The Virginia Judge 35, etc.

Barnett, Vince (1902–1977).
American character actor, usually of minor gangsters or downtrodden little men, from vaudeville. He was previously a professional insulter, hired to be be rude to people at parties.
Her Man 30. *Scarface* 32. I Cover the Waterfront 33. Springfield Rifle 35. Dancing Feet 36. A Star Is Born 37. Overland Trail 39. East Side Kids 40. A Dangerous Game 41. Baby Face Morgan 42. Kid Dynamite 43. The Killers 46. Big Town Scandal 48. Mule Train 50. Carson City 52. The Quiet Gun 57. The Rookie 59. Dr Goldfoot and the Bikini Machine 65. The Big Mouth 67. Crazy Mama 75, many others.

Barney Bear.
Ponderous, affable, dim-witted grizzly who was a star of MGM cartoons from 1939–54. His voice was supplied by Bill Bletcher, Rudolph Ising and Paul Frees.
The Bear that Couldn't Sleep 39. The Fishing Bear 40. The Flying Bear 41. Barney Bear's Victory Garden 42. Bah Wilderness 43. Bear Raid Warden 44. Busybody Bear 52. Heir Bear 53. Bird-Brain Bird Dog 54, etc.

Barnum, Phineas T. (1810–1891).
American showman who is alleged to have said 'There's one born every minute' of the people who flocked to see his freak shows. He became a multi-millionaire and co-founded the famous Barnum and Bailey Circus. He was played in *A Lady's Morals* 30 and *The Mighty Barnum* 35 by Wallace Beery; in *Rocket to the Moon* 67 by Burl Ives.

Baron, Auguste (1853–1938).
French inventor who patented a method of talking pictures (1896–99) and two multiscreen processes, Cinématorama in 1896 and Multirama in 1912, but failed to find backing for his ideas.

Baron Munchausen.
There has been a longish line of movies about the tall story-teller. Méliès made a version in 1911; Emile Cole in 1913; Hans Albers starred in a German version in 1943. Karl Zeman made a semi-animated fantasy in 1962, and John Neville starred in Terry Gilliam's expensive version in 1989. The real Baron (1720–97) was a German army officer, but the collection of stories written by Rudolph Raspe, first published in English in 1785, included much material from other sources.

Baroncelli, Jacques De (1881–1951).
French director, a former journalist, who made more than 80 films in a career that ran from the silent era until the late 40s.
La Maison de l'Espoir 15. Le Père Goriot 21. La Femme du Pantin 29. Michel Strogoff 37. La Duchesse de Langeais 42. Rocambole 48, etc.

Barr, Douglas (1931–).
English juvenile actor who also starred in the BBC's first radio comedy series aimed at teenagers, *It's Fine to Be Young* 48.
Hue and Cry 46. Fortune Lane 47. The Last Load 48. Dance Hall 50. Madeleine 50. One Good Turn 51, etc.

Barr, Jean-Marc (1960–).
French leading actor in international films. Bilingual, he has a French mother and an American father and trained as an actor in London.
The Frog Prince 85. King David 85. Hope and Glory 87. The Big Blue (Le Grand Bleu) 88. Le Brasier 90. Europa 91. The Plague (La Peste) 92. Iron Horsemen 94. Les Faussaires 94, etc.

Barr, Patrick (1908–1985).
British stage, screen and TV actor who played solid, dependable types from the 30s.
Norah O'Neale 34. The Return of the Scarlet Pimpernel 38. The Frightened Lady 41. The Blue Lagoon 48. Robin Hood 52. Singlehanded 53. Crest of the Wave 54. Saint Joan 57. Next to No Time 60. The Longest Day 62. Billy Liar 63. Ring of Spies 64. House of Whipcord 74, many others.

Barr, Roseanne:
see *Arnold, Roseanne*.

Barrat, Robert (1891–1970).
American character actor in films from silent days, usually as heavy western villain. In 1934 alone he appeared in 19 films.
Mayor of Hell 33. Wild Boys of the Road 33. Dark Hazard 34. Wonder Bar 34. Captain Blood 35. Dr Socrates 35. Trail of the Lonesome Pine 36. The Charge of the Light Brigade 36. The Life of Emile Zola 37. Souls at Sea 37. The Buccaneer 38. Union Pacific 39. Return of the Cisco Kid 39. Go West 40. Captain Caution 40. Riders of the Purple Sage 41. American Empire 42. They Came to Blow Up America 43. The Adventures of Mark Twain 44. Road to Utopia 45. They Were Expendable 45. The Time of Their Lives 46. Road to Rio 47. Joan of Arc 48. Canadian Pacific 49. The Baron of Arizona 50. Flight to Mars 51. Double Crossbones 51. Son of Ali Baba 52. Tall Man Riding 55, many others.

Barrault, Jean-Louis (1910–1994).
Celebrated French stage actor, in a few rewarding film roles. He was married to actress Madeleine Renaud.
Mademoiselle Docteur 36. *Drôle de Drame* 36. *La Symphonie Fantastique* 42. *Les Enfants du Paradis* 44. D'Homme à Hommes 48. La Ronde 50. Le Testament du Docteur Cordelier 59. The Longest Day 62. La Nuit de Varennes 83, etc.

Barrault, Marie-Christian (1944–).
French actress, best known for her work with Eric Rohmer. She is the niece of Jean-Louis Barrault.
My Night at Maud's (Ma Nuit Chez Maud) 68. Lancelot of the Lake (Lancelot du Lac) 74. Cousin Cousine (AAN) 75. Perceval 78. The Medusa Touch 78. Stardust Memories 80. Table for Five 83. A Love in Germany (Eine Liebe in Deutschland) 83. Swann in Love (Un Amour de Swann) 83. The Abyss (L'Oeuvre au Noir) 88. Gallant Ladies (Dames Galantes) 91. Necessary

Love (L'Amore Necessario) 91. La Prossima Volta Il Fuoco 93. Mad Love (Amour Fou) 94, etc.

Barreto, Bruno (1955–).
Brazilian director and screenwriter.
Tati, a Garota 73. Dona Flor and Her Two Husbands (Dona Flor e Seus Dois Maridos) 76. Amor Bandido 78. Lucia 81. Gabriela 83. Felizes para Sempre 84. The Story of Fausta 92, etc.

Barreto, Lima (1905–1982).
Brazilian film director and screenwriter, a former actor and journalist. Born in Casa Branca, he became a documentary film-maker in the 40s and 50s before making his feature debut with the first Brazilian film to gain an international reputation.
The Bandit (O Cangaçeiro) 53. A Primeira Missa 61, etc.

Barrett, Edith (1912–1977).
American character actress, usually in fey roles.
Ladies in Retirement 41. Jane Eyre 43. I Walked with a Zombie 43. The Song of Bernadette 43. The Swan 56, etc.

Barrett, James Lee (1929–1989).
American screenwriter.
The D.I. 58. The Greatest Story Ever Told (co-w) 65. The Truth About Spring 65. Shenandoah 65. Bandolero 68. The Green Berets 68. The Cheyenne Social Club (& p) 70. Smokey and the Bandit (co-w) 77, etc.

Barrett, Jane (1923–1969).
British leading lady.
The Captive Heart 45. Eureka Stockade 48. Time Gentlemen Please 52. The Sword and the Rose 53, etc.

Barrett, Judith (1914–). (Lucille Kelly).
American leading lady of a few 30s films.
Flying Hostess 36. Let Them Live 37. Armored Car 37. Illegal Traffic 38. Television Spy 39. The Great Victor Herbert 39. Road to Singapore 40. Women without Names 40, etc.

Barrett, Ray (1926–).
Australian leading actor in British TV and films.
The Sundowners 60. Touch of Death 62. Jigsaw 63. The Reptile 65. Revenge 71. Waterfront 83. Where the Green Ants Dream 84. Rebel 86, etc.
TV series: *The Troubleshooters* 66–71.

Barrett, Rona (1934–) (Rona Burnstein).
American gossip columnist who, centred in Hollywood for the television networks, has more or less inherited the mantle of Hedda and Louella.
Autobiography: 1974, *Miss Rona*.

¶ I'm not friends with the stars, because if I were I couldn't tell the truth about them. – *R.B.*
I'm really a pussycat – with an iron tail. – *R.B.*

Barrie, Amanda (1939–) (Amanda Broadbent).
British leading lady with TV experience.
Carry On Cleo 64. I Gotta Horse 65, etc.

Barrie, Barbara (1931–).
Pert American character actress.
One Potato Two Potato 64. Summer of My German Soldier (TV) 78. The Bell Jar 79. Breaking Away (AAN) 79. Private Benjamin 80. Real Men 87. End of the Line 88, etc.
TV series: Diana 73–74. Barney Miller 75–76. Breaking Away 80–81. Tucker's Witch 82–83. Reggie 83. Double Trouble 84–85.

Barrie, Sir J. M. (1860–1937).
British playwright whose work usually had a recognizable fey quality, which even survived the film versions.
The Admirable Crichton 17. Peter Pan 24 and 53. The Little Minister 34. What Every Woman Knows 34. Quality Street 37. Darling How Could You? ('Alice Sit by the Fire') 51. Forever Female 'Rosalind') 53, etc.

Barrie, John (1917–1980).
Heavily built British character actor with long repertory experience. Played *Sergeant Cork* on TV, and in the cinema is best remembered as the police inspector in *Victim* 63.

Barrie, Mona (1909–1964) (Mona Smith).
Australian 'second lead' actress, in Hollywood from early 30s.
Carolina 34. The House of Connelly 34. A Message to Garcia 36. I Met Him in Paris 37. When Ladies Meet 41. Cairo 42. Storm over Lisbon 44. I Cover Big Town 47. Strange Fascination 52. Plunder of the Sun 53, many others.

Barrie, Wendy (1912–1978) (Wendy Jenkins).
Bright British leading lady who went to Hollywood in 1934 but found only mediocre roles. Had her own TV show in 1948, and was later active in local radio.
It's a Boy (GB) 32. *The Private Life of Henry VIII* (GB) 32. For Love or Money 34. A Feather in Her Hat 35. Love on a Bet 36. Dead End 37. I Am the Law 38. The Hound of the Baskervilles 39. Five Came Back 39. The Saint Takes Over 40. Who Killed Aunt Maggie? 40. The Gay Falcon 41. Eyes of the Underworld 42. Women in War 42. Forever and a Day 43. It Could Happen to You (guest appearance) 53. Summer Holiday 63. The Moving Finger 63, etc.

Barrier, Edgar (1907–1964).
American character actor with stage experience.
Escape 40. Arabian Nights 42. Phantom of the Opera 43. Flesh and Fantasy 44. *A Game of Death* 45. Macbeth 48. To the Ends of the Earth 48. Cyrano de Bergerac 50. Princess of the Nile 54. On the Double 61. Irma la Douce 63, many others.

barring clause.
The part of an exhibitor's contract with a renter preventing him from showing new films before other specified cinemas in the area. The showing of a film in London may thus prevent its exhibition elsewhere within a radius of fifty miles or more.

Barron, Keith (1934–).
British leading actor of the angry young man type; mostly on TV.
Baby Love 69. Melody 70. The Fire Chasers 70. The Man Who Had Power Over Women 70. She'll Follow You Anywhere 71. Nothing but the Night 73. The Land that Time Forgot 75. Voyage of the Damned 76. The Elephant Man 80, etc.
TV series: All Night Long 94.

Barron, Steve (1956–).
British director who began with pop videos. He is the son of Zelda Barron.
Electric Dreams 84. Bulldance 89. Teenage Mutant Ninja Turtles 90. Coneheads 93.

Barron, Zelda.
British director.
Secret Places 84. Shag 88.

Barry, Don (1912–1980) (Donald Barry d'Acosta).
Rugged American actor, in Hollywood from 1939

after stage experience and immediately popular as hero of second-feature westerns. Sometimes known as Donald 'Red' Barry. Committed suicide.
Night Waitress 36. The Crowd Roars 38. Calling All Marines 39. Remember Pearl Harbor 42. The Chicago Kid 45. The Dalton Gang 49. Jesse James' Women (& d) 53. I'll Cry Tomorrow 55. Walk on the Wild Side 62. Fort Utah 66. Bandolero 68. Shalako 68. Dirty Dingus Magee 70. Junior Bonner 72. Hustle 75. Orca 77. The Swarm 78, etc.
TV series: Surfside Six 60. Mr Novak 63.

Barry, Gene (1921–) (Eugene Klass).
Poised and debonair American leading man who also does a song and dance act. Films routine, but TV has kept him busy.
■ The Atomic City 52. The Girls of Pleasure Island 52. *The War of the Worlds* 53. Those Redheads from Seattle 53. Alaska Seas 54. *Red Garters* 54. *Naked Alibi* 54. Soldier of Fortune 55. The Purple Mask 55. The Houston Story 56. Back From Eternity 56. The 27th Day 57. China Gate 57. Ain't No Time for Glory (TV) 57. Forty Guns 57. Hong Kong Confidential 58. *Thunder Road* 58. Maroc 7 67. Prescription Murder (TV) 67. Istanbul Express (TV) 68. Subterfuge 69. Do You Take This Stranger? (TV) 70. The Devil and Miss Sarah (TV) 71. The Second Coming of Suzanne 73. Guyana, Crime of the Century 79. The Adventures of Nellie Bly (TV) 81. The Girl, The Gold Watch and Dynamite (TV) 81.
TV series: Our Miss Brooks 55. *Bat Masterson* 58–60. *Burke's Law* 63–65. *The Name of the Game* 68–70. The Adventurer 72. Aspen 77. Burke's Law 94.

Barry, Iris (1895–1969).
Founder-member of the London Film Society (1925); director of New York Museum of Modern Art Film Library from 1935; president of the International Federation of Film Archives 1946; author of books on the film.

¶ Film is a machine for seeing more than meets the eye. – I.B.

Barry, Joan (1903–1989).
British leading lady of the early 30s, chiefly known for dubbing Anny Ondra's voice in *Blackmail*.
The Card 22. The Rising Generation 28. The Outsider 31. Rich and Strange 31. Ebb Tide 32. Sally Bishop 32. Rome Express 32. Mrs Dane's Defence 34, etc.

Barry, John (1933–) (J. B. Prendergast).
British composer. He was formerly married to actress Jane Birkin.
Beat Girl 59. Never Let Go 60. Dr No (md) 62. The Amorous Prawn 62. The L-shaped Room 62. *From Russia with Love* 63. Zulu 63. The Man in the Middle 64. Goldfinger 64. The Ipcress File 65. The Knack 65. Thunderball 65. King Rat 65. The Chase 66. *Born Free* (AA) 66. The Wrong Box 66. The Quiller Memorandum 66. Petulia 68. Boom 68. Deadfall 68. The Lion in Winter (AA) 68. Midnight Cowboy 69. Murphy's War 71. They Might Be Giants 71. Mary, Queen of Scots (AA) 71. Diamonds Are Forever 72. The Tamarind Seed 73. The Man with the Golden Gun 74. King Kong 76. The Deep 77. The White Buffalo 77. The Betsy 78. Moonraker 79. The Black Hole 79. Raise the Titanic 80. Somewhere in Time 80. Superman 2 80. Body Heat 81. Hammett 82. Francis 82. Octopussy 83. Out of Africa (AA) 85. Jagged Edge 86. Peggy Sue got Married 86. The Living Daylights 87. Hearts of Fire 87. Masquerade 88. Dances with Wolves 90. Chaplin (AAN) 92. My Life 93. Indecent Proposal 93. Ruby Cairo 93. The Specialist 94, etc.

Barry, John (1935–1979).
Anglo-American production designer.
A Clockwork Orange 73. Phase IV 73. Lucky Lady 75. Star Wars 77. Superman 78. Superman 2 80. The Empire Strikes Back 80, etc.

Barry, Julian.
American screenwriter.
Secret Agent Fireball 66. Rhinoceros 74. Lenny (AAN) 74. The River 84, etc.

Barry, Philip (1896–1949).
American playwright, several of whose sophisticated comedies have been filmed.
Holiday 30 and 38. The Animal Kingdom 32 (remade as One More Tomorrow 46). The Philadelphia Story 40. Without Love 45.

Barry, Wesley (1907–).
American child actor, on screen from the age of six, who later became an assistant director of 'B' movies and retired in the 40s.
Rebecca of Sunnybrook Farm 13. The Country Kid 23. Battling Bunyon 24. Sunny Skies 30. Daddy Long Legs 31. Night Life of the Gods 35. The Plough and the Stars 36, etc.

Barrymore, Diana (1921–1960).
American actress, daughter of John Barrymore. She made a few mediocre films in the early 40s but was not a successful leading lady and later succumbed to alcoholism. Her autobiography *Too Much Too Soon* was filmed in 1958 with Dorothy Malone (and Errol Flynn as John Barrymore).
■ Eagle Squadron 42. *Between Us Girls* 42. Nightmare 42. Frontier Badmen 43. Fired Wife 43. *Ladies Courageous* 44.

Barrymore, Drew (1975–).
American child actress of the 80s, now attempting more adult roles. She is the daughter of John Barrymore Jnr.
Autobiography: 1989, *Little Girl Lost*, with Todd Gold.
E.T. 82. Firestarter 84. Irreconcilable Differences 84. Cat's Eye 84. A Conspiracy of Love (TV) 87. Far from Home 89. See You in the Morning 89. Guncrazy 92. Doppelganger 92. Motorama 92. Poison Ivy 92. Beyond Control: The Amy Fisher Story (TV) 93. Wayne's World 2 93. Bad Girls 94. Inside the Goldmine 94. Mad Love 95, etc.
TV series: 2000 Malibu Road 92.

Barrymore, Ethel (1879–1959) (Edith Blythe).
Distinguished American actress of regal presence; sister of Lionel and John, daughter of Maurice Barrymore, Made a few silents, then remained on Broadway until 1944 when she made her home in Hollywood.
Autobiography: 1956, *Memories*.
■ The Nightingale 14. The Final Judgement 15. The Awakening of Helen Ritchie 16. Kiss of Hate 16. The White Raven 17. The Lifted Veil 17. The Eternal Mother 17. The American Widow 17. Life's Whirlpool 17. The Call of Her People 17. Our Miss McChesney 18. The Divorcee 19. Rasputin and the Empress (only film appearance with her brothers) 32. *None but the Lonely Heart* (AA) 44. The Spiral Staircase (AAN) 46. *The Farmer's Daughter* 47. Moss Rose 47. The Paradine Case (AAN) 48. Night Song 48. Moonrise 49. Portrait of Jennie 49. The Great Sinner 49. That Midnight Kiss 49. Pinky (AAN) 49. The Red Danube 49. The Secret of Convict Lake 51. *Kind Lady* 51. It's a Big Country 52. *Deadline* 52. Just for You 52. The Story of Three Loves 53. Main Street to Broadway 53. *Young at Heart* 54. Johnny Trouble 57.
✪ For spending her later years portraying

Hollywood's idea of the indomitable old lady with a heart of gold. *The Farmer's Daughter*.

Barrymore, John (1882–1942) (John Blythe). Celebrated American stage and screen actor, brother of Ethel and Lionel Barrymore. A famous matinée idol with a 'great profile', he became a famous romantic movie star of the 20s but later squandered his talents in inferior comedies caricaturing his own alcoholism and debauchery. A great personality and a splendid if often misguided talent.

Autobiography: 1926, *Confessions of an Actor*.

Biographies: 1944, *Good Night Sweet Prince* by Gene Fowler. 1977, *Damned in Paradise* by John Kobler.

Barrymore was lampooned on film by Fredric March in *The Royal Family of Broadway*, and portrayed by Errol Flynn in *Too Much Too Soon* and Jack Cassidy in *W. C. Fields and Me*.

■ Are You a Mason? 13. An American Citizen 13. The Man from Mexico 14. The Dictator 15. The Incorrigible Dukane 16. The Lost Bridegroom 16. The Red Widow 16. *Raffles* 17. On the Quiet 18. Here Comes the Bride 18. Test of Honour 19. *Dr Jekyll and Mr Hyde* 20. The Lotus Eater 21. *Sherlock Holmes* 22. *Beau Brummell* 24. *The Sea Beast* 26. *Don Juan* 26. When a Man Loves 27. *The Beloved Rogue* 27. *Tempest* 28. Eternal Love 29. *Show of Shows* (first talkie: recites Richard III) 29. General Crack 29. The Man from Blankley's 30. *Moby Dick* 30. *Svengali* 31. The Mad Genius 31. *Arsène Lupin* 32. *Grand Hotel* 32. State's Attorney 32. *A Bill of Divorcement* 32. *Rasputin and the Empress* 32. *Topaze* 33. *Reunion In Vienna* 33. *Dinner at Eight* 33. Night Flight 33. *Counsellor at Law* 33. Long Lost Father 34. *Twentieth Century* 34. *Romeo and Juliet* (as Mercutio) 36. *Maytime* 37. Bulldog Drummond Comes Back (as the inspector) 37. Night Club Scandal 37. Bulldog Drummond's Revenge 37. Bulldog Drummond's Peril 37. *True Confession* 38. Romance in the Dark 38. *Marie Antoinette* 38. Spawn of the North 38. Hold that Co-Ed 38. *The Great Man Votes* 39. *Midnight* 39. The Great Profile 40. Invisible Woman 41. World Premiere 41. Playmates 42.

~A colour test he made for *Hamlet* in 1933 allegedly remains in New York's Museum of Modern Art.

✪ For a few performances of fine swashbuckling, for a few more of ripe ham, and as an awful warning of what can happen to a star who becomes too sure that the world is his oyster. *Twentieth Century*.

¶ I like to be introduced as America's foremost actor. It saves the necessity of further effort. – *J.B.*

My head is buried in the sands of tomorrow, while my tail feathers are singed by the hot sun of today. – *J.B.*

I'm fifty years old and I want to look like Jackie Cooper's grandson. – *J.B.*

If you stay in front of the movie camera long enough, it will show you not only what you had for breakfast but who your ancestors were. – *J.B.*

I've done everything three times. The fourth time around becomes monotonous. – *J.B.*

The good die young – because they see no point in living if you have to be good. – *J.B.*

Student to lecturer: Tell me, Mr Barrymore, in your view did Ophelia ever sleep with Hamlet?' J.B. to student, after much thought: 'Only in the Chicago company . . .'

Katharine Hepburn after finishing *A Bill of Divorcement*: 'Thank goodness I don't have to act with you any more!' J.B., sweetly: 'I didn't know you ever had, darling . . .'

J.B., flinging a fish at a coughing audience: 'Busy

yourselves with that, you damned walruses, while the rest of us get on with the play!'

A producer's wife at a Hollywood party, finding J.B. relieving himself in a corner of the ladies' room: 'Mr Barrymore, this is for ladies!' J.B., turning around without buttoning up: 'So, madam, is this!'

'My memory is full of beauty: Hamlet's soliloquies, Queen Mab's speech, the Song of Solomon. Do you expect me to clutter up all that with this horse shit?' (When asked why he required idiot boards in the studio, having perfect recall elsewhere.)

He moved through a movie scene like an exquisite paper knife. – *Heywood Broun*

Die? I should say not, old fellow. No Barrymore would allow such a conventional thing to happen to him. – *J.B. during his last illness*

This is a man who went through all the genres, starting with vaudeville – he was a song and dance man – classical theatre, the great American Hamlet, the silent movies, straight through into talking pictures. Nobody else did all that. Nobody. – *Nicol Williamson*

What I really have in common with Jack Barrymore is a lack of vocation. He himself played the part of an actor because that was the role he'd been given. – *Orson Welles*

Famous line (*Twentieth Century*): 'I close the iron door on you!'

Barrymore, John, Jnr (1932–) (John Drew Barrymore).
American actor, son of John Barrymore and Dolores Costello. Usually plays weaklings. He is the father of actress Drew Barrymore.

The Sundowners 50. The Big Night 51. Thunderbirds 52. While the City Sleeps 56. Night of the Quarter Moon 59. The Boatmen 59. The Cossacks 60. Nights of Rasputin 61. War of the Zombies 63, etc.

Barrymore, Lionel (1878–1954) (Lionel Blythe). Celebrated American character actor, brother of Ethel and John Barrymore. His career was almost entirely devoted to films, including some direction; from the early 30s he was a familiar and well-loved member of the MGM galaxy, playing sentimental crotchety grandpas and churlish millionaires. From 1938, arthritis and two falls forced him to act from a wheelchair.

Autobiography: 1951, *We Barrymores*.

■ Friends 09. Fighting Blood 11. Judith of Bethulia 11. The New York Hat 12. The Seats of the Mighty 14. Under the Gaslight 14. Wildfire 15. A Modern Magdalen 15. The Curious Conduct 15. The Flaming Sword 15. Dora 15. A Yellow Streak 15. The Exploits of Elaine 15. Dorian's Divorce 16. The Quitter 16. The Upheaval 16. The Brand of Cowardice 16. His Father's Son 17. The End of the Tour 17. The Millionaire's Double 17. Life's Whirlpool 17. The Valley of Night 19. The Devil's Garden 20. The Copperhead 20. The Master Mind 20. Jim the Penman 21. The Great Adventure 21. Face in the Fog 22. Boomerang 22. Enemies of Women 23. Unseeing Eyes 23. The Eternal City 24. America 24. Meddling Women 24. The Iron Man 25. Children of the Whirlwind 25. The Girl Who Wouldn't Work 25. Fifty Fifty 25. I am the Man 25. The Wrongdoers 25. The Barrier 26. *The Bells* 26. The Splendid Road 26. The Temptress 26. Brooding Eyes 26. The Lucky Lady 26. Paris at Midnight 26. Women Love Diamonds 27. The Show 27. Body and Soul 27. The 13th Hour 27. Drums of Love 27. Love 27. *Sadie Thompson* 28. West of Zanzibar 28. Decameron Nights 28. The Lion and the Mouse 28. Roadhouse 28. The River

Woman 28. Alias Jimmy Valentine (first talkie) 29. Mysterious Island 29. Hollywood Revue 29. Confession (d only) 29. Madame X (AAN d only) 29. His Glorious Night (d only) 29. The Unholy Night (d only) 29. The Rogue Song (d only) 30. Free and Easy 30. Ten Cents a Dance (d only) 31. *A Free Soul* (AA) 31. The Yellow Ticket 31. Guilty Hands 31. Mata Hari 31. *The Man I Killed* 32. *Arsène Lupin* 32. *Grand Hotel* 32. Washington Masquerade 32. *Rasputin and the Empress* (as Rasputin) 32. Sweepings 33. Looking Forward 33. The Stranger's Return 33. Dinner at Eight 33. One Man's Journey 33. Night Flight 33. Christopher Bean 33. Should Ladies Behave? 33. This Side of Heaven 34. Carolina 34. The Girl from Missouri 34. Treasure Island 34. David Copperfield 34. The Little Colonel 35. Mark of the Vampire 35. Public Hero Number One 35. The Return of Peter Grimm 35. *Ah Wilderness* 35. The Voice of Bugle Ann 36. The Road to Glory 36. *The Devil Doll* 36. The Gorgeous Hussy 36. Camille 37. *A Family Affair* (first of Hardy Family series) 37. Captains Courageous 37. Saratoga 37. Navy Blue and Gold 37. A Yank at Oxford 38. Test Pilot 38. *You Can't Take It With You* 38. *Young Dr Kildare* (start of series as Dr Gillespie) 38. Let Freedom Ring 39. Calling Dr Kildare 39. *On Borrowed Time* 39. The Secret of Dr Kildare 39. Dr Kildare's Strange Case 40. Dr Kildare Goes Home 40. Dr Kildare's Crisis 40. The Bad Man 41. The Penalty 41. The People vs Dr Kildare 41. Dr Kildare's Wedding Day 41. Lady Be Good 41. Dr Kildare's Victory 41. *Calling Dr Gillespie* 42. Dr Gillespie's New Assistant 42. Tennessee Johnson 43. Dr Gillespie's Criminal Case 43. Thousands Cheer 43. A Guy Named Joe 43. Three Men in White 44. Since You Went Away 44. Between Two Women 45. The Valley of Decision 45. *Three Wise Fools* 46. *It's a Wonderful Life* 46. The Secret Heart 46. *Duel in the Sun* 46. Dark Delusion 47. *Key Largo* 48. Down to the Sea in Ships 49. Malaya 50. Right Cross 50. Bannerline 51. Lone Star 52. Main Street to Broadway 53.

~Lionel once wrote a novel: *Mr Cantonwine, a Moral Tale*.

✪ For having a go at everything in sight, even female impersonation; and for becoming Hollywood's omnipresent crotchety grandpa. *You Can't Take It with You*.

Barsacq, Leon (1906–1969).
Russian art director and set designer, long in France.

La Marseillaise 38. Lumière d'Eté 43. *Les Enfants du Paradis* 44. L'Idiot 46. Le Silence est d'Or 47. *La Beauté du Diable* 50. Les Belles de Nuit 52. Les Diaboliques 55. Les Grandes Maneuvres 55. The Ambassador's Daughter (US) 56. Porte des Lilas 57. The Longest Day 62. The Visit 64. Phèdre 69, many others.

Barsi, Judith (1977–1988).
American child actress. Killed by her father.

Eye of the Tiger 86. Jaws: The Revenge 87. Slamdance 87. The Land before Time (voice) 88. All Dogs Go to Heaven (voice) 89, etc.

Barstow, Stan (1928–).
British north country novelist whose *A Kind of Loving* was successfully filmed. Some of his other material has been adapted for television.

Bart, Lionel (1930–) (Lionel Begleiter).
London-born lyricist and composer who can't read music but has been phenomenally successful with West End musicals such as *Fings Ain't What They Used To Be*, *Oliver!*, *Blitz* and *Maggie May*. Has written songs and scores for films since 1957; *Oliver!* was filmed in 1968.

...rtel, Paul (1938–).
...merican actor and director.
...Private Parts (d) 72. Death Race 2000 (d) 75. Eat
...y Dust (a) 76. Cannonball (adw) 76. Grand Theft
...to (a) 77. Eating Raoul (ad) 81. Lust in the Dust
... Not for Publication 84. Longshot 85. Scenes
...m the Class Struggle in Beverly Hills 89.
...remlins 2: The New Batch (a) 89. The Pope Must
...e (US: The Pope Must Diet) (a) 91. Desire and
...ll at Sunset Motel (a) 92. Shelf Life (a) 93.
...cting on Impulse (a) 93, etc.

...arthelmess, Richard (1895–1963).
...esentable American leading man who went
...raight from college into silent films. Griffith
...ed him memorably, and in 1921 he formed his
...wn company and was popular until the advent
... talkies, which made his innocent image seem
...d-fashioned and condemned him to insipid
...aracter roles.
...Gloria's Romance 16. Camille 17. The Eternal
...n 17. The Moral Code 17. Rich Man Poor Man
...s. The Hope Chest 19. Boots 19. The Girl Who
...ayed Home 19. Three Men and a Girl 19. Peppy
...lly 19. Broken Blossoms 19. I'll Get Him Yet 19.
...carlet Days 19. The Idol Dancer 20. The Love
...ower 20. Way Down East 20. Experience 21.
...l'able David 21. The Seventh Day 22. Sonny 22.
...e Bond Boy 22. The Bright Shawl 23. The
...ighting Blade 23. Twenty One 24. The Enchanted
...ottage 24. Classmates 24. New Toys 25. Soul Fire
...5. Shore Leave 25. The Beautiful City 25. Just
...uppose 26. Ranson's Folly 26. The Amateur
...entleman 26. The White Black Sheep 26. The
...atent Leather Kid (AAN) 27. The Drop Kick 27.
...e Noose (AAN) 28. Kentucky Courage 28.
...heels of Chance 28. Out of the Ruins 28. Scarlet
...eas 28. Weary River 29. Drag 29. Young
...owheres 29. Show of Shows 29. Son of the Gods
... The Dawn Patrol 30. The Lash 31. Way Down
...ast 31. The Finger Points 31. The Last Flight 31.
...lias the Doctor 32. The Cabin in the Cotton 32.
...entral Airport 33. Heroes for Sale 33. Massacre
...3. A Modern Hero 34. Midnight Alibi 34. Spy of
...apoleon 35. Four Hours to Kill 35. Only Angels
...ave Wings 39. The Man Who Talked Too Much 40.
...e Mayor of 44th Street 42. The Spoilers 42.

He has the most beautiful face of any man who
ever went before a camera. – Lillian Gish

...artholomew, Freddie (1924–1992) (Frederick
...ewellyn).
...npeccably well-bred British child actor whose
...ccess in Hollywood films of the 30s delighted
...derly aunts the world over. His somewhat toffee-
...osed image fell from favour during the war and
...s an adult he moved out of show business into
...dvertising.
...Fascination (GB) 30. Lily Christine (GB) 32.
...avid Copperfield 35. Anna Karenina 35.
...rofessional Soldier 35. Little Lord Fauntleroy 36.
...he Devil is a Sissy 36. Lloyds of London 36.
...aptains Courageous 37. Kidnapped 38. Lord Jeff 38.
...esten Darling 38. Spirit of Culver 38. Two Bright
...oys 39. The Swiss Family Robinson 40. Tom Brown's
...chooldays 40. Naval Academy 41. Cadets on Parade
...2. A Yank at Eton 42. The Town Went Wild 44.
...epia Cinderella 51. St Benny the Dip 51.

...artlam, Dorothy (1908–).
...nglish leading actress and novelist, a former
...ancer who began in films as an extra in 1925. As
... result of winning a beauty contest, she obtained
...eading roles with British Lion in the late 20s,
...etiring in the mid-30s, soon after her first novel,
...ontrary-Wise, was published.
...The Flying Squad 29. The Ringer 31. Birds of a

Feather 31. We Dine at Seven 31. The Fires of
Fate 32. Call Me Mame 33. Up for the Derby 33.
On Thin Ice 33, etc.

Bartlett, Hall (1922–).
American independent producer, director and
screenwriter whose films seldom seem quite good
enough to be independent about.
■ Navajo 52. Unchained (& wd) 55. Drango (& wd)
56. Zero Hour (& d) 57. All the Young Men (&
d) 60. The Caretakers (& d) 64. A Global Affair 64.
Sol Madrid 68. Changes (d) 69. The Wild Pack (d)
72. Jonathan Livingston Seagull (& d, co-w) 73.
The Children of Sanchez (d) 78. Leaving Home (d)
86.

Bartlett, Richard.
American director.
The Lonesome Trail 55. I've Lived Before 56.
Rock Pretty Baby 56. Joe Dakota 57. Slim Carter
57. Money, Women and Guns 58, etc.

Bartlett, Sy (1900–1978) (Sacha Baraniev).
American screenwriter, and more recently
producer.
The Big Brain (w) 33. Boulder Dam (w) 35.
Coconut Grove 38. Road to Zanzibar (co-w) 41.
Bullet Scars 42. The Princess and the Pirate 44. 13
Rue Madeleine 46. Down to the Sea in Ships 49.
Twelve O'Clock High (w) 49. That Lady (wp) 55. The
Big Country (w) 57. A Gathering of Eagles (wp) 63.
Che (p) 69, etc.

Bartok, Eva (1926–) (Eva Sjöke).
Agreeable Hungarian leading lady in international
films. She was formerly married to actor Curt
Jurgens.
Autobiography: 1959, Worth Living For.
A Tale of Five Cities 51. Venetian Bird 52. The
Crimson Pirate 52. Front Page Story 54. Ten
Thousand Bedrooms 57. Operation Amsterdam 59.
SOS Pacific 60. Beyond the Curtain 60. Blood and
Black Lace 64, etc.

Barton, Buzz (1914–1980).
American character actor, a child star in early
westerns, from rodeo.
The Boy Rider 28. Apache Kid's Escape 30. The
Lone Defender (serial) 32. Mystery Trooper 32.
Powersmoke Range 35. The Tonto Kid 35. In the
Heat of the Night 67. In Cold Blood 67, etc.

Barton, Charles (1902–1981).
Routine American director, long at Universal.
■ Wagon Wheels 34. Car 99 35. Rocky Mountain
Mystery 35. The Last Outpost (co-d) 35.
Timothy's Quest 36. And Sudden Death 36.
Nevada 36. Rose Bowl 36. Murder with Pictures 36.
The Crime Nobody Saw 37. Forlorn River 37.
Thunder Train 37. Born to the West 38. Behind
Prison Gates 39. Five Little Peppers and How They
Grew 39. My Son is Guilty 40. Five Little Peppers
at Home 40. Island of Doomed Men 40. Babies for
Sale 40. Out West with the Peppers 40. Five Little
Peppers in Trouble 40. Nobody's Children 40. The
Phantom Submarine 40. The Big Boss 41. The
Richest Man in Town 41. Harmon of Michigan 41.
Two Latins from Manhattan 41. Sing for your
Supper 41. Honolulu Lu 41. Shut My Big Mouth
42. Tramp Tramp Tramp 42. Hello Anapolis 42.
Parachute Nurse 42. Sweetheart of the Fleet 42. A
Man's World 42. Lucky Legs 42. The Spirit of
Stanford 42. Laugh Your Blues Away 42. Reveille
with Beverly 43. Let's Have Fun 43. She Has What
It Takes 43. What's Buzzin Cousin 43. Is Everybody
Happy 43. What a Woman 43. Beautiful but Broke
44. Hey Rookie 44. Jam Session 44. Louisiana
Hayride 44. Men in her Diary 45. White Tie and

Tails 45. The Time of Their Lives 46. Smooth as Silk
46. The Wistful Widow of Wagon Gap 47. Buck
Privates Come Home 47. Mexican Hayride 48.
Abbott and Costello Meet Frankenstein 48. The Noose
Hangs High 48. Free for All 49. Africa Screams 49.
Abbott and Costello Meet the Killer 49. The
Milkman 50. Double Crossbones 50. Ma and Pa
Kettle at the Fair 52. Dance with Me Henry 56.
The Shaggy Dog 59. Toby Tyler 60. Swinging Along
62.

Barton, Dee.
American composer.
Play Misty for Me 71. High Plains Drifter 73.
Thunderbolt and Lightfoot 74, etc.

Barton, James (1890–1962).
Grizzled, good-humoured American character
actor, a veteran of burlesque and Broadway.
Captain Hurricane 35. Shepherd of the Hills 41.
The Time of Your Life 48. Yellow Sky 49. The
Daughter of Rosie O'Grady 50. Wabash Avenue
50. Here Comes the Groom 51. Golden Girl 51.
The Naked Hills 57. Quantez 57. The Misfits 61, etc.

Bartosch, Berthold (1893–1968).
Austro-Hungarian animator, best known for his
symbolic L'Idée 34.

Barty, Billy (1925–).
American dwarf actor who has been seen in many
films from Gold Diggers of 1933 to Under the Rainbow
81.
Rumpelstiltskin 87. Willow 88. Life Stinks 91.
TV series: The Spike Jones Show 54. Circus Boy
56–58. The Spike Jones Show 57. Ace Crawford,
Private Eye 82.

Barwood, Hal (1940–).
American director and screenwriter, most recently
involved in designing video games for George
Lucas's software company LucasArts, including
Indiana Jones and the Fate of Atlantis.
The Sugarland Express (co-w) 74. The Bingo
Long Traveling All-Stars & Motor Kings (co-w) 76.
MacArthur (co-w) 77. Corvette Summer (co-w)
78. Dragonslayer (co-w) 81. Warning Sign (co-
w, d) 85, etc.

Baryshnikov, Mikhail (1948–).
Latvian ballet dancer who made his American film
debut in The Turning Point (AAN) 77 and
consolidated this in White Nights 85, Dancers 87.
The Cabinet of Dr Ramirez 91. Company Business
91.

I'm not the first straight dancer or the last.
Anyway, it has nothing to do with art. – M.B.

Barzman, Ben (1911–1989).
Canadian writer with Hollywood experience; in
Britain from early 50s.
True to Life 42. The Boy with Green Hair 48. He
Who Must Die 56. Time without Pity 57. Blind Date
59. The Ceremony 63. The Heroes of Telemark 65.
The Blue Max 66, etc.

baseball
has been the subject for occasional films since
1899, when Casey at the Bat was first made. (It
turned up again in 1927 with Wallace Beery.)
Biopics of famous baseball personalities include The
Stratton Story (James Stewart), The Babe Ruth Story
(William Bendix), The Pride of the Yankees (Gary
Cooper as Lou Gehrig), The Winning Team (Ronald
Reagan as G. C. Alexander), The Pride of St Louis
(Dan Dailey as Dizzy Dean), Fear Strikes Out
(Anthony Perkins as Jim Piersall), The Jackie

Robinson Story and *Babe*, with John Goodman as Babe Ruth. Serious dramatic films about the sport include *The Bush Leaguer, Slide Kelly Slide, The Big Leaguer, The Natural* and *Field of Dreams*. Baseball's biggest scandal, involving the Chicago White Sox of 1919, was treated sympathetically in *Eight Men Out*. There has been a fantasy, *Angels in the Outfield*, and a who-done-it, *Death on the Diamond*. Musicals are led by *Take Me Out to the Ball Game* and *Damn Yankees*. Comedies include *Elmer the Great, Alibi Ike, Fast Company, Rhubarb, It Happens Every Spring, Speedy* (Harold Lloyd), *College* (Buster Keaton), *Ladies' Day, The Bad News Bears* and its sequels, *Major League* and *A League of Their Own*, about a female team. Baseball stadiums have provided memorable scenes in films on other subjects: *The FBI Story, Beau James, The Satan Bug, Experiment in Terror*, etc.

Basehart, Richard (1914–1984).
Thoughtful American leading actor who somehow never achieved his expected stardom; equally adept at honesty, villainy and mental disturbance. Many TV appearances. He was married to Valentina Cortese.
■ Cry Wolf 47. Repeat Performance 47. *He Walked by Night* 48. Roseanna McCoy 49. *The Black Book* 49. Tension 49. Outside the Wall 50. *Fourteen Hours* 51. The House on Telegraph Hill 51. Fixed Bayonets 51. Decision Before Dawn 51. The Stranger's Hand 53. Titanic 53. La Strada 54. The Good Die Young 54. La Reprise de Justice 54. La Vena d'Oro 55. Cartouche 55. Canyon Crossroads 55. Il Bidone (The Swindlers) 55. The Extra Day 56. *Moby Dick* 56. The Intimate Stranger 56. *Time Limit* 57. So Soon to Die (TV) 57. Arrivederci Dimas 57. *The Brothers Karamazov* 58. L'Ambiteuse 58. Jons und Erdme 59. Five Branded Women 60. Portrait in Black 60. For the Love of Mike 60. Passport to China 61. The Savage Guns 61. Tierra Brutal 62. *Hitler* (title role) 63. Kings of the Sun 63. The Satan Bug 65. The Sole Survivor (TV) 69. The Death of Me Yet (TV) 71. City Beneath the Sea (One Hour to Doomsday) (TV) 71. Assignment Munich (TV) 72. The Bounty Man (TV) 72. Escape of the Birdmen (TV) 72. Chato's Land 72. Rage 72. Maneater (TV) 73. And Millions Will Die 73. How the West Was Won (TV) 75. Mansion of the Doomed 76. The Island of Dr Moreau 77. WEB (TV) 78. The Bastard (TV) 78. Being There 79. The Great Georgia Bank Hoax 79. Marilyn, the Untold Story (TV) 80. Knight Rider (TV) 82.
TV series: *Voyage to the Bottom of the Sea* 64–67.

Basevi, James
Anglo-American art director and special effects wizard, at Fox from the mid-20s.
The Big Parade 25. The Hurricane 38. Wuthering Heights (AAN) 39. The Long Voyage Home 40. The Westerner (AAN) 40. Tobacco Road 41. The Ox-Bow Incident 43. The Gang's All Here (AAN) 43. The Song of Bernadette (AA) 43. Lifeboat 44. Jane Eyre 44. Spellbound 45. The Keys of the Kingdom (AAN) 45. Duel in the Sun 46. My Darling Clementine 46. Boomerang! 47. Fort Apache 48. Mighty Joe Young 49. She Wore a Yellow Ribbon 49. My Man and I 52. East of Eden 54. The Searchers 56, many others.

Basinger, Kim (1953–).
Sultry American leading actress, often in oversexed roles. She is married to Alec Baldwin.
■ Hard Country 81. Killjoy (TV) 81. Mother Lode 82. The Man Who Loved Women 83. Never Say Never Again 83. The Natural 84. Fool for Love 85. Nine and a Half Weeks 85. No Mercy 86. Blind Date 87. Nadine 87. My Stepmother Is an Alien 88. Batman 89. The Marrying Man (aka Too Hot

to Handle) 91. Final Analysis 92. The Real McCoy 93. Wayne's World 2 93. The Getaway 94. Prêt-à-Porter 94.
TV series: Dog and Cat 79. From Here to Eternity 80.

¶ You have to be a little unreal to be in this business. – *K.B.*
I don't have any friends in this business at all. That Mafia guy John Gotti's best friend is the one who stabbed him in the back. Hollywood is a lot like that. It's like the Mafia. – *K.B.*

Baskett, James (1904–1948).
American character actor best known for his performance as Uncle Remus in *Song of the South* 48.

Basquette, Lina (1907–1994).
American leading lady of the 20s, former child star and dancer. Her lively private life included seven husbands.
Autobiography: 1990, *Lina: DeMille's Godless Girl*.
Juvenile Dancer 16. Prince for a Day 17. Penrod 22. Ranger of the North 27. Wheel of Chance 28. Show Folks 28. *The Godless Girl* 29. Dude Wrangler 30. Hard Hombre 31. Morals for Women 31. Phantom Express 32. Ebb Tide 37. Four Men and a Prayer 38, etc.

Bass, Alfie (1920–1987).
Pint-sized British character comedian, adept at cockney/Jewish roles.
Johnny Frenchman 45. Holiday Camp 47. It Always Rains on Sunday 47. The Hasty Heart 49. *The Lavender Hill Mob* 51. *The Bespoke Overcoat* 55. A Kid for Two Farthings 55. A Tale of Two Cities 57. I Only Arsked 59. The Millionairess 60. Alfie 66. The Fearless Vampire Killers 67. The Magnificent Seven Deadly Sins 72. Moonraker 79, etc.
TV series: The Army Game 57–62. Bootsie and Snudge 60–63. Are You Being Served? 79.

Bass, Ronald.
American screenwriter.
Code Name: Emerald 85. Black Widow 87. Gardens of Stone 87. Rain Man (co-w, AA) 88. Joy Luck Club (co-w) 93. When a Man Loves a Woman (co-w) 94, etc.

Bass, Sam (1851–1878).
American western adventurer, played by Howard Duff in *Calamity Jane and Sam Bass*.

Bass, Saul (1920–).
American graphic designer and director, best known for creating title sequences for some 50 films, including many by Otto Preminger. He also designed the detailed storyboards and directed the shower sequence in Hitchcock's *Psycho*, directed racing scenes for John Frankenheimer's *Grand Prix* and the final battle in *Spartacus*.
AS DIRECTOR: Why Man Creates (short) (AA) 68. Phase IV 74, etc.
AS TITLE DESIGNER: Carmen Jones 54. The Shrike 55. The Man with the Golden Arm 55. The Seven Year Itch 55. Around the World in 80 Days (closing animated credit sequence) 56. Vertigo 58. The Big Country 58. Bonjour Tristesse 58. North by Northwest 59. Anatomy of a Murder 59. Psycho 60. Exodus 60. Ocean's Eleven 60. A Walk on the Wild Side 62. It's a Mad Mad Mad Mad Mad World 63. Nine Hours to Rama 63. Bunny Lake Is Missing 65. The Human Factor 79. Broadcast News 87. Big 88. The War of the Roses 89. Cape Fear 91. The Age of Innocence 93, etc.

Basserman, Albert (1867–1952).
Distinguished German stage actor who came to Hollywood as refugee in 1939 and played sympathetic roles.
■ Der Andere 13. Voruntersuchung 31. The Last Days Before the War 32. Kadetten 33. Ein Gewisser Herr Gran 33. Alraune 33. Letzte Liebe 38. Le Famille Lefrancois 39. Dr Ehrlich's Magic Bullet 40. *Foreign Correspondent* (AAN) 40. A Dispatch from Reuters 40. Moon Over Burma 40. Knute Rockne 40. Escape 40. *The Shanghai Gesture* 41. The Great Awakening 41. New Wine 41. A Woman's Face 41. The Moon and Sixpence 42. Invisible Agent 42. Once Upon a Honeymoon 42. Fly by Night 42. Desperate Journey 42. Good Luck Mr Yates 43. Passport to Heaven 43. Reunion in France 43. Madame Curie 44. Since You Went Away 44. *Rhapsody in Blue* 45. Strange Holiday 46. The Searching Wind 46. The Private Affairs of Bel Ami 47. Escape Me Never 47. *The Red Shoes* (GB) 48.
✪ For bringing to Hollywood a suggestion of the unique strength of the European theatre. *The Shanghai Gesture*.

Bassett, Angela (c. 1962–).
American leading actress, from the stage. She played Tina Turner in the biopic *What's Love Got to Do with It?*
Boyz N The Hood 91. Malcolm X 93. *What's Love Got to Do with It?* (AAN) 93. Strange Days 95, etc.

Bassey, Shirley (1937–).
Torrid British-born cabaret singer whose film appearances have always been as a performer.

Bassler, Robert (1903–).
American producer.
My Gal Sal 42. *The Black Swan* 43. The Lodger 44. Hangover Square 45. Thunder in the Valley 47. *The Snake Pit* 48. Thieves' Highway 49. Halls of Montezuma 50. Kangaroo 52. Beneath the Twelve Mile Reef 53. Suddenly 54, etc.

Bassman, George (1914–).
American composer, working for MGM from the mid-30s and 40s.
A Day at the Races 37. Babes in Arms 39. Go West 40. Lady Be Good 41. The Big Store 41. The Canterville Ghost 44. The Clock 45. The Postman Always Rings Twice 46. Little Mister Jim 47. The Joe Louis Story 53. Ride the High Country 62. Mail Order Bride 63, etc.

Bastedo, Alexandra (1946–).
Leading lady of Canadian, Italian and English ancestry.
Thirteen Frightened Girls 63. Inside Daisy Clover 66. Casino Royale 67. The Ghoul 75. The Blood-Spattered Bride 80, etc.
TV series: *The Champions* 67.

Batchelor, Joy (1914–1991).
British animator, wife of John Halas and co-founder of Halas and Batchelor Cartoon Films.

Bate, Anthony (1929–).
Smooth English character actor, mostly on television. He trained at the Central School of Speech and Drama and was on stage from 1953.
Stopover Forever 64. Act of Murder 64. Ghost Story (aka Madhouse Mansion) 74. Bismarck 76. Philby, Burgess and Maclean (TV) 80. Give My Regards to Broad Street 83. Eminent Domain 90, etc.

Bateman, Jason (1969–).
American actor, from television as a juvenile. He is the brother of Justine Bateman.

Can You Feel Me Dancing? 85. Teen Wolf Too
. Breaking the Rules 92. A Taste for Killing 92,
.
TV series: Little House on the Prairie 81–82.
ver Spoons 82–84. It's Your Move 84–85.
alerie 86–87. The Hogan Family 88–91.

ateman, Justine (1966–).
merican actress, from television as a juvenile. She
the sister of Jason Bateman.
Can You Feel Me Dancing? 85. Satisfaction 88.
e Fatal Image (TV) 90. The Closer 91. Primary
otive 92. Deadbolt 92. The Night We Never Met
, etc.
TV series: Family Ties 82–89.

ates, Alan (1934–).
ading British actor of stage and screen: tends to
ay thoughtful toughs with soft centres.
The Entertainer 59. A Kind of Loving 62. Whistle
wn the Wind 62. The Caretaker 63. The Running
an 63. Nothing But the Best 64. Zorba the Greek 65.
eorgy Girl 66. King of Hearts 67. Far from the
adding Crowd 67. The Fixer (AAN) 68. Women in
ve 69: Three Sisters 70. The Go-Between 70. A
ay in the Death of Joe Egg 71. Impossible Object
. Butley 73. In Celebration 74. Royal Flash 75.
e Collection (TV) 76. An Unmarried Woman 77.
e Shout 78. The Rose 79. Very Like a Whale (TV)
. Nijinsky 80. Quartet 81. The Return of the
oldier 82. Britannia Hospital 82. An Englishman
broad (TV) 83. A Voyage Around My Father (TV)
. Dr Fischer of Geneva (TV) 83. Duet For One 86.
Prayer for the Dying 87. We Think the World
You 88. Force Majeure 89. 102 Boulevard
aussman (TV) 90. Docteur M. 90. Hamlet 90.
ister Frost 90. Secret Friends 91. Silent Tongue
.

ates, Barbara (1925–1969).
merican leading lady, former model and ballet
ncer. Committed suicide.
This Love of Ours 45. The Fabulous Joe 48. June
ride 48. The Inspector General 49. Cheaper by the
ozen 49. All About Eve 50. Belles on Her Toes
2. Rhapsody 54. House of Secrets (GB) 56. Town
Trial (GB) 57. Apache Territory 58, etc.
TV series: It's a Great Life 54–55

ates, Florence (1888–1954) (Florence Rabe).
merican character actress, adept at friendly or
onstrous matrons. A former lawyer, she was
rsuaded by Alfred Hitchcock to play the role for
hich she is best remembered, and remained much
demand for a decade.
The Man in Blue 37. Rebecca 40. Calling All
usbands 40. Son of Monte Cristo 40. Hudson's Bay
. Kitty Foyle 40. Road Show 41. Love Crazy 41.
e Chocolate Soldier 41. Strange Alibi 41. The
evil and Miss Jones 41. The Tuttles of Tahiti 42.
e Moon and Sixpence 42. My Heart Belongs to
addy 42. Mexican Spitfire at Sea 42. We Were
ancing 42. Slightly Dangerous 43. His Butler's
ster 43. They Got Me Covered 43. Mister Big 43.
eaven Can Wait 43. Mr Lucky 43. Since You
ent Away 44. The Mask of Dimitrios 44. Kismet
. Belle of the Yukon 44. The Racket Man 44.
aratoga Trunk 45. Tahiti Nights 45. Tonight and
ery Night 45. Sanantonio 45. Out of This World
5. Claudia and David 46. Cluny Brown 46. The
iary of a Chambermaid 46. Whistle Stop 46. The
me the Place and the Girl 46. The High Window
7. Love and Learn 47. Desire Me 47. The Secret Life
Walter Mitty 47. Texas Brooklyn and Heaven 48.
inter Meeting 48. The Inside Story 48. River Lady
8. My Dear Secretary 48. Portrait of Jennie 48. I
emember Mama 48. A Letter to Three Wives 48.
e Judge Steps Out 49. The Girl from Jones Beach

49. On the Town 49. Belle of Old Mexico 50.
County Fair 50. The Second Woman 51. Lullaby of
Broadway 51. The Tall Target 51. Havana Rose 51.
Father Takes the Air 51. The Whistle at Eaton Falls
51. The San Francisco Story 52. Les Miserables
52. Paris Model 53. Main Street to Broadway 53.
~In 1914, when she was 26, F.B. was the first
woman lawyer in Texas.

Bates, Granville (1882–1940).
American general purpose supporting actor of the
30s: storekeepers, doctors and grandpas.
Jealousy 29. The Smiling Lieutenant 31. Woman
Wanted 35. 13 Hours by Air 36. They Won't Forget
37. Nancy Steele is Missing 37. Wells Fargo 37. Go
Chase Yourself 38. Gold is Where You Find It 38.
The Great Man Votes 39. Pride of the Blue Grass
39. Of Mice and Men 39. Jesse James 39. My
Favorite Wife 40. The Mortal Storm 40. Brother
Orchid 40, many others.

Bates, H. E. (1905–1974).
British novelist who dabbled in the cinema. The
Purple Plain was filmed; The Darling Buds of May was
filmed as The Mating Season and formed the basis
of a successful TV series from 1990. Fair Stood the
Wind for France was done on television; but he co-
scripted Summer Madness.

Bates, Kathy (1948–).
American character actress, notable as the crazed
fan in Misery.
Straight Time 78. Come Back to the Five and
Dime, Jimmy Dean, Jimmy Dean 82. Summer Heat
87. Arthur 2: On the Rocks 88. High Stakes (aka
Melanie Rose) 89. Signs of Life 89. Men Don't
Leave 90. Dick Tracy 90. White Palace 90. Misery
(AA) 90. Fried Green Tomatoes at the Whistle
Stop Café 91. The Road to Mecca 91. At Play in
the Fields of the Lord 91. Shadows and Fog 92.
Prelude to a Kiss 92. A Home of Our Own 93.
North 94. Curse of the Starving Class 94, etc.

Bates, Michael (1920–1978).
British character actor who specialized in stupid
policemen and other caricatures.
Carrington VC 55. I'm All Right Jack 59.
Bedazzled 67. Here We Go Round the Mulberry Bush
67. Salt and Pepper 68. Don't Raise the Bridge
Lower the River 68. Hammerhead 68. Patton 70.
The Rise and Rise of Michael Rimmer 70. A
Clockwork Orange 71. No Sex Please, We're British
73, etc.
TV series: It Ain't Half Hot Mum 73–77.

Bates, Ralph (1940–1991).
Incisive British character actor who played
Caligula on TV and took the natural step to
Hammer horrors.
The Horror of Frankenstein 70. Lust for a
Vampire 70. Dr Jekyll and Sister Hyde 71. Fear in
the Night 73. Persecution 74. I Don't Want to be
Born 75. Letters to an Unknown Lover 84, etc.
TV series: Poldark, Penmarric, Dear John.

Bath, Hubert (1883–1945).
British composer.
Blackmail 29. The 39 Steps 35. Rhodes of Africa
36. A Place of One's Own 44. Love Story 45, etc.

bathtubs,
though especially associated with Cecil B. De Mille,
have been a favourite Hollywood gimmick from
early silent days. But De Mille undressed his
heroines with the most showmanship, whether
it was Gloria Swanson in Male and Female,
Claudette Colbert in her asses' milk in The Sign of
the Cross (emulated years later by Frances Day in

Fiddlers Three) or Paulette Goddard in Unconquered.
Other ladies who have bathed spectacularly
include Joan Crawford in The Women, Deanna
Durbin in Can't Help Singing, Jean Harlow in Red
Dust, Phyllis Haver in The Politic Flapper, Joan
Collins in The Wayward Bus, Elke Sommer in The
Wicked Dreams of Paula Schultz, Gina Lollobrigida in
Belles de Nuit, Carroll Baker in Harlow and Sophia
Loren (who had Gregory Peck hiding in her
shower) in Arabesque. Not that the men have had
it all their own way: Roger Livesey in Colonel Blimp
and Gary Cooper in Love in the Afternoon suffered
in the steamroom; and all the actors who have
played coal miners, including Trevor Howard in
Sons and Lovers and Donald Crisp in How Green Was
My Valley, know how it feels to be scrubbed all
over. Marat in Marat/Sade spent the whole film in
a tub. The most bathed male star is probably Cary
Grant, who had a tub in The Howards of Virginia,
a shower in Mr Blandings Builds His Dream House,
another shower, fully clothed this time, in
Charade, and a Japanese geisha bath in Walk, Don't
Run. And Hitchcock, with Psycho, still takes the prize
for the most memorable shower scene.

Batman.
An American comic strip character created in 1939
by Bob Kane, Batman was a personable
millionaire who, with his young helper Robin,
donned fancy dress to fight the evil forces in
society, and zoomed about in a 'batmobile' with
many a pow and a splat. His chief enemies were
the Riddler, the Penguin, the Joker and
Catwoman. He came to the big screen in two
serials, and was played in 1943 by Lewis Wilson
and in 1949 by Robert Lowery. A TV series in
1965–67 starred Adam West with Burt Ward, and
the villains were played by Frank Gorshin,
Burgess Meredith, Cesar Romero and Lee
Meriwether. A feature version emerged in 1966. In
1989 a new version transformed him into a semi-
psychotic character, with Michael Keaton in the
title role. A sequel, Batman Returns, followed in
1992, and Batman Forever, with Val Kilmer replacing
Keaton, in 1995.

Bators, Stiv (1950–1990) (Steve Bators).
American singer with the 70s punk group Dead
Boys and occasional actor. Died after being hit by
a car.
Polyester 81. Tapeheads 89.

Battle, John Tucker.
American screenwriter.
Captain Eddie 45. So Dear to My Heart 48. The
Frogmen 51. A Man Alone 55. Lisbon 56, etc.

Bauchens, Anne (1882–1967).
American editor, almost always for De Mille.
The Squaw Man 18. Don't Change Your
Husband 19. The Affairs of Anatol 21. The Ten
Commandments 23. King of Kings 27. Dynamite
29. The Sign of the Cross 32. Cleopatra 34. The
Crusade 35. The Buccaneer 38. North West
Mounted Police (AA) 40. Reap the Wild Wind 42.
Love Letters 45. Unconquered 47. Samson and
Delilah 49. The Greatest Show on Earth 52. The
Ten Commandments 56, many others.

Bauer, Belinda (1956–).
Australian actress, a former model, in American
films, usually in off-beat roles.
Winter Kills 79. Success 79. Fugitive from the
Empire (TV) 81. Sins of Dorian Gray (TV) 82.
Timerider 83. Flashdance 83. Samson and Delilah
(TV) 84. The Rosary Murders 87. The Game of
Love 87. UHF 89. Act of Piracy 90. Robocop 2 90.
Necronomicon 93, etc.

Bauer, Steven (1956–) (Steven Echevarria).
Cuban character actor in Hollywood.

Scarface 83. Thief of Hearts 84. Running Scared 86. Sword of Gideon 86. The Beast 88. Gleaming the Cube 89. A Row of Crows 90. Sweet Poison 91. False Arrest (TV) 91. Raising Caine 92, etc.

Baum, L. Frank (1856–1919).
American author of *The Wizard of Oz*, 1900, and other adventures set in the mythical kingdom. He brought out the book himself after every publisher turned it down, adapted it as a Broadway musical and financed early silent film versions, setting up the Oz Film Manufacturing Company in 1914 and briefly opening his own studio in Hollywood.

The Wizard of Oz 08. The Road to Oz 09. His Majesty the Tin Scarecrow of Oz 14. The Patchwork Girl of Oz 14. The Magic Cloak of Oz 14. The Wizard of Oz 25. The Wizard of Oz 39. The Wiz 78, etc.

Baum, Vicki (1896–1960).
Austrian novelist whose chief gift to Hollywood was the much-filmed and well imitated *Grand Hotel*, which she herself revamped as *Hotel Berlin*.
Autobiography: 1964, *It Was All Quite Different*.

Baur, Harry (1880–1943).
Celebrated French actor of stage and screen.

Shylock 10. La Voyante 23. David Golder 31. Poil de Carotte 32. Golgotha 34. Moscow Nights 35. Crime and Punishment 35. Taras Bulba 35. Un Carnet de Bal 37. The Rebel Son 38. Volpone 39. L'Assassinat du Père Noel 41. Symphonie eines Lebens 42, etc.

Bava, Lamberto (1944–).
Italian director of horror and action movies, the son of Mario Bava.

Macabre (Macabro) 80. Blastfighter 84. Monster Shark (Shark Rosso nell'Oceano) 84. Demons (Demoni) 85. Demons 2 (Demoni 2) 86. Le Foto di Gioia 87. The Returners 92, etc.

Bava, Mario (1914–1980).
Italian director, former photographer, of period muscleman epics and pseudo-British horror stories, revered by the *cognoscenti* for his tongue-in-cheek attitude towards some of them.

Black Sunday (wd, ph) 60. Hercules in the Centre of the Earth (wd, ph) 61. Erik the Conqueror (wd) 63. The Evil Eye (wd, ph) 63. *Black Sabbath* (wd) 63. *Blood and Black Lace* (wd, ph) 64. Planet of Blood (d) 65. Dr Goldfoot and the Girl Bombs (d) 66. Curse of the Dead (wd) 67. *Diabolik* (wd) 68. The Antecedent (d) 71, etc.

Bavier, Francis (1905–1989).
Motherly American actress, mainly on TV and best known for her Emmy award-winning performance as Aunt Bee on *The Andy Griffith Show* 60–68.

The Day the Earth Stood Still 51. The Lady Says No 51. Horizons West 52. Benji 74, etc.

TV series: It's a Great Life 54–56. The Eve Arden Show 57–58. Mayberry R.F.D. 68–70.

Bax, Sir Arnold (1883–1953).
British composer.
■ Malta GC 43. Oliver Twist 48. Journey into History 48.

Baxley, Barbara (1927–1990).
American character actress.

The Badlanders 58. The Savage Eye 60. All Fall Down 62. Countdown 67. No Way to Treat a Lady 68. The Impostor (TV) 74. Nashville 75. Norma Rae 79, etc.

Baxley, Craig R.
American director of action films.

Action Jackson 88. I Come in Peace (aka Dark Angel) 91. Stone Cold 91, etc.

Baxter, Alan (1908–1976).
Cold-eyed American second lead of the 40s; graduated to colonels and tough executives.

Mary Burns Fugitive 35. The Last Gangster 37. Gangs of New York 38. Each Dawn I Die 39. Santa Fe Trail 40. Saboteur 42. Submarine Base 43. Winged Victory 44. The Set Up 49. The Devil's Weed 49. End of the Line (in Britain) 56. The True Story of Jesse James 57. The Mountain Road 60. Judgment at Nuremburg 61. This Property is Condemned 66. Willard 71, etc.

Baxter, Anne (1923–1985).
American leading lady who usually played shy and innocent but proved equally at home as a schemer. Trained for the stage but was starring in Hollywood at seventeen. After 1960 found the going tough.

Autobiography: 1977, *Intermission*.
■ Twenty Mule Team 40. The Great Profile 40. Charley's Aunt 41. Swamp Water 41. The Pied Piper 42. *The Magnificent Ambersons* 42. Crash Dive 43. *Five Graves to Cairo* 43. North Star 43. The Sullivans 44. The Eve of St Mark 44. Sunday Dinner for a Soldier 44. *Guest in the House* 45. A Royal Scandal 45. Smoky 46. Angel on My Shoulder 46. *The Razor's Edge* (AA) 46. Blaze of Noon 47. Homecoming 48. The Walls of Jericho 48. The Luck of the Irish 48. Yellow Sky 48. You're My Everything 49. A Ticket to Tomahawk 49. *All About Eve* (AAN) 50. Follow the Sun 51. The Outcasts of Poker Flat 52. My Wife's Best Friend 52. Full House 52. I Confess 53. The Blue Gardenia 53. Carnival Story 54. Bedevilled 55. One Desire 55. The Spoilers 55. The Come On 56. The Ten Commandments 56. Three Violent People 57. *Chase a Crooked Shadow* 57. Summer of the Seventeenth Doll 60. Mix Me a Person 61. Cimarron 61. A Walk on the Wild Side 62. The Family Jewels 65. Frontier Woman 66. The Busy Body 67. Companions in Nightmare (TV) 67. Stranger on the Run (TV) 68. The Challengers (TV) 68. The Tall Women 68. Marcus Welby MD (TV pilot) 69. Ritual of Evil 69. The Catcher (TV) 71. Fools Parade 71. The Late Liz 71. If Tomorrow Comes (TV) 71. Lisa Bright and Dark (TV) 72. The Moneychangers (TV) 76. Jane Austen in Manhattan 80. East of Eden (TV) 81.

TV series: Marcus Welby, MD 69–70. Hotel 83–85.

Baxter, Beryl (1926–) (Beryl Ivory).
British leading lady who was groomed for stardom but starred in only one film, and that notoriously poor Idol of Paris 46.

Subsequently: The Man with the Twisted Lip 51. Counterspy 53.

Baxter, Jane (1909–) (Feodora Forde).
Gentle-mannered British actress of stage and screen.

The Constant Nymph 32. The Clairvoyant 34. We Live Again (US) 35. The Ware Case 39. Ships with Wings 41. The Flemish Farm 43. Death of an Angel 51, etc.

Baxter, John (1896–1975).
Influential British producer-director of vigorous rough-and-ready dramas and comedies of the 30s and 40s which pointed the way to 50s realism and had an amiable style of their own.

Doss House 32. Song of the Plough 32. Lest We Forget 34. Music Hall 35. Say It with Flowers 36. Men of Yesterday 37. Crooks Tour 39. *Love on the Dole* 40. *The Common Touch* 41. *Let the People Sing* 42. *When We are Married* 43. The Shipbuilders 45. The Second Mate 50. Judgment Deferred 51. Ramsbottom Rides Again 56, many others including Old Mother Riley and Flanagan & Allen comedies.

Baxter, Les (1922–).
American composer.

Hot Blood 55. The Black Sheep 56. Macabre 58. Goliath and the Barbarians 59. *House of Usher* 60. The Pit and the Pendulum 61. Panic in Year Zero 62. Tales of Terror 62. *The Raven* 63. The Comedy of Terrors 63. Muscle Beach Party 64. Dr G and the Bikini Machine 65. Wild in the Streets 68. Flare-Up 69. The Dunwich Horror 70. Cry of the Banshee 70. Frogs 72. I Escaped from Devil's Island 73. Savage Sisters 74. Born Again 78. The Beast Within 82, etc.

Baxter, Meredith:
see *Birney, Meredith Baxter*.

Baxter, Stanley (1926–).
Rubber-faced Scottish comedian and impressionist of stage, screen and TV.
■ Geordie 55. *Very Important Person* 61. Crooks Anonymous 62. *The Fast Lady* 63. And Father Came Too 63. Joey Boy 65.

¶ I'm the best known anonymity in the business. – S.B.

Baxter, Warner (1891–1951).
Distinguished-looking American leading man with stage experience. Popular hero of silent melodrama; survived transition to talkies.
■ Her Own Money 14. All Woman 18. Lombardi Ltd. 19. Cheated Hearts 21. First Love 21. The Love Charm 21. Sheltered Daughters 22. If I were Queen 22. The Girl in His Room 22. A Girl's Desire 22. The Ninety and Nine 22. Her Own Money (remake) 22. Blow Your Own Horn 23. In Search of a Thrill 23. St Elmo 23. Alimony 23. Christine of the Hungry Heart 24. The Female 24. The Garden of Weeds 24. His Forgotten Wife 24. Those Who Dance 24. The Golden Bed 25. Air Mail 25. The Awful Truth 25. The Best People 25. Rugged Water 25. A Son of His Father 25. Welcome Home 25. Mannequin 26. Miss Brewster's Millions 26. Mismates 26. Aloma of the South Seas 26. *The Great Gatsby* 26. The Runaway 26. The Telephone Girl 27. The Coward 27. Drums of the Desert 27. Singed 27. Danger Street 28. Three Sinners 28. *Ramona* 28. Craig's Wife 28. The Tragedy of Youth 28. A Woman's Way 28. Linda 29. Far Call 29. Thru Different Eyes 29. Behind that Curtain 29. Romance of the Rio Grande 29. *In Old Arizona* (AA) 29. West of Zanzibar 29. Happy Days 29. The Arizona Kid 30. Renegades 30. Such Men are Dangerous 30. The Cisco Kid 31. The Squaw Man 31. Doctors' Wives 31. Their Mad Moment 31. *Daddy Long Legs* 31. Surrender 31. Six Hours to Live 32. Man About Town 32. Amateur Daddy 32. Paddy the Next Best Thing 33. *42nd Street* 33. Dangerously Yours 34. I Loved You Wednesday 34. Penthouse 34. Stand Up and Cheer 34. *Broadway Bill* 34. As Husbands Go 34. Such Women are Dangerous 34. Grand Canary 35. Hell in the Heavens 35. Under the Pampas Moon 35. *One More Spring* 35. King of Burlesque 35. *Prisoner of Shark Island* 35. *The Road to Glory* 36. To Mary with Love 36. White Hunter 36. Robin Hood of El Dorado 36. Slave Ship 37. Vogues of 1938 37. Wife Doctor and Nurse 37. Kidnapped 38. I'll Give a Million 38. Wife Husband and Friend 39. Barricade 39. The Return of the Cisco Kid 39. Earthbound 40. Adam Had Four Sons 41. Crime

Doctor 43. The Crime Doctor's Strangest Case 43. Lady in the Dark 44. Shadows in the Night 44. The Crime Doctor's Courage 45. The Crime Doctor's Warning 45. Just Before Dawn 46. The Crime Doctor's Man Hunt 46. The Millerson Case 47. The Crime Doctor's Gamble 47. A Gentleman from Nowhere 48. Prison Warden 49. The Devil's Henchman 49. The Crime Doctor's Diary 49. State Penitentiary 50.

Baye, Nathalie (1948–).
French leading actress.

Day for Night 73. The Green Room 78. A Girl from Lorraine 80. La Balance 82. The Return of Martin Guerre 82. Beethoven's Nephew 85. De Guerre Lasse 87. Massacre Play (Gioco al Massacro) 89. C'est la Vie (La Baule-les-pins) 90. La Voix 92. Mensonge 93. And the Band Played On (TV) 93, etc.

Bayes, Nora (1880–1928) (Dora Goldberg).
American vaudeville singer, impersonated by Ann Sheridan in the biopic *Shine On Harvest Moon* 44.

Bayldon, Geoffrey (1924–).
Lanky British character actor with a penchant for absent-minded or eccentric types.

The Stranger Left No Card 53. Dracula 58. Libel 60. The Webster Boy 62. A Jolly Bad Fellow 64. King Rat 65. *Sky West and Crooked* 65. *To Sir With Love* 66. Casino Royale 67. Otley 69. The Raging Moon 70. Scrooge 71. Asylum 72. Bullshot 83. Madame Sousatzka 88, etc.

Bayne, Beverly (1894–1982) (Pearl von Name).
American silent screen star, especially when married to Francis X. Bushman.

Graustark 15. A Virginia Romance 16. Romeo and Juliet 16. The Voice of Conscience 17. The Age of Innocence 24. Eve's Loves 25, etc.

Bazelli, Bojan.
American cinematographer.

China Girl 87. Patty Hearst 88. Tapeheads 88. King of New York 90. The Rapture 91. Deep Cover 92. Body Snatchers 93. Kalifornia 93. Sugar Hill 93. Surviving the Game 94, etc.

Bazin, Andre (1918–1958).
French critic who wrote books on Welles, de Sica and Renoir: 'the spiritual father of the New Wave'. Founded 'Cahiers du Cinema'.

Bazlen, Brigid (1944–1989).
Israeli leading lady of a few international films.

King of Kings (as Salome) 61. The Honeymoon Machine 61. How the West Was Won 62.
TV series: Too Young to Go Steady 59.

Beach, Rex (1877–1949).
American novelist whose books set in the Klondike, where he lived for a while, have attracted film-makers hoping to strike it rich. *The Spoilers* (aka *Alaska*) has been filmed five times: in 14, 23, 30, 42 and 55.

The Silver Horde 30. Son of the Gods 30 and 42. The Avengers (from Don Careless) 50. The World in His Arms 52.

Beacham, Stephanie (1947–).
British leading lady.

The Games 69. The Nightcomers 71. Dracula AD 1972 72. House of Whipcord 76. Schizo 77. Seminoid 80. The Wolves of Willoughby Chase 88. Troop Beverly Hills 89. Foreign Affairs (TV) 93, etc.

TV series: Tenko 82. Sorrell and Son 84. Connie 85. The Colbys 85. Napoleon and Josephine 87. Dynasty 88–89.

Beal, John (1909–) (Alexander Bliedung).
American stage actor whose look of boyish innocence was useful in the 30s but tended to hamper him subsequently.

Another Language 33. Hat Coat and Glove 34. *The Little Minister* 34. Les Misérables 35. *Laddie* 35. Break of Hearts 35. The Man Who Found Himself 37. Double Wedding 37. Port of Seven Seas 38. I Am The Law 38. *The Cat and the Canary* 39. Ellery Queen and the Perfect Crime 41. The Great Commandment 42. Edge of Darkness 43. Key Witness 47. Alimony 49. My Six Convicts 52. Remains to be Seen 53. That Night 57. The Vampire 57. Ten Who Dared 61. Amityville 3-D 83, etc.

TV series: The Nurses 62–67. Another World 64. The Adams Chronicles 67.

Beals, Jennifer (1963–).
American leading lady.

Flashdance (in which she did *not* do the dancing) 83. The Bride 85. The Gamble (La Partita) 88. Split Decisions 88. Vampire's Kiss 88. Sons 89. Docteur M. 90. Blood and Concrete 91. Day of Atonement (Le Grand Pardon 2) 92. In the Soup 92. Mrs Parker and the Vicious Circle 94, etc.

TV series: 2000 Malibu Road 92.

Bean, Judge Roy (1823–1902).
American Western badman, a self-appointed lawmaker who kept himself in whisky from his fines. Played by Walter Brennan in *The Westerner* 40; by Edgar Buchanan in a TV series, *Judge Roy Bean* 50; and by Paul Newman in *The Life and Times of Judge Roy Bean* 72.

Bean, Sean (1958–).
British leading actor, from television.

Caravaggio 86. Stormy Monday 88. War Requiem 88. The Field 90. Clarissa (TV) 91. Patriot Games 92. Sharpe's Rifles (TV) 93. Sharpe's Eagle (TV) 93. Lady Chatterley (TV) 93. A Woman's Guide to Adultery (TV) 93. Sharpe's Company (TV) 94. Shopping 94. Black Beauty 94, etc.

Beard, John.
English production designer.

The Wildcats of St Trinians 80. An Unsuitable Job for a Woman 81. Digital Dreams 83. Eureka 83. Brazil 83. Absolute Beginners 86. Siesta 87. The Last Temptation of Christ 88. Erik the Viking 89. Splitting Heirs 93. The Browning Version 94, etc.

Beard, Matthew 'Stymie' (1925–1981).
American actor, as a child in the Our Gang comedy shorts of the late 20s and 30s, and later in supporting roles.

Uncle Tom's Cabin 27. Two Gun Man from Harlem 38. Broken Strings 40. The Return of Jesse James 40. Fallen Angel 45. Truck Turner 74. The Buddy Holly Story 78. East of Eden 80, etc.

Béart, Emmanuelle (1965–).
French leading actress. She is the daughter of French singer Guy Béart. She has a daughter by French actor Daniel Auteuil.

Manon des Sources 87. Date with an Angel 87. Captain Fracassa's Journey (Il Viàggio di Capitan Fracassa) 90. La Belle Noiseuse 91. I Don't Kiss (J'Embrasse Pas) 91. Un Coeur en Hiver 91. Ruptures 93. L'Enfer 94. Haute Epoque 94, etc.

¶ There is no Hollywood now. – *E.B.*
I could never become a slave to the movie machine. I must be captain of my own ship. That to me is the only imperative. – *E.B.*

The Beatles.
This Liverpudlian pop group achieved astonishing popularity in the early 60s, but the pressures of success caused a split and the members went their rich but somewhat malcontented ways. They were *John Lennon* (1940–1980), *George Harrison* (1943–), *Paul McCartney* (1942–) and *Ringo Starr* (Richard Starkey) (1940–).
FILMS TOGETHER: *A Hard Day's Night* 64. Help! 65. Let It Be 70. They also lent their music and cartoon images to *Yellow Submarine* 67 and a subsequent TV series.
SEPARATELY: Lennon was in *How I Won The War* 67; Starr in *Candy* 68, *The Magic Christian* 70, *That'll Be the Day* 73, *Caveman* 81, *Give My Regards to Broad Street* 84, together with the film's producer, Paul McCartney.

¶ I see the Beatles have arrived from England. They were forty pounds overweight, and that was just their hair. – *Bob Hope, 1964*

Beaton, Sir Cecil (1904–1980).
British photographer and designer who advised on many films, his greatest achievements probably being *Gigi* 58 and *My Fair Lady* 64.
Biography: 1985, *Cecil Beaton* by Hugo Vickers; 1994, *Loving Garbo* by Hugo Vickers.
Kipps 41. Major Barbara 41. Anna Karenina 47. An Ideal Husband 48. The Doctor's Dilemma 59. On a Clear Day You Can See Forever 70.

Beatty, Clyde (1903–1965).
American animal trainer and circus owner who made a few film appearances.
■ The Big Cage 33. The Lost Jungle 34. Darkest Africa 36. Africa Screams 49. Ring of Fear 54.

Beatty, Ned (1937–).
Chubby American character actor.
■ Deliverance 72. The Life and Times of Judge Roy Bean 72. Footsteps (TV) 72. The Thief Who Came to Dinner 73. White Lightning 73. The Marcus-Nelson Murders (TV) 73. Dying Room Only (TV) 73. The Execution of Private Slovik (TV) 74. The Last American Hero 74. Attack on Terror (TV) 75. The Deadly Tower (TV) 75. W. W. and the Dixie Dancekings 75. Nashville 75. All the President's Men 76. *Network* (AAN) 76. Silver Streak 76. The Big Bus 76. Mikey and Nicky 76. Alambrista 77. Tail Gunner Joe (TV) 77. Lucan (TV) 77. Exorcist II 77. Shenanigans 77. Gray Lady Down 78. Superman 78. A Question of Love 78. Promises in the Dark 79. Wise Blood 79. *Friendly Fire* (TV) 79. 1941 79. Success 79. Guyana Tragedy (TV) 80. Hopscotch 80. The Incredible Shrinking Woman 81. Superman 2 81. The Toy 82. A Woman Called Golda (TV) 82. Stroker Ace 83. Touched 83. Restless Natives 84. Back to School 86. The Big Easy 86. The Fourth Protocol 87. Rolling Vengeance 87. The Trouble with Spies 87. After the Rain 88. Midnight Crossing 88. Physical Evidence 88. Purple People Eater 88. Shadows in the Storm 88. Switching Channels 88. The Unholy 88. Ministry of Vengeance 89. Time Trackers 89. Twist of Fate 89. Chattahoochee 89. Tennessee Nights 89. Big Bad John 90. Captain America 90. A Cry in the Wild 90. Repossessed 90. Going Under 90. *Hear My Song* 91. Angel Street 91. Illusions 91. Prelude to a Kiss 92. Ed and His Dead Mother 93. Rudy 93. The Legend of O. B. Taggart 94. Radioland Murders 94.

TV series: Szysznyk 77–78. Homicide: Life on the Street 93.

Beatty, Robert (1909–1992).
Rugged, good-humoured Canadian leading man long resident in Britain.
San Demetrio, London 43. Appointment with Crime 46. *Odd Man Out* 46. *Against the Wind* 47. Counterblast 48. Another Shore 48. Captain Horatio Hornblower R.N. 51. The Square Ring 53. *Albert R.N.* 53. The Gentle Gunman 53. Tarzan and the Lost Safari 57. Something of Value 57. The Shakedown 59. The Amorous Prawn 62. 2001: A Space Odyssey 68. Where Eagles Dare 69. Man at the Top 73. Golden Rendezvous 77. The Spaceman and King Arthur 79. The Amateur 81. Superman III 83. Meeting at Reykjavik (TV) (as Ronald Reagan) 87, etc.
TV series: *Dial 999* 57–58.

Beatty, Warren (1937–) (Warren Beaty).
Unruly American leading actor of the post-Brando school, with a flair for psychological maladjustment. Brother of Shirley Maclaine. He married actress Annette Bening in 1992.
■ *Splendour in the Grass* 61. The Roman Spring of Mrs Stone 61. *All Fall Down* 62. *Lilith* 65. *Mickey One* 65. Promise Her Anything 66. Kaleidoscope 66. *Bonnie and Clyde* (& p) (AAN) 67. The Only Game in Town 69. McCabe and Mrs Miller 71. Dollars 72. The Parallax View 74. Shampoo (& p, co-w) (AAN) 75. The Fortune 75. *Heaven Can Wait* (& p, w, co-d) (AAN) 78. *Reds* (& pd, co-w) (AAd, AANa) 81. Ishtar 87. Dick Tracy (& pd) 90. Bugsy (AAN) 91. Love Affair (& d) 94.
TV series: The Many Loves of Dobie Gillis 55–59.

¶ I'm old, I'm young, I'm intelligent, I'm stupid. My tide goes in and out. – *W.B.*

Movies are fun, but they're not a cure for cancer. – *W.B.*

Warren has an interesting psychology. He has always fallen in love with girls who have just won, or just been nominated for, an Oscar . . . Anyone who comes close to him loses a few feathers. He tends to maul you. – *Leslie Caron*

He was insatiable. Three, four, five times a day was not unusual for him, and he was able to accept telephone calls at the same time. – *Joan Collins*

Beaudine, William (1892–1970).
Prolific American director of silent family films and, later, second features. In two years in England in the 30s he directed 13 films.
Penrod and Sam 23. Little Annie Rooney 25. *Sparrows* 26. The Life of Riley 27. The Cohens and Kellys in Paris 28. Home James 28. The Girl from Woolworth's 29. The Lady Who Dared 31. *Penrod and Sam* 31. Three Wise Girls 32. The Crime of the Century 33. The Old-Fashioned Way 34. Says O'Reilly to Macnab (in Britain) 37. Torchy Gets Her Man 38. Torchy Blane in Chinatown 39. Broadway Big Shot 42. The Mystery of the 13th Guest 43. Black Market Babies 46. Kidnapped 48. Blue Grass of Kentucky 50. Westward Ho the Wagons 56. Lassie's Greatest Adventure 63. Billy the Kid versus Dracula 66, etc.

¶ I've been moderate in everything. I never set out to break any records. – *W.B.*

Beaumont, Charles (1929–1967).
American writer, chiefly of science fiction.
Queen of Outer Space 58. The Intruder 61. Night of the Eagle 62. The Haunted Palace 63. Seven Faces of Dr Lao 64. Mister Moses 65, etc.

Beaumont, Harry (1888–1966).
American director, at his peak in the 20s.
A Man and His Money 19. Lord and Lady Algy 19. *Main Street* 23. Beau Brummell 24. Babbitt 24. The Lover of Camille 24. *His Majesty Bunker Bean* 25. *Our Dancing Daughters* 28. *Broadway Melody* (AAN) 29. Lord Byron of Broadway 30. The Florodora Girl 30. Our Blushing Brides 30. Dance Fools Dance 31. Faithless 32. *When Ladies Meet* 33. Enchanted April 35. The Girl on the Front Page 36. When's Your Birthday? 37. Maisie Goes to Reno 44. Twice Blessed 45. The Show-Off 47, many others.

Beaumont, Hugh (1909–1982).
American second lead and second-feature hero.
Flight Lieutenant 42. The Seventh Victim 43. Objective Burma 45. The Blue Dahlia 46. Bury Me Dead 47. Railroaded 49. Mr Belvedere Rings the Bell 52. Mississippi Gambler 53. The Mole People 57. The Human Duplicators 65, etc.
TV series: Leave It To Beaver 57–62.

Beaumont, Lucy (1873–1937).
English character actress, from the London and New York stage, in Hollywood from the 20s.
Ashes of Vengeance 23. The Crowd 28. Sonny Boy 29. A Free Soul 31. Condemned to Live 35. The Devil Doll 36. The Maid of Salem 37, etc.

Beaumont, Susan (1936–) (Susan Black).
British leading lady of a few 50s films.
Jumping for Joy 55. High Tide at Noon 57. Innocent Sinners 58. Carry On Nurse 59. Web of Suspicion 59, etc.

Beavers, Louise (1902–1962).
American actress who played innumerable happy housekeepers.
Coquette 29. Girls About Town 32. What Price Hollywood 32. She Done Him Wrong 33. *Imitation of Life* (her best role) 35. Rainbow on the River 36. The Last Gangster 37. Made For Each Other 39. No Time for Comedy 40. Reap the Wild Wind 42. Dubarry was a Lady 43. Delightfully Dangerous 46. *Mr Blandings Builds His Dream House* 48. My Blue Heaven 50. Teenage Rebel 56. The Goddess 58. The Facts of Life 61, many others.
TV series: *Beulah* 50.

Famous line (*Mr Blandings*): 'If you ain't eatin' Wham, you ain't eatin' ham!'

Beck, John (1943–).
American leading man.
The Silent Gun (TV) 69. Lawman 71. The Unexpected Mrs Pollifax 72. Pat Garrett and Billy the Kid 73. Sidekicks (TV) 74. The Law (TV) 74. The Call of the Wild (TV) 76. The Big Bus 76. Sky Riders 76. Audrey Rose 77. The Other Side of Midnight 77. Wheels (TV) 78. The Time Machine (TV) 78. The Great American Traffic Jam (TV) 80. Deadly Illusion 87. Fire and Rain (TV) 89. A Row of Crows 90, etc.
TV series: Flamingo Road 80–82. Dallas 83–85.

Beck, Michael (1948–).
American leading man.
Holocaust (TV) 77. Mayflower (TV) 78. The Warriors 79. Xanadu 80. Alcatraz (TV) 81. Triumphs of a Man Called Horse 84. Rear View Mirror (TV) 84. Blackout 85. Deadly Game (TV) 91, etc.

Becker, Harold.
American director, a former photographer.
The Onion Field 79. The Black Marble 80. Taps 81. Vision Quest 85. The Boost 88. Sea of Love 89. Malice 93, etc.

Becker, Jacques (1906–1960).
French director, mainly of civilized comedies, an assistant to Jean Renoir for most of the 30s.
Goupi Mains Rouges 42. Falbalas 44. *Antoine et Antoinette* 47. Rendezvous de Juillet 49. *Edouard et Caroline* 50. *Casque d'Or* 51. Rue de l'Estrapade 52. *Touchez Pas au Grisbi* 53. Ali Baba 55. The Adventures of Arsène Lupin 56. Montparnasse Nineteen 57. The Hole 60, etc.

Becker, Jean (1933–).
French director, son of Jacques Becker.
Echappement Libre 62. Pas de Caviar pour Tante Olga 64. Tendre Voyou 66, etc.

Beckett, Scotty (1929–1968).
Soulful-looking American child actor of the 30s and 40s; one-time member of 'Our Gang'.
Whom the Gods Destroy 34. Dante's Inferno 35. The Charge of the Light Brigade 36. Marie Walewska 38. *The Bluebird* 40. *King's Row* 42. The Youngest Profession 43. *Ali Baba and the Forty Thieves* 43. Junior Miss 45. *The Jolson Story* (as young Jolson) 46. A Date with Judy 48. Battleground 49. Corky 51. Three for Jamie Dawn 56, many others.

Beckinsale, Kate (1974–).
English actress, the daughter of actor Richard Beckinsale. She made her first film while still a student at Oxford University.
One against the Wind (TV) 91. Much Ado about Nothing 93. Uncovered 94. Cold Comfort Farm (TV) 95.

Beckinsale, Richard (1947–1979).
British comedy leading man, in several TV series.
Three for All 74. Porridge 79.
Film: The Lovers 72.

Beckley, Tony (1928–1980).
British actor, often seen as young thug.
The Penthouse 67. Chimes at Midnight 67. The Long Day's Dying 68. The Lost Continent 68. Get Carter 71. Sitting Target 72. Gold 74. The Return of the Pink Panther 74. Diagnosis Murder 75. Revenge of the Pink Panther 78. When a Stranger Calls 79, etc.

Beckwith, Reginald (1908–1965).
Chubby British character actor, whose high voice and impeccable timing were a constant delight. Also wrote successful plays, e.g. *Boys in Brown, A Soldier for Christmas*.
Voice in the Night 41. *Scott of the Antarctic* 48. Another Man's Poison 51. Mr Drake's Duck 52. *Genevieve* 53. *The Runaway Bus* 54. Dance Little Lady 55. *The Captain's Table* 58. The Thirty-Nine Steps 59. Double Bunk 61. The Password is Courage 62. Never Put It in Writing 64. A Shot in the Dark 64. Mister Moses 65, many others.

Beddoe, Don (1903–1991).
American character actor with genial, sometimes startled, look; in hundreds of films, often as sheriff, reporter or cop.
Golden Boy 39. *The Face Behind the Mask* 41. Talk of the Town 42. Crime Inc. 45. O.S.S. 46. The Best Years of Our Lives 46. The Farmer's Daughter 47. Dancing in the Dark 49. Carrie 51. Night of the Hunter 55. *Saintly Sinners* (lead role) 61. *Jack the Giant Killer* (as a leprechaun) 62. Texas Across the River 66. The Impossible Years 68. Generation 69. How Do I Love Thee 70. Nickel Mountain 85, many others.

Bedelia, Bonnie (1946–).
American leading lady.
The Gypsy Moths 69. They Shoot Horses Don't They? 70. *Lovers and Other Strangers* 70. The Strange Vengeance of Rosalie 72. Hawkins on Murder (TV) 73. The Big Fix 78. Heart Like a Wheel 83. Between Friends (TV) 83. Death of an Angel 85. The Stranger 87. Die Hard 88. Fat Man and Little Boy (GB: The Shadowmakers) 89. Die Hard 2 90. Presumed Innocent 90. Somebody Has to Shoot the Picture 91. The Fire Next Time (TV) 93. Needful Things 93, etc.

Bedford, Brian (1935–).
British stage actor who has been in a few films.
Miracle in Soho 58. The Angry Silence 59. The Punch and Judy Man 63. The Pad 66. Grand Prix 67. Robin Hood (voice) 73, etc.
TV series: Coronet Blue 67.

Bedi, Kabir (1945–).
Stalwart Indian leading man of the late 70s.
Swashbuckler 76. The Thief of Baghdad (TV) 78. Ashanti 78. Octopussy 83. Terminal Entry 87. The Beast 88, etc.
TV series: Sandokan the Great 76.

Bedoya, Alfonso (1904–1957).
Mexican character actor whose beaming face could provide comedy or menace.
The Treasure of the Sierra Madre (as the bandit) 47. The Pearl 48. Streets of Laredo 49. The Black Rose 50. Sombrero 52. California Conquest 52. The Stranger Wore a Gun 53. Ten Wanted Men 55. *The Big Country* 57, etc.

The Bee Gees.
Three British brothers who as pop singers challenged the record of the Beatles and had an even more extravagant life style. A succession of hits culminated in their original score for *Saturday Night Fever*, which put them in the multimillionaire category. They are *Barry* (born Douglas) 1947–), *Maurice* and *Robin* (both born 1949). Sergeant Pepper's Lonely Hearts Club Band 78.

Beebe, Ford (1888–1978).
American director of low-budget westerns, second features and serials – over 200 of them from 1916.
Laughing at Life 33. *Flash Gordon's Trip to Mars* 38. *Riders of Death Valley* 41. Night Monster 42. The Invisible Man's Revenge 44. Enter Arsène Lupin 44. Bomba the Jungle Boy 49, etc.

Beecher, Janet (1884–1955) (J. B. Meysenburg).
American character actress usually seen in ladylike roles. Retired 1943.
Gallant Lady 33. The President Vanishes 34. The Mighty Barnum 34. The Dark Angel 35. Love Before Breakfast 36. The Thirteenth Chair 37. Rosalie 37. Judge Hardy's Children 38. Yellow Jack 38. Man of Conquest 39. The Mark of Zorro 40. Bitter Sweet 40. The Lady Eve 41. Silver Queen 42. Reap the Wild Wind 42. Mrs Wiggs of the Cabbage Patch 42. Henry Aldrich Gets Glamour 43, many others.

Beeny, Christopher (1941–).
Self-effacing English character actor who began on stage in 1951 and was in films as a child. Born in London, he played Lennie, the young son, in Britain's first TV soap opera, *The Grove Family*. He gave up acting in the 60s, returning in the 70s.
The Kidnappers 53. The Long Memory 53. Trouble in Store 53. Child's Play 54. Doctor in Distress 63, etc.
TV series: The Grove Family 54–57. Upstairs Downstairs 71–75. Miss Jones and Son 77–78. The Rag Trade 77–79. In Loving Memory 79–86.

Beery, Noah (1884–1946).
American character actor, half-brother of Wallace Beery and one of the silent screen's most celebrated villains.
The Mormon Maid 18. *The Mark of Zorro* 20. The Sea Wolf 20. Tol'able David 21. The Spoilers 22. The Coming of Amos 25. Beau Geste 26. *Don Juan* 26. Beau Sabreur 27. The Four Feathers 29. Noah's Ark 29. Tol'able David 30. The Drifter 31. Out of Singapore 32. She Done Him Wrong 33. King of the Damned (GB) 35. Our Fighting Navy (GB) 37. The Girl of the Golden West 38. Isle of Missing Men 42. This Man's Navy 45, many others.

Beery, Noah, Jnr (1913–1994).
American character actor, son of Noah Beery. Started as child actor, and later played easy-going country cousins.
The Mark of Zorro 20. Heroes of the West 26. Father and Son 29. Jungle Madness 31. The Road Back 37. Only Angels Have Wings 39. Of Mice and Men 40. Riders of Death Valley 41. Prairie Chickens 43. Gung Ho 44. Red River 48. Rocketship XM 50. White Feather 55. Inherit the Wind 60. The Seven Faces of Dr Lao 64. Incident at Phantom Hill 65. Little Fauss and Big Halsy 70. Walking Tall 73. The Best Little Whorehouse in Texas 82, many others.
TV series: Circus Boy 56–57. Custer 67. Doc Elliot 74. The Rockford Files 74–80. The Quest 83.

Beery, Wallace (1885–1949).
American character star with circus and musical comedy experience, long under contract to MGM. Started as a grotesque female impersonator and tried every kind of part before acquiring his best remembered persona: tough, ugly, slow-thinking and easy-going. Half-brother of Noah Beery.
SELECTED SILENT FILMS: Teddy at the Throttle 16. The Unpardonable Sin 19. The Virgin of Stamboul 20. The Last of the Mohicans 21. *Robin Hood* (as King Richard) 22. *Richard the Lion-Hearted* 23. The Sea Hawk 24. So Big 24. *The Lost World* (as Professor Challenger) 25. The Wanderer 25. Volcano 26. We're in the Navy Now 26. Casey at the Bat 27. Fireman Save My Child 27. Partners of Crime 28. Beggars of Life 28, many others.
■ SOUND FILMS: Chinatown Nights 29. River of Romance 29. *The Big House* (AAN) 30. Way for a Sailor 30. Billy the Kid 30. A Lady's Morals 30. *Min and Bill* 30. The Secret Six 31. Hell Divers 31. *The Champ* (AA) 31. *Grand Hotel* 32. Flesh 32. Dinner at Eight 33. Tugboat Annie 33. *The Bowery* 33. *Viva Villa* 34. *Treasure Island* (as Long John Silver) 34. *The Mighty Barnum* 34. West Point of the Air 35. China Seas 35. O'Shaughnessy's Boy 35. *Ah Wilderness* 35. A Message to Garcia 36. Old Hutch 36. Good Old Soak 37. *Slave Ship* 37. Bad Man of Brimstone 38. Port of Seven Seas 38. Stablemates 38. Sergeant Madden 39. *Stand Up and Fight* 39. Thunder Afloat 39. The Man from Dakota 40. Twenty Mule Team 40. Wyoming 40. Barnacle Bill 41. The Bad Man 41. The Bugle Sounds 42. Jackass Mail 42. Salute to the Marines 43. Rationing 44. *Barbary Coast Gent* 44. This Man's Navy 45. Bad Bascomb 46. The Mighty McGurk 47. A Date with Judy 48. Alias a Gentleman 48. Big Jack 49.

¶ I never let anyone sucker me, not even for a nickel. – *W.B.*
Like my dear old friend Marie Dressler, my ugly mug has been my fortune. – *W.B.*
He always made me feel uncomfortable. – *Jackie Cooper*
Beery's a son of a bitch, but he's *our* son of a bitch. – *Louis B. Mayer*

Beeson, Paul (1921–).
British cinematographer.
Dunkirk 58. Greyfriars Bobby 61. In Search of the Castaways 62. The Moonspinners 64. To Sir with Love 66. Moon Zero Two 69. Kidnapped 70. Jane Eyre 71. A Warm December 73. The Mutations 74. One of our Dinosaurs is Missing 75. Escape from the Dark 76. Candleshoe 77. The Spaceman and King Arthur 79. Silver Dream Racer 80. Hawk the Slayer 80. Raiders of the Lost Ark 81. Never Say Never Again 83. Indiana Jones and the Temple of Doom 84. Santa Claus 85. Jane and the Lost City 87, etc.

Beethoven, Ludwig van (1770–1827).
German classical composer who in view of his total deafness and unattractive physique has been surprisingly frequently portrayed in movies: by Harry Baur in *Beethoven* 36; Albert Basserman in *New Wine* 41; Rene Deltgen in *Whom the Gods Love* 41; Karl Bochm in *The Magnificent Rebel* 60 and Wolfgang Reichmann in *Beethoven's Nephew* 88; Gary Oldman in *Imortal Beloved* 95.

Begley, Ed (1901–1970).
Blustery American character actor with radio and stage experience; usually seen as jovial uncle or man at the end of his tether.
■ Big Town 47. Boomerang 47. Deep Waters 48. Sitting Pretty 48. The Street with No Name 48. Sorry Wrong Number 48. Tulsa 49. It Happens Every Spring 49. The Great Gatsby 49. Backfire 50. Stars in my Crown 50. Wyoming Mail 50. Convicted 50. Saddle Tramp 50. Dark City 50. Lady from Texas 51. On Dangerous Ground 51. You're In the Navy Now 51. Deadline 52. Boots Malone 52. The Turning Point 52. What Price Glory 52. Lone Star 52. *Patterns* 56. *Twelve Angry Men* 57. *Odds Against Tomorrow* 59. The Green Helmet 61. *Sweet Bird of Youth* (AA) 62. The Unsinkable Molly Brown 64. The Oscar 66. Warning Shot 66. *Billion Dollar Brain* 67. Firecreek 67. Wild in the Streets 68. Hang 'Em High 68. The Violent Enemy 69. The Silent Gun (TV) 69. The Dunwich Horror 69. The Road to Salina 71.
TV series: Leave It to Larry 52.

Begley, Ed, Jnr (1949–).
American character actor.
Now You See Him Now You Don't 72. Cockfighter 74. Stay Hungry 76. Blue Collar 78. The Concorde–Airport 79 79. This is Spinal Tap 80. The In-Laws 81. Young Doctors in Love 82. Protocol 84. Streets of Fire 85. Amazon Women on the Moon 87. The Accidental Tourist 88. Scenes from the Class Struggle in Beverly Hills 89. She-Devil 89. Meet the Applegates 91. Dark Horse 92. Rave Review 94, etc.
TV series: Roll Out! 73–74. St Elsewhere 81–88. The Ed Begley Jnr Show 89. Parenthood 92.

Behan, Brendan (1923–1964).
Irish dramatist whose flamboyant behaviour often hit the headlines in the 50s; his only play to be filmed was *The Quare Fellow*.

Behrman, S. N. (1893–1973).
American playwright and screenwriter.
He Knew Women (oa) 30. *Queen Christina* 33. Cavalcade 33. *Anna Karenina* 35. Biography of a Bachelor Girl (oa) 35. A Tale of Two Cities 35. Parnell 37. Conquest 37. *No Time for Comedy* (oa) 40. Waterloo Bridge 40. Two-Faced Woman 41. The Pirate (oa) 48. Quo Vadis 51. *Me and the Colonel* (& oa) 56, etc.

Beich, Albert (1919–).
American radio and film writer.

Girls in Chains 44. The Perils of Pauline 47. The Bride Goes Wild 48. Key to the City 50. The Lieutenant Wore Skirts 55. Dead Ringer 64, etc.

Beiderbecke, Leon Bix (1903–1931).
Jazz cornettist, also a pianist and composer, who played with the Wolverines and the Paul Whiteman orchestra. A legendary figure for his brilliant improvisations and short, alcoholic life, he was the subject of a biopic, *Bix*, made by Italian director Pupi Avati in 1991, and a documentary, *Bix*, made by Brigette Berman in 1981. Dorothy Baker's novel *Young Man with a Horn*, filmed by Michael Curtiz in 1950, is very loosely based on his life, apart from the happy ending, although the soundtrack trumpet by Harry James is closer to that of the equally alcoholic and almost as accomplished jazz trumpeter Bunny Berigan (1908–42), who replaced Beiderbecke in Whiteman's orchestra.

Beineix, Jean-Jacques (1946–).
Chic French director. He gave up medical studies to become an assistant director and also directs TV commercials.
Diva 82. The Moon in the Gutter 83. Betty Blue 86. Roselyne and the Lions 88. IP5: The Island of Pachyderms 92, etc.

¶ I'm an anxious person in an anxious world. – J-J.B.

Bekassy, Stephen (1910–).
Hungarian stage actor who came to Hollywood in the 40s.
A Song to Remember (as Liszt) 45. Arch of Triumph 48. Black Magic 49. Fair Wind to Java 53. Hell and High Water 54. Interrupted Melody 55. The Light in the Forest 58. Bachelor Flat 61. The Four Horsemen of the Apocalypse 62, etc.

Bel Geddes, Barbara (1922–) (Barbara Geddes Lewis).
American stage actress who makes occasional films, usually as nice placid girls.
■ The Gangster 47. The Long Night 47. *I Remember Mama* (AAN) 48. Blood on the Moon 48. Caught 49. Panic in the Streets 50. *Fourteen Hours* 51. Vertigo 58. The Five Pennies 59. Five Branded Women 60. By Love Possessed 61. The Todd Killings 70. Summertree 71.
TV series: Dallas 78–90.

Belafonte, Harry (1927–).
Handsome American ballad singer who has acted strikingly in several films.
■ Bright Road 53. Carmen Jones 54. *Island in the Sun* 57. The World the Flesh and the Devil 59. *Odds Against Tomorrow* 59. The Angel Levine 70. Buck and the Preacher 72. Uptown Saturday Night 74. First Look 84. The Player (as himself) 92.

Belasco, Leon (1902–1988).
Wiry Russian-born small-part player of excitable balletmasters, head-waiters, landlords, etc.
The Best People (debut) 26. Topper Takes a Trip 39. The Mummy's Hand 40. Nothing But the Truth 41. Pin-Up Girl 44. The New Adventures of Don Juan 48. Call Me Madam 53, many others.
TV series: My Sister Eileen.

Belita (1924–) (Gladys Jepson-Turner).
British ice-skating and dancing star who made a few Hollywood films.
Ice Capades 41. Silver Skates 43. Suspense 46. The Hunted 47. Never Let Me Go 53. Invitation to the Dance 56. Silk Stockings 57, etc.

Bell, Ann (1939–).
British character actress who was always welcome but never reached the top.
Flat Two 62. Dr Terror's House of Horrors 64. To Sir with Love 66. The Witches 66. The Shuttered Room 66. The Reckoning 69. The Statue 70. Spectre (TV) 77. Very Like a Whale (TV) 80. Champions 84, etc.

Bell, James (1891–1973).
American character actor, usually in benevolent roles.
I Am a Fugitive from a Chain Gang 32. White Woman 33. I Walked with a Zombie 42. The Spiral Staircase 45. Brute Force 47. The Violent Hour 50. The Glenn Miller Story 54. The Lonely Man 57. Twilight of Honor 63, many others.

Bell, Marie (1900–1985) (Marie-Jeanne Bellon-Downey).
Distinguished French actress who appeared in a few well-remembered films.
Madame Recamier 28. *Le Grand Jeu* 34. La Garçonne 35. *Carnet de Bal* 37. La Charrette Fantôme 40. Colonel Chabert 43. La Bonne Soupe 64. Hotel Paradiso 66, etc.

Bell, Monta (1891–1958).
American director whose peak was in the 20s.
A Woman of Paris (co-d) 23. Broadway after Dark 24. The Snob 24. *The Torrent* 25. The King on Main Street 27. After Midnight (& w) 27. Man Woman and Sin (& w) 27. The Bellamy Trial 29. East is West 30. Men in White 33. West Point of the Air 35. China's Little Devils 45, etc.

Bell, Rex (1905–1962) (George F. Beldam).
American cowboy star of the 30s: left Hollywood to become Lieut.-Governor of Nevada. Married Clara Bow.
Pleasure Crazed 29. True to the Navy 30. Lightnin' 30. Tombstone 42. Lone Star 52, many others.
TV series: Cowboys and Injuns 50.

Bell, Tom (1932–).
Gaunt British leading man.
The Kitchen 61. *Payroll* 61. HMS Defiant 62. *The L-Shaped Room* 62. A Prize of Arms 63. Ballad in Blue 65. *He Who Rides a Tiger* 66. The Long Day's Dying 68. In Enemy Country (US) 68. Lock Up Your Daughters 69. *All the Right Noises* 69. Quest for Love 71. The Spy's Wife 71. Royal Flash 75. Holocaust (TV) 78. Wish You Were Here 87. Resurrected 88. Red King, White Knight (TV) 89. The Krays 90. Let Him Have It 91. Prospero's Books 91. Angels (TV) 92. Prime Suspect 3 (TV) 93, etc.
TV series: Out 78. Hope It Rains 91–92.

Bellah, James Warner (1899–1976).
American screenwriter, mainly on historical themes; former war correspondent.
Fort Apache 48. She Wore a Yellow Ribbon 49. Rio Grande 50. Rio Bravo 55. The Sea Chase (co-w) 55. Sergeant Rutledge 59. A Thunder of Drums 61. The Man Who Shot Liberty Valance (co-w) 62, etc.

Bellamy, Earl (1917–).
Routine American director, much involved in TV series.
Blackjack Ketchum, Desperado 56. Fluffy 65. Gunpoint 65. Incident at Phantom Hill 66. Seven Alone 74. Part Two Walking Tall 75. Sidewinder One 77. Speedtrap 78. Magnum Thrust 81, etc.

Bellamy, Madge (1899–1990) (Margaret Philpott).
American general-purpose actress of the 20s, a former dancer and beauty queen.
Autobiography: 1990, *Darling of the Twenties*.
Lorna Doone 23. Bertha the Sewing Machine Girl 27. *Mother Knows Best* 28, etc.

Bellamy, Ralph (1904–1991).
Soft-voiced, serious-looking American leading man of stage and screen who in the 30s became typecast as the simple-minded rich man who never got the girl. In fact he played most kinds of parts, including detectives and villains, and later became a highly respected stage actor. He was given an honorary Oscar in 1987.
■ The Secret Six 31. The Magnificent Lie 31. Surrender 31. Forbidden 32. West of Broadway 32. Disorderly Conduct 32. Young America 32. Rebecca of Sunnybrook Farm 32. The Woman in Room 13 32. Wild Girl 32. Air Mail 32. Almost Married 32. Second Hand Wife 32. Parole Girl 33. Destination Unknown 33. Picture Snatcher 33. Narrow Corner 33. Below the Sea 33. Headline Shooters 33. Flying Devils 33. Blind Adventure 33. Ace of Aces 33. Ever in My Heart 33. Spitfire 34. This Man Is Mine 34. Once to Every Woman 34. One Is Guilty 34. Before Midnight 34. The Crime of Helen Stanley 34. Girl in Danger 34. Woman in the Dark 34. Helldorado 35. The Wedding Night 35. Rendezvous at Midnight 35. Air Hawks 35. Eight Bells 35. The Healer 35. Gigolette 35. Navy Wife 35. Hands Across the Table 35. Dangerous Intrigue 36. The Final Hour 36. Roaming Lady 36. Straight from the Shoulder 36. Wild Brian Kent 36. Counterfeit Lady 37. The Man Who Lived Twice 37. *The Awful Truth* (in which his 'other man' stereotype was sealed) (AAN) 37. Let's Get Married 37. The Crime of Dr Hallet 38. Fools for Scandal 38. Boy Meets Girl 38. Carefree 38. Girls' School 38. Trade Winds 38. Let Us Live 38. *Blind Alley* 39. Smashing the Spy Ring 39. Coast Guard 39. *His Girl Friday* (in which the Ralph Bellamy type was amiably mocked) 40. Flight Angels 40. Brother Orchid 40. Queen of the Mob 40. Dance Girl Dance 40. Public Deb Number One 40. Ellery Queen Master Detective (title role) 40. Meet the Wildcat 40. Ellery Queen's Penthouse Mystery 41. Footsteps in the Dark 41. Affectionately Yours 41. Ellery Queen and the Perfect Crime 41. Dive Bomber 41. Ellery Queen and the Murder Ring 41. The Wolf Man 41. The Ghost of Frankenstein 42. Lady in a Jam 42. Men of Texas 42. The Great Impersonation 42. Stage Door Canteen 43. Guest in the House 44. Delightfully Dangerous 45. Lady on a Train 45. The Court Martial of Billy Mitchell 55. *Sunrise at Campobello* (as FDR) 60. The Professionals 66. Rosemary's Baby 68. Wings of Fire (TV) 68. The Immortal (TV) 69. Doctors' Wives 71. Cancel My Reservation 72. Something Evil (TV) 72. The Log of the Black Pearl (TV) 75. Adventures of the Queen (TV) 75. Search for the Gods (TV) 75. Murder on Flight 502 (TV) 75. McNaughton's Daughter (TV) 76. Nightmare in Badham County (TV) 76. The Boy in the Plastic Bubble (TV) 76. Once an Eagle (TV) 76. The Moneychangers (TV) 76. Testimony of Two Men (TV) 77. Charlie Cobb: Nice Night for a Hanging (TV) 77. Westside Medical (TV) 77. Oh God 77. Wheels (TV) 78. The Clone Master (TV) 78. The Millionaire (TV) 78. Billion Dollar Threat (TV) 79. Condominium (TV) 79. Power (TV) 79. The Memory of Eva Ryker (TV) 83. *The Winds of War* (TV) 83. *Trading Places* 83. Space (TV) 85. Disorderlies 87.
TV series: Man Against Crime 49–53. The Eleventh Hour 64. The Survivors 69. The Most Deadly Game 69. Hunter 77.
⊙ For solid service and the occasional gleam of brilliance.

¶ One day in Hollywood I read a script in which the character was described as 'charming but ull – a typical Ralph Bellamy type'. I promptly eaded for New York to find a part with guts. – *R.B.*

ellaver, Harry (1905–   ).
.merican character actor, often seen as cop, small-me gangster or cabby.
   Another Thin Man 40. The House on 92nd treet 45. No Way Out 50. The Lemon Drop Kid 1. From Here to Eternity 53. Love Me or Leave Ae 55. Serenade 56. Slaughter on Tenth Avenue 7. The Old Man and the Sea 58. One Potato Two otato 64. A Fine Madness 66. Madigan 67. God old Me To 76. Demon 77. Blue Collar 78. Hero t Large 80, etc.
   TV series: *Naked City* 58–63.

eller, Kathleen (1955–   ).
.merican leading lady.
   Godfather II 74. The Betsy 78. Mary White (TV) 9. Something for Joey (TV) 80. Are You in the Iouse Alone? (TV) 82. Touched by Love 83. urfacing 84. Cloud Waltzing (TV) 87. Time rackers 88, etc.
   TV series: Dynasty 82–84.

ellocchio, Marco (1939–   ).
alian director.
   Fists in the Pocket 65. China is Near 67. In the ame of the Father 71. Triumphal March 76. Les eux Fertiles 77. Salto nel Vuoto 79. Henry IV 84. evil in the Flesh 85. La Visione del Sabba 87. The entence (La Condanna) 91. Il Sogno della Farfalla 4, etc.

ellon, Yannick (1924–   ).
rench director and screenwriter, a former editor. lthough she made shorts from the mid-40s, she id not direct her first feature until 1972. Her films nd to deal with the troubled lives of women.
   Quelque Part, Quelqu'un 72. La Femme de Jean 4. Rape of Love (L'Amour Violé) 78. La Triche 4. Les Enfants du Désordre 89, etc.

elmondo, Jean-Paul (1933–   ).
nteresting but unhandsome French leading actor.
   Dimanche . . . Nous Volerons 56. Les Tricheurs 8. Un Drôle de Dimanche 58. Sois Belle et Tais-oi 58. A Double Tour 59. *A Bout de Souffle* 59. Aoderato Cantabile 60. La Viaccia 60. Leon Morin, riest 61. Two Women 61. Cartouche 62. *Un Singe n Hiver* 62. Cent Milles Dollars au Soleil 63. *That Aan from Rio* 64. Weekend in Dunkirk 65. Pierrot Fou 65. Les Tribulations d'un Chinoise en Chine 5. Is Paris Burning? 66. Tendre Voyou 66. Le oleur 67. The Brain 68. Ho! 68. The Mississippi Aermaid 69. A Man I Like 69. Le Casse 71. coundrel in White 72. Le Magnifique 73. taviksy 74. The Night Caller 75. L'Alpageur 76. e Corps de Mon Ennemi 76. L'Animal 77. Le uignolo 80. Le Marginal 83. Vultures 83. Hold-p 85. Le Solitaire 86. Der Glückspitz 88. Inconnu dans la Maison 92. Les Misérables du Xème Siècle 95, etc.

¶ Hell, everybody knows that an ugly guy with a good line gets the chicks. – *J.P.B.*
New blood, new looks, new vitality, new uidism, new eroticism, new normality for that alady-ridden strain of today's neurotic actors. *Marlene Dietrich*
Wrong or right I suppose he represents France. *Daniel Boulander*

elmore, Bertha (1882–1953).
mple British character comedienne, a British

Margaret Dumont whose dignity was inevitably shattered.
   Are You a Mason? 33. Going Gay 34. Broken Blossoms 36. In the Soup 37. Over She Goes 38. Yes Madam 39, etc.

Belmore, Lionel (1867–1953).
Portly British character actor in Hollywood in the 30s.
   The Antique Dealer 15. Madame X 20. Oliver Twist 22. Red Lights 23. The Sea Hawk 24. Never the Twain Shall Meet 25. Bardelys the Magnificent 26. Sorrell and Son 27. King of Kings 27. Rose Marie 28. The Love Parade 29. Monte Carlo 30. Alexander Hamilton 31. Frankenstein 31. Vanity Fair 32. So Big 32. The Vampire Bat 33. Cleopatra 34. Vanessa 34. The Count of Monte Cristo 34. Cardinal Richelieu 35. Clive of India 35. Little Lord Fauntleroy 36. Maid of Salem 37. The Prince and the Pauper 37. Tower of London 39. Son of Frankenstein 39. My Son My Son 40, many others.

Beloin, Edmund (1910–1992).
American comedy writer with radio experience.
   Buck Benny Rides Again 40. Love Thy Neighbour 40. Because of Him 45. The Great Lover (& p) 49. A Connecticut Yankee in King Arthur's Court 49. The Sad Sack 57. G.I. Blues 60. All in a Night's Work 61, etc.

Belson, Jerry.
American screenwriter and director.
   How Sweet It Is 68. Smile 76. Fun with Dick and Jane 77. The End 78. Smokey and the Bandit II (co-w) 80. Jekyll and Hyde . . . Together Again 82 (wd). Surrender (wd) 87. Always 89, etc.

Belushi, James (1954–   ).
American leading man whose popularity does not travel much beyond America. He is the brother of John Belushi.
   Mutant Video 76. Thief 81. Trading Places 83. Man with One Red Shoe 85. Salvador 85. About Last Night . . . 86. Little Shop of Horrors 86. Jumpin' Jack Flash 86. The Principal 87. Real Men 87. Red Heat 88. K-9 89. Who's Harry Crumb? 89. Homer and Eddie 89. To Forget Palermo (Dimenticare Palermo) 89. Mr Destiny 90. Taking Care of Business (GB: Filofax) 90. Only the Lonely 91. Curly Sue 91. Once Upon a Crime 92. Traces of Red 92. Diary of a Hit Man 92. Once Upon a Crime 92. Royce 94. Parallel Lives (TV) 94, etc.
   TV series: Working Stiffs 79. Wild Palms 93.

Belushi, John (1949–1982).
Overweight American comic actor from television satire shows. Died from an overdose of drugs. A biography, *Wired*, by Bob Woodward, was filmed in 1989 with Michael Chiklis as Belushi.
■ National Lampoon's Animal House 78. Going South 78. 1941 79. Old Boyfriends 79. The Blues Brothers 80. Continental Divide 81. Neighbours 81.
¶ A good man, but a bad boy. – *Dan Aykroyd*

Bemberg, Maria Luisa (1917–   ).
Argentinian film director and screenwriter on feminist themes who made her first feature film when she was in her 50s. She has also been active in the theatre as a producer.
■ Crónica de una Señora (w) 70. Triángulo de Cuatro (w) 74. Moments (Momentos) 80. Nobody's Wife (Señora de Nadie) 82. Camila (AAN) 84. Miss Mary 86. I, the Worst of All (Yo, la Peor de Todas) 90. We Don't Want to Talk about It (De Eso No Se Habla) 93.

Benacerraf, Margot (1926–   ).
Venezuelan film director who studied in Paris and made two acclaimed films in the 50s before retiring, despite offers of work.
■ Reveron (doc) 52. Araya 58.

Benchley, Peter (1940–   ).
American novelist, fashionable in Hollywood for his one real hit. Grandson of Robert Benchley.
   Jaws 75. The Deep 77. The Island 80.

Benchley, Robert (1889–1945).
American magazine humourist who exploited the small problems of twentieth-century living. He appeared in many films as a lovable bumbler, usually trying to explain something very complicated or to control a patently unmanageable situation. Benchley made many amusing shorts consisting of lectures by him on matters of science or domestic harmony. One of them, *How to Sleep* (1935), won an Academy Award. In *Mrs Parker and the Vicious Circle* (1994) he is played by Campbell Scott.
   Biography: 1946, *Robert Benchley* by his son Nathaniel.
■ FEATURE APPEARANCES: Headline Shooter 33. Dancing Lady 33. Rafter Romance 34. Social Register 34. China Seas 35. Piccadilly Jim 36. Live Love and Learn 37. Broadway Melody of 1938 37. Hired Wife 40. *Foreign Correspondent* 40. Nice Girl 41. *The Reluctant Dragon* 41. You'll Never Get Rich 41. Three Girls about Town 41. Bedtime Story 41. Take a Letter Darling 42. The Major and the Minor 42. *I Married a Witch* 42. Flesh and Fantasy 43. Young and Willing 43. Song of Russia 43. The Sky's the Limit 43. Her Primitive Man 44. National Barn Dance 44. See Here Private Hargrove 44. Practically Yours 44. Janie 44. Pan Americana 45. *It's In the Bag* 45. Weekend at the Waldorf 45. Kiss and Tell 45. Duffy's Tavern 45. The Stork Club 45. *Road to Utopia* 45. The Bride Wore Boots 46. Snafu 46. Janie Gets Married 46. Blue Skies 46.
✪ For assuming a subtly fantasticated screen version of his own cosmopolitan personality, and delighting the world by doing so. *Road to Utopia.*

¶ In Milwaukee last month a man died laughing at one of his own jokes. That's what makes it so tough for us outsiders. We have to fight home competition. – *R.B.*
   It took me fifteen years to discover that I had no talent for writing. But by then I couldn't give it up because I was too famous. – *R.B.*
   Benchley tended to spend his later years drinking in Hollywood's Garden of Allah hotel. When he finally left to go east he pointedly refrained from favouring a hated doorman. 'Sir,' said the man, 'aren't you going to remember me?' 'Sure,' said Benchley, 'I'll write you every day.'
   Leaving a restaurant, Benchley approached what appeared to be a uniformed commissionaire and muttered: 'Get me a taxi.' The man bridled and said: 'Sir, I am a rear admiral in the United States Navy.' 'Really,' said Benchley. 'Then get me a battleship.'

Bendix, William (1906–1964).
Familiar American character actor who usually played the tough guy with the heart of gold; his broken nose, raucous Brooklyn accent and air of amiable stupidity endeared him to a generation.
■ Woman of the Year 42. The McGuerins from Brooklyn 42. Brooklyn Orchid 42. Wake Island (AAN) 42. *The Glass Key* (as a murderous thug) 42. Who Done It? 42. Star Spangled Rhythm 42. The Crystal Ball 43. Taxi Mister 43. China 43. Hostages 43. Guadalcanal Diary 43. *Lifeboat* 43. *The Hairy Ape* 44. Abroad with Two Yanks 44. Greenwich

Village 44. It's in the Bag 45. Don Juan Quilligan 45. A Bell for Adano 45. Sentimental Journey 45. *The Blue Dahlia* 46. The Dark Corner 46. Two Years Before the Mast 46. White Tie and Tails 46. I'll Be Yours 46. Blaze of Noon 47. Calcutta 47. The Web 47. Where There's Life 47. Variety Girl 47. *The Time of Your Life* 48. Race Street 48. The Babe Ruth Story 48. *The Life of Riley* 49. A Connecticut Yankee in King Arthur's Court 49. *The Big Steal* 49. Streets of Laredo 49. Cover Up 49. Johnny Holiday 49. Kill the Umpire 50. Gambling House 50. Submarine Command 51. *Detective Story* 51. Macao 52. A Girl in Every Port 52. Blackbeard the Pirate 52. Dangerous Mission 54. Crashout 55. Battle Stations 56. The Deep Six 58. Idol on Parade (GB) 59. The Rough and the Smooth (GB) 59. Boy's Night Out 62. Johnny Nobody (GB) 62. The Young and the Brave 63. For Love or Money 63. Law of the Lawless 64. The Phony American 64. Young Fury 65.

TV series: *The Life of Riley* 53–58. Overland Stage 60.

¶ Neanderthal man reincarnated in Brooklyn. – *David Shipman*

Benedek, Barbara.
American screenwriter.
The Big Chill (co-w, AAN) 83. Immediate Family 89. Men Don't Leave (co-w) 90, etc.

Benedek, Laslo (1907–1992).
Hungarian director in Hollywood; output surprisingly meagre.
■ The Kissing Bandit 48. Port of New York 49. Storm over the Tiber 52. *Death of a Salesman* 52. *The Wild One* 54. Bengal Brigade 54. Kinder Mütter und ein General (Ger.) 55. Affair in Havana 57. Moment of Danger (GB) 62. Namu the Killer Whale (& p) 66. The Daring Game 68. The Night Visitor 71. Assault on Agathon 74.

Benedict, Billy (1906–).
American character actor who in his youth was one of the original 'Bowery Boys'; now plays cabbies, bartenders, etc.
Doubting Thomas 35. Way Down East 35. Ramona 36. Libeled Lady 36. That I May Live 37. King of the Newsboys 38. Little Tough Guys in Society 38. Newsboys' Home 39. Code of the Streets 39. Call a Messenger 39. The Bowery Boy 40. My Little Chickadee 40. The Mad Doctor 41. Lady in a Jam 42. Clancy Street Boys 43. Adventures of the Flying Cadets 43. Follow the Leader 44. Docks of New York 45. Hollywood and Vine 45. Spook Busters 46. The Hucksters 47. Hard Boiled Mahoney 47. Fighting Fools 49. Ghost Chasers 51. Last Train from Gun Hill 59. Lover Come Back 61. The Hallelujah Trail 65. Hello Dolly 69. The Sting 73. Farewell My Lovely 75. Won Ton Ton 76, many others.

Benedict, Dirk (1945–) (D. Niewoehner).
Standard-type American leading man with mainly television experience.
Journey from Darkness (TV) 75. Cruise into Terror (TV) 78. Scavenger Hunt 79. Underground Aces 81. Body Slam 87. Blue Tornado 90. Shadow Force 92, etc.
TV series: Chopper One 74. Battlestar Galactica 78. The A Team 83–87.

Benedict, Richard (1916–1984) (Riccardo Benedetto).
American leading man, usually in second features; sometimes played the heavy.
Till the End of Time 46. Crossfire 47. City Across the River 49. State Penitentiary 50. Ace in the

Hole 51. Okinawa 52. The Juggler 53. Hoodlum Empire 55. The Shrike 55. Monkey on my Back 57. Ocean's Eleven 60, etc.

Benet, Stephen Vincent (1898–1943).
American poet and novelist whose *The Devil and Daniel Webster* was filmed as *All that Money Can Buy*. His *The Sobbin' Women* was the basis of the musical *Seven Brides for Seven Brothers*, filmed in 1954.

Ben Hur.
There were several silent versions of Lew Wallace's semi-biblical adventure novel. Best known is MGM's lavish spectacular of 1926, directed by Fred Niblo with Ramon Navarro and Francis X. Bushman; it was reissued with sound effects in 1931. In 1959 it was remade by MGM and William Wyler, with Charlton Heston and Stephen Boyd: the greatest praise went to the chariot race sequence directed by Andrew Marton with the assistance of Yakima Canutt.

Benigni, Roberto (1952–).
Italian comedian, director, screenwriter and actor who was picked to star in a new *Pink Panther* movie. His *Johnny Stecchino* set box-office records in Italy.
I Love You Berlinguer (Berlinguer ti Voglio Bene) (a) 77. Tu mi Turbi (a, wd) 83. Non ci Resta che Piangere (a, wd) 84. Down by Law (a) 86. The Little Devil (Il Piccolo Diavolo) 87 (a, wd). The Voice of the Moon (La Voce della Luna) (a) 90. Johnny Stecchino (a, wd) 91. Night on Earth (a) 91. Son of the Pink Panther (a) 93. The Monster (Le Monstre) (a, co-w, d) 94, etc.

Bening, Annette (1958–).
American leading actress. She is married to actor and director Warren Beatty.
The Great Outdoors 88. Valmont 89. Grifters (AAN) 90. Postcards from the Edge 90. Guilty by Suspicion 90. Regarding Henry 91. Bugsy 91. Love Affair 94, etc.

Benjamin, Arthur (1893–1960).
Anglo-Australian composer.
The Man Who Knew Too Much 34. The Scarlet Pimpernel 34. Turn of the Tide 35. Under the Red Robe 36. Master of Bankdam 47. An Ideal Husband 48. Above Us the Waves 55. Naked Earth 57, etc.

Benjamin, Richard (1938–).
Diffident-seeming American leading man who now concentrates on directing. Married Paula Prentiss in 1961.
Thunder over the Plains 53. *Goodbye Columbus* 69. Catch 22 70. *Diary of a Mad Housewife* 70. Marriage of a Young Stockbroker 71. Portnoy's Complaint 72. The Last of Sheila 73. Westworld 73. The Sunshine Boys 76. House Calls 78. Scavenger Hunt 79. The First Family 80. How to Beat the High Cost of Living 80. The Last Married Couple in America 80. Saturday the 14th 81. My Favorite Year (d only) 82, etc. Racing with the Moon (d only) 83. City Heat (d only) 84. The Money Pit (d only) 85. Little Nikita (d only) 88. My Stepmother Is an Alien 88. Downtown (d only) 90. Mermaids (d only) 90. Made in America (d only) 93. Milk Money (d) 94, etc.
TV series: He and She 67. Quark 78.

¶ If you are married to an actress and your wife is getting all the calls, it's very hard on the ego. – *R.B.*

Bennent, David (1966–).
Swiss child actor, best known for playing the boy Oskar in *The Tin Drum* 79.
Legend 86, etc.

Bennet, Spencer Gordon (1893–1987).
American silent actor and stuntman who became a famous director of serials and made 52 in all.
Rogue of the Rio Grande 30. Mysterious Pilot 37. Arizona Bound 42. Batman and Robin 48. Atom Man vs Superman 50. Adventures of Sir Galahad 51. Brave Warrior (feature) 52. The Atomic Submarine (feature) 60. The Bounty Killer (feature) 65, many others.

Bennett, Alan (1934–).
British dramatist, screenwriter and occasional actor who first gained fame as one of the four performers in *Beyond the Fringe*, a satirical revue of the 60s that also featured Peter Cook, Dudley Moore and Jonathan Miller.
Autobiography: 1994, *Writing Home*.
AS WRITER: An Englishman Abroad (TV) 83. A Private Function 84. Prick Up Your Ears 87. 102 Boulevard Haussmann (TV) 90. A Question of Attribution (TV) 91. The Madness of King George 95.

¶ My claim to literary fame is that I used to deliver meat to a woman who became T.S. Eliot's mother-in-law. – *A.B.*

Bennett, Alma (1889–1958).
American silent-screen vamp.
Why Men Leave Home 14. The Silent Lover 16. The Dawn of a Tomorrow 19. Smiling Jim 22. Three Jumps Ahead 23. The Face on the Barroom Floor 23. Why Men Leave Home 24. The Lost World 25. The Light of Western Stars 25. Don Juan's Three Nights 26. Long Pants 27. Compassion 27. The Grain of Dust 28. Two Men and a Maid 29. Midnight Daddies 30, etc.

Bennett, Arnold (1867–1931).
British novelist, little of whose work has been filmed. *Buried Alive* has, however, been seen in several versions, under its own title, as *The Great Adventure*, as *His Double Life*, and as *Holy Matrimony*. British studios filmed *The Card* with Alec Guinness and less successfully *Dear Mr Prohack* with Cecil Parker.

Bennett, Barbara (1902–1958).
American leading lady of a few 20s films. Sister of Constance and Joan Bennett.
Syncopation 29. Mother's Boy 29. Love Among the Millionaires 30, etc.

Bennett, Belle (1891–1932).
American leading lady of the silent screen.
A Soul in Trust 18. His Supreme Moment 25. If Marriage Fails 25. *Stella Dallas* 25. The Fourth Commandment 27. The Way of All Flesh 27. Mother Machree 28. The Iron Mask 29. Courage 30. Recaptured Love 31. The Big Shot 31, etc.

Bennett, Billy (1887–1942).
English music-hall comedian and monologuist, billed as 'Almost a Gentleman', who appeared in films of the 20s and 30s. Born in Liverpool, the son of an acrobat, he also partnered James Carew and, later, Albert Whelan, in a black-face act, Alexander and Mose, on radio and in the halls.
Robin Hood 22. The Amateur Gentleman 26. Radio Parade of 1935 35. Soft Lights and Sweet Music 36. Calling All Stars 37. Almost a Gentleman 38. Young Man's Fancy 39, etc.

¶ Nobody who ever saw him is likely to forget that rubicund, unaesthetic countenance, that black, plastered quiff, that sergeant-major's moustache, that dreadful dinner-jacket, that well-used dickey and seedy collar, the too-short

rousers, the hobnail boots, the red silk
handkerchief tucked into the waistcoat, the
continual perspiration which was the outward
and visible sign of a mind struggling for expression
– these things will not be forgotten – *James Agate*

Bennett, Bruce (1909–) (Herman Brix).
Athletic American leading man who started in
films by playing Tarzan and subsequently settled
down as a familiar flannel-suited second lead. Used
his own name until 1940.

Student Tour 34. *The New Adventures of Tarzan*
35 (re-edited 1938 as *Tarzan and the Green Goddess*).
Danger Patrol 37. Before I Hang 40. Atlantic
Convoy 42. The More the Merrier 43. Sahara 43.
Mildred Pierce 45. The Treasure of the Sierra
Madre 47. Silver River 48. Task Force 49. The
Doctor and the Girl 49. Without Honor 50. Sudden
Fear 52. Dream Wife 53. Strategic Air Command
55. Three Violent People 57. The Outsider 61,
many others.

Bennett, Charles (1899–).
British screenwriter who worked on some of
Hitchcock's 30s films and later moved to
Hollywood. Usually worked in collaboration.
Recently he was busy rewriting *Blackmail* for a
forthcoming remake. He claims to be 'the oldest
working screenwriter of all time'.

Blackmail 29. The Man Who Knew Too Much
34. *The Thirty-nine Steps* 35. Secret Agent 36.
Sabotage 37. King Solomon's Mines 37. The Young
in Heart 38. Balalaika 39. *Foreign Correspondent*
(AAN) 40. Joan of Paris 42. Reap the Wild Wind
42. The Story of Dr Wassell 44. Ivy 47. Madness of
the Heart (& d) 48. Black Magic 49. Where Danger
Lives 51. The Green Glove 52. No Escape (& d) 53.
The Story of Mankind 57. The Lost World 60. Five
Weeks in a Balloon 62. War Gods of the Deep 65,
etc.

Bennett, Compton (1900–1974) (Robert
Compton-Bennett).
British director, former editor.
■ *The Seventh Veil* 45. The Years Between 46.
Daybreak 48. My Own True Love 49. *That Forsyte
Woman* 49. *King Solomon's Mines* 50. So Little Time
52. The Gift Horse 52. It Started in Paradise 52.
Desperate Moment 53. That Woman Opposite 57.
After the Ball 57. The Flying Scot 57. Beyond the
Curtain 60. How to Undress in Public Without
Undue Embarrassment 65.

Bennett, Constance (1904–1965).
Glamorous American star of the 30s, adept at
worldly roles; sister of Barbara and Joan Bennett.
■ Reckless Youth 22. Evidence 22. What's Wrong
with the Women? 22. Cytherea 24. Into the Net
24. *The Goose Hangs High* 25. Married 25. Code of
the West 25. My Son 25. My Wife and I 25. *The
Goose Woman* 25. Sally Irene and Mary 25.
Wandering Fires 25. The Pinch Hitter 26. This
Thing Called Love 29. Son of the Gods 30. Rich
People 30. Common Clay 30. *Three Faces East* 30.
Sin Takes a Holiday 30. The Easiest Way 31. Born
to Love 31. The Common Law 31. Bought 31. Lady
with a Past 32. *What Price Hollywood?* 32. Two
Against the World 32. Rockabye 32. Our Betters 33.
Bed of Roses 33. After Tonight 33. *Moulin Rouge*
33. Affairs of Cellini 34. Outcast Lady 34. After
Office Hours 35. Everything is Thunder (GB) 36.
Ladies in Love 36. *Topper* (as a ghost) 37. *Merrily
We Live* 38. Service de Luxe 38. Topper Takes a
Trip 38. Tailspin 39. *Escape to Glory* 40. Law of the
Tropics 41. *Two-Faced Woman* 41. Wild Bill Hickok
Rides 41. Sin Town 42. Madame Spy 42. Paris
Underground 46. Centennial Summer 46. *The
Unsuspected* 47. Smart Woman 48. Angel on the

Amazon 49. As Young as You Feel 51. It Should
Happen to You 53. *Madame X* 65.

¶ She seemed to me the quintessence of a movie
star. Everything about her shone – her
burnished head, her jewels, her famous smile, her
lovely long legs, and the highly publicised fact
that she pulled down 30,000 bucks a week. – *David
Niven*

Bennett, Enid (1895–1969).
Australian leading lady in Hollywood films of the
20s.

Princess in the Dark 17. The Vamp 18. The
Haunted Bedroom 19. Hairpins 20. Her Husband's
Friend 21. Robin Hood 22. Scandalous Tongues
22. The Courtship of Miles Standish 23. The Sea
Hawk 24. A Woman's Heart 26. The Wrong Mr
Wright 27. Good Medicine 29. Skippy 31. Meet
Dr Christian 39. Strike Up the Band 40, many
others.

Bennett, Hywel (1944–).
Welsh leading man who has usually played roles
requiring a feigning of innocence.
■ *The Family Way* 66. Twisted Nerve 68. *The Virgin
Soldiers* 69. The Buttercup Chain 70. Loot 71. Percy
71. Endless Night 72. Alice's Adventures in
Wonderland 72. The Love Ban 72. Malice
Aforethought (TV) 79. Tinker Tailor Soldier Spy
(TV) 79. Murder Elite (TV) 85. Deadline 87.
Deadly Advice 94.

TV series: *Shelley* 80–85.

Bennett, Jill (1930–1990).
Unusual-looking British actress who generally
played emancipated roles. Committed suicide. She
was formerly married to John Osborne (1970–77).

Autobiography: 1983, *Godfrey: A Special Time
Remembered* (about her relationship with actor Sir
Godfrey Tearle).

Moulin Rouge 53. Hell Below Zero 54. *Lust for
Life* 56. The Criminal 60. The Skull 65. *The Nanny*
65. *Inadmissible Evidence* 68. *The Charge of the Light
Brigade* 68. Julius Caesar 70. I Want What I Want
71. Mister Quilp 75. Full Circle 77. For Your Eyes
Only 81. Britannia Hospital 82. Lady Jane 86.
Hawks 89. The Sheltering Sky 90, etc.

¶ My idea of heaven is to be eternally rehearsing.
– *J.B.*

Bennett, Joan (1910–1990).
Popular American leading lady of the 30s and 40s,
one of the most attractive stars of her time. Sister
of Barbara and Constance Bennett. She was
formerly married to producer Walter Wanger.

Autobiography: 1970, *The Bennett Playbill*.
■ The Valley of Decision 15. Power 28. The Divine
Lady 29. Bulldog Drummond 29. Three Live Ghosts
29. Disraeli 29. Mississippi Gambler 29. Puttin' On
the Ritz 30. Crazy that Way 30. Moby Dick 30.
Maybe It's Love 30. Scotland Yard 30. Many a Slip
31. Doctors' Wives 31. Hush Money 31. She
Wanted a Millionaire 32. Careless Lady 32. The
Trial of Vivienne Ware 32. Weekends Only 32. Wild
Girl 32. Me and My Gal 32. Arizona to Broadway
32. *Little Women* 33. The Pursuit of Happiness 34.
The Man Who Reclaimed His Head 34. *Private
Worlds* 35. Mississippi 35. Two for Tonight 35. The
Man Who Broke the Bank at Monte Carlo 35. She
Couldn't Take It 35. Thirteen Hours by Air 36.
Big Brown Eyes 36. Two in a Crowd 36. Wedding
Present 36. Vogues of 1938 37. I Met My Love
Again 38. The Texans 38. Artists and Models
Abroad 38. Trade Winds 39. The Man in the Iron
Mask 39. *The Housekeeper's Daughter* 39. Green Hell
40. The House across the Bay 40. The Man I

Married 40. Son of Monte Cristo 40. She Knew All
the Answers 41. *Man Hunt* 41. Wild Geese Calling
41. Confirm or Deny 42. Twin Beds 42. The Wife
Takes a Flyer 42. Girl Trouble 42. Margin for Error
43. *The Woman in the Window* 44. Nob Hill 45.
Scarlet Street 45. Colonel Effingham's Raid 46. *The
Macomber Affair* 47. The Secret Beyond the Door
47. The Woman on the Beach 47. The Scar 47.
The Reckless Moment 49. *Father of the Bride* 50. For
Heaven's Sake 50. Father's Little Dividend 51. The
Guy Who Came Back 51. Highway Dragnet 54.
We're No Angels 55. There's Always Tomorrow
56. Navy Wife 56. Desire in the Dust 60. House of
Dark Shadows 70. Inn of the Damned 71. Gidget
Gets Married (TV) 71. The Eyes of Charles Sand
(TV) 72. Suspiria 77. Suddenly, Love (TV) 78.
Divorce Wars (TV) 82.

TV series: Too Young to Go Steady 59. Dark
Shadows 66–71.

¶ The golden age is gone, and with it most of the
people of great taste. It doesn't seem to be fun
any more. – *J.B.*, 1984.

My film career faded. A man can go on playing
certain roles till he's 60. But not a woman. – *J.B.*

Bennett, John (1928–).
Swarthy British character actor.

The Challenge 59. *The Barber of Stamford Hill* 62.
Kaleidoscope 66. The Forsyte Saga (TV) 68. The
House that Dripped Blood 70. The House in
Nightmare Park 73. Hitler, the Last Ten Days (as
Goebbels) 74. The Message 77. Eye of the Needle
81. Antonia and Jane (TV) 91, etc.

Bennett, Marjorie (1894–1982).
American character actress, in films since early
silent experience as a bathing beauty.

Monsieur Verdoux 47. Limelight 52. Young at
Heart 55. *Whatever Happened to Baby Jane?* 62. Mary
Poppins 64. Charley Varrick 73. Mother, Jugs and
Speed 76, many others.

Bennett, Richard (1873–1944).
Dapper American stage actor, a leading figure of
his day; father of Barbara, Constance and Joan
Bennett. Film appearances rare.

The Eternal City 23. The Home Towners 28.
Arrowsmith 32. *If I Had a Million* (as the millionaire)
32. Nana 34. *The Magnificent Ambersons* 42. Journey
into Fear 43, etc.

Bennett, Richard Rodney (1936–).
British composer.

Interpol 57. Indiscreet 58. Only Two Can Play
61. Billy Liar 63. One Way Pendulum 64. The
Nanny 65. Far from the Madding Crowd 67. Secret
Ceremony 68. Figures in a Landscape 70. Nicholas
and Alexandra (AAN) 71. Lady Caroline Lamb 72.
Voices 73. Murder on the Orient Express (AAN) 74.
Permission to Kill 75. Sherlock Holmes in New
York 77. Equus 77. Yanks 79. Brinks 79. The
Return of the Soldier 82. Murder with Mirrors (TV)
84. The Ebony Tower (TV) 84. Enchanted April 91.
Four Weddings and a Funeral 94, etc.

Bennett, Tony (1926–) (Antonio Benedetto).
Heavyweight Italian-American ballad singer,
famous for leaving his heart in San Francisco.
Principal film appearance in *The Oscar*.

Benny, Jack (1894–1974) (Benjamin Kubelsky).
Celebrated American comedian of radio, TV and
occasional films. His inimitable reproachful look,
his pretence of meanness and his much maligned
violin are among the trademarks which kept him
popular for forty years. He graduated from

burlesque, and later married his radio leading lady Mary Livingstone (Sadye Marks).

Biographies: 1976, *Jack Benny* by Irving Fein. 1978, *Jack Benny* by Mary Livingstone Marks and others.

Autobiography: 1990, *Sunday Nights at Seven: The Jack Benny Story.*

■ *Hollywood Revue of 1929* 29. Chasing Rainbows 30. Medicine Man 30. Transatlantic Merry-Go-Round 34. Broadway Melody of 1936 35. It's in the Air 35. The Big Broadcast of 1937 36. College Holiday 36. Artists and Models 37. Artists and Models Abroad 38. Man About Town 39. Buck Benny Rides Again 39. Love Thy Neighbour 40. *Charley's Aunt* 41. *To Be or Not To Be* (an outstanding performance) 42. George Washington Slept Here 42. The Meanest Man in the World 43. Hollywood Canteen 44. *It's in the Bag* 45. *The Horn Blows at Midnight* 45. A Guide for the Married Man 67.

TV series: *The Jack Benny Show* 50–65.

~Benny also made gag appearances in Without Reservations 47. Beau James 57. It's a Mad Mad Mad Mad World 63.

¶ Hold-up Man: 'Your money or your life! Come on, come on, hurry up!' Benny: 'I'm thinking it over!'
He couldn't ad-lib a belch after a Hungarian dinner. – *Fred Allen* (in jest)
He didn't just stand on the stage. He owned it. – *Bob Hope*

Benoît-Lévy, Jean (1883–1959).
French director who also wrote books on cinema.
La Maternelle 33. Hélène 37. La Mort du Cygne 38. Fire in the Straw 43, etc.

Benson, George (1911–1983).
British character actor of stage, screen and TV, the nervous 'little man' of countless films.
Keep Fit 37. Convoy 40. The October Man 48. Pool of London 50. The Man in the White Suit 51. The Captain's Paradise 53. Doctor in the House 54. Value for Money 56. Dracula 58. A Jolly Bad Fellow 64. A Home of Your Own 65. The Creeping Flesh 72, etc.

Benson, Lucille (1914–1984).
American character actress.
The Fugitive Kind 60. Little Fauss and Big Halsy 70. Duel 71. Cactus in the Snow 72. Tom Sawyer 73. Huckleberry Finn 74. Reflections of Murder 74, etc.
TV series: Nashville 99 77. Bosom Buddies 80–81.

Benson, Martin (1918–).
British character actor often seen as a smooth foreign-looking crook.
The Blind Goddess 49. West of Zanzibar 54. The King and I (US) 56. Windom's Way 58. The Three Worlds of Gulliver 60. Cleopatra 62. Behold a Pale Horse 64. Goldfinger 64. The Secret of My Success 65. Pope Joan 72. The Omen 76. Mohammed 77. The Sea Wolves 80. Sphinx 81, many others.
TV series: Sword of Freedom 57.

Benson, Robby (1956–) (Robert Segal).
American leading man, on stage from the age of five.
Jory 73. *Jeremy* 73. *Death Be Not Proud* (TV) 75. Lucky Lady 76. The Death of Richie (TV) 76. One on One (& co-w) 77. The End 78. Ice Castles 78. Walk Proud 79. Die Laughing 80. Tribute 80. The Chosen 81. National Lampoon Goes to the Movies 82. City Limits 85. Rent-A-Cop 88. White Hot (& d) 88. Modern Love (& wd) 90. Beauty and the Beast (voice) 91. Invasion of Privacy 92. The Webbers 93, etc.
TV series: Tough Cookies 86.

¶ I was into show business straight from the womb. – *R.B.*
Cute as Bambi and twice as smarmy. – *An anonymous critic*

Benson, Sally (1900–1972).
American screenwriter, former film critic and novelist.
Shadow of a Doubt (co-w) 43. Meet Me in St Louis (oa) 44. Junior Miss (oa) 45. Anna and the King of Siam (co-w, AAN) 46. Come to the Stable (co-w) 49. No Man of Her Own (co-w) 50. The Farmer Takes a Wife (co-w) 53. Summer Magic (co-w) 63. Joy in the Morning (co-w) 65. The Flying Nun (co-w) 66.

Bentine, Michael (1922–).
Anglo-Peruvian comedian, popular on stage and TV, who has made several unsuccessful attempts to film his goonish style of humour, for example in *The Sandwich Man* 66.

Bentivoglio, Fabrizio (1957–).
Italian leading actor, from the stage.
Masoch 80. Salomè 85. Via Montenapoleone 85. Marrakech Express 88. Turné 89. Italia-Germania 4 a 3 90. Americano Rosso 91, etc.

Bentley, Irene (1904–1965).
American leading actress of the 30s who made a few films and then suddenly dropped from sight.
My Weakness 33. Smoky 33. Frontier Marshall 33.

Bentley, John (1916–).
British leading man who left the stage in 1946 to play in innumerable low-budget crime dramas, including series about Paul Temple and The Toff.
Hills of Donegal 47. Calling Paul Temple 48. The Happiest Days of Your Life 49. The Lost Hours 51. The Scarlet Spear 53. Golden Ivory 55. Istanbul (US) 58. Submarine Seahawk 59. The Singer Not the Song 60. Mary Had a Little 61. The Fur Collar 63, many others.
TV series: African Patrol 59.

Bentley, Thomas (c. 1880–195*).
British director, former Dickensian impersonator, who began in films by making silent versions of several Dickens novels.
Young Woodley 30. *Hobson's Choice* 31. The Scotland Yard Mystery 33. *Those Were the Days* 34. The Old Curiosity Shop 35. Music Hath Charms 35. Marigold 38. The Middle Watch 39. Lucky to Me 39. Old Mother Riley's Circus 41, many others.

Benton, Robert (1932–).
American magazine writer and art director who teamed up with David Newman to become co-screenwriter of such movies as *Bonnie and Clyde* (AAN), There Was a Crooked Man, What's Up Doc, and Superman.
AS DIRECTOR: Bad Company (& co-w) 70. The Late Show (& co-w) (AAN) 77. *Kramer vs Kramer* (AA) 79. Still of the Night 82. Places of the Heart (AAw, AANd) 84. Nadine (wd) 87. The House on Carroll Street 88. Billy Bathgate 91. Nobody's Fool (wd) 94.

¶ The success of *Bonnie and Clyde* made me very miserable. It's some deep-seated neurosis I have. – *R.B.*

Beranger, André (1895–1973).
Australian Shakespearean actor who joined D. W. Griffith in Hollywood and appeared in mainly silent films.
The Birth of a Nation 15. Intolerance 16. Manhattan Madness 16. Broken Blossoms 19. The Bright Shawl 23. Beau Brummell 24. The Grand Duchess and the Waiter 26. Fig Leaves 26. Strange Cargo 29. Surrender 31. Mama Loves Papa 33. Over My Dead Body 42. Road House 48, many others.

Berard, Christian (1902–1949).
Noted French theatrical designer who was responsible for the art direction of three of Cocteau's films.
La Belle et la Bête 47. L'Aigle à Deux Têtes 47. Les Parents Terribles 48.

Berenger, Tom (1950–).
Brooding American leading man in the John Garfield mould.
Johnny We Hardly Knew Ye (TV) 77. Butch and Sundance 79. Flesh and Blood (TV) 80. The Dogs of War 81. The Big Chill 83. Eddie and the Cruiser 83. Platoon (AAN) 86. Someone to Watch Over Me 87. Betrayed 88. Last Rites 88. Shoot to Kill 88. Born on the Fourth of July 89. The Field 90. Shattered 91. At Play in the Fields of the Lord 91. Sniper 93. Sliver 93. Gettysburg 93. Major League II 94. Chasers 94, etc.

Berens, Harold.
English comedian and character actor, much on the radio, especially the long-running show *Ignorance Is Bliss* (1946–53).
Candelight in Algeria 43. The Man from Morocco 45. Up for the Cup 50. A Kid for Two Farthings 55. The Big Money 56. The Pure Hell of St Trinian's 59. What a Whopper! 61. Live Now, Pay Later 62. Mozambique 66. The Magic Christian 70. Straight On till Morning 72. Trail of the Pink Panther 82. Hear My Song 91, etc.
~Catchphrase: What a geezer!

Berenson, Marisa (1947–).
International fashion model who has appeared in films.
Death in Venice 72. Cabaret 72. Barry Lyndon 75. Killer Fish 78. Naked Sun 80. S.O.B. 81. Secret Diary of Sigmund Freud 84. Night of the Cyclone 90. White Hunter, Black Heart 90. Night of the White Rabbit 92. The Fugitives 93, etc.
¶ My ultimate goal is to become a saint. – *M.B.*

Beresford, Bruce (1940–).
Australian director and screenwriter.
The Adventures of Barry Mackenzie 72. Barry Mackenzie Holds His Own 74. Side by Side 75. Don's Party 76. *The Getting of Wisdom* 77. Money Movers 78. *Breaker Morant* (AAN) 80. The Club 80. Puberty Blues 81. Tender Mercies (AAN) 82. King David 84. The Fringe Dwellers 85. Crimes of the Heart 86. Aria (co-d) 87. *Driving Miss Daisy* (d) (AA) 89. Her Alibi (d) 89. *Mister Johnson* (wd) 90. *Black Robe* (d) 91. Rich in Love (d) 93. A Good Man in Africa 94. Silent Fall 94, etc.

Beresford, Harry (1864–1944).
British general-purpose actor in Hollywood from silent days.
The Quarterback 26. Charles Chan Carries On 31. So Big 32. Dr X 32. The Sign of the Cross 32. Murders in the Zoo 33. Dinner at Eight 33. Cleopatra 34. The Little Minister 34. Seven Keys to Baldpate 35. David Copperfield 35. Follow the

Fleet 36. The Prince and the Pauper 37. They Won't Forget 37, many others.

Berg, Gertrude (1899–1966) (Gertrude Edelstein). Plump American character actress famous on TV and radio as Molly of the Goldberg family. She appeared in a film version, *Molly* 51, also in another TV series, *Mrs G Goes to College* 61.

Bergdahl, Victor (1878–1939).
Swedish animator of the silent era.

Bergen, Candice (1946–).
Stylish American leading lady, daughter of Edgar Bergen. She married film director Louis Malle in 1980.
   Autobiography: 1984, *Knock Wood*.
■ *The Group* 66. The Sand Pebbles 66. The Day the Fish Came Out 67. Vivre Pour Vivre 67. The Magus 68. Getting Straight 70. Soldier Blue 70. The Adventures 70. *Carnal Knowledge* 71. The Hunting Party 71. T R Baskin 72. 11 Harrowhouse 74. Bite the Bullet 75. The Wind and the Lion 76. The Cassandra Crossing 76. The Domino Principle 77. A Night Full of Rain 77. Oliver's Story 78. Starting Over (AAN) 79. Rich and Famous 81. Gandhi 82. Stick 84. Hollywood Wives (TV) 85.
TV series: Murphy Brown 88–91.

¶ There are moments when I perceive us as being on the brink of another dark age, a media blitzkrieg of mindlessness. – *C.B.*

   It takes a long time to grow up. Longer than they tell you. – *C.B.*

Bergen, Edgar (1903–1978).
Mild-mannered Swedish-American ventriloquist, manipulator of Charlie McCarthy and Mortimer Snerd (special AA 1937); latterly a character actor.
   The Goldwyn Follies 38. Letter of Introduction 38. *You Can't Cheat an Honest Man* 39. *Charlie McCarthy Detective* 39. Look Who's Laughing 41. Here We Go Again 42. Stage Door Canteen 43. Song of the Open Road 44. *I Remember Mama* 48. The Hanged Man 64. One Way Wahine 66. Don't Make Waves 67. The Homecoming (TV) 70, etc.

¶ I'm one of those people who always needs a mountain to climb. When I get up a mountain as far as I think I'm going to get, I try to find another mountain. – *P.B.*

Berger, Helmut (1944–) (Helmut Steinberger).
Handsome Austrian actor who gives a sinister edge to his performances.
   The Damned 69. Un Beau Monstre 70. The Garden of the Finzi-Continis 71. Dorian Gray 72. Ash Wednesday 73. Ludwig 73. Conversation Piece 75. The Romantic Englishwoman 75. Madam Kitty 77. Roses of Danzig 79. Heroin 80. Victory 83. Code Name Emerald 85. Tunnel 85. Les Prédateurs de la Nuit 87. Er-Sie-Es 89. Never in Life (Nie im

Leben) (& co-w, d) 91. The Laughter of Maca Daracs (Das Lachen der Maca Daracs) 91. Once Arizona (Einamal Arizona) 91. Ludwig 1881 93, etc.
   TV series: Dynasty 83–84.

Berger, Ludwig (1892–1969) (Ludwig Bamberger).
German director who made some international films.
   Ein Glas Wasser 22. The Waltz Dream 26. The Woman from Moscow (US) 28. Sins of the Fathers 29. Die Meistersinger 29. The Vagabond King (US) 30. Playboy of Paris 30. Waltz Time in Vienna 33. Three Waltzes 39. The Thief of Baghdad (GB/US) 40. Ballerina (Fr.) 50, etc.

Berger, Nicole (1934–1967).
French leading lady.
   Juliette 52. Game of Love 54. Le Premier Mai 57. Love is My Profession 58. Les Dragueurs 59. Shoot the Pianist 62, etc.

Berger, Senta (1941–).
Austrian leading lady in international films.
   Die Lindenwirtin vom Donaus Trand (debut) 57. The Journey 59. The Secret Ways 61. The Good Soldier Schweik 62. Sherlock Holmes and the Deadly Necklace 62. The Victors 63. Major Dundee 65. The Glory Guys 65. Cast a Giant Shadow 66. The Quiller Memorandum 67. Our Man in Marrakesh 67. The Ambushers 67. Treasure of San Gennaro 68. De Sade 69. Ludwig 72. The Scarlet Letter 72. Der Reigen 73. The Swiss Conspiracy 75. Cross of Iron 77. The Two Lives of Mattia Pascal (Le Due Vite di Mattia Pascal) 84. The Flying Devils 85. Killing Cars 86. Swiss Cheese 87, etc.

Berger, William (1928–).
Austrian-born leading actor, mainly in Italian films.
   The Man with the Balloons (It.) 65. The Murder Clinic (It.) 66. The Day the Fish Came Out (Ger.) 67. Every Bastard a King (It.) 70. Sabata (It.) 70. Today We Kill, Tomorrow We Die (It.) 71. Superfly TNT (US) 73. Three Tough Guys (It.) 74. Oil (It.) 78. Hercules (It.) 83. Day of the Cobra (It.) 84. Hercules II (It.) 85. Tex and the Lord of the Deep (It.) 85. The Berlin Affair (Ger.) 85. Hell Hunters 87, etc.

Bergerac, Jacques (1927–).
French leading man, former lawyer, in Hollywood from 1953. He was formerly married to actresses Ginger Rogers and Dorothy Malone.
   Les Girls 57. Gigi 58. Thunder in the Sun 59. The Hypnotic Eye 60. Taffy and the Jungle Hunter 65, etc.

Bergere, Ouida (1885–1974).
American scriptwriter of the 20s (*On with the Dance*, *The Cheat*, etc.) who also acted in a few films before marrying Basil Rathbone and becoming Hollywood's most lavish hostess.

Berggren, Thommy (1937–).
Swedish leading actor.
   Sunday in September 63. Raven's End 63. *Elvira Madigan* 67. The Adventurers 70. Joe Hill 71. Giliap 73. Kristoffers Hus 79. Broken Sky 82. The Mountain on the Other Side of the Moon 83. *Strindberg* (TV) 85. *Gosta Berlings Saga* (TV) 86, etc.

Berghof, Herbert (1909–1990).
Austrian character actor long on American stage, also as drama teacher; films rare.
   Assignment Paris 52. *Five Fingers* 52. Red Planet Mars 52. Fräulein 58. Cleopatra 62. Harry and

Tonto 74. Those Lips Those Eyes 80. Times Square 83. Target 85, etc.

Bergin, Patrick (1954–).
Irish leading actor in international films, a former teacher.
   The Courier 87. Taffin 88. Mountains of the Moon 90. Robin Hood 90. Sleeping with the Enemy 91. Highway to Hell 91. The Humming-Bird (TV) 92. Map of the Human Heart 92. Love Crimes 92. Patriot Games 92. Highway to Hell 92. Frankenstein (TV) 93. Map of the Human Heart 93. Soft Deceit 95, etc.

Berglund, Sven (1881–1937).
Swedish inventor with claims to be the first person to record sound on film by an optical process, which he worked on from 1906–11 and demonstrated in the 20s in Stockholm and Berlin. He also worked on stereoscopic film in the 30s before committing suicide.

Bergman, Alan (1925–).
Lyricist and songwriter in collaboration with his wife Marilyn.
   The Thomas Crown Affair (AA) 68. The Happy Ending (AAN) 69. Pieces of Dreams (AAN) 70. Sometimes a Great Notion (AAN) 71. The Life and Times of Judge Roy Bean (AAN) 71. The Way We Were (AA) 73. Ode to Billy Joe 75. Same Time Next Year (AAN) 78. The Promise (AAN) 79. Best Friends (AAN) 82. Tootsie (AAN) 82. Yes, Giorgio (AAN) 82. Never Say Never Again 83. Yentl (AA) 83. Micki and Maude 84. Big 88. Shirley Valentine (AAN) 89. Welcome Home 89, many others.

Bergman, Andrew (1945–).
American screenwriter and director. He is the author of *We're in the Money: Depression America and Its Films* (1971), which was first written as a doctoral thesis at the University of Wisconsin.
   Blazing Saddles (co-w) 74. The In-Laws (w) 79. So Fine (wd) 81. Oh God! You Devil (w) 84. Fletch (w) 85. Big Trouble (w) 86. Fletch Lives 89. The Freshman (wd) 90. Soapdish (co-w) 91. Honeymoon in Vegas (wd) 92. It Could Happen to You 94. The Scout (co-w) 94, etc.

Bergman, Daniel (1962–).
Swedish director, the son of Ingmar Bergman.
   Sunday's Child 92.

Bergman, Henry (1868–1946).
American comedy actor, the heavy villain in many a Chaplin film from *His New Job* in 1915 to *The Great Dictator* in 1940.

Bergman, Ingmar (1918–).
Swedish writer-director who divides his time between stage and film. In the late 50s his films had world-wide impact because of their semi-mystic, under-explained themes and bravura presentation by a repertory of excellent actors and cameramen; more recently his work has become austere and withdrawn.
   Autobiography: 1988, *The Magic Lantern*; 1994, Images: *My Life in Film*.
   Biographies include: 1962, *Ingmar Bergman* by Peter Cowie. 1964, *The Personal Vision of Ingmar Bergman* by Jorn Donner. 1968, *Ingmar Bergman* by Brigitta Steene. 1969, *The Silence of God* by Arthur Gibson. 1969, *Ingmar Bergman* by Robin Wood. 1971, *Cinema Borealis* by Vernon Young. Various screenplays have been published.
■ Crisis 45. It Rains on Our Love 46. A Ship Bound for India 47. Night is Our Future 47. Port of Call 48. *Prison* 48. *Thirst* 49. Till Gladje 49. Summer Interlude 50. Sant Hander inte Har 50.

Waiting Women 52. Summer with Monika 52. *Sawdust and Tinsel* 53. A Lesson in Love 54. Journey into Autumn 55. *Smiles of a Summer Night* 55. *The Seventh Seal* 56. *Wild Strawberries* (AAN) 57. So Close to Life 58. *The Face (The Magician)* 58. *The Virgin Spring* (AA) 59. The Devil's Eye 60. *Through a Glass Darkly* (AA) 61. *Winter Light* 62. *The Silence* 63. Now About these Women 64. *Persona* 66. The Hour of the Wolf 67. The Shame 68. The Rite (TV) 69. The Touch 70. A Passion 70. *Cries and Whispers* (AAN) 72. Scenes from a Marriage (TV) 74. The Magic Flute (TV) 75. Face to Face (TV) (AAN) 76. The Serpent's Egg 77. Autumn Sonata (AAN) 78. From the Life of the Marionettes 80. *Fanny and Alexander* (AAN) 82. After the Rehearsal 84. The Best Intentions (w) 92. Sunday's Child (w) 92.
😒 For his obsessional realization of a bleak but bracing vision of the world. *The Seventh Seal.*

¶ The theatre is like a faithful wife. The film is the great adventure – the costly, exacting mistress. – *I.B.*

I have a morbid sense of humour. I'm very open and frank, and sometimes that is a mistake. – *I.B.*

To shoot a film is to organize a complete universe. – *I.B.*

I'm not a writer. My plays and scripts are skeletons awaiting sinew. – *I.B.*

Bergman, Ingrid (1915–1982).
Gifted Swedish leading actress who went to Hollywood in 1938 and became an international star. In 1948 her romance with Roberto Rossellini (qv) caused a return to Europe where she appeared in mainly inferior films; Hollywood's door opened to her again in 1956.
Biography: 1986, *As Time Goes By* by Laurence Leamer.
■ Munkbrogreven 34. Branningar 35. Swedenhielms 35. Valborgsmassoafton 35. Pa Solsidan 36. *Intermezzo* 36. *En Kvinnas Ansikte* 38. En Enda Natt 38. Dollar 38. Die Vier Gesellen 38. *Intermezzo* (US remake) 39. Juninatten 40. Rage in Heaven 41. Adam Had Four Sons 41. Dr Jekyll and Mr Hyde 41. *Casablanca* 43. *For Whom the Bell Tolls* (AAN) 43. *Gaslight* (AA) 44. *The Bells of St Mary's* (AAN) 45. *Spellbound* 45. *Saratoga Trunk* 45. *Notorious* 46. Arch of Triumph 48. *Joan of Arc* (AAN) 48. Under Capricorn 49. Stromboli 50. Europa 51. We the Women 53. Journey to Italy 54. Joan at the Stake 54. Fear 54. *Anastasia* (AA) 56. Paris Does Strange Things 57. *Indiscreet* 58. *The Inn of the Sixth Happiness* 58. Goodbye Again 61. The Visit 64. The Yellow Rolls-Royce 64. Fugitive in Vienna 67. *Cactus Flower* 69. A Walk in the Spring Rain 70. From the Mixed Up Files of Mrs Basil E. Frankweiler 74. Murder on the Orient Express (AA, BFA) 74. A Matter of Time 76. Autumn Sonata (AAN) 78. A Woman Called Golda (TV) 82.
😌 For the ease with which in the 40s she conquered international audiences with her presentation of innocent strength and beauty. *Spellbound.*

¶ I have no regrets. I wouldn't have lived my life the way I did if I was going to worry about what people were going to say. – *I.B.*

It's not whether you really cry. It's whether the audience thinks you are crying. – *I.B.*

Sweden's greatest export since Garbo! – *publicity*

Famous line (from *For Whom the Bell Tolls*): 'Where do the noses go?'

Famous line (from *Indiscreet*): 'How dare he make love to me and not be a married man?'

Bergman, Marilyn (1929–).
Lyricist and songwriter in collaboration with her husband Alan.
The Thomas Crown Affair (AA) 68. The Happy Ending (AAN) 69. Pieces of Dreams (AAN) 70. Sometimes a Great Notion (AAN) 71. The Life and Times of Judge Roy Bean (AAN) 71. The Way We Were (AA) 73. Ode to Billy Joe 75. Same Time Next Year (AAN) 78. The Promise (AAN) 79. Best Friends (AAN) 82. Tootsie (AAN) 82. Yes, Giorgio (AAN) 82. Never Say Never Again 83. Yentl (AA) 83. Micki and Maude 84. Big 88. Shirley Valentine (AAN) 89. Welcome Home 89, many others.

Bergman, Sandahl (1951–).
American actress.
All That Jazz 79. Xanadu 80. Conan the Barbarian 82. She 83. Getting Physical 84. Red Sonja 85. Programmed to Kill 86. Stewardess School 86. Kandyland 87. Hell Comes to Frogtown 88. Raw Nerve 91. Loving Lulu 92. Lipstick Camera 93, etc.

Bergner, Elisabeth (1898–1986) (Elizabeth Ettel). German leading actress who settled in Britain in the 30s and married Paul Czinner (qv). Her fey gamine character quickly dated, but she was an undoubted star.
■ Der Evangelimann 24. Nju 24. Der Geiger von Florenz 26. Liebe 27. Queen Louisa 28. Dona Juana 28. Fraulein Else 29. Ariane 31. *Der Traumende Mund* 32. Ariane (GB) 33. *Catherine the Great* (GB) 34. *Escape Me Never* (GB) (AAN) 35. As You Like It (GB) 36. Dreaming Lips (GB) 37. Stolen Life (GB) 39. Paris Calling (US) 41. Die Glucklichen Jahre der Thorwalds (Ger.) 62. Cry of the Banshee (GB) 70. Courier to the Tsar (GB) 71. Der Fussganger (Ger.) 73. Whitsun Holiday (Ger.) 79.

Berke, William (1903–1958).
American director of second features.
Minesweeper 43. The Falcon in Mexico 44. Splitface 46. Jungle Jim 48. Deputy Marshal 49. Zamba the Gorilla 49. I Shot Billy the Kid (& p) 50. Four Boys and a Gun (& p) 55. Cop Hater (& p) 57, etc.

Berkeley, Ballard (1904–1988).
British light actor of stage and screen.
The Chinese Bungalow 30. London Melody 35. The Outsider 38. In Which We Serve 42. They Made Me a Fugitive 47. The Long Dark Hall 51. Three Steps to the Gallows 56. See How They Run 57. Star! 68. The Wildcats of St Trinian's 80. Bullshot 83. National Lampoon's European Vacation 85, etc.

Berkeley, Busby (1895–1976) (William Berkeley Enos).
American song and dance director who in the early 30s invaded Hollywood from Broadway and developed the spectacular, kaleidoscopic girlie numbers which became a feature of all musicals, quickly dated, and were joyously rediscovered in the 60s. Below, (m) signifies that Berkeley directed the musical sequences only. His occasional dramatic films were inconsiderable.
■ *Whoopee* (m) 30. Kiki (m) 31. Palmy Days (m) 31. Flying High (m) 31. Night World (m) 32. Bird of Paradise (m) 32. *The Kid from Spain* (m) 32. *Forty Second Street* (m) 33. *Gold Diggers of 1933* (m) 33. She Had to Say Yes 33. *Footlight Parade* (m) 33. *Roman Scandals* (m) 33. *Wonder Bar* (m) 34. *Fashions of 1934* (m) 34. Twenty Million Sweethearts (m) 34. *Dames* (m) 34. *Gold Diggers of 1935* 35. Go into Your Dance (m) 35. Bright Lights 35. In Caliente (m) 35. I Live for Love 35. Stars Over Broadway 35. Stage Struck 36. Gold Diggers of 1937 (m) 37. The

Go-Getter 37. The Singing Marine (m) 37. Varsity Show (m) 37. Hollywood Hotel 37. Men are Such Fools 38. Gold Diggers in Paris (m) 38. Garden of the Moon 38. Comet over Broadway 38. They Made Me a Criminal 39. Broadway Serenade (m) 39. *Babes In Arms* 39. Fast and Furious 39. Forty Little Mothers 40. *Strike Up the Band* 40. Blonde Inspiration 41. *Ziegfeld Girl* (m) 41. *Lady Be Good* (m) 41. Babes on Broadway 41. Born to Sing (m) 41. *For Me and My Gal* 42. Girl Crazy (m) 43. *The Gang's All Here* 43. Cinderella Jones 46. Romance on the High Seas (m) 48. *Take Me Out to the Ball Game* 49. Two Weeks with Love (m) 50. Call Me Mister (m) 51. Two Tickets to Broadway (m) 51. Million Dollar Mermaid (m) 52. Small Town Girl (m) 53. Easy to Love (m) 53. Rose Marie (m) 54. Jumbo (m) 62.
😌 For pushing to the limit the decorative possibilities of chorus girls, grand pianos, and optical processes. *Dames.*

¶ In an era of breadlines, depression and wars, I tried to help people get away from all the misery . . . to turn their minds to something else. I wanted to make people happy, if only for an hour. – *B.B.*

His vitality and ingenuity transcended the limitations of his sensibility, and he bequeathed to posterity an entertaining record of the audacity of an escapist era. – *Andrew Sarris, 1968*

If anybody wants to know what can be done with the camera, tell him to study every shot Busby Berkeley ever made. – *Gene Kelly*

Berkeley, Sir Lennox (1903–1989).
British composer.
Only feature film score: Hotel Reserve 44.

Berkoff, Steven (1937–).
Intense British dramatist, writer and actor, often in villainous roles on screen.
Autobiography: 1994, *Overview* (essays).
A Clockwork Orange 71. Nicholas and Alexandra 71. Barry Lyndon 75. The Passenger 75. Outland 81. Octopussy 83. Beverly Hills Cop 84. Rambo: First Blood II 85. Revolution 85. Absolute Beginners 86. Under the Cherry Moon 86. Underworld 86. Prisoner of Rio 88. Streets of Yesterday 89. The Krays 90. My Forgotten Man (a) 93. Decadence (a, wd) 94, etc.

Berlanga, Luis (1921–).
Spanish director.
Welcome Mr Marshall 52. Calabuch 56. The Executioner 63. Vivan los Novios 70. Life Size 77. Nacional III 83. La Vaquilla 85. Moros y Cristianos 87. Todos a la Carcel 94, etc.

Berle, Milton (1908–) (Mendel Berlinger).
Brash American vaudeville and TV comedian who never quite found his niche in the movies. In silents from 1914 (as the child clinging to Marie Dressler's knee in *Tillie's Punctured Romance*).
Autobiography: 1974, *Milton Berle, an Autobiography.*
New Faces of 1937 37. Radio City Revels 38. Tall, Dark and Handsome 41. Sun Valley Serenade 41. Rise and Shine 41. A Gentleman at Heart 42. Whispering Ghosts 42. Over My Dead Body 42. *Margin for Error* 43. *Always Leave Them Laughing* (based on his autobiography) 49. Let's Make Love 60. *It's a Mad Mad Mad Mad World* 63. The Oscar 65. The Loved Ones 65. Don't Worry We'll Think of a Title 66. The Happening 67. Who's Minding the Mint? 67. Where Angels Go Trouble Follows 68. For Singles Only 68. Hieronymus Merkin 69. Seven in Darkness (TV) 70. Evil Roy Slade (TV) 71. Lepke 75. The Legend of Valentino (TV) 75. Won Ton Ton 76. The Muppet Movie 80. Broadway

Danny Rose 84. Smorgasbord 85. Driving Me Crazy 92, etc.

¶ The thief of bad gags. – *Anon*
    He's been on TV for years and I finally figured out the reason for his success. He never improved. – *Steve Allen*

Berlin

has seemed to film-makers a grim grey city, and history provides obvious reasons for this. Standard attitudes are shown in *The Murderers Are Amongst Us, Germany Year Zero, Four Men in a Jeep, Hotel Berlin, Berlin Express, The Man Between, Night People, The Big Lift, I Am a Camera, The Spy Who Came in from the Cold, The Man Who Finally Died, A Prize of Gold, The Quiller Memorandum, Cabaret, Escape from East Berlin, Funeral in Berlin*. But some people have found fun there, notably Billy Wilder in *People on Sunday, A Foreign Affair* and *One Two Three*; and in 1928 Walter Ruttman's stylishly kaleidoscopic documentary, *Berlin: Symphony of a Great City*, showed the place and its people to be just as sympathetic as anywhere else if they are understandingly portrayed.

Berlin, Irving (1888–1989) (Israel Baline).
Prolific American composer and lyricist of tuneful popular songs.
    Biography: 1990, *As Thousands Cheer* by Laurence Bergreen.
    The Awakening 28. The Coconuts 29. Hallelujah 29. Putting on the Ritz 30. Mammy 30. Reaching for the Moon 31. Kid Millions 34. *Top Hat* 35. *Follow the Fleet* 36. *On the Avenue* 37. *Alexander's Ragtime Band* (AAN) 38. Carefree 38. Second Fiddle 39. Louisiana Purchase 42. Holiday Inn (AAN, story) 42. *This Is the Army* (in which he also appeared and sang 'Oh How I Hate to Get Up in the Morning') 43. *Blue Skies* 46. *Easter Parade* 48. *Annie Get Your Gun* 50. *Call Me Madam* 53. *There's No Business Like Show Business* 54. *White Christmas* 54. Sayonara 57, etc.
◆ For dominating three decades of musicals with an apparently endless barrage of tuneful melodies. *Alexander's Ragtime Band.*

Berlin, Jeannie (1949–)
American actress, daughter of Elaine May.
■ On a Clear Day You Can See Forever 70. Getting Straight 70. Move 70. The Strawberry Statement 70. The Baby Maker 70. Bone 72. Why 72. Portnoy's Complaint 71. *The Heartbreak Kid* (AAN) 73. Sheila Levine 75. In the Spirit (& co-w) 90.

Berlinger, Warren (1937–)
American stage and film actor, usually seen as chubby innocent.
    Teenage Rebel 56. Three Brave Men 57. Platinum High School 60. The Wackiest Ship in the Army 61. All Hands on Deck 61. Billie 65. Thunder Valley 67. The Shaggy D.A. 76. The Magician of Lublin 79. The World According to Garp 82. Free Ride 86. Hero (GB: Accidental Hero) 92, etc.
    TV series: The Joey Bishop Show 61. The Funny Side 71. A Touch of Grace 73. Operation Petticoat 78. Free Ride 86. Take Two 87. Outlaw Force 88. Going Bananas 88. Ten Little Indians 90. Hero (GB: Accidental Hero) 92, etc.

Berman, Monty (1913–)
British second feature producer, former cinematographer.
    Jack the Ripper (& d) 56. The Flesh and the Fiends 59. Sea of Sand 59. Blood of the Vampire 60. What a Carve Up 61. *The Hellfire Club* 61, many others.

TV series: *The Saint, Gideon's Way*, The Baron, The Champions, Department S, Randall and Hopkirk (Dec'd), The Adventurer, etc.

Berman, Pandro S. (1905–)
Distinguished American producer who spent many years at both RKO and MGM, and maintained a high standard of product.
    Morning Glory 32. *The Gay Divorcee* 34. The Little Minister 34. *Top Hat* 35. Sylvia Scarlett 36. Mary of Scotland 36. *Winterset* 36. Quality Street 37. *Stage Door* 37. Room Service 38. *The Hunchback of Notre Dame* 39. *Ziegfeld Girl* 41. Somewhere I'll Find You 42. The Seventh Cross 44. National Velvet 44. Undercurrent 46. *The Three Musketeers* 48. Madame Bovary 49. *Father of the Bride* 50. Ivanhoe 52. The Prisoner of Zenda 52. *The Blackboard Jungle* 55. Tea and Sympathy 56. Jailhouse Rock 57. The Brothers Karamazov 58. Butterfield 8 60. Sweet Bird of Youth 62. *The Prize* 63. A Patch of Blue 65, many others.
◆ For a lifetime of unobtrusive professionalism. *The Hunchback of Notre Dame.*

Berman, Shelley (1926–)
American cabaret monologuist who has made a few film appearances.
■ *The Best Man* 64. The Wheeler Dealers 64. Divorce American Style 67. Every Home Should Have One (GB) 70. Son of Blob 72. Think Dirty 78. Rented Lips 88. Teen Witch 89.
    TV series: Mary Hartman, Mary Hartman 77–78.

Bern, Paul (1889–1932) (Paul Levy).
American director whose suicide soon after his marriage to Jean Harlow is still a subject of controversy. (Because MGM executive.) Played in *Harlow* by Peter Lawford.
    The North Wind's Malice 20. Worldly Goods 24. Tomorrow's Love 25. The Dressmaker from Paris 25. Grounds for Divorce 25, etc.

¶ You understand that last night was only a comedy. – *from P.B.'s suicide note*

Bernard, James (1925–)
British composer with a predilection for horror themes. Co-authored film script, *Seven Days to Noon* 50.
    The Quatermass Experiment 55. X the Unknown 56. The Curse of Frankenstein 57. Dracula 58. Windom's Way 58. The Hound of the Baskervilles 59. Kiss of the Vampire 62. The Gorgon 64. The Plague of the Zombies 65. She 65. The Torture Garden 67. Scars of Dracula 70. Frankenstein and the Monster from Hell 72. The Legend of the Seven Golden Vampires 73. Murder Elite (TV) 85, etc.

Bernard, Raymond (1891–1977).
French director.
    Le Petit Café 19. Le Miracle des Loups 24. The Chess Player 27. Tarkanova 30. Les Misérables 34. Le Coupable 37. J'étais Une Aventurière 38. Les Otages 39. Un Ami Viendra Ce Soir 46. Maya 50. Le Jugement du Dieu 52. La Dame aux Camélias 53. Les Fruits de l'Eté 55. Le Septième Commandement 57. Le Septième Ciel 58, etc.

Bernardi, Herschel (1923–1986).
Balding, beaming American general-purpose actor, often seen as cop or gangster.
    Green Fields 37. Crime Inc. 45. Miss Susie Slagle's 46. Stakeout on Dope Street 58. The Savage Eye 60. A Cold Wind in August 61. Irma La Douce 63. The Honey Pot 67. But I Don't Want

to Get Married (TV) 71. No Place to Run (TV) 72. No Deposit No Return 76. The Front 76, etc.
    TV series: Peter Gunn 58–60. *Arnie* 70–71. Hail to the Chief 85.

Bernds, Edward (1905–)
American second feature director, former sound mixer.
    Blondie Hits the Jackpot 49. Harem Girl (& w) 52. Spy Chasers 55. World Without End (& w) 56. Quantrill's Raiders 58. Return of the Fly (& w) 59. The Three Stooges in Orbit 62. Tickle Me (w only) 65. Prehistoric Valley 66, many others.

Berners, Lord (1883–1950).
British composer.
■ Halfway House 44. Champagne Charlie (song arrangement only) 44. Nicholas Nickleby 47.

Bernhard, Jack (1913–)
American second feature director.
    Decoy 46. Appointment with Murder 48. Search for Danger 49. Alaska Patrol 49. The Second Face 50, etc.

Bernhard, Sandra (1955–)
American comedian, actress, singer, model, satirist and exhibitionist. *Without You I'm Nothing* is a film of her off-Broadway one-woman show.
    Autobiography: 1988, *Confessions of a Pretty Lady.*
    King of Comedy 82. Track 29 88. Casual Sex? 88. Without You I'm Nothing (& co-w) 90. Hudson Hawk 91. Truth or Dare (aka In Bed with Madonna) 91. Dallas Doll 94, etc.

Bernhardt, Curtis (Kurt) (1899–1981).
German director; on arrival in Hollywood in 1940, he was generally assigned to 'women's pictures' and approached them with variable style.
    Three Loves 29. Thirteen Men and a Girl 31. Die Letzte Kompagnie 32. The Beloved Vagabond (GB) 36. My Love Came Back 40. Lady with Red Hair 40. Million Dollar Baby 41. Juke Girl 42. Happy Go Lucky 43. *Devotion* 44. Conflict 45. My Reputation 45. *A Stolen Life* 46. *Possessed* 47. High Wall 47. The Doctor and the Girl 49. Payment on Demand (& w) 51. Sirocco 51. The Blue Veil 51. Miss Sadie Thompson 53. *Beau Brummell* 54. Interrupted Melody 55. Gaby 56. Stefanie in Rio 60. *Kisses for My President* (& p) 64, etc.

Bernhardt, Sarah (1844–1923) (Rosalie Bernard).
Famous French stage tragedienne who lent dignity if nothing else to early silent films, and even continued working in them after her leg was amputated. After seeing herself in *Queen Elizabeth*, which in America helped found the fortunes of Paramount, she is reputed to have said: 'Mr Zukor, you have put me in pickle for all time!' She was played in *The Incredible Sarah* by Glenda Jackson.
    Biography: 1976, *Sarah Bernhardt* by William Emboden.
■ Hamlet's Duel 00. Tosca 08. La Dame aux Camélias 11. *Queen Elizabeth* 12. Adrienne Lecouvreur 13. Jeanne Doré 14. Mères Françaises 17. La Voyante 23.

¶ The film audience could see her only as a figure of fun, a dumb creature jerking her sawdust heart around in a puppet world. – *Alistair Cooke*

Bernie, Ben (1891–1943) (Benjamin Anzelvitz).
American bandleader who worked up a publicity feud with Walter Winchell and consequently appeared in a film or two.
■ Shoot the Works 34. Stolen Harmony 35. *Wake Up and Live* 37. Love and Hisses 37.

Bernsen, Corbin (1954–).
American leading actor, from television.
Eat My Dust! 76. King Kong 76. S.O.B. 81. Dead Aim 87. Hello Again 87. Disorganised Crime 89. Major League 89. Bert Rigby, You're a Fool 89. Shattered 91. Frozen Assets 92. Guns of Honor (TV) 94. Major League II 94. The New Age 94, etc.
TV series: L.A. Law 86–93.

Bernstein, Charles (1943–).
American composer, mostly for TV films.
Hex 73. White Lightning 73. Mr Majestyk 74. Trackdown 76. Gator 76. Viva Knieval 77. Love at First Bite 79. The Entity 82. Cujo 83. A Nightmare on Elm Street 84. Deadly Friend 86. Dudes 87, etc.

Bernstein, Elmer (1922–).
American composer-conductor.
Saturday's Hero 51. Sudden Fear 52. Cat Women of the Moon 53. *The Man with the Golden Arm* (AAN) 55. The Ten Commandments 56. *The Sweet Smell of Success* 57. The Tin Star 57. God's Little Acre 58. The Buccaneer 59. *The Magnificent Seven* 60. Summer and Smoke (AAN) 61. A Walk on the Wild Side 62. To Kill a Mockingbird (AAN) 62. Baby the Rain Must Fall 65. The Sons of Katie Elder 65. The Reward 65. Return of the Seven (AAN) 66. Hawaii (AAN) 66. *Thoroughly Modern Millie* (AA) 67. A Cannon for Cordoba 70. The Shootist 76. National Lampoon's Animal House 76. Zulu Dawn 79. Airplane 80. The Great Santini 80. Saturn Three 80. An American Werewolf in London 81. Honky Tonk Freeway 81. Going Ape 81. Five Days One Summer 82. The Chosen 82. Class 82. Trading Places (AAN) 83. Ghostbusters 84. Legal Eagles 85. A Night in the Life of Jimmy Reardon 85. Spies Like Us 86. The Black Cauldron 86. Three Amigos! 86. Funny Farm 88. The Good Mother 88. Dad 88. My Left Foot 89. The Grifters 90. The Field 90. Oscar 91. Rambling Rose 91. Cape Fear (md) 91. The Babe 92. The Cemetery Club 93. Mad Dog and Glory 93. Lost in Yonkers 93. The Age of Innocence (AAN) 93. The Good Son 93, etc.

Bernstein, Leonard (1918–1990).
American concert musician, conductor and composer.
On the Town 49. On the Waterfront 54. West Side Story 61.

Bernstein, Lord (1899–1993) (Sidney Bernstein).
British executive and producer, founder and chairman of the Granada group, including a television station and a cinema circuit. Founder member of the Film Society (1924). First to institute Saturday morning shows for children and to research audience preferences. During World War II, films adviser to the Ministry of Information and SHAEF.
Produced three films with Alfred Hitchcock as director: *Rope* 48, *Under Capricorn* 49. *I Confess* 52.

Bernstein, Walter (1919–).
American screenwriter.
That Kind of Woman 59. A Breath of Scandal 60. *Fail Safe* 64. The Train (co-w) 64. The Money Trap 66. The Molly Maguires 70. The Front (AAN) 76. Semi Tough 77. The Betsy 78. Yanks 79. Little Miss Marker (d only) 80. The House on Carroll Street 88, etc.

Berri, Claude (1934–).
French writer-director and producer, usually of stories with a Jewish background. Acted in some of them.
■ Les Baisers (one episode) 64. La Chance et l'Amour 64. *Le Vieil Homme et l'Enfant* 67. Mazel Tov 68. La Pistonnée 70. Le Cinéma de Papa 71. Le Sex Shop 72. Male of the Century 75. La Première Fois 76. Un Moment d'Egarement 78. Tess (p, AAN) 79. Je Vous Aime 80. *Jean de Florette* 86. *Manon des Sources* 86. Uranus 90. *Germinal* 93.

Berry, Chuck (1926–) (Charles Edward Berry).
American singer, guitarist and songwriter of rhythm and blues and rock music. In films playing himself.
Rock, Rock, Rock 56. Mr Rock and Roll 57. Go, Johnny Go! 58. Jazz on a Summer's Day (concert) 59. Let the Good Times Roll (concert) 73. American Hot Wax 78. Chuck Berry Hail! Hail! Rock 'n' Roll (concert) 87, etc.

Berry, Halle (1968–).
American leading actress, a former model and beauty queen, who was Miss USA in 1987.
The Last Boy Scout 91. Jungle Fever 91. Boomerang 91. Queen (TV) 91. Strictly Business 91. Father Hood 93. The Program 93. The Flintstones 94, etc.
TV series: Living Dolls 89.

Berry, John (1917–).
American director with stage experience. Blacklisting in the 50s kept him away from Hollywood for a decade.
■ Cross My Heart 45. From This Day Forward 46. Miss Susie Slagle's 46. Casbah 48. Tension 49. He Ran All the Way 51. C'est Arrivé à Paris 52. Ça Va Barder (Fr.) 55. The Great Lover (Don Juan) (Fr.) 55. Je Suis un Sentimental (Fr.) 55. Tamango 57. Oh Que Mambo (It.) 59. Maya 66. A Tout Casser 67. Claudine 74. Thieves 77. The Bad News Bears Go to Japan 78. Angel on My Shoulder (TV) 80. Sister, Sister (TV) 82. Honeyboy (TV) 82. Le Voyage à Paimpol 85. Maldonne 85. A Captive in the Land 90.

Berry, Jules (1883–1951) (Jules Paufichet).
Saturnine French character actor.
The Crime of Monsieur Lange 34. Carrefour 39. *Le Jour Se Lève* 39. *Les Visiteurs du Soir* 42. La Symphonie Fantastique 47, etc.

Berry, Ken (1933–).
American actor often seen on TV as birdlike comic hero.
Wake Me When The War Is Over (TV) 70. The Reluctant Heroes (TV) 71. Herbie Rides Again 74. Mountain Man 77. The Cat from Outer Space 78, etc.
TV series: F Troop 65–67. Mayberry RFD 68–71. Mama's Family 83–89.

Berry, Richard (1950–).
Saturnine French leading actor. He studied at the Paris Conservatoire and worked with La Comédie Française before concentrating on films from the 80s.
La Gifle 74. La Balance 82. Le Grand Pardon 82. Une Chambre en Ville 83. Caged Heart 85. L'Addition 85. A Man and a Woman: 20 Years Later 86. Honeymoon 87. Mayrig 91. Day of Atonement (Le Grand Pardon II) 92. Adultère Mode d'Emploi 95, etc.

Berthomieu, André (1903–1960).
French director, former assistant to Julien Duvivier and author of a book on cinema grammar.
Ces Dames aux Chapeaux Verts 29. *Le Crime de Sylvestre Bonnard* 30. Mon Ami Victor 31. L'Aristo 34. La Flamme 36. The Girl in the Taxi (GB) 37. Les Nouveaux Riches 38. L'Inconnue de Monte Carlo 39. La Neige sur le Pas 41. L'Ange de la Nuit 44. J'ai 17 Ans 45. Gringalet 46. La Femme Nue 49. Chacun son Tour 51. Scènes de Ménage 54. La Joyeuse Prison 56. Préméditation 60, many others.

Berti, Marina (1928–).
Italian leading lady in occasional international films.
Prince of Foxes 49. Deported 50. Quo Vadis 51. Queen of Sheba 53. Abdullah the Great 56. Ben Hur 59. Tyrant of Syracuse 62. Cleopatra 62. Swordsman of Siena 63. Moses (TV) 76. Jesus of Nazareth (TV) 77.

Bertini, Francesca (1888–1985) (Elena Vitiello).
Italian leading lady of the silent period, a model of screen beauty and fashion.
La Dea del Mare 04. Il Trovatore 09. Salome 13. Assunta Spina 15. Tosca 17. Romeo and Juliet 20. Resurrection 20. La Donna Nuda 22. Monte Carlo 28. Odette 28. Dora 43, many others.

Berto, Juliet (1947–1990).
French leading actress and occasional screenwriter who turned to directing before her death from cancer.
Two or Three Things I Know About Her 66. La Chinoise 67. Weekend 67. Le Gai Savoir 68. Camarades 70. The Big Shots 72. Celine and Julie Go Boating (& w) 73. Summer Run 74. Mr Klein 76. Bastien, Bastienne 76. Snow (Neige) (& wd) 81. Cap Canaille (& d) 83. Havre (wd) 86. Un Amour à Paris 87. Une Vie Suspendue 88, etc.

Bertolucci, Bernardo (1940–).
Italian writer-director, a former romanticist and poet who turned increasingly to censorable themes.
■ The Grim Reaper 62. *Before the Revolution* 64. Love and Anger (part) 67. Partner 68. *The Spider's Stratagem* 70. The Conformist 70. *Last Tango in Paris* (AAN) 72. 1900 76. La Luna 79. Tragedy of a Ridiculous Man 81. *The Last Emperor* (AA) 87. The Sheltering Sky 90. Little Buddha 93.

Bertolucci, Giuseppe (1947–).
Italian director and screenwriter. The younger brother of Bernardo Bertolucci, he began as a documentary film-maker and has worked on the scripts of some of his brother's films.
1900 (co-w) 76. I Love You Berlinguer (Berlinguer ti Voglio Bene) 77. La Luna (co-w) 79. Secrets Secrets (Segreti Segreti) 85. It's an Odd Life (Strana la Vita) 88. The Camels (I Cammelli) 88. Love at Work (Amori in Corso) 89. Especially on Sundays (La Domenica Specialmente) (co-d) 91, etc.

Besch, Bibi (1942–) (Bibiara Besch).
Austrian-born character actress, in America. She is the daughter of actress Gusti Huber (1914–) and the mother of actress Samantha Mathis.
Peter Lundy and the Medicine Hat Stallion (TV) 77. The Pack 77. Hardcore 79. Meteor 79. The Promise 79. Death of a Centrefold (TV) 81. Star Trek II: The Wrath of Khan 82. The Beast Within 82. The Lonely Lady 83. Date with an Angel 87. Tremors 89. Kill Me Again 89. Crazy from the Heart (TV) 91, etc.
TV series: Secrets of Midland Heights 80–81. The Hamptons 83.

Bessell, Ted (1935–).
American comic character actor.
Billie 65. Don't Drink the Water 69. Two on a Bench (TV) 71. Your Money or Your Wife (TV) 72. Breaking Up Is Hard to Do (TV) 79, etc.
TV series: It's a Man's World 62. Gomer Pyle 65–66. That Girl 66–71. Hail to the Chief 85.

Besser, Joe (1907–1988).
Rotund American burlesque comic who in the 50s became one of the Three Stooges in their declining days.

Besserer, Eugenie (1870–1934).
American character actress.

The Count of Monte Cristo 12. Scarlet Days 19. The Sin of Martha Queed 21. The Rosary 22. Her Reputation 23. The Price She Paid 24. A Fool and His Money 25. The Millionaire Policeman 26. *The Jazz Singer* (as Jolson's mother) 27. Two Lovers 28. Madame X 29. Thunderbolt 29. In Gay Madrid 30. To the Last Man 33, many others.

Bessie, Alvah (1904–1985).
American screenwriter, blacklisted in 1949 as one of the Hollywood Ten (qv).

The Very Thought of You 44. Hotel Berlin 45. Objective Burma (AAN) 45, etc.

Besson, Luc (1959–).
French director and screenwriter with a fascination for the sea.

The Last Battle (Le Dernier Combat) 83. Subway 85. Kamikaze (co-d) 87. The Big Blue 88. Nikita (aka La Femme Nikita) 90. Atlantis 91. Leon (US: The Professional) 94, etc.

best boy.
Term used to describe the assistant to the chief electrician, or gaffer, on a film set.

Best, Edna (1900–1974).
Soft-spoken, maternal British actress, once married to Herbert Marshall. Went to Hollywood in 1939 and stayed.

Tilly of Bloomsbury 21. A Couple of Down and Outs 23. Escape 30. *Tilly of Bloomsbury* 30. The Calendar 31. *Michael and Mary* 32. The Faithful Heart 32. *The Man Who Knew Too Much* 34. Sleeping Partners 37. *South Riding* 38. Prison without Bars 39. *Intermezzo* 39. *The Swiss Family Robinson* 40. A Dispatch from Reuters 40. The Late George Apley 46. The Ghost and Mrs Muir 47. The Iron Curtain 48, etc.

Best, James (1926–).
American general-purpose actor, often in westerns as sly ranch-hand.

Winchester 73 50. Kansas Raiders 51. Francis Goes to West Point 52. Seven Angry Men 55. Gaby 56. The Left Handed Gun 58. The Mountain Road 60. Shock Corridor 63. Three on a Couch 66. Firecreek 67. Ode to Billy Joe 76. Rolling Thunder 77. The End 78. Hooper 78, etc.

TV series: The Dukes of Hazzard 79.

Best, Richard (1916–).
British editor.

Desert Victory 43. Fame is the Spur 47. Mine Own Executioner 48. The Magic Box 51. The Dam Busters 54. Ice Cold in Alex 58. The Double Man 66. Otley 68. Please Sir 71. Dominique 77.

The Best Remaining Seats
by Ben M. Hall. A book covering the golden age of the American picture palace; published in 1961.

Best, Willie (1916–1962).
Goggle-eyed American comedian, once known as Sleep'n Eat and later the prototype frightened manservant.

Feet First 30. The Monster Walks 32. Kentucky Kernels 33. Little Miss Marker 34. Murder on a Honeymoon 35. Jalna 35. The Littlest Rebel 35. Mummy's Boys 36. Thank You Jeeves 36. Super Sleuth 37. Blondie 38. Merrily We Live 38.

Vivacious Lady 38. At the Circus 39. I Take This Woman 40. *The Ghost Breakers* 40. Road Show 41. High Sierra 41. The Body Disappears 41. The Smiling Ghost 41. Busses Roar 42. The Hidden Hand 42. Cabin in the Sky 43. Thank Your Lucky Stars 43. Home in Indiana 44. Hold That Blonde 45. The Bride Wore Boots 46. Red Stallion 47. The Shanghai Chest 48. South of Caliente 51, many others.

TV series: My Little Margie 52–54. Trouble with Father 50–55.

Beswick, Martine (1941–).
British pin-up, decorative in occasional films.

From Russia with Love 62. Thunderball 65. One Million Years BC 66. The Penthouse 67. Dr Jekyll and Sister Hyde 71. Seizure 74. The Happy Hooker Goes to Hollywood 80. Melvin and Howard 80. Balboa 86. Cyclone 87. Evil Spirits 91. Trancers II 91. Wide Sargasso Sea 93, etc.

Bettger, Lyle (1915–).
American screen actor who started in 1946 as leading man but seemed more at home in villainous roles.

No Man of Her Own 50. Union Station 50. The First Legion 51. All I Desire 53. The Greatest Show on Earth 53. The Sea Chase 55. Gunfight at the OK Corral 57. Guns of the Timberland 60. Town Tamer 65. Nevada Smith 66. The Fastest Guitar Alive 68. The Seven Minutes 71. M Station Hawaii (TV) 80. many others.

TV series: Court of Last Resort 57. Grand Jury 58–59.

Betty Boop.
Doll-like cartoon creation, a wide-eyed gold-digging flapper created by animator Grim Natwick for Max Fleischer in the 1932 cartoon *Any Rags*. She was censored by Will H. Hays in 1935. She was developed from a dog who appeared in *Dizzy Dishes* in 1930, in which she was chased by Fleischer's dog star Bimbo, who first appeared in the early 20s. The cartoons she featured in were wildly imaginative and usually made comments on the social follies of their time; in the 70s they became popular through compilation features. She was based on the 'boop-a-doop' singer Helen Kane, with her voice being provided by Mae Questel.

Betz, Carl (1920–1978).
American leading man who moved from films to TV.

The President's Lady 53. Inferno 53. Vicki 53. Dangerous Crossing 53. Spinout 66, etc.

TV series: *The Donna Reed Show* 58–65. *Judd for the Defense* 67–68.

Bevan, Billy (1887–1957) (William Bevan Harris).
Wide-eyed, moustachioed silent screen comedian, an Australian who moved to Hollywood and became one of Mack Sennett's troupe. Later played many small parts, often that of a bewildered policeman.

Easy Pickings 27. Riley the Cop 28. *Journey's End* 30. Sky Devils 32. *Cavalcade* 33. Alice in Wonderland 33. Limehouse Blues 34. *Dracula's Daughter* 36. Captain Fury 39. The Long Voyage Home 40. Dr Jekyll and Mr Hyde 41. The Picture of Dorian Gray 45. Cluny Brown 46. The Black Arrow 48, many others.

Bevans, Clem (1879–1963) (Clement Blevins).
Long-faced and latterly white-haired American character actor who played a long succession of grandfathers, doorkeepers, oldest inhabitants and gold prospectors.

Way Down East 35. Of Human Hearts 38. Abe

Lincoln in Illinois 40. *Saboteur* 42. The Human Comedy 43. Captain Eddie 45. The Yearling 46. The Paleface 48. Streets of Laredo 49. *Harvey* 50. The Stranger Wore a Gun 53. The Kentuckian 55, etc.

Bewes, Rodney (1937–).
Chubby British comedy actor.

Billy Liar 63. Decline and Fall 68. Spring and Port Wine 70. Alice's Adventures in Wonderland 72. The Likely Lads 76. Jabberwocky 77. The Spaceman and King Arthur 79. Saint Jack 79, etc.

TV series: *The Likely Lads* 65–69. Dear Mother Love Albert 70–72. *Whatever Happened to the Likely Lads* 73.

Bey, Turhan (1920–) (Turhan Selahattin Sahultavy Bey).
Dapper Turkish leading man who had a good run in Hollywood during World War II in the absence on war service of more dynamic stars. Later became a stills photographer and moved to Vienna.

Footsteps in the Dark 41. Drums of the Congo 42. The Mummy's Tomb 42. Arabian Nights 42. White Savage 43. Background to Danger 43. The Mad Ghoul 43. Ali Baba and the Forty Thieves 43. Dragon Seed 44. Bowery to Broadway 44. The Climax 44. Frisco Sal 44. A Night in Paradise 46. Out of the Blue 47. Adventures of Casanova 48. Song of India 49. Prisoners of the Casbah 53. Stolen Identity (p only) 53, etc.

Beymer, Richard (1939–).
American child actor who in the early 60s seemed about to turn into a major juvenile lead, but somehow never made it. Also a TV director.

So Big 52. Indiscretion of an American Wife 52. Johnny Tremain 57. The Diary of Anne Frank 59. High Time 60. *West Side Story* 61. Five Finger Exercise 62. *Hemingway's Adventures of a Young Man* 62. The Longest Day 62. The Stripper 62. Cross Country 83. Silent Night, Deadly Night 3: Better Watch Out! 89. My Girl 2 94, etc.

TV series: Paper Dolls 84. Twin Peaks 90.

Bezzerides, A. I. (1908–) (Albert Isaac Bezzerides).
American screenwriter.

They Drive by Night 40. Northern Pursuit 43. *Thieves' Highway* 49. Sirocco 51. On Dangerous Ground 52. Beneath the 12 Mile Reef 53. Track of the Cat 54. *Kiss Me Deadly* 55. The Angry Hills 59, etc.

Bianchi, Daniela (1942–).
Italian leading lady.

Love is My Profession 59. Sword of El Cid 62. *From Russia With Love* 63. The Balearic Caper 66. Weekend Italian Style 68. The Dirty Heroes 68, etc.

Biberman, Abner (1909–1977).
American character actor who spent many years playing Red Indian braves and dastardly dagoes before turning into a director. He worked mainly as a TV director from the 50s.

Gunga Din 39. His Girl Friday 40. South of Pago Pago 40. South of Tahiti 41. Broadway 42. The Leopard Man 43. Salome Where She Danced 45. Captain Kidd 45. Back to Bataan 50. Elephant Walk 54. The Golden Mistress 54. The Price of Fear (d) 56. Above All Things 57. Gun for a Coward (d) 57, many others especially in TV.

Biberman, Herbert J. (1900–1971).
American director whose career was harmed by his political convictions. Married Gale Sondergaard.

One Way Ticket 35. Meet Nero Wolfe 36. King of Chinatown (w only) 38. *The Master Race* (& d) 44. New Orleans (w only) 47. Abilene Town (p only) 46. Salt of the Earth (& w) 53. Slaves (& w) 69, etc.

The Bible.

The extravaganza which claimed to be the 'film of the book' was conceived by Dino de Laurentiis as a nine-hour survey by several directors. It turned up in 1966 as a slow plod through Genesis by and with John Huston. Of the hundreds of films which have been inspired by the Old Testament stories, some of the most memorable are *The Private Life of Adam and Eve, Sodom and Gomorrah, Green Pastures, A Story of David, David and Bathsheba, Samson and Delilah, The Prodigal, The Ten Commandments* (two versions), *Salome, Esther and the King* and *The Story of Ruth.* For the New Testament, see under *Christ;* the immediate effects of whose life have been treated in such assorted films as *The Robe, Demetrius and the Gladiators, The Sign of the Cross, The Big Fisherman, Quo Vadis, Ben Hur, Spartacus, Fabiola, Barabbas, The Silver Chalice,* and *The Fall of the Roman Empire,* not to mention Lord Grade's six-hour *Jesus of Nazareth* for TV (a 'sequel' to his *Moses*). All this activity sparked off in 1978 a rather naive American TV series, *Greatest Heroes of the Bible.*

Bickford, Charles (1889–1967).

Rugged American character actor who sometimes played stubborn or unscrupulous roles but more often projected sincerity and warmth.

Autobiography: 1965, *Bulls, Balls, Bicycles and Actors.*

■ Dynamite 29. South Sea Rose 29. Hell's Heroes 29. *Anna Christie* 30. The Sea Bat 30. Passion Flower 30. River's End 31. The Squaw Man 31. East of Borneo 31. Pagan Lady 31. Men in Her Life 31. Panama Flo 32. *Thunder Below* 32. Scandal for Sale 32. The Last Man 32. Vanity Street 32. No Other Woman 33. Song of the Eagle 33. This Day and Age 33. White Woman 33. Little Miss Marker 34. A Wicked Woman 34. A Notorious Gentleman 35. Under Pressure 35. The Farmer Takes a Wife 35. East of Java 35. The Littlest Rebel 35. Rose of the Rancho 35. Pride of the Marines 36. The Plainsman 36. Night Club Scandal 37. Thunder Trail 37. Daughter of Shanghai 37. High, Wide and Handsome 37. Gangs of New York 38. Valley of the Giants 38. The Storm 39. Stand Up and Fight 39. Romance of the Redwoods 39. Street of Missing Men 39. Our Leading Citizen 39. One Hour to Live 39. Mutiny in the Big House 39. Thou Shalt Not Kill 39. *Of Mice and Men* 40. The Girl from God's Country 40. South to Karanga 40. Queen of the Yukon 40. *Riders of Death Valley* (serial) 41. Burma Convoy 41. Reap the Wild Wind 42. Tarzan's New York Adventure 42. Mr Lucky 43. *The Song of Bernadette* (AAN) 43. Wing and a Prayer 44. Captain Eddie 45. Fallen Angel 45. *Duel in the Sun* 46. *The Farmer's Daughter* (AAN) 47. The Woman on the Beach 47. *Brute Force* 47. The Babe Ruth Story 47. Four Faces West 48. *Johnny Belinda* (AAN) 48. Command Decision 48. Roseanna McCoy 49. Whirlpool 49. *Treason* (as Cardinal Mindzenty) 49. Branded 50. Riding High 50. Jim Thorpe – All American 51. The Raging Tide 51. Elopement 51. The Last Posse 53. *A Star is Born* 54. Prince of Players 55. Not as a Stranger 55. The Court Martial of Billy Mitchell 55. You Can't Run Away from It 56. Mister Cory 57. So Soon to Die (TV) 57. *The Big Country* 58. The Unforgiven 60. Days of Wine and Roses 62. Della (TV) 64. *A Big Hand for the Little Lady* 66.

bicycling.

A trade term for the sharing, usually illegally, of one print between two theatres: the manager had to make frequent bicycle trips!

Biddle, Adrian.

British cinematographer.

The Duellists 77. Aliens 86. The Princess Bride 87. Willow 88. The Tall Guy 90. Thelma and Louise (AAN) 91. 1492: Conquest of Paradise 92. Judge Dredd 95, etc.

Biehn, Michael (1956–).

American character actor, often in action films.

Coach 78. Hog Wild 80. The Fan 81. Lords of Discipline 83. The Terminator 84. Aliens 86. Rampage 87. In a Shallow Grave 88. The Seventh Sign 88. The Abyss 90. Navy SEALS 90. Terminator 2 91. K2 91. Timebomb 91. A Taste for Killing 92. Deadfall 93. Tombstone 94, etc.

TV series: The Runaways 78.

big business

was outside the range of silent movie-makers, but in the 30s, usually personified by Edward Arnold, it became a useful villain for the comedies and dramas of social conscience. A switch was made in *Dodsworth,* in which the businessman became an innocent abroad; but not until the growing affluence of the 50s did Hollywood think it worth while to probe into the personal lives of those who occupy the corridors of power. Then in quick succession we had *Executive Suite, Woman's World, Patterns of Power, The Power and the Prize* and *The Man in the Grey Flannel Suit;* while the inevitable knocking process began as early as *The Man in the White Suit* and continued with *The Solid Gold Cadillac, Cash McCall, Ice Palace, The Apartment, The Wheeler Dealers, Wall Street, Other People's Money* and *The Hudsucker Proxy.*

bigamists

have been prevented by the censorship codes from achieving hero status in more than a few films; perhaps it is significant that although the Italian film called *The Bigamist* is a comedy, the American one is a solemn affair. Over the years, however, scriptwriters have achieved some sympathy and humour for the characters played by William Bendix in *Don Juan Quilligan,* Alec Guinness in *The Captain's Paradise,* Clifton Webb in *The Remarkable Mr Pennypacker,* Rex Harrison in *The Constant Husband,* Jean-Claude Drouot in *Le Bonheur* and Leo McKern in *Decline and Fall.*

Bigas Luna (1946–) (José Juan Bigas Luna).

Spanish writer and director. Born in Barcelona, he worked as a graphic designer and wrote fiction before beginning to make short films in the early 70s. His feature films tend to be low-budget and are often on sexual themes.

Tatoo (Tatuaje) 76. Bilbao, una Historia del Amor (wd) 78. Poodle (Caniché) 79. Reborn (Renacer) 82. Lola 85. Anguish (Angoixa) 87. Las Edades de Lulu 91. Jamón, Jamón 92. Golden Balls (Huevos de Oro) 93. The Tit and the Moon (La Tita y la Luna) 94, etc.

Bigelow, Kathryn (1951–).

American director and screenwriter who began as an artist.

The Loveless (co-d) 81. Near Dark 87. Blue Steel 89. Point Break 91, etc.

¶ Movies can be cathartic. I think that they can transform you, they're kind of windows on to another universe that you can't experience in any other context. – K.B.

Biggers, Earl Derr (1884–1933).

American crime novelist, whose chief gift to the movies was Charlie Chan (qv). Also wrote original story of *The Millionaire* 31, and the much filmed play *Seven Keys to Baldpate.*

Bikel, Theodore (1924–).

Heavily-built Viennese actor, guitarist and singer; can play most nationalities. International stage, TV, cabaret and film work.

The African Queen 51. The Love Lottery 54. The Pride and the Passion 57. The Defiant Ones (AAN) 58. The Blue Angel 59. A Dog of Flanders 60. My Fair Lady 64. Sands of the Kalahari 65. The Russians Are Coming, The Russians Are Coming 66. My Side of the Mountain 68. Darker than Amber 70. The Little Ark 71. Victory at Entebbe (TV) 76. Very Close Quarters 84. See You in the Morning 89. Shattered 91. Benefit of the Doubt 93, etc.

Bill, Tony (1940–).

American light leading man, now concentrating on producing and directing.

Come Blow Your Horn 63. None But the Brave 65. Marriage on the Rocks 66. Ice Station Zebra 68. Castle Keep 69. Flap 70. Shampoo 75. Pee-Wee's Big Adventure 85, etc.

AS PRODUCER: Deadhead Miles 70. Steelyard Blues 70. The Sting 73. Hearts of the West 75. Shampoo 75, etc.

AS DIRECTOR: My Bodyguard 80. Six Weeks 82. Love Thy Neighbour (TV) 84. Five Corners (& p) 87. Heist (TV) 89. Crazy People 90. Baboon Heart (& p) 92. Untamed Heart (& p) 93. A Home of Our Own 93. Next Door (TV) 94.

billing.

The official credits for a film, usually stating the relative sizes of type to be accorded to title, stars, character actors, etc.

Billington, Kevin (1933–).

British director, from TV.

Interlude 68. The Rise and Rise of Michael Rimmer 70. The Light at the Edge of the World 71. And No One Could Save Her (TV) 72. Voices 74. The Good Soldier (TV) 83, etc.

Billy the Kid,

the historical, homicidal western gunslinger, has frequently been turned by the movies into some kind of hero. A favourite character of the silents, he has been seen also in numerous talkie versions. Johnny Mack Brown played him on the wide screen in *Billy the Kid* 30; pious Roy Rogers was the star of *Billy the Kid Returns* 39; in 1940 Robert Taylor was *Billy the Kid;* and in 1943 (or so) came *The Outlaw,* with a happy ending for Jack Buetel who played Billy. In 1949 Audie Murphy played Billy in *The Kid from Texas;* 1950 brought *I Shot Billy the Kid* with Don Barry; 1954 *The Law Versus Billy the Kid* with Scott Brady; 1955 *The Parson and the Outlaw* with Anthony Dexter; 1958 *The Left-Handed Gun* with Paul Newman; in 1966 we were even offered *Billy the Kid Meets Dracula;* and in 1974 Sam Peckinpah's *Pat Garrett and Billy the Kid* added new refinements of violence. He was turned into a teen hero by Emilio Estevez in *Young Guns* and *Young Guns II* in 1989–90. There were also scores of second features in the 30s and 40s, with Bob Steele or Buster Crabbe as Billy; whose real name incidentally was William Bonney and who died in 1881 at the age of 21.

Bilon, Michael (1948–1983).

American dwarf actor who played the title role in some of the scenes of *E.T. – the Extra-Terrestrial.*

Under the Rainbow 81.

Binder, Maurice (1925–1991).
American title artist in Britain, chiefly known for designing the graphics of the James Bond films.
 Indiscreet 58. The Mouse that Roared 59. The Grass is Greener 60. *Dr No* 62. Repulsion 64. The Chase 66. Bedazzled 67. The Private Life of Sherlock Holmes 71. Gold 74. Shout at the Devil 76. The Sea Wolves 80, etc.

Bing, Herman (1889–1947).
Plump, explosive German comedy actor, former assistant to F. W. Murnau; in Hollywood from 1929. Committed suicide.
 Married in Hollywood 29. The Guardsman 31. Dinner at Eight 33. The Black Cat 34. Rose Marie 36. The Great Ziegfeld 36. Champagne Waltz 37. The Great Waltz 38. Sweethearts 38. The Devil with Hitler 42. Where Do We Go from Here? 45. Rendezvous 24 46, many others.

Binns, Edward (Ed) (1916–1990).
Solid but unremarkable American character actor.
 Teresa 51. The Scarlet Hour 56. Twelve Angry Men 57. Compulsion 59. North by Northwest 59. Fail Safe 64. Chubasco 67. Patton 69. Oliver's Story 79, etc.
 TV series: Brenner 59–64. The Nurses 62–64. It Takes a Thief 69–70.

Binoche, Juliette (1964–).
French actress in international films. She won the best actress award at the 1993 Venice Film Festival and a French César for *Three Colours: Blue.* She is also an artist and in 1994 exhibited work done in collaboration with designer Christian Fenouillat.
 Liberty Belle 81. Les Nanas 84. Family Life 84. Rendezvous 85. Bad Blood (Mauvais Sang) 86. The Unbearable Lightness of Being 88. Les Amants du Pont-Neuf 91. Damage 92. Trois Couleurs: Rouge 92. Wuthering Heights 92. *Three Colours: Blue* (Trois Couleurs: Bleu) 93. Three Colours: White (Trois Couleurs: Blanc) 94, etc.

Binyon, Claude (1905–1978).
American writer-director.
 The Gilded Lily (w) 35. I Met Him in Paris (w) 37. Sing You Sinners (w) 38. Arizona (w) 40. Suddenly It's Spring (w) 44. *The Saxon Charm* (wd) 48. Family Honeymoon (w) 49. Mother Didn't Tell Me (w) 50. Stella (wd) 50. Aaron Slick from Punkin Crick (wd) 52. *Dreamboat* (wd) 52. You Can't Run Away from It (w) 56. North to Alaska (w) 60. Satan Never Sleeps (w) 62. Kisses for My President (w) 64, etc.

biograph.
(1) An old name for a cinema projector. (2) The name of Britain's first public cinema, near Victoria Station, London, opened 1905. (3) The name of D. W. Griffith's New York studios, 1903–10.

biopic.
A contraction of 'biographical picture', i.e. a film about the life of a real person. For examples see under *Composers, Courtesans, Entertainers, Explorers, Inventors, Kings and Queens, Painters, Politicians, Scientists, Soldiers, Spies, Sportsmen, Writers.*

Birch, Paul (c. 1900–1969).
Burly American character actor.
 The War of the Worlds 53. Rebel without a Cause 55. When Gangland Strikes 56. *Not of This Earth* 57. The Dark at the Top of the Stairs 60. The Man Who Shot Liberty Valance 62. It's a Mad Mad Mad Mad World 63. Welcome to Hard Times 67, etc.
 TV series: Cannonball 58.

Bird, Norman (1919–).
British character actor, usually of underdogs.
 An Inspector Calls 54. *The League of Gentlemen* 59. *Victim* 62. The Hill 65. Sky West and Crooked 65. The Wrong Box 66. A Dandy in Aspic 68. The Virgin and the Gypsy 70. The Rise and Rise of Michael Rimmer 70. Ooh . . . You Are Awful 73. The Slipper and the Rose 76. The Medusa Touch 77. The Final Conflict 81. Queenie (TV) 87, many others.

Bird, Richard (1895–).
British light actor who played genial middle-aged roles in the 30s, from the stage.
 Tilly of Bloomsbury 31. Mimi 35. Sensation 37. The Terror (& d) 38. The Door with Seven Locks 40. Halfway House 44. Forbidden 49. Alive and Kicking 58. Death Trap 62. Dr Strangelove 63. Masque of the Red Death 64. The Knack 65, many others.

birds
fit nicely into the glamorous romantic backgrounds of which Hollywood used to be so fond, but a few particular examples have been malevolent, including *The Vulture,* the owner of *The Giant Claw,* the carnivorous birds which nearly pecked *Barbarella* to death, and of course *The Birds* which turned on the human race in Hitchcock's 1963 movie. (In the various versions of Edgar Allan Poe's *The Raven,* the title character has been almost irrelevant.) Other notable birds have been seen in *Treasure Island, Birdman of Alcatraz, The Pigeon That Took Rome, Run Wild Run Free, The Bluebird, Kes, Doctor Dolittle,* and *Bill and Coo;* and in the cartoon field one must remember with affection Donald and Daffy Duck, Tweetie Pie, the Road Runner, and an assortment of other feathered friends. The heroes of *Brewster McCloud* and several other films thought they were birds; *Jonathan Livingston Seagull* was. *Mr Drake's Duck* and his Disney lookalike *The Million Dollar Duck* laid extremely valuable eggs. The pelican in *Storm Boy* stole the show from the hero; and the birds in *Tawny Pipit* and *Conflict of Wings* upset whole countrysides.

Birell, Tala (1908–1959) (Natalie Bierle).
Polish-Austrian leading lady who made some international films, then settled in Hollywood.
 Man in a Cage (GB) 30. Doomed Battalion 32. The Captain Hates the Sea 34. Crime and Punishment 35. Bringing Up Baby 38. Seven Miles from Alcatraz 42. The Song of Bernadette 43. Mrs Parkington 44. Song of Love 47. The House of Tao Ling 47, etc.

Birkett, Michael (1929–) (Lord Birkett).
British producer, mainly of specialized entertainments.
 The Caretaker 63. The Soldier's Tale 64. Modesty Blaise (associate) 66. The Marat/ Sade 66. A Midsummer Night's Dream 68. King Lear 70, etc.

Birkin, Andrew.
English screenwriter and director, the brother of Jane Birkin. He is also the biographer of James Barrie.
 The Pied Piper (co-w) 72. Flame 75. The Final Conflict 81. Kind David (co-w) 85. The Name of the Rose (co-w) 86. Burning Secret (wd) 88. Fields of Honor (co-w) 90. Salt on Our Skin (co-w, d) 93. The Cement Garden (d) 93, etc.

Birkin, Jane (1946–).
English leading lady, former model, who has been seen to most advantage in continental productions. She was formerly married to composer John Barry

and is the mother of Charlotte Gainsbourg. Married French director Jacques Doillon.
 Blow Up 66. Les Chemins de Katmandou 69. Romance of a Horsethief 71. Don Juan 73. Private Projection 73. Sept Morts sur Ordonnance 75. Catherine and Co. 75. Le Diable au Coeur 75. Death on the Nile 78. Evil Under the Sun 82. Love on the Ground (L'Amour par Terre) 84. Beethoven's Nephew 85. Dust 85. Leave All *Fair* 85. These Foolish Things (Daddy Nostalgie) 90. La Belle Noiseuse 91, etc.

Birney, David (1939–).
American leading man.
 Caravan to Vaccares 74. Trial by Combat 76. Prettykill 87.
 TV series: Bridget Loves Bernie 73. Serpico 76. St Elsewhere 82. Glitter 84.

Birney, Meredith Baxter (1947–).
American leading actress, mostly on TV. Wife of David Birney; formerly known as Meredith Baxter.
 Stand Up and Be Counted 71. Ben 72. The Cat Creature (TV) 73. The Stranger Who Looks Like Me (TV) 74. The Night That Panicked America (TV) 75. Target Risk (TV) 75. All the President's Men 76. The November Plan (TV) 76. Bittersweet Love 76. Beulah Land (TV) 80, etc.
 TV series: *Bridget Loves Bernie* 72. Family 76. *Family Ties* 82–89.

Biro, Lajos (1880–1948).
Hungarian screenwriter with Hollywood experience in the 20s followed by much work for Korda in Britain.
 Forbidden Paradise 24. The Last Command (AAN) 27. The Way of All Flesh 28. Service for Ladies 32. *The Private Life of Henry VIII* 32. Catherine the Great 34. *The Scarlet Pimpernel* 34. Sanders of the River 35. The Divorce of Lady X 37. The Drum 38. The Four Feathers 39. *The Thief of Baghdad* 40. Five Graves to Cairo 43. A Royal Scandal 45, etc.: mostly in collaboration.

Biroc, Joseph F. (1903–).
American cinematographer.
 It's a Wonderful Life (co-ph) 46. Magic Town 47. Roughshod 49. Without Warning 52. The Tall Texan 53. Down Three Dark Streets 54. Nightmare 56. Run of the Arrow 56. Attack 57. The Ride Back 57. The Amazing Colossal Man 57. Home Before Dark 58. Hitler 61. The Devil at Four o'Clock 61. Bye Bye Birdie 63. Bullet for a Badman 64. Hush Hush Sweet Charlotte 64. I Saw What You Did 65. The Flight of the Phoenix 65. The Russians Are Coming, The Russians Are Coming 66. The Killing of Sister George 68. Whatever Happened to Aunt Alice? 69. Too Late the Hero 69. The Legend of Lylah Clare 69. The Grissom Gang 71. The Organization 71. Emperor of the North Pole 73. Blazing Saddles 74. The Longest Yard 74. The Towering Inferno (co-ph, AA) 74. The Choirboys 77. Beyond the Poseidon Adventure 79. Airplane 80. All the Marbles 81. Airplane 2: the Sequel 82, etc.

Birrell, Tala (1908–1959).
Viennese leading actress, of German and Polish extraction, a protégée of Max Reinhardt, who began in German films before her unsuccessful Hollywood career, often in second features, after which she retired and returned to Europe.
 The Doomed Battalion (Berge in Flammen) (Ger.) 31. Nagana 33. Crime and Punishment 35. Bringing Up Baby 38. The Song of Bernadette 43. Women in Bondage 44. Mrs Parkington 44. The

Power of the Whistler 45. Dangerous Millions 46. Song of Love 47. Homicide for Three 49, etc.

Birt, Daniel (1907–1955).
British director, former editor: busy in late 40s.
The Three Weird Sisters 48. No Room at the Inn 49. The Interrupted Journey 49. Circumstantial Evidence 52. Background 53, etc.

Bischoff, Samuel (1890–1975).
American producer, with Warners in 30s, Columbia in 40s, subsequently independent.
The Charge of the Light Brigade 36. A Slight Case of Murder 37. Submarine Zone 41. You'll Never Get Rich 41. Appointment in Berlin 43. None Shall Escape 44. Mr District Attorney 47. Pitfall 48. Mrs Mike 50. The System 53. The Phenix City Story 55. Operation Eichmann 61. King of the Roaring Twenties 61. The Strangler 64, many others.

Bishop, Ed (1942–).
American leading man in Great Britain. Starred in TV's *UFO* series and subsequently served as a handy transatlantic voice.
The War Lover 62. The Mouse on the Moon 63. 2001: A Space Odyssey 68. Doppelganger (aka Journey to the Far Side of the Sun) 69. Diamonds Are Forever 71. The Devil's Web 74. Brass Target 78. Saturn 3 80. The Lords of Discipline 83. Restless Natives 85, etc.

Bishop, Joey (1918–) (Joseph Abraham Gottlieb).
American TV comedian who has made few film appearances.
The Naked and the Dead 58. Sergeants Three 63. Texas Across the River 66. A Guide for the Married Man 67. Who's Minding the Mint? 67. The Delta Force 86. Betsy's Wedding 90, etc.
TV series: The Joey Bishop Show 61–64, 67–69.

Bishop, Julie (1914–) (Jacqueline Brown).
American leading lady of routine films; also known as Jacqueline Wells.
Alice in Wonderland 33. The Bohemian Girl 36. The Nurse's Secret 41. Northern Pursuit 43. Rhapsody in Blue 45. Sands of Iwo Jima 49. Westward the Women 52. The High and the Mighty 54. The Big Land 57, many others.
TV series: My Hero 52.

Bishop, Terry (1917–1981).
British director. Much TV work.
You're Only Young Twice 52. Jim Driscoll's Donkey 54. Light Fingers 57. Model for Murder 58. Cover Girl Killer 59. Danger Tomorrow 60. The Unstoppable Man 61, etc.

Bishop, William (1918–1959).
American leading man, mostly in routine features.
Pillow to Post 46. The Romance of Rosy Ridge 47. Anna Lucasta 49. Lorna Doone 51. Cripple Creek 52. The Boss 56. The Oregon Trail 59, etc.
TV series: It's a Great Life 54.

Bissell, James D. (1951–).
American production designer.
E.T. – the Extra-Terrestrial 82. The Last Starfighter 84. The Falcon and the Snowman 85. Harry and the Hendersons 87. Twins 88. Always 89. Arachnophobia 90. The Rocketeer 91. Dennis the Menace (GB: Dennis) 93, etc.

Bissell, Whit (1909–).
American character actor who played anything from attorneys to garage attendants.
Holy Matrimony 43. Another Part of the Forest

47. It Should Happen to You 53. The Young Stranger 57. I Was a Teenage Frankenstein 58. The Time Machine 60. Hud 63. Seven Days in May 64. Covenant with Death 67. Airport 69. The Salzburg Connection 72. Soylent Green 73. Psychic Killer 75. Casey's Shadow 78, many others.
TV series: Bachelor Father 59–61. Time Tunnel 66.

Bisset, Jacqueline (1944–).
British leading lady, in American films.
■ The Knack 64. Arrivederci Baby 65. Cul de Sac 66. Casino Royale 67. Two for the Road 67. The Sweet Ride 67. Capetown Affair 67. The Detective 68. Bullitt 68. The First Time 68. L'Echelle Blanche (Fr.) 69. Secret World 69. Airport 69. *The Grasshopper* 70. The Mephisto Waltz 71. Believe in Me 71. Secrets 71. Judge Roy Bean 72. Stand Up and Be Counted 72. Le Magnifique 73. La Nuit Américaine 73. The Thief Who Came to Dinner 73. Murder on the Orient Express 74. The Spiral Staircase 75. End of the Game 76. St Ives 76. The Sunday Woman 76. The Deep 77. The Greek Tycoon 78. Someone Is Killing the Great Chefs of Europe 78. When Time Ran Out 80. Rich and Famous 81. Together 84. Inchon 82. Class 83. Under the Volcano 84. Anna Karenina (TV) 84. Forbidden (TV) 85. High Season 87. La Maison de Jade 88. Amoureuse 89. Scenes from the Class Struggle in Beverly Hills 89. Wild Orchid 90. The Maid 91. C'e Kim Novak al Telefano 92. Les Marmottes (Fr.) 93.

¶ I'm fascinated by a man with a twinkle in his eye. – *J.B.*

Bitzer, Billy (1874–1944) (George William Bitzer).
American cameraman who worked with D. W. Griffith on his most important films and is credited with several major photographic developments.
The New York Hat 12. Judith of Bethulia 13. Birth of a Nation 15. Intolerance 16. Hearts of the World 18. Broken Blossoms 19. Way Down East 21. America 24. The Struggle 30, many others.

Bixby, Bill (1934–1993).
Diffident American light leading man who turned to directing TV movies.
Lonely Are the Brave 62. Irma la Douce 63. Under the Yum Yum Tree 64. Ride Beyond Vengeance 66. Spinout 67. Speedway 68. Congratulations It's a Boy (TV) 71. The Couple Takes a Wife (TV) 72. Barbary Coast (pilot) (&d) (TV) 75. The Apple Dumpling Gang 75. The Invasion of Johnson County (TV) 76. Kentucky Fried Movie 77. The Incredible Hulk (TV) 77. The Incredible Hulk Returns (TV) 88. Trial of the Incredible Hulk (TV) (& d) 89. Death of the Incredible Hulk (TV) (& d) 90. Baby of the Bride (TV) (d) 91. Another Pair of Aces: Three of a Kind (TV) (d) 91. The Woman Who Loved Elvis (TV) (d) 93, etc.
TV series: The Joey Bishop Show 62. *My Favourite Martian* 63–66. The Courtship of Eddie's Father 69–70. The Magician 73. The Incredible Hulk 79–81. Goodnight Beantown 83.

Biziou, Peter.
Welsh cinematographer now working in Hollywood. He began in advertising, shooting commercials for director Alan Parker.
Hier, Aujourd'hui, Demain 68. Bugsy Malone 76. Monty Python's Life of Brian 79. Time Bandits 81. Pink Floyd – The Wall 82. Another Country 84. 9½ Weeks 86. Mississippi Burning (AA) 88. A World Apart 88. Rosencrantz and Guildenstern Are Dead 91. City of Joy 92. Damage 92. In the

Name of the Father 93. The Road to Wellville 94, etc.

Bjork, Anita (1923–).
Swedish actress who made only two English-speaking appearances.
Road to Heaven 42. Woman without a Face 47. The Realm of Men 49. *Miss Julie* 51. Secrets of Women 51. Night People (US) 52. Song of the Scarlet Flower 56. Of Love and Lust 57. The Phantom Carriage 58. Good Friends and Faithful Neighbours 60. The Lady in White 62. Square of Violence 63. Loving Couples 64. Adalen 31 69, etc.

Bjornstrand, Gunnar (1909–1986).
Distinguished Swedish character actor.
The False Millionaire 31. Panic 39. An Adventurer 42. A Night in the Harbour 43. Frenzy 44. It Rains on Our Love 46. Night Is My Future 47. The White Cat 50. Waiting Women 52. Sawdust and Tinsel 53. *Smiles of a Summer Night* 55. Seventh Heaven 56. *The Seventh Seal* 57. Wild Strawberries 57. *The Face* 58. The Devil's Eye 60. Through a Glass Darkly 61. Winter Light 63. Loving Couples 64. Persona 66. The Sadist 66. The Red Mantle 67. The Shame 68. The Rite 69. The Pistol 74. Face to Face 76. Tabu 77. Autumn Sonata 78. The Farewell 81. Fanny and Alexander 82, etc.

black comedy
finds humour in serious matters such as death, neurosis and sex perversion. In recent years it has become almost normal, though such films as *A Clockwork Orange* still cause controversy. We were once less sophisticated: in the early 30s, for instance, the comedy element in horror films such as James Whale's *The Bride of Frankenstein* and *The Old Dark House* was not understood, and even now is difficult to maintain on the same level, though Hammer films make sporadic attempts in this direction, and Roger Corman was rather more successful in *The Raven*. (Roman Polanski failed spectacularly in *The Fearless Vampire Killers*.) Comedies of murder date back to *The Front Page* and *Boudu Sauvé des Eaux*, with a progression through *Drôle de Drame*, *A Slight Case of Murder*, *Arsenic and Old Lace*, *Monsieur Verdoux*, *Kind Hearts and Coronets*, *The Red Inn*, *The Criminal Life of Archibaldo de la Cruz*, *The Naked Truth*, *She'll Have to Go*, *Candy* and *The Assassination Bureau*. Death and funerals have been the subject of jest in *Here Comes Mr Jordan*, *Too Many Crooks*, *The Loved One*, *The Wrong Box*, *Loot*, and *Harold and Maude*. On the level of social behaviour, there is black humour in *Who's Afraid of Virginia Woolf?*, *The Anniversary* and *The Honey Pot*, while Luis Buñuel castigates society through similar means in most of his films, notably *El*, *The Exterminating Angel* and *The Diary of a Chambermaid*. *Dr Strangelove* managed to laugh at the destruction of the world. Finally, Laurel and Hardy understood one aspect of the genre in their many grotesque jokes involving physical distortion. Elements of black comedy are to be found in an increasing number of modern films, notably those of Billy Wilder, John Huston and Alfred Hitchcock, and in the adventures of James Bond.

Black, Isobel (1943–).
British character actress.
Kiss of the Vampire 62. The Magnificent Two 67. David Copperfield (TV) 70. 10 Rillington Place 70. Twins of Evil 71, etc.

Black, Karen (1942–) (Karen Ziegeler).
American leading lady.
■ You're a Big Boy Now 67. Hard Contract 68. Easy Rider 69. Five Easy Pieces (AAN) 70. A

Gunfight 71. Drive He Said 71. Born to Win 71. Cisco Pike 71. Portnoy's Complaint 72. The Pyx 73. Rhinoceros 73. The Outfit 73. Little Laura and Big John 73. The Great Gatsby 74. Airport 75 75. Law and Disorder 75. Trilogy of Terror (TV) 75. The Day of the Locust 75. Nashville 75. Family Plot 76. Ace Up My Sleeve 76. Burnt Offerings 76. Killer Fish 78. Capricorn One 78. The Last Word 79. The Rip-Off 79. In Praise of Older Women 79. The Number 79. The Naked Sun 79. Separate Ways 81. Chanel Solitaire 81. Come Back to the Five and Dime, Jimmy Dean, Jimmy Dean 82. Can She Bake a Cherry Pie 83. Growing Pains 83. Martin's Day 84. Savage Dawn 84. Invaders from Mars 86. It's Alive III: Island of the Alive 87. Eternal Evil 87. Hostage 87. Dixie Lanes 88. The Invisible Kid 88. Homer and Eddie 89. Out of the Dark 89. Zapped Again 89. Twisted Justice 90. Night Angel 90. Judgement 91. Evil Spirits 91. Rubin and Ed 91. Club Fed 91. Blood Money 91. Haunting Fear 91. The Player 92. Caged Fear 92. Children of the Night 92. The Double O Kid 92. The Trust 93.

¶ My God, there aren't any more movie stars, which is terrific with me, it's very healthy. A lot of love now occurs in this business, people helping each other to do good work, getting high on each other's success. Isn't that great? – K.B.

Black Maria.
In the history of film this evocative phrase for a police van has a secondary meaning, being the nickname given to Edison's first portable studio.

Black, Noel (1937–).
American director who graduated to features from shorts.

Pretty Poison 68. Cover Me Babe 70. Jennifer on My Mind 71. A Man, a Woman and a Bank 79. The Other Victim (TV) 81. Private School 83. Quarterback Princess (TV) 83. A Conspiracy of Love (TV) 87, etc.

Black, Shane.
American screenwriter. He reportedly received $1.45m for his script for The Last Boy Scout and $4m in 1994 for his script The Long Kiss Goodnight (reportedly to be directed by Renny Harlin and starring Geena Davis), which Variety characterized as containing 'the grossest dialogue, grisliest killings, most sadistic torture scenes and most mean-spirited heavies'.

Lethal Weapon 87. The Monster Squad 87. Lethal Weapon 2 (story) 89. The Last Boy Scout 92. The Last Action Hero (co-w) 93.

Black, Stanley (1913–).
British bandleader and composer, responsible for scoring nearly 200 films.

Rhythm Racketeers 36. Mrs Fitzherbert 47. It Always Rains on Sunday 47. Laughter in Paradise 50. The Trollenberg Terror 57. Hell Is a City 60. The Young Ones 61. Summer Holiday 63. City Under the Sea 65. Crossplot 69, etc.

blackface.
A vaudeville adjective for comedians or singers who found their best appeal in 'Negro' disguise, i.e. with faces entirely blacked save for thick lips. Among the singers Al Jolson was perhaps the most famous exponent of this art, with Eddie Cantor a close second; the style derived from the minstrel shows which toured America from the mid-nineteenth century and which are clearly depicted in Jolson's Mammy and Swanee River. Dockstader's minstrels are recreated in The Jolson Story, and Dan Emmet's in Dixie; while Judy

Garland and Mickey Rooney created their own blackface troupe in Babes in Arms. Among blackface comics there were Moran and Mack, the 'two black crows'; and others who made themselves black for comic effect were Betty Grable and June Haver in The Dolly Sisters, Myrna Loy in Ham and Eggs at the Front, Gene Wilder in Silver Streak, Buster Keaton in College, Marion Davies in Going Hollywood, Fred Astaire in Swing Time, Dan Dailey in You're My Everything, and Chick Chandler in The Big Shot. In Watermelon Man, on the other hand, Godfrey Cambridge appeared in whiteface, as did Lenny Henry in True Identity.

blacklisting:
see The Hollywood Ten.

Blackman, Honor (1926–).
British leading lady, a Rank 'charm school' product submerged in 'English rose' roles from 1946 until a TV series fitted her up with kinky suits and judo tactics.

Fame is the Spur 47. Quartet 48. Diamond City 49. So Long at the Fair 50. The Rainbow Jacket 53. Breakaway 55. A Night to Remember 58. The Square Peg 58. A Matter of Who 61. Goldfinger 64. The Secret of My Success 65. Life at the Top 65. Moment to Moment 65. A Twist of Sand 68. Shalako 68. The Last Grenade 69. The Virgin and the Gypsy 70. Fright 71. Something Big 71. To the Devil a Daughter 75. The Cat and the Canary 78, etc.

TV series: The Avengers 60–63. The Upper Hand 90–93.

Blackman, Joan (1938–).
American leading lady of the 60s.

Visit to a Small Planet 61. The Great Imposter 61. Blue Hawaii 62. Twilight of Honor 63. Intimacy 66. Daring Game 68. Macon County Line 74, etc.

Blackmer, Sidney (1895–1973).
Suave American character actor, often seen as politician or high-class crook but also capable of sympathetic roles.

A Most Immoral Lady 29. Kismet 30. Little Caesar 30. Once a Sinner 31. Cocktail Hour 33. The Count of Monte Cristo 34. The President Vanishes 34. The Little Colonel 35. Smart Girl 35. Early to Bed 36. A Doctor's Diary 37. This is My Affair 37. Charlie Chan at Monte Carlo 37. The Last Gangster 37. Trade Winds 38. Hotel for Women 39. I Want a Divorce 40. Love Crazy 41. The Feminine Touch 41. The Panther's Claw 42. Quiet Please Murder 42. Murder in Times Square 43. Duel in the Sun 46. My Girl Tisa (as Teddy Roosevelt) 48. People Will Talk 51. Johnny Dark 54. High Society 56. Tammy and the Bachelor 57. How to Murder Your Wife 65. Covenant with Death 67. Rosemary's Baby 68, many others.

blacks
in films have only slowly attained equal status with whites. In early silents they were invariably depicted as slaves, a fact encouraged by the several popular versions of Uncle Tom's Cabin. If a film had a black role of consequence, it was usually played by a white man in blackface. But blacks began to make their own films for their own audiences, and still do, though these seldom get a general showing. The first all-black film was Darktown Jubilee in 1914 . . . the year that Griffith made The Birth of a Nation, with its strong anti-black bias. Griffith atoned for this in The Greatest Thing in Life 18, in which a white soldier and a black embraced, but in 1922 he again incurred the wrath of colour-sensitive critics by making One Exciting Night, the

first film to boast the quickly stereotyped figure of the terrified black manservant. Early talkies included such all-black films as Hearts in Dixie and Vidor's Hallelujah, and in 1933 Paul Robeson appeared in a version of Eugene O'Neill's The Emperor Jones. Much of the interest of Imitation of Life 34 centred on the problems of black servant Louise Beavers and her half-white daughter. In 1936 the screen version of Green Pastures, depicting the simple black's idea of the Bible, was widely acclaimed but tended to perpetuate a patronizing attitude. The feeling of the South for its blacks was strongly outlined in They Won't Forget 37 and Gone with the Wind 39. Stormy Weather 42 and Cabin in the Sky 43 were all-black musicals in Hollywood's best manner, but Tales of Manhattan 42 was retrogressive in showing blacks as inhabitants of a vast shanty town. In Casablanca 42, however, Dooley Wilson was accepted on equal terms by Humphrey Bogart. Disney's Song of the South 46, despite an engaging performance by James Baskett, brought back the old Uncle Remus image. The post-war period generally permitted the emergence of serious black actors like James Edwards and Sidney Poitier, and films on racial themes such as Intruder in the Dust and Pinky. At last, in 1965, came films in which a black could play a straight part utterly unrelated to his colour. Poitier did so in The Bedford Incident, then used colour defiantly in In the Heat of the Night and Guess Who's Coming to Dinner. Remakes of well known 'white' movies were one way to bring in a wide range of coloured actors: The Lost Man (Odd Man Out), Uptight (The Informer), Cool Breeze (The Asphalt Jungle). Even Barefoot in the Park became a black TV series. The subject was rather self-consciously aired in such films as Change of Mind, Watermelon Man, The Landlord and Medium Cool. In 1970 came Cotton Comes to Harlem, perhaps the first black thriller with no chip on its shoulder; in 1972 the seal of approval was set up by Shaft, a violent private-eye thriller with an all-black cast which proved not only acceptable to all audiences but highly commercial. The floodgates opened and before 1972 was out we even had Blacula and Blackenstein. Wholly black films which followed included Sounder, The Autobiography of Miss Jane Pittman (TV), Uptown Saturday Night, Let's Do It Again; and in 1977 a sensational impact was achieved by a TV serialization of Alex Haley's Roots, by watching which half of America sought to atone for centuries of bad white behaviour towards the blacks. Redd Foxx, a nightclub comedian, became a TV star in the 70s in Sanford and Son, based on the British series Steptoe and Son, followed by Sanford and the Redd Foxx Show in the 80s. At the same time, another comedian, Richard Pryor, was making a similar impact in films, particularly when teamed with Gene Wilder in Silver Streak and Stir Crazy. Following him came the fast-talking, self-confident Eddie Murphy, a hit on the TV show Saturday Night Live while still in his teens. The film 48 Hours established him as a Hollywood star, and Beverly Hills Cop confirmed his position as a big box-office attraction, although Harlem Nights, his attempt at writing and directing as well as acting, was not a success. Robert Townsend, also a comedian, turned his frustrations in Hollywood to comic account in Hollywood Shuffle, which also featured the talents of Keenan Wayans, who wrote, directed and starred in I'm Gonna Git You Sucka, a send-up of the 'blaxploitation' movies of the 70s, a genre which still lives on in the films of actor-director Fred Williamson. From the mid-80s the talented director, actor and writer Spike Lee created a series of provocative, socially-conscious films dealing with uneasy relationships between white and black: She's Gotta Have It, School Daze, Do

The Right Thing, Mo' Better Blues, Jungle Fever, Malcolm X, and *Crooklyn.* Lee's cinematographer, Ernest Dickerson, turned director with the powerful *Juice,* and the young John Singleton became the first director to be nominated for an Oscar for his first film with *Boyz N the Hood,* which probed into the reasons for the wasted lives of members of Los Angeles street gangs. Director Melvin Van Peebles had made one of the earliest and most significant films of black experience with *Sweet Sweetback's Baadasssss Song* in 1971. Twenty years later, his son Mario directed *New Jack City,* a violent anti-drug thriller that may have made a new star of rap performer Ice T. Actor Bill Duke returned to a Chester Himes novel to direct *A Rage in Harlem* in 1991, and followed it with *Deep Cover* in 92. Actors escaping from stereotyped roles include Wesley Snipes, Forest Whitaker, Danny Glover, Whoopi Goldberg and Morgan Freeman.

Britain, less affected by black problems, moved in parallel fashion: in the early 30s, films of *The Kentucky Minstrels;* then Paul Robeson dominating somewhat insulting material in *Sanders of the River* and subsequently earning three or four serious film vehicles of his own; the post-war attempt to understand in *Men of Two Worlds;* and problem pictures like *Simba,* about the Mau-Mau, and *Flame in the Streets,* about the prospect of a black in an East End family. The racism of British movies of the 30s is visible in the 90s on afternoon and late-night television screenings, where actors can still be seen putting coal-dust on their faces to pass as black, and you can still hear dialogue such as 'Whitemail? What's whitemail?' 'Blackmailing a nigger.' Comedian Lenny Henry is Britain's nearest equivalent to Eddie Murphy, though his success is so far confined to television. Director and writer Isaac Julien dealt with black experience in Britain in *Young Soul Rebels.*

Blackton, J. Stuart (1868–1941).
British pioneer producer who spent years in America working with Edison. He was one of the founders of Vitagraph, an important producer in the first days of cinema.

Raffles 05. The Life of Moses 10. The Battle Cry of Peace 15. Womanhood 16. The Glorious Adventure (in Prizmacolour) 21. On the Banks of the Wabash 23. The Clean Heart 24. The Beloved Brute 24. Gypsy Cavalier 24. Tides of Passion 25. The Happy Warrior 25. Bride of the Storm 30, many others.

Blackwell, Carlyle (1888–1955).
American stage matinée idol, in demand for romantic roles during the 20s; his declamatory style could scarcely survive the coming of sound.

Uncle Tom's Cabin 09. The Key to Yesterday 14. The Restless Sex 20. Sherlock Holmes 22. The Beloved Vagabond 23. Bulldog Drummond 23. She 25. The Wrecker 29. The Crooked Billet 30. The Calling of Dan Matthews 35, many others.

Blades, Ruben (1948–).
Panamanian leading actor, screenwriter, musician and composer, in America. He studied law and has political ambitions to become a future president of his country.

The Last Fight 83. Beat Street 84. Crossover Dreams 85. Critical Condition 87. Fatal Beauty 87. Homeboy 88. The Milagro Beanfield War 88. Oliver and Company (s) 88. Disorganized Crime 89. The Heart of the Deal 90. Mo' Better Blues 90. Predator 2 90. The Two Jakes 90. Crazy from the Heart 91. Color of Night 94, etc.

Blain, Gérard (1930–).
French leading actor once thought of as a

continental equivalent of James Dean. After a period of retirement he emerged again as a serious director.

Les Fruits Sauvages 54. Le Temps des Assassins 56. Crime and Punishment 56. Les Mistons 58. *Le Beau Serge* 58. *Les Cousins* 59. The Hunchback of Notre Dame 60. The Dauphins 60. Gold of Rome 61. Hatari (US) 62. La Bonne Soupe 64. Un Homme de Trop 67. Les Amis (w, d only) 71. Le Pélican (& w, d) 73. The American Friend 77. Utopia (w, d only) 78. Le Rebelle (w, d only) 80, etc.

Blaine, Vivian (1921–) (Vivienne Stapleton).
Vivacious American leading lady and personable songstress. Made comparatively few films, her greatest success being on Broadway.

■ Thru Different Eyes 42. Girl Trouble 42. He Hired the Boss 43. Jitterbugs 43. Greenwich Village 44. Something for the Boys 44. Nob Hill 45. *State Fair* 45. Doll Face 45. If I'm Lucky 46. *Three Little Girls in Blue* 46. Skirts Ahoy 52. Main Street to Broadway 53. *Guys and Dolls* 55. Public Pigeon Number One 57. Katie, Portrait of a Centerfold (TV) 78. The Dark 78. The Cracker Factory (TV) 79. Sooner or Later (TV) 79. Parasite 82. I'm Going to Be Famous 83.

Blair, Betsy (1923–) (Elizabeth Boger).
American character actress who often plays shy or nervous women.

■ The Guilt of Janet Ames 47. A Double Life 47. *Another Part of the Forest* 48. The Snake Pit 48. Mystery Street 50. Kind Lady 51. *Marty* (BFA, AAN) 55. Calle Mayor (Sp.) 56. Il Grido (It.) 57. The Halliday Brand 57. All Night Long (GB) 61. A Delicate Balance 73.

Blair, George (1906–1970).
American second feature director.

Duke of Chicago 49. Flaming Fury 49. Daughter of the Jungle 49. Insurance Investigator 51. Jaguar 55. The Hypnotic Eye 60, many others.

Blair, Janet (1921–) (Martha Lafferty).
Vivacious American leading lady of co-features in the 40s.

■ *Three Girls About Town* 41. Blondie Goes to College 42. Two Yanks in Trinidad 42. Broadway 42. *My Sister Eileen* 42. Something to Shout About 43. Once Upon a Time 44. Tonight and Every Night 45. Tars and Spars 46. Gallant Journey 46. The Fabulous Dorseys 47. I Love Trouble 48. The Black Arrow 48. The Fuller Brush Man 48. Public Pigeon Number One 57. Boys' Night Out 62. *Night of the Eagle* (GB) 62. The One and Only Genuine Original Family Band 68.

TV series: Caesar's Hour 56–57. *The Smith Family* 71–72.

Blair, Linda (1959–).
American juvenile lead of the 70s who made a spectacular beginning as a possessed child.

The Sporting Club 71. *The Exorcist* (AAN) 74. Born Innocent (TV) 74. Sarah T, Portrait of a Teenage Alcoholic (TV) 75. Airport 75 75. Sweet Hostage (TV) 76. Victory at Entebbe (TV) 76. Exorcist II: The Heretic 78. Roller Boogie 79. Hell Night 81. Chained Heat 81. Savage Streets 82. Night Patrol 82. Red Heat 83. Savage Island 85. Nightforce 87. Grotesque 88. Silent Assassins 88. Up Your Alley 88. Bad Blood 89. Witchcraft 89. A Woman Obsessed 89. The Chilling 89. Moving Target 89. Zapped Again 89. Bail Out 90. Repossessed 90. Moving Target 90. Dead Sleep 90. The Fatal Bond 91, etc.

Blake, Amanda (1929–1989) (Beverly Neill).
American supporting actress. Died of AIDS.

Duchess of Idaho 50. Stars in My Crown 50. Lili 53. Sabre Jet 53. A Star is Born 54. About Mrs Leslie 54. High Society 56. Betrayal (TV) 74, etc.

TV series: *Gunsmoke* (as Kitty) 55–75.

Blake, Howard.
British composer.

An Elephant Called Slowly 71. The Odd Job 78. Riddle of the Sands 79. Flash Gordon (co-m) 80. Amityville II: The Possession (US) 82. Amityville 3-D (US) 83. The Lords of Discipline (US) 83. A Month in the Country 87, etc.

Blake, Katherine (1928–1991).
South African actress in Britain, mostly on TV: Anne of the Thousand Days 70, etc.

Blake, Madge (1900–1969).
American supporting actress.

Between Midnight and Dawn 50. Singin' in the Rain 52. The Long Long Trailer 54. Batman 66, etc.

Blake, Marie (1896–1978) (Blossom MacDonald).
American small-part actress, sister of Jeanette MacDonald. Played the receptionist in the Dr Kildare movie series of the early 40s. Changed her billing to her married name, Blossom Rock, in the 50s.

Mannequin 37. Young Dr Kildare 38. The Women 39. They Knew What They Wanted 39. A Child Is Born 40. I Married a Witch 42. Abbott and Costello in Hollywood 45. The Snake Pit 49. Love Nest 51. From the Terrace 60, many others.

TV series: The Addams Family (as Grandmama) 64–66.

Blake, Robert (1933–) (Michael Gubitosi).
American child actor who later attracted some unusual adult roles.

Andy Hardy's Double Life 43. The Horn Blows at Midnight 45. Treasure of Sierra Madre 47. Revolt in the Big House 58. Battle Flame 59. The Purple Gang 60. The Greatest Story Ever Told 65. *In Cold Blood* 67. *Tell Them Willie Boy Is Here* 69. Corky 72. Electra Glide in Blue 73. Coast to Coast 80. Second Hand Hearts 80. Blood Feud (TV) 83, etc.

TV series: The Richard Boone Show 64. *Baretta* 74–77. Hell Town 85.

Blake, Whitney.
American character actress, mother of Meredith Baxter.

Deadline Midnight 59. The Boy Who Stole the Elephant (TV) 70. Strange Homecoming (TV) 74. The Betsy 78, etc.

TV series: Hazel 61–65.

Blakeley, John E. (1889–1958).
British producer-director of low-budget Lancashire comedies.

■ Dodging the Dole 36. Somewhere in England 40. Somewhere in Camp 42. Somewhere on Leave 42. Demobbed 44. Under New Management 46. Home Sweet Home 46. Cup Tie Honeymoon 48. Holiday with Pay 48. Somewhere in Politics 49. What a Carry On 49. School for Randle 49. Over the Garden Wall 50. Let's Have a Murder 50. It's a Grand Life 53.

Blakeley, Tom (1918–1984).
British producer of second features.

Love's a Luxury 58. Tomorrow at Ten 62. Devils of Darkness 65. Island of Terror 66, etc.

Blakely, Colin (1930–1987).
Stocky British stage actor, in occasional films.
  Saturday Night and Sunday Morning 60. This Sporting Life 62. The Informers 63. The Long Ships 64. A Man for All Seasons 66. The Spy with a Cold Nose 67. *The Day the Fish Came Out* 67. Charlie Bubbles 67. The Vengeance of She 68. *Decline and Fall* 68. Alfred the Great 69. *The Private Life of Sherlock Holmes* (as Watson) 70. Something to Hide 72. Young Winston 72. Murder on the Orient Express 74. Galilco 74. Love Among the Ruins (TV) 74. It Shouldn't Happen to a Vet 76. Equus 77. The Day Christ Died (TV) 80. Loophole 80. Nijinsky 80. The Dogs of War 81. Evil Under the Sun 82. The Red Monarch (TV) 83. Paradise Postponed (TV) 86.

Blakely, Susan (1948–   ).
American leading lady; former model.
  ■ Savages 72. The Lords of Flatbush 74. The Towering Inferno 74. Report to the Commissioner 75. Shampoo 75. Capone 75. *Rich Man Poor Man* (TV) 76. Secrets (TV) 77. Savages 78. Make Me an Offer (TV) 80. A Cry for Love (TV) 80. Oklahoma City Dolls (TV) 80. The Concorde – Airport 79 79. The Bunker (TV) 81. Will There Really be a Morning? (TV) 83. Over the Top 87. Out of Sight, Out of Her Mind 89. My Mom's a Werewolf 89. Wildflower (TV) 91. Tous les Jours Dimanche (Fr.) 94.

Blakemore, Michael (1928–   ).
Australian director, mostly on English stage.
  A Personal History of the Australian Surf 81. Privates on Parade 82. Country Life (a, wd) 94.

Blakley, Ronee (1946–   ).
American pop singer who has made acting appearances.
  Nashville (AAN) 75. Renaldo and Clara 78. The Driver 78. She Came to the Valley 79. The Baltimore Bullet 80. Lightning Over Water 81. The Private Files of J. Edgar Hoover 77. Good Luck Miss Wyckoff 79. A Nightmare on Elm Street 84. I Played for You 85. Return to Salem's Lot 87. Someone to Love 87. Student Confidential 87. Murder by Numbers 89, etc.

Blanc, Jean-Pierre (1942–   ).
French director.
  La Vieille Fille 71. Un Ange au Paradis 73. D'Amour et d'Eau Fraiche 75, etc.

Blanc, Mel (1908–1989).
The voice of Warner Brothers' cartoon characters, including Bugs Bunny, Sylvester and Tweetie Pie. Made occasional cameo appearances in films.
  Neptune's Daughter 49. Kiss Me Stupid 64, etc.
  TV series: The Jack Benny Show 50–65. The Bugs Bunny Show (voices) 60–62. The Flintstones (voices of Barney Rubble and Dino) 60–66. The Jetsons (voices) 63–63. Where's Huddles (voice) 70. The Bugs Bunny/Roadrunner Show (voices) 76. Buck Rogers in the 25th Century (voice of Twiki) 79–81.

Blanc, Michel (1952–   ).
Balding leading French actor, from the theatre, who made his reputation in comic roles. He is also a writer and director. He won the screenplay award at the 1994 Cannes Film Festival for *Gross Fatigue*.
  Walk in the Shadow (Marche à l'Ombre) (d) 84. The Fugitives (Les Fugitifs) 86. Evening Dress (Tenue de Soirée) 86. I Hate Actors! 86. Story of Women (Une Affaire de Femmes) 88. Monsieur Hire 89. Chambre à Part 89. Strike It Rich 90. Uranus 90. Merci la Vie 91. Prospero's Books 91.

The Favour, the Watch and the Very Big Fish (Rue Saint-Sulpice) 91. Toxic Affair 93. Grosse Fatigue (& d) 94, etc.

Blanchar, Pierre (1892–1963).
Distinguished French screen and stage actor.
  Jocelyn 23. L'Atlantide 31. Le Diable en Bouteille 34. Crime and Punishment 35. Mademoiselle Docteur 36. L'Affaire du Courrier de Lyon 37. *Un Carnet de Bal* 37. La Symphonie Pastorale 40. Pontcarral 42. Rififi Chez les Femmes 58, etc.

Blanchard, Mari (1927–1970) (Mary Blanchard).
Decorative American leading lady of 50s co-features.
  Mr Music 50. Ten Tall Men 51. Veils of Baghdad 53. Black Horse Canyon 54. *Destry* 55. The Crooked Web 56. The Return of Jack Slade 56. Jungle Heat 57. No Place to Land 58. Don't Knock the Twist 62. McLintock 63. Twice Told Tales 64, etc.

Blanchard, Terence (1962–   ).
American composer and jazz trumpeter who has scored four of Spike Lee's films. Born in New Orleans, he played with Art Blakey's Jazz Messengers in the 80s before leading his own band.
  School Daze 87. Do the Right Thing 89. Jungle Fever 91. Malcolm X 92. Sugar Hill 94. The Inkwell 94. Crooklyn 94. Trial by Jury 94.

Blandick, Clara (1880–1962).
American character actress, often seen as sensible servant or no-nonsense aunt. Committed suicide.
  The Girl Said No 30. Huckleberry Finn 31. The Wet Parade 32. One Sunday Afternoon 33. Broadway Bill 34. The Gorgeous Hussy 36. A Star is Born 37. Huckleberry Finn 39. *The Wizard of Oz* (as Aunt Em) 39. It Started with Eve 41. Can't Help Singing 44. A Stolen Life 46. Life with Father 47. The Bride Goes Wild 48. Love That Brute 50, many others.

Blane, Ralph (1914–   ) (Ralph Uriah Hunsecker).
American composer and lyricist who with his partner Hugh Martin (1914–   ) was responsible for *Best Foot Forward* and *Meet Me in St Louis*.

Blane, Sally (1910–   ) (Elizabeth Jung).
American leading lady of the early 30s; sister of Loretta Young.
  Sirens of the Sea 27. Rolled Stockings 27. The Vagabond Lover 29. Little Accident 30. Once a Sinner 31. Ten Cents a Dance 31. Disorderly Conduct 31. I am a Fugitive from a Chain Gang 32. Advice to the Lovelorn 33. The Silver Streak 35. One Mile from Heaven 37. Charlie Chan at Treasure Island 39. A Bullet for Joey 54, many others.

Blangsted, Folmar (1904–1982).
American editor.
  The Doughgirls 44. Rhapsody in Blue 45. Cry Wolf 47. Flamingo Road 49. Distant Drums 51. The Charge at Feather River 53. A Star is Born 54. A Cry in the Night 56. Rio Bravo 59. Taras Bulba 63. The War Lord 65. Camelot 67. The Forbin Project 70. Man of La Mancha 72. Oklahoma Crude 73, many others.

Blanke, Henry (1901–1981).
German-American producer, long at Warner.
  Female 33. *The Story of Louis Pasteur* 35. Satan Met a Lady 36. The Petrified Forest 36. Green Pastures 36. The Life of Emile Zola 37. Jezebel 38. *The Adventures of Robin Hood* 38. Juarez 39. The Old Maid 39. The Sea Hawk 40. *The Maltese Falcon*

41. Old Acquaintance 43. The Mask of Dimitrios 44. Deception 46. The Treasure of the Sierra Madre 47. The Fountainhead 49. Come Fill the Cup 51. King Richard and the Crusaders 54. Serenade 56. Too Much Too Soon 58. *The Nun's Story* 59. Ice Palace 60. Hell is for Heroes 62, many others.

Blankfort, Michael (1907–1982).
American screenwriter, former Princeton professor.
  Blind Alley 39. Adam Had Four Sons 40. Texas 41. Flight Lieutenant 42. An Act of Murder 48. Broken Arrow 50. Halls of Montezuma 51. My Six Convicts 52. The Juggler (from his novel) 53. Untamed 55. Tribute to a Bad Man 56. The Vintage 57. The Other Man (TV) 70. A Fire in the Sky (TV) 78, etc.

Blasetti, Alessandro (1900–1987).
Italian director mainly associated with comedy and spectaculars.
  Sole 29. Nero 30. Resurrection 31. The Old Guard 33. The Countess of Parma 37. *Four Steps in the Clouds* 42. A Day of Life 46. Fabiola 48. *First Communion* 50. Altri Tempi (Infidelity) 52. Europe by Night 59. I Love You Love 61, many others.

Blatt, Edward A. (1905–1991).
Russian-born American stage director who worked briefly for Warners in the 40s.
  ■ Between Two Worlds 44. Escape in the Desert 45. Smart Woman 48.

Blatty, William Peter (1928–   ).
American screenwriter.
  The Man from the Diners' Club 63. A Shot in the Dark 64. John Goldfarb Please Come Home 65. Promise Her Anything 66. What Did You Do in the War Daddy? 66. Gunn 67. The Great Bank Robbery 69. Darling Lili 69. The Exorcist (& w, p, oa) (AA script) 73. The Ninth Configuration (& w, oa) 80. 'Killer' Kane (wd) 80. The Exorcist III (wd) 90, etc.

Blaustein, Julian (1913–   ).
American producer.
  Broken Arrow 50. Mister 880 50. Take Care of My Little Girl 51. Desiree 54. Storm Center 56. Bell Book and Candle 58. The Wreck of the Mary Deare 59. Two Loves 61. The Four Horsemen of the Apocalypse 62. Khartoum 66. Three into Two Won't Go 69, etc.

Blech, Hans Christian (1925–   ).
German character actor, occasionally in international films.
  L'Affaire Blum 49. Decision Before Dawn 51. The Longest Day 62. The Visit 63. The Saboteur 65. Battle of the Bulge 65. The Bridge at Remagen 69. Dirty Hands (Les Innocents aux Main Sales) 76. The Wrong Move 78, etc.

Blessed, Brian (1937–   ).
Massive British character actor, originally 'Fancy Smith' in TV's *Z Cars*.
  Brotherly Love 70. The Trojan Women 71. Man of La Mancha 72. Henry VIII and His Six Wives 73. I Claudius (TV) 76. Flash Gordon 80. High Road to China 83. War and Remembrance (TV) 88. Henry V 89. Robin Hood: Prince of Thieves 91. Prisoners of Honor 92. Back in the USSR 92, etc.

Bletcher, William (Billy) (1894–1979).
Small, deep-voiced American comic actor, from vaudeville. He made his film debut in 1913, was in many of Max Sennett's two-reel comedies and partnered Billy Gilbert in some 30s shorts. He also appeared in Our Gang comedies as Spanky

McFarland's father and supplied the voice of the Big Bad Wolf for Walt Disney's *Three Little Pigs*.

Billy Jim 22. The Dude Cowboy 26. Top Speed 30. The Midnight Patrol 33. Babes in Toyland 34. Destry Rides Again 39. Boss of Rawhide 51. The Patsy 64. Hello Dolly! 69, etc.

Blier, Bernard (1916–1989).
French actor who made a virtue of his plumpness and baldness.

Hôtel du Nord 38. *Quai des Orfèvres* 47. *Dédée d'Anvers* 47. L'École Buissonière 48. Manèges (The Wanton) 49. Souvenirs Perdus 50. Les Misérables 57. Les Grandes Familles 58. Le Cave se Rebiffe 61. Les Saintes Nitouches 63. A Question of Honour (Italy) 66. Breakdown (& d) 67. Catch Me a Spy 71. The Tall Blond Man with One Black Shoe 74. Chez Victor 76. Le Compromis 78. Buffet Froid 80. Passione d'Amore 82, etc.

Blier, Bertrand (1939–).
French director, son of Bernard Blier.

Hitler Connais Pas 62. Les Valseurs 74. Femmes Fatales 76. *Préparez Vos Mouchoirs* (AA) 78. *Buffet Froid* 80. Beau Père 81. My Best Friend's Girl 83. Separate Rooms (Nôtre Histoire) 84. Ménage (Tenue de Soirée) 86. Trop Belle pour Toi 89. Merci la Vie 91. Un, Deux, Trois, Soleil 93. Gross Fatigue (story) 94, etc.

blimp.
A soundproof cover fixed over a camera during shooting to absorb running noise.

blindness,
a tragic affliction, has generally been treated by film-makers with discretion, though not without sentimentality. Typical is Herbert Marshall as the blind pianist in *The Enchanted Cottage*, dispensing words of wisdom with piano music in the background and the sounds of nature through the open door. Other sympathetic blind roles include Cary Grant in *Wings in the Dark*; Irene Dunne (later Jane Wyman) in *Magnificent Obsession*; Ronald Colman (later Fredric March) in *The Dark Angel*; Colman also in *The Light That Failed*; Ralph Richardson (later Laurence Harvey) in *The Four Feathers*; James Cagney in *City for Conquest*; Ida Lupino in *On Dangerous Ground*; Arthur Kennedy in *Bright Victory*; Patricia Neal in *Psyche* 59 64; John Garfield in *Pride of the Marines*; Michele Morgan in *La Symphonie Pastorale*; Virginia Cherrill in *City Lights*; Elizabeth Hartmann in *A Patch of Blue*; Michael Wilding in *Torch Song*; and Nicol Williamson in *Laughter in the Dark*. More sinister blind characters came in *Saboteur* and *Victim*; while blind detectives, not forgetting TV's *Longstreet*, include Edward Arnold in *Eyes in the Night* and *The Hidden Eye*, Van Johnson in *23 Paces to Baker Street*, Dick Powell (briefly blinded by cordite fumes) in *Murder My Sweet*; and Karl Malden in *Cat o' Nine Tails*.

In thrillers, terrified blind heroines have been useful: Patricia Dainton in *Witness in the Dark*, Audrey Hepburn in *Wait Until Dark* and Mia Farrow in *Blind Terror*. Other tricks with blind characters were played in *Faces in the Dark* and *Silent Dust*, in both of which the hero's condition helped him to outwit his assailants; and *Tread Softly Stranger*, where the murderer gave himself away through fear of the only witness – who turned out to be blind. *Afraid of the Dark* had a blind woman threatened by a serial killer while *Blink* dealt with a woman who may have witnessed a murder as she regained her sight. Genuinely blind actors include Esmond Knight (temporarily) playing a sighted role in *The Silver Fleet*, and Ray Charles in *Ballad in Blue*. A nice ironic point was made in

Bride of Frankenstein, where O. P. Heggie as a blind hermit was the only human being who did not fear the monster.

Other films involving blindness include *Night Song, Destiny, Man in the Dark*, and the thrice-made *Magnificent Obsession*. Finally, in *The Day of the Triffids*, almost everyone on earth was blinded.

Blinn, Holbrook (1872–1928).
American silent star.

Rosita 23. Janice Meredith 24. Yolanda 25. Zander the Great 27, many others.

Bliss, Sir Arthur (1891–1975).
British composer who occasionally scored films.

■ *Things to Come* 36. Conquest of the Air 38. Men of Two Worlds 46. Christopher Columbus 49. The Beggar's Opera 53. Welcome the Queen 54. Seven Waves Away 56.

Blitzstein, Marc (1905–1964).
American composer. Film music for documentaries, including Spanish Earth 38, Native Land 42.

Bloch, Robert (1917–1994).
American screenwriter dealing almost exclusively in horror themes with trick endings.

Psycho (oa) 60. The Cabinet of Caligari 62. Strait Jacket 63. *The Night Walker* 64. The Psychopath 66. The Deadly Bees 66. The Torture Garden 67. The House that Dripped Blood 70. Asylum 72, etc.

block booking.
A system supposedly illegal but still practised, whereby a renter forces an exhibitor to book a whole group of mainly mediocre films in order to get the one or two he wants.

Blocker, Dan (1928–1972).
Heavyweight American character actor.

Come Blow Your Horn 63. Lady in Cement 68. The Cockeyed Cowboys of Calico County 69, etc.

TV series: Cimarron City 58. Bonanza (as Hoss Cartwright) 59–72.

Blomberg, Erik (1913–).
Finnish director, a former cinematographer, whose first feature won the prize for the best fairy-tale film at the Cannes Film Festival in 1953. From the mid-60s, he worked in television.

The White Reindeer (Valkoinen Peura) 52. The Engagement (Kilhaus) 55. The Wedding Night (Hääyö) 62, etc.

Blomfield, Derek (1920–1964).
British boy actor of the 30s.

Emil and the Detectives 35. Turn of the Tide 35. The Ghost of St Michael's 41. Alibi 42. Night and the City 50. Hobson's Choice 54. It's Great to be Young 56. Carry On Admiral 57, etc.

Blondell, Joan (1909–1979).
Amiable American comedienne who played reporters, gold-diggers or the heroine's dizzy friend in innumerable comedies and musicals of the 30s. Later graduated to occasional character roles.

Autobiographical novel 1972: *Center Door Fancy*.
■ Sinner's Holiday 30. The Office Wife 30. Other Men's Women 30. Illicit 31. My Past 31. Millie 31. The Reckless Hour 31. Big Business Girl 31. Night Nurse 31. Public Enemy 31. Blonde Crazy 31. Union Depot 32. The Crowd Roars 32. The Famous Ferguson Case 32. *Miss Pinkerton* 32. Big City Blues 32. Make Me a Star 32. The Greeks Had a Word for Them 32. Three on a Match 32. Central Park 32. Broadway Bad 33. Lawyer Man 33. Blondie Johnson 33. *Gold Diggers of 1933* 33.

Goodbye Again 33. *Footlight Parade* 33. Havana Widows 33. *Convention City* 33. Kansas City Princess 34. Smarty 34. I've Got Your Number 34. He Was Her Man 34. *Dames* 34. The Travelling Saleslady 34. Broadway Gondolier 35. We're in the Money 35. Miss Pacific Fleet 35. Colleen 36. Sons o' Guns 36. Bullets or Ballots 36. *Stage Struck* 36. *Three Men on a Horse* 36. Gold Diggers of 1937 37. The King and the Chorus Girl 37. The Perfect Specimen 37. Back in Circulation 37. *Stand-In* 37. There's Always a Woman 38. Off the Record 38. East Side of Heaven 39. The Kid from Kokomo 39. Good Girls Go to Paris 39. The Amazing Mr Williams 39. Two Girls on Broadway 40. I Want a Divorce 40. *Topper Returns* 41. Model Wife 41. *Three Girls Around Town* 42. Lady for a Night 42. Cry Havoc 43. *A Tree Grows in Brooklyn* 44. Don Juan Quilligan 45. Adventure 46. The Corpse Came cod 47. Nightmare Alley 47. Christmas Eve 47. For Heaven's Sake 50. The Blue Veil (AAN) 51. The Opposite Sex 56. Lizzie 57. This Could be the Night 57. The Desk Set 58. Will Success Spoil Rock Hunter 58. Angel Baby 61. Advance to the Rear 63. The Cincinatti Kid 66. Paradise Road 66. Ride Beyond Vengeance 66. Waterhole Three 67. Stay Away Joe 68. Kona Coast 68. The Phynx 70. Support Your Local Gunfighter 71. Winner Take All 75. Death at Love House (TV) 76. Opening Night 77. Battered (TV) 78. The Rebels (TV) 78. Grease 79. The Champ 79.

TV series: Here Come the Brides 68–69. Banyon 72.

Bloom, Claire (1931–).
British leading actress who came to the screen via the Old Vic. She married novelist Philip Roth in 1990; previous husbands were Rod Steiger (1959–69) and producer Hillard Elkins (1969–72).

Autobiography: 1982, *Limelight and After: The Education of an Actress*.
■ The Blind Goddess 48. *Limelight* 52. Innocents in Paris 52. The Man Between 53. Richard III 56. Alexander the Great 56. The Brothers Karamazov 58. *Look Back in Anger* 59. The Buccaneer 59. Brainwashed (Ger.) 60. The Chapman Report 61. The Wonderful World of the Brothers Grimm 63. *The Haunting* 63. 80,000 Suspects 63. Il Maestro di Vigevano 64. The Outrage 64. High Infidelity 65. *The Spy Who Came in from the Cold* 66. Charly 68. Three into Two Won't Go 69. The Illustrated Man 69. A Severed Head 69. The Going Up of David Lev (TV) 71. Red Sky at Morning 71. A Doll's House 73. Islands in the Stream 77. Backstairs at the White House (TV) 79. Clash of the Titans 81. Brideshead Revisited (TV) 81. Shadowlands (TV) 85. Hold the Dream (TV) 86. Queenie (TV) 87. Sammy and Rosie Get Laid 87. Crimes and Misdemeanors 89. The Princess and the Goblin (voice) 92.

¶ I think that few professions have so much to do with chance and so little to do with the calculation of will. – *C.B.*
She could not be more beautiful without upsetting the balance of nature. – *Walter Kerr*

Bloom, Harold Jack.
American screenwriter.

The Naked Spur (co-w) 53. Magnificent Obsession 54. Last of the Pharaohs (co-w) 55. A Gunfight 71. Hardcase (co-w) 72.

Bloom, Jeffrey.
American screenwriter and director.

Snow Job (co-w) 72. Dogpound Shuffle (w) 74. 11 Harrowhouse (w) 74. Swashbuckler (w) 76. The Stick Up (wd) 78. Blood Beach (wd) 81. Nightmares (co-w) 83. Flowers in the Attic (wd) 87, etc.

Boom, John (1935–).
English film editor, a former script reader for Rank.
Funeral in Berlin 66. Georgy Girl 67. The Lion
in Winter 68. Travels with My Aunt 72. The Ritz
6. Orca 77. Who'll Stop the Rain (aka Dog
Soldiers) 78. Magic 79. Dracula 79. The French
Lieutenant's Woman (AAN) 81. Gandhi (AA) 82.
Betrayal 83. A Chorus Line (AAN) 85. Black Widow
7. Bright Lights, Big City 88. Jacknife 89.
Everybody Wins 90. Air America 90. Prague 91.
Damage 92. A Foreign Field (TV) 93, etc.

Boom, Verna (1939–).
American leading lady.
Medium Cool 69. The Hired Hand 71. High
Plains Drifter 72. Badge 373 73. Where Have All
the People Gone? (TV) 74. Sarah T (TV) 75. The
Blue Knight (TV) 75. Heroes 77. Contract on Cherry
Street (TV) 77. National Lampoon's Animal House
8. Playing for Time (TV) 80. The Journey of
Natty Gann 85. After Hours 85. The Last
Temptation of Christ 89, etc.

Boop.
To cover a splice in the sound track, usually with
thick 'blooping ink'.

Blore, Eric (1887–1959).
British comic actor with stage experience; went to
Hollywood and played unctuous/insulting butlers
and eccentric types in many films.
A Night Out and a Day In 20. The Great Gatsby
6. Laughter 30. My Sin 31. Tarnished Lady 31.
Flying Down to Rio 33. The Gay Divorcee 34.
Limehouse Blues 34. Behold My Wife 34. Folies
Bergère 34. To Beat the Band 35. The Good Fairy
5. Diamond Jim 35. The Casino Murder Case 35.
I Live My Life 35. Top Hat 35. I Dream Too Much
5. Seven Keys to Baldpate 35. Two in the Dark 36.
The Ex Mrs Bradford 36. Swing Time 36. The
Smartest Girl in Town 36. Sons o' Guns 36.
Piccadilly Jim 36. The Soldier and the Lady 37.
Quality Street 37. Shall We Dance? 37. Breakfast
for Two 37. Hitting a New High 37. It's Love I'm
After 37. Joy of Living 38. Swiss Miss 38. A
Desperate Adventure 38. Island of Lost Men 39.
$1000 Dollars a Touchdown 39. A Gentleman's
Gentleman 39. Music in My Heart 40. The Man
Who Wouldn't Talk 40. The Lone Wolf Strikes 40
and ten other Lone Wolf adventures 40–47, all
as the butler). Till We Meet Again 40. South of Suez
0. The Boys from Syracuse 40. The Earl of
Puddlestone 40. The Lady Eve 41. Road to Zanzibar
1. Redhead 41. Lady Scarface 41. New York Town
1. The Shanghai Gesture 41. Sullivan's Travels
1. Three Girls About Town 41. The Moon and
Sixpence 42. Confirm or Deny 42. Happy Go Lucky
3. The Sky's the Limit 43. Forever and a Day 43.
Holy Matrimony 43. Submarine Base 43. San
Diego I Love You 44. Penthouse Rhythm 45. Men
in Her Diary 45. Easy to Look At 45. Kitty 45.
Two Sisters from Boston 46. Abie's Irish Rose 46.
Winter Wonderland 47. Romance on the High
Seas 48. Love Happy 49. Ichabod and Mr Toad
voice of Toad) 49. Fancy Pants 50. Bowery to
Bagdad 54.

Famous line (Top Hat): 'We are Jones, sir.'

blow up.
To magnify an image, either a photograph for
background purposes, or a piece of film (e.g. from
16mm to 35mm).

Blue, Ben (1901–1975) (Benjamin Bernstein).
Lanky, rubber-limbed American comedian with
vaudeville experience; sporadically in films, usually
in cameos.

College Rhythm 33. Follow Your Heart 36. High
Wide and Handsome 37. College Swing 38. Paris
Honeymoon 39. For Me and My Gal 42. Thousands
Cheer 43. Easy to Wed 46. One Sunday
Afternoon 48. It's a Mad Mad Mad Mad World 63.
The Russians are Coming, The Russians are Coming 66.
A Guide for the Married Man 67. Where Were You
When the Lights Went Out? 68, etc.

Blue, Monte (1890–1963).
Burly American silent hero who later appeared in
innumerable bit roles.
Intolerance 16. Till I Come Back to You 18.
Pettigrew's Girl 19. The Affairs of Anatol 21.
Orphans of the Storm 22. Main Street 23. The
Marriage Circle 24. The Black Swan 24. Other
Women's Husbands 26. Other Men's Wives 26. So
This is Paris 26. Wolf 's Clothing 27. White Shadows
of the South Seas 28. Tiger Rose 29. Isle of Escape
30. The Flood 31. The Stoker 32. Wagon Wheels
34. Lives of a Bengal Lancer 34. G Men 35. Souls
at Sea 37. Dodge City 39. Geronimo 40. Across the
Pacific 42. The Mask of Dimitrios 44. Life with
Father 47. The Iroquois Trail 50. Apache 54,
many others.

Blum, Daniel (1900–1965).
American writer, editor and collector; annually
produced Theatre World and Screen World annuals.

Bluteau, Lothaire.
French-Canadian leading actor.
Jesus of Montreal 91. Black Robe 91. The Touch
92. Orlando 92. Le Confessionale 95, etc.

Bluth, Don (1938–).
Director of animation who first worked for Disney
before setting up his own company in the 80s to
restore old-fashioned standards to the medium,
with mixed results. In 1994, he signed a long-
term deal with Fox.
Pete's Dragon 77. The Rescuers 77. The Secret
of Nimh 82. An American Tail 86. The Land Before
Time 88. All Dogs Go to Heaven 89. Rock-a-
Doodle 91. Thumbelina 94. A Troll in Central
Park (p, co-d) 95, etc.

Blyden, Larry (1925–1975).
American comic actor, on TV and in supporting
roles.
The Bachelor Party 57. Kiss Them for Me 57. On
a Clear Day You Can See Forever 70, etc.
TV series: Harry's Girls 63.

Blystone, John G. (1892–1938).
American director, former actor.
Dick Turpin 25. Seven Chances 25. Ankles
Preferred 27. Mother Knows Best 28. The Sky
Hawk 29. Tol'able David 30. Charlie Chan's
Chance 32. Shanghai Madness 33. Hell in the
Heavens 34. The Magnificent Brute 36. Woman
Chases Man 37. Swiss Miss 38. Blockheads 38,
many others.

Blyth, Ann (1928–).
Diminutive American songstress and leading lady
who after opera training got her screen break in
Donald O'Connor musicals, then graduated to
dramatic roles.
Chip Off the Old Block 44. The Merry
Monahans 44. Babes on Swing Street 44. Bowery
to Broadway 44. Mildred Pierce (as the abominable
daughter) (AAN) 45. Swell Guy 46. Brute Force 47.
Killer McCoy 47. A Woman's Vengeance 47.
Another Part of the Forest 48. Mr Peabody and the
Mermaid 48. Red Canyon 49. Once More My
Darling 49. Top o' the Morning 49. Free For All 49.
Our Very Own 50. The Great Caruso 51. Katie Did

It 51. Thunder on the Hill 51. I'll Never Forget You
51. The Golden Horde 51. The World in his Arms
51. One Minute to Zero 52. Sally and Saint Anne
52. All the Brothers were Valiant 53. Rose Marie
54. The Student Prince 54. The King's Thief 55.
Kismet 55. Slander 57. The Buster Keaton Story
57. The Helen Morgan Story 57.

Blythe, Betty (1893–1972) (Elizabeth Blythe
Slaughter).
American leading lady of the silent era.
Nomads of the North 20. Queen of Sheba 21.
Chu Chin Chow 23. The Folly of Vanity 24. She
25. The Girl from Gay Paree 27. Glorious Betsy 28.
A Daughter of Israel 28. Eager Lips 30. Tom Brown
of Culver 32. Only Yesterday 33. Ever Since Eve
34. The Gorgeous Hussy 36. Gangster's Boy 38.
Honky Tonk 41. Jiggs and Maggie in Society 47.
My Fair Lady 64, many others.

Blythe, John (1921–).
British character actor, often of spiv types.
This Happy Breed 44. Holiday Camp 48. Vote
for Huggett 49. Worm's Eye View 51. The Gay
Dog 54. Foxhole in Cairo 60. A Stitch in Time 64.
The Bed Sitting Room 69, many others.

Boam, Jeffrey.
American screenwriter.
Straight Time 78. The Dead Zone 83. Innerspace
87. The Lost Boys 87. Funny Farm 88. Indiana
Jones and the Last Crusade 89. Lethal Weapon 2
89. Lethal Weapon 3 92, etc.

Boardman, Chris.
American composer.
The Color Purple (co-m, AAN) 85. Johnny Ryan
(TV) 90, etc.

Boardman, Eleanor (1898–1991).
Sympathetic American leading lady of the late
silent period, who never seemed happy in sound
films and retired in 1934. Was married variously
to King Vidor and Harry D'Abbadie D'Arrast.
The Stranger's Banquet 22. Gimme 23. Souls
for Sale 23. Vanity Fair (as Amelia Sedley) 23.
Three Wise Fools 23. Day of Faith 23. True as Steel
24. Wine of Youth 24. The Turmoil 24. Sinners
in Silk 24. So This Is Marriage 24. The Silent
Accuser 24. Wife of the Centaur 24. The Way of a
Girl 25. Proud Flesh 25. Exchange of Wives 25.
The Only Thing 25. The Circle 25. Memory Lane
26. The Auction Block 26. Bardeleys the
Magnificent 26. Tell It to the Marines 26. The
Crowd 28. Diamond Handcuffs 28. She Goes to War
29. Mamba 30. Redemption 30. The Great Meadow
31. The Flood 31. Women Love Once 31. The
Squaw Man 31. It Happened in Spain 34.

Bochner, Hart (1956–).
Canadian character actor, the son of Lloyd
Bochner.
Islands in the Stream 76. Breaking Away 79.
Rich and Famous 81. The Wild Life 84. Supergirl
84. Apartment Zero 88. Die Hard 88. Fellow
Traveller 90. Mr Destiny 90. And the Sea Will Tell
(TV) 91. Mad at the Moon 92. The Innocent 92.
Batman: Mask of the Phantasm (voice) 94, etc.

Bochner, Lloyd (1924–).
Canadian leading man, mostly on TV but in
occasional films.
Drums of Africa 63. The Night Walker 64. Sylvia
65. Harlow 65. Point Blank 67. Tony Rome 67. The
Detective 68. The Young Runaways 68. The Horse
in the Grey Flannel Suit 69. Ulzana's Raid 72. Mazes
and Monsters (TV) 83. The Lonely Lady 87. Crystal

Heart 87. Millennium 89. The Naked Gun 2½: The Smell of Fear 91. Morning Glory 93, etc.

TV series: Hong Kong 60. The Richard Boone Show 64. Dynasty 81–82.

Bock, Jerry (1928–).

American song composer who with lyricist Sheldon Harnick (1924–) wrote *Fiddler on the Roof*.

Bodard, Mag (1927–).

Swedish producer in France; a rare example of a woman in this job.

The Umbrellas of Cherbourg 64. The Young Girls of Rochefort 66. *Le Bonheur* 66. Mouchette 67. Benjamin 67. Le Viol 68. La Chinoise 68. *Peau d'Ane* 71, etc.

Bode, Ralph (Ralf D. Bode).

American cinematographer.

Saturday Night Fever 77. Slow Dancing in the Big City 78. Rich Kids 79. Coal Miner's Daughter (AAN) 80. Dressed to Kill 80. Raggedy Man 81. A Little Sex 82. Gorky Park 83. Firstborn 84. Bring on the Night 85. Violets Are Blue 86. The Whoopee Boys 86. The Big Town 87. Critical Condition 87. The Accused 88. Distant Thunder 88. Cousins 89. The Long Way Home 89. Uncle Buck 89. One Good Cop 91. Leaving Normal 92. Love Field 92. Made in America 93. George Balanchine's The Nutcracker 93. Gypsy (TV) 93. Bad Girls 94, etc.

Bodeen, De Witt (1908–1988).

American screenwriter.

The Seventh Victim 43. *The Curse of the Cat People* 44. The Enchanted Cottage 44. *I Remember Mama* 47. Mrs Mike 50. Twelve to the Moon 58. Billy Budd 62, etc.

Boehm, Karlheinz (1927–).

German leading actor who appeared in British and American films during the 60s.

Peeping Tom 60. Too Hot to Handle 60. Come Fly with Me 62. The Magnificent Rebel 62. The Wonderful World of the Brothers Grimm 62. Forever My Love 62. Rififi in Tokyo 63. The Venetian Affair 67. Martha 74. Fox and his Friends 75. Die Tannerhütt 76, etc.

Boehm, Sydney (1908–1990).

American screenwriter, a reliable hand at crime stories.

High Wall 48. *The Undercover Man* 49. Side Street 50. Mystery Street 50. *Union Station* 50. When Worlds Collide 52. The Savage 53. *The Big Heat* 53. The Secret of the Incas 54. Rogue Cop 54. Black Tuesday 54. Violent Saturday 55. The Tall Men 55. Hell on Frisco Bay 55. The Revolt of Mamie Stover 56. Harry Black 58. A Woman Obsessed (& p) 59. *Seven Thieves* (& p) 60. Shock Treatment 64. Sylvia 65. Rough Night in Jericho 67, etc.

Boetticher, Budd (1916–) (Oscar Boetticher).

American director, former bullfighter. Has not risen above a few striking co-features, but cineastes have made him the centre of a cult.

Autobiography: 1971, *When in Disgrace*.

The Missing Juror 44. Assigned to Danger 47. Sword of D'Artagnan 51. *The Bullfighter and the Lady* (& wp) 51. Red Ball Express 52. Bronco Buster 52. Horizons West 52. East of Sumatra 53. Wings of the Hawk 53. The Man from the Alamo 53. The Magnificent Matador (& w) 55. The Killer is Loose 56. Seven Men from Now 56. Decision at Sundown 57. The Tall T 57. Buchanan Rides Alone 58. Ride Lonesome 59. Westbound 59. *The Rise and Fall of Legs Diamond* 60. *Arruza* 68. A Time for Dying 69, etc.

boffins

are research scientists working on hush-hush government projects. Their problems have been dramatized in such films as *The Small Back Room*, *School for Secrets*, *Suspect*, *The Man in the Moon*, *The Satan Bug*, *The Andromeda Strain*, *The Atomic City* and *The Forbin Project*.

Bogarde, Sir Dirk (1921–) (Derek Van Den Bogaerd).

British leading actor of Dutch descent. In the 60s he moved to France and became a star of films by Visconti, Fassbinder, Cavani and other European directors. At the beginning of his career, he turned down an offer from Fox, who wanted to turn him into its new Spanish star and marry him off to one of its starlets, and instead signed a contract with Rank. He is also a novelist.

Autobiographies: 1977, *A Postillion Struck by Lightning*. 1978, *Snakes and Ladders*. 1983, *An Orderly Man*. 1994, *A Short Walk from Harrods*.

Biography: 1974, *The Films of Dirk Bogarde* by Margaret Hinxman.

■ Esther Waters 47. Once a Jolly Swagman 48. *Quartet* 48. Dear Mr Prohack 49. Boys in Brown 49. So Long at the Fair 49. The Woman in Question 50. The Blue Lamp 50. Blackmailed 51. Penny Princess 51. The Gentle Gunman 52. Hunted 52. *Doctor in the House* 53. Appointment in London 53. They Who Dare 53. Desperate Moment 53. Simba 54. The Sea Shall Not Have Them 54. *The Sleeping Tiger* 54. For Better For Worse 54. Doctor at Sea 55. *Cast a Dark Shadow* 55. Doctor at Large 56. *The Spanish Gardener* 56. Ill Met By Moonlight 57. Campbell's Kingdom 58. The Wind Cannot Read 58. *A Tale of Two Cities* 58. The Doctor's Dilemma 59. Libel 59. Song Without End (as Liszt) (US) 60. The Angel Wore Red 60. The Singer Not the Song 60. *Victim* 61. We Joined the Navy (cameo) 62. HMS Defiant 62. The Password is Courage 63. I Could Go On Singing 63. The Mind Benders 63. *The Servant* (BFA) 63. Hot Enough for June 64. Doctor in Distress 64. *King and Country* 64. The High Bright Sun 65. *Darling* (BFA) 65. Modesty Blaise 66. Accident 67. Our Mother's House 67. Sebastian 67. The Fixer 68. Oh What a Lovely War 69. *The Damned* 69. Justine 69. *Death in Venice* 70. The Serpent 72. The Night Porter 74. Permission to Kill 75. Providence 77. A Bridge Too Far 77. Despair 78. The Patricia Neal Story (TV) 81. May We Borrow Your Husband? (TV) 85. The Vision 87. These Foolish Things (Daddy Nostalgie) 90.

¶ I love the camera and it loves me. Well, not very much sometimes. But we're good friends – *D.B.*

I'll only work with new people. If you stick with your contemporaries, you're dead. – *D.B.*

I'm still in the shell, and you're not going to crack it, ducky. – *D.B. to Russell Harty in TV interview, 1986*

I've got a good left profile and a very bad right profile. I was the Loretta Young of my day. I was only ever photographed on the left-hand profile. – *D.B.*

I was as scrawny as a plucked hen. The Rank Organization did supply me with dumb-bells. All I did was put on two sweaters and then put my shirt on. – *D.B.*

Famous line (*Darling*): 'Your idea of fidelity is not having more than one man in bed at the same time.'

Bogart, Humphrey (1899–1957).

American leading actor who became one of Hollywood's imperishable personalities, a cynical

but amiable tough guy in a trench coat who summed up all the *films noirs* of the 40s, after a long apprenticeship playing gangsters.

Several biographies have been published, but none catch the full flavour of the man who influenced millions. The best are by Nathaniel Benchley, Jonah Ruddy, Clifford McCarty and Ezra Goodman.

■ A Devil with Women 30. Up the River 30. Body and Soul 30. Bad Sister 30. Women of All Nations 31. A Holy Terror 31. Love Affair 32. Big City Blues 32. Three on a Match 32. Midnight 34. *The Petrified Forest* (his stage role as gangster Duke Mantee) 36. Two Against the World 36. Bullets or Ballots 36. China Clipper 36. Isle of Fury 36. The Great O'Malley 37. Black Legion 37. San Quentin 37. *Marked Woman* 37. Kid Galahad 37. *Dead End* 37. Stand In 37. Swing Your Lady 38. Men Are Such Fools 38. The Amazing Dr Clitterhouse 38. Racket Busters 38. *Angels with Dirty Faces* 38. Crime School 38. King of the Underworld 39. The Oklahoma Kid 39. Dark Victory 39. You Can't Get Away with Murder 39. *The Roaring Twenties* 39. The Return of Dr X (as a vampire) 39. Invisible Stripes 39. Virginia City 40. It All Came True 40. Brother Orchid 40. They Drive by Night 40. *High Sierra* 41. The Wagons Roll at Night 41. *The Maltese Falcon* (his archetypal performance) 41. All Through the Night 42. The Big Shot 42. *Across the Pacific* 42. Casablanca (AAN) 42. Action in the North Atlantic 43. Thank Your Lucky Stars 43. *Sahara* 43. *To Have and Have Not* 43. Passage to Marseilles 44. Conflict 45. *The Big Sleep* 46. The Two Mrs Carrolls 47. Dead Reckoning 47. Dark Passage 47. *The Treasure of the Sierra Madre* 47. *Key Largo* 48. Knock on any Door 49. Tokyo Joe 49. Chain Lightning 50. In a Lonely Place 50. *The Enforcer* 51. Sirocco 51. *The African Queen* (AA) 52. Deadline 52. Battle Circus 53. *Beat the Devil* 54. *The Caine Mutiny* (AAN) 54. Sabrina 54. *The Barefoot Contessa* 54. We're No Angels 55. The Left Hand of God 55. The Desperate Hours 55. The Harder they Fall 56.

~Bogart also appeared in a 1930 short, *Broadway's Like That*; and he made uncredited gag appearances in *Two Guys from Milwaukee* 46, *Always Together* 48, *Road to Bali* 52, *The Love Lottery* 53.

🟢 For contriving to represent both Action Man and Thinking Man of the early 40s; and for taking both these roles with a large pinch of salt. *Casablanca*.

¶ To some extent Bogart tended to live his film roles. As Dave Chase the Hollywood restaurateur once said:

Bogart's a helluva nice guy till 11.30 p.m. After that he thinks he's Bogart.

So in a way his aptest quotes are from his movies. As Rick in *Casablanca*:

I stick my neck out for nobody.

Or as Sam Spade in *The Maltese Falcon*:

Don't be so sure I'm as crooked as I'm supposed to be.

And:

When you're slapped, you'll take it and like it!

Truman Capote commented:

He was an actor without theories (well, one: that he should be highly paid), without temper but not without temperament; and because he understood that discipline was the better part of artistic survival, he lasted, he left his mark.

Stanley Kramer saw through him:

He was playing Bogart all the time, but he was really just a big sloppy bowl of mush.

One feels that this hits the nail pretty squarely on the head: Bogie was a nice guy who enjoyed a good grouch. About, for instance, the untrained beefcake stars of the early 50s, many of them picked up for tests from sidewalks and gas stations:

Shout 'gas' around the studios today, and half the young male stars will come running.

bout acting theorists:
Do I subscribe to the Olivier school of acting? Ah, nuts. I'm an actor. I just do what comes naturally.

bout the industry:
I don't hurt the industry. The industry hurts itself, by making so many lousy movies – as if General Motors deliberately put out a bad car.

nd:
I made more lousy pictures than any actor in history.

nd about life:
The trouble with the world is that everybody in it is about three drinks behind.

ther actors, perhaps, knew him better than he new himself. Edward G. Robinson:
I always felt sorry for him – sorry that he had imposed upon himself the character with which he had become identified.

nd Katharine Hepburn:
His yes meant yes, his no meant no. There was no bunkum about Bogart.

amous lines:
(*The Maltese Falcon*) 'Don't be so sure I'm as rooked as I'm supposed to be.'
'Let's talk about the black bird.'
'We didn't exactly believe your story, Miss Shea, we believed your 200 dollars. You paid us nore than if you'd been telling the truth, and nough more to make it all right.'
'Yes, angel, I'm gonna send you over.'

Across the Pacific) 'When you're slapped, you're onna take it and like it.'

Casablanca) 'I came to Casablanca for the waters.' But we're in the middle of the desert.' 'I was nisinformed.'
'Louis, I think this is the beginning of a beautiful riendship.'

The Big Sleep) 'I don't mind if you don't like my nanners. I don't like them myself. They're pretty ad. I grieve over them on long winter evenings.'

Bogart, Paul (1919–).
American director.
■ Halls of Anger 68. Marlowe 69. In Search of America (TV) 70. The Skin Game 71. Cancel My Reservation 71. Class of '44 73. Tell Me Where It Hurts (TV) 74. Winner Take All (TV) 75. Mr Ricco 5. Oh God You Devil 84. Torch Song Trilogy 88.

Bogdanovich, Peter (1939–).
American director with a penchant for reworking raditional themes; former film critic.
Biography: 1992, *Picture Shows: The Life and Films f Peter Bogdanovich* by Andrew Yule.
■ Voyage to the Planet of Prehistoric Women (as Derek Thomas') 68. *Targets* (& w) 68. *The Last Picture Show* (& w, AAN) 71. *What's Up Doc?* (& w) 72. Paper Moon 73. Daisy Miller (& p) 74. At Long Last Love 75. Nickelodeon 77. Saint Jack 79. They All Laughed 31. Mask 84. Illegally Yours 88. Texasville 90. Noises Off 92. The Thing Called Love 93.

Bogeaus, Benedict (1904–1968).
American independent producer, formerly in real estate; his films were mildly interesting though eccentric.
The Bridge of San Luis Rey 44. Captain Kidd 45. The Diary of a Chambermaid 45. Christmas Eve 47. The Macomber Affair 47. Johnny One Eye 49.

Passion 54. Slightly Scarlet 56. The Most Dangerous Man Alive 61, etc.

Bogosian, Eric (1953–).
American dramatist, actor and screenwriter, noted for his one-man shows.
Born in Flames 82. Special Effects 85. Funhouse (concert) 87. Talk Radio (co-w) 88. Suffering Bastards 89. Sex, Drugs, Rock & Roll (& w) 91.

Bohnen, Roman (1894–1949).
American character actor usually seen as hard-working immigrant types.
Vogues of 1938 37. Of Mice and Men 40. So Ends Our Night 41. Appointment for Love 41. Edge of Darkness 43. Mission to Moscow 43. The Song of Bernadette 43. *The Hitler Gang* 44. A Bell for Adano 45. The Strange Love of Martha Ivers 46. Mr Ace 46. The Best Years of Our Lives 46. Brute Force 47. Arch of Triumph 48. Night Has a Thousand Eyes 48, etc.

Bohr, José (1901–1994).
Chilean leading actor, screenwriter, director and songwriter. He worked in Chile at the transition from silent to sound films, starred in the first Spanish-language film made in Hollywood, *Shadows of Glory*, and spent the 30s and 40s making films in Mexico before working in Venezuela, Cuba and Argentina.
Como por un Tubo 19. Shadows of Glory (Sombras de Gloria) 29. Marijuana, the Green Monster (Mariguana, El Mónstruo Verde) 35. Flor del Carmen 44. My Silver Spurs (Mis Espuelas de Plata) 48. La Cadena Infinita 49. El Gran Circo Chamorro 55. Un Chileno en España 62, many more.

Bohringer, Richard (1942–).
French leading actor, screenwriter and novelist. He began directing in the 90s.
L'Italien des Roses 72. Beau Masque (w) 72. Les Conquistadores 75. The Last Metro 80. Diva 81. La Bête Noire 83. Cap Canaille 83. Cent Francs l'Amour 85. Subway 85. Kamikaze 86. Le Grand Chemin 87. La Soule 88. The Cook, the Thief, His Wife and Her Lover 89. Stan the Flasher 90. Dien Bien Phu 91. Vézaz 91. La Reine Blanche 91. Gallant Ladies (Dames Galantes) 91. City for Sale (Ville à Vendre) 91. Wonderful Times (Une Epoque Formidable) 91. L'Accompagnatrice 92. C'est Beau une Ville la Nuit (wd) 92. Tango 93. La Lumière des Etoiles Mortes 94. Le Parfum d'Yvonne 94. L'Amour Est un Jeu d'Enfant 94. The Smile (Le Sourire) 94. Le Cri du Coeur 94. Fric-Frac 95, etc

Bohringer, Romane.
French leading actress, the daughter of Richard Bohringer.
Savage Nights 93. A Cause d'Elle 93. Mina Tannenbaum 94. Adultère Mode d'Emploi 95, etc.

Bois, Curt (1900–1991).
Dapper German comedy actor, long in Hollywood playing head-waiters and pompous clerks.
Tovarich 37. Hollywood Hotel 38. *The Great Waltz* 38. Boom Town 40. Bitter Sweet 40. Hold Back the Dawn 41. Casablanca 42. The Desert Song 43. The Spanish Main 45. *The Woman in White* 48. The Great Sinner 49. Fortunes of Captain Blood 50. *Herr Puntilla and His Servant Matti* (Ger.) 54. Wings of Desire 87, many others.

Boisrond, Michel (1921–).
French director.
Mamzelle Pigalle 56. Une Parisienne 57. Come Dance with Me 59. Love and the Frenchwoman

60. Comment Reussir en Amour 62. Comment Epouser un Premier Ministre 64. L'Homme Qui Valait de Milliards 68. The Tender Moment 69. On Est Toujours Trop Bon avec des Femmes 71. Le Petit Poucet 72. Tell Me You Love Me 74. Catherine and Company 75, etc.

Boisset, Yves (1939–).
French director.
A Cop 70. Cobra 71. L'Attentat 72. Coplan Saves His Skin 72. Une Folle à Tuer 75. The Sheriff 76. The Purple Taxi 78. La Femme Flick 80. Le Prix du Danger 83. Canicule 84. Radio Corbeau 88. The Predators (Les Carnassiers) 91. Double Identity 91. La Nuit du Herrison 93, etc.

Bolam, James (1938–).
Gritty English actor, mainly on television. Born in Sunderland, he trained at the Central School of Speech and Drama.
The Kitchen 61. A Kind of Loving 62. Otley 69. Crucible of Terror 71. Straight on Till Morning 72. O Lucky Man 73. In Celebration 74. The Likely Lads 76. The Limbo Connection (TV) 79. As You Like It (TV) 80. The Plague Dogs (voice) 82, etc.
TV series: *The Likely Lads* 65–69. *Whatever Happened to the Likely Lads?* 73. *When the Boat Comes In* 75–77. *Only When I Laugh* 79–83. The Beiderbecke Affair 85. Room at the Bottom 86–87. The Beiderbecke Tapes 87. The Beiderbecke Connection 88. Second Thoughts 92–94.

Boland, Bridget (1904–1988).
British playwright and screenwriter.
Gaslight 39. Spies of the Air 40. The Lost People 48. The Prisoner 54. War and Peace 56. Anne of the Thousand Days (co-w, AAN) 69, etc.

Boland, Mary (1880–1965).
American stage tragedienne who in middle age settled in Hollywood and played innumerable fluttery matrons: appeared in a series of domestic comedies with Charles Ruggles.
The Edge of the Abyss 16. His Temporary Wife 18. Personal Maid 31. *If I Had a Million* 32. *Three-Cornered Moon* 33. Four Frightened People 34. *Down to Their Last Yacht* 34. *Ruggles of Red Gap* 35. Early to Bed 36. Wives Never Know 36. Mama Runs Wild 37. Little Tough Guys in Society 38. *The Women* 39. New Moon 40. *Pride and Prejudice* (as Mrs Bennett) 40. In Our Time 44. Nothing But Trouble 44. Julia Misbehaves 48. Guilty Bystander 50, many others.

Boles, John (1895–1969).
American operetta singer who apart from musicals proved himself useful to Hollywood as a well-behaved 'other man'.
■ So This Is Marriage 24. Excuse Me 25. The Loves of Sunya 27. The Shepherd of the Hills 28. We Americans 28. The Bride of the Colorado 28. Fazil 28. The Water Hole 28. Virgin Lips 28. Man-made Woman 28. Romance of the Underworld 28. The Last Warning 29. *The Desert Song* 29. Scandal 29. Rio Rita 29. Song of the West 30. Captain of the Guard 30. *The King of Jazz* 30. One Heavenly Night 30. Resurrection 31. Seed 31. Frankenstein (as Victor, friend of the family) 31. Good Sport 31. Careless Lady 31. *Back Street* 32. Six Hours to Live 32. Child of Manhattan 32. My Lips Betray 33. *Only Yesterday* 33. I Believed in You 34. Music in the Air 34. Beloved 34. Bottoms Up 34. Stand Up and Cheer 34. The Life of Vergie Winters 34. Wild Gold 34. The Age of Innocence 34. The White Parade 34. Orchids to You 34. Curly Top 35. Redheads on Parade 35. The Littlest Rebel 35. Rose of the Rancho 36. A Message to Garcia 36. Craig's Wife 36. As Good as Married 37. *Stella Dallas* 37. Fight for

Your Lady 37. She Married an Artist 38. Romance in the Dark 38. Sinners in Paradise 38. The Road to Happiness 42. Between Us Girls 42. Thousands Cheer 43. Babes in Bagdad 52.

Boleslawski, Richard (1889–1937) (Boleslaw Ryszart Srzednicki).
Polish stage director, formerly with the Moscow Arts Theatre, who came to Hollywood in 1930 and made a few stylish movies.
■ Three Meetings (USSR) 17. Treasure Girl 30. The Last of the Lone Wolf 31. Woman Pursued 31. The Gay Diplomat 31. Rasputin and the Empress 32. Storm at Daybreak 33. Beauty for Sale 33. Fugitive Lovers 33. Men in White 34. Operator 13 34. *The Painted Veil* 34. *Clive of India* 35. *Les Misérables* 35. O'Shaughnessy's Boy 35. *Metropolitan* 35. Three Godfathers 36. *Theodora Goes Wild* 36. *The Garden of Allah* 36. The Last of Mrs Cheyney 37.

Bolger, Ray (1904–1987).
Rubber-legged American eccentric dancer, a stage star who made too few films.
■ The Great Ziegfeld 36. *Rosalie* 37. Sweethearts 38. *The Wizard of Oz* (as the scarecrow) 39. Sunny 41. Stage Door Canteen 43. Four Jacks and a Jill 44. *The Harvey Girls* 46. *Look for the Silver Lining* 49. *Where's Charley?* 52. April in Paris 52. Babes in Toyland 60. The Daydreamer 66. The Entertainer (TV) 75. The Captains and the Kings (TV) 76. Heaven Only Knows (TV) 79. The Runner Stumbles 79. Just You and Me Kid 79. That's Dancing 84.
TV series: Where's Raymond 52.

Bolkan, Florinda (1941–) (Florinda Suares Bulcao).
Spanish-Indian leading lady.
Candy 68. The Damned 69. Investigation of a Citizen 70. The Last Valley 70. The Anonymous Venetian 71. Detective Belli 71. Romance 71. The Island 72. A Man to Respect 72. Lizard in a Woman's Skin 72. Hearts and Minds 74. Royal Flash 75. The Right to Love 76. Day that Shook the World 78. The Word 78. Collector's Item 89, etc.

Bolling, Claude (1930–).
French composer and jazz pianist.
Bonjour Cinéma 55. Men and Women (L'Homme à Femmes) 60. The Hands of Orlac 62. Cadet l'Eau Douce 69. Borsalino 70. Catch Me a Spy 71. Borsalino and Co. 74. Tell Me You Love Me (Dis-moi que Tu M'Aimes) 74. Le Gitan 75. Les Passagers 76. Silver Bears 78. California Suite 78. The Awakening 80. Willie and Phil 80. Le Léopard 83. Bay Boy 84. On ne Meurt que Deux Fois 85. La Rumba 87, etc.

Bolling, Tiffany (1947–).
American leading lady.
Kingdom of the Spiders 77. Bonnie's Kids 82. Ecstasy 84. Love Scenes 84, etc.
TV series: The New People 69–70.

Bologna, Joseph (1936–).
American actor who with his wife Renee Taylor usually writes his own material.
Lovers and Other Strangers (co-w only) (AANw) 70. Made for Each Other 71. Honor Thy Father (TV) 73. Mixed Company 74. Woman of the Year (TV) 75. The Big Bus 76. Chapter Two 79. Blame It On Rio 84. The Woman in Red 84. Transylvania 6–5000 85. It Had To Be You (wd) 89. Coup de Ville 90. Alligator II: The Mutation 91. Revenge of the Nerds IV: Nerds in Love (TV) 94, etc.
TV series: Rags to Riches 87.

Bolognini, Mauro (1922–).
Italian director.
Wild Love 55. Young Husbands 58. La Notte Brava 59. Il Bell'Antonio 60. La Viaccia 61. Senilita 62. Le Bambole 65. I Tre Volti 65. The Oldest Profession 67. Arabella 67. That Splendid November 68. Metello 70. Bubu 71. Down the Ancient Stairs 75. Black Journal 77. La Vera Storia della Signora Camelie 80. La Venexiana 85. Mosca Addio 87. A Time of Indifference (TV) 88. Husbands and Lovers 92, etc.

Bolt, Ben (1952–).
English director, the son of Robert Bolt.
Rainy Day Woman (TV) 86. The Big Town 87. Scarlet and Black (TV) 93, etc.

Bolt, Robert (1924–1995).
British playwright who turned to screenwriting and direction. Actress Sarah Miles was his second wife (1967–1976) and his fourth in 1988.
Lawrence of Arabia (AA) 62. *Doctor Zhivago* (AA) 65. *A Man For All Seasons* (AAN) 66. Ryan's Daughter 70. Lady Caroline Lamb (& d) 72. The Bounty 84. The Mission 86.

Bolton, Guy (1884–1979).
American playwright and screenwriter, often associated with P.G. Wodehouse.
Grounds for Divorce 25. The Love Doctor 29. The Love Parade 30. Girl Crazy (oa) 32. Ladies Should Listen (oa) 34. Anything Goes (oa) 35. Rosalie (oa) 37. Weekend at the Waldorf 45. Anastasia (oa) 56, etc.

Bonanova, Fortunio (1893–1969).
Spanish opera singer and impresario who after managing his own repertory company in America in the 30s, settled in Hollywood to play excitable foreigners.
Careless Lady 32. Podoroso Caballero 36. Tropic Holiday 38. La Immaculada 39. I Was an Adventuress 40. *Citizen Kane* (as the music teacher) 41. Blood and Sand 41. The Black Swan 42. Five Graves to Cairo 43. For Whom the Bell Tolls 43. Going My Way 44. Double Indemnity 44. Monsieur Beaucaire 46. The Fugitive 47. Whirlpool 50. September Affair 51. The Moon is Blue 53. An Affair to Remember 57. Thunder in the Sun 59. The Running Man 63. Million Dollar Collar 69, many others.

Bond, Derek (1919–).
British light leading man with varied pre-film experience including the Grenadier Guards.
The Captive Heart 46. *Nicholas Nickleby* (title role) 47. *Scott of the Antarctic* 48. Broken Journey 48. The Weaker Sex 48. Christopher Columbus 49. Marry Me 49. Uncle Silas 50. The Hour of Thirteen 52. Stranger from Venus 54. Svengali 55. Trouble in Store 55. Gideon's Day 58. The Hand 60. Saturday Night Out 64. Wonderful Life 64. Press for Time 66. When Eight Bells Toll 71, etc.

Bond, Gary (1940–).
British leading man.
Zulu 64. Anne of the Thousand Days 70. *Outback* 70, etc.

Bond, James, III.
American actor, screenwriter and producer-director.
The Fish that Saved Pittsburg (a) 79. The Sky Is Gray (a) (TV) 80. Def by Temptation (a, p, wd) 90, etc.

Bond, Julian (1930–).
British writer, mainly for TV. *A Man of Our Times,*

Love for Lydia, Fair Stood the Wind for France, Th Far Pavilions, Strangers and Brothers.
Films: The Shooting Party 84. The Whistle Blower 87.

Bond, Lilian (1910–1991).
British leading lady in American films of the 30s
Just a Gigolo 31. Fireman Save My Child 32. T Old Dark House 32. Hot Pepper 33. Affairs of a Gentleman 34. China Seas 35. The Housekeeper' Daughter 39. The Westerner 40. The Picture of Dorian Gray 45. Man in the Attic 54. Pirates of Tripoli 55, etc.

Bond, Sudie (1923–1984).
American character actress in wisecracking roles.
A Thousand Clowns 65. Cold Turkey 70. They Might Be Giants 72. Come Back to the 5 and Dim Jimmy Dean, Jimmy Dean 82. Tomorrow 83. Silkwood 83. I Am the Cheese 83, etc.
TV series: Temperatures Rising 73–74. Flo 80– 81.

Bond, Tommy (1927–).
American child actor who played Butch in the Ou Gang comedies of the 30s; he also appeared in a few features before quitting acting in the early 50
Kid Millions 34. City Streets 38. A Little Bit of Heaven 40. Man from Frisco 44. Call Me Mister 5 etc.

Bond, Ward (1903–1960).
Burly American actor who from the coming of sound distinguished himself in small roles, especially in John Ford films; but it took TV to make him a star.
The Big Trail 30. When Strangers Marry 33. Devil Dogs of the Air 35. You Only Live Once 37 The Oklahoma Kid 39. Young Mr Lincoln 39. Gon with the Wind 39. The Grapes of Wrath 40. *Tobac Road* 41. The Maltese Falcon 41. Gentleman Jim 42. A Guy Named Joe 43. They Were Expendabl 45. My Darling Clementine 46. Fort Apache 48. *Wagonmaster* 50. *The Quiet Man* 52. Blowing Wild 53. The Long Gray Line 55. *The Searchers* 56. *Th Wings of Eagles* 57. *The Halliday Brand* 57. *Rio Bra* 59, many others.
TV series: Wagon Train 57–60.

Bondarchuk, Sergei (1920–1994).
Russian actor and director.
The Young Guards (a) 48. The Grasshopper (a) 55. Othello (a) 56. *Destiny of a Man* (ad) 59. *War and Peace* (ad) (AA) 64. *Waterloo* (d) 70. They Fought for Their Country 75. The Steppe 78. Ten Days That Shook the World 82. Boris Godunov 8(Quiet Flows the Don 92, etc.

Bondi, Beulah (1889–1981) (Beulah Bondy).
Distinguished American character actress who from early middle age played cantankerous or kindly old ladies.
■ Street Scene 31. Arrowsmith 31. Rain 32. The Stranger's Return 33. Christopher Bean 33. Finishing School 34. The Painted Veil 34. Two Alone 34. Registered Nurse 34. Ready for Love 34. Bad Boy 35. The Good Fairy 35. The Invisible Ray 36. The Trail of the Lonesome Pine 36. The Moon's Our Home 36. The Case Against Mrs Ame 36. Hearts Divided 36. The Gorgeous Hussy (AAN) 36. *Maid of Salem* 37. *Make Way for Tomorro* 37. The Buccaneer 38. Of Human Hearts (AAN) 38 Vivacious Lady 38. The Sisters 38. On Borrowed Time 39. Mr Smith Goes to Washington 39. The Underpup 39. Remember the Night 40. *Our Town* 40. The Captain is a Lady 40. Penny Serenade 41 Shepherd of the Hills 41. One Foot in Heaven 41 Tonight We Raid Calais 43. Watch on the Rhine 43

Love a Soldier 44. She's a Soldier Too 44. Our
Hearts Were Young and Gay 44. And Now
Tomorrow 44. The Very Thought of You 44. *The
Southerner* 45. Back to Bataan 45. Breakfast in
Hollywood 46. Sister Kenny 46. *It's a Wonderful
Life* 46. High Conquest 47. The Sainted Sisters 48.
The Snake Pit 48. So Dear to My Heart 48. The
Life of Riley 49. Reign of Terror 49. Mr Soft Touch
49. The Baron of Arizona 50. The Furies 50. Lone
Star 52. Latin Lovers 53. *Track of the Cat* 54. Back
from Eternity 56. The Unholy Wife 57. The Big
Fisherman 59. A Summer Place 59. *Tammy Tell
Me True* 61. The Wonderful World of the Brothers
Grimm 62. Tammy and the Doctor 63. She Waits
(TV) 71.

B.B. always said that her great regret was being
passed over for the role of Ma Joad in *The Grapes of
Wrath.*

Bonerz, Peter (1938–).
American comic actor and director.
Funnyman (a, co-w) 67. Medium Cool (a) 69.
Catch-22 (a) 70. Fuzz (a) 72. Serial (a) 80. Nobody's
Perfekt (a, d) 81. Police Academy VI: City Under
Siege (d) 89, etc.
TV series: The Bob Newhart Show 72–78. 9 to
5 82–83.

Bonet, Lisa (1967–).
American actress, born in San Francisco. She is
best known for her television role as Denise in
The Cosby Show.
Angel Heart 87. Bank Robber 93. Lights Out 93.
TV series: The Cosby Show 84–91. A Different
World 87–88.

Bonham Carter, Helena (1966–).
British leading lady.
Lady Jane 84. A Room with a View 85. Maurice
87. The Vision 87. La Maschera 88. Francesco 89.
Getting It Right 89. Hamlet 90. Where Angels Fear
to Tread 91. Howards End 92. Mary Shelley's
Frankenstein 94.

I hate this image of me as a prim Edwardian.
I want to shock everyone. – H.B.C.

Bonnaire, Sandrine (1967–).
French leading actress.
To Our Loves (A Nos Amours) 83. Sans Toi ni
Loi 85. Police 85. Sous le Soleil de Satan 87.
Monsieur Hire 89. Prisoner of the Desert (Captive
du Désert) 90. Towards Evening (Verso Sera) 90.
The Sky Above Paris (Le Ciel de Paris) 91. Prague
92. The Plague (La Peste) 92. Jeanne la Pucelle
94. Confidences d'un Inconnu 95. La Nuit des
Cerfs-Volants 95, etc.

Bonner, Margerie (1905–1983).
American actress, in silent films, often westerns,
as a juvenile. She was the second wife (1940–57)
of novelist Malcolm Lowry, serving as a model for
the character of Yvonne, a former film star, in his
novel *Under the Volcano*, filmed in 1984 with
Jacqueline Bisset in the role, and for Primrose
Wilderness in his posthumously published *Dark as
the Grave wherein My Friend Is Laid*.

Bonnot, Françoise (1939–).
French editor, now working in international films.
Guns for San Sebastian 68. Z (AA) 69. The
Confession 70. State of Siege 73. Special Section 75.
The Tenant 76. Black and White in Colour 76.
The Cassandra Crossing 77. I Sent a Letter to My
Love 80. Missing 82. Hannah K 83. Swann in Love
84. Year of the Dragon 85. The Sicilian 87. Fat
Man and Little Boy (GB: The Shadowmakers) 89.
1492: Conquest of Paradise 92, etc.

Bono, Sonny (1935–) (Salvatore Bono).
American actor, a former pop singer and
songwriter. Together with his then-wife Cher he
had several hits as Sonny and Cher. He later
became mayor of Palm Springs.
Good Times 67. Murder on Flight 502 (TV) 75.
Escape to Athena 79. Airplane II: The Sequel 82.
Balboa (TV) 82. Troll 85. Dirty Laundry 87.
Hairspray 88. Under the Boardwalk 89, etc.
TV series: The Sonny and Cher Comedy Show
71–74. The Sonny Comedy Revue 74. The Sonny
and Cher Show 76–77.

Bonomo, Joe (1902–1978).
Muscular American strongman of silent pictures,
often in serials. In films from 1911, he retired
with the coming of sound and turned to
merchandising physical fitness.
Autobiography: 1968, *The Strongman*.
The Hunchback of Notre Dame 23. Beasts of
Paradise (serial) 23. The Iron Man (serial) 24. The
Flaming Frontier 26. Heroes of the Wild (serial)
27. The Phantom of the West (serial) 31. Island of
Lost Souls 33, etc.

boo-boos
occur even in the best-regulated movies;
sometimes they pass the eagle eye of editor and
director and find their way into the release version.
Here are a few which have delighted me.
▶ In *Carmen Jones*, the camera tracks with
Dorothy Dandridge down a shopping street, and
the entire crew is reflected in the windows she
passes.
▶ In *The Invisible Man*, when the naked but
invisible hero runs from the police but is given
away by his footprints in the snow, the
footprints are of shoes, not feet.
▶ In *The Wrong Box*, the roofs of Victorian London
are disfigured by TV aerials.
▶ In *The Viking Queen*, one character is plainly
wearing a wrist watch.
▶ In *One Million Years BC*, all the girls wear false
eyelashes.
▶ In *The Group*, set in the 30s, there are several
shots of the Pan Am building in New York, built
in the 60s.
▶ In *Stagecoach*, during the Indian chase across
the salt flats one can see the tracks of rubber
tyres.
▶ In *Decameron Nights*, Louis Jourdan as Paganino
the Pirate stands on the deck of his
fourteenth-century ship . . . and down a hill in
the distance trundles a large white truck.
▶ In *Camelot*, the character played by Lionel
Jeffries first meets King Arthur about an hour
into the movie; yet twenty minutes earlier he
is plainly visible at the king's wedding.
▶ In *Son of Frankenstein*, Basil Rathbone during a
train journey draws attention to the weirdly
stunted trees . . . one of which passes by three
times during the conversation.
▶ In *Castle of Fu Manchu*, one of the leading
characters is referred to in the film as Ingrid,
in the synopsis as Anna, and in the end credits
as Maria.
▶ In *Tea and Sympathy*, a pair of china dogs are
back to back in a general view of the scene, but
face to face in the close-ups.
▶ In *Dracula*, Bela Lugosi refers to Whitby as 'so
close to London'. It is in fact 243 miles away.
▶ In *The Yellow Mountain* and *A Man Alone*, both
westerns set in the last century, aeroplane
vapour trails can be seen in the sky.
▶ In *The King and I*, while Yul Brynner is singing
'Puzzlement' he is wearing an earring in some
shots but not in others.
▶ In *Emma Hamilton* (1969) Big Ben is heard to
strike in 1804, fifty years before it was built.
▶ In *The Lodger* (1944) London's Tower Bridge is
shown, ten years before it was built.
▶ In *Hello Dolly*, set at the turn of the century, a
modern car lies derelict by the side of the
railway track.
▶ In *Anatomy of a Murder*, Lee Remick in the café
scene wears a dress, but when she walks outside
she is wearing slacks.
▶ In *Hangover Square*, the introductory title gives
the date of the action as 1899, but shortly
thereafter a theatre programme shows 1903.
▶ In *Queen Christina*, the famous final close-up
apparently has the wind blowing in two
directions at once, one to get the boat under
way and the other to arrange Garbo's hair to
the best advantage.
▶ In *The Desk Set*, Katharine Hepburn leaves her
office carrying a bunch of white flowers. By the
time she reaches the pavement they are pink.
▶ In *Knock on Wood*, Danny Kaye turns a corner
in London's Oxford Street, and finds himself in
Ludgate Hill, three miles away.
▶ In *23 Paces to Baker Street*, Van Johnson has an
apartment in Portman Square, with a river view
which seems to be that of the Savoy Hotel two
miles away.
▶ In *Triple Cross*, a World War II newspaper bears
a headline about the cost of Concorde going up
again.
▶ In *The Lady Vanishes*, Miss Froy writes her name
in the steam on a train window, but two or three
shots later the writing is quite different and in
another place.
▶ In *The Eddie Cantor Story*, the scene is set in
1904, but Eddie sings 'Meet Me Tonight in
Dreamland' which was not written till 1909.
▶ Similarly, in *Thoroughly Modern Millie*, clearly
set in 1922 per the song title, one of the big
numbers is 'Baby Face', written in 1926.
▶ In *Miracle on 34th Street*, a camera shadow
follows Edmund Gwenn and John Payne as
they walk across a square.
▶ In *Broken Lance*, Katy Jurado's dress changes
colour in alternate shots as she stands in a
doorway talking to Spencer Tracy at the
gate.
▶ In *North by Northwest*, Cary Grant's only suit
during his stay in Chicago is a different colour
out in the prairie from back at the hotel.
Hitchcock said this was because of different
kinds of lighting which were used.
▶ In *Mysterious Island*, set in 1860, an air balloon
rises above a nest of TV aerials.
▶ In *The Alamo*, mobile trailers are clearly seen
in the battle sequences, and a falling stuntman
lands on a mattress.
▶ In *North to Alaska* during a fistfight, John
Wayne loses his toupee and then regains it.
▶ In *The Green Berets*, the sun sets in the east
during the final shot.
▶ In *The Scalphunters*, set in the 1800s, Ossie Davis
mentions the planet Pluto, which was not
discovered until 1930.
▶ In *Annie*, set in 1933, characters go to Radio
City Music Hall and see *Camille*, which was not
made until 1937.
▶ In *Yankee Doodle Dandy*, the *Lusitania* is sunk
and there is a newspaper picture showing a ship
with two funnels. The *Lusitania* had four
funnels.
▶ In the same film a luggage label with a picture
of Nelson's Column bears the legend 'Nelson
Square Hotel'.
▶ In *Brief Encounter*, Celia Johnson runs through
a downpour but remains dry.
▶ In *National Lampoon's Animal House*, the word

Satan written on a blackboard looks totally different in adjacent shots.

► In *Quadrophenia*, clearly set in 1964, a cinema is showing Warren Beatty in *Heaven Can Wait*, made fourteen years later.

► In *Carrie*, the final dream was projected backwards to achieve the right effect. But in the background a car is also moving backwards . . .

► In *Halloween*, which is set in Illinois, all the cars have California number plates.

► In *The Birds*, the creatures which pursue the children cast no shadows.

► In *Cain and Mabel*, a workman walks across a sound stage during a production number.

► In *The Band Wagon*, during the train ride to Baltimore, the scenery is dark on one side and light on the other.

► In *Knock on Wood*, a policeman rushes upstairs wearing a helmet, and into a room wearing a peaked cap.

► In *Silk Stockings*, a typewriter shown on a table vanishes in the reverse shot taken from the balcony.

► In *Fire Maidens from Outer Space*, Sidney Tafler in a T-shirt glances down at his watch, and we get an insert of a watch on a fully-sleeved arm.

► In *Genevieve*, Kenneth More comes out of a pub carrying a pint of beer, which has become a half pint by the time he reaches his table.

► In *The Band Wagon*, a theatre is shown on its canopy as the Alcott; but on the programme it says the Stratton.

► In *Meet Me In St Louis*, during the Trolley Song, one of the extras calls 'Hi, Judy!' Judy Garland's character name is Esther.

► In *The Adventures of Robin Hood*, Errol Flynn takes a bite at a complete leg of mutton. In the next shot, only a bone is left.

► In *Round Midnight*, which is set in the 50s, there is a shot of New York's World Trade Center towers, which were built much later.

► In *Camelot*, Richard Harris plays one scene with a Band-Aid on his neck.

► In *North by Northwest*, a small boy (who has obviously been to rehearsal) puts his fingers in his ears *before* Eva Marie Saint picks up a gun to shoot Cary Grant.

► In *Mysterious Island*, during the air balloon sequence, it is raining *above* the clouds.

► In *The Smallest Show on Earth*, although the cinema is supposedly in the north of England, a taxi arriving at it stops outside Hammersmith station.

► In *The Corn is Green*, the villagers are all said to be illiterate, but they cluster round to read a poster.

Booke, Sorrell (1926–1994).
Chubby American character actor.
Gone are the Days 63. Fail Safe 64. Black Like Me 64. Lady in a Cage 64. Up the Down Staircase 67. Slaughterhouse Five 71. The Take 72. The Iceman Cometh 73. Bank Shot 74. Special Delivery 76. Freaky Friday 77. The Other Side of Midnight 77, etc.

books on the cinema:
see list at end of book.

boom.
A 'long arm' extending from the camera unit and carrying a microphone to be balanced over the actors so that sound can be picked up in a semi-distant shot. A 'camera boom' is a high movable platform strong enough to support the entire camera unit.

Boone, Daniel (1734–1820).
American pioneer and Indian scout who helped to open up Kentucky and Missouri. He has been frequently portrayed in films, notably by George O'Brien (*Daniel Boone*, 1936), David Bruce (*Young Daniel Boone*, 1950) and Bruce Bennett (*Daniel Boone, Trail Blazer*, 1956). In 1964 began a long-running TV series, *Daniel Boone*, starring Fess Parker.

Boone, Pat (1934–).
Gentle-mannered American pop singer of the 50s; never quite made it as a straight actor, perhaps because he paraded his lack of private vices.
■ *Bernardine* 57. April Love 57. Mardi Gras 58. *Journey to the Centre of the Earth* 59. All Hands on Deck 61. State Fair 62. The Yellow Canary 63. The Main Attraction 63. The Horror of it All (GB) 63. Never Put it in Writing (GB) 64. Goodbye Charlie 64. The Greatest Story Ever Told 65. The Perils of Pauline 67. The Pigeon (TV) 69. The Cross and the Switchblade 70.

Boone, Richard (1917–1981).
Craggy American character actor, often in menacing roles.
■ Halls of Montezuma 51. Call Me Mister 51. The Desert Fox 51. Return of the Texan 52. Red Skies of Montana 52. Kangaroo 52. The Way of a Gaucho 52. Man on a Tightrope 53. *Vicki* 53. *The Robe* 53. City of Bad Men 53. Beneath the Twelve-Mile Reef 53. The Siege at Red River 54. Dragnet 54. The Raid 54. Battle Stations 55. *Man Without a Star* 55. Ten Wanted Men 55. Robbers' Roost 55. Star in the Dust 56. Away All Boats 56. Lizzie 57. Garment Center 57. The Tall T 57. I Bury the Living 58. *The Alamo* 60. A Thunder of Drums 61. *Rio Conchos* 64. *The War Lord* 65. Hombre 67. Kona Coast 68. The Night of the Following Day 69. *The Arrangement* 69. Madron 70. *The Kremlin Letter* 70. Big Jake 71. In Broad Daylight (TV) 72. A Tattered Web 72. Goodnight My Love (TV) 72. Deadly Harvest 72. The Great Niagara (TV) 74. Against a Crooked Sky 75. The Shootist 76. God's Gun 77. The Big Sleep 78. Winter Kills 79. The Bushido Blade 79.
TV series: *Medic* 54–55. *Have Gun Will Travel* 57–62. *The Richard Boone Show* 63. Hec Ramsey 72–74.

Boorman, John (1933–).
British director, from TV.
Autobiography: 1985, *Money into Light: The Emerald Forest, a Diary.*
■ Catch Us if You Can 65. *Point Blank* (US) 67. *Hell in the Pacific* (US) 69. Leo the Last 70. *Deliverance* (AAN) 72. Zardoz (& w) 74. Exorcist II: The Heretic 77. Long Shot (as actor, in the role of himself) 78. Excalibur 81. Dream One (p only) 82. The Emerald Forest (& p) 85. *Hope and Glory* (& p) (AAN) 87. Where the Heart Is (p, wd) 90. I Dreamt I Woke Up (doc) 91.

Booth, Anthony (1937–).
British general-purpose actor: everything from Nazis to layabouts.
Mix Me a Person 62. The L-Shaped Room 62. Of Human Bondage 64. Till Death Us Do Part 68. Girl With a Pistol 69. The Garnett Saga 72, etc.
TV series: *Till Death Us Do Part* 67–71.

Booth, Edwina (1909–1991) (Josephine Constance Woodruff).
American leading lady of the late 20s, best known for catching jungle fever while filming in Africa for *Trader Horn* 30. She retired shortly after.

Booth, Harry.
British director, former editor.

Blitz on Britain 59. A King's Story 64. On the Buses 71. Mutiny on the Buses 72. Go for a Take 72, etc.

Booth, James (1930–) (David Geeves-Booth).
British character actor who can play innocent or villainous, now in America.
The Trials of Oscar Wilde 60. The Hellions 61. In the Doghouse 62. Sparrows Can't Sing 63. French Dressing 63. *Zulu* 64. The Secret of My Success 65. Ninety Degrees in the Shade 66. *Robbery* 67. The Bliss of Mrs Blossom 68. The Man Who Had Power Over Women 70. Darker Than Amber 70. Macho Callahan 71. Revenge 71. That'll Be the Day 74. Brannigan 75. Airport 77 77. Wheels (TV) 78. It's Not the Size that Counts 79. The Jazz Singer 80. Zorro the Gay Blade 81. The Cowboy and the Ballerina (TV) 84. Bad Guys 85. Programmed to Kill 87. American Ninja 4: The Annihilator 91, etc.

Booth, Karin (1923–1992) (aka Katherine Booth).
American leading lady of second features.
Big City 48. Last of the Buccaneers 50. The Texas Rangers 50. Cripple Creek 52. Let's Do It Again 53. Seminole Uprising 55. The Crooked Sky (GB) 57. Beloved Infidel 59, etc.

Booth, Margaret (1898–).
Distinguished American editor, long at MGM, latterly as supervisor. She was given an honorary Oscar in 1977.
Memory Lane 26. The Bridge of San Luis Rey 29. Cuban Love Song 31. New Moon 31. Susan Lenox 31. Strange Interlude 31. Bombshell 33. Dancing Lady 33. The Barretts of Wimpole Street 34. Mutiny on the Bounty 35. Camille 36. Romeo and Juliet 36. The Way We Were 73. The Sunshine Boys 76. Murder by Death 76. California Suite 78. Annie 82, many others.

Booth, Shirley (1898–1992) (Thelma Ford Booth).
Distinguished American stage actress who came to the screen for a few middle-aged roles.
■ *Come Back Little Sheba* (AA) 52. About Mrs Leslie 53. Main Street to Broadway 53. Hot Spell 57. *The Matchmaker* 59. The Smugglers (TV) 68.
TV series: *Hazel* 61–65. A Touch of Grace 73.

Boothe, Powers (1949–).
Powerful American lead actor, on TV in the mid-80s as Philip Marlowe.
A Cry for Love (TV) 80. Cruising 81. *Guyana Tragedy* (TV) 81. Southern Comfort 81. Chandlertown (TV) 83. Red Dawn 84. The Emerald Forest 85. Extreme Prejudice 87. By Dawn's Early Light 89. Tombstone 94. Blue Sky (made 91) 94, etc.

Borchers, Cornell (1925–) (Cornelia Bruch).
German leading actress, in a few international films.
The Big Lift 50. The Divided Heart (BFA) 55. Never Say Goodbye 56. Istanbul 57. Oasis 60, etc.

Borden, Lizzie (1954–).
American director and screenwriter of independent films, a former editor.
Born in Flames 82. Working Girls 86. Love Crimes 92. Erotique (co-d) 94.

Borden, Olive (1907–1947) (Sybil Tinkle).
American leading lady of the 20s. She failed to make the transition to sound and died in poverty, an alcoholic.
Dressmaker from Paris 25. Three Bad Men 26. Fig Leaves 26. The Joy Girl 26. Pajamas 26. Gang

ar 28. Virgin Lips 28. Love in the Desert 29. ance Hall 29. Hello Sister 30, etc.

ordoni, Irene (1895–1953).
orsican-American revue comedienne who left roadway to make only three films.
 Show of Shows 28. Paris 30. Louisiana Purchase .

oreham Wood.
British studio fourteen miles north of London, site originally chosen by John M. East (1860–)24), a stage and silent screen actor. It opened in)14 as Neptune Films, which folded in 1921; the ages were later taken over by Ideal, Rock, British ational, and Associated Television. MGM and BPC also had studios in nearby Elstree.

org, Veda Ann (1915–1973).
american character actress, the archetypal hard-)iled blonde of a hundred second features.
 Three Cheers for Love 36. Alcatraz Island 37. he Loved a Fireman 38. Café Hostess 39. Glamour r Sale 40. The Pittsburgh Kid 41. Duke of the avy 42. Isle of Forgotten Sins 43. Smart Guy 44. Vhat a Blonde 45. Mildred Pierce 45. Accomplice). Big Town 47. Blonde Savage 48. Forgotten Vomen 49. The Kangaroo Kid 50. Big Jim McLain 2. Three Sailors and a Girl 53. Bitter Creek 54. uys and Dolls 55. Frontier Gambler 56. The earmakers 58. Thunder in the Sun 59. lamo 60, many others.

orgia, Cesare (1476–1507) and **Lucretia** (1480–)19).
he son and daughter of Pope Alexander VI were 3spected of several family murders. On screen they ave been played as melodramatic figures, notably MacDonald Carey and Paulette Goddard (*Bride Vengeance* 49), Orson Welles (*Prince of Foxes* 49), dro Armendariz and Martine Carol (*Lucretia orgia* 52), and Franco Fabrizi and Belinda Lee *ights of Lucretia Borgia* 59). In 1981 the BBC roduced a risible mini-series on the subject, with dolfo Celi unintelligible as the founder of the clan.

orgnine, Ernest (1915–) (Ermes Borgnino).
orceful American character actor who after stage id TV work was typecast by Hollywood as a eavy until *Marty* gave him star status.
 China Corsair 51. The Whistle at Eaton Falls 51. he Mob 51. *From Here to Eternity* 53. The Stranger Vore a Gun 53. Demetrius and the Gladiators 54. he Bounty Hunter 54. Johnny Guitar 54. Vera ruz 54. *Bad Day at Black Rock* 54. Run for Cover 5. *Marty* (AA, BFA) 55. Violent Saturday 55. The ast Command 55. The Square Jungle 56. Jubal 6. *The Catered Affair* 56. *The Best Things in Life Are ree* 56. Three Brave Men 57. *The Vikings* 58. The adlanders 58. Torpedo Run 58. The Rabbit Trap 8. Man on a String 60. *Pay or Die* 60. Go Naked the World 61. Summer of the Seventeenth Doll . Les Guerrilleros (Sp.) 61. Il Re de Poggioreale .) 61. Il Giudizio Universale (It.) 61. Seduction the South (It.) 62. Barabbas 62. McHale's Navy . The Flight of the Phoenix 65. The Oscar 66. he Dirty Dozen 67. Chuka 67. Ice Station Zebra 68. he Split 68. The Legend of Lylah Clare 68. The Vild Bunch 69. Suppose They Gave a War and obody Came 69. Vengeance is Mine (It.) 69. The dventurers 70. Bunny O'Hare 71. Hannie aulder 71. Rain for a Dusty Summer 71. The rackers (TV) 71. Willard 71. Tough Guy 72. The evengers 72. What Happened to the Mysterious r Foster? (TV) 72. The Poseidon Adventure 72. mperor of the North Pole 73. The Neptune Factor 3. Law and Disorder 74. Sunday in the Country 4. Twice in a Lifetime (TV) 74. The Devil's Rain

75. Cleaver and Haven (TV) 76. Hustle 76. Shoot 76. The Prince and the Pauper 77. Jesus of Nazareth (TV) 77. The Greatest 77. Convoy 78. The Black Hole 79. The Double McGuffin 79. All Quiet on the Western Front (TV) 79. When Time Ran Out 80. Escape from New York 81. High Risk 81. Deadly Blessing 81. Superfuzz 81. Blood Feud (TV) 82. Young Warriors 83. Masquerade (TV) 83. Airwolf (TV) 84. The Last Days of Pompeii (TV) 84. Codename Wildgeese 84. The Manhunt 84. The Dirty Dozen – The Next Mission (TV) 85. Skeleton Coast 88. Spike of Bensonhurst 88. Laser Mission 89. Turnaround 89. Ski School 89. Any Man's Death 90. Moving Target 90. Appearances (TV) 90. Mistress (as himself) 92. The Legend of O. B. Taggart 94.
 TV series: *McHale's Navy* 62–65. Future Cop 76. Airwolf 84–86.

Boris, Robert.
American screenwriter and director.
 Electra Glide in Blue (w) 73. Some Kind of Hero (co-w) 82. Doctor Detroit (co-w) 83. Oxford Blues (wd) (GB) 84. Steele Justice (wd) 87. Buy and Cell (d) 89, etc.

Boros, Ferike (1880–1951).
Hungarian actress in Hollywood.
 Little Caesar 30. Svengali 31. Huddle 32. Humanity 33. The Fountain 34. Make Way for Tomorrow 37. Love Affair 39. Argentine Nights 40. Caught in the Draft 41. Once Upon a Honeymoon 42. The Doughgirls 44. The Specter of the Rose 46, etc.

Borowczyk, Walerian (1923–).
Polish writer-director, formerly animator, living in France.
 The Theatre of M. and Mme Kobal 67. Goto, Island of Love 68. *Blanche* 72. Immoral Tales 74. The Story of Sin 74. La Bête 75. The Streetwalker 76. Dr Jekyll and the Women 81. L'Art d'Aimer 83. Emmanuelle 5 86. Cérémonie d'Amour 86, etc.

Borradaile, Osmond (1898–).
Canadian cinematographer, in Hollywood from 1916 and later in Britain.
 The Private Life of Henry VIII (2nd unit) 33. Sanders of the River (2nd unit) 35. The Scarlet Pimpernel (2nd unit) 35. Elephant Boy (2nd unit) 36. The Drum (2nd unit) 38. *The Four Feathers* (2nd unit) 39. *The Thief of Bagdad* (co-ph) 40. *The Overlanders* 46. The Macomber Affair 47. Bonnie Prince Charlie 48. *Scott of the Antarctic* 48. I Was a Male War Bride 49. The Trap 66, etc.

Borsche, Dieter (1909–1982).
German character actor.
 Alles weg'n dem Hund (debut) 35. Die Nachtwache 49. Die Grosse Versuchung 52. Ali Baba (Fr.) 54. Die Barrings 55. A Time to Love and a Time to Die (US) 58. Scotland Yard vs Dr Mabuse 63. Lady Hamilton 63, etc.

Borsos, Phillip (1953–1995).
Canadian director. Died from leukemia.
 The Grey Fox 83. The Mean Season 84. One Magic Christmas 85. Bethune 89. Far From Home: The Adventures of Yellow Dog 95, etc.

Borzage, Frank (1893–1962).
American director who favoured a soft, sentimental approach to romantic dramas.
SILENT FILMS INCLUDE: Humoresque 20. Get Rich Quick Wallingford 21. Children of the Dust 23. Secrets 24. The Circle 25. The Marriage Licence 26. Seventh Heaven (AA) 27. Street Angel 28. The River 29.

■ SOUND FILMS: Song o' My Heart 30. *Liliom* 30. Doctors' Wives 31. Young as You Feel 31. Bad Girl (AA) 32. After Tomorrow 32. Young America 32. *A Farewell to Arms* 32. Secrets 33. *Man's Castle* 33. No Greater Glory 34. Little Man What Now? 34. Flirtation Walk 34. Living on Velvet 35. Stranded 35. Shipmates Forever 35. *Desire* 36. Hearts Divided 36. The Green Light 37. *History Is Made at Night* 37. Big City 38. Mannequin 38. *Three Comrades* 38. The Shining Hour 39. Disputed Passage 39. *Strange Cargo* 40. *The Mortal Storm* 40. Flight Command 41. *Smilin' Through* 41. The Vanishing Virginian 42. Seven Sweethearts 42. Stage Door Canteen 43. His Butler's Sister 43. Till We Meet Again 44. The Spanish Main 45. I've Always Loved You 46. Magnificent Doll 46. That's My Man 47. *Moonrise* 49. China Doll 58. The Big Fisherman 59.

¶ *History Is Made at Night* is not only the most romantic tragedy in the history of the cinema but also a profound exposition of Borzage's commitment to love over probability. – *Andrew Sarris, 1968*

Bosco, Philip (1930–).
American character actor. Born in Jersey City, he is a noted New York stage actor.
 Requiem for a Heavyweight 62. A Lovely Way to Die 68. Trading Places 83. The Pope of Greenwich Village 84. Heaven Help Us 85. Flanagan 85. Walls of Glass 85. The Money Pit 86. Children of a Lesser God 86. Suspect 87. Three Men and a Baby 87. Another Woman 88. Working Girl 88. The Dream Team 89. The Luckiest Man in the World 89. Blue Steel 90. Quick Change 90. FX/2 – The Deadly Art of Illusion 91. True Colors 91. Angie 94. Milk Money 94, etc.

Bose, Lucia (1931–).
Italian leading lady, former beauty queen.
 No Peace Among the Olives 50. Cronaca di un Amore 51. Girls of the Spanish Steps 52. Death of a Cyclist (Sp.) 54. Le Testament d'Orphée 61. Lumière 76, etc.

Bosley, Tom (1927–).
Plump American character actor with stage and TV experience.
 The Street with No Name 46. Call Northside 777 48. The World of Henry Orient 64. *Love with the Proper Stranger* 64. Divorce American Style 67. The Secret War of Harry Frigg 67. Yours Mine and Ours 68. To Find a Man 72. Gus 76. O'Hara's Wife 81. The Jesse Owens Story (TV) 84. Private Sessions (TV) 85. Million Dollar Mystery 87. Fire and Rain 89. Wicked Stepmother 89, etc.
 TV series: *Debbie* 69. Happy Days 75.

Bost, Pierre:
see *Aurenche, Jean.*

The Boston Strangler:
see *DeSalvo, Albert.*

Bostwick, Barry (1945–).
Personable, easy-going leading man of the 70s, sometimes with a startling resemblance to James Stewart.
■ Jennifer on My Mind 71. Janice 72. The Chadwick Family (TV) 74. The Rocky Horror Picture Show 75. The Wrong Damn Film 75. The Quinns (TV) 77. Movie Movie 78. Murder by Natural Causes (TV) 79. Once Upon a Family (TV) 80. Moviola (TV) (as John Gilbert) 80. Scruples (TV) 80. Megaforce 82. George Washington (title role) (TV) 84. A Woman of Substance (TV) 84. Deceptions (TV) 85. Jailbait: Betrayed by Innocence (TV) 90. Weekend at Bernie's II 93.

Praying Mantis (TV) 93. Eight Hundred Leagues down the Amazon 93. Danielle Steel's Once in a Lifetime (TV) 94.

TV series: Foul Play 80. War and Remembrance 88.

Bosustow, Stephen (1911–1981).
Founder of UPA cartoons (1943) after working as artist for Disney and others. Later won Academy Awards for creation of Gerald McBoing Boing and Mr Magoo.

Boswell, Connee (1907–1976).
American band singer, a polio victim who recovered sufficiently to continue her career.
Artist and Models 37. Kiss the Boys Goodbye 40. Syncopation 41, etc.

Bosworth, Hobart (1867–1943).
American character actor with stage experience: films from 1909.
The Country Mouse 14. Joan the Woman 16. Oliver Twist 16. Below the Surface 20. Vanity Fair 23. Captain January 24. Zander the Great 25. The Big Parade 25. The Blood Ship 27. A Woman of Affairs 29. Mammy 30. The Miracle Man 32. Lady for a Day 33. The Crusades 35. Bullets for O'Hara 41. Sin Town 42, many others.

Boteler, Wade (1891–1943).
American general-purpose small-part actor.
An Old Fashioned Boy 19. The Ghost Patrol 23. High School Hero 26. Top Sergeant Mulligan 28. College Lovers 30. Death Kiss 32. Belle of the Nineties 34. Whipsaw 36. You Only Live Once 37. In Old Chicago 38. Thunder Afloat 39. Castle on the Hudson 40. Kathleen 41. I Was Framed 42. Hi Buddy 43. The Last Ride 44, many others.

Botkin, Perry, Jnr (1933–).
American composer.
Bless the Beasts and Children (co-ph) 72. Skyjacked 72. Lady Ice 72. Your Three Minutes Are Up 73. Tarzan the Ape Man 81. Dance of the Dwarves 83. Silent Night, Deadly Night 84. Weekend Warriors 86. Ordinary Heroes 86. Windmill of the Gods (TV) 88, etc.

Bottin, Rob (1959–).
American special effects and make-up designer. He worked with Rick Baker before setting up on his own.
Piranha 78. Rock 'n' Roll High School 79. The Fog (& a) 80. Humanoids from the Deep 80. The Howling 81. The Thing 82. Explorers 85. Legend (AAN) 86. Innerspace 87. Robocop 87. Witches of Eastwick 87. The Great Outdoors 88. Robocop 2 90. Total Recall (AA) 90. Bugsy 91. Basic Instinct 92. Robocop 3 93, etc.

Bottoms, Joseph (1954–).
American juvenile of the 70s.
The Dove 74. Crime and Passion 76. Holocaust (TV) 78. The Black Hole 79. Cloud Dancer 80. King of the Mountain 81. Surfacing 84. Blind Date 84. Celebrity 85. Open House 86. Born to Race 88. Inner Sanctum 91. Liars Edge 92, etc.

Bottoms, Sam (1955–).
American leading man, youngest of the Bottoms brothers.
The Last Picture Show 71. Class of '44 73. Zandy's Bride 74. Savages (TV) 74. The Outlaw Josey Wales 76. Cage without a Key (TV) 77. Apocalypse Now 79. Bronco Billy 80. Prime Risk 84. After School 88. Hunter's Blood 87. Return to Eden 89. Ragin' Cajun 90. Dolly Dearest 92. The Trust 93, etc.

Bottoms, Timothy (1951–).
Leading American juvenile actor of the early 70s who has found few comparable adult roles.
Johnny Got His Gun 71. *The Last Picture Show* 71. Love, Pain and the Whole Damned Thing 73. The Paper Chase 73. The White Dawn 74. The Crazy World of Julius Vrooder 74. The Moneychangers (TV) 76. Operation Daybreak 76. A Small Town in Texas 76. Rollercoaster 77. Return Engagement (TV) 78. Hurricane 79. The Other Side of the Mountain Part Two 79. *East of Eden* (TV) 80. The High Country 81. Hambone and Hillie 83. Love Leads the Way (TV) 85. Invaders from Mars 86. The Land of Faraway 87. The Drifter 88. Husbands, Wives, Money and Murder 89. Return to the River Kwai 89. The Fantasist 89. The Gift of Love 90. Istanbul 90. Texasville 90. Digger 93, etc.

Bouchet, Barbara (1943–) (Barbara Gutscher).
German-American glamour girl.
In Harm's Way 65. Agent for HARM 66. Casino Royale 67. Danger Route 68. Down the Ancient Stairs 75. House of a Thousand Pleasures 76, etc.

Bouchey, Willis (1895–1977).
American character actor, often seen as judge or reluctant sheriff.
Elopement 51. Suddenly 54. Johnny Concho 56. The Last Hurrah 58. Sergeant Rutledge 60. Where Love has Gone 64. Support Your Local Sheriff 69, many others.

Bouchier, Chili (1909–) (Dorothy Irene Bouchier).
British leading lady, mainly on the London stage, where she was still active in her 80s.
Autobiography: 1968, *For Dogs and Angels*.
■ A Woman in Pawn 27. Shooting Stars 28. Maria Marten 28. Dawn 28. Chick 28. Palais de Danse 28. You Know What Sailors Are 28. Warned Off 28. The Silver King 29. City of Play 29. Downstream 29. Enter the Queen 30. The Call of the Sea 30. Kissing Cup's Race 30. Brown Sugar 31. *Carnival* 31. *The Blue Danube* 32. Ebb Tide 32. The King's Cup 33. Summer Lightning 33. Purse Strings 33. It's a Cop 34. To Be a Lady 34. The Office Wife 34. Death Drives Through 35. Royal Cavalcade 35. The Mad Hatters 35. Honours Easy 35. Lucky Days 35. Get Off My Foot 35. Mr Cohen Takes a Walk 35. The Ghost Goes West 36. Faithful 36. Where's Sally 36. Southern Roses 36. *Gypsy* 36. Mayfair Melody 37. The Minstrel Boy 37. Change for a Sovereign 37. The Singing Cop 38. The Dark Stairway 38. *Mr Satan* 38. The Return of Carol Deane 38. Everything Happens to Me 38. The Mind of Mr Reeder 39. My Wife's Family 41. Facing the Music 41. Murder in Reverse 45. The Laughing Lady 46. Mrs Fitzherbert 47. *The Case of Charles Peace* 48. Old Mother Riley's New Venture 49. The Wallet 52. The Counterfeit Plan 57. The Boy and the Bridge 59. Dead Lucky 60. Catch a Fallen Star (TV) 87.
TV series: Flip 91.

Boulting, Ingrid (1947–) (Ingrid Munnik).
South African leading lady who made less than a dazzling impact in *The Last Tycoon* 76.

Boulting, John (1913–1985) and **Roy** (1913–).
Twin Britishers who after varied experience set up as writer-producer-directors of films with something to say. After World War II they became somewhat more conventional, and the early 50s were barren, but then they came up with a highly successful series of comedies pillorying national institutions. In the 60s they became directors of British Lion Films, with commercially successful

but otherwise disappointing results. (Although they have produced and directed alternately, neither showed a particular style, and their films below are treated as joint efforts unless mentioned otherwise.)
■ Consider Your Verdict 37. Inquest 38. Trunk Crime 38. *Pastor Hall* 39. *Thunder Rock* 42. *Desert Victory* (Roy) 44. Burma Victory (Roy) 45. *Journey Together* (John) 45. *Fame is the Spur* 46. *Brighton Rock* 46. *The Guinea Pig* 49. *Seven Days to Noon* 50. The Magic Box 51. High Treason (Roy) 52. Sailor of the King (Roy) 53. Seagulls Over Sorrento 54. Josephine and Men 54. *Private's Progress* 55. *Brothers in Law* 56. Run for the Sun (Roy) 56. *Lucky Jim* 57. Happy is the Bride 57. Carlton Browne of the F.O. 58. *I'm All Right Jack* 59. Suspect 60. A French Mistress 61. *Heavens Above* 63. Rotten to the Core 65. The Family Way 66. Twisted Nerve 68. There's a Girl in My Soup (Roy) 70. Endless Night 72. Soft Beds and Hard Battles (Roy) 73. The Last Word (Roy) 79.
◎ For raising the sights of British films in the 40s and later for devising a strain of satirical comedy. *I'm All Right Jack.*

Boulton, David.
British cinematographer.
The Password Is Courage 62. The Haunting 63. Children of the Damned 65. The Secret of My Success 65. It 66. The Great Waltz 72, etc.

Bouquet, Carole (1957–).
French leading actress and model of classic beauty
That Obscure Object of Desire 77. Buffet Froid 79. For Your Eyes Only 81. Le Bon Roi Dagobert 84. Rive Droite, Rive Gauche 85. Special Police 85 New York Stories 89. Trop Belle pour Toi (Too Beautiful for You) 89. Tango 93. A Business Affair 94. Grosse Fatigue 94, etc.

Bouquet, Michel (1926–).
French general-purpose actor, notably in the film of Claude Chabrol.
Monsieur Vincent 47. Manon 49. La Tour de Nesle 55. Katia 60. An Orchid for the Tiger 65. The Road to Corinth 67. The Bride Wore Black 68. The Mississippi Mermaid 69. Borsalino 70. Just Before Nightfall 71. Malpertuis 72. The Serpent 73. Les Suspects 74. Beyond Fear 75. Le-Jouet 77. La Raison d'Etat 78. Toto Le Héros 91, etc.

Bourgignon, Serge (1928–).
French director of style but little substance.
Sundays and Cybele (AA) 62. The Reward 65. Two Weeks in September 67. The Picasso Summer 69. My Kingdom for a Horse (doc) 86. The Fascination 87, etc.

Bourgoin, Jean (1913–).
French cinematographer.
La Marseillaise 38. Goupi Mains Rouges 43. Voyage Surprise 46. Dedée d'Anvers 47. Manèges 50. Justice est Faite 50. Nous Sommes Tous des Assassins 52. Confidential Report 55. *Mon Oncle* 58 *Black Orpheus* 59. The Counterfeit Traitor 62. Gigo 62. The Longest Day 62. Germinal 63. Pas Question le Samedi 65. Qui 70. La Chambre Rouge 73, many others.

Bourne, Mel.
Production designer, often for Woody Allen's films.
Annie Hall 77. Interiors (AAN) 78. The Greek Tycoon 78. Manhattan 79. Stardust Memories 80 Windows 80. Thief 81. A Midsummer Night's Sex Comedy 82. Zelig 83. Broadway Danny Rose 84. The Natural (AAN) 84. Manhunter 86. F/X 86. Fatal Attraction 87. Cocktail 89. Rude Awakening

. Reversal of Fortune 90. The Fisher King 91. an Trouble 92. Indecent Proposal 93. Angie 94, c.

ourneuf, Philip (1912–1979).
merican supporting stage actor of the older hool. Films few.
Winged Victory 44. Joan of Arc 49. The Big ght 51. Beyond a Reasonable Doubt 56. emingway's Adventures of a Young Man 62. The rrangement 69. The Molly Maguires 70, etc.

ourvil (1917–1970) (André Raimbourg).
iminutive, expressive French comic actor.
La Ferme du Pendu 45. Mr Peek-a-boo 51. *La aversée de Paris* 56. The Mirror Has Two Faces 58. ie Green Mare's Nest 69. Tout l'Or du Monde ?. Heaven Sent 63. The Secret Agents 65. The Big ree 66. *The Sucker* 66. Don't Look Now 67. The ain 68. Monte Carlo or Bust 69. The Red Circle), many others.

ow, Clara (1905–1965).
merican leading lady, the 'It' girl of the 20s: her ms depicted the gay young flapper generation and r wide-eyed vivacity was tremendously popular r a time, but she came to grief through trying to arallel her screen image in her private life.
Biography: 1989, *Clara Bow: Running Wild* by avid Stenn.
Beyond the Rainbow 22. Down to the Sea in hips 22. Enemies of Women 23. Maytime 23. The aring Years 23. Grit 24. Black Oxen 24. Poisoned aradise 24. Daughters of Pleasure 24. Wine 24. mpty Hearts 24. This Woman 24. Black Lightning !. Capital Punishment 25. Helen's Babies 25. ie Adventurous Sex 25. My Lady's Lips 25. arisian Love 25. Eve's Lover 25. Kiss Me Again 25. ie Scarlet West 25. The Primrose Path 25. The astic Age 25. The Keeper of the Bees 25. Free to ove 25. The Best Bad Man 25. Lawful Cheaters 5. Two Can Play 26. The Runaway 26. *Mantrap* 5. Kid Boots 26. The Ancient Mariner 26. My idy of Whim 26. Dancing Mothers 26. The hadow of the Law 26. It 27. Children of Divorce 7. Rough House Rosie 27. *Wings* 27. Hula 27. et Your Man 27. Red Hair 28. Ladies of the Mob 3. The Fleet's In 28. Three Weekends 28. The 'ild Party 29. The Saturday Night Kid 29. angerous Curves 29. Paramount on Parade 30. rue to the Navy 30. Love Among the Millionaires). Her Wedding Night 30. No Limit 31. Kick In 31. all Her Savage 32. Hoopla 33.

¶ She danced even when her feet were not moving. – *Adolph Zukor*
Being a sex symbol is a heavy load to carry, specially when one is tired, hurt and bewildered. C.B.
Her life and career still seem to have been reamed up by one of her scriptwriters. – *David hipman*

owdon, Dorris (1915–).
merican leading lady who abruptly retired to arry Nunnally Johnson.
Down on the Farm 38. Young Mr Lincoln 39. rums Along the Mohawk 39. *The Grapes of Wrath* as Rosasharn) 40. The Moon Is Down 42.

ower, Dallas (1907–).
ritish producer. Originally sound recordist, editor nd writer, he became director of BBC TV 1936– 9, supervisor of Ministry of Information film roduction 1940–42. Associate producer *As You ike It* 36, *Henry V* 44, etc.; produced *Sir Lancelot*, V series.
s DIRECTOR: Alice in Wonderland (Fr.) 50. The

Second Mrs Tanqueray 52. Doorway to Suspicion 57.

Bowers, William (1916–1987).
American screenwriter.
My Favorite Spy 42. Night and Day 46. *The Web* 47. Black Bart 48. Larceny 48. *The Gunfighter* 50. Cry Danger 51. *The Mob* 51. Split Second 53. *Five Against the House* 55. The Best Things in Life are Free 56. *The Sheepman* 58. Alias Jesse James 59. *The Last Time I Saw Archie* 61. Advance to the Rear 64. *Support Your Local Sheriff* 69, etc.

Bowie, David (1947–) (David Robert Jones).
Bizarrely decorated British pop singer who makes curious forays into film acting.
■ The Man Who Fell to Earth 76. Just a Gigolo 78. The Hunger 83. Merry Christmas Mr Lawrence 83. Ziggy Stardust and the Spiders from Mars 83 (recorded 73). Into the Night 84. Absolute Beginners 85. Labyrinth 86. The Last Temptation of Christ 88. When the Wind Blows (title song) 88. UHF 89. The Linguini Incident 92. Twin Peaks: Fire Walk with Me 92.

¶ I get offered so many bad movies. And they're all raging queens or transvestites or Martians. – *D.B.*, 1983
I'm an instant star. Just add water and stir. – *D.B.*

Bowie, Jim (1796–1836).
American folk hero who invented the Bowie knife and died at the Alamo. He was played in *The Iron Mistress* by Alan Ladd, in *The Last Command* by Sterling Hayden, in *The First Texan* by Jeff Morrow, in *Davy Crockett* by Kenneth Tobey, in *Man of Conquest* by Robert Armstrong, in *Comanche Territory* by Macdonald Carey, and in *The Alamo* by Richard Widmark. A TV series called *The Adventures of Jim Bowie* 60 starred Scott Forbes.

Bowie, Les (1913–1979).
British special effects technician especially noted for matte shots.
Great Expectations 46. The Red Shoes 48. Star Wars 76. Superman 78. Many Hammer films.

Bowker, Judy (1954–).
British leading lady.
Brother Sun Sister Moon 73. Count Dracula (TV) 78. Clash of the Titans 81. East of Elephant Rock 81. The Shooting Party 85, etc.

Bowman, Lee (1910–1979).
Well-groomed American light leading man with stage experience; found a desultory career in films.
Three Men in White 36. I Met Him in Paris 37. Love Affair 39. Miracles for Sale 39. Florian 40. Buck Privates 41. Kid Glove Killer 42. Three Hearts for Julia 43. Cover Girl 44. *The Impatient Years* 44. Tonight and Every Night 45. The Walls Came Tumbling Down 46. Smash-Up 47. The House by the River 50. Double Barrel Miracle 55. Youngblood Hawke 64, etc.
TV series: Ellery Queen 50.

Box, Betty E. (1920–).
British producer, sister of Sydney Box and once assistant to him. For many years she turned out comedies and dramas with box office appeal but little cinematic flavour, usually in association with director Ralph Thomas.
Miranda 48. Here Come the Huggetts 49. *Doctor in the House* 53. The Iron Petticoat 56. A Tale of Two Cities 58. The Thirty-nine Steps 59. No Love for Johnnie 61. A Pair of Briefs 63. No My Darling

Daughters 63. The High Bright Sun 65. Deadlier than the Male 66. The High Commissioner 68. Percy 70. The Love Ban 72. Percy's Progress 74, many others.

Box, John (1920–).
British production designer.
Lawrence of Arabia (AA) 62. *Doctor Zhivago* (AA) 65. *A Man For All Seasons* 66. *Oliver* (AA) 68. The Looking Glass War (p only) 69. *Nicholas and Alexandra* (AAN) 71. Travels with my Aunt (AAN) 73. Rollerball 74. *The Great Gatsby* 74. Sorcerer 76. A Passage to India 84. Murder by the Book (TV) 90. Black Beauty 94. First Knight 95, etc.

Box, Muriel (1905–1991).
British director, producer and screenwriter, also a playwright, novelist and publisher. Having failed to become a professional actress, she began as a continuity girl, started directing documentaries in the 40s and feature films from 1950. She was married to producer and screenwriter Sydney Box (1935–68) and Lord Gardiner, a former Lord Chancellor.
Autobiography: 1974, *Odd Woman Out*.
AS SCREENWRITER (with Sydney Box): 29 Acacia Avenue 45. *The Seventh Veil* (AA) 45. The Years Between 46. The Man Within (& p) 47. Dear Murderer (& p) 47. Holiday Camp 47. The Brothers 47. Easy Money 48. Daybreak 48. A Girl in a Million (& p) 50, etc.
AS DIRECTOR: The Happy Family (& w) 52. Street Corner (& w) 53. The Beachcomber 54. To Dorothy a Son 54. Simon and Laura 55. A Novel Affair (Passionate Stranger) (& w) 56. The Truth about Women (& w) 57. Subway in the Sky 58. Too Young to Love (& w) 59. Rattle of a Simple Man 64, etc.

Box, Sydney (1907–1983).
British writer-producer who had considerable success in the decade after World War II.
The Seventh Veil (co-w, AA) 46. The Years Between 47. *Holiday Camp* 47. Jassy 47. *The Brothers* 48. Dear Murderer 48. *Quartet* 48. Don't Take It to Heart (p only) 48. Broken Journey 48. Daybreak 49. A Girl in a Million 50. So Long at the Fair (p only) 51. *The Prisoner* 55, etc.

boxing.
Actual prizefighters whose lives have been fictionalized on film include Jim Corbett (Errol Flynn in *Gentleman Jim*), John L. Sullivan (Greg McClure in *The Great John L*), Joe Louis (Coley Wallace in *The Joe Louis Story*), Rocky Graziano (Paul Newman in *Somebody Up There Likes Me*), and Jack Johnson (James Earl Jones in *The Great White Hope*). Purely fictional boxing films have tended to emphasize the corruption of the fight game: *The Ring, The Square Ring, The Square Jungle, Iron Man, Kid Galahad, Kid Nightingale, The Champ, The Crowd Roars, Body and Soul, The Set Up, Champion, Golden Boy, No Way Back, The Good Die Young, Run With the Wind, The Harder They Fall,* and from Europe *Walkover* and *Boxer*. Boxing comedy is rare once one discounts the Joe Palooka series, but most comedians have taken part in boxing sequences: Abbott and Costello in *Meet the Invisible Man*, Harold Lloyd in *The Milky Way*, Danny Kaye in *The Kid from Brooklyn*, Chaplin in *The Champion*, etc. The only boxing fantasy was *Here Comes Mr Jordan*, in which Robert Montgomery's soul was transferred into that of a prizefighter. The most violent boxing film was undoubtedly *Raging Bull*, in which Robert de Niro put on fifty pounds to play the ageing Jake La Motta.

Boxleitner, Bruce (1950–).
American leading man, mostly on TV.
  Six Pack Annie 75. Kiss Me Kill Me (TV) 76.
Tron 82. Diplomatic Immunity 91. Breakaway 91.
Murderous Vision 91. Kuffs 92. The Babe 92, etc.
  TV series: How the West Was Won 76. Bring
'em Back Alive 82. Scarecrow and Mrs King 83.

Boyd, Don (1948–).
British independent producer and director.
AS PRODUCER: Sweet William 78. Hussy 78. The
Tempest 78. Blue Suede Shoes 79. Scum 79. Great
Rock and Roll Swindle 80. Honky Tonk Freeway
81. Scrubbers 82. Unsuitable Job for a Woman 83.
Captive 85. Aira 86. Last of England 87. War
Requiem 89, etc.
AS DIRECTOR: Intimate Reflections 75. East of
Elephant Rock 76. Twenty-One 91. Kleptomania
93, etc.

Boyd, Dorothy (1907–).
English leading actress of the 30s, who began as
an extra.
  Easy Virtue 27. The Constant Nymph 28. Too
Many Crooks 30. Third Time Lucky 31. The Girl
in the Night 31. A Shot in the Dark 33. Ace of
Spades 35. Ticket of Leave 36. Pearls Bring Tears
37. Shadowed Eyes 39, etc.

Boyd, Russell (1944–).
Australian cinematographer.
  The Man from Hong Kong 75. Picnic at Hanging
Rock 75. Summer of Secrets 76. Break of Day 77.
The Last Wave 77. Dawn 79. Chain Reaction 80.
Gallipoli 81. Starstruck 82. The Year of Living
Dangerously 82. Tender Mercies 83. Phar Lap 84.
A Soldier's Story 84. Mrs Soffel 85. Between Wars
85. Crocodile Dundee 86. High Tide 87. Burke and
Wills 87. The Rescue 88. Crocodile Dundee II 88.
In Country 89. Almost an Angel 90. Sweet Talker
91. White Men Can't Jump 92, etc.

Boyd, Stephen (1928–1977) (William Millar).
Irish leading man in international films; fairly
popular during the 60s.
■ Born for Trouble 55. An Alligator Named Daisy
55. A Hill in Korea 56. The Man Who Never Was (as
the German spy) 56. Seven Waves Away 57. Island
in the Sun 57. Seven Thunders 57. Heaven Fell
That Night 57. The Bravados 58. Ben Hur (as
Messala) 59. Woman Obsessed 59. The Best of
Everything 59. The Big Gamble 61. The Inspector
62. Jumbo 62. Imperial Venus 63. The Fall of the
Roman Empire 64. The Third Secret 64. Genghis
Khan 64. The Oscar 66. Fantastic Voyage 66. The
Bible 66. The Caper of the Golden Bulls 67.
Assignment K 68. Shalako 68. Slaves 69. Carter's
Army (TV) 71. The Hands of Cormac Joyce (TV)
71. Key West (TV) 72. Hannie Caulder 72. The Man
Called Noon 73. Marta 74. Kill, Kill, Kill 74. Those
Dirty Dogs 74. Evil in the Deep 75. The Lives of
Jenny Dolan (TV) 75. Left Hand of the Law 76.
The Squeeze 77. The Devil Has Seven Faces 77.
Impossible Love 77.

Boyd, William (1895–1972).
Unassuming American leading man, in films from
1919, internationally famous from 1934 as cowboy
hero Hopalong Cassidy, in which guise he made
scores of second features and TV episodes.
  Why Change Your Wife? 19. The Temple of
Venus 23. Changing Husbands 24. The Volga
Boatmen 26. King of Kings 27. Two Arabian Knights
27. Skyscraper 28. The Leatherneck 29. The Benson
Murder Case 30. The Spoilers 30. The Painted
Desert 31. Murder by the Clock 31. Lucky Devils
33. Port of Lost Dreams 34. Hopalong Cassidy 35,

many others, but all subsequent films as Cassidy;
last in 1948.

Boyd, William (1952–).
English novelist and screenwriter.
  Stars and Bars 88. Tune in Tomorrow (aka Aunt
Julia and the Scriptwriter) 90. Mister Johnson 91.
Chaplin 92. A Good Man in Africa (from his novel)
94.

Boyd, William 'Stage' (1890–1935).
American stage actor, so known to distinguish him
from his Hopalong Cassidy namesake.
  Sky Devils 32. Painted Woman 32. Oliver Twist
(as Sikes) 33, etc.

Boyer, Charles (1899–1978).
Gentlemanly French romantic actor in
international films: went to Hollywood first in
1929, and later gained a reputation as the screen's
'great lover'. Committed suicide following the
death of his wife of 44 years.
  Biography: 1964, Charles Boyer by Larry
Swindell.
■ L'Homme du Large 20. Chantelouve 21. Le
Grillon du Foyer 22. L'Esclave 23. La Ronde
Infernale 27. Le Capitain Fracasse 27. La Barcarolle
d'Amour 28. Le Procès de Mary Dugan 28. The
Big House (French version) 30. The Magnificent
Lie 31. Tumultes 31. Red-headed Woman 32. The
Man from Yesterday 32. F.P.I. (French version) 32.
The Only Girl 33. L'Impervier 33. The Battle (as a
Japanese) 34. Caravan 34. Liliom 35. Private
Worlds 35. Break of Hearts 35. Shanghai 35. Le
Bonheur 36. The Garden of Allah 36. Mayerling 37.
Tovarich 37. Conquest (as Napoleon) (AAN) 37.
History is Made at Night 37. Algiers (AAN) 38. Orage
38. Love Affair 39. When Tomorrow Comes 39.
Le Corsaire 39. All This and Heaven Too 40. Les
Amoureux 40. Back Street 41. Hold Back the Dawn
41. Appointment for Love 41. Tales of Manhattan
42. The Constant Nymph 43. Flesh and Fantasy
(& p) 43. Gaslight (AAN) 44. Confidential Agent
45. Together Again 45. Cluny Brown 46. Arch of
Triumph 48. A Woman's Vengeance 48. The
Thirteenth Letter 51. The First Legion 52. The
Happy Time 52. Thunder in the East 53. Madame de
. . . 53. The Cobweb 55. Lucky to Be a Woman 55.
Paris Palace Hotel 56. Nana 56. Around the World
in Eighty Days 56. La Parisienne 58. The Buccaneer
58. Maxime 58. Fanny (AAN) 62. The Four
Horsemen of the Apocalypse 62. Les Démons de
Minuit 62. Love is a Ball 63. Adorable Julia 64. A
Very Special Favour 64. How to Steal a Million 66.
Is Paris Burning? 66. Casino Royale 67. Barefoot in
the Park 68. The April Fools 69. The Madwoman of
Chaillot 69. The Day the Hot Line Got Hot 69. Lost
Horizon 73. Stavisky 74. A Matter of Time 76.
  TV series: Four Star Theatre 56. The Rogues 64.
✪ For capitalizing on the accepted image of the
romantic Frenchman and proving that he could
also act. Love Affair.

¶ We got a French actor here on a 6-month
  option, but I'm letting him go home because
nobody can understand the guy's accent.–Irving
Thalberg, 1932.

Famous line (which he never actually said in
Algiers): 'Come with me to the Casbah.'

Boyer, François (1920–).
French screenwriter, also novelist.
  Le Point du Jour 49. Jeux Interdits (& oa) 52.
Chiens Perdus sans Collier 55. Le Joueur 58. Les
Magiciennes 60. Un Singe en Hiver 62. War of the
Buttons 62. Weekend in Dunkirk 64. The 25th Hour
67. Mords Pas On t'Aime 76, etc.

Boyer, Jean (1901–1965).
French director.
  Monsieur, Madame et Bibi 32. Un Mauvais
Garçon 36. Circonstances Attenuantes 39. Serena
40. Romance de Paris 41. Bolero 42. La Bonne
Etoile 43. La Femme Fatale 45. Les Aventures de
Casanova 47. All Roads Lead to Rome 49. Le Rosi
de Madame Husson 50. Le Passe-Muraille 51.
Coiffeur pour Dames 52. Femmes de Paris 53.
J'avais Sept Filles 54. Fernandel the Dressmaker
56. Sénéchal le Magnifique 57. Nina 58. Coup de
Bamboo 62. Relaxe-toi Chérie 64, many others.

Boyle, Catherine (1929–) (Caterina di
Francavilla).
Winsome Italian-English TV personality who has
made a few film appearances.
  Not Wanted on Voyage 52. Intent to Kill 56. Th
Truth About Women 57, etc.

Boyle, Danny.
Scottish director, from television and theatre.
  Shallow Grave 94.

Boyle, Lara Flynn (1970–).
American actress.
  Poltergeist III 88. How I Got into College 89.
Dead Poets Society 89. The Rookie 90. May Win
91. Mobsters 91. Eyes of the Storm 91. Wayne's
World 92. Equinox 92. The Dark Backward 92.
Where the Day Takes You 92. Red Rock West 93
The Temp 93. Threesome 94. Baby's Day Out 94
The Road to Wellville 94, etc.
  TV series: Twin Peaks 90.

¶ I don't mind playing 'the girlfriend'. I figure I
  go from girlfriend parts to wife parts to moth
parts to grandmother parts. That's how it works,
isn't it? – L.F.B.

Boyle, Peter (1933–).
Rotund, balding American character actor, a
former Christian Brother who became a key
performer in fashionable films of his time.
■ The Virgin President 68. Medium Cool 69. Joe
70. Diary of a Mad Housewife 70. T.R. Baskin 71
The Candidate 72. Steelyard Blues 73. Slither 73.
Kid Blue 73. The Friends of Eddie Coyle 73. The
Man Who Could Talk to Kids (TV) 73. Crazy Joe
74. Young Frankenstein (as the monster) 74. Taxi
Driver 76. Swashbuckler 76. Tail Gunner Joe (TV)
(as Senator Joe McCarthy) 77. FIST 78. Superma
78. Beyond the Poseidon Adventure 79. Brink's
79. From Here to Eternity (TV) 79. Hardcore 79.
In God We Trust 80. Where the Buffalo Roam 80
Outland 81. Hammett 82. Yellowbeard 83. Johnn
Dangerously 84. Morons from Outer Space 85.
Turk 182 85. The In Crowd 87. Surrender 87.
Walker 87. Funny 88. Red Heat 88. The Dream
Team 89. Speed Zone 89. Men of Respect 90.
Solar Crisis 90. Kickboxer II 91. Rubin & Ed 91.
Royce 94. Killer 94. The Shadow 94. The Santa
Clause 94.
  TV series: Comedy Tonight 70. Joe Bash 86.
Midnight Caller 88–91.

Boyle, Robert (1910–).
American production designer.
  The Thrill of it All 63. The Birds 63. Marnie 64
The Russians are Coming, The Russians are Comi
66. How to Succeed in Business 67. In Cold Bloo
67. The Thomas Crown Affair 68. Gaily Gaily 69
The Landlord 70. Fiddler on the Roof 71. Portnoy
Complaint 72. Mame 74. The Shootist 76. The B
Fox 78. Winter Kills 79. Private Benjamin 80. Th
Best Little Whorehouse in Texas 82. Table for Fi
83. Staying Alive 83. Rhinestone 84. Explorers 8

Jumpin' Jack Flash 86. Dragnet 87. Troop Beverly Hills 89, etc.

Bozzuffi, Marcel (1929–1988).
Balding French character actor.
Z 69. The American 69. The Lady in the Car 70. The French Connection 71. Images 72. Nightmare for a Killer 72. Caravan to Vaccares 76. La Grande Bourgeoise 77. La Cage aux Folles 79. La Cage au Folles II 81, etc.

Brabin, Charles (1883–1957).
British film director who made a career in Hollywood but retired early.
Stella Maris 18. So Big 23. Twinkletoes 26. Hard Boiled Haggerty 27. The Bridge of San Luis Rey 29. Call of the Flesh 30. Sporting Blood 31. Beast of the City 32. The Mask of Fu Manchu 32. Stage Mother 33. A Wicked Woman 34, many others.

Brabourne, John (1924–   ) (Lord Brabourne).
British producer, in films from 1950.
Harry Black 58. Sink the Bismarck 60. HMS Defiant 62. The Mikado 66. Tales of Beatrix Potter 71. Murder on the Orient Express 74. Death on the Nile 78. The Mirror Crack'd 80. Evil Under the Sun 82. A Passage to India 84. Little Dorrit 87, etc.

Bracco, Lorraine (1954–   ).
American leading actress and former model. She was formerly married to actor Harvey Keitel.
The Pickup Artist 87. Someone to Watch Over Me 87. The Dream Team 89. GoodFellas (AAN) 90. Switch 91. Talent for the Game 91. Medicine Man 92. Radio Flyer 92. Traces of Red 92. Scam 93. Even Cowgirls Get the Blues 93. Being Human 94. Getting Gotti (TV) 94, etc.

Brach, Gérard (1927–   ).
French screenwriter who has often worked with Roman Polanski.
Repulsion 65. Cul-de-Sac 66. The Fearless Vampire Killers 67. The Tenant 76. Tess 79. I Sent a Letter to My Love (Chère Inconnue) 80. The Quest for Fire 81. L'Africain 83. Maria's Lovers 85. Jean de Florette 86. Manon des Sources 86. The Name of the Rose 86. Pirates 86. Shy People 87. Frantic 88. The Bear (L'Ours) 89. The Lover (L'Amant) 91. I Divertimenti della Vita Privata 91. Bitter Moon 92, etc.

Bracken, Eddie (1920–   ).
American comic actor, popular in the 40s as the nervous hayseed type; made his best films for Preston Sturges. Later found stage success.
Too Many Girls 40. Life with Henry 41. Reaching for the Sun 41. Caught in the Draft 41. Sweater Girl 42. The Fleet's In 42. Star Spangled Rhythm 42. Happy Go Lucky 43. Young and Willing 43. The Miracle of Morgan's Creek 43. Hail the Conquering Hero 44. Rainbow Island 44. Out of This World 45. Bring on the Girls 45. Duffy's Tavern 45. Hold That Blonde 45. Ladies' Man 47. Fun on a Weekend 47. The Girl from Jones Beach 49. Summer Stock 50. Two Tickets to Broadway 51. We're Not Married 52. About Face 52. A Slight Case of Larceny 53. National Lampoon's Vacation 83. Oscar 91. Home Alone 2: Lost in New York 92. Rookie of the Year 93. Baby's Day Out 94.

Brackett, Charles (1892–1969).
American writer-producer, of generally sophisticated material; enjoyed long association with Billy Wilder.
Tomorrow's Love (oa) 25. Pointed Heels (oa) 29. Secrets of a Secretary (oa) 31. Enter Madame (w) 35. Piccadilly Jim (w) 36. Bluebeard's Eighth Wife (w) 38. Midnight (w) 39. Ninotchka (w, AAN) 39.

Arise My Love (w) 40. Hold Back the Dawn (co-w, AAN) 41. The Major and the Minor (w) 42. Five Graves to Cairo (wp) 43. The Uninvited (p) 43. The Lost Weekend (wp) (AA) 45. To Each His Own (wp, AAN) 46. A Foreign Affair (wp, AAN) 48. Sunset Boulevard (wp) (AA) 50. Niagara (wp) 52. Titanic (wp) 52. Woman's World (p) 54. The King and I (p) 56. Ten North Frederick (p) 58. Journey to the Centre of the Earth (wp) 59. State Fair (p) 61, many others.

Brackett, Leigh (1915–1978).
American lady screenwriter.
The Big Sleep 46. Rio Bravo 59. 13 West Street 62. Hatari 62. El Dorado 67. Rio Lobo 70. The Long Goodbye 73. The Empire Strikes Back 80, etc.

Brackman, Jacob.
American screenwriter.
The King of Marvin Gardens 72. Times Square 80, etc.

Bradbury, Ray (1920–   ).
American science fiction writer who has dabbled in films.
It Came from Outer Space (oa) 53. The Beast from 20,000 Fathoms (oa) 54. Moby Dick (w) 56. Fahrenheit 451 (oa) 66. The Illustrated Man (oa) 69. Something Wicked This Way Comes 83. Little Nemo: Adventures in Slumberland 92, etc.

Bradbury, Robert North.
American director and screenwriter of low-budget action films, mainly westerns and including many of John Wayne's early films. He was the father of western actor Bob Steele (qv), who also starred in some of his films.
The Faith of the Strong 19. Desert Rider 23. Davy Crockett at the Fall of the Alamo 26. Hidden Valley 32. Breed of the Border 33. Blue Steel 34. Man from Utah 34. Alias John Law 35. Dawn Rider 35. Desert Trail 35. Headin' for the Rio Grande 36. Riders of the Rockies 37. Trouble in Texas 37, many others.

Braddell, Maurice (1901–1990).
English leading actor, dancer, playwright, screenwriter and producer. Born in Singapore and educated at Charterhouse and Oxford, he studied at RADA and toured America with Mrs Patrick Campbell's company, trying and failing to find work in Hollywood. On his return to London, he worked as an assistant producer on The Battles of Coronel and Falkland Islands 27, before becoming a film actor and writer, retiring after the Second World War to settle in New York as a picture restorer, and briefly returning to the screen in some Andy Warhol movies.
A Window in Piccadilly 28. Dawn 28. Not Quite a Lady 28. Master and Man 29. Wolves 30. School for Scandal 30. Her Reputation 31. Men of Tomorrow 32. This Week of Grace (co-w) 33. Love, Life and Laughter (co-w) 34. Things to Come 36. It's You I Want (oa) 36. Where's That Fire (story) 39. Sleep Walk 64. Flesh 68. Women in Revolt 72, etc.

Braden, Bernard (1916–1993).
Canadian TV personality, in Britain since 1938. Occasional film appearances. Long married to Barbara Kelly.
Autobiography: 1990, The Kindness of Strangers.
Love in Pawn 52. The Full Treatment 61. The Day the Earth Caught Fire 62. The War Lover 63, etc.

Bradford, Richard.
Thickset American character actor.

The Chase 66. The Missouri Breaks 76. Goin' South 78. More American Graffiti 79. Panic on Page One (TV) 79. Running Hot (aka Highway to Hell) 83. The Trip to Bountiful 85. Legend of Billie Jean 85. The Untouchables 87. Little Nikita 88. The Milagro Beanfield War 88. Night Game 89. The Heart of Dixie 89. Internal Affairs 90. Ambition 91. Cold Heaven 92, etc.
TV series: Man in a Suitcase 68.

Bradley, David (1919–   ).
American director who showed promise as an amateur but never seemed to make it professionally.
■ Peer Gynt 41. Julius Caesar 50. Talk About a Stranger 52. Dragstrip Riot 58. Twelve to the Moon 60. Madmen of Mandoras 64.

Bradley, Doug (1954–   ).
English actor, known for playing the Cenobite Pinhead in the Hellraiser series of horror films. Born in Liverpool, he began in experimental theatre.
Hellraiser 87. Hellbound: Hellraiser II 88. Hellraiser III: Hell on Earth 92.

Bradley, Scott.
American musical director and composer, scoring cartoons, especially Tom and Jerry, after joining MGM in 1934.

Bradna, Olympe (1920–   ).
Slightly built French circus performer who had a brief Hollywood career following a stage tour, and retired on marriage to an American.
■ Three Cheers for Love 36. College Holiday 36. Last Train from Madrid 37. Souls at Sea 37. Stolen Heaven 38. Say It in French 38. The Night of Nights 39. South of Pago Pago 40. Highway West 41. Knockout 41. International Squadron 41.

Brady, Alice (1892–1939).
American stage actress who in her last few years made many films, either as a fluttery society matron or as a drab housewife.
■ As Ye Sow 14. The Boss 15. The Cup of Chance 15. The Lure of Women 15. La Bohème 16. Bought and Paid for 16. Betsy Ross 17. Maternity 17. Woman and Wife 18. A Dark Lantern 19. The Fear Market 19. Out of the Chorus 21. Little Italy 21. The Land of Hope 21. Dawn of the East 21. Hush Money 21. Anna Ascends 21. Missing Millions 21. The Snow Bride 23. The Leopardess 23. When Ladies Meet 33. Broadway to Hollywood 33. Beauty for Sale 33. Stage Mother 33. Should Ladies Behave? 33. Miss Fane's Baby is Stolen 34. The Gay Divorcee 34. Let 'em Have It 34. Gold Diggers of 1935 35. Lady Tubbs 35. Metropolitan 35. The Harvester 35. My Man Godfrey (AAN) 36. Go West Young Man 36. Mind Your Own Business 36. Three Smart Girls 37. Call It a Day 37. Mama Steps Out 37. Mr Dodd Takes the Air 37. One Hundred Men and a Girl 37. Merry Go Round of 1938 38. In Old Chicago (AA) 38. Joy of Living 38. Goodbye Broadway 38. Zenobia 39. Young Mr Lincoln 39.

Brady, Scott (1924–1985) (Gerald Tierney).
Tough-looking American leading man of the 50s, brother of Lawrence Tierney.
Canon City 48. He Walked by Night 48. Port of New York 49. Undercover Girl 50. Kansas Raiders 51. The Model and the Marriage Broker 52. Perilous Journey 53. Johnny Guitar 54. Gentlemen Marry Brunettes 55. Mohawk 56. The Maverick Queen 56. They Were So Young 58. Battle Flame 59. Black Spurs 65. Castle of Evil 66. Red Tomahawk 67. Doctors' Wives 70. Nightmare in Wax 70.

Dollars 71. The China Syndrome 79. The Winds of War (TV) 83, many others.

TV series: Shotgun Slade 59–60.

Braeden, Eric (1942–) (Hans Gudegast).
German general-purpose actor in international films.

Colossus of Rhodes 57. The Law and Jake Wade 59. Escape from the Planet of the Apes 70. Lady Ice 73. The Ultimate Thrill 74. Death Scream 75. The Adulteress 77. Happily Ever After 82. The Ambulance 90, etc.

TV series: The Rat Patrol 66–68.

Braga, Sonia (1951–).
Brazilian leading actress in international films and a star of stage and TV in her native country.

Dona Flor and Her Two Husbands 77. I Love You 81. Gabriela 83. Kiss of the Spider Woman 85. The Man Who Broke 1,000 Chains (TV) 87. The Milagro Beanfield War 88. Moon over Parador 88. The Rookie 90. Roosters 93. The Burning Season (TV) 94, etc.

Bragg, Melvyn (1939–).
English screenwriter, novelist and television presenter.

Isadora (co-w) 68. Play Dirty (co-w) 69. The Music Lovers (w) 71. Jesus Christ Superstar (co-w) 73. A Time to Dance (oa) (TV) 92.

Brahm, John (1893–1982) (Hans Brahm).
German director who in the 30s moved first to Britain, then to Hollywood. Films generally competent, but routine.
■ ENGLISH-SPEAKING FILMS: Scrooge 35. The Last Journey 35. *Broken Blossoms* (British remake) 36. Counsel for Crime 37. Penitentiary 38. Girls' School 38. Let Us Live 39. Rio 39. *Escape to Glory* 40. Wild Geese Calling 41. *The Undying Monster* 42. Tonight We Raid Calais 42. Wintertime 43. The Lodger 44. *Hangover Square* 44. Guest in the House 44. *The Locket* 46. *The Brasher Doubloon* 47. Singapore 47. The Thief of Venice 49. Face to Face 52. The Miracle of Fatima 52. The Diamond Queen 53. The Mad Magican 54. Special Delivery 55. Bengazi 55. So Soon to Die (TV) 57. A Death of Princes (TV) 61. Hot Rods to Hell 67.

¶ His quiet virtues of visual tastefulness and dramatic balance were unable to sustain his career. – *Andrew Sarris, 1968*

Braithwaite, Dame Lilian (1873–1948).
Distinguished British stage actress in occasional films.
■ The World's Desire 15. The Climax 15. Masks and Faces 15. The Woman Who Was Nothing 16. Justice 16. The Gay Lord Quex 16. Dombey and Son 16. Because 18. The Chinese Puzzle 19. General Post 20. Castles in Spain 20. Downhill 27. Carnival 31. Man of Mayfair 31. The Chinese Puzzle 32. *A Man About the House* 47.

Brakhage, Stan (1933–).
American underground film-maker.

Interim 51. Desistfilm 54. Nightcats 56. Flesh of Morning 57. An Intercourse 59. The Dead 60. Mothlight 63. Black Vision 65. Lovemaking 68. Sexual Meditations 70. Fox Fire Child Watch 71, many others.

Brambell, Wilfrid (1912–1985).
British character actor, specializing in grotesques. Celebrated on TV as old Steptoe in *Steptoe and Son* (64–73); film appearances usually cameos.

Autobiography: 1976, *All Above Board.*

39 Steps 35. Another Shore 48. Dry Rot 56.

Serious Charge 58. What a Whopper 61. *In Search of the Castaways* 62. The Three Lives of Thomasina 63. *A Hard Day's Night* 64. Crooks in Cloisters 64. Where the Bullets Fly 66. Witchfinder General 68. Steptoe and Son 72. Steptoe and Son Ride Again 73. Holiday on the Buses 74. Sword of the Valiant 83, etc.

Bramble, A. V. (c. 1880–1963).
British director, former actor.

Fatal Fingers 16. Wuthering Heights 18. The Will 21. The Card 22. Chick 28. Shooting Stars (p & co-d) 28. The Man Who Changed His Name 29. Mrs Dane's Defence 33. An Outcast of the Islands (a only) 51, etc.

Branagh, Kenneth (1960–).
Belfast-born British leading actor, director and dramatist. He also runs his own classical theatre company. He married actress Emma Thompson in 1989.
■ Fortunes of War (TV) 87. A Month in the Country 87. *Henry V* (a, d) (AAN) 89. Dead Again (a, d) 91. Peter's Friends (a, d) 92. Swing Kids (a) 92. *Much Ado about Nothing* (a, d) 93. Mary Shelley's Frankenstein (a, d) 94.

Branch, Sarah (1938–).
British leading lady of the early 60s.

Sands of the Desert 60. Hell is a City 61. Sword of Sherwood Forest 61, etc.

Brand, Max (1892–1944) (Frederick Faust).
American popular novelist whose major bequests to Hollywood were *Destry Rides Again* and the Dr Kildare books. Killed in action as a war correspondent.

Brand, Neville (1921–1992).
Thickset American actor with stage and TV experience; often seen as Red Indian or gangster. In films from 1948 after ten years in the US Army; he was the fourth most decorated soldier.

D.O.A. 49. Halls of Montezuma 51. Stalag 17 53. *Riot in Cell Block Eleven* 54. Mohawk 55. The Tin Star 57. Cry Terror 58. Five Gates to Hell 59. *The Scarface Mob* (as Al Capone) 60. Huckleberry Finn 60. Birdman of Alcatraz 62. That Darn Cat 65. The Desperados 69. The Train Robbers 73. Scalawag 74. The Mad Bomber 75. Eaten Alive 76. The Quest (TV) 76. Captains Courageous (TV) 77. The Ninth Configuration 80. Without Warning 80. Alligator 80. Evils of the Night 85, many others.

TV series: The Untouchables 59–62 (as Al Capone). Laredo 66–67.

Brandauer, Klaus Maria (1944–).
Austrian actor and director, in international films.

Mephisto 82. Never Say Never Again 83. *Colonel Redl* 85. Out of Africa (AAN) 85. Quo Vadis (TV) 85. Streets of Gold 86. The Lightship 86. Burning Secret 89. Hanussen 89. Georg Elser – Einer au Deutschsland (& d) 89. Seven Minutes (& d) 89. The Russia House 90. White Fang 91. Becoming Colette 92. Mario and the Magician (Mario und der Zauberer) (d) 94, etc.

Brando, Jocelyn (1919–).
American character actress, sister of Marlon Brando; film appearances rare.

The Big Heat 53. China Venture 53. Nightfall 56. The Explosive Generation 61. The Ugly American 63. Bus Riley's Back in Town 65. The Chase 66. A Question of Love (TV) 78, etc.

Brando, Marlon (1924–).
Unsmiling American leading actor whose prototype is the primitive modern male; he has

however attempted a wide range of parts which have not always suited his 'method' technique and mumbling accent.

Autobiography: 1994, *Brando: Songs My Mother Never Taught Me.*

Biographies: 1974, *Brando* by René Jordan. 1991, *Conversations with Brando* by Lawrence Grobel. 1991, *Brando: A Life in Our Times* by Richard Schickel. 1994, *Brando: The Biography* by Peter Manso. 1994, *Marlon Brando: A Portrait* by Paul Ryan.

Autobiography: 1994, *Brando: Songs My Mother Taught Me.*
■ *The Men* 50. *A Streetcar Named Desire* (AAN) 51 *Viva Zapata* (BFA, AAN) 52. *Julius Caesar* (as Mar Antony) (BFA, AAN) 53. *The Wild One* 53. *On the Waterfront* (AA, BFA) 54. Desirée (as Napoleon) 54 Guys and Dolls 55. *The Teahouse of the August Moo* 56. Sayonara (AAN) 57. *The Young Lions* 58. The Fugitive Kind 60. One Eyed Jacks (also directed) 60. Mutiny on the Bounty (as Fletcher Christian) 62. The Ugly American 63. Bedtime Story 64. Th Saboteur 65. *The Chase* 66. The Appaloosa 66. A Countess from Hong Kong 67. Reflections in a Golden Eye 67. Candy 68. The Night of the Following Day 68. Queimada 70. The Nightcomer 71. *The Godfather* (AA) 72. *Last Tango in Paris* (AAN 72. The Missouri Breaks 76. Superman 78. Roots the New Generations (TV) 79. Apocalypse Now 79. The Formula 80. A Dry White Season (AAN) 89. The Freshman 90. Christopher Columbus: Th Discovery 92.

¶ Acting is an empty and useless profession. – *M.B.*

Most of the time he sounds like he has a mout full of wet toilet paper. – *Rex Reed*

I have eyes like those of a dead pig. – *M.B.*

Acting is the expression of a neurotic impulse. It's a bum's life. Quitting acting, that's the sign of maturity. – *M.B.*

Once you're a star actor, people start asking yo questions about politics, astronomy, archaeology, and birth control. – *M.B.*

An actor's a guy who, if you ain't talking abou him, ain't listening. – *M.B.*

I'm not interested in making an assessment of myself and stripping myself for the general public to view. – *M.B.*

I think I would have liked to be a caveman, a neolithic person. – *M.B.*

Too much success can ruin you as surely as too much failure. – *M.B.*

He was deeply rebellious against the bourgeois spirit, the over-ordering of life. – *Elia Kazan*

Democracy is a fine way to run a country, but it's a hell of a way to make pictures. – *Lillian Hellman after working with Brando on The Chase*

An angel as a man, a monster as an actor. – *Bernardo Bertolucci*

He was in a unique position. He could have don anything. But he didn't choose to. – *Rod Steiger*

No actor of my generation has possessed greate natural gifts; but none other has transported intellectual falsity to higher levels of hilarious pretension. – *Truman Capote*

The once-beautiful, most distinguished actor of our time has turned into a self-loathing slob and left a lot of human wreckage in his wake. – *Peter Manso*

Famous line (*On The Waterfront*): 'I coulda had class. I coulda been a contender.'

Brandon, Henry (1912–1990) (Henry Kleinbach).
American character actor, a reliable menace for thirty years.

Babes in Toyland (as Barnaby) 34. The Garden c

...ah 36. I Promise to Pay 37. Son of Monte Cristo
... Edge of Darkness 43. Canon City 48. Scarlet
...gel 52. Scared Stiff 53. Vera Cruz 54. The
...archers 56. The Buccaneer 58. Two Rode
...gether 61. *Where the North Wind Blows* 75, many
...hers.

...randon, Michael (1945–).
...merican leading man.
...Lovers and Other Strangers 70. Four Flies on
...ey Velvet 73. FM 78. A Vacation in Hell 79.
...tween Two Brothers (TV) 81. Deadly Messages
...V) 83, etc.
...TV series: Emerald Point 83. Dempsey and
...akepeace 84–86.

...rantford, Mrs Aggie (1884–*).
...glish character actress, on the stage from the
...e of seven, who made child stars of her two
...ildren, Aggie (1915–), whose career lasted
...m the age of two to 12, usually in films with her
...other; and Mickey Brantford (qv), who started
...the age of three.
...A Will and a Way 22. Second to None 26. Heroes
...the Mine 32. Everything Is Rhythm 36.
...cqueline 56, etc.

...rantford, Mickey (1911–).
...hletic English juvenile star of the 20s and 30s,
...films from 1915. He was the son of Mrs Aggie
...antford.
...The Man the Army Made 15. The Road to
...aven 22. The Knockout 23. Afraid of Love 25.
...e Rolling Road 27. Sexton Blake, Gambler 28.
...spense 30. A 'Yell' of a Night 32. My Old Dutch
... The Phantom Light 35. The Last Journey 35.
...vice Branded 36. Darby and Joan 37, etc.

...ass, Tinto (1933–).
...lian director, mainly of soft-core porn, whose
...st-known film is Caligula.
...Book: 1981, *Ultimate Porno* by PierNico Solinas
...n the making of *Caligula*).
...Chi Lavora è Perduto 63. La Mia Signora (co-d)
... Yankee 66. Nerosubianco 69. Dropout 72.
...Jrlo 72. Salon Kitty 76. Caligula 77. Action 79.
... Chiave 85. Miranda 85. Snack Bar Budapest 88.
...prika 91. Cosi Fan Tutte 92. The Voyeur
...'Uomo che Guarda) (& a) 94, etc.

All directors are voyeurs. Anybody who looks
at the world through a hole is a voyeur. By
...finition. – *T.B.*
The difference between pornography and
...oticism is not whether you see a penetration or
...u don't see it; it is how you show it. – *T.B.*
I put two big balls and a big cock between the
...s of Italian cinema. – *T.B.*
First I look at the bottom of an actress. A bottom
...ver lies. – *T.B.*

...asselle, Keefe (1923–1981).
...merican light leading man who made little
...adway in movies but later, with the help of James
...ubrey of CBS, became a television producer who
...veral unsuccessful shows such as *The Baileys of
...lboa* and *Mr Broadway*. He wrote a bitter novel
...out his experiences and called it *The Cannibals*.
...Janie 44. River Gang 45. Railroaded 47. Not
...anted 48. Dial 1119 50. A Place in the Sun 51.
...nnerline 51. It's a Big Country 52. Skirts Ahoy
... *The Eddie Cantor Story* (title role) 53. Three
...ung Texans 54. Mad at the World 55. Battle
...ations 56. West of Suez 57. If You Don't Stop It
...u'll Go Blind 77.

...asseur, Claude (1936–).
...ench actor, son of Pierre Brasseur.

Eyes without a Face 60. Les Menteurs 61. The
Vanishing Corporal 62. Germinal 63. Bande à Part
64. Un Homme de Trop 67. Portrait of Marianne
70. Such a Gorgeous Kid Like Me 72. Seins de
Glace 74. Aggression 75. Pardon Mon Affaire 76.
Une Histoire Simple 78. Ils Sont Grands Ces Petits
79. Josepha 81. La Boum 2 82. La Crime 83. Palace
84. Dandin 88. Dancing Machine 90. Dirty Like
an Angel (Sale comme un Ange) 91. Ville à Vendre
91. Le Souper 93. A Linha do Horizonte 93. Delit
Mineur 94, many others.

Brasseur, Pierre (1903–1972) (P. Espinasse).
Distinguished French stage actor in occasional
films from 1925.
Claudine à l'École 28. Café de Paris 33. *Quai des
Brumes* 38. Lumière d'Été 42. *Les Enfants du Paradis*
44. Les Portes de la Nuit 46. Julie de Carneilhan
50. Bluebeard 51. Porte des Lilas 55. Eyes without
a Face 59. Il Bell' Antonio 60. Deux Heures à Tuer
65. A New World 66. King of Hearts 67. Birds in
Peru 68, etc.

Braunstein, Joseph:
see *Larraz, José Ramón*.

Bray, Robert (1917–1983).
American actor of the strong silent type.
Blood on the Moon 48. Warpath 52. Bus Stop
56. The Wayward Bus 57. My Gun is Quick (as
Mike Hammer) 58. Never So Few 60, etc.
TV series: Man from Blackhawk 54. Stagecoach
West 60. Lassie 67–68.

Brazil
has had a very patchy production history. One of
its best directors, Alberto Cavalcanti, spent most of
his career abroad, and failed in the 50s to spark
local production. Despite subsequent attempts,
the best-known Brazilian film is still 1953's
O'Cangaceiro (The Bandit). Its only rival is Hector
Babenco's *Pixote* 81. The country's film production
came to a virtual stop in 1990 with the abolition
of Emrafilme, the state finance board, but resumed
on a smaller scale in 1994 when government grants
were resumed and tax incentives offered to film-
makers.

Brazzi, Rossano (1916–1994).
Handsome Italian romantic lead who apart from
local work appeared in some successful
international films.
Volcano 48. *Little Women* 49. *Three Coins in the
Fountain* 54. The Barefoot Contessa 54. *Summertime*
55. The Story of Esther Costello 57. Legend of the
Lost 57. Interlude 57. *South Pacific* 58. A Certain
Smile 58. Count Your Blessings 59. The Light in
the Piazza 62. Rome Adventure 62. Dark Purpose
64. The Battle of the Villa Fiorita 65. The Christmas
That Almost Wasn't (& d) 66. The Bobo 67.
Woman Times Seven 67. Krakatoa 68. The Italian
Job 69. Honeymoon with a Stranger (TV) 69. The
Survivors (TV 69. The Adventures 70. Psychout for
Murder 70. The Great Waltz 72. Master of Love
74. The White Telephone 76. The Final Conflict
81. The Voice 82. Fear City 84. Final Justice 85.
Formula for a Murder 86. The Third Solution 89.
Christopher Columbus 91, etc.
TV series: The Survivors 69–70.

break figure.
A specified amount of takings after which an
exhibitor pays a greater percentage to the renter.
For the protection of both parties many contracts
are on a sliding scale, with the exhibitor paying
anything from 25% to 50% of the gross according
to the business he does.

breakaway furniture
is specially constructed from balsa wood for those
spectacular saloon brawls in which so much damage
is apparently done to stars and stunt men.

Breakston, George (1922–1973).
American who, born in France, went to Hollywood
as a child and acted for several years; later went
to Africa and produced many routine adventure
films and TV series, usually with British backing.
AS ACTOR: Great Expectations 34. Mrs Wiggs of the
Cabbage Patch 34. The Dark Angel 35. Love Finds
Andy Hardy 38. Jesse James 35. The Courtship of
Andy Hardy 42, etc.
AS PRODUCER: Urubu 48. Tokyo File 212 51. The
Scarlet Spear (& d) 54. Golden Ivory 55. Escape
in the Sun 56. Woman and the Hunter 57. Shadow
of Treason (& d) 63. The Boy Cried Murder (& d)
66, etc.

Brecher, Irving (1914–).
American radio writer who moved on to
Hollywood and received solo credit for two Marx
Brothers scripts.
New Faces of 1937 37. *At the Circus* 39. Go West
40. Shadow of the Thin Man 41. Dubarry was a
Lady 53. *Meet Me in St Louis* (AAN) 44. Yolanda
and the Thief 45. Summer Holiday 47. The Life
of Riley (& pd) 49. Somebody Loves Me (& d) 52.
Cry for Happy 61. Sail a Crooked Ship (& d) 61.
Bye Bye Birdie 63, etc.
TV series: The People's Choice 56–58.

Brecht, Bertolt (1898–1956).
German poet and playwright whose 'alienation
method' (by which audiences are forced by various
theatrical devices to remember that they are
watching a play) has been influential on films from
Citizen Kane to *Alfie*. His *Dreigroschenoper*, based on
The Beggar's Opera, has been filmed twice; films
have also been made of *Mother Courage*, *Herr
Puntila* and *Galileo*. His sole Hollywood credit is for
the script of *Hangmen Also Die*.

Breck, Peter (1930–).
American general-purpose actor.
The Beatniks 60. Shock Corridor 63. The
Crawling Hand 63. A Man for Hanging 72. Benji
74. Highway 61 91, etc.
TV series: Black Saddle 58–59. The Big Valley
65–68. The Secret Empire 79. Also episodes of
Maverick (as Bat Masterson).

Breen, Bobby (1927–).
American boy singer of the 30s; later gave up films
for night club work.
Let's Sing Again 36. Rainbow on the River 36.
Make a Wish 37. Hawaii Calls 37. Breaking the Ice
38. Fisherman's Wharf 39. Way Down South 39.
Johnny Doughboy 43, etc.

Breen, Joseph (1890–1965).
American executive, for many years administrator
of the Production Code. See: *censorship*

Breen, Richard L. (1919–1967).
American scenarist. Former president of
Screenwriters' Guild.
A Foreign Affair (co-w, AAN) 48. Miss Tatlock's
Millions 49. The Model and the Marriage Broker
51. Niagara 53. Titanic (AA) 53. Dragnet 54. Pete
Kelly's Blues 55. Stopover Tokyo (& d) 57. Wake
Me When It's Over 60. Captain Newman 63. Do
Not Disturb 65. Tony Rome 67, many others.

Breese, Edmund (1871–1936).
American character actor, from the stage.
The Song of the Wage Slave 15. Luck 23. The

Brown Derby 26. Sonny Boy 29. Tol'able David 30. All Quiet on the Western Front 30. Mata Hari 32. Cabin in the Cotton 32. International House 33. Duck Soup 33. Treasure Island 34. The Marriage Bargain 35, etc.

Bregman, Martin (1926–).
American producer. In 1992 he formed M & M Productions with Michael Caine.

Serpico 73. Dog Day Afternoon 75. The Next Man 76. The Seduction of Joe Tynan 79. Simon 80. The Four Seasons 81. Venom 82. Eddie Macon's Run 83. Scarface 83. Sweet Liberty 86. A New Life 88. Sea of Love 89. Betsy's Wedding 90. Blue Ice 92. Carlito's Way 93, etc.

Bremer, Lucille (1922–).
American dancer. MGM groomed her for stardom in the 40s, but her career was brief.
■ Meet Me in St Louis 44. *Yolanda and the Thief* 45. *Ziegfeld Follies* 45. Till the Clouds Roll By 46. Dark Delusion 47. Adventures of Casanova 48. Ruthless 48. Behind Locked Doors 48.

Brendel, El (1890–1964).
Mild-mannered American comic actor, a fake Swede from vaudeville with an attractive way of fracturing the English language.

The Campus Flirt 26. Wings 27. *Sunny Side Up* 29. The Big Trail 30. *Just Imagine* 30. Mr Lemon of Orange 30. Delicious 31. Hot Pepper 33. My Lips Betray 33. God's Country and the Woman 37. Little Miss Broadway 38. *If I Had My Way* 40. Captain Caution 40. Machine Gun Mama 44. The Beautiful Blonde from Bashful Bend 49. The She Creature 56, many others.

Brennan, Eileen (1935–).
Brassy American character actress.
■ Divorce American Style 67. The Last Picture Show 71. Playmates (TV) 72. The Blue Knight (TV) 73. Scarecrow 73. The Sting 73. Daisy Miller 74. My Father's House (TV) 75. The Night That Panicked America (TV) 75. At Long Last Love 75. Hustle 75. Murder by Death 76. The Death of Richie (TV) 77. All That Glitters (TV) 77. Last of the Cowboys 77. The Great Smokey Roadblock 78. FM 78. The Cheap Detective 78. My Old Man (TV). 79. Black Beauty 79. *Private Benjamin* (AAN) 80. When the Circus Came to Town (TV) 80. The Funny Farm 82. Pandemonium 82. Clue 85. The Fourth Wise Man 85. Blood Vows – the Story of a Mafia Wife (TV) 87. The New Adventures of Pippi Longstocking 88. Rented Lips 88. Sticky Fingers 88. It Had To Be You 89. Stella 90. Texasville 90. White Palace 90.

TV series: All that Glitters 77. 13 Queens Boulevard 79. A New Kind of Family 79–80. Private Benjamin 81–82 (cancelled because of her car accident). Off the Rack 85. Blossom 91.

Brennan, Michael (1912–).
'Tough guy' British supporting actor, in films from 1932.

The Clouded Yellow 50. Ivanhoe 52. Trouble in Store 56. The Day They Robbed the Bank of England 60. Thunderball 65. Lust for a Vampire 70, many others.

Brennan, Walter (1894–1974).
Popular American character actor who played toothless old men in his 30s, and was still a star in his 70s. Best remembered as a countrified wit, he also played villains and city slickers.
■ The Long Long Trail 29. The Shannons of Broadway 29. Smiling Guns 29. King of Jazz 30. One Hysterical Night 30. Dancing Dynamite 31. Neck and Neck 31. Law and Order 32. Texas

Cyclone 32. Two Fisted Law 32. All American 32. Parachute Jumper 32. The Fourth Horseman 32. Strange Justice 32. Man of Action 33. Fighting for Justice 33. Sing Sinner Sing 33. Strange People 33. Silent Men 33. One Year Later 33. Goldie Gets Along 33. The Invisible Man 33. Good Dame 34. Half a Sinner 34. Great Expectations 34. The Crosby Case 34. Northern Frontier 35. The Wedding Night 35. Bride of Frankenstein 35. Lady Tubbs 35. Man on the Flying Trapeze 35. Metropolitan 35. Barbary Coast 35. Seven Keys to Baldpate 35. These Three 36. Three Godfathers 36. The Moon's Our Home 36. Fury 36. The Prescott Kid 36. *Come and Get It* (AA) 36. Banjo on My Knee 36. She's Dangerous 36. When Love Is Young 37. The Affair of Cappy Ricks 37. Wild and Woolly 37. *The Adventures of Tom Sawyer* 38. The Buccaneer 38. The Texans 38. Mother Carey's Chickens 38. *Kentucky* (AA) 38. The Cowboy and the Lady 38. The Story of Vernon and Irene Castle 38. They Shall Have Music 39. *Stanley and Livingstone* 39. Joe and Ethel Turp Call on the President 39. Northwest Passage 40. *The Westerner* (as Judge Roy Bean) (AA) 40. This Woman Is Mine 41. Nice Girl 41. *Meet John Doe* 41. *Sergeant York* (AAN) 41. *Swamp Water* 41. Rise and Shine 41. Pride of the Yankees 42. Stand by for Action 42. Slightly Dangerous 43. Hangmen Also Die 43. North Star 43. Home in Indiana 43. *To Have and Have Not* 44. The Princess and the Pirate 44. Dakota 45. A Stolen Life 46. Centennial Summer 46. Nobody Lives Forever 46. *My Darling Clementine* (as Old Clanton) 46. Driftwood 47. Scudda Hoo Scudda Hay 48. Red River 48. Blood on the Moon 48. The Green Promise 49. The Great Dan Patch 49. Brimstone 49. Task Force 49. Singing Guns 50. A Ticket to Tomahawk 50. Curtain Call at Cactus Crick 50. The Showdown 50. Surrender 50. Best of the Bad Men 51. Along the Great Divide 51. The Wild Blue Yonder 51. Return of the Texan 52. Lure of the Wilderness 52. Sea of Lost Ships 53. The Far Country 54. Drums Across the River 54. Four Guns to the Border 54. At Gunpoint 55. Bad Day at Black Rock 55. *Come Next Spring* 56. Glory 56. Goodbye My Lady 56. The Proud Ones 56. Tammy and the Bachelor 57. The Way to the Gold 57. God Is My Partner 57. *Rio Bravo* 59. How the West Was Won 62. Those Calloways 64. The Oscar 66. *Who's Minding the Mint?* 67. The Gnome-mobile 67. The One and Only Genuine Original Family Band 67. Support Your Local Sheriff 69. The Over the Hill Gang (TV) 70. The Young Country (TV) 70. Two for the Money (TV) 71. The Over the Hill Gang Rides Again (TV) 71. Smoke in the Wind 71. Home for the Holidays (TV) 72.

TV series: *The Real McCoys* 57–63. Tycoon 64. *The Guns of Will Sonnett* 67–68. To Rome with Love 69.
◉ For long and spirited service, with and without his teeth. *The Westerner*.

Brenner, Albert. (1926–).
American production designer.

The Hustler 61. The Pawnbroker 65. Point Blank 67. Bullitt 68. Monte Walsh 70. Summer of '42 71. Scarecrow 73. The Sunshine Boys (AAN) 75. The Missouri Breaks 76. Silent Movie 76. The Turning Point (AAN) 77. California Suite (AAN) 78. Only When I Laugh 81. Two of a Kind 83. Unfaithfully Yours 84. 2010 (AAN) 84. Sweet Dreams 85. Monster Squad 87. The Presidio 88. Baja Oklahoma 88. Beaches (AAN) 88. Pretty Woman 90. Backdraft 91. Frankie and Johnny 91. Mr Saturday Night 92. The Program 93, etc.

Brenner, Jules.
American cinematographer.

Johnny Got His Gun 71. The Glass House (TV)

72. Dillinger 73. Posse 75. Outlaw Blues 77. Whe You Comin' Back Red Ryder? 79. The Last Word 79. The Return of the Living Dead 85. Teen Wolf Too 87. 1969 88. Sins of the Mother (TV) 91, etc

Brenon, Herbert (1880–1958).
Irish director, in Hollywood after stage experience a big name of the 20s.

Ivanhoe 13. The Kreuzer Sonata 15. War Bride 16. The Passing of the Third Floor Back 18. The Sig on the Door 21. The Spanish Dancer 23. *Peter Pa* 24. A Kiss for Cinderella 24. *Beau Geste* 26. *Sorrel and Son* (GB) (AAN) 27. The Great Gatsby 27. Laugh Clown Laugh 28. The Rescue 29. Beau Ide 29. Oliver Twist 33. Wine Women and Song 34. The Housemaster (GB) 38. At the Villa Rose (GB 38. Yellow Sands (GB) 38. The Flying Squadron (GB) 40, etc.

Brent, Eve (1930–).
American leading lady who played Jane in *Tarzan Fight for Life* 55. *Tarzan and the Trappers* 57.

Brent, Evelyn (1899–1975) (Mary Elizabeth Riggs)
American leading lady of the silent era; made a few talkies, then retired apart from some bit part in the 40s.

The Other Man's Wife 19. The Shuttle of Life (GB) 20. Sybil (GB) 21. Married to a Mormon (GB) 22. Silk Stocking Sal 24. Smooth as Satin 2 Love 'Em and Leave 'Em 26. Queen of Diamond 26. *Underworld* 27. Beau Sabreur 28. A Night of Mystery 28. The Mating Call 28. *Broadway* 29. *Slightly Scarlet* 30. Madonna of the Streets 30. Th Pagan Lady 31. The World Gone Mad 33. Home c the Range 35. Night Club Scandal 37. Mr Wong Detective 38. The Mad Empress 40. The Seventh Victim 43. Bowery Champs 44. The Golden Eye 48, many others.

Brent, George (1904–1979) (George Brent Nola
Irishman who went to Hollywood and after year as a tough hero developed into a light leading ma very effective against strong actresses such as Be Davis and Myrna Loy.
■ SOUND FILMS: Under Suspicion 30. Lightning Warrior 31. Homicide Squad 31. Once a Sinner 31. Fair Warning 31. Charlie Chan Carries On 31 Ex Bad Boy 31. So Big 32. The Rich Are Always With Us 32. Weekend Marriage 32. Miss Pinkerto 32. Purchase Price 32. The Crash 32. They Call I Sin 32. Luxury Liner 33. *Forty Second Street* 33. Th Keyhole 33. Lilly Turner 33. Baby Face 33. Female 33. Stamboul Quest 34. Housewife 34. Desirable 34. *The Painted Veil* 34. Living on Velve 35. Stranded 35. *Front Page Woman* 35. The Goos and the Gander 35. Special Agent 35. In Person 3 The Right to Live 35. Snowed Under 35. The Golden Arrow 36. The Case Against Mrs Ames 3 Give Me Your Heart 36. More than a Secretary 3 God's Country and the Woman 37. The Go-gette 37. Mountain Justice 37. Gold Is Where You Fin It 37. Submarine D-1 37. *Jezebel* 38. Racket Busters 38. Secrets of an Actress 38. Wings of th Navy 39. *Dark Victory* 39. The Old Maid 39. *The Rai Came* 39. The Man Who Talked Too Much 40. Th We Meet Again 40. The Fighting 69th 40. South Suez 40. Adventure in Diamonds 40. Honeymoo for Three 41. *The Great Lie* 41. They Dare Not Lo 41. International Lady 41. Twin Beds 42. The Ga Sisters 42. In This Our Life 42. You Can't Escape Forever 42. Silver Queen 42. Experiment Perilou 44. *The Affairs of Susan* 45. My Reputation 45. Th *Spiral Staircase* 45. Tomorrow Is Forever 46. Love Come Back 46. Temptation 46. Slave Girl 47. O of the Blue 47. The Corpse Came COD 47. Christmas Eve 47. Luxury Liner 48. Angel on th Amazon 48. Red Canyon 49. Illegal Entry 49. K

om Cleveland 49. Bride for Sale 49. FBI Girl 51. he Dark Page (GB) 51. Montana Belle 52. Tangier ncident 53. Born Again 78.

TV series: Wire Service 56.

For behaving like the perfect gentleman in ompany with some extremely difficult ladies. *The ains Came.*

rent, Romney (1902–1976) (Romulo Larralde). apper Mexican actor in British films in the 30s, ter elsewhere.

East Meets West 36. Dreaming Lips 37. School r Husbands 37. Under the Red Robe 37. Dinner t the Ritz (& w) 37. Let George Do It 40. The dventures of Don Juan 48. The Virgin Queen 55. on't Go Near the Water 57. The Sign of Zorro 58, tc.

reon, Edmund (1882–1951) (Edmund cLaverty). eaming, monocled British stage actor, often seen s amiable bumbler. In Hollywood from late 20s, ritain 1933–42.

The Dawn Patrol 30. I Like Your Nerve 31. *Three en in a Boat* 33. No Funny Business 33. The Scarlet impernel 35. Keep Fit 37. A Yank at Oxford 38. oodbye Mr Chips 39. The Outsider 39. She Shall ave Music 42. Gaslight 44. Casanova Brown 44. *he Woman in the Window* 45. *Dressed To Kill* 46. orever Amber 47. Enchantment 48. Challenge to assie 50. At Sword's Point 51, etc.

resler, Jerry (1912–1977). merican independent producer.

Main Street after Dark 44. Bewitched 45. The Veb 47. *Another Part of the Forest* 48. The Flying Aissile 50. The Mob 51. Assignment Paris 52. izzie 57. *The Vikings* 58. Gidget Goes Hawaiian 61. Diamond Head 63. Major Dundee 65. Pussycat ussycat I Love You 70, etc.

ressart, Felix (1890–1949). erman character actor in Hollywood from late 0s, usually in downtrodden comic roles; a enuine original.

Drei von der Tankstelle 31. Der Wahre Jakob 1. Das Alte Lied 31. Nie Weider Liebe 31. Eine reundin so Goldig wie Du 31. Der Schrecken der arnison 32. Hirsekorn Greift Ein 32. Der Herr uervorsteher 32. Holzapfel Weiss Alles 33. Drei age Mittelarrest 33. Der Sohn der Weissen Berge 3. Der Glueckszylinger 34. Und Wer Kuesst Aich? 35. Three Smart Girls Grow Up 39. Bridal uite 39. Swanee River 39. *Ninotchka* 39. The Shop round the Corner 40. It All Came True 40. Edison he Man 40. Third Finger Left Hand 40. Bitter weet 40. Comrade X 40. Escape 40. Ziegfeld Girl 0. Blossoms in the Dust 41. Married Bachelor 41. athleen 41. Mr and Mrs North 41. *To Be or Not Be* 42. Crossroads 42. Iceland 42. Three Hearts or Julia 43. Song of Russia 43. Above Suspicion 3. Greenwich Village 44. The Seventh Cross 44. londe Fever 44. Dangerous Partners 44. Without ove 45. Ding Dong Williams 46. I've Always oved You 46. The Thrill of Brazil 46. Her Sister's ecret 46. A Song Is Born 48. Portrait of Jennie 8. Take One False Step 49.

resslaw, Bernard (1933–1993). ritish comic actor who sprang to fame as giant-ized dope in TV series *The Army Game* 57–62 but roved lacking in big-screen star quality.

I Only Arsked 57. Too Many Crooks 58. The Ugly uckling 59. Morgan 66. Carry On Screaming 66. p Pompeii 70. Vampira 74. One of our Dinosaurs Missing 76. Hawk the Slayer 80. Krull 83, many thers in small roles.

Bresson, Robert (1907–). Elusive French writer-director of austere, introspective, low-budget films.

■ Les Anges du Péché 43. *Les Dames du Bois de Boulogne* 44. *Le Journal d'un Curé de Campagne* 50. Un Condamné à Mort s'est Echappé 56. Pickpocket 59. The Trial of Joan of Arc 62. Au Hasard Balthazar 66. Mouchette 67. Une Femme Douce 69. Quatre Nuits d'un Rêveur 71. Lancelot du Lac 74. Le Diable Probablement 77. L'Argent 83.

¶ A film is not a spectacle: it is pre-eminently a style. – *R.B.*

Brest, Martin (1951–). American director.

Hot Tomorrows 78. Going in Style 79. Beverly Hills Cop 84. Midnight Run 88. Scent of a Woman (AAN) 92, etc.

Bretherton, David. American film editor, on the staff of Twentieth Century-Fox for 20 years.

The Living Swamp 55. The Dark Wave 56. Peyton Place 57. Ten North Frederick 58. Let's Make Love 60. Return to Peyton Place 61. State Fair 62. The Sandpiper 65. Villa Rides 68. On a Clear Day You Can See Forever 69. Lovers and Other Strangers 70. Cabaret (AA) 72. Slither 73. Westworld 74. The Man in the Glass Booth 75. Silver Streak 76. Coma 78. Winter Kills 79. The Big Red One 80. Cannery Row 82. Love Lines 84. Clue 85. Lionheart 86. The Pick-Up Artist 87. Sea of Love 89. Malice 93, etc.

Bretherton, Howard (1896–1969). American director of second features.

Hills of Kentucky 27. The Redeeming Sin 29. Isle of Escape 30. The Match King 32. Ladies They Talk About 33. The Return of the Terror 34. The Leathernecks Have Landed 36. It Happened Out West 37. The Girl Who Dared 44. Prince of Thieves 48. Whip Law 50, many others.

Brett, Jeremy (1935–) (Jeremy Huggins). British light leading man, best known for playing Sherlock Holmes in the 80s TV series.

War and Peace 56. The Wild and the Willing 61. The Very Edge 63. *My Fair Lady* 64. The Medusa Touch 77. Florence Nightingale (TV) 84. Deceptions (TV) 84. Mad Dogs and Englishmen 95, etc.

Brialy, Jean-Claude (1933–). French leading man.

Éléna et les Hommes 56. Lift to the Scaffold 57. Le Beau Serge 58. The Four Hundred Blows 59. Tiré au Flanc 61. La Chambre Ardente 62. The Devil and Ten Commandments 62. La Ronde 64. Un Homme de Trop 67. King of Hearts 67. Le Rouge et le Noir 70. Claire's Knee 71. The Phantom of Liberty 74. Catherine and Company 75. Le Point de Mire 77. Robert et Robert 78. La Banquière 80. The Judge and the Assassin 81. The Demon of the Isle 83. Sarah 83. Pinot, Simple Flic 84. Grand Guignol 86. Inspector Lavardin 86. Les Innocents 87. Le Cop 2 (Ripoux contre Ripoux) 89. S'en Fout La Mort 89. August (Août) 91. Queen Margot (La Reine Margot) 94, etc.

ALSO DIRECTED: Eglantine 72. Closed Shutters 73. Un Amour de Pluie 74, etc.

Brian, David (1914–1993). Stalwart American second lead, a former song-and-dance man who came to Hollywood in 1949 and sank into a groove of toughness and reliability, with a streak of villainy when required.

Flamingo Road 49. Beyond the Forest 49. *Intruder*

in the Dust 49. The Damned Don't Cry 50. Breakthrough 50. Inside Straight 51. This Woman is Dangerous 52. Million Dollar Mermaid 52. The High and the Mighty 54. Timberjack 55. The First Travelling Saleslady 56. The Rabbit Trap 59. A Pocketful of Miracles 61. How the West was Won 62. The Rare Breed 68. The Destructors 69. The Seven Minutes 71, many others.

TV series: *Mr District Attorney* 54–55. The Immortal 70.

Brian, Mary (1908–) (Louise Dantzler). Charming American leading lady of the 20s; her roles diminished with sound and finally petered out.

Peter Pan (as Wendy) 24. The Little French Girl 25. Brown of Harvard 26. Beau Geste 26. Running Wild 27. Shanghai Bound 27. Harold Teen 28. Varsity 28. The Man I Love 29. *The Virginian* 29. The Light of Western Stars 30. *The Royal Family of Broadway* 30. *The Front Page* 31. Blessed Event 32. Girl Missing 33. College Rhythm 34. Charlie Chan in Paris 35. Killer at Large 36. The Amazing Quest of Ernest Bliss (GB) 36. Navy Bound 37. Calaboose 43. The Dragnet 48, many others.

Briant, Shane (1946–). British general purpose actor, mainly in Australia.

Demons of the Mind 70. Straight on till Morning 71. Captain Kronos 72. Frankenstein and the Monster from Hell 72. Moving Targets 87. True Colors 87. Cassandra 87. Grievous Bodily Harm 89. Till There Was You 90, etc.

Brice, Fanny (1891–1951) (Fanny Borach). American Jewish entertainer who made a virtue of her plainness. Screen appearances rare, but four films were based on her life: *Broadway thro' a Keyhole* 33, *Rose of Washington Square* 38, *Funny Girl* 68, *Funny Lady* 75.

Biography: 1992, *Fanny Brice – the Original Funny Girl* by Herbert G. Goldman.

■ *My Man* 28. Night Club 29. Be Yourself 30. The Great Ziegfeld 36. Everybody Sing 38. Ziegfeld Follies 45.

Brickman, Marshall (1941–). American screenwriter and director.

Sleeper (co-w) 73. *Annie Hall* (co-w) (AA) 77. *Manhattan* (co-w) (AAN) 79. Simon (& d) 80. Lovesick (& d) 83. The Manhattan Project (& d) 86. For the Boys (d) 91. Manhattan Murder Mystery (co-w) 93. Intersection (co-w) 94, etc.

Bricusse, Leslie (1931–). British lyricist and composer.

Charley Moon 56. Stop the World I Want to Get Off 65. Doctor Dolittle (AA) 67. Goodbye Mr Chips (AAN) 69. Scrooge (AAN) 70. Willie Wonka and the Chocolate Factory (AAN) 71. Revenge of the Pink Panther 78. Superman 78. The Sea Wolves 80. Victor/Victoria 82. Babes in Toyland (TV) 86. Bullseye! 91, etc.

Bridge, Al (1891–1957). Gravel-voiced American character actor chiefly memorable in Preston Sturges comedies.

Christmas in July 40. The Palm Beach Story 42. *Hail the Conquering Hero* 44, etc.

Bridges, Alan (1928–). British director, from TV.

■ *An Act of Murder* 65. *Invasion* 66. The Lie (TV) 70. The Hireling 73. Brief Encounter (TV) 75. Out of Season 75. Summer Rain (Can.) 76. The Return of the Soldier 82. The Shooting Party 84. Displaced Person (TV) 85. Apt Pupil 88.

Bridges, Beau (1941–).
American leading man, son of Lloyd Bridges.
　Force of Evil 48. The Red Pony 49. The Incident 67. For Love of Ivy 68. *Gaily Gaily* 69. *The Landlord* 70. Adam's Woman 70. The Christian Licorice Store 71. Hammersmith is Out 72. Child's Play 72. Loving Molly 73. The Other Side of the Mountain 75. Medical Story (TV) 75. One Summer Love 76. Swashbuckler 76. Two Minute Warning 76. Greased Lightning 77. The Fifth Musketeer 77. The Four Feathers (TV) 78. The President's Mistress (TV) 78. Norma Rae 79. The Child Stealer (TV) 79. The Runner Stumbles (TV) 79. Honky Tonk Freeway (TV) 81. Love Child 82. Night Crossing 82. Dangerous Company (TV) 82. Heart Like a Wheel 83. Witness for the Prosecution (TV) 84. Space 85. The Red Light Sting (TV) 86. The Wild Pair (& d) 87. Seven Hours to Judgement (& d) 88. The Fabulous Baker Boys 89. The Iron Triangle 89. Signs of Life 89. Daddy's Dyin', Who's Got the Will? 90. Married to It 91. The Positively True Adventures of the Alleged Texas Cheerleader-Murdering Mom (TV) 93. Sidekicks 93. Secret Sins of the Father (& d) (TV) 94, etc.
　TV series: Ensign O'Toole 62–64. United States 80.

Bridges, James (1936–1993).
American writer-director, a former actor.
■ The Appaloosa (co-w only) 66. The Forbin Project (w only) 70. The Baby Maker 70. The Paper Chase (AANw) 73. September 30, 1955 77. The China Syndrome (AANw) 79. Urban Cowboy 80. Mike's Murder 82. Perfect 84. Bright Lights, Big City 88. White Hunter, Black Heart (w) 90.

Bridges, Jeff (1949–).
American leading man of the early 70s, son of Lloyd Bridges.
■ Halls of Anger 70. In Search of America (TV) 70. The Last Picture Show (AAN) 71. Fat City 71. Bad Company 72. The Last American Hero 73. Lolly Madonna XXX 73. The Iceman Cometh 73. Thunderbolt and Lightfoot (AAN) 74. Rancho de Luxe 75. *Hearts of the West* 75. Stay Hungry 76. King Kong 76. Somebody Killed Her Husband 79. Winter Kills 79. Success 79. Heaven's Gate 80. Cutter's Way 81. Tron 82. Kiss Me Goodbye 82. Against All Odds 83. Starman (AAN) 84. Jagged Edge 85. 8 Million Ways to Die 85. The Morning After 86. Nadine 87. Tucker: The Man and His Dream 88. The Fabulous Baker Boys 89. See You in the Morning 89. Texasville 90. The Fisher King 91. American Heart 92. The Vanishing 93. Fearless 93. Blown Away 94. Wild Bill 95.

Bridges, Lloyd (1913–).
American general-purpose actor and sometimes leading man who, over 30 years, has brought a sense of integrity to many westerns and melodramas.
　Here Comes Mr Jordan 41. The Lone Wolf Takes a Chance 41. Atlantic Convoy 42. The Heat's On 43. The Master Race 44. Strange Confession 45. Miss Susie Slagle's 46. Canyon Passage 46. Ramrod 47. Sixteen Fathoms Deep 48. Moonrise 49. *Home of the Brave* 49. Trapped 49. Rocketship XM 50. The White Tower 50. *Try and Get Me* 51. Little Big Horn 51. The Whistle at Eaton Falls 51. High Noon 52. Plymouth Adventure 52. City of Bad Men 53. The Tall Texan 53. The Limping Man (GB) 54. Apache Woman 55. Wetbacks 56. The Rainmaker 56. *The Goddess* 58. Around the World Under the Sea 66. Attack on the Iron Coast 68. *The Love War* (TV) 70. The Silent Gun (TV) 70. To Find a Man 72. Haunts of the Very Rich (TV) 72. Trouble Comes to Town (TV) 73. Running Wild 73. Crime Club (TV) 73. Death Race (TV) 73. Stowaway to

the Moon (TV) 75. The Return of Joe Forrester (TV) 75. Roots (TV) 77. Telethon (TV) 77. The Great Wallendas (TV) 78. The Critical List (TV) 78. Airplane 80. Grace Kelly (TV) 82. Weekend Warriors 86. The Wild Pair 87. Cousins 89. Joe Versus the Volcano 90. Hot Shots! 91. Devlin 92. Honey, I Blew Up the Kid 92. Hot Shoes! Part Deux 93. Run of Hearts 93. Secret Sins of the Father (TV) 94. Blown Away 94, etc.
　TV series: Sea Hunt 57–60. The Lloyd Bridges Show 62. *The Loner* 65. San Francisco International 70. Joe Forrester 75. Paper Dolls 85.

Bridie, James (1888–1951) (Osborne Henry Mavor).
Pawky Scottish dramatist whose works were more suited to stage than screen. Two films which did result were *Flesh and Blood* (from *A Sleeping Clergyman*) and *Folly to Be Wise* (from *It Depends What You Mean*).

Briel, Joseph Carl (1870–1926).
American composer who wrote and arranged the music to accompany silent films, including several by D. W. Griffith. In the process he created the first hit song from a movie score: the love theme from *The Birth of a Nation* for scenes between the Little Colonel and Elsie Stoneman, published as 'The Perfect Song', which later became the theme tune of the radio show *Amos 'n' Andy*.
　Queen Elizabeth 12. The Prisoner of Zenda 13. The Birth of a Nation 15. The Lily and the Rose 15. Intolerance 16. The Dramatic Life of Abraham Lincoln 23. America 24, etc.

Briers, Richard (1934–).
British comic character actor, a farceur who inherited the mantle of Ralph Lynn and was popular on TV.
　Girls at Sea 58. The Girl on the Boat 62. Fathom 67. Rentadick 72. A Chorus of Disapproval 89. Henry V 90. Much Ado about Nothing 93. Skallagrigg (TV) 94, etc.
　TV series: Marriage Lines 63–66. Birds on the Wing 71. The Good Life 75–78. The Other One 77–79. Goodbye Mr Kent 82. Ever Decreasing Circles 84–89. All in Good Faith 85–88. If You See God, Tell Him 93.

¶ At drama school I played Hamlet and all the usual things one does. Then I got into the real world and realised I only had a one-string fiddle, a single talent – an instinctive sense of comedy timing. – *R.B.*

I know the word 'bumbling' often comes up when people discuss me. I don't mind, but I prefer 'obsessive'. – *R.B.*

Briggs, Harlan (1880–1952).
American small-part actor.
　Dodsworth 36. A Family Affair 37. One Wild Night 38. Calling Dr Kildare 39. Abe Lincoln in Illinois 40. One Foot in Heaven 41. Tennessee Johnson 43. State Fair 45. A Double Life 48. Carrie 52, many others.

Briggs, Johnny (1935–).
British character actor, often a cockney on the wrong side of the law, best known for the role of Mike Baldwin in the TV soap opera *Coronation Street*.
　Hue and Cry 47. Cosh Boy 53. Diplomatic Corpse 58. Light Up the Sky 60. 633 Squadron 64. Perfect Friday 70. Carry On Behind 75, etc.

Briley, John (1925–).
American-born screenwriter in Britain.
　Postman's Knock 61. Children of the Damned

64. Pope Joan 72. That Lucky Touch 75. Eagle's Wing 79. *Gandhi* (AA) 82. Cry Freedom 87. Christopher Columbus: The Discovery 92, etc.

Brimley, Wilford (1934–).
American character actor who plays wise, rough-edged old gents and hovers just below the star level.
　The Electric Horseman 79. Brubaker 79. Borderline 80. The China Syndrome 80. Heaven's Gate 80. Death Valley 82. Absence of Malice 82. Tender Mercies 83. Ten to Midnight 83. Country 84. Hotel New Hampshire 84. The Natural 84. American Justice 85. Cocoon 85. Thompson's Last Run (TV) 85. Remo Williams 85. Act of Vengeance (TV) 86. American Justice (aka Jackals) 86. Thompson's Last Run (TV) 86. End of the Line 87. Cocoon: The Return 88. Eternity 90. The Firm 93. Hard Target 93, etc.
　TV series: Our House 86–88.

Brinegar, Paul (1925–).
American character actor, a long-time mainstay of television westerns, including the trail cook Wishbone in *Rawhide*.
　Larceny 48. The Gal Who Took the West 49. The Captive City 51. Human Desire 54. How to Make a Monster 58. Charro! 69. High Plains Drifter 73. Maverick 94, etc.
　TV series: The Life and Legend of Wyatt Earp 56–58. Rawhide 59–66. Lancer 69–70. Matt Houston 82–83.

Brissac, Virginia (1894–1979).
American supporting actress, a familiar face in mother and neighbour roles.
　A Tree Grows in Brooklyn 44. Monsieur Verdoux 47. The Snake Pit 48. Cheaper by the Dozen 50. Rebel Without a Cause 55, many others.

Brisson, Carl (1895–1958) (Carl Pedersen).
Danish leading man who made films in Britain.
　The Ring 28. The Manxman 29. The American Prisoner 29. Song of Soho 30. Murder at the Vanities 34. All the King's Horses 35, etc.

Brisson, Frederick (1912–1984).
Danish producer with long experience in Britain (pre-39) and Hollywood. Married Rosalind Russell and subsequently masterminded her appearances.
■ The Velvet Touch 48. Never Wave at a WAC 53. The Girl Rush 55. The Pajama Game 57. Damn Yankees 58. Five Finger Exercise 62. Under the Yum Yum Tree 63. Generation 69. Mrs Pollifax – Spy 71.

The British Empire
has provided a useful background for innumerable movies: some comic, some tragic, but most of them plain adventurous. The Elizabethan Adventurers roistered through films like *The Sea Hawk*, *The Virgin Queen* and *Seven Seas to Calais;* the westward voyage occupied *Plymouth Adventure;* Australia provided the canvas for *Under Capricorn*, *Robbery Under Arms* and *Botany Bay; Mutiny on the Bounty* showed the British in the South Seas; Africa was the subject of *Zulu*, *The Four Feathers*, *Khartoum*, *Sundown*, *Rhodes of Africa*, *The Sun Never Sets* and (for the anti-British view) *Ohm Krüger;* and favourite of all far-flung outposts, India provided splendid terrain for such adventures as *The Drum*, *Northwest Frontier*, *Gunga Din*, *King of the Khyber Rifles*, *The Rains Came*, *Charge of the Light Brigade* and *Lives of a Bengal Lancer*. When the Empire was at its height, one could view the British influence as benevolent (*Pacific Destiny*), maiden-auntish (*Sanders of the River*), or merely acquisitive (*Victoria the Great*).

The inevitable break-up was rather less well
covered. Even American independence has been
played down by Hollywood producers with an eye
on the British market, though of course it comes
into such films as *Last of the Mohicans, Lafayette,
Daniel Boone,* and even Disney's *Ben and Me.*
Emergent Africa was the theme of *Men of Two
Worlds* as long ago as 1946, but between that and
the independent state depicted in *Guns at Batasi*
came the Mau Mau period shown in *Simba, Safari*
and *Something of Value. The High Bright Sun* dealt
with Cyprus; *The Planter's Wife* and *The Seventh
Dawn* with Malaya; *Exodus, Judith* and *Cast a Giant
Shadow* with Israel; scores of films with the Irish
troubles; *Bhowani Junction* and *Nine Hours to Rama*
with India. But the emergence of new states is a
painful business as a rule, and most of these films
give the impression of so much tasteless picking
at sore points. The unexpected 1982 success of
Gandhi may, however, begin a more serious process
of revaluing imperial history.
    See also: *Ireland.*

British Film Academy.
An organization founded in 1946 'for the
advancement of the film'. Since 1959 it has been
amalgamated with the Society of Film and
Television Arts. Its award statuette is noted in this
book by the letters BFA. See Appendix for full
listing.

British Film Commission.
An organization set up in 1992 and funded by the
British government to provide information and
services to international film and television
companies to encourage the use of British
technicians, artists, facilities and locations. The first
British Film Commissioner is Sydney Samuelson,
who began working in the cinema industry in
1939.

British Film Institute.
Partly government-subsidized organization
founded in 1933 'to encourage the use and
development of cinema as a means of
entertainment and instruction'. Includes the
National Film Archive (founded 1935) and the
National Film Theatre (founded after the 1951
Festival of Britain). Also library, information
section, stills collection, film distribution agency,
lecture courses, etc. Chief publication: *Sight and
Sound.*

British Lion Film Corporation.
A film production company of the 20s which, in
the 30s, became mainly a distributor of cheap
American product but was revived after World
War II by the control of Alexander Korda, then by
Michael Balcon, the Boulting Brothers and Frank
Launder and Sidney Gilliat. It merged in 1976
with EMI.

Britt, May (1933–) (Maybritt Wilkens).
Swedish leading lady, in a few Hollywood films.
She was married to Sammy Davis Jnr (1960–68).
The Affairs of a Model 52. La Lupa 54. *The Young
Lions* 58. The Hunters 58. The Blue Angel 59.
Murder Inc. 60. Secrets of Woman 61. Haunts 77,
etc.

Brittany, Morgan (1951–) (Suzanne Caputo).
American child actress, later leading lady.
Gypsy 62. The Birds 63. Marnie 64. Yours, Mine
and Ours 68. The Day of the Locust 75. Gable and
Lombard 76. Samurai (TV) 79. Death Car on the
Freeway (TV) 79. Stunt Seven (TV) 80. The
Prodigal 83. LBJ: The Early Years (TV) 88, etc.
TV series: Dallas 81–84. Glitter 84–85.

Britten, Baron Benjamin of Aldeburgh
(1913–1976).
Distinguished English composer, pianist and co-
founder of the Aldeburgh Festival, who scored
several documentaries in the 30s and one feature
film. He was made a life peer in 1976.
    Coal Face (doc) 35. Night Mail (doc) 36. Love
from a Stranger 37. Village Harvest (doc) 38, etc.

Britton, Barbara (1920–1980) (Barbara
Brantingham Czukor).
American leading lady of the 40s who went
straight from college to Hollywood.
    Secret of the Wastelands 40. Louisiana Purchase
41. Wake Island 42. Reap the Wild Wind 42. So
Proudly We Hail 43. *Till We Meet Again* 44. The
Story of Dr Wassell 44. The Great John L. 45.
Captain Kidd 45. The Virginian 46. The Fabulous
Suzanne 47. Gunfighters 47. Albuquerque 48. I
Shot Jesse James 49. Champagne for Caesar 50.
Bandit Queen 50. The Raiders 52. Bwana Devil
53. The Spoilers 55, etc.
    TV series: Mr and Mrs North 52–54.

Britton, Pamela (1923–1974).
Lightweight American actress, mainly familiar as
TV's *Blondie* and in the *My Favorite Martian* series.
    Anchors Aweigh 45. Key to the City 50. If It's
Tuesday This Must Be Belgium 74, etc.

Britton, Tony (1924–).
British stage, screen and TV actor of quiet and
polished style.
    Salute the Toff 52. Loser Take All 57. The
Birthday Present 57. Operation Amsterdam 58.
The Rough and the Smooth 59. Suspect 60. Stork
Talk 61. The Break 63. There's a Girl in My Soup
70. Sunday Bloody Sunday 71. The Day of the
Jackal 73. Night Watch 74. The People That Time
Forgot 76. Agatha 79, etc.
    TV Series: Father Dear Father 68–73. Robin's
Nest 77–81. Don't Wait Up 83–84.

Broadbent, Jim.
English character actor.
    The Good Father 87. Life Is Sweet 91. *The Crying
Game* 92. Enchanted April 92. Wide-Eyed and
Legless (TV) 93. Widow's Peak 94. The Wedding
Gift 94. Princess Caraboo 94. *Bullets over Broadway*
94, etc.
    TV series: Gone to the Dogs 91. Gone to See 92.

Broccoli, Albert R. ('Cubby') (1909–).
American independent producer resident in
London since 1951; successful as co-chief of
Warwick Productions and later the James Bond
films.
    Hell Below Zero 54. The Black Knight 54.
Cockleshell Heroes 55. Zarak 56. Fire Down
Below 57. The Man Inside 59. *Dr No* 62. Call Me
Bwana 63. From Russia with Love 63 (and
subsequent Bond films). Chitty Chitty Bang Bang
68, many others.

Brocka, Lino (1940–1991).
Leading Filipino director whose best films focus on
social deprivation in his homeland. He gained
international recognition in 1978 when *Insiang*
was shown at the Cannes Film Festival. He died
in a car crash.
    Wanted: Perfect Mother 70. Cherry Blossoms
72. Manila in the Claws of Light 75. Insiang 77.
Jaguar 79. Hello Young Lovers 81. Caught in the
Act 82. My Country: In Desperate Straits 84.
Macho Dancer 88. I Carry the World 88, many
others.

Brockwell, Gladys (1894–1929).
American leading actress of silent films. Died as a
result of a car crash.
    Double Trouble 15. Oliver Twist 22. The
Hunchback of Notre Dame 23. Unmarried Wives
24. The Last Frontier 26. Seventh Heaven 27.
Lights of New York 28. The Argyle Case 29. The
Drake Case 29, etc.

Broderick, Helen (1890–1959).
Wry-faced American stage comedienne whose
wisecracks enlivened many 30s comedies. Mother
of Broderick Crawford.
■ Fifty Million Frenchmen 31. *Top Hat* 35. To Beat
the Band 35. Love on a Bet 36. Murder on the
Bridle Path 36. Swing Time 36. The Bride Walks
Out 36. Smartest Girl in Town 36. We're on the
Jury 37. Meet the Missus 37. Life of the Party 37.
Radio City Revels 38. She's Got Everything 38. The
Rage of Paris 38. The Road to Reno 38. Service de
Luxe 38. Stand Up and Fight 39. Naughty but
Nice 39. Honeymoon in Bali 39. The Captain Is a
Lady 40. No No Nanette 40. Virginia 41. Nice Girl
41. Father Takes a Wife 41. Are Husbands
Necessary 42. Stage Door Canteen 43. Chip Off the
Old Block 44. Her Primitive Man 44. Three Is a
Family 44. Love Honor and Goodbye 45. Because
of Him 46.

Broderick, James (1927–1982).
Worried-looking American character actor.
    The Group 66. Alice's Restaurant 69. The Taking
of Pelham One Two Three 74. Dog Day Afternoon
75. The Shadow Box (TV) 80, etc.
    TV series: Brenner 59. *Family* 76–80.

Broderick, Matthew (1962–).
American leading actor, from the stage. He is the
son of James Broderick.
    Max Dugan Returns 82. *War Games* 83.
Ladyhawke 84. On Valentine's Day 85. Ferris
Bueller's Day Off 86. Project X 87. Biloxi Blues 88.
Torch Song Trilogy 88. Family Business 89. Glory
89. The Freshman 90. Out on a Limb 92. The Night
We Never Met 93. A Life in the Theatre 93. Mrs
Parker and the Vicious Circle 94. The Lion King
(voice) 94. The Road to Wellville 94. Infinity (&
d) 95, etc.

Brodie, Steve (1919–1992) (John Stevens).
Tough-looking American leading man and
character actor, mainly in second features.
    This Man's Navy 45. Young Wife 46. Trail Street
47. Home of the Brave 49. Winchester 73 50. Only
the Valiant 51. Lady in the Iron Mask 52. The Beast
from Twenty Thousand Fathoms 53. The Caine
Mutiny 54. Gun Duel in Durango 57. Three Came
to Kill 60. Of Love and Desire 63, etc.

Brodine, Norbert (1893–1970).
Distinguished American cinematographer.
SELECTED SILENT FILMS: Almost a Husband 19. The
Invisible Power 21. A Blind Bargain 22. Brass 23.
The Sea Hawk 24. The Eagle of the Sea 25. Paris at
Midnight 26. The Clown 27. Beware of Bachelors
28. Her Private Affair 29.
■ SOUND FILMS: Rich People 29. This Thing Called
Love 29. The Divorcee 30. Holiday 30. Let Us Be
Gay 30. Beyond Victory 31. The Guardsman 31.
Pagan Lady 31. The Passionate Plumber 32. Beast
of the City 32. Night Court 32. Bachelor's Affairs
32. Unashamed 32. Wild Girl 32. Uptown New York
32. The Death Kiss 32. Whistling in the Dark 33.
Clear All Wires 33. Made on Broadway 33.
Broadway to Hollywood 33. Deluge 33. Counsellor
at Law 33. The Crosby Case 34. Love Birds 34.
Little Man What Now 34. The Human Side 34.
There's Always Tomorrow 34. Cheating Cheaters

34. The Good Fairy 35. Princess O'Hara 35. She Gets Her Man 35. Lady Tubbs 35. The Affair of Susan 36. Don't Get Personal 36. Nobody's Fool 36. *Libeled Lady* 36. Nobody's Baby 37. Pick a Star 37. *Topper* 37. *Merrily We Live* 37. Swiss Miss 38. There Goes My Heart 38. Topper Takes a Trip 39. Captain Fury 39. The Housekeeper's Daughter 39. Of Mice and Men 39. *One Million Years BC* 40. Turnabout 40. Captain Caution 40. Model Wife 41. Road Show 41. Lady for a Night 41. Dr Gillespie's Criminal Case 43. The Dancing Masters 43. The Bullfighters 45. Don Juan Quilligan 45. *The House on 92nd Street* 45. Sentimental Journey 46. Somewhere in the Night 46. *Thirteen Rue Madeleine* 46. *Kiss of Death* 47. *Boomerang* 47. Sitting Pretty 48. I Was a Male War Bride 49. *Thieves' Highway* 49. *The Frogmen* 51. The Desert Fox 51. Five Fingers 52.

Brodney, Oscar (1905–   ).
American comedy writer, former lawyer. With Universal from the 40s, working mainly on routine series and light costume dramas.

When Johnny Comes Marching Home 43. Are You With It? 48. Yes Sir That's My Baby 49. Francis 50. Little Egypt 53. The Glenn Miller Story 54. Lady Godiva 55. Tammy and the Bachelor 57. Bobbikins (GB) (& p) 59. Tammy and the Doctor 63. The Brass Bottle 64. I'd Rather Be Rich 64, etc.

Brodszky, Nicholas (1905–1958).
Russian-born composer, long in America and Britain.

French Without Tears 39. Quiet Wedding 40. The Way to the Stars 45. A Man About the House 47. The Toast of New Orleans 50. Latin Lovers 53. The Opposite Sex 56, etc.

Brody, Estelle (1904–   ).
French-Canadian actress and dancer who became a star of British silent films in the late 20s, returning as a character actress in the 50s.

White Heat 26. Mademoiselle from Armentieres 26. Hindle Wakes 27. Sailors Don't Care 28. Kitty 29. Me and the Boys 29. The Plaything 29. Lili Marlene 51. Safari 56. The Story of Esther Costello 57. Never Take Sweets from a Stranger 60, etc.

Brolin, James (1940–   ).
American leading man.

Take Her She's Mine 63. Goodbye Charlie 64. Von Ryan's Express 65. Morituri 65. Our Man Flint 67. The Boston Strangler 68. Short Walk to Daylight (TV) 72. Skyjacked 72. Westworld 73. Trapped (TV) 73. Class of 63 (TV) 73. *Gable and Lombard* (as Gable) 76. The Car 77. Steel Cowboy (TV) 78. The Amityville Horror 79. High Risk 81. Pee-Wee's Big Adventure 85. Bad Jim 89. Finish Line 89. Backstab 90. And the Sea Will Tell (TV) 91. Gas Food Lodging 92. Paper Hearts 93. Ted & Venus 93. Gunsmoke: The Long Ride (TV) 93. Relative Fear 94. Parallel Lives (TV) 94, etc.

TV series: *Marcus Welby MD* 69–75. Hotel 83–88.

Bromberg, J. Edward (1903–1951).
Plump, wide-eyed Hungarian actor, in America from infancy; usually in gentle roles.
■ Under Two Flags 36. Sins of Man 36. The Crime of Dr Forbes 36. Girls' Dormitory 36. Star for a Night 36. Ladies in Love 36. Reunion 36. Stowaway 36. Fair Warning 37. That I May Live 37. Seventh Heaven 37. Charlie Chan on Broadway 37. Second Honeymoon 37. Mr Moto Takes a Chance 37. The Baroness and the Butler 38. One Wild Night 38. Four Men and a Prayer 38. Sally, Irene and Mary 38. Rebecca of Sunnybrook Farm 38. I'll Give a

Million 38. *Suez* 38. Jesse James 39. Wife, Husband and Friend 39. *Hollywood Cavalcade* 39. Three Sons 39. Strange Cargo 40. The Return of Frank James 40. *The Mark of Zorro* 40. Hurricane Smith 41. Dance Hall 41. The Devil Pays Off 41. Pacific Blackout 42. Invisible Agent 42. Life Begins at 8.30 42. Tennessee Johnson 42. Reunion in France 42. Halfway to Shanghai 42. Lady of Burlesque 43. Phantom of the Opera 43. Son of Dracula 43. Chip Off the Old Block 44. Voice in the Wind 44. Easy to Look At 45. The Missing Corpse 45. Pillow of Death 45. Salome Where She Danced 45. The Walls Came Tumbling Down 46. Tangier 46. Cloak and Dagger 46. Queen of the Amazons 47. Arch of Triumph 48. *A Song Is Born* 48. I Shot Jesse James 49. Guilty Bystander 50.

Bromberger, Herve (1918–1993).
French director, a former journalist; influenced later 'New Wave' directors, including Godard and Truffaut.

Identité Judiciaire 51. Les Fruits Sauvages 54. Les Loups dans la Bergerie 60. Mort Où Est Ta Victoire? 64, etc.

Bromfield, John (1922–   ) (Farron Bromfield).
American second lead; leading man of second features. He was formerly married to actress Corinne Calvet.

Harpoon 48. Rope of Sand 49. Paid in Full 50. The Furies 50. Flat Top 52. Easy to Love 53. Ring of Fear 53. Crime Against Joe 55. Manfish 56. Hot Cars 57, etc.

TV series: Sheriff of Cochise 56–57. U.S. Marshal 58–59.

Bromfield, Louis (1896–1956).
American popular novelist. *The Rains Came* was twice filmed; *Mrs Parkington* once. *It All Came True* and *Johnny Vagabond* were both taken from Bromfield stories.

Bromiley, Dorothy (1935–   ).
British leading lady of very few films.

The Girls of Pleasure Island (US) 53. It's Great to be Young 55. A Touch of the Sun 56. The Criminal 60, etc.

Bron, Eleanor (1934–   ).
Bloomsburyish British TV revue actress.

Help 65. Alfie 66. Two for the Road 67. Women in Love 69. Turtle Diary 85. Deadly Advice 94. Black Beauty 94, etc.

Bronson, Betty (1906–1971) (Elizabeth Bronson).
Lively American leading lady of the 20s; did not succeed in talkies.

Peter Pan (title role) 24. The Golden Princess 25. Are Parents People? 25. A Kiss for Cinderella 26. *Ben Hur* 26. The Cat's Pajamas 26. Everybody's Acting 27. Brass Knuckles 27. *The Singing Fool* 28. Companionate Marriage 28. Sonny Boy 29. The Locked Door 29. Medicine Man 30. The Yodelling Kid from Pine Ridge 37. Who's Got the Action? 62. Blackbeard's Ghost 67. Evel Knievel 71, etc.

Bronson, Charles (1920–   ) (Charles Buchinski).
Sombre-looking, deep-featured American character actor who can deal with a variety of types, from Russian to Red Indian, from villainous to sturdily heroic. At the age of fifty he suddenly became a star.

You're In the Navy Now 51. Pat and Mike 52. House of Wax 53. Apache 54. *Drumbeat* 54. Vera Cruz 54. Target Zero 55. Jubal 56. Run of the Arrow 57. Machine Gun Kelly 57. When Hell Broke Loose 58. Never So Few 59. *The Magnificent Seven* 60. A Thunder of Drums 61. Lonely are the

Brave 62. The Great Escape 63. The Sandpiper 65● Battle of the Bulge 65. This Property is Condemned 66. *The Dirty Dozen* 67. Guns for San Sebastian 68● Adieu l'Ami 68. Once Upon a Time in the West 69. Rider in the Rain 69. Twinky 69. Violent City (It.) 70. You Can't Win Them All 70. Cold Sweat 71. *Chato's Land* 72. The Mechanic 72. *The Valach Papers* 72. Wild Horses 73. The Stone Killer 73. Mr Majesty 74. *Death Wish* 74. Breakout 75. *Hard Times* 75. Breakheart Pass 76. From Noon Till Three 76. St Ives 76. Raid on Entebbe (TV) 76. Telefon 77. The White Buffalo 77. Love and Bullet● 79. Cabo Blanco 80. Borderline 80. Death Hunt 81. Death Wish II 82. Ten to Midnight 83. The Evil That Men Do 84. Death Wish III 85. Assassination 86. Death Wish IV 87. Messenger of Death 88. Kinjite 89. The Indian Runner 91. N● Return 91. The Sea Wolf (TV) 93. Death Wish V: The Face of Death 94, etc.

TV series: Man with a Camera 58–59. Redigo 63. The Travels of Jamie McPheeters 64.

¶ Someday I'd like a part where I can lean my elbow against a mantelpiece and have a cocktai – C.B.

I guess I look like a rock quarry that someone has dynamited – C.B.

Acting is the easiest thing I've ever done. I gues● that's why I'm stuck with it. – C.B.

Bronson, Lillian (1902–   ).
American character actress.

Happy Land 43. A Tree Grows in Brooklyn 44. The Hucksters 47. The Next Voice You Hear 51. Walk on the Wild Side 62. The Americanization ● Emily 64, many others.

Bronston, Samuel (1909–1994).
Russian-born American independent producer who in 1959 set up a studio in Madrid and made several international epics but ran into financial difficulty.

Jack London 43. A Walk in the Sun 46. John Paul Jones 59. King of Kings 60. El Cid 61. Fifty Five Days at Peking 62. The Fall of the Roman Empire 64. Circus World 64. Savage Pampas (co-p) 66, etc.

Brontë, Charlotte (1816–1855).
British novelist whose *Jane Eyre* has been frequently filmed, most recently in 1934 with Virginia Bruce and Colin Clive, in 1944 with Joan● Fontaine and Orson Welles, and in 1971 with Susannah York and George C. Scott. Its central situation, of a governess in the house of a mysterious but romantic tyrant, has also been frequently plagiarized.

Brontë, Emily (1818–1848).
British novelist, sister of Charlotte Brontë, and author of *Wuthering Heights*, much filmed in Britain before the definitive 1939 version. A somewhat romantic film about the sisters was filmed in 194● under the title *Devotion*, with Olivia de Havilland as Charlotte and Ida Lupino as Emily.

Brook, Clive (1887–1974) (Clifford Brook).
Distinguished British leading man of stage and screen, for forty years the perfect gentleman (with very occasional caddish lapses). Popular in Hollywood in the 20s and early 30s.
■ A Debt of Honour 19. Trent's Last Case 20. Kissing Cup's Race 20. Her Penalty 20. The Loudwater Mystery 21. Daniel Deronda 21. A Sportsman's Wife 21. Sonia 21. Christie Johnston● 21. Woman to Woman 21. Through Fire and Water 22. This Freedom 22. Out to Win 22. The Reverse of the Medal 23. The Royal Oak 23. The

oney Habit 24. The White Sheik 24. Recoil 24.
ae Wine of Life 24. The Passionate Adventure
4. Human Desires 24. Christine of the Hungry
eart 24. The Mirage 24. When Love Grows Cold
5. Enticement 25. The Social Exile 25. Playing
ith Souls 25. If Marriage Fails 25. The Woman
ater 25. Compromise 25. Seven Sinners 25. The
ome Maker 25. The Pleasure Buyers 25. Three
aces East 26. Why Girls Go Back Home 26. For
limony Only 26. You Never Know Women 26.
ae Popular Sin 26. Afraid to Love 27. Barbed
ire 27. *Underworld* 27. Hula 27. The Devil Dancer
7. French Dressing 27. Midnight Madness 28. The
ellow Lily 28. The Perfect Crime 28. Forgotten
aces 28. Interference 29. A Dangerous Woman
9. *The Four Feathers* 29. Charming Sinners 29. The
eturn of Sherlock Holmes 29. The Laughing
ady 29. Slightly Scarlet 30. Paramount on Parade
0. Sweethearts and Wives 30. Anybody's
oman 30. Scandal Sheet 31. East Lynne 31.
arnished Lady 31. The Lawyer's Secret 31. Silence
1. Twenty Four Hours 31. Husband's Holiday 31.
anghai Express 32. The Man from Yesterday 32.
ae Night of June 13th 32. *Sherlock Holmes* 32.
ake Me a Star 32. *Cavalcade* 33. Midnight Club
3. Gallant Lady 33. If I Were Free 34. Where
nners Meet 34. Let's Try Again 34. The Love
ffair of the Dictator 35. Dressed to Thrill 35. The
onely Road 36. Love in Exile 36. *Action for Slander*
7. The Ware Case 38. *Return to Yesterday* 40.
onvoy 40. Freedom Radio 41. Breach of Promise
1. The Flemish Farm 43. Shipbuilders 43. *On
pproval* 44 (also d). The List of Adrian Messenger
3.

¶ Hollywood is a chain gang and we lose the will
to escape. The links of the chain are forged
ot with cruelties but with luxuries. – *C.B. 1933*

rook, Faith (1922–).
ritish actress of stage, screen and TV; daughter of
live Brook.
Jungle Book 42. Uneasy Terms 48. Wicked as
hey Come 56. Chase a Crooked Shadow 57. The
hirty-Nine Steps 59. To Sir With Love 66. North
ea Hijack 80. The Sea Wolves 80. The Razor's
dge 83. Sins (TV) 86. The Two Mrs Grenvilles
V) 86, etc.

rook, Lesley (1916–).
ritish leading lady of a few sentimental dramas
f the 40s.
The Vulture 37. Dead Men Tell No Tales 39. Rose
f Tralee 41. Variety Jubilee 42. I'll Walk Beside
ou 43. The Trojan Brothers 46. House of Darkness
8, etc.

rook, Lyndon (1926–).
ritish actor of stage, screen and TV; son of Clive
rook.
Train of Events 49. The Purple Plain 54. Reach
or the Sky 56. Innocent Sinners 58. Song
ithout End (US) 60. Invasion 66. Pope Joan 72.
he Hireling 73. Plenty 85. Defence of the Realm
5, etc.

rook, Sir Peter (1925–).
ritish stage director whose film experiments have
een largely unsuccessful.
The Beggar's Opera 52. Moderato Cantabile 60.
ord of the Flies 63. The Marat-Sade 66. Tell Me
ies 67. King Lear 70. Meetings with Remarkable
Men 77. Carmen 83. The Mahabharata 89.

¶ We've had an enormous amount of trips into
people's private visions. They're played out:
's exactly what's true of nudity, when you've
een one you've seen them all. – *P.B.*

Brook-Jones, Elwyn (1911–1962).
Thickset British character actor usually seen in
villainous roles.
Dangerous Moonlight 40. Tomorrow We Live
42. Odd Man Out 46. The Three Weird Sisters 48.
I'll Get You For This 50. Beau Brummell 54. The
Pure Hell of St Trinian's 61, etc.

Brooke, Hillary (1914–) (Beatrice Peterson).
Statuesque, blonde American leading lady of 40s
co-features; on TV in the 50s in the much revived
Abbott and Costello series.
New Faces of 1937. Eternally Yours 39.
Unfinished Business 41. Sherlock Holmes and the
Voice of Terror 42. Lady in the Dark 44. Practically
Yours 44. Ministry of Fear 44. *The Woman in Green*
45. Road to Utopia 45. Strange Journey 46. Big
Town 47. Big Town After Dark 47. Let's Live Again
48. Africa Screams 49. The Admiral was a Lady 50.
Insurance Investigator 51. Confidence Girl 52.
Abbott and Costello Meet Captain Kidd 52.
Mexican Manhunt 53. Dragon's Gold 54. The
House Across the Lake (GB) 54. Bengazi 55.
Spoilers of the Forest 57, many others.
TV series: My Little Margie 52–55. The Abbott
and Costello Show 53–54.

Brooke-Taylor, Tim (1940–).
British light comedian, one of The Goodies. Mostly
on radio and TV.
Twelve Plus One 70. The Statue 70. Willy
Wonka and the Chocolate Factory 70.

Brooks, Albert (1947–) (Albert Einstein).
American director, actor and screenwriter of
sharply observed comedies. He is the son of radio
comedian Parkyakarkus (Harry Einstein).
Taxi Driver (a) 76. Real Life 79. Private
Benjamin (a) 80. Modern Romance 81. Twilight
Zone: The Movie (a) 83. Unfaithfully Yours (a) 84.
Lost in America 85. Broadcast News (a) (AAN) 87.
Defending Your Life 91. I'll Do Anything 94. The
Scout (& co-w) 94, etc.

Brooks, Geraldine (1925–1977) (Geraldine
Stroock).
Intense young American actress of the 40s; never
fulfilled her promise. She was married to writer
Budd Schulberg.
Possessed 47. Cry Wolf 47. The Younger Brothers
49. *The Reckless Moment* 49. Challenge for Lassie
50. Volcano 50. The Green Glove 52. Street of
Sinners 56. Johnny Tiger 66, etc.
TV series: Faraday and Co. 73. The Dumplings
76.

Brooks, Hazel (1924–).
American second lead of the mid-40s. She was
formerly married to art director Cedric Gibbons.
Body and Soul 47. Sleep My Love 48.

Brooks, James L. (1940–).
American writer-director and producer.
Terms of Endearment (AAw, AAd) 83.
Broadcast News (wd) (AAN) 87. Big (p) 88. Say
Anything (p) 89. The War of the Roses (p) 89. I'll
Do Anything (p, wd) 94, etc.

Brooks, Jean (1921–).
Stylish-looking American leading lady who
worked briefly for RKO in the 40s.
The Seventh Victim 43. The Leopard Man 43.
The Falcon and the Co-Eds 44. Two O'Clock
Courage 46. The Falcon's Alibi 46, etc.

Brooks, Leslie (1922–) (Leslie Gettman).
American leading lady of the 40s.
Undercover Agent 42. Nine Girls 44. Tonight

and Every Night 45. The Cobra Strikes 48. Romance
on the High Seas 48, etc.

Brooks, Louise (1906–1985).
American leading lady of the 20s who made her
best films in Germany and remained an attractive
critical enigma.
Autobiography: 1982, *Lulu in Hollywood* (with
Hollis Alpert).
■ The Street of Forgotten Men 25. The American
Venus 26. A Social Celebrity 26. It's the Old Army
Game 26. The Show Off 26. Just Another Blonde
26. Love 'em and Leave 'em 27. Evening Clothes
27. Rolled Stockings 27. The City Gone Wild 27.
Now We're in the Air 27. *A Girl in Every Port* 28.
Beggars of Life 28. *Pandora's Box* (Ger.) 29. The
Canary Murder Case 29. *Diary of a Lost Girl* (Ger.)
30. Prix de Beauté (Fr.) 30. It Pays to Advertise
31. God's Gift to Women 31. Empty Saddles 36.
When You're in Love 36. King of Gamblers 37.
Overland Stage Raiders 38.

¶ Not one woman exerted more magic, not one
had her genius of interpretation. – *Ado Kyrou,
1957*

Her favourite form of exercise was walking off
a movie set, which she did with the insouciance
of a little girl playing hopscotch. – *Anita Loos*

Brooks, Mel (1926–) (Melvin Kaminsky).
American writer-producer-director of off-beat
comedies.
■ The Producers 68. Putney Swope (a only) 69.
The Twelve Chairs (also acted) 70. *Blazing Saddles*
(also acted) 74. *Young Frankenstein* 74. Silent Movie
(also acted) 76. High Anxiety (also acted) 78. The
Muppet Movie (a only) 79. History of the World
Part One (also acted) 81. To Be or Not to Be (pa)
83. Spaceballs 87. Life Stinks 91. Robin Hood: Men
in Tights (a, p, wd) 93. The Little Rascals (a) 94.

¶ If you got it, flaunt it. – *M.B.*
When I write, I keep Tolstoy around because
I want great limits. I want big thinking. – *M.B.*
The death of Hollywood is Mel Brooks and
special effects. If Mel Brooks had come up in my
time he wouldn't have qualified to be a busboy.
– *Joseph L. Mankiewicz*

Brooks, Phyllis (1914–) (Phyllis Weiler).
Blonde American leading lady of co-features in the
30s and 40s.
I've Been Around 34. McFadden's Flats 35. You
Can't Have Everything 37. Rebecca of Sunnybrook
Farm 38. Charlie Chan in Reno 39. Slightly
Honourable 40. *The Shanghai Gesture* 41. Hi Ya Sailor
43. The Unseen 45. High Powered 45, etc.

Brooks, Rand (1918–).
American leading man, usually in minor films.
Gone with the Wind 39. Florian 40. Son of
Monte Cristo 41. Joan of Arc 47. The Steel Fist 52.
Man from the Black Hills 56. Comanche Station
60. The Sex Symbol (TV) 74, etc.
TV series: Rin Tin Tin 54–56.

Brooks, Ray (1939–).
British leading man with repertory experience.
HMS Defiant 62. Play it Cool 62. Some People
63. *The Knack* 65. Daleks Invasion Earth 2150 AD
66. Alice's Adventures in Wonderland 72. Tiffany
Jones 73. House of Whipcord 74. Tiffany Jones 76.
Death of an Expert Witness (TV) 85, etc.
TV series: Growing Pains 92–93.

Brooks, Richard (1912–1992).
American writer-director whose reputation was
somewhat higher than his films seem to justify.

However, he wrote one of the best novels about Hollywood, *The Producer*.

■ White Savage (w only) 42. Cobra Woman (w only) 44. Swell Guy (w only) 46. The Killers (co-w only) 46. Brute Force (w only) 47. Crossfire (oa only) 47. To the Victor (w only) 48. Key Largo (w only) 48. Any Number Can Play (w only) 49. *Crisis* 50. Mystery Street (w only) 50. Storm Warning (co-w only) 50. The Light Touch 51. Deadline 52. Battle Circus 52. The Last Time I Saw Paris (d only) 54. Take the High Ground (d only) 54. The Flame and the Flesh (d only) 54. *The Blackboard Jungle* (AANw) 55. *The Last Hunt* 56. The Catered Affair (d only) 56. Something of Value 57. The Brothers Karamazov 58. Cat on a Hot Tin Roof (AANw, d) 58. *Elmer Gantry* (AAw) 60. Sweet Bird of Youth 62. Lord Jim (& p) 65. The Professionals (& p) (AANw, d) 66. *In Cold Blood* (& p) (AANw, d) 67. The Happy Ending (& p) 70. Dollars (& p) 72. Bite The Bullet (& p) 75. Looking for Mr Goodbar 77. Wrong Is Right 82. Fever Pitch 85.

¶ Although most of his films display something of value on first viewing, none can take the high ground in retrospect. – *Andrew Sarris, 1968*

Brophy, Edward S. (1895–1960).
American character actor, often a gangster or a very odd kind of valet: a rotund, cigar-chewing little man in a bowler hat, oddly likeable despite his pretence of toughness.

Those Three French Girls 30. *The Champ* 31. Freaks 32. What, No Beer? 33. *The Thin Man* 34. Death on the Diamond 34. Mad Love (miscast as a murderer) 35. Remember Last Night 35. Strike Me Pink 36. Kelly the Second 36. *A Slight Case of Murder* 37. You Can't Cheat an Honest Man 39. Calling Philo Vance 40. Buy Me That Town 41. All Through the Night 42. Broadway 42. Cover Girl 44. The Thin Man Goes Home 44. The Falcon in San Francisco (and series) 45. *Wonder Man* 45. It Happened on Fifth Avenue 47. *The Last Hurrah* 58, many others.

Brosnan, Pierce (1951–).
Irish leading man of the matinée-idol type. In 1994, he was chosen to replace Timothy Dalton as James Bond.

The Long Good Friday 80. The Manions of America (TV) 81. Nancy Astor (TV) 81. Nomads 85. The Fourth Protocol 86. Noble House (TV) 87. The Deceivers 88. Taffin 88. The Heist (TV) 89. Mister Johnson 90. Victim of Love 91. Murder 101 (TV) 91. The Lawnmower Man 92. Live Wire 92. Mrs Doubtfire 93. Don't Talk to Strangers (TV) 94. Love Affair 94. Golden Eye 95, etc.

TV series: Remington Steele 82–87.

¶ I don't see myself as a hunk of the month – *P.B.*
A new Cary Grant, sexy but suave, manly though mannered, with subtlety instead of slapstick. – *People*

brothels
were reasonably prominent in silent films, but the Hays Code banished them and for many years one had to look to the French for such revelations as were to be found in *Le Plaisir* and *Adua et sa Compagnie*. In the 60s, however, the doors opened. Comic Victorian brothels were shown in *The Assassination Bureau* and *The Best House in London*, and a French version in *Lady L. Ulysses* showed the Dublin version. *A House is not a Home* told the 'true' story of Polly Adler. The brothel in *The Balcony* was symbolic, in *House of a Thousand Dolls* fantastic, in *How Sweet It Is* charming, in *Games That Lovers Play* whimsical, in *The Last Detail* grimly realistic. *Walk on the Wild Side* concentrated on the depressing aspects and even sported a lesbian madam. *Pretty Baby* had a young girl growing up in a brothel and being sold for the night to the highest bidder. Nowadays every western has one, notably *Waterhole Three, Five Card Stud, Hang 'em High, McCabe and Mrs Miller, Dirty Dingus Magee, The Cheyenne Social Club, The Ballad of Cable Hogue*, and *Unforgiven*; nor are police thrillers such as *Badge 343* complete without them.

Brough, Mary (1863–1934).
British character comedienne usually seen as battleaxe or suspicious landlady, especially in the Aldwych farces. In films from 1914.

The Amazing Quest of Ernest Bliss 20. Squibs Wins the Calcutta Sweep 22. A Sister to Assist 'er 22 and 27. Dawn 28. *Rookery Nook* 30. On Approval 30. Tons of Money 31. Plunder 31. A Night Like This 32. Thark 32. *A Cuckoo in the Nest* 33. Up to the Neck 33. Turkey Time 33, etc.

Broughton, Bruce (1945–).
American composer, from television.

Ice Pirates 83. The Prodigal 84. Silverado (AAN) 85. Young Sherlock Holmes 85. Sweet Liberty 86. The Monster Squad 87. Square Dance 87. Harry and the Hendersons 87. Big Shots 87. The Presidio 88. The Rescue 88. Moonwalker 88. Last Rites 88. Jacknife 89. Betsy's Wedding 90. The Rescuers Down Under 90. All I Want for Christmas 91. Honey, I Blew Up The Kid 92. Homeward Bound: The Incredible Journey 93. So I Married an Axe Murderer 93. Holy Matrimony 94. Tombstone 94. Baby's Day Out 94, etc.

Brown, Barry (1951–1978).
American leading man who shot himself.

Flesh 68. Halls of Anger 70. Escape of the Birdmen (TV) 71. The Great Northfield Minnesota Raid 71. Bad Company 72. Daisy Miller 74. The Disappearance of Aimee (TV) 76. Piranha 78, etc.

Brown, Blair (1948–).
American leading lady.

The Choirboys 77. Wheels (TV) 78. And I Alone Survived (TV) 78. The Child Stealer (TV) 79. Altered States 80. One Trick Pony 80. Continental Divide 81. Kennedy (TV) (as Jackie) 83. A Flash of Green 84. Stealing Home 88. Strapless 88. Passed Away 92, etc.

Brown, Bruce (1938–).
American director, cinematographer and editor, mainly of surfing documentaries, from 1958. *The Endless Summer* was a surprising box-office success, earning more than $30 million.

The Endless Summer 66. On Any Sunday (AAN) 71. The Endless Summer II 94.

Brown, Bryan (1947–).
Australian leading actor. He is married to actress Rachel Ward.

Newsfront 79. Breaker Morant 79. The Chant of Jimmie Blacksmith 80. Winter of Our Dreams 81. A Town Like Alice (TV) 81. Far East 82. The Thorn Birds (TV) 83. Kim (TV) 83. Give My Regards to Broad Street 84. Parker 85. Eureka Stockade (TV) 85. The Empty Beach 85. F/X 85. Rebel 85. The Good Wife 86, Taipan 86. The Shiralee (TV) 87. Cocktail 88. Gorillas in the Mist 88. Blood Oath 90. Sweet Talker (& story) 91. FX2 – the Deadly Art of Illusion 91. Blame It On The Bellboy 92. Devlin 92. The Last Hit (TV) 93, etc.

Brown, Charles D. (1887–1948).
Bland-faced American character actor who played scores of detectives, officials and executives.

The Dance of Life 29. Murder by the Clock 31. The Woman I Stole 33. It Happened One Night 34. Thoroughbreds Don't Cry 37. Charlie Chan in Reno 39. The Grapes of Wrath 39. Fingers at the Window 42. Jam Session 44. The Killers 46. Merton of the Movies 47, many others.

Brown, Clarence (1890–1987).
American director, with MGM and Garbo for many years; most at home with sentimental themes and busy pictorial values.

■ The Great Redeemer 20. The Last of the Mohicans 20. The Light in the Dark 22. Don't Marry for Money 23. The Acquittal 23. The Signal Tower 24. Butterfly 24. Smouldering Fires 25. *The Eagle* 25. The Goose Woman 25. Kiki 26. Flesh and the Devil 26. Trail of 98 28. A Woman of Affairs 29. Wonder of Women 29. Navy Blues 29. *Anna Christie* (AAN) 30. Romance (AAN) 30. Inspiration 31. A Free Soul 31. Possessed 31. Emma 32. Lett Lynton 32. The Son Daughter 32. Looking Forward 33. Night Flight 33. Sadie McKee 34. Chained 34. *Anna Karenina* 35. Ah Wilderness 35. Wife Versus Secretary 36. The Gorgeous Hussy 36. Conquest 37. Of Human Hearts 38. Idiot's Delight 38. *The Rains Came* 39. Edison the Man 40. Come Live with Me (& p) 41. They Met in Bombay 41. *The Human Comedy* (& p) (AAN) 43. The White Cliffs of Dover 44. National Velvet (AAN) 44. *The Yearling* (AAN) 46. Song of Love (& p) 47. *Intruder in the Dust* (& p) 49. To Please a Lady (& p) 50. Angels in the Outfield (& p) 51. It's a Big Country (part) 51. When in Rome (& p) 51. Plymouth Adventure 52. Never Let Me Go (p only) 53.

✪ For persuading a commercially minded studio to let his films represent its cultural pretensions. *Intruder in the Dust.*

¶ His career is not without a certain amiability in its evolution from German Expressionism to American Gothic. – *Andrew Sarris, 1968*

Brown, David (1916–).
American producer, a New York journalist who became story editor at Fox and later joined Richard Zanuck in Zanuck-Brown, which made *The Sting* and *Jaws*.

Jaws 2 78. The Island 80. The Verdict (AAN) 82. Cocoon 85. Cocoon: The Return 88. Driving Miss Daisy (AA) 89, etc.

Brown, Ed.
American cinematographer.

The Hot Rock 72. Lovin' Molly 74. The Education of Sonny Carson 74, etc.

Brown, George H. (1913–).
British producer, former production manager.

Sleeping Car to Trieste 48. The Chiltern Hundreds 50. The Seekers 54. Jacqueline 56. Dangerous Exile 57. Tommy the Toreador 60. Murder at the Gallop 63. Guns at Batasi 64. The Trap 66. Finders Keepers 66. Assault 70. Revenge 71. Innocent Bystanders 72. Open Season 74, etc.

Brown, Georg Stanford (1943–).
American character actor and TV director.

The Comedians 67. Dayton's Devils 68. Bullitt 68. The Forbin Project 70. The Man 72. Wild in the Sky 72. Roots (TV) 77. The Night the City Screamed (TV) 80. In Defense of Kids (TV) 83. The Jesse Owens Story (TV) 84, etc.

TV series: The Rookies 72–74.

Brown, Georgia (1933–1992) (Lilian Klot).
British cabaret songstress in occasional films.

The Fixer 67. Lock Up Your Daughters 69. The Raging Moon 71. Nothing but the Night 73. The Bawdy Adventures of Tom Jones 76. The Seven Per Cent Solution 77, etc.

Brown, Harry (1917–1986).
American novelist and screenwriter, mainly on war themes.

The True Glory (co-w) 45. A Walk in the Sun (oa) 46. Arch of Triumph 48. Sands of Iwo Jima (AAN) 49. A Place in the Sun (co-w, AA) 51. Bugles in the Afternoon 52. The Sniper (co-w) 52. Eight Iron Men 52. All the Brothers Were Valiant (co-w) 53. D-Day Sixth of June (co-w) 56. Between Heaven and Hell (co-w) 57. El Dorado (oa) 66, etc.

Brown, Harry Joe (1892–1972).
American producer with long experience in all branches of show business; latterly concentrated on Randolph Scott westerns.

Parade of the West (d only) 30. Madison Square Garden (d only) 32. Sitting Pretty (d only) 33. Captain Blood 35. Alexander's Ragtime Band 38. The Rains Came 39. Young People 40. Western Union 41. Knickerbocker Holiday (& d) 44. Gunfighters 47. Fortunes of Captain Blood 50. Hangman's Knot 52. Three Hours to Kill 54. Screaming Mimi 58. Ride Lonesome 59, many others.

Brown, James (1920–1992).
Stalwart American supporting actor, in many westerns of the 40s and 50s.

The Forest Rangers 42. Corvette K225 44. Objective Burma 45. The Fabulous Texan 47. Sands of Iwo Jima 50. Springfield Rifle 52. The Woman They Almost Lynched 53. A Star Is Born 54. The Police Dog Story 61. Irma La Douce 63. Town Tamer 65. Whiffs 75. Mean Johnny Barrows 76, etc.

TV series: Rin Tin Tin 54–56.

Brown, Jim (1935–).
American leading man, former athlete.
■ Rio Conchos 64. The Dirty Dozen 67. Dark of the Sun 68. The Split 68. Ice Station Zebra 68. Riot 68. 100 Rifles 69. Tick Tick Tick 70. The Grasshopper 70. El Condor 70. Kenner 71. Black Gunn 72. Slaughter 72. Slaughter's Big Rip-off 73. I Escaped from Devil's Island 73. The Slams 74. Three the Hard Way 74. Take a Hard Ride 75. Kid Vengeance 77. Fingers 78. One Down Two to Go 81. Pacific Inferno 84. Slam Dunk 87. The Running Man 87. I'm Gonna Git You Sucka 88. L.A. Heat 88. Crack House 89. L.A. Vice 89. Twisted Justice 90. Deadly Avenger 92.

Brown, Joe (1941–).
Amiable British pop singer, in occasional films.
What a Crazy World 63. Three Hats for Lisa 65, etc.

Brown, Joe E. (1892–1973).
Wide-mouthed American star comedian of the 30s, with background in circus, vaudeville and basketball.

Autobiography: 1956, Laughter is a Wonderful Thing.
■ Crooks Can't Wait 28. Me, Gangster 28. Road House 28. Dressed to Kill 28. The Circus Kid 28. Hit of the Show 28. Take Me Home 28. Burlesque 28. Don't Be Jealous 28. In Old Arizona 29. Sunny Side Up 29. Molly and Me 29. Sally 29. My Lady's Past 29. On with the Show 29. Painted Faces 29. The Cockeyed World 29. The Ghost Talks 29. Protection 29. Up the River 30. Maybe It's Love 30.

Song of the West 30. Born Reckless 30. City Girl 30. Hold Everything 30. The Lottery Bride 30. Top Speed 30. Going Wild 31. Local Boy Makes Good 31. Broadminded 31. Sit Tight 31. The Tenderfoot 32. Fireman Save My Child 32. You Said a Mouthful 32. Elmer the Great 32. Son of a Sailor 32. The Circus Clown 34. Six Day Bike Rider 34. A Very Honourable Guy 34. A Midsummer Night's Dream 35. Alibi Ike 35. Bright Lights 36. Polo Joe 36. Sons of Guns 36. Earthworm Tractors 36. Fit for a King 37. When's Your Birthday 37. Flirting with Fate 38. The Gladiator 38. Wide Open Faces 38. Beware Spooks 39. One Thousand Dollars a Touchdown 39. So You Won't Talk 40. Shut My Big Mouth 42. The Daring Young Man 42. Joan of Ozark 42. Chatterbox 43. Pin Up Girl 44. Hollywood Canteen 44. Casanova in Burlesque 44. The Tender Years 49. Showboat 51. Around the World in 80 Days 56. Some Like It Hot 59. A Comedy of Terrors 63. It's a Mad Mad Mad Mad World 63.

Brown, John (Johnny) Mack (1904–1974).
American leading man of the 30s, former football star.

The Bugle Call 26. The Divine Woman 27. Our Dancing Daughters 28. Coquette 29. Jazz Heaven 29. Billy the Kid 30. The Secret Six 31. The Last Flight 31. Saturday's Millions 33. Female 33. Belle of the Nineties 34. Riding the Apache Trail 36. Wells Fargo 37. Bad Man from Red Butte 40. Ride 'Em Cowboy 41. The Right to Live 45. Stampede 49. Short Grass 50. The Bounty Killer 65. Apache Uprising 65, many others.

Brown, John Moulder:
see Moulder Brown, John.

Brown, Karl (1897–1990).
American cinematographer of the 20s; retired early.

Autobiography: 1976, Adventures with D.W. Griffith.
The Birth of a Nation (2nd unit) 15. The Fourteenth Man 20. Gasoline Gus 21. The Dictator 22. The Covered Wagon 23. Ruggles of Red Gap 23. Merton of the Movies 24. Beggar on Horseback 25. Pony Express 25. Mannequin 26, etc.

Brown, Nacio Herb (1896–1964).
American light composer who usually supplied the music for Arthur Freed's lyrics: 'Broadway Melody', 'Singin' in the Rain', 'Good Morning', 'You Are My Lucky Star', many others.

The Broadway Melody 29. Good News 30. Going Hollywood 33. Student Tour 34. Broadway Melody of 1936 35. Broadway Melody of 1938 37. Greenwich Village 44. Singin' in the Rain 52, etc.

Brown, Pamela (1917–1975).
British stage actress in occasional films, usually in haughty or eccentric roles. She was married to Paul Copley.

One of Our Aircraft Is Missing 42. I Know Where I'm Going 45. Tales of Hoffman 51. The Second Mrs Tanqueray 52. Personal Affair 53. Richard III 56. The Scapegoat 59. Becket 64. Secret Ceremony 68. Wuthering Heights 70. On a Clear Day You Can See Forever 70. Lady Caroline Lamb 72. Dracula (TV) 73, etc.

Brown, Phil (1916–1973).
American second lead, usually in diffident roles; moved to Europe in 1950.

I Wanted Wings 41. Calling Dr Gillespie 42. The Impatient Years 44. Without Reservations 46. The Killers 46. If You Knew Susie 48. Moonrise 49. Obsession 50. The Green Scarf 54. Camp on Blood

Island 58. The Bedford Incident 65. Tropic of Cancer 69, etc.

Brown, Robert (c. 1918–).
Burly British actor of stage, TV and film who played 'M' in the Bond films of the 80s.

Helen of Troy 55. A Hill in Korea 56. Campbell's Kingdom 57. Ben Hur 59. Sink the Bismarck 60. The Masque of the Red Death 64. One Million Years BC 66. Private Road 71. Warlords of Atlantis 78. Octopussy 83. A View to a Kill 85. The Living Daylights 87. Licence to Kill 89, etc.

TV series: Ivanhoe 57.

Brown, Robert N. (aka Toby Brown).
American editor.

The Mack 73. Damien: Omen II 78. The Amityville Horror 79. Brubaker 80. The Beast Within 82. The Pope of Greenwich Village 84. The Lost Boys 87. Cousins 89. Vital Signs 90. Flatliners 90. Dying Young 91. Lethal Weapon 3 92, etc.

Brown, Rowland (1901–1963).
American director whose career waned curiously after a promising start.
■ Quick Millions 31. Hell's Highway 32. Blood Money 33. The Devil is a Sissy (co-w only) 37.

Brown, Roy 'Chubby' (1945–) (Royston Vasey).
Northern English comic, a former drummer, billed as 'the rudest, crudest, filthiest comedian in the world'. He made his first film, which was publicized as 'the most offensive movie known to man', following the success of three videos of his stage act, which are said to have sold 750,000 copies.

UFO: The Movie 93.

¶ All I want to do is make people laugh, and I've found if you tell men about the size of women's tits and arses, they laugh; if you tell women about men's sexual exploits, their little bollocks, not being circumcised, women laugh. – R.C.B.

Brown, Tom (1913–1990).
American juvenile lead of the 30s; the 'boy next door' type. Re-emerged in the 60s as one of the villagers in the long-running TV series Gunsmoke.

The Hoosier Schoolmaster 24. The Lady Lies 29. Queen High 30. Tom Brown of Culver 32. Three Cornered Moon 33. Judge Priest 34. Anne of Green Gables 34. Freckles 35. I'd Give My Life 36. Maytime 37. In Old Chicago 38. Duke of West Point 38. Sergeant Madden 39. Sandy is a Lady 40. The Pay Off 43. The House on 92nd Street 45. Buck Privates Come Home 47. Duke of Chicago 49. The Quiet Gun 57, many others.

TV series: Mr Lucky 59–60.

Brown, Vanessa (1928–) (Smylla Brind).
American juvenile leading lady of a few late 40s films; usually demure.

Margie 46. The Late George Apley 47. Mother Wore Tights 47. The Foxes of Harrow 47. The Heiress 49. Tarzan and the Slave Girl 50. The Bad and the Beautiful 52. Rosie 68. Bless the Beasts and Children 71. The Witch Who Came from the Sea 76, etc.

TV series: My Favourite Husband 54. Rosie 67. Bless the Beasts and Children 71. The Witch Who Came from the Sea 75, etc.

Brown, Wally (1898–1961).
American comedian, a fast-talking vaudevillian who teamed with Alan Carney (qv) in a few comedy second features of the 40s.

Adventures of a Rookie 44. Rookies in Burma

44. Step Lively 44. Zombies on Broadway 45. Genius at Work 45. As Young As You Feel 51. The High and the Mighty 54. The Absent-minded Professor 61, etc.

TV series: Cimarron City 58.

Browne, Coral (1913–1991).
Australian stage actress long in Britain, usually in worldly comedy roles; films few. She married actor Vincent Price in 1974.

The Amateur Gentleman 36. Black Limelight 38. Let George Do It 40. Piccadilly Incident 46. *Auntie Mame* (US) 58. The Roman Spring of Mrs Stone 61. Dr Crippen 64. *The Killing of Sister George* 68. Theatre of Blood 73. The Drowning Pool 75. An Englishman Abroad (TV) 83. American Dreamer 84. Dreamchild 85, etc.

TV series: Time Express 79.

Browne, Irene (1891–1965).
British stage actress, usually in dignified roles; films few.

The Letter 29. Cavalcade 33. Berkeley Square 33. The Amateur Gentleman 36. Pygmalion 38. The Prime Minister 40. *Quartet* 48. Madeleine 50. All at Sea 57. Rooney 58, etc.

Browne, Leslie (1958–).
American ballet dancer and occasional actress.

The Turning Point (AAN) 77. Nijinksy 80. Dancers 87, etc.

Browne, Roscoe Lee (1925–).
American character actor, a former athlete.

The Connection 62. The Cool World 64. *Topaz* 69. *The Liberation of L. B. Jones* 70. The Cowboys 72. Cisco Pike 72. Superfly Two 73. Logan's Run 76. Twilight's Last Gleaming 77. Nothing Personal 80. Jumpin' Jack Flash 86. Legal Eagles 86. Moon 44 91. The Mambo Kings 92. Eddie Presley 93. Naked in New York 93, etc.

TV series: McCoy 75–76. Miss Winslow and Son 79. Soap 80–81. Falcon Crest 88.

Browning, Ricou (1930–).
American diver and stuntman who became a specialist in underwater direction for Ivan Tors.

The Creature from the Black Lagoon (also played title role) 54. Flipper 63. Around the World Under the Sea 66. Lady in Cement 68, etc.

Browning, Tod (1882–1962).
American director remembered chiefly for his horror films of the 20s and early 30s; revaluation has made them less striking than once was thought.

The Brazen Beauty 18. The Virgin of Stamboul 20. Under Two Flags 22. The White Tiger 23. The Unholy Three 25. The Mystic (& w) 25. The Unknown 27. *London After Midnight* 27. West of Zanzibar 28. Where East is East 29. The Thirteenth Chair 29. The Unholy Three (sound remake) 30. *Dracula* 30. Iron Man 31. *Freaks* 32. Fast Workers 33. Mark of the Vampire 35. *The Devil Doll* 36. Miracles for Sale 39, etc.

Brownlow, Kevin (1938–).
British producer-director who made his first film, *It Happened Here*, on a shoestring budget over seven years. It was released in 1966. Published 1969 *The Parade's Gone By*, a collection of interviews with silent movie stars. His 1975 film *Winstanley* was a clever but cheerless historical reconstruction; his 1979 book *The War, The West and The Wilderness* was another classic tome of research into silent filming.

TV series: *Hollywood* 79.

Bruce, Brenda (1918–).
British stage, TV and occasionally screen actress.

Millions Like Us 43. They Came to a City 45. Piccadilly Incident 46. My Brother's Keeper 48. Marry Me 52. The Final Test 53. Law and Disorder 57. Nightmare 63. The Uncle 65. That'll Be the Day 73. Swallows and Amazons 74. All Creatures Great and Small 74. Steaming 81. December Bride 90. Splitting Heirs 93. Harnessing Peacocks (TV) 93, etc.

Bruce, David (1914–1976) (Marden McBroom).
American light leading man familiar in Universal films during World War II.

The Sea Hawk 40. Singapore Woman 42. The Mad Ghoul 43. Ladies Courageous 44. Christmas Holiday 44. Can't Help Singing 44. Salome Where She Danced 45. Lady on a Train 45. Prejudice 49. Masterson of Kansas 55, etc.

TV series: Beulah 52.

Bruce, George (1898–).
American screenwriter.

Navy Blue and Gold 37. The Crowd Roars 38. The Duke of West Point 38. The Man in the Iron Mask 39. Son of Monte Cristo 40. South of Pago Pago 40. The Corsican Brothers 41. Miss Annie Rooney 42. Stand By for Action 43. Salute to the Marines 43. Two Years Before the Mast 46. Killer McCoy 47. Walk a Crooked Mile 48. Rogues of Sherwood Forest 50. Lorna Doone 51. Valentino 51. Kansas City Confidential 53. Solomon and Sheba 59, many others.

Bruce, Lenny (1926–1966) (Leonard Alfred Schneider).
Dirty-talking American nightclub comedian, a nine-day wonder who was impersonated on film by Dustin Hoffman in *Lenny*.

¶ Lenny, despite what his cultists and the Hoffman movie said, was dirty and sick. He had no redeeming social values. – *James Bacon*

Bruce, Nigel (1895–1953).
Tubby British comedy actor, mainly in Hollywood from 1934; usually played well-meaning upper-class buffoons, and was the screen's most memorable Dr Watson.

■ Red Aces 29. Birds of Prey 30. The Squeaker 31. Escape 31. The Calendar 31. Lord Camber's Ladies 32. The Midshipmaid 32. Channel Crossing 32. I Was a Spy 33. Springtime for Henry 34. Stand Up and Cheer 34. Coming Out Party 34. Murder in Trinidad 34. The Lady is Willing 34. Treasure Island 34. The Scarlet Pimpernel 35. *Becky Sharp* 35. Jalna 35. She 35. The Man Who Broke the Bank at Monte Carlo 35. The Trail of the Lonesome Pine 36. Under Two Flags 36. The White Angel 36. The Charge of the Light Brigade 36. Follow Your Heart 36. Make Way for a Lady 36. The Man I Married 36. Thunder in the City 37. The Last of Mrs Cheyney 37. The Baroness and the Butler 38. Kidnapped 38. Suez 38. *The Hound of the Baskervilles* 39. The Adventures of Sherlock Holmes 39. The Rains Came 39. *Rebecca* 40. Adventure in Diamonds 40. *The Bluebird* 40. Susan and God 40. Lillian Russell 40. A Dispatch from Reuters 40. Hudson's Bay 40. Playgirl 41. Free and Easy 41. The Chocolate Soldier 41. This Woman is Mine 41. Suspicion 41. Roxie Hart 42. This Above All 42. Eagle Squadron 42. Sherlock Holmes and the Voice of Terror 42. Sherlock Holmes and the Secret Weapon 42. Journey for Margaret 42. Sherlock Holmes in Washington 43. Crazy House (cameo) 43. Forever and a Day 43. Lassie Come Home 43. Sherlock Holmes Faces Death 43. Follow the Boys 44. The Pearl of Death 44. Spider

Woman 44. Gypsy Wildcat 44. *The Scarlet Claw* 44. *Frenchman's Creek* 44. Son of Lassie 45. *House of Fear* 45. The Corn is Green 45. The Woman in Green 45. Pursuit to Algiers 45. Terror by Night 46. Dressed to Kill 46. The Two Mrs Carrolls 47. The Exile 47. Julia Misbehaves 48. Vendetta 50. Savage Drums 51. Hong Kong 51. Bwana Devil 53. *Limelight* 53. World for Ransom 53.
🟢 For regrettably but amusingly fixing the image of the upper-class English dodderer. *Rebecca.*

Bruce, Tony (1910–1937).
Scottish leading actor, who left the Navy to star in Anthony Asquith's *Tell England* 31.

Mr Bill the Conqueror 32. Brother Alfred 32. Lucky Girl 32. Diamond Cut Diamond 32. Men of Tomorrow 32. Windjammer 35, etc.

Bruce, Virginia (1910–1982) (Helen Virginia Briggs).
American light leading lady of the 30s.

Woman Trap 29. The Love Parade 29. Safety in Numbers 30. Hell Divers 31. The Wet Parade 32. Kongo 32. Jane Eyre (title role) 34. Dangerous Corner 34. Escapade 35. Metropolitan 35. The Great Ziegfeld 36. Born to Dance 36. Between Two Women 37. Arsène Lupin Returns 38. Yellow Jack 38. Society Lawyer 39. Flight Angels 40. Invisible Woman 41. Pardon My Sarong 42. Careful Soft Shoulders 42. Action in Arabia 44. Love Honour and Goodbye 45. Night Has a Thousand Eyes 48. The Reluctant Bride (GB) 52. Strangers When We Meet 60, many others.

Bruckheimer, Jerry.
American producer, formerly in advertising. With his partner Don Simpson he headed a company that produced some of the biggest box-office successes of the 80s for Paramount Pictures.

Farewell My Lovely 75. March or Die 77. American Gigolo 80. Defiance 80. Thief 81. Cat People 82. Young Doctors in Love 82, etc.
CO-PRODUCTIONS (with Don Simpson): Flashdance 83. Beverly Hills Cop 84. Thief of Hearts 84. Top Gun 86. Beverly Hills Cop II 87. Days of Thunder 90. The Ref 94, etc.

Bruckman, Clyde (1894–1955).
American writer-director of many silent comedies, especially associated with Keaton, Lloyd and Fields.

Sherlock Jnr (w) 24. *The Navigator* (w) 24. *The General* (wd) 27. *Feet First* (wd) 30. *Movie Crazy* (d) 32. The Man on the Flying Trapeze (d) 35, many others.

Brummell, Beau (1778–1840).
A famous British dandy and politician who has been the subject of two biopics: in 1924 with John Barrymore (directed by Harry Beaumont) and in 1954 with Stewart Granger (directed by Curtis Bernhardt).

Brunel, Adrian (1892–1958).
British director with pleasant reputation in the 20s as an intellectual at large.
Autobiography: 1952, *Nice Work.*

Bookworms (short) 20. The Bump (short) 20. *The Man without Desire* 23. Crossing the Great Sagrada (short) 24. *Blighty* 27. *The Constant Nymph* 27. The Vortex 28. While Parents Sleep 35. The City of Beautiful Nonsense 35. Prison Breaker 36. The Lion Has Wings 39. The Girl Who Forgot 40, etc.

Brunius, Jacques (1906–1967).
French actor, once critic and assistant to Clair and Renoir; later resident in Britain.

L'Age d'Or 30. Partie de Campagne 37. Sea

Devils 53. To Paris with Love 55. Orders to Kill 58, etc.

Bruns, George (1913–).
American composer whose film scores have almost all been for Disney.

Davy Crockett, King of the Wild Frontier 55. Sleeping Beauty (AAN) 59. One Hundred and One Dalmatians 60. Babes in Toyland (AAN) 61. The Sword in the Stone (AAN) 63. The Jungle Book 67. The Love Bug 69. The Aristocats 70. Robin Hood 73. Herbie Rides Again 74, etc.

Bryan, Dora (1923–) (Dora Broadbent).
British stage and film comedienne, specializing in warm-hearted tarts of the cockney or northern variety.

Autobiography: 1987, *According to Dora*.

Odd Man Out 46. The Fallen Idol 48. The Cure for Love 48. The Blue Lamp 50. High Treason 51. Lady Godiva Rides Again 51. Mother Riley Meets the Vampire 52. Time Gentlemen Please 53. Fast and Loose 54. See How They Run 55. Cockleshell Heroes 56. The Green Man 57. Desert Mice 59. The Night We Got the Bird 60. *A Taste of Honey* (BFA: leading role) 61. The Great St Trinian's Train Robbery 66. The Sandwich Man 66. Two a Penny 68. Hands of the Ripper 71. Up the Front 72. Screamtime 83. Apartment Zero 88, etc.

TV series: Mother's Ruin 94.

Bryan, Jane (1918–) (Jane O'Brien).
Sympathetic American leading lady of the later 30s.

■ The Case of the Black Cat 36. Marked Woman 37. Kid Galahad 37. Confession 37. A Slight Case of Murder 38. *The Sisters* 38. Girls on Probation 38. Brother Rat 38. Each Dawn I Die 39. The Old Maid 39. These Glamour Girls 39. *We are Not Alone* 39. Invisible Stripes 40. Brother Rat and a Baby 40.

Bryan, John (1911–1969).
British producer and production designer.

Great Expectations (des) (AA) 46. Pandora and the Flying Dutchman (des) 51. *The Card* 52. The Purple Plain 54. The Spanish Gardener (& w) 56. Windom's Way 57. The Horse's Mouth 58. There Was a Crooked Man 60. Tamahine 62. After the Fox 66. The Touchables 68, etc.

Bryant, Michael (1928–).
Serious-looking British character actor of stage and TV; films occasional.

Life for Ruth 62. The Mindbenders 63. Goodbye Mr Chips 69. Nicholas and Alexandra (as Lenin) 71. Gandhi 81. Sakharov (TV) 84. Girly 87, etc.

Bryant, Nana (1888–1955).
Dignified but friendly American character actress who usually played middle-class mums or rich patrons.

A Feather in Her Hat 35. Theodora Goes Wild 36. Mad About Music 38. Espionage Agent 39. Nice Girl 41. Calling Dr Gillespie 42. The Song of Bernadette 43. Brewster's Millions 45. The Unsuspected 47. Harvey 50. Bright Victory 51. About Mrs Leslie 54. The Private War of Major Benson 55, many others.

TV series: Our Miss Brooks 55.

Brynner, Yul (1915–1985) (Youl Bryner).
Bald-headed international star of somewhat mysterious background: variously alleged to have originated in Switzerland and Russia, but assuredly American by adoption. A Broadway stage success, especially as the king in *The King and I*; long dominant in films though not easy to cast.

■ Port of New York 49. *The King and I* (AA) 56.

The Ten Commandments 56. *Anastasia* 56. *The Brothers Karamazov* 58. The Buccaneer 58. The Journey 58. The Sound and the Fury 59. Solomon and Sheba 59. Once More with Feeling 60. Surprise Package 60. *The Magnificent Seven* 60. The Testament of Orpheus 60. Escape from Zahrain 62. *Taras Bulba* 62. Kings of the Sun 63. Flight from Ashiya 64. *Invitation to a Gunfighter* 64. The Saboteur 65. Cast a Giant Shadow 66. Return of the Seven 66. The Poppy is Also a Flower 66. Triple Cross 66. The Double Man 67. The Long Duel 67. Villa Rides 68. The Madwoman of Chaillot 69. The File of the Golden Goose 69. The Battle of Neretva 70. Indio Sabata 70. The Magic Christian 70. The Light at the Edge of the World 71. Romance of a Horsethief 71. Adios Sabata 71. Catlow 72. Fuzz 72. The Serpent 72. Westworld 73. The Ultimate Warrior 74. Futureworld 76. Anger in his Eyes (Italian) 76.

TV series: *Anna and the King* 72.

☺ For proving that bald is beautiful at the box-office. *The Magnificent Seven*.

¶ People don't know my real self and they're not about to find out. – *Y. B.*

B.S.C.
British Society of Cinematographers, a professional society founded in the 50s, similar in aims to the A.S.C. (qv).

Buchan, John (1875–1940).
British adventure novelist oddly neglected by the cinema apart from *The Thirty-nine Steps*, no version of which bears much resemblance to the original; and a 1927 version of *Huntingtower*.

Buchanan, Edgar (1902–1979).
Jovial American character actor, in innumerable westerns and rustic dramas as hayseed, crooked judge, comic side-kick or straight villain.

My Son is Guilty 39. Arizona 40. The Richest Man in Town 41. The Desperados 42. Destroyer 43. Buffalo Bill 44. The Fighting Guardsman 45. Abilene Town 46. Framed 47. The Black Arrow 48. The Best Man Wins 48. Red Canyon 49. Devil's Doorway 50. The Great Missouri Raid 51. The Big Trees 52. Shane 53. Human Desire 54. Day of the Badman 57. The Sheepman 58. Edge of Eternity 60. Cimarron 61. Ride the High Country 62. McLintock 63. The Rounders 65. Welcome to Hard Times 67. Benji 75, many others.

TV series: Hopalong Cassidy 51–52. Judge Roy Bean 53. Petticoat Junction 63–69. Cade's County 71.

Buchanan, Jack (1891–1957).
Debonair British entertainer, a memorable song-and-dance man of stage and screen in the 20s and 30s: good-looking, long-legged, nasal of voice and debonair in appearance.

Biography: 1978, *Top Hat and Tails* by Michael Marshall.

■ Bulldog Drummond's Third Round 25. Happy Landing 25. Toni 27. Confetti 28. Paris 29. Show of Shows 29. *Monte Carlo* 30. Goodnight Vienna 32. A Man of Mayfair 32. Yes Mr Brown 32. Magic Night 32. *Brewster's Millions* 33. That's a Good Girl 33. That Girl 34. Come out of the Pantry 35. Sons o'Guns 35. When Knights were Bold 36. Limelight 36. Smash and Grab 37. Break the News 37. This'll Make You Whistle 37. The Sky's the Limit 38. *The Gang's All Here* 39. Alias the Bulldog 39. The Middle Watch 39. Bulldog Sees It Through 40. *The Band Wagon* 53. As Long as They're Happy 53. Josephine and Men 55. The Diary of Major Thompson 56.

Buchholz, Horst (1933–).
German leading man, in occasional international films.

Marianne de Ma Jeunesse (debut) 54. Himmel Ohne Sterne 55. King in Shadow 56. The Confessions of Felix Krull 57. Resurrection 58. *Tiger Bay* 59. *The Magnificent Seven* 60. Fanny 61. *One Two Three* 61. Nine Hours to Rama 63. The Empty Canvas 64. Marco the Magnificent 65. That Man in Istanbul 66. Cervantes 66. L'Astragale 68. The Great Waltz 72. The Catamount Killing 75. Raid on Entebbe (TV) 77. Avalanche Express 79. Aphrodite 81. Sahara 83. Code Name: Emerald 85. Aces: Iron Eagle III 92. Faraway, So Close! (In Weiter Ferne, So Nah) 93, etc.

Buchman, Sidney (1902–1975).
American writer-producer of good commercial films.

Matinée Ladies (oa) 27. *The Sign of the Cross* (co-w) 32. I'll Love You Always (w) 35. The King Steps Out (w) 36. *Theodora Goes Wild* (w) 36. *Mr Smith Goes to Washington* (w) 39. The Howards of Virginia (w) 40. *Here Comes Mr Jordan* (w) (AA) 41. *The Talk of the Town* (co-w, AAN) 42. *A Song to Remember* (wp) 45. Over 21 (p) 45. Jolson Sings Again (wp, AANw) 49. Saturday's Hero (w) 51. Cleopatra (w) 63. *The Group* (wp) 66, many others.

Buck, Frank (1888–1950).
American explorer who made several animal films. In 1982 Buck was impersonated by Bruce Boxleitner in a short-lived TV series called *Bring 'Em Back Alive*, based in 1939 Singapore and involving Buck with spies as well as animals.

Appeared in *Africa Screams* 50.

Bring 'Em Back Alive 32. Fang and Claw 36. Jungle Menace 37. Jacare, Killer of the Amazon 42, etc.

Buck, Jules (1917–).
American producer who in the late 50s came to Britain and founded Keep Films with Peter O'Toole.

Fixed Bayonets 51. Treasure of the Golden Condor 53. The Day They Robbed the Bank of England 60. *Becket* 64. Great Catherine 66. The Ruling Class 71, etc.

Buck, Pearl (1892–1973).
American novelist and missionary to the Far East. Works filmed include *The Good Earth*, *Dragon Seed*, *Satan Never Sleeps*.

Buckland, Wilfred (1866–1946).
American art director, with claims to be the first so employed in films. A successful stage designer, he joined Famous Players Lasky in 1914 and worked from Cecil B. De Mille's early films, becoming involved not only in design but in using lighting for dramatic effect. Committed suicide after killing his mentally ill son.

Squaw Man 14. The Ghost Breaker 14. The Virginian 14. Carmen 15. Joan the Woman 16. Stella Maris 18. The Squaw Man 18. Conrad in Search of His Youth 20. Adam's Rib 23. Almost Human 27, many others.

Buckler, Hugh (1870–1936).
English actor, in Hollywood from the 30s. He was the father of actor John Buckler (qv). Both were drowned in a car accident.

The Garden of Resurrection 19. Duke's Son 20. Guy Fawkes 23. Crash Donovan 36. Last of the Mohicans 36. Jungle Princess 36. Lost Horizon 37, etc.

Buckler, John (1896–1936).
English actor who accompanied his father Hugh (qv) to Hollywood in the 30s and died with him in a car accident.

David Copperfield 35. Eight Bells 35. The Black Room 35. Tarzan Escapes 36. The Unguarded Hour 36.

Buckley, Betty (1947–).
American actress and singer, from the Broadway stage.

Carrie 76. Tender Mercies 83. Frantic 88. Another Woman 88, etc.

TV series: Eight Is Enough 77–81.

Buckner, Robert (1906–).
American screenwriter, later producer.

Gold is Where You Find It 38. Jezebel 38. The Oklahoma Kid 39. *Dodge City* 39. Virginia City 39. *Santa Fe Trail* 40. Dive Bomber 41. Yankee Doodle Dandy (AAN) 42. Gentleman Jim (p) 42. Mission to Moscow (p) 43. Confidential Agent (& p) 45. Rogues' Regiment (& p) 48. Sword in the Desert (& p) 49. Bright Victory (& p) 51. Love Me Tender 56. From Hell to Texas (& p) 58. Return of the Gunfighter 68, etc.

Bucquet, Harold S. (1891–1946).
English director in Hollywood.

Young Dr Kildare 39. *On Borrowed Time* 39. The Secret of Dr Kildare 39. We Who Are Young 40. Dr Kildare Goes Home 40. The Penalty 41. Kathleen 41. Calling Dr Gillespie 42. The War Against Mrs Hadley 42. The Adventures of Tartu (GB) 43. Dragon Seed 44. Without Love 45, etc.

Budd, Roy (1949–1993).
British composer and jazz pianist.

Soldier Blue 70. Zeppelin 71. Get Carter 71. Flight of the Doves 71. Pulp 72. The Stone Killer 73. The Internecine Project 74. Paper Tiger 75. Sinbad and the Eye of the Tiger 77. The Wild Geese 78. The Sea Wolves 80. Who Dares Wins 82. Wild Geese II 85. Field of Honor 86, etc.

Buetel, Jack (1917–1989).
American western leading man who was little seen after a highly publicized debut.

The Outlaw (as Billy the Kid) 43. Best of the Badmen 51. The Half Breed 52. Jesse James' Women 54. Mustang 59, etc.

TV series: Judge Roy Bean 53.

Bugs Bunny.
Warners' famous cartoon character, the wise-cracking Brooklynesque rabbit who maintained his aplomb in all situations. Voiced by Mel Blanc. Catchphrase: 'What's up Doc?' First appearance in A Wild Hare 40, although he evolved from a rabbit seen earlier in Porky's Hare Hunt 37; 'retired' 1963; reappeared in 70s as 'compère' of TV specials grouping his old cartoons.

Biography: 1990, *Bugs Bunny: Fifty Years and Only One Grey Hare* by Joe Adamson.

AA 1958: *Knightly Knight Bugs*.

~One of Bugs' creators claimed that the character was inspired by the sight of Clark Gable eating a carrot in *It Happened One Night*.

Bujold, Geneviève (1942–).
French-Canadian leading lady.

French Can Can 56. La Guerre est Finie 63. King of Hearts 67. Isabel 67. Act of the Heart 70. *Anne of the Thousand Days* (as Anne Boleyn) (AAN) 70. Earthquake 74. Obsession 76. Swashbuckler 76. Alex and the Gypsy 76. Another Man, Another Chance 77. Murder by Decree 78. Coma 78. Final Assignment 80. Monsignor 81. Tightrope 84.

Choose Me 85. Trouble in Mind 85. Dead Ringers 88. The Moderns 88. False Identity 90. Rue du Bac 91. The Dance Goes On 91. Paper Wedding 91. Oh, What a Night 92. An Ambush of Ghosts 93. Mon Amie Max 94, etc.

Bukowski, Charles (1920–).
Hard-drinking American poet, chronicler of the low life, and occasional screenwriter.

Tales of Ordinary Madness (oa) 83. Love Is a Dog From Hell (oa) 87. Barfly (w) 87. Cold Moon (oa) 91.

Bull, Peter (1912–1984).
Portly British character actor often in haughty, aggressive or explosively foreign roles.

Autobiography: 1959, *I Know the Face but . . .*

Sabotage 37. The Ware Case 39. The Turners of Prospect Road 47. Oliver Twist 48. Saraband for Dead Lovers 48. The African Queen 51. The Malta Story 53. Footsteps in the Fog 55. Tom Jones 63. Dr Strangelove 63. The Old Dark House 63. Dr Dolittle 67. Lock Up Your Daughters 69. The Executioner 70. Up the Front 72. Alice's Adventures in Wonderland 72. Joseph Andrews 77. The Brute 78. Yellowbeard 83, many others.

Bulldog Drummond.
'Sapper' (Herman Cyril McNeile) created this famous character, an amateur James Bond of the 20s with old-fashioned manners and an army background, based on his friend Gerard Fairlie (qv). First portrayed on screen by Carlyle Blackwell in 1922; later by Jack Buchanan (1925 and 1940), Ronald Colman (1928 and 1934), Kenneth McKenna (1930), Ralph Richardson (1934), Atholl Fleming in Jack Hulbert's *Bulldog Jack* (1935), John Lodge (1937), Ray Milland (1937), John Howard, in eight films (1937–39), Ron Randell, in two films (1947), Tom Conway, in two films (1948), Walter Pidgeon in *Calling Bulldog Drummond* (1951) and Richard Johnson in *Deadlier than the Male* (1966) and *Some Girls Do* (1968).

bullfights
have understandably not been a popular ingredient of English-speaking films, apart from the romanticism of the two versions of *Blood and Sand* and the cynicism of *The Last Flight* 31 and *The Sun Also Rises*. Several Continental films, including *The Moment of Truth*, have tried to convey the mystique of bullfighting, but it has more often been seen as a background for suspense films (*The Caper of the Golden Bulls*) and comedy (*The Kid from Spain*, Laurel and Hardy in *The Bullfighters* and *Tommy the Toreador*, Abbott and Costello in *Mexican Hayride*, Peter Sellers in *The Bobo*, etc.). The three more recent American attempts to make a serious drama on the subject (*The Bullfighter and the Lady*, *The Brave Bulls* and *The Magnificent Matador*) were notably unpopular, while *Arruza* by Budd Boetticher (himself an ex-bullfighter) was never properly finished.

Bullock, Sandra (1966–).
American actress.

Who Shot Pat? (aka Who Shot Patakango?) 90. Bionic Showdown: The Six-Million Dollar Man and the Bionic Woman (TV) 91. Fire on the Amazon 91. Love Potion #9 92. Demolition Man 93. The Vanishing 93. The Thing Called Love 93. Wrestling Ernest Hemingway 93. Speed 94, etc.

TV series: Working Girl 90.

❡ My goal is to create small films that we are crazy about. – S.B.

Buloff, Joseph (1899–1985).
American actor of stage and screen. Born in Lithuania, he went to America in the late 20s and first worked with the Yiddish Art Theatre in New York.

Let's Make Music 40. Carnegie Hall 47. The Loves of Carmen 48. A Kiss in the Dark 49. Somebody Up There Likes Me 56. Silk Stockings 57, etc.

Bumstead, Henry (1915–).
American production designer.

The Man Who Knew Too Much 56. Vertigo (AAN) 58. The Great Impostor 60. To Kill a Mockingbird (AA) 62. Father Goose 64. The War Lord 65. Tell Them Willie Boy Is Here 69. Topaz 69. Slaughterhouse Five 71. High Plains Drifter 73. The Sting (AA) 73. The Front Page 74. Family Plot 76. Slapshot 77. Same Time Next Year 78. A Little Romance 79. The Concorde – Airport '79 79. The World According to Garp 82. The Little Drummer Girl 84. Psycho III 86. A Time of Destiny 88. Ghost Dad 90. Almost an Angel 90. Cape Fear 91. Unforgiven 92. A Perfect World 93, many others.

Bunnage, Avis (1923–1990).
Exuberant English character actress, from the stage.

Espresso Bongo 59. Saturday Night and Sunday Morning 60. Loneliness of the Long Distance Runner 62. Sparrows Can't Sing 63. Tom Jones 63. A Study in Terror 65. The Wrong Box 66. Gandhi 82. The Krays 90, etc.

Bunny, John (1863–1915).
British actor who became the funny fat man of early American silent comedy; made more than 150 shorts, usually with Flora Finch.

Buñuel, Luis (1900–1983).
Spanish writer-director who worked in France in the 20s and 30s, made many films in Mexico 1945–60, then returned to Europe. A once-notorious surrealist, his later films mocked hypocrisy and the shows of religion.

Autobiography: 1984, *My Last Breath*.

Biographies: 1963, by Adonis Kyrou. 1967, by Raymond Durgnat. 1993, *Objects of Desire: Conversations with Luis Buñuel* by José de la Colina and Tomás Pérez.

■ Un Chien Andalou 28. L'Age d'Or 30. Land without Bread 32. Grand Casino 46. El Gran Calavera 49. Los Olvidados 50. Suzana la Perverse 50. La Hija del Engaño 51. Una Mujer Sin Amor 51. Subida al Cielo 51. The Brute 52. Wuthering Heights 52. Robinson Crusoe 52. El 53. La Ilusión Viaja en Tranvía 53. El Rio y La Muerte 54. The Criminal Life of Archibaldo de la Cruz 55. La Mort en ce Jardin 56. Cela S'Appelle L'Aurore 58. La Fièvre Monte à El Pao 59. Nazarin 59. The Young One 60. Viridiana 61. The Exterminating Angel 62. Diary of a Chambermaid 64. Belle de Jour 66. Simon of the Desert 66. The Milky Way 69. Tristana (AAN) 70. The Discreet Charm of the Bourgeoisie (AAN) 72. The Phantom of Liberty 74. That Obscure Object of Desire 77.

✪ For making surrealism irresistible by mixing it with deft film-making techniques and suave direction of actors. The Discreet Charm of the Bourgeoisie.

❡ I've always found insects exciting. – L.B.

Buono, Victor (1938–1982).
Massively bulky American character actor who moved to films via the amateur theatre.

■ Whatever Happened to Baby Jane? (AAN) 62. Fou

for Texas 63. *The Strangler* 64. Robin and the Seven Hoods 64. The Greatest Story Ever Told 65. Hush Hush Sweet Charlotte 65. Young Dillinger 65. The Silencers 66. Who's Minding the Mint? 67. Beneath the Planet of the Apes 69. In the Name of our Father (It.) 69. The Wrath of God 72. The Mad Butcher 72. Crime Club (TV) 72. Goodnight My Love (TV) 72. Northeast of Seoul 74. Arnold 75. Brenda Starr (TV) 75. High Risk (TV) 76. Man from Atlantis (TV) 77. The Evil 78. Return of the Mod Squad (TV) 79. Backstairs at the White House (TV) 79. The Man with Bogart's Face 80.

Burden, Hugh (1913–1985).
British character actor.
  One of Our Aircraft is Missing 41. The Way Ahead 44. Fame is the Spur 46. Sleeping Car to Trieste 48. The Malta Story 53. No Love for Johnnie 61. Funeral in Berlin 66. The Statue 71. Blood from the Mummy's Tomb 71. The House in Nightmare Park 73, etc.

Burge, Stuart (1918–).
British director, from TV.
■ There Was a Crooked Man 60. Uncle Vanya 63. Othello 65. The Mikado 67. Julius Caesar 70.

Burgess, Anthony (1917–1993) (John Burgess Wilson).
British novelist whose chief contribution to the cinema is *A Clockwork Orange*.

Burgess, Dorothy (1907–1961).
American actress, from the New York stage, who went to Hollywood to star opposite Warner Baxter in *In Old Arizona* 29. Subsequently, she played leading roles in second features.
  Cleopatra 30. Malay Nights 32. Orient Express 34. Manhattan Butterly 35. I Want a Divorce 40. Lady for a Night 41. The Lone Star Ranger 42. Girls in Chains 43, etc.

Burgon, Geoffrey.
British composer.
  Life of Brian 79. Dogs of War 80. Brideshead Revisited (TV) 82. Turtle Diary 85. Bleak House (TV) 85. A Foreign Field (TV) 93, etc.

Burke, Alfred (1918–).
British stage, screen and TV actor usually in cold, unsympathetic or other-worldly roles.
  Touch and Go 56. The Man Upstairs 58. The Angry Silence 59. Children of the Damned 64. The Nanny 65. One Day in the Life of Ivan Denisovitch 71. The House on Garibaldi Street (TV) 79, etc.
  TV series: Public Eye 69–73.

Burke, Billie (1885–1970) (Mary William Ethelbert Appleton Burke).
American stage star who married Florenz Ziegfeld; Myrna Loy played her in *The Great Ziegfeld*. After a few early silents she settled in Hollywood in the 30s and played variations on the dithery matron role she made her own.
  Autobiographies: 1949, *With a Feather on my Nose.* 1959, *With Powder on My Nose.*
■ Gloria's Romance 16. Peggy 16. The Land of Promise 17. The Mysterious Miss Terry 17. Arms and the Girl 18. Eve's Daughter 18. Let's Get a Divorce 18. In Pursuit of Polly 18. The Make Believe Wife 18. Good Gracious Annabelle 19. The Misleading Widow 19. Sadie Love 19. Wanted, a Husband 19. Away Goes Prudence 20. The Frisky Mrs Johnson 21. The Education of Elizabeth 21. *A Bill of Divorcement* 32. Christopher Strong 33. *Dinner at Eight* 33. Only Yesterday 33. Finishing School 34. Where Sinners Meet 34. We're Rich Again 34. Forsaking all Others 34. Society Doctor

35. After Office Hours 35. Becky Sharp 35. Doubting Thomas 35. *A Feather in Her Hat* 35. She Couldn't Take It 35. Splendour 35. My American Wife 36. Piccadilly Jim 36. Craig's Wife 36. Parnell 36. *Topper* 37. The Bride Wore Red 37. Navy Blue and Gold 37. Everybody Sing 38. *Merrily We Live* (AAN) 38. *The Young in Heart* 38. Topper Takes a Trip 38. Zenobia 39. Bridal Suite 39. The Wizard of Oz 39. Eternally Yours 39. Remember 39. And One Was Beautiful 40. Irene 40. Dulcy 40. Hullaballoo 40. The Captain is a Lady 40. The Ghost Comes Home 40. The Wild Man of Borneo 41. Topper Returns 41. One Night in Lisbon 41. *The Man Who Came to Dinner* 41. What's Cookin'? 42. In This Our Life 42. They All Kissed the Bride 42. Girl Trouble 42. Hi Diddle Diddle 42. Gildersleeve on Broadway 43. You're a Lucky Fellow Mr Smith 43. So's Your Uncle 45. *The Cheaters* 45. Swing Out Sister 45. Breakfast in Hollywood 46. The Bachelor's Daughters 46. The Barkleys of Broadway 49. And Baby Makes Three 49. Father of the Bride 50. The Boy from Indiana 50. Three Husbands 51. Father's Little Dividend 51. Small Town Girl 53. The Young Philadelphians 59. Sergeant Rutledge 60. Pepe 60.
  TV series: Doc Corkle 52.

Famous line (*The Wizard of Oz*): 'Close your eyes and tap your heels together three times. And think to yourself, there's no place like home.'

Burke, James (1886–1968).
Irish-American character actor who played more New York cops than he could count.
  A Lady's Profession 33. Little Miss Marker 34. Ruggles of Red Gap 35. Song and Dance Man 36. Dead End 37. Dawn Patrol 38. At the Circus 39. Ellery Queen Master Detective 40. The Maltese Falcon 41. Army Surgeon 42. A Night to Remember 43. The Horn Blows at Midnight 45. Two Years Before the Mast 46. Nightmare Alley 47. June Bride 48. Copper Canyon 50. Lone Star 52. Lucky Me 54, many others.

Burke, Johnny (1908–1964).
American songwriter who often supplied lyrics for Jimmy Van Heusen's music. 'Pennies from Heaven', 'Moonlight Becomes You', 'Swinging on a Star' (AA 44), many others.

Burke, Kathleen (1913–1980).
American leading lady who made a few 30s appearances after being dubbed 'the panther woman' in 1932's *Island of Lost Souls.*

Burke, Marie (1894–1988) (Marie Holt).
British actress, mostly on stage.
  After the Ball 33. Odette 50. The Constant Husband 55. The Snorkel 58. Rattle of a Simple Man 64, etc.

Burke, Martyn.
Canadian director.
  The Clown Murders 76. Power Play 78. The Last Chase 81.

Burke, Patricia (1917–).
British actress, daughter of Marie Burke.
  The Lisbon Story 45. The Trojan Brothers 45. Love Story 46. While I Live 47. Forbidden 49. The Happiness of Three Women 60. Spider's Web 60. The Day the Fish Came Out 67, etc.

Burke, Paul (1926–).
American leading man, who on TV projected integrity with great success but has done few movies.
  South Sea Woman 53. Screaming Eagles 56.

Valley of the Dolls 67. The Thomas Crown Affair 68. Daddy's Gone a-Hunting 69. Lt Schuster's Wife (TV) 72. Psychic Killer 75. Little Ladies of the Night (TV) 77. Wild and Wooly (TV) 78. Beach Patrol (TV) 79. The Red Light Sting 84, etc.
  TV series: Harbormaster 57. Five Fingers 59. Noah's Ark 60. Naked City 60–63. Twelve o'Clock High 67. Dynasty 83. Hot Shots 86–87.

Burke, Robert (1961–).
American actor.
  The Unbelievable Truth 90. Rambling Rose 91. Dust Devil 92. Robocop 3 92. A Far Off Place 93. Tombstone 94, etc.

Burke, Thomas (1886–1945).
English novelist and essayist, noted for his stories set in Limehouse, London's Chinese quarter. His essay 'The Comedian' in his *City of Encounters* was described by Chaplin's biographer David Robinson as 'the most searching and perceptive portrait ever written' of Charlie Chaplin.
  Broken Blossoms (from The Chink and the Child) 19 and 36. Dream Street (from Gina of Chinatown) 21. Curlytop (from Twelve Golden Curls) 24, etc.

Burks, Robert (1910–1968).
American cinematographer.
■ Make Your Own Bed 44. Escape in the Desert 45. To the Victor 48. A Kiss in the Dark 49. *The Fountainhead* 49. Beyond the Forest 49. Task Force 49. The Glass Menagerie 50. Close to My Heart 51. *Strangers on a Train* 51. Tomorrow Is Another Day 51. *Come Fill the Cup* 51. *The Enforcer* 51. The Miracle of Our Lady of Fatima 51. Room for One More 52. Mara Maru 52. The Desert Song 53. This Is Love 53. Hondo 53. *I Confess* 53. The Boy from Oklahoma 54. Dial M for Murder 54. *Rear Window* 54. *To Catch a Thief* (AA) 55. The Trouble with Harry 56. The Man Who Knew Too Much 56. The Vagabond King 56. The Wrong Man 57. The Spirit of St Louis (co-ph) 58. *Vertigo* 58. The Black Orchid 59. *North by Northwest* 59. But Not for Me 59. The Rat Race 60. The Great Impostor 61. The Pleasure of His Company 61. *The Music Man* 62. *The Birds* 63. Marnie 64. Once a Thief 65. A Patch of Blue 66. A Covenant with Death 67. Waterhole Three 67.

burlesque.
A word of Italian origin which came to mean an acted 'spoof' of a serious subject. In America it was applied to what the British would call music hall of variety, and eventually connoted striptease and low comedians. It died out as an institution in the 30s: Mamoulian's film *Applause* 29 gives a vivid picture of its latter days. George Watters and Arthur Hopkins' play *Burlesque*, popular in the 20s, concerns a comedian who leaves his long-suffering wife for other women and the demon rum. It was filmed three times, most recently as *When My Baby Smiles at Me* 48, with Betty Grable and Dan Dailey. The heyday of burlesque was also evoked in *The Night They Raided Minsky's* 68, in *Lady of Burlesque* and in *Gypsy.*

Burlinson, Tom (1956–).
Australian leading actor.
  The Man from Snowy River 82. Phar Lap 84. Flesh + Blood 85. King Solomon's Mines 86. Windrider 86. The Time Guardian 87. Return to Snowy River 88. Showdown at Williams Creek 91, etc.

Burnaby, Davy (1881–1949).
Heavyweight, monocled British entertainer.
  The Co-optimists 29. Three Men in a Boat 33.

Are You a Mason? 34. Boys Will Be Boys 35. Feather Your Nest 37. Many Tanks Mr Atkins 39. etc.

burned out.
Cinematographer's jargon for 'over-exposed'.

Burness, Pete (1910–).
American animator who worked his way through *The Little King* and *Tom and Jerry* to U.P.A. and *Bullwinkle*.

Burnett, Carol (1933–).
Lanky, long-faced American revue and television star who, despite being a household word at home, hasn't made much of an impression in the overseas market.
■ Who's Been Sleeping in My Bed? 63. Pete 'n' Tillie 72. The Front Page 74. A Wedding 78. The Grass Is Always Greener Over the Septic Tank (TV) 78. *Friendly Fire* (TV) 79. Health 80. The Four Seasons 81. Chu Chu and the Philly Flash 81. Annie 82. Between Friends 83. Noises Off 92. Seasons of the Heart (TV) 94.
TV series: Stanley 56. The Garry Moore Show 60s. *The Carol Burnett Show* 70s. Mama's Family 83–84.

¶ How many people do you know who can make a lot of money by crossing their eyes and doing pratfalls? – *C.B.*
Celebrity was a long time in coming; it will go away. Everything goes away. – *C.B.*

Burnett, Charles (1944–).
American director and screenwriter.
Killer of Sheep 77. My Brother's Wedding 83. Bless Their Little Hearts 84. To Sleep with Anger 90. The Glass Shield (wd) 94, etc.

Burnett, Frances Hodgson (1849–1924).
English novelist whose screen contributions include the much-filmed children's stories *Little Lord Fauntleroy* and *The Secret Garden*. *A Little Princess* made a solid vehicle for Shirley Temple.

Burnett, W. R. (1899–1982).
American writer of gangster novels and screenplays which have been influential.
Little Caesar (oa) 30. *Scarface* (oa) 32. Dr Socrates (oa) 35. *High Sierra* (oa) 40. Wake Island (co-w, AAN) 42. Crash Dive (w) 43. Nobody Lives Forever (w) 46. The Asphalt Jungle (oa) 50. Captain Lightfoot (w) 54. Sergeants Three (w) 62, many others.

Burnette, Smiley (1911–1967) (Lester Alvin Burnette).
Tubby American character comedian who for many years made low-budget westerns as the side-kick of Charles Starrett or Gene Autry.
TV series: Petticoat Junction 63–67.

Burns, Bob ('Bazooka') (1893–1956).
Folksy American comedian and humorist who after radio success appeared in several light films.
The Big Broadcast of 1937 37. Waikiki Wedding 37. Wells Fargo 37. The Arkansas Traveler 38. Tropic Holiday 38. Our Leading Citizen 39. Alias the Deacon 40. Belle of the Yukon 44, etc.

Burns, Catherine (1945–).
American young character actress of the 70s.
■ Me Natalie 69. *Last Summer* (AAN) 69. Red Sky at Morning 71. The Catcher (TV) 71. Night of Terror (TV) 72. Two for the Money (TV) 72. Amelia Earhart (TV) 76. The Word (TV) 78.

Burns, David (1902–1971).
American character actor who often played the hero's buddy, the villain's henchman, or a fast-talking agent.
The Queen's Affair (GB) 34. The Sky's the Limit (GB) 38. A Girl Must Live (GB) 38. Knock On Wood 54. Deep in My Heart 55. Let's Make Love 60. The Tiger Makes Out 67. Who is Harry Kellerman? 71, etc.

Burns, George (1896–) (Nathan Birnbaum).
American vaudeville comedian who married his partner Gracie Allen (qv) and spent many successful years on radio and TV, puffing philosophically at his cigar as he suffered her harebrained schemes. At the age of eighty he again became a big star and a national institution.
Autobiographies: 1955, *I Love Her, That's Why.* 1976, *Living It Up.*
■ The Big Broadcast 32. College Humor 33. International House 33. Six of a Kind 34. We're Not Dressing 34. Many Happy Returns 34. Love in Bloom 35. The Big Broadcast of 1936 35. Here Comes Cookie 35. College Holiday 36. A Damsel in Distress 37. College Swing 38. Honolulu 39. *The Sunshine Boys* (AA) 75. *Oh God* 77. Sergeant Pepper's Lonely Hearts Club Band 78. Just You and Me Kid 79. Two of a Kind 79. Oh God Book Two 80. Going in Style 80. Oh God Book Three 83. Oh God! You Devil 84. 18 Again! 88.
TV series: The Burns and Allen Show 50–57. The George Burns Show 59–60. Wendy and Me 64.

¶ My husband will never chase another woman. He's too fine, too decent, too old. – *Gracie Allen, 1960*
Acting is all about honesty. If you can fake that, you've got it made. – *G.B.*

Burns, Mark (1936–).
British leading man.
The Charge of the Light Brigade 67. The Adventures of Gerard 70. A Day on the Beach 70. Death in Venice 70. A Time for Loving 72. Juggernaut 74. The Maids 75. The Stud 78. The Bitch 79. The Wicked Lady 83, etc.

Burns, Michael (1947–).
American leading man of the 60s.
The Wizard of Baghdad 60. Mr Hobbs Takes a Vacation 62. The Raiders 64. Forty Guns to Apache Pass 66. The Mad Room 68. Thumb Tripping 72. The Magnificent Magical Magnet of Santa Mesa (TV) 77, etc.
TV series: Wagon Train 63–65.

Burns, Ralph (1922–).
American musical director and composer, a former jazz pianist and arranger for bandleader Woody Herman.
Cabaret (md) (AA) 72. Lenny 74. Lucky Lady 75. New York, New York 77. Movie Movie 78. All That Jazz (md) (AA) 79. Urban Cowboy 80. Annie (md) (AAN) 82. My Favorite Year 82. National Lampoon's Vacation 83. Star 80 83. The Muppets Take Manhattan 84. Perfect 85. A Chorus Line (md) 85. Moving Violations 85. In the Mood (aka The Woo Woo Kid) 87. Bert Rigby, You're a Fool 89. All Dogs Go to Heaven 89, etc.

Burns, Wilfred (1917–).
British composer.
Fools Rush In 49. Thunder Over Tangier 57. Till Death Us Do Part 68. Dad's Army 71, etc.

Burr, Raymond (1917–1993).
Heavily-built Canadian leading man who for years played Hollywood heavies and then achieved TV stardom as Perry Mason.
■ Without Reservations 46. San Quentin 46. Code of the West 47. Desperate 47. Pitfall 48. Raw Deal 48. Fighting Father Dunne 48. Ruthless 48. Sleep My Love 48. The Adventures of Don Juan 48. Walk a Crooked Mile 48. Station West 48. I Love Trouble 48. Criss Cross 49. Bride of Vengeance 49. Black Magic 49. Abandoned 49. The Red Light 49. Love Happy 49. Unmasked 50. Borderline 50. Key to the City 50. *A Place in the Sun* 51. His Kind of Woman 51. Bride of the Gorilla 51. New Mexico 51. M 51. FBI Girl 51. The Whip Hand 51. Meet Danny Wilson 52. Mara Maru 52. Horizons West 52. The Blue Gardenia 53. Fort Algiers 53. Bandits of Corsica 53. Tarzan and the She Devil 53. Serpent of the Nile 54. Casanova's Big Night 54. Gorilla at Large 54. Khyber Patrol 54. *Rear Window* 54. Passion 54. Thunder Pass 54. They Were So Young 55. You're Never Too Young 55. Count Three and Pray 55. A Man Alone 55. The Brass Legend 56. Please Murder Me 56. Godzilla 56. Great Day in the Morning 56. The Secret of Treasure Mountain 56. A Cry in the Night 56. Ride the High Iron 56. Crime of Passion 57. Affair in Havana 57. Desire in the Dust 60. P.J. 68. 77 Park Avenue (TV) 77. The Jordan Chance (TV) 78. Tomorrow Never Comes 78. Love's Savage Fury (TV) 79. Out of the Blue 80. The Curse of King Tut's Tomb (TV) 80. The Return 80. The Night the City Screamed (TV) 80. Peter and Paul (TV) 81. Airplane II: the Sequel 82. Perry Mason Returns (TV) 85 (and several subsequent TV movies). Gojira 85. Delirious 91.
TV series: *Perry Mason* 57–65. *Ironside* 67–74. Kingston: Confidential 77. Centennial 78.

Burroughs, Edgar Rice (1875–1950).
American novelist, the creator (in 1914) of *Tarzan of the Apes*.

¶ I am one of those fellows who have few adventures. I always get to the fire after it's out. – *E.R.B.*

Burroughs, William S. (1914–).
American novelist whose *Naked Lunch* was filmed by David Cronenberg in 1991. An influential, experimental writer, using cinematic techniques in his work, he has featured in documentaries about the Beat generation and made cameo appearances as an actor. He also scripted and appeared in some short underground films directed by Antony Balch in the 60s: *Towers Open Fire, The Cut-Ups, Bill and Tony*, and *William Buys a Parrot*, which have been released on video-cassette.
AS HIMSELF: This Song for Jack 83. Burroughs 83. Heavy Petting 83. What Happened to Kerouac? 85. The Beat Generation – an American Dream 87.
AS ACTOR: Chappaqua 66. Twister 89. Drugstore Cowboy 89. The Bloodhounds of Broadway 89. Wax, or the Discovery of Television among the Bees 92.

¶ The cut-up method brings to writers the collage, which has been used by painters for fifty years, and used by the moving and still camera. In fact all street shots from movie or still cameras are by the unpredictable factors of passers-by and juxtaposition cut-ups. – *W.B.*
I went through about six analysts. I was too much for them. I wore 'em out. – *W.B.*

Burrows, Abe (1910–1985) (Abram Borowitz).
American librettist: *Guys and Dolls, Can Can, Silk Stockings, How to Succeed in Business*, etc.

Burstall, Tim (1929–).
English producer, director and screenwriter in Australia who began as a documentary film-maker.

Two Thousand Weeks 69. Stork 71. Alvin Purple 73. Petersen 74. End Play (& w) 75. Eliza Fraser 76. The Last of the Knucklemen (& w) 79. Attack Force Z 82. Duet for Four 82. The Naked Country 84. Kangaroo 86. Great Expectations – the Untold Story 87. Nightmare at Bitter Creek (TV) 88, etc.

Burstyn, Ellen (1932–) (Edna Gilhooley).
Leading American actress, acting under the name of Ellen McRae in the 60s.
■ Goodbye Charlie 64. For Those Who Think Young 65. Pit Stop 69. Tropic of Cancer 69. Alex in Wonderland 70. The Last Picture Show (AAN) 71. *The Exorcist* (AAN) 73. Harry and Tonto 74. *Alice Doesn't Live Here Any More* (AA) 75. Providence 77. Same Time Next Year (AAN) 78. A Dream of Passion 78. Resurrection (AAN) 80. Silence of the North 82. The People vs Jean Harris (TV) 83. The Ambassador 84. Surviving (TV) 85. Twice in a Lifetime 85. Dear America 87. Hello Actors Studio 87. Hanna's War 88. Dying Young 91. Grand Isle 91. The Cemetery Club 93. When a Man Loves a Woman 94. Getting Out (TV) 94. Getting Gotti (TV) 94.

TV series: The Iron Horse 67–68. The Ellen Burstyn Show 86–87.

¶ Acting feels like a congenital condition to me – it's in my genes. – *E.B.*

Burton, Geoff.
Australian cinematographer turned director, associated with the films of John Duigan.

The Fourth Wish 75. Storm Boy 76. Born to Run 76. The Picture Show Man 77. Blue Fin 78. Stir 80. The Year My Voice Broke 87. The Time Guardian 87. Romero 89. Bangkok Hilton (TV) 90. Flirting 92. Wide Sargasso Sea 93. Bedevil 93. The Nostradamus Kid 93. Frauds 93. Sirens 94. The Sum of Us (& co-d) 94, etc.

Burton, LeVar (1958–).
American character actor who played the young Kunta Kinte in TV's *Roots*.

Billy: Portrait of a Street Kid (TV) 77. Looking for Mr Goodbar 77. Guyana Tragedy (TV) 80. The Hunter 80. The Supernaturals 86. The Midnight Hour 86, etc.

Burton, Richard (1925–1984) (Richard Jenkins).
Welsh leading actor whose dark, brooding good looks did not bring him immediate film success either in Britain or in Hollywood. His 1963 marriage to Elizabeth Taylor, however, helped him climb to the crest of what these days passes for stardom, as did their subsequent divorces and reunions. High living and a kind of contempt for his work kept him from the heights of both serious achievement and popular acclaim.

Biography: 1986, *Burton, the Man Behind the Myth* by Penny Junor; 1988, *Rich: The Life of Richard Burton* by Melvyn Bragg.
■ The Last Days of Dolwyn 48. Now Barabbas was a Robber 49. Waterfront 50. The Woman with No Name 50. Green Grow the Rushes 51. *My Cousin Rachel* (AAN) 52. The Robe 53. The Desert Rats 53. Prince of Players 54. The Rains of Ranchipur 55. *Alexander the Great* 56. Seawife 57. Bitter Victory 58. *Look Back in Anger* 59. The Bramble Bush 59. Ice Palace 60. The Longest Day 62. *Cleopatra* 62. *The V.I.P.s* 63. *Becket* (AAN) 64. *The Night of the Iguana* 64. The Sandpiper 65. *The Spy Who Came in from the Cold* (AAN) 65. *Who's Afraid of Virginia Woolf?* (AAN) 66. *The Taming of the Shrew* 67. Dr Faustus

(& co-d) 67. The Comedians 67. Boom 68. Where Eagles Dare 68. Candy 68. *Staircase* 69. *Anne of the Thousand Days* (as Henry VIII) (AAN) 70. Raid on Rommel 71. Villain 71. Under Milk Wood 71. The Assassination of Trotsky 72. Hammersmith is Out 72. Bluebeard 72. Divorce His, Divorce Hers (TV) 73. Sutjeska (Yug.) 73. Massacre in Rome 74. The Klansman 74. The Voyage 74. Brief Encounter (TV) 75. Exorcist II: The Heretic 77. Equus (AAN) 77. The Medusa Touch 77. The Wild Geese 78. Sergeant Steiner 79. Absolution 79. Tristan and Isolt 80. Circle of Two 80. Wagner, 83. 1984 84. Ellis Island (TV) 84.

¶ I've done the most awful rubbish in order to have somewhere to go in the morning. – *R.B.*

When I played drunks I had to remain sober because I didn't know how to play them when I was drunk. – *R.B.*

An actor is something less than a man, while an actress is something more than a woman. – *R.B.*

Certainly most movie executives were making love to the starlets. But then, so were most of us actors. – *R.B. of Hollywood in the 50s*

The Burtons offered me a drink and rolled in a liquor cart from the bedroom which was its permanent abode, and the conversation afterwards was limited to a discussion of twentieth-century poetry. – *William Fadiman*

There is no longer any novelty in watching the sad disintegration of his acting career. – *Roger Ebert*

Who could take that scruffy arrogant buffoon seriously? – *Eddie Fisher*

Cable from Laurence Olivier to Burton at the height of the *Cleopatra* scandal: 'Make up your mind, dear heart. Do you want to be a great actor or a household word?' – Burton, replying: 'Both.'

Burton, Robert (1895–1964).
American character actor who played many executives, sheriffs and detectives.

Inferno 53. The Big Heat 54. Riot in Cell Block Eleven 56. Spirit of St Louis 57. Birdman of Alcatraz 62, many others.

TV series: Kings Row 55.

Burton, Tim (1960–).
American director, a former Disney animator.

Book: *Burton on Burton*, edited by Mark Salisbury.

Pee-Wee's Big Adventure 85. Beetlejuice 88. *Batman* 89. *Edward Scissorhands* 90. Batman Returns 92. Tim Burton's The Nightmare Before Christmas (p, story, characters) 93. Cabin Boy (p) 94. *Ed Wood* (p, d) 94, etc.

Burton, Wendell (1947–).
American character actor.

The Sterile Cuckoo 69. Fortune and Men's Eyes 70. Being There 79. East of Eden (TV) 81, etc.

Burum, Stephen H.
American cinematographer.

Pacific High 80. Death Valley 82. The Escape Artist 82. The Entity 83. The Outsiders 83. Something Wicked This Way Comes 83. Rumble Fish 83. Uncommon Valor 83. Body Double 84. St Elmo's Fire 85. The Bride 85. 8 Million Ways to Die 86. Nutcracker: The Motion Picture 86. The Untouchables 87. Arthur 2: On the Rocks 88. Casualties of War 89. War of the Roses 89. He Said, She Said 91. Man Trouble 92. Carlito's Way 93. The Shadow 94, etc.

Burwell, Carter.
American composer, associated with the films of the Coen brothers.

Blood Simple 84. Psycho III 86. Raising Arizona

87. Pass the Ammo 88. It Takes Two 88. Beat 88. Checking Out 89. Miller's Crossing 90. Doc Hollywood 91. Barton Fink 91. Storyville 92. Buffy the Vampire Slayer 92. Waterland 92. This Boy's Life 93. Kalifornia 93. A Dangerous Woman 93. Wayne's World 2 93. The Hudsucker Proxy 94. It Could Happen to You 94, etc.

Buscemi, Steve (1958–).
American character actor, in oddball roles.

No Picnic 86. Parting Glances 86. Sleepwalk 86. Force of Circumstance 87. Heart 87. Heart of Midnight 88. Vibes 88. Bloodhounds of Broadway 89. Mystery Train 89. New York Stories 89. Slaves of New York 89. King of New York 90. Miller's Crossing 90. Zandalee 90. Tales from the Darkside: The Movie 90. Billy Bathgate 91. Barton Fink 91. Reservoir Dogs 92. In the Soup 92. Crisscross 92. Ed and His Dead Mother 93. Rising Sun 93. Airheads 94. Floundering 94. The Hudsucker Proxy 94. Somebody to Love 94, etc.

Busch, Mae (1897–1946).
Cynical-looking Australian-born leading lady of Hollywood silents who later became an excellent foil for Laurel and Hardy in some of their best two-reelers.

The Grim Game 19. The Devil's Pass-key 20. *Foolish Wives* 21. The Christian (GB) 23. Nellie the Beautiful Cloak Model 24. Married Flirts 24. The Unholy Three 25. San Francisco Nights 27. While the City Sleeps 28. A Man's Man 29. Wicked 31. *Come Clean* 31. Scarlet Dawn 32. Their First Mistake 32. Sucker Money 33. Sons of the Desert 33. The Private Life of Oliver the Eighth 34. The Bohemian Girl 36. Daughter of Shanghai 37. Prison Farm 38. Women without Names 40. Ziegfeld Girl 40. The Blue Dahlia 46. Ladies' Man 47, many others.

Busch, Niven (1903–1991).
American novelist and screenwriter. He left Hollywood in 1952 to teach. He was married to actress Teresa Wright (1942–52).

Babbitt (w) 34. In Old Chicago (w, AAN) 38. The Westerner (w) 40. Duel in the Sun (oa) 46. Pursued (w) 47. The Furies (oa) 50. The Moonlighter (oa & w) 52. Treasure of Pancho Villa (w) 56, etc.

buses
have often provided a dramatic background for film plots. *Man-Made Monster* and *The October Man* began with bus accidents, and one of the stories in *Dead of Night* ended with one. Strangers met on a bus in *Friday the Thirteenth*, *It Happened One Night*, *San Diego I Love You* (in which Buster Keaton defied regulations by driving his bus along the seashore), *Bus Stop* and *The Wayward Bus*. Parting at the bus station was featured in *Orchestra Wives*, *Dark Passage*, *Two Tickets to Broadway*, and *Rattle of a Simple Man;* romances were conducted on a bus in *Violent Playground* and *Underground;* a trap was set for a criminal in a bus station in *Down Three Dark Streets*. Passengers on buses broke into song in *Keep Your Seats Please*, *Ride 'Em Cowboy* and *Summer Holiday*. As for comedy effects using buses, there was the little boy whose head stuck in the bus wheel in *Monsieur Hulot's Holiday*, Will Hay driving a bus round a race-track in *Ask a Policeman*, Bob Hope wrecking an Irish bus outing in *My Favourite Blonde*, Frankie Howerd losing his way in the fog in *The Runaway Bus*, Richard Burton escorting his matrons on a bus tour in *The Night of the Iguana*, and Laurel and Hardy driving a bus on to a roller coaster in *The Dancing Masters* . . . among others. The only comedies about bus crews were the spinoffs from the British TV series *On the Buses*. *The*

Big Bus was a spoof on disaster movies. *Speed* 94 made a runaway bus big box-office.

Busey, Gary (1944–).
American leading actor.

Dirty Little Billy 72. Lolly Madonna XXX 73. The Last American Hero 73. The Execution of Private Slovik (TV) 74. Thunderbolt and Lightfoot 74. The Law (TV) 74. The Gumball Rally 76. A Star Is Born 76. Straight Time 77. Big Wednesday 78. The Buddy Holly Story (AAN) 78. Carny 80. D.C. Cab 83. The Bear 84. Insignificance 85. Silver Bullet 85. Eye of the Tiger 86. Lethal Weapon 87. Let's Get Harry 87. Bulletproof 87. Hider in the House 89. Predator 2 90. Point Break 91. Ganglands 91. Wild Texas Wind 91. My Heroes Have Always Been Cowboys 91. You and Me 91. Canvas 92. South Beach 92. The Player 92. Vengeance 93. The Firm 93. Rookie of the Year 93. Double Suspicion 94. Surviving the Game 94. Chasers 94. Drop Zone 94, etc.

TV series: The Texas Wheelers 74.

Bush, Billy 'Green'.
American character actor of the 70s.

40 Carats 73. Electra Glide in Blue 74. Alice Doesn't Live Here Any More 74. Mackintosh and T. J. 75. Tom Horn 80. The River 84. Critters 86. The Deliberate Stranger (TV) 86. Elvis and Me (TV) 88. Friday the Thirteenth Part IX: Jason Goes to Hell 93, etc.

Bush, Dick (1931–).
British cinematographer.

Savage Messiah 73. Mahler 74. Tommy 74. In Celebration 74. The Legacy 78. Yanks 79. One Trick Pony 80. Little Gloria . . . Happy At Last (TV) 82. Victor Victoria 83. Crimes of Passion 85. The Journey of Natty Gann 85. Nazi Hunter (TV) 86. The Lair of the White Worm 88. Little Monsters 89. Staying Together 89. Switch 91, etc.

Bushell, Anthony (1904–).
Bland-faced British leading man of the 30s who started his career in Hollywood; later turned to playing occasional brigadiers and concentrated his efforts on production.

Disraeli 29. *Journey's End* 30. Three Faces East 30. Five Star Final 31. A Woman Commands 32. I Was a Spy 33. The Ghoul 33. Soldiers of the King 33. The Scarlet Pimpernel 34. Dark Journey 37. Farewell Again 37. The Return of the Scarlet Pimpernel 38. The Lion Has Wings 39. Hamlet (co-p only) 48. The Angel with the Trumpet (& d) 49. The Miniver Story 50. The Long Dark Hall (& pd) 51. High Treason 51. Who Goes There? 52. The Red Beret 53. The Purple Plain 54. The Battle of the River Plate 56. Richard III (co-p only) 56. The Wind Cannot Read 57. The Terror of the Tongs 61. The Queen's Guards 63, etc.

Bushman, Francis X. (1883–1966).
Heavily-built American leading actor of the silent era, once known as the handsomest man in the world. After a return to the stage, made a brief comeback in 1926 and later played bit parts in unsuitable films of the 60s.

The Magic Wand 12. The Spy's Defeat 13. One Wonderful Night. 14. Under Royal Patronage 14. Graustark 15. The Return of Richard Neal 15. Romeo and Juliet 15. The Great Secret 16. Red White and Blue Blood 17. Social Quicksands 18. The Masked Bride 25. *Ben Hur* (as Messala) 26. The Lady in Ermine 27. The Thirteenth Juror 27. The Grip of the Yukon 29. Once a Gentleman 30. Hollywood Boulevard 36. David and Bathsheba 51. Sabrina 54. The Story of Mankind 57. The Ghost in the Invisible Bikini 66, many others.

¶ All the people love you, but I can't even have the love of half the people. – *President Taft*
His is the best known name and face in the world. – *Arthur Brisbane*

business
is just as essential as art or entertainment to the continuance of movies: and the greatest moguls are those who have had an eye to all three.

¶ Hollywood's trade, which is dreams at so many dollars per thousand feet, is managed by businessmen pretending to be artists and by artists pretending to be businessmen. In this queer atmosphere, nobody stays as he was; the artist begins to lose his art, and the businessman becomes temperamental and overbalanced. – *J. B. Priestley, 1937*
No picture can be considered a success unless it appeals to the matinee trade. When you've got a picture women want to see, the men will have to go along. But a woman can always keep a man away from a picture that only attracts him. – *Irving Thalberg, 1933*
That wasn't the ending I wanted for *Blackmail*, but I had to change it for commercial reasons. – *Alfred Hitchcock*
We are in this business primarily to provide entertainment, but in doing so we do not dodge the issue if we can also provide enlightenment. – *Darryl F. Zanuck*
In certain pictures I do hope they will leave the cinema a little enriched, but I don't make them pay a buck and a half and then ram a lecture down their throats. – *Billy Wilder*
You can fool all the people all the time if the advertising is right and the budget is big enough. – *Joseph E. Levine*
This isn't exactly a stable business. It's like trying to stand up in a canoe with your pants down. – *Cliff Robertson*
Business has been bad lately. The other night I rang up a local theatre and asked, what time does the main feature start? The manager replied: 'What time can you get here?' – *Bob Hope*

Bussières, Raymond (1907–1982).
Long-faced, mournful-looking French character actor.

Nous les Gosses 41. Les Portes de la Nuit 46. Quai des Orfèvres 47. Alice au Pays des Merveilles 51. Ma Pomme 51. Casque d'Or 52. Justice est Faite 52. Belles de Nuit 54. Porte des Lilas 55. Paris Palace Hotel 58. Fanny 61. Paris When It Sizzles 64. Up from the Beach 65. Drôles de Zèbres 77. Les Sous-Doues 80, many others.

Butcher, Ernest (1885–1965).
British character actor who spent a lifetime playing mild little men.

Variety Jubilee 42. Tawny Pipit 43. My Brother Jonathan 48, many others.

Butler, Artie.
American composer.

The Harrad Experiment 73. For Pete's Sake 74. It's Showtime 76. The Rescuers 78. Angel on My Shoulder (TV) 80. American Dream (TV) 81. Grease 2 82. O'Hara's Wife 82. Copacabana (TV) 85. Classified Love (TV) 86, etc.

Butler, Bill (1931–).
American cinematographer.

The Rain People 69. Drive He Said 71. The Conversation 74. *Jaws* 75. *One Flew over the Cuckoo's Nest* (AAN) 75. Alex and the Gypsy 76. Demon Seed 77. Damien: Omen II 78. Capricorn One 78. Grease 78. Rocky II 78. Can't Stop the Music 80.

Stripes 81. A Little Sex 82. Rocky III 82. The Sting II 83. Beer 85. Rocky IV 85. Big Trouble 86. Biloxi Blues 88. Child's Play 88. Graffiti Bridge 90. Hot Shots! 91. Cop and a Half 93. Sniper 93. Beethoven's 2nd 93, etc.

Butler, David (1894–1979).
American director of light entertainments: occasional promise but little fulfilment. Former actor.

High School Hero 27. Win That Girl 28. *Sunny Side Up* 29. *Just Imagine* 30. *A Connecticut Yankee* 31. Business and Pleasure 32. Hold Me Tight 33. Bottoms Up 34. Bright Eyes 34. The Little Colonel 35. The Littlest Rebel 35. Captain January 36. White Fang 36. Ali Baba Goes to Town 37. Kentucky 38. East Side of Heaven 39. That's Right You're Wrong (& p) 39. If I Had My Way (& p) 40. You'll Find Out (& p) 40. *Caught in the Draft* 41. *Road to Morocco* (AAN) 42. Wake Island (AAN) 42. They Got Me Covered 43. *Thank Your Lucky Stars* 43. Shine on Harvest Moon 44. The Princess and the Pirate 44. San Antonio 45. Two Guys from Milwaukee 46. My Wild Irish Rose 47. Two Guys from Texas 48. Look for the Silver Lining 49. The Daughter of Rosie O'Grady 50. Tea for Two 50. Lullaby of Broadway 51. Painting the Clouds with Sunshine 51. Where's Charley? 52. By the Light of the Silvery Moon 53. *Calamity Jane* 53. King Richard and the Crusaders 54. Glory (& p) 56. The Right Approach 61. C'mon Let's Live a Little 67, etc.

Butler, Frank (1890–1967).
British-born writer, long in Hollywood.

College Humor 33. Babes in Toyland 34. Strike Me Pink 36. Road to Singapore 40. Road to Morocco (AAN) 42. Wake Island (AAN) 42. Going My Way (AA) 44. Incendiary Blonde 45. The Perils of Pauline 47. Whispering Smith 49. Strange Lady in Town 55, many others.

Butler, Michael (1944–).
American cinematographer.

Charley Varrick 74. Harry and Tonto 74. The Car 77. The Gauntlet 77. Telefon 77. Wanda Nevada 79. A Small Circle of Friends 80. The Cannonball Run 81. Megaforce 82. Dance of the Dwarfs 83, etc.

Butler, Robert (1927–).
American director, from TV.

Guns in the Heather 69. The Computer Wore Tennis Shoes 69. The Barefoot Executive 71. Scandalous John 71. Death Takes a Holiday (TV) 71. Now You See Him Now You Don't 71. The Blue Knight (TV) 73. James Dean (TV) 76. In the Glitter Palace (TV) 77. Hot Lead and Cold Feet 78. Night of the Juggler 80. Up the Creek 83. Moonlighting (TV) 85. Out on a Limb (TV) 87. Out of Time (TV) 88, etc.

butlers.
Hollywood has always been fascinated by butlers, especially those who give an impression of British imperturbability. Actors notably benefiting from this penchant include Arthur Treacher (who played Jeeves on film in the 30s), Robert Greig, Charles Coleman, Aubrey Mather, Melville Cooper, Halliwell Hobbes, Barnett Parker, Alan Mowbray and Eric Blore (whose butlers usually had a kind of suppressed malevolence). The catch-phrase 'the butler did it' was, however, seldom true of murder mysteries, though Bela Lugosi played some very sinister servants in the 40s, Richard Haydn was guilty of at least one murder in *And Then There Were None*; the butler in *The Hound of the Baskervilles* certainly had something to hide. Another villainous 'man's man' was Philip Latham in *Dracula Prince of Darkness*: he lured the count's

victims. Comedy butlers are led by Charles Laughton as *Ruggles of Red Gap* and by Edward Brophy, who often played an American imitation of the real thing, Richard Hearne in *The Butler's Dilemma*, Edward Rigby in *Don't Take It to Heart*, and Laurel and Hardy who in *A Chump at Oxford* took literally an instruction to 'serve the salad undressed'. Jack Buchanan pretended to be his own butler in *Lord Richard in the Pantry*, and William Powell and David Niven, who both played *My Man Godfrey*, had their own reasons for going into service. Other butlers with something to hide were found in *White Tie and Tails* and *The Baroness and the Butler*, and in *Spring in Park Lane* Michael Wilding was a mysterious footman. In *The Fallen Idol* Ralph Richardson's butler was almost arrested for a murder he didn't commit. Perhaps television gave us the most famous butler of all: Gordon Jackson as Hudson in *Upstairs Downstairs*.

Butrick, Merrit (1960–1989).
American actor, best known for playing William Shatner's son in two *Star Trek* movies. He died of AIDS.

Zapped! 82. Star Trek II: The Wrath of Khan 82. Star Trek III: The Search for Spock 84. Wired to Kill 86. When the Bough Breaks 86. Shy People 87. Death Spa 87, etc.

Butterworth, Charles (1896–1946).
Balding American comic actor who through the 30s played his own style of shy upper-class bachelor, never getting the girl and sometimes drowning his sorrows in drink.
■ The Life of the Party 30. Illicit 30. The Bargain 31. Side Show 31. The Mad Genius 31. Beauty and the Boss 32. *Love Me Tonight* 32. Manhattan Parade 32. The Nuisance 33. Penthouse 33. My Weakness 33. The Cat and the Fiddle 34. Student Tour 34. Forsaking All Others 34. *Bulldog Drummond Strikes Back* (as Algy) 34. Hollywood Party 34. *Ruggles of Red Gap* 34. The Night Is Young 35. Baby-Face Harrington 35. Orchids to You 35. Magnificent Obsession 35. The Moon's Our Home 36. Half Angel 36. We Went to College 36. Rainbow on the River 36. Swing High Swing Low 37. Every Day's a Holiday 37. Thanks for the Memory 38. Let Freedom Ring 39. The Boys from Syracuse 40. Second Chorus 40. Road Show 41. Blonde Inspiration 41. Sis Hopkins 41. What's Cookin' 42. A Night in New Orleans 42. Give Out Sisters 42. Always a Bridesmaid 43. The Sultan's Daughter 43. This Is the Army 43. The Bermuda Mystery 44. Dixie Jamboree 44. Follow the Boys 44.
¶ I fell flat on my flute. – *C.B. in Love Me Tonight*

Butterworth, Donna (1956–).
American child actress.
The Family Jewels 65. Paradise Hawaiian Style 66.

Butterworth, Peter (1919–1979).
British comedian usually seen as well-meaning bumbler.
William Comes to Town 49. Penny Princess 51. Mr Drake's Duck 52. Carry On series 58–77. The Ritz 76. Carry On Emmanuelle 78, many others.

Buttolph, David (1902–).
American composer.
Show Them No Mercy 35. Nancy Steele is Missing 37. Four Sons 40. *The Mark of Zorro* 40. Tobacco Road 41. Moontide 42. My Favorite Blonde 42. Crash Dive 43. The Hitler Gang 44. The House on 92nd Street 45. Somewhere in the Night 46. Kiss of Death 47. Rope 48. Roseanna McCoy 49. Three Secrets 50. The Enforcer 51. My Man and I

52. *House of Wax* 53. Secret of the Incas 54. The Lone Ranger 56. The Big Land 57. The Horse Soldiers 59. Guns of the Timberland 60. The Man from Galveston 64, many others.

Buttons, Red (1919–) (Aaron Chwatt).
American vaudeville and TV comic who graduated to strong supporting roles in occasional movies.
■ Winged Victory 44. *Sayonara* (AA) 57. Imitation General 58. The Big Circus 59. One, Two, Three 61. Hatari 62. Five Weeks in a Balloon 62. The Longest Day 62. A Ticklish Affair 63. Your Cheating Heart 65. Up from the Beach 65. Harlow 65. Stagecoach 66. Breakout (TV) 67. *They Shoot Horses Don't They?* 69. Who Killed Mary What's Her Name? 71. The Poseidon Adventure 72. Louis Armstrong, Chicago Style 75. The New Original Wonder Woman (TV) 75. Gable and Lombard 76. Viva Knievel 77. Pete's Dragon 77. Telethon (TV) 78. Vegas (TV pilot) 78. Movie Movie 78. The Users (TV) 78. C.H.O.M.P.S. 79. When Time Ran Out 80. The Dream Merchants 80. Reunion at Fairborough (TV) 85. 18 Again! 88. Into Thin Air 89. The Ambulance 90. It Could Happen to You 94.
TV series: The Red Buttons Show 52. The Double Life of Henry Phyfe 66. Knots Landing 87.

Buttram, Pat (1917–1994).
American comic character actor who usually plays hayseeds. He replaced Smiley Burnette as Gene Autry's sidekick in his later westerns. Married actress Sheila Ryan in 1952.
National Barn Dance 44. Beyond the Purple Hills 50. Mule Train 50. Blue Canadian Rockies 52. Twilight of Honor 63. Roustabout 64. The Sweet Ride 67. The Gatling Gun (aka King Gun) 72. Robin Hood (voice) 73. Choices 81. Back to the Future III 90, etc.
TV series: Gene Autry Show 50–56. Green Acres 65–71.

Butts, Dale (1910–1991).
American composer, almost entirely for Republic.
Flame of the Barbary Coast 45. Catman of Paris 46. The Plunderers 48. Sea of Lost Ships 53. Santa Fe Passage 55. Affair in Reno 57, many others.

Buzzell, Edward (1897–1985).
American director of competent but not very individual output; former musical comedy actor.
Virtue 32. Ann Carver's Profession 33. Cross Country Cruise 34. Transient Lady 35. The Luckiest Girl in the World 36. As Good as Married 37. Fast Company 38. Honolulu 39. *At the Circus* 39. Go West 40. Married Bachelor 41. Ship Ahoy 42. The Youngest Profession 43. Keep Your Powder Dry 45. *Easy to Wed* 46. Three Wise Fools 46. Song of the Thin Man 47. Neptune's Daughter 49. A Woman of Distinction 50. Confidentially Connie 53. Ain't Misbehavin' (& w) 55. Mary Had a Little (GB) 61, etc.

Buzzi, Ruth (1936–).
American comedienne who came to the fore as the frustrated spinster in TV's *Laugh-In*.
Freaky Friday 77. The Villain 79. Chu Chu and the Philly Flash 81. The Being 83. Surf II 84. Bad Guys 86. Dixie Lanes 88. My Mom's a Werewolf 89. Up Your Alley 89. Digging Up Business 91, etc.
TV series: That Girl 67–68.

Bygraves, Max (1922–).
British entertainer who has played in several films. Autobiography: 1976, *I Wanna Tell You a Story*.
Skimpy in the Navy 49. Tom Brown's Schooldays 50. Charley Moon 56. A Cry from the Streets 57. Bobbikins 59. Spare the Rod 61. The Alf Garnett Saga 72, etc.

Byington, Spring (1893–1971).
American stage actress who settled in Hollywood in the 30s and played a long succession of bird-brained wives, scatty matrons, gossip columnists, and loving mums.
Little Women (as Marmee) 33. Werewolf of London 35. Way Down East 35. Mutiny on the Bounty 35. Ah Wilderness 35. Every Saturday Night (and ensuing Jones Family series: qv) 36. Dodsworth 36. Theodora Goes Wild 36. It's Love I'm After 37. The Adventures of Tom Sawyer 38. Jezebel 38. *You Can't Take It with You* (AAN) 38. The Story of Alexander Graham Bell 39. A Child is Born 40. The Bluebird 40. Meet John Doe 41. The Devil and Miss Jones 41. When Ladies Meet 41. Roxie Hart 42. *Rings on Her Fingers* 42. Presenting Lily Mars 43. Heaven Can Wait 43. The Heavenly Body 44. I'll Be Seeing You 45. The Enchanted Cottage 45. Dragonwyck 46. Singapore 47. BF's Daughter 48. In the Good Old Summertime 49. Louisa 50. Walk Softly Stranger 50. According to Mrs Hoyle 51. Because You're Mine 52. The Rocket Man 54. Please Don't Eat the Daisies 60, many others.
TV series: *December Bride* 54–58. Laramie 59–62.

¶ TV keeps me young because it keeps me busy, keeps my mind alert, my senses sharp and my interest up. – *S.B., 1959*

Byrd, Ralph (1909–1952).
Tough-looking American leading man, mainly in second features.
Hell Ship Morgan 31. Dick Tracy 38. Desperate Cargo 41. Guadalcanal Diary 43. Mark of the Claw 47. The Redhead and the Cowboy 51, etc.
TV series: Dick Tracy 51.

Byrne, David (1952–).
Scottish-born musician, composer and director, in America. He was vocalist and leader of the rock band Talking Heads.
Something Wild (s) 86. True Stories (a, wd, m) 86. The Last Emperor (co-m, AA) 87. Married to the Mob (m) 88. David Byrne Live: Between the Teeth (concert) (co-d, m) 93.

Byrne, Eddie (1911–1981).
Irish character actor, in British films.
Odd Man Out 46. The Gentle Gunman 52. *Time Gentlemen Please* (leading role) 53. A Kid for Two Farthings 55. The Admirable Crichton 57. The Mummy 59. The Bulldog Breed 60. Mutiny on the Bounty 62. Devils of Darkness 65. Island of Terror 66. Stardust 74, many others.

Byrne, Gabriel (1950–).
Irish leading man and producer. He married actress Ellen Barkin in 1988.
The Outsider 79. Excalibur 81. The Keep 83. Hannah K 83. Reflections 83. Christopher Columbus (TV) 83. Defence of the Realm 85. Gothic 86. Lionheart 87. Siesta 87. Julia and Julia 87. Hello Again 87. The Courier 87. A Soldier's Tale 88. Diamond Skulls 89. Miller's Crossing 90. Shipwrecked (Haakon Haaakonsen) 91. Christopher Columbus 91. Cool World 92. Into the West 92. A Dangerous Woman 93. Point of No Return 93. In the Name of the Father (p) 93. A Simple Twist of Fate 94. Trial by Jury 94. Little Women 94, etc.

Byrnes, Edd (1933–) (Edward Breitenberger).
American TV juvenile of the 50s; never quite made it in movies.
Darby's Rangers 58. Up Periscope 59. Yellowstone Kelly 59. The Secret Invasion 64.

Payment in Blood 69. Twirl (TV) 81. Erotic Images 85. Back to the Beach 87. Mankillers 87, etc.

TV series: 77 Sunset Strip 58–63. Sweepstakes 79.

Byron, Arthur (1872–1943).
American character actor.

The Mummy 32. Mayor of Hell 33. Marie Galante 34. Fog Over Frisco 34. Oil for the Lamps of China 35. Prisoner of Shark Island 36, many others.

Byron, Lord (1788–1824) (George Gordon).
English poet who has been played on the screen by Dennis Price in The Bad Lord Byron, by Richard Chamberlain in Lady Caroline Lamb, by Gavin Gordon in The Bride of Frankenstein, and by Noel Willman in Beau Brummell. Gabriel Byrne played him in Gothic, the story of his time in Switzerland with Shelley and Mary Shelley which resulted in her creation of Frankenstein, which has also been the subject of two further films, Frankenstein Unbound and Rowing with the Wind.

Byron, Kathleen (1922–).
British leading actress of the 40s; on stage and screen.

The Young Mr Pitt 41. The Silver Fleet 43. A Matter of Life and Death 46. Black Narcissus (as a mad nun) 46. The Small Back Room 48. Madness of the Heart 49. The Reluctant Widow 50. Four Days 51. The Gambler and the Lady 52. Hand in Hand 60. Night of the Eagle 62. Private Road 71. Twins of Evil 71. One of Our Dinosaurs is Missing 76, etc.

Byron, Marion (1911–1985) (Miriam Bilenkin).
American leading actress whose first role was opposite Buster Keaton in Steamboat Bill Jnr 28; retired at the end of the 30s.

Broadway Babies 29. Forward Pass 29. Playing Around 30. The Matrimonial Bed (GB: A Matrimonial Problem) 30. The Heart of New York 32. Love Me Tonight 32. Five of a Kind 38, etc.

Byron, Walter (1899–1972) (Walter Butler).
British leading man who had success in America.

White Heat 26. Passion Island 27. The Awakening 28. The Sacred Flame 29. Queen Kelly 29. Not Damaged 30. The Dancers 30. The Last Flight 31. Roar of the Dragon 32. Society Girl 32. British Agent 34. Folies Bergere 35. Mary of Scotland 36. Trade Winds 38, many others.

Byrum, John (1947–).
American writer-director. He created the TV sitcom Winnetka Road 94.
■ Inserts (GB) 75. Mahogany (w only) 75. Harry and Walter Go to New York (w only) 76. Heartbeat 79. Sphinx (w only) 81. The Razor's Edge 84. The Whoopee Boys 86.

aan, James (1939–).
merican leading man who has not quite made
e front rank, but continues promising.
Irma La Douce 63. Lady in a Cage 64. The Glory
uys 65. Red Line 7000 65. El Dorado 67. Games
7. Journey to Shiloh 68. Countdown 68.
ubmarine XI 68. The Rain People 69. Rabbit Run
). Man Without Mercy 70. *Brian's Song* (TV) 71.
R. Baskin 72. *The Godfather* (AAN) 72. Slither 73.
inderella Liberty 75. Freebie and the Bean 75.
he Gambler 75. Funny Lady 75. Godfather Two
ameo) 74. Rollerball 75. The Killer Elite 76.
arry and Walter Go to New York 76. A Bridge
oo Far 77. Another Man, Another Chance 77.
omes a Horseman 78. Chapter Two 79. Hide in
lain Sight (& d) 80. Les Uns et les Autres 81. Thief
1. Bolero 81. Kiss Me Goodbye 82. Gardens of
one 87. Alien Nation 88. Dick Tracy 90. Misery
0. The Dark Backward 91. For the Boys 91.
oneymoon in Vegas 92. The Program 93.

My acting technique is to look up at God just
before the camera rolls and say, 'Give me a
reak.' – J.C.

abanne, Christy (1888–1950).
merican silent film director for Griffith and
airbanks; declined to second features when talkies
ame.
Enoch Arden 15. Flirting with Fate 16. Reckless
outh 22. Youth for Sale 24. The Masked Bride 27.
ltars of Desire 27. Hotel Continental 32. Daring
aughters 33. A Girl of the Limberlost 34. Keeper
f the Bees 35. The Last Outlaw 36. Criminal
awyer 37. Mutiny on the Blackhawk 39. The
Mummy's Hand 40. Scattergood Baines 41. Drums
f the Congo 42. Keep 'Em Slugging 43. Scared
o Death 46. Robin Hood of Monterey 47. Back
rail 48, many others.

able.
A method of disseminating television programmes
y underground cable whose fibres can
ccommodate a great many channels, none of
hem subject to interference from the others. From
he mid-70s it became highly popular in America
ecause of poor airwave reception in many areas;
s a subscription service it also screened fewer
ommercials and most of its movies were uncut.
These advantages however did not apply in most
other countries, where it had a slower start.

able cars
ave added excitement to the climax of many a
ilm adventure, notably *Night Train to Munich, The
rollenberg Terror, Edge of Eternity, Second Chance,
Where Eagles Dare, Hannibal Brooks* and *The Double
Man*. In 1979 Irwin Allen made a four-hour TV
suspenser, *Hanging by a Thread*, entirely about a
able car accident; but it failed to thrill.

Cabot, Bruce (1904–1972) (Etienne Pelissier de
Bujac).
Square-jawed American hero of many a 30s action
adventure; later turned up as a western villain.
Roadhouse Murder 32. *King Kong* 33. Murder
on the Blackboard 34. Let 'Em Have It 35. Show
Them No Mercy 35. Fury 36. Legion of Terror 37.
Love Takes Flight 37. Smashing the Rackets 38.
Homicide Bureau 39. Dodge City 39. Captain
Caution 40. The Flame of New Orleans 41. Wild
Bill Hickok Rides 42. The Desert Song 43. Salty
O'Rourke 45. Fallen Angel 46. Angel and the
Badman 47. Sorrowful Jones 49. Fancy Pants 50.
Best of the Badmen 51. Kid Monk Baroni 52. The
Quiet American 58. John Paul Jones 59. The
Comancheros 61. Hatari 62. Law of the Lawless 64.
Cat Ballou 65. The War Wagon 67. The Green
Berets 68. Big Jake 71. Diamonds are Forever 71,
many others.

Cabot, Sebastian (1918–1977).
Weighty British character actor who became
popular on American TV as the incarnation of the
pompous but amiable Englishman.
Secret Agent 36. Love on the Dole 41. The
Agitator 45. They Made Me a Fugitive 47. Dick
Barton Strikes Back 48. Old Mother Riley's Jungle
Treasure 50. Ivanhoe 52. Babes in Baghdad 52.
Romeo and Juliet 54. *Kismet* 55. Dragoon Wells
Massacre 57. Terror in a Texas Town 58. The Time
Machine 60. Twice Told Tales 63. The Family
Jewels 65, etc.
TV series: *Checkmate* 59–61. *A Family Affair* 66–
70. Ghost Story 73.

Cabot, Susan (1927–1986) (Harriet Shapiro).
American leading lady of the 50s.
The Enforcer 50. Flame of Araby 51. Battle at
Apache Pass 52. Duel at Silver Creek 52. Ride Clear
of Diablo 54. Fort Massacre 58. The Wasp Woman
60, etc.

Cabrera, Sergio.
Colombian film director. *The Strategy of a Snail* was
the biggest box-office success of the year in
Colombia, out-drawing *Jurassic Park*.
The Strategy of a Snail (La Estrategia del
Caracol) 93.

Cacavas, John (1930–).
American composer.
Redneck 72. Horror Express 72. The Satanic
Rites of Dracula 74. Airport 75 75. Airport 77 77.
Murder at the World Series (TV) 77. Superdome
(TV) 78. Hangar 18 80. Separate Ways 81. The
Executioner's Song 82. A Time to Die 83. They're
Playing with Fire 84. Jessie (TV) 84. The Dirty
Dozen: The Deadly Mission (TV) 87. The Dirty
Dozen: The Fatal Mission (TV) 88. Colombo Goes
to the Guillotine (TV) 89. Murder in Paradise (TV)
90, etc.

Cacoyannis, Michael (1922–).
Greek director, trained in England.
Windfall in Athens 53. Stella 54. A Girl in Black
55. A Matter of Dignity 57. One Last Spring 59. The
Wastrel 61. Electra 62. *Zorba the Greek* (AAN) 64.
The Day the Fish Came Out 67. The Trojan Women
71. Iphigenia 76. Sweet Country (b & w) 86. Up,
Down and Sideways 92. Pano Kato Ke Plagios 93,
etc.

Cadell, Jean (1884–1967).
Sharp-faced Scottish character actress, typically
cast as acidulous spinster and latterly dowager.
The Loves of Robert Burns 30. Fires of Fate 33.
David Copperfield (as Mrs Micawber) 34. Love from
a Stranger 37. *Pygmalion* 38. Quiet Wedding 40.
The Young Mr Pitt 42. Dear Octopus 43. I Know
Where I'm Going 45. Jassy 47. *Whisky Galore* 48.
Madeleine 50. The Late Edwina Black 51. Marry
Me 52. Rockets Galore 56. *A Taste of Money* (leading
role) 62, many others.

Caesar, Adolph (1934–1986).
American actor who made an impression in *A
Soldier's Story* 85, and received an Academy
Award nomination.
The Color Purple 85. Club Paradise 86.

Caesar, Irving (1895–).
American song composer and lyricist.
No No Nanette, Hit the Deck, Wonder Bar, etc.

Caesar, Sid (1922–).
American comedian, seldom in films but a big TV
hit of the 50s, especially in *Your Show of Shows*.
■ Tars and Spars 45. The Guilt of Janet Ames 47.
It's a Mad Mad Mad Mad World 63. A Guide for
the Married Man 67. The Busy Body 67. Ten from
Your Show of Shows 74. Airport 75 75. Silent
Movie 76. The Cheap Detective 78. Grease 78. The
Fiendish Plot of Fu Manchu 80. History of the World
Part One 81. Grease 2 82. Cannonball Run 2 83.
Over the Brooklyn Bridge 83. Stoogemania 86. The
Emperor's New Clothes 87.

Cage, Nicolas (1964–) (N. Coppola).
American leading actor. He is the nephew of
director Francis Ford Coppola.
Rumblefish 83. Racing with the Moon 83. The
Cotton Club 84. Birdy 85. Raising Arizona 87.
Vampire's Kiss 88. Never on Tuesday 89. Time to
Kill (Tempo di Uccidere) 89. Firebirds 90. Wild
at Heart 90. Zandalee 90. Le Raccourci 91.
Honeymoon in Vegas 92. Red Rock West 93. Amos
& Andrew 93. Deadfall 93. Guarding Tess 94. It
Could Happen to You 94, etc.

Cagney, James (1899–1986).
American leading actor whose cocky walk and
punchy personality took him out of the
vaudeville chorus to become one of the most
memorable stars of the 30s and 40s.
Autobiography: 1976, *Cagney by Cagney*.
■ Sinners' Holiday 30. Doorway to Hell 30. The
Steel Highway 30. The Millionaire 31. Other
Men's Women 31. *The Public Enemy* 31. Smart
Money 31. Blonde Crazy 31. Taxi 32. The Crowd
Roars 32. Winner Take All 32. Hard to Handle 33.
The Picture Snatcher 33. Mayor of Hell 33. *Footlight
Parade* 33. *Lady Killer* 33. Jimmy the Gent 34. He
was her Man 34. Here Comes the Navy 34. The
St Louis Kid 34. *Devil Dogs of the Air* 35. G-Men 35.
The Irish in Us 35. *A Midsummer Night's Dream* (as
Bottom) 35. The Frisco Kid 35. Ceiling Zero 35.
Great Guy 36. Something to Sing About 37. *Boy
Meets Girl* 38. *Angels with Dirty Faces* (AAN) 38. The

Oklahoma Kid 39. Each Dawn I Die 39. *The Roaring Twenties* 39. The Fighting 69th 40. Torrid Zone 40. City for Conquest 40. *Strawberry Blonde* 41. The Bride Came C.O.D. 41. Captains of the Clouds 42. *Yankee Doodle Dandy* (AA; as George M. Cohan) 42. Johnny Come Lately 43. Blood on the Sun 45. 13 Rue Madeleine 46. *The Time of Your Life* 48. *White Heat* 49. West Point Story 50. Kiss Tomorrow Goodbye 50. Come Fill the Cup 51. Starlift 51. What Price Glory? 52. A Lion is in the Streets 53. Run for Cover 55. Love Me or Leave Me (AAN) 55. The Seven Little Foys (guest) 55. *Mister Roberts* 55. Tribute to a Bad Man 56. These Wilder Years 56. *Man of a Thousand Faces* (as Lon Chaney) 57. Short Cut to Hell (d only) 58. Never Steal Anything Small 59. Shake Hands with the Devil 59. The Gallant Hours 60. *One Two Three* 61. Arizona Bushwhackers (narrator only) 68. Ragtime 81. Terrible Joe Moran (TV) 84.
🌑 For refining the image of the irrepressible Irishman; for inventing a unique form of dancing; and, whether as gangster or cop, for providing work for a thousand imitators. *Yankee Doodle Dandy*.

¶ He can't even put a telephone receiver back on the hook without giving the action some special spark of life. – *Time*
There's not much to say about acting but this. Never settle back on your heels. Never relax. If you relax, the audience relaxes. And always mean everything you say. – *J.C.*
Cagney has an inspired sense of timing, an arrogant style, a pride in the control of his body and a conviction and lack of self-consciousness that is unique in the deserts of the American cinema. – *Lincoln Kirstein, 1932*
He can do nothing which is not worth watching. – *Graham Greene*
I'm sick of carrying guns and beating up women. – *J.C., 1931.*
I admire him for quitting when he was at the top. – *Robert Redford*

Famous line *(White Heat):* 'Made it, Ma – top of the world!'

Famous line (*Yankee Doodle Dandy):* 'My mother thanks you, my father thanks you, my sister thanks you – and I thank you.'

Cagney, Jeanne (1919–1984) (Jean Cagney).
American actress, in occasional films: sister of James Cagney.
Golden Gloves 40. Yankee Doodle Dandy 42. The Time of Your Life 48. Don't Bother to Knock 52. A Lion is in the Streets 53. Man of a Thousand Faces 57. Town Tamer 65, etc.

Cagney, William (1902–1988).
American producer, brother of James Cagney.
Johnny Come Lately 43. Blood on the Sun 45. The Time of Your Life 48. Kiss Tomorrow Goodbye 50. A Lion is in the Streets 53, etc.

Cahn, Edward L. (1899–1963).
American director of second features.
Homicide Squad 31. *Law and Order* 32 (his best film, with Walter Huston as Wyatt Earp). Confidential 35. Main Street After Dark 44. The Checkered Coat 48. Prejudice 48. Experiment Alcatraz (& p) 51. The Creature with the Atom Brain 58. Girls in Prison 56. Curse of the Faceless Man 58. Guns, Girls and Gangsters 58. It, The Terror from Beyond Space 58. Riot in a Juvenile Prison 61. Beauty and the Beast 62. Incident in an Alley 63, many others.

Cahn, Sammy (1913–1993) (Samuel Cohen).
American lyricist who has written many film songs, usually with James Van Heusen. Won Academy Awards for four songs: 'Three Coins in the Fountain', 'High Hopes', 'All the Way' and 'Call Me Irresponsible'.
Autobiography: 1974, *I Should Care*.
Tonight and Every Night 44. Anchors Aweigh 45. Wonder Man 45. West Point Story 50. April in Paris 53. The Court Jester 55. A Touch of Class 73, etc.

Cain, Christopher (1943–) (Bruce Doggett).
American director and screenwriter.
Brother, My Song 76. The Buzzard 76. Grand Jury 77. Sixth and Main 77. The Stone Boy 84. That Was Then . . . This Is Now 85. Where the River Runs Black 86. The Principal 87. Young Guns 88. Pure Country 92. The Next Karate Kid 94, etc.

Cain, James M. (1892–1977).
American novelist of the hard-boiled school; also worked in Hollywood.
She Made Her Bed (oa) 34. Stand Up and Fight (w) 38. When Tomorrow Comes (oa) 39. *Double Indemnity* (oa) 44. Gypsy Wildcat (w) 44. *Mildred Pierce* (oa) 45. *The Postman Always Rings Twice* (oa) 46, 81. Serenade (oa) 56. Butterfly 85, etc.

Caine, Michael (1933–) (Maurice Micklewhite).
British light leading man with effective mild manner and deliberately unconcealed cockney origin. Played for years in second features before his international appeal was discovered. He now runs his own production company, M & M Productions, in partnership with Martin Bregman.
Autobiography: 1993, *What's It All About*.
How to Murder a Rich Uncle 56. A Hill in Korea 56. Blind Spot 58. The Key 58. Passport to Shame 58. The Wrong Arm of the Law 62. Solo for Sparrow 62, etc.
■ COMPLETE FROM 1963: *Zulu* 64. *The Ipcress File* 65. *Alfie* (AAN) 66. The Wrong Box 66. Gambit 66. Funeral in Berlin 66. Woman Times Seven 67. Hurry Sundown 67. Billion Dollar Brain 67. Deadfall 68. The Magus 68. Play Dirty 68. The Italian Job 69. The Battle of Britain 69. Too Late the Hero 69. The Last Valley 70. *Get Carter* 71. Zee and Co 71. Kidnapped 72. Pulp 72. *Sleuth* (AAN) 73. The Black Windmill 73. The Marseilles Contract 74. The Wilby Conspiracy 75. Peeper 75. The Romantic Englishwoman 75. The Man Who Would Be King 76. Harry and Walter Go To New York 76. The Eagle Has Landed 76. A Bridge Too Far 77. Silver Bears 77. Swarm 78. Ashanti 78. *California Suite* 78. Beyond the Poseidon Adventure 79. Dressed to Kill 80. The Island 80. The Hand 81. Victory 81. Deathtrap 82. *Educating Rita* (AAN) 83. The Honorary Consul 83. The Jigsaw Man 83. Blame It On Rio 84. Water 84. The Holcroft Covenant 84, *Hannah and Her Sisters* (AA) 86. Sweet Liberty 86. Half Moon Street 86. The Whistle Blower 86. Mona Lisa 86. The Fourth Protocol 86. Jaws – The Revenge 87. Surrender 87. Dirty Rotten Scoundrels 88. Without a Clue 88. Mr Destiny 90. A Shock to the System 90. Bullseye! 91. Noises Off 92. Blue Ice 92. A Muppet Christmas Carol 92. On Deadly Ground 93.

¶ I'll always be there because I'm a skilled professional actor. Whether or not I've any talent is beside the point. – *M.C.*
John Wayne once advised me, talk low, talk slow and don't talk too much. And then I went and made *Sleuth*. – *M.C.*
I'm a sort of boy next door. If that boy has a good scriptwriter. – *M.C.*

You get paid the same for a bad film as you do for a good one. – *M.C.*

Calamity Jane (c. 1848–1903) (Martha Jane Canary).
This rootin' tootin' shootin' woman of the Old West has been glamorized many times for the movies, notably by Jean Arthur in *The Plainsman* 36, Frances Farmer in *Badlands of Dakota* 41, Jane Russell in *The Paleface* 48, Yvonne de Carlo in *Calamity Jane and Sam Bass* 49, Evelyn Ankers in *The Texan Meets Calamity Jane* 50, Doris Day in *Calamity Jane* 53, Judi Meredith in *The Raiders* 64 and Abby Dalton in *The Plainsman* 66.

Calder-Marshall, Anna (1949–).
British leading actress.
Pussycat Pussycat I Love You 70. *Wuthering Heights* 70. Zulu Dawn 79. Two Faces of Evil 82, etc.

Caldwell, Erskine (1903–1987).
American novelist who attacked social injustice in several novels which by their sensationalism earned him a fortune. *Tobacco Road* was filmed as a farce; *God's Little Acre* had to be taken straight.

Calhern, Louis (1895–1956) (Carl Vogt).
Distinguished American stage actor who was in films occasionally from silent days and later became one of MGM's elder statesmen.
■ What's Worth While? 21. The Blot 21. Too Wise Wives 21. Women, Wake Up 22. The Last Moment 23. Stolen Heaven 31. Road to Singapore 31. Blonde Crazy 31. They Call It Sin 32. Night After Night 32. Okay America 32. Afraid to Talk 32. The Woman Accused 33. Twenty Thousand Years in Sing Sing 33. Frisco Jenny 33. Strictly Personal 33. World Gone Mad 33. Diplomaniacs 33. Duck Soup 33. Affairs of Cellini 34. Man with Two Faces 34. The Count of Monte Cristo 34. Sweet Adeline 34. The Arizonian 34. Woman Wanted 35. The Last Days of Pompeii 35. The Gorgeous Hussy 36. Her Husband Lies 36. The Life of Emile Zola 37. Fast Company 38. Juarez 39. Fifth Avenue Girl 39. Charlie McCarthy Detective 39. I Take this Woman 40. Dr Ehrlich's Magic Bullet 40. Heaven Can Wait 43. Nobody's Darling 43. Up in Arms 44. The Bridge of San Luis Rey 44. Notorious 46. Arch of Triumph 48. The Red Pony 49. The Red Danube 49. *Annie Get Your Gun* (as Buffalo Bill) 50. Nancy Goes to Rio 50. *The Asphalt Jungle* 50. Devil's Doorway 50. A Life of Her Own 50. *The Magnificent Yankee* (AAN) 50. Two Weeks with Love 50. Man with a Cloak 51. It's a Big Country 51. Invitation 52. We're Not Married 52. Washington Story 52. *The Prisoner of Zenda* 52. Confidentially Connie 53. Remains To Be Seen 53. Julius Caesar (title role) 53. Latin Lovers 53. Main Street to Broadway 53. Rhapsody 54. Executive Suite 54. The Student Prince 54. Men of the Fighting Lady 54. Betrayed 54. Athena 54. The Blackboard Jungle 55. The Prodigal 55. Forever Darling 56. High Society 56.

Calhoun, Rory (1922–) (Francis Timothy Durgin).
Amiable American leading man of 50s action films did not make the first rank.
Something for the Boys 44. The Red House 47. Miraculous Journey 48. Massacre River 49. Rogue River 50. I'd Climb the Highest Mountain 51. *With a Song in My Heart* 52. Powder River 53. How to Marry a Millionaire 53. Four Guns to the Border 54. Dawn at Socorro 54. Treasure of Pancho Villa 55. The Spoilers 55. Raw Edge 56. The Big Caper 57. The Hired Gun 57. The Colossus of Rhodes 60. Marco Polo 61. A Face in the Rain 62. The Gun Hawk 64. Apache Uprising 65. Finger on the Trigger 67. Dayton's Devils 68. Night of the

Lepus 72. Avenging Angel 84. Hell Comes to Frogtown 88. Pure Country 92, many others.

TV series: The Texan 58–59. The Blue and the Grey 82.

Callahan, Gene (1908–1990).
American production designer.

America, America (AA) 63. The Cardinal (AAN) 63. The Group 65. The Last Tycoon (AAN) 76. Julia 77. Eyes of Laura Mars 78. Bloodbrothers 79. Whose Life Is It, Anyway? 81. Grease 2 82. Jagged Edge 85. Children of a Lesser God 86. Black Widow 87. Little Nikita 88. Arthur 2: On the Rocks 88. Steel Magnolias 89. The Man in the Moon 91, etc.

Callan, Michael (1935–) (Martin Caliniff).
American leading man, former dancer.

They Came to Cordura 58. The Flying Fontaines 59. Mysterious Island 61. Bon Voyage 62. The Interns 63. The Victors 63. Cat Ballou 65. You Must Be Joking 65. Lepke 75. The Cat and the Canary 78. Freeway 88, etc.

TV series: Occasional Wife 66.

Callard, Kay.
Canadian leading lady in Britain in the 50s.

They Who Dare 54. Find the Lady 56. Intent to Kill 58. Freedom to Die 62, etc.

TV series: Knight Errant 58–60.

Callas, Maria (1923–1977) (Maria Kalogeropolos).
Celebrated Greek-American opera singer who in 1971 played the non-singing role of *Medea*.

Calleia, Joseph (1897–1975) (Joseph Spurin-Calleja).
Humorous but often sinister Maltese character actor who after world tours as an opera singer settled in Hollywood in the 30s and played several distinguished roles.

His Woman 31. Public Hero Number One 35. After the Thin Man 36. Winner Take All 37. Algiers 38. Juarez 39. Five Came Back 39. Golden Boy 39. My Little Chickadee 40. The Monster and the Girl 41. Jungle Book 42. *The Glass Key* 42. For Whom the Bell Tolls 43. The Conspirators 44. Gilda 46. Lured 47. Four Faces West 48. Noose (GB) 48. Vendetta 50. Branded 51. Valentino 51. When in Rome 52. Treasure of Pancho Villa 55. Hot Blood 56. Serenade 56. Wild is the Wind 57. Touch of Evil 58. Cry Tough 59. The Alamo 60. Johnny Cool 63, many others.

Calley, John (1930–).
American production executive who was appointed president of United Artists in 1993. He was president of production at Warner Brothers from 1975–80.

The Americanization of Emily (co-p) 64. Wheeler Dealer 64. Topkapi (co-p) 64. The Cincinatti Kid (co-p) 65. Tne Loved One (co-p) 65. Don't Make Waves 67. Ice Station Zebra 68. Catch 22 (co-p) 70. Postcards from the Edge (co-p) 90, etc.

Callow, Simon (1949–).
British stage actor, in occasional films. He now concentrates on directing, mainly for the stage. He is the author of a biography of Charles Laughton 87 and *Being An Actor* 85, a book that challenged the autocracy of directors.

Autobiography: 1991, *Shooting the Actor*.

■ Amadeus 84. A Room with a View 86. Maurice 87. Mr & Mrs Bridge 90. Postcards from the Edge 90. The Ballad of the Sad Café (d) 91. Soft Top, Hard Shoulder 92. Howards End 92. Femme Fatale (TV) 93. Four Weddings and a Funeral 94.

TV series: Little Napoleons 94.

Calloway, Cab (1907–1994) (Cabell Calloway).
High-spirited American band leader and entertainer, in occasional films.

Autobiography: 1976, *Of Minnie the Moocher and Me*.

The Big Broadcast 32. International House 33. The Singing Kid 36. Manhattan Merry Go Round 37. *Stormy Weather* 43. Sensations of 1945 44. St Louis Blues 58. The Cincinnati Kid 65. A Man Called Adam 66. The Blues Brothers 80, etc.

Calthrop, Donald (1888–1940).
Slightly-built British stage actor whose film appearances were usually as nervy villains.

The Gay Lord Quex 18. Nelson 19. *Shooting Stars* 27. *Blackmail* 29. Atlantic 30. Murder 30. The Bells 31. Number Seventeen 32. The Ghost Train 32. Rome Express 32. I Was a Spy 33. Friday the Thirteenth 33. Sorrell and Son 34. The Clairvoyant 34. Scrooge 35. Broken Blossoms 36. Fire Over England 36. Dreaming Lips 37. Let George Do It 40. Major Barbara 40, etc.

Calvert, E. H. (1873–1941).
American silent screen director who later had a second career as an actor, usually in military roles.
AS DIRECTOR: One Wonderful Night 14. The Slim Princess 15. The Man Trail 15. The Outer Edge 15. A Daughter of the City 15, etc.
AS ACTOR: The House of Pride 12. Vultures of Society 16. The Silent Partner 23. Inez from Hollywood 24. Sally 25. Ella Cinders 26. Rookies 27. The Wizard 27. Legion of the Condemned 28. The Canary Murder Case 29. The Virginian 29. The Love Parade 30. The Benson Murder Case 30. Beyond Victory 31. The Mysterious Rider 33. Here Comes the Groom 34. The Oregon Trail 36, many others.

Calvert, Phyllis (1915–) (Phyllis Bickle).
British leading lady of the forties, former child actress; usually played good girls.

Two Days to Live 39. They Came by Night 39. Charley's Big-hearted Aunt 40. Let George Do It 40. *Kipps* 41. The Young Mr Pitt 42. Uncensored 42. *The Man in Grey* 43. *Fanny by Gaslight* 44. Two Thousand Women 44. *Madonna of the Seven Moons* 44. They Were Sisters 45. Men of Two Worlds 46. The Magic Bow 46. The Root of All Evil 47. Time Out of Mind (US) 47. *My Own True Love* (US) 48. Broken Journey 48. Appointment with Danger (US) 49. The Golden Madonna 49. The Woman with No Name 50. Mr Denning Drives North 51. *Mandy* 52. The Net 53. It's Never Too Late 55. Child in the House 56. Indiscreet 58. Oscar Wilde 60. The Battle of the Villa Fiorita 65. Twisted Nerve 68. Oh What a Lovely War 69. The Walking Stick 69, etc.

TV series: Kate 70–71.

Calvet, Corinne (1925–) (Corinne Dibos).
French leading lady, a statuesque blonde who had some success in Hollywood in the early 50s.

Autobiography: 1983, *Has Corinne Been a Good Girl?*

La Part de l'Ombre 45. Rope of Sand 49. When Willie Comes Marching Home 50. On the Riviera 51. What Price Glory? 52. Powder River 53. Flight to Tangier 53. The Far Country 54. So This Is Paris 55. The Plunderers of Painted Flats 58. Bluebeard's Ten Honeymoons 60. Hemingway's Adventures of a Young Man 62. Apache Uprising 65. Dr Heckle and Mr Hype 80. The Death of the Heart 86, etc.

Calvin, Henry (1918–1975) (Wimberly Calvin Goodman Jnr).
Rotund American comedy actor who for a while appeared in Disney films imitating Oliver Hardy.

Babes in Toyland 60. Toby Tyler 63.

TV series: Zorro.

Cambern, Donn.
American editor.

2000 Years Later 69. Easy Rider 69. The Last Picture Show 71. Blume in Love 73. The Hindenberg 75. Hooper 78. Time after Time 79. The Cannonball Run 81. Romancing the Stone (AAN) 84. Harry and the Hendersons 87. Twins 88. Ghostbusters II 89. The Bodyguard 92, etc.

Cambridge, Godfrey (1929–1976).
American comic actor.

The Last Angry Man 59. Gone are the Days 63. The Busy Body 67. The President's Analyst 67. Bye Bye Braverman 68. The Biggest Bundle of' Them All 68. *Watermelon Man 70. Cotton Comes to Harlem* 70. The Biscuit Eater 72. Come Back Charleston Blue 72. Whiffs 75, etc.

cameo.
A word coined (in its cinematic sense) by Mike Todd when persuading famous stars to accept walk-on parts for *Around the World in Eighty Days*.

Camerini, Mario (1895–1981).
Italian director of the old commercial school.

The House of Pulcini 24. Kiff Tebbi 27. Rotaie 29. Giallo 33. Il Grande Appello 36. Il Signor Max 37. Il Documento Fatale 39. Una Romantica Avventura 40. I Promessi Sposi 41. Due Lettere Anonime 45. The Captain's Daughter 47. Molti Sogni per le Strade 48. Il Brigante Musolino 50. Wife for a Night 51. Ulysses 54. The Miller's Wife 55. Primo Amore 58. Via Margutta 60. And Suddenly It's Murder 60. Kali-Yug Goddess of Vengeance 63. Don Camillo and Modern Youth 72, many others.

Cameron, Earl (1925–).
Jamaican actor seen in many British films.

Pool of London 50. Emergency Call 51. The Heart of the Matter 53. Simba 55. Safari 56. Sapphire 59. Flame in the Streets 61. Guns at Batasi 64. Thunderball 65. Battle beneath the Earth 68. Mohammed 77, etc.

Cameron, James (1954–).
Canadian-born action film director and screenwriter who began as an art director for Roger Corman. He runs his own production company, Lightstorm Entertainment, with his partner, producer Lawrence Kasanoff, and signed a five-year deal in 1992 with Fox to produce 12 films. He was formerly married to producer Gale Anne Hurd and director Kathryn Bigelow. He has a daughter by actress Linda Hamilton. Founded his own computer effects company, Digital Domain, in the mid-90s.

Piranha II: The Spawning 83. *The Terminator* 84. Rambo: First Blood Part II (w) 85. Aliens 86. The Abyss 89. *Terminator 2: Judgment Day* 91. True Lies (p, wd) 94. Strange Days (co-w) 95, etc.

❡ I would never do anything as merciful as firing anyone. – *J.C.*

If you're going to hang out with Jim, you better have your life insurance. – *Bill Paxton*

Cameron, John (1944–).
British composer.

Poor Cow 67. The Ruling Class 68. Kes 70. Every Home Should Have One 70. All the Right Noises 71. A Touch of Class 73. Scalawag 73. Night Watch 73. Out of Season 75. Great Scout and Cathouse Thursday 76. Nasty Habits 77. The Thief of Baghdad 78. Sunburn 79. Lost and Found 79.

The Mirror Crack'd 80. Who? 82. The Jigsaw Man 84. Jack the Ripper (TV) 88. Jekyll and Hyde (TV) 90, etc.

Cameron, Rod (1910–1983) (Nathan Cox).
Rugged Canadian star of many a Hollywood second feature; originally labourer, engineer, and stand-in for Fred MacMurray.
Christmas in July 40. Northwest Mounted Police 40. The Monster and the Girl 41. The Remarkable Andrew 42. Wake Island 42. Gung Ho 43. Boss of Boom Town 44. Salome Where She Danced 45. The Runaround 46. The Bride Wasn't Willing 46. The Plunderers 48. Panhandle 49. The Sea Hornet 51. Ride the Man Down 53. Escapement (GB) 57. The Gun Hawk 63. The Bounty Killer 65. Old Firehand (Ger.) 66. The Last Movie 71. Evel Knievel 71. Jessie's Girls 76, many others.
TV series: City Detective 53–54. Coronado 9 59. State Trooper 57–59.

Cammel, Donald.
British screenwriter and director.
Duffy 68. *Performance* (co-d) 70. Demon Seed (d) 77. Tilt (w) 79. White of the Eye (wd) 87. Centrifuge (w) 90, etc.

Camp, Colleen (1953–).
American actress.
Battle for the Planet of the Apes 73. Smile 75. Funny Lady 75. Apocalypse Now 79. Game of Death 79. They All Laughed 82. Valley Girls 83. Joy of Sex 84. Police Academy 2: Their First Assignment 85. D.A.R.Y.L. 85. Clue 85. Police Academy 3: Back in Training 86. Police Academy 4: Citizens on Patrol 87. Track 29 88. Wicked Stepmother 89. The Vagrant 91. Wayne's World 92, etc.

Camp, Joe (1939–).
American director of independent family films: *Benji, For the Love of Benji,* etc.

Campanella, Joseph (1927–).
American stage and TV actor who makes occasional film appearances.
Murder Inc. 61. The Young Lovers 64. The St Valentine's Day Massacre 67. Ben 72. Journey from Darkness (TV) 75. Meteor 79. Plutonium Incident (TV) 80. Steele Justice 87. Down the Drain 89. Body Chemistry 90. Club Fed 91. No Retreat No Surrender 3: Blood Brothers 91. Ninja Dragons 92, etc.
TV series: The Nurses 64–65. Mannix 67–68. The Lawyers 69–72. The Colbys 85–86.

Campanile, Pasquale Festa (1927–1986).
Italian director.
The Chastity Belt 67. The Girl and the General 68. The Libertine 69. La Calandria 72. When Women Lost Their Tails 72. Rugantino 73. Soldier of Fortune 75. Autostop 77. Amante 78. Gege Bellevita 79, etc.

Campbell, Beatrice (1923–1980).
British leading lady.
Wanted for Murder 46. Things Happen at Night 48. Silent Dust 48. Last Holiday 50. The Mudlark 50. Laughter in Paradise 51. Grand National Night 53. Cockleshell Heroes 55, etc.

Campbell, Bruce.
American actor, the clean-cut hero of horror movies.
Evil Dead 83. Crimewave 86. Evil Dead II 87. Maniac Cop 88. Moontrap 90. Mindwarp 92. Army of Darkness: The Medieval Dead 93. The Hudsucker Proxy 94, etc.

Campbell, Colin (1883–1966).
Diminutive Scottish character actor, long in Hollywood.
Tillie's Tomato Surprise 15. Where Lights are Low 21. The Grail 23. The White Monkey 25. Big Boy 30. Alice in Wonderland 33. San Francisco Docks 41. Mrs Miniver 42. The Lodger 44. Moss Rose 47. The Fan 49. Abbott and Costello Meet the Keystone Kops 55. The Lost World 60. My Fair Lady 64.

Campbell, Colin (1937–).
Young British proletarian actor of the 60s.
Saturday Night Out 63. The Leather Boys 63. The High Bright Sun 65.

Campbell, Eric (1878–1917).
Scottish actor who played the bearded heavy in some of Chaplin's most famous two-reelers 1916–17: *Easy Street, The Cure, The Adventurer,* etc.

Campbell, Glen (1935–).
American pop singer, venturing into films.
True Grit 69. Norwood 69. Uphill All the Way 85. Rock-a-Doodle (voice) 90, etc.

Campbell, Judy (1916–) (Judy Gamble).
British leading lady of stage and TV; film appearances infrequent. She is the mother of actress Jane Birkin.
Saloon Bar 40. Breach of Promise 41. The World Owes Me a Living 44. Green for Danger 46. Bonnie Prince Charlie 48. There's a Girl in My Soup 70. Forbush and the Penguins 71. Dust to Dust (TV) 85, etc.

Campbell, Martin.
New Zealand-born director, who made his name working for British television.
Reilly – Ace of Spies (TV) 81. Charlie (TV) 83. Edge of Darkness (TV) 85. Frankie and Johnnie (TV) 85. Criminal Law 88. Defenseless 91. No Escape 94, etc.

Campbell, Mrs Patrick (1865–1940) (Beatrice Tanner).
Leading British stage actress, the original Eliza in *Pygmalion,* who spent her last years playing supporting roles in Hollywood. Marie Dressler caricatured her as Carlotta Vance in *Dinner at Eight.*
■ The Dancers 30. Riptide 34. One More River 34. Outcast Lady 34. Crime and Punishment 35.

¶ 'She has an ego like a raging tooth.' – *W. B. Yeats*
(Reported conversation) 'You are handsome enough to be in pictures.' – 'But Mrs Campbell, my name is Joseph Schildkraut.' – 'Never mind, you can change it.'

Famous line (when offered the role of the pawnbroker in *Crime and Punishment*): 'I could not possibly become a tradesperson.'

Campbell, Patrick (1913–1980).
British humorist and screenplay writer, the latter usually with Vivienne Knight.
Captain Boycott 47. Helter Skelter 50. The Oracle 54. Lucky Jim 57. Go to Blazes 62. Girl in the Headlines 63, etc.

Campbell, William (1926–).
American actor, often seen as personable villain or friend of the hero.
The Breaking Point 50. The People against O'Hara 52. Escape from Fort Bravo 53. The High and the Mighty 54. Man without a Star 55. Cell

2455 Death Row (as Caryl Chessman) 55. Backlash 56. Eighteen and Anxious 57. The Naked and the Dead 58. The Young Racers 63. The Secret Invasion 64. Hush Hush Sweet Charlotte 64. Dementia 13 65. Blood Bath 66. Black Gunn 72. Dirty Mary Crazy Larry 74, etc.
TV series: Cannonball 58–59. Dynasty 84–85. Crime Story 86–88.

Campion, Jane (1955–).
New Zealand director and screenwriter.
Sweetie 89. An Angel at My Table 90. The Piano (AAw, AANd) 93.

Campos, Rafael (1936–1985).
Dominican actor best remembered for *The Blackboard Jungle* 55.
TV series: Rhoda 77–78. Centennial 78–79. V 83.

Camus, Marcel (1912–1982).
French director, a former art teacher, who worked as an assistant to Henri Decoin, Alexandre Astruc and others. He made his first short in 1950 and achieved international success with *Black Orpheus* one of several films he made in Brazil and which starred his wife, Marpessa Dawn.
Mort et Fraude 56. Black Orpheus (Orfeu Negro) (AA) 58. Os Bandeirantes 60. Le Chant du Monde 65. Vivre la Nuit 68. Le Mur de l'Atlantique 70. Otalia de Bahia 77, etc.

Canada
has made strenuous efforts through the years to promote a native film industry, but the trouble has been that its best talents are easily siphoned off to Hollywood or Britain, and few genuinely Canadian films have earned world acclaim; among those to raise interest have been *Mon Oncle Antoine* and *The Apprenticeship of Duddy Kravitz.*
The National Film Board of Canada, however, has had a stimulating effect on world documentary especially when under the leadership of John Grierson: and Norman McLaren's experimental cartoons are enjoyed the world over.
Films wholly or largely set in Canada have included *Saskatchewan, Quebec, Northwest Mounted Police, The Canadians, River's End, The Naked Heart, Northern Pursuit, Island in the Sky, Hudson's Bay, Rose Marie* and *Jalna.* Until the end of the 70s the best of them was probably the wartime *49th Parallel,* but the 80s brought new efforts in the direction of international co-production, and although the first fruits seemed heavily influenced by current Hollywood fashion, signs of a new vitality have undoubtedly emerged.
The Canadian government has made half-hearted attempts to encourage the local industry to escape American domination, but with little success. Some excellent talents, however, emerged towards the end of the 80s. The French-Canadian director Denys Arcand attracted international attention with his *The Decline of the American Empire* 86 and, especially, *Jesus of Montreal* 89. And Atom Egoyan's more experimental *Family Viewing* 87, *Speaking Parts* 89, and *The Adjuster* 91 have found appreciative art-house audiences.

Canale, Gianna Maria (1927–).
Italian leading lady, occasionally seen in international films.
Rigoletto 49. Go For Broke 51. The Man from Cairo 53. Theodora Slave Empress 54. The Silent Enemy 58. The Whole Truth 58. Queen of the Pirates 60. Scaramouche 63. The Marauder 65, etc.

Canary, David (1938–).
American western actor who played for a while in

oth *Wagon Train* and *Bonanza* before concentrating n daytime soap operas.

Hombre 67. Sharks' Treasure 74. Posse 75. The ain Curse (TV) 78, etc.

Candy, John (1950–1994).
ulky Canadian actor and writer in Hollywood, ften as a good-natured slob.

The Silent Partner 78. Lost and Found 79. Stripes 1. Brewster's Millions 84. Splash! 84. Summer ental 84. Volunteers 85. Little Shop of Horrors 7. Planes, Trains and Automobiles 87. Spaceballs 7. The Great Outdoors 88. Hot to Trot 88. Uncle uck 89. Who's Harry Crumb? 89. The Rescuers own Under (voice) 90. Only the Lonely 91. elirious 91. Career Opportunities 91. Nothing but rouble 91. JFK 91. Once Upon a Crime 92. Cool unnings 93. Rookie of the Year (uncredited) 93. ostage for a Day (TV) (& d) 94. Canadian Bacon 4. Wagons East! 94, etc.

TV series: Second City TV 77–79. SCTV Network 0 81–83.

Cannes.
A Riviera watering place which since the late orties has housed a film festival having more to o with commerce than with art. Rex Reed escribed it as a place 'where you lie on the beach nd look at the stars – or vice versa.' See Appendix or a full list of its awards.

Cannibalism
as been featured in such documentaries as *The ky Above, The Mud Below*, but it is rare in fiction ilms, although it is becoming much more ommon. Apart from the Swedish short *Midvinterblot*, the main examples are from the 70s: *Welcome to Arrow Beach* and *Survive!*, a low-budget ilm based on the true story of the cannibalistic survivors of a South American plane crash. It was emade in 92 as *Alive!* By then, the films *Manhunter* 36 and *The Silence of The Lambs* 91 had made a popular bogeyman of Dr Hannibal Lecter, a serial killer who feasted on his victims. Cannibalism also featured in the climax of Peter Greenaway's art- house hit *The Cook, the Thief, His Wife and Her Lover* 39. From the 60s onwards, eaters of human flesh had become a familiar ingredient of horror movies, notably in the cult success *Texas Chainsaw Massacre* 74 and its sequels. But it also found its way into more mainstream films, including *The 'burbs* and *Parents*, showing that no taboo is proof against the predations of producers.

Canning, Victor (1911–1986).
British detective novelist whose works have often been filmed.

Spy Hunt 50. The Golden Salamander 51. Venetian Bird 53. The House of the Seven Hawks 59. Masquerade 63. Family Plot 76.

Cannon and Ball (Tommy Derbyshire, 1938– ; Robert Harper, 1944–).
British comedians from the working-men's club circuit. First film, *The Boys in Blue* 83.

Cannon, Danny (1968–).
English director and screenwriter who went to work for Hollywood after his first film.

Young Americans (co-w, d) 93. Judge Dredd (d) 95.

Cannon, Dyan (1938–) (Samile Diane Friesen).
American leading actress who tends to play floozies. She was married to Cary Grant (1965–68).

The Rise and Fall of Legs Diamond 59. *Bob and Carol and Ted and Alice* (AAN) 69. Doctors' Wives 70. The Anderson Tapes 71. The Love Machine 71.

Such Good Friends 72. Shamus 72. The Last of Sheila 73. Child Under a Leaf 75. Revenge of the Pink Panther 77. *Heaven Can Wait* (AAN) 78. Lady of the House (TV) 79. Coast to Coast 80. Honeysuckle Rose 80. Deathtrap 82. Author! Author! 82, etc. Master of the Game (TV) 83. Jenny's War (TV) 84. Caddyshack II 88. The End of Innocence (& wd) 90. Jailbirds (TV) 90. The Pickle 93, etc.

Cannon, Esma (1896–1972).
Diminutive British character actress often seen in bit parts. Notable in *Sailor Beware* 56.

Cannon, J. D. (1922–).
Cold-eyed American character actor.

An American Dream 66. Cool Hand Luke 67. Cotton Comes to Harlem 70. Lawman 71. Testimony of Two Men (TV) 77. Killing Stone (TV) 78. Ike (TV) 79. Raise the Titanic 80. Walking through the Fire (TV) 80. Death Wish 2 81. Street Justice 89, etc.

TV series: McCloud 71–76. Call to Glory 84– 85.

Cannon, Robert (1901–1964).
American animator, a leading figure at UPA during the formative period and the designer of simplified, witty cartoons like *Gerald McBoing Boing* and *Christopher Crumpet*.

Canonero, Milena.
Italian costume designer, in Hollywood.

A Clockwork Orange 71. Barry Lyndon (AA) 75. Midnight Express 78. The Shining 80. Chariots of Fire (AA) 81. The Hunger 83. The Cotton Club 84. Give My Regards to Broad Street 84. Out of Africa (AAN) 85. Barfly 87. Haunted Summer 88. Tucker: The Man and His Dream (AAN) 88. Dick Tracy (AAN) 90. Godfather III 90. Single White Female 92, etc.

Canova, Diana (1953–).
American light actress, daughter of Judy Canova.

The First Nudie Musical 76. Love Boat II (TV) 77. With This Ring (TV) 78. Night Partners 93, etc.

TV series: Soap 77–80. But I'm a Big Girl Now 81. Foot in the Door 83. Throb 86.

Canova, Judy (1916–1983) (Juliet Canova).
American hillbilly comedienne whose strident yodelling and cornfed humour enlivened a number of forties programmers.

■ In Caliente 35. Broadway Gondolier 35. Going Highbrow 35. Artists and Models 37. Thrill of a Lifetime 37. Scatterbrain 40. Sis Hopkins 41. Puddin'head 41. Sleepytime Gal 42. True to the Army 42. Joan of Ozark 42. Chatterbox 43. Sleepy Lagoon 43. Louisiana Hayride 44. Hit the Hay 45. Singin' in the Corn 45. Honeychile 51. Oklahoma Annie 52. The WAC from Walla Walla 52. Untamed Heiress 54. Carolina Cannonball 55. Lay That Rifle Down 55. The Adventures of Huckleberry Finn 60.

Cantinflas (1911–1993) (Mario Moreno).
Mexican clown, acrobat and bullfighter who made unambitious local comedies for years and was briefly beckoned by Hollywood in the 50s. Immensely popular in Spanish-speaking countries. In Mexican films from 1936.

Neither Blood Nor Sand 41. Romeo and Juliet 44. *Around the World in Eighty Days* 56. *Pepe* 59, many others.

Cantor, Eddie (1892–1964) (Edward Israel Itskowitz).
Rolling-eyed American vaudeville entertainer

whose inimitable high-toned voice and sprightly movement made him a big Hollywood star of the 30s. He later made a huge hit in radio, and wrote several autobiographical books including *Take My Life* (1957), *The Way I See It* (1959) and *As I Remember Them* (1962). He appeared briefly in a 1953 biopic, *The Eddie Cantor Story*, in which he was played by Keefe Brasselle, and in 1956 received an Academy Award 'for distinguished service to the film industry'.

■ Kid Boots 26. Special Delivery 27. Glorifying the American Girl 29. *Whoopee* 30. Palmy Days 31. *The Kid from Spain* 32. *Roman Scandals* 33. Kid Millions 34. Strike Me Pink 35. Ali Baba Goes to Town 37. Forty Little Mothers 40. *Thank Your Lucky Stars* 43. *Show Business* 44. If You Knew Susie 48. The Story of Will Rogers (guest) 52.

¶ Another bride; another groom;
   Another sunny honeymoon;
   Another season; another reason
   For makin' whoopee . . .
   – Cantor's most famous song

Canty, Marietta (1906–1986).
American character actress.

The Searching Wind 46. Home Sweet Homicide 47. Father of the Bride 50. The I Don't Care Girl 53. My Foolish Heart 50, etc.

Canutt, Yakima (1895–1986) (Enos Edward Canutt).
American stuntman and second unit director specializing in action. A former rodeo rider, who won world championships in 1917, 19, 20, and 23, he turned to stunts with the coming of sound, performing them in innumerable westerns, including many of John Wayne's early films. He then used his expertise as a second unit director in epic films and was awarded an Oscar in 1966.

Autobiography: 1980, *Stunt Man*.

Lightning Bryce (serial) 19. 'Scar' Hanan 25. Lonesome Trail 30. Westward Bound 31. Two-Fisted Justice 32. Fighting Texans 33. West of the Divide 34. The Last Days of Pompeii 35. San Francisco 36. Riders of the Dawn 37. Stage Coach (including as the Indian who jumps on the lead horse of the coach and is shot by Wayne) 39. Man of Conquest 39. Gone with the Wind (including doubling Gable driving a one-horse hack through the burning streets of Atlanta) 39. Dark Command 40. They Died with Their Boots On 41. Gentleman Jim 42. The Devil's Doorway 50. Only the Valiant 51. Ivanhoe 53. Mogambo 53. Knights of the Round Table 53. Westward Ho, the Wagons 55. Old Yeller 57. Ben Hur 59. Spartacus 60. El Cid 61. The Fall of the Roman Empire 64. Cat Ballou 65. Khartoum 66. Where Eagles Dare 67. A Man Called Horse 69. Rio Lobo 70. Equus 76, etc.

¶ It doesn't matter how great the stunt is, what matters is what gets on film. – Y.C.
You don't have to be crazy in the picture business, but it sure helps. – Y.C.

Capaldi, Peter.
Scottish leading actor and screenwriter.

Local Hero 83. The Love Child 87. Lair of the White Worm 88. Dangerous Liaisons 88. Soft Top, Hard Shoulder (& w) 92. Prime Suspect 3 (TV) 93. Captives 94, etc.

Capellani, Albert (1870–1931).
French director of silent films, in Hollywood from 1915.

Camille 15. La Vie de Bohème 16. Daybreak 17.

The Red Lantern 19. The Fortune Teller 20. The Young Diana 22. Sisters 22, etc.

Capone, Al (1899–1947).
Italian–American gangster, the king of Chicago during the roaring 20s. Has been impersonated many times on screen, notably by Paul Muni (*Scarface*), Edward G. Robinson (*Little Caesar*), Rod Steiger (*Al Capone*), Neville Brand (*The Scarface Mob*), Jason Robards (*The St Valentine's Day Massacre*), Robert De Niro (*The Untouchables*).

¶ It was ironic that he, who was guilty of committing countless murders, had to be punished merely for failing to pay taxes on the money he had made by murder. – *Herbert Hoover*

Capote, Truman (1924–1984) (Truman Persons).
Diminutive, boyish American Southern short-story writer, novelist, playwright and screenwriter, who achieved literary fame at the age of 21 with his first book, *Other Voices, Other Rooms*. Late in life, when corpulent and alcoholic though retaining his curiously high-pitched voice, he starred in *Murder by Death* 76. His lovers are said to have included Errol Flynn and John Garfield.
   Beat the Devil (co-w) 53. Breakfast at Tiffany's (oa) 61. The Innocents (co-w) 61. In Cold Blood (oa) 67.

¶ I'd rather be a friend of mine than an enemy. – *T.C.*
   The trouble with most actors (*and* actresses) is that they are dumb. And, in many instances, the dumbest are the most gifted. – *T.C.*
   A work of art is the one mystery, the one extreme magic; everything else is either arithmetic or biology. – *T.C.*
   The most perfect writer of a generation. – *Norman Mailer*

Capra, Frank (1897–1991).
Italian-American director who is justly celebrated for a stylish handful of 30s and 40s comedies demonstrating a whimsical attachment to the common man and to the belief that even the nastiest of us can be human if given a chance. His best films are masterpieces of timing and organization, but his career ended with sentimental and flabby remakes of his own successes.
   Autobiography: 1971, *The Name Above the Title*.
   Biography: 1992, *Frank Capra: The Catastrophe of Success* by Joseph McBride.
■ The Strong Man 26. Tramp Tramp Tramp 26. Long Pants 27. For the Love of Mike 27. That Certain Feeling 28. So This is Love 28. The Matinée Idol 28. The Way of the Strong 28. Say it with Sables 28. Submarine 28. Power of the Press 28. The Younger Generation 29. The Donovan Affair 29. Flight 29. Ladies of Leisure 30. Rain or Shine 30. Dirigible 31. The Miracle Woman 31. Forbidden 31. *Platinum Blonde* 32. *American Madness* 32. The Bitter Tea of General Yen 32. *Lady for a Day* (AAN) 33. *It Happened One Night* (AA) 34. Broadway Bill 34. *Mr Deeds Goes to Town* (AA) 36. *Lost Horizon* 37. *You Can't Take It With You* (AA) 38. *Mr Smith Goes to Washington* (AAN) 39. *Meet John Doe* 41. *Why We Fight* (war documentaries) 42–44. Arsenic and Old Lace 44. *It's a Wonderful Life* (AAN) 46. State of the Union 48. Riding High 50. Here Comes the Groom 51. A Hole in the Head 59. Pocketful of Miracles 61.
✪ For presenting an amiable if mythical picture of Mr Joe Smith American, and for doing so with great style. *It's a Wonderful Life*.

¶ He has achieved his effects mainly through a brilliantly fluid editing style, a command of masses of people, and a constantly moving camera. – *Charles Higham*
   I made some mistakes in drama. I thought drama was when the actors cried. But drama is when the audience cries. – *F.C.*
   The obligatory scene in most Capra films is the confession of folly in the most public manner possible. – *Andrew Sarris*

Capshaw, Kate (1953–   ) (Katherine Nail).
American leading actress, a former teacher. Married to Steven Spielberg.
   A Little Sex 82. Best Defence 84. Dreamscape 84. *Indiana Jones and the Temple of Doom* 84. Windy City 84. Power 86. SpaceCamp 86. The Quick and the Dead (TV) 87. Internal Affairs (TV) 88. Black Rain 89. Love at Large 90. Love Affair 94. Next Door (TV) 94, etc.

Capucine (1933–1990) (Germaine Lefebvre).
Lean and beautiful French model who was leading lady of a number of international films. Committed suicide.
   Song without End 60. North to Alaska 60. A Walk on the Wild Side 62. *The Pink Panther* 63. The Seventh Dawn 64. What's New Pussycat? 65. The Honey Pot 67. The Queens 67. Fräulein Doktor 68. Satyricon 69. Red Sun 72. Jaguar Lives 78. Arabian Adventure 79. Martin Eden (TV) 79. Trail of the Pink Panther 82. Curse of the Pink Panther 83.

¶ I'm weary, always weary these days. I'd like to work, but the enthusiasm is gone. But then, so are the opportunities. – *C. in 1989*

car crashes
have been responsible for the deaths of several film actors including James Dean, Charles Butterworth, and Ernie Kovacs.

Cara, Irene (1957–   ).
American actress and singer.
   Aaron Loves Angela 75. Sparkle 76. Fame 80. City Heat 84. D.C. Cab 84. Certain Fury 85. Killing Them Softly 85. Busted Up 86. For Us, the Living 88, etc.

Carax, Leos (1962–   ).
French director and screenwriter, a former critic.
   Boy Meets Girl 84. Bad Blood (Mauvais Sang) 86. Les Amants du Pont-Neuf 91, etc.

Cardiff, Jack (1914–   ).
Superb British colour cinematographer who became an indifferent director of routine films.
AS CINEMATOGRAPHER: *Wings of the Morning* 37. *The Four Feathers* 39. *Western Approaches* 44. Caesar and Cleopatra 45. *A Matter of Life and Death* 46. *Black Narcissus* (AA) 46. *The Red Shoes* 48. Pandora and the Flying Dutchman 51. The Barefoot Contessa 54. *War and Peace* (AAN) 56. The Vikings 58. Fanny (AAN) 61. The Prince and the Pauper 77. The Fifth Musketeer 78. Death on the Nile 78. Avalanche Express 79. The Awakening 80. Ghost Story 81. The Dogs of War 81. The Far Pavilions (TV) 83. Conan the Destroyer 84. The Last Days of Pompeii (TV) 85. Taipan 86. Million Dollar Mystery 87. Call from Space 89, etc.
■ AS DIRECTOR: Intent to Kill 58. Beyond This Place 59. Scent of Mystery 60. *Sons and Lovers* (AAN) 60. My Geisha 62. The Lion 62. The Long Ships 64. Young Cassidy 65. The Liquidator 65. Dark of the Sun 67. Girl on a Motorcycle (& p, ph) 69. The Mutations 74. Penny Gold 74. Ride a Wild Pony 76.

Cardinale, Claudia (1939–   ).
Italian leading lady who was given the international star build-up but did not quite manage the front rank.
   Persons Unknown 58. Upstairs and Downstairs (GB) 58. Il Bell' Antonio 59. Rocco and his Brothers 60. Cartouche 61. The Leopard 62. Eight and a Half 63. *The Pink Panther* 63. Circus World 64. Vaghe Stella dell'Orsa 65. Blindfold 65. Lost Command 66. The Professionals 66. Don't Make Waves 67. The Queens 67. Day of the Owl 68. To Hell with Heroes 68. Once Upon a Time in the West 69. A Fine Pair 69. Adventures of Brigadier Gerard 70. Popsy Pop 70. The Red Tent 71. Papal Audience 71. Days of Fury 73. Conversation Piece 76. Midnight Pleasures 76. Escape to Athena 78. The Salamander 80. Burden of Dreams 82. Princess Daisy (TV) 83. Henry IV 84. Woman of Wonders 85. History 86. A Man in Love (Un Homme Amoureux) 87. Blu Elettrico 88. Mother (Mayrig) 91. Act of Contrition (Atto di dolore) 91. 588 rue Paradis 92. Son of the Pink Panther 93. Elles ne Pensent qu'à Ça 94, etc.

Carere, Christine (1930–   ) (Christine de Borde).
French leading lady who had a brief Hollywood career.
   Olivia 50. Les Collégiennes 57. A Certain Smile 57. Mardi Gras 58. A Private's Affair 59. I Deal in Danger 66, etc.

Carette (1897–1966) (Julien Carette).
Dapper French character actor.
   L'Affaire est dans le Sac 32. La Grande Illusion 37. La Bête Humaine 38. La Marseillaise 38. *La Règle du Jeu* 39. Adieu Léonard 43. Sylvie et le Fantôme 45. Les Portes de la Nuit 46. *Occupe-Toi d'Amélie* 49. *The Red Inn* 51. Éléna et les Hommes 55. Archimède le Clochard 59. The Green Mare's Nest 61, many others.

Carew, Arthur Edmund (1894–1937).
American character actor. Committed suicide.
   Rio Grande 20. The Ghost Breaker 22. Trilby 23. The Phantom of the Opera 25. The Torrent 26. Uncle Tom's Cabin 27. The Cat and the Canary 27. Sweet Kitty Bellairs 30. Doctor X 32. The Mystery of the Wax Museum 33. Charlie Chan's Secret 36, many others.

Carew, James (1876–1938).
American actor, on stage from 1897. He moved to England, where he made his stage debut in 1905 and was in films from 1913, often as the villain. The third husband of actress Dame Ellen Terry, he also partnered comedian Billy Bennett in Alexander and Mose, a black-face act on radio and music hall in the early 30s.
   The Fool 13. The Rajah's Tiara 14. Justice 17. The Kinsman 19. Alf 's Button 20. Mr Justice Raffles 22. High Treason 29. Guilt 31. Royal Cavalcade 35. The Improper Duchess 36. Wings over Africa 36. Jericho (aka Dark Sands) 37. Glamour Girl 38, etc.

Carewe, Edwin (1883–1940) (Jay Fox).
American director of silent films noted for their pictorial beauty, a former hobo.
   The Final Judgment 15. The Trail to Yesterday 18. Shadow of Suspicion 19. Rio Grande 20. Son of the Sahara 24. Resurrection 27. Ramona 28. Evangeline 29. The Spoilers 30. Are We Civilized? 34, etc.

Carey, Harry (1878–1947).
American leading man of silent westerns who later became a character actor in quiet dependable roles.

Riding the Trail 11. Travellin' On 14. Two Guns 17. The Outcasts of Poker Flat 19. Desperate Trails 20. Man to Man 22. Roaring Rails 24. The Texas Trail 25. Trail of 98 27. *Trader Horn* 30. Law and Order 32. Barbary Coast 35. Sutter's Gold 36. Kid Galahad 37. King of Alcatraz 38. *Mr Smith Goes to Washington* (AAN) 39. They Knew What They Wanted 40. The Spoilers 42. Happy Land 43. The Great Moment 44. Duel in the Sun 46, many others.

Carey, Harry, Jnr (1921–).
American light actor, son of Harry Carey; followed his father's example and was seen mostly in westerns.

Pursued 47. Red River 48. So Dear to My Heart 49. Wagonmaster 50. Rio Grande 50. Island in the Sky 53. The Long Gray Line 55. The Searchers 56. The River's Edge 57. Rio Bravo 59. The Great Imposter 61. Alvarez Kelly 66. Bandolero 68. One More Time 71. A Man from the East 74. Nickelodeon 76. The Long Riders 80. Endangered Species 82. Princess Daisy (TV) 83. The Whales of August 87. Illegally Yours 88. Breaking In 89. Back to the Future III 90. Tombstone 94, many others.

Carey, Joyce (1898–1993) (Joyce Lawrence).
British stage actress, daughter of Lilian Braithwaite; made a few silent films then appeared more regularly as upper-class ladies in the 40s and 50s.

God and the Man 21. The Newcomers 25. *In Which We Serve* 42. Blithe Spirit 45. *The Way to the Stars* 45. *Brief Encounter* 45. The October Man 48. London Belongs to Me 48. The Chiltern Hundreds 49. The Astonished Heart 50. Happy Go Lovely 51. Cry the Beloved Country 52. The End of the Affair 55. The Eyes of Annie Jones 63. A Nice Girl Like Me 69. The Black Windmill 74, etc.

Carey, Leonard (1893–1977).
British character actor in Hollywood in the forties, best remembered as old Ben in *Rebecca* 40.

Carey, Macdonald (1913–1994).
American leading man, usually the sympathetic good guy in routine romantic comedy-dramas.

Dr Broadway 42. Wake Island 42. Shadow of a Doubt 43. Suddenly It's Spring 46. Dream Girl 47. East of Java 49. Streets of Laredo 49. The Lawless 50. Copper Canyon 50. Let's Make It Legal 51. My Wife's Best Friend 52. Stranger at My Door 56. Blue Denim 59. The Damned (GB) 61. Tammy and the Doctor 63. Broken Sabre 65. End of the World 77. It's Alive III 87, etc.

TV series: Dr Christian 56. Lock Up 59–65. Days of Our Lives 73–94.

Carey, Olive (1896–1988) (Olive Fuller Golden).
American actress who had leading roles in silent films, retired soon after her marriage to Harry Carey in 1920 and returned later as a character actress, often in the films of John Ford.

Storm Country 14. Trader Horn 30. The Searchers 56. Run of the Arrow 56. Gunfight at the O.K. Corral 57. Two Rode Together 61, etc.

Carey, Phil (Philip) (1925–).
American leading man of the rugged but good-humoured type, in routine films of the 50s and 60s; latterly in senior officer roles.

Operation Pacific 51. *Pushover* 54. Mister Roberts 55. Port Afrique 56. *Wicked As They Come* 56. Screaming Mimi 58. Tonka 59. The Time Travellers 64. The Great Sioux Massacre (as Custer) 65. The Seven Minutes 71. Fighting Mad 76, many others.

TV series: 77th Bengal Lancers 56. Philip Marlowe 59. Laredo 66–67.

Carey, Timothy (1929–1994).
Heavy-eyed American character actor, often a loathsome villain.

Hellgate 52. Alaska Seas 54. The Killing 56. Paths of Glory 57. One-Eyed Jacks 61. Reprieve 62. The World's Greatest Sinner (& wd) 62. Bikini Beach 64. Waterhole Three 67. Head 68. Minnie and Moskowitz 71. The Conversation 73. The Killing of a Chinese Bookie 75. Speedtrap 77. Fast Walking 82. D.C. Cab 85. Echo Park 86, etc.

Carfagno, Edward C.
American art director.

Best Foot Forward 43. The Secret Heart 46. Neptune's Daughter 49. Quo Vadis 51. The Story of Three Loves 52. The Bad and the Beautiful (AA) 53. Julius Caesar (AA) 53. Ben Hur (AA) 59. Ada 61. The Cincinnati Kid 65. The Shoes of the Fisherman 69. Skyjacked 73. The Man Who Loved Cat Dancing 73. The Hindenburg 75. The Last Hard Men 76. Gable and Lombard 76. Demon Seed 77. Looking for Mr Goodbar 77. Meteor 79. Time After Time 79. Little Miss Marker 80. Beulah Land (TV) 81. Wrong is Right 83. Sudden Impact 83. All of Me 84. Tightrope 84. City Heat 84. Pale Rider 85. Ratboy 86. Heartbreak Ridge 86. Bird 88. The Dead Pool 88. Pink Cadillac 89, etc.

Cargill, Patrick (1918–).
Impeccable British farce actor with long stage experience.

The Cracksman 63. This is my Street 63. A Stitch in Time 64. *A Countess from Hong Kong* 66. Inspector Clouseau 68. Every Home Should Have One 70. Up Pompeii 71. Father Dear Father 73. The Picture Show Man (Austr.) 77, etc.

TV series: *Father Dear Father* 68–73, 77. The Many Wives of Patrick 77–78.

Cariou, Len (1939–).
Canadian leading actor.

A Little Night Music 77. The Four Seasons 81. Who'll Save Our Children? (TV) 82. Killer in the Mirror (TV) 86. Louisiana (TV) 87. Lady in White 88. The Sea Wolf (TV) 93. Witness to the Execution (TV) 94, etc.

Carle, Gilles (1929–).
Canadian director.

Red 69. Bernadette 72. La Tête de Normande St Onge 75. Fantastica 80. Les Plouffe 81. Maria Chapdelaine 83. The Crime of Ovide Plouffe (co-d) 85. Scalp 85. La Guêpe 86, etc.

Carle, Richard (1871–1941) (Charles Carleton).
American character actor.

Zander The Great 25. Eve's Leaves 26. The Understanding Heart 27. Madame X 28. Brothers 30. One Hour With You 32. Morning Glory 33. Caravan 34. The Ghost Walks 35. Anything Goes 36. One Rainy Afternoon 36. True Confession 37. Persons in Hiding 39. The Great McGinty 40. The Uncertain Feeling 41, many others.

Carlei, Carlo (1962–).
Italian director who went to Hollywood after his first feature.

Captain Cosmos (short) 90. Flight of the Innocent (La Corsa dell'Innocente) 92, etc.

Carlin, George (1937–).
American comedian in occasional films.

With Six You Get Egg Roll 68. Car Wash 76. Outrageous Fortune 87. Bill & Ted's Excellent Adventure 89. Bill & Ted's Bogus Journey 91. The Prince of Tides 91, etc.

TV series: That Girl 66–67.

Carlin, Lynn (1930–).
American character actress.

Faces (AAN) 68. Tick Tick Tick 70. *Taking Off* 71. Wild Rovers 71. Battle Beyond the Stars 80. Forbidden Love (TV) 82. Superstition 82, etc.

TV series: James at 15 77–78.

Carlino, Lewis John (1932–).
American screenwriter.

The Brotherhood 68. Reflection of Fear 71. The Mechanic 72. Crazy Joe 74. The Sailor Who Fell from Grace with the Sea (& d, p) 76. I Never Promised You a Rose Garden 77. Resurrection 80. The Great Santini (& d) 80. Class (d only) 83. Haunted Summer 88, etc.

Carlisle, Kitty (1915–) (Catherine Holzman).
American operatic singer, briefly with MGM in the 30s. She was married to Moss Hart.

Autobiography: 1988, *Kitty*.

■ Murder at the Vanities 34. She Loves Me Not 34. Here is my Heart 34. *A Night at the Opera* 35. Hollywood Canteen 44. Radio Days 87.

Carlisle, Mary (1912–).
American leading lady of the 30s.

Justice for Sale 32. College Humor 33. One Frightened Night 35. Love in Exile 36. Dr Rhythm 38. Call a Messenger 40. Baby Face Morgan 42. Dead Men Walk 43, etc.

Carlo-Rim (1905–1989) (Jean-Marius Richard).
French writer-director, mainly of Fernandel comedies.

L'Armoire Volante 47. Les Truands (Lock Up the Spoons) 56. Le Petit Prof 59, etc.

Carlos, Wendy (1941–).
American composer, a former engineer, born Walter Carlos, and a pioneer in the use of synthesizers.

■ A Clockwork Orange 71. The Shining 80. Tron 82.

Carlsen, Henning (1927–).
Danish director and screenwriter, a former documentary film-maker and cinema manager.

Dilemma 62. The Cats (Kattorna) 64. Hunger (Sult) 66. We Are All Demons (Klabautermanden) 69. Oh, to Be on the Bandwagon! (Man sku' Vaere Noget ved Musikken) 72. A Happy Divorce (En Lykkelig Skilsmisse) 75. Did Somebody Laugh? (Hör, Var der Ikke en, Som Lo?) 78. Your Money or Your Life (Pengene eller Livet) 82. The Wolf at the Door (Oviri) 86. Two Green Feathers 95, etc.

Carlson, Richard (1912–1977).
American leading man of the 40s, mainly in routine films; played the diffident juvenile so long that he had nothing to give to mature roles.

The Young in Heart 38. Winter Carnival 39. The Ghost Breakers 40. No No Nanette 40. Back Street 41. Hold That Ghost 41. *The Little Foxes* 41. White Cargo 42. Presenting Lily Mars 43. So Well Remembered 47. Behind Closed Doors 48. King Solomon's Mines 50. The Blue Veil 51. Valentino 51. Whispering Smith Hits London 52. The Magnetic Monster 53. It Came from Outer Space 53. All I Desire 53. Riders to the Stars (& d) 54. The Creature from the Black Lagoon 54. Four Guns to the Border (d only) 54. Three for Jamie Dawn 56. The Helen Morgan Story 57. Appointment with a Shadow (d only) 59. Kid Rodelo (& d) 66. The Power 68. The Valley of Gwangi 69, many others.

TV series: I Led Three Lives 52. Mackenzie's Raiders 58.

Carlson, Veronica (1944–).
British leading lady, mainly in screamies.
Dracula has Risen from the Grave 68.
Frankenstein must be Destroyed 69. The Horror
of Frankenstein 70. Pussycat Pussycat I Love You
70. The Ghoul 75, etc.

Carmel, Roger C. (1929–1986).
Rotund American character actor. Died of a drug
overdose.
Goodbye Charlie 64. The Silencers 66. Gambit
66. The Venetian Affair 66. Skullduggery 69.
Thunder and Lightning 77.
TV series: Fitz and Bones 81.

Carmen.
Prosper Mérimée's high-romantic tale of a fatal
gypsy whose worthless attractions wreck men's
lives was promptly turned by Bizet into an opera
which has been filmed many times, notably as
Carmen Jones 54. The straight dramatic story,
however, probably holds the record for the number
of film versions it has spawned:

France	1909	with Victoria Lepanto
Spain	1910	actress unknown
US	1913	Marguerite Snow
US	1913	Marion Leonard
Spain	1914	actress unknown
US	1915	Geraldine Farrar
US	1915	Edna Purviance (*Burlesque on Carmen*)
US	1916	Theda Bara
US	1918	Pola Negri
US	1921	Raquel Miller
US	1927	Dolores del Rio
France	1942	Vivianne Romance
US	1948	Rita Hayworth
US/WG	1966	Uta Levke

Carmet, Jean (1921–1994).
French character actor, usually in ordinary roles.
He appeared in some 200 movies. He won two
Césars as best actor and was awarded a César for
lifetime achievement in 1993.
Les Enfants du Paradis 45. The Little Theatre of
Jean Renoir 71. The Tall Blond Man with One
Black Shoe (Le Grand Blond avec une Chaussure
Noire) 74. Return of the Tall Blond Man with One
Black Shoe 74. Black and White in Colour (La
Victoire en Chantant) 76. Violette 78. Buffet Froid
(US: Cold Cuts) 79. Les Misérables 82. Secret
Sorceress 87. Obsession 88. Merci la Vie 92. La Nuit
des Cerfs-Volants 95, etc.

¶ In my imagination, I have been recasting my
old films and casting all the films I never made,
and the male star is always Jean Carmet. – *Jean
Renoir*

Carmichael, Hoagy (1899–1981) (Hoaglund
Howard Carmichael).
American song composer and lyricist, best known
for 'Stardust' and 'In the Cool, Cool, Cool of the
Evening' (AA 1951). Also a slow-speaking actor
of light supporting roles, usually involving his
singing at the piano.
Autobiographies: 1946, *The Stardust Road*. 1965,
Sometimes I Wonder.
AS ACTOR/PERFORMER: To Have and Have Not 44.
Canyon Passage 46. *The Best Years of Our Lives* 46.
Young Man with a Horn 50. Belles on Their Toes
52. Timberjack 55, etc.
TV series: Laramie 59–62.

Carmichael, Ian (1920–).
British light leading man, adept at nervous
novices; long experience in revue. Trained at

RADA, he was on stage from 1939 and in films
from 1947.
Meet Mr Lucifer 54. The Colditz Story 54. Storm
over the Nile 55. *Simon and Laura* 55. *Private's
Progress* 55. *Brothers in Law* 57. *Lucky Jim* 57. Happy
is the Bride 57. The Big Money 57. Left, Right
and Centre 59. *I'm All Right, Jack* 59. School for
Scoundrels 60. Light Up the Sky 60. Double Bunk
61. The Amorous Prawn 62. Hide and Seek 63.
Heavens Above 63. Smashing Time 67. The
Magnificent Seven Deadly Sins 71. From Beyond
the Grave 75. The Lady Vanishes 79. Diamond
Skulls (aka Dark Obsession) 89, etc.

Carminati, Tullio (1894–1971) (Count Tullio
Carminati de Brambilla).
Italian romantic actor who had a modest career in
British and American as well as European films.
The Bat 26. Three Sinners 28. Moulin Rouge 33.
One Night of Love 34. *The Three Maxims* 35. Safari
40. The Golden Madonna 49. La Beauté du Diable
51. Roman Holiday 53. Saint Joan 57. El Cid 61.
The Cardinal 63, many others.

Carne, Judy (1939–) (Joyce Botterill).
Pert British actress who found fame as the 'sock it
to me' girl in Hollywood's *Laugh-In* TV series. She
was married to actor Burt Reynolds (1966–69).
A Pair of Briefs 63. The Americanization of Emily
64. All the Right Noises 69. Only with Married Men
74, etc.
TV series: Fair Exchange 62. The Baileys of
Balboa 64. Love on a Rooftop 66. Laugh-In 67–72.

Carné, Marcel (1909–).
Certainly the most brilliant of French directors
1937–45; his career later suffered a semi-eclipse.
■ Jenny 36. *Drôle de Drame* 37. *Quai des Brumes*
38. Hôtel du Nord 38. *Le Jour Se Lève* 39. *Les
Visiteurs du Soir* 42. *Les Enfants du Paradis* 44. Les
Portes de la Nuit 46. La Marie du Port 48. Juliette
Ou La Clef des Songes 51. Thérèse Racquin 53.
L'Air de Paris 54. Le Pays d'Où Je Viens 56. Les
Tricheurs 58. Terrain Vague 60. Du Mouron pour
les Petits Oiseaux 62. Three Rooms in Manhattan
65. The Young Wolves 68. Les Assassins de l'Ordre
71. La Vie a Belles Dents (w only) 80. La Bible
(wd) 84.
❂ For creating, almost single-handedly, the
images of French *film noir* in the 30s. *Les Enfants du
Paradis*.

¶ The precise mood of the period – a sense of
fatalism enveloping a pair of doomed lovers,
drably poetic urban settings – is to be found in his
work. – *Roy Armes*

Carney, Alan (1911–1973).
American comedy supporting actor who in the
mid-40s made some second features with Wally
Brown (qv). His solo appearances were sparse.
Mr Lucky 43. The Pretender 47. Lil Abner 59.
It's a Mad Mad Mad Mad World 63. The Love
Bug Rides Again 73, etc.

Carney, Art (1918–).
American comedy actor, popular on TV, especially
from 1955 in *The Honeymooners*.
Pot O'Gold 41. The Yellow Rolls Royce 64. A
Guide for the Married Man 67. *Harry and Tonto* (AA)
74. Won Ton Ton 76. Lanigan's Rabbi (TV) 76. *The
Late Show* 77. Movie Movie 78. Sunburn 79.
Roadie 80. Steel 80. St Helens 81. Take This Job
and Shove It 81. Firestarter 84. The Naked Face 84.
Izzy and Moe (TV) 85. Night Friend 88. The Last
Action Hero 93, etc.

Carney, George (1887–1947).
British character actor of stage and screen, on
screen from 1916.
Say It With Flowers 34. Father Steps Out (title
role) 37. The Stars Look Down 39. Convoy 40. *Love
on the Dole* 41. The Common Touch 41. Tawny Pipit
44. I Know Where I'm Going 45. Good Time Girl
47, etc.

¶ The embodiment of the commonplace civilian
turned warrior. – *James Agate*

carnivals:
see *funfairs*.

Carnovsky, Morris (1897–1992).
Distinguished American stage actor, with long
experience in Jewish theatre. Films regrettably
few.
■ The Life of Emile Zola 37. Tovarich 37. Edge of
Darkness 43. Address Unknown 44. The Master
Race 44. Our Vines Have Tender Grapes 45,
Rhapsody in Blue 45. Cornered 45. Miss Susie
Slagle's 45. *Dead Reckoning* 47. Dishonored Lady
47. Joe Palooka in The Knockout 47. Saigon 48.
Maneater of Kumaon 48. Siren of Atlantis 48. Gun
Crazy 49. Thieves' Highway 49. Western Pacific
Agent 50. Cyrano de Bergerac 50. The Second
Woman 51. A View from the Bridge 62. The
Gambler 74.

Carol, Martine (1922–1967) (Maryse Mourer).
French leading lady popular in undressed roles in
the early 50s.
Voyage Surprise 48. *Caroline Chérie* 50. A Night
with Caroline 52. *Lucrezia Borgia* 52. The Bed 53.
The Beach 54. Nana 55. *Lola Montes* 55. Action of
the Tiger 57. Ten Seconds to Hell 59. Le Cave Se
Rebiffe 61. Hell is Empty 66, etc.

Carol, Sue (1906–1982) (Evelyn Lederer).
American leading lady of the early 30s. Widow of
Alan Ladd.
Is Zat So? 27. Girls Gone Wild 29. Dancing
Sweeties 30. Her Golden Calf 30. Graft 31. Secret
Sinners 34. A Doctor's Diary 37, etc.

Caron, Leslie (1931–).
French leading lady and dancer who after being
discovered by Gene Kelly followed a successful
English-speaking career in light drama and
comedy. She was married to director Peter Hall
(1957–65).
■ *An American In Paris* 51. Man with a Cloak 51.
Glory Alley 52. The Story of Three Loves 53. *Lili*
(BFA, AAN) 53. The Glass Slipper 54. Daddy
Longlegs 55. Gaby 56. *Gigi* 58. The Doctor's
Dilemma 58. The Man Who Understood Women
59. The Subterraneans 60. Austerlitz 60. *Fanny* 61.
Guns of Darkness 62. *The L-Shaped Room* (BFA,
AAN) 62. Three Fables of Love 63. Father Goose
64. A Very Special Favour 65. Promise Her
Anything 66. Is Paris Burning? 66. Head of the
Family 68. Madron 69. Purple Night 71. Chandler
72. QB VII (TV) 74. The Man Who Loved Women
77. Valentino 77. Sérail 77. Goldengirl 79. Tous
Vedettes 80. The Contract 80. Imperatives 82.
Master of the Game (TV) 84. Dangerous Moves
85. The Genius 85. Courage Mountain 89.
Guerriers et Captives 89. Damage 92.

Carpenter, Carleton (1926–).
American light leading man groomed by MGM in
the early 50s.
Lost Boundaries 48. Father of the Bride 50.
Summer Stock 51. Fearless Fagan 53. Sky Full of
Moon 53. Take the High Ground 53. Up Periscope
59. Some of My Best Friends Are 71.

Carpenter, John (1948–).
American director who in the late 70s swiftly carved a niche for himself with scary but derivative horror thrillers.

The Resurrection of Broncho Billy (short) (AA) 9. *Dark Star* 74. *Assault on Precinct 13* 76. Someone's Watching Me (TV) 77. Halloween 78. Eyes of Laura Mars (w only) 78. Elvis (TV) 79. The Fog 79. Escape from New York (& co-w) 81. Halloween II (co-w, co-p only) 81. The Thing 82. Halloween III (co-p only) 83. Christine 83. Starman 84. Big Trouble in Little China 86. Something Wild (a only) 86. Black Moon Rising (w) 86. Prince of Darkness (d, m) 87. The House on Carroll Street (a) 88. They Live (wd, m) 88. Memoirs of an Invisible Man 92. In the Mouth of Madness 95, many others.

¶ Movies are pieces of film stuck together in a certain rhythm, an absolute beat, like a musical composition. The rhythm you create affects the audience. – *J.C.*

Real life is scarier than any movie these days. – *J.C.*

Carpenter, Paul (1921–1964).
Canadian leading man long in Britain as hero of scores of second features.

School for Secrets 46. Albert RN 53. Night People 54. The Sea Shall Not Have Them 55. Fire Maidens from Outer Space 56. The Iron Petticoat 56. Jet Storm 59. Murder Reported 60. Call Me Bwana 63, etc.

Carpenter, Russell.
American cinematographer.

Sole Survivor 84. The Wizard of Speed and Time 88. Critters 2: The Main Course 88. Lady in White 88. Cameron's Closet 89. Death Warrant 90. The Perfect Weapon 91. The Lawnmower Man 92. Hard Target 93. True Lies 94, etc.

Carpi, Fiorenzo (1918–).
Italian composer.

Zazie (Zazie dans le Métro) (Fr.) 60. A Very Private Affair 62. Italian Secret Service 68. Equinozio 71. La Vacanza 72. La Chair de l'Orchidée (Fr.) 74. Salon Kitty 76, etc.

Carr, Allan (1941–).
Chubby American impresario associated with *Grease, La Cage aux Folles* and the unsuccessful *Can't Stop the Music.*

Carr, Darleen (1950–).
American leading lady mainly familiar in TV series: *The John Forsythe Show, The Smith Family, The Oregon Trail,* etc.

Monkeys Go Home 66. The Impossible Years 68. The Beguiled 70. Runaway (TV) 73. Young Joe the Forgotten Kennedy (TV) 77, etc.

Carr, Jane (1909–1957) (Rita Brunstrom).
British leading lady, in occasional films.

Taxi to Paradise 33. Lord Edgware Dies 37. Lilac Domino 37. The Lady from Lisbon 37. It's Not Cricket 48. 36 Hours 54, etc.

Carr, John Dickson (1905–1977).
American detective story writer, curiously few of whose many novels have been adapted for the screen.

Man with a Cloak 51. That Woman Upstairs 52. Dangerous Crossing 52, etc.

Carr, Mary (1874–1973).
Leading American character actress of the 20s; the archetypal white-haired old mother.

Mrs Wiggs of the Cabbage Patch 19. *Over the Hill to the Poorhouse* 20. Silver Wings 22. Why Men Leave Home 24. The Wizard of Oz 25. Jesse James 27. Lights of New York 28.Beyond Victory 31. Change of Heart 34. East Side of Heaven 36. Friendly Persuasion 56, many others.

Carr, Thomas (1907–).
American director, mainly of second-feature westerns. Went into TV.

Bandits of the Badlands 45. Red River Renegades 46. Code of the Saddle 47. Colorado Ranger 50. Wyoming Roundup 52. Captain Scarlett 53. The Bowery Boys Meet the Monsters 54. Bobby Ware Is Missing 55. Three for Jamie Dawn 56. The Tall Stranger 57. Gunsmoke in Tucson 58. Cast a Long Shadow 59. Sullivan's Empire 67, many others.

Carradine, David (1936–) (John Arthur Carradine).
Lanky sad-eyed American character actor, son of John Carradine.

The Violent Ones 67. Young Billy Young 69. The McMasters 70. Macho Callahan 71. Boxcar Bertha 72. You and Me (& d) 73. Mean Streets 73. Death Race 2000 75. Cannonball 76. *Bound for Glory* 76. Carquake 77. Thunder and Lightning 77. The Silent Flute 78. Cloud Dancer 80. The Long Riders 80. Safari 3000 82. The Winged Serpent 82. Mr Horn 82. Lone Wolf McQuade 82. Armed Response 86. North and South (TV) 86. Wheels of Terror 87. The Misfit Brigade 87. Warlords 88. Crime Zone 88. Future Force 89. Wizards of the Lost Kingdom II 89. Bird on a Wire 90. Future Zone 90. Think Big 90. Evil Toons 91. Deadly Surveillance 91. You and Me (d) 91. Roadside Prophets 92. Animal Instincts 92. Night Rhythms 92, etc.

TV series: *Shane* 66. *Kung Fu* 72–75. Kung Fu: The Legend Continues 93.

¶ David Carradine is about as good a martial artist as I am an actor. – *Chuck Norris*

Carradine, John (1906–1988) (Richmond Reed Carradine).
Gaunt American actor who scored a fine run of character roles in the 30s and 40s but later sank to mad doctors in cheap horror movies, touring meanwhile with one-man Shakespeare readings. Played 1930–35 under the name John Peter Richmond.

Tol'able David 30. The Sign of the Cross 32. Cleopatra 34. Bride of Frankenstein 35. Dimples 36. The Prisoner of Shark Island 36. The Garden of Allah 36. Winterset 36. Captains Courageous 36. The Last Gangster 37. The Hurricane 37. Alexander's Ragtime Band 38. Jesse James 39. Drums along the Mohawk 39. *Five Came Back* 39. *Stagecoach* 39. Brigham Young 40. *The Grapes of Wrath* 40. Blood and Sand 41. Man Hunt 41. Son of Fury 42. Hitler's Madman (as Heydrich) 43. Gangway for Tomorrow 43. *Bluebeard* (title role) 44. The Invisible Man's Revenge 44. It's In the Bag 45. *House of Frankenstein* (as Dracula) 45. Fallen Angel 45. House of Dracula 45. The Face of Marble 46. The Private Affairs of Bel Ami 47. C – Man 49. Casanova's Big Night 54. The Egyptian 54. The Kentuckian 55. The Black Sleep 56. The Ten Commandments 56. Hell Ship Mutiny 57. The Last Hurrah 58. The Cosmic Man 59. Sex Kittens go to College 60. Invasion of the Animal People 62. *The Man Who Shot Liberty Valance* 62. Cheyenne Autumn 64. Billy the Kid vs Dracula 66. Hillbillies in a Haunted House 67. The Fiend with the Electronic Brain 67. The Astro-Zombies 68. The Good Guys and the Bad Guys 69. Bigfoot 69. The McMasters 70. The Seven Minutes 71. Boxcar

Bertha 72. The House of the Seven Corpses 73. Silent Night Bloody Night 74. The Shootist 76. The Sentinel 77. The Bees 78. The Boogey Man 80. The Scarecrow 82. The House of Long Shadows 83. Evils of the Night 85. Peggy Sue Got Married 86. The Tomb 87, many others.

Carradine, Keith (1950–).
American leading man of the 70s, half brother of David Carradine. He is the father of actress Martha Plimpton.

■ A Gunfight 71. McCabe and Mrs Miller 71. Hex 73. Emperor of the North 73. The Godchild (TV) 74. Thieves Like Us 74. Nashville (AA song) 75. Lumiere 76. Welcome to L.A. 77. Pretty Baby 78. An Almost Perfect Affair 79. Old Boyfriends 79. The Long Riders 80. Southern Comfort 81. Maria's Lovers 83. Choose Me 85. Chiefs (TV) 85. Scorned and Swindled (TV) 85. Blackout 86. Half a Lifetime 86. Backfire 87. The Inquiry (L'Inchiesta) 87. The Moderns 88. Sans Espoir de Retour 88. Cold Feet 89. My Dear Doctor Grasler (Mio Caro Dottor Gräsler) 89. Daddy's Dyin', Who's Got the Will? 90. The Ballad of the Sad Café 91. The Bachelor 91. Payoff 91. You and Me 91. Crisscross 92. Andre 94. Mrs Parker and the Vicious Circle 94.

Carradine, Robert (1954–).
American leading man, youngest son of John Carradine (brother of Keith, half-brother of David).

The Cowboys 72. Mean Streets 73. Aloha Bobby and Rose 75. You and Me 75. Jackson County Jail 76. Cannonball 76. Orca 77. Coming Home 78. The Big Red One 80. Heartaches 82. Wavelength 83. Revenge of the Nerds 84. Number One with a Bullet 87. Revenge of the Nerds II 87. All's Fair 89. Buy and Cell 89. Revenge of the Nerds IV: Nerds in Love (TV) 94, etc.

Carré, Ben (1883–1978).
American art director.

The Blue Bird 18. *Phantom of the Opera* 25. Mare Nostrum 25. *Don Juan* 26. The Jazz Singer 27. *Dante's Inferno* 35, many others.

Carrera, Barbara (1947–).
Nicaraguan leading lady of smouldering personality.

Puzzle of a Downfall Child 70. The Master Gunfighter 75. Embryo 76. The Island of Dr Moreau 78. Never Say Never Again 83. Wild Geese II 84. Love at Stake 87. The Underachievers 88. Loverboy 89. Wicked Stepmother 89, etc.

TV series: Dallas 85–86.

Carrera, Carlos (1962–).
Mexican director and screenwriter.

Benjamin's Wife (La Mujer de Benjamin) (co-w, d) 91. A Conjugal Life (La Vida Conyugal) (co-w, d) 92.

Carreras, Sir James (1909–1990).
British production executive, former exhibitor; chairman of Hammer Films.

¶ All Roman Catholic countries are wonderful for business. In Hammer films the crucifix wins every time. In Spain and Italy, when the monster is defeated by the sign of the cross, the audience stands up and cheers. – *J.C.*

Carreras, Michael (1927–1994).
British producer-director for Hammer Films. Son of James Carreras.

Blackout (p) 54. The Snorkel (p) 57. Ten Seconds to Hell (p) 58. Passport to China (pd) 61. The Two Faces of Dr Jekyll (d) 61. Maniac (d) 62.

What a Crazy World (d) 63. The Curse of the Mummy's Tomb (d) 64. She (p) 65. One Million Years BC (p) 67. The Lost Continent (pd) 68, etc.

Carrere, Tia (1967–   ) (Althea Janairo).
American actress and singer, born in Honolulu.
   Nightmare 87. Aloha Summer 88. Showdown in Little Tokyo 91. Harley Davidson and the Marlboro Man 91. Wayne's World 92. Rising Sun 93. Wayne's World 2 93. True Lies 94, etc.
   TV series: General Hospital 82–83.

Carrey, Jim (1962–   ) (aka James Carrey).
Canadian comic actor in Hollywood, best known for appearing in the 90s television series In Living Color until Ace Ventura, Pet Detective was a surprise hit. Overnight his fee for a film role increased from $450,000 to a reported $7m.
   Club Med 83. Finders Keepers 84. Once Bitten 85. Peggy Sue Got Married 86. Earth Girls Are Easy 89. Pink Cadillac 89. Ace Ventura, Pet Detective 94. The Mask 94. Dumb and Dumber 95. Batman Forever 95, etc.
   TV series: The Duck Factory 84.

¶ I tend to stay up late, not because I'm partying but because it's the only time of day when I'm alone and don't have to be on, performing. – J.C.

Carrick, Edward (1905–   ) (Edward Anthony Craig).
British art director, son of Edward Gordon Craig.
   Autumn Crocus 34. Jump for Glory 36. Captain Boycott 47. The Divided Heart 54. Tiger Bay 59. What a Crazy World 63. The Nanny 65, many others.

Carrière, Jean-Claude (1931–   ).
French screen writer who began by collaborating with Tati and Etaix.
   Book: 1994, The Secret Language of Film.
   Belle de Jour 66. Hotel Paradiso 66. Le Voleur 67. Borsalino 67. The Milky Way (La Voie Lactée) 69. Taking Off 70. The Discreet Charm of the Bourgeoisie 72. The Phantom of Liberty (Le Fantôme de la Liberté) 74. Le Gang 76. That Obscure Object of Desire 77. The Tin Drum 79. Circle of Deceit (Die Flaschung) 81. Danton 82. The Return of Martin Guerre (Le Retour de Martin Guerre) 82. Swann in Love (Un Amour de Swann) 83. The Tragedy of Carmen 83. Max, My Love 86. The Mahabharata 89. Valmont 89. At Play in the Fields of the Lord 91, etc. (Usually in collaboration.)

Carriere, Mathieu (1950–   ).
German leading actor in international films.
   Young Torless (Der Junge Törless) 66. Bluebeard 72. India Song (Fr.) 75. Coup de Grace 78. La Passante 83. Benvenuta (Bel.) 83. A Woman in Flames (Die Flambierte Frau) 84. The Bay Boy (Can.) 85. Shining Through (US) 92. Dieu que les Femmes Sont Amoureuses (Fr.) 94, etc.

Carrillo, Leo (1880–1961).
American light character actor. A Spanish Californian from a wealthy landowning family, he enjoyed many years in Hollywood as an assortment of amiably talkative fellows, usually in fractured English.
   Mr Antonio 29. Hell Bound 31. Girl of the Rio 31. The Broken Wing 32. Moonlight and Pretzels 33. Manhattan Melodrama 34. In Caliente 35. The Gay Desperado 36. History Is Made at Night 37. Blockade 38. Rio 39. Lillian Russell 40. Horror Island 41. Riders of Death Valley 41. Sin Town 42. Top Sergeant 43. Ghost Catchers 44. Mexicana 45. The Fugitive 47. The Gay Amigo 48. Pancho Villa Returns 50, many others.
   TV series: The Cisco Kid 51–55.

¶ Ze female of ze species she is a-deadlier zan ze male. – L. C. in History Is Made at Night

Carroll, Diahann (1935–   ) (Carol Diahann Johnson).
American entertainer and actress. She is married to singer Vic Damone.
   Carmen Jones 54. Porgy and Bess 59. Goodbye Again 60. Paris Blues 61. Hurry Sundown 67. The Split 68. Claudine (AAN) 74. The Five Heartbeats 91, etc.
   TV series: Julia 68–70. Dynasty 85–

Carroll, Joan (1932–   ) (Joan Felt).
American child star of the 40s.
   Primrose Path 40. Laddie 41. Petticoat Larceny 43. Meet Me in St Louis 44. Tomorrow the World 45. The Bells of St Mary's 46, etc.

Carroll, John (1906–1979) (Julian La Faye).
Latin-American leading man with a decent singing voice but not much personality.
   ■ Marianne 29. Devil May Care 29. Hearts in Exile 29. Rogue Song 30. Dough Boys 30. Monte Carlo 30. New Moon 30. Reaching for the Moon 30. Go into Your Dance 35. Hi Gaucho 35. The Accusing Finger 36. Murder on the Bridle Path 36. Muss 'Em Up 36. We Who Are About to Die 37. Zorro (serial) 37. Death in the Air 37. Rose of the Rio Grande 38. I am a Criminal 38. Only Angels Have Wings 39. Wolf Call 39. Congo Maisie 40. Phantom Raiders 40. Susan and God 40. Hired Wife 40. Go West 40. Sunny 41. This Woman is Mine 41. Lady be Good 41. Rio Rita 42. Pierre of the Plains 42. Flying Tigers 42. Hit Parade of 1943 42. The Youngest Profession 43. Bedside Manner 45. A Letter for Evie 45. Fiesta 47. Wyoming 47. The Fabulous Texan 47. The Flame 47. Old Los Angeles 48. I Jane Doe 48. Angel in Exile 48. The Avengers 50. Surrender 50. Hit Parade of 1951 50. Belle Le Grande 52. The Farmer Takes a Wife 53. Geraldine 53. The Reluctant Bride 55. Decision at Showdown 57. Plunderers of Painted Flats 59.

Carroll, Leo G. (1892–1972).
Distinguished, dry-faced British character actor long based in Hollywood; usually played doctors, judges or academics.
   ■ What Every Woman Knows 34. Sadie McKee 34. Outcast Lady 34. Stamboul Quest 34. The Barretts of Wimpole Street 34. Murder on a Honeymoon 35. The Right to Live 35. Clive of India 35. The Casino Murder Case 35. London by Night 37. Captains Courageous 37. A Christmas Carol 38. The Private Lives of Elizabeth and Essex 39. Wuthering Heights 39. Bulldog Drummond's Secret Police 39. Charlie Chan in the City of Darkness 39. Tower of London 39. Rebecca 40. Charlie Chan's Murder Cruise 40. Waterloo Bridge 40. Scotland Yard 41. Bahama Passage 41. This Woman is Mine 41. Suspicion 41. The House on 92nd Street 45. Spellbound 45. Forever Amber 47. Time Out of Mind 47. Song of Love 47. The Paradine Case 48. So Evil My Love 48. Enchantment 48. The Happy Years 50. Father of the Bride 50. The First Legion 51. Strangers on a Train 51. The Desert Fox 51. The Snows of Kilimanjaro 52. The Bad and the Beautiful 52. Rogues' March 52. Treasure of the Golden Condor 52. Young Bess 53. We're No Angels 55. Tarantula 55. The Swan 56. North by Northwest 59. The Parent Trap 61. One Plus One 61. The Prize 63. That Funny Feeling 65. The Spy with My Face 66. One of Our Spies Is Missing 66. One Spy Too Many 66.

TV series: Topper 53–54. Going My Way 62. The Man from U.N.C.L.E. (as Mr Waverly) 64–67.

Carroll, Lewis (1832–1898) (Charles Lutwidge Dodgson).
British writer, an Oxford lecturer in mathematics who wrote Alice in Wonderland. His poem Jabberwocky from Through the Looking Glass inspired the film of the same name.

Carroll, Madeleine (1906–1987) (Marie Madeleine Bernadette O'Carroll).
British leading lady of the 30s and 40s; her gentle well-bred air made her popular in Hollywood for a while.
   ■ The Guns of Loos 28. The First Born 28. What Money Can't Buy 29. The American Prisoner 29. Atlantic 30. Young Woodley 30. Escape 30. The W Plan 30. Madame Guillotine 31. Kissing Cup's Race 31. French Leave 31. The Written Law 31. Fascination 32. School for Scandal 33. Sleeping Car 33. I Was a Spy 33. The World Moves On 34. Love of a Dictator 35. The Thirty-nine Steps 35. The Case Against Mrs Ames 36. Secret Agent 36. The General Died at Dawn 36. Lloyds of London 36. On the Avenue 37. The Prisoner of Zenda 37. It's All Yours 38. Blockade 38. Honeymoon in Bali 39. Café Society 39. My Son My Son 40. Safari 40. Northwest Mounted Police 40. Virginia 41. One Night in Lisbon 41. Bahama Passage 42. My Favourite Blonde 42. White Cradle Inn 46. Don't Trust Your Husband 48. The Fan 49.

Carroll, Nancy (1906–1965) (Ann La Hiff).
Warmly-remembered American leading lady of early talkie musicals and light dramas.
   Biography: 1969, The Films of Nancy Carroll by Paul L. Nemcek.
   ■ Ladies Must Dress 27. Abie's Irish Rose 28. Easy Come Easy Go 28. Chicken à la King 28. The Water Hole 28. Manhattan Cocktail 28. The Shopworn Angel 29. The Wolf of Wall Street 29. Sin Sister 29. Close Harmony 29. The Dance of Life 29. Illusion 29. Sweetie 29. Dangerous Paradise 30. Honey 30. Paramount on Parade 30. The Devil's Holiday (AAN) 30. Follow Through 30. Laughter 30. Stolen Heaven 31. The Night Angel 31. Personal Maid 31. Broken Lullaby 32. Wayward 32. Scarlet Dawn 32. Hot Saturday 32. Undercover Man 32. Child of Manhattan 33. The Woman Accused 33. The Kiss Before the Mirror 33. I Love that Man 33. Springtime for Henry 34. Transatlantic Merry-go-round 34. Jealousy 34. I'll Love You Always 35. After the Dance 35. Atlantic Adventure 35. There Goes My Heart 38. That Certain Age 38.

Carry On films.
This long-running series that became as much a British institution as fish and chips began with an army farce, Carry On Sergeant, scripted by Norman Hudis from an unpublished play by R. F. Delderfield, and directed by Gerald Thomas. Among the cast were Kenneth Williams, Charles Hawtrey and Kenneth Connor, who were to become Carry On regulars. Over the years the plots gradually disappeared under an accumulation of old jokes which grew steadily bluer, especially when, after the first six, Talbot Rothwell replaced Hudis as the writer; after his death the last four were written by various hands but failed to recapture the flavour of the earlier movies. An amalgam of music-hall humour and end-of-pier farces, the films' makeshift construction was evident even with the later use of colour, and they never raised their sights as high as satire. All were directed by Thomas and produced by Peter Rogers on as low a budget as

possible. A Sussex beach stood in for the Sahara in Carry On, Follow That Camel and a Welsh mountainside for the Khyber Pass. Apart from Williams, Hawtrey and Connor, the regulars included Sid James, Bernard Bresslaw, Jim Dale, Joan Sims, Barbara Windsor, Hattie Jacques, Terry Scott, Patsy Rowlands, Jack Douglas and Peter Butterworth, with occasional guests such as Harry H. Corbett, Fenella Fielding, Juliet Mills and even Phil Silvers. The music for the first four was written by Bruce Montgomery and for the remainder, apart from the final film, by Eric Rogers.

The sequence was: Carry On Sergeant 58; Carry On Nurse (a surprising hit in the US) 59; Carry On Teacher 59; Carry On Constable 60; Carry On Regardless 60; Carry On Cruising (the first in colour) 62; Carry On Cabby (bw) 63; Carry On Jack (colour, the first by Talbot Rothwell) 64; Carry On Spying (bw) 64; Carry On Cleo (colour, as were all subsequent films) 64; Carry On Cowboy 65; Carry On Screaming 66; Carry On – Don't Lose Your Head 66; Carry On – Follow That Camel 66; Carry On Doctor 68; Carry On up the Khyber 68; Carry On Again Doctor 69; Carry On Camping 69; Carry On up the Jungle 70; Carry On Loving 70; Carry On Henry 71; Carry On at Your Convenience 71; Carry On Abroad 72; Carry On Matron 72; Carry On Girls 73; Carry On Dick (Rothwell's last) 74; Carry On Behind (scripted by Dave Freeman) 75; Carry On England (scripted by Jack Seddon and David Pursall) 76; Carry On Emmannuelle (scripted by Lance Peters) 78; Carry On Columbus (scripted by Dave Freeman) 92.

¶ I am convinced that audiences do not like change; they like the same thing over and over again. – Peter Rogers
They were all alike, weren't they? We made 31 films out of one gag. – Peter Rogers
This is v. odd, the way that Carry Ons are just starting to get mentioned: why are they suddenly fashionable? They're even trying to justify the bad scripts now! and talk about the classlessness of them. What hogwash! You can only call a mess a mess. – Kenneth Williams, 1964
The film was Carry On Abroad and I was featured doing all the old crap. Looking at this rubbish you realise that nothing has changed! British sit-coms all consist of the same routines, jokes, and dirt. Very depressing. – Kenneth Williams, 1988
If I had to think of one reason why the Carry Ons matter so much, it's because they really aren't recuperable for proper culture. Like the Crazy Gang, like George Formby, like Frank Randle, they display a commitment to bodily functions and base desires that will always render them irreducibly vulgar, inescapably Not Art. – Andy Medhurst, Sight and Sound, 1992

Carson, Charles (1886–1977).
British character actor of stage and screen, seen utterly as distinguished old gentlemen.
Leap Year 32. Sanders of the River 35. Victoria the Great 37. Dark Journey 37. Quiet Wedding 40. Pink String and Sealing Wax 45. Cry the Beloved Country 52. Reach for the Sky 56. The Trials of Oscar Wilde 60, many others.

Carson, Jack (1910–1963).
Beefy Canadian comedy actor; a former vaudevillian, he usually played 'smart guys' who were really dumber than the suckers they tried to con.
You Only Live Once 37. Stage Door 37. Stand In 37. Too Many Wives 37. It Could Happen To You 37. Music for Madame 37. The Toast of New York 37. Reported Missing 37. The Saint in New York

37. Vivacious Lady 37. Mr Doodle Kicks Off 38. Crashing Hollywood 38. She's Got Everything 38. Night Spot 38. Law of the Underworld 38. This Marriage Business 38. Having Wonderful Time 38. Maids Night Out 38. Everybody's Doing It 38. Quick Money 38. Bringing Up Baby 38. Go Chase Yourself 38. Carefree 38. Destry Rides Again 39. The Kid from Texas 39. Mr Smith Goes to Washington 39. Legion of Lost Flyers 39. The Escape 39. The Honeymoon's Over 39. The Girl in 313 40. Shooting High 40. Young As You Feel 40. Enemy Agent 40. Parole Fixer 40. Alias the Deacon 40. Queen of the Mob 40. Sandy Gets His Man 40. Love Thy Neighbour 40. Lucky Partners 40. I Take this Woman 40. Typhoon 40. The Strawberry Blonde 41. Mr and Mrs Smith 41. Love Crazy 41. The Bride Came COD 41. Navy Blues 41. Blues in the Night 41. The Male Animal 42. Gentleman Jim 42. Larceny Inc. 42. Wings for the Eagle 42. The Hard Way 42. Princess O'Rourke 43. Thank Your Lucky Stars 43. Shine On Harvest Moon 44. Arsenic and Old Lace 44. The Doughgirls 44. Make Your Own Bed (leading role) 44. Roughly Speaking 45. Mildred Pierce 45. One More Tomorrow 46. The Time The Place and The Girl 46. Two Guys from Milwaukee 46. Love and Learn 47. April Showers 48. Romance on the High Seas 48. Two Guys from Texas 48. John Loves Mary 49. My Dream is Yours 49. It's a Great Feeling 49. Bright Leaf 50. Mr Universe 51. The Groom Wore Spurs 51. The Good Humor Man 51. Dangerous When Wet 53. Phffft! 54. Red Garters 54. A Star is Born 54. Ain't Misbehavin' 54. The Bottom of the Bottle 56. The Magnificent Roughnecks 56. The Tattered Dress 57. Cat on a Hot Tin Roof 58. Rally Round the Flag Boys 58. The Tarnished Angels 58. The Bramble Bush 60. King of the Roaring Twenties 61. Sammy the Way Out Seal (TV) 62.

Famous line (Mildred Pierce): 'Oh boy! I'm so smart it's a disease!'

Carson, Jeannie (1928–) (Jean Shufflebottom).
Vivacious British entertainer who became popular in America and then surprisingly retired.
Love in Pawn 51. As Long as They're Happy 54. An Alligator Named Daisy 56. Rockets Galore 57. Seven Keys 62, etc.
TV series: Hey Jeannie! 56.

Carson, John (1927–).
British character actor with a James Mason-like voice. Much on TV, especially heard on commercials.
The Plague of the Zombies 67. The Man Who Haunted Himself 70. Taste the Blood of Dracula 70. Captain Kronos Vampire Hunter 72, etc.

Carson, Johnny (1925–).
American comedian and late-night talk show host. He retired in 1992.
¶ He's an anaesthetist. Prince Valium. – Mort Sahl

Carson, Kit (1809–1868).
American western frontiersman and guide who became a legendary figure and has been portrayed in several films, notably Kit Carson 39, in which he was played by Jon Hall (also on TV by Bill Williams).

Carson, L. M. 'Kit'.
American screenwriter, occasional actor and director. He is divorced from actress Karen Black.
David Holzman's Diary 67. The Lexington Experience 70. The American Dreamer (wd) 71. The Last Word 79. Breathless 83. Chinese Boxes

84. Paris, Texas 84. The Texas Chainsaw Massacre Part 2 86. Running on Empty 88 (a), etc.

Carstairs, John Paddy (1912–1970) (John Keys). British director, usually of light-hearted subjects; also comic novelist and painter. Son of Nelson Keys (qv).
Autobiographies: 1942, Honest Injun. 1945, Hadn't We the Gaiety. 1946, Kaleidoscope and a Jaundiced Eye.
The Saint in London 39. Spare a Copper 40. He Found a Star 40. Dancing with Crime 46. Sleeping Car to Trieste 48. The Chiltern Hundreds 49. Made in Heaven 52. Trouble in Store 53. Up to His Neck 54. Up in the World 56. Just My Luck 57. The Square Peg 58. Tommy the Toreador 59. Sands of the Desert 60. Weekend with Lulu 61, many others.

Carsten, Peter (1929–) (Pieter Ransenthaler).
German character actor in America.
Mr Superinvisible 73, etc.

Carter, Ann (1936–).
American child star of the 40s.
I Married a Witch 42. North Star 43. Curse of the Cat People 44. The Two Mrs Carrolls 46. Song of Love 47. A Connecticut Yankee in King Arthur's Court 49, etc.

Carter, Ben (1911–1947).
American character actor.
Gone with the Wind 39. Maryland 40. Tin Pan Alley 40. Chad Hanna 40. Reap the Wild Wind 42. The Harvey Girls 46, etc.

Carter, Benny (1907–).
American composer, arranger and multi-instrumentalist, one of the finest jazz alto saxophonists.
A Man Called Adam 66. Buck and the Preacher 72. Manhunter (TV) 74. Louis Armstrong – Chicago Style (TV) 76, etc.

Carter, Helena (1923–) (Helen Rickerts).
American leading lady of second features in the 40s; former model.
Time Out of Mind 46. River Lady 48. Double Crossbones 51. The Golden Hawk 52. Invaders from Mars 53, etc.

Carter, Jack (1922–) (John Chakrin).
American nightclub and TV comic of the 50s.
The Horizontal Lieutenant 62. Viva Las Vegas 63. The Extraordinary Seaman 64. Hustle 75. The Amazing Dobermans 76. Rainbow (TV) 78. Alligator 80. Ecstasy 84. Hambone and Hillie 84. Death Blow 87. Red Nights 87. Deadly Embrace 88. Sexpot 88, etc.

Carter, Janis (1921–1994) (J. Dremann).
American leading lady of minor films in the 40s; former radio experience.
Cadet Girl 41. Notorious Lone Wolf 43. Paula 44. The Fighting Guardsmen 45. I Love Trouble 47. The Woman on Pier 13 49. My Forbidden Past 51. Flying Leathernecks 51. The Half-Breed 52, etc.

Carter, Mrs Leslie (1862–1937) (Caroline Louise Dudley).
American stage actress, a protégée of David Belasco; a 1940 biopic, Lady with Red Hair, starred Miriam Hopkins. Film appearances rare.
■ Du Barry 15. The Heart of Maryland 15. The Vanishing Pioneer 34. Rocky Mountain Mystery 34.

Carter, Nell (1948–).
American comedy actress and singer.

Hair 79. Back Roads 81. Modern Problems 81, etc.

TV series: Lobo 80–81. Gimme a Break 81–87. You Take the Kids 90–91.

cartoon:

a film composed of animated drawings, carefully varied to give the appearance of motion. Gertie the Dinosaur, who appeared in 1909, is thought to be the first cartoon character; Mutt and Jeff followed soon after. In the 20s, Pat Sullivan's Felix the Cat and Max Fleischer's Out of the Inkwell series vied for popularity until both were ousted by Walt Disney, who with Ub Iwerks created Mickey Mouse and his familiar friends. In the 30s, Disney went on to Silly Symphonies, Fleischer to Popeye. Other creations were Woody Woodpecker (Walter Lantz), Mighty Mouse, Heckle and Jeckle, Tom and Jerry (Hanna-Barbera for MGM) and Bugs Bunny. Disney's Donald Duck became more popular than Mickey. In the 40s, David Hand made British cartoons for the Rank Organisation, but they were not commercially successful. The 50s brought U.P.A. with their new refined lines, intellectual conceptions and sophisticated jokes; Mr Magoo and Gerald McBoing Boing led the new characters but quickly palled. Then the needs of television led to innumerable cartoon series which for the sake of economy had to be only semi-animated and had little vitality; the best of them were The Flintstones and Yogi Bear. These series proliferated into hundreds and not until 1972 did anyone try an adult cartoon series, Hanna-Barbera's Wait Till Your Father Gets Home.
■ Feature-length cartoons were started by Disney in 1937 with Snow White and the Seven Dwarfs; Fleischer responded in 1939 with Gulliver's Travels. Disney's outstanding serious cartoon was Fantasia 40, an interpretation of classical music. Later, French and Japanese cartoons flooded the market, but inspiration was lacking in most of them. Halas and Batchelor's British Animal Farm was a fair summation of Orwell's fable, but their later attempts to interpret Gilbert and Sullivan failed. In recent years the cartoon has been put to every kind of serious and comic purpose, including propaganda and advertising, and many prizewinners have come from Europe. Ralph Bakshi's ruderies of Fritz the Cat were startling, but he atoned with his careful rendering of Lord of the Rings.

Cartwright, Veronica (1949–).

American leading lady.

The Children's Hour 62. The Birds 63. Inserts 77. Going South 78. Invasion of the Body Snatchers 78. Alien 79. Guyana Tragedy (TV) 80. Prime Suspect (TV) 81. The Right Stuff 83. My Man Adam 85. Flight of the Navigator 86. Wisdom 86. The Witches of Eastwick 87. Valentino Returns 88. False Identity 90. Dead in the Water 91, etc.

TV series: Daniel Boone 64–70.

Caruso, Anthony (1913–).

American character actor, usually seen as menace.

Johnny Apollo 40. Sunday Punch 42. Objective Burma 45. Wild Harvest 47. Bride of Vengeance 49. Tarzan and the Slave Girl 50. The Iron Mistress 52. Phantom of the Rue Morgue 54. Hell on Frisco Bay 56. The Badlanders 58. The Most Dangerous Man Alive 61. Young Dillinger 65. Flap 70. Zebra Force 76. Claws 77, many others.

Caruso, David (1955–).

Red-haired American leading actor, best known so far as Detective John Kelly in NYPD Blue. His salary per film is currently reportedly $1m.

Without Warning 80. An Officer and a

Gentleman 82. First Blood 82. Thief of Hearts 84. Blue City 86. China Girl 87. Twins 88. King of New York 90. Hudson Hawk 91. Mad Dog and Glory 93. Kiss of Death 95, etc.

TV series: NYPD Blue 93–94.

Caruso, Enrico (1873–1921).

Celebrated Italian operatic tenor who appeared in a few silent films, for which he was paid $100,000 a time, and was played by Mario Lanza in The Great Caruso 51.

My Cousin 18. A Splendid Romance 18, etc.

Carver, Louise (1869–1956) (Louise Spilger Murray).

American character actress, a famous silent comedienne.

The Extra Girl 23. Shameful Behaviour 26. The Fortune Hunter 27. The Man from Blankley's 30. The Big Trail 30. Side Show 31. Hallelujah I'm a Bum 33. Every Night at Eight 35, etc.

Carver, Lynne (1909–1955) (Virginia Reid Sampson).

American general-purpose actress.

Roberta 35. Maytime 37. A Christmas Carol 38. Calling Dr Kildare 39. Charley's Aunt 41. Tennessee Johnson 42. Law of the Valley 44. Crossed Trails 48, etc.

Carvey, Dana (1955–).

American actor and writer, best known for his performance as Garth in Wayne's World on the TV show Saturday Night Live, which became a successful film series.

Tough Guys 86. Moving 88. Opportunity Knocks 90. Wayne's World (& co-w) 92. Wayne's World 2 (& co-w) 93. Clean Slate 94. The Road to Wellville 94, etc.

TV series: One of the Boys 82. Blue Thunder 84.

Cary, Tristram (1925–).

British composer, the third son of novelist Joyce Cary, many of whose scores incorporate electronic music. Educated at Oxford and Trinity College of Music, London, he founded the electronic music studio at the Royal College of Music in the mid-60s and set up his own electronic music facility in England before moving to Australia, where he became Dean of Music at Adelaide University in the 80s. He now runs Tristram Cary Creative Music Services. Author of the Illustrated Compendium of Musical Technology, 1992. Apart from features, he has scored many documentaries.

The Ladykillers 55. Time without Pity 55. Town on Trial 56. The Flesh Is Weak 57. Tread Softly Stranger 58. She Didn't Say No 58. The Little Island (cartoon) 58. The Boy Who Stole a Million 61. The Prince and the Pauper 62. Sammy Going South 63. The Silent Playground 63. Daylight Robbery 64. Quatermass and the Pit 67. A Twist of Sand 67. Blood from the Mummy's Tomb 72. The Fourth Wish 76, etc.

Casanova, Giovanni (1725–1798).

The celebrated Italian lover, whose career was much romanticized during his lifetime and afterwards, was a popular cinema figure although until the 70s his exploits had to be bowdlerized. Principal films are as follows:

France 1946:	Les Aventures de Casanova, Georges Guetary	
US 1948:	The Adventures of Casanova, Arturo de Cordova	
Italy 1955:	Casanova, Gabriele Ferzetti	
Italy 1965:	Casanova 70, Marcello Mastroianni	

Italy 1969:	Casanova the Venetian, Leonard Whiting	
Italy/West Germany/ France 1977:	The Rise and Rise of Casanova, Tony Curtis	
UK 1971:	Casanova (TV serial by Dennis Potter), Frank Finlay	
Italy 1977:	Fellini's Casanova, Donald Sutherland	
Italy 1978:	The Return of Casanova, Giulio Boseti	

And in 1954 Vincent Price played Casanova in a Bob Hope spoof, Casanova's Big Night.

Casares, Maria (1922–) (Maria Casares Quiroga).

Dark-eyed, solemn-looking French-Spanish character actress.

Les Enfants du Paradis 43. Les Dames du Bois de Boulogne 44. La Chartreuse de Parme 47. Bagarres 48. Orphée (as Death) 49. Le Testament d'Orphée 59. The Rebel Nun 74. Flavia 76. Blanche et Marie 85. De Sable et de Sang 88. La Lectrice 88. Les Chevaliers de la Table Ronde 90, etc.

case histories

from medical files, which would once have been considered pretty dull plot material, have recently been presented quite starkly to paying audiences who appear to have relished them. In the 40s, Lady in the Dark was a richly decorated trifle, and even The Snake Pit and Mandy had subsidiary love interest, but in more recent years we have had such unvarnished studies as El (paranoiac jealousy), Pressure Point (fascist tendencies), A Child is Waiting (mentally handicapped children), Life Upside Down (withdrawal), The Collector (sex fantasies), Repulsion, In Cold Blood, 10 Rillington Place and The Boston Strangler (homicidal mania), Bigger Than Life (danger from drugs). The Three Faces of Eve and Lizzie (split personality), Marnie (frigidity), Morgan (infantile regression), and Family Life. At least the pretence of studying a case history relieves writers of the responsibility of providing a dramatic ending.

See also: dreams; fantasy; amnesia.

Caserini, Mario (1874–1920).

Italian director of silent epics, a former actor and artist.

Othello 07. Romeo and Juliet 08. Beatrice Cenci 09. Hamlet 10. Lucrezia Borgia 10. Dante e Beatrice 12. The Last Days of Pompeii (Gli Ultimi Giorni di Pompei) 13. Resurrection 17. Il Miracolo 19. La Modella 20, etc.

Casey, Bernie (1939–).

American character actor, a former professional football player.

Tick Tick Tick 69. Black Gunn 72. Cornbread Earl and Me 75. Brothers 77. Sharky's Machine 81. Revenge of the Nerds 84. Spies Like Us 85. Steele Justice 87. Backfire 88. Rent-A-Cop 88. Bill & Ted's Excellent Adventure 89. Another 48 Hrs 90. The Cemetery Club 93. The Glass Shield 94, etc.

TV series: Harris and Company 79. Bay City Blues 83.

Cash, Jim.

American screenwriter, often in collaboration with Jim Epps Jnr.

Top Gun (co-w) 86. Legal Eagles (co-w) 86. The Secret of My Success (co-w) 86. Turner & Hooch (co-w) 89, etc.

Cash, Johnny (1932–).

American country singer.

Five Minutes to Live 62. A Gunfight 70. The Pride

Jesse Hallam (TV) 80. Murder in Coweta County
. The Baron and the Kid 84. Stagecoach (TV) 86.
st Days of Frank and Jesse James (TV) 86, etc.

ash, Rosalind (1938–   ).
merican leading lady.
  Klute 71. The Omega Man 71. The All-
merican Boy 71. The New Centurions 72.
ckey and Boggs 72. Melinda 72. Uptown
turday Night 74. Amazing Grace 74. Hit the
en Man 75. Dr Black, Mr Hyde 76. The Monkey
stle 76. The Class of Miss McMichael 78.
ashpoint (TV) 79. Guyana Tragedy (TV) 80.
rong is Right 82. Death Drug 83. The
lventures of Buckaroo Banzai across the Eighth
mension 84. The Offspring (aka From a
hisper to a Scream) 86, etc.

aspary, Vera (1899–1987).
merican romantic crime novelist.
  The Night of June 13th (oa) 32. I'll Love You
ways (w) 35. Scandal Street (oa) 38. Lady from
uisiana (w) 41. *Laura* (oa) 44. Claudia and David
) 46. Bedelia (oaw) 46. A Letter to Three Wives
) 48. Three Husbands (oaw) 51. The Blue
rdenia (oa) 53. Bachelor in Paradise (oa) 61,
c.

asper, the Friendly Ghost.
e happy baby ghost created by producer Joseph
riolo and animator Seymour Wright in 1945
as popular through the 50s and as a star of
ildren's television in the 60s. A live action feature
arring Christina Ricci and Eric Idle was released
1995.
  The Friendly Ghost 45. There's Good Boos
night 48. A-Haunting We Will Go 49. Casper
mes to Clown 51. Deep Boo Sea 52. Frightday
e 13th 53. Zero the Hero 54. Casper Genie 54.
ide and Shriek 55. Ground Hog Play 56. Ghost
Honor 57. Heir Restorer 58. Not Ghoulty 59.
asper's Birthday 59, etc.

ass, Henry (1902–1989).
ritish director with stage experience as actor and
oducer.
  Lancashire Luck 37. 29 Acacia Avenue 45. The
lass Mountain 48. No Place for Jennifer 49. Last
oliday 50. Young Wives' Tale 51. Windfall 55.
lood of the Vampire 59. The Hand 60. Give a Dog
Bone 66, etc.

ass, Maurice (1884–1954).
merican character actor of Russian origin; often
ayed old men.
  Two for Tonight 35. Charlie Chan at the Opera
7. Son of Monte Cristo 40. Blood and Sand 41.
harley's Aunt 41. Up in Arms 44. Angel on My
oulder 46. Spoilers of the North 47. We're Not
arried 52, many others.

ass, Peggy (1925–   ).
merican comedy actress, mainly on Broadway:
ms few.
  The Marrying Kind 52. *Auntie Mame* (AAN) 58.
idget Goes Hawaiian 62. If It's Tuesday This Must
e Belgium 69. Age of Consent 69. Paddy 70.
heaters 84. Tales from the Darkside 85, etc.
  TV series: The Hathaways 61–62. Women in
rison 87–88.

assavetes, John (1929–1989).
ight, intense American actor who played a
ariety of parts and later became an experimental
rector. He was married to actress Gena
owlands.
  Taxi 54. The Night Holds Terror 55. Crime in
e Streets 56. Edge of the City 57. Saddle the

Wind 58. Virgin Island 58. The Webster Boy 61.
Shadows (d only) 61. Too Late Blues (d only) 62. A
Child is Waiting (d only) 62. The Killers 64. The
Dirty Dozen (AAN) 67. Affair in Havana 67. The
Devil's Angels 67. Rosemary's Baby 68. *Faces* (w,
d only) (AANw) 68. Bandits in Rome (It.) 69. If
It's Tuesday This Must be Belgium 69. Husbands
(& w, d) 70. Machine Gun McCain 70. *Minnie and
Moskowitz* (& w, d) 71. A Woman Under the
Influence (w, d only) (AAN) 74. Capone 75. Two
Minute Warning 76. Mikey and Nicky 76. Opening
Night (& w, d) 78. The Killing of a Chinese Bookie
(w, d only) 78. Brass Target 78. The Fury 78. Flesh
and Blood (TV) 80. Gloria (w, p, d only) 80.
Whose Life is it Anyway? 81. Tempest 82. The
Incubus 82. Love Streams (w, p, d) 83. Marvin and
Tige 83. Big Trouble 84.
  TV series: *Johnny Staccato* 59.

¶ People have forgotten how to relate or respond
  . . . what I'm trying to do with my movies is
build something audiences can respond to. – *J.C.*
  When I started making films, I wanted to make
Frank Capra pictures. But I've never been able to
make anything but these crazy, tough pictures.
You are what you are. – *J.C.*
  As a director, too much of the time he is groping
when he should be gripping. – *Andrew Sarris, 1968*
  One of the most garrulous noncomformists in
show business. – *Anon*

Cassel, Jean-Pierre (1932–   ) (Jean-Pierre
Crochon).
French leading man.
  Les Jeux de l'Amour 60. L'Amant de Cinq Jours
61. The Vanishing Corporal 62. La Ronde 64. Those
Magnificent Men in Their Flying Machines 65. Les
Fêtes Galantes 65. Is Paris Burning? 66. Jeu de
Massacre 67. Baxter 71. The Discreet Charm of the
Bourgeoisie 72. The Three Musketeers 74.
Murder on the Orient Express 74. That Lucky
Touch 75. The Four Musketeers 75. Grandison
78. Who Is Killing the Great Chefs of Europe 78.
La Vie Continue 81. The Trout (La Truite) 82.
Tranches de Vie 84. Mangeclous 88. Mister Frost
90. The Favour, The Watch and The Very Big Fish
(Rue Saint-Sulpice) 91. The Maid 91. In Heaven
as on Earth (Sur la Terre, comme au Ciel) 92.
Pétain 93, etc.

Cassel, Seymour (1935–   ).
American character actor associated with the films
of John Cassavetes.
  Too Late Blues 61. The Killers 64. The Sweet
Ride 68. Faces (AAN) 68. The Revolutionary 70.
Minnie and Moskowitz 71. The Last Tycoon 76. The
Killing of a Chinese Bookie 78. Convoy 78.
California Dreaming 79. The Mountain Men 80.
Love Streams 84. Eye of the Tiger 86. Tin Men 87.
Colors 88. Plain Clothes 88. Wicked Stepmother
89. Cold Dog Soup 90. Dick Tracy 90. White Fang
91. In the Soup 92. Diary of a Hit Man 92. Indecent
Proposal 93. Boiling Point 93. When Pigs Fly 93.
Handgun 94. Chasers 94. When Pigs Fly 94. It
Could Happen to You 94. Dark Side of Genius 94.
There Goes My Baby 94. Imaginary Crimes 94, etc.

cassettes.
In 1970–71 the show business world awaited a
revolution which despite enormous expense and
drum-beating failed to happen at the time. The
idea was to make available one's favourite film,
or any other kind of entertainment, in
miniaturized cartridge form which could be played
back whenever one wished through new
equipment. Unfortunately international agreement
on the type of hardware could not be achieved,
and none of the prototype gadgets were compatible.

Moreover the trade was still busy selling colour
TV, so by general consensus the new miracle was
deferred until the 80s, when under the name
'video', and with fewer competing systems, it was
a success beyond the industry's wildest dreams or
fears. By 1984 one in every five homes had the
equipment, and films new and old were cheaply
available on hire from a myriad of local shops.
The British success with the system caused more
cinema closures, but was not equalled in other
countries.

Cassidy, David (1950–   ).
American actor who enjoyed fame on the
television series *The Partridge Family* 70–74,
together with his step-mother Shirley Jones, and
was the teeny-boppers' favourite singer in the
early 70s. He retired for three years in the mid-
70s, began recording again in the 80s but has so
far not regained his early success. He is the son of
Jack Cassidy and actress Evelyn Ward.
  The Spirit of '76 90.
  TV series: David Cassidy – Man Undercover 78–
79.

Cassidy, Jack (1926–1976).
American light actor, mostly on TV; husband of
Shirley Jones and father of David Cassidy.
  Look in any Window 62. FBI Code 98 64. Guide
for the Married Man 67. Your Money or Your
Wife (TV) 72. Phantom of Hollywood (TV) 74. The
Eiger Sanction 75. W. C. Fields and Me (as John
Barrymore) 76, etc.
  TV series: He and She 67.

Cassidy, Joanna (1944–   ) (Joanna Caskey).
American leading lady.
  The Laughing Policeman 73. The Outfit 73. Bank
Shot 74. Stunts 77. Blade Runner 82. Under Fire
83. Hollywood Wives (TV) 85. Club Paradise 86.
The Fourth Protocol 87. Who Framed Roger Rabbit
88. 1969 89. The Package 89. May Wine 90. Where
the Heart Is 90. All-American Murder 91. Lonely
Hearts 91. The Tommyknockers (TV) 93, etc.
  TV series: The Roller Girls 78. 240-Robert 79–
80. The Family Tree 83. Buffalo Bill 83–84.
Codename Foxfire 85. Hotel Malibu 94.

Cassidy, Ted (1932–1979).
Giant-size American character actor who became
popular in 1964 as Lurch the butler in TV's *The
Addams Family*.
  Mackenna's Gold 68. Harry and Walter Go to
New York 76. The Last Remake of Beau Geste 77,
etc.

Casson, Sir Lewis (1875–1969).
Leading English actor, on stage from 1900, who
made a few films. Husband of Sybil Thorndike.
  Crime on the Hill 33. Midshipman Easy 35.
Rhodes of Africa 36. Victoria the Great 37. Sixty
Glorious Years 38. The Winslow Boy 48. Shake
Hands with the Devil 59, etc.

cast.
The actors in a movie.

Castel, Lou.
Italian leading actor, in European films.
  Fists in the Pocket (I Pugni in Tasca) 65. A Bullet
for the General (El Chucho, Quién Sabe?) 66.
Paranoia (aka A Beautiful Place to Kill) 69. In the
Name of the Father (In Nome del Padre) 71. The
Scarlet Letter (Der Scharlachrote Buchstabe)
(Ger.) 73. The Cassandra Crossing 76. The
American Friend (Ger.) 77. The Eyes, the Mouth
(Gli Occhi, la Bocca) 82. Trauma (Ger.) 83. Rorret
87. Treasure Island (L'Île au Trésor) (Fr.) 91. Year

of the Gun (US) 91. La Naissance de l'Amour (Fr.) 93. Manila Paloma Blanca 93, etc.

Castellani, Renato (1913–1985).
Italian director.

Un Colpo di Pistola 41. My Son the Professor 46. E Primavera 50. Due Soldi di Speranza 51. Romeo and Juliet (GB) 54. Nella Città l'Inferno 59. Il Brigante 61. Mare Matto 62. Three Nights of Love 64. Sotto il Cielo Stellato 66. Ghosts Italian Style 67. Una Breva Stagione 69. Leonardo da Vinci (TV) 72, etc.

Castellano, Richard (1931–1988).
Fat Italian-American character actor who came to fame in Lovers and Other Strangers (AAN) 69.

A Fine Madness 66. The Godfather 72. Honor Thy Father (TV) 73. Night of the Juggler 80.

TV series: The Super 72. Joe and Sons 75–76. Gangster Chronicles 81.

Castelnuovo, Nino (1937–).
Italian leading man.

La Garçonnière 60. Escapade in Florence 62. Les Parapluies de Cherbourg 64. Camille 2000 69, etc.

Castelnuovo-Tedesco, Mario (1895–1968).
Italian composer in America.

The Return of the Vampire 44. The Black Parachute 44. And Then There Were None 45. Night Editor 46. Time out of Mind 47. Mark of the Avenger 51, etc.

casting.
To the old Hollywood, casting usually meant type-casting, or bending the character to suit the star. In the 70s, stars became less important, and leading actors became more chameleon-like. Even so, many best-remembered performances have been given by actors who were second or third choice. The original requirement for Dracula was Paul Muni, not Bela Lugosi. Clark Gable was thought of for Tarzan. Greta Garbo was asked to play Dorian Gray as a woman. Gloria Swanson's role in Sunset Boulevard was first offered to Mae West. Humphrey Bogart got High Sierra and The Maltese Falcon only because George Raft turned them down. Robert Montgomery, Fredric March, Carole Lombard and Myrna Loy all turned down It Happened One Night before Gable and Colbert accepted. Carole Lombard however benefited when Miriam Hopkins turned down Twentieth Century. Olivier's role as Maxim de Winter in Rebecca was first offered to William Powell and Ronald Colman. Doris Day was offered Mrs Robinson in The Graduate. Lana Turner gave way to Lee Remick on Anatomy of a Murder. Bette Davis would have been Scarlett O'Hara if she hadn't thought Errol Flynn was to play Rhett. George Jessel would have starred in The Jazz Singer if his demands had been less outrageous. Danny Thomas would have starred in The Jolson Story if he had agreed to have his nose shortened. Marlon Brando, Montgomery Clift and Paul Newman were all sought for East of Eden before James Dean got the role. Bette Davis played Margo in All About Eve only because Claudette Colbert gave it up. Ingrid Bergman was second choice to Vera Zorina for For Whom the Bell Tolls. Jack Nicholson took over from Rip Torn in Easy Rider, Marlon Brando from Montgomery Clift in On The Waterfront. Bette Davis turned down Mildred Pierce and Joan Crawford grabbed it. Olivia de Havilland, not Vivien Leigh, was first choice for A Streetcar named Desire. Ingrid Bergman won Oscars for Gaslight, first offered to Hedy Lamarr, and Anastasia, intended for Jennifer Jones; but she turned down The Farmer's Daughter and To Each His Own, which won Oscars for Loretta Young and Olivia de Havilland. If Grace

Kelly hadn't become Princess of Monaco, she would have played in Cat on a Hot Tin Roof and Designing Woman, not Elizabeth Taylor or Lauren Bacall. William Holden got Sunset Boulevard after Montgomery Clift said no. Frank Sinatra walked out of Carousel: Gordon MacRae took over. Ginger Rogers replaced the ailing Judy Garland in The Barkleys of Broadway. Deborah Kerr got From Here to Eternity when Joan Crawford withdrew. Vivien Leigh thought herself too young to play the role in Suddenly Last Summer which went to Katharine Hepburn. Shirley Temple was wanted for Judy Garland's role in The Wizard of Oz; W. C. Fields was to have been the wizard, but argued over money. Fields himself only got Micawber in David Copperfield because Charles Laughton walked out after two days of filming.

¶ Casting: deciding which of two faces the public is least tired of. – Anonymous definition

I couldn't go on forever being Little Miss Fixit who burst into song. – Deanna Durbin

No matter what roles I play, I can't get Caligari out of my system. – Conrad Veidt

I was a thirteen-year-old boy for thirty years. – Mickey Rooney

After The Wizard of Oz I was typecast as a lion, and there aren't all that many parts for lions. – Bert Lahr

If I made Cinderella, the audience would be looking for the body in the coach. – Alfred Hitchcock

They get to know your face too well out there in Hollywood, and you're finished. – Ethel Griffies

Aren't you tired, Spence, of always playing Spencer Tracy?
– What am I supposed to do, play Bogart?

Castle, Don (1919–1966).
American leading man of 40s second features.

Love Finds Andy Hardy 38. I Take this Woman 40. Power Dive 41. Tombstone 42. The Guilty 47. The Invisible Wall 47, etc.

Castle, Irene, Vernon (Irene Foote, Vernon Blythe).
A dancing team who were highly popular in American cabaret 1912–17. Irene (1893–1969) was American, Vernon (1893–1918) was British. Apart from some 1914 shorts, their only feature together was The Whirl of Life 15; but Irene alone made a number of dramatic films, especially after Vernon's death in an air crash: Patria 17, The Hillcrest Mystery 18, The Invisible Bond 19, The Broadway Bride 21, No Trespassing 22, etc. In 1939 Fred Astaire and Ginger Rogers appeared in The Story of Vernon and Irene Castle; in 1958 Irene published an autobiography, Castles in the Air.

Castle, John (1940–).
British character actor.

The Lion in Winter 68. The Promise 69. Antony and Cleopatra 71. Man of La Mancha 72. The Incredible Sarah 77. The Three Hostages (TV) 78. Eagle's Wing 79. Night Shift 80. Second Star to the Right 80. King David 85. Lost Empires (TV) 86, etc.

Castle, Mary (1931–).
American leading lady of the 60s.

Criminal Lawyer 51. Eight Iron Men 52. The Lawless Breed 53. The Jailbreakers 61, etc.

Castle, Nick (1910–1968).
American dance director.

Swanee River 39. Hellzapoppin 42. Royal Wedding 47. Red Garters 54, many others.

Castle, Nick (1947–).
American screenwriter and director, the son of choreographer Nick Castle.

Skatetown U.S.A. (w) 79. Pray TV (w) 80. Escape from New York (co-w) 81. The Last Starfighter (d) 84. The Boy Who Could Fly (wd) 86. Tap (wd) 89. Dennis the Menace (GB: Denni 93, etc.

Castle, Peggie (1927–1973).
American leading lady of 50s second features.

Mr Belvedere Goes to College 49. Buccaneer's Girl 50. Air Cadet 51. I the Jury 53. The Long Wait 54. Jesse James' Women 54. Target Zero 55 Bury Me Dead 57. Seven Hills of Rome 58, etc.

TV series: Lawman 58–61.

Castle Rock Entertainment.
Hollywood production company co-founded by director Rob Reiner. Now a subsidiary of the Turner Broadcasting System, it has plans to become a distributor also.

Castle, Roy (1932–1994).
British light entertainer, in occasional films.

Dr Terror's House of Horrors 66. Dr Who and the Daleks 66. Carry On Up the Khyber 71. Legen of the Werewolf 75, etc.

Castle, William (1914–1977) (William Schloss).
American director of second features (1941–57) who became a cheerful purveyor of gimmicky horror films involving give-away insurance policies, mobile skeletons, tingling seats, etc; these he not only produced and directed but introduced in the Hitchcock manner.

Autobiography: 1976, Step Right Up! . . . I'm Gonna Scare the Pants off America.

■ The Chance of a Lifetime 43. Klondyke Kate 4: The Whistler 44. When Strangers Marry 44. She's a Soldier Too 44. The Mark of the Whistler 44. Voic of the Whistler 46. Just Before Dawn 46. Mysteriou Intruder 46. The Return of Rusty 46. The Crime Doctor's Manhunt 46. The Crime Doctor's Gambl 47. Texas Brooklyn and Heaven 48. The Gentleman from Nowhere 48. Johnny Stool Pigeon 49. Undertow 49. It's a Small World 50. The Fat Man 51. Hollywood Story 51. Cave of Outlaws 51. Serpent of the Nile 53. Fort Ti 53. Conquest of Cochise 53. Slaves of Babylon 53. Charge of the Lancers 54. Drums of Tahiti 54. Jess James vs the Daltons 54. Battle of Rogue River 54. The Iron Glove 54. The Saracen Blade 54. Th Law vs Billy the Kid 54. Masterson of Kansas 54. The Americano 55. New Orleans Uncensored 55. The Gun that Won the West 55. Duel on the Mississippi 55. The Houston Story 56. Uranium Boom 56. Macabre 58. House on Haunted Hill 59. The Tingler 59. Thirteen Ghosts 60. Homicidal 61. Sardonicus 61. Zotz! 62. Thirteen Frightened Girl 63. The Old Dark House 63. Strait Jacket 64. The Night Walker 64. I Saw What You Did 65. Let's Kill Uncle 66. The Busy Body 67. The Spirit is Willing 67. Rosemary's Baby (p only) 68. Project 68. The Sex Symbol (TV) (as actor) 74. Shanks (8 p) 74. Shampoo (as actor) 75. Bug (p only) 75. Da of the Locust (as actor) 75.

TV series: Ghost Story 72.

catchphrases
¶ Although Garbo got into the act with 'I want to be alone' and Boyer impersonators have had a ball with a line Boyer never spoke, 'Come with me to the Casbah', it is comedians who devise and need readily identifiable catchphrases, so that audiences have something to laugh at without even being warmed up. Here are a few which should be immediately recognized:

Diminutive Arthur Askey came up with
    I thank you (pronounced Ay Theng Yow)
nd was annoyed when Cyril Fletcher used the
ight variation
    Thanking you . . .
s well as:
    Dreaming oh my darling love of thee.
andy Powell had
    Can you hear me, mother?
eorge Formby contracted this, in moments of
ress, to
    Ohh, muvver!
hen he wasn't telling everyone that it had
    Turned out nice again!
lanagan and Allen's most notable trade mark was
mply
    Oi!
hile Will Hay perfected a sniff, Max Miller
owever told his audiences:
    There'll never be another!
nd when they laughed at his floral suit, asked:
    Well, what if I am?
Vhen Old Mother Riley needed help, she
reamed:
    Mrs Ginocchi, SOS!
nd of her errant daughter she inevitably
emanded:
    Where've you been, who've you been with,
    what've you been doing, and why?
obb Wilton reminisced about
    The day war broke out
nd Tommy Trinder called his audience
    You lucky people!
ruce Forsyth also gets on chummily with his
udience, asking for applause with
    Didn't he do well?
ack Warner was worried for his property:
    Mind my bike . . .
nd Robertson Hare always anticipated disaster:
    Oh, calamity!
choolmasterish Jimmy Edwards told his audience
    Wake up at the back there!
Vhile Ben Lyon was constantly afraid that his
other-in-law in the audience might take
mbrage at any insulting lines from the stage:
    Not you, momma, sit down!
he famous radio series It's That Man Again
ractically consisted of catchphrases, including
    Can I do you now, sir?
    Don't forget the diver . . .
    After you, Claude . . . no, after you,
    Cecil . . .
    I go, I come back.
    Good morning, nice day.
    I don't mind if I do.
    Boss, boss, sumpn terrible's happened . . .
    This is Funf speaking . . .
fter ITMA's demise, other radio shows caught on
 the idea, Arthur Askey producing
    Hello, playmates!
    Before your very eyes.
    Don't be filthy.
nd
    These jokes are free for pantomime!
am Costa was recognized by:
    Good morning, sir, was there something?
While Take It from Here also added its share of
hrases to the language:
    Gently, Bentley.
    A mauve one.
    Clumsy clot.
    Oh, Eth . . . oh, Ron . . .
lore recently, Frankie Howerd has wished his
udiences:
    And the best of luck!
lax Bygraves has asserted himself:
    I've arrived, and to prove it, I'm here.

Tough heroes have been getting in on the act. Clint
Eastwood's
    Make my day
has become a cliché that has even found its way
on to T-shirts. And there's Arnold 'The Terminator'
Schwarzenegger with:
    I'll be back.

Cates, Gilbert (1934–) (Gilbert Katz).
American director with Broadway and TV
experience.
■ I Never Sang for My Father 69. To All My Friends
on Shore (TV) 71. Summer Wishes, Winter
Dreams 73. The Affair (TV) 73. Johnny We Hardly
Knew Ye (TV) 77. The Promise 79. Oh God Book
Two 80. The Last Married Couple in America 80.
Backfire 87. Fatal Judgement (TV) 88. My First Love
(TV) 88.

Cates, Phoebe (1963–).
American leading lady who after modelling
experience became an instant star in 1984 as the
heroine of the TV mini-series Lace. She married
actor Kevin Kline in 1990.
    Fast Times at Ridgemont High 82. Paradise 82.
Private School 83. Gremlins 84. Date with an Angel
87. Bright Lights, Big City 88. Shag 88. Heart of
Dixie 89. Gremlins 2: The New Batch 90. Drop
Dead Fred 91. Bodies, Rest and Motion 93. Princess
Caraboo 94, etc.

Catherine the Great (1729–1798).
'mother of all the Russias', has appeared in the
following screen personifications:

Pola Negri	Forbidden Paradise 24
Marlene Dietrich	The Scarlet Empress 34
Elisabeth Bergner	Catherine the Great 34
Tallulah Bankhead	A Royal Scandal 45
Viveca Lindfors	Tempest 58
Bette Davis	John Paul Jones 59
Hildegarde Neff	Catherine of Russia 62
Jeanne Moreau	Great Catherine 68

What a pity that Mae West's play Catherine Was
Great never reached the screen . . .

Catlett, Walter (1889–1960).
Bespectacled American comedian with long
vaudeville experience; his flustered gestures often
characterized inept crooks, commercial travellers,
or Justices of the Peace.
    Second Youth 24. Summer Bachelors 29. Why
Leave Home? 29. Palmy Days 31. Rain 32. Mama
Loves Papa 33. The Captain Hates the Sea 34. Mr
Deeds Goes to Town 36. On the Avenue 37.
Bringing Up Baby 38. Pop Always Pays 40. Horror
Island 41. Yankee Doodle Dandy 42. They Got Me
Covered 43. Ghost Catchers 44. I'll Be Yours 47.
Look for the Silver Lining 49. Here Comes the Groom
51. Father Takes the Air 51. Friendly Persuasion
56, many others.

Caton-Jones, Michael (1958–).
Scottish-born director, now working in
Hollywood.
    Scandal 89. Memphis Belle 90. Doc Hollywood
91. This Boy's Life 92. Rob Roy 95.

¶ When I'm shooting I become a monstrous
    exhibitionist egomaniac. It's quite weird,
because you have to play the role of being a
director. It's not necessarily because that's what you
believe in, but it's what other people want out of
you. I kind of debunk the whole thing by mincing
around with a riding crop and whacking people
with it and barking orders. – M.C.-J.
    Hollywood really is an industry about making
money, not making films. – M.C.-J.

Catto, Max (1907–1992).
Popular British adventure novelist.
    Daughter of Darkness (oa) 48. A Prize of Gold
(oa) 54. West of Zanzibar (w) 54. Trapeze (oa) 56.
Seven Thieves (oa) 60. The Devil at Four o'Clock
(oa) 61. Mister Moses (oa) 65. Murphy's War 71,
etc.

Cattrall, Kim (1956–).
British-born actress, on stage and screen in Canada
and America as well as England.
    Rosebud 75. Porky's 81. Police Academy 84. City
Limits 84. Big Trouble in Little China 86.
Mannequin 87. Masquerade 88. Return of the
Musketeers 89. Brown Bread Sandwiches 89.
Bonfire of the Vanities 90. Star Trek VI: The
Undiscovered Country 91. Split Second 92,
etc.

Caulfield, Joan (1922–1991).
Demure American leading lady of the 40s.
■ Miss Susie Slagle's 46. Monsieur Beaucaire 46.
Blue Skies 46. Dear Ruth 47. Welcome Stranger 47.
The Unsuspected 47. The Sainted Sisters 48.
Larceny 48. Dear Wife 50. The Petty Girl 50. The
Lady Says No 51. The Rains of Ranchipur 55. Cattle
King 63. Red Tomahawk 66. Buckskin 68.
    TV series: My Favorite Husband 53. Sally 57.

Caulfield, Maxwell (1959–).
British leading actor in Hollywood.
    Grease 2 82. Electric Dreams 84. The Boys Next
Door 85. The Supernaturals 86. Sundown 88.
Mind Games 89. Fatal Sky 90. Exiled 91. Animal
Instincts 92. Alien Intruder 93. Gettysburg 93.
Inevitable Grace 94, etc.

Cavalcanti, Alberto (1897–1982).
Brazilian director who made interesting films in
several countries but never quite achieved a
masterpiece.
    Rien que les Heures 26. En Rade 27. Sea Fever 29.
North Sea 38. Men of the Lightship 41. Went the
Day Well? 42. Champagne Charlie 45. Dead of
Night (part) 45. Nicholas Nickleby 47. They Made Me
a Fugitive 47. The First Gentleman 48. For Them
that Trespass 49. O Canto do Mar (Braz.) 53. Herr
Puntila (Ger.) 55. La Prima Notte (It.) 58. Yerma
(It.) 62, etc.

Cavanagh, Paul (1895–1964).
Suave British actor who went to Hollywood in the
20s and spent the rest of his career playing elegant
villains, understanding husbands, and murder
victims.
    The Runaway Princess 29. Grumpy 30. The
Devil to Pay 30. The Squaw Man 31. The Devil's
Lottery 32. A Bill of Divorcement 32. The Kennel
Murder Case 33. Tarzan and his Mate 34. The
Notorious Sophie Lang 34. Goin' to Town (opposite
Mae West) 35. Champagne Charlie 36. Romance
in Flanders 37. Crime over London 38. Reno 39.
The Case of the Black Parrot 40. Maisie was a Lady
41. The Strange Case of Dr RX 42. The Hard Way
43. The Scarlet Claw 44. The Man in Half Moon
Street 44. House of Fear 45. The Verdict 46.
Humoresque 46. Ivy 47. You Gotta Stay Happy 48.
The Iroquois Trail 50. House of Wax 53.
Casanova's Big Night 54. The Purple Mask 55.
Francis in the Haunted House 56. Diane 57. The
Four Skulls of Jonathan Drake 59, many others.

Cavanaugh, Hobart (1886–1950).
Mild-mannered, bald and bespectacled American
character actor usually seen as clerk, nervous
husband or frightened caretaker.
    San Francisco Nights 27. I Cover the Waterfront
33. Convention City 33. Housewife 34. I Sell

Anything 34. Don't Bet on Blondes 35. A Midsummer Night's Dream 35. Stage Struck 36. Cain and Mabel 36. Reported Missing 37. *Rose of Washington Square* (as a double act with Al Jolson) 39. An Angel from Texas 40. Meet the Chump 41. Horror Island (as the villain) 41. The Magnificent Dope 42. Sweet Rosie O'Grady 43. Kismet 44. Black Angel 46. You Gotta Stay Happy 48. Stella 50, many others.

Cavani, Lilana (1937–).
Italian director.
■ Night Encounter 61. Philip Pétain 64. Francis of Assisi 66. Galileo 68. The Cannibals 69. The Hospital 71. The Night Porter 74. Beyond Evil 77. The Berlin Affair 85. St Francis of Assisi 89. Dove Sieta? Io Sono Qui 93.

Cawthorn, Joseph (1868–1949).
American character actor of the 30s.
Very Confidential 27. Silk Legs 28. Jazz Heaven 29. The Taming of the Shrew 29. Dixiana 30. Kiki 31. White Zombie 32. Love me Tonight 32. Whistling in the Dark 33. Housewife 34. The Last Gentleman 34. Go into Your Dance 35. Naughty Marietta 35. The Great Ziegfeld 36. Lillian Russell 40. The Postman Didn't Ring 42, many others.

Cayatte, André (1909–1989).
French lawyer who became writer-director of films with something to say.
Justice Est Faite 50. *Nous Sommes Tous les Assassins* 52. An Eye for an Eye 56. The Mirror Has Two Faces 57. The Crossing of the Rhine 60. La Vie Conjugale 63. A Trap for Cinderella 65. Die of Loving 70, etc.

Cazale, John (1936–1978).
American character actor. Died of cancer.
The Godfather 72. The Conversation 74. The Godfather Part II 74. Dog Day Afternoon 75. *The Deer Hunter* 78, etc.

Cazenove, Christopher (1945–).
British leading man, mostly on TV.
Royal Flash 74. East of Elephant Rock 75. Zulu Dawn 79. Eye of the Needle 80. From a Far Country 80. The Letter (TV) 81. Heat and Dust 82. Mata Hari 83. Jenny's War (TV) 84. Lace II (TV) 85. The Fantasist 86. Souvenir 88. Three Men and a Little Lady 90. Hold My Hand, I'm Dying 90, etc.
TV series: Dynasty 86–88. A Fine Romance 89.

Cecchi d'Amico, Suso (1914–) (Giovanna Cecchi d'Amico).
Italian screenwriter.
Vivere in Pace 46. Bicycle Thieves 49. Miracle in Milan 51. Bellissima 51. Le Amiche 55. Rocco and His Brothers 60. Salvatore Giuliano 61. The Leopard 63. Casanova 70 65. The Stranger 67. Brother Sun, Sister Moon 72. Ludwig 73. La Storia 86. Stradivari 89. The Dark Illness (Il Male Oscuro) 89. Parenti e Serpenti 92. La Fine E'Nota 93. Cari Fottutussimi Amici 94, many others.

Cecil, Henry (1902–1976).
British novelist, a county court judge who poked fun at the vagaries of the British legal system in a series of amusing but rather overstretched books, of which *Brothers in Law* was successfully filmed.

Cecil, Jonathan (1939–).
British light comic actor usually seen as gangling ineffective types.
The Yellow Rolls-Royce 64. Otley 68. The Private Life of Sherlock Holmes 71. Barry Lyndon 75. Rising Damp 80. History of the World Part One 81. Dead Man's Folly (TV) 85. Second Victory 86.

Murder in Three Acts (TV) 86. Little Dorrit 87. Tchin-Tchin 91, etc.

cel.
The sheet of celluloid on which cartoon animators draw their foreground actions, one cel per film frame.

Celi, Adolfo (1922–1986).
Solidly-built Italian character actor who followed a Brazilian stage career by playing villains in international films.
Escape into Dreams 50. *That Man from Rio* 64. Von Ryan's Express 65. *Thunderball* 65. El Greco 66. Grand Prix 67. The Honey Pot 67. The Bobo 67. Grand Slam 68. Fragment of Fear 70. Murders in the Rue Morgue 71. Hitler – The Last Ten Days 73. And Then There Were None 75. The Next Man 76. Sandokan 77. Cafe Express 79. The Borgias (TV) 82, etc.

Cellier, Frank (1884–1948).
British stage actor who seemed to frown a lot and usually played unsympathetic types.
Soldiers of the King 33. The Thirty-nine Steps 35. Rhodes of Africa 36. Tudor Rose 36. Non Stop New York 37. Sixty Glorious Years 38. The Ware Case 39. Quiet Wedding 40. Love on the Dole 41. Give Us the Moon 44. Quiet Weekend 46. The Blind Goddess 48, etc.

Cenobites.
Demons from hell that feature in the work of author Clive Barker and which have appeared in three films: *Hellraiser*; *Hellbound: Hellraiser II*; *Hellraiser III*. The best known is Pinhead, so called because the contours of his face are marked out by pins stuck in his flesh.

censorship.
Each country has found it necessary to apply its own rules for film producers; in Britain and America at least these rules were drawn up and enforced at the request of the industry itself. The British Board of Film Censors was founded in 1912. It has now changed its name to the British Board of Film Classification and covers material released on video-cassette as well as films. For many years films were classified as 'U' (for universal exhibition) or 'A' (adults and accompanied children only) or (from 1933) 'H' (horrific; prohibited for persons under 16). In 1951, with the growing emphasis on sex, 'H' was replaced by 'X', which includes sex *and* horror. In the 60s 'X' came to mean over 18, 'AA' no one under 14, and 'A' was simply a warning to parents (children could still get in unaccompanied). The current ratings system is 'U', suitable for children; 'PG', parental guidance advised; '12', suitable for persons over the age of 12; '15', only suitable for persons over the age of 15; and '18', only suitable for adults. In America, the Arbuckle scandal of 1921 precipitated the founding of the 'Hays Office' (named after its first paid president) by the Motion Picture Producers and Distributors of America. The first Production Code was issued in 1930 and has undergone constant amendment especially since *The Moon is Blue* 53, and very rapidly indeed since *Room at the Top* 59; in 1966 *Who's Afraid of Virginia Woolf?* almost swamped it completely and a revised, broadened code was issued. In 1968 this was replaced by a new rating system: 'X', 'R' (restricted), 'PG' (parental guidance advised) and 'G' (general audience). In the 90s the 'X' rating was replaced by an 'NC-17' rating. The independent and very strict Catholic Legion of Decency was founded in 1934 and issues its own classifications;

it recently changed its name to the National Catholic Office for Motion Pictures.
Best books: Murray Schumach's *The Face on the Cutting Room Floor*, Doug McClelland's *The Unkindest Cuts*, Leonard J. Leff and Jerold L. Simmons's *The Dame in the Kimono: Hollywood's Censorship and the Production Code* (1990), and Tom Dewe Mathews' *Censored* (1994).

¶ We are paid to have dirty minds. – *John Trevelyan, British censor, 1968*
Any film that isn't fit to be shown to my youngest child isn't fit to be shown to anybody. – *Chicago Chief of Police, 1936*
The Seashell and the Clergyman is apparently meaningless. If it has any meaning, it is doubtless objectionable. – *British Board of Film Censors, 192?*
Travesties of religious rites . . . references to royalty . . . hangings or executions either serious . . . comic . . . political propaganda . . . too much shooting . . . intoxication . . . cruelty . . . companionate marriage . . . free love . . . immodesty . . . vamping . . . vulgar noises . . . harsh screams . . . the divinity . . . life after death . . . British officers shown in an unflattering light . . . – *themes banned by the British censor, 1930*
The cinema needs continual repression of controversy if it is to stave off disaster. – *Lord Tyrrell, Chairman of British Board of Film Censors, 1936*
They can't censor the gleam in my eye. – *Charles Laughton, told that incest had been removed from his role in The Barretts of Wimpole Street*
The inanities blessed by the Hays Office are more genuinely corrupting than any pornography. – *Joseph Wood Krutch*
It is in the interest of producers to maintain a certain moral standard since, if they don't do this, the immoral films won't sell. – *Jean Renoir*
Hollywood buys a good story about a bad girl and changes it to a bad story about a good girl. – *Anon, 1930s*
The Hays Office warned us that we couldn't show the heroine as a prostitute. We had to put a sewing machine in her apartment, so in that way she was not a whore but a seamstress. – *Fritz Lang on Man Hunt*
The industry must have towards that sacred thing, the mind of a child, towards that clean virgin thing, that unmarked slate, the same responsibility, the same care about the impressions made on it, that the best clergyman or the most inspired teacher of youth would have. – *Will Hays, 1930s*
Will Hays is my shepherd, I shall not want, He maketh me to lie down in clean postures. – *Gene Fowler*
Hollywood must never permit censorship to collapse. It's far too good for the box office. – *Claude Binyon*
What critics call dirty in our movies, they call lusty in foreign films. – *Billy Wilder*
In a novel a hero can lay ten girls and marry a virgin for the finish. In a movie, this is not allowed. The hero, as well as the heroine, has to be a virgin. The villain can lay anyone he wants, have as much fun as he wants cheating and stealing, getting rich and whipping the servants. But you have to shoot him in the end. When he falls with a bullet in his forehead, it is advisable that he clutch at the Gobelin tapestry on the library wall and bring it down over his head like a symbolic shroud. Also, covered by such a tapestry, the actor does not have to hold his breath while being photographed as a dead man. – *Herman J. Mankiewicz, 1930s*
I don't like censorship, but nor do I like the absence of it. – *Robert Rossen, 1950s*

The trouble with censors is they worry if a girl has cleavage. They ought to worry if she hasn't any. – *Marilyn Monroe, 1950s*

Nowadays when a film is awarded the production seal the producer cries: 'Where have we failed?' – *Bob Hope, 1962*

They are doing things on the screen now that I wouldn't do in bed. If I could. – *Bob Hope, 1965*

They are doing things on the screen now that the French don't even put on postcards. – *Bob Hope, 1970*

The Americans are nice people, but right now they're behaving like small boys who've just discovered what sex is. – *John Trevelyan, British Board of Film Censors, 1970*

The only censor is the audience, which will decide whether it wants it and how soon it gets fed up with it. – *Lord Eccles, Minister for the Arts, 1972*

Central Casting.
The talent agency through whose doors passed many unknowns who stayed that way. In the 30s the Hollywood office had a sign above the door: DON'T TRY TO BECOME AN ACTOR. FOR EVERY ONE WE EMPLOY, WE TURN AWAY THOUSANDS.

Cervantes, Miguel de (1547–1616).
Spanish novelist whose *Don Quixote* has been much filmed.

Cervi, Gino (1901–1974).
Stocky Italian character actor.

Frontier 34. An Ideal Marriage 39. Four Steps in the Clouds 42. Fabiola 47. Furia 48. *The Little World of Don Camillo* (as the mayor) 51. OK Nero 52. Three Forbidden Stories 53. Indiscretion 53. Maddalena 53. The Return of Don Camillo 54. Wife for a Night 55. The Naked Maja 59. Wild Love 60. The Revolt of the Slaves 61. Becket 64, many others.

Chabrol, Claude (1930–).
Variable but generally distinguished French director, credited with starting the *nouvelle vague*.
Le Beau Serge 58. Les Cousins 59. A Double Tour 59. Les Bonnes Femmes 60. Les Godelureaux 60. The Third Lover 61. The Seven Deadly Sins (part) 61. Les Plus Belles Escroqueries du Monde (part) 61. Ophelia 62. Landru 62. Paris vu Par (part) 64. Le Tigre se Parfume à la Dynamite 64. Le Tigre Aime a Chair Fraîche 65. Marie Chantal 65. Line of Demarcation 66. The Champagne Murders 67. The Road to Corinth 68. *Les Biches* 68. La Femme Infidèle 69. *The Beast Must Die* 69. La Rupture 70. *The Butcher* 70. Just Before Nightfall 71. La Decade Prodigieuse 71. Blood Wedding 71. Ten Days' Wonder 72. The Wolf Trap 72. Scoundrel in White 72. Ophelia 73. Nada 73. Innocents with Dirty Hands 73. Une Partie de Plain 73. Les Magiciens 73. Le Banc de la Desolation 74. Folies Bourgeoise 77. Alice 77. Violette Nozière 78. Il Etait Un Musicien 78. Fantomas I (TV) 78. Fantomas IV (TV) 78. Monsieur Prokoviev (TV) 78. La Bouche a l'Oreille 78. Les Menteurs 79. Blood Relatives 79. Le Cheval d'Orgueil 80. Les Fantômes du Chapelier 81. Le Sang des Autres 83. Cop au Vin 84. Inspector Lavardin 86. Le Cri du Hibou 87. Masques 87. Story of Women (Une Affaire de Femmes) 88. Docteur M. 89. Quiet Days in Clichy (Jours Tranquilles à Clichy) 90. Madame Bovary 91. Sam Suffit (a) 91. Betty 92. Hell (L'Enfer) 94.

Chaffey, Don (1917–1990).
British director; started in art department at Gainsborough in the early 40s.

Time is My Enemy 53. The Girl in the Picture 56. The Flesh is Weak 57. A Question of Adultery 58. *The Man Upstairs* 59. Danger Within 59. Dentist in the Chair 60. Greyfriars Bobby 60. Nearly a Nasty Accident 60. A Matter of Who 61. The Prince and the Pauper 62. *Jason and the Argonauts* 63. A Jolly Bad Fellow 64. One Million Years BC 66. The Viking Queen 67. A Twist of Sand 68. Creatures the World Forgot 71. Persecution 73. Pete's Dragon 77. The Gift of Love (TV) 78. The Magic of Lassie 78. C.H.O.M.P.S. 79. Lassie; the New Beginning (TV) 79. Strike Force (TV) 79. Hollywood Beat (TV) 84. International Airport (TV) 85, etc.

Chagrin, Francis (1905–1972).
Russian-born composer in films (mostly British) from 1934; composed over 200 scores.

Last Holiday 50. An Inspector Calls 54. The Colditz Story 55. The Snorkel 58. Danger Within 59. Greyfriars Bobby 60. In the Cool of the Day 63, etc.

Chahine, Youssef (1926–).
Egyptian director. He studied acting in America and gave Omar Sharif his start in movies. Following a heart attack in the 70s, he turned to directing an autobiographical trilogy that began with *Alexandria . . . Why?*

Father Amine (Baba Amine) 50. The Nile's Son (Ibn el Nil) 51. Struggle in the Valley (Sera'a fil Wadi) 53. Struggle on the Pier (Sera'a fil Mina) 55. Cairo Station (Bab el Haded) 58. Saladin (El Naser Salah el Dine) 64. The Land (El Ard) 69. The Sparrow (Al Asfour) 73. Alexandria . . . Why? (Iskendria . . . Leh?) 78. An Egyptian Story (Hadota Misreya) 82. Alexandria, More and More (Iskendria Kaman Wakaman) 89. Alexandria Now and Forever (Alexandrie Encore et Toujours) 90, etc.

Chakiris, George (1933–).
American dancer (from the chorus) and leading man; his star blazed for a while in the early 60s.

Brigadoon 54. Two and Two Make Six (GB) 60. *West Side Story* (AA) 61. Diamond Head 63. Kings of the Sun 63. Flight from Ashiya 64. 633 Squadron 64. The High Bright Sun (GB) 65. Is Paris Burning? 66. The Young Girls of Rochefort 67. The Big Cube 69. Return to Fantasy Island (TV) 78. Why Not Stay for Breakfast (GB) 80. Pale Blood 91, etc.

Chaliapin, Feodor (1873–1938).
Russian opera singer who appeared in two films and was played by Ezio Pinza in *Tonight We Sing*.
Pskovityanka 15. *Don Quixote* 33.

Challis, Christopher (1919–).
Distinguished British cinematographer.
Theirs is the Glory 46. End of the River 47. *The Small Back Room* 48. Tales of Hoffman 50. Gone to Earth 50. The Elusive Pimpernel 52. *Genevieve* 53. Angels One Five 53. 24 Hours in a Woman's Life 53. Saadia 54. The Story of Gilbert and Sullivan 54. Twice Upon a Time 54. Malaga 54. The Flame and the Flesh 54. Oh Rosalinda 55. Quentin Durward 55. Raising a Riot 55. The Battle of the River Plate 56. Footsteps in the Fog 56. III Met By Moonlight 56. The Spanish Gardener 56. Miracle in Soho 56. Windom's Way 56. Floods of Fear 57. Rooney 57. Sink the Bismarck 60. The Grass is Greener 61. Surprise Package 61. The Captain's Table 62. Never Let Go 62. Blind Date 62. Flame in the Streets 63. HMS Defiant 64. Five Golden Hours 64. The Long Ships 64. Those Magnificent Men in Their Flying Machines 64. *The Victors* 65. A Shot in the Dark 65. The Americanization of Emily 65. Return from the Ashes 65. *Arabesque* 66. Two for the Road 67. Kaleidoscope 67. A Dandy in Aspic 68. Chitty Chitty Bang Bang 69. Staircase 69. The Private Life of Sherlock Holmes 71. Villain 71.

Catch Me a Spy 71. Mary Queen of Scots 72. Follow Me 72. The Boy Who Turned Yellow 72. The Little Prince 74. Mister Quilp 75. The Incredible Sarah 76. The Deep 77. Force Ten From Navarone 78. The Riddle of the Sands 79. The Mirror Crack'd 80. Evil Under the Sun 81. Top Secret 84. Secrets 84. Steaming 84.

Chamberlain, Cyril (1909–1974).
British small-part player often seen as average man, policeman or dull husband.

This Man in Paris 39. London Belongs to Me 48. Trouble in Store 53. Blue Murder at St Trinian's 58. Carry On Constable 60, many others.

Chamberlain, Richard (1935–).
Boyish-looking American leading man who used his success in a TV series to establish himself as a serious international actor.
The Secret of the Purple Reef 60. A Thunder of Drums 62. Twilight of Honor 63. Joy in the Morning 65. Petulia 68. The Madwoman of Chaillot 69. Julius Caesar 70. *The Music Lovers* (as Tchaikovsky) 70. *Lady Caroline Lamb* (as Byron) 72. The Last of the Belles (TV) 74. The Three Musketeers 74. The Towering Inferno 75. *The Slipper and the Rose* 76. The Count of Monte Cristo (TV) 76. The Man in the Iron Mask (TV) 77. The Last Wave 78. Swarm 78. Shogun (TV) 80. Murder by Phone 82. *The Thorn Birds* (TV) 83. King Solomon's Mines 85. Raoul Wallenberg. Lost Hero (TV) 85. Allan Quatermain and the Lost City of Gold 86. The Bourne Identity (TV) 88. The Return of the Musketeers 89. Night of the Hunter (TV) 91. Aftermath 91.

TV series: Dr Kildare 61–66.

Champion.
The name given to Gene Autry's steed, known as the 'World's Wonder Horse'. There were three of them: the first Champion was in films in the 30s; the second and third, who were father and son, were in films of the 40s and early 50s. They also appeared on the TV series The Gene Autry Show 47–54, and in the children's TV series Autry produced, *The Adventures of Champion* (aka *Champion the Wonder Horse*), 55–56.

Champion, Gower (1919–1980).
American dancer who appeared with his then wife Marge in several musicals of the early 50s; later turned director.

Till the Clouds Roll By (solo) 46. Mr Music 50. *Show Boat* 51. Lovely to Look At 52. Give a Girl a Break 53. Jupiter's Darling 55. Three for the Show 55. My Six Loves (d) 63. Bank Shot (d) 74, etc.

Champion, Gregg.
American director.

Short Time 90. The Cowboy Way 94.

Champion, Marge (1923–) (Majorie Belcher).
American dancer who teamed with her then husband Gower (qv). Solo appearances include *The Story of Vernon and Irene Castle* 39; later appeared as character actress.

The Swimmer 67. The Party 68.

Chan, Jackie (1954–) (Chan Kwong Sang).
Hong Kong actor, director and writer of martial arts movies who has appeared in more than 100 films. Trained in classical Chinese theatre, he first worked as a stuntman and still does his own stunts, suffering many injuries as a result.

Eagle Shadow Fist 71. Fists of Fury (& d) 73. Dragon Fist 78. Fantasy Mission Force 78. Half a Loaf of King-Fu 78. The Fearless Hyena (& d) 79. Young Master (& d) 79. Dragon Lord 82. Project

A 83. Police Story (& d) 85. The Fearless Hyena Part II (& d) 86. The Armour of God (& d) 86. Project A Part II 87. The Brothers 87. Police Story – Part II 88. Miracle (Keitsik) 89. Police Story 3: Supercop 93. Drunken Master II (Tsui Kun II) 94, many others.

¶ The Buster Keaton of Hong Kong. – *Movieline magazine*

Chan, Michael Paul.
American character actor.

Thief 81. The Goonies 85. Thousand Pieces of Gold 90. Rapid Fire 92. Falling Down 93. Heaven and Earth 93. Maverick 94, etc.

Chance, Naomi (1930–).
Stylish British leading lady who appeared sporadically in the 50s.

Dangerous Voyage 53. The Saint's Return 54. Operation Bullshine 59. The Trials of Oscar Wilde 60, etc.

chanchada.
Term used to describe a genre of popular Brazilian films that mixes love stories with comedy and colourfully staged musical numbers, usually involving the samba. The form was created by Watson Macedo (1918–81), a Brazilian director, screenwriter and art director, in his musicals of the 40s and 50s, particularly *Carnaval No Fogo* 49. It includes parodies of Hollywood movies, such as Carlos Manga's *Matar ou Correr*, based on *High Noon*.

Chandler, Chick (1905–1988).
Wiry American hero or second lead of many a second feature in the 30s and 40s.

Melody Cruise 33. Murder on a Honeymoon 35. Woman Wise 36. Born Reckless 37. Alexander's Ragtime Band 38. Time Out for Murder 38. Hotel for Women 39. Hollywood Cavalcade 39. Honeymoon Deferred 40. Cadet Girl 41. Hot Spot 41. The Big Shot 42. He Hired the Boss 43. Irish Eyes are Smiling 44. Seven Doors to Death 44. The Chicago Kid 45. Do You Love Me? 46. Lost Continent 47. Family Honeymoon 49. The Great Rupert 50. Aaron Slick from Punkin Crick 52. Battle Cry 55. The Naked Gun 58. It's a Mad Mad Mad Mad World 63, many others.

TV series: Soldiers of Fortune 55.

Chandler, George (1899–1985).
American character actor, an ex-vaudevillian who specialized in sly or comically nervous roles.

The Light of Western Stars 30. Blessed Event 32. Hi Nellie 34. Fury 36. Three Men on a Horse 36. Nothing Sacred 37. Jesse James 39. Arizona 41. *Roxie Hart* 42. It Happened Tomorrow 44. This Man's Navy 45. Dead Reckoning 47. Kansas Raiders 50. Hans Christian Andersen 52. The High and the Mighty 54. Spring Reunion 57. Dead Ringer 64. One More Time 71, many others.

Chandler, Helen (1906–1965).
American leading lady of the 30s: her early retirement through personal problems robbed Hollywood of an interesting personality.

■ The Music Master 27. Joy Girl 27. Mother's Boy 29. Salute 29. The Sky Hawk 29. A Rough Romance 30. Outward Bound 30. Mother's Cry 30. *Dracula* 31. Daybreak 31. *The Last Flight* 31. Salvation Nell 31. Fanny Foley Herself 31. A House Divided 32. Vanity Street 32. Behind Jury Doors 32. Christopher Strong 33. Alimony Madness 33. Dance Hall Hostess 33. Goodbye Again 33. The Worst Woman in Paris 33. Long Lost Father 34. Midnight Alibi 34. Unfinished Symphony (GB)

35. It's a Bet (GB) 35. Radio Parade (GB) 35. Mr Boggs Steps Out (GB) 37.

Chandler, Jeff (1918–1961) (Ira Grossel).
American leading man with the unusual attraction of prematurely grey hair; carved a solid niche for himself by playing an Indian, but his films seldom rose above co-feature level.

■ Johnny O'Clock 47. Invisible Wall 47. Roses are Red 47. Mr Belvedere Goes to College 49. Sword in the Desert 49. Abandoned 49. *Broken Arrow* (as Cochise) (AAN) 50. Two Flags West 50. Deported 50. Bird of Paradise 51. Smuggler's Island 51. Iron Man 51. Flame of Araby 51. The Battle at Apache Pass 52. Yankee Buccaneer 52. Red Ball Express 52. Because of You 52. The Great Sioux Uprising 53. East of Sumatra 53. Yankee Pasha 54. War Arrow 54. Sign of the Pagan 54. Foxfire 55. The Female on the Beach 55. The Spoilers 55. Toy Tiger 55. Away all Boats 56. Pillars of the Sky 56. Drango 57. The Tattered Dress 57. *Jeanne Eagels* 57. Man in the Shadow 57. The Lady Takes a Flyer 58. Raw Wind in Eden 58. Stranger in my Arms 59. Thunder in the Sun 59. Ten Seconds to Hell 59. The Jayhawkers 59. The Plunderers 60. A Story of David (TV) 60. Return to Peyton Place 61. Merrill's Marauders 61.

Chandler, Joan (1923–1979).
American leading lady, briefly featured in the 40s.

Humoresque 47. The Street with No Name 48. Rope 49, etc.

Chandler, John Davis (1937–).
American character player usually seen as neurotic, twitching villain.

The Young Savages 61. Mad Dog Coll (title role) 61. Major Dundee 65. Once a Thief 65. The Good Guys and the Bad Guys 69. Barquero 70. Shootout 71. Capone 75. Jaws of Death 76. Whiskey Mountain 77, etc.

Chandler, Lane (1899–1972) (Robert Oakes).
American western character actor.

Open Range 27. Texas Tornado 34. Two Gun Justice 38. Sundown Jim 42. Northwest Stampede 48. Montana 50. Requiem for a Gunfighter 65, many others.

Chandler, Raymond (1888–1959).
American crime novelist to whom literary acclaim came late in life. Several films and a TV series were based on the exploits of his cynical but incorruptible private eye Philip Marlowe.

The Falcon Takes Over (oa) 42. Time to Kill (oa) 42. *Double Indemnity* (co-w, AAN) 44. And Now Tomorrow 44. The Unseen 45. *Murder My Sweet* (oa) 45. *The Big Sleep* (oa) 46. *The Lady in the Lake* (oa) 46. The Blue Dahlia (AANw) 46. The Brasher Doubloon (oa) 47. *Strangers on a Train* (w) 51. Marlowe (oa) 69. The Long Goodbye (oa) 72. Farewell my Lovely (oa) 76. The Big Sleep (oa) 79.

TV series: Philip Marlowe 59.

¶ The making of a motion picture is an endless contention of tawdry egos, almost none of them capable of anything more creative than credit stealing and self promotion. – *R.C.*

He looked as inconspicuous as a tarantula on a slice of angel food. – *Farewell my Lovely*

The edges of the folded handkerchief in her breast pocket looked sharp enough to slice bread. – *The Lady in the Lake*

She had a lot of face and chin. She had pewter-coloured hair set in a ruthless permanent, a hard beak and large moist eyes with the sympathetic expression of wet stones. There was lace at her throat, but it was the kind of throat that would

have looked better in a football sweater. – *The High Window*

Chaney, Lon (1883–1930) (Alonzo Chaney).
American star character actor, known as 'the man of a thousand faces' because of his elaborate disguises in macabre roles; hence the joke, 'Don't step on that spider, it might be Lon Chaney.' A 195█ biopic, *Man of a Thousand Faces*, starred James Cagney.

■ Where the Forest Ends 14. The Chimney Swee█ 15. The Oyster Dredger 15. The Stool Pigeon 15. Fires of Rebellion 17. Triumph 17. That Devil Bateese 18. Riddle Gawne 18. The Kaiser, Beast of Berlin 18. Paid in Advance 19. The Rap 19. The Unholy Three 19. *The Miracle Man* 19. False Faces 19. Victory 19. The Wolf Breed 19. The Wicked Darling 19. Nomads of the North 19. Treasure Island 20. Daredevil Jack 20. *The Penalty* 21. Outside the Law 21. The Ace of Hearts 21. Bit o' Life 21. For Those We Love 21. The Night Rose 21. The Trap 22. Quincy Adams Sawyer 22. Shadows 22. *A Blind Bargain* 22. Flesh and Blood 22. Voices of the City 22. The Light in the Dark 22. Oliver Twist 22. *The Hunchback of Notre Dame* 23. The Shock 23. All the Brothers were Valiant 23. While Paris Sleeps 23. He Who Gets Slapped 24. The Next Corner 24. *The Phantom of the Opera* 25. The Tower of Lies 25. The Monster 25. *The Unholy Three* 25. The Black Bird 26. The Road to Mandalay 26. Tell it to the Marines 26. Mr Wu 27█ The Unknown 27. Mockery 27. *London After Midnight* 27. The Big City 28. Laugh Clown Laugh 28. While the City Sleeps 28. West of Zanzibar 28█ The Thunder 29. Where East is East 29. The Unholy Three 30.

✪ For becoming an international household word through his ability to distort his own body and hide it under layers of disguise. *The Phantom of the Opera*

¶ My whole career has been devoted to keeping people from knowing me. – *L.C.*

Chaney, Lon, Jnr (1906–1973) (Creighton Chaney).
Massive American character actor, who largely followed his father's type of role in progressively inferior films, with many bit parts. In *Man of a Thousand Faces* he was played by Roge█ Smith.

Bird of Paradise 32. Lucky Devils 33. Sixteen Fathoms Deep 34. The Life of Vergie Winters 35. Accent on Youth 35. Wife, Doctor and Nurse 37. Love and Hisses 37. Charlie Chan on Broadway 37█ Road Demon 38. Mr Moto's Gamble 38. Jesse James 39. Frontier Marshal 39. *Of Mice and Men* (his best performance, as Lennie) 39. One Million BC 40. Northwest Mounted Police 40. Man Made Monster 41. *The Wolf Man* 41. North to the Klondike 42. *The Ghost of Frankenstein* (as the monster) 42. The Mummy's Tomb 42. Frankenstein Meets the Wolf Man 43. Son of Dracula 43. Ghost Catchers 44. Weird Woman 44█ Dead Man's Eyes 44. House of Frankenstein 45. Strange Confession 45. My Favourite Brunette 47█ Sixteen Fathoms Deep 48. *Abbott and Costello Meet Frankenstein* 48. Captain China 49. Once a Thief 50. Behave Yourself 51. High Noon 52. A Lion is in the Streets 53. Casanova's Big Night 54. Not as a Stranger 55. Manfish 56. The Black Sleep 56. Cyclops 57. The Defiant Ones 58. The Alligator People 59. The Haunted Palace 63. Witchcraft 64. Apache Uprising 66. Hillbillies in a Haunted House 67. Buckskin 68, many others.

TV series: *The Last of the Mohicans* (as Chingachgook) 56.

Chaney, Norman 'Chubby' (1918–1936).
American child actor who replaced Joe Cobb as
the plump boy in the Our Gang comedies of the
mid-20s and early 30s. Died of glandular problems.

Change-over.
Transition from one reel of film to another during
projection. A reel originally lasted ten minutes but
most 35mm projectors now take 20 or 30 minutes.
Change-over cues are given in the form of dots
which appear on the top right-hand corner of the
screen a standard number of seconds before the
end of the reel.

Chang-Ho, Bae (1953–).
South Korean director, often causing local
controversy.
People in the Slums (Kkobang Dongne
Saramdul) 82. Whale Hunter (Gorae Sanyan) 84.
Deep Blue Day (Gipgo Purun Bam) 85. Hwang Jin-
86. Our Sweet Days of Youth 87, etc.

Changwei, Gu (1957–).
Chinese cinematographer. He studied at the
Beijing Film Academy and went to work at the
Xi'an studios. He has worked on three of director
Chen Kaige's films.
The Beach 84. The Magic Braid 86. The King of
Children 87. *Red Sorghum* 88. Ju Dou 90. Life
on a String 91. *Farewell My Concubine* (AAN) 93,
etc.

Channing, Carol (1921–).
Vivacious American cabaret comedienne whose
films have been few.
Paid in Full 50. The First Travelling Saleslady
56. *Thoroughly Modern Millie* (AAN) 67. Skidoo 69.
Shinbone Alley (voice) 71. Thumbelina (voice) 94.

I am terribly shy, but of course no one believes
me. Come to think of it, neither would I. –
C.C.

She never just enters a room. Even when she
comes out of the bathroom, her husband applauds. –
George Burns

Channing, Stockard (1944–) (Susan Stockard).
Tomboy-type American leading lady, mainly on
television.
The Girl Most Likely To (TV) 73. The Fortune
75. Sweet Revenge 76. The Big Bus 76. Lucan 77.
The Cheap Detective 78. Grease 78. Silent Victory
(TV) 79. The Fish That Saved Pittsburgh 79. Safari
3000 82. Without a Trace 83. Heartburn 86. The
Men's Club 86. A Time of Destiny 88. Staying
Together 89. Meet the Applegates 90. Married to
It 93. Six Degrees of Separation (AAN) 93. David's
Mother (TV) 94.

Chapin, Billy (1943–).
American child actor of the 50s.
Cluny Brown 48. Tobor the Great 53. Naked
Alibi 54. There's No Business Like Show Business
54. A Man Called Peter 55. Violent Saturday 55.
Night of the Hunter 55. Tension at Table Rock 56,
etc.

Chaplin, Sir Charles (1889–1977).
A legendary figure in his own lifetime despite a
comparatively limited output, this British
pantomimist went to the US in 1910 with Fred
Karno's troupe and was invited to join the Keystone
company; later also worked for Essanay and
Mutual, and these early two-reelers are held by
many to be superior to the later, more pretentious
features which he produced himself. Honorary AA
1971. A biopic, *Chaplin*, appeared in 1992, directed
by Richard Attenborough with Robert Downey Jnr
in the title role.
Autobiographical books: 1922, *My Trip Abroad.*
1930, *My Wonderful Visit.* 1964, *My Autobiography.*
1974, *My Life in Pictures.*
Other books: 1951, *The Little Fellow* by Peter
Cotes and Thelma Nicklaus. 1952, *The Great Charlie*
by Robert Payne. 1961, *Charlie Chaplin* by
Theodore Huff. 1966, *My Life with Chaplin* by Lita
Grey Chaplin. 1974, *Charlie Chaplin. His Life and
Art* by William Dodgson Bowman. 1977, *Sir Charlie*
by Edwin P. Hoyt. The best biography is 1985,
Chaplin by David Robinson.
■ SHORTS: Making a Living 14. Kid Auto Races at
Venice (in which he first wore the improvised
tramp costume in which he later became famous)
14. Mabel's Strange Predicament 14. Between
Showers 14. A Film Johnnie 14. Tango Tangle 14.
His Favorite Pastime 14. Cruel Cruel Love 14. The
Star Boarder 14. Mabel at the Wheel 14. Twenty
Minutes of Love 14. The Knockout 14. Tillie's
Punctured Romance 14. Caught in a Cabaret 14.
Caught in the Rain 14. A Busy Day 14. The Fatal
Mallet 14. Her Friend the Bandit 14. Mabel's Busy
Day 14. Mabel's Married Life 14. Laughing Gas
14. The Property Man 14. The Face on the
Barroom Floor 14. Recreation 14. The Masquerader
14. His New Profession 14. The Rounders 14. The
New Janitor 14. These Love Pangs 14. Dough and
Dynamite 14. Gentlemen of Nerve 14. His Musical
Career 14. His Trysting Place 14. Getting
Acquainted 14. His Prehistoric Past 14. His New
Job 15. A Night Out 15. The Champion 15. In the
Park 15. A Jitney Elopement 15. *The Tramp* 15. By
the Sea 15. Work 15. A Woman 15. The Bank
15. Shanghaied 15. A Night in the Show 15.
Carmen 16. Police 16. The Floorwalker 16. The
Fireman 16. The Vagabond 16. One a.m. 16. The
Count 16. *The Pawnshop* 16. Behind the Screen
16. *The Rink* 16. *Easy Street* 17. *The Cure* 17. *The
Immigrant* 17. *The Adventurer* 17. Triple Trouble 18.
A Dog's Life 18. The Bond 18. *Shoulder Arms* 18.
Sunnyside 19. A Day's Pleasure 19. *The Idle Class*
21. Pay Day 22.
■ FEATURES: *The Kid* 20. The Pilgrim 23. A Woman
of Paris (directed only) 23. *The Gold Rush* 24. *The
Circus* (AA) 28. *City Lights* 31. *Modern Times* 36. *The
Great Dictator* (AANw) 40. *Monsieur Verdoux* 47.
Limelight 52. A King in New York (GB) 57. A
Countess from Hong Kong (GB) 66.
🟢 For combining precision of comedy technique
with a sentimental view of the common man
which pleased the millions of oppressed and
disarmed sophisticated criticism. *Easy Street.*

The son of a bitch is a ballet dancer!
So pronounced W.C. Fields, having been
urged to sit through and enjoy a Chaplin movie.
Fields promptly realized that the Chaplin brand of
comic art was not only more popular than his own,
but one which it was impossible for him to
emulate. He continued:
He's the best ballet dancer that ever lived, and
if I get a good chance I'll strangle him with my
bare hands . . .
Many people have been jealous of Chaplin's
success, partly because he was never modest about
it. His poverty-stricken childhood made him
mercenary, and once at the top he displayed a
private personality it was difficult to like. Even his
friend Mary Pickford called him:
That obstinate, suspicious, egocentric,
maddening and lovable genius of a problem child.
And Chaplin had never found a way of making
friends with his public. Even in his autobiography
he seemed at pains to present himself
unsympathetically, as when he recalled telling
Mack Sennett:
The public doesn't line up outside the box
office when your name appears as they do for
mine.
His memories of his manifold romantic activities
are tastelessly presented:
Like everyone else's, my sex-life went in cycles.
Sometimes I was potent, other times
disappointing.
In the more intimate details his phrasing is curious
to say the least:
[She was] a big handsome woman of twenty-
two, well built, with upper regional domes
immensely expansive and made alluring by an
extremely low décolleté summer dress which,
on the drive home, evoked my libidinous
curiosity . . .
His willingness to prognosticate on matters of
which he plainly knows little, such as the true
authorship of the Shakespeare plays, is often
foolhardy:
I can hardly think it was the Stratford boy.
Whoever wrote them had an aristocratic
personality.
His philosophy is usually naïve, as in his much-
attacked defence of murder in *Monsieur Verdoux:*
Wars, conflict, it's all business. One murder
makes a villain. Millions, a hero. Numbers
sanctify . . .
Determined to make his clown a tragic hero, he is
frequently guilty of relentless sentimentality. The
opening title of *The Kid* runs:
A picture with a smile and perhaps a tear.
As Hannen Swaffer once said:
His gospel is like Mary Pickford's: the hope of a
little child.
Billy Wilder was more caustic:
When he found a voice to say what was on his
mind, he was like a child of eight writing lyrics
for Beethoven's Ninth.
He frequently over-estimated himself. Of *The Great
Dictator* he declared:
I made this picture for the Jews of the world.
He was a poor loser. Having been forced to leave
the United States, which made him rich and to
which he owed a large amount in back taxes, he
stated:
I have no further use for America. I wouldn't
go back there if Jesus Christ was President.
Over the years he had alternately denied and
proclaimed his Jewishness. This was a typical
announcement of the late 40s:
I am not a Jew! I am a citizen of the world! I
am not a communist! I am a peacemonger!
A rather limited attitude is struck in his remark
about Negroes:
They have suffered too much ever to be funny
to me.
(Yet Chaplin's own comedy derives from poverty
and deprivation.) He took credit for every aspect
of his films, and frequently denied it to those who
helped him most. Yet he was not an inventive
director:
I am the unusual and do not need camera
angles.
Cinematographer Karl Struss said of him:
He has no knowledge of camera direction. His
films are completely theatre.
Yet there is no denying that Chaplin managed very
well by feeding his own self-importance. He used
to say:
You have to believe in yourself, that's the secret.
And as late as 1960:
I remain one thing and one thing only, and that
is a clown. It places me on a far higher plane than
any politician.
In a sense he was right. Despite all Chaplin's
failings, his tramp is an archetypal creation which
strikes a chord in everybody and will live as long

as films can be preserved. Chaplin always knew the virtue of simplicity:

All I need to make a comedy is a park, a policeman and a pretty girl.

That was in 1916, and ambition soon overtook him. Colleen Moore in her autobiography *Silent Star* tells that in 1922 a producer was contemplating a life of Christ, and Chaplin demanded audience and became very excited:

I want to play the role of Jesus. I'm a logical choice. I look the part. I'm a Jew. And I'm a comedian . . . And I'm an atheist, so I'd be able to look at the character objectively . . .

The funny thing is, he was very likely right. But Andrew Sarris saw the other side of his psyche:

He will die as he has lived, an unregenerate classicist who believes in making movies he can feel in his frayed lace valentine heart.

While nobody denied his business acumen, least of all Sam Goldwyn:

Chaplin is no business man – all he knows is that he can't take anything less.

And Douglas Fairbanks in 1925 saw the emotional force of his screen personality:

He shows one inadequate man struggling against all the forces of nature.

Chaplin's essential trouble was that he could never take advice. That he needed it was shown by his remark during pre-production of the truly awful *A Countess from Hong Kong:*

A millionaire falling in love with a prostitute. What better story could they want than that?

Chaplin, Geraldine (1944–).
Actress daughter of Charles Chaplin.

Doctor Zhivago 65. A Countess from Hong Kong 66. Stranger in the House 67. Peppermint Frappé (Sp.) 67. I Killed Rasputin 68. Honeycomb (Sp.) 69. The Hawaiians 70. Zero Population Growth 72. Innocent Bystanders 72. The Three Musketeers 74. *Nashville* 75. Buffalo Bill and the Indians 76. Roseland 77. Welcome to L.A. 77. Cria! 77. The Word (TV) 78. Remember My Name 78. The Mirror Crack'd 80. Les Uns et les Autres 80. Voyage en Douce 81. Life is a Novel 81. Bolero 82. Love on the Ground 83. Buried Alive 84. Gentille Alouette 85. White Mischief 87. The Moderns 88. Je Veux Rentrer à la Maison 89. Return of the Musketeers 89. The Children 90. Buster's Bedroom 91. The Milky Way (La Via Lactea) 92. Chaplin 92. A Foreign Field (TV) 93. The Age of Innocence 93. Words upon the Window Pane 94, etc.

Chaplin, Saul (1912–) (Saul Kaplan).
American song-writer, arranger and producer.

Rookies on Parade (c) 41. Time Out for Rhythm (c) 41. *An American in Paris* (arr) (AA) 51. *Seven Brides for Seven Brothers* (arr) (AA) 54. Can Can (p) 59. *West Side Story* (p) 61. *The Sound of Music* (p) 65. Star! (p) 68. That's Entertainment, Part Two (p) 76, etc.

Chaplin, Syd (1885–1965).
British comedian, elder brother of Charles Chaplin; popular internationally in the 20s.

A Submarine Pirate 15. Shoulder Arms 18. King Queen Joker 21. Her Temporary Husband 23. The Perfect Flapper 24. Charley's Aunt 25. Oh What a Nurse 26. The Better 'Ole 27. The Missing Link 27. A Little Bit of Fluff 28, etc.

Chaplin, Sydney (1926–).
Actor son of Charles Chaplin; has not achieved the distinction of which he seems capable.

Limelight 52. Confession 55. Land of the Pharaohs 55. Four Girls in Town 56. Quantez 57. Follow that Man 61. A Countess from Hong Kong 66. The Sicilian Clan 70, etc.

Chapman, Edward (1901–1977).
British character actor of solid dependable types, corrupt aldermen and northern millowners.

Juno and the Paycock 29. Murder 30. The Skin Game 31. *Things to Come* 35. Rembrandt 36. The Man Who Could Work Miracles 37. The Citadel 38. The Proud Valley 39. The Briggs Family 40. They Flew Alone 42. Ships with Wings 42. *The October Man* 47. *It Always Rains on Sunday* 47. Mr Perrin and Mr Traill 49. *The Card* 52. Folly to be Wise 53. A Day to Remember 54. His Excellency 55. School for Scoundrels 60. Oscar Wilde (as Queensberry) 60. A Stitch in Time 63. Joey Boy 64, many others.

Chapman, Graham (1941–1989).
British character comedian, a member of the Monty Python group (qv) who also had a go on his own.

The Odd Job 78. Yellowbeard 83.

Chapman, Lonny (1920–).
American character actor.

Young at Heart 54. Baby Doll 57. The Birds 63. The Reivers 69. The Cowboys 71. Where the Red Fern Grows 74. Moving Violation 76. Norma Rae 79, etc.

Chapman, Marguerite (1916–).
Dependable American heroine of many 40s co-features.

Charlie Chan at the Wax Museum 40. The Body Disappears 41. Parachute Nurse 42. Destroyer 43. My Kingdom for a Cook 43. Pardon My Past 45. The Walls Came Tumbling Down 46. Mr District Attorney 47. Coroner Creek 48. Kansas Raiders 50. Man Bait 51. Flight to Mars 51. The Seven Year Itch 55. The Amazing Transparent Man 61, etc.

Chapman, Matthew (1950–).
American screenwriter and director.

Hussy (wd) 80. Stranger's Kiss (wd) 84. Slow Burn (wd) (TV) 86. Heart of Midnight (wd) 89. Consenting Adults (w) 92. Color of Night (co-w) 94, etc.

Chapman, Michael (1935–).
American cinematographer.

The Last Detail 73. The White Dawn 73. Taxi Driver 76. The Front 76. Fingers 78. Invasion of the Body Snatchers 78. The Last Waltz 78. Hardcore 79. The Wanderers 79. Raging Bull (AAN) 80. Personal Best 82. Dead Men Don't Wear Plaid 82. The Lost Boys 87. Shoot to Kill 88. Scrooged 88. Ghostbusters II 89. Quick Change 90. Kindergarten Cop 90. Rising Sun 93. The Fugitive (AAN) 93, etc.

character actor.
Usually thought of as one who does not play romantic leads.

Charisse, Cyd (1922–) (Tula Ellice Finklea).
Stylish, long-legged American dancer and heroine of MGM musical dramas of the 50s.

Autobiography: 1976, *The Two of Us* (with Tony Martin, her husband).
■ Mission to Moscow 43. Something to Shout About 43. Ziegfeld Follies 45. The Harvey Girls 46. Three Wise Fools 46. Till the Clouds Roll By 46. Fiesta 47. *The Unfinished Dance* 47. On an Island with You 48. Words and Music 48. The Kissing Bandit 49. East Side West Side 49. Tension 49. Mark of the Renegade 51. The Wild North 52. Singin' in the Rain 52. Sombrero 53. Easy to Love 53. The Band Wagon 53. Brigadoon 54. Deep in My Heart 54. It's Always Fair Weather 55. Meet Me in Las Vegas 56.

Invitation to the Dance 57. Silk Stockings 57. Twilig for the Gods 58. Party Girl 58. Black Tights 60. Fiv Golden Hours 61. *Two Weeks in Another Town* 62. The Silencers 67. Maroc 7 67. Assassination in Rome 67. Call Her Mom (TV) 72. Warlords of Atlantis 78. Portrait of an Escort (TV) 80. Swimsu (TV) 89. Visioni Privati 90.
~She missed the lead in *Easter Parade* when she broke a leg, and in *An American in Paris* when sh was pregnant.

Charles I
of England (1600–1649) (reigned 1625–1649) has not been a popular screen figure. Alec Guinne in *Cromwell* provided the nearest to a full-length portrait; cameos were given by Hugh Miller in *The Vicar of Bray* and Robert Rietty in *The Scarlet Blade.*

Charles II
of England (1630–1685) (reigned 1660–1685) has been a popular screen figure, attracting the talents of Cedric Hardwicke in *Nell Gwyn*, Vincen Price in *Hudson's Bay*, George Sanders in *Forever Amber*, and Douglas Fairbanks Jnr in *The Exile.*

Charles, Maria (1929–) (Maria Zena Schneider) Diminutive British redhead, familiar as Jewish matron in TV's *Agony.*
■ Folly to Be Wise 52. The Deadly Affair 66. Ey of the Devil 67. The Return of the Pink Panther 74. Great Expectations (TV) 75. Cuba 79. Victor Victoria 82.

Charleson, Ian (1954–1990).
British leading actor. He died of AIDS.

Chariots of Fire 81. Gandhi 82. Greystoke 84. Th Sun Also Rises (TV) 84. Car Trouble 85.

Charlesworth, John (1935–1960).
British teenage actor of the 50s.

Tom Brown's Schooldays 51. Scrooge 51. John of the Fair 54. Yangtse Incident 57. The Angry Silence 59, etc.

Charlie Chan
Earl Derr Biggers' polite oriental detective with th large family and an even more plentiful supply of wise and witty sayings was first featured by Hollywood in a 1926 serial; George Kuwa played him.

Kamiyama Sojin played him once in 1928, E. Park once in 1929, Warner Oland sixteen times (1931–37), Sidney Toler twenty-two times (1938–47) and Roland Winters six times (1948– 52). J. Carrol Naish then took over for thirty-nin TV films (1957), and in 1971 Ross Martin appeare as Chan in a TV feature. 1972 brought an animate TV cartoon series, *Charlie Chan and the Chan Clan.* Chan was voiced by Keye Luke, who had played Chan's number two son so often in the 30s. A ve is best drawn over the so-called spoof of 1981's *Charlie Chan and the Curse of the Dragon Queen*, in which Peter Ustinov took over the role of the famous detective.

The 'classic' Chan films were as follows:

1929: *Behind That Curtain*
1931: *Charlie Chan Carries On, The Black Camel*
1932: *Charlie Chan's Chance, Charlie Chan's Greates Case*
1934: *Charlie Chan's Courage, Charlie Chan in London*
1935: *Charlie Chan in Paris, Charlie Chan in Egypt, Charlie Chan in Shanghai*
1936: *Charlie Chan's Secret, Charlie Chan at the Circus, Charlie Chan at the Racetrack, Charli Chan at the Opera*

1937: *Charlie Chan at the Olympics, Charlie Chan on Broadway*
1938: *Charlie Chan at Monte Carlo* (last Oland), *Charlie Chan in Honolulu*
1939: *Charlie Chan in Reno, Charlie Chan at Treasure Island, Charlie Chan in the City of Darkness*
1940: *Charlie Chan in Panama, Charlie Chan's Murder Cruise, Charlie Chan in the Wax Museum, Murder over New York*
1941: *Dead Men Tell, Charlie Chan in Rio*
1942: *Castle in the Desert* (after which the series moved from Fox to Monogram and consequently lower budgets)

Charlot, André (1882–1956).
French producer of intimate star revues in London and New York in the 20s. Later played small parts in Hollywood films.

Charpin, Fernand (1887–1944).
Plump French character actor, from the stage. He is best known for his role as the rich widower who marries the pregnant Fanny in Marcel Pagnol's trilogy of films set in Marseilles, his birthplace.
    Marius 31. *Fanny* 32. César 36. They Were Five (La Belle Équipe) 36. Pépé Le Moko 36. The Baker's Wife (La Femme du Boulanger) 38. The Well-Digger's Daughter (La Fille du Puisatier) 41, etc.

Charrel, Erik (1894–1974).
German producer best known abroad for *Congress Dances* 31, which he also directed.

Charteris, Leslie (1907–1993) (Leslie Charles Bowyer Yin).
Chinese-English crime novelist, creator of 'the Saint' (qv).

Charters, Spencer (1878–1943).
American character actor; usually played rural fellows who may have been deaf but not too dumb to outsmart the city slicker. Committed suicide.
    Little Old New York 3. Janice Meredith 24. Whoopee 30. The Bat Whispers 30. The Front Page 31. The Match King 32. Female 33. Wake up and Dream 34. It's a Gift 34. The Ghost Walks 34. The Raven 35. Colleen 36. Banjo on my Knee 36. Mountain Music 37. In Old Chicago 38. Professor Beware 38. Topper Takes a Trip 38. Jesse James 39. Drums Along the Mohawk 39. Alias the Deacon 40. Our Town 40. Tobacco Road 41. The Remarkable Andrew 42. Juke Girl 42, many others.

Chartoff, Robert (1933–).
American producer, usually with Irwin Winkler.
    The Split 68. Leo the Last 69. They Shoot Horses Don't They? 69. The Mechanic 72. Up the Sandbox 72. The Gambler 74. Nickelodeon 76. Rocky (AA) 76. New York New York 77. Comes a Horseman 78. Rocky II 79. Raging Bull (AAN) 80. True Confessions 81. Rocky III 82. The Right Stuff (AAN) 83. Rocky IV 85. Rocky V 90, etc.

the chase
has always been a standard ingredient of film-making, providing a foolproof way of rounding off a comedy or thriller in good style. In silent days it was necessary to every comedian, from the Keystone Kops to Buster Keaton, while westerns inevitably concluded with the goodies chasing the baddies, and even *Intolerance* has a four-stranded chase finale. Sound comedies began by using the chase sparingly, but René Clair's *Le Million* 32 was a superbly sustained example of the fuller orchestration now possible, and later sophisticated comedies like *It Happened One Night, Sullivan's*

Travels, The Runaround, Sex and the Single Girl, Good Neighbour Sam and *What's Up Doc?* have not disdained using the chase as a basic theme; nor of course have broader comedians such as Harold Lloyd, W.C. Fields, Laurel and Hardy and Abbott and Costello, and Stanley Kramer devised a super chase in the marathon *It's a Mad Mad Mad Mad World* 63, to be rivalled in 1965 by *The Great Race*. Most of the old chase gags were crammed into the finale of *A Funny Thing Happened on the Way to the Forum* 67. Ealing comedies of the late 40s and early 50s (*The Lavender Hill Mob, Whisky Galore, The Man in the White Suit, A Run For Your Money*) also used chases brilliantly to broaden their shafts of satire.
    More serious films using the chase theme include: *You Only Live Once, Stagecoach, Out of the Past, High Sierra, They Live By Night, Odd Man Out, The Capture, The Chase, Tell Them Willie Boy Is Here, Figures in a Landscape*, and the innumerable versions of *Les Misérables*, which also sparked off five television series: *The Fugitive, Run For Your Life, Branded, Run Buddy Run*, and *Kung Fu*. Thrillers which have featured exciting chases include *The Thirty-nine Steps* and *North by Northwest, The Naked City, Robbery, Bullitt, Vanishing Point, The French Connection, Puppet on a Chain, Dirty Mary Crazy Larry, Race with the Devil, Escape from Zahrain* and *The Seven-Ups*.

Chase, Borden (1900–1971).
American screenwriter.
    Under Pressure 35. Blue White and Perfect 41. Destroyer 43. Flame of the Barbary Coast 45. Tycoon 47. Montana 48. Red River (AAN) 48. The Great Jewel Robber 50. Lone Star 51. Bend of the River 52. The World in his Arms 52. Man without a Star 55. Backlash 56. Night Passage 57. Gunfighters of Casa Grande 65, many others.

Chase, Charley (1893–1940) (Charles Parrott).
Toothbrush-moustached American comedian who made many two-reel comedies from 1924, usually as henpecked husband. Brother of James Parrott.
■ COMPLETE TALKIE SHORTS: The Big Squawk 29. Leaping Love 29. Snappy Sneezer 29. Crazy Feet 29. Stepping Out 29. Great Gobs 29. The Real McCoy 30. Whispering Whoopee 30. All Teed Up 30. Fifty Million Husbands 30. Fast Work 30. Girl Shock 30. Dollar Dizzy 30. Looser than Loose 30. High Cs 30. Thundering Tenors 31. *The Pip from Pittsburgh* 31. Rough Seas 31. One of the Smiths 31. The Panic Is On 31. Skip the Maloo 31. What a Bozo 31. The Hasty Marriage 31. The Tabasco Kid 32. The Nickel Nurser 32. In Walked Charley 32. First in War 32. Young Ironsides 32. Good Grief 32. Now We'll Tell One 32. Mr Bride 32. *Fallen Arches* 32. Nature in the Wrong 33. His Silent Racket 33. Arabian Tights 33. Sherman Said It 33. Midsummer Mush 33. *Luncheon at Twelve* 33. The Cracked Iceman 34. Four Parts 34. I'll Take Vanilla 34. Another Wild Idea 34. It Happened One Day 34. Something Simple 34. You Said a Hatful 34. Fate's Fathead 34. *The Chases of Pimple Street* 34. Okay Toots 35. Poker at Eight 35. Southern Exposure 35. The Four Star Boarder 35. Nurse to You 35. Manhattan Monkey Business 35. Public Ghost Number One 35. Life Hesitates at 40 36. The Count Takes the Count 36. Vamp Till Ready 36. *On the Wrong Trek* 36. *Neighborhood House* 36. The Grand Hooter 37. From Bad to Worse 37. The Wrong Miss Wright 37. Calling All Doctors 37. The Big Squirt 37. Man Bites Lovebug 37. Time Out for Trouble 38. The Mind Needer 38. Many Sappy Returns 38. The Nightshirt Bandit 38. Pie à la Maid 38. The Sap Takes a Rap 39. The Chump Takes a Bump 39. *Rattling Romeo* 39. Skinny the Moocher 39. Teacher's Pest 39. The

Awful Good 39. *The Heckler* 40. South of the Boudoir 40.
~Feature appearance: Sons of the Desert 33.

Chase, Chevy (1943–) (Cornelius Crane Chase).
American light leading man. He hosted an unsuccessful late-night TV chat show for Fox in 1993.
    Tunnelvision 76. *Foul Play* 78. O Heavenly Dog 80. Seems Like Old Times 80. Under the Rainbow 81. Modern Problems 81. National Lampoon's Vacation 83. Deal of the Century 83. Fletch 85. National Lampoon's European Vacation 85. Spies Like Us 85. Three Amigos 86. Caddyshack II 88. The Couch Trip 88. Funny Farm 88. Fletch Lives 89. National Lampoon's Christmas Vacation 89. Nothing but Trouble 91. Memoirs of an Invisible Man 92. Cops and Robbersons 94, etc.

¶ I guess I look so straight and normal nobody expects me to pick my nose and fall. – C.C.

Chase, Ilka (1900–1978).
American columnist who occasionally brightened films.
    Autobiographies: 1945, *Past Imperfect*. 1948, *Free Admission*.
    Why Leave Home? 29. South Sea Rose 29. Free Love 30. The Animal Kingdom 32. Soak the Rich 36. Stronger than Desire 39. *Now Voyager* 42. No Time for Love 43. Miss Tatlock's Millions 48. Johnny Dark 54. The Big Knife 55. Ocean's Eleven 60, etc.
    TV series: The Trials of O'Brien 65.

Chase, James Hadley (1906–1985) (René Raymond).
British author of violent crime stories, set in the United States via a slang dictionary and a vivid imagination. His most famous, *No Orchids for Miss Blandish*, was filmed in 1948 and again, as *The Grissom Gang*, in 1971. Other films: *I'll Get You for This* 49, *The Man in the Raincoat* 56, *Young Girls Beware* 58, *What Price Murder* 58, *Eve* 63.

Chase, Mary (1907–1981).
American playwright best known for her whimsical comedy *Harvey*, filmed with James Stewart.

Chattaway, Jay.
American composer, mainly for action and horror movies.
    Maniac 81. The Big Score 83. Vigilante 83. Missing in Action 84. Invasion U.S.A. 85. Maniac Cop 87. Red Scorpion 89. Relentless 89. Bar Sinister 90. Maniac Cop II 90. Rich Girl 91, etc.

Chatterton, Ruth (1893–1961).
Dignified American leading lady, popular in 20s and 30s after stage success; later had success as novelist.
■ Sins of the Fathers 28. The Doctor's Secret 29. The Dummy 29. *Madame X* (AAN) 29. Charming Sinners 29. The Laughing Lady 29. Sarah and Son (AAN) 30. Paramount on Parade 30. The Lady of Scandal 30. Anybody's Woman 30. The Right to Love 30. Unfaithful 31. The Magnificent Lie 31. Once a Lady 31. Tomorrow and Tomorrow 32. The Rich are Always with Us 32. The Crash 32. Frisco Jenny 33. Lilly Turner 33. Female 33. Journal of a Crime 33. Lady of Secrets 36. Girls' Dormitory 36. *Dodsworth* 36. The Rat (GB) 38. A Royal Divorce (GB) 38.

Chauvel, Charles (1897–1959).
Australian writer-producer-director.
    In the Wake of the Bounty 33. Forty Thousand

Horsemen 42. The Rats of Tobruk 48. The Rugged O'Riordans 48. Jedda 53, many others.

Chayevsky, Paddy (1923–1981) (Sidney Stuchevsky).
Distinguished but latterly somewhat hysterical American writer whose greatest success was in TV.
　Autobiography: 1978, *Altered States*.
■ As Young as You Feel (oa) 51. *Marty* (AA) 55. The Catered Affair (oa) 56. *The Bachelor Party* 57. The Goddess (AANw) 58. Middle of the Night (oa) 59. The Americanization of Emily (w) 64. *The Hospital* (w) (AA) 71. *Network* 76. Altered States 80 (as Sidney Aaron).
~His non-Jewish first name is said to originate from his pretending in the army to be Catholic so as to go to mass rather than do fatigues.

Chaykin, Maury.
Canadian character actor.
　The Kidnapping of the President 80. Death Hunt 81. Soup for One 82. Of Unknown Origins 83. Mrs Soffel 84. Harry and Son 84. Highpoint 84. Wild Thing 87. Twins 88. Caribe 88. Iron Eagle II 88. Stars and Bars 88. Breaking In 89. Dances with Wolves 90. Mr Destiny 90. Where the Heart Is 90. The Adjuster 91. George's Island 91. My Cousin Vinny 92. Hero (GB: Accidental Hero) 92. Sommersby 93. Camilla 93. Josh and S.A.M. 93. Money for Nothing 93. Whale Music 94, etc.

Checker, Chubby (1941–) (Ernest Evans).
Endlessly gyrating American pop singer-dancer, briefly popular in the early 60s.
　Twist Around the Clock 62. Don't Knock the Twist 62. Calendar Girl 93, etc.

Chee-Ak.
Eskimo cinematographer, writer and actor. Born in Alaska, he was cameraman for Danish explorer Knud Rasmussen's film *Teddy Bear* 23. He went to Hollywood to work as cameraman on *Iceberg* and *Frozen Justice* 30, and co-wrote and starred in *Igloo* 32, set in the Arctic, for Universal, but it failed at the box-office.

Cheech and Chong:
see *Chong, Thomas, Marin, Richard 'Cheech'*.

Chekhov, Anton (1860–1904).
Introspective Russian writer whose plays about the melancholies of the upper classes have been frequently filmed, though never very commercially. Sidney Lumet's version of *The Seagull*, with Simone Signoret and James Mason, was perhaps the gamest try.

Chekhov, Michael (1891–1955).
Russian character actor who set up drama schools in London and New York; films sparse.
■ Song of Russia 44. In Our Time 44. *Spellbound* (AAN) 45. *Spectre of the Rose* 46. Cross My Heart 46. Abie's Irish Rose 46. Arch of Triumph 47. Invitation 51. Holiday for Sinners 52. Rhapsody 54.

Chelsom, Peter (1956–).
English actor, director and screenwriter. Studied at the Central School of Speech and Drama and was on stage from 1978.
　The Ringer (a) 78. An Englishman Abroad (a) (TV) 83. Indian Summer (a) 87. *Hear My Song* (co-w, d) 91, etc.

Chen, Joan (1961–) (Chen Chong).
Chinese actress, who began her career at the age of 14 and studied at the Shanghai Film Studio. She moved to America in 1981, and majored in film

production at California State University before resuming her career, first on television.
　Dim Sum: A Little Bit of Heart 85. James Clavell's Tai-Pan 86. The Night Stalker 87. The Last Emperor 87. Salute of the Jugger (aka The Blood of Heroes) 90. Wedlock 90. Hollywood Zen 92. Turtle Beach 92. The Joy Luck Club 93. You Seng (HK) 93. Heaven and Earth 93. On Deadly Ground 94. Golden Gate 94. Judge Dredd 95, etc.
　TV series: Twin Peaks 90.

Chenal, Pierre (1903–1990) (Pierre Cohen).
French director.
　Crime and Punishment 35. The Late Mathias Pascal 36. *Alibi* 37. Le Dernier Tournant 39. Sirocco 45. Clochemerle 48. Native Son (US) 51. Sinners of Paris 59, etc.

Cher (1946–) (Cher Bono, formerly Cherilyn Sarkisian).
American pop singer, once of Sonny and Cher, now turned actress. She has a daughter, Chastity, by Sonny Bono, and a son, Elijah Blue, by Gregg Allman.
　Biography: 1991, *Totally Uninhibited: The Life and Wild Times of Cher* by Lawrence J. Quirk.
■ Good Times 68. Come Back to the Five and Dime, Jimmy Dean, Jimmy Dean 83. Silkwood (AAN) 83. Mask 85. The Witches of Eastwick 87. Moonstruck (AA) 87. Suspect 87. Mermaids 90.

¶ I'm scared to death of being poor. It's like a fat girl who loses 500 pounds but is always fat inside. I grew up poor and will always feel poor inside. It's my pet paranoia. – *C*.
　Men are luxuries, not necessities. – *C*.
　When you take away those wild wings, there's an honest, complex screen presence underneath. – *New York Times*

Cherkassov, Nicolai (1903–1966).
Russian leading actor of epic hero stature.
　Autobiography: 1957, *Notes of a Soviet Actor*.
■ Baltic Deputy 37. *Peter the Great* 37. Ski Battalion 38. The Man with the Gun 38. *Alexander Nevsky* 38. Friends 39. Captain Grant's Children 39. Lenin in October 39. General Suvorov 41. *Ivan the Terrible Part One* 42. In the Name of Life 42. Ivan the Terrible Part Two 44. Spring 48. The First Front 49. Ivan Pavlov 50. Mussorgsky 51. Rimsky Korsakov 54. *Don Quixote* 53.

Cherrill, Virginia (1908–).
American leading lady, a society girl who had a brief film career in the early 30s. She was formerly married to Cary Grant (1934–35).
■ City Lights (as the blind girl) 31. Girls Demand Excitement 31. The Brat 31. Delicious 31. Fast Workers 33. The Nuisance 33. Charlie Chan's Greatest Case 32. White Heat 34. What Price Crime 35. Troubled Waters 35.

Cherry, Helen (1915–).
Cool and gracious British actress, mostly on stage; wife of Trevor Howard.
　The Courtneys of Curzon Street 48. Adam and Evelyn 49. Morning Departure 50. Young Wives' Tale 51. Castle in the Air 53. Three Cases of Murder 55. High Flight 57. The Naked Edge 61. Flipper's New Adventure 64. Hard Contract 69. 11 Harrowhouse 74, etc.

Chesebro, George (1888–1959).
American star of silent westerns who became a sidekick to Ken Maynard, Gene Autry and Tex Ritter in cowboy movies of the 30s and 40s.
　Hands Up (serial) 18. Rustler's Ranch 26. Tex Takes a Holiday 32. In Old Santa Fe 34. Laramie

Kid 35. Tumbling Tumbleweeds 35. Red River Valley 36. Roamin' Wild 36. Starlight over Texas 38. Gun Code 40. The Renegade 43. Boss of Rawhide 44. Return of the Lash 47. Cheyenne Takes Over 47. Stage to Mesa City 48. Gunslingers 50. The Kid from Amarillo 51. Last of the Comanches 53, many others.

Chester, Hal E. (1921–).
American teenage actor who, as Hally Chester, was one of the 'Little Tough Guys' in 1938–40. Later became producer and settled in Europe.
　Joe Palooka Champ 46. The Underworld Story 50. The Highwayman 53. Crashout 55. The Bold and the Brave 56. Night of the Demon 57. School for Scoundrels 60. Hide and Seek 64. The Secret War of Harry Frigg 67. The Double Man 67, etc.

Chesterton, G.K. (1874–1936).
English novelist and journalist, an irrepressible wit whose chief bequest to the cinema is the clerical detective Father Brown, played in movies by Walter Connolly and Alec Guinness and on TV by Heinz Ruhmann and Kenneth More.

Cheung, Leslie (Zhang Guorong).
Hong Kong leading actor, a former pop singer.
　A Chinese Ghost Story 88. Rouge 88. A Chinese Ghost Story II 89. Once a Thief 90. Days of Being Wild 90. Farewell My Concubine (Bawang Bie Ji) 93. The Bride with White Hair (aka Jiang-Hu: Between Love and Glory) 93. The Eagle Shooting Heroes: Dong Cheng Xi Jiu 93, etc.

Chevalier, Albert (1861–1923).
British actor and songwriter who found fame in the music halls from the 1890s as 'The Coster Laureate' singing Cockney songs. His best-known, 'My Old Dutch', was the basis of a silent film, in which he starred, and a movie made in 1934 with Gordon Harker and Betty Balfour.
　The Middleman 15. The Bottle 15. My Old Dutch 15. A Fallen Star 16, etc.

¶ He and his songs are as immortal as the cliffs of Dover. – *W. Macqueen-Pope*

Chevalier, Maurice (1888–1972).
Inimitable French singing entertainer, known throughout the world for his accent, his straw hat and his jutting lower lip. Became famous in Paris revues of the 20s, went to Hollywood in the 30s, remained in Europe in the 40s, then re-emerged as an international star. Special Academy Award 1958 'for his contributions to the world of entertainment for more than half a century'.
　Autobiographies: 1949, *The Man in the Straw Hat*. 1960, *With Love*. 1972, *I Remember It Well*.
　Biography: 1993, *Thank Heaven For Little Girls* by Edward Behr.
■ SOUND FILMS: Innocents in Paris 29. *The Love Parade* (AAN) 30. Paramount on Parade 30. The Big Pond (AAN) 30. Playboy of Paris 30. The Smiling Lieutenant 31. *One Hour With You* 32. Love Me Tonight 32. Bedtime Story 33. The Way to Love 33. The Merry Widow 34. *Folies Bergère* 35. L'Homme du Jour 36. Avec Le Sourire 36. Break the News 36. The Beloved Vagabond 37. Pièges 39. *Le Silence est d'Or* 47. Le Roi 49. Ma Pomme 50. J'Avais Sept Filles 55. Love in the Afternoon 57. *Gigi* 58. Count Your Blessings 59. Can Can 59. Black Tights 60. A Breath of Scandal 60. Pepe 60. *Fanny* 61. Jessica 62. *In Search of the Castaways* 62. A New Kind of Love 63. Panic Button 64. I'd Rather be Rich. Monkeys Go Home 67.
❂ For his incomparable technique as a singing entertainer; and for cheering up two widely

separate generations of the international audience. *Love Me Tonight*.

¶ Love the public the way you love your mother. — *M.C.*

The 70-odd years young Maurice Chevalier takes his place beside children and animals as one of the great scene stealers of all times. — *Mike Connelly*

Chevallier, Gabriel (1895–1969).
French novelist whose chief gift to the film world was *Clochemerle*, about the furore caused by the building of a public lavatory in a French village.

Chew, Richard.
American editor.
The Conversation 74. One Flew over the Cuckoo's Nest (AAN) 76. Star Wars (AA) 77. Goin' South 78. My Favorite Year 82. Real Genius 85. Where the River Runs Black 86. Clean and Sober 88. Men Don't Leave 90. Late for Dinner 91. Singles (& co-p) 92, etc.

Cheyney, Peter (1896–1951).
British mystery writer who created Lemmy Caution and Slim Callaghan, some of whose adventures were filmed.
Deputy Drummer (w) 32. Uneasy Terms (w) 48. Meet Mr Callaghan (w) 50. Diplomatic Courier 52. Alphaville 65.

Chiari, Mario (1909–1989).
Italian production designer.
Miracle in Milan 51. The Golden Coach 54. Neapolitan Fantasy 54. I Vitelloni 54. The Sea Wall 56, etc.

Chiari, Walter (1924–1992) (Walter Annichiarico).
Italian comic actor, occasionally in international films.
Bellissima 51. OK Nero 51. The Moment of Truth 53. Nana 56. The Little Hut 57. Bonjour Tristesse 58. Pepote 58. Chimes at Midnight 66. They're a Weird Mob 66. Squeeze a Flower 69. The Valachi Papers 72. Tracce di Vita Amorosa 91, etc.

Chiba, Sonny (1939–   ) (Shinichi Chiba).
Japanese actor, star of violent martial arts movies, in films from 1961. He formed his own martial arts school to train stuntmen and fight choreographers for film work.
Terror beneath the Sea 70. The Bodyguard 70. Street Fighter 75. Return of the Street Fighter 76. The Killing Machine 76. Kowloon Assignment 77. The Street Fighter's Last Revenge 77. Champion of Death 78. Sister Streetfighter 78. Hunter in the Dark 80. Virus 82. Shogun's Ninja 83. Legend of the Eight Samurai 84. Aces: Iron Eagle III 92. Resort to Kill 93, etc.

Chief Thundercloud (1899–1955) (Victor Daniels).
American Indian actor who began in films as a stuntman.
Ramona 36. Union Pacific 38. Western Union 41. The Falcon Out West 44. Unconquered 47. The Half Breed 51, many others.

Chief Thundercloud (1901–1967) (Scott Williams).
American actor of Indian descent who appeared in many second feature westerns and played Tonto on radio.

Chihara, Paul (1938–   ).
American composer, also scoring many television movies.

Death Race 2000 75. Sweet Revenge 76. I Never Promised You a Rose Garden 77. The Bad News Bears Go to Japan 77. Prince of the City 81. The Legend of Walks Far Woman 82. The Survivors 83. Manimal (TV) 83. Impulse 84. The Morning After 86. Jackals 86. A Walk on the Moon 87. The Killing Time 87. Crossing Delancey 88. Penn and Teller Get Killed 89, etc.

child stars
have been popular with every generation of filmgoers. Throughout the 20s Mary Pickford stayed at the top by remaining a child as long as, and after, she could; with only slight competition from Baby Peggy, Madge Evans, Dawn O'Day (later Anne Shirley) and Wesley Barry. Stronger competitors, perhaps, were Junior Coghlan and, around 1930, Junior Durkin; strongest of all was Jackie Coogan, immortalized by Chaplin as *The Kid* in 1920 and subsequently cast in all the standard juvenile roles. The child comedians who composed *Our Gang* for Hal Roach started in the 20s and went on, with cast changes, into the 40s: best remembered of them are Joe Cobb, Jean Darling, Johnny Downs, Mickey Daniels, Farina, Spanky Macfarland, Alfalfa Switzer, Darla Hood and Buckwheat Thomas.

Jackie Cooper also started in *Our Gang* but became a star in his own right after playing in *The Champ* and *Skippy*. In the early 30s his main rival was Dickie Moore, a lad of somewhat gentler disposition. Soon both were displaced in popular favour by Freddie Bartholemew in *David Copperfield*; but no boy could hold a candle to the multi-talented prodigy Shirley Temple, a star in 1933 at the age of five. She captivated a generation in a dozen or more hurriedly-produced sentimental comedies, and neither the angelic British Binkie Stuart nor the mischievous Jane Withers could cast the same spell.

Noting a splendid performance by twelve-year-old Robert Lynen in the French *Poil de Carotte*, we next encounter the still irrepressible Mickey Rooney, who popped up variously as Puck, Andy Hardy or a one-man-band. Then in 1937, the year that the Mauch twins appeared in *The Prince and the Pauper*, an MGM short called *Every Sunday* introduced two singing teenage girls, Deanna Durbin and Judy Garland, who went on to achieve enormous popularity in maturing roles until both were overtaken by personal difficulties. Another child who went on to musical stardom was vaudeville-bred Donald O'Connor, first seen in *Sing You Sinners*. But little more was seen of Tommy Kelly, who played *Tom Sawyer*, or Ann Gillis, or Terry Kilburn, or even Roddy McDowall until he re-emerged as a character actor twenty-five years later.

The early 40s saw Edith Fellows as a good girl and Virginia Weidler, so marvellous in *The Philadelphia Story*, as a bad one. Baby Sandy appeared in a few comedies, as had Baby Le Roy ten years earlier; neither was seen on screen after the toddler stage. Two infant Dead-End Kids, Butch and Buddy, roamed mischievously through several Universal comedies. Margaret O'Brien and Peggy Ann Garner were two truly remarkable child actresses who never quite managed the transition to adult stardom. Teenagers Ann Blyth and Peggy Ryan partnered Donald O'Connor in many a light musical. Other child actors of the period were Ted Donaldson, Diana Lynn, Darryl Hickman and Sharyn Moffett, while Skippy Homeier gave an electrifying performance as the young Nazi in *Tomorrow the World*. In the post-war years Europe contributed Ivan Jandl in *The Search*; Britain had George Cole and Harry Fowler for cockney roles, Jeremy Spenser for well-bred ones,

Anthony Wager and Jean Simmons in *Great Expectations*, and very memorable performances from Bobby Henry in *The Fallen Idol* and John Howard Davies in *Oliver Twist*. Hollywood responded with thoughtful Claude Jarman, tearful Bobs Watson, spunky Bobby Driscoll and Tommy Rettig, and pretty little misses Gigi Perreau and Natalie Wood.

The 50s brought William (now James) Fox in *The Magnet*, Brigitte Fossey and Georges Poujouly in *Les Jeux Interdits*, Mandy Miller in *Mandy*, Vincent Winter and Jon Whiteley in *The Kidnappers*, Brandon de Wilde in *Shane*, and Patty McCormack as the evil child in *The Bad Seed*. In 1959 Hayley Mills embarked on a six-year reign (somewhat outshone in *Whistle down the Wind* by Alan Barnes); the similar and equally capable American actress Patty Duke confined herself principally to stage and TV apart from *The Miracle Worker*. Then there have been Disney's over-wholesome Tommy Kirk and Annette Funicello, Fergus McClelland in *Sammy Going South*, Jean-Pierre Léaud in *The Four Hundred Blows*, William Dix in *The Nanny*, Matthew Garber and Karen Dotrice in *Mary Poppins*, Deborah Baxter in *A High Wind in Jamaica*, Mark Lester and Jack Wild in *Oliver*, Tatum O'Neal in *Paper Moon*, Linda Blair in *The Exorcist*, Ando in *Paper Tiger*, Kim Richards and Ike Eisenmann in *Escape to Witch Mountain*, Ricky Schroder in *The Champ* . . . and more moppets are inevitably waiting in the wings, though the recent tendency has been for them to make one appearance and disappear from the boards.

One exception has been Bonnie Bedelia's nephew Macaulay Culkin, who starred in the most successful of all comedies, *Home Alone*, which was his fourth film, and commanded a fee of $5 million for the sequel. Lukas Haas, who played the wide-eyed seven-year-old boy in *Witness*, has gone on to make another eight or so films with great success. Perhaps it is significant that Jodie Foster, one of the few to have made the successful transition from child star to adult actress, chose to make her début as a director in 91 with *Little Man Tate*, a film about the problems of gifted children.

childhood portrayed by grown-ups
was instanced by Joan Fontaine in *Letter from an Unknown Woman*; by Ginger Rogers in *The Major and the Minor*; by Ginger Rogers and Alan Marshal in *Tom Dick and Harry*; by Ginger Rogers and Cary Grant in *Monkey Business*; and by Jack Buchanan, Fred Astaire and Nanette Fabray in the 'Triplets' number in *Band Wagon*. One might also add Judy Garland in *The Wizard of Oz*: she was seventeen when she played Dorothy.

Children's Film Foundation.
British company formed in 1951 to produce and distribute specially devised entertainment films for children's Saturday matinées. Sponsored by trade organizations.

Childress, Alvin (1907–1986).
American character actor who made occasional films, best known for playing Amos in the TV series *Amos 'n' Andy* 51–53.
Anna Lucasta 58. The Man in the Net 59. The Bingo Long Traveling All-Stars and Motor Kings 76. Sister, Sister (TV) 82, etc.

Chiles, Linden (1934–   ).
American character actor who usually plays well-educated types.
Sanctuary 61. A Rage to Live 64. Texas across the River 67. Death Be Not Proud (TV) 75. Who Is the Black Dahlia? (TV) 75. Deadline Assault (aka

Act of Violence) 79. Red Flag: The Ultimate Game (TV) 81. Forbidden World (aka Mutant) 82, etc.
TV series: Convoy 65. James at 15 77–78.

Chiles, Lois (1950–).
American leading lady of the late 70s.
The Way We Were 73. The Great Gatsby 74. Death on the Nile 78. Coma 78. Moonraker 79. Courage 84. Sweet Liberty 85. Creepshow 2 87. Broadcast News 87. Twister 88. Until the End of the World (Bis ans Ende der Welt) 91. Diary of a Hit Man 92. Lush Life 93, etc.
TV series: Dallas 82–84.

Chilly Willy.
Cheerful, quick-witted penguin who starred in 35 cartoons from 1953–72, produced by Walter Lanz and released by Universal. He enjoyed his greatest success when animated briefly by Tex Avery.
Chilly Willy 53. I'm Cold (AAN) 54. Hot and Cold 55. The Big Snooze 57. Polar Pests 58. Clash and Carry 61. Fish and Chips 63. Snow Place Like Home 66. Hot Time on Ice 67. Chilly's Cold War 70. The Rude Intruder 72, etc.

Chin, Tsai (c. 1938–).
Chinese leading lady in international films.
Autobiography: 1990, *Daughter of Shanghai*.
The Face of Fu Manchu 65. Invasion 66. The Brides of Fu Manchu 66. You Only Live Twice 67. Rentadick 72. The Joy Luck Club 93, etc.

China
was making films of a kind early in the century, but development of the industry was sporadic until the 50s, when the communists churned out many propaganda dramas. In recent years, though, the so-called Fifth Generation of Chinese directors has produced films of world class, notably Chen Kaige's *Yellow Earth*, *King of the Children* and *Life on a String*, and Zhang Yimou's *Red Sorghum*, *Jou Dou* and *Raise the Red Lantern*, which starred Gong Li. These films came from the Xi'an Studios, which were under the direction of Wu Tianming, himself a director (*The Old Well*), but most of the directors' best efforts were either given a very restricted release in China or banned altogether. Zhang Yimou turned to Japan and Taiwan to finance his films, and Wu Tianming and Chen Kaige left for America at the end of the 80s, so the blossoming of an indigenous Chinese cinema may have been a short one.

Ching, William (1912–1989).
American general-purpose actor of the 40s.
Something in the Wind 47. D.O.A. 50. Belle le Grand 51. Pat and Mike 52. Scared Stiff 53, etc.
TV series: Our Miss Brooks 55–56.

Chirgwin, G. H. (1855–1922) (George Chirgwin).
English black-faced comedian and one-string fiddle-player who performed in music halls as a child with his brothers. In the 1870s he went solo as 'The White-Eyed Kaffir', so-called because he painted a diamond shape around his right eye white when he made up. He twice filmed *The Blind Boy*, based on his most popular song and intended to be shown synchronized to his recording.
■ Chirgwin in his Humorous Business 1896. Chirgwin Plays a Scotch Reel 1896. The Blind Boy 1900. The Blind Boy 1917.

Chitty, Eric (1906–1977).
British character actor who spent many years playing crotchety little men, notably in the TV series *Please Sir*.
Contraband 40. Raising a Riot 55. Doctor Zhivago 65. The Railway Children 70. Great

Expectations 75. A Bridge Too Far 77, many others.

Chlumsky, Anna (1981–).
American child actress, a former model.
My Girl 91. My Girl 2 94. Trading Mom 94.

Chodorov, Edward (1904–1988).
American screenwriter and dramatist. He was blacklisted in 1953 for refusing to co-operate with the House Un-American Activities Committee.
The World Changes 33. Kind Lady 35. The Story of Louis Pasteur (co-w) 35. Yellow Jack 38. Undercurrent 46. The Hucksters 47. Roadhouse 48, etc.

Chodorov, Jerome (1911–).
American writer, usually with Joseph Fields.
Louisiana Purchase 41. My Sister Eileen 42. Junior Miss 45. Happy Anniversary 59 (all from their plays), etc.

Chomsky, Marvin (1929–).
American director of efficient but nondescript style.
■ Assault on the Wayne (TV) 70. *Family Flight* (TV) 71. Evel Knievel 71. Mongo's Back in Town (TV) 71. Fireball Forward (TV) 72. Female Artillery (TV) 73. The FBI vs Alvin Karpis (TV) 74. Mrs Sundance (TV) 74. Attack on Terror (TV) 74. Kate McShane (TV) 75. A Matter of Wife and Death (TV) 75. Murph the Surf 75. Brinks: the Great Robbery (TV) 76. Law and Order (TV) 76. *Roots* (co-d) (TV) 76. Danger in Paradise (TV) 77. Little Ladies of the Night (TV) 77. MacKintosh and TJ 77. Good Luck Miss Wyckoff 78. *Holocaust* 78. Hollow Image 79. King Crab 80. Dr Franken 80. Attica (TV) 80. Evita Peron (TV) 81. My Body My Child (TV) 82. Inside the Third Reich (TV) 82. Nairobi Affair (TV) 84. Tank 84. Robert Kennedy and his Times (TV) 85.

Chong, Rae Dawn (1962–).
Canadian-born actress. She is the daughter of Thomas Chong.
Quest for Fire 79. Commando 85. The Color Purple 85. Choose Me 86. Soul Man 86. The Principal 87. The Squeeze 87. Walking After Midnight 88. The Borrower 89. Far Out, Man! 90. Amazon 90. Tales from the Darkside: The Movie 91. Time Runner 92. Amberwaves 93. Boulevard (& w) 94. Boca 94, etc.

Chong, Thomas (1938–).
Canadian guitarist, actor, director and screenwriter who formed a coarse comic double-act with Richard 'Cheech' Marin, which split up in 1985. He is the father of actress Rae Dawn Chong.
Up in Smoke (a) 79. Cheech & Chong's Next Movie (a, wd) 80. Cheech & Chong's Nice Dreams (a, wd) 81. Things Are Tough All Over (a, wd) 82. Cheech & Chong: Still Smokin' (a, wd) 83. Yellowbeard (a) 83. Cheech & Chong's The Corsican Brothers (a, wd) 84. After Hours (a) 85. Tripwire (a) 89. Far Out, Man! (a, wd) 90. Life after Sex (a) 91. Ferngully . . . the Last Rainforest (voice) 92, etc.

Chopin, Frédéric (1810–1849).
Polish pianist and composer most famous in film circles for his love affair with the eccentric Georges Sand. ('Frederic, stop composing that Polonaise jangle!' said Merle Oberon to Cornel Wilde in *A Song to Remember*.) His chief cinematic interpreters have been as follows:

1935	*Un Amour de Frédéric Chopin*	Jean Servais
1945	*A Song to Remember*	Cornel Wilde
1951	*The Young Chopin*	Czeslaw Wollejko
1960	*Song Without End*	Alex Davion
1975	*Lisztomania*	Ken Colley
1991	*Impromptu*	Hugh Grant

Chopra, Joyce (1938–).
American director.
Smooth Talk 86. The Lemon Sisters 89.

Chouraqui, Elie (1950–).
French director.
Mon Premier Amour 78. Love Songs (Paroles et Musique) 84. Man on Fire 87. Miss Missouri 90. Les Marmottes 94, etc.

Choureau, Etchika (1923–).
French leading lady.
Children of Love 53. The Fruits of Summer 55. Lafayette Escadrille (US) 57. Darby's Rangers (US) 58, etc.

Chow, Raymond (1929–).
Chinese producer who in the early 80s expanded his interests from kung fu action films, through his Golden Harvest group, to international vehicles such as *The Cannonball Run*, *The Return of the Soldier* and *Teenage Mutant Ninja Turtles*.

Chrétien, Henri (1879–1956).
French inventor of the anamorphic lens subsequently used in CinemaScope and allied processes.

Christ
on the screen was for many years a controversial subject: film-makers have usually preferred to imply his presence by a hand, a cloak, or simply reactions of onlookers. However, even in the first ten years of cinephotography there were several versions of his life, and in 1912 Robert Henderson played the role in a 'super' production of *From the Manger to the Cross*. In 1916 came *Civilisation*, with George Fisher as Christ on the battlefields, and in the same year *Intolerance*, in which Howard Gaye was Jesus. In 1927 Cecil B. de Mille's *King of Kings* had H. B. Warner in the role; any offence was minimized by having his first appearance a misty fade-in as the blind girl regains her sight. In 1932 Duvivier made *Golgotha*, with Robert le Vigan; twenty years then went by before Christ's next appearance on the screen, played by a non-professional, Robert Wilson, in a sponsored movie called *Day of Triumph*. In 1961 Jeffrey Hunter appeared as Christ in *King of Kings*, which was unfortunately tagged by the trade *I Was a Teenage Jesus*. George Stevens' disappointing 1965 colossus, *The Greatest Story Ever Told*, cleverly cast Swedish Max von Sydow in the part; in the same year came Pasolini's *The Gospel According to St Matthew*, with Enrique Irazoqui; and in 1969 Buñuel cast Bernard Verley as Christ in *The Milky Way*. Christ-like figures of various kinds have been found in such films as *The Passing of the Third Floor Back*, *The Fugitive*, *Strange Cargo* and *The Face*; while films about the direct influence of Christ's life include *Quo Vadis*, *The Last Days of Pompeii*, *Ben Hur*, *Barabbas*, *The Wandering Jew* and *The Robe*, in which the voice of Christ was provided by Cameron Mitchell. The most recent Christs have been in the modernized pop-operas *Godspell* and *Jesus Christ Superstar*; a TV series, *Jesus of Nazareth*; a TV movie with a literal slant, *The Day Christ Died*; and Martin Scorsese's *The Last Temptation of Christ*.

Christensen, Benjamin (1879–1959).
Danish director whose career faded after a sojourn in Hollywood.

The Mysterious X 13. The Night of Revenge 15. Häxan (Witchcraft through the Ages) 21. Seine Frau Die Unbekannte 23. The Devil's Circus 25. Mockery 27. The Hawk's Nest 28. Seven Footprints to Satan 29, many others.

Christian, Linda (1923–) (Blanca Rosa Welter). Mexican-born leading lady who appeared in a few international films. She was Tyrone Power's second wife, then married into European nobility.
Holiday in Mexico 46. Green Dolphin Street 47. Tarzan and the Mermaids 48. The Happy Time 52. Athena 54. Thunderstorm 56. The House of Seven Hawks 59. The VIPs 63. How to Seduce a Playboy 66, etc.

Christian, Paul:
see *Hubschmid, Paul.*

Christian-Jaque (1904–1994) (Christian Maudet). French writer-director, former journalist.
Les Disparus de Saint-Agil 38. La Symphonie Fantastique 42. Sortilèges 44. *Un Revenant* 46. D'Homme à Hommes 48. Souvenirs Perdus 50. Bluebeard 51. *Fanfan la Tulipe* 51. Lucrezia Borgia 52. Adorables Creatures 52. Nana 54. Si Tous les Gars du Monde (Race for Life) 55. Babette Goes to War 59. Madame Sans Gêne 61. The Black Tulip 63. The Secret Agents (The Dirty Game) (co-director) 66. The Saint Versus . . . 66. Two Tickets to Mexico (Dead Run) 67. La Ville a Belles Dents 80. Carne, l'Homme à la Caméra 85, etc.

Christians, Mady (1900–1951) (Margarethe Marie Christians).
Austrian-born stage actress in occasional Hollywood films.
The Waltz Dream (GB) 26. Slums of Berlin 27. The Runaway Princess (GB) 29. A Wicked Woman 35. Escapade 36. Seventh Heaven 37. Heidi 37. Address Unknown 44. All My Sons 48. Letter from an Unknown Woman 48, etc.

Christie, Dame Agatha (1891–1976) (Mary Clarissa Miller).
Best-selling British mystery novelist and playwright whose innumerable puzzle plots have furnished film-makers with relatively few, and usually forgettable, movies. In *Agatha* 79, a fiction based on a mysterious episode in her real life, she was played by Vanessa Redgrave. Her work has also been turned into television films and series, most notably featuring her two eccentric detectives, Miss Marple and Hercule Poirot (qqv).
Autobiography: 1977, *An Autobiography.*
Biography: 1984, *Agatha Christie* by Janet Morgan.
Book: 1993, *The Films of Agatha Christie* by Scott Palmer.
■ Die Abenteuer GmbH (from The Secret Adversary) 28. The Passing of Mr Quinn 28. Alibi 31. Black Coffee 31. Lord Edgware Dies 34. Love from a Stranger 37 and 47. And Then There Were None 45 and, as Ten Little Indians, 65, 75, 89. Witness for the Prosecution 57. The Spider's Web 60. Murder She Said 62. Murder at the Gallop 63. Murder Most Foul 64. The Alphabet Murders 66. Endless Night 72. Murder on the Orient Express 74. Death on the Nile 78. The Mirror Crack'd 80. Evil under the Sun 82. Ordeal by Innocence 85.

¶ I'm a sausage machine, a perfect sausage machine. – A.C.
An archaeologist is the best husband a woman can have. The older she gets, the more interested he is in her. – A.C.
~A mysterious episode in her own life was fictitiously cleared up in *Agatha* 79.

Christie, Al (1886–1951).
American comedy producer, mainly of two-reelers, in Hollywood from 1914 and a rival of Mack Sennett.
Features include *Tillie's Punctured Romance* 17, *Up in Mabel's Room* 26; produced and directed *Charley's Aunt* 25.

Christie, Audrey (1912–1989).
American supporting actress.
Deadline 52. Carousel 56. Splendor in the Grass 61. The Unsinkable Molly Brown 64. The Ballad of Josie 68. Mame 73, etc.

Christie, Howard (1912–1992).
American producer.
Lady on a Train 44. Abbott and Costello Meet the Invisible Man 50. The Purple Mask 55. Away All Boats 56. Gunfight at Abilene 60. Nobody's Perfect 68, etc.

Christie, Julie (1940–).
Striking British leading actress whose choice of roles has not always been fortunate.
■ Crooks Anonymous 62. The Fast Lady 63. *Billy Liar* 63. Young Cassidy 64. *Darling* (AA, BFA) 65. *Doctor Zhivago* 65. Fahrenheit 451 66. Far From the Madding Crowd 67. Petulia 68. In Search of Gregory 69. The Go-Between 71. McCabe and Mrs Miller (AAN) 71. *Don't Look Now* 74. Shampoo 75. Nashville 75. Demon Seed 77. Heaven Can Wait 78. Memoirs of a Survivor 82. The Return of the Soldier 82. The Gold Diggers 83. Heat and Dust 83. Power 86. Miss Mary 86. Power 86. Secret Obsession 88. Fools of Fortune 90. The Railway Station Man 92.

Christine, Virginia (1917–).
American character actress.
Edge of Darkness 42. The Mummy's Curse 45. The Killers 46. Cyrano de Bergerac 50. Never Wave at a WAC 53. Not as a Stranger 55. Nightmare 56. Invasion of the Body Snatchers 56. The Careless Years 58. Judgment at Nuremberg 61. The Prize 63. Guess Who's Coming to Dinner 67, etc.

Christmas
has provided a favourite sentimental climax for many a film. Films wholly based on it include *The Holly and the Ivy, Tenth Avenue Angel, Miracle on 34th Street, White Christmas, Christmas Eve, Christmas in Connecticut, The Bishop's Wife, I'll Be Seeing You,* and the many versions of *Scrooge.* There were happy Christmas scenes in *The Bells of St Mary, The Inn of the Sixth Happiness, The Man Who Came to Dinner, Holiday Inn, Since You Went Away, Three Godfathers, It's a Wonderful Life, Young at Heart, Meet Me in St Louis, On Moonlight Bay, Little Women, The Cheaters, Desk Set* and *Young at Heart* among others; while unhappy Christmases were spent in *Things to Come, Full House* ('The Gifts of the Magi'), *The Apartment, Meet John Doe, The Glenn Miller Story, The Christmas Tree, Christmas Holiday,* and *The Victors.* (Nor was there much for the characters in *The Lion in Winter* to celebrate at the Christmas court of 1189.)
Santa Claus himself put in an appearance in *Miracle on 34th Street* (played by Edmund Gwenn), *The Lemon Drop Kid* (played by Bob Hope), *The Light at Heart* (played by Monty Woolley), and *Robin and the Seven Hoods* (played by the Sinatra clan). Disney features him in *Babes in Toyland* and a short cartoon, *The Night Before Christmas;* and in their 1934 version of *Babes in Toyland* Laurel and Hardy found him an irate employer.
Christmas was celebrated in unlikely settings in *Knights of the Round Table, Conquest of Space, Scott*

of the Antarctic, Encore ('Winter Cruise'), Destination Tokyo (in a submarine), The Nun's Story (in a Congo Mission), and Black Narcissus (in an Indian nunnery).

Christopher, Dennis (1955–) (Dennis Carelli). American leading man.
The Boys in Company C 77. A Wedding 78. Breaking Away 79. California Dreaming 80. Fade to Black 80. Chariots of Fire 81. Don't Cry It's Only Thunder 82. Flight of the Spruce Goose 86. Jake Speed 86. Alien Predator 87. A Sinful Life 89. Doppelganger 92. Plughead Rewired: Circuitry Man II 94, etc.

Chrystall, Belle (1911–).
British leading lady of the 30s.
Hindle Wakes 31. Friday the Thirteenth 33. Edge of the World 38, etc.

Chukrai, Grigori (1920–).
Russian director.
The Forty First 56. Ballad of a Soldier 59. Clear Sky 61. There Was an Old Man and an Old Woman 65. People! 66. Pamyat 71. La Vita è Bella 82, etc.

churches
have provided a setting for many pretty secular-minded films, from the various versions of *The Hunchback of Notre Dame* to the use of a church as a refuge during a flood in *When Tomorrow Comes.* Other memorable moments include Bogart confessing the plot of *Dead Reckoning* to a priest; Robert Donat's sermon in *Lease of Life* and Orson Welles' in *Moby Dick;* the scandalous confessions in *Les Jeux Interdits* and the dramatic one in *I Confess;* the murder of Becket; the bombed but well-used churches in *Mrs Miniver* and *Sundown;* the thing in the rafters of Westminster Abbey in *The Quatermass Experiment;* the attempted murder in Westminster Cathedral in *Foreign Correspondent* and the fall from the church tower in *Vertigo;* the spies in the mission chapel in *The Man Who Knew Too Much;* the arrest of *Pastor Hall;* Arturo de Cordova going mad during a service in *El;* the church-tower climax of *The Stranger;* the Russian services in *Ivan the Terrible* and *We Live Again;* Cagney dying on the church steps in *The Roaring Twenties;* the church used as refuge against the Martians in *The War of the Worlds;* the church used for a town meeting in *High Noon;* the Turkish mosque and espionage rendezvous in *From Russia with Love;* the comic rifling of offertory boxes in *Heaven Sent;* the finale of *Miracle in the Rain* in the church porch; the meeting in church of the protagonists in *The Appaloosa;* the characters finally trapped in a church in *The Exterminating Angel;* the churches swept away by the elements in *The Hurricane* and *Hawaii;* the church rendezvous in *Alice's Restaurant;* the church with the moving statue in *The Miracle of the Bells;* and all the many films in which the protagonists are *priests, monks* and *nuns* (qv).

Churchill, Berton (1876–1940).
Forceful Canadian stage actor who in later years settled in Hollywood and played stern bosses and fathers.
Tongues of Flame 24. Nothing but the Truth 29. Secrets of a Secretary 31. The Rich are Always with Us 32. American Madness 32. Master of Men 33. Hi Nellie 34. Dames 34. Babbitt 34. Page Miss Glory 35. Parole 36. Parnell 37. The Singing Marine 37. Sweethearts 38. *Stagecoach* (as the absconding banker) 39. The Way of All Flesh 40. Turnabout 40, many others.

Churchill, Diana (1913–1994).
British leading lady, mostly on stage. Multiple sclerosis brought her career to an end. Married to actors Barry K. Barnes and Mervyn Johns.

School for Husbands 36. Housemaster 38. House of the Arrow 40. Eagle Squadron (US) 44. Scott of the Antarctic 48. The History of Mr Polly 49, etc.

Churchill, Donald (1930–1991).
British light actor who developed from callow young men to eccentric middle-aged creations. Also wrote many TV scripts.

Victim 60. The Wild Affair 63, etc.

TV series (a, w) include Bulldog Breed 62. Never a Cross Word 68. Moody and Pegg 63. Spooner's Patch 80.

Churchill, Frank (1901–1942).
American composer, always with Disney and the author of several hit songs.

Three Little Pigs ('Who's Afraid of the Big Bad Wolf?') 33. *Snow White and the Seven Dwarfs* 37. *Dumbo* 41. *Bambi* 42, etc.

Churchill, Marguerite (1910–).
Pert American leading lady of the 30s, now retired and living in Europe. She was married to actor George O'Brien (1933–48).

The Valiant 29. Seven Faces 29. Born Reckless 30. The Big Trail 30. Charlie Chan Carries On 31. Quick Millions 31. Forgotten Commandments 32. Girl without a Room 33. The Walking Dead 36. Dracula's Daughter 36. Legion of Terror 36, etc.

Churchill, Sarah (1914–1982).
British actress, daughter of Sir Winston Churchill.

He Found a Star 40. All Over the Town 47. *Royal Wedding* (US) 51. Serious Charge 58, etc.

Churchill, Sir Winston (1874–1965).
British statesman and author who has been the subject of a major documentary, *The Finest Hours* 64, and a TV series, *The Valiant Years* 60. He was impersonated by Dudley Field Malone in *Mission to Moscow* 43, by Patrick Wymark in *Operation Crossbow* 65, by a number of Russian actors in various propaganda pieces, by Simon Ward in *Young Winston* 72, by Nigel Stock in *A Man Called Intrepid* 79 and by Wensley Pithey in *Ike* 79.

¶ He would rather make love to a word than to a woman. – *Ingrid Bergman*

Chytilova, Vera (1929–).
Czech director. A former model, she studied at the Prague Film School. Always controversial, she was forbidden to make films in the early 70s.

Another Way of Life 63. Pearls at the Bottom (co-d) 66. Daisies (Sedmikrásky) 66. The Apple Game (Hra o Jablko) 76. Panel Story 79. Calamity (Kalamita) 80. The Very Late Afternoon of a Faun 84. Wolf 's Lair (Vlcíbouda) 86. The Jester and the Queen (Sasek a Kralovna) 88. Dedictvi Aneb Kurvahosigutntag 93, etc.

Ciampi, Yves (1921–1982).
French director.

Suzanne et Ses Brigands 50. Un Grand Patron 51. L'Esclave 53. Les Héros Sont Fatigués 55. Typhoon over Nagasaki 57. Qui Etes-vous Monsieur Sorge 60. Le Ciel sur la Tête 62. A Quelques Jours 69, etc.

Ciannelli, Eduardo (1887–1969).
Italian character actor, long in Hollywood; his finely-etched features and incisive speech were usually employed in villainous roles, but he could also strike sympathetic chords.

Reunion in Vienna 33. The Scoundrel 35. *Winterset* 36. Marked Woman 37. Law of the Underworld 38. Gunga Din 39. Foreign Correspondent 40. The Mummy's Hand 40. They Met in Bombay 41. Cairo 42. They Got Me Covered 43. *The Mask of Dimitrios* 44. The Conspirators 44. Dillinger 45. Wife of Monte Cristo 46. Perilous Holiday 47. The Creeper 48. Rapture 50. The People Against O'Hara 51. Volcano 53. Mambo 55. Helen of Troy 55. Houseboat 58. The Visit 64. Mackenna's Gold 68. The Brotherhood 68. The Secret of Santa Vittoria 69, many others.

TV series: *Johnny Staccato* 59.

Cicognini, Alessandro (1906–).
Italian composer.

Four Steps in the Clouds 42. Shoeshine 46. Bicycle Thieves 48. I Miscrabili 48. Tomorrow is Too Late 50. Miracle in Milan 51. Don Camillo 52. Umberto D 52. Due Soldi di Speranza 52. Gold of Naples 54. Ulysses 54. Summer Madness 55. The Black Orchid 58, etc.

Cilento, Diane (1933–).
Versatile Australian leading actress whose talent has not been fully tested in movies. She was married to Sean Connery (1962–73) and is the mother of actor Jason Connery.

Wings of Danger 52. The Angel who Pawned Her Harp 54. The Passing Stranger 54. Passage Home 55. The Woman for Joe 56. *The Admirable Crichton* 57. Jet Storm 59. The Full Treatment 60. The Naked Edge 61. I Thank a Fool 62. *Tom Jones* (AAN) 63. The Third Secret 64. *Rattle of a Simple Man* 64. The Agony and the Ecstasy 65. *Hombre* 67. Negatives 68. Zero Population Growth 72. The Wicker Man 73. Hitler: the Last Ten Days 74. For the Term of His Natural Life (TV) 82. The Boy Who Had Everything 84. Winner Takes All 86, etc.

Cimino, Michael (1940–).
American screenwriter/director.
■ Silent Running (co-w) 72. Magnum Force (co-w) 73. Thunderbolt and Lightfoot (wd) 74. *The Deer Hunter* (wd) (AA) 78. Heaven's Gate (wd) 80. The Year of the Dragon 85. The Sicilian 87. Desperate Hours 90.

¶ Films are home movies of your past. – *M.C.*

Cinecittà.
Large film studios in Rome, built in 1935, that have been at the centre of the Italian film industry and have also housed such international blockbusters as *Ben Hur* 59 and *Cleopatra* 63.

Cinecolor.
A two-colour process that was a cheaper alternative to Technicolor and so was used on many 'B' pictures in the 30s and 40s. The film had an orange-red emulsion on one side and a blue-green emulsion on the other.

the cinema
¶ A few fragments of thought:
The cinema, like the detective story, makes it possible to experience without danger all the excitement, passion and desirousness which must be suppressed in a humanitarian ordering of society. – *C.G. Jung*

It has no boundary . . . it is a ribbon of dream. – *Orson Welles*

The most collaborative of the arts. – *Dore Schary*

Truth twenty-four times a second. – *Jean-Luc Godard*

Of all the arts, the cinema is the most important for us. – *V.I. Lenin*

That temple of sex, with its goddesses, its guardians and its victims . . . – *Jean Cocteau*

An uncomfortable way of watching television. – *Sheila Black*

The film is not an art but a super tabloid for young and old, moron and genius. Her sister muses are the comic strips, the pulp magazines, the radio and all other forms of entertainment based on democratic rather than aesthetic principles. – *Howard Collins (manager in 1953 of Roxy Theatre, NY)*

Of course a film should have a beginning, a middle and an end. But not necessarily in that order. – *Jean-Luc Godard*

I always think that watching films is very like dreaming. – *John Boorman*

Whoever it was who first thought the cinema was an art, he should have kept his mouth shut. Not that it isn't, but there are so many terrible instances of films made specifically to be art which come perilously close to making us doubt the whole proposition. – *John Russell Taylor*

The film does best when it concentrates on a single character. It does *The Informer* superbly. It tends to lose itself in the ramifications of *War and Peace*. – *Budd Schulberg*

The finished product is not finished when the actor is. The work is completed by a pair of shears. – *Josef von Sternberg*

Editing is the foundation of the film art. – *Pudovkin*

Get a director and a writer and leave them alone. That's how the best pictures get made. – *William Wellman*

Any attempt in America to make a film a work of art must be hailed. Usually, in the same breath, it must be farewelled. – *John Simon*

The American film mind, though it can deal competently enough with the stupendous, cannot help vulgarizing any scene which approaches the intimate. – *James Agate*

Collectively the audience is, in the matter of aesthetic, totally uneducated. They gape before the screen today as the thirteenth-century playgoer gaped at the morality play. – *James Agate again, in 1921*

Most Hollywood comedies are so vulgar, witless and dull that it is preposterous to write about them in any publication not meant to be read while chewing gum. – *Wolcott Gibbs*

Cinema is an improvement on life. – *François Truffaut*

If you want art, don't mess about with movies. Buy a Picasso. – *Michael Winner*

The movies languish as a fine art because the men who determine what is to get into them haven't the slightest visible notion that such a thing as a fine art exists. – *H. L. Mencken, 1927*

Film-making has now reached the same stage as sex – it's all technique and no feeling. – *Penelope Gilliatt in the 80s*

cinema vérité
A fashionable term of the 60s for what used to be called candid camera. A TV-style technique of recording life and people as they are, in the raw, using handheld cameras, natural sound and the minimum of rehearsal and editing. Chiefly applied to *Chronique d'une Eté* 61, *Le Joli Mai* 62, and the documentaries of Richard Leacock and the Maysles brothers.

cinemas
have only rarely provided a background for film situations. A Hollywood première and a sneak preview were shown in *Singin' in the Rain*, and *The Oscar* revealed all about the Academy Awards ceremony. Characters in *Sherlock Junior*, *Borderlines*

and *Merton of the Movies* (Red Skelton version) clambered on to the stage while a film was showing. Projectionists were featured in *Clash by Night, The Blob, The Great Morgan,* and *Hellzapoppin;* also in *The Smallest Show on Earth,* the only film concerned with the running of a cinema as its main plot unless one counts *The Last Picture Show* in which the small-town cinema is an essential background to the character development. Fred Allen in *It's in the Bag* had a terrible time trying to find a seat in a full house; Dillinger was killed coming out of a cinema in *The F.B.I. Story;* Bogart was nearly shot in a Chinese cinema in *Across the Pacific,* and Anthony Perkins met Valli in a Siamese one in *This Angry Age (The Sea Wall).* A cinema was used as a rendezvous for spies in *The Traitors* and *Sabotage;* a church was used as a cinema in *Sullivan's Travels* when chain-gang convicts watched Mickey Mouse. Mark Stevens and Joan Fontaine in *From This Day Forward* visited a news cinema but were too much in love to heed the warnings of impending war. Louis Jourdan and Linda Christian watched Valentino at the local in *The Happy Time,* and astronauts watched Bob Hope in a space station in *Conquest of Space.* Deanna Durbin got a murder clue in a cinema in *Lady on a Train;* and in *Bullets or Ballots* Humphrey Bogart took Barton MacLane to see a documentary about his nefarious career. Ray Danton in *The Rise and Fall of Legs Diamond* excused himself during a performance to rob the shop next door. The monster in *The Tingler* escapes into a silent cinema. Linda Hayden in *Baby Love* was accosted in a cinema. Robert Cummings in *Saboteur* started a riot in Radio City Music Hall, on the stairs of which Danny Kaye sang in *Up in Arms.* Fredric March watched a Thomas Ince silent at the local nickelodeon in *One Foot in Heaven.* In *Brief Encounter,* Celia Johnson and Trevor Howard thought the organist was the best part of the programme. Polly Bergen in *The Caretakers* went crazy and climbed up in front of the screen. *Bonnie and Clyde* found time between robberies to see a *Gold Diggers* movie. In *Eye Witness* a cinema manager was killed during the Saturday night performance; and in *Targets* a killer was apprehended by Boris Karloff at a drive-in. A drive-in was used as a rendezvous in *White Heat* and a 42nd Street cinema was a homosexual rendezvous in *Midnight Cowboy. Cinema Paradiso* was a love-letter to a small-town cinema and its projectionist. Home movies figured most notably in *Rebecca* and *Adam's Rib.*

See also: *excerpts, theatres.*

CinemaScope

Wide-screen process copyrighted by Fox in 1953 and first used in *The Robe;* invented many years earlier by Henri Chrétien. Other companies either adopted it or produced their own trade name: WarnerScope, SuperScope, etc. Basically, the camera contains an anamorphic lens which 'squeezes' a wide picture on to a standard 35mm frame (which has a breadth/height ratio of 4:3 or 1.33:1). This, when projected through a complementary lens, gives a picture ratio on screen of 2.55:1 with stereophonic magnetic sound, or 2.35:1 with optical sound. Directors found the new shape awkward to compose for, the easiest way of handling it being to park the camera and let the actors move, a reversion to early silent methods. Although wide screens are said to have helped the box office, they have effectively prevented the full use of cinematic techniques. Oddly enough Fox in the mid-60s quietly dropped their own system and moved over to Panavision.

¶ The wide, wide screen may have saved the industry, but it came close to killing the art. Hear these justified cries of woe.

The worst shape ever devised. – *Rouben Mamoulian*

It's fine if you want a system that shows a boa constrictor to better advantage than a man. – *George Stevens*

A wide screen makes a bad film twice as bad. – *Samuel Goldwyn*

It is a formula for a funeral, or for snakes, but not for human beings. – *Fritz Lang*

It wrecked the art of film for a decade. – *Leon Shamroy*

Why not keep the screen the same size and reduce the size of the audience? – *Irving Brecher*

There was a time when all I looked for was a good story, but nowadays everything has to look the size of Mount Rushmore, and the actors in close-up look as though they belong there. – *Fritz Lang*

Processed by De Luxe, it made all films look like very cheap colour advertisements in magazines. – *James Mason*

It resulted in a collapse of visual quality even more disastrous than that which accompanied the dawn of sound. – *Charles Higham*

Cinematograph Exhibitors' Association.
The British theatre-owners' protective association, founded in 1912 with 10 members. In 1922 there were 2000, in 1950, 4000.

cinematographer.
Lighting cameraman or chief photographer.

Cinemobile.
A massive truck into which everything necessary for location shooting, including dressing rooms and toilets, can be packed.

Cinerama.
Extra-wide-screen system, invented by Fred Waller. Three projectors, electronically synchronized, were used to put the picture on the screen in three sections: this gave a disturbing wobble at the joins, though the range of vision was sometimes magnificently wide, as in the aerial shots and roller coaster sequence in *This is Cinerama* 52. After ten years of scenic but cinematically unremarkable travelogues (*Cinerama Holiday, Seven Wonders of the World, Search for Paradise,* etc.), the first story film in the process, *How the West Was Won,* was made in 1962. Shortly afterwards the three-camera system was abandoned in favour of 'single-lens Cinerama' which is virtually indistinguishable from CinemaScope except for the higher definition resulting from using wider film. 'Cinemiracle', a similar process, was short-lived.

The released Cinerama features were:
This is Cinerama 52. Cinerama Holiday 55. Seven Wonders of the World 56. Search for Paradise 57. South Seas Adventure 58. The Wonderful World of the Brothers Grimm 62. How the West Was Won 62. It's a Mad Mad Mad Mad World (single lens) 63. Circus World 64. The Best of Cinerama 64. Battle of the Bulge 65. Grand Prix 66. Cinerama's Russian Adventure 66. Ice Station Zebra 68. Custer of the West 68. 2001: A Space Odyssey 68. Krakatoa – East of Java 69.

Cioffi, Charles (1935–).
American character actor.
Klute 71. The Don is Dead 73. The Thief who Came to Dinner 73. Crazy Joe 74. The Next Man 76. The Other Side of Midnight 77. Dog and Cat (TV) 77. Time after Time 79. Missing 82. All the

Right Moves 83. Remo Williams: The Adventure Begins 85. Newsies (GB: News Boys) 92, etc.
TV series: Assignment Vienna 72. Get Christy Love 74. Kojak 89–90.

Cipriani, Stelvio.
Italian composer.
The Stranger Returns (El Precio de un Hombre) 66. La Belva 70. La Polizia Ringrazia 72. Blondy 75. Frankenstein – Italian Style 76. Vudu Baby 79. City of the Walking Dead 80. Sweet Sins 81. La Voce 82. Piranha II: The Spawning (US) 83. La Classe 84. Rage 84. Rage of Honor (US) 87, etc.

circuit.
A chain of cinemas under the same ownership, often playing the same release programme.

circuses,
according to the cinema, are full of drama and passion behind the scenes. So you would think if you judged from *Variety, Freaks, The Wagons Roll at Night, The Greatest Show on Earth, The Big Show, The Big Circus, Sawdust and Tinsel, Circus of Horrors, Tromba, Four Devils, The Three Maxims, Trapeze, Captive Wild Woman, Ring of Fear, Charlie Chan at the Circus, A Tiger Walks, Circus World, The Trojan Brothers, Circus of Fear, Berserk, The Dark Tower, He Who Gets Slapped, Flesh and Fantasy, Man on a Tightrope, Chad Hanna, Pagliacci, Far From the Madding Crowd,* and *Vampire Circus.* But there is a lighter side, as evidenced by *Doctor Dolittle, Yo Yo, Jumbo, High Wide and Handsome, Lady in the Dark, Life is a Circus, The Marx Brothers at the Circus, Three Rings Circus,* Chaplin's *The Circus, The Great Profile, You Can't Cheat an Honest Man, Road Show, Merry Andrew,* and *Toby Tyler.*

TV series have included *Circus Boy, Frontier Circus* and *The Greatest Show on Earth.*

Cissé, Souleymane Oumar (1940–).
Malian director. He studied cinema in Moscow from 1963–69 before returning to his homeland to make documentaries for the Ministry of Information.
The Young Girl (Den Moussa) 74. Work (Baara) 78. The Wind (Finye) 82. The Light (Yeleen) 87.

Clair, René (1898–1981) (René Chomette).
Distinguished French director of light comedy; he brought to the screen a nimble command of technique, an optimistic outlook, and a total lack of malice or message.
Novel: 1925, Star Turn.
■ Paris Qui Dort 23. Entr'acte 24. La Fantôme du Moulin Rouge 24. Le Voyage Imaginaire 25. La Proie du Vent 26. Les Deux Timides 28. *An Italian Straw Hat* 28. Sous les Toits de Paris 29. *Le Million* 31. A Nous la Liberté 31. Le Quatorze Juillet 33. Le Dernier Milliardaire 34. The Ghost Goes West 35. Break the News 36. The Flame of New Orleans 41. *I Married a Witch* 42. Forever and a Day (part) 43. It Happened Tomorrow 44. *And Then There Were None* 45. Le Silence est d'Or 47. La Beauté du Diable 49. *Les Belles de Nuit* 52. Les Grandes Manoeuvres 55. Porte des Lilas 56. Tout l'Or du Monde 60. Love and the Frenchwoman (part) 60. Les Quatres Vérités (part) 62. Les Fêtes Galantes 65.
◑ For creating films in which, by a dextrous combination of sound and picture, the feet of the characters appeared never to touch the ground. *Le Million.*

¶ Once too good to be called even the French Lubitsch, he now seems more like the French Mamoulian. – *Andrew Sarris, 1968*
A film-maker who would sooner raise a soufflé than roast an ox. – *Alexander Walker*

Claire, Ina (1892–1985) (Ina Fagan).
American stage actress who made occasional films.
The Puppet Crown 15. Wild Goose Chase 15. Polly with a Past 20. The Awful Truth 29. The Royal Family of Broadway 31. Rebound 31. The Greeks Had a Word for Them 32. Ninotchka 39. Claudia 43, etc.

clairvoyance
on the screen seems to have caused a remarkable amount of suffering to Edward G. Robinson: he was haunted by the effects of a prophecy in *Flesh and Fantasy*, *Nightmare* and *Night Has a Thousand Eyes*. Other frightened men for similar reasons were Claude Rains in *The Clairvoyant*, Dick Powell in *It Happened Tomorrow*, George Macready in *I Love a Mystery*, Mervyn Johns in *Dead of Night*, and Michael Hordern in *The Night My Number Came Up*.

Clampett, Bob (1914–1985).
American animator, in at or near the birth of Bugs Bunny, Porky Pig, Daffy Duck and Tweety, who went on to work in television, creating *Time for Beany* (1949–59) and *Beany and Cecil* (1959–67).
Lady Play Your Mandolin 31. The Lone Stranger and Porky 38. Jeepers Creepers 39. Falling Hare 43, etc.

Clancy, Tom (1947–).
Best-selling American writer of technological thrillers featuring CIA agent Jack Ryan. Alec Baldwin starred as Ryan in the first film; subsequently the role has been played by Harrison Ford.
The Hunt for Red October 90. Patriot Games 92. Clear and Present Danger 94.

¶ Giving your book to Hollywood is like turning your daughter over to a pimp. – *T.C.*

clapperboard.
A hinged board recording film details. At the beginning of each 'take' it is held before the camera for identification and then 'clapped' to make a starting point in the sound track. This point is then synchronized with the image of the closed board.

Clapton, Eric (1945–).
British rock guitarist, singer and composer. He was a member of the 60s groups The Yardbirds and Cream.
AS PERFORMER: Tommy 75. The Last Waltz 78. Eric Clapton and Friends (concert) 86, etc.
AS COMPOSER: The Hit 84. Edge of Darkness (TV) 86. Lethal Weapon 87. Homeboy 88. Lethal Weapon 2 89. Communion 89. Rush 91. Lethal Weapon 3 92, etc.

Clare, Mary (1894–1970).
British character actress, latterly in formidable matron roles.
Becket 24. Hindle Wakes 31. The Constant Nymph 33. The Clairvoyant 34. The Passing of the Third Floor Back 35. Young and Innocent 37. The Lady Vanishes 38. A Girl Must Live 39. Old Bill and Son 40. *Mrs Pym of Scotland Yard* (title role) 40. Next of Kin 42. *The Night Has Eyes* 42. The Hundred-Pound Window 44. The Three Weird Sisters 48. *Oliver Twist* 48. Moulin Rouge 53. Mambo 55. The Price of Silence 59, many others.

Clarence, O. B. (1870–1955).
British stage actor who played benevolent doddering roles in a number of films.
Liberty Hall 14. Perfect Understanding 32. Friday the Thirteenth 33. The Scarlet Pimpernel 34. Seven Sinners 36. Pygmalion 38. Inspector Hornleigh

Goes To It 41. Penn of Pennsylvania 42. On Approval 43. A Place of One's Own 44. Great Expectations (as the aged P) 46. Uncle Silas 47, many others.

Clark, Bob (1941–).
American director.
■ Children Shouldn't Play with Dead Things 72. Black Christmas 72. Breaking Point 76. Murder by Decree 78. Tribute 80. Porky's 82. Porky's II 83. A Christmas Story 83. Rhinestone 84. Turk 182 85. From the Hip 87. Loose Cannons 89. It Runs in the Family 94.

Clark, Bobby (1888–1960).
Bouncy American vaudeville comedian who with Paul McCullough made thirty-six two-reel comedies for RKO between 1928 and 1936, when McCullough died. Clark made only one solo film appearance, in *The Goldwyn Follies* 38.

Clark, Candy (1947–).
American leading lady of the 70s.
Fat City 72. American Graffiti (AAN) 73. The Man Who Fell to Earth 76. I Will, I Will, For Now 76. Citizen's Band 77. When You Comin' Back, Red Ryder? 79. More American Graffiti 79. Blue Thunder 83. Amityville 3-D 83. Hambone and Hilie 84. Stephen King's Cat's Eye 85. At Close Range 86. The Blob 88. Cool as Ice 91, etc.

Clark, Cliff (1893–1953).
Short, stocky American character actor who played tough sheriffs and police inspectors in 40s co-features.
Mr Moto's Gamble 38. Kentucky 39. Honolulu 39. The Grapes of Wrath 40. Double Alibi 40. Manpower 41. Kid Glove Killer 42. The Falcon's Brother 42. The Falcon in Danger 43. The Falcon out West 44. Bury Me Dead 47. Deep Waters 48. The Men 50. Cavalry Scout 51. The Sniper 52, many others.

Clark, Dane (1915–) (Bernard Zanville).
Pint-sized American tough guy of the 40s, a poor man's Garfield.
Tennessee Johnson 43. Destination Tokyo 43. The Very Thought of You 44. God is My Co-Pilot 45. A Stolen Life 46. Her Kind of Man 46. That Way with Women 47. Deep Valley 47. Whiplash 48. *Moonrise* 49. Barricade 50. Without Honour 50. Highly Dangerous (GB) 50. Go Man Go (& co-p) 53. Port of Hell 54. The Toughest Man Alive 55. Murder by Proxy (GB) 55. This Man is Armed 56. The Outlaw's Son 57. The McMasters 70. Say Goodbye, Maggie Cole (TV) 72. Murder on Flight 502 (TV) 75. James Dean (TV) 76. The Woman Inside 81. Blood Song 82. Last Rites 88, etc.
TV series: Justice 52. Bold Venture 54. Wire Service 56. The New Perry Mason 73.

Clark, Ernest (1912–).
British character actor of all media, usually in cold, tight-lipped roles.
Private Angelo 49. Doctor in the House 53. Beau Brummell 54. The Dam Busters 55. Time without Pity 57. A Tale of Two Cities 58. Sink the Bismarck 60. Nothing but the Best 64. Arabesque 66. Salt and Pepper 68. Gandhi 82, many others.

Clark, Fred (1914–1968).
Bald-domed American character comedian, usually in explosive roles.
■ The Unsuspected 47. Ride the Pink Horse 47. Hazard 48. Cry of the City 48. Two Guys from Texas 48. Fury at Furnace Creek 48. Alias Nick Beal 49. Flamingo Road 49. The Younger Brothers 49. Task Force 49. White Heat 49. The Lady Takes a

Sailor 49. *Sunset Boulevard* 50. The Eagle and the Hawk 50. Return of the Frontiersman 50. The Jackpot 50. Mrs O'Malley and Mr Malone 50. The Lemon Drop Kid 51. Hollywood Story 51. A Place in the Sun 51. Meet Me After the Show 51. Three for Bedroom C 52. Dreamboat 52. The Stars are Singing 53. The Caddy 53. How to Marry a Millionaire 53. Here Come the Girls 53. Living It Up 54. Abbott and Costello Meet the Keystone Kops 54. Daddy Longlegs 55. How to be Very Very Popular 55. The Court Martial of Billy Mitchell 55. Miracle in the Rain 56. The Birds and the Bees 56. *The Solid Gold Cadillac* 56. Back from Eternity 56. Joe Butterfly 57. The Fuzzy Pink Nightgown 57. *Don't Go Near the Water* 57. Mardi Gras 58. Auntie Mame 58. The Mating Game 59. It Started with a Kiss 59. Visit to a Small Planet 60. Bells are Ringing 60. Zotz 62. Boys' Night Out 62. Hemingway's Adventures of a Young Man 62. Move Over Darling 63. John Goldfarb Please Come Home 64. The Curse of the Mummy's Tomb (GB) 65. Sergeant Deadhead 65. Dr Goldfoot and the Bikini Machine 65. When the Boys meet the Girls 65. War Italian Style 67. The Horse in the Grey Flannel Suit 68. Skidoo 68. I Sailed to Tahiti with an All-Girl Crew 68.
TV series: *The Double Life of Henry Phyfe* 65. Also with Burns and Allen for several seasons.

Clark, Harvey (1886–1936).
American character actor, usually in comic roles, from the stage and vaudeville.
The Innocence of Lizette 16. The Kiss 21. Alias Julius Caesar 22. The Roughnecks 24. Black Paradise 26. Camille 27. The Olympic Hero 28. Seven Keys to Baldpate 29. Man Trouble 30. Cracked Nuts 31. The Big Shot 32. Red-Headed Woman 32. West of Singapore 33. Alice in Wonderland 33. Countess of Monte Cristo 34. Three Godfathers 36. The Singing Cowboy 36. History Is Made at Night 37. Spawn of the North 38, etc.

Clark, James B. (1908–).
American director, former editor.
Under Fire 57. Sierra Baron 58. The Sad Horse 59. A Dog of Flanders 60. One Foot in Hell 60. The Big Show 60. Misty 61. Flipper 63. Island of Blue Dolphins 64. And Now Miguel 66. My Side of the Mountain 68. The Little Ark 71, etc.

Clark, Jim (1931–).
British editor.
The Grass is Greener 61. The Innocents 61. Charade 63. The Pumpkin Eater 64. Darling 65. Zee and Co. 72. The Day of the Locust 75. Marathon Man 76. Yanks 79. Agatha 79. Honky Tonk Freeway 81. The Killing Fields (AA) 84. The Frog Prince 84. The Mission 86. Meeting Venus 90. This Boy's Life 93. A Good Man in Africa 94. Radio Inside 94, etc.
ALSO DIRECTOR: ■ The Christmas Tree 68. Every Home Should Have One 70. Rentadick 72. Madhouse 74.

Clark, Ken.
American supporting actor, usually in tough roles.
The Proud Ones 56. Between Heaven and Hell 56. Attack of the Giant Leeches 58. Hercules Against the Barbarians 64. From the Orient with Fury 65, many others.

Clark, Marguerite (1883–1940).
American heroine of the silent screen, a rival for Mary Pickford in waif-like and innocent roles. Retired 1921.
Wildflower 14. The Goose Girl 15. Molly Make-Believe 16. Snow White 17. Prunella 18. Mrs Wiggs

of the Cabbage Patch 18. Girls 19. All-of-a-Sudden Peggy 20. Scrambled Wives 21.

Clark, Matt. (1936–).
American character actor, mostly as western villain.

Will Penny 67. Monte Walsh 70. Emperor of the North 73. Hearts of the West 75. Kid Vengeance 77. Brubaker 80. The Legend of the Lone Ranger 81. Honkytonk Man 82. Love Letters 82. Country 84. Return to Oz 84. Tuff Turf 84. Out of the Darkness (TV) 85. The Quick and the Dead (TV) 87. The Horror Show 89, etc.

Clark, Petula (1932–).
British child actress who later made it big as a singer and settled in France.
■ Medal for the General 44. Murder in Reverse 45. I Know Where I'm Going 45. London Town 46. Strawberry Roan 47. Here Come the Huggetts 48. Vice Versa 48. Easy Money 48. Don't Ever Leave Me 49. Vote for Huggett 49. The Huggetts Abroad 50. Dance Hall 50. The Romantic Age 50. White Corridors 51. Madame Louise 51. Made in Heaven 52. The Card 52. The Runaway Bus 54. The Gay Dog 54. The Happiness of Three Women 55. Track the Man Down 56. That Woman Opposite 57. Daggers Drawn 64. Finian's Rainbow 68. Goodbye Mr Chips 69. Never Never Land 81.

Clark, Robert (1905–1984).
British executive, longtime director (resigned 1969) of Associated British Picture Corporation. Former lawyer; producer of many ABPC films including The Hasty Heart, The Dam Busters, etc.

Clark, Susan (1940–).
Canadian leading lady in Hollywood.
■ Banning 67. Madigan 68. Coogan's Bluff 68. Something for a Lonely Man (TV) 68. The Challengers (TV) 68. The Forbin Project 69. Tell Them Willie Boy Is Here 69. Skullduggery 69. Valdez Is Coming 70. The Skin Game 71. The Astronaut (TV) 71. Showdown 73. Trapped (TV) 73. Airport 75 74. The Midnight Man 74. The Apple Dumpling Gang 75. Babe (TV) 75. Night Moves 75. Amelia Earhart (TV) 76. Murder by Decree 78. Promises in the Dark 79. City on Fire 79. The North Avenue Irregulars 80. Double Negative 80. Nobody's Perfekt 81. Porky's 82. Maid in America (TV) 82.
TV series: Webster 83–88.

Clarke, Alan (1935–1990).
British director, from television, noted for his films of tough working-class life.
Scum 79. Contact (TV) 85. Made in Britain (TV) 83. Billy the Kid and the Green Baize Vampire 85. Rita, Sue and Bob, Too 87. The Firm (TV) 90, etc.

¶ I wouldn't make a film with the edge written out. – A.C.

Clarke, Arthur C. (1917–).
British science fiction writer who provided the basis for 2001: A Space Odyssey (AAN). Non-fiction interests include the popular science TV series of 1981, Arthur C. Clarke's Mysterious World.

Clarke, Charles G. (1899–1983).
American cinematographer.
The Light That Failed 23. Friendly Enemies 25. Whispering Smith 26. Upstream 27. The Exalted Flapper 29. So This Is London 30. The Cat and the Fiddle 34. Tarzan and His Mate 34. The Return of the Cisco Kid 39. Moontide 42. Guadalcanal Diary 43. Margie 46. Miracle on 34th Street 47. The Iron

Curtain 48. Sand 49. The Big Lift 50. Destination Gobi 53. Prince of Players 55. Carousel 56. The Barbarian and the Geisha 58. The Sound and the Fury 59. Return to Peyton Place 59. Madison Avenue 62, many others.

Clarke, Mae (1910–1992).
Pert American leading lady at her peak in the early 30s; from musical comedy. She may be best remembered for having a grapefruit ground into her face by James Cagney in Public Enemy. She was also the inspiration for Lorelei Lee in Anita Loos's Gentlemen Prefer Blondes.
Big Time 29. Fall Guy 30. The Front Page 31. Public Enemy 31. Waterloo Bridge 31. Frankenstein 31. Night World 32. The Penguin Pool Murder 32. Parole Girl 33. Penthouse 33. Lady Killer 33. Nana 34. The Silk Hat Kid 35. Wild Brian Kent 36. Trouble in Morocco 37. Women in War 40. Sailors on Leave 41. Flying Tigers 42. Here Come the Waves 44. Kitty 45. Daredevils of the Clouds 48. Annie Get Your Gun 50. The Great Caruso 51. Because of You 52. Women's Prison 55. Mohawk 56. Ask Any Girl 59. Big Hand for a Little Lady 66. Thoroughly Modern Millie 67, many others.

Clarke, Margi (1954–).
British actress, a former TV presenter.
Letter to Brezhnev 85. Helsinki Napoli All Night Long 87. I Hired a Contract Killer 90. Blonde Fist 91, etc.
TV series: Making Out 89–91. The Good Sex Guide 93–94.

Clarke, Shirley (1925–).
American director of the New York cinema vérité school.
The Connection 60. Cool World 63. Portrait of Jason 67, etc.

Clarke, Stanley (1951–).
American composer and bassist, a founding member of the 70s jazz group Return to Forever, and the Clark/Duke Project and Animal Logic.
Book of Love 91. Boyz N The Hood 91. Cool as Ice 91. The Five Heartbeats 91. Watch It 93. What's Love Got to Do with It? 93. Little Big League 94, etc.

Clarke, T. E. B. (1907–1989).
British screenwriter, former journalist; associated with the heyday of Ealing comedy.
Autobiography: 1974, This Is Where I Came In.
Johnny Frenchman 45. Against the Wind 46. Hue and Cry 46. Passport to Pimlico (AAN) 48. The Blue Lamp 50. The Lavender Hill Mob (AA) 51. The Titfield Thunderbolt 53. Barnacle Bill 57. Law and Disorder 58. Gideon's Day 58. Sons and Lovers (AAN) 60. The Horse Without a Head 63. A Man Could Get Killed 66, etc.

Clarke-Smith, D. A. (1888–1959).
British character actor, mainly on stage.
Atlantic 30. The Ghoul 33. Warn London 34. Sabotage 36. The Flying Fifty-Five 39. Frieda 47. Quo Vadis 51. The Baby and the Battleship 56, etc.

Clavell, James (1922–1994).
Australian writer of Anglo-Irish descent.
The Fly 58. Five Gates to Hell (& pd) 58. Walk Like a Dragon (& pd) 60. The Sweet and the Bitter (wpd) (Can.) 62. The Great Escape 63. The Satan Bug 65. King Rat (oa) 65. To Sir With Love (& pd) 66. Where's Jack? (& pd) 69. Shogun (TV) 80.

¶ I'm not a novelist, but a storyteller. I'm not a literary figure at all. – J.C.

Claxton, William F. (1914–).
American director.
Fangs of the Wild 55. The Quiet Gun 57. Desire in the Dust 60. Law of the Lawless 64. Night of the Lepus 72, etc.

Clay, Andrew Dice (1958–) (Andrew Clay Silverstein).
Controversial American comedian.
Making the Grade 84. Pretty in Pink 86. Amazon Women on the Moon 86. Casual Sex? 88. The Adventures of Ford Fairlane 90. Dice Rules 91. Brain Smasher 93, etc.

Clay, Nicholas (1946–).
British leading man.
The Night Digger 71. The Darwin Adventure 75. Tristan and Isolde 76. Zulu Dawn 78. Excalibur 81. Lady Chatterley's Lover 81. Evil under the Sun 82. Hound of the Baskervilles (TV) 83. Lionheart 87, etc.

Clayburgh, Jill (1944–).
American leading lady of the 70s. She married dramatist and screenwriter David Rabe in 1979.
■ The Wedding Party 69. The Telephone Book 71. Portnoy's Complaint 72. The Thief Who Came to Dinner 73. The Terminal Man 74. The Art of Crime (TV) 74. Hustling (TV) 74. Griffin and Phoenix (TV) 76. Gable and Lombard (as Lombard) 76. Silver Streak 76. Semi-Tough 77. An Unmarried Woman (AAN) 78. La Luna 79. Starting Over (AAN) 79. It's My Turn 80. First Monday in October 81. I'm Dancing as Fast as I Can 82. Hannah K 83. Where Are The Children? 85. Shy People 87. Beyond the Ocean 90. Day of Atonement (Le Grand Pardon 2) 92. Whispers in the Dark 92. Naked in New York 93.

Clayton, Ethel (1884–1966).
American silent star actress.
Her Own Money 12. The College Widow 15. Pettigrew's Girl 19. Sham 21. If I Were Queen 22. The Remittance Woman 23. Wings of Youth 25. Mother Machree 28. Hit the Deck 30. Continental 32. Secrets 33. Artists and Models 37. The Buccaneer 38. Ambush 39, many others.

Clayton, Jack (1921–1995).
British producer-director who worked his way up through the industry.
■ The Bespoke Overcoat (pd) 55. Three Men in a Boat (p) 56. Room at the Top (AANd) 58. The Innocents (d) 61. The Pumpkin Eater (d) 64. Our Mother's House (d) 67. The Great Gatsby (d) 74. Something Wicked This Way Comes 83. The Lonely Passion of Judith Hearne 87. Memento Mori (TV) 92.

¶ I don't believe in being fashionable. Try to be, and you're usually out of date before you start. – J.C.

Cleese, John (1939–).
Tall British comic actor, often on TV satirizing familiar types.
Interlude 68. The Best House in London 68. The Rise and Rise of Michael Rimmer 70. And Now for Something Completely Different 71. The Love Ban 72. Monty Python and the Holy Grail 74. The Life of Brian 79. The Secret Policeman's Ball 80. Time Bandits 82. Privates on Parade 82. Monty Python and the Meaning of Life 83. Yellowbeard 83. Clockwise 85. A Fish Called Wanda (& p, w) (AAN) 88. The Big Picture 89. Erik the Viking 89. Bullseye! 90. An American Tail: Fievel Goes West (voice) 91. Splitting Heirs 93. Mary Shelley's Frankenstein 94. The Jungle Book 95, etc.
TV series: Fawlty Towers 75, 79.

¶ Filming is like a long air journey: there's so much hanging around and boredom that they keep giving you food. – *J.C.*

Clemens, Brian (1931–).

British screenwriter especially associated with *The Avengers;* author of many TV thrillers.

Station Six Sahara 64. The Corrupt Ones 64. And Soon the Darkness 70. See No Evil 71. Dr Jekyll and Sister Hyde 71. Captain Kronos Vampire Hunter (&d) 72. The Golden Voyage of Sinbad 73. The Watcher in the Woods 80, etc.

Clemens, William (1905–).

American director of second features.

■ Man Hunt 36. The Law in Her Hands 36. The Case of the Velvet Claws 36. Down the Stretch 36. Here Comes Carter 37. Once a Doctor 37. The Case of the Stuttering Bishop 37. Talent Scout 37. The Footloose Heiress 37. Missing Witnesses 37. Torchy Blane in Panama 38. Accidents Will Happen 38. Mr Chump 38. Nancy Drew Detective 38. Nancy Drew Reporter 39. Nancy Drew Trouble Shooter 39. Nancy Drew and the Hidden Staircase 39. The Dead End Kids on Dress Parade 39. Calling Philo Vance 40. King of the Lumberjacks 40. Devil's Island 40. She Couldn't Say No 41. Knockout 41. The Night of January 16th 41. A Night in New Orleans 42. Sweater Girl 42. Lady Bodyguard 43. The Falcon in Danger 43. The Falcon and the Co-Eds 43. The Falcon Out West 44. Crime by Night 44. The Thirteenth Hour 47.

Clément, Aurore.

French leading actress.

Lacombe Lucien 73. Caro Michele 76. Apocalypse Now 79. Lovers and Liars 79. Paris, Texas 84. Le Livre de Marie. Stan the Flasher 90. Eline Vere 91. Pas d'Amour sans Amour 92, etc.

Clement, Dick (1937–).

British writer-director.

The Jokers (co-w) 67. *Otley* (co-w, d) 69. A Severed Head (d) 70. Villain (w) 71. Catch Me a Spy (co-w, d) 71. The Likely Lads 76. The Prisoner of Zenda (w) 79. Porridge (wd) 79. Bullshot (d) 83. Water (d) 84. Vice Versa (co-w) 88. The Commitments (co-w) 91, etc.

Clément, René (1913–).

Distinguished French director whose later films have disappointed.

■ *Bataille du Rail* 43. Les Maudits 46. Le Père Tranquille 46. Au Dela des Grilles 49. Le Château de Verre 50. *Les Jeux Interdits* 51. Knave of Hearts (GB) 53. *Gervaise* 55. The Sea Wall 56. Plein Soleil 59. Quelle Joie de Vivre 61. The Day and the Hour 63. The Love Cage 65. Is Paris Burning? 66. Rider on the Rain 69. The House under the Trees 71. And Hope to Die 72. Wanted: Babysitter 75.

Clementi, Pierre (1941–).

French leading actor.

The Leopard 63. *Belle de Jour* 67. Benjamin 68. The Milky Way 68. Pigsty 70. The Conformist 71. Steppenwolf 74. Les Apprentis Sorciers 77. La Chanson de Roland 78. Zoo-Zero 78. L'Amour des Femmes 81. Le Pont du Nord 81. Quartet 81. Exposed 83. Canicule 84. Clash 84. A L'ombre de la Canaille Bleue (& wd) 86. Hard to Be a God 89, etc.

Clements, Sir John (1910–1988).

Distinguished British actor-manager, on stage from 1930. He married actress Kay Hammond in 1946.

Ticket of Leave 35. Things to Come 36. Rembrandt 36. Knight Without Armour 36.

South Riding 38. The Housemaster 39. *The Four Feathers* 39. Convoy 40. This England 41. Ships with Wings 41. Tomorrow We Live 42. Undercover 42. They Came to a City 45. Call of the Blood (& wpd) 47. The Silent Enemy 57. *The Mind Benders* 63. Oh What a Lovely War 69. Gandhi 82, etc.

Clements, Stanley (1926–1981).

American actor familiar in the 40s as tough teenager.

Tall Dark and Handsome 41. Going My Way 44. Salty O'Rourke 45. Bad Boy 49. Jet Job 52. Robbers' Roost 55. Up in Smoke 59. Saintly Sinners 61. Tammy and the Doctor 63, many others.

Cleopatra (69–30 BC).

The sultry Egyptian queen has been portrayed in many films, notably in a Méliès trick film of 1899; by unspecified American actresses in 1908 and 1909; by Helen Gardner in 1911; by Theda Bara in 1917; by Claudette Colbert in the de Mille version of 1934; by Vivien Leigh in Pascal's 1945 *Caesar and Cleopatra;* by Rhonda Fleming in *Serpent of the Nile* 1953; by Hedy Lamarr in *The Story of Mankind* 1957; by Elizabeth Taylor in the well-publicized 1962 version; and by Amanda Barrie in a spoof, *Carry On Cleo,* in 1963. There seems to be something about the lady that encourages waste, for the Leigh version was Britain's most expensive film and the Taylor version the world's; in neither case did the money show on the screen.

Cleveland, George (1886–1957).

American character actor, typically cast as grizzled old prospector.

Keeper of the Bees 35. Revolt of the Zombies 36. Goldtown Ghost Riders 38. Port of Missing Girls 38. Mutiny in the Big House 39. Call Out the Marines 41. The Spoilers 42. Woman of the Town 44. Can't Help Singing 44. Dakota 45. The Runaround 46. The Wistful Widow of Wagon Gap 47. Please Believe Me 50. Trigger Jnr 52. Untamed Heiress 54, many others.

TV series: *Lassie* 55–57.

Cliff, Laddie (1891–1937) (Clifford Perry).

British light comedian and composer.

The Co-Optimists 29. Sleeping Car 33. Happy 33, etc.

cliffhanger.

Trade name for a serial, especially an episode ending in an unresolved situation which keeps one in suspense till next time.

Clifford, Graeme.

Australian director and screenwriter, a former film editor.

AS EDITOR: Don't Look Now 74. The Rocky Horror Picture Show 76. The Man Who Fell to Earth 76. F.I.S.T. 78. Convoy 78. The Postman Always Rings Twice 81, etc.

AS DIRECTOR: Frances 82. Burke & Wills (& w) 85. Gleaming the Cube 88. Turn of the Screw (TV) 89. Ruby Cairo 93, etc.

Clift, Montgomery (1920–1966).

Romantic American leading actor of stage and screen, usually in introspective roles; his career was jeopardized in 1956 by a car accident which somewhat disfigured him.

Biographies: 1977, *Monty* by Robert La Guardia. 1978, *Montgomery Clift* by Patricia Bosworth.

■ *The Search* 48. *Red River* 48. The Heiress 49. The Big Lift 50. *A Place in the Sun* (AAN) 51. I Confess 53. *From Here to Eternity* (AAN) 53. Indiscretion of an American Wife 54. Raintree County 57. The Young Lions 58. Lonelyhearts 59. Suddenly Last

Summer 59. Wild River 60. The Misfits 60. Judgment at Nuremberg (AAN) 61. *Freud* 63. The Defector 66.

Clifton, Elmer (1890–1949).

American director, mainly of second features; started as an actor with Griffith.

Boots 19. Nugget Nell 19. Mary Ellen Comes to Town 21. Down to the Sea in Ships 22. The Wreck of the Hesperus 27. Virgin Lips 28. Six Cylinder Love 31. Crusade against Rackets 37. Isle of Destiny 40. Swamp Woman 41. Seven Doors to Death 44. Not Wanted 49, many others.

Cline, Edward (1892–1961).

American comedy director who began with the Sennett bathing beauties.

Summer Girls 18. Three Ages 23. Captain January 24. Old Clothes 25. *Sherlock Junior* 26. Let it Rain 27. Soft Cushions 27. Ladies Night in a Turkish Bath 27, etc.

■ SOUND FILMS INCOMPLETE: Broadway Fever 29. His Lucky Day 29. The Forward Pass 29. In the Next Room 30. Sweet Mama 30. Leathernecking 30. Hook Line and Sinker 30. The Widow from Chicago 30. Cracked Nuts 31. The Naughty Flirt 31. The Girl Habit 31. *Million Dollar Legs* 32. Parole Girl 33. So This is Africa 33. Peck's Bad Boy 34. The Dude Ranger 34. When a Man's a Man 35. The Cowboy Millionaire 35. It's a Great Life 35. F Man 36. On Again Off Again 37. Forty Naughty Girls 37. High Flyers 37. Hawaii Calls 38. Go Chase Yourself 38. Breaking the Ice 38. Peck's Bad Boy with the Circus 38. *My Little Chickadee* 40. The Villain Still Pursued Her 40. *The Bank Dick* 40. Meet the Chump 41. Cracked Nuts 41. Hello Sucker 41. *Never Give a Sucker an Even Break* 41. Snuffy Smith 32. What's Cookin' 42. Private Buckaroo 42. Give Out Sisters 42. Behind the Eight Ball 42. He's My Guy 43. Crazy House 43. Swingtime Johnny 44. Ghost Catchers 44. Slightly Terrific 44. Moonlight and Cactus 44. Night Club Girl 44. See My Lawyer 45. Penthouse Rhythm 45. Bringing Up Father 46. Jiggs and Maggie in Society 48. Jiggs and Maggie in Court 48.

Clitheroe, Jimmy (1916–1973).

Diminutive (4 ft 2 ins tall) English comedian, who spent a lifetime playing a naughty schoolboy, mainly on his long-running radio show *The Clitheroe Kid* 58–72, and occasionally in films.

Old Mother Riley in Business 40. Much Too Shy 42. Rhythm Serenade 43. Somewhere in Politics 49. School for Randle 49. Stars in Your Eyes 56. Rocket to the Moon 67, etc.

Clive, Colin (1898–1937) (Clive Greig).

British leading man who looked older than his years; in Hollywood from 1930, playing fraught, serious roles. Died of TB complicated by alcoholism.

■ *Journey's End* 30. Frankenstein (title role) 31. The Stronger Sex (GB) 31. Lily Christine (GB) 32. Christopher Strong 33. Looking Forward 33. The Key 34. *Jane Eyre* (as Rochester) 34. One More River 34. Clive of India 35. The Right to Live 35. *The Bride of Frankenstein* 35. The Girl from Tenth Avenue 35. Mad Love 35. The Man who Broke the Bank at Monte Carlo 35. *History is Made at Night* 37. The Woman I Love 37.

Clive, E. E. (1879–1940).

British character actor who came late in life to Hollywood and played a succession of sour-faced but often amiable butlers, burgomasters and statesmen, with a sprinkling of lower orders.

■ The Invisible Man 33. The Poor Rich 34. The Gay Divorcee 34. Long Lost Father 34. One More

River 34. Riptide 34. Bulldog Drummond Strikes Back 34. Charlie Chan in London 34. The Mystery of Edwin Drood 35. *The Bride of Frankenstein* 35. Remember Last Night 35. We're in the Money 35. Gold Diggers of 1935 35. Stars Over Broadway 35. A Tale of Two Cities 35. Captain Blood 35. Atlantic Adventure 35. Father Brown Detective 35. Sylvia Scarlett 35. The Widow from Monte Carlo 35. The King Steps Out 36. Little Lord Fauntleroy 36. Love Before Breakfast 36. Dracula's Daughter 36. The Unguarded Hour 36. Trouble for Two 36. Piccadilly Jim 36. All American Champ 36. Libeled Lady 36. Tarzan Escapes 36. Isle of Fury 36. *The Charge of the Light Brigade* 36. Cain and Mabel 36. Palm Springs 36. Ticket to Paradise 36. Lloyds of London 36. The Dark Hour 36. Live, Love and Learn 36. They Wanted to Marry 37. Maid of Salem 37. Bulldog Drummond Escapes 37. *Bulldog Drummond Comes Back* 37. Bulldog Drummond's Revenge 37. Ready Willing and Able 37. It's Love I'm After 37. On the Avenue 37. Love Under Fire 37. Danger Love at Work 37. *Personal Property* 37. Night Must Fall 37. The Emperor's Candlesticks 37. Beg Borrow or Steal 37. Arsène Lupin Returns 38. The First Hundred Years 38. The Last Warning 38. Kidnapped 38. Gateway 38. Submarine Patrol 38. Bulldog Drummond's Peril 38. Bulldog Drummond in Africa 38. Arrest Bulldog Drummond 39. I'm from Missouri 39. The Little Princess 39. Bulldog Drummond's Secret Police 39. Man About Town 39. Bulldog Drummond's Bride 39. The Hound of the Baskervilles 39. Rose of Washington Square 39. The Adventures of Sherlock Holmes 39. The Honeymoon's Over 39. Raffles 39. Bachelor Mother 39. The Earl of Chicago 40. Congo Maisie 40. Pride and Prejudice 40. Foreign Correspondent 40.

Cloche, Maurice (1907–1990).
French director, in films (as documentarist) from 1933.
     La Vie est Magnifique 38. Monsieur Vincent 47. Cage aux Filles 48. Né de Père Inconnu 50. Les Filles de la Nuit 57. Coplan, Secret Agent 64. Mais Toi, Tu Es Pierre 71. Hommes de Rose (TV) 77, etc.

Cloerec, René (1911–).
French composer.
     Douce 43. Le Diable au Corps 46. The Red Inn 51. Occupe-Toi d'Amélie 51. La Blé en Herbe 53. En Cas de Malheur 57, many others.

Clooney, Rosemary (1928–).
Breezy American cabaret singer who made a few film appearances. A TV movie, *Rosie*, was filmed in 1982. She was married to José Ferrer (1953– 67) and is the mother of actor Miguel Ferrer.
     Autobiography: 1977, *This for Remembrance*.
■ The Stars are Singing 53. Here Come the Girls 53. *Red Garters* 54. *White Christmas* 54. Deep in My Heart 54.

Cloquet, Ghislain (1924–1981).
Belgian cinematographer.
     Night and Fog (Nuit et Brouillard) 55. The Fire Within (Le Feu Follet) 63. Mickey One 65. Au Hasard, Balthazar 66. The Young Girls of Rochefort 67. Une Femme Douche 69. Donkey Skin (Peau d'âne) 70. Pouce 71. Rendez-vous à Bray 71. Belle 73. Love and Death 75. Monsieur Albert 75. Tess (AA) 79. I Sent a Letter to My Love (Chère Inconnue) 80. Four Friends 81, etc.

Close, Glenn (1947–).
American leading actress. She played the role of Norma Desmond in Los Angeles and on Broadway

in Andrew Lloyd Webber's musical version of *Sunset Boulevard*.
     The World According to Garp (AAN) 82. The Big Chill (AAN) 84. Something about Amelia (TV) 84. The Natural (AAN) 84. Maxie 85. *Jagged Edge* 85. *Fatal Attraction* (AAN) 87. Dangerous Liaisons (AAN) 88. Light Years (voice) 88. Immediate Family 89. Hamlet 90. Reversal of Fortune 90. Meeting Venus 90. The House of the Spirits 94. The Paper 94. Mary Roberts 95, etc.

¶ Mine is not a face that can take care of itself. If I want to look beautiful in movies I have to have help with lighting and camera angles. – *G.C.*

close-up.
Generally applied to a head-and-shoulders shot of a person or any close shot of an object. The first close-up is said to be that of Fred Ott sneezing in an Edison experimental film of 1900. See: *long shot*.

Clothier, William H. (1903–).
American cinematographer.
     Sofia 48. Confidence Girl 52. Track of the Cat 54. Blood Alley 55. The Man in the Vault 56. The Horse Soldiers 59. The Alamo 60. The Deadly Companions 61. The Man Who Shot Liberty Valance 62. A Distant Trumpet 64. Cheyenne Autumn 64. Shenandoah 65. The Way West 67. The War Wagon 67. Firecreek 67. The Devil's Brigade 68. Hellfighters 68. The Cheyenne Social Club 70. Big Jake 71. The Train Robbers 73, etc.

Clouse, Robert.
American director.
     Happy Mothers Day, Love George (w only) 73. Enter the Dragon 73. Golden Needles 74. Black Belt Jones 74. The Ultimate Warrior (wd) 74. The Pack 77. The Amsterdam Kill 78. The Big Brawl 80. Force Five 81. Night Eyes 83. Dark Warrior 84. Gymkata 85. China O'Brien 89, etc.

Cloutier, Suzanne (1927–).
French-Canadian leading lady. She was married to Peter Ustinov (1954–71).
     Temptation (US) 46. Au Royaume des Cieux 47. Juliette ou la Clef des Songes 50. Othello 51. Derby Day (GB) 51. Moulin Rouge 53. Romanoff and Juliet (US) 61, etc.

Clouzot, Henri-Georges (1907–1977).
French writer-director, noted for suspense melodramas.
     Un Soir de Rafle (w) 31. Le Dernier des Six (w) 41. Les Inconnus dans la Maison (w) 42. L'Assassin Habite au 21 (wd) 42. *Le Corbeau* (wd) 43. *Quai des Orfèvres* (wd) 47. Manon (wd) 49. Retour à la Vie (wd) 49. *The Wages of Fear* (wd) 53. *Les Diaboliques* (wd) 54. The Picasso Mystery (wd) 56. Les Espions (wd) 57. The Truth (wd) (AA) 60. La Prisonnière (wd) 70. L'Enfer (co-w) 94, etc.

Clouzot, Vera (1921–1960).
Portuguese actress, wife of H. G. Clouzot.
     The Wages of Fear 53. Les Diaboliques 54. Les Espions 57, etc.

Clunes, Alec (1912–1970).
British stage actor who made occasional film appearances.
     Convoy 40. Saloon Bar 40. Melba 53. Quentin Durward 56. *Richard III* 56. Tomorrow at Ten 62, etc.

Clunes, Martin (1963–).
English comic actor and director.
     Staggered (a, d) 94. An Evening with Gary Lineker (TV) 94.

TV series: Men Behaving Badly 92–94. Demob 93.

Clurman, Harold (1901–1980).
American stage director chiefly associated with New York's Group Theatre of the 30s. Directed one very pretentious film: *Deadline at Dawn* 46.
     Autobiography: 1974, *All People Are Famous*.

Clute, Chester (1891–1956).
American character comedian. His startled look, small stature, tiny moustache and bald pate made him an inimitable henpecked husband or harassed clerk in scores of films.
     Dance Charlie Dance 37. Rascals 38. Annabel Takes a Tour 38. Dancing Co-Ed 39. Hired Wife 40. She Couldn't Say No 41. Yankee Doodle Dandy 42. Chatterbox 43. Arsenic and Old Lace 44. Guest Wife 45. Angel on my Shoulder 46. Something in the Wind 47. Mary Ryan Detective 50, many others.

Clyde, Andy (1892–1967).
Scottish acrobatic comedian, long in Hollywood as western side-kick and hero of innumerable two-reelers, often as grizzled, toothless old fool.
     The Goodbye Kiss 28. Million Dollar Legs 32. The Little Minister 34. McFadden's Flats 35. Two in a Crowd 36. Abe Lincoln in Illinois 39. The Green Years 46, many others.
     TV series: The Real McCoys 57–60. Lassie 63. No Time for Sergeants 64–65.

Clyde, June (1909–1987).
American musical comedy actress who played leading roles in the 30s and character parts thereafter. She was working in vaudeville, billed as Baby Tetrazzini, from the age of eight and was in Britain from the mid-30s. Married to director Thornton Freedland.
     Tanned Legs 29. Hit the Deck 30. Arizona (GB: The Virtuous Wife) 31. Back Street 32. Steady Company 32. Cohens and Kellys in Hollywood 32. Radio Patrol 32. Only Yesterday 33. A Study in Scarlet 33. Dance Band (GB) 35. Charing Cross Road (GB) 35. She Shall Have Music (GB) 35. School for Husbands (GB) 37. Unfinished Business 41. Sealed Lips 41. Hi Ya, Chum (GB: Everything Happens to Us) 43. Treasure Hunt (GB) 52. The Love Lottery (GB) 53. After the Ball (GB) 57. The Story of Esther Costello 57, etc.

coal mines
and the bravery of the men who work in them formed a theme which commanded the respect of cinema audiences for many years. Apart from Kameradschaft (the French-German border), Black Fury (US), and The Molly Maguires (US), all the major films on this subject have been about Britain: *The Proud Valley, The Stars Look Down, How Green Was My Valley, The Citadel, The Corn is Green, The Brave Don't Cry, Sons and Lovers, Women in Love.*

Coates, Anne V. (1925–).
British editor.
     Grand National Night 53. Lost 56. The Horse's Mouth 59. Tunes of Glory 60. Lawrence of Arabia (AA) 63. Becket (AAN) 64. The Bofors Gun 68. The Adventurers 70. Bequest to the Nation 73. Murder on the Orient Express 74. The Eagle Has Landed 76. The Legacy 79. The Elephant Man (AAN) 80. Ragtime 81. The Bushido Blade 81. Greystoke: The Legend of Tarzan, Lord of the Apes 84. Lady Jane 86. Farewell to the King 89. What About Bob? 91. Chaplin 92. In the Line of Fire (AAN) 93, etc.

Coates, Eric (1886–1957).
British composer.
■ The Old Curiosity Shop 35. Nine Men 43. The Dam Busters 55. High Flight 57.

Cobb, Irvin S. (1876–1944).
American humorous writer who appeared in a few films and was touted as another Will Rogers after that actor's death.
■ Pardon My French 21. Peck's Bad Boy 21. The Five Dollar Baby 22. The Great White Way 24. Turkish Delight 27. *Steamboat Round the Bend* 34. Everybody's Old Man 36. Pepper 36. Hawaii Calls 38. The Arkansas Traveller 38. The Young in Heart 38.

Cobb, Joe (1917–).
American child actor, the original fat boy in the Our Gang comedy shorts in the 20s and early 30s.

Cobb, Lee J. (1911–1976) (Leo Jacoby).
Powerful American character actor who forsook stage for screen.
■ North of the Rio Grande 37. Ali Baba Goes to Town 37. Rustler's Valley 37. Danger on the Air 38. The Phantom Creeps 39. *Golden Boy* 39. Men of Boys' Town 41. This Thing Called Love 41. Paris Calling 42. Tonight We Raid Calais 43. Buckskin Frontier 43. *The Moon is Down* 43. The Song of Bernadette 43. Winged Victory 44. *Anna and the King of Siam* 46. Boomerang 47. Johnny O'Clock 47. Captain from Castile 47. Call Northside 777 48. The Miracle of the Bells 48. The Luck of the Irish 48. *The Dark Past* 48. Thieves' Highway 49. The Man Who Cheated Himself 50. Sirocco 51. The Family Secret 51. The Fighter 52. The Tall Texan 53. Yankee Pasha 54. Gorilla at Large 54. *On the Waterfront* (AAN) 54. Day of Triumph 54. The Racers 55. The Road to Denver 55. The Left Hand of God 55. *The Man in the Grey Flannel Suit* 56. Miami Exposé 56. *Twelve Angry Men* 57. The Garment Jungle 57. The Three Faces of Eve 57. The Brothers Karamazov (AAN) 58. Man of the West 58. Party Girl 58. The Trap 59. Green Mansions 59. But Not for Me 59. Exodus 60. The Four Horsemen of the Apocalypse 62. How the West Was Won 62. *Come Blow Your Horn* 63. Our Man Flint 66. In Like Flint 67. Il Giorno della Civetta (It.) 67. Mackenna's Gold 68. Coogan's Bluff 68. They Came to Rob Las Vegas 68. The Liberation of L. B. Jones 70. Macho Callahan 70. Lawman 70. Heat of Anger (TV) 71. Double Indemnity (TV) 73. The Exorcist 73. The Man Who Loved Cat Dancing 73. Dr Max (TV) 74. The Great Ice Rip-Off (TV) 74. Trapped Beneath the Sea (TV) 74. That Lucky Touch 75. Blood, Sweat and Fear (It.) 75.
TV series: *The Virginian* 62–66. The Young Lawyers 70.

Cobb, Ty (1886–1961) (Tyrus Raymond Cobb).
Legendary American baseball player and occasional actor in baseball movies. A biopic of his life was made in 1994 by Ron Shelton starring Tommy Lee Jones.
Somewhere in Georgia in 16 16. The Ninth Innings 42. Angels in the Outfield 51.

Cobert, Bob (1926–).
American composer who has also scored television movies.
Ladybug, Ladybug 63. House of Dark Shadows 70. Night of Dark Shadows 71. Dracula (TV) 74. Burnt Offerings 76. Scalpel 76. The Scarlet Pimpernel (TV) 82. The Winds of War (TV) 83. War and Remembrance (TV) 89, etc.

Coborn, Charles (1852–1945) (Colin McCallum).
British music-hall artiste famous for his longevity and his rendering of 'The Man Who Broke the Bank at Monte Carlo'.
Say it with Flowers 34. Music Hall 35. Variety Jubilee 41, etc.

Coburn, Charles (1877–1961).
Distinguished American actor. A stage star for many years, he came late in life to Hollywood and delighted audiences for another twenty years in roles of crusty benevolence.
■ Boss Tweed 33. The People's Enemy 35. Of Human Hearts 38. Vivacious Lady 38. Yellow Jack 38. Lord Jeff 38. Idiot's Delight 39. The Story of Alexander Graham Bell 39. Made for Each Other 39. *Bachelor Mother* 39. Stanley and Livingstone 39. In Name Only 39. Road to Singapore 40. Florian 40. Edison the Man 40. Three Faces West 40. The Captain is a Lady 40. *The Lady Eve* 41. *The Devil and Miss Jones* (AAN) 41. Our Wife 41. Unexpected Uncle 41. H. M. Pulham Esq. 41. Kings Row 41. In This Our Life 42. George Washington Slept Here 42. *The More the Merrier* (AA) 43. The Constant Nymph 43. *Heaven Can Wait* 43. Princess O'Rourke 43. My Kingdom for a Cook 43. *Knickerbocker Holiday* 44. Wilson 44. The Impatient Years 44. Together Again 44. A Royal Scandal 45. Rhapsody in Blue 45. Over 21 45. Colonel Effingham's Raid 45. Shady Lady 45. *The Green Years* (AAN) 46. Lured 47. BF's Daughter 48. The Paradine Case 48. Green Grass of Wyoming 48. Impact 49. Yes Sir That's My Baby 49. Everybody Does It 49. The Doctor and the Girl 49. The Gal who Took the West 49. Louisa 50. Peggy 50. Mr Music 50. The Highwayman 51. *Monkey Business* 52. *Has Anybody Seen My Gal?* 52. Gentlemen Prefer Blondes 53. Trouble along the Way 53. The Long Wait 54. The Rocket Man 54. How to Be Very Very Popular 55. The Power and the Prize 56. Around the World in Eighty Days 56. Town on Trial 57. The Story of Mankind 57. How to Murder a Rich Uncle 57. Stranger in My Arms 59. The Remarkable Mr Pennypacker 59. John Paul Jones (as Benjamin Franklin) 59. Pepe 60.
🌑 For becoming a beloved international star after the age of sixty. *The More the Merrier*.
Famous line (to Marilyn Monroe, playing his secretary in *Monkey Business*): 'Find someone to type this.'

Famous line (to Barbara Stanwyck in *The Lady Eve*): 'We must be crooked but never common.'

Coburn, James (1928–).
American leading man of lithe movement and easy grin; career has been patchy.
■ Ride Lonesome 59. Face of a Fugitive 59. *The Magnificent Seven* 60. Hell is for Heroes 62. The Great Escape 63. *Charade* 63. The Man from Galveston 64. The Americanization of Emily 64. Major Dundee 65. A High Wind in Jamaica 65. The Loved One 65. *Our Man Flint* 66. What Did You Do in the War, Daddy? 66. Dead Heat on a Merry Go Round 66. In Like Flint 67. Waterhole Three 67. The President's Analyst 67. Duffy 68. Candy 68. Hard Contract 68. Blood Kin 69. *A Fistful of Dynamite* 71. The Carey Treatment 72. The Honkers 72. A Reason to Live, A Reason to Die 72. Pat Garrett and Billy the Kid 73. The Last of Sheila 73. Harry in Your Pocket 73. The Internecine Project (GB) 74. Bite the Bullet 75. Hard Times 75. The Last Hard Men 75. Midway 76. Sky Riders 76. Cross of Iron 77. The Dain Curse (TV) 78. California Suite 78. Firepower 79. The Muppet Movie 79. Goldengirl (TV) 79. Loving Couples 80. The Baltimore Bullet 80. Mr Patman 80. Looker 81. High Risk 81. Malibu (TV) 83.

Digital Dreams 83. Draw! 84. Sins of the Father (TV 85. Martin's Day 85. The Lions Roar 85. The Leonski Incident 85. Death of a Soldier 86. Walking after Midnight 88. Call from Space 89. Train to Heaven (Tag Till Himlen) 89. Young Gun II 90. Hudson Hawk 91. Deadfall 93. Sister Act 2: Back in the Habit 93. Ray Alexander: A Taste for Justice (TV) 94. Maverick 94.
TV series: Klondike 60. Acapulco 61. Darkroom 81–82.

Coca, Imogene (1908–).
American TV and revue comedienne. Rare film appearances.
Under the Yum Yum Tree 64. Rabbit Test 78. The Return of the Beverly Hillbillies (TV) 81. National Lampoon's Vacation 83. Nothing Lasts Forever 84 Buy and Cell 89, etc.
TV series: *Grindl* 63. It's About Time 66.

Cochise (c. 1818–1874).
Peace-loving Apache Indian chief who became a prominent cinema character after Jeff Chandler played him in *Broken Arrow* 50, and later in *Battle at Apache Pass* 52 and *Taza Son of Cochise* 53. John Hodiak took over for *Conquest of Cochise* 53. Previously, Antonio Moreno had played him in *Valley of the Sun* and Miguel Inclan in *Fort Apache*. Michael Ansara took over in the TV series *Broken Arrow*.

Cochran, Steve (1917–1965) (Robert Cochran).
American leading man, usually a good-looking heavy, in mainly poor films.
Wonder Man 45. The Best Years of Our Lives 46. The Chase 46. The Kid from Brooklyn 47. A Song is Born 48. White Heat 49. The Damned Don't Cry 50. *Storm Warning* 50. The Tanks are Coming 51. Operation Secret 52. The Desert Song 53. Carnival Story 54. *Come Next Spring* 56. The Weapon (GB) 56. I, Mobster 58. The Beat Generation 59. The Deadly Companions 61. Of Love and Desire 63. Mozambique 65, etc.

Coco, James (1928–1987).
Chubby American comic actor.
■ Ensign Pulver 64. Generation 69. End of the Road 70. The Strawberry Statement 70. Tell Me That You Love Me Junie Moon 70. A New Leaf 71. Such Good Friends 71. Man of La Mancha 72. *The Wild Party* 75. Murder by Death 76. Bye Bye Monkey 78. The Cheap Detective 78. Charleston 78. Scavenger Hunt 79. Wholly Moses 80. Only When I Laugh (AAN) 81. The Muppets Take Manhattan 84. Hunk 87. The Chair (aka Hot Seat) 89. That's Adequate 90.
TV series: Calucci's Department 73. The Dumplings 76.

Cocteau, Jean (1889–1963).
Fanciful French poet and writer who occasionally dabbled in cinema with effective if slightly obscure results.
■ Le Sang d'un Poète (wd) 30. La Comédie du Bonheur (w) 40. Le Baron Fantôme (w) 43. L'Eternel Retour (w) 43. Les Dames du Bois de Boulogne (co-w) 44. *La Belle et la Bête* (w, co-d) 46. Ruy Blas (w) 47. L'Aigle á Deux Têtes (d) 48. Les Parents Terribles (wd) 48. Les Enfants Terribles (w) 50. *Orphée* (wd) 50 *Le Testament d'Orphée* (wd) 59. La Princesse de Clèves (w) 60. Thomas l'Imposteur (w) 65.
🌑 For bringing a unique visual imagination to the cinema. *Orphée*.

¶ A film is a petrified fountain of thought. – *J.C.*

odee, Ann (1890–1961).
elgian-born character actress in Hollywood who
ayed a variety of middle-aged roles for many
ears.
  Hi Gaucho 35. Captain Caution 40. Old
quaintance 44. The Other Love 47. On the
iviera 51. Kiss Me Kate 53. Daddy Long Legs 55.
an Can 59, etc.

ody, Iron Eyes (1915–).
merican Indian actor.
  The Iron Horse 24. Ride 'Em Cowboy 42. The
aleface 48. Broken Arrow 50. Sitting Bull 54.
he Great Sioux Massacre 67. El Condor 70, many
hers.

ody, Lew (1884–1934) (Louis Coté).
martly-dressed American leading man of the
ient screen; his French accent affected his sound
areer. He was married to actresses Mabel
ormand and Dorothy Dalton.
  Comrade John 15. The Demon 18. *Don't Change
our Husband* 19. The Sign on the Door 21. Secrets
f Paris 22. Within the Law 23. *Rupert of Hentzau*
itle role) 23. The Shooting of Dan McGrew 24.
xchange of Wives 25. Adam and Evil 27. On Ze
oulevard 27. Beau Broadway 28. What a Widow
0. Dishonoured 31. Sporting Blood 31. The
enderfoot 32. Sitting Pretty 33. Shoot the Works
4, many others.

ody, William Frederick (Buffalo Bill)
846–1917).
merican guide, Indian scout and buffalo hunter,
ho discovered he could make an easier living
laying himself on-stage and in 'Buffalo Bill's Wild
Vest', a show which toured America and, later,
urope. Famous for having killed and scalped
hief Yellow Hand in single combat, he did much
o create the myths that formed the basis of
estern movies. He is said to have invented the
ndian war whoop, with the hand flapping over
he mouth, to add excitement to his shows and
o that it could be heard over the sound of gunfire.
le featured sharp-shooting cowboys and battles
etween marauding Indians and western
nmigrants with their wagons drawn in a circle
n real life, attacks on wagon trains usually came
hen they were spread out across the plains). He
ave employment to Wild Bill Hickok, Annie
akley and Sitting Bull, and can claim to have been
ne of the first film-makers of faction – fiction
ased on fact. In 1913, he formed the W. F. Cody
istorical Pictures Company to re-create major
vents in the history of the American West, using,
here possible, the actual participants. His first and
nly film, of which a few minutes survive, was
ased on the massacre of the Sioux at Wounded
Knee, and was distributed by Essanay, the
ompany formed by 'Bronco Billy' Anderson. He
as been played in movies by James Ellison in
he Plainsman 36, Joel McCrea in *Buffalo Bill* 42,
ouis Calhern in *Annie Get Your Gun* 50, Charlton
leston in *Pony Express* 52, Clayton Moore in *Buffalo
ill in Tomahawk Territory* 53, Gordon Scott in
uffalo Bill (Ger.) 64, Guy Stockwell in *The
lainsman* 66 and Paul Newman in *Buffalo Bill and
he Indians* 76. He was a favourite hero of silent
movies.
  Biography: 1973, *Buffalo Bill: The Noblest
Vhiteskin* by John Burke.

¶ Making a film is harder to organize and run
than three circuses. – *W.C.*
  The doc says I've got thirty-six hours. Let's forget
bout it and play some cards. – *W.C. on his death-
ed*

Perhaps the handsomest American of all time.
– *Gene Fowler*

Coe, Barry (1934–).
American juvenile actor of the 50s.
  On The Threshold of Space 56. Peyton Place 57.
The Bravados 58. One Foot in Hell 60. The 300
Spartans 62, etc.
  TV series: Follow the Sun 61.

Coe, Fred (1914–1979).
American producer-director from stage and TV.
  The Left-handed Gun (p) 58. The Miracle
Worker (p) 62. A Thousand Clowns (pd) 65. Me
Natalie (d) 69, etc.

Coe, Peter (1929–1987).
British director with stage experience.
  Lock Up Your Daughters 69.

Coen, Ethan (1958–).
American screenwriter and producer who works
in collaboration with his brother Joel.
  Blood Simple 84. Crimewave 85. Raising
Arizona 87. Miller's Crossing 90. Barton Fink 91.
The Hudsucker Proxy (p, co-w) 94, etc.

Coen, Franklin (1912–).
American screenwriter.
  This Island Earth (co-w) 55. The Train (co-w)
64. Alvarez Kelly 66, etc.

Coen, Joel (1955–).
American director and screenwriter who works in
partnership with his brother Ethan.
  Blood Simple 84. Crimewave (co-w only) 85.
Raising Arizona 87. Miller's Crossing 90. Barton
Fink 91. The Hudsucker Proxy (co-w, d) 94, etc.

co-feature.
A moderate-budget production designed (or fated)
to form equal half of a double bill.

Coffee, Lenore (1900–1984).
American screenwriter, in films from 1919.
  Autobiography: 1973, *Storyline.*
  Ladyfingers 21. East Lynne 25. Chicago 28.
Arsène Lupin 32. Suzy 36. Four Daughters (AAN)
38. The Way of All Flesh 40. The Gay Sisters 42.
Tomorrow Is Forever 46. Beyond the Forest 49.
Lightning Strikes Twice 51. Sudden Fear 52. Young
at Heart 55. The End of the Affair 55. Cash McCall
60, etc.

Coffin, Tristram (1912–1990).
American actor, a villain in many a 'B' western.
  No Greater Sin 41. Blackmail 47. Outrage 50.
Undercover Girl 50, etc.
  TV series: 26 Men 56.

Coghlan, Junior (1916–) (Frank Coghlan).
American boy star of the 20s; previously played
baby roles.
  Autobiography: 1992, *They Still Call Me Junior.*
  Slide, Kelly, Slide 26. The Country Doctor 27.
River's End 31. Penrod and Sam 32. Boys'
Reformatory 39. The Adventures of Captain
Marvel (serial) 40. Henry Aldrich for President
41. The Sand Pebbles 66.

Cohan, George M. (1878–1942).
Dapper American actor-dancer-author-composer
of the Broadway stage. Songs include: 'Mary's a
Grand Old Name', 'Give My Regards to Broadway',
'Over There', 'Yankee Doodle Dandy'; plays
include the much-filmed *Seven Keys to Baldpate.*
FILM APPEARANCES: Broadway Jones 16. Hit-the-
Trail Holiday 18. The Phantom President 32. Gambling

34, etc. Was impersonated by James Cagney in a
biopic, *Yankee Doodle Dandy* 42, and in *The Seven
Little Foys* 55.

¶ Whatever you do, kid, always serve it with a
little dressing. – *G.M.C. to Spencer Tracy*
  I don't care what you say about me so long as
you spell my name right. – *G.M.C.*

Cohen, Herman (1928–1985).
American producer and director of low-budget
horror films.
  I Was a Teenage Werewolf 57. Konga 61. Black
Zoo 63. Berserk 68. Crooks and Coronets 69. Trog
70. Craze 73, etc.

Cohen, Larry (1938–).
American creator of 'realist' horror films.
  Bone 72. It's Alive (wpd) 76. Demon (wpd) 77.
The Private Files of J. Edgar Hoover 77. Dial Rat for
Terror (Housewife) (wpd) 80. It Lives Again (wpd)
80. The Winged Serpent 81. Perfect Strangers
(wd) 83. Scandalous (story) 84. Special Effects
(wd) 85. The Stuff (wd) 85. Best Seller (w) 87.
Deadly Illusion (wd) 87. It's Alive III: Island of the
Alive (wd) 87. Return to Salem's Lot (wd) 87.
Maniac Cop (w) 88. Wicked Stepmother (wd) 89.
Maniac Cop 2 (w) 90. The Ambulance (wd) 90.
Brute Force (wd) 92. Guilty as Sin 93, etc.

Cohen, Norman (1936–1983).
Irish director.
■ Brendan Behan's Dublin 67. The London
Nobody Knows 68. Till Death Us Do Part 68. Dad's
Army 70. Adolf Hitler, My Part in His Downfall
72. Stand Up Virgin Soldiers 77.

Cohen, Rob (1949–).
American producer and director, mainly of
episodes of such TV series as *Miami Vice* and
thirtysomething. He began producing for the
Motown Corporation before setting up the
Badham-Cohen Group with director John
Badham.
AS PRODUCER: Mahogany 75. The Bingo Long
Traveling All-Stars and Motor Kings 76. Scott Joplin
76. Almost Summer 77. Thank God It's Friday 77.
The Wiz 78. The Razor's Edge 84. Light of Day
86. The Witches of Eastwick 87. Ironweed 87.
Disorganized Crime 89. The Hard Way 90, etc.
AS DIRECTOR: A Small Circle of Friends 80.
Scandalous 84. Dragon: The Bruce Lee Story (co-
w, d) 93.

Cohl, Emile (1857–1938) (Emile Courte).
Pioneer French cartoonist of the 1908–18 period.
  Fantasmagorie 08. Les Allumettes Animées 09.
Don Quichotte 09. Aventures d'une Bout de Papier
11. Monsieur Stop 13. Snookums (series) (US)
13–15. Les Pieds Nickelés 18, many others.

Cohn, Arthur (1928–).
Swiss producer.
  The Sky Above the Mud Below 63. Woman
Times Seven 67. Sunflower 70. *The Garden of the
Finzi-Continis* (AA) 71. Wolf of the Seven Seas 74.
Black and White in Colour (co-p, AA) 76.
Dangerous Moves (AA) 84. American Dream 90,
etc.

Cohn, Harry (1891–1958).
American executive, chief of Columbia Pictures
(qv) for many years; a former song-plugger and
vaudevillian who built the company in 1924,
reputedly from his sales of a film called *Traffic in
Souls*. He was the model for the character of
producer Marcus Hoff in Clifford Odets's *The Big
Knife*, filmed by Robert Aldrich in 1955.

Biography: 1967, *King Cohn* by Bob Thomas.
✪ For enjoying his career as an ogre and for bringing a Poverty Row studio up to the big time. *Gilda*.

¶ When the big boss of Columbia Studios died in 1958, you could take your pick of brickbats and bouquets. The most famous tasteless comment came from Red Skelton on hearing of the huge crowds at Cohn's funeral:

It proves what they always say: give the public what they want to see, and they'll come out for it.

Then there was Hedda Hopper:

You had to stand in line to hate him.

And George Jessel:

He was a great showman, and he was a son of a bitch.

And Elia Kazan:

He liked to be the biggest bug in the manure pile.

And Samuel Goldwyn:

He never learned how to live.

And Budd Schulberg:

He was the meanest man I ever knew – an unreconstructed dinosaur.

But Cohn had a few defenders. There was Artie Shaw:

He was a lovable old pirate.

And, surprisingly, Ethel Barrymore:

He knew the score.

One thing was sure, Cohn thoroughly enjoyed his long tyranny. He said once:

Gower Street is paved with the bones of my executive producers.

And again:

I don't have ulcers: I give them.

Despite his frequent ill-treatment of actors and other creative people, he always averred:

I kiss the feet of talent.

He was disappointed in the treatment he got back from the stars he had created:

I have never met a grateful performer in the movies.

He maintained his confidence in his own ability:

Great pictures make great stars. This girl (Novak) has had five hit pictures. Send me your mother or your aunt and we will do the same for them.

He certainly knew what he wanted, and he had a long record of success. One of his mottoes was:

Let Rembrandt make character studies, not Columbia.

He once said to Daniel Taradash:

Promise me you'll never make a picture where the characters walk out of the room backward.

He claimed:

All I need to make pictures is an office.

In a more self-knowing mood, he admitted:

If I wasn't head of a studio, who would talk to me?

But he concluded:

It's better than being a pimp.

He once expounded his entire philosophy to Robert Parrish, who had asked to be allowed to direct good pictures:

I make fifty-two pictures a year here. Every Friday the front door opens on Gower Street and I spit a picture out. A truck picks it up and takes it away to the theatres, and that's the ball game. Now, if that door opens and I spit and nothing comes out, you and everybody else around here is out of work. So let's cut this crap about only good pictures . . . I run this place on the basis of making *one* good picture a year. I'll lay everything on the line for that one. I don't care if it's Capra, or Ford, or Riskin, or Milestone – that's the good one. The rest of the time I just have to keep spitting out.

As Frank Sinatra said:

He had a sense of humour like an open grave.

~Columbia was once known as the Pine Tree Studio (because it has so many Cohns).

cokuloris.

A palette with random irregular holes, placed between lights and camera to prevent glare and give a better illusion of real-life light and shadow.

Colbert, Claudette (1905–) (Lily Claudette Chauchoin).

French leading lady who went to America as a child and became one of Hollywood's most durable and versatile light actresses of the golden age, most typically cast in smart emancipated roles.

■ For the Love of Mike 28. The Hole in the Wall 29. The Lady Lies 29. The Big Pond 30. Young Man of Manhattan 30. Manslaughter 30. Honour among Lovers 31. The Smiling Lieutenant 31. Secrets of a Secretary 31. His Woman 31. The Wiser Sex 32. Misleading Lady 32. The Man from Yesterday 32. The Phantom President 32. *The Sign of the Cross* (as Poppaea) 32. Tonight is Ours 33. I Cover the Waterfront 33. *Three-Cornered Moon* 33. The Torch Singer 33. Four Frightened People 34. *It Happened One Night* (AA) 34. Cleopatra 34. *Imitation of Life* 34. The Gilded Lily 35. Private Worlds (AAN) 35. She Married Her Boss 35. The Bride Comes Home 35. Under Two Flags 36. Maid of Salem 37. I Met Him in Paris 37. Tovarich 37. Bluebeard's Eighth Wife 38. Zaza 39. *Midnight* 39. It's a Wonderful World 39. Drums along the Mohawk 39. Boom Town 40. *Arise My Love* 40. Skylark 41. Remember the Day 41. *The Palm Beach Story* 42. So Proudly We Hail 43. No Time for Love 43. *Since You Went Away* (AAN) 44. Practically Yours 45. Guest Wife 45. Tomorrow is Forever 46. Without Reservations 46. The Secret Heart 46. *The Egg and I* 47. Sleep My Love 48. Family Honeymoon 49. Bride for Sale 49. *Three Came Home* 50. The Secret Fury 50. Thunder on the Hill 51. Let's Make it Legal 51. The Planter's Wife (GB) 52. Love and the Frenchwoman 54. Si Versailles M'était Conté 55. Texas Lady 55. Parrish 60. The Two Mrs Grenvilles (TV) 86.

✪ For being more than a match for her male stars through twenty years of romantic comedy. *Midnight*.

Famous line (*Midnight*): 'The moment I saw you, I had an idea you had an idea.'

the Cold War

has occupied the cinema right from Churchill's Fulton speech in 1948. For three years diehard Nazis had been the international villains par excellence, but a change was required, and Russians have been fair game ever since, in films like *The Iron Curtain, Diplomatic Courier, I Was a Communist for the FBI, I Married a Communist, The Big Lift, Red Snow, The Red Danube, Red Menace, Red Planet Mars, The Journey, From Russia With Love* and innumerable pulp spy thrillers, as well as such classier productions as *The Third Man, The Man Between* and *The Spy Who Came in from the Cold*. Rather surprisingly none of these caused much escalation of tension between the nations, and cooler feelings have permitted comedies like *One Two Three, Dr Strangelove* and *The Russians are Coming, The Russians are Coming*; while such terrifying panic-button melodramas as *Fail Safe* and *The Bedford Incident* are probably our best guarantee that the dangers are realized on both sides.

Cole, Dennis (1940–).

American general purpose actor who plays almost entirely on television.

Powderkeg (TV) 70. The Connection (TV) 73. Barbary Coast (TV) 74. Cave-In (TV) 79. Amateur Night 85. Pretty Smart 87. Dead End City 88, etc.

TV series: *The Felony Squad* 66–68. Lancer 68–69. Bearcats 71.

Cole, George (1925–).

British comedy actor who made his film debut as a cockney child evacuee; usually plays the befuddled innocent. Best known, though, as a bumbling con-man in the TV series *Minder*.

Cottage to Let 41. Henry V 44. *Quartet* 48. Morning Departure 50. Laughter in Paradise 50. Lady Godiva Rides Again 51. Scrooge 51. *Top Secret* 51. Will Any Gentleman? 52. Happy Ever After 53. Our Girl Friday 53. The Belles of St Trinian's 54. A Prize of Gold 55. The Weapon 56. It's a Wonderful World 56. The Green Man 57. Blue Murder at St Trinian's 58. Too Many Crooks 58. The Bridal Path 59. The Pure Hell of St Trinian's 60. Cleopatra 62. Dr Syn 63. One-Way Pendulum 64. The Legend of Young Dick Turpin 65. The Great St Trinian's Train Robbery 66. The Vampire Lovers 70. Fright 71. Take Me High 73. The Bluebird 76. Blott on the Landscape (TV) 85. Mary Reilly 95, etc.

TV series: Don't Forget to Write 77–79. Minder 79–94. The Bounder 82–83. Heggerty Haggerty 84–85. Comrade Dad 86. Root into Europe 92.

Cole, Jack (1914–1974).

American dancer and choreographer.

Moon Over Miami (d) 41. Kismet (d) 44. Tonight and Every Night (ch) 45. The Jolson Story (ch) 46. On the Riviera (ch) 51. Designing Woman (dch) 55. Let's Make Love (ch) 61, etc.

Cole, Lester (1904–1985).

American screenwriter. One of the blacklisted Hollywood Ten.

If I Had a Million 32. The President's Mystery 34. The Crime of Dr Hallet 36. The Invisible Man Returns 39. Hostages 42. None Shall Escape 44. Objective Burma 45. Blood on the Sun 45. The Romance of Rosy Ridge 47. High Wall 48. Operation Eichmann (as Lewis Copley) 61, etc.

Cole, Michael (1945–).

American leading man, mostly on television.

The Last Child (TV) 71. Beg Borrow or Steal (TV) 73. Evening in Byzantium (TV) 78. Nickel Mountain 85, etc.

TV series: *The Mod Squad* 68–72.

Cole, Nat King (1919–1965) (Nathaniel Coles).

American pianist and singer who made occasional film appearances.

The Blue Gardenia 53. St Louis Blues (as W. C. Handy) 58. The Night of the Quarter Moon 59. *Cat Ballou* 65, etc.

Cole, Sidney (1908–).

British producer, a former editor who worked at Ealing through its finest hours. Subsequently produced Black Beauty (72) and Dick Turpin (78) for TV.

Coleman, Charles (1885–1951).

Australian character actor in Hollywood; almost always played the perfect portly butler.

That's my Daddy 28. Bachelor Apartment 31. Gallant Lady 33. Down to Their Last Yacht 34. Poor Little Rich Girl 36. That Certain Age 38. Mexican Spitfire 39. It Started with Eve 41. Twin Beds 42. The Whistler 44. The Runaround 46. The Imperfect Lady 47, many others.

Coleman, Charlotte (1968–).

English actress who began as a child on the

television series *Educating Marmalade* and *Worzel Gummidge*, the daughter of actress Anne Beach.
Oranges Are Not the Only Fruit (TV) 90. Four Weddings and a Funeral 94.

Coleman, Cy (1929–).
American song composer, usually with lyricist Carolyn Leigh (1926–83).
Spartacus 60. Father Goose 64. The Troublemaker 64. The Art of Love 65. Sweet Charity (from his stage musical) (AAN) 69. The Heartbreak Kid (song) 72. Garbo Talks 84. Blame It on Rio (song) 84. Power 86. Family Business 89, etc.

Coleman, Dabney (1932–).
American comic actor, usually the heavy.
This Property Is Condemned 66. I Love My Wife 70. The Brotherhood of the Bell (TV) 70. Bad Ronald (TV) 74. Returning Home (TV) 75. Maneaters Are Loose (TV) 78. North Dallas Forty 79. How to Beat the High Cost of Living 80. Melvin and Howard 80. *Nine to Five* 80. Nothing Personal 80. On Golden Pond 81. Young Doctors in Love 82. Tootsie 82. War Games 83. The Muppets Take Manhattan 84. Cloak and Dagger 85. The Man with One Red Shoe 85. Dragnet 87. Hot to Trot 88. Short Time 90. Where the Heart Is 90. Meet the Applegates 90. Clifford 91. Amos & Andrew 93. The Beverly Hillbillies 93. Clifford 94, etc.
TV series: That Girl 66–70. Mary Hartman, Mary Hartman 76. Forever Fernwood 77. Buffalo Bill 83. Drexell's Class 91.

Coleman, Gary (1968–).
American juvenile actor, star of TV's *Diff'rent Strokes*.
On the Right Track 81. Jimmy the Kid 82. The Kid with the Broken Halo (TV) 82. The Kid with the 200 IQ (TV) 82. Jimmy the Kid 82. The Fantastic World of D. C. Collins (TV) 83. Playing with Fire (TV) 84.

Coleman, Nancy (1917–).
American leading lady of the 40s, usually in timid roles.
Kings Row 42. Dangerously They Live 42. The Gay Sisters 42. Desperate Journey 42. Edge of Darkness 43. In Our Time 44. *Devotion* (as Anne Brontë) 45. Her Sister's Secret 46. Mourning Becomes Electra 47. That Man from Tangier 53. Slaves 68, etc.

Colette (1873–1954) (Sidonie-Gabrielle Colette).
French writer, usually on sex themes.
Claudine á l'Ecole 38. Gigi 48 and 58. Julie de Carnelihan 50. L'Ingénue Libertine 51. Ripening Seed 54.

Colicos, John (1928–).
Canadian character actor in occasional films.
Anne of the Thousand Days 70. Raid on Rommel 71. Red Sky at Morning 71. Doctors' Wives 71. The Wrath of God 72. Scorpio 73. Drum 76. Breaking Point 76. Phobia 80. The Changeling 80. The Postman Always Rings Twice 81, etc.
TV series: Battlestar Galactica 78.

Colin, Jean (1905–1989).
British leading lady of the 30s; appearances sporadic.
The Hate Ship 30. Compromising Daphne 30. *The Mikado* 39. Bob's Your Uncle 41. Laxdale Hall 54, etc.

Colin, Sid (1920–1989).
British TV comedy scriptwriter.
I Only Arsked 58. The Ugly Duckling 59. Up Pompeii 70. Up the Chastity Belt 71. Up the Front 72. Percy's Progress 74, etc.

Colla, Richard A. (1918–).
American director.
Zigzag 70. *Fuzz* 72. Live Again, Die Again (TV) 74. The Tribe (TV) 74. The UFO Incident (TV) 75. Olly Olly Oxen Free 78. Battlestar Galactica 79. Stingray (TV) 85. That Secret Sunday (TV) 86. Something Is Out There (TV) 88, etc.

Colleano, Bonar (1924–1958) (Bonar Sullivan).
Wisecracking American actor, from family of acrobats; worked chiefly in Britain.
The Way to the Stars 45. A Matter of Life and Death 46. While the Sun Shines 46. Good Time Girl 47. One Night With You 48. Sleeping Car to Trieste 48. Pool of London 50. A Tale of Five Cities 52. Eight Iron Men (US) 52. The Sea Shall Not Have Them 55. Interpol 57. No Time To Die 58, etc.

colleges:
see *universities*.

Collier, Constance (1878–1955) (Laura Constance Hardie).
Distinguished British stage actress who spent her later years in Hollywood playing great ladies with caustic tongues and eccentric habits.
Autobiography: 1929, *Harlequinade*.
■ Intolerance 16. The Code of Marcia Gray 16. Macbeth 16. Bleak House 20. The Bohemian Girl 22. *Our Betters* 33. Dinner at Eight 33. Peter Ibbetson 34. Shadow of Doubt 35. Anna Karenina 35. Girls' Dormitory 36. Professional Soldier 36. Little Lord Fauntleroy 36. Thunder in the City 37. Wee Willie Winkie 37. *Stage Door* 37. She Got What She Wanted 37. A Damsel in Distress 37. Zaza 39. Susan and God 40. Half a Sinner 40. Weekend at the Waldorf 45. *Kitty* 45. Monsieur Beaucaire 46. The Dark Corner 46. The Perils of Pauline 47. *An Ideal Husband* 47. Rope 48. The Girl from Manhattan 48. Whirlpool 50.

Collier, John (1901–1980).
British writer of polished macabre stories; his screen work was sporadic.
Sylvia Scarlett 35. Her Cardboard Lover 42. Deception 46. Roseanna McCoy 49. The Story of Three Loves 53. I Am a Camera 55. The War Lord 65, etc.

Collier, Lois (1919–) (Madelyn Jones).
American leading lady of 40s 'B' pictures.
A Desperate Adventure 38. The Phantom Plainsman 42. Cobra Woman 44. Weird Woman 44. Ladies Courageous 44. The Naughty Nineties 45. The Crimson Canary 45. The Cat Creeps 46. A Night in Casablanca 46. Slave Girl 47. Out of the Storm 48. Miss Mink of 1949 49. Flying Disc Man from Mars 51. Missile Monsters 58, etc.
TV series: Boston Blackie 51–53.

Collier, William (1866–1944) (William Senior).
American stage actor, usually of comedy character roles; moved to Hollywood in 1929.
Six Cylinder Love 31. The Cheater 34. Josette 38. Thanks for the Memory 38. Invitation to Happiness 39. There's Magic in Music 41, many others.

Collier, William 'Buster' Jnr (1902–1987).
Handsome American leading man of silents who retired in the 30s to become an agent. His father was actor William Collier.
The Bugle Call 16. The Sea Hawk 24. The Wanderer 25. The Lion and the Mouse 28. New Orleans 29. Little Caesar 31. Cimarron 31. The Story of Temple Drake 33. The People's Enemy 35, etc.

Collin, John (1931–).
British character actor.
Star! 68. Before Winter Comes 69. Innocent Bystanders 72. Tess 79, etc.

Collinge, Patricia (1892–1974).
Irish-American stage actress who made occasional film appearances.
The Little Foxes (AAN) 41. Shadow of a Doubt 43. Casanova Brown 44. Teresa 51. The Nun's Story 58, etc.

Collings, David (1940–).
British character actor, much on TV.
Scrooge (as Bob Cratchit) 70. Elizabeth R (TV) 71. Mahler 74. Hennessy 75. The 39 Steps 78.

Collins, Alfred.
English comic actor, from music hall, and pioneer director, specializing in chase films. His approach was in advance of most of his contemporaries, using a mobile camera and close-ups to good effect.
The Runaway Match 03. Welshed – A Derby Day Incident 03. Rip Van Winkle 03. Two Little Vagabonds 03. Mutiny on a Russian Battleship 05. This Little Girl and That Little Girl 07. The Coster's Phantom Fortune 10. Algie's Expensive Stick 12, etc.

Collins, Anthony (1893–1964).
British composer.
The Rat 37. Victoria the Great 37. Sixty Glorious Years 38. Nurse Edith Cavell 40. The Courtneys of Curzon Street 47. Odette 50. Derby Day 52. Laughing Anne 53, etc.

Collins, Cora Sue (1927–).
American child star of the 30s.
They Just Had to Get Married 33. Queen Christina 33. Torch Singer 34. The Scarlet Letter 35. Anna Karenina 35. Magnificent Obsession 36. The Adventures of Tom Sawyer 38, etc.

Collins, Eddie (1884–1940).
American character comedian from Vaudeville; crowded a few films into his last years.
In Old Chicago 38. Kentucky Moonshine 38. Charlie Chan in Honolulu 38. Young Mr Lincoln 39. Hollywood Cavalcade 39. *The Bluebird* 39. The Return of Frank James 40.

Collins, Gary (1938–).
Easy-going American leading man, familiar on television in the 70s; the lead in *Born Free* (series).
The Pigeon that Took Rome 62. Airport 69. Killer Fish 77. Hangar 18 80, etc.
Other TV series: The Wackiest Ship in the Army 65. The Iron Horse 66. The Sixth Sense 72.

Collins, Jackie (1939–).
British light novelist, sister of Joan Collins. Works filmed include *The World Is Full of Married Men, The Stud, The Bitch*.

Collins, Joan (1933–).
British leading lady whose sultry charms won her parts in an assortment of international films.
Autobiography: 1978, *Past Imperfect*.
I Believe in You 52. Cosh Boy 53. Our Girl Friday 53. Turn the Key Softly 53. The Good Die Young 54. Land of the Pharaohs 55. The Virgin Queen 55. The Girl in the Red Velvet Swing 55. The Opposite Sex 56. The Wayward Bus 57. Island in the Sun 57. Sea Wife 57. The Bravados 58. Rally Round the Flag Boys 58. Seven Thieves 60. Road to Hong Kong 62. Warning Shot 66. Heironymus Merkin 69. The Executioner 69. Subterfuge 69. Up

in the Cellar 70. Drive Hard, Drive Fast (TV) 70. Quest for Love 71. Revenge 71. Tales That Witness Madness 73. Alfie Darling 74. I Don't Want to Be Born 75. The Moneychangers (TV) 76. Empire of the Ants 77. The Stud 78. The Bitch 79. Game for Vultures 79. Sunburn 79. Nutcracker 82. The Wild Women of Chastity Gulch (TV) 82. The Making of a Male Model (TV) 83. Her Life as a Man (TV) 84. The Cartier Affair (TV) 85. Sins (TV) 85. Monte Carlo (TV) 86. Decadence 93, etc.

TV series: *Dynasty* 81–89.

¶ Dynasty was the opportunity to take charge of my career rather than walking around like a library book waiting to be loaned out. – *J.C.*

She appears to have the world by the balls, but underneath she's trying to solve the problem of loneliness, which I think is the universal problem of all rich people. – *J.C.* (of her character in *The Bitch*)

Even when you win the rat race, you're still a rat. – *J.C.*

The secret of having a personal life is not answering too many questions about it. – *J.C.*

Collins, Lewis (1946–).
British leading man familiar from TV's *The Professionals* 78–80.

Who Dares Wins 82. Jack the Ripper (TV) 88, etc.

Collins, Pauline (1940–).
English leading actress, from the stage and television. She is married to actor John Alderton, with whom she starred in three TV series.

Shirley Valentine (AAN) 89. City of Joy 92.

TV series: Upstairs Downstairs 71–73. No, Honestly 74. Thomas and Sarah 78. Forever Green 89–91.

Collins, Phil (1951–).
British singer, songwriter, drummer and actor. A member of the rock band Genesis, he began as a child actor, playing the Artful Dodger in the stage musical *Oliver!*

A Hard Day's Night 64. Chitty Chitty Bang Bang 69. Against All Odds (AAN for song). 84. Eric Clapton and Friends (concert) 86. The Return of Bruno 87. Buster (& song) (AAN) 88. Hook 91. Frauds 93. And the Band Played On (TV) 93, etc.

Collins, Ray (1890–1965).
American stage actor who came to Hollywood with Orson Welles, stayed to play kindly uncles and political bosses.

■ The Grapes of Wrath 40. *Citizen Kane* (as Boss Jim Geddes) 41. The Big Street 42. Highways by Night 42. The Navy Comes Through 42. The Commandos Strike at Dawn 42. *The Magnificent Ambersons* 42. The Human Comedy 43. Slightly Dangerous 43. Crime Doctor 43. Salute to the Marines 43. Whistling in Brooklyn 43. See Here Private Hargrove 43. The Hitler Gang 44. The Eve of St Mark 44. The Seventh Cross 44. Barbary Coast Gent 44. Can't Help Singing 44. Roughly Speaking 45. The Hidden Eye 45. Miss Susie Slagle's 45. Leave Her to Heaven 45. Up Goes Maisie 46. A Night in Paradise 46. Badman's Territory 46. Boys' Ranch 46. Crack-Up 46. Three Wise Fools 46. Two Years Before the Mast 46. The Return of Monte Cristo 46. The Best Years of Our Lives 46. *The Bachelor and the Bobbysoxer* 47. Red Stallion 47. The Swordsman 47. The Senator Was Indiscreet 47. Homecoming 48. A Double Life 48. Good Sam 48. For the Love of Mary 48. The Man from Colorado 48. Command Decision 48. Red Stallion in the Rockies 48. Hideout 49. It Happens Every Spring 49. The Fountainhead 49. The Heiress 49.

Free for All 49. Francis 49. Paid in Full 50. Kill the Umpire 50. The Reformer and the Redhead 50. Summer Stock 50. You're in the Navy Now 51. Ma and Pa Kettle Back on the Farm 51. Vengeance Valley 51. Reunion in Reno 51. I Want You 51. The Racket 51. Invitation 52. Dreamboat 52. Young Man with Ideas 52. The Desert Song 53. Ma and Pa Kettle at the Fair 53. Column South 53. Ma and Pa Kettle on Vacation 53. The Kid from Left Field 53. Bad for Each Other 53. Rose Marie 54. Athena 54. The Desperate Hours 55. Texas Lady 55. Never Say Goodbye 56. The Solid Gold Cadillac 56. Spoilers of the Forest 57. Touch of Evil 58. I'll Give My Life 61.

TV series: Halls of Ivy 54. Perry Mason 57–65.

Collins, Russell (1897–1965).
Hardened-looking American character actor.

Shockproof 49. Niagara 53. Miss Sadie Thompson 53. Bad Day at Black Rock 55. Soldier of Fortune 56. The Enemy Below 57. The Matchmaker 58. Fail Safe 64, etc.

TV series: The Detectives 59–61. Many Happy Returns 64.

Collins, Wilkie (1824–1889).
British novelist, credited with being the inventor of the detective story via *The Moonstone*, whose complications have resisted filming. *The Woman in White* however was filmed with some fidelity in 1947.

Collinson, Peter (1938–1980).
British director who quickly slumped from arty pretentiousness to routine thrillers.

■ The Penthouse 67. Up the Junction 68. The Long Day's Dying 68. *The Italian Job* 69. You Can't Win 'em All 70. Fright 71. Straight on till Morning 72. Innocent Bystanders 72. The Man Called Noon 73. Open Season 74. And Then There Were None 74. The Spiral Staircase 75. The Sell Out 75. Tomorrow Never Comes 77. Tigers Don't Cry 77. The House on Garibaldi Street (TV) 79. The Earthling 80.

Collyer, June (1907–1968) (Dorothy Heermance).
American leading lady in a few light films of the early 30s; married Stuart Erwin.

Woman Wise 27. East Side West Side 28. Charley's Aunt 31. Alexander Hamilton 31. The Ghost Walks 35, etc.

TV series: The Stuart Erwin Show 53.

Colman, Edward (1905–).
American cinematographer who began work as an assistant cameraman in 1924 and worked almost exclusively for Disney after he became a director of photography.

The DI 57. Black Patch 57. Shaggy Dog 59. –30– (aka Deadline Midnight) 59. The Absent-Minded Professor (AAN) 60. Big Red 61. Babes in Toyland 61. Son of Flubber 62. Savage Sam 62. Mary Poppins (AAN) 64. Those Calloways 64. The Monkey's Uncle 64. That Darn Cat 65. The Ugly Dachshund 65. The Adventures of Bullwhip Griffin 65. The Gnome-Mobile 66. The Happiest Millionaire 67. The Love Bug 68, etc.

Colman, Ronald (1891–1958).
Distinguished British romantic actor whose gentle manners, intelligence and good looks thrilled two generations. Turned to acting after World War I wounds, and went to Hollywood in 1920.

Biography: 1975, *A Very Private Person* by Juliet Benita Colman.

■ The Toilers 19. A Son of David 19. The Snow in the Desert 19. The Black Spider 20. Anna The Adventuress 20. Handcuffs or Kisses 21. The

Eternal City 23. *The White Sister* 23. Twenty Dollars a Week 24. Tarnish 24. Romola 24. Her Night of Romance 24. A Thief in Paradise 24. His Supreme Moment 25. The Sporting Venus 25. Her Sister from Paris 25. *The Dark Angel* 25. Stella Dallas 25. Lady Windermere's Fan 25. Kiki 26. *Beau Geste* 26. The Winning of Barbara Worth 26. The Night of Love 27. The Magic Flame 27. The Lovers 28. The Rescue 29. *Bulldog Drummond* (AAN) 29. Condemned (AAN) 29. *Raffles* 30. The Devil to Pay 30. The Unholy Garden 31. *Arrowsmith* 31. Cynara 32. The Masquerader 33. Bulldog Drummond Strikes Back 34. Clive of India 35. The Man who Broke the Bank at Monte Carlo 35. *A Tale of Two Cities* 35. Under Two Flags 36. *Lost Horizon* 37. *The Prisoner of Zenda* 37. If I were King 38. The Light that Failed 39. Lucky Partners 40. My Life with Caroline 41. *The Talk of the Town* 42. *Random Harvest* (AAN) 42. Kismet 44. The Late George Apley 47. *A Double Life* (AA) 48. Champagne for Caesar 50. Around the World in Eighty Days 56. The Story of Mankind 57.

TV series: *Halls of Ivy* 54.

✪ For conquering world audiences by steadfastly playing the old-fashioned British gentleman adventurer in a number of elegant guises. *The Prisoner of Zenda.*

¶ He is as ingratiating when he talks as when he was silent. – *New York Times, 1929*

He led the perfect colonial life in Hollywood. The longer he stayed there the more English he got – but he never wanted to go home. – *Douglas Fairbanks Jnr*

Before God I'm worth 35 dollars a week. Before the motion picture industry I'm worth anything you can get. – *R.C.* (to his agent)

He is an excellent director's dummy. He has no personality of his own, only an appearance. – *Alleged screen test report*

When Colman looks at the camera, the whole world knows what he is thinking. – *New Yorker, 1937*

Colombier, Michel (1939–).
French composer, mainly for American films.

L'Arme à Gauche 65. Dirty Money (Un Flic) 72. Paul and Michelle 74. Steel 80. Against All Odds 84. Purple Rain 84. White Nights 85. The Money Pit 86. Ruthless People 86. The Golden Child 86. Surrender 87. The Couch Trip 88. Satisfaction 88. Loverboy 89. Who's Harry Crumb? 89. Impulse 90. New Jack City 91. Strictly Business 91. Diary of a Hit Man 92. Deep Cover 92. Folks! 92. Posse 93. The Program 93. Major League II 94, etc.

Colonna, Jerry (1903–1986).
American comic actor with strong, high-pitched voice, walrus moustache and bulging eyes.

College Swing 38. Little Miss Broadway 38. Road to Singapore 40. Sis Hopkins 41. True to the Army 42. Star-Spangled Rhythm 42. Ice Capades 42. Atlantic City 44. It's in the Bag 45. Road to Rio 47. Kentucky Jubilee 51. Meet Me in Las Vegas 56. Andy Hardy Comes Home 58, etc.

colour
prints of a primitive kind were made as long ago as 1898. During the next few years many films were hand-coloured by stencil, and two unsatisfactory processes. KinemaColor and Gaumont colour, were tried out. D. W. Griffith in *The Birth of a Nation* 14 developed the French practice of tinting scenes for dramatic effect: blue for night, orange for sunshine, etc. In 1918 red-and-green Technicolor was tried out along with half a dozen other processes. 1921: Prizmacolour was used for the British historical film *The Great Adventure*. 1923: de

ille used a colour sequence in *The Ten
mmandments.* 1926: *The Black Pirate* was shot in
vo-colour Technicolor. 1932: first three-colour
echnicolor film, Disney cartoon *Flowers and Trees*
A). 1934: colour used in dramatic sequences of
* Cucaracha* and *The House of Rothschild.* 1935: first
ature film entirely in three-strip colour, *Becky
arp.* 1937: first British Technicolor feature,
ings of the Morning. 1939: two-colour Cinecolor,
ry cheap, became popular for low-budget
esterns. 1942: Technicolor introduced monopack
rocess, using one negative instead of three and
aking equipment less cumbersome and more
exible. 1948: Republic adopted Trucolor. 1949:
nscocolor, later to become Metrocolor, used on
he Man on the Eiffel Tower. 1951: Supercinecolor
colours) adopted by Columbia in *Sword of Monte
risto.* 1952: Eastmancolor used in *Royal Journey;*
arners adopted it as Warnercolor. 1954: Fox
dopted De Luxe Color.
Today, with new colours springing up all the
me, effectiveness seems to depend not on the
ademark but on how well the film is shot,
rocessed and printed.

olour sequences
a otherwise black-and-white movies were used
t first experimentally (see above) but have also
een employed for dramatic effect. Early examples
iclude *The Ten Commandments* 23, *Ben Hur* 26,
he Wedding March 28, *Chasing Rainbows* 30; many
f the early sound musicals went into colour for
ieir final number, and this went on as late as *Kid
iillions* 35. *Victoria the Great* 37 had colour for the
nal 'Empress of India' scenes. *The Wizard of Oz* 39
ad the Oz scenes in colour and the Kansas scenes
a sepia. *Irene* 40 went into colour for the 'Alice
lue Gown' number – which made the second
alf of the film anti-climactic. *The Moon and
ixpence* 42 blazed into colour for the fire at the end
. . and the same director, Albert Lewin, used a
milar trick whenever the picture was shown in
he Picture of Dorian Gray 44. *A Matter of Life and
eath* 45 had earth in colour, heaven in a rather
netallic monochrome. *Task Force* 49 went into
olour for its final battle reels, most of which
onsisted of blown-up 16mm war footage. *The
ecret Garden* 49 played the same trick as *The
Vizard of Oz.* The *Solid Gold Cadillac* 56 had a few
nal feet of colour to show off the irrelevant car
f the title. In 1958 *I Was a Teenage Frankenstein*
evived the old dodge of colour for the final
onflagration. In *Cleo de 5 à 7* only the ominous
arot cards were in colour; in *The House of Rothschild*
nly the court finale. In *If,* nobody was ever able
› work out why black-and-white alternated with
olour until someone guessed that the producers
ept on running out of money as shooting
rogressed. And *Is Paris Burning?* 66 used colour
or the climactic victory sequence, having been
orced into black-and-white for the rest of the
novie by the necessity of using old newsreel
ootage. In few of the above cases has reissue
rinting maintained the original intention: printing
hort sequences in colour is time-consuming. See
lso: *tinting.*

Colpi, Henri (1921–).
French editor.
Night and Fog 55. The Picasso Mystery 56.
Hiroshima Mon Amour 59. Last Year in Marienbad
51. Les Fruits de Passion 81. Le Grand Frère 83,
nany others.
■ ALSO DIRECTOR: Une Aussi Longue Absence 61.
Codine 63. Mona 66. Heureux Qui Comme Ulysse
70. Mysterious Island 73. Bilitis 76. Rue des
Archives 87.

Coltrane, Robbie (1950–).
Portly Scottish comic actor.
Flash Gordon 80. Subway Riders 81. Britannia
Hospital 82. Scrubbers 82. Ghost Dance 83. Krull
83. Loose Connections 83. Chinese Boxes 84.
Defence of the Realm 85. Revolution 85.
Supergrass (TV) 85. Absolute Beginners 86.
Caravaggio 86. Mona Lisa 86. Eat the Rich (TV) 87.
The Fruit Machine 88. Midnight Breaks 88.
Slipstream 89. Bert Rigby, You're a Fool 89.
Henry V (as Falstaff) 90. Nuns on the Run 90.
Perfectly Normal 90. The Pope Must Die (US: The
Pope Must Diet) 91. Alive and Kicking (TV) 91.
Oh, What a Night 92. The Adventures of Huck Finn
93. Boswell and Johnson's Tour of the Western
Isles (TV) 93, etc.
TV series: Tutti Frutti 87. Coltrane in a Cadillac
93. *Cracker* 93– .

Columbia Pictures.
American production and distribution company
long considered one of the 'little two' (the other
being Universal) against the 'big five' (MGM, RKO,
Fox, Warner and Paramount). Columbia originated
with one man, Harry Cohn, who founded it in
1924 after a career as a salesman and shorts
producer. Throughout the 30s and 40s he turned
out competent co-features and second features,
apart from prestige pictures such as the Capra
comedies and an ill-fated Kramer deal; he was also
prepared to spend big money on certainties such
as Rita Hayworth and *The Jolson Story.* From the
late 40s, with films like *All the King's Men, Born
Yesterday* and *From Here to Eternity,* the company
began to pull itself into the big-time, and when
Cohn died in 1958 it was one of the leaders of
international co-production, with such major films
to its credit as *On the Waterfront* and *The Bridge on
the River Kwai,* with *Lawrence of Arabia* and *A Man
For All Seasons* to come. It also produces and
distributes TV films through its subsidiary Screen
Gems (Columbia Television). In 1990, the Japanese
company Sony paid $3.4 billion for the company.
Peter Guber and Jon Peters were installed to run
the organization, but Peters soon left to resume
life as an independent producer. Since then, the
studio has had mixed fortunes. It has had moderate
successes, such as *A League of Their Own, A Few Good
Men, In The Line of Fire* and *Philadelphia,* but it also
had many misses, culminating in the disaster of *The
Last Action Hero* starring Arnold Schwarzenegger,
which turned out to be not the expected
blockbuster but a dismal flop. In 1994 Peter Guber
followed Jon Peters' example and quit to become
an independent producer.
Books: 1967, *King Cohn* by Bob Thomas. *Hail
Columbia* by Rochelle Larkin. 1989, *The Columbia
Story* by Clive Hirschhorn. 1991, *The Columbia
Checklist* by Leo D. Martin.

Columbo, Russ (1908–1934) (Ruggerio de
Rudolpho Columbo).
American violinist, vocalist, songwriter and
bandleader who appeared in a few films. Died in a
shooting accident.
Wolf Song 29. The Street Girl 29. Hellbound 31.
Broadway through a Keyhole 33. Wake Up and
Dream 34, etc.

Columbus, Chris (1959–).
American director who began as a screenwriter on
films produced by Steven Spielberg. *Home Alone* is
the third most successful film so far made, having
grossed more than $500 million worldwide.
Gremlins (w) 84. Reckless (w) 84. The Goonies
(w) 85. Young Sherlock Holmes (w) 85. Adventures
in Babysitting (d) 87. Heartbreak Hotel (wd) 88.
Home Alone (d) 90. Only the Lonely (wd) 91. Home

Alone 2: Lost in New York 92. Mrs Doubtfire (co-
w, d) 93, etc.

Columbus, Christopher (1451–1506).
The explorer, born in Genoa, enjoyed a brief burst
of screen fame 500 years after his epic voyage to
America with three films: *1492: Discovery of
Paradise,* in which he was played by a French
actor, Gérard Depardieu, *Christopher Columbus: The
Discovery,* in which he was played by a Franco-Greek
actor, George Corraface, and *Carry On Columbus,* in
which he was played by an English actor, Jim
Dale. In 1949, in *Christopher Columbus,* he was
played by Fredric March.

Colvig, Vance (1892–1967).
American actor who spent most of his career at
the Disney studio and became the voice for Pluto
and Goofy. He was also co-author of the song
'Who's Afraid of the Big Bad Wolf?'

combined print.
One on which both sound and picture (always
produced separately) have been 'married', i.e. a
standard print as shown in cinemas.
See also: *double-headed print.*

Comden, Betty (1918–) (Elizabeth Cohen).
American screenwriter who has collaborated with
Adolph Green on books and lyrics of many
Broadway shows and films.
Good News 47. The Barkleys of Broadway 49.
On the Town 49. Singin' in the Rain 52. Band
Wagon (AAN) 54. It's Always Fair Weather (AAN)
55. Auntie Mame 58. What a Way to Go 64, etc.

comedy:
see *comedy teams; crazy comedy; light comedians;
satire; sex; social comedy; slapstick.*

comedy teams
in the accepted sense began in vaudeville, but,
depending so much on the spoken word, could
make little headway in films until the advent of
the talkies. Then they all tried, and many (Amos 'n
Andy, Gallagher and Shean, Olsen and Johnson)
didn't quite make it, at least not immediately.
Laurel and Hardy, who had been successful in
silents by the use of mime, adapted their methods
very little and remained popular; during the 30s
they were really only challenged by Wheeler and
Woolsey, whose style was more frenetic, and
briefly by Burns and Allen. From 1940 the cross-
talking Abbott and Costello reigned supreme, with
an occasional challenge from Hope and Crosby
and the splendid *Hellzapoppin* from Olsen and
Johnson. Then came Martin and Lewis, who
didn't appeal to everybody, Rowan and Martin,
who in 1957 didn't appeal to anybody, and
sporadic attempts to popularize such teams as
Brown and Carney and Allen and Rossi. In
Britain, comedy teams were popular even in poor
films: the best of them were Jack Hulbert and
Cicely Courtneidge, Tom Walls and Ralph Lynn,
Lucan and MacShane ('Old Mother Riley'),
Arthur Askey and Richard Murdoch, and the Crazy
Gang, a bumper fun bundle composed of
Flanagan and Allen, Naughton and Gold, and
Nervo and Knox. One should also mention Basil
Radford and Naunton Wayne, not cross-talkers but
inimitable caricaturists of the Englishman abroad;
and others, not strictly comedians, who raised a
lot of laughs together: Edmund Lowe and Victor
McLaglen, Slim Summerville and ZaSu Pitts, Joan
Blondell and Glenda Farrell, George Sidney and
Charlie Murray, Marie Dressler and Polly Moran,
Wallace Beery and Raymond Hatton, James

Cagney and Pat O'Brien. Recent teams include Morecambe and Wise and Cannon and Ball.

See: 1970, *Movie Comedy Teams* by Leonard Maltin.

Of larger groups, among the most outstanding are Our Gang, the Keystone Kops, the Marx Brothers, the Three Stooges, the Ritz Brothers, Will Hay with Moore Marriott and Graham Moffat, the 'Carry On' team, the Beatles and the Monty Python team.

See also: *romantic teams*.

¶ Nobody should try to play comedy unless they have a circus going on inside. – *Ernst Lubitsch*

Comencini, Luigi (1916–).
Italian director.

Bambini in Città 46. Proibito Rubare 48. The Mill on the Po (co-writer only) 49. La Città Si Difende (co-writer only) 51. Persiane Chiuse 51. Bread, Love and Dreams (& w) 53. Bread, Love and Jealousy 54. Mariti in Città 58. Bebo's Girl 63. Le Bambole (part) 65. Misunderstood 67. Casanova 69. Le Avventure di Pinocchio 72. Sunday Woman 76. Till Marriage Us Do Part 77. Il Gatto 78. Traffic Jam (L'Ingorgo) 79. They All Loved Him 80. Cercasi Gesu 82. The Boy from Calabria 87. La Bohème 88. Merry Christmas, Happy New Year (Buon Natale, Buon Anno) (& co-w) 89. Bread and Wine (Pane e Vino) 92, etc.

Comer, Anjanette (1942–).
American leading lady.

Quick Before It Melts 65. The Loved One 65. The Appaloosa 66. Banning 66. Guns for San Sebastian 68. Rabbit, Run 70. The Firechasers (TV) 70. The Baby 73. Lepke 74. Fire Sale 77, etc.

Comerford, Joe.
Irish director and screenwriter.

Reefer and the Model 88. High Boot Benny 94.

Comfort, Lance (1908–1966).
British director, formerly cameraman.

Penn of Pennsylvania 41. Hatter's Castle 41. When We Are Married 42. Old Mother Riley, Detective 42. Daughter of Darkness (& p) 45. Great Day 45. Silent Dust 48. Portrait of Clare 50. Eight o'Clock Walk 54. At the Stroke of Nine 57. Make Mine a Million 58. The Ugly Duckling 59. Touch of Death 62. Tomorrow at Ten 62. Devils of Darkness 65, many others.

Directed many episodes of TV series, especially *Douglas Fairbanks Presents* which he also co-produced.

comic strips
in newspapers have always been avidly watched by film producers with an eye on the popular market. Among films and series so deriving are the following:

Gertie the Dinosaur (cartoon series) 19; The Gumps (two-reelers) 23–28; *Bringing Up Father* 16 (drawn), 20 (two-reeler), 28 (feature with J. Farrell MacDonald and Marie Dressler), 45 (series of 'Jiggs and Maggie' features with Joe Yule and Renée Riano); *The Katzenjammer Kids* (cartoon series) 17 and 38, *Krazy Kat* (various cartoons 16–38); *Ella Cinders* (with Colleen Moore) 22; *Tillie the Toiler* (with Marion Davies) 27; *Skippy* (with Jackie Cooper) 30; *Little Orphan Annie* 32 (with Mitzi Green) and 38 (with Ann Gillis); *Joe Palooka* 34 (with Stu Erwin) and 47–51 (with Joe Kirkwood); *Blondie* (with Penny Singleton) 38–48; *Gasoline Alley* (with James Lydon) 51; *L'il Abner; Popeye; Jungle Jim* 49–54; *Prince Valiant* 54; *Up Front* 51–53; *Felix the Cat* (GB) 40; *Dick Barton* (GB) in various personifications; *Jane* (GB) in an

abysmal 1949 second feature; and, of course, *Modesty Blaise* 66, *Batman* 66, *Barbarella* 68, and *Fritz the Cat* 71.

Strip characters whose adventures were turned into Hollywood serials during the 30s and 40s include *Tailspin Tommy, Mandrake the Magician, Don Winslow of the Navy, Jet Jackson Flying Commando, Flash Gordon, Batman, Buck Rogers in the 25th century, Brick Bradford* ('in the centre of the earth'), *Chandu, Superman, Dick Tracy* (also in 40s features), *The Lone Ranger* and *Red Ryder*.

In the late 70s comic strip characters became popular TV action heroes, and until the balloon burst audiences were overwhelmed by the antics of *The Incredible Hulk, Wonder Woman, Buck Rogers in the 25th Century*, etc., following on the success of TV's own creations in this vein, *The Six Million Dollar Man, Bionic Woman* and *The Man from Atlantis*.

Comingore, Dorothy (1913–1971).
American actress who made few films but will always be remembered as the second Mrs Kane. Formerly known as Kay Winters and Linda Winters. Committed suicide.

■ Campus Cinderella 38. Comet over Broadway 38. Prison Train 38. Trade Winds 38. Blondie Meets the Boss 39. North of the Yukon 39. Scandal Sheet 39. Mr Smith Goes to Washington 39. Café Hostess 39. Pioneers of the Frontier 40. *Citizen Kane* 41. The Hairy Ape 44. Any Number Can Play 49. The Big Night 51.

communism
has always been treated by Hollywood as a menace. In the 30s one could laugh at it, in *Ninotchka* and *He Stayed for Breakfast*. Then in World War II there was a respite during which the virtues of the Russian peasantry were extolled in such films as *Song of Russia* and *North Star*. But with the Cold War, every international villain became a Commie instead of a Nazi, and our screens were suddenly full of dour dramas about the deadliness of 'red' infiltration: *I Married a Communist, I Was a Communist for the FBI, The Red Menace, The Iron Curtain, Trial, My Son John, Walk East on Beacon, The Red Danube, Red Snow, Red Planet Mars, Blood Alley, Big Jim McLain, The Manchurian Candidate*. In the early 60s a documentary compilation of red aggression was released under the title *We'll Bury You*. The British never seemed to take the peril seriously, though the agitator in *The Angry Silence* was clearly labelled red.

Famous line: 'Communism,' said the butler in *Soak the Rich*, 'is the growing pains of the young.'

Como, Perry (1912–) (Pierino Como; aka Nick Perido).
American popular singer of Italian ancestry and barber apprenticeship. His deceptively relaxed manner made him immensely popular on television in the 60s and 70s.

■ Something for the Boys 44. Doll Face 45. If I'm Lucky 46. Words and Music 48.

¶ The audience knows I'm not going to do anything after all these years to upset them. – *P.C.*

I'm convinced that his voice comes out of his eyelids. – *Oscar Levant*

compilation films
have become commonplace on TV through such series as *Twentieth Century, Men of Our Time* and *The Valiant Years*, all using library material to evoke a pattern of the past. Thanks to the careful preservation of original documentary material,

film-makers have been able, over the last thirty years or so, to give us such films on a wide variety of subjects and to develop an exciting extra dimension of film entertainment which also serves a historical need.

The first outstanding efforts in this direction were made by H. Bruce Woolfe in his 20s documentaries of World War I, mixing newsreel footage with reconstructed scenes. In 1940 Cavalcanti assembled his study of Mussolini, *Yellow Caesar*; and in 1942 Frank Capra, working for the US Signal Corps, gave a tremendous fillip to the art of the compilation film with his 'Why We Fight' series. Paul Rotha's *World of Plenty* 43 was a clever study of world food shortages using all kinds of film material including animated diagrams and acted sequences. In 1945 Carol Reed and Garson Kanin, in *The True Glory*, gave the story of D-Day to Berlin an unexpected poetry, and in 1946 Don Siegel in his short *Hitler Lives* showed all too clearly what a frightening potential the compilation form had as propaganda. Nicole Védrès in 1947 turned to the more distant past and in *Paris 1900* produced an affectionate portrait of a bygone age; Peter Baylis followed this with *The Peaceful Years*, covering the period between the two wars. In 1953 Stuart Legg's *Powered Flight* traced the history of aviation.

The Thorndikes, working in East Germany, started in 1956 their powerful series *The Archives Testify*, attributing war crimes to West German officials; this aggressive mood was followed in their *Du und Mancher Kamerad* ('The German Story') and *The Russian Miracle*, though in the latter case they seemed somewhat less happy in praising than in blaming. In 1959 George Morrison's *Mise Eire* graphically presented the truth of the much-fictionalized Irish troubles; and in 1960 came the first of the films about Hitler, Erwin Leiser's *Mein Kampf*, to be sharply followed by Rotha's *The Life of Adolf Hitler* and Louis Clyde Stoumen's rather fanciful *Black Fox*. Jack Le Vien, producer of the last-named, went on to make successful films about Churchill (*The Finest Hours*) and the Duke of Windsor (*A King's Story*). Now every year the compilations come thick and fast. From France, *Fourteen-Eighteen*; from BBC TV, twenty-six half-hours of *The Great War*; from Granada TV, *The Fanatics* (suffragettes), *The World of Mr Wells* (H.G. that is) and a long-running weekly series, *All Our Yesterdays*, which consisted entirely of old newsreels; from Associated-British, *Time to Remember*, a series devoting half an hour to each year of the century; from Italy, *Allarmi Siam' Fascisti*, a history of the fascist movement; from Japan, *Kamikaze*, about the suicide pilots; from France, Rossif's *Mourir à Madrid* and *The Fall of Berlin*. The list will be endless, because even though every foot of old newsreel were used up, one could begin again, using different editing, juxtaposition and commentary to achieve different effects.

Best book on the subject: Jay Leyda's *Films Beget Films*.

In the late 50s there began a pleasing fashion for compilations of scenes from fictional films on a theme. This began with Robert Youngson's masterly evocations of silent slapstick: *The Golden Age of Comedy, When Comedy Was King*, etc. TV series such as *Silents Please* and *Hollywood and the Stars* followed suit. In the 70s MGM had an immense success with *That's Entertainment*, compiled from its past successes, and also brought out *The Big Parade of Comedy*. Twentieth-Century-Fox turned its backlog into a television series, *That's Hollywood*; and for a while wherever one looked in Hollywood there was at least one studio cutting room devoted to turning over and reassembling highlights of the past.

See also: *documentary*.

composers

have frequently been lauded on cinema screens, usually in storylines which bore little relation to their real lives, and the films were not often box-office successes. Here are some of the subjects of musical biopics:
- George Frederick Handel (1685–1759): Wilfred Lawson, *The Great Mr Handel* 42.
- Wolfgang Amadeus Mozart (1756–91): Stephen Haggard, *Whom the Gods Love* 36; Hannes Steltzer, *Die Kleine Nachtmusik* 39; Gino Cervi, *Eternal Melody* 39; Oskar Werner, *The Life of Mozart* 56; Tom Hulce, *Amadeus* (84).
- Ludwig van Beethoven (1770–1827): Albert Basserman, *New Wine* 41; Ewald Balser, *Eroica* 49; Karl Boehm, *The Magnificent Rebel* 60; Gary Oldman, *Immortal Beloved* 95.
- Niccolò Paganini (1782–1840): Stewart Granger, *The Magic Bow* 47.
- Franz Schubert (1797–1828): Nils Asther, *Love Time* 34; Richard Tauber, *Blossom Time* 34; Hans Jaray, *Unfinished Symphony* 35; Alan Curtis *New Wine* 41; Tino Rossi, *La Belle Meunière* 47; Claude Laydu, *Symphony of Love* 54; Karl Boehm, *Das Dreimaederlhaus* 58.
- Vincenzo Bellini (1801–35): Phillips Holmes, *The Divine Spark* 35.
- Hector Berlioz (1803–69): Jean-Louis Barrault, *La Symphonie Fantastique* 40.
- Frederic Chopin (1810–49): Jean Servais, *Adieu* 35; Cornel Wilde, *A Song to Remember* 44; Czeslaw Wollejko, *The Young Chopin* 52; Alexander Davion, *Song Without End* 60.
- Robert Schumann (1810–56): Paul Henreid, *Song of Love* 47.
- Franz Liszt (1811–86): Stephen Bekassy, *A Song to Remember* 44; Henry Daniell, *Song of Love* 47; Will Quadflieg, *Lola Montez* 55; Dirk Bogarde, *Song Without End* 60; Henry Gilbert, *Song of Norway* 70; Roger Daltrey, *Lisztomania* 75.
- Richard Wagner (1813–83): Alan Badel, *Magic Fire* 56; Trevor Howard, *Ludwig* 73; Richard Burton, *Wagner* 83.
- Johann Strauss Jnr (1825–99): Esmond Knight, *Waltzes from Vienna* 33; Anton Walbrook, *Vienna Waltzes* 34. Fernand Gravet, *The Great Waltz* 38; Kerwin Matthews, *The Waltz King* 60; Horst Buchholz, *The Great Waltz* 72.
- Stephen Foster (1826–64): Don Ameche, *Swanee River* 39; Bill Shirley, *I Dream of Jeannie* 52.
- Johannes Brahms (1833–97): Robert Walker, *Song of Love* 47.
- W. S. Gilbert (1836–1911) and Arthur Sullivan (1842–1900): Nigel Bruce and Claud Allister, *Lillian Russell* 41; Robert Morley and Maurice Evans, *The Story of Gilbert and Sullivan* 53.
- Peter Ilich Tchaikovsky (1840–93): Frank Sundstrom, *Song of My Heart* 47; Innokenti Smoktunovsky, *Tchaikovsky* 69; Richard Chamberlain, *The Music Lovers* 70.
- Edvard Grieg (1843–1907): Toralv Maurstad, *Song of Norway* 70.
- Nikolai Rimsky-Korsakov (1844–1908): Jean-Pierre Aumont, *Song of Scheherezade* 47.
- John Philip Sousa (1854–1932): Clifton Webb, *Stars and Stripes Forever* 52.
- Victor Herbert (1859–1924): Walter Connolly, *The Great Victor Herbert* 39; Paul Maxey, *Till the Clouds Roll By* 46.
- Gustav Mahler (1860–1911): Robert Powell, *Mahler* 74.
Leslie Stuart (1866–1928): Robert Morley, *You Will Remember* 40.
- W. C. Handy (1873–1948): Nat King Cole, *St Louis Blues* 58.
- Jerome Kern (1885–1945): Robert Walker, *Till the Clouds Roll By* 46.
- Sigmund Romberg (1887–1951): Jose Ferrer, *Deep in My Heart* 54.
- Irving Berlin (1888–   ): Tyrone Power, *Alexander's Ragtime Band* 38.
- Cole Porter (1892–1964): Cary Grant, *Night and Day* 45.
- George Gershwin (1898–1937): Robert Alda, *Rhapsody in Blue* 45.

The list of biopics of lesser modern composers would be long indeed.

composite print:

see *combined print* for which it is an alternative term.

Compson, Betty (1897–1974).

American leading lady of the 20s, in Christie comedies from 1915. The first of her three husbands was director James Cruze.

The Miracle Man 19. Kick In 22. Woman to Woman (GB) 23 and 29. The Enemy Sex 24. The Fast Set 26. The Barker (AAN) 28. Docks of New York 28. The Great Gabbo 29. On with the Show 30. The Gay Diplomat 31. Destination Unknown 33. Laughing Irish Eyes (GB) 36. A Slight Case of Murder 38. Strange Cargo 40. Mr and Mrs Smith 41. Claudia and David 46. Hard-Boiled Mahoney 47. Here Comes Trouble 48, many others.

Compton, Fay (1894–1978).

British stage actress who made occasional film appearances.

She Stoops to Conquer 14. One Summer's Day 17. The Labour Leader 17. A Woman of No Importance 21. The Old Wives' Tale 21. Mary Queen of Scots 22. This Freedom 23. Robinson Crusoe 27. Fashions in Love (US) 29. Tell England 31. Autumn Crocus 34. The Mill on the Floss 35. The Prime Minister 41. Odd Man Out 46. London Belongs to Me 48. Laughter in Paradise 50. Othello 52. Aunt Clara 54. The Story of Esther Costello 57. The Haunting 63. The Virgin and the Gypsy 70, many others.

Compton, Joyce (1907–   ) (Eleanor Hunt).

American light second lead of the 30s.

Syncopating Sue 26. Dangerous Curves 29. Three Rogues 31. Only Yesterday 33. Magnificent Obsession 35. The Toast of New York 37. Balalaika 39. City for Conquest 40. Blues in the Night 42. Pillow to Post 45. Grand Canyon 51, etc.

Compton, Juliette (1902–   ).

American actress, a performer in Ziegfeld's Follies who came to England to appear in Cochran's revues and starred in local films before returning to America in 1929.

The Wine of Life (GB) 24. Bulldog Drummond's Third Round (GB) 25. Nell Gwyn (GB) 26. The Intruder (GB) 28. Anybody's Woman 30. Strangers in Love 32. Westward Passage 32. Peg o' My Heart 33. Berkeley Square 33. The Count of Monte Cristo 34. Irene 40. That Hamilton Woman (GB: Lady Hamilton) 41, etc.

computers

from the mid-70s became so commonplace as barely to rate a mention, forming the basis of such films as *Rollover* and *War Games* and TV series such as *Knight Rider* and *Whiz Kids*. Some of their earlier uses in film, however, were in Disney's *The Computer Wore Tennis Shoes*; in the unpleasant *Demon Seed*; in space fiction such as *The Forbin Project*, *2001* and *Dark Star*; in *Billion Dollar Brain*; and in a rather advanced TV movie of 1971 called *Paper Man*. In the beginning, computers tended to be regarded as evil, machines that wanted to control people, as in *Superman III* or *Electric Dreams*. But as computers became familiar objects in many homes, and computer and video games grew in popularity, and in turn were often based on hit movies, attitudes changed. Disney's *Tron* tried to capitalize on computer games, as did *Interface*, in which a game turned into reality. The appeal of *The Lawnmower Man* depended on its stunning computer graphics and its simulation of the latest technology of 'virtual reality', a computer-generated world with which people can interact. Androids – half-men, half-computers – emerged as popular heroes in such films as *Robocop* and *The Terminator 2*. By 92, the tail was beginning to wag the dog, with computer games on compact disk incorporating film clips, and the Nintendo game *Super Mario Brothers* being turned into a movie starring Bob Hoskins.

Conaway, Jeff (1950–   ).

American general-purpose actor.

Jennifer on My Mind 71. The Eagle Has Landed 76. Grease 78. Breaking Up Is Hard to Do (TV) 79. For the Love of It (TV) 80. Covergirl 83. The Patriot 86. Elvira, Mistress of the Dark 88. Ghost Writer 89. The Banker 89. The Sleeping Car 90, etc.

TV series: Taxi 78–82.

concentration camps,

until long after World War II, were thought too harrowing a subject for film treatment; but a few serious reconstructions have emerged, notably *The Last Stage* (Poland) 48, *Kapo* (Italy) 60, *Passenger* (Poland) 61, and *One Day in the Life of Ivan Denisovitch* 71, while the shadow of Auschwitz hangs over *The Diary of Anne Frank* 59 and *The Pawnbroker* 64. An alleged British concentration camp in South Africa was depicted in the Nazi film *Ohm Krüger* 42. The best documentary on the subject was probably Resnais' *Night and Fog*. In 1978 TV included much footage on the subject in *Holocaust*, which was quickly followed by *Playing for Time*. *Shoah* (1986) used no archive footage at all, but spent its nine hours in long interviews with survivors. *Triumph of the Spirit* told the true story of a boxer's survival in Auschwitz.

concerts

of serious music naturally figure largely in films about the lives of composers (qv), and also in those concerned to show off living musicians: *They Shall Have Music, Music for Millions, Battle for Music, Tonight We Sing, Carnegie Hall, A Hundred Men and a Girl, Rhapsody in Blue*. In the 40s a string of romantic films were centred on classical musicians and had concert climaxes: *Dangerous Moonlight, Love Story, The Seventh Veil, Intermezzo, The Great Lie*; this style later returned in *Interlude*. Other dramatic and comic concerts were featured in *Unfaithfully Yours, Tales of Manhattan, The Man Who Knew Too Much, The World of Henry Orient, The Bride Wore Black, Counterpoint* and *Deadfall*. The most influential film concert was certainly *Fantasia*, and the most poignant probably Myra Hess's recital in the blitz-beset National Gallery in *Listen to Britain*.

Condon, Jackie (1913–1977).

American child actor, one of the original members of the Our Gang comedies of the 20s.

Condon, Richard (1915–   ).

American screenwriter and novelist of paranoid thrillers that have become successful movies. He is a former publicist for Walt Disney.

The Oldest Confession (from novel *The Happy Thieves*) 61. The Manchurian Candidate (oa) 62. Winter Kills (oa) 79. Prizzi's Honor (co-w) 85, etc.

confidence tricksters

have figured as minor characters in hundreds of films, but full-length portraits of the breed are few and choice. Harry Baur in *Volpone* and Rex Harrison in *The Honey Pot;* Roland Young, Billie Burke, Janet Gaynor and Douglas Fairbanks Jnr in *The Young in Heart;* Gene Tierney, Laird Cregar and Spring Byington in *Rings on Her Fingers;* Tyrone Power in *Nightmare Alley* and *Mississippi Gambler;* Mai Zetterling in *Quartet;* Paul Newman in *The Hustler;* Charles Coburn and Barbara Stanwyck in *The Lady Eve;* David Niven and Marlon Brando in *Bedtime Story;* George C. Scott in *The Flim Flam Man;* Richard Attenborough and David Hemmings in *Only When I Larf;* James Garner in *The Skin Game;* Newman and Robert Redford in *The Sting;* Ryan and Tatum O'Neal in *Paper Moon;* James Coburn in *Dead Heat on a Merry-go-Round;* Joe Mantegna in *House of Games,* demonstrating how to do it to a bemused Lindsay Crouse; Steve Martin and Michael Caine in *Dirty Rotten Scoundrels;* John Cusack, Annette Bening and Angelica Huston in *The Grifters.*

Coninx, Stijn (1957–).
Belgian director.
Hector 87. Koko Flanel 89. Daens (AAN) 92, etc.

Conklin, Chester (1888–1971) (Jules Cowles).
American silent slapstick comedian, in innumerable short comedies for Keystone and Sennett; features rarer.
Greed 24. Rubber Heels 27. Gentlemen Prefer Blondes 28. Her Majesty Love 31. Hallelujah I'm a Bum 33. *Modern Times* 36. Hollywood Cavalcade 39. The Great Dictator 40. Hail the Conquering Hero 44. The Perils of Pauline 47. Big Hand for a Little Lady 66, etc.

Conklin, Heinie (1880–1959) (Charles Conklin).
American character comedian, one of the original Keystone Kops.

Conlin, Jimmy (1884–1962).
Birdlike little American character comedian, in many films, notably those of Preston Sturges.
College Rhythm 33. And Sudden Death 36. Sullivan's Travels 41. The Palm Beach Story 42. Ali Baba and the Forty Thieves 44. Mad Wednesday 47. The Great Rupert 50. Anatomy of a Murder 59, many others.

Connaughton, Shane.
Irish dramatist, screenwriter and occasional actor.
My Left Foot (co-w, AAN) 89. The Miracle (a) 91. The Playboys (co-w) 92. O Mary This London (TV) 94, etc.

Connell, Richard (1893–1949).
American writer whose chief bequest to Hollywood was his short story 'The Most Dangerous Game' (qv), filmed in 1932 (aka *The Hounds of Zaroff*) and remade several times. He also provided the original story for other films: *Seven Faces* 29. *F Man* 36. *Brother Orchid* 40. Meet John Doe (AAN) 41. Two Girls and a Sailor (co-w, AAN) 44.

Connelly, Christopher (1944–1988).
American light leading man, mostly on television.
Corky 72. Benji 74. Hawmps 76. The Norsemen 78, etc.
TV series: Peyton Place 64–69. Paper Moon 74.

Connelly, Jennifer (1970–).
American juvenile actress.
Once upon a Time in America 84. Creepers 85. Labyrinth 86. Seven Minutes in Heaven 86. Some Girls 88. The Hot Spot 90. The Rocketeer 91. Career Opportunities (aka One Wild Night) 91. Of Love and Shadows 94, etc.

Connelly, Marc (1890–1980).
American playwright whose *The Green Pastures* was influentially filmed in 1936. He occasionally contributed to screenplays, e.g. *I Married a Witch;* and other movies based on his work are *Merton of the Movies*, *Make Me a Star*, *Dulcy* and *Beggar on Horseback*, all from the late 20s and early 30s.

Connery, Jason (1962–).
British actor, the son of actors Sean Connery and Diane Cilento.
Lords of Discipline 82. Dream One 83. The Boy Who Had Everything 83. Winner Takes All 86. Tank Malling 88. Bye Bye Baby 88. Casablanca Express 89. The Secret Life of Ian Fleming (TV) 90. Jamila 94, etc.
TV series: Robin of Sherwood 88–89.

Connery, Neil (1938–).
British leading man who made a brief appearance; Sean Connery's brother.
Operation Kid Brother 66. The Body Stealers 70, etc.

Connery, Sean (1930–) (Thomas Connery).
Virile Scots leading man who shot to fame as James Bond and has since cornered the market in gruffly indomitable characters.
Biographies: 1993, *Sean Connery* by John Parker. 1993, *Sean Connery: Neither Shaken nor Stirred* by Andrew Yule.
■ No Road Back 55. Time Lock 56. Hell Drivers 57. Action of the Tiger 57. Another Time Another Place 58. Darby O'Gill and the Little People 59. Tarzan's Greatest Adventure 59. Frightened City 60. On the Fiddle 61. The Longest Day 62. *Doctor No* 62. From Russia With Love 63. Woman of Straw 64. Marnie 64. *Goldfinger* 64. *The Hill* 65. Thunderball 65. A Fine Madness 66. You Only Live Twice 67. Shalako 68. The Molly Maguires 69. The Red Tent 69. The Anderson Tapes 71. Diamonds are Forever 71. The Offence 72. Zardoz 74. Ransom 74. Murder on the Orient Express 74. The Wind and the Lion 75. The Man Who Would Be King 76. Robin and Marian 76. The Next Man 76. A Bridge Too Far 77. The First Great Train Robbery 78. Meteor 79. Cuba 79. Outland 81. Time Bandits 81. Five Days One Summer 82. Wrong is Right 82. Never Say Never Again 83. Sword of the Valiant 83. Highlander 85. The Name of the Rose 86. The Untouchables (AA) 87. Memories of Me 88. The Presidio 88. Indiana Jones and the Last Crusade 89. The Hunt for Red October 90. The Russia House 90. Highlander II – the Quickening 90. Robin Hood: Prince of Thieves 91. Medicine Man 92. Rising Sun 93. A Good Man in Africa 94. Dragonheart 95. First Knight 95.

¶ I have always hated that damn James Bond. I'd like to kill him. – *S.C.*
With the exception of Lassie, he's the only person I know who's never been spoiled by success. – *Terence Young*

Connick, Harry, Jnr (1967–).
American singer, songwriter, pianist and actor.
When Harry Met Sally (s) 89. Memphis Belle (a, s) 90. The Godfather Part III (s) 90. Little Man Tate (a) 91, etc.

Connolly, Billy (1942–).
Scatological Scottish comedian, often hard to understand for Sassenachs, now in America.
Big Banana Feet 77. Absolution 78. Water 84. Blue Money (TV) 84. Absolution 88. Crossing the Line 92. Indecent Proposal 93. Down among the Big Boys (TV) 93, etc.
TV series: Head of the Class 90–92. Billy 92.

¶ I set out to be a cross between Lenny Bruce and Robert the Bruce – my main thrust was the body and its functions and malfunctions – the absurdity of the thing. – *B.C.*

Connolly, Walter (1887–1940).
Chubby American character actor who spent his last years in films playing rasping millionaires and choleric editors.
■ No More Orchids 32. Washington Merry Go Round 32. Man Against Woman 32. Lady for a Day 33. East of Fifth Avenue 33. The Bitter Tea of General Yen 33. Paddy the Next Best Thing 33. Master of Men 33. Man's Castle 33. *It Happened One Night* 34. Once to Every Woman 34. Eight Girls in a Boat 34. Twentieth Century 34. Whom the Gods Destroy 34. Servants Entrance 34. Lady by Choice 34. Broadway Bill 34. The Captain Hates the Sea 34. White Lies 34. *Father Brown Detective* 35. She Couldn't Take It 35. So Red the Rose 35. One Way Ticket 35. The Music Goes Round 36. *Soak the Rich* 36. The King Steps Out 36. Libeled Lady 36. The Good Earth 37. Nancy Steele is Missing 37. Let's Get Married 37. The League of Frightened Men 37. First Lady 37. *Nothing Sacred* 37. Penitentiary 38. Start Cheering 38. Four's a Crowd 38. Too Hot to Handle 38. The Girl Downstairs 39. The Adventures of Huckleberry Finn 39. Bridal Suite 39. Good Girls Go to Paris 39. Coast Guard 39. Those High Gray Walls 39. *Fifth Avenue Girl* 39. *The Great Victor Herbert* 39.

¶ I am sitting here, Mr Cook, toying with the idea of cutting out your heart and stuffing it like an olive! – *W.C. in Nothing Sacred*

Connor, Edric (1915–1968).
British West Indian actor and singer.
Cry the Beloved Country 52. Moby Dick 56. Fire Down Below 57. Four for Texas 63. Nobody Runs Forever 68, many others.

Connor, Kenneth (1918–1993).
British radio and TV comedian adept at nervous or shy roles. A mainstay of the 'Carry On' film series.
There Was a Young Lady 53. The Black Rider 55. Davy 57. Carry On Sergeant 58. Carry On Nurse 59. Dentist in the Chair 60. Carry On Constable 60. What a Carve-up 61. Gonks Go Beat 65. Carry On England 76. Carry On Emmanuelle 78, etc.

Connor, Kevin (1937–).
British director, former editor.
■ The Land That Time Forgot 75. From Beyond the Grave 75. At the Earth's Core 76. Dirty Knight's Work 76. The People That Time Forgot 77. Warlords of Atlantis 78. Arabian Adventure 79. Motel Hell 80. The House Where Evil Dwells 82. Master of the Game (TV) 84. The Return of Sherlock Holmes (TV) 87. What Price Victory (TV) 88. Dirty Dozen: Danko's Dozen (TV) 88. Great Expectations (TV) 89. The Hollywood Detective (TV) 89.

Connors, Chuck (1921–1992) (Kevin Connors).
Tough guy American hero/villain, his thin smile being adaptable to friendship or menace.

Pat and Mike 52. South Sea Woman 53. Naked Alibi 54. Target Zero 55. Three Stripes in the Sun 55. Designing Woman 57. Geronimo 62. Move Over Darling 63. Synanon 65. Broken Sabre 65. Ride Beyond Vengeance 66. Captain Nemo and the Underwater City 69. Kill 'Em All and Come Back Alone 70. The Deserter 70. Pancho Villa 71. Embassy 72. Soylent Green 72. The Mad Bomber 72. 99 44/100% Dead 74. Banjo Hackett (TV) 76. Nightmare in Badham County (TV) 76. Roots (TV) 77. The Night They Took Miss Beautiful (TV) 77. Standing Tall (TV) 78. The Tourist Trap 79. Airplane 2: The Sequel 82. Summer Camp Nightmare 85. Terror Squad 87. Kill and Enjoy 88. Skinheads 88. Trained to Kill 88. Taxi Killer 88. Once Upon a Texas Train (aka Texas Guns) (TV) 88. Jump 89. Critical Action 90. High Desert Kill 90. Salmonberries 91. Three Days to a Kill 92, etc.

TV series: *Rifleman* 57–61. Arrest and Trial 63. Branded 64–65. Cowboy in Africa 67. The Thrillseekers 72. The Yellow Rose 83.

Connors, Mike (1925–) (Kreker Ohanian).
American action hero of films and TV. Formerly known as Touch Connors.

Sudden Fear 52. The Ten Commandments 56. Where Love has Gone 64. Good Neighbour Sam 64. Situation Hopeless but not Serious 65. Harlow 65. *Stagecoach* 66. Kiss the Girls and Make them Die 67. The Killer who Wouldn't Die (TV) 76. S.S. Casino (TV) 79. Avalanche Express 79. Too Scared to Scream 85. Fist Fighter 88, etc.

TV series: *Tightrope* 57. *Mannix* 67–74. Today's FBI 81.

Conrad, Con (1891–1938) (Conrad K. Dober).
American song composer whose 'The Continental' in 1934 won the first song Oscar.

Broadway 29. Happy Days 30. Palmy Days 31. The Gay Divorcee 34. Reckless 35. The Great Ziegfeld 36. The Story of Vernon and Irene Castle 39, etc.

Conrad, Jess (1940–).
British pop singer and lightweight actor.

Too Young to Love 59. Konga 61. The Boys 62. The Golden Head 65. Hell is Empty 67. The Assassination Bureau 69. Absolute Beginners 86, etc.

Conrad, Joseph (1857–1924) (Teodor Josef Konrad Korzeniowski).
Polish-Ukrainian novelist, former seaman, who settled in Britain.

Lord Jim 26 and 65. Sabotage 37. Victory 30 and 40. An Outcast of the Islands 52. Laughing Anne 53. The Duellists 77.

Conrad, Michael (1925–1983).
Giant-sized American character actor.

The War Lord 65. Sol Madrid 67. The Todd Killings 70. The Longest Yard 74. Baby Blue Marine 76, etc.

TV series: Delvecchio 76. *Hill Street Blues* 81–84.

Conrad, Robert (1935–) (Conrad Robert Falk).
Short but personable American leading man who never carried his TV popularity over to the big screen.

■ Palm Springs Weekend 63. Young Dillinger 65. The DA: Murder One (TV) 69. Weekend of Terror (TV) 70. The DA: Conspiracy to Kill (TV) 71. Five Desperate Women (TV) 71. The Adventures of Nick Carter (TV) 72. The Last Day (TV) 75. Live a Little Steal a Lot 75. Smash-up on Interstate Five (TV) 77. Sudden Death 77. Centennial (TV) 78. The Wild Wild West Revisited (TV) 79. Breaking Up Is Hard to Do (TV) 80. Wrong Is Right 82. Will

(TV) 82. Confessions of a Married Man (TV) 84. Falling for the Stars 85. Two Fathers' Justice (TV) 85. Assassin (TV) 86, etc.

TV series: Hawaiian Eye 59–62. *The Wild Wild West* 65–68. Assignment Vienna 72. Ba Ba Black Sheep 76–77. The Duke 79. A Man Called Sloan 79. Jesse Hawkes 89.

Conrad, William (1920–1994).
Heavily-built American radio writer and actor who came to Hollywood to play unpleasant villains, but later became a producer-director.

The Killers (a) 46. Arch of Triumph (a) 48. One Way Street (a) 50. Cry Danger (a) 51. Lone Star (a) 52. The Naked Jungle (a) 54. *Johnny Concho* (a) 56. The Ride Back (a) 57. Two on a Guillotine (pd) 64. Brainstorm (pd) 65. Chamber of Horrors (p) 66. An American Dream (p) 67. Covenant with Death (p) 67. Countdown (p) 68. The Brotherhood of the Bell (a) (TV) 70. O'Hara US Treasury (a) (TV) 71. Night Cries (a) (TV) 78. Keefer (a) (TV) 79. The Mikado (a) (TV) 82. Side Show (d) 84, etc.

TV series (as actor): *Cannon* 71–76. Nero Wolfe 81.

Conried, Hans (1917–1982).
Tall, weedy American comic actor with precise diction and a richly variable voice.

Dramatic School 37. Crazy House 43. Mrs Parkington 44. The Senator Was Indiscreet 47. My Friend Irma 49. The Twonky 53. *The Five Thousand Fingers of Doctor T* 53. Bus Stop 56. Rockabye Baby 58. The Patsy 64. The Brother O'Toole 73. Oh God Book Two 80, many others.

TV series: The Danny Thomas Show 58–64. The Bullwinkle Show (voice) 61–62. Make Room for Granddaddy 70–71. The Tony Randall Show 77–78. American Dream 81.

Conroy, Frank (1890–1964).
British stage actor who went to Hollywood in the early 30s, generally played domestic tyrants.

The Royal Family of Broadway 30. Grand Hotel 32. Call of the Wild 35. Wells Fargo 37. *The Ox-Bow Incident* 42. Naked City 48. Lightning Strikes Twice 51. The Last Mile 59, etc.

Conroy, Pat (1945–).
American novelist.

The Water Is Wide (from Conrack) 74. The Great Santini 81. The Lord of Discipline 82. The Prince of Tides 91.

Constanduros, Mabel (1880–1957).
English character actress, screenwriter and dramatist, best known for creating the cockney Buggins family on radio and records. In films from silents and radio from 1925.

Hello Radio 32. Radio Parade 33. Where's George? 35. Rose of Tralee 42. Variety Jubilee (co-w) 43. My Ain Folk 44. A Medal for the General 44. 29 Acacia Avenue (oa) 45. Caravan 46. This Man Is Mine (co-w) 46. Holiday Camp (co-w) 47. Easy Money 48, etc.

Constantine, Eddie (1917–1993).
Tough American actor popular in France where he plays Peter Cheyney heroes in crime films.

SOS Pacific 59. Treasure of San Teresa 60. Riff Raff Girls 62. Alphaville 65. Beware of a Holy Whore 71. The Long Good Friday 80. Box Office 83. Soap Bubbles 85. Macaroni Blues 86. Helsinki, Napoli All Night Long 88. The Return of Lemmy Caution 88. Europa 91. Germany Nine Zero (Allemagne Neuf Zero) 91, many others.

Constantine, Michael (1927–) (Constantine Joanides).
Greek-American character actor, mostly on TV.

The Last Mile 59. The Hustler 61. Island of Love 63. Beau Geste 66. Hawaii 66. Skidoo 68. If it's Tuesday This Must Be Belgium 69. The Reivers 69. Peeper 74. Voyage of the Damned 76. Raid on Entebbe (TV) 77. The North Avenue Irregulars 79, etc.

TV series: Hey Landlord. Room 222. Sirota's Court. Amanda's 83.

Conte, Richard (1911–1975) (Nicholas Conte).
Amiable Italian-American action hero in films of varying merit; often seen as oppressed hero or sympathetic gangster.

■ Heaven with a Barbed Wire Fence 39. *Guadalcanal Diary* 43. The Purple Heart 44. *A Walk in the Sun* 45. A Bell for Adano 45. Captain Eddie 45. The Spider 45. Somewhere in the Night 46. 13 Rue Madeleine 46. The Other Love 47. Call Northside 777 48. Cry of the City 48. Appointment with Murder 48. Thieves' Highway 49. Big Jack 49. *House of Strangers* 49. Whirlpool 49. The Sleeping City 50. Under the Gun 50. Hollywood Story 51. The Raging Tide 51. Thief of Damascus 52. The Fighter 52. The Raiders 52. Desert Legion 53. The Blue Gardenia 53. Slaves of Babylon 53. Highway Dragnet 54. A Race for Life 54. Target Zero 55. The Big Combo 55. Bengazi 55. New York Confidential 55. The Big Tip-Off 55. I'll Cry Tomorrow 55. Full of Life 56. The Brothers Rico 57. Little Red Monkey 57. This Angry Age 58. They Came to Cordura 59. Ocean's Eleven 60. Pepe 60. Who's Been Sleeping in My Bed? 63. The Eyes of Annie Jones 64. Circus World 64. Synanon 65. Stay Tuned for Terror 65. The Greatest Story Ever Told 65. Assault on a Queen 65. Tony Rome 66. Hotel 67. Lady in Cement 68. Operation Cross Eagle 69. Explosion 70. The Godfather 72.

TV series: The Four Just Men 59. The Jean Arthur Show 66.

Conti, Albert (1887–1967) (Albert de Conti Cedassamare).
Austrian actor in American films. He began as assistant director to Eric von Stroheim on *The Merry-Go-Round.*

The Eagle 25. The Merry Widow 25. Show People 28. Madame Satan 30. Morocco 30. Freak 32. Suez 38. Gateway 38, etc.

Conti, Bill (1943–).
American composer.

Blume in Love 73. Harry and Tonto 74. Next Stop Greenwich Village 76. *Rocky* 76. Citizen's Band 77. F.I.S.T. 78. An Unmarried Woman 78. Paradise Alley 78. The Big Fix 78. Hurricane 79. Rocky II 79. Gloria 80. Private Benjamin 80. For Your Eyes Only 81. Victory 81. I the Jury 82. Rocky III 82. Split Image 82. The Right Stuff (AA) 83. Unfaithfully Yours 84. The Karate Kid 84. Mass Appeal 85. Nomads 85. Rocky IV 85. The Boss's Wife 86. F/X 86. The Karate Kid Part II 86. Broadcast News 87. Happy New Year 87. Cohen and Tate 88. A Night in the Life of Jimmy Reardon 88. The Karate Kid Part III 89. Lean on Me 89. Lock Up 89. The Fourth War 90. Rocky V 90. Year of the Gun 91. Necessary Roughness 91. Nails 92. The Adventures of Huck Finn 93. Blood In Blood Out 93. Rookie of the Year 93. 8 Seconds 94. The Next Karate Kid 94. The Scout 94, etc.

Conti, Tom (1941–).
Saturnine British actor, mostly on stage and TV.

Flame 74. Galileo 74. Eclipse 76. Full Circle 76. The Glittering Prizes (TV) 76. The Duellists 77. Blade on the Feather (TV) 80. The Wall (TV) 80. Merry Christmas Mr Lawrence 83. *Reuben Reuben* (AAN) 83. American Dreamer 84. Saving Grace 84. Miracles 85. Heavenly Pursuits 85. Nazi Hunter (TV) 86. Beyond Therapy 87. Shirley Valentine 89. That Summer of White Roses 89. Two Brothers Running 89. Shattered 90. Someone Else's America 94, etc.

¶ A film set is just a never-ending hell. – *T.C.*

continuity.
The development of cinematic narrative from beginning to end of a film. If continuity is good the audience will be carried smoothly from one scene to another without disturbing breaks or lapses of detail.

contrast.
The tone range in a print. Heavy contrast results in 'soot and whitewash', i.e. blurry blacks and burnt-out whites.

Converse, Frank (1938–).
American general-purpose actor.
Hurry Sundown 67. Hour of the Gun 67. A Tattered Web (TV) 70. Dr Cook's Garden (TV) 73. The Rowdyman 72. Cruise into Terror (TV) 78. The Bushido Blade 79. Mystery at Fire Island 81. The Pilot 82. Spring Fever 83. Anne of Avonlea (TV) 87. Everybody Wins 90. Primary Motive 92, etc.
TV series: Coronet Blue 67. NYPD 67–68. *Movin' On* 74–75. The Family Tree 83.

Convertino, Michael.
American composer.
Children of a Lesser God 86. The Hidden 87. Bull Durham 88. Queen of Hearts 89. The End of Innocence 90. Aspen Extreme 93. Bodies, Rest & Motion 93. Wrestling Ernest Hemingway 93, etc.

Conway, Gary (1936–) (Gareth Carmody).
American light leading man.
I was a Teenage Frankenstein (as the monster) 57. Young Guns of Texas 62. Black Gunn 72. Once is not Enough 75. The Farmer (& p) 77. American Ninja II (& co-w) 86. Liberty and Bash 90, etc.
TV series: *Burke's Law* 63–65. Land of the Giants 68–69.

Conway, Jack (1887–1952).
American action director, launched as acting member of D. W. Griffith's stock company; long with MGM.
■ The Old Armchair 12. Bond of Fear 18. Because of a Woman 18. Little Red Decides 18. Her Decision 18. You Can't Believe Everything 18. Diplomatic Mission 19. Desert Law 19. Riders of the Dawn 20. Lombardi Limited 20. Dwelling Place of Light 21. The Money Changers 21. The Spenders 21. The Kiss 21. A Daughter of the Law 21. Step On It 22. A Parisian Scandal 22. The Millionaire 22. Across the Deadline 22. Another Man's Shoes 22. Don't Shoot 22. The Long Chance 22. The Prisoner 23. Sawdust 23. Quicksands 23. What Wives Want 23. Trimmed in Scarlet 23. Lucretia Lombard 23. The Trouble Shooter 24. The Heart Buster 24. The Roughneck 25. The Hunted Woman 25. The Only Thing 25. Brown of Harvard 26. Soul Mates 26. The Understanding Heart 27. Twelve Miles Out 27. Quicksands 27. The Smart Set 28. Bringing Up Father 28. While the City Sleeps 28. Alias Jimmy Valentine 29. *Our Modern Maidens* 29. Untamed 29. They Learned about Women 29. *The Unholy Three* 30. New Moon 30. The Easiest Way 31. Just a Gigolo 31. *Arsène Lupin* 32. But the Flesh is Weak 32. Red-headed Woman 32. Hell Below 33. The

Nuisance 33. The Solitaire Man 33. *Viva Villa* 34. The Girl from Missouri 34. The Gay Bride. 34. One New York Night 35. *A Tale of Two Cities* 35. *Libeled Lady* 36. Saratoga 37. *A Yank at Oxford* 38. Too Hot to Handle 38. Let Freedom Ring 39. Lady of the Tropics 39. *Boom Town* 40. Love Crazy 40. Honky Tonk 40. Crossroads 42. Assignment in Brittany 43. Dragon Seed 44. High Barbaree 47. *The Hucksters* 47. Julia Misbehaves 48.

Conway, Morgan (1900–1981).
Tough-guy American actor of 40s 'B' pictures, chiefly notable as the screen's first Dick Tracy.
Looking for Trouble 34. Crime Ring 38. Blackwell's Island 39. Brother Orchid 40. Sing Your Worries Away 42. Jack London 44. *Dick Tracy* 45. Badman's Territory 46. Dick Tracy vs Cueball 46, many others.

Conway, Tim (1933–).
American television comic who found a niche in Disney films.
McHale's Navy 64. The World's Greatest Athlete 73. The Apple Dumpling Gang 75. Gus 76. The Billion Dollar Hobo 77. The Apple Dumpling Gang Rides Again 79. The Prize Fighter 79. The Private Eyes 80. The Long Shot 85. Dorf and the First Games of Mount Olympus 87, etc.
TV series: McHale's Navy 62–65. The Tim Conway Show 70. Later with Carol Burnett. Ace Crawford 83.

Conway, Tom (1904–1967) (Thomas Sanders).
British light leading man, brother of George Sanders; well-liked as 'the Falcon' in the 40s, but his career declined very suddenly. He began drinking heavily and died in poverty.
Sky Murder 40. The Trial of Mary Dugan 41. Grand Central Murder 42. *The Falcon's Brother* 42. *Cat People* 42. I Walked with a Zombie 43. The Falcon Strikes Back 43. The Seventh Victim 43. The Falcon Out West 44 (and five other Falcon adventures ending in 1946). Criminal Court 46. Repeat Performance 47. One Touch of Venus 48. Confidence Girl 52. Park Plaza 505 (GB) 53. Barbados Quest (GB) 55. The Last Man to Hang (GB) 56. The She-Creature 56. Twelve to the Moon 60. What a Way to Go (unbilled) 64, many others.
TV series: Mark Saber 52–54. The Betty Hutton Show 59.

Conyers, Darcy (1919–1973).
British director, former actor.
Ha'penny Breeze (& p) 52. The Devil's Pass (& w, p) 56. The Night We Dropped a Clanger 60. Nothing Barred 61. In the Doghouse 62, etc.

Cooder, Ry (1947–).
American guitarist, singer and composer of blues-tinged scores.
Goin' South (s) 78. The Long Riders 80. Southern Comfort 81. The Border 81. Streets of Fire 84. Paris, Texas 84. Alamo Bay 85. Brewster's Millions 85. Crossroads 86. Blue City 86. Extreme Prejudice (md) 87. Johnny Handsome 90. Geronimo: An American Legend 93, etc.

Coogan, Jackie (1914–1984).
American child actor of the 20s who achieved outstanding star status but later reappeared as a less appealing adult in minor roles. He was married to Betty Grable (1937–39).
The Kid 20. *Peck's Bad Boy* 21. *Oliver Twist* 21. My Boy 22. Trouble 22. Daddy 23. Circus Days 23. Long Live the King 24. A Boy of Flanders 24. The Rag Man 24. Little Robinson Crusoe 25. Johnny Get Your Gun 25. Old Clothes 25. Johnny Get Your Hair Cut 26. The Bugle Call 27. Buttons 27. Tom

Sawyer 30. Huckleberry Finn 31. Home on the Range 35. College Swing 38. Kilroy Was Here 47. Outlaw Women 52. Lost Women 56. High School Confidential 58. A Fine Madness 66. The Shakiest Gun in the West 68. Marlowe 69. Cahill 73. The Escape Artist 82, many others.
TV series: Cowboy G-Men 52. McKeever and the Colonel 62. *The Addams Family* 64 (as Uncle Fester).

Coogan, Keith (1970–) (Keith Franklin).
Young American actor. He is the grandson of Jackie Coogan.
Adventures in Babysitting 87. Hiding Out 87. Cheetah 89. Under the Boardwalk 89. Cousins 89. Book of Love 90. Toy Soldiers 91. Don't Tell Mom the Babysitter's Dead 91, etc.

Cook, Clyde (1891–1984).
Australian clown and dancer who played in many Mack Sennett comedies and settled in California. Subsequently played character roles.
Soldiers of Fortune 19. Skirts 21. The Eskimo 22. He Who Gets Slapped 24. The Winning of Barbara Worth 26. Good Time Charley 27. The Spieler 28. The Taming of the Shrew 29. Sunny 30. Blondie of the Follies 32. Oliver Twist 33. Barbary Coast 35. Kidnapped 38. The Little Princess 39. The Sea Hawk 40. White Cargo 42. To Each His Own 46. Pride of Maryland 51, many others.

Cook, Donald (1900–1961).
American stage leading man who never quite made it in Hollywood.
The Public 31. The Mad Genius 31. The Man Who Played God 32. Frisco Jenny 33. Long Lost Father 34. Gigolette 35. Show Boat 36. Two Wise Maids 37. Bowery to Broadway 44. Patrick the Great 45. Our Very Own 50, etc.
TV series: Too Young to Go Steady 59.

Cook, Elisha, Jnr (1903–).
American character actor adept at cowards and neurotics.
Her Unborn Child 30. Two in a Crowd 36. Pigskin Parade 36. Love Is News 37. Breezing Home 37. Wife, Doctor and Nurse 37. Danger Love at Work 37. Life Begins in College 37. They Won't Forget 37. The Devil Is Driving 37. My Lucky Star 38. Submarine Patrol 38. Three Blind Mice 38. Grand Jury Secrets 39. Newsboy's Home 39. He Married His Wife 40. Stranger on the Third Floor 40. Public Deb Number One 40. Love Crazy 40. Tin Pan Alley 40. Man at Large 41. Sergeant York 41. Ball of Fire 41. *The Maltese Falcon* (as Wilmer the gunsel) 41. *I Wake Up Screaming* 41. A Gentleman at Heart 42. In This Our Life 42. Sleepytime Gal 42. A-Haunting We Will Go 42. Manila Calling 42. Hellzapoppin 42. Wildcat 42. Casanova Brown 44. *Phantom Lady* 44. Up in Arms 44. Dark Mountain 44. *Dark Waters* 44. Dillinger 44. Why Girls Leave Home 44. *The Big Sleep* 46. Blonde Alibi 46. Cinderella Jones 46. The Falcon's Alibi 46. Joe Palooka Champ 46. Two Smart People 46. Born to Kill 47. The Fall Guy 47. The Long Night 47. The Gangster 47. Flaxy Martin 49. The Great Gatsby 49. Behave Yourself 51. Don't Bother to Knock 51. I the Jury 53. Thunder over the Plains 53. *Shane* 53. The Outlaw's Daughter 54. Drum Beat 54. Timberjack 55. The Indian Fighter 55. Trial 55. *The Killing* 56. Accused of Murder 56. The Lonely Man 57. Voodoo Island 57. Baby Face Nelson 57. Plunder Road 57. Chicago Confidential 57. House on Haunted Hill 58. Day of the Outlaw 59. Platinum High School 60. College Confidential 60. One-Eyed Jacks 61. Papa's Delicate Condition 63. The Haunted Palace

3. Black Zoo 63. Johnny Cool 63. Blood on the
arrow 64. The Glass Cage 64. Welcome to Hard
imes 67. Rosemary's Baby 68. The Great Bank
Robbery 69. El Condor 70. The Movie Murderer
TV) 70. Night Chase (TV) 70. The Great Northfield
Minnesota Raid 72. Blacula 72. The Night Stalker
TV) 72. Emperor of the North Pole 73. Electra Glide
n Blue 73. The Outfit 73. The Black Bird 75.
Messiah of Evil 75. Winterhawk 75. St Ives 76.
Mad Bull (TV) 77. 1941 79. The Champ 79. Leave
Em Laughing (TV) 80. Carny 80. Tom Horn 80.
Harry's War 80. Salem's Lot 80. Hammett 82. This
Girl for Hire 84. National Lampoon Goes to the
Movies 84, etc.

¶ As he has grown older, the vulnerable look has
congealed in his face so that his very presence
has become an open invitation to destroy him.
Ian Cameron

Cook, Fielder (1923–).
American TV director who makes occasional films.
Patterns of Power 56. Home is the Hero (Eire) 59.
Big Hand for a Little Lady 66. How to Save a Marriage
7. Prudence and the Pill 68. Teacher Teacher (TV)
9. Who Killed the Mysterious Mr Foster? (TV) 70.
Goodbye Raggedy Ann (TV) 71. Eagle in a Cage
1. The Hands of Cormac Joyce (TV) 72. Miracle
n 34th Street (TV) 73. From the Mixed Up Files
f Mrs Basil E. Frankenweiler 73. This Is the West
hat Was (TV) 74. Judge Horton and the Scottsboro
oys (TV) 76. Beauty and the Beast (TV) 77. Too
ar to Go (TV) 79. I Know Why the Caged Bird
ings (TV) 79. Family Reunion (TV) 81. Evergreen
TV) 85. A Special Friendship (TV) 87, etc.

Cook, Joe (1890–1959) (Joseph Lopez).
American comic in Broadway musicals and revues
f the 20s, 30s and 40s, and star of the movie
ersion of his 1928 stage success *Rain and Shine*,
which was directed in 1930 by Frank Capra, who
urned it into a drama without music. A comedian
with a broad grin and an original line in nonsense
atter, he was also a multi-instrumentalist, knife-
hrower, expert shot, rope-spinner, juggler, slack-
ire walker and acrobat, skills which he
emonstrated in the film.

Cook, Peter (1937–1995).
ritish cabaret comedian and writer.
The Wrong Box 66. Bedazzled 67. A Dandy in
spic 68. Monte Carlo or Bust 69. The Bed Sitting
oom 69. The Rise and Rise of Michael Rimmer
0. The Adventures of Barry Mackenzie 72. The
ound of the Baskervilles 77. Yellowbeard 83.
upergirl 84. Whoops Apocalypse 86. Mr Jolly
ives Next Door 87. The Princess Bride 87. Without
Clue 88. Getting It Right 89. Great Balls of Fire
9. Kokoda Crescent (w) 89. Black Beauty 94.
TV series: The Two of Us 81.

Cool J, LL
ee LL Cool J.

Coolidge, Martha (1946–).
merican director and screenwriter. She trained
s an actress and began as a documentary film-
aker.
Not a Pretty Picture (& w) 76. Valley Girl 83.
oy of Sex 84. City Girl (& w) 84. Real Genius
5. Plain Clothes 88. That's Adequate (a) 90.
ambling Rose 91. Crazy in Love 92. Lost in
onkers 93. Angie 94, etc.

Coombe, Carol (1911–1966).
Blonde Australian leading actress who came to
ritain in 1930 and starred in several films of the
ecade.

P.C. Josser 31. The Sport of Kings 31. Sally in
Our Alley 31. The Ringer 31. Tilly of Bloomsbury
31. The Ghost Train 31. The Strangler 32. Double
Bluff 33. The Man without a Face 35. Woman to
Woman 46, etc.

Coop, Denys (1920–1981).
British cameraman.
A Kind of Loving 61. Billy Liar 63. This Sporting
Life 63. One Way Pendulum 64. King and Country
65. Bunny Lake Is Missing 65. The Double Man
67. My Side of the Mountain 68. 10 Rillington Place
70. Superman (AA visual effects) 78, etc.

Cooper, Ben (1930–).
American light juvenile lead, mainly in westerns.
The Woman They almost Lynched 52. Perilous
Journey 53. Johnny Guitar 54. Jubilee Trail 54.
The Eternal Sea 55. The Last Command 56. *The
Rose Tattoo* 57. Chartroose Caboose 60. Gunfight
at Comanche Creek 64. Arizona Raiders 65. Red
Tomahawk 67, many others.

Cooper, Frederick (1890–1945).
Ferrety-looking British character actor who
managed a few choice roles.
Thunder Rock 42. The Great Mr Handel 42.
Henry V (as Nym) 44, etc.

Cooper, Gary (1901–1961) (Frank J. Cooper).
Slow-speaking, deep-thinking American leading
man, a long-enduring Hollywood star who
always projected honest determination. Was
cowboy and cartoonist before becoming a film
extra; progressed to two-reelers and became a star
in his first feature, *The Winning of Barbara Worth*
26. Special Academy Award 1960 'for his many
memorable screen performances and for the
international recognition he, as an individual, has
gained for the film industry'.
■ The Thundering Herd 25. Wild Horse Mesa 25.
The Lucky Horseshoe 25. The Vanishing American
25. The Eagle 25. The Enchanted Hill 26. Watch
Your Wife 26. It 27. Children of Divorce 27. Arizona
Bound 27. Wings 27. Nevada 27. The Last Outlaw
27. Beau Sabreur 28. Legion of the Condemned 28.
Doomsday 28. Half a Bride 28. *Lilac Time* 28. The
First Kiss 28. Shopworn Angel 28. Wolf Song 29.
The Betrayal 29. The Virginian 29. Only the Brave
29. The Texan 29. Seven Days' Leave 30. A Man
from Wyoming 30. Paramount on Parade 30. The
Spoilers 30. Morocco 30. Fighting Caravans 31. I
Take This Woman 31. His Woman 31. The Devil
and the Deep 32. *A Farewell to Arms* 32. *City Streets*
32. If I Had a Million 32. One Sunday Afternoon
33. Alice in Wonderland (as the White Knight)
33. Today We Live 33. Design for Living 34. Peter
Ibbetson 34. Operator Thirteen 34. The Wedding
Night 35. *Lives of a Bengal Lancer* 35. Now and
Forever 35. Desire 36. *Mr Deeds Goes to Town*
(AAN) 36. The General Died at Dawn 36. *The
Plainsman* 36. Souls at Sea 37. The Adventures of
Marco Polo 38. Bluebeard's Eighth Wife 38. The
Cowboy and the Lady 39. *Beau Geste* 39. The Real
Glory 39. *The Westerner* 40. Northwest Mounted
Police 40. *Meet John Doe* 41. *Sergeant York* (AA) 41.
Ball of Fire 41. Pride of the Yankees (AAN) 42. *For
Whom the Bell Tolls* (AAN) 43. The Story of Dr
Wassell 44. Saratoga Trunk 44. Casanova Brown
44. Along Came Jones (& p) 45. Cloak and Dagger
46. Unconquered 47. Variety Girl 47 (cameo).
Good Sam 48. The Fountainhead 49. Task Force 49.
It's a Great Feeling 49 (cameo). Bright Leaf 50.
Dallas 50. You're in the Navy Now 51. Distant
Drums 51. Springfield Rifle 52. *High Noon* (AA) 52.
Return to Paradise 52. Blowing Wild 53. Garden
of Evil 54. *Vera Cruz* 54. The Court Martial of Billy
Mitchell 55. Alias Jesse James 55 (cameo).

Friendly Persuasion 56. Love in the Afternoon 56.
Ten North Frederick 58. Man of the West 58. They
Came to Cordura 59. The Hanging Tree 59. The
Wreck of the Mary Deare 59. The Naked Edge (GB)
61.
⊙ For his sheer domination of the Hollywood
scene for the first twenty years of the talkies. *Mr
Deeds Goes to Town*.

¶ The most underrated actor I ever worked
with
said Henry Hathaway. Fred Zinnemann put it
another way:
   He had magic. The only time he was in trouble
   was when he tried to act.
   He was a poet of the real
said Clifford Odets. Whatever that means, it would
have embarrassed Cooper. Perhaps Carl Sandburg
put it another way:
   One of the most beloved illiterates this country
   has ever known.
Cooper had no very high estimate of his own
talent:
   People ask me how come you been around so
   long. Well, it's through playing the part of Mr
   Average Joe American.
He had Mr Average Joe's reputed insularity:
   From what I hear about communism, I don't
   like it because it isn't on the level.
He distrusted the socialism of plays like *Death of a
Salesman*:
   Sure there are fellows like Willy Loman, but you
   don't have to write plays about them.
He enjoyed his niche:
   Until I came along, all the leading men were
   handsome, but luckily they wrote a lot of
   stories about the fellow next door.
For a man without acting training, he managed
very well. King Vidor thought that:
   He got a reputation as a great actor just by
   thinking hard about the next line.
Coop's own explanation was simpler:
   To get folks to like you, I figured you sort of had
   to be their ideal. I don't mean a handsome knight
   riding a white horse, but a fellow who answered
   the description of a right guy.
Richard Arlen summed up:
   Coop just likes people, it's as simple as that.
But Richard Zanuck latched on to another Cooper
essential: he was part of the great outdoors:
   You could never put Coop in a small hat and
   get your money back.

Famous line (*Sergeant York*): 'Folks back home
used to say I could shoot a rifle before I was weaned.
They was exaggerating some.'

Famous line (*The Virginian*): 'If you want to call
me that, smile.'

Famous line (*For Whom the Bell Tolls*): 'A man fights
for what he believes in, Fernando.'

Cooper, George A. (1916–).
British character actor of vengeful types.
Miracle in Soho 56. Violent Playground 58. Tom
Jones 63. Nightmare 64. Life at the Top 65. The
Strange Affair 68, etc.

Cooper, Dame Gladys (1888–1971).
Distinguished, gracious British stage actress who
essentially began her film career in Hollywood at
the age of 52, subsequently airing her warm
aristocratic personality in many unworthy roles
and a few good ones.
Autobiography: 1931, *Gladys Cooper*.
Biography: 1953, *Without Veils* by Sewell Stokes.

■ Masks and Faces 17. The Sorrows of Satan 17. My Lady's Dress 18. The Bohemian Girl 22. Bonnie Prince Charles 23. Dandy Donovan 31. The Iron Duke 35. *Rebecca* 40. Kitty Foyle 40. That Hamilton Woman 41. The Black Cat 41. The Gay Falcon 41. This Above All 42. Eagle Squadron 42. *Now Voyager* (AAN) 42. Forever and a Day 43. Mr Lucky 43. Princess O'Rourke 43. The Song of Bernadette (AAN) 43. The White Cliffs of Dover 44. Mrs Parkington 44. The Valley of Decision 45. Love Letters 45. The Green Years 46. The Cockeyed Miracle 46. Green Dolphin Street 47. Beware of Pity 47. The Bishop's Wife 47. Homecoming 48. The Pirate 48. The Secret Garden 49. Madame Bovary 49. Thunder on the Hill 51. At Sword's Point 52. The Man Who Loved Redheads 54. *Separate Tables* 58. The List of Adrian Messenger 63. *My Fair Lady* (AAN) 64. The Happiest Millionaire 67. A Nice Girl Like Me 69.

TV series: *The Rogues* 64.

Cooper, Jackie (1921–).
'Little tough guy' American child actor who in adult life found roles getting rarer and became a powerful TV executive.
Autobiography: 1981, *Please Don't Shoot My Dog.*
■ *Our Gang* shorts 27–28. Movietone Follies 28. Sunny Side Up 29. *Skippy* (AAN) 31. Young Donovan's Kid 31. *The Champ* 31. Sooky 31. When a Feller Needs a Friend 32. Divorce in the Family 32. Broadway to Hollywood 33. *The Bowery* 33. *Treasure Island* 34. Peck's Bad Boy 34. Lone Cowboy 34. Dinky 35. O'Shaughnessy's Boy 35. Tough Guy 36. The Devil is a Sissy 36. Boy of the Streets 37. White Banners 38. That Certain Age 38. Gangster's Boy 38. Newsboys' Home 39. Scouts to the Rescue 39. Spirit of Culver 39. Streets of New York 39. Two Bright Boys 39. What a Life 39. The Big Guy 39. Seventeen 40. The Return of Frank James 40. Gallant Sons 40. Life with Henry 41. Ziegfeld Girl 41. Her First Beau 41. Glamour Boy 41. Syncopation 42. Men of Texas 42. The Navy Comes Through 42. Where are your Children? 44. Stork Bites Man 47. Kilroy Was Here 47. French Leave 48. Everything's Ducky 61. Shadow on the Land (TV) 68. The Astronaut (TV) 71. The Love Machine 71. Maybe I'll Come Home in the Spring (TV) 71. Stand Up and Be Counted (d only) 72. Chosen Survivors 74. The Day the Earth Moved (TV) 74. The Invisible Man (TV) 75. Mobile Two (TV) 75. Superman 78. Superman II 80. Superman III 83. Superman IV 87.

TV series: The People's Choice 56–58. Hennessey 59–71. Mobile One 75.

Cooper, James Fenimore (1789–1851).
American adventure novelist whose 'westerns' include *The Last of the Mohicans, The Pathfinder* and *The Deerslayer,* all frequently filmed.

Cooper, Melville (1896–1973).
British comedy character actor, long in Hollywood playing pompous upper-class idiots.
■ The Calendar 31. Black Coffee 31. Two White Arms 32. Forgin' Ahead 33. Leave It To Me 33. To Brighton with Gladys 33. The Private Life of Don Juan 34. The Scarlet Pimpernel 34. The Bishop Misbehaves (US from now on) 35. The Gorgeous Hussy 36. The Last of Mrs Cheyney 37. Thin Ice 37. The Great Garrick 37. Tovarich 37. Women Are Like That 37. *The Adventures of Robin Hood* (as Sheriff of Nottingham) 38. Gold Diggers in Paris 38. Four's a Crowd 38. Hard to Get 38. The Dawn Patrol 38. Comet over Broadway 38. Dramatic School 38. Garden of the Moon 38. I'm from Missouri 39. Blind Alley 39. The Sun Never Sets 39. Two Bright Boys 39. Rebecca 40. Too Many Husbands 40. *Pride and Prejudice* (his best role, as the pompous

Mr Collins) 40. Murder over New York 40. Submarine Zone 40. The Flame of New Orleans 41. The Lady Eve 41. Scotland Yard 41. You Belong to Me 41. This Above All 42. The Affairs of Martha 42. Random Harvest 42. Life Begins at 8.30 42. The Immortal Sergeant 43. Hit Parade of 1943 43. Holy Matrimony 43. My Kingdom for a Cook 43. Heartbeat 46. 13 Rue Madeleine 46. The Imperfect Lady 47. Enchantment 48. The Red Danube 49. Love Happy 49. And Baby Makes Three 49. The Underworld Story 50. Father of the Bride 50. Let's Dance 50. The Petty Girl 50. It Should Happen to You 53. Moonfleet 55. The King's Thief 55. Diane 55. Bundle of Joy 56. Around the World in 80 Days 56. The Story of Mankind 57. From the Earth to the Moon 58.

Cooper, Merian C. (1893–1973).
American executive producer associated with many adventurous films. Special Academy Award 1952 'for his many innovations and contributions to the art of the motion picture'.
Grass 25. Chang 27. The Four Feathers 29. *King Kong* 33. The Last Days of Pompeii 35. The Toy Wife 38. Fort Apache 48. Mighty Joe Young 49. Rio Grande 50. The Quiet Man 52. *This is Cinerama* 52. The Searchers 56, etc.

Cooper, Miriam (1892–1976).
American silent screen actress who married Raoul Walsh.
Autobiography: 1978, *Dark Lady of the Silents.*
A Blot on the Scutcheon 11. When Fate Frowned 14. The Birth of a Nation 15. His Return 15. The Woman and the Law 18. Kindred of Dust 22. Her Accidental Husband 23, many others.

Cooper, Richard (1893–1947).
English character actor, on stage from 1913 and notable in the title role of *Charley's Aunt.* In films from 1929, usually in muddle-headed roles.
At the Villa Rose 29. Enter the Queen 30. Black Coffee 31. The First Mrs Fraser 32. Home Sweet Home 33. Lord Edgware Dies 34. The Black Abbot 34. That's My Uncle 35. Shipyard Sally 39. Inspector Hornleigh Goes to It 41, etc.

Cooper, Stuart (1942–).
American director who got his first breaks in Britain.
Little Malcolm and his Struggle against the Eunuchs 74. Overlord 75. The Disappearance 77. A.D. (TV) 84. The Long Hot Summer (TV) 85. Christmas Eve (TV) 86. The Fortunate Pilgrim (TV) 88, etc.

Cooper, Violet Kemble (1886–1961).
British stage actress who appeared in a few Hollywood films in the 30s.
Our Betters 33. Vanessa 34. David Copperfield (as Miss Murdstone) 35. The Invisible Ray 36. Romeo and Juliet 36, etc.

Cooper, Wilkie (1911–).
British cinematographer, once a child actor.
The Rake's Progress 45. Green for Danger 46. Captain Boycott 47. London Belongs to Me 48. Stage Fright 50. The Admirable Crichton 57. Jason and the Argonauts 63. One Million Years BC 66, etc.

Coote, Robert (1909–1982).
British stage character actor who filmed mainly in Hollywood; familiar in amiable silly-ass roles.
Sally in Our Alley 31. *A Yank at Oxford* 38. Gunga Din (US) 39. You Can't Fool Your Wife 40. The Commandos Strike at Dawn 43. A Matter of Life and Death 46. The Ghost and Mrs Muir 47.

Forever Amber 47. Bonnie Prince Charlie 48. The Three Musketeers 48. The Elusive Pimpernel 50. Rommel, Desert Fox 51. *The Prisoner of Zenda* 52. The Constant Husband 55. Othello (as Roderigo) 55. The Swan 56. Merry Andrew 58. The League of Gentlemen 59. The Golden Head 65. A Man Could Get Killed 66. The Swinger 66. Prudence and the Pill 68. Up the Front 72. Theatre of Bloo 73. Institute for Revenge (TV) 79, etc.
TV series: *The Rogues* 64.

Cope, Kenneth (1931–).
British TV actor, usually of Liverpudlian types.
The Criminal 60. The Damned 62. Genghis Khan 65. Dateline Diamonds 65. She'll Follow You Anywhere 71, etc.
TV series: Coronation Street. Randall and Hopkirk (Deceased).

Copeland, Stewart (1952–).
American drummer and composer, in England as a child, and a founder of the rock band Police.
Rumble Fish 83. Out of Bounds 86. Wall Street 87. Talk Radio 88. She's Having a Baby 88. See N Evil, Hear No Evil 88. Hidden Agenda 90. The First Power 90. Highlander 2 90. Wide Sargasso Sea 9 Airborne 93. Bank Robber 93. Rapa Nui 94. Fres 94. Surviving the Game 94, etc.

Copland, Aaron (1900–1990).
American composer.
■ The City 39. Of Mice and Men (AAN) 39. Our Tow (AAN) 40. North Star (AAN) 43. Fiesta 47. *The Re Pony* 49. The Heiress (AA) 49. Something Wild 6

Copley, Peter (1915–).
British stage actor who makes occasional film appearances, usually in quiet, downtrodden or slightly sinister roles.
The Golden Salamander 49. The Card 52. The Sword and the Rose 53. Foreign Intrigue 56. Victim 61. King and Country 64, etc.

Coppel, Alec (1910–1972).
Australian playwright and screenwriter.
Over the Moon (w) 39. Obsession (oa) 46. Mr Denning Drives North (w) 51. The Captain's Paradise (AANw) 53. The Gazebo (oa) 59. Momen to Moment (w) 66. The Bliss of Mrs Blossom (w) 69.

Coppola, Carmine (1910–1991).
American composer, musician and conductor, th father of Francis Ford Coppola and Talia Shire, an the grandfather of actor Nicolas Cage.
Tonight for Sure 61. Finian's Rainbow 68. The Godfather Part II (co-m) (AA) 74. Apocalypse No 79. The Black Stallion 79. The Outsiders 83. Bloc Red 86. Gardens of Stone 87. Tucker: The Man ar His Dream 88. New York Stories 89. The Godfathe Part III (AAN for song) 90, etc.

¶ My father had a slogan he always used to tell us – and it's a good slogan: Steal from the bes – *Francis Ford Coppola*

Coppola, Francis Ford (1939–).
American writer-director who graduated from nudie movies.
Biography: 1989, *Coppola* by Peter Cowie.
■ Dementia 63. This Property Is Condemned (w 65. Is Paris Burning? (w) 66. *You're a Big Boy No* (wd) 67. Finian's Rainbow (d) 68. The Rain Peop (wd) 69. Patton (w only) (AA) 71. *The Godfather* (co-w) (AAN) 72. American Graffiti (p only) 73. The Great Gatsby (w only) 74. The Conversation (wd, p) 74. The Godfather Part Two (wd, p) (AA 74. Apocalypse Now (BFA, AAN) 79. One from

ae Heart (wd, p) 82. Hammett (p) 82. The Escape rtist (p) 82. The Outsiders 83. Rumblefish 83. eggy Sue Got Married 86. Gardens of Stone 87. ionheart (p) 87. Tough Guys Don't Dance (p) 87. owaqqatsi (p) 88. Tucker: The Man and His ream (d) 88. New York Stories (co-d, co-w) 89. he Godfather Part III (wd, p) (AAN) 90. Bram roker's Dracula 92. The Secret Garden (p) 93.

I bring to my life a certain amount of mess. – F.F.C.

If you don't bet, you don't have a chance to win. F.F.C.

Basically, both the Mafia and America feel they re benevolent organizations. And both the Mafia nd America have their hands stained with blood om what it is necessary to do to protect their ower and interests. – F.F.C.

I probably have genius. But no talent. – F.F.C.

He is his own worst enemy. If he directs a little omance, it has to be the biggest, most overdone ttle romance in movie history. – Kenneth Turan

opyright.
ritish law relating to film copyright is notably ague, but in practice the owner of a film is rotected against piracy for fifty years. In America opyright must be renewed in the 28th year, which as resulted in some fatal errors: e.g. MGM now ave no control over Till the Clouds Roll By because ney forgot to renew it, and Chaplin renewed only he version of The Gold Rush including his specially omposed 40s music track.

Coquillon, John.
ritish cinematographer.
Witchfinder General 68. Scream and Scream gain 69. The Oblong Box 69. Triple Echo 72. Cross f Iron 77. The Four Feathers (TV) 78. The 39 Steps 8. Final Assignment 80. The Changeling 80. The mateur 82. The Osterman Weekend 83. Master f the Game (TV) 83. The Last Place on Earth TV) 84. Clockwise 85. Absolution 88, etc.

Corbett, Glenn (1929–1993) (Glenn Rothenburg). American second lead.
The Fireball 50. Man on a String 60. The Mountain Road 60. All the Young Men 60. Homicidal 61. Pirates of Blood River (GB) 61. henandoah 65. Big Jake 71. Dead Pigeon on eethoven Street (WG) 72. The Stranger 73. Ride n a Pink Car 74. Nashville Girl 76, etc.
TV series: It's a Man's World 62–63. Route 66 3–64. The Road West 66–67. Dallas 83–84.

Corbett, Gretchen (1947–).
American character actress, mostly on TV.
Out of It 70. Let's Scare Jessica to Death 71. The Savage Bees (TV) 76. The Other Side of the Mountain Part Two 78. Secrets of Three Hungry Wives (TV) 78. Jaws of Satan 81, etc.
TV series: The Rockford Files 74–80.

Corbett, Harry H. (1925–1982).
British stage actor who played tough guys, regional ypes and maniacs in an assortment of films efore gaining great TV popularity in Steptoe and Son; subsequently starred in a number of nsatisfactory comedy vehicles.
Floods of Fear 57. Nowhere to Go 58. Cover Girl Killer 60. Sammy Going South 62. What a Crazy World 63. Ladies Who Do 63. The Bargee 64. Rattle f a Simple Man 64. Joey Boy 65. The Sandwich Man 66. Carry On Screaming 66. Crooks and Coronets 69. The Magnificent Seven Deadly Sins 71. Steptoe and Son 72, etc.

Corbett, Leonora (1907–1960).
British stage actress who made few films.
Heart's Delight 32. The Constant Nymph 33. Friday the Thirteenth 33. Farewell Again 36. Anything to Declare 38. Under Your Hat 40, etc.

Corbett, Ronnie (1930–).
Pint-sized British TV comedian, one of the Two Ronnies.
Rockets Galore 58. Casino Royale 67. Some Will Some Won't 70. The Rise and Rise of Michael Rimmer 70. No Sex Please We're British 73, etc.

Corbiau, Gerard (1941–).
Belgian director, from television, particularly of musical programmes.
The Music Teacher (AAN) 88. L'Année de l'Éveil 91. Farinelli il Castrato 95, etc.

Corbucci, Sergio (1927–1990).
Italian director.
Duel of the Titans 61. Son of Spartacus 62. The Slave 63. Minnesota Clay 64. Django 65. The Hellbenders 66. The Campanieros 71. Il Bestione 74. La Mazzetta 78. I Don't Understand You Anymore 80. I'm Getting Myself a Yacht 81. Super Fuzz 81. My Darling, My Dearest 82. Sing Sing 83. Sono un Fenomeno Paranormale 86. Rimini Rimini 87. Grazie Commissario 88, etc.

Corby, Ellen (1913–) (Ellen Hansen).
American character actress specializing in nosy neighbours and prim spinsters.
The Dark Corner 46. The Spiral Staircase 46. I Remember Mama (AAN) 48. Fighting Father Dunne 48. Madame Bovary 49. On Moonlight Bay 51. About Mrs Leslie 54. The Seventh Sin 57. Macabre 58. Visit to a Small Planet 60. The Strangler 64. The Gnome-Mobile 67, many others.
TV series: Please Don't Eat the Daisies 65. The Waltons 72–81.

Corcoran, Donna (1942–).
American child actress of the 50s.
Angels in the Outfield 51. Don't Bother to Knock 52. Scandal at Scourie 53. Dangerous when Wet 53. Gypsy Colt 54. Violent Saturday 55, etc.

Corcoran, Kevin (1949–).
American child actor of the 50s and 60s who turned producer in the 70s.
Untamed 55. Old Yeller 59. The Shaggy Dog 59. Toby Tyler 60. The Swiss Family Robinson 61. Babes in Toyland 62. Bon Voyage 63. Savage Sam 64. A Tiger Walks 65, etc.

Cord, Alex (1931–) (Alexander Viespi).
Italian-American leading man.
Synanon 65. Stagecoach 66. The Brotherhood 68. Stiletto 69. Dead or Alive 69. The Last Grenade 69. The Dead Are Alive 72. Genesis II (TV) 73. Chosen Survivors 74. Sidewinder One 77. Greyeagle 77. Beggarman, Thief (TV) 79. Goliath Awaits (TV) 81. Jungle Warriors 84. A Girl to Kill For 90. Street Asylum 90. To Be the Best 93, etc.
TV series: W.E.B. 78. Cassie and Company 82. Airwolf 84–86.

Corda, Maria (1902–c. 1965) (Maria Farcas).
Hungarian actress, in films from 1921. She began as a dancer with the Royal Opera, Budapest, and was the first wife of producer and director Alexander Korda.
Dance Fever (Ger.) 21. A Modern Dubarry (Ger.) 21. The Last Days of Pompeii (It.) 26. The Guardsman (US) 27. The Private Life of Helen of Troy (US) 27. Tesha (GB) 28. Love and the Devil (US) 29, etc.

Corday, Mara (1932–) (Marilyn Watts).
American leading lady of the 50s.
Sea Tiger 52. So This Is Paris 54. Man Without a Star 55. The Quiet Gun 57. The Black Scorpion 57. The Gauntlet 77. Pink Cadillac 89, etc.

Corday, Paula (1924–1992) (aka Paule Croset and Rita Corday).
Anglo-Swiss leading lady who went to Hollywood in the 40s.
The Falcon Strikes Back 43. The Body Snatcher 45. The Exile 47. Sword of Monte Cristo 51. Because You're Mine 52. The French Line 54, etc.

Cordell, Frank (1918–1980).
British composer.
The Voice of Merrill 52. The Rebel 60. Khartoum 66. Ring of Bright Water 69. Cromwell 71. A Choice of Weapons 76, etc.

Cording, Harry (1891–1954).
British supporting actor in Hollywood, usually as tough, blunt types.
The Knockout 25. Captain of the Guard 30. Forgotten Commandments 33. The Crusades 35. Mutiny on the Bounty 35. Sutter's Gold 36. The Prince and the Pauper 37. The Adventures of Robin Hood 38. The Hound of the Baskervilles 39. The Wolf Man 41. Arabian Nights 42. Lost in a Harem 44. The House of Fear 45. Terror by Night 46. A Woman's Vengeance 48. Samson and Delilah 49. Mask of the Avenger 51. Road to Bali 52. Titanic 53. Demetrius and the Gladiators 54. East of Eden 55, many others.

Cordy, Raymond (1898–1956) (R. Cordiaux).
French comedy actor, especially seen in René Clair's films.
Le Million 31. À Nous la Liberté 31. Le Quatorze Juillet 33. Le Dernier Milliardaire 34. Ignace 37. Les Inconnus dans la Maison 42. Le Silence est d'Or 46. La Beauté du Diable 49. Les Belles de Nuit 52. Les Grandes Manoeuvres 55, etc.

Corey, Jeff (1914–).
Gaunt American supporting actor seen as farmer, gangster, junkie, wino, convict, cop, and even Wild Bill Hickok.
All that Money Can Buy 41. My Friend Flicka 43. The Killers 46. Brute Force 47. Home of the Brave 49. Bright Leaf 50. Rawhide 51. Red Mountain 52. The Balcony 63. Lady in a Cage 64. Mickey One 65. The Cincinnati Kid 65. Seconds 66. In Cold Blood 67. True Grit 69. Little Big Man 71. Catlow 72. Paper Tiger 75. Oh God 77. Butch and Sundance: The Early Days 79. Battle Beyond the Stars 80. The Sword and the Sorcerer 82. Conan the Destroyer 84. Creator 85. Bird on a Wire 90. Pay Off 91. Ruby Cairo 93. Surviving the Game 94. Color of Night 94, many others.
TV series: Hell Town 85.

Corey, Wendell (1914–1968).
American leading actor who usually played solid dependable types.
■ Desert Fury 47. I Walk Alone 47. The Search 48. Maneater of Kumaon 48. Sorry Wrong Number 48. The Accused 48. Any Number Can Play 49. The File on Thelma Jordan 49. Holiday Affair 49. No Sad Songs for Me 50. The Furies 50. Harriet Craig 50. The Great Missouri Raid 50. Rich Young and Pretty 51. The Wild Blue Yonder 51. The Wild North 52. Carbine Williams 52. My Man and I 52. Laughing Anne (GB) 53. Jamaica Run 53. Hell's Half Acre 54. Rear Window 54. The Big Knife 55. The Bold and the Brave 56. The Killer is Loose 56. The Rack 56. The Rainmaker 56. Loving You 57. The Light in the Forest 58. Alias Jesse James 59.

Blood on the Arrow 64. Agent for Harm 65. Waco 66. Women of the Prehistoric Planet 66. Picture Mommy Dead 66. Red Tomahawk 67. Cyborg 2087 67. The Astro Zombies 68. Buckskin 68.

TV series: Harbor Command 57. Peck's Bad Girl 59. The Eleventh Hour 62.

Corfield, John (1893–).
British producer in films from 1929; co-founder of British National Films with Lady Yule and J. Arthur Rank.

Turn of the Tide 35. Laugh It Off 40. Gaslight 40. Headline 42. Bedelia 46. The White Unicorn 47. My Sister and I 48, etc.

Corman, Gene (1927–).
American producer, brother of Roger Corman.

Tower of London 62. The Secret Invasion 64. Tobruk 66. You Can't Win 'Em All 70, etc.

Corman, Roger (1926–).
American producer and director who during the 50s made a record number of grade Z horror films, then presented an interesting series of Poe adaptations; when he seemed poised for better things his career as a director slowed and he turned to producing low-budget exploitation movies and distributing foreign films. Among those who began their careers working for him are Martin Scorsese, Francis Ford Coppola, Peter Bogdanovich, Jack Nicholson, Monte Hellman, Jonathan Demme, Joe Dante, Jonathan Sayles, Ron Howard, Gale Anne Hurd and James Cameron.

Autobiography: 1990, *How I Made a Hundred Movies in Hollywood and Never Lost a Dime*.
■ Five Guns West 55. Apache Woman 55. The Day the World Ended 56. Swamp Woman 56. The Gunslinger 56. Oklahoma Woman 56. It Conquered the World 56. Naked Paradise 57. Attack of the Crab Monsters 57. *Not of this Earth* 57. The Undead 57. Rock all Night 57. Carnival Rock 57. Teenage Doll 57. Sorority Girl 57. The Viking Women and the Sea Serpent 57. War of the Satellites 57. Machine Gun Kelly 58. Teenage Caveman 58. She-Gods of Shark Reef 58. I Mobster 59. Wasp Woman 59. *A Bucket of Blood* 59. Ski Troop Attack 60. *House of Usher* 60. The Little Shop of Horrors 60. The Last Woman on Earth 60. Creature from the Haunted Sea 60. Atlas 60. The Pit and the Pendulum 61. The Premature Burial 62. *The Intruder* 62. Tales of Terror 62. Tower of London 62. *The Raven* 63. The Young Racers 63. The Haunted Palace 63. The Terror 63. X – The Man with X-ray Eyes 63. *The Masque of the Red Death* 64. Secret Invasion 64. *The Tomb of Ligeia* 65. The Wild Angels 66. The St Valentine's Day Massacre 67. The Trip 67. Bloody Mama 70. Gas-s-s! 70. Von Richthofen and Brown 71. Boxcar Bertha (p only) 72. I Escaped from Devil's Island (co-p only) 73. Big Bad Mama 74. Cockfighter (p only) 74. Grand Theft Auto (p only) 77. Thunder and Lightning (p only) 77. Piranha (p only) 78. St Jack (p only) 78. Battle Beyond the Stars (p only) 80. Humanoids from the Deep (p only) 80. Smokey Bites the Dust (p only) 81. Forbidden World (p only) 82. Love Letters (p) 83. Space Raiders (p) 83. Suburbia (p) 83. The Warrior and the Sorceress (p) 83. Deathstalker (p) 84. Streetwalkin' (p) 85. Amazons (p) 87. Big Bad Mama II (p) 88. Daddy's Boys (p) 88. Dangerous Love (p) 88. The Drifter (p) 88. Nightfall (p) 88. Not of This Earth (p) 88. Watchers (p) 88. Andy Colby's Incredibly Awesome Adventure (p) 89. The Lawless Land (p) 89. The Masque of the Red Death (p) 89. Stripped to Kill II (p) 89. The Terror Within (p) 89. Time Trackers (p) 89. Two to Tango (p) 89. Wizards of the Lost Kingdom II (p) 89. Back to Back (p) 90. Bloodfist II (p) 90. A Cry in the Wild (p)

90. Full Fathom Five (p) 90. The Haunting of Morella (p) 90. Overexposed (p) 90. Primary Target (p) 90. Frankenstein Unbound (co-w, d) 90. Silk 2 (p) 90. Streets (p) 90. Transylvania Twist (p) 90. Watchers II (p) 90. Welcome to Oblivion (p) 90. Hollywood Boulevard II (p) 91. The Terror Within II (p) 91. Dracula Rising (p) 92. In the Heat of Passion (p) 92. Reflections on a Crime (p) 94. Cheyenne Warrior (p) 94.

¶ I've never made the film I wanted to make. No matter what happens, it never turns out exactly as I hoped. – *R.C.*

Poe writes the first reel or the last reel. Roger does the rest. – *James H. Nicholson*

All my films have been concerned simply with man as a social animal. – *R.C., 1970*

I think there is always a political undercurrent in my films. With the exception of *The Intruder*, I tried not to put it on the surface. – *R.C.*

To one degree or another, almost all films finally adhere to the Corman policy. So many of them do have an enormous amount of action; the sex is there; the laughs are there; and, sometimes, to some degree, the social statement is there as well. *The Godfather* films are the most expensive Roger Corman films ever made, and I think that everyone's trying to exploit that formula, one way or another. But most people are less candid about it than Roger is. – *Jonathan Demme*

He once said, 'Martin, what you have to get is a very good first reel because people want to know what's going on. Then you need a very good last reel because people want to hear how it all turns out. Everything else doesn't really matter.' Probably the best sense I have ever heard in the movies. – *Martin Scorsese*

Corneau, Alain (1943–).
French director and screenwriter, usually of thrillers. He trained at the national film school, IDHEC, before going to America to collaborate on a script with novelist Jim Thompson. He also worked as an assistant to Roger Corman, Marcel Camus and Costa-Gavras.

France S.A. 74. La Menace 77. Série Noire 79. Choice of Arms (Le Choix des Armes) 81. Fort Saganne 84. Nocturne Indien 89, etc.

Cornelius, Henry (1913–1958).
British director with a subtle comedy touch.
■ It Always Rains on Sunday (co-w only) 47. *Passport to Pimlico* 48. The Galloping Major (& w) 51. *Genevieve* 53. I Am a Camera 55. Next to No Time 57. Law and Disorder 58.

Cornell, John (1941–).
Australian producer and director. A former journalist, he went on to work in television and discovered and managed comedian Paul Hogan.

Crocodile Dundee (p) 86. Crocodile Dundee II (p, d) 88. Almost an Angel (p) 90, etc.

Cornfield, Hubert (1929–).
American director.
■ Sudden Danger 56. Lure of the Swamp 57. Plunder Road 59. *The Third Voice* 59. Angel Baby (co-d) 61. Pressure Point 62. Night of the Following Day 68. Les Grands Moyens 76.

Corraface, Georges (1953–).
French-born leading actor, of Greek parents. He studied law in Paris before becoming an actor.

Mahabharata 89. Impromptu 90. Not without My Daughter 91. Columbus: The Discovery 92. Pasiones Turcas 94, etc.

Corri, Adrienne (1930–) (Adrienne Riccoboni)
Tempestuous red-headed British leading lady of Italian descent.

The River 51. The Kidnappers 53. Devil Girl fro Mars 54. *Lease of Life* 54. Make Me an Offer 54. The Feminine Touch 55. Three Men in a Boat 56 Corridors of Blood 58. The Rough and the Smoo 59. The Hellfire Club 61. The Tell-Tale Heart 61. A Study in Terror 65. Bunny Lake is Missing 65. The Viking Queen 67. Moon Zero Two 69. A Clockwork Orange 71. Vampire Circus 72. Madhouse 74, etc.

TV series: Sword of Freedom 57.

Corrigan, Douglas 'Wrong Way' (1907–).
American aviator who in 1939 left New York for Los Angeles and landed in Ireland, thus deservin the title Wrong Way Corrigan. In the same year he played himself in the film *The Flying Irishman*.

Corrigan, Lloyd (1900–1969).
Chubby American character actor, usually in jovi roles; also directed some films in the 30s.

The Splendid Crime 25. Daughter of the Drago (d) 31. The Broken Wing (d) 32. Murder on a Honeymoon (d) 35. The Dancing Pirate (d) 36. Night Key (d) 37. Young Tom Edison 40. *The Gho Breakers* 40. The Great Man's Lady 42. Since You Went Away 44. The Bandit of Sherwood Forest 4 Stallion Road 47. Cyrano de Bergerac 50. Son of Paleface 52. The Bowery Boys Meet the Monster 54. Hidden Guns 57. The Manchurian Candidate 62, many others.

TV series: Willy 54–55. Happy 60–61. Hank 65–66.

Corrigan, Ray 'Crash' (1903–1976) (Ray Benard).
American leading man, hero of innumerable second feature westerns.

The Three Mesquiteers 36. Wild Horse Rodeo 38. The Purple Vigilantes 38. Three Texas Steers 39. West of the Pinto Basin 40. Wrangler's Roost 41. Rock River Renegades 42, etc.

TV series: Crash Corrigan's Ranch 50.

Cort, Bud (1950–) (Walter Edward Cox).
American actor with a tendency to play demente youths.

M*A*S*H 70. The Travelling Executioner 70. Brewster McCloud 70. *Harold and Maude* 72. Why Shoot the Teacher 77. Hitler's Son 78. Die Laughing 80. She Dances Alone 82. Love Letters 83. Electric Dreams 84. Maria's Lovers 84. Invade from Mars 86. Love at Stake 87. Out of the Dark 88. Brain Dead 89. Ted and Venus (& d) 92, etc.

Cortese, Valentina (1924–).
Italian leading lady in international films. She wa married to Richard Basehart.

The Glass Mountain 48. Thieves' Highway 49. Malaya 50. The House on Telegraph Hill 51. Les Misérables 52. The Barefoot Contessa 54. Le Amiche 55. Magic Fire 56. Calabuch 58. Barabba 62. The Visit 64. Juliet of the Spirits 65. The Leger of Lylah Clare 68. Day for Night (La Nuit Américaine) (AAN) 73. When Time Ran Out 80. The Adventures of Baron Munchhausen 88. Buster's Bedroom 91. Sparrow (Storia di una Capinera) 93, etc.

Cortez, Ricardo (1899–1977) (Jake Kranz).
American leading man, groomed in the 20s as a Latin lover in the Valentino mould. Later developed outside interests and quit movies after a sojourn in routine roles.

Sixty Cents an Hour 23. Pony Express 24. *The Torrent* 26. *The Sorrows of Satan* 27. The Private Lif

Helen of Troy 27. Behind Office Doors 28. Ten
nts a Dance 31. Melody of Life 32. The Phantom
Crestwood 33. *Wonder Bar* 34. Special Agent 35.
e Walking Dead 36. Talk of the Devil (GB) 36.
r Moto's Last Warning 38. City Girl (d only) 38.
ee, Blonde and Twenty One (d only) 40. World
emière 40. I Killed That Man 42. Make Your
wn Bed 44. The Locket 46. Blackmail 47. The
st Hurrah 58, many others.

ortez, Stanley (1908–   ) (Stanley Kranz).
nerican cinematographer, brother of Ricardo
ortez; in Hollywood from silent days.
Four Days Wonder 37. The Wildcatter 37.
mored Car 37. The Black Doll 38. Lady in the
orgue 38. Danger on the Air 38. Personal
cretary 38. The Last Express 38. For Love or
oney 38. The Forgotten Woman 39. They Asked
r It 39. Hawaiian Nights 39. Risky Business 39.
ugh It Off 39. Alias the Deacon 39. The
atherpushers 40. Meet the Wildcat 40. Love
onor and Oh Baby 40. The Black Cat 40. A
angerous Game 41. San Antonio Rose 41.
oonlight in Hawaii 41. Badlands of Dakota 41.
mbay Clipper 42. Eagle Squadron 42. *The
agnificent Ambersons* 42. Flesh and Fantasy 43.
e Powers Girl 43. Since You Went Away (co-
) 44. Smash-Up 47. The Secret Beyond the Door
. Smart Woman 48. The Man on the Eiffel Tower
. Underworld Story 50. The Admiral was a Lady
. The Basketball Fix 51. Fort Defiance 51.
odels Inc 52. Abbott and Costello Meet Captain
dd 52. The Diamond Queen 53. Dragon's Gold
. Shark River 53. Riders to the Stars 54. Black
esday 54. *The Night of the Hunter* 55. Man from
l Rio 56. Top Secret Affair 57. The Three Faces
Eve 57. Thunder in the Sun 59. Vice Raid 60.
e Angry Red Planet 60. Dinosaurus 60. Back
reet 61. Shock Corridor 63. The Candidate 64.
ghtmare in the Sun 64. The Naked Kiss 65. The
avy vs the Night Monsters 66. The Ghost in the
visible Bikini 66. Blue 68. The Bridge at
magen 69. The Date 71. Do Not Fold, Spindle
Mutilate (TV) 72. Another Man, Another
ance (co-ph) 77.

orti, Alex (1933–1993).
ench-born director and screenwriter of Austrian
scent, in international films.
The Refusal (Der Verweigerung) 72. The
ndemned (Totstellen) 75. A Woman's Pale
ue Handwriting (& w) 84. God Does Not Believe
Us Anymore (An Uns Glaubt Gott Nicht Mehr)
. Sante Fe 85. Welcome in Vienna (& w) 86.
e King's Whore (& w) 90, etc.

osby, Bill (1937–   ).
merican leading man and TV personality.
To All My Friends on Shore (& p) (TV) 71.
ckey and Boggs 72. Uptown Saturday Night 74.
t's Do It Again 76. Mother, Jugs and Speed 76.
Piece of the Action 77. Top Secret (TV) 78.
alifornia Suite 79. Leonard Part 6 87. Ghost Dad
. The Meteor Man 93. I Spy Returns (TV) 94,
c.
TV series: *I Spy* 66–68. The Bill Cosby Show 69–
, 72–73, 84–92. Fat Albert and the Cosby Kids
. Cos 76. The Cosby Mysteries 94–   .

osma, Vladimir (1940–   ).
manian-born composer who has worked in
ance since the 60s.
Alexander 68. Maldonne 68. Le Distrait 70. The
ll Blond Man with One Black Shoe 72. Pleure
s la Bouche Pleine 73. Salut l'Artiste 73. The
ad Adventures of Rabbi Jacob 74. Lucky Pierre
a Moutarde me Monte au Nez) 74. The Return
the Tall Blond Man with One Black Shoe 74. The

Pink Telephone (Le Téléphone Rose) 75. Dracula
and Son 76. Pardon Mon Affaire (Un Eléphant Ča
Trompe Enormément) 76. Pardon Mon Affaire
Too! (Nous Irons Tous au Paradis) 77. Anne 78. The
Getaway (La Deborade) 79. La Boum 80. Diva 82.
La Boum II 83. Just the Way You Are 84. Asterix
vs Caesar 85. Judith Krantz's Till We Meet Again
(TV) 89. The Jackpot (La Totale!) 91. Cuisine et
Dépendances 93. Le Mari de Léon 93. Cache Cash
94, etc.

Cosmatos, George Pan (1941–   ).
Greek director of international adventures.
Massacre in Rome 74. The Cassandra Crossing
77. Escape to Athena 79. Rambo: First Blood II 84.
Cobra 85. Leviathan 89. Tombstone 94, etc.

¶ My pictures appeal all round the world. I do
slick American pictures with a European
sensitivity. – *G.P.C.*

Cossart, Ernest (1876–1951).
Portly British actor, inevitably cast by Hollywood
in butler roles.
The Scoundrel 35. Desire 36. The Great Ziegfeld
36. Angel 37. Zaza 39. The Light That Failed 39.
Tom Brown's Schooldays 40. *Charley's Aunt* 41.
Casanova Brown 44. Cluny Brown 46. John Loves
Mary 49, many others.

Cossins, James (1933–   ).
British character actor, usually of pompous,
flustered type.
The Anniversary 68. Lost Continent 68. Melody
70. Villain 71, etc.

Costa-Gavras (1933–   ) (Constantin Costa-
Gavras).
Russo-Greek director, in France from childhood.
■ The Sleeping Car Murders 65. Un Homme de
Trop 67. 'Z' (AAN) 68. L'Aveu 70. State of Siege
72. Special Section 75. Missing (AA co-w) 82.
Hannah K 83. Conseil de Femme 86. Betrayed 88.
Music Box 89. La Petite Apocalypse 93.

Costello, Dolores (1905–1979).
Gentle American silent screen heroine, in films
from 1911; married John Barrymore.
Lawful Larceny 23. *The Sea Beast* 25. Bride of the
Storm 26. When a Man Loves 27. Old San Francisco
27. Glorious Betsy 28. The Redeeming Sin 29.
Noah's Ark 29. Show of Shows 29. Second Choice
30. Expensive Women 31. Little Lord Fauntleroy
36. King of the Turf 39. *The Magnificent Ambersons*
42. This is the Army 43, many others.

Costello, Helene (1903–1957).
American silent screen leading lady, sister of
Dolores Costello, in films from 1912. Her first
husband was actor Lowell Sherman.
The Man on the Box 25. Bobbed Hair 25. Don
Juan 26. In Old Kentucky 27. *Lights of New York*
28. Midnight Taxi 28. The Circus Kid 28. Show of
Shows 29. Riffraff 35, etc.

Costello, Lou (1906–1959) (Louis Cristillo).
Dumpy American comedian, the zanier half of
Abbott and Costello. For films, see *Bud Abbott*.
Costello finally made one on his own, *The Thirty-
Foot Bride of Candy Rock* 59.

Costello, Maurice (1877–1950).
American matinée idol, the father of Dolores and
Helena Costello, in films from 1907.
A Tale of Two Cities 11. The Night Before
Christmas 12. Human Collateral 20. Conceit 21.
Glimpses of the Moon 23. The Mad Marriage 25.

Camille 27. Hollywood Boulevard 36. Lady from
Louisiana 41, many others.

Costner, Kevin (1955–   ).
American leading actor who scored a big hit with
his first attempt at directing.
Biographies: 1991, *Kevin Costner* by Todd Keith.
1993, *Kevin Costner – A Life on Film* by Adrian
Wright.
Night Shift 82. Table For Five 83. Testament 83.
American Flyers 84. Fandango 84. Silverado 85.
Sizzle Beach 86. The Untouchables 87. No Way
Out 87. Bull Durham 88. Field of Dreams 89.
Dances with Wolves (& d) (AAd, AANa) 90.
Revenge 90. Robin Hood: Prince of Thieves 91. JFK
91. The Bodyguard 92. A Perfect World 93. Rapa
Nui (p) 94. Wyatt Earp (& p) 94. Waterworld (& p)
95, etc.

Cottafavi, Vittorio (1914–   ).
Italian director, mainly of cut-rate spectaculars.
Has won critical approval for stylish handling of
some of them.
Revolt of the Gladiators 58. The Legions of
Cleopatra 59. The Vengeance of Hercules 60.
Hercules Conquers Atlantis 61, etc.

Cotten, Joseph (1905–1994).
Tall, quiet American leading man, former drama
critic and Broadway stage star. His second wife was
actress Patricia Medina.
Autobiography: 1987, *Vanity Will Get You
Somewhere*.
■ Citizen Kane 41. Lydia 41. *The Magnificent
Ambersons* 42. *Journey into Fear* 42. *Shadow of a
Doubt* 43. Hers to Hold 43. Gaslight 44. Since You
Went Away 44. Love Letters 45. *I'll Be Seeing You*
45. Duel in the Sun 46. The Farmer's Daughter 47.
Portrait of Jennie 48. Under Capricorn 49. Beyond
the Forest 49. *The Third Man* 49. Two Flags West
50. Walk Softly Stranger 50. September Affair 50.
Half Angel 51. Man with a Cloak 51. Peking
Express 52. Untamed Frontier 52. The Steel Trap
52. Niagara 52. Blueprint for Murder 53. Special
Delivery 54. The Bottom of the Bottle 55. The Killer
is Loose 56. The Halliday Brand 56. From the Earth
to the Moon 58. Touch of Evil (uncredited cameo)
58. The Angel Wore Red 60. The Last Sunset 61.
Hush Hush Sweet Charlotte 64. The Money Trap
65. The Great Sioux Massacre 65. The Tramplers
66. The Oscar 66. The Hell-benders 67. Jack of
Diamonds 67. Brighty 67. Some May Live (TV) 67.
Petulia 68. Days of Fire (It.) 68. Keene 69. Cutter's
Trail (TV) 69. The Lonely Profession (TV) 69.
Latitude Zero 69. The Grasshopper 70. Do You
Take This Stranger (TV) 70. The Abominable Dr
Phibes 71. City Beneath the Sea (TV) 71.
Doomsday Voyage 71. Tora! Tora! Tora! 71. White
Comanche 71. Lady Frankenstein 71. Baron
Blood 72. Assault on the Wayne (TV) 72. The
Screaming Woman (TV) 72. The Devil's Daughter
(TV) 72. The Scientific Cardplayer 72. Soylent
Green 73. A Delicate Balance 73. The Lindbergh
Kidnapping Case (TV) 76. Twilight's Last Gleaming
76. Airport 77 77. Caravans 78. Churchill and the
Generals (TV) 79. Island of Mutations 79. Guyana,
Crime of the Century 79. The Survivor 80.
Heaven's Gate 80. The Hearse 80. Delusion 81. The
House Where Evil Dwells 82.
TV series: The 20th Century Fox Hour (as host)
55–56. The Joseph Cotten Show 56–57.
Hollywood and the Stars 63–64.

¶ I didn't care about the movies, really. I was tall.
I could talk. It was easy to do. – *J.C.*
I'm afraid you'll never make it as an actor. But
as a star, I think you might well hit the jackpot.
– *Orson Welles*

Cotton, Carolina.
Singing leading lady of westerns of the 40s and
early 50s, opposite Ken Curtis and Gene Autry;
she later worked as a school teacher.
Song of the Prairie 45. Singing on the Trail 46.
Cowboy Blues (GB: Beneath the Starry Skies) 46.
Blue Canadian Rockies 52. Apache Country 52,
etc.

Cotton, Oliver (1944–).
Darkly brooding English character actor, mainly
on stage, from 1965, and TV.
Here We Go round the Mulberry Bush 67.
Firefox 82. Eleni 85. The Sicilian 87. Hiding Out
87. Columbus: The Discovery 92, etc.
TV series: Robin of Sherwood 85–86.
Westbeach 93.

Couffer, Jack (1922–).
American director with a penchant for natural
history.
■ Nikki, Wild Dog of the North (co-d) 61. Ring of
Bright Water 69. The Darwin Adventure 72.
Jonathan Livingston Seagull (ph) 73. The Last
Giraffe 79.

Coulouris, George (1903–1989).
British character actor, in America 1930–50;
usually in explosive roles.
Christopher Bean 33. All This and Heaven Too
40. The Lady in Question 40. *Citizen Kane* 41. This
Land is Mine 43. *Watch on the Rhine* 43. Between
Two Worlds 44. The Master Race 44. Hotel Berlin
45. Confidential Agent 45. The Verdict 46. Sleep
My Love 47. A Southern Yankee 48. *An Outcast of
the Islands* 51. Doctor in the House 53. The
Runaway Bus 54. I Accuse 57. Womaneater 59.
Conspiracy of Hearts 60. King of Kings 61. The
Skull 65. Arabesque 66. The Assassination Bureau
69. Blood from the Mummy's Tomb 71. Papillon
73. Mahler 74. Murder on the Orient Express 74.
The Antichrist 75. The Ritz 76. The Long Good
Friday 80, many others.

Coulter, Michael.
English cinematographer, closely associated with
director Bill Forsyth.
That Sinking Feeling 79. Gregory's Girl 82. The
Good Father 87. Housekeeping 87. The Dressmaker
88. Breaking In 89. Diamond Skulls (aka Dark
Obsession) 89. Bearskin: An Urban Fairytale 89.
Monster in a Box 92. Being Human 94. The Neon
Bible 95, etc.

Courant, Curt.
German cinematographer who did his best work
elsewhere.
Quo Vadis 24. Woman in the Moon 29. Perfect
Understanding (GB) 33. Amok 34. The Man Who
Knew Too Much (GB) 34. The Iron Duke (GB) 35.
Broken Blossoms (GB) 36. La Bête Humaine 38.
Louise 39. Le Jour Se Lève 39. De Mayerling à
Sarajevo 40. Monsieur Verdoux (US) 47. It
Happened in Athens 61, etc.

Courcel, Nicole (1930–) (Nicole Andrieux).
French leading lady of warm personality.
La Marie du Port 49. Versailles 53. La Sorcière
55. The Case of Dr Laurent 56. Sundays and
Cybele 62, etc.

Court, Hazel (1926–).
Red-headed British leading lady; moved into
horror films and went to live in Hollywood.
Champagne Charlie 44. Dear Murderer 46. My
Sister and I 48. It's Not Cricket 48. Bond Street
50. The Curse of Frankenstein 56. The Man Who
Could Cheat Death 59. Doctor Blood's Coffin 60.

The Premature Burial 62. The Masque of the Red
Death 64, etc.
TV series: Dick and the Duchess 57.

Courtenay, Syd.
British comic actor and screenwriter. A sketch
writer from 1919 for Leslie Fuller, with whom he
worked in revue, he began in films in 1930,
writing, and appearing in, Fuller's low-budget
comedies.
Not So Quiet on the Western Front (a, w) 30.
Why Sailors Leave Home (a, story) 30. Kiss Me
Sergeant (co-w) 30. Bill's Legacy (co-w) 31.
Tonight's the Night (a, co-w) 31. What a Night (a,
story) 31. Poor Old Bill (a, story) 31. Hawleys of
High Street (co-w) 33. Pride of the Force (a, co-w)
33. Lost in the Legion (a, co-w) 34. Doctor's Orders
(story) 34. Cotton Queen (a, co-w) 35. Captain
Bill (co-w) 35. Everything Is Rhythm (co-w) 36.
The Man behind the Mask 36. Boys Will Be Girls
(a, co-w) 37. Darby and Joan (w) 37. Sing as You
Swing (w) 37. The Reverse Be My Lot (w) 38,
etc.

Courtenay, Tom (1937–).
Lean British actor specializing in under-privileged
roles.
Billy Liar 63. Private Potter 62. *The Loneliness of
the Long Distance Runner* 63. King and Country 64.
Operation Crossbow 65. King Rat 65. Doctor
Zhivago (AAN) 65. The Night of the Generals 66.
The Day the Fish Came Out 67. A Dandy in Aspic
68. *Otley* 69. One Day in the Life of Ivan Denisovitch
71. Catch Me a Spy 71. *The Dresser* (AAN) 83.
Happy New Year 87. Leonard Part 6 87. The Last
Butterfly 90. Let Him Have It 91, etc.

¶ There just doesn't seem to be a market for
something with aspiration any more. – *T.C.*

courtesans
have always been viewed by the cinema through
rose-coloured glasses. There have been
innumerable films about Madame du Barry,
Madame Sans Gêne and Nell Gwyn; Garbo played
Camille and Marie Walewska as well as Anna
Christie; even Jean Simmons had a shot at
Napoleon's *Désirée*, and Vivien Leigh was a
decorative Lady Hamilton. Martine Carol played
Lola Montes in the Max Ophüls film, Yvonne de
Carlo in *Black Bart* (in which she became involved
in western villainy during an American tour).
See also: *prostitutes*.

Courtland, Jerome (1926–).
Gangling young American lead of 40s comedies,
now working as a producer.
Kiss and Tell 45. Man from Colorado 48.
Battleground 49. The Barefoot Mailman 52. The
Bamboo Prison 55. Tonka 59. O Sole Mio (It.) 60.
Mary Read, Pirate (It.) 61. Thanis, Son of Attila (It.)
61. Black Spurs 65. Diamonds on Wheels (d only)
73. Pete's Dragon (co-p only) 77, etc.
TV series: Tales of the Vikings 60.

Courtneidge, Dame Cicely (1893–1980).
British comedienne; wife of Jack Hulbert. On stage
from 1901; her great vitality made her a musical
comedy favourite.
Autobiography: 1953, *Cicely*.
■ Elstree Calling 30. *The Ghost Train* 31. *Jack's the
Boy* 32. Happy Ever After 32. Aunt Sally 33.
Soldiers of the King 33. Falling for You 33. Things
are Looking Up 34. Me and Marlborough 35.
Everybody Dance 36. Take my Tip 37. *Under Your
Hat* 40. Miss Tulip Stays the Night 56. The Spider's
Web 60. *The L-Shaped Room* 62. Those Magnificent

Men in their Flying Machines 65. The Wrong Bo
66. Not Now Darling 72.

¶ When I was in Delhi,
I lay on my — hm, hm,
In a flat-bottomed canoe.
They all called me barmy,
But I know the army!
The nation depends on you!
– sung by C.C. in Under Your Hat

courtroom scenes
have been the suspenseful saving grace of more
films than can be counted; and they also figure
some of the best films ever made.
British courts best preserve the ancient aura of
the law; among the films they have figured in ar
*London Belongs to Me, The Paradine Case, Eight
O'Clock Walk, Life for Ruth, Twenty-one Days,
Brothers in Law, The Winslow Boy, Witness for the
Prosecution, The Blind Goddess* and *The Dock Brief.*
The last four are based on stage plays, as are the
American *Madame X, Counsellor at Law,* and *The Tr
of Mary Dugan.* Other American films depending
heavily on courtroom denouements include *They
Won't Believe Me, The Unholy Three, The Mouthpiec
Boomerang, They Won't Forget, The Missing Juror,
Trial, The Young Savages, The Criminal Code, To Ki
a Mockingbird, Criminal Lawyer, Fury, The Lawyer,
Free Soul, The Seven Minutes, The People Against
O'Hara, The Lady from Shanghai, Twilight of Honou
An American Tragedy* (and its remake *A Place in th
Sun*), the several Perry Mason films, *Young Mr
Lincoln,* and *Philadelphia.* These, even the last-
named, were fictional: genuine cases were
reconstructed in *I Want to Live, Cell 2455 Death Ro
Compulsion, Inherit the Wind, Dr Ehrlich's Magic
Bullet, The Witches of Salem, The Trials of Oscar Wila
Judgment at Nuremberg, The Life of Emile Zola, Dr
Crippen, Captain Kidd, Landru* and *The Case of Char
Peace.* Comedy courtroom scenes have appeared
*I'm No Angel, Mr Deeds Goes to Town, You Can't Ta
It With You, Roxie Hart, My Learned Friend, Adam
Rib, Pickwick Papers, Brothers in Law, What's Up
Doc?, Star!* and *A Pair of Briefs.*
Films in which special interest has centred on
the jury include *Twelve Angry Men, Murder (Enter
Sir John), Perfect Strangers (Too Dangerous to Love),
Justice est Faite* and *The Monster and the Girl* (in
which the criminal brain inside the gorilla murde
the jurors at his trial one by one). Ghostly juries
figured in *All That Money Can Buy* and *The
Remarkable Andrew.* The judge has been the key
figure in *The Judge Steps Out, Talk of the Town, Th
Bachelor and the Bobbysoxer,* and *Destry Rides Agair
and we are constantly being promised a film of
Henry Cecil's *No Bail for the Judge. Anatomy of a
Murder* remains the only film in which a real judg
(Joseph E. Welch) has played a fictional one. A
lady barrister (Anna Neagle) had the leading rol
in *The Man Who Wouldn't Talk.*
Specialized courts were seen in *M* (convened b
criminals), *Saint Joan* and *The Hunchback of Notre
Dame* (church courts), *Black Legion* (Ku Klux Klar
The Devil's Disciple (18th-century military court),
Kind Hearts and Coronets (a court of the House of
Lords), *The Wreck of the Mary Deare* (mercantile),
Cone of Silence (civil aviation), *A Tale of Two Cities*
and *The Scarlet Pimpernel* (French Revolutionary
courts). Courts in other countries were shown ir
*The Lady in Question, The Count of Monte Cristo, Cra
in the Mirror, A Flea in Her Ear, La Vérité,* and *Can
Can* (French); *The Purple Heart* (Japanese); *The
Fall of the Roman Empire* (ancient Roman); *The Sp
Who Came in from the Cold* (East German); and
Shoeshine (Italian). Coroners' courts were feature
in *Inquest, My Learned Friend* and *Rebecca.*
Courts martial figured largely in *The Caine*

Mutiny, Time Limit, The Man in the Middle, Across the Pacific, The Rack, Carrington VC, The Court Martial of Billy Mitchell and *A Few Good Men*. There was also a TV series called *Court Martial (Counsellors at War* in the US).

Heavenly courts were convened in *A Matter of Life and Death, Outward Bound* and *The Flight That Disappeared;* while other fantasy courts appeared in *Rashomon, Morgan, One Way Pendulum, Alice in Wonderland, The Balcony, The Wonderful World of the Brothers Grimm, The Trial, All That Money Can Buy,* and *The Remarkable Andrew*. The court in *Planet of the Apes* is perhaps best classed as prophetic, along with that in *1984*.

TV series based on trials and lawyers include *The Law and Mr Jones, Harrigan and Son, Sam Benedict, The Trials of O'Brien, Perry Mason, Arrest and Trial, The Defenders, The D.A., The Verdict is Yours, Judd for the Defense, Owen Marshall, Petrocelli, Adam's Rib* and *L.A. Law*.

Cousteau, Jacques-Yves (1910–).
French underwater explorer and documentarist.
The Silent World 56. World Without Sun 64, etc.

Coutard, Raoul (1924–).
French cinematographer.
Ranuntcho 50. A Bout de Souffle 59. Shoot the Pianist 60. *Lola* 60. *Jules et Jim* 61. Vivre Sa Vie 61. Bay of Angels 62. Les Carabiniers 63. Silken Skin 63. Pierrot le Fou 65. Made in USA 66. Sailor from Gibraltar 66. The Bride Wore Black 67. 'Z' 68. L'Aveu 70. L'Explosion 70. Embassy 72. The Jerusalem File 72. A Pain in the A . . . 73. Le Crabe-Tambour 77. Le Légion Saute sur Kolwezi (d only) 80. Passion 82. SAS à San Salvador (d) 82. First Name: Carmen (Prénom Carmen) 83. La Garce 84. Max, Mon Amour 86. Fuegos 87. Burning Beds (Brennende Betten) 88. Bethune: The Making of a Hero 90. La Femme Fardée 90. Dien Bien Phu 91. La Naissance de l'Amour 93. Faut Pas Rire du Bonheur 94, etc.

coverage.
All the shots that comprise the photography from various angles of a particular scene in a film.

Cowan, Jerome (1897–1972).
American character actor with an easy manner. In films from 1936 (*Beloved Enemy:* out of character as a fanatical Irishman). He played hundreds of supporting roles, typically in *The Maltese Falcon* 41 as the detective killed while searching for the mysterious Floyd Thursby; played the lead in *Crime by Night* 43, Find The Blackmailer 44. Latterly graduated from jealous rivals to executives, from lawyers to judges.
Claudia and David 46. The Unfaithful 47. Miracle on 34th Street 48. June Bride 48. The Fountainhead 49. Young Man with a Horn 50. Dallas 51. The System 53. Visit to a Small Planet 60. Frankie and Johnny 65. The Gnome-Mobile 67. The Comic 69, many others.
TV series: The Tab Hunter Show 60. Tycoon 64.

Cowan, Lester (1907–1990).
American producer from 1934.
My Little Chickadee 39. Ladies in Retirement 41. The Story of G.I. Joe 45. Love Happy 50. Main Street to Broadway 52, etc.

Cowan, Maurice (1891–1974).
British producer of mainly routine films.
Derby Day 52. Turn the Key Softly 55. The Gypsy and the Gentleman 57, etc.

Coward, Sir Noël (1899–1973).
British actor-writer-composer-director, the bright young man of international show business in the 20s and 30s.
Autobiographies: 1933, *Present Indicative*. 1949, *Future Indefinite*.
Biographies: 1969, *A Talent to Amuse* by Sheridan Morley. 1976, *The Life of Noël Coward* by Cole Lesley. Coward was portrayed in 1968, *Star!* by Dan Massey. *The Noël Coward Diaries* were published in 1982.
■ Hearts of the World (a) 18. Private Lives (oa) 31. Cavalcade (oa) 33. Tonight is Ours (oa) 33. Bitter Sweet (oa) 33 and 40. Design for Living (oa) 34. *The Scoundrel* (a) 35. In Which We Serve (awpd) (AA special award, AANp, AANw) 41. We Were Dancing (oa) 42. *Blithe Spirit* (oa) 45. This Happy Breed (oa) 45. *Brief Encounter* (oa) 46. The Astonished Heart (a) 49. Meet Me Tonight (oa) 50. Around the World in Eighty Days (a) 56. *Our Man in Havana* (a) 59. Surprise Package (a) 60. Paris When it Sizzles (a) 64. Bunny Lake is Missing (a) 65. Boom (a) 66. The Italian Job (a) 69.
☻ For displaying, if only intermittently, a wholly professional talent to amuse. *In Which We Serve*.

¶ Destiny's tot. – *Alexander Woollcott*

Cowen, William J. (1883–1964).
American director.
■ Kongo 32. Oliver Twist 33. Woman Unafraid 34.

Cowl, Jane (1884–1950).
American leading stage actress who made very few film appearances.
■ The Garden of Lies 15. The Spreading Dawn 17. Once More My Darling 49. No Man of Her Own 49. The Secret Fury 50. Payment on Demand 50.

Cox, Alex (1954–).
British director and screenwriter with a cult reputation. He studied law at Oxford and film at Bristol University before going to America for further film studies. He now lives and works in Mexico and presents the BBC-TV film series *Moviedrome*.
Repo Man (wd) 84. Sid and Nancy (wd) 86. Straight to Hell (wd) 87. Walker (d) 87. Highway Patrolman (El Patrullero) (d) 92. Dead Beat (a) 94. The Queen of the Night 94.

¶ If you're a fascist in Hollywood, you work with great regularity. If you're not, you don't – so I don't. – *A.C.*
There is no place in Hollywood for certain directors. It has to do with the big corporations owning the studios and being tied into the military-industrial complex, or the Mafia. – *A.C.*
The movie business feels it must support war and encourage white yuppies to have babies. If you don't buy into that, you are ultimately excluded. – *A.C.*

Cox, Brian (1946–).
Scottish classical theatre actor and director, in occasional films.
Autobiographies: 1989, *From Salem to Moscow: An Actor's Odyssey*. 1992, *The Lear Diaries*.
Nicholas and Alexandra 71. In Celebration 75. Manhunter 86. Shoot for the Sun 86. Hidden Agenda 90. The Lost Language of Cranes (TV) 91. Sharpe's Rifles (TV) 93. Sharpe's Eagle (TV) 93. Iron Will 94. Rob Roy 95, etc.

¶ Big audiences in Britain are mind-dead. The best British audience I ever played to was in Broadmoor asylum. – *B.C.*

Cox, Courtenay (1964–).
American actress.
Misfits of Science (TV) 85. Masters of the Universe 87. Cocoon: The Return 88. Down Twisted 89. The Prize Pulitzer (TV) 89. Curiosity Kills (TV) 90. Mr Destiny 90. Shaking the Tree 92. The Opposite Sex and How to Live with Them 93, etc.

Cox, Jack (1896–) (John Jaffray Cox).
Distinguished British cinematographer who became a director of photography in 1920. His career ranged from being Alfred Hitchcock's cameraman on his early movies to photographing the popular comedies of Norman Wisdom in the late 50s.
A Romance of Wastdale 20. The Four Feathers 21. Guy Fawkes 23. The Ring 27. The Farmer's Wife 28. Champagne 28. The Manxman 29. Blackmail 29. Almost a Honeymoon 30. Juno and the Paycock 30. Murder! 30. The Skin Game 31. Number Seventeen 32. Arms and the Man 32. Rich and Strange (aka East of Shanghai) 32. The Man Who Changed His Mind 36. Dr Syn 37. The Lady Vanishes 38. They Came by Night 39. The Ghost Train 41. We Dive at Dawn 43. Madonna of the Seven Moons 44. The Wicked Lady 45. Idol of Paris 48. The Cure for Love 49. Mr Drake's Duck 50. Jumping for Joy 55. Up in the World 56. The Big Money 56. Just My Luck 57. The Square Peg 58, etc.

Cox, Paul (1940–).
Dutch-born director and screenwriter, a former photographer who settled in Australia in 1965.
Illuminations 76. Inside Looking Out 77. Kostas 79. Lonely Hearts 82. Man of Flowers 84. My First Wife 84. Death and Destiny 85. Cactus 86. Vincent: The Life and Death of Vincent van Gogh 87. Island 89. The Golden Braid 90. A Woman's Tale 91. Exile (wd, e) 94. Erotic Tales (co-d) 94, etc.

Cox, Ronny (1938–).
American character actor with stage background.
The Happiness Cage 72. *Deliverance* 72. Bound for Glory 76. The Car 77. The Onion Field 79. Taps 81. The Beast Within 82. Robocop 87. Steele Justice 87. Loose Cannons 89. One Man Force 89. Captain America 90. Total Recall 90, etc.
TV series: Apple's Way 74. Spencer 84–85. Cop Rock 90.

Cox, Vivian (1915–).
British producer.
Father Brown 54. The Prisoner 55. Bachelor of Hearts 58, etc.

Cox, Wally (1924–1973).
American comic actor, usually seen as the bespectacled, weedy character he played in the TV series *Mr Peepers*.
■ State Fair 62. Spencer's Mountain 63. Fate Is the Hunter 64. The Bedford Incident 65. Morituri 65. The Yellow Rolls-Royce 65. A Guide for the Married Man 67. The One and Only Genuine Original Family Band 68. The Boatniks 70. The Cockeyed Cowboys of Calico County 70. Up Your Teddy Bear 70.
TV series: Mr Peepers 52–55. The Adventures of Hirman Holiday 56–57. Underdog (voice) 64–73.

Coyote, Peter (1942–) (Peter Cohon).
American leading actor with stage experience.
Tell Me a Riddle 80. Die Laughing 80. Southern Comfort 81. The Pursuit of D. B. Cooper 81. E.T. – the Extraterrestrial 82. Endangered Species 82. Out 82. Cross Creek 83. Slayground 84. The

Legend of Billie Jean 85. Jagged Edge 85. Outrageous Fortune 87. Season of Dreams (aka Stacking) 87. Baja Oklahoma 88. Heart of Midnight 88. The Man Inside 90. Keeper of the City 91. Crooked Hearts 91. Exposure 91. Blind Judgement 91. Living a Lie 91. Bitter Moon 92. Kika 93. That Eye, the Sky 94, etc.

Crabbe, Buster (1907–1983) (Clarence Linden Crabbe).
American Olympic athlete who became leading man of 'B' pictures.
  King of the Jungle 33. Tarzan the Fearless 33. Nevada 36. *Flash Gordon's Trip to Mars* 38. Buck Rogers 39. Queen of Broadway 43. Caged Fury 48. Gunfighters of Abilene 59. Arizona Raiders 65, many others.
  TV series: Captain Gallant 55–57.

Crabe, James (c. 1931–1989).
American cinematographer.
  Zigzag 70. Save the Tiger 72. W.W. and the Dixie Dancekings 72. Rocky 76. Players 79. The China Syndrome 79. How to Beat the High Cost of Living 80. The Baltimore Bullet 80. The Formula (AAN) 80, etc.

Crabtree, Arthur (1900–1975).
British director, former cameraman.
  Madonna of the Seven Moons 44. They Were Sisters 45. Dear Murderer 46. Caravan 46. The Calendar 48. Lili Marlene 50. Hindle Wakes 52. The Wedding of Lili Marlene 53. West of Suez 57. Morning Call 58. Horrors of the Black Museum 59, etc.

Craig, Alec (1878–1945).
Scottish character actor in Hollywood; often played misers, moneylenders and downtrodden roles.
  Mutiny on the Bounty 35. Mary of Scotland 36. Winterset 36. Vivacious Lady 38. Tom Brown's Schooldays 40. Cat People 42. Holy Matrimony 43. Lassie Come Home 43. Spider Woman 44. Kitty 46, many others.

Craig, Edward Gordon (1872–1966) (Henry Edward Wardell).
British stage designer, father of Edward Carrick (qv). Though not directly employed in films, his stage designs were influential to people like William Cameron Menzies and Anton Grot.

Craig, H. A. L. (1925–1978) (Harold).
British screenwriter.
  Anzio 68. Waterloo 70. Mohammed 77, etc.

Craig, James (1912–1985) (John Meador).
American leading man, usually the good-natured but tough outdoor type.
  Thunder Trail 37. The Buccaneer 38. The Man They Could Not Hang 39. Zanzibar 40. Kitty Foyle 40. *All that Money Can Buy* (the 'Faust' role, and his best) 41. Valley of the Sun 41. The Omaha Trail 42. The Human Comedy 43. Lost Angel 43. Kismet 44. Our Vines Have Tender Grapes 45. Boys Ranch 45. Little Mister Jim 46. Northwest Stampede 48. Side Street 50. Drums in the Deep South 51. Hurricane Smith 52. Fort Vengeance 53. While the City Sleeps 56. Four Fast Guns 59. The Hired Gun 67, many others.

¶ I was out there in Hollywood on vacation, and I saw a lot of people making movies. If they could do it, why couldn't I? – *J.C.*

Craig, Michael (1929–) (Michael Gregson).
British light leading man, a former crowd artist

groomed by the Rank Organization; later attempted more ambitious roles before settling in Australia.
  Malta Story 53. The Love Lottery 54. Yield to the Night 56. House of Secrets 56. High Tide at Noon 57. Campbell's Kingdom 58. The Silent Enemy 58. Nor the Moon by Night 58. Sea of Sand 58. Sapphire 59. Upstairs and Downstairs 59. *The Angry Silence* (& w) 59. Cone of Silence 60. Doctor in Love 60. Mysterious Island 61. *Payroll* 61. A Pair of Briefs 62. Life for Ruth 62. The Iron Maiden 62. Stolen Hours 63. Of a Thousand Delights (Vaghe Stella dell'Orsa) 65. Life at the Top 65. Modesty Blaise 66. Sandra (It.) 66. *Star!* 68. The Royal Hunt of the Sun 69. Twinky 69. Brotherly Love 70. A Town Called Bastard 71. Vault of Horror 73. The Emigrants (TV) 77. The Timeless Land (TV) 77. Turkey Shoot 82. Stanley 83, etc.

Craig, Stuart.
English production designer.
  Saturn 3 80. The Elephant Man (AAN) 80. Gandhi (AA) 82. Greystoke: The Legend of Tarzan, Lord of the Apes 84. Cal 84. The Mission (AAN) 86. Cry Freedom 87. Stars and Bars (co-pd) 88. Dangerous Liaisons (AA) 88. Chaplin 92. The Secret Garden 93. Shadowlands 93, etc.

Craig, Wendy (1934–).
British comedy actress, especially on TV in *Not in Front of the Children, And Mother Makes Three, Nanny,* etc.
  The Mind Benders 63. The Servant 63. The Nanny 65. Just Like a Woman 66. I'll Never Forget Whatshisname 67. Joseph Andrews 77, etc.
  TV series: Brighton Belles 93.

Craig, Yvonne (1941–).
American leading lady, now retired.
  The Young Land 60. By Love Possessed 61. Seven Women from Hell 62. Kissin' Cousins 64. One Spy Too Many 66. In Like Flint 67, etc.
  TV series: Batman (as Batgirl) 67–68.

Craigie, Jill (1914–).
British documentary director.
  The Way We Live 46. Blue Scar 48. The Million Pound Note (w only) 51. Windom's Way (w only) 57, etc.

Crain, Jeanne (1925–).
American leading lady of the 40s; usually the personification of sweetness and light.
  ■ The Gang's All Here 43. Home in Indiana 44. In the Meantime Darling 44. Winged Victory 44. *State Fair* 45. Leave Her to Heaven 45. Centennial Summer 46. *Margie* 46. Apartment for Peggy 48. You Were Meant for Me 48. A Letter to Three Wives 49. The Fan 49. *Pinky* (AAN) 49. Cheaper by the Dozen 50. Take Care of My Little Girl 51. People Will Talk 51. The Model and the Marriage Broker 52. Belles on Their Toes 52. Full House 52. Dangerous Crossing 53. City of Bad Men 53. Vicki 53. Duel in the Jungle (GB) 54. Man Without a Star 55. Gentlemen Marry Brunettes 55. The Second Greatest Sex 55. The Fastest Gun Alive 56. The Tattered Dress 57. The Joker is Wild 58. Guns of the Timberland 60. Twenty Plus Two 61. Queen of the Nile (It.) 61. With Fire and Sword (It.) 61. Pontius Pilate (It.) 61. Madison Avenue 62. 52 Miles to Terror 64. The Night God Screamed 71. Skyjacked 72.

Cramer, Rychard (1889–1960).
Malevolent-looking American character actor, a memorable foil for Laurel and Hardy in *Scram, Saps at Sea,* etc. He later played heavies in 'B' westerns.

Crane, Bob (1929–1978).
American light comic actor, popular in TV series *Hogan's Heroes.* He was murdered.
  ■ Return to Peyton Place 61. Mantrap 61. The Wicked Dreams of Paula Schultz 68. Superdad 74. Gus 76.

Crane, Richard (1919–1969).
American juvenile lead of the 40s.
  Susan and God 40. This Time for Keeps 42. Happy Land 43. None Shall Escape 44. Captain Eddie 45. Behind Green Lights 46. Triple Threat 48. Dynamite 49. The Last Outpost 51. The Neanderthal Man 53. The Eternal Sea 55. The Deep Six 58. The Alligator People 59. House of the Damned 63. Surf Party 64, etc.
  TV series: Surfside Six 61–62.

crane shot.
A high-angle shot in which the camera travels up, down or laterally while mounted on a travelling crane.

Crane, Stephen (1871–1900).
American novelist who crystallized aspects of the Civil War in *The Red Badge of Courage.*

Cranham, Kenneth (1944–).
British leading actor, mainly on stage and television.
  Oliver! 68. All the Way Up 70. Brother Sun, Sister Moon 73. Joseph Andrews 77. Reilly, Ace of Spies (TV) 83. Hellbound: Hellraiser II 88. Oranges Are Not the Only Fruit (TV) 90. Prospero's Books 91. Chimera (TV) 93, etc.
  TV series: Shine on Harvey Moon 85–87.

Cravat, Nick (1911–1994).
Small, agile American actor, once Burt Lancaster's circus partner.
  The Flame and the Arrow 51. The Crimson Pirate 52. King Richard and the Crusaders 54. Three-Ring Circus 55. Kiss Me Deadly 55. Davy Crockett 56. Run Silent, Run Deep 59. The Scalphunters 68. Ulzana's Raid 72. The Island of Dr Moreau 77, etc.

Craven, Frank (1875–1945).
American stage character actor who spent his later years in Hollywood; typically cast as kindly pipe-smoking philosopher.
  ■ We Americans 28. The Very Idea 29. State Fair 33. That's Gratitude 34. He Was Her Man 34. Let's Talk It Over 34. City Limits 34. Funny Thing Called Love 34. *Barbary Coast* 35. Car 99 35. Vagabond Lady 35. Small Town Girl 36. The Harvester 36. Penrod and Sam 37. Blossoms on Broadway 37. You're Only Young Once 37. Penrod and his Twin Brother 38. Our Neighbours the Carters 39. Miracles for Sale 39. Dreaming Out Loud 40. City for Conquest 40. *Our Town* (his stage role) 40. The Lady from Cheyenne 41. The Richest Man in Town 41. In This Our Life 41. *Thru Different Eyes* 42. Pittsburgh 42. Girl Trouble 42. Son of Dracula 43. Harrigan's Kid 43. Jack London 43. The Human Comedy 43. Keeper of the Flame 43. Destiny 44. My Best Gal 44. They Shall Have Faith 44. The Right to Live 45. Colonel Effingham's Raid 45.

Craven, Gemma (1950–).
Irish-born leading lady of the 70s.
  ■ The Slipper and the Rose 76. Why Not Stay for Breakfast 79. Wagner 83. Double X 92. The Mystery of Edwin Drood 93.
  TV series: Pennies from Heaven 77.

Craven, Wes (1949–).

American director of horror movies, a former academic.

Summer of Fear 78. The Hills Have Eyes 79. Deadly Blessing 81. A Nightmare on Elm Street 84. Deadly Friend 86. Flowers in the Attic (w) 87. A Nightmare on Elm Street III: Dream Warriors (p, story) 87. The Serpent and the Rainbow (d) 88. Shocker (wd, a) 89. The People under the Stairs (wd) 91. Wes Craven's New Nightmare (wd, a) 94, etc.

Crawford, Andrew (1917–).

Scottish character actor.

The Brothers 46. Dear Murderer 47. London Belongs to Me 48. Morning Departure 50. Shadow of the Cat 61, etc.

Crawford, Anne (1920–1956) (Imelda Crawford).

British leading lady with gentle, humorous personality.

They Flew Alone (debut) 42. The Peterville Diamond 42. The Dark Tower 42. The Hundred-Pound Window 43. Millions Like Us 43. Two Thousand Women 44. They Were Sisters 45. Caravan 46. Bedelia 46. Master of Bankdam 47. Daughter of Darkness 48. The Blind Goddess 48. It's Hard To Be Good 49. Tony Draws a Horse 49. Thunder on the Hill (US) 50. Street Corner 52. Knights of the Round Table 53. Mad about Men 55, etc.

Crawford, Broderick (1911–1986).

Beefy American character actor, son of Helen Broderick; began by playing comic stooges and gangsters, with acting performances coming later; after a long spell in TV his popularity waned.

Woman Chases Man 37. The Real Glory 39. Eternally Yours 39. Beau Geste 39. Slightly Honorable 40. When the Daltons Rode 40. The Black Cat 41. Butch Minds the Baby 42. Broadway 42. Sin Town 42. *The Runaround* 46. Slave Girl 47. The Flame 47. The Time of Your Life 48. Anna Lucasta 49. *All the King's Men* (AA) 50. *Born Yesterday* 51. The Mob 51. Lone Star 52. Scandal Sheet 52. Last of the Comanches 52. Stop You're Killing Me 52. Night People 54. Human Desire 54. Down Three Dark Streets 54. New York Confidential 55. Il Bidone (The Swindlers) 55. Not as a Stranger 55. The Fastest Gun Alive 56. The Decks Ran Red 58. Up from the Beach 65. The Oscar 66. The Texican 66. Red Tomahawk 66. The Vulture 67. Embassy 72. Terror in the Wax Museum 73. Smashing the Crime Syndicate 73. Mayday at 40,000 Feet (TV) 77. *The Private Files of J. Edgar Hoover* 78. A Little Romance 79. There Goes the Bride 80. Liar's Moon 82, etc.

TV series: *Highway Patrol* 55–58. King of Diamonds 61. The Interns 70.

¶ My trademarks are a hoarse, grating voice and the face of a retired pugilist: small narrowed eyes set in puffy features which look as though they might, years ago, have lost on points. – *B.C.*

Crawford, Howard Marion:

see *Marion Crawford, Howard.*

Crawford, Joan (1904–1977) (Lucille le Sueur; known for a time as Billie Cassin).

American leading lady; one of Hollywood's most durable stars, first as a flapper of the jazz age and later as the personification of the career girl and the repressed older woman. Few of her films have been momentous, but she has always been 'box office', especially with women fans, who liked to watch her suffering in mink.

Autobiography: 1962, *A Portrait of Joan.*

In 1978 her adopted daughter Christine Crawford published *Mommie Dearest*, which painted her as a monster and caused a sensation. A film version of the book was released in 1981, with Faye Dunaway playing J.C.

■ Pretty Ladies 25. The Only Thing 25. Old Clothes 25. Sally, Irene and Mary 25. The Boob 25. Paris 25. Tramp Tramp Tramp 26. The Taxi Dancer 27. Winners of the Wilderness 27. The Understanding Heart 27. The Unknown 27. Twelve Miles Out 27. Spring Fever 27. West Point 28. Rose Marie 28. Across to Singapore 28. The Law of the Range 28. Four Walls 28. *Our Dancing Daughters* 28. Dream of Love 28. The Duke Steps Out 29. Our Modern Maidens 29. Hollywood Revue 29. Untamed 29. Montana Moon 30. Our Blushing Brides 30. Paid 30. Dance Fools Dance 31. Laughing Sinners 31. This Modern Age 31. Possessed 31. Letty Lynton 32. *Grand Hotel* 32. Rain 32. Today We Live 33. *Dancing Lady* 33. Sadie McKee 34. Chained 34. Forsaking All Others 34. No More Ladies 35. I Live My Life 35. *The Gorgeous Hussy* 36. Love on the Run 36. The Last of Mrs Cheyney 37. The Bride Wore Red 37. Mannequin 38. The Shining Hour 38. Ice Follies 39. *The Women* 39. Strange Cargo 40. Susan and God 40. *A Woman's Face* 41. When Ladies Meet 41. They All Kissed the Bride 42. Reunion in France 42. Above Suspicion 43. Hollywood Canteen 44. *Mildred Pierce* (AA) 45. *Humoresque* 46. *Possessed* (AAN) 47. Daisy Kenyon 47. Flamingo Road 49. The Damned Don't Cry 50. Harriet Craig 50. Goodbye My Fancy 51. This Woman is Dangerous 52. *Sudden Fear* (AAN) 52. Torch Song 53. Johnny Guitar 54. The Female on the Beach 55. Queen Bee 55. Autumn Leaves 56. The Story of Esther Costello (GB) 57. The Best of Everything 59. *Whatever Happened to Baby Jane?* 62. The Caretakers 63. Strait Jacket 64. Della (TV) 64. I Saw What You Did 65. The Karate Killers (TV) 67. Berserk (GB) 67. Night Gallery (TV pilot) 69. Trog 70.

✪ For sheer determination. *Mildred Pierce.*

¶ Everybody imitated my fuller mouth, my darker eyebrows. But I wouldn't copy anybody. If I can't be me, I don't want to be anybody. I was born that way. – *J.C.*

The most important thing a woman can have, next to her talent of course, is her hairdresser. – *J.C.*

Inactivity is one of the great indignities of life. The need to work is always there, bugging me. – *J.C.*

I never go out unless I look like Joan Crawford the movie star. If you want to see the girl next door, go next door. – *J.C.*

Whenever she came to the realisation that the men she loved simply didn't come back, she compensated by adopting children. – *Hedda Hopper*

The best time I ever had with her was when I pushed her downstairs in *Baby Jane*. – *Bette Davis*

With her emergence as a film star she dieted off her excess weight, lowered her voice range by several tones, was taught how to dress by Adrian and how to enter a room by Douglas Fairbanks Jnr. And she never let up in her quest for self-improvement. – *Radie Harris*

She was a mean, tipsy, powerful, rotten-egg lady. – *Mercedes McCambridge*

She's like that old joke about Philadelphia. First prize four years with Joan. Second, eight. – *Franchot Tone*

I tried to be a good listener. I decided that was what she wanted all along – not so much a friend as an audience. – *June Allyson*

Famous line (*The Female on the Beach*): 'I wouldn't

have you if you were hung with diamonds – upside down!'

Crawford, John (1926–).

Forgettable American leading man.

Cyrano de Bergerac 50. Actors and Sin 52. Slaves of Babylon 53. Battle of Royne River 54. Orders to Kill 58. John Paul Jones 59. Floods of Fear 59. Hell is a City 60. The 300 Spartans 62. Captain Sinbad 63. The Americanization of Emily 64, etc.

TV series: The Waltons 72–81.

Crawford, Johnny (1946–).

American actor, mainly on television as a juvenile. He began as a child, was a Mickey Mouse Club Mousketeer in the mid-50s, and in the 60s made a few hit records during a spell of television fame, playing Chuck Connors' son in the series *The Rifleman* 58–63. From the mid-60s he worked in rodeos and now concentrates on his singing, leading his own big band and playing music from the 30s.

Courage of Black Beauty 57. Indian Paint 64. Village of the Giants 65. El Dorado 67. Outlaw Blues 77. The Great Texas Dynamite Chase 77. Kenny Rogers as The Gambler Part II: The Adventure Continues (TV) 83, etc.

Crawford, Kathryn (1908–1980) (Kathryn Crawford Moran).

American leading actress and singer, from the Broadway stage, who quit films in the early 30s. She was married to Wesley Ruggles.

The Kid's Clever 29. King of the Rodeo 29. The Climax 30. Red Hot Rhythm 30. Hide Out 30. Safety in Numbers 30. King of Jazz 30. Flying High 31. Grand Hotel 32. New Morals for Old 32, etc.

Crawford, Michael (1942–) (Michael Dumble-Smith).

Lively British comedy lead, former child actor, now best known for stage musicals.

Soap Box Derby 50. Blow Your Own Trumpet 54. Two Living One Dead 62. The War Lover 63. Two Left Feet 63. *The Knack* 65. A Funny Thing Happened on the Way to the Forum 66. *The Jokers* 66. How I Won the War 67. *Hello Dolly* 69. The Games 69. Hello Goodbye 70. Alice's Adventures in Wonderland 72. Condorman 81. Once Upon a Forest 93, etc.

TV series: Sir Francis Drake 62. *Some Mothers Do 'Ave 'Em* 74–79. Chalk and Cheese 79.

crazy comedy

has two distinct meanings in the cinema. On one hand it encompasses the Marx Brothers, *Hellzapoppin* and custard pies; for this see *Slapstick*. On the other it means the new kind of comedy which came in during the 30s, with seemingly adult people behaving in what society at the time thought was a completely irresponsible way. The Capra comedies, for instance, are vaguely 'agin' the government', upholding Mr Deeds' right to give away all his money and play the tuba, the Vanderhofs' right not to work, and Mr Smith's right to be utterly honest. This endearing eccentricity permeated many of the funniest and most modern comedies of the period. William Powell and Myrna Loy in *The Thin Man* were a married couple who upheld none of the domestic virtues. In *Libeled Lady* four top stars behaved like low comedians. In *My Man Godfrey* a rich man pretended to be a tramp and so reformed a party of the idle rich who found him during a 'scavenger hunt'. *Theodora Goes Wild*, *I Met Him in Paris* and *Easy Living* had what we would now call 'kooky' heroines. In *True Confession* Carole Lombard confessed to a murder she hadn't done, and was told by John Barrymore that she would 'fry'; in *Nothing Sacred* she pretended to be dying of an obscure disease and was socked on the jaw by Fredric March. Hal Roach introduced comedy ghosts, played by two of Hollywood's most sophisticated stars, in *Topper*, and followed it up with two sequels as well as three individual and endearingly lunatic comedies called *The Housekeeper's Daughter* (a battle of fireworks), *Turnabout* (a husband and wife exchange bodies) and *Road Show* (an asylum escapee runs a travelling circus). *The Awful Truth* had no respect for marriage; *You Can't Take It With You* had no respect for law, business, or the American way of life. A film called *Bringing Up Baby* turned out to be about a leopard and a brontosaurus bone; *Boy Meets Girl* was a farcical send-up of Hollywood; and *A Slight Case of Murder* had more corpses than characters. *The Women* had its all-female cast fighting like tiger-cats. *Road to Singapore* began as a romantic comedy but degenerated into snippets from Joe Miller's gag-book; and any Preston Sturges film was likely to have pauses while the smart and witty hero and heroine fell into a pool. In *Here Comes Mr Jordan* the hero was dead after five minutes or so and spent the rest of the film trying to get his body back.

The genre was by this time well established, and although America's entry into the war modified it somewhat it has remained fashionable and popular ever since. A 1966 film like *Morgan* may seem rather startling, but in fact it goes little further in its genial anarchy than *You Can't Take It With You*; only the method of expression is different. What modern crazy comedies lack is the clear pattern which produced so many little masterpieces within a few years: even direct imitations like *What's Up Doc?* fail to produce the same results.

The Crazy Gang.
Three pairs of British music hall comedians made up this famous group which was enormously popular on stage from 1935 till 1962. Bud Flanagan (qv) and Chesney Allen (qv); Jimmy Nervo (James Holloway) (1890–1975) and Teddy Knox (1896–1974) and Charlie Naughton (1887–1976) and Jimmy Gold (1886–1967).
■ OK for Sound 37. Alf 's Button Afloat 38. The Frozen Limits 39. Gasbags 40. Life is a Circus 54.

Creasey, John (1908–1973).
British thriller writer, author under various pseudonyms of more than six hundred books. Creator of the Toff, the Baron and Gideon of Scotland Yard.

credits.
Titles at beginning or end of film (nowadays very often five minutes *after* the beginning) listing the names of the creative talents concerned.

creeping title.
One which moves up (or sometimes across) the screen at reading pace. Also known as *roller title.*

Cregar, Laird (1916–1944).
Heavyweight American character actor who had a tragically brief but impressive career in a rich variety of roles.
■ Granny Get Your Gun 40. Oh Johnny How You Can Love 40. Hudson's Bay 40. Blood and Sand 41. *Charley's Aunt* 41. *I Wake Up Screaming* 41. Joan of Paris 42. Rings on Her Fingers 42. This Gun for Hire 42. *Ten Gentlemen from West Point* 42. *The Black Swan* 42. Hello Frisco Hello 43. *Heaven Can Wait* 43. Holy Matrimony 43. *The Lodger* 44. Hangover Square 44.

☯ For providing such a memorable gallery of middle-aged characters while still in his early 20s. *The Black Swan.*

Crehan, Joseph (1884–1966) (Charles Wilson).
American character actor, often as sheriff or cop.
Stolen Heaven 31. Before Midnight 33. Identity Parade 34. Boulder Dam 36. Happy Landing 38. Stanley and Livingstone 39. The Roaring Twenties 39. Brother Orchid 40. Texas 42. Phantom Lady 44. Deadline at Dawn 46. The Foxes of Harrow 48. Red Desert 54, many others.

Creme, Lol (1947–).
British director and musician. He was guitarist and vocalist with the 70s rock band 10CC, and also produces music videos.
The Lunatic 92.

Cremer, Bruno (1929–).
French leading actor.
The 317th Platoon (La 317ème Section) 65. Is Paris Burning? (Paris Brûle-t-il?) 68. Sorcerer (US) 77. A Simple Story (Histoire Simple) 79. Josepha 82. Hail Mary (Je Vous Salue Marie) 83. Tenue de Soirée (aka Menage) 86. Taxi de Nuit (Fr.) 94, etc.

Crenna, Richard (1926–).
American leading man, formerly boy actor on radio and TV.
Red Skies of Montana 52. It Grows on Trees 52. Over Exposed 56. John Goldfarb Please Come Home 65. Made in Paris 65. The Sand Pebbles 66. Wait until Dark 67. Star! 68. Marooned 69. The Deserter 70. Thief (TV) 71. Doctors' Wives 71. Red Sky at Morning 71. Catlow 72. The Man Called Noon 73. Double Indemnity (TV) 73. Nightmare (TV) 75. Breakheart Pass 76. Dirty Money (Fr.) 77. Body Heat 81. *Table for Five* 83. Rambo: First Blood 2 86. The Flamingo Kid 86. Rambo III 88. Leviathan 89. And the Sea Will Tell (TV) 91. A Place to Be Loved (TV) 93. Hot Shots! Part Deux 93, etc.
TV series: Our Miss Brooks 52–56. The Real McCoys 57–62. Slattery's People 64–65. All's Fair 76. It Takes Two 83. Gabriel's Fire 91–92.

Crews, Laura Hope (1880–1942).
American stage actress who played character parts in many films, usually as fluttery matron.
Charming Sinners 29. New Morals for Old 32. Escapade 35. *Camille* 36. Thanks for the Memory 38. *Gone with the Wind* (as Aunt Pittypat) 39. The Bluebird 40. The Flame of New Orleans 41. One Foot in Heaven 41, many others.

Cribbins, Bernard (1928–).
British comedy character actor and recording star. Played light support roles in several films.
Two Way Stretch 60. The Girl on the Boat 62. The Wrong Arm of the Law 62. Carry On Jack 63. Crooks in Cloisters 64. She 65. The Sandwich Man 66. Daleks Invasion Earth 2150 A.D. 66. The Railway Children 70. Frenzy 72. The Water Babies 78. Dangerous Davies (TV) 81. Carry On Columbus 92, etc.

Crichton, Charles (1910–).
British director, former editor. Latterly directing TV episodes.
For Those in Peril 44. Dead of Night (part) 45. Painted Boats 45. *Hue and Cry* 46. Against the Wind 47. Another Shore 48. Train of Events 49. Dance Hall 50. *The Lavender Hill Mob* 51. Hunted 52. *The Titfield Thunderbolt* 53. The Love Lottery 54. The Divided Heart 54. The Man in the Sky 56. Law and Disorder 57. Floods of Fear (& w) 58. The Battle of the Sexes 59. The Boy Who Stole a Million 60. The Third Secret 63. He Who Rides a

Tiger 65. A Fish Called Wanda (& story) (AAN) 88, etc.
TV series: Dick Turpin 78.

Crichton, Michael (1942–).
American novelist and screenwriter. He studied at Harvard and lectured in anthropology at Cambridge before qualifying as a doctor at the Harvard Medical School and then turning to writing.
The Andromeda Strain (oa) 71. The Carey Treatment (oa) 72. The Terminal Man (oa) 72. *Pursuit* (oa, d) (TV) 72. *Westworld* (wd) 73. Coma (d) 77. The Great Train Robbery (wd) 78. Looker (wd) 80. Runaway 84. Physical Evidence 88. Jurassic Park (co-w from his novel) 93. Rising Sun (co-w from his novel) 93. Disclosure (oa) 94, etc.

¶ One of the definitions of intelligence is that you don't make the same mistake twice. – M.C.

criminals
– real-life ones – whose careers have been featured in films include Burke and Hare (*The Flesh and the Fiends, Burke and Hare*), Cagliostro (*Black Magic*), Al Capone (*Little Caesar, The Scarface Mob, Al Capone*), Caryl Chessman (*Cell 2455 Death Row*), Crippen (*Dr Crippen*), John Wilkes Booth (*Prince of Players*), Jack the Ripper (*The Lodger, A Study in Terror, Jack the Ripper*, many others), Landru (*Landru, Bluebeard, Monsieur Verdoux, Bluebeard's Ten Honeymoons*), Leopold and Loeb (*Rope and Compulsion*), Christie (*10 Rillington Place*), Charles Peace (*The Case of Charles Peace*), Dick Turpin (qv), Jesse James (qv), Vidocq (*A Scandal in Paris*), Robert Stroud (*Birdman of Alcatraz*), Barbara Graham (*I Want to Live*), Rasputin (qv), Eddie Chapman (*Triple Cross*), the Kray brothers (*The Krays*), and the various American public enemies of the 30s: *Bonnie and Clyde, Dillinger, Baby Face Nelson, Bloody Mama* (Barker), *A Bullet for Pretty Boy* (Floyd), etc. The clinical 60s also brought accounts of the motiveless murderers of *In Cold Blood* and of *The Boston Strangler*. Criminal movements have been very well explored in fictional films, especially the Mafia, the Thugs, Murder Inc. and the racketeers and bootleggers of the 20s.

Crisp, Donald (1880–1974).
Distinguished British screen actor, in Hollywood from 1906; worked with D. W. Griffith and directed some silents, but from 1930 settled on acting and played mainly stern character roles.
Home Sweet Home 14. The Birth of a Nation 15. Broken Blossoms 19. Why Smith Left Home (d) 19. The Bonnie Brier Bush (d) 21. The Mark of Zorro (d) 22. Ponjola (d) 23. *Don Q Son of Zorro* (ad) 25. The Black Pirate 26. Man Bait (d) 27. Stand and Deliver (d) 28. The Return of Sherlock Holmes 29. Runaway Bride (d) 30. Svengali 31. Red Dust 32. Crime Doctor 34. The Little Minister 34. Mutiny on the Bounty 35. Mary of Scotland 36. Beloved Enemy 36. Parnell 37. Jezebel 38. The Sisters 38. *The Dawn Patrol* 38. Wuthering Heights 39. The Old Maid 39. *Brother Orchid* 40. The Sea Hawk 40. Dr Jekyll and Mr Hyde 41. *How Green Was My Valley* (AA) 41. The Gay Sisters 42. Lassie Come Home 43. *The Uninvited* 44. National Velvet 44. Valley of Decision 45. Ramrod 47. Whispering Smith 49. Bright Leaf 50. Prince Valiant 54. The Man from Laramie 55. Saddle the Wind 58. The Last Hurrah 58. Pollyanna 60. Greyfriars Bobby 61. Spencer's Mountain 63, many others.

Crisp, Quentin (1909–) (Denis Pratt).
English eccentric and wit, artist's model, writer, film critic and occasional actor. He is the author of

a best-selling autobiography, *The Naked Civil Servant*, which detailed his homosexuality and was turned into a successful TV drama in 1975. It led to his performing one-man shows in Britain and America. He now lives in New York.

Book: 1989, *How to Go to the Movies: A Guide for the Perplexed*.

■ Hamlet (as Polonius) 77. An Evening with Quentin Crisp (TV) 83. The Bride 85. Orlando (as Queen Elizabeth I) 93. Natural Born Crazies 94.

¶ I took a friend to see *King Kong* (the first time around). During a dramatic episode in which a certain Miss Wray lay gibbering across Mr Kong's wrist, my friend, in a voice shrill with irritation, cried out, 'I can't think what he sees in her.' – Q.C.

What keeps a woman young and beautiful is not repeated surgery but perpetual praise. – Q.C.

If we go to the movies often enough and in a sufficiently reverent spirit, they will become more absorbing than the outer world, and the problems of reality will cease to burden us. – Q.C.

If Quentin Crisp had never existed, it is unlikely that anyone would have had the nerve to invent him. – *The Times*

Cristal, Linda (1934–) (Victoria Maya). Argentinian leading lady, in Hollywood from 1956.

Comanche 56. The Fiend Who Walked the West 58. The Perfect Furlough 58. Cry Tough 59. The Alamo 60. Panic in the City 68. Mr Majestyk 74, etc.

TV series: The High Chaparral 67–71.

Cristaldi, Franco (1924–1992). Italian producer of good reputation. He was formerly married to actress Claudia Cardinale.

La Pattuglia Sperduta 53. La Sfida 59. L'Assassino 60. Salvatori Giuliano 61. Divorce Italian Style 61. The Red Tent 69. In the Name of the Father (In Nome del Padre) 71. Lady Caroline Lamb 72. Amarcord (AA) 73. Christ Stopped at Eboli (Cristo Si è Fermato a Eboli) 78. Ratataplan 79. And the Ship Sails On (E la Nave Va) 83. The Name of the Rose 86. Cinema Paradiso (AA) 88. Vanille Fraise 89. C'era un Castello con 40 Cani 90, etc.

Cristiani, Gabriella (1949–). Italian film editor.

La Luna 79. The Tragedy of a Ridiculous Man 82. The Last Emperor (AA) 87. High Season 88. Francesco 89. The Sheltering Sky 90, etc.

Criswell (1907–1982) (Charles Criswell King). Psychic of newspapers and television, best remembered for his portentous narration to Ed Wood's *Plan 9 from Outer Space* 58, intoning, 'My friends, can your hearts stand the shocking facts about grave robbers from outer space?'

Night of the Ghouls 59. Orgy of the Dead 65, etc.

critics
¶ Very little film criticism is quotable: at its best it is an expression of personality rather than wit. The reviews one remembers tend to be the scathing ones, especially those dismissive one-liners which are really unforgivable but linger over the arch of years:

No Leave, No Love. No comment.

I Am a Camera. Me no Leica.

Lost in a Harem. But with Abbott and Costello.

Aimez-vous Brahms? Brahms, oui.

Ben Hur. Loved Ben, hated Hur.

Samson and Delilah. A movie for de Millions.

Bill and Coo. By conservative estimate, one of the God-damnedest things ever seen.

The authors of these pearls are now, by me, forgotten, with the exception of the last, which came from the pen of James Agee, a lamented American writer whose economical, literate reviews delighted all film enthusiasts in the 40s and established a few Hollywood reputations. His collected reviews should all be read with affection; here we can spare room for five of his more waspish put-downs:

Random Harvest. I would like to recommend this film to those who can stay interested in Ronald Colman's amnesia for two hours and who could with pleasure eat a bowl of Yardley's shaving soap for breakfast.

During the making of *Pin Up Girl* Betty Grable was in an early stage of pregnancy – and everyone else was evidently in a late stage of paresis.

Tycoon. Several tons of dynamite are set off in this picture – none of it under the right people.

You Were Meant For Me. That's what you think.

Star Spangled Rhythm. A variety show including everyone at Paramount who was not overseas, in hiding or out to lunch.

A few more moments of invective. First, *Variety* on Hedy Lamarr's independent production *The Strange Woman*:

Hedy bit off more than she could chew, so the chewing was done by the rest of the cast, and what was chewed was the scenery.

And Pamela Kellino on *The Egyptian*:

One of those great big rotten pictures Hollywood keeps on turning out.

And Stanley Kauffmann on *Isadora*:

This long but tiny film . . .

And the *New Statesman* (Frank Hauser) on *Another Man's Poison*:

Like reading Ethel M. Dell by flashes of lightning.

And the *Saturday Evening Post* on *Macabre*:

It plods along from its opening scene in a funeral parlor to its dénouement in a graveyard, unimpeded by the faintest intrusion of good taste, literacy, or sense.

And Don Herold on *The Bride Walks Out*:

You've seen this a million times on the screen, but they keep on making it, and folks keep asking me why I am so dyspeptic regarding the cinema. Because I have judgment, is the answer.

And John Simon on *Camelot*:

This film is the Platonic idea of boredom, roughly comparable to reading a three-volume novel in a language of which one knows only the alphabet.

And David Lardner on *Panama Hattie*:

This film needs a certain something. Possibly burial.

And Judith Crist on *Five Card Stud*:

So mediocre that you can't get mad at it.

And Charles Champlin on *The Missouri Breaks*:

A pair of million dollar babies in a five and ten cent flick.

Now for some self-criticism. Joseph L. Mankiewicz on his own movie *Cleopatra*:

This picture was conceived in a state of emergency, shot in confusion, and wound up in blind panic.

He also called it:

The toughest three pictures I ever made.

Ethel Barrymore, when asked her opinion of *Rasputin and the Empress*, in which she co-starred with her brothers Lionel and John, replied:

I thought I was pretty good, but what those two boys were up to I'll never know.

Erich Von Stroheim, reminiscing on his own much-mutilated picture *Greed*:

When ten years later I saw the film myself, it was like seeing a corpse in a graveyard.

Otto Preminger on *Saint Joan*:

My most distinguished flop. I've had much less distinguished ones.

And Victor Fleming, director of *Gone with the Wind*, refusing David O. Selznick's offer of a percentage of the profits instead of salary:

Don't be a damn fool, David. This picture is going to be one of the biggest white elephants of all time.

Philip French on *Carry on Emmanuelle*:

Put together with an almost palpable contempt for its audience, this relentless sequence of badly written, badly timed dirty jokes is surely one of the most morally and aesthetically offensive pictures to emerge from a British studio.

Similarly misguided was Adolph Zukor when he first read the script of *Broken Blossoms*:

You bring me a picture like this and want money for it? You may as well put your hand in my pocket and steal it. It isn't commercial. Everyone in it dies.

I can recall only three memorable items of praise. Cecilia Ager on *Citizen Kane*:

It's as though you had never seen a movie before.

Terry Ramsaye on *Intolerance*:

The only film fugue.

And Woodrow Wilson on *The Birth of a Nation*:

Like writing history with lightning. And it's all true.

My own favourite critiques also include Sarah Bernhardt's enthusiastic remark when she saw her 1912 version of *Queen Elizabeth*:

Mr Zukor, you have put the best of me in pickle for all time.

And the comment of macabre New Yorker cartoonist Charles Addams, when asked his opinion after the première of *Cleopatra*:

I only came to see the asp.

And the anonymous reviewer of a Jack Benny violin concert:

Jack Benny played Mendelssohn last night. Mendelssohn lost.

Come to that, another anonymous gentleman had a pretty good definition of critics:

Yawning as a profession.

Channing Pollock defined a critic as:

A legless man who teaches running.

To Whitney Balkett he was:

A bundle of biases held together by a sense of taste.

And to Ken Tynan:

A man who knows the way but can't drive a car.

Mel Brooks was scathing:

Critics can't even make music by rubbing their back legs together.

R. W. Emerson was dismissive:

Taking to pieces is the trade of those who cannot construct.

Perhaps the wisest reflection on the critics was made by Rouben Mamoulian:

The most important critic is Time.

Crocker, Barry.
Australian leading man.

Squeeze a Flower 69. The Adventures of Barry Mackenzie 72. Barry Mackenzie Holds His Own 74.

Crockett, Davy (1786–1836).
American trapper and Indian scout who became a legendary hero and a politician before dying at the Alamo (qv). He has been portrayed on film by George Montgomery (*Indian Scout*), Fess Parker (*Davy Crockett, Davy Crockett and the River Pirates*), Arthur Hunnicutt (*The Last Command*) and John Wayne (*The Alamo*), among others.

Crombie, Donald (1942–).
Australian director.
Caddie 76. The Irishman 78. Cathy's Child 79. The Killing of Angel Street 81. Kitty and the Bagman 82. Robbery under Arms (co-d) (TV) 85. Playing Beatie Bow 86. The Heroes (TV) 88. The Saint in Australia (TV) 89. The River Kings (TV) 91. Rough Diamonds 94, etc.

Crompton, Richmal (1890–1969).
British writer for children, author of the 'William' books which have been filmed from time to time.

Cromwell, John (1888–1979).
Distinguished American director with stage background.
■ The Dummy (acted only) 29. The Mighty 29. The Dance of Life 29. Close Harmony 29. Street of Chance 30. Tom Sawyer 30. The Texan 30. For the Defense 30. Scandal Street 31. Rich Man's Folly 31. Vice Squad 31. Unfaithful 31. The World and the Flesh 31. Sweepings 33. The Silver Cord 33. Double Harness 33. Ann Vickers 33. Spitfire 34. This Man is Mine 34. *Of Human Bondage* 34. The Fountain 34. Jalna 35. Village Tale 35. I Dream Too Much 35. Little Lord Fauntleroy 36. To Mary With Love 36. Banjo on My Knee 36. *The Prisoner of Zenda* 37. *Algiers* 38. Made for Each Other 38. In Name Only 39. Abe Lincoln in Illinois 39. Victory 40. So Ends Our Night 41. Son of Fury 42. *Since You Went Away* 44. The Enchanted Cottage 45. *Anna and the King of Siam* 46. Dead Reckoning 47. Night Song 47. Caged 50. The Company She Keeps 51. The Racket 51. Top Secret Affair (a only) 57. The Goddess 58. The Scavengers 60. A Matter of Morals 61. *Three Women* (a only) 77. *A Wedding* (a only) 78.

Cromwell, Oliver (1599–1658).
The Puritan Protector of England during the Civil War has been shown on screen as a repressed rather than a heroic figure, as follows:

1937	*The Vicar of Bray*	George Merritt
1949	*Cardboard Cavalier*	Edmund Willard
1958	*The Moonraker*	John Le Mesurier
1968	*Witchfinder General*	Patrick Wymark
1970	*Cromwell*	Richard Harris

Cromwell, Richard (1910–1960) (Roy Radebaugh).
American leading man, gentle hero of early sound films. He was married to Angela Lansbury.
■ Tol'able David 30. Fifty Fathoms Deep 31. Shanghaied Love 31. Maker of Men 31. That's My Boy 32. Emma 32. The Strange Love of Molly Louvain 32. Age of Consent 32. Tom Brown of Culver 32. This Day and Age 33. Hoopla 33. Above the Clouds 34. Carolina 34. Among the Missing 34. Name the Woman 34. When Strangers Meet 34. Most Precious Thing in Life 34. *Lives of a Bengal Lancer* 35. McFadden's Flats 35. Life Begins at Forty 35. Men of the Hour 35. Unknown Woman 35. Annapolis Farewell 35. Poppy 36. Our Fighting Navy (GB) 37. The Road Back 37. The Wrong Road 37. Jezebel 38. Come On Leathernecks 38. Storm Over Bengal 38. Young Mr Lincoln 39. Enemy Agent 40. The Villain Still Pursued Her 40. Village Barn Dance 40. Parachute Battalion 41. Riot Squad 42. Baby Face Morgan 42. Bungalow 13 48.

Cronenberg, David (1943–).
Canadian director of outlandish and generally over-the-top horror films.
Autobiography: 1992, *Cronenberg on Cronenberg* (edited by Chris Radley).
Biography: 1994, *David Cronenberg: A Delicate Balance* by Peter Morris.

Crimes of the Future 70. Squirm 74. Shivers 75. Rabid 77. The Brood 80. Scanners 81. Videodrome 83. The Dead Zone 83. The Fly 86. Dead Ringers 88. Nightbreed (a only) 90. Naked Lunch 91. M. Butterfly 93, etc.

¶ My dentist said to me the other day, I've enough problems in my life, so why should I see your films? – *D.C.*
A friend of mine saw *Videodrome*, said he really liked it, and added, you know someday they're going to lock you up. – *D.C.*
I don't have a moral plan. I'm a Canadian. – *D.C.*
He works from his dreams. If he'd just dream a little more normally, I'd love to work with him again. – *James Woods*

Cronenweth, Jordan.
American cinematographer.
Brewster McCloud 70. Play it as it Lays 72. Zandy's Bride 74. The Front Page 74. Handle With Care 77. Rolling Thunder 77. Altered States 80. Cutter's Way 81. Blade Runner 82. Best Friends 82. Peggy Sue Got Married (AAN) 86. Gardens of Stone 87. State of Grace 90. Get Back 91. Final Analysis 92, etc.

Cronin, A. J. (1896–1981).
British novelist, former doctor.
Grand Canary 34. The Citadel 38, 83 (TV). The Stars Look Down 39. Shining Victory 41. Hatter's Castle 41. The Keys of the Kingdom 44. The Green Years 46. The Spanish Gardener 56.
TV series: Dr Finlay's Casebook 59–66.

Cronjager, Edward (1904–1960).
American cinematographer.
The Quarterback 26. The Virginian 30. Cimarron 31. Roberta 35. The Gorilla 39. *Hot Spot* 41. *Heaven Can Wait* 43. Canyon Passage 46. The House by the River 50. Treasure of the Golden Condor 53. Beneath the Twelve-Mile Reef 53, many others.

Cronyn, Hume (1911–) (Hume Blake).
Canadian character actor of stage and screen; married Jessica Tandy.
Autobiography: 1991, *A Terrible Liar.*
■ *Shadow of a Doubt* 43. Phantom of the Opera 43. The Cross of Lorraine 43. *The Seventh Cross* (AAN) 44. Main Street After Dark 44. *Lifeboat* 44. A Letter for Evie 45. The Sailor Takes a Wife 45. The Green Years 46. The Postman Always Rings Twice 46. Ziegfeld Follies 46. The Beginning or the End 47. *Brute Force* 47. The Bride Goes Wild 48. Top o' the Morning 49. People Will Talk 51. Crowded Paradise 56. *Sunrise at Campobello* 60. Cleopatra 63. Hamlet 64. Gaily Gaily 69. The Arrangement 70. There Was a Crooked Man 70. The Parallax View 74. Conrack 74. Rollover 80. Honky Tonk Freeway 81. The World According to Garp 82. Brewster's Millions 84. Impulse 84. Cocoon 85. The Thrill of Genius 85. Batteries Not Included 87. Cocoon: The Return 88. Camilla 93. To Dance with the White Dog (TV) 93. The Pelican Brief 93.

¶ To act you must have a sense of truth and some degree of dedication. – *H.C.*

Crosbie, Annette (1934–).
British character actress, popular on TV as Catherine of Aragon and Queen Victoria.
The Public Eye 72. The Slipper and the Rose 76. Hawk the Slayer 80. Ordeal by Innocence 84. The Pope Must Die (US: The Pope Must Diet) 91, etc.

Crosby, Bing (1903–1977) (Harry Lillis Crosby).
Star American crooner of the 30s and 40s; former

band singer, later an agreeable comedian, romantic lead and straight actor.
Autobiography: 1953, *Call Me Lucky.*
Biography: 1982, *The Hollow Man* by Robert F. Slatzer.
■ King of Jazz 30. Check and Double Check 31. Reaching for the Moon 31. Confessions of a Co-Ed 31. The Big Broadcast 32. College Humor 33. Too Much Harmony 33. Going Hollywood 33. We're Not Dressing 34. She Loves Me Not 34. Here is My Heart 34. *Mississippi* 35. Two for Tonight 35. The Big Broadcast of 1936 36. *Anything Goes* 36. Rhythm on the Range 36. Pennies from Heaven 36. Waikiki Wedding 37. Double or Nothing 37. Dr Rhythm 38. *Sing You Sinners* 38. Paris Honeymoon 39. East Side of Heaven 39. The Star Maker 39. *Road to Singapore* 40. If I Had My Way 40. Rhythm on the River 40. Road to Zanzibar 41. Birth of the Blues 41. *Holiday Inn* 42. Road to Morocco 42. Star Spangled Rhythm 43. Dixie 43. *Going My Way* (AA) 44. Here Come The Waves 45. Duffy's Tavern 45. Road to Utopia 45. The Bells of St Mary's (AAN) 45. Blue Skies 46. Variety Girl 47. Welcome Stranger 47. Road to Rio 47. The Emperor Waltz 48. A Connecticut Yankee in King Arthur's Court 49. Top o' the Morning 49. Riding High 50. Mr Music 50. Here Comes the Groom 51. Just for You 52. Road to Bali 52. Little Boy Lost 53. White Christmas 54. *The Country Girl* (AAN) 54. Anything Goes 56. High Society 56. Man on Fire 57. Say One for Me 59. High Time 60. Pepe 60. Road to Hong Kong 62. Robin and the Seven Hoods 64. Stagecoach 66. Dr Cook's Garden (TV) 70.
TV series: The Bing Crosby Show 64.
✪For his songs; and for his acceptance as a member of everybody's family over a fifty-year career. *Holiday Inn.*

¶ Honestly, I think I've stretched a talent which is so thin it's almost transparent over a quite unbelievable term of years. – *B.C.*
He was an average guy who could carry a tune. – *B.C.'s own epitaph*
Once or twice I've been described as a light comedian. I consider this the most accurate description of my abilities I've ever seen. – *B.C.*
~Crosby made gag appearances in a number of films, including *My Favorite Blonde, The Princess and the Pirate, My Favorite Brunette, Scared Stiff* and *Let's Make Love.*
~~Crosby also appeared in six Mack Sennett two-reelers of the early 30s; and his voice was heard in *Out of this World* 45 and *Ichabod and Mr Toad* 49.

Crosby, Bob (1913–1993).
American bandleader, brother of Bing.
Let's Make Music 40. Reveille with Beverly 43. See Here Private Hargrove 44. Two Tickets to Broadway 51. The Five Pennies 59, etc.

Crosby, Floyd (1899–1985).
American cinematographer who worked on everything from documentary to horror thrillers.
■ *Tabu* (AA) 31. *The River* (co-ph) 37. The Fight for Life 40. My Father's House 47. Of Men and Music 50. The Brave Bulls 51. *High Noon* 52. Man in the Dark 53. The Steel Lady 53. Man Crazy 53. Stormy 54. The Snow Creature 54. The Monster from the Ocean Floor 54. The Fast and the Furious 54. Five Guns West 55. The Naked Street 55. Shack out on 101 55. Hell's Horizon 55. Apache Woman 55. Naked Paradise 56. She Gods of Shark Reef 56. Attack of the Crab Monsters 56. Rock All Night 56. Reform School 57. Teenage Doll 57. Ride out for Revenge 57. Hell Canyon Outlaws 57. Carnival Rock 57. War of the Satellites 57. Suicide Battalion 58. Cry Baby Killer 58. Machine Gun

Kelly 58. The Old Man and the Sea (co-ph) 58. Wolf Larsen 58. Hot Rod Gang 58. Teenage Caveman 58. I Mobster 59. Crime and Punishment USA 59. The Miracle of the Hills 59. The Wonderful Country 59. Blood and Steel 59. The Rookie 60. Twelve Hours to Kill 60. *House of Usher* 60. The High Powered Rifle 60. Walk Tall 60. Freckles 60. Operation Bottleneck 61. The Pit and the Pendulum 61. A Cold Wind in August 61. The Purple Hills 61. The Little Shepherd of Kingdom Come 61. The Gambler Wore a Gun 61. Seven Women from Hell 62. The Explosive Generation 62. Woman Hunt 62. The Premature Burial 62. The Two Little Bears 62. Tales of Terror 62. The Firebrand 62. The Broken Land 62. Terror at Black Falls 62. *The Raven* 63. Black Zoo 63. Yellow Canary 63. The Young Racers 63. X – the Man with X-ray Eyes 63. The Comedy of Terrors 64. Bikini Beach 64. Pajama Party 64. The Haunted Palace 64. Raiders from beneath the Sea 65. Beach Blanket Bingo 65. How to Stuff a Wild Bikini 65. Sergeant Deadhead 65. Sallah 65. Fireball 500 66. The Cool Ones 67.

Croset, Paule:
see *Corday, Paula*.

Crosland, Alan (1894–1936).
Routine American director who happened to handle two innovative films. A former actor, he died of injuries sustained in a car crash.
Enemies of Women 23. Under the Red Robe 23. Three Weeks 24. Bobbed Hair 25. *Don Juan* (first film with synchronized music) 26. The Beloved Rogue 27. Old San Francisco 27. *The Jazz Singer* (first film with talking sequences) 27. Glorious Betsy 28. General Crack 29. Song of the Flame 30. Captain Thunder 31. Weekends Only 32. The Case of the Howling Dog 34. Lady Tubbs 35. The Great Impersonation 35, many others.

Crosman, Henrietta (1861–1944).
American stage actress, a grande dame who made a few films.
■ The Unwelcome Mrs Hatch 14. How Molly Made Good 15. Broadway Broke 23. Wandering Fires 25. *The Royal Family of Broadway* 30. Pilgrimage 33. Three on a Honeymoon 34. Carolina 34. Such Women Are Dangerous 34. Among the Missing 34. The Curtain Falls 34. Menace 34. Elinor Norton 35. The Right to Live 35. *The Dark Angel* 35. Hitch Hike to Heaven 36. Charlie Chan's Secret 36. The Moon's Our Home 36. Girl of the Ozarks 36. Follow Your Heart 37. Personal Property 37.

Cross, Ben (1948–).
British leading man of somewhat lugubrious countenance.
Chariots of Fire 81. The Citadel (TV) 83. The Far Pavilions (TV) 83. The Assisi Underground 85. The Unholy 88. Steal the Sky 88. Paperhouse 89. Nightlife (TV) 89. Live Wire 92. Cold Sweat 93. Symphony 93. The Ascent 94. First Knight 95, etc.
TV series: Dark Shadows 91.

cross cutting.
Interlinking fragments of two or more separate sequences so that they appear to be taking place at the same time. One of the most famous examples is the climax of *Intolerance* which intertwines four stories; and in more modern times *The Godfather* crosscut a murder with a baptism.

Cross, Eric (1902–).
British cinematographer.
Make Up 37. Song of Freedom 38. The First of the Few 42. Don't Take It To Heart 44. The Chance of a Lifetime 49. Hunted 52. The

Kidnappers 53. Private's Progress 55. The One That Got Away 57. Behind the Curtain 60, many others.

Crosse, Rupert (1927–1973).
American actor best remembered for *The Reivers* (AAN) 68, and for the TV series *Partners*.

Crossley, Syd (1885–1960).
British music-hall comedian who played comic supporting roles in many films. In US in 20s.
Keep Smiling 25. Fangs of the Wild 28. Atlantic 29. Tonight's the Night 31. Those were the Days 34. Dandy Dick 35. Music Hath Charms 36. The Ghost Goes West 36. Silver Blaze 37. Penny Paradise 38, many others.

Crothers, Rachel (1878–1958).
American playwright; works much filmed.
When Ladies Meet 33 and 41. As Husbands Go 34. Splendour 35. Mother Carey's Chickens 38. Susan and God 40, etc.

Crothers, Scatman (1910–1986) (Sherman Crothers).
American character actor with a penchant for comedy.
Between Heaven and Hell 56. Lady in a Cage 64. Hello Dolly 69. The Great White Hope 70. Lady Sing the Blues 72. The Fortune 74. One Flew Over the Cuckoo's Nest 75. The Shootist 76. Silver Streak 77. Scavenger Hunt 79. Bronco Billy 80. The Shining 80. Twilight Zone 83. The Journey of Natty Gann 85, etc.
TV series: Chico and the Man 74–77. One of the Boys 82. Casablanca 83. Morning Star, Evening Star 86.

Crouse, Lindsay (1948–).
American leading lady, daughter of Russel Crouse. She was formerly married to director and writer David Mamet.
All the President's Men 76. Between the Lines 77. Slapshot 77. The Verdict 82. Iceman 82. Places in the Heart (AAN) 85. House of Games 87. Communion, a True Story 89. Desperate Hours 90. Chantilly Lace (TV) 93. Being Human 94. Parallel Lives (TV) 94, etc.

Crouse, Russel (1893–1966).
American librettist, usually with *Howard Lindsay* (1888–1968). Their musicals to have been filmed include *Anything Goes, Call Me Madam* and *The Sound of Music*. Non-musicals: *Life with Father, State of the Union*, etc.

Crowden, Graham (1922–).
Scottish character actor, often in querulous or eccentric roles. Born in Edinburgh, he first worked as a stage manager and in repertory and has been a member of the Royal National Theatre Company and the Royal Shakespeare Company.
Don't Bother to Knock 61. Nil Carborundum (TV) 62. One Way Pendulum 64. Morgan 66. If . . . 68. The Virgin Soldiers 69. Leo the Last 70. Up the Chastity Belt 71. The Ruling Class 72. O Lucky Man 73. Jabberwocky 77. For Your Eyes Only 81. Britannia Hospital 82. Company of Wolves 85. Out of Africa 85, etc.
TV series: нмs Paradise 64. A Very Peculiar Practice 86–88. Waiting for God 90–93.

Crowe, Cameron (1957–).
American screenwriter and director, a former journalist.
Fast Times at Ridgemont High (w) 82. The Wild Life (w) 84. Say Anything (wd) 89. Singles (wd) 92. Sessions (wd) 92, etc.

Crowe, Russell.
Australian leading actor.
Blood Oath 90. The Crossing 90. Proof 91. Spotswood (aka The Efficiency Expert) 91. *Romper Stomper* 92. Love in Limbo 92. Hammers over the Anvil 93. The Silver Brumby 93. For the Moment (Can.) 94, etc.

Crowley, Pat (1929–).
American leading lady of the 50s.
Forever Female 53. Money from Home 54. Red Garters 54. There's Always Tomorrow 55. Hollywood or Bust 56. Key Witness 60. To Trap a Spy 64. A Family Upside Down (TV) 78, etc.
TV series: Please Don't Eat the Daisies 65–66. Joe Forrester 75. Dynasty 86.

Crowther, Bosley (1905–1981).
American film critic. Long with the *New York Times*.

Cruickshank, Andrew (1907–1988).
Scottish stage actor who appeared in a number of films, usually as doctor or judge. A national figure on TV as Dr Cameron in *Dr Finlay's Casebook* 59–66.
Auld Lang Syne 37. The Mark of Cain 47. Paper Orchid 49. Your Witness 50. The Cruel Sea 53. Richard III 56. Innocent Sinners 58. Kidnapped 60. *There Was a Crooked Man* 60. El Cid 61. Murder Most Foul 64, etc.

Cruise, Tom (1962–) (Thomas Cruise Mapother).
American leading actor. He married actress Nicole Kidman in 1990. His current fee per film is reported to be $15m.
■ Endless Love 81. Taps 81. Losin' It 83. All the Right Moves 83. The Outsiders 83. Risky Business 84. Legend 84. *Top Gun* 85. *The Color of Money* 86. Cocktail 88. Rain Man 88. *Born on the Fourth of July* (AAN) 89. Days of Thunder 90. Far and Away 92. A Few Good Men 92. The Firm 93. Interview with the Vampire 94.

¶ Hollywood didn't create Tom Cruise so that he could do *Rain Man* and *Born on the Fourth of July*. Hollywood created him to make twelve *Top Guns*, and it will replace him if he doesn't. – *Joe Queenan*
He's no more my Vampire Lestat than Edward G. Robinson is Rhett Butler. – *Anne Rice*

Crumb, Robert (1943–).
American comic-book artist who emerged from underground publications of the 60s. He is the creator of Fritz the Cat, the randy hero of two animated features, *Fritz the Cat* 72, directed by Ralph Bakshi, and *The Nine Lives of Fritz the Cat* 74, directed by Robert Taylor. (Crumb disowned both movies.) A two-hour documentary on his life, *Crumb*, was released in 1994, directed by Terry Zwigoff.

Crutchley, Rosalie (1921–).
Striking, lean-featured British stage actress who makes occasional film appearances.
Take My Life 47. Give Us This Day 49. Quo Vadis 51. Make Me an Offer 55. The Spanish Gardener 56. *A Tale of Two Cities* (as Madame Lafarge) 58. Beyond This Place 59. Sons and Lovers 60. Freud 62. The Girl in the Headlines 63. Behold a Pale Horse 64. Jane Eyre (TV) 70. Blood from the Mummy's Tomb 71. Who Slew Auntie Roo? 71. Man of La Mancha 72. Mahler 74. Smiley's People (TV) 82. Eleni 85, etc.

Cruz, Brandon (1962–).
American child actor of the 70s.
But I Don't Want to Get Married (TV) 70. The

Going Up of David Lev (TV) 72. The Bad News Bears 76. The One and Only 78, etc.

TV series: *The Courtship of Eddie's Father* 69–71.

Cruze, James (1884–1942) (Jens Cruz Bosen). Danish-American silent screen actor who broke his leg and turned to direction.
AS ACTOR: A Boy of Revolution 11. She 11. The Star of Bethlehem 12. Joseph in the Land of Egypt 14. *The Million Dollar Mystery* (serial) 14. The Twenty Million Dollar Mystery (serial) 15. Nan of Music Mountain 17. Too Many Millions 18, etc.
AS DIRECTOR: Too Many Millions 18. The Dollar a Year Man 21. One Glorious Day 22. The Dictator 22. *The Covered Wagon* 23. Hollywood 23. Ruggles of Red Gap 23. To the Ladies 23. Merton of the Movies 24. The Goose Hangs High 25. *Beggar on Horseback* 25. Pony Express 25. *Old Ironsides* 26. The Mating Call 27. The Great Gabbo 29. Salvation Nell 31. *Washington Merry Go Round* 32. I Cover the Waterfront 33. David Harum 34. Helldorado 34. *Sutter's Gold* 36. Prison Nurse 38. Gangs of New York 38, many others.

Crystal, Billy (1947–).
American stand-up comic and writer turned light leading man. His one-man shows have been released on video.

Rabbit Test 78. Enola Gay: The Men, the Mission, the Atomic Bomb (TV) 80. This Is Spinal Tap 83. Running Scared 86. The Princess Bride 87. Throw Momma from the Train 88. Memories of Me 88. When Harry Met Sally 89. City Slickers 91. Mr Saturday Night (& d) 92. City Slickers II: The Legend of Curly's Gold 94. Forget Paris 95, etc.

TV series: Soap 77–81.

Cuaron, Alfonso (1961–).
Mexican director.

Tale of Love and Hysteria (Solo con Tu Pareja) 91.

Cuba
produced its first film in 1897, but native film-making was swamped by American imports until the Communist revolution of 1959, when a politically conscious programme was begun. Tomas Alea is the best known Cuban director.

Cucciolla, Ricardo (1932–).
Italian leading actor.

Italia Brava Gente 65. Grand Slam 67. Sacco and Vanzetti 71, etc.

Cugat, Xavier (1900–1990).
Chubby, beaming Spanish-American bandleader and caricaturist, a feature of many MGM musicals of the 40s.

Autobiography: 1948, *Rumba Is My Life*.

You Were Never Lovelier 42. Two Girls and a Sailor 44. Holiday in Mexico 46. This Time for Keeps 47. A Date with Judy 48. Neptune's Daughter 49. Chicago Syndicate 55, etc.

Cukor, George (1899–1983).
American director, from the Broadway stage; proved to be one of Hollywood's most reliable handlers of high comedy and other literate material.

Biography: 1991, *A Double Life: Director George Cukor* by Patrick McGilligan.
■ Grumpy (co-d) 30. Virtuous Sin (co-d) 30. The Royal Family of Broadway 30. Tarnished Lady 30. Girls About Town 31. *One Hour with You* (with Lubitsch) 32. *What Price Hollywood?* 32. A Bill of Divorcement 32. Rockabye 32. Our Betters 33. *Dinner at Eight* 33. Little Women (AAN) 33. *David Copperfield* 34. Sylvia Scarlett 35. Romeo and Juliet

36. *Camille* 36. *Holiday* 38. Zara 39. *The Women* 39. Susan and God 40. *The Philadelphia Story* (AAN) 40. A Woman's Face 41. Two-faced Woman 41. Her Cardboard Lover 42. *Keeper of the Flame* 43. Gaslight 44. Winged Victory 44. Desire Me (co-d) 47. A Double Life (AAN) 47. *Adam's Rib* 49. Edward My Son (GB) 49. A Life of Her Own 50. Born Yesterday (AAN) 50. The Model and the Marriage Broker 52. The Marrying Kind 52. Pat and Mike 52. The Actress 53. It Should Happen to You 53. *A Star is Born* 54. Bhowani Junction 56. Les Girls 57. Wild is the Wind 57. Heller in Pink Tights 59. Song Without End (part) 60. Let's Make Love 61. The Chapman Report 62. *My Fair Lady* (AA) 64. Justine 69. Travels with My Aunt 73. Love Among the Ruins (TV) 75. The Bluebird 76. The Corn Is Green (TV) 79. Rich and Famous 81.
⦿For adding to Hollywood a sense of light culture; and for his discretion in handling a score of the film colony's more temperamental ladies. *The Philadelphia Story*.

¶ His films vary drastically in their visual texture, their style reposing mainly in the theatrically accomplished handling of the actors. – *Charles Higham*

When a director has provided polished tasteful entertainments of a high order consistently over a period of thirty years, it is clear that said director is much more than a mere entertainer. – *Andrew Sarris*

Culkin, Kieran.
American juvenile actor, the brother of Macaulay Culkin.

Father of the Bride 91. Home Alone II: Lost in New York 92. Nowhere to Run 93. It Runs in the Family 94.

Culkin, Macaulay (1980–).
American juvenile actor who became a star with *Home Alone*, the most successful movie comedy yet made. He was reportedly paid $5 million and 5 per cent of the gross to appear in the sequel.

Rocket Gibraltar 88. Uncle Buck 89. See You in the Morning 89. Home Alone 90. Jacob's Ladder (uncredited cameo) 90. My Girl 91. Only the Lonely 91. Home Alone 2: Lost in New York 92. The Good Son 93. George Balanchine's The Nutcracker 93. Getting Even with Dad 94. The Pagemaster 94. Richie Rich 94, etc.

Culp, Robert (1930–).
American leading man.

P.T. 109 62. The Raiders 63. Sunday in New York 64. Rhino! 64. *Bob and Carol and Ted and Alice* 69. Hannie Caulder 71. Hickey and Boggs (& d) 72. See the Man Run (TV) 72. The Castaway Cowboy 74. A Cry for Help (TV) 75. Inside Out 75. Sky Riders 76. The Great Scout and Cathouse Thursday 76. Breaking Point 76. Word Games (TV) 79. Goldengirl 79. Turk 182 84. The Blue Lightning (TV) 86. The Gladiator (TV) 86. Big Bad Mama II 87. Silent Night, Deadly Night 3: Better Watch Out! 89. Timebomb 91. The Pelican Brief 93. I Spy Returns (TV) 94, etc.

TV series: Trackdown 57. *I Spy* 65–67. *The Greatest American Hero* 81–82.

Culver, Roland (1900–1984).
British stage actor of impeccable English types, usually comic.

77 Park Lane 32. Nell Gwyn 34. Paradise for Two 37. *French Without Tears* (his stage role) 39. *Quiet Wedding* 40. Night Train to Munich 40. Talk about Jacqueline 42. *On Approval* 43. Dear Octopus 43. *Dead of Night* 45. Wanted for Murder 46. To Each His Own (US) 47. Down to Earth (US) 47. The

Emperor Waltz (US) 48. Isn't It Romantic? 48. *Trio* (as Somerset Maugham) 50. The Holly and the Ivy 54. The Man Who Loved Redheads 55. Touch and Go 57. Bonjour Tristesse 58. The Yellow Rolls-Royce 64. A Man Could Get Killed 65. Fragment of Fear 70. Bequest to the Nation 73. The Word (TV) 78, many others.

Cummings, Constance (1910–) (Constance Halverstadt).
American stage actress, long resident in England.

The Criminal Code (US) 31. The Guilty Generation (US) 31. Movie Crazy (US) 32. Channel Crossing 32. Broadway thro' a Keyhole (US) 33. Glamour 34. Looking for Trouble 34. Remember Last Night? (US) 35. Seven Sinners 36. *Busman's Honeymoon* 40. This England 41. The Foreman Went to France 42. *Blithe Spirit* 45. John and Julie 55. The Intimate Stranger 56. The Battle of the Sexes 59. Sammy Going South 62. In the Cool of the Day 63, etc.

Cummings, Irving (1888–1959).
American director, former actor; in films from 1909.

SELECTED SILENT FILMS: As Man Desires 25. The Johnstown Flood 26. The Brute 27, etc.
■ In Old Arizona (AAN) 29. Behind That Curtain 29. Cameo Kirby 30. On the Level 30. A Devil with Women 30. A Holy Terror 31. *The Cisco Kid* 31. Attorney for the Defense 32. Night Club Lady 32. Man Against Woman 32. Man Hunt 33. The Woman I Stole 33. The Mad Game 33. I Believed in You 34. Grand Canary 34. The White Parade 34. It's a Small World 35. Curly Top 35. Nobody's Fool 36. Poor Little Rich Girl 36. Girls Dormitory 36. White Hunter 36. Vogues of 1938 37. Merry go Round of 1938 37. Little Miss Broadway 38. Just Around the Corner 38. *The Story of Alexander Graham Bell* 38. *Hollywood Cavalcade* 39. Everything Happens at Night 39. *Lillian Russell* 40. Down Argentine Way 40. *That Night in Rio* 41. Belle Starr 41. Louisiana Purchase 41. My Gal Sal 42. Springtime in the Rockies 42. Sweet Rosie O'Grady 43. What a Woman 44. The Impatient Years 44. *The Dolly Sisters* 45. Double Dynamite 51.

Cummings, Jack (1900–1989).
American producer, especially of musicals; long with MGM.

The Winning Ticket 35. Born to Dance 36. Go West 40. Ship Ahoy 42. Bathing Beauty 44. Neptune's Daughter 49. Three Little Words 50. Lovely to Look At 52. Kiss Me Kate 53. Seven Brides for Seven Brothers 54. Many Rivers to Cross 55. The Teahouse of the August Moon 56. The Blue Angel 59. Can Can 60. Bachelor Flat 62. Viva Las Vegas 64, many others.

Cummings, Quinn (1967–).
American actress, from television, born in Hollywood.

Night Terror (TV) 76. The Goodbye Girl (AAN) 77. The Babysitter (TV) 80. Listen to Me 89, etc.

TV series: Big Eddie 75. Family 78–80. Hail to the Chief 85.

Cummings, Robert (1908–1990).
American light leading man of the 40s.

The Virginia Judge 35. Forgotten Faces 36. Last Train from Madrid 37. Souls at Sea 37. Three Smart Girls Grow Up 38. Rio 39. Spring Parade 40. The Devil and Miss Jones 41. Moon over Miami 41. *It Started with Eve* 41. *Kings Row* 41. Saboteur 42. Princess O'Rourke 43. You Came Along 45. The Bride Wore Boots 46. The Chase 46. Heaven Only Knows 47. The Lost Moment 47. Sleep My Love 48. The Accused 48. Paid in Full 50. For Heaven's

Sake 50. The Barefoot Mailman 51. Marry Me Again 53. Lucky Me 54. Dial M for Murder 54. How to be Very Very Popular 55. My Geisha 62. Beach Party 63. What a Way to Go 64. *The Carpetbaggers* 64. Promise Her Anything 66. Stagecoach 66. 5 Golden Dragons 67. Partners in Crime (TV) 73, many others.

TV series: My Hero 52. *The Bob Cummings Show* 54–61. My Living Doll 64.

Cummins, Peggy (1925–).
British leading lady, former teenage star.

Dr O'Dowd 39. The Late George Apley (US) 47. Moss Rose (US) 47. Green Grass of Wyoming (US) 48. Escape (US) 48. My Daughter Joy 50. Who Goes There? 52. To Dorothy a Son 54. The March Hare 55. Night of the Demon 57. Dentist in the Chair 60. In the Doghouse 62, etc.

Cunard, Grace (1893–1967) (Harriet Jeffries).
American silent serial queen.

The Broken Coin 13. The Purple Mask 15. Peg o' the Ring 18. The Last Man on Earth 24. Untamed 29. Resurrection 31. Ladies They Talk About 33, many others.

Cundey, Dean.
American cinematographer.

Bare Knuckles 78. Halloween 78. Roller Boogie 79. Rock 'n' Roll High School 79. The Fog 80. Galaxina 80. Without Warning 80. Halloween II 81. Escape from New York 81. Angels Brigade 81. The Thing 82. Halloween III: Season of the Witch 82. Separate Ways 83. Psycho II 83. Romancing the Stone 84. Back to the Future 85. Warning Sign 85. Big Trouble in Little China 86. Project X 87. Big Business 88. Who Framed Roger Rabbit (AAN) 88. Road House 89. Back to the Future Part II 89. Back to the Future Part III 90. Nothing but Trouble 91. Hook 91. Death Becomes Her 92. Jurassic Park 93. The Flintstones 94, etc.

Cundieff, Rusty.
American director, screenwriter and actor, a former stand-up comedian.

Hollywood Shuffle (a) 87. House Party 2 (co-w) 91. *Fears of a Black Hat* (a, wd) 93, etc.

Cunningham, Cecil (1888–1959).
American character actress, usually in hard or wisecracking roles.

Their Own Desire 29. Monkey Business 31. Mata Hari 31. The Impatient Maiden 32. Blonde Venus 32. Baby Face 33. The Life of Vergie Winters 34. Come and Get It 36. Artists and Models 37. College Swing 38. Lady of the Tropics 39. Lillian Russell 40. New Moon 40. Back Street 41. Blossoms in the Dust 41. I Married an Angel 42. Twin Beds 42. The Hidden Hand 42. Du Barry Was a Lady 43. Wonder Man 45. Saratoga Trunk 45. My Reputation 46. The Bride Goes Wild 48, many others.

Cunningham, Sean S. (1941–).
American horror film director and producer.

Together 71. Here Come the Tigers 78. Manny's Orphans 79. Friday the 13th 80. A Stranger Is Watching 82. Spring Break 83. The New Kids (& p) 85. House (p) 86. House II (p) 87. Deepstar Six 89. My Boyfriend's Back (p) 93.

Cuny, Alain (1908–1994).
Tall, imposing French actor, in occasional films. He directed his first film at the age of 83.

Les Visiteurs du Soir 42. Il Cristo Proibito 50. The Hunchback of Notre Dame 56. Les Amants 58. The Milky Way 68. Satyricon 69. Valparaiso Valparaiso 70. Emmanuelle 74. Il Contesto 75. Cadaveri

Eccelenti 76. Christ Stopped at Eboli 79. Les Jeux de la Comtesse 80. Basileus Quartet 81. Camille Claudel 89. The Annunciation of Marie (L'Annonce Faîte à Marie) (& d) 91. Farewell Sweet War (Uova di Garofano) 92, etc.

Cupito, Suzanne:
see *Brittany, Morgan*.

Currie, Finlay (1878–1968) (Finlay Jefferson).
Veteran Scottish actor with stage and music-hall experience.

The Case of the Frightened Lady 32. Rome Express 32. Edge of the World 38. The Bells Go Down 42. *Great Expectations* (as Magwitch) 46. *Sleeping Car to Trieste* 48. *The History of Mr Polly* 49. Trio 50. Treasure Island 50. *The Mudlark* (as John Brown) 51. Quo Vadis 51. Kangaroo 51. *People Will Talk* (US) 52. Ivanhoe 52. Rob Roy 53. Treasure of the Golden Condor 53. Captain Lightfoot 54. Beau Brummell 54. The End of the Road (leading role) 54. Make Me an Offer 55. King's Rhapsody 56. Around the World in 80 Days 56. Saint Joan 57. Zarak 57. The Little Hut 57. Naked Earth 57. Dangerous Exile 57. Ben Hur (US) 59. Tempest 59. Solomon and Sheba 59. The Angel Wore Red 60. Huckleberry Finn 60. Kidnapped 60. Five Golden Hours 61. Francis of Assisi 61. The Inspector 62. Hand in Hand 62. The Amorous Prawn 62. Corridors of Blood 63. The Cracksman 63. West Eleven 63. The Three Lives of Thomasina 63. Billy Liar 63. The Fall of the Roman Empire 64. Who Was Maddox? (leading role) 64. The Battle of the Villa Fiorita 65. Bunny Lake is Missing 65, etc.

Curry, Tim (1946–).
British actor, hard to cast but with a wide range.

The Rocky Horror Picture Show 74. Will Shakespeare (TV) (title role) 76. The Shout 77. Times Square 80. Oliver Twist (TV) 81. Annie 82. The Ploughman's Lunch 83. Baby 83. Legend 85. Clue 86. Pass the Ammo 87. The Hunt for Red October 90. Stephen King's It (TV) 91. Oscar 91. Ferngully . . . the Last Rainforest (voice) 92. Passed Away 92. Home Alone 2: Lost in New York 92. Ferngully . . . The Last Rainforest (voice) 92. National Lampoon's Loaded Weapon 1 93. The Three Musketeers 93. The Shadow 94, etc.

Curtin, Valerie.
American actress and screenwriter, formerly married to director Barry Levinson, with whom she has collaborated on scripts. She also wrote for the TV series *The Mary Tyler Moore Show* and *Phyllis*.

AS ACTRESS: Alice Doesn't Live Here Anymore 74. Silver Streak 76. Mother, Jugs and Speed 76. Silent Movie 76. All the President's Men 76. Different Story 78. A Christmas without Snow (TV) 80. Down and Out in Beverly Hills 85. Maxie 85. Big Trouble 86, etc.

AS WRITER: . . . And Justice for All (AAN) 79. Inside Moves 80. Best Friends 82. Unfaithfully Yours 84. Toys 92.

TV series: 9 to 5 82–83, 86–88.

Curtis, Alan (1909–1953) (Harold Neberroth).
American leading man, and sometimes villain, of many 'B' pictures of the 40s.

Walking on Air 36. Winterset 36. Mannequin 38. Hollywood Cavalcade 39. Buck Privates 40. The Great Awakening 41. Two Tickets to London 43. Hitler's Madman 43. *Phantom Lady* 44. Destiny 44. The Invisible Man's Revenge 44. The Naughty Nineties 45. Philo Vance's Gamble 48. The Masked Pirate 50, etc.

Curtis, Dan (1928–).
American producer specializing in horror themes for TV.

Dark Shadows (serial) 66. The Night Strangler (TV) 72. *The Norliss Tapes* (TV) 73. Dracula (TV) (& d) 73. Kolchak, the Night Stalker (TV series) 74. Supertrain (TV) 79, etc.

AS DIRECTOR: House of Dark Shadows 70. Burnt Offerings 76. Melvin Purvis G-Man (TV) 77. The Raid on Coffeyville (TV) 79. *The Winds of War* (& p) 83. War and Remembrance (TV) 88–89. Me and the Kid 93.

Curtis, Jackie (1947–1985).
Transvestite actor, best known for roles in Andy Warhol's films. Born in New York, he was also a dramatist, providing Robert De Niro with a notable success in his off-Broadway play *Glamour, Glory and Gold* in 1968. Died of a drug overdose.

Flesh 68. WR: Mysteries of the Organism 71. Women in Revolt 72. Underground U.S.A. 80. Burroughs (doc) 84, etc.

¶ It's much easier to be a weird girl than a weird guy. – J.C.

Curtis, Jamie Lee (1958–).
American leading lady who seemed to get stuck in horrors. Daughter of Tony Curtis and Janet Leigh.

Operation Petticoat (TV) 78. Halloween 79. Prom Night 80. Terror Train 80. The Fog 80. Halloween II 81. Road Games 81. Love Letters 83. Trading Places 83. Grandview USA 84. Perfect 85. Amazing Grace and Chuck 87. Un Homme Amoureux 87. Dominick and Eugene 88. A Fish Called Wanda 88. Blue Steel 89. Queen's Logic 91. My Girl 91. Forever Young 92. My Girl 2 94. Mother's Boys 94. True Lies 94, etc.

TV series: Operation Petticoat 78.

Curtis, Ken (1916–1991) (Curtis Gates).
American singing cowboy of the 40s and later a character actor, mainly in John Ford's westerns. He began as a singer with big bands, including those of Tommy Dorsey and Shep Fields.

Song of the Prairie 45. Lone Star Moonlight 46. Call of the Forest 49. Rio Grande 50. Mr Roberts 55. The Searchers 56. The Last Hurrah 58. Escort West 59. Two Rode Together 61. Cheyenne Autumn 64. Pony Express Rider 76, many others.

TV series: Ripcord 61–63. Gunsmoke (as Festus Haggen) 64–75. The Yellow Rose 83–84.

Curtis, Richard.
British comedy screenwriter, from television. He was co-writer of the *Blackadder* television series starring Rowan Atkinson and also wrote for *Not the Nine O'Clock News*.

The Tall Guy 89. *Four Weddings and a Funeral* 94.

¶ Whatever your script is like, no matter how much rewriting you do, if the punters don't want to sleep with the star, you may never be asked to write another one. – R.C.

Curtis, Tony (1925–) (Bernard Schwarz).
Bouncy American leading man of 50s actioners who constantly sought a wider range. He was married to Janet Leigh (1951–62); their daughter is Jamie Lee Curtis.

Novel: 1977, *Kid Andrew Cody and Julie Sparrow*. Autobiography: 1994, *Tony Curtis* (with Barry Paris).

■ Criss Cross 49. City Across the River 49. The Lady Gambles 49. Johnny Stool Pigeon 49. Francis 49. I was a Shoplifter 50. Sierra 50. Kansas Raiders 50. Winchester 73 50. *The Prince Who Was a Thief* 51. Flesh and Fury 52. No Room for the Groom

52. Son of Ali Baba 52. *Houdini* 53. The All American 53. Forbidden 53. Beachhead 54. The Black Shield of Falworth 54. Johnny Dark 54. So This is Paris 54. The Purple Mask 54. Six Bridges to Cross 55. The Square Jungle 55. *Trapeze* 56. The Rawhide Years 56. Mister Cory 57. The Midnight Story 57. *Sweet Smell of Success* 57. *The Vikings* 58. Kings go Forth 58. *The Defiant Ones* 58. The Perfect Furlough 58. *Some Like It Hot* 59. Operation Petticoat 59. Pepe 60. Who Was That Lady? 60. The Rat Race 60. *Spartacus* 60. The Great Imposter 60. The Outsider 61. Forty Pounds of Trouble 62. Taras Bulba 62. The List of Adrian Messenger 63. Captain Newman MD 63. Wild and Wonderful 64. Goodbye Charlie 64. Sex and the Single Girl 64. *The Great Race* 65. Boeing Boeing 65. Not With My Wife You Don't 66. Drop Dead Darling 67. Don't Make Waves 67. The Chastity Belt 68. *The Boston Strangler* 68. Those Daring Young Men in their Jaunty Jalopies 69. You Can't Win Them All 70. Suppose They Gave a War and Nobody Came 71. Third Girl from the Left (TV) 73. Lepke 75. Casanova 76. The Count of Monte Cristo (TV) 76. The Last Tycoon 76. The Manitou 78. Scarlett 78. The Bad News Bears Go to Japan 78. Little Miss Marker 80. The Mirror Crack'd 80. The Scarlett O'Hara Wars (TV) 81. Inmates (TV) 81. Portrait of a Showgirl (TV) 82. Brain Waves 83. Insignificance (TV) 85. King of the City 85. The Last of Philip Banter 86. Midnight 88. Welcome to Germany 88. Lobster Man from Mars 89. Walter and Carlo/Amerika 89. Prime Target 91. Center of the Web 92. Naked in New York 93.

TV series: *The Persuaders* 71. McCoy 75. Vegas 78.

¶ I had to be careful where I went because I was a Jew, because I was young and because I was handsome. It made me wiry and erratic and paranoid, which is what I still am. Always on guard. – *T.C.*

Curtiz, Michael (1888–1962) (Mihaly Kertesz). Hungarian director of more than sixty films in Europe before settling in Hollywood, where he made some of the smoothest spectacles and melodramas of the 30s and 40s and also became famous for his fractured English.

■ ENGLISH-SPEAKING FILMS: The Third Degree 26. A Million Bid 27. The Desired Woman 27. Good Time Charley 27. Tenderloin 28. *Noah's Ark* 28. Hearts in Exile 29. Glad Rag Doll 29. The Madonna of Avenue A 29. The Gamblers 29. *Mammy* 30. Under a Texas Moon 30. The Matrimonial Bed 30. Bright Lights 30. A Soldier's Plaything 30. River's End 30. God's Gift to Women 31. The Mad Genius 31. The Woman from Monte Carlo 32. Alias the Doctor 32. The Strange Love of Molly Louvain 32. *Doctor X* 32. Cabin in the Cotton 32. Twenty Thousand Years in Sing Sing 33. *The Mystery of the Wax Museum* 33. The Keyhole 33. Private Detective 33. Goodbye Again 33. The Kennel Murder Case 33. Female 33. Mandalay 34. British Agent 34. Jimmy the Gent 34. The Key 34. *Black Fury* 35. The Case of the Curious Bride 35. *Front Page Woman* 35. Little Big Shot 35. *Captain Blood* 35. The Walking Dead 36. *The Charge of the Light Brigade* 36. Mountain Justice 37. Stolen Holiday 37. Kid Galahad 37. The Perfect Specimen 37. Gold is Where You Find It 38. *The Adventures of Robin Hood* 38. *Four Daughters* (AAN) 38. Four's a Crowd 38. *Angels with Dirty Faces* (AAN) 38. Dodge City 39. Daughters Courageous 39. Four Wives 39. Elizabeth and Essex 39. *The Sea Hawk* 40. Santa Fe Trail 41. Dive Bomber 41. *The Sea Wolf* 41. Captains of the Clouds 42. *Yankee Doodle Dandy* 42. *Casablanca* (AA) 42. Mission to Moscow

43. This is the Army 43. Passage to Marseilles 44. Janie 44. Roughly Speaking 45. *Mildred Pierce* 45. Night and Day 46. Life with Father 47. The Unsuspected 47. Romance on the High Seas 48. My Dream is Yours 49. Flamingo Road 49. The Lady Takes a Sailor 49. Young Man with a Horn 50. Bright Leaf 50. The Breaking Point 51. Jim Thorpe – All American 51. Force of Arms 51. I'll See You in My Dreams 52. The Story of Will Rogers 52. The Jazz Singer 53. Trouble Along the Way 53. The Boy from Oklahoma 54. The Egyptian 54. White Christmas 54. We're No Angels 55. The Scarlet Hour 56. The Vagabond King 56. The Best Things in Life are Free 56. The Helen Morgan Story 57. The Proud Rebel 58. King Creole 58. The Hangman 59. The Man in the Net 59. The Adventures of Huckleberry Finn 60. A Breath of Scandal 60. Francis of Assisi 61. The Comancheros 62.

✪ For the striking Teutonic influence which he brought to a score of 30s melodramas; and for the apparent ease with which he handled top action films in a language which did not come easily to him. *Casablanca*.

¶ Bring on the empty horses! – *instruction attributed to M.C.*

This man Cole Porter, he sticked to purpose of making good music, come hell or hayride. – *M.C. of his film Night and Day*

When one speaks of a typical Warners film in the 30s and 40s, one is generally speaking of a typical Curtiz film of those periods. – *Andrew Sarris, 1968*

Curwood, James Oliver (1878–1927).
American journalist and author of novels about the outdoor life.

River's End 40. The Gold Hunters (from Trail of the Yukon) 49. Kazan the Wolf Dog 49. The Wolf Hunters 49. Snow Dog 51. Back to God's Country 53. Northern Patrol 54. Nikki, Wild Dog of the North (from Nomads of the North) 62, etc.

Curzon, George (1896–1976).
British stage actor, in occasional films from early 30s, usually in aristocratic or sinister roles.

The Impassive Footman 32. Lorna Doone 35. *Young and Innocent* 37. Sexton Blake and the Hooded Terror 38. Uncle Silas 47. Harry Black 58, etc.

Cusack, Cyril (1910–1993).
Diminutive Irish actor with fourteen years' Abbey Theatre experience. Film debut as child in 1917.

Odd Man Out 47. The Blue Lagoon 48. The Elusive Pimpernel 50. The Blue Veil (US) 51. Soldiers Three (US) 51. The Man Who Never Was 56. *Jacqueline* 56. The Spanish Gardener 56. Ill Met by Moonlight 57. Floods of Fear 58. Shake Hands with the Devil 59. A Terrible Beauty 59. The Waltz of the Toreadors 62. Eighty Thousand Suspects 63. The Spy Who Came in from the Cold 65. I Was Happy Here 66. *Fahrenheit 451* 66. The Taming of the Shrew 67. Oedipus the King 67. Galileo (It.) 68. David Copperfield 69. King Lear 70. Harold and Maude (US) 71. The Day of the Jackal 73. The Homecoming 73. The Abdication 74. Execution Squad 76. An Eye for an Eye 78. Strumpet City (TV) 80. Tristam and Isolt 81. True Confessions 81. Menace Unseen (TV) 88. Little Dorrit 88. My Left Foot 89. The Fool 90. Memento Mori (TV) 92. Far and Away 92. As You Like It 92, many others.

Cusack, Joan (1962–).
American actress, often in comic roles. She is the sister of actor John Cusack.

My Bodyguard 80. Class 83. Grandview USA 84. Sixteen Candles 84. The Allnighter 87. Broadcast News 87. Married to the Mob 88. Stars and Bars 88. Working Girl (AAN) 88. Men Don't Leave 90. My Blue Heaven 90. The Cabinet of Dr Ramirez 91. Toys 92. Bram Stoker's Dracula 92. Addams Family Values 93. Corrina, Corrina 94, etc.

Cusack, John (1966–).
American leading actor.

Class 83. Grandview USA 84. Sixteen Candles 84. Stand by Me 86. Broadcast News 87. Eight Men Out 88. Fat Man and Little Boy (GB Shadow Makers) 89. Say Anything 89. Grifters 90. True Colors 91. Shadows and Fog 91. Roadside Prophets 92. Bob Roberts 92. Map of the Human Heart 92. Money for Nothing 93. Bullets over Broadway 94. Floundering 94. The Road to Wellville 94, etc.

Cusack, Sinead (1948–).
Irish leading lady, daughter of Cyril Cusack.

■ David Copperfield 69. Alfred the Great 69. Hoffman 70. Revenge 71. Tam Ling 71. The Last Remake of Beau Geste 77. Bad Behaviour 93. The Cement Garden 93. Sparrow (Storia di una Capinera) 93. Uncovered 94.

Cushing, Peter (1913–1994).
British character actor of stage, TV and screen. His slightly fussy manner at first confined him to mild roles, but since allying himself with the Hammer horror school he has dealt firmly with monsters of all kinds.

Autobiographies: 1986, *An Autobiography*. 1988, *Past Forgetting*.

■ The Man in the Iron Mask (US) 39. A Chump at Oxford (US) 39. Vigil in the Night (US) 40. Laddie (US) 40. They Dare Not Love (US) 41. Women in War (US) 42. *Hamlet* (as Osric) 47. Moulin Rouge 53. The Black Night 54. The End of the Affair 55. Magic Fire (US) 56. Time Without Pity 56. Alexander the Great 56. *The Curse of Frankenstein* 57. Violent Playground 57. The Abominable Snowman 57. *Dracula* 58. The Revenge of Frankenstein 58. Suspect 59. The Hound of the Baskervilles 59. John Paul Jones (US) 59. The Mummy 59. Cone of Silence 60. Brides of Dracula 60. The Hellfire Club 61. Fury at Smugglers Bay 61. The Flesh and the Fiends 61. Sword of Sherwood Forest 61. The Naked Edge 61. Captain Clegg 62. *Cash on Demand* 63. The Man Who Finally Died 63. The Gorgon 64. The Evil of Frankenstein 64. Dr Terror's House of Horrors 65. She 65. Dr Who and the Daleks 65. Island of Terror 66. Daleks Invasion Earth 66. The Skull 66. Frankenstein Created Woman 67. The Blood Beast Terror 67. Some May Live (TV) 67. Night of the Big Heat 67. The Torture Garden 67. Corruption 68. Frankenstein Must Be Destroyed 69. Scream and Scream Again 69. The House that Dripped Blood 70. The Vampire Lovers 70. One More Time 70. I Monster 70. Twins of Evil 71. Incense for the Damned 71. Dracula AD 1972 72. Dr Phibes Rises Again 72. Nothing But the Night 72. *Tales from the Crypt* 72. The Creeping Flesh 73. Asylum 73. Fear in the Night 73. The Satanic Rites of Dracula 73. Frankenstein and the Monster from Hell 73. From Beyond the Grave 74. The Beast Must Die 74. Horror Express 74. Shatter 74. The Legend of the Seven Golden Vampires 74. And Now the Screaming Starts 74. Madhouse 74. The Ghoul 75. Legend of the Werewolf 75. La Grande Trouille 75. Shock Waves 75. Trial by Combat 76. The Uncanny 76. The Devil's Men 76. At the Earth's Core 76. Battle Flag 77. Star Wars 77. The Great Houdinis (TV) 77. Hitler's Son 78. Arabian Adventure 79. A Touch of the Sun 79. Monster Island 81. The House of Long Shadows 83. The

Masks of Death (TV) (as Sherlock Holmes) 85. Biggles 86.

¶ If I played Hamlet, they'd call it a horror film. – P.C.

custard pies

as a comic weapon were evolved in music hall by Fred Karno and at the Keystone studio around 1915, and most silent comedians relied heavily on them. In the 30s Mack Sennett staged a splendid one for a nostalgic farce called *Keystone Hotel*. Other notable pie fighters have included Laurel and Hardy in *The Battle of the Century* 28; the whole cast of *Beach Party* 63; and most of the cast of *The Great Race* 64 and *Smashing Time* 65.

Custer, Bob (1898–1974) (Raymond Anthony Glenn).

American leading actor in westerns, a former engineer and cowboy.

Trigger Finger 24. The Dude Cowboy 26. Cactus Trails 27. Arizona Days 29. Riders of the Rio Grande 29. Code of the West 30. Riders of the North 31. Under Texas Skies 31. Mark of the Spur 32. The Law of the Wild (serial) 34. Ambush Valley 36, many others.

Custer, George Armstrong (1839–1876).

American major-general whose romantic eccentricities and foolish death at Little Big Horn have been favourite screen fodder. The screen Custers include Dustin Farnum in *Flaming Frontier* 26, Frank McGlynn in *Custer's Last Stand* 36, Ronald Reagan in *Santa Fe Trail* 40, Addison Richards in *Badlands of Dakota* 41, Errol Flynn in the large-scale Custer biopic *They Died with Their Boots On* 41, James Millican in *Warpath* 51, Sheb Wooley in *Bugles in the Afternoon* 52, Britt Lomond in *Tonka* 58, Phil Carey in *The Great Sioux Massacre*

65, Robert Shaw in *Custer of the West* 67, Leslie Nielsen in *The Plainsman* (TV) and Richard Mulligan in *Little Big Man* 70. There has also been a TV series, *The Legend of Custer*, with Wayne Maunder.

cut.

Noun: abrupt transition from one shot to another, the first being instantaneously replaced by the second (as opposed to a wipe or a dissolve). Verb: to edit a film, or (during production) to stop the camera running on a scene.

cutaway.

An intervening shot allowing an editor to change the focus of action, e.g. clouds or a clock face.

Cuthbertson, Allan (1920–1988).

Australian actor in Britain, adept at supercilious roles.

Carrington VC 55. Law and Disorder 57. *Room at the Top* 58. Tunes of Glory 60. Term of Trial 62. The Informers 63. The Seventh Dawn 64. Life at the Top 65. Press for Time 66. The Winds of War (TV) 83, many others.

cutting copy.

The first print assembled from the 'rushes'. When this is deemed satisfactory, the negative will be cut to match it, and release prints made.

Cutts, Graham (1885–1958).

British director, eminent in silent days.

Flames of Passion 24. Woman to Woman 26. The Rat 27. The Sign of Four 32. Aren't Men Beasts? 37. Just William 39, etc.

Cutts, Patricia (1926–1974).

British child actress and leading lady. Daughter of Graham Cutts.

Self Made Lady 31. Just William's Luck 49. Your Witness 50. The Man Who Loved Redheads 55. Merry Andrew 58. The Tingler (US) 58. Private Road 71, etc.

Cybulski, Zbigniew (1927–1967).

Polish leading actor.

■ A Generation 54. Ashes and Diamonds 58. The Eighth Day of the Week 59. Pociag 59. He, She or It 62. Love at Twenty 62. Silence 63. How to be Loved 63. To Love 64. Salto 65. *The Saragossa Manuscript* 65. Jowita 67.

~Wajda's *Everything for Sale* was inspired by his accidental death.

cyclorama.

A smooth, curved giant screen at the back of the set, cunningly lit to give the impression of daylight.

Czechoslovakian

films were almost unknown in Western countries until recently, when the gentle realistic comedies of Milos Forman (*Peter and Pavla, A Blond in Love*) began winning festival prizes. Other notable Czech films include Pavel Juráček's *Josef Kilian*, Jan Kádar and Elmar Klos's *The Shop on the High Street*, and Jan Nemec's *Diamonds of the Night* and Jiři Menzel's *Capricious Summer*.

Czinner, Paul (1890–1972).

Hungarian producer-director, long in Britain: husband of Elisabeth Bergner. From 1955 he concentrated on films of opera and ballet, using multiple cameras.

Der Traumende Mund 32. Catherine the Great 33. Escape Me Never 35. As You Like It 36. Dreaming Lips 37. Stolen Life 39. The Bolshoi Ballet 55. The Royal Ballet 59. Der Rosenkavalier 61. Romeo and Juliet 66, etc.

D

Da Costa, Morton (1914–1989) (Morton
Tecosky).
American director of stage musicals and three
films.
■ Auntie Mame 58. *The Music Man* 62. Island of
Love 64.

Da Silva, Howard (1909–1986) (Harold
Silverblatt).
Tough, suspicious-looking American character
actor with stage experience. Graduated from bit
parts to a peak in the late 40s, then had McCarthy
trouble.
Abe Lincoln in Illinois 39. The Sea Wolf 41. The
Big Shot 43. *The Lost Weekend* 45. The Blue Dahlia
46. Blaze of Noon 47. Unconquered 47. They Live
by Night 48. The Great Gatsby 49. Three
Husbands 50. Fourteen Hours 51. M 51. David and
Lisa 62. The Outrage 65. Nevada Smith 66.' '1776'
72. The Great Gatsby 74. Mommie Dearest (as
Louis B. Mayer) 81, etc.

Dade, Frances (1910–1968).
Blonde American leading actress of the early 30s,
on stage from the age of 16.
Grumpy 30. Dracula 31. Seed 31. Mother's
Millions 31. Pleasure 31. The She-Wolf 31.
Daughter of the Dragon 31, etc.

Dade, Stephen (1909–   ).
British cinematographer, in films from 1927.
We'll Meet Again 42. Caravan 46. The Brothers
47. Snowbound 49. A Question of Adultery 57.
Bluebeard's Ten Honeymoons 60. Zulu 64. City
under the Sea 65. The Viking Queen 66, many
others.

Dafoe, Willem (1955–   ).
American leading actor with powerful presence,
from experimental and off-Broadway theatre.
Heaven's Gate 80. The Loveless 81. New York
Nights 82. The Hunger 83. Streets of Fire 84.
Roadhouse 66 84. To Live and Die in L.A. 85.
Platoon (AAN) 86. The Hitchhiker I (TV) 87. Off
Limits (aka Saigon) 88. The Last Temptation of
Christ 88. Mississippi Burning 88. Born on the
Fourth of July 89. Triumph of the Spirit 89. Cry-
Baby 90. Wild at Heart 90. Flight of the Intruder
91. Light Sleeper 91. White Sands 92. Faraway, So
Close! (In Weiter Ferne, So Nah) 93. Body of
Evidence 93. Tom and Viv 94. The Night and the
Moment 94, etc.

Daffy Duck.
Witty, manic duck who was a star of Warner
Looney Tunes and Merrie Melodies cartoons from
1937 and evolved into a mischief-making foil to
Bugs Bunny and Porky Pig. He is said to have been
modelled on Harpo Marx, although he was far
more loquacious and developed a spluttering
speech impediment in the 50s. He was voiced by
Mel Blanc.
Porky's Duck Hunt 37. The Daffy Doc 38. A Coy
Decoy 41. To Duck or Not to Duck 43. The Stupid
Cupid 44. Ain't That Ducky 45. Birth of a Notion
47. Wise Quackers 49. Rabbit Fire 51. Rabbit

Seasoning 52. Duck Dodgers in the 24½th Century
53. A Star Is Bored 56. Robin Hood Daffy 58. The
Abominable Snow-Rabbit 61. The Iceman
Ducketh 64. Moby Duck 65. Daffy's Diner 67. The
Duckorcist 87. Night of the Living Duck 88, etc.

D'Agostino, Albert S. (1893–1970).
American art director, in Hollywood from early
silent days; with RKO 1936–58.
The Raven 35. Mr and Mrs Smith 41. The
Enchanted Cottage 44. Notorious 46. The Woman
on the Beach 47. Mourning Becomes Electra 48.
Clash by Night 51. Androcles and the Lion 53.
Back from Eternity 56, many others.

Dagover, Lil (1897–1980) (Marta Maria Liletts).
Distinguished German actress.
The Cabinet of Dr Caligari 19. Destiny 21. Dr
Mabuse Der Spieler 22. Chronicles of the Grey
House 24. Tartuffe 26. Hungarian Rhapsody 27.
The White Devil 30. Congress Dances 31. Kreuzer
Sonata 35. Fredericus 39. Die Fussganger 73, Karl
May 74, etc.

Daguerre, Louis (1787–1851).
French pioneer of photography; his original
copper-plated prints were known as *daguerrotypes*.

Dahl, Arlene (1924–   ).
Red-haired American leading lady, former model;
also beauty columnist.
■ Life with Father 47. *My Wild Irish Rose* 47. The
Bride Goes Wild 48. A Southern Yankee 48. Reign
of Terror 49. Scene of the Crime 49. Ambush 49.
The Outriders 50. Three Little Words 50. Watch
the Birdie 50. Inside Straight 51. No Questions
Asked 51. Caribbean 52. Jamaica Run 53. Desert
Legion 53. Sangaree 53. The Diamond Queen 53.
Here Come the Girls 54. Woman's World 54.
Bengal Brigade 54. Slightly Scarlet 56. Wicked as
They Come (GB) 56. Fortune is a Woman (GB)
57. *Journey to the Centre of the Earth* 59. Kisses for
My President 64. The Land Raiders 69. The Road
to Khatmandu 69.
TV series: One Life to Live 82. Night of the
Warrior 91.

¶ With enthusiasm anything is possible. – *A.D.*
I considered the years in Hollywood nothing
but an interim. What I always wanted was to be a
musical comedy star. – *A.D.*

Dahl, John.
American director and screenwriter.
Kill Me Again (wd) 89. Red Rock West (wd) 93.
The Last Seduction (d) 94.

¶ Film noir is endlessly fascinating to me. I'm a
movie buff, and I like to make films that movie
fans like. – *J.D.*
It's only in the last thirty years that we've had
all these Hollywood movies where they desperately
want you to fall in love with the main character.
I mean, who in a Shakespearean play did you
ever want to take home and have dinner with?

They were brooding, upset, frustrated, twisted,
neurotic people. – *J.D.*

Dahl, Roald (1916–1990).
Norwegian writer of British adoption; switched
from children's books to macabre short stories. He
was married to actress Patricia Neal (1953–83).
You Only Live Twice 67. Chitty Chitty Bang
Bang 69. Willy Wonka and the Chocolate Factory
70. Danny the Champion of the World (oa) 89.
The Witches (oa) 90, etc.
TV series (which he also introduced): *Roald
Dahl's Tales of the Unexpected* 79.

Dahlbeck, Eva (1920–   ).
Swedish actress, often in Ingmar Bergman's films.
Waiting Women 52. The Village (GB) 53. Smiles
of a Summer Night 55. So Close to Life 61. Now
About These Women 64. Loving Couples 64.
Les Creatures 65. The Red Mantle 67. People
Meet 69, etc.

Dailey, Dan (1914–1978).
Lanky American actor-dancer with wide
experience in vaudeville and cabaret.
The Mortal Storm 40. Duley 40. Ziegfeld Girl 41.
Moon over Her Shoulder 41. Lady Be Good 41.
Panama Hattie 42. Give Out Sisters 42. *Mother Wore
Tights* 47. *Give My Regards to Broadway* 48. You
Were Meant for Me 48. When My Baby Smiles at
Me (AAN) 48. Chicken Every Sunday 49. My Blue
Heaven 50. *When Willie Comes Marching Home* 50.
A Ticket to Tomahawk 50. I Can Get It for You
Wholesale 51. Call Me Mister 51. Pride of St Louis
51. What Price Glory? 52. Meet Me at The Fair 53.
There's No Business Like Show Business 54. *It's
Always Fair Weather* 55. Meet Me in Las Vegas 56.
The Best Things in Life are Free 56. The Wings of
Eagles 56. Oh Men, Oh Women 57. The Wayward
Bus 57. Pepe 60. Hemingway's Adventures of a
Young Man 62. The Private Files of J. Edgar Hoover
77, many others.
TV series: The Four Just Men 59. The Governor
and J.J. 69. Faraday and Company 73.

dailies:
see *rushes*.

Dainton, Patricia (1930–   ).
British leading lady who started as a teenager.
Don't Ever Leave Me 49. The Dancing Years 50.
Castle in the Air 52. Operation Diplomat 54. The
Passing Stranger 57. Witness in the Dark 60, etc.

Dalby, Amy (1888–1969).
British character actress who normally on screen
played ageing spinsters.
The Wicked Lady 45. The Man Upstairs 57. The
Lamp in Assassin Mews 62. *The Secret of My Success*
65. Who Killed the Cat? 66. The Spy with a Cold
Nose 67, etc.

Dale, Charles (1881–1971) (Charles Marks).
American vaudevillian who, with Joe Smith
(c. 1884–1981), made up Smith and Dale, the
inspiration for *The Sunshine Boys*.

■ Manhattan Parade 31. The Heart of New York 32. Two Tickets to Broadway 51.

Dale, Esther (1885–1961).
American character actress usually a motherly soul, nurse or grandma.

Crime without Passion 34. Curly Top 35. Fury 36. Dead End 37. Prison Farm 38. Tell No Tales 39. The Mortal Storm 40. Back Street 41. North Star 43. Margie 44. Stolen Life 46. The Egg and I 47. Ma and Pa Kettle 49. No Man of Her Own 50. Ma and Pa Kettle at the Fair 52. The Oklahoman 57, many others.

Dale, Jim (1935–) (James Smith).
British pop singer turned light comedian and member of the 'Carry On' team. Nominated for an Oscar for writing the lyrics to the title tune for *Georgy Girl* 64.

Raising the Wind 62. Carry On Spying 64. Carry On Cleo 65. The Big Job 65. Carry On Cowboy 66. Carry On Screaming 66. Lock Up Your Daughters 69. *The National Health* 73. Digby 73. Joseph Andrews 77. *Pete's Dragon* 77. Bloodshy 79. The Spaceman and King Arthur 79. Scandalous 84. Adventures of Huckleberry Finn 85. Carry On Columbus 92, etc.

Dalen, Zale (1947–).
Canadian director, born in the Philippines.
Skip Tracer 77. Hounds of Nôtre Dame 80. Hollywood North 87. Terminal City Ricochet 90, etc.

Daley, Cass (1915–1975) (Catherine Dailey).
American comedienne whose shouted songs and acrobatic contortions were a feature of several light musicals of the 40s.

The Fleet's In 41. Star Spangled Rhythm 42. Crazy House 43. Out of This World 45. Ladies' Man 46. Here Comes the Groom 51. Red Garters 54. The Spirit Is Willing 67, etc.

Dali, Salvador (1904–1989).
Spanish surrealist painter who collaborated with Luis Buñuel in making two controversial films: *Un Chien Andalou* 29 and *L'Age d'Or* 30. Later designed the dream sequence for *Spellbound* 45.

Dalio, Marcel (1900–1983) (Israel Mosche Blauschild).
Dapper French comedy actor, frequently in Hollywood.

La Grande Illusion 37. Pepe le Moko 37. *La Règle du Jeu* 39. Unholy Partners 41. Casablanca 42. The Song of Bernadette 43. Temptation Harbour (GB) 46. On the Riviera 51. *The Happy Time* 52. The Snows of Kilimanjaro 52. Lucky Me 54. Sabrina Fair 54. Miracle in the Rain 56. Pillow Talk 59. Can Can 59. Jessica 62. Wild and Wonderful 63. Lady L 65. The 25th Hour 67. How Sweet It Is 68. Catch 22 70. The Mad Adventures of Rabbi Jacob 73. L'Ombre de Château 76. Brigade Mondaine 80, many others.

Dall, Evelyn (c. 1914–).
American nightclub singer who appeared in some British film extravaganzas of the 40s.

He Found a Star 41. King Arthur Was a Gentleman 42. Miss London Ltd 43. Time Flies 44, etc.

Dall, John (1918–1971).
American stage leading man; played in occasional films.
■ For the Love of Mary 45. *The Corn Is Green* (AAN). Something in the Wind 47. *Rope* 48. Another Part of the Forest 48. Gun Crazy 49. The

Man Who Cheated Himself 50. Spartacus 60. Atlantis the Lost Continent 61.

Dalle, Béatrice (1965–).
French leading actress.
Betty Blue 86. Charlie Spencer 86. The Witches' Sabbath (La Visione del Sabba) 88. Les Bois Noirs 89. Chimère 89. The Beautiful Story (La Belle Histoire) 91. Night on Earth 91. La Fille de l'Air 92. I Can't Sleep (J'ai Pas Sommeil) 94. Six Days Six Nights (A la Folie) 94, etc.

Dallesandro, Joe (1948–).
American actor who gained fame as the object of desire in Andy Warhol's films.

The Loves of Ondine 67. Flesh 68. Lonesome Cowboys 68. Trash 70. Heat 72. Andy Warhol's Frankenstein 73. Blood for Dracula 74. The Gardener 74. Black Moon 75. Seeds of Evil 76. Merry Go Round 83. The Cotton Club 84. Critical Condition 87. Sunset 88. Private War 89. The Hollywood Detective (TV) 89. Cry-Baby 90. Double Revenge 90. Wild Orchid II: Two Shades of Blue 92. Sugar Hill 93, etc.

¶ I don't know whether I'll ever become a household name in America, but my big thing is to land that television series that goes 50 episodes and you sit at home and collect the cheques. – *J.D. in 1993*

D'Almeida, Neville (1941–).
Brazilian director who spent some time studying film in the United States.

Jardin de Guerra 70. Lady on the Bus (A Dama de Lotaçao 78. Rio Babilonia 82, etc.

Dalrymple, Ian (1903–1989).
British writer-producer.

South Riding (w only) 38. The Citadel (w only) 38. The Lion Has Wings 39. Once a Jolly Swagman 46. The Woman in the Hall 48. The Wooden Horse 50. The Heart of the Matter 52. Three Cases of Murder 55. The Admirable Crichton 57. A Cry from the Streets 58. Mix Me a Person 62. Calamity the Cow 67, etc.

Dalton, Abby (1932–).
American actress, a former model who first appeared in low-budget teen movies in the late 50s.

Viking Woman and the Sea Serpent 57. Rock All Night 57. Stakeout on Dope Street 58. Cole Younger, Gunfighter 58. Girls on the Loose 58. The Plainsman 66. A Whale of a Tale 76, etc.

TV series: Hennesey 59–62. The Joey Bishop Show 62–65. Falcon Crest 81–86.

Dalton, Audrey (1934–).
British leading lady in Hollywood.

My Cousin Rachel 52. The Girls of Pleasure Island 53. Titanic 53. Casanova's Big Night 54. The Prodigal 55. Separate Tables 58. Mr Sardonicus 62. The Bounty Killer 65, etc.

Dalton, Dorothy (1894–1972).
American silent screen leading lady with stage experience.

The Disciple 14. Black is White 20. Moran of the Lady Letty 22. The Crimson Challenge 22. Fogbound 23. The Moral Sinner 24. The Lone Wolf 24, etc.

Dalton, Timothy (1946–).
Saturnine British stage actor in occasional films.

The Lion in Winter 68. *Wuthering Heights* 70. Mary Queen of Scots 71. Lady Caroline Lamb 72. Sextette 78. Agatha 79. Flash Gordon 80. Chanel Solitaire 81. Mistral's Daughter (TV) 84. Florence

Nightingale (TV) 84. The Doctor and the Devils 85. Sins (TV) 85. *The Living Daylights* (as James Bond) 87. Hawks 88. Licence to Kill 89. Brenda Starr 90. The King's Whore 90. The Rocketeer 91. Naked in New York 93. Scarlett (TV) 94, etc.

Daltrey, Roger (1944–).
British rock singer, composer, actor and producer. The lead singer with The Who, he was given dramatic roles by Ken Russell.
■ Tommy 74. Lisztomania 75. The Legacy 79. McVicar 80. Murder: Ultimate Grounds for Divorce 85. Mack the Knife 89. Buddy's Song (& p, m) 90. Teen Agent 91. Lightning Jack 94.

¶ Of course, chicks keep popping up. When you're in a hotel, a pretty young lady makes life bearable. – *R.D.*

Daly, James (1918–1978).
American stage actor; film appearances rare.
■ The Court Martial of Billy Mitchell 55. The Young Stranger 57. I Aim at the Stars 60. Planet of the Apes 68. The Big Bounce 68. The Five Man Army 69. Wild in the Sky 72. The Resurrection of Zachary Wheeler 73.

TV series: Foreign Intrigue 53–54. *Medical Center* 69–76.

Daly, John (1937–).
British independent producer and distributor, who moved to America in the 80s. A former journalist and actor, and David Hemmings' manager, he founded Hemdale Film Corporation, of which he was chairman, in 1967 with Hemmings, who sold his interest four years later.

Melody 71. Where Does It Hurt? 71. Triple Echo 72. Images 72. The Amazing Mr Blunden 72. Cattle Annie and Little Britches 80. Race for the Yankee Zephyr 81. Carbon Copy 81. Yellowbeard 83. Terminator 84. Return of the Living Dead 85. Platoon (AA) 86. At Close Range 86. Salvador 86. Hoosiers 86. The Last Emperor (AA) 87. Buster 88. Miracle Mile 89. Out Cold 89. Chattahoochee 90. Hidden Agenda 90. Bright Angel 91, etc.

Daly, Mark (1887–1957).
British character actor, on stage from 1906, in films from 1930, often as cheerful tramp.

The Private Life of Henry VIII 32. A Cuckoo in the Nest 33. The Ghost Goes West 36. Wings of the Morning 37. Next of Kin 42. Bonnie Prince Charlie 49. Lease of Life 54. The Shiralee 57, many others.

Daly, Tyne (1946–).
American leading lady. She is the daughter of James Daly.

John and Mary 69. Angel Unchained 70. Heat of Anger (TV) 71. Play It as It Lays 72. The Entertainer (TV) 75. The Enforcer 76. Telefon 77. Speedtrap 77. The Women's Room (TV) 80. Zoot Suit 82. Your Place or Mine (TV) 83. Movers and Shakers 85. The Aviator 85, etc.

TV series: Cagney and Lacey 82.

D'Amato, Joe (1936–) (Aristide Massaccesi).
Prolific Italian director of quickie exploitation movies that reach international audiences on video-cassette. His output, made under such pseudonyms as Steve Benson, Michael Wotruba, David Hills and Kevin Mancuso, ranges from horror to fantasy and soft-core pornography, including a *Black Emanuelle* series in the 70s.

Heroes in Hell (Eroi all'Inferno) 67. Kneel Bastard (Inginocchiate) 72. Black Emanuelle (Emanuelle Nera) 73. Emanuelle and the Last Cannibals (Emanuelle e gli Ultimi Cannibali;

aka Trap Them and Kill Them) 77. Beyond the Darkness (Buio Omega) 79. Grim Reaper (Anthropophagus) 81. Ator the Fighting Eagle (Ator I'Invincible) 82. Ator the Invincible – the Return (aka Blade Master) 83. 2020 Texas Gladiators (Texas 2000) 84. Buried Alive 84. Quest for the Mighty Sword 90. Return from Death 91. Love Appurtenance 92, many others.

¶ I like to manipulate intestines, pieces of meat, vital organs. Is there a limit? Not at all! – J. D'A.
There's little doubt that sitting through one of Joe's efforts is as near to brain death as a film viewer can get. – Stefan Jaworzyn, Shock Xpress

Damiani, Damiano (1922–).
Italian director.
The Empty Canvas 64. A Bullet for the General 66. Confessions of a Police Captain 71. The Tempter 74. The Genius 75. I Am Afraid 77. Goodbye and Amen 78. L'Ultimo Nome 79. Time of Jackals 80. Amityville II: The Possession 82. Attaco alla Poivra 85. The Inquiry (L'Inchiesta) 87. Massacre Play (Gioco al Massacro) (& co-w) 89. Angel of Death (L'Angelo con la Pistola) 92, etc.

Damiano, Gerald.
American director of hard-core porn movies.
Deep Throat 73. The Devil in Miss Jones 73. The Story of Joanna 75. Let My Puppets Come 77. Throat – 12 Years After 84, etc.

Damita, Lili (1901–1994) (Lilliane Carré).
French leading lady who made a few American films and married Errol Flynn (1935–42). Her death certificate gave her age as 85.
The Rescue 28. The Bridge of San Luis Rey 29. The Cockeyed World 29. The Match King 31. This Is the Night 32. Goldie Gets Along 33. The Frisco Kid 35. L'Escadrille de la Chance (Fr.) 36, etc.

Damon, Cathryn (1933–1987).
American comedy actress who played the slightly more sensible sister in TV's Soap.
Friendships, Secrets and Lies (TV) 80. How to Beat The High Cost of Living 80.

Damon, Mark (1933–) (Alan Mark Harris).
American leading man in routine films, now a producer in Europe.
Between Heaven and Hell 56. The Fall of the House of Usher 60. The Young Racers 63. Anzio 68. There Is No Thirteen 77. The Choirboys (co-p only) 77, etc.

Damone, Vic (1928–) (Vito Farinola).
American light leading man and singer. He was married to actress Pia Angeli (1955–59) and married singer Diahann Carroll in 1987.
Rich, Young and Pretty 51. The Strip 51. Athena 53. Deep in My Heart 55. Kismet 55. Hell to Eternity 60, etc.

Dampier, Claude (1879–1955) (Claude Cowan).
British comedian noted for nasal drawl and country yokel characterization. Long on stage and music hall.
Biography: 1978, Claude Dampier, Mrs Gibson and Me by Billie Carlyle (his wife and partner on the halls).
Boys Will Be Boys 35. Mr Stringfellow Says No 37. Riding High 39. Don't Take It to Heart 44. Meet Mr Malcolm 53, etc.

Damski, Mel (1946–).
American director, working mainly in television.

Yellowbeard 83. Mischief 85. Happy Together 90.

Dana, Bill (1924–).
American television comedian who used to play Mexicans.
Rossetti and Ryan (TV) 77. A Guide for the Married Woman 78. The Hungry Reunion 81. Lena's Holiday 91, etc.
TV series: The Bill Dana Show 62–65. No Soap Radio 82. Zorro and Son 83.

Dana, Leora (1923–1983).
American general purpose actress.
Three-Ten to Yuma 57. Kings Go Forth 58. Some Came Running 58. Pollyanna 60. A Gathering of Eagles 63. Shoot the Moon 82, etc.

Dana, Viola (1897–1987) (Violet Flugrath).
American silent screen actress, usually in light comedy and fashionable drama.
Molly the Drummer Boy 14. Rosie O'Grady 17. A Chorus Girl's Romance 20. The Willow Tree 20. Open All Night 24. Merton of the Movies 24. Winds of Chance 25. Kosher Kitty Kelly 26. The Sisters 29, etc.

dance bands.
in the 30s and 40s were so popular as to be stars in their own films: Henry Hall's in Music Hath Charms, Kay Kyser's in half a dozen films including That's Right You're Wrong, Paul Whiteman's in King of Jazz, Tommy and Jimmy Dorsey's in The Fabulous Dorseys. Also frequently on hand to assist the stars were the bands of Glenn Miller, Xavier Cugat, Woody Herman and Harry James, to name but a few. In the 50s bands became too expensive to maintain, but The Glenn Miller Story and The Benny Goodman Story reawakened interest.

Dance, Charles (1946–).
British leading actor.
■ Saigon (TV) 83. The Jewel in the Crown (TV) 84. For Your Eyes Only 84. Plenty 86. Good Morning Babylon 86. Out on a Limb (TV) 87. The Golden Child 87. Hidden City 87. White Mischief 87. Pascali's Island 88. Alien 3 92. The Last Action Hero 93. Century 93. China Moon 94. Nanook (Kablooak) 94. Shortcut to Paradise (Sp.) 94.

Dandridge, Dorothy (1923–1965).
American leading lady, former child actress. Died of a drug overdose.
A Day at the Races 37. Lady from Louisiana 41. Drums of the Congo 42. Bright Road 52. Carmen Jones (AAN) 54. Island in the Sun 57. The Decks Ran Red 58. Porgy and Bess 59. Tamango 59. Moment of Danger 60, etc.

Dane, Karl (1886–1934) (Karl Daen).
Lanky Danish character actor who almost accidentally became a popular comedian at the end of the silent period, but could not survive sound. Committed suicide.
Lights of Old Broadway 25. The Big Parade 25. The Scarlet Letter 26. The Red Mill 27. Rookies 27. Baby Mine 28. Circus Rookies 28. Alias Jimmy Valentine 28. Speedway 29. Montana Moon 30. The Big House 30. Billy the Kid 30, etc.

Daneman, Paul (1925–).
British light leading man, mainly on stage.
The Clue of the New Pin 61. Zulu 64. How I Won the War 67. Oh What a Lovely War 69, etc.
TV series: Spy Trap.

D'Angelo, Beverly (1953–).
American leading lady.

Every Which Way but Loose 78. Hair 79. Coal Miner's Daughter 80. Paternity 81. Honky Tonk Freeway 81. The Woo Woo Kid 87. Trading Hearts 88. High Spirits 88. Cold Front 89. National Lampoon's Christmas Vacation 89. Pacific Heights 90. Daddy's Dyin', Who's Got the Will? 90. The Miracle 90. The Pope Must Die (US: The Pope Must Diet) 91. Lonely Hearts 91. Man Trouble 92. Lightning Jack 94. Menendez: A Killing in Beverly Hills (TV) 94, etc.

Dangerfield, Rodney (1921–) (Jacob Cohen).
American comedian and screenwriter.
The Projectionist 71. Caddyshack 80. Easy Money (& w) 83. Back to School (& story) 86. Moving 88. Rover Dangerfield 91. Ladybugs 92. Natural Born Killers 94, etc.

Daniel, Rod.
American director.
Teen Wolf 85. Stranded (TV) 86. Like Father Like Son 87. K-9 89. The Super 91. Ace Ventura: Pet Detective 92. Beethoven's 2nd 93, etc.

Daniell, Henry (1894–1963).
Incisive, cold-eyed British stage actor, a popular Hollywood villain of the 30s and 40s.
■ Jealousy 29. The Awful Truth 29. The Last of the Lone Wolf 30. Path of Glory 34. The Unguarded Hour 36. Camille 36. Under Cover of Night 37. The Thirteenth Chair 37. The Firefly 37. Madame X 37. Holiday 38. Marie Antoinette 38. The Private Lives of Elizabeth and Essex 39. We Are Not Alone 39. All This and Heaven Too 40. The Sea Hawk 40. The Great Dictator 40. The Philadelphia Story 40. A Woman's Face 41. Dressed to Kill 41. Four Jacks and a Jill 41. The Feminine Touch 41. Castle in the Desert 42. Random Harvest 42. Sherlock Holmes and the Voice of Terror 42. Reunion in France 42. The Great Impersonation 42. Nightmare 42. Mission to Moscow 43. Sherlock Holmes in Washington 43. Watch on the Rhine 43. Jane Eyre 43. The Suspect 44. The Chicago Kid 45. Hotel Berlin 45. The Woman in Green 45. The Body Snatcher 45. Captain Kidd 45. The Bandit of Sherwood Forest 46. Song of Love 47. The Exile 47. Siren of Atlantis 48. Wake of the Red Witch 48. The Secret of St Ives 49. Buccaneer's Girl 50. The Egyptian 54. The Prodigal 55. Diane 55. The Man in the Grey Flannel Suit 56. Lust for Life 56. Les Girls 57. The Story of Mankind 57. The Sun Also Rises 57. Witness for the Prosecution 57. Mr Cory 57. From the Earth to the Moon 58. The Four Skulls of Jonathan Drake 59. Voyage to the Bottom of the Sea 61. The Comancheros 61. Madison Avenue 62. The Notorious Landlady 62. Five Weeks in a Balloon 62. The Chapman Report 62. My Fair Lady 64.

Famous Line (The Philadelphia Story): 'I understand we understand each other.'

Daniels, Bebe (1901–1971) (Virginia Daniels).
American leading lady of the silent screen. Film debut at seven; played opposite Harold Lloyd and became a popular star; later married Ben Lyon, moved to Britain and appeared with their family on radio and TV.
Male and Female 19. Why Change Your Wife? 20. The Affairs of Anatol 21. Pink Gods 22. Unguarded Women 24. Monsieur Beaucaire 24. Campus Flirt 26. She's a Sheik 27. Rio Rita 29. Alias French Gertie 30. Reaching for the Moon 30. The Maltese Falcon 31. Forty-Second Street 33. Counsellor at Law 33. The Return of Carol Deane 35. Hi Gang (GB) 40. Life with the Lyons (GB) 53. The Lyons in Paris (GB) 55, etc.

Daniels, Jeff (1955–).
Clean-cut American leading actor.
Ragtime 81. Terms of Endearment 83. The Purple Rose of Cairo 85. Something Wild 86. Radio Days 87. The House on Carroll Street 88. Love Hurts 89. Arachnophobia 90. Welcome Home, Roxy Carmichael 91. The Butcher's Wife 91. There Goes the Neighborhood (aka Paydirt) 92. Gettysburg 93. Speed 94, etc.

Daniels, Mickey (1914–1970).
American actor, one of the original kids in the Our Gang comedies of the 20s. He retired in the early 40s to work as an engineer.
This Day and Age 33. Magnificent Obsession 35. The Great Ziegfeld 36, etc.

Daniels, William (1895–1970).
Distinguished American cinematographer, associated with the films of Greta Garbo.
■ Foolish Wives 21. Merry Go Round (co-ph) 23. Helen's Babies (co-ph) 24. *Greed* (co-ph) 25. Women and Gold 25. The Merry Widow (co-ph) 25. Bardelys the Magnificent 26. The Boob 26. Dance Madness (co-ph) 26. *Flesh and the Devil* 26. Money Talks 26. Monte Carlo 26. The Temptress (co-ph) 26. The Torrent 26. Altars of Desire 27. Captain Salvation 27. Love 27. On Ze Boulevard 27. Tillie the Toiler 27. The Actress 28. Bringing Up Father 28. Dream of Love 28. Lady of Chance 28. The Latest from Paris 28. The Mysterious Lady 28. Sally's Shoulders 28. A Woman of Affairs 28. *The Kiss* 29. The Last of Mrs Cheyney 29. Their Own Desire 29. The Trial of Mary Dugan 29. Wild Orchids 29. Wise Girls 29. Anna Christie 30. Montana Moon 30. Romance 30. Strictly Unconventional 30. Strangers May Kiss 31. The Great Meadow 31. Inspiration 31. A Free Soul 31. Susan Lenox 31. *Mata Hari* 32. Lovers Courageous 32. Grand Hotel 32. As You Desire Me 32. Skyscraper Souls 32. Rasputin and the Empress 33. The White Sister 33. Dinner at Eight 33. The Stranger's Return 33. Broadway to Hollywood 33. Christopher Bean 33. *Queen Christina* 33. The Barretts of Wimpole Street 34. The Painted Veil 34. Naughty Marietta 35. *Anna Karenina* 35. Rendezvous 35. Rose Marie 36. Romeo and Juliet 36. *Camille* 36. Personal Property 37. Broadway Melody of 1938 37. Double Wedding 37. The Last Gangster 37. Beg Borrow or Steal 37. Marie Antoinette 38. Three Loves Has Nancy 38. Dramatic School 38. Idiot's Delight 39. Stronger Than Desire 39. Ninotchka 39. Another Thin Man 39. The Shop Around the Corner 40. The Mortal Storm 40. New Moon 40. So Ends Our Night 41. Back Street 41. They Met in Bombay 41. Shadow of the Thin Man 41. Dr Kildare's Victory 41. *Keeper of the Flame* 42. Girl Crazy 42. Brute Force 47. Lured 47. *The Naked City* (AA) 48. For the Love of Mary 48. Family Honeymoon 48. The Life of Riley 49. Illegal Entry 49. Abandoned 49. The Gal who Took the West 49. Woman in Hiding 49. Winchester 73 50. Harvey 50. Deported 50. Thunder on the Hill 51. Bright Victory 51. The Lady Pays Off 51. When in Rome 52. Pat and Mike 52. Glory Alley 52. Plymouth Adventure 52. Never Wave at a WAC 53. Forbidden 53. Thunder Bay 53. *The Glenn Miller Story* 53. War Arrow 54. The Far Country 54. Six Bridges to Cross 55. Foxfire 55. The Shrike 55. Strategic Air Command 55. The Girl Rush 55. The Benny Goodman Story 55. Away All Boats (co-ph) 56. The Unguarded Moment 56. Istanbul 56. Night Passage 57. Interlude 57. My Man Godfrey 57. Voice in the Mirror 57. Cat on a Hot Tin Roof 58. Some Came Running 59. Stranger in My Arms 59. A Hole in the Head 60. Never So Few 60. Can Can 60. Ocean's Eleven 60. All the Fine Young Cannibals 60. Come September 61. Jumbo 62.

How the West was Won (co-ph) 63. Come Blow Your Horn 63. The Prize 63. Robin and the Seven Hoods (& p) 64. Von Ryan's Express 65. Marriage on the Rocks 65. Assault on a Queen (& p) 66. In Like Flint 67. Valley of the Dolls 67. The Impossible Years 68. Marlowe 68. The Maltese Bippy 69. Move 70.

¶ We try to tell the story with light, and the director tells it with action. – W.D.

Daniels, William (1927–).
Dapper American stage actor who came to films and TV in mid-career.
Family Honeymoon 49. A Thousand Clowns 65. The President's Analyst 67. *The Graduate* 67. Two for the Road 67. Marlowe 69. 1776 (as John Adams) 72. The Parallax View 74. Black Sunday 77. The One and Only 78. Sunburn 79. The Blue Lagoon 80. All Night Long 81. Reds 81. Blind Date 87. Her Alibi 89, many others.
TV series: *Captain Nice* 66. The Nancy Walker Show 76. Freebie and the Bean 80. *St Elsewhere* 82.

Daniely, Lisa (1930–).
Anglo-French leading lady.
Lili Marlene 50. Hindle Wakes 51. The Wedding of Lili Marlene 53. Tiger by the Tail 55. The Vicious Circle 57. An Honourable Murder 60. The Lamp in Assassin Mews 62, etc.

Danischewsky, Monja (1911–1994).
Russian writer-producer, in Britain since 20s. Publicist and writer for Ealing 1938–48. Produced *Whisky Galore* 48. *The Galloping Major* 50. *The Battle of the Sexes* 61, etc. Screenplays, *Topkapi* 64. *Mister Moses* 65.
Autobiography: 1966, *White Russian, Red Face*. 1972, *Out of My Mind*.

Danish cinema.
was one of the first to start production. Nordisk studios were founded in 1906 and from 1910 to 1915 Danish films were as internationally popular as those of any country in the world. But the talent was all drained away, first by the merger with Germany's UFA studios in 1917 and later by a steady trek to Hollywood. Carl Dreyer, one of the wanderers, later returned to Denmark and made there such major films as *Day of Wrath* and *Order;* but no Danish school ever emerged again. In recent years some Danish directors have gained international recognition, notably Bille August with *Pelle the Conqueror*, Gabriel Axel with *Babette's Feast* – both Oscar winners for the best foreign film in consecutive years – and Lars von Trier with *Europa*.

Dankworth, John (1927–).
British bandleader who has written scores.
The Criminal 60. Saturday Night and Sunday Morning 60. The Servant 64. Return from the Ashes 65. Accident 67. The Last Grenade 69. Ten Rillington Place 70. Loser Take All 89, etc.

Danner, Blythe (1944–).
American young actress of the 70s.
■ Dr Cook's Garden (TV) 70. 1776 72. To Kill a Clown 72. Lovin' Molly 74. The Last of the Belles (TV) 74. Sidekicks (TV) 74. Hearts of the West 75. Futureworld 76. A Love Affair: The Eleanor and Lou Gehrig Story (TV) 78. Are You in the House Alone? (TV) 78. *Too Far to Go* (TV) 79. The Great Santini 80. Man, Woman and Child 83. Brighton Beach Memoirs 86. One Art 87. Another Woman 88. Alice 90. Mr & Mrs Bridge 90. The Prince of Tides 91. Husbands and Wives 92. Oldest Living Confederate Widow Tells All (TV) 94.

TV series: Adam's Rib 73.

Danning, Sybil (1950–).
Blonde Austrian actress, in glamorous roles in forgettable films.
Swedish Love Games (Urlaubsreport) 71. Bluebeard 72. The Three Musketeers 73. The Four Musketeers 74. The Prince and the Pauper 77. Meteor 79. Battle beyond the Stars 80. The Salamander 81. Jungle Warriors 84. The Seven Magnificent Gladiators 85. Howling II . . . Your Sister Is a Werewolf 86. Private Property (aka Young Lady Chatterley II) 86. Reform School Girls 86. The Tomb 86. Warrior Queen 87. Amazon Women on the Moon 87, etc.

¶ What I am is the new dream girl – one who has both body and intelligence. – S.D.

Dano, Royal (1922–1994).
American general-purpose supporting actor.
■ Undercover Girl 49. Under the Gun 50. *The Red Badge of Courage* (as The Tattered Man) 51. Flame of Araby 51. Bend of the River 52. Johnny Guitar 54. The Far Country 55. The Trouble with Harry 55. Tribute to a Bad Man 55. Santiago 56. Moby Dick 56. Tension at Table Rock 56. Crime of Passion 57. Trooper Hook 57. All Mine to Give 57. Man in the Shadow 57. Saddle the Wind 57. Handle with Care 58. Man of the West 58. Never Steal Anything Small 59. These Thousand Hills 59. Hound Dog Man 59. Face of Fire 59. Huckleberry Finn 60. Cimarron 60. Posse from Hell 61. King of Kings 61. Savage Sam 61. Seven Faces of Dr Lao 64. Gunpoint 66. The Dangerous Days of Kiowa Jones (TV) 66. Welcome to Hard Times 67. The Last Challenge 67. Day of the Evil Gun 68. If He Hollers Let Him Go 68. The Undefeated 69. Backtrack (TV) 69. Run Simon Run (TV) 70. Moon of the Wolf (TV) 72. The Great Northfield Minnesota Raid 72. The Culpepper Cattle Company 72. Howzer 72. Ace Eli and Rodger of the Skies 73. Cahill 73. Electra Glide in Blue 73. Big Bad Mama 74. The Wild Party 75. Huckleberry Finn (TV) 75. Capone 75. Manhunter (TV) 76. Drum 76. Messiah of Evil 76. The Outlaw Josey Wales 76. The Killer Inside Me 76. Murder in Peyton Place (TV) 77. Donner Pass (TV) 78. Strangers (TV) 79. Take This Job and Shove It 81. Hammett 82. Something Wicked This Way Comes 83. The Right Stuff 83. Teachers 84. Red-Headed Stranger 86. Ghoulies II 88. Once Upon a Texas Train (aka Texas Guns) 88. Cocaine Wars 89. Spaced Invaders 90. The Dark Half 93.

Danova, Cesare (1926–1992).
Italian leading man, often in Hollywood.
The Captain's Daughter 47. The Three Corsairs 52. Don Juan 55. The Man Who Understood Women 59. Cleopatra 63. Viva Las Vegas 64. Chamber of Horrors 66. Che 69. Tentacles 77, etc.
TV series: Garrison's Gorillas 67.

Danson, Ted (1947–).
Tall, craggy American leading man.
The Onion Field 79. Body Heat 81. Creepshow 82. Something about Amelia (TV) 84. Little Treasure 85. Just between Friends 85. A Fine Mess 86. Three Men and a Baby 87. Cousins 89. Dad 89. Three Men and a Little Lady 90. Made in America 93. Getting Even with Dad 94. Pontiac Moon 94, etc.
TV series: Somerset 74–76. *Cheers* 82–93.

Dante, Joe (1946–).
American director, associated with Steven Spielberg. He is a former journalist who began his career cutting trailers for Roger Corman's movies.

Hollywood Boulevard (co-d) 76. Piranha 78. The Howling 80. Twilight Zone – the Movie (co-d) 83. *Gremlins* 84. Explorers 85. Amazon Women on the Moon (co-d) 87. Innerspace 87. The 'burbs 89. Gremlins II: The New Batch 90. Sleepwalkers (a) 92. *Matinee* 93, etc.

¶ We did all kinds of things in trailers to help sell films. We had a famous exploding helicopter shot from one of those Filipino productions that we'd cut in every time a trailer was too dull because that was always exciting. – *J.D.*

Dante, Michael (1935–) (Ralph Vitti).
American 'second lead' with a screen tendency to villainy.
Fort Dobbs 58. Westbound 59. Seven Thieves 60. Kid Galahad 62. The Naked Kiss 64. Harlow 65. The Farmer 77. Cruise Missile 78. Beyond Evil 80. The Big Score 83. Cage 89. Crazy Horse and Custer – the Untold Story 90, etc.

Dantine, Helmut (1917–1982).
Lean good-looking Austrian actor, in US from 1938. Latterly an executive with the Joseph M. Schenk organization.
International Squadron 41. *Mrs Miniver* 41. Passage to Marseilles 44. Hotel Berlin 45. Escape in the Desert 45. Northern Pursuit 45. Shadow of a Woman 46. Whispering City 48. Call Me Madam 53. Stranger from Venus (GB) 54. War and Peace 56. Fraulein 57. Thundering Jets (d only) 58. Operation Crossbow 65. Garcia 74, etc.

Danton, Ray (1931–1992).
Tall, dark American leading man with radio experience.
Chief Crazy Horse 52. The Spoilers 55. I'll Cry Tomorrow 55. *Too Much Too Soon* 58. *The Rise and Fall of Legs Diamond* 59. Ice Palace 60. A Fever in the Blood 61. *The George Raft Story* 61. The Chapman Report 62. The Longest Day 62. Sandokan the Great (It.) 63. Tiger of Terror (It.) 64. The Spy Who Went into Hell (Ger.) 65. The Deathmaster (d only) 72. The Centrefold Girls 74, etc.
TV series: The Alaskans 59–60.

D'Antoni, Philip (1929–).
American producer for cinema and TV.
The French Connection (AA) 71. The Connection (TV) 73. Mr Inside Mr Outside (TV) 73. The Seven-Ups (& d) 74, etc.

Danvers-Walker, Bob (1907–1990).
A radio and television announcer, he was the distinctive voice of British Pathé newsreels from 1940–70.

The Danziger Brothers (Edward and Harry).
American producers who after making *Jigsaw* 46 and two or three other films came to England, set up New Elstree Studios and spent 15 years producing hundreds of second features and TV episodes, hardly any worth recalling.

Darabont, Frank.
American screenwriter and director.
A Nightmare on Elm Street 3: Dream Warriors (co-w) 87. The Blob (co-w) 88. The Fly II (co-w) 89. Buried Alive (d) (TV) 90. *The Shawshank Redemption* (wd) 94. Mary Shelley's Frankenstein (w) 94, etc.

D'Arbanville, Patty (1951–).
American actress, a former model, who began her career in one of Andy Warhol's underground films.

Flesh 68. Rancho Deluxe 75. Bilitis 77. Big Wednesday 78. Time after Time 79. The Main Event 79. The Fifth Floor 80. Hog Wild 80. Modern Problems 81. Real Genius 85. The Boys Next Door 85. Fresh Horses 88. Call Me 88. Wired 89. Frame-Up II: The Cover-Up 92, etc.

Darby, Ken (1909–1992).
American composer and arranger.
Song of the South 46. So Dear to My Heart 48. Rancho Notorious 52. The Robe 53. The Egyptian 54. Bus Stop (AAN) 56. The King and I (AA) 56. South Pacific (AAN) 58. Hound Dog Man 59. Porgy and Bess (AA) 59. Flower Drum Song (AAN) 61. How the West Was Won (AAN) 62. The Greatest Story Ever Told 65. Camelot (AA) 67, many others.

Darby, Kim (1947–) (Deborah Zerby).
American leading lady.
Bus Riley's Back in Town 65. A Time for Giving 69. *True Grit* 69. Norwood 69. The Grissom Gang 71. Rich Man Poor Man (TV) 76. The One and Only 78. The Pink Telephone 78. The Last Convertible (TV) 79. Better Off Dead 85. Teen Wolf Too 87, etc.

Darc, Mireille (1938–) (M. Aigroz).
French leading lady.
Tonton Flingueurs 64. Galia 65. Du Rififi à Paname 66. Weekend 67. Jeff 68. Blonde from Peking 68. There was Once a Cop 72. The Tall Blond Man With One Black Shoe 74.

Darcel, Denise (1925–) (Denise Billecard).
French leading lady, in Hollywood from 1947.
To the Victor 48. Battleground 49. Tarzan and the Slave Girl 50. Westward the Women 51. Dangerous When Wet 53. Flame of Calcutta 53. Vera Cruz 54. Seven Women from Hell 62, etc.

D'Arcy, Alex (1908–) (Alexander Sarruf).
Egyptian light actor who has appeared in films of many nations.
Champagne 28. A Nous la Liberté 31. La Kermesse Héroïque 35. The Prisoner of Zenda 37. Fifth Avenue Girl 39. Marriage Is a Private Affair 44. How to Marry a Millionaire 53. Soldier of Fortune 56. Way Way Out 66. The St Valentine's Day Massacre 67. Blood of Dracula's Castle (as Dracula) 69. The Seven Minutes 71, etc.

D'Arcy, Roy (1894–1969) (Roy F. Guisti).
American actor who hovered on the edge of stardom during the 20s and was in second features in the 30s, usually as a villain. Born in San Francisco, he was educated at the University of Jena, Germany, and worked in South America before becoming an actor in New York.
The Merry Widow 25. La Bohème 26. Trelawney of the Wells 26. King of the Khyber Rifles 26. The Gay Deceiver 26. Adam and Evil 27. The Actress 28. A Woman of Affairs 29. Romance 30. Sherlock Holmes 32. Whispering Shadows (serial) 33. Flying Down to Rio 33. Orient Express 34. Outlawed Guns 35. Revolt of the Zombies 36. Captain Calamity 36. Chasing Danger 39, etc.

Darden, Severn (1929–).
American comedy character actor.
Dead Heat on a Merry Go Round 67. The President's Analyst 67. Luv 68. Pussycat Pussycat I Love You 70. Vanishing Point 71. The Hired Hand 71. Cisco Pike 71. The War Between Men and Women 72. Who Fears the Devil 74. In God We Trust 79. Why Would I Lie 80. Saturday the 14th 81. Real Genius 85. Back to School 86, etc.
TV series: Mary Hartman, Mary Hartman 77–78. Beyond Westworld 80. Take Five 87.

Darien, Frank (c. 1878–1955).
American character actor often seen as meek or downtrodden little man.
Five Star Final 31. The Miracle Man 32. Professional Sweetheart 33. Marie Galante 34. Brides are Like That 36. Love Finds Andy Hardy 38. At the Circus 39. *The Grapes of Wrath* 40. Hellzapoppin 42. Tales of Manhattan 42. The Outlaw 43. Bowery to Broadway 44. Kiss and Tel 45. Claudia and David 46. You Gotta Stay Happy 46. Merton of the Movies 47. The Flying Saucer 50 many others.

Darin, Bobby (1936–1973) (Walden Robert Cassotto).
American pop singer who alternated lightweight appearances with more serious roles. He was married to Sandra Dee.
Come September 60. Pepe 60. Too Late Blues 61. *Pressure Point* 62. Captain Newman MD (AAN) 63. That Funny Feeling 65. Gunfight at Abilene 67. Stranger in the House 67. The Happy Ending 69, etc.

Daring, Mason.
American composer, often for the films of John Sayles.
Return of the Secaucus Seven 80. The Brother from Another Planet 84. Matewan 87. Eight Men Out 88. The Laserman 88. Little Vegas 90. City of Hope 91. Wild Hearts Can't Be Broken 91. Passion Fish 92. The Secret of Roan Inish 94, etc.

Darling, Candy (1949–1974) (James Hope Slattery).
Transvestite star, best known for roles in Andy Warhol's movies. Born in Massapequa, Long Island, he also appeared in European films and on stage. Died of leukaemia.
Flesh 68. Der Tod der Maria Malibran (TV) 71. Women in Revolt 72. Silent Night, Bloody Night 73, etc.

¶ Candy didn't want to be a perfect woman – that would be too simple, and besides it would give her away. What she wanted was to be a woman with all the little problems that a woman has to deal with – runs in her stocking, runny mascara, men that left her. – *Andy Warhol*

Darling, William (1882–1963) (Wilhelm Sandorhazi).
Hungarian-American art director, long with Twentieth Century-Fox.
A Question of Honor 22. Seven Faces 29. Renegades 30. *Cavalcade* (AA) 43. In Old Kentucky 35. The Littlest Rebel 35. Under Two Flags 36. Lloyds of London 36. On the Avenue 37. *The Rains Came* 39. The Song of Bernadette (AA) 43. The Keys of the Kingdom 44. Anna and the King of Siam (AA) 46, etc.

Darnborough, Anthony (1913–).
British producer.
The Calendar 47. Quartet 48. The Astonished Heart 50. The Net 52. To Paris with Love 55. The Baby and the Battleship 56, etc.

Darnell, Linda (1921–1965) (Monetta Eloisa Darnell).
Wide-eyed American leading lady of the 40s. Died in a fire.
■ Hotel for Women 39. Daytime Wife 39. Stardust 40. Brigham Young 40. The Mark of Zorro 40. Chad Hanna 40. Blood and Sand 41. Rise and Shine 41. The Loves of Edgar Allan Poe 42. The Song of Bernadette (as the Virgin Mary) 43. City Without Men 43. Buffalo Bill 44. *It Happened Tomorrow* 44.

Summer Storm 44. Sweet and Lowdown 44. The Great John L 45. Fallen Angel 45. Hangover Square 45. Anna and the King of Siam 46. Centennial Summer 46. My Darling Clementine 46. Forever Amber 47. The Walls of Jericho 48. Unfaithfully Yours 48. A Letter to Three Wives 48. Slattery's Hurricane 49. Everybody Does It 49. No Way Out 50. Two Flags West 50. The Thirteenth Letter 51. The Lady Pays Off 51. The Guy who Came Back 51. Saturday Island 52. Night Without Sleep 52. Blackbeard the Pirate 52. Second Chance 53. This Is My Love 54. Forbidden Women (It.) 55. The Last Five Minutes (It.) 56. Dakota Incident 56. Zero Hour 57. Homeward Borne (TV) 57. Black Spurs 65.

D'Arrast, Harry D'Abbabie (1893–1968). American director of the 20s, with a reputation for style.
■ Service for Ladies 27. A Gentleman of Paris 27. Serenade 27. The Magnificent Flirt 28. Dry Martini 28. Raffles (part) 30. *Laughter* (AA co-story) 30. Topaze 33. It Happened in Spain 34.

Darren, James (1936–) (James Ercolani). American leading man whose appeal seems to have waned with maturity although he is still seen occasionally on TV.
Rumble on the Docks 56. Operation Mad Ball 57. Gidget 59. Let No Man Write My Epitaph 60. *The Guns of Navarone* 61. Diamondhead 63. For Those Who Think Young 64. Venus in Furs 70. The Boss's Son 78, etc.
TV series: Time Tunnel 66. T.J. Hooker 83.

Darrieux, Danielle (1917–).
Vivacious French leading lady, in films since 1931.
Le Bal 32. *Mayerling* 36. *The Rage of Paris* (US) 38. *Battement de Coeur* 39. Premier Rendezvous 44. *Occupe-Toi d'Amélie* 49. La Ronde 50. Le Plaisir 51. Rich, Young and Pretty (US) 51. Five Fingers (US) 52. Adorables Créatures 52. *Madame De* 53. Alexander the Great (US) 55. Le Rouge et le Noir 57. Marie Octobre 58. Lady Chatterley's Lover 59. Murder at 45 RPM 61. The Greengage Summer (GB) 61. Landru 63. L'Or du Duc 65. Le Dimanche de la Vie 66. The Young Girls of Rochefort 67. L'Homme à la Buick 67. Birds in Peru 68. The Lonely Woman 75. L'Année Sainte 76. La Cavaleur 79. At the Top of the Stairs 83. The Scene of the Crime 86. Bille en Tête 89. Le Jour de Rois 90, many others.

Darro, Frankie (1918–1976) (Frank Johnson). Tough-looking little American actor, former child and teenage player; star of many second features.
So Big 24. The Cowboy Cop 26. Long Pants 27. The Circus Kid 28. The Mad Genius 31. Wild Boys of the Road 33. Broadway Bill 34. Charlie Chan at the Race Track 36. Racing Blood 37. Chasing Trouble 39. Laughing at Danger 40. Freddie Steps Out 45. Heart of Virginia 48. Across the Wide Missouri 51. Operation Petticoat 59. Hook, Line and Sinker 68, many others.

Darrow, Clarence (1857–1938). Celebrated American defence lawyer, impersonated by Orson Welles in *Compulsion* 58, and by Spencer Tracy in *Inherit the Wind* 60. In the 70s Henry Fonda played him in a one-man stage and TV show.

Darrow, John (1907–1980) (Harry Simpson). American light leading man of the 20s and 30s, who later became an agent.
High School Hero 27. Girls Gone Wild 29. Hell's Angels 30. The Lady Refuses 31. Ten Nights in a Bar-Room 31. The All American 32. Midshipman

Jack 33. Monte Carlo Nights 34. A Notorious Gentleman 35. Crime over London (GB) 36, etc.

Darvi, Bella (1927–1971) (Bayla Wegier). Polish-French leading lady, in a few Hollywood films after being discovered by Darryl Zanuck. Committed suicide.
■ Hell and High Water 54. The Egyptian 54. The Racers 55. Je Suis Un Sentimental 55. Sinners of Paris 59. Lipstick 65.

Darwell, Jane (1880–1967) (Patti Woodward). American character actress, usually in warm-hearted motherly roles.
Rose of the Rancho 14. Brewster's Millions 20. Tom Sawyer 30. Back Street 32. Design for Living 34. Life Begins at Forty 35. Captain January 36. Slave Ship 37. Three Blind Mice 38. Jesse James 39. The Rains Came 39. Gone with the Wind 39. *The Grapes of Wrath* (AA: as the indomitable Ma Joad) 40. *All That Money Can Buy* 41. Private Nurse 41. The Ox Bow Incident 43. The Impatient Years 44. *Captain Tugboat Annie* (title role) 46. My Darling Clementine 46. Three Godfathers 48. Wagonmaster 50. Caged 50. The Lemon Drop Kid 51. Fourteen Hours 51. We're Not Married 52. The Sun Shines Bright 52. Hit the Deck 55. The Last Hurrah 58. Mary Poppins 64, many others.
✪ For the sheer maternal strength of her characterizations. *The Grapes of Wrath*.

Famous line (*The Grapes of Wrath*): 'Can't nobody lick us, pa. We're the people.'

Dash, Stacey (1966–).
American actress.
Enemy Territory 87. Moving 88. Tennessee Nights 89. Mo' Money 92, etc.
TV series: TV 101 88–89.

Dassin, Jules (1911–).
American director, former radio writer and actor. Joined MGM 1941 to direct shorts (including a two-reel version of *The Tell-Tale Heart*); moved to features; left for Europe during the McCarthy witch hunt of the late 40s.
■ Nazi Agent 42. The Affairs of Martha 42. Reunion in France 42. Young Ideas 43. The Canterville Ghost 44. A Letter for Evie 44. Two Smart People 46. *Brute Force* 47. *Naked City* 48. *Thieves' Highway* (& a) 49. Night and the City (GB) 50. *Rififi* (also acted, as Perlo Vita) 54. He Who Must Die 56. Where the Hot Wind Blows 58. *Never on Sunday* (also acted) (AAN) 60. Phaedra 62. Topkapi 64. 10.30 p.m. Summer 66. Survival 68. Uptight 68. Promise at Dawn 70. Dream of Passion 78. Circle of Two 80.

Daugherty, Herschel.
American director, from TV.
The Light in the Forest 58. The Raiders 63. Winchester 73 (TV) 67. The Victim (TV) 72. Twice in a Lifetime (TV) 74, etc.

Dauphin, Claude (1903–1978) (Claude Franc-Nohain). Dapper French actor of stage and screen: in films from 1930.
Entrée des Artistes 38. Battement de Coeur 39. Les Deux Timides 42. English Without Tears (GB) 44. Deported (US) 50. Le Plaisir 51. Casque d'Or 52. Little Boy Lost (US) 53. Innocents in Paris (GB) 54. Phantom of the Rue Morgue (US) 54. The Quiet American (US) 58. The Full Treatment 60. Lady L 65. Two for the Road 67. Hard Contract 69. Rosebud 75. The Tenant 76, many others.
TV series: Paris Precinct.

Davenport, A. Bromley (1867–1946). Eton-educated English character actor who made his stage debut in *Siberia* in 1892 and was in films from 1920.
The Great Gay Road 20. Bonnie Prince Charlie 23. What the Butler Saw 24. Roses of Picardy 27. Too Many Crooks 30. Glamour 31. Mischief 32. Mr Bill the Conqueror 32. The Return of Raffles 32. A Shot in the Dark 33. The Warren Case 34. The Scarlet Pimpernel 35. The Cardinal 36. Owd Bob 38. Jamaica Inn 39. Love on the Dole 41. Old Mother Riley's Ghosts 41. The Young Mr Pitt 42. When We Are Married 43. The Way Ahead 44, etc.

Davenport, Doris (1915–1980). American leading lady, formerly a Goldwyn Girl. Played several bit parts, but was prominent only in *Kid Millions* 35, *The Westerner* 40, *Behind the News* 40. Her career ended after she was injured in a car crash that left her with a limp.

Davenport, Dorothy (1895–1977) (aka Dorothy Reid). Silent screen actress, often opposite her husband Wallace Reid, who turned to directing, writing and producing after his death in 1923.
Her Indian Hero 09. The Intruder 13. Fruit of Evil 14. The Fighting Chance 20. Every Woman's Problem 21. Human Wreckage 23. Broken Laws (& p) 24. The Earth Woman (p) 26. Linda (pd) 29. Suçker Money (d) 33. Road to Ruin (co-w, d) 34. Prison Break (w) 38. The Haunted House (w) 40. Redhead 41. Who Killed Doc Robbin? 48. Footsteps in the Fog 55, etc.

Davenport, Harry (1866–1949). American character actor; long stage career, then in Hollywood as chucklesome, benevolent old man.
■ Her Unborn Child 30. My Sin 31. His Woman 32. Get That Venus 33. Three Cheers for Love 34. The Scoundrel 35. Three Men on a Horse 36. The Case of the Black Cat 36. King of Hockey 36. Fly Away Baby 36. The Life of Emile Zola 37. Under Cover of Night 37. Her Husband's Secretary 37. White Bondage 37. They Won't Forget 37. Mr Dodd Takes the Air 37. First Lady 37. The Perfect Specimen 37. Paradise Express 37. As Good as Married 37. Armored Car 37. Wells Fargo 37. Fit for a King 37. Gold is Where You Find It 38. Saleslady 38. The Sisters 38. The Long Shot 38. The First Hundred Years 38. Marie Antoinette 38. The Cowboy and the Lady 38. Reckless Living 38. The Rage of Paris 38. Tailspin 38. Young Fugitives 38. *You Can't Take It With You* 38. The Higgins Family 38. Orphans of the Street 38. Made for Each Other 39. My Wife's Relatives 39. Should Husbands Work 39. The Covered Trailer 39. Money to Burn 39. Exile Express 39. Death of a Champion 39. The Story of Alexander Graham Bell 39. Juarez 39. Gone with the Wind 39. *The Hunchback of Notre Dame* 39. Dr Ehrlich's Magic Bullet 40. Granny Get Your Gun 40. Too Many Husbands 40. Grandpa Goes to Town 40. Lucky Partners 40. I Want a Divorce 40. All This and Heaven Too 40. Foreign Correspondent 40. That Uncertain Feeling 41. I Wanted Wings 41. Hurricane Smith 41. The Bride Came COD 41. One Foot in Heaven 41. King's Row 41. *Son of Fury* 42. Larceny Inc 42. Ten Gentlemen from West Point 42. Tales of Manhattan 42. Heading for God's Country 43. We've Never Been Licked 43. Riding High 43. *The Ox Bow Incident* 43. The Amazing Mrs Holliday 43. Gangway for Tomorrow 43. Government Girl 43. Jack London 43. Princess O'Rourke 43. *Meet Me In St Louis* 44. The Impatient Years 44. The Thin Man Goes Home 44. Kismet 44. Music for Millions 45. *The Enchanted*

Forest 45. Too Young to Know 45. This Love of Ours 45. She Wouldn't Say Yes 45. Courage of Lassie 46. Blue Sierra 46. A Boy a Girl and a Dog 46. Faithful in My Fashion 46. Three Wise Fools 46. War Brides 46. Lady Luck 46. Claudia and David 46. Pardon My Past 46. Adventure 46. The Farmer's Daughter 47. That Hagen Girl 47. Stallion Road 47. Keeper of the Bees 47. Sport of Kings 47. The Fabulous Texan 47. *The Bachelor and the Bobbysoxer* 47. Three Daring Daughters 48. The Man from Texas 48. For the Love of Mary 48. That Lady in Ermine 48. The Decision of Christopher Blake 48. Down to the Sea in Ships 49. Little Women 49. Tell It To the Judge 49. *That Forsyte Woman* 49. Riding High 50.

✪ For being everybody's cheerful grandpa. *The Hunchback of Notre Dame*.

Davenport, Nigel (1928–).
Breezy, virile British actor, much on TV.
Peeping Tom 59. In the Cool of the Day 63. A High Wind in Jamaica 65. Sands of the Kalahari 65. Where the Spies Are 66. *A Man for All Seasons* 67. Red and Blue 67. Play Dirty 68. Sinful Davey 69. *The Virgin Soldiers* 69. The Royal Hunt of the Sun 69. No Blade of Grass 71. Villain 71. *Living Free* 72. Mary Queen of Scots 72. Dracula (TV) (as Van Helsing) 73. Phase IV 73. The Island of Dr Moreau 77. An Eye for an Eye 78. Zulu Dawn 79. Nighthawks 81. Strata 82. Greystoke: The Legend of Tarzan, Lord of the Apes 84. Caravaggio 86. Without a Clue 88, etc.
TV series: *Prince Regent* (as George III) 79.

Daves, Delmer (1904–1977).
American writer-producer-director with highly miscellaneous experience. Writer with MGM from 1933, writer-director with Warners from 1943.
Destination Tokyo (wd) 43. The Red House (wd) 47. *Dark Passage* (wd) 47. Broken Arrow (d) 50. Bird of Paradise (wd) 51. Never Let Me Go (d) 53. Demetrius and the Gladiators (d) 54. Jubal (wd) 56. The Last Wagon (wd) 56. *3.10 to Yuma* (d) 57. Cowboy (wd) 58. The Hanging Tree (d) 59. Parrish (wd) 61. Spencer's Mountain (wpd) 62. Youngblood Hawke (wd) 64. The Battle of the Villa Fiorita (wpd) 65, many others.

¶ He remains the property of those who can enjoy stylistic conviction in an intellectual vacuum. – *Andrew Sarris, 1968*

Davi, Robert (1953–).
Burly American actor, usually in menacing roles.
The Goonies 85. Wild Thing 87. License to Kill 89. Maniac Cop 2 90. Amazon 90. Predator 2 90. Legal Tender 90. Illicit Behaviour 91. The Taking of Beverly Hills 91. Center of the Web 92. Christopher Columbus: The Discovery 92. Wild Orchid 2: Two Shades of Blue 92. Maniac Cop 3 93. Night Trap (aka Mardi Gras for the Devil) 93. Son of the Pink Panther 93. The November Men 93. Cops and Robbersons 94, etc.
TV series: The Gangster Chronicles 81.

Daviau, Allen.
American cinematographer.
E.T. – the Extraterrestrial (AAN) 82. Twilight Zone – the Movie 83. Harry Tracy 83. The Falcon and the Snowman 85. The Color Purple (AAN) 86. Harry and the Hendersons 87. Empire of the Sun (AAN) 87. Avalon (AAN) 90. Defending Your Life 91. Bugsy 91. Fearless 93, etc.

David, Hal (1921–).
American lyricist and collaborator with Burt Bacharach (qv for credits). He is the brother of Mack David.
Autobiography: 1968, *What The World Needs Now.*

David, Mack (1912–1993).
American songwriter, in Hollywood from 1949, often in collaboration with Jerry Livingston. He is the brother of Hal David.
Cinderella (AAN) 49. At War with the Army 50. Sailor Beware 51. Jumping Jacks 52. Scared Stiff 53. The Hanging Tree (AAN) 59. Bachelor in Paradise (AAN) 61. Walk on the Wild Side (AAN) 62. It's a Mad, Mad, Mad, Mad World (AAN) 63. Hush, Hush Sweet Charlotte (AAN) 64. Cat Ballou (AAN) 65. Hawaii (AAN) 66, etc.

David, Saul (1921–).
American producer.
Von Ryan's Express 65. Our Man Flint 65. Fantastic Voyage 67. Skullduggery 69. The Black Bird 75. Logan's Run 76.

David, Thayer (1926–1978) (David Thayer Hersey).
American character actor.
A Time to Love and a Time to Die 58. *Journey to the Centre of the Earth* 59. The Story of Ruth 60. The Eiger Sanction 74. The Duchess and the Dirtwater Fox 76. Meet Nero Wolfe (TV) 77. House Calls 78, etc.

Davidovich, Lolita (1962–) (aka Lolita David).
Canadian actress of Yugoslavian descent.
Adventures in Babysitting 1987. The Big Town 1987. Blaze 89. Object of Beauty 91. The Inner Circle (El Proiezionista) 91. Money Men 92. Raising Cain 92. Boiling Point 93. Younger and Younger 93. Intersection 94. Cobb 94, etc.

¶ I'm Yugoslavian. They're passionate but not really ambitious. Life is eating and drinking and children. – *L.D.*

Davidson, Boaz (1943–).
Israeli director.
Azit the Paratrooper Dog 72. Lupo Goes to New York 77. Lemon Popsicle 81. Going Steady (Lemon Popsicle II) 81. Hot Bubblegum (Lemon Popsicle III) 82. The Last American Virgin 82. Private Popsicle (Lemon Popsicle IV) 82. Dutch Treat 86. Going Bananas 87. Salsa 88. American Cyborg: Steel Warrior 94, etc.

Davidson, Jaye.
British actor whose role as a transvestite surprised the hero, and the audience, of *The Crying Game*.
The Crying Game (AAN) 93. Stargate 94.

Davidson, John (1886–1968).
American character actor, a piercing-eyed, white-haired villain of the 20s and 30s.
The Green Cloak 15. The Spurs of Sybil 18. The Bronze Bell 21. Under Two Flags 22. Monsieur Beaucaire 24. Kid Gloves 29. Arsène Lupin 32. Dinner at Eight 33. Hold That Girl 34. The Last Days of Pompeii 35. Mr Moto Takes a Vacation 38. Arrest Bulldog Drummond 38. Miracles for Sale 39. Captain Marvel 41. Captain America 44. The Purple Monster Strikes 45. Shock 46. Daisy Kenyon 47. A Letter to Three Wives 48. Oh You Beautiful Doll 49. A Gathering of Eagles 63, many others.

Davidson, John (1941–).
American light singer and leading man, mostly on television.
The Happiest Millionaire 67. The One and Only Genuine Original Family Band 68. Coffee, Tea or Me (TV) 73. The Mitera Targets (TV) 78. Shell Game (TV) 78. The Concorde – Airport '79 79. The Squeeze 87, etc.
TV series: The Entertainers. Kraft Music Hall. The Girl with Something Extra. That's Incredible.

Davidson, Max (1875–1950).
American slapstick comedian of 20s two-reelers, spotlighted in *Laurel and Hardy's Laughing Twenties*.

Davidson, William B. (1888–1947).
American character actor, in hundreds of small roles, usually as pompous, lecherous or overbearing businessman.
A Modern Cinderella 17. The Capitol 19. Partners of the Night 20. Adam and Eva 23. Women and Gold 25. The Gaucho 28. For the Defense 30. Sky Devils 32. Fog over Frisco 34. Dangerous 35. Earthworm Tractors 36. Easy Living 37. Love on Toast 38. Indianapolis Speedway 39. Maryland 40. My Little Chickadee 40. Juke Girl 42. Up in Arms 44. See My Lawyer 45. My Darling Clementine 46. The Farmer's Daughter 47, many others.

Davidtz, Embeth.
South African-born actress in America.
Army of Darkness 92. Deadly Matrimony (TV) 92. Schindler's List 93. Murder in the First 94, etc.

Davies, Betty Ann (1910–1955).
British stage actress, usually in tense roles; occasional films from early 30s.
Chick 34. Kipps 41. It Always Rains on Sunday 47. The History of Mr Polly 49. *Tri* 50. Cosh Boy 52. Grand National Night 53. The Belles of St Trinian's 54, etc.

Davies, Jack (1913–1994).
British comedy scriptwriter, busy since 1932 on Will Hay and Norman Wisdom comedies, 'Doctor' series, etc. Father of John Howard Davies.
Laughter in Paradise 51. Top Secret 52. An Alligator Named Daisy 56. *Very Important Person* 61. *The Fast Lady* 62. Those Magnificent Men in Their Flying Machines 65. Gambit 66. Monte Carlo 68. Doctor in Trouble 70. Paper Tiger 75, many others.

Davies, John Howard (1939–).
British child actor, who became a BBC TV director.
Oliver Twist 48. The Rocking-Horse Winner 50. Tom Brown's Schooldays 51, etc.

Davies, Marion (1897–1961) (Marion Douras).
American leading lady famous less for her rather mediocre films than for being the protégée of William Randolph Hearst the newspaper magnate, who was determined to make a star out of her. She enjoyed moderate success 1917–36, then retired.
Pictorial autobiography: 1975, *The Times We Had,* collated by Pamela Pfau.
Biography: 1973, *Marion Davies* by Fred Lawrence Guiles.
■ Runaway Romany 17. Cecilia of the Pink Roses 18. The Burden of Proof 18. Getting Mary Married 19. The Cinema Murder 19. The Dark Star 19. The Belle of New York 19. The Restless Sex 20. April Folly 20. Enchantment 21. Buried Treasure 21. The Bride's Play 22. Beauty Worth 22. When Knighthood was in Flower 22. The Young Diana 22. Daughter of Luxury 22. Little Old New York 22. Adam and Eva 23. Janice Meredith 24. Yolanda 24. Lights of Old Broadway 25. Zander the Great 25. Beverly of Graustark 26. Quality Street 27. The Fair Co-ed 27. The Red Mill 27. Tillie the Toiler 27. The Cardboard Lover 28. The Patsy 28. *Show People* 28. Hollywood Revue 29. Marianne 29. The

ay Nineties 29. Not so Dumb 30. The Floradora
irl 30. It's a Wise Child 31. Five and Ten 31.
achelor Father 31. Polly of the Circus 32. Blondie
the Follies 32. The Dark Horse 32. Peg O'My
eart 33. Operator 13 34. Going Hollywood 34.
ge Miss Glory 35. Hearts Divided 36. Cain and
abel 36. Ever Since Eve 37.

Upon my honour
I saw a madonna
Sitting alone in a niche
Above the door
Of the glamorous whore
Of a prominent son-of-a-bitch.
– *attributed to Dorothy Parker on seeing the elaborate
ressing room built by W. R. Hearst for M.D. at MGM*
With me it was 5 per cent talent and 95 per cent
ublicity. – *M.D.*
She was quite a comedian, and would have been
star in her own right without the cyclonic Hearst
ublicity. – *Charles Chaplin*

Davies, Rupert (1916–1976).
ritish character actor, formerly in small roles,
en famous as TV's Maigret.
The Key 58. Sapphire 59. The Uncle 65. The Spy
Vho Came in from the Cold 65. Brides of Fu
Manchu 66. House of a Thousand Dolls 67.
Vitchfinder General 68. Waterloo 70. Zeppelin 71,
tc.
TV series: Sailor of Fortune 56.

Davies, Terence (1945–).
ritish director of autobiographical films of
orking-class life in the 50s. He left school at 15
nd worked as a clerk for 12 years before raising
he money to make his first short.
Terence Davies Trilogy (The Children 76;
Madonna and Child 80; Death and
ransfiguration 83). Distant Voices, Still Lives 88.
he Long Day Closes 92. The Neon Bible 95, etc.

Cinema is not valid for me if it's just people
talking their way through a plot. I couldn't
et interested in all that. I just get bored, because
hat's not real cinema at all. It's talking pictures.
T.D.
The great thing in life is to be very beautiful and
ery stupid. – *T.D.*
I believe Mr Davies went to film school –
resumably not for long. – *Ken Russell*

Davies, Valentine (1905–1961).
american screenwriter.
Three Little Girls in Blue 46. *Miracle on 34th Street*
AA original story) 47. You Were Meant for Me
8. Chicken Every Sunday 48. It Happens Every
pring 49. On the Riviera 51. The Glenn Miller
tory 53. *The Benny Goodman Story* (& d) 55. The
ridges at Toko-Ri 55. Strategic Air Command 55.
Bachelor in Paradise 61, etc.

Davies, Windsor (1930–).
British comedy character actor who rather
verdoes the blustering sergeant-major act.
The Alphabet Murders 65. Hammerhead 67. Sex
Clinic 71. Mister Quilp 74. Carry on Behind 74. Not
Now Comrade 76, etc.
TV series: It Ain't Half Hot, Mum 73–77.

Davion, Alexander (1929–).
Anglo-French leading man, mostly on stage and
American TV.
Song without End (as Chopin) 60. Paranoiac 63.
Valley of the Dolls 67. The Royal Hunt of the Sun
9. Incense for the Damned 71, etc.
TV series: Gideon's Way 64. The Man Who
Never Was 66. Custer 67. Bloodsuckers 70, etc.

Davis, Andrew.
American director and screenwriter, a former
cinematographer.
Over the Edge (ph) 79. Stony Island (wd) 80.
The Final Terror 83. Code of Silence 85. Above
the Law (wd) 88. The Package 89. Under Siege 92.
The Fugitive 93, etc.

Davis, Bette (1908–1989) (Ruth Elizabeth Davis).
Inimitably intense American dramatic actress; a
box-office queen for ten years from 1937, she
later played eccentric roles.
Autobiographies: 1962, *The Lonely Life*. 1975,
Mother Goddam (with Whitney Stone).
Biographies: 1991, *No Guts, No Glory:
Conversations with Bette Davis* by Whitney Stone.
1992, *Bette Davis* by Barbara Leaming.
■ Bad Sister 31. Seed 31. Waterloo Bridge 31.
Way Back Home 31. The Menace 31. *The Man Who
Played God* 32. Hell's House 32. So Big 32. The Rich
are Always with Us 32. The Dark Horse 32. The
Cabin in the Cotton 32. Three on a Match 32. Twenty
Thousand Years in Sing Sing 32. Parachute Jumper
32. The Working Man 33. Ex Lady 33. Bureau of
Missing Persons 33. Fashions of 1934 34. The Big
Shakedown 34. Jimmy the Gent 34. Fog over
Frisco 34. *Of Human Bondage* 34. Housewife 34.
Bordertown 34. The Girl from Tenth Avenue 35.
Front Page Woman 35. Special Agent 35. *Dangerous*
(AA) 35. The Petrified Forest 36. The Golden
Arrow 36. Satan Met a Lady 36. Marked Woman
37. Kid Galahad 37. That Certain Woman 37. It's
Love I'm After 37. *Jezebel* (AA) 38. The Sisters 38.
Dark Victory (AAN) 39. Juarez 39. *The Old Maid* 39.
The Private Lives of Elizabeth and Essex 39. All This
and Heaven Too 40. *The Letter* (AAN) 40. *The Great
Lie* 41. The Bride Came COD 41. *The Little Foxes*
(AAN) 41. *The Man Who Came to Dinner* 41. In This
Our Life 42. *Now Voyager* (AAN) 42. Watch on
the Rhine 43. Thank Your Lucky Stars 43. Old
Acquaintance 43. *Mr Skeffington* (AAN) 44.
Hollywood Canteen 44. *The Corn is Green* 45. A
Stolen Life 46. Deception 46. Winter Meeting 48.
June Bride 48. Beyond the Forest 49. *All About Eve*
(AAN) 50. Payment on Demand 51. Another
Man's Poison 51. Phone Call from a Stranger 52.
The Star (AAN) 52. The Virgin Queen 55. The
Catered Affair 56. Storm Center 56. John Paul
Jones 59. The Scapegoat 59. A Pocketful of
Miracles 61. *Whatever Happened to Baby Jane?*
(AAN) 62. Dead Ringer 64. The Empty Canvas
64. Where Love Has Gone 64. *Hush Hush Sweet
Charlotte* 64. The Nanny 65. The Anniversary 68.
Connecting Rooms 69. Bunny O'Hare 71. Madame
Sin (TV) 71. The Scientific Cardplayer 72. The Judge
and Jake Wyler (TV) 73. Scream Pretty Peggy (TV)
74. Burnt Offerings 76. The Disappearance of Aimée
(TV) 76. The Dark Secret of Harvest Home (TV)
78. Return from Witch Mountain 78. Death on
the Nile 78. Strangers (TV) 79. White Mama (TV)
79. The Watcher in the Woods 80. Skyward (TV)
81. Family Reunion (TV) 81. *Little Gloria . . . Happy
at Last* (TV) 82. A Piano for Mrs Cimino (TV) 82. Hotel
(TV) 83. Right of Way (TV) 83. *The Whales of August*
87.
✪ For her ten-year domination of the 'woman's
picture'. *The Great Lie.*

For a girl with no looks, Bette Davis rose fast
to the top and stayed there a long time. When
she first arrived in Hollywood the official greeter
missed her at the station, and his later excuse
was:
No one faintly like an actress got off the train.
Carl Laemmle is credited with two waspish
remarks about her:
I can't imagine any guy giving her a tumble.
And:

She has as much sex appeal as Slim
Summerville.
She herself confesses:
When I saw my first film test I ran from the
projection room screaming.
She finally settled for a career without glamour:
I was the first star who ever came out of the
water looking wet.
Nobody knew what I looked like because I
never looked the same way twice.
Determination carried her through. As her later
husband Gary Merrill said:
Whatever Bette had chosen to do in life, she
would have had to be the top or she couldn't
have endured it.
She admitted this herself:
If Hollywood didn't work out I was all prepared
to be the best secretary in the world.
As David Zinman summarizes:
All she had going for her was her talent.
But by 1937 she was at the top of the tree, dishing
out hell to those who had dished it out to her.
Said her once co-star Brian Aherne:
Surely no one but a mother could have loved
Bette Davis at the height of her career.
E. Arnot Robertson in 1935 had expressed a similar
feeling in a different way:
She would probably have been burned as a
witch if she had lived two or three hundred
years ago. She gives the curious feeling of being
charged with power which can find no
ordinary outlet.
By the early 50s she was no longer a bankable star,
and work was suddenly in short supply. She
inserted a full-page ad in the Hollywood trade
papers:
MOTHER OF THREE: divorcee; American. Twenty
years experience as an actress in motion pictures.
Mobile still and more affable than rumour
would have it. Wants steady employment in
Hollywood. (Has had Broadway.) References
upon request.
She reflected bitterly on her career at the top:
I was the only star they allowed to come out of
the water looking wet.
Jack L. Warner however remembered her with
affection:
An explosive little broad with a straight left.
But despite all difficulties she persevered, and was
still acting as she neared eighty. Vincent Canby said:
Her career has been recycled more often than
the average rubber tyre.

Famous line (*Cabin in the Cotton*): 'I'd like to kiss
yuh, but I just washed my hair.'

Famous line (*All About Eve*): 'Fasten your seat belts,
it's going to be a bumpy night.'

Famous line (*Old Acquaintance*): 'There comes a
time in every woman's life when the only thing
that helps is a glass of champagne.'

Famous line (*Now Voyager*): 'Oh, Jerry, don't let's
ask for the moon: we have the stars.'
~One story has it that she named the awards
statuette Oscar because its backside resembled that
of her first husband, Ham Oscar Nelson.

Davis, Brad (1949–1991).
American leading actor. Died of AIDS.
Midnight Express 77. A Small Circle of Friends 80.
Chariots of Fire 81. Querelle 84. Chiefs (TV) 84.
Robert Kennedy and his Times (TV) 84. Blood Ties
86. Cold Steel 87. Rosalie Goes Shopping 89.
Hangfire 90. Child of Light (TV) 91, etc.

Davis, Carl (1936–).
American composer in Britain, best known for his

silent film scores: *Napoleon, The Crowd,* Hollywood TV series, etc.

The Bofors Gun 68. Up Pompeii 71. Rentadick 72. Man Friday 75. The Sailor's Return 77. The French Lieutenant's Woman (BFA) 81. The Far Pavilions (TV) 81. King David 85. Scandal 89. The Rainbow 89. Frankenstein Unbound 90. The Trial 94. Widow's Peak 94, etc.

Davis, Desmond (1927–).
British director, former cameraman.
■ *Girl with Green Eyes* 64. The Uncle 65. *I Was Happy Here* 66. Smashing Time 67. A Nice Girl Like Me 69. Clash of the Titans 81. The Sign of Four (TV) 83. The Country Girls (TV) 83. Ordeal by Innocence 84. Camille (TV) 84. Freedom Fighter (TV) 88. The Man Who Lived at the Ritz (TV) 88.

Davis, Gail (1925–) (Betty Jeanne Grayson).
American leading lady of westerns, opposite Gene Autry in 15 films and many episodes of his TV show; she also had her own TV series, produced by Autry, and appeared in his rodeo.
Cow Town 50. Valley of Fire 51. Blue Canadian Rockies 52. Goldtown Ghost Riders 52. The Old West 52. On Top of Old Smoky 53. Winning of the West 53, etc.
TV series: Annie Oakley 53–56.

Davis, Geena (1957–).
Tall American leading actress, a former model, usually in off-beat roles. Married director Renny Harlin in 1993. She was formerly married to actor Jeff Goldblum.
Tootsie 82. Fletch 84. Transylvania 6–5000 84. The Fly 86. Beetlejuice 88. The Accidental Tourist (AA) 88. Earth Girls Are Easy 89. Quick Change 90. Thelma and Louise (AAN) 91. Hero 92. A League of Their Own 92. Speechless 94, etc.
TV series: Buffalo Bill 83–84. Sara 85.

¶ It seems that if a woman has a job in a movie now, she's cold and gets no sex – or if she does have sex, then she's either going to be punished for it or she's a psycho killer. – *G.D.*
A feminist spirit in the body of a goddess. – *Premiere*

Davis, James (Jim) (1915–1981).
Burly American actor who, despite star billing opposite Bette Davis, subsided quickly into second-feature westerns.
White Cargo 42. Swing Shift Maisie 43. Gallant Bess 46. The Fabulous Texan 47. *Winter Meeting* 48. Brimstone 49. Cavalry Scout 52. Woman of the North Country 52. The Fighting 7th 52. The Last Command 54. Timberjack 55. The Maverick Queen 56. Alias Jesse James 59. Fort Utah 66. Rio Lobo 70. Big Jake 71. The Honkers 72. Bad Company 72. Monte Walsh 72. The Deputies (TV) 76. The Choirboys 77. Comes a Horseman 78. The Day Time Ended 80, many others.
TV series: Stories of the Century. *Rescue 8. The Cowboys.* Dallas 78–80.

Davis, Joan (1907–1961).
Rubber-faced American comedienne, in show business from infancy, who enlivened many routine musicals of the 30s and 40s.
■ Millions in the Air 35. Bunker Bean 35. The Holy Terror 36. On the Avenue 37. Time Out for Romance 37. Wake Up and Live 37. Angel's Holiday 37. You Can't Have Everything 37. The Great Hospital Mystery 37. Sing and Be Happy 37. *Thin Ice* 37. Life Begins in College 37. Love and Kisses 37. Sally, Irene and Mary 38. Josette 38. My Lucky Star 38. *Hold that Coed* 38. Just Around

the Corner 38. Tailspin 39. Daytime Wife 39. Too Busy to Work 39. Free, Blonde and Twenty One 40. Manhattan Heartbeat 40. Sailor's Lady 40. For Beauty's Sake 41. Sun Valley Serenade 41. *Hold that Ghost* 41. Two Latins from Manhattan 42. Yokel Boy 42. Sweetheart of the Fleet 42. He's My Guy 43. Two Señoritas from Chicago 43. Around the World 43. *Show Business* 44. Beautiful but Broke 44. Kansas City Kitty 44. She Gets Her Man 45. *George White's Scandals* 45. She Wrote the Book 46. If You Knew Susie 48. The Traveling Saleswoman 50. Love that Brute 50. The Groom Wore Spurs 51. Harem Girl 53.
TV series: I Married Joan 52–56.

Davis, Sir John (1906–1993).
British executive, a former accountant who became chairman of the Rank Organization. After the artistic extravagance of the mid-40s, he imposed financial stability; but subsequent film production was comparatively routine and in the late 60s dwindled to nothing as the group was diversified into other fields.

Davis, Judy (1955–).
Australian leading lady.
My Brilliant Career (BFA) 79. Winter of Our Dreams 81. Hoodwink 81. Heatwave 82. Who Dares Wins 82. A Woman Called Golda (TV) 82. A Passage to India (AAN) 84. Kangaroo 86. High Tide 87. Georgia 88. Impromptu 89. Alice 90. Barton Fink 91. Where Angels Fear to Tread 91. Naked Lunch 91. *Husbands and Wives* (AAN) 92. The Ref 94. Dark Blood 94. The New Age 94, etc.

¶ She's the patron saint of modern emotions. – *Michael Tolkin*

Davis, Lilian Hall (1896–1933) (aka Lillian Hall-Davis).
Blonde English leading actress of the silent era and star of two of Hitchcock's early movies. Born in London, she was in films from childhood, but failed to make the transition to sound and committed suicide.
The Admirable Crichton 18. The Better 'Ole 18. The Honey Pot 20. The Game of Life 22. Brown Sugar 22. The Faithful Heart 22. A Royal Divorce 23. The Knock Out 23. Pagliacci 23. Should a Doctor Tell 23. Quo Vadis? 24. Roses of Picardy 27. The Ring 27. Blighty 27. The Farmer's Wife 28. Many Waters 31. Volga Volga 33, etc.

Davis, Martin S. (1927–).
American production executive. He resigned as chairman and chief executive of Paramount in April 1994.

Davis, Miles (1926–1991).
Innovative American jazz trumpeter, composer and actor. He was married to actress Cicely Tyson (1981–89).
Lift to the Scaffold (Ascenseur pour l'Echafaud) (m) 57. Jack Johnson (m) 71. Siesta (m) 87. Dingo – Dog of the Desert (a, m) 91.

Davis, Nancy (1921–) (Anne Frances Robbins).
American leading lady of a few 50s films; married Ronald Reagan.
Shadow on the Wall 50. The Doctor and the Girl 50. Night into Morning 51. It's a Big Country 53. Donovan's Brain 53. Crash Landing 57. Hellcats of the Navy 59, etc.

Davis, Ossie (1917–).
American actor of massive presence.
No Way Out 50. The Joe Louis Story 53. Gone Are the Days (& w) 63. *The Hill* 65. *The Scalphunters*

68. Sam Whiskey 69. Slaves 69. Cotton Comes [t]Harlem (d only) 70. Kongi's Harvest (d only) 71[?]Black Girl (d only) 72. Malcolm X 72. Gordon's War (d only) 73. Let's Do It Again 75. Hot Stuff 7[?]Harry and Son 83. Avenging Angel 84. School Daze 88. Do the Right Thing 89. Joe versus the Volcano 90. Jungle Fever 91. Gladiator 92. Que [?](TV) 93. Grumpy Old Men 93. Ray Alexander: [?]Taste for Justice (TV) 94. The Stand (TV) 94. Th[e]Client 94, etc.

Davis, Sammi (1964–).
British actress.
Mona Lisa 86. Hope and Glory 87. Lionheart [?]A Prayer for the Dying 87. Consuming Passions 88. The Lair of the White Worm 88. The Rainbo[w]89. Chernobyl: The Final Warning (TV) 91. Shad[e]of China 91, etc.

Davis, Sammy, Jnr (1925–1990).
American singer and entertainer, a bundle of vitality who described himself as 'a one-eyed Jewish Negro'. His second wife was actress Mai Britt (1960–67).
Autobiographies: 1966, Yes I Can. 1980, *Hollywood in a Suitcase.* 1989, *Why Me?*
■ Rufus Jones for President (debut) 29. Season Greetings 30. The Benny Goodman Story 56. *Anna Lucasta* 58. *Porgy and Bess* 59. *Ocean's Eleve[n]*60. Pepe 60. A Raisin in the Sun 61. Sergeants Thr[ee]62. Convicts Four 62. Nightmare in the Sun 63. Johnny Cool 63. Robin and the Seven Hoods 64[?]The Threepenny Opera 65. A Man Called Adam 66. Salt and Pepper 68. Sweet Charity 68. Man without Mercy 69. Gone with the West 69. The Pigeon (TV) 70. One More Time 70. The Tracke[r](TV) 71. Diamonds Are Forever 71. Poor Devil (T[V]73. Cinderella at the Palace (TV) 78. Stop the World I Want to Get Off 78. Little Moon and Ju[?]McGraw 78. The Cannonball Run 81. Heidi's Song 82. Cracking Up 83. Cannonball Run II 84[?]Moon over Parador 88. Tap 89.

Davis, Stringer (1896–1973).
Gentle-mannered British character actor who wa[s]usually to be found playing small roles in the film[s]of his wife Margaret Rutherford.
The Happiest Days of Your Life 50. Curtain Up 53. Murder Most Foul 62. Murder Ahoy 64, etc.

Davis, Tamra (1962–).
American director, from rock videos.
Guncrazy 92. CB4 93.

¶ Most of Hollywood's so-called women's movi[es]are based on men's fantasies. – *T.D.*

Davison, Bruce (1946–).
Slightly-built young American character actor.
Last Summer 69. The Strawberry Statement 7[0]*Willard* 71. The Jerusalem File 71. Ulzana's Raid 72. Mame 73. The Affair (TV) 73. Mother, Jugs and Speed 76. Short Eyes 77. Brass Target 78. High Risk 81. Crimes of Passion 84. Spies Like U[s]85. The Ladies Club 86. The Misfit Brigade 86. Longtime Companion (AAN) 90. Steel and Lace 91. Oscar 91. An Ambush of Ghosts 93. Short Cuts 93. Six Degrees of Separation 93, etc.
TV series: Hunter 85–86. Harry and the Hendersons 90–92.

D'Avril, Yola (1907–).
French actress and dancer who went to North America in the 20s, arriving in Hollywood in the mid-20s, where she first worked as an extra.
Lady Be Good 28. *All Quiet on the Western Fron[t]*30. The Bad One 30. The Man from Yesterday 3[?]I Met Him in Paris 37. Little Boy Lost 53, etc.

...aw, Evelyn (1912–1970).
...merican leading lady of the 30s.
...Something to Sing About 37. Panamint's Bad
...an 38, etc.

...awson, Anthony (1916–   ).
...an-faced British character actor.
...The Way to the Stars 45. The Queen of Spades
... The Long Dark Hall 51. Dial M for Murder
...S) 54. Midnight Lace (US) 60. Seven Seas to
...lais (US) 63, etc.

...awson, Anthony M.:
...e *Margheriti, Antonio.*

...awson, Marion (1889–1975).
...nglish actress who began as an opera singer and
...vitched to comedy when her voice failed. Her
...reen career faltered after she lost an eye in an
...cident with fireworks in 1932.
...The Last Coupon 32. His Wife's Mother 32. The
...ve Nest 33. A Political Party 34. Save a Little
...unshine 38, etc.

...awson, Ralph (1897–   ).
...merican editor.
...Lady of the Night 25. The Singing Fool 28.
...utward Bound 30. Girl Missing 33. The Story of
...ouis Pasteur 35. A Midsummer Night's Dream 35.
...nthony Adverse 36. The Adventures of Robin
...ood 38. Ivy 47. All My Sons 48. Undertow 49.
...arvey 50. Island in the Sky 53. The High and
...e Mighty 54, many others.

...ay, Clarence (1874–1935).
...merican humorist whose light pieces about his
...mily were the basis for the apparently immortal
...ay *Life with Father,* which was successfully filmed
... 1947.

...ay, Dennis (1921–1988) (Eugene Patrick McNulty).
...merican singer and light actor of the 40s and 50s,
...ost familiar from Jack Benny's radio and TV
...now.
...Buck Benny Rides Again 40. Music in
...anhattan 44. One Sunday Afternoon 48. I'll Get
...y 50. Golden Girl 51. The Girl Next Door 53, etc.

...ay, Doris (1924–   ) (Doris Kappelhoff).
...ivacious American dance-band singer who
...chieved instant star status in 1948 and preserved
...er eminence by transferring to a brand of
...nocent sex comedy which was all her own and
...eased the 60s.
...Biographies: 1976, *Doris Day, Her Own Story* by
...E. Hotcher. 1992, *Doris Day* by Eric Braun.
...*Romance on the High Seas* 48. My Dream is Yours
...9. It's a Great Feeling 49. Young Man with a
...orn 50. Tea for Two 50. West Point Story 50.
...*torm Warning* 50. Lullaby of Broadway 51. *On
...Moonlight Bay* 51. I'll See You in My Dreams 51.
...tarlift 51. The Winning Team 52. April in Paris 52.
...y the Light of the Silvery Moon 53. Calamity Jane
...3. Lucky Me 54. *Young at Heart* 55. Love Me or
...eave Me 55. The Man Who Knew Too Much 56.
...ulie 56. *The Pajama Game* 57. Teacher's Pet 58. The
...unnel of Love 58. It Happened to Jane 59. *Pillow
...alk* (AAN) 59. Please Don't Eat the Daisies 60.
...Midnight Lace 60. Lover Come Back 62. *That Touch
...f Mink* 62. Jumbo 62. The Thrill of It All 63. Move
...ver Darling 63. Send Me No Flowers 64. Do Not
...isturb 65. The Glass Bottom Boat 66. Caprice 67.
...he Ballad of Josie 68. Where Were You When
...he Lights Went Out? 68. With Six You Get Egg
...oll 68.
...TV series: *The Doris Day Show* 68–72. Doris Day's
...est Friends 85.
...¶ For her box-office domination of 60s comedies

by playing the perennial virgin. *That Touch of Mink.*

¶ I've been around so long I can remember Doris
Day before she was a virgin. – *Groucho Marx*
She thinks she doesn't get old. She told me once
it was her cameraman who was getting older. She
was going to fire him. – *Joe Pasternak*
Just about the remotest person I know. – *Kirk
Douglas*
No one guessed that under all those dirndls
lurked one of the wildest asses in Hollywood. – *Ross
Hunter*
My doctor won't let me watch Doris Day. I have
a family history of diabetes. – *Marvin Kitman*
Underneath her wholesome exterior beat the
heart of a true sex goddess and a very strong
woman. – *Debbie Harry*

Day, Ernest (1927–   ).
British cinematographer and occasional director.
Running Scared 72. Visit to a Chief 's Son 74.
Ghost in a Noonday Sun 74. Made 75. The Song
Remains the Same 76. The Revenge of the Pink
Panther 78. Sphinx 80. Green Ice (co-d) 81. Waltz
across Texas (d) 83. A Passage to India (AAN) 84.
Superman IV: The Quest for Peace 87. Burning
Secret 88. Parents 88, etc.

Day, Frances (1907–1984) (Frances Victoria
Schenk).
American revue star, in London from 1925.
■ The Price of Divorce 27. OK Chief 30. Big
Business 30. The First Mrs Frazer 32. Two Hearts
in Waltztime 34. The Girl from Maxim's 34.
Temptation 34. Oh Daddy 34. Public Nuisance No. 1
36. You Must Get Married 36. Dreams Come True
36. Who's Your Lady Friend? 37. The Girl in the
Taxi 37. Kicking the Moon Around 38. Room for
Two 40. *Fiddlers Three* (as Poppea) 44. Tread Softly
52. There's Always a Thursday 57. Climb up the
Wall 60.

¶ Little Day, you've had a busy man. – *Bud
Flanagan, when F.D. turned up for rehearsals
looking decidedly shaggy*

Day, Jill (1932–1990).
British pop singer and leading lady.
Always a Bride 54. All for Mary 56.

Day, Josette (1914–1978) (J. Dagory).
French leading lady.
Allo Berlin, Ici Paris 32. La Fille du Puisatier 40.
La Belle et la Bête 45. Les Parents Terribles 48. Four
Days' Leave 50, etc.

Day, Laraine (1917–   ) (Laraine Johnson).
American leading lady of the 40s, with stage
experience.
Autobiographical book 1952: *Day With The
Giants.*
Stella Dallas 37. Scandal Street 38. Border G-
Men 38. *Young Dr Kildare* (and others in the
series) 39. My Son, My Son 40. *Foreign
Correspondent* 40. *The Trial of Mary Dugan* 41.
Unholy Partners 41. Fingers at the Window 41.
Journey for Margaret 42. Mr Lucky 43. The Story
of Dr Wassell 43. Bride by Mistake 44. Those
Endearing Young Charms 45. Keep Your Powder
Dry 45. *The Locket* 46. Tycoon 47. My Dear
Secretary 48. I Married a Communist 49. Without
Honour 49. The High and the Mighty 54. Toy Tiger
56. Three for Jamie Dawn 57. The Third Voice 59.
Murder on Flight 502 (TV) 75. Return to Fantasy
Island (TV) 78, etc.

Day, Richard (1896–1972).
American production designer.

We Live Again 35. *The Dark Angel* (AA) 35.
Dodsworth (AA) 36. *The Little Foxes* 41. How Green
Was My Valley (AA) 41. This Above All (AA) 42.
My Gal Sal (AA) 43. *A Streetcar Named Desire* (AA)
51. On the Waterfront (AA) 54. Exodus 60. The
Greatest Story Ever Told 65. The Chase 66. Valley
of the Dolls 67. Tora! Tora! Tora! 70, etc.

Day, Robert (1922–   ).
British director, former cameraman.
The Green Man 57. Grip of the Strangler 58.
First Man into Space 58. Corridors of Blood 59.
Bobbikins 59. Two-Way Stretch 60. The Rebel 61.
Operation Snatch 62. Tarzan's Three Challenges 64.
She 65. Tarzan and the Valley of Gold 66. Tarzan
and the Great River 67. Ritual of Evil (TV) 69. The
House on Greenapple Road (TV) 70. Banyon (TV)
70. In Broad Daylight (TV) 71. Mr and Mrs Bo Jo
Jones (TV) 71. Death Stalk (TV) 75. Switch (TV)
75. Having Babies (TV) 76. Logan's Run (TV) 77.
The Initiation of Sarah (TV) 77. The Grass Is
Always Greener Over the Septic Tank (TV) 78.
Murder by Natural Causes (TV) 79. Walking Through
the Fire (TV) 79. The Man with Bogart's Face 80.
Peter and Paul (TV) 81. Running Out (TV) 83.
Hollywood Wives (TV) 85. Love, Mary (TV) 85. The
Quick and the Dead (TV) 87. Higher Ground (TV)
88, etc.

Day, Vera (1939–   ).
Bubbly blonde British actress.
Dance Little Lady 52. A Kid for Two Farthings
55. It's a Great Day 56. Hell Drivers 57. Quatermass
II 57. The Prince and the Showgirl 57. Up the
Creek 58. I Was Monty's Double 58. Too Many
Crooks 59. Watch It Sailor 61. Saturday Night Out
63, etc.

Day-Lewis, Daniel (1957–   ).
British leading actor.
Gandhi 83. The Bounty 84. My Beautiful
Laundrette 85. A Room with a View 85. Nanou
87. Stars and Bars 88. The Unbearable Lightness
of Being 88. Eversmile, New Jersey 89. My Left
Foot (AA) 89. The Last of the Mohicans 92. The
Age of Innocence 93. *In the Name of the Father* (AAN)
93, etc.

De Anda, Peter (1940–   ).
American leading man of the 70s.
Cutter (TV) 72. Come Back Charleston Blue 72.
The New Centurions 72, etc.

De Angelis, Guido.
Italian composer, in collaboration with Maurizio
De Angelis.
They Call Me Trinity 70. Trinity Is Still My Name
71. All the Way Boys 73. Run Run Joe 74. Zorro
75. Keoma (The Violent Breed) 76. Charleston 78.
Killer Fish 79. Between Miracles 79. Safari Express
80. The Immortal Bachelor 80. Great White 82.
Blue Paradise 82. Yor, the Hunter from the Future
83. Body Beat 89, etc.

De Angelis, Maurizio.
Italian composer, in collaboration with Guido De
Angelis (qv for films).

De Antonio, Emile (1920–1989).
American experimental documentarist.
Point of Order 64. Rush to Judgment 67. America
Is Hard to See 68. In the Year of the Pig 69. Milhouse
71. Painters Painting 73. Underground 76. In the
King of Prussia 82. Mr Hoover and I 89, etc.

De Banzie, Brenda (1915–1981).
British character actress who got her big chance

on the edge of middle age; later played flouncy matrons.

The Long Dark Hall 51. I Believe in You 52. *Hobson's Choice* 54. The Purple Plain 54. What Every Woman Wants 54. A Kid for Two Farthings 55. The Man Who Knew Too Much 56. The Thirty-nine Steps 59. *The Entertainer* 60. Flame in the Streets 61. The Mark 61. The Pink Panther 63. Pretty Polly 67, etc.

De Benning, Burr.
American character actor.

Beach Red 67. Sweet November 69. City Beneath the Sea (TV) 71. St Ives 76. The Incredible Melting Man 77. Hanging by a Thread (TV) 79. A Nightmare on Elm Street 5: The Dream Child 89, etc.

De Bont, Jan (1943–).
Dutch cinematographer turned director, in Hollywood from the mid-80s. *Speed*, his first feature, was a success, his asking price as director rising to $4m.

Turkish Delight (Turks Fruit) 73. Katie's Passion (Keetje Tippel) 75. Max Havelaar 76. Private Lessons 81. I'm Dancing as Fast as I Can 82. Cujo 83. All the Right Moves 83. The Fourth Man (De Vierde Man) 83. Flesh and Blood 85. The Jewel of the Nile 85. Ruthless People 86. The Clan of the Cave Bear 86. Who's That Girl? 87. Leonard Part 6 87. Die Hard 88. Black Rain 89. Bert Rigby, You're a Fool 89. The Hunt for Red October 90. Flatliners 90. Basic Instinct 92. Shining Through 92. Lethal Weapon 3 92. Speed (d) 94, etc.

De Borba, Dorothy (1925–).
American child actress, in the Our Gang comedies 1930–35.

De Bray, Yvonne (1889–1954).
French character actress, in films from 1943.
Gigi 48. Les Parents Terribles 49. Olivia 50. Caroline Cherie 50. Nous Sommes Tous des Assassins 52, etc.

De Broca, Philippe (1933–).
French director and screenwriter who first worked as an assistant to François Truffaut and Claude Chabrol.

■ Les Jeux de l'Amour 60. Le Farceur 60. The Seven Deadly Sins (part) 61. L'Amant de Cinq Jours 61. Cartouche 62. Les Veinards (part) 63. *That Man from Rio* 63. Un Monsieur de Compagnie 64. Tribulations Chinoise en Chine 65. The Oldest Profession 67. King of Hearts 67. Devil by the Tail 68. Give Her the Moon 70. Le Poudre d'Escampette 71. Chère Louise 72. Le Magnifique 73. Dear Inspector 77. Psy 80. On à Volé tu Cuisse de Jupiter 80. Louisiana 84. The Gypsy 85. Chouans! 88. The 1001 Nights (Sheherazade) (wd) 90. The Keys of Paradise (Les Clés du Paradis) 91.

De Brulier, Nigel (1878–1948).
British actor in Hollywood: career waned with sound.

Intolerance 16. The Four Horsemen of the Apocalypse 21. The Three Musketeers (as Richelieu) 21. Salome 23. The Hunchback of Notre Dame 23. Ben Hur 26. Wings 27. Noah's Ark 29. The Iron Mask 29. Moby Dick 31. Rasputin and the Empress 32. Mary of Scotland 36. The Garden of Allah 36. The Hound of the Baskervilles 39. One Million B.C. 40. The Adventures of Captain Marvel 48, many others.

De Camp, Rosemary (1913–).
American character actress specializing in active motherly types.

Cheers for Miss Bishop 41. Jungle Book 42. This is the Army 43. *The Merry Monahans* 44. *Rhapsody in Blue* 44. From this Day Forward 46. Nora Prentiss 47. Night unto Night 49. The Big Hangover 50. *On Moonlight Bay* 51. By the Light of the Silvery Moon 53. Many Rivers to Cross 55. Thirteen Ghosts 60. Blind Ambition (TV) 79. Saturday the 14th 81, etc.

TV series: The Life of Riley. *The Bob Cummings Show*. That Girl.
~Miss De Camp was thirteen years James Cagney's junior – but in *Yankee Doodle Dandy* she played his mother.

De Carlo, Yvonne (1922–) (Peggy Middleton).
Canadian leading lady, a star in the 40s of Hollywood's most outrageous easterns and westerns.

Salome Where She Danced 45. Frontier Gal 45. Song of Scheherezade 47. Brute Force 47. Slave Girl 47. Black Bart (as Lola Montez) 48. Casbah 48. River Lady 48. *Criss Cross* 49. Calamity Jane and Sam Bass 49. The Desert Hawk 50. Tomahawk 51. Hotel Sahara 51. Scarlet Angel 52. Sea Devils 52. Sombrero 53. The Captain's Paradise 53. Passion 54. Magic Fire 56. The Ten Commandments 56. Death of a Scoundrel 56. Band of Angels 57. McLintock 63. Law of the Lawless 64. Munster Go Home 66. The Power 68. The Seven Minutes 71. Guyana Cult of the Damned 80. The Man with Bogart's Face 80. Liar's Moon 82. Flesh and Bullets 85. A Masterpiece of Murder (TV) 86. American Gothic 88. Oscar 91, etc.

TV series: *The Munsters* 64–65.

De Casalis, Jeanne (1897–1966).
British revue comedienne and character actress, best known as radio's 'Mrs Feather' in dithery telephone monologues. She was married to Colin Clive.

Autobiography: 1953, *Things I Don't Remember*.
Settled out of Court 25. The Arcadians 27. Nell Gwyn 34. Cottage to Let 41. Charley's Big Hearted Aunt 41. Those Kids from Town 42. Medal for the General 44. This Man Is Mine 46. Woman Hater 48, etc.

De Cordoba, Pedro (1881–1950).
American stage actor, lean and often sinister, in many silent and sound films.

Carmen 15. Maria Rosa 16. Runaway Romany 20. Young Diana 22. The Crusades 35. Anthony Adverse 36. The Light That Failed 39. The Ghost Breakers 40. The Mark of Zorro 40. Son of Fury 42. For Whom the Bell Tolls 43. The Beast with Five Fingers 47. When the Redskins Rode 50, etc.

De Cordova, Arturo (1908–1973) (Arturo Garcia).
Mexican leading man with flashing grin and impudent eyes. Popular in Mexico since 1935; made a few Hollywood films in the 40s.

For Whom the Bell Tolls 43. Hostages 43. *Frenchman's Creek* 44. Incendiary Blonde 44. A Medal for Benny 45. Masquerade in Mexico 45. The Flame 47. New Orleans 47. The Adventures of Casanova 48. El (Mex.) 51. Kill Him for Me 53, etc.

De Cordova, Frederick (1910–).
American director with stage and TV experience.

■ Too Young to Know 45. Her Kind of Man 46. That Way with Women 47. Love and Learn 47. Always Together 47. Wallflower 48. For the Love of Mary 48. The Countess of Monte Cristo 48. Illegal Entry 49. The Gal Who Took the West 49. Buccaneer's Girl 50. Peggy 50. The Desert Hawk

50. Bedtime for Bonzo 51. Katie Did It 51. Littl[e] Egypt 51. Finders Keepers 51. Here Come the Nelsons 52. Bonzo Goes to College 52. Yankee Buccaneer 53. Column South 53. I'll Take Swe[d] 65. Frankie and Johnny 66.

De Corsia, Ted (1904–1973).
American character actor with long vaudeville experience; usually played surly villains.

The Lady from Shanghai 47. *Naked City* 48. Th[e] Enforcer 51. Vengeance Valley 51. Man In the D[...] 53. Twenty Thousand Leagues Under The Sea 5[...] The Big Combo 55. Slightly Scarlet 56. The Kill[i] 56. Baby Face Nelson 57. Gunfight at the O.K. Corral 57. Blood on the Arrow 61. The Quick G[...] 64. Nevada Smith 66. Five Card Stud 68, many others.

TV series: Steve Canyon 57–60.

De Courville, Albert (1887–1960).
British stage director who directed a few film comedies.

Wolves 30. The Midshipmaid 32. This is the I 33. Things Are Looking Up 34. The Case of Gab[...] Perry 35. Seven Sinners 36. Crackerjack 38. The Lambeth Walk 38. An Englishman's Home 39, etc.

DeCuir, John (1918–).
American production designer.

Naked City 48. The Snows of Kilimanjaro 51. Call Me Mister 52. The King and I 56. South Pac[...] 57. Cleopatra 62. The Agony and the Ecstasy 65 Hello Dolly 69. The Great White Hope 70. Once [it] is not Enough 75. Raise the Titanic 80. Dead Me[...] Don't Wear Plaid 82. Ghostbusters 84. Jo Jo Danc[...] Your Life Is Calling 86. Legal Eagles 86, etc.

DEFA (Deutsche Film Aktiengesellschaft[)]
The East German party line film production company which absorbed UFA in 1946.

De Filippo, Eduardo (1900–1984) (Eduardo Passarelli).
Italian actor and director of many and varied talents.

Tre Uomini in Frac (a) 32. Il Capello a Tre Pun[...] (a) 40. In Campagna e Caduta una Stella (w, d, [...] 40. Il Sogno di Tutti (a) 40. La Vita Ricomincia [...] 45. Assunta Spina (w) 47. Napoli Milionaria (w, d, a) 50. Altri Tempi (a) 51. Filumena Marturan[...] (w, d, a) 51. The Girls of the Spanish Steps (a) 5[...] Villa Borghese (a) 53. Napoletani a Milano (w, d, a) 53. Questi Fantasmi (w, d, a) 54. Fortunella (d, a) 58. Raw Wind in Eden (a) 58. Ghosts of Rome (a) 60. Shoot Loud, Louder, I Don't Understand (w, d, a) 66, many others.

De Forest, Lee (1873–1961).
American inventor, pioneer of many developments in wireless telegraphy, also the De[...] Forest Phonofilm of the 20s, an early experimen[...] in synchronized sound.

De Funes, Louis (1908–1983).
French character comedian.

Lock up the Spoons 56. Femmes de Paris 58. Taxi 59. A Pied à Cheval et en Spoutnik 61. The[...] Sucker 65. Fantomas 66. Don't Look Now 67. Jo 71. The Mad Adventures of Rabbi Jacob 73. Up [...] a Tree 75. What's Cooking in Paris 77. Les Charlo[...] 79. L'Avare 80, many others.

De Govia, Jackson.
American production designer.

Boulevard Nights 79. Butch and Sundance, the Early Years 79. It's My Turn 80. My Bodyguard 80. Spacehunter: Adventures in the Forbidden

e 83. Red Dawn 84. Remo Williams: The
venture Begins 85. 'Night, Mother 86. Nobody's
l 86. Roxanne 87. Punchline 88. Die Hard 88.
Country 89. Dad 89. Sister Act 92, etc.

Grasse, Robert (1900–1971).
erican cinematographer, with RKO from 1934.
hree Pals 26. Fury of the Wild 29. Break of
arts 35. *Stage Door* 37. The Story of Vernon and
ne Castle 39. Bachelor Mother 39. Kitty Foyle
Forever and a Day 43. Step Lively 44. *The Body
atcher* 45. The Miracle of the Bells 48. Home of
Brave 49. The Men 50. Chicago Calling 52,
ny others.

Grasse, Sam (1875–1953).
nadian leading actor, often in villainous roles.
films from 1912.
irth of a Nation 16. Intolerance 16. The Scarlet
r 17. Robin Hood (as Prince John) 22. The
oilers 23. The Black Pirate 26. King of Kings 27.
e Farmer's Daughter 28. Wall Street 29.
ptain of the Guard 30, etc.

Grunwald, Anatole (1910–1967).
tish producer, in films since 1939.
French Without Tears (w) 39. Quiet Wedding
) 40. The First of the Few (w) 41. The Demi-
radise 42. The Way to the Stars 45. The Winslow
y (& w) 48. The Holly and the Ivy (& w) 54.
e Doctor's Dilemma 58. Libel (& w) 61. Come
y with Me 62. The VIPs 63. The Yellow Rolls-
yce 64. Stranger in the House 67, many others.

Grunwald, Dmitri (1914–1990).
tish producer, brother of Anatole de Grunwald.
The Dock Brief 62. Perfect Friday 67. Connecting
oms 69. The Last Grenade 69. Murphy's War
, That Lucky Touch 75, etc.

Haven, Carter (1887–1977).
nerican stage star who appeared in a few silent
ms. His son *Carter de Haven Jnr* (1910–1979) was
roduction manager, especially for Chaplin.

Haven, Gloria (1924–).
nerican soubrette, films mostly light musicals of
enduring quality.
Modern Times 36. The Great Dictator 40. Susan
d God 40. Keeping Company 41. Two Faced
oman 41. The Penalty 41. *Best Foot Forward* 43.
ousands Cheer 43. Broadway Rhythm 44. *Two
rls and a Sailor* 44. Step Lively 44. The Thin Man
es Home 44. Between Two Women 45. Summer
liday 48. Scene of the Crime 49. The Doctor and
Girl 49. Yes Sir That's My Baby 49. The Yellow
b Man 50. Three Little Words 50. Summer Stock
. I'll Get By 50. Two Tickets to Broadway 51.
wn among the Sheltering Palms 53. So This Is
ris 55. The Girl Rush 55. Call Her Mom (TV) 72.
ho Is the Black Dahlia? (TV) 75. Banjo Hackett
V) 76. Sharon, Portrait of a Mistress 77. Evening
Byzantium (TV) 78. The Legend of O. B. Taggart

TV series: Ryan's Hope 75. Nakia 79.

Havilland, Olivia (1916–).
ritish-born leading lady, sister of Joan Fontaine.
Hollywood from teenage as leading lady of
medy, romance and costume drama; later
roved herself an actress.
Semi-autobiography: 1960, *Every Frenchman Has
ne.
A Midsummer Night's Dream* 35. The Irish in Us
5. Alibi Ike 35. Captain Blood 35. Anthony
dverse 36. The Charge of the Light Brigade 36.
all It a Day 36. The Great Garrick 36. It's Love
m After 37. Gold Is Where You Find It 37. Four's

a Crowd 38. *The Adventures of Robin Hood* 38. Hard
To Get 38. Wings of the Navy 39. Dodge City 39.
Gone with the Wind (AAN) 39. Elizabeth and Essex
39. Raffles 40. My Love Came Back 40. Santa Fe
Trail 40. Strawberry Blonde 41. Hold Back the
Dawn (AAN) 41. They Died with Their Boots On
41. The Male Animal 42. In This Our Life 42.
Government Girl 43. Thank Your Lucky Stars 43.
Princess O'Rourke 43. The Well-Groomed Bride 45.
Devotion (as Charlotte Brontë) 46. *The Dark Mirror*
46. *To Each His Own* (AA) 46. *The Snake Pit* (AAN)
47. *The Heiress* (AA) 49. My Cousin Rachel 52. That
Lady 55. Not as a Stranger 55. The Ambassador's
Daughter 56. The Proud Rebel 58. Libel (GB) 60.
The Light in the Piazza 62. Lady in a Cage 64.
Hush Hush Sweet Charlotte 64. The Adventurers 69.
Pope Joan 72. The Screaming Woman (TV) 72. The
Fifth Musketeer 77. Airport 77 77. The Swarm 78.
Roots: The Next Generation (TV) 79. Murder Is Easy
(TV) 82. Charles and Diana: A Royal Romance
(TV) (as the Queen Mother) 82.
◆ For her development from a charming leading
lady to a star actress of some distinction. *The Dark
Mirror.*

Famous line (*The Heiress*): 'Yes, I can be very cruel.
I have been taught by masters.'

De Heer, Rolf (1957–).
Dutch-born screenwriter and director, in
Australia. He worked for the Australian
Broadcasting Commission in a variety of jobs
before studying at the Australian Film and TV
School.
Tail of a Tiger 84. Incident at Raven's Gate 88.
Dingo 91. *Bad Boy Bubby* 93.

De Jesus, Luchi (1923–1984).
American composer and arranger.
Slaughter 72. A Time for Love 74. Black Belt
Jones 74. Thieves 77, etc.

De Keyzer, Bruno.
French cinematographer in international films.
A Sunday in the Country (Un Dimanche à la
Campagne) 84. 'Round Midnight 86. Little Dorrit
88. Beatrice 88. Reunion (L'Ami Retrouvé 89. Life
and Nothing But (La Vie et Rien d'Autre) 89.
December Bride (GB) 91. Impromptu (GB) 91.
War of the Buttons (GB) 94. The Queen of the Night
94, etc.

De La Motte, Marguerite (1902–1950).
American leading lady of silent films.
The Mark of Zorro 20. The Three Musketeers
21. When a Man's a Man 24. The Beloved Brute
24. Red Dice 26. The Unknown Soldier 26. The
Iron Mask 28. Woman's Man 34. Reg'lar Fellers 42,
etc.

De La Patelliere, Denys (1921–).
French director.
Le Défroque (w only) 52. Les Aristocrates 56.
Retour de Manivelle 57. Les Grandes Familles 59.
Marco the Magnificent 65. Du Rififi à Paname 66.
Black Sun 66, etc.

De La Tour, Frances (1944–).
Angular British character actress who plays both
comedy and drama.
Country Dance 69. Every Home Should Have
One 70. Our Miss Fred 72. To the Devil a
Daughter 76. Wombling Free 77. Rising Damp 80.
Genghis Cohen (TV) 93, etc.
TV series: Rising Damp 74–78. Every Silver
Lining 93. Downwardly Mobile 94.

De Lane Lea, William (1900–1964).
British executive, pioneer of sound dubbing
processes.

De Laurentiis, Dino (1919–).
Italian producer who made a stab at Hollywood in
the 70s.
Bitter Rice 48. Ulysses 52. La Strada 54. Barabbas
62. The Bible 65. Kiss the Girls and Make Them
Die 67. Anzio 68. Barbarella 68. Waterloo 69. Wild
Horses 73. Death Wish 74. King Kong 76. The White
Buffalo 77. King of The Gypsies 78. Hurricane 79.
The Brinks Job 79. Flash Gordon 80. Ragtime 81.
Conan the Barbarian 82. Fighting Back 82. The
Bounty 84. Dune 85. Cat's Eye 85. Manhunter
86. Desperate Hours 90, etc.

De Luise, Dom (1933–).
Rotund American comedy star who became one
of the Mel Brooks repertory company.
The Glass Bottom Boat 65. The Twelve Chairs
70. Blazing Saddles 73. Sherlock Holmes' Smarter
Brother 75. Silent Movie 76. The World's Greatest
Lover 78. The End 78. Hot Stuff (& d) 79. The
Muppet Movie 79. Fatso 80. Smokey and the
Bandit II 80. The Last Married Couple in America
80. Wholly Moses 80. The Cannonball Run 81.
History of the World Part One 81. The Best Little
Whorehouse in Texas 82. Happy (TV) 83. Johnny
Dangerously 84. Haunted Honeymoon 86. Going
Bananas 87. Spaceballs 87. Oliver and Company
(voice) 88. All Dogs Go to Heaven (voice) 89.
Loose Cannons 89. Happily Ever After 90. Driving
Me Crazy 91. An American Tail: Fievel Goes West
(voice) 91. Robin Hood: Men in Tights 93.
Munchie Strikes Back 94. A Troll in Central Park
(voice) 94. The Silence of the Hams (It.) 94, etc.
TV series: Lotsa Luck 73.

¶ I'm actually a thin serious person but I play fat
and funny, but only for the movies. – D. De L.

DeLuxe Color
is the Twentieth Century-Fox version of
Eastmancolor but usually comes out decidedly blue.

De Madeiros, Maria (1965–) (Maria de
Almeida).
Portuguese leading actress, in international films
from the 90s.
Henry and June 90. Meeting Venus 91. Tous les
Jours Dimanche 94. Des Feux Mal Éteints 94. Two
Brothers, My Sister (Tres Irmaos) 94, etc.

De Marney, Derrick (1906–1978).
Good-looking British actor with stage experience.
Music Hall 35. Things to Come 36. *Young and
Innocent* 37. Victoria the Great (as Disraeli) 37.
Blonde Cheat (US) 38. The Spider 39. The Lion
Has Wings 40. Dangerous Moonlight 40. The First
of the Few 42. Latin Quarter (& co-p) 46. Uncle
Silas 47. Sleeping Car to Trieste 48. She Shall Have
Murder (& p) 50. Meet Mr Callaghan (& p) 54.
Private's Progress 55. Doomsday at Eleven 62. The
Projected Man 66, etc.

De Marney, Terence (1909–1971).
British actor with stage experience, brother of
Derrick de Marney. Died after falling under a
train.
The Mystery of the Marie Celeste 36. I Killed
the Count 38. Dual Alibi 46. No Way Back 49.
Uneasy Terms 49. The Silver Chalice (US) 55.
Death Is a Woman 66. All Neat in Black Stockings
69, etc.

De Maupassant, Guy (1850–1893).
French short storywriter. Work filmed includes

Diary of a Madman, Une Vie, Le Rosier de Madame Husson, and many versions of *Boule de Suif.*

De Mille, Cecil B. (1881–1959).

American producer-director, one of Hollywood's pioneers and autocrats. Notable in the 20s for sex comedies, in the 30s and 40s for action adventures, then for biblical epics; all now seem very stolid, but were enormously successful in their day.

Autobiography: 1959.

■ *The Squaw Man* 13. The Virginian 14. The Call of the North 14. What's His Name 14. The Man from Home 14. Rose of the Rancho 14. The Girl of the Golden West 15. The Warrens of Virginia 15. The Unafraid 15. The Captive 15. Wild Goose Chase 15. The Arab 15. Chimmie Fadden 15. Kindling 15. Maria Rosa 15. Carmen 15. Temptation 15. Chimmie Fadden Out West 15. *The Cheat* 15. The Golden Chance 16. The Trail of the Lonesome Pine 16. Joan the Woman 16. The Heart of Nora Flynn 16. The Dream Girl 16. A Romance of the Redwoods 17. The Little American 17. The Woman God Forgot 17. The Devil Stone 17. The Whispering Chorus 18. Old Wives for New 18. We Can't Have Everything 18. Till I Come Back to You 18. The Squaw Man 18. Don't Change Your Husband 19. For Better for Worse 19. Male and Female 19. Why Change your Wife? 20. Something to Think About 20. Forbidden Fruit 21. *The Affairs of Anatol* 21. Fool's Paradise 22. Saturday Night 22. Manslaughter 22. Adam's Rib 23. *The Ten Commandments* 23. Triumph 24. Feet of Clay 24. The Golden Bed 25. The Road to Yesterday 25. The Volga Boatmen 26. *King of Kings* 27. The Godless Girl 28. Dynamite 29. Madame Satan 30. The Squaw Man 31. *The Sign of the Cross* 32. This Day and Age 33. Four Frightened People 34. Cleopatra 34. *The Crusades* 35. *The Plainsman* 36. The Buccaneer 38. *Union Pacific* 39. Northwest Mounted Police 40. *Reap The Wild Wind* 42. The Story of Dr Wassell 44. Unconquered 47. Variety Girl (actor) 47. Samson and Delilah 49. Sunset Boulevard (as actor) 50. The Greatest Show on Earth (AAp, AANd) 52. The Ten Commandments 56. The Buccaneer (p only) 59.
☻ For making himself an unseen star by imposing the personality of an autocratic schoolmaster on a variety of somewhat dubious material. *The Sign of the Cross.*

¶ Ready when you are, Mr De Mille. It's the tag-line of a long shaggy dog story, the purpose of which is to establish de Mille as the producer of enormous, stagey biblical epics. Towards the end of his life he did submerge himself in this role, but his career embraced almost every kind of movie. Whatever the show, he made a success of it, and he was respected throughout Hollywood as a disciplinarian who always got his films out under budget. There was a joke during World War II:
Anyone who leaves de Mille for the armed forces is a slacker.
He is credited with sending back a writer's script and attaching a terrifying cover note:
What I have crossed out I didn't like.
What I haven't crossed out I am dissatisfied with.
He exercised supreme control over his stars, and once said to Paulette Goddard:
Remember you are a star. Never go across the alley even to dump garbage unless you are dressed to the teeth.
He told his staff:
You are here to please me. Nothing else on earth matters.
He went to extreme lengths to prove his authority. Arthur Miller thought:

I never met such an egotist in my life.
Even if he was wrong and knew it, once he said it it had to be.
His brother William was awed by his ambition and achievement:
The trouble with Cecil is that he always bites off more than he can chew—and then chews it.
The same William cast a wry eye on Cecil's first Bible picture in the 20s:
Having attended to the underclothes, bathrooms and matrimonial irregularities of his fellow citizens, he now began to consider their salvation.
Even when Cecil dealt with heavenly themes, he kept his feet on earth. He said to a scriptwriter:
It's just a damn good hot tale, so don't get a lot of thees, thous and thums on your mind.
His comparative ignorance of his favourite subject provoked a much-repeated clerihew:
Cecil B. De Mille
Much against his will
Was persuaded to keep Moses
Out of the Wars of the Roses.
He saw the Bible as a ready-made script factory:
Give me any couple of pages of the Bible and I'll give you a picture.
He took neither credit nor blame for his themes:
I didn't write the Bible and didn't invent sin.
He was also quite clear where his support lay:
I make my pictures for people, not for critics.
His approach to actresses was on similarly direct lines. In 1934, when he thought of Claudette Colbert as Cleopatra, he said to her:
How would you like to be the wickedest woman in history?
But he knew that what really mattered to a movie is not the star but the producer:
A picture is made a success not on a set but over the drawing board.
Action was another essential ingredient:
I will trade you forty gorgeously beautiful Hawaiian sunsets for one good sock in the jaw.
He chuckled at the result of his labours:
Every time I make a picture the critics' estimate of American public taste goes down ten per cent.
Typical reaction was Pauline Kael's:
He made small-minded pictures on a big scale.
But Graham Greene had a soft spot for him:
There has always been a touch of genius as well as absurdity in this warm-hearted sentimental salvationist.
He remained true to the literary tradition of Cooper's Leatherstocking Tales and to the dramatic conventions of David Belasco. – *Andrew Sarris, 1968*
I learned an awful lot from him by doing the opposite. – *Howard Hawks*
He wore baldness like an expensive hat, as though it were out of the question for him to have hair like other men. – *Gloria Swanson*
He didn't make pictures for himself or for the critics. He made them for the public. – *Adolph Zukor*

De Mille, Katherine (1911–) (Katherine Lester).

American leading lady of the 30s. She was married to actor Anthony Quinn (1937–55).
Viva Villa 34. Call of the Wild 35. Ramona 36. Banjo on My Knee 37. Blockade 38. Reap the Wild Wind 42. The Story of Dr Wassell 44. Unconquered 47. The Gamblers 50, etc.

De Mille, William (1878–1955).

American director. Elder brother of Cecil B. De Mille, with theatrical background.
Nice People 22. Craig's Wife 28. Captain Fury (p only) 39, etc.

DeMornay, Rebecca (1962–).

American actress. She was educated in Austria and England (at Summerhill School).
One from the Heart 82. Testament 83. Risky Business 84. The Trip to Bountiful 85. Runaway Train 85. The Slugger's Wife 85. The Murders in the rue Morgue (TV) 86. Beauty and the Beast 87.... And God Created Woman 87. Feds 88. Dealers 89. By Dawn's Early Light (TV) 90. An Inconvenient Woman (TV) 91. Backdraft 91. The Hand that Rocks the Cradle 92. Guilty as Sin 93. The Three Musketeers 93. Getting Out (TV) 94, etc.

¶ My mother told me: 'If you do not find a way of earning a living, a man will pay for the roo over your head and he's going to tell you what to do.' I've never forgotten that. I do not want anyone telling me how to live or saying what I can do or can't do or who I can or cannot see. – *R. DeM*
In the best of all worlds and on the best of all days the last thing I like to do at night is feel the physical embrace of someone I love. – *R. DeM.*

De Niro, Robert (1943–).

Leading American actor, usually in downbeat roles.
■ Greetings 68. Sam's Song 69. The Wedding Party 69. Hi Mom 70. Bloody Mama 70. Born to Win 71. The Gang that couldn't Shoot Straight 7! Jennifer on my Mind 71. *Bang the Drum Slowly* 73. *Mean Streets* 73. The Godfather Part Two (AA) 74. Taxi Driver (AAN) 76. The Last Tycoon 76. 1900 76. New York New York 77. *The Deer Hunte* 78. *Raging Bull* (for which he became fifty pound overweight) (AA) 80. True Confessions 81. King of Comedy 83. Once Upon a Time in America 84 Falling in Love 85. Brazil 85. The Mission 86. Ange Heart 87. The Untouchables 87. Midnight Run 88 Jacknife 89. We're No Angels 89. Awakenings (AAN) 90. *GoodFellas* 90. Stanley and Iris 90. Guilty by Suspicion 91. Backdraft 91. *Cape Fear* 9! Mistress 92. This Boy's Life 92. Night and the Cit 92. A Bronx Tale (& d) 93. This Boy's Life 93. A Bronx Tale (& p, d) 93. Mad Dog and Glory 93. Mary Shelley's Frankenstein (as the creature) 94.
☻ For becoming the best film actor of his generation. *Raging Bull.*

¶ There is a mixture of anarchy and discipline i the way I work. – *R. de N.*
After my first movies, I gave interviews. Then I thought, what's so important about where I wen to school, and hobbies . . . what does any of that have to do with acting, with my own head? – *R. d N.*

De Oliveira, Manoel (1908–).

Portuguese director of features and documentarie a former racing driver, trapeze artist and businessman.
Aniki-Bobo 42. The Passion of Jesus (Acto de Primavera) 63. Amor de Perdição (Fr.) 78. Francisc 81. The Satin Slipper (Fr.) 85. Mon Cas 86. The Cannibals (Os Canibais) 88. The Divine Comedy (La Divina Comedia) 91. The Day of Despair (O Dia do Desespero) 92. Vale Abraao 93. Blindman's Buff (A Caixa) 94, etc.

De Ossorio, Amando (1925–).

Spanish director of horror movies, best known fc his movies about the blind dead – corpses of the Knights Templar who rise from their graves to attack the living.
Fangs of the Living Dead (Malenka, la Nipote del Vampiro) 68. Tomb of the Blind Dead (La Noche del Terror Ciego) 71. Return of the Blind Dead (El Ataque de los Muertos sin Ojos) 72.

When the Screaming Stops (Las Garras de Lorelei) 72. Horror of the Zombies (El Buqué Maldito) 73. Night of the Sorcerers (La Noche de los Brujos) 73. Night of the Death Cult (La Noche de las Gaviotas) 74, etc.

De Palma, Brian (1940–).

American director who began in the satirical underground school, then graduated to glossy shock/horrors, usually in clever imitation of somebody else's style.

Murder à la Mode (& w) 68. *Greetings* 68. The Wedding Party 69. Dionysus 70. Hi Mom 70. Get to Know Your Rabbit 72. Sisters 73. Phantom of the Paradise (& w) 74. Obsession 76. *Carrie* 76. The Fury 78. Home Movies 79. Dressed to Kill 80. Blow Out 81. Scarface 83. Body Double 84. Wise Guys 86. *The Untouchables* 87. Casualties of War 89. Bonfire of the Vanities 90. Father's Day 92. Raising Cain 92. Carlito's Way 93.

¶ A superb cinematic talent unable to do more than play doctor with his toy implements. – *Sunday Times, 1981*

My films deal with a stylized, expressionistic world that has a kind of grotesque beauty about it. – *B. de P.*

I don't see scary films. I certainly wouldn't see my films. – *B. de P.*

De Putti, Lya (1901–1931).

Aristocratic Hungarian actress and ballet dancer who began her film career in Germany before going to America in the mid-20s. Died from pneumonia.

The Hindu Tombstone (Das Indische Grabmal) (Ger.) 21. Othello (Ger.) 22. Die Fledermaus (Ger.) 23. Variety (Vareite) (Ger.) 25. God Gave Me Twenty Cents (US) 26. The Sorrows of Satan (US) 26. The Heart Thief (US) 27. Midnight Rose (US) 28. Buck Privates (US) 28. The Scarlet Lady (US) 28. The Informer (US) 29, etc.

De Rochemont, Louis (1899–1978).

American producer, from the world of newsreel. Devised *The March of Time* 34; later produced semi-documentaries like *The House on 92nd Street* 46 and *Boomerang* 47; and was involved in many ventures including Cinerama and Cinemiracle.

DeSalvo, Albert (1931–1973).

Serial killer known as The Boston Strangler who was the subject of a biopic of the same name starring Tony Curtis and directed by Richard Fleischer in 1968. DeSalvo raped and murdered at least 13 women (he claimed to have raped many hundreds) in the early 60s. He was committed to a mental institution in 1967 and was stabbed to death in his cell.

De Santis, Giuseppe (1917–).

Italian director.

Caccia Tragica 47. *Bitter Rice* (AANw) 49. *No Peace among the Olives* 50. Rome Eleven O'Clock 51. A Husband for Anna 53. Men and Wolves 56. La Garconnière 60. Italiani Brava Gente 64. Un Apprezzato Professionista di Sicuro Avvenire 71, etc.

De Santis, Joe (1909–1989).

American character actor who often played alienate gangsters.

Slattery's Hurricane 49. Man with a Cloak 51. The Last Hunt 56. Tension at Table Rock 57. And Now Miguel 66. The Professionals 66. Blue 68, etc.

De Santis, Pasqualino.

Italian cinematographer who has worked with

such directors as Robert Bresson, Luchino Visconti and Francesco Rosi.

Romeo and Juliet (AA) 68. The Damned (Götterdämmerung) (co-p) 69. Death in Venice (Morte a Venezia) 71. The Assassination of Trotsky 72. Lancelot du Lac 74. Conversation Piece (Gruppo di Famiglia in un Interno) 74. Illustrious Corpses (Cadaveri Eccellenti) 75. L'Innocente 76. Christ Stopped at Eboli 79. Three Brothers 80. Bizet's Carmen 84. Sheena, Queen of the Jungle 84. Harem 85. Salome 86. Chronicle of a Death Foretold (Cronica di una Morte Annunciata) 87. High Frequency 89. To Forget Palermo (Dimenticare Palermo) 89. Music for Old Animals (Musica per Animali) 90, etc.

De Sarigny, Peter (1911–).

South African-born producer, in Britain from 1936.

The Malta Story 53. Simba 55. True as a Turtle 56. Never Let Go 61, etc.

De Seta, Vittorio (1923–).

Italian director, mainly of shorts until *Bandits at Orgosolo* 62.

De Sica, Vittorio (1901–1974).

Italian actor and director, in the latter respect an important and skilful realist. Well known in Italy in the 30s, but not elsewhere until after World War II.

Teresa Venerdi (d) 41. I Bambini ci Guardino (d) 42. *Shoeshine* (AA) (d) 46. *Bicycle Thieves* (AA) (d) 48. *Miracle in Milan* (d) 50. *Umberto D* (d) 52. *Madame De* (a) 52. Stazione Termini (Indiscretion) (d) 52. Bread, Love and Dreams (a) 53. Gold of Naples (d) 54. A Farewell to Arms (a, AAN) 57. Il Generale della Rovere (a) 59. Two Women (d) 61. The Condemned of Altona (d) 63. Yesterday, Today and Tomorrow (d) (AA) 64. Marriage Italian Style (d) 64. A New World (d) 66. The Biggest Bundle of Them All (a) 66. After the Fox (d) 66. Woman Times Seven (d) 67. The Shoes of the Fisherman (a) 68. A Place for Lovers (d) 69. Sunflower (d) 70. *The Garden of the Finzi-Continis* (d, AA) 71. The Voyage (d) 73, etc.

TV series as actor: *The Four Just Men* (GB) 59.
☯ For a half-dozen splendid films dotting a very variable career. *Miracle in Milan.*

¶ A fine actor, a polished hack, and a flabby whore – not necessarily in that order. – *Stanley Kauffmann*

De Souza, Edward (1933–).

British leading man, mostly on stage.

The Roman Spring of Mrs Stone 61. The Phantom of the Opera 62. Kiss of the Vampire 63, etc.

De Souza, Steven E.

American screenwriter.

48 Hours 82. The Return of Captain Invincible 83. Commando 85. The Running Man 87. Seven Hours to Judgement 88. Die Hard 88. Bad Dreams 88. Die Hard 2 90. Hudson Hawk 91. Ricochet 92. The Flintstones (co-w) 94. Beverly Hills Cop III 94, etc.

De Sylva, Buddy (1895–1950).

American lyricist, one-third of songwriting team Brown, Henderson and De Sylva, whose story was told in *The Best Things in Life Are Free*. Shows filmed include *Big Boy, Good News*. As B. G. De Sylva, he later became head of production for Paramount Studios, and in *Star Spangled Rhythm* was spoofed by Walter Abel (as G. B. de Soto).

De Toth, André (1912–).

Hungarian-American director, mainly of routine actioners. Oddly enough, directed one of the first 3-D films; having only one eye, he could not see the effect.

Autobiography: 1994, *Fragments: Portraits from the Inside.*

■ Ot Ora forty (Hung.) 38. Ketlany Azultean (Hung.) 38. Har Het Bologsag (Hung.) 38. Semmelweis (Hung.) 38. Balalaika (Hung.) 39. Toprini Nasz (Hung.) 39. Passport to Suez 43. None Shall Escape 44. *Dark Waters* 44. Ramrod 47. The Other Love 47. Pitfall 48. Slattery's Hurricane 49. Man in the Saddle 51. Carson City 52. Springfield Rifle 52. Last of the Comanches 52. *House of Wax* 53. The Stranger Wore a Gun 53. Thunder Over the Plains 53. Crime Wave 54. Riding Shotgun 54. Tanganyika 54. The Bounty Hunter 54. The Indian Fighter 55. Monkey on My Back 57. Hidden Fear 57. The Two Headed Spy (GB) 59. Day of the Outlaw 59. Man on a String 60. Morgan the Pirate 61. The Mongols 62. Gold for the Caesars 64. Play Dirty (GB) 69.

DeTreaux, Tamara (1959–1990).

Tiny (31 ins) American actress who played E.T. in some scenes of the film.

Ghoulies 85. Rockula 90. The Linguini Incident 92, etc.

De Vinna, Clyde (1892–1953).

American cinematographer.

SELECTED SILENTS: The Raiders 16. Madam Who 18. Leave it to Me 20. Yellow Men and Gold 22. The Victor 23. Ben Hur (co-ph) 26. California 27. White Shadows in the South Seas (co-ph) (AA) 28. The Pagan 29.

■ SOUND FILMS: *Trader Horn* 31. The Great Meadow (co-ph) 31. Shipmates 31. Politics 31. Tarzan the Ape Man (co-ph) 32. Bird of Paradise (co-ph) 32. Eskimo 33. Tarzan and His Mate (co-ph) 34. *Treasure Island* 34. West Point of the Air 35. The Last of the Pagans 35. Ah Wilderness 35. Old Hutch 36. Good Old Soak 36. Bad Man of Brimstone 38. Of Human Hearts 38. Fast Company 38. The Girl Downstairs 39. Bridal Suite 39. Blackmail 39. They All Come Out 39. Twenty Mule Team 40. Phantom Raiders 40. Wyoming 40. The Bad Man 41. The People vs Dr Kildare 41. Barnacle Bill 41. Tarzan's Secret Treasure 41. The Bugle Sounds 41. Jackass Mail 41. Whistling in Dixie 42. The Immortal Sergeant 43. Within these Walls 45. The Caribbean Mystery 45. It's a Joke Son 47. Sword of the Avenger 48. The Jungle 52.

De Vito, Danny (1944–).

Diminutive and aggressive American character actor, often in venal roles, who began directing in the 90s.

■ Dreams of Glass 68. La Mortadella 72. Hurry Up, Or I'll Be 30 73. Scalawag 73. One Flew Over the Cuckoo's Nest 75. The Van 77. The World's Greatest Lover 77. Goin' South 78. Going Ape! 81. Terms of Endearment 83. Johnny Dangerously 84. The Ratings Game (& d) (TV) 84. Romancing the Stone 84. The Jewel of the Nile 85. Head Office 86. My Little Pony: The Movie 86. Ruthless People 86. Wise Guys 86. Throw Momma from the Train (& d) 87. Tin Men 87. Twins 88. Wars of the Roses (& d) 89. Other People's Money 91. Batman Returns 92. Hoffa (& d) 92. Jack the Bear 93. Look Who's Talking Now (voice) 93. Renaissance Man 94. Junior 94.

TV series: Taxi 78–83.

¶ If you're my height and look the way I do and you don't have an abundance of ego and self-esteem, you become a basket case, one of life's prime losers, because height and looks and suave and all those qualities are worshipped. – *D. de V.*

De Vol, Frank (1925–).
American composer.

The Big Knife 55. Kiss Me Deadly 55. Attack 56. Pillow Talk (AAN) 59. Whatever Happened to Baby Jane? 62. McLintock 63. Hush Hush Sweet Charlotte (AAN) 64. Send Me No Flowers 64. Cat Ballou 65. The Flight of the Phoenix 65. Guess Who's Coming to Dinner (AAN) 67. The Dirty Dozen 67. Krakatoa East of Java 68. Ulzana's Raid 71. The Longest Yard 74. Doc Savage 75. The Choirboys 77. The Frisco Kid 79. Herbie Goes Bananas 80 . . . All the Marbles 81, etc.

De Vorzon, Barry.
American composer.

The Warriors 79. The Ninth Configuration 80. Xanadu 80. Looker 81. Tattoo 81. Tarzan, the Ape Man 82. Jekyll and Hyde . . . Together Again 82. Stick 85. Night of the Creeps 86. Exorcist III 90, etc.

De Wilde, Brandon (1942–1972).
American child actor, later juvenile lead. Died in a car accident.

■ *The Member of the Wedding* 52. *Shane* (AAN) 53. Goodbye My Lady 56. Night Passage 57. The Missouri Traveller 58. Blue Denim 59. All Fall Down 62. *Hud* 63. In Harm's Way 65. Those Calloways 65. The Deserter 70. Wild in the Sky 72.

TV series: Jamie 54.

De Wolfe, Billy (1907–1974) (William Andrew Jones).
Toothy, moustachioed American comedy actor, formerly dancer, with vaudeville and night club experience. (Famous act: a lady taking a bath.)

Dixie 43. Blue Skies 46. *Dear Ruth* 47. Dear Wife 50. Tea for Two 50. Lullaby of Broadway 51. *Call Me Madam* 53. Billie 65. The World's Greatest Athlete 73, etc.

TV series: The Pruitts of Southampton 67. Good Morning World 67. The Queen and I 69. The Debbie Reynolds Show 69. The Doris Day Show 70–71.

De Wolff, Francis (1913–1984).
Bearded, burly British character actor.

Adam and Evelyne 48. Under Capricorn 49. Treasure Island 50. Scrooge 51. Ivanhoe 53. The Master of Ballantrae 53. Geordie 55, many others.

De Young, Cliff (1945–).
American general-purpose actor.

Sunshine (TV) 73. Harry and Tonto 74. The Night that Panicked America (TV) 75. The Lindbergh Kidnapping Case (TV) (title role) 76. Blue Collar 78. King (TV) (as Bobby Kennedy 78. Shock Treatment 81. The Hunger 83. Protocol 84. F/X 85. Flight of the Navigator 87. Crackdown 90. Nails 92. Revenge of the Red Baron 94. Infinity 95, etc.

TV series: Sunshine 75. Centennial 78–79. Master of the Game 84.

Deacon, Brian (1949–).
British general-purpose actor.

Triple Echo 73. Vampire 74. Lillie (TV) 78. A Zed and Two Noughts 86, etc.

Deacon, Richard (1922–1984).
Bald, bespectacled American character actor who usually played comic snoops.

Abbott and Costello Meet the Mummy 55. The Power and the Prize 56. The Remarkable Mr Pennypacker 58. Blackbeard's Ghost 68. Piranha 78, many others.

TV series: Leave It to Beaver 57–63. *Dick Van Dyke* 61–66. Mothers-in-law 67–68.

deaf mutes
have been movingly portrayed by Jane Wyman in *Johnny Belinda*, Mandy Miller in *Mandy*, Harry Bellaver in *No Way Out*, and Alan Arkin *The Heart Is a Lonely Hunter*. Dorothy McGuire in *The Spiral Staircase* was mute but not deaf; Patty Duke in *The Miracle Worker* was deaf but could make sounds.

Deakins, Roger (1949–).
British cinematographer.

Before Hindsight 77. Blue Suede Shoes 80. Another Time, Another Place 83. 1984 84. Return to Waterloo 85. Defence of the Realm 85. Shadey 85. Sid and Nancy 86. Kitchen Toto 87. Personal Services 87. White Mischief 87. Pascali's Island 88. Stormy Monday 88. Air America 90. Mountains of the Moon 90. The Long Walk Home 90. Air America 90. Barton Fink 91. Homicide 91. Thunderheart 92. The Secret Garden 93. The Hudsucker Proxy 94. The Shawshank Redemption 94. Rob Roy 95, etc.

Dean, Basil (1888–1978).
British stage producer who also directed several important films for Associated Talking Pictures, which he founded. He was also responsible for the formation in wartime of the organization of travelling entertainers, ENSA, often known disrespectfully as Every Night Something Awful, but standing in fact for Entertainments National Service Association.

Autobiography: 1973, *Mind's Eye*.

The Impassive Footman 32. The Constant Nymph (& co-w) 33. Java Head 34. Sing As We Go 34. Lorna Doone 35. Twenty-One Days 39, etc.

Dean, Eddie (1907–) (Edgar D. Glossup).
American star of western second features in the 30s and 50s.

Renegade Trail 39. Sierra Sue 41. Romance of the West 47. Hawk of Powder River 50, many others.

Dean, Isabel (1918–) (Isabel Hodgkinson).
British stage actress, usually in upper-class roles: very occasional film appearances.

The Passionate Friends 47. Twenty-four Hours of a Woman's Life 52. The Story of Gilbert and Sullivan 53. Out of the Clouds 55. Virgin Island 58. The Light in the Piazza 62. A High Wind in Jamaica 65. Inadmissible Evidence 68. Catch Me a Spy 71. Five Days One Summer 82. Weather in the Streets 84, etc.

Dean, James (1931–1955).
Moody young American actor who after a brief build-up in small roles was acclaimed as the image of the mid-50s; his tragic death in a car crash caused an astonishing world-wide outburst of emotional necrophilia. A biopic, *The James Dean Story*, was patched together in 1957.

Biographies: 1956, *James Dean* by William Bast. 1974, *James Dean: The Mutant King* by David Dalton. 1975, *James Dean* by John Howlett. 1982, *James Dean: A Portrait* by Roy Schatt. 1994, *James Dean: Boulevard of Broken Dreams* by Paul Alexander.

■ Has Anybody Seen My Gal? 51. Sailor Beware 51. Fixed Bayonets 52. Trouble Along the Way 53. *East of Eden* (AAN) 55. *Rebel Without A Cause* 55. *Giant* (AAN) 56.

¶ Another dirty shirt-tail actor from New York. – *Hedda Hopper*

He was sad and sulky. You kept expecting him to cry. – *Elia Kazan*

Dean, Julia (1878–1952).
American stage actress who made a few movies after she retired to California.

How Molly Made Good 15. Curse of the Cat People 44. O.S.S. 46. Nightmare Alley 48. People Will Talk 51. Elopement 51, etc.

Dean, Loren (1969–).
American juvenile actor.

Plain Clothes 88. Say Anything 89. Billy Bathgate (title role) 91.

Dean, Man Mountain (1899–1963).
American wrestler who played comedy roles in a few films.

Reckless 35. The Gladiator 36. Surprise Package 60, etc.

Dean, Priscilla (1896–1987).
American star of silent films, on stage from the age of four and in films from the age of 12, notably for Universal.

Even as You and I 17. The Hand that Rocks the Cradle 17. She Hired a Husband 18. The Wicked Darling 19. The Exquisite Thief 19. Pretty Smooth 19. The Virgin of Stamboul 20. Outside the Law 21. Reputation 21. Under Two Flags 22. The Flame of Life 23. Drifting 23. The White Tiger 23. The Storm Daughter 24. Slipping Wives 26. Behind Stone Walls 32, etc.

Dear, William.
American director.

Time Rider 83. Harry and the Hendersons 87. If Looks Could Kill 91. Angels in the Outfield 94, etc.

Dearden, Basil (1911–1971).
British director, former editor. Began by co-directing Will Hay's last films for Ealing, then formed a writer-producer-director partnership with Michael Relph. Killed in a car crash.

■ The Black Sheep of Whitehall (co-d) 41. The Goose Steps Out (co-d) 42. The Bells Go Down 43. My Learned Friend (co-d) 43. The Halfway House 44. They Came to a City 44. Dead of Night (part) 45. *The Captive Heart* 46. Frieda 47. Saraband for Dead Lovers 48. Train of Events (co-d) 49. *The Blue Lamp* 50. Cage of Gold 50. Pool of London 51. I Believe in You (co-d) 52. The Gentle Gunman 52. The Square Ring 53. The Rainbow Jacket 54. Out of the Clouds (co-d) 55. The Ship That Died of Shame (co-d) 55. Who Done It (co-d) 56. The Smallest Show on Earth 57. Violent Playground 58. *Sapphire* 59. *The League of Gentlemen* 60. Man in the Moon 60. The Secret Partner 61. *Victim* 61. All Night Long (co-d) 62. Life for Ruth 62. The Mind Benders 63. A Place to Go 63. Woman of Straw 64. Masquerade 65. Khartoum 66. Only When I Larf 68. The Assassination Bureau 69. The Man Who Haunted Himself 70.

¶ He was a master film-maker. If we'd have had the right atmosphere in which he could have worked, he would have been a top one. – *Dirk Bogarde*

Dearden, James (1949–).
British director and screenwriter. He is the son of Basil Dearden.

Fatal Attraction (w) 87. Pascali's Island 88. A Kiss before Dying, 91, etc.

Dearing, Edgar (1893–1974).
American character actor, often seen as tough cop.
Thanks for Everything 35. Swing Time 37. Miss Annie Rooney 42, many others.

Death
has always fascinated film-makers, though the results have often appeared undergraduate-ish, as fantasy tends to look when brought down to a mass-appeal level. Death has been personified in *Death Takes a Holiday* by Fredric March and in the 1971 TV remake by Monte Markham, in *On Borrowed Time* by Cedric Hardwicke, in *Here Comes Mr Jordan* by Claude Rains, in *Orphée* by Maria Casares, in *The Seventh Seal* by Bengt Ekerot, by Richard Burton in *Boom*, by George Jessel in *Heironymous Merkin* and by several actors in *The Masque of the Red Death*. In *Devotion*, Ida Lupino as Emily Brontë dreamed of death on horseback coming to sweep her away; in *The Bluebird* Shirley Temple ventured into the land of the dead to see her grandparents. Most of the characters in *Thunder Rock*, and all in *Outward Bound* (remade as *Between Two Worlds* and later varied for TV as *Haunts of the Very Rich*) were already dead at the start of the story. Other films to involve serious thought about death include *Dark Victory, Jeux Interdits, All the Way Home, Sentimental Journey, No Sad Songs for Me, One Way Passage, Paths of Glory, Wild Strawberries*, and *Ikuru. Flatliners* and *The Rapture* both dealt with experiences after death.
Comedies taking death lightly included *A Slight Case of Murder, Kind Hearts and Coronets, The Trouble with Harry, Too Many Crooks, The Criminal Life of Archibaldo de la Cruz, Send Me No Flowers, The Assassination Bureau, The Loved One, The Wrong Box, Arrivederci Baby, Kiss the Girls and Make Them Die, Arsenic and Old Lace, Une Journée Bien Rempliée*, and *Weekend at Bernie's*.

Debucourt, Jean (1894–1958) (J. Pelisse).
French character actor with long stage experience.
Le Petit Chose 22. La Chute de la Maison Usher 28. Douce 43. Le Diable au Corps 46. Occupe-Toi d'Amélie 49, etc.

Decae, Henri (1915–1987).
Distinguished French cinematographer.
Le Silence de la Mer 49. Les Enfants Terribles 49. Crève-Coeur 52. Bob le Flambeur 55. Lift to the Scaffold 57. Le Beau Serge 58. A Double Tour 59. Les Quatre Cents Coups 59. Les Cousins 59. Plein Soleil 59. Les Bonnes Femmes 60. Léon Morin, Priest 61. Sundays and Cybele 62. Dragées au Poivre 63. Viva Maria 65. Weekend at Dunkirk 65. Night of the Generals 66. Le Voleur 67. The Comedians 67. Castle Keep 69. The Sicilian Clan 70. The Light at the Edge of the World 71. Bobby Deerfield 77. The Island 80. Exposed 83, etc.

Decker, Diana (1926–).
Bright, blonde, American leading lady, in Britain from 1939; became known through toothpaste commercials ('Irium, Miriam?').
Fiddlers Three 44. Meet Me at Dawn 48. Murder at the Windmill 49. Is Your Honeymoon Really Necessary? 53. Lolita 62. Devils of Darkness 65, etc.
TV series: Mark Saber 54

Deckers, Eugene (1917–1977).
French character actor who played Continental types in British films after 1946.
Sleeping Car to Trieste 48. The Elusive Pimpernel 50. The Lavender Hill Mob 51. Father Brown 54. Port Afrique 56. Northwest Frontier 59. Lady L 66. The Limbo Line 68, many others.

Decoin, Henri (1896–1969).
French director, in films since 1929.
Abus de Confiance 37. Les Inconnus dans la Maison 42. La Fille du Diable 46. Three Telegrams 50. The Truth about Bebe Donge 52. The Lovers of Toledo 53. Razzia sur la Chnouf 55. Charmants Garçons 57. The Face of the Cat 58. Outcasts of Glory 64, many others.

Dee, Frances (1907–) (Jean Dee).
American leading lady of the 30s, long married to Joel McCrea; a former extra, she was chosen by Chevalier to play opposite him in her first speaking role.
Playboy of Paris 30. An American Tragedy 31. Rich Man's Folly 32. King of the Jungle 33. Becky Sharp 35. If I Were King 38. So Ends Our Night 41. Meet the Stewarts 42. I Walked with a Zombie 43. Happy Land 43. Bel Ami 48. Four Faces West 48. Payment on Demand 51. Because of You 53. Mr Scoutmaster 53. Gypsy Colt 54, etc.

Dee, Ruby (1924–) (Ruby Ann Wallace).
American actress.
No Way Out 50. Tall Target 51. Go Man Go 53. Edge of the City 57. Take a Giant Step 59. *A Raisin in the Sun* 61. The Balcony 62. Buck and the Preacher 72. Black Girl 72. Cat People 82. Do the Right Thing 89. Jungle Fever 91. A Cop and a Half 93. The Stand (TV) 94, etc.

Dee, Sandra (1942–) (Alexandra Zuck).
Petite American leading lady, former model.
Until They Sail 57. The Reluctant Debutante 58. Gidget 59. *Imitation of Life* 59. A Summer Place 59. Portrait in Black 60. Romanoff and Juliet 61. Come September 62. Tammy and the Doctor 63. Take Her She's Mine 64. That Funny Feeling 65. A Man Could Get Killed 66. Doctor, You've Got to be Kidding 67. Rosie 68. The Daughters of Joshua Cabe (TV) 72. Houston We've Got a Problem (TV) 74. Manhunter (TV) 76. Fantasy Island (TV) 77, etc.

Deed, André (1884–1938) (Andre Chapuis).
French actor and director who was probably cinema's first comedian. A music-hall acrobat and singer, he entered films in 1905, when he was discovered by Charles Pathé, to become one of the screen's first stars, though hardly any of his films survive. He was known by different names in different countries: Boireau in France, Foolshead in Britain, Cretinetti in Italy, and Toribio in Spain. His popularity ending with the coming of sound, he became night-watchman at the Pathé studios and died forgotten.
Boireau Déménage 05. Cretinetti al Cinema 11. Boireau Domestique 13. Graine au Vent 28, etc.

Deeley, Michael (1931–).
British producer, a former EMI executive.
The Case of the Mukkinese Battlehorn 61. One Way Pendulum 64. Robbery 67. The Italian Job 69. Murphy's War 70. The Man Who Fell to Earth 75. Nickelodeon 76. The Deer Hunter 78, etc.

deep focus.
Dramatic camera technique which brings both foreground and background objects into equal focus and clarity; notably used in *Citizen Kane* and *Hamlet*.

definitions
¶ A selection, chosen for entertainment rather than instruction.
Agent: A guy who is sore because an actor gets ninety per cent of what he makes.

Casting: Deciding which of two faces the public is least tired of.
Disneyland: The biggest people trap ever built by a mouse.
Double feature: A show that enables you to sit through a picture you don't care to see, so you can see one you don't like. — *Henry Morgan*
Epic: The easiest kind of picture to make badly. — *Charlton Heston*
It: The indefinable something. – *Elinor Glyn*, creator of 'It'
Musicals: A series of catastrophes ending with a floor show. – *Oscar Levant*
Oomph: The sound a fat man makes when he bends over to tie his laces in a phone booth. – *Ann Sheridan*
Romanoff's Restaurant: A place where a man can take his wife and family and have a lovely seven-course meal for $3,400. – *George Jessel*
Starlet: Any woman under thirty not actively employed in a brothel.
Television: A medium, so called because it is neither rare nor well done. – *Ernie Kovacs*

Defoe, Daniel (1659–1731).
English writer whose work included the oft-filmed *Robinson Crusoe*; also *Moll Flanders*, which the 1965 film resembled but slightly.

DeFore, Don (1917–1993).
American second lead, the good guy or dumb hearty westerner of dozens of forgettable films in the 40s and 50s.
You Can't Escape Forever 42. A Guy Named Joe 43. Thirty Seconds Over Tokyo 44. The Affairs of Susan 45. You Came Along 45. Ramrod 47. Romance on the High Seas 48. Too Late for Tears 48. My Friend Irma 49. Dark City 50. The Guy Who Came Back 51. She's Working Her Way Through College 52. Battle Hymn 57. The Facts of Life 61. A Rare Breed (TV) 81, etc.
TV series: Ozzie and Harriet 52–58. Hazel 61–65.

Degermark, Pia (1949–).
Swedish leading lady in international films.
Elvira Madigan 67. The Looking Glass War 71, etc.

Degregorio, Eduardo (1942–).
Argentinian-born screenwriter and director who has lived in France since the mid-60s.
The Spider's Stratagem (La Strategia del Ragno) (co-w) 70. Celine and Justine Go Boating (Celine et Justine Vont en Bateau) (co-w) 74. Serail (d) 76, etc.

Dehlavi, Jamil.
Pakistani director.
The Blood of Hussain 80. Immaculate Conception (GB) 92.

Dehn, Paul (1912–1976).
British screenwriter, former film critic.
Seven Days to Noon 51. Orders to Kill 58. *Goldfinger* 64. The Spy Who Came in from the Cold 65. The Deadly Affair 66. The Taming of the Shrew 67. Beneath the Planet of the Apes (and two sequels) 67. Fragment of Fear (& p) 69. Murder on the Orient Express 74, etc.

Dehner, John (1915–1992) (John Forkum).
American character actor, usually as sympathetic smart alec or dastardly villain, a former animator, from radio.
Captain Eddie 45. The Secret of St Ives 49. Last of the Buccaneers 50. Lorna Doone 51. Scaramouche 52. Apache 54. Carousel 56. The

Left-handed Gun (as Pat Garrett) 58. Timbuktu 59. The Chapman Report 62. Critic's Choice 63. Youngblood Hawke 63. Stiletto 69. Support Your Local Gunfighter 71. Fun with Dick and Jane 77. The Boys from Brazil 78. The Right Stuff 83. Creator 84. Jagged Edge 85, etc.

TV series: The Westerner 60. The Roaring Twenties 60–62. The Baileys of Balboa 64–65. The Doris Day Show 71–73. Temperatures Rising 73–74. Big Hawaii 77. Young Maverick 79–80. Enos 80–81.

Deighton, Len (1929–).
British writer of convoluted spy thrillers.

The Ipcress File (oa) 65. Funeral in Berlin (oa) 66. Billion Dollar Brain (oa) 67. Only When I Larf (w) 68. Spy Story 76, etc.

Deitch, Donna (1945–).
American director who first attracted attention by making a lesbian affair a box-office success in *Desert Hearts*. She studied as an artist before attending film school and began by making documentaries. She appears in a documentary on women film-makers, *Calling the Shots* 88.

Woman to Woman (doc) 75. The Great Wall of Los Angeles (doc) 78. Desert Hearts 85. The Women of Brewster Place (TV) 89. Angel of Desire 94, etc.

Dekker, Albert (1905–1968).
Dutch-American stage actor of long experience; film career disappointing. Hanged himself.

■ The Great Garrick 37. Marie Antoinette 38. The Last Warning 38. She Married an Artist 38. The Lone Wolf in Paris 38. Extortion 38. Paris Honeymoon 39. Never Say Die 39. Hotel Imperial 39. Beau Geste 39. The Man in the Iron Mask 39. The Great Commandment 39. Dr Cyclops 40. Strange Cargo 40. Rangers of Fortune 40. Seven Sinners 40. You're the One 41. Blonde Inspiration 41. Reaching for the Sun 41. Buy Me That Town 41. Honky Tonk 41. *Among the Living* 41. Night in New Orleans 42. Wake Island 42. Once Upon a Honeymoon 42. Star Spangled Rhythm 42. The Lady Has Plans 42. In Old California 42. Yokel Boy 42. The Forest Rangers 42. Woman of the Town 43. War of the Wildcats 43. Buckskin Frontier 43. The Kansan 43. Experiment Perilous 44. Incendiary Blonde 45. Hold that Blonde 45. Salome Where She Danced 45. The French Key 46. *The Killers* 46. California 46. Suspense 46. The Pretender 47. Gentleman's Agreement 47. Wyoming 47. Cass Timberland 47. Slave Girl 47. The Fabulous Texan 47. Fury at Furnace Creek 48. Lulu Belle 48. Search for Danger 49. Bride of Vengeance 49. Tarzan's Magic Fountain 49. The Kid from Texas 50. Destination Murder 50. The Furies 50. As Young as You Feel 51. Wait till the Sun Shines Nellie 52. The Silver Chalice 54. East of Eden 55. Kiss Me Deadly 55. Illegal 55. She Devil 57. These Thousand Hills 59. Middle of the Night 59. The Wonderful Country 59. Suddenly Last Summer 59. The Sound and the Fury 59. Come Spy with Me 67. The Wild Bunch 69.

Dekker, Fred (1959–).
American screenwriter and director.

Night of the Creeps 86. Monster Squad 87. Teen Agent (story) 91. Ricochet (story) 91. Robocop 3 (co-w, d) 93.

Del Giudice, Filippo (1892–1961).
Italian producer who settled in England and became managing director of Two Cities Films.

French without Tears 39. In Which We Serve 42. Henry V 44. The Way Ahead 44. Blithe Spirit

45. Odd Man Out 47. The Guinea Pig 48, many others.

Del Rio, Dolores (1905–1983) (Dolores Asunsolo).
Mexican leading lady with aristocratic background; beautiful and popular star of the 20s and 30s. Her second husband was Cedric Gibbons.

Joanna (debut) 25. High Stepper 26. What Price Glory? 27. *The Loves of Carmen* 27. Resurrection 28. Evangeline 29. The Bad One 30. The Dove 31. Bird of Paradise 32. Flying Down to Rio 33. Wonder Bar 34. Madame Du Barry 34. Lancer Spy 37. *Journey into Fear* 42. Portrait of Maria 45. The Fugitive 47. *Cheyenne Autumn* 64. Once upon a Time 67, many others.

Del Ruth, Roy (1895–1961).
Very competent American director, former gag writer for Mack Sennett.

■ SOUND FILMS: Conquest 29. The Desert Song 29. The Hottentot 29. Gold Diggers of Broadway 29. The Aviator 29. Hold Everything 30. The Second Floor Mystery 30. Three Faces East 30. The Life of the Party 30. My Past 31. Divorce Among Friends 31. *The Maltese Falcon* 31. Side Show 31. Blonde Crazy 31. Taxi 32. Beauty and the Boss 32. Winner Take All 32. *Blessed Event* 32. Employees Entrance 33. The Mind Reader 33. The Little Giant 33. Captured 33. Bureau of Missing Persons 33. *Lady Killer* 33. Bulldog Drummond Strikes Back 34. Upperworld 34. Kid Millions 34. *Folies Bergere* 35. Broadway Melody of 1936 35. *Thanks a Million* 35. It Had to Happen 36. Private Number 36. Born to Dance 36. *On the Avenue* 37. Broadway Melody of 1938. Happy Landing 38. My Lucky Star 38. Tail Spin 39. The Star Maker 39. Here I Am A Stranger 39. He Married His Wife 40. *Topper Returns* 41. The Chocolate Soldier 41. Maisie Gets Her Man 42. Dubarry was a Lady 43. Broadway Rhythm 44. Barbary Coast Gent 44. It Happened on Fifth Avenue 47. The Babe Ruth Story 48. The Red Light 49. Always Leave Them Laughing 49. West Point Story 50. On Moonlight Bay 51. Starlift 51. About Face 52. Stop You're Killing Me 52. Three Sailors and a Girl 53. Phantom of the Rue Morgue 54. The Alligator People 59. Why Must I Die 60.

Del Toro, Guillermo (1965–).
Mexican director and screenwriter, from television, a former assistant to Jaime Humberto Hermosillo and a special effects and make-up expert, studying in the US under Dick Smith. He is also the author of a study of Alfred Hitchcock.

Invasion (TV) 90. Cronos 93, etc.

Delair, Suzy (1916–).
Vivacious French entertainer, in several films.

Quai des Orfèvres 47. Lady Paname 49. Robinson Crusoe Land 50. Gervaise 55. Rocco and his Brothers 60. Is Paris Burning? 66, etc.

Delaney, Shelagh (1939–).
British playwright whose chief contributions to the screen are *A Taste of Honey* and *Charlie Bubbles*.

The Railway Station Man 92.

Delannoy, Jean (1908–).
French director, formerly journalist and cutter.

La Symphonie Pastorale 40. *L'Eternel Retour* 43. Les Jeux Sont Faits 47. *Dieu a Besoin des Hommes* 49. Le Garçon Sauvage 51. The Moment of Truth 52. Marie Antoinette 56. Notre Dame de Paris 56. Maigret Sets a Trap 57. Le Soleil des Voyous 67, many others.

Delany, Dana (1956–).
American actress.

Almost You 84. Where the River Runs Black 86.

Moon over Parador 88. Masquerade 88. Patty Hearst 88. Housesitter 92. Light Sleeper 92. Tombstone 94. Exit to Eden 94, etc.

TV series: China Beach 88–91. Wild Palms 93.

Delderfield, Ronald Frederick (1912–1972).
English playwright and novelist of provincial domestic life, a former journalist.

Autobiographies: 1951, *Nobody Shouted Author.* 1956, *Bird's Eye View.*

All over Town (oa) 48. Worm's Eye View (w) 50. Glad Tidings (oa) 52. Where There's a Will (w) 53. Now and Forever (w) 56. On the Fiddle (oa) 61, etc.

TV series: The Adventures of Ben Gunn 56.

Delerue, Georges (1925–1992).
French composer.

Hiroshima Mon Amour 58. Les Jeux de L'Amour 60. Une Aussi Longue Absence 61. Shoot the Piani 61. Jules et Jim 61. Silken Skin 63. The Pumpkin Eater 64. Viva Maria 65. A Man for All Seasons 6. The 25th Hour 67. Interlude 68. Women in Love 69. Anne of the Thousand Days (AAN) 69. The Conformist 70. The Horseman 70. The Day of the Dolphin (AAN) 73. The Slap 74. Julia (AAN) 77. Tendre Poulet 77. Get Out Your Handkerchiefs 7. A Little Romance (AA) 79. Love on the Run 79. True Confessions 81. Partners 82. The Escape Arti 82. Exposed 83. Agnes of God 85. Salvador 86. Platoon 86. The Lonely Passion of Judith Hearne 87. The House on Carroll Street 88. Biloxi Blues 88. Twins 88. Beaches 88. Steel Magnolias 89. Show of Force 90. Curly Sue 91. Black Robe 91. Dien Bien Phu 92. Memento Mori (TV) 92, many others.

Delevanti, Cyril (1887–1975).
British-born stage actor who played aged gentlemen for many years.

Red Barry 38. Man Hunt 41. Son of Dracula 4. Ministry of Fear 45. Forever Amber 47. Land of th Pharaohs 55. Bye Bye Birdie 63. Mary Poppins 6. *Night of the Iguana* 64. The Greatest Story Ever To 65. Counterpoint 67. The Killing of Sister George 68. Bedknobs and Broomsticks 71. Black Eye 73, many others.

Delfont, Bernard (1910–1994) (Lord Delfont, formerly Barnet Winogradsky).
British show business entrepreneur, brother of Lord Grade; mainly involved in live entertainmen until the 70s when he came to head the EMI entertainment complex.

Delgado, Roger (1918–1973).
English character actor, of Spanish and French parents, in aristocratic and villainous roles, best known as The Master in the TV series *Dr Who*. Educated at the London School of Economics, he began acting in regional repertory. Died in a car crash.

The Captain's Paradise 53. Star 53. Storm over the Nile 56. Battle of the River Plate 56. Sea Fury 58. First Man in Space 59. The Stranglers of Bombay 60. The Terror of the Tongs 61. The Singe Not the Song 61. The Road to Hong Kong 62. The Running Man 63. Masquerade 65. Khartoum 66. The Mummy's Shroud 67. The Assassination Bureau 69. Anthony and Cleopatra 73, etc.

TV series: Sir Francis Drake 62.

Dell, Dorothy (1915–1934) (Dorothy Goff).
American beauty queen whose film career was cu short by a car crash.

■ Wharf Angel 34. Little Miss Marker 34. Shoot the Works 34.

ell, Gabriel (1920–1988) (Gabriel del Vecchio).
merican actor, one of the original Dead End Kids
v) who in the 60s emerged as a TV character
tor.

ell, Jeffrey (1904–1985).
ritish comedy writer, author in the 30s of *Nobody
rdered Wolves*, a satirical novel of the film
dustry.
Sanders of the River (co-w) 35. The Saint's
acation 41. Thunder Rock (co-w) 42. *Don't Take
to Heart* (& d) 44. It's Hard to Be Good (& d) 48.
e Dark Man (& d) 50. Brothers-in-Law (co-w)
. Lucky Jim (co-w) 58. Carlton-Browne of the
O. (& co-d) 59. A French Mistress (co-w) 61.
tten to the Core (co-w) 65. The Family Way
o-w) 66, etc.

elli Colli, Tonino (1923–).
istinguished Italian cinematographer, noted for
s work with Sergio Leone and Pier Paolo Pasolini.
Il Paese senza Pace 42. Toto a Colori 51. Le
ouge et le Noir 54. Accattone 61. Mama Roma
2. The Gospel According to St Matthew (Il
angelo Secondo Matteo) 64. The Hawks and the
parrows (Uccellacci e Uccellini) 66. The Good, the
ad and the Ugly 66. La Mandragola 66. Once
pon a Time in the West 68. Pigsty (Porcile) 69.
ussycat, Pussycat I Love You 70. The Decamaron
0. The Canterbury Tales 71. Lacombe, Lucien 73.
alo, or the 120 Days of Sodom 75. Seven Beauties
6. The Purple Taxi (Un Taxi Mauve) 77. Viva
alia 78. Sunday Lovers 80. Tales of Ordinary
Madness (Storie di Ordinaria Follia) 81.
renchcoat 83. Once Upon a Time in America 84.
inger and Fred 86. The Name of the Rose 86. The
oice of the Moon (La Voce della Luna) 90. The
frican (L'Africana) 91. Bitter Moon 92. En
uivant la Comète 94, many others.

elluc, Louis (1892–1924).
oneer French director of the 20s, associated with
e impressionist school.
■ Fièvre 21. La Femme de Nulle Part 22.
'Innondation 24.

Delon, Alain (1935–).
omantic-looking French leading man.
Plein Soleil 59. Rocco and his Brothers 60. The
clipse 61. The Leopard 62. The Big Snatch 63. The
lack Tulip 64. The Yellow Rolls-Royce 64. The
ove Cage 65. Once a Thief 65. Lost Command
6. Is Paris Burning? 66. Texas Across the River
6. Les Aventuriers 66. Histories Extraordinaires 67.
iabolically Yours 67. Samurai 67. Girl on a
Motorcycle 67. La Piscine 67. Jeff 68. Borsalino 70.
he Sicilian Clan 70. The Red Circle 70. Red Sun
1. The Assassination of Trotsky 72. Scorpio 72.
irty Money 72. Borsalino and Co. 73. Shock 74.
he Investigator 74. The Gypsy 75. Zorro 75. Mr
lein 76. Farewell Friend 77. The Concorde–
irport 79 79. Harmonie 79. Trois Hommes à
battre 80. *Swann in Love* 84. Cop's Honour 85.
he Passage 86. New Wave (Nouvelle Vague) 89.
ancing Machine 90. Casanova 91. Dérapage 92.
'Ours en Peluche 94, etc.

Delon, Nathalie (1938–) (Francine Canovas).
rench leading actress.
Le Samourai 67. La Sorelle 69. When Eight Bells
oll 71. Bluebeard 72. The Romantic
nglishwoman 75. Sweet Lies (& d) 88, etc.

Delorme, Daniele (1926–) (Gabrielle Girard).
rench leading lady.
Gigi 48. La Cage aux Filles 49. Sans Laisser
l'Adresse 51. Tempi Nostri 54. Prisons de Femmes

58. La Guerre des Boutons (p only) 62. Pardon
Mon Affaire 77, etc.

Delpy, Julie (1969–).
Young French leading actress.
Bad Blood (Mauvais Sang) 86. Beatrice (La
Passion Béatrice) 86. Europa, Europa 91. Voyager
92. The Three Musketeers 93. Younger and
Younger 93. Killing Zoe 94. Three Colours: White
(Trois Couleurs: Blanc) 94. Before Sunrise 95, etc.

Del Toro, Guillermo (1965–).
Mexican director and screenwriter, from
television, a former assistant to Jaime Humberto
Hermosillo and a special effects and make-up
expert, studying in the US under Dick Smith. He is
also the author of a study of Alfred Hitchcock.
■ Invasion (TV) 90. Cronos 93, etc.

Delvaux, André (1926–).
Belgian director.
The Man Who Had His Hair Cut Short 67. Un
Soir un Train 68. *Rendezvous at Bray* 73, etc.

Demarest, William (1892–1983).
American character actor, an 'old pro' with vast
vaudeville experience before film debut in 1927.
The Jazz Singer 27. Fingerprints 27. The Murder
Man 35. Wedding Present 36. Rosalie 38. Mr Smith
Goes to Washington 39. Tin Pan Alley 40. The
Great McGinty 40. *Sullivan's Travels* 41. The Palm
Beach Story 42. *Hail the Conquering Hero* 43. *The
Miracle of Morgan's Creek* (as Officer Kockenlocker)
43. Once upon a Time 44. Pardon My Past 45.
Along Came Jones 45. *The Jolson Story* (AAN) 46.
The Perils of Pauline 47. On Our Merry Way 49.
Jolson Sings Again 50. *The First Legion* 51. Riding
High 51. Dangerous When Wet 52. Escape from
Fort Bravo 53. Jupiter's Darling 54. The Rawhide
Years 56. Son of Flubber 63. It's a Mad Mad Mad
Mad World 63. That Darn Cat 65. The McCullochs
75. Won Ton Ton 76, many others.
TV series: Wells Fargo 56–58. Love and
Marriage 59. My Three Sons 67–71.
✪ For his reliability in a wide variety of roles, and
for his ability to be instantly recognized and
welcomed by people who didn't know his name.
Hail the Conquering Hero.

Demick, Irina (1937–).
Franco-Russian leading lady in international films.
The Longest Day 62. Those Magnificent Men in
Their Flying Machines 65. Up From The Beach
65. Cloportes 65. Prudence and the Pill 68, etc.

Demme, Jonathan (1944–).
American director. He is a former critic, film
publicist for Joseph Levine and screenwriter and
producer for Roger Corman's New World
Productions.
■ Angels Hard As They Come (p, co-w) 71. The
Hot Box (p, co-w) 72. Black Mama, White Mama
(co-w) 72. Caged Heat (wd) 74. Crazy Mama 75.
Fighting Mad (wd) 76. Citizens Band 77. Last
Embrace 79. *Melvin and Howard* 80. Swing Shift
84. Stop Making Sense 84. Swimming to Cambodia
87. Something Wild 87. Married to the Mob 88.
The Silence of the Lambs (AA) 91. Cousin Bobby
92. Philadelphia 93.

¶ I don't care what I get remembered for – or
don't get remembered for. That's no interest to
me whatsoever. I just love making movies. – *J.D.*

Demme, Ted.
American director.
Who's the Man 93. The Ref 94, etc.

Demongeot, Mylene (1936–).
Blonde French leading lady, briefly flaunted as sex
symbol.
Les Enfants de L'Amour 54. It's a Wonderful
World (GB) 56. *The Witches of Salem* 56. Bonjour
Tristesse 57. Upstairs and Downstairs (GB) 59. The
Giant of Marathon 60. Gold for the Caesars 62.
Uncle Tom's Cabin (Ger.) 65. Fantomas 66. The
Vengeance of Fantomas 67. The Private Navy of
Sgt O'Farrell 68. By the Blood of Others 77. La
Piste du Télégraphe (In the Wind's Eye) 94, etc.

Dempsey, Patrick (1966–).
American juvenile actor.
Heaven Help Us 85. Meatballs III 86. In the
Mood (aka The Woo Woo Kid) 87. Can't Buy Me
Love 87. In a Shallow Grave 88. Some Girls 88.
Lover Boy 89. Happy Together 90. Coupe de Ville
90. Run 91. Mobsters 91. Face the Music 92. JFK:
Reckless Youth (TV) 93. Bank Robber 93. With
Honors 94, etc.
TV series: Fast Times 86.

Dempster, Austin.
British cinematographer.
Bedazzled 67. Otley 69. The Looking Glass War
69, etc.

Dempster, Carol (1901–1991).
American leading lady of the silent screen,
especially for D. W. Griffith.
Scarlet Days 19. The Love Flower 20. Dream
Street 21. *One Exciting Night* 22. America 24. Isn't
Life Wonderful? 24. That Royle Girl 26. The
Sorrows of Satan 26, etc.

Demy, Jacques (1931–1990).
French director. He was married to director Agnes
Varda.
■ *Lola* 60. The Seven Deadly Sins (part) 61. La
Baie des Anges 62. *Les Parapluies de Cherbourg* 64.
The Young Girls of Rochefort 67. The Model Shop
(US) 70. Peau d'Ane 71. The Pied Piper 72. The
Slightly Pregnant Man 73. Lady Oscar 79.

Dench, Dame Judi (1934–).
British stage actress. She is married to actor
Michael Williams.
Biography: 1985, *Judi Dench* by Gerald Jacobs.
■ The Third Secret 64. A Study in Terror 65. He
Who Rides a Tiger 66. Four in the Morning (BFA)
66. A Midsummer Night's Dream 68. Luther 73.
Dead Cert 74. Saigon – Year of the Cat (TV) 83.
Wetherby 84. 84 Charing Cross Road 87. A
Handful of Dust 88. Henry V 90.
TV series: A Fine Romance 81–84.

Deneuve, Catherine (1943–) (Catherine
Dorleac).
French leading lady, sister of Françoise Dorleac.
Vice and Virtue 62. *Les Parapluies de Cherbourg*
64. *Repulsion* (GB) 65. Das Liebeskarussell (Who
Wants to Sleep?) 65. Les Créatures 66. The Young
Girls of Rochefort 67. *Belle de Jour* 67. Benjamin
68. Manon 70 68. Mayerling 68. The April Fools
(US) 69. The Mississippi Mermaid 69. *Tristana* 70.
Peau d'Ane 71. The Lady in Red Boots 74. Hustle
76. Le Sauvage 76. L'Argent des Autres 78. Ils
Sont Grands ces Petits 79. Le Dernier Metro 80.
The Hunger 83. Abattre 80. The African 84. Fort
Saganne 85. The Scene of the Crime 86. Indochine
92. La Reine Blanche 92. My Favourite Season (Ma
Saison Préférée) 93. Les Demoiselles Ont Eu 25
Ans (doc) 93, etc.

¶ She is the man I would have liked to be.
– *Gérard Depardieu*

Denham.
An English village north of London where in 1936 Korda opened a huge film studio which was later taken over by the Rank Organisation but closed in the 50s so that production could be concentrated at Pinewood a few miles away.

Denham, Maurice (1909–).
British character actor with stage experience from 1934.
It's Not Cricket 48. London Belongs to Me 48. The Spider and the Fly 50. The Million Pound Note 54. Simon and Laura 55. Checkpoint 56. Night of the Demon 57. Our Man in Havana 59. Sink the Bismarck 60. HMS Defiant 62. The Seventh Dawn 64. Hysteria 65. The Alphabet Murders 65. After the Fox 66. The Midas Run 69. The Virgin and the Gypsy 70. Countess Dracula 70. Nicholas and Alexandra 71. Luther 73. Shout at the Devil 75. Julia 77. 84 Charing Cross Road 87. Memento Mori (TV) 92, many others.

Denham, Reginald (1894–1983).
British playwright (usually with Edward Percy) who also directed several films.
Borrow a Million 34. Death at Broadcasting House 34. The Price of Wisdom 35. Lucky Days 35. The House of the Spaniard 36. Kate Plus Ten 38. Anna of Brooklyn 59, etc.

Denis, Prince (1900–1984).
Diminutive French-born actor and circus performer who played the Mayor of the Munchkins in *The Wizard of Oz* 39.
Three Wise Fools 46. The Greatest Show on Earth 52.

Denison, Michael (1915–).
British leading man with firm but gentle manner; married to Dulcie Gray.
Autobiography: 1973, *Overture and Beginners.*
Tilly of Bloomsbury 40. Hungry Hill 46. *My Brother Jonathan* 47. *The Glass Mountain* 47. The Blind Goddess 48. The Importance of Being Earnest 51. Angels One Five 51. The Franchise Affair 52. The Tall Headlines 52. Landfall 53. The Truth about Women 57. Faces in the Dark 61. Dark River 90. Shadowlands 93, etc.

Denmark:
see *Danish cinema.*

Dennehy, Brian (1938–).
Heavily built American character actor, mostly on television.
■ Johnny We Hardly Knew Ye (TV) 77. It Happened at Lakewood Manor (TV) 77. Semi Tough 77. Foul Play 78. Ruby and Oswald (TV) 78. A Death in Canaan (TV) 78. A Real American Hero (as Buford Pusser) (TV) 78. Pearl (TV) 79. Silent Victor (TV) 79. '10' 79. Butch and Sundance 79. Little Miss Marker 80. A Rumour of War (TV) 80. Split Image 82. First Blood 82. Gorky Park 83. Never Cry Wolf 83. Cocoon 85. Silverado 85. Twice in a Lifetime 85. Legal Eagles 86. The Belly of an Architect 87. Best Seller 87. Dear America 87. Cocoon: The Return 88. Miles from Home 88. Return to Snowy River Part II 88. Indio 89. Perfect Witness (TV) 89. Last of the Finest 89. Seven Minutes 89. Presumed Innocent 90. Rising Sun 90. FX2 – the Deadly Art of Illusion 91. To Catch a Killer (TV) 91. Gladiator 92. Foreign Affairs (TV) 93. Murder in the Heartland (TV) 93.
TV series: *Big Shamus Little Shamus* 79. Star of the Family 82. Birdland 94.

Denner, Charles (1926–).
French leading actor.

Landru 62. *Life Upside Down* 63. The Sleeping Car Murder 66. The Two of Us 68. The Bride Wore Black 68. A Gorgeous Bird Like Me 72. And Now My Love 75. The Man Who Loved Women 77. Le Coeur a L'Envers 80, etc.

Denning, Richard (1914–) (Louis A. Denninger).
American leading man who from 1937 played light romantic roles and manly athletes.
Hold 'Em Navy 37. Persons in Hiding 38. Union Pacific 39. Golden Gloves 40. Adam Had Four Sons 41. Beyond the Blue Horizon 42. The Glass Key 42. Seven Were Saved 46. Black Beauty 46. Caged Fury 48. No Man of Her Own 48. Weekend with Father 50. Scarlet Angel 51. Hangman's Knot 53. The Creature from the Black Lagoon 54. Assignment Redhead (GB) 56. The Black Scorpion 57. Twice Told Tales 63, many others, mainly second features.
TV series: Mr and Mrs North 53–54. The Flying Doctor 59. Michael Shayue 60. Karen 64. Hawaii Five-O (occasionally) 68–79.

Dennis, Sandy (1937–1992) (Sandra Dale Dennis).
American leading actress.
■ Splendour in the Grass 61. *Who's Afraid of Virginia Woolf?* (AA) 66. Up the Down Staircase 67. The Fox 68. Sweet November 68. That Cold Day in the Park 69. A Touch of Love 69. The Out-of-Towners 69. The Only Way Out Is Dead 70. Something Evil (TV) 71. Mr Sycamore 75. Nasty Habits 76. God Told Me To 76. Three Sisters 77. Perfect Gentlemen (TV) 78. The Four Seasons 81. Come Back to the Five and Dime, Jimmy Dean, Jimmy Dean 82. The Execution (TV) 84. 976-EVIL 88. Another Woman 88. Parents 89. The Indian Runner 91.

¶ She has made an acting style out of post-nasal drip. – *Pauline Kael on S.D.*
When you finish an acting stint, there's nothing except money. You have to keep going, giving the best you've got, to get something intangible. – *S.D.*

Denny, Reginald (1891–1967) (Reginald Leigh Daymore).
British actor, on stage from childhood. From 1919 starred in many Hollywood action comedies and when sound came in began to play amiable stiff-upper-lip Britishers. More or less retired after 1950 to devote time to his aircraft company.
49 East 20. Footlights 21. *The Leather Pushers* 22. The Abysmal Brute 23. *Skinner's Dress Suit* 25. Oh Doctor 26. California Straight Ahead 27. Embarrassing Moments 29. Madame Satan 30. Private Lives 32. Of Human Bondage 34. Anna Karenina 35. Romeo and Juliet 36. Several Bulldog Drummond films 37–38 (as Algy). *Rebecca* (as Frank Crawley) 40.· Sherlock Holmes and the Voice of Terror 42. Love Letters 45. The Macomber Affair 47. The Secret Life of Walter Mitty 47. *Mr Blandings Builds His Dream House* (as Mr Simms) 48. Abbott and Costello Meet Dr Jekyll and Mr Hyde 53. Around the World in Eighty Days 56. Fort Vengeance 59. Cat Ballou 65. Batman 66, many others.

Dent, Vernon (1894–1963).
American character actor, a pompous butt for the Three Stooges in many of their two-reelers.

dentists
are seldom popular chaps, but Preston Sturges made a film about one of them, the inventor of laughing gas: The Great Moment. The Counterfeit Traitor had a spy dentist. Sinister dentists were found in The Man Who Knew Too Much (original

version), The Secret Partner, and Footsteps in the Dark, and a comic one, in the person of Bob Hope in The Paleface. Dentistry is the subject of two Britis farces: Dentist in the Chair and Dentist on the Job. W. C. Fields once made a film of his sketch The Dentist; and Laurel and Hardy in Leave 'Em Laughing were overcome by laughing gas. The most notable dentist hero was in the twice remad One Sunday Afternoon; and the most villainous dentist is certainly Laurence Olivier in Marathon Man. The dentist with the most hectic private life was Walter Matthau in Cactus Flower. The oddest was Daniel Day-Lewis as a motorcycling enthusias for dental hygiene in Eversmile, New Jersey.

Denver, Bob (1935–).
American TV comedian.
Take Her She's Mine 63. For Those Who Think Young 64. Who's Minding the Mint? 67. The Swee Ride 67. Do You Know The One About the Travelling Saleslady 68, etc.
TV series: Dobie Gillis 59–62. Gilligan's Island 64–66. The Good Guys 68. Dusty's Trail 73. High School U.S.A. (TV) 83. Back to the Beach 87, etc.

Denver, John (1943–) (Henry John Deutschendor Jnr).
American guitarist, singer and songwriter.
Oh God! 77. Fire and Ice (narrator) 87. Foxfire (TV) 87, etc.

Depardieu, Gérard (1948–).
Burly, ubiquitous French leading actor who has made more than 70 films. He left home at 13 to work in a variety of menial jobs, was sometimes in trouble with the police, and turned to acting in his late teens.
Le Tueur 71. L'Affaire Dominici 72. Deux Hommes dans la Ville 73. Les Valseuses 74. Stavisky 74. Vincent François Paul et les Autres 75. La Dernière Femme 76. 1900 76. Le Camion 77. Get Out Your Handkerchiefs 78. Le Sucre 78. Le Dernier Metro 80. Mon Oncle d'Amérique 80. The Woman Next Door 81. Danton 82. The Moo in the Gutter 83. Fort Saganne 85. Jean de Florette 85. Street of Departures 86. Under the Su of Satan 87. Camille Claudel 88. Drôle d'Endroit pour une Rencontre 88. Deux 88. Too Beautiful for You (Trop Belle pour toi) 89. Je Veux Rentrer à la Maison 89. Cyrano de Bergerac (AAN) 90. Green Card 90. Uranus 90. Merci la Vie 91. Every Morning of the World (Tous les Matins du Monde 91. Mon Père, Ce Héros 91. 1492: The Discovery 92. Hélas pour Moi 93. Germinal 93. My Father, the Hero (US) 94. A Simple Formality (Una Pura Formalita) 94. Le Colonel Chabert 94. Elisa 95, etc

¶ Having to confront policemen and judges is ar excellent way to train your imagination. In a few seconds you have to improvise a role with talent and emotion. – G.D.
There appears to be nothing he cannot do well on the screen. – New York Times
I sometimes think I shall never view/A French film lacking Gérard Depardieu. – John Updike

department stores
have usually been a background for comedy. New York store backgrounds have often shown the native superiority of the working girl to snobbish shopwalkers and obtuse management, as in Bachelo Mother and its remake Bundle of Joy, The Devil and Miss Jones and Manhandled 24. Broader comedy elements were to the fore in Miracle on 34th Street, Modern Times, The Big Store, Who's Minding the Store?, Fitzwilly and How to Save a Marriage. British comedies with store settings include Kipps, The

owded Day, Laughter in Paradise, Keep Fit, and *ruble in Store.*

epp, Johnny (1963–).
merican leading actor, often in fey or eccentric
es. Born in Owensboro, Kentucky, he played
a rock group, The Kids, before turning to acting
the mid-80s.
A Nightmare on Elm Street 84. Private Resort
, Platoon 86. Cry-Baby 90. Edward
issorhands 90. Arizona Dream 92. Benny & Joon
, What's Eating Gilbert Grape? 93. Ed Wood
, etc.
TV series: 21 Jump Street 87–90.

I don't pretend to be Captain Weird. I just do
what I do. – *J.D.*
Feet are fascinating, don't you think? They tell
u so much about people. – *J.D.*

eray, Jacques (1927–).
ench director.
Le Gigolo 60. Rififi in Tokyo 61. Symphony for
Massacre 63. Our Man in Marrakesh 66. The
imming Pool 69. Borsalino 70. The Outside Man
, Flic Story 75. Le Gang 77. A Butterfly on the
oulder 78. Trois Hommes à Abattre 80. Le
arginal 83. On ne Meurt que Deux Fois 85.
glements de Comptes 86. Maladie d'Amour 87.
Solitaire 87. Les Bois Noirs 89. Netchaiev est de
tour 91. Dérapage 92. L'Ours en Peluche 94, etc.

erek, Bo (1957–) (Mary Cathleen Collins).
merican pin-up who rather curiously caused a
ess sensation in her first starring film. Wife of
hn Derek.
Orca Killer Whale 77. '10' 79. A Change of
asons 80. Tarzan the Ape Man 81. Fantasies 81.
elero 84. Hot Chocolate 92. Sognando La
lifornia (It.) 93. Woman of Desire 94.

erek, John (1926–) (Derek Harris).
merican light leading man.
I'll Be Seeing You 45. *Knock on any Door* 49. All
e King's Men 49. *Rogues of Sherwood Forest* 50.
ask of the Avenger 51. Scandal Sheet 51. Mission
er Korea 53. The Adventures of Hajji Baba 54.
ince of Players 55. Run for Cover 55. The Leather
int 56. The Ten Commandments 56. Omar
ayyam 57. Prisoner of the Volga 60. Exodus 60.
ghtmare in the Sun 64. Once Before I Die (& d)
. Childish Things (& d) 69. Tarzan the Ape Man
ph) 81. Fantasies (& ph) 81. Bolero 84. Ghosts
n't Do It 90, etc.
TV series: Frontier Circus 61.

ern, Bruce (1936–).
merican general-purpose actor, usually seen as
ugh guy or psychotic. He is the father of actress
ura Dern.
Wild River 60. Marnie 64. The Wild Angels 66.
e Trip 67. The War Wagon 67. Will Penny 68.
stle Keep 69. Number One 69. They Shoot
rses Don't They? 69. Bloody Mama 70. The
credible Two-headed Transplant 70. Drive He
id 71. The Cowboys 72. *Silent Running* 72. The
ng of Marvin Gardens 72. The Laughing
liceman 73. The Great Gatsby 74. Posse 75.
mily Plot 75. Smile 75. Black Sunday 76. Won
n Ton 77. *Coming Home* (AAN) 78. The Driver
, Middle Age Crazy 80. Tattoo 81. Harry Tracy
. That Championship Season 82. On the Edge
. The Big Town 87. 1969 88. World Gone Wild
. The 'burbs 89. After Dark, My Sweet 91.
ggstown (aka Midnight Sting) 92. Amelia
rhart: The Final Flight (TV) 94. Wild Bill 95,
.
TV series: Stony Burke 62.

¶ I've played more psychotics and freaks and
dopers than anyone. – *B.D.*

Dern, Laura (1966–).
American actress of the 80s, daughter of Bruce
Dern.
Teachers 84. Mask 85. Smooth Talk 86. Blue
Velvet 86. Haunted Summer 88. Fat Man and
Little Boy (GB: The Shadowmakers) 89. Wild at
Heart 90. Rambling Rose 91. Jurassic Park 93. A
Perfect World 93, etc.

Derr, Richard (1917–1992).
American leading man, usually in minor films.
Ten Gentlemen from West Point 42. Tonight We
Raid Calais 43. The Secret Heart 47. Joan of Arc
48. When Worlds Collide 51. Something to Live
For 52. Terror Is a Man 59. Three in the Attic 68.
The Drowning Pool 75, etc.

Deruddere, Dominique (1957–).
Belgian director, a former assistant cameraman.
Crazy Love (aka Love Is a Dog from Hell) 87.
Wait until Spring, Bandini 89.

Desailly, Jean (1920–).
French leading man.
Le Voyageur de la Toussaint 42. Sylvie et la
Fantôme 45. *Occupé-Toi d'Amélie* 49. Les Grandes
Manoeuvres 55. Maigret Sets a Trap 59. Le Doulos
62. *Le Peau Douce* 64. The Twenty-Fifth Hour 66.
Un Flic 72. The Assassination of Trotsky 72. Le
Cavaleur 74. Pile ou Face 80. Le Professionel 81.
Le Fou du Roi 84, etc.

DeSalvo, Albert (1931–1973).
Serial killer known as The Boston Strangler who
was the subject of a biopic of the same name
starring Tony Curtis and directed by Richard
Fleischer in 1968. DeSalvo raped and murdered at
least 13 women (he claimed to have raped many
hundreds) in the early 60s. He was committed to
a mental institution in 1967 and was stabbed to
death in his cell.

Deschanel, Caleb (1944–).
American cinematographer.
The Black Stallion 79. More American Graffiti
79. Being There 79. The Escape Artist (d) 82. The
Right Stuff (AAN) 83. The Natural (AAN) 84. The
Slugger's Wife 85. It Could Happen to You 94,
etc.

desert islands
have provided the locale of many a film adventure.
Robinson Crusoe has been filmed several times, with
two variations in *Robinson Crusoe on Mars*
and *Lt Robin Crusoe USN. Treasure Island* too has
survived three or four versions, to say nothing of
imitations like *Blackbeard the Pirate* and parodies
such as *Abbott and Costello Meet Captain Kidd* and
*Old Mother Riley's Jungle Treasure. The Admirable
Crichton* is perhaps the next most overworked
desert island story, with *The Swiss Family Robinson*
following on. Dorothy Lamour found a few desert
islands in films like *Typhoon* and *Aloma of the South
Seas;* the inhabitants of *The Little Hut* had one
nearly to themselves; Joan Greenwood and co.
were marooned on a rather special one in
Mysterious Island. Our Girl Friday played the theme
for sex; *Dr Dolittle* found educated natives on one;
Cary Grant lived on one as a reluctant spy in *Father
Goose; Sea Wife, Lord of the Flies* and *The Day the Fish
Came Out* were three recent but not very successful
attempts to take the theme seriously; *Hell in the
Pacific* was one that did work. *The Blue Lagoon* was
treated decorously in the 50s and sexily in the 80s.

A comic TV series on the subject was *Gilligan's
Island* 64–66; a serious one, *The New People* 69.

deserts
have figured in many a western, from *Tumbleweed*
to *Mackenna's Gold.* Other films which have paid
particularly respectful attention to the dangers that
too much sand can provide include *The Sheik* and
*Son of the Sheik, Greed, The Lost Patrol, The Garden
of Allah, Sahara, Five Graves to Cairo, Ice Cold in
Alex, Sea of Sand, Desert Rats, Play Dirty, An Eye for
an Eye, Inferno, Zabriskie Point, The Sabre and the
Arrow, Legend of the Lost, The Ten Commandments,
She, Lawrence of Arabia, The Black Tent, Oasis, Sands
of The Kalahari, The Flight of the Phoenix, Garden of
Evil* and *The Professionals.*

Desmond, Florence (1905–1993) (Florence
Dawson).
British dancer and impersonator, seen in many
stage revues but few films.
Autobiography: 1953, *Florence Desmond by
Herself.*
The Road to Fortune 30. Sally in Our Alley 31.
No Limit 35. *Keep Your Seats Please* 37. Hoots Mon
40. Three Came Home (US) 50. Charley Moon 56.
Some Girls Do 68, etc.

Desmond, William (1878–1949) (William
Mannion).
Irish leading man of the American silent screen,
mostly in westerns.
The Sunset Trail 24. Blood and Steel 26. Tongues
of Scandal 29. Hell Bent for Frisco 31. Flying Fury
33. Arizona Days 36, etc.

Desmonde, Jerry (1908–1967).
British character actor with long music-hall
experience, a perfect foil for comedians from Sid
Field to Norman Wisdom.
London Town 46. Cardboard Cavalier 48. Follow
a Star 59. A Stitch in Time 63. The Early Bird 65,
many others.

Desni, Tamara (1913–).
Russian-born, British-resident leading lady.
Jack Ahoy 34. Fire over England 36. The
Squeaker 37. Traitor Spy 40. Send for Paul Temple
46. Dick Barton at Bay 50, etc.

Desny, Ivan (1922–).
Continental leading man, in films from 1948.
Madeleine (GB) 50. La Putain Respectueuse 52.
Lola Montes 55. Anastasia 56. The Mirror Has Two
Faces 58. The Magnificent Rebel 60. Das
Liebeskarussel (Who Wants to Sleep?) 65. The
Mystery of Thug Island 66. I Killed Rasputin 68.
Mayerling 68. The Adventures of Gerard 70. Paper
Tiger 75. The Marriage of Maria Braun 78.
Bloodline 79. The Lady without Camelias 80.
Quicker than the Eye 88, etc.

Detmers, Maruschka (1961–).
Dutch actress, in international films.
First Name: Carmen (Prénom Carmen) 83. Devil
in the Flesh 86. Hanna's War 88. Le Brasier 90. The
Mambo Kings 92. Love in the Strangest Way (Elle
N'Oublient Jamais) (Fr.) 94, etc.

Deutch, Howard.
American director, from rock videos.
Pretty in Pink 86. Some Kind of Wonderful 87.
The Great Outdoors (aka Big Country) 88. Article
99 92. Getting Even with Dad 94, etc.

Deutsch, Adolph (1897–1980).
American composer associated with Warner and
MGM.

The Smiling Lieutenant 31. The Great Garrick 37. Indianapolis Speedway 39. The Fighting 69th 40. They Drive by Night 40. *The Maltese Falcon* 41. High Sierra 41. Across the Pacific 42. The Mask of Dimitros 43. Uncertain Glory 44. Intruder in the Dust 49. Father of the Bride 50. The Long Long Trailer 53. The Rack 56. Tea and Sympathy 56. The Matchmaker 57. Les Girls 57. Some Like It Hot 59. The Apartment 60, many others.

Deutsch, David (1926–1992).
British producer, in films from 1949. Son of Oscar Deutsch who founded the Odeon circuit.
Blind Date 59. Nothing But the Best 64. Catch Us If You Can 65. Lock Up Your Daughters 69, etc.

Deutsch, Ernst (1890–1969).
German character actor.
Die Rache der Toten (debut) 16. The Golem 20. Lady Godiva 21. The Marriage of Corbal (GB) 35. Nurse Edith Cavell (US) 39. The Man I Married (US) 40. So Ends Our Night (US) 41. The Third Man (GB) 49. Der Wasserdoktor 58, etc.

Deutsch, Helen (1907–1992).
American screenwriter and dramatist.
The Seventh Cross 44. National Velvet 45. Loves of Carmen 48. King Solomon's Mines 50. Kim 50. Lili (AAN) 53. I'll Cry Tomorrow 55. Forever Darling 56. The Unsinkable Molly Brown 64. Valley of the Dolls 67, etc.

Devane, William (1939–).
Craggy, toothy American leading actor who rode the crest for a while in the late 70s.
■ The Pursuit of Happiness 71. My Old Man's Place 71. McCabe and Mrs Miller 71. Mortadella 71. Irish Whiskey Rebellion 73. The Bait (TV) 73. Crime Club (TV) 73. *Missiles of October* (TV) (as John F. Kennedy) 73. Report to the Commissioner 75. *Fear on Trial* (TV) (as John Henry Faulk) 75. *Family Plot* 76. Marathon Man 76. Red Alert (TV) 77. Black Beauty (TV) 77. The Bad News Bears in Breaking Training 77. Rolling Thunder 77. *From Here to Eternity* (TV) 79. Yanks 79. The Dark 79. Honky Tonk Freeway 81. Testament 83. Jane Doe (TV) 84. Timestalkers 87. Vital Signs 90.
TV series: Knots Landing 84–88.

Devereaux, Ed.
Australian character actor who in addition to starring in the *Skippy* TV series appeared in some international films.
Floods of Fear 58. Carry on Regardless 61. The Wrong Arm of the Law 63. They're a Weird Mob 66. The Nickel Queen 71. Barry Mackenzie Holds His Own 74. Pressure 75, etc.

the devil
has made frequent appearances in movies. There were versions of *Faust* in 1900, 1903, 1904, 1907, 1909, 1911, 1921 and 1925, the last of these featuring Emil Jannings as Mephistopheles. Later variations on this theme include *The Sorrows of Satan* 27, with Adolphe Menjou; *All That Money Can Buy* 41, with Walter Huston as Mr Scratch; *Alias Nick Beal* 49, with Ray Milland; *La Beauté du Diable* 50 with Gérard Philipe; *Damn Yankees* 58 with Ray Walston; *Bedazzled* 67 with Peter Cook; and *Doctor Faustus* 68 with Andreas Teuber. In other stories, Satan was played by Helge Nissen in *Leaves From Satan's Book* 20, Jules Berry in *Les Visiteurs du Soir* 42, Alan Mowbray in *The Devil with Hitler* 42, Rex Ingram in *Cabin in the Sky* 43, Laird Cregar in *Heaven Can Wait* 43, Claude Rains in *Angel on My Shoulder* 46, Stanley Holloway in *Meet Mr Lucifer* 53, Richard Devon in *The Undead* 56, Vincent Price in *The Story of Mankind* 57, Cedric Hardwicke in

Bait 54, Vittorio Gassman in *The Devil in Love* 67, Stig Järrel in *The Devil's Eye* 60, Donald Pleasence in *The Greatest Story Ever Told* 65, Burgess Meredith in *Torture Garden* 68, Pierre Clementi in *The Milky Way* 68, Ralph Richardson in *Tales From the Crypt* 71. In the Swedish *Witchcraft through the Ages* 21, the devil was played by the director, Benjamin Christensen. Devil worship has been the subject of *The Black Cat* 34, *The Seventh Victim* 43, *Night of the Demon* 57, *Back from the Dead* 57, *The Witches* 66, *Eye of the Devil* 66, *The Devil Rides Out* 68, *Rosemary's Baby* 68; while the last-named presaged a rash of diabolically-inspired children in *The Exorcist, I Don't Want to be Born, It's Alive, Devil Within Her* and *The Omen*.

Deville, Michel (1931–).
French director.
Ce Soir ou Jamais 60. L'Appartement de Filles 63. Benjamin 67. Bye Bye Barbara 69. The Bear and the Doll 71. La Femme en Bleu 73. Love at the Top 74. L'Apprenti Salaud 77. Le Dossier 51 79. Le Voyage en douce 80. Eaux Profondes 81. La Petite Bande 83. Peril en la Demeure 84. Death in a French Garden 86. Le Paltoquet 86. The Reader (La Lectrice) 88. Nuit d'Été en Ville 90. Toutes Peines Confondues 92. Aux Petits Bonheurs 93, etc.

Devil's Island,
the French Guianan penal colony, has intermittently fascinated film-makers. Apart from the versions of the Dreyfus case (*Dreyfus, The Life of Emile Zola, I Accuse*), there have been Ronald Colman in *Condemned to Devil's Island*, Donald Woods in *I Was a Prisoner on Devil's Island*, Boris Karloff in *Devil's Island*, Clark Gable in *Strange Cargo*, Humphrey Bogart in *Passage to Marseilles*, Bogart and company in *We're No Angels*, Eartha Kitt in *Saint of Devil's Island*, Steve McQueen in *Papillon*, and Jim Brown in *I Escaped From Devil's Island*. The prison colony opened in 1852 and closed in 1946.

Devine, Andy (1905–1977).
Fat, husky-voiced American character comedian, seen in innumerable westerns.
We Americans 28. Hot Stuff 29. Law and Order 32. Midnight Mary 33. Stingaree 34. Way Down East 35. Romeo and Juliet 36. A Star is Born 37. In Old Chicago 37. *Stagecoach* 39. When the Daltons Rode 40. Badlands of Dakota 41. Sin Town 42. Crazy House 43. Ghost Catchers 44. Frisco Sal 45. Canyon Passage 46. The Vigilantes Return 47. Old Los Angeles 48. *The Red Badge of Courage* 51. New Mexico 51. Montana Belle 52. Island in the Sky 53. Pete Kelly's Blues 55. The Adventures of Huckleberry Finn 60. Two Rode Together 61. The Man who Shot Liberty Valance 62. It's a Mad Mad Mad Mad World 63. Zebra in the Kitchen 65. The Ballad of Josie 68. A Whale of a Tale 77, many others.
TV series: *Wild Bill Hickok* 51–54. Andy's Gang 57. Flipper 64.

Devon, Laura (1940–).
American leading lady from TV.
Goodbye Charlie 65. Red Line 7000 66. Gunn 67, etc.

Devry, Elaine (1935–).
American leading lady.
Mantrap 61. Diary of a Madman 63. Guide for the Married Man 67. The Boy Who Cried Werewolf 73, etc.

Dewaere, Patrick (1946–1982).
French leading man. Committed suicide.

Les Mariés de l'An II 70. Going Places 73. Get Out Your Handkerchiefs 78. Coup de Tête 78. Psy 80. Hotel of the Americas 81. Plein Sud 81. Paradise for All 83, etc.

Dewhurst, Colleen (1924–1991).
American general-purpose actress most notable fo her stage performances, especially in the plays of Eugene O'Neill. She was twice married to actor George C. Scott (1960–65, 1967–72).
■ The Nun's Story 59. Man on a String 60. A Fir Madness 63. The Last Run 71. The Cowboys 72. McQ 74. The Story of Jacob and Joseph (TV) 74. Annie Hall 77. Ice Castles 78. Silent Victory (TV) 79. Studs Lonigan (TV) 79. When a Stranger Call 79. Final Assignment 80. Tribute 80. Guyana Tragedy (TV) 80. A Perfect Match (TV) 81. The Dead Zone 83. The Boy Who Could Fly 86. Lantern Hill 89. Termini Station 89. Bed and Breakfast 90. Dying Young 91.

Dexter, Anthony (1919–) (Walter Fleischmann American leading man with stage experience. Cas as Rudolph Valentino, he never lived down the ta and his subsequent roles have been in small-scal action dramas and science-fiction quickies.
Valentino 51. The Brigand 52. Captain John Smith and Pocahontas 53. Captain Kidd and the Slave Girl 54. Fire Maidens from Outer Space (GB 54. He Laughed Last 56. The Parson and the Outlaw (as Billy the Kid) 57. Twelve to the Moor 59. Thoroughly Modern Millie 67, etc.

Dexter, Brad (1917–).
American character actor often seen as a tough hoodlum.
The Asphalt Jungle 50. Macao 52. Untamed 55 The Oklahoman 57. The Magnificent Seven 60. Taras Bulba 62. Bus Riley's Back in Town 64. Vo Ryan's Express 65. Blindfold 66. The Naked Runne (p only) 67. The Lawyer (p only) 69. Winter Kills 79, etc.

Dexter, John (1925–1990).
British director, a former actor. He was also a theatre and opera director, notably with Britain's National Theatre.
Autobiography: 1993, *The Honourable Beast*.
■ The Virgin Soldiers 69. Sidelong Glances of a Pigeon Kicker 70. I Want What I Want 71.

Dexter, Maury (1927–).
American producer-director of second features.
The Third Voice (p) 60. Harbour Lights (pd) 63 The Day Mars Invaded Earth (pd) 63. House of th Damned (pd) 63. The Naked Brigade (d) 65. The Outlaw of Red River (pd) 65. Maryjane (pd) 68. Hell's Belles (pd) 70, etc.

Dey, Susan (1952–).
American juvenile actress of the 70s.
Skyjacked 72. Terror on the Beach (TV) 73. Cag without a Key (TV) 75. Mary Jane Harper Cried Last Night (TV) 77. First Love 77. The Comeback Kid 80. Looker 81. Sunset Limousine (TV) 83. Love Leads the Way (TV) 84. Echo Park 86. The Trouble with Dick 88. That's Adequate 90, etc.
TV series: The Partridge Family 70–74. Emeral Point 83. L.A. Law 86.

Dhery, Robert (1921–) (Robert Foulley).
Dapper French cabaret comedian and pantomimist.
Les Enfants du Paradis 44. Sylvie et la Fantôme 45. La Patronne (d only) 49. *Ah, Les Belles Bacchantes* (Femmes de Paris) (& w, p) 54. La Bell Américaine (& w, p) 61. Allez France (& w, p) 64.

e Petit Baigneur (& w, p) 67. A Time for Loving
1. Malevil 80, etc.

Dhiegh, Khigh (1910–1991).
Oriental American character actor familiar on TV
as the evil villain of *Hawaii Five-O*.
    The Manchurian Candidate 62. Judge Dec (TV)
7, etc.

DiCaprio, Leonardo (1974–).
American leading young actor.
    Critters 3 91. Incident at Oglala 92. This Boy's
Life 93. What's Eating Gilbert Grape (AAN) 93,
etc.

Di Palma, Carlo (1925–).
Italian cinematographer and occasional director
whose international reputation was made in the
mid-60s. Recently he has worked in America for
Woody Allen.
    Ivan 54. The Lady Killer of Rome (L'Assassino)
61. Omicron 63. Red Desert (Deserto Rosso) 64.
Blow-Up 66. The Appointment (US) 69. The
Pacifist (La Pacifista) 71. Teresa la Ladra (d) 73.
Amo non Amo 79. The Black Stallion Returns (US)
83. Hannah and Her Sisters (US) 86. Off Beat (US)
86. Radio Days (US) 87. September 87. The Secret
of My Success (US) 87. Alice (US) 90. Shadows and
Fog 92. Husbands and Wives 92. Manhattan
Murder Mystery 93. Bullets over Broadway 94, etc.

Di Venanzo, Gianni (1920–1966).
Italian cinematographer, in films from 1941.
    Amore in Città 53. L'Amiche 55. Il Grido 57. I
Soliti Ignoti 58. Salvatore Giuliano 61. La Notte 61.
L'Eclisse 62. Eva 62. *Eight and a Half* 63. *Juliet of
the Spirits* 65, etc.

Diamond, I. A. L. (1915–1988) (Itek Dommnici,
later Isadore Diamond).
Romanian-American screenwriter, his best work
being in collaboration with Billy Wilder.
    Murder in the Blue Room 44. Never Say
Goodbye 46. Always Together 47. The Girl from
Jones Beach 49. Something for the Birds 52. That
Certain Feeling 56. Love in the Afternoon 57. Merry
Andrew 58. *Some Like It Hot* 59. *The Apartment* (AA)
60. *One Two Three* 61. Irma la Douce 63. Kiss Me
Stupid 64. The Fortune Cookie 66. Cactus Flower
69. *The Private Life of Sherlock Holmes* 70. Avanti
72. The Front Page 74. Fedora 78, etc.

Diamond, Neil (1941–).
American pop singer who failed to break into the
movies in 1981 with *The Jazz Singer*.

¶ I'm not there to entertain people. We're there
to do something together. – N.D.

Diaz, Cameron (1973–).
American actress, a former model.
    The Mask 94.

Dick Barton.
Tough British special agent, created by Edward J.
Mason, who was the hero of a popular radio
programme 1946–51, and three low-budget films
starring Don Stannard. In 1978, Tony Vogel
played him in an unsuccessful television series.
    Dick Barton, Special Agent 48. Dick Barton
Strikes Back 49. Dick Barton at Bay 50.

Dick, Douglas (1920–).
Innocent-looking American 'second lead', now a
psychologist.
    The Searching Wind 46. Saigon 47. The Accused
48. Home of the Brave 49. The Red Badge of

Courage 51. The Gambler from Natchez 55. The
Oklahoman 57. North to Alaska 60, etc.

Dick, Philip K. (1928–1982).
American science-fiction writer of dark fables
whose stories have been the basis of two
memorable movies.
    Blade Runner (from *Do Androids Dream of Electric
Sheep?*) 82. Total Recall (from *We Can Remember It
for You Wholesale*) 90.

Dick Tracy.
The lantern-jawed detective of the comic strips
made sporadic film appearances, notably when
impersonated by Ralph Byrd or Morgan Conway
in a number of 40s second features and serials.
In 1951 Byrd starred in a TV series. Tracy also
appeared in a TV cartoon series in the 50s, in *TV
Funnies* in 1971, and in the big-budget film of
1990, starring Warren Beatty.

Dickens, Charles (1812–1870).
Prolific British novelist whose gusto in
characterization and plot-weaving made his books
ideal cinema material until the last decade when
producers seem to have thought them old-
fashioned. Most filmed has perhaps been *A
Christmas Carol*, usually personified as *Scrooge*; but
Oliver Twist runs it a close second. There had been
several early silent versions of *David Copperfield*
before Cukor's splendid 1934 version, and *The Old
Curiosity Shop* was popular as the basis of one-reelers
before the talkie versions with Hay Petrie (1935)
and Anthony Newley (1975). *A Tale of Two Cities*
had been a popular stage play under the title *The
Only Way*; after many early versions it was directed
as a spectacular by Frank Lloyd in 1917, with
William Farnum; as a British silent in 1926, with
Martin Harvey; as a vehicle for Ronald Colman in
1935; and in a rather uninspired British version of
1958 starring Dirk Bogarde. A 1969 all-star version
of *David Copperfield* was primarily intended for
American TV.
■ Other Dickens novels less frequently filmed
include *The Mystery of Edwin Drood*, once as an early
British silent, again in Hollywood in 1935, with
Claude Rains as John Jasper, and again in Britain
in 1993 with Robert Powell; *Great Expectations*,
which had two silent versions, a rather dull
Hollywood remake of 1934 and the magnificent
David Lean version of 1946; *Dombey and Son*, under
the title *Rich Man's Folly*, starring George Bancroft
in 1931; *Nicholas Nickleby*, the only picturization
of which was the patchy Ealing version of 1947,
though the Royal Shakespeare Company's epic
stage production has been released on video; and
The Pickwick Papers, seen in various potted versions
in silent days and in Noel Langley's superficial
version of 1952.
    Dickens' novels which were filmed in the silent
period but not since sound include *The Cricket on the
Hearth*, *Martin Chuzzlewit*, *Our Mutual Friend* and
Barnaby Rudge. *Little Dorrit* was made in Germany
in 1933 with Anny Ondra, and in 1987 by the
Richard Brabourne group at a 6-hour length with
a cast headed by Alec Guinness.

Dickerson, Ernest (1953–).
American cinematographer closely associated with
director Spike Lee. He studied as an architect and
worked as a photographer before entering films.
He began writing and directing in the 90s.
    The Brother from Another Planet 84. Krush
Groove (aka Rap Attack) 85. She's Gotta Have It
86. Enemy Territory 87. Eddie Murphy 'Raw' 87.
School Daze 88. Do the Right Thing 89. Ava and
Gabriel 89. Mo' Better Blues 90. Def by Temptation
90. The Laserman 90. Jungle Fever 91. Sex, Drugs,

Rock & Roll 91. Juice (wd) 92. Cousin Bobby 92.
Malcolm X 92. The Untouchables (TV) (d) 93.
Surviving the Game (d) 94, etc.

Dickinson, Angie (1932–) (Angeline Brown).
Capable American leading lady, former beauty
contest winner, in films from 1954.
■ Lucky Me 54. Man with the Gun 55.
Tennessee's Partner 55. The Return of Jack Slade
55. Gun the Man Down 56. Hidden Guns 56. The
Black Whip 56. Tension at Table Rock 56. Shootout
at Medicine Bend 57. Calypso Joe 57. China Gate
57. I Married a Woman 58. Cry Terror 58. Rio
Bravo 59. The Bramble Bush 60. Ocean's Eleven
60. A Fever in the Blood 61. The Sins of Rachel
Cade 62. Rome Adventure 62. Jessica 62. Captain
Newman MD 63. The Killers (TV) 64. The Art of
Love 65. The Chase 66. Cast a Giant Shadow 66.
Point Blank 67. The Last Challenge 67. Sam
Whiskey 69. Young Billy Young 69. Some Kind of
a Nut 69. The Love War (TV) 70. Thief (TV) 71.
Pretty Maids All in a Row 71. The Resurrection of
Zachary Wheeler 71. See the Man Run (TV) 71.
The Norliss Tapes (TV) 73. The Outside Man 73.
Pray for the Wildcats (TV) 74. Big Bad Mama 74.
Labyrinth 79. Pearl (TV) 79. Dressed to Kill 80.
Death Hunt 80. Klondike Fever 80. Charlie Chan
and the Curse of the Dragon Queen 81. Death
Hunt 81. Big Bad Mama II 88. Once Upon a Texas
Train (aka Texas Guns) 88. Even Cowgirls Get the
Blues 93.
    TV series: Police Woman 75–78. Cassie and Co.
81.

¶ I dress for women, and undress for men. – A.D.

Dickinson, Desmond (1902–).
British cinematographer.
    Detective Lloyd (serial) 31. Men of Two Worlds
45. Fame is the Spur 46. *Hamlet* 47. The History
of Mr Polly 49. Morning Departure 50. The
Browning Version 52. The Importance of Being
Earnest 52. Carrington VC 55. Orders to Kill 58.
City of the Dead 60. Sparrows Can't Sing 63. A
Study in Terror 65. Circus of Blood 67. Decline
and Fall 68. Who Slew Auntie Roo? 71. The Fiend
71, etc.

Dickinson, Thorold (1903–1984).
British director, in films from 1925. Retired to
teach film theory at Slade School, London.
    Book 1971: *A Discovery of Cinema*.
■ The High Command 36. The Arsenal Stadium
Mystery 39. *Gaslight* 39. The Prime Minister 41.
Next of Kin 41. Men of Two Worlds 45. *The Queen
of Spades* 48. The Secret People 52. Hill 24 Doesn't
Answer 55.

Dickson, Dorothy (1894–).
American musical comedy star who spent most of
her career in Britain.
    Money Mad 17. Channel Crossing 32. Danny
Boy 34. Sword of Honour 39, etc.

Dickson, Gloria (1916–1945) (Thais Dickerson).
American leading lady of the 30s. Died of
asphyxiation from a fire.
    They Won't Forget 37. Racket Busters 38. No
Place to Go 39. They Made Me a Criminal 39. I
Want a Divorce 40. The Big Boss 41. Affairs of
Jimmy Valentine 42. Lady of Burlesque 43, etc.

Dickson, Paul (1920–).
British director, hailed for documentaries: *The
Undefeated* 49, *David* 51. His feature films have been
less distinguished: *Satellite in the Sky* 56. *The
Depraved* 57, many second features and TV episodes.

Didion, Joan (1934–).
American screenwriter, novelist and essayist. She is married to writer John Gregory Dunne, with whom she has collaborated on film scripts.

Panic in Needle Park (co-w) 71. Play It as It Lays (oa, co-w) 71. A Star Is Born (co-w) 76. True Confessions (co-w) 81.

Dieges, Carlos (1940–).
Brazilian director, screenwriter and poet, a former film critic.

Ganga Zumba 64. Xica da Silva 76. Bye Bye Brazil 79. Quilombo 84. Subway to the Stars (Um Trem para as Estrelas) 86. Dias Melhores Virao 91, etc.

Dierkes, John (1905–1975).
Gaunt American supporting actor.

Macbeth 48. *The Red Badge of Courage* 51. Shane 53. The Naked Jungle 54. Jubal 56. The Alamo 60. The Comancheros 61. The Haunted Palace 63, many others.

Dieterle, William (1893–1972) (Wilhelm Dieterle).
Distinguished German director, long in Hollywood; at his best, an incomparable master of crowd scenes and pictorial composition. Formerly an actor in Germany, e.g. in Leni's *Waxworks*.
■ Die Heilige und ihr Narr 26. The Weavers 29. Behind the Altar 29. The Dance Goes On 31. *The Last Flight* 31. Her Majesty Love 31. Man Wanted 32. Jewel Robbery 32. The Crash 32. Six Hours to Live 32. Scarlet Dawn 32. Lawyer Man 32. Grand Slam 33. Adorable 33. Devils in Love 33. Female 33. From Headquarters 33. Fashions of 1934 34. Fog Over Frisco 34. Madame du Barry 34. The Firebird 34. The Secret Bride 35. Dr Socrates 35. *A Midsummer Night's Dream* 35. *The Story of Louis Pasteur* 35. Concealment 35. Men on Her Mind 36. The White Angel 36. Satan Met a Lady 36. The Great O'Malley 37. Another Dawn 37. *The Life of Emile Zola* (AAN) 37. Blockade 38. Juarez 39. *The Hunchback of Notre Dame* 39. *Dr Ehrlich's Magic Bullet* 40. A Dispatch from Reuters 40. *All That Money Can Buy* 41. Syncopation 42. Tennessee Johnson 42. Kismet 44. *I'll Be Seeing You* 44. Love Letters 45. This Love of Ours 45. The Searching Wind 47. The Accused 48. *Portrait of Jennie* 48. Rope of Sand 49. Paid in Full 50. Dark City 50. September Affair 50. Volcano 50. Peking Express 51. Red Mountain 51. Boots Malone 52. The Turning Point 52. Salome 53. Elephant Walk 54. Magic Fire 56. Omar Khayyam 57. Dubrowsky (Yug.) 58. Mistress of the World (Ger.) 60. The Confession 66.
✪ For marshalling the tricks of his trade with spectacular professionalism. *Portrait of Jennie*.

¶ One day I walked on to his set, he was directing some young children. He wasn't getting what he wanted. He grabbed a child by her arms, swung her in the air and, screaming in German, forcibly placed her in a new position. He took his hands off the child and she fainted dead away. I left wondering what directing was about. – *Don Siegel*

Dietrich, Marlene (1901–1992) (Maria Magdalena von Losch).
German singer-actress long in America, a legend of glamour despite many poor films and her domination in the 30s by the heavy style of Josef Von Sternberg.

Biographies: 1955, *Blonde Venus* by Leslie Frewin. 1984, *Dietrich* by Alexander Walker. 1992, *Marlene Dietrich* by Maria Riva (her daughter). 1992, *Marlene Dietrich* by Stephen Bach. 1992, *Blue Angel: The Life of Marlene Dietrich* by Donald Spoto.

■ Der Mensch am Wege 23. The Tragedy of Love 24. Der Sprung ins Leben 24. Joyless Street 25. Manon Lescaut 26. Cafe Electric 26. A Modern Dubarry 27. Sein Groesster Bluff 27. Der Jux Baron 27. Princess Olala 28. I Kiss Your Hand Madame 28. Die Frau nach der Man Sich Sehnt 28. Das Schiff der Verlorenen Menschen 29. Gefahren der Brautzeit 30. *The Blue Angel* 30. Morocco (AAN) 30. Dishonoured 31. *Shanghai Express* 32. Blonde Venus 32. Song of Songs 33. *The Scarlet Empress* 34. The Devil Is a Woman 35. *Desire* 36. The Garden of Allah 36. Knight Without Armour (GB) 37. Angel 37. *Destry Rides Again* 39. Seven Sinners 40. The Flame of New Orleans 41. Manpower 41. The Lady Is Willing 42. The Spoilers 42. Pittsburgh 42. Follow the Boys 44. Kismet 44. Martin Roumagnac (Fr.) 46. Golden Earrings 47. *A Foreign Affair* 48. Stage Fright (GB) 50. No Highway (GB) 51. Rancho Notorious 52. The Monte Carlo Story 53. Around the World in Eighty Days 56. Witness for the Prosecution 57. Touch of Evil 58. Judgement at Nuremberg 61. Paris When It Sizzles 64. Just a Gigolo 78.
✪ For enjoying being a legend. *Destry Rides Again*.

¶ If she had nothing but her voice, she could break your heart with it. But she also has that beautiful body and the timeless loveliness of her face. – *Ernest Hemingway*

Age cannot wither her, nor custom stale her infinite sameness – *David Shipman*

I have a child and I have made a few people happy. That is all. – *M.D.*

The relationship between the make-up man and the film actor is that of accomplices in crime – *M.D.*

There is a lack of dignity to film stardom. – *M.D.*

She has sex but no positive gender. Her masculinity appeals to women and her sexuality to men. – *Ken Tynan*

The legs aren't so beautiful, I just know what to do with them. – *M.D.*

I never ever took my career seriously. – *M.D.*

I was an actress. I made my films. Finish. – *M.D.*

You should be afraid of life, yes, but not of death. Then you know nothing more. It's all over. – *M.D.*

It took more than one man to change my name to Shanghai Lily. – *M.D. in Shanghai Express*

See what the boys in the back room will have
And tell them I'm having the same.
See what the boys in the back room will have
And give me the poison they name.
And if I die, don't bring a preacher
To witness all my follies and my shame;
Just see what the boys in the back room will have
And tell them I sighed –
And tell them I cried –
And tell them I died of the same! – *M.D. in Destry Rides Again*

Dietz, Howard (1896–1983).
American librettist and writer, with MGM from its inception. Best film score: *The Band Wagon* 53.
Autobiography: 1974, *Dancing in the Dark*.

Diffring, Anton (1918–1989).
German actor, in British films from 1951; often the villainous Nazi or the protagonist of a horror film.

State Secret 50. *Albert RN* 53. The Sea Shall Not Have Them 55. The Colditz Story 55. *I Am a Camera* 56. *The Man Who Could Cheat Death* 59. Circus of Horrors 60. Incident at Midnight 63. The Heroes of Telemark 65. Fahrenheit 451 66. The Double Man 67. Counterpoint (US) 67. Where Eagles Dare 68. Zeppelin 71. The Swiss Conspiracy 75. Operation Daybreak 76. Vanessa 76. Valentino 77, etc.

Digges, Dudley (1879–1947).
Versatile Irish character actor, with Abbey Theatre experience; played a variety of good roles in Hollywood in the 30s.
■ Condemned 29. Outward Bound 30. Upper Underworld 30. *The Maltese Falcon* 31. The Ruling Voice 31. Alexander Hamilton 31. Devotion 31. The Hatchet Man 32. The Strange Case of Clara Deane 32. Roar of the Dragon 32. The First Year 32. Tess of the Storm Country 32. The King's Vacation 33. Mayor of Hell 33. Silk Express 33. The Narrow Corner 33. The Invisible Man 33. The Emperor Jones 33. Before Dawn 33. Fury of the Jungle 34. Caravan 34. The World Moves On 34. Massacre 34. What Every Woman Knows 34. I am a Thief 34. Notorious Gentleman 35. Kind Lady 35. *Mutiny on the Bounty* 35. China Seas 35. The Bishop Misbehaves 35. Three Live Ghosts 36. The Voice of Bugle Ann 36. The Unguarded Hour 36. *The General Died at Dawn* 36. Valiant is the Word for Carrie 36. Love is News 37. *The Light that Failed* 39. The Fight for Life 40. *Raffles* 40. Son of Fury 42. The Searching Wind 46.

Dighton, John (1909–).
British writer, in films from 1935.
Let George Do It 40. Nicholas Nickleby 47. Saraband for Dead Lovers 48. *Kind Hearts and Coronets* 49. *The Happiest Days of Your Life* (from his own play) 49. The Man in the White Suit (co-w, AAN) 51. Roman Holiday (co-w, AAN) 53. Summer of the Seventeenth Doll 60, many others.

Dignam, Basil (1905–1979).
British character actor, in innumerable small parts, often as barrister or other professional man.
His Excellency 53. Brothers in Law 57. Room at the Top 58. The Silent Partner 61. Life for Ruth 63. Victim 62, etc.

Dignam, Mark (1909–1989).
British character actor, brother of Basil Dignam. Also played professional men.
Murder in the Cathedral 52. The Maggie 54. The Prisoner 55. Sink the Bismarck 60. No Love for Johnnie 62. Hamlet 69, etc.

Diller, Phyllis (1917–).
Zany, grotesque American comedienne who has had trouble adapting her TV style to movies.
■ Splendor in the Grass 60. Boy Did I Get a Wrong Number 66. Eight on the Lam 67. The Private Navy of Sergeant O'Farrell 68. Did You Hear the One about the Travelling Saleslady? 68. The Adding Machine (GB) 69. Pink Motel 82. The Bone Yard 90. Wisecracks (doc) 92. The Perfect Man 93. The Silence of the Hams (It.) 94.
TV series: The Pruitts of Southampton 66. The Beautiful Phyllis Diller Show 68.

¶ It's a good thing that beauty is only skin deep, or I'd be rotten to the core. – *P.D.*

I have an agreement with Bob Hope. I don't make fun of his nose and he doesn't ridicule my body. – *P.D.*

My house used to be haunted, but the ghosts haven't been back since the night I tried on all my wigs. – *P.D.*

Dilley, Leslie.
British production designer, from TV.
The Last Remake of Beau Geste 77. Star Wars (AA) 77. Superman 78. Alien (AAN) 79. The Empire Strikes Back (AA) 80. An American

Werewolf in London 81. Raiders of the Lost Ark (AA) 81. Eureka 83. Never Say Never Again 83. Invaders from Mars 86. Legend 86. Stars and Bars 88. The Abyss (AAN) 89. Guilty by Suspicion 91. What About Bob? 91. Honey, I Blew Up the Kid 3. Monkey Trouble 94, etc.

Dillinger, John (1903–1934).
American gangster of the 30s, public enemy number one; he was shot after leaving a cinema (where he had seen *Manhattan Melodrama*). He has been played in *Dillinger* 45 by Lawrence Tierney, in *Young Dillinger* 64 by Nick Adams, and in *Dillinger* 3 by Warren Oates.

Dillman, Bradford (1930–   ).
Lean American actor, a staple of TV movies and series.
A Certain Smile 58. *Compulsion* 59. Circle of Deception 61. Francis of Assisi 61. A Rage to Live 5. The Helicopter Spies 67. The Bridge at Remagen 69. Suppose They Gave a War and Nobody Came 71. Brother John 71. Escape from the Planet of the Apes 71. The Way We Were 73. The Iceman Cometh 73. Mastermind 77. The Lincoln Conspiracy (as John Wilkes Booth) 77. The Swarm 78. Piranha 78. Guyana Cult of the Damned 80. Sudden Impact 83. The Treasure of the Amazon 85, etc.
TV series: Court Martial (GB) 65, many guest appearances; King's Crossing 82. Falcon Crest 2–83.

Dillon, Carmen (1908–   ).
British art director.
The Five Pound Man 37. Quiet Wedding 41. The Demi Paradise 43. *Henry V* 44. The Way to the Stars 45. *Hamlet* 48. Cardboard Cavalier 49. The Importance of Being Earnest 52. *Richard III* 56. A Tale of Two Cities 58. Carry on Constable 60. The Chalk Garden 64. Accident 67. The Go Between 1. Bequest to the Nation 73, many others.

Dillon, John Francis (1887–1934).
American director.
Children of the Ritz 29. Sally 29. Kismet 30. The Finger Points 31. The Cohens and Kellys in Hollywood 32. Call Her Savage 32. Humanity 33. The Big Shakedown 34, etc.

Dillon, Kevin (1965–   ).
American actor, the brother of Matt Dillon.
Heaven Help Us (GB: Catholic Boys) 85. Platoon 86. The Rescue 88. The Blob 88. War Party 89. Immediate Family 89. The Doors 91. A Midnight Clear 91. No Escape 94, etc.

Dillon, Matt (1964–   ).
American leading actor.
Liar's Moon 82. Tex 82. The Outsiders 84. Rumble Fish 84. The Flamingo Kid 85. Target 85. Rebel 85. Native Son 86. The Big Town (aka The Arm) 87. Dear America 87. Kansas 88. Bloodhounds of Broadway 89. Drugstore Cowboy 89. A Kiss before Dying 91. Singles 92. Golden Gate 92. The Saint of Fort Washington 93. Mr Wonderful 93. Golden Gate 94. 2 Die 4 94, etc.

Dillon, Melinda (1939–   ).
American leading actress.
The April Fools 69. Slapshot 77. Close Encounters of the Third Kind 77. Bound for Glory 78. The Critical List (TV) 78. F.I.S.T. 78. Reunion (TV) 80. Absence of Malice 81. Harry and the Hendersons 87. Spontaneous Combustion 89. Nightbreak (TV) 89. Staying Together 89. Captain America 90, etc.

¶ She gives off a lovely light. – *Steven Spielberg*

Dillon, Robert.
American screenwriter.
Prime Cut 72. 99 and 44/100 per cent Dead 74. French Connection II 75. The River 84. Revolution 85. The Survivalist 86, etc.

Dinehart, Alan (1886–1944).
American supporting actor who played many bluff-businessman roles.
The Brat 31. Street of Women 32. Rackety Rax 32. Supernatural 33. Cross Country Cruise 34. Jimmy the Gent 34. The Cat's Paw 34. Dante's Inferno 35. Your Uncle Dudley 35. Thanks a Million 35. Charlie Chan at the Race Track 36. Step Lively Jeeves 37. Ali Baba Goes to Town 37. Rebecca of Sunnybrook Farm 38. Second Fiddle 39. Slightly Honorable 39. Girl Trouble 42. Fired Wife 43. Moon over Las Vegas 44. The Whistler 44. Oh What a Night 44, many others.

Dinelli, Mel (1912–1991).
American screenwriter.
The Spiral Staircase 46. House by the River 50. Beware My Lovely 52. Jeopardy 53. Lizzie 57, etc.

Dingle, Charles (1887–1956).
American stage actor who made occasional screen appearances, usually in cheerfully wicked roles.
■ One Third of a Nation 33. *The Little Foxes* 41. Unholy Partners 41. Johnny Eager 42. Calling Dr Gillespie 42. Are Husbands Necessary 42. The Talk of the Town 42. George Washington Slept Here 42. Tennessee Johnson 42. Somewhere I'll Find You 42. Edge of Darkness 43. Someone to Remember 43. She's for Me 43. The Song of Bernadette 43. Home in Indiana 44. National Barn Dance 44. Together Again 44. A Medal for Benny 45. Here Come the Co-eds 45. Guest Wife 45. Cinderella Jones 46. Wife of Monte Cristo 46. Centennial Summer 46. Three Wise Fools 46. Sister Kenny 46. The Beast with Five Fingers 46. Duel in the Sun 46. My Favorite Brunette 47. Welcome Stranger 47. The Romance of Rosy Ridge 47. State of the Union 48. If You Knew Susie 48. A Southern Yankee 48. Big Jack 49. Never Wave at a WAC 52. Call Me Madam 53. The President's Lady 53. Half a Hero 53. The Court Martial of Billy Mitchell 55.

Dinner, Michael (1953–   ).
American director, a former songwriter and musician, most recently working in television.
Miss Lonelyhearts (TV) 83. Heaven Help Us (GB: Catholic Boys) 85. Off Beat 86. Hot to Trot 88.

dinosaurs
have been a cinematic favourite since the earliest days of cinema, when Winsor McCay appeared with his cartoon creation Gertie in 1909. But it was *The Lost World* 25 which proved to be the template for virtually all the succeeding dinosaur films. This silent movie adaptation of Conan Doyle's novel of an isolated plateau where prehistoric monsters survived improved on the original. Where that had a pterodactyl loose in London, the film sent a brontosaurus rampaging through the streets, attacking Tower Bridge (special effects by Willis O'Brien). It was a scene that became a standard in most subsequent movies, from the Japanese series that began with *Godzilla, King of the Monsters!* 54, in which Tokyo was flattened, to *Gorgo*, which brought a monster swimming up the Thames to rescue its offspring; *Behemoth the Sea Monster* 58, which was just another *Beast from Twenty Thousand Fathoms*, also gave London a going-over. The *Godzilla* (qv) movies, in which the beast

progressed from ravening monster to a saviour of mankind, also drew on the dinosaur battles from *King Kong* 33, in which O'Brien refined the stop-motion techniques he used in *The Lost World*. The problem of getting man and dinosaur into the same setting was solved in many ways: *One Million BC* simply ignored the anachronism, using lizards optically enlarged and a stuntman in a suit for its creatures, and covering elephants with fur to pass as mastodons; its footage was to turn up in later, low-budget efforts, such as Bert I. Gordon's *King Dinosaur* 55. *Unknown Island* 48, *The Land that Time Forgot* and its sequel *The People that Time Forgot* used a similar amnesiac low-budget approach. Hammer's remake *One Million Years BC* used stop-motion for the beasts, although the film is remembered, if at all, for Raquel Welch in a fur bikini. Hammer also made *When Dinosaurs Ruled the Earth* 70, which again relied on the sex appeal of its leading lady. Others used nuclear power to revive the long-dead creatures, including *The Beast from Twenty Thousand Fathoms*, with special effects by Ray Harryhausen. *The Land Unknown* 57 put them in a lost, underground world beneath the Pole, as did *Journey to the Center of the Earth* 59, which again used real lizards (ignoring modern thinking which believes that dinosaurs are related to birds rather than reptiles), and *The Last Dinosaur* 77. Lizards again turn up in the 60s remake of *The Lost World*. *Jurassic Park* was scientifically more advanced, using modern techniques of DNA cloning to bring the creatures back; it once again made dinosaurs monster box-office (special effects by Stan Winston and others), although the mutated creatures of *Super Mario Bros* proved that special effects were not enough on their own to make a successful film, and Roger Corman's attempt to cash in on the craze with *Carnosaur* proved to be no more than a throwback to 50s monster films. There have been two dinosaur westerns, *The Beast of Hollow Mountain* 56 and *The Valley of the Gwangi* 68. Only one animated film has used dinosaurs to good effect: Walt Disney's *Fantasia*, although they were also to be found in Steven Spielberg's jokey *We're Back: A Dinosaur's Story*, and *The Land before Time*.
Books: 1988, *Beasts and Behemoths: Prehistoric Creatures in the Movies* by Roy Kinnard. 1992, *When Dinosaurs Ruled the Screen* by Marc Shapiro. 1993, *The Illustrated Dinosaur Movie Guide* by Stephen Jones.

The Dionne Quins (1934–   )
appeared in two films, *Reunion* 36 and *The Country Doctor* 36. They were *Cecile, Annette, Emilie* (d. 1954), *Marie* (d. 1970), *Yvonne*.

director.
Normally the most influential creator of a film, who may not only shoot scenes on the studio floor but also supervise script, casting, editing, etc., according to his standing. In more routine films these functions are separately controlled.

¶ A selection of directional attitudes:
I feel very strongly that the director is supposed to be the boss. Art was never created by democracy. – *Charlton Heston*
Don't get excited. Obstacles make a better picture. – *Victor Fleming*
You can have all the philosophy you like: if a film doesn't come across in graphic terms, it falls short. – *Rouben Mamoulian*
There is no suspense like the suspense of a delayed coition. – *D. W. Griffith*
I don't try to guess what a million people will like. It's hard enough to know what I like. – *John Huston*

Always cast against the part and it won't be boring. – *David Lean*

Film-making has become a kind of hysterical pregnancy. – *Richard Lester*

I am never quite sure whether I am one of the cinema's elder statesmen or just the oldest whore on the beat. – *Joseph L. Mankiewicz*

The best films are best because of nobody but the director. – *Roman Polanski*

I renew myself at the fountain of the past. – *François Truffaut*

I regard actors as marionettes, as pieces of colour in my canvas. – *Josef von Sternberg*

You should think of each shot you make as the most important one in the film. – *Henry Blanke*

I have never made a picture to please me. Do you imagine I'd make a film like *Tammy* for me? – *Ross Hunter*

The director is the channel through which a motion picture reaches the screen. – *King Vidor*

The director is the only man besides your husband who can tell you how many of your clothes to take off. – *Betty Blythe*

No one can pretend to be a film director unless he also does his own editing. – *Orson Welles*

Shooting a film is like taking a stagecoach ride in the old west. At first you look forward to a nice trip. Later you just hope to reach your destination. – *François Truffaut*

It's the best job in picture business because when you're a director, you're God. And you know, that's the best job in town. – *Burt Lancaster*

It's not a film-maker's job to explain his technique, but to tell his story the best way he can. – *Mike Nichols*

Each picture has some sort of rhythm which only the director can give it. He has to be like the captain of a ship. – *Fritz Lang*

Am I a cult director? Yeah, I love all of that. I want to join the cult of the 100 to 200 million grossers and still make an artistic picture. – *Samuel Fuller*

I like stylization. I try to get away with as much as possible until people start laughing at it. – *Brian de Palma*

Dior, Christian (1905–1957).
French fashion designer who worked occasionally in films.

Stage Fright 50. The Indiscretion of an American Wife (AAN) 54. The Ambassador's Daughter 54, etc.

directors' appearances
in films are comparatively few. Hitchcock remains the unchallengeable winner, with moments in over thirty of his fifty-odd films, including the confined *Rope* (in which his outline appears on a neon sign) and *Lifeboat* (in which he can be seen in a reducing ad. in a newspaper). Preston Sturges can be glimpsed in *Sullivan's Travels*, and in *Paris Holiday*, as a French resident, gets a whole scene to himself. John Huston, uncredited, plays a tourist in *The Treasure of the Sierra Madre* and a master of foxhounds in *The List of Adrian Messenger*; he has more recently begun to take sizeable credited roles, e.g. in *The Cardinal* and *The Bible*. The Paramount lot became a familiar scene in many 40s pictures, with notable guest appearances by Mitchell Leisen in *Hold Back the Dawn* and Cecil B. de Mille in *Sunset Boulevard, The Buster Keaton Story, Star-Spangled Rhythm, Variety Girl, Son of Paleface* and others. Jean Cocteau played an old woman in *Orphée* and appeared throughout *The Testament of Orphée*. Nicholas Ray was the American ambassador in *55 Days at Peking*. Jules Dassin played major roles in *Rififi* (as Perlo Vita) and *Never on Sunday*, as did Jean Renoir in *La Règle du Jeu*.

Hugo Fregonese was a messenger in *Decameron Nights*, Samuel Fuller a Japanese cop in *House of Bamboo*. Others who can be glimpsed in their own work include Tony Richardson in *Tom Jones*, Michael Winner in *You Must Be Joking*, George Marshall in *The Crime of Dr Forbes*, Frank Borzage in *Jeanne Eagels*, Robert Aldrich in *The Big Knife*, Ingmar Bergman in *Waiting Women*, King Vidor in *Our Daily Bread*, William Castle (producer) in *Rosemary's Baby*, Claude Chabrol in *Les Biches* and *The Road to Corinth*, and Joseph Losey in *The Intimate Stranger* (which he made under the name of Joseph Walton). Huston, Polanski, Truffaut and Bondartchuk are among those who have played major roles in their own and other films.

disaster films
have always been popular. In the 30s large crowds flocked to see *Tidal Wave, San Francisco, The Last Days of Pompeii, In Old Chicago* and *The Rains Came*. World War II was disaster enough for the 40s, but the 50s brought *Titanic, A Night to Remember*, and *Invasion USA*, and the 60s *The Devil at Four O'Clock* and *Krakatoa East of Java*. It was the 70s, however, that found the killing of large numbers of people to be really top box office. *Earthquake* and *The Towering Inferno* were giants of their kind, and even though *The Hindenberg* was not clever enough to attract, there were plenty of successful imitators: *The Swarm, Avalanche, Meteor*, etc. TV contributions include *Smash-up on Interstate Five, Hanging by a Thread, The Death of Ocean View Park* and *Disaster on the Coastliner*.

disguise
has featured in many hundreds of films, and was in the 20s the perquisite of Lon Chaney, all of whose later films featured it. Lon Chaney Jnr has also had a tendency to it, as had John Barrymore; while most of the Sherlock Holmes films involved it. Other notable examples include Henry Hull in *Miracles for Sale*; Donald Wolfit in *The Ringer*; Marlene Dietrich in *Witness for the Prosecution*; Jack Lemmon and Tony Curtis in *Some Like It Hot*; Alec Guinness in *Kind Hearts and Coronets*; Peter Sellers in *The Naked Truth* and *After the Fox*; Rod Steiger in *No Way to Treat a Lady*; Tony Randall in *Seven Faces of Dr Lao*; John Barrymore in *Bulldog Drummond Comes Back*; Michael Caine in *Sleuth*; Dustin Hoffman in *Tootsie*; and practically the entire cast of *The List of Adrian Messenger*. Extensions of disguise are the split personality films: *Dr Jekyll and Mr Hyde, Lizzie, The Three Faces of Eve, Sybil, Darkman*.

See also: *transvestism; multiple roles.*

Dishy, Bob.
American character actor.

The Tiger Makes Out 67. Lovers and Other Strangers 70. The Big Bus 76. The First Family 80. The Last Married Couple in America 80. Author! Author! 82. Brighton Beach Memoirs 86, etc.

Diskant, George E. (1907–1965).
American cinematographer.

Riff Raff 47. The Narrow Margin 50. On Dangerous Ground 51. The Bigamist 53, many others.

Disney, Walt (1901–1966).
American animator and executive whose name is a household word all over the world. Formerly a commercial artist, he produced his first Mickey Mouse cartoon in 1928, using his own voice; also Silly Symphonies, one of which (*Flowers and Trees* 33) was the first film in full Technicolor. Donald Duck first appeared in 1936. First full-length

cartoon: *Snow White and the Seven Dwarfs* 37, followed by *Pinocchio* 39, *Fantasia* 40, *Dumbo* 41, *Bambi* 42, *The Three Caballeros* (combining cartoon and live action) 44, *Cinderella* 50, *Alice in Wonderland* 51, *Peter Pan* 53, *Lady and the Tramp* 5, *The Sleeping Beauty* 59, *One Hundred and One Dalmatians* 61, *The Sword in the Stone* 63, *Winnie the Pooh and the Honey Tree* 66, *The Jungle Book* 67, *The Aristocats* 70, *Robin Hood* 73, *The Rescuers* 77, *The Black Cauldron* 85, *The Great Mouse Detective* 86, *Little Mermaid* 89, *The Rescuers Down Under* 90, *Beauty and the Beast* (AAN) 91, *Aladdin* 92, *The Lion King* 94, *Pocahontas* 95. Firs live-action feature *Treasure Island* 50, followed by a plentiful supply including westerns (*Westward Ho the Wagons, The Nine Lives of Elfego Baca*), adventure classics (*Kidnapped, Dr Syn*), animal yarns (*Greyfriars Bobby, Old Yeller, The Incredible Journey*), cosy fantasies with music (*In Search of th Castaways, Mary Poppins*), trick comedies (*The Absent-Minded Professor, Son of Flubber*) and plain old-fashioned family fun (*Bon Voyage, The Ugly Dachshund*). The patchiness of these films has mea that although the Disney label is still a sure sign of suitability for children, it no longer necessarily indicates quality of any other kind. In 1948 begu the irresistible series of 'True-Life Adventures' (cleverly jazzed-up animal documentaries containing much rare footage) and in 1953 came the first feature of this kind, *The Living Desert*; the series has unfortunately died out in films. In 1994, *The Lion King* became the company's top-grossing animated film, and one of the all-time top ten box-office successes in America, taking more than $220m at the box-office. Disney's other recent animated films have also been successes, with *Aladdin* grossing $217.4m and *Beauty and the Beas* $145.8m, although Disney's first, *Snow White and the Seven Dwarfs*, remains among its top hits, havin taken $175.3m over the years.

Disney's long list of Academy Awards are all fo shorts, apart from 'special awards' for *Snow White Fantasia, The Living Desert* and *The Vanishing Prairi* They include a special award for creating *Mickey Mouse* 32. *Three Little Pigs* 33. *The Tortoise and the Hare* 34. *Three Orphan Kittens* 35. *The Old Mill* 37. *Ferdinand the Bull* 38. *The Ugly Duckling* 39. *Lend a Paw* 41. *Der Fuhrer's Face* 42. *Seal Island* 48. *Beave Valley* 50. *Nature's Half Acre* 51. *Water Birds* 52. *To Whistle Plunk and Boom* 53. *Bear Country* 53. *The Alaskan Eskimo* 53. *Men against the Arctic* 55. *The Wetback Hound* 57. *White Wilderness* 58. *Ama Girls* 58. *The Horse with the Flying Tail* 60. *Winnie the Poo and the Blustery Day* 68, etc.

A biography, *Walt Disney*, was published in 195 by his daughter Diane, and in 1968 came Richard Schickel's iconoclastic *The Disney Version*, with Marc Elliot's even more iconoclastic *Walt Disney: Hollywood's Dark Prince* being published in 1993. A massive informational tome is Christopher Finch's *The Art of Walt Disney* 73. Further information was contained in 1973 in *Disney Animation: The Illusion of Life*, by Frank Thomas and Ollie Johnston.

◎ For creating a whole new world of magic as a corrective to the real one. *Pinocchio.*

¶ I love Mickey Mouse more than any woman I've ever known. – *W.D.*

Disney has the best casting. If he doesn't like an actor, he just tears him up. – *Alfred Hitchcock*

At the bottom line he was a down-to-earth farmer's son who happened to be a genius. – *War Kimball*

Disraeli, Benjamin (1804–1881).
Novelist and prime minister; has been notably portrayed on screen by George Arliss in 1921 and

1930 (in each case his wife Florence Arliss played Mrs Disraeli), by Derrick de Marney in *Victoria the Great* 37 and *Sixty Glorious Years* 38, by John Gielgud in *The Prime Minister* 40; and by Alec Guinness in *The Mudlark* 50. In a rather dismal 1978 TV series he was played by Ian McShane.

dissolve (or mix).
A change of scene accomplished by gradually exposing a second image over the first while fading the first away.

distributor (or renter).
A company which, for a percentage of the profits or a flat fee, undertakes to rent a film to exhibitors on the producing company's behalf. Originally major producers like MGM, Warner and Paramount distributed their own films exclusively, but with the rise of independent producers the situation has become much more fluid, with distributors bidding for the films they consider most likely to succeed at the box office and tying up successful producers to long-term contracts.

¶ It's easy enough to make fun of a distributor today, but how can you help but feel sorry for the poor bastard? He's faced with the daily decision whether or not to commit large sums of capital to producers who want to make pictures for release a year from now. Now, we all realize that exhibitors haven't a clue about what the kids want to see today. How can anyone possibly know what kids will want to see a year from now? – *Arthur Mayer*

Divine (1945–1988) (Harris Glenn Milstead).
Obese American transvestite who became notorious for eating dog's droppings in *Pink Flamingos* and was a regular in the films of John Waters.
Biography: 1993, *Not Simply Divine* by Bernard Jay.
Mondo Trasho 69. Multiple Maniacs 70. Pink Flamingos 72. Female Trouble 74. Polyester 81. Trouble in Mind 85. Lust in the Dust 85. Out of the Dark 88. Hairspray 88, etc.

¶ Of course, the last thing my parents wanted was a son who wears a cocktail dress that glitters, but they've come around to it. – *D.*

Dix, Richard (1894–1949) (Ernest Brimmer).
Stalwart American leading man of the 20s and 30s, after which his vehicles declined.
Dangerous Curve Ahead 21. Fools First 22. The Sin Flood 22. The Christian (GB) 23. Souls for Sale 23. Icebound 24. Unguarded Women 24. Too Many Kisses 25. The Lady Who Lied 25. *The Vanishing American* 25. The Quarterback 26. Shanghai Bound 27. Sporting Goods 28. Moran of the Marines 28. Nothing but the Truth 29. *Seven Keys to Baldpate* 29. Shooting Straight 30. Cimarron (AAN) 31. The Public Defender 31. The Lost Squadron 32. Roar of the Dragon 32. The Great Jasper 33. Ace of Aces 33. Stingaree 34. West of the Pecos 34. The Arizonian 35. The Tunnel (GB) 35. Special Investigator 36. The Devil's Playground 37. The Devil is Driving 37. Sky Giant 38. Man of Conquest 39. Here I am a Stranger 39. Cherokee Strip 40. Badlands of Dakota 41. Tombstone 42. Eyes of the Underworld 42. The Kansan 43. Top Man 43. The Ghost Ship 43. The Whistler 44. Mark of the Whistler 44. The Thirteen Hour 47, many others.

Dix, William (1956–).
British child actor of the 60s.
The Nanny 65. Doctor Dolittle 67.

Dixon, Adele (1908–1992).
British musical comedy actress and singer, rarely in films.
Uneasy Virtue 31. The Happy Husband 32. Calling the Tune 36. Banana Ridge 41. Woman to Woman 47, etc.

Dixon, Donna (1957–).
American actress. Married Dan Aykroyd.
Margin for Murder (TV) 81. Doctor Detroit 83. Spies Like Us 85. The Couch Trip 87. Lucky Stiff 88. Speed Zone 88. It Had to Be You 89. Wayne's World 92, etc.
TV series: Bosom Buddies 80–82. Berrengers 85.

Dixon, Jean (1896–1981).
American stage actress, in a few films.
The Lady Lies 29. The Kiss Before the Mirror 33. Sadie McKee 34. She Married Her Boss 35. My Man Godfrey 36. You Only Live Once 37. Joy of Living 38. *Holiday* 38, etc.

Dixon, Thomas (1864–1946).
American Baptist minister who wrote the anti-Negro novel *The Clansman*, on which Griffith's *The Birth of a Nation* was based.

Djola, Badja.
American actor, a former dancer, usually in villainous roles.
Penitentiary 79. The Main Event 79. The Lightship 86. The Serpent and the Rainbow 88. Mississippi Burning 88. A Rage in Harlem 91. The Last Boy Scout 91. The Waterdance 92. Who's the Man 93. Heaven's Prisoners 95, etc.

Dmytryk, Edward (1908–).
American director, in films from 1923. After years of second features he gained a reputation as a stylist with some tough adult thrillers of the 40s; but after years of exile due to the McCarthy witch-hunt his more ambitious recent films have seemed impersonal.
Autobiography: 1979, *It's a Hell of a Life but Not a Bad Living*.
■ The Hawk 35. Television Spy 39. Emergency Squad 40. Golden Gloves 40. Mystery Sea Raider 40. Her First Romance 40. The Devil Commands 41. Under Age 41. Sweetheart of the Campus 41. Blonde from Singapore 41. Confessions of Boston Blackie 41. Secrets of the Lone Wolf 41. Counter Espionage 42. Seven Miles from Alcatraz 42. Hitler's Children 43. The Falcon Strikes Back 43. Behind the Rising Sun 43. Captive Wild Woman 43. Tender Comrade 44. *Murder My Sweet* 44. Back to Bataan 45. Cornered 46. Till the End of Time 46. *Crossfire* (AAN) 47. So Well Remembered (GB) 47. Obsession (GB) 48. Give Us This Day (GB) 49. Mutiny (Fr.) 52. The Sniper 52. Eight Iron Men 52. The Juggler 53. *The Caine Mutiny* 54. Broken Lance 54. The End of the Affair (GB) 54. Soldier of Fortune 55. The Left Hand of God 55. The Mountain (& p) 56. Raintree County 57. The Young Lions 58. Warlock 59. The Blue Angel 59. The Reluctant Saint (It.) 61. A Walk on the Wild Side 62. The Carpetbaggers 63. Where Love Has Gone 64. *Mirage* 65. Alvarez Kelly 66. Anzio 68. Shalako 68. Bluebeard 72. The Human Factor 75. He Is My Brother 76.

¶ My lifelong ambition has been to spend my money as soon as I can get it. – *E.D.*

Dobbs, Lem (1961–).
American screenwriter who took his pseudonym from the character played by Humphrey Bogart in *The Treasure of the Sierra Madre*. He is the son of artist R. B. Kitaj.

Hider in the House 89. The Hard Way 91. Kafka 91, etc.

¶ I think the phrase 'ignorant talentless scum' is best to characterize the people involved in *Hider in the House* at every level. – *L.D.*
The age of the superstar director is over. I think that's bad for us; it's one reason movies aren't good any more. Directors aren't as powerful or as famous. – *L.D.*

Dobie, Alan (1932–).
British leading actor, usually in astringent roles on stage or TV.
Seven Keys 62. The Comedy Man 64. The Long Day's Dying 68. Alfred the Great 69. The Chairman 69, etc.

Dobson, Tamara (1947–).
American leading lady.
Cleopatra Jones 73. Cleopatra Jones and the Casino of Gold 75. Norman Is That You? 76. Murder at the World Series (TV) 77. Chained Hat 83. Amazons (TV) 84, etc.

Dr Christian
was the kindly country doctor hero, played by Jean Hersholt, of a number of unambitious little films which came out between 1938 and 1940, based on a radio series and inspired by the publicity surrounding Dr Dafoe, who delivered the Dionne Quins in 1934. In 1956 Macdonald Carey featured in a TV series of the same name, but he played the nephew of the original Dr Christian.

Dr Mabuse.
The criminal mastermind was created by novelist Norbert Jacques and first filmed in 1922 by Fritz Lang in the two-part *Doctor Mabuse, the Gambler* (*Doktor Mabuse, der Spieler*), starring Rudolf Klein-Rogge, who repeated the role in Lang's 1933 sound film *The Testament of Dr Mabuse* (*Das Testament des Dr Mabuse*), which was banned by the Nazis and led to Lang fleeing to America. He returned to West Germany in 1960 to make the less successful *The Thousand Eyes of Dr Mabuse* (*Die Tausend Augen des Dr Mabuse*) with Wolfgang Preiss in the role. In 1990, Claude Chabrol updated Jacques' original novel in *Docteur M* (aka *Club Extinction*), starring Alan Bates, but the story no longer seemed plausible.

Dr Who.
Ageless time traveller with a time machine, the Tardis, disguised as a police box. Created by producer Sydney Newman as a science-fiction TV series in 1963, its mixture of fantasy, adventure and comedy captured the imagination of the nation and became almost required viewing in the 60s, especially in adventures involving the Daleks, aliens encased in what looked like mobile pepperpots, whose conversation consisted mainly of 'Exterminate! Exterminate!' Also featuring men in rubber suits as aliens, its popularity waned as some odd choices were made in casting the title role, and its run of 695 episodes ended in 1989. It gave rise to a stage play and two dull films starring Peter Cushing as the Doctor. On TV the role was played by William Hartnell (with Richard Hurndall substituting for him after his death in one episode featuring five incarnations of the Doctor), Patrick Troughton, Jon Pertwee, Tom Baker, Peter Davison, Colin Baker, and Sylvester McCoy. In 1994, Steven Spielberg announced that his company would produce a new television series.
Dr Who and the Daleks 65. Daleks: Invasion Earth 2150 AD 66.

Doctorow, E. L. (1931–).
American novelist whose *Ragtime* created an original, almost cinematic, method of prose storytelling which simply could not be afforded in the disappointing film version. There was an earlier film of his *Welcome to Hard Times*. His *Billy Bathgate* was filmed in 91.

doctors
(in the medical sense) have been crusading heroes of many movies: fictional epics that come readily to mind include *Arrowsmith, The Citadel, Magnificent Obsession, Private Worlds, Men in White, The Green Light, Disputed Passage, Yellow Jack, The Last Angry Man, Not as a Stranger, Johnny Belinda, The Girl in White, The Doctor and the Girl, Green Fingers, The Outsider, The Crime of Dr Forbes, The Interns, The New Interns, The Young Doctors, Behind the Mask, Doctor Zhivago,* and *White Corridors.* A few have even commanded whole series to themselves: *Dr Kildare, Dr Christian, Dr Gillespie, The Crime Doctor.* Once-living doctors have received the accolade of a Hollywood biopic: *The Story of Louis Pasteur, Dr Ehrlich's Magic Bullet, Prisoner of Shark Island* (Dr Mudd), *L'Enfant Sauvage* (Dr Jean Retard), *The Story of Dr Wassell, Il Est Minuit Dr Schweizer.* Many less single-minded films have had a background of medicine and doctors as leading figures: *The Nun's Story, King's Row, No Way Out, People Will Talk, The Hospital.* More or less villainous doctors were found in *The Flesh and the Fiends, Frankenstein, Dr Socrates, Dr Jekyll and Mr Hyde, Green for Danger, Dr Cyclops, The Hands of Orlac, Dr Goldfoot, The Amazing Dr Clitterhouse,* and *Malice.*
    TV series on medical subjects have included *Medic* 54–55. *Ben Casey* 60–65. *Dr Kildare* 61–66. *Dr Christian* 56. *Dr Hudson's Secret Journal* 55–56. *The Nurses* 62–63. *The Doctors and the Nurses* 64. *Marcus Welby MD* 69. *The Bold Ones* 68–72. *Police Surgeon* 72. *St Elsewhere* 82. *Ryan's Four* 83.
    See also: *hospitals.*

documentary
was not coined as a word until 1929, but several famous films, including Ponting's *With Scott to the Antarctic,* Lowell Thomas' *With Allenby in Palestine,* and Flaherty's *Nanook of the North,* had before 1921 brought an attitude to their reportage which made them more than mere travel films. In Britain during the 20s, H. Bruce Woolfe made a series of painstaking and still evocative reconstructions of the battles of World War I; while Cooper and Schoedsack went even further afield for the exciting material in *Grass* and *Chang.* 1928 brought Eisenstein's *The General Line,* a brilliant piece of farming propaganda, and Turin's *Turksib,* a showy account of the building of the Turko-Siberian railway. John Grierson, who invented the term 'documentary', made in 1929 a quiet little two-reeler about Britain's herring fleet, and called it *Drifters;* for the next ten years Britain's official and sponsored film units produced such brilliant results as *Shipyard, Coalface, Housing Problems, Song of Ceylon, North Sea* and *Night Mail.* In 1931 Vigo made his satirical documentary *A Propos de Nice,* and shortly afterwards Eisenstein was at work on his never-finished *Thunder over Mexico,* brilliant fragments of which survive as *Time in the Sun.* Travel films by explorers like the Martin Johnsons proliferated during the 30s; Flaherty spent two uncomfortable years off the Irish coast to make his *Man of Aran,* and later produced in India the semi-fictional *Elephant Boy.* Pare Lorenz produced cinematic poetry out of America's geographical problems in *The Plow that Broke the Plains* and *The River.*
    World War II stimulated documentarists to new urgency and new techniques, brilliantly

exemplified by Frank Capra's *Why We Fight* series for the US Signal Corps, turning unpleasant facts into breathtaking entertainment. With a predictably understated approach the British units produced a more sober but equally stirring series of reports on the war (*Western Approaches, Desert Victory, Target for Tonight*) and the home front (*Listen to Britain, Fires Were Started, A Diary for Timothy*), many of them directed by Britain's first documentary poet, Humphrey Jennings. The two countries combined resources to present a brilliant, high-flying compilation film about the last year of war, *The True Glory.*
    Since 1945 the use of documentary for advertising (often very subtly) and teaching has so proliferated that no simple line of development can be shown. Television has relentlessly explored and elaborated every technique of the pioneers, with special attention to 'action stills', compilation films, and hard-hitting popular journalist approaches such as NBC's White Paper series and Granada's *World in Action.* Entertainment films devised a popular blend of fact and fiction in such neo-classics as *Boomerang, The House on 92nd Street* and *Naked City.* At last documentary was accepted as an agreeable blend of instruction and pleasure; and in the changed environment Flaherty's lyrical *Louisiana Story* seemed slow and solemn.
    Book: *Documentary, a History of the Non-fiction film,* by E. Barnouw, was published by OUP in 1974.

¶ The story of the documentary movement is the story of how, not without a scar or two, we got by. – *John Grierson*

Dodd, Claire (1908–1973).
Pert supporting actress or second lead of the 30s.
    Our Blushing Brides 30. An American Tragedy 31. The Match King 32. *Hard to Handle* 33. Footlight Parade 33. Babbitt 34. *The Case of the Curious Bride* 35. The Glass Key 35. The Case of the Velvet Claws 36. Three Loves Has Nancy 38. Charlie Chan in Honolulu 38. The Black Cat 41. The Mad Doctor of Market Street 42, many others.

Doherty, Shannen (1971–).
American leading actress, on television as a child and best known for her role as Brenda Walsh in the series *Beverly Hills 90210.*
    Night Shift 82. Girls Just Want to Have Fun 85. Heathers 89. Freeze Frame 92, etc.
    TV series: Little House on the Prairie 82–83. Our House 86–88.

Doillon, Jacques (1944–).
French director and screenwriter, often of films dealing with the problems of youth, a former film editor.
    L'An 01 (co-d) 72. Les Doigts dans la Tête (co-w, d) 74. Un Sac de Billes (co-w, d) 75. La Drôlesse (wd) 79. La Fille Prodigue (wd) 81. La Pirate (wd) 84. La Vie de Famille (co-w, d) 85. Comédie (co-w, d) 87. La Vengeance d'une Femme (wd) 90. Le Petit Criminal (wd) 90. Amoureuse (wd) 91. Le Jeune Werther (wd) 92. Germaine and Benjamin (Du Fond au Coeur – Germaine et Benjamin) (wd) 94, etc.

Dolan, Robert Emmett (1906–1972).
American composer, in Hollywood from 1941.
    Scores include: Birth of the Blues 41. Going My Way 44. The Bells of St Mary's 45. My Son John 51, etc. Produced White Christmas 54. Anything Goes 56, etc.

Dolby system.
A method of improving the sound quality of optical

sound tracks by reducing background noise and hiss, first used for tape recordings. The Dolby stereo system creates four sound tracks.

Doldinger, Klaus.
German composer.
    The Boat (Das Boot) 81. Die Wilden Fuenziger 83. The Neverending Story (co-m) 84. Me and Him 89, etc.

Doleman, Guy (1923–).
Australian character actor, in British films.
    Phantom Stockade 53. The Shiralee 57. The Ipcress File 65. Thunderball 65. The Idol 66, etc.

Dolenz, George (1908–1963).
Dullish Trieste-born leading man who played leads in some Hollywood films from 1941.
    Unexpected Uncle 41. Enter Arsène Lupin 45. Vendetta 50. My Cousin Rachel 53. The Purple Mask 55. The Four Horsemen of the Apocalypse 62, many others.
    TV series: The Count of Monte Cristo 55.

Dolenz, Mickey (1945–).
American child actor, the son of George Dolenz, who became a member of the pop group The Monkees. He provided voices for TV cartoons in the 70s and later became a TV producer in Britain.
    Head 69.
    TV series: Circus Boy 56–58. The Monkees 66–68.

dolly.
A trolley on which a camera unit can be soundlessly moved about during shooting: can usually be mounted on rails. A 'crab dolly' will move in any direction.

Dolly, Jenny (1893–1941), and **Rosie** (1893–1970) (Janszieka and Roszika Deutsch).
European-American twins who became a world famous singing act and in 1918 starred in *The Million Dollar Dollies.* Jenny committed suicide. In 1946 Betty Grable and June Haver portrayed them in *The Dolly Sisters.*

Domergue, Faith (1925–).
American leading lady, launched in 1950 with a publicity campaign which misfired. However, she played competently in a number of films.
    Vendetta 50. Where Danger Lives 50. This Island Earth 55. California 63. Prehistoric Planet Women 66. One on Top of the Other 70. Legacy of Blood 71. The House of the Seven Corpses 73, etc.

Domingo, Placido (1941–).
Spanish operatic tenor, who makes occasional films.
    Autobiography: 1984, *My First Forty Years.*
    La Traviata 82. Carmen 84. Otello 86.

Dommartin, Solveig (1961–).
French leading actress, often in the films of Wim Wenders.
    Wings of Desire 88. Until the End of the World 91. Faraway, So Close! (In Weiter Ferne, So Nah) 93, etc.

Don Juan.
The amorous adventures of this legendary rascal, a heartless seducer created in stories by Gabriel Tellez (1571–1641), have been filmed several times, notably with John Barrymore in 1927, Douglas Fairbanks Snr in 1934, Errol Flynn in 1948 and (of all people) Fernandel in 1955. Versions of the opera, *Don Giovanni,* are legion: the

most elaborate was directed by Joseph Losey in 1979.

Don Quixote.

There have been many screen versions of Cervantes' picaresque novel about the adventures of the addled knight and his slow but faithful lieutenant Sancho Panza . . . but none have been entirely successful because the genius of the book is a purely literary one. There was a French production in 1909; an American one in 1916 directed by Edward Dillon; a British one in 1923 directed by Maurice Elvey and starring Jerrold Robertshaw with George Robey. In 1933 Pabst made a British film of the story with Chaliapin and (again) George Robey; meanwhile a Danish director, Lau Lauritzen, had done one in 1926. The next batch of Quixotes began in 1947 with Rafael Gil's Spanish version; but the Russian production of 1957, directed by Kozintsev with Cherkassov in the title role, was probably the best of all. Orson Welles filmed sections of his own version, which it looks as though we may never see, though edited versions are being screened at festivals; a Jugoslavian cartoon version appeared in 1961; in 1962 Finland, of all nations, contributed its own Quixote, directed by Eino Ruutsalo; and in 1972 the BBC and Universal made a TV film with Rex Harrison. The popular stage musical *Man of la Mancha*, filmed in 1972, is based on the life of author Miguel de Cervantes (1547–1616) and its correlation with that of his hero. There followed in 1973 a ballet version with Rudolph Nureyev.

Donaggio, Pino (1941–) (Giuseppe Donaggio).
Italian composer.
Don't Look Now 73. Carrie 76. Piranha 78. The Black Cat 80. Dressed to Kill 80. The Howling 81. The Fan 81. Hercules 83. Body Double 84. Hercules II 85. Déjà Vu 85. The Berlin Affair 85. Crawlspace 86. Dancers 87. The Barbarians 87. Hotel Colonial 87. Zelly and Me 88. Appointment with Death 88. Phantom of Death 89. Night Game 89. Meridian – Kiss of the Beast 90. Tchin Tchin 91. Trauma 93. Dove Siete? Io Sono Qui 93. Giovanni Falcone 93. Oblivion 94, etc.

Donahue, Troy (1937–) (Merle Johnson).
American beefcake hero of the 60s.
Tarnished Angels 57. This Happy Feeling 58. The Perfect Furlough 59. Imitation of Life 59. A Summer Place 59. The Crowded Sky 61. *Parrish* 61. Susan Slade 61. Rome Adventure 62. Palm Springs Weekend 63. A Distant Trumpet 64. My Blood Runs Cold 65. Rocket to the Moon 67. Sweet Saviour 71. Godfather Part II 74. The Legend of Frank Woods 77. Malibu (TV) 83. Cyclone 87. Deadly Prey 87. Hawkeye 87. Hollywood Cop 87. A Woman Obsessed 88. Sexpot 88. Dr Alien 88. Assault at the Party Nerds 89. Bad Blood 89. The Chilling 89. Cry-Baby 90. Omega Cop 90. Terminal Force 90. Shock 'em Dead 91. The Pamela Principle 92, etc.
TV series: Hawaiian Eye 59–60. Surfside Six 60–62.

Donald Duck.
Belligerent Disney cartoon character who was introduced in 1934 in *The Wise Little Hen*, was quickly streamlined and became more popular than Mickey Mouse. Still going strong.

Donald, James (1917–1993).
British stage actor who has been in occasional films since 1941; usually plays a man of conscience rather than action.
The Missing Million 41. In Which We Serve 42. The Way Ahead 44. Broken Journey 47. *The Small*

Voice 47. Trottie True 49. *White Corridors* 51. Brandy for the Parson 51. The Gift Horse 52. The Pickwick Papers 52. The Net 53. Beau Brummell 54. Lust for Life 56. *The Bridge on the River Kwai* 57. The Vikings 58. The Great Escape 63. King Rat 65. Cast a Giant Shadow 66. *The Jokers* 67. Hannibal Brooks 69. David Copperfield 69. The Royal Hunt of the Sun 69. The Big Sleep 78, etc.

Donaldson, Roger (1945–).
Australian director who made films in New Zealand before going to work in Hollywood.
Sleeping Dogs 77. Smash Palace 81. The Bounty 84. Marie 85. Deceit 86. No Way Out 87. Cocktail 88. Cadillac Man 90. White Sands 92. The Getaway 94, etc.

Donaldson, Ted (1933–).
American child star of the 40s.
Once upon a Time 44. *A Tree Grows in Brooklyn* 45. For the Love of Rusty 47 (and others in this series). The Decision of Christopher Blake 48. Phone Call from a Stranger 52, etc.

Donaldson, Walter (1893–1947).
American composer who wrote the music for *Whoopee!*, a Broadway musical starring Eddie Cantor that Samuel Goldwyn turned into a movie with virtually the same cast in 1930. The film version retained only three of the original 16 songs, dropping, among others, 'Love Me or Leave Me'. His Hollywood output includes 'You' and 'You Never Looked So Beautiful Before' for *The Great Ziegfeld* 30, and 'Did I Remember' for *Suzy* 36.

Donat, Peter (1928–).
Canadian character actor.
My Old Man's Place 71. The Godfather Part II 74. Russian Roulette 75. The Hindenburg 75. F.I.S.T. 78. A Different Story 78. The China Syndrome 79. Mazes and Monsters 82. The Bay Boy 84. Honeymoon 87. Tucker: The Man and His Dream 88. The War of the Roses 89. School Ties 92. The Babe 92, etc.

Donat, Robert (1905–1958).
Distinguished British stage actor (of Polish descent) with an inimitably melodious voice; he made some impressive films despite asthma which blighted his career.
Biography: 1985, *Mr Chips: The Life of Robert Donat* by Kenneth Barrow.
■ Men of Tomorrow 32. That Night in London 32. Cash 32. The Private Life of Henry VIII 33. *The Count of Monte Cristo* 34. *The Thirty-Nine Steps* 35. *The Ghost Goes West* 36. Knight without Armour 37. *The Citadel* (AAN) 38. *Goodbye Mr Chips* (AA) 39. *The Young Mr Pitt* 42. The Adventures of Tartu 43. Perfect Strangers 45. Captain Boycott (guest appearance) 47. *The Winslow Boy* 48. The Cure for Love (& d) 50. The Magic Box 50. Lease of Life 55. Inn of the Sixth Happiness 58.
✪ For the ethereal quality, partly caused by illness, of a few of his greatest performances. *Goodbye Mr Chips.*

Donath, Ludwig (1900–1967).
Austrian character actor busy in America from the 30s.
The Strange Death of Adolf Hitler 43. *The Jolson Story* 46. Cigarette Girl 47. Jolson Sings Again 50. The Great Caruso 51. Sins of Jezebel 53. Torn Curtain 66, many others.

Donati, Danilo (1926–).
Italian costume and production designer, from television and the theatre.

The Mandrake (La Mandragola) (cos) 65. The Gospel according to St Matthew (cos) 64. The Taming of the Shrew (cos) 67. Oedipus Rex (cos) 67. Romeo and Juliet (AAcos) 68. Medea (cos) 69. The Decameron (cos) 71. Brother Sun, Sister Moon (cos) 72. Amarcord (cos) 73. Casanova (AAcos) 76. Hurricane (pd) 79. Flash Gordon (pd) 80. Red Sonja (cos, pd) 85. Ginger and Fred (cos) 86. Intervista (co-ad) 87. Francesco (pd) 89. En Suivant la Comète (pd) 94, etc.

Donehue, Vincent J. (1916–1966).
American stage director who came to Hollywood to make *Lonelyhearts* 59. *Sunrise at Campobello* 60.

Donen, Stanley (1924–).
American director, former dancer; later branched out from musicals to sophisticated comedies and thrillers.
■ On The Town (co-d) 49. Royal Wedding 51. Fearless Fagan 51. Give a Girl a Break 51. Love is Better than Ever 52. *Singin' in the Rain* (co-d) 52. Seven Brides for Seven Brothers 54. Deep in My Heart 54. It's Always Fair Weather (co-d) 55. *Funny Face* 57. *The Pajama Game* (& co-p) 57. Kiss Them for Me 57. *Indiscreet* (& p) 58. Damn Yankees (& co-p) 58. Once More with Feeling (& p) 60. Surprise Package (& p) 60. The Grass is Greener (& p) 61. *Charade* (& p) 63. Arabesque (& p) 66. Two for the Road (& p) 67. Bedazzled (& p) 67. Staircase (& p) 69. The Little Prince (& p) 73. Lucky Lady (& p) 76. Movie Movie 78. Saturn Three 80. Blame It on Rio 85.

Donfeld.
American costume designer.
Days of Wine and Roses (AAN) 62. They Shoot Horses, Don't They? (AAN) 69. Tom Sawyer (AAN) 73. The China Syndrome 79. Prizzi's Honor (AAN) 85. Next of Kin 89. Gladiator 92, etc.

Doniger, Walter (1917–).
American writer.
Mob Town 41. Red Sundown 49. Cease Fire 52. The Steel Jungle (& d) 56. Madonna Red 78, etc.

Donlan, Yolande (1920–).
American leading lady who had great success on the British stage as the dumb blonde in *Born Yesterday*; settled in England and married Val Guest.
Autobiography: 1976, *Shake the Stars Down*.
Turnabout 41. Miss Pilgrim's Progress 50. *Mr Drake's Duck* 50. Penny Princess 51. They Can't Hang Me 55. *Expresso Bongo* 59. Jigsaw 62. Eighty Thousand Suspects 63. Seven Nights in Japan 76, etc.

Donlevy, Brian (1899–1972).
Irish-American leading man, later character actor, in Hollywood after stage experience; characteristically in fast-talking tough roles with soft centres.
Mother's Boy 28. Barbary Coast 35. In Old Chicago 38. We're Going To Be Rich (GB) 38. Jesse James 39. *Beau Geste* (as the evil sergeant) (AAN) 39. *Destry Rides Again* 39. *The Great McGinty* (leading role) 40. Brigham Young 40. The Great Man's Lady 40. A Gentleman after Dark 41. Billy the Kid 41. The Remarkable Andrew 41. Wake Island 42. *The Glass Key* 42. Nightmare 42. Hangmen Also Die 43. The Miracle of Morgan's Creek 43. *An American Romance* 44. Two Years Before the Mast 44. The Virginian 45. The Trouble with Women 46. The Beginning or the End 47. Kiss of Death 47. The Lucky Stiff 48. Shakedown 50. Hoodlum Empire 52. The Woman They Almost Lynched 53. The Big Combo 55. The Quatermass Experiment (GB) 55.

A Cry in the Night 56. Quatermass II (GB) 56. Cowboy 58. Never So Few 59. The Errand Boy 61. Curse of the Fly (GB) 65. How to Stuff a Wild Bikini 65. The Fat Spy 66. Waco 66. Rogues' Gallery 67, etc.

TV series: Dangerous Assignment 52.

Donnell, Jeff (1921–1988) (Jean Marie Donnell). Pert American actress who played the heroine's friend in many routine comedies of the 40s, and later played mothers.

A Night to Remember 43. He's My Guy 45. In a Lonely Place 50. Thief of Damascus 52. Sweet Smell of Success 57. Gidget Goes Hawaiian 61. The Iron Maiden (GB) 62. Stand Up and Be Counted 72. The Amazing Spiderman (TV) 77, etc.

TV series: The George Gobel Show 56. Matt Helm 75.

Donnelly, Donal (1931–).
Irish stage actor, in occasional films.

The Rising of the Moon 57. Shake Hands with the Devil 59. Young Cassidy 65. The Knack 65. Up Jumped a Swagman 65. Waterloo 70. The Dead 87, etc.

Donnelly, Dorothy (1880–1928).
American stage actress who became lyricist and librettist for Sigmund Romberg, and was played by Merle Oberon in *Deep in My Heart* 54.

Donnelly, Ruth (1896–1982).
American character actress, a wisecracking girlfriend in the 30s, latterly in maternal roles.

Rubber Heels 27. Transatlantic 31. Ladies They Talk About 33. Footlight Parade 33. Convention City 33. Wonder Bar 34. Alibi Ike 35. Mr Deeds Goes to Town 36. More than a Secretary 36. *A Slight Case of Murder* 38. *Holiday* 38. Mr Smith Goes to Washington 39. My Little Chickadee 39. Rise and Shine 41. Pillow to Post 45. Cinderella Jones 46. *The Snake Pit* 48. I'd Climb the Highest Mountain 51. The Spoilers 55. Autumn Leaves 56. The Way to the Gold 57, many others.

Donner, Clive (1926–).
British director, former editor, in films since 1942, directing since the mid-50s.
■ The Secret Place 56. Heart of a Child 57. A Marriage of Convenience 59. The Sinister Man 60. Some People 62. The Caretaker 63. *Nothing But the Best* 63. What's New Pussycat? 65. Luv 67. *Here We Go Round the Mulberry Bush* 67. Alfred the Great 69. Vampira 74. Spectre (TV) 76. Rogue Male (TV) 76. The Three Hostages (TV) 77. She Fell Among Thieves (TV) 78. The Thief of Baghdad (TV) 78. The Nude Bomb 80. Charlie Chan and the Curse of the Dragon Queen 81. Oliver Twist (TV) 82. The Scarlet Pimpernel (TV) 82. Arthur the King (TV) 83. Agatha Christie's Dead Man's Folly (TV) 86. Babes in Toyland (TV) 86. Stealing Heaven 88.

Donner, Jörn (1933–).
Finnish writer-director, producer and novelist, who worked in Sweden as a film critic and also directed four features there in the mid-60s before returning to his homeland.

Sunday in September 63. *To Love* 65. Black on White 67. Portraits of Women 69. Anna 70. Fuck Off! Images of Finland (doc) 71. Tenderness 72. Man Cannot Be Raped 78. Dirty Story 85, etc.

Donner, Richard (1939–).
American director.

X-15 62. Salt and Pepper (GB) 68. Twinky (GB) 69. *The Omen* 76. Superman 78. Superman II (uncredited) 80. Inside Moves 80. The Final Conflict 81. The Toy 82. Ladyhawke 84. Lethal

Weapon 87. Scrooged 88. Lethal Weapon 2 89. Lethal Weapon 3 92. Radio Flyer 92. Dave (p) 93. Maverick 94, etc.

D'Onofrio, Vincent (1960–).
American leading actor.

Full Metal Jacket 87. Adventures in Babysitting 87. Mystic Pizza 88. Signs of Life 89. Salute of the Jugger (aka The Blood of Heroes) 90. Naked Tango 90. Crooked Hearts 91. Dying Young 91. JFK 91. The Player 92. Salt on Our Skin 93. Household Saints 93. Mr Wonderful 93. Being Human 94. Ed Wood (as Orson Welles) 94. Imaginary Crimes 94. Strange Days 95, etc.

Donohoe, Amanda (1965–).
British leading actress.

Castaway 86. Foreign Body 86. The Lair of the White Worm 88. Diamond Skulls 89. The Rainbow 89. Tank Malling 89. Paper Mask 90. It's Nothing Personal (TV) 93. A Woman's Guide to Adultery (TV) 93. The Madness of King George 95, etc.

TV series: L.A. Law 90–92.

Donohue, Jack (1908–1984).
American director, former Ziegfeld Follies dancer. Worked on many MGM musicals.

The Yellow Cab Man 50. Watch the Birdie 51. Calamity Jane (dances only) 53. Lucky Me 54. Babes in Toyland 61. Marriage on the Rocks 65. Assault on a Queen 66, etc.

Donovan, Jason (1969–).
Australian leading actor and singer, on television from the age of 11. Best known for playing Scott in the television soap opera *Neighbours*, he is the son of actor Terence Donovan.

Blood Oath 90. Shadows of the Heart (TV) 90. Rough Diamonds 94.

Donovan, King (1919–1987).
American general-purpose actor, usually in support roles; a frequent TV guest star.

Cargo to Capetown 50. The Beast from Twenty Thousand Fathoms 53. *Invasion of the Body Snatchers* 56. The Hanging Tree 59, many others.

TV series: The Bob Cummings Show 54. Please Don't Eat the Daisies 66.

Donovan, Terence.
Australian actor, much on television, including roles in the two best-known Australian soaps, *Home and Away* and *Neighbours*. He is the father of actor Jason Donovan.

The Getting of Wisdom 77. Money Movers 79. The Man from Snowy River 82. Breaker Morant 88, etc.

Donskoi, Mark (1901–1981).
Russian director celebrated for his 'Maxim Gorki trilogy'.

The Pigeon 29. Alien Shore 30. Fire 31. *The Childhood of Maxim Gorki* 38. *My Apprenticeship* 39. *My Universities* 40. How the Steel Was Tempered 42. The Rainbow 44. The Village Teacher 47. Mother 56. The Gordeyev Family 59. A Mother's Heart 66. A Mother's Devotion 67. Nadyezhda 73, many others.

Doohan, James (1920–).
Canadian-born character actor best known for playing Scotty, the chief engineer of Starship *Enterprise*, in *Star Trek*.

The Wheeler Dealers 63. The Satan Bug 65. Bus Riley's Back in Town 65. Pretty Maids All in a Row 71. Star Trek: The Motion Picture 79. Star Trek II: The Wrath of Khan 82. Star Trek III: The Search for Spock 84. Star Trek IV: The Voyage Home 86.

Star Trek V: The Final Frontier 89. Star Trek VI: The Undiscovered Country 91. Double Trouble 92. Story Book 94. Star Trek: Generations 94, etc.

TV series: Star Trek 66–68. Jason of Star Command 78–79.

Dooley, Paul (1928–).
American character actor associated chiefly with the films of Robert Altman.

Slapshot 77. A Wedding 78. A Perfect Couple 79. Breaking Away 79. Rich Kids 79. Health 80. Popeye 80. Paternity 81. Endangered Species 82. Kiss Me Goodbye 82. Going Berserk 83. Big Trouble 84. Sixteen Candles 85. O.C. and Stiggs 87. Last Rites 88. Flashback 90. Shakes the Clown 91, etc.

Doonan, Patric (1925–1958).
British stage and screen actor, usually in honest, put-upon roles. Son of comedian George Doonan. Committed suicide.

Once a Jolly Swagman 48. The Blue Lamp 50. The Gentle Gunman 52. The Net 53. Seagulls over Sorrento 54. Cockleshell Heroes 55, many second features.

dope sheet.
A list of the contents of a piece of film, usually applied to newsreel libraries.

Dor, Karin (1938–).
German leading lady.

Treasure of Silver Lake 62. Winnetou II 64. The Face of Fu Manchu 65. You Only Live Twice 67. Topaz 69. Live and Let Die 73, etc.

Doran, Ann (1914–).
American character actress, often a friend of the heroine.

Penitentiary 38. Blondie 38. Blue, White and Perfect 42. The More the Merrier 43. Fear in the Night 46. The Snake Pit 48. Rebel without a Cause 55. The Man Who Turned to Stone 58. The Rawhide Trail 60. Rosie 67. First Monday in October 81, many others.

TV series: *Longstreet* 71. Shirley 79.

Dorff, Stephen.
American actor.

The Gate 87. I Know My First Name Is Steven (TV) 89. A Son's Promise (TV) 90. An Ambush of Ghosts 93. Judgment Night 93. Backbeat 94. S.F.W. 94, etc.

TV series: What a Dummy 90–91.

Dorff, Steve.
American composer. He also wrote the theme for the TV series *Uncle Buck* 90–91.

Every Which Way but Loose 78. Bronco Billy 80. Honky Tonk Freeway 81. Honkytonk Man 82. Cannonball Run II 84. Stick 85. Ratboy 86. Back to the Beach 87. My Best Friend Is a Vampire 88. Pink Cadillac 89. Pure Country 92, etc.

Dorfmann, Robert (1912–).
French producer.

Jeux Interdits 52. Road to Salina 69. The Red Circle 70. Red Sun 71. Papillon 73, etc.

Dorleac, Françoise (1941–1967).
French leading lady, killed in car crash. Sister of Catherine Deneuve.

That Man from Rio 64. Genghis Khan 65. Where the Spies Are 65. Cul de Sac (GB) 66. The Young Girls of Rochefort 67. Billion Dollar Brain 67, etc.

Dorn, Dolores (1935–) (D. Dorn-Heft).
American stage actress briefly in Hollywood.

Phantom of the Rue Morgue 54. Uncle Vanya 8. Underworld USA 60. 13 West Street 62. Tell Me Riddle 80, etc.

Dorn, Philip (1905–1975) (Frits van Dongen). Dutch stage actor who went to Hollywood in 1940 and was used mainly in sincere refugee or thoughtful professional roles: returned to Holland in the 50s, later settled in California.

Ski Patrol 40. *Escape* 40. Ziegfeld Girl 41. Tarzan's Secret Treasure 41. Calling Dr Gillespie 41. *Random Harvest* 42. Reunion in France 42. Chetniks 43. *Passage to Marseilles* 44. Blonde Fever 44. Escape in the Desert 45. I've Always Loved You 46. *I Remember Mama* 48. Panther's Moon 49. Sealed Cargo 51, etc.

Dorne, Sandra (1925–).
British 'platinum blonde', often in tawdry roles.
Eyes That Kill 45. Once a Jolly Swagman 48. The Beggars' Opera 51. Roadhouse Girl 54. The Gelignite Gang 56. The Iron Petticoat 57. Orders to Kill 58. The Devil Doll 64. All Coppers Are . . . 72. Eat the Rich 87, etc.

Doro, Marie (1882–1956) (Marie Steward).
American leading lady of the silent screen, one of Zukor's 'Famous Players'.
The Morals of Marcus 15. The White Pearl 15. Oliver Twist (title role) 16. The Heart of Nora Flynn 16. The Wood Nymph 16. The Mysterious Princess 19. Twelve Ten 19. Maid of Mystery 20, etc.

Dörrie, Doris (1955–).
German director and screenwriter.
Straight through the Heart (Mitten ins Herz) 83. In the Belly of the Whale (Im Innern des Wals) 84. Men . . . (Manner . . .) 85. Paradise (Paradies) 86. Me and Him (US) 88. Money (Geld) 89. Happy Birthday, Türke! 91. Nobody Loves Me (Keiner Liebt Mich) 95, etc.

Dors, Diana (1931–1984) (Diana Fluck).
British 'blonde bombshell' who played good-time girls from the mid-40s.
Wrote several catchpenny memoirs.
The Shop at Sly Corner 46. Holiday Camp 47. Dancing with Crime 47. My Sister and I 48. Peggy and the Pownall Case 48. *Oliver Twist* 48. Good Time Girl 48. The Calendar 49. Here Come the Huggetts 49. Vote for Huggett 49. It's Not Cricket 49. A Boy a Girl and a Bike 49. Diamond Lily 49. Dance Hall 50. Lady Godiva Rides Again 51. Worm's Eye View 51. The Last Page 52. My Wife's Lodger 52. The Weak and the Wicked 52. Is Your Honeymoon Really Necessary? 52. It's a Grand Life 53. The Great Game 53. The Saint's Return 54. Value for Money 55. A Kid for Two Farthings 55. Miss Tulip Stays the Night 55. As Long as They're Happy 55. *Yield to the Night* 56. I Married a Woman (US) 56. The Unholy Wife (US) 56. The Long Haul 57. The Love Specialist (It.) 57. Tread Softly, Stranger 58. Passport to Shame 59. On the Double (US) 60. Scent of Mystery (US) 60. The Big Bankroll (US) 61. Mrs Gibbons' Boys 62. West Eleven 63. Allez France 64. The Sandwich Man 66. Berserk 67. Danger Route 67. Hammerhead 68. Baby Love 69. There's a Girl in My Soup 70. Deep End 71. Hannie Caulder 71. The Pied Piper 71. Every Afternoon 72. Nothing but the Night 72. The Amazing Mr Blunden 72. The Amorous Milkman 72. Theatre of Blood 73. Steptoe and Son Ride Again 73. Craze 73. Rosie 74. Steaming 85, etc.

D'Orsay, Fifi (1904–1983) (Yvonne Lussier).
Vivacious Canadian leading lady of Hollywood films in the early 30s.
Hot for Paris 30. *Just Imagine* 31. Silk Stockings 32. Wonder Bar 34. Accent on Youth 45. Wild and Wonderful 63. The Art of Love 65, many others.

Dorsey, Jimmy (1904–1957) and **Tommy** (1905–1956).
American bandleaders and brothers; individually they decorated many musicals of the 40s, and came together in a biopic, The Fabulous Dorseys 46.

Dorziat, Gabrielle (1880–1979) (G. Sigrist).
French character actress, in films from 1922.
Mayerling 36. La Fin du Jour 39. Premier Rendezvous 41. *Les Parents Terribles* 48. Manon 49. Little Boy Lost 53. Act of Love 54. Les Espions 57. Germinal 63, etc.

Dostoievsky, Fyodor (1821–1881).
Russian writer, chiefly of doom-laden novels, of which the most frequently-filmed is Crime and Punishment; there have also been attempts at The Idiot, The Brothers Karamazov, White Nights, The Great Sinner, Pyriev and others.

Dotrice, Karen (1955–).
British child actress who matured gracefully.
Daughter of Roy Dotrice.
The Three Lives of Thomasina 63. Mary Poppins 64. The Gnome-Mobile 67. Joseph Andrews 77. The Thirty-Nine Steps 79, etc.

Dotrice, Michele (1947–).
British leading actress, mostly on TV. Daughter of Roy Dotrice.
And Soon the Darkness 70. Jane Eyre (TV) 73. Not Now Comrade 76, etc.

Dotrice, Roy (1923–).
British stage actor with a strong line in senile impersonation.
The Heroes of Telemark 65. A Twist of Sand 68. Lock Up Your Daughters 69. One of Those Things 71. Nicholas and Alexandra 71. Family Reunion (TV) 82. Amadeus 84. Eliminators 85. Young Harry Houdini (TV) 87. Carmilla (TV) 89. Suburban Commando 91. The Cutting Edge 92, etc.
TV series: Space 1999 75–77.

double exposure.
This occurs when two or more images are recorded on the same piece of film. Used for trick shots when two characters played by the same actor have to meet; also for dissolves, dream sequences, etc.

double-headed print.
One in which sound and picture are recorded on separate pieces of film, usually at cutting copy stage or before OK is received to make combined negative.

double take.
A form of comic reaction to a piece of news or situation. The subject at first fails to take it in, and after a few moments the penny drops with a start. Cary Grant and Oliver Hardy were among the prime exponents of the device, but the comedian who really brought it to the point of art was James Finlayson, who not only had the most pronounced reactions but added a slow withdrawal of the head, calling the entire effect a 'double take and fade away'.

Doucet, Catherine (1875–1958) (Catherine Green).
American stage actress of imposing presence; played dowagers in a few films.
As Husbands Go 33. Little Man What Now 34. Accent on Youth 35. Millions in the Air 35. *These Three* 36. Poppy 36. When You're in Love 37. It Started with Eve 41. Nothing But the Truth 41. Family Honeymoon 49, etc.

Douglas, Angela (1940–).
British general-purpose actress.
Shakedown 59. Some People 61. The Comedy Man 63. Carry On Cowboy 64. Carry On Follow That Camel 66. Carry On up the Khyber 67. Maroc 7 68. Digby 74.

Douglas, Bill (1937–1991).
Scottish director and screenwriter. A former miner, and an astringent chronicler of working-class life, he devoted his first three films to an autobiographical account of his tough early years. He also taught at Britain's National Film and Television School.
Book: 1993, *Bill Douglas, A Lanternist's Account*, edited by Eddie Dick, Andrew Noble and Duncan Petrie.
Childhood 72. My Ain Folk 73. My Way Home 78. Comrades 86, etc.

¶ Never show the audience something they can imagine better than you can show it. – *B.D.*

Douglas, Donald (1905–1945) (Douglas Kinleyside).
Quiet-spoken American actor, usually seen as smooth villain or 'good loser'.
Men in White 34. Alexander's Ragtime Band 38. Whistling in the Dark 41. The Crystal Ball 43. Show Business 44. Farewell My Lovely 44. Club Havana 45. Gilda 46, etc.

Douglas, Donna (1933–) (Doris Smith).
Chirpy American blonde supporting player who found fame and fortune 1962–71 as Ellie Mae in TV's *The Beverly Hillbillies*.
Career 62. Lover Come Back 62. Frankie and Johnny 66, etc.

Douglas, Gordon (1909–1993).
American director, former comedy writer for Hal Roach. Jobs have grown in importance but talent remains routine.
Saps at Sea 40. Broadway Limited 41. The Devil with Hitler 43. Zombies on Broadway 45. If You Knew Susie 48. The Doolins of Oklahoma 49. Kiss Tomorrow Goodbye 50. Only the Valiant 51. I Was a Communist for the FBI 51. Come Fill the Cup 51. Mara Maru 52. The Iron Mistress 53. So This is Love 53. The Charge at Feather River 53. *Them* 54. Young at Heart 54. Sincerely Yours 55. The Big Land 56. Bombers B-52 58. Yellowstone Kelly 59. The Sins of Rachel Cade 60. Gold of the Seven Saints 61. Follow That Dream 62. Call Me Bwana 63. Robin and the Seven Hoods 64. Rio Conchos 64. Sylvia 65. Harlow 65. Stagecoach 66. Way Way Out 66. In Like Flint 67. Chuka 67. Tony Rome 67. *The Detective* 68. Lady in Cement 68. Skullduggery 69. Viva Knievel 77, etc.

Douglas, Jack (1927–).
British comedian who has appeared exclusively in *Carry Ons*. Much on TV.

Douglas, Kirk (1916–) (Issur Danielovitch Demsky).
American leading actor with stage experience; started playing weaklings and gangsters but

graduated to tense, virile, intelligent heroes in films of many kinds.

■ *The Strange Love of Martha Ivers* 46. *Out of the Past* 47. I Walk Alone 47. My Dear Secretary 47. Mourning Becomes Electra 47. The Walls of Jericho 48. A Letter to Three Wives 48. *Champion* (AAN) 49. Young Man with a Horn 50. The Glass Menagerie 51. *Ace in the Hole* 51. Along the Great Divide 51. *Detective Story* 51. The Big Trees 52. The Big Sky 52. The Bad and the Beautiful (AAN) 52. The Story of Three Loves 53. The Juggler 53. Act of Love 54. Ulysses (It.) 54. Twenty Thousand Leagues under the Sea 54. Man without a Star 55. The Racers 55. The Indian Fighter 55. *Lust for Life* (as Van Gogh) (AAN) 56. Top Secret Affair 57. Gunfight at the OK Corral (as Doc Holiday) 57. *Paths of Glory* 57. The Vikings 58. Last Train from Gun Hill 58. The Devil's Disciple 59. *Spartacus* 60. Town Without Pity 61. The Last Sunset 61. Strangers When We Meet 61. *Lonely Are the Brave* 62. Two Weeks in Another Town 62. *The List of Adrian Messenger* 63. For Love or Money 63. The Hook 63. *Seven Days in May* 64. In Harm's Way 65. The Heroes of Telemark 65. *Cast a Giant Shadow* 66. Is Paris Burning? 66. The Way West 67. The War Wagon 67. A Lovely Way to Die 68. The Brotherhood 68. The Arrangement 69. There Was a Crooked Man 70. A Gunfight 71. The Light at the Edge of the World 71. Catch Me a Spy 71. A Man to Respect 72. Scalawag (& d) 73. Mousey (TV) 73. Posse (& d) 75. Once is not Enough 75. The Moneychangers (TV) 76. Victory at Entebbe (TV) 76. Holocaust 2000 77. The Fury 78. Saturn Three 79. Home Movies 79. The Villain 79. The Final Countdown 80. The Man from Snowy River 82. Remembrance of Love (TV) 82. Eddie Macon's Run 83. Tough Guys 86. Oscar 91. Vézaz 91.
✪ For determination and intelligence above the call of duty. *Ace in the Hole.*

¶ My kids never had the advantage I had. I was born poor. – *K.D.*

I want my sons to surpass me, because that's a form of immortality. – *K.D.*

I've made a career of playing sons of bitches. – *K.D.*

He's wanted to be Burt Lancaster all his life. – *John Frankenheimer*

Champion established the essential Kirk Douglas persona – a ruthless, selfish, fiercely driven upstart. – *Stephen Farb and Marc Green, Hollywood Royalties*

Kirk never makes an effort towards people. He's pretty much wrapped up in himself. – *Doris Day*

Famous line (*Ace in the Hole*): 'I'm a thousand a day man, Mr Boot. You can have me for nothing.'
~The name of Douglas's company is Bryna. It was his mother's forename.

Douglas, Lloyd C. (1877–1951).
American best-selling novelist; a doctor who did not begin writing till in his 50s. Films of his books include *The Green Light, Magnificent Obsession, The Robe, White Banners, Disputed Passage, The Big Fisherman.*

Douglas, Melvyn (1901–1981) (Melvyn Hesselberg).
Suave, polished American leading man of the 30s and 40s, most at home in a dinner jacket with an elegant lady on his arm; later spent some years on Broadway and emerged as a fine character actor.
■ Tonight or Never 31. Prestige 32. The Wiser Sex 32. Broken Wing 32. As You Desire Me 32. *The Old Dark House* 32. Nagana 33. The Vampire Bat 33. Counsellor at Law 33. Woman in the Dark 34. *Dangerous Corner* 34. People's Enemy 35. She Married Her Boss 35. Mary Burns Fugitive 35.

Annie Oakley 35. *The Lone Wolf Returns* 35. And So They Were Married 36. The Gorgeous Hussy 36. Theodora Goes Wild 36. Women of Glamour 37. Captains Courageous 37. *I Met Him In Paris* 37. Angel 37. I'll Take Romance 37. There's Always a Woman 38. Arsène Lupin Returns 38. The Toy Wife 38. Fast Company 38. *That Certain Age* 38. The Shining Hour 38. There's That Woman Again 38. Tell No Tales 38. Good Girls Go to Paris 39. The Amazing Mr Williams 39. *Ninotchka* 39. Too Many Husbands 40. He Stayed for Breakfast 40. Third Finger Left Hand 40. This Thing Called Love 41. That Uncertain Feeling 41. A Woman's Face 41. Our Wife 41. Two Faced Woman 41. They All Kissed the Bride 42. Three Hearts for Julia 43. Sea of Grass 47. The Guilt of Janet Ames 47. *Mr Blandings Builds His Dream House* 48. My Own True Love 48. A Woman's Secret 49. The Great Sinner 49. My Forbidden Past 51. On the Loose 51. Billy Budd 62. *Hud* (AA) 63. Advance to the Rear 64. The Americanization of Emily 64. Rapture 65. Hotel 67. Companions in Nightmare (TV) 67. *I Never Sang for My Father* (AAN) 69. Hunters are for Killing (TV) 70. Death Takes a Holiday (TV) 71. The Going Up of David Lev (TV) 71. One is a Lonely Number 72. The Candidate 72. Death Squad (TV) 73. Murder or Mercy? (TV) 74. The Tenant 76. Twilight's Last Gleaming 76. The Seduction of Joe Tynan 79. Tell Me a Riddle 79. Being There (AA) 79. The Changeling 81. Ghost Story 81.

TV series: Steve Randall 52. Hollywood Confidential 54.

✪ For perfecting the image of the smart-spoken 30s playboy. *Ninotchka.*

¶ The Hollywood roles I did were boring: I was soon fed up with them. It's true they gave me a world-wide reputation I could trade on, but they also typed me as a one-dimensional non-serious actor. – *M.D.*

Douglas, Michael (1944–).
American leading man, son of Kirk Douglas.
Biographies: 1993, *Michael Douglas* by Alan Lawson. 1994, *Acting on Instinct* by John Parker.
Hail Hero 70. Adam at 6 a.m. 70. Summertree 71. When Michael Calls (TV) 72. Napoleon and Samantha 72. One Flew Over the Cuckoo's Nest (co-p only) (AA) 75. Coma 78. Running 79. The China Syndrome 80. It's My Turn 80. The Star Chamber 83. Romancing the Stone 84. A Chorus Line 85. Jewel of the Nile 86. Fatal Attraction 87. Wall Street (AA) 87. Black Rain 89. The War of the Roses 89. Flatliners (p) 90. Shining Through 92. Basic Instinct 92. *Falling Down* 93. Made in America (co-p) 93. Disclosure 94, etc.
TV series: *The Streets of San Francisco* 72–75.

¶ The exciting thing about making movies today is that everything is up for grabs. And you had better grab. – *M.D., 1980*

Revenge is a very good motivation if you can direct it. It's healthy. Very healthy. – *M.D.*

Unlike me, he never had to worry about making a living, but he has worked hard, never forgetting to help others. – *Kirk Douglas*

Douglas, Paul (1907–1959).
Burly American actor with unexpected comedy sense.
■ A Letter to Three Wives 48. It Happens Every Spring 49. Everybody Does It 49. The Big Lift 50. Love that Brute 50. Panic in the Streets 50. *Fourteen Hours* 51. The Guy who Came Back 51. Angels in the Outfield 51. When in Rome 52. Clash by Night 52. We're Not Married 52. Never Wave at a WAC 52. Forever Female 53. *Executive Suite* 54. The

Maggie 54. Green Fire 54. *Joe Macbeth* 55. The Leather Saint 56. *The Solid Gold Cadillac* 56. The Gamma People 56. This Could Be the Night 57. Beau James 57. Fortunella (It.) 58. The Mating Game 59.

Douglas, Robert (1909–) (Robert Douglas Finlayson).
British stage leading man who made some home-grown films during the 30s; moved to Hollywood after the war and played mainly suave villains in routine melodramas, then went into TV direction.
P.C. Josser 31. The Blarney Stone 34. The Street Singer 36. The Challenge 38. Over the Moon 39, etc; war service: The End of the River 47. The Decision of Christopher Blake 48. The New Adventures of Don Juan 48. Sons of the Musketeers 51. Ivanhoe 52. The Prisoner of Zenda 52. Fair Wind to Java 53. King Richard and the Crusaders 54. The Virgin Queen 55. The Scarlet Coat (as Benedict Arnold) 55. Night Train to Paris (GB) (d only) 64, etc.

Dourif, Brad (1950–).
American character actor.
One Flew Over the Cuckoo's Nest (AAN) 75. Gruppenbild mit Dame 77. The Eyes of Laura Mars 78. Wise Blood 79. Studs Lonigan 79. Guyana Tragedy (TV) 80. Heaven's Gate 80. Ragtime 81. Dune 84. Blue Velvet 86. Impure Thoughts 86. Fatal Beauty 87. Mississippi Burning 88. Medium Rare 89. Grim Prairie Tales 90. Hidden Agenda 90. Graveyard Shift 90. London Kills Me 91. Jungle Fever 91. Scream of Stone 91. Body Parts 91. Amos & Andrew 93. Trauma 93. Color of Night 94, etc.

Douy, Max (1914–).
French production designer, often for the films of Claude Autant-Lara.
Falbalas 45. Ladies of the Park (Les Dames du Bois de Boulogne) 46. Devil in the Flesh (Le Diable au Corps) 47. Keep an Eye on Amelia (aka Oh, Amelia!) (Occupe-Toi d'Amélie) 49. The Red Inn (L'Auberge Rouge) 51. The Ripening Seed (aka The Game of Love) (Le Blé en Herbe) 53. Scarlet and Black (Le Rouge et le Noir) 54. A Pig across Paris (aka Four Bags Full) (La Traversée de Paris 56. Love Is My Profession (En Cas de Malheur) 58. The Gambler (Le Joueur) 58. The Green Mare's Nest (La Jument Verte) 59. Thou Shalt Not Kill (Non Uccidere) 61. Topkapi 64. Woman in White (Le Journal d'une Femme en Blanc) 65, etc.

Dove, Billie (1904–) (Lilian Bohny).
American leading lady of the 20s; could not adapt to sound.
Beyond the Rainbow 22. Polly of the Follies 22. Wanderer of the Wasteland 24. The Black Pirate 26. One Night at Susie's 28. Painted Angel 30. Blondie of the Follies 32. Diamond Head 62, etc.

Dovzhenko, Alexander (1894–1956).
Russian writer-director, former teacher; in films since 1925.
Arsenal 29. *Earth* 30. Ivan 32. Aerograd 35. Life in Blossom 47, etc.

Dow, Peggy (1928–) (Peggy Varnadow).
American leading lady who before retiring to marry made a strong impression in several films of the early 50s.
■ Undertow 49. Woman in Hiding 50. Showdown 50. The Sleeping City 50. *Harvey* 50. Reunion in Reno 51. You Never Can Tell 51. *Bright Victory* 51. I Want You 51.

Dowd, Nancy (1944–).
American screenwriter.

Slapshot 77. Coming Home 78. Swing Shift 83. Happy New Year 87. Let It Ride 89.

Dowling, Constance (1923–1969).
American leading lady who flowered briefly in the 40s. She was married to producer Ivan Tors.
Knickerbocker Holiday 44. Up in Arms 44. The Flame 47. Gog 54, etc.

Dowling, Doris (1921–).
American leading lady, sister of Constance Dowling. Briefly in Hollywood character roles, then moved to Italy.
The Lost Weekend 45. The Blue Dahlia 46. Bitter Rice 48. Othello 51. Running Target 58, etc.
TV series: My Living Doll 64.

Dowling, Eddie (1894–1976) (Joseph Nelson Goucher).
American singer, comedian and director of the Broadway stage; appeared only in silent films.

Dowling, Joan (1929–1954).
British teenage actress who failed to get mature roles.
Hue and Cry 46. No Room at the Inn 48. Landfall 49. Pool of London 51. Woman of Twilight 52, etc.

Down, Lesley-Anne (1954–).
British leading lady of the late 70s; made her name on TV in Upstairs, Downstairs.
All the Right Noises 69. Assault 70. Scalawag 74. The Pink Panther Strikes Again 76. A Little Night Music 77. The Betsy 78. The One and Only Original Phyllis Dixey (TV) 78. The Great Train Robbery 79. Hanover Street 79. Rough Cut 80. Sphinx 81. Murder Is Easy (TV) 81. The Hunchback of Notre Dame (TV) 82. Nomads 84. The Last Days of Pompeii (TV) 84. Arch of Triumph (TV) 85. North and South (TV) 86. Night Trap (aka Mardi Gras for the Devil) 93. Death Wish V: The Face of Death 94. Munchie Strikes Back 94, etc.

Downey, Robert (1936–).
American independent director and screenwriter of small, quirky films.
Putney Swope (wd) 69. Greaser's Palace (wd) 72. Up the Academy (d) 80. America (wd) 82. Rented Lips (d) 88, etc.

Downey, Robert, Jnr (1965–).
American leading actor, the son of Robert Downey.
America 82. Baby It's You 82. Firstborn 84. Tuff Turf 85. Weird Science 85. Back to School 86. Less than Zero 87. The Pick-Up Artist 87. 1969 88. Johnny Be Good 88. Rented Lips 88. True Believer 89. Chances Are 89. Air America 90. That's Adequate 90. Soapdish 91. Chaplin (AAN) 92. Heart and Souls 93. Short Cuts 93. Natural Born Killers 94. Only You 94, etc.

Downs, Cathy (1924–1976).
American leading lady of a few 40s films.
Diamond Horseshoe 45. My Darling Clementine 46. The Noose Hangs High 48. Short Grass 50. Gobs and Gals 52. Missile to the Moon 59, etc.
TV series: Joe Palooka 54.

Downs, Johnny (1913–1994).
American light leading man and dancer, former member of 'Our Gang'. He later became a presenter of children's TV programmes.
The Clock Strikes Eight 35. Melody Girl 40. All-American Co-Ed 41. Harvest Melody 44. The Right to Love 45. Cruising Down the River 53, many others.

Doyle, Sir Arthur Conan (1859–1930).
British novelist and creator of Sherlock Holmes (qv). His other chief bequest to the screen is the twice-filmed The Lost World.

Doyle, David (1925–).
American character actor.
Parades 72. Lady Liberty 72. The Comeback 77. Love or Money 88. Ghost Writer 89, etc.
TV series: Bridget Loves Bernie 73. Charlie's Angels 76–80.

Doyle, Laird (1907–1936).
American screenwriter.
Oil for the Lamps of China 35. The Prince and the Pauper 36. Another Dawn 37. Strangers on Honeymoon (GB) 37, etc.

Doyle, Patrick.
Scottish composer and occasional actor, who often scores Kenneth Branagh's films. After studying at the Royal Scottish Academy of Music and Drama, he became a teacher and then wrote music for the stage, including work for Branagh's Renaissance Theatre Company. He played the role of the court singer Balthazar in Much Ado about Nothing.
Henry V 89. Shipwrecked 90. Dead Again 91. Into the West 92. Much Ado about Nothing 93. Indochine 93. Needful Things 93, etc.

Doyle, Roddy (1958–).
Irish novelist and screenwriter of Dublin working-class life. He won the Booker Prize in 1993 for his novel Paddy Clarke Ha Ha Ha.
The Commitments (oa) 91. The Snapper (w) 93. The Family (w) (TV) 94.

Dozier, William (1908–1991).
American producer, former talent agent. With RKO, Columbia and Goldwyn in 40s; independently made Two of a Kind 51. Harriet Craig 53; then into TV.

Drach, Michel (1930–1990).
French director.
Amélie ou le Temps d'Aimer 60. Diamond Safari 65. Elise ou la Vraie Vie 69. Les Violons du Bal 73. Parlez-moi d'Amour 75. Le Passé Simple 77, etc.

Dracula.
The Transylvanian vampire count created by Bram Stoker in his novel published 1897 has been on the screen in many manifestations. Max Schreck played him in Murnau's German silent Nosferatu 23. Bela Lugosi first donned the cloak for Universal's Dracula 31, was not in Dracula's Daughter 36 but reappeared as one of Dracula's relations in Return of the Vampire 44 and played the Count in Abbott and Costello Meet Frankenstein 48. Lon Chaney starred in Son of Dracula 44; John Carradine took over in House of Frankenstein 45 and House of Dracula 45; Francis Lederer had a go in The Return of Dracula 58. Also in 1958 came the British remake of the original Dracula (Horror of Dracula) with Christopher Lee; David Peel was one of the Count's disciples in Brides of Dracula 60 and Noel Willman another in Kiss of the Vampire 63; while Lee ingeniously reappeared in 1965 as Dracula Prince of Darkness, in 1968 in Dracula Has Risen from the Grave, in 1969 in Taste the Blood of Dracula, and in 1970 in Scars of Dracula. In the same year Ingrid Pitt was Countess Dracula and 1972 brought Vampire Circus. Meanwhile the Count had American rivals in Count Yorga, in The House of Dark Shadows and in Blacula. (Hollywood in 1957 had produced a lady vampire in Blood of Dracula, and in 1965 Billy the Kid Meets Dracula. Polanski's failed

satire of 1967, The Fearless Vampire Killers, had Ferdy Mayne as Von Krolock, who was Dracula in all but name.) Dracula AD 1972 and The Satanic Rites of Dracula were further variations on the main theme, both with Mr Lee; while Jack Palance in 1973 did a TV film version of the original story for Dan Curtis. It seemed that the Count, though officially dead, was unlikely ever to lie down for long; but no one could have been prepared for the profusion of Dracula variations of the late 70s, by which time Hammer had given up participating. Klaus Kinski aped Schreck in a remake of Nosferatu. George Hamilton appeared in a sexy spoof, Love at First Bite. Laurence Olivier played Van Helsing to Frank Langella's Dracula. Would it never end? No, it wouldn't. Francis Ford Coppola's Bram Stoker's Dracula in 1992 began another frenzied cycle of vampire movies.
Books: 1987, The Dracula Scrapbook by Peter Haining. 1990, Hollywood Gothic by David J. Skal.
See also: Vampires.

drag:
see female impersonation.

Drago, Billy.
American actor, usually in exploitation movies.
Invasion USA 85. The Untouchables 87. Freeway 88. Hero and the Terror 88. Prime Suspect 88. Dark before Dawn 89. Delta Force 2: Operation Stranglehold 90. Martial Law 2: Undercover 91. Guncrazy 92, etc.

Dragon, Carmen (1914–1984).
American composer, arranger and conductor.
Cover Girl (AA) 44. Mr Winkle Goes to War 44. Dishonored Lady 47. The Time of Your Life 48. Kiss Tomorrow Goodbye 50. When in Rome 52. Invasion of the Body Snatchers 56, etc.

Dragoti, Stan (1932–).
American director.
Dirty Little Billy 73. Love at First Bite 78. Mr Mom 83. The Man with One Red Shoe 85. She's Out of Control 89. Necessary Roughness 91, etc.

Drake, Alfred (1914–1992) (Alfredo Capurro).
Italian-American singer-dancer popular in Broadway shows.
Tars and Bars 46. Trading Places 83. The Life and Adventures of Santa Claus (voice) 85.

Drake, Betsy (1923–).
American leading lady, formerly on stage; married for a time to Cary Grant (1949–62).
Every Girl Should Be Married 48. Pretty Baby 50. The Second Woman 51. Room for One More 52. Clarence the Cross-Eyed Lion 65. Players 79, etc.

Drake, Charles (1914–) (Charles Ruppert).
American actor usually found in dullish, good-natured 'second leads'.
Dive Bomber 41. The Man Who Came to Dinner 41. Yankee Doodle Dandy 42. Air Force 43. You Came Along 44. Conflict 45. A Night in Casablanca 45. Whistle Stop 46. Tarzan's Magic Fountain 49. Harvey 50. Gunsmoke 52. It Came from Outer Space 53. The Glenn Miller Story 53. All That Heaven Allows 55. The Price of Fear 56. The Third Day 65. Valley of the Dolls 67. The Swimmer 68. The Arrangement 69. The Seven Minutes 71, many others.
TV series: Rendezvous (GB) 61.

Drake, Charlie (1925–) (Charles Springall).
Diminutive British TV comedian with high-pitched voice and tendency to acrobatic slapstick.

Sands of the Desert 60. Petticoat Pirates 61. The Cracksman 63. Mister Ten Per Cent 66. Filipina Dreamgirls (TV) 91, etc.

Drake, Dona (1914–1989) (Rita Novella).
Mexican singer, dancer and general livewire, former band vocalist as Rita Rio.
Aloma of the South Seas 41. Road to Morocco 42. Salute for Three 43. The House of Tao Ling 47. So This Is New York 48. Beyond the Forest 49. Valentino 51. Princess of the Nile 54, etc.

Drake, Fabia (1904–1990) (F. D. McGlinchy).
British stage and screen character actress: usually played battleaxes.
Autobiography: 1978, *Blind Fortune.*
Meet Mr Penny 38. All over the Town 48. Young Wives' Tales 51. Fast and Loose 54. The Good Companions 57. Valmont 89, many others.

Drake, Frances (1908–   ).
American leading lady of the 30s.
The Jewel 33. Bolero 34. Ladies Should Listen 34. Forsaking All Others 34. *Les Misérables* 35. Mad love 35. The Invisible Ray 36. And Sudden Death 36. Love Under Fire 37. There's Always a Woman 38. It's a Wonderful World 39. I Take This Woman 40, etc.

Drake, Tom (1918–1982) (Alfred Alderdice).
American actor, the 'boy next door' of many a 40s film.
Two Girls and a Sailor 44. Meet Me in St Louis 44. *The Green Years* 46. I'll Be Yours 47. Master of Lassie 48. Never Trust a Gambler 51. Sudden Danger 55. The Sandpiper 65. Red Tomahawk 67. The Spectre of Edgar Allan Poe 72. The Return of Joe Forrester (TV) 75, etc.

Draper, Peter (1925–   ).
British playwright and screenwriter.
The System 64. I'll Never Forget Whatshisname 67. The Buttercup Chain 70, etc.

Drayton, Alfred (1881–1949) (Alfred Varick).
Bald British actor who in later life often played comedy villains in stage farces co-starring Robertson Hare.
Iron Justice 15. A Little Bit of Fluff 19. Honeypot 20. A Scandal in Bohemia 25. The Squeaker 30. The W Plan 31. The Calendar 31. Friday the Thirteenth 33. Jack Ahoy 34. The Crimson Circle 36. So This Is London 38. A Spot of Bother 40. The Big Blockade 42. They Knew Mr Knight 44. The Halfway House 44. *Nicholas Nickleby* (as Squeers) 47. Things Happen at Night 48, etc.

dreams,
with their opportunities for camera magic and mystery, are dear to Hollywood's heart. The first film with dream sequences followed by a psychological explanation was probably Pabst's *Secrets of a Soul;* the trick caught on very firmly in such later pictures as *Lady in the Dark, A Matter of Life and Death, Spellbound, Dead of Night, Fear in the Night, Farewell My Lovely, The Secret Life of Walter Mitty, Possessed, Dream Girl, Three Cases of Murder* and *The Night Walker.* In *Vampyr* and *Wild Strawberries* the hero dreamed of his own funeral; and in *Devotion* Ida Lupino dreamed of death as a man on horseback coming across the moor to sweep her away. Recently, flashbacks have become less fashionable than a story told as in a series of daydreams by the main character, the past mingling with the present, as in *Death of a Salesman* and *I Was Happy Here. Roman Scandals, A Connecticut Yankee at the Court of King Arthur, Ali Baba Goes to Town, Fiddlers Three* and *Dreaming* are but five

examples of the many comedies in which a character has been knocked on the head and dreams himself back in some distant time.
In the mid-40s such films as *The Woman in the Window, The Strange Affair of Uncle Harry* and *The Horn Blows at Midnight* set the fashion for getting the hero out of some impossible situation by having him wake up and find he'd been dreaming. This was scarcely fair in adult films, though it had honourable origins in *Alice in Wonderland* and *The Wizard of Oz.* Nor is there much excuse for the other favourite script trick of having one's cake and eating it, as in *Portrait of Jennie* and *Miracle in the Rain,* when some ghostly occurrence to the hero is passed off as a dream until he finds some tangible evidence – a scarf, a coin or some other memento – that it was real.
The closest a film dream came to coming true was in *The Night My Number Came Up,* when the foreseen air crash was narrowly averted. In the brilliantly clever frame story of *Dead of Night,* the hero dreams he will commit a murder, and does, only to wake up and find the whole sequence of events beginning again: he is caught in an endless series of recurring nightmares. *A Nightmare on Elm Street* developed the idea of dreams becoming real, with its sadistic child murderer haunting the horrific dreams of a group of teenagers who burned him to death, only to find that the power of their emotions brings him back to life. Its many sequels continued the nightmare until it became quite soporific. The notion was developed with more subtlety in *Paperhouse,* in which a young girl dreams her drawings into existence.
See also: *fantasy.*

Dreier, Alex (1916–   ).
Rotund American character actor, former news presenter.
Chandler 72. The Carey Treatment 72. Murdock's Gang (TV) 74.

Dreier, Hans (1884–1966).
German art director, primarily associated with Lubitsch and, like him, long in Hollywood.
The Hunchback of Notre Dame 23. *Forbidden Paradise* 24. The Love Parade 29. *Dr Jekyll and Mr Hyde* 31. *Trouble in Paradise* 32. *Cleopatra* 34. Desire 36. Bluebeard's Eighth Wife 38. Dr Cyclops 39. Reap the Wild Wind 42. For Whom the Bell Tolls 43. *Lady in the Dark* 43. Incendiary Blonde 45. The Emperor Waltz 48. Samson and Delilah 49. *Sunset Boulevard* 50. A Place in the Sun 51, many others.
⊙ For ingeniously influencing fashions for interior decoration in the early 30s. *Trouble in Paradise.*

Dreifuss, Arthur (1908–1993).
German-born American director of second features, former child conductor and choreographer.
■ Mystery in Swing 40. Reg'lar Fellers 41. Baby Face Morgan 42. Boss of Big Town 42. The Payoff 42. Sarong Girl 43. Melody Parade 43. Campus Rhythm 43. Nearly Eighteen 43. The Sultan's Daughter 43. Ever Since Venus 44. Eadie was a Lady 45. Booked on Suspicion 45. Boston Blackie's Rendezvous 45. The Gay Señorita 45. Prison Ship 45. Junior Prom 46. Freddie Steps Out 46. High School Hero 46. Vacation Days 47. Betty Co-Ed 47. Little Miss Broadway 47. Two Blondes and a Redhead 47. Sweet Genevieve 47. Glamor Girl 48. Mary Lou 48. I Surrender Dear 48. An Old Fashioned Girl 49. Manhattan Angel 49. Shamrock Hill 49. There's a Girl in My Heart 49. Life Begins at 17 58. The Last Blitzkrieg 58. Juke Box Rhythm 58. *The Quare Fellow* 62. Riot on Sunset Strip 67.

The Love Ins 67. For Singles Only 68. A Time to Sing 68. The Young Runaways 68.

Dreiser, Theodore (1871–1945).
Serious American novelist, a social realist who was popular in the early part of the century. Films of his books include *An American Tragedy* (remade as *A Place in the Sun*), *Jennie Gerhardt* and *Carrie.*

Dresdel, Sonia (1909–1976) (Lois Obee).
British stage actress usually cast in masterful roles.
The World Owes Me a Living 42. While I Live 47. This Was a Woman 47. The Fallen Idol 48. The Clouded Yellow 50. The Third Visitor 51. Now and Forever 54. The Trials of Oscar Wilde 60. Lady Caroline Lamb 72, etc.

Dresser, Louise (1881–1965) (Louise Kerlin).
American character actress of the 30s, former vaudevillian.
Prodigal Daughters 23. The Eagle 25. Not Quite Decent 27. A Ship Comes In (AAN) 27. Mammy 30. State Fair 33. The Scarlet Empress 34. Maid of Salem 37, etc.

Dressler, Marie (1869–1934) (Leila Von Koerber).
Canadian-born comedy character actress, the heavyweight heroine of silent comedy and star of MGM comedy-dramas of the early 30s.
Autobiographical books: 1924, *The Life Story of an Ugly Duckling.* 1934, *My Own Story.*
■ *Tillie's Punctured Romance* 14. Tillie's Tomato Surprise 15. Tillie's Nightmare 15. The Scrublady 17. The Agonies of Agnes 18. The Red Cross Nurse 18. The Callahans and the Murphys 27. Breakfast at Sunrise 27. The Joy Girl 27. Bringing Up Father 28. The Patsy 28. The Divine Lady 29. The Vagabond Lovers 29. Hollywood Revue of 1929. Road Show 29. Chasing Rainbows 30. One Romantic Night 30. Let Us Be Gay 30. Derelict 30. *Anna Christie* 30. Caught Short 30. The Swan 30. The March of Time 30. Call of the Flesh 30. The Girl Said No 30. *Min and Bill* (AA) 30. Reducing 31. Politics 31. *Emma* (AAN) 32. Prosperity 32. *Tugboat Annie* 33. *Dinner at Eight* 33. Christopher Bean 33.
⊙ For turning her unlikely personality into true star quality at an advanced age. *Dinner at Eight.*

¶ I'm too homely for a prima donna and too ugly for a soubrette. – *M.D.*
You're only as good as your last picture. – *M.D.*
I have been known to grande dame it, at times. – *M.D.*

Dreville, Jean (1906–   ).
French director.
Cage aux Rossignols 43. La Ferme du Pendu 46. Le Visiteur 47. Operation Swallow (The Battle for Heavy Water) 47. Les Casse-Pieds 48. Horizons Sans Fin 53. A Pied a Cheval et en Spoutnik 58. Normandie-Niemen 60. Lafayette 61. The Sleeping Sentry 66, etc.

Drew, Ellen (1915–   ) (Terry Ray).
American light leading lady of the 40s.
College Holiday 36. Hollywood Boulevard 36. Night of Mystery 37. Murder Goes to College 37. The Buccaneer 38. You and Me 38. Sing you Sinners 38. If I Were King 38. Geronimo 39. French Without Tears 39. *Christmas In July* 40. The Mad Doctor 41. Our Wife 41. The Remarkable Andrew 42. The Impostor 44. China Sky 45. Isle of the Dead 46. Johnny O'Clock 47. The Swordsman 47. The Crooked Way 49. Davy Crockett Indian Scout 50. The Great Missouri Raid 50. The Outlaw's Son 57, many others.

Drew, Mr and Mrs Sidney (1864–1919 and 1868–1925) (Sidney White and Lucille McVey). American stage actors who appeared in a number of very popular middle-class domestic film comedies.

Duplicity 16. Hypochondriacs 17. Henry's Ancestors 17. Her First Love 17. His Deadly Calm 17. His First Love 18. A Youthful Affair 18. Romance and Rings 19. Once a Mason 19. Harold the Last of the Saxons 19. The Charming Mrs Chase 20, etc.

Dreyer, Carl (1889–1968). Celebrated Danish director whose later works were few but notable.
■ Praesidenten 20. *Leaves from Satan's Book* 20. Praesteenken 21. Elsker Hverandre 22. Once Upon a Time 22. Michael 24. Du Skal Aere Din Hustru 25. *The Passion of Joan of Arc* 28. *Vampyr* 32. *Day of Wrath* 43. Tva Manniskor 45. *Ordet* 55. Gertrud 64.

Dreyfus, Alfred (1859–1935). The French officer unjustly sentenced to Devil's Island in 1885 for selling secrets, but reprieved by Zola's advocacy, has been played on screen by Cedric Hardwicke in *Dreyfus* (GB 1930) (Fritz Kortner in the German version), by Joseph Schildkraut in *The Life of Emile Zola* (US 1937) and by Jose Ferrer in *I Accuse* (GB 1957).

Dreyfuss, Richard (1947–). American leading man in Hollywood. Over-indulgence in drink and drugs brought a break in his career in the early 80s.
■ The Graduate 67. Hello Down There 68. The Young Runaways 69. Dillinger 73. The Second Coming of Suzanne 73. *American Graffiti* 73. *The Apprenticeship of Duddy Kravitz* 74. *Jaws* 75. Inserts 75. Victory at Entebbe (TV) 76. Close Encounters of the Third Kind 77. The Goodbye Girl (AA, BFA) 77. The Big Fix 78. The Competition 80. Whose Life Is It Anyway? 81. Down and Out in Beverly Hills 85. Stand By Me 86. Stakeout 87. Tin Men 87. Nuts 87. Moon over Parador 88. Always 89. Let It Ride 89. Postcards from the Edge 90. Once Around 90. Rosencrantz and Guildenstern Are Dead 90. What about Bob? 91. Prisoner of Honor 92. Lost in Yonkers 93. Another Stakeout 93. Silent Fall 94.

¶ Behind all art is ego, and I am an artist and I am unique. – R.D.
I enjoyed the journey to the top but then found myself disappointed. – R.D.
The motion picture business is run by corporate thieves. – R.D.
Working is better than snorting. – R.D.

Driscoll, Bobby (1937–1968). American boy actor of the 40s and 50s; AA 1949 as best child actor. He died in poverty, a drug addict.
Lost Angel 43. The Sullivans 44. From This Day Forward 46. So Goes My Love 46. Song of the South 46. If You Knew Susie 48. So Dear to My Heart 48. *The Window* 49. *Treasure Island* 50. *The Happy Time* 52. Peter Pan (voice) 53. The Scarlet Coat 55, etc.

¶ I was carried on a satin cushion and then dropped in a garbage can. – B.D.

Drivas, Robert (1938–1986). American leading man, mainly on TV.
Where It's At 69. Janice 73. Road Movie 74. God Told Me To 76. Demon 77, etc.

drive-in.
A cinema in the open air, with loudspeakers relaying the sound track into your car.

Droopy.
Stony-faced, lugubrious bloodhound star of MGM cartoons. Created by Tex Avery, he was inspired by Wallace Wimple, of the popular radio comedy *The Fibber McGee and Molly Show*, played by Bill Thompson, who first supplied the voice for Droopy.
Dumb Hounded 43. The Shooting of Dan McScrew 45. Señor Droopy 49. Caballero Droopy 52. Dixieland Droopy 54. Millionaire Droopy 56. One Droopy Knight (AAN) 57. Sheep Wrecked 58, etc.

Dru, Joanne (1923–) (Joanne la Coque). American leading lady of the 40s, formerly model.
Abie's Irish Rose 46. *Red River* 48. *All the King's Men* 49. She Wore a Yellow Ribbon 49. Wagonmaster 50. Vengeance Valley 51. Return of the Texan 52. Thunder Bay 53. Three Ring Circus 54. Sincerely Yours 55. The Light in the Forest 58. September Storm 60. Sylvia 65. Supersnooper 80, etc.
TV series: Guestward Ho 61.

drug addiction,
long forbidden by the Hays Code, even in Sherlock Holmes films (though it featured in Chaplin's *Easy Street* in 1917), has recently been the subject of many intense reforming movies such as *The Man with the Golden Arm*, *A Hatful of Rain*, *Bigger than Life*, *Monkey on My Back* and *Synanon*. *Confessions of an Opium Eater*, on the other hand, is a throwback to the Hollywood films of the 20s, when almost every adventure involved a chase through a Chinatown opium den. The addiction has provided plots for many thrillers about the tireless efforts of agents of the US Narcotics Bureau: *Johnny Stool Pigeon*, *To the Ends of the Earth*, *Sol Madrid*, *The Poppy is Also a Flower*, *The French Connection*, etc. In the late 60s drugs began to be advocated as a permissible opting out, or to be freely and seriously discussed, in such films as *The Trip*, *Chappaqua* and *Beyond the Valley of the Dolls*; *Panic in Needle Park*; *Born to Win*; *Believe in Me*; *Jennifer on my Mind*; and *Lenny*.

drunk scenes
have been the delight of many actors as well as audiences. Who can judge between the charms of the following? Greta Garbo in *Ninotchka*; Robert Montgomery in *June Bride*; Jean Arthur in *Mr Smith Goes to Washington*; Laurel and Hardy in *The Bohemian Girl* and *Scram*; Lionel Barrymore in *A Free Soul*; Eva Marie Saint in *That Certain Feeling*; Errol Flynn in *The Sun Also Rises*; Katharine Hepburn in *The Desk Set*; Leslie Caron in *Father Goose*; Fredric March in *There Goes My Heart*; Lee Marvin in *Cat Ballou* (accompanied by a drunken horse); Albert Finney in *Saturday Night and Sunday Morning*; Alan Bates in *A Kind of Loving*; Bette Davis in *Dark Victory*; Claudia Cardinale in *The Pink Panther*; Charles Laughton in *Hobson's Choice*; Katharine Hepburn in *The Philadelphia Story* and *State of the Union*; Lucille Ball in *Yours Mine and Ours*; Arthur Askey in *The Love Match*; Dan Dailey in *It's Always Fair Weather*; Vanessa Redgrave in *Isadora*; Julie Andrews in *Star!*; Dudley Moore in *Arthur*; Dean Martin and Tony Curtis in *Who Was That Lady?* Martin indeed has deliberately built himself an off-screen alcoholic reputation, as did W. C. Fields.
See also: *alcoholics*.

Drury, Allen (1918–). American novelist, whose *Advise and Consent* became one of the better film exposés of Washington.

Drury, James (1934–). American second lead and TV western star.
Forbidden Planet 56. Love Me Tender 56. Bernardine 57. Pollyanna 60. Ride the High Country 62. The Young Warriors 65, etc.
TV series: *The Virginian* 62–69, Firehouse 74.

dry ice.
A chemical substance which in water produces carbon dioxide gas and gives the effect of a low-hanging white ground mist, very effective in fantasy sequences.

Dryburgh, Stuart (1953–). New Zealand cinematographer, associated with the films of Jane Campion.
An Angel at My Table 90. The Piano (AAN) 93.

Dryhurst, Edward (1904–1989) (Edward Roberts). British producer, former writer, in films from 1920.
Autobiographies: 1987, *Gilt off the Gingerbread*. 1987, *Who Needs Enemies?*
So Well Remembered 47. Master of Bankdam 48. Noose 48. While I Live 49. Castle in the Air 52, etc.

DTS
stands for Digital Theatre Systems, a new sound recording and playback system launched by Universal Pictures and used first for *Jurassic Park* in 1993. The sound is stored on a compact disk which is synchronized with the film.

Du Barry, Madame (1741–1793). The French courtesan and mistress of Louis XV whose life was ended on the guillotine was a favourite role for many actresses, though Lubitsch's 1919 German film starring Pola Negri is probably still the best. Other actress who have played the role include Mrs Leslie Carter in *Du Barry* 15; Theda Bara in *Du Barry* 17; Norma Talmadge in *Du Barry, Woman of Passion* 30; Dolores del Rio in *Madame Du Barry* 34; Lucille Ball in *Du Barry Was a Lady* 43; and Martine Carol in *Mistress Du Barry* 54.

Du Maurier, Daphne (1907–1989). Best-selling British novelist of whose works *Rebecca*, *Jamaica Inn*, *Frenchman's Creek*, *The Years Between*, *Hungry Hill*, *My Cousin Rachel*, *The Scapegoat*, *The Birds* and *Don't Look Now* have been filmed.

Du Maurier, Sir Gerald (1873–1934). British stage actor who appeared in occasional films.
■ Masks and Faces 16. Escape 30. Lord Camber's Ladies 32. I Was a Spy 33. Catherine the Great 34. The Scotland Yard Mystery 34. Jew Suss 34.

Du Prez, John.
British composer.
Bullshot! 83. Monty Python's The Meaning of Life 83. A Private Function 84. She'll Be Wearing Pink Pajamas 84. Once Bitten 85. Personal Services 87. A Fish Called Wanda 88. A Chorus of Disapproval 89. Teenage Mutant Ninja Turtles 90. Teenage Mutant Ninja Turtles II: The Secret of the Ooze 91. Teenage Mutant Ninja Turtles III: The Turtles Are Back . . . in Time 92, etc.

dubbing

has several shades of meaning within the general one of adding sound (effects, music, song, dialogue) to pictures already shot. It can mean re-recording; or replacing original language dialogue by a translation; or having someone else provide top notes for a star who can't sing. Here is an incomplete list of singers who provided uncredited voice-overs for actors who couldn't quite measure up.

Band Wagon India Adams for Cyd Charisse, *The Belle of New York* Anita Ellis for Vera-Ellen, *Brigadoon* Carole Richards for Cyd Charisse, *Call Me Madam* Carole Richards for Vera-Ellen, *Cover Girl* Nan Wynn for Rita Hayworth, *Down to Earth* Anita Ellis for Rita Hayworth, *Gigi* Betty Wand for Leslie Caron, *Gilda* Nan Wynn for Rita Hayworth, *The Great Ziegfeld* Allan Jones for Dennis Morgan, *Gypsy* Lisa Kirk for Rosalind Russell, *Happy Go Lovely* Eve Boswell for Vera-Ellen, *The Helen Morgan Story* Gogi Grant for Ann Blyth, *Interrupted Melody* Eileen Farrell for Eleanor Parker, *The Jolson Story* Al Jolson for Larry Parks, *The King and I* Marni Nixon for Deborah Kerr, *Meet Me in St Louis* Arthur Freed for Leon Ames, *The Merry Widow* Trudy Erwin for Lana Turner, *My Fair Lady* Marni Nixon for Audrey Hepburn, *Orchestra Wives* Pat Friday for Lynn Bari, *Pal Joey* Jo Ann Greer for Rita Hayworth, *South Pacific* Muriel Smith for Juanita Hall, *South Pacific* Giorgio Tozzi for Rossano Brazzi, *Showboat* Annette Warren for Ava Gardner, *A Song Is Born* Jeri Sullivan for Virginia Mayo, *The Sound of Music* Bill Lee for Christopher Plummer, *State Fair* (1945) Lorraine Hogan for Jeanne Crain, *To Have and Have Not* (believe it or not) Andy Williams for Lauren Bacall, *Torch Song* India Adams for Joan Crawford, *West Side Story* Marni Nixon for Natalie Wood, *West Side Story* Jim Bryant for Richard Beymer, *West Side Story* Betty Wand for Rita Moreno, *White Christmas* Trudy Stevens for Vera-Ellen, *With a Song in My Heart* Jane Froman for Susan Hayward.

Dubbing of speaking parts is comparatively rare, but note Joan Barry for Anny Ondra in *Blackmail* and Angela Lansbury for Ingrid Thulin in *The Four Horsemen of the Apocalypse*.

Dubbins, Don (1929–1991).

American second lead of the 50s.

From Here to Eternity 53. Tribute to a Bad Man 56. These Wilder Years 57. From the Earth to the Moon 58. The Enchanted Island 58. The Prize 63. The Illustrated Man 69, etc.

Duchin, Eddy (1909–1951).

American pianist and bandleader, best remembered for being impersonated by Tyrone Power in *The Eddy Duchin Story*.

■ Mr Broadway 32. Coronado 35. Hit Parade 37.

Dudgeon, Elspeth (1871–1955).

British stage actress who made her first appearance on screen disguised as an old man.

The Old Dark House (as John Dudgeon) 32. The Moonstone 34. Becky Sharp 35. Camille 36. The Great Garrick 37. Mystery House 38. Pride and Prejudice 40. Random Harvest 42. The Canterville Ghost 44. If Winter Comes 47. The Paradine Case 48. The Great Sinner 49, etc.

Dudikoff, Michael (1954–).

American leading actor in action movies.

The Black Marble 77. Bloody Birthday 80. I Ought to Be in Pictures 82. Tron 82. Making Love 82. Bachelor Party 84. American Ninja 85. Avenging Force 86. Radioactive Dreams 86. American Ninja 2: The Confrontation 87. Platoon

Leader 87. River of Death 90. American Ninja 4: The Annihilation 91. The Human Shield 92, etc.

Dudley-Ward, Penelope (1919–1982).

British leading lady of the 40s.

The Case of the Frightened Lady 39. The Demi-Paradise 43. The Way Ahead 44, etc.

Duel, Pete (1940–1972) (Peter Deuel).

American leading man. Died of a gunshot wound, an apparent suicide.

A Time for Giving 69. Cannon for Cordoba 70. The Young Country (TV) 71, etc.

TV series: Love on a Rooftop 66. *Alias Smith and Jones* 70.

duels

are fought in hundreds of low-budget action dramas, but the well-staged ones are rare enough to be recounted. Basil Rathbone fought Errol Flynn in *The Adventures of Robin Hood* (and later spoofed the occasion in *The Court Jester*). He also lost to Tyrone Power in *The Mark of Zorro*; Flynn also encountered Rathbone in *Captain Blood* and Henry Daniel in *The Sea Hawk*. Douglas Fairbanks Snr fought duels in *The Mark of Zorro*, *The Black Pirate* and others; Douglas Fairbanks Jnr was a memorable opponent for Ronald Colman in *The Prisoner of Zenda* (later restaged for James Mason and Stewart Granger and mimicked by Tony Curtis and Ross Martin in *The Great Race*) and duelled again in *The Corsican Brothers*. Granger also duelled with Mason in *Fanny by Gaslight*, but used pistols this time; it was back to foils again for *Scaramouche* and *Swordsman of Siena*. John Barrymore fought splendid duels in his silent films, notably *Don Juan* and *General Crack*, later opposing Rathbone in *Romeo and Juliet*. In the 40s Cornel Wilde became fencer in chief, in such films as *Bandit of Sherwood Forest*, *Forever Amber* and *Sons of the Musketeers*. All the versions of *The Three Musketeers* involved duelling, but Gene Kelly turned it into a splendid series of acrobatic feats. Paul Henreid duelled in *The Spanish Main*, Larry Parks in *The Swordsman*, Fredric March in *The Buccaneer*, Charlton Heston in *El Cid*, Louis Hayward in half a dozen low-budgeters. In more serious films Ferrer duelled in *Cyrano de Bergerac* and Olivier in *Hamlet*, and there was a pistol duel in the Russian *War and Peace* and the Italian *Colpi di Pistola*. The most recent major films to feature duels are *Barry Lyndon*, *Royal Flash* and the ultimate *The Duellists*.

Duff, Howard (1917–1990).

American actor with stage experience; usually played good-looking but shifty types.

Brute Force 47. *Naked City* 48. All My Sons 48. Calamity Jane and Sam Bass 50. Woman in Hiding 50. Shakedown 50. Steel Town 52. Women's Prison 54. While the City Sleeps 56. Boys' Night Out 62. Sardanapalus the Great (It.) 63. The Late Show 77. In the Glitter Palace (TV) 78. A Wedding 78. Kramer vs Kramer 79. Double Negative 80. Oh God Book Two 80. No Way Out 87, etc.

TV series: Mr Adams and Eve 56–57. Dante 60. The Felony Squad 66–68. Flamingo Road 80–81.

Duffell, Peter (1924–).

British director.

The House that Dripped Blood 71. England Made Me 72. Inside Out 75. The Far Pavilions (TV) 84. Letters to an Unknown Lover (TV) 85. Inspector Morse 88. Genghis Khan 92, etc.

Dugan, Dennis (1948–).

American leading man, usually in rather clumsy comic roles; much on TV.

Harry and Walter Go to New York 76. The

Spaceman and King Arthur 79. Empire Inc 84. Shadow Chasers 85, etc.

TV series: Richie Brockelman 77. Empire 84. Shadow Chasers 85–86.

Dugan, Tom (1889–1955).

American supporting comic actor, often seen as Irish cop or minor criminal.

Sharp Shooters 27. Lights of New York 28. Sonny Boy 29. Bright Lights 31. Doctor X 32. Grand Slam 33. Palooka 34. Princess O'Hara 35. Pick a Star 37. Four Daughters 38. The Housekeeper's Daughter 39. The Ghost Breakers 40. The Monster and the Girl 41. To Be Or Not To Be 42. Bataan 43. Up in Arms 44. Bringing Up Father 46. Good News 47. Take Me Out to the Ball Game 49. The Lemon Drop Kid 51, many others.

Duggan, Andrew (1923–1988).

American character actor of stalwart types.

Patterns 56. The Bravados 58. The Chapman Report 62. FBI Code 98 66. The Secret War of Harry Frigg 67. The Skin Game 71. Jigsaw (TV) 72. The Bears and I 74. It's Alive 77. The Private Files of J. Edgar Hoover 78, etc.

TV series: Bourbon Street Beat 59. Room for One More 61. Twelve O'Clock High 65–67. Lancer 68–69.

Duggan, Pat (1910–).

American producer, former performer and writer.

Red Garters 54. The Vagabond King 56. The Search for Bridey Murphy 56. The Young Savages 61, etc.

Duhamel, Antoine (1925–).

French composer.

Gala 62. Un Amour de Guerre 64. Pierrot le Fou 65. Fugue 66. Weekend 68. Stolen Kisses (Baisers Volés) 68. Mississippi Mermaid (La Sirène du Mississippi) 69. The Wild Child (L'Enfant Sauvage) 69. Bed and Board (Domicile Conjugal) 71. L'Acrobate 75. Twisted Obsession 90. These Foolish Things (Daddy Nostalgie) 90, etc.

Duigan, John.

English-born director and screenwriter, in Australia from the early 60s.

The Firm Man 75. The Trespassers 76. Mouth to Mouth 78. Dimboola 79. Winter of Our Dreams 81. Far East 82. One Night Stand 84. The Year My Voice Broke 87. Romero 89. Flirting 91. Wide Sargasso Sea 93. Sirens 94, etc.

Dukakis, Olympia (1931–).

American actress, mainly on the stage.

Lilith 64. Twice a Man 64. John and Mary 69. Death Wish 74. Rich Kids 79. The Wanderers 79. The Idolmaker 80. Flanagan 85. Moonstruck (AA) 87. Working Girl 88. Dad 89. Look Who's Talking 90. Steel Magnolias 90. In the Spirit 90. Look Who's Talking Too 91. Fire in the Dark 91. Over the Hill 92. The Cemetery Club 93. Look Who's Talking Now 93. Digger 93. I Love Trouble 94, etc.

TV series: Tales from the City 93.

Duke, Bill (1943–).

American director and actor, usually as a heavy, from television, where he also directed episodes of *Falcon Crest*, *Hill Street Blues* and *Miami Vice*.

An American Gigolo (a) 80. The Killing Floor (d) 84. Commando (a) 85. Predator (a) 87. No Man's Land (a) 87. Action Jackson (a) 88. Bird on a Wire (a) 91. A Rage in Harlem (d) 91. Deep Cover (d) 92. The Cemetery Club (d) 93. Menace II Society (a) 93. Sister Act 2 (d) 93, etc.

TV series: Palmerstown, USA 80–81.

Duke, Daryl.
Canadian director in Hollywood.

The Psychiatrist (TV) 70. Happiness Is a Warm Clue (TV) 73. The President's Plane Is Missing (TV) 73. I Heard the Owl Call My Name (TV) 73. Payday 73. A Cry for Help (TV) 75. *Griffin and Phoenix* (TV) 76. The Silent Partner 78. Hard Feelings 82. *The Thorn Birds* (TV) 83. Florence Nightingale (TV) 84. Tai-pan 86. Fatal Memories (TV) 92, etc.

Duke, Ivy (1895–).
Star of British silent screen; married to Guy Newall.

The Garden of Resurrection 18. The Lure of Crooning Water 20. The Persistent Lover 22. The Starlit Garden 23. The Great Prince Shan 24. A Knight in London 29, etc.

Duke, Patty (1946–).
American child actress who found difficulty in graceful adaptation to adult roles. Former wife of John Astin.

■ I'll Cry Tomorrow 55. Somebody Up There Likes Me 56. Country Music Holiday 57. The Goddess 58. Happy Anniversary 59. 4-D Man 59. The Power and the Glory (TV) 62. *The Miracle Worker* (AA) 62. Billie 65. Valley of the Dolls 67. Me Natalie 69. My Sweet Charlie (TV) 70. Two on a Bench (TV) 71. If Tomorrow Comes (TV) 71. She Waits (TV) 71. You'll Like My Mother 72. Deadly Harvest (TV) 72. Nightmare (TV) 73. Captains and the Kings (TV) 76. A Family Upside Down (TV) 78. The Swarm 78. Hanging by a Thread (TV) 79. The Miracle Worker (TV) 79. Before and After (TV) 80. Best Kept Secrets (TV) 84. Prelude to a Kiss 92.

TV series: *The Patty Duke Show* 63–65. It Takes Two 82. Hail to the Chief 85.

Duke, Vernon (1903–1969) (Vladimir Dubelsky).
Russian-American song composer. Shows filmed include *Cabin in the Sky*, but he wrote mostly for revue.

Dukes, David (1945–).
American leading man.

A Fire in the Sky (TV) 77. A Little Romance 79. The First Deadly Sin 80. Only when I Laugh 81. Without a Trace 83. The Winds of War (TV) 83. Space 85. The Men's Club 86. Catch the Heat 87. Date with an Angel 87. See You in the Morning 89. Snow Kill 90. She Woke Up 92, etc.

Dulac, Germaine (1882–1942) (G. Saisset-Schneider).
French woman director.

Ames de Fous 18. Le Diable dans la Ville 24. The Seashell and the Clergyman 26. Theme and Variations 30, etc.

Dullea, Keir (1936–).
American leading man, usually in roles of nervous tension.

The Hoodlum Priest 61. David and Lisa 62. Mail Order Bride 64. The Thin Red Line 64. Bunny Lake is Missing 65. Madame X 66. The Fox 68. De Sade 69. 2001: A Space Odyssey 69. Last of the Big Guns 73. Paperback Hero 73. Paul and Michelle 74. Black Christmas 75. Full Circle 77. Leopard in the Snow 78. Brave New World (TV) 79. Brain Waves 83. 2010 84. The Next One 85. Oh, What a Night 92, etc.

Dumas, Alexandre, père (1802–1870).
Highly industrious French novelist, mainly of swashbuckling adventures. Films resulting include several versions of *The Count of Monte Cristo* and *The Three Musketeers, The Man in the Iron Mask, The Fighting Guardsman* and *The Black Tulip*.

Dumas, Alexandre fils (1824–1895).
French novelist best known for *Camille*, which has been filmed several times.

Dumbrille, Douglass (1890–1974).
Canadian character actor, long in Hollywood and typecast as smooth, suave villain of many a 'B' picture and an admirable foil for many great comedians.

His Woman 31. That's My Boy 32. Elmer the Great 33. Voltaire 33. Lady Killer 34. Broadway Bill 34. Naughty Marietta 35. Crime and Punishment 35. Lives of a Bengal Lancer 35. *Mr Deeds Goes to Town* 36. *A Day at the Races* 37. The Firefly 37. Ali Baba Goes to Town 37. Mr Moto on Danger Island 38. The Three Musketeers 39. Charlie Chan at Treasure Island 39. *The Big Store* 41. Ride 'Em Cowboy 42. Lost in a Harem 44. The Frozen Ghost 45. *Road to Utopia* 45. The Cat Creeps 46. Christmas Eve 47. Alimony 49. Riding High 50. Son of Paleface 52. Jupiter's Darling 55. The Ten Commandments 56. The Buccaneer 58. Shock Treatment 63, many others.

TV series: China Smith 52–55. The Life of Riley 53–58. The Phil Silvers Show 63. Petticoat Junction 64–65.

Dumke, Ralph (1900–1964).
Heavily-built American supporting actor.

All the King's Men 49. Mystery Street 50. The Mob 51. Lili 53. Rails into Laramie 54. The Solid Gold Cadillac 56. The Buster Keaton Story 57, etc.

Dumont, Margaret (1889–1965) (Margaret Baker).
American character comedienne, the stately butt of many a comedian, notably Groucho Marx ('Ah, Mrs Rittenhouse, won't you . . . lie down?).

■ *The Coconuts* 29. *Animal Crackers* 30. The Girl Habit 30. *Duck Soup* 33. The Gridiron Flash 34. Fifteen Wives 34. Kentucky Kernels 34. *A Night at the Opera* 35. Orchids to You 35. Rendezvous 35. The Song and Dance Man 36. Anything Goes 36. *A Day at the Races* 37. The Life of the Party 37. High Flyers 37. Youth on Parole 37. Wise Girl 37. Dramatic School 39. *At the Circus* 39. *The Big Store* 41. Never Give a Sucker an Even Break 41. For Beauty's Sake 41. Born to Sing 41. Sing Your Worries Away 42. Rhythm Parade 42. About Face 42. The Dancing Masters 43. Bathing Beauty 44. Seven Days Ashore 44. Up in Arms 44. The Horn Blows at Midnight 45. Diamond Horseshoe 45. Sunset in El Dorado 45. The Little Giant 46. Susie Steps Out 46. Three for Bedroom C 52. Stop You're Killing Me 53. Shake Rattle and Rock 56. Auntie Mame 58. Zotz! 62. What a Way to Go 64.

TV series: My Friend Irma 52–54.

☻For suffering beyond the call of comic duty. *A Day at the Races.*

Duna, Steffi (1913–1992) (Stephanie Berindey).
Hungarian dancer who appeared in some dramatic roles in the 30s.

The Indiscretions of Eve 31. La Cucaracha 35. The Dancing Pirate 36. Anthony Adverse 36. Pagliacci 37. Waterloo Bridge 40. River's End 41, etc.

Dunaway, Faye (1941–).
American leading lady.

Biography: 1986, *Faye Dunaway* by Allan Hunter.

■ Hurry Sundown 67. The Happening 67. *Bonnie and Clyde* (AAN) 67. The Thomas Crown Affair 68. The Extraordinary Seaman 69. A Place for Lovers 69. The Arrangement 69. Little Big Man 70. Puzzle of a Downfall Child 71. Doc 71. The Deadly Trap 71. Oklahoma Crude 73. The Three Musketeers 73. Chinatown (AAN) 74. The Four Musketeers 74. The Towering Inferno 74. 3 Days of the Condor 75. Voyage of the Dammed 76. *Network* (AA) 76. The Disappearance of Aimée (TV) 76. The Eyes of Laura Mars 78. The Champ 79. The First Deadly Sin 80. Mommie Dearest 81. Evita Peron (TV) 82. The Wicked Lady 83. Christopher Columbus (TV) 84. Supergirl 84. Ordeal by Innocence 85. Barfly 87. Burning Secret 88. Midnight Crossing 88. The Gamble (La Partita) 88. The Handmaid's Tale 89. Crystal or Ash, Fire or Wind, as Long as It's Love (In una Notte di Chiaro di Luna) 89. Wait until Spring, Bandini 89. Silhouette 90. Christopher Columbus 91. Scorchers 91. Arizona Dream 92. The Temp 93.

¶ A star today has to take charge of every aspect of her career. There are no studios left to do it for you. – F.D.

Dunbar, Adrian (1958–).
Irish actor and screenwriter.

■ A World Apart 87. The Dawning 88. My Left Foot 89. *Hear My Song* (& w) 91. Force of Duty (TV) 92. The Crying Game 92. A Woman's Guide to Adultery (TV) 93. Widow's Peak 94.

Dunbar, Dixie (1915–1991) (Christina Dunbar).
American dancer and light lead, in films of the 30s.

George White's Scandals 34. King of Burlesque 36. Sing Baby Sing 36. Rebecca of Sunnybrook Farm 38. Alexander's Ragtime Band 38, etc.

Duncan, Archie (1914–1979).
Burly Scottish actor, the 'Little John' of TV's Robin Hood series.

Operation Diamond 47. The Bad Lord Byron 48. The Gorbals Story 51. Robin Hood 53. The Maggie 53. Laxdale Hall 54. Johnny on the Run 56. Harry Black 56. Lancelot and Guinevere 63. Ring of Bright Water 69, etc.

Duncan, Arletta (1914–1938).
American actress and singer, on the stage as a child, who was given a seven-year contract by Universal after winning a trip to Hollywood in a photographic contest. Committed suicide by jumping from the 'Hollywoodland' sign.

Frankenstein 31. Law and Order 32. Back Street 32. The Unexpected Father 32. Night World 32. Fast Companions 32, etc.

Duncan, David (1913–).
American screenwriter.

Sangaree 53. The Black Scorpion 57. The Thing that Couldn't Die 58. Monster on the Campus 58. The Leech Woman 60. The Time Machine 60.

Duncan, Isadora (1878–1927).
Flamboyant American dancer. Died when her scarf caught in the wheel of a car. She was the subject of a biopic, *Isadora* (US: *The Loves of Isadora*) 58, directed by Karel Reisz and starring Vanessa Redgrave.

Duncan, Rosetta (1900–1959).
American vaudeville performer with her sister Vivian as the Duncan Sisters, who made only two films: an unsuccessful silent from their long-running stage show, based on *Uncle Tom's Cabin* (with Rosetta blacked up as Topsy), which they were still performing in the 40s, and one successful talkie.

Topsy and Eva 27. It's a Great Life 29.

Duncan, Sandy (1946–).
Tomboyish American leading lady.
■ Million Dollar Duck 71. *Star Spangled Girl* 71. Roots (TV) 77. The Cat from Outer Space 78. Rock-a-Doodle (voice) 90.
TV series: *Funny Face* 71.

Duncan, Vivian (1902–1986).
American vaudeville performer with her sister Rosetta Duncan (qv). She was married to Nils Asther.

Dundas, David.
English composer.
Withnail and I 87. How to Get Ahead in Advertising 89, etc.

Dunham, Duwayne.
American editor turned director.
AS EDITOR: Return of the Jedi 83. The Mean Season 85. Blue Velvet 86. Mad House 90. Wild at Heart 90. Twin Peaks (TV) 90, etc.
AS DIRECTOR: Homeward Journey: The Incredible Journey 93.

Duning, George (1919–).
American music director and composer.
The Corpse Came COD 46. To the Ends of the Earth 48. The Dark Past 49. No Sad Songs for Me 50. The Mob 51. Paula 52. Salome 53. The Man from Laramie 55. Bell Book and Candle 58. Houseboat 58. The Last Angry Man 59. The World of Suzie Wong 61. Toys in the Attic 63. Dear Brigitte 65. Any Wednesday 66. Terror in the Wax Museum 73. The Man with Bogart's Face 80. Goliath Awaits (TV) 81, many others.

Dunlap, Paul.
American composer, mainly for low-budget movies.
The Baron of Arizona 50. The Steel Helmet 50. Little Big Horn 51. Park Row 52. Loophole 54. Fort Yuma 55. The Broken Star 56. Dance with Me, Henry 56. Apache Warrior 57. I Was a Teenage Werewolf 57. I Was a Teenage Frankenstein 57. Blood of Dracula 57. Frankenstein – 1970 58. The Four Skulls of Jonathan Drake 59. The Rookie 59. The Angry Red Planet 60. Shock Corridor 63. The Naked Kiss 64. Castle of Evil 66. The Money Jungle 68, many others.

Dunn, Emma (1875–1966).
British character actress, long in Hollywood, typically as housekeeper.
Old Lady 31 20. Pied Piper Malone 23. Side Street 29. Bad Sister 31. Hard to Handle 33. The Glass Key 35. Mr Deeds Goes to Town 36. Thanks for the Memory 38. Son of Frankenstein 39. The Great Dictator 40. Ladies in Retirement 41. I Married a Witch 42. It Happened Tomorrow 44. Life with Father 47. The Woman in White 48, many others.

Dunn, James (1905–1967).
Genial American leading man of the 30s; later seized one good acting chance but slipped into low-budget westerns.
Bad Girl 31. Over the Hill 31. Sailor's Luck 33. Hold Me Tight 33. Stand Up and Cheer 34. Baby Take a Bow 34. Bright Eyes 34. The Daring Young Man 35. Don't Get Personal 36. Mysterious Crossing 37. Shadows over Shanghai 38. Government Girl 43. *A Tree Grows in Brooklyn* (AA) 45. That Brennan Girl 46. Killer McCoy 48. The Golden Gloves Story 50. The Bramble Bush 60. The Nine Lives of Elfego Baca 62. Hemingway's Adventures of a Young Man 62. The Oscar 66, etc.
TV series: It's A Great Life 54.

Dunn, Michael (1935–1973) (Gary Neil Miller).
American dwarf actor. Found dead, a possible suicide, while filming The Abdication.
Ship of Fools 65. You're a Big Boy Now 67. No Way to Treat a Lady 68. Madigan 68. Boom 68. Justine 69. Murders in the Rue Morgue 71. Goodnight My Love (TV) 72. The Mutations 74, etc.

Dunne, Dominique (1959–1982).
American actress, the sister of Griffin Dunne. Killed by a former boyfriend.
Magic on Love Island 80. Poltergeist 82. The Shadow Riders (TV) 82. Haunting of Harrington House (TV) 82, etc.

Dunne, Griffin (1955–).
American leading man of the 80s.
■ Head over Heels 79. The Fan 81. An American Werewolf in London 81. Cold Feet 83. Almost You 84. Johnny Dangerously 84. After Hours 85. Who's That Girl? 87. The Big Blue (Le Grand Bleu) 88. Me and Him 88. Running on Empty 88. White Palace 90. Once Around 91. My Girl 91. Straight Talk 92. The Pickle 93. I Like It Like That 94. Quiz Show 94.

Dunne, Irene (1898–1990).
Gracious American leading lady of the 30s and 40s, usually in sensible well-bred roles.
■ Leathernecking 30. *Cimarron* (AAN) 31. The Great Lover 31. Consolation Marriage 31. Bachelor Apartment 31. *Back Street* 32. Symphony of Six Million 33. Thirteen Women 32. No Other Women 33. The Secret of Madame Blanche 33. The Silver Cord 33. *Ann Vickers* 33. If I Were Free 34. This Man is Mine 34. Stingaree 34. The Age of Innocence 34. Sweet Adeline 35. *Roberta* 35. *Magnificent Obsession* 35. Show Boat 36. *Theodora Goes Wild* (AAN) 36. *The Awful Truth* (AAN) 37. High Wide and Handsome 37. Joy of Living 38. *Love Affair* (AAN) 39. Invitation to Happiness 39. When Tomorrow Comes 39. *My Favourite Wife* 40. Penny Serenade 41. Unfinished Business 41. Lady in a Jam 42. A Guy Named Joe 43. The White Cliffs of Dover 44. Together Again 45. Over Twenty One 45. *Anna and the King of Siam* 46. Life with Father 47. I Remember Mama (AAN) 48. Never a Dull Moment 50. *The Mudlark* (as Queen Victoria) 51. It Grows on Trees 52.
✪ For epitomizing the American lady of a gentler, more romantic age than ours. *Love Affair.*

Dunne, John Gregory (1932–).
American screenwriter, novelist and essayist. He is also the author of *The Studio* (1970), a study of Twentieth Century Fox during the year it was making *Dr Dolittle* and *Star!* He is married to Joan Didion (qv), with whom he has collaborated on his film scripts.
Panic in Needle Park (co-w) 71. Play It as It Lays (co-w) 71. A Star Is Born (co-w) 76. True Confessions (oa, co-w) 81.

¶ The truly absorbing aspect of the motion picture ethic, of course, is that it affects not only motion picture people but almost everyone alive in the United States today. By adolescence, children have been programmed with a set of responses and life lessons learned almost totally from motion pictures, television and the recording industry. – *J.G.D.*

Dunne, Philip (1908–1992).
American screenwriter and director.
Student Tour 34. The Last of the Mohicans 36. Lancer Spy 37. Suez 38. Stanley and Livingstone 39. The Rains Came 39. Swanee River 39. How

Green was My Valley (AAN) 41. The Late George Apley 47. Forever Amber 47. The Luck of the Irish 48. Pinky 49. David and Bathsheba (AAN) 51. The Robe 53. Prince of Players (& pd) 55. Hilda Crane (& d) 56. Ten North Frederick (& d) 58. Blue Denim (& d) 59. Lisa (d only) 62. The Agony and the Ecstasy 65. Blindfold (& d) 66, many others.

Dunning, George (1920–1979).
Canadian animator whose main feature work was *The Yellow Submarine.*

Dunning, Ruth (1911–1983).
British character actress, mainly on TV.

Dunnock, Mildred (1904–1991).
American character actress specializing in motherly types.
The Corn is Green 45. Kiss of Death 47. *Death of a Salesman* (AAN) 51. Viva Zapata 52. The Jazz Singer 53. Love Me Tender 56. Baby Doll (AAN) 56. Peyton Place 57. The Nun's Story 57. Cat on a Hot Tin Roof 58. Butterfield 8 60. Something Wild 61. Sweet Bird of Youth 62. Behold a Pale Horse 64. Seven Women 66. Whatever Happened to Aunt Alice? 69. Murder or Mercy (TV) 74. The Spiral Staircase (GB) 75. The Pickup Artist 87, etc.

dupe negative.
One made from the original negative (via a lavender print) to protect it from wear by producing too many copies.

duping (lavender) print.
A high-quality print made from the original negative. From it dupe negatives can be made.

Dupont, E.A. (1891–1956) (Ewald André).
German director who moved with unhappy results to Britain and Hollywood.
Baruh 23. *Variety* 26. Love Me and the World Is Mine 27. Moulin Rouge 28. *Piccadilly* 28. Atlantic 30. Ladies Must Love 33. The Bishop Misbehaves 35. Forgotten Faces 36. Hell's Kitchen 39. The Scarf (& w) 50. The Neanderthal Man 53. Return to Treasure Island 54. Magic Fire (co-w only) 56, etc.

Dupree, Minnie (1873–1947).
American character actress seen infrequently as sweet old lady.
Night Club 29. *The Young in Heart* 38. Anne of Windy Poplars 40, etc.

Duprez, June (1918–1984).
British leading lady who moved to Hollywood in the 40s.
The Crimson Circle 36. The Spy in Black 38. The Four Feathers 39. The Thief of Baghdad 41. None But the Lonely Heart (US) 44. *And Then There Were None* (US) 45. Calcutta (US) 46. That Brennan Girl (US) 47. The Kinsey Report (US) 61, etc.

Dupuis, Paul (1916–1976).
French-Canadian leading man popular in British films in the late 40s.
Johnny Frenchman 45. The White Unicorn 47. Sleeping Car to Trieste 48. Passport to Pimlico 49. The Reluctant Widow 50, etc.

Durante, Jimmy 'Schnozzle' (1893–1980).
Long-nosed, well-loved American comedian with long career in vaudeville and nightclubs. Film appearances spasmodic, and most successful when involving his old routines: 'Umbriago', 'Ink-a-dink', etc.
Biographies: 1951, *Schnozzola* by Gene Fowler. 1963, *Goodnight Mrs Calabash* by William Cahn.

■ Roadhouse Nights 30. The New Adventures of Get-Rich-Quick Wallingford 31. Cuban Love Song 31. The Passionate Plumber 32. The Wet Parade 32. Speak Easily 32. The Phantom President 33. Blondie of the Follies 33. Meet the Baron 33. What No Beer 33. Hell Below 33. Broadway to Hollywood 33. George White's Scandals 34. Hollywood Party 34. Joe Palooka 34. She Learned About Sailors 34. Strictly Dynamite 34. Student Tour 34. Carnival 35. Land without Music (GB) 36. Sally, Irene and Mary 38. Start Cheering 38. Little Miss Broadway 38. Melody Ranch 40. *You're in the Army Now* 40. *The Man who Came to Dinner* 41. Two Girls and a Sailor 44. Music for Millions 45. *Two Sisters from Boston* 46. It Happened in Brooklyn 47. This Time for Keeps 47. On an Island with You 48. The Great Rupert 50. The Milkman 50. Beau James 57. Pepe 60. The Last Judgment 61. *Jumbo* 62. It's a Mad Mad Mad Mad World (cameo) 63.

TV series: The Jimmy Durante Show 54–56.

¶ Everybody wants to get into de act! – *J.D., catchphrase*

Dere's a million good-looking guys in the world, but I'm a novelty. – *J.D.*

Goodnight, Mrs Calabash, wherever you are. – *J.D., closing words of music-hall act* (Mrs Calabash was his pet name for his late wife)

I don't split infinitives. When I go to work on 'em, I break 'em up into little pieces. – *J.D.*

Duras, Marguerite (1914–   ) (Marguerite Donnadieu).
French director, screenwriter, novelist and dramatist, born in French Indochina. Her award-winning autobiographical novel *L'Amant* (*The Lover*) was turned into a hit movie in France in 1991.

The Sea Wall (Barrage contre le Pacifique) (oa) 57. Hiroshima Mon Amour (w) 59. Moderato Cantabile (w) 60. The Long Absence (Une Aussi Longue Absence) 61. 10.30 p.m. Summer (w) 66. La Musica (w, co-d) 66. The Sailor from Gibraltar (oa) 67. Destroy, She Said (Détruire, Dit-elle) (wd) 69. Jaune de Soleil (wd) 71. Nathalie Granger (wd) 73. La Femmes du Gau (wd) 74. India Song (a, wd) 75. Entire Days in the Trees (Entières dans les Arbres) (wd) 77. Baxter, Vera Baxter (wd) 77. Le Navire Night (wd) 79. Aurelia Steiner (wd) 79. Les Enfants (w, co-d) 85, etc.

Durbin, Deanna (1921–   ) (Edna Mae Durbin).
Canadian girl-singer who won instant world-wide success as a teenage star; her career faltered after ten years when weight problems added to a change in musical fashion brought about her premature retirement. Special Academy Award 1938 'for bringing to the screen the spirit and personification of youth'. Long retired and living in France.
■ Every Sunday 36. *Three Smart Girls* 36. *One Hundred Men and a Girl* 37. *Mad about Music* 38. *That Certain Age* 38. Three Smart Girls Grow Up 39. First Love 39. It's a Date 39. Spring Parade 40. Nice Girl 40. *It Started with Eve* 41. The Amazing Mrs Holliday 42. Hers to Hold 43. His Butler's Sister 43. Christmas Holiday 44. *Can't Help Singing* 44. Lady on a Train 45. Because of Him 45. I'll Be Yours 46. Something in the Wind 47. Up in Central Park 47. For the Love of Mary 48.

◯ For pleasing world audiences by making the character she despised: 'Little Miss Fixit who bursts into song.' *That Certain Age.*

¶ Just as a Hollywood pin-up represents sex to dissatisfied erotics, so I represented the ideal

daughter millions of fathers and mothers wished they had. – *D.D. in 1959*

She is one of those personalities whom the world will insist on regarding as its private property. – *Joe Pasternak, her producer*

Durfee, Minta (1897–1975).
American leading lady of knockabout comedies 1914–16, including some with Chaplin. Married Roscoe Arbuckle and retired, but much later played bit parts.

Durkin, Junior (1915–1935) (Trent Durkin).
American juvenile player who was Huck Finn in *Tom Sawyer* 30 and *Huckleberry Finn* 31. On stage from the age of two, he died in a car crash.

Durning, Charles (1933–   ).
Burly American TV actor who slowly gained a star footing in movies.
■ Harvey Middleman Fireman 65. I Walk the Line 70. Hi Mom 70. Deadhead Miles 72. Dealing 72. Sisters 72. The Connection (TV) 73. The Sting 73. The Front Page 74. Dog Day Afternoon 75. The Hindenburg 75. The Trial of Chaplin Jensen (TV) 75. Queen of the Stardust Ballroom (TV) 75. Switch (TV) 75. Captains and the Kings (TV) 76. Breakheart Pass 76. Harry and Walter Go to New York 76. Twilight's Last Gleaming 77. Special Olympics (TV) 78. *The Choirboys* 78. The Greek Tycoon 78. An Enemy of the People 78. The Fury 78. F.I.S.T. 79. Studs Lonigan (TV) 79. The Muppet Movie 79. North Dallas Forty 79. Tilt 79. Starting Over 79. When a Stranger Calls 79. Die Laughing 80. The Final Countdown 80. True Confessions 81. Sharkey's Machine 81. *The Best Little Whorehouse in Texas* (AAN) 82. Tootsie 82. To Be or Not to Be (AAN) 83. Two of a Kind 83. Side by Side 83. Mass Appeal 84. Stick 85. The Man with One Red Shoe 85. Stand Alone 85. Private Conversations 85. Tough Guys 86. Happy New Year 87. A Tiger's Tale 87. The Rosary Murders 87. Cop 88. Far North 88. Brenda Starr 89. Cat Chaser 89. Etoile 89. Dick Tracy 90. Fatal Sky 90. Project: Alien 90. V.I. Warshawski 91. Brenda Starr 92. The Music of Chance 93. The Hudsucker Proxy 94.

Dury, Ian (1942–   ).
British actor, singer and composer. He was leader of the rock bands Kilburn & The High Roads and The Blockheads in the 70s and 80s.
AS ACTOR: Radio On 79. Number One 84. Pirates 86. Rocinante 86. Hearts of Fire 87. Red Ants 87. The Raggedy Rawney 88. The Cook, the Thief, His Wife and Her Lover 89. Bearskin 89. Split Second 92.
AS SONGWRITER: Take It or Leave It 81. Real Genius 85. Brennende Betten 88.

Duryea, Dan (1907–1968).
Laconic, long-faced American character actor often typecast as whining villain.
■ *The Little Foxes* 41. Ball of Fire 41. Pride of the Yankees 42. That Other Woman 42. Sahara 43. Man from Frisco 44. Ministry of Fear 44. None but the Lonely Heart 44. *The Woman in the Window* 44. Main Street After Dark 44. Mrs Parkington 45. The Great Flamarion 45. Lady on a Train 45. Scarlet Street 45. Along Came Jones 45. The Valley of Decision 45. *Black Angel* 46. White Tie and Tails 46. Black Bart 48. River Lady 48. *Another Part of the Forest* 48. Larceny 48. Criss Cross 49. Manhandled 49. Too Late for Tears 49. Johnny Stoolpigeon 50. One Way Street 50. The Underworld Story 50. Winchester 73 50. Al Jennings of Oklahoma 50. *Chicago Calling* 51. Sky Commando 53. Thunder Bay 53. 36 Hours 53. World for Ransom 54. Ride Clear of Diablo 54. Silver Lode 54. This is My Love 54. Rails in to Laramie 54. The Marauders 55.

Foxfire 55. Storm Fear 56. Battle Hymn 57. The Burglar 57. Night Passage 57. Slaughter on Tenth Avenue 57. Kathy O 58. Platinum High School 60. Six Black Horses 62. He Rides Tall 64. Taggart 64. Walk a Tightrope 64. Do You Know This Voice? 64. The Bounty Killer 65. Incident at Phantom Hill 65. *The Flight of the Phoenix* 65. The Hills Run Red 67. Stranger on the Run (TV) 67. Five Golden Dragons 67. The Bamboo Saucer 68.

TV series: China Smith 58. Peyton Place 68.

¶ The crime movie equivalent of an absolute bounder. – *Ian Cameron*

Duse, Elèonora (1858–1924).
Eminent Italian tragedienne whose one film appearance was in *Cenere* 16.

¶ Something quite different is needed. I'm too old for it. Isn't it a pity. – *E.D. after making her film*

Dussollier, André (1946–   ).
French leading actor.
And Now My Love 74. Perceval le Gallois 78. A Gorgeous Bird Like Me (US: Such a Gorgeous Kid Like Me) (Une Belle Fille comme Moi) 72. Le Beau Mariage 82. Three Men and a Cradle (Trois Hommes et un Couffin) 85. De Sable et de Sang (Blood and Sand) 87. Un Coeur en Hiver 92. Les Marmottes 93. Montparnasse-Pondichery 94. Aux Petits Bonheurs 94. Le Colonel Chabert 94, etc.

Dutta, Dulal (1925–   ).
Indian editor, who worked on all of Satyajit Ray's films.
Pather Panchali 55. Aparajito 56. The Music Room (Jalsaghar) 58. The World of Apu 59. Three Daughters (Teen Kanya) 61. Kanchenjungha 62. Mahanagar 63. Nayak 66. Days and Nights in the Forest 69. Company Limited 71. Distant Thunder 73. The Middle Man 75. The Chess Players 77. Deliverance 81. The Home and the World 84. An Enemy of the People (Ganasatru) 89, etc.

Dutton, Charles S. (1951–   ).
American character actor.
No Mercy 86. Crocodile Dundee II 88. Runaway (TV) 89. An Unremarkable Life 89. Jacknife 89. Q & A 90. Alien³ 92. Mississippi Masala 92. Rudy 93. Surviving the Game 94, etc.
TV series: Roc 91–92.

Duvall, Robert (1930–   ).
American character actor, often seen as nervous villain.
Biography: 1985, *Robert Duvall: Hollywood Maverick* by Judith Slawson.
Captain Newman MD 63. To Kill a Mockingbird 63. The Chase 65. Bullitt 68. The Rain People 69. True Grit 69. M*A*S*H 70. Lawman 71. *The Godfather* (AAN) 72. The Great Northfield Minnesota Raid 72. Joe Kidd 72. The Godfather Part Two 74. The Outfit 74. Breakout 75. Killer Elite 76. Network 76. The Seven Per Cent Solution (as Dr Watson) 76. The Greatest 77. The Eagle Has Landed 77. The Betsy 78. Ike (TV) 79. Apocalypse Now (BFA, AAN) 79. The Great Santini (AAN) 80. True Confessions 81. The Pursuit of D. B. Cooper 81. Tender Mercies (AA) 83. The Stone Boy 84. The Natural 84. The Lightship 85. Hotel Colonial 87. Let's Get Harry 87. Colors 88. The Handmaid's Tale 89. Days of Thunder 90. A Show of Force 90. Rambling Rose 91. Newsies (GB: The News Boys) 92. *Falling Down* 93. Geronimo: An American Legend 93. Wrestling Ernest Hemingway 93. The Paper 94, etc.

¶ Being a star is an agent's dream, not an actor's. – *R.D.*

Duvall, Shelley (1949–).
American actress.
Brewster McCloud 70. McCabe and Mrs Miller 71. Thieves Like Us 74. Nashville 75. Three Women 77. Annie Hall 77. The Shining 80. Popeye 80. Time Bandits 81. Roxanne 87. Suburban Commando 91, etc.

Duvivier, Julien (1896–1967).
Celebrated French director of the 30s whose touch seemed to falter after a wartime sojourn in Hollywood.
Hacadelma 19. Poil de Carotte 25 and 32. David Golder 30. Maria Chapdelaine 33. Le Golem 35. La Belle Equipe 36. *Pépé Le Moko* 37. *Un Carnet de Bal* 37. The Great Waltz (US) 38. *La Fin du Jour* 39. La Charrette Fantôme 39. Lydia (US) 41. Tales of Manhattan (US) 42. Flesh and Fantasy (US) 43. The Imposter (US) 44. *Panique* 46. Anna Karenina (GB) 48. Au Royaume des Cieux 49. Sous le Ciel de Paris 51. *Don Camillo* 52. La Fête à Henriette 54. L'Affaire Maurizius 54. Voici le Temps des Assassins 55. The Man in the Raincoat 57. Pot-Bouille 57. Marie Octobre 59. La Femme et le Pantin 59. La Grande Vie 61. La Chambre Ardente 62. Chair de Poule 63, etc.

Dvorak, Ann (1912–1979) (Ann McKim).
Smart but sensitive American leading lady of the 30s.
Hollywood Revue 29. Way out West 30. The Guardsman 31. This Modern Age 31. The Crowd Roars 32. *Scarface* 32. The Strange Love of Molly Louvain 32. Three on a Match 32. The Way to Love 33. Heat Lightning 34. Housewife 34. I Sell Anything 34. G Men 35. Folies Bergère 35. *Dr Socrates* 35. We Who Are About to Die 36. Racing Lady 37. The Case of the Stuttering Bishop 37. Merrily We Live 38. Blind Alley 39. Café Hostess 40. Girls of the Road 40. Squadron Leader X (GB) 41. This Was Paris (GB) 42. Escape to Danger 44. Flame of the Barbary Coast 45. Abilene Town 46. The Long Night 47. The Walls of Jericho 48. A Life of Her Own 50. I Was an American Spy 51. The Secret of Convict Lake 51, etc.

Dwan, Allan (1885–1981).
Veteran American director, former writer; he competently handled commercial movies of every type.
Wildflower 14. The Good Bad Man 15. Manhattan Madness 16. A Modern Musketeer 18. Luck of the Irish 20. *Robin Hood* 22. Big Brother 23. Zaza 23. Manhandled 24. Stage Struck 25. *The Iron Mask* 29. Man to Man 31. Mayor of Hell 33. Human Cargo 36. Heidi 37. Suez 38. The Three Musketeers (Ritz Brothers version) 39. Trail of the Vigilantes 40. Rise and Shine 41. Abroad with Two Yanks 44. Up in Mabel's Room 44. Brewster's Millions 45. Getting Gertie's Garter 46. Angel in Exile 48. *Sands of Iwo Jima* 49. The Wild Blue Yonder 51. Montana Belle 52. The Woman They Almost Lynched 53. Silver Lode 54. Tennessee's Partner 55. Hold Back the Night 56. Slightly Scarlet 56. The River's Edge 56. The Most Dangerous Man Alive 61, many others.

¶ If you get your head up above the mob, they try to knock it off. If you stay down, you last forever. – *A.D.*

Dwyer, Leslie (1906–1986).
Plump cockney character actor, in films from childhood.
The Fifth Form at St Dominic's 21. The Flag Lieutenant 31. The Goose Steps Out 41. The Way Ahead 44. Night Boat to Dublin 46. When the Bough Breaks 48. The Calendar 48. Midnight Episode 50. Laughter in Paradise 51. Hindle Wakes 52. Where There's a Will 53. Act of Love 54. Left, Right and Centre 59. I've Gotta Horse 64, many others.

Dyall, Franklin (1874–1950).
British stage actor from 1894, in films from 1930. He was the father of Valentine Dyall.
Atlantic 30. The Ringer 32. The Private Life of Henry VIII 33. The Iron Duke 35. Fire Over England 36. Bonnie Prince Charlie 49, etc.

Dyall, Valentine (1908–1985).
Gaunt British actor with resounding voice, famous as radio's wartime 'Man in Black'. Son of stage actor Franklin Dyall. Film debut *The Life and Death of Colonel Blimp* 43; later in many supporting roles, notably Henry V 44. Caesar and Cleopatra 45. Brief Encounter 45. Vengeance Is Mine 48. City of the Dead 60. The Haunting 63. The Horror of It All 65, etc.

Dyer, Anson (1876–*).
Pioneer British cartoonist: many entertainment shorts, also work for government departments.

Dykstra, John (1947–).
Special effects expert. After working as an assista[nt] to Douglas Trumbull, he founded Industrial Ligh[t] and Magic with George Lucas before leaving to s[et] up his own company, Apogee.
Silent Running 71. Star Wars (AA) 77. Avalanche Express 78. Star Trek: The Motion Picture (AAN) 79. Caddyshack 80. Firefox 82. Lifeforce 86. Invaders from Mars 87. My Stepmother Is an Alien 88, etc.

Dylan, Bob (1941–) (Robert Allen Zimmerman).
American singer in occasional films.
Don't Look Back 66. Pat Garrett and Billy the Kid 73. Renaldo and Clara 78. Hearts of Fire 87, etc.

dynamic frame.
A concept invented in 1955 by an American, Glenn Alvey: the screen was maximum size, i.e. CinemaScope, but individual scenes were to be masked down to whatever ratio suited them best, e.g. rather narrow for a corridor. Only one experimental British film, a version of H. G. Wells *The Hole in the Wall*, was made in dynamic frame, which proved distracting and has in any case bee[n] overtaken by multiscreen experiments of the 60s.

Dyneley, Peter (1921–1977).
British character actor.
Beau Brummell 54. The Young Lovers 55. The Split 60. Call Me Bwana 63. Chato's Land 72, etc.

Dysart, Richard (1929–).
American character actor.
Petulia 68. The Terminal Man 74. The Hindenburg 75. Being There 79. Bitter Harvest 81. The Thing 82. The Falcon and the Snowman 85. Mask 85. Pale Rider 85. Wall Street 87. Back t[o] the Future Part III 90, etc.
TV series: L.A. Law 86–93.

Dzundza, George (1945–)
Burly American character actor.
The Deer Hunter 78. Brubaker 80. A Long Way Home 81. Honky Tonk Freeway 81. Streamers 83. Act of Passion 83. Best Defence 84. Brotherly Love (TV) 85. No Mercy 86. Glory Years (TV) 87. No Way Out 87. The Beast 88. White Hunter, Black Heart 89. Impulse 89. The Butcher's Wife 91. Basic Instinct 92, etc.

Eady, David (1924–).
British director.
　The Bridge of Time (documentary) 52. Three Cases of Murder (one story) 55. In the Wake of a Stranger 58. Faces in the Dark 60, etc.

Eagels, Jeanne (1894–1929).
American leading lady of the 20s; her private life was highly publicized and Kim Novak played her in a 1957 biopic.
　Biography: 1930, *The Rain Girl* by Edward Doherty.
■ The World and the Woman 16. Fires of Youth 17. Under False Colours 17. The Cross Bearer 18. Man, Woman and Sin 27. The Letter (AAN) 29. Jealousy 29.

Ealing Studios
This famous little studio in suburban west London now houses the BBC. In its heyday in the 40s and 50s it was the independent home of scores of well-paced comedies featuring the likes of Will Hay and George Formby, and from 1948 on aspired a little higher, to quiet comedies of the English character, usually featuring a downtrodden group who rebelled against authority. The resulting films, including *The Lavender Hill Mob*, *My Darling Galore* and *The Titfield Thunderbolt*, became known the world over. The credit for these films is largely due to Michael Balcon as impresario and often to T. E. B. Clarke as writer; but results were less happy when the studio tackled epic themes such as *Scott of the Antarctic* and *The Cruel Sea*, though it certainly brought off non-comic subjects like *Dead of Night* and *Mandy*. See Charles Barr's 1977 book, *Ealing Studios*; also Michael Balcon's *A Lifetime of Films* and George Perry's *Forever Ealing*.
　A collection of Ealing posters, edited by David Wilson, was published in 1983 under the title *Projecting Britain*.

Earl, Merie (1889–1984).
American character actress who began her career in her mid-70s.
　Cat Ballou 65. Fitzwilly 67. Gaily, Gaily 69. Norwood 70. Crazy Mama 75. Fatso 80. Going Ape! 81, etc.
　TV series: The Jerry Reed When You're Hot You're Hot Hour 72. The Waltons 73–79.

Earles, Harry (1902–1985).
German-American midget who appeared in *The Unholy Three* 25 and 30, Baby Mine 26, Do It Again 27, *Freaks* 32, *The Wizard of Oz* 39.

Earp, Wyatt (1848–1929).
American frontier marshal, the most famous lawman of the wild west. Screen impersonations of him include Walter Huston in *Law and Order* 31, George O'Brien in *Frontier Marshal* 35, Randolph Scott in *Frontier Marshal* 39, Richard Dix in *Tombstone* 42, Henry Fonda in *My Darling Clementine* 46, Joel McCrea in *Wichita* 55, Burt Lancaster in *Gunfight at the OK Corral* 57, James Stewart in *Cheyenne Autumn* 64, James Garner in *Hour of the Gun* 67, Harris Yulin in *Doc* 70, Kurt

Russell in *Tombstone* 94, Kevin Costner in *Wyatt Earp* 94. There was also a long-running TV series starring Hugh O'Brian.

Easdale, Brian (1909–).
British composer.
　GPO Film Unit shorts 34–38. Ferry Pilot 42. Black Narcissus 46. The Red Shoes (AA) 48. An Outcast of the Islands 51. The Battle of the River Plate 56. Peeping Tom 60, etc.

Eason, B. Reeves (1886–1956).
American action director, mostly of second features. SELECTED SILENT FILMS: Moon Rider 20. *Ben Hur* (chariot race) 26.
■ SOUND FILMS: The Lariat Kid 29. Winged Horseman 29. Troopers Three 30. The Roaring Ranch 30. Trigger Tricks 30. Spurs 30. The Galloping Ghost 31. The Sunset Trail 32. Honor of the Press 32. The Heart Punch 32. Cornered 33. Behind Jury Doors 33. Alimony Madness 33. Revenge at Monte Carlo 33. Her Resale Value 33. Dance Hall Hostess 33. Red River Valley 36. Land Beyond the Law 37. Empty Holsters 37. Prairie Thunder 37. Sergeant Murphy 38. The Kid Comes Back 38. Daredevil Drivers 38. Call of the Yukon 38. Blue Montana Skies 39. Mountain Rhythm 39. Men with Steel Faces 40. Murder in the Big House 42. Spy Ship 42. Truck Busters 43. Rimfire 49.
　Also directed action scenes in major films, notably *The Charge of the Light Brigade* 36.

The East Side Kids.
Set up in 1939 by Monogram as a Poverty Row challenge to the Dead End Kids, the original team consisted of Hally Chester, Harris Berger, Frankie Burke, Donald Hines, Eddie Brian and Sam Edwards. They were later joined by Bobby Jordan and Leo Gorcey from Dead End, and within a few years elements of both rival gangs were absorbed into the Bowery Boys.

Eastman, George (1854–1932).
American pioneer of cinematography: invented the roll film, which made him a millionaire.

Eastwood, Clint (1930–).
American leading man who after TV success made his big screen name in Italian westerns, then returned to Hollywood and became one of the big action stars of the late 60s. From the 70s he also began to produce and direct.
　Biographies: 1977, *Clint Eastwood, the Man behind the Myth* by Patrick Agan. 1983, *Clint Eastwood* by Gerald Cole and Peter Williams. 1992, *Clint Eastwood: Sexual Cowboy* by Douglas Thompson. Book: 1993, *Clint Eastwood, A Cultural Production* by Paul Smith.
■ Revenge of the Creature 55. Francis in the Navy 55. Lady Godiva 55. Tarantula 55. Never Say Goodbye 56. The First Travelling Saleslady 56. Star in the Dust 56. Escapade in Japan 57. Ambush at Cimarron Pass 58. Lafayette Escadrille 58. *A Fistful of Dollars* 64. *For a Few Dollars More* 65. *The Good the Bad and the Ugly* 66. The Witches 67. Hang 'em High 68. *Coogan's Bluff* 68. Where Eagles Dare 69.

Paint Your Wagon 69. Kelly's Heroes 70. Two Mules for Sister Sara 70. The Beguiled 71. *Play Misty for Me* (& d) 71. *Dirty Harry* 71. Joe Kidd 72. Breezy (d only) 73. High Plains Drifter (& d) 73. Magnum Force 73. Thunderbolt and Lightfoot 74. The Eiger Sanction (& d) 75. The Outlaw Josey Wales (& d) 76. The Enforcer 76. The Gauntlet (& d) 77. Every Which Way but Loose 78. Escape from Alcatraz 79. Any Which Way You Can 80. Bronco Billy (& d) 80. Firefox 82. Honky Tonk Man 82. Sudden Impact 83. Tightrope 84. City Heat 84. Pale Rider 85. Heartbreak Ridge (& d) 86. Bird (p, d) 88. The Dead Pool (& p) 88. Thelonius Monk: Straight No Chaser (p) 88. Pink Cadillac 89. The Rookie (& d) 90. White Hunter, Black Heart (& p, d) 90. *Unforgiven* (& p, d) (AAp, d, AANa) 92. In the Line of Fire 93. A Perfect World (& d) 93. The Bridges of Madison County (a, d) 95.
　TV series: *Rawhide* 58–65.
✪ For being the cynical tough guy the 70s seemed to want. *Dirty Harry*.

¶ I like to play the line and not wander too far to either side. If a guy has just had a bad day in the mines and wants to see a good shoot-'em-up, that's great. – *C.E.*
　My involvement goes deeper than acting or directing. I love every aspect of the creation of motion pictures and I guess I'm committed to it for life. – *C.E.*
　Whatever success I've had is due to a lot of instinct and a little luck. – *C.E.*
　I've always had the ability to say to the audience, watch this if you like, and if you don't, take a hike. – *C.E.*
　I try to approach film intellectually – how it moves me. If you start below the intellectual level, I think you're starting without the nucleus. – *C.E.*
　I've never worked with a guy who was less conscious of his good image. – *Don Siegel of C.E.*

Eaton, Mary (1901–1948).
American leading lady whose brief teaming with Ziegfeld and the Marx Brothers makes her career a footnote at least to film history.
■ His Children's Children 23. Broadway after Dark 24. *Glorifying the American Girl* 29. *The Coconuts* 29.

Eaton, Shirley (1936–).
Pneumatic blonde British leading lady.
　Doctor at Large 56. Sailor Beware 57. Carry on Sergeant 58. Carry on Nurse 59. What a Carve Up 62. The Girl Hunters 63. Goldfinger 64. Rhino 65. Ten Little Indians 65. Around the World Under the Sea 66. Eight on the Lam 67. Sumuru 68, many others.

Eberhardt, Mignon G. (1899–).
American detective novelist, several of whose works were filmed.
　While the Patient Slept 30. The Murder of Dr Harrigan 36. Murder by an Aristocrat 36. The Great Hospital Mystery 37. Mystery House 38, etc.

Eberhardt, Thom.
American director.

Sole Survivor 84. Night of the Comet 84. Without a Clue 88. Gross Anatomy 89. Captain Ron 92.

Ebsen, Buddy (1908–) (Christian Rudolf Ebsen). American actor-dancer of the 30s, usually in 'countrified' parts; later emerged as a character actor and achieved his greatest success in a long-running TV series.

Broadway Melody 1936. Captain January 36. Born to Dance 36. Banjo on My Knee 36. The Girl of the Golden West 38. Four Girls in White 39. Parachute Battalion 41. Sing Your Worries Away 42. Thunder in God's Country 51. Night People 54. Red Garters 54. Davy Crockett 55. Attack 56. Breakfast at Tiffany's 61. The Interns 62. Mail Order Bride 64. The One and Only Genuine Original Family Band 68. The Daughters of Joshua Cabe (TV) 72. Horror at 37,000 Feet (TV) 72. The President's Plane is Missing (TV) 74. Smash-up on Interstate Five (TV) 77. Leave Yesterday Behind (TV) 78. The Bastard (TV) 78. *The Critical List* (TV) 81. The Return of the Beverly Hillbillies (TV) 81. The Beverly Hillbillies 93, etc.

TV series: Northwest Passage 57. *The Beverly Hillbillies* 62–70. Barnaby Jones 72–80. Matt Houston 85.

~Ebsen was to have played the Tin Man in *The Wizard of Oz*, but was badly affected by the aluminium dust in the make-up.

Eburne, Maude (1875–1960).
Diminutive American character actress who usually played frowning matrons and nosey neighbours.

The Bat Whispers 30. The Guardsman 31. The Vampire Bat 33. Lazy River 34. *Ruggles of Red Gap* 35. Champagne Waltz 37. Meet Doctor Christian 39. West Point Widow 41. Bowery to Broadway 44. The Suspect 45. Mother Wore Tights 47. Arson Inc. 50, many others.

Eck, Johnnie (1909–1981).
American actor, born with a body that ended at the waist, and one of the stars of Tod Browning's *Freaks* 32. He also appeared in *Tarzan, the Ape Man* 32.

Eddy, Helen Jerome (1897–1990).
American character actress who retired early. Always in high class films.

Rebecca of Sunnybrook Farm 16. The March Hare 21. The Country Kid 23. The Dark Angel 25. Camille 27. The Divine Lady 29. Skippy 31. Mata Hari 31. Madame Butterfly 32. The Bitter Tea of General Yen 33. Riptide 34. Keeper of the Bees 35. Stowaway 36. Winterset 36. The Garden of Allah 36. Outside the Law 38. Strike Up the Band 40, many others.

Eddy, Nelson (1901–1967).
Romantic American actor-singer with opera background; famous on screen for series of operettas with Jeanette MacDonald.

■ Broadway to Hollywood 31. Dancing Lady 33. Student Tour 34. *Naughty Marietta* 35. *Rose Marie* 36. *Maytime* 37. Rosalie 37. The Girl of the Golden West 38. *Sweethearts* 38. Let Freedom Ring 39. Balalaika 39. *New Moon* 40. Bitter Sweet 40. The Chocolate Soldier 41. I Married an Angel 43. Phantom of the Opera 43. Knickerbocker Holiday 44. Make Mine Music (voice only) 46. Northwest Outpost 47.

~Eddy and MacDonald were rudely known in some quarters as The Singing Capon and The Iron Butterfly.

Edel, Uli (1947–) (Ulrich Edel).
German director.

The Little Soldier 70. Tommi Kehrt Zurück 72. Oisthalter 75. Christiane F. 81. Last Exit to Brooklyn 89. Body of Evidence 92, etc.

Edelman, Herb (1930–).
Bald, lanky American character actor, usually in comic roles.

In Like Flint 67. Barefoot in the Park 67. The Odd Couple 68. The Front Page 74. The Yakuza 75. Charge of the Model-Ts 77. Smorgasbord 83, etc.

TV series: The Good Guys 68. Strike Force 81. Nine to Five 82. St Elsewhere 83–

Edelman, Louis F. (1901–1976).
American producer.

Once upon a Time 44. White Heat 48. I'll See You in My Dreams 52, etc.

TV series include *Wyatt Earp* and *The Big Valley*.

Edelman, Randy.
American composer.

Outside In 72. Executive Action 73. Feds 88. Twins 88. Troop Beverly Hills 89. Ghostbusters II 89. Quick Change 90. Come See the Paradise 90. V.I. Warshawski 92. Shout 92. Drop Dead Fred 92. Dragon: The Bruce Lee Story 93. Gettysburg 93. Beethoven's 2nd 93. Angels in the Outfield (p) 94. The Mask 94, etc.

Eden, Barbara (1934–) (Barbara Huffman).
American leading lady, former chorine.

Back from Eternity 56. Twelve Hours to Kill 60. Flaming Star 60. Voyage to the Bottom of the Sea 61. Five Weeks in a Balloon 62. The Wonderful World of the Brothers Grimm 63. The Brass Bottle 64. Seven Faces of Dr Lao 64. The Feminist and the Fuzz (TV) 71. The Woman Hunter (TV) 72. A Howling in the Woods (TV) 72. The Amazing Dobermans 76. Harper Valley PTA 78. Chattanooga Choo Choo 84. The Stepford Children (TV) 87. Her Wicked Ways (TV) 90, etc.

TV series: How to Marry a Millionaire 58. I Dream of Jeannie 65–70. Harper Valley PTA 81.

Edens, Roger (1905–1970).
American musical supervisor who moulded many MGM musicals, often as associate to producer Arthur Freed. Academy Awards for Easter Parade 48. On the Town 49. Annie Get Your Gun 50. Produced Deep in My Heart 55. Funny Face 56. Hello Dolly 69, etc.

Edeson, Arthur (1891–1970).
American cinematographer.

Wild and Woolly 17. *Robin Hood* 23. *The Thief of Baghdad* 24. *The Lost World* 25. The Bat 26. The Patent Leather Kid 27. In Old Arizona 28. *All Quiet on the Western Front* 30. Frankenstein 31. The Old Dark House 32. *The Invisible Man* 33. Mutiny on the Bounty 35. They Won't Forget 37. Each Dawn I Die 39. They Drive by Night 40. Sergeant York 41. *The Maltese Falcon* 41. *Casablanca* 42. Thank Your Lucky Stars 43. The Mask of Dimitrios 44. The Fighting O'Flynn 48, many others.

Edgar, Marriott (1880–1951).
British comedy scenarist, in films from 1935. Worked on many of the best vehicles of Will Hay and the Crazy Gang.

Good Morning Boys 36. Oh Mr Porter 38. Alf's Button Afloat 38. The Frozen Limits 39. The Ghost Train 41, many others; later on children's films. Also author of the 'Sam Small' and 'Albert' monologues made famous by Stanley Holloway.

edge numbers.
Serial numbers printed along the edge of all film material to assist identification when re-ordering sections.

Edison, Thomas Alva (1847–1931).
American inventor of the phonograph and the incandescent lamp, among over a thousand other devices including the kinetoscope (a combined movie camera and projector), edge perforations and 35 mm gauge.

Biopics: *Young Tom Edison* 39 with Mickey Rooney; *Edison the Man* 40 with Spencer Tracy.

editor.
Technician who assembles final print of film from various scenes and tracks available; works closely under director's control except in routine pictures.

¶ Editing is crucial. Imagine James Stewart looking at a mother nursing her child. You see the child, then cut back to him. He smiles. Now Mr Stewart is a benign old gentleman. Take away the middle piece of film and substitute a girl in a bikini. Now he's a dirty old man. – *Alfred Hitchcock*

Edouart, Farciot (1895–1980).
American special effects man, with Paramount for many years.

Alice in Wonderland 33. Lives of a Bengal Lancer 35. Sullivan's Travels 41. Reap the Wild Wind 42. Unconquered 47. Ace in the Hole 51. The Mountain 56, many others.

Edwards, Anthony (1962–).
American leading actor.

Fast Times at Ridgemont High 82. Heart Like a Wheel 82. Revenge of the Nerds 84. Gotcha! 85. The Sure Thing 85. Top Gun 86. Revenge of the Nerds II 87. Summer Heat 87. Mr North 88. Miracle Mile 89. How I Got into College 89. Hawks 89. Downtown 90. Landslide 92. Pet Sematary II 92. The Client 94, etc.

TV series: It Takes Two 82–83.

Edwards, Blake (1922–) (William Blake McEdwards).
American writer-producer-director with a leaning for all kinds of comedy. Married to Julie Andrews, who now appears mainly in his films, not always to her own advantage.

■ Panhandle (a, w) 47. All Ashore (w) 53. Cruising down the River (w) 53. Drive a Crooked Road (w) 54. Sound Off (w) 54. Bring Your Smile Along (w) 55. My Sister Eileen (w) 55. He Laughed Last (wd) 55. Mr Cory (wd) 56. Operation Mad Ball (w) 57. This Happy Feeling (wd) 58. The Perfect Furlough (wd) 58. Operation Petticoat (d) 59. High Time (d) 60. Breakfast at Tiffany's (d) 61. Experiment in Terror (d) 62. Notorious Landlady (w) 62. *Days of Wine and Roses* (d) 62. The Pink Panther (wd) 63. A Shot in the Dark (wd, p) 64. *The Great Race* (wd, p) 64. Soldier in the Rain (w) 64. What Did You Do in the War, Daddy? (wd, p) 66. Waterhole Three (p) 67. Gunn (d, p) 67. The Party (wd, p) 68. Darling Lili (wd, p) 69. Wild Rovers (wd, p) 71. The Carey Treatment (wd, p) 72. The Tamarind Seed (wd) 74. The Return of the Pink Panther (wd, p) 74. The Pink Panther Strikes Again (wd, p) 76. Revenge of the Pink Panther (wd, p) 78. '10' (wd, p) 79. S.O.B. (wd, p) 81. Trail of the Pink Panther (wd, p) 82. Curse of the Pink Panther (wd, p) 83. The Man Who Loved Women (wd) 83. Micki and Maude (d) 84. A Fine Mess (d) 86. That's Life! (d) 87. Blind Date (d) 87. Sunset (wd) 88. Skin Deep (wd) 89. Switch (wd) 91. Son of the Pink Panther (wd) 93.

TV series: Richard Diamond. Dante. Peter Gunn (all as creator).

¶ Make 'em redecorate your office. That's primary, to let them know where you stand. Then, when you're shooting interior sequences, use your own interior decorator and set dresser. That way, everything on the set will fit your house when you're finished. – *B.E.*

Edwards, Cliff (1895–1971).
Diminutive American entertainer known as 'Ukelele Ike'.
  Hollywood Revue 29. Parlour Bedroom and Bath 31. Hell Divers 31. Flying Devils 33. Red Salute 35. Bad Guy 39. Pinocchio (voice of Jimmy Cricket) 40. The Monster and the Girl 41. The Falcon Strikes Back 43. She Couldn't Say No 45. The Avenging Rider 53, many others.

Edwards, Henry (1882–1952).
Gentlemanly British romantic lead of the 20s; later directed some films and came back to acting as amiable elderly man.
  Broken Threads 18. The Amazing Quest of Ernest Bliss 22. A Lunatic at Large 23. *The Flag Lieutenant* 26. Fear 27. Three Kings 28. Call of the Sea 31. The Flag Lieutenant (talkie) 31. The Barton Mystery (d) 32. General John Regan 33. Discord Driven (d) 33. Scrooge (d) 35. Juggernaut (d) 37. Spring Meeting (d) 41. Green for Danger 46. Oliver Twist 48. London Belongs to Me 48. Madeleine 50. The Long Memory 52, many others.

Edwards, Hilton (1903–1982).
Irish producer and impresario, long with the Abbey Theatre. In 1953 made *Return to Glennascaul* and in 1961 appeared in *Victim*. Also on TV in Orson Welles' *Filming Othello*.

Edwards, J. Gordon (1867–1925).
American director of silent epics, especially for Theda Bara.
  Anna Karenina 15. Under Two Flags 16. Cleopatra 17. Salome 18. The Queen of Sheba 21. Nero 22. The Shepherd King 23, many others.

Edwards, James (1922–1970).
American actor, on stage from 1945.
  The Set-Up 49. *Home of the Brave* 49. The Member of the Wedding 52. The Caine Mutiny 54. The Phoenix City Story 55. Men in War 57. The Sandpiper 65, etc.

Edwards, Jimmy (1920–1988).
Moustachioed British comedian of stage, radio and TV.
  Autobiography: 1953, *Take It from Me*.
  Murder at the Windmill 48. Treasure Hunt 52. Three Men in a Boat 55. Bottoms Up 60. Nearly a Nasty Accident 61. Rhubarb 70, etc.

Edwards, Meredith (1917–   ).
Balding Welsh character actor with stage experience.
  A Run for Your Money 50. The Blue Lamp 50. Girdle of Gold 53. The Cruel Sea 53. The Long Arm 56. The Trials of Oscar Wilde 60. Only Two Can Play 61. This Is My Street 64. The Great St Trinian's Train Robbery 66. Fame Is the Spur (TV) 82, etc.

Edwards, Penny (1919–   ).
American light leading lady of the 40s.
  Let's Face It 43. That Hagen Girl 47. Two Guys from Texas 48. The Wild Blue Yonder 51. Street Bandits 52. Powder River 53, etc.

Edwards, Vince (1928–   ) (Vincento Eduardo Zoino).
American leading man of the tough/sincere kind.
  Mr Universe 51. Hiawatha 52. The Killing 56. City of Fear 58. *Murder by Contract* 59. The Victors 63. The Devil's Brigade 68. Hammerhead 68. The Desperadoes 69. The Mad Bomber 72. The Power and the Passion (TV) 79. Space Raiders 83. Cellar Dweller 87. The Gumshoe Kid 89, etc.
  TV series: *Ben Casey* 60–65. Matt Lincoln 70.

Edzard, Christine.
British director of meticulously researched historical films.
  Stories from a Flying Trunk 79. Biddy 83. Little Dorrit, Part I: Nobody's Fault 87. Little Dorrit, Part II: Little Dorrit's Story 87. The Fool 90. As You Like It 92, etc.

Egan, Eddie (1924–   ).
Burly American policeman whose exploits were the basis of *The French Connection*. He subsequently left the force and played small parts in films.
  TV series: Joe Forrester 75. Eischied 79.

Egan, Peter (1946–   ).
British TV leading man who has sporadically appeared on stage and in films.
  The Hireling 73. Callan 74. Hennessy 75. Chariots of Fire 81. A Woman of Substance (TV) 84. The Perfect Spy (TV) 87.
  TV series: Lillie (as Oscar Wilde) 78. Prince Regent 79. Ever Decreasing Circles 85–88.

Egan, Richard (1921–1987).
Virile American leading man once thought likely successor to Clark Gable but who was mainly confined to westerns and action dramas.
  The Damned Don't Cry 49. Undercover Girl 50. Split Second 52. Demetrius and the Gladiators 54. Wicked Woman 54. Gog 54. Underwater 55. Untamed 55. Violent Saturday 55. The View from Pompey's Head 55. Seven Cities of Gold 55. Love Me Tender 56. Tension at Table Rock 56. These Thousand Hills 58. A Summer Place 59. Pollyanna 60. Esther and the King 60. The 300 Spartans 62. The Destructors 66. Chubasco 68. The Big Cube 69. The Day of the Wolves (TV) 72. The Sweet Creek County War 79, etc.
  TV series: Empire 62. Redigo 64.

Ege, Julie (1943–   ).
Decorative Norwegian leading lady in British films of the 70s.
  Every Home Should Have One 70. Up Pompeii 70. Creatures the World Forgot 71. The Magnificent Seven Deadly Sins 71. Rentadick 72. The Garnett Saga 72. Not Now Darling 73. Craze 73. The Mutations 74, etc.

Eggar, Samantha (1939–   ).
British leading lady, in international films.
■ The Wild and the Willing 62. Dr Crippen 63. Doctor in Distress 63. Psyche 59 63. *The Collector* (AAN) 65. Return from the Ashes 65. Walk Don't Run 66. Doctor Dolittle 67. The Molly Maguires 69. The Walking Stick 69. The Lady in the Car 70. The Light at the Edge of the World 72. The Dead Are Alive 72. A Name for Evil 72. Double Indemnity (TV) 73. All the Kind Strangers (TV) 74. The Seven Per Cent Solution 76. The Killer Who Wouldn't Die (TV) 76. Why Shoot the Teacher? 77. The Uncanny 77. Welcome to Blood City 77. Ziegfeld: The Man and His Women (TV) 78. Hagen (TV pilot) 79. The Brood 79. The Exterminator 80. Demonoid 81. Hot Touch 82. For the Term of His Natural Life 85. Ragin' Cajun 90. Dark Horse 92.

Round Numbers 92. A Case for Murder (TV) 93. Inevitable Grace 94.
  TV series: *Anna and the King* 72.

Eggby, David.
Australian cinematographer.
  Mad Max 79. Kansas 88. The Salute of the Jugger 90. Quigley Down Under 90. Warlock 91. Harley Davidson and the Marlboro Man 91. The Paper 94, etc.

Eggleston, Colin.
Australian director of adventure and horror movies.
  Long Weekend 79. Bellamy 80. Sky Pirates 86. Cassandra 87. Innocent Prey 88. The Wicked 89, etc.

Egoyan, Atom (1961–   ).
Armenian director and screenwriter, in Canada.
  Next of Kin 85. Family Viewing 87. Speaking Parts 89. Montreal Sextet (co-d) 91. The Adjuster 91. Calendar 93. Exotica 94, etc.

¶ The difference between a Hollywood film and what I do is this: in mainstream films, you're encouraged to forget that you're watching a movie, whereas in my films, you're always encouraged to remember that you're watching a collection of designed images. – *A.E.*

Eichhorn, Lisa (1952–   ).
American actress who studied drama in Britain and works in both countries.
  The Europeans 79. Yanks 79. Who Would I Lie? 80. Cutter's Way 81. The Weather in the Streets 83. Wildrose 84. Opposing Force 86. Grim Prairie Tales 90. Moon 44 90. The Vanishing 93. King of the Hill 93, etc.

Eidelman, Cliff (1964–   ).
American composer and conductor.
  Silent Night 88. To Die For 89. Triumph of the Spirit 89. Strike It Rich (co-w) 90. Crazy People 90. The Meteor Man 93. Untamed Heart 93. My Girl 2 94. Picture Bride 94. A Simple Twist of Fate 94, etc.

8mm.
A substandard gauge used mostly by amateurs. Sound used to require 9.5mm, but recently 'super 8' was introduced.

Eikenberry, Jill (1947–   ).
American leading lady of the early 80s.
  The Deadliest Season (TV) 77. A Night Full of Rain 77. Butch and Sundance 79. Hide in Plain Sight 80. Arthur 81. Sessions 83. Manhattan Project 86. Cast the First Stone (TV) 89. Chantilly Lace (TV) 93. Parallel Lives (TV) 94, etc.
  TV series: Nurse 82. LA Law 86–   .

Eilbacher, Lisa (1947–   ).
American leading lady.
  The War between Men and Women 72. Wheels (TV) 78. The Winds of War (TV) 83. Beverly Hills Cop 84. Monte Carlo (TV) 86. Leviathan 89. Living a Lie 91. Live Wire (TV) 92, etc.
  TV series: The Texas Wheelers 74–75. The Hardy Boys Mysteries 77. Ryan's Four 83. Me and Mom 85.

Eilers, Sally (1908–1978).
Quiet-spoken American leading lady of the 30s. She was briefly married to cowboy star Hoot Gibson (1930–33).
  The Goodbye Kiss 28. She Couldn't Say No 30. Quick Millions 31. The Black Camel 31. Over the

Hill 31. State Fair 33. She Made Her Bed 34. Alias Mary Dow 34. Strike Me Pink 35. Talk of the Devil 36. Danger Patrol 37. Nurse from Brooklyn 38. They Made Her a Spy 39. Full Confession 39. I Was a Prisoner on Devil's Island 41. A Wave a WAC and a Marine 44. Coroner Creek 48. Stage to Tucson 50, many others.

Eisenmann, Ike (1962–).
American child actor of the 70s.
    Escape to Witch Mountain 74. Banjo Hackett (TV) 76. Return from Witch Mountain 78. The Hound of Hell (TV) 79, etc.
    TV series: Fantastic Journey 77.

Eisenstein, Sergei (1898–1948).
Russian director, one of the cinema giants.
    Biographies: 1952, *Sergei Eisenstein* by Marie Seton. 1966, *Eisenstein* by Yon Barna.
    Books published include: 1942, *The Film Sense*. 1948, *Notes of a Film Director*. 1949, *Film Form*.
■ *Strike* 24. *The Battleship Potemkin* 25. *October* (Ten Days That Shook the World) 27. *The General Line* 28. *Que Viva Mexico* (unfinished: sections later released under this title and as *Time in the Sun*) 32. *Alexander Nevsky* 38. *Ivan the Terrible* 42–46.
✪ For virtually inventing montage, and for using the grammar of film-making more vividly and purposefully than almost anyone else. *Alexander Nevsky*.

Eisinger, Jo.
American screenwriter.
    The Spider 45. Gilda 46. The Sleeping City 50. Night and the City 51. The System 53. Bedevilled 55. The Poppy is Also a Flower (Danger Grows Wild) 66. The Jigsaw Man 84, many others.

Eisler, Hanns (1898–1962).
Austrian composer, who also collaborated with Brecht on plays and songs. Born in Leipzig, he studied music in Vienna under Arnold Schoenberg and left Germany in 1933, moving to the United States in the late 30s to lecture, teach, and to work in Hollywood. He fell foul of the Un-American Activities Committee in the late 40s and was deported, going to live and work in East Germany, where he wrote that country's national anthem.
    Book: 1947, *Composing for Films*.
    Kuhle Wampe (Ger.) 32. Song of Heroes (USSR) 32. New Earth (Netherlands) 34. Le Grand Jeu (Fr.) 34. Our Russian Front (co-m) 41. Hangmen Also Die 43. None but the Lonely Heart 43. Jealousy 45. The Spanish Main 45. Deadline at Dawn 46. A Scandal in Paris (aka Thieves' Holiday) 46. Monsieur Verdoux 47. The Woman on the Beach 47. So Well Remembered 47. Herr Puntila and His Servant Matti (Herr Puntila und Sein Knecht Matti (Aus.) 55. Night and Fog (Nuit et Brouillard) (Fr.) 55. Les Arrivistes (Fr.) 60, many others.

¶ Once or twice a year I write a motion picture. It interests me and I need the money – H.E.
Hanns Eisler is the Karl Marx of Communism in the musical field. – *Robert E. Stripling, chief investigator of the Un-American Activities Committee*

Eisley, Anthony (1925–).
American general-purpose actor.
    The Naked Kiss 64. Frankie and Johnny 65. Journey to the Centre of Time 67. Star! 68. Blood of Frankenstein 70. The Doll Squad 73. Secrets (TV) 77, etc.
    TV series: Hawaiian Eye 59–73. Capitol 82–84.

Eisner, Lotte H. (1896–1983).
German film historian.

Most noted book: *The Haunted Screen*.

Eisner, Michael (1942–).
American production executive. He is chairman, chief executive officer and president of the Walt Disney Company.

Ekberg, Anita (1931–).
Statuesque Swedish blonde who decorated a number of films in various countries.
    The Golden Blade 53. Blood Alley 55. Artists and Models 55. Back from Eternity 56. War and Peace 56. Zarak 56. Interpol 57. Sign of the Gladiator 58. La Dolce Vita 59. The Mongols 60. Boccaccio 70 61. Summer is Short (Sw.) 62. Il Comandante (It.) 63. Call Me Bwana 63. Four for Texas 63. The Alphabet Murders 65. Who Wants to Sleep (Das Liebeskarussel) 65. Way Way Out 66. The Glass Sphinx 67. If It's Tuesday, This Must Be Belgium 69. The Divorcee 70. The Clowns 70. Fangs of the Living Dead 73. Gold of the Amazon Women (TV) 79, etc.

Ekk, Nikolai (1902–1976).
Russian director.
    The Road to Life 31. The Nightingale 36. A Night in May 41, etc.

Ekland, Britt (1942–) (Britt-Marie Eklund).
Swedish leading lady in international films. She was formerly married to Peter Sellers.
    Too Many Thieves (TV) 66. After the Fox 66. The Bobo 67. The Double Man 68. The Night They Raided Minsky's 68. Stiletto 69. Percy 71. Get Carter 71. A Time for Loving 71. Night Hair Child 71. Baxter 72. Endless Night 72. Asylum 72. The Wicker Man 73. The Man with the Golden Gun 73. Royal Flash 74. The Ultimate Thrill 74. Casanova 77. High Velocity 77. King Solomon's Treasure 77. The Great Wallendas (TV) 77. Ring of Passion (TV) 79. Satan's Mistress 82. Moon in Scorpio 88. Scandal 89. The Children 90, etc.

¶ The ideal man doesn't exist. A husband is easier to find. – *B.E.*
    I said I don't sleep with married men, but what I meant was I don't sleep with happily married men. – *B.E.*

Ekman, Gosta (1890–1948).
Swedish leading actor.
    Charles XII 24. Faust 26. Intermezzo 36, etc.

El Santo
Silver-masked Mexican wrestler who was a star of the ring and of more than 50 cheap, popular and profitable adventure movies in which he defeated crooks, monsters, vampires, werewolves and extra-terrestrials. He first appeared in films in *Santo – El Enmascarado de Plata* 52, but the series proper began in 1961 with *Santo versus the Diabolic Brain* and ended in 1982 with *Santo versus the Television Assassin*. It was probably not always the same actor behind the mask. Most often, it was Rodolfo Guzmán Huerta (qv), but Eric del Castillo may have taken the role in some of the films. Occasionally El Santo was paired with a rival masked wrestler, Blue Demon (El Demonio Azul), played by Alejandro Cruz. In versions of the films dubbed into English, the character is sometimes renamed Samson.

Elam, Jack (1916–).
Laconic, swarthy American character actor, often seen as western villain or sinister comic relief.
    Rawhide 50. Kansas City Confidential 52. The Moonlighter 53. Vera Cruz 54. Moonfleet 55. Kiss Me Deadly 55. *Gunfight at the OK Corral* 57. Baby

Face Nelson 57. Edge of Eternity 59. The Comancheros 62. The Rare Breed 66. The Way West 67. Firecreek 67. Once Upon a Time in the West 69. Support Your Local Sheriff 69. Rio Lob 70. Support Your Local Gunfighter 71. A Knife f the Ladies 74. Creature from Black Lake 76. Grayeagle 77. Lacy and the Mississippi Queen (TV) 78. The Villain 79. The Sacketts (TV) 79. T Cannonball Run 80. Jinxed! 82. Cannonball Run 83. The Aurora Encounter 86. Hawken's Breed 8 Big Bad John 90. Suburban Commando 91. The Giant of Thunder Mountain 91, etc.
    TV series: *The Dakotas* 62. Temple Houston 63. The Texas Wheelers 77. Struck by Lightning (as t Frankenstein monster) 79.

Eldredge, John (1917–1960).
Mild-looking American actor usually cast as weakling brother or bland schemer.
    The Man with Two Faces 34. Persons in Hidin 38. Blossoms in the Dust 41. The French Key 47 Champagne for Caesar 50. Lonely Hearts Bandits 52. The First Travelling Saleslady 56, many other

Eldridge, Florence (1901–1988) (Florence McKechnie).
Distinguished American stage actress, wife of Fredric March. Film appearances occasional.
    Six Cylinder Love 23. The Studio Murder Mystery 29. The Matrimonial Bed 30. The Story Temple Drake 33. Les Misérables 35. Mary of Scotland (as Elizabeth I) 36. *An Act of Murder* 48. *Another Part of the Forest* 48. Christopher Columbu 49. Inherit the Wind 60, etc.

Eldridge, John (1904–1961).
British documentary and feature director.
    Waverley Steps 47. Three Dawns to Sydney 49 Brandy for the Parson 51. Laxdale Hall 53. Conflict of Wings 54, etc.

the electric chair
has figured prominently in innumerable gangster and prison movies, notably *Two Seconds*, *Twenty Thousand Years in Sing Sing*, *Angels with Dirty Faces* and *The Last Mile*. *Front Page Woman* concentrated on the reporters ushered in to watch. The death cell scenes in *Double Indemnity* were deleted befor the film's release. The most horrific sequence of this kind was the gas chamber climax of *I Want To Live*.

electronovision.
A much-touted form of transfer from videotape t film, thought likely to save money in putting great stage performances on to the big screen.
    Unfortunately it proved technically and aesthetically unacceptable, and the two features shot in it in 1965 are only interesting if one can ignore the technical shortcomings. They are *Harlo* with Carol Lynley and *Hamlet* with Richard Burton.

Elektrotachyscope.
A device for displaying motion pictures, patented in 1887 by the Polish inventor Ottomar Anschutz who also took the photographs of the movement of people and animals it showed.

elephants
have come closest to starring roles in *Zenobia*, *Elephant Boy* and *Hannibal Brooks;* but they were the subject of concern in *Chang*, *Where No Vultures Fly Elephant Walk*, *Maya*, and *Roots of Heaven*, and Tarzan and Dorothy Lamour (in her jungle days) usually had one around as a pet. (*Tarzan Goes to India* had a splendid elephant stampede.) Circus

elephants were stars of *Jumbo,* and above all of *Dumbo.*

Eles, Sandor (1936–).
Hungarian leading man in Britain.
   The Naked Edge 61. The Evil of Frankenstein 64. And Soon the Darkness 70. Countess Dracula 70. The Greek Tycoon 78, etc.

elevators:
see lifts.

Elfand, Martin (1937–).
American producer.
   Serpico 73. Dog Day Afternoon 75. It's My Turn 80. An Officer and a Gentleman 82. King David 85. Clara's Heart 86. A Talent for the Game 90, etc.

Elfman, Danny (1954–).
American musician, composer and singer with the rock band Oingo Boingo, who has scored the movies so far made by director Tim Burton. He also composed the theme music for the TV series *The Simpsons.*
   Forbidden Zone 80. Pee-Wee's Big Adventure 85. Back to School 86. Wisdom 86. Summer School 87. Hot to Trot 88. Beetlejuice 88. Midnight Run 88. Big Top Pee-Wee 88. Scrooged 88. Batman 89. Nightbreed 90. Dick Tracy 90. Darkman 90. Edward Scissorhands 90. Article 99 92. Batman Returns 92. Sommersby 93. Tim Burton's The Nightmare before Christmas (& voice) 93. Black Beauty 94. To Die For 94, etc.

Elg, Taina (1931–).
Finnish leading lady in international films.
   The Prodigal 55. Diane 56. Gaby 56. Les Girls 57. Imitation General 57. Watusi 58. The Thirty-Nine Steps 59, etc.

Elias, Michael (1940–).
American director and screenwriter, a former actor and comedian. He worked in television as a writer and producer on such shows as *The Mary Tyler Moore Show, All in the Family,* and *Head of the Class.*
   The Jerk (co-w) 79. The Frisco Kid (co-w) 79. Serial (co-w) 80. Young Doctors in Love (co-w) 82. Lush Life (wd) 93.

Eliot, T. S. (1888–1965).
American poet who lived mainly in England. His play *Murder in the Cathedral* was his only work adapted for the cinema. A biopic about his first unhappy marriage, *Tom and Viv,* was released in 1994, with Willem Dafoe and Miranda Richardson in the title roles.

Elizabeth I,
Queen of England (1533–1603), has been notably played by Sarah Bernhardt in *Queen Elizabeth* 12; by Flora Robson in *Fire Over England* 36 and *The Sea Hawk* 40; by Florence Eldridge in *Mary of Scotland* 36; by Bette Davis in *Elizabeth and Essex* 39 and *The Virgin Queen* 55; by Agnes Moorehead in *The Story of Mankind* 57; by Irene Worth in *Seven Seas to Calais* 63; by Catherine Lacey in *The Fighting Prince of Donegal* 65, and by Glenda Jackson in a 1971 TV series followed by *Mary Queen of Scots* 72; Jean Simmons played the young queen in *Young Bess* 53; Jean Kent had the role in the TV series *Sir Francis Drake;* Quentin Crisp played it in *Orlando* 92.

Elizondo, Hector (1936–).
American character actor, mainly on stage.
   Pocket Money 71, Stand Up and Be Counted 72. The Taking of Pelham One Two Three 74. Report

to the Commissioner 75. Thieves 77. Cuba 79. American Gigolo 80. The Fan 81. Young Doctors in Love 82. The Flamingo Kid 84. Courage (TV) 86. Nothing in Common 86. Leviathan 89. Frankie and Johnny 91. Necessary Roughness 91. Lunatics: A Love Story 91. Final Approach 92. There Goes the Neighborhood (aka Paydirt) 92. Samantha 92. Being Human 94. Exit to Eden 94. Beverly Hills Cop III 94. Getting Even with Dad 94, etc.
   TV series: Freebie and the Bean 80. Casablanca 83. The Flamingo Kid (aka Pablo) 84. Private Resort 85. Nothing in Common 86. Chicago Hope 94.

Ellenshaw, Peter (c. 1914–).
British special effects artist and production designer, with Disney since 1950.
   Things to Come 36. Victoria the Great 37. The Drum 38. A Matter of Life and Death 45. The Red Shoes 48. Treasure Island 50. *20,000 Leagues Under the Sea* 54. Johnny Tremain 57. Darby O'Gill and the Little People 59. In Search of the Castaways 61. *Mary Poppins* 64. The Island at the Top of the World 74. *The Black Hole* 79, etc.

Ellery Queen.
The fictional American detective was played by four actors between 1935 and 1943: Donald Cook, Eddie Quillan, Ralph Bellamy and William Gargan. The name is a pseudonym for two authors: Frederick Dannay (1905–82) and Manfred Lee (1905–71). In 1971 Peter Lawford turned up in a TV movie, *Don't Look Behind You,* and in 1975 there was a TV series with Jim Hutton, following a 1954 one with George Nader.

Ellington, Duke (1899–1974) (Edward Kennedy Ellington).
Celebrated American jazz bandleader, composer and pianist.
   Hit Parade 37. New Faces 37. Reveille with Beverly 43. Anatomy of a Murder 59. Paris Blues 61. Change of Mind (m only) 69, etc.

Elliot, Laura (1929–).
American supporting actress.
   Special Agent 49. Paid in Full 50. *Strangers on a Train* 51. When Worlds Collide 52. Jamaica Run 53. About Mrs Leslie 54, etc.

Elliott, Denholm (1922–1992).
British stage and screen actor, often of well-mannered ineffectual types, latterly in more sophisticated roles. Died of AIDS.
   Biography; 1994, *Denholm Elliott – Quest for Love* by Susan Elliott with Barry Turner.
   Dear Mr Prohack 49. The Sound Barrier 52. The Cruel Sea 53. The Heart of the Matter 53. They Who Dare 54. The Night My Number Came Up 55. Pacific Destiny 56. Scent of Mystery (Holiday in Spain) 59. Station Six Sahara 63. *Nothing But the Best* 64. The High Bright Sun 65. You Must Be Joking 65. King Rat 65. Alfie 66. The Spy with a Cold Nose 67. Maroc 7 67. *Here We Go Round the Mulberry Bush* 67. The Night They Raided Minsky's 68. Too Late the Hero 69. The Rise and Rise of Michael Rimmer 70. Percy 70. Quest for Love 71. A Doll's House 73. Madame Sin 73. The Apprenticeship of Duddy Kravitz 75. Robin and Marian 75. Russian Roulette 76. A Bridge Too Far 77. The Boys from Brazil 78. Saint Jack 79. Cuba 79. Bad Timing 80. Sunday Lovers 80. Raiders of the Lost Ark 81. The Missionary 82. Brimstone and Treacle 82. Trading Places 83. The Razor's Edge 84. A Private Function (BFA) 84. A Room With a View (AAN) 85. Defence of the Realm (BFA) 85. Maurice 87. The Happy Valley (TV) 87. September 87. The Bourne Identity 88. Stealing Heaven 88.

Indiana Jones and the Last Crusade 89. Killing Dad 89. Return to the River Kwai 89. Toy Soldiers 91. Scorchers 91. Noises Off 92, etc.

Elliott, Robert (1879–1951).
Irish leading man of American silents.
   Spirit of Lafayette 17. Resurrection 18. A Woman There Was 19. A Virgin Paradise 21. Man and Wife 23. Romance of the Underworld 28. Thunderbolt 29. The Divorcee 30. Five Star Final 31. Phantom of Crestwood 32. Crime of the Century 33. Girl of the Limberlost 34. Circumstantial Evidence 35. Trade Winds 38. Gone with the Wind 39. Captain Tugboat Annie 45, many others.

Elliott, Sam (1944–).
American leading man of the 70s.
■ The Games 70. Frogs 72. Molly and Lawless John 72. The Blue Knight (TV) 73. I Will Fight No More Forever (TV) 75. Evel Knievel (TV) 75. Lifeguard 76. Once an Eagle (TV) 77. The Last Convertible (TV) 79. Aspen (TV) 79. The Sacketts (TV) 79. The Legacy 79. Wild Times (TV) 80. Murder in Texas (TV) 81. The Shadow Riders (TV) 82. Travis McGee (TV) 82. Mask 85. Fatal Beauty 87. Shakedown (aka Blue Jean Cop) 88. Prancer 89. Road House 89. Sibling Rivalry 90. Rush 91. Gettysburg 93. Tombstone 94.

Elliott, Stephan (1964–).
Australian director and screenwriter.
   Frauds 93. *The Adventures of Priscilla, Queen of the Desert* 94.

Elliott, 'Wild Bill' (1904–1965) (Gordon Elliott).
Burly American leading man of the 20s who later appeared in many second feature westerns and mysteries.
   The Private Life of Helen of Troy 27. Broadway Scandals 28. The Great Divide 31. Wonder Bar 34. False Evidence 40. Blue Clay 42. The Plainsman and the Lady 46. The Fabulous Texan 48. Hellfire 49. The Longhorn 51. Dial Red O 55. Chain of Evidence 57, etc.

Ellis, Don (1933–1978).
American composer, former jazz trumpeter.
   Moon Zero Two 69. The French Connection 71. The Seven Ups 73. French Connection II 75. Ruby 77, etc.

Ellis, Edward (1872–1952).
American stage character actor who made a number of films in the 30s, usually as stern father or judge.
   I Am a Fugitive from a Chain Gang 32. From Headquarters 33. The President Vanishes 34. The Return of Peter Grimm 35. Fury 36. Maid of Salem 37. *A Man to Remember* 38. Three Sons 39. A Man Betrayed 41. The Omaha Trail 42, etc.

Ellis, Mary (1900–) (Mary Elsas).
American leading lady and singer famous in British stage musicals, especially those of Ivor Novello.
   Bella Donna 34. Paris Love Song 35. All the King's Horses 35. Glamorous Night 36. The Three Worlds of Gulliver 61, etc.

Ellis, Patricia (1916–1970) (Patricia Gene O'Brien).
American leading lady of the 30s.
   Three on a Match 32. 42nd Street 33. Picture Snatcher 33. The St Louis Kid 34. The Case of the Lucky Legs 34. Boulder Dam 36. Melody for Two 37. Blockheads 38. Back Door to Heaven 39. Fugitive at Large 39, etc.

Ellis, Ruth (1927–1955).
The last woman to be hanged for murder in Britain has been the subject of two films: *Yield to the Night* (US: *Blonde Sinner*) 56, starring Diana Dors, and *Dance with a Stranger* 85, starring Miranda Richardson.

Ellis, Vivian (1904–).
British song composer and lyricist. Shows filmed include *Mr Cinders* and *Under Your Hat*, but most of his tinkly tunes aired only on the London stage.

Ellison, James (1910–) (James Ellison Smith).
Genial American leading man, mainly seen in routine westerns.
The Play Girl 32. Hopalong Cassidy 35. The Plainsman (as Buffalo Bill) 36. Vivacious Lady 38. Fifth Avenue Girl 39. Ice Capades 41. Charley's Aunt 41. The Undying Monster 42. I Walked with a Zombie 43. The Ghost Goes Wild 46. Calendar Girl 47. Last of the Wild Horses 48. Lone Star Lawman 50. Dead Man's Trail 52, etc.

Elmer Fudd.
Warner Brother's cartoon star. An adversary of Bugs Bunny, Elmer is a constantly frustrated wabbit-hunter noted for his deer-stalker hat, double-barrelled shotgun, and his inability to pronounce the letter 'r'. He made his debut in 1939 in a Tex Avery cartoon.
Dangerous Dan McFoo 39. Wabbit Twouble 41. An Itch in Time 43. Hare Remover 46. Hare Do 49. Rabbit Fire 51. Rabbit Seasoning 52. Robot Rabbit 53. Hare Brush 55. Pre-Hysterical Hare 58. What's My Lion? 61, etc.

Elmes, Frederick (1947–).
American cinematographer.
The Killing of a Chinese Bookie 76. Eraserhead 78. Opening Night 79. Valley Girl 83. Blue Velvet 86. Allan Quatermain and the Lost City of Gold 87. Heaven 87. River's Edge 87. Permanent Record 88. Moonwalker 89. Wild at Heart 90. Night on Earth 92. The Saint of Fort Washington 93. Trial by Jury 94, etc.

Elmes, Guy (1920–).
British writer.
The Planter's Wife (co-w) 51. The Stranger's Hand 53. Across the Bridge (co-w) 57. Swordsman of Siena 62. A Face in the Rain 63. El Greco 66. The Night Visitor 71, etc.

Elphick, Michael (1946–).
Heavy-set British character actor of all media.
Fraulein Doktor 67. Cry of the Banshee 69. Blind Terror 70. O Lucky Man 73. The Elephant Man 80. Privates on Parade 83. Gorky Park 83. Masada (TV) 83. Hitler's SS (TV) 84. Ordeal by Innocence 85. Supergrass 85. Little Dorrit 87. Buddy's Song 90. Let Him Have It 91, etc.
TV series: Boon 85–90. Three Up Two Down 85–87. Harry 93– .

Elsom, Isobel (1893–1981) (Isobel Reed).
British stage actress who starred in over 60 early British romantic films; went to Hollywood in the late 30s and played innumerable great ladies.
A Debt of Honour 19. Dick Turpin's Ride to York 22. The Sign of Four 23. The Wandering Jew 23. The Love Story of Aliette Brunon 24. Stranglehold 30. Illegal 31. *Ladies in Retirement* 41. You Were Never Lovelier 42. Between Two Worlds 44. The Unseen 45. Of Human Bondage 46. Ivy 47. Love from a Stranger 47. Monsieur Verdoux 47. Desiree 54. 23 Paces to Baker Street 57. The Miracle 59. Who's Minding the Store? 63. My Fair Lady 64, many others.

Elstree Studios.
Production complex at Borehamwood, north of London, started in the 20s by British International, which later became Associated British (qv). After many vicissitudes the facilities and library passed into the hands of Thorn-EMI, who sold out in the 80s to Cannon, who sold off the library to Weintraub. In 1982 Patricia Warren wrote a useful book: *Elstree, the British Hollywood*.

Eltinge, Julian (1882–1941) (William J. Dalton).
American female impersonator who appeared in a few silent films.
The Countess Charming 17. Over the Rhine 18. Madame Behave 24, etc.

Elton, Sir Arthur (1906–1973).
British producer especially associated with documentary; GPO Film Unit 34–37, Ministry of Information 37–45, Shell Film Unit 45 on. Founder Film Centre, governor BFI, etc.

Elton, Ben (1959–).
English stand-up comedian, actor, writer, novelist and playwright. He studied drama at Manchester University and gained fame performing at London's Comedy Store, on television in *The Ben Elton Show*, and as co-writer of the popular TV series *The Young Ones* (1982–84) and *Blackadder* (1983–89), and writer of *Filthy Rich and Catflap* 87.
Stark (a, w from his novel) (TV) 93. Much Ado about Nothing (a) 93.

¶ I do feel sorry for my mum. For years she thought she had a fairly reasonable, moderately pleasant child, and it turns out she had a hypocritical, foul-mouthed, self-righteous wanker. – B.E.
His anxiety levels make Woody Allen look like a Zen Master. – *Guardian*

Elvey, Maurice (1887–1967) (William Folkard).
Veteran British director of over 300 features.
Maria Marten 12. Comradeship 18. Nelson 19. At the Villa Rose 20. The Elusive Pimpernel 20. The Hound of the Baskervilles 21. Dick Turpin's Ride to York 22. The Love Story of Aliette Brunon 24. The Flag Lieutenant 26. Hindle Wakes 27. Balaclava 28. High Treason 30. The School for Scandal 30. Sally in Our Alley 31. In a Monastery Garden 31. The Water Gypsies 32. The Lodger 32. The Wandering Jew 33. The Clairvoyant 34. *The Tunnel* 34. Heat Wave 35. The Return of the Frog 37. For Freedom 39. Room for Two 39. Under Your Hat 40. The Lamp Still Burns 43. The Gentle Sex (co-d) 43. Medal for the General 44. Salute John Citizen 44. *Beware of Pity* 46. The Third Visitor 51. My Wife's Lodger 52. Fun at St Fanny's 55. Dry Rot 56, many others.

Elwes, Cary (1962–).
British actor.
Another Country 84. The Bride 85. Lady Jane 86. The Princess Bride 87. Glory 89. Days of Thunder 90. Hot Shots! 91. Bram Stoker's Dracula 92. The Crush 93. Robin Hood: Men in Tights 93, etc.

Ely, Ron (1938–) (Ronald Pierce).
American athlete who was television's Tarzan and starred in one other movie, *Doc Savage* 75.
Slavers 78.
TV series: The Aquanauts 61.

Emerson, Eric (1946–1975).
Boyish American dancer, a star of Andy Warhol's films. He was found dead in a New York street, apparently the victim of a hit-and-run accident, though Warhol thought that he probably died of a drug overdose.
The Chelsea Girls 66. Lonesome Cowboys 68. Heat 72.

Emerson, Faye (1917–1983).
American socialite leading lady popular for a time in the 40s following her marriage to Elliot Roosevelt, son of the President (1944–50). Retired to Majorca in the 60s.
Between Two Worlds 44. The Mask of Dimitrios 44. Hotel Berlin 45. Danger Signal 45. Nobody Lives Forever 46. Guilty Bystander 50. A Face in the Crowd 57, etc.
TV series: Faye Emerson Show 50. Faye Emerson's Wonderful Town 51–52.

Emerson, Hope (1897–1960).
Brawny 6'2" American character actress, in films from early 30s.
Smiling Faces 32. Cry of the City 48. Adam's Rib 49. Caged (AAN) 50. Casanova's Big Night 54. The Day They Gave Babies Away 56. Rock a Bye Baby 58, many others.
TV series: Doc Corkle 52. Peter Gunn 58–60.

Emerson, Keith (1944–).
English composer and keyboard player, a former member of the rock groups Nice and Emerson, Lake and Palmer.
Inferno (US) 80. Nighthawks (US) 81. Best Revenge (Can.) 83. Murderock, Uccide a Passo di Danza (It.) 84, etc.

Emerton, Roy (1892–1944).
Long-nosed British character actor: an eminently hissable villain.
The Sign of Four 32. Java Head 34. Lorna Doone (as Carver) 35. Doctor Syn 38. The Drum 38. Busman's Honeymoon 40. The Thief of Baghdad 40. The Man in Grey 43. Henry V 44, etc.

Emery, Dick (1918–1983).
Chubby British TV comedian with a flair for disguise.
Autobiography: 1974, *In Character*.
Light Up the Sky 60. A Taste of Money 62. The Wrong Arm of the Law 63. Baby Love 69. *Ooh You Are Awful* 72, etc.

Emery, Gilbert (1875–1945) (Gilbert Emery Bensley Pottle).
British character actor long in Hollywood as police commissioners, lords of the manor, etc.
Behind that Curtain 29. The Royal Bed 30. A Farewell to Arms 32. The House of Rothschild 34. One More River 34. Clive of India 35. Magnificent Obsession 35. Dracula's Daughter 36. A Man to Remember 38. Nurse Edith Cavell 39. Raffles 39. Rage in Heaven 41. That Hamilton Woman 41. The Loves of Edgar Allan Poe 42. Between Two Worlds 44. The Brighton Strangler 45, many others.

Emery, John (1905–1964).
American stage and screen actor of suave and sometimes Mephistophelean types.
Here Comes Mr Jordan 41. Spellbound 45. Blood on the Sun 45. The Woman in White 48. The Gay Intruders 48. Let's Live Again 49. The Mad Magician 54. Ten North Frederick 57. Youngblood Hawke 64, many others.

Emhardt, Robert (1914–1994).
American character actor, short and tubby; once understudied Sydney Greenstreet.
The Iron Mistress 52. 3.10 to Yuma 57. Underworld USA 60. The Stranger 61. Kid Galahad 62. *The Group* 66. Where Were You When

he Lights Went Out? 68. Lawman 71. Alex and the
ypsy 76, etc.

imlyn, Endaf (1945–).
Welsh director and screenwriter, from television.
   One Full Moon 91. Leaving Lenin 93.

immer, Luciano (1918–).
Italian director.
   Domenica d'Agosto 50. The Girls of the Spanish
teps 52. The Bigamist 56, etc.

immerich, Roland.
German director.
   Making Contact 85. Hollywood Monster 87.
Moon 44 89. Universal Soldier 92. Stargate 94,
tc.

immett, E. V. H. (1902–1971).
Jrgent-voiced commentator, film editor,
screenwriter and producer, a former journalist. He
was the voice of Gaumont-British News in the 30s
antil the mid-40s and Universal News in the 50s,
and can also be heard as narrator in Carry On Cleo
14. He also produced features at Ealing from
946–50.
   Sabotage (co-w) 36. Young Man's Fancy (co-w)
19, etc.

imney, Fred (1900–1980).
Heavyweight British comedian, characterized by a
growl, a cigar, and a top hat.
   Brewster's Millions 35. Yes Madam 39. Just
William 40. Let the People Sing 42. Fun at
St Fanny's 56. San Ferry Ann 65. The Sandwich
Man 66. Lock Up Your Daughters 69, etc.

the end of the world
has been fairly frequently considered in movies,
and not only in panic button dramas like Dr
Strangelove, The Bedford Incident and Fail Safe.
Movement of the earth was threatened in The Day
the Earth Stood Still and stopped (by Roland Young)
n The Man Who Could Work Miracles. Plague very
nearly ended everything in Things to Come. Danger
from other planets looming perilously close was
only narrowly averted in Red Planet Mars, while in
When Worlds Collide and The Day the Earth Caught
Fire the worst happened. Another kind of danger
was met in Crack in the World. The Martians nearly
got us in The War of the Worlds. In Five there were
only five people left alive, in The World, the Flesh
and the Devil only three, and in On the Beach none
at all.

Endfield, Cy (1914–).
American director, in films since 1942. Made
second features until 1951; thereafter resident in
Britain.
   Gentleman Joe Palooka 47. Stork Bites Man (&
w) 47. The Argyle Secrets (& w) 48. Underworld
Story 50. The Sound of Fury 51. Tarzan's Savage
Fury 52. The Search 55. Child in the House 56. Hell
Drivers 57. Sea Fury 58. Jet Storm 59. Mysterious
Island 61. Zulu 63. Sands of the Kalahari 65. De
Sade 69. Universal Soldier 71. Zulu Dawn (co-w)
79, etc.

Endore, Guy (1900–1970).
American screenwriter and novelist.
   Mark of the Vampire 35. Mad Love 35. The
Raven 35. The Devil Doll 36. The League of
Frightened Men 37. Carefree 38. The Story of G.I.
Joe (AAN) 45. Whirlpool (oa) 49. He Ran All the
Way 51. Curse of the Werewolf (oa) 61, etc.

Engel, Morris (1918–).
American producer-director of off-beat semi-
professional features.
   The Little Fugitive 53. Lovers and Lollipops 55.
Weddings and Babies 58.

Engel, Samuel G. (1904–1984).
American producer, a former screenwriter.
   Earthbound (w) 40. Scotland Yard (w) 41. My
Darling Clementine 46. Sitting Pretty 48. Rawhide
50. Belles on Their Toes 52. Daddy Long Legs 55.
Boy on a Dolphin 57. The Story of Ruth 60. The
Lion 62, many others.

English, John (1903–1969).
British director of second features, long in
America; a specialist in serials.
   Arizona Days 37. Drums of Fu Manchu 40.
Captain Marvel 41. King of the Texas Rangers 41.
Captain America 44. Don't Fence Me In 45. The
Phantom Speaks 45. Murder in the Music Hall
46. Loaded Pistols 48. Riders in the Sky 49. Valley
of Fire 51, many others.

Englund, George H. (1926–).
American producer-director.
   The World, the Flesh and the Devil (p) 59. The
Ugly American (pd) 62. Signpost to Murder (d)
64. Dark of the Sun (p) 67. Zachariah (d) 70.
Snowjob (d) 71. A Christmas to Remember (d)
(TV) 78. Dixie: Changing Habits (d) (TV) 83. The
Vegas Strip War (d) (TV) 84, etc.

Englund, Ken (1914–1993).
American writer, in films from 1938.
   Good Sam 47. The Secret Life of Walter Mitty
48. The Caddy 53. The Vagabond King 56, etc.

Englund, Robert (1948–).
American character actor who became a mild cult
after playing the demoniacal Freddy in Nightmare
on Elm Street and its sequels.
   Buster and Billie 74. The Great Smokey
Roadblock 76. St Ives 76. A Star Is Born 76. Blood
Brothers 78. Galaxy of Terror 81. 976-EVIL (d) 88.
The Phantom of the Opera 89. The Adventures
of Ford Fairlane 90. Dance Macabre 91. Wes
Craven's New Nightmare 94, etc.
   TV series: V 84–85. Downtown 86–87. Freddy's
Nightmares (host) 88–90.

Ennis, Skinnay (1907–1963).
American bandleader and vocalist who appeared
in such 30s films as College Swing, Sleepytime Gal
and Follow the Band.

Eno, Brian (1948–).
English composer and keyboard player, a founder-
member of Roxy Music.
   Land of the Minotaur (co-m) 76. Dune (co-m)
84. For All Mankind (doc) 89, etc.

Enoch Arden
was a character in a Tennyson poem who came
back to his family after having been long
supposed dead. Films with an 'Enoch Arden'
theme include Tomorrow Is Forever (with Orson
Welles), The Years Between (with Michael
Redgrave), My Two Husbands (with Fred
MacMurray) and its remake Three for the Show
(with Jack Lemmon), My Favourite Wife (with
Irene Dunne) and its remake Move Over Darling
(with Doris Day), Piccadilly Incident (with Anna
Neagle), Return from the Ashes (with Ingrid Thulin),
Desire Me (with Robert Mitchum), Laura (with
Gene Tierney), Man Alive (with Pat O'Brien), and
The Man from Yesterday (with Clive Brook). D. W.

Griffith in 1910 and 1911 made short versions of
the original story.

Enrico, Robert (1931–).
French director.
   Incident at Owl Creek 64. Au Coeur de la Vie
65. La Belle Vie 65. Les Aventuriers 67. Zita 67.
Ho! 68. Rum Runner 76. The Old Gun 76.
L'Empreinte des Géants 80. For Those I Loved 83.
Zone Rouge 86. The French Revolution (co-d) 89,
etc.

Enright, Ray (1896–1965).
American director, former editor and Sennett
gagman. Films mostly routine.
   Tracked by the Police 27. Dancing Sweeties 30.
Havana Widows 33. Twenty Million Sweethearts
34. Dames 34. Alibi Ike 35. Miss Pacific Fleet 35.
Earthworm Tractors 36. Slim 37. Swing Your Lady
37. Gold Diggers in Paris 38. Angels Wash Their
Faces 39. On Your Toes 39.

entertainers,
including actors and impresarios, have frequently
been the subject of biopics, and if all their stories
have seemed much the same, that is Hollywood's
fault rather than theirs. Here is a reasonably
comprehensive list:
   Always Leave Them Laughing Milton Berle, After
the Ball Pat Kirkwood as Vesta Tilley, Bound for
Glory David Carradine as Woody Guthrie, The
Buddy Holly Story Gary Busey, The Buster Keaton Story
Donald O'Connor, Champagne Charlie Tommy
Trinder as George Leybourne and Stanley
Holloway as the Great Vance, Chaplin Robert
Downey Jnr as Charlie Chaplin, The Dolly Sisters
Betty Grable & June Haver, The Doors Val Kilmer
as Jim Morrison, The Eddie Cantor Story Keefe
Brasselle, The Fabulous Dorseys Tommy and Jimmy
Dorsey, W. C. Fields and Me Rod Steiger as W. C.
Fields, The Five Pennies Danny Kaye as Red Nichols,
Frances Jessica Lange as Frances Farmer, Funny Girl
Barbra Streisand as Fanny Brice, Gable and Lombard
James Brolin and Jill Clayburgh, The Gene Krupa
Story Sal Mineo, The Glenn Miller Story James
Stewart, Great Balls of Fire Dennis Quaid as Jerry
Lee Lewis, The Great Caruso Mario Lanza, The Great
Ziegfeld William Powell, Gypsy Natalie Wood as
Gypsy Rose Lee, Harlow Carroll Baker/Carol
Lynley, The Helen Morgan Story Ann Blyth, Houdini
Tony Curtis, The I Don't Care Girl Mitzi Gaynor as
Eva Tanguay, Incendiary Blonde Betty Hutton as
Texas Guinan, Interrupted Melody Eleanor Parker as
Marjorie Lawrence, Jeanne Eagels Kim Novak, The
Joker is Wild Frank Sinatra as Joe E. Lewis, The Jolson
Story Larry Parks, La Bamba Lou Diamond Phillips
as Richie Valens, A Lady's Morals Grace Moore as
Jenny Lind, Lady Sings the Blues Diana Ross as
Billie Holliday, Lady With Red Hair Miriam Hopkins
as Mrs Leslie Carter and Claude Rains as David
Belasco, Leadbelly Roger E. Mosley, Lenny Dustin
Hoffman as Lenny Bruce, Lillian Russell Alice
Faye, Look for the Silver Lining June Haver as
Marilyn Miller, Love Me or Leave Me Doris Day as
Ruth Etting, Man of a Thousand Faces James Cagney
as Lon Chaney, Melba Patrice Munsel, Peg of Old
Drury Anna Neagle as Peg Woffington, Prince of
Players Richard Burton as Edwin Booth, The Seven
Little Foys Bob Hope as Eddie Foy, Shine on Harvest
Moon Ann Sheridan as Nora Bayes, Somebody Loves
Me Betty Hutton as Blossom Seeley, So This Is Love
Kathryn Grayson as Grace Moore, Star! Julie
Andrews as Gertrude Lawrence and Daniel Massey
as Noël Coward, The Story of Vernon and Irene Castle
Fred Astaire and Ginger Rogers, The Story of Will
Rogers Will Rogers Jnr, Tonight We Sing David Wayne
as Sol Hurok, Too Much Too Soon Dorothy Malone
as Diana Barrymore and Errol Flynn as John

Barrymore, *With a Song in My Heart* Susan Hayward as Jane Froman, *Yankee Doodle Dandy* James Cagney as George M. Cohan, *Young Man With a Horn* Kirk Douglas as Bix Beiderbecke, *Your Cheatin' Heart* George Hamilton as Hank Williams.

Movies made for TV include: *Bud and Lou* Buddy Hackett and Harvey Korman as Abbott and Costello, *Elvis* Kurt Russell as Presley, *Elvis and Me* Dale Midkiff as Elvis, *James Dean* Stephen McHattie, *The Jayne Mansfield Story* Loni Anderson with Arnold Schwarzenegger as Mickey Hargitay, *The Legend of Valentino* Franco Nero, *Liberace* Andrew Robinson, *Liberace: Behind the Music* Victor Garber, *Marilyn: The Untold Story* Catherine Hicks as Monroe, *Rainbow* Andrea McArdle as the young Judy Garland, *Rita Hayworth: The Love Goddess* Lynda Carter, *Sophia Loren: Her Own Story* Sophia Loren as herself and her mother, John Gavin as Cary Grant, Edmund Purdom as Vittorio De Sica.

Enyedi, Ildikó.
Hungarian director and screenwriter.
My Twentieth Century 90. Magic Hunter (Buvos Vadas) (co-w, d) 94, etc.

Ephron, Henry (1912–1992).
American screenwriter who invariably worked as a team with his wife Phoebe Ephron (1914–71). He also produced a few films.
Bride by Mistake 44. Always Together 46. John Loves Mary 49. *The Jackpot* 50. On the Riviera 51. Belles on Their Toes 52. There's No Business Like Show Business 54. Daddy Long Legs 55. Carousel (& p) 56. The Best Things in Life Are Free (p only) 56. Desk Set 57. Take Her, She's Mine 63. Captain Newman MD (AAN) 63, etc.

Ephron, Nora (1941–).
American screenwriter and novelist, particularly witty on the traumas of marriage, who has now turned to directing. She is the daughter of screenwriters Phoebe and Henry Ephron, who wrote the plays *Three's a Family* about her childhood and *Take Her, She's Mine* about her life at college.
Silkwood (AAN) 83. Heartburn 86. Cookie 89. When Harry Met Sally (AAN) 89. My Blue Heaven 90. This Is My Life (wd) 92. Sleepless in Seattle (co-w, d) (AANw) 93. Lifesavers (co-w, d) 94.

¶ I know that people are afraid of me . . . Sometimes it's helpful. The opposite of it is something I'm not interested in, which is that people think they can walk all over you – and when you're a screenwriter, people think that anyway. – N.E.
When you're a director, everyone wants a piece of you; they want to know what you think of the tablecloth. I loved nothing more than being asked 10,000 questions in one day. – N.E.

epic film.
Term used to describe a film directed and designed on a spectacular scale, focusing on the actions of a great hero and featuring a cast of thousands. The style has fallen out of favour in recent times, mainly due to the fiasco of *Cleopatra* 63 and the increasing cost of elaborate sets and large casts, so that the continuing appetite for spectacle is now supplied by movies that concentrate on violent action, such as car chases and crashes, and special effects. Favourite settings for epic films have included Rome (*Ben Hur*, *Spartacus* and dozens of movies from Italian directors) and Biblical times, in the productions of Cecil B. De Mille. More modern history featured in D. W. Griffith's *Birth of a Nation* 15 and in the work of the last master of the epic

form, David Lean's, *Lawrence of Arabia* 62 and *Dr Zhivago* 65.
Books: 1984, *The Epic Film* by Derek Elley. 1992, *Epic Films: Casts, Credits and Commentary on over 250 Historical Spectacle Movies* by Gary A. Smith.

epidemics
featured memorably in *Jezebel*, *Yellow Jack*, *Arrowsmith*, *The Rains Came*, *Forever Amber*, *Panic in the Streets*, *The Killer that Stalked New York*, *Elephant Walk No Blade of Grass*, *The Andromeda Strain*, *Eighty Thousand Suspects*, *The Omega Man*, *Things to Come*, *Isle of the Dead*, *The Satan Bug* and *The Seventh Seal*.

episodic films
in a sense have always been with us – *If I Had a Million*, after all, came out in 1932, and *Intolerance* in 1916 – but it was in the 40s, possibly spurred by the all-star variety films intended to help the war effort, that they achieved their greatest popularity. Julien Duvivier, who had made *Un Carnet du Bal* in Paris, remade it in Hollywood as *Lydia* and followed it with *Tales of Manhattan* which was linked by a tailcoat and *Flesh and Fantasy* which was linked by the ramblings of a club bore. The stories in *Forever and a Day* were held together by a house, *Easy Money* by football pools, *Train of Events* by a railway accident, *Meet Mr Lucifer* by television. Then came the author complex: *Quartet* (Somerset Maugham), *Le Plaisir* (Maupassant), *Meet Me Tonight* (Noël Coward). The French took over with films like *The Seven Deadly Sins*, *The Devil and Ten Commandments*, *Life Together*; and the Italians were at it with *Four Kinds of Love*, *Made in Italy* and *The Queens*. For English-speaking markets the form was killed in the mid-50s by the advent of the half-hour TV play, but the 60s saw a brief revival with *How the West Was Won* and *The Yellow Rolls-Royce*. The 80s showed signs: the Italians were at it again with *Sunday Lovers* and Hollywood assigned four directors to one story each for *Twilight Zone*.

epitaphs
¶ Over the years, a few stars have been nudged by the press into composing their own epitaphs. Herewith a selection of this grave humour.
▶ *W. C. Fields:* On the whole, I'd rather be in Philadelphia.
▶ *Cary Grant:* He was lucky – and he knew it.
▶ *Edward Everett Horton:* A nice part – only four 'sides', but good company and in for a long run.
▶ *Lionel Barrymore:* Well, I've played everything but a harp.
▶ *Hedy Lamarr:* This is too deep for me.
▶ *Dorothy Parker:* Excuse my dust.
▶ *Warner Baxter:* Did you hear about my operation?
▶ *William Haines:* Here's something I want to get off my chest.
▶ *Lewis Stone:* A gentleman farmer goes back to the soil.
▶ *Constance Bennett:* Do not disturb.
▶ *Wallace Ford:* At last I get top billing.
▶ *Preston Sturges:*
Now I've laid me down to die
I pray my neighbours not to pry
Too deeply into sins that I
Not only cannot here deny
But much enjoyed as time flew by . . .

Epps, Jack, Jnr.
American screenwriter, often in collaboration with Jim Cash.
Top Gun (co-w) 86. Legal Eagles (co-w) 86. The

Secret of My Success (co-w) 86. Turner & Hooch (co-w) 89, etc.

Epstein, Jean (1897–1953).
French director since 1922; also wrote books on film theory.
Cœur Fidèle 23. The Fall of the House of Usher 28. Finis Terrae 28. Mor Vran 30. His sister *Marie Epstein* (1899–) often worked with him, and herself directed La Maternelle 33. La Mort du Cygne 38, etc.

Epstein, Julius J. (1909–) and Philip G. (1909–1952).
American twin screenwriters.
Four Daughters (AAN) 38. Four Wives 39. No Time for Comedy 40. Strawberry Blonde 41. The Man Who Came to Dinner 41. *Casablanca* (AA) 4 Mr Skeffington (& p) 44. Romance on the High Seas 48. My Foolish Heart 49. Forever Female 53 The Last Time I Saw Paris 54.
JULIUS ALONE: The Tender Trap 55. Tall Story 60. Take a Giant Step (& p) 61. Fanny 61. Send Me N Flowers 64. Any Wednesday (& p) 66. Pete 'n Tilli (& p) (AAN) 72. Reuben Reuben (AAN) 83, etc.

Erdman, Richard (1925–).
American actor who began playing callow youths later taking rather crustier roles; now a director for TV.
Thunder across the Pacific 44. Objective Burma 45. The Men 50. The Happy Time 52. Benghazi 55. Bernardine 57. Saddle the Wind 58. Namu th Killer Whale 66. The Brothers O'Toole (d only) 73. Heidi's Song 82, others.
TV series: The Tab Hunter Show 60.

Erice, Victor (1940–).
Spanish director.
Los Desafios 69. Spirit of the Beehive 73. El Su 83. El Sol del Membrillo 92, etc.

Erickson, Leif (1911–1986) (William Anderson).
American 'second lead', former singer. In unspectacular roles from 1935.
Wanderer of the Wasteland 35. College Holiday 36. Ride a Crooked Mile 38. Nothing But the Truth 41. Eagle Squadron 42. Sorry, Wrong Number 48 Fort Algiers 50. Carbine Williams 52. On the Waterfront 54. The Fastest Gun Alive 56. Tea and Sympathy 57. Straitjacket 63. Mirage 65. Twilight' Last Gleaming 76, many others.
TV series: High Chaparral 67–71.

Ericson, John (1926–) (Joseph Meibes).
German-born leading man, long in America.
Teresa (debut) 51. Rhapsody 54. Green Fire 54. Bad Day at Black Rock 54. The Return of Jack Slade 55. Forty Guns 57. Pretty Boy Floyd 59. Under Ten Flags 60. The Seven Faces of Dr Lao 64. The Destructors 66. Operation Bluebook 67. Bedknobs and Broomsticks 71. Hustler Squad 76. Crash 77. Zone of the Dead 78. Primary Target 89 etc.
TV series: Honey West 65.

Errol, Leon (1881–1951).
Australian comedian who in 1910 left medicine for Broadway musical comedy and vaudeville, lately becoming familiar to filmgoers as twitchy, bald-pated, henpecked little man in innumerable 30s two-reelers and a number of features, mainly unworthy of his talents.
Paramount on Parade 30. Only Saps Work 30. One Heavenly Night 30. Alice in Wonderland 33. *We're Not Dressing* 34. Princess O'Hara 35. Make a Wish 37. *Mexican Spitfire* (first of a series with Lupe Velez in which Errol appeared as the drunken Lord

ping) 39. Pop Always Pays 40. Six Lessons from ...adame la Zonga 41. Never Give a Sucker an Even ...eak 41. Higher and Higher 43. Hat Check ...ney 44. The Invisible Man's Revenge 44. What ...londe 45. Mama Loves Papa 45. Joe Palooka ...amp (first of another series) 46. The Noose ...ngs High 48, etc.

For bringing a breath of inspired vaudeville to ...me pretty tired Hollywood formats, and for ...venting Lord Epping. *Mexican Spitfire.*

...skine, Chester (1905–1986).
...nerican writer-producer-director.
...Call it Murder (pd) 34. The Egg and I (wpd) 47.
...l My Sons (wp) 48. Take One False Step (co-wpd)
... Androcles and the Lion (wd) 53. Witness to
...urder (wp) 57. The Wonderful Country (p) 59,
...

...win, Stuart (1903–1967).
...nerican character comedian, who usually played
...r Average or the hero's faithful but slow-
...inking friend.
...Mother Knows Best 28. The Trespasser 29.
...veetie 29. Men Without Women 30. Dude
...nch 31. Misleading Lady 32. International
...use 33. Palooka 34. After Office Hours 35. All
...nerican Chump 36. *Pigskin Parade* (AAN) 36.
...im 37. Three Blind Mice 38. Hollywood Cavalcade
... Our Town 40. Cracked Nuts 41. Blondie for
...ctory 42. He Hired the Boss 43. The Great Mike
...s. Pillow to Post 45. Killer Dill 47. Strike it Rich
...s. Father is a Bachelor 50. For the Love of Mike
...s. Son of Flubber 64. The Misadventures of
...erlin Jones 64, many others.
...TV series: *The Trouble with Father* 53. The
...reatest Show on Earth 63. The Bing Crosby
...ow 65.

...skimos
...ve seldom been seriously tackled by the cinema.
...ocumentaries abound, from *Nanook of the North*
... Eskimo, and *Ukaliq* is a charming cartoon of
...skimo folklore, but the fictional stuff such as
...vage Innocents and *The White Dawn* has been dull
...d unsympathetic. The most authentic was
...obably *Igloo* 32, starring Chee-Ak (qv), but it
...iled to attract audiences, as did the more recent
...adows of the Wolf (aka *Agaguk*) 93.

...smond, Carl (1906–) (Willy Eichberger).
...ood-looking Austrian actor usually in haughty
... arrogant roles, first in Britain and later in
...ollywood.
...Evensong 33. Invitation to the Waltz 37. Dawn
...atrol 38. Thunder Afloat 39. Pacific Rendezvous
...2. The Story of Dr Wassell 43. *Ministry of Fear* 44.
...ddress Unknown 44. Without Love 45. This Love
... Ours 45. Catman of Paris 46. Smash-Up 47.
...Jalk a Crooked Mile 48. The Desert Hawk 50.
...Iystery Submarine 51. The World in His Arms 52.
...rom the Earth to the Moon 58. Thunder in the
...un 59. Agent for Harm 66. Morituri 66, etc.

...smond, Jill (1908–1990).
...ritish leading lady of the 30s, later in Hollywood.
...he was married to Laurence Olivier (1930–40).
...The Skin Game 31. Ladies of the Jury 32. No
...unny Business 32. This Above All 42. Random
...arvest 42. The White Cliffs of Dover 44. The
...andit of Sherwood Forest 46. Escape 48. Night
...eople 54. A Man Called Peter 55, etc.

...sposito, Giancarlo (1958–).
...merican actor.
...Sweet Lorraine 87. School Daze 88. Do the Right
...hing 89. King of New York 90. Mo' Better Blues

90. Night on Earth 91. Bob Roberts 92. Amos & Andrew 93, etc.

Esquivel, Laura (1950–).
Mexican screenwriter and novelist. She is married to actor and director Alfonso Arau.
Like Water for Chocolate (Como Agua para Chocolate) (oa, w) 92. Estrellita Marinera 94.

Essanay.
A production company formed in 1907 by G. K. Spoor and G. M. Anderson (S and A). Mainly remembered for enormous output of early westerns and for Chaplin's first comedies.

Essex, David (1947–).
British pop singer.
■ Assault 70. Carry on Henry 71. All Coppers Are . . . 71. That'll Be The Day 73. Stardust 74. Silver Dream Racer 80.

Essex, Harry (1910–).
American writer.
Boston Blackie and the Law 43. He Walked by Night 48. The Killer That Stalked New York 50. Kansas City Confidential 52. It Came from Outer Space 53. I The Jury (& d) 55. Mad at the World (& d) 56. The Lonely Man 57. The Sons of Katie Elder (co-w) 64, many others; also many TV episodes.

establishing shot.
Opening shot of sequence, showing location of scene or juxtaposition of characters in action to follow.

Estabrook, Howard (1884–1978).
American screenwriter.
The Four Feathers 28. Hell's Angels 30. *Cimarron* (AA) 31. A Bill of Divorcement 32. The Masquerader 33. David Copperfield 34. International Lady 39. The Bridge of San Luis Rey 44. The Human Comedy 45. The Girl from Manhattan 48. Lone Star 51. The Big Fisherman 59, many others.

Estevez, Emilio (1962–).
American leading man, son of Martin Sheen.
Tex 82. Repo Man 84. The Breakfast Club 84. St Elmo's Fire 84. That was Then . . . This is Now 85. Maximum Overdrive 86. Wisdom 86. Stakeout 87. Young Guns 88. Never on Tuesday 89. Men at Work (& wd) 90. Young Guns II 90. Freejack 92. The Mighty Ducks 92. National Lampoon's Loaded Weapon 1 93. Another Stakeout 93. Judgment Night 93. D2: The Mighty Ducks 94, etc.

Estrada, Erik (1949–).
American leading man of Puerto Rican descent.
The New Centurions 74. Trackdown 76. Fire! (TV) 77. Hour of the Assassin 87. Caged Fury 90. The Last Riders 90. Do or Die 91. The Divine Enforcer 91. National Lampoon's Loaded Weapon 1 93. Final Goal 94, etc.
TV series: *Chips* 77–82.

Estridge, Robin (1920–).
British screenwriter.
Above Us the Waves 54. The Young Lovers 54. Campbell's Kingdom 57. Northwest Frontier 59. Escape from Zahrain 62. Eye of the Devil 67, etc.

Eszterhas, Joe (1944–).
Hungarian-born American screenwriter. A former journalist, he writes scripts that tend to reflect current social concerns. He received a reported $3 million for his script for *Basic Instinct*.
F.I.S.T. 78. Flashdance 83. Jagged Edge 85. Big

Shots 87. Hearts of Fire 87. Betrayed 88. Checking Out 89. Music Box 89. Basic Instinct 92. Crossing the Line 92. Nowhere to Run (co-w) 93. Sliver 93, etc.

Etaix, Pierre (1928–).
French mime comedian, former circus clown and assistant to Tati.
Rupture (short) 61. Happy Anniversary (short) 61. The Suitor 62. Yo Yo 65. As Long As You Have Your Health 67. Le Grand Amour 69. Henry and June 90, etc.

Etting, Ruth (1896–1978).
American popular singer of the 20s, a version of whose life was told in 1955 in *Love Me or Leave Me.* Very briefly on screen.
■ Roman Scandals 33. Hips Hips Hooray 33. Gift of Gab 34.

Eustache, Jean (1938–1981).
French director and screenwriter. A former film editor, he also acted in Godard's *Weekend* and Wender's *The American Friend.* He committed suicide.
Les Mauvaises Fréquentations 63. Le Père Noel a les Yeux Bleus 66. Le Cochon 70. Numéro Zéro 71. The Mother and the Whore (La Maman et la Putain) 73. Mes Petites Amoureuses 74. Une Sale Histoire 77. Le Jardin des Délices de Jerome Bosch 79. Offre d'Emploi 80, etc.

Eustrel, Anthony (1903–1979).
British character actor.
The Silver Fleet 43. Caesar and Cleopatra 45. The Robe 53, etc.

Evans, Barry (1945–).
British light leading man.
Here We Go Round the Mulberry Bush 67. Die Screaming Marianne 71, etc.
TV series: Mind Your Language 77–81.

Evans, Clifford (1912–1985).
Welsh actor with stage experience. In films from 1936, at first as leading man and latterly as character actor.
Ourselves Alone 36. The Mutiny on the Elsinore 37. The Luck of the Navy 39. The Proud Valley 39. His Brother's Keeper 39. The Saint Meets the Tiger 40. *Love on the Dole* 41. Penn of Pennsylvania 41. Suspected Person 42. *The Foreman Went to France* 42; war service; The Silver Darlings 47. While I Live 48. Valley of Song 52. The Gilded Cage 55. Passport to Treason 56. Violent Playground 58. SOS Pacific 60. Curse of the Werewolf 62. Kiss of the Vampire 63. The Long Ships 64. Twist of Sand 69. One Brief Summer 70, etc.
TV series: Stryker of the Yard. The Power Game 65–67, etc.

Evans, Dale (1912–) (Frances Octavia Smith).
American leading lady of the 40s, former band singer; appeared frequently with Roy Rogers, and in 1947 married him.
Orchestra Wives 42. Swing Your Partner 43. Casanova in Burlesque 44. The Yellow Rose of Texas 44. Utah 45. Belles of Rosarita 45. My Pal Trigger 46. Apache Rose 47. Slippy McGee 48. Susanna Pass 49. Twilight in the Sierras 50. Trigger Jnr 51. Pals of the Golden West 51. Roy Rogers: King of the Cowboys (doc) 91, many others.
TV series: The Roy Rogers Show 51–56.

Evans, Dame Edith (1888–1976).
Distinguished British stage actress who made occasional films.

Biographies 1977: *Ned's Girl* by Bryan Forbes. *Edith Evans: A Personal Memoir* by Jean Batters.
■ A Welsh Singer 15. East is East 15. *The Queen of Spades* 48. *The Last Days of Dolwyn* 48. *The Importance of Being Earnest* 51. Look Back in Anger 59. The Nun's Story 59. Tom Jones (AAN) 63. The Chalk Garden (AAN) 64. Young Cassidy 65. *The Whisperers* (BFA, AAN) 67. Fitzwilly (US) 68. Prudence and the Pill 68. Crooks and Coronets 69. The Madwoman of Chaillot 69. David Copperfield 69. Scrooge 70. A Doll's House 73. Craze 73. QB VII (TV) 74. The Slipper and the Rose 76. Nasty Habits 76.

¶ As a young actress I always had a rule. If I didn't understand a line I always said it as though it were improper. – *E.E.*
Comedy, dear, is just like blowing powder puffs out of a cannon. – *E.E.*
Acting with her was heaven. It was like being in your mother's arms. – *Sir Michael Redgrave*

Evans, Fred (1889–1951).
English comic actor and director, from music hall, who was one of the earliest stars of British cinema, notably in the character of 'Pimple' (renamed 'Flivver' in America). In films from 1910, he made his first Pimple short in 1912 and turned out between 10 and 30 a year until his last, *Pimple's Three Musketeers*, in 1922. In the 30s and 40s, he worked as an extra in films. He was the nephew of Will Evans (qv) and was a member of a famous family of music-hall performers and clowns.

Evans, Gene (1922–).
Stocky American actor in demand for heavy roles since 1947.
Berlin Express 48. Park Row 52. Donovan's Brain 53. The Golden Blade 53. Hell and High Water 54. The Sad Sack 57. Operation Petticoat 59. Apache Uprising 65. Support Your Local Sheriff 69. The Ballad of Cable Hogue 70. Walking Tall 73. Devil Times Five 82, etc.
TV series: My Friend Flicka 57. Matt Helm 75. Spencer's Pilots 76.

Evans, Joan (1934–) (Joan Eunson).
American actress who played teenage roles in the early 50s, now working in education.
Our Very Own 50. On the Loose 51. Roseanna McCoy 51. Skirts Ahoy 52. Edge of Doom 54. The Fortune Hunter 54. No Name on the Bullet 59. The Flying Fontaines 60, etc.

Evans, Joe (1891–1967).
English music-hall performer who starred in many comedy shorts from 1912–18 and also appeared in the films of his brother Fred 'Pimple' Evans (qv).

Evans, Josh (1971–).
American actor, director and writer, the son of Robert Evans and Ali McGraw.
Dream a Little Dream 89. Born on the Fourth of July 89. Ricochet 90. The Doors 90. Inside the Goldmine (& co-w, d) 94, etc.

Evans, Linda (1943–).
Blonde American leading lady.
Twilight of Honor 63. Those Calloways 64. Female Artillery (TV) 73. The Klansman 74. Mitchell 75. Nowhere to Run (TV) 78. Avalanche Express 79. The Gambler Part Two (TV) 83. *The Last Frontier* (TV) 86. She'll Take Romance 90, etc.
TV series: The Big Valley 65–69. Hunter 77. *Dynasty* 81–88.

Evans, Madge (1909–1981).
American actress, a child star of silent days, pretty

heroine of mainly unremarkable films in the 30s.
The Sign of the Cross 14. The Burglar 16. Classmates 24. Son of India 29. Lovers Courageous 30. The Greeks Had a Word for Them 32. Hallelujah I'm a Bum 33. Dinner at Eight 33. Grand Canary 34. David Copperfield 34. The Tunnel (GB) 35. Piccadilly Jim 37. The Thirteenth Chair 37, etc.

Evans, Maurice (1901–1989).
Eloquent Welsh actor who, long in America, distinguished himself on the Broadway stage.
White Cargo 30. Raise the Roof 30. Wedding Rehearsal 32. Scrooge (GB) 35. Kind Lady 51. The Story of Gilbert and Sullivan (as Sullivan) 53. Androcles and the Lion (as Caesar) 53. Macbeth (title role) 59. The War Lord 65. Jack of Diamonds 67. Planet of the Apes 67. Rosemary's Baby 68. Terror in the Wax Museum 73, etc.
TV series: Bewitched 68–71.

Evans, Norman (1901–1962).
British north-country music hall comedian famous for toothless characterization and female impersonation.
Demobbed 45. Under New Management 46. Over the Garden Wall 50, etc.

Evans, Ray (1915–).
American songwriter, in Hollywood from 1945 in partnership with Jay Livingston.
'Buttons and Bows' (AA 48), 'Que Sera Sera' (AA 56), many others.

Evans, Rex (1903–1969).
British character actor in Hollywood. Often played stately butlers, as in *The Philadelphia Story* 40. Other appearances include *Camille* 36, *It Should Happen to You* 53, *The Matchmaker* 58. Ran an art gallery in his spare time.

Evans, Robert (1930–).
Bland-faced American juvenile of the 50s; gave up acting to become a Paramount production executive, then went independent. He was formerly married to Ali McGraw.
Autobiography: 1994, *The Kid Stays in the Picture*.
Lydia Bailey 52. *The Man of a Thousand Faces* (as Irving Thalberg) 57. The Sun Also Rises 57. The Fiend Who Walked the West (title role) 58. The Best of Everything 59. Desperate Hours 90, etc.
AS PRODUCER: Chinatown 74. The Great Gatsby 74. Marathon Man 76. Black Sunday 77. Players 79. Popeye 80. Urban Cowboy 80. The Cotton Club 84. The Two Jakes 90. Sliver 93, etc.

Evans, Will (1867–1931).
English comic actor, notable pantomime dame at Drury Lane, and playwright, who filmed many of his classic music-hall slapstick sketches and appeared in the silent shorts of his nephew Fred Evans. He was the co-author of *Tons of Money*, the long-running and influential farce of the 20s which was filmed in 1930.
They Do Such Things at Brighton 1899. Will Evans the Living Catherine Wheel 1899. The Jockey 07. Harnessing a Horse 13. Whitewashing the Ceiling 14. Building a Chicken House 14. Moving a Piano 14. A Study in Skarlit 15, etc.

Eve, Trevor (1951–).
Slightly-built British leading man who became popular from 1979 as TV's radio station detective *Shoestring*.
Dracula 79. Jamaica Inn (TV) 82. Lace (TV) 84. The Corsican Brothers (TV) 84. Scandal 88. In the Name of the Father 93.
TV series: Shadow Chasers 85.

Evein, Bernard (1929–).
French art director.
Les Amants 57. Les Jeux de L'Amour 60. Zazie dans le Métro 61. Lola 61. Cléo de 5 à 7 62. La Baie des Anges 62. Le Feu Follet 63. The Umbrell of Cherbourg 64. Do You Like Women? 64. Viva Maria 65. The Young Girls of Rochefort 67. Woman Times Seven 67, etc.

Evelyn, Judith (1913–1967) (J. E. Allen).
American stage actress; often played neurotic women.
The Egyptian 54. Rear Window 54. Hilda Cran 56. The Tingler 59, etc.

Everest, Barbara (1890–1968).
British stage actress who appeared in many films latterly in motherly roles.
Lily Christine 31. The Wandering Jew 33. The Passing of the Third Floor Back 35. He Found a Star 40. Mission to Moscow (US) 43. Jane Eyre (US) 43. The Uninvited (US) 44. The Valley of Decision (US) 45. Wanted for Murder 46. Frieda 47. Madeleine 49. Tony Draws a Horse 51. The Ma Who Finally Died 62, etc.

Everett, Chad (1936–) (Raymond Cramton).
Handsome American leading man of the 60s; film unremarkable.
Claudelle Inglish 61. The Chapman Report 62. Get Yourself a College Girl 65. The Singing Nun 66. First to Fight 67. The Last Challenge 67. The Firechasers (TV) 70. The French Atlantic Affair (TV) 79. Airplane 2: The Sequel 82. Fever Pitch 85. Heroes Stand Alone 89. Jigsaw Murders 89. The Rousters (TV) 90, etc.
TV series: *Medical Center* 69–75. Hagen 79. The Rousters 83. McKenna 94–95.

Everett, Rupert (1959–).
British leading man, usually in aristocratic roles, and novelist.
Princess Daisy (TV) 83. *Another Country* 84. Dance with a Stranger 85. The Right Hand Man 8 Duet for One 86. Hearts of Fire 87. Gli Occhiali d'Oro 87. Tolerance 89. The Comfort of Stranger 90. Dellamorte Dellamore (It.) 94. The Madness King George 95, etc.

Evers, Jason (1922–) (Herbert Evers).
American general-purpose actor.
A Piece of the Action 77.
TV series: Wrangler 60. Channing 63–64.

Ewell, Tom (1909–1994) (S. Yewell Tompkins).
American comic actor with wide stage experienc
Adam's Rib 49. A Life of Her Own 50. An America Guerilla in the Philippines 50. Mr Music 50. Finders Keepers 51. Up Front 51. Back at the Fro 52. Abbott and Costello Lost in Alaska 52. *The Sev Year Itch* 55. The Lieutenant Wore Skirts 55. The Great American Pastime 56. The Girl Can't Help It 57. A Nice Little Bank that Should be Robbed 58. Tender is the Night 61. State Fair 62. Suppos They Gave a War and Nobody Came 70. To Find A Man 72. They Only Kill Their Masters 72. The Great Gatsby 74. Promise Him Anything (TV) 75 etc.
TV series: *The Tom Ewell Show* 60–61. Baretta 75–78. Best of the West 81–82.

excerpts
from films are sometimes incorporated into othe films in which characters go to a cinema or wate television. So in *Hollywood Cavalcade* Don Ameche watched a rough-cut of *The Jazz Singer*, just as te years later Larry Parks in *Jolson Sings Again* watched a rough-cut of himself in *The Jolson Stor*

n unidentified silent comedy was being played in he room below when the first murder took place n *The Spiral Staircase*; Linda Christian and Louis ourdan saw *Son of the Sheik* at their local in *The Happy Time*, and Fredric March and his son watched a William S. Hart film in *One Foot in Heaven*. risoners watched *Wings of the Navy* during *Each Dawn I Die* and *The Egg and I* during *Brute Force*; nd the chain gang in *Sullivan's Travels* roared with aughter at a Mickey Mouse cartoon. Footage from *Phantom of the Opera* was shown in *Hollywood Story*, from *Comin' thru' the Rye* in *The Smallest Show on Earth*, from *Tol'able David* in *The Tingler*, from *Queen Kelly* in *Sunset Boulevard*, from *Camille* in *Bridge to the Sun*, from *Destination Tokyo* in *Operation Pacific*, and from *Boom Town* in *Watch the Birdie*. Other movies shown in 'cinemas' in later films include: *Uncle Tom's Cabin* in *Abbott and Costello Meet the Keystone Kops*; *Gold Diggers of 1933* in *Bonnie and Clyde*; *Crossroads* in *The Youngest Profession*; *Casablanca* in *First to Fight*; *Red River* in *The Last Picture Show*; *Hell Divers* in *The Wings of Eagles*; *Task Force* in *White Heat*; *The Walking Dead* in *Ensign Pulver*; *Tin Pan Alley* in *Wing and a Prayer*; *Now Voyager* in *Summer of '42*; *Red Dust* in *Heavy Traffic*; various Bogart films in *Play It Again Sam*; *Caprice* in *Caprice* (Doris Day went to the movies, saw herself on the screen, and didn't like it). In *Two Weeks in Another Town*, which had a plot pretty close to that of *The Bad and the Beautiful*, Kirk Douglas watched himself in – *The Bad and the Beautiful!* The Bette Davis character in *Whatever Happened to Baby Jane?* was criticized as a bad actress on the strength of clips from early Bette Davis movies, *Ex-Lady* and *Parachute Jumper*. In the same film Joan Crawford watched herself on TV in *Sadie McKee*; and in *Walk Don't Run* there was a flash of James Stewart dubbed in Japanese in *Two Rode Together*. Finally the cosmonauts on their space station in *Conquest of Space* were entertained by a showing of *Here Come the Girls* ... thus showing, as one critic remarked, that in 50 years' time TV will still be relying on old movies!

Other uses for old footage in new films include such gags as Bob Hope in *Road to Bali* meeting up with Humphrey Bogart in *The African Queen*; and economy dictates such measures as the ten-minute chunk of *The Mummy* at the beginning of *The Mummy's Hand* and the use in *Singin' in the Rain*, as part of a 'new' picture in production, of sequences from Gene Kelly's version of *The Three Musketeers*. Similarly bits of *The Sheik* were in *Son of the Sheik*, and *Topper* in *Topper Takes a Trip*. Great chunks of the *Joan of Arc* battles turned up in *Thief of Damascus*, as did *The Black Knight* in *Siege of the Saxons* and *The Four Feathers* in *Storm Over the Nile* and *East of Sudan*. Universal's *Sword of Ali Baba* used so much footage from their *Ali Baba and the Forty Thieves* that one actor had to be engaged to replay his original part! It was, however, wit rather than

economy that persuaded Preston Sturges to open *Mad Wednesday* with the last reel of *The Freshman* and the Boris Karloff clips were central to the concept of *Targets*. As for *Dead Men Don't Wear Plaid*, the new footage was constructed entirely to fit in with clips from old movies, so that the hero appeared to be taking part in 40s scenes with the likes of Dorothy Lamour and Alan Ladd.

exchange.

An American enterprise: a middleman business which for a commission deals with the small exhibitors of an area on behalf of major renters.

exploitation.

A trade word covering all phases of publicity, public relations and promotion.

exploitation film.

A term used to describe low-budget movies of a sensational kind that either focus on some headline-making social phenomenon or attempt to cash in on a current box-office success. Sex, horror and fantasy are the predominant subject matters. Sometimes the title or the poster comes first, and the movie is made to match it. Such films flourished from the early 60s when drive-in cinemas provided double-bills and there was a new youthful audience for rock 'n' roll and biker movies. One of the most successful companies in the field was AIP, run by Samuel Arkoff and Jack Nicholson. The most notable exponent of the form has been producer and director Roger Corman, who began by supplying films for AIP to distribute before setting up his own production companies. Many of today's most successful directors, writers and cinematographers began by making films for Corman. That may, in part, be the reason why in recent years Hollywood studios have been turning out what are in effect big-budget exploitation movies, such as *Terminator 2*, and have also followed the exploitation movie-makers' habit of recycling their successes, as witness the seemingly endless succession of sequels to *A Nightmare on Elm Street*, *Halloween*, etc. As the subject matter of exploitation movies is now part of mainstream cinema, and there are fewer cinemas in which to show such movies, the likelihood is that the day of the exploitation film is nearly over. Its main market is now video, with films bypassing the cinema entirely, or being given very restricted releases in the hope of garnering publicity for their video-release. It is possible, however, that the growth in soft-core pornography for satellite and cable TV will provide its practitioners with a continuing market.

explorers

have inspired many documentaries but

surprisingly few features except wholly fictitious ones like *Trader Horn*, *She* and *The Lost World*. *Marco Polo* has thrice been dealt with, and *Christopher Columbus* got the full Rank treatment as well as featuring in the satirical *Where Do We Go from Here?* The Pilgrim Fathers were the heroes of *Plymouth Adventure*, and Drake of *Seven Seas to Calais*. Lewis and Clark in *The Far Horizons* were played by Fred MacMurray and Charlton Heston. *Scott of the Antarctic* was played by John Mills, and Amundsen in *The Red Tent* by Sean Connery; Pierre Radisson in *Hudson's Bay* by Paul Muni; Cortez in *Captain from Castile* by César Romero; Pizarro in *The Royal Hunt of the Sun* by Robert Shaw; Junipero Serra in *Seven Cities of Gold* by Michael Rennie. *Penn of Pennsylvania* and *Stanley and Livingstone* were in the practical sense explorers, though driven by other motives; *Aguirre Wrath of God* seemed to be driven chiefly by greed.

expressionism.

A term indicating the fullest utilization of cinematic resources to give dramatic larger-than-life effect, as in *Citizen Kane* or, in a different way, *The Cabinet of Dr Caligari*. In a secondary sense it also allows the fullest expression to be given, by the above means, to states of emotion.

exterior.

A shot taken in normal lighting outside the studio.

Exton, Clive (1930–).

British dramatist who wrote notable television plays in the 60s and turned to screenwriting with less happy results.

No Fixed Abode (TV) 59. The Big Eat (TV) 62. A Place to Go 63. The Trial of Dr Fancy (TV) 64. Night Must Fall 64. Isadora (co-w) 68. Entertaining Mr Sloane 69. Ten Rillington Place 70. Running Scared (co-w) 72. The House in Nightmare Park (co-w) 73. Doomwatch (made 71) 76. The Awakening (co-w) 80. Red Sonja (co-w) 85, etc.

TV series: The Crezz 77. Dick Barton – Special Agent 79. Jeeves and Wooster 92–93.

extra.

A crowd player with no lines to speak.

Eythe, William (1918–1957).

American leading man of the 40s.

The Ox-Bow Incident 42. The Song of Bernadette 43. The Eve of St Mark 44. A Royal Scandal 45. The House on 92nd Street 45. Meet Me at Dawn 47. Customs Agent 50, etc.

Eziashi, Maynard.

British leading actor.

Mr Johnson 90. Twenty-One 91. Bopha! 93. A Good Man in Africa 94, etc.

F

Fabares, Shelley (1944–).
American juvenile leading lady of the early 60s. Niece of Nanette Fabray.

Never Say Goodbye 56. Summer Love 58. Ride the Wild Surf 64. Girl Happy 65. Hold On 66. Spinout 66. Clambake 67. The Great American Traffic Jam 80. Love or Money 88, etc.

TV series: The Donna Reed Show 58–63. The Brian Keith Show 72–74. The Practice 76–77. Mary Hartman, Mary Hartman 77–78. Highcliffe Manor 79. One Day at a Time 81–84.

Fabian (1942–) (Fabian Forte Bonaparte).
American teenage idol, singer and guitarist.

The Hound Dog Man (debut) 59. North to Alaska 60. Mr Hobbs Takes a Vacation 62. Dear Brigitte 65. Ten Little Indians 65. Fireball 500 66. The Devil's Eight 68. A Bullet for Pretty Boy 70. Lovin' Man 72, Little Laura and Big John 73. Kiss Daddy Goodbye 81, etc.

Fabian, Françoise (1932–) (Michele Cortes de Leone y Fabianera).
Spanish leading actress who has made several forays into international films.

Mamzelle Pigalle 56. Fernandel the Dressmaker 56. The Fanatics 57. Maigret Sees Red 63. Le Voleur 67. *Belle de Jour* 67. *Ma Nuit Chez Maud* 70. La Bonne Année 73. Down the Ancient Stairs 75. Salut l'Artiste 76. Madame Claude 77. Reflections in a Dark Sky (Riflessi in un Cielo Scuro) 91, etc.

Fabray, Nanette (1920–) (Nanette Fabares).
American comedy actress and singer, former child star of 'Our Gang' comedies.

Adult films: Elizabeth and Essex 39. Band Wagon 53. The Happy Ending 69. Amy 81. Personal Exemptions 88, etc.

TV series: Peck's Bad Girl 59. Caesar's Hour 64.

Fabre, Saturnin (1884–1961).
French character actor.

Pépé le Moko 37. Il Etait Neuf Celibataires 42. Un Ami Viendra Ce Soir 46. Les Portes de la Nuit 46. Clochemerle 52. La Fête à Henriette 54, etc.

Fabri, Zoltan (1917–1994).
Hungarian director.

The Storm 52. Merry-Go-Round 55. Professor Hannibal 56. The Brute 59. The Last Goal 61. Twenty Hours 65. The Paul Street Boys 68. One Day More One Day Less 73. Hungarians 77. Balint Fabian Meets God 80. Requiem 82, etc.

Fabrizi, Aldo (1905–1990).
Italian character actor, known abroad.

Open City 45. Vivere in Pace 47. First Communion 50. Cops and Robbers, 54. Altri Tempi 55. The Angel Wore Red 60. The Birds the Bees and the Italians 65. Made in Italy 68.

fade in.
Gradual emergence of a scene from blackness to full definition; opposite of *fade out*.

Fahey, Jeff (1956–).
American leading actor.

Silverado 85. Psycho III 86. Backfire 87. Split Decisions 88. True Blood 89. The Last of the Finest 90. Impulse 90. White Hunter, Black Heart 90. Body Parts 91. Iron Maze 91. The Lawnmower Man 92. Sketch Artist 92. Freefall 94. Woman of Desire 94. Wyatt Earp 94, etc.

Fain, Sammy (1902–1987) (Samuel Feinberg).
American composer, a former vaudeville performer, whose songs featured in many Hollywood films.

Young Man of Manhattan 30. Footlight Parade 33. Sweet Music 35. Meet the People 44. Call Me Mister 51. Alice in Wonderland 51. The Jazz Singer 53. Peter Pan 53. Calamity Jane (AAs) 53. Love Is a Many Splendored Thing (AA title s) 55. Hollywood or Bust 56. April Love 57. The Big Circus 59, etc.

Fairbanks, Douglas (1883–1939) (Douglas Ullman).
Swashbuckling American star of the silent screen, the acrobatic, zestful, ever-smiling hero of many comedies and costume adventures, almost all of which he produced himself. Despite long stage experience, sound did not suit him, and his 30s films showed a marked decline. He had a famous marriage with Mary Pickford, and in 1919, with Chaplin and Griffith, they were co-founders of United Artists Film Corporation. Posthumous AA 1939 'for his unique and outstanding contribution to the international development of the motion picture'.

Biographies: 1953, The Fourth Musketeer by Elton Thomas. 1976, The Fairbanks Album by Richard Schickel. 1977, His Majesty the American by John C. Tibbetts and James M. Welsh.

■ The Lamb 15. Double Trouble 15. His Picture in the Papers 16. The Habit of Happiness 16. The Good Bad Man 16. Reggie Mixes In 16. Flirting with Fate 16. The Mystery of the Leaping Fish 16. The Half Breed 16. Manhattan Madness 16. American Aristocracy 16. The Matrimaniac 16. The Americano 16. In Again Out Again 17. Wild and Woolly 17. Down to Earth 17. The Man from Painted Post 17. Reaching for the Moon 17. A Modern Musketeer 18. Headin' South 18. Mr Fix-It 18. Say Young Fellow 18. Bound in Morocco 18. He Comes Up Smiling 18. Arizona (& wd) 18. Knickerbocker Buckaroo 19. His Majesty the American 19. When the Clouds Roll By 20. The Mollycoddle 20. *The Mark of Zorro* (& w) 20. The Nut (& w) 21. *The Three Musketeers* 21. *Robin Hood* (& w) 21. *The Thief of Baghdad* (&w) 23. *Don Q Son of Zorro* 25. *The Black Pirate* 26. The Gaucho (& w) 27. The Iron Mask (& w) 29. The Taming of the Shrew 29. Reaching for the Moon 30. Around the World in Eighty Minutes (& w) 31. Mr Robinson Crusoe 32. The Private Life of Don Juan 34.

For giving his high spirits to a world which needed them. *The Black Pirate.*

¶ Quotes about the elder Fairbanks all point the same way; despite his comparatively short stature, he was much larger than life.

He has such verve. We can use his body, said D. W. Griffith.
From that day Fairbanks kept himself in rigorous training, believing that:
The man that's out to do something has to kee in high gear all the time.
He managed. An anonymous critic in 1920 put hi finger on the Fairbanks magic:
He smiles, and you feel relieved.
Alistair Cooke called him:
A sort of Ariel,
and added:
At a difficult period in American history, Douglas Fairbanks appeared to know all the answers.
Director Allan Dwan commented:
Stunt men have had to imitate him and it alway looked like a stunt when they did it. With him it always looked right.
But Mary Pickford, who should know, had a minority view:
In his private life Douglas always faced a situation in the only way he knew, by running away from it.

Fairbanks, Douglas, Jnr (1909–).
American leading man who has spent much time in Britain; of more conventional debonair mould than his father, he spent as much time in drawing rooms as on castle battlements, but was at home in any surroundings. During the early 50s, produced and sometimes played in innumerable TV half-hours under the title *Douglas Fairbanks Presents.*

Biography: 1955, *Knight Errant* by Brian Connell.

■ Party Girl 20. Stephen Steps Out 23. Air Mail 25. Wild Horse Mesa 25. Stella Dallas 25. The American Venus 25. Padlocked 26. Manbait 26. Is Zat So? 27. A Texas Steer 27. The Barker 28. A Woman of Affairs 28. *The Jazz Age* 29. Fast Life 29. Our Modern Maidens 29. The Careless Age 29. The Forward Pass 29. Show of Shows 29. Loose Ankle 30. *The Dawn Patrol* 30. Little Accident 30. The Way of All Men 30. *Outward Bound* 30. Little Caesar 30. One Night at Susie's 30. Chances 31. I Like Your Nerve 31. Union Depot 32. It's Tough to be Famous 32. Love is a Racket 32. Parachute Jumper 32. The Narrow Corner 33. *Morning Glory* 33. Captured 33. The Life of Jimmy Dolan 33. *Catherine the Great* 34. Success at any Price 34. Mim 35. The Amateur Gentleman 35. Accused 36. Jump for Glory 36. *The Prisoner of Zenda* (as Rupert of Hentzau) 37. Joy of Living 38. The Rage of Paris 38. Having Wonderful Time 38. *The Young in Hear* 38. *Gunga Din* 39. The Sun Never Sets 39. Rulers of the Sea 39. Green Hell 40. Safari 40. Angels ove Broadway 40. The Corsican Brothers 41. *Sinbad th Sailor* 47. The Exile 47. That Lady in Ermine 48. The Fighting O'Flynn 49. *State Secret* 50. Mr Drake's Duck 51. The Crooked Hearts (TV) 72. Ghost Story 81. The Hostage Tower (TV) 81.

Fairbrother, Sydney (1873–1941) (S. Tapping).
British character actress, in films occasionally from
1916.
   Iron Justice 16. The Third String 31. Chu Chin
Chow 33. The Crucifix 34. The Last Journey 36.
King Solomon's Mines (as Gagool) 37. Little Dolly
Daydream 38, etc.

Fairchild, Morgan (1950–) (Patsy McClenny).
American leading lady.
   The Initiation of Sarah (TV) 78. Murder in Music
City (TV) 79. The Dream Merchants (TV) 80. The
Seduction 82. Campus Man 87. Midnight Cop 88.
The Haunting of Sarah Hardy (TV) 89. Mob Boss
90. Sherlock Holmes and the Leading Lady (TV)
91, etc.
   TV series: Flamingo Road 80–81.

Fairchild, William (1918–).
British screenwriter.
   Morning Departure 50. An Outcast of the Islands
51. The Gift Horse 52. The Net 53. The Malta Story
53. Front Page Story 54. John and Julie (& d) 54.
Value for Money 57. The Silent Enemy (& d) 58.
Star! 68. Embassy 72. Invitation to the Wedding
85, etc.

Fairhurst, Lyn (1920–).
British writer.
   Band of Thieves 62. Touch of Death 63. Be My
Guest 64. Devils of Darkness 65, etc.

Fairlie, Gerard (1899–1983).
British novelist and screenwriter. A former Guards
officer, army heavyweight boxing champion and
rugby player, he was a model for Bulldog
Drummond, who was created by his friend 'Sapper'
Lt-Col. H. C. McNeile). Fairlie wrote seven
Drummond novels after McNeile's death and ran
a commando training school during the Second
World War.
   Shot in the Dark (oa) 33. Bulldog Jack (co-w)
34. Jack Ahoy! (co-w) 34. Open All Night 34. The
Ace of Spades 35. Forever England (co-w) 35. The
Mad 35. Lazybones 35. The Big Noise 36. The
Lonely Road (co-w) 36. Troubled Waters 36.
Calling Bulldog Drummond (oa, co-w) 51, etc.

fairy tales:
see fantasy.

Faith, Adam (1940–) (Terence Nelhams).
British pop singer turned actor, popular as the
cheerful cockney crook in the TV series Budgie in
1971.
   Never Let Go 60. Beat Girl 61. Mix Me a Person
62. Stardust 74. Yesterday's Hero 79. McVicar 80.
Murder on the Orient Express (TV) 85, etc.
   TV series: Love Hurts 91–92.

Faith, Percy (1908–1976).
American orchestral conductor and composer.
   Love Me or Leave Me 55, I'd Rather Be Rich 64, The
Oscar 66.

Faithfull, Geoffrey (1893–1979).
British cinematographer and occasional director,
with Hepworth from 1908.
   For You Alone (d) 44. The Lavender Hill Mob
51. Corridors of Blood 59. Village of the Damned
60. On the Beat 62, etc.

Faithfull, Marianne (1947–).
British leading lady and singer.
   Autobiography: 1994, Faithfull.
   I'll Never Forget Whatshisname 67. Girl on a
Motorcycle 68. Hamlet 69. Ghost Story 74. When
Pigs Fly 93. Shopping 94, etc.

Falconetti (1901–1946) (Marie Falconetti).
French stage actress, unforgettable in her only
film, The Passion of Joan of Arc 28.

Falk, Peter (1927–).
Fast-talking, cast-eyed American actor from the
off-Broadway stage.
   Wind Across the Everglades 58. The Bloody Brood
59. Pretty Boy Floyd 59. The Secret of the Purple
Reef 60. Murder Inc. (AAN) 60. Pocketful of
Miracles (AAN) 61. Pressure Point 62. The
Balcony 63. It's a Mad Mad Mad Mad World 63.
Robin and the Seven Hoods 64. The Great Race 65.
Italiano Brava Gente 65. Too Many Thieves (TV)
66. Penelope 66. Luv 67. Prescription Murder (TV)
(his first appearance as Columbo) 67. Anzio 68.
Castle Keep 69. Machine Gun McCain 70. A Step
Out of Line (TV) 70. Husbands 70. Operation Snafu
70. Ransom for a Dead Man (start of Columbo
series) (TV) 71. A Woman Under the Influence 76.
Murder by Death 76. Griffin and Phoenix (TV) 76.
Mikey and Nicky 76. The Brinks Job 78. The Cheap
Detective 78. The In-Laws 79. All the Marbles 81.
Big Trouble 84. Happy New Year 87. The Princess
Bride 87. Vibes 88. Cookie 89, In the Spirit 89.
Columbo Goes to the Guillotine (TV) 89. Tune in
Tomorrow (aka Aunt Julia and the Scriptwriter)
90. Motion and Emotion. Columbo Goes to College
(TV). Columbo: Grand Deception (TV) 90.
Faraway, So Close! (In Weiter Ferne, So Nah) 93,
etc.
   TV series: The Trials of O'Brien 65. Columbo 71–
78.

Falkenburg, Jinx (1919–) (Eugenia Falkenburg).
Tall, good-looking American model who made a
few light comedies and musicals in the 40s.
   Autobiography: 1951, Jinx.
   Two Latins from Manhattan 42. Sing for Your
Supper 42. Lucky Legs 43. Tahiti Nights 44. Talk
about a Lady 46, etc.

The Fall of the House of Usher.
This grisly tale by Edgar Allan Poe was filmed by
Jean Epstein in 1928, by Americans Melville
Webber and James Watson in the same year, by
British semi-professionals in 1950, by Roger
Corman in 1960, and by Allan Burkinshaw in
1988.

falling
is, of all man's inherited fears, the one most
spectacularly played on by Hollywood, where the
shot of the villain's hand slipping away from the
hero's frenzied grasp, followed by a quick-fading
scream, has become a screen stereotype. Harold
Lloyd's skyscraper comedies played on this fear, as
have the films of many comedians since; in The
Horn Blows at Midnight, for instance, Jack Benny is
only one of six people hanging on to each other's
coat-tails from the top of a high building. All
circus films, and that includes The Marx Brothers at
the Circus, base one or two of their thrills on trapeze
acts that might go wrong. And whenever a villain
starts climbing upwards, as Ted de Corsia did in
Naked City, or along a ledge, as the same accident-
prone Ted de Corsia did in The Enforcer, the
audience grits its teeth and waits for the inevitable.
The whole action of Fourteen Hours was based on
the question whether a potential suicide would or
would not jump from a ledge.
   Some of the screen's most spectacular falls
include Walter Abel's in Mirage, the key to the
whole action; Agnes Moorehead's (through a
window) in Dark Passage; Charlotte Henry's in Alice
in Wonderland; Cedric Hardwicke's in Hunchback of
Notre Dame; W. C. Fields' (from an aeroplane) in
Never Give a Sucker an Even Break; Alan Ladd's

(through a roof) in The Glass Key; Slim Pickens'
(on the bomb) in Dr Strangelove; Eleanor Parker's
in An American Dream; King Kong's (from the top of
the Empire State Building); William Bendix's from
a skyscraper in The Dark Corner. To Alfred
Hitchcock, falls are a speciality: Edmund Gwenn
fell from Westminister Cathedral in Foreign
Correspondent, Norman Lloyd from the torch of the
Statue of Liberty in Saboteur, while Vertigo not only
boasted three falls but based its entire plot on the
hero's fear of heights. Falls under trains and buses
are legion, but in The Well a little girl fell down an
old wellshaft, in The List of Adrian Messenger a
victim fell to his death in a lift (as did characters
in Hotel and House of Wax, while in Ivy Joan
Fontaine fell down a lift shaft), in Somerset
Maugham's Encore an acrobat hoped to fall safely
into a water tank; and an unnamed gentleman
was pushed out of The High Window by Florence
Bates.

Faltermeyer, Harold.
American composer.
   Thief of Hearts 84. Beverly Hills Cop 84. Fletch
85. Top Gun 86. Fire and Ice 87. Fatal Beauty 87.
Beverly Hills Cop II 87. The Running Man 87.
Fletch Lives 89. Tango & Cash 89. Kuffs 92, etc.

the family
is the centre of most people's lives, so naturally
there have been many memorable film families.
Those popular enough to have warranted a series
include the Joneses, the Hardys, the Huggetts, the
Wilkinses of Dear Ruth, The Cohens and the Kellys,
the Bumsteads of Blondie and the Four Daughters
saga. World War II brought a sentimental
attachment to the family which in Hollywood
expressed itself in Happy Land, The Human Comedy,
Our Town, The Happy Time, Since You Went Away,
Meet Me in St Louis, A Genius in the Family, The
Sullivans and The Best Years of Our Lives; in Britain,
Salute John Citizen, The Holly and the Ivy, Dear
Octopus, Quiet Wedding, This Man is Mine. Semi-
classical treatments of the theme include Cavalcade,
The Swiss Family Robinson, Pride and Prejudice, Little
Women, Scrooge and Whiteoaks. Odd families,
ranging from the merely sophisticated to the
downright bizarre, were seen in Three Cornered
Moon, The Old Dark House, The Royal Family of
Broadway, My Man Godfrey, You Can't Take It With
You, The Young in Heart, The Little Foxes, Tobacco
Road, The Bank Dick, House of Strangers, An Inspector
Calls, Sweethearts, Treasure Hunt, Holiday, The
Philadelphia Story, The Anniversary, and The Lion in
Winter. Vaudeville families were seen in Yankee
Doodle Dandy, The Merry Monahans, The Seven Little
Foys, The Buster Keaton Story and There's No Business
Like Show Business. There has been a fashion for
the large family, started by Cheaper by the Dozen
and Chicken Every Sunday in 1949 and reprised by
With Six You Get Egg Roll and Yours Mine and Ours
in 1968 and a TV series The Brady Bunch in 1969.
Other charming families have included those in
Our Vines Have Tender Grapes, Background, The
Happy Family, Four Sons, The Holly and the Ivy, Made
in Heaven, 29 Acacia Avenue, Little Murders, Never
Too Late, This Happy Breed and My Wife's Family; but
the most memorable family of all is likely to
remain the Joads in The Grapes of Wrath, unless it
is one of the real families put under the microscope
by American and British TV.

Famous Players.
A production company founded by Adolph Zukor
in New York in 1912, following his success in
distributing Sarah Bernhardt in Queen Elizabeth.
The motif was 'famous players in famous plays'
which could not work too well as the films were

silent; but the tag caught on and the company did well enough. It was later absorbed into Paramount.

Fanck, Arnold (1889–1974).
German director, renowned for mountaineering films.
■ Wunder des Schneeschuhs 19. Kampf mit dem Berge 21. Der Heilige Berg 25. Der Grosse Sprung 27. The White Hell of Pitz Palu (co-d) 29. Storm over Mont Blanc 30. Der Weisse Rausch 31. SOS Iceberg 33. Der Ewige Traum 34. Die Tochter des Samurai 37. Ein Robinson 40.

Fanny.
Originally one of Marcel Pagnol's 1932–34 trilogy (the others: *Marius* and *César*) about the Marseilles waterfront, this tale of a girl left pregnant by a sailor was almost unrecognizable in the MGM version *Port of Seven Seas* 38. The film was subsequently turned into a stage musical, and in 1960 Joshua Logan filmed this – but deleted the songs. The stars were Leslie Caron, Maurice Chevalier, and Charles Boyer.

fans
have been with us as long as the star system. One way of describing them is as people who adore an actor whatever he's doing and whether he's good or not. Another definition is: 'People who tell an actor he's not alone in the way he feels about himself.' Judy Garland once played a fan when she sang 'Dear Mr Gable'; and MGM made a whole movie about them, called *The Youngest Profession*. *The Fan* who pursued Lauren Bacall was quite another matter, a homicidal lunatic; and Eve in *All About Eve* was another fan who didn't do her star any good.

fantasy
has always been a popular form of cinema entertainment because the camera can lie so well, and trick work is most easily used in an unrealistic or fanciful story. The early films of Méliès and his innumerable imitators set a high standard and were still popular when the sombre German classics of the 20s – *The Golem, Nosferatu, Faust, Warning Shadows, The Niebelungen Saga, Metropolis* – awakened filmgoers to the possibilities of the medium for sustaining impossible situations throughout a whole serious feature.

Although Ince's *Civilisation* showed Christ on the battlefields, and the 20s brought such films as *The Four Horsemen of the Apocalypse, The Lost World* and *The Sorrows of Satan*, Hollywood did not fully explore the possibilities of fantasy until sound. Then in quick succession picturegoers were startled by *Outward Bound, Dracula, Frankenstein, Berkeley Square, King Kong* and *The Invisible Man*. *The Scoundrel*, with Noël Coward, was the forerunner of the few serious ghost films: *The Uninvited, The Return of Peter Grimm, Earthbound, The Ghost and Mrs Muir, Portrait of Jennie, The Haunting*, etc. Comic ghosts have, of course, been legion, notably in the *Topper* films, *The Ghost Breakers, I Married a Witch, The Canterville Ghost, The Man in the Trunk, The Remarkable Andrew, Thirteen Ghosts, The Spirit Is Willing, Blackbeard's Ghost, Wonder Man*, and so on. There were even singing ghosts in *Maytime, Bitter Sweet* and *Carousel*. Britain's contributions to the genre were few but choice: *The Ghost Goes West, Blithe Spirit, Things to Come, The Man Who Could Work Miracles, A Matter of Life and Death, Dead of Night*.

In 1936 *Green Pastures* showed the Negro view of heaven, and *On Borrowed Time* three years later paved the way for the heavenly comedies of the 40s: *Here Comes Mr Jordan, That's the Spirit, A Guy Named Joe, Heaven Can Wait, Down to Earth, The Horn Blows at Midnight, You Never Can Tell*, even *Ziegfeld Follies* (in which Ziegfeld's shade wrote in his diary 'Another *heavenly* day . . .'). For many years the last in this vein was *Carousel* 56; but 1968 brought *Barbarella* with its slightly tarnished angel, and *The Adding Machine* had its own perverse view of the hereafter. Meanwhile objects with magical properties were well served in *Alf's Button Afloat, A Thousand and One Nights, The Thief of Baghdad, Turnabout* and *The Picture of Dorian Gray*.

Among the many fairy tales filmed are *The Bluebird, The Wizard of Oz, Alice in Wonderland, The Glass Slipper, Tom Thumb, Mary Poppins* and a selection in *Hans Christian Andersen* and *The Wonderful World of the Brothers Grimm*. Disney's cartoon versions included *Pinocchio, Dumbo, The Sleeping Beauty, Cinderella, Peter Pan*, and, of course, *Snow White and the Seven Dwarfs*, which was cannily adapted for grown-ups by Billy Wilder as *Ball of Fire. Lost Horizon* was a kind of grown-up fairy tale too; and *The Red Shoes* as shown was certainly not for children. Original fairy tales for both categories were *The Luck of the Irish*, with Cecil Kellaway as a leprechaun, and *Miracle on 34th Street*, with Edmund Gwenn as Santa Claus. Modern fairy tales adapted for the screen include: *Chitty Chitty Bang Bang, Mary Poppins, Bedknobs and Broomsticks* and *Willy Wonka and the Chocolate Factory*.

In France during the occupation Marcel Carné made *Les Visiteurs du Soir*, a medieval fantasy with allegorical overtones, and after the war poet Jean Cocteau once again turned his attention to the cinema with such results as *La Belle et la Bête, Love Eternal, Orphée*, and *The Testament of Orphée*. More recently Albert Lamorisse has produced fantasies like *Crin Blanc* and *The Red Balloon*. Japan electrified the world with *Rashomon* and other strange, fanciful, stylized entertainments; Russia contributed many solidly-staged versions of old legends like *Sadko* and *Epic Hero and the Beast (Ilya Muromets)*.

Since 1950, when in Hollywood Dick Powell played an Alsatian dog in *You Never Can Tell* and James Stewart in *Harvey* had a white rabbit six feet high which the script could never quite categorize as fact or hallucination, fantastic elements have been infiltrating into supposedly realistic films to such an extent that it is now difficult to separate them, especially in the films of Fellini, Antonioni, Tony Richardson, Richard Lester and Robert Altman.

See also: *dreams; horror; prophecy; space exploration*.

Fantoni, Sergio (1930–).
Italian leading man in international films.
Esther and the King 60. The Prize 63. Kali-Yug Goddess of Vengeance 63. Von Ryan's Express 65. Do Not Disturb 65. What Did You Do in the War, Daddy? 66. Hornet's Nest 70. Bad Man's River 71. The Belly of an Architect 87, etc.

Fapp, Daniel (1921–).
American cinematographer.
Kitty 45. Golden Earrings 47. Bride of Vengeance 49. Union Station 50. Knock on Wood 54. Living It Up 54. Desire under the Elms 58. One, Two, Three 61. West Side Story (AA) 61. I'll Take Sweden 65. Our Man Flint 66. Lord Love a Duck 66. Sweet November 67. Ice Station Zebra (AAN) 68. Marooned (AAN) 69, many others.

Faragoh, Francis Edward (1898–1992).
American screenwriter, often in collaboration.
Her Private Affair 29. *Little Caesar* (AAN) 31. *Frankenstein* 31. The Last Man 32. Becky Sharp 35. The Return of Peter Grimm 35. The Dancing Pirate 36. My Friend Flicka 43. Renegades 46. Easy Come Easy Go 47, etc.

farce
was once called 'tragedy with its trousers down'. Like melodrama, it presents exaggerated accounts of things that might happen in life. Comedy is more plausible than farce, but farce is often more enjoyable, involving more happenings, more chases, more doors slamming, more misunderstandings and mistaken identities. Good farce must be played with great style, and no lapses are permitted until the curtain comes down. Major exponents in Britain have been the Aldwych team of Tom Walls, Ralph Lynn and Robertson Hare and the Whitehall team headed by Brian Rix. In Hollywood good farce has been more occasional, but one might highlight *Nothing Sacred, To Be or Not to Be, Topper Returns, Love Crazy* and *The Palm Beach Story* (or almost anything else by Preston Sturges, who so delighted in controlled disorder). France gave us Fernandel and Pierre Etaix. The real trouble with farce on film is that it needs an audience: watched cold, it can often seem merely silly, and great stage farces such as Feydeau's *Hotel Paradiso* don't really translate.

Farentino, James (1938–).
American leading man, mostly on TV.
Psychomania 64. Ensign Pulver 64. The War Lord 65. The Pad 66. Banning 67. Rosie 68. Me Natalie 69. The Story of a Woman 70. Jesus of Nazareth (TV) 77. Son-Rise (TV) 79. The Final Countdown 80. Dead and Buried 81. Evita Peron (TV) 81. Licence to Kill 84. Family Sins (TV) 87. Her Alibi 88, etc.
TV series: The Bold Ones 69–71. Cool Million 7 Dynasty 81–82.

Farewell, My Lovely.
Raymond Chandler's thriller of private eye Philip Marlowe searching for the girlfriend of an ex-convict was first filmed as vehicle for George Sanders' suave detective The Falcon (based on a character created by Michael Arlen) in *The Falcon Takes Over* 42. It was more faithfully and successfully remade two years later as *Murder, My Sweet* (aka *Farewell, My Lovely*), starring Dick Powell. In 1975, Dick Richards made another good version with Robert Mitchum in the lead.

A Farewell to Arms.
Hemingway's tough-romantic anti-war novel has been filmed twice: in 1933 by Frank Borzage, with Gary Cooper and Helen Hayes, and in 1958 by Charles Vidor, with Rock Hudson and Jennifer Jones. Neither version was a triumph artistically, but the first proved more popular than the second, which was badly inflated by David O. Selznick in a pseudo-epic.

Fargas, Antonio (1943–).
Puerto Rican actor who became popular as Huggy Bear in TV's *Starsky and Hutch*.
Putney Swope 69. Shaft 71. Cleopatra Jones 7 The Gambler 74. Car Wash 76. Next Stop Greenwich Village 76. Pretty Baby 78. The Ambush Murders (TV) 82. Florida Straits (TV) 8 I'm Gonna Git You, Sucka 88. Night of the Shark 89. The Borrower 89, etc.

Fargo, James (1938–).
American director.
The Enforcer 86. Every Which Way But Loose 78. Caravans 79. Game for Vultures (UK) 80. Forced Vengeance 82. Voyage of the Rock Aliens (aka When the Rain Begins to Fall) 84. Born to Race 88. Riding the Edge 89, etc.

arina, Dennis (1944–).
American character actor, a former detective who
spent 18 years in the Chicago police.
    Thief 81. Code of Silence 85. Manhunter (aka
Red Dragon) 86. Midnight Run 88. The Hillside
Strangler (TV) 89. Men of Respect 91. Street
Crimes 92. Another Stakeout 93. Striking Distance
3, etc.
    TV series: Crime Story 86–88.

armer, Frances (1914–1970).
American leading lady of the 30s who trained in
New York's Group Theatre, found Hollywood
distasteful and retired prematurely through ill-
health and family pressures.
    In 1972 a posthumous autobiography, *Will There
'ver Be a Morning*, was published. This was also the
title of a TV movie in 1983, in which she was
portrayed by Susan Blakely. In the same year
Jessica Lange played her in a theatrical film,
Frances.
    Too Many Parents 36. Border flight 36. Rhythm
on the Range 36. *Come and Get It* 36. The Toast of
New York 37. Exclusive 37. Ebb Tide 37. Ride a
Crooked Mile 38. South of Pago Pago 40. Flowing
Gold 40. World Première 41. Badlands of Dakota
-1. Among the Living 41. Son of Fury 42. The
arty Crashers 58.

The nicest thing I can say about Frances Farmer
is that she is unbearable. – *William Wyler*
Cinderella goes back to the ashes on a liquor-
licked highway. – *Louella Parsons*

armer, Mimsy (1945–).
American leading lady of the 60s.
    Spencer's Mountain 63. Bus Riley's Back in
own 65. Hot Roads to Hell 67. The Devil's Angels
-7. Move 69. Road to Salina 69. Four Flies on Gray
Velvet 71. La Legion saute sur Kolwesi 80.

arnon, Robert (1917–).
Canadian composer.
    Spring in Park Lane 48. Captain Horatio
Hornblower 51. Gentlemen Marry Brunettes 55. All
or Mary 56. The Little Hut 57. Road to Hong Kong
2. The Truth About Spring 65. Shalako 68. Bear
sland 79, etc.

arnsworth, Richard (1919–).
American character actor, a former stuntman.
    The Duchess and the Dirtwater Fox 76. Comes
a Horseman (AAN) 78. Tom Horn 80. Resurrection
0. *The Grey Fox* 82. Waltz Across Texas 83. The
Natural 84. Rhinestone 84. Sylvester 85. Space Rage
7. Havana 90. The Two Jakes 90. Misery 91.
Highway to Hell 92. The Fire Next Time (TV) 93.
The Getaway 94. Lassie 94, etc.

arnum, Dustin (1870–1929).
American cowboy star of silent days. Brother of
William Farnum.
    The Squaw Man 13. The Virginian 14. The
Scarlet Pimpernel 17. The Corsican Brothers 19.
Flaming Frontier 26, etc.

arnum, Franklyn (1876–1961).
American leading man of the silent screen,
especially westerns; appeared in more than a
thousand films.

arnum, William (1876–1953).
American leading man of the silent screen.
    The Spoilers 14. Les Misérables 17. The Lone Star
Ranger 19. If I Were King 20. A Stage Romance
2. The Man Who Fights Alone 24. The Painted
Desert 31. Supernatural 33. The Crusades 35. The

Spoilers 42. Captain Kidd 45. Samson and Delilah
49. Jack and the Beanstalk 52, many others.

Farr, Derek (1912–1986).
British leading man of stage and screen, married
to Muriel Pavlow; former schoolmaster.
    The Outsider 40. Spellbound 40. Quiet Wedding
40. Quiet Weekend 46. Wanted for Murder 46.
Teheran 47. Bond Street 48. Noose 48. Silent Dust
49. Man on the Run 49. Young Wives' Tale 51.
Reluctant Heroes 52. The Dam Busters 55. Town
on Trial 56. Doctor at Large 57. The Truth About
Women 58. Attempt to Kill 61. The Projected Man
66. Thirty is a Dangerous Age Cynthia 68, etc.

Farr, Felicia (1932–).
American leading lady. She married actor Jack
Lemmon in 1962.
    Timetable 56. Jubal 56. 3.10 to Yuma 57. The
Last Wagon 57. Hell Bent for Leather 60. Kiss Me
Stupid 64. The Venetian Affair 67. Charley Varrick
73, etc.

Farr, Jamie (1936–) (Jamiel Farah).
Long-nosed American character actor who
reached his greatest comic heights in TV's *M*A*S*H*
and *Aftermash*.
    Ride Beyond Vengeance 65. Who's Minding the
Mint? 67. With Six You Get Egg Roll 68. The Blue
Knight (TV) 73. The Cannonball Run 81.
Cannonball Run II 84. Happy Hour 87. Curse II:
The Bite 88. Scrooged 88. Speed Zone! 89, etc.

Farrar, David (1908–).
Tall, virile-looking British leading man whose
career faltered when he went to Hollywood and
played villains.
    Autobiography: 1948, *No Royal Road*.
    Return of a Stranger 38. The Sheepdog of the
Hills 41. Suspected Person 41. Danny Boy 42. The
Night Invader 42. The Dark Tower 43. They Met
in the Dark 44. The World Owes Me a Living 44.
Meet Sexton Blake (title role) 44. The Echo
Murders 45. The Lisbon Story 46. The Trojan
Brothers 46. *Black Narcissus* 46. Frieda 47. *Mr Perrin
and Mr Traill* 48. *The Small Back Room* 48. Diamond
City 49. Night Without Stars 51. The Golden Horde
(US) 51. Gone to Earth 52. Duel in the Jungle
54. The Black Shield of Falworth (US) 54. Lilacs
in the Spring 55. The Sea Chase (US) 55. Lost 56.
I Accuse 57. Solomon and Sheba (US) 59. John
Paul Jones (US) 59. Beat Girl 60. The 300 Spartans
62, etc.

Farrar, Geraldine (1882–1967).
American operatic star who, unexpectedly,
appeared for Samuel Goldwyn as heroine of silent
films.
    Carmen 15. Maria Rosa 16. The Devil Stone 17.
Joan the Woman 17. Flame of the Desert 19. The
Riddle Woman 20, etc.

Farrell, Charles (1901–1990).
Gentle-mannered American leading man of the
20s; formed a well-liked romantic team with Janet
Gaynor. Retired in middle age to become Mayor
of Palm Springs.
    The Ten Commandments 23. Wings of Youth
25. Old Ironsides 26. *Seventh Heaven* 27. Street Angel
28. Lucky Star 29. Sunny Side Up 29. High Society
Blues 30. Liliom 30. Merely Mary Ann 31. Tess
of the Storm Country 32. Aggie Appleby, Maker
of Men 33. Change of Heart 34. Fighting Youth
35. Moonlight Sonata (GB) 37. Tailspin 39. The
Deadly Game 42, etc.
    TV series: My Little Margie 52–54. The Charlie
Farrell Show 56, 60.

Farrell, Charles (1901–1988).
Irish character actor who played bit parts in British
films from childhood.
    Creeping Shadows 31. Meet Mr Penny 38. Meet
Sexton Blake 44. Night and the City 50. The Sheriff
of Fractured Jaw 58. Oh! What a Lovely War 69.
The Abominable Dr Phibes 71, etc.

Farrell, Glenda (1904–1971).
American leading lady and comedienne of the 30s,
often seen as wisecracking reporter; made a
comeback in the 50s as character actress.
    Little Caesar (debut) 30. Three on a Match 31.
I Am a Fugitive from a Chain Gang 32. *The Mystery
of the Wax Museum* 32. Hi Nellie 33. Gold Diggers
of 1935 35. In Caliente 36. *Torchy Blane in
Chinatown* (and ensuing series) 39. Johnny Eager
41. A Night for Crime 42. Heading for Heaven 47.
I Love Trouble 48. Apache War Smoke 52. Girls
in the Night 52. Susan Slept Here 54. The Girl in
the Red Velvet Swing 55. The Middle of the Night
59. Kissing Cousins 64. The Disorderly Orderly 64.
Tiger by the Tail 68, many others.

Farrell, James T. (1904–1979).
Irish-American novelist best known for his twice-
filmed Studs Lonigan trilogy.

Farrell, Sharon (1946–).
American general-purpose actress.
    Kiss Her Goodbye 59. Forty Pounds of Trouble
63. A Lovely Way to Die 68. Marlowe 69. The
Reivers 69. Quarantined (TV) 70. The Love
Machine 71. The Eyes of Charles Sand (TV) 72.
It's Alive 76. The Last Ride of the Dalton Gang
(TV) 79. The Stunt Man 80. One Man Force 89,
etc.

Farrow, John (1904–1963).
Stylish Australian director, former research
scientist; in Hollywood from the mid-30s. Also
wrote many of his own scripts.
    Men in Exile 37. West of Shanghai 37. She
Loved a Fireman 38. Little Miss Thoroughbred 38.
My Bill 38. Broadway Musketeers 38. Women in
the Wind 39. The Saint Strikes Back 39. Sorority
House 39. *Five Came Back* 39. Full Confession 39.
Reno 39. Married and in Love 40. A Bill of
Divorcement 40. Wake Island 42. The Commandos
Strike at Dawn (& w) 43. China 43. *The Hitler
Gang* (& w) 44. You Came Along 45. Two Years
Before the Mast (& w) 46. California 46. Easy Come
Easy Go 47. Blaze of Noon 47. Calcutta 47. *The Big
Clock* 48. Night Has a Thousand Eyes 48. Beyond
Glory 48. *Alias Nick Beal* 49. Red Hot and Blue 49.
Where Danger Lives 50. Copper Canyon 50. *His
Kind of Woman* (& w) 51. Submarine Command
51. Ride Vaquero 53. *Plunder of the Sun* 53. Botany
Bay 53. Hondo 54. A Bullet is Waiting 54. The Sea
Chase (& w) 55. Back from Eternity 56. Around
the World in Eighty Days (co-w) (AA) 56. The
Unholy Wife 57. John Paul Jones (& w) 59.

Farrow, Mia (1945–) (Maria Farrow).
American leading lady, daughter of John Farrow
and Maureen O'Sullivan. She married Frank
Sinatra (1966–68) and André Previn (1970–79)
and has a son by Woody Allen.
    Biography: 1990, *Mia Farrow* by Sam Rubin and
Richard Taylor.
    Guns at Batasi 64. A Dandy in Aspic 67.
Rosemary's Baby 68. Secret Ceremony 68. John
and Mary 69. See No Evil 71. Follow Me 72.
Goodbye Raggedy Ann (TV) 72. Scoundrel in White
72. The Great Gatsby 73. Full Circle 77. *Death on
the Nile* 78. A Wedding 78. Avalanche 78. The
Hurricane 79. A Midsummer Night's Sex Comedy
82. Zelig 83. Broadway Danny Rose 84. Supergirl

84. The Purple Rose of Cairo 85. Hannah and Her Sisters 86. Radio Days 87. September 87. Another Woman 88. Crimes and Misdemeanors 89. New York Stories 89. Alice 90. Shadows and Fog 92. Widows' Peak 94.

TV series: Peyton Place 64–67.

¶ If I seem to be running, it's because I'm pursued. – *M.F.*

Fasano, John.
American director of low-budget features and writer of big-budget action movies.

Black Roses (d) 88. The Jitters (d) 89. Another 48 Hrs (co-w) 90, etc.

fashions
were the basis of many a woman's film of the 30s: *Roberta, Fashions of 1934, Vogues of 1938.* Later attempts to recapture this interest had an air of *déjà vu: Maytime in Mayfair, It Started in Paradise, Lucy Gallant, Designing Woman.* But the wheel turns, and the 70s brought *Mahogany* and the 80s *Chanel Solitaire.*

Fassbinder, Rainer Werner (1946–1982).
Fashionable German director of the 70s, usually with something despairing to say about the current state of society.

Biography: 1987, *Love Is Colder than Death* by Robert Katz and Peter Berling.

Gods of the Plague 69. Katzelmacher 69. The Pedlar of Four Seasons 71. The Bitter Tears of Petra Von Kant 72. Wild Game 73. Martha 73. Effi Briest 74. Fear Eats the Soul 74. Fox 75. Fear 75. Mother Kusters Goes to Heaven 75. Tenderness of the Wolves 75. Chinese Roulette 76. Satan's Brew 76. Despair 77. The Marriage of Maria Braun 78. In a Year with 13 Moons 78. Berlin Alexanderplatz 79, etc.

¶ I hope to build a house with my films. Some of them are the cellar, some are the walls, and some are the windows. But I hope in time there will be a house. – *R.W.F.*

He was a genius. And geniuses are notoriously loony, because it's a very fine line between madness and genius. – *Dirk Bogarde*

Fast, Howard (1914–).
American historical novelist, Works filmed include *Freedom Road, The Last Frontier, Spartacus, The Immigrants.*

fast motion:
see *accelerated motion.*

fastest money-making movies:
Jurassic Park holds the record, taking more than $100m at the American box-office in nine days in 1993. In 1989, *Batman* took 10 days to reach that mark, while *Batman Returns* took 11 days in 1992.

Father Brown.
The only British attempt to film the adventures of G. K. Chesterton's tubby detective in 1958 was a civilized comedy with all concerned on the same wavelength. A quietly witty script by Thelma Schnee, polished direction by Robert Hamer, and high-comedy acting by Alec Guinness, Peter Finch, Joan Greenwood, and Ernest Thesiger made it a film with a rare flavour. On television, Kenneth More played the role in a 1974 series. In 1934 Walter Connolly played the role in a Hollywood second feature, *Father Brown Detective.* In West Germany, Heinz Ruhmann played the role in two 60s films, and Josef Meinrad in a 1969 TV

series. In 1980 Barnard Hughes played the priest on TV in *The Girl in the Park.*

Faulds, Andrew (1923–).
British character actor and MP.

The Card 52. The One That Got Away 56. Payroll 61. Jason and the Argonauts 64. The Prince and the Pauper 65. The Devils 70. The Music Lovers 71. Mahler 74. Lisztomania 76, etc.

Faulkner, W. G. (1864–*).
English journalist, a former teacher, with claims to being the first regular newspaper film critic in Britain. He reviewed films for the London *Evening News* from 1910–21.

Faulkner, William (1897–1962).
Distinguished American novelist. Works filmed include *Sanctuary, Intruder in the Dust, The Sound and the Fury.* Also collaborated on screenplays:

Road to Glory 36. To Have and Have Not 44. The Big Sleep 46. Land of the Pharaohs 55, etc.

¶ It's not Hollywood's fault. The writer is not accustomed to money. It goes to his head and destroys him. – *W.F.*

Faust, Johann (1488–1541).
These at least are the approximate dates of a German conjurer, the scanty details of whose wandering life were the basis of plays by Marlowe (1593) and later Goethe (1808) which turned into classics. The theme of the man who sells his soul to the Devil in exchange for a rich full life has been seen in innumerable film versions, including many musical ones based on Gounod's opera, and a puppet one from Czechoslovakia. The first straight version was made in France in 1905; the most famous silent version is Murnau's of 1926, with Emil Jannings and Gosta Ekman. 1941 brought Dieterle's *All That Money Can Buy,* from Stephen Vincent Benet's *The Devil and Daniel Webster;* René Clair's version, *La Beauté du Diable,* followed in 1949, *Alias Nick Beal* in the same year, Autant-Lara's *Marguerite de la Nuit* in 1955, *Damn Yankees* in 1958 and Richard Burton's *Dr Faustus* in 1967. There were modernized versions in France 63, USA 64 and Rumania 66, and a Spanish version of 1957, *Faustina,* in which the hero becomes a heroine. The latest variations on the theme are *Bedazzled* 67, a comic extravaganza with Peter Cook as the tempter and Dudley Moore as the tempted and *Hammersmith Is Out* 72 with Richard Burton and Peter Ustinov.

Favio, Leonardo (1938–).
Argentinian director, a former actor, singer and circus performer. Born in Mendoza, he began in films in 1958 and became a leading actor in the films of Leopoldo Torre-Nilsson, who encouraged him to start directing. His career was interrupted from 1976–83 when the military government prevented him from working.

El Ángel de España (a) 58. El Secuestrador (a) 58. Fin de Fiesta (a) 60. La Terraza (a) 63. Crónica de un Niño Solo 65. El Dependiente 69. Juan Moreira 73. Nazareno Cruz y El Lobo 75. Soñar, Soñar 76, etc.

Fawcett, Farrah (1947–) (formerly Farrah Fawcett-Majors).
American pin-up who enjoyed brief success as one of the original 1976 *Charlie's Angels.*
■ A Man I Like 67. Myra Breckinridge 70. The Feminist and the Fuzz (TV) 71. The Great American Beauty Contest (TV) 73. Murder on Flight 502 (TV) 75. Logan's Run 76. Somebody Killed Her Husband 78. Sunburn 78. Strictly

Business 79. The Helper 79. Saturn Three 79. The Cannonball Run 80. Extremities 86. Unfinished Business (TV) 86. Between Two Women (TV) 86. Nazi Hunter: The Beata Klarsfeld Story 86. Poor Little Rich Girl (TV) 87. See You in the Morning 88. Margaret Bourke-White (TV) 88. Small Sacrifices (TV) 89. The Substitute Wife (TV) 94.

TV series: Good Sports 91.

¶ Marriages that last are with people who do not live in Los Angeles. – *F.F.*

I was always serious. But nobody would take me seriously. – *F.F.*

She is uniquely suited to play a woman of limited intelligence. – *Harry and Michael Medved*

Fay, Frank (1894–1961).
American light actor and vaudeville star who made a few undistinguished films. He was married to Barbara Stanwyck.

Show of Shows 29. God's Gift to Women 31. Stars over Broadway 35. They Knew What They Wanted 40. Spotlight Scandals 43. Love Nest 51, etc.

¶ The 32 model lover – built for speed, style and endurance. – *Warner's publicity*

Faye, Alice (1912–) (Ann Leppert).
American leading lady of the 30s and 40s, once a singer with Rudy Vallee's band. Her wry expression tended to limit her roles, but she was a key star of her time and commanded a loyal following.
■ George White's Scandals 34. Now I'll Tell 34. She Learned about Sailors 34. 365 Nights in Hollywood 34. George White's 1935 Scandals 35. Every Night at Eight 35. Music Is Magic 35. King of Burlesque 36. Poor Little Rich Girl 36. Sing Baby Sing 36. Stowaway 36. On the Avenue 37. Wake Up and Live 37. You Can't Have Everything 37. You're a Sweetheart 37. Sally Irene and Mary 38. *In Old Chicago* 38. *Alexander's Ragtime Band* 38. Tailspin 39. *Rose of Washington Square* 39. *Hollywood Cavalcade* 39. Barricade 39. Little Old New York 40. *Lillian Russell* 40. Tin Pan Alley 40. That Night in Rio 41. The Great American Broadcast 41. Weekend in Havana 41. *Hello Frisco Hello* 43. The Gang's All Here 43. Fallen Angel 45. State Fair 62. The Magic of Lassie 78.

Faye, Julia (1896–1966).
American actress. A former Max Sennett Bathing Beauty, she played important roles in De Mille's early pictures.

As in Days of Old 15. The Squaw Man 18. Male and Female 19. The Ten Commandments 23. The King of Kings 29. The Squaw Man 31. Only Yesterday 33. Union Pacific 39. North West Mounted Police 40. Reap the Wild Wind 42. Samson and Delilah 49. The Greatest Show on Earth 52. The Ten Commandments 56. The Buccaneer 58, etc.

Faylen, Frank (1907–1985) (Frank Ruf).
American character actor with stage experience. Played scores of bartenders, gangsters, sheriffs, cops, etc., from 1936.

Bullets or Ballots 36. The Grapes of Wrath 40. Top Sergeant Mulligan 42. *The Lost Weekend* (his best role, as the male nurse) 45. Blue Skies 46. Road to Rio 47. Detective Story 51. Riot in Cell Block Eleven 54. Killer Dino 58. The Monkey's Uncle 65. Funny Girl 68, many others.

TV series: Dobie Gillis 59–62.

Fazan, Adrienne.
American editor.

The Bride Wore Red 37. Barbary Coast Gent 44.

e Kissing Bandit 48. *An American in Paris* 51.
gin' in the Rain 52. Deep in My Heart 54.
itation to the Dance 56. *Gigi* (AA) 58. The
zebo 59. Two Weeks in Another Town 62. This
perty is Condemned 66. The Comic 69, many
ers.

zenda, Louise (1895–1962).
erican leading lady of the Mack Sennett era:
hing beauty, slapstick comedienne, later a
aracter actress.
he Beautiful and Damned 22. Main Street 23.
eaper to Marry 25. Bobbed Hair 25. The Bat
The Red Mill 27. The Terror 28. Riley the Cop
Noah's Ark 29. The Desert Song 29. No No
nette 30. Leathernecking 30. Cuban Love Song
Alice in Wonderland 33. Wonder Bar 34.
leen 36. The Road Back 37. Swing Your Lady
The Old Maid 39, many others.

I.
e US governmental crime-fighting agency was
up in 1924 by J. Edgar Hoover and became
nous for its heroic stand against the public
mies of the 30s, when its agents became known
G-Men. Surface glamour concealed an
mensely painstaking organization relying
avily on science, but only the glamour was
wn in such films as *Show 'Em No Mercy, G-Men,*
sons in Hiding, Let 'Em Have It, The FBI Story, FBI
l, Parole Fixer, Confessions of a Nazi Spy, FBI Code
Walk East on Beacon and *Queen of the Mob. The*
use on 92nd Street in 1945 gave the best impression
the FBI at work, but its sequel *The Street with No*
me reverted to stereotype, which was maintained
Quinn Martin's nine-year TV series. In 1978,
e *Private Files of J. Edgar Hoover* provided a rather
erficial exposé.

aring, Kenneth (1902–1961).
nerican novelist of urban cynicism: *The Big Clock*
his chief contribution to the screen.

ature film.
rmally accepted to mean a (fictional)
tertainment film of more than 3000 feet in
gth (approx. 34 minutes). Anything less than
s is technically a 'short'. *NB:* In journalism and
evision a 'feature' usually means a *non*-fiction
icle or documentary.

atured players.
ose next in importance to the stars: usually
led after the title.

deration of Film Societies.
itish organization which issues information and
anges screening for film societies; also
blishes magazine *Film*.

gté, Ernst (1900–1976).
rman production designer, in Hollywood from
early 30s.
The General Died at Dawn 36. The Palm Beach
ory 42. I Married a Witch 42. Five Graves to Cairo
. Frenchman's Creek (AA) 44. Concerto 47.
gel and the Badman 47, etc.

hmiu, Bekim (1932–).
alwart Slav leading man in international films.
The Happy Gypsies 66. *The Adventurers* 70. The
serter 71. Permission to Kill 75. Black Sunday
. Madam Kitty 77, etc.

hr, Rudi (1911–).
rman-American editor.
Invisible Enemies (GB) 35. Honeymoon for
ree 41. Desperate Journey 42. Watch on the

Rhine 43. The Conspirators 44. Humoresque 46.
Possessed 47. Key Largo 48. The Inspector
General 49. House of Wax 53. Dial M for Murder
54, many others.

Feiffer, Jules (1929–).
American satirical strip cartoonist, venturing into
screenwriting.
Little Murders 71. Carnal Knowledge 71. Popeye
80. I Want to Go Home 89, etc.

Feist, Felix E. (1906–1965).
American director, at first of short subjects
including Pete Smith Specialities; in Hollywood
from 1928.
■ Stepping Sisters 32. The Deluge 33. All By
Myself 43. You're a Lucky Fellow Mr Smith 43.
This is the Life 44. Pardon My Rhythm 44. Reckless
Age 44. George White's Scandals 45. The Devil
Thumbs a Ride (& w) 47. The Winner's Circle 47.
The Threat 49. Treason 49. The Golden Gloves
Story 50. The Man Who Cheated Himself 50.
Tomorrow is Another Day 51. The Basketball Fix
51. This Woman is Dangerous 52. The Big Trees
52. The Man Behind the Gun 52. Donovan's
Brain 53. Pirates of Tripoli 55.

Fejos, Paul (1893–1963).
Hungarian director, in America from 1923.
The Last Moment 27. Lonesome 28. Erik the
Great 29. Broadway 29. The Big House (co-d) 30.
Maria (Hung.) 32. The Golden Smile (Dan.) 35. A
Handful of Rice (Swedish) 38.

Feld, Fritz (1900–1993).
Dapper German character comedian, once stage
director for Max Reinhardt; long in Hollywood
playing temperamental head waiters and clerks in
more than 400 films.
Broadway 29. I Met Him in Paris 37. Bringing
Up Baby 38. Idiot's Delight 39. *At the Circus* (as
Jardinet) 39. Sandy is a Lady 40. *World Première*
41. Iceland 42. Phantom of the Opera 43. The Great
John L 45. Catman of Paris 46. The Secret Life of
Walter Mitty 47. My Girl Tisa 48. Mexican
Hayride 49. The Jackpot 50. Full House 52. The
Patsy 64. Barefoot in the Park 67. Hello Dolly 69.
The Love Bug Rides Again 73. Silent Movie 76.
The World's Greatest Lover 77. History of the
World Part One 81, many others.

Feldman, Andrea (1948–1972).
American actress in Andy Warhol's films. She
committed suicide, leaving a note that read, 'I am
going for the big time. Heaven.'
The Imitation of Christ 67. Trash 69. Heat 70.

Feldman, Charles K. (1904–1968) (Charles
Gould).
American producer, former lawyer and talent
agent.
Pittsburgh 42. Follow the Boys 44. To Have and
Have Not 44. The Big Sleep 46. Red River 48. The
Red Pony 49. A Streetcar Named Desire 51. The
Seven Year Itch 54. A Walk on the Wild Side 62.
The Seventh Dawn 64. What's New Pussycat? 65.
The Group 66. Casino Royale 67, etc.

Feldman, Corey (1971–).
American juvenile actor, performing in
commercials from the age of three.
Time after Time 79. Friday the 13th – the Final
Chapter 84. Gremlins 84. Friday the 13th Part V: A
New Beginning 85. The Goonies 85. Stand by Me
86. The Lost Boys 87. License to Drive 88. The
'burbs 89. Dream a Little Dream 89. Teenage
Mutant Ninja Turtles 90. Edge of Honor 91.
Meatballs IV 92. Round Trip to Heaven 92. Blown

Away 93. Lipstick Camera 94. National
Lampoon's Last Resort 94, etc.
TV series: The Bad News Bears 79–80.
Madame's Place 82.

Feldman, Marty (1933–1983).
Pop-eyed British TV comic who from writing TV
comedy scripts became a limited but well-known
international star in his own right.
Every Home Should Have One 69. Young
Frankenstein 73. The Adventures of Sherlock
Holmes' Smarter Brother 75. Silent Movie 76. The
Last Remake of Beau Geste 77. High Anxiety 78.
Sex with a Smile 79. In God We Trust 80.
Yellowbeard 83, etc.

Feldon, Barbara (1939–).
American leading lady of the 70s who came to
notice on TV.
Fitzwilly 67. Playmates (TV) 72. Smile 74. Let's
Switch (TV) 75. No Deposit No Return 76. A
Vacation in Hell (TV) 79. Get Smart: The Movie
(TV) 89, etc.
TV series: *Get Smart* 65–69.

Feldshuh, Tovah (1952–).
American leading lady who came to the fore in
Holocaust (TV) 78 but then failed to justify her
promise.
Scream Pretty Peggy (TV) 73. The Amazing
Howard Hughes (TV) 77. Terror out of the Sky
(TV) 78. The Triangle Factory Fire Scandal (TV)
79. Cheaper to Keep Her 80. The Women's Room
(TV) 80. The Idolmaker 80. Daniel 83. Brewster's
Millions 85. The Blue Iguana 88. A Day in October
(En Dag Oktober) 91, etc.

Felix (the Cat).
Cartoon creation of Pat Sullivan, a perky and
indestructible character highly popular in the 20s;
in the 50s revived for TV by other hands in more
streamlined style. An unsuccessful full-length
feature, directed by Tibor Hernadi, was released in
89.

Felix, Maria (1915–).
Mexican actress of strong personality.
The Kneeling Goddess 47. Dona Diabla 49. Mare
Nostrum 50. Messalina 52. The Kidnapping 52.
French Can Can 53. Les Héros Sont Fatigués 55,
many Mexican films.

Felix, Seymour (1892–1961).
American dance director, in films since 1929.
The Great Ziegfeld (AA) 36. Alexander's
Ragtime Band 38. Cover Girl 44. The I Don't Care
Girl 52, many others.

Fell, Norman (1924–).
Sad-looking American character actor.
Ocean's Eleven 61. Pork Chop Hill 59. Bullitt 68.
If It's Tuesday This Must Be Belgium 69. The Stone
Killer 73. Guardian of the Wilderness 76. On the
Right Track 81. Paternity 81. Transylvania 6–500
85. Stripped to Kill 87, etc.
TV series: 87th Precinct 61–64. The Man from
UNCLE 68. Dan August 71. Needles and Pins 74.
Three's Company 77–78. The Ropers 79–80, etc.

Fellini, Federico (1920–1993).
Fashionable and influential Italian director,
formerly cartoonist. Film actor and writer from
1941. He was married to actress Giulietta Masina.
Awarded an honorary Oscar for lifetime
achievement in 1993.
Biographies: 1977, *Fellini the Artist* by Edward
Murray. 1986, *Fellini: A Life* by Hollis Alpert. 1992,

The Cinema of Federico Fellini by Peter Bondanella. 1993, *Fellini* by John Baxter.

■ AS DIRECTOR: Lights of Variety 50. The White Sheik 50. I Vitelloni 53. *La Strada* (AA, AANw) 54. Il Bidone 55. Notti di Cabiria (AA) 57. *La Dolce Vita* (AAN) 59. Boccaccio 70 (part) 62. *Eight and a Half* (AAN) 63. Juliet of the Spirits 65. Histoires Extraordinaires (part) 68. *Satyricon* (AAN) 69. The Clowns 70. Fellini Roma 72. Amarcord (AAN) 74. Casanova 77. City of Women 81. And the Ship Sails On 83. *Ginger and Fred* 85. Federico Fellini's Intervista 87. Voices of the Moon (La Voce della Luna) 90.

¶ I always direct the same film. I can't distinguish one from another. – *F.F.*

Our dreams are our real life. – *F.F.*

Although my father wanted me to become an engineer and my mother a bishop, I myself am quite content to have succeeded in becoming an adjective. – *F.F.*

Fellowes, Rockliffe (1885–1950).
Canadian general-purpose actor in Hollywood films of silent days.

The Easiest Way 17. In Search of a Sinner 20. The Spoilers 23. The Garden of Weeds 24. East of Suez 25. Syncopating Sue 26. The Taxi Dancer 27. The Third Degree 27. The Charlatan 29. Outside the Law 30. Monkey Business 31. Lawyer Man 32. The Phantom Broadcast 33. The Black Page 34, many others.

Fellows, Edith (1923–).
American teenage star of the 30s.

Riders of Death Valley 32. Jane Eyre 34. Pennies from Heaven 36. Five Little Peppers 38. Five Little Peppers in Trouble 41. Girls' Town 42. Her First Romance 47, etc.

Fellows, Robert (1903–1969).
American producer.

Virginia City 39. They Died with Their Boots On 41. The Spanish Main 45. A Yankee in King Arthur's Court 49. Hondo 54. The High and the Mighty 54, etc.

Felmy, Hansjoerg (1931–).
German leading man.

Der Stem von Afrika (debut) 56. Wir Wunderkinder 58. Buddenbrooks 59. Station Six Sahara 63. Torn Curtain 66.

Felton, Felix (1912–1972).
English character actor, from radio.

Lady Godiva Rides Again 51. The Pickwick Papers 52. Doctor in the House 54. Doctor at Sea 55. Around the World in Eighty Days 56. Pacific Destiny 56. Just My Luck 57. The Two Faces of Dr Jekyll 60. Licensed to Kill 65. Chitty Chitty Bang Bang 68, etc.

Felton, Verna (1890–1966).
American character actress, often seen as neighbour or busybody.

The Gunfighter 50. New Mexico 52. Picnic 55. Little Egypt 55. The Oklahoman 57, etc.

TV series: December Bride 54–59. Pete and Gladys 60.

female impersonation:
see *transvestism*.

Fenn, Sherilyn (1964–).
American leading actress.

Out of Control 85. Just One of the Guys 85. Thrashin' 86. The Wraith 86. Zombie High 87. Two Moon Junction 88. Crime Zone 88. True Blood 89.

Wild at Heart 90. Meridian (Kiss of the Beast) 90. Backstreet Dreams 90. Of Mice and Men 92. Ruby 92. Diary of a Hit Man 92. Desire and Hell at Sunset Motel 92. Boxing Helena 93. Three of Hearts 93. Fatal Instinct 93, etc.

TV series: Twin Peaks 90.

Fennell, Albert (1920–1988).
British producer best known for TV's *The Avengers* and *The Professionals*.

The Green Scarf 54. Next to No Time 57. Tunes of Glory 59. The Innocents 61. Night of the Eagle 62. And Soon the Darkness 71. Dr Jekyll and Sister Hyde 71. The Legend of Hell House 73, etc.

Fenton, Frank (1906–1957) (Frank Fenton-Morgan).
American general-purpose supporting actor.

Lady of Burlesque 42. Buffalo Bill 44. Magic Town 46. Red River 48. Island in the Sky 53. Emergency Hospital 56. Hellbound 58, many others.

Fenton, George (c. 1952–).
British composer, from TV.

Hitting Town (TV) 76. Gandhi (AAN) 82. Company of Wolves 84. 84 Charing Cross Road 87. Cry Freedom (AAN) 87. High Spirits 88. The Dressmaker 88. White Mischief 87. Dangerous Liaisons (AAN) 88. We're No Angels 89. Memphis Belle 90. White Palace 90. The Fisher King 91. Final Analysis 92. Hero (GB: Accidental Hero) 92. Groundhog Day 93. Born Yesterday 93. Shadowlands 93. China Moon 94. Interview with a Vampire 95, etc.

Fenton, Leslie (1902–1978).
British-born director of Hollywood 'B' pictures. (Former actor in many silent films and early talkies including *What Price Glory?*, *The Man I Love*, *Broadway*, *Public Enemy*, *F.P.I.* etc.)

■ *Tell No Tales* 39. Stronger than Desire 39. The Man from Dakota 40. The Golden Fleecing 40. The Saint's Vacation 41. Tomorrow the World 46. Pardon my Past 46. On Our Merry Way (co-d) 48. Saigon 48. Lulu Belle 48. Whispering Smith 48. Streets of Laredo 49. The Redhead and the Cowboy 50.

Feore, Colm.
Canadian leading actor.

Blades of Courage (TV) 88. Personals (TV) 90. Beautiful Dreamers 90. *Thirty-Two Short Films about Glenn Gould* 93, etc.

Ferber, Edna (1887–1968).
American novelist, some of whose works were filmed.

Biography: 1978, *Ferber* by Julia Goldsmith Gilbert.

Our Mrs McChesney 18. Mother Knows Best 28. Showboat 29, 35 and 51. The Royal Family of Broadway 31. Cimarron 31 and 61. So Big 32 and 53. Dinner at Eight 33. Come and Get It 36. Stage Door (with George S. Kaufman) 38. Saratoga Trunk 43. Giant 56. Ice Palace 59.

Ferguson, Elsie (1883–1961).
American leading lady of silent melodramas about the upper classes. Popular 1918–27, then retired.

Barbary Sheep 17. The Lie 18. Song of Songs 18. A Society Exile 19. His House in Order 20. Sacred and Profane Love 21. Outcast 22, etc.

Ferguson, Frank (1899–1978).
Toothy American character actor, often in comic bit parts.

This Gun for Hire 42. The Miracle of the Bells

48. Abbott and Costello Meet Frankenstein 49. Elopement 51. Johnny Guitar 54. Andy Hardy Comes Home 58. Raymie 60, many others.

TV series: My Friend Flicka 56. Peyton Place 6 68.

Ferguson, Larry.
American screenwriter and director.

St Helens 81. Highlander 86. Beverly Hills Co II 87. The Presidio 88. The Hunt for Red Octobe 90. Nails 92. Alien 3 92. Fixing the Shadow (w 92, etc.

Ferman, James (1930–).
British executive, former television director; sin 1975 secretary of the British Board of Film Cens (now renamed the British Board of Film Classification).

¶ The instinctive good taste of the artist usuall prevents him from indulging in unnecessaril explicit detail. But we are faced too rarely with t work of first-class artists. – *J.F.*

Fernandel (1903–1971) (Fernand Contandin).
Rubber-faced French comedian with toothy grin and music-hall background. Films usually 'naugh but nice.'

Regain (Harvest) 37. Un Carnet de Bal 37. *Fri Frac* 39. *La Fille du Puisatier* 40. *The Red Inn* 51. Forbidden Fruit 52. The *Don Camillo* series from 1952. *The Sheep Has Five Legs* 54. Paris Holiday 5 The Cow and I 59. Croesus 60. La Cuisine au Beurre 63. Le Voyage du Père 66. L'Homme a la Buick 67, Heureux qui comme Ulysse 69, etc.

Fernández, Emilio (1904–1986).
Prolific Mexican director, few of whose films ha been seen abroad.

Isle of Passion 41. Maria Candelaria 44. The Pea 45. Rio Escondido 47. Maclovia 48. The Torch 5 Bring Me the Head of Alfredo Garcia (a) 74. Breakout 75. México Norte 77. Erótica 78, etc.

Ferrara, Abel (1952–).
American director of action films and, under the name of Jimmy Laine, occasional actor. He has directed episodes of *Miami Vice* for TV.

The Driller Killer (& a) 79. Ms 45 (& a) 81. Fea City 84. China Girl 87. Cat Chaser 89. King of Ne York 90. Bad Lieutenant 92. Body Snatchers 93. Snake Eyes 93, etc.

Ferrell, Conchata (1943–).
American character actress.

A Death in Canaan (TV) 78. *Heartland* 80. The Girl Called Hatter Fox (TV) 80. The Seduction of Miss Leona (TV) 81. Rape and Marriage (TV) 81 Where the River Runs Black 86. Deadly Intentio . . . Again (TV) 91. Heaven and Earth 93, etc.

TV series: Hot L Baltimore 75. B.J. and the Be 79–80. McClain's Law 81–82. E/R 84–85. A Peaceable Kingdom 89. L.A. Law 92.

Ferréol, Andréa.
French leading actress, in international films.

Blow-Out (La Grande Bouffe) 73. The Day of the Jackal 73. The Tin Drum 79. The Last Metro 8 Three Brothers (Tre Fratelli) 81. The Night of Varennes (La Nuit de Varennes) 82. The Two Liv of Mattia Pascal (Le Due Vite di Mattia Pascal) 8 A Zed and Two Noughts 85. The Sleazy Uncle (L Zio Indegno) 89. Stroke of Midnight (US) 91. A Linha do Horizonte 93. Domenica 94, many othe

Ferrer, José (1912–1992) (José Vicente Ferrer y Centron).
Distinguished American stage actor of Puerto

Rican origin; film career spotty but interesting. His third wife was singer Rosemary Clooney (1953–62). Their son Miguel is an actor.

■ *Joan of Arc* (as the Dauphin) (AAN) 48. Whirlpool 49. Crisis 50. *Cyrano de Bergerac* (AA) 50. Anything Can Happen 52. *Moulin Rouge* (as Toulouse Lautrec) (AAN) 53. Miss Sadie Thompson 53. The Caine Mutiny 54. Deep in My Heart 54. The Shrike (& d) (GB) 56. Cockleshell Heroes (& d) (GB) 56. The Great Man (& wd) 56. I Accuse (& d) 58. The High Cost of Loving (d) 58. Return to Peyton Place (d only) 61. State Fair (d only) 62. Lawrence of Arabia 62. Nine Hours to Rama 63. Stop Train 349 64. Cyrano contre d'Artagnan (Fr.) 64. The Greatest Story Ever Told 65. *Ship of Fools* 65. Enter Laughing 67. Cervantes 67. The Aquarians (TV) 70. Banyon (TV) 71. Cross Current (TV) 71. The Missing Are Deadly (TV) 73. The Marcus Nelson Murders (TV) 73. Order to Kill 75. Medical Story (TV) 75. Roman Grey (TV) 75. E Lollipop 75. The Big Bus 76. Voyage of the Damned 76. The Sentinel 77. Crash 77. The Private Files of J. Edgar Hoover 78. Dracula's Dog 78. The Swarm 78. Natural Enemies 79. The Big Brawl 80. The French Atlantic Affair (TV) 79. Gideon's Trumpet (TV) 80. The Dream Merchants (TV) 80. Bloody Birthday 80. Evita Peron (TV) 81. Blood Feud (TV) 82. A Midsummer Night's Sex Comedy 82. Blood Tide 82. To Be or Not to Be 83. Dune 84. The Evil That Men Do 84. Ingrid (TV) 85. Blood and Orchids (TV) 85.

TV series: Bridges to Cross 85.

Ferrer, Mel (1917–).
Sensitive-looking American leading man, former radio producer and writer.

Girl of the Limberlost (d only) 45. *Lost Boundaries* 49. The Secret Fury (d only) 50. Vendetta (d only) 50. Born to Be Bad 50. The Brave Bulls 51. *Scaramouche* 52. Rancho Notorious 52. Lili 53. Knights of the Round Table (GB) 54. Saadia 54. Oh! Rosalinda (GB) 55. War and Peace 56. The Vintage 57. The Sun Also Rises 57. Fräulein 58. The World, the Flesh and the Devil 59. Green Mansions (d only) 59. Blood and Roses 61. The Fall of the Roman Empire 64. Sex and the Single Girl 64. El Greco 65. Wait until Dark (p only) 67. Every Day's a Holiday (& wd, p) (Sp.) 67. A Time for Loving (& p) 71. Embassy (p only) 72. W (p only) 73. Brannigan 75. Eaten Alive 77. The Norseman 78. The Fifth Floor 80. The Top of the Hill (TV) 80. The Memory of Eva Ryker (TV) 81. Fugitive Family (TV) 81. Lili Marlene 81. Eye of the Widow 91, etc.

TV series: Behind the Screen 81–82. Falcon Crest 81–84.

Ferrer, Miguel (1955–).
American character actor, the son of José Ferrer and Rosemary Clooney.

The Last Horror Film 81.... And They're Off 82. The Evil that Men Do 83. Heartbreaker 83. Star Trek III: The Search for Spock 84. Flashpoint 84. Robocop 87. Deepstar Six 88. The Guardian 90. Broken Badges (TV) 90. Innocent Blood 91. Twin Peaks: Fire Walk with Me 92. The Harvest 92. Scam 93. Point of No Return 93. Hot Shots! Part Deux 93. Another Stakeout 93. Blank Check 94. The Stand (TV) 94, etc.

Ferreri, Marco (1928–).
Italian director.

El Pisto (Sp.) 56. The Wheelchair (Sp.) 60. Queen Bee 63. The Bearded Lady 64. Wedding March 65. *Dillinger Is Dead* 68. Liza 72. *Blowout* 73. The Last Woman 76. The Future Is Woman 84. I Love You 86. Y'a Bon les Blancs 87. House of

Smiles (La Casa del Sorriso) 91. The Flesh (La Carne) 91. Diario di un Vizio 93, etc.

¶ The master of bad taste – *Sunday Times*

Ferrero, Anna Maria (1931–) (Anna Maria Guetra).
Italian leading lady of the 50s, now retired.

The Sky Is Red (Il Cielo è Rosso) 49. Giuseppe Verdi 53. The Golden Falcon (Il Falco d'Oro) 55. War and Peace (US) 56. Bad Girls Don't Cry (La Notte Brava) 59. The Hunchback of Rome (Il Gobbo) 60. Controsesso 64, etc.

Ferretti, Dante (1943–).
Italian production designer, frequently on the films of Pier Paolo Pasolini and Federico Fellini.

Medea 69. The Decameron 71. The Canterbury Tales 72. The Arabian Nights 74. The Night Porter 74. Salo or the 120 Days of Sodom 75. Orchestra Rehearsal (Prova d'Orchestra) 78. City of Women (Città delle Donne) 80. Tales of Ordinary Madness (Storie di Ordinaria Follia) 81. Ginger and Fred 86. The Name of the Rose 86. The Adventures of Baron Munchausen (AAN) 88. The Voice of the Moon (La Voce della Luna) 90. Hamlet (AAN) 90. The Age of Innocence (AAN) 93. Interview with the Vampire 94, many others.

Ferretti, Robert A.
American editor.

Gymkata 85. Out of Control 85. Tango & Cash (co-e) 89. Die Hard 2 (co-e) 91. Out for Justice (co-e) 91. Showdown in Little Tokyo (co-e) 91. Under Siege 92. On Deadly Ground 94, etc.

Ferrigno, Lou (1952–).
Muscular American actor, a former Mr Universe and footballer, who gained fame on TV as the green Incredible Hulk 78–82.

Pumping Iron (doc) 77. Hercules 83. Hercules II 85. Desert Warrior 88. The Cage 88. All's Fair 89. Sinbad of the Seven Seas 89. Liberty & Bash 90. The Making of 'And God Spoke' 94, etc.

Ferris, Barbara (1940–).
British leading lady.

Catch Us If You Can 66. Interlude 68. A Nice Girl Like Me 69. A Chorus of Disapproval 89, etc.

Ferzetti, Gabriele (1925–) (Pasquale Ferzetti).
Italian leading man.

William Tell 48. Cuore Ingrato 51. Three Forbidden Stories 52. Puccini 54. Le Amiche 55. Donatello 56. L'Avventura 59. Torpedo Bay 64. Once Upon a Time in the West 69. On Her Majesty's Secret Service 69. Hitler – The Last Ten Days 73. The Night Porter 74. A Matter of Time 76. End of the Game 76. Julia and Julia 87, etc.

festivals.
Since World War II a great many cities round the world have derived excellent publicity from annual film festivals. Producers, distributors and actors in search of accolades now diligently trek each year to Cannes, Venice, Berlin, Mar del Plata, Cork, Edinburgh, Karlovy Vary, San Sebastian, Moscow, etc., while London and New York offer résumés in October.

Fetchit, Stepin (1892–1985) (Lincoln Perry).
Gangly, slow-moving American comedian, popular in films of the 30s.

In Old Kentucky 29. Stand Up and Cheer 33. Steamboat Round the Bend 35. Charlie Chan in Egypt 35. Dimples 36. On the Avenue 37. Zenobia

39. Bend of the River 52. The Sun Shines Bright 53, many others.

Feuillade, Louis (1873–1925).
Newly-rediscovered and fêted French director who made marathon silent serials about master criminals.

Fantomas 13. Les Vampires 15. Judex (remade by Franju 63) 16–17. Tih Minh 18. Parisette 21, etc.

Feuillère, Edwige (1907–) (Edwige Cunati).
Distinguished French actress, a leading member of the Comédie Française.

Le Cordon Bleu 30. Topaze 32. I Was An Adventuress 38. Sans Lendemain 40. La Duchesse de Langeais 42. *L'Idiot* 46. L'Aigle a Deux Têtes 47. Woman Hater (GB) 48. *Olivia* 50. Adorable Creatures 52. *Le Blé en Herbe* 53. The Fruits of Summer 54. En Cas de Malheur (Love Is My Profession) 57. Crime Doesn't Pay 62. Do You Like Women? 64, etc.

Feydeau, Georges (1862–1921).
French writer of stage farces, many of which have become classics and are often filmed, the best cinematic examples being *Occupe Toi d'Amelie* 49 and *Hotel Paradiso* 66.

Feyder, Jacques (1885–1948) (Jacques Frederix).
French director, former actor; married Françoise Rosay.

L'Atlantide 21. Crainquebille 22. Thérèse Raquin 28. *Les Nouveaux Messieurs* 29. The Kiss (US) 29. Le Grand Jeu 34. *La Kermesse Héroique* 35. Knight without Armour (GB) 37. Les Gens du Voyage 38. La Loi du Nord 39. Une Femme Disparait 41. Macadam (supervised only) 45, etc.

Fiander, Lewis (1938–).
Australian-born stage and TV actor in Britain.

Dr Jekyll and Sister Hyde 71. The Abdication 73. Death is Child's Play 75. Sweeney 2 78. The Doctor and the Devils 86, etc.

F.I.D.O.
The Film Industry Defence Organization, a body formed by British renters and exhibitors to prevent old feature films being sold to television. It collapsed in 1964 after five years during which no renter dared sell his product for fear of reprisals.

Fiedel, Brad (1951–).
American composer.

The Calendar Girl Murders (TV) 83. The Terminator 84. Compromising Positions 85. Fright Night 85. Desert Bloom 86. Popeye Doyle (TV) 86. Let's Get Harry 86. The Big Easy 87. Nowhere to Hide 87. The Serpent and the Rainbow 88. The Accused 88. Fright Night Part 2 89. True Believer 89. Immediate Family 89. Blue Steel 90. Gladiator 92. The Real McCoy 93. Blink 94. True Lies 94, etc.

Fiedler, John (1925–).
Mild, bespectacled American character actor.

Twelve Angry Men 57. Stage Struck 58. That Touch of Mink 62. The World of Henry Orient 64. Kiss Me Stupid 64. Fitzwilly 67. The Odd Couple 68. True Grit 69. Making It 71. The Shaggy D.A. 76. The Cannonball Run 81. Savannah Smiles 82, etc.

TV series: The Bob Newhart Show 73–78. Kolchak: The Night Stalker 74–75. Buffalo Bill 83–84.

Field, Betty (1918–1973).
American character actress who played a variety of roles from neurotic girls to slatternly mums.

■ What a Life 39. *Of Mice and Men* 39. Seventeen 40. Victory 40. The Shepherd of the Hills 41. Blues in the Night 41. *Kings Row* 42. Are Husbands Necessary? 42. Flesh and Fantasy 43. The Great Moment 44. Tomorrow the World 44. *The Southerner* 45. The Great Gatsby 49. Picnic 55. Bus Stop 56. Peyton Place 57. The Hound Dog Man 59. Butterfield 8 60. Bird Man of Alcatraz 62. Seven Women 65. How to Save a Marriage 68. Coogan's Bluff 68.

Field, Chelsea.
American actress.
　Prison 88. Skin Deep 89. Harley Davidson & the Marlboro Man 91. Last Boy Scout 91. Hotel Room (TV) 93. The Dark Half 93. Andre 94. Royce 94, etc.
　TV series: The Bronx Zoo 88. Nightingales 89. Capital News 90.

Field, Mary (1896–1968).
British executive long associated with films specially made for children. From 1926 worked as continuity girl, editor, etc., also directed some instructional films, including the *Secrets of Nature* series. Well-known writer and lecturer on social aspects of film.

Field, Mary (c. 1905–　).
American character comedienne, usually as prissy spinster.
　Wild Geese Calling 41. *Ball of Fire* 41. The Affairs of Susan 45. A Song Is Born 48. Sitting Pretty 48, etc.

Field, Rachel (1894–1942).
American novelist.
■ All This and Heaven Too 40. And Now Tomorrow 44. Time Out of Mind 47.

Field, Sally (1946–　) (S. F. Mahoney).
Diminutive American actress who played the lead in TV series: *Gidget* 65, *The Flying Nun* 67–69. The Girl with Something Extra 73.
　The Way West 67. Home for the Holidays (TV) 72. Maybe I'll Come Home in the Spring (TV) 72. Marriage Year One (TV) 72. Stay Hungry 76. Sybil (TV: Emmy) 76. Smokey and the Bandit 77. Heroes 77. Hooper 78. The End 78. *Norma Rae* (AA) 79. Smokey and the Bandit II 80. Back Roads 81. Absence of Malice 81. Kiss Me Goodbye 82. *Places in the Heart* (AA) 84. Murphy's Romance 85. Surrender 87. Punchline 88. Steel Magnolias 89. Not Without My Daughter 91. Soapdish 91. Mrs Doubtfire 93. Forrest Gump 94, etc.

Field, Shirley Ann (1938–　).
British leading lady with stage experience; career waned after a promising start.
　Dry Rot 56. Once More with Feeling 59. The Entertainer 59. *Saturday Night and Sunday Morning* 60. The Man in the Moon 60. The Damned 61. The War Lover 62. Lunch Hour 63. Kings of the Sun (US) 63. Doctor in Clover 66. *Alfie* 66. My Beautiful Laundrette 85. Shag 88. Getting It Right 89. The Rachel Papers 89. Hear My Song 91. Lady Chatterley (TV) 92. Lady Chatterley (TV) 93. UFO: The Movie 93. At Risk 94, etc.

Field, Sid (1904–1950).
British comedian who after years in music-hall became West End star in 1943. First film, *London Town* 46, valuable as record of his sketches; second and last, *Cardboard Cavalier* 48, a patchy historical farce.
　Biography: 1975, *What a Performance!* by John Fisher.

¶ It took me thirty years to become an overnight star. – *S.F.*

~Catchphrase: What a per*form*ance!

Field, Virginia (1917–1992) (Margaret Cynthia Field).
British-born second lead of Hollywood films in the 40s.
　The Primrose Path (GB) 35. Lloyds of London 37. Lancer Spy 38. Waterloo Bridge 40. Hudson's Bay 41. The Perfect Marriage 46. Dial 1119 50. The Big Story 58. The Earth Dies Screaming 65, many others.

Fielding, Fenella (1930–　).
Anglo-Rumanian leading lady, usually in outrageously exaggerated roles on stage and TV.
　In the Doghouse 62. The Old Dark House 63. Doctor in Clover 66. Carry on Screaming 66. Arrivederci Baby 66. Lock Up Your Daughters 69, etc.

Fielding, Henry (1707–1754).
Influential English novelist whose chief bequests to films have been *Tom Jones*, *Lock Up Your Daughters* (indirectly) and *Joseph Andrews*.

Fielding, Jerry (1922–1980).
American composer.
　Advise and Consent 62. The Wild Bunch (AAN) 69. Johnny Got His Gun 71. Lawman 71. The Nightcomers 71. Straw Dogs 71. Chato's Land 72. Bring Me the Head of Alfredo Garcia 74. The Outlaw Josey Wales 76. Demon Seed 77. Semi-Tough 77. The Big Sleep 78. Beyond the Poseidon Adventure 79. Escape from Alcatraz 80. High Midnight (TV) 80, etc. Much TV, including *Hogan's Heroes*, *McMillan and Wife*, The Bionic Woman.

Fielding, Marjorie (1892–1956).
British stage actress who usually played strict but kindly gentlewomen. Repeated her stage role in *Quiet Wedding* 40 and was subsequently in many films.
　The Demi-Paradise 43. Quiet Weekend 46. Spring in Park Lane 47. The Conspirator 49. The Chiltern Hundreds 49. The Franchise Affair 50. The Lavender Hill Mob 51. Mandy 52. Rob Roy 53, etc.

Fields, Benny (1894–1959) (Benjamin Geisenfeld).
American vaudevillian whose career was linked with Blossom Seeley. Their story was told (more or less) in *Somebody Loves Me*.
■ Mr Broadway 33. The Big Broadcast of 1937 36. Minstrel Man 44.

Fields, Freddie (1923–　).
American agent and producer.
　Lipstick 76. Looking for Mr Goodbar 77. American Gigolo 80. Wholly Moses 80. Victory 81. The Fever 85. Crimes of the Heart 86. Glory 89, etc.

Fields, Dame Gracie (1898–1979) (Grace Stansfield).
British singer and comedienne whose Lancashire humour and high spirits helped working-class audiences through the 30s Depression. An inimitable voice and personality.
　Autobiography: 1960, *Sing As We Go*.
■ Sally in our Alley 31. Looking on the Bright Side 32. This Week of Grace 33. Love Life and Laughter 33. *Sing As We Go* 34. Look Up and Laugh 35. Queen of Hearts 36. The Show Goes On 37. We're Going to Be Rich 38. Keep Smiling 38. Shipyard Sally 39. Stage Door Canteen 43. *Holy Matrimony* 43. Molly and Me 45. Paris Underground 45.
☻ For keeping a nation cheerful. *Sing As We Go.*

Fields, Stanley (1884–1941) (Walter L. Agnew).
American character actor, former prizefighter and vaudevillian.
　Mammy 30. Little Caesar 30. Island of Lost Souls 32. Kid Millions 35. Way Out West 37. Algiers 38. New Moon 40, many others.

Fields, Verna (1918–1982).
American editor.
　The Savage Eye 60. Studs Lonigan 60. Medium Cool 69. What's Up Doc? 72. American Graffiti 73. Paper Moon 73. *Jaws* (AA) 75, etc.

Fields, W. C. (1879–1946) (William Claude Dukinfield).
Red-nosed, gravel-voiced, bottle-hitting, misogynist American comedian around whose intolerance and eccentric habits many legends have been built. After a hard life as a tramp juggler, his off-beat personality found a niche in silent films, though sound was necessary to his full flowering as a screen personality. Many of his routines were made up as he went along; once he sold for $25,000 a storyline written on the back of an envelope.
　Books on him include: 1949, *W. C. Fields, His Follies and Fortunes* by Robert Lewis Taylor. 1960, *The Films of W. C. Fields* by Donald Deschner. Rod Steiger impersonated him in an inaccurate 1976 film of his life, *W. C. Fields and Me*, from a book by his mistress Carlotta Monti.
■ Pool Sharks 15. Janice Meredith 24. Sally of the Sawdust 25. That Royle Girl 26. It's the Old Army Game 26. So's Your Old Man 26. The Potters 27. Running Wild 27. Two Flaming Youths 27. Tillie's Punctured Romance 27. Fools for Luck 28. The Golf Specialist 30. Her Majesty Love 31. Million Dollar Legs 32. If I Had a Million 32. The Dentist 32. The Fatal Glass of Beer 32. The Pharmacist 33. The Barber Shop 33. International House 33. Tillie and Gus 33. Alice in Wonderland (as Humpty Dumpty) 33. Six of a Kind 34. You're Telling Me 34. The Old-Fashioned Way 34. Mrs Wiggs of the Cabbage Patch 34. *It's a Gift* 34. David Copperfield (as Micawber) 34. Mississippi 35. The Man on the Flying Trapeze 35. Poppy 36. The Big Broadcast of 1938 37. You Can't Cheat an Honest Man 39. *My Little Chickadee* 40. *The Bank Dick* 40. Never Give a Sucker an Even Break 41. Follow the Boys 44. Song of the Open Road 44. Sensations of 1945 44.
☻ For making a disreputable character almost entirely sympathetic; and for moments of inspired surrealism. *It's a Gift.*

¶ Today the centre of a cult which would have astonished him, W. C. Fields was one of life's genuine oddballs, able to see the funny side of his own misanthropy and to turn it to commercial use. In most of his films he was strait-jacketed, but the few he controlled personally are uniquely Fieldsian, anarchic and paceless, fantasticated versions of his unyielding private life with a few in-jokes for good measure. They feature such characters as:
　J. Frothingham Waterbury
　Ogg Ogilvie
　Filthy McNasty
　Ouliotta Haemoglobin
　F. Snoopington Pinkerton
　Elmer Prettywillie
　T. Frothingwell Bellows
　A. Pismo Clam
　Ambrose Wolfinger
　Egbert Souse
　Cuthbert J. Twillie
　Larson E. Whipsnade
Fields' own pseudonyms, either for professional

se on his screenplays or merely to conceal a new —ank account, include:

Primrose Magoo
Mahatma Kane Jeeves
Otis Criblecoblis
Ampico J. Steinway
Charles Bogle
Felton J. Satchelstern

—e had a splendid command of the English —nguage which effectively silenced criticisms when —e was cast as Micawber in *David Copperfield*. His —asal delivery and orotund phrasing were imitated —e world over, and they are essential to the —ffectiveness of such oft-quoted lines as:

I must have a drink of breakfast.

—r:

Somebody left the cork out of my lunch.

—r (of an elderly lady dressed to kill):

She's all done up like a well-kept grave.

—r:

I exercise extreme self control. I never drink anything stronger than gin before breakfast.

—r:

If at first you don't succeed, try again. Then quit. No use being a damn fool about it.

—r:

There's an Ethiopian in the fuel supply.

—r:

I never vote for anyone. I always vote against.

—is oaths were splendid, consisting of such —atered-down versions of profanity as 'Godfrey —aniel!' or 'Great Mother of Pearl!' He was indeed —profane and outlandish man. When his lady —eighbour in Beverly Hills came out to —emonstrate with him for standing in the middle of —is new green lawn and shooting the singing birds —ith a rifle, he is alleged to have growled:

I'll go on shooting the bastards till they learn to shit green . . .

—When another lady, an inquiring journalist this —ime, asked why he never drank water, he gave —he simple reason:

Fish fuck in it.

—He occasionally mentioned to acquaintances that —e was involved in charity work, and when asked —what charity he would murmur: 'The F.E.B.F.' —When an explanation of the initials was requested, —t was given as:

Fuck Everyone but Fields.

—As his biographer Robert Lewis Taylor said:

His main purpose seemed to be to break as many rules as possible and cause the maximum amount of trouble for everybody.

—He hated children and animals, and once said of a —churlish friend:

Anyone who hates small dogs and children can't be all bad.

—t is of course alleged that when co-starring with —Baby Le Roy he spiked the infant's milk with gin, —and when Le Roy proved unfit for further work —hat day stalked around yelling:

The kid's no trouper!

—He hated women too:

Women are like elephants. I like to look at them but I wouldn't want to own one.

—and:

A woman drove me to drink. I never had the courtesy to thank her for it.

But he was essentially impartial:

I am free of all prejudices. I hate everybody equally.

Fiennes, Ralph (1963–   ).

British leading actor, from the theatre.

A Dangerous Man – Lawrence after Arabia (TV) —91. Wuthering Heights 92. The Baby of Macon —93. Schindler's List (AAN) 93. Quiz Show 94. **Strange Days 95.**

¶ I am sure acting is a deeply neurotic thing to do. I veer away from trying to understand why I do it. – R.F.

Fierstein, Harvey (1954–   ).

American actor and screenwriter, from the theatre.

Garbo Talks (a) 84. Apology (a) 86. Torch Song Trilogy (a, w) 88. Tidy Endings (a, oa) 88. The Harvest 93. Mrs Doubtfire (a) 93.

Figgis, Mike (1950–   ).

British director, screenwriter and musician, now in Hollywood. He first worked in experimental theatre in Britain.

The House (TV) 85. Stormy Monday (wd, m) 88. Internal Affairs (d, m) 89. Liebestraum 91 (wd, m). Mr Jones 93. The Browning Version 94.

fights

provide the climax to many a film, but only the outstandingly staged ones remain in the mind. The slugging match between the two heroes of *The Spoilers* became a tradition, as each of the five versions tried to outdo the previous one. John Wayne had many fighting triumphs, notably against Victor McLaglen in *The Quiet Man; McLintock* and *North to Alaska* seemed at times to have more brawling than dialogue. Spoof fights were probably topped by the saloon brawl in *The Great Race;* serious ones by the solemn allegorical punch-up in *The Big Country*. Other good western fights are found in *Shane, The Sheepman,* and (between Dietrich and Una Merkel) in *Destry Rides Again*. For viciousness within a serious picture the waterfront fights in *Edge of the City* and *On the Waterfront* take some beating.

Figueroa, Gabriel (1907–   ).

Mexican cinematographer who worked in Hollywood with Gregg Toland and on Luis Buñuel's Mexican films.

The Fugitive 47. Maclovia 50. Night of the Iguana 64. Kelly's Heroes 70, etc.

film-making

is not too frequently used as a background for movies, as movies about movies are thought to be bad box office. Certainly not too many of the following were big hits: *OK for Sound, The Best Pair of Legs in the Business, Go for a Take, The Comedy Man, The Bad and the Beautiful, Two Weeks in Another Town, It's a Great Feeling, Shooting Stars, Pick a Star, A Star is Born, The Carpetbaggers, Eight and a Half, Hellzapoppin, Day for Night, Stand In, Singin' In The Rain, Abbott and Costello Meet the Keystone Kops, Gable and Lombard, Harlow, W.C. Fields and Me, The Big Knife, Once in a Lifetime, Wonderful Life, Hollywood Cavalcade, Hollywood Boulevard, Hollywood Story, Nickelodeon, The Last Tycoon, Everything for Sale, The Stunt Man, Crimes and Misdemeanors, The Big Picture, The Player.*

film noir.

A French phrase meaning *dark film*. It was probably first applied to the moody, downbeat character melodramas of the late 30s, such as *Quai des Brumes* and *Le Jour se Lève,* but it soon came to be thought of as applying chiefly to the American urban crime film of the 40s, for instance *Double Indemnity, Laura, Scarlet Street* (based on a French original) and the versions of Raymond Chandler novels.

Books: 1980 (revised 1988), *Film Noir: An Encyclopedic Reference Guide,* edited by Alain Silver and Elizabeth Ward. 1984, *Dark City: The Film Noir* by Spencer Selby.

Films include:

The Maltese Falcon 41. Johnny Eager 42. The Glass Key 42. Double Indemnity 44. Laura 44.

Murder, My Sweet (aka Farewell My Lovely) 44. Ministry of Fear 44. Mildred Pierce 45. Scarlet Street 45. Gilda 46. The Big Sleep 46. The Blue Dahlia 46. The Chase 46. Notorious 46. The Postman Always Rings Twice 46. Crossfire 47. Lady in the Lake 47. He Walked by Night 48. The Big Clock 48. Key Largo 48. The Naked City 48. White Heat 49. Follow Me Quietly 49. The Asphalt Jungle 50. D.O.A. 50. Gun Crazy 50. Ace in the Hole 51. M 51. The Prowler 51. Beware, My Lovely 52. Clash by Night 52. Angel Face 53. The Big Heat 53. The Hitch-Hiker 53. Drive a Crooked Road 54. Witness to Murder 54. The Big Knife 55. Kiss Me Deadly 55. The Killing 56. Sweet Smell of Success 57. Touch of Evil 58. The Crimson Kimono 59. Odds against Tomorrow 59. Underworld USA 61. Cape Fear 62. The Manchurian Candidate 62. The Servant 63. Marlowe 69. The Friends of Eddie Coyle 73. Chinatown 74. Farewell My Lovely 75. Taxi Driver 76. The Driver 78. Body Heat 81. The Postman Always Rings Twice 81. Blood Simple 84. Backfire 88. Miller's Crossing 90. The Grifters 90. The Two Jakes 90. Cape Fear 91. The Last Seduction 94.

film society.

A club formed to show high-quality revivals and new films not normally found in public cinemas.

films à clef

are those which appear to be fiction but are really based on factual cases with the names changed. The obvious example is *Citizen Kane,* which parallels the career of William Randolph Hearst. Others are *The Great Dictator,* in which Hynkel is obviously Hitler; *Compulsion,* based on the Leopold and Loeb murder; *Inherit the Wind,* about the Scopes monkey trial; *The Moon and Sixpence,* in which Charles Strickland stands in for Paul Gauguin; *The Man Who Came to Dinner,* in which Sheridan Whiteside is Alexander Woollcott, Banjo is Harpo Marx, and Beverly Carlton is Noël Coward; *Young Cassidy,* drawn from the early life of Sean O'Casey; *All About Eve,* in which Margo Channing was said to be Tallulah Bankhead and Addison de Witt George Jean Nathan; *Twentieth Century,* in which Oscar Jaffe is an amalgam of Jed Harris and David Belasco; *All the King's Men* and *A Lion is in the Streets,* both essentially about Huey Long; *The Lost Moment,* in which the old lady is allegedly Claire Clairemont, the aged mistress of Byron; *The Adventurers,* in which the characters are supposedly based on Porfirio Rubirosa, Barbara Hutton, Aristotle Onassis and Maria Callas; *The Carpetbaggers,* plainly about Howard Hughes; *Little Caesar,* who was clearly Al Capone; *Major Barbara,* in which Adolphus Cusins was Gilbert Murray; *Call Me Madam,* based on the exploits of Perle Mesta; *The Winslow Boy,* based on the Archer–Shee case, with Sir Robert Morton standing in for Sir Edward Carson; *An American Tragedy,* from the real life Chester Gillette murder case; *Monsieur Verdoux,* who was Landru; *Death of a Scoundrel,* from the career of Charles Rubenstein; *The Prisoner,* inspired by the sufferings of Cardinal Mindzenty; *Fame is the Spur,* in which Homer Radshaw was Ramsay MacDonald; and if you like, *Dr Jekyll and Mr Hyde,* whose story was inspired by the burglarious second life of Deacon William Brodie; or even any Sherlock Holmes story, as Holmes was modelled on Dr Joseph Bell. *Where Love Has Gone* was modelled on the Lana Turner case in which her daughter murdered her lover; and *Imitation of Life* also reflected the Turner career, as *Dancing Lady* and *Torch Song* reflected Joan Crawford's. *The Barefoot Contessa* was vaguely drawn from Rita Hayworth's international goings-on, though the star who played her, Ava Gardner, was also no slouch in the fun department. *Bombshell* was an obvious echo of Jean Harlow's own troubles with hangers-on. *I Could Go on Singing* featured Judy Garland clearly playing herself; *The Devil Is a Woman* can be seen as Sternberg's farewell to Dietrich (with Lionel Atwill playing himself), just as Orson Welles cast himself as bedevilled by his then wife Rita Hayworth in *The Lady from Shanghai*. The leading roles in *Will Success Spoil Rock Hunter?*, *After the Fox*, *The Band Wagon*, *Blondie of the Follies* and *Kiss Me Stupid* were clearly based on those who played them: Jayne Mansfield, Victor Mature, Fred Astaire, Marion Davies and Dean Martin. The same can be said of Gloria Swanson in *Sunset Boulevard*, Bette Davis in *The Star*, Errol Flynn in *The Sun Also Rises*, Hedy Lamarr in *The Female Animal*, Marlene Dietrich in *No Highway*, John Wayne in *The Shootist*, John Barrymore in *The Great Profile* and Zero Mostel in *The Front*. *The Goddess* reflected Marilyn Monroe's marriage with Joe Di Maggio. *Flight for Freedom*, though not using Amelia Earhart's name, gave a fictional solution to the aviatrix's real-life disappearance. *Funny Girl* was the official biography of Fanny Brice, but *Rose of Washington Square* also had lots of similarities. *All About Eve*'s leading character, Margo Channing, according to its creator, was based on Elisabeth Bergner. *New York New York* seemed to be taken from Doris Day's autobiography. *Smash-Up* was allegedly based on the drinking problems of Bing Crosby's first wife Dixie Lee, just as *Written on the Wind* had connections with the suicide of Libby Holman's first husband. Evangelist Aimee Semple McPherson was clearly impersonated by Barbara Stanwyck in *The Miracle Woman* and by Jean Simmons in *Elmer Gantry*. Columnist Walter Winchell was parodied in several Lee Tracy vehicles – Tracy even looked like him – and also by Burt Lancaster in *Sweet Smell of Success*. The Robert Ryan character in *Caught* was allegedly based on Howard Hughes. Bette Midler in *The Rose* is obviously Janis Joplin. *The Greek Tycoon* is clearly inspired by Aristotle Onassis and Jackie Kennedy. In *It's Tough to Be Famous*, Douglas Fairbanks Jnr could only be Charles Lindbergh. James Cagney and Pat O'Brien in *Boy Meets Girl* were inspired by Charles MacArthur and Ben Hecht. In *The Last Tycoon*, Robert de Niro was Irving Thalberg. Anne Baxter in *You're My Everything* was Clara Bow. The sliding marriage in *A Star Is Born* could have been based on Al Jolson and Ruby Keeler, or on John Gilbert and Greta Garbo. Patty Duke in *Valley of the Dolls* was Judy Garland. And so on.

Finch, Flora (1869–1940).
British-born actress, formerly on stage; famous as John Bunny's partner in early film comedies. After his death in 1915 she formed her own production company and was in many silent films of the 20s.

Finch, Jon (1941–   ).
British leading man.
    The Vampire Lovers 70. Horror of Frankenstein 71. Macbeth 71. Sunday Bloody Sunday 71. Frenzy 72. Lady Caroline Lamb 72. The Final Programme 73. Diagnosis: Murder 74. A Faithful Wife (Fr.) 75. The Man with the Green Cross (Sp.) 76. Battleflag (Sp.) 76. Death on the Nile 78. El Barracho (Sp.) 78. Breaking Glass 80. Peter and Paul (TV) 81. Riviera (TV) 82. Giro City (TV) 85. La Più Bella del Reame 89, etc.

Finch, Peter (1916–1977) (William Mitchell).
British leading actor in British and US films. Born in London, he was brought up in France and Australia. In films in Australia from 1937, he made his stage debut in 1939, as a stooge to a comedian,

and was on the British stage from 1949. Married three times, he had much-publicized affairs with actresses Kay Kendall, Vivien Leigh and Mai Zetterling, among others. His off-stage and - screen antics, as a hard-drinking womanizer, sometimes obscured his abilities as one of the best film actors of his time.
    Biographies: 1979, *Peter Finch* by Trader Faulkner. 1980, *Finchy: My Life* by Peter Finch with Yolande Finch. 1980, *Finch, Bloody Finch* by Elaine Dundy.
■ The Magic Shoes 35. Dad and Dave Come to Town 37. Red Sky at Morning 37. Mr Chedworth Steps Out 38. Rats of Tobruk 44. The Power and the Glory 45. A Son Is Born 46. Eureka Stockade 47. Train of Events 49. The Wooden Horse 50. The Miniver Story 50. *Robin Hood* (as Sheriff) 51. The Heart of the Matter 53. The Story of Gilbert and Sullivan 53. Elephant Walk 54. *Father Brown* (as Flambeau) 54. Make Me an Offer 54. The Dark Avenger 55. Passage Home 55. Josephine and Men 55. *Simon and Laura* 55. The Battle of the River Plate (as Langsdorff) 56. *A Town Like Alice* (BFA) 56. The Shiralee 56. Robbery Under Arms 57. Windom's Way 57. Operation Amsterdam 58. Kidnapped 59. *The Nun's Story* 59. The Sins of Rachel Cade 60. *The Trials of Oscar Wilde* (BFA) 60. *No Love for Johnnie* (BFA) 61. I Thank a Fool 62. In the Cool of the Day 63. Girl with Green Eyes 64. The Pumpkin Eater 64. Judith 65. The Flight of the Phoenix 65. 10.30 pm Summer 67. *Far from the Madding Crowd* 67. The Legend of Lylah Clare 68. The Red Tent 69. *Sunday Bloody Sunday* (BFA, AAN) 71. Something to Hide 72. England Made Me 72. *Lost Horizon* 73. A Bequest to the Nation 73. The Abdication 73. *Network* (AA, BFA) 76. Raid on Entebbe (TV) 77.

¶ Good acting should teach people to understand rather than judge. – *P.F.*
    An Australian outlaw character, wild and unruly, who despised himself for having become an actor – *Mai Zetterling*
    He was a piss-pot and a hell-raiser, but he was also a happy drunk, a gigglebum and very, very good company. – *Yolande Finch*
    My first and lasting impression of Finchie was of a withdrawn man with a quiet assurance in his own ability as a remarkable actor which belied his vulnerability. – *Trader Faulkner*
    He was a deeply complex man. Film acting is not just acting, it's catching something about the essence of a personality very often, and I think that's what makes someone extraordinary in movies, and it was Peter's complexity that was inescapable. I remember sometimes he'd suddenly stop and say, 'I've lost it! I've lost it! Please don't let's do any more!' – *John Schlesinger*

Famous line (*Network*): 'I want you to get up right now and go to the window, open it and stick your head out and yell "I'm mad as hell, and I'm not going to take this any more!" '

Fincher, David (1965–   ).
American director, from TV commercials and music videos, who made his debut as director with a movie costing more than $50 million.
    Alien³ 92.

fine grain print.
One of high quality stock (avoiding the coarseness of silver salt deposit); used for making dupe negatives.

Fine, Larry (1911–1975) (Laurence Feinberg).
American comedian, one of the Three Stooges (qv).

Finklehoffe, Fred F. (1911–1977).
American writer-producer.
    Brother Rat (co-w & co-w original stage play) 39. For Me and My Gal (co-w) 42. Meet Me in St Louis (co-w, AAN) 44. The Egg and I (co-wp) 47. At War with the Army (co-wp) 50, etc.

Finland
has produced many films for internal consumption, but its films have not enjoyed the international success of its neighbours Sweden and Denmark. Until the mid-80s, the best-known Finnish film was probably Edvin Laine's *The Unknown Soldier* 55, although Jorn Donner's *A Sunday in September* 63 also found an audience outside Finland. Then the Kaurismaki Brothers, Mika and Aki, began to attract attention with their output. Both make at least a film a year, taking it in turns to use the same crew. Aki Kaurismaki has filmed in America and England, attracting an art-house audience for his *The Match Girl* 89, *Leningrad Cowboys Go America* 89 and *I Hired a Contract Killer* 90. But perhaps the best-known Finnish director is Renny Harlin, who works in Hollywood.

Finlay, Frank (1926–   ).
British stage and TV actor who has made tentative screen appearances.
    Life for Ruth 62. The Informers 63. Othello (as Iago) (AAN) 65. Robbery 67. Inspector Clouseau 68. Twisted Nerve 68. Cromwell 69. Assault 71. Gumshoe 71. Danny Jones 71. Sitting Target 72. Shaft in Africa 73. The Three Musketeers 74. The Four Musketeers 75. Murder by Decree 79. Enigma 82. The Ploughman's Lunch 83. Arch of Triumph (TV) 84. The Key 85. Sakharov 85. Life Force 85. In the Secret State (TV) 86. The Return of the Musketeers 89. King of the Wind 89. Cthulhu Mansion 92. An Exchange of Fire (TV) 93. Sparrow (Storia di una Capinera) 93, etc.
    TV successes include The Last Days of Hitler (title role), Casanova (title role) and Bouquet of Barbed Wire.

Finlayson, James (1877–1953).
Scottish comic actor who went to Hollywood in early silent days and became an indispensable comic villain, known for the exaggerated reaction known as a 'double take and fade away'. A memorable opponent for Laurel and Hardy.
    Small Town Idol 21. Ladies Night in a Turkish Bath 28. Lady Be Good 28. The Dawn Patrol 30. *Big Business* 30. Pardon Us 31. Fra Diavolo 33. Our Relations 36. *Way Out West* 37. Blockheads 38. The Flying Deuces 39. The Perils of Pauline 47. Grand Canyon Trail 48. Royal Wedding 51, many others.

Finnerman, Gerald Perry (1931–   ).
American photographer, mostly in television.
    Night Gallery (TV) 69. The Lost Man 69. Brother John 70. They Call Me Mr Tibbs 70. Joe Forrester (TV) 76. Salvage (TV) 78. Ziegfeld the Man and His Women (TV) 78. That Man Bolt 78. The Dream Merchants (TV) 80. Smorgasbord 83, etc.

Finney, Albert (1936–   ).
Leading British actor whose comparatively few films have tended to be controversial.
    Biography: 1992, *Albert Finney in Character* by Quentin Falk.
■ The Entertainer 59. *Saturday Night and Sunday Morning* 60. *Tom Jones* (AAN) 63. The Victors 63. Night Must Fall (& p) 63. Two for the Road 67. *Charlie Bubbles* (& p, d) 68. The Picasso Summer 69. Scrooge 70. Gumshoe (& p) 71. Alpha Beta 73. Murder on the Orient Express (as Hercule Poirot)

(AAN) 74. The Duellists 77. Wolfen 80. Looker 80. Loophole 80. Annie 82. Shoot the Moon 82. The Dresser (AAN) 83. Under the Volcano (AAN) 84. The Biko Inquest (TV) 85. Orphans 87. Miller's Crossing 90. The Playboys 92. Rich in Love 93. A Man of No Importance 94. The Browning Version 94.

Finney, Jack (1911–) (Walter Braden Finney). American science-fiction author whose *The Body Snatchers* has been filmed three times, notably by Don Siegel in 1956. The catch-penny title obscured the most subtle film in the 50s science-fiction cycle, with no visual horror whatever, about a small town whose population is taken over by duplicates from outer space.

Invasion of the Body Snatchers (oa) 56, 74, 92. House of Numbers (oa) 57. Good Neighbour Sam (oa) 65. Assault on a Queen (oa) 66.

Fiorentino, Linda (1958–).
American leading actress.
After Hours 85. Gotcha! 85. Vision Quest 85. Wildfire 88. The Moderns 88. Neon Empire (TV) 89. Queen's Logic 91. Shout 91. Strangers 91. All Shook Up 91. Acting on Impulse 93. *The Last Seduction* 94, etc.

Firbank, Ann.
British actress, usually in refined roles.
Behind the Mask 58. Nothing Barred 61. The Servant 63. Darling 65. Accident 67. A Severed Head 70. Sunday Bloody Sunday 71. Asylum 74. Stories from a Flying Trunk 79, etc.

fire
is a standard part of the melodramatist's equipment, whether it be used for disposing of country houses with too many memories (*Dragonwyck*, *Rebecca*, *The Lost Moment*, *The Fall of the House of Usher*, *The Tomb of Ligeia*, *Gone with the Wind*) or whole cities (*Forever Amber*, *In Old Chicago*, *Quo Vadis*, *City on Fire*). Sometimes, as in *House of Wax*, it makes a splendid starting point; though to judge from *She* one can't rely on its life-prolonging qualities. Its use in realistic films is rare, though cases of arson were seriously studied in *On the Night of the Fire* and *Violent Playground*. The fires of hell were most spectacularly recreated in the 1935 version of *Dante's Inferno*. Comedies about firemen include *Where's That Fire?* (Will Hay), *Fireman Save My Child*, *Harvey Middleman Fireman*, and *Go to Blazes* (Dave King); and firemen who start fires instead of putting them out are prophesied in *Fahrenheit 451*. Oil fires were spectacularly depicted in *Tulsa*, *Wildcat*, and *Hellfighters*. The classic study of conventional firemen remains *Fires Were Started*; TV series which took up the theme include *Emergency*, *Firehouse* and *London's Burning*. For many, the greatest screen fire will be the burning of Atlanta in *Gone with the Wind*, but *The Towering Inferno* was probably the most spectacular. *Backdraft* is another where the flames stole the picture. *Endless Love* was brought to an end by a pyromaniac, *Firestarter* dealt with a psychic who could set anything ablaze, while *Quest for Fire* dealt with a Stone Age tribe who weren't able to set anything alight after their fire went out. Finally, fire was always a splendid aid for serial producers, as the oft-used title 'Next Week: Through the Flames' may suggest.
See also: *forest fires*.

firing squads
have figured chiefly in films about World War I (*Paths of Glory*, *King and Country*) or those telling the lives of spies (*Mata Hari*, *Nurse Edith Cavell*, *Carve Her Name With Pride*). Other uses have been

in *Dishonoured*, *The Fugitive*, *Custer of the West*, *The Victors*, *The Long Ride Home*, *Reach for Glory*, *The Counterfeit Traitor* and *The Ceremony*; and firing squads were given a comic effect in *The Captain's Paradise*, *Casino Royale*, *Morgan* and *The Ambushers*.

First National
was a Hollywood company founded in 1917. During the next 12 years it was very active, with films featuring Chaplin, Pickford, Milton Sills and Richard Barthelmess. In 1929 it was taken over by Warner Brothers, who however kept the name going for certain product until the mid-30s.

Firstenberg, Sam (1950–).
Israeli director of action and martial arts movies.
One More Chance 81. Revenge of the Ninja 83. Ninja III: The Domination 84. Breakin' 2: Electric Boogaloo 84. American Ninja 85. Avenging Force 86. American Ninja 2: The Confrontation 87. Night of the Eagles 89. One More Chance 90. Delta Force 3: The Killing Game 91. American Samurai 92. Cyborg Cop 2 94, etc.

Firth, Colin (1960–).
British leading man.
Camille (TV) 84. Dutch Girls (TV) 85. Lost Empires (TV) 86. Apartment Zero 88. Valmont 89. Wings of Fame 90. Femme Fatale 91. Hostages (TV) 93. The Hour of the Pig 93, etc.

Firth, Peter (1953–).
British juvenile character lead of the late 70s.
■ Brother Sun, Sister Moon 71. Diamonds on Wheels 73. Aces High 76. Equus (AAN) 77. Joseph Andrews 77. When You Coming Home, Red Ryder? 79. Tess 80. The Aerodrome (TV) 83. Life Force 85. Letter to Brezhnev 85. Lifeforce 85. A State of Emergency 86. Born of Fire 87. Prisoner of Rio 88. Deadly Triangle 89. Tree of Hands 89. Burndown 90. The Hunt for Red October 90. The Rescuers Down Under (voice) 90. The Pleasure Principle 91. Prisoner of Honor 92. Shadowlands 93. White Angel 93, etc.
TV series: Heartbeat 94.

Fishburne, Larry (1961–).
American actor who began as an 11-year-old on the TV soap opera *One Life to Live*.
Fast Break 79. Apocalypse Now 79. Willy and Phil 80. Rumble Fish 83. The Cotton Club 84. The Color Purple 85. Quicksilver 86. Band of the Hand 86. Gardens of Stone 87. A Nightmare on Elm Street 3: Dream Warriors 87. School Daze 88. Red Heat 88. King of New York 90. Boyz N the Hood 91. Deep Cover 92. *What's Love Got to Do with It* (AAN) 93. Searching for Bobby Fischer (GB: Innocent Moves) 93. Bad Company 94, etc.

Fischbeck, Harry.
American cinematographer.
Wives of Men 18. The Devil 21. The Green Goddess 23. Monsieur Beaucaire 24. A Sainted Devil 24. Cobra 25. Sally of the Sawdust 25. That Royle Girl 25. The Sorrows of Satan 26. Serenade 27. Manhattan Cocktail 28. The Canary Murder Case 29. The Mysterious Dr Fu Manchu 29. Ladies Love Brutes 30. The Spoilers 30. Working Girls 31. Lady and Gent 32. Terror Aboard 33. Search for Beauty 34. Double Door 34. Millions in the Air 35. The Jungle Princess 36. John Meade's Woman 37. Bulldog Drummond's Revenge 37. Prison Farm 38. Persons in Hiding 39. Parole Fixer 40, many others.

Fischer, Gunnar (1911–).
Swedish cinematographer who has worked on most of Ingmar Bergman's films.
Smiles of a Summer Night 55. The Seventh Seal

56. Wild Strawberries 57. The Face 58. The Devil's Eye 60. Siska 62. Min Kara Ar En Ros 63. Adamson i Sverige 66. Made in Sweden 68. Miss and Mrs Sweden 69. Parade 74, etc.

Fischer, O.W. (1915–1973).
Leading Austrian actor, in films since 1936 but hardly known outside Germany.
Sommerliebe 42. Seven Letters 44. Heidelberger Romanze 51. Der Traumende Mund 52. The Heart Plays False 53. Ludwig II (title role) 54. El Hakim 57. Arms and the Man 58. Uncle Tom's Cabin 65, many others.

Fischinger, Oskar (1900–1967).
German animator who predated *Fantasia* in his attempt to illustrate music with abstract forms.
Composition in Blue 33. Allegretto 36. Motion Painting Number One 47, etc.

Fisher, Carrie (1956–).
American leading lady of routine talent, daughter of Debbie Reynolds and Eddie Fisher. She is also a screenwriter and novelist.
■ Shampoo 75. Star Wars 77. Mr Mike's Mondo Video 78. The Empire Strikes Back 80. The Blues Brothers 80. Under the Rainbow 81. Return of the Jedi 83. Garbo Talks 84. The Man with One Red Shoe 85. Hannah and Her Sisters 86. Hollywood Vice Squad 86. Amazon Women on the Moon 87. The Time Guardian 87. Appointment with Death 88. The 'burbs 89. Loverboy 89. She's Back 89. When Harry Met Sally 89. Postcards from the Edge (w) 90. Sibling Rivalry 90. Drop Dead Fred 91. Soapdish 91. Sweet Revenge 91. This Is My Life 92.

¶ I always wanted to do what my mother did – get all dressed up, shoot people, fall in the mud. I never considered anything else. – C.F.

Fisher, Eddie (1928–).
American nightclub singer and actor. He was married to Debbie Reynolds and Elizabeth Taylor.
Bundle of Joy 56. Butterfield 8 60, etc.

Fisher, Gerry (1926–).
British cinematographer.
AS OPERATOR: The Devil's Disciple 59. Suddenly Last Summer 60. Night Must Fall 63. Guns at Batasi 64. Modesty Blaise 66.
AS CINEMATOGRAPHER: Accident 67. Sebastian 68. Interlude 68. The Go-Between 70. Macho Callahan 71. See No Evil 71. The Amazing Mr Blunden 72. A Bequest to the Nation 73. S.P.Y.S. 74. Juggernaut 74. The Romantic Englishwoman 75. Aces High 76. Mr Klein 77. The Last Remake of Beau Geste 77. The Island of Dr Moreau 77. Fedora 78. Don Giovanni 79. Wise Blood 79. The Ninth Configuration 80. Wolfen 81. Victory 81. Yellowbeard 82. The Holcroft Covenant 84. Highlander 85. Man on Fire 87. Running on Empty 88. Dead Bang 89. Black Rainbow 89. The Fourth War 90. The Exorcist III 90. Company Business 91. Diggstown (GB: Midnight Sting) 92. The Positively True Adventures of the Alleged Texas Cheerleader-Murdering Mom (TV) 93. Cops and Robbersons 94, etc.

Fisher, Joely.
American actress and singer, the daughter of Connie Stevens and Eddie Fisher.
I'll Do Anything 94.

Fisher, Terence (1904–1980).
British director, former editor, in films from 1933. Work mainly routine; latterly associated with

Hammer horror. Also worked for TV, especially *Douglas Fairbanks Presents*.

Biography: 1991, *The Charm of Evil: The Life and Films of Terence Fisher* by Wheeler Winston Dixon.

To the Public Danger 47. Portrait from Life 48. Marry Me 49. The Astonished Heart 49. So Long at the Fair 50. Home to Danger 51. Kill Me Tomorrow 55. The Curse of Frankenstein 56. Dracula 57. The Hound of the Baskervilles 58. Brides of Dracula 59. The Two Faces of Dr Jekyll 60. The Phantom of the Opera 62. The Gorgon 64. Dracula, Prince of Darkness 65. Island of Terror 66. The Devil Rides Out 68. Frankenstein and the Monster from Hell 73, etc.

Fisk, Jack (1945–).
American production designer who has turned to directing. He married actress Sissy Spacek in 1974.

Badlands 73 (pd). Phantom of the Paradise (pd) 74. Carrie (pd) 76. Days of Heaven (pd) 78. Movie Movie (pd) 78. Raggedy Man (d) 81. Violets Are Blue (d) 86. Daddy's Dyin', Who's Got the Will? (d) 90, etc.

Fiske, Minnie Maddern (1866–1932).
American stage actress who made two silent films.
■ Tess of the D'Urbervilles 13. Vanity Fair 15.

Fisz, Benjamin (1922–1989).
Polish-born independent producer, long in England.

Hell Drivers 57. Sea Fury 58. On the Fiddle 61. Heroes of Telemark (co-p) 65. The Battle of Britain (co-p) 69. A Town Called Bastard 71, etc.

Fitzgerald, Barry (1888–1961) (William Shields).
Diminutive Irish character actor who found his way to Hollywood and eventually achieved star status, usually in irascible or whimsical 'Oirish' roles.
■ Juno and the Paycock 30. When Knights were Bold 36. *The Plough and the Stars* 36. *Ebb Tide* 37. Bringing Up Baby 38. Marie Antoinette 38. Four Men and a Prayer 38. The Dawn Patrol 38. The Saint Strikes Back 39. Pacific Liner 39. Full Confession 39. *The Long Voyage Home* 40. San Francisco Docks 41. The Sea Wolf 41. How Green Was My Valley 41. Tarzan's Secret Treasure 41. The Amazing Mrs Holliday 43. Two Tickets to London 43. Corvette K225 43. *Going My Way* (AA) 44. I Love a Soldier 44. None but the Lonely Heart 44. Incendiary Blonde 45. *And Then There Were None* 45. Duffy's Tavern 45. The Stork Club 45. Two Years Before the Mast 46. California 46. Easy Come Easy Go 47. Welcome Stranger 47. Variety Girl 47. The Sainted Sisters 48. *The Naked City* 48. Miss Tatlock's Millions 48. Top o' the Morning 49. The Story of Seabiscuit 49. Union Station 50. Silver City 51. *The Quiet Man* 52. Happy Ever After 54. The Catered Affair 56. *Rooney* 57. Broth of a Boy 59.

Fitzgerald, Ella (1918–).
American singer and entertainer.

Ride 'Em Cowboy 41. Pete Kelly's Blues 55. St Louis Blues 56. Let No Man Write My Epitaph 60, etc.

Fitzgerald, F. Scott (1896–1940).
American novelist and chronicler of 'the jazz age'; was played by Gregory Peck in a biopic, *Beloved Infidel*, in 1959. Films of his work include *The Great Gatsby, The Last Tycoon, Tender is the Night*; his one complete screenplay is *Three Comrades*. In his novel *The Last Tycoon* the character of Monroe Stahr is mainly based on MGM's 'boy wonder' producer Irving Thalberg. Fitzgerald was a model for the

alcoholic writer Manley Halliday in Budd Schulberg's novel *The Disenchanted*.

In the 70s Fitzgerald was played on TV by Richard Chamberlain and Jason Miller.

¶ Scott was different. Most writers came there because they knew there was lots of money. But he was the only one who thought films could be an art form – *Budd Schulberg*

Fitzgerald, Geraldine (1914–).
Irish leading lady who played in British films from 1935; went to Hollywood in 1939 but had rather disappointing roles. In her 60s made a stage comeback as a folk singer.

Turn of the Tide 35. The Mill on the Floss 36. Dark Victory 39. *Wuthering Heights* (AAN) 39. Till We Meet Again 40. Flight from Destiny 41. The Gay Sisters 42. Watch on the Rhine 43. Ladies Courageous 44. *Wilson* 44. Uncle Harry 45. Three Strangers 46. O.S.S. 46. Nobody Lives Forever 47. So Evil My Love (GB) 48. Ten North Frederick 58. The Fiercest Heart 61. The Pawnbroker 65. Rachel Rachel 69. The Last American Hero 73. Harry and Tonto 74. Echoes of a Summer 76. Yesterday's Child (TV) 77. The Quinns (TV) 77. Arthur 81. The Mango Tree 82. Easy Money 83. Kennedy (TV) 83. The Link 85. Poltergeist II: The Other Side 86, etc.

Fitzgerald, Tara (1968–).
English leading actress of stage and screen.

Hear My Song 91. The Camomile Lawn (TV) 92. Sirens 94. A Man of No Importance 94. The Englishman Who Went up a Hill but Came down a Mountain 95, etc.

Fitzgerald, Walter (1896–1976) (Walter Bond).
British character actor, on stage from 1922, films from 1930.

Murder at Covent Garden 30. This England 40. Squadron Leader X 41. Strawberry Roan 45. Mine Own Executioner 47. Treasure Island 50. Pickwick Papers 52. Personal Affair 53. Lease of Life 54. Cockleshell Heroes 55. Something of Value 57. Third Man on the Mountain 59. HMS Defiant 62, many others.

Fitzmaurice, George (1885–1940).
American director of French origin, noted in the 20s for visual style.

A Society Exile 19. On with the Dance 20. Experience 21. *Belladonna* 23. Cytherea 24. *The Dark Angel* 25. Son of the Sheik 26. Rose of the Golden West 27. *Lilac Time* 28. His Captive Woman 29. Tiger Rose 29. The Devil to Pay 30. One Heavenly Night 30. The Unholy Garden 31. Mata Hari 32. As You Desire Me 32. Petticoat Fever 36. The Emperor's Candlesticks 37. Arsène Lupin Returns 38. Adventure in Diamonds 40, many others.

Fitzpatrick, James A. (1902–1980).
American documentarist, who from 1925 produced and narrated innumerable travel shorts ('Fitzpatrick Traveltalks'), invariably concluding 'And so we leave . . .' Wrote, produced and directed one feature, *Song of Mexico* 45.

Fix, Paul (1901–1983) (Paul Fix Morrison).
American general-purpose actor who played hundreds of sheriffs, ranchers, doctors, etc., from the 20s.

The First Kiss 28. Ladies Love Brutes 30. The Last Mile 32. Zoo in Budapest 33. Little Man What Now? 34. Prisoner of Shark Island 36. Souls at Sea 37. News Is Made at Night 39. The Ghost Breakers 40. In Old Oklahoma 43. Dakota 45. Tycoon 47. California Passage 50. Hondo 53. The High and

the Mighty 54. Blood Alley 55. Giant 56. To Kill a Mockingbird 63. Shenandoah 65. Nevada Smith 66. El Dorado 67. The Day of the Evil Gun 68. Something Big 71. Grayeagle 77. Wanda Nevada 80, many others.

TV series: The Rifleman 57–61.

The Flag Lieutenant.
The stiff-upper-lip stage melodrama by W. P. Drury and Lee Trevor, about the intrepid exploits of a naval officer in an outpost of empire, was filmed as a silent in 1919 with George Wynn, and in 1926 with Henry Edwards. In 1932 Edwards appeared in a sound remake with Anna Neagle as his leading lady.

Flagg, Cash:
see *Steckler, Ray Dennis*.

Flagg, Fannie (1941–).
American TV comedienne, notably in *The New Dick Van Dyke Show*.

Five Easy Pieces 70. Some of My Best Friends Are 71. Stay Hungry 76. Sex and the Married Woman (TV) 77. Rabbit Test 78. Grease 78. My Best Friend Is a Vampire 88, etc.

Flagstad, Kirsten (1895–1962).
Norwegian operatic soprano whose only film appearance was, surprisingly, in *The Big Broadcast of 1938*.

Flaherty, Robert (1884–1951).
Very influential American documentary pioneer, originally an explorer; noted for superb visual sense. Claude Massot's *Nanook* (*Kabloonak*) in 1994 recreated Flaherty's expedition to the Arctic, and starred Charles Dance as Flaherty.

Biographies: 1953, *The World of Robert Flaherty* by Richard Griffith. 1963, *The Innocent Eye* by Arthur Calder-Marshall.
■ Nanook of the North 20. The Pottery Maker 25. Moana (co-d) 26. 24-Dollar Island 27. *White Shadows in the South Seas* (co-d) 28. Tabu (co-d) 31. Industrial Britain (co-d) 33. *Man of Aran* 34. *Elephant Boy* (co-d) 37. The Land 42. Louisiana Story (AANw) 48.

¶ I took it to the biggest of the distributors first – Paramount. When the film was over, they all pulled themselves together and got up in a rather dull way, I thought, and silently left the room. The manager came up to me and very kindly put his arm around my shoulders and told me that he was terribly sorry, but it was a film that just couldn't be shown to the public – *R.F. on Nanook of the North*

His films slip so easily into the stream of fictional cinema that they hardly seem like documentaries at all. – *Andrew Sarris*

World-famous and world-loved, his standing in his own profession was nil. You might suppose that a master film director who would work for a salary normally paid an assistant would be in great demand, but that is not the way of things in the film world. – *Richard Griffith*

Flanagan, Bud (1896–1968) (Reuben Weinthrop).
Genial British comedian, long teamed with Chesney Allen (qv for list of films); they formed part of the Crazy Gang. Wrote and sang catchy, sentimental songs: 'Hometown', 'Underneath the Arches', 'Umbrella Man', 'Strolling'.

Flanagan, Fionnula (Fionnuala) (1941–).
Irish-American character actress, mostly in TV.

Ulysses 67. *Rich Man Poor Man* (TV) 76. Nightmare in Badham County (TV) 76. Mary

White (TV) 77. Young Love First Love (TV) 79. Mr Patman 80. Through Naked Eyes (TV) 83. Scorned and Swindled (TV) 84. Youngblood 86. Mad at the Moon 92. Money for Nothing 93. White Mile (TV) 94, etc.

TV series: How the West Was Won 79.

Flanders, Ed (1934–).
American character actor and Truman impersonator.

Goodbye Raggedy Ann (TV) 71. Indict and Convict (TV) 74. The Legend of Lizzie Borden (TV) 75. Eleanor and Franklin (TV) 76. *The Amazing Howard Hughes* (TV) 77. MacArthur 77. Collision Course (TV) 77. Backstairs at the White House (TV) 79. The Ninth Configuration 80. Salem's Lot (TV) 80. True Confessions 81. The Pursuit of D. B. Cooper 81. Special Bulletin (TV) 83. Exorcist III 90, many others.

TV series: St Elsewhere 82–88.

Flannery, Susan (1943–).
American general-purpose actress, from TV soap opera *Days of Our Lives*.

The Towering Inferno 74. The Moneychangers (TV) 76. The Gumball Rally 76. Anatomy of a Seduction (TV) 79. Women in White (TV) 79, etc.

Flash Gordon.
American newspaper strip hero whose exploits were featured in three famous Hollywood serials starring Buster Crabbe. In the original *Flash Gordon* 36 our hero and his friends saved the Earth from collision with another planet at the cost of being stranded there at the mercy of the wicked Emperor Ming. *Flash Gordon's Trip to Mars* 38 and *Flash Gordon Conquers the Universe* 40 were compounded of similar elements. The directors respectively were Frederick Stephani; Ford Beebe and Robert Hill; and Ray Taylor. A softcore spoof, *Flesh Gordon*, appeared in 1974. In 1980 Dino de Laurentiis presented a lavish but empty remake of the original, and in the following year came a cartoon remake from Filmation.

flashback.
A break in chronological narrative during which we are shown events of past time which bear on the present situation. The device is as old as the cinema: you could say that *Intolerance* was composed of four flashbacks. As applied to more commonplace yarns, however, with the flashback narrated by one of the story's leading characters, the convention soared into popularity in the 30s until by 1945 or so a film looked very dated indeed if it was not told in retrospect. In the 50s flashbacks fell into absolute disuse, but are now creeping back into fashion again. Some notable uses are:

The Power and the Glory 33, which was advertised as being in 'Narratage' because Ralph Morgan spoke a commentary over the action. *Bride of Frankenstein* 35, which was narrated by Elsa Lanchester as Mary Shelley; the gag was that she also played the monster's mate. *The Great McGinty* 40, in which the flashback construction revealed the somewhat corrupt leading figures finally as penniless, thus mollifying the Hays Office. *Rebecca* 40, in which the introductory narrative, while revealing that Manderley was to go up in flames, also comforted in the knowledge that the hero and heroine would be saved. *Citizen Kane* 41, the complex structure of which was so influential that a whole host of pictures followed in which we tried to get at the truth about a character already dead, by questioning those who knew him: cf. *The Killers, The Rake's Progress, The Moon and Sixpence,*

The Bridge of San Luis Rey, The Woman in Question, Letter from an Unknown Woman, Rashomon, The Great Man, even *Doctor Zhivago. Hold Back the Dawn* 41, in which Charles Boyer as a penniless refugee visited Paramount Studios and sold his story to Mitchell Leisen. *The Mummy's Hand* 41, in which the ten-minute chunk telling how the mummy came to be buried alive was lifted straight from the 1932 film *The Mummy*. (Such economies have become commonplace.) *Roxie Hart* 42, in which George Montgomery told a twenty-year-old tale about a notorious lady who at the end of the film was revealed as the mother of his large family. *Ruthless* 48, a tortuous Zachary Scott melodrama, reviewed as follows by the British critic C. A. Lejeune:

> Beginning pictures at the end
> Is, I'm afraid, a modern trend;
> But I'd find *Ruthless* much more winning
> If it could end at the beginning.

Road to Utopia 45, in which Hope and Lamour appeared as old folks telling the story; as a pay-off their 'son' appeared, looking just like Crosby, and Hope told the audience: 'We adopted him.' *Passage to Marseilles* 44, a complex melodrama ranging from Devil's Island to war-torn Britain; it has flashbacks within flashbacks *within flashbacks*. In *Dead of Night* 45, all the characters told supernatural experiences to a psychiatrist, who was then murdered by one of them; the murderer then woke up with no recollection of his nightmare, and proceeded to meet all the other characters again as though for the first time, being caught in an endless series of recurring dreams. *Enchantment* 47, and later *Death of a Salesman* 52, and many films up to *I Was Happy Here* 66, in which characters walk straight out of the present into the past, dispensing with the boring 'I remember' bit. *Edward My Son* 49 and *Teahouse of the August Moon* 56, in which characters step out of the play to tell the story to the audience. *Dead Reckoning* 47, in which Humphrey Bogart confesses the entire plot to a priest. *Kind Hearts and Coronets* 49, in which the story springs from the memoirs of a murderer being written on the night before his execution. *Sunset Boulevard* 50, in which the story is told by the dead hero. *An Inspector Calls* 54, in which a supernatural figure visits a family to make them remember their harsh treatment of a girl who has committed suicide. *Repeat Performance* 47, in which a desperate husband relives the events of the year, leading up to his predicament, and gets a chance to change the outcome. *A Woman's Face* 41, in which the story was based on the recollections of eight courtroom witnesses. *The Locket* and *Lust for Gold*, in which complex flashbacks framed and divided the action.

If the format is to catch on again it will have to be more deftly used than in two 60s films: *Ride Beyond Vengeance*, with its completely irrelevant framing story about a census-taking, and *Lady L*, in which the framing story with the characters as old folks is only marginally less inept than the basic one. Two big-scale musicals, *Star!* and *Funny Girl*, have flashbacks with style but little purpose, and *Little Big Man* barely used its framework except to show that Dustin Hoffman can play a 121-year-old.

Flavin, James (1906–1976).
Irish-American supporting actor, usually as genial or bewildered cop.

King Kong 33. The Grapes of Wrath 40. Cloak and Dagger 46. Desert Fury 47. Mighty Joe Young 50. Fighter Attack 55. Mister Roberts 55. The Last Hurrah 58. It's a Mad Mad Mad Mad World 63. Cheyenne Autumn 64. Bullwhip Griffin 67, many others.

fleapit.
An affectionate British term for the kind of tatty little cinema in which, it was sometimes alleged, the management loaned a hammer with each ticket.

Fleetwood, Susan (1944–).
Scottish leading actress, mainly on stage and TV.

Clash of the Titans 81. The Sacrifice 86. White Mischief 87. Dream Demon 88. The Krays 90. A Few Short Journeys of the Heart (TV) 94, etc.

Fleischer, Max (1889–1972).
Austrian-born cartoonist and producer, long in Hollywood. Created Betty Boop, Koko, Out of the Inkwell series, Popeye the Sailor, etc. His brother *Dave Fleischer* (1894–1979) worked as his administrative head.

Gulliver's Travels 39. Mr Bug Goes to Town 41.

Fleischer, Richard (1916–).
American director, son of Max Fleischer; former shorts producer. His films usually sound more interesting than they prove to be.

Autobiography: 1994, *Just Tell Me When to Cry: A Memoir*.

■ Child of Divorce 46. Banjo 47. Bodyguard 48. So This Is New York 49. Make Mine Laughs 49. Trapped 49. Follow Me Quietly 49. The Clay Pigeon 49. The Armored Car Robbery 50. *The Narrow Margin* 51. *The Happy Time* 52. Arena 53. *Twenty Thousand Leagues under the Sea* 54. Violent Saturday 55. The Girl in the Red Velvet Swing 55. Bandido 56. Between Heaven and Hell 56. *The Vikings* 57. These Thousand Hills 58. Compulsion 59. Crack in the Mirror 60. The Big Gamble 61. Barabbas 62. *Fantastic Voyage* 66. Doctor Dolittle 67. *The Boston Strangler* 68. Che! 69. Tora! Tora! Tora! 70. The Last Run 70. Blind Terror 70. The New Centurions 71. 10 Rillington Place 71. Soylent Green 72. The Don is Dead 73. Mr Majestyk 74. The Spikes Gang 74. Mandingo 75. The Incredible Sarah 76. The Prince and the Pauper 77. Ashanti 78. The Jazz Singer 80. Tough Enough 82. Amityville 3-D 83. Conan, King of Thieves 84. Conan the Destroyer 85. Red Sonja 86. Million Dollar Mystery 87.

Fleiss, Noah (1984–).
American child actor, from television and the stage, a former model.

Josh and S.A.M. 93.

Fleming, Eric (1924–1966).
Taciturn American general-purpose actor. Died by drowning.

Conquest of Space 55. Fright 57. Curse of the Undead 59. The Glass Bottom Boat 66, etc.

TV series: Rawhide (as Gil Favor, trail boss) 58–65.

Fleming, Ian (1888–1969).
Australian-born character actor, long in British films as doctors, civil servants, solicitors, etc. A memorable Dr Watson in the 30s series with Arthur Wontner as Sherlock Holmes.

Second to None 26. The School for Scandal 30. The Sleeping Cardinal 31. The Missing Rembrandt 32. The Triumph of Sherlock Holmes 35. The Crouching Beast 35. Jump for Glory 37. The Nursemaid who Disappeared 39. The Butler's Dilemma 43. George in Civvy Street 45. Quartet 48. The Woman in Question 50. The Voice of Merrill 52. The Seekers 54. High Flight 57. Bluebeard's Ten Honeymoons 60. No My Darling Daughter 61. The Boys 63. The Return of Mr Moto 65, many others.

Fleming, Ian (1908–1964).
Creator of James Bond, whose exploits have been so successfully filmed from the novels.

Fleming, Rhonda (1922–   ) (Marilyn Louis).
Red-haired American leading lady of the 40s and 50s.

When Strangers Marry 43. Spellbound 45. The Spiral Staircase 45. Adventure Island 46. Out of the Past (Build My Gallows High) 47. A Yankee in King Arthur's Court 49. Cry Danger 50. The Redhead and the Cowboy 51. The Great Lover 51. Little Egypt 52. The Golden Hawk 52. Serpent of the Nile 53. Inferno 53. Yankee Pasha 54. The Killer Is Loose 56. Slightly Scarlet 56. Gunfight at the OK Corral 57. Gun Glory 57. Home Before Dark 58. Alias Jesse James 59. The Big Circus 59. Run For Your Wife 66. The Nude Bomb 80, etc.

Fleming, Victor (1883–1949).
American director, long with MGM: he was in charge of a few outstanding films, but they seemed to succeed for other reasons.
■ When the Clouds Roll By 20. The Mollycoddle 20. Mamma's Affair 21. Woman's Place 22. Red Hot Romance 22. The Lane That Had No Turning 22. Anna Ascends 22. Dark Secrets 23. Law of the Lawless 23. To the Last Man 23. Call of the Canyon 23. Empty Hands 24. The Code of the Sea 24. A Son of His Father 25. Adventure 25. The Devil's Cargo 25. Lord Jim 25. The Blind Goddess 26. *Mantrap* 26. Rough Riders 27. The Way of all Flesh 27. Hula 27. Abie's Irish Rose 28. The Awakening 28. Wolf Song 29. *The Virginian* 29. Common Clay 30. Renegades 30. Around the World in Eighty Minutes 31. *The Wet Parade* 32. *Red Dust* 32. The White Sister 33. Bombshell 33. *Treasure Island* 34. Reckless 35. The Farmer Takes a Wife 35. Captains Courageous 37. *Test Pilot* 38. *The Wizard of Oz* 39. Gone with the Wind (AA) (with assistance) 39. *Dr Jekyll and Mr Hyde* 41. Tortilla Flat 42. A Guy Named Joe 43. Adventure 45. Joan of Arc 48.

Flemyng, Gordon (1934–   ).
British director, from TV.
Solo for Sparrow 62. Five to One 63. Dr Who and the Daleks 65. Great Catherine 68. The Split 68. The Last Grenade 69. A Good Human Story (TV) 77. Mirage (TV) 78. Cloud Waltzer (TV) 87, etc.

Flemyng, Robert (1912–   ).
British actor who usually plays attractive professional men. On stage from 1931, films from 1936 (*Head Over Heels*).
The Guinea Pig 49. The Blue Lamp 50. The Holly and the Ivy 52. The Man Who Never Was 55. Funny Face (US) 56. Windom's Way 57. A Touch of Larceny 59. The Terror of Dr Hitchcock (It.) 63. The Deadly Affair 66. The Spy with a Cold Nose 67. The Blood Beast Terror 67. Young Winston 72. Travels with my Aunt 73. The Medusa Touch 77. The 39 Steps 78. Kafka 91. Shadowlands 94, etc.

Fletcher, Bramwell (1904–1988).
British light leading man of the 30s.
Chick 30. To What Red Hell 30. Raffles (US) 31. Svengali (US) 31. The Mummy (US) 32. The Scarlet Pimpernel 34. Random Harvest (US) 42. White Cargo (US) 42. The Immortal Sergeant (US) 42, etc.

Fletcher, Cyril (1913–   ).
British comedian and entertainer who has made appearances in a few films.
Yellow Canary 43. Nicholas Nickleby 47. A Piece of Cake 48, etc.

Fletcher, Dexter (1966–   ).
British juvenile actor, in films from 1972.
Bugsy Malone 76. Les Misérables (TV) 78. The Long Good Friday 80. The Elephant Man 80. The Bounty 84. Revolution 85. Caravaggio 86. Lionheart 87. Gothic 86. The Raggedy Rawney 87. When the Whales Came 89. The Rachel Papers 89. Exit Genua 89. The Mad Monkey 90. All Out 91, etc.

Fletcher, Louise (1934–   ).
American character actress.
Thieves Like Us 74. Russian Roulette 75. *One Flew Over the Cuckoo's Nest* (AA) 75. Exorcist II: The Heretic 77. *The Cheap Detective* 78. Thou Shalt Not Commit Adultery (TV) 78. The Lady in Red 79. Natural Enemies 79. The Magician of Lublin 79. The Lucky Star 80. Mama Dracula (Fr.) 80. Strange Behaviour 81. *Brainstorm* 83. Firestarter 84. The Boy Who Could Fly 85. Invaders from Mars 86. Best of the Best 89. In a Child's Name 92. Tryst 94. Tollbooth 94, etc.

Flicker, Theodore J. (1930–   ).
American director, former Greenwich Village satirist.
The Troublemaker 64. The President's Analyst 68. Up in the Cellar (& w) 70. Playmates (TV) 72. Guess Who's Sleeping in My Bed (TV) 73. Just a Little Inconvenience (TV) 77. Last of the Good Guys (& w) 78. Where the Ladies Go (TV) 80. Soggy Bottom USA 82, etc.

The Flintstones.

An animated TV suburban situation comedy set in the Stone Age, created by Bill Hanna and Joe Barbera, was turned into a feature film using actors in 1994. In the cartoon version, Fred Flintstone was voiced by Alan Reed, his wife Wilma by Jean Vanderpyl, and their pet dinosaur, Dino, by Mel Blanc, who also supplied the voice for their neighbour Barney Rubble. Broadcast from 1960–66 and often repeated, it owed much to an earlier TV sitcom, *The Honeymooners*, starring Jackie Gleason, and became the longest-running animated show on television; its spin-offs included *The Flintstone Kids*, broadcast in the late 80s. In the feature film, John Goodman appeared as Fred, Rosie O'Donnell as Wilma, and Rick Moranis as Barney.

Flippen, Jay C. (1898–1971).
Bulky American character actor with vaudeville background; often seen as cop, sergeant or sheriff.
Marie Galante 34. Intrigue 48. Love that Brute 50. Flying Leathernecks 51. Bend of the River 52. The Wild One 53. The Far Country 55. Oklahoma 55. *The Killing* 56. Night Passage 57. From Hell to Texas 58. Studs Lonigan 60. Cat Ballou 65. Firecreek 67. Hellfighters 68. The Seven Minutes 71, many others.
TV series: Ensign O'Toole 62.

Flon, Suzanne (1923–   ).
French leading actress.
La Cage aux Filles 49. La Belle Image 51. Moulin Rouge 53. Mr Arkadin 55. *Thou Shalt Not Kill* 61. A Monkey in Winter 62. The Trial 62. The Train 64. Le Soleil des Voyous 67. Le Silencieux 73. Mr Klein 76. Blackout 77. Comme un Boomerang 77. L'Eté meurtrier 83, etc.

Florey, Robert (1900–1979).
French-born director, in Hollywood since 1921.
The Romantic Age 27. The Coconuts 29. *The Murders in the Rue Morgue* 32. Ex Lady 33. The Woman in Red 34. Hollywood Boulevard 36. Hotel Imperial 38. The Face Behind the Mask 40. Lady Gangster 42. Dangerously They Live 43. God Is My Co-Pilot 44. *The Beast with Five Fingers* 46. Monsieur Verdoux (co-d) 47. Rogues' Regiment 48. Outpost in Morocco 48. Johnny One Eye 49. The Gangster We Made 50, many second features; latterly directed hundreds of TV films. Also wrote several scripts, including work on *Frankenstein* 31.

Flowers, Bess (1900–1984).
American bit-part player, 'queen of the Hollywood extras', who appeared in literally hundreds of films between 1922 and 1962.

Fluellen, Joel (1908–1990).
American character actor. Committed suicide.
Two Guys from Milwaukee 46. The Burning Cross 47. You're in the Navy Now 51. Affair in Trinidad 52. The Decks Ran Red 59. A Raisin in the Sun 61. The Chase 66. The Skin Game 71. The Bingo Long Travelling All Stars and Motor Kings 76, many others.

Flynn, Errol (1909–1959).
Tasmanian leading man who led an adventurous life on and off screen and by his handsome impudence maintained a world-wide following for nearly twenty years before hard living got the better of him.
Wrote two autobiographical books: 1934, *Beam Ends* and 1959, *My Wicked Wicked Ways*, and a novel, 1952, *Showdown*; one of several biographies was 1977, *The Life and Crimes of Errol Flynn* by Lionel Godfrey.
■ In the Wake of the Bounty (as Fletcher Christian) 33. Murder at Monte Carlo (GB) 34. The Case of the Curious Bride 34. Don't Bet on Blondes 35. *Captain Blood* 35. *The Charge of the Light Brigade* 36. The Green Light 36. The Prince and the Pauper 37. Another Dawn 37. The Perfect Specimen 37. *The Adventures of Robin Hood* 38. Four's a Crowd 38. The Sisters 38. The Dawn Patrol 38. Dodge City 39. Elizabeth and Essex 39. Virginia City 39. *The Sea Hawk* 40. Santa Fe Trail 40. Footsteps in the Dark 41. Dive Bomber 41. *They Died with Their Boots On* 41. Desperate Journey 42. *Gentleman Jim* 42. Edge of Darkness 43. Northern Pursuit 43. Thank Your Lucky Stars 43. Uncertain Glory 44. Objective Burma 45. San Antonio 45. Never Say Goodbye 45. Cry Wolf 46. Escape Me Never 47. Silver River 47. The New Adventures of Don Juan 48. *That Forsyte Woman* (as Soames) 49. Montana 50. Rocky Mountain 50. Kim 51. The Adventures of Captain Fabian (& w) 51. Mara Maru 52. Against All Flags 52. The Master of Ballantrae (GB) 53. Crossed Swords (It.) 53. Lilacs in the Spring (GB) 55. The Dark Avenger (GB) 55. King's Rhapsody (GB) 56. The Big Boodle 56. Istanbul 57. The Sun Also Rises 57. *Too Much Too Soon* (as John Barrymore) 58. Roots of Heaven 58. Cuban Rebel Girls 59.
TV series: Errol Flynn Theatre 57.
☻ For living several lives in half of one, and almost getting away with it. *The Adventures of Robin Hood.*

¶ He was one of the wild characters of the world, said Ann Sheridan. His wicked wicked ways were well known, but nobody ever admitted to disliking him for them; perhaps because, as Jack L. Warner said:
To the Walter Mittys of the world he was all the heroes in one magnificent, sexy, animal package.
Yakima Canutt added:
I think any man who had his appeal for women would have played it just the way he did – a bit wild.
Henry King's view was that

He loved to talk about how much he could drink and the women he'd made love to, but most of it was just the rationalizations of a disappointed moralist.

ette Davis said:

Basically a nice man, and very honest about the fact that he knew he didn't have much talent.

d drinking cronies like David Niven (who shared ith him a house called Cirrhosis-by-the-sea) d Peter Finch later talked of him with affection. ewis Milestone perhaps exaggerated slightly hen he said:

His faults harmed no one but himself.

ut even the people he did jar against seem to ave borne him little ill-will, with the possible xception of the Australian creditors from whom e escaped before going to Hollywood. In a later roadcast to the people down under, he said vially:

If there's anyone listening to whom I owe money, I'm prepared to forget it if you are.

ene Autry said:

He spent more time on a bar stool, or in court, or in the headlines, or in bed, than anyone I knew.

nd David Niven summed up his own experience:

The great thing about Errol was that you knew precisely where you were with him – because he *always* let you down.

 lot of people certainly looked at him and tut- utted. Herbert Wilcox thought that:

His love of life defeated his ability as an artist.

nd Leslie Mallory described his life as:

A fifty-year trespass against good taste.

here were other ways of looking at his behaviour. ne of his wives, Nora Eddington, said rather roudly:

He wasn't afraid of anything, particularly if there was a challenge to it.

ome of the things he did were a reaction against eing under-employed:

I felt like an impostor, taking all that money for reciting ten or twelve lines of nonsense a day.

e defended himself blithely:

The public has always expected me to be a playboy, and a decent chap never lets his public down.

nd:

Women won't let me stay single, and I won't let myself stay married.

e exaggerated cheerfully in the cause of publicity:

I allow myself to be understood as a colourful fragment in a drab world.

ut he was determined to have a good time:

I'll live this half of my life, I don't care about the other half.

e gleefully acknowledged his troubles:

My difficulty is trying to reconcile my gross habits with my net income.

nd at the end he could say:

I've had a hell of a lot of fun, and I've enjoyed every minute of it.

At his passing, Tony Britton cabled Trevor Howard:

Old Errol died laughing. Can you beat that?

Famous line (*The Adventures of Robin Hood*): 'It's injustice I hate, not the Normans.'

Famous line (*Desperate Journey*): 'Now for Australia and a crack at those Japs!'

~He made an uncredited cameo appearance in Always Together 47.

Flynn, Joe (1925–1974).

American character comedian, much on TV.

Did You Hear the One about the Travelling Saleslady? 68. Million Dollar Duck 71. Superdad 74, etc.

TV series: McHale's Navy 62–65.

Flynn, John.

American director.

■ The Sergeant 68. The Jerusalem File 72. The Outfit 73. Rolling Thunder 77. Defiance 80. Marilyn, the Untold Story (TV) 80. Touched 83. Best Seller 87. Escape 89. Out for Justice 91. Nails (TV) 92. Brainscan 94.

Flynn, Sean (1941–1970).

Athletic American leading man, son of Errol Flynn.

Son of Captain Blood 62. Duel at Rio Grande 62. Five Ashore in Singapore, etc.

Foch, Nina (1924–   ) (Nina Fock).

Cool, blonde, Dutch-born actress, long in America. Also associate director of George Stevens' *The Diary of Anne Frank*.

■ The Return of the Vampire 43. Nine Girls 43. Cry of the Werewolf 44. Shadows in the Night 44. A Song to Remember 44. I Love a Mystery 44. Escape in the Fog 45. Prison Ship 45. *My Name Is Julia Ross* 45. Johnny o'Clock 46. The Guilt of Janet Ames 48. The Dark Past 49. Undercover Man 50. *An American in Paris* 51. Young Man with Ideas 51. Scaramouche 52. Fast Company 53. Sombrero 53. *Executive Suite* (AAN) 54. Four Guns to the Border 54. You're Never Too Young 55. Illegal 55. The Ten Commandments 56. Three Brave Men 57. Spartacus 60. Cash McCall 60. Prescription Murder (TV) 67. Gidget Grows Up (TV) 69. Such Good Friends 71. Female Artillery (TV) 73. Salty 73. The Great Houdinis (TV) 76. Mahogany 76. Jennifer 78. Child of Glass (TV) 78. Ebony, Ivory and Jade (TV) 78. Rich and Famous 81. Shadow Chasers (TV) 85. Dixie Lanes 87. Skin Deep 89. Sliver 93. Morning Glory 93.

fog

has been a godsend to many a cinematic entertainment, whether it's the genuine pea-souper inseparable from Hollywood's idea of London, or the ankle-high white mist which used to distinguish heaven and dream sequences. Fog can provide a splendid dramatic background, especially in horror-thrillers like *Dracula, The Wolf Man* and *The Cat and the Canary;* but too often it is simply imposed on a film to force a particular atmosphere, as in *Footsteps in the Fog, Fog over Frisco, Fog Island, Winterset, Out of the Fog* and *The Notorious Landlady. Barbary Coast* seemed to be permanently enveloped in fog, as did the village in *Sherlock Holmes and the Scarlet Claw:* while in *The Adventures of Sherlock Holmes* London had fog in May! Fog was dramatically used in *The VIPs* and *The Divorce of Lady X* (for bringing people together in a hotel); in *The Runaway Bus* (for bringing people together in an abandoned village); in *Midnight Lace* (for masking the identity of the voice threatening Doris Day); in *Twenty-Three Paces to Baker Street* (for hampering the villain but not the blind hero); in *Alias Nick Beal* (as a background for the devil's materialization); in *The Lost Continent* (as a nauseous yellow background for the weird community); in *Random Harvest* (as a means for the hero's escape); and in the various versions of *The Sea Wolf* (for causing the accident that brings hero and heroine together on Wolf Larsen's boat). Even comedies find it useful: the chase through fog in *After the Fox* results in happy confusion. Oddly enough John Carpenter's film *Fog* made insufficient use of its titular commodity.

Foghorn Leghorn.

Boastful rooster from the Deep South, a star of Warner Brothers' Merrie Melodies and Looney Tunes cartoons. His voice was supplied by Mel Blanc.

Walky Talky Hawky (AAN) 46. The Foghorn Leghorn 48. Leghorn Swoggled 51. All Fowled Up 55. The High and the Flighty 56. Fox Terror 57. A Broken Leghorn 59. Strangled Eggs 61. Banty Raids 63, etc.

Foley artist.

A sound effects specialist, named after Jack Foley, who is credited for creating the techniques for adding post-production sound effects to enhance the action on the screen.

Foley, James.

American director and screenwriter.

Reckless 84. At Close Range 86. Who's That Girl 87. After Dark, My Sweet 90. Glengarry Glen Ross 92, etc.

Folies Bergère.

This innocuous 1935 musical comedy was written by Bess Meredith and Hal Long as a vehicle for Maurice Chevalier, who played a dual role; at the climax his double had to masquerade as his wife as himself. It was too good an idea not to be used again. In 1941 came *That Night in Rio* with Don Ameche; in 1951, there was *On the Riviera* with Danny Kaye. Kaye apparently liked it so much that he had it altered a little and it served for *On the Double* 61 as well.

Folsey, George J. (1898–1988).

American cinematographer who was nominated 13 times for Academy Awards for cinematography.

The Fear Market 20. Born Rich 24. *Applause* 29. The Smiling Lieutenant 31. Reckless 35. *The Great Ziegfeld* 36. The Shining Hour 38. Lady Be Good 41. Meet Me in St Louis 44. A Guy Named Joe 44. Under the Clock 45. The Green Years (AAN) 46. Green Dolphin Street (AAN) 47. State of the Union 48. Take Me Out to the Ball Game 48. The Great Sinner 49. *Adam's Rib* 49. Man with a Cloak 51. Million Dollar Mermaid 53. Executive Suite (AAN) 54. Seven Brides for Seven Brothers (AAN) 55. The Fastest Gun Alive 56. Imitation General 58. I Passed for White 60. The Balcony (AAN) 63, etc.

Fonda, Bridget (1964–   ).

American actress, the daughter of Peter Fonda.

You Can't Hurry Love 88. Aria 88. Shag 88. Scandal 89. Strapless 89. The Godfather Part III 90. Roger Corman's Frankenstein Unbound 90. Drop Dead Fred 91. Leather Jackets 91. Iron Maze 91. Out of the Rain 91. Doc Hollywood 91. Single White Female 92. Bodies, Rest and Motion 92. Singles 92. Bodies, Rest & Motion 93. Point of No Return 93. Little Buddha 93. It Could Happen to You 94. Camilla 94. The Road to Wellville 94, etc.

Fonda, Henry (1905–1982).

American leading actor who used to play gauche young fellows and graduated to roles of amiable wisdom. Long stage experience; father of Jane and Peter Fonda.

■ The Farmer Takes a Wife 35. Way Down East 35. I Dream Too Much 36. The Trail of the Lonesome Pine 36. *The Moon's Our Home* 36. Spendthrift 36. Wings of the Morning (GB) 37. You Only Live Once 37. Slim 37. That Certain Woman 37. I Met My Love Again 37. Jezebel 38. Blockade 38. Spawn of the North 38. The Mad Miss Manton 38. Jesse James 39. Let Us Live 39. The Story of Alexander Graham Bell 39. *Young Mr Lincoln* 39. Drums Along the Mohawk 39. The Grapes of Wrath (AAN) 40. Lilian Russell 40. The Return of Frank James 40. Chad Hanna 40. *The Lady Eve* 41. Wild

Geese Calling 41. You Belong to Me 41. The Male Animal 42. Rings on Her Fingers 42. The Big Street 42. Tales of Manhattan 42. The Magnificent Dope 42. The Immortal Sergeant 42; *The Ox Bow Incident* 43; war service; *My Darling Clementine* (as Wyatt Earp) 46. The Long Night 47. The Fugitive 47. Daisy Kenyon 47. On Our Merry Way 48. Fort Apache 48; long absence on stage; Mister Roberts 55. The Wrong Man 56. War and Peace 56. *Twelve Angry Men* (BFA) (& p) 57. *Stage Struck* 57. The Tin Star 57. Warlock 59. The Man Who Understood Women 59. Advise and Consent 61. The Longest Day 62. How the West Was Won 62. Spencer's Mountain 63. The Best Man 64. *Fail Safe* 64. The Dirty Game 64. Sex and the Single Girl 64. The Battle of the Bulge 65. The Rounders 65. In Harm's Way 65. Big Hand for a Little Lady 66. Welcome to Hard Times 67. Firecreek 67. Stranger on the Run (TV) 67. Madigan 68. Yours, Mine and Ours 68. The Boston Strangler 68. Once upon a Time in the West 69. Too Late the Hero 69. There Was a Crooked Man 70. The Cheyenne Social Club 70. Sometimes a Great Notion 71. The Red Pony (TV) 72. The Serpent 72. The Alpha Caper (TV) 73. Ash Wednesday 73. My Name Is Nobody (It.) 73. Inside Job 75. Midway 76. Captains and the Kings 76. Tentacles 77. Rollercoaster 77. The Great Smokey Roadblock 78. The Swarm 78. Home to Stay (TV) 78. Fedora 78. Roots: The Next Generations (TV) 79. Wanda Nevada 79. Gideon's Trumpet (TV) 79. City on Fire 79. Meteor 79. *On Golden Pond* (AA) 81.

TV series: The Deputy 59–60. The Smith Family 70–71.

🌑 For being a 40-year paradox: a self-effacing star. *Twelve Angry Men*.

¶ I ain't really Henry Fonda. Nobody could have that much integrity. – *H.F.*

A lean, stringy, dark-faced piece of electricity walked out on the screen and he had me. I believed my own story again. – *John Steinbeck on watching The Grapes of Wrath*

~In 1980 Fonda was given an honorary Oscar 'in recognition of his brilliant accomplishments'.

Fonda, Jane (1937–).
American leading lady, daughter of Henry Fonda. Stage and modelling experience. She was married to director Roger Vadim (1965–73).

Biography: 1991, *Citizen Jane: The Turbulent Life of Jane Fonda* by Christopher Andersen.
■ Tall Story (debut) 60. Walk on the Wild Side 61. The Chapman Report 62. Period of Adjustment 62. In the Cool of the Day 63. Sunday in New York 63. La Ronde 64. Joy House 65. Cat Ballou 65. The Chase 66. Any Wednesday 66. The Game is Over (Fr.) 66. Hurry Sundown 67. Barefoot in the Park 67. Histoires Extraordinaires 67. Barbarella 68. They Shoot Horses Don't They? (AAN) 69. *Klute* (AA) 71. F.T.A. (& p) 72. Tout va Bien 72. Steelyard Blues 72. A Doll's House 74. The Bluebird 76. Fun with Dick and Jane 77. Julia (BFA, AAN) 77. Coming Home (AA) 78. California Suite 78. Comes a Horseman 79. The China Syndrome (BFA, AAN) 80. The Electric Horseman 80. Nine to Five 81. On Golden Pond (AAN) 81. Rollover 81. The Dollmaker (TV) 84. Agnes of God 85. The Morning After (AAN) 86. Leonard, Part 6 87. Old Gringo (& p) 89. Stanley and Iris 90.

¶ Being a movie star is not a purpose. – *J.F.*
I'm hard-working. Honest. – *J.F.*

Fonda, Peter (1939–).
American actor, son of Henry Fonda.
Tammy and the Doctor 63. The Victors 63. Lilith

64. The Wild Angels 66. The Trip 67. *Easy Rider* (& p) 69. The Last Movie 71. The Hired Hand (& d) 71. Two People 73. Dirty Mary Crazy Larry 74. Open Season 74. Race with the Devil 75. Killer Force 75. Fighting Mad 76. 92 in the Shade 76. Futureworld 76. Outlaw Blues 77. High Ballin' 78. Wanda Nevada (& d) 79. The Hostage Tower (TV) 80. Cannonball Run 81. Split Image 82. Peppermint Freedom 84. Certain Fury 85. Come the Day 85. Hawker 86. The Long Voyage 88. The Rose Garden 89. Fatal Mission 90. South Beach 92. Deadfall 93. Molly & Gina 94. Nadja 94, etc.

¶ Civilization has always been a bust. – *P.F.*

Fonseca, Gregg.
American production designer.
Eyes of Fire 84. A Nightmare on Elm Street 84. Critters 85. Johnny Be Good 88. Honey, I Shrunk the Kids 89. The Guardian 89. Shattered 91. Wayne's World 92. Coneheads 93. Wayne's World 2 93.

Fontaine, Joan (1917–) (Joan de Havilland; sister of Olivia).
British-born leading actress, in America from childhood. Became typed as a shy English rose; later made efforts to play sophisticated roles.

Autobiography: 1978, *No Bed of Roses*.
■ No More Ladies 35. Quality Street 37. You Can't Beat Love 37. Music for Madame 37. Maid's Night Out 38. A Damsel in Distress 38. Blonde Cheat 38. The Man Who Found Himself 38. The Duke of West Point 38. Sky Giant 38. Gunga Din 39. Man of Conquest 39. The Women 39. *Rebecca* (AAN) 40. *Suspicion* (AA) 41. This Above All 42. The Constant Nymph (AAN) 43. *Jane Eyre* 43. *Frenchman's Creek* 44. The Affairs of Susan 45. *From This Day Forward* 46. Ivy 47. The Emperor Waltz 48. Kiss the Blood off My Hands 48. *Letter from an Unknown Woman* 48. You Gotta Stay Happy 48. Born To Be Bad 50. September Affair 50. Darling How Could You? 51. Something To Live For 52. Ivanhoe 52. Decameron Nights (GB) 53. Flight to Tangier 53. The Bigamist 53. Casanova's Big Night 54. Serenade 56. Beyond a Reasonable Doubt 56. Island in the Sun 56. Until They Sail 57. A Certain Smile 58. Tender Is the Night 61. Voyage to the Bottom of the Sea 61. The Devil's Own (The Witches) (GB) 66. The Users (TV) 79.
🌑 For successfully playing several variations on what was clearly a limited theme. *Rebecca*.

¶ If you keep marrying as I do, you learn everybody's hobby. – *J.F.*

Famous line (*Rebecca*): 'Last night I dreamed I went to Manderley again.'

Fontanne, Lynn (1887–1983).
Celebrated British-born stage actress, long in America and the wife of Alfred Lunt. Never really took to the screen.
■ The Man Who Found Himself 25. Second Youth 26. The Guardsman (AAN) 32. Stage Door Canteen 43.

footage.
Length of a film expressed in feet.

Foote, Horton (1916–).
American screenwriter and dramatist.
To Kill a Mockingbird (AA) 62. Baby, the Rain Must Fall 65. The Chase 66. Hurry, Sundown 67. Fools Parade 71. Tomorrow 72. Tender Mercies (AA) 83. 1918 84. On Valentine's Day 86. The Trip to Bountiful (AAN) 85. Convicts 91. Of Mice and Men 92, etc.

Foran, Dick (1910–1979) (Nicholas Foran).
Burly American leading man of light comedies and westerns in the early 40s; often played the good guy who didn't get the girl.
Stand Up and Cheer 34. Shipmates Forever 35. The Petrified Forest 36. The Perfect Specimen 37. Four Daughters 38. Daughters Courageous 39. The Mummy's Hand 40. Horror Island 41. Butch Minds the Baby 42. He's My Guy 43. Guest Wife 45. Fort Apache 48. El Paso 49. Al Jennings of Oklahoma 51. Chicago Confidential 57. Atomic Submarine 60. Taggart 64, many others.
TV series: OK Crackerby 65.

Forbes, Bryan (1926–) (John Clarke).
Lively British small-part actor who became a useful scriptwriter, director and production executive. He is also a novelist. Married actress Nanette Newman.
Autobiographies: 1976, *Notes for a Life*. 1992, *A Divided Life*.
■ AS ACTOR: The Small Back Room 48. All Over the Town 48. Dear Mr Prohack 49. The Wooden Horse 50. Green Grow the Rushes 51. Appointment in London 52. Sea Devils 53. Wheel of Fate 53. The Million Pound Note 54. *An Inspector Calls* 54. Up to his Neck 54. The Colditz Story 54. Passage Home 55. Now and Forever 55. The Quatermass Experiment 55. The Last Man to Hang 55. The Extra Day 56. It's Great to be Young 56. The Baby and the Battleship 56. Satellite in the Sky 56. Quatermass II 57. The Key 58. I Was Monty's Double 58. Yesterday's Enemy 59. *The League of Gentlemen* 59. The Guns of Navarone 61. A Shot in the Dark 64. The Slipper and the Rose 76. International Velvet 78.
■ AS WRITER/PRODUCER/DIRECTOR: Cockleshell Heroes (w) 56. The Baby and the Battleship (w) 56. The Black Tent (w) 56. House of Secrets (w) 56. *I Was Monty's Double* (w) 58. The Captain's Table (w) 59. The Angry Silence (w) 59. *The League of Gentlemen* (w) 60. Man in the Moon (w) 60. *Whistle down the Wind* (d) 61. Only Two Can Play (w) 62. Station Six Sahara (w) 62. *The L-Shaped Room* (wd) 62. Of Human Bondage (w) 64. The High Bright Sun (w) 64. Seance on a Wet Afternoon (wd) 64. King Rat (wd) 65. The Wrong Box (pd) 66. The Whisperers (wd) 67. Deadfall (wd) 67. The Madwoman of Chaillot (d) 69. The Raging Moon (wd) 70. The Stepford Wives (d) 74. The Slipper and the Rose (wd) 76. International Velvet (wd) 78. Sunday Lovers (d part) 80. Jessie (TV) (d) 80. Better Late Than Never 82. The Naked Face (d) 85. The Endless Game (d) 89. Chaplin (co-w) 92.

¶ I may not have come up the hard way, but I have come up the whole way. – *B.F.*

An actor must have arrogance, conceit . . . I would never have made it as an actor, but I still have that conceit. – *B.F.*

If you treat the production of films like the production of shoes, you end up with Hush Puppies – *B.F.*

I wish Bernie Delfont had had the courage of my convictions more often. – *B.F., of his period as production controller at EMI*

I knew I was there at Elstree to be shot at, but I never found time to be fitted for a bullet-proof vest. – *B.F.*

He perpetually pursues the anticliché only to arrive at anticlimax. – *Andrew Sarris, 1968*

Forbes, Mary (1882–1974).
British character actress in Hollywood, usually as haughty society lady.
Sunny Side Up 29. A Farewell to Arms 32. Blonde Bombshell 33. Les Misérables 35. Wee Willie Winkie 37. The Awful Truth 37. Always

Goodbye 38. You Can't Take It With You 38. The Adventures of Sherlock Holmes 40. This Above All 42. The Picture of Dorian Gray 44. Ivy 47. You Gotta Stay Happy 48. The Ten Commandments 56, many others.

Forbes, Meriel (1913–) (M. Forbes-Robertson).
British stage actress, wife of Sir Ralph Richardson.
   Borrow a Million 35. Young Man's Fancy 39. Come on George 39. The Gentle Sex 43. The Captive Heart 46. Home at Seven 52. Oh What a Lovely War 69.

Forbes, Ralph (1902–1951) (Ralph Taylor).
British leading man who became a Hollywood star in the late 20s.
   The Fifth Form at St Dominics (GB) 21. Beau Geste 26. Mr Wu 29. The Trail of '98 30. Bachelor Father 31. Smilin' Through 32. The Barretts of Wimpole Street 33. The Three Musketeers 36. Romeo and Juliet 36. If I Were King 39. Elizabeth and Essex 39. Frenchman's Creek 44, etc.

Forbes, Scott (1921–).
Minor American leading man of the 50s.
   Rocky Mountain 50. Raton Pass 51. Operation Pacific 51. Subterfuge 68. The Mind of Mr Soames 70, many others.

Forbstein, Leo F. (1892–1948).
American musical director, credited on all Warner sound films up to 1948.

Ford, Alexander (1908–1980).
Polish director who made films from 1930. Best known abroad: *The Young Chopin* 51. *Five Boys from Barska Street* 53. *Knights of the Teutonic Order* 60.

Ford, Cecil (1911–1980).
Former Irish actor who turned production manager on some notable films: *Moby Dick* 56. *Around the World in Eighty Days* 56. *The Bridge on the River Kwai* 57. *The Inn of the Sixth Happiness* 58.
   Produced: *The Guns of Navarone* 61. *633 Squadron* 64, others.

Ford, Constance (1929–1993).
American general-purpose actress of the 50s.
   The Last Hunt 56. A Summer Place 59. Home from the Hill 60. Claudelle Inglish 61. All Fall Down 62. The Cabinet of Caligari 62. The Caretaker 63, etc.

Ford, Dorothy (1923–).
Tall American leading lady of the 40s and 50s.
   An American Romance 44. Here Come the Coeds 45. Love Laughs at Andy Hardy 47. Three Godfathers 49. One Sunday Afternoon 49. Jack and the Beanstalk 52. The High and the Mighty 54, etc.

Ford, Faith (1964–).
Perky American actress, best known for her role as Corky Sherwood Forrest in the television sitcom *Murphy Brown*.
   'You Talkin' To Me?' 87. North 94.
   TV series: The Popcorn Kid 87.

Ford, Francis (1883–1953) (Francis O'Fearna).
American character actor, often seen as grizzled, cheery westerner; formerly star of early silents and serials. Brother of John Ford.
   The Deserter 12. The Invader 13. The Broken Coin 15. Charlie Chan's Greatest Case 33. The Informer 35. Prisoner of Shark Island 36. In Old Chicago 38. Drums Along the Mohawk 39. Lucky Cisco Kid 40. The Ox-Bow Incident 42. The Big

Noise 44. My Darling Clementine 46. Wagonmaster 50. The Sun Shines Bright 52, many others.

Ford, Glenn (1916–) (Gwyllyn Ford).
Stocky Canadian-born star of Hollywood dramas; from the early 40s he radiated integrity and determination, and continued his stardom into tortured middle-aged roles.
■ Heaven with a Barbed Wire Fence 39. My Son is Guilty 39. Convicted Woman 40. Men Without Souls 40. Babies for Sale 40. Blondie Plays Cupid 40. The Lady in Question 40. So Ends Our Night 41. Texas 41. Go West Young Lady 41. The Adventures of Martin Eden 42. Flight Lieutenant 42. The Desperadoes 43. Destroyer 43. *Gilda* 46. A Stolen Life 46. Framed 47. The Mating of Millie 48. The Loves of Carmen 48. The Return of October 48. The Man from Colorado 48. The Undercover Man 49. Mr Soft Touch 49. Lust for Gold 49. The Doctor and the Girl 49. The White Tower 50. Convicted 50. The Redhead and the Cowboy 50. The Flying Missile 50. Follow the Sun 51. The Secret of Convict Lake 51. The Green Glove 52. Affair in Trinidad 52. Young Man with Ideas 52. Time Bomb 53. The Man from the Alamo 53. Plunder of the Sun 53. *The Big Heat* 53. Appointment in Honduras 53. Human Desire 54. The Americano 55. The Violent Men 55. *The Blackboard Jungle* 55. Interrupted Melody 55. Trial 55. Ransom 56. Jubal 56. *The Fastest Gun Alive* 56. The Teahouse of the August Moon 56. *3.10 to Yuma* 57. Don't Go Near the Water 57. Cowboy 58. *The Sheepman* 58. Imitation General 58. Torpedo Run 58. It Started with a Kiss 59. The Gazebo 59. Cimarron 60. Cry for Happy 61. Pocketful of Miracles 61. The Four Horsemen of the Apocalypse 62. Experiment in Terror 62. Love is a Ball 63. The Courtship of Eddie's Father 63. Advance to the Rear 64. Fate is the Hunter 64. Dear Heart 64. The Rounders 65. The Money Trap 66. Is Paris Burning? 66. Rage 67. The Last Challenge 67. A Time for Killing 67. Day of the Evil Gun 68. Heaven with a Gun 69. Smith! 69. Brotherhood of the Bell (TV) 70. Santee 73. Jarrett (TV) 73. The Disappearance of Flight 412 (TV) 74. Punch and Jody (TV) 74. The Greatest Gift (TV) 75. Midway 76. Once an Eagle (TV) 76. Evening in Byzantium (TV) 78. Superman 78. The Sacketts (TV) 79. Beggarman Thief (TV) 80. Happy Birthday to Me 81. Virus 82. Casablanca Express 89. Border Shootout 90. Raw Nerve 91.
   TV series: *Cade's County* 71. Holvak 75.

¶ If they tried to rush me, I'd always say I've only got one other speed, and it's slower. – G.F.
I've never played anyone but myself on screen. – G.F.

Ford, Harrison (1892–1957).
American leading man of the silent screen.
   The Mysterious Mrs M. 17. Food for Scandal 20. Foolish Wives 22. Janice Meredith 24. That Royle Girl 25. Up in Mabel's Room 26. The Girl in the Pullman 27. Three Weekends 28. Love in High Gear 32, many others.

Ford, Harrison (1942–).
American action lead who became a star of major movies in the late 70s. His 1993/94 earnings were $44m according to *Forbes* magazine, and in 1994 he was voted Star of the Century by American exhibitors.
■ Dead Heat on a Merry Go Round 66. A Time for Killing 67. Luv 67. Journey to Shiloh 68. Getting Straight 70. The Intruders (TV) 70. Zabriskie Point 70. American Graffiti 73. The Conversation 74. Dynasty (TV) 76. The Possessed (TV) 77. Heroes 77. *Star Wars* 77. Force Ten from Navarone 78. Apocalypse Now (bit) 79. Hanover

Street 79. The Frisco Kid 79. The Empire Strikes Back 80. *Raiders of the Last Ark* 81. Blade Runner 82. Return of the Jedi 83. Indiana Jones and the Temple of Doom 84. Witness (AAN) 85. The Mosquito Coast 87. Frantic 87. Working Girl 88. Indiana Jones and the Last Crusade 89. Presumed Innocent 90. Regarding Henry 91. Patriot Games 92. The Fugitive 93. Clear and Present Danger 94.

¶ Before, I was grateful for a job, almost any job. Now, I'm apprehensive, but I know I have other options, and when I ask for the money, they pay it. It's that simple. – H.F.
I don't use any particular method. I'm from the let's pretend school of acting. – H.F.

Ford, John (1895–1973) (Sean O'Fearna).
Distinguished Irish-American director who from 1917 made over 125 features, many of them silent westerns. In the 30s he built up to a handful of incomparable human dramas; in the 40s he turned towards roving, brawling, good-natured outdoor action films using a repertory of his favourite actors. His best films are milestones, but he disclaimed any artistic pretensions.
   Biography: 1982, *The Unquiet Man* by Dan Ford (grandson).
SELECTED SILENT FILMS: The Tornado 17. A Woman's Fool 18. Bare Fists 19. The Wallop 21. Silver Wings 22. The Face on the Bar Room Floor 23. *The Iron Horse* 24. Lightnin' 25. Three Bad Men 26. Four Sons 28. Mother Machree 28. Riley the Cop 28. Strong Boy 29.
■ SOUND FILMS: Black Watch 29. Salute 29. *Men Without Women* 30. Born Reckless 30. Up the River 30. The Seas Beneath 30. The Brat 31. *Arrowsmith* 31. Air Mail 32. Flesh 32. Pilgrimage 33. Doctor Bull 33. *The Lost Patrol* 34. The World Moves On 34. *Judge Priest* 34. *The Whole Town's Talking* 35. *The Informer* (AA) 35. Steamboat Round the Bend 35. Prisoner of Shark Island 36. Mary of Scotland 36. The Plough and the Stars 36. Wee Willie Winkie 37. *The Hurricane* 37. Four Men and a Prayer 38. Submarine Patrol 38. *Stagecoach* (AAN) 39. *Young Mr Lincoln* 39. *Drums Along the Mohawk* 39. *The Grapes of Wrath* (AA) 40. The Long Voyage Home 40. *Tobacco Road* 41. *How Green Was My Valley* (AA) 41. Why We Fight and other war documentaries 42–45. They Were Expendable 45. *My Darling Clementine* 46. The Fugitive 47. Fort Apache 48. Three Godfathers 48. *She Wore A Yellow Ribbon* 49. When Willie Comes Marching Home 50. Wagonmaster 50. Rio Grande 50. This is Korea 51. *The Quiet Man* (AA) 52. What Price Glory? 52. Mogambo 53. *The Sun Shines Bright* 54. The Long Gray Line 55. Mister Roberts (co-d) 55. *The Searchers* 56. The Wings of Eagles 57. The Rising of the Moon 57. *The Last Hurrah* 58. Gideon's Day 59. The Horse Soldiers 59. Sergeant Rutledge 60. Two Rode Together 61. The Man Who Shot Liberty Valance 62. How the West Was Won (part) 63. Donovan's Reef 63. Cheyenne Autumn 64. Young Cassidy (part) 64. Seven Women 66.
✪ For half-a-dozen simply marvellous films. *The Grapes of Wrath*.

¶ Anybody can direct a picture once they know the fundamentals. Directing is not a mystery, it's not an art. The main thing about directing is: photograph the people's eyes. – J.F.
It's no good asking me to talk about art. – J.F.
He developed his craft in the 20s, achieved dramatic force in the 30s, epic sweep in the 40s, and symbolic evocation in the 50s. – *Andrew Sarris, 1968*
He never once looked in the camera when we worked together. You see, the man had bad eyes, as long as I knew him, but he was a man whose

veins ran with the business. – *Arthur Miller, photographer*

Knockabout comedy and tragedy co-exist with perfect ease in his work, which throughout a long career shows a clear development and progression. – *John M. Smith*

He had instinctively a beautiful eye for the camera. But he was also an egomaniac. – *Henry Fonda*

His films look entirely different one from another, the style emerging rather from a personal response to people: affectionate, warm, with a rural decency and intimacy. – *Charles Higham*

Ford, Paul (1901–1976) (Paul Ford Weaver).
American character actor best known on TV as the harassed colonel in the Bilko series and star of *The Baileys of Balboa*.

The House on 92nd Street 45. Lust for Gold 49. Perfect Strangers 50. *The Teahouse of the August Moon* 56. The Matchmaker 58. Advise and Consent 61. *The Music Man* 62. *Never Too Late* 65. Big Hand for a Little Lady 66. The Russians Are Coming, The Russians Are Coming 66. The Spy with a Cold Nose (GB) 67. The Comedians 67, etc.

Ford, Wallace (1898–1966) (Sam Grundy).
British general-purpose actor who went to Hollywood in the early 30s and after a few semi-leads settled into character roles.

Freaks 32. Lost Patrol 34. *The Informer* 35. OHMS (GB) 36. The Mummy's Hand 40. Inside the Law 42. Shadow of a Doubt 43. The Green Years 46. Embraceable You 48. *Harvey* 50. The Nebraskan 53. Destry 55. Johnny Concho 56. The Last Hurrah 58. A Patch of Blue 66, etc.

TV series: The Deputy 59.

Forde, Eugene (1898–1986).
American director of second features, former silent-screen actor.

Charlie Chan in London 33. Buy Me That Town 41. Berlin Correspondent 42. Jewels of Brandenberg 46. Invisible Wall 47, many others.

Forde, Florrie (1876–1940).
Australian actress and singer who became a top music-hall performer in Britain from the late 1890s with songs that featured a catchy chorus, including 'Down at the Old Bull and Bush' and 'It's a Long Way to Tipperary'.

Say It with Flowers 34. My Old Dutch 34. Royal Cavalcade 35, etc.

Forde, Walter (1897–1984) (Thomas Seymour).
British director, formerly a popular slapstick comedian of the silents: *Wait and See, Would You Believe It*, many shorts, one of which was featured in *Helter Skelter* 49. Directed some high-speed farces and several thrillers and melodramas.

The Silent House 28. Lord Richard in the Pantry 30. *The Ghost Train* 31. Jack's the Boy 32. *Rome Express* 32. Orders Is Orders 33. Jack Ahoy 34. Chu Chin Chow 34. *Bulldog Jack* 35. King of the Damned 35. Land Without Music 36. The Gaunt Stranger 38. The Four Just Men 39. Inspector Hornleigh on Holiday 39. *Saloon Bar* 40. Sailors Three 40. The Ghost Train 41. Atlantic Ferry 41. Charley's Big-Hearted Aunt 41. *It's That Man Again* 42. Time Flies 44. Master of Bankdam 47. Cardboard Cavalier 48, many others.

the Foreign Legion
has been taken reasonably seriously in the three versions of *Beau Geste*, the two versions of *Le Grand Jeu, Beau Sabreur, China Gate, Rogue's Regiment, Ten Tall Men*, and *The Legion's Last Patrol*. It was sent up something wicked by Laurel and Hardy in *Beau Hunks* and *The Flying Deuces;* by Abbott and Costello *In the Foreign Legion;* and by the Carry On gang in *Follow That Camel*.

Foreman, Carl (1914–1984).
American writer-producer-director, latterly resident in Britain after being blacklisted.

So This Is New York (w) 48. The Clay Pigeon (w) 49. Home of the Brave (w) 49. *Champion* (AANw) 49. The Men (AANw) 50. Cyrano de Bergerac (w) 50. *High Noon* (w) 52. *The Bridge on the River Kwai* (AAw) 57. The Key (wp) 58. *The Guns of Navarone* (wp) (AAN) 61. The Victors (wpd) 63. Born Free (p) 65. Mackenna's Gold (p) 68. The Virgin Soldiers (p) 69. Young Winston (wp) (AAN) 72. Force Ten from Navarone (p) 78. When Time Ran Out (co-w) 80.

Foreman, John (1925–1992).
American producer, former agent.

WUSA 70. They Might Be Giants 71. The Effect of Gamma Rays on Man in the Moon Marigolds 72. The Life and Times of Judge Roy Bean 72. The Man Who Would Be King 75. The First Great Train Robbery 78. Prizzi's Honor 85, etc.

Forest, Mark (1933–) (Lou Degni).
American athlete and gymnast who appeared in many Italian muscle-man epics.

■ Goliath and the Dragon 60. Maciste the Mighty (Son of Samson) 60. The Strongest Man in the World 61. Death in the Arena 62. Goliath and the Sins of Babylon 63. The Terror of Rome Against the Son of Hercules 63. Hercules Against the Sons of the Sun 64. The Lion of Thebes 64. Hercules Against the Barbarians 64. Hercules Against the Mongols 64. Kindar the Invulnerable 64.

forest fires
have made a roaring climax for many films including *The Blazing Forest, Red Skies of Montana, Guns of the Timberland, The Bluebird, The Big Trees* and *Ring of Fire*. None was more dramatic than the cartoon version in *Bambi*.

Forester, C. S. (1899–1966).
British adventure novelist. Works filmed include *Captain Horatio Hornblower, The African Queen, Payment Deferred, The Pride and the Passion* ('The Gun').

Forman, Milos (1932–).
Czech director of realistic comedies.
Autobiography: 1994, *Turnaround – A Memoir* with Jan Novak.

■ Peter and Pavla 64. *A Blonde in Love* 65. The Fireman's Ball 68. *Taking Off* (US) 71. *One Flew Over the Cuckoo's Nest* (AA) 75. *Hair* 79. Ragtime 81. Amadeus (AA) 83. Valmont 89.

❡ One of the criteria of casting was that we couldn't afford to have a prick in the company. – *M.F., on One Flew Over the Cuckoo's Nest*

Formby, George (1904–1961) (George Booth).
British north-country comedian with a toothy grin and a ukelele, long popular in music halls.
Biography: 1974, *George Formby* by Alan Randal and Ray Seaton.

■ Boots Boots (debut) 33. Off the Dole 34. *No Limit* 35. Keep Your Seats Please 36. Feather Your Nest 37. Keep Fit 37. I See Ice 38. It's in the Air 38. Trouble Brewing 39. Come On, George 39. *Let George Do It* 40. Spare a Copper 41. Turned Out Nice Again 41. South American George (dual role) 42. Much Too Shy 42. Get Cracking 43. Bell-Bottom George 43. He Snoops To Conquer 44. I Didn't Do It 45. George in Civvy Street 46.

Forrest, Frederic (1936–).
American leading man of the 70s.

■ Where the Legends Die 72. The Don Is Dead 74. The Conversation 74. The Gravy Train 74. Larry (TV) 74. Promise Him Anything (TV) 75. Permission to Kill 75. The Missouri Breaks 77. It Lives Again 79. Apocalypse Now 79. The Rose (AAN) 79. One from the Heart 82. Hammett 82. Saigon – Year of the Cat (TV) 83. Valley Girl 83. The Stone Boy 84. Best Kept Secrets (TV) 84. Return 85. Where are the Children? 85. Stacking 87. Valentino Returns 87. Quo Vadis 88. Tucker: The Man and His Dream 88. Cat Chaser 89. Music Box 89. The Two Jakes 90. Falling Down 93. Trauma 93. Against the Wall (TV) 94. Chasers 94. Hidden Fears 94. Before the Night 94. Lassie 94.

Forrest, Sally (1928–) (Katharine Scully Feeney).
American leading lady of the early 50s.

Not Wanted 49. Mystery Street 50. Never Fear 50. Hard Fast and Beautiful 51. Excuse My Dust 51. The Strange Door 51. The Strip 51. Son of Sinbad 55. Ride the High Iron 56. While the City Sleeps 56, etc.

Forrest, Steve (1924–) (William Forrest Andrews).
American leading man, brother of Dana Andrews.

The Bad and the Beautiful 52. Phantom of the Rue Morgue 54. Prisoner of War 54. Bedevilled 55. The Living Idol 57. Heller in Pink Tights 60. The Yellow Canary 63. Rascal 69. The Wild Country 71. Wanted the Sundance Woman (TV) 76. North Dallas Forty 79. The Manions of America (TV) 81. Malibu (TV) 83. Hollywood Wives (TV) 84. Spies Like Us 85. Amazon Women on the Moon 87, etc.

TV series: The Baron 65. S.W.A.T. 75–76. Dallas 86.

Forst, Willi (1903–1980) (Wilhelm Frohs).
Austrian director and actor.

Maskerade (wd) 34. Bel Ami (a, wd) 39. Operette (a, wd) 40. Wiener Maedelin (a, w) 45. The Sinner (wd) 50. Vienna, City of My Dreams (d) 57, etc.

Forster, E. M. (1879–1970).
British novelist who stopped writing fiction in 1924. His novels, with the exception of *The Longest Journey*, have all been filmed in a mood of nostalgic Edwardiana.

A Passage to India (d David Lean) 84. A Room with a View (d James Ivory) 85. Maurice (d James Ivory) 87. Where Angels Fear to Tread (d Charles Sturridge) 91. Howards End (d James Ivory) 92.

Forster, Robert (1941–).
Sardonic-looking American leading man with echoes of John Garfield.

■ Reflections in a Golden Eye 67. The Stalking Moon 68. Justine 69. Medium Cool 69. Pieces of Dreams 70. Cover Me Babe 72. Death Squad (TV) 73. The Don Is Dead 73. Nakia (TV) 74. Stunts 77. Avalanche 78. Standing Tall 78. The Black Hole 79. Alligator 80. Vigilante 83. Goliath Awaits (TV) 84. Hollywood Harry (& pd) 85. Once a Hero 88. The Banker 89. Peacemaker 90. Satan's Princess 90.

TV series: *Banyon* 71.

Forster, Rudolph (1884–1968).
German leading actor of heavy personality, seen abroad chiefly in *Die Dreigroschenoper (The Threepenny Opera*; as Macheath) 32.

Forsyth, Bill (1947–).
Scottish writer-director who met with instant success for his small local comedies. He moved to

llywood in the late 80s, but failed to find a ceptive audience for his pawky sense of amour. *Being Human*, made at a cost of $20m, as a box-office flop.

That Sinking Feeling 80. *Gregory's Girl* 81. Local ero 83. Comfort and Joy 84. Housekeeping (US) . Breaking In (US) 89. Being Human (US) 94.

The thing about Hollywood is the mind-set that prevails. It works from the assumption that if u're in the movie business, you want all those ople to like your film, you want to win an Oscar d you want to make a $100 million gross. That's hat having a career in the industry means. *B.F.*

The only ambitions I have for the films I make that they're appreciated as poetical works. ther film is too crude a medium to handle that else I can't make it do these things. If something esn't work over a period of time you tend not be so interested in it. In a way my perception film has been reduced. – *B.F.*

My problem is that 40 per cent of me wants to ake an entertaining film and 60 per cent of me ants to subvert the idea of movies. It's actually t a very happy way to work. – *B.F.*

orsyth, Bruce (1927–) (Bruce Forsyth Johnson). ouncy, beaming, British TV comedian whose film pearances have been scant.

Star! 68. Hieronymus Merkin 69. The lagnificent Seven Deadly Sins 71. Bedknobs and roomsticks 71.

orsyth, Frederick (1938–). ritish writer of adventure thrillers, most of which ave been picked up as screen material: *The Day of e Jackal, The Odessa File, The Dogs of War, The ourth Protocol.*

I've yet to be convinced that the film business is a profession for adults. – *F.F.*

orsyth, Rosemary (1944–). merican leading actress.

Shenandoah (debut) 65. The War Lord 65. Texas cross the River 66. Where It's At 69. Whatever appened to Aunt Alice? 69. How Do I Love Thee? 0. City Beneath the Sea (TV) 71. One Little ndian 73. Black Eye 74. Gray Lady Down 78, etc.

orsythe, John (1918–) (John Freund). mooth American leading man with Broadway xperience.

Destination Tokyo 43. Captive City 52. Escape rom Fort Bravo 53. The Trouble with Harry 56. *The mbassador's Daughter* 56. See How They Run (TV) 4. Kitten with a Whip 65. Madame X 66. In Cold lood 67. Topaz 69. The Happy Ending 69. Murder nce Removed (TV) 71. The Healers (TV) 75. The eather and Father Gang (TV) 77. The Users (TV) 9. And Justice for All 79. Sizzle (TV) 81. crooged 88, etc.

TV series: Bachelor Father 57–61. The John orsythe Show 65. To Rome with Love 69–70. harlie's Angels (voice only) 76–80. *Dynasty* 81– 6.

I can't afford to bulge. Being a 64-year-old sex symbol is a hell of a weight to carry. – *J.F.*

Forsythe, William. urly American actor, often as a villain.

Cloak and Dagger 84. Once upon a Time in America 84. Savage Dawn 84. The Lightship 85. The Long Hot Summer (TV) 87. Raising Arizona 87. Extreme Prejudice 87. Weeds 87. Patty Hearst

88. Dead-Bang 89. Torrents of Spring (It./Fr.) 89. Dick Tracy 90. Career Opportunities 91. Out for Justice 91. Stone Cold 91. The Waterdance 91. The Gun in Betty Lou's Handbag 92, etc.

TV series: The Untouchables (as Al Capone) 92– 93.

Fosse, Bob (1927–1987). American dancer who became a Broadway director.

Biography: 1989, *Razzle Dazzle: The Life and Work of Bob Fosse* by Kevin Boyd Grubb.

■ Give a Girl a Break 52. The Affairs of Dobie Gillis 52. Kiss Me Kate 53. My Sister Eileen (& ch) 55. *The Pajama Game* (ch only) 57. Damn Yankees (ch only) 58. *Sweet Charity* (directed and choreographed) 68. *Cabaret* (d, ch) (AA) 72. Lenny (AANd) 74. The Little Prince (a only) 75. *All That Jazz* (allegedly based on his life) (d, ch) (AAN) 79. Star 80 (wd) 83.

Fossey, Brigitte (1945–). French actress.

Jeux Interdits 52. Le Grand Meaulnes 67. Adieu l'Ami 68. M comme Mathieu 71. Un Mauvais Fils 80. Enigma 82. The Last Butterfly 90. Les Enfants du Naufrageur 92, etc.

Foster, Barry (1931–). British light actor, usually figuring as comic relief, but popular on TV as the Dutch detective Van der Valk.

Sea of Sand 56. Yesterday's Enemy 59. King and Country 64. The Family Way 66. Robbery 67. Twisted Nerve 68. Ryan's Daughter 70. Frenzy 72. Divorce His Divorce Hers (TV) 73. The Sweeney 77. The Three Hostages (TV) 78. The Wild Geese 78. Smiley's People (TV) 81. A Woman Called Golda (TV) 82. Heat and Dust 83, To Kill a King 84. The Whistle Blower 86, etc.

Foster, Dianne (1928–) (D. Laruska). Canadian leading lady who has made British and American films.

The Quiet Woman (GB) 51. Isn't Life Wonderful? (GB) 53. Drive a Crooked Road (US) 54. The Kentuckian (US) 55. The Brothers Rico (US) 57. Gideon's Day (GB) 58. The Last Hurrah (US) 58. King of the Roaring Twenties (US) 61. Who's Been Sleeping in My Bed (US) 63, etc.

Foster, Jodie (1962–). Child actress in precocious roles who has matured successfully and become a director.

Tom Sawyer 73. One Little Indian 73. *Alice Doesn't Live Here Any More* 74. *Bugsy Malone* 76. *Taxi Driver* (AAN) 76. The Little Girl Who Lives Down the Lane 76. Candleshoe 77. Freaky Friday 77. Carny 80. Foxes 80. O'Hara's Wife 81. Svengali (TV) 82. The Blood of Others 84. Hotel New Hampshire 84. Five Corners 87. Siesta 87. The Accused (AA) 88. Stealing Home 88. Catchfire (aka Backtrack) 89. *Silence of the Lambs* (AA) 91. Little Man Tate (& d) 91. Shadows and Fog 91. Sommersby 93. Maverick 94. Nell 94, etc.

TV series: Bob and Carol and Ted and Alice 73. Paper Moon 74.

I believe women should be sexual. And why not? What a great thing to be: a sexual woman, coming of age and discovering sensuality and the intoxification of it. I've seen so many movies about women who don't like sex and really don't want to have sex, or have that posey stuff in Calvin Klein ads. Well, that's just not true and I'm sick of that myth being out there. What I'd like to do is develop movies that better reflect my generation of women. – *J.F.*

Foster, Julia (1941–). British leading lady.

The Small World of Sammy Lee 63. Two Left Feet 63. The System 64. The Bargee 64. One-Way Pendulum 64. Alfie 66. Half a Sixpence 67. All Coppers Are 72. The Great McGonagall 74. F. Scott Fitzgerald in Hollywood (TV) 76. The Thirteenth Reunion 81, etc.

Foster, Lewis (1899–1974). American director, former Hal Roach gag writer; won an Oscar in 1939 for the original story of *Mr Smith Goes to Washington.*

The Lucky Stiff (& w) 48. Manhandled (& w) 49. Captain China 49. The Eagle and the Hawk (& w) 49. Crosswinds 51. Those Redheads from Seattle (& w) 53. Top of the World 55. The Bold and the Brave 56. Tonka (& w) 58, etc.

Foster, Meg (1948–). American leading lady with striking blue eyes, mostly on TV.

The Death of Me Yet (TV) 71. Sunshine (TV) 73. Things in Their Season (TV) 74. James Dean (TV) 76. A Different Story 79. The Legend of Sleepy Hollow 79. Carny 80. Guyana Tragedy (TV) 81. Ticket to Heaven 81. The Osterman Weekend 83. The Emerald Forest 85. The Wind 87. Masters of the Universe 87. They Live 88. Tripwire 89. Blind Fury 89. Relentless 89. Stepfather II 89. Backstab 90. To Catch a Killer (TV) 92. Hidden Fears 94. Oblivion 94, etc.

TV series: Sunshine 73. Cagney and Lacey 82– 84.

Foster, Norman (1900–1976). American leading man of the early 30s; became a director and had a rather patchy career.

Gentlemen of the Press 29. It Pays to Advertise 31. Reckless Living 31. Alias the Doctor 32. Skyscraper Souls 32. State Fair 33. Professional Sweetheart 33. Orient Express 34. Behind the Green Lights 35. High Tension 36. I Cover Chinatown (& d) 36.

■ DIRECTED ONLY: Fair Warning 37. Think Fast Mr Moto 37. Thank You Mr Moto 37. Walking Down Broadway 38. Mysterious Mr Moto 38. Mr Moto Takes a Chance 38. Mr Moto's Last Warning 39. Charlie Chan in Reno 39. Mr Moto Takes a Vacation 39. *Charlie Chan at Treasure Island* 39. Charlie Chan in Panama 40. Viva Cisco Kid 40. Ride Kelly Ride 41. Scotland Yard 41. *Journey Into Fear* 42. Rachel and the Stranger 48. Kiss the Blood off My Hands 48. Tell It to the Judge 49. Father is a Bachelor 50. Woman on the Run 50. Navajo 52. Sky Full of Moon 52. Sombrero 53. Davy Crockett 55. Davy Crockett and the River Pirates 56. The Nine Lives of Elfego Baga 58. The Sign of Zorro 60. Indian Paint 66. Brighty 67.

Foster, Preston (1901–1970). Handsome American leading man of the 30s, former clerk and singer.

Nothing But the Truth (debut) 30. Life Begins 31. *The Last Mile* 31. Wharf Angel 34. The Informer 35. The Last Days of Pompeii 35. Annie Oakley 36. The Plough and the Stars 37. First Lady 38. News Is Made at Night 38. Geronimo 39. Moon over Burma 40. Northwest Mounted Police 40. Unfinished Business 41. Secret Agent of Japan 42. My Friend Flicka 43. The Bermuda Mystery 44. The Valley of Decision 45. The Last Gangster 45. The Harvey Girls 46. Ramrod 47. Green Grass of Wyoming 48. Tomahawk 49. The Tougher They Come 51. The Big Night 52. Kansas City Confidential 53. I the Jury 55. Destination 60,000 58. Advance to the Rear 64. The Time Travellers 65. Chubasco 68, many others.

TV series: Waterfront 54–55. Gunslinger 60.

Foster, Stephen (1826–1864).
American songwriter of popular sentimental ballads: 'Old Folks at Home', 'Beautiful Dreamer', etc. Impersonated on screen by Douglass Montgomery in *Harmony Lane* 35, Don Ameche in *Swanee River* 39, and Bill Shirley in *I Dream of . Jeannie* 52.

Foster, Susanna (1924–) (Suzan Larsen).
American operatic singer and heroine of several 40s films.
The Great Victor Herbert 40. *There's Magic in Music* 41. The Hard Boiled Canary 42. Top Man 43. *Phantom of the Opera* 43. The Climax 44. Bowery to Broadway 44. This Is the Life 44. Frisco Sal 45. That Night with You 45, etc.

Fotopoulos, Vassilis (1934–).
Greek production designer, from the stage.
America America (GB: The Anatolian Smile) 63. Zorba the Greek (AA) 64. You're a Big Boy Now 67, etc.

Foulger, Byron (1900–1970).
American small-part actor, the prototype of the worried, bespectacled clerk.
The Prisoner of Zenda 37. Edison the Man 40. Sullivan's Travels 41. Since You Went Away 44. Champagne for Caesar 49. The Magnetic Monster 53. The Long Hot Summer 59. The Gnome-Mobile 67, many others.
TV series: Captain Nice 67. Petticoat Junction 68–70.

Fowlds, Derek (1937–).
British comedy character actor, usually in unassuming roles.
The Smashing Bird I Used to Know 69. Hotel Paradiso 66. Tower of Evil 71. Over the Hill 92, etc.
TV series: The Basil Brush Show 69–73. Yes Minister 80–85. Yes Prime Minister 86–90. Heartbeat 93–94.

Fowler, Gene (1890–1960).
American writer, close friend of John Barrymore and author of his biography, *Good Night Sweet Prince*.

Fowler, Gene, Jnr.
American director.
■ I Was a Teenage Werewolf 56. Gang War 58. Showdown at Boot Hill 58. I Married a Monster from Outer Space 59. Here Come the Jets 59. The Rebel Set 59. The Oregon Trail 59.

Fowler, Harry (1926–).
British cockney actor on screen since the early 40s, often in cameo roles.
Those Kids from Town 42. Champagne Charlie 44. Hue and Cry 46. For Them That Trespass 48. I Believe in You 52. Pickwick Papers 53. Home and Away 56. Idol on Parade 59. Ladies Who Do 63. Doctor in Clover 66. The Prince and the Pauper 77. Chicago Joe and the Showgirl 89, many others.
TV series: The Army Game, Our Man at St Mark's.

Fowler, Hugh (c. 1904–1975).
American editor.
Les Misérables 52. Gentlemen Prefer Blondes 53. The Last Wagon 56. Say One for Me 59. The Lost World 60. The List of Adrian Messenger 63. Stagecoach 66. Planet of the Apes 67. Patton (AA) 70. The Life and Times of Judge Roy Bean 72, many others.

Fowles, John (1926–).
British novelist whose slightly mystic themes have generally attracted film-makers, though not always with satisfactory results: *The Collector, The Magus, The French Lieutenant's Woman*.

Fowley, Douglas (1911–).
American character actor often seen as nervous or comic gangster.
Let's Talk it Over 34. Crash Donovan 36. Charlie Chan on Broadway 37. Mr Moto's Gamble 38. Dodge City 39. Ellery Queen Master Detective 40. Tanks a Million 41. Jitterbugs 42. The Kansan 43. One Body Too Many 44. The Hucksters 47. If You Knew Susie 48. Battleground 49. Edge of Doom 50. Criminal Lawyer 51. *Singin' in The Rain* (as the hysterical director) 52. The High and the Mighty 54. Macumba Love (p and d only) 59. Desire in the Dust 60. Barabbas 62. From Noon till Three 76. The White Buffalo 77, many others.
TV series: The Life and Legend of Wyatt Earp (as Doc Holliday) 56–61. Pistols and Petticoats 66. Gunsmoke 68–74.

The Fox.
Name of an actor-detective played by Red Skelton in three films directed by S. Sylvan Simon. He plays an actor who plays The Fox, hero of a radio series, and finds himself called upon to solve crimes in the real world. The character Skelton plays resembles that projected by Bob Hope in many of his films of the period – a wisecracking coward who nevertheless comes good and gets the girl (played in Skelton's films by Ann Southern).
Whistling in the Dark 41. Whistling in Dixie 42. Whistling in Brooklyn 43.

Fox and the Crow.
Stars of Columbia Pictures' (1941–47) and UPA's (1948–50) cartoons. Created by Frank Tashlin, Fox was voiced by Frank Graham and Crow by Paul Frees.
The Fox and the Grapes 41. Woodman Spare That Tree 42. Slay It with Flowers 43. The Dream Kids 44. Treasure Jest 45. Tooth or Consequences 47. Robin Hoodlum (AAN) 48. Magic Fluke (AAN) 49. Punchy De Leon 50, etc.

Fox, Bernard.
British character actor in Hollywood: plays a rather stiff gent of the old school.
Soho Incident 56. The Safecracker 58. Honeymoon Hotel 64. Star 68. Big Jake 71. The Hound of the Baskervilles (TV) (as Dr Watson) 72. Herbie Goes to Monte Carlo 77, etc.

Fox, Charles (1940–).
American composer.
Barbarella (co-m) 67. Goodbye Columbus 69. Star Spangled Girl 71. The Laughing Policeman 73. The Other Side of the Mountain 75. Foul Play 78. Nine to Five 80. Why Would I Lie 80. Zapped! 82. Love Child 82. Strange Brew 83. National Lampoon's European Vacation 85. Longshot 86. Parent Trap 87. Love at Stake 88. Short Circuit II 88. The Gods Must Be Crazy II 89. It Had to Be You 89, etc.
Much TV including Happy Days, The Love Boat.

Fox, Edward (1937–).
Diffident British leading man of the 70s.
The Naked Runner 67. The Long Duel 67. Oh What a Lovely War 69. Skullduggery 69. The Breaking of Bumbo 70. The Go-Between 71. *The Day of the Jackal* 73. Doll's House 73. Galileo 74. The Squeeze 77. A Bridge Too Far 77. The Cat and the Canary 78. Force Ten From Navarone 78. *Edward and Mrs Simpson* (TV) 78. The Mirror Crack'd 80.

Gandhi 82. Never Say Never Again 83. The Dress 83. The Shooting Party 84. The Bounty 84. Wile Geese 2 85. Return to the River Kwai 89. They Never Slept 90. Robin Hood 90, etc.

Fox, James (1939–).
British leading man, who usually plays a weaklin Once a child actor, notable in *The Magnet* 50 (as William Fox). Returned to acting 1982 after a te year break in good works. Brother of Edward Fo and very similar in style.
Autobiography: 1983, *Comeback*.
The Loneliness of the Long Distance Runner 6 The Servant 63. Tamahine 64. Those Magnifice Men in Their Flying Machines 65. King Rat 65. The Chase 65. Thoroughly Modern Millie 67. Duffy 68. Isadora 68. Arabella 69. Performance 7 Runners 83. A Passage to India 84. Greystoke 84 Absolute Beginners 85. The Whistle Blower 86. High Season 87. Boys in the Island 89. Farewell to the King 89. She's Been Away 89. Russia Hou 90. A Question of Attribution (TV) 91. Afraid of t Dark 91. As You Like It 92. Hostage 92. Patriot Games 92. The Remains of the Day 93. Heart of Darkness (TV) 94. The Dwelling Place (TV) 94. Doomsday Gun (TV) 94. Clockwork Mice 95, etc
TV series: The Choir 95.

Fox, Kerry (1968–).
New Zealand leading actress, now resident in Australia.
An Angel at My Table 90. The Last Days of Che Nous 92. Mr Wroe's Virgins (TV) 93. Friends 94. Shallow Grave 94, etc.

Fox, Michael J. (1961–).
Canadian leading man in Hollywood who plays younger than his years.
Midnight Madness 80. Class of 84 83. *Back to t Future* 85. Teen Wolf 85. Poison Ivy (TV) 85. The Secret of my Success 87. Light of Day 87. Bright Lights, Big City 88. Back to the Future II 89. Casualties of War 89. Back to the Future III 90. Doc Hollywood 91. The Hard Way 91. The Concierge 92. Where the Rivers Flow North 93. Life with Mikey 93, etc.
TV series: Palmerstown USA 80–81. *Family Tie* 82–89.

Fox, Sidney (1910–1942).
American leading lady of the early 30s.
Bad Sister 31. The Mouthpiece 32. Once In a Lifetime 32. Murders in the Rue Morgue 32. Midnight 34, etc.

Fox, Wallace (1898–1958).
American director.
The Amazing Vagabond 29. Cannonball Expres 32. Powdersmoke Range 35. The Last of the Mohicans (co-d) 36. Racing Lady 37. Pride of the Plains 40. Bowery Blitzkrieg 41. Kid Dynamite 43. Riders of the Santa Fe 44. Mr Muggs Rides Again 45. Gunman's Code 46. Docks of New Yor 48. Six Gun Mesa 50. Montana Desperado 51, many others.

Fox, William (1879–1952) (Wilhelm Fried).
Hungarian-American pioneer and executive, the Fox of Twentieth Century-Fox. Moved from the garment industry into exhibition, production and distribution.
Biography: 1933, *Upton Sinclair Presents William Fox*.

¶ I always bragged of the fact that no second of those contained in the twenty-four hours eve passed but that the name of William Fox was on the screen, being exhibited in some theatre in some part of the world. – *W.F.*

Foxwell, Ivan (1914–).
British producer, in films since 1933.

No Room at the Inn 47. The Intruder 51. The Colditz Story 54. Manuela 56. A Touch of Larceny 59. Tiara Tahiti 62. The Quiller Memorandum 66. Decline and Fall (also wrote) 68, etc.

Foxworth, Robert (1941–).
American general-purpose actor.

The New Healers (TV) 72. Frankenstein (TV) 73. The Devil's Daughter (TV) 73. The Questor Tapes (TV) 74. Mrs Sundance (TV) 74. James Dean (TV) 76. Treasure of Matecumbe 76. It Happened at Lake Wood Manor (TV) 77. Death Moon (TV) 78. Damien: Omen II 78. Prophecy 79. The Black Marble 80. Double Standard (TV) 88. Beyond the Stars 89, etc.

TV series: Storefront Lawyers 70–71. Falcon Crest 81–89.

Foxx, Redd (1922–1991) (John Elroy Sanford).
American vaudevillian who became a 70s star in the long-running *Sanford and Son*.

Norman, Is That You? 76. Harlem Nights 89.

TV series: Sanford and Son 72–77. Redd Foxx 77–78. Sanford 80–81. The Redd Foxx Show 86.

Foy, Bryan (1895–1977).
American producer, mostly of low budgeters at Warner. Wrote song, 'Mr Gallagher & Mr Shean'; and was the oldest of the 'seven little Foys'.

The Home Towners (d) 28. Little Old New York (d) 28. The Gorilla (d) 31. Berlin Correspondent 42. Guadalcanal Diary 43. Doll Face 46. Trapped 49. Breakthrough 50. Inside the Walls of Folsom Prison 51. The Miracle of Fatima 52. *House of Wax* 53. The Mad Magician 54. Women's Prison 55. Blueprint for Robbery 61. PT 109 63, many others.

Foy, Eddie, Snr (1854–1928) (Edward Fitzgerald).
Famous American vaudeville comedian who made few film appearances but was several times impersonated by Eddie Foy Jnr: in *Yankee Doodle Dandy, Wilson, Bowery to Broadway*, etc. Bob Hope played him in *The Seven Little Foys*. Films include A Favourite Fool 15.

Foy, Eddie, Jnr (1905–1983).
American vaudeville entertainer, son of another and one of the 'seven little Foys'.

Fugitive from Justice 40. The Farmer Takes a Wife 53. Lucky Me 54. *The Pajama Game* 57. Bells Are Ringing 60. Thirty Is a Dangerous Age, Cynthia 67, etc.

TV series: Fair Exchange 63.

foyer cards.
Elaborate, oversized stills with coloured borders bearing credits, all designed for lobby display. A collection of them by John Kobal was published in 1983: it bore the wince-making title *Foyer Pleasure*.

Fraker, William A. (1923–).
American cinematographer.

Games 67. The Fox 67. The President's Analyst 67. *Bullitt* 68. Rosemary's Baby 68. Paint Your Wagon 69. *Monte Walsh* (& d) 70. Day of the Dolphin 73. Lipstick 76. Exorcist II: The Heretic 77. Looking for Mr Goodbar (AAN) 77. American Hot Wax 78. Heaven Can Wait (AAN) 78. Hard Contract 78. 1941 (AAN) 79. Old Boyfriends 79. Hollywood Knights 80. Sharkey's Machine 81. The Legend of the Lone Ranger (d only) 81. The Best Little Whorehouse in Texas 82. War Games

(AAN) 83. Protocol 84. Murphy's Romance (AAN) 85. Burglar 87. Baby Boom 87. Chances Are 89. An Innocent Man 89. The Freshman 90. Memoirs of an Invisible Man 92. There Goes My Baby 94, etc.

frame.
A single picture on a strip of film. At normal sound projection speed, 24 frames are shown each second.

France's
national film history falls into a pattern of clearly-defined styles. First of note was that of Louis Feuillade, whose early serials had tremendous panache. In the 20s came René Clair, with his inimitable touch for fantastic comedy, and a little later Jean Renoir, whose view of the human comedy was wider but equally sympathetic. Sacha Guitry contributed a series of rather stagey but amusing high comedies; Jean Vigo in his brief career introduced surrealism. Marcel Pagnol made a number of self-indulgent regional comedies which were hugely enjoyable but had little to do with cinema. Then beginning in the 30s came an unsurpassed group of adult entertainments from the writer-director team of Jacques Prévert and Marcel Carné; these were widely copied by less talented hands and the resulting stream of sex dramas, seldom less than competent, preserved the legend of the naughty French. Other notable directors were Julien Duvivier, the romantic; Jacques Becker, at his happiest in comedy; and Jacques Feyder, who generally made melodramas with flashes of insight. Henri-Georges Clouzot developed into the French Hitchcock, and Cocteau's art films reached a wide public. In the 40s Robert Bresson, René Clément and Jacques Tati all began to make themselves felt. The 50s were in danger of becoming a dull period, with no new talent of note, when the 'new wave' (qv) changed the whole direction of French film-making and made some of the older hands look suddenly and undeservedly old-fashioned. Directors well-regarded in the 60s include Jacques Demy, François Truffaut, Jean-Luc Godard, Louis Malle, Jean-Pierre Melville, Claude Chabrol, Claude Lelouch and Georges Franju; in the 70s, Eric Rohmer, Jacques Deray, Yves Boisset, Costa-Gavras, Bertrand Blier and Jacques Rivette; in the 80s, Maurice Pialat, though he had been making films since the 60s, Claude Berri, influential as a producer as well as a director, Diane Kurys, Bertrand Tavernier, Jean-Jacques Annaud and Patrice Leconte. Coline Serrau, a former actress, demonstrated a gift for comedy that attracted the attention of Hollywood. Younger talents include Jean-Jacques Beineix, Leos Carax, and Luc Besson.

Among French male stars of note are Raimu, Michel Simon, Harry Baur, Fernandel, Louis Jouvet, Jean Gabin, Pierre Fresnay, Jean-Louis Barrault, Gérard Philippe, Pierre Brasseur, Maurice Chevalier, Charles Boyer, Yves Montand, Jean-Paul Belmondo, Alain Delon, Patrick Dewaere, Philippe Noiret, Michel Blanc and Gérard Depardieu. Of the women, the most influential have been Ginette Leclerc, Michele Morgan, Danielle Darrieux, Arletty, Simone Signoret, Brigitte Bardot, Jeanne Moreau, Françoise Dorleac, Catherine Deneuve, Miou Miou, Anne Girardot, Isabelle Adjani and Isabelle Huppert. The new generation of actresses emerging in the 90s includes Charlotte Gainsbrough, Emmanuelle Béart, Juliette Binoche and Julie Delpy.

France, C. V. (1868–1949).
British stage character actor, most typically seen

in films as dry lawyer or ageing head of household.

Lord Edgware Dies 35. Scrooge 35. Victoria the Great 37. A Yank at Oxford 38. If I Were King (US) 39. Night Train to Munich 40. Breach of Promise 41. The Halfway House 44, etc.

Francen, Victor (1888–1977).
Belgian stage actor, occasionally in French films from 1921, but most familiar in Hollywood spy dramas during World War II.

Crépuscule d'Epouvante 21. Après l'Amour 31. Nuits de Feu 36. Le Roi 36. J'Accuse 38. Sacrifice d'Honneur 38. La Fin du Jour 39. Tales of Manhattan 42. Mission to Moscow 43. Devotion 43. The Mask of Dimitrios 44. The Conspirators 44. Passage to Marseilles 44. Confidential Agent 45. The Beast with Five Fingers 46. La Nuit s'achève 49. The Adventures of Captain Fabian 51. Hell and High Water 54. Bedevilled 55. A Farewell to Arms 58. Fanny 61. Top-Crack 66, many others.

franchise.
A term used to describe a film that provides opportunities for more of the same: that lends itself to sequels or features a character who can appear in several more films, often virtually indistinguishable from the original. There are low-rent franchises, such as *Nightmare on Elm Street* or *Friday the 13th*, and big-budget ones such as *James Bond, Superman, Batman* and *Lethal Weapon*. Such series have been around since the early days of films, beginning with serials like *The Perils of Pauline* and such series as *Tarzan*, but they used to be largely confined to the low-budget end of film-making; these days creating a franchise seems to be the main preoccupation of mainstream Hollywood producers and directors. Apart from the films themselves, franchises also lend themselves to merchandising (qv). The term derives from business, and results from films being seen as the artistic equivalent of fast food.

Franciosa, Anthony (Tony) (1928–)
(Anthony Papaleo).
Italian-American leading actor with lithe movement and ready grin. He was married to actress Shelley Winters (1957–60).

A Face in the Crowd (debut) 57. This Could Be the Night 57. *A Hatful of Rain* (his stage role) (AAN) 57. Wild Is the Wind 58. *The Long Hot Summer* 58. The Naked Maja 59. Career 59. The Story on Page One 59. Go Naked in the World 60. Period of Adjustment 62. Rio Conchos 64. The Pleasure Seekers 65. A Man Could Get Killed 65. Assault on a Queen 66. The Swinger 66. Fathom (GB) 67. The Sweet Ride 68. In Enemy Country 68. A Man Called Gannon 68. Across 110th Street 72. The Drowning Pool 75. The World Is Full of Married Men (GB) 79. Firepower 79. Death Wish II 82. Unsane (Tenebrae) 82. Stagecoach (TV) 86. Death House 88. Ghostwriter 89. Backstreet Dreams 90. Double Threat 92, etc.

TV series: Valentine's Day 64. *The Name of the Game* 68–70. Search 72. Matt Helm 75.

Francis.
The talking mule of several Universal comedies (1950–56) was the direct ancestor of TV's talking palomino *Mister Ed*, also produced by Arthur Lubin. Francis' first master was Donald O'Connor, but later Mickey Rooney took over the reins. Francis was 'voiced' by Chill Wills, Ed by Allan Lane.

Francis, Alec B. (1869–1934).
British-born character actor in Hollywood films as elderly gentleman.

Flame of the Desert 19. Smiling Through 22.

Three Wise Fools 23. Charley's Aunt 25. Tramp Tramp Tramp 26. The Terror 28. Outward Bound 30. Arrowsmith 31. The Last Mile 32. Oliver Twist 33. Outcast Lady 34, many others.

Francis, Anne (1930–).
American leading lady of several 50s films: formerly model, with radio and TV experience.

Summer Holiday (debut) 48. So Young So Bad 50. Elopement 52. Lydia Bailey 52. Susan Slept Here 54. Bad Day at Black Rock 54. The Blackboard Jungle 55. Forbidden Planet 56. Don't Go Near the Water 57. Girl of the Night 60. The Satan Bug 65. Funny Girl 68. The Love God 69. More Dead than Alive 70. Pancho Villa 71. Haunts of the Very Rich (TV) 72. A Masterpiece of Murder (TV) 86, etc.

TV series: Honey West 65. My Three Sons 71.

Francis, Arlene (1908–) (Arlene Kazanjian).
American TV personality who has appeared in a few films.

Stage Door Canteen 43. All My Sons 48. One Two Three 61. The Thrill of it All 63, etc.

Francis, Connie (1938–) (Concetta Franconero).
American pop singer who had some light films built around her. She dubbed the singing voice of Freda Holloway in *Jamboree* 57, and Tuesday Weld in *Rock, Rock, Rock* 57.

Where the Boys Are 63. Follow the Boys 64. Looking for Love 65, etc.

Francis, Derek (1923–1984).
Portly British character actor, often in self-important roles.

Bitter Harvest 63. Ring of Spies 64. The Comedy Man 64. Carry on Camping 69. To the Devil a Daughter 75. Jabberwocky 77, etc.

Francis, Freddie (1917–).
British cinematographer who turned to direction with less distinguished results.

Mine Own Executioner 47. Time without Pity 57. Room at the Top 59. Sons and Lovers (AA) 60. The Innocents 61. The French Lieutenant's Woman 80. The Elephant Man 81. Dune 85. Code Name: Emerald 85. Dark Tower 87. Clara's Heart 88. Her Alibi 89. Brenda Starr 89. Glory (AA) 89. The Plot to Kill Hitler (TV) 90. Cape Fear 91. The Man in the Moon 91. School Ties 92. A Life in the Theatre 93. Princess Caraboo 94, etc.
AS DIRECTOR ONLY: Two and Two make Six 61. Vengeance 62. Paranoiac 63. Nightmare 63. The Evil of Frankenstein 64. Traitor's Gate 65. The Skull 65. The Deadly Bees 66. They Came from Beyond Space 66. The Torture Garden 67. Dracula has Risen from the Grave 68. Mumsy Nanny Sonny and Girlie 69. Tales from the Crypt 71. Asylum 72. Tales that Witness Madness 73. Legend of the Werewolf 74. The Doctor and the Devils 86. Dark Tower 87, etc.

Francis, Ivor (c. 1911–1986).
American character actor who played self-important or bumbling types.

I Love My Wife 70. The Late Liz 71. The World's Greatest Athlete 73. Superdad 74. The Prisoner of Second Avenue 75. The North Avenue Irregulars 78, etc.

TV series: Gilligan's Island 64–67. Dusty's Trail 73.

Francis, Karl.
Welsh director.

The Mouse and the Woman 81. Giro City 82. The Happy Alcoholic 84. Boy Soldier (TV) 86. Angry Earth (TV) 90. Rebecca's Daughters 91, etc.

TV series: Judas and the Gimp (p, wd) 93.

Francis, Kay (1899–1968) (Katherine Gibbs).
Ladylike, serious-faced American star of women's films in the 30s.
■ Gentlemen of the Press 29. The Coconuts 29. Dangerous Curves 29. Illusion 29. The Marriage Playground 29. Behind the Makeup 30. *Street of Chance* 30. Paramount on Parade 30. A Notorious Affair 30. Raffles 30. For the Defence 30. Let's Go Native 30. The Virtuous Sin 30. Passion Flower 30. Scandal Sheet 31. Ladies' Man 31. The Vice Squad 31. Transgression 31. Guilty Hands 31. Twenty-Four Hours 31. Girls about Town 31. The False Madonna 32. Strangers in Love 32. Man Wanted 32. Street of Women 32. Jewel Robbery 32. *One Way Passage* 32. *Trouble in Paradise* 32. *Cynara* 32. The Keyhole 33. Storm at Daybreak 33. Mary Stevens MD 33. I Loved a Woman 33. The House on 56th Street 33. Mandalay 34. Wonder Bar 34. Doctor Monica 34. British Agent 34. Stranded 34. The Goose and the Gander 35. Living on Velvet 35. I Found Stella Parish 35. *The White Angel* (as Florence Nightingale) 36. Give Me Your Heart 36. Stolen Holiday 37. Confession 37. Another Dawn 37. First Lady 37. Women Are Like That 38. My Bill 38. Secrets of an Actress 38. Comet over Broadway 38. King of the Underworld 39. Women in the Wind 39. In Name Only 39. It's a Date 40. Little Men 40. When the Daltons Rode 40. Play Girl 40. The Man Who Lost Himself 40. *Charley's Aunt* 41. The Feminine Touch 41. Always in My Heart 42. Between Us Girls 42. Four Jills in a Jeep 44. Divorce 45. Allotment Wives 45. Wife Wanted 46.

Francis, Robert (1930–1955).
American leading man whose budding career was cut short by an air crash.

The Caine Mutiny 54. The Long Gray Line 55, etc.

Franciscus, James (1933–1991).
American leading man.

Four Boys and a Gun 56. I Passed for White 60. The Outsider 61. The Miracle of the White Stallions 63. Youngblood Hawke 64. The Valley of Gwangi 69. Marooned 69. Beneath the Planet of the Apes 69. Cat O'Nine Tails 71. The Dream Makers (TV) 75. The Amazing Dobermans 76. The Greek Tycoon 78. When Time Ran Out 80. Jacqueline Bouvier Kennedy (TV) 81. Butterfly 81. The Great White 82. The Courageous 82. Secret Weapons (TV) 85, etc.

TV series: Naked City 58. Mr Novak 63–64. Longstreet 71. Hunter 77.

Francks, Don (1932–).
Canadian singer whose first notable film role was in *Finian's Rainbow* 68.

My Bloody Valentine 81. Terminal Choice 85. The Christmas Wife (TV) 88, etc.

Franco, Jess (Jesús).
Prolific Spanish director, mainly of exploitation and horror movies of extremely variable quality, usually ranging from bad to abysmal. He has made as many as eight features a year under several pseudonyms, including Jess Frank, Clifford Brown, and Frank Hollman, and was an assistant to Orson Welles on his unfinished *Don Quixote*.

Dr Orloff's Monster 64. The Diabolical Dr Z (Miss Muerte) 65. Attack of the Robots 66. Succubus (aka Necronomicon) 67. The Castle of Fu Manchu (El Castillo de Fu Manchu) 68. Deadly Sanctuary 68. Kiss and Kill 68. 99 Women 69. Venus in Furs 69. Mrs Hyde (Sie Toetete in Extase) 70. Lesbian Vampires (Vampyros Lesbos)

70. De Sade 70 70. Bram Stoker's Count Dracula (aka Count Dracula) (El Conde Dracula) 70. Virgin among the Living Dead 71. Dracula Prisoner of Frankenstein (US: The Screaming Dead) (Dracula contra Frankenstein) 72. Jack the Ripper 76. Ilsa the Wicked Warden (& a) 78. Revenge in the House of Usher (El Hundimiento de la Casa Usher) 83. Faceless 88, many others.

Franju, Georges (1912–1987).
French director, former set designer. Co-founder of Cinémathèque Française. Best-known documentaries: *Le Sang des Bêtes* 49. *Hôtel des Invalides* 51. *Le Grand Melies* 51. Features: *La Tête contre les Murs (The Keepers)* 58. *Eyes without a Face* 59. Spotlight on a Murderer 61. *Thérèse Desqueyroux* 62. Judex 63. Thomas the Impostor 64. Les Rideaux Blancs 65.

Frank, Charles (1910–).
British director, former dubbing expert.

Uncle Silas 47. Intimate Relations 53, etc.

Frank, Christopher (1943–1993).
British-born director and screenwriter, based in France.

Josepha 81. The Year of the Jellyfish 84. Love in the Strangest Way (Elles N'Oublient Pas) 94, etc.

Frank, Fredric M. (1911–1977).
American scriptwriter.

The Greatest Show on Earth (co-w, AA) 52. The Ten Commandments (co-w) 56. El Cid (co-w) 61, etc.

Frank, Gerold (1907–).
American 'ghost writer' who co-authored the autobiographies of such luminaries as Sheilah Graham, Lillian Roth and Diana Barrymore.

Frank, Harriet:
see *Ravetch, Irving*.

Frank, Melvin (1913–1988).
American comedy scriptwriter and latterly producer/director.
WITH NORMAN PANAMA: My Favourite Blonde 42. Thank Your Lucky Stars 43. Road to Utopia (AAN) 45. Monsieur Beaucaire 46. *Mr Blanding Builds His Dream House* 48. The Reformer and the Redhead 50. Above and Beyond 52. Knock on Wood (AAN) 54. White Christmas 56. That Certain Feeling 56. Li'l Abner 59. *The Facts of Life* 61. Road to Hong Kong 62. Strange Bedfellows 65, etc.
SOLO: A Funny Thing Happened on the Way to the Forum (wp) 66. Buona Sera Mrs Campbell (wpd) 68. A Touch of Class (wpd) 72. The Prisoner of Second Avenue (pd) 75. The Duchess and the Dirtwater Fox (wpd) 76. Lost and Found (wpd) 79.

Frankau, Ronald (1894–1951).
British stage and radio comedian with an 'idle rich' characterization.

The Calendar 31. His Brother's Keeper 39. Double Alibi 46. The Ghosts of Berkeley Square 47, etc.

¶ To the pure *nothing* is pure. – R.F.

Frankel, Benjamin (1906–1973).
British composer. Scores include:

The Years Between 46. The Seventh Veil 46. Mine Own Executioner 47. Sleeping Car to Trieste 48. Appointment with Venus 51. The Importance of Being Earnest 52. A Kid For Two Farthings 55. Simon and Laura 55. Happy is the Bride 58. Libel

9. Guns of Darkness 62. Night of the Iguana 64.
.attle of the Bulge 65, etc.

rankel, Cyril (1921–1973).
british director, former documentarist with Crown
ilm Unit.
Devil on Horseback 54. Make Me an Offer 55.
's Great To Be Young 56. No Time for Tears 57.
he Didn't Say No 58. Alive and Kicking 58. Never
ake Sweets from a Stranger 61. Don't Bother To
nock 61. On the Fiddle 61. The Very Edge 63.
he Witches (The Devil's Own) 66. The Trygon
actor 67. Permission to Kill 75, etc.

rankenheimer, John (1930–).
bullient American director, formerly in TV.
■ The Young Stranger 57. The Young Savages 61.
.ll Fall Down 61. The Manchurian Candidate 62.
irdman of Alcatraz 62. Seven Days in May 64. The
rain 64. Seconds 66. Grand Prix 67. The
xtraordinary Seaman 68. The Fixer 68. The Gypsy
Moths 69. I Walk the Line 70. The Horsemen 71.
mpossible Object 73. The Iceman Cometh 73. 99
14/100 Dead 74. French Connection II 75. Black
Sunday 76. Prophecy 79. The Challenge 82. The
holcroft Covenant 85. 52 Pick-Up 86. Dead Bang
19. The Fourth War 90. Year of the Gun 91.
Against the Wall (TV) 94. The Burning Season (TV)
14.

Frankenstein.
The man/monster theme was explored in
American movies of 1908 (with Charles Ogle) and
1916 (Life Without Soul); also in Italy in 1920
Master of Frankenstein). The 1931 Hollywood film,
written by Robert Florey and directed by James
Whale, borrowed as much from Wegener's The
Golem 22 as from Mary Shelley's early 19th-
century novel; but despite censorship problems the
elements jelled, with Boris Karloff a great success
as the monster composed from dead bits and
pieces, and a legend was born. Sequels included
Bride of Frankenstein 35. Son of Frankenstein 39.
Ghost of Frankenstein 41. Frankenstein Meets the Wolf
Man 43. House of Frankenstein 45. House of Dracula
45. Abbott and Costello Meet Frankenstein 48; among
those who took over from Karloff were Lon
Chaney, Bela Lugosi and Glenn Strange. In 1956
the original story was remade in Britain's Hammer
Studios under the title The Curse of Frankenstein;
colour and gore were added, and sequels, with
various monsters, came thick and fast: The Revenge
of Frankenstein 58. The Evil of Frankenstein 63.
Frankenstein Created Woman 67. Frankenstein Must
Be Destroyed 69. Horror of Frankenstein 70.
Frankenstein and the Monster from Hell 73. A
variation on the original monster make-up was
used by Fred Gwynne in the TV comedy series,
The Munsters 64–65. There have also been several
recent American, Japanese and Italian attempts to
cash in on the name of Frankenstein in cheap
exploitation pictures: I Was a Teenage Frankenstein
57. Frankenstein 1970 58. Frankenstein Versus the
Space Monsters 65. Frankenstein Conquers the World
68. Lady Frankenstein 70, etc. In 1973 a four-hour
TV version called Frankenstein: The True Story
(which it could scarcely be) was co-authored by
Christopher Isherwood but proved merely a
laborious reworking of the earlier films, with
occasional references back to the book, but no
humour. Films about Mary Shelley's creation of
Frankenstein appeared towards the end of the 80s:
Haunted Summer, Gothic and Frankenstein Unbound,
and Mary Shelley's Frankenstein, directed by
Kenneth Branagh with Robert De Niro as the
monster, appeared in 1994.
Book: 1994, The Illustrated Frankenstein Movie
Guide by Stephen Jones.

Franklin, Carl (1930–).
American director, a former actor on stage and
television.
Nowhere to Run (d) 88. Eye of the Eagle II:
Inside the Enemy (d) 89. Full Fathom Five (d) 90.
Eye of the Eagle III (a) 91. One False Move (d) 91.
Laurel Avenue (TV) 93, etc.
TV series (as actor): Caribe 75. Fantastic Journey
77. McClain's Law 81–82.

Franklin, Pamela (1949–).
British juvenile actress of the 60s.
The Innocents 61. The Lion 62. The Third Secret
64. The Nanny 65. Our Mother's House 67. The
Night of the Following Day 68. The Prime of Miss
Jean Brodie 69. Sinful Davey 69. David
Copperfield 69. And Soon the Darkness 70.
Necromancy 72. The Legend of Hell House 73.
Food for the Gods 76, etc.

Franklin, Richard (1948–).
Australian director.
■ Belinda 72. Loveland 73. The True Story of
Eskimo Nell (aka Dick Down Under) 75. Fantasm
77. Patrick 78. Road Games 81. Psycho II 83. Cloak
and Dagger 84. Link 86. FX/2: The Deadly Art of
Illusion 91. Hotel Sorrento 94.

Franklin, Sidney (1893–1972).
American producer-director, in Hollywood since
leaving school. Academy Award 1942 'for
consistent high achievement'.
Martha's Vindication (d) 16. Heart o' the Hills
(d) 19. Dulcy (d) 23. Beverly of Graustark (d) 26.
The Last of Mrs Cheyney (d) 29. Private Lives (d)
31. The Guardsman (d) 32. Smiling Through (d)
32. Reunion in Vienna (d) 33. The Barretts of
Wimpole Street (d) 33. The Dark Angel (d) 35.
The Good Earth (AANd) 37. On Borrowed Time
(p) 39. Waterloo Bridge (p) 40. Mrs Miniver (p) 42.
Random Harvest (p) 42. The White Cliffs of Dover
(p) 44. The Yearling (p) 46. The Miniver Story (p)
50. Young Bess (p) 54. The Barretts of Wimpole
Street (d) 57, many others.

Franklyn, Leo (1897–1975).
English character actor, mainly on the stage in
musical comedy, revue and farce. In films from
the early 30s in Australia. Father of actor William
Franklyn.
Two Minutes Silence 34. I've Got a Horse 38.
The Same to You 59. The Night We Dropped a
Clanger 59. The Night We Got the Bird 60, etc.

Franklyn, William (1926–).
Smooth British character actor, popular on TV.
Quatermass II 57. Fury at Smugglers' Bay 58.
Pit of Darkness 62. The Legend of Young Dick
Turpin 64. The Intelligence Men 65. The Satanic
Rites of Dracula 73. Splitting Heirs 93, etc.

Frankovich, Mike (1910–1992).
American producer, a former sports commentator
and screenwriter. During the 50s he ran Columbia's
British organization, and in the 60s became their
head of world production, then turned
independent again. He was the adopted son of Joe
E. Brown and married to Binnie Barnes.
Fugitive Lady 51. Decameron Nights 53.
Footsteps in the Fog 55. Joe Macbeth 56.
Marooned 69. Bob and Carol and Ted and Alice
69. Cactus Flower 69. Butterflies are Free 72. Forty
Carats 73. The Shootist 76, etc.

Franz, Arthur (1920–).
American leading man, latterly character actor;
radio, stage and TV experience.
Jungle Patrol (debut) 48. Sands of Iwo Jima 49.

Abbott and Costello Meet the Invisible Man 51. The
Sniper 52. Eight Iron Men 52. The Caine Mutiny
54. The Unholy Wife 57. Running Target 58.
Hellcats of the Navy 59. Alvarez Kelly 66. Anzio
68. Sisters of Death 77. That Championship Season
82, etc.

Franz, Dennis (1944–).
American character actor, best known for his TV
roles as a tough cop, from the stage.
Dressed to Kill 80. Blow Out 81. Psycho 2 83.
Body Double 84. Kiss Shot 89. The Package 89. Die
Hard 2 90, etc.
TV series: Chicago Story 82. Bay City Blues 83.
Hill Street Blues 85–87. NYPD Blue 93–95.

Franz, Eduard (1902–1983).
American character actor, often seen as foreign
dignitary, Jewish elder, or psychiatrist.
The Iron Curtain 48. Francis 50. The Thing 51.
The Jazz Singer 52. Dream Wife 53. Broken Lance
54. The Ten Commandments 56. Man Afraid 57.
A Certain Smile 58. The Story of Ruth 60. Hatari
62. The President's Analyst 67, many others.
TV series: The Breaking Point 63. Zorro 78.

Fraser, Bill (1908–1987).
British comic character actor, TV's 'Snudge'. Wide
stage experience; film parts since 1938 usually bits
till latterly.
Meet Me Tonight 52. The Americanization of
Emily 65. Joey Boy 65. Masquerade 65. I've Gotta
Horse 65. Up the Chastity Belt 71. That's Your
Funeral 72, etc.

Fraser, Brendan (1969–).
American leading actor. The son of Canadian
parents, he studied theatre at the Cornish College
of the Arts in Seattle.
Dogfight 91. Encino Man (GB: California Man)
92. School Ties 92. Twenty Bucks 93. With
Honors 94. Airheads 94. The Scout 94. The Passion
of Darkly Noon 95, etc.

Fraser, John (1931–).
British leading man with stage experience,
sporadically in films.
The Good Beginning 53. Touch and Go 55. The
Good Companions 57. Tunes of Glory 59. The Trials
of Oscar Wilde (as Lord Alfred Douglas) 60. El Cid
61. Fury at Smugglers' Bay 61. The Waltz of the
Toreadors 62. Repulsion 65. Operation Crossbow
65. Isadora 68. Schizo 77, etc.

Fraser, Liz (1933–).
British character actress, specializing in dumb
cockney blondes.
Wonderful Things 58. I'm All Right, Jack 59.
Two-Way Stretch 60. The Rebel 61. Double Bunk
61. Carry On Regardless 61. The Painted Smile
61. Raising the Wind 62. Live Now
Pay Later 63. The Americanization of Emily 64.
The Family Way 66. Up the Junction 68. Dad's
Army 70. Confessions of a Driving Instructor 76.
Confessions from a Holiday Camp 77. Chicago Joe
and the Showgirl 88, etc.

Fraser, Moyra (1923–).
Australian comedienne in British stage and TV.
Here We Go Round the Mulberry Bush 67.
Prudence and the Pill 68. The Boy Friend 71, etc.

Fraser, Richard (1913–1971).
Scottish-born leading man of some American
second features in the 40s.
How Green Was My Valley 41. The Picture of
Dorian Gray 44. Fatal Witness 46. The Cobra
Strikes 48. Alaska Patrol 51, etc.

Fraser, Ronald (1930–).
Stocky British character actor, in films and TV since 1954.

The Sundowners 59. The Pot Carriers 62. The Punch and Judy Man 63. Crooks in Cloisters 64. The Beauty Jungle 64. The Flight of the Phoenix 65. The Whisperers 67. The Killing of Sister George 68. Sinful Davey 69. Too Late the Hero 69. The Rise and Rise of Michael Rimmer 70. The Magnificent Seven Deadly Sins 71. Rentadick 72. Ooh You Are Awful 72. Swallows and Amazons 74. Paper Tiger 75. The Wild Geese 78. Trail of the Pink Panther 82. Absolute Beginners 86. Let Him Have It 91. The Mystery of Edwin Drood 93, etc.

Frawley, James (1937–).
American director.

The Christian Licorice Store 70. Kid Blue 73. Delancey Street 75. The Eddie Capra Mysteries (pilot) (TV) 76. The Big Bus 76. The Muppet Movie 79. The Great American Traffic Jam (TV) 80. Fraternity Vacation 85, etc.

Frawley, William (1887–1966).
Stocky, cigar-chewing American comedy character actor from vaudeville, in innumerable films as taxi driver, comic gangster, private detective or incompetent cop.

Moonlight and Pretzels 33. Crime Doctor 34. Alibi Ike 35. Desire 36. High Wide and Handsome 37. Professor Beware 38. Persons in Hiding 39. One Night in the Tropics 40. Footsteps in the Dark 42. *Roxie Hart* 42. Whistling in Brooklyn 43. Going My Way 44. Lady on a Train 45. The Crime Doctor's Manhunt 46. Miracle on 34th Street 47. The Babe Ruth Story 48. East Side West Side 49. Kill the Umpire 50. The Lemon Drop Kid 51. Rancho Notorious 52. Safe at Home 62, etc.

TV series: *I Love Lucy* 51–60. My Three Sons 60–63.

Frayn, Michael (1933–).
British dramatist, novelist and occasional screenwriter, a former journalist.

Clockwise 86. Noises Off (oa) 92.

Frazee, Jane (1918–1985) (Mary Jane Frehse).
Vivacious American singer and leading lady of minor musicals in the 40s.

Buck Privates 41. Moonlight in Havana 42. When Johnny Comes Marching Home 42. Practically Yours 44. Swing and Sway 44. Kansas City Kitty 45. Incident 48. Rhythm Inn (last appearance) 51, etc.

TV series: Beulah 52.

Frears, Stephen (1931–).
British director. Born in Leicester, he studied law at Cambridge University, worked at the Royal Court Theatre as assistant to Lindsay Anderson, and then joined the BBC, directing documentaries and drama before making his first feature in 1971.

Gumshoe 71. Saigon–Year of the Cat (TV) 83. The Hit 84. *My Beautiful Laundrette* 85. Prick Up Your Ears 87. Sammy and Rosie Get Laid 87. Dangerous Liaisons 88. *The Grifters* (AAN) 90. Hero (GB Accidental Hero) 92. *The Snapper* (TV) 93. Mary Reilly 95, etc.

¶ Being English drives you barmy. – S.F.
    What happened to self-doubt? That was the basis of my generation – doubt mixed with confidence. – S.F.

Frechette, Mark (1947–1975).
American leading man of *Zabriskie Point*; subsequently died in prison.

Freda, Riccardo (1909–) (aka Robert Hampton, George Lincoln, Willy Pareto).
Egyptian-Italian director who brings some style to exploitation pictures; former art critic.

Les Misérables 46. Theodora, Slave Express 54. I Vampiri 57. The Giant of Thessaly 61. The Terror of Dr Hitchcock 62. The Spectre 63. Le Due Orfanelle 66. Coplan FX18 (Coplan, Secret Agent FX18) 66. La Morte non Conta i Dollari 67. A Doppia Faccia 69. L'Iguana della Lingua di Fuoco 70. L'Ossessione che Uccide (Murder Obsession) 80, etc.

Frederick, Lynne (1953–1994).
British leading lady, widow of Peter Sellers. She was briefly married to David Frost.

No Blade of Grass 70. Vampire Circus 71. Henry VIII and His Six Wives 72. Schizo 76. Voyage of the Damned 76. The Prisoner of Zenda 79, etc.

Frederick, Pauline (1885–1938) (Pauline Libbey).
American leading lady of silent days.

Bella Donna 15. The Slave Island 16. Sleeping Fires 17. Her Final Reckoning 18. The Peace of Roaring River 19. *Madame X* 20. La Tosca 21. Married Flirts 24. Her Honour the Governor 26. Mumsie (GB) 27. On Trial 28. The Sacred Flame 29. This Modern Age 31. The Phantom of Crestwood 32. My Marriage 36. Thank You Mr Moto 38, etc.

Fredericks, Ellsworth.
American cinematographer.

Invasion of the Body Snatchers 56. The Friendly Persuasion 56. Sayonara 57. High Time 60. Seven Days in May 64. Pistolero 66. The Power 67. Mister Buddwing 67, etc.

Free Cinema.
A term applied to their own output by a group of British documentarists of the 50s, e.g. Lindsay Anderson, Karel Reisz. Their aim was to make 'committed' films which cared about the individual and the significance of the everyday. The resulting films were not always better than those produced by professional units with more commercial intent. The most notable were *O Dreamland, Momma Don't Allow, The March to Aldermaston, Every Day Except Christmas* and *We Are the Lambeth Boys*, the two latter films being sponsored by commercial firms.

¶ As film-makers we believe that:
    No film can be too personal.
The image speaks. Sound amplifies and comments. Size is irrelevant.
Perfection is not an aim.
An attitude means a style. A style means an attitude.
– *statement of belief, signed by the members of Free Cinema and written by Lindsay Anderson in 1956*

Freed, Alan (1922–1965).
American disc-jockey, the self-styled 'King of Rock 'n' Roll', which is a term he claimed to have coined. A tireless promoter of the music, he appeared as himself in several 50s films. His career was ruined at the end of that decade following accusations that he had accepted bribes to play records. Two movies have been made about his life: *Mister Rock and Roll*, in which he starred, and *American Hot Wax* 78, in which he was played by Tim McIntire.

■ Rock around the Clock 56. Don't Knock the Rock 56. Mister Rock and Roll 57. Rock Rock Rock 57. Go Johnny Go (& p) 58.

Freed, Arthur (1894–1973) (Arthur Grossman).
American producer, mainly of musicals for MGM, many of them featuring his own lyrics.

Hold Your Man (ly only) 33. Hollywood Party (ly only) 34. Broadway Melody of 1936 (ly only). Broadway Melody of 1938 (ly only). *Babes In Arms* (& ly) 39. Strike Up the Band 40. Lady Be Good (& ly) 41. Cabin in the Sky 43. Meet Me in St Louis 44. Ziegfeld Follies 46. The Pirate 48. *On the Town* 49. Annie Get Your Gun 50. Showboat 51. *An American in Paris* 51. Singin' in The Rain (& ly) 52. *Band Wagon* 53. Kismet 55. Invitation to the Dance 56. *Gigi* 58. Bells are Ringing 60. The Light in the Piazza 62, many others.

Freed, Bert (1919–).
Burly American character actor.

Why Must I Die? 60. Fate Is the Hunter 64. P.J 67. Billy Jack 71. Till Death 77. Barracuda 79, etc

Freedman, Jerrold (1919–).
American director.

Kansas City Bomber 72. Borderline 80. Native Son 86. The Comeback (TV) 89, etc.

Freeland, Thornton (1898–1987).
American director, former cameraman.

Three Live Ghosts 29. Whoopee 30. *Flying Down to Rio* 33. Brewster's Millions (GB) 35. The Amateur Gentleman (GB) 36. Jericho (GB) 37. The Gang's All Here (GB) 39. Over the Moon (GB) 39. Too Many Blondes 41. Meet Me at Dawn 47. The Brass Monkey (Lucky Mascot) (GB) 48. Dear Mr Prohack (GB) 49, etc.

Freeman, Al, Jnr (1934–).
American leading man, a regular on the daytime soap opera *One Life to Live*.

Black Like Me 64. Dutchman 67. The Detective 68. Finian's Rainbow 68. Castle Keep 69. The Lost Man 70. A Fable (& d) 71. Seven Hours to Judgment 88. The Defense Never Rests (TV) 90. Malcolm X 92, etc.

TV series: Hot L Baltimore 75. Roots 79.

Freeman, Everett (1911–1991).
American writer, usually in collaboration.

Larceny Inc. 42. Thank Your Lucky Stars 43. The Secret Life of Walter Mitty 47. Million Dollar Mermaid 52. My Man Godfrey 57. The Glass Bottom Boat 66. Where Were You When the Lights Went Out? (& co-p) 68. Zigzag 70, many others.

Freeman, Howard (1899–1967).
American character actor, usually in comic roles as businessman on the make.

Pilot Number Five 43. Once Upon a Time 44. Take One False Step 49. Scaramouche 52. Remains To Be Seen 53. Dear Brigitte 65, many others.

Freeman, Joan (1941–).
American general-purpose actress.

The Remarkable Mr Pennypacker 58. Come September 61. The Rounders 65. The Fastest Guitar Alive 66. The Reluctant Astronaut 67, etc.

Freeman, Kathleen (1919–).
American character actress.

Naked City 47. Lonely Heart Bandits 52. Bonzo Goes To College 52. Full House 52. Athena 54. The Fly 58. The Ladies' Man 61. The Disorderly Orderly 65. Three on a Couch 66. Support Your Local Gunfighter 71. Stand Up and Be Counted 72. The Blues Brothers 80. Innerspace 87. Gremlins 2: The New Batch 90, etc.

TV series: Topper 53. Mayor of the Town 54–55. It's about Time 66–67. The Beverly Hillbillies 69–71. Funny Face 71. Lotsa Luck 73–74.

Freeman, Leonard (1921–1974).
American TV producer best known for *Hawaii Five-O*.

Freeman, Mona (1926–) (Monica Freeman).
American leading lady, at her peak as a troublesome teenager in the 40s.
■ National Velvet 44. Our Hearts Were Young and Gay 44. Till We Meet Again 44. Here Come the Waves 44. Together Again 44. Roughly Speaking 45. Junior Miss 45. Danger Signal 45. Black Beauty 46. That Brennan Girl 46. Our Hearts Were Growing Up 46. Variety Girl 47. *Dear Ruth* 47. Mother Wore Tights 47. Isn't It Romantic? 48. Streets of Laredo 49. The Heiress 49. Dear Wife 49. Branded 50. Copper Canyon 50. I Was a Shoplifter 50. Dear Brat 51. Darling How Could You? 51. The Lady from Texas 51. Flesh and Fury 52. Jumping Jacks 52. Angel Face 52. Thunderbirds 52. Battle Cry 55. The Road to Denver 55. The Way Out (GB) 56. Before I Wake (GB) 56. Hold Back the Night 56. Huk 56. Dragoon Wells Massacre 57. The World Was His Jury 58.

Freeman, Morgan (1937–).
American character actor, a former dancer.
Brubaker 80. Eyewitness 80. Harry and Son 84. Teachers 84. That Was Then . . . This Is Now 85. Street Smart (AAN) 87. Clean and Sober 88. Driving Miss Daisy (AAN) 89. Glory 89. Johnny Handsome 89. Lean on Me 89. Bonfire of the Vanities 90. Robin Hood: Prince of Thieves 91. The Power of One 92. Unforgiven 92. The Positively True Adventures of the Alleged Texas Cheerleader-Murdering Mom (TV) 93. Bopha! (d) 93. The Shawshank Redemption 94. Outbreak 95, etc.

Freeman, Paul (1943–).
British character actor, often as a villain.
The Dogs of War 81. Raiders of the Lost Ark 81. The Sender 82. The Long Good Friday 82. An Unsuitable Job for a Woman 82. Shanghai Surprise 86. A World Apart 88. Prisoner of Rio 89. Aces: Iron Eagle III 92. Pretty Princess (It.) 93, etc.

Freeman, Robert (c. 1935–).
British director, former fashion director and title artist (*A Hard Day's Night, Help*).
The Touchables 68. World of Fashion (short) 68. L'Echelle Blanche 69.

freeze frame.
A printing device whereby the action appears to 'freeze' into a still, this being accomplished by printing one frame many times.

Fregonese, Hugo (1908–1987).
Argentine-born director, former journalist, in Hollywood from 1945.
One-Way Street 50. Saddle Tramp 51. Apache Drums 51. Mark of the Renegade 52. My Six Convicts 52. The Raid 53. Decameron Nights 53. Blowing Wild 54. The Man in the Attic 54. Black Tuesday 54. Seven Thunders (GB) 57. Harry Black 58. Marco Polo 61. Apaches Last Battle (Old Shatterhand) (Ger.) 64. Savage Pampas (Sp.) 66, etc.

Freleng, Friz (1906–1994) (Isidore Freleng).
American director of cartoons whose creations include Speedy Gonzales, Yosemite Sam, and the Pink Panther. Born in Kansas City, he began working in animated films in 1924 and was among the first animators to work for Walt Disney, although the association was a brief one. In the 30s he became head animator and later a director at Warner, where he remained until the early 60s, apart from two unhappy years at MGM in the late 30s. With David De Patie, he set up his own cartoon production company, De Patie-Freleng Enterprises, before returning to Warner in 1980.
Wicked West 29. Bosko in Person 33. Bing Crosbyana 36. Sweet Sioux 37. A Star Is Hatched 38. Poultry Pirates 38. You Ought to Be in Pictures 40. Hiawatha's Rabbit Hunt (AAN) 41. Rhapsody in Rivets (AAN) 41. Pigs in a Polka (AAN) 42. Greetings Bait (AAN) 43. Life with Feathers (AAN) 45. Hare Trigger 45. Tweetie Pie (AA) 47. Sandy Claws (AAN) 54. Speedy Gonzales (AA) 55. Birds Anonymous (AA) 57. Show Biz Bugs 57. Knighty Knight Bugs (AA) 58. Mexicali Shmoes (AAN) 59. Mouse and Garden (AAN) 60. Pied Piper of Guadalupe (AANp) 61. The Pink Phink (AA) 64. The Pink Blueprint (AANp) 66. Friz Freleng's Looney Looney Bugs Bunny Movie (compilation) 81. Bugs Bunny's 3rd Movie: 1001 Rabbit Tales (compilation) 82. Daffy Duck's Movie: Fantastic Island (compilation) 83. Porky Pig in Hollywood (compilation, co-d) 86, many others.

French, Harold (1897–1982).
British stage actor and producer, in films since 1931.
Biographies: 1970, *I Swore I Never Would*. 1972, *I Thought I Never Could*.
AS DIRECTOR: The House of the Arrow 39. Jeannie 41. Unpublished Story 42. The Day Will Dawn 42. Secret Mission 42. *Dear Octopus* 43. English Without Tears 44. Mr Emmanuel 44. Quiet Weekend 46. My Brother Jonathan 47. The Blind Goddess 48. Quartet (part) 48. The Dancing Years 49. Trio (part) 50. Encore (part) 51. The Hour of 13 52. Isn't Life Wonderful 53. Rob Roy 53. Forbidden Cargo 54. The Man Who Loved Redheads 55, etc.

French, Leslie (1899–).
Diminutive British character player.
This England 41. *Orders to Kill* 58. The Leopard 63. More than a Miracle 67. Death in Venice 70, etc.

French, Valerie (1931–1990).
British actress, in occasional Hollywood films.
Jubal 56. Garment Center 57. Decision at Sundown 57. The Four Skulls of Jonathan Drake 59. Shalako 68, etc.

Frend, Charles (1909–1977).
British director.
AS EDITOR: Waltzes from Vienna 33. Secret Agent 36. Sabotage 37. Young and Innocent 37. The Citadel 38. Goodbye Mr Chips 39. Major Barbara 40, etc.
■ AS DIRECTOR: The Big Blockade 42. The Foreman Went to France 42. *San Demetrio London* (& w) 43. Johnny Frenchman 45. Return of the Vikings 45. The Loves of Joanna Godden 47. Scott of the Antarctic 48. A Run for Your Money 49. The Magnet 49. *The Cruel Sea* 53. Lease of Life 54. The Long Arm 56. Barnacle Bill 58. Cone of Silence 60. Girl on Approval 62. Torpedo Bay 62. The Shy Bike 67.

Fresnay, Pierre (1897–1975) (Pierre Laudenbach).
Distinguished French stage actor who made many films.
Marius (debut) 31. Fanny 32. César 34. The Man Who Knew Too Much (GB) 34. *La Grande Illusion* 37. Le Corbeau 43. *Monsieur Vincent* 47. *God Needs Men* 50. The Fanatics 57, many others.

Freud, Sigmund (1856–1939).
Viennese physician who became the virtual inventor of psychoanalysis and the discoverer of sexual inhibition as a mainspring of human behaviour; a gentleman, therefore, to whom Hollywood has every reason to be grateful. A biopic *Freud* 62 was directed by John Huston starring Montgomery Clift.

Freund, Karl (1890–1969).
Czech-born cinematographer, famous for his work in German silents like The Last Laugh 24.
Metropolis 26. Variety 26. Berlin 27, etc.
SINCE IN USA: *The Mummy* (& d) 33. Moonlight and Pretzels (d only) 33. Madame Spy (d only) 33. Mad Love (d only) 35. Camille 36. *The Good Earth* (AA) 37. Marie Walewska 38. Pride and Prejudice 40. The Seventh Cross 44. Key Largo 48. Bright Leaf 50, many others.

Frewer, Matt (1958–).
American actor, best known for his role as Max Headroom on television.
Max Headroom (TV) 84. Supergirl 84. Speed Zone 88. Far from Home 89. Honey, I Shrunk the Kids 89. Short Time 90. The Taking of Beverly Hills 91, etc.
TV series: Max Headroom 87.

Frey, Leonard (1938–1988).
American character actor. He died of AIDS.
The Magic Christian 70. Tell Me That You Love Me Junie Moon 70. *The Boys in the Band* 70. Fiddler on the Roof (AAN) 71. Shirts/Skins (TV) 73. Where the Buffalo Roam 80.
TV series: Best of the West 81.

Frey, Sami (1937–) (Samuel Frei).
French leading actor, in films from a teenager.
Cleo from 5 to 7 61. The Outsiders (aka Band of Outsiders) (Bande à Part) 64. César and Rosalie 72. Sweet Movie 75. Nea 78. The Little Drummer Girl 84. Blood and Sand (aka Sand and Blood) (De Sable et de Sang) 87. La Fille de D'Artagnan 94, etc.

Fricker, Brenda (1944–).
Irish character actress.
My Left Foot (AA) 89. The Field 90. Utz (TV) 91. Home Alone 2: Lost in New York 92. So I Married an Axe Murderer 93. Seekers (TV) 93. Angels in the Outfield 94. Deadly Advice 94. A Man of No Importance 94, etc.
TV series: Casualty 86–90.

Friderici, Blanche (1870/78–1933).
American character actress of stark, dour presence.
Trespassing 22. Sadie Thompson 28. Jazz Heaven 29. Billy the Kid 30. Kismet 30. Night Nurse 31. Murder by the Clock 31. Mata Hari 31. Love Me Tonight 32. A Farewell to Arms 32. If I Had a Million 32. Flying down to Rio 33. It Happened One Night 34, many others.

Fried, Gerald (1928–).
American composer, mainly for TV.
Killer's Kiss 55. Terror in a Texas Town 58. A Cold Wind in August 60. The Cabinet of Caligari 62. One Potato Two Potato 64. The Killing of Sister George 68. Too Late the Hero 69. The Grissom Gang 71. Soylent Green 73. Roots (TV) 76. Testimony of Two Men (TV) 77. Foul Play 78. Little Darlings 80. Nine to Five 80, many others.

Friedhofer, Hugo (1902–1981).
American composer.
The Adventures of Marco Polo 38. China Girl 42. The Lodger 44. The Woman in the Window 45. *The Best Years of Our Lives* (AA) 46. The Bishop's Wife 47. Joan of Arc 48. Broken Arrow 50. Ace in the Hole 51. Above and Beyond 52. Vera Cruz 54. The Rains of Ranchipur 55. The Harder They Fall

**56. One-Eyed Jacks 59. The Secret Invasion 64. The Red Baron 71. Die Sister Die 78, etc.

Friedkin, William (1939–).
American director and screenwriter, from TV. Formerly married to actresses Jeanne Moreau and Lesley-Anne Down.
Biography: 1990, *Hurricane Billy* by Nat Segaloff.
Good Times 67. The Birthday Party 68. The Night They Raided Minsky's 68. The Boys in the Band 70. *The French Connection* (AA) 71. *The Exorcist* (AAN) 73. Sorcerer 77. The Brinks Job 79. Cruising 80. Deal of the Century 84. To Live and Die in L.A. 85. Rampage 87. The Guardian 90. Blue Chips 94, etc.

¶ By the time a film of mine makes it into the theatres, I have a love-hate relationship with it. There is always something I could have done to make it better. – *W.F.*

Friedman, Seymour (1917–).
American second feature director.
Trapped by Boston Blackie 48. Prison Warden 49. Customs Agent 50. Criminal Lawyer 51. Son of Dr Jekyll 51. Escape Route (co-d) (GB) 53. Secret of Treasure Mountain 56, etc.

Friedman, Stephen.
American producer.
Loving Molly (& w) 73. Little Darlings 80. Hero at Large 80. Eye of the Needle 81. All of Me 84. Creator 85. Enemy Mine 85. The Big Easy 87. Miss Firecracker 89, etc.

Friels, Colin (1954–).
Scottish-born leading man, in Australia. He is married to actress Judy Davis.
Hoodwink 81. Monkey Grip 82. Buddies 83. Malcolm 86. Kangaroo 86. High Tide 87. Ground Zero 87. Warm Nights on a Slow Moving Train 87. Grievous Bodily Harm 88. Darkman 90. Dingo 90. Weekend with Kate 90. Class Action 91. The Nostradamus Kid 93. Stark (TV) 93. A Good Man in Africa 94, etc.

Friend, Philip (1915–1987).
British leading man with stage experience.
Pimpernel Smith 41. Next of Kin 42. The Flemish Farm 43. Great Day 45. My Own True Love (US) 48. Panthers' Moon (US) 50. The Highwayman (US) 51. Background 53. Son of Robin Hood 59. Stranghold 62, etc.

Friese-Greene, William (1855–1921).
Pioneer British inventor who built the first practical movie camera in 1889. Died penniless; his life was the subject of *The Magic Box* 51.
Biography: 1948, *Friese-Greene, Close-Up of an Inventor* by Ray Allister.

Friml, Rudolf (1879–1972).
Czech-American composer of operettas which were frequently filmed: *The Firefly, Rose Marie, The Vagabond King*, etc.

Frings, Ketti (1909–1981) (Catherine Frings).
American scenarist.
Hold Back the Dawn (& original novel) 41. Guest in the House 44. The Accused 48. Dark City 50. Because of You 52. Come Back Little Sheba 53. Foxfire 55, etc.

Frinton, Freddie (1911–1968).
English comedian of stage, TV and films, best known for playing opposite Thora Hird in the 60s TV series *Meet the Wife.*
Trouble in the Air 48. Force's Sweetheart 53.

Stars in Your Eyes 56. Make Mine Mink 60. What a Whopper 61!, etc.

Fritsch, Willy (1901–1973).
Popular German leading man, in films since 1921.
The Spy 28. Congress Dances 31. Drei Von Der Tankstelle 31 (and 55). Amphitryon 35. Film Ohne Titel 47, many others.

Fritz the Cat.
Randy feline, created by cartoonist Robert Crumb (qv), who appeared in various magazines of the 60s and was the star of two animated adult features:
Fritz the Cat 72. The Nine Lives of Fritz the Cat 74.

Frobe, Gert (1913–1988).
German character actor first seen abroad as the downtrodden little man of *Berliner Ballade* 48; later put on weight and emerged in the 60s as an international semi-star, usually as villain.
Ewiger Walzer 54. Double Destin 54. The Heroes Are Tired 55. He Who Must Die 56. The Girl Rosemarie 58. Menschen im Hotel 59. The Thousand Eyes of Dr Mabuse 60. The Longest Day 62. Die Dreigroschenoper 63. The Testament of Dr Mabuse 64. *Goldfinger* 64. Those Magnificent Men in Their Flying Machines 65. Is Paris Burning? 66. Du Rififi à Paname 67. I Killed Rasputin 67. Rocket to the Moon 67. Monte Carlo or Bust 69. Dollars 71. Ludwig 72. And Then There Were None 75. The Serpent's Egg 77. Bloodline 79. Le Coup de Parapluie 80, etc.

Froeschel, George (1891–1979).
Viennese-American scriptwriter, long in Hollywood; often one of a team.
Waterloo Bridge 40. The Mortal Storm 40. Mrs Miniver (co-w, AA) 42. Random Harvest (AAN) 42. The White Cliffs of Dover 44. Command Decision 48. The Miniver Story 50. Scaramouche 52. Never Let Me Go 53. Betrayed 54. Quentin Durward 55. Me and the Colonel 58, many others.

Frohlich, Gustav (1902–1987).
German actor (from *Metropolis* 26) and director (*The Sinner* 51, etc.). Few of his films have been exported.
Asphalt 29. Stadt Anatol 36. Der Grosse König 41, etc.

From Caligari to Hitler.
This 'psychological history of the German film' by Siegfried Kracauer was first published in 1946 and quickly became the standard work on its subject. It embraces Nazi propaganda films as well as the silent classics of the 20s.

Froman, Jane (1907–1980).
American band-singer, whose heroic resumption of her career following an air crash was portrayed in *With a Song in My Heart*, in which she was played by Susan Hayward.

Frome, Milton (1911–1989).
American comedy character actor, often in bad-tempered bits.
You're Never Too Young 55. Short Cut to Hell 59. I'd Rather Be Rich 64. The St Valentine's Day Massacre 67. The Strongest Man in the World 75, etc.

Frontière, Dominic (1931–).
American composer.
The Marriage Go Round 60. Hero's Island 62. The Outer Limits (TV) 63. Billie 65. The Invaders (TV) 67. Hang 'Em High 68. Popi 69. Chisum 70. Cancel My Reservation 72. Hammersmith is Out

72. Freebie and the Bean 74. Brannigan 75. The Gumball Rally 76. Washington Behind Closed Doors (TV) 77. The Stunt Man 80. Modern Problems 81. Roar 81. The Aviator 87. Color of Night 94, etc.

frost
on movie windows is usually produced from a mixture of Epsom salts and stale beer.

Frost, Sir David (1939–).
Britain's Mr Television of the 60s, later exported to America; mixes entertainment shows with hard-hitting political interviews, and latterly financed a number of rather indifferent movies.
The Rise and Rise of Michael Rimmer 70. The Slipper and the Rose 76.

¶ He has risen without trace. – *Kitty Muggeridge*
Hello, good evening, and welcome. – *catchphrase*

Frost, Sadie.
English actress. Married actor Gary Kemp.
Diamond Skulls 91. Bram Stoker's Dracula 92. Splitting Heirs 93. The Cisco Kid (TV) 94. Shopping 94. Magic Hunter (Buvos Vadas) 94, etc.

Fruet, William (1933–).
Canadian director.
Death Weekend 76. Search and Destroy 79. Funeral Home 81. Baker County U.S.A. 82. Spasms 83. Bedroom Eyes 84. Killer Party 86. Blue Monkey 87, etc.

Fry, Stephen (1957–).
English actor, writer, comedian and novelist. Born in Hampstead, London, he was educated at Cambridge University and began working in TV in 1980 and films from 1985. He often collaborates with Hugh Laurie (qv), a partnership that began with the Cambridge Footlights revue of 1981. He also scripted the revival of the long-running stage musical *Me and My Girl.*
The Good Father 85. A Fish Called Wanda 88. The Secret Policeman's Other Ball 88. A Handful of Dust 88. The Common Pursuit (TV) 92. Peter's Friends 92.
TV series: Blackadder 84–91. This Is David Lander 88. A Bit of Fry and Laurie 89–92. Jeeves and Wooster 90–93. Stalag Luft 93.

Frye, Dwight (1899–1943).
American character actor who made a corner in crazed hunchbacks.
■ The Night Bird 27. Doorway to Hell 30. Man to Man 31. The Maltese Falcon 31. *Dracula* 31. The Black Camel 31. *Frankenstein* 31. By Whose Hand 32. Attorney for the Defense 32. The Invisible Man 33. Strange Adventure 33. Western Code 33. The Vampire Bat 33. The Circus Queen Murder 33. King Solomon of Broadway 33. The Crime of Dr Crespi 33. The Great Impersonation 35. Atlantic Adventure 35. Bride of Frankenstein 35. Florida Special 36. Alibi for Murder 36. The Man who Found Himself 36. Something to Sing About 36. Beware of Ladies 37. The Shadow 37. Great Guy 37. Sea Devils 37. Renfrew of the Royal Mounted 37. Invisible Enemy 38. Fast Company 38. Adventure in Sahara 38. Who Killed Gail Preston 38. Sinners in Paradise 38. Conspiracy 39. Son of Frankenstein 39. The Man in the Iron Mask 39. I Take This Woman 39. Gangs of Chicago 40. Phantom Raiders 40. Drums of Fu Manchu 40. Sky Bandits 40. Mystery Ship 41. Son of Monte Cristo 41. The People vs Dr Kildare 41. Blonde from Singapore 41. The Devil Pays Off 41. Prisoner of Japan 42. The Ghost of Frankenstein 42.

Sleepytime Gal 42. Danger in the Pacific 42. Frankenstein meets the Wolf Man 43. Dead Men Walk 43. Submarine Alert 43. Hangmen Also Die 43. Dangerous Blondes 43.

Fryer, Robert (1920–).
American producer, former casting director.
   The Boston Strangler 68. The Prime of Miss Jean Brodie 69. Myra Breckinridge 69. The Salzburg Connection 71. Travels with My Aunt 73. The Abdication 73. Voyage of the Damned 76.

Fu Manchu.
Sax Rohmer's oriental master-criminal was played by Harry Agar Lyons in a series of British two-reelers in the 20s. Warner Oland played him in *The Mysterious Fu Manchu* 29, *The Return of Fu Manchu* 30 and *Daughter of the Dragon* 31; Boris Karloff in *Mask of Fu Manchu* 32, and Henry Brandon in *Drums of Fu Manchu* 41. Otherwise he was oddly neglected until the 60s series starring Christopher Lee, beginning with *The Face of Fu Manchu* 65 and *Brides of Fu Manchu* 66: it degenerated into shambling nonsense.

Fuchs, Daniel (1909–1993).
American screenwriter and novelist, a former teacher. Born in Brooklyn, he went to Hollywood after his early novels, based on his childhood, failed to find a big enough readership.
   The Big Shot (co-w) 42. The Hard Way 42. Between Two Worlds (w) 44. Love Me or Leave Me (AA) 55. Jeanne Eagels 57, etc.

Fuest, Robert (1927–).
British director, from TV.
■ Just Like a Woman 66. And Soon the Darkness 70. Wuthering Heights 70. The Abominable Dr Phibes 71. Dr Phibes Rises Again 72. The Final Programme (& w) 73. The Devil's Rain (US) 76. The Revenge of the Stepford Wives (TV) 80. Aphrodite 82.

Fujicolor.
Japanese colour film first used in 1955. Fuji's ultra-high-speed colour negative film was given an Academy Award of Merit in 1981, and was used to film the international success *Das Boot*, directed by Wolfgang Petersen.

Fujimoto, Tak.
Japanese-American cinematographer.
   Remember My Name 78. Last Embrace 79. Borderline 80. Melvin and Howard 80. Where the Buffalo Roam 80. Heart Like a Wheel 83. Swing Shift 84. Ferris Bueller's Day Off 86. Pretty in Pink 86. Something Wild 86. Backfire 87. Cocoon: The Return 88. Married to the Mob 88. Sweethearts Dance 88. Miami Blues 90. The Silence of the Lambs 91. Philadelphia 93, etc.

Fulci, Lucio (1927–).
Italian general-purpose director who gained some international attention with horror films in the 80s.
   I Ladri 59. Le Massaggiatrici 62. I Maniaci 64. Beatrice Cenci 69. La Pretora 76. Zombi 2 (aka Zombie Flesh Eaters) 79. City of the Living Dead (Paura nella Città dei Morti Viventi) 80. The Black Cat (Il Gatto Nero di Park Lane) 80. Manhattan Baby 82. House of Doom (co-d) (TV) 89. Nightmare Concert 90. Voices from the Deep 90, many others.

¶ I find much of what I film very repugnant. But it has to be done. – L.F.
Italy's last great sleaze merchant. – *The Dark Side*

Fuller, Leslie (1889–1948).
Beefy British concert-party comedian who was popular in broad comedy films of the 30s.
■ Not So Quiet on the Western Front 30. Kiss Me Sergeant 30. Why Sailors Leave Home 30. Old Soldiers Never Die 31. Poor Old Bill 31. What a Night 31. The Last Coupon 32. Old Spanish Customers 32. Tonight's the Night 32. Hawleys of the High Street 33. The Pride of the Force 33. A Political Party 34. The Outcast 34. Lost in the Legion 34. Doctor's Orders 34. Strictly Illegal 35. Captain Bill 35. The Stoker 35. One Good Turn 36. Boys Will Be Girls 37. The Middle Watch 39. Two Smart Men 40. My Wife's Family 41. Front Line Kids 42. What Do We Do Now 45.

Fuller, Mary (1887–1973).
Popular American star of silent films who disappeared from view in 1917 and was forgotten until her death in a Washington mental hospital.
   Frankenstein 10. What Happened to Mary (serial) 12. Under Southern Skies 15. The Strength of the Week 16. Public Be Damned 17. The Long Trail 17, etc.

Fuller, Robert (1934–).
American leading man, mostly on TV.
   Return of the Seven 66. Incident at Phantom Hill 67. The Hard Ride 70. The Gatling Gun 72. Mustang Country 76. Donner Pass: The Road to Survival (TV) 78. Maverick 94, etc.
   TV series: Laramie 59–62. Wagon Train 62–63. Emergency 72–77.

Fuller, Samuel (1912–).
American writer-director who has also produced most of his own pictures, which have normally been violent melodramas on topical subjects.
■ I Shot Jesse James 49. The Baron of Arizona 50. Fixed Bayonets 51. The Steel Helmet 51. Park Row 52. Pickup on South Street 52. Hell and High Water 54. House of Bamboo 55. Run of the Arrow 55. China Gate 56. Forty Guns 57. Verboten 58. The Crimson Kimono 59. Underworld USA 60. Merrill's Marauders 62. Shock Corridor 64. The Naked Kiss 66. Shark 67. Dead Pigeon on Beethoven Street 72 (West Ger.). The American Friend (acted only) 77. The Big Red One 80. White Dog 82. Thieves after Dark (Les Voleurs de la Nuit) 84. Let's Get Harry (story) 87. A Return to Salem's Lot (a) 87. Helsinki Napoli All Night Long (a) 88. Street of No Return (Sans Espoir de Retour) 89. Tell Me Sam (a) 89. Bohemian Life (La Vie de Bohème) (a) 92. Petrified Garden (a) 93. Somebody to Love (a) 94.

Fullerton, Fiona (1955–).
British juvenile actress of the 70s.
   Run Wild Run Free 69. Nicholas and Alexandra 71. Alice's Adventures in Wonderland 72. Gauguin the Savage (TV) 80. A View to a Kill 85. Shaka Zulu (TV) 87. Hold the Dream (TV) 87. The Secret Life of Ian Fleming (TV) 90, etc.

Fulton, John P. (1902–1965).
American special effects photographer, responsible for the tricks in most of the *Invisible Man* series and other fantasy movies.

funerals
provided a starting point for *The Third Man*, *Frankenstein*, *The Great Man*, *Death of a Salesman*, *The Bad and the Beautiful*, *Citizen Kane*, and *Keeper of the Flame*; figured largely in *The Premature Burial*, *The Mummy*, *The Fall of the House of Usher*, *The Counterfeit Traitor*, *Funeral in Berlin*, *The Godfather*, *The Glass Key*, *I Bury the Living*, *Miracle in Milan*, *Doctor Zhivago* and *Hamlet*; and formed a

climax for *Our Town* and *Four Weddings and a Funeral*. In *Vampyr* and *Wild Strawberries* the hero dreamed of his own funeral; and in *Holy Matrimony* Monty Woolley attended his own funeral, having arranged to have his valet's body mistaken for his. Funerals were taken lightly in *I See a Dark Stranger*, *Little Caesar*, *Kind Hearts and Coronets*, *Too Many Crooks*, *A Comedy of Terrors*, *Charade*, *The Wrong Box*, *I Love You Alice B. Toklas*, *Robin and the Seven Hoods*, *Monsieur Hulot's Holiday*, *Entr'acte*, *Ocean's Eleven*, *Comrade X*, *What a Way to Go*, *The Private Life of Sherlock Holmes*, and above all *The Loved One*.

funfairs
have provided fascinating settings for many a bravura film sequence. *The Wagons Roll at Night*, *Nightmare Alley*, *Dante's Inferno*, *Rollercoaster* and *The Ring* were set almost entirely on fairgrounds. Tawdry or 'realistic' funfairs were shown in *Jeanne Eagels*, *Saturday Night and Sunday Morning*, *East of Eden*, *Picnic*, and *Inside Daisy Clover*; glamorized or sentimentalized ones cropped up in *The Wolf Man*, *My Girl Tisa*, *State Fair*, *Roseanna McCoy*, *The Great Ziegfeld* and *Mr and Mrs Smith*. Musicals like *On the Town*, *On the Avenue*, *Coney Island*, *Centennial Summer*, *State Fair* and *Down to Earth* had funfair sequences and they are also used to excellent advantage in thrillers:
   Brighton Rock, *Spider Woman*, *Horrors of the Black Museum*, *Gorilla at Large*, *The Third Man*, *Lady from Shanghai*, *Strangers on a Train*. Naturally funfairs are also marvellous places for fun: though not for Eddie Cantor in *Strike Me Pink*, Tony Curtis in *Forty Pounds of Trouble*, Laurel and Hardy in *The Dancing Masters*, or Bob Hope (fired from a cannon) in *Road to Zanzibar*. *The Beast from 20,000 Fathoms* was finally cornered in a funfair; *Dr Caligari* kept his cabinet in one. The star who made the most of a funfair sequence was undoubtedly Mae West as the carnival dancer in *I'm No Angel*, in which she delivered her famous line: 'Suckers!'

Funicello, Annette (1942–).
American leading lady, former juvenile actress; was host of Disney's TV Mickey Mouse Club, and in his films is known simply as 'Annette'.
   Johnny Tremain 57. The Shaggy Dog 61. Babes in Toyland 61. The Misadventures of Merlin Jones 63. Bikini Beach 64. The Monkey's Uncle 65. Fireball 500 66. Back to the Beach 87, etc.

Funt, Allen (1914–).
American TV trickster who appeared for years on *Candid Camera* and in 1970 produced and starred in a film version, *What Do You Say to a Naked Lady?*
   Money Talks (d) 71.

Furie, Sidney J. (1933–).
Canadian director with a restless camera; came to Britain 1959, Hollywood 1966.
■ A Dangerous Age 57. A Cool Sound from Hell 58. The Snake Woman 60. Doctor Blood's Coffin 61. During One Night 61. Three on a Spree 61. The Young Ones 61. The Boys 61. The Leather Boys 63. Wonderful Life 64. *The Ipcress File* 65. Day of the Arrow 65. The Appaloosa 66. The Naked Runner 67. The Lawyer 69. Little Fauss and Big Halsy 70. Lady Sings the Blues 72. Hit 73. Sheila Levine Is Dead and Living in New York 75. Gable and Lombard 76. The Boys in Company C 77. The Entity 82. Purple Hearts 84. Iron Eagle 85. Superman IV 87. Iron Eagle II 88. The Taking of Beverly Hills 91. Ladybugs 92.
   TV series: Hudson's Bay 59.

Furlong, Edward (1977–).
American teenage actor.
   Terminator 2: Judgment Day 91. American

Heart 93. A Home of Our Own 94. Brainscan 94. Little Odessa 94, etc.

Furneaux, Yvonne (1928–   ).
French leading lady in British films.
  Meet Me Tonight 52. The Dark Avenger 55. Lisbon 56. The Mummy 59. La Dolce Vita 59. Enough Rope (Fr.) 63. *Repulsion* 64. The Scandal (Fr.) 66, etc.

Furrer, Urs (1934–1975).
Swiss-born American cinematographer.
  Pigeons 70. Desperate Characters 71. Shaft 71. Shaft's Big Score 72. Dr Cook's Garden (TV) 72. The Seven Ups 73, etc.

Furse, Judith (1912–1974).
British character actress who often played district nurses, matrons, heavy schoolmistresses, etc.
  Goodbye Mr Chips 39. English Without Tears 44. Black Narcissus 46. The Man in the White Suit 51. Doctor at Large 57. Serious Charge 59. Carry On Regardless 61. Carry On Spying 64. Sinful Davy 69. The Adventures of Barry McKenzie 72, etc.

Furse, Margaret (1911–1974).
British costume designer.
  Oliver Twist 48. The Mudlark 50. The Inn of the Sixth Happiness 58. Sons and Lovers 60. Young Cassidy 64. Anne of the Thousand Days 70. Mary Queen of Scots 72. Love Among the Ruins (TV) 75, etc.

Furse, Roger (1903–1972).
British stage designer.
  Henry V (costumes only) 44. The True Glory 45. Odd Man Out 47. Hamlet 47. Ivanhoe 52. Richard III 56. The Prince and the Showgirl 57. Saint Joan 57. Bonjour Tristesse 58. The Roman Spring of Mrs Stone 61. Road to Hong Kong 62, etc.

Furst, Anton (1944–1991) (Anthony Francis Furst).
British production designer who trained as an architect and first worked on elaborate laser-light shows for rock concerts. He left Britain to work in Hollywood in the late 80s and committed suicide there.
  Lady Chatterley's Lover 81. An Unsuitable Job for a Woman 81. The Company of Wolves 85. The Frog Prince 85. Full Metal Jacket 87. High Spirits 88. Batman (AA) 89. Awakenings 90, etc.

Furst, Stephen (1954–   ).
Plump American character actor who has also turned to writing and directing.
  National Lampoon's Animal House 78. Swim Team 79. Getting Wasted 80. Midnight Madness 80. The Unseen 80. Up the Creek 84. The Dream Team 89. Magic Kid 2 (& co-w, d) 93, etc.

Furthman, Jules (1888–1966).
Seminal American writer, usually in collaboration.
  Treasure Island 20. The Way of All Flesh 27. *Shanghai Express* 32. *Mutiny on the Bounty* (AAN) 35. Spawn of the North 38. Only Angels Have Wings 39. The Outlaw 43. To Have and Have Not 44. The Big Sleep 46. Nightmare Alley 48. Jet Pilot 50 (released 57). Peking Express 51, many others.

Fury, Billy (1941–1983) (Ronald Wycherly).
British pop singer.
  ■ Play it Cool 62. I've Gotta Horse 65. That'll Be the Day 73.

Fusco, Giovanni (1906–1968).
Italian composer, especially associated with Antonioni.
  Cronaca di un Amore 50. Le Amiche 51. Il Grido 57. Hiroshima Mon Amour 59. L'Avventura 59. The Eclipse 62. The Red Desert 64. The War is Over 66, etc.

Fyffe, Will (1884–1947).
Pawky Scots comedian, famous in the halls for his song 'I Belong to Glasgow'.
  Happy 34. Annie Laurie 36. Cotton Queen 37. Owd Bob 38. The Mind of Mr Reeder 39. Rulers of the Sea (US) 39. For Freedom 40. Neutral Port 40. Heaven Is Round the Corner 44. The Brothers 47, etc.

Gaal, Franceska (1904–1972) (Fanny Zilveritch). Hungarian leading lady who made three American films: The Buccaneer 38. Paris Honeymoon 39. The Girl Downstairs 39.

Gabel, Martin (1912–1986). Balding, rotund American character actor, mostly on stage.

The Lost Moment (d only) 47. Fourteen Hours 51. M 51. The Thief 52. Tip on a Dead Jockey 57. Marnie 64. Lord Love a Duck 66. Divorce American Style 67. Lady in Cement 68. There was a Crooked Man 70. The Front Page 75. The First Deadly Sin 80, etc.

Gabel, Scilla (1937–). Buxom Italian leading lady in international films. Queen of the Pirates 60. Village of Daughters 62. Sodom and Gomorrah 62. Revenge of the Gladiators 65. Modesty Blaise 66, etc.

Gabin, Jean (1904–1976) (Alexis Moncourgé). Distinguished French actor, former Folies Bergères extra, cabaret entertainer, etc. His stocky virility and world-weary features kept him a star from the early 30s.

Chacun sa Chance 30. Mephisto 31. Paris Beguin 31. Gloria 31. Tout Ca ne vaut pas l'Amour 31. Coeur de Lilas 32. La Belle Marinère 32. Les Gaités de l'Escadron 32. La Foule Hurle 33. L'Etoile de Valencia 33. Adieu les Beaux Jours 33. Le Tunnel 33. De Haut en Bas 33. Au Bout du Monde 34. Zouzou 34. Maria Chapdelaine 34. Bassage Interdit 35. Variétés 35. Golgotha 35. La Bandera 36. La Belle Equipe 36. Les Bas-Fonds 36. Pépé le Moko 37. La Grande Illusion 37. Le Messager 37. Gueule d'Amour 37. Quai des Brumes 38. La Bête Humaine 38. Le Recif de Corail 38. Le Jour se Lève 39. Remorques 41. Moontide (US) 42. The Imposter (US) 42. Martin Roumagnac 46. Miroir 47. Au Dela des Grilles 49. La Marie du Port 50. It's Easier for a Camel (It.) 51. Victor 51. Night is My Kingdom 51. Le Plaisir 52. The Truth about Bébé Donge 52. Bufere 53. La Vierge du Rhin 53. Leur Dernière Nuit 53. Touchez Pas au Grisbi 54. L'Air de Paris 54. Napoleon 55. French Can Can 55. Razzia sur la Chnouff 55. Port of Desire 55. Lost Dogs 56. Important People 56. Gas-Oil 56. Voici le Temps des Assassins 56. Pig Across Paris 56. Le Sang à la Tête 56. Crime and Punishment 56. Le Rouge est Mis 57. Les Misérables 57. The Case of Dr Laurent 58. Le Désordre et la Nuit 58. Maigret Sets a Trap 58. En Cas de Malheur 58. Les Grandes Familles 58. The Tramp 59. Maigret et l'Affaire Saint-Fiacre 59. Rue des Prairies 59. Le Baron de l'Ecluse 60. Les Vieux de la Vieille 61. Le Président 61. Le Cave se Rebiffe 61. A Monkey in Winter 62. Le Gentleman d'Epsom 62. Mélodie en Sous-sol 63. Maigret Sees Red 63. Monsieur 64. The Ungrateful Age 65. God's Thunder 65. Rififi in Panama 66. Le Jardinier d'Argenteuil 67. Le Soleil des Voyous 67. Le Pacha 67. The Tattooed Man 68. Fin de Journée 69. The Sign of the Bull 69. The Sicilian Clan 70. La Horse 70. Le Drapeau Noir Flotte sur la Marmite 71. Le Tueur 72. Le Chat 72. L'affaire

Dominici 73. Deux Hommes dans la Ville 74. Verdict 74. L'Année Sainte 76.

⚙ For forcing such a wide range of roles, without ever losing sympathy, to fit his own dominant personality. Quai des Brumes.

Gable, Christopher (1940–). British actor, ex-ballet dancer.

Women in Love 69. The Music Lovers 70. The Boy Friend 71. The Slipper and the Rose 76. The Lair of the White Worm 88. The Rainbow 88, etc.

Gable, Clark (1901–1960). American leading man who kept his popularity for nearly thirty years, and was known as the 'king' of Hollywood. His big ears were popular with caricaturists; his impudent grin won most female hearts.

■ Forbidden Paradise 24. The Merry Widow 25. The Pacemakers 25. The Plastic Age 25. North Star 26. The Painted Desert 30. The Easiest Way 31. Dance Fools Dance 31. A Free Soul 31. The Finger Points 31. The Secret Six 31. Laughing Sinners 31. Night Nurse 31. Sporting Blood 31. Susan Lenox 32. Possessed 32. Hell's Divers 32. Polly of the Circus 32. Red Dust 32. Strange Interlude 32. No Man of Her Own 32. The White Sister 32. Dancing Lady 33. Hold Your Man 33. Night Flight 33. It Happened One Night (AA) 34. Men in White 34. Manhattan Melodrama 34. Chained 34. After Office Hours 35. Forsaking All Others 35. Mutiny on the Bounty 35. China Seas 35. Call of the Wild 35. Wife Versus Secretary 36. San Francisco 36. Cain and Mabel 36. Love on the Run 37. Parnell 37. Saratoga 37. Test Pilot 38. Too Hot to Handle 38. Idiot's Delight 39. Gone with the Wind 39. Strange Cargo 40. Boom Town 40. Comrade X 40. They Met in Bombay 41. Honky Tonk 41. Somewhere I'll Find You 41; war service; Adventure 45. The Hucksters 47. Homecoming 48. Command Decision 48. Any Number Can Play 49. Key to the City 50. To Please a Lady 50. Across the Wide Missouri 51. Lone Star 52. Never Let Me Go (GB) 53. Mogambo 53. Betrayed 54. The Tall Men 55. Soldier of Fortune 55. The King and Four Queens 56. Band of Angels 57. Teacher's Pet 58. Run Silent Run Deep 58. But Not for Me 59. It Started in Naples 59. The Misfits 61.

⚙ For effortlessly maintaining a Hollywood legend, and for doing so with cheerful impudence. Gone with the Wind.

¶ The King of Hollywood? He modestly disclaimed the title, but there was sense to it: he always seemed to be in charge. As the New York Times said:

Gable was as certain as the sunrise. He was consistently and stubbornly all man.

He said himself:

The only reason they come to see me is that I know life is great – and they know I know it.

And again:

I'm no actor and I never have been. What people see on the screen is me.

What they saw, they liked. Publicity man Ralph Wainwright said:

All of his life people turned around to stare at him.

This was remarkable considering his famous physical drawback, well phrased by Howard Hughes:

His ears made him look like a taxicab with both doors open.

Milton Berle called him:

The best ears of our lives.

It didn't stop him from influencing the world, and not only the female half of it. Historian Frederick Lewis Allen recalled that:

When Clark Gable in It Happened One Night disclosed that he wore no undershirt, the knitwear manufacturers rocked from the shock to their sales.

But Gable disclaimed his sexual reputation:

Hell, if I'd jumped on all the dames I'm supposed to have jumped on – I'd have had no time to go fishing.

Eve Arden remembered:

He used to claim that he was very dull in bed.

Carole Lombard confirmed this:

Listen, he's no Clark Gable at home.

And her husband nodded ruefully:

I can't emote worth a damn.

David Selznick knew the secret:

Gable has enemies all right, but they all like him.

Gable himself summed up:

This King stuff is pure bull. I eat and drink and go to the bathroom just like anybody else. I'm just a lucky slob from Ohio who happened to be in the right place at the right time.

And seven years after his death, Joan Crawford could say:

He was king of an empire called Hollywood. The empire is not what it was – but the king has not been dethroned, even after death.

Famous line (It Happened One Night): 'Behold the walls of Jericho!'

Famous line (Gone with the Wind): 'Frankly, my dear, I don't give a damn.'

Gabor, Eva (1919–). Hungarian leading lady, sister of Zsa Zsa Gabor. Autobiography: 1954, Orchids and Salami.

Pacific Blackout 41. Forced Landing 41. A Royal Scandal 45. Wife of Monte Cristo 46. Song of Surrender 49. The Mad Magician 54. Tarzan and the Slave Girl 54. The Truth about Women 56. Gigi 58. A New Kind of Love 63. Youngblood Hawke 63. The Princess Academy 87. The Rescuers Down Under (voice) 90, etc.

TV series: Green Acres 65–70. Bridges to Cross 86.

Gabor, Zsa Zsa (1919–) (Sari Gabor). Exotic international leading lady, Miss Hungary of 1936, who has decorated films of many nations. Autobiographies: 1961, My Story. 1991, One Lifetime Is Not Enough.

Lovely To Look At (US) 52. Lili (US) 53. Moulin Rouge (GB) 53. Public Enemy Number One (Fr.) 54. Diary of a Scoundrel (US) 56. The Man Who

Wouldn't Talk (GB) 57. Touch of Evil (US) 58. Queen of Outer Space (US) 59. Arrivederci Baby 66. Picture Mommy Dead (US) 66. Up the Front (GB) 72. Won Ton Ton, the Dog Who Saved Hollywood 75. Frankenstein's Great Aunt Tillie 85. Smart Alec (aka Movie Maker) 86. A Nightmare on Elm Street 3: Dream Warriors 87. Happily Ever After (voice) 90. The Naked Gun 2½: The Smell of Fear 91, etc.

¶ I believe in large families: every woman should have at least three husbands. – Z.Z.G.

I never hated a man enough to give him his diamonds back. – Z.Z.G.

Husbands are like fires: they go out if unattended. – Z.Z.G.

She's an expert housekeeper. Every time she gets divorced, she keeps the house. – *Henny Youngman*

Her face is inscrutable, but I can't vouch for the rest of her. – *Oscar Levant*

Gabriel, Peter (1950–   ).
British composer and singer, a co-founder of the rock band Genesis.
Birdy (m) 84. The Last Temptation of Christ (m) 88.

Gabrilovich, Yevgeny (1898–1993).
Russian screenwriter and founder of the national screenwriting school.
The Last Night (Poslednaya Noch) (co-w) 37. Girl No. 217 (Chelovek No. 217) (co-w) 44. In the Name of Life (Vo Imya Zhizni) (co-w) 47. The Return of Vasili Bortnikov (co-w) 53. The Communist (Kommunist) 58. Stories about Lenin (Rasskazi o Lenine) (co-w) 58. Lenin in Poland 66. Your Contemporary (Tvoi Sovremyonnik) 67. The Beginning (Nachalo) (co-w) 70. Strange Woman (Strannaya Zhenshchina) 78. Declaration of Love (Obyasneniye v Liubvi) (oa) 79, etc.

gaffer.
The chief electrician on a film, responsible for operating the lights under the instructions of the cinematographer or director of photography.

Gahagan, Helen (1900–1980).
American actress who limited herself to just one film: the title role in the 1935 version of *She*. Married Melvyn Douglas.

Gaillard, Bulee 'Slim' (1916–1991).
American jazz vocalist, multi-instrumentalist and dancer, born in Cuba. An eccentric performer of his own hit nonsense songs, often using an invented language called 'Vout', he appeared as himself in occasional films and on British TV in the 80s.
Star Spangled Rhythm 42. Hellzapoppin 42. Almost Married 42. Go, Man, Go 54. Too Late Blues 62. Absolute Beginners 86, etc.

Gainsborough.
A British film company of the 30s, associated with costume drama and Aldwych farces. Subsequently merged with Rank. Its trademark showed actress Glennis Lorrimer as Mrs Siddons in Thomas Gainsborough's portrait, turning to smile at the audience. She was the daughter of Harry Ostrer, co-founder of the company.

Gainsbourg, Charlotte (1972–   ).
Young French leading actress, the daughter of actors Serge Gainsbourg and Jane Birkin.
Words and Music (Paroles et Musique) 84. L'Effrontée 86. Charlotte Forever 86. The Little Thief (La Petite Voleuse). Night Sun (Il Sole Anche di Notte) 90. Merci la Vie 91. Autobus (Aux Yeux

du Monde) 91. L'Amoureuse 92. The Cement Garden 93, etc.

Gainsbourg, Serge (1929–1991) (Lucien Ginzburg).
French singer, composer, director and actor whose songs, full of a direct sexuality, often caused controversy. His daughter Charlotte, by actress Jane Birkin, is a leading French actress.
Game for Six Lovers (L'Eau à la Bouche) (m) 60. Revolt of the Slaves (a) 61. Strip-Tease (m) 63. Comment Trouvez-vous Ma Soeur? (m) 64. The Defector (L'Espion) (m) 66. Manon 70 (m) 66. L'Horizon (m) 67. Le Jardinier d'Argenteuil (m) 67. La Pacha (m) 68. Paris n'Existe pas (m) 68. The Marriage Came Tumbling Down (Ce Sacré Grand-père) (a, m) 68. Mr Freedom (a, m) 69. Cannabis (m) 70. The Romance of a Horse Thief (m) 71. Le Sex Shop (m) 73. Je t'Aime Moi non plus (wd, m) 75. Goodbye Emmanuelle (m) 77. The French Woman (Madame Claude) (m) 79. Je Vous Aime (a) 80. Equator (Equateur) (d, m) 83. Evening Dress (Tenue de Soirée) (m) 86. Charlotte Forever (d) 86. Stan the Flasher (d) 90, etc.

Gale, Bob (1952–   ).
American screenwriter, in collaboration with director Robert Zemeckis.
I Wanna Hold Your Hand 78. 1941 79. Used Cars 80. Back to the Future (AAN) 85. Back to the Future II 89. Back to the Future III 90. Looters 92.

Galeen, Henrik (1881–1949).
Dutch writer-director, a leading figure of German silent cinema.
The Student of Prague (wd) 12. *The Golem* (wd) 14. *The Golem* (w) 20. Nosferatu (w) 22. Waxworks (w) 25. The Student of Prague 26. Alraune 27. After the Verdict 30. Salon Dora Greene 36, many others.

Gallagher, Peter (1955–   ).
American leading actor, in films from 1980.
The Idolmaker 80. Summer Lovers 82. Dreamchild 85. My Little Girl 87. High Spirits 88. sex, lies and videotape 89. Tune In Tomorrow (aka Aunt Julia and the Scriptwriter) 90. An Inconvenient Woman 91. Late for Dinner 91. Watch It 93. Short Cuts 93. Malice 93. The Hudsucker Proxy 94. Mother's Boys 94. Mrs Parker and the Vicious Circle 94. White Mile (TV) 94, etc.
TV series: Skag 80.

Gallagher, Skeets (1891–1955).
Cheerful American vaudevillian, in some films of the early talkie period.
The Racket 28. It Pays to Advertise 31. Merrily We Go to Hell 32. Riptide 34. Polo Joe 37. Idiot's Delight 39. Zis Boom Bah 42. The Duke of Chicago 50, etc.

Gallian, Ketti (1913–1959).
French leading lady in America; films few.
■ Marie Galante 34. Under the Pampas Moon 35. Espionage 37. Shall We Dance 37.

Gallico, Paul (1897–1976).
American novelist whose work has been much adapted.
Wedding Present 36. Joe Smith American 42. Pride of the Yankees (AAN) 42. The Cock 45. Never Take No for an Answer 52. Lili 53. Merry Andrew 58. Next to No Time 58. The Three Lives of Thomasina 63. The Snow Goose (TV) 71. The Poseidon Adventure 72, etc.

Galligan, Zach (1963–   ).
American leading actor.
Nothing Lasts Forever 84. Gremlins 84. Waxwork 88. Rebel Storm 90. Mortal Passions 90. Gremlins 2: The New Batch 90. Psychic 91. Waxwork II: Lost in Time 92. Warlock: The Armageddon 93. Ice 94, etc.

Gallo, George.
American screenwriter and director.
Wise Guys (w) 86. Midnight Run (w) 88. Relentless (a) 89. 29th Street (co-w, d) 91, etc.

Gallo, Mario (1878–1945).
Italian-born musician who became one of the pioneers of Argentinian cinema, making El Fusilamiento de Dorrego, the country's first feature film using professional actors, in 1908. He continued making films, most of which are now lost, until 1919.

Gallone, Carmine (1886–1973).
Veteran Italian director who ranged from opera to action epics.
Pawns of Passion 28. Un Soir de Rafle 30. My Heart Is Calling 34. Madame Butterfly 39. Manon Lescaut 40. La Traviata 47. Faust and the Devil 49. La Forza del Destino 51. Tosca 56. Michael Strogoff 59. Carthage in Flames 59, many others.

Galloway, Don (1937–   ).
American TV leading man, familiar in *Ironside*.
The Rare Breed 66. Rough Night in Jericho 67. The Ride to Hangman's Tree 67. Lt Schuster's Wife (TV) 72. The Big Chill 83. Two Moon Junction 88, etc.

Gallu, Samuel (1918–   ).
American director, former opera singer.
Theatre of Death 66. The Man Outside 67. The Limbo Line 68.

Galsworthy, John (1867–1933).
British novelist who wrote about the upper middle class. Works filmed include *Escape* 30 and 48. *The Skin Game* 31. *Loyalties* 34. *Twenty-one Days* 39. *The Forsyte Woman* 49, etc.

Galton, Ray (1930–   ).
British comedy writer; with Alan Simpson, co-author of successful TV series, e.g. *Hancock's Half Hour*, *Steptoe and Son*; films include *The Rebel* 61. *The Wrong Arm of the Law* 62. *The Bargee* 64. *The Spy with a Cold Nose* 67, etc.

Galvani, Dino (1890–1960).
Distinguished-looking Italian actor, in films (mainly British) from 1908.
Atalantic 30. In a Monastery Garden 32. Midnight Menace 35. Mr Satan 38. It's That Man Again (as Signor So-So) 42. Sleeping Car to Trieste 49. Father Brown 54. Checkpoint 57. Bluebeard's Ten Honeymoons 60, many others.

Gam, Rita (1928–   ).
American stage leading lady in occasional films.
The Thief 52. Sign of the Pagan 54. Night People 54. Magic Fire 55. Mohawk 56. King of Kings 61. Klute 71. Such Good Friends 71. Noah – the Deluge (TV) 79. Distortions 87. Midnight 89, etc.

gambling,
in the indoor sport sense, is quite a preoccupation of film-makers. Gregory Peck in *The Great Sinner* played a man who made a great career of it, as did James Caan in *The Gambler* and George Segal in *California Split*; while in *The Queen of Spades* Edith Evans learnt the secret of winning at cards from

he devil himself. Other suspenseful card games were played in *The Cincinnati Kid*, *Lucky Jordan*, *The Lady Eve*, *Hazard*, and *Big Hand for a Little Lady*; snooker pool was the game in *The Hustler* and *The Color of Money*; old-time Mississippi river-boats were the setting for *Mississippi Gambler*, *The Naughty Nineties*, *Frankie and Johnny* and a sequence in *The Secret Life of Walter Mitty*. Roulette, however, is the most spectacular and oft-used film gambling game, seen in *The Shanghai Gesture*, *Robin and the Seven Hoods*, *Ocean's Eleven*, *The Big Snatch*, *Doctor No*, *La Baie des Anges*, *Quartet* (the 'Facts of Life' sequence), *Seven Thieves*, *The Las Vegas Story*, *The Only Game in Town*, *The Big Sleep*, *Gilda*, *Kaleidoscope*, and many others. Second features with such titles as *Gambling House*, *Gambling Ship* and *Gambling on the High Seas* were especially popular in the 40s. Musically, the filmic high-point was undoubtedly the 'oldest established permanent floating crap game in New York' number in *Guys and Dolls*. This stemmed from the writings of Damon Runyon, also adapted in such films as *Sorrowful Jones* and *The Lemon Drop Kid*. The most comic game on film was perhaps the hand of poker played between Judy Holliday and Broderick Crawford in *Born Yesterday*.

Gambon, Michael (1940–).
British stage actor, in occasional films.

The Beast Must Die 74. Turtle Diary 85. The Singing Detective (TV) 88. Paris by Night 88. The Cook, the Thief, His Wife and Her Lover 89. A Dry White Season 89. The Rachel Papers 89. Mobsters 91. Toys 92. Clean Slate 94. The Browning Version 94. A Man of No Importance 94, etc.

TV series: Maigret 92.

Gamley, Douglas (1924–).
Australian composer in Britain.

The Admirable Crichton 57. Gideon's Day 59. Watch It Sailor 61. The Horror of It All 64. Spring and Port Wine 70. Tales from the Crypt 72. Asylum 72. The Vault of Horror 73. And Now the Screaming Starts 73. From Beyond the Grave 73. Madhouse 74. The Beast Must Die 74. The Land that Time Forgot 75. The Monster Club 81, etc.

Gance, Abel (1889–1981).
French producer-director, in films since 1910. Pioneer of wide-screen techniques.

Baberousse 16. J'Accuse 19 and 37. La Roue 21. Napoleon 27. La Fin du Monde 31. Lucrezia Borgia 35. Une Grande Amour de Beethoven 36. Paradis Perdu 39. La Tour de Nesle 54. The Battle of Austerlitz 60, etc.

~Gance's *Napoleon* had sterling qualities which were never properly noted because of its length, its wide-screen reels, and the fact that silents were overwhelmed by sound soon after its release. In the late 70s, however, film scholar Kevin Brownlow assembled a five-hour version to which Thames TV added a newly commissioned musical score; in this version it was shown again triumphantly in the early 80s, in all the capitals of the world.

gangsters,
a real-life American menace of the 20s, provided a new kind of excitement for early talkies like *Little Caesar* and *Public Enemy*, which told how their heroes got into criminal activities but didn't rub in the moral very hard. The pace of the action, however, made them excellent movies, and critics defended them against religious pressure groups. *Quick Millions*, *Scarface*, *Lady Killer*, *The Little Giant* and *Public Enemy's Wife* were among the titles which followed; then Warner Brothers cleverly devised a way of keeping their thrills while mollifying the protesters: they made the policeman

into the hero, in films like *G-Men*, *I Am the Law*, *Bullets or Ballots*. By 1938 it seemed time to send up the whole genre in *A Slight Case of Murder*, with its cast of corpses, and in the later *Brother Orchid* the gangster-in-chief became a monk; yet in 1940 the heat had cooled off sufficiently to allow production of *The Roaring Twenties*, one of the most violent gangster movies of them all. The war made gangsters old-fashioned, but in the late 40s Cagney starred in two real psychopathic toughies, *White Heat* and *Kiss Tomorrow Goodbye*. After that the fashion was to parody gangsterism, in *Party Girl*, *Some Like It Hot*, and a couple of Runyon movies; but the success of a French film called *Rififi* and a TV series called *The Untouchables* left the field wide open for redevelopment. Successes in the 60s included *Bonnie and Clyde*, *The St Valentine's Day Massacre*, *Pay or Die*, *The Rise and Fall of Legs Diamond*, *King of the Roaring Twenties*, and from the French *Borsalino* and various *Rififi* sequels. The 70s brought British gang violence in *Get Carter*, *Villain*, *The Squeeze* and *Sweeney*, and in 1972 the gigantic success of *The Godfather* spawned sequels, rivals (*The Valachi Papers*) and parodies (*The Gang That Couldn't Shoot Straight*). Britain showed that it could make gangster movies in the American style with *The Long Good Friday*, but there were few successors, although *The Krays* followed the fortunes of its most notorious criminals. Alan Parker's *Bugsy Malone* parodied the Chicago gangster movies by having one acted by kids armed with pop guns, but the era continued to fascinate film-makers. Sergio Leone's epic *Once Upon a Time in America*, hacked about by its producers on its first release, became available on video-cassette in an uncut version. Brian De Palma remade *Scarface* as a film about Hispanic gangsters, and turned *The Untouchables* into a big-screen success. Coppola's examination of the Mafia was extended into *The Godfather II* and *III*, while Marlon Brando parodied his title role in *The Freshman*. Martin Scorsese had a hit with *GoodFellas* while Shakespeare's *Macbeth* was turned into a gangland movie in *Men of Respect*. Jonathan Demme found some humour in the subject of a Mafia widow fleeing the gangs in *Married to the Mob*. In the 90s, the hot subject became the gangs' involvement in drug-dealing. Abel Ferrera's *The King of New York* traced the rise of a white drug baron and his black confederates taking over from the Mafia, while *New Jack City* showed a gang turning an apartment block into a fortified drug factory. It was almost a relief to return to the simpler antics of the 50s in Bill Duke's *A Rage in Harlem*.

Gann, Ernest K. (1910–).
American adventure novelist. Films of his work include *The High and the Mighty*, *Blaze of Noon*, *Fate Is the Hunter*.

Ganz, Bruno (1941–).
Swiss leading actor, in international films, from German experimental theatre.

Rece Do Gory 67. Lumière 75. The Marquise of O 76. The American Friend (Der Amerikanische Freund) 77. The Boys from Brazil 78. Nosferatu 78. Der Erfinder 80. A Girl from Lorraine (La Provinciale) 80. Circle of Deceit (Die Falschung) 81. In the White City (Dans la Ville Blanche) 82. Wings of Desire (Der Himmel über Berlin) 87. Strapless 89. Especially on Sunday (La Domenica Specialmente) 91. The Last Days of Chez Nous 91. Success (Erfolg) 91. Night on Fire 92. Prague 92. Faraway, So Close! (In Weiter Ferne, So Nah) 93, etc.

Ganz, Lowell (1948–).
American comedy screenwriter, in collaboration with Babaloo Mandel.

Nightshift 82. Splash 84. Spies Like Us 85. Gung Ho 86. Vibes 88. Parenthood 89. City Slickers 91. Mr Saturday Night 92. A League of Their Own 92. City Slickers II: The Legend of Curly's Gold 94, etc.

Ganzer, Alvin.
American second-feature director.

The Girls of Pleasure Island (co-d) 53. The Leather Saint 56. When the Boys Meet the Girls 65. Three Bites of the Apple 67, etc.

Garas, Kaz (1940–).
American leading man.

The Last Safari 68. Ben 72. Final Mission 84. Naked Vengeance 85, etc.

Garber, Matthew (1956–1977).
British child actor.

The Three Lives of Thomasina 63. Mary Poppins 64. The Gnome-Mobile 67.

Garbo, Greta (1905–1990) (Greta Gustafson).
Swedish leading actress who was taken to Hollywood by her director Mauritz Stiller and became a goddess of the screen, her aloof beauty carefully nurtured by MGM through the late 20s and early 30s. Her early retirement enhanced the air of mystery which has always surrounded her. Special Academy Award 1954 'for her unforgettable screen performances'.

Biographies: 1954, *Garbo* by John Bainbridge. 1970, *Garbo* by Norman Zierold. 1992, *Conversations with Greta Garbo* by Sven Broman. 1994, *Loving Garbo* by Hugo Vickers.
■ Peter the Tramp 22. The Atonement of Gösta Berling 24. Joyless Street 25. The Torrent 26. The Temptress 26. *Flesh and the Devil* 27. Love 27. The Mysterious Lady 27. The Divine Woman 28. The Kiss 29. A Woman of Affairs 29. Wild Orchids 29. The Single Standard 29. *Anna Christie* (AAN) 30. Romance (AAN) 30. Inspiration 31. Susan Lennox 31. Mata Hari 31. *Grand Hotel* 32. As You Desire Me 32. Queen Christina 33. The Painted Veil 34. *Anna Karenina* 35. Camille (AAN) 36. Conquest 37. *Ninotchka* (AAN) 39. Two Faced Woman 41.
✪ For stretching a mystery over twelve splendid years and for knowing when to quit. *Queen Christina*.

¶ Boiled down to essentials, she is a plain mortal girl with large feet.
So wrote Herbert Kretzmer, sick of the 'sphinx' image, which in the early 30s was overpowering.
Alistair Cooke called her:
Every man's harmless fantasy mistress. She gave you the impression that, if your imagination had to sin, it could at least congratulate itself on its impeccable taste.
Life in 1928 hailed her thus:
She is the dream princess of eternity, the knockout of the ages.
Richard Watts Jnr called her:
That fascinating, inscrutable, almost legendary personage . . .
The *New York Mirror* said:
Her alluring mouth and volcanic, slumbrous eyes stimulate men to such passion that friendships collapse.
Graham Greene in his review of *Conquest* defined her:
A great actress? Oh, undoubtedly, one wearily assents, but what dull pompous films they make for her, hardly movies at all so retarded are they by her haggard equine renunciations, the slow consummation of her noble adulteries!
To Clare Boothe Luce she was:

A deer in the body of a woman, living resentfully in the Hollywood zoo.

A 1929 critic said:

She is a woman who marches to some unstruck music, unheard by the rest of us.

Rouben Mamoulian thought her:

A wonderful instrument.

Even the sensible Lilian Gish considered that:

Garbo's temperament reflected the rain and gloom of the long dark Swedish winters.

More recently Ken Tynan remarked:

What when drunk one sees in other women, one sees in Garbo sober.

Remoteness was part of her charm. To Fredric March:

Co-starring with Garbo hardly constituted an introduction.

To James Wong Howe, the famous cameraman:

She was like a horse on the track. Nothing, and then the bell goes, and something happens.

But the image always had its knockers, including the lady herself:

I never said, I want to be alone. I only said I want to be let alone.

(She did say it actually, but in *Grand Hotel*.) She added:

My talent falls within definite limits. I'm not a versatile actress.

She also said with a smile:

I'm a woman who's unfaithful to a million men.

But the fact is, men were not her fans. It was women who queued to see her suffer. J. Robert Rubin of MGM noted in wonder:

Garbo was the only one we could kill off. The Shearer and Crawford pictures had to end in a church, but the public seemed to enjoy watching Garbo die.

George Cukor, who directed her several times, thought:

She is a fascinating actress but she is limited. She must never create situations. She must be thrust into them. The drama comes in how she rides them out.

When she suddenly retired in 1941, her reason, given much later, was:

I had made enough faces.

And:

Being in the newspapers is awfully silly to me. I have nothing to contribute.

David Niven commented:

The longer she stayed away, the stranger and stranger the Garbo myth grew.

In the 70s, thirty years after her retirement, her movies were still making money all over the world and the lady herself was front-page news. You can't kill a legend. And it wasn't the movies that kept the interest; as Richard Whitehall remarked:

Subtract Garbo from most of her films, and you are left with nothing.

Isobel Quigley remained undecided:

I can't make up my mind whether Garbo was a remarkable actress or simply a person so extraordinary that she made everything she did, including acting, seem remarkable.

C. Aubrey Smith's appraisal was the oddest of all:

She's a rippin' gel.

If you're going to die on screen, you've got to be strong and in good health. – *G.G.*

Famous line (*Ninotchka*): 'Don't make an issue of my womanhood.'

Famous line (*Anna Christie*): 'Gimme visky, ginger ale on the side. And don't be stingy, baby.'

Famous line (*Queen Christina*): 'I have been memorizing this room. In the future, in my memory, I shall live a great deal in this room.'

Garcia, Andy (1956–) (Andrés Arturo García-Menéndez).

Cuban-born American leading actor.

Blue Skies Again 83. A Night in Heaven 83. The Lonely Guy 84. The Mean Season 85. 8 Million Ways to Die 86. Stand and Deliver 87. The Untouchables 87. American Roulette 88. Black Rain 89. A Show of Force 90. Internal Affairs 90. The Godfather, Part III (AAN) 90. Dead Again 91. Hero 92. Jennifer 8 92. Cachao . . . Como Su Ritmo No Hay Dos (doc) (p, d) 93. When a Man Loves a Woman 94, etc.

¶ I spent seven years without working, so if they're making cop movies, I'll play cops. I got two kids to bring up. – *A.G.*

Garcia Márquez, Gabriel (1928–).

Colombian novelist and screenwriter. Born in Aracataca, he worked as a journalist, and began writing novels after he came to Europe in the 50s. A leading exponent of Magic Realism, he won the Nobel Prize for literature in 1982.

In This Town There Are No Thieves (En Este Pueblo No Hay Ladrones) (oa) 65. The Year of the Plague (El Año de la Peste) (co-w) 79. La Viuda de Montiel (oa) 80. El Mar del Tiempo Perdido (oa) 81. My Dearest Maria (María de Mi Corazón) (oa, co-w) 82. Erendira (oa, w) 82. Time to Die (Tiempo de Morir) (w) 85. Chronicle of a Death Foretold (Cronaca di una Morte Annuciata) (oa) 87. Letters from the Park (Cartas del Parque) (oa) 88, etc.

The Garden of Allah.

Robert Hichen's novel, about a sophisticated woman whose husband turns out to be an escaped Trappist monk, was filmed as a silent in 1917, with Tom Santschi and Helen Ware, and again in 1927 with Ivan Petrovich and Alice Terry. The 1936 sound remake had excellent early colour, elegant direction by Richard Boleslawski, and exotic performances from Charles Boyer and Marlene Dietrich.

Gardenia, Vincent (1922–1992) (Vincent Scognamiglio).

American comic character actor.

Mad Dog Coll 61. A View from the Bridge 61. The Pursuit of Happiness 71. Cold Turkey 71. Hickey and Boggs 72. Bang the Drum Slowly (AAN) 73. *Death Wish* 74. The Front Page 74. Greased Lightning 77. Fire Sale 77. Heaven Can Wait 78. Home Movies 79. The Dream Merchants (TV) 80. Death Wish II 81. *Kennedy* (as J. Edgar Hoover) (TV) 83. Little Shop of Horrors 86. Moonstruck (AAN) 87. Cavalli Si Nasce 89. Age-Old Friends (TV) 89. Skin Deep 89, etc.

Gardiner, Reginald (1903–1980).

British actor who perfected the amiable silly ass type, in Hollywood from 1936.

The Lovelorn Lady 32. Borrow a Million 34. *Born to Dance* 36. Everybody Sing 37. Marie Antoinette 38. Sweethearts 39. *The Great Dictator* 40. My Life with Caroline 41. *The Man Who Came to Dinner* 41. Captains of the Clouds 42. The Immortal Sergeant 43. Molly and Me 44. Christmas in Connecticut 45. Cluny Brown 46. Fury at Furnace Creek 48. Wabash Avenue 50. Halls of Montezuma 51. The Black Widow 54. Ain't Misbehavin' 55. The Birds and the Bees 56. Mr Hobbs Takes a Vacation 62. Do Not Disturb 65. Sergeant Deadhead 66, many others.

TV series: The Pruitts of Southampton 66.

Famous line (*The Man Who Came to Dinner*): 'I've

very little time, and so the conversation will be entirely about me, and I shall love it.'

Gardner, Arthur (1910–) (Arthur Goldberg).

American independent producer, of Levy-Gardner-Laven, a former actor.

Without Warning 52. Down Three Dark Streets 54. Geronimo 62. The Glory Guys 65. The Scalphunters 68. The McKenzie Break 70. The Hunting Party 71. Kansas City Bomber 72. Brannigan 75. Gator 76, etc.

TV series include: Rifleman, The Detectives, Law of the Plainsman, The Big Valley.

Gardner, Ava (1922–1990).

American leading lady of the 40s and 50s, once voted the world's most beautiful woman.

Autobiography: 1991, *Ava: My Story*.

Biographies: 1960, *Ava* by David Hanna. 1984, *Ava Gardner* by John Daniell.

■ We Were Dancing 42. Joe Smith American 42. Sunday Punch 42. This Time for Keeps 42. Calling Dr Gillespie 42. Kid Glove Killer 42. Pilot No. 5 43. Hitler's Madman 43. Ghosts on the Loose 43. Reunion in France 43. Dubarry was a Lady 43. Young Ideas 43. Lost Angel 43. Swing Fever 44. Music for Millions 44. Three Men in White 44. Blonde Fever 44. Maisie Goes to Reno 44. Two Girls and a Sailor 44. She Went to the Races 45. Whistle Stop 46. *The Killers* 46. *The Hucksters* 47. Singapore 47. One Touch of Venus 48. The Great Sinner 49. East Side West Side 49. The Bribe 49. My Forbidden Past 51. *Show Boat* 51. *Pandora and the Flying Dutchman* 51. Lone Star 52. The Snows of Kilimanjaro 52. Ride Vaquero 53. *Mogambo* (AAN) 53. Knights of the Round Table 53. *The Barefoot Contessa* 54. Bhowani Junction 56. The Little Hut 57. *The Sun Also Rises* 57. The Naked Maja 59. On the Beach 59. The Angel Wore Red 60. 55 Days at Peking 63. Seven Days in May 64. *The Night of the Iguana* 64. The Bible 66. Mayerling 68. Tam Lin 70. Judge Roy Bean 72. Earthquake 74. Permission to Kill 75. The Bluebird 76. The Cassandra Crossing 77. The Sentinel 77. City on Fire 79. The Kidnapping of the President 80. Priest of Love 81.

TV series: Knots Landing 85.

¶ A lady of strong passions, one of them rage. – *Mickey Rooney (former husband)*

Although no one believes me, I have always been a country girl, and still have a country girl's values. – *A.G.*

Gardner, Ed (1901–1963).

American radio comic who starred in the 1945 film version of his series *Duffy's Tavern*.

Gardner, Erle Stanley (1889–1970).

American best-selling crime novelist, the creator of Perry Mason (qv).

Gardner, Joan (1914–).

British leading lady of the 30s who married Zoltan Korda.

Men of Tomorrow 32. Catherine the Great 34. The Scarlet Pimpernel 35. The Man Who Could Work Miracles 36. Dark Journey 39. The Rebel Son (last to date) 39, etc.

Garfein, Jack (1930–).

American stage and screen director, married to Carroll Baker (1955–69).

The Strange One 57. Something Wild 62.

Garfield, Allen (1939–) (aka Allen Goorwitz).

Heavy-set American character actor.

Get to Know Your Rabbit 72. Slither 73. Busting 74. The Long Goodbye 74. The Conversation 74.

he Front Page 74. Nashville 76. Mother Jugs and
peed 76. Gable and Lombard (as Louis B. Mayer)
0. Brinks 79. One Trick Pony 80. The Stunt Man
0. Continental Divide 81. One from the Heart
2. The Black Stallion Returns 83. Get Crazy 83.
he Cotton Club 84. Desert Bloom 86. Beverly Hills
op II 87. Let It Ride 89. Night Visitor 90. Dick
racy 90. Club Fed 91. Until the End of the World
is ans Ende der Welt) 91. Family Prayers 93. Les
atriotes (Fr.) 94, etc.

arfield, Brian. (1921–   ).
merican screenwriter and novelist. *Death Wish*,
s novel of a lone vigilante, was filmed by
lichael Winner and so far has spawned three
quels. He is the author of *Western Films, A
omplete Guide* (1982).
  Death Wish (oa) 74. The Last Hard Men 76.
opscotch (co-w) 80. The Stepfather (co-story) 87.

arfield, John (1913–1952) (Julius Garfinkle).
merican leading actor, usually in aggressive or
mbittered roles; formerly a star of New York's
ftish Group Theatre.
  Biography: 1978, *John Garfield* by James Beaver.
  Four Daughters (AAN) 38. Blackwell's Island 38.
hey Made Me a Criminal 39. Juarez 39. Daughters
ourageous 39. Dust Be My Destiny 39. Four
/ives (cameo) 39. Saturday's Children 40. East of
liver 40. Castle on the Hudson 40. Flowing
old 40. *The Sea Wolf* 41. Out of the Fog 41. Tortilla
lat 42. Dangerously They Live 42. Air Force 43.
he Fallen Sparrow 43. Thank Your Lucky Stars 43.
etween Two Worlds 44. Hollywood Canteen
ameo) 44. Destination Tokyo 44. Pride of the
larines 45. Nobody Lives Forever 46. *The Postman
lways Rings Twice* 46. Humoresque 46. Body and
oul (AAN) 47. Gentleman's Agreement 47. We Were
trangers 48. Force of Evil 49. Jigsaw (cameo) 49.
nder My Skin 50. The Breaking Point 50. He Ran
ll the Way 51.

¶ Projected on the screens of the world, he was
  the Eternal Outsider, obliged to glimpse Paradise
ut not to dwell there. – *Larry Swindell*
  His feeling never changed that he was mandated
y the American public to go in there and keep
unching for them. – *Clifford Odets*
  Garfield is alleged to have turned down the role
  Kowalski in *A Streetcar Named Desire*.

arfunkel, Arthur (1941–   ).
merican pop singer, half of Simon and Garfunkel;
ccasional actor.
  Catch 22 70. Carnal Knowledge 71. Bad Timing
9. Good to Go 86.

argan, Ed (1902–1964).
merican character actor, brother of William
argan; often seen as comedy cop or prizefighter's
lanager.
  Gambling Ship 33. Belle of the Nineties 34. Miss
acific Fleet 35. My Man Godfrey 36. Big City 37.
ateway 38. Another Thin Man 39. Road to
ngapore 40. A Date with the Falcon 41. Over My
ead Body 42. Hit the Ice 43. The Falcon Out West
4. The Bullfighters 45. Wonder Man 45. Gallant
ess 46. Little Miss Broadway 47. You Gotta Stay
appy 48. Red Light 49. Belle of Old Mexico 51.
edtime for Bonzo 51, many others, often in one-
ne or one-shot roles.

argan, William (1905–1979).
merican light leading man of the 30s and 40s,
sually in 'good guy' roles; retired when left
oiceless after operation. Brother of Ed Gargan.
  Autobiography: 1969, *Why Me?*
  The Misleading Lady 32. *Rain* 32. The Story of

Temple Drake 33. Four Frightened People 34. Black
Fury 35. The Milky Way 36. You Only Live Once
37. The Crowd Roars 38. *The Housekeeper's
Daughter* 39. Turnabout 40. *They Knew What They
Wanted* (AAN) 40. Bombay Clipper 41. Miss
Annie Rooney 42. The Canterville Ghost 44. The
Bells of St Mary's 45. Till the End of Time 46. Night
Editor 46. The Argyle Secrets 48. Miracle in the
Rain 56, many others.
  TV series: *Martin Kane* 57.

Garland, Beverly (1926–   ) (Beverly Fessenden).
Pert and pretty leading lady of some 50s
Hollywood films; more successful on TV.
  DOA 49. The Glass Web 53. The Miami Story 54.
The Desperate Hours 55. It Conquered the World
56. Not of this Earth 56. The Joker is Wild 57. The
Alligator People 59. Twice Told Tales 63. Pretty
Poison 68. The Mad Room 69. Airport 75 74. Roller
Boogie 79. It's My Turn 80, etc.
  TV series: Mama Rosa 50. *Decoy* 57. The Bing
Crosby Show 64. My Three Sons 69–72. Scarecrow
and Mrs King 87.

Garland, Judy (1922–1969) (Frances Gumm).
American entertainer and leading lady who for
many years radiated the soul of show business.
The child of vaudeville performers, on stage from
five years old, she later seemed unable to stand
the pace of her own success; but her resultant
personal difficulties only accentuated the loyalty of
her admirers. Special Academy Award 1939 'for
her outstanding performance as a screen
juvenile'.
  Biographical books include: 1971, *The Other Side
of the Rainbow* by Mel Tormé. 1993, *Judy Garland*
by David Shipman. 1993, *Judy Garland – World's
Greatest Entertainer* by John Fricke.
■ Every Sunday (short) 36. Pigskin Parade 36.
Broadway Melody of 1938 37. Thoroughbreds
Don't Cry 38. Everybody Sing 38. Listen Darling
38. Love Finds Andy Hardy 38. *The Wizard of Oz*
39. *Babes in Arms* 39. Andy Hardy Meets a
Debutante 39. Strike Up the Band 40. Little Nellie
Kelly 40. Ziegfeld Girl 41. Life Begins for Andy
Hardy 41. Babes on Broadway 41. *For Me and My
Gal* 42. Presenting Lily Mars 42. Girl Crazy 42.
Thousands Cheer (guest) 43. *Meet Me in St Louis* 44.
Ziegfeld Follies 45. *The Clock* 45. The Harvey Girls
46. Till the Clouds Roll By (guest) 46. The Pirate
47. *Easter Parade* 48. Words and Music (guest) 48.
In the Good Old Summertime 49. Summer Stock
50. *A Star Is Born* (AAN) 54. Judgment at
Nuremberg (AAN) 60. A Child Is Waiting 62. I
Could Go On Singing (GB) 63.
✪ For her incredible voice; and for drawing
cathartic tears as much by her own life as by her
performances. *The Wizard of Oz*.

¶ If I'm such a legend, why am I so lonely? – *J.G.*
  I had the stage mother of all time. If I wasn't
well, and didn't want to go on, she'd yell 'Get out
on that stage or I'll tie you to the bedpost.' – *J.G.*
  I didn't know her well, but after watching her
in action I didn't want to know her well. – *Joan
Crawford*
  An angel with spurs. – *Joe Pasternak, producer*
  You see that girl? She used to be a hunchback.
You see what I've made her into? – *Louis B. Mayer*
  Her mental attitude may have been pathetic but
it turned her into a great bore. – *Anita Loos*

Famous line (*The Wizard of Oz*): 'If I ever go looking
for my heart's desire again, I won't look any further
than my own backyard, because if it isn't there, I
never really lost it to begin with.'

Garmes, Lee (1897–1978).
Distinguished American cinematographer, in
Hollywood from 1916.
  The Grand Duchess and the Waiter 26. The
Private Life of Helen of Troy 27. Disraeli 29. Lilies
of the Field 30. Whoopee 30. Morocco 30.
Dishonoured 31. City Streets 31. An American
Tragedy 31. *Shanghai Express* (AA) 32. *Scarface* 32.
Smilin' Through 32. *Zoo in Budapest* 33. Crime
without Passion 34. The Scoundrel 34. Dreaming
Lips (GB) 37. Gone with the Wind (co-ph)
(uncredited) 39. Angels over Broadway 40. *Lydia*
41. Jungle Book 42. Guest in the House 44. Since
You Went Away 44. *Love Letters* 45. *Duel in the Sun*
46. The Spectre of the Rose (& co-p) 46. The
Secret Life of Walter Mitty 47. The Paradine Case
48. Our Very Own 50. Detective Story 51. Actors
and Sin (& co-d) 52. The Desperate Hours 55. Land
of the Pharaohs 55. The Big Fisherman 59.
Hemingway's Adventures of a Young Man 62.
Lady in a Cage 64. Big Hand for a Little Lady 66.
How to Save a Marriage 68, etc.
✪ For his contributions to black-and-white
photography, and especially for the effects he
created with 'north light'. *Zoo in Budapest*.

¶ A cameraman is often the saviour of a film. His
  lighting can be the main factor in its success.
– *L.G.*

Garner, James (1928–   ) (James Baumgarner).
Amiable, good-looking American leading man of
the 60s; showed a sense of humour among the
action and romance, but did not quite measure up
as a substitute for Clark Gable.
■ Toward the Unknown 56. The Girl He Left
Behind 56. Shoot out at Medicine Bend 57.
Sayonara 57. Darby's Rangers 58. Up Periscope 59.
Cash McCall 59. The Children's Hour 62. Boys'
Night Out 62. *The Great Escape* 63. *The Thrill of It
All* 63. The Wheeler Dealers 63. Move Over
Darling 63. *The Americanization of Emily* 64. *Thirty
Six Hours* 64. The Art of Love 65. Duel at Diablo
66. A Man Could Get Killed 66. Mister Buddwing
66. Grand Prix 66. Hour of the Gun (as Wyatt Earp)
67. The Pink Jungle 68. How Sweet It Is 68. *Support
Your Local Sheriff* 69. Marlowe 69. A Man Called
Sledge 70. *The Skin Game* 71. Support Your Local
Gunfighter 71. They Only Kill Their Masters 72.
One Little Indian 73. The Castaway Cowboy 74.
The New Maverick (TV) 78. Health 80. The Fan
81. Victor/Victoria 82. The Long Summer of
George Adams (TV) 82. Tank 84. Murphy's
Romance (AAN) 85. Space (TV) 85. Sunset 88. My
Name Is Bill W (TV) 89. Decoration Day (TV) 90.
Barbarians at the Gate (TV) 93. Fire in the Sky 93.
Breathing Lessons (TV) 94. *Maverick* 94.
  TV series: *Maverick* 57–71. Nichols 71. The
Rockford Files 74–80. Bret Maverick 81.

¶ I became an actor by accident; I'm a
  businessman by design. – *J.G.*
  I am an actor. I hire out. I am not afraid of
hurting my image. – *J.G.*
  He is a master at playing dumb while
maintaining a sense of shrewdness and dignity.
He always throws us off guard. He is the macho
stud who makes fun of himself; he is the scaredy-
cat we know will not let us down in the end.
– *Esquire*

Garner, Peggy Ann (1931–1984).
American child star of the 40s; Academy Award
1945 as 'outstanding child actress'. Did not make
it as adult star.
■ Little Miss Thoroughbred 38. Blondie Brings Up
Baby 39. In Name Only 39. Abe Lincoln in Illinois
40. The Pied Piper 42. Eagle Squadron 42. *Jane*

Eyre 44. *A Tree Grows in Brooklyn* 45. The Keys of the Kingdom 45. Nob Hill 45. Junior Miss 45. Home Sweet Homicide 46. Daisy Kenyon 47. Thunder in the Valley 47. The Sign of the Ram 48. The Lovable Cheat 49. Bomba the Jungle Boy 49. The Big Cat 49. Teresa 51. The Black Widow 54. Eight Witnesses 54. The Black Forest 54. The Cat 67. A Wedding 78.

Garnett, Tay (1894–1977).
American director, a light professional talent.
Autobiography: 1974, *Light Up Your Torches and Pull on Your Tights.*
■ Celebrity 28. The Spieler 28. Flying Fools 29. Oh Yeah 29. Officer O'Brien 30. *Her Man* (& w) 30. Bad Company 31. *One Way Passage* (& w) 32. Prestige 32. Okay America 32. Destination Unknown 33. SOS Iceberg 33. China Seas (& w) 35. She Couldn't Take It 35. Professional Soldier 35. Love is News (& w) 37. *Slave Ship* (& w) 37. Stand In 37. Joy of Living 38. Trade Winds (& w) 38. Eternally Yours (& p) 39. Slightly Honorable (& wp) 40. Seven Sinners 40. Cheers for Miss Bishop (& w) 41. My Favorite Spy 42. Bataan 43. The Cross of Lorraine 43. Mrs Parkington 44. The Valley of Decision 45. The Postman Always Rings Twice 46. Wild Harvest 47. A Connecticut Yankee in King Arthur's Court 49. The Fireball (& w) 50. Soldiers Three 51. Cause for Alarm 51. One Minute to Zero 52. Main Street to Broadway 53. The Black Knight 54. Seven Wonders of the World 56. A Terrible Beauty 60. Cattle King 63. The Delta Factor 70. The Timber Tramps 73.

Garnett, Tony (1936–).
British producer.
■ *Kes* 69. The Body 70. *Family Life* 71. Prostitute 80. Handgun (& d) 82.

Garr, Teri (1949–).
American leading lady.
Oh God 77. Close Encounters of the Third Kind 77. Mr Mike's Mondo Video 78. The Black Stallion 79. Honky Tonk Freeway 81. Wrong Is Right 82. One from the Heart 82. Tootsie (AAN) 82. The Sting II 82. The Black Stallion Returns 83. Mr Mom 83. Firstborn 84. After Hours 85. Full Moon in Blue Water 88. Out Cold 88. Let It Ride 89. Short Time 90. Waiting for the Light 90. Mom and Dad Save the World 92. The Whole Shebang (TV) 93, etc.
TV series: Girl with Something Extra 73–74. The Sonny and Cher Comedy Hour 73–74. The Sonny Comedy Revue 74. Good and Evil 91.

Garrett, Betty (1919–).
Peppy American singer and actress with musical comedy experience.
■ Big City (debut) 46. Words and Music 48. Take Me Out to the Ball Game 48. Neptune's Daughter 49. *On the Town* 49. My Sister Eileen 55. The Shadow on the Window 57.
TV series: All in the Family 73–75. Laverne and Shirley 76.

Garrett, Oliver H.P. (1897–1952).
American screenwriter.
Forgotten Faces 28. *Street of Chance* 30. She Couldn't Take It 35. One Third of a Nation 39. The Man I Married 40. Flight for Freedom 43. Duel in the Sun 46. Dead Reckoning 47. Sealed Cargo 51, etc.

Garrett, Otis (c. 1895–1941).
American director.
■ The Black Doll 37. The Last Express 38. Personal Secretary 38. Danger on the Air 38. *Lady in the Morgue* 38. The Witness Vanishes 39. The Mystery

of the White Room 39. Exile Express 39. Margie 40. Sandy Gets Her Man 41.

Garrett, Pat (1850–1908).
American western adventurer who allegedly, as sheriff, shot Billy the Kid (qv). Actors who have played him include Wallace Beery in *Billy the Kid* 30, Thomas Mitchell in *The Outlaw* 43, Charles Bickford in *Four Faces West* 48, Frank Wilcox in *The Kid from Texas* 50, John Dehner in *The Left-Handed Gun* 58, Glenn Corbett in *Chisum* 70, James Coburn in *Pat Garrett and Billy the Kid* 73.
On TV, Barry Sullivan was Garrett in *The Tall Men.*

Garrick, David (1717–1779).
Famous English actor who has been impersonated on screen by Cedric Hardwicke in *Peg of Old Drury* 34 and Brian Aherne in *The Great Garrick* 37.

Garrick, John (1902–1966) (Reginald Doudy).
British stage actor of the 20s and 30s; made some film appearances, usually as 'the other man'.
The Lottery Bride (US) 31. Chu Chin Chow 33. Rocks of Valpre 35. Sunset in Vienna 37. The Great Victor Herbert (US) 39, etc.

Garrison, Sean (1937–).
American leading man of the 60s.
Moment to Moment 66. Banning 67, etc.
TV series: Dundee and the Culhane 67.

Garson, Greer (1908–).
Red-haired Anglo-Irish leading lady who after stage experience was cast as Mrs Chipping in *Goodbye Mr Chips* (AAN) 39 and promptly went to Hollywood, where her gentle aristocratic good looks enabled her to reign as a star for ten years.
■ Remember 39. Pride and Prejudice 40. *Blossoms in the Dust* (AAN) 41. When Ladies Meet 41. *Mrs Miniver* (AA) 42. *Random Harvest* 42. Madame Curie (AAN) 43. Mrs Parkington (AAN) 44. The Valley of Decision (AAN) 45. Adventure 45. Desire Me 47. Julia Misbehaves 48. *That Forsyte Woman* 49. The Miniver Story 50. The Law and the Lady 51. Scandal at Scourie 52. Julius Caesar 53. Her Twelve Men 53. Strange Lady in Town 54. Sunrise at Campobello (as Eleanor Roosevelt) (AAN) 60. Pepe 60. The Singing Nun 66. The Happiest Millionaire 67. Little Women (TV) 78.

¶ If you're going to be typed, there are worse moulds in which you can be cast. – *G.G.*
One of the most richly syllabled queenly horrors of Hollywood. – *Pauline Kael*
Metro's Glorified Mother. – *Anon*
The mixture of Irish charm, natural red-haired beauty and her unceasing capacity to project the shopgirl's vision of the great lady made her an incontestable star in a decade that required a staunch, wholesome ideal. – *New Yorker*
After Greer Garson they stopped trying to make English stars out here. – *Anna Lee, 1983*

Garvin, Anita (1907–1994).
American actress, a charming foil to Laurel and Hardy and Charley Chase in many comedy shorts from 1918. She was a Mack Sennett Bathing Beauty at the age of 12 and became a Ziegfeld girl a year later. She also made a few features before retiring in the early 40s.
The Snow Hawk 25. Why Girls Love Sailors 27. With Love and Hisses 27. The Battle of the Century 27. From Soup to Nuts 28. A Pair of Tights 28. Red Hot Rhythm 29. Trent's Last Case 29. Dynamite 29. Blotto 30. Be Big 31. A Chump at Oxford 40, etc.

Garwood, Norman.
British production designer.
The Missionary 81. Time Bandits 81. Brimston and Treacle 82. Bullshot 83. Red Monarch 83. Water 84. Brazil (AAN) 85. Shadey 85. Link 86. The Princess Bride 87. Glory (AAN) 89. Misery 9 Hook (AAN) 91. Being Human 94, etc.

Gary, Lorraine (1937–).
American general-purpose actress.
Jaws 75. I Never Promised You a Rose Garder 77. Jaws II 78. 1941 79. Just You and Me Kid 7 Jaws – the Revenge 87.

Gary, Romain (1914–1980).
French novelist. Chief films from his work are *T Roots of Heaven* and *Lady L*; his autobiography, *Promise at Dawn*, was also filmed.

Gaslight.
Patrick Hamilton's stage suspense thriller, about Victorian wife deliberately being driven insane b her murderous husband, was perfectly filmed in Britain in 1940 by Thorold Dickinson with Anto Walbrook, Diana Wynyard, and Frank Pettingell MGM promptly bought and destroyed the negativ and in 1944 produced an opulent and inferior remake with Charles Boyer, Ingrid Bergman (AA and Joseph Cotten, directed by George Cukor. I Britain this version was known as *The Murder in Thornton Square*; prints of the original did surviv and have been shown in America as *Angel Street*.

Gasnier, Louis J. (1882–1963).
American director: mostly of foreign language versions.
Darkened Rooms 29. The Lawyer's Secret 31. Forgotten Commandments 32. Gambling Ship 3 The Last Outpost 35. Bank Alarm 37. Murder or the Yukon 40. Fight On Marines 42, etc.

Gassman, Vittorio (1922–).
Italian actor and matinée idol, in occasional film since 1946.
Bitter Rice 48. Sombrero (US) 53. Rhapsody (US) 54. War and Peace 56. Tempest 57. The Lo Specialist 60. Barabbas 62. The Devil in Love 66 Woman Times Seven 67. Lucky Thirteen 70. We All Loved Each Other So Much 73. Scent of a Woman 75. The Prophet 76. A Wedding 78. Quintet 79. The Nude Bomb 80. La Terrazzo 80. Turno 81. Sharkey's Machine 81. Tempest 82. L Vie est un Roman 83. The Family (La Famiglia) 87. To Forget Palermo (Dimenticare Palermo) 89 The Sleazy Uncle (Lo Zio Indegno) 89. The 1001 Nights (Sheherazade) 90. I Divertimenti della Vi Privata 91. I Won't Disturb You (Tolgo il Disturb 91. The Long Winter (El Largo Invierno) 92. When We Were Repressed (Quando eravamo Repressi) 92. The Bible: Abraham (TV) 93, etc.

Gassner, Dennis (1948–).
American production designer.
The Hitcher 86. Wisdom 86. In the Mood 87. Like Father Like Son 87. Field of Dreams 88. Ear Girls Are Easy 88. Miller's Crossing 90. Barton Fi (AAN) 91. Bugsy (AA) 91. Hero (GB: Accidental Hero) 92. The Hudsucker Proxy 94, etc.

Gastoni, Lisa (1935–).
Italian leading lady in British films of the 50s.
The Runaway Bus 54. Man of the Moment 55 The Baby and the Battleship 56. Intent to Kill 58 Hello London 59. Passport to China 64. Maddale 72. The Last Days of Mussolini 74, etc.

Gates, Larry (1915–).
American character actor, often seen as small-town merchant or middle-aged good guy.

Has Anybody Seen My Gal? 52. The Girl Rush 54. Invasion of the Body Snatchers 56. Jeanne Eagels 57. Cat on a Hot Tin Roof 58. One Foot in Hell 60. The Hoodlum Priest 62. Toys in the Attic 63. The Sand Pebbles 67. Airport 69. Funny Lady 75, etc.

Gates, Nancy (1926–).
American leading lady of the 40s and 50s.

The Great Gildersleeve 42. The Spanish Main 45. The Atomic City 52. The Member of the Wedding 53. Suddenly 54. The Search for Bridey Murphy 56. The Brass Legend 56. Death of a Scoundrel 56. Some Came Running 59. Comanche Station 60, etc.

Gateson, Marjorie (1891–1977).
American character actress of dignified mien.

The Beloved Bachelor 31. Silver Dollar 32. Cocktail Hour 33. Lady Killer 33. Big Hearted Herbert 34. Your Uncle Dudley 35. The Milky Way 36. Wife versus Secretary 36. First Lady 37. Stablemates 38. Geronimo 39. Pop Always Pays 40. Submarine Zone 41. Rings on Her Fingers 42. The Youngest Profession 43. Ever Since Venus 44. One More Tomorrow 46. Passage West 51. The Caddy 53, many others.

Gaudio, Tony (1885–1951) (Gaetono Gaudio).
Italian cinematographer, long in Hollywood.

The Mark of Zorro 20. Secrets 24. The Temptress 25. Two Arabian Knights 27. *Hell's Angles* 30. Sky Devils 32. Bordertown 35. The Story of Louis Pasteur 35. *Anthony Adverse* (AA) 36. *The Life of Emile Zola* 37. *The Adventures of Robin Hood* 38. Juarez 39. *The Letter* 40. The Great Lie 41. The Constant Nymph 43. A Song to Remember 45. Love From a Stranger 47. The Red Pony 49, many others.

Gauge, Alexander (1914–1960).
Heavyweight British actor, Friar Tuck in TV's *Robin Hood* series.

The Interrupted Journey (debut) 49. Murder in the Cathedral 51. Pickwick Papers 52. Fast and Loose 54. Martin Luther 55. The Iron Petticoat 56. The Passing Stranger 57, etc.

Gaumont, Leon (1863–1946).
Pioneer French inventor, producer and exhibitor. Founder of Gaumont Studios at Shepherds Bush, also Gaumont circuit, both later sold to Rank. Invented sound on disc in 1902.

Gaup, Nils (1955–).
Lapp director and screenwriter, a former actor in Norway.

Pathfinder (Ofelas) (AAN) 1987. Shipwrecked (Hakon Hakonsen) 91. Head above Water 93, etc.

Gautier, Dick (1939–).
American leading man of the 70s.

Wild in the Sky 72. Fun with Dick and Jane 77. Billy Jack Goes to Washington 78. Marathon 80. Glitch! 88, etc.

TV series: *Here We Go Again* 71.

Gavin, John (1928–).
American leading man. He became Ambassador to Mexico during President Reagan's administration.

A Time to Live and a Time to Die 58. Imitation of Life 59. Spartacus 60. Psycho 60. A Breath of Scandal 61. Back Street 61. Romanoff and Juliet 61. Thoroughly Modern Millie 67. The Madwoman of Chaillot 69. Pussycat Pussycat I

Love You 70. Rich Man Poor Man (TV) 76. Jennifer 78. Sophia Loren: Her Own Story (TV) 80, etc.

TV series: Destry 64. Convoy 65.

Gawthorne, Peter (1884–1962).
Splendidly pompous-looking British stage actor, often seen as general, admiral or chief constable in comedies of the 30s.

Sunny Side Up (US) 29. Charlie Chan Carries On (US) 31. Jack's the Boy 32. The Iron Duke 35. Wolf 's Clothing 36. Alf 's Button Afloat 38. *Ask a Policeman* 40. Much Too Shy 42. The Case of Charles Peace 49. Five Days 54, many others.

Gaxton, William (1893–1963) (Arturo Gaxiola).
American entertainer who made a few film appearances.

Fifty Million Frenchmen 31. Something to Shout About 42. Best Foot Forward 43. Tropicana 44. Diamond Horseshoe 45, etc.

Gay, John (1924–).
American writer.

Run Silent Run Deep 58. The Four Horsemen of the Apocalypse (co-w) 62. The Hallelujah Trail 65. No Way to Treat a Lady 68. Soldier Blue 70. Sometimes a Great Notion 71. Hennessy 75. A Matter of Time 76, etc.

Gay, Noel (1898–1954) (Richard Moxon Armitage).
British composer of musicals and songs for stage and screen. His song 'Tondelayo', featured in *White Cargo*, was the first to be synchronized with the action in a British talking picture.

White Cargo (s) 28. The Camels Are Coming (s) 34. Me and Marlborough (s) 35. Okay for Sound (s) 37. Father Knew Best (s) 37. Sailors Three (aka Three Cockeyed Sailors) (s) 40, etc.

Gaye, Gregory (1900–).
American character actor.

Dodsworth 36. Hollywood Boulevard 36. Ninotchka 39. Cash 42. The Bachelor and the Bobbysoxer 47. The Eddy Duchin Story 56. Auntie Mame 58, etc.

Gaynes, George (1917–) (George Jongejans).
Finnish-born character actor, in America, a former opera singer; best known for playing the senile police chief in the *Police Academy* series.

The Group 65. Doctors' Wives 70. The Way We Were 73. Nickelodeon 76. Washington: Behind Closed Doors 77. Dead Men Don't Wear Plaid 79. Altered States 80. Tootsie 82. To Be or Not to Be 83. It Came upon the Midnight Clear 84. Micki & Maude 84. Police Academy 84. Police Academy 2: Their First Assignment 85. Police Academy 3: Back in Training 86. Police Academy 4: Citizens on Patrol 88. Police Academy 5: Assignment Miami Beach 88. Police Academy 6: City under Siege 89. Stepmonster 92. Vanya on 42nd Street 94, etc.

TV series: Rich Man, Poor Man – Book II 76–77. Punky Brewster 84–86. The Days and Nights of Molly Dodd 89–91.

Gaynor, Janet (1906–1984) (Laura Gainer).
American leading lady of the 20s and 30s, immensely popular in simple sentimental films, especially when teamed with Charles Farrell. Played in many short comedies and westerns before achieving star status. She was married to costume designer Adrian and producer Paul Gregory.
■ The Johnstown Flood 26. The Shamrock Handicap 26. The Midnight Kiss 26. The Blue Eagle 26. The Return of Peter Grimm 26. *Seventh Heaven* (AA) 27. *Sunrise* (AA) 27. Two Girls Wanted 27. Street Angel (AA) 28. Four Devils 29. Christina

29. Lucky Star 29. Sunny Side Up 29. Happy Days 30. High Society Blues 30. The Man Who Came Back 30. *Daddy Longlegs* 31. Merely Mary Ann 31. Delicious 31. The First Year 32. Tess of the Storm Country 32. *State Fair* 33. Adorable 33. Paddy the Next Best Thing 33. Carolina 34. Change of Heart 34. Servants' Entrance 34. One More Spring 35. The Farmer Takes a Wife 35. Small Town Girl 36. Ladies in Love 36. *A Star Is Born* (AAN) 37. Three Loves Has Nancy 38. *The Young in Heart* 38. Bernardine 57.

Famous line (*A Star Is Born*): 'Hello, everybody. This is Mrs Norman Maine.'

Gaynor, Mitzi (1930–) (Francesca Mitzi von Gerber).
American light leading lady with singing and dancing talents.
■ My Blue Heaven 50. Take Care of My Little Girl 51. *Golden Girl* 51. We're Not Married 51. Bloodhounds of Broadway 51. The I Don't Care Girl 53. Down Among the Sheltering Palms 53. Three Young Texans 54. There's No Business Like Show Business 54. Anything Goes 56. The Birds and the Bees 56. The Joker is Wild 57. Les Girls 57. *South Pacific* 58. Happy Anniversary 59. Surprise Package 60. For Love or Money 63. For the First Time 69.

Gayson, Eunice (1931–).
British leading lady, also on stage.

Dance Hall 50. Street Corner 53. Out of the Clouds 54. Zarak 57. The Revenge of Frankenstein 58. Dr No 62. From Russia with Love 63.

Gazzara, Ben (1930–) (Biago Gazzara).
American actor, usually of rebellious types.
■ The Strange One 57. *Anatomy of a Murder* 59. The Young Doctors 61. Convicts Four 62. The Captured City 62. A Rage to Live 65. If It's Tuesday This Must Be Belgium 69. The Bridge at Remagen 69. Husbands 70. When Michael Calls (TV) 71. The Passionate Thief 71. Pursuit (TV) 72. Fireball Forward (TV) 72. The Family Rico (TV) 72. Indict and Convict (TV) 73. The Neptune Factor 73. Maneater (TV) 73. QB VII 74. Capone 75. High Velocity 76. The Sicilian Connection 76. Voyage of the Damned 76. The Killing of a Chinese Bookie 76. The Death of Richie (TV) 77. The Trial of Lee Harvey Oswald (TV) 77. Opening Night 77. Saint Jack 79. Bloodline 79. They all Laughed 81. Inchon 81. Tales of Ordinary Madness 83. The Girl From Trieste 83. An Early Frost (TV) 85. The Professor 86. Il Giorno Prima 87. Secret Obsession (La Mémoire Tatouée) 88. Quicker than the Eye 88. Road House 89. Beyond the Ocean (Oltre l'oceano) (& co-w, d) 90. Forever 91. Els de Davant (Sp.) 94. Parallel Lives (TV) 94.

TV series: *Arrest and Trial* 63. *Run for Your Life* 65–67.

Gazzo, Michael V. (1923–).
American character actor, screenwriter and playwright.

A Hatful of Rain (co-w, from his play) 57. King Creole (co-w) 58. Godfather Part II (AAN) 74. Black Sunday 77. King of the Gypsies 78. Love and Bullets 79. The Fish that Saved Pittsburg 79. Kill Castro 80. Alligator 80. Fear City 84. Cookie 89, etc.

Geer, Will (1902–1978) (William Ghere).
American character actor with a penchant for sinister old men.

The Misleading Lady 32. Deep Waters 48. Intruder in the Dust 49. Broken Arrow 50. The Tall Target 51. Salt of the Earth 53. Advise and Consent

61. *Seconds* 66. In Cold Blood 67. Bandolero 68.
The Reivers 70. Brother John 70. Napoleon and
Samantha 72. Executive Action 73. Jeremiah
Johnson 73. Moving Violation 76. Billion Dollar
Hobo 78, etc.
TV series: *The Waltons* 72–78.

Geesink, Joop (1913–1984).
Dutch puppeteer who in the late 30s made several
shorts under the general heading of 'Dollywood'.

Geeson, Judy (1948–).
British leading lady who started with sexy teenage
roles.
Berserk 67. To Sir With Love 67. Here We Go
Round the Mulberry Bush 67. Prudence and the
Pill 68. Hammerhead 68. Three into Two Won't
Go 69. The Executioner 69. 10 Rillington Place 70.
One of Those Things 71. Who Killed the
Mysterious Mr Foster? (TV) 71. Doomwatch 72.
Fear in the Night 72. Brannigan 75. The Eagle Has
Landed 76. Dominique 78. Inseminoid (aka
Horror Planet) 80. The Plague Dogs (voice) 82.
Young Goodman Brown 93, etc.
TV series: Danger UXB 79.

Geeson, Sally (1950–).
British juvenile actress of the 60s, sister of Judy
Geeson.
■ What's Good for the Goose 68. Cry of the
Banshee 70. The Oblong Box 70. Forbush and the
Penguins 71. Carry on Abroad 72. Bless This House
73 (and TV series). Carry on Girls 74.

Geffen, David (1943–).
American producer and record company head, a
former agent. Born in Brooklyn, he founded the
Asylum record label in 1970 before becoming a
top executive at Warner in the mid-70s. He then
taught music at Yale, started another record
company, and became an independent producer.
He set up his own studio in 1994 with partners
Jeffrey Katzenberg and Steven Spielberg.
Personal Best 82. Lost in America 85. Little Shop
of Horrors 86. Beetlejuice 88. Interview with the
Vampire 94, etc.

Gein, Ed (1906–1984).
American murderer who was the model for the
character of Norman Bates in *Psycho*, Robert
Bloch's novel filmed by Alfred Hitchcock and
followed by three sequels from other directors, all
starring Anthony Perkins. His characteristics were
also used for the character of James 'Buffalo Bill'
Gumb, played by Ted Levine in *Silence of the
Lambs*, filmed by Jonathan Demme from Thomas Harris's
novel. Gein was a solitary mother-dominated
farmer who wanted to change sex. He killed two
women, dressed in female clothing and wore the
skins of dead women, taken from corpses he dug
up. Following his trial in 1957 he was committed
to an asylum.

Gelin, Daniel (1921–).
French leading man with stage experience. In films
since 1941.
Rendezvous de Juillet 49. *Edouard et Caroline* 50.
La Ronde 50. Les Mains Sales 51. Rue de l'Estrapade
53. Les Amants du Tage (The Lovers of Lisbon) 54.
The Man Who Knew Too Much (US) 55.
Charmants Garçons 57. There's Always a Price Tag
58. Carthage in Flames 60. The Season for Love
65. Black Sun 66. Le Souffle au Coeur 71. Far from
Dallas 72. Trop c'est Trop 74. Nous Irons Tous au
Paradis 77. Mister Frost 90. Un Type Bien 91. Les
Marmottes 93, etc.

Gemma, Giuliano (1940–).
Italian leading man of spaghetti westerns.
The Titans 62. Goliath and the Sins of Babylon
63. Adios Gringo 65. A Pistol for Ringo 65. Day
of Anger 67. A Man to Respect 72. The Great Battle
78. Corleone 85, etc.

Gemora, Charlie (1903–1961).
American character actor with an unusual
speciality: playing gorillas. He also played aliens.
The Gorilla 39. At the Circus 39. The War of the
Worlds 53. Phantom of the Rue Morgue 54. I
Married a Monster from Outer Space 58. Jack the
Giant Killer 62, etc.

Genina, Augusto (1892–1957).
Italian pioneer director.
La Gloria 13. Prix de Beauté 30. The White
Squadron 35. Bengasi 42. Heaven Over the Marshes
49. Three Forbidden Stories 52. Maddalena 54.
Frou Frou 55, many others.

Genn, Leo (1905–1978).
Bland British character actor, formerly a practising
barrister.
Immortal Gentleman 35. Dream Doctor 36.
Jump for Glory 37. Kate Plus Ten 38. Contraband
40. The Way Ahead 44. *Henry V* 44. Caesar and
Cleopatra 45. *Green for Danger* 46. Mourning
Becomes Electra (US) 48. The Velvet Touch (US)
48. *The Snake Pit* (US) 48. The Wooden Horse 50.
The Miniver Story 50. *Quo Vadis* (AAN) 51.
Plymouth Adventure (US) 52. Personal Affair 53.
The Green Scarf 55. Beyond Mombasa 56. Lady
Chatterley's Lover (Fr.) 56. Moby Dick 56. I
Accuse 57. No Time to Die 58. Too Hot to Handle
60. The Longest Day 62. Fifty-Five Days at Peking
62. Ten Little Indians 65. Circus of Fear 67.
Connecting Rooms 69. Die Screaming Marianne
70. The Mackintosh Man 73. The Martyr 76, etc.

Gentlemen Prefer Blondes.
Anita Loos's comic novel about a gold-digging 20s
chorus girl on the make in the millionaire set was
filmed in 1928 by Mal St Clair, with Ruth Taylor
and Alice White, then in 1953 by Howard Hawks
with Marilyn Monroe and Jane Russell. Hawks's
film was followed in 1955 by a sequel of sorts,
Gentlemen Marry Brunettes, directed by Richard Sale
and starring Jane Russell and Jeanne Crain.

George, Chief Dan (1899–1981). (Geswanouth
Slaholt)
Canadian Indian actor.
■ Smith! 69. *Little Big Man* (AAN) 70. Alien
Thunder 73. Harry and Tonto 74. The Bears and I
74. The Outlaw Josey Wales 76. Shadow of the
Hawk 76. Americathon 79. Spirit of the Wind 80.

George, Christopher (1929–1983).
American TV leading man.
El Dorado 68. Tiger by the Tail 69. Escape (TV)
69. The Immortal (TV) 69. Man on a String (TV)
72. I Escaped from Devil's Island 73. Grizzly 76.
Day of the Animals 77. Whiskey Mountain 77.
Mortuary 83, etc.
TV series: The Rat Patrol 66. The Immortal 69,
etc.

George, Gladys (1900–1954) (Gladys Clare).
American leading actress with stage experience.
■ Red Hot Dollars 20. Home Spun Folks 20. The
Easy Road 21. Chickens 21. The House that Jazz
Built 21. Straight is the Way 34. *Valiant Is the World
for Carrie* (AAN) 36. They Gave Him a Gun 37.
Madame X 37. Love is a Headache 38. Marie
Antoinette 38. *The Roaring Twenties* 39. Here I Am
a Stranger 39. I'm from Missouri 39. A Child is

Born 40. The Way of all Flesh 40. The House
Across the Bay 40. *The Maltese Falcon* 41. The Lady
from Cheyenne 41. Hit the Road 41. The Hard
Way 42. Nobody's Darling 43. The Crystal Ball 43
Minstrel Man 44. Christmas Holiday 44. Steppin
In Society 45. The Best Years of Our Lives 46.
Millie's Daughter 47. Alias a Gentleman 48.
Flamingo Road 49. Undercover Girl 50. Bright Lea
50. He Ran all the Way 51. Detective Story 51.
Lullaby of Broadway 51. Dark City 51. Silver City
53. It Happens Every Thursday 54.

George, Grace (1879–1961).
American stage actress whose one film, in 1943,
was *Johnny Come Lately*.

George, Heinrich (1893–1946).
German leading man of the 20s.
Kean 21. Lady Hamilton 21. Lucretia Borgia 22
Metropolis 26. Dreyfus 30. Jew Suss 40. The
Postmaster 40. Kolberg 45.

George, Lynda Day (1944–) (formerly Lynda
Day).
American leading lady of the 70s. Started in TV's
Petticoat Junction; wife of Christopher George.
The Sound of Anger (TV) 68. The House on
Greenapple Road (TV) 70. Chisum 71. Set This
Town on Fire (TV) 71. She Cried Murder (TV) 73
The Trial of Chaplain Jensen (TV) 75. Murder at
the World Series (TV) 77. Cruise into Terror (TV)
78. Casino (TV) 80. The Junkman 82. Mortuary
83, many others.

George, Muriel (1883–1965).
Plump, motherly British character actress who
often played charladies or landladies. Music-hall
background.
His Lordship (debut) 32. Yes Mr Brown 33. Dr
Syn 37. A Sister to Assist 'Er (leading role) 38.
Quiet Wedding 40. Dear Octopus 43. The Dancing
Years 49. Simon and Laura 55, many others.

George, Screaming Mad (Joji Tani).
Japanese-born director and special effects make-
up expert in horror movies.
A Nightmare on Elm Street 4: The Dream Maste
(sfx) 88. The Guyver (co-d) 91. Bride of Re-
Animator (sfx) 91. Society (sfx) 92. Necronomico
(sfx) 93, etc.

George, Susan (1950–).
British leading lady, former child actress; usually
typed as sexpot. Also now involved in production
Billion Dollar Brain 67. The Strange Affair 68.
Twinky 68. All Neat in Black Stockings 69. Spring
and Port Wine 69. The Looking Glass War 69. Die
Screaming Marianne 70. Eye Witness 70. Fright
71. The Straw Dogs 71. Dirty Mary Crazy Larry
73. Sonny and Jed 74. Mandingo 75. Out of
Season 75. A Small Town in Texas 76. Tintorea
77. Tomorrow Never Comes 78. Enter the Ninja
81. Venom 82. The Jigsaw Man 84. Lightning 86.
Stealing Heaven (p) 88. The Lifeguard 88. That
Summer of White Roses (& p) 89, etc.
TV series: Stay Lucky 93.

Gerald, Jim (1889–1958) (Jacques Guenod).
French actor, in occasional films from 1911.
An Italian Straw Hat 27. La Chant au Marin 31
French Without Tears (as le professeur) 39. Boule
de Suif 45. The Crimson Curtain 52. Father Brown
54. Fric Frac en Dentelles 57, etc.

Gerald McBoing Boing.
A smiling little boy who could only make sounds
created by author Dr Seuss and the hero of four
UPA cartoons. The spareness of line and sharpnes

f wit, particularly in the first of the series, ontrasted happily with Disney's chocolate-box eriod.

Gerald McBoing Boing (AA) 51. Gerald McBoing oing's Symphony 53. How Now Boing Boing 54. erald McBoing Boing on the Planet Moo (AA) 6.

Gerard, Gil (1940–).
merican leading man who generates a little isdom amid the derring-do.

Airport 77 76. Ransom for Alice (TV) 77. Killing tone (TV) 78. Buck Rogers in the Twentieth entury (TV) 79. Hear No Evil (TV) 83, etc.

TV series: Buck Rogers 80–81.

Gerasimov, Sergei (1906–1985).
ussian director, best known abroad for *And uietly Flows the Don* 57. Formerly an actor.

Geray, Steve (1904–1973) (Stefan Gyergyay).
Iungarian character actor of stage and screen, sually seen as mild-mannered little fellow. In ondon from 1934, Hollywood from 1941.

Dance Band 34. Inspector Hornleigh 39. Man at arge 41. *The Moon and Sixpence* (as Dirk Stroeve) 2. Night Train from Chungking 43. The Mask of imitrios 44. *So Dark the Night* (leading role) 46. ilda 46. I Love Trouble 48. The Big Sky 52. Call Me Madam 53. The Birds and the Bees 56. Count our Blessings 59. Dime with a Halo 63, many thers.

Gere, Richard (1949–).
American leading man of the late 70s. He is narried to model Cindy Crawford. In 1994, ollowing an article in a French magazine, they ook a full-page advertisement in *The Times*, osting £17,500, to announce, 'We are eterosexual and monogamous and take our ommitment to each other very seriously'.

Report to the Commissioner 75. Strike Force TV) 75. Baby Blue Marine 76. Looking for Mr oodbar 77. Days of Heaven 78. Bloodbrothers 78. anks 79. American Gigolo 79. An Officer and a entleman 82. The Honorary Consul 83. reathless 83. The Cotton Club 84. King David 5. Power 85. No Mercy 86. Miles from Home 88. nternal Affairs 90. Pretty Woman 90. Rhapsody in August (Hachigatsu-no Kyoshikyoku) 91. Final nalysis 92. Mr Jones 93. Sommersby 93. And he Band Played On (TV) 93. Intersection 94. First night 95.

¶ I'm still like this guy who, like, washed his dad's car. I don't feel like I'm some sort of arefied species of creature. – *R.G.*

Gering, Marion (1901–1977).
olish-Russian director with long stage xperience; in America from 1925.

The Devil and the Deep 32. Madame Butterfly 3. Jennie Gerhardt 33. Thirty Day Princess 34. umba 35. Lady of Secrets 36. Thunder in the City GB) 37. She Married an Artist 38. Sarumba (& o-p) 50, etc.

Germaine, Mary (1933–).
ritish leading lady of the 50s.

Laughter in Paradise 51. Where's Charley? 52. Vomen of Twilight 53. The Green Buddha (last to ate) 54, etc.

German cinema
ad its most influential period in the years ollowing World War I, when depression and espair drove directors into a macabre fantasy vorld and produced films like *The Golem, The Cabinet

---

of Dr Caligari, Nosferatu, Warning Shadows* and *Waxworks;* it is also notable that many of the makers of these films later went to Hollywood and exerted a strong influence there. G. W. Pabst was somewhat more anchored to reality, apart from the stylish *Die Dreigroschenoper;* Fritz Lang seemed primarily interested in the criminal mentality, though he produced masterworks of prophecy and Teutonic legend. With the advent of Hitler most of Germany's genuine creative talent was forced abroad; the main achievements of the 30s were Leni Riefenstahl's colossal propaganda pieces *Triumph of the Will* and *Olympische Spiele.* The anti-British war-time films have their interest, but the post-war German cinema was not producing competent thrillers and comedies for the home market. In the 70s however a new realistic school developed in the hands of Rainer Fassbinder, Werner Herzog, etc. Other notable directors who emerged at this time included Alexander Kluge, Jean-Marie Straub, Volker Schlöndorff, Wim Wenders and Hans Jürgen Syberberg. Margarethe von Trotta was one of the few women directors to come to the fore, although she was joined in the 80s by Doris Dörrie. Commercial success was enjoyed in the 80s by Wolfgang Petersen with *The Boat* and by Percy Adlon with his English-language film *Bagdad Café*, featuring Marianne Sägebrecht, who had starred in his earlier *Sugarbaby.* Another German director fascinated by America was Uli Edel with his *Last Exit to Brooklyn.* Michael Verhoeven received international acclaim for *The Nasty Girl.* Notable German players include Werner Krauss, Conrad Veidt, Emil Jannings, Marlene Dietrich, Anton Walbrook, Gert Frobe and, in the 70s, Hanna Schygulla, star of many of Fassbinder's films. The Austrian-born actor Klaus Maria Brandauer, who trained in Germany, became an international star in the 80s following his performance as the Nazis' favourite actor in *Mephisto* 81.

Germi, Pietro (1914–1974).
Italian director, in films since 1945.

In the Name of the Law 49. The Road to Hope 50. Man of Iron 56. Maledetto Imbroglio (A Sordid Affair) 59. Divorce Italian Style (AAN) 61. Seduced and Abandoned 63. The Birds, the Bees and the Italians 65. Alfredo Alfredo 73, many others.

Geronimo (1829–1909).
Apache Indian chief who dealt destruction to the whites.

Memorably impersonated by Chief Thundercloud in *Geronimo* 38, Jay Silverheels in *The Battle at Apache Pass* 52, Chuck Connors in *Geronimo* 62, Wes Studi in *Geronimo: An American Legend* 93.

Gerrard, Gene (1892–1971) (Eugene O'Sullivan).
British music-hall comedian with engaging light style: starred in several comedy musicals of the 30s.

Let's Love and Laugh 31. *My Wife's Family* 31. *Out of the Blue* (& d) 31. Let Me Explain Dear (& d) 32. The Love Nest 33. It's a Bet 35. No Monkey Business 35. Where's Sally? 36. Glamour Girl 37, etc.

Gershenson, Joseph (1904–).
Russian musician, long in US. In films from 1920; head of Universal music department from 1941. Not himself a composer.

Gershwin, George (1898–1937) (Jacob Gershowitz).
American popular composer of scores of songs and concert pieces.

Contributed to many films. His biography was told in *Rhapsody in Blue* 45, and his music was

---

used exclusively in *An American in Paris* 51. Three hitherto unpublished songs were even used in *Kiss Me Stupid* 64.

¶ His was a modernity that reflected the civilization we live in as excitingly as the headline in today's newspaper. – *Ira Gershwin*

He was a child of his age who never became old enough to outlive his usefulness. – *Charles Schwartz*

Gershwin, Ira (1896–1983) (Israel Gershowitz).
American lyricist, brother of George Gershwin. He wrote for stage from 1918, films from 1931.

Delicious 31. Goldwyn Follies 39. Cover Girl 44. An American in Paris 51. Kiss Me Stupid 64, many others.

Gertie the Dinosaur.
Early American cartoon character created by Winsor McKay in 1909.

Gertsman, Maury (c. 1910–).
American cinematographer.

Strange Confession 45. Terror by Night 46. Singapore 47. Rachel and the Stranger 48. One Way Street 50. Meet Danny Wilson 52. The World in My Corner 55. Kelly and Me 57. Gunfight in Abilene 66, many others.

Gertz, Jami (1965–).
American leading actress.

Endless Love 81. Alphabet City 84. Sixteen Candles 84. Mischief 85. Crossroads 86. Quicksilver 86. Solarbabies 86. Less than Zero 87. The Lost Boys 87. Listen to Me 89. Renegades 89. Silence Like Glass (Zwei Frauen) 89. Don't Tell Her It's Me 90. Sibling Rivalry 90, etc.

Gessner, Nicolas (1931–).
Hungarian-born director who has worked in France, Germany, Canada and Hollywood.

Diamonds Are Brittle (Un Milliard dans un Billard) (Fr.) 65. The Peking Blonde (Fr.) 67. Twelve Plus One (Fr.) 69. The Little Girl Who Lives down the Lane 76. It Rained All Night the Day I Left (Can.) 79. Quicker than the Eye (Fr.) 89. Tennessee Nights 89. Twist of Fate 91, etc.

Getchell, Robert.
American screenwriter.

■ Alice Doesn't Live Here Any More 74. Bound for Glory 76. Mommie Dearest (co-w) 81. Sweet Dreams 85. Stella 90. This Boy's Life (co-w) 93. Point of No Return (co-w) 93. The Client (co-w) 94.

Getty, Balthazar (1975–).
American teenage actor.

Lord of the Flies 90. Young Guns II 90. My Heroes Have Always Been Cowboys 91. The Pope Must Die (US: The Pope Must Diet) 91. Red Hot 92. Where the Day Takes You 92. Dead Beat 94. Don't Do It 94. Natural Born Killers 94. Judge Dredd 95, etc.

Getty, Estelle (1923–) (Estelle Scher).
American character actress, from the stage and best known for her role as Sophia in the TV series *Golden Girls.*

Mask 85. Mannequin 87. Stop! Or My Mom Will Shoot 92, etc.

Ghatak, Ritwik (1925–1976).
Indian director, screenwriter and author, from the theatre. A Communist, he was hospitalized for schizophrenia in the 70s and died from alcoholic poisoning.

The Citizen (Nagarik) 53. Pathetic Fallacy (Ajantrik) 58. The Runaway (Bari Theke Paliye) 59. The Cloud Capped Star (Meghe Dhaka Tara) 60. E Flat (Komal Gandhar) 61. Subarnarekha 65. A River Called Titah (Titash Ekti Nadir Naam) 73. Reason, Argument and Story (Jukti Takko Ar Gappo) 74, etc.

Gherardi, Pietro (1909–1971).
Italian production and costume designer.
Daniele Cortis 46. Her Favourite Husband 50. Nights of Cabiria (Le Notti di Cabiria) 56. Big Deal on Madonna Street 58. La Dolce Vita (AAN) 59. 8½ (AAN) 63. Juliet of the Spirits (AAN) 65. The Appointment 69. Quemada! 69, many others.

Ghose, Goutam (1950–).
Indian director and screenwriter, a former maker of documentaries.
Our Land (Ma Bhoomi) 79. The Occupation (Dakhai) 82. The Crossing (Paar) 84. The Voyage Beyond (Antarjali Yatra) 88. Boatman of the River Padma (Padma Nadir Majhi) 93. The Kite (Patang) 94, etc.

The Ghost Breaker.
This American stage thriller by Paul Dickey and Charles W. Goddard, about an heiress's voodoo-haunted castle, was filmed in 1915 with H. B. Warner and in 1922, directed by Alfred E. Green, with Wallace Reid. In 1940 George Marshall directed a talkie version as a vehicle for Bob Hope, and the result was an oddly successful combination of laughs and horror, with contributions from Willie Best, Paulette Goddard and Paul Lukas. (The title, incidentally, was made plural.) In 1953 Marshall remade it, with remarkable fidelity to the 1940 script, as a vehicle for Dean Martin and Jerry Lewis under the title Scared Stiff, with Lizabeth Scott and Carmen Miranda; the results were hardly stimulating.

The Ghost Train.
This hugely successful British stage comedy-thriller by Arnold Ridley (also an actor best known for playing Private Godfrey in the long-running television series Dad's Army), about stranded passengers at a lonely Cornish station being used by gun-runners, was first filmed in 1928, directed by Geza Bolvary, with Guy Newall as the silly-ass hero who turns out to be a policeman. A talkie version followed in 1931 with Jack Hulbert, directed by Walter Forde, who also directed the 1941 remake in which the leading role was split between Arthur Askey and Richard Murdoch.

ghosting.
Another word for dubbing, especially when a star apparently singing is actually miming to the voice of the real artist.
See also: dubbing.

Ghostley, Alice (1926–).
American revue comedienne and character actress.
New Faces 54. To Kill a Mockingbird 62. My Six Loves 63. The Flim Flam Man 67. Viva Max 68. Ace Eli and Rodger of the Skies 72. Not for Publication 84, etc.

ghosts:
see fantasy.

Giallelis, Stathis (1939–).
Greek actor who went to Hollywood.
America America 63. Cast a Giant Shadow 66. The Eavesdropper 67, etc.

Giannini, Giancarlo (1942–).
Italian leading actor.
Rita the Mosquito 66. Anzio 68. The Secret of Santa Vittoria 69. The Pizza Triangle 70. The Seduction of Mimi 72. The Sensual Man 73. Swept Away 74. Seven Beauties (AAN) 76. The Innocent 76. A Night Full of Rain 77. Travels with Anita 79. Suffer or Die 79. American Dreamer 84. Fever Pitch 85. Saving Grace 86. Ternosecco (& d) 86. Snack Bar Budapest 88. Blood Red 89. Brown Bread Sandwiches 89. New York Stories 89. The Sleazy Uncle (Lo Zio Indegno) 89. Le Raccourci 91. Black Heart (Nero come il Cuore) 91. Once Upon a Crime 92. Colpo di Coda 92. Giovanni Falcone 93. Come Due Coccodrilli 94, etc.

giants
are infrequently encountered in films, but Harold Lloyd met one in Why Worry?, as did Abbott and Costello in Lost in a Harem. Costello also met The Thirty Foot Bride of Candy Rock, not to be confused with The Attack of the Fifty Foot Woman. Then there was The Giant of Marathon, and Glenn Langan played The Amazing Colossal Man in two films. Back to Abbott and Costello again: it was they who appeared with Buddy Baer in Jack and The Beanstalk.

Gibbons, Cedric (1893–1960).
American art director; worked for Edison 1915–17, Goldwyn 1918–24, MGM 1924 on. Co-directed one film, Tarzan and His Mate 34. Designed the 'Oscar' statuette.
The Bridge of San Luis Rey (AA) 29. The Merry Widow (AA) 34. Pride and Prejudice (AA) 40. Blossoms in the Dust (AA) 41. Gaslight (AA) 44. The Yearling (AA) 46. Little Women (AA) 49. An American in Paris (AA) 51, many others.

Gibbs, Anthony (1925–).
British editor.
Oscar Wilde 60. A Taste of Honey 61. Tom Jones 63. The Knack 64. Petulia 68. Performance 70. Fiddler on the Roof 71. Jesus Christ Superstar 74. Juggernaut 75. Rollerball 75. A Bridge Too Far 77. F.I.S.T. 78. The Dogs of War 81. Ragtime 81. Dune 84. Tai-Pan 86. Stealing Home 88. In Country 89, many others.

Gibbs, Gerald (c. 1910–).
British cinematographer.
Whisky Galore 49. Fortune Is a Woman 57. The Man Upstairs 58. The Leather Boys 63. A Jolly Bad Fellow 64. Mister Ten Per Cent 67, etc.

Gibbs, Michael (1937–) (Michael Irving).
South African-born composer, arranger, jazz trombonist, pianist and bandleader, in America from the mid-70s and since busy there and in Europe.
Heat 87. Housekeeping 87. American Roulette 88. Riding the Edge 89. Breaking In 89. Iron & Silk 91. Whore 91. Close My Eyes 91. Century 93. Being Human 94, etc.

Gibney, Sheridan (1903–1988).
American screenwriter.
I Am a Fugitive from a Chain Gang 32. The World Changes 33. The Story of Louis Pasteur (AA) 36. Green Pastures 36. Letter of Introduction 38. Disputed Passage 39. Cheers for Miss Bishop 41. Once Upon a Honeymoon 42. Our Hearts Were Young and Gay 44. The Locket 47, etc.

Gibson, Alan (1938–1987).
Canadian director in Britain.
■ Crescendo 69. Goodbye Gemini 70. Dracula AD 1972 72. The Satanic Rites of Dracula 73. Crash 77.

Churchill and the Generals (TV) 79. A Woman Called Golda (TV) 82. Witness for the Prosecution (TV) 82. Martin's Day 84.

Gibson, Brian (1944–).
British director, from TV.
Breaking Glass 80. Poltergeist II: The Other Side 86. The Josephine Baker Story (TV) 90. What's Love Got to Do with It? 93, etc.

Gibson, Helen (1892–1977) (Rose August Wenger).
American leading lady of the silent screen; of Swiss descent; married to Hoot Gibson. Former stuntgirl. Appeared in Hollywood Story 51.
The Hazards of Helen (serial) 15. No Man's Woman 20. The Wolverine 21, etc.

Gibson, Henry (1935–).
Diminutive American comedy character actor who came to the fore in TV's Laugh-In.
Kiss Me Stupid 64. Evil Roy Slade (TV) 72. Nashville 75. The Last Remake of Beau Geste 78. Amateur Night at the Dixie Bar and Grill (TV) 79. A Perfect Couple 79. Health 80. The Blues Brothers 80. The Incredible Shrinking Woman 81. Monster in the Closet 86. Innerspace 87. Long Gone (TV) 87. Switching Channels 88. Tune in Tomorrow (aka Aunt Julia and the Scriptwriter) 90. etc.

Gibson, Hoot (1892–1962) (Edward Richard).
American cowboy hero of silent films; in Hollywood from 1911 after real cowpunching experience. Films good-humoured but not memorable. He ended his career as a greeter at a Los Angeles night-club. His third wife was actress Sally Eikis.
The Hazards of Helen 15. The Cactus Kid 19. The Denver Dude 22. Surefire 24. Galloping Fury 27. Points West 29. Spirit of the West 32. Powdersmoke Range 33. Sunset Range 35. The Marshal's Daughter 53. The Horse Soldiers 59. Ocean's Eleven 61, many others.
~Allegedly, his name became Hoot because he loved to go owl-hunting.

Gibson, Mel (1956–).
American-born leading actor, in Australia from childhood. After graduating from the National Institute of Dramatic Arts in 1977, he began in the theatre before the Mad Max movies catapulted him to stardom.
■ Summer City 77. Tim 79. Mad Max 79. Gallipoli 81. Mad Max II (US: The Road Warrior) 81. Attack Force Z 82. The Year of Living Dangerously 83. The Bounty 84. The River 84. Mrs Soffel 84. Mad Max Beyond Thunderdome 85. Lethal Weapon 87. Tequila Sunrise 88. Lethal Weapon 2 89. Air America 90. Bird on a Wire 90. Hamlet 90. Lethal Weapon 3 92. The Man without a Face (& d) 93. Maverick 94. Braveheart (& d) 95. Pocahontas (voice) 95.

Gibson, Wynne (1899–1987).
American leading lady, from the chorus.
Nothing But the Truth 30. Ladies of the Big House 32. I Give My Love 34. The Captain Hates the Sea 34. Gangs of New York 38. Café Hostess 40. The Falcon Strikes Back 43, many others.

Gidding, Nelson (1915–).
American screenwriter.
I Want to Live (AAN) 58. Odds against Tomorrow 59. Nine Hours to Rama 61. The Inspector 62. The Haunting 64. Lost Command 66. The Andromeda Strain 70. The Hindenburg 75. Beyond the Poseidon Adventure 79. Wheels of Terror 87, etc.

Gidget.
An American teenager of the early 60s, a kind of female Andy Hardy. The first film was released in 1959 and starred Sandra Dee. Then in 1961 came *Gidget Goes Hawaiian* with Deborah Walley, and in 1963 *Gidget Goes to Rome* with Cindy Carol. In 1969 and 1971 there were TV movies called *Gidget Grows Up* with Karen Valentine, and *Gidget Gets Married* with Monie Ellis; in 1972 came a cartoon version, *Gidget Makes the Wrong Connection*. In 1965 there was also a TV series with Sally Field.

Giehse, Therese (1898–1975).
German stage actress whose occasional films included *Kinder, Mutter und Ein General* 58 and *Black Moon* 75.

Gielgud, Sir John (1904–   ).
Distinguished British stage actor who has made occasional films.
   Autobiographies: 1953, *Early Stages*. 1972, *Distinguished Company*. 1979, *An Actor and His Times*.
■ Who Is the Man? 24. The Clue of the New Pin 29. Insult 32. The Good Companions 32. Secret Agent 36. The Prime Minister (as Disraeli) 40. *Julius Caesar* (as Cassius) 53. Richard III 56. The Barretts of Wimpole Street 57. Saint Joan 57. Becket (AAN) 64. The Loved One 65. Chimes at Midnight 66. Around the World in Eighty Days 56. Sebastian 67. *The Charge of the Light Brigade* 68. Assignment to Kill 68. The Shoes of the Fisherman 58. Oh What a Lovely War 69. Julius Caesar 70. Eagle in a Cage 71. Probe (TV) 72. Lost Horizon 73. Frankenstein, the True Story (TV) 73. QB VII (TV) 74. 11 Harrowhouse 74. Luther 74. Gold 74. *Murder on the Orient Express* 74. Galileo 75. Aces High 76. Joseph Andrews 77. *Providence* 77. Murder by Decree 79. Les Misérables (TV) 79. A Portrait of the Artist as a Young Man 79. Caligula 79. The Human Factor 79. The Elephant Man 80. The Formula 80. The Seven Dials Mystery (TV) 80. Marco Polo (TV) 80. *Arthur* (AA) 81. Sphinx 81. Lion of the Desert 81. Chariots of Fire 81. Priest of Love 81. *Brideshead Revisited* (TV) 81. Gandhi 82. Wagner (TV) 82. The Conductor 82. The Scarlet and the Black (TV) 82. Inside the Third Reich (TV) 82. The Wicked Lady 83. Invitation to a Wedding 83. Wagner 83. The Shooting Party 84. Scandalous 84. The Far Pavilions (TV) 84. The Master of Ballantrae (TV) 84. Camille (TV) 85. Romance on the Orient Express (TV) 86. The Whistle Blower 86. Plenty 86. War and Remembrance (TV) 88. Barbablu Barbablu 88. Appointment with Death 88. Arthur 2: On the Rocks 88. Getting It Right 89. Strike It Rich 89. Prospero's Books 91. Shining Through 92. The Power of One 92. First Knight 95.

Gifford, Alan (1905–1989).
American character actor in British films.
   It Started in Paradise 52. Lilacs in the Spring 54. The Iron Petticoat 56. A King in New York 57. Too Young to Love 60. Carry On Cowboy 66. Arrivederci Baby 66. Phase IV 73, etc.

Gifford, Frances (1922–1994).
American leading lady of the 40s, trained as a lawyer. Career subsequently halted by ill-health.
   Hold That Woman 40. Jungle Girl 41. My Son Alone 42. Tarzan Triumphs 43. She Went to the Races 45. Little Mister Jim 46. Luxury Liner 48. Riding High 49. Sky Commando 53, etc.

Gigli, Beniamino (1890–1957).
Famous Italian tenor who starred in several films.
   Forget Me Not 35. Ave Maria 37. Pagliacci 42. Night Taxi 50, etc.

gigolos
are figures from another age, when women could be imposed on, but they were memorably played by David Niven in *Dodsworth*, Montgomery Clift in *The Heiress*, Fred MacMurray in *The Lady is Willing*, Burt Lancaster in *Sorry Wrong Number*, William Holden in *Sunset Boulevard*, Van Johnson in *Invitation*, Bekim Fehmiu in *The Adventurers*, Jon Voight in *Midnight Cowboy*, Charles Grodin in *The Heartbreak Kid*, Helmut Berger in *Ash Wednesday*, David Bowie in *Just a Gigolo* and Richard Gere in *American Gigolo*.

Gilbert, Billy (1893–1971).
American character comedian usually seen as a fat, excitable Italian. In films since 1929, after vaudeville experience; a memorable stooge for Laurel and Hardy, the Three Stooges and the Marx Brothers.
   Noisy Neighbours (debut) 29. The Music Box 32. Sutter's Gold 37. Snow White and the Seven Dwarfs (as the voice of Sneezy) 37. Blockheads 38. Destry Rides Again 39. *The Great Dictator* (as Goering) 40. *His Girl Friday* 40. Tin Pan Alley 41. Anchors Aweigh 45. Down among the Sheltering Palms 52. Five Weeks in a Balloon 62, many others.

Gilbert, Brian.
British director, from television.
   Sharma and Beyond (TV) 84. The Frog Prince (aka French Lesson) 84. Vice Versa 88. Not without My Daughter 91. Tom and Viv 94, etc.

Gilbert, Herschel Burke (1918–   ).
American composer and conductor.
   Mr District Attorney 47. Shamrock Hill 49. There's a Girl in My Heart 49. Three Husbands 50. The Scarf 51. Without Warning 52. The Ring 52. The Thief (AAN) 52. No Time for Flowers 52. Sabre Jet 53. Vice Squad 53. Riot in Cell Block Eleven 54. Carmen Jones (AAN) 54. While the City Sleeps 56. Beyond a Reasonable Doubt 56. The Naked Hills 56. No Place to Hide 56. Slaughter on Tenth Avenue 57. Crime and Punishment USA 59. Sam Whiskey 69. I Dismember Mama 72, etc.

Gilbert, John (1895–1936) (John Pringle).
American leading man of the 20s. From a theatrical family, he worked his way from bit parts to romantic leads, but sound revealed his voice to be less dashing than his looks. The character of the alcoholic Norman Maine in *A Star Is Born* was based on him.
   Biography: 1985, *Dark Star* by Leatrice Gilbert Fountain with John R. Maxim.
■ Hell's Hinges 16. Bullets and Brown Eyes 16. The Apostle of Vengeance 16. The Phantom 16. The Eye of the Night 16. Shell 43 16. The Princess of the Dark 16. Happiness 16. The Millionaire Vagrant 16. Golden Rule Kate 16. Hater of Men 17. The Devil Dodger 17. Nancy Comes Home 18. More Trouble 18. Shackled 18. Three X Gordon 18. Wedlock 18. The Mask 18. The Dawn of Understanding 18. White Heather 19. The Busher 19. Heart o' the Hills 19. The Red Viper 19. Should Women Tell? 19. Widow By Proxy 19. The Servant in the House 20. The Great Redeemer 20. The White Circle 20. Deep Waters 21. Ladies Must Live 21. Gleam o' Dawn 22. Monte Cristo 22. Arabian Love 22. The Yellow Stain 22. Honor First 22. Calvert's Valley 22. The Love Gambler 22. While Paris Sleeps 22. Truxten King 23. The Madness of Youth 23. Saint Elmo 23. *Cameo Kirby* 23. A California Romance 23. Just Off Broadway 24. The Wolf Man 24. A Man's Mate 24. The Lone Ranch 24. Romance Ranch 24. His Hour 24. He Who Gets Slapped 24. The Snob 24. The Wife of the Centaur

25. *The Merry Widow* 25. *The Big Parade* 25. La Boheme 26. Bardelys the Magnificent 26. *Flesh and the Devil* 27. The Show 27. Twelve Miles Out 27. *Love* 27. Man, Woman and Sin 28. The Cossacks 28. Four Walls 28. Marks of the Devil 28. A Woman of Affairs 29. Desert Nights 29. Hollywood Revue 29. His Glorious Night (the talkie which killed his romantic image) 29. Redemption 30. Way for a Sailor 30. Gentleman's Fate 30. The Phantom of Paris 31. West of Broadway 32. Downstairs 32. Fast Workers 33. Queen Christina 33. The Captain Hates the Sea 35.

Gilbert, Lewis (1920–   ).
British director, former actor and documentarist.
■ The Little Ballerina 47. Marry Me (w only) 49. Once a Sinner 50. There Is Another Sun 50. The Scarlet Thread 51. Emergency Call 52. Time Gentlemen Please 52. Cosh Boy 53. Johnny on the Run 53. Albert RN 53. The Sea Shall Not Have Them 54. *The Good Die Young* 54. Cast a Dark Shadow 55. *Reach for the Sky* 56. The Admirable Crichton 57. Carve Her Name with Pride 57. A Cry from the Streets 58. Ferry to Hong Kong 59. *Sink The Bismarck* 60. Light Up the Sky 60. The Greengage Summer 61. HMS Defiant 62. The Seventh Dawn 64. Alfie 66. You Only Live Twice 67. The Adventurers 70. Friends (& w) 71. Paul and Michelle 73. Operation Daybreak 75. Seven Nights in Japan 76. The Spy Who Loved Me 77. Moonraker 79. Educating Rita 83. Not Quite Jerusalem·84. Shirley Valentine 89. Stepping Out 91.

¶ Paramount backed *Alfie* because it was going to be made for £500,000, normally the sort of money spent on executives' cigar bills. – L.G.

Gilbert, Olive (1898–1981).
Welsh contralto, in opera and musical comedy.
■ Glamorous Night 37. The Dancing Years 50. King's Rhapsody (voice only) 55.

Gilbert, Paul (1917–1976) (Paul MacMahon).
American comedy dancer, former trapezist.
   So This Is Paris 55. The Second Greatest Sex 55. You Can't Run Away from It 56. Women of the Prehistoric Planet 66, etc.
   TV series: The Duke 54.

Gilbert, W. S. (1836–1911) (William Schwenck).

Sullivan, Sir Arthur (1842–1900).
Celebrated British composers (words and music respectively) of the Savoy operas of the 80s, most cherished for their comic aspects and still performed all over the world by the D'Oyly Carte Company. Many film versions have been made, notably of *The Mikado*. In 1954 came a moderate biopic, *The Story of Gilbert and Sullivan*, with Robert Morley and Maurice Evans.

Gilbreth, Elizabeth (1908–   ).
American author of *Cheaper by the Dozen* and *Belles on Their Toes*, two books of reminiscences which centre on her father, who tried to apply his time-and-motion-study techniques to bringing up his large family.

Gilchrist, Connie (1901–1985) (Rose Gilchrist).
American character actress of stage and screen.
   Billy the Kid 41. The Hucksters 47. A Letter to Three Wives 49. The Man in the Grey Flannel Suit 56. Some Came Running 58. Auntie Mame 59. Say One For Me 59. A House Is Not a Home 64. Sylvia 65. Tickle Me 65. Fuzz 70, etc.
   TV series: Long John Silver 55.

Giler, David.
American screenwriter with many TV credits.
■ Myra Breckinridge (co-w) 70. The Parallax
View (co-w) 74. The Black Bird (& d) 75. Fun
with Dick and Jane (co-w) 77. Alien (co-w) 79.
Southern Comfort (co-w) 81. The Money Pit 86.
Aliens (co-story) 86.

Gilford, Jack (1907–1990) (Jacob Gellman).
American comic actor with long stage career.
Hey Rookie 53. Main Street to Broadway 53. A
Funny Thing Happened on the Way to the Forum
66. Mister Buddwing 66. Enter Laughing 67. The
Happening 67. Who's Minding the Mint? 67. They
Might Be Giants 71. Catch 22 71. Save the Tiger
(AAN) 73. Harry and Walter Go to New York 76.
Wholly Moses 80. Caveman 81. Hotel (TV) 82.
Cocoon 85. Cocoon: The Return 88. Arthur 2 On
the Rocks 88, etc.
TV series: Paul Sand in Friends and Lovers 74–
75. Apple Pie 78. The Duck Factory 84.

Gill, Basil (1877–1955).
British leading actor in silent films, from the stage.
Henry VIII 11. The Admirable Crichton 18. God's
Good Man 19. The Worldlings 20. High Treason 29.
The School for Scandal 30. The Wandering Jew
33. The Immortal Gentleman 35. Rembrandt 36.
Knight without Armour 37. St Martin's Lane (aka
Sidewalks of London) 38. The Citadel 38.
Dangerous Medicine 38, etc.

Gill, Maude.
English character actress, from the stage, best
known for playing the role of Thirza Tapper in
the long-running *The Farmer's Wife*, which she
repeated on (silent) film for Hitchcock.
Autobiography: 1938, *See the Players*.
The Farmer's Wife 28. Glorious Youth 28. The
Price of Divorce 28. Under the Greenwood Tree
29. A Sister to Assist 'Er 30. Excess Baggage 33.
Lilies of the Field 34. Look Up and Laugh 35. Love
at Sea 36. Keep Your Seats Please 36, etc.

¶ I have met with a certain amount of
recognition. For years I was well known to the
army of fierce little boys who guard the outer
offices of theatrical agents as a woman to whom
they had to say at once: 'Sorry! Nothing doing.'
– *M.G.*
Once an uncomplimentary friend asked me if I
preferred the Films to acting! – *M.G.*

Gilles, Genevieve (1946–) (Genevieve
Gillaizeau).
French leading lady, protégée of Darryl Zanuck.
■ World of Fashion (short) 67. Hello – Goodbye
69.

Gillespie, John Birks 'Dizzy' (1917–1993).
Distinguished and innovative American jazz
trumpeter, composer, singer and actor.
Jazz Is Our Religion (doc) 72. A Night in Havana:
Dizzy Gillespie in Cuba (doc) 90. The Winter in
Lisbon (a, m) 92.

Gillette, William (1855–1937).
American stage actor famous for his
personification of *Sherlock Holmes*, which he played
on film in 1916.

Gilliam, Terry (1940–).
American director/animator, one of the Monty
Python team (qv).
AS DIRECTOR: Jabberwocky 76. Time Bandits 81.
Brazil 85. The Adventures of Baron
Munchhausen 88. The Fisher King 91.

Gilliat, Leslie (1917–).
British producer, brother of Sidney Gilliat, with
whom he usually works.

Gilliat, Sidney (1908–1994).
British comedy screenwriter usually in
collaboration with Frank Launder (qv); they also
produced most of their films since the 40s.
Rome Express 33. *Friday the Thirteenth* 33. Jack
Ahoy 34. Chu Chin Chow 34. Bulldog Jack 35.
Where There's a Will 36. Seven Sinners 36. Take
My Tip 37. *A Yank at Oxford* 38. *The Lady Vanishes*
38. The Gaunt Stranger 38. Jamaica Inn 39. Ask a
Policeman 39. They Came by Night 40. *Night Train
to Munich* 40. Kipps 41. *The Young Mr Pitt* 42.
Millions Like Us (& d) 43. *Waterloo Road* (& d) 44.
The Rake's Progress (& d) 45. *Green for Danger* (& d)
46. London Belongs to Me (& d) 48. State Secret
(& d) 50. The Story of Gilbert and Sullivan (& d)
53. The Constant Husband (& d) 55. Fortune is a
Woman (& d) 57. Left Right and Centre (& d) 59.
Only Two Can Play (& d) 62. The Great St Trinian's
Train Robbery (& d) 65. Endless Night 72, etc.

Gilliatt, Penelope (1933–1993).
British critic and screenwriter. She was the third
wife of playwright John Osborne.
Sunday Bloody Sunday (AAN) 72.

Gillie, Jean (1915–1949).
British leading lady, former chorine.
School for Stars 35. Brewster's Millions 35.
While Parents Sleep 36. Sweet Devil 38. Tilly of
Bloomsbury 40. Sailors Don't Care 40. The Gentle
Sex 43. *Tawny Pipit* 44. Decoy (US) 47. The
Macomber Affair (US) 47, etc.

Gillin, William (1868–1942).
English showman who became one of the first
travelling cinema operators in the north of
England in the 1900s. From the 1910s he turned
to performing as a ventriloquist, using a dummy
that walked off the stage on its own at the end of
his act.

Gilling, John (1912–1984).
British writer-director who turned out dozens of
crime and adventure pot-boilers after the war.
The Greed of William Hart (w) 48. The Man
from Yesterday (wd) 49. No Trace (wd) 50. Mother
Riley Meets the Vampire (wd) 52. The Voice of
Merrill (d) 52. The Gamma People (wd) 55.
Odongo (wd) 56. Interpol (wd) 57. High Flight (d)
57. The Man Inside (wd) 58. Idol on Parade (d)
59. The Flesh and the Fiends (wd) 59. The
Challenge (wd) 60. Fury at Smuggler's Bay (wd)
61. Shadow of the Cat (wd) 62. Pirates of Blood
River (wd) 62. The Scarlet Blade (wd) 63. The
Brigand of Kandahar (wd) 64. The Plague of the
Zombies (wd) 65. The Mummy's Shroud (wd) 67,
many others.

Gillingwater, Claude (1870–1939).
American stage actor who came to films to play
irascible old men. Committed suicide.
Little Lord Fauntleroy 21. Dulcy 23. Daddies 24.
Daddy Long Legs 31. The Captain Hates the Sea
34. A Tale of Two Cities 36. Prisoner of Shark
Island 36. Conquest 37. Café Society 39, etc.

Gillis, Ann (1927–) (Alma O'Connor).
American child star of the 30s; adult roles routine.
Now retired and living in Belgium.
The Garden of Allah 37. Off to the Races 37. *The
Adventures of Tom Sawyer* 38. The Underpup 39.
Little Men 40. Nice Girl 41. In Society 44. Since
You Went Away 44. Janie Gets Married 46. 2001:
A Space Odyssey 68, etc.

Gillmore, Margalo (1897–1986).
American stage actress in occasional films.
Wayward 32. Perfect Strangers 50. The Law and
the Lady 51. Skirts Ahoy 52. Woman's World 54.
Gaby 56. High Society 56, etc.

Gilmore, Lowell (1907–1960).
British general-purpose actor.
The Picture of Dorian Gray 44. Calcutta 47. Dream
Girl 48. Tripoli 50. Lone Star 52. Plymouth
Adventure 52. Saskatchewan 54, etc.

Gilmore, Peter (1931–).
British light actor, familiar on TV as the hero of
The Onedin Line.
Bomb in the High Street 61. Carry on Jack 64.
Doctor in Clover 66. My Lover My Son 69. The
Abominable Dr Phibes 71. Warlords of Atlantis 78
etc.

Gilmore, Stuart (1913–1971).
American editor.
Arrest Bulldog Drummond 38. The Lady Eve 41.
Sullivan's Travels 41. The Palm Beach Story 42.
The Miracle of Morgan's Creek 43. Hail the
Conquering Hero 44. Road to Utopia 45. Vendetta
50. The French Line 54. Underwater 55. Journey
to the Center of the Earth 59. The Alamo 60. Hata
62. A Rage To Live 65. Hawaii 66. Thoroughly
Modern Millie 67. Sweet Charity 69. Airport 70.
The Andromeda Strain 71, many others.
■ AS DIRECTOR: The Virginian 46. Hot Lead 51.
Captive Women 52. The Half Breed 52. Target 52

Gilmore, Virginia (1919–1986) (Sherman Poole).
American leading lady of the 40s; films routine.
Winter Carnival 39. Laddie 40. Swamp Water
41. The Loves of Edgar Allan Poe 42. Orchestra
Wives 42. Chetniks 43. Wonder Man 45. Close U
48. Walk East on Beacon 52, etc.

Gilroy, Frank D. (1925–).
American playwright, screenwriter and director.
Autobiography: 1993, *I Wake Up Screening!*
The Fastest Gun Alive 56. The Gallant Hours 66
The Subject Was Roses 68. The Only Game in Tow
69. Desperate Characters (& d) 71. From Noon til
Three (& d) 74. Once in Paris (& d) 78. Jinxed
82. The Gig (& d) 85. The Luckiest Man in the
World (& d) 89, etc.

Gilson, René (1931–).
French director.
■ L'Escadron Volapuk 70. On n'Arrête pas le
Printemps 71. La Brigade 73. Juliette et l'Air du
Temps 76. Ma Blonde Entends-tu dans la Ville 8

gimmicks.
There are those who would classify such
developments as 3-D, CinemaScope and even
talkies under this heading. The genuine gimmick
however is a more fleeting affair, a momentary
method for getting audiences into cinemas for
reasons that have little to do with the quality of
the film. William Castle is the established master
For *Macabre* he offered free insurance if one died
of heart failure. For *Homicidal*, a fright break befor
the climax when cowards could leave – and even
get their money back if they could stand to go
home without learning the awful secret. For *The
House on Haunted Hill*, 'Emergo', in which a
skeleton on wires shot above the audience's hea
at a suitable point in the film. For *The Tingler*, a
device which wired up certain seats to give peop
a small electric shock. In competition, the
producers of *Chamber of Horrors* thought up the
fear flasher and the horror horn to warn weak
spirits when a nasty moment was coming.

ingold, Hermione (1897–1987).
ritish revue comedienne and writer who
lighted in grotesque characters. Born in
ndon, she began on stage at the age of 10 and
as in films from the mid-30s, moving to
merica in 1951. Her second husband was the
reenwriter and lyricist Eric Maschwitz.
Autobiographies: 1958, *The World Is Square.*
988, *How to Grow Old Disgracefully.*
  Someone at the Door 36. Meet Mr Penny 39.
e Butler's Dilemma 43. Cosh Boy 52. *Pickwick*
pers 52. Our Girl Friday 53. Around the World
 Eighty Days 56. Bell, Book and Candle (US) 58.
gi (US) 58. *The Music Man* (US) 61. I'd Rather Be
ch (US) 64. Harvey Middlemann, Fireman (US)
. Munster Go Home (US) 66. Banyon (TV) 71.
Little Night Music 76. Garbo Talks 84, etc.

¶ I had all the schooling any actress needs. I
  learned enough to sign contracts. – *H.G.*
  The trouble with men is that there aren't enough
 them. – *H.G.*
  The nearest my mother ever came to telling me
e facts of life was the day she called me to her
om and said she had something important to tell
e. After a good deal of embarrassed coughing,
e spluttered, 'Don't ever sit down on a strange
vatory seat'. – *H.G.*
  I believe in trying everything once – except
ountry dancing and incest. – *H.G.*
  An amalgam of Groucho Marx and Tallulah
ankhead. – *S. J. Perelman*

Girard, Bernard (1930–).
merican director.
 Ride Out for Revenge 57. Green Eyed Blonde
7. The Party Crashers 58. As Young as we Are
8. A Public Affair 62. Dead Heat on a Merry Go
ound 68. The Mad Room 69. The Happiness
age 72. Gone with the West 75.

Girard, François (1963–).
anadian film director.
 32 Short Films about Glenn Gould 93.

Girard, Remy.
anadian leading actor.
 The Decline of the American Empire 86. Jesus
f Montreal 89. La Florida 93, etc.

Girardot, Annie (1931–).
rench leading lady.
 Thirteen at Table 56. Maigret Sets a Trap 58.
Vice and Virtue 63. Vivre pour Vivre 67. Les
Gauloises Bleues 68. Dillinger Is Dead 69. A Man
Like 69. The Novices 70. Traitement de Choc 73.
The Slap 76. Une Robe Noire pour un Tueur 80.
Le Coeur a l'Envers 80. La Vie Continue 81, All
Night Long 81. Memories, Memories 84.
Departure, Return 85. L'Autre Enigma 86. Cinq
Jours en Juin 89. Comédie d'Amour 89. Merci la
Vie 91. Toujours Seuls 91. Les Braqueuses 94, etc.

Girardot, Etienne (1856–1939).
Dapper Anglo-French character actor, in many
American plays and films.
 The Violin of Monsieur 12. The Kennel Murder
Case 33. *Twentieth Century* 34. Clive of India 35.
Metropolitan 35. Go West Young Man 36. *The
Great Garrick* 37. Professor Beware 38. The
Hunchback of Notre Dame 39. Isle of Destiny 40,
many others.

Girotti, Massimo (1918–).
Italian leading man.
 Obsession 42. Caccia Tragica 47. Fabiola 47.
Bellissima 51. Aphrodite 57. Theorem 68. Mr
Klein 76. Cagliostro 76, etc.

Gish, Annabeth (1970–) (Anne Elizabeth Gish).
American actress.
 Desert Bloom 86. Hiding Out 87. Mystic Pizza
88. Shag: The Movie 89. When He's Not a
Stranger (TV) 89. Coupe de Ville 90. Silent Cries
(TV) 93. Wyatt Earp 94, etc.

Gish, Dorothy (1898–1968) (Dorothy de Guiche).
Famous American silent star, in films for D. W.
Griffith from 1912: *Hearts of the World, Orphans of
the Storm*, etc. On stage between 1928 and 1944.
Our Hearts Were Young and Gay 44. The Whistle
at Eaton Falls 51. The Cardinal 63, etc.

Gish, Lillian (1899–1993) (Lillian de Guiche).
Famous American silent star, sister of Dorothy
Gish, and also a D. W. Griffith discovery, on stage
as a child and in films from 1912. From mid-20s
spent much time on stage, but filmed occasionally.
Directed one film, Remodelling Her Husband 21.
She was given a special Academy Award in 1970.
 Autobiography: 1969, *The Movies, Mr Griffith,
and Me.*
 Birth of a Nation 14. Intolerance 16. *Broken
Blossoms* 18. *Way Down East* 20. Orphans of the
Storm 22. The Scarlet Letter 26. Annie Laurie 27.
His Double Life 34. The Commandos Strike at
Dawn 43. Miss Susie Slagle's 46. *Duel in the Sun*
(AAN) 46. Portrait of Jennie 48. *Night of the Hunter*
55. Orders to Kill 58. The Unforgiven 59. Follow
Me Boys 66. Warning Shot 66. The Comedians 67.
Twin Detectives (TV) 76. Hambone and Hillie 85.
Sweet Liberty 85. The Whales of August 87, etc.
☼ For her early stardom and her later
graciousness; and for achieving the longest acting
career in show business. *Way Down East.*

¶ You know, when I first went into the movies
  Lionel Barrymore played my grandfather. Later
he played my father and finally he played my
husband. If he had lived, I'm sure I would have
played his mother. That's the way it is in
Hollywood. The men get younger and the women
get older. – *L.G.*
  Fans always write asking why I didn't smile
more in films. I did in *Annie Laurie*, but I can't recall
that it helped much. – *L.G.*
  I can't remember a time when I wasn't acting,
so I can't imagine what I would do if I stopped now.
– *L.G.*
  I don't care for modern films – all crashing cars
and close-ups of people's feet. – *L.G.*
  I've never been in style, so I can't go out of style.
– *L.G.*

Gist, Robert (1924–).
American general-purpose actor; turned director
once, then went into TV.
 Jigsaw 49. I Was a Shoplifter 50. The Band
Wagon 53. D Day Sixth of June 56. Operation
Petticoat 59. Blueprint for Robbery 61. An
American Dream (d only) 66, etc.

Givenchy, Hubert de (1927–).
French fashion designer who worked on
occasional movies.
 Funny Face (AAN) 57. Breakfast at Tiffany's 61.
The VIPs 63, etc.

Givens, Robin (1964–).
Sultry American actress who studied medicine
before being tempted by TV roles. She was married
briefly to heavyweight boxer Mike Tyson.
 The Wiz 78. Fort Apache, The Bronx 81. A Rage
in Harlem 91. Boomerang 92. Foreign Student 94.
Blankman 94, etc.
 TV series: Head of the Class 86. Angel Street 92.

Givney, Kathryn (1897–1978).
American general-purpose character actress.
 Isn't It Romantic? 48. Operation Pacific 51.
Three Coins in the Fountain 54. Guys and Dolls
55. The Wayward Bus 57. The Man in the Net 59,
etc.

Givot, George (1903–1984).
American character actor, usually in hearty roles.
 When's Your Birthday 37. Marie Walewska 38.
Dubarry Was a Lady 43. Riff Raff 46. Captain Blood
Fugitive 52. Miracle in the Rain 56, etc.

Glaser, Paul Michael (1943–).
American leading man who leaped to fame as
Starsky in TV's *Starsky and Hutch* (1975–79), but
subsequently found roles scarce. He began
directing in the 80s.
 Fiddler on the Roof 71. Butterflies Are Free 72.
Trapped Beneath the Sea (TV) 74. The Great
Houdinis (TV) 77. Phobia 80. Wait till Your Mother
Gets Home (TV) 81. Princess Daisy (TV) 82. Single
Bars, Single Women (TV) 84. Amazons (TV) (d)
84. Band of the Hand (d) 86. The Running Man (d)
87. The Cutting Edge (d) 92. The Air Up There (d)
94, etc.
 TV series: Love Is a Many Splendoured Thing
69–70. Love of Life 71–72.

The Glass Key.
Dashiell Hammett's novel of a politician saved
from a murder charge has been turned into two
lively thrillers, in 1935 with George Raft and Claire
Dodd and directed by Frank Tuttle, and in 1942
with Alan Ladd and Veronica Lake, directed by
Stuart Heisler.

Glass, Ned (1905–1984).
Crusty American character actor.
 Storm Warning 50. Back from the Dead 57.
Experiment in Terror 62. Blackbeard's Ghost 68.
Save the Tiger 72, etc.
 TV series: Bridget Loves Bernie 73.

Glass, Philip (1937–).
American composer.
 Koyaanisqatsi 82. Mishima: A Life in Four
Chapters 85. Hamburger Hill 87. Powaqqatsi 88.
The Thin Blue Line 88. The Church (s) 90. A Brief
History of Time (TV) 91, etc.

glass shot.
Usually a scenic shot in which part of the
background is actually painted on a glass slide held
in front of the camera and carefully blended with
the action. In this way castles, towns, etc. may be
shown on a location where none exist, without
the expense of building them.

Glasser, Albert (1916–).
American composer.
 Call of the Jungle 44. The Cisco Kid in Old
Mexico 45. Law of the Lash 47. The Gay Amigo 49.
I Shot Jesse James 49. The Treasure of Monte
Cristo 49. I Shot Billy the Kid 50. The Neanderthal
Man 52. Top Banana 54. Huk 56. The Amazing
Colossal Man 57. Monster from Green Hell 57.
When Hell Broke Loose 58. Teenage Caveman 58.
The Boy and the Pirates 60. The Unbelievable 66.
The Cremators 72, many others.

Gleason, Jackie (1916–1987).
Heavyweight American TV comedian who as a
young man played small movie roles, then
returned as a star but never found his niche.
 Biographies: 1956, *The Golden Ham* by Jim
Bishop. 1992, *The Great One: The Life and Legend
of Jackie Gleason* by William A. Henry III.

Navy Blues 41. Orchestra Wives 42. Springtime in the Rockies 42. The Desert Hawk 50. *The Hustler* (as Minnesota Fats) (AAN) 61. Gigot (& w) 62. Requiem for a Heavyweight 62. Papa's Delicate Condition 63. Soldier in the Rain 63. Skidoo 68. How to Commit Marriage 69. Don't Drink the Water 69. How Do I Love Thee? 70. Mr Billion 77. Smokey and the Bandit 77. Smokey and the Bandit II 80. The Sting II 82. Smokey and the Bandit III 83. The Toy 83. Izzy and Moe (TV) 85, etc.

TV series: The Life of Riley 49. *The Honeymooners* 49–54. The Jackie Gleason Show 64–70.

¶ I'm no alcoholic, I'm a drunkard. The difference is, drunkards don't go to meetings. – *J.G.*

I have no use for humility, I am a fellow with an exceptional talent. – *J.G.*

Jackie's consistent: he's got a fat mouth and a fat belly. – *Joe Namath*

Gleason, James (1886–1959).
American character actor noted for hard-boiled comedy roles, usually in Brooklynese. On stage from infancy; also wrote several plays.

A Free Soul 30. Her Man 30. Oh Yeah (& oa) 30. Orders Is Orders (GB) 33. Murder on the Bridle Path 36. The Higgins Family 38. On Your Toes 39. Meet John Doe 41. *Here Comes Mr Jordan* (AAN) 41. A Guy Named Joe 43. Arsenic and Old Lace 44. *Once Upon a Time* 44. A Tree Grows in Brooklyn 44. This Man's Navy 45. Captain Eddie 45. Down to Earth 47. The Bishop's Wife 48. The Life of Riley 49. Come Fill the Cup 51. *Suddenly* 54. The Last Hurrah 58, many others.

TV series: The Life of Riley 54–57 (as postman). ✪ For adding a little comic acid to any number of routine comedies. *Here Comes Mr Jordan.*

Gleason, Joanna (1950–   ) (Joanna Hall).
Canadian actress in Hollywood films.

Hannah and Her Sisters 86. Heartburn 86. Crimes and Misdemeanours 89. FX/2 91. For Richer, for Poorer (TV) 92, etc.

Gleason, Lucille (1886–1947).
American character actress, wife of James Gleason, with whom she often appeared.

The Shannons of Broadway 29. Nice Women 32. Beloved 33. Klondike Annie 36. First Lady 37. *The Higgins Family* (& four subsequent episodes) 38. Lucky Partners 40. The Clock 45, etc.

Gleason, Russell (1908–1945).
American juvenile actor, son of James and Lucille Gleason. Died following a fall from a hotel window.

Strange Cargo 29. All Quiet on the Western Front 30. Nice Women 32. Private Jones 33. Off to the Races 37. Big Business (as Jones Family member) 37. *The Higgins Family* (& four subsequent episodes) 38. News Is Made at Night 39. Unexpected Uncle 41. Salute to the Marines 43. The Adventures of Mark Twain 44, etc.

Glen, Iain (1961–   ).
Scottish leading actor.

Paris by Night 88. Mountains of the Moon 89. Silent Scream 89. Rosencrantz and Guildenstern Are Dead 90. Fools of Fortune 90. Adam Bede (TV) 91. Young Americans 93, etc.

Glen, John (1932–   ).
British director, a former editor.

For Your Eyes Only 81. Octopussy 83. A View to a Kill 85. The Living Daylights 87. Licence to Kill 89. Aces: Iron Eagle III 92. Christopher Columbus: The Discovery 92, etc.

Glenn, Roy, Snr (1905–1971).
American character actor.

Bomba and the Jungle Girl 52. The Golden Idol 54. Written on the Wind 56. A Raisin in the Sun 61. Dead Heat on a Merry Go Round 67. *Guess Who's Coming to Dinner?* 67. Escape from the Planet of the Apes 71, many others.

Glenn, Scott (1942–   ).
American leading man.

Hex 73. Fighting Mad 76. Apocalypse Now 79. Urban Cowboy 80. Personal Best 82. The Challenge 82. The Right Stuff 83. Wild Geese 84. The River 84. Silverado 85. Wild Geese II 85. Gangland 87. Man on Fire 87. Off Limits 88. Miss Firecracker 89. The Hunt for Red October 90. The Silence of the Lambs 91. Backdraft 91. My Heroes Have Always Been Cowboys 91. The Player 92. Shadowhunter 93. Slaughter of the Innocents 93, etc.

Glennon, Bert (1893–1967).
Distinguished American cinematographer.

Ramona 16. The Torrent 20. *The Ten Commandments* 23. Woman of the World 26. The Patriot 28. Java Head 34. *The Hurricane* 37. *Drums along the Mohawk* 39. *Stagecoach* 39. They Died with Their Boots On 41. Dive Bomber 41. Destination Tokyo 44. The Red House 47. *Wagonmaster* 50. Operation Pacific 50. The Big Trees 52. House of Wax 53. The Mad Magician 54. Sergeant Rutledge 60, many others.

Glenville, Peter (1913–   ).
British stage director who has made occasional films, usually of theatrical successes.

■ The Prisoner 54. Me and the Colonel 58. Summer and Smoke 60. Term of Trial 61. *Becket* (AAN) 64. Hotel Paradiso 66. The Comedians 67.

Glickenhaus, James (1950–   ).
American screenwriter, producer and director. In 1987 he founded with Lenny Shapiro the production and distribution company Shapiro Glickenhaus Entertainment.

The Astrologer (aka The Suicide Cult) 77. The Exterminator 80. The Soldier 82. The Protector 85. Shakedown (aka Blue Jean Cop) 88. McBain 91. Slaughter of the Innocents (wd) 93. Time Master 93, etc.

¶ Home video is a blessing, but it's also a terrible liability. We can't just become people that make films for video, because then no more big films will get made. – *J.G.*

Globus, Yoram (1941–   ).
Israeli film producer in partnership with Menahem Golan (qv) until 1989. He now runs his own production company. He formed a new production company with Menahem Golan in 1993.

Glover, Brian (1934–   ).
British character actor (also occasional writer).

Kes 69. Mister Quilp 75. Jabberwocky 75. Trial by Combat 76. The First Great Train Robbery 78. An American Werewolf in London 81. Britannia Hospital 82. Laughterhouse (w) 84. Company of Wolves 84. Kafka 91. Alien³ 92. Leon the Pig Farmer 91, etc.

Glover, Crispin (1964–   ).
American juvenile actor.

My Tutor 82. Friday the 13th – the Final Chapter 83. Racing with the Moon 84. Teachers 84. Back to the Future 85. At Close Range 86. River's Edge 87. Twister 89. Where the Heart Is 90. Wild at Heart 90. Ruben and Ed 91. Little Noises 91. Hotel Room (TV) 93. Even Cowgirls Get the Blues 93. What's Eating Gilbert Grape 93. Chasers 94, etc.

Glover, Danny (1947–   ).
American actor.

Escape from Alcatraz 79. Chu Chu and the Philly Flash 81. Out 82. Iceman 84. Place in the Heart 84. The Stand-In 84. The Color Purple 85. Silverado 85. Witness 85. Lethal Weapon 87. BAT 21 88. Lethal Weapon 2 89. Predator 2 90. To Sleep with Anger 90. Flight of the Intruder 91. A Rage in Harlem 91. Pure Luck 91. Grand Canyon 92. Lethal Weapon 3 92. The Saint of Fort Washington 93. Queen (TV) 93. Bopha! 93. Angels in the Outfield 94, etc.

Glover, John (1944–   ).
American character actor, often as a heavy.

Shamus 72. Annie Hall 77. Last Embrace 79. Brubaker 80. Melvin and Howard 80. The Evil that Men Do 84. White Nights 84. 52 Pick-Up 86. The Chocolate War 88. Scrooged 88. Traveling Man (TV) 89. Gremlins 2: The New Batch 90. Robocop 2 90, etc.

Glover, Julian (1935–   ).
British general-purpose actor chiefly on stage and TV.

Tom Jones 63. Girl with Green Eyes 64. I Was Happy Here 66. Alfred the Great 69. The Adding Machine 69. Wuthering Heights 70. Nicholas and Alexandra 71. Dead Cert 74. Juggernaut 75. The Brute 77. For Your Eyes Only 81. Heat and Dust 83. Cry Freedom 87. The Fourth Protocol 87. Heart of Fire 87. Indiana Jones and the Last Crusade 89. Tusks 90. King Ralph 91, etc.

Glyn, Elinor (1864–1943).
Extravagant British romantic novelist whose 'daring' *Three Weeks* was filmed in Hollywood in 1924 and proved both sensational and influential. Her grandson Anthony Glyn wrote her biography in 1968. She invented the catchword 'It' for sex appeal, and this in 1926 was made the basis of a movie which brought fame to Clara Bow and in which Miss Glyn consented to appear.

Glynne, Mary (1898–1954).
British stage actress of the well-bred school.

The Cry of Justice 19. The Hundredth Chance 20. The Good Companions (as Miss Trant) 32. Emil and the Detectives 34. Scrooge 35. The Heirloom Mystery (last film) 37, etc.

Gobel, George (1919–1991).
American TV comedian of 'little man' appeal.

■ The Birds and the Bees 56. I Married a Woman 57. The Invisible Woman (TV) 83. The Fantastic World of D. C. Collins (TV) 84.

TV series: The George Gobel Show 54–60. Harper Valley PTA 80.

Goblin.
Italian rock group whose music has featured in horror movies.

Deep Red (Profundo Rosso) 76. Suspiria 77. Dawn of the Dead 79. Patrick 79. Alien Contamination 80. Night of the Zombies 80. Buried Alive 81. Creepers (Phenomena) 85, etc.

Godard, Jean-Luc (1930–   ).
Semi-surrealist French writer-director of the 'new wave', his talent often muffled by incoherent narrative.

A Bout de Souffle (Breathless) (d only) 60. Une Femme Est Une Femme 61. Vivre Sa Vie 62. Le Petit Soldat 63. Les Carabiniers 63. Bande à Part 64. Une Femme Mariée 64. Alphaville 65. Pierrot

Le Fou 66. Made in USA 66. Weekend 67. One Plus One 69. Numero Deux 75. Comment Ça Va 76. Ici et Ailleurs 77. Sauve Qui Peut 80. Passion 82. First Name: Carmen (Prénom Carmen) 83. Detective 85. Hail Mary (Je Vous Salue, Marie) 85. Aria (co-d) 87. King Lear 87. Soigne Ta Droite 87. Nouvelle Vague 89. Germany Nine Zero (Allemagne Neuf Zéro) 91. Hélas pour Moi 93. JLG/JLG – Self-Portrait in December 94, etc.

¶ My aesthetic is that of the sniper on the roof. – *J.L.G.*

The cinema is truth 24 times a second. – *J.L.G.*

You don't make a movie, the movie makes you. – *J.L.G.*

Since Godard's films have nothing to say, perhaps we could have 90 minutes' silence instead of each of them. – *John Simon*

Goddard, Alf (1897–1981).
English character actor in cockney roles, often comic, from the stage. Born in London, he was a former boxer and began in films as a stuntman.

The Sign of Four 23. White Heat 26. Hindle Wakes 27. Sailors Don't Care 28. You Know What Sailors Are 28. Alf 's Button 30. East Lynne on the Western Front 31. Lost in the Legion 34. Strictly Illegal 35. The Scarlet Pimpernel 37. King Solomon's Mines 37. The Squeaker 37. Bank Holiday 38. St Martin's Lane 38. Murder in Soho 39. The Young Mr Pitt 42. The Way Ahead 44. The Way to the Stars 45. Innocents in Paris 53, many others.

Goddard, Paulette (1911–1990) (Marion Levy).
Pert, pretty American leading lady of the early 40s; started as a Goldwyn girl, married Charlie Chaplin and Burgess Meredith, and when her not inconsiderable career petered out married Erich Maria Remarque.

Biography: 1986, *Paulette* by Joe Morella and Edward Epstein.

■ The Girl Habit 31. The Mouthpiece 32. The Kid from Spain 32. Modern Times 36. The Young in Heart 38. Dramatic School 38. The Women 39. *The Cat and the Canary* 39. *The Ghost Breakers* 40. The Great Dictator 40. Northwest Mounted Police 40. Second Chorus 40. Pot o' Gold 41. Nothing But the Truth 41. Hold Back the Dawn 41. The Lady Has Plans 42. *Reap The Wild Wind* 42. The Forest Rangers 42. Star Spangled Rhythm 43. The Crystal Ball 43. So Proudly We Hail (AAN) 43. Standing Room Only 44. I Love a Soldier 44. Duffy's Tavern 45. Kitty 45. *The Diary of a Chambermaid* 46. Suddenly It's Spring 47. Variety Girl 47. Unconquered 47. An Ideal Husband (GB) 47. On Our Merry Way 48. Hazard 48. Bride of Vengeance 49. Anna Lucasta 49. The Torch 50. Babes in Baghdad 52. Vice Squad 53. Paris Model 53. Sins of Jezebel 53. Charge of the Lancers 54. The Stranger Came Home (GB) 54. Time of Indifference 66. The Snoop Sisters (TV) 72.

Goddard, Willoughby (1932–).
Heavyweight British character actor, mostly on TV.

In the Wake of a Stranger 59. The Wrong Box 66. The Charge of the Light Brigade 68. Young Sherlock Holmes 85, etc.

TV series: *William Tell* 57.

Godden, Rumer (1907–).
Much-filmed British novelist.

Black Narcissus 46. Enchantment 48. The River 51. The Greengage Summer 61. Battle of the Villa Fiorita 65, etc.

Godfrey, Bob (1921–).
British animator: shorts include *Polygamous*

Polonius, The Do-It-Yourself Cartoon Kit, The Plain Man's Guide to Advertising, Great, etc.

Godfrey, Peter (1899–1970).
British stage actor and producer who in the 30s directed two quickies, subsequently went to Hollywood and remained to direct routine films.

■ The Lone Wolf Spy Hunt 39. Unexpected Uncle 41. Highways by Night 42. Make Your Own Bed 44. Hotel Berlin 45. Christmas in Connecticut 45. One More Tomorrow 46. The Two Mrs Carrolls 47. Cry Wolf 47. That Hagen Girl 47. Escape Me Never 47. *The Woman in White* 48. The Decision of Christopher Blake 48. The Girl from Jones Beach 49. One Last Fling 49. Barricade 50. The Great Jewel Robber 50. He's a Cockeyed Wonder 50. One Big Affair 52. Please Murder Me 56.

Godsell, Vanda (1918–1990).
British character actress, usually in blowsy roles.

The Large Rope 54. Hour of Decision 57. Hell Is a City 60. This Sporting Life 63. The Earth Dies Screaming 64. Who Killed the Cat? 66. The Pink Panther Strikes Again 76. Trail of the Pink Panther 82, etc.

Godunov, Alexander (1950–).
Russian ballet dancer who defected and turned actor in the occasional film.

Witness 85. The Money Pit 86. Die Hard 88. Waxwork 2: Lost in Time 91. The Runestone 91, etc.

Godzilla.
A Japanese monster creation first seen in the film of that name in 1955.

Apparently closely related to *Tyrannosaurus rex*, he has since suffered at the hands of King Kong and the Thing in inferior sequels. He remained rather plainly a man in a rubber suit.

Godzilla's screen appearances:
Godzilla 54
Gigantis the Fire Monster 55
King Kong vs Godzilla 62
Godzilla vs the Thing 64
Ghidrah the Three Headed Monster 64
Monster Zero 65
Godzilla vs the Sea Monster 66
Son of Godzilla 67
Destroy all Monsters 68
Godzilla's Revenge 69
Godzilla vs the Smog Monster 71
Godzilla on Monster Island 72
Godzilla vs Megalon 73
Godzilla vs the Cosmic Monster 74
Terror of Mechagodzilla 75
Godzilla '85 85
Godzilla vs Biollante 89
Godzilla vs King Ghidorah 91
Godzilla vs Mothra 92

Goehr, Walter (*–1960).
British composer.

Amateur Gentlemen (co-m) 36. Great Expectations 47. Lucky Nick Cain 51. Betrayed 54, etc.

Goetz, Ben (1891–1979).
American executive, long with MGM and in charge of their British studios in the 40s.

Goetz, William (1903–1969).
American producer, in films since 1923, chiefly with Fox and Universal. As independent, he latterly produced the following:

The Man from Laramie 55. Sayonara 57. They Came to Cordura 58. Me and the Colonel 58. Song without End 60, etc.

Goff, Ivan (1910–).
Australian-born screenwriter; usually in collaboration with Ben Roberts (qv).

My Love Came Back 40. *White Heat* 49. Captain Horatio Hornblower 51. Come Fill the Cup 51. Full House 52. King of the Khyber Rifles 53. Green Fire 54. Serenade 56. Man of a Thousand Faces 57. Shake Hands with the Devil 59. Portrait in Black 60, etc.

TV series: The Rogues 64. Charlie's Angels 75. Time Express 79.

Golan, Gila (c. 1940–).
Hollywood leading lady of indeterminate background, being a European war orphan of probably Polish-Jewish parentage.

Ship of Fools 65. Our Man Flint 66. Three on a Couch 66. The Valley of Gwangi 69, etc.

Golan, Menahem (1929–) (Menahem Globus).
Flamboyant Israeli producer, director and screenwriter noted for quantity rather than quality. He trained in stage-management in London, became a theatre director in Israel, and began his film career working for Roger Corman. With his cousin Yoram Globus he ran Noah Films in Israel and then, from 1979–89, the international Cannon Group. The partnership foundered and he now heads a new production company, the 21st Century Film Corporation, with plans to produce programmes for 'erotic TV'. He formed a new production company with Yoram Globus in 1993.

Biography: 1986, *Hollywood a Go-go* by Andrew Yule.

AS PRODUCER: Sallah (AAN) 64. The House on Chelouche Street (AAN) 73. Lemon Popsicle 77. Going Steady – Lemon Popsicle II 78. Hot Bubblegum 81. Death Wish 2 81. Lady Chatterley's Lover 81. Body and Soul 81. The Last American Virgin 82. That Championship Season 82. The Wicked Lady 83. Revenge of the Ninja 83. Breakin' 84. Sahara 84. Hot Chili 85. Hot Resort 85. The Ambassador 85. Maria's Lovers 85. Missing in Action 2 85. Invasion U.S.A. 85. Death Wish 3 85. King Solomon's Mines 85. Fool for Love 85. Runaway Train 85. Ordeal by Innocence 85. The Assisi Underground 85. Delta Force 86. Murphy's Law 86. Otello 86. 52 Pickup 86. Firewalker 86. The Naked Cage 86. P.O.W.: The Escape 86. Avenging Force 86. Assassination 87. Allan Quatermain and the Lost City of Gold 87. Number One with a Bullet 87. Street Smart 87. Superman IV: The Quest for Peace 87. Masters of the Universe 87. Dancers 87. Barfly 87. Shy People 87. Tough Guys Don't Dance 87. Hero and The Terror 88. Messenger of Death 88. King Lear 88. Going Bananas 88. Apppointment with Death 88. Kinjite (Forbidden Subjects) 89. The Phantom of the Opera 89. Cyborg 89. Manifesto 89. The Forbidden Dance 90. Night of the Living Dead 90. The Fifth Monkey 90. Crazy Joe 92. Mad Dog Coll 92. Invader 92. The Finest Hour 92. Emmanuelle 7 92, etc.

AS DIRECTOR: El Dorado 63. Trunk to Cairo 67. Tevye and His Seven Daughters 68. What's Good for the Goose 69. Margo 70. Lupo! 70. Kazablan 73. Diamonds 75. Lepke 75. Entebbe: Operation Thunderbolt (AAN) 77. The Magician of Lublin 79. The Apple 80. Enter the Ninja 81. Delta Force 86. Over the Top 87. Hanna's War 88. Mack the Knife 89. Hit the Dutchman 92, etc.

¶ If you make an American film with a beginning, a middle and an end, with a budget of less than five million dollars, you must be an idiot to lose money. – *M.G.*

We have some good news. We didn't buy anything today. – *M.G. (Cannes 1986)*

Gold, Ernest (1921–).
Viennese-American composer.

Girl of the Limberlost 45. The Falcon's Alibi 46. Unknown World 51. Jennifer 53. The Naked Street 55. Too Much Too Soon 57. On the Beach 59. Exodus (AA) 60. Inherit the Wind 60. Judgment at Nuremberg 60. A Child Is Waiting 62. Pressure Point 62. It's a Mad Mad Mad Mad World 63. Ship of Fools 65. The Secret of Santa Vittoria 69. Small Miracle (TV) 73. Betrayal (TV) 74. Cross of Iron 77. Fun with Dick and Jane 77. The Runner Stumbles 79. Tom Horn 80. Safari 3000 82. Dreams of Gold (TV) 86. Gore Vidal's Lincoln (TV) 88, etc.

Gold, Jack (1930–).
British TV director who moved into films.
■ *The Bofors Gun* 68. The Reckoning 69. The National Health 73. *Catholics* (TV) 73. Who? 74. Man Friday 75. *The Naked Civil Servant* (TV) 75. Aces High 76. The Medusa Touch 77. Charlie Muffin (TV) 79. The Sailor's Return (TV) 79. Praying Mantis (TV) 82. Sakharov 84. The Chain 85. Escape from Sobibor (TV) 86. Ball-Trap on the Côte Sauvage 89. The Last Romantics (TV) 90.

Gold, Jimmy:
see *The Crazy Gang*.

Goldbeck, Willis (1899–1979).
American director, former writer (co-author of *Freaks*).
Dr Gillespie's New Assistant 42. Between Two Women 44. She Went to the Races 45. Love Laughs at Andy Hardy 46. Johnny Holiday 50. Ten Tall Men 51, etc.

Goldberg, Whoopi (1949–) (Caryn Johnson).
American actress, often in comic roles.
The Color Purple (AAN) 85. Jumpin' Jack Flash 87. Fatal Beauty 87. Burglar 87. Clara's Heart 87. The Telephone 88. Beverly Hills Brats 89. Homer and Eddie 89. Ghost (AA) 90. The Long Walk Home 90. Soapdish 91. Kiss Shot 91. Change of Heart 92. The Player 92. Sarafina! 92. Sister Act 92. Made in America 93. National Lampoon's Loaded Weapon 1 93. Naked in New York 93. Sister Act 2: Back in the Habit 93. The Lion King (voice) 94. The Little Rascals 94. Corrina, Corrina 94. The Pagemaster (voice) 94. Star Trek: Generations 94, etc.

¶ I worked in strip joints – but I never got my clothes off. People were screaming: 'Don't do it!' – *W.G.*

I'm really glad we do what we do, man. We are amazing! – *W.G. at the Oscars, 1994*

Goldblatt, Stephen.
British cinematographer, now working in Hollywood.
Breaking Glass 80. Outland 81. The Return of the Soldier 82. The Hunger 83. The Cotton Club 84. Young Sherlock Holmes 85. Lethal Weapon 87. Everybody's All American 88. Lethal Weapon 2 89. Joe versus the Volcano 90. For the Boys 91. The Prince of Tides (AAN) 91. Consenting Adults 92. The Pelican Brief 93, etc.

Goldblum, Jeff (1952–).
Lanky American leading man, rather difficult to cast. He was formerly married to actress Geena Davis.
California Split 74. Death Wish 74. Nashville 75. Next Stop Greenwich Village 76. Between the Lines 77. Invasion of the Body Snatchers 78. Remember

My Name 78. Thank God It's Friday 78. Escape from Athena 79. The Big Chill 83. Buckaroo Banzai 84. Silverado 85. Into the Night 85. Transylvania 6–5000 85. *The Fly* 86. Beyond Therapy 87. Life Story (TV) 87. Vibes 88. Earth Girls Are Easy 89. The Mad Monkey (El Mono Loco) 89. The Tall Guy 89. Mister Frost 90. The Favour, the Watch and the Very Big Fish (Rue Saint-Sulpice) 91. Deep Cover 92. Shooting Elizabeth 92. Jurassic Park 93. Lush Life 93, etc.
TV series: Tenspeed and Brown Shoe 81.

Golden, Michael (1913–).
British character actor.
Send for Paul Temple 46. Hungry Hill 47. Escape 48. The Blue Lamp 50. The Green Scarf 55. Murder She Said 62, etc.

Goldenberg, Billy (1936–).
American composer, mainly for TV films.
The Grasshopper 69. Red Sky at Morning 70. Duel (TV) 71. The Marcus Nelson Murders (TV) 72. The Last of Sheila 73. Reflections of Murder (TV) 73. The Domino Principle 76. Scavenger Hunt 78. King (TV) 78. Haywire (TV) 81. The Diary of Anne Frank (TV) 82. Reuben Reuben 83. Rage of Angels (TV) 83. The Sun Also Rises (TV) 84. Kane and Abel (TV) 85. Rage of Angels: The Story Continues (TV) 86. 18 Again 88. People Like Us (TV) 90, many others.
Several TV series include Kojak, Columbo, McCloud, Harry O, Executive Suite.

¶ Movies are a group endeavour, and people don't want to know that. They want to know that Clint Eastwood is really Superman and Richard Attenborough is Plato reincarnated. – *B.G.*

Goldenthal, Elliot.
American composer.
Pet Sematary 89. Drugstore Cowboy 89. Alien³ 92. Demolition Man 93, etc.

Golding, Louis (1896–1958).
English novelist and screenwriter. Born in Manchester, he was educated at Oxford University.
Cotton Queen (co-w) 37. Proud Valley (co-w) 38. Freedom Radio (w) 40. Mr Emmanuel (co-w, oa) 45. Five Silver Daughters (co-w) 44. The Silver Cat (co-w) 47. Theirs Is the Glory (co-w) 47. The Call of the Blood (co-w) 47, etc.

Goldman, Bo (1932–).
American screenwriter. He first worked in TV as a producer and writer.
One Flew over the Cuckoo's Nest (AA) 76. The Rose 79. Melvin and Howard (AA) 80. Shoot the Moon 82. Swing Shift 83. Little Nikita 88. Dick Tracy 90. Scent of a Woman 92, etc.

Goldman, James (1927–).
American playwright and screenwriter.
The Lion in Winter (oa & w) (AAN) 68. *They Might Be Giants* 71. Nicholas and Alexandra 72. Robin and Marian 75. White Nights (co-w) 85, etc.

Goldman, William (1931–).
American screenwriter and novelist.
Autobiographies: 1985, *Adventures in the Screen Trade*. 1990, *Hype and Glory*.
Soldier in the Rain (oa) 63. Masquerade 65. Harper 66. No Way to Treat a Lady (oa) 67. *Butch Cassidy and the Sundance Kid* (AA) 69. The Hot Rock 71. The Great Waldo Pepper 75. All the President's Men 76. Marathon Man (& oa) 77. A Bridge Too Far 77. Magic (& oa) 78. Butch and Sundance: The Early Days 79. Heat (& oa) 87. The Princess Bride (& oa) 87. Misery 90. Year of the

Comet 92. Chaplin (co-w) 92. Memoirs of an Invisible Man 92. Maverick 94, etc.

¶ Nobody knows anything. – *W.G. on the film business*

Goldner, Charles (1900–1955).
Austrian character actor, in Britain from the 30s.
Room for Two 40. Brighton Rock 47. One Night With You 48. Third Time Lucky 48. Give Us This Day 49. Black Magic 49. Shadow of the Eagle 50. *The Captain's Paradise* 54, etc.

Goldoni, Lelia (c. 1938–).
American actress.
Shadows 59. Hysteria 64. The Italian Job 69. Alice Doesn't Live Here Any More 74. The Day of the Locust 75. Baby Blue Marine 76. Bloodbrothers 78. Invasion of the Body Snatchers 78. The Disappearance of Sister Aimee (TV) 79. Scruples (TV) 81, etc.

Goldsmith, Jerry (1929–) (Jerrald Goldsmith).
American composer.
Black Patch 57. City of Fear 59. Lonely Are the Brave 62. Freud (AAN) 63. The Prize 63. Seven Days in May 64. Lilies of the Field 64. In Harm's Way 65. A Patch of Blue (AAN) 65. The Trouble with Angels 66. Stagecoach 66. The Blue Max 66. Seconds 66. The Sand Pebbles (AAN) 66. In Like Flint 67. Planet of the Apes (AAN) 68. Patton (AAN) 70. Tora! Tora! Tora! 71. The Mephisto Waltz 71. Papillon (AAN) 73. The Reincarnation of Peter Proud 75. Chinatown (AAN) 75. The Wind and the Lion (AAN) 75. The Omen (AA) 76. Islands in the Stream 77. MacArthur 77. Capricorn One 78. The Boys from Brazil (AAN) 78. Coma 78. Magic 78. Alien 79. Star Trek: the Motion Picture (AAN) 79. The First Great Train Robbery 80. The Final Conflict 81. Outland 81. Raggedy Man 81. Poltergeist (AAN) 82. Psycho II 83. Under Fire (AAN) 83. Gremlins 84. King Solomon's Mines 85. Poltergeist 2 85. Hoosiers (AAN) 86. Extreme Prejudice 86. Innerspace 87. Lionheart 87. Criminal Law 88. Rambo III 88. The 'burbs 89. Leviathan 89. Star Trek V: The Final Frontier 89. Warlock 89. Gremlins 2: The New Batch 90. The Russia House 90. Total Recall 90. Sleeping with the Enemy 90. Not without My Daughter 91. Medicine Man 92. Basic Instinct 92. Matinee 93. The Vanishing 93. Dennis the Menace (GB: Dennis) 93. Rudy 93. Malice 93. Six Degrees of Separation 93. Angie 94. Bad Girls 94. The River Wild 94, etc.
TV series: Twilight Zone. Dr Kildare. The Man from UNCLE. The Waltons, etc.

Goldstein, Robert (1903–1974).
American producer, with Twentieth Century-Fox for many years.

Goldstone, James (1931–).
American director, from TV.
■ The Inheritors (TV) 64. Scalplock (TV) 66. Ironside (TV pilot) 67. Jigsaw (TV) 68. Shadow Over Elveron (TV) 68. A Clear and Present Danger (TV) 69. A Man Called Gannon 69. Winning 69. Brother John 70. Red Sky at Morning 71. The Gang that Couldn't Shoot Straight 72. They Only Kill Their Masters 72. Cry Panic (TV) 74. Dr Max (TV) 74. Things in Their Season (TV) 74. Eric (TV) 75. Journey from Darkness (TV) 75. Swashbuckler 76. Rollercoaster 77. When Time Ran Out 80.

Goldstone, Richard (1912–).
American producer.
The Outriders 50. Inside Straight 51. The Tall Target 51. The Devil Makes Three 52. Cinerama's

South Seas Adventure 58. No Man Is an Island (&
wd) 62. The Sergeant 68, etc.

Goldthwait, Bobcat (1962–).
Manic American comedian and actor.
Police Academy 2: Their First Assignment 85.
Police Academy 3: Back in Training 86. One Crazy
Summer 86. Burglar 87. An Evening with Bob
Goldthwait: Share the Warmth (concert) 87. Police
Academy 4: Citizens on Patrol 87. Hot to Trot 88.
Scrooged 88. Little Vegas 90. Shakes the Clown
(& wd) 92, etc.

Goldwyn, Samuel (1882–1974) (Samuel Goldfish).
Polish-American producer, in Hollywood from
1910. Co-produced *The Squaw Man* (1913); a top
producer ever after, with a high reputation for
star-making; he always refused to make any but
family films.
Biographies: 1937, *The Great Goldwyn* by Alva
Johnston. 1976, *Samuel Goldwyn Presents* by Alvin
H. Marill. 1976, *Goldwyn* by Arthur Marx.
■ FILMS SINCE SOUND: *Bulldog Drummond* 29.
Condemned 29. Raffles 30. One Heavenly Night 30. The Devil To Pay 30. Street
Scene 31. The Unholy Garden 31. Tonight or Never
31. *Arrowsmith* 31. The Greeks Had a Word for
Them 32. Cynara 32. The Kid from Spain 32. The
Masquerader 33. *Roman Scandals* 33. Nana 34. We
Live Again 34. Kid Millions 34. The Wedding
Night 35. The Dark Angel 35. Barbary Coast 35.
Splendor 35. Strike Me Pink 36. These Three 36.
Dodsworth 36. Come and Get It 36. Beloved Enemy
36. Woman Chases Man 37. *Hurricane* 37. Stella
Dallas 37. *Dead End* 37. The Adventures of Marco
Polo 38. The Goldwyn Follies 38. The Cowboy and
the Lady 38. The Real Glory 39. *Wuthering Heights*
39. They Shall Have Music 39. Raffles 40. *The
Westerner* 40. *The Little Foxes* 41. Ball of Fire 41. The
Pride of the Yankees 41. They Got Me Covered
43. North Star 43. Up in Arms 44. The Princess
and the Pirate 44. Wonder Man 45. The Kid from
Brooklyn 46. *The Best Years of Our Lives* 46. The
Secret Life of Walter Mitty 47. The Bishop's Wife
47. A Song Is Born 48. Enchantment 48. Roseanna
McCoy 49. My Foolish Heart 49. Our Very Own
50. Edge of Doom 50. I Want You 51. Hans
Christian Andersen 52. Guys and Dolls 55. Porgy
and Bess 59.
☉ For giving the appearance of culture and
refinement while keeping his standards modest
though irreproachable. *Wuthering Heights.*

¶ He was the archetypal movie mogul: the glove
salesman from Minsk who became more
American than apple pie and founded his credo
on the family audience. His maxims included:
Motion pictures should never embarrass a man
when he brings his wife to the theatre,
and:
I seriously object to seeing on the screen what
belongs in the bedroom.
He was proud of his art:
The picture makers will inherit the earth.
As an executive, he certainly knew his own mind:
A producer shouldn't get ulcers: he should give
them,
and:
I was always an independent, even when I had
partners,
and:
In this business it's dog eat dog, and nobody's
going to eat me.
He was a great showman:
What we want is a story that starts with an
earthquake and works its way up to a climax . . .
But his logic was all his own:
I don't care if it doesn't make a nickel. I just

want every man, woman and child in America
to see it!
That was about *The Best Years of Our Lives*. He
disdained subtlety. When a harassed publicist
devised a campaign that began:
The directing skill of Rouben Mamoulian, the
radiance of Anna Sten and the genius of
Samuel Goldwyn have combined to bring you
the world's greatest entertainment . . .
Goldwyn nodded approval:
That's the kind of advertising I like. Just the
facts. No exaggeration . . .
He is said to have telegraphed Eisenstein as
follows:
Have seen your picture (*The Battleship Potemkin*)
and enjoyed it very much. Should like you to
do something of the same kind, but cheaper, for
Ronald Colman.
With this kind of gall, it is not surprising that
intellectuals like Robert Sherwood continued to
relish his company:
I find I can live with Sam just as one lives with
high blood pressure.
Did he really coin all the famous Goldwynisms
which have filled so many books? Not all of them,
perhaps. One doubts the authenticity of:
Directors are always biting the hand that lays
the golden egg,
and:
In two words: im-possible,
and:
Tell me, how did you love the picture?
and:
We have all passed a lot of water since then.
But I imagine Goldwyn probably did say, rather
wittily:
Gentlemen, kindly include me out,
and:
Let's bring it up to date with some snappy
nineteenth-century dialogue,
and:
Anyone who goes to a psychiatrist should have
his head examined,
and:
I had a great idea this morning, but I didn't like
it,
and:
A verbal contract isn't worth the paper it's
written on.
His film appreciation was untutored but vivid, like
his speaking style:
When everybody's happy with the rushes, the
picture's always a stinker,
he once said; and he can't have been alone among
Hollywood producers in vowing:
I'd hire the devil himself if he'd write me a good
story.
Lindsay Anderson summed him up in 1974:
There are lucky ones whose great hearts,
shallow and commonplace as bedpans, beat in
instinctive tune with the great heart of the
public, who laugh as it likes to laugh, weep the
sweet and easy tears it likes to weep . . .
Goldwyn is blessed with that divine confidence
in the rightness (moral, aesthetic, commercial)
of his own intuition – and that I suppose is the
chief reason for his success.
Goldwyn had in fact summed up himself rather
nicely:
I am a rebel. I make a picture to please me. If it
pleases me, there is a chance it will please
others. But it has to please me first.
And his son Samuel Goldwyn Jnr was taught the
value of his legacy:
With every picture he made, my father raised
the money, paid back the bank, and kept
control of the negative. He said, you be
careful of these films: some people will tell you

they're not worth anything, but don't you
believe it.

Goldwyn, Samuel, Jnr (1926–).
American producer, son of Samuel Goldwyn.
The Man with the Gun 55. Sharkfighters 56. The
Proud Rebel 58. Huckleberry Finn 60. The Young
Lovers (& d) 65. Cotton Comes to Harlem 70.
Come Back Charleston Blue 72. The Golden Seal
83. A Prayer for the Dying 87. Mystic Pizza 88, etc.

Goldwyn, Tony (1960–).
American actor, the son of producer Samuel
Goldwyn Jnr.
Gaby – a True Story 87. Ghost 90. Traces of Red
92. The Pelican Brief 93. Doomsday Gun (TV) 94,
etc.

The Golem.
This legend of a clay monster being brought to life
by a rabbi to save persecuted Jews was first filmed
in 1914; a classic version followed in 1920, written
and directed by Henrik Galeen and Paul Wegener,
who also played the Golem. Brilliant Grimm-like
medieval sets, photographed by Karl Freund, make
the second part of the film still fresh and both in
detail and general development it was closely
copied in *Frankenstein* 31. The story was remade
in France in 1936 (with Harry Baur) and in
Czechoslovakia in 1953, and in 1922 a British film
called *It* borrowed the idea.

Golino, Valeria (1966–).
Italian leading actress, also in international films.
Blind Date 84. My Dearest Son (Figlio Mio
Infinamente Caro) 85. Dumb Dicks (Asilo di Polizia)
86. Love Story (Storia d'Amore) 86. Big Top Pee-
Wee 88. Rain Man 88. Torrents of Spring 89. The
King's Whore 90. Three Sisters (Paura e Amore)
90. Hot Shots! 91. The Indian Runner 91. Year of
the Gun 91. Tracce di Vita Amorosa 91. Hot Shots!
Part Deux 93. Clean Slate 94. Come Due
Coccodrilli 94. Immortal Beloved 94, etc.

Golitzen, Alexander (1907–).
Russian-born production designer, in Hollywood
from the mid-30s, who spent most of his career
at Universal Studios.
The Call of the Wild 35. Foreign Correspondent
(AAN) 40. Sundown (AAN) 41. Arabian Nights
(AAN) 42. The Phantom of the Opera (AA) 43.
The Climax (AAN) 44. Letter from an Unknown
Woman 48. Seminole 53. The Glenn Miller Story
54. The Far Country 55. The Incredible Shrinking
Man 57. A Time to Love and a Time to Die 58.
Imitation of Life 59. Spartacus (AA) 60. Flower
Drum Song (AAN) 61. That Touch of Mink (AAN)
62. To Kill a Mockingbird (AA) 62. Gambit (AAN)
66. Coogan's Bluff 68. Sweet Charity (AAN) 69.
Airport (AAN) 70. Play Misty for Me 71.
Earthquake (AAN) 74, many others.

Gombell, Minna (1900–1973) (also known as
Winifred Lee and Nancy Carter).
American character actress of the 30s and 40s,
usually in hard-boiled roles.
Doctors' Wives (debut) 31. The Thin Man 34.
Babbitt 35. Banjo on My Knee 37. The Great Waltz
38. The Hunchback of Notre Dame 39. Boom Town
40. A Chip Off the Old Block 44. Man Alive 46.
Pagan Love Song 51. I'll See You in My Dreams
52, etc.

Gomez, Nick (1963–).
American director, a former editor and musician.
Trust (e) 90. Laws of Gravity (d) 92.

Gomez, Thomas (1905–1971).
Bulky American stage character actor who became
a familiar villain or detective in Hollywood films.
■ Sherlock Holmes and the Voice of Terror 42.
Arabian Nights 42. Pittsburgh 42. Who Done It 42.
White Savage 43. Corvette K 225 43. Frontier
Badmen 43. Crazy House 43. The Climax 44.
Phantom Lady 44. Dead Man's Eyes 44. Follow
the Boys 44. In Society 44. Bowery to Broadway
44. Can't Help Singing 45. Patrick the Great 45.
I'll Tell the World 45. The Daltons Ride Again 45.
Frisco Sal 45. A Night in Paradise 45. Swell Guy
46. *The Dark Mirror* 46. Singapore 47. *Ride the Pink
Horse* (AAN) 47. Captain from Castile 47. Johnny
O'Clock 47. Casbah 48. Angel in Exile 48. Key Largo
48. *Force of Evil* 48. Come to the Stable 49.
Sorrowful Jones 49. That Midnight Kiss 49. The
Woman on Pier 13 49. Kim 50. The Toast of New
Orleans 50. The Eagle and the Hawk 50. The
Furies 50. Anne of the Indies 51. The Harlem
Globetrotters 51. The Sellout 51. The Merry Widow
52. Macao 52. Pony Soldier 52. Sombrero 53. The
Gambler from Natchez 54. The Adventures of
Haiiji Baba 54. The Looters 55. The Magnificent
Matador 55. Las Vegas Shakedown 55. Night
Freight 55. Trapeze 56. The Conqueror 56. John
Paul Jones 59. But Not for Me 59. Summer and
Smoke 61. Stay Away Joe 68. Beneath the Planet
of the Apes 70.
   TV series: Life with Luigi 52.

Gonzalez, Myrtle (1891–1918).
American star of Vitagraph silents. Died of
pneumonia.
   The Spell 13. The Ebony Casket 15. The Secret
of the Swamp 16. The End of the Rainbow 16.
Captain Alvarez 17. Mutiny 17, etc.

The Good Companions.
J. B. Priestley's sprawling comic novel of English
life was filmed by Victor Saville in rather primitive
style in 1932, but its very naiveté remains
infectious, and there are attractive performances by
Edmund Gwenn, Jessie Matthews, Max Miller and
others. It was remade in 1957 by J. Lee-
Thompson, with Eric Portman and Janette Scott,
with only fair success. A nine-hour TV version with
music in 1980 missed the bus at every stop.

Goodbye Mr Chips.
This sentimental biography of a schoolmaster,
from James Hilton's novel, was a highly
successful product of MGM's short-lived British
studio under Michael Balcon (1937–39), directed
by Sam Wood and enhanced by a brilliant
performance from Robert Donat (AA). It was
remade in 1969 as an overlong and lifeless semi-
musical starring Peter O'Toole (AAN), directed by
Herbert Ross; and in 1983 as a six-part BBC TV
serial, with Roy Marsden.

Gooding, Cuba, Jnr.
American actor.
   Boyz N The Hood 91. Gladiator 92. Judgment
Night 93. Lightning Jack 94. Outbreak 95, etc.

Goodliffe, Michael (1914–1976).
British stage actor often cast as officer, professional
man or diplomat.
   The Small Back Room (debut) 48. The Wooden
Horse 50. Rob Roy 53. The Adventures of Quentin
Durward 55. The Battle of the River Plate 56. A
Night To Remember 58. Sink the Bismarck 60.
The Trials of Oscar Wilde 60. Jigsaw 62. The
Seventh Dawn 64. The Man with the Golden Gun
73, many others.
   TV series: Sam 73–75.

Goodman, Benny (1909–1986).
American clarinettist and bandleader, the 'King of
Swing'.
   Hollywood Hotel 38. Hello Beautiful 42. The
Gang's All Here 44. Sweet and Lowdown 44. A Song
Is Born 48, etc.
   Provided the music for The Benny Goodman
Story 55, in which he was portrayed by Steve
Allen.

Goodman, David Zelag.
American screenwriter.
   Lovers and Other Strangers (AAN) 69. Monte
Walsh 70. Straw Dogs 71. Man on a Swing 73.
Farewell My Lovely 74. Logan's Run 76. March or
Die 77. The Eyes of Laura Mars 78. Freedom Road
(TV) 79. Fighting Back 82. Man, Woman and Child
83. Sheena 84, etc.

Goodman, John (1952–).
Heavyweight American actor, often in comic roles,
from the stage.
   Eddie Macon's Run 83. The Survivors 83.
C. H. U. D. 84. Revenge of the Nerds 84. Maria's
Lovers 85. Sweet Dreams 85. The Big Easy 86. True
Stories 86. Burglar 87. Raising Arizona 87.
Punchline 88. Everybody's All-American 88. The
Wrong Guys 88. Sea of Love 89. Always 89.
Arachnophobia 90. Stella 90. King Ralph 91.
Barton Fink 91. The Babe 92. Born Yesterday 92.
Matinee 93. Born Yesterday 93. We're Back! A
Dinosaur's Story (voice) 93. The Flintstones 94,
etc.
   TV series: Roseanne 88– .

¶ I'm not a major player. I just turn up and do
my job. – *J.G.*

Goodman, Miles.
American composer.
   Skatetown USA 79. The Man Who Wasn't There
83. Table for Five (co-w) 83. Footloose 84. Teen
Wolf 85. La Bamba (co-m) 86. Real Men 87. Like
Father Like Son 87. Dirty Rotten Scoundrels 88.
Vital Signs 90. Opportunity Knocks 90. Funny
about Love 90. Problem Child 90. The Super 91.
What about Bob? 91. He Said, She Said 91.
Housesitter 92. Blankman 94. Getting Even with
Dad 94, etc.

Goodrich, Frances (1891–1984).
American screenwriter, almost always in
collaboration with her husband Albert Hackett.
   The Secret of Madame Blanche 33. *The Thin Man*
(AAN) 34. Ah Wilderness 35. Naughty Marietta 35.
After the Thin Man (AAN) 36. Another Thin Man
39. The Hitler Gang 44. Lady in the Dark 44. *It's
a Wonderful Life* (AAN) 46. The Pirate 48. Summer Holiday
48. Easter Parade 49. *Father-of the Bride* (AAN) 50.
Father's Little Dividend 51. The Long Long Trailer
54. Seven Brides for Seven Brothers (AAN) 55. The
Diary of Anne Frank 60. Five Finger Exercise 62,
etc.

Goodwin, Bill (1910–1958).
American character actor, usually of genial type in
routine films.
   Wake Island 42. So Proudly We Hail 43. Bathing
Beauty 44. Spellbound 45. House of Horrors 46.
The Jolson Story 46. Heaven Only Knows 47. Jolson
Sings Again 49. Tea for Two 50. The Atomic Kid
54. The Big Heat 54. The Opposite Sex 56, etc.

Goodwin, Harold (1917–).
British character actor usually seen as cockney
serviceman or small-time crook.
   Dance Hall 50. The Card 52. The Cruel Sea 53.
The Dam Busters 55. Sea of Sand 58. The Mummy

59. The Bulldog Breed 61. The Comedy Man 63.
The Curse of the Mummy's Tomb 64. Frankenstein
Must Be Destroyed 69, many others.

Goodwin, Ron (1929–).
British composer.
   I'm All Right Jack 59. The Trials of Oscar Wilde
60. Postman's Knock 62. Murder She Said 62.
Lancelot and Guinevere 63. 633 Squadron 64.
Operation Crossbow 65. Those Magnificent Men
in Their Flying Machines 65. The Alphabet
Murders 65. Where Eagles Dare 68. Battle of
Britain 70. Frenzy 72. The Happy Prince 74. One
of Our Dinosaurs Is Missing 75. Candleshoe 77.
Force Ten from Navarone 78. Unidentified Flying
Oddball 79. Clash of Loyalties 83. Valhalla 85, etc.

Goodwins, Leslie (1899–1969).
British-born director, in Hollywood for many
years. Films mainly routine second features.
   'Mexican Spitfire' series 39–44.
   Glamour Boy 39. Pop Always Pays 40. Silver
Skates 43. Murder in the Blue Room 44. What a
Blonde 45. The Mummy's Curse 46. Gold Fever
52. Fireman Save My Child 54. Paris Follies of
1956 56.

Goofy.
Dim-witted, optimistic, enthusiastic dog created by
Walt Disney's animators in the 30s, with Art Babbitt
contributing most to the development of his
character. For much of his career, his voice was
supplied by Pinto Colvig.
   Goofy and Wilbur 39. The Art of Skiing 41. How
to Swim 42. How to Play Football (AAN) 44.
Hockey Homicide 45. Foul Hunting 47. Goofy
Gymnastics 47. How to Ride a Horse 50. Two-Gun
Goofy 52. How to Sleep 53. Aquamania 61.
Goofy's Freeway Trouble 65, etc.

Goolden, Richard (1895–1981).
British character actor, on stage and screen for
many years, usually in henpecked or bewildered
roles; created the radio character of Old Ebenezer
the night watchman.
   Whom the Gods Love 38. Meet Mr Penny 38.
Mistaken Identity 43, etc.

Goorwitz, Allen:
see *Garfield, Allen.*

Gorcey, Bernard (1888–1955).
American character actor and ex-vaudevillian,
father of Leo Gorcey, with whom he often appeared
in the Bowery Boys series.
   Abie's Irish Rose 28. The Great Dictator 40. Out
of the Fog 41. No Minor Vices 49. Pick-Up 51,
many others.

Gorcey, Leo (1915–1969).
Pint-sized American second feature star, one of the
original Dead End Kids; his screen personality was
that of a tough, fast-talking, basically kindly
Brooklyn layabout, and he developed this in scores
of routine films, mostly under the Bowery Boys
banner.
   Dead End 37. Mannequin 38. Crime School 38.
Angels With Dirty Faces 38. Hell's Kitchen 39. Angels
Wash Their Faces 39. Invisible Stripes 40. Pride of
the Bowery 40. Spooks Run Wild 41. Mr Wise
Guy 42. Destroyer 43. Midnight Manhunt 45.
Bowery Bombshell 46. Spook Busters 46. Hard
Boiled Mahoney 47. Jinx Money 48. Angels in
Disguise 49. Lucky Losers 50. Crazy over Horses
51. No Holds Barred 52. Loose in London 52. The
Bowery Boys Meet the Monsters 54. Bowery to
Bagdad 55. Crashing Las Vegas 56. The Phynx 69,
many others.

Gordon, Bert (1898–1974).
American radio comedian. Known as The Mad
Russian, he made a few films in the 40s.

Gordon, Bert I. (1922–).
American producer-director of small independent
horror exploitation films.
　The Beginning of the End 57. The Amazing
Colossal Man 57. Cyclops 57. The Boy and the
Pirates 60. The Magic Sword 62. Picture Mommy
Dead 66. How to Succeed with Sex (wd only) 69.
Necromancy (pd) 73. The Mad Bomber 75. Food
of the Gods 76. Empire of the Ants 77. The
Coming 81. Doing It 84. The Big Bet 86.
Malediction 89. Satan's Princess 90, etc.

Gordon, Bruce (1919–).
American character actor, invariably a heavy.
　Love Happy 50. The Buccaneer 58. Rider on a
Dead Horse 61. Slow Run 68, etc.
　TV series: *The Untouchables* (as Frank Nitti) 59–
62. Run Buddy Run 66.

Gordon, C. Henry (1882–1940).
American character actor, often seen as maniacally
evil villain or Indian rajah.
　Charlie Chan Carries On 31. Rasputin and the
Empress 32. Mata Hari 32. Lives of a Bengal
Lancer 35. The Charge of the Light Brigade 36. The
Return of the Cisco Kid 38. Kit Carson 40. Charlie
Chan at the Wax Museum 40, etc.

Gordon, Colin (1911–1972).
British light comedy actor, on stage from 1931;
often seen as mildly cynical civil servant or
schoolmaster.
　Bond Street 47. The Winslow Boy 48. The Man
in the White Suit 51. *Folly to Be Wise* 52. Escapade
55. The Safecracker 58. Please Turn Over 59. Night
of the Eagle 62. The Pink Panther 63. The Family
Way 66. Casino Royale 67, many others.

Gordon, Dexter (1923–1990).
Hard-blowing jazz tenor saxophonist and
occasional actor. He played a musician somewhat
like himself (though actually based on pianist Bud
Powell) in *Round Midnight*. In *Unchained*, his music
was dubbed by saxophonist Georgie Auld.
　Unchained 55 (a). Round Midnight (AAN) (a,
m) 86. Awakenings (a) 91.

Gordon, Gale (1905–) (Gaylord Aldrich).
Plump, fussy American comedy actor, best known
on TV.
　Here We Go Again 42. A Woman of Distinction
50. Don't Give Up the Ship 59. Visit to a Small
Planet 60. Sergeant Deadhead 65. Speedway 68.
The 'burbs 89, etc.
　TV series: My Favorite Husband 53–54. Our
Miss Brooks 52–56. The Brothers 57. Dennis the
Menace 59–63. *The Lucy Show* 62–68. Life with
Lucy 86.

Gordon, Gavin (1906–1970).
American general-purpose actor.
　Romance (lead) 30. The Bitter Tea of General
Yen 32. The Scarlet Empress 34. Bride of
Frankenstein 35. Windjammer 38. Paper Bullets
41. Centennial Summer 46. Knock on Wood 54.
The Bat 59, etc.

Gordon, Hal (1894–1946).
Hearty British comedy actor, often seen as good-
natured foil to star comedian.
　Adam's Apple 31. Happy 34. Captain Bill 36.
Keep Fit 37. It's in the Air 38. Old Mother Riley,
Detective 43. Give Me the Stars 45 (last
appearance), etc.

Gordon, Keith (1961–).
American actor, screenwriter, producer and
director.
AS ACTOR: Home Movies 79. All That Jazz 79.
Dressed to Kill 80. Kent State (TV) 81. Silent
Rebellion 82. Single Bars, Single Women (TV) 84.
Static (& co-w, p) 89. Christine 84. Legend of Billie
Jean 85. Combat Academy 86. Back to School 86.
AS DIRECTOR: The Chocolate War (wd) 88. A
Midnight Clear (wd) 92. Wild Palms (TV) (co-d)
93, etc.

Gordon, Lawrence (1934–).
American producer who veers between films and
television (where he was the original producer of
Burke's Law).
　Dillinger 73. Hard Times 75. Rolling Thunder 77.
Hooper 78. The Driver 78. The End 78. The
Warriors 79. Xanadu 80. Paternity 81. 48 Hours
82. Streets of Fire 84. Brewster's Millions 85.
Predator 87. Die Hard 88. Field of Dreams 89. Die
Hard II 90. Predator 2 90. The Rocketeer 91, etc.

Gordon, Leo (1922–).
Thick-set American character actor, usually in
tough-guy roles.
　China Venture 53. Riot in Cell Block 11 53.
Seven Angry Men 55. The Conqueror 55. The Man
Who Knew Too Much 56. Cry Baby Killer (& w)
57. The Big Operator 59. The Stranger 62. The
Terror (& w) 63. The Haunted Palace 64. Beau
Geste 66. Tobruk (& w) 66. The St Valentine's Day
Massacre 67. You Can't Win 'Em All 71. Rage 80.
Bog 84, etc.
　TV series: Enos 81.

Gordon, Mack (1904–1959).
American lyricist.
　Tin Pan Alley 40. Lillian Russell 40. Sun Valley
Serenade ('Chattanooga Choo Choo') 41.
Orchestra Wives ('Kalamazoo') 42. Mother Wore
Tights 47. Wabash Avenue 50, etc.

Gordon, Mary (1882–1963).
Tiny Scottish character actress in Hollywood; best
remembered as the perfect Mrs Hudson in many a
Sherlock Holmes film.
　The Home Maker 25. The Black Camel 31. The
Little Minister 34. The Bride of Frankenstein 35.
The Plough and the Stars 36. Kidnapped 38. The
Hound of the Baskervilles 39. Tear Gas Squad 40.
Appointment for Love 41. The Mummy's Tomb
42. Sherlock Holmes Faces Death 43. The Woman
in Green 45. Little Giant 46. The Invisible Wall 47,
many others.

Gordon, Michael (1909–1993).
American director with stage experience.
■ Boston Blackie Goes to Hollywood 42.
Underground Agent 42. One Dangerous Night 43.
Crime Doctor 43. *The Web* 47. Another Part of the
Forest 48. An Act of Murder 48. The Lady
Gambles 49. Woman in Hiding 49. Cyrano de
Bergerac 50. I Can Get It for You Wholesale 51.
The Secret of Convict Lake 51. Wherever She Goes
53. *Pillow Talk* 59. Portrait in Black 60. Boys' Night
Out 62. For Love of Money 63. Move Over Darling
63. A Very Special Favor 65. Texas across the
River 66. The Impossible Years 68. How Do I Love
Thee? 70.

Gordon, Richard (1921–) (Gordon Ostlere).
British comic novelist whose accounts of hospital
life were a staple of British comedy in the 50s and
60s and gave rise to the TV series *Doctor in the House*
70–73. The films were all directed by Ralph
Thomas and the first established Dirk Bogarde as
Britain's most popular actor.

Doctor in the House 54. Doctor at Sea 55. Doctor
at Large 57. Doctor in Love 60. Doctor in Distress
63. Doctor in Clover 66. Doctor in Trouble 70.

Gordon, Ruth (1896–1985) (Ruth Gordon Jones).
Distinguished American stage actress who wrote
several screenplays with her husband Garson
Kanin, saw two of her own plays filmed, and had
a long, sporadic career as film actress.
■ AS WRITER: Over 21 (oa/solo) 45. *A Double Life*
48. *Adam's Rib* (AAN) 49. The Marrying Kind 51.
Pat and Mike (AAN) 52. The Actress (oa/solo) 53.
Rosie (oa/solo) 58.
■ AS ACTRESS: Camille 15. The Wheel of Life 16.
Abe Lincoln in Illinois 40. Dr Ehrlich's Magic Bullet
40. Two Faced Woman 41. Edge of Darkness 43.
Action in the North Atlantic 43. Inside Daisy Clover
(AAN) 66. Lord Love a Duck 66. *Rosemary's Baby*
(AA) 68. Whatever Happened to Aunt Alice? 69.
Where's Poppa? 70. *Harold and Maude* 72. Isn't It
Shocking? (TV) 73. Panic 75. The Big Bus 76. The
Great Houdinis (TV) 76. Look What Happened to
Rosemary's Baby (TV) 76. Prince of Central Park
(TV) 77. Boardwalk 78. Perfect Gentlemen (TV)
78. *Every Which Way but Loose* 78. My Bodyguard
80. Any Which Way You Can 80. Don't Go to Sleep
(TV) 83. Jimmy the Kid 83. Maxie 85. Delta Pi
85.

Gordon, Steve (1938–1982).
American writer-director.
　The One and Only (co-p, w) 78. Arthur (wd)
80.

Gordon, Stuart (1947–).
American director and screenwriter of horror
films, from the theatre.
　Re-Animator 85. From Beyond 86. Dolls 87.
Daughter of Darkness (TV) 89. Robojox (aka
Robot Jox) 89. Honey, I Shrunk the Kids (co-w)
89. The Pit and the Pendulum 90. Body Snatchers
(w) 92. Chicago Cops 92. Fortress 92. Honey, I
Blew Up the Kid (p) 92. Fortress 93. Body Snatchers
(co-w) 93, etc.

¶ One of the great things about genre movies is
that as long as you follow the rules of the genre
you can do anything you want and say anything
you want. There's a tremendous amount of
freedom. – *S.G.*
　Horror films are really the subconscious of the
movies. – *S.G.*

Gordon-Sinclair, John (1962–).
Scottish actor, a former electrician, who starred in
Bill Forsyth's comedy *Gregory's Girl*.
　That Sinking Feeling 79. *Gregory's Girl* 80.
Britannia Hospital 82. Local Hero 83. The Girl in
the Picture 86. Erik the Viking 89, etc.
　TV series: Hot Metal 86–88. Nelson's Column 94.

Gore, Michael.
American composer.
　Fame (AA) 80. Terms of Endearment (AAN) 83.
Pretty in Pink 86. Don't Tell Her It's Me 90. The
Butcher's Wife 91. Defending Your Life 91, etc.

Goretta, Claude (1929–).
Swiss director.
　The Invitation 73. *The Lacemaker* 77. La
Provenciale (A Girl from Lorraine) 80. La Morte de
Mario Ricci 82. Si le Soleil ne Revenait pas 87. Le
Rapport du Gendarme (TV) 87. Guillaume T – la
Fouine 92, etc.

Goring, Marius (1912–).
British stage and screen actor adept at neurotic or
fey roles.

Consider Your Verdict (debut) 36. Rembrandt 37. *The Case of the Frightened Lady* 38. *A Matter of Life and Death* 45. The Red Shoes 48. Mr Perrin and Mr Traill 49. So Little Time 52. *Ill Met by Moonlight* 57. Exodus 60. The Inspector (Lisa) 62. Up From the Beach 65. Girl on a Motorcycle 68. Subterfuge 69. First Love 70. Zeppelin 71. Holocaust (TV) 78. Strike It Rich 89, etc.

TV series: The Scarlet Pimpernel 54. The Expert 68–70, 74.

Gorky, Maxim (1868–1936) (Alexei Maximovitch Peshkov).
Russian writer whose autobiography was filmed by Donskoi as *The Childhood of Maxim Gorky*, *Out in the World* and *My Universities*. Other filmed works include *The Lower Depths* (many times) and *The Mother*.

Gorman, Cliff (1936–).
American leading man of the 70s.
Justine 69. The Boys in the Band 70. Cops and Robbers 73. Rosebud 75. An Unmarried Woman 78. All That Jazz 79. Night of the Juggler 80. Angel 84, etc.

Gorney, Karen Lynn (1945–).
American leading lady who was top-billed with Travolta in *Saturday Night Fever* 77.

Gorris, Marleen (1948–).
Dutch director and screenwriter of features with a feminist slant.
A Question of Silence (De Stilte Rond Christine M) 81. Broken Mirrors (Gebrokene Spiegels) 84. The Last Island 91.

Gorshin, Frank (1933–).
Wiry American impressionist and character actor, popular as 'The Riddler' in TV's *Batman* series.
The True Story of Jesse James 57. Warlock 59. Studs Lonigan 60. Ring of Fire 61. The George Raft Story 61. Batman 66. Sky Heist (TV) 75. Underground Aces 81. Hot Resort 85. Hollywood Vice Squad 86. Upper Crust 88. Midnight 89. Sweet Justice 92. The Meteor Man 93, etc.

Gortner, Marjoe (1944–).
American evangelist turned actor (following a 1972 documentary on his life called *Marjoe*).
■ The Marcus Nelson Murders (TV) 73. Earthquake 74. The Gun and the Pulpit (TV) 74. Food of the Gods 76. Bobbie Joe and the Outlaw 76. Sidewinder One 77. Viva Knievel 77. Acapulco Gold 78. Starcrash 79. When You Comin' Back Red Ryder 79. Hellhole 85. American Ninja III 89. Fire, Ice and Dynamite 91. Wild Bill 95.
TV series: Falcon Crest 86–87.

Gorton, Assheton.
British production designer.
The Knack . . . and How to Get It 65. Blow Up 66. The Bed Sitting Room 69. Get Carter 71. The French Lieutenant's Woman (AAN) 81. Legend 85. Lost Angels 89. For the Boys 91. Rob Roy 95, etc.

Gosho, Heinosuke (1901–1981).
Japanese director, best known for *Four Chimneys* 52. *Adolescence* 55. *When a Woman Loves* 59.

Gossett, Lou (1936–) (aka Louis Gossett Jnr).
American character actor of striking presence.
Companions in Nightmare (TV) 68. The Landlord 70. The River Niger 72. It's Good to Be Alive (TV) 74. Sidekicks (TV) 74. Delancey Street (TV) 75. Roots (TV) 77. The Choirboys (TV) 77. The Deep (TV) 77. Little Ladies of the Night (TV) 78. To Kill a Cop (TV) 78. The Critical List (TV)

78. *The Lazarus Syndrome* (TV) (and series) 79. Backstairs at the White House (TV) 79. This Man Stands Alone (TV) 79. Don't Look Back (TV) 81. *An Officer and a Gentleman* (AA) 82. Sadat (TV) 83. Jaws 3-D 83. Finders Keepers 84. Enemy Mine 85. Iron Eagle 85. Firewalker 86. The Principal 87. Iron Eagle II 88. The Punisher 89. Cover Up 90. Toy Soldiers 91. Keeper of the City 91. Diggstown (GB: Midnight Sting) 92. Monolith 93. Blue Chips 94. Flashfire 94. Ray Alexander: A Taste for Justice (& p) (TV) 94. A Good Man in Africa 94. Curse of the Starving Class 94, etc.
TV series: The Powers of Matthew Starr 82.

Gotell, Walter (1924–).
British character actor, often as Nazi or KGB menace.
Treasure of San Teresa 59. The Guns of Navarone 61. The Damned 61. Our Miss Fred 72. The Spy Who Loved Me 77. The Boys from Brazil 78. For Your Eyes Only 80. Basic Training 86, etc.

Gottlieb, Carl (1938–).
American screenwriter, with TV comedy experience.
Jaws 75. Which Way Is Up 77. Jaws 2 78. The Jerk 79. Caveman (& d) 81. Doctor Detroit 83. Jaws 3-D 83, etc.

Gottschalk, Ferdinand (1869–1944).
Bald-domed English character actor in Hollywood.
Zaza 26. Grand Hotel 32. The Sign of the Cross 32. Les Misérables 35. The Garden of Allah 36, many others.

Goudal, Jetta (1898–1985).
French leading lady of American silent films.
The Bright Shawl 24. Open All Night 24. Spanish Love 25. Road to Yesterday 25. The Coming of Amos 25. 3 Faces East 26. White Gold 27. Forbidden Woman 28. Her Cardboard Lover 28. Lady of the Pavements 30. Business and Pleasure 32, etc.

Gough, Michael (1917–).
Tall British stage (since 1936) and screen (since 1946) actor; has recently gone in for homicidal roles.
Blanche Fury (debut) 46. The Small Back Room 48. The Man in the White Suit 51. Richard III 56. Dracula 57. Horrors of the Black Museum 58. The Horse's Mouth 59. Konga 61. Black Zoo 63. Dr Terror's House of Horrors 65. Circus of Blood 67. Trog 70. The Corpse 70. The Go-Between 70. Henry VIII and His Six Wives 72. Horror Hospital 73. The Boys from Brazil 78. Suez 1956 (TV) (as Anthony Eden) 79. The Dresser 83. Memed My Hawk 83. Out of Africa 85. Let Him Have It 91. Batman Returns 92. Wittgenstein 93. The Age of Innocence 93. The Hour of the Pig 93. Nostradamus 94. Uncovered 94, many others.

Gould, Elliott (1938–) (Elliot Goldstein).
American actor whose very unhandsomeness made him the man for the early 70s.
■ The Confession 66. The Night They Raided Minsky's 68. *Bob and Carol and Ted and Alice* (AAN) 69. M*A*S*H 70. Getting Straight 70. Move 70. I Love My Wife 70. The Touch 70. Little Murders 71. The Long Goodbye 72. Busting 73. S.P.Y.S. 74. California Split 74. Who? 74. Nashville 74. Whiffs 76. I Will . . . I Will . . . for Now 76. Harry and Walter Go to New York 76. Mean Johnny Barrows 76. A Bridge Too Far 77. Matilda 78. The Silent Partner 78. Capricorn One 78. Escape to Athena 79. The Lady Vanishes 79. The Muppet Movie 79. Falling in Love Again 80. The Last Flight of Noah's Ark 80. Dirty Tricks 81. The Devil

and Max Devlin 81. Rites of Marriage (TV) 82. The Muppets Take Manhattan 84. The Naked Face 84. Inside Out 86. I Miei Primi Quarant'Anni 87. Der Joker 87. Dangerous Love 88. The Telephone 88. The Lemon Sisters 89. Night Visitor 89. Scandalo Segreto 89. Massacre Play (Gioco al Massacro) 89. Dead Men Don't Die 90. I Won't Disturb You (Tolgo il Disturbo) 91. Bugsy 91. Exchange Lifeguards (Aus.) 93. The Glass Shield 94.
TV series: E. R. 84. Together We Stand 86.

¶ Success didn't change me. I was distorted *before* I became a star. – *E.G.*

Gould, Harold (1923–).
American light character actor, a former drama teacher.
He and She 69. Where Does It Hurt? 71. Love and Death 75. Silent Movie 76. The Big Bus 76. Feather and Father (TV) 77. *Washington: Behind Closed Doors* (TV) 77. The Feather and Father Gang 77. Seems Like Old Times 80. The Man in the Santa Claus Suit (TV) 80. Moviola (TV) 80. The Dream Chasers 84. The Fourth Wise Man 85, etc.
TV series: He & She 67–68. Rhoda 74–78. The Feather and Father Gang 77. Park Place 81. Foot in the Door 83. Under One Roof 85. Singer & Sons 90.

Gould, Jason (1966–).
American actor, the son of Barbra Streisand and Elliott Gould.
The Big Picture 88. Listen to Me 89. The Prince of Tides 91, etc.

Gould, Morton (1913–).
American composer (and conductor).
Delightfully Dangerous 42. Cinerama Holiday 55. Holocaust (TV) 77.

Goulding, Alfred J. (1896–1972).
American director; active with Harold Lloyd in the 20s and later with Laurel and Hardy (*A Chump at Oxford*).

Goulding, Edmund (1891–1959).
British director in Hollywood; a safe handler of the big female stars of the 30s and 40s.
■ Sun Up 25. Sally, Irene and Mary 25. Paris 26. Women Love Diamonds 26. Love 27. *The Trespasser* (& w) 29. The Devil's Holiday (& w) 30. Paramount on Parade (part) 30. Reaching for the Moon (& w) 30. The Night Angel (& w) 31. *Grand Hotel* 32. Blondie of the Follies 32. Riptide 34. The Flame Within (& wp) 35. That Certain Woman (& w) 37. White Banners 38. The Dawn Patrol 38. *Dark Victory* 39. *The Old Maid* 39. We Are Not Alone 39. Till We Meet Again 40. *The Great Lie* 41. Forever and a Day (co-d) 43. The Constant Nymph 43. *Claudia* 43. Of Human Bondage 46. *The Razor's Edge* 46. *Nightmare Alley* 47. Everybody Does It 49. Mister 880 50. We're Not Married 52. Down Among the Sheltering Palms 53. Teenage Rebel 56. Mardi Gras 58.

Goulet, Robert (1933–) (Stanley Applebaum).
Canadian singer and leading man, with experience mainly on TV.
Honeymoon Hotel 63. I'd Rather Be Rich 64. Underground 70. Atlantic City USA 80. Scrooged 88. The Naked Gun 2½: The Smell of Fear 91, etc.
TV series: The Blue Light 64.

governesses
have most frequently been personified by Deborah Kerr: in *The King and I*, *The Innocents*, and *The Chalk Garden*. Julie Andrews runs a close second with *Mary Poppins* and *The Sound of Music*; as does Bette

avis with *All This and Heaven Too* and *The Nanny*. oan Fontaine's contribution to the gallery was *Jane yre*, and Susannah York later followed in her ootsteps.

Gowers, Patrick (1936–). nglish composer.

The Virgin and the Gypsy 70. A Bigger Splash '5. Stevie 78. Smiley's People (TV) 82. Sorrel and on (TV) 86. Whoops Apocalypse 86. The Hound f the Baskervilles (TV) 88, etc.

Gowland, Gibson (1872–1951). nglish character actor in mainly American films.

The Promise 17. Blind Husbands 19. Ladies Must ove 21. Shifting Sands 23. *Greed* 24. The 'hantom of the Opera 25. Don Juan 26. Topsy and va 27. Rose Marie 28. The Mysterious Island 29. he Sea Bat 30. Doomed Battalion 32. SOS Iceberg 3. The Secret of the Loch 34. The Mystery of the Marie Celeste 36. Cotton Queen 37, many others.

Gozzi, Patricia (1950–). rench juvenile actress of the 60s.

Sundays and Cybele 62. Rapture 65, etc.

Grable, Betty (1916–1973). American leading lady who personified the peaches-and-cream appeal which was required in he 40s but which later seemed excessively bland. She performed efficiently in a series of light musicals and dramas, and was the most famous pin-up of World War II.

Let's Go Places 30. New Movietone Follies of 1930 30. Whoopee 30. Kiki 31. Palmy Days 31. The Greeks had a Word for Them 32. The Kid from Spain 32. Child of Manhattan 32. Probation 32. Hold 'Em Jail 32. Cavalcade 33. What Price Innocence 33. Student Tour 34. *The Gay Divorcee* 34. The Nitwits 35. Old Man Rhythm 35. Collegiate 35. Follow the Fleet 36. Pigskin Parade 36. Don't Turn 'Em Loose 36. This Way Please 37. Thrill of a Lifetime 37. College Swing 38. Give Me a Sailor 38. Campus Confessions 38. Man About Town 39. Million Dollar Legs 39. The Day the Bookies Wept 39. *Down Argentine Way* 40. *Tin Pan Alley* 40. *Moon Over Miami* 41. A Yank in the RAF 41. *I Wake Up Screaming* 41. Footlight Serenade 42. Song of the Islands 42. Springtime in the Rockies 42. *Coney Island* 43. Sweet Rosie O'Grady 43. Four Jills in a Jeep 44. Pin Up Girl 44. Diamond Horseshoe 45. The Dolly Sisters 45 The Shocking Miss Pilgrim 47. *Mother Wore Tights* 47. That Lady in Ermine 48. When My Baby Smiles at Me 48. The Beautiful Blonde from Bashful Bend 49. Wabash Avenue 50. My Blue Heaven 50. Call Me Mister 51. Meet Me After the Show 51. The Farmer Takes a Wife 53. *How To Marry A Millionaire* 53. Three for the Show 54. How to be Very Very Popular 55.

There are two reasons why I'm in show business, and I'm standing on both of them. – *B.G.*

I'm strictly an enlisted man's girl. – *B.G.*

There's nothing mysterious about me. – *B.G.*

I don't think Betty would want an Oscar on her mantelpiece. She has every Tom, Dick and Harry at her feet. – *Nunnally Johnson*

Grace, Nickolas (1949–). English character actor, mainly on stage. In films from 1974.

Sleepwalker 75. City of the Dead 78. Europe after the Rain 80. Heat and Dust 83. Salome's Last Dance 87. Just Ask for Diamond (aka Diamond's Edge) 88. Dream Demon 88. Tom and Viv 94, etc.

Grade, Lew (Lord Grade) (c. 1906–) (Lewis Winogradsky).
British impresario, brother of Lord Delfont, long in charge of Associated Television, latterly producing feature films for family audiences.

Autobiography: 1987, *Still Dancing*.

Biographies: 1982, *My Fabulous Brothers* by Rita Grade Freeman. 1984, *The Grades* by Hunter Davies. 1987, *Last of a Kind: The Sinking of Lew Grade* by Quentin Falk and Dominic Prince.

Voyage of the Damned 76. March or Die 77. The Cassandra Crossing 77. The Boys from Brazil 78. Movie Movie 78. Firepower 79. Raise the Titanic 80. *On Golden Pond* 81. The Great Muppet Caper 81. Green Ice 81. The Legend of the Lone Ranger 81. Barbarosa 81. The Salamander 82. Sophie's Choice 82. The Dark Crystal 82, etc.

All my shows are great. Some of them are bad, but they're all great. – *L.G.*

I intend to produce more feature films than any major studio in the world. I am only 68 and just beginning. By the time I am 70, British films will rule the world. – *L.G.*

It would have been cheaper to lower the Atlantic. – *L.G. on Raise the Titanic*

Lew Grade only did what everyone else did before him, which was to lose money on British films. People may not have liked the films he made. But he went out and slogged away and got money for hundreds and thousands of British actors, directors and technicians. I think the man should be applauded for that. – *Michael Winner*

grading:
the laboratory process of matching the density and brightness of each shot to the next.

Graetz, Paul (1901–1966).
Franco-Austrian independent producer.

Le Diable au Corps 46. Monsieur Ripois (Knave of Hearts) 53. Is Paris Burning? 66, etc.

Graham, Morland (1891–1949).
Stocky Scottish character actor, on stage and screen from 20s.

The Scarlet Pimpernel 35. Jamaica Inn 39. Old Bill and Son (as Old Bill) 40. The Ghost Train 41. The Shipbuilders 44. The Brothers 47. Bonnie Prince Charlie 48. Whisky Galore 48, etc.

Graham, Sheilah (1904–1988) (Lilly Shiel).
British gossip columnist in America, companion of F. Scott Fitzgerald. Author of *Beloved Infidel*, *The Garden of Allah*, etc.

Graham, William (c. 1930–).
American director, from TV. (Sometimes billed as William A. Graham.)

The Doomsday Flight (TV) 66. Waterhole Three 67. Then Came Bronson (TV) 68. Submarine X1 68. Change of Habit 69. Thief (TV) 71. *Birds of Prey* (TV) 73. Get Christie Love (TV) 74. Trapped Beneath the Sea (TV) 74. 21 Hours at Munich (TV) 76. *Minstrel Man* (TV) 77. *The Amazing Howard Hughes* (TV) 77. Contract on Cherry Street (TV) 77. And I Alone Survived (TV) 78. Transplant (TV) 79. Guyana Tragedy (TV) 81. Harry Tracy 81. Mothers Against Drunk Drivers (TV) 82. Mussolini: The Untold Story (TV) 85. The Last Days of Frank and Jesse James (TV) 86. Proud Men 87. Street of Dreams 88, etc.

Grahame, Gloria (1924–1981) (Gloria Hallward).
Blonde American leading lady, usually in off-beat roles.

Blonde Fever (debut) 44. Without Love 45. It's a Wonderful Life 46. It Happened in Brooklyn 47. Merton of the Movies 47. Song of the Thin Man 47. *Crossfire* (AAN) 47. Roughshod 48. A Woman's Secret 48. *In a Lonely Place* 50. *The Bad and the Beautiful* (AA) 52. Macao 52. Sudden Fear 52. The Glass Wall 53. Man on a Tightrope 53. Prisoners of the Casbah 53. The Greatest Show on Earth 53. Naked Alibi 54. *The Big Heat* 54. The Good Die Young (GB) 54. Human Desire 55. The Man Who Never Was (GB) 55. Not as a Stranger 55. The Cobweb 55. Oklahoma 56. Ride Out for Revenge 57. Odds Against Tomorrow 59. Ride Beyond Vengeance 66. The Todd Killings 70. Black Noon (TV) 71. Chandler 72. The Loners 72. Blood and Lace 72. Tarot 73. Mama's Dirty Girls 74. The Girl on the Late Late Show (TV) 75. Rich Man Poor Man (TV) 76. Mansion of the Doomed 76. Seventh Avenue (TV) 77. Head Over Heels 79. Melvin and Howard 80. A Nightingale Sang in Berkeley Square 80.

Grahame, Margot (1911–1982).
British leading lady of the 30s, with stage experience.

The Love Habit 30. Rookery Nook 30. Sorrell and Son 34. The Three Musketeers (US) 36. Michael Strogoff (US) 37. The Shipbuilders 44. Broken Journey 48. The Romantic Age 49. Venetian Bird 52. Orders Are Orders 55. Saint Joan 57, etc.

Grainer, Ron (1922–1981).
Australian composer in Britain.

A Kind of Loving 62. Nothing But the Best 64. To Sir with Love 67. Lock Up Your Daughters 68. In Search of Oregon 70. The Omega Man 71. Yellow Dog 73. I Don't Want to Be Born 76, many others.

Grainger, Edmund (1906–1981).
American producer and executive, long with RKO. Specialized in quality action pictures.

Diamond Jim 35. Sutter's Gold 36. International Squadron 41. Wake of the Red Witch 48. Sands of Iwo Jima 49. Flying Leathernecks 50. One Minute to Zero 52. Treasure of Pancho Villa 55. Green Mansions 59. Home from the Hill 60. Cimarron 61, many others.

A Grammar of the Film,
by Raymond Spottiswoode. First published in 1935, this book remains an essential theoretical study of film technique.

Granach, Alexander (1890–1945).
Polish character actor who went to Hollywood in the late 30s.

Biography: 1945, *There Goes an Actor*.

Warning Shadows 23. Kameradschaft 31. Ninotchka 39. Hangmen Also Die 43. For Whom the Bell Tolls 43. The Hitler Gang 44. A Voice in the Wind 44. The Seventh Cross 44, etc.

Grand Hotel.
The Hollywood all-star film *par excellence* and an Oscar-winner as best film of 1932, from Vicki Baum's novel. Directed by Edmund Golding, it allowed effective parts for Garbo, the Barrymore brothers, Joan Crawford, and Wallace Beery. It was remade in 1945 as *Weekend at the Waldorf* with no impact whatsoever. A 1959 West German remake, *Menschen im Hotel*, had Michele Morgan in Garbo's role and O. W. Fischer in John Barrymore's.

Granger, Dorothy (1912–1995).
American actress, a foil to Laurel and Hardy, Charley Chase, and W. C. Fields, and Leon Errol's wife in a series of comedy shorts.

Hog Wild 30. The Laurel-Hardy Murder Case 30. One Good Turn 31. The Dentist 32. Crime Rave 39. When the Daltons Rode 40. Twin Husbands 46. Killer Dill 47. New York Confidential 55. Raintree Country 57, etc.

Granger, Farley (1925–).
American leading man who began his film career straight from school.

North Star (debut) 43. They Live By Night 47. *Rope* 48. *Strangers on a Train* 51. Hans Christian Andersen 52. Senso (Italian) 53. The Girl in the Red Velvet Swing 55. Rogues' Gallery 68. Something Creeping in the Dark (It.) 71. The Serpent 72. Confessions of a Sex Maniac (It.) 72. They Call Me Trinity (It.) 72. The Man Called Noon 73. Arnold 75. Black Beauty (TV) 78. The Imagemaker 85. The Whoopee Boys 86, etc.

Granger, Stewart (1913–1993) (James Lablanche Stewart).
British leading man, on stage from 1935.
Autobiography: 1981, *Sparks Fly Upward*.
■ A Southern Maid 33. Give Her a Ring 34. So This Is London 38. Convoy 40. Secret Mission 42. Thursday's Child 43. *The Man in Grey* 43. The Lamp Still Burns 43. Fanny by Gaslight 43. *Waterloo Road* 44. *Love Story* 44. Madonna of the Seven Moons 44. *Caesar and Cleopatra* 45. Caravan 46. The Magic Bow (as Paganini) 46. *Captain Boycott* 47. Blanche Fury 48. Saraband for Dead Lovers (as Koenigsmark) 48. Woman Hater 49. Adam and Evelyne 49. *King Solomon's Mines* (US) 50. The Light Touch (US) 51. Soldiers Three 51. The Wild North 52. *Scaramouche* (US) 52. The Prisoner of Zenda (US) 52. Young Bess (US) 53. Salome (US) 53. All the Brothers Were Valiant (US) 54. *Beau Brummell* (US) 54. Green Fire (US) 55. Moonfleet (US) 55. Footsteps in the Fog 55. Bhowani Junction 56. The Last Hunt (US) 56. Gun Glory 57. The Little Hut 57. The Whole Truth 58. Harry Black and the Tiger 58. North to Alaska (US) 60. The Secret Partner 61. Sodom and Gomorrah 62. Swordsman of Siena (It.) 62. The Legion's Last Patrol (It.) 63. Among Vultures (Ger.) 64. The Secret Invasion 64. The Crooked Road 65. Der Oelprinz (Ger.) 65. Mission Hong Kong 65. Requiem for a Secret Agent 66. Glory City 66. Where Are You Taking that Woman? 66. The Trygon Factor 67. The Last Safari 67. The Flaming Frontier 68. The Hound of the Baskervilles (TV) (as Holmes) 71. The Wild Geese 77. The Royal Romance of Charles & Diana (TV) 82. Hell Hunters 88.
TV series: The Men from Shiloh 70.

¶ I've never done a film I'm proud of. – *S.G.*

Grangier, Gilles (1911–).
French director.
Le Cavalier Noir 44. L'Amour Madame 52. Archimède le Clochard 58. Le Cave Se Rebiffe 61. La Cuisine au Beurre 63. Train d'Enfer 65. L'Homme à la Buick 67. Fin de Journée 69, etc.

Grant, Arthur (1915–1972).
British cinematographer.
Hell Is a City 60. Jigsaw 62. Eighty Thousand Suspects 63. The Tomb of Ligeia 64. Blood from the Mummy's Tomb 71, etc.

Grant, Cary (1904–1986) (Archibald Leach).
Debonair British-born leading man with a personality and accent all his own; varied theatrical experience before settling in Hollywood. Special AA 1969.
Biographies: 1989, *Cary Grant: The Lonely Heart*

by Charles Higham and Roy Moseley. 1991, *Evenings with Cary Grant* by Nancy Nelson.
■ This Is the Night 32. Sinners in the Sun 32. Hot Saturday 32. Merrily We Go to Hell 32. The Devil and the Deep 32. Madame Butterfly 33. Blonde Venus 33. *She Done Him Wrong* 33. Alice in Wonderland (as the Mock Turtle) 33. The Eagle and the Hawk 33. Woman Accused 33. Gambling Ship 33. I'm No Angel 33. Thirty Day Princess 34. Born To Be Bad 34. Kiss and Make Up 34. Enter Madame 34. Ladies Should Listen 34. Wings in the Dark 35. The Last Outpost 35. Sylvia Scarlett 35. Big Brown Eyes 35. Suzy 36. Wedding Present 36. The Amazing Quest of Mr Ernest Bliss (GB) 36. When You're in Love 36. *The Awful Truth* 37. The Toast of New York 37. *Topper* 37. *Bringing Up Baby* 38. Holiday 38. *Gunga Din* 39. Only Angels Have Wings 39. In Name Only 39. *My Favorite Wife* 40. The Howards of Virginia 40. *His Girl Friday* 40. *The Philadelphia Story* 40. Penny Serenade (AAN) 41. Suspicion 41. Talk of the Town 42. Once upon a Honeymoon 42. Destination Tokyo 43. Mr Lucky 43. Once upon a Time 44. None But the Lonely Heart (AAN) 44. *Arsenic and Old Lace* 44. Night and Day (as Cole Porter) 45. Notorious 46. *The Bachelor and the Bobbysoxer* 47. The Bishop's Wife (as an angel) 48. Every Girl Should Be Married 48. *Mr Blandings Builds His Dream House* 48. I Was a Male War Bride 49. Crisis 50. People Will Talk 51. Room for One More 52. Monkey Business 52. Dream Wife 53. To Catch a Thief 55. The Pride and the Passion 57. *An Affair to Remember* 57. Kiss Them for Me 57. *Indiscreet* (GB) 58. Houseboat 58. *North by Northwest* 59. Operation Petticoat 59. The Grass Is Greener 60. That Touch of Mink 62. Charade 63. Father Goose 64. Walk Don't Run 66.
☉ For being the world's most admired sophisticated man for twenty-five years. *Mr Blandings Builds His Dream House.*

¶ When a journalist wired his agent 'How old Cary Grant?', Grant himself replied: 'Old Cary Grant fine. How you?'
Everyone tells me I've had such an interesting life, but sometimes I think it's been nothing but stomach disturbances and self-concern. – *C.G.*
I improve on misquotation. – *C.G.*
I think making love is the best form of exercise. – *C.G.*
I'd like to have made one of those big splashy Technicolor musicals with Rita Hayworth. – *C.G.*
The drama in a Cary Grant movie is always seeing whether the star can be made to lose his wry, elegant and habitual aplomb. – *Richard Schickel*
A completely private person, totally reserved, and there is no way into him. – *Doris Day*
Cary's enthusiasm made him search for perfection in all things, particularly the three that meant most to him – film-making, physical fitness and women. – *David Niven*

Grant, Hugh (1960–).
English leading actor. Born in London, he was educated at Oxford University and began his career on the stage and as a comedian. The success of *Four Weddings and a Funeral* made him a star.
Maurice 87. White Mischief 87. The Dawning 88. The Lair of the White Worm 88. La Nuit Bengali 88. Impromptu 89. The Big Man 90. Bitter Moon 92. Night Train to Munich 92. The Remains of the Day 93. *Four Weddings and a Funeral* 94. Sirens 94. An Awfully Big Adventure 95. The Englishman Who Went up a Hill but Came Down a Mountain 95, etc.

¶ He is a very bright man. He will not suffer fools gladly. – *Mike Newell*

He's found something that's gone from the movies: the intelligent comic leading man. – *Duncan Kenworthy*

Grant, James Edward (1902–1966).
American writer.
Whipsaw 35. We're Going to Be Rich 38. Belle of the Yukon 44. The Great John L. 45. Angel and the Bad Man (& d) 46. Sands of Iwo Jima 49. Big Jim McLain 52. Hondo 54. Ring of Fear (co-w, d) 54. The Sheepman (AAN) 58. The Alamo 60. McLintock 63, etc.

Grant, Kathryn (1933–) (Olive Grandstaff).
American leading lady who retired to marry Bing Crosby.
Arrowhead 53. Living it Up 54. The Phoenix City Story 55. Mister Cory 56. Gunman's Walk 58. Operation Mad Ball 58. The Seventh Voyage of Sinbad 58. The Big Circus 60, etc.

Grant, Kirby (1914–1985) (K. G. Horn).
Dutch-Scottish-American leading man, former bandleader.
Red River Range 39. Ghost Catchers 44. The Lawless Breed 47. Trail of the Yukon 50. Snow Dog 51. Yukon Gold 52. The Court Martial of Billy Mitchell 55. Yukon Vengeance 55, etc.
TV series: Sky King 53–54.

Grant, Lawrence (1870–1952).
British character actor in American films.
The Great Impersonation 21. His Hour 24. The Grand Duchess and the Waiter 26. Doomsday 28. The Canary Murder Case 29. *Bulldog Drummond* 29. The Cat Creeps 30. Daughter of the Dragon 31. The Unholy Garden 31. Jewel Robbery 32. The Mask of Fu Manchu 32. Grand Hotel 32. Shanghai Express 32. Queen Christina 33. By Candlelight 34. Nana 34. Werewolf of London 34. The Devil is a Woman 35. Little Lord Fauntleroy 36. The Prisoner of Zenda 37. Bluebeard's Eighth Wife 38. Son of Frankenstein 39. Women in War 40. Dr Jekyll and Mr Hyde 41. Confidential Agent 45, many others.

Grant, Lee (1927–) (Lyova Rosenthal).
Dynamic American stage actress, sporadically seen in films. She turned to directing in the 80s. She is the mother of Dinah Manoff.
■ AS ACTRESS: *Detective Story* (AAN) 51. Storm Fear 55. Middle of the Night 59. The Balcony 63. An Affair of the Skin 63. Terror in the City 66. Divorce American Style 67. In the Heat of the Night 67. Valley of the Dolls 67. Buona Sera Mrs Campbell 68. The Big Bounce 69. Perilous Voyage 69. Marooned 69. There Was a Crooked Man 70. *The Landlord* (AAN) 70. Night Slaves (TV) 70. Plaza Suite 71. *The Neon Ceiling* (TV) 71. Ransom for a Dead Man (TV) 71. Lt Schuster's Wife (TV) 72. Portnoy's Complaint 72. Partners in Crime (TV) 73. What Are Best Friends For (TV) 73. The Internecine Project 74. Shampoo (AA) 75. Voyage of the Damned (AAN) 76. Airport 77 77. The Spell (TV) 77. The Mafu Cage 77. The Swarm 78. Damien: Omen II 78. Backstairs at the White House (TV) 79. When You Comin' Back Red Ryder 79. You Can't Go Home Again (TV) 79. Tell Me a Riddle (d only) 80. Little Miss Marker 80. Charlie Chan and the Curse of the Dragon Queen 81. Visiting Hours 82. Will There Really Be a Morning? (TV) 83. Teachers 84. The Big Town 87. Calling the Shots 88. Staying Together (d) 89. Defending Your Life 91.
AS DIRECTOR: Tell Me a Riddle 80. A Matter of Sex (TV) 84. Nobody's Child (TV) 86. Staying Together 89. Women on Trial (TV) 92, etc.

Grant, Richard E. (1957–).
British leading actor, born in Swaziland.
Honest, Decent and True 85. Withnail and I 87.
Hidden City 87. How to Get Ahead in Advertising
88. Killing Dad 89. Warlock 89. Henry and June
90. Mountains of the Moon 90. Hudson Hawk 91.
L.A. Story 91. The Player 92. Bram Stoker's
Dracula 92. Suddenly Last Summer (TV) 93. The
Age of Innocence 93, etc.

Granville, Bonita (1923–1988).
American child actress of the 30s; adult career
gradually petered out but she became a producer.
Westward Passage 32. Cradle Song 33. Ah
Wilderness 35. *These Three* (AAN) 36. Maid of Salem
37. Call It a Day 37. Merrily We Live 38. Nancy
Drew Detective (and subsequent series) 38.
Angels Wash Their Faces 39. Escape 40. H.M.
Pulham Esq. 41. The Glass Key 42. Now Voyager
42. *Hitler's Children* 43. Youth Runs Wild 44. Love
Laughs at Andy Hardy 46. The Guilty 47. Treason
50. The Lone Ranger 56. Lassie's Greatest
Adventure (p) 63, etc.
TV series: Lassie (p) 55–67.

Grapewin, Charley (1869–1956).
American character actor best remembered in
movies for his range of grizzled old gentlemen.
Only Saps Work 30. The Night of June 13th 32.
Heroes for Sale 33. Judge Priest 34. Ah Wilderness
35. Alice Adams 35. Libelled Lady 36. The Good
Earth 37. Captains Courageous 37. Big City 37.
Three Comrades 38. The Wizard of Oz 39. *The
Grapes of Wrath* 40. Ellery Queen Master Detective
40. *Tobacco Road* (as Jeeter Lester) 41. They Died
with Their Boots On 41. Crash Dive 42. The
Impatient Years 44. Gunfighters 47. Sand 49.
When I Grow Up 51, many others.

Grault, Jean (1924–).
French screenwriter.
Jules et Jim 61. The Wild Child (L'Enfant
Sauvage) 70. The Story of Adele H. 75. Mon Oncle
d'Amérique (AAN) 80. L'Amour à Mort 84. Life Is
a Bed of Roses (La Vie est un Roman) 84. Les
Années 80s (co-w) 85. The Mystery of Alexina
(co-w) 85. Australia 89, etc.

Grauman, Sid (1879–1950).
Showbiz-loving American impresario, he of the
Chinese Theater on Hollywood Boulevard.

Grauman, Walter (1922–).
American director, from TV.
Lady in a Cage 63. 633 Squadron 64. A Rage to
Live 65. I Deal in Danger 66. The Last Escape 69.
Force Five (TV) 75. Most Wanted (TV) 76. Are You
in the House Alone? (TV) 78. Pleasure Palace (TV)
80. Scene of the Crime (TV) 85. Shakedown on
the Sunset Strip (TV) 88, etc.
TV series include The Untouchables, Naked City,
Route 66, The Felony Squad.

Graves, Peter (1926–) (Peter Aurness).
American leading man, usually in 'B' action
pictures; brother of James Arness.
Rogue River (debut) 50. Fort Defiance 52. Red
Planet Mars 52. Stalag 17 53. Beneath the Twelve-
Mile Reef 53. Black Tuesday 55. It Conquered the
World 56. Wolf Larsen 59. A Rage to Live 65. The
Ballad of Josie 67. The Five Man Army 68. Call to
Danger (TV) 73. The President's Plane Is Missing
(TV) 73. Scream of the Wolf (TV) 74. The
Underground Man (TV) 74. Where Have All the
People Gone (TV) 74. Dead Man on the Run (TV)
75. Disaster in the Sky (TV) 77. The Rebels (TV)
79. Airplane 80. Death Car on the Freeway (TV)
80. The Memory of Eva Ryker (TV) 81. Airplane 2:

the Sequel 82. Savannah Smiles 82. The Winds of
War (TV) 83. Number One with a Bullet 87, etc.
TV series: Fury 55–59. Whiplash 60. Court
Martial (Counsellors at War) 66. Mission Impossible
66–72.

Graves, Peter (1911–1994).
British light leading man, tall and suave, usually
in musical comedy.
Kipps (debut) 41. King Arthur Was a Gentleman
42. Bees in Paradise 44. I'll Be Your Sweetheart 44.
Waltz Time 45. The Laughing Lady 46. Spring Song
47. Mrs Fitzherbert (as the Prince Regent) 47.
Spring in Park Lane 48. Maytime in Mayfair 49.
Derby Day 52. Lilacs in the Spring 54, etc. Latterly
in cameo roles, e.g. The Wrong Box 66, The Slipper
and the Rose 76.

Graves, Ralph (1901–1977).
American silent star of heroic roles. Later became
writer and producer of minor films.
Talkies include: Submarine 28. Dirigible 30.
Ladies of Leisure 30.

Graves, Rupert (1963–).
British actor usually in upper-class roles.
A Room with a View 86. Maurice 87. A Handful
of Dust 88. The Children 90. Where Angels Fear
to Tread 91. Damage 92. The Madness of King
George 95, etc.

Graves, Teresa (1944–).
American leading lady.
Black Eye 73. Get Christie Love (TV) (and series)
74. Vampira 74.

Gravet, Fernand (1904–1970) (Fernand Martens).
Debonair French leading man with some
Hollywood experience.
Bitter Sweet 33. The Great Waltz 38. Fools for
Scandal 38. Le Dernier Tournant 38. La Ronde
50. Short Head 53. How to Steal a Million 66. The
Madwoman of Chaillot 69, etc.

Gray, Allan (1904–ʔ).
Polish-born composer in Britain.
Emil and the Detectives (Ger.) 36. The Life and
Death of Colonel Blimp 43. *A Matter of Life and Death*
45. Mr Perrin and Mr Traill 48. *The African Queen*
51. The Planter's Wife 52, etc.

Gray, Billy (1938–).
American juvenile actor of the 50s, latterly
working as a motorcycle racer.
Specter of the Rose 46. Fighting Father Dunne
49. *On Moonlight Bay* 52. The Day the Earth Stood
Still 52. The Seven Little Foys 55. Two for the
Seesaw 62, etc.
TV series: Father Knows Best 54–60.

Gray, Carole (1940–).
South African leading lady in British films of the
60s.
The Young Ones 61. Curse of the Fly 64. Rattle
of a Simple Man 64. Island of Terror 66, etc.

Gray, Charles (1928–) (Donald M. Gray).
British stage and TV actor usually seen in smooth,
unsympathetic roles.
The Entertainer 60. The Man in the Moon 61.
Masquerade 65. The Night of the Generals 66. The
Secret War of Harry Frigg (US) 67. *The Devil Rides
Out* 68. The File of the Golden Goose 69.
Cromwell 69. *Diamonds Are Forever* 71. The Beast
Must Die 74. Seven Nights in Japan 76. The Seven
Per Cent Solution (as Mycroft Holmes) 76. Silver
Bears 77. The Legacy 78. The Mirror Crack'd 80.

The Jigsaw Man 84. An Englishman Abroad (TV)
84. Dreams Lost, Dreams Found (TV) 87, etc.

Gray, Colleen (1922–) (Doris Jensen).
American leading lady of the 40s.
Kiss of Death 47. Nightmare Alley 47. Fury at
Furnace Creek 48. *Red River* 48. Sand 49. Riding
High 50. The Sleeping City 51. Kansas City
Confidential 52. Sabre Jet 53. Arrow in the Dust
54. The Killing 56. Hell's Five Hours 57. The Leech
Woman 60. Town Tamer 65. PJ 68, etc.
TV series: Window on Main Street 61.

Gray, Dolores (1924–).
Statuesque American singer-dancer, on stage in
musical comedy (played *Annie Get Your Gun* in
London).
■ It's Always Fair Weather 54. Kismet 55. The
Opposite Sex 56. Designing Woman 57.

Gray, Donald (1914–1978) (Eldred Tidbury).
One-armed British leading man, former radio
actor and announcer; best known as TV's Mark
Saber.
Strange Experiment 37. The Four Feathers 39.
Idol of Paris 48. Saturday Island (Island of Desire)
52. Timeslip 55. Satellite in the Sky 56, etc.

Gray, Dulcie (1919–) (Dulcie Bailey).
Gentle-mannered British leading lady, married to
Michael Denison.
A Place of One's Own 44. They Were Sisters 45.
Mine Own Executioner 47. The Glass Mountain
48. Angels One Five 51. A Man Could Get Killed
65, etc.

Gray, Gary (1936–).
American boy actor of the 40s.
A Woman's Face 41. Address Unknown 44. The
Great Lover 47. Rachel and the Stranger 48.
Father Is a Bachelor 49. The Next Voice You Hear
50. The Painted Hills 51. The Party Crashers 58,
many others.

Gray, Gilda (1901–1959) (Marianna Michalska).
Polish dancer who went to America and is credited
with inventing the shimmy.
Aloma of the South Seas 26. The Devil Dancer
28. Rose Marie 36, etc.

Gray, Nadia (1923–1994) (Nadia Kujnir-Herescu).
Russian-Rumanian leading lady, in European and
British films.
The Spider and the Fly 49. Night Without Stars
51. Valley of Eagles 51. Neapolitan Fantasy 54.
Folies Bergères 56. The Captain's Table 58.
Parisienne 59. La Dolce Vita 59. Maniac 63. Two
for the Road 67. The Naked Runner 67, etc.

Gray, Sally (1916–) (Constance Stevens).
Popular British screen heroine of the 30s and 40s,
with stage experience from 1925.
School for Scandal 30. Radio Pirates 35. Cheer
Up! 36. The Saint in London 38. The Lambeth
Walk 38. Dangerous Moonlight 40. Carnival 46.
Green for Danger 46. They Made Me a Fugitive 47.
The Mark of Cain 48. Silent Dust 49. Obsession
49. Escape Route 52, etc.

Gray, Simon (1936–).
British dramatist, novelist and screenwriter. He is
also a university lecturer in English.
Butley 74. A Month in the Country 87. Common
Pursuit (TV) 91. Running Late (TV) 93. Femme
Fatale (TV) 93, etc.

Gray, Spalding (1941–).
American character actor and writer who turned

a small part in *The Killing Fields* into a witty one-man show, *Swimming to Cambodia*, filmed by Jonathan Demme.

Heavy Petting 83. The Killing Fields 84. True Stories 86. Hard Choices 86. Swimming to Cambodia (& w) 87. Beaches 88. Clara's Heart 88. Stars and Bars 88. Monster in a Box (& w) 91. Straight Talk 92. Twenty Bucks 93. The Pickle 93. King of the Hill 93. The Paper 94, etc.

Graysmark, John.
British production designer.

Young Winston (AAN) 72. The Big Sleep 78. Flash Gordon 80. Ragtime (AAN) 81. The Lords of Discipline 83. The Bounty 84. Duet for One 87. Superman IV: The Quest for Peace 87. Gorillas in the Mist 88. White Hunter, Black Heart 90. Robin Hood: Prince of Thieves 91. White Sands 92. So I Married an Axe Murderer 93. Blown Away 94, etc.

Grayson, Godfrey.
British second-feature director, especially for the Danzigers.

Room to Let 50. To Have and to Hold 51. The Fake 53. Black Ice 57. High Jump 59. Spider's Web 60. So Evil So Young 61. She Always Gets Their Man 62, etc.

Grayson, Kathryn (1922–) (Zelma Hedrick).
American singing star in Hollywood from 1941 (as one of Andy Hardy's dates).
■ Andy Hardy's Private Secretary 40. Andy Hardy's Spring Fever 41. The Vanishing Virginian 41. Rio Rita 42. Seven Sweethearts 42. Thousands Cheer 43. Anchors Aweigh 45. Two Sisters from Boston 46. Ziegfeld Follies 46. Till the Clouds Roll By 46. It Happened in Brooklyn 47. The Kissing Bandit 48. The Midnight Kiss 49. The Toast of New Orleans 50. Grounds for Marriage 50. *Show Boat* 51. Lovely to Look At 52. The Desert Song 53. So This Is Love (as Grace Moore) 53. *Kiss Me Kate* 53. The Vagabond King 55. That's Entertainment Two 76.

Grazer, Brian (1951–).
American producer, a former agent, now in partnership with director Ron Howard.

Night Shift 82. Splash 83. Real Genius 84. Spies Like Us 85. Armed and Dangerous (& story) 86. Like Father, Like Son 87. Parenthood 89. The Dream Team 89. Kindergarten Cop 90. Problem Child 90. Cry-Baby 90. Backdraft 91. Closet Land 91. My Girl 91. The Doors 91. Far and Away 91, etc.

Graziano, Rocky (1921–1990) (Thomas Rocco Barbella).
World middleweight boxing champion whose 1955 autobiography, *Somebody Up There Likes Me*, was filmed in 1956 starring Paul Newman. He became a TV actor and a regular on variety shows in the 50s and 60s, and wrote another volume of autobiography, *Somebody Down Here Likes Me Too*, in 1981.

Mr Rock and Roll 57. Teenage Millionaire 61. Tony Rome 67, etc.

¶ I get a real belt out of this racket where I get paid because people laugh instead of stand up and scream for me to belt somebody. – *R.G.*

The Great Adventure.
Arnold Bennett's play and novel, *Buried Alive*, about a famous painter who assumes the identity of his valet and falls in love, was first filmed in England in 1915 with Henry Ainley in the lead. It was remade in America in 1921 with Lionel Barrymore; in 1933 came *His Double Life* with Roland Young and Lillian Gish as the lovers. The best version, emphasizing the comedy and retitled *Holy Matrimony*, came in 1943, directed by John Stahl, with a script by Nunnally Johnson, and pairing Monty Woolley with Gracie Fields.

Great Britain
had been making films for more than 50 years when finally a 'British school' emerged capable of influencing world production. Hollywood films had invaded British cinemas during World War I, and British audiences liked them; so the battle for power was won with only faint stirrings of resistance. British films were tepid, shoddy, stilted, old-fashioned in acting and production; and for many years they were kept that way by short-sighted government legislation, intended to help the industry, ensuring that at least a proportion (usually a third) of local product must be shown in every British cinema. Thus began the long list of 'quota quickies', deplorable 'B' pictures whose producers knew they could not fail to get their money back. In the mid-30s, Britain was producing 200 films a year, but they reflected nothing of life and offered little in the way of entertainment.

Exceptions to this general rule were the suspense thrillers of Alfred Hitchcock; a couple of promising dramas from Anthony Asquith; some well-produced entertainments from Victor Saville, such as *The Good Companions* and *South Riding*; Herbert Wilcox's popular view of such historical figures as Nell Gwyn and Queen Victoria; and the ambitious and often masterly, but not particularly British, productions of Alexander Korda, whose *Rembrandt* and *Things to Come* could still justify their inclusion in any list of the world's ten best. The British music-hall tradition also survived remarkably well in skilful low-budget productions with such stars as Gracie Fields, George Formby, Will Hay and the Crazy Gang; the two directors most concerned, Marcel Varnel and Walter Forde, had much to tell anyone who cared to listen about the art of screen comedy, as had writers Val Guest, Frank Launder and Sidney Gilliat.

In 1939 MGM had achieved three notable British productions – *A Yank at Oxford, Goodbye Mr Chips* and *The Citadel* – but the war swept away all plans and British studios started anew. Their renaissance began through the splendid documentaries of Humphrey Jennings, Harry Watt and Basil Wright, graduates of the GPO Film Unit which had been turning out excellent short films in the 30s but failing to secure cinema bookings for them. The strong feelings of national pride and urgency percolated to the fiction film, first in stories of social comment (*The Proud Valley, The Stars Look Down, Love on the Dole*), then in topical entertainments like Carol Reed's *Night Train to Munich* and Thorold Dickinson's *Next of Kin*. Noël Coward's *In Which We Serve* came as a revelation of style and substance, and what it did for the navy was done for the army by Reed's *The Way Ahead* and for the air force by Asquith's *The Way to the Stars*. The home front was covered with equal sensitivity by Launder and Gilliat's *Millions Like Us*, Leslie Howard's *The Gentle Sex*, and Coward's *This Happy Breed*.

Even non-war films had a fresh impetus. Gabriel Pascal made an excellent *Major Barbara* to follow the success of his 1938 *Pygmalion*. Dickinson's *Gaslight*, Reed's *Kipps*, and Asquith's *Quiet Wedding* were all excellent of their kind. The new team of Michael Powell and Emeric Pressburger brought a fresh command and insight to some unlikely but ambitious themes in *The Life and Death of Colonel Blimp* and *A Matter of Life and Death*. Korda supplied *The Thief of Baghdad, Lady Hamilton* and *Perfect Strangers*. The Boulting Brothers followed up *Pastor Hall* with the thoughtful *Thunder Rock*. Launder and Gilliat followed the realistic *Waterloo Road* with sparkling comedy-dramas (*The Rake's Progress, I See a Dark Stranger*), and a classic who-done-it (*Green for Danger*). Gainsborough Studios turned out several competent costume dramas on the Hollywood model. In 1945 the future of British films seemed bright indeed with Olivier's *Henry V*, Coward and Lean's *Blithe Spirit*, and Ealing Studios' supernatural omnibus *Dead of Night* earning popular approval, and such films as *Brief Encounter* and *Odd Man Out* in the works.

In the next few years the industry was beset by financial problems and diminishing audiences. Then Britain's leading film magnate, J. Arthur Rank, set out to conquer by means which proved regrettable. Originally attracted to the cinema as a means for spreading the Methodist religion, he now determined to impress world markets by a series of enormously expensive and generally arty productions, few of which recovered their costs: *Caesar and Cleopatra* is the most notorious. The more modestly-budgeted pictures proved to have little to say now that the end of the war had removed their main subject; and with exceptions like *Mine Own Executioner, The Red Shoes*, and *The Third Man* the field was thin until the celebrated Ealing comedies (*Passport to Pimlico, Whisky Galore, The Man in the White Suit, Kind Hearts and Coronets*) began to attract world audiences. But these too had their day, and all through the 50s British studios were trying in vain to find subjects to replace them. During this period many stars found their way to Hollywood, and then gradually began to drift back as kingpins of international co-productions, ventures which seldom turned out very happily. It was not till the relaxed hand of censorship permitted *Room at the Top, Saturday Night and Sunday Morning, The Leather Boys, Tom Jones, Georgy Girl, Blow Up*, James Bond and *Alfie* that British films at last set the world afire by showing just what you could get away with if you did it with sufficient skill and truth. Unfortunately even sex and violence must pall . . . so what next? The stopgap answer of the late 60s and early 70s was low comedy, much of it borrowed from TV; but that couldn't last, and didn't. By 1980 so many cinemas had closed that it was impossible to make ends meet on films for English consumption alone, and British studios and unions had priced themselves out of the international market. It remained for enterprising financiers such as Goldcrest to stimulate international palates with what would once have seemed very unlikely themes (*Chariots of Fire, Gandhi*); between these occasional high-spots good reviews were achieved for a number of outspoken low-budget realistic dramas, most of them partly financed by the new television Channel Four, which aired them after a usually brief run in cinemas. Cinema was no longer a mass entertainment, but a means of attracting specific minorities.

With the local film industry worsening each year, and the government giving only grudging help, much British talent settled for Hollywood. The British directors there included Alan Parker, Ridley Scott, Tony Scott, Franc Roddam, Adrian Lyne, Mike Figgis and Mike Jackson. British actors like Jeremy Irons and Anthony Hopkins were winning Oscars, but in American films. The few directors left in Britain made low-budget films, with Ken Russell turning out some cheap horrors. The will seemed to have gone. John Boorman's essentially English *Hope and Glory* was mainly inanced by foreign money. Even when some notable local films were made, like Ken Loach's *Riff-Raff* and Peter Chelsom's *Hear My Song*, British distributors could hardly be bothered to show them in the cinemas. Only Richard Attenborough, with his biopic of Charlie Chaplin (with an American star, Robert Downey, in the title role), seemed to be able to continue to work on a large scale. Yet, against the odds, some distinctive films did emerge, including Kenneth Branagh's *Henry V*, Peter Greenaway's *The Cook, the Thief, His Wife and Her Lover* and *Prospero's Books*, Christine Edzard's *Little Dorrit*, Peter Medak's *The Krays*, with a script by Philip Ridley, Derek Jarman's *Edward II* and Terence Davies's *Distant Voices, Still Lives* and *The Long Day Closes*.

The Great Gatsby.
F. Scott Fitzgerald's mordant story of an ex-gangster who meets his death among the Long Island high-livers was filmed in 1926 with Warner Baxter, in 1949 with Alan Ladd, and in 1974 with Robert Redford. The first was by all accounts the most successful, the second being merely surprising for biting off more than it could chew, and the third swamped by decoration and overlength.

The Great Impersonation.
E. Phillips Oppenheim's cunningly constructed spy thriller was filmed in 1921 with James Kirkwood; in 1935 with Edmund Lowe; and in 1942 with Ralph Bellamy.

The Great Movie Stars,
by David Shipman. These three volumes (the first subtitled *The Golden Years*, the second *The International Years*, the third *The Independent Years*) comprise more than four hundred and fifty witty though capsuled accounts of star careers, with every film given an appropriate if passing mention.

Greco, Juliette (1927–).
French singer who acted in several films both at home and abroad.
Au Royaume des Cieux 49. The Green Glove 52. *The Sun Also Rises* 57. Naked Earth 58. Roots of Heaven 59. Whirlpool 59. Crack in the Mirror 60, etc.

Greece
has had a film industry since 1912, but its development has been affected by political upheavals, and the results have had little international appeal, the best known directors being Michael Cacoyannis and Greg Tallas. The personality of Melina Mercouri and the music of Mikis Theodorakis were, however, more successfully exported. In the 80s, the only new director to emerge to international acclaim was Theodorous Angelopoulos, a former critic, with *The Beekeeper* and *Landscape in the Mist*.

Green, Adolph (1915–).
American writer of books and lyrics for many Broadway shows and musical films, usually with Betty Comden (qv).

Green, Alfred E. (1889–1960).
American director of mainly routine but generally competent films; in Hollywood from 1912.
Little Lord Fauntleroy 20. Ella Cinders 23. Through the Back Door 26. The Green Goddess 30. Old English 31. Smart Money 31. Disraeli 31. The Rich Are Always with Us 32. Parachute 33. Dangerous 35. Duke of West Point 38. South of Pago Pago 40. Badlands of Dakota 41. Meet the Stewarts 42. A Thousand and One Nights 44. The Jolson Story 46. The Fabulous Dorseys 47. They Passed This Way 48. Four Faces West 48. Cover Up 49. Invasion USA 52. The Eddie Cantor Story 53, many others.

Green, Danny (1903–).
Heavyweight British character actor usually in cheerful – or sometimes menacing – cockney roles. Appeared in some American silents.
Crime over London 37. Fiddlers Three 44. The Man Within 47. No Orchids for Miss Blandish 48. Little Big Shot 52. A Kid for Two Farthings 55. The Lady Killers 55. Beyond This Place 59, many others.

Green, David (1948–).
British director, from television.
Car Trouble 86. Buster 88. Fire Birds 90.

Green, Guy (1913–).
British cinematographer who became a useful director.
AS CINEMATOGRAPHER: In Which We Serve 42. The Way Ahead 44. *Great Expectations* (AA) 46. Take My Life 47. *Oliver Twist* 48. Captain Horatio Hornblower 51. The Beggar's Opera 52. Rob Roy 53, etc.
■ AS DIRECTOR: River Beat 54. Portrait of Alison 55. Lost 56. House of Secrets 56. The Snorkel 58. Sea of Sand 58. SOS Pacific 59. *The Mark* 60. The Angry Silence 60. The Light in the Piazza 62. Diamond Head 63. A Patch of Blue 65. Pretty Polly 67. The Magus 68. A Walk in the Spring Rain 70. Luther 73. Once Is Not Enough 75. The Devil's Advocate 77. Strong Medicine (TV) 85.

Green, Harry (1892–1958).
American comedian, primarily on stage; former lawyer.
Close Harmony 31. Bottoms Up 34. The Cisco Kid and the Lady 37. Star Dust 40. Joe MacBeth (GB) 55. A King in New York (GB) 57, etc.

Green Hornet, The.
A masked crime-fighter, who used a gas gun to incapacitate criminals, on US radio 36–52, and hero of the film serials *The Green Hornet* 40, starring Gordon Jones, and *The Green Hornet Strikes Again* 41, starring Warren Hull. A TV series 66–67 starred Van Williams and featured Bruce Lee as his Japanese assistant, Kato. The Green Hornet, otherwise Britt Reid, was the nephew of John Reid, better known as The Lone Ranger; both were creations of radio producer George W. Trendle and writer Fran Striker.

Green, Hughie (1920–).
Canadian actor in Britain, former juvenile, then popular TV quizmaster and talent scout.
Little Friend 34. Midshipman Easy 36. Tom Brown's Schooldays (US) 39. If Winter Comes (US) 48. Paper Orchid 49, etc.

Green, Jack N.
American cinematographer, mainly for Clint Eastwood's movies.
Heartbreak Ridge 86. Like Father, Like Son 87. The Dead Pool 88. Bird 88. Pink Cadillac 89. Race for Glory 89. White Hunter, Black Heart 90. The Rookie 90. Love Crimes 92. Rookie of the Year 93. A Perfect World 93, etc.

Green, Janet (1914–).
British screenwriter.
The Clouded Yellow 49. Cast a Dark Shadow (oa) 54. Lost 55. The Long Arm 56. *Sapphire* (BFA) 59. Midnight Lace (oa) 60. Life for Ruth 62. *Victim* 62. Seven Women 66, etc.

Green, Johnny (1908–1989).
American composer, band leader, songwriter; in Hollywood from 1933.
Scored Easter Parade (AA) 47. An American in Paris (AA) 51. Oliver (AA) 68. They Shoot Horses, Don't They? (AAN) 69, many others.

Green, Martyn (1899–1975).
British light opera singer, with the D'Oyly Carte Company for many years; settled in America.
Autobiography: 1952, *Here's a How De Do*.
■ *The Mikado* 39. The Story of Gilbert and Sullivan 53. A Lovely Way to Die 68.

Green, Mitzi (1920–1969) (Elizabeth Keno).
American child performer of the 30s.
Honey 30. Tom Sawyer 30. Little Orphan Annie 32. Transatlantic Merry-Go-Round 34, etc.: later appeared in Lost in Alaska 52. Bloodhounds of Broadway 52.
TV series: So This is Hollywood 54.

Green, Nigel (1924–1972).
Dominant British character actor with stage experience.
Reach for the Sky 56. Bitter Victory 58. The Criminal 60. Jason and the Argonauts 63. *Zulu* 64. *The Ipcress File* 65. The Face of Fu Manchu 65. The Skull 66. Let's Kill Uncle (US) 66. *Deadlier than the Male* 66. Tobruk (US) 67. Africa Texas Style 67. Play Dirty 68. Wrecking Crew (US) 69. The Kremlin Letter 69. Countess Dracula 70. The Ruling Class 71, etc.
TV series: William Tell 57.

Green, Philip (1917–).
British composer.
The March Hare 54. John and Julie 55. Rooney 57. Innocent Sinners 58. Operation Amsterdam 59. Sapphire 59. The Bulldog Breed 61. Victim 62. It's All Happening (& co-p) 63. The Intelligence Men 65. Masquerade 65, etc.

Green, Walon (1936–).
American screenwriter and director.
The Wild Bunch (AAN) 69. Sorcerer 77. The Brinks Job 78. The Secret Life of Plants (& d) 78. The Border 82. Solarbabies 86. Crusoe 88. Robocop 2 90, etc.

Greenaway, Peter (1942–).
British director and screenwriter who has moved from the experimental to the near-mainstream without altering his style.
The Falls 80. Act of God 81. The Draughtsman's Contract 83. A Zed and Two Noughts 85. Drowning by Numbers 88. *The Cook, the Thief, His Wife and Her Lover* 89. A TV Dante (TV) 90. *Prospero's Books* 91. The Baby of Macon 92. Darwin 93. The Pillow Book 95, etc.

¶ I do feel for me that cinema has somehow ceased to be a spectator sport. I get tremendous excitement out of making it rather than watching it. – *P.G.*
We live in a time of excess – excess population, excess information – *P.G.*
What is it about Greenaway's films that makes the flesh crawl? I think it's his apparent loathing of the human race. – *Ken Russell*

Greenberg, Adam.
Polish cinematographer, working in Hollywood.
Diamonds 75. The Passover Plot 77. Operation Thunderbolt 77. The Big Red One 80. Lemon Popsicle 80. Teen Mothers (aka Seed of Innocence) 80. Paradise 82. 10 to Midnight 83. The Terminator 84. The Ambassador 85. Once Bitten

85. Wisdom 86. Iron Eagle 86. La Bamba 87. Near Dark 87. Jocks 87. Three Men and a Baby 87. Spellbinder 88. Alien Nation 88. Turner & Hooch 89. Worth Winning 89. Love Hurts 90. Ghost 90. Three Men and a Little Lady 90. Terminator 2 91. Sister Act 92. Toys 92. Dave 93. Renaissance Man 94. North 94. First Knight 95, etc.

Greenberg, Gerald (1936–).
American editor.
Bye Bye Braverman 68. The Boys in the Band 70. The French Connection (AA) 71. The Seven Ups 73. The Taking of Pelham One Two Three 75. The Missouri Breaks 76. Apocalypse Now (AAN) 79. Dressed to Kill 80. Heaven's Gate 80. Scarface 83. Body Double 84. Wise Guys 86. The Untouchables 87. The Accused 88. Awakenings 90. For the Boys 91. School Ties 92, etc.

Greenberg, Stanley R.
American screenwriter.
Welcome Home Johnny Bristol (TV) 72. Skyjacked 72. Soylent Green 73. The Missiles of October (TV) 73. The Silence (TV) 76. Blind Ambition (TV) 79. FDR, the Last Years (TV) 81, etc.

Greene, Clarence (1918–).
American writer-producer, usually in collaboration with Russel Rouse.
The Town Went Wild 45. D.O.A. 48. The Well (AAN) 51. New York Confidential 55. A House Is Not a Home 64. The Oscar 66. Caper of the Golden Bulls 67, etc.
TV series: Tightrope 57.

Greene, David (1921–).
British director, former small-part actor; became a TV director in Canada and the US.
■ The Shuttered Room 66. Sebastian 68. The Strange Affair 68. I Start Counting (& p) 69. The People Next Door 70. Madame Sin (TV) 72. Godspell 73. Ellery Queen (TV) 75. Rich Man Poor Man (TV) (co-d) 76. Roots (co-d) (TV) 77. Lucan (TV pilot) 77. The Man in the Iron Mask (TV) 77. Gray Lady Down 78. The Trial of Lee Harvey Oswald (TV) 78. Friendly Fire (TV) 79. A Vacation in Hell (TV) 80. Hard Country 81. World War III (TV) 81. Ghost Dancing (TV) 81. Prototype (TV) 83. The Guardian (TV) 84. Sweet Revenge (TV) 84. Fatal Vision (TV) 84. Guilty Conscience (TV) 85. Miles to Go (TV) 86. Vanishing Act (TV) 86. The Betty Ford Story (TV) 87. Night of the Hunter (TV) 91.

Greene, Graham (1904–1991).
Distinguished British novelist who provided material for many interesting films.
Book: 1990, Travels in Greeneland: The Cinema of Graham Greene by Quentin Falk.
Stamboul Train (Orient Express) 34. This Gun for Hire 42. The Ministry of Fear 43. Confidential Agent 45. The Man Within 46. Brighton Rock 47. The Fugitive 48. The Fallen Idol (AAN) 48. The Third Man 49. The Heart of the Matter 53. The Stranger's Hand 54. The End of the Affair 55. The Quiet American 58. Our Man in Havana 59. The Comedians 67. Travels with My Aunt 73, etc.

Greene, Graham.
Native American (Indian) actor.
Dances with Wolves (AAN) 90. Clearcut 91. Thunderheart 92. Medicine River 92. Benefit of the Doubt 93. Cooperstown (TV) 93. Camilla 93. Maverick 94. North 94, etc.

Greene, Leon.
Stalwart British supporting actor, former opera singer.
A Funny Thing Happened on the Way to the Forum 67. The Ritz 76. The Seven Per Cent Solution 76, etc.

Greene, Lorne (1915–1987).
Solidly-built Canadian character actor, best known for his role as Ben Cartwright in the TV series Bonanza 59–73, and his similar role as Commander Adama in Battlestar Galactica 78–80.
The Silver Chalice 54. Tight Spot 55. Autumn Leaves 56. Peyton Place 57. The Gift of Love 58. The Trap 58. Legacy of a Spy (TV) 68. The Harness (TV) 71. Earthquake 74, etc.
TV series: Sailor of Fortune 56. Bonanza (as Ben Cartwright) 59–73. A Funny Thing Happened on the Way to the Forum 67. Griff 74. The Ritz 76. The Seven Per Cent Solution 76. Battlestar Galactica 78–80. Code Red 81.

Greene, Max (1896–1968) (Mutz Greenbaum).
German cinematographer, long in Britain.
The Stars Look Down 39. Hatter's Castle 41. Spring in Park Lane 48. Maytime in Mayfair 49. Night and the City 50, etc.

Greene, Richard (1918–1985).
Good-looking, lightweight British leading man with brief stage experience before 1938 film debut resulted in Hollywood contract.
■ Four Men and a Prayer 38. My Lucky Star 38. Submarine Patrol 38. Kentucky 38. The Little Princess 38. The Hound of the Baskervilles 39. Stanley and Livingstone 39. Here I Am a Stranger 39. Little Old New York 40. I Was an Adventuress 40. Unpublished Story 42. Flying Fortress 42. Yellow Canary 43. Don't Take It to Heart 45. Gaiety George 46. Forever Amber 47. The Fighting O'Flynn 48. The Fan 48. That Dangerous Age 49. Now Barabbas 49. The Desert Hawk 50. My Daughter Joy 50. Shadow of the Eagle 50. Lorna Doone 51. Black Castle 51. Rogue's March 53. Captain Scarlet 53. Bandits of Corsica 54. Contraband Spain 55. Beyond the Curtain 60. Sword of Sherwood Forest 61. Dangerous Island 67. Blood of Fu Manchu 68. Kiss and Kill 69. Tales from the Crypt 72.
TV series: Robin Hood 55–59.

Greene, W. Howard (–1956).
American colour cinematographer.
Trail of the Lonesome Pine 36. The Garden of Allah 36. A Star is Born 37. Nothing Sacred 37. The Adventures of Robin Hood 38. Jesse James 39. Elizabeth and Essex 39. Northwest Mounted Police 40. Blossoms in the Dust 41. The Jungle Book (AAN) 42. Arabian Nights 42. Phantom of the Opera (AA) 43. Ali Baba and the Forty Thieves 44. Can't Help Singing 44. Salome Where she Danced 45. A Night in Paradise 46. Tycoon 47. High Lonesome 50. Quebec 51. The Brigand 52. Gun Belt 53, etc.

Greenleaf, Raymond (1892–1963).
American character actor, usually seen as benevolent elderly man.
Storm Warning 51. Angel Face 53. Violent Saturday 54. When Gangland Strikes (leading role) 56. The Story on Page One 60, many others.

Greenstreet, Sydney (1879–1954).
Immense British stage actor long in America; a sensation in his first film, made at the age of 61, he became a major star of the 40s.
■ The Maltese Falcon (AAN) 41. They Died with Their Boots On 41. Across the Pacific 42. Casablanca

42. Background to Danger 42. Passage to Marseilles 44. Between Two Worlds 44. The Mask of Dimitrios 44. The Conspirators 44. Hollywood Canteen 44. Pillow to Post 45. Conflict 45. Christmas in Connecticut 45. Three Strangers 46. Devotion (as Thackeray) 46. The Verdict 46. That Way with Women 47. The Hucksters 47. The Woman in White 48. The Velvet Touch 48. Ruthless 48. Flamingo Road 49. It's a Great Feeling 49. Malaya 50.
☺ For his inimitable chuckle; and for the sheer improbability of his success. The Maltese Falcon

¶ By gad, sir, you're a fellow worth knowing, a character. No telling what you'll say next, except that it'll be something astonishing. – S.G. in The Maltese Falcon
I distrust a man who says when. He's got to be careful not to drink too much, because he's not to be trusted when he does. Well, sir, here's to plain speaking and clear understanding. You're a close-mouthed man?
– No, I like to talk.
– Better and better. I distrust a close-mouthed man. He generally picks the wrong time to talk, and says the wrong things. Talking's something you can't do judiciously, unless you keep in practice. – Ibid.

Greenwald, Maggie (1955–).
American director, a former editor and dancer.
Home Remedy 87. The Kill Off 89. The Ballad of Little Joe 93.

Greenwood, Charlotte (1890–1978).
Tall American comedienne and eccentric dancer, on stage from 1905.
Autobiography: 1947, Never Too Tall.
Jane 18. Baby Mine 27. So Long Letty 30. Palmy Days 32. Down Argentine Way 40. Springtime in the Rockies 43. Up in Mabel's Room 44. Home in Indiana 47. Peggy 50. Dangerous when Wet 52. Glory 55. Oklahoma 56. The Opposite Sex 56, etc.

Greenwood, Jack (1919–).
British producer, responsible for second-feature crime series: Edgar Wallace, Scales of Justice, Scotland Yard, etc.

Greenwood, Joan (1921–1987).
Plummy-voiced British leading lady of the 40s. She was married to André Morell.
■ John Smith Wakes Up 40. My Wife's Family 40. He Found a Star 41. The Gentle Sex 42. They Knew Mr Knight 44. Latin Quarter 44. A Girl in a Million 45. The Man Within 46. The October Man 47. The White Unicorn 47. Saraband for Dead Lovers 48. The Bad Lord Byron 48. Whisky Galore 49. Kind Hearts and Coronets 49. Flesh and Blood 50. The Man in the White Suit 50. Young Wives' Tale 51. Mr Peek-a-Boo 51. The Importance of Being Earnest 52. Knave of Hearts 54. Father Brown 54. Moonfleet (US) 55. Stage Struck (US) 57. Mysterious Island 62. The Amorous Prawn 62. Tom Jones 63. The Moon Spinners 64. Girl Stroke Boy 71. The Uncanny 77. The Hound of the Baskervilles 78. The Water Babies 78. Little Dorrit 88.

¶ She speaks her lines as though suspecting in them some hidden menace that she can't quite identify. – Karel Reisz

Greenwood, John (1889–1975).
British composer.
To What Red Hell? 30. The Constant Nymph 33. Elephant Boy 37. Pimpernel Smith 41. San Demetrio, London 44. Frieda 47. Quartet 48. The Last Days of Dolwyn 48. Trio 50. The Gentle Gunman 52, many others.

Greenwood, Walter (1903–1974).
British writer who chronicled industrial life, notably in *Love On the Dole*.

Greer, Howard (1886–1964).
American costume designer, in films from 1923 and chief designer at Paramount from 1924–27 before establishing his own salon in Hollywood.
  Autobiography: 1949, *Designing Male*.
  The Spanish Dancer 23. The Cheat 23. The Covered Wagon 23. The Ten Commandments 24. Coquette 29. Hell's Angels 30. The Animal Kingdom 32. Page Miss Glory 35. Bringing Up Baby 38. When Tomorrow Comes 39. Christmas Holiday 44. Spellbound 45. Holiday Affair 49. The French Line 54, etc.

¶ For every luscious bloom there's been a fat, sharp thorn. – *H.G.*

Greer, Jane (1924–) (Bettyjane Greer).
Cool American leading lady of the 40s; could play good-humoured dames, well-bred ladies or *femmes fatales*.
■ Pan Americana 45. Two o'Clock Courage 45. George White's Scandals 45. Dick Tracy 45. The Falcon's Alibi 46. Bamboo Blonde 46. Sunset Pass 46. Sinbad the Sailor 46. *They Won't Believe Me* 47. *Out of the Past* 47. Station West 48. *The Big Steal* 49. You're in the Navy Now 51. The Company She Keeps 51. The Prisoner of Zenda 52. Desperate Search 52. You for Me 52. The Clown 53. Down among the Sheltering Palms 53. *Run for the Sun* 56. *Man of a Thousand Faces* 57. Where Love Has Gone 64. Billie 65. The Outfit 74. The Shadow Riders (TV) 82. Against All Odds 84.

Gregg, Colin (1947–).
British director.
  Remembrance 82. Lamb 85. We Think the World of You 88.

Gregg, Everley (1898–1959).
British character actress.
  The Private Life of Henry VIII 32. The Ghost Goes West 36. Pygmalion 38. Brief Encounter 45, etc.

Gregg, Hubert (1914–).
British songwriter, screenwriter, and light actor, married to Pat Kirkwood. On stage from 1933, films from 1942.
  In Which We Serve 42. 29 Acacia Avenue 45. Vote for Huggett 49. Robin Hood 52. The Maggie 54. Simon and Laura 55. Stars in My Eyes 57, etc.

Gregor, Nora (c. 1890–1949).
Austrian leading lady.
  The Trial of Mary Dugan (US) 29. His Glorious Night (US) 30. *La Règle du Jeu* (Fr.) 39, etc.

Gregory, James (1911–).
American character actor with stage experience, a familiar Hollywood 'heavy' or senior cop.
  Naked City 48. The Frogmen 51. The Scarlet Hour 56. The Young Stranger 57. Al Capone 59. Two Weeks in Another Town 62. *The Manchurian Candidate* 62. P.T. 109 63. A Distant Trumpet 64. The Sons of Katie Elder 65. A Rage To Live 65. *The Silencers* 66. Clambake 68. The Hawaiians 70. Million Dollar Duck 71. Shootout 71. The Main Event 79, etc.
  TV series: The Lawless Years 59. Barney Miller 81.

Gregory, Paul (c. 1905–) (Jason Lenhart).
American impresario who teamed with Charles Laughton in the 40s to present dramatized

readings: also produced *Night of the Hunter* 55, which Laughton directed, and *The Naked and the Dead* 58.

Gregson, John (1919–1975).
Scottish leading man, a likeable and dependable star of British comedies and action dramas in the 50s.
■ Saraband for Dead Lovers 48. Scott of the Antarctic 48. Whisky Galore 49. The Hasty Heart 49. Train of Events 49. Treasure Island 50. Cairo Road 50. *The Lavender Hill Mob* 51. Angels One Five 51. *The Brave Don't Cry* 51. Venetian Bird 52. The Holly and the Ivy 52. The Titfield Thunderbolt 53. *Genevieve* 53. The Weak and the Wicked 53. Conflict of Wings 54. To Dorothy a Son 54. The Crowded Day 54. Above Us the Waves 55. Value for Money 55. Three Cases of Murder 55. *Jacqueline* 56. The Battle of the River Plate 56. True as a Turtle 56. Miracle in Soho 57. *Rooney* 57. Sea of Sand 58. *The Captain's Table* 58. SOS Pacific 59. Faces in the Dark 60. Hand in Hand 60. Treasure of Monte Cristo 61. Frightened City 61. *Live Now Pay Later* 62. Tomorrow at Ten 62. The Longest Day 62. The Night of the Generals 66. Fright 71.
  TV series: Gideon's Way 64. Shirley's World 71.

Greig, Robert (1880–1958).
Australian character actor, long in Hollywood; the doyen of portly pompous butlers.
  Animal Crackers 30. Tonight or Never 31. Love Me Tonight 32. Trouble in Paradise 32. Horse Feathers 32. Merrily We Go to Hell 33. Pleasure Cruise 33. Clive of India 35. Lloyds of London 36. Easy Living 37. Algiers 38. No Time for Comedy 40. The Lady Eve 41. Sullivan's Travels 42. *The Moon and Sixpence* 42. I Married a Witch 42. The Palm Beach Story 42. The Great Moment 44. The Picture of Dorian Gray 45. The Cheaters 45. Unfaithfully Yours 48, many others.

Greist, Kim (1958–).
American actress.
  C.H.U.D. 84. Brazil 85. Manhunter 86. Throw Momma from the Train 87. Punchline 88. Why Me? 90. Payoff 91. Duplicates 92. Homeward Bound: The Incredible Journey 93, etc.

Grémillon, Jean (1901–1959).
French director with limited but interesting output since 1929.
  Remorques 39. Lumière d'Eté 42. Pattes Blanches 48, etc.

Grenfell, Joyce (1910–1979) (Joyce Phipps).
Angular British comedienne adept at refined gaucherie; a revue star and solo performer, on stage from 1939.
  The Demi-Paradise 42. The Lamp Still Burns 43. While the Sun Shines 46. The Happiest Days of Your Life 49. Stage Fright 50. *Laughter in Paradise* 51. Genevieve 53. The Million Pound Note 54. The Belles of St Trinian's 54. Happy Is the Bride 57. Blue Murder at St Trinian's 58. The Pure Hell of St Trinian's 60. The Old Dark House 63. The Americanization of Emily 64. The Yellow Rolls-Royce 64, etc.

Greville, Edmond (1906–1966).
French director; assistant to Dupont on *Piccadilly* 30, to Clair on *Sous les Toits de Paris* 32.
  Remous 34. Mademoiselle Docteur 37. L'Ille du Péché 39. Passionelle 46. Noose (GB) 48. The Romantic Age (GB) 49. But Not in Vain (also wrote and produced) (GB) 49. Port du Désir 56. Guilty (GB) 56. Beat Girl (GB) 60. The Hands of Orlac (GB) 61. Les Menteurs 61, etc.

Grey, Jennifer (1960–).
American actress, the daughter of Joel Grey.
  Red Dawn 84. The Cotton Club 84. American Flyers 85. Ferris Bueller's Day Off 86. Dirty Dancing 87. Light Years 88. Bloodhounds of Broadway 89. The Sixth Family 90. Stroke of Midnight 91. A Case for Murder (TV) 93, etc.

Grey, Joel (1932–) (Joe Katz).
American singing entertainer who took a long time to hit stardom, managed it on the New York stage in *Cabaret*, but proved difficult to cast.
■ About Face 52. Come September 63. Man on a String (TV) 71. *Cabaret* (AA) 72. Man on a Swing 74. Buffalo Bill and the Indians 76. The Seven Per Cent Solution 76. Remo Williams . . . the Adventure Begins 85. Kafka 91. The Music of Chance 93.

Grey, Lita (1908–) (Lillita MacMurray).
American juvenile actress of the 20s who appeared with Chaplin, became his child bride, and is the mother of Sydney Chaplin. In the late 60s, wrote *My Life with Chaplin*.

Grey, Nan (1918–1993) (Eschal Miller).
American leading lady of the late 30s; married to singer Frankie Laine.
  Dracula's Daughter 36. Three Smart Girls 36. Three Smart Girls Grow Up 38. Tower of London 39. The Invisible Man Returns 40. Sandy Is a Lady 41, etc.

Grey, Virginia (1917–).
American leading lady of minor films in the 30s and 40s.
  Uncle Tom's Cabin (debut) 27. Misbehaving Ladies 31. Secrets 33. Dames 34. The Firebird 34. The Great Ziegfeld 36. Rosalie 37. Test Pilot 38. The Hardys Ride High 39. Hullaballoo 40. Blonde Inspiration 41. The Big Store 41. Grand Central Murder 42. Idaho 43. Strangers in the Night 44. Blonde Ransom 45. House of Horrors 46. Unconquered 47. Who Killed Doc Robbin? 48. Jungle Jim 49. Slaughter Trail 51. Desert Pursuit 52. Target Earth 54. The Last Command 55. Crime of Passion 56. The Restless Years 58. Portrait in Black 60. Back Street 61. Black Zoo 63. Love Has Many Faces 65. Madame X 66. Rosie 68. Airport 69, many others.

Grey, Zane (1875–1939).
American novelist whose western yarns provided the basis of hundreds of silent and sound movies. He lacked sophistication, but as late as 1960 TV had its *Zane Grey Theatre*.

Grieco, Richard (1964–).
American leading actor in teen-oriented movies, from television.
  If Looks Could Kill 91. Mobsters 91. Tomcat: Dangerous Desires 93. Born to Run (TV) 93.
  TV series: 21 Jump Street 88–89. Booker 89–90.

Griem, Helmut (1940–).
German leading man in international films.
  The Damned 69. The Mackenzie Break 70. *Cabaret* 72. Ludwig 73. Voyage of the Damned 76. Sergeant Steiner 79. Children of Rage 82. Malou 83, etc.

Grier, David Alan.
American actor.
  Streamers 83. A Soldier's Story 84. From the Hip 87. Off Limits 87. Loose Cannons 90. Boomerang 92. In the Army Now 94. Blankman 94, etc.

Grier, Pam (1949–).
American leading lady.

Beyond the Valley of the Dolls 70. Twilight People 72. Blacula 72. Hit Man 72. Coffy 74. Black Mama White Mama 74. The Arena 74. Sheba Baby 75. Friday Foster 75. Drum 76. Greased Lightning 77. Fort Apache, the Bronx 81. Something·Wicked This Way Comes 83. Badge of the Assassin 85. On the Edge 86. Tough Enough 87. Naked Warriors 87. Above the Law 88. The Package 89. Class of 1999 90. Bill & Ted's Bogus Journey 91. Posse 93, etc.

Grier, Roosevelt (1932–).
American footballer, cousin of Pam Grier; makes occasional showbiz appearances.

The Thing with Two Heads 72. Skyjacked 72. Evil in the Deep 76.

Grierson, John (1898–1972).
Distinguished British documentarist. Founded Empire Marketing Board Film Unit 30. GPO Film Unit 33; Canadian Film Commissioner 39–45, etc. Produced *Drifters* 29. *Industrial Britain* 33. *Song of Ceylon* 34. *Night Mail* 36, etc. In 1957–63 he had his own weekly TV show *This Wonderful World* showing excerpts from the world's best non-fiction films.

Gries, Tom (1922–1977).
American director (also producer and co-writer) with varied Hollywood experience from 1946 and much TV.
■ Hell's Horizon 55. The Girl in the Woods 58. Will Penny (& w) 68. 100 Rifles 69. Number One 69. The Hawaiians 70. Fools 71. Earth II (TV) 71. Call to Danger (TV) 72. The Glass House (TV) 72. Journey through Rosebud 72. Migrants (TV) 73. Lady Ice 73. QB VII (TV) 74. Breakout 75. Breakheart Pass 76. Helter Skelter (TV) 76. The Greatest 77.

Griffies, Ethel (1878–1975) (Ethel Woods).
Angular British character actress, in Hollywood for many years.

Waterloo Bridge 31. Love Me Tonight 32. The Mystery of Edwin Drood 35. Kathleen 37. We are Not Alone 39. Irene 40. Great Guns 41. *Time to Kill* 42. Jane Eyre 44. The Horn Blows at Midnight 45. Devotion 46. The Homestretch 47. The Birds 63. *Billy Liar* (GB) 63, many others.

Griffin, Josephine (1928–).
British leading lady.

The Weak and the Wicked 54. The Purple Plain 54. The Man Who Never Was 56. The Spanish Gardener (last to date) 56, etc.

Griffith, Andy (1926–).
Tall, slow-speaking American comic actor, adept at wily country-boy roles.

A Face in the Crowd (debut) 57. No Time for Sergeants 58. Onionhead 58. Winter Kill (TV) 73. Hearts of the West 75. *Washington: Behind Closed Doors* (TV) 76. The Girl in the Empty Grave (TV) 77. Deadly Game (TV) 77. Centennial (TV) 78. From Here to Eternity (TV) 79. Roots: The Next Generations (TV) 79, etc. Fatal Vision (TV) 85, etc. Next Generations (TV) 79.

TV series: The Andy Griffith Show 60–68. The Headmaster 70. Salvage 78. Matlock 86– .

Griffith, Corinne (1898–1979).
American leading lady of the 20s.

The Yellow Girl 22. Six Days 23. Lilies of the Field 24. Love's Wilderness 24. The Marriage Whirl 25. Infatuation 25. Syncopating Sue 26. Three Hours 27. The Garden of Eden 28. The Divine Lady 29. Saturday's Children 29. Back Pay 30. Lily Christine 30. Papa's Delicate Condition (oa only) 52, etc.

Griffith, D. W. (1875–1948) (David Wark).
American film pioneer, the industry's first major producer-director; he improved the cinema's prestige, developed many aspects of technique, created a score of stars, and was only flawed by his sentimental Victorian outlook, which in the materialistic 20s put him prematurely out of vogue and in the 30s out of business.

Best biographies: 1969, *The Movies, Mr Griffith, and Me* by Lillian Gish. 1984, *D. W. Griffith and the Birth of Film* by Richard Schickel.

SELECTED EARLY FILMS: For the Love of Gold 08. The Song of the Shirt 08. Edgar Allan Poe 09. The Medicine Bottle 09. The Drunkard's Reformation 09. The Cricket on the Hearth 09. What Drink Did 09. The Violin Maker of Cremona 09. Pippa Passes 09. In the Watches of the Night 09. Lines of White on a Sullen Sea 09. Nursing a Viper 09. The Red Man's View 09. In Old California 10. Ramona 10. In the Season of Buds 10. The Face at the Window 10. The House with Closed Shutters 10. The Usurer 10. The Chink at Golden Gulch 10. Muggsy's First Sweetheart 10. The Italian Barber 10. The Manicure Lady 11. What Shall We Do with Our Old? 11. *The Lonedale Operator* 11. The Spanish Gypsy 11. Paradise Lost 11. Enoch Arden 11. Through Darkened Vales 11. The Revenue Man and the Girl 11. A Mender of Nets 12. The Goddess of Sagebrush Gulch 12. The Old Actor 12. *Man's Genesis* 12. The Sands of Dee 12. *The Musketeers of Pig Alley* 12. My Baby 12. *The New York Hat* 12. The God Within 12. The One She Loved 12. The Mothering Heart 13. The Sheriff's Baby 13. The Battle at Elderbrush Gulch 13. *Judith of Bethulia* 13. The Escape 14. The Avenging Conscience 14. The Mother and the Law 14. Home Sweet Home 14, many others.
■ FROM 1915: *The Birth of a Nation* 15. Intolerance 16. *Hearts of the World* 18. The Great Love 18. The Greatest Thing in Life 18. A Romance of Happy Valley 19. *Broken Blossoms* 19. The Girl Who Stayed at Home 19. True Heart Susie 19. Scarlet Days 19. The Greatest Question 19. The Idol Dancer 20. The Love Flower 20. *Way Down East* 20. Dream Street 21. *One Exciting Night* 22. *Orphans of the Storm* 22. The White Rose 23. America 24. Isn't Life Wonderful 25. Sally of the Sawdust 26. That Royle Girl 26. *The Sorrows of Satan* 26. Drums of Love 28. The Battle of the Sexes 28. Lady of the Pavements 29. Abraham Lincoln 30. The Struggle 31. One Million Years BC (reputed contribution) 39.
✪ For enduring the fate of most monuments, and for deserving the tribute in the first place, despite being a personality with clearly unlikeable aspects. *Intolerance.*

¶ Remember how small the world was before I came along. I brought it all to life: I moved the whole world onto a 20-foot screen. – *D.W.G.*

He did what he did genuinely, and straight from the heart. His best films are passionate and tender, terrifying and pregnant, works of art certainly, and products too of an imagination far ahead of its time. – *Paul O'Dell*

It is time D. W. Griffith was rescued from the pedestal of an outmoded pioneer. The cinema of Griffith, after all, is no more outmoded than the drama of Aeschylus. – *Andrew Sarris, 1968*

He was the first to photograph thought, said Cecil B. de Mille. It was quite a compliment. But Griffith was full of contradictions. His brain was progressive, his emotions Victorian. For a few years the two aspects were able to join in public favour, but he could not adapt himself to the brisker pace of the 20s, when he made many such blinkered and stubborn pronouncements as:

We do not want now and we never shall want the human voice with our films.

When the inevitable happened in 1928 he declared:

We have taken beauty and exchanged it for stilted voices.

He could be tactless too, as when in 1918 he commented:

Viewed as drama, the war is somewhat disappointing.

Yet this was the man of whom Gene Fowler could say:

He articulated the mechanics of cinema and bent them to his flair.

Lilian Gish, a great admirer of Griffith, said:

He inspired in us his belief that we were working in a medium that was powerful enough to influence the whole world.

To Mack Sennett:

He was my day school, my adult education program, my university . . . (but) he was an extremely difficult man to know.

He said himself:

The task I'm trying to achieve above all is to make you see . . .

He knew his own value, as many an actor found when asking for a rise:

It's worth a lot more than money to be working for me!

This was true enough up to the time of *The Birth of a Nation*, which President Wilson described as:

Like writing history with lightning.

But it became less so after the box-office flop of *Intolerance*, which Gene Fowler called:

The greatest commercial anticlimax in film history.

He became an embarrassment to Hollywood because his ideas seemed outmoded; in the 30s he scarcely worked at all. When he died in 1948 Hedda Hopper, recalling the marks made by stars in the wet cement at Hollywood's Chinese Theater, said:

Griffith's footprints were never asked for, yet no one has ever filled his shoes . . .

And James Agee added:

There is not a man working in movies, nor a man who cares for them, who does not owe Griffith more than he owes anyone else.

Ezra Goodman commented:

At Griffith's funeral, the sacred cows of Hollywood gathered to pay him homage. A week before, he probably could not have gotten any of them on the telephone.

It is said indeed that death had to come before such tributes as Frank Capra's:

Since Griffith·there has been no major improvement in the art of film direction.

And Carmel Myers':

He was the umbrella that shaded us all.

And John Simon's:

Griffith did for film what Sackville and Norton, the authors of *Gorboduc*, did for drama.

Griffith, Edward H. (1894–1975).
American director.

Scrambled Wives 21. Unseeing Eyes 23. Bad Company 25. Afraid to Love 27. Paris Bound 29. Holiday 30. Rebound 31. The Animal Kingdom 32. Another Language 33. Biography of a Bachelor Girl 35. No More Ladies 35. Ladies in Love 36. Café Metropole 37. Café Society 39. Safari 40. Virginia 40. One Night in Lisbon 41. Bahama Passage 42. The Sky's the Limit 43. Perilous Holiday 46, etc.

Griffith, Hugh (1912–1980).
Flamboyant Welsh actor, former bank clerk.

Neutral Port (debut) 40; war service; The Three Weird Sisters 48. London Belongs to Me 48. The Last Days of Dolwyn 48. A Run for Your Money 49. Laughter in Paradise 51. The Galloping Major 51. The Beggar's Opera 52. *The Titfield Thunderbolt* 53. The Sleeping Tiger 54. Passage Home 55. *Lucky Jim* 57. Ben Hur (AA) 59. The Day They Robbed the Bank of England 60. Exodus 61. The Counterfeit Traitor 62. Tom Jones (AAN) 63. The Bargee 64. Moll Flanders 65. Oh Dad, Poor Dad 66. Sailor from Gibraltar 66. How to Steal a Million 66. The Chastity Belt 67. Oliver 68. The Fixer 68. Start the Revolution Without Me 69. Cry of the Banshee 70. Wuthering Heights 70. The Abominable Dr Phibes 71. Who Slew Auntie Roo? 72. What 72. Craze 73. Take Me High 73. Luther 75. Loving Cousins 76. Joseph Andrews 77. The Last Remake of Beau Geste 77. The Passover Plot 77, many others.

Griffith, James (1919–).
American general-purpose actor.
Bright Leaf 50. Rhubarb 51. The Law vs Billy the Kid (as Pat Garrett) 54. Anything Goes 56. The Big Fisherman 59. The Amazing Transparent Man 61, etc.

Griffith, Kenneth (1921–).
Sharp-eyed Welsh actor of stage and screen, often the envious 'little man'.
Love on the Dole 41. The Shop at Sly Corner 45. Bond Street 48. High Treason 50. Lucky Jim 57. I'm All Right, Jack 59. Circus of Horrors 59. *Only Two Can Play* 61. Rotten to the Core 65. The Bobo 67. The Whisperers 67. Revenge 71. The House in Nightmare Park 73. Remembrance 82. The Englishman Who Went up a Hill but Came Down a Mountain 95, many others.

Griffith, Melanie (1957–).
American leading actress, the daughter of Tippi Hedren. She married actor Don Johnson (1976–77) and, following another divorce, remarried him in 1989.
Night Moves 75. The Drowning Pool 76. Body Double 84. Fear City 85. Something Wild 86. The Milagro Beanfield War 88. Cherry 2000 88. Stormy Monday 88. Working Girl (AAN) 88. In the Spirit 90. The Bonfire of the Vanities 90. Pacific Heights 90. Paradise 91. Shining Through 92. Born Yesterday 93. Milk Money 94. Nobody's Fool 94, etc.
TV series: Once an Eagle 76–77. Carter Country 78–79.

¶ There's a bit of a stripper in every woman. – *M.G.*

The instantly recognisable Griffith Girl: a trashy babe in black underpant and matching garter belt with a squeaky voice, a butt that is not to be trifled with, and a heart as wide as Asia. – *Joe Queenan*

Griffith, Raymond (1894–1937).
Dapper American comedian of the 20s.
Fools First 22. The Eternal Three 23. Changing Husbands 24. Poisoned Paradise 24. Open All Night 24. Miss Bluebeard 24. A Regular Fellow 25. *Fine Clothes* 25. *Hands Up* 25. Wet Paint 26. You'd Be Surprised 27. Time to Love 27. Wedding Bills 27. All Quiet on the Western Front (as the dying soldier) 30, etc.

Griffith, Richard (1912–1969).
American film critic and curator of New York's Museum of Modern Art.

Griffith, Thomas Ian (1960–).
American actor, producer and screenwriter, in action movies.
The Karate Kid Part III (a) 89. Night of the Warrior (p, w) 91. Ulterior Motives (a) 92. Excessive Force (a, p, w) 93, etc.

Griffiths, Jane (1929–1975).
British leading lady of the 50s.
The Million Pound Note 54. The Green Scarf 54. Dead Man's Evidence 62. The Traitors 63, etc.

Griffiths, Linda.
Canadian leading actress, dramatist and screenwriter.
Lianna 83. Overdrawn at the Memory Bank 83. Reno and the Doc 84. The Darling Family (& w) 94, etc.

Griffiths, Richard (1947–).
Sizeable British actor.
Greystoke 84. Gorky Park 84. A Private Function 85. Shanghai Surprise 86. Withnail and I 87. King Ralph 91. The Naked Gun 2½: The Smell of Fear 91. Blame It on the Bellboy 92. Guarding Tess 94, etc.
TV series: Bird of Prey 84. Nobody's Perfect 80–82. Ffizz 87–89. A Kind of Living 88–90. Pie in the Sky 94–95.

Griggs, Loyal (1906–1978).
American cinematographer.
Shane (AA) 53. Elephant Walk 54. We're No Angels 55. The Ten Commandments 56. The Hangman 59. Walk Like a Dragon 60. The Slender Thread 66. Hurry Sundown 67. P. J. 68, many others.

Grimault, Paul (1905–1994).
French animator. Le Petit Soldat 47, many shorts.

Grimes, Gary (1955–).
American juvenile lead of the 70s.
■ *Summer of 42* 71. The Culpepper Cattle Co. 72. Class of 44 73. Cahill 73. The Spikes Gang 74. Once an Eagle (TV) 76. Gus 76.

Grimes, Stephen (1927–1988).
American production designer.
Reflections in a Golden Eye 67. Ryan's Daughter 71. Murder by Death 76. The Electric Horseman 79. Urban Cowboy 80. Out of Africa 85, etc.

Grimes, Tammy (1934–).
American comedy actress who never really made it in the movies. She is the mother of Amanda Plummer.
■ Three Bites of the Apple 67. Arthur Arthur 69. The Other Man (TV) 70. Play It As It Lays 72. The Borrowers (TV) 73. Horror at 37,000 Feet (TV) 73. Somebody Killed Her Husband 78. You Can't Go Home Again (TV) 79. The Runner Stumbles 79. Can't Stop the Music 80. America 86. Mr North 88.

Grimm, Jakob (1785–1863) and **Wilhelm** (1786–1859).
German writers of philology and – especially – fairy tales. The latter are familiar throughout the world and have been the basis of many children's films by Walt Disney and others. A thin biopic, The Wonderful World of the Brothers Grimm, was made in 1962.

Grimm, Oliver (1948–).
German child actor of the 50s.
My Name is Nicki 52. Father Needs a Wife 52.

My Father the Actor 56. Kleiner Mann – ganz gross 57, etc.

Grinde, Nick (1891–1979).
American director.
Excuse Me 25. Upstage 26. Beyond the Sierra 28. *The Bishop Murder Case* 30. Good News 30. This Modern Age 31. Vanity Street 32. Ladies Crave Excitement 35. Public Enemy's Wife 36. White Bondage 37. King of Chinatown 39. The Man They Could Not Hang 39. Behind the Door 40. Hitler Dead or Alive 43. Road to Alcatraz 45, etc.

grip.
A technician who builds or arranges the film set; a specialized labourer. The chief grip on a picture is usually credited as 'Key Grip'.

Grisham, John (1955–).
American best-selling novelist, a former lawyer. He was paid $2.25m for the film rights to The Client and a record $3.75m for the film rights to The Chamber before it was written. Film rights in his 1989 novel A Time to Kill were sold for around $6m in 1994.
The Firm 92. The Pelican Brief 93. The Client 94.

Grizzard, George (1928–).
American stage actor, usually in sneaky roles in films.
From the Terrace 60. *Advise and Consent 62.* Warning Shot 66. Happy Birthday Wanda June 71. Travis Logan DA (TV) 71. Indict and Convict (TV) 74. The Stranger Within (TV) 74. Attack on Terror (TV) 75. The Lives of Jenny Dolan (TV) 75. Comes a Horseman 78. The Night Rider (TV) 79. Firepower 79. Seems Like Old Times 80. Wrong Is Right 82. Bachelor Party 84, etc.
TV series: Studio 5-B 89.

Grock (1880–1959) (Adrien Wettach).
Swiss clown who made a few silent films in Britain, and later in Germany. A biopic, *Farewell Mr Grock*, was made in 1954.

Grodin, Charles (1935–).
American leading man.
■ Rosemary's Baby 68. Sex and the College Girl 70. Catch 22 70. *The Heartbreak Kid 72.* 11 Harrowhouse 74. King Kong 76. Thieves 77. Heaven Can Wait 78. Just You and Me (TV) 78. The Grass Is Always Greener Over the Septic Tank (TV) 78. Sunburn 79. Real Life 79. It's My Turn 80. Seems Like Old Times 80. The Great Muppet Caper 81. The Incredible Shrinking Woman 81. The Lonely Guy 83. Movers and Shakers 84. The Woman in Red 84. The Last Resort 86. Ishtar 87. The Couch Trip 88. Midnight Run 88. You Can't Hurry Love 88. Taking Care of Business 90. Clifford 91. Beethoven 92. Dave 93. So I Married an Axe Murderer 93. Beethoven's 2nd 93. Heart and Souls 93. Clifford 94. It Runs in the Family 94.

¶ He keeps threatening to be funny but he rarely makes it. – *Pauline Kael*

Grosbard, Ulu (1929–).
Belgian-American director, former diamond-cutter and Broadway director.
■ The Subject Was Roses 68. Who Is Harry Kellerman and Why Is He Saying Those Terrible Things About Me? 71. Straight Time 78. True Confessions 81. Falling in Love 84. Georgia 95.

Gross, Charles.
American composer, mainly for TV movies.

The Group 65. Valdez Is Coming 71. Heartland 79. Sweet Dreams 85. Punchline 88. Turner & Hooch 89. Air America 90, etc.

Gross, Larry.
American screenwriter.
Headin' for Broadway (co-w) 80. 48 Hrs (co-w) 82. Streets of Fire (co-w) 84. Another 48 Hrs (co-w) 90. Geronimo (co-w) 93.

Grossmith, George (1874–1935).
British musical comedy star who appeared in a few films.
■ Women Everywhere 30. Service for Ladies 32. Wedding Rehearsal 32. The Girl from Maxim's 33. Princess Charming 34.

Grot, Anton (1884–1974) (Antocz Franziszek Groszewski).
Polish art director, in Hollywood from the 20s: the driving force of Warner's 30s dream machine.
Robin Hood 20. The Thief of Bagdad 24. Don Q Son of Zorro 25. The Volga Boatmen 26. White Gold 27. Show Girl 28. Her Private Life 30. *Svengali* 31. *Little Caesar* 31. The Mad Genius 32. *Doctor X* 32. Gold Diggers of 1933 33. *The Mystery of the Wax Museum* 33. Captain Blood 35. Anthony Adverse 35. *A Midsummer Night's Dream* 35. The Life of Emile Zola 37. *Juarez* 39. *The Sea Hawk* 40. *The Sea Wolf* 41. The Conspirators 44. *Mildred Pierce* 45. *Possessed* 47. *The Unsuspected* 47. Backfire 50, many others.
❻ For putting his unmistakable stamp on so many films whose visuals linger in the memory. *The Mystery of the Wax Museum.*

Group 3.
A British production company set up in 1951 by the National Film Finance Corporation. In charge were John Baxter, John Grierson and Michael Balcon, and their aim was to make low-budget films employing young talent. The venture was regarded with suspicion by the trade, and the results were not encouraging – a string of mildly eccentric comedies and thrillers lucky to get second-feature circuit bookings. Some of the titles: *Judgement Deferred, Brandy for the Parson, The Brave Don't Cry, You're Only Young Twice, The Oracle, Laxdale Hall, Time Gentlemen Please.*

Gruber, Frank (1904–1969).
American screenwriter.
Death of a Champion (oa) 39. The Kansan (oa) 43. *The Mask of Dimitrios* 44. Terror by Night 47. Fighting Man of the Plains 49. The Great Missouri Raid 51. Denver and Rio Grande 52. Hurricane Smith 52. Backlash (oa) 56. The Big Land (oa) 57. Town Tamer 65. Arizona Raiders (oa) 67, etc.
TV: created *Tales of Wells Fargo.*

Gruenberg, Louis (1884–1964).
Russian-American composer.
Stagecoach (co-w) 39.

Gruendgens, Gustav (1899–1963).
German stage actor and director; films occasional.
M (a) 31. Pygmalion (a) 35. Capriolen (d) 37. Friedemann Bach (a) 41. Faust (ad) 61.

Grune, Karl (1890–1962).
Czech-Austrian director in German films.
The Street 23. At the Edge of the World 27. Waterloo 28. Abdul the Damned (GB) 35. Pagliacci (GB) 37, etc.

Gruner, Olivier (1960–).
French star of American action movies, a former marine and kick-boxing champion. Born in Paris,

he worked as a model in TV commercials before moving to the USA.
Angel Town 89. Nemesis 93. Zero Hour 94.

Grusin, Dave (1934–).
American composer.
Divorce American Style 67. The Graduate 67. Candy 68. The Mad Room 69. Tell them Willie Boy is Here 69. The Pursuit of Happiness 71. The Great Northfield Minnesota Raid 72. Bobby Deerfield 77. The Goodbye Girl 77. The Cheap Detective 78. Heaven Can Wait (AAN) 78. The Champ (AAN) 79. And Justice for All 79. The Electric Horseman 79. My Bodyguard 80. On Golden Pond (AAN) 81. Absence of Malice 81. Reds 81. The Little Drummer Girl 84. Falling in Love 84. The Goonies 85. Lucas 86. Ishtar 87. The Milagro Beanfield War (AA) 88. Tequila Sunrise 88. A Dry White Season 89. The Fabulous Baker Boys (AAN) 89. Bonfire of the Vanities 90. Look Who's Talking Too 90. Havana 90. For the Boys 91. The Firm (AAN) 93, etc.

Guard, Dominic (1956–).
British juvenile actor of the 70s.
The Go-Between 70. The Hands of Cormac Joyce (TV) 72. Bequest to the Nation 73. The Count of Monte Cristo (TV) 74. Picnic at Hanging Rock 75. Gandhi 82. A Woman of Substance (TV) 84. Absolution 88. The Man Who Lost His Shadow 91, etc.

Guardino, Harry (1925–).
Leading American TV actor, in occasional films.
Houseboat 58. Pork Chop Hill 59. The Five Pennies 59. King of Kings 61. Hell is for Heroes 62. Rhino 64. Bullwhip Griffin 67. Madigan 68. Lovers and Other Strangers 69. Red Sky at Morning 71. Dirty Harry 71. Capone 75. St Ives 76. The Enforcer 76. Street Killing (TV) 76. Rollercoaster 77. Goldengirl (TV) 79. Any Which Way You Can 80. The Neon Empire 89, etc.
TV series: The Reporter 64. Monty Nash 71.

Guare, John (1938–).
American dramatist and screenwriter. Born in New York, he studied at the Yale School of Drama.
Taking Off (co-w) 71. Atlantic City (AANw) 81. Six Degrees of Separation (w, from his play) 93.

Guareschi, Giovanni (1908–1968).
Italian author of the 'Don Camillo' stories about a parish priest's comic struggles with a communist mayor. Several were filmed with Fernandel and Gino Cervi.

Guber, Peter (1939–).
Producer whose Guber-Peters production company, formed in partnership with Jon Peters, enjoyed success in the 80s. He is now head of Columbia, following its takeover by Sony in 1989.
The Deep 77. Midnight Express 78. An American Werewolf in London 81. Six Weeks 82. The Color Purple 85. The Clan of the Cave Bear 86. Innerspace 87. The Witches of Eastwick 87. Gorillas in the Mist 88. Rain Man 88. Batman 89. The Bonfire of the Vanities 90, etc.

Guerra, Ruy (1931–).
Brazilian director, playwright, actor and composer. Born in Mozambique and educated in France, he lived in Brazil from the late 50s to the mid-60s, leaving to settle in Mozambique, where he founded the National Institute of Cinema and made that country's first feature film in 1980.
Os Cafajestes 62. Os Fuzis 64. Sweet Hunters 69. Mueda, Memoria e Massacre 80. Erendira 82. Opera do Malandro 86. Kuarup 89, etc.

Guerra, Tonino (1920–).
Italian screenwriter and novelist who wrote five films for Antonioni.
La Notte 61. L'Avventura 61. Red Desert 65. Casanova '70 (AAN) 65. Blow-Up (AAN) 66. Zabriskie Point 70. Amarcord (AAN) 74. Un Papillon sur l'Epaule 78. The Night of the Shooting Stars (La Notte di San Lorenzo) 82. And the Ship Sails On 83. Nostalgia 84. Henry IV 85. Ginger and Fred 86. Good Morning Babylon 86. The Beekeeper (O Melissokomos) 86. Chronicle of a Death Foretold 87. To Forget Palermo (Dimenticare Palermo) 89. The Dark Illness (Il Male Oscuro) 89. Stanno Tutti Bene 90. Journey of Love (Viàggio d'Amore) 91. Especially on Sundays (La Domenica Specialmente) 91, many others.

Guest, Christopher (1948–).
American actor and screenwriter turned director. He married actress Jamie Lee Curtis in 1984.
The Hot Rock 72. Girlfriends 78. The Long Riders 80. Heartbeeps 81. This Is Spinal Tap (& w) 84. Little Shop of Horrors 86. The Princess Bride 87. Beyond Therapy 87. Sticky Fingers 88. The Big Picture (wd) 89. Attack of the 50 Ft Woman (TV) (d) 93, etc.

Guest, Val (1911–) (Valmond Guest).
British writer-producer-director, former journalist. Worked on screenplays of 30s comedies for Will Hay, Arthur Askey, the Crazy Gang, etc. Married to Yolande Donlan.
SCREENPLAYS, MOSTLY IN COLLABORATION: The Maid of the Mountains 32. Good Morning Boys 36. Okay for Sound 37. *Oh Mr Porter* 38. Convict 99 38. *Alf's Button Afloat* 38. Band Waggon 39. The Frozen Limits 39. Old Bones of the River 39. Ask a Policeman 40. Charley's Aunt 40. Gasbags 40. Inspector Hornleigh Goes to It 41. *The Ghost Train* 41. Back Room Boy 42. London Town 46. Paper Orchid 49 etc.
■ AS DIRECTOR (usually writer also): Miss London Ltd. 43. Bees in Paradise 44. Give Us the Moon 44. I'll Be Your Sweetheart 45. Just William's Luck 47. William Comes to Town 48. Murder at the Windmill 49. Miss Pilgrim's Progress 50. The Body Said No 50. *Mr Drake's Duck* 51. Penny Princess 52. *The Runaway Bus* 54. Life with the Lyons 54. Men of Sherwood Forest 54. Dance Little Lady 54. They Can't Hang Me 54. The Lyons in Paris 55. Break in the Circle 55. *The Quatermass Experiment* 55. It's A Wonderful World 55. The Weapon 56. Carry On Admiral 57. *Quatermass II* 57. The Abominable Snowman 57. Camp on Blood Island 58. Up the Creek 58. Life is a Circus 59. Yesterday's Enemy 59. *Expresso Bongo* 60. Further Up the Creek 60. Hell is a City 60. The Full Treatment 60. The Day the Earth Caught Fire 62. Jigsaw 63. 80,000 Suspects 63. The Beauty Jungle 64. Where the Spies are 65. Casino Royale (wd) 67. Assignment K 67. When Dinosaurs Ruled the World 68. Tomorrow 70. Au Pair Girls 72. Confessions of a Window Cleaner 74. The Diamond Mercenaries 76. Dangerous Davies (TV) 80. The Boys in Blue 83. Possession (TV) 84. The Scent of Fear (TV) 85.

Guetary, Georges (1915–) (Lambros Worloou).
Greek/Egyptian singer who became popular in French cabaret and musical comedy. Only American film: An American in Paris 51.

Guffey, Burnett (1905–1983).
Distinguished American cinematographer.
Cover Girl 44. Johnny O'Clock 46. Gallant Journey 46. The Reckless Moment 48. *All the King's Men* 49. In a Lonely Place 50. The Sniper 52. *From Here to Eternity* (AA) 53. Human Desire 55. The

Harder They Fall 56. Edge of Eternity 59. Birdman of Alcatraz 62. King Rat 65. *Bonnie and Clyde* (AA) 67. The Split 68. The Madwoman of Chaillot 69. The Great White Hope 70, etc.

Guilaroff, Sydney (1910–).
American star hairdresser, long at MGM.

Guild, Nancy (1925–).
American leading lady.
Somewhere in the Night 46. The High Window 47. Give My Regards to Broadway 49. Abbott and Costello Meet the Invisible Man 51. Francis Covers the Big Town 54. Such Good Friends 71, etc.

Guilfoyle, Paul (1902–1961).
American character actor usually in sly or sinister roles.
Special Agent 36. Blind Alibi 38. Time to Kill 42. Sweetheart of Sigma Chi 46. Miss Mink of 1949. Mighty Joe Young 50. Torch Song 52. Julius Caesar 53. Valley of Fury 55, many others.
AS DIRECTOR: Captain Scarface 53. A Life at Stake 54. Tess of the Storm Country 60.

Guillaume, Robert (1930–) (Robert Williams).
Handsome American leading man and comedian, former opera singer.
Seems Like Old Times 80. The Kid with the Broken Halo (TV) 82. The Kid with the 200 I.Q. (TV) 83. Prince Jack 84. They Still Call Me Bruce 86. Wanted: Dead or Alive 86. Fire and Rain 89. The Meteor Man 93. The Lion King (voice) 94, etc.
TV series: *Soap* 77–80. *Benson* 79–86.

Guillermin, John (1925–).
English director and screenwriter. Born in London of French parents, he was educated at Cambridge University and produced and directed documentaries in Paris before returning to England in the late 40s, moving to Los Angeles in the early 60s, after the success of *Waltz of the Toreadors*.
■ Torment 49. Smart Alec 50. Never Let Go (w) 50. Two on the Tiles 51. Four Days 51. Song of Paris 52. Miss Robin Hood 52. Operation Diplomat 53. Adventure in the Hopfields 54. The Crowded Day 54. Thunderstorm 55. Double Jeopardy 55. *Town on Trial* 56. The Whole Truth 57. *I Was Monty's Double* 58. Tarzan's Greatest Adventure 59. The Day They Robbed The Bank of England 60. Never Let Go (& w) 60. Waltz of the Toreadors 62. Tarzan Goes to India 62. Guns at Batasi 64. Rapture 65. *The Blue Max* 66. P.J. 68. House of Cards 68. The Bridge at Remagen 69. El Condor 70. Skyjacked 72. Shaft in Africa 74. The Towering Inferno (co-d) 74. King Kong 76. Death on the Nile 78. Mr Patman 80. Crossover 83. Sheena Queen of the Jungle 84. King Kong Lives 86.

the guillotine,
that French instrument of execution, cast its shadow over a variety of films including *Marie Antoinette, A Tale of Two Cities, Uncertain Glory, The Scarlet Pimpernel,* and *Mad Love.* The Carry On gang managed to make fun with it in *Don't Lose Your Head.* Private guillotines were employed for diabolical purposes in *The Mystery of the Wax Museum, House of Wax, Chamber of Horrors* and *Two on a Guillotine.*

Guinan, Texas (1886–1934) (Mary Louise Guinan).
Canadian star entertainer of 20s speakeasies: her catchphrase was 'Hello, sucker!', and she was one of Broadway's most prominent attractions. Betty Hutton played her in *Incendiary Blonde* 45.
■ The Gun Woman 18. Little Miss Deputy 19. I am the Woman 21. The Stampede 21. Queen of the Night Clubs 29. Glorifying the American Girl 29. Broadway through a Keyhole 33.

Guinness, Sir Alec (1914–).
Distinguished British stage actor, who in the late 40s started a spectacular film career, first as a master of disguise, then as a young hero and later as any character from an Arab king to Hitler. Honorary Oscar 1979 'for advancing the art of screen acting'.
Autobiography: 1985, *Blessings in Disguise.*
■ Evensong 33. Great Expectations (as Herbert Pocket) 46. *Oliver Twist* (as Fagin) 48. *Kind Hearts and Coronets* (playing eight roles) 49. A Run for Your Money 49. Last Holiday 50. *The Mudlark* (as Disraeli) 50. *The Lavender Hill Mob* (AAN) 51. *The Man in the White Suit* 51. *The Card* 52. The Captain's Paradise 52. The Malta Story 53. *Father Brown* 54. To Paris with Love 54. The Prisoner 55. The Ladykillers 55. The Swan 56. Barnacle Bill 57. *The Bridge on the River Kwai* (AA, BFA) 57. The Scapegoat 58. The Horse's Mouth (& w) (AAN) 58. Our Man in Havana 59. *Tunes of Glory* 60. A Majority of One 61. HMS Defiant 62. Lawrence of Arabia 62. The Fall of the Roman Empire 64. Situation Hopeless but Not Serious 64. Doctor Zhivago 66. Hotel Paradiso 66. The Quiller Memorandum 66. The Comedians 67. Cromwell (as Charles I) 69. Scrooge 70, Hitler: The Last Ten Days (as Hitler) 73. Brother Sun and Sister Moon 73. Murder by Death 76. Star Wars (AAN) 77. Tinker Tailor Soldier Spy (TV) 79. The Empire Strikes Back 80. Raise the Titanic 80. Little Lord Fauntleroy (TV) 80. Smiley's People (TV) 82. Lovesick 83. A Passage to India 84. Monsignor Quixote (TV) 85. Little Dorrit (AAN) 87. A Handful of Dust 88. Kafka 91. A Foreign Field (TV) 93.
✿ For a multitude of disguises in which he never allowed humanity to be swamped by dexterity. *Father Brown.*

¶ I gave my best performances, perhaps, during the war – trying to be an officer and a gentleman. – *A.G.*
I don't know what else I could do but pretend to be an actor. – *A.G.*
Once I've done a film, it's finished. I never look at it again. – *A.G.*

Guiol, Fred (1898–1964).
American director, mainly of second features; also worked as assistant on many of George Stevens's pictures.
Live and Learn 30. The Cohens and Kellys in Trouble 33. The Nitwits 35. Hayfoot 41. Here Comes Trouble 48. Giant (co-w, AAN) 56, many others.

Guitry, Sacha (1885–1957).
Distinguished French writer-director, in films occasionally over a long period.
Autobiography: 1956, *If Memory Serves.*
Biography: 1968, *The Last Boulevardier* by James Harding.
Ceux de Chez Nous 15. Les Deux Couverts 32. Bonne Chance 35. Le Roman d'un Tricheur 36. Quadrille 38. Ils Etaient Neuf Célibataires 39. Donne-moi tes yeux 43. Le Comedien 49. Deburau 51. Versailles 54. Napoleon 55. La Vie à Deux 57, etc.

Gulager, Clu (1928–).
American leading man, mostly on TV.
The Killers (TV) 64. Winning 69. The Last Picture Show 71. The Glass House (TV) 72. Footsteps (TV) 72. Call to Danger (TV) 73. McQ 74. The Killer Who Wouldn't Die (TV) 76. The Other Side of Midnight 77. A Force of One 79. Touched by Love 80. The Return of the Living Dead 85. Hunter's Blood 86. The Offspring 86. Eddie Presley 93, etc.
TV series: The Tall Man 60–61. The Virginian 64–68. The Survivors 69. San Francisco International 70.

Gulliver's Travels.
Jonathan Swift's savage allegory was naturally seen by Hollywood as merely a child's fantasy. Max Fleischer's 1939 feature cartoon seemed at the time to have as much charm and skill as a Disney production, but it has worn disappointingly. Jack Sher's 1960 live-action version, *The Three Worlds of Gulliver,* had neat trick-work but a less than absorbing screenplay. Peter Hunt's 1977 version had Richard Harris as Gulliver in an otherwise lacklustre animated film.

Gulpilil, David (1954–).
Australian actor, memorable as the aborigine youth in Nicolas Roeg's *Walkabout.* He is also head of an aboriginal dance company.
Walkabout 71. Mad Dog Morgan 76. Storm Boy 76. The Last Wave 77. Blue Fin 78. Long Weekend 78. Crocodile Dundee 86. Dark Age 88. Until the End of the World (Bis ans Ende der Welt) 91, etc.

Güney, Yilmaz (1937–1984).
Leading Turkish actor and screenwriter who turned to directing after serving terms of imprisonment for his left-wing political activities. He supervised films in the mid-70s from his prison cell, escaped in 1981, lost his Turkish citizenship as a result, and died from cancer shortly afterwards.
My Name Is Kerim 67. Bride of the Earth 68. An Ugly Man 69. Hope 70. Tomorrow Is the Final Day 71. Pain 71. The Father 71. Anxiety (co-d) 74. The Poor Ones (co-d) 75. Yol (supervised direction by Serif Goren) 82. The Wall 83, etc.

Gunfight at the OK Corral.
The celebrated, if semi-legendary, confrontation between Wyatt Earp and the Clanton Gang in 1881 at Tombstone, Arizona has been filmed several times, notably in the film of the same name in 1957, with Burt Lancaster as Earp and Kirk Douglas as Doc Holliday, roles played in *My Darling Clementine* 46 by Henry Fonda and Victor Mature, in *Tombstone* 94 by Kurt Russell and Val Kilmer, and in *Wyatt Earp* 94 by Kevin Costner and Dennis Quaid. Randolph Scott also played Earp in an earlier version, *Frontier Marshall* 39, and the TV series *Wyatt Earp* starred Hugh O'Brian.

Gunga Din.
Rudyard Kipling's narrative poem of the north-west frontier was rewritten in 1939 by Joel Sayre and Fred Guiol as a rousing combination of high adventure and barrack-room comedy, directed by George Stevens and starring Douglas Fairbanks Jnr, Cary Grant, and Victor McLaglen. In 1951, *Soldiers Three,* directed by Tay Garnett with Stewart Granger, David Niven, and Walter Pidgeon, amounted almost to a remake; while in 1961 John Sturges directed Frank Sinatra, Dean Martin, and Peter Lawford in a pastiche called *Sergeants Three,* set in the American West.

Gunn, Gilbert (c. 1912–).
British director, former documentarist.
The Elstree Story 51. The Strange World of Planet X 57. Girls at Sea 58. Operation Bullshine 59. What a Whopper 62, etc.

Gunn, Moses (1929–).
American actor.

The Great White Hope 70. Carter's Army (TV) 70. The Wild Rovers 71. Shaft 72. The Hot Rock 72. Haunts of the Very Rich (TV) 73. Rollerball 75. Remember My Name 78. The Ninth Configuration 80. Ragtime 81. Amityville II 82. Firestarter 84. Heartbreak Ridge 86.

TV series: The Cowboys 74. Roots 77. Good Times 77. The Contender 80. Father Murphy 80–81. A Man Called Hawk 89.

Gurie, Sigrid (1911–1969) (S. G. Haukelid).
American/Norwegian leading lady of the late 30s.
The Adventures of Marco Polo 38. Algiers 38. Rio 40. Three Faces West 40. Dark Streets of Cairo 41. A Voice in the Wind 44. Sword of the Avenger 48, etc.

Guthrie, A. B. (1901–1991).
American Western novelist and screenwriter, a former journalist, three of whose novels were filmed.
The Big Sky (oa) 52. Shane (AAN) 53. The Kentuckian 55. These Thousand Hills (oa) 59. The Way West (oa) 67.

Guthrie, Arlo (1947–).
American ballad singer, son of another (Woody Guthrie, whose story was told in *Bound for Glory*).
Alice's Restaurant 69. Roadside Prophets 92, etc.

Gutowski, Gene (1925–).
Polish producer with US TV experience.
Four Boys and a Gun 56. Station Six Sahara (GB) 63. Repulsion (GB) 65. Cul-de-Sac (GB) 66. The Fearless Vampire Killers (GB) 66, etc.

Guttenberg, Steve (1958–).
American leading actor.
The Chicken Chronicles 77. Players 79. Diner 81. Police Academy 84. Police Academy II 85. Cocoon 85. Bad Medicine 85. Short Circuit 86. The Bedroom Window 86. Police Academy 4: Citizens on Parade 87. Surrender 87. Three Men and a Baby 87. Cocoon: The Return 88. High Spirits 88. Don't Tell Her It's Me 90. Three Men and a Little Lady 90, etc.
TV series: Billy 79. No Soap, Radio 82.

Guy-Blaché, Alice (1873–1968).
French film director with claims to have been the world's first female director and possibly the world's first director. A secretary to Léon Gaumont, she began by making demonstration films for the company. With her cameraman-husband, Herbert Blaché, she went to America in 1910, set up her own companies and continued directing there until she returned to France in 1922.
The Cabbage Fairy (La Fée aux Choux) 1896. La Vie du Christ 06. Fra Diavolo 12. In the Year 2000 12. Michael Strogoff 14. Tarnished Reputations 20, many others.

Guzman, Pato (1933–1991).
American production designer.

I Love You Alice B. Toklas 68. Bob and Carol and Ted and Alice 69. Alex in Wonderland 70. Blume in Love 73. An Unmarried Woman 78. The In-Laws 79. Hide in Plain Sight 80. Willie and Phil 80. Tempest 82. Moscow on the Hudson 84. Down and Out in Beverly Hills 86. Enemies, a Love Story 89. Scenes from a Mall 91, etc.

Gwenn, Edmund (1875–1959).
Stocky English stage actor who in middle age became a Hollywood film star and gave memorable comedy portrayals into his 80s.
■ SILENT FILMS: The Real Thing at Last 16. Unmarried 20. The Skin Game 20.
■ SOUND FILMS: How He Lied to Her Husband 31. Money for Nothing 31. Condemned to Death 31. Frail Women 31. Hindle Wakes 31. Tell Me Tonight 32. The Admiral's Secret 32. Love on Wheels 32. *The Skin Game* 32. *The Good Companions* 33. I Was a Spy 33. Early to Bed 33. Cash 33. Smithy 33. *Friday the Thirteenth* 33. Marooned 33. Java Head 34. Spring in the Air 34. Channel Crossing 34. Passing Shadows 34. Waltzes from Vienna 34. Father and Son 34. Warn London 34. The Bishop Misbehaves 35. Sylvia Scarlett 35. The Walking Dead 36. Anthony Adverse 36. All American Chump 36. Mad Holiday 36. *Laburnum Grove* 36. Parnell 37. A Yank at Oxford 38. *South Riding* 38. Penny Paradise 38. An Englishman's Home 38. Cheer Boys Cheer 39. The Earl of Chicago 40. Madmen of Europe 40. The Doctor Takes a Wife 40. *Pride and Prejudice* 40. *Foreign Correspondent* (rare villainous role) 40. Scotland Yard 41. Cheers for Miss Bishop 41. The Devil and Miss Jones 41. *Charley's Aunt* 41. One Night in Lisbon 41. A Yank at Eton 42. The Meanest Man in the World 43. Forever and a Day 43. *Lassie Come Home* 43. *Between Two Worlds* (his original 'Outward Bound' stage role) 44. The Keys of the Kingdom 45. Bewitched 45. Dangerous Partners 45. She Went to the Races 45. Of Human Bondage 46. Undercurrent 46. *Miracle on 34th Street* (AA) 47. Thunder in the Valley 47. Life with Father 47. Green Dolphin Street 47. Apartment for Peggy 48. Hills of Home 48. Challenge to Lassie 49. A Woman of Distinction 50. Louisa 50. *Pretty Baby* 50. *Mister 880* (AAN) 50. For Heaven's Sake 50. Peking Express 51. Sally and St Anne 52. Bonzo Goes to College 52. Les Misérables 52. Something for the Birds 52. Mister Scoutmaster 52. The Bigamist 53. *Them* 54. The Student Prince 54. *The Trouble with Harry* 55. It's a Dog's Life 55. Calabuch 57.
✪ For having the talent for remaining a star into his 80s, and the discretion not always to insist on star billing. *Pride and Prejudice*.

Gwynn, Michael (1916–1976).
British stage actor in occasional films.
The Runaway Bus 54. The Secret Place 57. The Revenge of Frankenstein (as the monster) 58. Village of the Damned 60. The Virgin Soldiers 69, etc.

Gwynne, Anne (1918–) (Marguerite Gwynne Trice).
American leading lady of the 40s, former model.

Sandy Takes a Bow 39. Jailhouse Blues 41. The Strange Case of Doctor RX 42. Weird Woman 44. House of Frankenstein 45. Fear 46. The Ghost Goes Wild 46. Dick Tracy Meets Gruesome 48. Call of the Klondike 51. Breakdown 52. The Meteor Monster 57, etc.

Gwynne, Fred (1926–1993).
Lanky, lugubrious American comic actor who appeared in TV series: Car 54 Where Are You? 61–62 and The Munsters 64–65.
On the Waterfront 54. Munster Go Home 66. Captains Courageous (TV) 77. La Luna 78. Simon 80. The Cotton Club 84. Fatal Attraction 87. Ironweed 87. The Secret of My Success 87. Disorganized Crime 89. Pet Sematary 89. Shadows and Fog 91. My Cousin Vinny 92, etc.

Gyllenhaal, Stephen (1949–).
American director, from TV.
A Certain Fury 85. The Abduction of Kari Swenson (TV) 87. Paris Trout 91. Waterland 92. A Dangerous Woman 93, etc.

Gynt, Greta (1916–) (Greta Woxholt).
Norwegian leading lady, popular in British films of the 40s.
The Arsenal Stadium Mystery 39. Dark Eyes of London 39. The Common Touch 41. Tomorrow We Live 42. It's That Man Again 42. Mr Emmanuel 44. London Town 46. Dear Murderer 47. Take My Life 47. The Calendar 48. Mr Perrin and Mr Traill 48. Shadow of the Eagle 50. Soldiers Three (US) 51. Forbidden Cargo 54. Bluebeard's Ten Honeymoons 60. The Runaway 66, many others.

Gyöngyössy, Imre (1930–1994).
Hungarian director, screenwriter, playwright and poet. Imprisoned in the early 50s, he later studied at the Budapest Academy of Film and Television and collaborated on films with his wife, the writer Katalin Petényi, and Barna Kabay, who co-wrote and co-directed their later work. In the late 70s, they moved to work from Munich.
Palm Sunday (wd) 69. You Are Naked 72. Sons of Fire 73. A Quite Ordinary Life (doc) 77. The Revolt of Job (AAN) 82. Homeless 90. Freedom of the Death (Holtak Szabadsaga) 93. Death in Shallow Water (Halal A Sekely Vizben) 94, etc.

gypsies
have not been a favourite subject for movies but glamorized versions have turned up in *Gypsy Wildcat*, *Golden Earrings*, *Caravan*, *Hot Blood*, and *The Man in Grey*. Something closer to the real thing, perhaps, was on view in *Sky West and Crooked*, *The Gypsy and the Gentleman*, and *Alex and the Gypsy*, while TV failed to get going a gypsy detective series called *Roman Grey*. The screen's most memorable gypsy was probably Maria Ouspenskaya as Maleva in *The Wolf Man* and *Frankenstein Meets the Wolf Man*. The most authentic were probably in Hungary's *I Even Met Happy Gypsies*.

Haanstra, Bert (1916–).
Dutch documentarist.

Mirror of Holland 50. The Rival World 55. Rembrandt Painter of Man 56. Glass 58. Fanfare (feature) 58. Zoo 62. The Human Dutch 64. The Voice of the Water 66, etc.

Haas, Charles (1918–).
American director.

Star in the Dust 56. Screaming Eagles 56. Showdown at Abilene 56. Summer Love 58. Wild Heritage 58. The Beat Generation 59. The Big Operator 59. Girls' Town 59. Platinum High School 60, etc.

Haas, Dolly (1910–1994).
German leading lady of the 30s, in a few international films.

Dolly's Way to Stardom 30. Liebes-commando 32. Der Page vom Dalmasse Hotel 34. *Broken Blossoms* (GB) 36. Spy of Napoleon (GB) 37. I Confess (US) 53, etc.

Haas, Hugo (1901–1968).
Czech character actor, in Hollywood from the late 40s; later took to writing and directing low-budget melodramas as vehicles for himself.

Skeleton on Horseback 39. Summer Storm 44. A Bell for Adano 45. Dakota 45. Holiday in Mexico 46. The Foxes of Harrow 47. My Girl Tisa 48. King Solomon's Mines 50. Vendetta 50. The Girl on the Bridge (& wd) 51. Pickup (& wd) 51. Strange Fascination (& wd) 52. Thy Neighbour's Wife (& wd) 53. Hold Back Tomorrow (& wd) 55. The Other Woman (& wd) 55. Edge of Hell (& wd) 56. *Lizzie* (& wd) 57. Born to be Loved (& wd) 59. Night of the Quarter Moon (& wd) 59. Paradise Alley (& wd) 61, etc.

Haas, Lukas (1976–).
American juvenile actor.

Testament 83. Witness 85. Solarbabies 86. Lady in White 88. The Wizard of Loneliness 88. Music Box 89. See You in the Morning 89. Gettysburg 90. Rambling Rose 91. Alan & Naomi 92. Leap of Faith 92, etc.

Hack, Shelley (1948–).
American actress, a former teenage model.

Annie Hall 77. If I Ever See You Again 78. King of Comedy 82. Single Bars, Single Women (TV) 85. Troll 85. The Stepfather 85. Blind Fear 89. A Casualty of War (TV) 90. The Finishing Touch 92, etc.

TV series: Charlie's Angels 79–80. Cutter to Houston 83. Jack and Mike 86–87.

Hackathorne, George (1895–1940).
American light actor of the later silents.

The Last of the Mohicans 20. The Little Minister 21. Merry Go Round 23. Magnificent Obsession 35. Gone with the Wind 39, many others.

Hackett, Albert (1900–).
American writer, usually with his wife Frances

Goodrich (qv). He began as an actor in silent films, together with his brother, Raymond Hackett.

Hackett, Buddy (1924–) (Leonard Hacker).
Tubby American comedian with vaudeville experience.

Walking My Baby Back Home 53. God's Little Acre 58. *The Music Man* 62. *It's a Mad Mad Mad Mad World* 63. The Golden Head 65. The Love Bug 69. The Good Guys and the Bad Guys 69. Bud and Lou (TV) 78. Scrooged 88. The Little Mermaid (voice) 89, etc.

TV series: Stanley 56.

Hackett, Joan (1934–1983).
American leading lady usually seen in unglamorous roles.

■ *The Group* 66. Will Penny 67. Support Your Local Sheriff 69. Assignment to Kill 69. The Other Man (TV) 70. How Awful About Allan (TV) 70. The Young Country (TV) 71. Five Desperate Women (TV) 71. The Rivals 73. The Last of Sheila 73. Class of 63 (TV) 73. Reflections of Murder (TV) 74. The Terminal Man 74. Mackintosh and T.J. 75. Treasure of Matecumbe 76. Stonestreet (TV) 77. The Possessed (TV) 77. Pleasure Cove (TV) 79. Mr Mike's Mondo Video 79. The North Avenue Irregulars 79. One Trick Pony 80. The Long Days of Summer (TV) 80. Only When I Laugh (AAN) 81. The Long Summer of George Adams (TV) 82. The Escape Artist 82.

TV series: The Defenders 61–62. Another Day 78.

Hackett, Raymond (1902–1958).
American leading man who had brief popularity during the changeover from silent to sound.

The Loves of Sunya 28. Madame X 29. Our Blushing Brides 29. The Trial of Mary Dugan 30. The Sea Wolf 30. The Cat Creeps 31. Seed 31, etc.

Hackford, Taylor (1945–).
American director and producer who runs his own production company, New Visions Entertainment.

The Idolmaker 80. An Officer and a Gentleman 82. Against All Odds 83. White Nights 85. Hail! Hail! Rock 'n' Roll 87. La Bamba (p) 87. Everybody's All-American 88. Rooftops (p) 89. The Long Walk Home (p) 90. Mortal Thoughts (p) 91. Queen's Logic (p) 91. Sweet Talker (p) 91. Blood In, Blood Out (pd) 93. Dolores Claiborne 94, etc.

Hackman, Gene (1931–).
Virile American character actor who unexpectedly became a star of the early 70s.

■ Mad Dog Coll 61. Lilith 64. Hawaii 66. First to Fight 67. A Covenant with Death 67. Banning 67. *Bonnie and Clyde* (AAN) 67. The Split 68. Shadow on the Land (TV) 68. Riot 69. Downhill Racer 69. *I Never Sang for My Father* (AAN) 69. The Gypsy Moths 69. Marooned 70. Doctors' Wives 71. The Hunting Party 71. *The French Connection* (AA) 71. Cisco Pike 72. Prime Cut 72. The Poseidon Adventure 72. The Conversation 73. Scarecrow 73. Zandy's Bride 74. Young Frankenstein 74. Bite the

Bullet 75. French Connection II 75. Lucky Lady 75. Night Moves 76. The Domino Principle 77. A Bridge Too Far 77. March or Die 77. Superman 78. Superman II 80. All Night Long 81. Reds 81. Eureka 83. Two of a Kind 83. Uncommon Valor 83. Under Fire 83. Misunderstood 84. Target 85. Twice in a Lifetime 85. Hoosiers 86. No Way Out 87. Superman IV 87. Another Woman 88. BAT 21 88. Full Moon in Blue Water 88. Split Decisions 88. Mississippi Burning (AAN) 88. Loose Cannons 89. The Package 89. Narrow Margin 90. Postcards from the Edge 90. Loose Cannons 90. Company Business 91. Class Action 91. Unforgiven (AA) 92. Geronimo: An American Legend 93. The Firm 93. Wyatt Earp 94. Crimson Tide 95.

¶ People in the street still call me Popeye, and *The French Connection* was 15 years ago. I wish I could have another hit and a new nickname. – G.H.

Hackney, Alan (1924–).
British comedy writer.

Private's Progress 55. I'm All Right, Jack 59. Two-way Stretch (c-w) 60. Swordsman of Siena 62. You Must Be Joking 65, etc.

Haddon, Peter (1898–1962) (Peter Tildsley).
British light actor, usually in silly-ass roles.

Death at Broadcasting House 34. The Silent Passenger (as Lord Peter Wimsey) 35. Kate Plus Ten 38. Helter Skelter 49. The Second Mrs Tanqueray 54, etc.

Haden, Sara (1897–1981).
American actress of quiet, well-spoken parts, best remembered as the spinster aunt of the Hardy family.

Spitfire (debut) 34. Magnificent Obsession 35. First Lady 38. H. M. Pulham Esquire 41. Lost Angel 43. Mr Ace 45. Our Vines Have Tender Grapes 45. She-Wolf of London (as villainess) 46. The Bishop's Wife 48. A Life of her Own 50. A Lion is in the Streets 53. Andy Hardy Comes Home 58, many others.

Hadjidakis, Manos (1925–1994).
Greek composer.

Stella 55. A Matter of Dignity 57. *Never on Sunday* (AA) 59. America America 63. Blue 68. The Martlet's Tale 70. The Pedestrian 74. Sweet Movie 75. Honeymoon 79, etc.

Hadley, Reed (1911–1974) (Reed Herring).
American 'second lead'.

Fugitive Lady 38. The Bank Dick 41. Guadalcanal Diary 43. Leave Her to Heaven 46. The Iron Curtain 48. Captain from Castile 49. Dallas 51. Big House USA 55. The St Valentine's Day Massacre 68, etc.

TV series: Racket Squad 51–53. Public Defender 53–54.

Hageman, Richard (1882–1966).
Dutch-American composer.

If I Were King (AAN) 38. Stagecoach (co-m, AA)

39. The Howards of Virginia (AAN) 40. The Long Voyage Home (AAN) 40. This Woman Is Mine (AAN) 41. The Shanghai Gesture (AAN) 42. Fort Apache 48. Three Godfathers 48. She Wore a Yellow Ribbon 49. Wagon Master 50, etc.

Hagen, Jean (1924–1977) (Jean Verhagen). American comedy character actress, usually in Brooklynesque dames; also minor leading lady. Forced to retire in the mid-60s because of illness. ■ Side Street 49. *Adam's Rib* 49. Ambush 50. The Asphalt Jungle 50. A Life of Her Own 50. Night into Morning 50. No Questions Asked 51. *Singin' in the Rain* (a splendid performance as the silent star with the ghastly voice) (AAN) 52. Shadow in the Sky 52. Carbine Williams 52. Latin Lovers 53. Arena 53. Half a Hero 53. The Big Knife 55. Spring Reunion 57. The Shaggy Dog 59. Sunrise at Campobello 60. Panic in Year Zero 62. Dead Ringer 64.
TV series: The Danny Thomas Show 53–56.

Famous line (*Singin' in the Rain*): 'If we bring a little joy into your humdrum lives, we feel all our hard work ain't been in vain for nothin'.'

Hagen, Julius (1884–1939). British producer, a former actor, who founded Twickenhan Film Studios and Real Art Productions in 1929, in partnership with director Leslie Hiscott, to turn out 'quota quickies' to meet the legal requirement of the time for exhibitors to show British films. Directors and writers spent a fortnight writing a script and a fortnight shooting it. He persuaded many leading British actors and some Hollywood ones to appear in his films, including Sydney Howard, Leslie Fuller, Henry Kendall, Sir John Martin Harvey, Ivor Novello, Gracie Fields, Sir Seymour Hicks, Flanagan and Allen, Edward Everett Horton and Conrad Veidt. He hired D.W. Griffith to remake *Broken Blossoms* in sound, but Griffith walked out after a disagreement. He ran into trouble trying to make more expensive films and became bankrupt in 1938.
To What Red Hell 29. At the Villa Rose 30. Chin, Chin, Chinaman 31. Alibi 31. Bill's Legacy 31. The Lyons Mail 31. Condemned to Death 32. The Crooked Lady 32. The Lodger 32. Excess Baggage 33. This Week of Grace 33. The Wandering Jew 33. I Lived with You 33. The Black Abbot 34. Blind Justice 34. The Admiral's Secret 34. Bella Donna 34. Department Store 35. The Ace of Spades 35. A Fire Has Been Arranged 35. Scrooge 35. She Shall Have Music 35. The Triumph of Sherlock Holmes 35. The Last Journey 35. The Private Secretary 35. Broken Blossoms 36. Eliza Comes to Stay 36. Spy of Napoleon 36. Juggernaut 36. Beauty and the Barge 37. Silver Blaze 37. Clothes and the Woman 37. Underneath the Arches 37, etc.

Hagerty, Julie (1955–). American actress, a former model, usually in comic roles.
Airplane 80. Airplane II 82. A Midsummer Night's Sex Comedy 82. Bad Medicine 85. Goodbye New York 85. Lost in America 85. Aria 87. Beyond Therapy 87. Bloodhounds of Broadway 89. Rude Awakening 89. Reversal of Fortune 90. What About Bob? 91. Noises Off 92, etc.
TV series: Princesses 91.

Haggar, William (1851–1924). British pioneer producer, a former fairground showman who made short sensational films featuring himself and his family.
The Maniac's Guillotine 02. The Wild Man of Borneo 02. Mirthful Mary 03. A Dash for Liberty

03. The Sign of the Cross 04. The Life of Charles Peace 05. Desperate Footpads 07. Maria Marten 08. The Dumb Man of Manchester 08, etc.

Haggard, Sir H. Rider (1856–1925). British adventure novelist, whose most famous novel, *She*, has been filmed at least nine times. There have also been two versions of *King Solomon's Mines*, and two lightly disguised variants, *Watusi* and *King Solomon's Treasure*.

Haggard, Piers (1939–). British director.
Wedding Night 69. Satan's Skin 70. Pennies from Heaven (TV) 78. The Fiendish Plot of Dr Fu Manchu 80. Venom 82. A Summer Story (TV) 88. I'll Take Romance (TV) 90. The Lifeforce Experiment (TV) 94, etc.

Haggerty, Dan (1941–). Hefty American leading man, notably on TV in *The Legend of Grizzly Adams*.
The Tender Warrior 70. Hex 73. When the North Wind Blows 74. Starbird and Sweet William 75. Frontier Freemont 76. Desperate Women (TV) 79. Condominium (TV) 80. Grizzly Adams: The Mark of the Bear 91, etc.

Hagman, Larry (1931–). American comedy leading man, much on TV; son of Mary Martin.
Ensign Pulver 64. Fail Safe 64. In Harm's Way 65. The Group 65. Vanished (TV) 70. Up in the Cellar 70. Beware the Blob (TV) 71. A Howling in the Woods (TV) 72. The Alpha Caper (TV) 73. Stardust 74. Harry and Tonto 74. Mother Jugs and Speed 76. The Eagle Has Landed 76. Crash 77. The President's Mistress (TV) 78. Superman 78. SOB 81, etc.
TV series: I Dream of Jeannie 65–70. The Good Life 71. Here We Go Again 71. *Dallas* 78–88.

¶ People I meet really want me to be J.R., so it's hard to disappoint them. – *L.H.*
I was born with success. Lucky for me, I am able to handle it. Also, I damn well deserve it! – *L.H.*

Hagmann, Stuart (1939–). American director who turned to making TV commercials after the failure of his second feature.
The Strawberry Statement 70. Believe in Me 71, etc.

Haid, Charles (1943–). American actor, producer and director.
AS ACTOR: The Choirboys 77. Oliver's Story 78. Who'll Stop the Rain (aka Dog Soldiers) 78. Altered States 80. Twirl (TV) 81. Cop 88. Fire and Rain (TV) 89. Night Breed 90. Storyville 92, etc.
AS DIRECTOR: Iron Will 94.
TV series (as actor): Kate McShane 75. Delvecchio 76–77. Hill Street Blues 81–87.

Haigh, Kenneth (1929–). British stage actor, the original lead of *Look Back in Anger*, has tended to remain in angry young man roles.
My Teenage Daughter 56. High Flight 56. Saint Joan 57. Cleopatra 63. A Hard Day's Night 64. The Deadly Affair 66. A Lovely Way to Die (US) 68. Eagle in a Cage 71. Man at the Top 73. The Bitch 79, etc.
TV series: *Man at the Top* 71–73.

Hailey, Arthur (1920–). American novelist who rigorously researches specific milieux and weaves a plot through them.

Films of his work include *Hotel, Airport, The Moneychangers, Wheels, Flight into Danger* (which became *Zero Hour* and was parodied as *Airplane*).

Haim, Corey (1972–). Canadian-born juvenile lead, in commercials fro... the age of 11.
Firstborn 84. Murphy's Romance 85. Secret Admirer 85. Silver Bullet 85. Lucas 86. The Lost Boys 87. License to Drive 88. Watchers 88. Drea... a Little Dream 89. Dream Machine 90. Fast Getawa... 91. Prayer of the Rollerboys 91. Oh, What a Nig... 92. Double O Kid 92. Fast Getaway II 94. Nation... Lampoon's Last Resort 94, etc.

Haines, Randa. American director, from television.
Under This Sky (TV) 79. Something about Amelia (TV) 84. Children of a Lesser God 86. Th... Doctor 91. Wrestling Ernest Hemingway 93, etc.

Haines, William (1900–1973). American leading man of the silents.
Three Wise Fools 23. Tower of Lies 24. Brown... of Harvard 25. Tell It to the Marines 27. Alias Jimmy Valentine 28. Navy Blues 30. The Adventures of Get-Rich-Quick Wallingford 31. Th... Fast Life 33. The Marines Are Coming 35, etc.

Hajos, Karl (1889–1950). Hungarian-born composer, in America from the 20s.
Morocco 30. Werewolf of London 35. Hitler's Hangman 43. Summer Storm (AAN) 44. Dangerou... Intruder 45. Stars over Texas 46. Appointment with Murder 48. The Lovable Cheat 49. It's a Small World 50, etc.

Hakim, André (1915–). Egyptian-born producer, long in US.
Mr Belvedere Rings the Bell 52. The Man Wh... Never Was 56, etc.

Hakim, Robert (1907–). **Raymond** (1909– 1980). Egyptian-born brothers who were in and out of film production from 1927.
Pépé Le Moko 36. La Bête Humaine 38. Le Jou... Se Lève 39. The Southerner 44. Her Husband's Affairs 47. The Long Night 47. The Blue Veil 52. Belle de Jour 67. Isadora 68, many others.

Halas, John (1912–). Hungarian-born animator, long in Britain producing in association with his wife Joy Batchelor (1914–1992) a stream of efficient shor... cartoons, many sponsored by official organizations. FEATURES: *Animal Farm* 54. Ruddigore 67.

Hale, Alan (1892–1950) (Rufus Alan McKahan). Jovial American actor, a hero of silent action film... from 1911 and a familiar cheerful figure in score... of talkies.
The Cowboy and the Lady (debut) 11. The Fou... Horsemen of the Apocalypse 21. Robin Hood (as Little John) 22. The Covered Wagon 23. Main Street 24. She Got What She Wanted 27. The Ris... of Helga 30. So Big 32. It Happened One Night 34... The Last Days of Pompeii 35. Jump for Glory (GB... 36. Stella Dallas 37. *The Adventures of Robin Hood* (as Little John) 38. Dodge City 39. The Man in the Iron Mask 40. The Sea Hawk 40. Tugboat Annie Sails Again 41. *Strawberry Blonde* 41. Manpower 41. *Desperate Journey* 42. Action in the North Atlantic 43. Destination Tokyo 44. Hotel Berlin 45. Escape in the Desert 45. Night and Day 45. My Wild Irish Rose 47. Pursued 48. The New Adventures of Don Juan 48. *My Girl Tisa* 49.

Rogues of Sherwood Forest (as Little John) 50, many others.

⊙ For innumerable stalwart performances, including three as Little John. *The Adventures of Robin Hood.*

Hale, Alan, Jnr (1918–1990).
American character actor who bid fair to be his father's double.

To the Shores of Tripoli 42. One Sunday Afternoon 48. The Gunfighter 50. The Big Trees 52. Rogue Cop 54. Young at Heart 54. The Indian Fighter 55. The Killer is Loose 56, many others.

TV series: Biff Baker 52–53. *Casey Jones* 58. *Gilligan's Island* 64–67. The Good Guys 69.

Hale, Barbara (1922–).
Pleasant American leading lady of the 40s.

Higher and Higher 43. The Falcon in Hollywood 44. First Yank into Tokyo 45. Lady Luck 46. The Boy with Green Hair 48. The Window 48. *Jolson Sings Again* 49. The Jackpot 50. Lorna Doone 51. A Lion is in the Streets 53. Unchained 54. The Far Horizons 55. The Oklahoman 57. Airport 69. The Defence Never Rests 90, many others.

TV series: *Perry Mason* (as Della Street) 57–65.

Hale, Binnie (1899–1984) (Beatrice Mary Hale-Monro).
British revue comedienne of the 30s, sister of Sonnie Hale. Films rare.

This is the Life 34. The Phantom Light 35. Hyde Park Corner 36. Love from a Stranger 37. Take a Chance 37.

Hale, Creighton (1882–1965) (Patrick Fitzgerald).
American leading man of the 20s, sometimes in meek-and-mild comedy roles.

The Exploits of Elaine 15. The Thirteenth Chair 19. Way Down East 20. Trilby (as Little Billee) 23. *The Marriage Circle* 24. The Circle 25. Beverly of Graustark 26. Annie Laurie 27. *The Cat and the Canary* 27. Rose Marie 28. Holiday 30. The Masquerader 33. Hollywood Boulevard 36. The Return of Dr X 39. The Gorilla Man 42. Bullet Scars 45. The Perils of Pauline 47, many others.

Hale, Georgia (1903–1985).
American leading lady of the 20s.

The Gold Rush 24. The Salvation Hunters 25. The Great Gatsby 26. The Last Moment 48, etc.

Hale, Georgina (1943–).
Generally strident British actress.

Eagle in a Cage 70. The Devils 71. Mahler 74. Sweeney 2 78. The World Is Full of Married Men 78. McVicar 80. The Watcher in the Woods 80. Castaway 86, etc.

Hale, Jonathan (1891–1966) (J. Hatley).
American character actor, former consular attaché, in films from 1934, usually as mildly exasperated businessman or hero's boss. Committed suicide.

Lightning Strikes Twice 34. Alice Adams 35. Fury 36. The 'Blondie' series (as Mr Dithers) 38–50. Her Jungle Love 39. Johnny Apollo 40. Call Northside 777 48. The Steel Trap 52. The Night Holds Terror 56. Jaguar 58, many others.

Hale, Louise Closser (1872–1933).
American character actress with long stage experience.

The Hole in the Wall 29. Dangerous Nan McGrew 30. Platinum Blonde 31. Shanghai Express 32. Rasputin and the Empress 33. Today We Live 33. Dinner at Eight 33, etc.

Hale, Monte (1919–).
American western star of the 40s. Mostly with Republic.

Home on the Range 47. South of Rio 48. Rainbow Valley 49. The Missourians 50. Giant 56. The Chase 66. The Drifter 73. Guns of a Stranger 73, many others.

Hale, Richard (1893–1981).
American supporting actor.

The Other Love 47. All the King's Men 50. Scaramouche 52. Julius Caesar 53. Moonfleet 55. Pillars of the Sky 56. Ben Hur 59. Sergeants Three 62, etc.

Hale, Sonnie (1902–1959) (John Robert Hale-Monro).
British light comedian of the 30s, mostly on stage.
■ On with the Dance 27. The Parting of the Ways 27. Tell me Tonight 32. Happy Ever After 32. Friday the Thirteenth 33. Early to Bed 33. Evergreen 34. Wild Boy 34. My Song for You 34. My Heart is Calling 34. Are You a Mason? 34. Marry the Girl 35. First a Girl 35. It's Love Again 36. Head over Heels (d only) 37. Gangway (d only) 37. Sailing Along (d only) 38. The Gaunt Stranger 38. Let's Be Famous 39. Fiddlers Three 44. London Town 46.
~ *A French Mistress* 60 was based on his play.

Hale, William (1928–).
American director, from TV.

The Naked Hunt 58. Gunfight in Abilene 66. Journey to Shiloh 67. Stalk the Wild Child (TV) 76. One Shoe Makes It Murder (TV) 82. Lace (TV) 84. Lace 2 (TV) 85, etc.

Hale's Tours.
In 1902 at the St Louis Exposition, George C. Hale, ex-chief of the Kansas City Fire Department, had the bright idea of shooting a film from the back of a moving train and screening the result in a small theatre decorated like an observation car. During the screening bells clanged, train whistles sounded and the 'coach' rocked slightly. The idea was so successful that it toured for several years in the United States.

Haley, Bill (1926–1981).
American rock-and-roll musician and bandleader; Bill Haley and his Comets provided the title music for *The Blackboard Jungle* and starred in *Rock around the Clock*, which caused cinema riots in 1956. Also, Don't Knock the Rock 56.

Haley, Jack (1899–1979).
Diffident American light comedian, popular in the 30s and 40s.

Broadway Melody 27. Follow Thru 30. Sitting Pretty 33. The Girl Friend 35. *Poor Little Rich Girl* 36. Wake Up and Live 37. Pick a Star 37. Rebecca of Sunnybrook Farm 38. Hold that Co-Ed 38. *The Wizard of Oz* (as the Tin Man) 39. Moon over Miami 41. Beyond the Blue Horizon 42. F Man 42. Higher and Higher 43. Scared Stiff 44. George White's Scandals 45. People are Funny 45. Vacation in Reno 47. Norwood 69, etc.

Haley, Jack, Jnr (1934–).
American executive, best known for marrying Liza Minnelli and assembling *That's Entertainment* and *That's Dancing*. Directed *Norwood* 69 and *The Love Machine* 71.

Haley, Jackie Earle (1961–).
American juvenile of the 70s.

The Day of the Locust 74. Damnation Alley 75.

The Bad News Bears 76. The Bad News Bears in Breaking Training 77. Breaking Away 79. The Zoo Gang 85, etc.

TV series: Wait Till Your Father Gets Home (voice) 72–74.

Hall, Alexander (1894–1968).
American director from 1932, previously on Broadway.
■ Sinners in the Sun 32. Madame Racketeer 32. The Girl in 419 33. Midnight Club 33. Torch Singer 33. Miss Fane's Baby is Stolen 34. Little Miss Marker 34. The Pursuit of Happiness 34. Limehouse Blues 34. Going to Town 35. Annapolis Farewell 35. Give Us This Night 36. Yours for the Asking 36. Exclusive 37. There's Always a Woman 38. I am the Law 38. There's That Woman Again 38. The Lady's From Kentucky 39. Good Girls Go to Paris 39. The Amazing Mr Williams 39. The Doctor Takes a Wife 40. He Stayed for Breakfast 40. This Thing Called Love 40. *Here Comes Mr Jordan* (AAN) 41. Bedtime Story 41. They All Kissed the Bride 42. My Sister Eileen 42. The Heavenly Body 43. Once Upon a Time 44. She Wouldn't Say Yes 45. Down to Earth 47. The Great Lover 49. Love that Brute 50. Louisa 50. Up Front 51. Because You're Mine 52. Let's Do it Again 53. Forever Darling 56.

Hall, Anthony Michael (1968–).
American young leading actor, a former child actor on stage and TV.

Sixteen Candles 84. The Breakfast Club 85. Weird Science 85. Out of Bounds 86. Johnny Be Good 88. Edward Scissorhands 90. Into the Sun 92. Six Degrees of Separation 93, etc.

Hall, Charles (1899–1959).
Rotund English-born music-hall comic and character actor, a member of Fred Karno's troupe. In America from the early 20s, he appeared in more than 40 movies as an irascible foil to Laurel and Hardy.

Leave 'Em and Weep 27. College 27. Pardon Us 31. Sons of the Desert 34. Them Thar Hills 34. Tit for Tat 35. Swing Time 36. A Chump at Oxford 40. Saps at Sea 40. The Lodger 44. The Canterville Ghost 44. Hangover Square 45. Forever Amber 47. The Big Clock 48. The Vicious Years 51, many others.

Hall, Charles D. (1899–1968).
British-born production designer, long in Hollywood; a key craftsman of his time.

The Gold Rush 24. *The Phantom of the Opera* 25. The Cohens and the Kellys 26. *The Cat and the Canary* 27. The Man Who Laughs 28. The Circus 28. The Last Warning 29. *Broadway* 29. *All Quiet on the Western Front* 30. *Dracula* 31. Frankenstein 31. City Lights 32. *The Old Dark House* 32. *The Invisible Man* 33. By Candlelight 33. *The Bride of Frankenstein* 35. The Good Fairy 35. Showboat 36. *Modern Times* 36. My Man Godfrey 36. Captain Fury 39. Big House USA 55, etc.

⊙ For bringing to Hollywood Gothic a mixture of English and German artistic sensibilities.

Hall, Conrad L. (1926–).
American cinematographer.

Morituri (AAN) 65. Harper 66. The Professionals (AAN) 66. *Cool Hand Luke* 67. In Cold Blood (AAN) 67. Hell in the Pacific 69. *Butch Cassidy and the Sundance Kid* (AA) 69. Tell Them Willie Boy is Here 69. The Happy Ending 70. Fat City 72. The Day of the Locust (AAN) 75. Smile 75. Marathon Man 76. Black Widow 87. Tequila Sunrise 88. Class Action 91. Jennifer 8 92. Searching for Bobby Fischer (GB: Innocent Moves) (AAN) 93, etc.

Hall-Davis, Lillian:
see *Davis, Lilian Hall.*

Hall, Grayson (1927–1985).
American stage actress remembered for one film performance, in *Night of the Iguana* (AAN) 64.

Hall, Henry (1898–1989).
British bandleader of the 30s, popular on radio. Appeared in a few films including *Music Hath Charms* 36.
Autobiography: 1955, *Here's to the Next Time.*

Hall, Huntz (1920–) (Henry Hall).
Long-faced American character actor, the 'dumbbell' second lead of the original Dead End Kids and later of the Bowery Boys.
Dead End 37. Crime School 38. Angels with Dirty Faces 38. The Return of Doctor X 39. Give Us Wings 40. Spooks Run Wild 41. Private Buckaroo 42. Wonder Man 45. Bowery Bombshell 46. Bowery Buckaroos 47. Jinx Money 48. Angels in Disguise 49. Lucky Losers 50. Ghost Chasers 51. No Holds Barred 52. Loose in London 53. Paris Playboys 54. High Society 55. Dig That Uranium 56. Spook Chasers 57. In the Money 58. The Gentle Giant 67. The Love Bug Rides Again 73. The Escape Artist 82. Auntie Lee's Meat Pies 92, many others.
TV series: Chicago Teddy Bears 71.

Hall, James (1900–1940) (James Brown).
American leading man of the early talkie period.
The Campus Flirt 26. Stranded in Paris 27. Rolled Stockings 27. Four Sons 28. Smiling Irish Eyes 29. The Canary Murder Case 29. The Saturday Night Kid 29. Dangerous Nan McGrew 30. *Hells Angels* 30. Millie 31. The Good Bad Girl 31. Divorce Among Friends 31. Manhattan Tower 33, etc.

Hall, Jon (1913–1979) (Charles Locher).
Athletic American leading man who became a star in his first year as an actor but whose roles gradually diminished in stature; he retired to a photography business. Committed suicide.
Charlie Chan in Shanghai 36. Mind Your Own Business 36. The Girl from Scotland Yard 37. *The Hurricane* 37. Kit Carson 40. South of Pago Pago 40. Aloma of the South Seas 41. Eagle Squadron 42. Invisible Agent 42. Arabian Nights 42. White Savage 43. Ali Baba and the Forty Thieves 44. Cobra Woman 44. The Invisible Man's Revenge 44. San Diego I Love You 45. Sudan 45. The Michigan Kid 47. Last of the Redmen 47. Prince of Thieves 48. Deputy Marshal 49. Hurricane Island 50. When the Redskins Rode 51. Last Train from Bombay 52. The Beachgirls and the Monster (& d) 65. Five the Hard Way (co-p & ph only) 69, etc.
TV series: Ramar of the Jungle 52–53.

Hall, Juanita (1901–1968).
American character actress and singer, best remembered in the stage and screen versions of *South Pacific* (as Bloody Mary) and *Flower Drum Song.*

Hall, Ken G. (1901–1994).
Australian producer, director and screenwriter, head of Cinesound Productions, which was the busiest company of the 30s and 40s, turning out low-budget movies reflecting Australian life, four of them based on the exploits of the Rudd family. The company was later part-owned by J. Arthur Rank and thereafter concentrated on distribution and exhibition. Hall began as a journalist and a film publicist and went on to run Australia's first television station in 1956.

Autobiographies: 1977, *Directed by Ken G. Hall.* 1980, *Australian Film: The Inside Story.*
On Our Selection (co-w, d) 32. The Squatter's Daughter (p, d) 33. The Silence of Dean Maitland (p, d) 34. Grandad Rudd (p, d) 35. It Isn't Done (p, d) 37. Lovers and Luggers (p, d) 37. Tall Timbers (p, d) 37. Let George Do It (GB: In the Nick of Time) (p, d) 38. Dad and Dave Come to Town (GB: The Rudd Family Goes to Town) (p, story) 38. Gone to the Dogs (p, d) 39. Dad Rudd MP (p, d) 40. Kokoda Front Line (p) (AA doc) 42. Smithy (GB: Southern Cross, aka Pacific Adventure) (co-w, d) 46, etc.

Hall, Kevin Peter (1955–1991).
American actor and stand-up comedian, 7 feet 2 inches tall, who was best known for playing the role of a Bigfoot in the film *Harry and the Hendersons* 87, and in the first season of the subsequent TV series 90–91.
Highway to Hell 92.
TV series: Misfits of Science 85–86.

Hall, Sir Peter (1930–).
British theatrical producer who ventured into films. His first wife was actress Leslie Caron (1956–65).
Autobiographies: 1983, *Peter Hall's Diaries.* 1993, *Making an Exhibition of Myself.*
■ Work Is a Four-Letter Word 68. A Midsummer Night's Dream 68. Three Into Two Won't Go 69. Perfect Friday 70. The Homecoming 73. Akenfield 74.

Hall, Porter (1888–1953).
Wry-faced American character actor with stage experience before settling in Hollywood.
■ *The Thin Man* 34. Murder in the Private Car 34. The Case of the Lucky Legs 35. The Story of Louis Pasteur 35. The Petrified Forest 36. Too Many Parents 36. The Princess Comes Across 36. And Sudden Death 36. *The General Died at Dawn* 36. Satan Met a Lady 36. The Plainsman 36. Snowed Under 36. Let's Make a Million 37. Bulldog Drummond Escapes 37. Souls at Sea 37. Make Way for Tomorrow 37. King of Gamblers 37. Hotel Haywire 37. This Way Please 37. True Confession 37. Wild Money 37. Wells Fargo 37. Scandal Street 38. Stolen Heaven 38. Dangerous to Know 38. Bulldog Drummond's Peril 38. Prison Farm 38. King of Alcatraz 38. The Arkansas Traveller 38. Men with Wings 38. Tom Sawyer Detective 38. Mr Smith Goes to Washington 39. Grand Jury Secrets 39. They Shall Have Music 39. His Girl Friday 40. Dark Command 40. Arizona 40. Trail of the Vigilantes 40. Sullivan's Travels 41. The Parson of Panamint 41. Mr and Mrs North 41. The Remarkable Andrew 42. Butch Minds the Baby 42. A Stranger in Town 43. The Desperadoes 43. Woman of the Town 43. Standing Room Only 44. The Miracle of Morgan's Creek 44. Going My Way 44. Double Indemnity 44. The Great Moment 44. Mark of the Whistler 44. Blood on the Sun 45. Bring on the Girls 45. Kiss and Tell 45. *Murder He Says* 45. Weekend at the Waldorf 45. Unconquered 47. Miracle on 34th Street 47. Singapore 47. You Gotta Stay Happy 48. That Wonderful Urge 48. The Beautiful Blonde from Bashful Bend 49. *Intruder in the Dust* 49. Chicken Every Sunday 49. *Ace in the Hole* 51. The Half Breed 52. Carbine Williams 52. Holiday for Sinners 52. Pony Express 53. Vice Squad 53. Return to Treasure Island 54.

Hall, Thurston (1883–1958).
American character actor adept at choleric executives. Long stage experience; ran his own touring companies.

Cleopatra (as Mark Antony) 18. Theodora Goes Wild 36. Professor Beware 38. The Great McGinty 40. He Hired the Boss 43. Brewster's Millions 45. The Secret Life of Walter Mitty 47. Affair in Reno 56, many others.
TV series: Topper 53–54.

Hall, Willis (1929–).
British playwright and screenwriter (in collaboration with Keith Waterhouse).
The Long and the Short and the Tall 61. Whistle Down the Wind 61. A Kind of Loving 62. Billy Liar 63, etc.

Hallatt, May (1882–1969).
British character actress, mainly on stage.
No Funny Business 33. The Lambeth Walk 39. Painted Boats 45. *Black Narcissus* 46. The Pickwick Papers 52. *Separate Tables* 58. Make Mine Mink 60, etc.

Haller, Daniel (1928–).
American director, former art director on Roger Corman's Poe films, etc.
■ Die Monster Die 67. The Devil's Angels 68. The Wild Racers 68. Paddy 70. The Dunwich Horror 70. Pieces of Dreams 70. The Desperate Miles (TV) 75. Sword of Justice (TV pilot) 78. Little Women (TV) 78. Little Mo (TV) 78. Buck Rogers in the 25th Century 78. Follow That Car 81.

Haller, Ernest (1896–1970).
Distinguished American cinematographer.
Neglected Wives 20. Outcast 22. Stella Dallas 25. Weary River 29. The Dawn Patrol 31. The Emperor Jones 33. Dangerous 35. Jezebel 38. *Gone with the Wind* (AA) 39. Dark Victory 39. All This and Heaven Too 40. Saratoga Trunk 43. Mr Skeffington 44. *Mildred Pierce* 45. Humoresque 46. *My Girl Tisa* 47. The Flame and the Arrow 50. Rebel without a Cause 55. Back from the Dead 57. God's Little Acre 58. Man of the West 58. The Third Voice 59. Whatever Happened to Baby Jane? 62. Lilies of the Field 64. Dead Ringer 64, many others.

Halliday, John (1880–1947).
Suave and dapper Scottish actor, long in Hollywood.
■ The Woman Gives 20. East Side Sadie 29. Father's Sons 30. Recaptured Love 30. Scarlet Pages 30. Smart Women 31. Consolation Marriage 31. The Ruling Voice 31. Millie 31. Once a Sinner 31. Captain Applejack 31. Fifty Million Frenchmen 31. The Spy 31. Transatlantic 31. Men of Chance 32. The Impatient Maiden 32. The Age of Consent 32. Weekends Only 32. Bird of Paradise 32. Perfect Understanding 33. Terror Aboard 33. Bed of Roses 33. The House on 56th Street 33. Woman Accused 33. Return of the Terror 34. Housewife 34. A Woman's Man 34. Happiness Ahead 34. Registered Nurse 34. The Witching Hour 34. Desirable 34. Finishing School 34. Mystery Woman 35. The Dark Angel 35. The Melody Lingers On 35. Peter Ibbetson 35. Fatal Lady 36. Three Cheers for Love 36. *Hollywood Boulevard* 36. Arsène Lupin Returns 38. Blockade 38. That Certain Age 39. The Light that Failed 39. Hotel for Women 39. Intermezzo 39. *The Philadelphia Story* 40. Lydia 41. Escape to Glory 41.

Famous line (*The Philadelphia Story*): 'What most wives fail to realize is that their husbands' philandering has nothing to do with them.'

Halliwell, Leslie (1929–1989).
British critic, author and creator of two of cinema's best-loved reference books, *Halliwell's Film Guide* (from 1977) and *Halliwell's Filmgoer's Companion*

(from 1965). A former cinema manager and journalist, he was a film researcher for Britain's Granada TV, and went on to become programme buyer for the whole ITV network and, later, Channel 4. He wrote eleven other books, including *Halliwell's Hundred*, his choice of favourite films.

Autobiography: 1985, *Seats in All Parts*.

¶ It was an aroma compounded of soft plush and worn carpet and Devon violets and sweat. It was that scent, perhaps, which first made me a film fan; for it was to the Queen's in Bolton that I ventured on my first remembered visit to any cinema, one wet and windy afternoon in 1933, when I was four. – *L.H.*

Hallström, Lasse (1946–).
Swedish director.
Abba – the Movie 77. Father to Be 79. The Rooster 81. Happy We 83. My Life as a Dog (Mitt Liv Som Hund) (AAN) 85. The Children of Bullerby Village (Alla Vi Barn i Bullerby) 86. More about the Children of Bullerby Village (Mer Om Oss Barn i Bullerbyn) 87. Once Around 90. What's Eating Gilbert Grape? 93, etc.

Halop, Billy (1920–1976).
American actor, the erstwhile leader of the Dead End Kids; stardom failed to materialize, and he descended to bit parts.
Dead End 37. Crime School 38. Little Tough Guy 38. Angels with Dirty Faces 38. You Can't Get Away with Murder 39. Angels Wash Their Faces 39. Call a Messenger 39. Tom Brown's Schooldays 40. Hit the Road 41. Mob Town 41. Junior Army 43. Dangerous Years 47. Mister Buddwing 66. Fitzwilly 66, many others.
TV series: All in the Family 72–76.

Halperin, Victor (1895–*).
American director.
Party Girl 29. Ex Flame 30. *White Zombie* 32. Supernatural 33. I Conquer the Sea 36. Revolt of the Zombies 36. Nation Aflame 37. Torture Ship 39. Buried Alive 40. Girls' Town 42.

Halsey, Brett (1933–).
American leading man.
The Glass Web 53. Ma and Pa Kettle at Home 54. Cry Baby Killer 58. The Best of Everything 59. Desire in the Dust 60. Return to Peyton Place 61. Twice Told Tales 63. Spy in Your Eye 65. Where Does It Hurt? 72, etc.

Halton, Charles (1876–1959).
American character actor, inimitable as a sour-faced bank clerk, professor or lawyer.
Come and Get It 36. Penrod and Sam 37. Dead End 37. The Prisoner of Zenda 37. The Saint in New York 38. Room Service 38. Jesse James 39. Swanee River 39. Dodge City 39. Juarez 39. The Shop around the Corner 40. *Dr Cyclops* 40. Foreign Correspondent 40. Stranger on the Third Floor 40. The Westerner 40. Tobacco Road 41. The Smiling Ghost 41. *To Be or Not to Be* 42. Across the Pacific 42. Jitterbugs 43. Wilson 44. Rhapsody in Blue 45. The Best Years of Our Lives 46. Three Godfathers 48. The Nevadan 50. Here Comes the Groom 51. Carrie 52. Friendly Persuasion 56, many others.

Hambling, Gerry (1926–).
British film editor, a regular on the films of director Alan Parker, and a former sound editor.
The Whole Truth 58. The Bulldog Breed 60. The Early Bird 65. That Riviera Touch 68. Moses (TV)

75. Bugsy Malone 76. Midnight Express (AAN) 78. Fame (AAN) 80. Heartaches 82. Shoot the Moon 82. Pink Floyd the Wall 82. Another Country 84. Birdy 84. Invitation to the Wedding 85. Absolute Beginners 86. Leonard Part 6 87. Angel Heart 87. Mississippi Burning (AAN) 88. Lenny: Live and Unleashed 89. Come See the Paradise 90. The Commitments (AAN) 91. City of Joy 92. In the Name of the Father (AAN) 93. The Road to Wellville 94, etc.

Hamer, Gerald (1886–1973).
British character actor in Hollywood.
Swing Time 36. Bulldog Drummond's Bride 39. Sherlock Holmes Faces Death 43. The Scarlet Claw 44. The Sign of the Ram 48, etc.

Hamer, Robert (1911–1963).
British director, erratic but at his best impeccably stylish.
■ San Demetrio London (w only) 43. Dead of Night (mirror sequence & w) 45. Pink String and Sealing Wax 45. *It Always Rains on Sunday* (& w) 47. *Kind Hearts and Coronets* (& w) 49. The Spider and the Fly 49. His Excellency (& w) 52. The Long Memory (& w) 52. *Father Brown* 54. To Paris With Love 54. The Scapegoat 59. *School for Scoundrels* 60. A Jolly Bad Fellow (w only) 63.

Hamill, Mark (1952–).
American leading man.
■ Sarah T (TV) 75. Delancey Street (TV) 75. Eric (TV) 75. Mallory (TV) 76. The City (TV) 77. *Star Wars* 77. Corvette Summer 78. The Big Red One 79. The Empire Strikes Back 80. The Night the Lights Went Out in Georgia 81. Return of the Jedi 83. Slipstream 89. Black Magic Woman 91. Sleepwalkers 92. Time Runner 93. Batman: Mask of the Phantasm (voice) 94.

¶ I'm waiting for my body to catch up with my age. – *M.H.*
Acting in *Star Wars* I felt like a raisin in a giant fruit salad, and I didn't even know who the cantaloupes were. – *M.H.*

Hamilton, Ashley (1977–).
American teen actor, the son of George Hamilton.
Lost in Africa 94.

Hamilton, Bernie (1929–).
Burly American actor.
Let No Man Write My Epitaph 60. 13 West Street 62. Captain Sinbad 63. The Swimmer 67. The Lost Man 69. The Organization 71. Scream Blacula Scream 73. Bucktown 75, etc.
TV series: *Starsky and Hutch* 75–79.

Hamilton, Donald (1913–).
American thriller writer, creator of Matt Helm. The resulting films and TV series were undistinguished to say the least.

Hamilton, George (1939–).
American leading man, usually in serious roles.
Crime and Punishment USA (debut) 58. Home from the Hill 60. All the Fine Young Cannibals 60. Angel Baby 61. By Love Possessed 61. A Thunder of Drums 61. The Light in the Piazza 62. The Victors 63. *Act One* (as Moss Hart) 63. Viva Maria 65. Your Cheating Heart 65. Doctor, You've Got To Be Kidding 67. The Long Ride Home 67. Jack of Diamonds 67. The Power 67. Evel Knievel 72. The Man Who Loved Cat Dancing 73. Once Is Not Enough 75. The Dead Don't Die (TV) 75. Roots (TV) 77. The Strange Possession of Mrs Oliver (TV) 77. Killer on Board (TV) 77. The Users (TV) 78. Institute for Revenge (TV) 79. Love at First Bite (as

Dracula) 79. Zorro the Gay Blade 81. Love at Second Bite 90. The Godfather Part III 90. Doc Hollywood 91. Once Upon a Crime 92, etc.
TV series: The Survivors 69. Paris 7000 70. Dynasty 85. Spies 86.

Hamilton, Guy (1922–).
British director, former assistant to Carol Reed.
■ The Ringer 52. The Intruder 53. *An Inspector Calls* 54. The Colditz Story 54. Charley Moon 56. Manuela 57. The Devil's Disciple 58. A Touch of Larceny 59. The Best of Enemies 62. The Party's Over 63. The Man in the Middle 64. *Goldfinger* 64. Funeral in Berlin 66. The Battle of Britain 70. Diamonds are Forever 71. Live and Let Die 72. The Man with the Golden Gun 73. Force Ten from Navarone (also p) 78. The Mirror Crack'd 80. Evil under the Sun 82. Remo Williams . . . the Adventure Begins 85. Try This One On for Size (Fr.) 89.

Hamilton, John (1886–1958).
Chubby American character actor, in hundreds of small parts as judge, cop, lawyer.
Rainbow Riley 26. White Cargo 30. Legion of Terror 37. Rose of Washington Square 39. The Maltese Falcon (as district attorney) 41. Meet Miss Bobby Socks 44. Law of the Golden West 49. The Pace that Thrills 52. On the Waterfront 54, many others.
TV series: Superman 51–57.

Hamilton, Linda (1956–).
American actress.
Rape and Marriage: The Rideout Case (TV) 80. T.A.G. – the Assassination Game 82. The Terminator 84. Children of the Corn 84. Secret Weapons (TV) 85. King Kong Lives 86. Black Moon Rising 86. Mr Destiny 90. Terminator 2: Judgment Day 91. Silent Fall 94, etc.
TV series: Secrets of Midland Heights 81–82. King's Crossing 82. Beauty and the Beast 87–90.

Hamilton, Lloyd (1891–1935).
American silent slapstick comedian, in many two-reelers from 1914.

Hamilton, Margaret (1902–1985).
American character actress, a former kindergarten teacher who came to films via Broadway and usually played hatchet-faced spinsters or maids.
Another Language 33. These Three 36. Nothing Sacred 37. *The Wizard of Oz* 39. Invisible Woman 41. Guest in the House 44. Mad Wednesday 47. State of the Union 48. The Great Plane Robbery 50. Thirteen Ghosts 60. The Daydreamer 66. Rosie 67. The Anderson Tapes 71. Brewster McCloud 71, etc.

Hamilton, Murray (1923–1986).
American general-purpose actor.
Bright Victory 50. No Time for Sergeants 58. The FBI Story 59. Seconds 66. The Graduate 67. No Way to Treat a Lady 68. The Boston Strangler 68. If It's Tuesday This Must Be Belgium 69. The Way We Were 73. Jaws 75. Jaws 2 78. 1941 79. The Amityville Horror 79. Brubaker 80, etc.
TV series: Love and Marriage 59–60. The Man Who Never Was 66–67. Rich Man, Poor Man Book I 76. B.J. and the Bear 81. Hail to the Chief 85.

Hamilton, Neil (1899–1984).
Stalwart American leading man of silent days, a former model.
White Rose 23. America 24. Isn't Life Wonderful? 25. Beau Geste 26. The Great Gatsby 27. Why Be Good? 28. Keeper of the Bees 29. The Dawn Patrol 30. The Wet Parade 31. The Animal Kingdom 32. Tarzan the Ape Man 32. One Sunday

Afternoon 33. Tarzan and His Mate 34. Federal Fugitives 41. The Little Shepherd of Kingdom Come 61. Madame X 66, many others.

TV series: Hollywood Screen Test 48–53. That Wonderful Guy 49–50. Batman 65–67.

Hamilton, Patrick (1904–1962).
British novelist and playwright whose work inspired a small but significant group of films.
■ *Gaslight* 39 and 44. Hangover Square 44. Rope 49.

Hamlet.
William Shakespeare's play of an enigmatic prince slow to revenge his father's death has been filmed many times. Among the 19 silent versions are two female Hamlets, from Sarah Bernhardt in 1900, and from Asta Nielsen in 1920, as well as one by the leading Shakespearean actor of his time, Johnston Forbes-Robertson, in 1913. Laurence Olivier's 1948 version remains the most celebrated, winning Oscars for the best film, for him as best actor, for Roger Furse's art direction and costume design, and for Carmen Dillon's set decoration. A powerful Russian version appeared in 1964, starring Innokenti Smoktunovsky, directed by Grigori Kozintsev, and with music by Shostakovich. Nicol Williamson starred in an uneven version, directed by Tony Richardson, in 1969, and Mel Gibson took the role under Franco Zeffirelli's direction, in a version aimed at a young audience, in 1991. The role has been notably played on TV by Richard Chamberlain 70, Ian McKellen 72, and Derek Jacobi 80. The play's plot also turns up in Akira Kurosawa's *The Bad Sleep Well* 60, a story of corporate corruption, a western, *Johnny Hamlet* 72, and Aki Kaurismäki's *Hamlet Goes Business* 87, set in the rubber duck industry.

Hamlin, Harry (1952–   ).
American light leading man. He has a son by Ursula Andress.
Movie Movie 78. Studs Lonigan (TV) 79. Clash of the Titans 81. King of the Mountain 81. Dragonslayer 81. Making Love 82. Blue Skies Again 83. Maxie 85. Space (TV) 85. Laguna Heat 88. Dinner at Eight 89. Deceptions (TV) 90. Deadly Intentions . . . Again (TV) 91, etc.
TV series: L.A. Law 86–91.

Hamlisch, Marvin (1945–   ).
American composer and pianist.
The Swimmer 68. The April Fools 69. Flap 70. The Sting (AA) 73. The Way We Were (AAs, m) 73. The Prisoner of Second Avenue 75. The Spy Who Loved Me 77. Same Time Next Year 78. Ice Castles 79. Chapter Two 79. Starting Over 79. Ordinary People 80. Seems Like Old Times 80. Pennies from Heaven 81. The Fan 81. I Ought to Be in Pictures 82. Sophie's Choice (AAN) 82. Romantic Comedy 83. A Chorus Line 85. D.A.R.Y.L. 85. Three Men and a Baby 87. The January Man 88. Little Nikita 88. The Experts 89. Frankie and Johnny 91, etc.

¶ My whole life revolves around dessert. – *M.H.*
     To put something on the earth that wasn't there yesterday, that's what I like. – *M.H.*

Hammer Films.
British production company set up in 1947 which gained fame and fortune from its cycle of horror films, beginning in 1955 with *The Quatermass Experiment* (aka *The Creeping Unknown*). It revived the Frankenstein myth with *The Curse of Frankenstein* 56, and followed it with the first of its Dracula series a year later, making stars of Christopher Lee and Peter Cushing. The company

grew out of Exclusive Films, a distribution company formed by Will Hammer and Enrique Carreras, a Spaniard who had opened cinemas in London in 1913. Enrique's son, Sir James Carreras, and his grandson Michael, were the main forces behind Hammer's success, together with Hammer's son Tony Hinds, who produced and wrote scripts under the name of John Elder, and director Terence Fisher. Hammer announced its return to film production in 1994, planning to remake some of its previous successes. Among the films in development were *The Day the Earth Caught Fire*, to be directed by Renny Harlin, *The Devil Rides Out*, *The Quatermass Xperiment* and *Vlad the Impaler*.
Book: 1973, *The House of Horror* edited by Allen Eyles, Robert Adkinson and Nicholas Fry.

Hammer, Will (1887–*) (William Hinds).
British producer, one of the founders of Hammer Films.

Hammerstein II, Oscar (1895–1960).
Immensely successful American lyricist who wrote many stage musicals, usually with Richard Rodgers (qv). *The King and I, South Pacific, The Sound of Music*, etc.

Hammett, Dashiell (1894–1961).
American writer of detective novels and occasional screenplays.
City Streets (& w) 31. The Maltese Falcon 31. The Thin Man 34. The Glass Key 35. The Maltese Falcon 41. The Glass Key 42. Watch on the Rhine (AANw) 43, etc.
~Wim Wenders' film *Hammett*, which appeared in 1982, was a pastiche in which the real Hammett became one of his own detective creations. In the vein of the Chandler movies, but less entertaining, it had minority appeal.

Hammid, Alexander (c. 1910–   ) (Alexander Hackenschmied).
Czech documentarist in America.
Hymn of the Nations 46. Of Men and Music 51. To the Fair 65, etc.

Hammond, Kay (1909–1980) (Dorothy Standing).
Plummy-voiced British leading lady, mostly on stage; married to John Clements.
Children of Chance 30. A Night in Montmartre 31. Almost a Divorce 32. Out of the Blue 32. A Night Like This 32. Sally Bishop 32. Yes Madam 33. Sleeping Car 33. Bitter Sweet 33. Two on a Doorstep 36. Jeannie 41. *Blithe Spirit* (as Elvira) 45. Call of the Blood 48. Five Golden Hours 61, etc.

Hammond, Peter (1923–   ).
British juvenile player of the 40s; became a TV and film director.
They Knew Mr Knight 46. Holiday Camp 47. Fly Away Peter 48. Morning Departure 50. Vote for Huggett 50. The Adventurers 51. Spring and Port Wine (d only) 69, etc.
TV series: The Buccaneers 56–57.

Hampden, Walter (1879–1955) (Walter Hampden Dougherty).
American stage actor with a long career behind him when he came to Hollywood.
■ Warfare of the Flesh 17. The Hunchback of Notre Dame 39. All This and Heaven Too 40. North West Mounted Police 40. They Died with Their Boots On 41. Reap the Wild Wind 42. The Adventures of Mark Twain 44. All About Eve 50. The First Legion 51. Five Fingers 52. Sombrero 53. Treasure of the Golden Condor 53. The Silver

Chalice 54. Sabrina 54. Strange Lady in Town 55. The Prodigal 55. The Vagabond King 56.

Hampshire, Susan (1938–   ).
Talented British leading lady, somewhat handicapped by her own demureness.
■ Upstairs and Downstairs 59. Expresso Bongo 59. During One Night 61. The Long Shadow 61. The Three Lives of Thomasina 63. Night Must Fall 64. Wonderful Life 64. The Fighting Prince of Donegal 66. The Trygon Factor 67. Paris in August 67. Violent Enemy 69. Monte Carlo or Bust 69. David Copperfield (TV) 69. A Time for Loving 72. Living Free 72. Neither the Sea nor the Sand 72. Baffled (TV) 72. Malpertius 72. The Lonely Woman 76.
TV series: The Forsyte Saga (as Fleur) 68. *The Pallisers* 75.

Hampton, Christopher (1946–   ).
English dramatist and screenwriter.
A Doll's House 73. Tales from the Vienna Woods 81. Beyond the Limit 83. The Wolf at the Door 86. The Good Father 87. Dangerous Liaisons (AA) 88. Carrington (wd) 95. Mary Roberts (w) 95.

Hampton, Hope (1899–1982).
American leading lady of the silents.
The Bait 21. The Gold Diggers 23. Hollywood 23. The Truth about Women 24. Lover's Island 25. The Unfair Sex 26, etc.

Hampton, Louise (1881–1954).
British character actress.
Goodbye Mr Chips 39. Busman's Honeymoon 40. Bedelia 46, etc.

Hancock, Herbie (1940–   ) (Herbert Jeffrey Hancock).
American composer and musician, a leading jazz keyboard player who turned to electronic music in the 70s, soon after he began writing for films.
Blow-Up 66. The Spook Who Sat by the Door 73. Death Wish 74. A Soldier's Story 84. Jo Jo Dancer, Your Life Is Calling 86. Round Midnight (& a) (AAm) 86. Action Jackson 88. Colors 88. Harlem Nights 89.

Hancock, John (1939–   ).
American director.
■ Let's Scare Jessica to Death 73. Bang the Drum Slowly 74. Baby Blue Marine 76. California Dreaming 78. Weeds 87. Prancer 89.

Hancock, Sheila (1933–   ).
British comic actress of stage and TV.
Light Up the Sky 58. The Girl on the Boat 61. Night Must Fall 64. The Anniversary 67. Take a Girl Like You 70. Three Men and a Little Lady 90. A Business Affair 94, etc.
TV series: Brighton Belles 93.

Hancock, Tony (1924–1968).
Popular British radio and TV comedian. He committed suicide in Australia, leaving a note that said 'Things seemed to go wrong too many times'. He was the model for Lon Bracton, a self-destructive comedian, in J. B. Priestley's novel *London End*.
Biography: 1969, *Hancock* by Freddie Hancock and David Nathan.
■ Orders are Orders 61. The Rebel 61. The Punch and Judy Man 62. Those Magnificent Men in the Flying Machines 65. The Wrong Box 66.

¶ A comedian with a touch of genius who had no enemy except himself. – *J. B. Priestley*
An indifferent performer saved by two of the most brilliant scriptwriters of the decade, Galton

nd Simpson, whom he rejected. Thereafter, it was
l downhill. – *Kenneth Williams*

Hand, David (1900–1986).
merican animator, formerly with Disney; came
Britain 1945 to found a cartoon unit for Rank
with some pleasing results (*Musical Paintbox* series,
tc), but it was a financial failure and Hand
eturned to American in 1950.

Handke, Peter (1942–).
ustrian avant-garde dramatist, novelist,
creenwriter and director.
   The Goalkeeper's Fear of the Penalty Kick (Die
ngst des Tormanns beim Elfmeter) (w) 72.
Vrong Move (Falsche Bewegung) (w) 75. The
eft-Handed Woman (Die Linkshändige Frau)
wd) 77. Wings of Desire (Der Himmel über Berlin)
w) 87, etc.

Handl, Irene (1902–1987).
umpy British character comedienne, frequently
een as maid or charlady; became a star in her later
ears. She was also a novelist.
   Missing Believed Married 37. The Girl in the
Vews 41. Pimpernel Smith 41. Temptation
Iarbour 46. Silent Dust 48. One Wild Oat 51. The
elles of St Trinian's 54. A Kid for Two Farthings
6. Brothers in Law 57. *I'm All Right Jack* 59. Make
Mine Mink 60. The Rebel 61. Heavens Above 63.
Morgan 66. Smashing Time 67. On a Clear Day
ou Can See Forever 70. The Private Life of
herlock Holmes 71. For the Love of Ada 72.
Adventures of a Private Eye 76. Stand Up Virgin
oldiers 77, etc.
   TV series: *For the Love of Ada* 70–72. Maggie and
Ier 78–79.

Handley, Tommy (1894–1949).
Sritish radio comedian most famous for his long-
unning, morale-building *ITMA* series during World
Var II.
   Elstree Calling 30. Two Men in a Box 38. *It's
hat Man Again* 42. Time Flies 43. Tom Tom Topia
short) 46.

HandMade Films.
Sritish production company formed by Denis
)'Brien and former Beatle George Harrison. Among
ts successes have been *Monty Python's Life of Brian*
9, *The Long Good Friday* 80, *Time Bandits* 81, *A
rivate Function* 84, *Mona Lisa* 86, and *Withnail and
* 87.

nands.
he clutching hand was long a staple of
nelodrama; usually hairy, with long fingernails,
came out of shadowed panelling and menaced
he heroine in hundreds of thrillers such as *The
at and the Canary*. Severed hands were also a
avourite: passing fancies in most of the mummy
lms, they received more detailed attention in *The
east with Five Fingers*, *Chamber of Horrors*, *The
Iand*, and the various versions of *The Hands of
)rlac*.

Handy, W.C. (1873–1958) (William Christopher
Iandy).
Slind American blues pioneer; was impersonated
y Nat King Cole in *St Louis Blues*.

Haneke, Michael (1942–).
German director and screenwriter. Born in
Munich, he studied philosophy, psychology and
heatre in Vienna before entering television as a
criptwriter, from 1967, and as a director, from
974. He also works as a theatre director.
   The Seventh Continent (Der Siebente

Kontinent) 88. Benny's Video 92. 71 Fragments of
a Chronology of Chance (71 Fragmente Einer
Chronologie des Zufalls) 94.

Haney, Carol (1928–1964).
American dancer, former assistant to Gene Kelly.
■ Kiss Me Kate 53. Invitation to the Dance 54.
The Pajama Game 57.

Hanks, Tom (1957–).
American leading man of the 80s.
■ He Knows You're Alone 80. Bachelor Party 83.
Splash! 84. The Man with One Red Shoe 85.
Volunteers 85. The Money Pit 85. Nothing in
Common 86. Every Time We Say Goodbye 86.
Dragnet 87. Big (AAN) 88. Punchline 88. The
'burbs 89. Turner & Hooch 89. Bonfire of the
Vanities 90. Joe versus the Volcano 90. Radio Flyer
92. A League of Their Own 92. Sleepless in Seattle
93. *Philadelphia* (AA) 93. Forrest Gump 94.

Hanley, Jenny (1947–).
British light leading lady and television
personality, daughter of Dinah Sheridan and
Jimmy Hanley.
   Joanna 68. On Her Majesty's Secret Service 69.
Tam Lin 70. Scars of Dracula 72. The Private Life
of Sherlock Holmes 73. Soft Beds Hard Battles 74.
Alfie Darling 75, etc.

Hanley, Jimmy (1918–1970).
Former British child actor developed as 'the boy
next door' type by Rank in the 40s. He was on stage
from the age of 12 and a circus bareback rider at
14 before making his film debut when he was 16.
In the mid-50s he was presenter of a daily
television programme, *Jolly Good Time*, and a
consumer programme, *Jim's Inn*. The first of his
two wives was actress Dinah Sheridan. Their
daughter is actress Jenny Hanley (qv) and their
son, Jeremy Hanley, MP, became chairman of the
Conservative party in 1994.
   Little Friend 34. Boys Will Be Boys 35. Night
Ride 37. There Ain't No Justice 39. Salute John
Citizen 42. For You Alone 44. The Way Ahead 44.
Henry V 44. 29 Acacia Avenue 45. The Captive
Heart 46. Master of Bankdam 47. It Always Rains
on Sunday 48. It's Hard To Be Good 49. Here
Come the Huggetts (and ensuing series) 49–52.
The Blue Lamp 50. The Black Rider 54. The Deep
Blue Sea 56. Lost Continent 68, etc.

Hanna, William (1910–).
American animator who with his partner Joe
Barbera created Tom and Jerry for MGM, later
founding their own successful company creating
innumerable semi-animated series for TV:
Huckleberry Hound, Yogi Bear, The Flintstones,
The Jetsons, Wait Till Your Father Gets Home, etc.

Hannah, Daryl (1960–).
American leading lady.
   The Fury 78. Hard Country 81. Blade Runner
82. The Pope of Greenwich Village 84. Splash! 84.
Clan of the Cave Bear 86. Legal Eagles 86.
Roxanne 87. Wall Street 87. High Spirits 88. Crimes
and Misdemeanors 89. Steel Magnolias 89. At Play
in the Fields of the Lord 91. Memoirs of an Invisible
Man 92. Attack of the 50 Ft Woman (TV) 93.
Grumpy Old Men 93. The Little Rascals 94, etc.

Hannam, Ken (1929–).
Australian director who moved to England in the
late 60s to work as a television director.
   Sunday Too Far Away 74. Break of Day 76.
Summerfield 77. Dawn! 78.

Hannan, Peter (1941–).
Australian cinematographer, now working in
Britain.
   Eskimo Nell 71. Flame 74. The Haunting of Julia
77. The Stud 78. The Missionary 81. Brimstone and
Treacle 82. Monty Python's Meaning of Life 83.
The Razor's Edge 83. Blame It on Rio 83. Dance
with a Stranger 84. Turtle Diary 85. Insignificance
85. Half Moon Street 85. Club Paradise 85.
Withnail and I 87. The Lonely Passion of Judith
Hearne 87. A Handful of Dust 88. How to Get
Ahead in Advertising 89. Not without My
Daughter 91, etc.

Hanray, Lawrence (1874–1947).
British stage character actor of great dignity.
   The Private Life of Henry VIII 32. The Scarlet
Pimpernel 34. The Man Who Could Work
Miracles 36. Hatter's Castle 41, etc.

Hansberry, Lorraine (1930–1965).
American playwright, whose *A Raisin in the Sun*
was filmed.

Hansen, Juanita (1895–1961).
American leading lady of the silents, especially in
serials.
   His Pride and Shame 16. Secret of the Submarine
16. Dangers of a Bride 17. The Brass Bullet 18. The
Lost City 20. The Yellow Arm 21. Broadway
Madonna 22. The Jungle Princess 23, etc.

Hansen, Peter (1922–).
American general-purpose actor.
   Branded 50. When Worlds Collide 51. Darling
How Could You 53. Three Violent People 56. The
Deep Six 58. Harlow 65, etc.
   TV series: Mr Parkson 64–65. General Hospital
65– .

Hanson, Curtis.
American director.
   The Arousers 76. The Little Dragons 80. Losin'
It 83. The Bedroom Window 87. Bad Influence
90. The Hand that Rocks the Cradle 92. The River
Wild 94, etc.

Hanson, Lars (1887–1965).
Swedish stage actor who made silent films abroad
but after the coming of sound remained in Sweden.
   Ingeborg Holm (debut) 13. Dolken 16. Erotikon
19. The Atonement of Gosta Berling 24. The Scarlet
Letter (US) 26. The Divine Woman (US) 27. The
Wind (US) 28. The Informer (GB) 28, etc.

Harareet, Haya (1931–) (Haya Hararit).
Israeli leading lady. She is married to director Jack
Clayton.
   Hill 24 Does Not Answer 55. Ben Hur 59. The
Secret Partner 61. The Lost Kingdom 61. The
Interns 62. Our Mother's House (co-w only) 67,
etc.

Harburg, E. Y. (1896–1981) (Edgar 'Yip' Harburg).
American lyricist chiefly noted for the songs in *The
Wizard of Oz*; also wrote 'Brother Can You Spare
a Dime', 'Happiness Is a Thing Called Joe', 'Can't
Help Singing', 'Lydia the Tattooed Lady', 'Last Night
When We Were Young', 'April in Paris', 'How Are
Things in Glocca Morra', etc.

hard ticket.
A phrase used in the 60s to describe film exhibition
of the type once called 'road show': separate
performances, reserved seats, long runs and high
prices.

Hardin, Ty (1930–   ) (Orton Hungerford).
Muscular leading man, mostly on TV.

I Married a Monster from Outer Space 58. The Chapman Report 62. PT 109 63. Battle of the Bulge 65. Berserk (GB) 67. Custer of the West 68. The Last Rebel 71. Drums of Vengeance 77. Bad Jim 89. Born Killer 90, etc.

TV series: *Bronco* 58–61. Riptide 69.

¶ I'm really a very humble man. Not a day passes that I don't thank God for my looks and my talent. – T.H.

Harding, Ann (1902–1981) (Dorothy Gatley).
Gentlewomanly American leading lady of 30s romances. She was married to conductor and composer Werner Janssen (1937–63).
■ Paris Bound 29. Her Private Affair 29. Condemned 29. *Holiday* (AAN) 30. Girl of the Golden West 30. East Lynne 31. Devotion 31. Prestige 31. Westward Passage 32. The Conquerors 32. *The Animal Kingdom* 32. When Ladies Meet 33. Double Harness 33. Right to Romance 33. Gallant Lady 33. The Life of Vergie Winters 34. The Fountain 34. *Biography of a Bachelor Girl* 35. Enchanted April 35. The Flame Within 35. Peter Ibbetson 35. The Lady Consents 36. The Witness Chair 36. *Love from a Stranger* (GB) 37. Eyes in the Night 42. Mission to Moscow 43. North Star 43. Janie 44. Nine Girls 44. Those Endearing Young Charms 45. Janie Gets Married 46. It Happened on Fifth Avenue 47. Christmas Eve 47. The Magnificent Yankee 50. Two Weeks with Love 50. The Unknown Man 51. The Man in the Grey Flannel Suit 56. I've Lived Before 56. Strange Intruder 56.

Harding, Gilbert (1907–1960).
Explosive British TV personality who appeared in a few films.

The Gentle Gunman 52. Meet Mr Lucifer 53. As Long as They're Happy 55. An Alligator Named Daisy 55. Expresso Bongo 60, etc.

Harding, Lyn (1867–1952) (David Llewellyn Harding).
British stage actor who made a splendid 'heavy' in some films of the 20s and 30s.

The Barton Mystery 20. When Knighthood Was in Flower (as Henry VIII) 21. The Speckled Band (as Moriarty) 31. *The Triumph of Sherlock Holmes* (as Moriarty) 35. Spy of Napoleon 36. Fire Over England 36. Knight without Armour 37. *Goodbye Mr Chips* (as Chips' first headmaster) 39. The Prime Minister 40, etc.

Hardison, Kadeem (1965–   ).
American actor.

Rappin' 85. School Daze 88. I'm Gonna Git You Sucka 88. Dream Date (TV) 89. Def by Temptation 90. White Men Can't Jump 92, etc.

TV series: A Different World 87–92.

Hardwicke, Sir Cedric (1893–1964).
Distinguished British stage actor who settled in Hollywood and too frequently allowed his talents to be squandered on inferior material.

Autobiography: 1961, *A Victorian in Orbit*.
■ Nelson 26. Dreyfus 31. Rome Express 32. Orders is Orders 32. The Ghoul 33. *Nell Gwyn* (as Charles II) 34. The Lady is Willing 34. Jew Süss 34. King of Paris 34. Bella Donna 34. Peg of Old Drury 35. Les Misérables 35. *Becky Sharp* 35. Things to Come 36. Tudor Rose 36. Laburnum Grove 36. The Green Light 37. *King Solomon's Mines* (as Allan Quartermain) 37. *On Borrowed Time* (as Death) 39. *Stanley and Livingstone* (as Livingstone) 39. The Hunchback of Notre Dame (as Frollo) 39. The

Invisible Man Returns 40. *Tom Brown's Schooldays* (as Dr Arnold) 40. The Howards of Virginia 40. *Victory* 40. Suspicion 41. Sundown 41. The Ghost of Frankenstein 42. Valley of the Sun 42. Invisible Agent 42. The Commandos Strike at Dawn 42. Forever and a Day 43. *The Moon is Down* 43. The Cross of Lorraine 43. The Lodger 44. Wing and a Prayer 44. Wilson 44. The Keys of the Kingdom 45. Sentimental Journey 46. The Imperfect Lady 47. Ivy 47. Lured 47. Song of My Heart 47. A Woman's Vengeance 47. Beware of Pity 47. *Nicholas Nickleby* 47. Tycoon 47. *I Remember Mama* 48. *The Winslow Boy* 48. Rope 48. A Connecticut Yankee in King Arthur's Court 49. Now Barabbas 49. The White Tower 50. Mr Imperium 51. The Desert Fox 51. The Green Glove 52. Caribbean 52. Salome 53. Botany Bay 53. Bait 54. *Richard III* 55. Helen of Troy 55. Diane 56. Gaby 56. The Vagabond King 56. The Power and the Prize 56. The Ten Commandments 56. Around the World in Eighty Days 56. The Story of Mankind 57. Baby Face Nelson 57. Five Weeks in a Balloon 62. The Pumpkin Eater 64.

TV series: Mrs G Goes to College 61.

Hardwicke, Edward (1932–   ).
English actor in occasional films, the son of Sir Cedric Hardwicke. On stage from 1954, after training at RADA, he became a member of the National Theatre company in the 60s. On television, he has played Dr Watson to Jeremy Brett's Sherlock Holmes.

Hell below Zero 53. Othello 65. Otley 68. A Flea in Her Ear 68. The Day of the Jackal 73. Venom 81. Shadowlands 93, etc.

TV series: My Old Man 74–75.

Hardy, Forsyth (1910–1994).
Influential Scottish critic and writer. He was the first film critic of the *Scotsman* newspaper in 1929, one of the founders of *Film Quarterly* magazine in the 30s, and became the first director of the Edinburgh Film Festival, writing its history in *Slightly Mad and Full of Dangers* (1992). His other books include *Scotland in Film* (1990), and *John Grierson, A Documentary Biography*, and he also edited collections of Grierson's writings.

Hardy, Oliver (1892–1957).
Ample-figured American comedian, the fat half of the screen's finest comedy team, noted for his genteel pomposity, tie twiddle and long-suffering look at the camera.

Biographies: 1961, *Mr Laurel and Mr Hardy* by John McCabe. 1989, *Babe – the Life of Oliver Hardy* by John McCabe.

SELECTED SOLO APPEARANCES: Outwitting Dad 13. Playmates 15. Lucky Dog 17. He Winked and Won 17. The Chief Cook 18. The Three Ages 23. Rex, King of the Wild Horses 24. The Wizard of Oz (as the Tin Man) 24. The Nicklehopper 25. Zenobia 39. The Fighting Kentuckian 49. Riding High 50, many others.

■ LAUREL AND HARDY FILMS: Slipping Wives 26. With Love and Hisses 27. Sailors Beware 27. Do Detectives Think? 27. Flying Elephants 27. Sugar Daddies 27. Call of the Cuckoo 27. The Rap 27. Duck Soup 27. Eve's Love Letters 27. Love 'em and Weep 27. Why Girls Love Sailors 27. Should Tall Men Marry? 27. Hats Off 27. Putting Pants on Philip 27. *The Battle of the Century* 27. Leave 'em Laughing 28. From Soup to Nuts 28. *The Finishing Touch* 28. *You're Darn Tootin'* 28. Their Purple Moment 28. Should Married Men Go Home? 28. Early to Bed 28. *Two Tars* 28. Habeas Corpus 28. We Faw Down 28. Liberty 28. Wrong Again 29. That's My Wife 29. *Big Business* 29. *Double Whoopee* 29. Berth Marks 29. Men o'War 29. *The Perfect Day*

29. They Go Boom 29. Bacon Grabbers 29. Angora Love 29. Unaccustomed as We Are 29. Hollywood Revue of 1929 29. The Hoosegow 29. Nig[ht] Owls 30. Blotto 30. The Rogue Song (feature) 3[0]. Brats 30. Be Big 30. Below Zero 30. The Laurel an[d] Hardy Murder Case 30. Hog Wild 30. Another Fi[ne] Mess 30. Chickens Come Home 30. *Laughing Gra[vy]* 31. Our Wife 31. *Come Clean* 31. Pardon Us (feature) 31. One Good Turn 31. Beau Hunks 3[1.] Helpmates 31. Any Old Port 31. *The Music Box* (A[AN]) 32. The Chimp 32. *County Hospital* 32. Scram 32. Pack Up Your Troubles (feature) 32. Their First Mistake 32. *Towed in a Hole* 33. Twice Two 33. Me and My Pal 33. *Fra Diavolo* (feature) 33. *The Midnight Patrol* 33. *Busy Bodies* 33. *Dirty Work* 33. *Sons of the Desert* (feature) 33. Oliver the Eighth 3[4.] Hollywood Party (feature) 34. Going Bye Bye 34. *Them Thar Hills* 34. *Babes in Toyland* (feature) 34. Th[e] Live Ghost 34. *Tit for Tat* 35. The Fixer Uppers 3[5.] Thicker than Water 35. Bonnie Scotland (feature) 35. The Bohemian Girl (feature) 36. *Our Relation[s]* (feature) 36. *Way out West* (feature) 36. Pick a S[tar] (feature) 37. Swiss Miss (feature) 38. *Blockheads* (feature) 38. *The Flying Deuces* (feature) 39. *A Chump at Oxford* (feature) 40. Saps at Sea (featur[e]) 40. Great Guns (feature) 41. A Haunting We W[ill] Go (feature) 42. Air Raid Wardens (feature) 43. Jitterbugs (feature) 43. The Dancing Masters (feature) 43. The Big Noise (feature) 44. Nothin[g] but Trouble (feature) 44. The Bullfighters (featur[e]) 45. Robinson Crusoeland (Atoll K) (feature) 52.
■ COMPILATION FEATURES: The Golden Age of Comedy 58. When Comedy was King 60. Days o[f] Thrills and Laughter 61. Thirty Years of Fun 62. MGM's Big Parade of Comedy 65. Laurel and Hardy's Laughing Twenties 65. The Crazy World of Laurel and Hardy 66. The Further Perils of Laurel and Hardy 69. Four Clowns 69. The Best of Laurel and Hardy 74.

✪ For his many unique qualities, seen to best advantage in his partnership with Stan Laurel. *Blockheads*.

Hardy, Robert (1925–   ).
British character actor, mostly on TV.

The Spy Who Came in from the Cold 65. How I Won the War 67. 10 Rillington Place 70. The F[ar] Pavilions (TV) 84. The Shooting Party (TV) 84. Jenny's War (TV) 84. Middlemarch (TV) 94, etc.

TV series: *Elizabeth R* 71. All Creatures Great a[nd] Small 77–79. *Churchill: the Wilderness Years* 81. Hot Metal 86–88.

Hardy, Robin (1929–   ).
British director.

The Wicker Man 75. The Fantasist 86.

Hardy, Thomas (1840–1928).
British novelist of dour country stories. Works principally filmed, neither satisfactorily, are *Tess of the D'Urbervilles* and *Far from the Madding Crow[d]*.

Hare, David (1947–   ).
British playwright, screenwriter and director.

Licking Hitler (wd) 77. Saigon – Year of the C[at] (w) 83. Wetherby (wd) 85. Plenty (w) 85. Paris by Night (wd) 88. Strapless (wd) 89. Heading Home (w) 91. Damage (w) 92. The Secret Raptu[re] (wd) 93.

Hare, Lumsden (1875–1964).
Irish character actor, long in Hollywood.

Charlie Chan Carries On 31. Clive of India 35. She 35. Gunga Din 39. Rebecca 40. The Lodger 44. Challenge to Lassie 49. Julius Caesar 53. The Four Skulls of Jonathan Drake 59, many others.

Hare, Robertson (1891–1979).
Bald-headed British comedian, the put-upon little man of the Aldwych farces of the 20s and 30s, transferred intact from stage to screen.
Autobiography: 1958, *Yours Indubitably*.
Rookery Nook 30. A Cuckoo in the Nest 33. Thark 33. Fishing Stock 35. Aren't Men Beasts? 38. Banana Ridge 41. He Snoops To Conquer 45. Things Happen at Night 48. *One Wild Oat* 51. Our Girl Friday 53. Three Men in a Boat 56. The Young Ones 61, etc.

Harewood, Dorian (1951–   ).
American actor.
Sparkle 75. Gray Lady Down 77. Looker 81. Against All Odds 83. The Falcon and the Snowman 84. Full Metal Jacket 87. Pacific Heights 90. Solar Crisis 90, etc.
TV series: Roots: The Next Generation 79. Strike Force 81–82. Trauma Centre 83. Glitter 84–85. Trials of Rose O'Neill 91–92. Viper 93.

Hark, Tsui (1951–   ) (Xu Ke).
Vietnamese-born, Hong Kong-based director and producer.
The Butterfly Murders 79. We're Going to Eat You 80. Zu Warriors from the Magic Mountain 83. Shanghai Blues 84. Peking Opera Blues (Do Ma Dan) 86. A Chinese Ghost Story (Qian Nu Youhun) 87. A Better Tomorrow III 89. The Swordsman 90. A Chinese Ghost Story III 91. Once upon a Time in China (Wong Fei-hung) 91. Swordsman II (co-w, p) 92. Once upon a Time in China II (Wong Fei-Hung II) (wd) 92. Monkey King 93. The Iron Monkey (co-w, p) 93. Once Upon a Time in China III (wd) 93. Swordsman III (co-w, p) 93, etc.

Harker, Gordon (1885–1967).
British comic actor, the jutting-lipped cockney of many a 30s comedy.
The Ring (debut) 27. The Calendar 31. *Rome Express* 33. Friday the Thirteenth 33. Boys Will be Boys 35. Millions 37. The Return of the Frog 38. *Inspector Hornleigh* 40. *Saloon Bar* 41. Warn That Man 43. 29 Acacia Avenue 45. Things Happen at Night 48. Her Favourite Husband 50. The Second Mate 50. Derby Day 52. Small Hotel 58. Left, Right and Centre 59, etc.

Harlan, Kenneth (1895–1967).
American leading man of the silent screen.
Cheerful Givers 17. The Hoodlum 19. The Beautiful and the Damned 22. The Broken Wing 23. Bobbed Hair 24. Twinkletoes 26. San Francisco 36. Paper Bullets 41. The Underdog 44, many others.

Harlan, Otis (1865–1940).
Tubby American character actor with long stage experience.
What Happened to Jones? 25. Lightnin' 26. Man to Man 31. The Hawk 32. Married in Haste 34. Diamond Jim 35. A Midsummer Night's Dream 35. Mr Boggs Steps Out 38, many others.

Harlan, Russell (1903–1974).
American cinematographer, former stuntman.
Hopalong Rides Again 37. Stagecoach War 40. The Kansan 43. *A Walk in the Sun* 45. Red River 48. The Big Sky 52. *Riot in Cell Block Eleven* 54. The Blackboard Jungle 55. This Could Be the Night 57. Witness for the Prosecution 57. Run Silent Run Deep 58. King Creole 58. The Spiral Road 62. Hatari 62. To Kill a Mockingbird 62. Quick Before It Melts 65. Tobruk 66. Darling Lili 70, etc.

Harlan, Veit (1899–1964).
German director of Nazi propaganda.
Kreutzer Sonata 36. Jew Süss 40. Der Grosse Konig 41. Opfergang 43. Die Blaue Stunde 52. The Third Sex 57, etc.

Harlin, Renny (1959–   ) (Lauri Harjula).
Finnish director, now in Hollywood. He married actress Geena Davis in 1993.
Born American (& w) 86. A Nightmare on Elm Street Part 4: The Dream Master 88. Prison 88. The Adventures of Ford Fairlane 90. Die Hard II 90. Cliffhanger (& p) 93, etc.

¶ In Europe, film-making is perceived as an art form with marginal business possibilities, and in the US, film-making is a business with marginal artistic possibilities. – *R.H.*

Harline, Leigh (1907–1969).
American screen composer.
Snow White and the Seven Dwarfs (s) 37. Pinocchio (s) (AA) 39. His Girl Friday 40. The Pride of the Yankees (AAN) 42. You Were Never Lovelier (AAN) 42. The Sky's the Limit (AAN) 43. Johnny Come Lately (AAN) 43. The More the Merrier 43. Road to Utopia 45. The Farmer's Daughter 47. The Big Steal 49. Monkey Business 52. Broken Lance 54. The Wayward Bus 57. Ten North Frederick 58. Warlock 60. The Wonderful World of the Brothers Grimm (AAN) 62. Seven Faces of Dr Lao 63. Strange Bedfellows 64, etc.

Harling, W. Franke (1887–1958).
American composer.
One Hour with You 32. So Big 32. The Scarlet Empress 34. So Red the Rose 35. Souls at Sea 37. Stagecoach (co-m, AA) 39. Penny Serenade 41. The Lady Is Willing 42. Three Russian Girls (AAN) 44. The Bachelor's Daughter 46, etc.

Harlow, Jean (1911–1937) (Harlean Carpenter).
American leading lady and most sensational star of the early 30s, a wisecracking 'platinum blonde' with a private life to suit her public image.
Biographies: 1937, *Hollywood Comet* by Dentner Davies. 1964, *Harlow* by Irving Shulman.
■ Moran of the Marines 28. Double Whoopee (short) 29. The Unkissed Man 29. The Fugitive 29. Close Harmony 29. New York Nights 29. The Love Parade 29. Weak but Willing 29. Bacon Grabbers (short) 29. The Saturday Night Kid 29. The Love Parade 30. *Hell's Angels* 30. City Lights 31. The Secret Six 31. Iron Man 31. *Public Enemy* 31. Goldie 31. Platinum Blonde 31. Three Wise Girls 32. Beast of the City 32. *Red Headed Woman* 32. *Red Dust* 32. *Dinner at Eight* 33. Hold Your Man 33. *Bombshell* 33. The Girl from Missouri 34. Reckless 35. *China Seas* 35. Riffraff 35. Wife vs Secretary 35. Suzy 36. *Libelled Lady* 36. Personal Property 37. Saratoga 37. ✪ For combining a sophistication which she acted with an innocence which was her own. *Red Dust*.

¶ Would it shock you if I put on something more comfortable? – *Jean Harlow in Hell's Angels*
She didn't want to be famous. She wanted to be happy. – *Clark Gable*
A square shooter if ever there was one. – *Spencer Tracy*
Last lines of *Dinner at Eight:*
Jean Harlow: 'You know, the other day I read a book. It said that machinery is going to take the place of every profession.'
Marie Dressler: 'Oh, my dear: that's something you'll *never* have to worry about!'

Harlow, John (1896–   ).
British writer-director, former music-hall performer.
Spellbound (d) 40. Candles at Nine (d) 43. Meet Sexton Blake (d) 44. The Agitator (d) 45. Appointment with Crime (wd) 46. Green Fingers (wd) 47. *While I Live* (Dream of Olwen) (wd) 48. Old Mother Riley's New Venture (d) 49. Those People Next Door (d) 52, etc.

Harman, Hugh (1903–1982).
American animator who in the early 30s, with Rudolph Ising, formed Harman-Ising and made some brilliantly inventive cartoons for MGM. Later originated Merrie Melodies and Looney Tunes, and was cited by the Nobel Peace jury for *Peace on Earth* (1940).

Harmon, Mark (1951–   ).
Competent American leading man, difficult to distinguish from several others.
Eleanor and Franklin: the White House Years (TV) 77. Centennial 78. Comes a Horseman 78. Beyond the Poseidon Adventure 79. *The Dream Merchants* (TV) 80. Summer School 87. The Presidio 88. Worth Winning 89. Fourth Story (TV) 90. Till There Was You 91. Cold Heaven 92. Wyatt Earp 94, etc.
TV series: Flamingo Road 81–82.

Harolde, Ralf (1899–1974) (R. H. Wigger).
American supporting actor often seen as thin-lipped crook.
Night Nurse 32. A Tale of Two Cities 35. Horror Island 41. Baby Face Morgan 42. Farewell My Lovely (as the doctor) 44. Alaska Patrol (last film) 51, many others.

Harper, Gerald (1929–   ).
Aristocratic-looking British actor familiar on TV as *Adam Adamant* and *Hadleigh*.
The Admirable Crichton 57. A Night to Remember 58. The League of Gentlemen 59. The Punch and Judy Man 62. The Lady Vanishes 79, etc.

Harper, Jessica (1948–   ).
American leading lady.
Inserts 76. Suspiria 77. The Evictors 79. Shock Treatment 81. Pennies from Heaven 81. My Favorite Year 82. Big Man on Campus 89, etc.

Harper, Tess (1950–   ) (Tessie Jean Washam).
American actress.
Amityville: The Demon (aka Amityville 3-D) 83. Tender Mercies 83. Flashpoint 84. Crimes of the Heart (AAN) 86. Ishtar 87. Far North 88. Her Alibi 89. Criminal Law 89. Daddy's Dying . . . Who's Got the Will? 90. My Heroes Have Always Been Cowboys 91. The Man in the Moon 91. My New Gun 92, etc.

Harper, Valerie (1940–   ).
American leading comedy actress, a star of TV.
The Ones in Between 72. Freebie and the Bean 74. Thursday's Game (TV) 74. Night Terror (TV) 77. The Last Married Couple in America 79. Blame It on Rio 84. Drop-out Mother (TV) 88, etc.
TV series: *The Mary Tyler Moore Show* 70–73. *Rhoda* 74–78.

Harrelson, Woody (1962–   ).
American leading actor, best known for his role as Woody Boyd in the TV series *Cheers*.
Wildcats 86. Casualties of War 89. Ted and Venus 91. White Men Can't Jump 92. Indecent Proposal 93. The Cowboy Way 94. Natural Born Killers 94, etc.
TV series: Cheers 85–92.

Harrigan, William (1894–1966).
American general-purpose actor of the 30s and 40s.

On the Level 17. Cabaret 27. Nix on Dames 27. Born Reckless 30. Pick Up 33. The Invisible Man 33. G Men 35. The Silk Hat Kid 35. Federal Bullets 37. Hawaii Calls 38. Back Door to Heaven 39. The Farmer's Daughter 47. Flying Leathernecks 51. Street of Sinners 55, etc.

Harrington, Curtis (1928–).
American director who made experimental shorts before graduating to features.
■ Night Tide 63. Voyage to a Prehistoric Planet 64. Queen of Blood 66. Games 67. How Awful About Allan (TV) 70. What's the Matter with Helen? 71. Who Slew Auntie Roo? 73. The Cat Creature (TV) 73. Killer Bees (TV) 74. The Dead Don't Die (TV) 74. The Killing Kind 76. Ruby 77. Devil Dog (TV) 78. Mata Hari 85.

Harris, Barbara (1936–).
American leading lady.
A Thousand Clowns 65. Oh Dad . . . 66. Plaza Suite 71. Who Is Harry Kellerman . . . ? (AAN) 71. The War between Men and Women 72. Family Plot 76. Freaky Friday 77. Movie Movie 78. The Seduction of Joe Tynan 79. Second Hand Hearts 80. Night Magic 85. Peggy Sue Got Married 86. Dirty Rotten Scoundrels 88, etc.

Harris, Damian (1960–).
British director and screenwriter, the son of actor Richard Harris.
Otley (a) 68. The Rachel Papers (wd) 89. Deceived (d) 91. Bad Company 94.

Harris, Ed (1950–).
Dour American leading actor, from the stage. Married actress Amy Madigan.
Coma 77. Zombies 80. Borderline 80. Knightriders 81. Dream On 81. Creepshow 82. The Right Stuff 83. Under Fire 83. Swing Shift 84. Places in the Heart 84. Sweet Dreams 85. Alamo Bay 85. A Flash of Green 85. The Last Innocent Man 87. Walker 87. To Kill a Priest 89. Jackknife 89. The Abyss 89. State of Grace 90. Paris Trout 91. Glengarry Glen Ross 92. The Firm 93. Needful Things 93. China Moon 94. Milk Money 94, etc.

Harris, Jack (1905–1971).
British editor.
The Sleeping Cardinal 31. The Wandering Jew 33. The Face at the Window 39. Let the People Sing 42. This Happy Breed 44. Blithe Spirit 45. Brief Encounter 45. Great Expectations 46. Oliver Twist 48. Where No Vultures Fly 51. The Crimson Pirate 53. Indiscreet 58. The Sundowners 60. Billy Budd 62. The Chalk Garden 64. Three Sisters 70, many others.

Harris, James B. (1928–).
American producer and director, associated with director Stanley Kubrick.
The Killing 56. Paths of Glory 57. Lolita 62. The Bedford Incident (& d) 65. Some Call It Loving (& d) 71. Telefon 77. Fast Walking (& wd) 82. Cop (& wd) 88. Boiling Point (wd) 93, etc.

Harris, Jed (1900–1979) (Jacob Horowitz).
American theatrical impresario of the 30s and 40s, notorious for toughness and rudeness; lampooned in films *Twentieth Century* and *The Saxon Charm*. He was the model both for Walt Disney's Big Bad Wolf and Laurence Olivier's Richard III. Joseph Losey began as his assistant.

¶ The most loathsome man I'd ever met.
– *Laurence Olivier*
Fresh as poison ivy. – *Edna Ferber*
When I die, I want to be cremated and have my ashes thrown in Jed Harris's face. – *George S. Kaufman*

Harris, Joel Chandler (1848–1908).
American journalist and story writer who created the characters of Uncle Remus and Brer Rabbit, filmed by Disney in *Song of the South*.

Harris, Jonathan (1914–).
American character actor, popular in prissy roles in TV series *The Third Man* 59–61, *The Bill Dana Show* 63–64, *Lost in Space* 65–68.
Botany Bay 54. The Big Fisherman 59, etc.

Harris, Julie (1925–).
American stage actress, adept at fey roles. Films occasional.
■ *The Member of the Wedding* (AAN) 53. East of Eden 55. I Am a Camera 56. The Truth about Women 56. Sally's Irish Rogue 60. Requiem for a Heavyweight 62. *The Haunting* 63. Harper 66. You're a Big Boy Now 66. *Reflections in a Golden Eye* 67. The Split 68. The House on Greenapple Road (TV) 69. How Awful about Allan (TV) 70. The People Next Door 70. Home for the Holidays (TV) 72. The Greatest Gift (TV) 74. The Hiding Place 75. Voyage of the Damned 76. The Bell Jar 79. Backstairs at the White House (TV) 79. Bronte 83. Leaving Home 86. Gorillas in the Mist 88. The Woman He Loved (TV) 88. Too Good to Be True (TV) 88. Single Women, Married Men (TV) 89. The Dark Half (TV) 91. Paris Trout 91. Housesitter 92.
TV series: Thicker than Water 73. The Family Holvak 76. Knots Landing 81–87.

Harris, Julie.
British costume designer.
The Naked Edge 61. The Fast Lady 62. The Chalk Garden 64. The Wrong Box 65. Casino Royale 67. Goodbye Mr Chips 69. Live and Let Die 73. Rollerball 74. The Slipper and the Rose 76, many others.

Harris, Julius W.
American character actor.
Slaves 69. Incident in San Francisco (TV) 71. Shaft's Big Score 73. A Cry for Help (TV) 75. King Kong 76. Rich Man Poor Man (TV) 76. Victory at Entebbe (as Idi Amin) (TV) 76. Islands in the Stream 77. Looking for Mr Goodbar 77. Ring of Passion (TV) 78. The First Family 80. Missing Pieces (TV) 83. Crimewave 85. Prayer of the Rollerboys 91. Harley Davidson and the Marlboro Man 91, etc.

Harris, Mildred (1901–1944).
American leading lady of the silent era, first wife of Charles Chaplin.
Intolerance 15. Borrowed Clothes 18. Fool's Paradise 21. Fog 23. Unmarried Wives 24. My Neighbour's Wife 25. The Mystery Club 26. The Show Girl 27. Sea Fury 29. No No Nanette 30. Lady Tubbs 35. Reap the Wild Wind 42. The Story of Dr Wassell 44, etc.

Harris, Phil (1904–).
American bandleader and comic singer; in occasional films.
Melody Cruise 33. Man about Town 39. Buck Benny Rides Again 40. Here Comes the Groom 51. The Glenn Miller Story 54. The High and the Mighty 54. Anything Goes 56. The Wheeler Dealers 63. The Cool Ones 67. Robin Hood (voice) 73. Rock-a-Doodle (voice) 90, etc.

Harris, Richard (1932–).
Gaunt Irish leading actor. Usually cast as a rebel, he tries to match the part in real life.
■ Alive and Kicking 58. Shake Hands with the Devil 59. The Wreck of the Mary Deare 59. A Terrible Beauty 60. All Night Long 61. The Long the Short and the Tall 61. The Guns of Navarone 61. *Mutiny on the Bounty* 62. *This Sporting Life* (AAN 63. The Red Desert 64. I Tre Volti 64. Major Dunde 65. The Heroes of Telemark 65. The Bible 66. Hawaii 66. Caprice 66. *Camelot* (as King Arthur) 67 The Molly Maguires 69. A Man Called Horse 69. Bloomfield (& d) 70. *Cromwell* (title role) 70. The Snow Goose (TV) 71. Man in the Wilderness 71. The Deadly Trackers 73. 99 44/100 Dead 74. Juggernaut 75. Robin and Marian 75. The Return of a Man Called Horse 76. Echoes of a Summer 76 Gulliver's Travels 76. The Cassandra Crossing 77. Orca – Killer Whale 77. Golden Rendezvous 77. The Wild Geese 78. Game for Vultures 79. The Las Word 79. The Revengers 79. Your Ticket Is No Longer Valid 79. Highpoint 80. Tarzan the Ape Man 81. Triumphs of a Man Called Horse 82. Martin's Day 84. The Return 88. Mack the Knife 89. King of the Wind 89. *The Field* (AAN) 90. Patric Games 92. *Unforgiven* 92. Silent Tongue 93. The Bible: Abraham (TV) 93. Wrestling Ernest Hemingway 93.

¶ He's something of a fuck-up, no question.
– *Charlton Heston*
He hauls his surly carcass from movie to movie being dismembered. I'd just as soon wait till he's finished. – *Pauline Kael*

Harris, Robert (1900–).
British classical actor who has played occasional film roles.
How He Lied to Her Husband 31. The Life and Death of Colonel Blimp 43. The Bad Lord Byron 48. That Lady 55. Oscar Wilde 60. Decline and Fal 68, etc.

Harris, Robert H. (1911–1981).
American character actor, usually beaky, officious and unsympathetic.
Bundle of Joy 56. How to Make a Monster 58. America America 63. Mirage 65. Valley of the Dolls 67, etc.
TV series: The Goldbergs 56. Court of Last Resor 57–60.

Harris, Rosemary (1930–).
British leading lady, chiefly on stage.
Beau Brummel 54. The Shiralee 55. A Flea in Her Ear 68. Holocaust (TV) 77. The Boys from Brazi 78. The Chisholms (TV) 78. Crossing Delancey 88 The Bridge 91. Tom and Viv 93, etc.

Harris, Theresa (1910–1985).
American actress.
Morocco 30. Blood Money 33. Morning Glory 33. Jezebel 38. Santa Fe Trail 40. Blossoms in the Dust 40. I Walked with a Zombie 43. Three Little Girls in Blue 46. Neptune's Daughter 49. And Bab Makes Three 50. The Company She Keeps 51, many others.

Harris, Vernon (c. 1910–).
British screenwriter. He also scripted the 1938 BB radio series *Band Waggon* with Arthur Askey and Richard Murdoch.
Joy Ride (story) 35. Improper Duchess 36. Tropical Trouble 36. Albert RN (co-w) 53. The Se Shall Not Have Them (co-w) 55. Reach for the Sk 56. Ferry to Hong Kong 57. The Admirable Crichton 57. Light up the Sky 61. Oliver! (AAN) 68. Paul and Michelle (co-w) 75, etc.

Harrison, Doane (–1968).
American editor.
Youth and Adventure 25. Celebrity 28. The Spieler 29. Her Man 30. 13 Hours by Air 36. Midnight 39. Hold Back the Dawn 41. The Major and the Minor 42. Five Graves to Cairo 43. The Uninvited 44. The Lost Weekend 45. A Foreign Affair 48. Branded 50, etc.
Later associate producer for Billy Wilder.

Harrison, George (1943–   ).
English composer, musician and producer. Formerly guitarist for The Beatles, he runs the British production company HandMade Films with Denis O'Brien.
AS COMPOSER: Shanghai Surprise 86.
AS PERFORMER: A Hard Day's Night 64. Help 65. Magical Mystery Tour 67. The Concert for Bangladesh (concert) 72. The Rutles (TV) 78. Life of Brian 79, etc.
AS PRODUCER: Life of Brian 79. Time Bandits 81. Privates on Parade 83. Water 86. Withnail and I 87. Track 29 88. Powwow Highway 89. How to Get Ahead in Advertising 89. Cold Dog Soup 90. Nuns on the Run 90. The Raggedy Rawney 90, etc.

¶ I don't really think the film business is all it's cracked up to be . . . It's still much better being a guitar player. – G.H.

Harrison, Gregory (1950–   ).
American actor.
Trilogy of Terror (TV) 75. The Gathering (TV) 77. For Ladies Only 81. Razorback (Aus.) 84. Seduced (TV) 85. Oceans of Fire 86. The Hasty Heart 86. North Shore 87. Dangerous Pursuit 89. Bare Essentials (TV) 91. Body Chemistry II: Voice of a Stranger 91. Duplicates 92, etc.
TV series: Logan's Run 77–78. Centennial 78–79. Trapper John, M.D. 79–86. Falcon Crest 89–90. The Family Man 90–91. True Detectives 90–91.

Harrison, Joan (1911–1994).
British writer-producer, assistant for many years to Alfred Hitchcock. She was married to author Eric Ambler.
Jamaica Inn (w) 39. Rebecca (co-w, AAN) 40. Foreign Correspondent (co-w, AAN) 40. Suspicion (w) 41. Saboteur (w) 42. Dark Waters (w) 44. Phantom Lady (p) 44. Uncle Harry (p) 45. Ride the Pink Horse (p) 47. Circle of Danger (p) 51, etc.
TV series: Alfred Hitchcock Presents (p) 55–63.

Harrison, Kathleen (1898–   ).
British character actress, usually seen as a cockney but born in Lancashire. On stage from 1926; films made her an amiable, slightly dithery but warm-hearted national figure.
Hobson's Choice (debut) 31. The Ghoul 33. Broken Blossoms 36. Night Must Fall (US) 37. Bank Holiday 38. The Outsider 39. The Ghost Train 41. Kipps 41. In Which We Serve 42. Dear Octopus 43. Great Day 45. Holiday Camp 47. The Winslow Boy 48. Bond Street 48. Oliver Twist 48. Here Come the Huggetts (and ensuing series) 49–52. Waterfront 50. Scrooge 51. Pickwick Papers 52. Turn the Key Softly 53. Cast a Dark Shadow 54. Where There's a Will 54. Lilacs in the Spring 54. All for Mary 55. Home and Away 56. A Cry from the Streets 58. Alive and Kicking 58. Mrs Gibbons' Boys 62. West Eleven 63. Lock Up Your Daughters 69, many others.

Harrison, Linda (1945–   ).
American leading lady, briefly evident at

Twentieth Century-Fox: married Richard Zanuck.
Way Way Out 66. A Guide for the Married Man 67. Planet of the Apes 67. Airport 75 75.
TV series: Bracken's World 69–70.

Harrison, Sir Rex (1908–1990) (Reginald Carey).
Debonair British leading actor of pleasant if limited range, on stage since 1924; films only occasionally gave him the right material.
Autobiographies: 1974, Rex. 1991, A Damned Serious Business: My Life in Comedy.
Biographies: 1985, Rex Harrison by Allen Eyles. 1991, Rex Harrison by Nicholas Wapshott. 1992, Rex Harrison by Alexander Walker.
■ The Great Game 30. The School for Scandal 30. All at Sea 34. Get Your Man 34. Leave It to Blanche 35. Men Are Not Gods 36. Storm in a Teacup 37. School for Husbands 37. St Martin's Lane 38. The Citadel 38. Over the Moon 39. The Silent Battle 39. Ten Days in Paris 39. Night Train to Munich 40. Major Barbara 40. I Live in Grosvenor Square 45. Blithe Spirit 45. The Rake's Progress 46. Anna and the King of Siam (US) 46. The Ghost and Mrs Muir (US) 47. The Foxes of Harrow (US) 47. Unfaithfully Yours (US) 48. Escape 48. The Long Dark Hall 51. The Fourposter (US) 52. King Richard and the Crusaders (as Saladin) (US) 54. The Constant Husband 55. The Reluctant Debutante (US) 58. Midnight Lace (US) 60. The Happy Thieves (US) 62. Cleopatra (US) (AAN) 62. My Fair Lady (AA) (US) 64. The Yellow Rolls-Royce 64. The Agony and the Ecstasy (US) (as a medieval pope) 65. The Honey Pot (US) 67. Doctor Dolittle (US) 67. A Flea in Her Ear (US/Fr.) 68. Staircase 69. Don Quixote (TV) 72. The Prince and the Pauper 77. The Fifth Musketeer 77. Ashanti 78. Shalimar 78. Crossed Swords 78. A Time to Die 79.

¶ I'm now at the age where I've got to prove that I'm just as good as I never was. – R.H., 1980
If you weren't the finest light-comedy actor in the world next to me, you'd be good for only one thing – selling cars in Great Portland Street – Noel Coward to R.H.
A limited man, rather reppy, whose youthful good looks and some luck with the parts ensured a profitable career. – Kenneth Williams

Famous line (Blithe Spirit): 'If you're trying to compile an inventory of my sex life, I feel it only fair to warn you that you've omitted several episodes. I shall consult my diary and give you a complete list after lunch.'

Harrison, Richard.
American strongman in Italian spectaculars.
Executioner on the High Seas 61. Invincible Gladiator 61. Perseus against the Monsters 63. Spy Killers 65. Adventures of the Bengal Lancers 65. Vengeance 68. Commando Attack 70. The Way of the Godfather 73.

Harrold, Kathryn (1950–   ).
American leading lady.
Yes Giorgio 82. The Sender 82. Into the Night 84. McGruder and Loud (TV) 84. Raw Deal 86. Someone to Love 87. Raw Deal 86. Deadly Desire 91, etc.
TV series: MacGruder and Loud 85. The Bronx Zoo 87–88.

Harron, Robert (Bobby) (1894–1920).
American juvenile lead who joined D. W. Griffith's company almost from school; died in shooting accident.
Dr Skinum 07. Bobby's Kodak 08. Man's Genesis

12. The Birth of a Nation 15. Intolerance 16. Hearts of the World 18. True Heart Susie 19. Darling Mine 21, many others.

Harrow, Lisa (1943–   ).
New Zealand leading actress.
The Devil Is a Woman (It.) 75. It Shouldn't Happen to a Vet (GB) 76. The Final Conflict (US) 81. Under Capricorn (Aus.) 82. Shaker Run 85. The Last Days of Chez Nous (Aus.) 92. That Eye, the Sky (Aus.) 94, etc.

Harry Callahan.
The tough, maverick cop who imposes his own law and order on the world has been played by Clint Eastwood in five films: Dirty Harry 71, Magnum Force 73, The Enforcer 76, Sudden Impact 83, The Dead Pool 88. He made famous the phrase 'Make my day', addressed as a dare to a crook about to go for his gun. Other dialogue, from Dirty Harry (uncredited addition by John Milius to the script by Harry Julian Fink, Rita M. Fink, Dean Riesner):
'I know what you're thinking, punk. You're thinking, Did he fire six shots or only five? Now to tell you the truth I've forgotten myself in all this excitement. But being this is a .44 Magnum, the most powerful handgun in the world, and will blow your head clean off, you've got to ask yourself a question: Do I feel lucky? Well, do you, punk?'

Harry, Debbie (1954–   ) (Deborah Harry).
American actress and singer. She was the lead singer of the 70s rock band Blondie.
Roadie 80. Union City 81. Videodrome 83. The Foreigner 84. Forever Lulu 87. Hairspray 88. Satisfaction 88. New York Stories 89. Tales from the Darkside: The Movie 90. Intimate Stranger 91. Dead Beat 94, etc.

¶ I am now a shopaholic and I shop 'til I drop. It's more expensive than taking drugs but it's legal and fun. – D.H.

Harryhausen, Ray (1920–   ).
American trick film specialist and model-maker; invented 'Superdynamation'.
Book: 1972, Film Fantasy Scrapbook.
Mighty Joe Young 50. It Came from Beneath the Sea 52. Twenty Million Miles to Earth 57. The Three Worlds of Gulliver 60. Jason and the Argonauts 63. The First Men in the Moon 64. One Million Years BC 66. The Valley of Gwangi 69. The Golden Voyage of Sinbad 73. Sinbad and the Eye of the Tiger 77, etc.

Hart, Dolores (1938–   ) (D. Hicks).
American lady of a few films in the late 50s. Retired to become a nun.
Loving You 56. Wild is the Wind 57. Lonelyhearts 59. Sail a Crooked Ship 60. Lisa 62, etc.

Hart, Dorothy (1923–   ).
American second lead of the 50s.
Naked City 47. Take One False Step 49. Undertow 49. I Was a Communist for the FBI 51. Tarzan's Savage Fury 52, etc.

Hart, Harvey (1928–1989).
Canadian director, from TV, latterly in Hollywood.
■ Dark Intruder 65. Bus Riley's Back in Town 65. Sullivan's Empire 67. The Sweet Ride 68. The Young Lawyers (TV) 69. Fortune and Men's Eyes 71. The Pyx 73. Panic on the 5.22 (TV) 74. Can Ellen Be Saved? (TV) 74. Murder or Mercy? (TV) 74. Shoot 77. Goldenrod (TV) 77. Prince of Central Park 77. W.E.B. (TV) 78. Captains

Courageous (TV) 78. Standing Tall (TV) 78. Like
Normal People (TV) 79. The Aliens Are Coming
(TV) 79. East of Eden (TV) 81. The High Country
81. Massarati and the Brain (TV) 82. Born
Beautiful (TV) 82. Getting Even 83. Master of the
Game (TV) 84. Reckless Disregard (TV) 85. Beverly
Hills Madam (TV) 86. Stone Fox (TV) 87. Murder
Sees the Light (TV) 87. Passion and Paradise (TV)
89.

Hart, Lorenz (1895–1943).
American lyricist, mostly with Richard Rodgers as
composer. Shows filmed include *On Your Toes, Pal
Joey, The Boys from Syracuse.* Played by Mickey
Rooney in *Words and Music.*

Hart, Moss (1904–1961).
American playwright (usually in collaboration
with George S. Kaufman) and theatrical
producer. Wrote occasional screenplays.
Autobiography: 1958, *Act One* (filmed 1963).
Once in a Lifetime (oa) 32. You Can't Take It
With You (oa) 38. *The Man Who Came to Dinner* (oa)
41. George Washington Slept Here (oa) 42. Lady
in the Dark (oa) 44. Winged Victory (w) 44.
Gentleman's Agreement (AANw) 47. Hans Christian
Andersen (w) 52. A Star Is Born (w) 54. Prince of
Players (w) 55, etc.

Hart, Richard (1915–1951).
American leading man with a very brief
Hollywood career.
■ Green Dolphin Street 47. Desire Me 47. B.F.'s
Daughter 48. The Black Book 49.

Hart, William S. (1870–1946).
Mature, solemn-faced hero of innumerable silent
westerns; one of the key performers of the 20s. The
initial 'S' is variously reputed to have stood for
'Shakespeare' and 'Surrey'.
Autobiography: 1929, *My Life East and West.*
The Disciple 15. The Captive God 16. The Return
of Draw Egan 16. Hell's Hinges 17. Truthful Tolliver
17. Blue Blazes Rawden 18. Selfish Yates 18.
Riddle Gawne 18. The Border Wireless 18. Wagon
Tracks 18. The Poppy Girl's Husband 19. The Toll
Gate 20. Sand 20. Cradle of Courage 20. O'Malley
of the Mounted 21. White Oak 21. Travellin' On
22. Hollywood 23. Wild Bill Hickok 23. Singer Jim
McKee 24. *Tumbleweeds* 25, many others.

¶ His frequently austere look breathed dedication
to the West as a subject suited for all the artistic
possibilities of cinema. – *Allen Eyles*

Harte, Bret (1836–1902) (Francis Brett Harte).
American short-story writer who wandered the
old west. Works filmed include *The Outcasts of
Poker Flat, Tennessee's Partner.*

Hartford-Davis, Robert (1923–1977).
British producer-director, in films since 1939.
That Kind of Girl 62. The Yellow Teddybears 63.
Saturday Night Out 63. Black Torment 64. Gonks
Go Beat 65. The Sandwich Man 66. Corruption
68. The Smashing Bird I Used to Know 69. The
Fiend 71. Black Gunn (US) 72. The Take (US) 74,
etc.

Hartl, Karl (1899–   ).
Austrian director.
The Doomed Battalion 31. F.P.1 32. Gold 34.
The Gypsy Baron 35. The Man Who Was Sherlock
Holmes 37. Whom the Gods Love 42. The Angel
with the Trumpet 48. The Wonder Kid 51.
Journey into the Past 54. Mozart 55. Love Is Red
57, many others. Also scenarist for many of the
above.

Hartley, Hal.
American director, screenwriter and producer of
quirky low-budget movies.
The Unbelievable Truth 90. Trust 91. Surviving
Desire (TV) 92. Simple Men 92. Amateur 94.

Hartley, Mariette (1940–   ).
Under-used leading lady who makes an occasional
impression.
Ride the High Country 62. Drums of Africa 63.
Marooned 67. Barquero 70. The Return of Count
Yorga 71. Earth II (TV) 71. Sandcastles (TV) 72.
Genesis II (TV) 73. The Killer Who Wouldn't Die
(TV) 76. The Last Hurrah (TV) 77. Improper
Channels 81. No Place to Hide (TV) 82. 1969 89.
Encino Man (GB: California Man) 92, etc.
TV series: Peyton Place 65. The Hero 66–67.
Goodnight Beantown 83–84. WIOU 90–91.

Hartley, Richard.
British composer.
Galileo 75. The Romantic Englishwoman 75.
The Rocky Horror Picture Show 75. Aces High 75.
The Lady Vanishes 79. Bad Timing 80. Shock
Treatment 81. The Trout 82. Bad Blood 83. Sheena
84. Parker 85. Dance with a Stranger 85. The Good
Father 86. Soursweet 88. Consuming Passions 88.
The Tree of Hands 89. Dealers 89. She's Been Away
89. Afraid of the Dark 91. The Railway Station
Man 92. Princess Caraboo 94, etc.

Hartman, David (1937–   ).
Tall, gangling American leading man who after a
few years, mostly in television, gained a
permanent niche as anchorman for ABC's *Good
Morning America.*
The Ballad of Josie 68. Nobody's Perfect 69. Ice
Station Zebra 69. San Francisco International
(TV) 70. The Feminist and the Fuzz (TV) 71. I Love
a Mystery (TV) 73. You'll Never See Me Again (TV)
73. Miracle on 34th Street (TV) 74. The Island at
the Top of the World 75, etc.
TV series: The Bold Ones 69–71. Lucas Tanner
76.

Hartman, Don (1901–1958) (Samuel Hartman).
American comedy screenwriter.
The Gay Deception 35. The Princess Comes
Across 35. Waikiki Wedding 37. Tropic Holiday
38. Paris Honeymoon 39. The Star Maker 39. *Road
to Singapore* 40. Life with Henry 41. *Road to Zanzibar*
41. Nothing but the Truth 41. *Road to Morocco*
(AAN) 42. True to Life 42. Up in Arms 44. The
Princess and the Pirate 44. Down to Earth (& p)
47. It Had to be You (& d) 47. Every Girl Should
Be Married (& pd) 48. Mr Imperium (& d) 51.
Desire Under the Elms (p) 57. The Matchmaker
(p) 58, many others.

Hartman, Elizabeth (1941–1987).
American leading actress. Committed suicide.
A Patch of Blue (AAN) 66. The Group 66. You're
a Big Boy Now 67. The Fixer 68. The Beguiled
71. Walking Tall 73.

Hartman, Phil (1948–   ).
Canadian comedian and writer, best known as a
regular, from 1986, on the television series
Saturday Night Live.
Weekend Pass 84. Jumpin' Jack Flash 86. Three
Amigos 86. Blind Date 87. How I Got into College
89. Fletch Lives 89. Coneheads 93. So I Married
an Axe Murderer 93. Greedy 94, etc.
TV series: Our Time 85.

Hartnell, William (1908–1975).
Thin-lipped British character actor who rose
briefly to star status in the 40s after playing many

small-time crooks and tough sergeants. Popular on
TV in the 60s as the first Dr Who.
Follow the Lady 33. While Parents Sleep 35.
Midnight at Madame Tussaud's 36. Farewell Again
37. They Drive by Night 39. Flying Fortress 40.
Suspected Person 41. The Peterville Diamond 42.
The Bells Go Down 43. Headline 43. *The Way Ahead*
44. The Agitator 44. Murder in Reverse 45.
Strawberry Roan 46. Appointment with Crime 46.
Odd Man Out 46. Temptation Harbour 47. *Brighton
Rock* 47. Now Barabbas 49. The Lost People 49.
The Dark Man 50. The Magic Box 51. The Holly
and the Ivy 52. The Ringer 52. Will any
Gentleman? 53. Footsteps in the Fog 54. Private's
Progress 55. Hell Drivers 57. Carry on Sergeant 58.
Piccadilly Third Stop 60. This Sporting Life 62.
Heaven's Above 63, many others.

Harvey, Anthony (1931–   ).
British editor, later director.
AS EDITOR: Private's Progress 56. Happy is the Bride
58. The Angry Silence 60. Lolita 62. Dr
Strangelove 63. The Whisperers 67, etc.
■ AS DIRECTOR: Dutchman (& e) 66. The Lion in
Winter (AAN) 68. They Might be Giants 71. The
Glass Menagerie (TV) 73. The Abdication 74. The
Disappearance of Aimee (TV) 76. Players 79.
Eagle's Wing 79. Richard's Things (TV) 81.
Svengali (TV) 83. The Ultimate Solution of Grace
Quigley 85.

Harvey, Forrester (1880–1945).
Irish character actor, long in Hollywood.
The Lilac Sunbonnet 22. The Flag Lieutenant 26.
The Ring 27. The White Sheik 28. Sky Devils 32.
Tarzan the Ape Man 32. Red Dust 33. The Invisible
Man 33. The Painted Veil 34. The Mystery of
Edwin Drood 35. Jalna 35. Lloyds of London 36.
Personal Property 37. Kidnapped 38. Mysterious Mr
Moto 38. Let Us Live 39. Rebecca 40. A Chump at
Oxford 40. Little Nellie Kelly 40. The Wolf Man
41. Random Harvest 42. Scotland Yard Investigator
45, many others.

Harvey, Frank (1912–1981).
British playwright and screenwriter.
Saloon Bar (oa) 40. Things Happen at Night (oa)
48. Seven Days to Noon (w) 50. High Treason (w)
52. Private's Progress (w) 55. I'm All Right Jack
(w) 59. Heaven's Above (w) 63. No My Darling
Daughter (w) 63, etc.

Harvey, Laurence (1928–1973) (Larushka Mischa
Skikne).
Lithuanian-born leading man who worked his
way slowly from British second features to top
Hollywood productions, but was only briefly in
fashion.
Biographies: 1973, *The Prince* by Emmett and
Des Hickey. 1976, *One Tear is Enough* by Paulene
Stone.
House of Darkness 48. Man on the Run 48. The
Dancing Years 48. The Man from Yesterday 49.
Cairo Road 49. The Scarlet Thread 50. Landfall 50.
The Black Rose 50. There is Another Sun 51. A
Killer Walks 51. I Believe in You 52. Women of
Twilight 52. Innocents in Paris 53. Knights of the
Round Table 53. Romeo and Juliet 54. King
Richard and the Crusaders 54. The Good Die
Young 55. I Am a Camera 55. Storm over the Nile
56. Three Men in a Boat 57. After the Ball 57.
The Truth About Women 58. The Silent Enemy
58. *Room at the Top* (AAN) 59. Expresso Bongo 59.
The Alamo 60. Butterfield Eight 60. The Long and
the Short and the Tall 61. Two Loves 61. Summer
and Smoke 61. A Walk on the Wild Side 62. The
Wonderful World of the Brothers Grimm 63. A
Girl Named Tamiko 63. The Manchurian

Candidate 63. The Running Man 63. The Ceremony (& pd) 64. Of Human Bondage 64. The Outrage 64. Darling 65. Life at the Top 65. The Spy with the Cold Nose 66. A Dandy in Aspic 67. The Winter's Tale 68. Rebus 68. Kampf um Rom 69. He and She 69. The Magic Christian 70. WUSA 71. Flight into the Sun 72. Night Watch 73. Welcome to Arrow Beach 73, etc.

¶ He demonstrated conclusively that it is possible to succeed without managing to evoke the least audience interest or sympathy and to go on succeeding despite unanimous critical antipathy and overwhelming public apathy. – *David Shipman*

Life with him was exciting and funny, but he was consumed with a hunger to have everything – fame, fortune, all the riches of life. It was as if he knew there was only so much time alloted to him. – *Hermione Baddeley*

Harvey, Lilian (1906–1968).
British leading lady who in the 30s became star of German films.
Biography: 1974, *The Lilian Harvey Story* by Hans Borgen.
Leidenschaft 25. Die Tolle Lola 227. Drei von der Tankstelle 30. *Congress Dances* 31. Happy Ever After 32. My Weakness (US) 33. I Am Suzanne (US) 34. Invitation to the Waltz (GB) 35. Capriccio 38. Serenade (Fr.) (last film) 39, etc.

Harvey, Paul (1884–1955).
American character actor who often played the choleric executive or kindly father.
Advice to the Lovelorn 34. Rebecca of Sunnybrook Farm 38. Algiers 38. Stanley and Livingstone 39. Maryland 40. Pillow to Post 45. The Late George Apley 47. Father of the Bride 50. The First Time 52. Three for the Show 55, many others.

Harwood, Ronald (1934–).
South African-born dramatist and screenwriter, in England since 1951. He was formerly an actor with Sir Donald Wolfit's company.
Private Potter 62. Eyewitness 70. One Day in the Life of Ivan Denisovich 71. Operation Daybreak 75. The Dresser (AAN) 83. The Doctor and the Devils 85. Tchin Tchin 91. The Browning Version 94.

Haskell, Jimmy.
American composer, mainly for television movies since the 80s.
Love in a Goldfish Bowl 61. Wild on the Beach 65. Red Tomahawk 67. Zachariah 71. Night of the Lepus 72. Dirty Mary Crazy Larry 74. Joyride 77. Hard Country (co-m) 81. She's Back 89, etc.

Haskell, Peter (1934–).
American leading man.
The Ballad of Andy Crocker (TV) 69. The Eyes of Charles Sand (TV) 72. Phantom of Hollywood (TV) 73. Christina 74. The Night They Took Miss Beautiful (TV) 77. The Cracker Factory (TV) 79. Legend of Earl Durand 90. Child's Play 3 91, etc.
TV series: Bracken's World 69. Rich Man, Poor Man Book II 76–77. Rituals 84–85. The Law and Harry McGraw 87.

Haskin, Byron (1899–1984).
American director with a penchant for science fiction; some interesting films among the routine.
Cameraman and special effects expert through the 30s.
■ Matinée Ladies 27. Ginsberg the Great 27. Irish Hearts 27. The Siren 28. *I Walk Alone* 47. Maneater of Kumaon 48. Too Late for Tears 49.

Treasure Island 50. Tarzan's Peril 51. Warpath 51. Silver City 51. Denver and Rio Grande 52. *The War of the Worlds* 53. His Majesty O'Keefe 53. The Naked Jungle 54. Long John Silver 55. Conquest of Space 55. The First Texan 56. The Boss 56. From the Earth to the Moon 58. The Little Savage 59. Jet over the Atlantic 59. September Storm 60. Armored Command 61. *Captain Sinbad* 63. *Robinson Crusoe on Mars* 64. The Power 67.

Hasse, O.E. (1903–1978).
German character actor: dubbed the voices of Spencer Tracy and Paul Muni.
Peer Gynt 34. Rembrandt 42. Berliner Ballade 48. Epilog 50. Decision Before Dawn (US) 51. I Confess (US) 53. Canaris 54. Mrs Warren's Profession 59. State of Siege 72. Ice Age 75, etc.

Hasselhoff, David (1952–).
American leading man, mainly on television.
Revenge of the Cheerleaders 76. Star Crash (aka Stella Star) 78. Pleasure Cove (TV) 79. Cartier Affair (TV) 84. Terror at London Bridge (TV) 85. Witchery 88. The Final Alliance 89. Fire and Rain (TV) 89. Bail Out 90, etc.
TV series: The Young and the Restless 75–82. Semi-Tough 80. Knight Rider 82–86. Bay Watch 89– . Baywatch Nights 95– .

Hassett, Marilyn (1947–).
American leading lady.
Quarantined (TV) 70. They Shoot Horses Don't They? 72. *The Other Side of the Mountain* 76. Two Minute Warning 76. The Other Side of the Mountain: Part Two 77. The Bell Jar 79. Body Count 87. Messenger of Death 88, etc.

Hasso, Signe (1910–).
Swedish leading lady of the 40s, in Hollywood. Also a writer.
Assignment in Brittany 43. The Seventh Cross 44. *The House on 92nd Street* 45. Johnny Angel 45. A Scandal in Paris 46. Where There's Life 47. *To the Ends of the Earth* 48. A Double Life 48. Outside the Wall 50. Crisis 50. Picture Mommy Dead 66. Reflection of Fear 71. The Black Bird 75. I Never Promised You a Rose Garden 77, etc.

Hatcher, Terri.
American actress.
The Big Picture 89. Tango and Cash 89. Soapdish 91. Dead in the Water 91. Straight Talk 92. Brain Smasher 93, etc.
TV series: Lois & Clark: The New Adventures of Superman 93.

Hatfield, Hurd (1918–).
American leading man whose coldly handsome face proved to be his misfortune.
■ Dragon Seed 44. *The Picture of Dorian Gray* 45. The Diary of a Chambermaid 46. The Beginning or the End 47. The Unsuspected 47. The Checkered Coat 48. Joan of Arc 48. Chinatown at Midnight 48. Tarzan and the Slave Girl 50. Destination Murder 51. The Left Handed Gun 58. King of Kings 61. El Cid 61. Mickey One 65. The Boston Strangler 68. Thief (TV) 70. Von Richthofen and Brown 71. The Norliss Tapes (TV) 73. The Word (TV) 78. You Can't Go Home Again (TV) 79. Crimes of the Heart 86. Her Alibi 88.

Hathaway, Henry (1898–1985).
American director, in films (as child actor) from 1907. Acted till 1932, then directed westerns. Later became known as a capable handler of big action adventures and thrillers.
■ Wild Horse Mesa 32. Heritage of the Desert 33. Under the Tonto Rim 33. Sunset Pass 33. Man of

the Forest 33. To the Last Man 33. Come On Marines 34. The Last Round-Up 34. Thundering Herds 34. The Witching Hour 34. Now and Forever 34. *Lives of a Bengal Lancer* (AAN) 35. Peter Ibbetson 35. Trail of the Lonesome Pine 36. Go West Young Man 36. Souls at Sea 37. Spawn of the North 38. The Real Glory 39. Johnny Apollo 40. Brigham Young 40. Shepherd of the Hills 41. Sundown 41. Ten Gentlemen from West Point 42. China Girl 43. Home in Indiana 44. A Wing and a Prayer 44. Nob Hill 45. *The House on 92nd Street* 45. The Dark Corner 46. 13 Rue Madeleine 46. *Kiss of Death* 47. Call Northside 777 48. Down to the Sea in Ships 49. The Black Rose 50. You're in the Navy Now 51. Rawhide 51. Fourteen Hours 51. *Rommel, Desert Fox* 51. Diplomatic Courier 52. *Niagara* 52. White Witch Doctor 53. Prince Valiant 54. Garden of Evil 54. The Racers 54. The Bottom of the Bottle 55. Twenty-three Paces to Baker Street 56. Legend of the Lost 57. From Hell to Texas 58. A Woman Obsessed 59. Seven Thieves 60. *North to Alaska* 60. How the West Was Won (part) 62. Circus World 64. The Sons of Katie Elder 65. Nevada Smith 66. The Last Safari 67. Five Card Stud 68. True Grit 69. Raid on Rommel 71. Shootout 72.
✪ For long-standing professionalism in handling all types of subject. *The House on 92nd Street*.

¶ Being educated is making the pictures themselves, if you make it your business to pay attention. – *H.H.*

To be a good director you've got to be a bastard. I'm a bastard and I know it. – *H.H.*

His charm consists of minor virtues uncorrupted by major pretensions. – *Andrew Sarris*

Hatley, Thomas Marvin (1905–1986).
American composer who was musical director at the Hal Roach Studio 1930–39, scoring several Laurel and Hardy movies. In the 40s he quit films to play the piano in cocktail lounges.
Hog Wild 30. The Music Box 31. Sons of the Desert (song, 'Honolulu Baby') 33. Way Out West (AAN) 37. Pick a Star 37. Block-Heads (AAN) 38. There Goes My Heart (AAN) 38. Captain Fury 39. Topper Takes a Trip 39. A Chump at Oxford 40, etc.

Hattie, Hilo (1901–1979).
Hawaiian entertainer who in 1942 made her only Hollywood musical: *Song of the Islands*.

Hatton, Raymond (1887–1971).
American character actor, the comic side-kick of a hundred minor westerns; in Hollywood from 1911. Formed a comedy team with Wallace Beery 1926–29.
Oliver Twist 16. Whispering Chorus 18. Male and Female 19. Jes' Call Me Jim 20. The Affairs of Anatol 21. Ebb Tide 22. The Hunchback of Notre Dame 23. The Fighting American 24. In the Name of Love 25. Born to the West 26. *Behind the Front* 26. *We're In the Navy Now* 26. Fireman Save My Child 27, The Woman God Forgot 27. We're in the Air Now 27. Partners in Crime 28. Hell's Heroes 29. Midnight Mystery 30. Woman Hungry 31. The Squaw Man 31. Polly of the Circus 32. Terror Trail 33. Wagon Wheels 34. Laughing Irish Eyes 36. Roaring Timber 37. Love Finds Andy Hardy 38. Kit Carson 40. Tall in the Saddle 44. Black Gold 47. Operation Haylift 50. Shake Rattle and Rock 56. In Cold Blood 67, many others.

Hatton, Richard (1891–1931).
American star of silent westerns. Killed in a traffic accident.
Fearless Dick 22. Blood Test 23. Come On,

Cowboys 24. 'Scar' Hanan 25. He-Man's Country 26. Saddle Jumpers 27. The Boss of Rustler's Roost 28. The Vanishing Legion (serial) 31, etc.

¶ Hatton was strictly a city man and our nickname for him was 'Fearless Richard' since he was actually afraid to go out at night unless someone was with him. – *Yakima Canutt*

Hatton, Rondo (1894–1946).
American actor who suffered from facial and bodily deformity as a result of acromegaly; he was rather tastelessly cast as a monstrous killer in several low-budget mysteries of the early 40s.
■ Hell Harbor 30. In Old Chicago.38. Alexander's Ragtime Band 38. The Hunchback of Notre Dame 39. Captain Fury 39. Chad Hanna 40. Moon over Burma 40. The Big Guy 40. The Cyclone Kid 42. The Moon and Sixpence 42. Sleepy Lagoon 43. The Ox Bow Incident 43. *The Pearl of Death* 44. Raiders of Ghost City 44. The Princess and the Pirate 44. Johnny Doesn't Live Here Any More 44. The Royal Mounted Rides Again 45. Jungle Captive 45. Spider Woman Strikes Back 46. House of Horrors 46. The Brute Man 46.

Hauer, Rutger (1944–).
Dutch leading actor, now in international films.
Soldier of Orange 77. Blade Runner 82. Eureka 83. The Osterman Weekend 83. A Breed Apart 84. Ladyhawke 85. Flesh and Blood 85. The Hitcher 86. Wanted Dead or Alive 86. The Legend of the Holy Drinker (La Leggenda del Santo Brevitore) 88. Bloodhounds of Broadway 89. Blind Fury 89. The Salute of the Jugger 89. In una Notte di Chiaro di Luna 89. The Blood of Heroes 90. Wedlock 91. Split Second 92. Buffy the Vampire Slayer 92. Beyond Justice 92. Past Midnight 92. Arctic Blue 93. Amelia Earhart: The Final Flight (TV) 94. Surviving the Game 94. Nostradamus 94, etc.

The Haunted Screen,
by Lotte Eisner. First published in the 30s, this is a significant study of German cinema between 1913 and 1933, concentrating (according to its sub-title) on 'expressionism and the influence of Max Reinhardt'.

Hauser, Wings.
Powerful American leading man of low-budget action films, who turned to directing in the 90s. He began in TV soap operas.
Who'll Stop the Rain (aka Dog Soldiers) 78. Vice Squad 82. Homework 82. Deadly Force 83. Mutant 83. A Soldier's Story 84. The Long Hot Summer 86. Hostage 87. Tough Guys Don't Dance 87. The Wind 87. Nightmare at Noon 87. No Safe Haven 87. Dead Men Walking 88. Marked for Murder 89. Street Asylum 90. Reason to Die 90. Exiled 91. Pale Blood 91. Coldfire (& d) 91. Living to Die (& d) 91. In Between 92. Mind, Body and Soul 92. Frame-Up II: The Cover-Up 92, etc.
TV series: The Last Precinct 86. Lightning Force 91.

Havelock-Allan, Sir Anthony (1905–).
British producer.
This Man Is News 38. In Which We Serve (associate) 42. Blithe Spirit 45. Brief Encounter (co-w, AAN) 46. Great Expectations 46. Oliver Twist 48. The Small Voice 49. Never Take No for an Answer 51. The Young Lovers 54. Orders to Kill 58. The Quare Fellow 61. An Evening with the Royal Ballet 64. Othello 65. The Mikado 67, etc.

Haver, June (1926–) (June Stovenour).
American leading lady of the 40s, mostly in musicals; married Fred McMurray. Now retired.

■ The Gang's All Here 43. Home in Indiana 44. Irish Eyes Are Smiling 44. Where Do We Go from Here? 45. *The Dolly Sisters* 45. Three Little Girls in Blue 46. Wake Up and Dream 46. I Wonder Who's Kissing Her Now 47. Scudda Hoo Scudda Hay 48. Oh You Beautiful Doll 49. *Look for the Silver Lining* (as Marilyn Miller) 49. The Daughter of Rosie O'Grady 50. I'll Get By 50. Love Nest 51. The Girl Next Door 53.

Haver, Phyllis (1899–1960) (Phyllis O'Haver).
American leading lady of the silent screen, a former Sennett bathing beauty. Committed suicide.
Small Town Idol 20. Temple of Venus 23. Fig Leaves 25. Up in Mabel's Room 26. The Way of All Flesh 28. Hard Boiled 29. Hell's Kitchen 29, many others.

Havers, Nigel (1949–).
Elegant British actor.
Chariots of Fire 79. A Passage to India 84. Burke and Wills 86. The Whistle Blower 86. Empire of the Sun 87. Farewell to the King 89. Quiet Days in Clichy 90. The Burning Season (TV) 94, etc.
TV series: Don't Wait Up 83–85. The Charmer 87.

Havlick, Gene (c. 1895–1959).
American editor.
Beauty and Bullets 28. Madonna of the Streets 30. Shopworn 32. Broadway Bill 34. Mr Deeds Goes to Town 36. *Lost Horizon* (AA) 37. You Can't Take It with You 38. Mr Smith Goes to Washington 39. His Girl Friday 40. The Wife takes a Flyer 42. A Song to Remember 45. Relentless 48. Son of Dr Jekyll 51. Jungle Maneaters 54. Screaming Mimi 58, many others.

Havoc, June (1916–) (June Hovick).
American leading lady, former child actress; sister of Gypsy Rose Lee.
Autobiography: 1960, *Early Havoc.*
Four Jacks and a Jill 42. Brewster's Millions 45. The Story of Molly X 49. Once a Thief 50. A Lady Possessed 51. Three for Jamie Dawn 57. The Private Files of J. Edgar Hoover 78. Can't Stop the Music 80, etc.
TV series: Willy 54.

Hawke, Ethan (1970–).
American actor.
Explorers 85. Dead Poets Society 89. Dad 89. White Fang 90. A Midnight Clear 91. Mystery Date 91. Waterland 92. Alive 93. White Fang 2: Myth of the White Wolf 94. Reality Bites 94. Floundering 94. Before Sunrise 95, etc.

Hawkins, Jack (1910–1973).
Dominant British actor; after long apprenticeship, became an international star in middle age, but in 1966 lost his voice after an operation; his subsequent minor appearances were dubbed. His first wife was Jessica Tandy.
Autobiography: 1974, *Anything for a Quiet Life.*
Birds of Prey 30. The Lodger 32. The Good Companions 32. The Lost Chord 33. I Lived with You 33. The Jewel 33. A Shot in the Dark 33. Autumn Crocus 34. Death at Broadcasting House 34. *Peg of Old Drury* 35. Beauty and the Barge 37. The Frog 37. Who Goes Next 38. A Royal Divorce 38. Murder Will Out 39. The Flying Squad 40. Next of Kin 42. *The Fallen Idol* 48. Bonnie Prince Charlie 48. The Small Back Room 48. *State Secret* 50. The Black Rose 50. The Elusive Pimpernel 50. The Adventurers 51. No Highway 51. Home at Seven 51. *Angels One Five* 52. The Planter's Wife 52. Mandy 52. *The Cruel Sea* 53. Twice Upon a Time

53. The Malta Story 53. The Intruder 53. Front Page Story 54. The Seekers 54. The Prisoner 55. Touch and Go 55. Land of the Pharaohs 55. The Long Arm 56. The Man in the Sky 56. Fortune is a Woman 57. *The Bridge on the River Kwai* 57. Gideon's Day 58. The Two-Headed Spy 58. *The League of Gentlemen* 59. Ben Hur (US) 59. Two Loves (US) 61. Five Finger Exercise (US) 62. *Lawrence of Arabia* 62. Lafayette 63. *Rampage* (US) 63. Zulu 63. The Third Secret 64. Guns at Batasi 64. Masquerade 65. Lord Jim 65. Judith 65. Great Catherine 67. Shalako 68. Oh What a Lovely War 69. Monte Carlo or Bust 69. Waterloo 70. The Adventures of Gerard 70. Nicholas and Alexandra 71. Kidnapped 72. Young Winston 72. Theatre of Blood 73. Tales that Witness Madness 73, etc.
TV series: *The Four Just Men* 59.
◎ For humorously perpetuating the image of the friendly World War II officer. *The League of Gentlemen.*

Hawkins, Screamin' Jay (1929–) (Jalacy Hawkins).
Exuberant and eccentric American rhythm and blues singer and actor. He is a former Golden Gloves middleweight boxing champion.
American Hot Wax 78. Mystery Train 89. A Rage in Harlem 91, etc.

Hawks, Howard (1896–1977).
American director, at his best an incomparable provider of professional comedies and action dramas. In films from 1918, at first as writer and editor. Awarded an honorary Oscar as 'a master American filmmaker' in 1974.
Books include: 1962, *The Cinema of Howard Hawks* by Peter Bogdanovich. 1977, *Howard Hawks* by Robin Wood. 1982, *Hawks on Hawks* (devised by Joe McBride). 1982, *Howard Hawks, Storyteller* by Gerald Mast.
■ Tiger Love (w only) 24. The Road to Glory (& w) 26. Fig Leaves (& w) 26. The Cradle Snatchers 27. Paid to Love 27. A Girl in Every Port (& w) 28. Fazil 28. The Air Circus 28. Trent's Last Case (& w) 29. *The Dawn Patrol* 30. The Criminal Code 31. The Crowd Roars 32. *Scarface* 32. Tiger Shark 32. Today We Live 33. *Twentieth Century* 34. Viva Villa (part) 34. *Barbary Coast* 35. Ceiling Zero 36. Road to Glory 36. Come and Get It (co-d) 36. *Bringing Up Baby* 38. Only Angels Have Wings 39. *His Girl Friday* 40. Sergeant York (AAN) 41. Ball of Fire 41. Air Force 42. Corvette K 225 (p only) 44. *To Have and Have Not* 44. *The Big Sleep* 46. A Song Is Born 48. *Red River* 48. I Was a Male War Bride 49. The Thing from Another World (p only) 52. The Big Sky 52. Monkey Business 52. Full House (one episode) 52. Gentlemen Prefer Blondes 53. Land of the Pharaohs 55. *Rio Bravo* 59. Hatari 62. Man's Favourite Sport 64. Red Line 7000 65. El Dorado 66. Rio Lobo 70.
◎ For the remarkably consistent vigour with which he presented a man's world invaded by a woman. *His Girl Friday.*

¶ For me the best drama is one that deals with a man in danger. – *H.H.*
He stamped his remarkably bitter view of life on adventure, gangster and private eye melodramas, the kind of thing Americans do best and appreciate least. – *Andrew Sarris, 1968*

Hawn, Goldie (1945–).
American leading lady who scored as blonde dimwit on TV's *Laugh-In.*
■ The One and Only Genuine Original Family Band 68. *Cactus Flower* (AA) 69. *There's a Girl in My Soup* 70. Butterflies are Free 72. Dollars 72. The Sugarland Express 73. The Girl from Petrovka 74.

Shampoo 75. The Duchess and the Dirtwater Fox 76. Foul Play 78. Travels with Anita 79. Private Benjamin (AAN) 80. Seems Like Old Times 80. Best Friends 82. Protocol 84. Swing Shift 84. Wildcats 85. Overboard 87. Bird on the Wire 90. Deceived 91. Crisscross 92. Housesitter 92. Death Becomes Her 92.

TV series: Good Morning World 67.

Haworth, Jill (1945–).
British leading lady in Hollywood.
Exodus 60. In Harm's Way 65. It 66. Home for the Holidays (TV) 72. The Mutations 74.

Haworth, Ted (1917–).
American production designer.
Villa Rides 68. The Kremlin Letter 70. The Beguiled 71. Harry and Tonto 74. Telefon 77. Bloodline 79. Rough Cut 80. Death Hunt 81. Jinxed 82. Blame It on the Night 84. The Legend of Billie Jean 85. Poltergeist II: The Other Side 86. Batteries Not Included 87, etc.

Hawthorne, Nathaniel (1804–1864).
American novelist and short-story writer, of oppressive Puritan attitudes in New England. His *The Scarlet Letter*, about a woman accused of adultery, has been filmed at least five times, notably in 1926 with Lillian Gish and 1934 with Colleen Moore. *The House of Seven Gables* was transferred flatly to the screen in 1940, with a cast that included George Sanders, Margaret Lindsay and Vincent Price. His story 'Young Goodman Brown' was even less successfully filmed in 1993 by Peter George.

Hawthorne, Nigel (1929–).
British star character actor.
A Tale of Two Cities (TV) 80. The Hunchback of Notre Dame (TV) 81. Firefox 82. Gandhi 82. Dream Child 84. Turtle Diary 84. Jenny's War (TV) 84. The Chain 86. A Handful of Time (En Handfull Tid) 90. Demolition Man 93. The *Madness of King George* 95, etc.

TV series: Yes, Minister (as Sir Humphrey) 81– 87.

Hawtrey, Charles (1914–1988) (George Hartree).
Spindle-shanked British comic actor, long cast as ageing schoolboy in *Will Hay* and other comedies. In the 60s, a familiar member of the 'Carry On' team.
Good Morning Boys 37. Where's That Fire 40. The Goose Steps Out 42. A Canterbury Tale 44. The Galloping Major 50. Brandy for the Parson 52. *You're Only Young Twice* 53. Carry On Jack 54. Carry On Sergeant 58. Carry On Nurse 59. Carry On Cowboy 67. Carry On at Your Convenience 71. Carry On Abroad 72, many others.

Hay, Alexandra (1947–).
American leading lady.
Skidoo 68. The Model Shop 69. The Love Machine 71. 1000 Convicts and a Woman 71. How Come Nobody's on Our Side 73, etc.

Hay, Will (1888–1949).
British character comedian, one of the screen's greats; after many years in the music halls, starred in several incomparable farces playing variations on his favourite role of an incompetent, seedy schoolmaster. Born in Stockton-on-Tees, he worked as a book-keeper before beginning in the music halls in a schoolmaster sketch in 1909, later joining Fred Karno's troupe and becoming a star attraction from the mid-20s. In private life, he was an expert amateur astronomer who built his own observatory and wrote a book on the subject

(1935, *Through My Telescope*), a pilot and a linguist.
Biography: 1978, *Good Morning Boys* by Ray Seaton and Roy Martin.
■ Those Were the Days 34. Dandy Dick 34. Radio Parade 35. Boys will be Boys 35. Where There's a Will 36. Windbag the Sailor 36. *Good Morning Boys* 37. Convict 99 38. Hey Hey USA 38. *Old Bones of the River* 38. Oh Mr Porter 38. Ask a Policeman 39. Where's that Fire? 39. *The Ghost of St Michael's* 41. The Black Sheep of Whitehall 41. The Big Blockade 42. The Goose Steps Out 42. *My Learned Friend* 44.
☯ For developing an unforgettable comic persona which lives in the memory independently of his films; and for persuading us to root for that character despite its basically unsympathetic nature. *Oh Mr Porter.*

¶ A good comedy scenario is very near pathos. The character I play is really a very pathetic fellow. – *W.H.*

I've always found something funny in the idea of a hopelessly inefficient man blundering through a job he knows nothing about. – *W.H.*

For each one of us there comes a moment when death takes us by the hand and says: 'It is time to rest; you are tired; lie down and sleep; sleep well.' The day is gone and stars shine in the canopy of eternity. – *the last words Will Hay read before he died, which were inscribed at the foot of his grave*

Hayakawa, Sessue (1889–1973).
Japanese actor, a popular star of American silents; more recently in occasional character roles.
The Typhoon 14. *The Cheat* 15. Forbidden Paths 17. The Tong Man 19. Daughter of the Dragon 29. Tokyo Joe 49. Three Came Home 50. *The Bridge on the River Kwai* (AAN) 57. The Geisha Boy 59. The Swiss Family Robinson 60. Hell to Eternity 61, etc.

Hayasaka, Fumio (1914–1955).
Japanese composer, often for the films of Akira Kurosawa and Kenji Mizoguchi.
Drunken Angel (Yoidore Tenshi) 48. Rashomon 50. Meshi 51. Ikiru 52. Ugetsu 53. Sansho the Bailiff (Sansho Dayu) 54. Seven Samurai (Shichinin no Samurai) 54. A Story from Chikamatsu (Chikamatsu Monogatari) 54. I Live in Fear 55, etc.

Hayashi, Kaizo.
Japanese director and screenwriter.
Circus Boys (Ni Ju-Seiki Shonen Dokuhon) 89. Waga Jinsei Saisuku no Toki 94, etc.

Hayden, Harry (1884–1955).
Tubby American character actor who played scores of bankers, clergymen and unassuming family chaps.
I Married a Doctor 36. Black Legion 36. Ever Since Eve 37. Kentucky 38. Angels with Dirty Faces 38. Swanee River 39. Christmas in July 40. The Palm Beach Story 42. Up in Mabel's Room 44. The Killers 46. The Unfinished Dance 47. Intruder in the Dust 49. Double Dynamite 51. Army Bound 52, many others.

Hayden, Linda (1951–).
British leading lady; started by playing teenage sexpots.
Baby Love 69. Taste the Blood of Dracula 69. Satan's Skin 70. Something to Hide 72. Confessions of a Window Cleaner 74. Let's Get Laid 77, etc.

Hayden, Russell (1912–1981) (Pate Lucid).
American 'second string' leading man, for many

years Hopalong Cassidy's faithful sidekick. Later produced TV westerns.
Hills of Old Wyoming (debut) 37. Range War 39. Lucky Legs 42. 'Neath Canadian Skies 46. Seven Were Saved 47. Silver City 49. Valley of Fire 51, many others.
TV series: Cowboy G-Men 52. Judge Roy Bean 55.

Hayden, Sterling (1916–1986) (Sterling Walter Relyea).
Rangy American leading man and part-time explorer.
Autobiographies: 1963, *Wanderer*. 1978, *Voyage*.
Virginia 40. Bahama Passage 41. Blaze of Noon 47. El Paso 49. Manhandled 49. *The Asphalt Jungle* 50. Denver and Rio Grande 52. The Golden Hawk 52. The Star 52. So Big 53. Prince Valiant 54. Arrow in the Dust 54. Johnny Guitar 54. Suddenly 54. Timberjack 55. The Eternal Sea 55. The Last Command 55. *The Killing* 56. Crime of Passion 56. Five Steps to Danger 56. Zero Hour 57. Terror in a Texas Town 58. Dr Strangelove 63. Hard Contract 69. Loving 70. The Godfather 72. The Long Goodbye 73. Cobra 73. Deadly Strangers 74. Is It Any Wonder 75. 1900 77. King of the Gypsies 78. The Outsider 79. Winter Kills 79. Nine to Five 80. Venom 82. Lighthouse of Chaos 83. Voyager 84, etc.

¶ If I had the dough, I'd buy up the negative of every film I ever made . . . and start one hell of a fire. – *S.H.*

I don't think there are many other businesses where you can be paid good money and not know what you're doing. – *S.H.*

I started at the top and worked my way down. – *S.H.*

Haydn, Richard (1905–1985).
British revue star of the 30s, in Hollywood from 1941, usually in adenoidal character cameos. He performed in revue and on radio from the 30s as Professor Edwin Carp, the world's only fish mimic.
Ball of Fire (debut) 41. Charley's Aunt 41. Forever and a Day 43. And Then There Were None 45. *Cluny Brown* 46. *Sitting Pretty* 47. Miss Tatlock's Millions (& d) 48. Mr Music (& d) 50. Dear Wife (d only) 50. Jupiter's Darling 54. Please Don't Eat the Daisies 60. *The Lost World* 60. Mutiny on the Bounty 62. Five Weeks in a Balloon 62. The Sound of Music 65. Clarence the Cross-Eyed Lion 65. Bullwhip Griffin 66. Young Frankenstein 74, many others.

Haye, Helen (1874–1957) (Helen Hay).
Distinguished British stage actress (debut 1898), in occasional films, usually as kindly dowager.
Tilly of Bloomsbury 21. Atlantic 30. Congress Dances 31. *The Spy in Black* 39. Kipps 41. *Dear Octopus* 43. Anna Karenina 48. Richard III 56, many others.

Hayers, Sidney (1921–).
British director, in films since 1942. Former editor and second unit director.
■ Violent Moment 58. The White Trap 59. Circus of Horrors 59. Echo of Barbara 60. The Malpas Mystery 60. *Payroll* 61. *Night of the Eagle* 62. This Is My Street 63. Three Hats for Lisa 65. The Trap 66. Finders Keepers 66. The Southern Star 69. Mr Jerico 69. The Firechasers 70. Assault 71. Revenge 71. All Coppers Are . . . 72. Deadly Strangers 74. What Changed Charley Farthing 74. Diagnosis Murder (TV) 74. One Way 76. The Seekers (TV) 78. The Last Convertible (TV) 79. Condominium (TV) 80.

Hayes, Alfred (c. 1911–1985).
American screenwriter.

Paisa 46. Clash by Night 51. Teresa (co-w, AAN) 51. Act of Love 54. The Left Hand of God 55. The Double Man 67, etc.

Hayes, Allison (1930–1977) (Mary Jane Hayes).
American leading lady of a few films in the 50s.

Francis Joins the WACs 54. The Purple Mask 55. The Blackboard Jungle 55. Mohawk 56. The Zombies of Mora Tau 57. Attack of the Fifty-Foot Woman (title role) 58. Who's Been Sleeping in My Bed? 63. Tickle Me 65.

TV series: Acapulco 60.

Hayes, George 'Gabby' (1885–1969).
Bewhiskered American character comedian, in minor westerns from silent days.

The Rainbow Man 29. Beggars in Ermine 34. The Lost City 35. Three on the Trail 36. Mountain Music 37. Hopalong Rides Again 38. Gold is Where You Find It 38. Man of Conquest 39. Wagons Westward 40. Melody Ranch 41. In Old Oklahoma 43. Tall in the Saddle 44. Utah 45. My Pal Trigger 46. Wyoming 47. Return of the Badmen 48. El Paso 49. The Cariboo Trail 50, many others.

TV series: The Gabby Hayes Show 50.

Hayes, Helen (1900–1993) (Helen Hayes Brown).
Distinguished American stage actress who made a number of film appearances. She was married to writer Charles MacArthur.

Autobiographies: 1965, *A Gift of Joy*. 1969, *On Reflection*. 1981, *Twice Over Lightly*.

Biography: 1985, *Helen Hayes – First Lady of the American Theatre* by Kenneth Barrow.

The Weavers of Life 17. *The Sin of Madelon Claudet* (AA) 31. Arrowsmith 31. *A Farewell to Arms* 32. The Son Daughter 33. The White Sister 33. Another Language 33. Night Flight 33. What Every Woman Knows 34. Crime without Passion (unbilled) 34. Vanessa 35. Stage Door Canteen 43. My Son John 51. Main Street to Broadway 53. *Anastasia* 56. Third Man on the Mountain (unbilled) 59. *Airport* (AA) 69. Do Not Fold Spindle or Mutilate (TV) 71. Herbie Rides Again 73. The Snoop Sisters (TV) 73 (and series). One of Our Dinosaurs Is Missing 75. Victory at Entebbe (TV) 76. Candleshoe 77. A Family Upside Down (TV) 78. The Moneychangers (TV) 79. Murder Is Easy (TV) 82. A Caribbean Mystery (TV) 83. Murder with Mirrors (TV) 84, etc.

TV series: The Snoop Sisters 73–74.

¶ An actor's life is so transitory. Suddenly you're a building. – H.H. (on having a theatre named after her)

Hayes, Isaac (1942–).
American composer, singer and actor.

Shaft (AAs, AANm) 71. Shaft's Big Score (co-m) 72. Wattstax (doc) 73. Save the Children (doc) 73. Three Tough Guys (a, m) 74. Truck Turner (a, m) 74. Escape from New York 81. I'm Gonna Git You Sucka 88. Guilty as Charged 91. Prime Target 91. Robin Hood: Men in Tights 93. Posse 93. Acting on Impulse 93. It Could Happen to You 94. Oblivion 94, etc.

Hayes, John Michael (1919–).
American screenwriter.

Rear Window (AAN) 54. To Catch a Thief 55. The Trouble with Harry 56. Peyton Place (AAN) 57. *The Carpetbaggers* 63. Where Love Has Gone 64. Harlow 65. Judith 66. Nevada Smith 66. Iron Will (co-w) 94, etc.

Hayes, Margaret (1915–1977).
American character actress, also in TV and public relations.

The Blackboard Jungle 55. Violent Saturday 55. Omar Khayyam 57. Fraulein 57. Damn Citizen 58, etc.

Hayes, Melvyn (1935–).
British comedy character actor, a former child star who was part of Cliff Richards' support in *The Young Ones*, *Summer Holiday*, etc; later became familiar on TV in *It Ain't Half Hot Mum*.

The Curse of Frankenstein 56. No Trees in the Street 58. The Young Ones 61. Summer Holiday 62. Wonderful Life 64. A Walk with Love and Death 69. Love Thy Neighbour 73. Carry on England 76. Santa Claus 85, etc.

Hayes, Patricia (1910–).
British character actress, mainly in low-life comedy roles. Much on TV.

Candles at Nine 44. Nicholas Nickleby 46. The Love Match 54. The Battle of the Sexes 59. Goodbye Mr Chips 69. Love Thy Neighbour 73. The Corn Is Green (TV) 79. The Never Ending Story 84. Little Dorrit 87. The Last Island 91, etc.

Hayles, Brian (1930–1978).
British scriptwriter, from TV.

Warlords of Atlantis 78. Arabian Adventure 79.

Hayman, David (1950–).
Scottish director, a former actor.

AS ACTOR: A Sense of Freedom (TV) 79. Sid and Nancy 86. Heavenly Pursuits 86. Hope and Glory 87. Venus Peter 89, etc.

AS DIRECTOR: Silent Scream 90. Black and Blue (TV) 92. The Hawk 93. A Woman's Guide to Adultery (TV) 93, etc.

Haymes, Dick (1918–1980).
Argentine-born crooner, former radio announcer.

Irish Eyes Are Smiling (debut) 44. Diamond Horseshoe 45. *State Fair* 45. Do You Love Me? 46. The Shocking Miss Pilgrim 47. Up in Central Park 48. One Touch of Venus 48. St Benny the Dip 51. All Ashore 53. Betrayal (TV) 74, etc.

Haynes, Todd (1961–).
American independent director and editor. He first attracted attention with *Superstar: The Karen Carpenter Story*, a short made in 1987 about the pop singer's life and anorexic death, in which he used Barbie dolls instead of live actors.

Poison 1991.

Hays, Robert (1948–).
American leading man of the early 80s.

The Young Pioneers (TV) 76. Delta County USA (TV) 78. The Initiation of Sarah (TV) 78. The Fall of the House of Usher (TV) 79. Airplane 80. Take This Job and Shove It 81. Airplane 2: The Sequel 82. Trenchcoat 82. Touched 83. Cat's Eye 85. Murder by the Book 87. Honeymoon Academy 90. Fifty/Fifty 93, etc.

Hays, Will H. (1879–1954).
American executive, for many years (1922–45) president of the Motion Picture Producers and Distributors Association of America, and author of its high-toned Production Code (1930), which for many years put producers in fear of 'the Hays Office'.

Autobiography: 1955, *The Memoirs of Will Hays*.

¶ Good taste is good business. – W.H. (1930)

Hayter, James (1907–1983).
Portly, jovial British character actor, on stage from 1925, films from 1936.

Sensation 36. Sailors Three 41. School for Secrets 46. *Nicholas Nickleby* (as the Cheeryble twins) 47. The Blue Lagoon 48. *Trio* 50. Tom Brown's Schooldays 51. Robin Hood (as Friar Tuck) 52. *Pickwick Papers* (title role) 53. The Great Game 53. A Day to Remember 54. Touch and Go 56. Port Afrique 58. The Thirty-Nine Steps 59. Stranger in the House 67. Oliver 68. David Copperfield 69. Song of Norway 70, many others.

TV series: Are You Being Served? 78.

Haythorne, Joan (1915–) (Joan Haythornthwaite).
British stage actress, usually in aristocratic roles.

School for Secrets 46. Jassy 47. Highly Dangerous 50. Svengali 54. The Weak and the Wicked 54. The Feminine Touch 56. Three Men in a Boat 56. Shakedown 59. So Evil So Young 61, etc.

Hayton, Lennie (1908–1971).
American composer.

The Bugle Sounds 41. Meet the People 43. Salute to the Marines 43. The Harvey Girls 45. Summer Holiday 46. The Hucksters 47. The Pirate 48. Battleground 49. On the Town (co-w) (AA) 49. Inside Straight 51. Singin' in the Rain 52. Battle Circus 53. Star! (AAN) 68. Hello Dolly (co-w) (AA) 69, etc.

Hayward, Leland (1902–1971).
American talent agent and stage producer. Also produced films.

Mister Roberts 55. The Spirit of St Louis 57. The Old Man and the Sea 58, etc.

Hayward, Louis (1909–1985) (Seafield Grant).
Mild-mannered, South African-born leading man with stage experience; in Hollywood from 1935. He was formerly married to Ida Lupino.

■ Chelsea Life (GB) 33. The Man Outside (GB) 33. I'll Stick to You (GB) 33. The Thirteenth Candle (GB) 33. The Love Test (GB) 34. *Sorrell and Son* (GB) 34. The Flame Within 35. Anthony Adverse 36. The Luckiest Girl in the World 36. Midnight Intruder 37. The Rage of Paris 38. *The Saint in New York* 38. *Duke of West Point* 39. *The Man in the Iron Mask* 39. *My Son, My Son* 40. Son of Monte Cristo 40. Ladies in Retirement 41. And Then There Were None 45. Monte Cristo's Revenge 47. Young Widow 47. Repeat Performance 47. The Black Arrow 48. Walk a Crooked Mile 48. Pirates of Capri 49. The Fortunes of Captain Blood 50. House by the River 50. Son of Dr Jekyll 51. The Lady and the Bandit 51. Lady in the Iron Mask 52. Captain Pirate 52. Royal African Rifles 53. The Saint's Return (GB) 53. Duffy of San Quentin 54. *The Search for Bridey Murphy* 56. Chuka 67. Terror in the Wax Museum 73.

TV series: The Lone Wolf 53. The Pursuers 63. The Survivors 69.

Hayward, Susan (1918–1975) (Edythe Marrener).
Vivacious American leading lady, in films from 1938 after modelling experience: often in aggressive roles.

Biography: 1974, *Divine Bitch* by Doug McLelland.

■ Girls on Probation 38. Our Leading Citizen 39. $1000 A Touchdown 39. Beau Geste 39. Adam Had Four Sons 41. Sis Hopkins 41. Among the Living 41. Reap the Wild Wind 42. The Forest Rangers 42. I Married a Witch 42. Star Spangled Rhythm 42. Change of Heart 43. Jack London 43. Young and Willing 43. The Fighting Seabees 44. And Now Tomorrow 44. The Hairy Ape 44. **Canyon** assage 45. Deadline at Dawn 46. Smash-Up (AAN) 47. They Won't Believe Me 47. The Lost Moment 47. Tap Roots 48. The Saxon Charm 48. ulsa 49. *My Foolish Heart* (AAN) 49. House of trangers 49. I'd Climb the Highest Mountain 50. *Can Get It For You Wholesale* 51. Rawhide 51. David nd Bathsheba 51. *With a Song in My Heart* (AAN) 2. The Lusty Men 52. The Snows of Kilimanjaro 2. The President's Lady 53. White Witch Dóctor 3. Demetrius and the Gladiators 54. Garden of vil 54. Untamed 55. Soldier of Fortune 55. The onqueror 55. *I'll Cry Tomorrow* (as Lilian Roth) AAN) 55. Top Secret Affair 57. *I Want To Live* (as arbara Graham) (AA) 58. A Woman Obsessed 9. Thunder in the Sun 59. The Marriage-Go ound 60. Ada 61. Back Street 61. Stolen Hours GB) 63. I Thank a Fool (GB) 63. Where Love Has one 64. The Honey Pot 67. Valley of the Dolls 7. Fitzgerald and Pride (TV) 71. Heat of Anger TV) 71. The Revengers 72. Say Goodbye Maggie ole (TV) 72.

aywood, Chris.
nglish character actor, in Australia.
Newsfront 78. In Search of Anna 79. Kostas 79. he Clinic 82. Heatwave 82. The Return of aptain Invincible 82. Man of Flowers 83. trikebound 84. Razorback 84. A Street to Die 85. Malcolm 85. Burke and Wills 85. Dogs in Space 7. Manifesto 88. The Tale of Ruby Rose 88. merald City 89. Island 89. Quigley Down Under 0. Golden Braid 91. Sweet Talker 91. A Woman's ale 91. Alex 93. Exile 94. Erotic Tales 94, etc.
TV series: The Boys from the Bush 91.

Hayworth, Rita (1918–1987) (Margarita Carmen Cansino).
tar American leading lady and dancer of the 40s, often in tempestuous roles; on stage from six years old; of Latin and Irish ancestry. From 1980 her decline from Alzheimer's disease was well known. Lynda Carter played her in a 1983 TV movie, *Rita Hayworth: the Love Goddess*.
Biography: 1977, *Rita Hayworth, the Time, the Place and the Woman* by John Kobal.
■ Dante's Inferno 35. Under the Pampas Moon 35. Charlie Chan in Egypt 35. Paddy O'Day 35. Human Cargo 36. A Message to Garcia 36. Meet Nero Wolfe 36. Rebellion 36. Old Louisiana 37. Hit the Saddle 37. Trouble in Texas 37. Criminals of the Air 37. Girls Can Play 37. The Game that Kills 37. Paid to Dance 37. The Shadow 37. Who Killed Gail Preston? 38. There's Always a Woman 38. Convicted 38. Juvenile Court 38. Homicide Bureau 38. The Lone Wolf's Spy Hunt 39. Renegade Ranger 39. *Only Angels Have Wings* 39. Special Inspector 39. Music in My Heart 40. Blondie on a Budget 40. Susan and God 40. *The Lady in Question* 40. Angels over Broadway 40. *The Strawberry Blonde* 41. Affectionately Yours 41. Blood and Sand 41. *You'll Never Get Rich* 41. My Gal Sal 42. Tales of Manhattan 42. You Were Never Lovelier 42. *Cover Girl* 44. Tonight and Every Night 45. *Gilda* 46. Down to Earth 47. *The Lady from Shanghai* 48. The Loves of Carmen 48. Affair in Trinidad 52. Salome 53. *Miss Sadie Thompson* 53. Fire Down Below 57. *Pal Joey* 57. *Separate Tables* 58. They Came to Cordura 59. The Story on Page One 59. The Happy Thieves 62. Circus World 64. The Money Trap 66. The Poppy is also a Flower 67. The Rover 68. Sons of Satan 68. The Road to Salina 70. The Naked Zoo 71. The Wrath of God 72.
✪ For supplying the kind of glamour the 40s needed, and for doing it with the saving grace of humour. *Gilda*.

¶ Every man I knew had fallen in love with Gilda
‖ and wakened with me. – *R.H.*

A girl is . . . a girl. It's nice to be told you're successful at it. – *R.H.*
I haven't had everything from life. I've had too much. – *R.H.*
I never really thought of myself as a sex symbol – more as a comedienne who could dance. – *R.H.*

Hazell, Hy (1920–1970) (Hyacinth Hazel O'Higgins).
British revue and musical comedy artist.
Meet Me at Dawn 46. Paper Orchid 49. Celia 49. The Lady Craved Excitement 50. The Night Won't Talk 52. Up in the World 56. The Whole Truth 58, etc.

Hazlehurst, Noni.
Australian leading actress.
The Getting of Wisdom 77. Fatty Finn 80. *Monkey Grip* 82. Waterfront (TV) 83. Fran 85. Australian Dream 85. True Colours 87, etc.

HDTV,
High Definition Television, the latest development in television technology, which provides a better picture by increasing the resolution to 1,125 lines and having a screen with a similar ratio to the cinema. Future development may be held up by the failure of interested parties to agree on a standard; it seems likely that Europe will set a standard that differs from America and Japan in order to protect European manufacturers of electronic equipment. Japan began HDTV broadcasts in 1991, using an analog system. In the long term, as computers grow in importance in entertainment, it is more likely that the HDTV of the future will be digital. It has already attracted the attention of film-makers: Peter Greenaway used HDTV editing facilities to create the rich imagery of *Prospero's Books* 91, his version of Shakespeare's *The Tempest*, and Wim Wenders used it for his *Until the End of the World* (*Bis ans Ende der Welt*) 92.

Head, Edith (1907–1981).
American dress designer, in Hollywood from the 20s. First solo credit *She Done Him Wrong* 33; later won Academy Awards for The Heiress 49. Samson and Delilah 51. A Place in the Sun 52, etc; worked on Olly Olly Oxen Free 78. Appeared in *The Oscar* 66.
Autobiography: 1940, *The Dress Doctor*.

Head, Murray (1946–).
Young British actor of the 70s.
Sunday Bloody Sunday 71. Gawain and the Green Knight 73.

Headly, Glenne (1955–).
American leading actress, from the stage. She was formerly married to actor John Malkovich (1982–90).
Four Friends 81. Eleni 85. Fandango 85. Seize the Day 86. Making Mr Right 87. Nadine 87. Dirty Rotten Scoundrels 88. Paperhouse 88. Stars and Bars 88. Dick Tracy 90. Mortal Thoughts 91. Grand Isle 92. Ordinary Magic 93. Getting Even with Dad 94, etc.

Healey, Myron (1922–).
American general-purpose actor; Doc Holliday in the *Wyatt Earp* TV series.
I Dood It 43. The Man from Colorado 48. Salt Lake Raiders 50. Fort Osage 52. Rage at Dawn 55. Hell's Crossroads 57. Escape from Red Rock 58. Gunfight at Dodge City 59. Harlow 65. Mirage 65. True Grit 69. Which Way to the Front? 70. Devil Bear 75. The Incredible Melting Man 77. Ghost Fever 86. Pulse 87, many others.

Healy, Ted (1886–1937).
Tough-looking, cigar-chewing American vaudevillian who originated the Three Stooges and took them to Hollywood.
Soup to Nuts 30. Dancing Lady 33. The Band Plays On 34. Mad Love 35. San Francisco 36. Hollywood Hotel 37, etc.

Heard, John (1946–).
American general-purpose actor.
First Love 77. Between the Lines 79. Head over Heels 80. Heartbeat 80. Cutter's Way 81. Cat People 82. Best Revenge 83. C.H.U.D. 84. Too Scared to Scream 84. Heaven Help Us 85. After Hours 85. The Trip to Bountiful 85. Violated 86. The Telephone 87. Big 88. The Milagro Beanfield War 88. Betrayed 88. Beaches 88. The Package 89. Mindwalk 90. Rambling Rose 91. Deceived 91. Radio Flyer 92. Gladiator 92. There Was a Little Boy (TV) 93. In the Line of Fire 93. The Pelican Brief 93. Spoils of War (TV) 94, etc.

Hearne, Richard (1908–1979).
British acrobatic comedian, in music hall and circus practically from the cradle. Made occasional films, often in his character of 'Mr Pastry'.
Dance Band 35. Millions 37. Miss London Ltd 42. The Butler's Dilemma 43. One Night with You 48. Helter Skelter 49. Captain Horatio Hornblower 50. Madame Louise 51. Miss Robin Hood 52. Something in the City 53. Tons of Trouble 56, etc.

Hearst, William Randolph (1863–1951).
American newspaper magnate thought to have been the original of *Citizen Kane*. Also noted for pushing his protégée Marion Davies (qv) to film stardom by buying a production company solely for her vehicles.
Biography: 1961, *Citizen Hearst* by W. A. Swanberg.

Heartherton, Joey (1944–).
American leading lady, former child stage performer.
Twilight of Honor 64. Where Love Has Gone 64. My Blood Runs Cold 64. Bluebeard 72. The Happy Hooker Goes to Washington 77, etc.

heaven:
see *fantasy*.

Hecht, Ben (1894–1964).
American writer and critic with screenplay credits going back to silent days. Often worked in collaboration with Charles MacArthur.
Autobiographies: 1954, *A Child of the Century*. 1963, *Gaily Gaily*.
Biography: 1978, *The Five Lives of Ben Hecht* by Doug Fetherling.
Underworld (w) (AA) 29. The Great Gabbo (oa) 29. *The Front Page* (oa) 31. Topaze (w) 33. Twentieth Century (oa) 34. *Crime Without Passion* (wd) 34. *The Scoundrel* (wd) (AA) 35. Soak the Rich (wpd) 36. Nothing Sacred (w) 37. The Goldwyn Follies (w) 38. *Wuthering Heights* (co-w, AAN) 39. *Angels Over Broadway* (wpd) (AANw) 40. Lydia (w) 41. Tales of Manhattan (w) 42. The Black Swan (w) 42. *Spellbound* (w) 45. *Notorious* (AANw) 46. The Specter of the Rose (wpd) 46. Her Husband's Affairs (w) 47. The Miracle of the Bells (w) 48. Whirlpool (w) 49. Actors and Sin (wpd) 52. Monkey Business (w) 52. Miracle in the Rain (w) 56. Legend of the Lost (w) 58. Circus World (w) 64, etc.
✪ For being connected in some way with most of the enjoyable hard-boiled comedies and melodramas with which one associates Hollywood in the 30s and 40s. *Nothing Sacred*.

¶ Hollywood held the lure . . . tremendous sums of money for work that required no more effort than a game of pinochle. – *B.H.*

Movies are one of the bad habits that have corrupted our century. They have slipped into the American mind more misinformation in one evening than the Dark Ages could muster in a decade. – *B.H.*

A movie is never any better than the stupidest man connected with it. – *B.H.*

The movies are an eruption of trash that has lamed the American mind and retarded Americans from becoming cultured people. – *B.H.*

Hecht, Harold (1903–1985).
American producer, formerly dance director and literary agent. From 1947 produced jointly with Burt Lancaster and later James Hill.

Vera Cruz 54. Marty 55. Trapeze 56. Separate Tables 58. Taras Bulba 63. Cat Ballou 65. The Way West 67, etc.

Heckart, Eileen (1919–).
American character actress, mainly on stage.

Miracle in the Rain 56. The Bad Seed (AAN) 56. Somebody Up There Likes Me 57. Hot Spell 57. Heller in Pink Tights 60. Up the Down Staircase 68. No Way to Treat a Lady 68. Butterflies Are Free (AA) 72. Zandy's Bride 74. The Hiding Place 75. Burnt Offerings 77. Sunshine Christmas (TV) 77. Suddenly Love (TV) 78. Backstairs at the White House (TV) 79. White Mama (TV) 81. FDR: The Last Year (TV) 81. Heartbreak Ridge 86.

Heckerling, Amy (1954–).
American director and screenwriter, concentrating on low-brow comedies.

Fast Times at Ridgemont High 82. Johnny Dangerously 84. National Lampoon's European Vacation 85. Look Who's Talking (wd) 89. Look Who's Talking Too (wd) 90.

Heckle and Jeckle.
Crafty twin magpies, created by Paul Terry, the heroes of more than 50 Terrytoons cartoons. Although identical in appearance, Heckle spoke with a New York accent and Jeckle with a British one. Their voices were supplied by Dayton Allen, Ned Sparks, and Roy Halee.

The Talking Magpies 46. Flying South 47. Magpie Madness 48. Dancing Shoes 49. King Tut's Tomb 50. Movie Madness 52. Bargain Daze 53. Blue Plate Symphony 54. Miami Maniacs 56. Wild Life 59. Trapeze Please 60. Sappy New Year 61. Messed Up Movie Madness 66, etc.

Heckroth, Hein (1901–1970).
German art director who did work in Britain, mainly for Powell and Pressburger.

Caesar and Cleopatra 45. *A Matter of Life and Death* 46. *The Red Shoes* (AA) 48. Tales of Hoffman 51. The Story of Gilbert and Sullivan 53. The Battle of the River Plate 56. Torn Curtain (US) 66, etc.

Hedison, David (1926–) (Ara Heditsian, formerly known as Al Hedison).
American leading man, mostly on TV.

The Enemy Below 57. *The Fly* 58. Son of Robin Hood 59. The Lost World 60. Marines Let's Go 61. The Greatest Story Ever Told 65. Live and Let Die 73. The Cat Creature (TV) 73. Adventures of the Queen (TV) 75. The Lives of Jenny Dolan (TV) 75. Murder in Peyton Place (TV) 77. The Power Within (TV) 79. North Sea Hijack 80. The Naked Face 84. Smart Alec 85, License to Kill 89, etc.

TV series: *Five Fingers* 59–60. *Voyage to the Bottom of the Sea* 64–68. Dynasty II: The Colbys 85–87.

Hedley, Jack (1930–).
Amiable British leading man best remembered as TV's 'Tim Frazer'.

Room at the Top (debut) 59. Make Mine Mink 60. Lawrence of Arabia 62. In the French Style 63. The Scarlet Blade 63. *Of Human Bondage* 64. Witchcraft 65. The Anniversary 67. Goodbye Mr Chips 69. Brief Encounter (TV) 74. For Your Eyes Only 81. Sophia Loren (TV) 81. Three Kinds of Heat 87, etc.

TV series: Kate 70–71. Colditz 72–73. Who Pays the Ferryman 77. Hard Cases 88.

Hedren, Tippi (1935–) (Nathalie Hedren).
American leading lady, former TV model. She is the mother of actress Melanie Griffith.

■ *The Birds* 63. Marnie 64. A Countess from Hong Kong 66. The Man with the Albatross 69. Tiger by the Tail 69. Satan's Harvest 69. Mr Kingstreet's War 73. The Harrad Experiment 73. Roar 82. The Thrill of Genius 85. Foxfire Light 86. Deadly Spygames 89. Pacific Heights 90. In the Cold of the Night 91. Inevitable Grace 94. The Birds II: Land's End (TV) 94.

Heerman, Victor (1892–1977).
Anglo-American director, in US from boyhood.

■ Don't Ever Marry 20. The Poor Simp 20. A Divorce of Convenience 21. The Chicken in the Case 21. My Boy 22. John Smith 22. Love Is an Awful Thing 22. Rupert of Hentzau 23. Modern Matrimony 23. The Dangerous Maid 23. The Confidence Man 24. Old Home Week 25. Irish Luck 25. For Wives Only 26. Rubber Heels 26. Ladies Must Dress 27. Love Hungry 28. Personality 30. Paramount on Parade 30. *Animal Crackers* 30. Sea Legs 30.

Also screenwriter, usually in collaboration.

Heffron, Richard T. (1930–).
American director, from TV.

Newman's Law 73. Toma (TV pilot) 73. Outrage (TV) 73. The Rockford Files (TV pilot) 74. The Morning After (TV) 74. The California Kid (TV) 74. Locusts (TV) 74. I Will Fight No More Forever (TV) 75. Death Scream (TV) 75. Trackdown 76. Futureworld 76. Young Joe the Forgotten Kennedy (TV) 77. Outlaw Blues 77. See How She Runs (TV) 78. True Grit (TV) 78. A Rumor of War (TV) 80. Foolin' Around 80. I the Jury 82. Anatomy of an Illness (TV) 82. The French Revolution 89, etc.

Heflin, Van (1910–1971) (Emmett Evan Heflin).
Purposeful American leading man of the 40s; craggy character actor of the 50s and 60s.

■ A Woman Rebels 36. The Outcasts of Poker Flat 37. Flight from Glory 37. Saturday's Heroes 37. Annapolis Salute 37. Back Door to Heaven 39. *Santa Fe Trail* 40. The Feminine Touch 41. H. M. Pulham Esq 41. *Johnny Eager* (AA) 41. *Kid Glove Killer* 42. Seven Sweethearts 42. Grand Central Murder 42. Tennessee Johnson 42. Presenting Lily Mars 43. *The Strange Love of Martha Ivers* 46. Till the Clouds Roll By 46. Possessed 47. Green Dolphin Street 47. Tap Roots 48. B.F.'s Daughter 48. The Three Musketeers 48. Act of Violence 48. Madame Bovary 48. East Side 48. East Side West Side 49. Tomahawk 51. *The Prowler* 51. Weekend with Father 51. My Son John 52. Wings of the Hawk 53. *Shane* 53. Tanganyika 54. South of Algiers (GB) 54. The Raid 54. Woman's World 54. The Black Widow 54. Count Three and Pray 55. Battle Cry 55. *Patterns* 56. *3.10 to Yuma* 57. Gunman's Walk 58. They Came to Cordura 59. Tempest 59. Five Branded Women 60. Under Ten Flags 60. Cry of Battle 63. The Wastrel 64. To Be a Man 64. The Greatest Story Ever Told 65. Once a Thief 65. Stagecoach 66. The Man Outside (GB) 67. Each

Man for Himself 68. *Airport* 69. The Big Bounce 69. The Last Child (TV) 71.

Hefti, Neal (1922–).
American composer, a former big band musician and arranger for the bands of Woody Herman, Harry James and Count Basie. He also wrote the theme for the *Batman* TV series.

Sex and the Single Girl 65. How to Murder Your Wife 65. Boeing Boeing 65. Harlow 65. Synanon 65. Duel at Diablo 66. Lord Love a Duck 66. Barefoot in the Park 66. The Odd Couple 68. Last of the Red Hot Lovers 72. Won Ton Ton, the Dog Who Saved Hollywood 76, etc.

Heggie, O.P. (1879–1936).
Australian character actor of stage and, latterly, Hollywood screen.

The Mysterious Dr Fu Manchu 29. East Lynne 31. Smiling Through 32. Midnight 34. The Count of Monte Cristo 34. Bride of Frankenstein (as the blind hermit) 35. Prisoner of Shark Island 36, etc.

Heifits, Joseph (1904–).
Russian director, from 1928. Known in the 30s for *Baltic Deputy*, but did not come to Western notice again until *The Lady with the Little Dog* 59.

In the Town of S 65. Salute Marya 70, etc.

Heim, Alan.
American film editor.

The Twelve Chairs 70. Doc 71. Godspell 73. Lenny 74. Network (AAN) 76. Hair 79. All That Jazz (AA) 79. The Fan 81. So Fine 81. Star 80 83. Goodbye New York 85. She's Having a Baby 88. Funny Farm 88. Valmont 89. Quick Change 90. Billy Bathgate 91, etc.

Heindorf, Ray (1908–1980).
American musical director.

Hard to Get 38. Strawberry Blonde 41. Yankee Doodle Dandy (AA) 42. This Is the Army (AA) 43. Calamity Jane 53. A Star Is Born 54. The Music Man (AA) 62. Finian's Rainbow (AAN) 68, many others.

Heinz, Gerard (1903–1972).
German character actor, mainly in British movies.

Thunder Rock 42. Went the Day Well? 42. Caravan 46. His Excellency 51. The Man Inside 57. House of the Seven Hawks 59. The Guns of Navarone 61. The Cardinal 63. The Dirty Dozen 67, many others.

Heisler, Stuart (1894–1979).
Competent American director.

■ Straight from the Shoulder 36. Poppy 37. The Hurricane (co-d) 38. The Biscuit Eater 40. *The Monster and The Girl* 41. Among the Living 41. The Remarkable Andrew 42. *The Glass Key* 42. Along Came Jones 45. *Blue Skies* 46. Vendetta (co-d) 46. Smash Up 47. Tulsa 49. Tokyo Joe 49. Chain Lightning 50. Dallas 50. Storm Warning 50. Journey into Light 51. Saturday Island 52. *The Star* 53. Beachhead 54. This is My Love 54. I Died a Thousand Times 55. The Lone Ranger 56. The Burning Hills 56. Hitler 62.

Heiss, Carol (1940–).
German-Swiss skating star: she came to Hollywood for one movie, *Snow White and the Three Stooges* 61.

Held, Anna (1873–1918).
German singer-dancer who married Ziegfeld and starred in his early Follies. Luise Rainer portrayed her in *The Great Ziegfeld* and Barbara Parkins in

Ziegfeld, the Man and His Women. She made one film appearance in 1916: *Madame La Présidente.*

Held, Edward (1894–1985).
American set designer.
Lost Horizon 37. The Hurricane 38. The Goldwyn Follies 38. Wuthering Heights 39. Kings Row 41. Across the Pacific 42. Them 54, etc.

Held, Martin (1908–   ).
German leading actor.
Black Eyes 51. Captain from Kopenick 56. Roses for the Prosecutor 59. The Oldest Profession 67. The Serpent 72.

helicopters,
restricted in scope, have been put to sound dramatic use in two films about helicopter services, *Battle Taxi* and *Flight from Ashiya;* while their potential for thrill sequences was well explored in *The Bridges at Toko-Ri, Experiment in Terror, From Russia with Love, Arabesque, Caprice, You Only Live Twice, The Satan Bug, Fathom, The Las Vegas Story, Where Eagles Dare, Masquerade, Tarzan in the Valley of Gold, That Riviera Touch, The Wrecking Crew, Figures in a Landscape, Birds of Prey, Breakout, Russian Roulette* and *Apocalypse Now.* TV series on the subject include *Chopper One, Chopper Squad, Riptide, Blue Thunder* and *Air Wolf.*
See also: *airplanes.*

hell
has been used more figuratively than realistically in movies; but what passed for the real thing did appear in *Dante's Inferno, Heaven Can Wait, Hellzapoppin* and *Angel on My Shoulder,* not to mention a Sylvester cartoon called *Satan's Waitin'.*

Heller, Joseph (1923–   ).
American satirical novelist, whose *Catch 22* was rather unsatisfactorily filmed.
Dirty Dingus Magee (co-w) 70.

Heller, Lukas (1930–1988).
German-born screenwriter, associated chiefly with Robert Aldrich.
Whatever Happened to Baby Jane? 62. Hush Hush Sweet Charlotte (co-w) 64. The Dirty Dozen (co-w) 67. The Killing of Sister George 68. The Deadly Trackers 73. Damnation Alley (co-w) 77, etc.

Heller, Otto (1896–1970).
Czech-born cinematographer, in Britain since early 30s. Had more than 300 features to his credit.
The High Command 36. Tomorrow We Live 42. Mr Emmanuel 44. I Live in Grosvenor Square 45. *The Queen of Spades* 48. The Winslow Boy 48. Never Take No for an Answer 51. The Divided Heart 54. Manuela 57. The Light in the Piazza 62. West Eleven 63. The Ipcress File 65. Alfie 66. Funeral in Berlin 66. Duffy 68. Bloomfield 70, etc.

Hellinger, Mark (1903–1947).
American journalist who scripted some films and later turned producer.
Biography: 1952, *The Mark Hellinger Story* by Jim Bishop.
The Killers 46. Brute Force 47. Naked City (also narrated) 48.

Hellman, Jerome (1928–   ).
American producer, former agent.
■ The World of Henry Orient 64. A Fine Madness 66. *Midnight Cowboy* (AA) 69. The Day of the Locust 75. *Coming Home* (AAN) 78. Promises in the Dark (& d) 79. Mosquito Coast 86.

Hellman, Lillian (1907–1984).
American playwright who adapted much of her own work for the screen and also wrote other screenplays.
Autobiographies: 1969, *An Unfinished Woman.* 1974, *Pentimento,* which was filmed as *Julia.*
These Three 36. *The Little Foxes* (AAN) 41. Watch on the Rhine 43. North Star (AAN) 43. The Searching Wind 46. *Another Part of the Forest* 48. *The Children's Hour* 62. Toys in the Attic 63. The Chase 66. Julia 77, etc.

¶ I cannot and will not cut my conscience to fit this year's fashions. – *L.H.*

Hellman, Marcel (1898–1985).
Rumanian producer, long in Britain.
The Amateur Gentleman 36. Jeannie 41. Happy Go Lucky 51. Northwest Frontier 59. Moll Flanders 65, many others.

Hellman, Monte (1931–   ).
American director and producer whose career began promisingly and then petered out in a succession of abandoned projects. A former editor, he began in films working for Roger Corman.
■ The Beast from Haunted Cave 59. Flight to Fury 65. Back Door to Hell 65. The Shooting 65. Ride in the Whirlwind 66. Two Lane Blacktop 71. Cockfighter 74. China 9, Liberty 37 78. Iguana 88. Reservoir Dogs (p) 92.

Hello, Hollywood,
by Allen Rivkin and Laura Kerr. Published in 1962, this is a 600-page collection of essays and journalistic pieces about the movies, 'by the people who make them'. Required reading for addicts.

Helm, Brigitte (1906–   ) (Gisele Eve Schittenhelm).
German star actress of the 20s.
Metropolis 26. *The Loves of Jeanne Ney* 27. Alraune 28. Countess of Monte Cristo 31. L'Atlantide 31. Gold 33. The Blue Danube 34, etc.

Helm, Fay (1913–   ).
American actress.
Racket Busters 38. Dark Victory 39. A Child Is Born 40. Night Monster 42. Phantom Lady (title role) 44. Sister Kenny 46. The Locket 47, etc.

Helmond, Katherine (1933–   ).
Saucer-eyed American comedy actress.
Baby Blue Marine 74. Dr Max (TV) 74. Locusts (TV) 74. The Legend of Lizzie Borden (TV) 75. Family Plot 76. Little Ladies of the Night (TV) 77. Getting Married (TV) 79. Pearl (TV) 79. Time Bandits 81. Brazil 84. Shadey 85. Lady in White 88. Inside Monkey Zetterland 92, etc.
TV series: *Soap* 77–80.

Helpmann, Sir Robert (1909–1986).
Australian ballet dancer and actor of stage and screen, in Britain from 1930.
One of Our Aircraft Is Missing 42. Henry V 44. The Red Shoes 48. Tales of Hoffman 50. 55 Days in Peking 62. The Quiller Memorandum 66. Chitty Chitty Bang Bang 68. Alice's Adventures in Wonderland 72. Don Quixote (& co-d) 73, others.

Helton, Percy (1894–1971).
Chubby little American comedy actor; his round face expressed surprise and dismay in innumerable small roles.
Silver Wings 22. Miracle on 34th Street 47. The Set Up 49. My Friend Irma 49. Call Me Madam 52: A Star is Born 54. Butch Cassidy and the Sundance Kid 69, many others.

TV series: The Beverly Hillbillies 68–71.

Hemingway, Ernest (1899–1961).
Distinguished American novelist. Works filmed include *A Farewell to Arms* 32 and 57. *Spanish Earth* (orig sp, p) 37. *For Whom the Bell Tolls* 43. *The Killers* 46 and 64. *The Macomber Affair* 47. *The Snows of Kilimanjaro* 53. *The Sun Also Rises* 57. *The Old Man and the Sea* 58. *Adventures of a Young Man* 62. *To Have and Have Not* was filmed three times (inaccurately): in 1944, 1951 (as *The Breaking Point*) and 1956 (as *The Gun Runner*).
Book: 1981, *Hemingway and the Movies* by Frank M. Laurence.

Hemingway, Margaux (1955–   ).
American fashion model and occasional leading lady, granddaughter of Ernest Hemingway.
Lipstick 76. Killer Fish 80. They Call Me Bruce 82. Over the Brooklyn Bridge 83. The Killing Machine 85. La Messe en Si Mineur 90. Inner Sanctum 91. Deadly Rivals 92. Frame-Up II: The Cover-Up 92, etc.

Hemingway, Mariel (1961–   ).
American actress, sister of Margaux Hemingway.
Lipstick 76. I Want to Keep My Baby (TV) 76. Manhattan (AAN) 79. Personal Best 82. Star 80 83. Creator 84. The Mean Season 84. Superman IV 87. The Suicide Club 87. Sunset 88. Fire, Ice and Dynamite 90. Midnight Spy 90. Delirious 91, etc.

Hemmings, David (1941–   ).
Slightly-built British leading man who after appearing in many second features suddenly seemed to have the acceptable image for the late 60s.
No Trees in the Street 59. The Wind of Change 60. Some People 62. Live It Up 63. Dateline Diamonds 65. Eye of the Devil 66. *Blow Up* 66. Camelot 67. *The Charge of the Light Brigade* 68. A Long Day's Dying 68. Only When I Larf 68. Barbarella 68. Alfred the Great 69. The Walking Stick 69. Fragment of Fear 69. Unman, Wittering and Zigo 70. The Love Machine 71. Running Scared (d only) 72. Mister Quilp 75. The Squeeze 77. Islands in the Stream 77. The Prince and the Pauper 77. Just a Gigolo (& d) 78. Murder by Decree 79. Charlie Muffin (TV) 79. Race for the Yankee Zephyr (d only) 81. The Survivor (d only) 81. Man, Woman and Child 82. Calamity Jane (TV) 84. The Rainbow 89. Dark Horse (d) 92, etc.

Hempel, Anouska (Lady Weinberg).
Australian-born leading lady in Britain. She is now a hotelier and fashion designer.
On Her Majesty's Secret Service 69. Scars of Dracula 70. The Magnificent Seven Deadly Sins 71. Go for a Take 72. Slaves 73. Double Exposure 76, etc.

Henabery, Joseph (1886–1976).
American silent actor who played Lincoln in *The Birth of a Nation* and later directed Gish and Fairbanks.
His Majesty the American 19. A Sainted Devil 24, etc.

¶ If you'd had two or three years of motion pictures you were a pioneer, a veteran. You'd really been through the mill. You might have made a hundred and some pictures in that time – a one-reeler could be made in a day. – *J.H.*

Henderson, Florence (1934–   ).
American singer and actress with theatrical experience.
Song of Norway 70.

TV series: The Brady Bunch 69–73.

Henderson, Marcia (1930–1987).
American leading lady of the 50s.
Thunder Bay 53. The Glass Web 53. Naked Alibi 54. Back to God's Country 54, etc.

Henderson, Ray (1896–1970) (Raymond' Brost).
American composer, mainly with collaborators B. G. De Sylva and Lew Brown; the late 20s constituted their most successful period.

Hendrix, Wanda (1928–1981).
American leading lady.
Confidential Agent 45. Ride the Pink Horse 47. Miss Tatlock's Millions 48. Prince of Foxes 49. Captain Carey USA 50. The Highwayman 52. The Last Posse 53. The Black Dakotas 54. Johnny Cool 63. Stage to Thunder Rock 65, etc.

Hendry, Ian (1931–1984).
Virile, aggressive British leading actor, mostly on TV.
In the Nick 60. *Live Now Pay Later* 62. The Girl in the Headlines 63. Children of the Damned 63. This Is My Street 63. *The Beauty Jungle* 64. Repulsion 65. The Hill 65. The Sandwich Man 66. Casino Royale 67. Doppelganger 69. The Southern Star 69. The Mackenzie Break 70. Get Carter 71. The Jerusalem File 72. All Coppers are . . . 72. Tales from the Crypt 72. Theatre of Blood 73. Assassin 73. The Internecine Project 74. The Bitch 79. McVicar 80, etc.

Henenlotter, Frank.
American exploitation and horror film director and screenwriter.
Basket Case 82. Brain Damage 88. Basket Case 2 89. Frankenhooker 90. Basket Case 3 91, etc.

¶ Sleazy movies are my world. Give me $23 million and I'll give you 23 low-budget sex and horror films. – F.H.

Henie, Sonja (1912–1969).
Norwegian skating star who appeared in light Hollywood musicals of the 30s and 40s. Died of leukaemia.
Autobiography: 1940, *Wings on My Feet.*
■ One in a Million 36. Thin Ice 37. Happy Landing 38. My Lucky Star 38. Second Fiddle 39. Everything Happens at Night 39. Sun Valley Serenade 41. Iceland 42. Wintertime 43. It's a Pleasure 45. The Countess of Monte Cristo 48. Hello London (GB) 58.

¶ Sonja, you'll never go broke. All you have to do is hock your trophies. – *Radie Harris*

Henley, Beth (1952–).
American dramatist and screenwriter.
True Stories 86. Crimes of the Heart (AAN) 86. Nobody's Fool (& a) 86. Miss Firecracker 89.

Hennesy, Dale (–1981).
American production designer.
Everything You Always Wanted to Know About Sex 72. Sleeper 73. Young Frankenstein 74. Logan's Run 76. Norma Rae 79. The Competition 80. Wholly Moses 80. Annie 82, etc.

Henning-Jensen, Astrid (1914–).
Danish woman director, a former actress.
Denmark Grows Up 47. Krane's Bakery Shop 51. Ballet Girl 54. Unfaithful 66. Me and You 68. Winter Children (Vinterboern) (wd) 78. Street of My Childhood (Barndommens Gade) 86, etc.

Henreid, Paul (1908–1992) (Paul von Hernreid).
Austrian leading man of the 30s; fled to Britain, then to Hollywood, where his immobile good looks made him a suitable leading man, in the absence at war of home-grown talent, for a number of strong-willed leading ladies. In later life he directed the occasional film and many TV shows.
Autobiography: 1984, *Ladies' Man.*
Goodbye Mr Chips 39. *Night Train to Munich* 40. Joan of Paris 41. *Now Voyager* 42. Casablanca 42. In Our Time 44. Between Two Worlds 44. The Conspirators 44. The Spanish Main 45. Devotion 46. Of Human Bondage 46. Deception 46. Song of Love 47. The Scar 48. Rope of Sand 49. So Young So Bad 50. Last of the Buccaneers 50. For Men Only (& pd) 51. Thief of Damascus 52. Siren of Baghdad 53. Deep in My Heart (as Ziegfeld) 54. Pirates of Tripoli 55. A Woman's Devotion (& d) 57. Holiday for Lovers 59. The Four Horsemen of the Apocalypse 62. Dead Ringer (d only) 64. Operation Crossbow 65. The Madwoman of Chaillot 69. The Failing of Raymond (TV) 71. Mrs R (TV) 75. Exorcist II: The Heretic 77, etc.

¶ He looks as though his idea of fun would be to find a nice cold damp grave and sit in it.
– *Richard Winnington, 1946, of Henreid's performance in Of Human Bondage*

Henrey, Bobby (1939–).
British child actor, notable in *The Fallen Idol* 48. Retired after *The Wonder Kid* 50.

Henriksen, Lance.
Lean, intense American character actor, often as a villain, whose performances enliven many exploitation movies.
Dog Day Afternoon 75. Damien: Omen II 78. The Visitor 80. Prince of the City 81. Piranha 2: The Spawning 83. The Right Stuff 83. Savage Dawn 84. The Terminator 84. The Jagged Edge 85. Aliens 86. Near Dark 87. Pumpkinhead 88. Deadly Intent 88. The Hit List 88. The Horror Show 89. Johnny Handsome 89. Stone Cold 91. The Pit and the Pendulum (as Torquemada) 91. Alien³ 92. Super Mario Bros 93. Excessive Force 93. No Escape 94. Boulevard 94. Man's Best Friend 94. Color of Night 94, etc.

Henry Aldrich.
The accident-prone American teenager of the 40s series derived from Clifford Goldsmith's play *What a Life*, which was filmed in 1939 with Jackie Cooper in the role. *Life with Henry*, again with Cooper, followed in 1941, owing to the popularity of the radio series featuring Ezra Stone, who had played the part on Broadway. The series proper starred Jimmy Lydon, with Charles Smith as his friend Dizzy. Goldsmith then created *The Aldrich Family*, a TV situation comedy that ran from 1949–53, in which Henry was played by Robert Casey, Richard Tyler, Henry Girard, Kenneth Nelson and Bobby Ellis.
What a Life 39. Life with Henry 41. Henry Aldrich for President 41. Henry and Dizzy 42. Henry Aldrich, Editor 42. Henry Aldrich Gets Glamour 43. Henry Aldrich Swings It 43. Henry Aldrich Haunts a House 43. Henry Aldrich, Boy Scout 44. Henry Aldrich Plays Cupid 44. Henry Aldrich's Little Secret 44.

Henry, Buck (1930–) (B. Zuckerman).
Mild-looking American actor-writer of abrasive comedy.
The Troublemaker (w) 64. The Graduate (AANw) 67. Candy (w) 68. *Catch 22* (w) 70. The Owl and the Pussycat (w) 70. *Taking Off* (a) 71. The Day of the Dolphin (w) 73. The Man Who Fell

to Earth (w) 76. Heaven Can Wait (co-d, AAN) 78. Old Boyfriends (a) 79. The First Family (wd) 80. Gloria (a) 80. Eating Raoul (a) 82. Protocol (w) 84. Aria (a) 87. I Love N.Y. (w) 87. Dark Before Dawn (a) 88. Rude Awakening (a) 89. Tune in Tomorrow (aka Aunt Julia and the Scriptwriter) (a) 90. Defending Your Life (a) 91. The Lounge People (a) 91. The Linguini Incident (a) 91. Short Cuts (a) 93. Grumpy Old Men (a) 93. 2 Die 4 (w) 94, etc.

Henry, Charlotte (1913–1980).
American juvenile actress of the early 30s.
Rebecca of Sunnybrook Farm 32. Alice in Wonderland 33. Babes in Toyland 34. Charlie Chan at the Opera 37. Stand and Deliver 41, etc.

Henry, Justin (1971–).
American child star.
■ *Kramer vs Kramer* (AAN) 79. Tiger Town 84. Sixteen Candles 84. Martin's Day 85. Sweet Hearts Dance 88.

Henry, Lenny (1958–).
English stand-up comedian, successful on TV.
The Suicide Club 88. Lenny: Live and Unleashed (concert) 90. True Identity 91. Alive and Kicking (TV) 91, etc.
TV series: The Fosters 76. The Lenny Henry Show 87–89. Chef! 93–94.

Henry, Mike (1939–).
American ex-athlete who came to the screen briefly as Tarzan.
Tarzan and the Valley of Gold 65. Tarzan and the Great River 67. Tarzan and the Jungle Boy 68. Skyjacked 72. Adios Amigo 75. Smokey and the Bandit 77. Smokey and the Bandit II 80. Smokey and the Bandit III 83, etc.

Henry, O. (1862–1910) (William Sydney Porter).
American story writer who for the last ten years of his life wrote a weekly story for the *New York World*. A compendium of them was used in *O. Henry's Full House* 52, and there followed a TV series, *The O. Henry Playhouse* 56.

Henry, William (1918–).
American leading man, former child actor, later in callow roles.
Lord Jim 26. The Thin Man 34. Tarzan Escapes 36. Four Men and a Prayer 38. Blossoms in the Dust 41. Women in Bondage 44. Federal Man 49. Jungle Moonmen 54. Mister Roberts 54. The Lone Ranger and the Lost City of Gold 58. How the West Was Won 62. The Man Who Shot Liberty Valance 62. Donovan's Reef 63. Cheyenne Autumn 64. Taggart 64. Dear Brigitte . . . 65. El Dorado 67. Skin Game 71, etc.

Henson, Gladys (1897–1983) (Gladys Gunn).
Irish character actress often seen as plump, homely mum, or latterly grand-mum. On stage from 1910.
The Captive Heart 45. It Always Rains on Sunday 47. *London Belongs to Me* 48. *The Blue Lamp* 50. Lady Godiva Rides Again 51. Those People Next Door 52. Cockleshell Heroes 55. The Leather Boys 63, etc.

Henson, Jim (1936–1990).
American creator of the Muppets; actor, writer, director, and the voice of Kermit the Frog. The Muppets, created in 1954, featured on such TV series as *Sesame Street* from 1969, *The Muppet Show* 76–81, and *Fraggle Rock* 83–87. His Creature Shop also created animatronic creatures for films,

including *Teenage Mutant Ninja Turtles* and *The Witches*.

Biography: 1994, *Jim Henson – The Works* by Christopher Finch.

The Muppet Movie 79. The Great Muppet Caper (d) 81. The Dark Crystal (co-d) 82. The Muppets Take Manhattan 84. Labyrinth 86.

Henson, Leslie (1891–1957).
British stage comedian with bulging eyes; often in musical farces.

Autobiography: 1948, *Yours Faithfully*.

The Sport of Kings 30. It's a Boy 33. A Warm Corner 34. Oh Daddy 35. The Demi-Paradise 43. Home and Away 56, etc.

Henson, Nicky (1945–).
British general-purpose actor. He is the son of Leslie Henson.

Witchfinder General 68. There's a Girl in My Soup 70. All Coppers Are 71. Penny Gold 72. Vampira 74. The Bawdy Adventures of Tom Jones 76. Number One of the Secret Service 77. The Golden Triangle 80, etc.

Henze, Hans Werner (1926–).
Leading modern German composer who writes the occasional film score.

Muriel 63. Young Torless 66. The Lost Honour of Katharina Blum 75. Good for Nothing 78. Swann in Love 84. L'Amour à Mort 84. Comrades 86, etc.

Hepburn, Audrey (1929–1993) (Audrey Hepburn-Ruston).
Belgian-born star actress of Irish-Dutch parentage; after small parts in English films, rose rapidly to Hollywood stardom as elegant gamine. She was married to Mel Ferrer (1954–68).

Biographies: 1993, *Audrey Hepburn* by Sheridan Morley. 1993, *A Star Danced: The Life of Audrey Hepburn* by Robyn Karney. 1994, *Audrey: Her Real Story* by Alexander Walker.

■ One Wild Oat 51. Young Wives' Tale 51. Laughter in Paradise 51. The Lavender Hill Mob 51. Monte Carlo Baby 52. The Secret People 52. *Roman Holiday* (AA, BFA) 53. Sabrina (AAN) 54. *War and Peace* 56. *Funny Face* 57. Love in the Afternoon 57. *The Nun's Story* (BFA, AAN) 59. Green Mansions 59. The Unforgiven 60. Breakfast at Tiffany's (AAN) 61. The Children's Hour 62. Charade 63. Paris When It Sizzles 64. My Fair Lady 64. How to Steal a Million 66. Two for the Road 66. *Wait until Dark* (AAN) 67. Robin and Marian 76. Bloodline 79. They All Laughed 81. Love among Thieves (TV) 87. Always 89.

✪ For providing the 50s with a fashionable image between a tomboy and a lady (and oddly failing to combine the two in *My Fair Lady*). *Roman Holiday*.

Hepburn, Katharine (1907–).
Dominant American star actress with Bryn Mawr personality; one of the most durable, talented and likeable interpreters of emancipated feminine roles.

Autobiography: 1991, *Me*.

Biographies: 1973, *Tracy and Hepburn* by Garson Kanin. 1976, *Kate* by Charles Higham.

■ *A Bill of Divorcement* 32. Christopher Strong 33. *Morning Glory* (AA) 33. *Little Women* 33. Spitfire 34. Break of Hearts 34. The Little Minister 34. Alice Adams (AAN) 35. Sylvia Scarlett 35. Mary of Scotland 36. A Woman Rebels 36. Quality Street 37. *Stage Door* 37. *Bringing Up Baby* 38. *Holiday* 38. *The Philadelphia Story* (AAN) 40. *Woman of the Year* 42. Keeper of the Flame 42. Stage Door Canteen 43. Dragon Seed 44. Without Love 45. Undercurrent 46. Sea of Grass 47. Song of Love 47.

State of the Union 48. *Adam's Rib* 49. *The African Queen* (AAN) 51. *Pat and Mike* 52. Summertime (GB: Summer Madness) (AAN) 55. The Rainmaker (AAN) 56. The Iron Petticoat (GB) 56. *Desk Set* 57. *Suddenly Last Summer* (AAN) 59. *Long Day's Journey Into Night* (AAN) 62. *Guess Who's Coming to Dinner* (AA) 67. *The Lion in Winter* (AA, BFA) 68. The Madwoman of Chaillot 69. The Trojan Women 71. The Glass Menagerie (TV) 73. A Delicate Balance 73. Love Among the Ruins (TV) 74. Rooster Cogburn 75. Olly Olly Oxen Free 78. The Corn Is Green (TV) 79. On Golden Pond (AA, BFA) 81. The Ultimate Solution of Grace Quigley 84. Mrs Delafield Wants to Marry (TV) 86. Laura Lansing Slept Here (TV) 88. The Man Upstairs (TV) 92. Love Affair 94.

✪ For her unique qualities of understanding, diction and movement; and for winning two Oscars thirty years after being declared box-office poison. *The Philadelphia Story*.

¶ The screen's first lady has never had a lot to say for herself. Her most thoughtful piece of self-analysis was:

I was fortunate to be born with a set of characteristics that were in the public vogue.
Cecil Beaton was more poetic than kind in his description:

She has a face that belongs to the sea and the wind, with large rocking-horse nostrils and teeth that you just know bite an apple every day.
Robert Hopkins said of her physical angularity:

You could throw a hat at her, and wherever it hit, it would stick.
Tennessee Williams thought her a dream actress:

She makes dialogue sound better than it is by a matchless clarity and beauty of diction, and by a fineness of intelligence and sensibility that illuminates every shade of meaning in every line she speaks.
One feels too that she brings similar high standards to every corner of her life. She said of herself:

When I started out, I didn't have any desire to be an actress or to learn how to act. I just wanted to be famous.
Perhaps only chance kept her from being the first woman president. She obviously has the charm, as Garson Kanin says:

As the years go by she does not lose her old admirers, she goes on gaining new ones.
Other self-musings:

I've had a fascinating life. I don't think I'm the least bit peculiar, but people tell me I am.
And:

Acting is the most minor of gifts. After all, Shirley Temple could do it when she was four.
And:

We used to laugh so much then. Now everything is so solemn, so joyless. One must laugh. One cannot moan everlastingly.
And:

My privacy is my own. I am the one to decide whether it will be invaded.
And:

I am revered rather like an old building. Yet I still seem to be master of my fate. The boat may be only a canoe, but I'm paddling it.
Three final opinions from other people: first, Humphrey Bogart:

She talks at you as though you were a microphone . . . she lectured the hell out of me on temperance and the evils of drink. She doesn't give a damn how she looks. I don't think she tries to be a character. I think she *is* one.
And James Agate:

She has a cheekbone like a death's head

attached to a manner as sinister and aggressive as crossbones.
And our old friend anon:

A cross between Donald Duck and a Stradivarius.

Famous line (*Stage Door*): 'The calla lilies are in bloom again . . .'

Famous line (*The Philadelphia Story*): 'I'm going crazy. I'm standing here, on my own two hands, and going crazy.'

Famous line (*The African Queen*): 'Nature, Mr Allnut, is what we are put into this world to rise above.'

Hepton, Bernard (1925–).
Tall, serious-looking British character actor, mostly on TV (*Colditz*, *The Squirrels*, *Secret Army*).

Get Carter 71. Henry VIII and His Six Wives 71. Voyage of the Damned 76. Tinker Tailor Soldier Spy (TV) 79. Gandhi 82. Smiley's People (TV) 82. Mansfield Park (TV) 85. Eminent Domain 91, etc.

Hepworth, Cecil (1874–1953).
Pioneer British film producer-director. For many years had his own stock company of stars and was financially successful, though his films were old-fashioned and sentimental.

Wrote first book on cinema: 1897, *Animated Photography*.

Autobiography: 1951, *Came the Dawn*.

The Quarrelsome Anglers 98. Two Cockneys in a Canoe 99. Wiping Something off the Slate 00. How it Feels to be Run Over 00. The Glutton's Nightmare 01. Alice in Wonderland 03. Firemen to the Rescue 03. Rescued by Rover 05. Blind Fate 12. His Country's Bidding 14. The Canker of Jealousy 14. The Man Who Stayed at Home 15. Trelawney of the Wells 16. Annie Laurie 16. Comin' Through the Rye 16. Nearer My God to Thee 17. The Touch of a Child 18. The Forest on the Hill 19. Alf's Button 20. Wild Heather 21. The Pipes of Pan 22. Strangling Threads 22. *Comin' Through the Rye* (remake) 24. The House of Marney 26, many others.

Herbert, F. Hugh (1897–1957).
American comedy screenwriter.

Adam and Evil 27. Hotel Continental 32. If You Could Only Cook (oa) 35. That Certain Age (oa) 38. Melody Ranch 40. West Point Widow 41. Together Again 44. *Kiss and Tell* (& oa) 45. Home Sweet Homicide 46. *Margie* 46. Scudda Hoo Scudda Hay (& d) 48. *Sitting Pretty* 48. Our Very Own 50. The Girls of Pleasure Island (& d) 53. *The Moon is Blue* (& oa) 53. The Little Hut 57, many others.

Herbert, Holmes (1882–1956) (Edward Sanger).
British stage actor, on the Hollywood screen from 1917, usually in quiet British roles – butler, lawyer or clerk.

Gentlemen Prefer Blondes 27. The Terror 28. Dr Jekyll and Mr Hyde 32. The Mystery of the Wax Museum 33. Mark of the Vampire 35. Lloyds of London 37. Stanley and Livingstone 39. This Above All 42. The Uninvited 44. Sherlock Holmes and the Secret Code (Dressed to Kill) 46. David and Bathsheba 51. The Brigand 52, etc.

Herbert, Hugh (1887–1952).
American eccentric comedian, remembered for nervous 'woo woo' exclamation.

Caught in the Fog 28. Laugh and Get Rich 31. The Lost Squadron 32. Strictly Personal 33. Convention City 33. Wonder Bar 34. Dames 34. A Midsummer Night's Dream 35. One Rainy

Afternoon 36. Top of the Town 37. Gold Diggers in Paris 38. The Great Waltz 38. Eternally Yours 39. La Conga Nights 40. The Black Cat 41. *Hellzapoppin* 41. Cracked Nuts 42. Mrs Wiggs of the Cabbage Patch 42. There's One Born Every Minute 43. Kismet 44. Men in Her Diary 45. Carnegie Hall 46. A Song Is Born 48. The Beautiful Blonde from Bashful Bend 49. Havana Rose 51, many others.

Herbert, Percy (1925–1992).
British character actor, usually seen as cockney rating or private.
The Baby and the Battleship 56. The Bridge on the River Kwai 57. *Tunes of Glory* 61. Mysterious Island 62. Mutiny on the Bounty 63. One Million Years BC 66. Tobruk (US) 66. The Viking Queen 67. The Royal Hunt of the Sun 69. Man in the Wilderness 71. Captain Apache 71. Doomwatch 72. Craze 73. The Wild Geese 78. The Sea Wolves 80, etc.
TV series: Cimarron Strip 67.

Herbert, Victor (1859–1924).
Irish popular composer long dominant in New York; played by Walter Connolly in *The Great Victor Herbert* 39. Scores filmed include *The Red Mill* and *Naughty Marietta*.

Hercule Poirot.
Agatha Christie's short, fussy, fiercely moustachioed Belgian detective was first played by the tall, clean-shaven Austin Trevor in *Alibi* 31, *Black Coffee* 31, *Lord Edgware Dies* 34; Tony Randall was closer to Christie's creation in the otherwise dull *The Alphabet Murders* 66; Albert Finney received an Oscar nomination for his performance in the big-budget *Murder on the Orient Express* 74, which was the best of the Poirot films; Peter Ustinov took the role in *Death on the Nile* 78 and *Evil under the Sun* 82. He was first portrayed on stage by Francis L. Sullivan in 1940. On television, David Suchet has made the role his own in the series *Poirot* since 1989.

Herek, Stephen.
American director.
Critters 86. Bill and Ted's Excellent Adventure 87. Don't Tell Mom the Babysitter's Dead 91. Mighty Ducks 92. The Three Musketeers 93, etc.

Herlie, Eileen (1919–   ) (Eileen Herlihy).
Scottish stage actress who has made occasional films.
Hungry Hill (debut) 47. Hamlet 48. The Angel with the Trumpet 49. The Story of Gilbert and Sullivan 53. Isn't Life Wonderful? 53. For Better For Worse 54. She Didn't Say No 58. Freud 62. The Seagull 68.

Herlihy, James Leo (1927–1994).
American novelist, whose *All Fall Down* and *Midnight Cowboy* were fairly memorably filmed. Also acted in Blue Denim (oa) 59, In the French Style 63, Friends 81. Committed suicide.

Herman, Jerry (1932–   ).
American composer of popular shows; those filmed include *Hello Dolly* and *Mame*.

Herman, Pee-Wee:
see *Reubens, Paul.*

Hermosillo, Jaime Humberto (1942–   ).
Mexican director.
La Verdadera Vocación de Magdalena 71. Naufragio 78. Confidencias 82. Maria de Mi Corazón 83. Dona Herlinda and Her Two Sons 85.

Clandestino Destino 87. La Tarea 90. Encuentro Inesperado 93, etc.

Hernandez, Juano (1896–1970).
American character actor with powerful presence.
Intruder in the Dust 48. The Breaking Point 50. *Young Man with a Horn* 50. Kiss Me Deadly 55. Trial 55. Ransom 56. Something of Value 57. The Pawnbroker 64. The Extraordinary Seaman 68, etc.

Herrington, Rowdy.
American screenwriter and director.
■ Jack's Back (wd) 88. Road House (d) 89. Gladiator (d) 92. Striking Distance (co-w, d) 93.

Herrmann, Bernard (1911–1975).
American composer and orchestral conductor.
Biography: 1991, *A Heart at Fire's Center* by Steven C. Smith.
■ *Citizen Kane* 41. All that Money Can Buy (AA) 41. *The Magnificent Ambersons* 42. Jane Eyre 43. Hangover Square 45. Anna and the King of Siam 46. The Ghost and Mrs Muir 47. The Day the Earth Stood Still 51. On Dangerous Ground 51. Five Fingers 52. The Snows of Kilimanjaro 52. White Witch Doctor 53. Beneath the 12-mile Reef 53. King of the Khyber Rifles 53. Garden of Evil 54. The Egyptian 54. Prince of Players 55. The Kentuckian 55. *The Trouble with Harry* 56. The Man in the Grey Flannel Suit 56. The Man who Knew Too Much 56. The Wrong Man 57. A Hatful of Rain 57. Vertigo 58. The Naked and the Dead 58. The Seventh Voyage of Sinbad 58. *North by Northwest* 59. Blue Denim 59. Journey to the Centre of the Earth 59. *Psycho* 60. The Three Worlds of Gulliver 60. Mysterious Island 61. Cape Fear 61. Tender is the Night 62. Jason and the Argonauts 63. Marnie 64. Joy in the Morning 65. Fahrenheit 451 66. The Bride wore Black 67. Twisted Nerve 69. Obsessions 69. The Battle of Neretva 70. The Night Diggers 71. Endless Night 72. Sisters 73. It's Alive 74. Taxi Driver (AAN) 76. Obsession (AAN) 76. Cape Fear 91.
✪ For musical backing second to none. *All that Money Can Buy.*

Herrmann, Edward (1943–   ).
American character actor.
Lady Liberty 71. The Paper Chase 72. The Day of the Dolphin 73. The Great Gatsby 74. The Great Waldo Pepper 75. *Eleanor and Franklin* (as Franklin Roosevelt) (TV) 76. Eleanor and Franklin: The White House Years (TV) 77. The Betsy 78. A Love Affair: The Eleanor and Lou Gehrig Story (TV) 79. Freedom Road (TV) 79. The North Avenue Irregulars 79. Reds 81. Harry's War 81. A Little Sex 82. Annie (as FDR) 82, Mrs Soffel 84. Compromising Positions 84. The Man with One Red Shoe 85. The Lost Boys 87. Overboard 87. Big Business 88. Sweet Poison 91. Hero (GB: Accidental Hero) 92. Born Yesterday 93. A Foreign Field (TV) 93. My Boyfriend's Back 93. Foreign Student 94, etc.

Hersey, John (1914–1993).
American novelist, most famous for his pamphlet reportage, *Hiroshima*. Two novels were filmed: *A Bell for Adano* and *The War Lover*.

Hershey, Barbara (1948–   ).
American leading actress. From 1974–76 she was known as Barbara Hershey Seagull.
■ With Six You Get Eggroll 68. Heaven with a Gun 69. Last Summer 69. The Baby Maker 70. The Liberation of L.B. Jones 70. The Pursuit of Happiness 71. Boxcar Bertha 72. Dealing: Or the Berkeley-to-Boston Forty-Brick Lost-Bag Blues

72. Angela 73. The Crazy World of Julius Vrooder 74. Diamonds 75. You and Me 75. A Choice of Weapons 76. The Last Hard Man 76. The Stunt Man 80. Americana 81. Take this Job and Shove It 81. The Entity 82. The Right Stuff 83. The Natural 84. Hannah and Her Sisters 86. Hoosiers 86. Shy People 87. Tin Men 87. Beaches 88. The Last Temptation of Christ 88. A World Apart 88. Tune in Tomorrow (aka Aunt Julia and the Scriptwriter) 90. Paris Trout 91. You and Me 91. Defenseless 91. The Public Eye 92. Swing Kids 93. Falling Down 93. A Dangerous Woman 93. Splitting Heirs 93. The Bible: Abraham (TV) 93.
TV series: The Monroes 66–67.

Hershel.
American costume designer who worked for Twentieth Century-Fox (1936–42) and then MGM.
Quo Vadis (AAN) 51. Dream Wife (AAN) 53, etc.

Hershman, Joel (1961–   ).
American director.
Hold Me, Thrill Me, Kiss Me 93.

Hersholt, Jean (1886–1956).
Phlegmatic Danish character actor in Hollywood, in sub-Jannings roles.
Princess Virtue 16. The Four Horsemen of The Apocalypse 21. *Greed* 23. Stella Dallas 25. The Secret Hour 28. Abie's Irish Rose 28. The Rise of Helga 30. Transatlantic 31. *Grand Hotel* 32. The Mask of Fu Manchu 32. Christopher Bean 35. Mark of the Vampire 35, Seventh Heaven 35. The Country Doctor (as Dr Dafoe) 35. Crime of the Century 36. Heidi 37. Alexander's Ragtime Band 38. Meet Doctor Christian (and ensuing series) 38–40. They Meet Again 41. Stage Door Canteen 43. Dancing in the Dark 49. Run for Cover 55, others.

¶ Dr Christian is such a sweet sentimental fellow, I'd hate to be stuck with playing him for the rest of my life. – *J.H.*, 1954
~A much respected industry figure, he was largely responsible for the foundation of the Motion Picture Country Home and Hospital in Calabasas.

Hervey, Irene (1910–   ) (Irene Herwick).
American leading lady of light films in the 40s.
Three on a Honeymoon 34. East Side of Heaven 39. Destry Rides Again 39. Unseen Enemy 42. Half Way to Shanghai 43. My Guy 44. Mr Peabody and the Mermaid 49. Teenage Rebel 56. Going Steady 59. Cactus Flower 69. Play Misty for Me 71, etc.
TV series: Honey West 65.

Herz, Michael (1949–   ).
American director, writer and producer of low-budget exploitation movies, in collaboration with Lloyd Kaufman. He is vice-president of the production and distribution company Troma.
Squeeze Play! (co-d) 80. Waitress! (co-d) 82. The First Turn-On! 84. The Toxic Avenger (co-d) 84. The Toxic Avenger: Part II (co-d) 88. Troma's War (co-d) 88. Sgt Kabukiman N.Y.P.D. (co-d) 94, etc.

Herzog, Werner (1942–   ).
German director and screenwriter.
■ Signs of Life 67. Even Dwarfs Started Small 70. Fata Morgana 71. Land of Silence and Darkness 72. Aguirre Land of Silence and Darkness 72. *Aguirre Wrath of God* 73. The Enigma of Kaspar Hauser 74. Heart of Glass 76. Stroszek 77. Nosferatu 79. Wozzeck 79. *Fitzcarraldo* 82. Ballad of the Little

oldier 84. The Dark Glow of the Mountains 84.
Where the Green Ants Dream 85. Gasherbrum –
er Leuchtende Berg 85. Slave Coast (Cobra
erde) 88. Herdsmen of the Sun 88. Echos aus
inem Düsteren Reich 90. Scream of Stone (Schrei
us Stein) 91. Lessons in Darkness 92.

¶ I'm not out to win prizes – that's for dogs and
  horses. – *W.H.*

Heslop, Charles (1883–1966).
British comic actor, longtime star of stage farces.
   Waltzes from Vienna 33. The Lambeth Walk 39.
Flying Fortress 42. The Late Edwina Black 51.
Follow a Star 59.

Hessler, Gordon (1930–   ).
German-born director in Britain and Hollywood.
   The Last Shot You Hear 64. The Oblong Box (&
p) 69. Scream and Scream Again 70. Cry of the
Banshee (& p) 70. Murders in the Rue Morgue (&
p) 71. Embassy 72. Sinbad's Golden Voyage 73.
Scream Pretty Peggy (TV) 73. Skyway to Death
(TV) 74. A Cry in the Wilderness (TV) 74. The
Strange Possession of Mrs Oliver (TV) 77. The
Secrets of Three Hungry Wives (TV) 78. Wheels
of Terror 87. The Girl on a Swing 88, etc.

Heston, Charlton (1924–   ) (John Charlton
Carter).
Stalwart American leading actor with stage
experience; seemed likely for a time to become
typed in biblical and medieval epics.
   Autobiography: 1978, *An Actor's Life.*
■ Dark City 50. The Greatest Show on Earth 52.
The Savage 52. Ruby Gentry 52. The President's
Lady (as Andrew Jackson) 52. Pony Express 53.
Arrowhead 53. Bad for Each Other 54. The Naked
Jungle 54. The Secret of the Incas 54. The Far
Horizons 55. The Private War of Major Benson 55.
Lucy Gallant 55. *The Ten Commandments* (as Moses)
56. Three Violent People 56. Touch of Evil 58.
The Big Country 58. The Buccaneer 58. The Wreck
of the Mary Deare 59. Ben Hur (AA) 59. El Cid
61. The Pigeon that Took Rome 62. Diamond Head
62. 55 Days at Peking 63. The Greatest Story Ever
Told 65. Major Dundee 65. The Agony and the
Ecstasy (as Michelangelo) 65. *The War Lord* 65.
Khartoum (as General Gordon) 66. Counterpoint
67. *Planet of the Apes* 67. *Will Penny* 68. Number One
69. Beneath the Planet of the Apes 69. Julius
Caesar 70. The Hawaiians 70. The Omega Man
71. Antony and Cleopatra (& d) 71. Skyjacked 72.
Call of the Wild 72. Soylent Green 73. Earthquake
73. The Three Musketeers 73. The Four
Musketeers 74. Airport 75 74. The Last Hard Men
76. Two Minute Warning 76. Midway 76. Gray
Lady Down 77. The Prince and the Pauper 77. The
Awakening 80. The Mountain Men 80. Mother
Lode 82. Chiefs (TV) 83. Call from Space 89.
Treasure Island (TV) 89. Almost an Angel 90. Solar
Crisis (TV) 90. The Little Kidnappers (TV) 90.
Crucifer of Blood (TV) 91. Starfire 92. Tombstone
94. True Lies 94. In the Mouth of Madness 95.
TV series: The Colbys 85–86.

¶ A careful and successful actor, Heston has been
  blessed with the kind of impressive face and
physique that inevitably got him cast as a
succession of epic heroes. This was a mixed blessing
to his career. On the one hand, as he said:
   There's a special excitement in playing a man
   who made a hole in history large enough to be
   remembered centuries after he died.
Commercially, furthermore:
   If you can't make a career out of two de Milles,
   you'll never do it.
On the other hand:

After spending all of last winter in armour it's a
great relief to wear costume that bends.
Heston has continued to explore, without having
to resort to character parts. He knows however
that:
   The minute you feel you have given a faultless
   performance is the time to get out.
And:
   I have played three presidents, three saints and
   two geniuses. If that doesn't create an ego
   problem, nothing does.
Having played Antony (and lost) he still feels:
   The great roles are always Shakespearean.
and has found:
   It's hard living up to Moses.

Heston, Fraser C.
American director, producer and screenwriter, the
son of Charlton Heston.
   Treasure Island (p, wd) 89. The Crucifer of Blood
(d) (TV) 91. Needful Things (d) 93.

Hexum, Jon-Eric (1957–1984).
Handsome American leading man, a former
model. Died after accidentally shooting himself
on the set of his TV series.
   The Making of a Male Model (TV) 83. The Bear
84.
   TV series: Voyagers 82–83. Cover Up 84.

Heydt, Louis Jean (1905–1960).
American character actor, often seen as a man with
something to hide.
   Test Pilot 38. Each Dawn I Die 39. Gone with
the Wind 39. Dive Bomber 41. Our Vines Have
Tender Grapes 45. The Furies 50. The Eternal Sea
55, many others.

Heyer, John (1916–   ).
Australian documentarist, former cameraman;
with the Shell Film Unit 1948–56.
   The Back of Beyond 54. Playing with Water 54.
The Forerunner 57. Tumult Pond 62, etc.

Heyes, Douglas (1923–1993).
American director, from TV.
   Kitten with a Whip 65. Beau Geste 67. The
Highwayman (TV) 87, etc.

Heyman, John (1933–   ).
British agent and producer.
   Privilege 66. Boom! 68. Secret Ceremony 69.
Twinky 70. Bloomfield 71. The Go-Between 71, etc.

Heymann, Werner (1896–1961).
German composer who went to Hollywood.
   Spione 28. Congress Dances 31. Bluebeard's
Eighth Wife 38. Ninotchka 39. One Million BC
39. The Shop Around the Corner 40. That
Uncertain Feeling 41. To Be or Not to Be 42. Hail
the Conquering Hero 44. Knickerbocker Holiday
44. Kiss and Tell 45. Mad Wednesday 47. Tell It
to the Judge 49. Congress Dances (Ger.) 55, etc.

Heyward, Louis M. (Deke) (1920–   ).
American producer, especially associated with
horror films made in Europe for AIP.
   De Sade 69. Wuthering Heights 70. The
Abominable Dr Phibes 71. Murders in the Rue
Morgue 71, etc.

Heywood, Anne (1931–   ) (Violet Pretty).
British leading lady, former beauty contestant.
   Find the Lady 55. Checkpoint 56. Dangerous
Exile 56. The Depraved 57. Violent Playground
58. Floods of Fear 58. Upstairs and Downstairs 59.
A Terrible Beauty 60. Petticoat Pirates 61. Stork Talk
62. Vengeance 62. The Very Edge 62. Ninety

Degrees in the Shade 66. *The Fox* 68. The Chairman
69. The Awful Story of the Nun of Monza (It.) 69.
The Midas Run 69. I Want What I Want 71.
Trader Horn 73. The Nun and the Devil (It.) 73.
Good Luck Miss Wyckoff 79, etc.

Heywood, Pat (1927–   ).
British character actress.
   Romeo and Juliet 68. All the Way Up 69. 10
Rillington Place 71. Who Slew Auntie Roo? 72.
Wish You Were Here 87. Sparrow (Storia di una
Capinera) 93, etc.

Hibbert, Geoffrey (1922–1969).
British actor who played callow youths around
1940 but turned rather quickly into a character
man.
   Love on the Dole 41. The Common Touch 42. Next
of Kin 42. Orders to Kill 58. Crash Drive 59, etc.

Hibbs, Jesse (1906–1985).
American director, mainly of routine 'B' features.
■ The All American 53. Ride Clear of Diablo 54.
Black Horse Canyon 54. Rails into Laramie 54. The
Yellow Mountain 54. To Hell and Back 55. The
Spoilers 55. World in My Corner 56. Walk the
Proud Land 56. Joe Butterfly 57. Ride a Crooked
Trail 58.

Hibler, Winston (1911–1976).
American producer, almost entirely of wild life
material for Disney.

Hickey, William (1928–   ).
American character actor from the stage.
   A Hatful of Rain 57. The Producers 67. The
Boston Strangler 68. Little Big Man 70. A New
Leaf 71. The Sentinel 77. Wise Blood 79. Prizzi's
Honor (AAN) 85. The Name of the Rose 86. Bright
Lights, Big City 88. Da 88. Pink Cadillac 89. Sea of
Love 89. Mob Boss 90. My Blue Heaven 90. Tales
from the Darkside: The Movie 90. The Runestone
92. Tim Burton's The Nightmare before Christmas
(voice) 93, etc.

Hickman, Darryl (1931–   ).
American juvenile actor who was later seen in
heavy roles.
   The Grapes of Wrath 40. Hearts in Springtime
41. Boys' Ranch 45. Dangerous Years 46. Prisoner
of War 53. Tea and Sympathy 54. The Tingler 59.
Network 76. Sharky's Machine 81, etc.
   TV series: The Blue and the Gold 58.

Hickman, Dwayne (1934–   ).
American juvenile, former child actor.
   Captain Eddie 45. The Return of Rusty 46. The
Sun Comes Up 49. Rally Round the Flag Boys 59.
Beach Party 64. Cat Ballou 65. High School U.S.A.
83, many others.
   TV series: The Affairs of Dobie Gillis 59.

Hickman, Howard (1880–1949).
Chubby American supporting actor, often seen as
conventioneer, suburban husband or judge.

Hickok, Wild Bill (1837–1876).
American frontier gunfighter of wild west days,
frequently personified on screen. He was shot in
the back of the head while playing poker. His hand
is said to have consisted of aces and eights.
   Wild Bill Hickok 21: William S. Hart. *The
Plainsman* 36: Gary Cooper. *Badlands of Dakota* 41:
Richard Dix. *Wild Bill Hickok Rides* 41: Bruce Cabot.
Dallas 50: Reed Hadley. *Pony Express* 52: Forrest
Tucker. *Calamity Jane* 53: Howard Keel. *The Raiders*
55: Robert Culp. *The Plainsman* 66: Don Murray.
Little Big Man 70: Jeff Corey.

Guy Madison starred as Hickok in a TV series (51–54).

¶ Tell that longhaired son of a gun that I have no more use for him and his damned show business. – *W.B.H. on quitting Buffalo Bill's Wild West*

Hickox, Anthony.
British director, working in America. He is the son of director Douglas Hickox.
Waxwork 88. Sundown: The Vampire in Retreat 90. Waxwork II: Lost in Time 91. Hellraiser III: Hell on Earth 92. Warlock II: The Armageddon 93. Playback 94, etc.

Hickox, Douglas (1929–1988).
British director.
■ The Giant Behemoth (co-d) 58. Four Hits and a Mister 62. It's All Over Town 64. Just for You 64. Les Bicyclettes de Belsize 69. Entertaining Mr Sloane 70. Sitting Target 72. Theatre of Blood 73. Brannigan 75. Sky Riders 76. Zulu Dawn 79. The Hound of the Baskervilles (TV) 83. Mistral's Daughter (TV) 84. Blackout 85. Sins (TV) 86. I'll Take Manhattan (TV) 87.

Hickox, Sid (1895–1982).
American cinematographer, long with Warners.
The Little Giant 26. The Private Life of Helen of Troy 27. Lilac Time 28. The Gorilla 31. A Bill of Divorcement 32. Frisco Jenny 33. Dames 34. Special Agent 35. San Quentin 37. A Slight Case of Murder 38. Flowing Gold 40. The Big Shot 42. Edge of Darkness 43. To Have and Have Not 44. The Horn Blows at Midnight 45. The Big Sleep 46. Dark Passage 47. White Heat 49. Along the Great Divide 51. Them 54. Battle Cry 55, many others.

Hicks, Catherine (1951–).
American actress.
Marilyn: The Untold Story (as Marilyn Monroe) (TV) 80. Death Valley 81. Better Late than Never 83. Garbo Talks 84. The Razor's Edge 84. Star Trek IV: The Voyage Home 86. Peggy Sue Got Married 86. Laguna Heat (TV) 87. Like Father, Like Son 87. Secret Ingredient 88. Souvenir 88. She's out of Control 89. Spy (TV) 89, etc.
TV series: The Bad News Bears 79–80. Tucker's Witch 82–83.

Hicks, Russell (1895–1957).
American character actor who almost always played executive types. Actor and director from silent days; in hundreds of films.
Laughing Irish Eyes 36. In Old Chicago 38. The Three Musketeers 39. The Big Store 41. His Butler's Sister 43. Bandit of Sherwood Forest 46. Bowery Battalion 51. Seventh Cavalry 56, many others.

Hicks, Sir Seymour (1871–1949).
British stage farceur, also writer and producer. Occasional film appearances.
Autobiographies: 1930, *Between Ourselves*. 1939, *Me and My Missus*.
Always Tell Your Wife 22. Sleeping Partners 26. The Secret of the Loch 34. Vintage Wine 35. *Scrooge* 35. Pastor Hall 39. *Busman's Honeymoon* 40. Silent Dust 48, etc.

Hickson, Joan (1906–).
British character actress, in innumerable films as understanding mum or slightly dotty aunt. At the age of nearly 80, J.H. made a big hit on TV in adaptations of Agatha Christie's Miss Marple stories.
Widow's Might 34. Love from a Stranger 37. I See a Dark Stranger 45. The Guinea Pig 48. Seven

Days to Noon 50. The Card 52. The Man Who Never Was 56. Happy is the Bride 57. The Thirty-Nine Steps 59. Murder She Said 61. A Day in the Death of Joe Egg 70. Theatre of Blood 73. Clockwise 86. Century 93, many others.

Higgins, Colin (1941–1988).
American screenwriter and director. Died of AIDS.
Harold and Maude 71. Silver Streak 77. Foul Play (& d) 78. Nine to Five (& d) 80. The Best Little Whorehouse in Texas (co-w, d) 82.

Higgins, Jack (1929–).
British adventure novelist. Chief film of his work: *The Eagle Has Landed.*

Higgins, Ken (1919–).
British cinematographer.
French Dressing 63. Darling 65. The Virgin Soldiers 69. You Can't Win 'Em All 70.

Highsmith, Patricia (1921–1995).
American detective novelist. Works filmed include *Strangers on a Train, Purple Noon (The Talented Mr Ripley)* and *Enough Rope (The Blunderer).*

Hildyard, Jack (1908–1990).
British cinematographer.
School for Secrets 46. While the Sun Shines 46. Vice Versa 48. The Sound Barrier 52. Hobson's Choice 54. The Deep Blue Sea 55. Summertime 55. *The Bridge on the River Kwai* (AA) 57. The Journey 59. Suddenly Last Summer 59. The Millionairess 60. 55 Days at Peking 62. The VIPs 63. The Yellow Rolls Royce 64. Battle of the Bulge 66. Casino Royale 67. The Long Duel 67. Villa Rides 68. Topaz 70. Puppet on a Chain 71. The Beast Must Die 74. The Message 76. The Wild Geese 78. Lion of the Desert 80, etc.

Hill, Arthur (1922–).
Canadian actor, on British and American stage and screen.
Miss Pilgrim's Progress 49. I Was a Male War Bride 49. Salute the Toff 52. Life with the Lyons 54. The Deep Blue Sea 55. The Ugly American 63. In the Cool of the Day 63. Moment to Moment 65. *Harper* 66. Petulia 68. The Chairman 69. *The Andromeda Strain* 70. The Pursuit of Happiness 70. Futureworld 76. A Bridge Too Far 77. Hagen (TV) 79. Butch and Sundance 79. The Champ 79. A Little Romance 79. Dirty Tricks 81. Making Love 82. The Amateur 82. One Magic Christmas, etc.
TV series: *Owen Marshall Counsellor at Law* 71–73. Hagen 80.

Hill, Benny (1925–1992) (Alfred Hawthorne Hill).
British vaudeville comedian and mimic, star of an occasional TV variety show with the emphasis on smut. An astonishing success on late-night American TV in 1979 and thereafter.
■ Who Done It? 56. Light Up the Sky 59. Those Magnificent Men in Their Flying Machines 65. Chitty Chitty Bang Bang 68. The Italian Job 69. The Best of Benny Hill 74.

Hill, Bernard (1944–).
British actor.
It Could Happen to You 75. A Choice of Weapons 76. Gandhi 82. Runners 83. The Bounty 84. No Surrender 86. Bellman & True 87. Drowning by Numbers 88. Shirley Valentine 89. Mountains of the Moon 90. Double X 92. Olly's Prison (TV) 93. Telltale (TV) 93. Speaking in Tongues (TV) 94. Skallagrigg (TV) 94, etc.
TV series: Once upon a Time in the North 94.

Hill, Debra.
American producer and screenwriter.
Halloween (& w) 78. The Fog (& co-w) 80. Escape from New York 81. Halloween II (& co-w) 81. Halloween III 82. The Dead Zone 83. Head Office 85. Clue 85. Adventures in Babysitting 87. Big Top Pee-Wee 88. Heartbreak Hotel 88. The Fisher King 91, etc.

Hill, George (1888–1934).
American director. Married to screenwriter Frances Marion. Shot himself.
Through the Dark 23. The Midnight Express 24. Zander the Great 25. Tell It to the Marines 26. The Cossacks 28. The Flying Fleet 29. *The Big House* 30. Min and Bill 30. The Secret Six 31. Hell Divers 31. Clear All Wires 33, etc.

Hill, George Roy (1922–).
American director with New York stage background.
■ Period of Adjustment 63. Toys in the Attic 63. *The World of Henry Orient* 64. Hawaii 66. Thoroughly Modern Millie 67. *Butch Cassidy and the Sundance Kid* (AAN) 69. *Slaughterhouse Five* 72. The Sting (AA) 73. The Great Waldo Pepper 75. Slap Shot 77. A Little Romance 79. The World According to Garp 82. The Little Drummer Girl 84. Funny Farm 88.

¶ He is famous in the movie business for never picking up a check. His dress can best be described as nondescript, or perhaps janitorial. A producer who once worked on a project with him told me that George would brag that he bought his clothes at an army surplus store in Santa Monica, where he could get khaki pants for under ten dollars; in our brief contacts I never had any reason to doubt this. – *John Gregory Dunne*

Hill, Howard (1898–1975).
American archer who, besides making sports shorts in the 40s, 'doubled' for Errol Flynn in several films.

Hill, James (1919–1994).
British director, former documentarist.
Journey for Jeremy 47. The Stolen Plans (& w) 52. The Clue of the Missing Ape (& w) 53. *Giuseppina* (& w) (AA) 61. The Kitchen 62. The Dock Brief 62. Every Day's a Holiday 64. A Study in Terror 65. Born Free 66. Captain Nemo and the Underwater City 69. Black Beauty 71. The Belstone Fox 73. Christian the Lion (co-d) 74. The Young Visitors (TV) 84, etc.

Hill, James (1916–).
American producer.
Vera Cruz 54. The Kentuckian 55. Trapeze 56, etc.

Hill, Sinclair (1894–1945).
British director most eminent in the 20s.
The Tidal Wave 20. Don Quixote 23. Indian Love Lyrics 23. Boadicaca 25. Beyond the Veil 25. The Chinese Bungalow 26. The King's Highway 27. A Woman Redeemed 27. *The Guns of Loos* 28. *The Price of Divorce* 28. The First Mrs Fraser 30. The Man from Toronto 33. My Old Dutch 34. Follow Your Star 38, etc.

Hill, Steven (1922–) (Solomon Berg).
American stage actor.
A Lady without Passport 50. The Goddess 58. A Child is Waiting 62. The Slender Thread 67. It's My Turn 80. Yentl 83. Garbo Talks 84. Heartburn 86. Legal Eagles 86. Raw Deal 86. Between Two Women 86. Boost 88. Running on Empty 88.

hite Palace 90. Billy Bathgate 91. The Firm 93, c.

TV series: Mission Impossible 66–67. Law and rder 90– .

ill, Terence (1941–) (Mario Girotti).
alian leading man of spaghetti westerns.
The Leopard 63. Seven Seas to Calais 63. Blood ver 67. Boot Hill 69. They Call Me Trinity 70. an of the East 72. My Name is Nobody 73. Watch ut, We're Mad 74. Mr Billion 77. March or Die 7. Deux Super Flics 78. Super Fuzz 80. Renegade ke 87. Lucky Luke (& d) 91, etc.

ill, Walter (1942–).
merican director, producer and screenwriter of tion films.
Hickey and Boggs 72. The Thief Who Came to inner 72. The Getaway 72. The Mackintosh Man 3. The Drowning Pool 74. Hard Times (& d) 75. he Driver (& d) 78. The Warriors (& d) 78. The ong Riders (& d) 80. Southern Comfort (& co-w) 1. 48 Hours (co-w) 82. Brewster's Millions 84. treets of Fire 85. Crossroads 85. Aliens (p, story) 6. Blue City (p, w) 86. Extreme Prejudice (d) 86. ed Heat (wdp) 88. Johnny Handsome (d) 89. nother 48 Hrs (d) 90. Alien³ (p) 92. Trespass (d) 2. The Getaway (w) 93. Geronimo: An American egend (p, d) 93. Wild Bill (wd) 95.

illbillies
ecame a stereotype of the 30s cinema, and ubsequently made infrequent appearances before the enormous success of the TV series *The Real cCoys* 57–62 and *The Beverly Hillbillies* 62–70. lotable hillbillies through the years include the Kettles, Lum and Abner, the Weaver Brothers nd Elviry; the Ritz Brothers in *Kentucky Moonshine*; Annie in *Annie Get Your Gun*; and the haracters in *Roseanna McCoy, Thunder Road, Li'l bner, Guns in the Afternoon, Feudin' Fussin' and -Fightin', The Moonshine War, I Walk the Line,* and *oming Round the Mountain;* while the denizens of *obacco Road,* geographically not hillbillies, plendidly personified the image. Cartoon-wise, lmer Fudd in the Bugs Bunny series is an old-ashioned hillbilly, and Disney produced a twenty-minute version of *The Martins and the McCoys,* ollowed in 1975 by a TV movie, *The Hatfields and he McCoys.* In 1980 *Coal Miner's Daughter* brought o general notice the rags-to-riches story of singer Loretta Lynn, and in 1983 Cheryl Ladd plumbed a similar milieu in a TV movie, *Kentucky Woman.*

Hillcoat, John (1961–).
Australian director, also making rock videos.
Ghosts . . . of the Civil Dead 89.

Hiller, Arthur (1923–).
Canadian-American director, from TV.
■ Massacre at Sand Creek (TV) 56. Homeward Borne (TV) 57. The Careless Years 57. Miracle of the White Stallions 63. The Wheeler Dealers 63. The Americanization of Emily 64. Promise Her Anything 66. Penelope 66. Tobruk 67. The Tiger Makes Out 67. Popi 69. The Out-of-Towners 70. Love Story (AAN) 70. Plaza Suite 71. The Hospital 71. Man of La Mancha 72. The Crazy World of Julius Vrooder 74. The Man in the Glass Booth 75. W. C. Fields and Me 76. Silver Streak 76. Nightwing 79. The In-Laws 79. Making Love 82. Author! Author! 82. Romantic Comedy 83. The Lonely Guy 84. Teachers 84. Outrageous Fortune 87. See No Evil, Hear No Evil 89. Taking Care of Business (aka Filofax) 90. Married to It 91. The Babe 92.

Hiller, Wendy (1912–).
Distinguished British stage actress with inimitable voice and clarity of diction; her films have been fewer than one would like.
■ Lancashire Luck 37. Pygmalion (AAN) 38. *Major Barbara* 40. *I Know Where I'm Going* 45. An Outcast of the Islands 51. Single Handed 52. Something of Value 57. How to Murder a Rich Uncle 57. *Separate Tables* (AA) 58. Sons and Lovers 60. Toys in the Attic 63. *A Man for All Seasons* (AAN) 66. David Copperfield 69. Murder on the Orient Express 74. Voyage of the Damned 76. The Cat and the Canary 77. The Elephant Man 80. The Curse of King Tut's Tomb (TV) 80. Making Love 82. The Death of the Heart 86. The Lonely Passion of Judith Hearne 87.

Famous line (*Pygmalion*): 'Walk? Not bloody likely. I'm going to take a taxi.'

Famous line (*Pygmalion*): 'I washed me face and hands before I came, I did.'

Hillerman, John (1932–).
Dapper American actor, mainly of comedy roles.
Paper Moon 73. At Long Last Love 76. The Day of the Locust 76. Lucky Lady 77. Sunburn 79. History of the World Part One 81, etc.
TV series: The Betty White Show 77. Magnum 80–88.

Hilliard, Harriet (1914–) (Peggy Lou Snyder).
American leading lady of 30s romantic comedies and musicals. Married Ozzie Nelson and for 14 years from 1952 appeared with him in their weekly TV show *Ozzie and Harriet;* they also appeared with their family in the film *Here Come the Nelsons* 51.
Follow the Fleet 36. *She's My Everything* 38. *Sweetheart of the Campus* 41. *Canal Zone* 42. *Smash-up on Interstate Five* (TV) 76, etc.
TV series: *Ozzie's Girls* 73.

Hillier, Erwin (1911–).
British cinematographer.
The Lady from Lisbon 41. The Silver Fleet 43. Great Day 45. *I Know Where I'm Going* 45. London Town 47. *The October Man* 48. Mr Perrin and Mr Traill 49. Where's Charley? 52. *The Dam Busters* 55. Shake Hands with the Devil 59. A Matter of Who 62. Sammy Going South 63. Operation Crossbow 65. Sands of the Kalahari 65. Eye of the Devil 66. The Quiller Memorandum 66. The Shoes of the Fisherman 68, etc.

Hills, David:
see *D'Amato, Joe.*

Hillyer, Lambert (1889–).
American director of westerns which declined in stature after his days of writing and directing for William S. Hart.
The Toll Gate 20. *Travellin' On* 22. White Oak 23. *The Spoilers* 23. The Branded Sombrero 28. Beau Bandit 30. Master of Men 33. *Dracula's Daughter* 36. The Invisible Ray 37. Batman (serial) 41. Blue Clay 42. The Case of the Baby Sitter 47. Sunset Pass 49, many others.

Hilton, James (1900–1954).
British novelist whose work was turned by himself and others into several highly successful films. Also worked as scenarist on other films, including *Mrs Miniver* (AA) 42.
Knight without Armour 37. *Lost Horizon* 37. *Goodbye Mr Chips* 39, 69. We Are Not Alone 39. *Random Harvest* 42. The Story of Dr Wassell 43. So Well Remembered 47, etc.

¶ Tempted by Hollywood, a writer must decide whether he would rather say a little less exactly what he wants, to millions, or a little more exactly, to thousands. – J.H.

Himes, Chester (1909–1984).
Tough American thriller writer, a former convict, whose Harlem detectives Grave Digger Jones and Coffin Ed Johnson have featured in three films based on his novels.
Autobiographies: 1972, *The Quality of Hurt.* 1976, *My Life of Absurdity.*
Cotton Comes to Harlem 70. Come Back, Charleston Blue 72. A Rage in Harlem 91.

Hindle, Art (1948–).
Canadian leading man.
Black Christmas 75. A Small Town in Texas 76. Invasion of the Body Snatchers 78. The Clone Master (TV) 78. The Power Within (TV) 79. The Brood 79. Desperate Lives 82. The Man Who Wasn't There 83. The Surrogate 84. The Gunfighters (TV) 87. Into the Fire 87. Dixie Lanes 88, etc.

Hinds, Anthony (1922–).
British producer, in films since 1946, latterly associated with Hammer's horror films. Also writes screenplays under the name 'John Elder'.

Hinds, Samuel S. (1875–1948).
Dignified American character actor, formerly a lawyer for thirty-five years; specialized in kindly fathers and crooked lawyers.
Gabriel over the White House 33. She 35. Trail of the Lonesome Pine 36. Test Pilot 38. *You Can't Take It with You* 38. *Destry Rides Again* 39. The Strange Case of Doctor RX 41. The Spoilers 42. A Chip off the Old Block 44. The Boy with Green Hair 48, many others.

Hines, Gregory (1946–).
American actor/dancer.
Wolfen 81. The Cotton Club 84. White Nights 85. Running Scared 86. Off Limits 88. Tap 89. Eve of Destruction 90. A Rage in Harlem 91. Renaissance Man 94. White Man's Burden (d) 94, etc.

Hines, Johnny (1895–1970).
American star comedian of the 20s; roles declined as sound came in.
Little Johnny Jones 23. The Speed Spook 24. The Crackerjack 25. The Brown Derby 26. Home Made 27. The Runaround 31. Whistling in the Dark 32. Her Bodyguard 33. Society Doctor 35. Too Hot to Handle 38, etc.

Hingle, Pat (1923–).
Burly American character actor with stage and TV experience.
On the Waterfront 54. The Strange One 57. No Down Payment 57. Splendor in the Grass 61. The Ugly American 63. Invitation to a Gunfighter 64. Nevada Smith 66. Hang 'Em High 68. Bloody Mama 69. Norwood 69. W.U.S.A. 70. The Carey Treatment 72. One Little Indian 73. Running Wild 73. The Gauntlet 77. Norma Rae 79. Sudden Impact 83. Brewster's Millions 84. Maximum Overdrive 86. The Land Before Time (voice) 88. The Grifters 90. Not of This World 91. Batman Returns 92. Lightning Jack 94, etc.
TV series: Stone 80. Blue Skies 88.

Hird, Dame Thora (1913–).
British north-country character comedienne, mother of Janette Scott; often plays acidulous landladies, etc.
Autobiography: 1976, *Seen and Hird.*

The Black Sheep of Whitehall 41. Corridor of Mirrors 46. The Blind Goddess 48. Conspirator 50. The Long Memory 53. Simon and Laura 55. The Entertainer 60. *A Kind of Loving* 62. Rattle of a Simple Man 64. The Nightcomers 71. Memento Mori (TV) 92. The Wedding Gift (TV) 94, many others.

TV series: Meet the Wife. First Lady. Flesh and Blood. In Loving Memory. Hallelujah. Thora on the Straight and Narrow, etc.

Hirsch, Judd (1935–).
American character actor who nearly became a star.

The Law (TV) 74. Fear on Trial (TV) 75. The Legend of Valentino (TV) 75. The Keegans (TV) 78. King of the Gypsies 78. Sooner or Later (TV) 79. Ordinary People (AAN) 80. Without a Trace 83. Teachers 84. Running on Empty 88, etc.

TV series: Delvecchio 76–77. Taxi 82–83. Detective in the House 85. Dear John 88–92.

Hirsch, Paul.
American editor.

Phantom of the Paradise 74. Star Wars (AA) 77. Carrie 76. The Empire Strikes Back 80. Creepshow 82. Footloose 84. Ferris Bueller's Day Off 86. Planes, Trains and Automobiles 87. Steel Magnolias 89. Coup de Ville 90. Dutch (GB: Driving Me Crazy) 91. Raising Cain 92, etc.

Hirsch, Robert (1926–).
French character actor of the Comédie Française.

No Questions on Saturday 64. Kiss Me General 66, etc.

Hirschfeld, Gerald (1921–).
American cinematographer.

Goodbye Columbus 69. Last Summer 69. Diary of a Mad Housewife 71. Doc 71. Summer Wishes Winter Dreams 73. *Young Frankenstein* 74. The Car 77. The World's Greatest Lover 77. Americathon 79. The Bell Jar 79. Sunday Lovers 80. Neighbors 81. My Favorite Year 82. To Be or Not to Be 83. The House of God 84. Head Office 85. Malone 87. The Neon Empire 87. Child in the Night (TV) 90, etc.

Hiscott, Leslie (1894–1968).
British director, in films from 1919.

The Passing of Mr Quinn 28. Black Coffee 32. While London Sleeps 33. The Triumph of Sherlock Holmes 35. She Shall Have Music 35. Tilly of Bloomsbury 40. The Seventh Survivor 41. Welcome Mr Washington 44. The Time of His Life 52. Tons of Trouble 56, etc.

histories of the cinema
have generally been unrewarding. Shortest and best may be Arthur Knight's *The Liveliest Art* (1957 but later revised). In 1938 Bardeche and Brasillach wrote *The History of Motion Pictures* in French, but it didn't translate easily. Paul Rotha's *The Film Till Now* (first published in 1930 but revised in 1967 with a later section by Richard Griffith) is heavy with thought and strongest on documentary and the European schools. The American cinema is dealt with in Lewis Jacobs' *The Rise of the American Film* (1939/68) and the silent years were well covered, mainly from a business viewpoint, in *A Million and One Nights* (1926) by Terry Ramsaye. A more light-hearted account is Ezra Goodman's *The Fifty Year Decline and Fall of Hollywood* (1961). The centenary of the cinema, celebrated during 1994, 1995 and 1996 depending on your choice of dates for the beginning, brought more histories. The best is Robert Sklar's concise and comprehensive *Film: An International History of the*

Medium (1993). David Shipman's well-illustrated *Cinema: The First Hundred Years* (1993) supplemented his earlier two-volume *The Story of Cinema* (1982). Two useful guides are Louis Giannetti and Scotty Eyman's *Flashback: A Brief History of Film* (1986) and Gerald Mast's *A Short History of the Movies* (3rd edition, 1981). David Robinson's *World Cinema 1895–1980* provides a crisp international perspective, as does Basil Wright's *The Long View, An International History of Cinema* (1974). Peter Cowie in 1971 produced a two-volume anthology called *A Concise History of the Cinema*. Silent cinema has not been specially well documented, though Kevin Brownlow's *The Parade's Gone By* (1968) is a brilliant collection of interviews with its survivors, and *The Real Tinsel* (1970) by Bernard Rosenberg and Harry Silverstein does almost as good a job.

Of picture histories, the grand-daddy is Paul Rotha's *Movie Parade*, first published in 1936 and revised in 1950 with the help of Roger Manvell. Ernest Lindgren's *A Picture History of the Cinema* (1960) is excellent if somewhat highbrow. Daniel Blum's *A Pictorial History of the Silent Screen* and *A Pictorial History of the Talkies*, both much reprinted, are useful reminders but contain no comment. Idiosyncratic but certainly liveliest is *The Movies* by Arthur Mayer and Richard Griffith, which has never been out of print since it first appeared in 1957.

The History of the British Film
is the title of a multi-volume work of detailed research undertaken in the 40s by Rachael Low. Seven volumes have been published, bringing the story up to the 30s. Meanwhile Denis Gifford did a valiant job with his *The British Film Catalogue*, which currently covers 1895–1985. George Perry and Roy Armes have both produced concise histories, while Charles Oakley's *Where We Came In* is more on the business side.

Hitchcock, Sir Alfred (1899–1980).
British director, in Hollywood more or less since 1940. His name, his profile, and his lugubrious voice are a trademark around the world for suspense thrillers with a touch of impudence, using techniques which are purely cinematic; though of course he frequently fell below his own high standards. Of innumerable books written about him, the most detailed and typical is probably *Le Cinema Selon Hitchcock* by François Truffaut (1966, translated into English). Others include *Hitch* by John Russell Taylor (the 'official' biography); *Alfred Hitchcock* by George Perry; a Freudian analysis, *The Secret Life of Alfred Hitchcock* by Donald Spoto; and *Alfred Hitchcock – The Hollywood Years* by Joel Finler.

■ The Pleasure Garden 25. The Mountain Eagle 25. *The Lodger* 26. Downhill 27. Easy Virtue 27. *The Ring* 27. The Farmer's Wife 28. Champagne 28. The Manxman 29. *Blackmail* 29. Elstree Calling (sketches) 30. Juno and the Paycock 30. Murder 30. The Skin Game 31. Rich and Strange 31. *Number Seventeen* 32. Waltzes from Vienna 33. *The Man Who Knew Too Much* 34. *The Thirty-Nine Steps* 35. Secret Agent 36. Sabotage 37. Young and Innocent 37. *The Lady Vanishes* 38. Jamaica Inn 39. *Rebecca* (AAN) 40. *Foreign Correspondent* 40. Mr and Mrs Smith 41. Suspicion 41. Saboteur 42. *Shadow of a Doubt* 43. Lifeboat (AAN) 43. *Spellbound* (AAN) 45. *Notorious* 46. The Paradine Case 47. Rope 48. Under Capricorn 49. Stage Fright 50. *Strangers on a Train* 51. I Confess 53. Dial M For Murder 54. *Rear Window* (AAN) 54. To Catch a Thief 55. *The Trouble with Harry* 55. The Man Who Knew Too Much 56. The Wrong Man 57. Vertigo 58. *North by Northwest* 59. Psycho (AAN) 60. The Birds 63.

Marnie 64. Torn Curtain 66. Topaz 69. Frenzy 72. Family Plot 76.

TV series: *Alfred Hitchcock Presents* 55–61.
✪ For his understanding of the craft of the cinema; and for his virtuosity in expressing it. *Foreign Correspondent.*

¶ Hitch did not even have to build up his own legend: eager critics like Truffaut did it for him. The suspense master did, however, oblige the press with a variety of *bon mots* about himself and his work. Personally I like best his story of how he caused consternation in a crowded elevator by muttering very audibly to a friend:
 I didn't think the old man would bleed so much.
His little epigrams include:
 Drama is life with the dull bits left out.
and:
 Always make the audience suffer as much as possible.
and:
 There is no terror in a bang, only in the anticipation of it.
and:
 Terror is a matter of surprise; suspense, of forewarning.
and
 I've become a body of films, not a man. I *am* all those films.
and:
 A good film is when the price of the admission, the dinner and the babysitter was well worth it.
and:
 The cinema is not a slice of life, it's a piece of cake.
and:
 Sometimes you find that a film is liked only for its content, without any regard to the style or the manner in which the story is told. But that, after all, is the art of the cinema.
And his defence if the tricks don't work:
 All things considered, I think I'm doing well if I get the sixty per cent of my original conception on the screen.
He despised long dialogue sequences:
 A film-maker isn't supposed to say things. He's supposed to show them.
He despised actors too. One of his most widely publicized remarks was:
 Actors are cattle.
His current star, Carole Lombard, promptly led a troop of oxen onto the shooting stage and herself headed for home. Hitch thought it discreet to tell the press:
 I didn't say actors are cattle. What I said was, actors should be *treated* like cattle.
He clearly knew himself to be typecast as a mystery man:
 If I made *Cinderella*, the audience would be looking out for a body in the coach.
Perhaps his most quoted admission is:
 That was the ending I wanted for *Blackmail*, but I had to change it for commercial reasons.
Many tributes have been paid to him, but John Frankheimer's is all-embracing:
 Any American director who says he hasn't been influenced by him is out of his mind.
Cary Grant was happy with Hitch:
 He couldn't have been a nicer fellow. I whistled coming to work on his films.
Andrew Sarris saw Hitch's problem:
 His reputation has suffered from the fact that he has given audiences more pleasure than is permissible in serious cinema.
Doggedly into his 70s he continued to invent mayhem:
 When people say I'm 70 I say that's a confounded lie. I'm twice 35, that's all. Twice 35.

He had little reason for complaint:
Even my failures make money and become
classics a year after I make them.

And he continued to be a realist:
The length of the film should be directly related
to the endurance of the human bladder.

~In 1944 Hitch also directed two war
documentaries for the Ministry of Information: *Bon
Voyage* and *Aventure Malagache*.

Hitler, Adolf (1889–1945) (Adolf Schickelgruber).
German fascist dictator, subject of many screen
documentaries, notably *Mein Kampf* 63 and *The
Life of Adolf Hitler* 65. Actors who have
impersonated him include Chaplin in *The Great
Dictator* 40; Luther Adler in *The Magic Face* 51 and
The Desert Fox 52; Tom Dugan in *To Be or Not To Be*
42 and *Star Spangled Rhythm* 42; Ludwig Donath
in *The Strange Death of Adolf Hitler* 43; Albin Skoda
in *The Last Act* 55; Kenneth Griffith in *The Two-
Headed Spy* 58; Richard Baschart in *Hitler* 61; Billy
Frick in *Is Paris Burning?* 65; Sidney Miller in *Which
Way to the Front?* 69; Alec Guinness in *Hitler: The
Last Ten Days* 73. Most frequent Hitler-player,
however, is Robert Watson, who in the 40s seemed
to do little else; apart from an excellent serious
portrayal in *The Hitler Gang* 44, he supplied Hitler
walk-ons in *The Devil with Hitler* 42, *That Nazty
Nuisance* 43, *Hitler Dead or Alive* 43, *The Miracle of
Morgan's Creek* 44, *The Story of Mankind* 57, and
many others.

In the 80s television began to show renewed
interest in fanciful presentations of Hitler. Anthony
Hopkins played him in *The Bunker*; Derek Jacobi
in *Inside the Third Reich*; and Gunther Meisner in
The Winds of War.

¶ A psychopath who somehow found his way
from a padded cell to Potsdam. – *Malcolm
Muggeridge*

Hively, Jack (c. 1907–).
American director.
■ They Made Her a Spy 39. Panama Lady 39. The
Spellbinder 39. Three Sons 39. Two Thoroughbreds
39. The Saint's Double Trouble 40. The Saint Takes
Over 40. Anne of Windy Poplars 40. Laddie 40. The
Saint in Palm Springs 41. They Met in Argentina
41. Father Takes a Wife 41. Four Jacks and a Jill
41. Street of Chance 42. Are You With It? 48.
Starbird and Sweet William 76. The Adventures
of Huckleberry Finn (TV) 81. California Gold Rush
(TV) 81.

Hobart, Rose (1906–) (Rose Keefer).
American actress, usually in character roles.
Liliom 30. Dr Jekyll and Mr Hyde 32. Tower of
London 39. Nothing but the Truth 41. Ziegfeld Girl
41. The Soul of a Monster 44. The Farmer's
Daughter 46. Mickey 48, etc.

Hobbes, Halliwell (1877–1962).
British character actor, long the impeccable butler,
on stage from 1898, films from 1929 (after which
he lived in Hollywood).
Charley's Aunt 30. Dr Jekyll and Mr Hyde 32. *The
Masquerader* 33. Bulldog Drummond Strikes Back
35. Dracula's Daughter 36. *You Can't Take It with
You* 38. Lady Hamilton 41. *Sherlock Holmes Faces
Death* 43. If Winter Comes 47. That Forsyte
Woman 49. Miracle in the Rain 56, many others.

Hobbs, Jack (1893–1968).
British actor on screen from silent days, usually in
genial roles.
The Sin Game 30. Trouble in Store 34. No Limit
35. Millions 37. *It's in the Air* 38. Behind These
Walls 48. *Worm's Eye View* 51, etc.

Hobson, Valerie (1917–).
British leading lady with 'upper-class' personality.
■ Eyes of Fate 33. Two Hearts in Waltztime 34.
The Path of Glory 34. Badger's Green 34. Strange
Wives (US) 34. Rendezvous at Midnight (US) 35.
Werewolf of London (US) 35. Bride of Frankenstein
(US) (arguably in title role) 35. The Mystery of
Edwin Drood (US) 35. Chinatown Squad (US) 35.
The Great Impersonation (US) 35. Oh What a
Night 35. August Weekend (US) 36. Tugboat
Princess (US) 36. The Secret of Stamboul 36. No
Escape 36. Jump for Glory 37. The Drum 38. Q
Planes 39. *This Man is News* 38. This Man in Paris
39. *The Spy in Black* 39. The Silent Battle 39.
Contraband 40. Atlantic Ferry 41. Unpublished
Story 42. The Adventures of Tartu 43. The Years
Between 46. *Great Expectations* 46. Blanche Fury
47. The Small Voice 48. *Kind Hearts and Coronets* 49.
Train of Events 49. The Interrupted Journey 49.
The Rocking Horse Winner 49. *The Card* 51. Who
Goes There 52. Meet Me Tonight 52. The Voice of
Merrill 53. Background 53. Knave of Hearts 54.

Hoch, Winton C. (1905–1979).
American cinematographer, former research
physicist.
Dr Cyclops 40. Captains of the Clouds 42. So
Dear to My Heart 48. Joan of Arc (co-ph) (AA)
48. *She Wore a Yellow Ribbon* (AA) 49. Tulsa 49.
Halls of Montezuma 51. *The Quiet Man* (co-ph) (AA)
52. Mr Roberts 55. *The Searchers* 56. Darby O'Gill
and the Little People 59. The Lost World 60. Five
Weeks in a Balloon 62. *Robinson Crusoe on Mars* 64.
The Green Berets 68, etc.

Hodge, Patricia (1946–).
British actress, mainly on TV (*Jemima Shaw
Investigates*, etc).
Betrayal 83. The Death of the Heart 86. Sunset
88, etc.

Hodges, Ken (1922–).
British cinematographer.
Faces in the Dark 60. The Comedy Man 63. The
Jokers 67. Negatives 68. Every Home Should
Have One 70. A Day in the Death of Joe Egg 70.
The Ruling Class 72. Bedevilled 73. Flash Gordon
80, etc.

Hodges, Mike (1932–).
British director, from TV.
■ Suspect (TV) 69. Rumour (TV) 70. *Get Carter* 71.
Pulp 72. The Terminal Man (US) (& p) 73. Flash
Gordon 79. Morons from Outer Space 84. A Prayer
for the Dying 87. Black Rainbow 89.

Hodiak, John (1914–1955).
Serious-looking American leading man of the 40s,
of Ukrainian descent.
■ A Stranger in Town 43. I Dood It 43. Song of
Russia 43. Swing Shift Maisie 43. *Lifeboat* 44.
Marriage is a Private Affair 44. Maisie Goes to Reno
44. Sunday Dinner for a Soldier 44. You Can't Do
That to Me 44. *A Bell for Adano* 45. Ziegfeld Follies
46. The Harvey Girls 46. Somewhere in the Night
46. Two Smart People 46. The Arnelo Affair 47.
Love from a Stranger 47. Desert Fury 47.
Homecoming 48. Command Decision 48. Ambush
49. The Bribe 49. A Lady Without Passport 50.
Battleground 50. The Miniver Story 50. Night into
Morning 51. The People Against O'Hara 51.
Across the Wide Missouri 51. Battle Zone 52. The
Sellout 52. Conquest of Cochise 53. Ambush at
Tomahawk Gap 53. Mission over Korea 53.
Dragonfly Squadron 54. Trial 55. On the
Threshold of Space 56.

Hoellering, George (c. 1899–1980).
producer of *Hortobagy*, long in Britain as specialized
distributor and exhibitor; also producer of *Murder
in the Cathedral* 51.

Hoey, Dennis (1893–1960) (Samuel David Hyams).
British character actor, mostly in Hollywood; a
memorably obtuse Lestrade to Basil Rathbone's
Sherlock Holmes.
Tell England 30. The Good Companions 32. Chu
Chin Chow 34. The Wandering Jew 34.
Brewster's Millions 35. Maria Marten 36. This
Above All 42. Sherlock Holmes and the Secret
Weapon 42. Spider Woman 44. Pearl of Death 44.
House of Fear 45. Kitty 46. Where There's Life 47.
If Winter Comes 47. Wake of the Red Witch 48.
David and Bathsheba 51, many others.

Hoffe, Monckton (1880–1951) (Reaney Monckton
Hoffe-Miles).
Irish playwright and screenwriter, a former actor,
in England from the early 1900s. He went to
Hollywood to write for MGM in the mid-30s,
returning to Britain on the outbreak of the
Second World War to work in propaganda.
The Faithful Heart (oa) 22 and 32. Man without
Desire (idea) 23. The Hate Ship (co-w) 29. Under
the Greenwood Tree (co-w) 29. High Seas (story)
30. The Flame of Love (co-w) 30. Many Waters (w,
oa) 31. Michael and Mary (co-w) 31. Bitter Sweet
(co-w) 33. Little Damozel (oa) 33. The Queen's
Affair (aka The Runaway Queen) (co-w) 34. The
Mystery of Mr X (co-w) (US) 34. What Every
Woman Knows (co-w) (US) 34. London Melody
(w) 37. The Last of Mrs Cheyney (co-w) (US) 37.
The Emperor's Candlesticks (co-w) (US) 37.
Pagliacci (co-w) 36. Busman's Honeymoon (aka
Haunted Honeymoon) 40. The Lady Eve (story,
AAN) (US) 41. Daybreak (oa) 48, etc.

Hoffenstein, Samuel (1890–1947).
Lithuanian-American screenwriter, always in
collaboration.
An American Tragedy 31. *Dr Jekyll and Mr Hyde*
31. *Love Me Tonight* 32. Song of Songs 33. Marie
Galante 34. Desire 36. Conquest 38. The Great
Waltz 39. Lydia 41. Flesh and Fantasy (AAN) 43.
Phantom of the Opera 43. Laura 44. Cluny Brown
46. Give My Regards to Broadway 48.

Hoffman, Basil (1941–).
American character actor.
Lady Liberty 72. At Long Last Love 75. All the
President's Men 76. Close Encounters of the Third
Kind 77. The Electric Horseman 79. Ordinary
People 80. My Favorite Year 82. Lambada 89, etc.

Hoffman, Dustin (1937–).
Diffident American leading actor who suited the
mood of the late 60s and made a big comeback
in the early 80s.
■ Madigan's Millions 66. The Tiger Makes Out 67.
The Graduate (AAN) 67. *Midnight Cowboy* (AAN)
69. John and Mary 69. Little Big Man 70. Who is
Harry Kellerman . . . ? 71. Alfredo Alfredo 72.
Straw Dogs 72. Papillon 73. Lenny (AAN) 74. *All
the President's Men* 76. Marathon Man 76. Straight
Time 78. Agatha 79. *Kramer vs Kramer* (AA) 80.
Tootsie (AAN) 83. Death of a Salesman 85. Private
Conversations 85. Ishtar 87. Rain Man (AA) 88.
Family Business 89. Dick Tracy 90. Billy Bathgate
91. Hook 91. Hero 92. Outbreak 95.

¶ A good review from a critic is just another stay
of execution. – *D.H.*
I don't like the fact that I have to get older so
fast, but I like the fact that I'm ageing so well. – *D.H.*

Famous line (*The Graduate*): 'Mrs Robinson, if you don't mind my saying so, this conversation is getting a little strange.'

Hoffmann, Kurt (1912–).
German director, mainly of comedies.
   Quax der Bruch pilot 41. I Think Often of Piroschka 55. The Confessions of Felix Krull 57. Wir Wunderkinder 58, etc.

Hofschneider, Marco.
Young German actor.
   Europa Europa 91. Foreign Student 94, etc.

Hogan, James P. (1891–1943).
American director.
   Last Train from Madrid 37. Ebb Tide 38. The Texans 39. Power Dive 41. The Mad Ghoul 43. The Strange Death of Adolf Hitler 44, etc.

Hogan, Paul (1939–).
Australian comedian and screenwriter whose second film made him an international star. A former construction worker and Australian TV star, he married actress Linda Kozlowski in 1990.
   Anzacs 85. Crocodile Dundee (AAN) 86. Crocodile Dundee II 88. The Humpty Dumpty Man 89. Almost an Angel 90. Lightning Jack (& p, w) 94, etc.

Hogan, Paul J.
Australian director. He is married to producer and director Jocelyn Moorhouse.
   Muriel's Wedding 94.

Hogan, Terry 'Hulk' (1953–).
Beefy American wrestler turned actor, attempting to widen his range from tough-guy roles to comedies.
   No Holds Barred 89. Gremlins 2: The New Batch 90. Suburban Commando 91. Mr Nanny 93, etc.

¶ I'd like to be the John Wayne of the 90s. – *T.H.*

Hohl, Arthur (1889–1964).
Staring-eyed American character actor who often played rustic types.
   The Cheat 31. Island of Lost Souls 32. Man's Castle 33. Cleopatra 34. Show Boat 36. The Road Back 37. Kidnapped 38. Blackmail 39. Moontide 42. The Scarlet Claw 44. The Yearling 46. The Vigilantes Return 47, many others.

hokum.
A word allegedly derived from an Indian word for a stodgy food, it came to mean pure entertainment of a routine kind, usually involving fast action. From it came the adjective 'hokey'. It was not always applied in the pejorative sense: many of most people's favourite films are basically hokum, in that they do not advance the art, but they may show it at its professional best.

¶ Who invented hokum? Think how much money he'd have made from the film producers if he'd sold his invention on a royalty basis. – *Robert Sherwood*

Holbrook, Hal (1925–).
American general-purpose stage and TV actor, also Mark Twain impersonator.
   The Group 66. Wild in the Streets 68. A Clear and Present Danger (TV) 69. The People Next Door 70. Suddenly Single (TV) 71. *That Certain Summer* (TV) 72. Magnum Force 73. All the President's Men 76. Midway 76. Julia 77. Murder by Natural Causes (TV) 79. Natural Enemies 79. Capricorn One 79. The Legend of the Golden Gun (TV) 79. Fog

80. The Killing of the President 80. Creepshow 82. The Star Chamber 82. Behind Enemy Lines 85. Wall Street 87. Fletch Lives 89. Bonds of Love (TV) 93. The Firm 93, etc.
   TV series: *The Bold Ones* 70–71.

Holcomb, Rod.
American director, mainly for TV films.
   The Red Light Sting 84. Stark 85. Chase 85. Blind Justice 86. China Beach 88. Royce 94, etc.

Holden, Fay (1894–1973) (Fay Hammerton).
British stage actress who went to Hollywood in the 30s and found a niche as the mother of the Hardy family. Once known as Dorothy Clyde.
   Wives Never Know 36. Exclusive 37. Judge Hardy's Children 38. Sweethearts 38. The Hardys Ride High 39. Bitter Sweet 40. Andy Hardy's Private Secretary 41. Ziegfeld Girl 41. Blossoms in the Dust 41. Andy Hardy's Double Life 43. Andy Hardy's Blonde Trouble 44. Canyon Passage 46. Love Laughs at Andy Hardy 46. Samson and Delilah 49. The Big Hangover 50. Andy Hardy Comes Home 58, many others.

Holden, Gloria (1908–1991).
London-born leading lady, long in Hollywood.
   Dracula's Daughter (title role) 36. The Life of Émile Zola 37. Test Pilot 38. A Child Is Born 40. The Corsican Brothers 41. Behind the Rising Sun 43. The Hucksters 47. Dream Wife 53. The Eddy Duchin Story 57. This Happy Feeling 68, etc.

Holden, Joyce (1930–) (Jo Ann Heckert).
Blonde leading American actress and dancer, a former beauty queen. She worked first in Universal's pictures before moving to low-budget movies and retiring in the late 50s.
   The Milkman 50. Iron Man 51. You Never Can Tell 51. Bronco Buster 52. Girls in the Night 53. The Werewolf 56. Terror from the Year 5000 58, etc.

Holden, William (1872–1932).
American general-purpose actor of the late silent period, usually in small roles; no relation to the later William Holden.
   The First Kiss 28. Dynamite 30, etc.

Holden, William (1918–1981) (William Beedle).
Good-looking American leading man who hit his greatest popularity in the 50s.
■ *Golden Boy* 39. Invisible Stripes 40. Our Town 40. Those were the Days 40. Arizona 40. I Wanted Wings 41. Texas 41. The Fleet's In 42. The Remarkable Andrew 42. Meet the Stewarts 42. Young and Willing 43. Blaze of Noon 47. Dear Ruth 47. Variety Girl 47. *Rachel and the Stranger* 48. Apartment for Peggy 48. The Man from Colorado 48. The Dark Past 49. The Streets of Laredo 49. Miss Grant Takes Richmond 49. Dear Wife 49. Father is a Bachelor 50. *Sunset Boulevard* (AAN) 50. Union Station 50. *Born Yesterday* 50. Force of Arms 51. Submarine Command 51. Boots Malone 52. The Turning Point 52. *Stalag 17* (AA) 53. The Moon is Blue 53. Forever Female 53. Escape from Fort Bravo 53. Executive Suite 54. Sabrina 54. The Country Girl 54. The Bridges at Toko-Ri 54. *Love is a Many-Splendored Thing* 55. *Picnic* 55. The Proud and Profane 56. Toward the Unknown 56. *The Bridge on the River Kwai* 57. The Key 58. The Horse Soldiers 59. The World of Suzie Wong 60. Satan Never Sleeps 62. The Counterfeit Traitor 62. The Lion 62. Paris When it Sizzles 64. The Seventh Dawn 64. Alvarez Kelly 66. Casino Royale 67. The Devil's Brigade 68. The Christmas Tree 69. *The Wild Bunch* 69. Wild Rovers 71. The Revengers 72. The Blue Knight (TV) 72. Breezy 73. Open Season 74.

The Towering Inferno 74. *Network* (AAN) 76. 21 Hours at Munich (TV) 77. Ashanti 78. Damien: Omen II 78. Fedora 78. Escape to Athena 79. The Earthling 80. When Time Ran Out 80. S.O.B. 81.

¶ I'm a whore, all actors are whores. We sell ou² bodies to the highest bidder. – *W.H.*
   Take any picture you can. One out of four will be good, one out of ten will be very good, and one out of fifteen will get you an Academy Award – *W.H.*
   When you look at him, the map of the US is right there on his – face. – *Pete Martin*

Famous line (*Picnic*): 'I gotta get somewhere in this world. I just gotta.'

Holdridge, Lee (1944–).
American composer, also for television movies.
   Jonathan Livingston Seagull (co-m) 73. Jeremy 73. Mahogany (co-m) 75. Goin' Home 76. The Greatest (co-m) 77. French Postcards 78. Tilt 79. Oliver's Story (co-m) 79. The Beastmaster 82. Mr Mom 83. Splash 84. Micki and Maude 84. Sylvester 85. Walk Like a Man 87. Big Business 88. Old Gringo 89. Pastime 91, etc.

Holender, Adam.
American cinematographer.
   Midnight Cowboy 69. Puzzle of a Downfall Child 70. Panic in Needle Park 71. Promises in the Dark 79. The Seduction of Joe Tynan 79. Simon 80. The Idolmaker 80. Street Smart 87. To Kill a Priest 88. The Dream Team 89. Sea of Love 89. Fresh 94, etc.

Holiday, Billie (1915–1959) (Eleonora Harris).
American jazz singer, one of the great interpreters of popular song, who made one feature film, in the role of a maid. She worked as an extra in *The Emperor Jones* 33, and also made a short with Duke Ellington, *Symphony in Black* 35. In the biopic of her life, *Lady Sings the Blues* 75, she was played by Diana Ross. In the 50s, when the film was first mooted, it was reported that Lana Turner was being considered for the role.
   Autobiography: 1956, *Lady Sings the Blues*, with William Dufty.
   Biographies: 1975, *Billie's Blues* by John Chilton. 1987, *Billie Holiday* by John White. 1994, *Wishing on the Moon: The Life and Times of Billie Holiday* by Donald Clarke.
   New Orleans 47.

Holland
has produced two major documentarists: Joris Ivens and Bert Haanstra. At one time, Fons Rademakers was the only Dutch director to be known outside his home country. But Holland has produced one of the most controversial directors of the 90s in Paul Verhoeven, especially since his move to America in the mid-80s to make films like *Robocop*, *Total Recall* and *Basic Instinct*. Even before, with such films as *Spetters* and *The Fourth Man*, he attracted interest. His films have helped make international actors of Dutch stars Rutger Hauer, Jeroen Krabbé and Renée Soutendijk, and have also drawn attention to the talents of cinematographers Jost Vacano (German-born) and Jan de Bont. Maruschka Detmers is another whose talent has taken her away from her home country. Verhoeven is not the only Dutch director to have made an impact in recent years: Dick Maas, a busy producer-director, scored with his thriller *Amsterdamned*, and George Sluizer went to Hollywood to remake his chilling *The Vanishing*.

Holland, Agnieszka (1948–).
Polish director and screenwriter, now based in

France. After studying at the Prague Film School, she began as an assistant to director Krzysztof Zanussi and then worked with Andrzej Wajda.

Rough Treatment (Bez Znieczulenia) (w) 78. Provincial Actors (Aktorzy Prowincjonalni) (d) 80. The Fever (Goraczka) (d) 81. Woman on Her Own (Kobieta Samotna i Chromy) (d) 82. Danton (w) 83. Angry Harvest (Bittere Ernte) (wd) 85. To Kill a Priest (wd) 88. Korczak (w) 90. Europa, Europa (wd) 91. Olivier, Olivier (co-w, d) 92. The Secret Garden (d) 93, etc.

Holland, Tom (1943–).
American director and screenwriter.

The Beast Within (w) 82. Psycho II (w) 83. Class of '84 (co-w) 84. Cloak and Dagger (w) 84. Scream for Help (w) 84. Fright Night 85. Fatal Beauty 87. Child's Play 88. The Temp 93, etc.

Hollander, Frederick (1892–1976).
German song composer, long in America.

The Blue Angel 30. Desire 36. *Destry Rides Again* 39. The Man Who Came to Dinner 42. A Foreign Affair 48. The Five Thousand Fingers of Dr T 53, etc.

Holles, Antony (1901–1950).
British actor who often played excitable foreigners.

The Lodger 32. Brewster's Millions 35. Dark Journey 37. Neutral Port 41. Warn That Man 43. Carnival 46. Bonnie Prince Charlie 49. The Rocking-Horse Winner 50, many others.

Holliday, Doc (1849–1885).
American wild west character; a tubercular dentist and poker-player who oddly changed to the right side of the law when he teamed up with Wyatt Earp in *Tombstone*. Played inaccurately but picturesquely on screen by Cesar Romero in *Frontier Marshal* 39; Walter Huston in *The Outlaw* 41; Kent Taylor in *Tombstone* 42; Victor Mature in *My Darling Clementine* 46; James Griffith in *Masterson of Kansas* 55; Kirk Douglas in *Gunfight at the OK Corral* 57; Arthur Kennedy in *Cheyenne Autumn* 64; Jason Robards in *Hour of the Gun* 67; Stacy Keach in *Doc* 70; Val Kilmer in *Tombstone* 94; Dennis Quaid in *Wyatt Earp* 94; and Douglas Fowley in the TV series *Wyatt Earp*.

Holliday, Judy (1922–1965) (Judith Tuvim).
American revue star who shot to fame in the 50s as a slightly daffy blonde in a handful of well-scripted comedies.

Biography: 1982, *Judy Holliday* by Gary Casey.
■ Greenwich Village 44. Something for the Boys 44. Winged Victory 44. Adam's Rib 49. *Born Yesterday* (AA) 50. The Marrying Kind 52. *It Should Happen to You* 53. Phffft 54. *The Solid Gold Cadillac* 56. Full of Life 56. Bells are Ringing 60.

Holliman, Earl (1928–).
American general-purpose actor who can play innocent or villainous.

Destination Gobi 53. The Bridges at Toko-Ri 54. Broken Lance 54. The Big Combo 55. Forbidden Planet 56. Giant 56. The Rainmaker 56. Gunfight at OK Corral 57. Trooper Hook 57. Hot Spell 58. The Trap 59. Last Train from Gun Hill 59. Visit to a Small Planet 60. Summer and Smoke 61. Armored Command 61. The Sons of Katie Elder 65. Covenant with Death 67. Anzio 68. Smoke 69. Trapped (TV) 73. I Love You, Goodbye (TV) 74. Alexander: The Other Side of Dawn (TV) 77. Sharky's Machine 81. The Thorn Birds (TV) 82.

TV series: Hotel de Paree 59. The Wide Country 62. Police Woman 74–78.

Hollingsworth, John (1916–1963).
British conductor for many film scores of the 40s.

Holloway, Stanley (1890–1982).
British comedian, entertainer, singer and character actor with a long list of international credits in revue, musical comedy and variety as well as films. Born in London, he became a star with the concert party the Co-Optimists and was famous for his monologues delivered in a Yorkshire accent.

Autobiography: 1969, *Wiv a Little Bit of Luck*.
■ The Rotters 21. *The Co-Optimists* 30. Sleeping Car 33. The Girl from Maxim's 33. Lily of Killarney 34. Love at Second Sight 34. Sing as We Go 34. Road House 34. D'Ye Ken John Peel? 35. In Town Tonight 35. *Squibs* 35. Play Up the Band 35. Song of the Forge 36. *The Vicar of Bray* 36. Cotton Queen 37. Sam Small Leaves Town 37. Our Island Nation 37. Major Barbara 41. *Salute John Citizen* 42. *The Way Ahead* 44. *Champagne Charlie* 44. *This Happy Breed* 44. *The Way to the Stars* 45. *Brief Encounter* 45. Caesar and Cleopatra 45. Wanted for Murder 46. Carnival 46. Meet Me at Dawn 46. *Nicholas Nickleby* (as Mr Crummles) 47. Snowbound 48. Saraband for Dead Lovers 48. One Night With You 48. Noose 48. The Winslow Boy 48. *Hamlet* (as the gravedigger) 48. Another Shore 48. Passport to Pimlico 49. The Perfect Woman 49. Midnight Episode 50. One Wild Oat 50. *The Lavender Hill Mob* 51. Lady Godiva Rides Again 51. The Magic Box 51. The Happy Family 52. Meet Me Tonight 52. *The Titfield Thunderbolt* 52. *The Beggar's Opera* 53. A Day to Remember 53. *Meet Mr Lucifer* 53. Fast and Loose 53. An Alligator Named Daisy 55. Jumping for Joy 55. Alive and Kicking 58. No Trees in the Street 58. Hello London 58. *No Love for Johnnie* 61. On the Fiddle 61. *My Fair Lady* (as Doolittle) (AAN) 64. In Harm's Way 64. Ten Little Indians 64. The Sandwich Man 66. Mrs Brown You've Got a Lovely Daughter 68. Run a Crooked Mile (TV) 69. The Private Life of Sherlock Holmes 70. The Flight of the Doves 71. Up the Front 72. Journey into Fear 76.

TV series: Our Man Higgins 62.

Holloway, Sterling (1905–1992).
Slow-speaking American comic actor, usually of yokels or hillbillies. Busiest in the 30s; latterly the voice of many Disney characters.

Casey at the Bat 27. Alice in Wonderland 33. Life Begins at Forty 35. Professor Beware 38. The Bluebird 40. A Walk in the Sun 46. The Beautiful Blonde from Bashful Bend 49. Shake, Rattle and Rock 56. Live a Little Love a Little 68. Thunder and Lightning 77, many others.

TV series: The Life of Riley 53–58. Willie 55. The Baileys of Balboa 64.

Holly, Buddy (1936–1959) (Charles Hardin Holley).
Influential American rock singer and songwriter, killed in a plane crash while on tour with singer Richie Valens (qv). He was played by Gary Busey in the biopic *The Buddy Holly Story* 78.

Hollywood.
The American film city, nominally a suburb of Los Angeles, was founded in 1912 when a number of independent producers headed west from New York to avoid the effects of a patents trust. The site was chosen because of its nearness to the Mexican border in case of trouble, and because the weather and location possibilities were excellent. By 1913 Hollywood was established as the film-maker's Mecca, and continued so for forty years. Several factors combined in the late 40s to affect its unique concentration. Actors transformed themselves into independent producers and reduced the power of the 'front office'; stars now made the films they

liked instead of the ones to which they were assigned. The consequent break-up of many big studios, which now simply sold production space to independent outfits, weakened continuity of product. Each production now had to start from scratch; there was no longer a training ground for new talent, nor was the old production gloss always in evidence. The communist witch-hunt unfortunately drove many leading talents to Europe, and some found they preferred Shepperton or Cinecittà to California. The coming of CinemaScope, a device to halt the fall in box-office returns which resulted from the beginning of commercial TV, meant that real locations were now necessary, as studio sets would show up on the screen. So began the world-wide trekking now evident in American production: generally speaking only routine product and TV episodes are made in the film city itself, but each distribution set-up will have up to a dozen films being made in various parts of the globe.

Books about Hollywood include *Hello Hollywood* (1962) by Allen Rivkin and Laura Kerr; *Hollywood* (1974) by Garson Kanin; *The Hollywood Exiles* (1976) by John Baxter; *Hollywood and the Great Fan Magazines* (1970) by Martin Levin; *Hollywood the Haunted House* (1969) by Paul Mayersberg; *Flesh and Fantasy* (1978) by Penny Stallings; *This Was Hollywood* (1960) by Beth Day; *Gone Hollywood* (1979) by Christopher Finch and Linda Rosenkrantz; *The Pink Palace* (1978) by Sandra Lee Stuart; *The Garden of Allah* (1971) by Sheilah Graham; *The Shattered Silents* (1978) by Alexander Walker; *Some Time in the Sun* (1976) by Tom Dardis; *Hollywood the Dream Factory* (1951) by Hortense Powdermaker; *The Hollywood Studios* (1978) by Roy Pickard; *Hollywood Babylon* (1975) by Kenneth Anger. And some classics: *Hollywood, The Movie Colony, The Movie Makers* (1939) by Leo Rosten; *America at the Movies* (1945) by Margaret Farrand Thorp; *Picture* (1951) by Lillian Ross; *The Studio* (1968) by John Gregory Dunne; *Hollywood, the Pioneers* (1979) by Kevin Brownlow and John Kobal; *The Parade's Gone By* (1968) by Kevin Brownlow; *The Real Tinsel* (1970) by Bernard Rosenberg and Harry Silverstein; *The Fifty Year Decline and Fall of Hollywood* (1961) by Ezra Goodman; *City of Nets* (1986) by Otto Friedrich; *You'll Never Eat Lunch in This Town Again* (1991) by Julia Phillips; *Naked Hollywood: Money and Power in the Movies Today* (1990) by Nicholas Kent. Plus all the books about individual stars, directors, studios and producers, especially: *King Cohn* (1967) by Bob Thomas; *Memo from David O. Selznick* (1972) by Rudy Behlmer; and *David O. Selznick's Hollywood* (1980) by Richard Haver; *Showman: The Life of David O. Selznick* (1993) by David Thomson; *Goldwyn* (1989) by A. Scott Berg; *Frank Capra: The Catastrophe of Success* (1992) by Joseph McBride; *Merchant of Dreams: Louis B. Mayer, M.G.M., and the Secret Hollywood* (1993) by Charles Higham.

¶ The legendary film city – sometimes referred to as Sodom-by-the-Sea – seems far from glamorous to the casual visitor. Geographically, it is not a city at all but a mere suburban segment of a forty-mile-square jigsaw puzzle of dormitory areas which all run into each other. James Gleason, Dorothy Parker, and several other people are credited with calling Los Angeles:

Seventy-two suburbs in search of a city.
No matter who said it, it's still true. L.A. also remains a supreme example of man's inhumanity to man, the promised land that only humans have polluted. Even before the glorious climate was filtered through several layers of smog, the values were all wrong. The residents were almost all on the run from somewhere else, and tended to idle

their lives away under the sun, pursuing the buck when they could and taking the biggest for the best. Ethel Barrymore's first impressions, in 1932, were vivid:

The people are unreal. The flowers are unreal, they don't smell. The fruit is unreal, it doesn't taste of anything. The whole place is a glaring, gaudy, nightmarish set, built up in the desert.

The heat, the richness and the sweet smells are certainly enervating. Shirley Maclaine, hot from Broadway, saw the difference at once:

The most important deals in the movie industry are finalized on the sun-drenched turf of golf courses or around turquoise swimming pools, where the smell of barbecue sauce is borne on gentle breezes and wafts over the stereo system of houses that people seldom leave.

Cedric Hardwicke felt the danger:

God felt sorry for actors, so he gave them a place in the sun and a swimming pool. The price they had to pay was to surrender their talent.

There's always a price tag. Fred Allen knew it when he said:

California is a great place . . . if you happen to be an orange.

Someone else called it 'Siberia with palms'. Raymond Chandler aptly summed up L.A. as:

A city with all the personality of a paper cup.

Joe Frisco thought of it as:

The only town in the world where you can wake up in the morning and listen to the birds coughing in the trees.

Stephen Vincent Benet was even more picturesque:

Of all the Christbitten places in the two hemispheres, this is the last curly kink in the pig's tail.

Hollywood is superior to other parts of L.A. only by virtue of the dusty hills into which it nestles on its northern side. The fact that most comments on it are cynical seems inevitable in an industrial area where the product is an intangible dream. Human beings must get injured in the process, their souls bruised by the struggle for fame, their bodies tossed onto the junkheap the minute they pass their prime. Hollywood has always sought, and then misused, the services of great talent. In the early 30s so many New York actors and writers made the four-day train journey and shortly returned in dejection that a saying sprang up on Broadway:

Never buy anything in Hollywood that you can't put on the Chief.

Billie Burke, a longtime resident, declared that:

To survive there, you need the ambition of a Latin-American revolutionary, the ego of a grand opera tenor, and the physical stamina of a cow pony.

Moss Hart called Beverly Hills:

The most beautiful slave quarters in the world.

Nelson Algren had a brief but unhappy experience:

I went out there for a thousand a week, and I worked Monday and I got fired Wednesday. The fellow who hired me was out of town Tuesday.

Walter Pidgeon liked the system:

It was like an expensive, beautifully-run fan club. You didn't need to carry money. Your face was your credit card – all over the world.

But Dorothy Parker saw its dangers:

Hollywood money isn't money. It's congealed snow.

Hedda Hopper put it another way:

Our town worships success, the bitch goddess whose smile hides a taste for blood.

John Huston saw through the illusion:

Hollywood has always been a cage . . . a cage to catch our dreams.

George Jean Nathan gave the most all-embracing description:

Ten million dollars worth of intricate and ingenious machinery functioning elaborately to put skin on baloney.

Oscar Levant was bitter:

Strip the phoney tinsel off Hollywood and you'll find the real tinsel underneath.

Wilson Mizner thought it:

A trip through a sewer in a glass-bottomed boat, and varied this thought as:

A sewer with service from the Ritz Carlton.

Dudley Field Malone found it:

A town where inferior people have a way of making superior people feel inferior.

Elinor Glyn in 1927 wondered:

Where else in the world will you find a coloured cook bursting into the dining room to say 'You folks better hustle to dinner if you don't want the stuff to get cold'?

H.L. Mencken marvelled at its reputation:

Immorality? Oh, my God, Hollywood seemed to me to be one of the most respectable towns in America. Even Baltimore can't beat it.

Leo Rosten saw its lotus-land attraction:

Fortunes were made overnight, and along with the speculators, the oil men and the real estate promoters, another group came to the promised land – the old, the sick and the middle-aged, who came not to woo Mammon but to sit out their savings in the sun and die in the shadow of an annuity and an orange tree.

Herman Weinberg saw the dangers:

Whatever goes into the Hollywood grist mill, it comes out the same way. It is a meat-grinder that will take beef and suet, pheasant and turnips, attar of roses and limburger and turn it all into the same kind of hash that has served so many so well for so long.

To Ginger Rogers,

Hollywood is like an empty wastebasket.

To John Schlesinger,

An extraordinary kind of temporary place.

To Carrie Fisher,

You can't find true affection in Hollywood because everyone does the fake affection so well.

To Sylvester Stallone,

The only way to be a success in Hollywood is to be as obnoxious as the next guy.

To Rod Steiger,

A community of lonely people searching for even the most basic kind of stimulation in their otherwise mundane lives.

To Groucho Marx,

It provided the kind of luxury that exists today only for the sons of Latin-American dictators.

To Marilyn Monroe,

A place where they pay you 50,000 dollars for a kiss and 50 cents for your soul.

To Rex Reed,

A place where, if you don't have happiness, you send out for it.

Elinor Glyn was waspish about it:

When I arrived, spittoons were still being placed in rows down the centre of a set which was supposed to be the baronial hall of an old English castle.

Lana Turner survived the dream:

It was all beauty and it was all talent, and if you had it they protected you.

Josef Von Sternberg was downright cynical:

You can seduce a man's wife there, rape his daughter and wipe your hands on his canary, but if you don't like his movie, you're dead.

Lauren Bacall spoke from other people's experience:

The only place in the world where an amicable divorce means that each gets fifty per cent of the publicity.

Evelyn Keyes recalled:

The big studios were each headed by a Big Daddy who reigned supreme.

Louis Sherwin remembered:

They knew only one word of more than one syllable, and that was FILLUM.

Wilson Mizner, in similar vein:

What I like about Hollywood is that you can get along knowing only two words of English: swell and lousy.

He added:

I spent several years there, and I think all the heroes are in the audience.

An anonymous wag called it:

Paradise with a lobotomy.

But for Joseph L. Mankiewicz it had saving graces, in the 30s at least:

The old moguls were really impressed to know that Lion Feuchtwanger and Aldous Huxley and Thomas Mann were living in Pacific Palisades. They reached for things in those days. Even Bernard Shaw came out to look around. I don't think he'd come today.

Ernst Lubitsch saw another danger, that the dream might be dangerously more attractive than reality:

I've been to Paris France and I've been to Paris Paramount. Paris Paramount is better.

Some failed to relish the easy life. After a short stay in 1932 Sergei Eisenstein packed his bags. When asked at the station 'Are you coming back?' he replied:

No, I'm *going* back.

And an anonymous wag complained:

In Hollywood you can be forgotten while you're out of the room going to the toilet.

F. Scott Fitzgerald was whimsical about it:

I accepted the assignment with the resignation of a ghost assigned to a haunted house.

A character in Gavin Lambert's *The Slide Area* had a different slant:

The past is out of place here, mister. You don't feel it, you only feel the future.

To Grover Jones it was:

The only asylum run by the inmates.

Walter Winchell called it:

A town that has to be seen to be disbelieved.

And Marlon Brando dismissed it as:

A cultural boneyard.

Ken Murray loved it, but admitted it to be:

A place where you spend more than you make, on things you don't need, to impress people you don't like.

Ethel Barrymore was finally repelled:

It looks, it feels, as though it had been invented by a Sixth Avenue peepshow man.

And Sonny Fox summed it all up:

Hollywood is like a world's fair that's been up a year too long.

All such remarks spring mainly from the system. But perhaps the people were partly to blame.

I'll miss Hollywood. Of the twenty friends I thought I had, I'll miss the six I really had,

remarked Lauren Bacall wryly on her way to Broadway. And Errol Flynn once said:

They've great respect for the dead in Hollywood, but none for the living.

Richard Burton responded frankly to a question about Hollywood morals:

Certainly most movie executives were making love to starlets. But then, so were most of us actors.

Alfred Hitchcock, on the other hand, maintained:

We lead a very suburban life here. We're in bed by nine o'clock every night.

And that reminds one of the anonymous 30s complaint about Hollywood's fabled social life:

No matter how hot it gets during the day, there's nothing to do at night.

Anonymous too was the mogul-hater who averred:

There's nothing wrong with the place, that six first-class funerals wouldn't cure.

Nepotism was of course rife. When Louis B. Mayer appointed his daughter's husband William Goetz to a key position at MGM, someone cracked:

The son-in-law also rises.

And Ogden Nash devised a famous couplet about the head of Universal:

Uncle Carl Laemmle
Has a very large faemmle.

Ethics were out, as Dorothy Parker knew:

The only-ism Hollywood believes in is plagiarism.

Glamour and insincerity gave it the atmosphere of a luxury liner, as someone said in the 30s:

I have this terrible apprehension that suddenly the boat is going to dock and I shall never see any of you again.

Phyllis Batelli called it:

A place where great-grandmothers dread to grow old.

And there's an old saying:

In Hollywood the eternal triangle consists of an actor, his wife and himself.

(There is another version which runs 'an actor, his wife and his agent'. Take your choice.) Walter Winchell thought:

They shoot too many pictures and not enough actors.

One can hardly be surprised that people are false when the movies themselves were sham for so many years. Arthur Freed produced the Scottish fantasy *Brigadoon* on the MGM lot and defended himself by saying:

I went to Scotland and found nothing there that looks like Scotland.

A wise saying of Hollywood's heyday, by David O. Selznick:

Nothing here is permanent. Once photographed, life here is ended.

But the system had its rueful supporters. Orson Welles:

Hollywood's all right: it's the pictures that are bad.

Raymond Chandler:

If my books had been any worse I should not have been invited to Hollywood, and if they had been any better I should not have come.

An anonymous writer:

They ruin your stories. They trample on your pride. They massacre your ideas. And what do you get for it? A fortune.

Typically, Hollywood was often ignorant of the talent it had bought. Bert Lahr didn't make it until his third trip, and said wryly:

If you want to be a success in Hollywood, be sure and go to New York.

Richard Dyer McCann wrote truthfully:

The most familiar, solid, bedrock certainty in Hollywood is sudden change.

Certainly, the town depended on fashion, and its well-set ways were in themselves a mere fashion. By 1956, David Selznick found the place to be:

Like Egypt, full of crumbled pyramids.

Fred Allen had said in 1941 that:

Hollywood is a place where people from Iowa mistake each other for stars.

In the 50s the mistake became pardonable: male leads were required to look less like matinée idols and more like the slob next door, or the fellow at the gas station. Humphrey Bogart was heard to remark:

I came out here with one suit and everybody said I looked like a bum. Twenty years later

Marlon Brando comes out with only a sweatshirt and the town drools over him. That shows you how much Hollywood has progressed.

Hollywood was desperate in the face of TV and better living standards. One trend followed another: in the 60s, for instance, English actors became more fashionable than ever before, and Bob Hope quipped:

There'll always be an England, even if it's in Hollywood.

By the end of the 60s the old complaints were being repeated with a new veneer of resigned cynicism. Paul Mayersberg:

The desert of Southern California cannot be said to have created a religion, but it has contributed greatly to the development of a way of life that operates at the extremity of our civilization. When you reach Los Angeles you are as far West as you can go.

An anonymous agent:

You fail upwards here. A guy makes a ten-million-dollar picture, the thing is not that he's made a bomb [i.e. disaster] but that he's made a ten-million-dollar picture. So next time out, they give him a twelve-million-dollar picture.

David Mamet thought that only one rule governed the place:

Hollywood is the city of the modern gold rush, and money calls the turn. That is the first and last rule, as we know, of Hollywood – we permit ourselves to be treated like commodities in the hope that we may, one day, be treated like *valuable* commodities.

Whether Hollywood finally succeeds or goes under, it has had a fair run, long enough to confound two doubting remarks of 1915, by Carl Laemmle:

I hope I didn't make a mistake coming out here.

And D. W. Griffith:

It's a shame to take this country away from the rattlesnakes. Perhaps the rattlesnakes are just biding their time.

Hollywood on film

has generally been shown as the brassy, gold-digging, power-conscious society which, in the nature of things, it can hardly fail to be. There was a somewhat sentimental period in the 20s and 30s, with *Ella Cinders, Hollywood, Going Hollywood, Hollywood Cavalcade,* and *Hollywood Boulevard*; but satire had already struck in such films as *The Last Command, Merton of the Movies, Show People, The Lost Squadron, What Price Hollywood, LadyKiller, Something to Sing About, Once in a Lifetime, Stardust, Hollywood Hotel, Stand In, A Star Is Born* and *Boy Meets Girl.* The moguls didn't seem to mind the film city being shown as somewhat zany, as in *The Goldwyn Follies,* Disney's *Mother Goose Goes Hollywood, The Cohens and Kellys in Hollywood, Abbott and Costello in Hollywood, The Jones Family in Hollywood, Movie Crazy, Never Give a Sucker an Even Break,* and *Hellzapoppin*; but they preferred the adulatory attitude best expressed in *The Youngest Profession,* which concerned the autograph hunters who lay in wait at the studio exits.

During the 40s Paramount was the studio most addicted to showing itself off, though the front office can't have relished watching Preston Sturges bite the hand that fed him in *Sullivan's Travels.* The story of *Hold Back the Dawn* was supposedly told to sentimental Mitchell Leisen during a lunch break on the studio floor; Crosby and Hope based a score of gags on Paramount; and the studio was the setting for *Star Spangled Rhythm,* an all-star musical which encouraged other studios to emulate it, with Warner's *Thank Your Lucky Stars* and *It's a Great Feeling,* Universal's *Follow the Boys,*

the independent *Stage Door Canteen,* and later Paramount's less successful reprise, *Variety Girl.*

In 1950 *Sunset Boulevard* took a really sardonic look at the film city, and set a fashion for scathing movies like *The Star, The Bad and the Beautiful, The Barefoot Contessa* and *The Big Knife.* As though to atone, almost every studio threw in a light-hearted, nostalgic look at Hollywood's golden era: *Singin' in the Rain, The Perils of Pauline, Jolson Sings Again, The Eddie Cantor Story.* But in the last few years the only really affectionate review of Hollywood's past has been in the Cliff Richard musical *Wonderful Life,* though Jerry Lewis continued to paint zany pictures of studio life in *The Errand Boy, The Ladies' Man* and *The Patsy.* The rest was all denunciation and bitterness: *Hollywood Boulevard, Hollywood Story, The Wild Party, The Day of the Locust, Inserts, The Goddess, Two Weeks in Another Town, The Carpetbaggers, Harlow, Inside Daisy Clover, The Loved One, Whatever Happened to Baby Jane, The Legend of Lylah Clare, Myra Breckinridge, The Oscar* and the satiric *The Player.* A 1969 TV series, *Bracken's World,* was set in a film studio (Twentieth Century-Fox) and saw it as a kind of valley of the dolls – and the studio scenes in *that* movie were none too convincing.

See the book by Rudy Behlmer and Tony Thomas: 1975, *Hollywood's Hollywood, the Movies about the Movies.*

The Hollywood Ten.

Alvah Bessie, Herbert Biberman, Lester Cole, Edward Dmytryk, Ring Lardner Jnr, John Howard Lawson, Albert Maltz, Sam Ornitz, Adrian Scott and Dalton Trumbo were the famous band of writers, producers and directors who in 1947 refused to tell the Unamerican Activities Committee whether or not they were communists. All served short prison sentences and had difficulty getting work in Hollywood for several years.

Holm, Celeste (1919–).

Cool, calm, American stage actress whose films have usually provided her with wisecracking roles.
■ Three Little Girls in Blue 46. Carnival in Costa Rica 47. *Gentleman's Agreement* (AA) 47. Road House 48. *The Snake Pit* 48. Chicken Every Sunday 48. Come to the Stable (AAN) 49. Everybody Does It 49. A Letter to Three Wives (narrator only) 49. *All About Eve* (AAN) 50. Champagne for Caesar 50. The Tender Trap 55. High Society 56. Bachelor Flat 61. Cosa Nostra, Arch Enemy of the FBI (TV) 66. Doctor You've Got to be Kidding 67. The Delphi Bureau (TV) 72. Tom Sawyer 73. The Underground Man (TV) 74. Death Cruise (TV) 74. Captains and the Kings (TV) 76. Bittersweet Love 76. Love Boat II (TV) 78. The Private Files of J. Edgar Hoover 78. Backstairs at the White House (TV) 79. Midnight Lace (TV) 80. This Girl for Hire (TV) 83. Jessie (TV) 85. Three Men and a Baby 87. Murder by the Book (TV) 87. Polly (TV) 89.
TV series: Honestly Celeste 54. Nancy 70–71. Jessie 84. Falcon Crest 85.

Holm, Ian (1932–) (Ian Holm Cuthbert).

British stage actor recently emerging in films.
■ The Bofors Gun (BFA) 68. A Midsummer Night's Dream 68. The Fixer 68. Oh What a Lovely War 69. A Severed Head 70. Nicholas and Alexandra 71. Mary Queen of Scots 72. Young Winston 72. The Homecoming 73. Juggernaut 75. Shout at the Devil 76. Robin and Marian 76. Jesus of Nazareth (TV) 77. The Man in the Iron Mask (TV) 77. March or Die 77. Holocaust (TV) 77. Alien 79. The Lost Boys 79. SOS Titanic (TV) 79. All Quiet on the Western Front (TV) 80. Time Bandits (TV) 81. Chariots of Fire (BFA, AAN) 81. Return of the Soldier 82. Greystoke 84. Dance with

a Stranger 85. Wetherby 85. Brazil 85. Laughterhouse 85. Dreamchild 86. Another Woman 88. Henry V 89. Hamlet 90. Kafka 91. Naked Lunch 91. Blue Ice 92. The Hour of the Pig 93. The Madness of King George 95.

Holm, Sonia (1922–1974).
English leading lady of the late 40s.
　When the Bough Breaks 47. The Loves of Joanna Godden 47. Miranda 48. The Bad Lord Byron 49. The Crowded Day 54, etc.

Holmes, Phillips (1907–1942).
American juvenile lead who went straight from college to Hollywood; son of Taylor Holmes. His rather stiff personality soon lost its appeal. Died in a plane crash.
　■ Varsity 28. His Private Life 28. Illusion 29. The Wild Party 29. Stairs of Sand 29. The Return of Sherlock Holmes 29. Pointed Heels 29. Only the Brave 30. Paramount on Parade 30. The Devil's Holiday 30. Grumpy 30. Her Man 30. Man to Man 30. The Dancers 30. The Criminal Code 31. Stolen Heaven 31. Confessions of a Co-Ed 31. *An American Tragedy* 31. The Man I Killed 32. Two Kinds of Women 32. Make Me a Star 32. 70,000 Witnesses 32. Night Court 33. The Secret of Madame Blanche 33. Men Must Fight 33. Looking Forward 33. Storm at Daybreak 33. The Big Brain 33. Dinner at Eight 33. Penthouse 33. Beauty for Sale 33. Stage Mother 33. Private Scandal 34. Nana 34. Caravan 34. Great Expectations 34. Million Dollar Ransom 34. The Divine Spark 34. No Ransom 35. Ten Minute Alibi (GB) 35. Chatterbox 36. House of a Thousand Candles 36. General Spanky 36. The Dominant Sex (GB) 37. The Housemaster (GB) 38.

Holmes, Stuart (1887–1971).
American leading actor of silents who became a character performer after the coming of sound.
　How Mrs Murray Saved the Army 11. Life's Shop Window 14. The Scarlet Letter 17. The Four Horsemen of the Apocalypse 21. The Prisoner of Zenda 22. Tess of the D'Urbervilles 24. The Age of Innocence 24. Captain of the Guard 30. Sitting Pretty 33. The Case of the Velvet Claws 36. Dark Victory 39. The Adventures of Mark Twain 44. Shady Lady 45. The Ghost and Mrs Muir 47. A Letter to Three Wives 48. Copper Canyon 50. Singin' in the Rain 52. The Girl in the Red Velvet Swing 55. The Birds and the Bees 56. The Man Who Shot Liberty Valance 62, etc.

Holmes, Taylor (1872–1959).
Veteran American character actor with long stage experience; latterly seen as amiably crooked politician or convincing trickster.
　Efficiency Edgar's Courtship 17. Ruggles of Red Gap (title role) 18. One Hour of Love 28. The First Baby 36. Boomerang 47. Nightmare Alley 47. Father of the Bride 50. The First Legion 51. Beware My Lovely 52. The Maverick Queen 56, many others.

Holt, Charlene (1939–).
American leading lady, former star of TV commercials (and *The Tom Ewell Show*).
　Man's Favourite Sport? 64. Red Line 7000 66. El Dorado 67, etc.

Holt, Jack (1888–1951) (Charles John Holt II).
Tough-looking American leading man of silent and sound action films.
　A Cigarette – That's All 15. The Little American 16. The Woman Thou Gavest Me 18. Held by the Enemy 20. Bought and Paid For 22. Empty Hands 24. Wanderer of the Wasteland 25. Vengeance

28. Hell's Island 30. *Dirigible* 31. War Correspondent 32. Whirlpool 33. The Littlest Rebel 35. *San Francisco* 36. Passport to Alcatraz 40. Holt of the Secret Service 43. They Were Expendable 45. Flight to Nowhere 46. Brimstone 49. Task Force 49. Across the Wide Missouri 51, many others.

Holt, Jennifer (1920–) (Elizabeth Holt).
American leading lady of 'B' westerns; daughter of Jack Holt.
　Stick to Your Guns 42. Cheyenne Round up 43. Oklahoma Raiders 44. Buffalo Bill Rides Again 47. Tornado Range 48. Range Renegades 48, etc.

Holt, Nat (1892–1971).
American independent producer.
　Badman's Territory 46. Trail Street 47. Return of the Badmen 48. Fighting Man of the Plains 49. The Great Missouri Raid 51. Denver and Rio Grande 52. Pony Express 53. Flight to Tangier 53, etc.
　TV series: Tales of Wells Fargo 57–61. Overland Trail 60.

Holt, Patrick (1912–) (Patrick Parsons).
Bland British leading man of the 40s, later in character roles.
　The Return of the Frog 38. Sword of Honour 39. Convoy 41. Hungry Hill 47. Master of Bankdam 47. The Mark of Cain 48. Portrait from Life 49. Marry Me 49. Guilt is My Shadow 50. The Dark Avenger 55. Miss Tulip Stays the Night 56. Thunderball 65. Murderers' Row 66. Hammerhead 68. No Blade of Grass 71. Little (TV) 78. Playing Away 86. Loser Takes All 89, many others.

Holt, Seth (1923–1971).
British director, formerly editor and associate producer for Ealing.
　■ Nowhere to Go 58. Taste of Fear 61. Station Six Sahara 63. *The Nanny* 65. Danger Route 67. Monsieur Lecoq 68. Blood from the Mummy's Tomb 71.

¶ I always have a movie going on in my head. I dream in shots. It's getting those dreams out from your head and on to the floor that's the most difficult thing. – *S.H.*
　Film has much more in common with literature than, say, television. – *S.H.*
　The most ruthless director I've ever worked with next to William Wyler. – *Bette Davis*

Holt, Tim (1919–1973) (Charles John Holt III).
American leading man, son of Jack Holt. In films from 1937, and was hero of many low-budget westerns.
　History Is Made at Night 37. The Law West of Tombstone 38. Stagecoach 39. The Swiss Family Robinson 40. *The Magnificent Ambersons* 42. Hitler's Children 42. My Darling Clementine 46. *The Treasure of the Sierra Madre* 47. The Mysterious Desperado 49. His Kind of Woman 51. The Monster That Challenged the World 57, etc.

Homans, Robert E. (1874–1947).
Round-faced American character actor, in hundreds of movies, usually as country cop.
　Legally Dead 23. The Bandit Buster 26. Princess from Hoboken 27. Obey Your Husband 28. Isle of Lost Ships 29. Trigger Tricks 30. The Black Camel 31. Young America 32. She Done Him Wrong 33. The Woman in Red 35. Black Legion 36. Easy Living 37. The Amazing Dr Clitterhouse 38. The Grapes of Wrath 40. Honky Tonk 41. Night Monster 42. It Ain't Hay 43. Pin Up Girl 44. Captain Eddie 45. Girl on the Spot 46, many others.

Homeier, Skip (1929–) (George Vincent Homeier).
American child actor of the 40s, later in a variety of supporting roles.
　Tomorrow the World 44. Boys' Ranch 46. Mickey 48. The Gunfighter 50. Fixed Bayonets 51. Sailor Beware 52. Beachhead 54. At Gunpoint 56. Comanche Station 60. The Ghost and Mr Chicken 66. Starbird and Sweet William 76. The Greatest 77. Overboard (TV) 78. The Wild Wild West Revisited (TV) 79, etc.
　TV series: *Dan Raven* 60.

Homoki-Nagy, Istvan (1914–).
Hungarian naturalist who has made many films of wild life including *From Blossom Time Till Autumn Frost*.

Homolka, Oscar (1899–1978).
Viennese-born character actor, a fine 'heavy'. On stage from 1918, international films from mid-30.
　■ Dreyfus (Ger.) 30. Hokuspokus (Ger.) 30. Der Weg Nach Rio (Ger.) 31. Im Geheimdienst (Ger.) 31. Nachtkolonne (Ger.) 31. 1914 (Ger.) 31. Zwischen Nacht und Morgen (Ger.) 31. Die Nachte von Port Said (Ger.) 32. Moral und Liebe (Ger.) 32. Spione am Werk (Ger.) 33. Unsichbara Gegner (Austria) 33. *Rhodes of Africa* 35. *Sabotage* 36. Everything Is Thunder 36. Ebb Tide 37. Hidden Power 37. Seven Sinners 40. Comrade X 40. The Invisible Woman 41. Rage in Heaven 41. Ball of Fire 41. Mission to Moscow 43. Hostages 43. Code of Scotland Yard 47. *The Shop at Sly Corner* 47. *I Remember Mama* (AAN) 48. Anna Lucasta 49. The White Tower 50. Top Secret 52. The House of the Arrow 53. Prisoner of War 54. The Seven Year Itch 55. War and Peace 56. A Farewell to Arms 57. The Key 58. Tempest 58. Mr Sardonicus 61. Boy's Night Out 62. The Wonderful World of the Brothers Grimm 63. The Long Ships 64. Joy in the Morning 65. *Funeral in Berlin* 66. The Happening 67. Billion Dollar Brain 67. The Madwoman of Chaillot 69. Assignment to Kill 69. The Executioner 70. Song of Norway 70. The Tamarind Seed 74.

homosexuality
can be said to have arrived during the late 60s as a fit subject for the western cinema, producers having toyed gingerly with it for the previous three decades. During the 40s, there were clear intimations of it in *The Maltese Falcon*, *Victory*, and *Rope*. The 50s brought *Strangers on a Train*, *I Vitelloni*, *Serious Charge*, Germany's *The Third Sex*, and *Suddenly Last Summer*, and the decade was rounded off with two productions of the life of Oscar Wilde. *Cat on a Hot Tin Roof* 58 and *Spartacus* 60 were probably the last Hollywood movies to have homosexual inferences deliberately removed from the original. In 1962 the subject came right out into the open with *Victim*, a well-intentioned thriller about the blackmail of homosexuals; *A Taste of Honey* featured a sympathetic homosexual; and both *Advise and Consent* and *The Best Man* concerned allegations of homosexuality against American politicians. On the other hand *Lawrence of Arabia* was so reticent about its hero's sexual make-up that it was difficult to know what estimate was being made; but for good measure Peter O'Toole was raped a second time in *Lord Jim*. Universal romantic comedies now began to make fun of the subject: in *That Touch of Mink* Gig Young's psychiatrist thought he was in love with Cary Grant, and in *A Very Special Favour* Rock Hudson deliberately made Leslie Caron think him effeminate so that she would 'rescue him'. The floodgates were now open: in rapid succession we had *A View From the Bridge*, with its male kiss; *The*

Servant, with its odd relationship between master and man; *The Leather Boys; Stranger in the House; The Fearless Vampire Killers*, with its young homosexual bloodsucker; the miscast and unhappy *Staircase; The Detective*, which made New York appear to be a very gay city; *The Gay Deceivers*, in which two young men avoided the draft by pretending to be queer; *Reflections in a Golden Eye; Midnight Cowboy; The Boys in the Band*, the first sympathetic homosexual comedy; *The Boston Strangler* and *Funeral in Berlin*, with scenes in transvestite bars; *If, Young Woodley, Tea and Sympathy, Riot, The Sergeant* and *Villain*, which revealed camp goings-on in school, prison, the army and gangland. *Girl Stroke Boy* revealed the plight of parents who could not tell whether their son was engaged to a girl or a boy. In *Myra Breckinridge* homosexuality was almost lost in a welter of more spectacular perversions. Historical figures such as Richard the Lionheart and Tchaikovsky had their sexual pecadilloes explored in *The Lion in Winter* and *The Music Lovers*, and Billy Wilder jokingly investigated *The Private Life of Sherlock Holmes*. TV movies invaded the territory in 1973 with *That Certain Summer*. There wasn't much further to go, especially as 'gays' had their own porno films. 1978 brought the last curiosity: *A Different Story*, the love affair of a homosexual and a lesbian. There was a celebration of extraordinary individuals in TV's *The Naked Civil Servant, Kiss of the Spider Woman*, based on Manuel Puig's novel steeped in 40s Hollywood, and Harvey Fierstein's semi-autobiographical stage-hit *Torch Song Trilogy*, which had less impact in the cinema. It went hand in hand with the camp sensibility and frivolity of *The Rocky Horror Picture Show, La Cage aux Folles* and its sequels, some of Andy Warhol's films, like *Lonesome Cowboys*, and the work of John Waters. There was the particularly British repression and love across social classes exemplified by *A Month in the Country, Maurice*, based on E.M. Forster's long-unpublished novel, and *We Think the World of You*. The mood changed towards the end of the 80s as AIDS (not, of course, restricted to homosexuals) became more prevalent and began to kill many young and talented performers. *Early Frost*, made for TV, dealt with the problems of a lawyer explaining to his family that he is gay and dying from AIDS. Bill Sherwood made the much-praised *Parting Glances* on a similar theme, and the bigger-budget *Longtime Companion* explored the subject sympathetically. British director Derek Jarman reacted by making his films more militantly homosexual, culminating in his modern-dress version of Christopher Marlowe's *Edward II*. Younger directors, working outside the mainstream, proclaimed a 'New Queer Cinema', making films aimed at gay audiences or attempting to reclaim themes from mainstream cinema: Tom Kalin's *Swoon* ('Puts the Homo back in Homicide' according to its publicity) dealt with the Leopold-Loeb murder, tackled in *Rope and Compulsion*, from a specifically homosexual viewpoint; Todd Haynes's *Poison* contemplated sexual and social deviance with the equanimity of Jean Genet; Gregg Araki's *The Living End* had two HIV-positive homosexuals taking revenge on the straight world; Christopher Münch's *The Hours and the Times* dealt with Beatles manager Brian Epstein's love for John Lennon; Mark Rappaport's *Rock Hudson's Home Movies* took a witty look at the actor's performances from a gay perspective. Gus Van Sant enjoyed success with *My Private Idaho*, about a narcoleptic hustler; British director Isaac Julien's *Young Soul Rebels* had a black and white male couple as its protagonists; Spanish director Pedro Almodóvar's films, displaying a camp sensibility, were box-office hits around the world;

and Jonathan Demme's *Philadelphia* was an Oscar-winner in 1993, though it managed to upset many AIDS activists.

See also: *AIDS; lesbianism.*

Honda, Inoshiro (1911–1993).
Japanese director of monster movies.
Godzilla, King of the Monsters (Gojira) 54. Rodan 57. Battle in Outer Space 60. Mothra 62. Godzilla vs Mothra 64. Attack of the Mushroom People 64. King Kong Escapes 68. Godzilla's Revenge 69. Yog-Monster from Space 71, many others.

Hondo, Med (1936–) (Abid Mohamed Medoun Hondo).
Mauritanian director, a former actor in France.
Everywhere or Perhaps Nowhere (Partout ou Peut-être Nulle Part) 69. Soleil O 69. Your Neighbours the Niggers (Les Bicots-Nègres, Vos Voisins) 73. We'll Have the Whole of Eternity for Sleeping (Nous Aurons Toute la Mort pour Dormir) 77. West Indies 79. Sarraounia 86. 1871 (a) 89, etc.

Honegger, Arthur (1892–1955).
Swiss composer who worked on French and British pictures.
La Roue 22. Napoleon 27. Les Misérables 34. L'Idée 34. Mayerling 36. *Pygmalion* 38. *Pacific 231* 46.

Honkasalo, Pirjo (1947–).
Finnish director, a former photographer and cinematographer, who studied at the film department of the University of Philadelphia. She worked in collaboration with director Pekka Lehto (qv).
Their Age (short, co-d) 76. Flame Top (Tulipää) (co-d) 80. Da Capo (co-d) 85. Mysterion (doc, d) 91, etc.

Hood, Darla (1931–1979).
American actress and singer who played Darla in the Our Gang shorts of the mid-30s and early 40s.
The Bohemian Girl 36. Happy Land 43. The Helen Morgan Story 57. The Bat 59, etc.

Hoogersteijn, Solveig (1943–).
Swedish-born director who was brought up in Venezuela. She studied film in Germany before returning to work in Venezuela, where *Macu* was the biggest local box-office hit of the 80s.
Manoa 79. El Mar del Tiempo Perdido 81. Macu, the Policeman's Wife (Macu, la Mujer del Policia) 86, etc.

Hook, Henry.
British director.
Sins of the Fathers 82. The Kitchen Toto 87. Lord of the Flies 89, etc.

Hooks, Robert (1937–).
American leading man.
Sweet Love Bitter 66. Hurry Sundown 67. Crosscurrent (TV) 71. Trapped (TV) 73. Aaron Loves Angela 75. The Killer Who Wouldn't Die (TV) 76. Just an Old Sweet Song (TV) 76. Airport 77 77. To Kill a Cop (TV) 78. A Woman Called Moses (TV) 78. Backstairs at the White House (TV) 79. Hollow Image (TV) 79. Fast Walking 82, etc.
TV series: N.Y.P.D. 67.

Hooper, Tobe (1943–).
American horror director and screenwriter.
■ The Texas Chainsaw Massacre 74. Eaten Alive 76. Salem's Lot (TV) 79. The Funhouse 81. Poltergeist 82. Lifeforce 85. Invaders from Mars

86. Texas Chainsaw Massacre II 86. Spontaneous Combustion 89. Leatherface: The Texas Chainsaw Massacre III 90. I'm Dangerous Tonight 90. Sleepwalkers (a) 92.

Hoover, J. Edgar (1895–1972).
American executive, director of the Federal Bureau of Investigation from 1935. In 1939 Paramount made several low-budgeters drawn from his book *Persons in Hiding*; in 1959 he appeared briefly in *The FBI Story*. Subsequently he was impersonated by Erwin Fuller in *Lepke*, by Broderick Crawford in *The Private Files of J. Edgar Hoover*, by Sheldon Leonard in *The Brinks Job*, by Vincent Gardenia in *Kennedy* (TV) and by Ernest Borgnine in *Blood Feud* (TV).

Hopalong Cassidy,
the genial black-garbed hero of scores of western second features since 1935, was created by novelist Clarence E. Mulford. William Boyd (qv) was his only screen and TV personification.
Book: 1992, *Hopalong Cassidy* by Bernard A. Drew.

Hope, Anthony (1863–1933) (Sir Anthony Hope Hawkins).
British adventure novelist whose *The Prisoner of Zenda* and its sequel *Rupert of Hentzau* have frequently been filmed.

Hope, Bob (1903–) (Leslie Townes Hope).
Wisecracking American star comedian, a major name in entertainment for nearly forty years. Born in Britain, he spent years in American vaudeville and musical comedy before establishing himself as a big star of the 40s, usually as a comic coward who makes good. Special Academy Awards in 1940, 1944 and 1952, mainly in appreciation of his troop shows and charitable ventures.
Autobiographical books: 1958, *Have Tux Will Travel*. 1963, *I Owe Russia $2000*. 1976, *The Last Christmas Show*. 1977, *The Road to Hollywood*.
■ The Big Broadcast of 1938. College Swing 38. Give Me a Sailor 38. *Thanks for the Memory* 38. Never Say Die 39. Some Like It Hot 39. *The Cat and the Canary* 39. Road to Singapore 40. *The Ghost Breakers* 40. *Road to Zanzibar* 41. Caught in the Draft 41. Nothing But the Truth 41. Louisiana Purchase 41. *My Favorite Blonde* 42. *Road to Morocco* 42. Star Spangled Rhythm 42. They Got Me Covered 42. Let's Face It 43. The Princess and the Pirate 44. Road to Utopia 45. Monsieur Beaucaire 46. My Favorite Brunette 47. Where There's Life 47. Variety Girl 47. Road to Rio 48. *The Paleface* 48. Sorrowful Jones 48. The Great Lover 49. *Fancy Pants* 50. The Lemon Drop Kid 51. My Favorite Spy 51. Son of Paleface 52. Road to Bali 52. Off Limits 53. Here Come the Girls 53. Casanova's Big Night 54. The Seven Little Foys 55. That Certain Feeling 56. The Iron Petticoat 56. Beau James 57. Paris Holiday 58. Alias Jesse James 59. *The Facts of Life* 60. Bachelor in Paradise 61. Road to Hong Kong 62. Critics Choice 63. Call Me Bwana 63. A Global Affair 64. I'll Take Sweden 65. Boy Did I Get a Wrong Number 66. The Oscar 66. Eight on the Lam 67. The Private Navy of Sgt O'Farrell 68. How to Commit Marriage 69. Cancel My Reservation 72. The Muppet Movie (guest) 79. Masterpiece of Murder (TV) 85. The Best Show in Town 89. Entertaining the Troops 89.
🟡 For a string of bright comedies which perfectly suited the 40s. *The Cat and the Canary.*

❝ I was lucky, you know, I always had a beautiful girl and the money was good. Although I would have done the whole thing over for, oh, perhaps half. – B.H.

My wife raised the kids and I was the guest of honour. For years, they thought I was the meter man. – *B.H.*

Bob Hope is still about as funny as he ever was. I just never thought he was that funny in the first place. – *Chevy Chase (1980s)*

Famous line (*The Cat and the Canary*): 'I get goose pimples. Even my goose pimples get goose pimples.'

Famous line (*The Ghost Breakers*): 'The girls call me Pilgrim, because every time I dance with one I make a little progress.'

Hope, Vida (1918–1963).
British character actress, usually in comic proletarian roles; also stage director.
English Without Tears 44. Nicholas Nickleby 47. It Always Rains on Sunday 48. *The Man in the White Suit* 51. Lease of Life 54. Family Doctor 58, etc.

Hopkins, Anthony (1921–).
British composer.
Vice Versa 48. Decameron Nights 53. The Pickwick Papers 53. Cast a Dark Shadow 55. Billy Budd 62, etc.

Hopkins, Sir Anthony (1937–).
British leading actor, now in Hollywood. A gifted mimic, he dubbed Olivier's voice for extra scenes added to the 1990 re-release of *Spartacus*.
Biography: 1989, *Anthony Hopkins – Too Good to Waste* by Quentin Falk.
The Lion in Winter 68. The Looking Glass War 70. *When Eight Bells Toll* 71. Young Winston (as Lloyd George) 72. A Doll's House 73. All Creatures Great and Small 74. QB VII (TV) 74. The Girl from Petrovka 74. Juggernaut 74. The Lindbergh Kidnapping Case (TV) 76. Dark Victory (TV) 76. Victory at Entebbe (TV) 76. Audrey Rose 77. A Bridge Too Far 77. International Velvet 78. *Magic* 78. Mayflower (TV) 80. A Change of Seasons 80. The Elephant Man 80. The Bunker (as Hitler) (TV) 81. Peter and Paul (TV) 81. The Hunchback of Notre Dame (TV) 82. A Married Man (TV) 82. The Bounty 83. Mussolini and I (TV) 84. Hollywood Wives (TV) 85. Guilty Conscience (TV) 85. 84 Charing Cross Road 87. Desperate Hours 90. Spotswood 91. *The Silence of the Lambs* (AA) 91. *Howards End* 91. Freejack 92. The Trial 92. Bram Stoker's Dracula 92. Chaplin 92. The Trial 93. The Innocent 93. The Remains of the Day (AAN) 93. Shadowlands 93. Mario und der Zauberer 93. The Road to Wellville 94. Legends of the Fall 94. August (& d) 95, etc.

¶ I was lousy in school. Real screwed-up. A moron. I was antisocial and didn't bother with the other kids. A really bad student. I didn't have any brains. I didn't know what I was doing there. That's why I became an actor. – *A.H.*

I like to be centre-stage, taking the big parts. I'm not interested in being worthy. – *A.H.*

I am able to play monsters well. I understand monsters. I understand madmen. I can understand what makes people tick in these darker levels. – *A.H.*

Hopkins, Bo (1942–).
American action hero.
The Wild Bunch 69. Monte Walsh 70. The Culpeper Cattle Company 72. The Getaway 72. American Graffiti 73. White Lightning 73. The Nickel Ride 74. The Day of the Locust 75. Tentacles 77. Aspen (TV) 77. Thaddeus Rose and Eddie (TV) 78. Midnight Express 78. More American Graffiti 79. The Fifth Floor 80.

Plutonium Incident 82. Mutant 83. Nightmare at Noon 87. The Bounty Hunter 89. The Final Alliance 89. Trapper County War 89. Big Bad John 90. Center of the Web 92. Romeo Is Bleeding 92. The Ballad of Little Joe 93, etc.
TV series: Doc Elliott 73. Dynasty 80–81.

Hopkins, John (1931–).
British writer, mostly for TV.
The Virgin Soldiers (w) 69. The Offence (w) 72. Murder by Decree 78. The Holcroft Covenant 85. Torment (co-w) 86, etc.

Hopkins, Kenyon (1932–).
American composer.
Baby Doll 56. Twelve Angry Men 57. The Fugitive Kind 57. Wild in the Country 61. The Yellow Canary 63. Mister Buddwing 66. A Lovely Way to Die 69. Downhill Racer 69. The Tree 69, etc.

Hopkins, Miriam (1902–1972).
American leading lady of the 30s; her rather brittle style has dated.
■ Fast and Loose 30. The Smiling Lieutenant 31. Twenty Four Hours 31. *Dr Jekyll and Mr Hyde* 32. Two Kinds of Women 32. Dancers in the Dark 32. The World and the Flesh 32. *Trouble in Paradise* 32. *The Story of Temple Drake* 33. Design for Living 33. The Stranger's Return 33. All of Me 34. She Loves Me Not 34. The Richest Girl in the World 34. *Becky Sharp* (AAN) 35. Barbary Coast 35. Splendor 35. *These Three* 36. Men Are Not Gods (GB) 37. The Woman I Love 37. Woman Chases Man 37. Wise Girl 37. The Old Maid 39. Virginia City 40. *Lady With Red Hair* 41. A Gentleman after Dark 42. *Old Acquaintance* 43. The Heiress 49. The Mating Season 51. Carrie 52. The Outcasts of Poker Flat 52. The Children's Hour 62. Fanny Hill 65. The Chase 66.

Hopkins, Shirley Knight:
see *Knight, Shirley.*

Hopkins, Stephen (1958–).
Australian director working in Hollywood. He began as an art director and director of music videos in London.
Dangerous Game 88. A Nightmare on Elm Street 5: The Dream Child 89. Predator 2 90. Judgment Night 93. Blown Away 94, etc.

Hopper, Dennis (1935–).
American juvenile of the 50s who later blossomed into a fashionable actor and director.
I Died a Thousand Times 55. Rebel without a Cause 55. Giant 56. The Story of Mankind 57. Key Witness 60. Night Tide 63. The Sons of Katie Elder 65. The Trip 67. Cool Hand Luke 67. *Easy Rider* (& d) 69. The Last Movie (& wd) 71. Kid Blue (& d) 72. Mad Dog Morgan 76. The American Friend 77. Tracks 77. Apocalypse Now 79. Out of the Blue (& d) 80. The Osterman Weekend 83. The Inside Man 84. My Science Project 85. Blue Velvet 86. Hoosiers (AAN) 86. The Texas Chainsaw Massacre 2 86. Black Widow 87. The Pick-Up Artist 87. River's Edge 87. Colors (d) 88. Blood Red 88. Catchfire (aka Backtrack) (& d) 89. Chattahoochee 89. The Hot Spot (d) 90. The Indian Runner 91. Paris Trout 91. Doublecrossed (TV) 91. Eye of the Storm 91. Nails 92. Super Mario Bros 93. Boiling Point 93. Red Rock West 93. *True Romance* 93. Chasers (& d) 94. *Speed* 94. Waterworld 95, etc.
TV series: Medic 54–55.

Hopper, Hedda (1890–1966) (Elda Furry).
American general-purpose actress, mainly in silent

days; in later life became a powerful Hollywood columnist.
Autobiographies: 1952, *From Under My Hat.* 1963, *The Whole Truth and Nothing But.*
Biography: 1972, *Hedda and Louella* by George Eels.
Virtuous Wives 19. Heedless Moths 21. Sherlock Holmes 22. Has the World Gone Mad? 23. Reno 24. The Teaser 25. Don Juan 26. Wings 27. Harold Teen 28. His Glorious Night 29. Holiday 30. The Common Law 31. Speak Easily 32. Beauty For Sale 33. Little Man What Now? 34. Alice Adams 35. Dracula's Daughter 36. Topper 37. Thanks for the Memory 38. The Women 39. Queen of the Mob 40. Reap the Wild Wind 42. Sunset Boulevard 50. Pepe 60. The Oscar 66, many others.

¶ Nobody's interested in sweetness and light. – *H.H.*

Hopper, Jerry (1907–1988).
American director of routine action films and TV series.
■ The Atomic City 52. Hurricane Smith 52. Pony Express 53. Alaska Seas 54. The Secret of the Incas 54. Naked Alibi 54. Smoke Signal 55. The Private War of Major Benson 55. One Desire 55. The Square Jungle 55. Never Say Goodbye 56. Toy Tiger 56. The Sharkfighters 56. Everything but the Truth 56. The Missouri Traveller 58. Blueprint for Robbery 61. Madron 70.

Hopper, Victoria (1909–).
Canadian leading lady of a few British films of the 30s.
■ The Constant Nymph 33. *Lorna Doone* 34. Whom the Gods Love 36. Laburnum Grove 36. The Lonely Road 36. The Mill on the Floss 37. Escape from Broadmoor 38.

Hopper, William (1915–1970) (William Furry).
American general-purpose supporting actor, son of Hedda Hopper.
Footloose Heiress 37. Torchy Blane 38. Track of the Cat 54. Rebel Without a Cause 55. The Bad Seed 56. Twenty Million Miles to Earth (lead) 57, etc.
TV series: *Perry Mason* (as Paul Drake) 57–65.

Hopton, Russell (1900–1945).
American light leading man.
Ella Cinders 26. Street Scene 31. Night World 32. Lady Killer 33. He Was Her Man 34. Death from a Distance 35. High Wide and Handsome 37. The Saint Strikes Back 39. A Night of Adventure 44. Zombies on Broadway 45, etc.

Hordern, Sir Michael (1911–).
British character actor, on stage from 1937; film appearances usually as careworn official.
Autobiography: 1993, *A World Elsewhere.*
The Girl in the News (debut) 39; war service; School for Secrets 46. Mine Own Executioner 47. Good Time Girl 48. Passport to Pimlico 48. The Hour of Thirteen 51. The Heart of the Matter 53. The Baby and the Battleship 55. *The Spanish Gardener* 56. Sink the Bismarck 60. El Cid 61. The VIPs 63. Dr Syn 63. Genghis Khan 65. The Spy Who Came In from the Cold 66. Khartoum 66. *A Funny Thing Happened on the Way to the Forum* 66. The Taming of the Shrew 67. Where Eagles Dare 68. *The Bed-Sitting Room* 69. Anne of the Thousand Days 70. Futtock's End 70. Girl Stroke Boy 71. England Made Me 72. Alice's Adventures in Wonderland (as the Mock Turtle) 72. Theatre of Blood 73. The Mackintosh Man 73. Mister Quilp 74. Royal Flash 74. Lucky Lady 75. *The Slipper and the Rose* 76. Joseph Andrews 76. The Medusa

ouch 77. Shogun (TV) 80. Ivanhoe (TV) 81.
liver Twist (TV) 81. Gandhi 82. *The Missionary* 82.
ellowbeard 83. Lady Jane 84. Paradise Postponed
(V) 85. Scoop (TV) 87. Comrades 87. The Trouble
ith Spies 87. Diamond Skulls 89. The Fool 90.
lemento Mori (TV) 92. Middlemarch (TV) 94, etc.

orn, Camilla (1906–   ).
erman actress who had brief careers in
ollywood and Britain before retiring. She
eturned to acting in the 80s.
   Faust 26. Tempest 28. The Return of Raffles 32.
uck of a Sailor (GB) 34. The Last Story of
onigswald Castle 88, etc.

orn, Leonard (1926–1975).
merican director, from TV.
   Rogues' Gallery 68. The Magic Garden of Stanley
weetheart 70. Going All Out 71, etc.

ornbeck, William W. (1901–1983).
merican editor, with Mack Sennett until 1929,
vorking mainly on two-reel comedies.
   The Extra Girl 23. Roman Scandals 33. The
carlet Pimpernel 34. *Things To Come* 36. The Four
eathers 39. Lady Hamilton 42. *Why We Fight* series
3–45. *It's a Wonderful Life* 46. State of the Union
8. *A Place in the Sun* (AA) 51. Shane 53. Giant 56.
he Quiet American 58, many others.

ornblow, Arthur, Jnr (1893–1976).
merican producer, in Hollywood from 1926.
   Bulldog Drummond 29. Ruggles of Red Gap 34.
he Cat and the Canary 39. Gaslight 44. Weekend
t the Waldorf 45. The Hucksters 47. The Asphalt
ungle 50. Oklahoma 56. Witness for the
rosecution 57. The War Lover 63, many others.

orne, David (1898–1970).
ortly British character actor, mainly on stage;
lmost always in pompous roles.
   General John Regan 33. The Mill on the Floss
6. The First of the Few 42. The Seventh Veil 45.
he Rake's Progress 45. The Man Within 46. It's
lard To Be Good 49. Madeleine 50. Lust for Life
6. The Devil's Disciple 59, many others.

orne, Geoffrey (1933–   ).
British general-purpose actor.
   The Bridge on the River Kwai 57. Tempest 58.
Bonjour Tristesse 58, etc.

orne, James V. (1880–1942).
American director, in Hollywood from 1911. Made
ome of Laurel and Hardy's best two-reelers, and
ppeared as the villain in *Beau Hunks*.
   The Third Eye 20. American Manner 24. *College*
27. Bonnie Scotland 35. The Bohemian Girl 36. *Way
Out West* 37. Holt of the Secret Service 42, many
thers.

orne, Lena (1917–   ).
Lithe and sultry American singer whose best
appearances were in 40s musicals.
   Autobiographies: 1950, *In Person.* 1966, *Lena*
(with Richard Schickel).
¶ The Duke is Tops 38. Panama Hattie 42. *Cabin
in the Sky* 43. *Stormy Weather* 43. Thousands Cheer
43. I Dood It 43. Swing Fever 43. Broadway
Rhythm 44. Two Girls and a Sailor 44. Ziegfeld
Follies 46. Till the Clouds Roll By 46. Words and
Music 48. Duchess of Idaho 50. Meet Me in Las
Vegas 56. *Death of a Gunfighter* (dramatic role) 69.
The Wiz 78.

¶ In my early days I was a sepia Hedy Lamarr.
Now I'm black and a woman, singing my own
way. – *L.H.*

Horne, Victoria (c. 1920–   ).
American comedienne. She was married to Jack
Oakie.
   The Scarlet Claw 44. The Ghost and Mrs Muir
47. The Snake Pit 48. Abbott and Costello Meet the
Killer 49. *Harvey* 50. Affair with a Stranger 53, etc.

Horner, Harry (1910–1994).
Czech-born production designer with stage
experience in Vienna and New York.
   Our Town 40. *The Little Foxes* 41. A Double Life
47. *The Heiress* (AA) 49. Born Yesterday 50. *The
Hustler* (AA) 61. They Shoot Horses, Don't They?
(AAN) 69. Harry and Walter Go to New York 76.
Audrey Rose 77. Moment to Moment 78. The
Driver 78, etc.
AS DIRECTOR: Beware My Lovely 52. Red Planet
Mars 52. New Faces 54. A Life in the Balance
55. The Wild Party 56. Man from Del Rio 56,
etc.

Horner, James (1953–   ).
American composer.
   Battle beyond the Stars 80. Humanoids from the
Deep 80. Star Trek II: The Wrath of Khan 82. 48
Hours 82. Krull 83. Gorky Park 83. The Dresser
83. The Stone Boy 84. Star Trek III: The Search for
Spock 84. Commando 85. Aliens (AAN) 86. The
Name of the Rose 86. An American Tale 86.
Batteries Not Included 87. Willow 88. Red Heat
88. Cocoon: The Return 88. Field of Dreams (AAN)
89. Honey, I Shrunk the Kids 89. In Country 89.
Dad 89. Glory 89. I Love You to Death 90. Another
48 Hrs 90. Class Action 91. The Rocketeer
91. An American Tail: Fievel Goes West 91.
Thunderheart 92. Patriot Games 92. House of
Cards 93. Once upon a Forest 93. Searching for
Bobby Fischer 93. The Man without a Face 93.
Bopha! 93. Jack the Bear 93. Swing Kids 93. A Far
Off Place 93. We're Back! A Dinosaur's Story 93.
The Pelican Brief 93. Clear and Present Danger 94,
etc.

Hornung, E. W. (1866–1921).
British novelist, creator of the gentleman burglar
A.J. Raffles, who was impersonated on screen by
Ronald Colman and David Niven, and on
television by Anthony Valentine.

Horrocks, Jane (1964–   ).
British character actress, best known for her role
as an anorexic daughter in *Life Is Sweet*.
   The Dressmaker 88. Witches 90. Memphis Belle
90. Life Is Sweet 91. Bad Girl (TV) 92. Suffer the
Little Children (TV) 94. Deadly Advice 94. Second
Best 94, etc.
   TV series: Absolutely Fabulous 93–94.

horror
as a staple of screen entertainment really emanates
from Germany (although Edison shot a picture of
Frankenstein as early as 1908). Before World War
I Wegener had made a version of *The Golem*,
which he improved on in 1920: it was this second
version which directly influenced the Hollywood
horror school stimulated by James Whale. What
is surprising is that Hollywood took so long to
catch on to a good idea, especially as the Germans,
in depressed postwar mood, relentlessly turned
out such macabre films as *The Cabinet of Dr Caligari*
(with Veidt as a hypnotically-controlled
monster), *Nosferatu* (Murnau's brilliantly personal
account of Bram Stoker's 'Dracula'), *Waxworks*
(Leni's three-part thriller about Ivan the Terrible,
Haroun-al-Raschid and Jack the Ripper); *The
Hands of Orlac* and *The Student of Prague*. Most of
the talents involved were exported to Hollywood
by 1927; but the only horror film directly resulting

was Leni's *The Cat and the Canary*, which was a
spoof. California did encourage Lon Chaney, but
his films were grotesque rather than gruesome;
and John Barrymore had already been allowed in
1921 to impersonate *Dr Jekyll and Mr Hyde* (a role
to be played even more for horror by Fredric
March in 1932). By the end of the 20s, the
European horror film was played out except for
Dreyer's highly individual *Vampyr*; the ball was in
Hollywood's court.
   In 1930 Tod Browning filmed the stage version
of *Dracula*, using a Hungarian actor named Bela
Lugosi; shortly after, Robert Florey wrote and
James Whale directed a version of *Frankenstein* that
borrowed freely from *The Golem*. Both films (see
individual entries) were wildfire successes, and the
studio involved, Universal, set out on a steady and
profitable progress through a series of sequels. In
1932 Karloff appeared in *The Mummy*, and in 1933
Claude Rains was *The Invisible Man;* these characters
were added to the grisly band. In 1935 the studio
made *Werewolf of London*, which led five years
later to *The Wolf Man* giving Lon Chaney Jnr a
useful sideline. By 1945, despite the upsurge in
supernatural interest during the war, these
characters were thought to be played out, and in
the last two 'serious' episodes they appeared *en
masse*. In 1948 they began to meet Abbott and
Costello, which one would have thought might
ensure their final demise; but more of that later.
   Meanwhile other landmarks had been
established. Browning made the outlandish
Freaks, and in 1935 the spoof *Mark of the Vampire*.
James Whale in 1932 made *The Old Dark House*,
an inimitably entertaining mixture of disagreeable
ingredients. Warners in 1932 came up with *Doctor
X* and *The Mystery of the Wax Museum* (remade as
House of Wax) and later got some mileage out of *The
Walking Dead*. Paramount went in for mad doctors,
from *The Island of Dr Moreau* (Island of Lost Souls)
to *Doctor Cyclops*, and at the beginning of World
War II produced scary remakes of *The Cat and the
Canary* and *The Ghost Breakers*. RKO was busy with
King Kong and *She*, MGM with *The Devil Doll*. In the
early 40s Universal began a listless anthology series
under the title *Inner Sanctum*, and later failed in
The Creature from the Black Lagoon to add another
intriguing monster to their gallery. By far the most
significant extension of the genre was the small
group of depressive but atmospheric thrillers
produced by Val Lewton at RKO in 1942–45, the
best of them being *The Body Snatcher*, *The Cat
People* and *I Walked with a Zombie*.
   After the war, little was heard of horror until
the advent of science fiction in 1950. After this we
heard a very great deal of nasty visitors from other
planets (*The Thing, Invasion of the Body Snatchers*),
mutations (*The Fly, This Island Earth*), robots (*The
Day the Earth Stood Still, Forbidden Planet*) and giant
insects (*Them, Tarantula*). To please the teenage
audience, fly-by-night producers thought up
fantastic horror-comic variations and came up
with titles like *The Blob, I Married a Monster from
Outer Space* and *I Was a Teenage Werewolf;* such
crude and shoddy productions cheapened the genre
considerably. The Japanese got into the act with
rubber-suited monsters like *Godzilla* and *Rodan;*
then, surprisingly, it was the turn of the British.
Hammer Films, a small independent outfit with
an old Thames-side house for a studio, impudently
remade the sagas of Frankenstein, Dracula *et alia*,
and the results have been flooding the world's
screens for more than twenty years now, marked
by a certain bold style, lack of imagination, and
such excess of blood-letting that several versions
have to be made for each film (the bloodiest for
Japan, the most restrained for the home market).
Britain also produced commendable screen

versions of *The Quatermass Experiment* and other TV serials.

Since 1955 horror has been consistently in fashion, at least in the world's mass markets, and film-makers have been busy capping each other by extending the bounds of how much explicit physical shock and horror is permissible. (This, of course, does not make for good films.) If Franju was revolting in the detail of *Eyes Without a Face*, Hitchcock certainly topped him in *Psycho* and was himself outdone by William Castle in *Homicidal*, and by the perpetration in the 70s of films like *Blood Feast* and *Death Line*. (*Psycho* also gave the screen an inventive horror-writing talent in Robert Bloch, who has since been kept as busy as he could wish.) And the cheapjack American nasties at least provided a training ground for producer-director Roger Corman, who between 1960 and 1964 made a series of Poe adaptations much admired for style and enthusiasm if not for production detail. The trend in the early 70s was towards the compendiums of graveyard horror typified by *Tales from the Crypt* and *The House that Dripped Blood*, and towards such combinations of spoof and nastiness as *Theatre of Blood*, *Shivers* and *Squirm*.

The video craze of the early 80s revealed a significant and rather worrying minority of people who doted on excesses of horror, not only on the recent wave of teenage assassination thrillers like *Friday the Thirteenth*, *Hell Night* and *Terror Train*, but on 'nasties' such as *Driller Killer* and *I Spit on Your Grave*, which seemed to have been made explicitly for the new medium. This cheap rubbish, with neither style nor imagination, had nothing at all to do with the great achievements of the genre, though indications of talent were found by some in the work of John Carpenter (*Halloween*, etc.) and David Cronenberg (*The Brood*, etc.). The success of George Romero's *Night of the Living Dead* in 68 encouraged many similar low-budget horrors, some made by Romero himself. From the time of *An American Werewolf in London* 81, with its startling transformations from man to beast, make-up and special effects experts such as Rick Baker and Rob Bottin have grown in importance and some, like Chris Walas (*The Fly 2*) and Tom Savini (a remake of *Night of the Living Dead*), have even become directors. From the 80s, though, the predominant influence was that of novelist Stephen King. His first novel, *Carrie*, became a successful film in 74 and his second novel, *Salem's Lot*, became a TV movie in 79. After Stanley Kubrick made *The Shining*, based on his third novel, in 80, the pace quickened so that by the 90s even a seven-page short story was being turned into a full-length film, *The Lawnmower Man*, and King's name was above the titles and usually in bigger type than those of the stars. His British rival, novelist Clive Barker, turned director with *Hellraiser*, a film that has so far spawned two sequels and turned one of his hellish characters, Pinhead, into something of a cult figure – though nothing so far to rival the extraordinary and outlandish appeal for many of Freddy (Robert Englund), the child murderer of the *A Nightmare on Elm Street* series that ran through most of the 80s and into the 90s. By the mid-90s, Hammer was promising to remake its greatest hits and the genre was attracting notable actors and directors, with Francis Ford Coppola's big-budget and overblown *Bram Stoker's Dracula*, Mike Nichols directing *Wolf* with Jack Nicholson and Michelle Pfeiffer, and Kenneth Branagh making *Mary Shelley's Frankenstein*, which had Robert De Niro surprisingly stepping into Boris Karloff's built-up shoes.

Best books: 1968, *An Illustrated History of Horror Films* by Carlos Clarens; 1973, *A Pictorial History of Horror Films* by Denis Gifford; 1980, *Caligari's Children* by S. S. Prawer; 1988, *Nightmare Movies* by Kim Newman; 1994, *The Monster Show* by David J. Skal.

horses

have in several cases risen to the rank of star. All the great cowboy heroes had their familiar steed: Trigger for Roy Rogers, Topper for Hopalong Cassidy, Fritz for William S. Hart, Tarzan for Ken Maynard, Tony for Tom Mix, Silver for Buck Jones, Blackjack for Allan Rocky Lane, Koko for Rex Allen, White Flash for Tex Ritter, Champion for Gene Autry. Other movies strongly featuring horses have included *National Velvet*, *The Red Pony*, *Red Stallion*, *The Black Stallion*, *Crin Blanc*, *King of the Wild Horses*, *My Friend Flicka*, *Green Grass of Wyoming*, *Thunderhead Son of Flicka*, *Sand*, *Fury*, *Black Beauty*.

Horsfall, Bernard (1930–).
British character actor.

On Her Majesty's Secret Service 69. Gold 74. Shout at the Devil 76. Gandhi 82, etc.

Horsley, John (1920–).
British character actor, often seen as plain clothes man or executive.

Highly Dangerous 48. The Long Memory 51. The Runaway Bus 54. Father Brown 54. Above Us the Waves 55. Bond of Fear 56. The Comedy Man 64. The Fourth Protocol 87, etc.

Horton, Edward Everett (1886–1970).
American star comic actor with inimitable crooked smile and diffident manner; a favourite throughout the 20s, 30s and 40s.

Too Much Business 22. Ruggles of Red Gap (title role) 23. Marry Me 25. The Nutcracker 26. The Terror 28. Sonny Boy 29. The Hottentot 29. The Sap 29. Take the Heir 30. Holiday 30. Once a Gentleman 30. Kiss Me Again 31. The Front Page 31. Six Cylinder Love 31. *Trouble in Paradise* 32. A Bedtime Story 33. Soldiers of the King (GB) 33. *Alice in Wonderland* (as the Mad Hatter) 33. It's a Boy (GB) 34. The Merry Widow 34. *The Gay Divorcee* 35. The Devil is a Woman 35. In Caliente 35. *Top Hat* 35. Your Uncle Dudley 35. The Private Secretary (GB) 35. The Man in the Mirror (GB) 36. *Lost Horizon* 37. Shall We Dance? 37. Angel 37. The Great Garrick 37. Bluebeard's Eighth Wife 38. *Holiday* (repeat of 1930 role) 38. That's Right You're Wrong 39. Ziegfeld Girl 41. Sunny 41. *Here Comes Mr Jordan* 41. The Body Disappears 41. The Magnificent Dope 42. Forever and a Day 43. *Thank Your Lucky Stars* 43. The Gang's All Here 43. Her Primitive Man 44. *Summer Storm* 44. *San Diego I Love You* 44. Arsenic and Old Lace 44. Lady on a Train 45. Cinderella Jones 46. Down to Earth 47. Her Husband's Affairs 47. The Story of Mankind 57. *Pocketful of Miracles* 61. Sex and the Single Girl 64. The Perils of Pauline 67. 2000 Years Later 69. Cold Turkey 70, many others.

TV series: *F Troop* (as a Red Indian chief) 65.
🟡 For redeeming many a dull comedy by his superior twittering and double takes. *Trouble in Paradise*.

Horton, Robert (1924–) (Mead Howard Horton).
Good-looking American leading man who made it big on TV in the late 50s but could not manage the transfer to the big screen.

The Tanks are Coming 51. Bright Road 53. Prisoner of War 54. This Man is Armed 56. The Dangerous Days of Kiowa Jones 66. The Green Slime 69, etc.

TV series: Wagon Train 57–61. A Man Called Shenandoah 65.

Hoskins, Allen 'Farina' (1920–1980).
American comic actor and vaudeville performer, on screen from the age of 14 months. He played Farina in the Our Gang shorts of the 20s and 30s. In later life, he worked as a psychiatric technician.

You Said a Mouthful 32. The Mayor of Hell 33. The Life of Jimmy Dolan 33. After the Thin Man 36, etc.

Hoskins, Bob (1942–).
Stocky, untutored British character actor who made a big critical hit in TV's *Pennies from Heaven*.

Zulu Dawn 79. The Long Good Friday 80. Pink Floyd the Wall 82. The Honorary Consul 83. Mussolini and I (TV) 84. The Dunera Boys (TV) 84. Lassiter 84. The Cotton Club 84. Brazil 85. Sweet Liberty 85. *Mona Lisa* (AAN) 85. A Prayer for the Dying 87. The Lonely Passion of Judith Hearne 87. The Raggedy Rawney (& d) 88. *Who Framed Roger Rabbit* 88. Major League 89. Heart Condition 90. Mermaids 90. Shattered 91. Hook 91. The Favour, the Watch and the Very Big Fish (Rue Saint-Sulpice) 91. The Inner Circle 91. Passed Away 92. Super Mario Bros 93, etc.

hospitals

have been the setting of many films. *Life Begins* and its remake *A Child is Born* were set in the maternity wards, *No Time for Tears* in the children's wards. *Young Dr Kildare* started a whole series about a general hospital, and soon they were *Calling Dr Gillespie*. Other general hospital dramas include *White Corridors*, *The Lamp Still Burns*, *Behind the Mask*, *Life in Emergency Ward Ten*, *Emergency Hospital*; thrillers set among the wards include *Intent to Kill*, *The Sleeping City*, *Green for Danger* (the best of all), *Eye Witness* and *The Carey Treatment*, which last is in the vein of savage black humour evidenced in the early 70s by such films as *The Hospital* and *Where Does It Hurt?* Gentler hospital comedy has been found in *Doctor in the House*, *Twice Round the Daffodils*, *Trio*, and several episodes of the 'Carry On' series which have specialized in bedpan humour.

TV series on the subject include *Medic*, *The Nurses*, *The Doctors and the Nurses*, *Doctor Kildare*, *Ben Casey*, *Dr Hudson's Secret Journal*, *Dr Christian*, *General Hospital*, *West Side Medical*, *Trapper John*, *Quincy*, *St Elsewhere*.

Hossein, Robert (1927–).
French actor.

Rififi 55. The Wicked Go to Hell (& d) 55. Girls Disappear 58. La Musica 60. Enough Rope 63. Marco the Magnificent 65. I Killed Rasputin (& d) 68. The Burglars (& d) 71. Les Uns et les Autres 80. Les Misérables (d only) 82. Bolero 82. L'Affaire 94, etc.

hotels

have frequently formed a useful setting for films wanting to use the 'slice of life' technique. Thus *Grand Hotel*, *Hotel for Women*, *Stage Door*, *Hotel Berlin*, *Weekend at the Waldorf*, *Separate Tables* and *Hotel* itself; while *Ship of Fools* is a variation on the same theme. The hotel background was a valuable dramatic asset to films as varied as *The Last Laugh*, *The October Man*, *Don't Bother to Knock*, *Hotel du Nord*, *Pushover*, *Honeymoon Hotel*, *Room Service* (and its remake *Step Lively*), *Hotel Reserve*, *Hotel Sahara*, *The Horn Blows at Midnight*, *Hotel for Women*, *Hollywood Hotel*, *Paris Palace Hotel*, *Bedtime Story*, *The Best Man*, *The Greengage Summer*, *A Hole in the Head*, and *The Silence*. Hotel security did not prevent attempts on the hero's life in *Journey into Fear* and *Foreign Correspondent*. The most bewildering hotel was certainly that in *So Long at the Fair*; the most amusing hotel sequences may have been in

Ninotchka, *The Bellboy*, *Hotel Paradiso*, *A Flea in Her Ear* or *The Perfect Woman*. And hotels which had no accommodation to offer sparked off quite a few comedies during World War II, including *Government Girl*, *Standing Room Only* and *The More the Merrier* (later remade as *Walk Don't Run*). The hotel format endeared itself to television, which brought forth such variations as *Love Boat*, *Fantasy Island* and *Paradise Cove*; 1983 brought back *Hotel* itself, with shooting in San Francisco's Fairmont. The hotels no one would wish to revisit are those which sheltered Janet Leigh in *Psycho* and Jack Nicholson in *The Shining*.

Houdini, Harry (1873–1926) (Ehrich Weiss).
American escapologist and magician extraordinary, in films from 1918. A biopic in 1953 starred Tony Curtis, and a 1976 TV movie, *The Great Houdinis*, Paul Michael Glaser.

Biographies: 1969, *Houdini, the Unknown Story* by Christopher Milbourne. 1993, *The Life and Many Deaths of Harry Houdini* by Ruth Brandon.

The Master Mystery (serial) 18. The Grim Game 19. Terror Island 20. The Man from Beyond 21. Haldane of the Secret Service 23, etc.

Hough, John (1941–).
British director in international films.

■ Wolfshead 69. Eye Witness 70. Twins of Evil 71. Treasure Island 72. The Legend of Hell House 73. Dirty Mary Crazy Larry 74. Escape to Witch Mountain 75. Brass Target 78. The Watcher in the Woods 80. Triumphs of a Man Called Horse 82. The Incubus 82. Biggles 85. American Gothic 87. A Hazard of Hearts (TV) 87. Howling IV: The Original Nightmare 88. Dangerous Love (TV) 88. The Lady and the Highwayman (TV) 89.

Houghton, Katharine (1945–).
American leading lady of *Guess Who's Coming to Dinner* 67; niece of Katharine Hepburn.

Seeds of Evil 76. Eyes of the Amaryllis 82. Mr North 88. Billy Bathgate 91. Ethan Frome 92.

House, Billy (1890–1961).
Rotund American character actor, formerly trumpet player.

Smart Money 32. Merry Go Round 37. Bedlam 44. The Stranger 45. Trail Street 46. The Egg and I 47. Where Danger Lives 50. People Will Talk 51, etc.

Houseman, John (1902–1988) (Jacques Haussmann).
American producer. After varied experience, helped Orson Welles to found his Mercury Theatre in New York in 1937, later followed him to Hollywood; unexpectedly became a star actor in his 70s.

Autobiographies: 1972, *Runthrough*. 1980, *Front and Center*. 1983, *Final Dress*.

The Blue Dahlia 46. Letter from an Unknown Woman 48. They Live by Night 48. The Bad and the Beautiful 52. Julius Caesar 53. Executive Suite 54. Lust for Life 56. Two Weeks in Another Town 62. This Property is Condemned 66, etc.
AS ACTOR: Seven Days in May 64. *Paper Chase* (AA) 74. Three Days of the Condor 75. Rollerball 75. Meeting at Potsdam (TV) (as Churchill) 76. Fear on Trial (TV) 76. St Ives 76. Captains and the Kings (TV) 76. Washington Behind Closed Doors (TV) 77. Aspen (TV) 77. Tentacles 77. The Cheap Detective 78. Old Boyfriends 79. My Bodyguard 80. The Fog 80. Wholly Moses 80. Ghost Story 81. Murder by Phone 82. Another Woman 88, etc.
TV series: *The Paper Chase* 78 and 83. Silver Spoons 82.

houses
have been the dramatic center of many films: there was even one, *Enchantment*, in which the house itself told the story. The films of Daphne du Maurier's novels usually have a mysterious old house at the crux of their plots, as in *Rebecca*, *Frenchman's Creek*, *Jamaica Inn*, *My Cousin Rachel*. So in *Dragonwyck*; so in *House of Fear*; so, of course, in *Jane Eyre* and *Wuthering Heights*. Both *Citizen Kane* and *The Magnificent Ambersons* are dominated by unhappy houses, as is *Gaslight*. Thrillers set in lonely houses full of secret panels and hidden menace are exemplified by *The Spiral Staircase*, *The Black Cat*, *Night Monster*, *The House on Haunted Hill*, *The Cat and the Canary*, *The Ghost Breakers*, *The House that Dripped Blood*, *Whatever Happened to Baby Jane?* *The Beast with Five Fingers*, *Ladies in Retirement* and *And Then There Were None*. Haunted houses are rarer, but those in *The Uninvited*, *The Unseen*, *The Innocents*, *The Enchanted Cottage* and *The Haunting* linger vividly in the memory. So for a different reason does the Bates's house in *Psycho*: happier houses of note include the rose-covered cottage in *Random Harvest*, the family mansions of *Forever and a Day* and *Enchantment*, the red-decorated Denver house in *The Unsinkable Molly Brown*, the laboriously built country seat of *Mr Blandings Builds His Dream House*, the labour-saving modern house of *Mon Oncle*, the broken-down houses of *George Washington Slept Here* and *Father Came Too*, and dear old *Rookery Nook*. And filmgoers have various reasons to remember *The House on 92nd Street*, *The House on Telegraph Hill*, *House of Strangers*, *House of Horrors*, *House of Bamboo*, *House of Numbers*, *House of the Damned*, *House of the Seven Hawks*, *House of Women*, *House by the River*, *House of Dracula*, *House of Frankenstein*, *House of Wax*, *Sinister House*, *The Red House*, *Crazy House*, *The Old Dark House*, *The House of Usher*, *The House of the Seven Gables* and the house in *House* and *House II*. The house in *Malpertuis* brought little comfort; come to that, nor did the noble pile in *Brideshead Revisited*, or the crumbling property in *The Money Pit*.

Housman, Arthur (1888–1942).
American character actor, usually seen as incoherent but gentlemanly drunk in comedies of the early 30s.

Under the Red Robe 23. Manhandled 24. The Bat 26. Sunrise 27. Fools for Luck 28. The Singing Fool 28. Broadway 29. The Squealer 30. Five and Ten 31. *Scram* (Laurel and Hardy two-reeler) 32. She Done Him Wrong 33. Mrs Wiggs of the Cabbage Patch 34. Our Relations 36. Step Lively Jeeves 37. Go West 40. Billy the Kid 41, etc.

Houston, Donald (1923–1991).
Burly, capable Welsh leading man of the early 50s. Later a useful character actor.

■ The Blue Lagoon 48. A Run for Your Money 49. Dance Hall 50. My Death is a Mockery 51. Crow Hollow 52. The Red Beret 53. Small Town Story 53. The Large Rope 53. Devil's Point 54. The Happiness of Three Women 54. Doctor in the House 54. The Flaw 55. Double Cross 55. The Girl in the Picture 56. Find the Lady 56. Yangtse Incident 57. The Surgeon's Knife 57. A Question of Adultery 58. The Man Upstairs 58. Danger within 58. Room at the Top 58. The Mark 61. Twice Round the Daffodils 62. The Prince and the Pauper 62. Maniac 62. The Longest Day 62. The 300 Spartans 63. Doctor in Distress 63. Carry on Jack 63. 633 Squadron 64. A Study in Terror 65. The Viking Queen 66. Where Eagles Dare 68. My Lover My Son 70. Tales that Witness Madness 73. Voyage of the Damned 76. The Sea Wolves 80. Clash of the Titans 81. The Secret Adversary (TV) 82.

Houston, Glyn (1926–).
Welsh character actor, brother of Donald Houston; much on TV.

The Blue Lamp 50. Payroll 60. Solo for Sparrow (lead role) 62. The Secret of Blood Island 65. Invasion 66. Are You Being Served? 77. The Sea Wolves 80. The Mystery of Edwin Drood 93, etc.

Houston, Penelope.
English film critic, one of the founders of the influential Oxford University Film Society magazine *Sequence* (qv) in the mid-40s and later the editor of the British Film Institute's magazine *Sight and Sound* from 1956–90. Author of *The Contemporary Cinema* (1963).

Houston, Renée (1902–1980) (Katherina Houston Gribbin).
British vaudeville and revue artiste, once teamed with her sister Billie, later with Donald Stewart; more recently character actress of screen and TV.

Autobiography: 1974, *Don't Fence Me In*.

Mr Cinders 34. A Girl Must Live 38. Old Bill and Son 40. Two Thousand Women 44. The Belles of St Trinians 54. A Town Like Alice 56. *Time Without Pity* 57. The Horse's Mouth 59. The Flesh and the Friends 60. Three on a Spree 61. Repulsion 64. Carry On at Your Convenience 71. Legend of the Werewolf 71, etc.

Houston, Sam (1793–1863).
An American hero of the early days of Texas, played on film by Richard Boone in *The Alamo*, William Farnum in *The Conqueror*, Richard Dix in *Man of Conquest*, Moroni Olsen in *Lone Star*, Hugh Sanders in *The Last Command* and Joel McCrea in *The First Texan*.

Houston, Whitney (1963–).
American singer and actress, the daughter of soul singer Cissy Houston (1932–). Her debut, playing a singer, was a massive box-office success, as was her soundtrack album.

Biography: 1994, *Diva* by Jeffrey Bowman.
The Bodyguard 93.

Hovey, Tim (1945–1989).
American child actor of the mid-50s. Later on TV.

The Private War of Major Benson 55. Toy Tiger 56. Man Afraid 57, etc.

Howard, Alan (1937–).
British Shakespearean actor in occasional films.

Victim 61. Work Is a Four-Letter Word 68. Little Big Man 70. Strapless 88. The Return of the Musketeers 89. The Cook, the Thief, His Wife and Her Lover 89. Dakota Road 91. The Secret Rapture 93, etc.

Howard, Arthur (1910–).
British character actor, brother of Leslie Howard, often seen as schoolmaster, clerk, etc.

Passport to Pimlico 48. *The Happiest Days of Your Life* 49. The Intruder 53. The Shoes of the Fisherman 68. Zeppelin 70. Steptoe and Son 72. One of Our Dinosaurs Is Missing 75. The Missionary 82. Curse of the Pink Panther 83. Another Country 84, etc.

Howard, Curly (1906–1952) (Jerome Horowitz).
American comedy actor: the fat, bald member of The Three Stooges (qv).

Howard, Cy (1915–1993).
American director.

Lovers and Other Strangers 69. Every Little Crook and Nanny 72. Won Ton Ton (co-w only) 76.

Howard, Esther (1892–1965).
American character actress, usually in blowsy roles.

Ladies of the Big House 31. Ready for Love 35. Serenade 39. Sullivan's Travels 41. Farewell My Lovely 44. The Lady Gambles 49, etc.

Howard, James Newton.
American composer.

Head Office 86. Wildcats 86. Never Too Young to Die 86. 8 Million Ways to Die 86. Nobody's Fool 86. Tough Guys 86. Campus Man 87. Five Corners 87. Russkies 87. Promised Land 87. Off Limits 88. Some Girls 88. Everybody's All-American 88. Tap 89. Major League 89. The Package 89. Coupe de Ville 90. Pretty Woman 90. Flatliners 90. King Ralph 90. My Girl 91. The Man in the Moon 91. The Prince of Tides 91. Grand Canyon 91. American Heart 92. Alive 93. Falling Down 93. Dave 93. The Saint of Fort Washington 93. The Fugitive (AAN) 93. Intersection 94. Wyatt Earp 94. Outbreak 95, etc.

Howard, John (1913–1995) (John Cox).
Good-looking, useful American leading man of the 30s and 40s, mainly in routine films.

Annapolis Farewell 35. Soak the Rich 36. *Lost Horizon* 37. Bulldog Drummond Comes Back (and ensuing series) 37. Penitentiary 38. Prison Farm 38. Disputed Passage 39. Green Hell 40. *The Philadelphia Story* 40. The Invisible Woman 40. The Mad Doctor 41. Tight Shoes 41. The Undying Monster 42. Isle of Missing Men 43. Love from a Stranger 47. I Jane Doe 48. The Fighting Kentuckian 49. Experiment Alcatraz 51. The High and the Mighty 54. Unknown Terror 58, etc.

TV series: *Dr Hudson's Secret Journal* 55–56. Adventures of Seahawk 58.

Howard, Joyce (1922–).
British leading lady of the 40s.

Freedom Radio 40. Love on the Dole 41. The Gentle Sex 43. They Met in the Dark 43. Woman to Woman 46. Mrs Fitzherbert 47. Shadow of the Past 50, etc.

Howard, Kathleen (1879–1956).
Canadian character actress, former opera singer; memorable as W. C. Fields's frequent screen wife.

Death Takes a Holiday 34. You're Telling me 34. The Man on the Flying Trapeze 35. It's a Gift 35. Laura 44. The Late George Apley 47, etc.

Howard, Ken (1944–).
Hulking American leading man who came to the fore on TV.

■ Tell Me That You Love Me Junie Moon 70. Such Good Friends 71. The Strange Vengeance of Rosalie 72. *1776* 72. Superdome (TV) 78. The Critical List (TV) 78. A Great American Hero (TV) 80. The Victims (TV) 81. Second Thoughts 83. Always Ready (doc) 85. Anchors Aweigh (doc) 85. Citizen Soldiers (doc) 85. The Wild Blue Yonder (doc) 85. Pudd'nhead Wilson (TV) 87. Strange Interlude (TV) 90.

TV series: Adam's Rib 73. Manhunter 74. The White Shadow 78–81. It's Not Easy 83. Dynasty 85–86. Dynasty II: The Colbys 85–86.

Howard, Leslie (1893–1943) (Leslie Stainer).
Distinguished British actor of Hungarian origin; his image was that of the romantic intellectual who had only to ignore women to be idolized. He was equally successful in American films. Died when his plane was shot down in the Second World War.

Biography: 1959, *A Very Remarkable Father* by his daughter Ruth Howard.

■ *Outward Bound* 30. Never the Twain Shall Meet 31. A Free Soul 31. Five and Ten 31. Devotion 31. Service for Ladies 32. Smilin' Through 32. The Animal Kingdom 32. Secrets 33. Captured 33. *Berkeley Square* (AAN) 33. The Lady is Willing 34. *Of Human Bondage* 34. British Agent 34. *The Scarlet Pimpernel* 35. *The Petrified Forest* 36. Romeo and Juliet 36. It's Love I'm After 36. Stand-In 37. *Pygmalion* (& co-d) (AAN) 38. *Gone with the Wind* 39. *Intermezzo* 39. Pimpernel Smith (& pd) 41. 49th Parallel 41. *The First of the Few* (& oa, d) 42. The Gentle Sex (pd only) 43. The Lamp Still Burns (p only) 43.

☼ For having more Englishness than any pure Englishman, and for conquering world audiences with it. *Pygmalion.*

¶ He had a passion for England and the English ideal that was almost Shakespearean. – *C. A. Lejeune*

Famous line (*The Petrified Forest*): 'Let there be killing. All the evening I've had a feeling of destiny closing in.'

Famous line (*Pygmalion*): 'Where the devil are my slippers, Eliza?'

Howard, Moe (1895–1975) (Moses Horowitz).
American comedy actor, the fringed and violent member of The Three Stooges (qv).

Howard, Ron (1954–).
American child actor of the 60s who matured into a director, screenwriter and producer.

The Journey 59. The Music Man 62. The Courtship of Eddie's Father 63. Smoke 69. The Wild Country 71. American Graffiti 73. The Spikes Gang 75. The Shootist 76. Grand Theft Auto (& d) 77. More American Graffiti 79. Night Shift (d only) 82. Splash! (d only) 84. Cocoon (d only) 85. Gung Ho (d only) 85. No Man's Land (p) 87. Clean and Sober (p) 88. Vibes (p) 88. Willow (d) 88. The 'burbs (p) 89. Parenthood (d, story) 89. Closet Land (p) 91. Backdraft (d) 91. Far and Away (d) 92. The Paper (d) 94, etc.

TV series: The Andy Griffith Show 60–68. The Smith Family 71–2. Happy Days 74–80.

Howard, Ronald (1918–).
British actor, son of Leslie Howard; formerly a reporter.

Biography: 1980, *In Search of My Father.*

While the Sun Shines (debut) 46. The Queen of Spades 48. Tom Brown's Schooldays 51. Drango (US) 56. Babette Goes to War 59. Spider's Web 60. The Curse of the Mummy's Tomb 64. Africa Texas Style 67. The Hunting Party 71. Persecution 74. Take a Hard Ride 75, many others.

TV series: *Sherlock Holmes* 55. Cowboy in Africa 67.

Howard, Shemp (1891–1955) (Samuel Horowitz).
American character comedian, brother of Moe Howard of the Three Stooges and occasional substitute for him; usually played tramps and bartenders.

Soup to Nuts 30. Headin' East 37. *The Bank Dick* 40. Buck Privates 41. *Hellzapoppin* 41. Pittsburgh 42. Crazy House 43. Blondie Knows Best 46. Africa Screams 49, many others.

Howard, Sidney (1891–1939).
American playwright whose chief contributions to Hollywood were *The Late Christopher Bean, They Knew What They Wanted, Yellow Jack,* and most of the script of *Gone with the Wind* (for which he won a posthumous Oscar).

Howard, Sydney (1884–1946).
Plump British comedian famous for fluttering gestures. On stage from 1912, films from 1930.

■ Splinters 29. French Leave 30. Tilly of Bloomsbury 31. Almost a Divorce 31. *Up for the Cup* 31. Splinters in the Navy 31. The Mayor's Nest 32. It's a King 32. Up for the Derby 32. *Night of the Garter* 33. Trouble 33. It's a Cop 34. Transatlantic Merry Go Round (US) 34. Where's George? 35. *Fame* 36. Chick 36. Splinters in the Air 37. What a Man 37. Shipyard Sally 39. Tilly of Bloomsbury 40. Once a Crook 41. Mr Proudfoot Shows a Light 42. *When We Are Married* 43. Flight from Folly 45 ~Catchphrase: What's to do?

Howard, Trevor (1916–1988).
Distinguished British leading man, on stage from 1934; later concentrated on films. He was married for 44 years to actress Helen Cherry.

Biography: 1988, *Trevor Howard: A Gentleman and a Player* by Vivienne Knight.

■ The Way Ahead (debut) 44. The Way to the Stars 45. Brief Encounter 46. I See a Dark Stranger 46. *Green for Danger* 46. So Well Remembered 47. They Made Me a Fugitive 47. The Passionate Friends 48. *The Third Man* 49. The Golden Salamander 49. Odette 50. The Clouded Yellow 51. An Outcast of the Islands 52. The Gift Horse 52. *The Heart of the Matter* 53. The Lovers of Lisbon (Fr.) 54. The Stranger's Hand 54. Cockleshell Heroes 55. Around the World in Eighty Days 56. Run for the Sun (US) 56. Interpol 57. Manuela 57. *The Key* (BFA) 58. Roots of Heaven 59. Moment of Danger 60. Sons and Lovers (AAN) 60. *Mutiny on the Bounty* (as Captain Bligh) 62. The Lion 62. The Man in the Middle 64. Father Goose 64. Von Ryan's Express 65. Operation Crossbow 65. Morituri 65. The Liquidator 65. The Poppy is Also a Flower 66. Triple Cross 66. The Long Duel 67. Pretty Polly 68. *The Charge of the Light Brigade* 68. The Battle of Britain 69. Twinky 69. *Ryan's Daughter* 70. *The Night Visitor* 71. Catch Me a Spy 71. Mary Queen of Scots 72. Kidnapped 72. Pope Joan 72. Ludwig 72. The Offence 72. Catholics (TV) 73. Craze 73. A Doll's House 73. Persecution 74. 11 Harrowhouse 74. Who? 74. Death in the Sun 75. Conduct Unbecoming 75. Hennessy 75. The Bawdy Adventures of Tom Jones 76. Eliza Fraser 76. Aces High 76. Slaves 77. The Last Remake of Beau Geste 77. Stevie 77. Superman 78. Night Flight (TV) 78. Hurricane 79. Meteor 79. The Sea Wolves 80. Windwalker 80. Staying On (TV) 80. Light Years Away 81. Inside the Third Reich (TV) 82. The Deadly Game (TV) 82. Gandhi 82. The Missionary 82. Sir Henry at Rawlinson End 82. Sword of the Valiant 84. Foreign Body 85. White Mischief 87. The Unholy 87. The Dawning 88.

¶ I've been number two in films for donkey's years. – *T.H.*

Howard, William K. (1899–1954).
American director who made some interesting films in the 30s.

East of Broadway 24. Code of the West 25. Gigolo 26. The Main Event 27. The River Pirate 28. Live Love and Laugh 29. Scotland Yard 30. Don't Bet on Women 31. Transatlantic 31. *Sherlock Holmes* 32. *The Power and the Glory* 33. The Cat and the Fiddle 34. Evelyn Prentice 34. Vanessa 35. *Mary Burns Fugitive* 35. The Princess Comes Across 36. *Fire Over England* (GB) 36. Back Door to Heaven 39. Bullets for O'Hara 41. Johnny Come Lately 43, etc.

Howe, James Wong (1899–1976) (Wong Tung Jim).
Distinguished Chinese cinematographer, in Hollywood from 1917.

■ Drums of Fate 23. The Woman with Four Faces 23. Call of the Canyon 23. The Spanish Dancer 23. To the Last Man 23. The Trail of the Lonesome Pine 23. The Alaskan 24. The Breaking Point 24. The Side Show of Life 24. The Best People 25. The Charmer 25. The King on Main Street 25. Not So Long Ago 25. Mantrap 26. Padlocked 26. Sea Horses 26. The Song and Dance Man 26. The Rough Riders 27. Sorrell and Son 27. Four Walls 28. The Perfect Crime 28. Laugh Clown Laugh 28. Desert Nights 29. Today 30. The Criminal Code 31. Transatlantic 31. The Spider 31. The Yellow Ticket 31. Surrender 31. Dance Team 32. After Tomorrow 32. Amateur Daddy 32. Man about Town 32. Chandu the Magician 32. Hello Sister 33. Beauty for Sale 33. The Power and the Glory 33. The Show Off 34. *The Thin Man* 34. Hollywood Party 34. Stamboul Quest 34. Have a Heart 34. Biography of a Bachelor Girl 34. The Night is Young 35. Mark of the Vampire 35. The Flame Within 35. O'Shaughnessy's Boy 35. Three Live Ghosts 35. Whipsaw 36. Fire Over England 36. Farewell Again 36. Under the Red Robe 37. *The Prisoner of Zenda* 37. The Adventures of Tom Sawyer 37. Algiers 38. Comet Over Broadway 38. They Made Me a Criminal 39. The Oklahoma Kid 39. Daughters Courageous 39. Dust Be My Destiny 39. On Your Toes 39. Abe Lincoln in Illinois 39. *Dr Ehrlich's Magic Bullet* 40. Saturday's Children 40. Torrid Zone 40. City for Conquest 40. A Dispatch from Reuter's 40. The Strawberry Blonde 41. Shining Victory 41. Navy Blues 41. Out of the Fog 41. *King's Row* 41. Yankee Doodle Dandy 42. The Hard Way 42. Hangmen also Die 43. Air Force 43. North Star 43. Passage to Marseille 44. Objective Burma 45. Counterattack 45. Confidential Agent 45. Danger Signal 45. My Reputation 46. Nora Prentiss 47. Pursued 47. Body and Soul 47. Mr Blandings Builds His Dream House 48. The Time of Your Life 48. The Eagle and the Hawk 49. The Baron of Arizona 50. Tripoli 50. The Brave Bulls 51. He Ran All the Way 51. Behave Yourself 51. The Lady Says No 52. Main Street to Broadway 53. Come Back Little Sheba 54. The Rose Tattoo (AA) 55. *Picnic* 56. Death of a Scoundrel 56. Drango 56. *Sweet Smell of Success* 57. The Old Man and the Sea 58. Bell, Book and Candle 58. The Last Angry Man 59. The Story on Page One 60. Song without End 60. Tess of the Storm Country 61. *Hud* (AA) 63. The Outrage 64. The Glory Guys 65. This Property Is Condemned 66. *Seconds* (AAN) 67. Hombre 67. The Heart is a Lonely Hunter 69. The Molly Maguires 70. Last of the Mobile Hotshots 70. Funny Lady (AAN) 75.
Directed Go Man Go 52.
☺ For the visual sensitivity which is evident in every shot of every one of his films. *Kings Row*.

Howell, C. Thomas (1966–).
American young leading actor. He is married to actress Rae Dawn Chong.
■ The Outsiders 83. Grandview USA 84. Red Dawn 84. Tank 84. Secret Admirer 85. The Hitcher 86. Soul Man 86. A Tiger's Tale 87. Il Giovane Toscanini 88. The Return of the Musketeers 89. Far Out, Man 90. The Kid 90. Side Out 90. That Night 92. Nickel & Dime 92. To Protect and Serve 92. Acting on Impulse 93. Gettysburg 93. Playback 94. Teresa's Tattoo 94. Mad Dogs and Englishmen 95.
TV series: Two Marriages 83–84.

Howells, Ursula (1922–).
British actress, mainly on stage and TV. Film roles infrequent.
Flesh and Blood 51. The Constant Husband 55. They Can't Hang Me 55. The Long Arm 56. Dr Terror's House of Horrors 65. The Forsyte Saga

(TV) 67. Mumsy Nanny Sonny and Girly 68. Crossplot 69, etc.

Howerd, Frankie (1922–1992) (Francis Howard).
British eccentric comedian of stage and TV.
Autobiography: 1977, *On My Way I Lost It*.
■ *The Runaway Bus* 54. An Alligator Named Daisy 55. Jumping for Joy 55. The Ladykillers 55. A Touch of the Sun 56. Further Up the Creek 59. Watch It Sailor 61. The Cool Mikado 63. Mouse on the Moon 63. The Great St Trinian's Train Robbery 66. Carry On Doctor 68. Carry On Up the Jungle 69. *Up Pompeii* 70. Up the Chastity Belt 71. Up the Front 72. *The House in Nightmare Park* 73. Sergeant Pepper's Lonely Hearts Club Band 78.

Howes, Bobby (1895–1972).
Diffident, diminutive British leading man of stage musical comedies in the 30s.
■ The Guns of Loos 28. Third Time Lucky 31. Lord Babs 32. For the Love of Mike 32. Over the Garden Wall 34. Please Teacher 37. Sweet Devil 38. *Yes Madam* 38. Bob's Your Uncle 41. The Trojan Brothers 45. Happy Go Lovely 51. The Good Companions 57. Watch It Sailor 61.

Howes, Sally Ann (1930–).
British child actress of the 40s, later an occasional leading lady. Daughter of Bobby Howes.
■ *Thursday's Child* 43. Halfway House 44. *Dead of Night* 45. Pink String and Sealing Wax 45. Nicholas Nickleby 47. My Sister and I 48. Anna Karenina 48. *The History of Mr Polly* 48. Fools Rush In 49. Stop Press Girl 50. Honeymoon Deferred 51. The Admirable Crichton 57. Chitty Chitty Bang Bang 68. The Hound of the Baskervilles (TV) 72. Female Artillery (TV) 72. Death Ship 80.

Howlett, Noel (1901–1984).
British stage actor who appeared in small film roles from 1936, often as solicitor, auctioneer or civil servant.
A Yank at Oxford 46. Corridor of Mirrors 47. The Blind Goddess 49. Father Brown 54. The Scapegoat 59. Some Will Some Won't 70, etc.

Howlin, Olin (1896–1959) (formerly known as Olin Howland).
American character actor, in innumerable small film roles since the early talkies.
So Big 32. Nothing Sacred 37. This Gun for Hire 42. The Wistful Widow 47. Them 54. The Blob 58, etc.

Hoxie, Jack (1890–1965) (Hartford Hoxie).
American star of early westerns who quit with the coming of sound. A cowboy, born in Oklahoma, he won the national riding championship in 1914 and went to Hollywood to work as a stuntman.
Lightning Bryce (serial) 19. Dead or Alive 21. Riders of the Law 22. Red Warning 22. Desert Rider 23. The Man from Wyoming 24. Flying Hoofs 25. The Last Frontier 26. The Western Whirlwind 27. Gold 32. Outlaw Justice 33, etc.

Hoyt, Arthur (1873–1953).
American character actor who played mild or henpecked husband in hundreds of silent and sound movies.
Love Never Dies 16. The Grim Game 19. Camille 21. Kissed 22. Souls for Sale 23. Sundown 24. The Lost World 25. Shanghai Bound 27. The Criminal Code 31. Call Her Savage 32. Only Yesterday 33. Wake Up and Dream 34. The Raven 35. Mr Deeds Goes to Town 36. A Star Is Born 37. The Black Doll 38. East Side of Heaven 39. The Great McGinty 40. The Lady Eve 41. The Palm Beach Story 42. The Miracle of Morgan's Creek 44. Hail the Conquering

Hero 44. Mad Wednesday 47. Brute Force 47, many others.

Hoyt, John (1905–1991) (John Hoysradt).
Incisive American character actor, sometimes cast as German officer or stylish crook.
O.S.S. 46. *Rommel, Desert Fox* 51. New Mexico 52. When Worlds Collide 52. Androcles and the Lion 53. Julius Caesar 53. The Blackboard Jungle 55. Trial 55. The Conqueror 56. Six Inches Tall 58. Never So Few 60. Duel at Diablo 66. Flesh Gordon 74, many others.

Hsiao-Hsien, Hou (1947–).
Taiwanese director and screenwriter.
Green, Green Grass of Home 82. Growing Up 82. The Sandwich Man 83. The Boys from Fengkuei 83. A Summer at Grandpa's 85. A Time to Live and a Time to Die 85. Dust in the Wind 87. Daughter of the Nile 88. City of Sadness (Pei-ch'ing Ch'eng Shih) 89. Sunless Days 90. The Puppetmaster (Hsimeng Jensheng) 93, etc.

Hu, King (1931–) (Hu Chin Ch'uan).
Chinese producer and director, working in Hong Kong.
Sons of the Good Earth 64. A Touch of Zen 68. The Valiant Ones 74. Legend of the Mountain 78. The Wheel of Life 83. Reckless Swordsman 89, etc.

Hubbard, John (1914–1988).
American light leading man who starred in several Hal Roach comedies.
The Housekeeper's Daughter 39. *Turnabout* 40. Road Show 41. Gunfight at Comanche Creek 63. Fate Is the Hunter 64. Duel at Diablo 66. Herbie Rides Again 73, etc.
TV series: The Mickey Rooney Show 54–55. Don't Call Me Charlie 62–63.

Hubbard, Lucien (1888–1971).
American screenwriter.
The Perils of Pauline 14. Wild Honey 22. The Vanishing American 25. Wings 27. Smart Money (AANw) Five Star Final 31. 42nd Street 33. The Casino Murder Case (& p) 35. A Family Affair (& p) 37. Ebb Tide (p) 37. Nick Carter Master Detective (p) 39, etc.

Huber, Harold (1904–1959).
American character actor, former lawyer; often seen as sly crook or dumb detective.
The Bowery 33. The Thin Man 34. G-Men 35. San Francisco 36. A Slight Case of Murder 38. Kit Carson 40. The Lady from Chungking 43. Let's Dance 50, many others.
TV series: I Cover Times Square 50.

Hubert, Jean-Loup (1949–).
French director whose best films are semi-autobiographical.
L'Année Prochaine Si Tout Va Bien 81. La Smala 84. The Grand Highway (Le Grand Chemin) 87. La Reine Blanche 91. À Cause d'Elle 93, etc.

Hubert, Roger (1903–1964).
French cinematographer.
Napoléon 27. Fanny 32. J'Accuse 37. Le Baron Fantôme 43. Les Enfants du Paradis 45. Thérèse Raquin 53. Paris Holiday 58. Lafayette 62. La Bonne Soupe 64, many others.

Hubie and Bertie.
Cartoon mice created by Chuck Jones. Their voices were supplied by Mel Blanc and Stan Freberg.
The Aristo Cat 43. House-Hunting Mice 48. Mouse Wreckers (AAN) 49. Cheese Chasers 51. Mouse Warming 52, etc.

Hubley, John (1914–1977).
American animator, associated with the early days of UPA; a co-creator of Mr Magoo. Latterly worked on experimental documentary cartoons: *Of Stars and Men*, etc.

Hubley, Season (1951–   ).
American leading lady of the 70s. She was formerly married to actor Kurt Russell.

Lolly Madonna XXX 73. Catch My Soul 74. She Lives (TV) 74. Death Flight (TV) 77. Loose Change (TV) 78. Elvis (TV) 79. Hardcore 79. Escape from New York 81. Prettykill 87.

TV series: Kung Fu 74–75. Family 76–77. Blue Skies 88.

Hubschmid, Paul (1917–   ) (known in US as Paul Christian).
German-Swiss leading man, in international films; also on stage, especially as Higgins in *My Fair Lady*.

Maria Ilona 40. Baghdad 49. The Thief of Venice 52. The Beast from 20,000 Fathoms 53. Der Tiger von Eschnapur 59. Journey to the Lost City 60. Mozambique 66. *Funeral in Berlin* 66. Skullduggery 69, many others.

Hudd, Walter (1898–1963).
British character actor of stage and screen; usually played aloof characters and in 1936 was cast as T. E. Lawrence but the production was abandoned.

Rembrandt 36. Black Limelight 37. Elephant Boy 37. The Housemaster 38. Major Barbara 40. I Know Where I'm Going 45. Paper Orchid 49. Life For Ruth 62, etc.

Huddleston, David (1930–   ).
Oversized American actor, often found in westerns.

All the Way Home 63. A Lovely Way to Die 66. Slaves 69. Rio Lobo 70. Bad Company 72. Fools Parade 72. Brock's Last Case (TV) 73. The Gun and the Pulpit (TV) 74. The Oregon Trail (TV) 76. Blazing Saddles 76. Capricorn One 78. Kate Bliss and the Tickertape Kid (TV) 78. Smokey and the Bandit II 80. Santa Claus, the Movie 85. The Tracker 88, etc.

TV series: Tenafly 73–74. Petrocelli 74–76. The Kallikaks 77. Hizzonner 79.

Hudis, Norman (1923–   ).
English screenwriter, a former journalist, who is best known for scripting the first six Carry On comedies. Originally a playwright, he first worked in films at Pinewood as a trainee screenwriter. In the mid-60s he emigrated to America to write for television, including *The Man from U.N.C.L.E.* series.

The Tommy Steele Story 57. The Duke Wore Jeans 58. Carry On Sergeant 58. Carry On Nurse 59. Carry On Teacher 59. Please Turn Over 59. Carry On Constable 60. Carry On Regardless 60. Beware of the Children 60. Carry On Cruising 62. Twice around the Daffodils 62. The Karate Killers 67. How to Steal the World 68. Hot Resort (co-w) 85, etc.

Hudlin, Reggie (1961–   ).
American screenwriter and director. Educated at Harvard University, he worked in advertising and then produced music videos with his brother Warrington.

House Party (wd) 90. Bebe's Kids (w) 92. Boomerang (d) 92.

Hudlin, Warrington (1953–   ).
American producer and director, in partnership with his brother Reggie. Educated at Yale University, he co-founded the Black Filmmaker Foundation to distribute black independent films and videos.

House Party (p) 90. Bebe's Kids (p) 92. Boomerang (p) 92.

Hudson, Hugh (1936–   ).
British director, from TV commercials.
■ *Chariots of Fire* (AAN) 81. Greystoke 84. Revolution 86. Lost Angels (aka The Road Home) 89.

Hudson, Rochelle (1914–1972).
American leading lady who played *ingénue* roles in the 30s.

Laugh and Get Rich 30. She Done Him Wrong 33. Les Misérables 35. Way Down East 36. Smuggled Cargo 39. Island of Doomed Men 40. Meet Boston Blackie 41. Rubber Racketeers 42. Queen of Broadway 43. Skyliner 49. Rebel without a Cause 55. The Night Walker 65. Broken Sabre 65, etc.

Hudson, Rock (1925–1985) (Roy Scherer).
Giant-sized American leading man who did very well in Hollywood despite lack of acting training, moving from westerns to sob stories to sophisticated comedies. Died of AIDS.

Autobiography: 1986, *Rock Hudson His Story* (with Sara Davidson).
■ Fighter Squadron 48. Double Crossbones 48. Undertow 49. I Was a Shoplifter 50. One Way Street 50. Winchester 73 50. Peggy 50. The Desert Hawk 50. Shakedown 50. The Fat Man 50. Air Cadet 51. Tomahawk 51. Iron Man 51. Bright Victory 51. Bend of the River 52. Here Come the Nelsons 52. Scarlet Angel 52. Has Anybody Seen My Gal? 52. Horizons West 52. The Lawless Breed 52. Gun Fury 53. Seminole 53. Sea Devils (GB) 53. The Golden Blade 53. Back to God's Country 53. Taza Son of Cochise 53. *Magnificent Obsession* 54. Bengal Brigade 54. Captain Lightfoot 55. One Desire 55. All That Heaven Allows 55. Never Say Goodbye 56. *Giant* (AAN) 56. Battle Hymn 56. *Written on the Wind* 56. Four Girls in Town 56. Something of Value 57. *The Tarnished Angels* 57. A Farewell to Arms 57. Twilight for the Gods 58. This Earth is Mine 59. *Pillow Talk* 59. The Last Sunset 61. Come September 61. Lover Come Back 61. The Spiral Road 62. A Gathering of Eagles 63. Marilyn (narrator) 63. Man's Favourite Sport? 64. Send Me No Flowers 64. Strange Bedfellows 64. A Very Special Favor 65. Blindfold 66. *Seconds* 66. Tobruk 67. Ice Station Zebra 68. A Fine Pair 69. The Undefeated 69. Darling Lili 69. Hornet's Nest 70. Pretty Maids all in a Row 71. Showdown 73. Embryo 76. Avalanche 78. Wheels (TV) 78. The Mirror Crack'd 80. The Martian Chronicles (TV) 80. The Ambassador 84. The Vegas Strip War (TV) 84.

TV series: McMillan and Wife 71–75. McMillan 76. The Devlin Connection 82. Dynasty 85.

¶ I can't play a loser: I don't look like one. – *R.H.*
  I have no philosophy about acting or anything else. You just do it. And I mean that. You just do it. However, I can say that with ease after thirty-five years. – *R.H.*
  That big, lumpy Rock Hudson. – *James Dean*
  I call him Ernie because he's certainly no Rock. – *Doris Day*

Huerta, Rodolfo Guzmán (1920–1984).
Masked Mexican wrestler who was also the hero of a series of some 50 low-budget action films that enjoyed great popularity in his homeland for 21 years, from 1961, and occasionally reached international audiences in dubbed versions, usually when he battled against Frankenstein, Dracula, and other movie monsters. He was known as El Santo (qv).

El Enmascarado de Plata 52. Santo contra el Cerebro Diabólico 61. Samson versus the Vampire Woman (Santo en las Mujeres Vampiro) 61. Santo en la Venganza de las Mujeres Vampiro 69. Santo contra la Hija de Frankenstein 71. Santo y Blue Demon contra Dracula y el Hombre Loco 72. El Santo contra el Asesino de la Televisión 82, many others.

Huffaker, Clair (1927–1990).
American screenwriter.

Flaming Star 60. Seven Ways from Sundown 60. Rio Conchos 64. Tarzan and the Valley of Gold 65. The War Wagon 67. Hellfighters 69. The Deserter 71. Chino 76, etc.

Huffman, David (1945–1985).
American general-purpose actor. He was murdered.

F.I.S.T. 78. Ice Castles 78. The Onion Field 79. Blood Beach 81. Firefox 82.

The Huggetts.
Cheerful cockney family first featured in the film *Holiday Camp* 47. Its success inspired a radio series, *Meet the Huggetts*, featuring the film's two stars, Jack Warner and Kathleen Harrison, as Joe and Ethel Huggett, which ran from 1953–61, as well as three further films: *Here Come the Huggetts* 48, *Vote for Huggett* 48, *The Huggetts Abroad* 49.

Huggins, Roy (1914–   ).
American screenwriter, later TV producer.

I Love Trouble 48. The Lady Gambles 49. Sealed Cargo 51. Hangman's Knot (& d) 52. *Pushover* 54. A Fever in the Blood (& p) 61, etc.

TV series: *The Fugitive* (p) 63–66. Run for Your Life (p) 65–67, etc.

Hughes, Albert and Allen (1972–   ).
American twin directors.
Menace II Society 93.

Hughes, Barnard (1915–   ).
American character actor familiar on TV as Doc.

Midnight Cowboy 69. Where's Poppa 71. The Hospital 72. Rage 72. Sisters 73. Oh God 77. Best Friends 82. Tron 82. Maxie 85. The Lost Boys 87. Da 88. Doc Hollywood 91. Sister Act 2: Back in the Habit 93, etc.

TV series: Mr Merlin 81.

Hughes, Howard (1905–1976).
American businessman and celebrated recluse of eccentric habits; once an enthusiastic film-maker. A character based on him was played by George Peppard in *The Carpetbaggers* 64. Tommy Lee Jones played him in a 1977 TV movie, *The Amazing Howard Hughes*, and Jason Robards Jnr in *Melvin and Howard* in 1981. Other Hughes-like figures were seen in *Caught* (Robert Ryan). *The Barefoot Contessa* (Warren Stevens). *Harlow* (Leslie Nielsen) and *Diamonds are Forever* (Jimmy Dean).

Biographies: 1967, *The Bashful Billionaire* by Albert Gerber. 1967, *Howard Hughes* by John Keats. 1993, *Howard Hughes – The Secret Life* by Charles Higham.

Two Arabian Knights (p) 27. Hell's Angels (pd) 30. The Front Page (p) 31. *Scarface* (p) 32. Sky Devils 32. *The Outlaw* (pd) 43. Jet Pilot (p) 56. The Conqueror (p) 56, etc.

¶ There are two good reasons why men go to see her. Those are enough. – *H.H. on Jane Russell*
This is a very simple engineering problem. – *H.H., designing a bra for Jane Russell*

Hughes never fired anybody. If he wanted to get rid of somebody, he'd merely put somebody in over the guy. – *Sam Bischoff*

In his heyday he boasted of deflowering 200 virgins in Hollywood. He must have got them all. – *Jimmy the Greek*

Hughes, John (1950–).
American director, screenwriter and producer of films aimed primarily at a teenage audience. *Home Alone* is the most commercially successful of all film comedies and ranks third in the top box-office movies.

Sixteen Candles (wd) 84. The Breakfast Club (wd, p) 85. Weird Science (wd) 85. Ferris Bueller's Day Off (wd, p) 86. Pretty in Pink (w, p) 86. Planes, Trains and Automobiles (wd) 87. Some Kind of Wonderful (w, p) 87. The Great Outdoors (w, p) 88. She's Having a Baby (wd, p) 88. National Lampoon's Christmas Vacation (w, p) 89. Uncle Buck (wd, p) 89. Home Alone (w, p) 90. Career Opportunities (w, p) 91. Curly Sue (wd, p) 91. Home Alone 2: Lost in New York (w, p) 92. Dennis the Menace (w, p) 93. Baby's Day Out (w, p) 94. Miracle on 34th Street (w) 94, etc.

Hughes, Kathleen (1929–) (Betty von Gerlean).
Blonde American leading lady of the 50s.

Mother Is a Freshman 49. For Men Only 51. The Golden Blade 53. It Came from Outer Space 53. The Glass Web 53. Dawn at Socorro 54. Cult of the Cobra 55. Promise Her Anything 66. The President's Analyst 67, etc.

Hughes, Ken (1922–).
British director who has tackled a great variety of projects with variable success.

Wide Boy 52. Black Thirteen 53. The Brain Machine 53. Little Red Monkey 53. Confession (& w) 53. Timeslip (& w) 53. The House Across the Lake (& w) 54. Joe Macbeth (& w) 55. Wicked as They Come (& w) 56. The Long Haul 57. Jazzboat 60: In the Nick 60. *The Trials of Oscar Wilde* (& w) 60. The Small World of Sammy Lee (& w) 63. Of Human Bondage 64. Drop Dead Darling (& w) 66. Casino Royale (co-d) 67. Chitty Chitty Bang Bang (& w) 69. *Cromwell* (& w) 70. The Internecine Project 74. Alfie Darling 74. Sextette 77. Night School 80.

Hughes, Lloyd (1896–1958).
American leading man of the 20s.

The Turn in the Road 19. Hail the Woman 21. Tess of the Storm Country 22. *The Sea Hawk* 24. *The Lost World* 24. The Desert Flower 25. Ella Cinders 26. Loose Ankles 26. The Stolen Bride 27. The Mysterious Island 29. Moby Dick 30. Hell Bound 31. The Miracle Man 32. Harmony Lane 35. Romance of the Redwoods 39, many others.

Hughes, Mary Beth (1919–).
American leading lady of the 40s, mainly in second features.

These Glamour Girls 39. Lucky Cisco Kid 40. Orchestra Wives 42. *The Ox-Bow Incident* 43. I Accuse My Parents 44. Caged Fury 47. Gun Battle at Monterey 57. How's Your Love Life? 77, etc.

Hughes, Roddy (1891–1970).
Welsh character actor in films from 1934, often in roly-poly comedy roles.

The Stars Look Down 39. The Ghost of St Michael's 41. Hatter's Castle 41. Nicholas Nickleby 47. Scrooge 51. Sea Wife 57, etc.

Hughes, Wendy.
Australian leading actress.
■ Sidecar Racers 75. High Rolling 77. Newsfront 78. Kostas 78. *My Brilliant Career* 79. Touch and Go 80. Partners 81. A Dangerous Summer 81. Lonely Hearts 82. Careful, He Might Hear You 83. My First Wife 84. An Indecent Obsession 85. I Can't Get Started 85. Promises to Keep 86. Warm Nights on a Slow Moving Train 87. The Heist 89. Wild Orchid II: Two Shades of Blue 92. Princess Caraboo 94.

Hugo, Ian (Hugh Parker Guiler).
American director, cinematographer and editor of short, experimental films. Born in Boston, he was educated in Scotland and at Columbia University and from the mid-20s to the late 30s lived in Paris. By profession a successful banker and stockbroker, he was also an engraver and was married to writer Anaïs Nin. A retrospective of his work was shown at the Edinburgh Film Festival in 1970 and at the Museum of Modern Art, New York, in 1971. In *Henry and June* 90, a character based on him was played by Richard E. Grant.

Ai-Ye 50. Bells of Atlantis 52. Jazz of Lights 54. Melodic Inversion 58. Venice, Étude No. 1 62. The Gondola Eye 63 (revised 71). Through the Magiscope 69. Apertura 70, etc.

¶ The motion picture is potentially the greatest of all arts because it unites them all: sound, movement and a luminosity of colour that a painter could never achieve. – *I.H.*

Hulbert, Claude (1900–1963).
British 'silly ass' comedian, brother of Jack Hulbert.

Champagne 28. Naughty Husbands 30. A Night Like This 32. The Mayor's Nest 32. *Thark* 32. Radio Parade 33. A Cup of Kindness 34. *Bulldog Jack* 34. Wolf's Clothing 36. The Vulture 37. His Lordship Regrets 38. *Sailors Three* 40. *The Ghost of St Michael's* 41. The Dummy Talks 43. *My Learned Friend* 44. London Town 46. The Ghosts of Berkeley Square 47. Cardboard Cavalier 48. Fun at St Fanny's 55. Not a Hope in Hell 60, etc.

Hulbert, Jack (1892–1978).
Jaunty, long-chinned British light comedian, popular in films of the 30s. On stage from 1913, he was married to Cicely Courtneidge.

Autobiography: 1976, *The Little Woman's Always Right.*
■ Elstree Calling 30. *The Ghost Train* 31. Sunshine Susie 31. *Jack's the Boy* 32. Love on Wheels 32. Happy Ever After 32. Falling for You 33. Jack Ahoy 34. The Camels are Coming 34. *Bulldog Jack* 34. Jack of all Trades 36. Take My Tip 37. Paradise for Two 37. Kate Plus Ten 38. Under Your Hat 40. Into the Blue 51. The Magic Box 51. Miss Tulip Stays the Night 55. Spider's Web 60. The Cherry Picker 72. Not Now Darling 73.

Hulce, Tom (1953–).
Young American character actor of the 80s.
■ '9/30/55' 77. National Lampoon's Animal House 78. Those Lips, Those Eyes 80. Amadeus (AAN, as Mozart) 84. Echo Park 85. Slam Dance 87. Dominick and Eugene (aka Nicky and Gino) 88. Shadowman 88. Black Rainbow 89. Parenthood 89. Murder in Mississippi (TV) 90. The Inner Circle 91. Fearless 93. Mary Shelley's Frankenstein 94.

Hull, Henry (1890–1977).
Versatile American character actor.

The Volunteer 17. One Exciting Night 22. The Hoosier Schoolmaster 24. For Woman's Favour 24. Midnight 34. Great Expectations 34. *Werewolf of London* (leading role) 35. Yellow Jack 38. Boys' Town 38. The Great Waltz 38. Jesse James 39. Miracles for Sale 39. Judge Hardy and Son 39. My Son My Son 40. High Sierra 40. Lifeboat 43. Woman of the Town 44. Objective Burma 45. Mourning Becomes Electra 47. The Walls of Jericho 48. The Great Gatsby 49. Hollywood Story 51. Inferno 53. The Man with the Gun 55. The Proud Rebel 58. The Sheriff of Fractured Jaw 58. Master of the World 61. The Chase 66. Covenant with Death 67, many others.

Hull, Josephine (1884–1957) (Josephine Sherwood).
Bubbly little American stage actress who gave two memorable film performances.
■ After Tomorrow 32. Careless Lady 32. *Arsenic and Old Lace* 44. *Harvey* (AA) 50. The Lady from Texas 51.

Famous line (*Harvey*): 'Myrtle Mae, you have a lot to learn, and I hope you never learn it.'

Hull, Warren (1903–1974).
American leading man of many second features: also radio host of such serials as Mandrake the Magician and The Spider.

Miss Pacific Fleet 35. The Walking Dead 36. Night Key 37. Wagons Westward 40. Bowery Blitzkrieg 41, etc.

Hulme, Kathryn C. (1900–1981).
Author of *The Nun's Story*, which was filmed with Audrey Hepburn playing her.

Humberstone, H. Bruce (1903–1984).
American director, a competent craftsman of action films and musicals.

If I Had a Million (part) 32. The Crooked Circle 32. Charlie Chan in Honolulu 37. Pack Up Your Troubles 39. Lucky Cisco Kid 40. Tall, Dark and Handsome 41. *Sun Valley Serenade* 41. Hot Spot 41. To the Shores of Tripoli 42. *Hello, Frisco Hello* 43. *Wonder Man* 45. Three Little Girls in Blue 46. *Fury at Furnace Creek* 48. East of Java 49. Happy Go Lovely (GB) 51. She's Working Her Way Through College 52. The Desert Song 53. The Purple mask 55. Tarzan and the Lost Safari 57. Madison Avenue 61, etc.

Hume, Alan (1924–).
British cinematographer.

The Legend of Hell House 72. Carry on Girls 73. The Land that Time Forgot 74. Trial by Combat 76. Bear Island 80. The Eye of the Needle 81. For Your Eyes Only 81. Return of the Jedi 83. Octopussy 83. Supergirl 84. A View to a Kill 85. Lifeforce 85. Runaway Train 85. The Second Victory 87. Hearts of Fire 87. A Fish Called Wanda 88. Without a Clue 88. Shirley Valentine 89. Eve of Destruction 91, etc.

Hume, Benita (1906–1967).
British leading lady of the 30s; in Hollywood from 1935; retired to marry Ronald Colman.

The Constant Nymph 28. High Treason 29. Service for Ladies 32. The Flying Fool 32. Lord Camber's Ladies 33. Jew Süss 34. The Garden Murder Case 36. Tarzan Escapes 36. The Last of Mrs Cheyney 37. Peck's Bad Boy with the Circus 39, etc.

TV series: Halls of Ivy 55.

Hume, Kenneth (1926–1967).
British producer, former editor.

Cheer the Brave (wpd) 50. Hot Ice (wd) 51. Sail into Danger (wd) 57. Mods and Rockers (pd) 64. I've Gotta Horse (pd) 65, etc.

Humphries, Barry (1934–).
Australian entertainer.

The Adventures of Barry McKenzie 72. Barry McKenzie Holds His Own 74. The Getting of Wisdom 77. Les Patterson Saves the World 87, etc.

Hung, Samo (1952–) (Hong Jinbao).

Hong Kong director, screenwriter and plump but agile leading actor of martial arts and comedy movies. *Painted Faces* is an autobiographical film based on his life from the age of seven to 17, training as a member of a traditional Chinese theatre group, where a fellow pupil was his frequent co-star Jackie Chan (qv).

Warriors Two 79. Spooky Encounters (& d) 80. Ghost against Ghost (Gui da Gui) (& co-w, d) 81. Carry On Pickpocket 82. Prodigal Son 83. Winners and Sinners (& d) 83. The Dead and the Deadly 83. Wheels on Meals (& d) 84. Project A 84. Twinkle, Twinkle, Lucky Stars (& d) 85. Eastern Condors 87. Painted Faces 89. Pantyhose Hero 91. The Prisoner 91. The Eagle Shooting Heroes: Dong Cheng Xi Jiu (action director) 93, etc.

Hung, Tran Anh (1962–).

Vietnamese director, now resident in France.
Scent of Green Papaya (AAN) 93. Cyclo 95.

Hungary

has had one of the most flourishing film histories in Europe, and many of its talents found their way to Hollywood, including Michael Curtiz, Alexander Korda and Bela Lugosi. The native films were seldom exported, oddly enough, until after a strong Soviet influence made itself felt: Zoltan Fabri and Miklos Jancso are now respected names. Matra Meszaros, Jancso's former wife, has made some impressive semi-autobiographical films. Karoly Makk came to the fore in the mid-70s, while Istvan Szabo has transcended national boundaries to become a truly European director.

Hunnicutt, Arthur (1911–1979).

American actor of slow-speaking country characters.
Wildcat 42. Lust for Gold 49. Broken Arrow 50. The Red Badge of Courage 51. The Big Sky (AAN) 52. The French Line 54. The Last Command 55. The Kettles in the Ozarks 56. Apache Uprising 65. Cat Ballou 65. El Dorado 66. Million Dollar Duck 71. The Revengers 72. Harry and Tonto 74. The Spikes Gang 74. Moonrunners 75, etc.

Hunnicutt, Gayle (1942–).

American leading lady of the 60s.
■ The Wild Angels 66. P.J. 68. Marlowe 69. Eye of the Cat 69. Fragment of Fear 70. Freelance 70. Scorpio 72. The Legend of Hell House 72. Running Scared 72. Voices 73. Nuits Rouges 73. The Spiral Staircase 75. Blazing Magnum 76. The Sellout 76. Once In Paris 78. A Man Called Intrepid (TV) 79. The Martian Chronicles (TV) 79. Kiss of Gold (TV) 80. The Return of the Man from UNCLE (TV) 83. The First Modern Olympics (TV) 84. A Woman of Substance (TV) 85. Target 85. Strong Medicine (TV) 86. Dream West (TV) 86. Turnaround 87. Hard to Be a God 89. Silence Like Glass 89.

Hunt, Linda (1945–).

Diminutive American character actress.
The Year of Living Dangerously (AA) (as a man) 83. The Bostonians 84. Silverado 85. Eleni 85. Dune 85. Waiting for the Moon (as Alice B. Toklas) 87. She-Devil 89. Kindergarten Cop 90. Teen Agent 91. Younger and Younger 93. Twenty Bucks 93, etc.
TV series: Space Rangers 93.

Hunt, Marsha (1917–) (Marcia Hunt).

American leading lady who usually plays gentle characters.
Virginia Judge (debut) 35. Hollywood Boulevard 36. The Hardys Ride High 38. These Glamour Girls 39. *Pride and Prejudice* 40. Blossoms in the Dust 41. Kid Glove Killer 42. Seven Sweethearts 42. The Human Comedy 43. *Lost Angel* 43. None Shall Escape 43. Cry Havoc 44. The Valley of Decision 45. A Letter for Evie 45. Carnegie Hall 46. Take One False Step 49. Mary Ryan, Detective 50. The Happy Time 52. No Place to Hide 56. Blue Denim 59. The Plunderers 60. Johnny Got His Gun 71, etc.
TV series: Peck's Bad Girl 59.

Hunt, Martita (1900–1969).

British stage and screen actress who graduated from nosy spinsters to *grandes dames*.
I Was a Spy (debut) 33. Spare a Copper 39. The Man in Grey 43. The Wicked Lady 45. *Great Expectations* (as Miss Havisham) 46. The Ghosts of Berkeley Square 47. My Sister and I 48. The Fan 49. *Treasure Hunt* 52. Melba 53. Three Men in a Boat 56. Anastasia 56. *Brides of Dracula* 60. The Unsinkable Molly Brown 64. Bunny Lake Is Missing 65, many others.

Hunt, Peter (1928–).

British director, former editor.
■ On Her Majesty's Secret Service 69. Gulliver's Travels 73. Gold 74. Shout at the Devil 76. The Beasts are on the Streets (TV) 78. Flying High (TV) 79. Death Hunt 80. Rendezvous Hotel (TV) 81. The Last Days of Pompeii (TV) 83. Wild Geese II 85. Hyper Sapien 86. Assassination 87.

Hunter, Bill (1940–).

Australian leading actor.
The Man from Hong Kong 75. Eliza Fraser 76. Backroads 77. Newsfront 77. Hard Knocks 80. Gallipoli 80. Heatwave 82. Far East 82. The Return of Captain Invincible 82. The Hit (GB) 84. Street Hero 84. An Indecent Obsession 85. Rebel 85. Death of a Soldier 86. Fever 88. The Last Days of Chez Nous 92. Strictly Ballroom 92. Broken Highway 93. The Custodian 93. The Adventures of Priscilla, Queen of the Desert 94. Muriel's Wedding 94. Everynight . . . Everynight 94, etc.
TV series: The Dismissal 83.

Hunter, Evan (1926–) (Salvadore Lombino).

American novelist and screenwriter who also writes as Ed McBain.
The Blackboard Jungle (oa) 55. Strangers When We Meet (w) 60. The Young Savages (w) 61. The Birds (w) 63. Mister Buddwing (oa) 66. Walk Proud 79, etc.
TV series: 87th Precinct 61. The Chisholms 78.

Hunter, Glenn (1897–1945).

American leading man of the 20s.
The Case of Becky 21. The Country Flapper 22. Smilin' Through 22. Puritan Passions 23. *Merton of the Movies* 24. West of the Water Tower 24. The Pinch Hitter 25. For Beauty's Sake 41, etc.

Hunter, Holly (1958–).

American leading actress.
The Burning 81. Svengali (TV) 83. Swing Shift 84. Urge to Kill (TV) 84. The End of the Line 87. Crimes of the Heart 87. Raising Arizona 87. A Gathering of Old Men (aka Murder on the Bayou) (TV) 87. Broadcast News (AAN) 87. Animal Behavior 89. Always 89. Roe vs Wade (TV) 89. Miss Firecracker 89. Once Around 90. Crazy in Love 92. The Positively True Adventures of the Alleged Texas Cheerleader-Murdering Mom (TV) 93. The Firm (AAN) 93. *The Piano* (AA) 93, etc.

Hunter, Ian (1900–1975).

British actor of dependable characters; on stage from 1919, films soon after.
Mr Oddy 22. Not for Sale 24. Confessions 25. The Ring 27. Something Always Happens 31. The Sign of Four (as Dr Watson) 32. Death at Broadcasting House 34. A Midsummer Night's Dream (US) 35. The White Angel (US) 36. Call It a Day (US) 37. *52nd Street* (US) 38. The Adventures of Robin Hood (as King Richard) (US) 38. Tower of London (US) 39. Strange Cargo (US) 40. Bitter Sweet (US) 40. Billy the Kid (US) 41. *Dr Jekyll and Mr Hyde* (as Lanyon) (US) 41. A Yank at Eton (US) 42. Bedelia 46. White Cradle Inn 47. The White Unicorn 48. *Edward My Son* 49. Appointment in London 52. Don't Blame the Stork 53. The Battle of the River Plate 56. Fortune Is a Woman 57. Northwest Frontier 59. The Bulldog Breed 60. Dr Blood's Coffin 61. Guns of Darkness 63, many others.

Hunter, Jeffrey (1925–1969) (Henry H. McKinnies).

American leading man, in films from 1951 after radio experience.
Fourteen Hours (debut) 51. Red Skies of Montana 52. Singlehanded 53. White Feather 55. The Searchers 56. A Kiss Before Dying 56. The True Story of Jesse James 57. No Down Payment 57. The Last Hurrah 57. Hell to Eternity 60. *King of Kings* (as Jesus) 61. The Longest Day 62. Vendetta 65. Brainstorm 65. Custer of the West 66. The Private Navy of Sgt O'Farrell 68, many others.
TV series: Temple Houston 63.

Hunter, Kim (1922–) (Janet Cole).

Pert, dependable American leading lady who after brief stage experience started a rather desultory film career, not helped by being blacklisted in the 50s.
■ The Seventh Victim 43. Tender Comrade 43. When Strangers Marry 44. You Came Along 45. A Matter of Life and Death (GB) 45. A Canterbury Tale (GB) 46. *A Streetcar Named Desire* (AA) 51. *Deadline USA* 52. Anything Can Happen 52. Storm Center 56. The Young Stranger 57. Bermuda Affair 58. Money Women and Guns 58. Lilith 64. Planet of the Apes 67. The Swimmer 68. Beneath the Planet of the Apes 70. Dial Hot Line (TV) 70. In Search of America (TV) 71. Escape from the Planet of the Apes 71. The Magician (TV) 73. Unwed Father (TV) 74. Born Innocent (TV) 74. Bad Ronald (TV) 74. Ellery Queen (TV) 75. The Dark Side of Innocence (TV) 76. Once an Eagle (TV) 76. Backstairs at the White House (TV) 79. The Kindred 86. Two Evil Eyes 89.

Hunter, Ross (1921–) (Martin Fuss).

American producer; a former actor, he has specialized in remakes of glossy dramas from Hollywood's golden age, and has seldom failed to make hot commercial properties of them.
AS ACTOR: A Guy a Gal and a Pal 45. Sweetheart of Sigma Chi 47, The Bandit of Sherwood Forest 47. The Groom Wore Spurs 51, etc.
AS PRODUCER: Take Me to Town 53. *Magnificent Obsession* 54. One Desire 55. The Spoilers 55. All that Heaven Allows 56. Battle Hymn 57. My Man Godfrey 57. *Pillow Talk* 58. *Imitation of Life* 59. Portrait in Black 60. Tammy Tell Me True 61. Back Street 61. Flower Drum Song 61. The Thrill of it All 63. The Chalk Garden 64. Madame X 66. The Pad 66. *Thoroughly Modern Millie* 67. *Airport* (AAN) 69. Lost Horizon 73. The Lives of Jenny Dolan (TV) 76. A Family Upside Down (TV) 78. The Best Place to Be (TV) 78. Suddenly Love (TV) 79, etc.

¶ The way life looks in my pictures is the way I want life to be. I don't want to hold a mirror p to life as it is. I just want to show the part which attractive. – *R.H.*

Hunter, T. Hayes (1881–1944).
American director, in Britain in the 30s.
   Desert Gold 19. Earthbound 20. The Triumph of the Scarlet Pimpernel 29. The Silver King 29. The Frightened Lady 31. Sally Bishop 33. *The Ghoul* 33, etc.

Hunter, Tab (1931–   ) (Andrew Arthur Kelm).
Athletic American leading man, a teenage rave of the 50s.
   The Lawless (debut) 48. Saturday Island 52. Gun Belt 53. Return to Treasure Island 53. *Track of the Cat* 54. Battle Cry 55. The Sea Chase 55. The Burning Hills 56. The Girl He Left Behind 57. Gunman's Walk 57. *Damn Yankees* 58. That Kind of Woman 59. The Pleasure of His Company 60. The Golden Arrow (It.) 62. City under the Sea 65. Birds Do It 66. Hostile Guns 67. Judge Roy Bean 72. The Timber Tramps 73. Grease II 82. Pandemonium 82. Polyester 82. Lust in the Dust 85. Cameron's Closet 87. Grotesque 88. Out of the Dark 88, etc.
   TV series: The Tab Hunter Show 60.

Hunter, Tim.
American director.
   Tex 82. Sylvester 85. River's Edge 87. Paint It Black 89. The Saint of Fort Washington 93, etc.

Huntington, Lawrence (1900–1968).
British director, mainly of routine thrillers.
   Suspected Person (& w) 41. Night Boat to Dublin 41. *Wanted for Murder* 46. *The Upturned Glass* 47. When the Bough Breaks 48. *Mr Perrin and Mr Traill* 48. Man on the Run (& w) 49. The Franchise Affair (& w) 51. There Was a Young Lady (& w) 53. Contraband Spain (& w) 55. Stranglehold 62. The Fur Collar (& w, p) 63, etc.

Huntley, Raymond (1904–1990).
British character actor, often of supercilious types or self-satisfied businessmen; on stage from 1922, screen from 1934.
   Rembrandt 37. *Night Train to Munich* 40. The Ghost of St Michael's 41. School for Secrets 45. Mr Perrin and Mr Traill 48. Trio 50. Room at the Top 59. Only Two Can Play 62. Rotten to the Core 65. Hostile Witness 67. Destiny of a Spy (TV) 69. *That's Your Funeral* 73, many others.

Huppert, Isabelle (1955–   ).
French leading lady in international films.
   Faustine 71. Cesar and Rosalie 72. Les Valseuses 74. Rosebud 75. The Judge and the Assassin 76. *The Lacemaker* 77. *Violette Nozière* 78. Heaven's Gate 80. Sauve Qui Peut 80. Camp de Torchon 81. The Trout 82. Entre Nous (Coup de Foudre) 83. My Best Friend's Girl (La Femme de Mon Pote) 83. La Garce 84. Cactus 86. The Bedroom Window 87. Migrations 88. Malina 90. Madame Bovary 91. After Love (Après l'Amour) 92. Amateur 94. The Flood (L'Inondation) 94, etc.

Hurd, Gale Anne (1955–   ).
American producer and screenwriter. She was married to director James Cameron (1985–89).
   The Terminator (& w) 84. Aliens 86. Alien Nation 88. Bad Dreams 88. The Abyss 89. Downtown 90. Tremors 90. Terminator 2: Judgement Day 91. The Waterdance 92. Raising Cain 92. No Escape 94, etc.

Hurley, Elizabeth (1966–   ).
English leading actress, from television.
   Rowing with the Wind 87. Aria 88. Passenger

57 92. Beyond Bedlam 94. Mad Dogs and Englishmen 95, etc.

Hurndall, Richard (1910–1984).
Incisive British character actor.
   Joanna 67. I Monster 71. Royal Flash 75. The Prince and the Pauper 77, etc.

Hurok, Sol (1889–1974).
Distinguished American impresario whose life in classical music was recounted in *Tonight we Sing* 53.

Hurst, Brandon (1866–1947).
British character actor in Hollywood; better roles in silents than sound films.
   Legally Dead 23. *The Hunchback of Notre Dame* 23. He Who Gets Slapped 24. *The Thief of Baghdad* 24. The Grand Duchess and the Waiter 26. Love 27. Interference 29. A Connecticut Yankee 31. White Zombie 32. The Lost Patrol 34. The Charge of the Light Brigade 36. Mary of Scotland 36. If I Were King 38. Stanley and Livingstone 39. If I Had My Way 40. Dixie 43. Jane Eyre 44. House of Frankenstein 44. Devotion 46. Road to Rio 47, many others.

Hurst, Brian Desmond (1900–1986).
Irish director who made many kinds of film.
   Sensation 36. Glamorous Night 37. Prison Without Bars 39. On the Night of the Fire 40. *Dangerous Moonlight* 41. Alibi 42. The Hundred Pound Window 43. Theirs Is the Glory 45. Hungry Hill 47. The Mark of Cain 48. Tom Brown's Schooldays (p only) 51. *Scrooge* 51. The Malta Story 53. Simba 55. The Black Tent 56. Dangerous Exile 57. Behind the Mask 58. His and Hers 60. The Playboy of the Western World 62, etc.

Hurst, David (1925–   ).
Austrian actor who played some comedy roles in British films.
   The Perfect Woman 49. So Little Time 52. Mother Riley Meets the Vampire 52. As Long As They're Happy 53. The Intimate Stranger 56. After the Ball 57. Hello Dolly (US) 69, etc.

Hurst, Fannie (1889–1968).
American popular novelist, several of whose romantic novels, usually with a tragic finale, have been filmed more than once: Humoresque, Imitation of Life, Back Street, etc.

Hurst, Paul (1889–1953).
American character actor in hundreds of cameo roles from 1912, usually as gangster, bartender, outlaw or cop. Committed suicide.
   The Red Raiders 27. Tugboat Annie 32. Riff Raff 34. Gone with the Wind 39. Caught in the Draft 41. Jack London 44. Yellow Sky 49. The Sun Shines Bright 53, many others.

Hurst, Veronica (1931–   ).
British light leading lady of the 50s.
   Laughter in Paradise 51. Angels One Five 51. The Maze (US) 53. Will Any Gentleman? 53. The Yellow Balloon 54. Peeping Tom 58. Dead Man's Evidence 62. Licensed to Kill 64. The Boy Cried Murder 66, etc.

Hurt, John (1940–   ).
Off-beat British stage and film leading man.
   ■ The Wild and the Willing 62. This is my Street 63. *A Man for all Seasons* 66. The Sailor from Gibraltar 67. Before Winter Comes 69. Sinful Davey 69. In Search of Gregory 70. *10 Rillington Place* 71. Forbush and the Penguins 71. The Pied Piper 72. The Ghoul 74. Little Malcolm and His

Struggle against the Eunuchs 74. *The Naked Civil Servant* (TV) 75. I Claudius (TV) 76. East of Elephant Rock 78. The Disappearance 78. The Shout 78. *Midnight Express* (AAN) 78. Spectre (TV) 78. Alien 79. Heaven's Gate 80. *The Elephant Man* (BFA, AAN) 80. Night Crossing 81. History of the World Part One 81. Partners 82. The Osterman Weekend 83. Champions 84. 1984 84. The Hit 84. Success is the Best Revenge 84. Sunset People 84. Jake Speed 86. Rocinante 86. From the Hip 87. Aria 87. Spaceballs 87. Vincent – the Life and Death of Vincent van Gogh 87. White Mischief 87. Little Sweetheart 88. La Nuit Bengal 88. Deadline 89. Scandal 89. Windprints 90. Frankenstein Unbound 90. The Field 90. Resident Alien 91. King Ralph 91. Lapse of Memory (Mémoire Tranquée) 91. I Dreamt I Woke Up 91. Dark at Noon (La Terreur de Midi) 92. Even Cowgirls Get the Blues 93. Monolith 93. Thumbelina (voice) 94. Great Moments in Aviation 94. Second Best 94. Rob Roy 95. Wild Bill 95.
   TV series: The Storyteller 87–88.

¶ America only makes children's pictures. – *J.H.*
   Hollywood is simply geared to cheat you left, right and bloody centre. – *J.H.*

Hurt, Mary Beth (1948–   ) (Mary Supinger).
American leading lady.
   Head over Heels 82. The World According to Garp 82. Compromising Positions 85. D.A.R.Y.L. 85. Parents 89. Slaves of New York 89. Light Sleeper 91. Defenseless 91. My Boyfriend's Back 93. The Age of Innocence 93. Six Degrees of Separation 93, etc.

Hurt, William (1950–   ).
American leading actor.
   Altered States 80. Eyewitness 81. Body Heat 81. The Big Chill 83. Gorky Park 83. *Kiss of the Spider Woman* (AA, BFA) 85. Children of a Lesser God (AAN) 86. Broadcast News (AAN) 87. The Accidental Tourist 88. A Time of Destiny 88. Alice 90. I Love You to Death 90. The Doctor 91. Until the End of the World (Bis ans Ende der Welt) 91. The Plague (La Peste) 92. Mr Wonderful 93. Second Best 94. Trial by Jury 94. Confidences d'un Inconnu 95, etc.

Hussein, Waris (1938–   ).
Anglo-Indian director, mostly for TV.
   ■ A Touch of Love 68. Quackser Fortune 69. Melody 71. The Possession of Joel Delaney 72. The Six Wives of Henry VIII 72. Divorce His, Divorce Hers (TV) 73. *The Glittering Prizes* (TV) 75. *Edward and Mrs Simpson* (TV) 78. *Little Gloria . . . Happy at Last* (TV) 82. Winter of our Discontent (TV) 83. Arch of Triumph (TV) 84. Surviving 85. Copacabana (TV) 86. When the Bough Breaks (TV) 86. Intimate Contact (TV) 87. Downpayment on Murder (TV) 87. The Richest Man in the World: The Aristotle Onassis Story (TV) 88. Those She Left Behind (TV) 89. She Woke Up 92. The Clothes in the Wardrobe (aka The Summer House) (TV) 93.

Hussey, Olivia (1951–   ).
British leading lady, born in Argentina. She was married to actor Dean Paul Martin.
   ■ The Battle of the Villa Fiorita 65. Cup Fever 65. *Romeo and Juliet* 68. All the Right Noises 69. Summertime Killer 72. *Lost Horizon* 73. Black Christmas 75. Jesus of Nazareth (TV) 77. The Cat and the Canary 77. Death on the Nile 78. The Pirate (TV) 79. The Man with Bogart's Face 80. Turkey Shoot 81. Escape 2000 81. Virus 82. The Last Days of Pompeii (TV) 84. The Corsican Brothers (TV) 84. Distortions 87. The Goldsmith's Shop 87.

The Undeclared War 90. Psycho IV: The Beginning 90.

Hussey, Ruth (1914–   ) (Ruth Carol O'Rourke). Smart, competent, sometimes wisecracking American leading lady of the early 40s.
■ Madame X 37. Big City 37. Judge Hardy's Children 38. Man Proof 38. Marie Antoinette 38. Hold that Kiss 38. Rich Man Poor Girl 38. Time Out for Murder 38. Spring Madness 38. Honolulu 39. Within the Law 39. Maisie 39. The Women 39. Another Thin Man 39. Blackmail 39. *Fast and Furious* 39. Northwest Passage 40. Susan and God 40. *The Philadelphia Story* (AAN) 40. Flight Command 40. Free and Easy 41. Our Wife 41. Married Bachelor 41. *H. M. Pulham Esq* 41. Pierre of the Plains 42. Tennessee Johnson 42. Tender Comrade 43. *The Uninvited* 44. Marine Raiders 44. Bedside Manner 45. I Jane Doe 48. The Great Gatsby 49. Louisa 50. Mr Music 50. That's My Boy 51. Woman of the North Country 52. Stars and Stripes Forever 52. The Lady Wants Mink 53. The Facts of Life 60. My Darling Daughter's Anniversary (TV) 72.

Huston, Anjelica (1952–   ). American leading lady, daughter of John Huston.
Biography: 1992, *Anjelica Huston – The Lady and Her Legacy* by Martha Harris.
Sinful Davey 69. A Walk with Love and Death 69. The Last Tycoon 76. Swashbuckler 76. Frances 82. The Ice Pirates 83. *Prizzi's Honor* (AA) 85. Good to Go 86. The Dead 87. Gardens of Stone 87. A Handful of Dust 88. The Witches 89. Enemies: A Love Story (AAN) 89. Crimes and Misdemeanors 89. The Grifters (AAN) 90. The Addams Family 91. The Player 92. Family Pictures (TV) 93. Manhattan Murder Mystery 93. Addams Family Values 93. The Perez Family 95, etc.

Huston, Danny (1962–   ). American screenwriter and director, the son of John Huston.
Bigfoot (TV) 87. Mr North 88. Becoming Colette 92.

Huston, John (1906–1987). Unpredictable but occasionally splendid American director, son of Walter Huston.
Autobiography: 1981, *An Open Book*.
Biography: 1965, *King Rebel* by W. F. Nolan. 1990, *The Hustons* by Lawrence Grobel.
AS SCREENWRITER ONLY: Murders in the Rue Morgue 32. The Amazing Dr Clitterhouse 38. Jezebel 38. High Sierra 40. Dr Erlich's Magic Bullet (co-w, AAN) 40. Sergeant York (AAN) 41. Three Strangers 46, etc.
■ AS DIRECTOR: *The Maltese Falcon* (& w) 41. In This Our Life 42. Across the Pacific 42. Report from the Aleutians 43. Battle of San Pietro 45. Let There Be Light 45 (four other official war documentaries 44–45). *The Treasure of the Sierra Madre* (& w) (AA) 47. *Key Largo* (& w) 48. We Were Strangers 49. *The Asphalt Jungle* (& w) (AANw, d) 50. The Red Badge of Courage (& w) 51. *The African Queen* (& w) (AAN) 52. Moulin Rouge (& w) (AAN) 53. Beat the Devil (& w) 54. Moby Dick (& w) 56. Heaven Knows Mr Allison (& w) (AANw) 57. The Barbarian and the Geisha 58. The Roots of Heaven (& w) 58. The Unforgiven 60. The Misfits 60. *Freud* 62. The List of Adrian Messenger 63. *The Night of the Iguana* (& w) 64. The Bible 66. Casino Royale (part) 67. Reflections in a Golden Eye 67. Sinful Davey 69. A Walk with Love and Death 69. The Kremlin Letter 70. *Fat City* 72. Judge Roy Bean 72. The Mackintosh Man 73. The Man Who Would Be King 75. Wise Blood 79. Phobia 80. Victory 81. Annie 82. Under the

Volcano 84. *Prizzi's Honor* (AAN) 85. The Dead 87.
■ AS ACTOR: The Treasure of the Sierra Madre (uncredited) 47. The List of Adrian Messenger (uncredited) 63. *The Cardinal* (AAN) 63. *The Bible* (as Noah) 66. Casino Royale 67. Candy 68. A Walk with Love and Death 68. De Sade 69. The Kremlin letter 70. The Bridge and the Jungle 70. Myra Breckinridge 70. The Deserter 70. Man in the Wilderness 71. Judge Roy Bean 72. Battle for the Planet of the Apes 73. Chinatown 74. Breakout 75. The Wind and the Lion 75. Tentacles 77. Sherlock Holmes in New York (TV) 77. The Word (TV) 78. Winter Kills 79. The Visitor 79. Jaguar Lives 79. Head On 80. Love Sick 83. Young Giants 83.

¶ I don't try to guess what a million people will like. It's hard enough to know what I like. – J.H.
I fail to see any continuity in my work from picture to picture. – J.H.
I completely storyboarded *The Maltese Falcon* because I didn't want to lose face with the crew: I wanted to give the impression that I knew what I was doing. – J.H.
Most of us go through life searching for the unobtainable and if we do get it, we find it's unacceptable. – J.H.
There is nothing more fascinating – and more fun – than making movies. Besides, I think I'm finally getting the hang of it. – J.H. (1984)

Huston, Walter (1884–1950) (W. Houghston). Distinguished American character actor of stage and screen: latterly projected roguery and eccentricity with great vigour. He also played bit parts in his son John's first two films, as Captain Jacoby in *The Maltese Falcon* 41, and a bartender in *In This Our Life* 42. After his death his stage recording of 'September Song', played in *September Affair* 50, became a big hit.
■ Gentlemen of the Press 28. The Lady Lies 29. *The Virginian* 30. The Bad Man 30. The Virtuous Sin 30. *Abraham Lincoln* 30. The Criminal Code 31. Star Witness 31. The Ruling Voice 31. A Woman from Monte Carlo 31. A House Divided 32. *Law and Order* (as Wyatt Earp) 32. Beast of the City 32. The Wet Parade 32. Night Court 32. *American Madness* 32. Kongo 32. Rain 32. Hell Below 32. Gabriel over the White House 33. The Prizefighter and the Lady 33. Storm at Daybreak 33. Ann Vickers 33. Keep 'Em Rolling 33. The Tunnel (GB) 34. Rhodes of Africa (GB) 36. *Dodsworth* (AAN) 36. Of Human Hearts 38. The Light That Failed 39. *All that Money Can Buy* (as the devil) (AAN) 41. Swamp Water 41. The Shanghai Gesture 42. Always in My Heart 42. Yankee Doodle Dandy (AAN) 42. Mission to Moscow 42. Edge of Darkness 42. North Star 43. *The Outlaw* (as Doc Holliday) 43. Dragon Seed 44. *And Then There Were None* 45. Dragonwyck 46. Duel in the Sun 46. *The Treasure of the Sierra Madre* (AA) 47. Summer Holiday 47. The Great Sinner 49. The Furies 50.
☺ For star quality combined with acting ability; whatever the proportions, no audience could look away when he was on screen. *Dodsworth*.

¶ Son, give 'em a good show, and always travel first class. – W.H.
Hell, I ain't paid to make good lines sound good. I'm paid to make bad lines sound good. – W.H.

Famous line (*All that Money Can Buy*): 'A soul – a soul is nothing. Can you see it, smell it, touch it, no?'

Hutcheson, David (1905–1976). British light comedian who often played monocled silly-asses, mainly on stage.

This'll Make You Whistle 35. Sabotage at Sea 41. Convoy 42. School for Secrets 46. *Vice Versa* 48. Sleeping Car to Trieste 48. The Elusive Pimpernel 50. The Evil of Frankenstein 64. The National Health 73, etc.

Hutchins, Bobby 'Wheezer' (1920–1945). American child actor in the Our Gang comedies of the late 20s and early 30s. Died in an accident.

Hutchins, Will (1932–   ). Bland-faced American leading man who came to fame in 57–60 as TV's *Sugarfoot*.
No Time for Sergeants 58. Merrill's Marauders 62. The Shooting 66. Clambake 67, etc.

Hutchinson, Josephine (1903–   ). American actress who usually played sweet or maternal types.
Happiness Ahead 34. The Story of Louis Pasteur 36. Son of Frankenstein 39. Somewhere in the Night 46. Ruby Gentry 52. Miracle in the Rain 56. North By Northwest 59. Huckleberry Finn 60. Baby the Rain Must Fall 64. Nevada Smith 66. Rabbit Run 70, etc.

Huth, Harold (1892–1967). British light leading man of silent days; later became producer-director.
One of the Best 27. Balaclava 28. The Silver King 29. Leave it to Me 30. The Outsider 31. Sally Bishop 32. Rome Express 32. The Ghoul 33. The Camels are Coming 34. Take My Tip 37. Hell's Cargo (d) 39. East of Piccadilly (d) 40. Busman's Honeymoon (p) 40. Breach of Promise (d) 42. Love Story (p) 44. They Were Sisters (p) 45. Caravan (p) 46. Night Beat (pd) 47. My Sister and I (pd) 48. Look Before You Love (pd) 48. One Wild Oat (p) 51. Police Dog (p) 55. The Hostage (d) 56. Idol on Parade (p) 59. The Trials of Oscar Wilde (p) 60. The Hellions (p) 61, etc.

Hutton, Betty (1921–   ) (Betty Thornberg). Blonde and bouncy American leading lady of many singing/dancing light entertainments of the 40s.
■ *The Fleet's In* 42. Star Spangled Rhythm 42. Happy Go Lucky 43. Let's Face It 43. *The Miracle of Morgan's Creek* 44. And the Angels Sing 44. Here Come the Waves 44. *Incendiary Blonde* (as Texas Guinan) 45. Duffy's Tavern 45. The Stork Club 45. Cross My Heart 46. *The Perils of Pauline* 47. Dream Girl 48. Red Hot and Blue 49. *Annie Get Your Gun* 50. Let's Dance 50. Somebody Loves Me 52. The Greatest Show on Earth 52. Spring Reunion 57.

Hutton, Brian G. (1935–   ). American director.
■ Fargo 65. The Pad 66. Sol Madrid 67. *Where Eagles Dare* 68. Kelly's Heroes 70. Zee and Co 71. Night Watch 73. The First Deadly Sin 80. High Road to China 83. Ryder 89.

Hutton, Jim (1934–1979). American leading man who usually played gangly types.
A Time to Love and a Time to Die 58. Bachelor in Paradise 61. The Horizontal Lieutenant 62. The Honeymoon Machine 62. Period of Adjustment 63. The Hallelujah Trail 65. Never Too Late 65. Walk Don't Run 66. Who's Minding the Mint 67. The Green Berets 68. Hellfighters 69, etc.
TV series: Ellery Queen 74.

Hutton, Lauren (1943–   ) (Mary Hutton). American leading lady, a former model.
Little Fauss and Big Halsy 71. The Gambler 74. Welcome to L.A. 77. Viva Knievel 77. Someone's

Watching Me! (TV) 78. A Wedding 78. American Gigolo 80. Zorro the Gay Blade 81. Paternity 81. Lassiter 83. Once Bitten 85. Flagrant Desire 85. Marathon 87. Malone 87. Forbidden Sun 88. Fear 89. Guilty As Charged 91. Billions (Miliardi) 91. Missing Pieces 92. My Father, the Hero 94, etc.

TV series: The Rhinemann Exchange 77. Paper Dolls 84.

Hutton, Marion (1919–1987) (Marion Thornburg). American singer, with the Glenn Miller band; appeared in a few 40s musicals. Sister of Betty Hutton.

Orchestra Wives 42. Crazy House 44. In Society 44. Babes on Swing Street 45. Love Happy 50, etc.

Hutton, Robert (1920–1994) (Robert Bruce Winne).
American leading man of the 40s.

Destination Tokyo 44. Janie 44. Too Young To Know 45. Time Out of Mind 47. Always Together 48. The Steel Helmet 51. Casanova's Big Night 54. Invisible Invaders 58. Cinderfella 60. The Slime People (& pd) 62. The Secret Man (GB) 64. Finders Keepers (GB) 66. They Came from Beyond Space (GB) 68. Can Hieronymus Merkin Ever Forget Mercy Humpe and Find True Happiness 68. Cry of the Banshee 70. Trog 70. Tales from the Crypt 72, etc.

Hutton, Timothy (1960–).
Leading young American actor of the early 80s, son of Jim Hutton. He was married to actress Debra Winger (1986–89).

Ordinary People (AA) 80. Taps 81. Daniel 83. Iceman 84. The Falcon and the Snowman 85. Turk 182 85. Made in Heaven 87. A Time of Destiny 87. Everybody's All American (GB: When I Fall in Love) 88. Torrents of Spring 89. Q & A 90. The Temp 93. The Dark Half 93, etc.

Huxley, Aldous (1894–1963).
Distinguished British novelist who spent some time in Hollywood and worked on the screenplays of Pride and Prejudice 40 and Jane Eyre 43.

¶ His erudition was staggering. I never discovered how many languages he knew, but one day I found him in his office at MGM reading Persian. – Anita Loos

Huyck, Willard.
American screenwriter and director. He began as a reader for AIP.

American Graffiti (co-w only) 73. Lucky Lady (co-w only) 75. Messiah of Evil 75. French Postcards 79. Best Defence 84. Indiana Jones and the Temple of Doom (co-w only) 84. Howard the Duck 86. Radioland Murders (co-w) 94, etc.

Hyams, Leila (1905–1977).
Vivacious, blonde American leading lady of the 20s.

Sandra 24. Summer Bachelors 26. The Brute 27. The Wizard 27. Alias Jimmy Valentine 28. Spite Marriage 29. The Idle Rich 29. The Bishop Murder Case 30. The Big House 30. The Flirting Widow 30. Men Call It Love 31. The Phantom of Paris 31. Red Headed Woman 32. Freaks 32. Island of Lost Souls 32. Sing Sinner Sing 33. Affairs of a Gentleman 34. Ruggles of Red Gap 35. Yellow Dust 36, many others.

Hyams, Peter (1943–).
American director.

T.R. Baskin (w & p only) 71. The Rolling Man (TV) 72. Goodnight My Love (TV) 73. Busting (& w) 74. Our Time (& w) 74. Peeper 76. Telefon (co-w only) 77. Capricorn One (& w) 78. Hanover Street (& w) 79. The Hunter (& w) 80. Outland (& w) 81. The Star Chamber 83. 2010 84. Running Scared 86. The Presidio 88. Narrow Margin 90. Stay Tuned 92. Timecop 94, etc.

Hyde-White, Wilfrid (1903–1991).
Impeccably British character actor of stage and screen, mainly in comedy roles.

Murder by Rope 37. The Third Man 49. The Story of Gilbert and Sullivan 54. See How They Run 55. The Adventures of Quentin Durward 56. North-West Frontier 59. Carry On Nurse 59. Two-Way Stretch 61. My Fair Lady 64. John Goldfarb Please Come Home 64. You Must Be Joking 65. Ten Little Indians 65. The Liquidator 65. Our Man in Marrakesh 66. Chamber of Horrors 66. Skullduggery 69. Gaily Gaily 69. Fragment of Fear 70. A Brand New Life (TV) 73. The Great Houdinis (TV) 76. The Cat and the Canary 78. The Rebels (TV) 79. In God We Trust 80. Oh God Book Two 80. Damien: Leper Priest (TV) 80. The Toy 82, etc.

TV series: Peyton Place 67. The Associates 79–80. Buck Rogers in the 25th Century 81.

Hyer, Martha (1929–).
American light leading lady of the 50s, in mainly routine films.

The Locket 46. The Woman on the Beach 47. The Velvet Touch 48. The Clay Pigeon 49. The Lawless 50. Salt Lake Raiders 50. Abbott and Costello Go to Mars 52. So Big 53. Riders to the Stars 54. Sabrina 54. Francis in the Navy 55. Red Sundown 56. Battle Hymn 57. Mister Cory 57. My Man Godfrey 57. Paris Holiday 58. Houseboat 58. Some Came Running (AAN) 59. The Best of Everything 59. Ice Palace 60. The Last Time I Saw Archie 61. A Girl Named Tamiko 62. Wives and Lovers 63. The Carpetbaggers 64. The First Men in the Moon 64. The Sons of Katie Elder 65. The Chase 66. The Happening 67. Massacre at Fort Grant 68. Crossplot 69. Once You Kiss a Stranger 70, many others.

Hyland, Diana (1936–1977) (Diana Gentner).
American stage and TV actress. At her death she had just begun to star in the TV series Eight is Enough.

One Man's Way 64. The Chase 66. The Boy in the Plastic Bubble (TV) 76.

Hylands, Scott (1943–).
Canadian leading man.

Daddy's Gone A-Hunting 68. Fools 70. Earth II (TV) 71. Earthquake 74. Bittersweet Love 76. The Boys in Company C 77. With This Ring (TV) 78. Winds of Kitty Hawk (TV) 78. Tales of the Klondike: In a Far Country (TV) 81. A Savage Hunger 84, etc.

TV series: Night Heat 85–91.

Hylton, Jack (1892–1965).
British bandleader who appeared in two films: She Shall Have Music 35 and Band Wagon 40. Later impresario.

Hylton, Jane (1926–1979).
British actress, in films after 1945.

When the Bough Breaks 47. Here Come the Huggetts 49. It Started in Paradise 52. The Weak and the Wicked 53. House of Mystery 59, many others.

Hylton, Richard (1921–1962).
American actor with stage experience.

Lost Boundaries 48. The Secret of Convict Lake 51. Fixed Bayonets 51. The Pride of St Louis 52, etc.

Hyman, Dick (1927–).
American composer and jazz pianist who has scored three of Woody Allen's films.

Scott Joplin 77. Zelig 83. Broadway Danny Rose 83. Radio Days 87. Leader of the Band 87. Moonstruck 87. Alan & Naomi 92, etc.

Hyman, Eliot (1905–1980).
American entrepreneur who made a fortune from buying up Hollywood libraries for sale to television, notably Monogram and Warner. Formed Seven Arts, film financers and distributors.

Hyman, Kenneth (1928–).
American executive producer; formerly with Allied Artists and Seven Arts in Britain, now independent. Son of Eliot Hyman.

The Hound of the Baskervilles 59. The Roman Spring of Mrs Stone 61. Gigot 62. The Small World of Sammy Lee 63. The Hill 65. The Dirty Dozen 66, etc.

Hymer, Warren (1906–1948).
American character actor with stage experience; usually seen as dim-witted gangster.

Up the River 30. Charlie Chan Carries On 31. Twenty Thousand Years in Sing Sing 32. Kid Millions 35. San Francisco 36. Tainted Money 37. Destry Rides Again 39. Meet John Doe 41. Baby Face Morgan 42. Joe Palooka Champ 46, many others.

hypnosis
on the screen has mainly been a basis for melodrama. Svengali was its most demonic exponent, but others who followed in his footsteps were Jacques Bergerac in The Hypnotic Eye, Boris Karloff in The Climax, Bela Lugosi in Dracula, Charles Gray in The Devil Rides Out, Erich Von Stroheim in The Mask of Fu Manchu, Christopher Lee in The Face of Fu Manchu, Orson Welles in Black Magic, and José Ferrer in Whirlpool (in which, immediately after major surgery, he hypnotized himself into leaving his bed and committing a murder). In Fear in the Night and its remake Nightmare, De Forrest Kelley and Kevin McCarthy were hypnotized into becoming murderers. Comic uses are legion, the perpetrators including Lugosi in Abbott and Costello Meet Frankenstein, Karloff in The Secret Life of Walter Mitty, Gale Sondergaard in Road to Rio, the cast of How to be Very Very Popular, Yves Montand in On a Clear Day You Can See Forever, Alan Badel in Will Any Gentleman, Mildred Natwick in The Court Jester, and Pat Collins in Divorce American Style. The chief serious study of the subject has been Freud, though one might also count The Search for Bridey Murphy.

Hyson, Dorothy (1915–).
British leading lady of the 30s, with stage experience (mainly in Aldwych farces).

Soldiers of the King 33. The Ghoul 33. Turkey Time 33. Sing As We Go 34. A Cup of Kindness 34. Spare a Copper 40, etc.

Hytten, Olaf (1888–1955).
Scottish character actor in American films.

It Is The Law 24. The Salvation Hunters 27. Daughter of the Dragon 31. Berkeley Square 33. Becky Sharp 35. The Good Earth 37. The Adventures of Robin Hood 38. Our Neighbours The Carters 40. The Black Swan 42. The Lodger 44. Three Strangers 46. Perils of the Jungle 53, etc.

I

Ibbetson, Arthur (1922–).
British cinematographer.

The Horse's Mouth 58. The Angry Silence 59. The League of Gentlemen 60. *Tunes of Glory* 61. Whistle Down the Wind 61. The Inspector 62. Nine Hours to Rama 63. I Could Go On Singing 63. The Chalk Garden 64. Sky West and Crooked 65. A Countess from Hong Kong 66. Inspector Clouseau 68. Where Eagles Dare 68. The Walking Stick 69. Anne of the Thousand Days (AAN) 70. The Railway Children 70. Willie Wonka and the Chocolate Factory 71. A Doll's House 73. Frankenstein: The True Story (TV) 73. 11 Harrowhouse 74. It Shouldn't Happen to a Vet 76. A Little Night Music 77. The Medusa Touch 77. The Prisoner of Zenda 79. Hopscotch 80. Little Lord Fauntleroy (TV) 80. Witness for the Prosecution 83. Master of the Game (TV) 83. The Bounty 84. Santa Claus 84.

Ibert, Jacques (1890–1962).
French composer.

The Italian Straw Hat 28. Don Quixote 34. Golgotha 35. La Charrette Fantôme 38. Panique 47. Macbeth 48. Invitation to the Dance 56, etc.

Ibsen, Henrik (1828–1906)
Norwegian dramatist who against great opposition brought social problems to the stage. Works filmed include *A Doll's House, An Enemy of the People.*

Ibuse, Masui (1898–1993).
Distinguished Japanese novelist and short-story writer whose masterpiece *Black Rain* (*Kuroi Ame*) was filmed in 1988 by Shohei Imamura.

Ice Cube (1968–) (O'Shea Jackson).
American rap performer, lyricist and actor. Born in Los Angeles, he trained as an architectural draughtsman before becoming a member of the group NWA (Niggaz With Attitude) and went solo in 1990 with raps notorious for their misogyny and violence.

Boyz N The Hood 91. Trespass 93. The Glass Shield 94, etc.

Ice-T (1959–) (Tracey Marrow).
Controversial American rap performer, lyricist and actor, notorious for his record 'Cop Killer'. Born in New Jersey, he was involved in crime before turning to performing.

Autobiography: 1994, *The Ice Opinion.*

Breakin' 84. Listen Up: The Lives of Quincy Jones 90. New Jack City 91. Ricochet 91. Who's the Man 93. Trespass 93. Surviving the Game 94. Johnny Mnemonic 95.

¶ Those criminal activities in my youth have got me where I am today, man. That's why people don't fuck with me. They know I'm real. – *I.T.*

America is a vicious killing machine based on rip-offs, lies, cheating and murder . . . The pilgrims were some corrupt mothafuckas. – *I.T.*

Ichikawa, Kon (1915–).
Distinguished Japanese director and screenwriter.

The Heart 54. The Punishment Room 55. *The Burmese Harp* 55. Odd Obsessions 58. *Fires on the Plain* 59. The Sin 61. An Actor's Revenge 63. *Alone on the Pacific* 66. To Love Again 71. The Wanderers 73. I Am a Cat 75. The Inugami Family 76. Matababi 77. Queen Bee 78. The Devil's Island 78. The Phoenix 79. Actress 87. Taketori Monogatari 87. Noh Mask Murders (Tenkawa Densetsu Satsujin Jiken) 91. 47 Ronin (Shiju Shichinin No Shikaku) 94, etc.

Idle, Eric (1943–).
Comic actor and screenwriter, one of the members of Monty Python.

And Now for Something Completely Different 71. Monty Python and the Holy Grail 75. The Rutles (TV) (& d) 78. Monty Python's Life of Brian 79. Monty Python's The Meaning of Life 83. Yellowbeard 83. National Lampoon's European Vacation 85. Transformers – the Movie 86. The Adventures of Baron Munchausen 88. Nuns on the Run 90. Missing Pieces 92. Heirs and Graces 92. Mom and Dad Save the World 92. Splitting Heirs (a, w) 93, etc.

Ifield, Frank (1937–).
British-born ballad singer who grew up in Australia.

Only film: *Up Jumped a Swagman* 65.

Ifukube, Akira (1914–).
Japanese composer.

The Quiet Duel 49. Godzilla, King of the Monsters 54. Hiroshima 55. The Burmese Harp 56. Rodan 57. King Kong vs Godzilla 63. Destroy All Monsters 69. Yog, Monster from Space 71. Revenge of Mecha-Godzilla 77, many others.

Iglesias, Alex de las (1965–).
Spanish director and screenwriter, born in Bilbao.

Acción Mutante (co-w, d) 93.

Ihnat, Steve (1934–1972).
Czech-born general-purpose actor in Hollywood, mostly in TV. Died of a heart attack.

The Chase 66. Countdown 67. The Hour of the Gun 67. Kona Coast 68. Madigan 69. Fuzz 72. *The Honkers* (wd only) 72, etc.

Ihnen, Wiard (1897–1979).
American production designer.

Blonde Venus 32. Madame Butterfly 32. Duck Soup 33. Cradle Song 33. The Trumpet Blows 34. Becky Sharp 35. Go West Young Man 36. Hollywood Cavalcade 39. Jane Eyre 44. Wilson 44. Along Came Jones 45. Blood on the Sun 45. The Time of Your Life 48. I the Jury 53, etc.

Ikebe, Shinchiro.
Japanese composer.

Kagemusha 80. The Ballad of Narayama 83. Zegen 87. Akira Kurosawa's Dreams 90, etc.

Iles, Francis (1893–1970).
British crime novelist who also wrote as Anthony Berkeley. *Before the Fact* formed the basis for

Hitchcock's *Suspicion; Malice Aforethought* was filmed for television with Hywel Bennett.

Illing, Peter (1899–1966).
Austrian-born character actor, in British films since the 40s.

The End of the River 46. Eureka Stockade 48. I'll Get You for This 51. The Young Lovers 54. Zarak 56. Whirlpool 59. Sands of the Desert 60. The Twenty-fifth Hour 66, many others.

Image, Jean (1911–1989).
French animator, best known abroad for his cartoon feature *Johnny Lionheart (Jeannot l'Intrépide)* 50.

Imai, Tadashi (1912–1991).
Japanese director, a controversial figure for his attacks on social injustice from a communist viewpoint. The son of a priest, he began as a screenwriter in 1934 and became a director in 1939; his best films were made in the 50s and 60s.

The Blue Mountains (Aoi Sanmyaku) 49. Till We Meet Again (Mata au hi Made) 50. And Yet We Live (Dokkoi Ikiteru) 51. Troubled Waters (Nigorie) 53. Monument of Star Lilies (Himeyuri no To) 53. Darkness at Noon (Mahiru no Ankoku) 56. Rice (Kome) 57. Yoru no Tsuzumi (Night Drum) 58. Kiku to Isamu 59. The Old Women's Paradise (Nippon no Obachan) 62. Bushido: Samurai Saga (Bushido Zankoku Monogatari) 63. A Story from Echigo (Echigo Tsutsuishi Oyashiraczu) 64. A Woman Called En (En to iu Onna) 71. The Life of a Communist Writer (Takij Kobayashi) 74. His Younger Sister (Ani Imoto) 77. War and Youth (Senso to Seishun) 91, etc.

Imamura, Shohei (1926–).
Japanese director, a former assistant to Ozu. He began as an amateur actor and playwright. During the 70s he worked mainly in television. In the 80s he founded his own film school, the Japan Academy of Visual Arts (Nihon Eiga Gakko) in Tokyo.

Stolen Desire (Nusumareta Yokubo) 58. Endless Desire (Hateshi Naki Yokubo) 58. Pigs and Battleships (Buta to Gunkan) 61. The Insect Woman (Nippon Konchuki) 63. The Pornographers (Jinruigaku Nyumon) 66. The Profound Desire of the Gods (Kamigami no Fukaki Yokubo) 68. Vengeance Is Mine (Fukushu Suru wa Ware ni Ari) 79. The Ballad of Narayama (Narayamabushi) 83. Zegen 87. Black Rain 89, etc.

Imax.
A large-screen technology, developed in Canada, that provides an image three times bigger than 70mm systems, and which uses six magnetic soundtracks to drive loudspeakers surrounding its audience. So far there are some 80 cinemas in the world capable of utilizing the system. There is one in Britain, at the National Museum of Photography, Film and Television in Bradford, with a screen 52 x 64 feet, and the British Film Institute plans to open another in London in the near future. Imax was first shown at Expo '70 in

apan, but attracted wider interest following the
elease in 1992 of a concert film, *At the Max*,
directed by Julien Temple and featuring the rock
band The Rolling Stones. The system's name is
derived from a combination of the words Image
and Maximum.

mi, Tony (1937–).
British cinematographer.

The Raging Moon 69. Dulcima 70. The Slipper
and the Rose 76. International Velvet 78. Brass
Target 78. The Sea Wolves 80. Inside the Third
Reich (TV) 82. Little Gloria . . . Happy at Last (TV)
82. Night Crossing 82. Nate and Hayes 83. Princess
Daisy (TV) 83. Sakharov (TV) 84. A Christmas Carol
(TV) 84. Reunion at Fairborough (TV) 85. Oceans
of Fire 85. Enemy Mine 85. Not Quite Paradise
85. Queenie (TV) 87. Empire State 87. Buster 88.
Wired 89. Options 89. Firebirds 90. Fourth Story
(TV) 91. Shopping 94. etc.

impresarios
presented on film include Sol Hurok, by David
Wayne in *Tonight We Sing*; Rupert D'Oyly Carte,
by Peter Finch in *The Story of Gilbert and Sullivan*;
Walter de Frece, by Laurence Harvey in *After the
Ball*; David Belasco, by Claude Rains in *Lady With
Red Hair*; Lew Dockstatter, by John Alexander in
The Jolson Story; Noël Coward by Daniel Massey,
and André Charlot by Alan Oppenheimer, in
Star!; and Florenz Ziegfeld, by William Powell in
The Great Ziegfeld and by Walter Pidgeon in *Funny
Girl*. Of fictional impresarios, the most memorable
were those played by John Barrymore in *Maytime*
and Anton Walbrook in *The Red Shoes*.

impressionism.
Generally understood to mean contriving an effect
or making a point by building up a sequence from
short disconnected shots or scenes.

in-jokes
were especially frequent when Hollywood was a
parochial society, and many must have been so
private as to escape the general eye. The following,
however, seem reasonably typical. *The Black Cat*
(34): Boris Karloff as a devil worshipper has to be
heard reciting an invocation to Satan, which to
please the Hays Code is made up of such Latin
phrases as 'cave canem' (beware of the dog), 'cum
grano salis' (with a grain of salt), 'in vino veritas'
(in wine is truth) and 'reductio ad absurdum est'
(it is shown to be impossible). *Bride of Frankenstein*:
Ernest Thesiger repeats a line ('It's my only
weakness') from his previous role for the same
director in *The Old Dark House*. *Mad Love*: a statue
apparently comes to life, and a frightened onlooker
says 'It went for a little walk', which is a line used
of the monster in *The Mummy*, the same director's
previous film. *His Girl Friday*: Cary Grant refers
to the execution of a fellow named Archie Leach,
which is Grant's own real name.

Hellzapoppin: Olsen and Johnson see a sledge on
a film set and remark 'I thought they burned that',
a reference to Rosebud in *Citizen Kane*. *Song of the
Thin Man*: William Powell finds a razor blade and
remarks 'Somerset Maugham has been here', a
reference to the author's current best-seller *The
Razor's Edge*. *The Maltese Falcon* and *In This Our Life*:
Walter Huston plays uncredited bit parts under his
son John's direction (one of innumerable similar
instances). *On the Town*: Frank Sinatra is subjected
to good-nature joshing about his real-life marriage
to Ava Gardner. *Arise My Love*: Ray Milland, asked
whether he was a test pilot, replies 'No, that was
Clark Gable', referring to the recently released *Test
Pilot*. *Northern Pursuit*: Errol Flynn, then in the
middle of a real-life rape case, tells the heroine she

is the only girl he has ever loved, then looks at the
audience and says: 'What am I saying?' *How to
Marry a Millionaire*: Lauren Bacall, then married to
Humphrey Bogart, says in conversation 'That old
man in *The African Queen*, I'm crazy about him'.
The Big Store: Groucho tells the audience: 'This
scene should have been in Technicolor but Mr
Mayer said it was too expensive'. (Again, many
similar instances exist, notably in the *Road* films,
which are full of studio gags such as 'Paramount
will protect us 'cause we're signed for five more
years'.) *Another Dawn*: in the 30s, whenever a
cinema canopy was shown, it usually advertised a
non-existent film under this title; but in 1938
Warners were stuck for a title for their new Errol
Flynn film, so they irrelevantly and cynically called
it *Another Dawn*. *Some Like It Hot*: Tony Curtis has
to impersonate a millionaire and as part of the
disguise gives a devastatingly accurate impression
of Cary Grant's voice, only to be told scathingly by
Jack Lemmon 'Nobody talks like that!' In the same
movie, and also in *Singin' in the Rain*, a gangster
tosses a coin in imitation of George Raft in *Scarface*.
The VIPs: asked for her home phone number,
Elizabeth Taylor gives 'Grosvenor 7060', which is
the number of MGM's London office. *Star
Spangled Rhythm*: the harassed and excitable
producer played by Walter Abel is named G. B. de
Soto, in imitation of B. G. de Sylva, then a
Paramount producer. *The Wings of Eagles*: the film
director, John Dodge, is played by Ward Bond as
an imitation of John Ford, who directed *The Wings
of Eagles*. *Irma La Douce*: the pimps' union is called
the Mecs' Paris Protective Association, or MPPA,
which also stands for Motion Picture Producers
Association, an organization which gave director
Billy Wilder some trouble. *Caprice*: heroine Doris
Day goes to the movies and sees a Doris Day movie.
One Two Three: James Cagney threatens a girl with
a grapefruit, mimicking his own action thirty years
before in *Public Enemy*: he also steals from *Little
Caesar* the line 'Mother of mercy, is this the end of
Rico?' *The Entertainer*: reference is made to
Sergeant Ossie Morris; the film was photographed
by Ossie Morris. *Finian's Rainbow*: Fred Astaire has
a short speech which consists, with different
emphasis, of the words of one of his old songs. *The
House that Dripped Blood*: Geoffrey Bayldon as a mad
scientist is made up to look like Ernest Thesiger in
Bride of Frankenstein. *How to Marry a Millionaire*:
Betty Grable fails to recognize a Harry James
recording (she was married to him at the time).
For the First Time: there is reference to a convict
named Cocozza, which happens to be star Mario
Lanza's real name. *Connecting Rooms*: Bette Davis
passes a poster mentioning stage star Margo(t)
Channing, the name of the character she played
in *All About Eve*. (The name is also used for one of
the unseen characters in *Sleuth*.) *Pete 'n' Tillie*:
Walter Matthau takes his girl to a cinema showing
Lonely Are the Brave, one of his own earlier films.
Aaron Slick From Punkin Crick: a waiter in a café
scene calls 'Give that Perlberg-Seaton order special
attention'. (Perlberg and Seaton produced and
directed the film.) *Road to Utopia*: Bob Hope says
Bing Crosby's voice is 'just right for selling cheese',
a reference to Bing's then-current radio show,
Kraft Music Hall. *Godfather II*: Troy Donahue plays
a character called Merle Johnson, which is his own
real name. *Dames*: Dick Powell is told 'Miss Warren,
Miss Dubin and Miss Kelly are outside', a reference
to songwriters Al Dubin and Harry Warren and
dress designer Orry-Kelly. *Strange Boarders*: Tom
Walls sees a picture of Disraeli and says 'Good old
George, what a make-up', a reference to George
Arliss' penchant for playing historical characters.
What's New Pussycat: a stranger who bumps into
Peter O'Toole in a nightclub turns out to be

Richard Burton, who asks 'Don't you know me
from someplace?' *West of the Divide*: in this 1934
quickie western John Wayne assumes the identity
of a bandit whose image (i.e. his own) he sees on
a wanted poster. The poster appeared in two other
Wayne films that year. *A Chump at Oxford*: Laurel
and Hardy foil a raid on the Finlayson National
Bank, a clear reference to their favourite
supporting player, James of that ilk. *The Lady in
the Lake*: Crystal Kingsley, the character who never
appears because she is dead, is listed as being
played by Ellay Mort ('elle est morte'). *Gold
Diggers of 1933*: a songwriter is told, 'Dubin and
Warren are out! You're writing the score!' (Dubin
and Warren wrote the score.) *Weekend at the
Waldorf*: Walter Pidgeon imitates John Barrymore
and Ginger Rogers says, 'Why, that's right out of
Grand Hotel!' (from which *Weekend at the Waldorf*
was adapted). *Trent's Last Case*: Orson Welles, who
had played Othello in London a year previously,
says: 'I saw *Othello* in London last year, but the
fellow was not very good.' *The Howling*: most of the
characters bear the names of horror film directors.
Quo Vadis: Peter Ustinov as Nero says as he dies
'Is this the end of Nero?', echoing Edward G.
Robinson's line at the end of *Little Caesar*, 'Is this
the end of Rico?'

Ince, John (1887–1947).
American lead in silent films and a supporting
actor in the 30s and 40s. On stage as a child, he
was in films from 1913. The brother of Thomas
and Ralph Ince, he also directed and produced
some silent movies.

The Price of Victory (& d) 13. The House of Fear
(& d) 14. The Urchin (d) 15. The Planter (& d)
17. Madame Sphinx 18. Old Lady 31 (d) 20. Hate
22. If Marriage Fails (d) 25. The Great Jewel
Robbery (p, d) 26. Moby Dick 30. Passport to
Paradise 32. Texas Terror 35. Way out West 36. Mr
Smith Goes to Washington 39. Pride of the
Yankees 42. Wilson 44. The Best Years of Our
Lives 46. The Paradine Case 48. etc.

Ince, Ralph (1881–1937).
American leading man of the 20s who rather oddly
ended his career in Britain directing quota quickies.
He was killed in a car crash.
AS ACTOR: One Flag at Last 11. The Lady of the
Lake 12. The Land of Opportunity 20. The Sea Wolf
25. Bigger than Barnum's 26. Wall Street 29. Little
Caesar 30. The Big Gamble 31. The Hatchet Man
32. The Tenderfoot 32. Havana Widows 33, etc.
AS DIRECTOR: A Man's Home 21. Homeward Bound
23. A Moral Sinner 24. Smooth as Satin 25. Bigger
than Barnum's 26. South Sea Love 28. Lucky
Devils 33. What's in a Name? 34. Murder at Monte
Carlo 34. Blue Smoke 35. It's You I Want 35. Hail
and Farewell 36. The Vulture 36. The Man Who
Made Diamonds 37, many others.

Ince, Thomas (1882–1924).
American director, a contemporary of D. W.
Griffith and some say an equal innovator. On stage
from the age of six, he began in films as an actor
before becoming a director with Carl Laemmle's
company. He systematized production methods,
built his own studio and provided films of a high
quality. Died suddenly at the end of a weekend
aboard William Randolph Hearst's yacht,
officially of a heart attack brought on by acute
indigestion. There were rumours that he had been
shot by Hearst, who suspected that Ince had
seduced his mistress Marion Davies, that he died
accidentally, hit by a shot intended for Charlie
Chaplin, and that Louella Parsons owed her
position as a columnist for Hearst's papers to not
revealing the truth about the incident. He was the

brother of John and Ralph Ince (qqv). Best remembered now for *Custer's Last Fight* 12. *Civilization* 15. *Human Wreckage* 23.

incest

has scarcely been fashionable film fare, though the theatrical acceptance of it goes back to *Oedipus Rex* (filmed in 1969) and one supposes *The Bible* (filmed in 1966) which fails to explain how else Adam and Eve's two sons propagated the species. It has been implied in a handful of American films from *Scarface* to *Toys in the Attic*, and more or less clearly stated in *Mourning Becomes Electra*, *A View from the Bridge* and *Chinatown*. Its full flowering came with the British *Country Dance*, but as expected the French had beaten us to it with *Souffle au Coeur*, though it became more explicit in *La Luna*. *My Lover My Son* is another example. *Close My Eyes* deals with an affair between a brother and sister, as does *The Cement Garden*, *The Miracle* with a son unwittingly attracted to his mother.

The Incredible Journey

Sheila Burnford's story of two dogs and a cat who are left with a friend and make a journey of 250 miles across the Canadian wilderness to their old home was first filmed by Disney in 1963 with a voice-over narration by Rex Allen. It was remade in 1993 with the animals being voiced by Don Ameche as a labrador, Michael J. Fox as a terrier, and Sally Field as the cat.

independent producer.

One not employed by a studio or distributor, who raises his own finance and makes his own deals. For many years independent productions tended to lack big studio expertise, and Tallulah Bankhead is said to have remarked, after viewing one of them, 'I don't see what that producer has got to be so independent about.' Since the breakup of the big studios in the 50s, however, most productions have been 'independent', and as Billy Wilder remarked, 'You now spend eighty per cent of your time making deals and only twenty per cent making pictures.'

India

has provided the setting for English-speaking films mainly of the military kind: *King of the Khyber Rifles*, *The Drum*, *Lives of a Bengal Lancer*, *Gunga Din*, *Soldiers Three*, *The Charge of the Light Brigade* (1936 version), *Bengal Brigade*, and *Conduct Unbecoming*. Civilian interests were the concern of *They Met in Bombay*, *The Rains Came*, *Elephant Boy*, *Bhowani Junction*, *Monsoon*, *The River Song of India*, *Calcutta*, *Thunder in the East*, *Northwest Frontier*, *Nine Hours to Rama* and *The Guru*. Of native Indian films only a few have percolated to Western cinemas, mostly directed by Mehboob, Satyajit Ray, or James Ivory. In the 80s there was a sudden flowering of interest in the last days of the Raj, especially on television: thus *The Jewel in the Crown*, *The Far Pavilions*, *Mountbatten the Last Viceroy*, and in the cinema *Heat and Dust* and *A Passage to India*.

Indians:

see *Red Indians*.

Industrial Light and Magic.

Special effects company formed in 1975 by George Lucas and John Dykstra when making *Star Wars*. Dykstra later left to form his own special effects company.

The Empire Strikes Back 80. E.T. – the Extraterrestrial 82. Return of the Jedi 83. Indiana Jones and the Temple of Doom 84. Back to the Future 85. Backdraft 91. Terminator 2 91. Switch 91. Star Trek VI: The Undiscovered Country 91. Hook 91. Memoirs of an Invisible Man 92. Jurassic Park 93. The Meteor Man 93, etc.

the industry.

¶ Some moments of horse sense:
Every time you pick up the trades you seem to find there's some new man sitting in the chair at one of the studios. This game of musical chairs that the majors play with studio heads is ridiculous. – *Mike Frankovich*

I am frequently told that my films don't make money. Since I have averaged one film a year for thirty years – some of them expensive ones – I can only conclude that somebody is making money. – *Joseph Losey*

Isn't it funny
That films never seem to make money
When everyone in the racket
Obviously makes a packet? – *Basil Boothroyd*

The infant industry has taken the ribbons from her hair. She has put away some of her bright toys — she is growing up. She may have a child one day, and the child's name may be Television, but that's another story. – *Edmund Goulding, 1929*

Inescort, Frieda (1900–1976) (Frieda Wightman).

Scottish-born actress of well bred roles, once secretary to Lady Astor; on stage from 1922. Went to Hollywood to begin film career.

If You Could Only Cook 35. Call it a Day 37. Beauty for the Asking 38. Woman Doctor 39. Pride and Prejudice 40. The Amazing Mrs Holliday 43. The Return of the Vampire 43. The Judge Steps Out 47. Foxfire 55. The Crowded Sky 60, etc.

Inge, William (1913–1973).

American playwright, most of whose work has been translated to the screen.

Come Back Little Sheba 52. Picnic 56. Bus Stop 56. The Dark at the Top of the Stairs 60. Splendor in the Grass (w) 61. The Stripper 63. Good Luck Miss Wycoff 79, etc.

Ingels, Marty (1936–   ).

American character comedian. He has been married to actress Shirley Jones since 1977.

Ladies' Man 60. Armored Command 61. The Horizontal Lieutenant 62. Wild and Wonderful 64. The Busy Body 67. For Singles Only 68. How to Seduce a Woman 74, etc.

TV series: *I'm Dickens He's Fenster* 62.

Ingham, Barrie (1934–   ).

British light leading man and general-purpose actor.

Tiara Tahiti 62. Invasion 66. Dr Who and the Daleks 66. A Challenge for Robin Hood (title role) 68, etc.

Ingraham, Lloyd (1875–1956).

American director, screenwriter and leading actor of silent films, from 1912, who became a character actor in the sound era.

Aurora of the North (a) 14. The Missing Link (d) 15. Intolerance (a) 16. The Little Liar (d) 16. Wives and Other Wives (d) 18. The Girl in the Taxi 20. At the Sign of the Jack O'Lantern (wd) 21. A Front Page Story (a) 22. Going Up 23. Midnight Molly 25. Silver Comes Through (wd) 27. Jesse James (d) 27. Kit Carson (co-d) 28. Take the Heir (d) 30. Texas Gunfighter (a) 32. Sons of Steel (a) 35. Destry Rides Again (a) 39. Adventures of Red Ryder (a) (serial) 40. Never Give a Sucker an Even Break (a) 41. Blazing Guns (a) 43. Sudan (a) 45. Sister Kenny (a) 46. The Savage Horde (a) 50, etc.

Ingram, Rex (1892–1950) (Reginald Hitchcock).

Irishman who went to Hollywood and became first an actor and screenwriter, then a noted director of silent spectaculars. Married to Alice Terry.

Biography: 1980, *Rex Ingram* by Liam O'Leary.
AS ACTOR: The Great Problem 16. Reward of the Faithless 17. Under Crimson Skies 19. Trifling Women 22, etc.
AS DIRECTOR: *The Four Horsemen of the Apocalypse* 21. The Conquering Power 21. *The Prisoner of Zenda* 22. Where the Pavement Ends 23. Scaramouche 23. The Arab 24. *Mare Nostrum* 26. The Magician 26. The Garden of Allah 27. Baroud 31. Love in Morocco 33, etc.

Ingram, Rex (1895–1969).

Impressive actor, in films from 1929; former doctor.

■ Hearts in Dixie 29. The Sign of the Cross 32. King Kong 33. The Emperor Jones 33. Harlem After Midnight 34. Captain Blood 35. *The Green Pastures* (as De Lawd) 36. *Huckleberry Finn* 39. *The Thief of Bagdad* 40. The Talk of the Town 42. Sahara 43. Cabin in the Sky 43. Fired Wife 43. Dark Waters 44. A Thousand and One Nights 45. Moonrise 48. King Solomon's Mines 50. Tarzan's Hidden Jungle 55. The Ten Commandments 56. Congo Crossing 56. Hell on Devil's Island 57. God's Little Acre 58. Anna Lucasta 59. Escort West 59. Watusi 59. Desire in the Dust 60. Elmer Gantry 60. Your Cheating Heart 64. Hurry Sundown 67. Journey to Shiloh 67.

Ingster, Boris (c. 1913–   ).

American writer-director.

The Last Days of Pompeii (co-w) 35. Happy Landing (w) 38. Stranger on the Third Floor (d) 40. Paris Underground (w) 45. The Judge Steps Out (wd) 49. Forgery (d) 50. Something for the Birds (co-w) 52, etc.

insanity

in the cinema has usually been of the criminal kind: Robert Montgomery (and Albert Finney) in *Night Must Fall*, Keir Dullea in *Bunny Lake is Missing*, Bette Davis in *Whatever Happened to Baby Jane?* and *The Nanny*, Franchot Tone in *Phantom Lady*, George Brent in *The Spiral Staircase*, Joseph Cotten in *Shadow of a Doubt*, Edward G. Robinson in *The Sea Wolf*, Robert Ryan in *Beware My Lovely*, Ivan Kirov in *Spectre of the Rose*, Robert Mitchum in *Night of the Hunter*, Douglass Montgomery in *The Cat and the Canary*, Anthony Perkins in *Psycho*, Hywel Bennett in *Twisted Nerve*, Oliver Reed in *Paranoiac*, Brember Wills in *The Old Dark House* and hundreds of others. Indeed, most screen villains have been, if not psychopathic, at least subject to an *idée fixe*: and many a tortured hero has had a mad wife in the attic. Insanity has however been played quite frequently for comedy, notably in *Harvey*, *Miss Tatlock's Millions*, *The Criminal Life of Archibaldo de la Cruz* and *Drôle de Drame*. Serious studies of insanity and its effects are on the increase, not only through fictitious situations as shown in *A Bill of Divorcement*, *The Shrike*, *Suddenly Last Summer*, *Of Mice and Men*, *David and Lisa*, *Shock Corridor*, *Shock Treatment*, *Diary of a Madman*, *One Flew over the Cuckoo's Nest* and *Cul de Sac*, but also in more clinical investigations such as *The Snake Pit*, *El*, *Labyrinth*, *La Tête contre les Murs*, *Morgan*, *Pressure Point*, *A Child Is Waiting*, *Lilith* and *Repulsion*. A mixture of attitudes is found in the scientific fantasy of *Charly*; while *Bedlam* was a curious attempt at a horror film set entirely in an asylum, a setting later used by *The Marat/Sade*. In *King of Hearts* the insane are shown to be wiser than the rest, like Mr Dick in *David Copperfield*.

insects

on the screen have generally been of the

monstrous kind: *Tarantula, The Black Scorpion, The Wasp Woman, The Fly, Them,* and *The Monster That Challenged the World* come to mind. Of course, normal-sized ants can be monstrous enough if seen in quantity, as in *The Naked Jungle,* or if you are as small as *The Incredible Shrinking Man.* Giant spiders are perhaps the most popular breed: there was a particularly loathsome one in *The Thief of Baghdad.* But even normal-sized ones caused trouble in *Arachnophobia.* Friendly insects have included those who went to the 'ugly bug ball' in *Summer Magic;* and the dancing caterpillar of *Once upon a Time.* The most symbolic insect was certainly the butterfly in *All Quiet on the Western Front;* the most abundant, the locust in *The Good Earth.* A documentary feature about insects of the most dramatic kind was *The Hellstrom Chronicle.*

insert shot.
One inserted into a dramatic scene, usually for the purpose of giving the audience a closer look at what the character on screen is seeing, e.g. a letter or a newspaper headline.

Inspector Hornleigh.
A detective whose interrogation of witnesses always led to a slip that gave away the criminal. Created by Hans Priwin (aka John P. Wynn), he was first featured on radio in 1937, which led to magazine stories and a stage play, followed by three films starring Gordon Harker in the title role: *Inspector Hornleigh* 39; *Inspector Hornleigh on Holiday* 39; *Inspector Hornleigh Goes to It* 41. A later radio series in the late 50s and early 60s from the same writer featured an identical detective except that he was now called Inspector Scott, but he failed to make the transition to the cinema.

insults.
¶ A choice selection, from scripts and from life.
Tony Curtis, about having to make love to Marilyn Monroe:
It's like kissing Hitler.
George Sanders to Anne Baxter in *All About Eve:*
That I should want you at all suddenly seems to me the height of improbability.
Louis B. Mayer to Greta Garbo's agent:
Tell her that in America men don't like fat women.
Monty Woolley to Mary Wickes in *The Man Who Came to Dinner:*
You have the touch of a sex-starved cobra.
Charles Winninger to Fredric March in *Nothing Sacred:*
The hand of God reaching down into the mire couldn't elevate you to the depths of degradation.
And in the same movie, Walter Connolly to Fredric March:
I am sitting here, Mr Cook, toying with the idea of removing your heart and stuffing it – like an olive!
Billy Wilder, after listening to Cliff Osmond singing for a part:
You have Van Gogh's ear for music.
Jan Sterling to Kirk Douglas in *Ace in the Hole:*
I've met a lot of hard-boiled eggs in my time, but you – you're twenty minutes!
Walter Matthau to Barbra Streisand on the set of *Hello Dolly:*
I have more talent in my smallest fart than you have in your entire body.
And later:
I have no disagreement with Barbra Streisand. I was merely exasperated by her tendency towards megalomania.
Mae West of W. C. Fields during the filming of *My Little Chickadee:*

There's no one in the world quite like Bill – thank God.

interactive films
are a goal towards which many seem to be working, though few agree on what is exactly meant by the term. At the moment, it is used to describe computer games on CD-ROM which incorporate filmed sequences using actors, who usually do little more than set the scene or tell the player what to do next. Interaction by the player is usually limited to choosing between one of several alternative actions. In the future, as technology progresses, it may be possible for an audience to interact more directly with what is happening, by altering the outcome of the story to suit its own tastes or by taking over the role of director to give instructions to the participants.

¶ The interaction between two people communicating enriches while interactive storytelling is like masturbation as opposed to love-making – *Krzystof Zanussi*

inventors
have been the subject of many screen biographies; indeed, Don Ameche had to live down his invention of the telephone in *The Story of Alexander Graham Bell* and of the sub-machine gun in *A Genius in the Family.* Mickey Rooney appeared as *Young Tom Edison* and Spencer Tracy as *Edison the Man;* James Stewart was *Carbine Williams;* Robert Donat played William Friese-Greene, inventor of the movie camera, in *The Magic Box.* Joel McCrea in *The Great Moment* invented laughing gas; *The Sound Barrier* covered Sir Frank Whittle's invention of the jet engine, and *The Dam Busters* has Michael Redgrave as the inventor of the bouncing bomb, Dr Barnes Wallis. That prolific inventor Galileo was played in an Italian film by Cyril Cusack and more recently by Topol. In *I Aim At the Stars* Curt Jurgens was Wernher von Braun. Benjamin Franklin was portrayed not by an actor but by Disney's cartoonists in *Ben and Me.* Charles Coburn later took over in *John Paul Jones* and Howard da Silva in *1776.*

Ireland
to film-makers has rather too often meant 'the troubles', which were celebrated in *Beloved Enemy, The Informer, The Gentle Gunman, Shake Hands with the Devil,* and the films of Sean O'Casey's plays, including *Juno and the Paycock* and *The Plough and the Stars.* (Rod Taylor played O'Casey, lightly disguised, in *Young Cassidy.*) More romantic or whimsical views of Eire were expressed in *The Luck of the Irish, The Rising of the Moon, Top of the Morning, Broth of a Boy, Home is the Hero, The Quiet Man, I See a Dark Stranger, Happy Ever After, Hungry Hill, The Search for Bridey Murphy, Jacqueline, Rooney, Never Put It In Writing* and *Ulysses;* realism was sought in *Odd Man Out, Parnell, Captain Boycott, No Resting Place, A Terrible Beauty,* and *Ryan's Daughter.* The number of Irish characters on the screen is of course legion, the most numerous and memorable varieties being priests, drunks, New York cops, and Old Mother Riley. The new 'troubles' of the early 70s and 80s have been, at the time of writing, too horrifying to provoke much response from makers of fiction films, apart from a TV movie called *War of Children* and a low-budget American exploiter called *The Outsider.* Ken Loach's controversial *Hidden Agenda* is the best film so far to grapple with the political realities of the present situation. Some talented Irish directors and writers have come to the fore in the 80s, including Neil Jordan, Jim Sheridan and Pat O'Connor.

Ireland, Jill (1936–1990).
British leading lady of the 50s. She married David McCallum and, in 1968, Charles Bronson. She wrote *Life Wish,* detailing her battle against cancer, in 1987, and a further volume of autobiography: 1989, *Life Lines.*
Oh Rosalinda 55. Three Men in a Boat 55. Hell Drivers 57. Robbery under Arms 57. Carry On Nurse 59. Raising the Wind 61. Twice Round the Daffodils 62. Villa Rides (US) 68. Rider on the Rain (US) 70. The Mechanic (US) 72. Wild Horses (US) 73. The Valachi Papers (It.) 73. The Streetfighter 75. Breakheart Pass (US) 76. From Noon Till Three (US) 76. Death Wish II 82. Assassination 86, etc.
TV series: Shane 66.

¶ I'm in so many Charles Bronson films because no other actress will work with him. – *J.I.*

Ireland, John (1879–1962).
British composer whose only film score was *The Overlanders* (47).

Ireland, John (1914–1992).
Canadian leading man in Hollywood; a popular tough-cynical hero of the early 50s, he declined with unaccountable rapidity to bit parts and second features.
A Walk in the Sun 45. Behind Green Lights 46. The Gangster 47. Raw Deal 48. Red River 48. I Shot Jesse James 49. Anna Lucasta 49. The Doolins of Oklahoma 49. All the King's Men (AAN) 49. Cargo to Capetown 50. The Scarf 51. Red Mountain 51. Hurricane Smith 52. Outlaw Territory 53. Security Risk 54. *The Good Die Young* (GB) 54. Queen Bee 55. Gunfight at the OK Corral 57. Party Girl 58. No Place to Land 59. Spartacus 60. Brushfire 62. The Ceremony 63. The Fall of the Roman Empire 64. I Saw What You Did 65. Fort Utah 67. Caxambu 67. Arizona Bushwackers 68. One on Top of the Other 70. The House of the Seven Corpses 73. Welcome to Arrow Beach 75. The Swiss Conspiracy 76. Love and the Midnight Auto Supply 77. Madam Kitty 77. The Shape of Things to Come 79. Guyana 80. The Incubus 82, many others.
TV series: The Protectors 61.

Irene (1901–1962) (Irene Lenz-Gibbons).
American costume designer. Born in Brookings, South Dakota, she worked as an extra in Hollywood in the mid-20s before studying fashion design and opening her own dress shop on the UCLA campus. She was an established designer by the mid-30s, joining MGM in 1942, where she stayed, and later regretted it, for seven years before designing for a chain of boutiques, as well as creating clothes for many stars. Personal problems, allied to heavy drinking, led her to commit suicide.
The Animal Kingdom 32. Flying down to Rio 33. Mrs Parkington 44. Weekend at the Waldorf 45. The Postman Always Rings Twice 46. State of the Union 48. B.F.'s Daughter (AAN) 48. Key to the City 50. Midnight Lace (AAN) 60. A Gathering of Eagles 63, etc.

¶ So quiet she was – and expensive, Miss Don't-Melt-Ice-Cube. – *L. B. Mayer*

Iribé, Paul.
Paris fashion designer and artist who was brought to Hollywood by De Mille to create the costumes for Gloria Swanson in *Male and Female* 19 and went on to design several other of De Mille's films.
The Affairs of Anatol 20. The Ten Commandments 23. The Road to Yesterday 25. Madame Satan 30.

iris.
An adjustable diaphragm in the camera which opens or closes from black like an expanding or contracting circle, giving a similar effect on the screen. So called because it resembles the iris of the human eye.

Irons, Jeremy (1948–).
British leading man of the introspective type.
Nijinsky 80. *The French Lieutenant's Woman* 81. *Brideshead Revisited* (TV) 81. Moonlighting 82. The Captain's Doll (TV) 82. Betrayal 82. The Wild Duck 83. Swann in Love 84. The Mission 85. Dead Ringers 88. Australia 89. A Chorus of Disapproval 89. Reversal of Fortune (AA) 90. Kafka 91. Damage 92. Waterland 92. M. Butterfly 93. The House of the Spirits 94. *The Lion King* (voice) 94. Die Hard 3 95, etc.

¶ Actors often behave like children and so we're taken for children. I want to be grown-up. – *J.I.*

Ironside, Michael (1950–).
Canadian leading actor, in American movies from the mid-80s.
Scanners 80. Visiting Hours 81. Spacehunter: Adventures in the Forbidden Zone 83. The Falcon and the Snowman 85. Top Gun 86. Jo Jo Dancer, Your Life Is Calling 86. Nowhere to Hide 87. Extreme Prejudice 87. Watchers 88. Mindfield 89. Office Party 89. Total Recall 90. Highlander II – the Quickening 90. Deadly Surveillance 91. McBain 91. Neon City 91. Chaindance (& w, p) 91. Black Ice 92. Night Trap (aka Mardi Gras for the Devil) 93. Forced to Kill 93. Sweet Killing 93. Free Willy 93. Father Hood 93. The Next Karate Kid 94. Red Scorpion 2 94. The Glass Shield 94, etc.
TV series: V 84–85.

Irvin, John (1940–).
British director, from TV.
Tinker Tailor Soldier Spy (TV) 80. The Dogs of War 80. Ghost Story 81. Champions 84. Raw Deal 86. Hamburger Hill 87. Next of Kin 89. Robin Hood 90. Eminent Domain 91. Widow's Peak 94. Freefall 94, etc.

Irving, Amy (1953–).
American leading actress who trained in San Francisco and London. She is the former wife of director Steven Spielberg (1985–89).
Carrie 78. The Fury 79. Voices 79. Honeysuckle Rose 80. The Competition 80. Yentl (AAN) 83. Micki and Maude 84. Rumpelstiltskin 87. Crossing Delancey 88. Who Framed Roger Rabbit? (voice) 88. A Show of Force 90. An American Tail: Fievel Goes West (voice) 91. Benefit of the Doubt 93. Kleptomania 93, etc.

Irving, George (1874–1961).
American character actor, long on the Broadway stage, for some while a film director, and most memorable in middle-aged businessman roles.
The Jungle 14. Madonna of the Streets 24. Wild Horse Mesa 25. Craig's Wife 28. Thunderbolt 29. The Spoilers 30. Island of Lost Souls 32. Dangerous 35. Sutter's Gold 36. The Toast of New York 37. Bringing Up Baby 38. New Moon 40. Son of Dracula 43. Christmas Holiday 44. Magic Town 47, many others.

Irving, John (1942–).
American novelist whose *The World According to Garp* was filmed in 82 and his *The Hotel New Hampshire* in 84.

Irving, Washington (1783–1859).
American humorist and storyteller whose *Rip Van Winkle* and *The Legend of Sleepy Hollow* have been filmed at various times and in various ways.

Irwin, Mark.
Canadian cinematographer.
Starship Invasion 77. Blood and Guts 78. The Brood 79. Scanners 81. Night School 81. Videodrome 83. The Dead Zone 83. Spasms 83. The Protector 85. The Fly 86. Youngblood 86. The Blob 88. Love at Stake 88. I Come in Peace 90. Class of 1999 90. Paint It Black 90. Robocop 2 90. Passenger 57 92, etc.

Irwin, May (1862–1938).
American actress who appeared in one of the very first short films, *The Kiss* 96; her only other film was *Mrs Black Is Back* 14.

Isaak, Chris (1956–).
American singer, songwriter and actor.
Married to the Mob 88. The Silence of the Lambs 91. Twin Peaks: Fire Walk with Me 92. Little Buddha 93, etc.

Isham, Mark.
American composer.
Never Cry Wolf 83. Mrs Soffel 84. The Hitcher 86. Made in Heaven 87. The Moderns 88. Everybody Wins 90. Reversal of Fortune 90. Fire in the Sky 93. Short Cuts 93. Nowhere to Run 93. Made in America 93. Romeo Is Bleeding 93. The Getaway 94. Mrs Parker and the Vicious Circle 94. Quiz Show 94. Timecop 94. The Browning Version 94, etc.

Isherwood, Christopher (1904–1986).
English novelist of the 30s who wrote the stories on which *I Am a Camera* and *Cabaret* were based. He later settled in California and co-wrote a few screenplays:
Rage in Heaven 42. Forever and a Day 43. Diane 55. The Loved One 65. Sailor from Gibraltar 67. Frankenstein: The True Story (TV) 73.

¶ It's no good explaining to people why one lives in Hollywood. They either understand or they don't. – *C.I.*

Israel's
native films have been few owing to problems of finance and language: *Hill 24 Does Not Answer* 55 is still the most notable, though a few comedies have been exported. The country's problems however have been fully aired in *Exodus, Judith, Cast a Giant Shadow, QB VII* and *Raid on Entebbe*, while Ingrid Bergman appeared as *Golda Meir* in a mini series.

Italian cinema
was an international force in the early years of the century with spectaculars like *Cabiria* and *Quo Vadis*. It later succumbed to the power of Hollywood and was little heard from until the post-war realist movement brought de Sica to world eminence. *Bicycle Thieves* was the high-water mark of achievement; afterwards came a slow slide into the commercialism of the 50s, which however re-established Rome – and Cinecittà Studios – as a world force in film-making, together with the idiosyncratic fancies of Fellini and Antonioni. Many big Hollywood films were made on Italian locations, the familiar cut-rate spectaculars peopled by mythical strong-men along with the 'spaghetti westerns' which aped Hollywood traditions but added an extra helping of violence.

Dario Argento gained a following for his baroque thrillers and horror films. New life was signalled by Bernardo Bertolucci's *Before the Revolution* 64 and Marco Bellocchio's *Fist in His Pocket* 65. Bellocchio's later films have not travelled as well as Bertolucci's, who soon established himself as an international director with a series of films on sex and politics and sexual politics: *The Conformist* 70, *Last Tango in Paris* 72, *1900* 76, *La Luna* 79. More recently, he has made films of great beauty and less message. Other notable directors include Paolo and Vittorio Taviani, whose best work so far is *Padre Padrone* 77, and Ermanno Olmi. Among film composers, few can match the output or the style of Ennio Morricone, while Roberto Benigni has an international reputation as a comic actor, despite the failure of his *Son of the Pink Panther*.

Itami, Juzo (1933–).
Japanese director and screenwriter, a former actor.
The Funeral 84. Tampopo 86. A Taxing Woman (Marusa no Onna) 88. A Taxing Woman Too 89. The Gangster's Moll (Mimbo no Onna) 92. Daibyonin 93, etc.

Iturbi, José (1895–1980).
Spanish pianist and conductor who made his American concert debut in 1929; in the 40s he appeared in a number of MGM musicals and helped to popularize classical music.
■ Thousands Cheer 43. Two Girls and a Sailor 44. Music for Millions 44. A Song to Remember (dubbed piano for Cornel Wilde; his recording of a Chopin Polonaise sold over one million copies) 44. Anchors Aweigh 45. Holiday in Mexico 46. Three Daring Daughters 48. That Midnight Kiss 49.

Ivan, Rosalind (1884–1959).
American character actress, mainly on stage.
The Suspect 44. Three Strangers 46. The Corn Is Green 46. Ivy 47. The Robe 53. Elephant Walk 54, etc.

Ivano, Paul (1900–1984).
American cinematographer.
The Dancers 25. No Other Woman 28. Atlantic Flight 37. *The Shanghai Gesture* 41. See My Lawyer 44. Spider Woman Strikes Back 46. Champagne for Caesar 50. For Men Only 52. Hold Back Tomorrow 55. Lizzie 57. Chubasco 68, many others, especially second unit shooting.

Ivens, Joris (1898–1989).
Dutch writer-director best known for documentaries.
Autobiography: 1969, *The Camera and I.*
Rain 29. Zuidersee 30. New Earth 34. Spanish Earth 37. The 400 Millions 39. The Power and the Land 40. Song of the Rivers 53. The Threatening Sky 66. Une Histoire de Vent 88, etc.

Ives, Burl (1909–) (Burl Icle Ivanhoe).
American actor and ballad-singer, once itinerant worker and professional footballer. His paunchy figure, beard and ready smile are equally adaptable to villainous or sympathetic parts.
Smoky (debut) 46. East of Eden 54. *Cat on a Hot Tin Roof* 57. Wind Across the Everglades 58. *The Big Country* (AA) 58. Our Man in Havana 59. The Brass Bottle 64. Rocket to the Moon 67. The McMasters 70. The Only Way Out is Dead 70. Baker's Hawk 76. Just You and Me, Kid 79. Earthbound (TV) 81. Uphill All the Way 84. Poor

Little Rich Girl (TV) 88. Two Moon Junction 88,
etc.

TV series: O.K. Crackerby 65. The Bold Ones 69.

Ivory, James (1928–).
American director who began by making films in
India.

Book: 1992, *The Films of Merchant Ivory* by Robert
Emmet Long.
■ The Householder 62. *Shakespeare Wallah* 64.

The Guru 69. Bombay Talkie 70. Savages (US) 72.
The Wild Party (US) 75. Autobiography of a
Princess 75. Roseland 77. Hullaballoo over
Bonnie and George's Pictures 78. The
Europeans 79. Jane Austen in Manhattan 79.
Quartet 81. *Heat and Dust* 83. The Bostonians 84.
A Room with a View (AAN) 86. *Maurice* 87. Slaves
of New York 89. Mr & Mrs Bridge 90. *Howards
End* 91. The Remains of the Day (AAN) 93.
Jefferson in Paris 95.

Iwerks, Ub (1900–1971).
American animator, long associated with Disney
(he drew the first Mickey Mouse cartoon, *Plane
Crazy*). Formed own company in 1930 to create
Flip the Frog; went back to Disney 1940 as
director of technical research. AA 1959 for
improvements in optical printing, 1965 for
advancing techniques of travelling matte. Iwerks
did much of the complex trick-work for Hitchcock's
The Birds (AAN).

J

Jabor, Arnaldo (1940–).
Brazilian director, dramatist, poet and journalist.
Pindorama 70. Toda Nudez Será Castigada 72. Tudo Bem 78. I Love You (Eu Te Amo) 81.

Jack the Ripper.
The unknown murderer of London prostitutes in 1888–9 has stimulated several flights of film fancy. Pabst brought him in to carry off the heroine of *Pandora's Box* 28. Two years earlier Alfred Hitchcock had directed the first film adaptation of Mrs Belloc Lowndes' novel *The Lodger*, but in this version Ivor Novello was found not to be the Ripper after all. Further versions were offered by Maurice Elvey in 1932 (Ivor Novello), John Brahm in 1944 (Laird Cregar) and Hugo Fregonese in 1953 (Jack Palance as *The Man in the Attic*). Further slight variations were posed in *The Phantom Fiend* 35 and *The Strangler* 64, while the long-standing puzzle was 'solved' in *Jack the Ripper* 58, *A Study in Terror* 65 and a TV 'Thriller' episode called *Yours Truly Jack the Ripper*. The Ripper was used as an alibi in *Dr Jekyll and Sister Hyde* 71, and the sins of the fathers were passed on in *Hands of the Ripper* 72, with Angharad Rees as the Ripper's daughter. In the 70s there was a German variation with Klaus Kinski, and in *Time after Time* the Ripper landed in modern San Francisco via H. G. Wells' time machine. In 1988, a TV film starred Michael Caine as a policeman on the track of the killer.

Jackley, Nat (1909–1988).
Skinny, lisping-voiced, rubber-necked English comedian in occasional films. He began as a clog dancer with the Eight Lancashire Lads, an act that had earlier included Charlie Chaplin, and was the son of comedian George Jackley.
Demobbed 44. Stars in Your Eyes 57. Mrs Brown, You've Got a Lovely Daughter 68. Yanks 79. The Ploughman's Lunch 83, etc.

Jacks, Robert L. (1922–1987).
American producer, long with Fox.
Man on a Tightrope 53. White Feather 55. A Kiss Before Dying 56. Bandido 57. Roots of Heaven 59. Man in the Middle 64. Zorba the Greek 65. Bandolero 68, many others.

Jackson, Anne (1926–).
American actress, wife of Eli Wallach; films rare.
■ So Young So Bad 50. The Journey 59. Tall Story 60. The Tiger Makes Out 67. How to Save a Marriage 67. *The Secret Life of an American Wife* 68. Lovers and Other Strangers 70. Zigzag 70. Dirty Dingus Magee 70. The Angel Levine 70. Nasty Habits 76. The Bell Jar 79. The Shining 80. A Woman Called Golda (TV) 82. The Family Man 82. Blinded by the Light (TV) 82. Leave 'em Laughing (TV) 82. Sam's Son 84. Funny about Love 90. Folks! 92.

Jackson, Freda (1909–1990).
British character actress with a penchant for melodrama; on stage from 1934, films from 1942.
A Canterbury Tale 42. Henry V 44. Beware of Pity 46. Great Expectations 46. *No Room at the Inn* 47. Women of Twilight 49. The Crowded Day 53. Brides of Dracula 60. The Third Secret 64. Monster of Terror 65, etc.

Jackson, Glenda (1936–).
British star actress. She announced her retirement from acting after being elected Labour MP for Hampstead and Highgate at the 1992 British general election.
■ This Sporting Life 63. The Marat/Sade 66. Tell Me Lies 67. Negatives 68. *Women in Love* (AA) 69. The Music Lovers 70. *Sunday Bloody Sunday* (AAN) 71. The Boy Friend (uncredited) 71. Mary Queen of Scots (as Queen Elizabeth) 71. A Touch of Class (AA) 72. The Triple Echo 72. A Bequest to the Nation 73. The Maids 73. The Tempter 74. The Romantic Englishwoman 75. Hedda (AAN) 76. The Incredible Sarah 76. Nasty Habits 76. House Calls 77. The Class of Miss MacMichael 78. Stevie 78. Lost and Found 79. Health 80. Hopscotch 80. The Patricia Neal Story (TV) 81. Return of the Soldier 82. Giro City (TV) 83. Sakharov (TV) 84. Turtle Diary 85. Business as Usual 87. Salome's Last Dance 88. The Rainbow 89. Doombeach 90.
TV series: *Elizabeth R* 71.

¶ I had no real ambition about acting, but I knew there had to be something better than the bloody chemist's shop. – *G.J.*
She's an absolute dreamboat, the epitome of professionalism, a splendid actress, and she has all the make-up of a fully rounded person. – *Walter Matthau*
If she went into politics she'd be prime minister; if she went into crime she'd be Jack the Ripper. – *Roy Hodge (her former husband)*

Jackson, Gordon (1923–1990).
Scottish actor whose rueful expression got him typecast as a weakling; maturity brought more interesting roles.
The Foreman Went to France (debut) 42. Millions Like Us 43. Nine Men 43. San Demetrio, London 44. Pink String and Sealing Wax 45. The Captive Heart 46. Against the Wind 47. Eureka Stockade 48. *Whisky Galore* 48. The Lady with a Lamp 51. Meet Mr Lucifer 54. Pacific Destiny 56. *Tunes of Glory* 60. The Great Escape (US) 62. *The Ipcress File* 65. Cast a Giant Shadow (US) 66. The Fighting Prince of Donegal 66. The Prime of Miss Jean Brodie 69. Run Wild Run Free 69. Kidnapped 72. Russian Roulette 75. Spectre (TV) 77. The Medusa Touch 77. The Last Giraffe (TV) 79. A Town Like Alice (TV) 80. The Shooting Party 84. The Masks of Death 85. The Whistle Blower 86. My Brother Tom (TV) 86. Beyond Therapy 87. The Lady and the Highwayman (TV) 89, many others.
TV series: *Upstairs Downstairs* 70–75. The Professionals 77–81.

Jackson, Janet (1966–).
American actress and singer, the sister of Michael Jackson, on stage with her family from the age of six.
Poetic Justice 93.
TV series: The Jacksons 76–77. Good Times 77–

79. A New Kind of Family 79–80. Diff 'rent Strokes 81–82. Fame 84–85.

Jackson, Kate (1948–).
American leading lady.
The Seven Minutes 70. Night of Dark Shadows 71. Limbo 72. Satan's School for Girls (TV) 73. Killer Bees (TV) 74. Death Cruise (TV) 74. Death Scream (TV) 75. Death at Love House (TV) 76. James at 15 (TV) 77. Thunder and Lightning 77. Topper (TV) 79. *Jacqueline Bouvier Kennedy* (TV) 81. Thin Ice (TV) 81. Dirty Tricks 81. Making Love 82. Listen to Your Heart (TV) 83. Rage of Angels (TV) 83. Loverboy 89, etc.
TV series: Dark Shadows 67–71. The Rookies 71–74. *Charlie's Angels* 76–80. Scarecrow and Mrs King 83–87.

Jackson, Mary Ann (1923–).
American child actress, in the Our Gang comedies of the late 20s and early 30s.

Jackson, Michael (1958–).
Precocious American rock singer and songwriter, first as a member of the Jackson Five and then as a solo artist. Rich and reclusive, he has spent a fortune re-making his appearance with the aid of plastic surgeons. Promotional videos of his songs directed by, among others, John Landis and John Singleton have cost more than many feature films. In 1994, he married Elvis Presley's daughter, Marie Louise Presley.
Biography: 1994, *Michael Jackson Unauthorized* by Christopher Andersen.
Save the Children (concert) 73. The Wiz 78. Moonwalker 88.

Jackson, Mick.
British director, from television, now working in Hollywood.
Threads (TV) 85. Yuri Nosenk, KGB (TV) 86. A Very British Coup (TV) 88. Chattahoochee 90. L.A. Story 91. The Bodyguard 92. Clean Slate 94, etc.

Jackson, Pat (1916–).
British director, a war documentarist whose later output has been disappointing.
Ferry Pilot 41. *Western Approaches* 44. The Shadow on the Wall (US) 48. *White Corridors* 50. Something Money Can't Buy 52. The Feminine Touch 55. Virgin Island 58. Snowball 60. What a Carve Up 62. Seven Keys 62. Don't Talk to Strange Men 62. Seventy Deadly Pills 64, etc.

Jackson, Peter (1961–).
New Zealand director, screenwriter and producer whose low-budget visceral horror films have achieved cult status.
■ Bad Taste 87. Meet the Feebles 89. Braindead 92. Heavenly Creatures 94.

Jackson, Samuel L. (1949–).
American actor, from the stage.
Sea of Love 89. Do the Right Thing 89. GoodFellas 90. Jungle Fever 91. White Sands 92.

Patriot Games 92. Juice 92. Amos & Andrew 93. National Lampoon's Loaded Weapon 1 93. Menace II Society 93. Jurassic Park 93. Against the Wall (TV) 94. Fresh 94. Pulp Fiction 94. The New Age 94. Die Hard 3 95, etc.

Jackson, Selmer (1888–1971).
American character actor who played hundreds of unobtrusive fathers, doctors, scientists and executives.
Dirigible 31. Doctor X 32. The Witching Hour 34. Front Page Woman 35. The Westland Case 37. Stand Up and Fight 39. The Grapes of Wrath 40. It Started with Eve 41. It Ain't Hay 43. The Sullivans 44. The French Key 46. Mighty Joe Young 49. Elopement 51. Autumn Leaves 56. The Gallant Hours 60, many others.
~In 1940 alone Jackson appeared in 20 films.

Jackson, Thomas E. (1886–1967).
American character actor often seen as police officer.
Little Caesar 30. Doctor X 32. Terror Aboard 33. The Mystery of the Wax Museum 33. Call of the Wild 35. Hollywood Boulevard 36. The Westland Case 37. Torchy Gets Her Man 38. Golden Gloves 40. Law of the Tropics 41. The Woman in the Window 44. The Big Sleep 46. Dead Reckoning 47. Stars and Stripes Forever 52. Attack of the Fifty Foot Woman 58. Synanon 65, many others.

Jacob, Irène (1966–).
French leading actress.
Au Revoir les Enfants 87. La Bande des Quatre 89. The Double Life of Veronique 91. Claude 92. La Passion Van Gogh 93. The Secret Garden 93. Three Colours: Red (Trois Couleurs: Rouge) 94. La Prédiction 94. Le Moulin de Daudet 94, etc.

Jacobi, Derek (1938–).
British actor who played the lead in I Claudius on TV.
The Day of the Jackal 73. Blue Blood 74. The Odessa File 74. Philby, Burgess and Maclean (TV) 77. The Medusa Touch 77. The Human Factor 79. The Hunchback of Notre Dame (TV) (as Frollo) 82. Inside the Third Reich (TV) (as Hitler) 82. Enigma 82. Mr Pye 86. Little Dorrit 87. Henry V 89. The Fool 90. Dead Again 91. The Vision Thing (TV) 93, etc.
TV series: Brother Cadfael 94.

Jacobi, Lou (1913–).
Chubby American character actor.
Song without End 60. Irma la Douce 62. Everything you Always Wanted to Know about Sex 72. Roseland 77. Arthur 81. The Lucky Star 81. My Favorite Year 82. The Boss's Wife 86. Amazon Women on the Moon 87, etc.
TV series: Ivan the Terrible 76. Melba 86.

Jacobs, Arthur P. (1918–1973).
American independent producer, former publicist.
■ What a Way to Go 64. Dr Dolittle (AAN) 67. Planet of the Apes 68. The Chairman 69. Goodbye Mr Chips 69. Beneath the Planet of the Apes 69. Escape from the Planet of the Apes 71. Conquest of the Planet of the Apes 72. Tom Sawyer 73. Huckleberry Finn 73.

Jacobs, W. W. (1863–1943).
British short story writer: The Monkey's Paw has been filmed many times.

Jacobsson, Ulla (1929–1982).
Leading Swedish actress.
One Summer of Happiness 51. Smiles of a Summer Night 55. Love is a Ball 63. Zulu 64. The Heroes of Telemark 65, etc.

Jacoby, Scott (1956–).
American juvenile lead.
Baxter 72. Rivals 73. Love and the Midnight Auto Supply 77. The Little Girl Who Lives Down the Lane 77. Our Winning Season 78. To Die For 89. To Die For II 91, etc.

Jacques, Hattie (1924–1980).
Oversized British comedienne, well known at the Players' Theatre and on TV. In most of the 'Carry On' films. Married John Le Mesurier.
Nicholas Nickleby 47. Oliver Twist 48. Trottie True 49. The Pickwick Papers 52. Make Mine Mink 61. In the Doghouse 62. The Bobo 67. Crooks and Coronets 69, etc.

Jaeckel, Richard (1926–).
American actor, former Fox mail-boy, who made a name playing frightened youths in war films.
Guadalcanal Diary 43. Jungle Patrol 48. Sands of Iwo Jima 49. The Gunfighter 50. Come Back Little Sheba 52. The Violent Men 55. Attack! 55. 3.10 to Yuma 57. The Gallant Hours 60. Town without Pity 61. Four for Texas 63. Town Tamer 65. The Dirty Dozen 67. The Devil's Brigade 68. The Green Slime 69. Chisum 70. Sometimes a Great Notion (AAN) 71. Chosen Survivors 74. Grizzly 76. Day of the Animals 77. The Dark 79. Herbie Goes Bananas 80. All the Marbles 81. The Awakening of Candra (TV) 81. The Fix 84. Starman 84. Pacific Inferno (TV) 85. Black Moon Rising 86. Ghetto Blaster 89, etc.
TV series: Frontier Circus 61. Banyon 70. Firehouse 74. Salvage 77. At Ease 83. Spenser: for Hire 85–87. Baywatch 91– .

Jaeckin, Just (1940–).
French director and screenwriter of erotic movies that promise more than they deliver.
Emmanuelle 74. The Story of O 75. Madame Claude 79. The Last Romantic Lover (Le Dernier Amant Romantique) 80. Lady Chatterley's Lover 82. The Perils of Gwendoline 84, etc.

Jaeger, Frederick (1928–).
Anglo-German general-purpose actor.
The Black Tent 56. I Was Monty's Double 59. The Looking Glass War 69. Scorpio 72. The Seven Percent Solution 76. The Passage 78. Nijinsky 80, etc.

Jaffe, Carl (1902–1974).
Aristocratic-looking German actor, long in England.
Over the Moon 39. The Lion Has Wings 40. The Life and Death of Colonel Blimp 43. Gaiety George 46. Appointment in London 53. Operation Crossbow 65. The Double Man 67, many others.

Jaffe, Sam (1891–1984).
American character actor of eccentric appearance and sharp talent. On stage from 1916, films from 1933.
We Live Again 34. The Scarlet Empress 34. Lost Horizon (as the High Lama) 37. Gunga Din 39. Stage Door Canteen 43. 13 Rue Madeleine 46. Gentleman's Agreement 47. The Accused 48. Rope of Sand 49. The Asphalt Jungle (AAN) 50. Under the Gun 50. I Can Get It for You Wholesale 51. The Day the Earth Stood Still 51. All Mine to Give 57. Les Espions 57. The Barbarian and the Geisha 58. Ben Hur 59. A Guide for the Married Man 67. Guns for San Sebastian 68. The Great Bank Robbery 69. Night Gallery (TV) 69. Quarantined (TV) 70. The Kremlin Letter 70. The Old Man Who Cried Wolf (TV) 70. The Dunwich Horror 70. Who Killed the Mysterious Mr Foster? (TV) 71. Bedknobs and Broomsticks 71. QB VII (TV) 74. Battle Beyond the Stars 80. The End 81. Nothing Lasts Forever 82. On the Line 83, etc.
TV series: Ben Casey 60–64.

Jaffe, Stanley R. (1940–).
American producer. He is President and Chief Operating Officer of Paramount Communications.
Goodbye Columbus 69. Bad Company 72. The Bad News Bears 76. Kramer vs Kramer 78. Taps 81. Without a Trace (& d) 83. Racing with the Moon 84. Firstborn 84. Fatal Attraction (AAN) 87. The Accused 88. Black Rain 89, etc.

Jaffrey, Madhur (1933–).
Indian actress, best known now for her books and television series on Indian cooking. She was formerly married to Saeed Jaffrey.
Shakespeare Wallah 65. The Guru 69. Autobiography of a Princess 75. Heat and Dust 82. The Assam Garden 85. The Perfect Murder 88. Vanya on 42nd Street 94, etc.
TV series: Firm Friends 93–94.

Jaffrey, Saeed.
Exuberant Indian actor, in Britain. He studied at RADA, has acted with the National Theatre and also appeared in many Indian movies. He was formerly married to Madhur Jaffrey.
The Guru 69. The Man Who Would Be King 75. The Wilby Conspiracy 75. The Chess Players 77. Staying On (TV) 81. Gandhi 82. The Jewel in the Crown (TV) 83. The Razor's Edge 84. A Passage to India 84. My Beautiful Laundrette 85. The Deceivers 87. Masala 91, etc.
TV series: Tandoori Nights 85–87. Little Napoleons 94.

Jagger, Dean (1903–1991) (Dean Jeffries).
American star character actor of the 40s, usually in sympathetic roles; later seen as colonels, fathers, town elders, etc.
Women from Hell 29. College Rhythm 34. Home on the Range 34. Men without Names 35. Revolt of the Zombies 36. Exiled to Shanghai 37. Brigham Young (title role) 40. Western Union 41. The Men in Her Life 41. The Omaha Trail 42. North Star 43. When Strangers Marry 44. I Live in Grosvenor Square (GB) 45. Sister Kenny 46. Pursued 47. Twelve O'Clock High (AA) 49. Dark City 50. Denver and Rio Grande 52. It Grows on Trees 52. The Robe 53. Executive Suite 54. Bad Day at Black Rock 55. The Great Man 56. X the Unknown (GB) 57. The Proud Rebel 58. The Nun's Story 59. Elmer Gantry 60. Parrish 61. The Honeymoon Machine 62. First to Fight 67. Firecreek 68. The Kremlin Letter 70. The Brotherhood of the Bell (TV) 70. Vanishing Point 71. The Glass House (TV) 72. God Bless Dr Shagetz 77. End of the World 77. Alligator 80, many others.
TV series: Mr Novak 63–65.

Jagger, Mick (1943–).
Heavy-faced British pop idol whose film career didn't get off the ground.
■ Ned Kelly 69. Performance 70. Gimme Shelter 70. Burden of Dreams (doc) 82. The Nightingale (TV) 84. Freejack 92.

¶ He sees all women as tarts. – Bianca Jagger
Mick's approach to acting was, once he discovered what it was about, he wasn't interested. – James Fox
Though fire and energy snake out of Mick like electricity in concert, he can't produce them cold

as an actor. It's a problem with many rock performers. – *Tony Richardson*

Jaglom, Henry (1941–).
American writer-director of eccentric films.
■ A Safe Place 71. Tracks 72. Other People 79. Sitting Ducks (& a) 80. Can She Bake a Cherry Pie 83. Someone to Love 87. New Year's Day 89. Eating 90. Venice/Venice 92. Babyfever (co-w, d, e) 94.

Jakubowska, Wanda (1907–).
Polish director.
Soldier of Victory 43. The Last Stop 48. An Atlantic Story 54. Farewell to the Devil 56. Encounters in the Dark 60. The Hot Line 65. 150 Na Godzine 71, Bialy Mazur 73. Ludwik Warynski 78, etc.

James Bond,
the over-sexed one-man spy machine created by Ian Fleming, first came to the screen in the guise of Sean Connery in *Dr No* 62. Connery continued in *From Russia with Love* 63, *Goldfinger* 64, *Thunderball* 65, *You Only Live Twice* 67; David Niven appeared as 'Sir James' in *Casino Royale* 67. George Lazenby took over for *On Her Majesty's Secret Service* 69; Connery came back for *Diamonds Are Forever* 71; Roger Moore signed on for *Live and Let Die, The Man with the Golden Gun, The Spy Who Loved Me, Moonraker, For Your Eyes Only* and *Octopussy*. In 1983 Connery returned as Bond in *Never Say Never Again*. Moore's last outing, in 1985, was *A View to a Kill*. Timothy Dalton took over for 1987's *The Living Daylights* and 1989's *Licence to Kill*. Pierce Brosnan replaced him in 1994.

James, Brion (1945–).
American character actor, usually in menacing roles.
Southern Comfort 81. Blade Runner 82. 48 Hours 82. A Breed Apart 84. Enemy Mine 85. Flesh and Blood 85. Crime Wave 86. Armed and Dangerous 86. Steel Dawn 87. Nightmare at Noon 87. Dead Men Walking 88. Nightmare at Noon 88. Horror Show 89. Tango and Cash 89. Red Scorpion 89. Another 48 Hrs 90. Street Asylum 90. Mom 91. The Player 92. Black Magic (TV) 92. Time Runner 92. Future Shock 93. The Dark 93. Striking Distance 93. Cabin Boy 94. F.T.W. 94. Art Deco Detective 94, etc.

James, Clifton (1893–1963).
British character actor who so resembled Field Marshal Montgomery that during World War II he was hired to impersonate him and hoodwink the Germans, as told in the subsequent book and film, *I Was Monty's Double.*

James, Clifton (1921–).
Corpulent American character actor.
David and Lisa 64. Cool Hand Luke 67. Tick Tick Tick 70. Live and Let Die 72. The Man with the Golden Gun 73. The Bank Shot 74. Silver Streak 76. The Bad News Bears in Breaking Training 77. Superman II 80. Talk to Me 82. Where Are the Children? 85. Eight Men Out 88. The Bonfire of the Vanities 90. Carolina Skeletons (TV) 91, etc.
TV series: City of Angels 76. Lewis & Clark 81–82.

James, Harry (1916–1983).
American band-leader and trumpeter who appeared in occasional films. He was married to Betty Grable (1943–65).
Springtime in the Rockies 42. Best Foot Forward 43. Bathing Beauty 44. Do You Love Me 46.

Carnegie Hall 47. I'll Get By 50. The Benny Goodman Story 56, etc.

James, Henry (1843–1916).
American novelist who lived in Europe. Film versions include *Berkeley Square, The Lost Moment, The Heiress, The Innocents, Daisy Miller.*

¶ I've always been interested in people, but I've never liked them. – *H.J.*
Poor Henry James! He's spending eternity walking round and round a stately park and the fence is just too high for him to peep over and he's just too far away to hear what the countess is saying. – *Somerset Maugham*

James, Jesse (1847–1882).
American wild west outlaw who has acquired the legend of a Robin Hood but in fact plundered ruthlessly as head of a gang which also included his sanctimonious elder brother Frank James (1843–1915). Among the many screen personifications of Jesse are Tyrone Power in *Jesse James* 39; Lawrence Tierney in *Badman's Territory* 46; Macdonald Carey in *The Great Missouri Raid* 52; Audie Murphy in *Kansas Raiders* 53; Willard Parker in *The Great Jesse James Raid* 53; Robert Wagner in *The True Story of Jesse James* 56; Dale Robertson in *Fighting Man of the Plains* 59; Ray Stricklyn in *Young Jesse James* 60; Chris Jones in a TV series *The Legend of Jesse James* 65; Robert Duvall in *The Great Northfield Minnesota Raid* 72; James Keach in *The Long Riders* 80 (brother Stacy was brother Frank); and Clayton Moore in several Republic serials. Henry Fonda was in *The Return of Frank James* 40.

James, M. R. (1862–1936).
English ghost-story writer, an academic with a splendid command of language. *The Night of the Demon* is a fairly satisfactory film version of *Casting the Runes.*

James, Peter.
Australian cinematographer, now resident in Canada.
Caddie 76. The Irishman 78. The Wild Duck 84. Rebel 85. The Right Hand Man 87. Echoes of Paradise 89. Driving Miss Daisy 89. Mr Johnson 90. Black Robe 91. My Life 93, etc.

James, Sid (Sidney) (1913–1976).
Crumple-faced South African comedy actor, in Britain from 1946. A familiar face on TV and in scores of movies, including most of the 'Carry On' series from 1958.
Black Memory 46. Once a Jolly Swagman 48. The Man in Black 49. The Lavender Hill Mob 51. The Titfield Thunderbolt 53. Joe Macbeth 55. The Silent Enemy 57. Too Many Crooks 58. Tommy the Toreador 59. Double Bunk 60. What a Carve Up 62. The Big Job 65. Don't Lose Your Head 67. Bless This House 73, many others.
TV series: Taxi. Hancock 56–59. Citizen James. Bless This House 71–75.

Jameson, Jerry.
American director.
The Dirt Gang 72. The Bat People 74. The Elevator (TV) 74. The Secret Night Caller (TV) 74. Heatwave (TV) 74. Hurricane (TV) 74. Terror on the 40th Floor (TV) 75. The Deadly Tower (TV) 75. The Invasion of Johnson County (TV) 76. Airport 77 77. A Fire in the Sky 77. High Noon Part Two (TV) 78. Raise the Titanic 80. The Cowboy and the Ballerina (TV) 84. Fire and Rain (TV) 89, etc.

Jamison, Bud (1894–1944).
American character actor, a stock Columbia player who played the heavy in most of the Three Stooges two-reelers.

Jancso, Miklos (1921–).
Hungarian director.
Cantata 63. My Way Home 64. The Round Up 65. The Red and the White 67. Silence and Cry 68. Winter Wind 70. The Pacifist 71. Agnus Dei 71. Red Psalm 72. Electra 74. Private Vice and Public Virtue 76. Masterwork 77. Hungarian Rhapsody 79. Heart of a Tyrant 81. Huzsika (TV) 84. Omega Omega 85. Budapest (doc) 85. Dawn 86. Season of Monsters 87. Jezus Krisztus Horoszkopia 89. The Blue Danube Waltz (Kek Duna Keringo) 92, etc.

Jandl, Ivan (1941–1987).
Czech child actor whose sole performance as a war orphan in the tear-jerking *The Search*, opposite Montgomery Clift, won him an Academy Award for 'the outstanding juvenile performance of 1948'.

Jane Eyre.
Charlotte Bronte's novel of a governess who falls in love with her master, Rochester, a man with a guilty secret, has been popular with film-makers from the early years of the century, although no version has yet captured the romantic spirit of the original. Christy Cabanne tried in 1934 with a cast that included Virginia Bruce as Jane Eyre and Colin Clive as Rochester; it was followed in 1934 by a classier version starring Orson Welles and Joan Fontaine, directed by Robert Stevenson and with Aldous Huxley among its scriptwriters. In 1970 came another lacklustre attempt destined for TV showing and directed by Delbert Mann, with George C. Scott and Susannah York heading the cast. The newest version was directed by Franco Zeffirelli, with a script by Hugh Whitemore. Novelist Jean Rhys wrote a prequel, *Wide Sargasso Sea*, explaining how Rochester met and married his first wife, which was lushly filmed in 1992 by John Duigan. The theme was also explored earlier, in Jacques Tourneur's 1943 film *I Walked with a Zombie.*

Janis, Conrad (1928–).
American character actor; began as a teenage player of the 40s.
Snafu 45. Margie 46. The High Window 46. Beyond Glory 48. Keep it Cool 58. The Duchess and the Dirtwater Fox 76. Roseland 77. Oh God Book Two 80. Brewster's Millions 84. Nothing in Common 86, etc.
TV series: Quark 76. Mork and Mindy 78–80.

Janis, Elsie (1889–1956) (Elsie Bierbauer).
American musical comedy star who made a few silent movies such as *Betty in Search of a Thrill* and *A Regular Girl*; only talkie, *Women in War* 42.

Jankel, Annabel.
British director who works in collaboration with Rocky Morton.
The Max Headroom Story (co-d) (TV) 85. D.O.A. (co-d) 88. Super Mario Bros (co-d) 93.

Janney, Leon (1917–1980).
American child actor, a member of the original Our Gang.
Doorway to Hell 30. Penrod and Sam 31. Should Ladies Behave 32, etc.

Janni, Joseph (1916–1994).
Italian producer, in England from 1939.
The Glass Mountain 48. Romeo and Juliet 53. *A Town Like Alice* 56. *A Kind of Loving* 62. Darling 65.

Modesty Blaise 66. Far From the Madding Crowd 7. Poor Cow 68. Sunday Bloody Sunday (AAN) 71. Made 72. Yanks 79, etc.

Jannings, Emil (1882–1950) (Theodor Emil Janenz). Distinguished German actor, on stage from ten years old. Entered films through his friend Ernst Lubitsch.

Im Banne der Leidenschaft 14. Passionels Tagebuch 14. Frau Eva 15. Vendetta 16. Wenn vier Dasselbe Tun 17. Life Is a Dream 18. The Eyes of the Mummy 18. The Brothers Karamazov 18. Der Stier von Oliviera 18. Rose Bernd 18. Madame Dubarry 19. Anne Boleyn 20. Kohlhiesels Tochter 21. Danton 21. The Wife of the Pharaoh 21. Tragedy of Love 22. Ratten 22. Othello 23. Peter the Great 24. All for Gold 24. Quo Vadis 24. Nju 24. The Last Laugh 24. Waxworks 24. Tartuffe 25. Faust 26. Variety 26. The Way of All Flesh (US) (AA) 27. The Last Command (US) (AA) 28. The Street of Sin (US) 28. The Patriot (US) 28. The Sins of the Fathers (US) 29. The Betrayal (US) 29. The Blue Angel 30. Darling of the Gods 31. The Tempest 31. Le Roi Pausaole 32. Der Schwarze Walfisch 34. The Old and the Young King 35. Traumulus 35. Der Herrscher 37. The Broken Jug 37. Robert Koch 39. Ohm Kruger 40. Die Entlassung 42. An Old Heart Becomes Young Again 42. Where Is Kerr Belling 45.

For being the last ham of the old school to become an international star. The Blue Angel.

Nine people out of ten, if asked to say who is the greatest actor on the screen, would unhesitatingly reply Emil Jannings. – Lionel Collier, Picturegoer, 1929

Jansen, Pierre (1930–). French composer who has scored many of the films of Claude Chabrol.

Les Bonnes Femmes 60. Les Sept Péchés Capitaux 62. Ophélia 62. Bluebeard (Landru) 62. Les Plus Belles Escroqueries du Monde 64. Le Tigre Aime la Chair Fraîche 64. La 317 Section 65. La Ligne de Demarcation 66. The Champagne Murders (Le Scandale) 67. La Route de Corinthe 67. Les Biches 68. The Unfaithful Wife (La Femme Infidèle) 68. This Man Must Die (Que la Bête Meure) 69. Le Boucheur 69. La Rupture 70. Just before Nightfall (Juste avant la Nuit) 71. High Heels (Docteur Popaul) 72. Wedding in Blood (Les Noces Rouges) 73. Nada 74. Les Innocents aux Mains Sales 75. Nuit d'Or 76. The Lacemaker (La Dentellière) 77. Violette 78. L'Etat Sauvage 78. Le Cheval d'Orgeuil 80, etc.

Janssen, David (1930–1980) (David Meyer). American leading man, very successful on TV; film roles routine, persona doggedly glum.

Yankee Buccaneer 52. Chief Crazy Horse 54. The Square Jungle 55. Toy Tiger 56. The Girl He Left Behind 56. Hell to Eternity 60. Ring of Fire 61. Mantrap 61. King of the Roaring Twenties (as Arnold Rothstein) 61. My Six Loves 63. Warning Shot 67. The Green Berets 68. The Shoes of the Fisherman 68. Where It's At 69. A Time for Giving 69. Macho Callahan 70. Birds of Prey (TV) 73. Fer de Lance (TV) 74. Once Is Not Enough 75. Stalk the Wild Child (TV) 76. The Swiss Conspiracy 76. Two Minute Warning 76. Mayday at 40,000 Feet 77. Warhead 77. The Word (TV) 78. The Golden Gate Murders 79. High Ice (TV) 79. City in Fear (TV) 79, etc.

TV series: Richard Diamond 59. The Fugitive 63–66. O'Hara US Treasury 71. Harry O 73–75.

Janssen, Eileen (1937–). American child actress of the 40s.

The Green Years 46. About Mrs Leslie 54. The Search for Bridie Murphy 56, etc.

Janssen, Werner (1899–1990). American composer. He was married to actress Ann Harding (1937–63).

The General Died at Dawn (AAN) 36. Blockade (AAN) 38. Eternally Yours (AAN) 39. Slightly Honorable 40. Guest in the House 44. The Southerner (AAN) 45. Captain Kidd (AAN) 45. A Night in Casablanca 46. Ruthless 48, etc.

Japan

has a cinema tradition all of its own, based on No plays and samurai epics, both with a style quite alien to the West. The first breakthrough was made in the 50s by the vivid films of Kurosawa, such as Rashomon and Seven Samurai; other directors who came to be respected if not entirely understood are Gosho, Ozu, Mizoguchi, Ichikawa, Kinugasa, Kobayashi, Naruse and Kinoshita. In the 60s Japan produced a new wave of directors including Imamura, Oshima and Shinoda. Since then the former actor Juzo Itami has gained an international reputation for his comedies of Japanese life and customs. Some innovative animators, who have learned their craft working on popular comic-books, have displayed an approach far removed from the Disney tradition in animated films like Akira and Barefoot Gen. Younger Japanese directors are now incorporating the style in their live-action films. What the future holds, though, is uncertain now that many Japanese companies have been investing heavily in Hollywood following Sony's acquisition of Columbia Pictures.

Jarman, Claude, Jnr (1934–). American boy actor of the 40s.

The Yearling (special AA) 46. High Barbaree 47. Intruder in the Dust 49. Rio Grande 51. Fair Wind to Java 53. The Great Locomotive Chase 56, etc.

Jarman, Derek (1942–1994). British independent director and screenwriter, often on homosexual themes. He went to the Slade School of Fine Art and began as a painter, becoming a set and costume designer for ballet and opera. He started making short films in the early 70s and also directed pop videos in the 80s. He has continued to work outside the mainstream, making low-budget films: The Tempest cost £150,000. Died of AIDS.

The Devils (ad) 70. Sebastiane 76. Jubilee 78. The Tempest 79. In the Shadow of the Sun 72–80. Imagining October 84. The Angelic Conversation 85. Aria (co-d) 85. Caravaggio 86. The Last of England 86. War Requiem 89. The Garden 90. Edward II 91. Wittgenstein 93. Blue 93. Glitterbug 94.

Jarmusch, Jim (1953–). Off-beat, independent American director, screenwriter, musician and occasional actor.

Permanent Vacation 82. Stranger than Paradise 84. Down by Law 86. Mystery Train 89. Leningrad Cowboys Go America (a) 90. Night on Earth 91. In the Soup (a) 92, etc.

Jarre, Kevin. American screenwriter.

Rambo: First Blood Part II (story) 85. Glory 89. Tombstone 94, etc.

Jarre, Maurice (1924–). French composer.

Hôtel des Invalides 52. La Tête contre les Murs 59. Eyes without a Face 59. Crack in the Mirror 60. The Longest Day 62. Lawrence of Arabia (AA) 62.

Weekend at Dunkirk 65. Dr Zhivago (AA) 65. Is Paris Burning? 66. The Professionals 66. The 25th Hour 67. Five Card Stud 68. Isadora 68. The Damned 69. Ryan's Daughter 70. Ash Wednesday 74. Great Expectations (TV) 76. The Last Tycoon 76. Jesus of Nazareth (TV) 76. Mohammed 76. March or Die 77. Winter Kills 79. Resurrection 80. The Black Marble 80. Taps 81. Lion of the Desert 81. Young Doctors in Love 82. Firefox 82. The Year of Living Dangerously 83. A Passage to India (AA) 84. The Bride 84. Mistress (AAN, BFA) 84. Enemy Mine 85. Witness (AAN) 85. Mosquito Coast 86. Solarbabies 86. Tai-Pan 86. Fatal Attraction 86. No Way Out 87. Buster 88. Gorillas in the Mist (AAN) 88. Moon over Parador 88. Wildfire 88. Dead Poets Society 89. Enemies: A Love Story 89. Prancer 89. After Dark, My Sweet 90. Almost an Angel 90. Ghost 90. Jacob's Ladder 90. Solar Crisis 90. Only the Lonely 91. School Ties 92. Shadow of the Wolf (co-m) 93. Fearless 93. Mr Jones 93, etc.

Jarrott, Charles (1927–). British director, from TV.

Time to Remember 62. Anne of the Thousand Days 70. Mary Queen of Scots 72. Lost Horizon 73. The Dove 74. Escape from the Dark 76. The Other Side of Midnight 77. The Last Flight of Noah's Ark 79. Condorman 81. The Amateur 82. The Boy in Blue 85. Poor Little Rich Girl (TV) 87. The Women He Loved 88. Morning Glory (co-w) 93.

Jarvilaturi, Ilkka (1961–). Finnish director, now in America.

Kotia Pänö 89. Darkness in Tallinn (Tallinnan Pimeys) 93, etc.

Jarvis, Martin (1941–). British leading man in all media.

The Last Escape 70. Taste the Blood of Dracula 70. Ike (TV) 79. The Bunker (TV) 81. Who Dares Wins (US: The Final Option) 82. Buster 88, etc.

TV series: Rings on their Fingers 78–80.

Jason, David (1940–) (David White). British comedy character actor, mostly on radio and TV.

Under Milk Wood 73. Royal Flash 75. The Water Babies 78. The Odd Job 78. Porterhouse Blue (TV) 87. The Bullion Boys (TV) 93.

TV series: Open All Hours 76–85. A Sharp Intake of Breath 78–81. Only Fools and Horses 81–93. A Bit of a Do 88–90. The Darling Buds of May 91–93. A Touch of Frost 93.

Jason, Leigh (1904–1979). American director, mainly of second features.

The Price of Fear 28. Wolves of the City 29. High Gear 33. The Mad Miss Manton 38. Lady for a Night 39. Model Wife 41. Three Girls About Town 41. Nine Girls 44. Lost Honeymoon 46. Out of the Blue 48. Okinawa 52, etc.

Jason, Rick (1926–). American leading man of the 50s.

Sombrero 53. The Saracen Blade 54. The Lieutenant Wore Skirts 55. The Wayward Bus 57. The Witch Who Came from the Sea 76. Partners 82, etc.

TV series: The Case of the Dangerous Robin 60. Combat 62–67.

Jason, Sybil (1929–). South African child actress of the 30s.

Barnacle Bill (GB) 35. Little Big Shot (GB) 36. The Singing Kid (US) 36. The Little Princess (US) 39. The Bluebird (US) 40, etc.

Jason, Will (1899–1970)
American second feature director.
The Soul of a Monster 44. Thief of Damascus 52, many others.

Jaubert, Maurice (1900–1940).
French composer.
L'Affaire Est dans le Sac 32. Le Quatorze Juillet 33. Zéro de Conduite 33. L'Atalante 34. Drôle de Drame 37. Un Carnet de Bal 37. Quai des Brumes 38. Le Jour Se Lève 39. La Fin du Jour 39, etc.

Jay, Ernest (1894–1957).
British stage character actor.
Tiger Bay 34. Broken Blossoms 36. Don't Take It to Heart 44. Vice Versa 47. The History of Mr Polly 49. Edward My Son 49. I Believe in You 52. Who Done It? 55. The Curse of Frankenstein 56.

Jayne, Jennifer (1932–).
British leading lady.
Once a Jolly Swagman 48. The Blue Lamp 50. It's a Grand Life 53. The Man Who Wouldn't Talk 57. The Trollenberg Terror 58. Raising the Wind 61. On the Beat 63. The Liquidator 65. The Medusa Touch 78. The Jigsaw Man 83, etc.

Jayston, Michael (1935–) (Michael James).
British stage actor commanding reputable film roles.
■ Cromwell 70. Nicholas and Alexandra 71. Follow Me 72. Alice's Adventures in Wonderland 72. A Bequest to the Nation 73. Tales that Witness Madness 73. The Homecoming 73. Craze 73. The Internecine Project 74. She Fell Among Thieves (TV) 78. Tinker Tailor Soldier Spy (TV) 80. Dominique 78. Zulu Dawn 79.

jazz
has been featured in American movies since they began to talk; Al Jolson always acknowledged its influence on his style. Jazz bands featured as specialities through the 30s, but in the 40s began a line of films purporting to investigate the origins of jazz: Birth of the Blues, New Orleans, Syncopation and St Louis Blues. Fictional stories relying on a jazz background include Young Man with a Horn, Paris Blues, Pete Kelly's Blues, Blues in the Night, Cabin in the Sky, New Orleans, Round Midnight, Bird and Bix; while most of the famous dance bands of the 40s were to some extent indebted to the inspiration of jazz.

Jeakins, Dorothy.
American costume designer.
South Pacific 58. Let's Make Love 60. The Sound of Music (AAN) 65. The Hindenburg 71. The Way We Were (AAN) 73. The Betsy 78. On Golden Pond 81. The Dead (AAN) 87, etc.

Jean, Gloria (1927–) (Gloria Jean Schoonover).
Former American child singer, on screen from 1939 as second-feature rival to Deanna Durbin.
■ The Underpup 39. If I Had My Way 40. A Little Bit of Heaven 40. Never Give a Sucker an Even Break 41. What's Cookin'? 42. Get Hep to Love 42. It Comes Up Love 42. When Johnny Comes Marching Home 42. Mister Big 43. Moonlight in Vermont 44. Follow the Boys 44. Pardon My Rhythm 44. The Ghost Catchers 44. Reckless Age 44. Destiny 44. I'll Remember April 44. Easy to Look At 45. River Gang 45. Copacabana 47. I Surrender Dear 48. An Old Fashioned Girl 49. Manhattan Angel 49. There's a Girl in My Heart 50. Air Strike 55. The Ladies' Man 61.

Jean, Vadim (1966–).
British screenwriter and director.

Leon the Pig Farmer (co-d) 92. Beyond Bedlam (co-w, d) 94. Clockwork Mice (d) 95.

Jeanmaire, Zizi (Renee) (1924–).
Leading lady and ballet dancer, in occasional films.
Hans Christian Andersen 52. Anything Goes 56. Folies Bergère 56. Charmants Garçons 57. Black Tights 60, etc.

Jeans, Isabel (1891–1985).
British stage actress, invariably in aristocratic roles.
Tilly of Bloomsbury 21. The Rat 25. Downhill 27. Easy Virtue 28. Sally Bishop 33. Tovarich (US) 38. Suspicion (US) 41. Banana Ridge 41. Great Day 45. It Happened in Rome 57. Gigi 58. A Breath of Scandal 60. Heavens Above 63, etc.

Jeans, Ursula (1906–1973) (Ursula McMinn).
British stage actress, long married to Roger Livesey; in occasional films.
The Gypsy Cavalier (debut) 31. Cavalcade 33. Dark Journey 37. Mr Emmanuel 44. The Woman in the Hall 46. The Weaker Sex 48. The Dam Busters 55. Northwest Frontier 59. The Queen's Guards 61. The Battle of the Villa Fiorita 65, etc.

Jeanson, Henri (1900–1970).
French writer, a former actor and critic.
Pepe le Moko 37. Un Carnet de Bal 37. Prison Without Bars 38. Carmen 42. Paname (d) 50. Nana 55. L'Affaire d'une Nuit 60, etc.

Jeayes, Allan (1885–1963).
British stage actor of dignified heavy presence; played supporting roles in many films.
The Impassive Footman 32. The Scarlet Pimpernel 34. Rembrandt 37. Elephant Boy 37. The Four Feathers 39. The Thief of Bagdad 40. The Man Within 46. Saraband for Dead Lovers 48. Waterfront 50, many others.

Jefford, Barbara (1930–).
British stage actress, more recently in films.
Ulysses 67. The Bofors Gun 68. A Midsummer Night's Dream 68. The Shoes of the Fisherman 68. Lust for a Vampire 70. And the Ship Sails On 84. When the Whales Came 89. Where Angels Fear to Tread 91, etc.

Jeffrey, Peter (1929–).
British general-purpose actor.
Becket 64. If 67. The Abominable Dr Phibes 71. The Horsemen 71. Dr Phibes Rises Again 72. The Odessa File 74. Midnight Express 78. The Adventures of Baron Munchausen 89. Middlemarch (TV) 94, etc.

Jeffreys, Anne (1923–) (Anne Carmichael).
American leading lady of the 40s, formerly in opera. She married actor Robert Sterling, her second husband, in 1956.
I Married an Angel 42. Step Lively 44. Dillinger 45. Riff Raff 47. Return of the Badmen 49. Boys Night Out 62. Panic in the City 68, etc.
TV series: Topper 53. Love That Jill 58.

Jeffries, Fran (1939–) (Frances Makris).
American singer and actress, born in California. She appeared as a singer on the TV variety show Spotlight in 1967.
The Buccaneer 58. The Pink Panther 63. Sex and the Single Girl 64. A Talent for Loving 69, etc.

Jeffries, Lionel (1926–)
Bald British character comedian, who rose to co-star status, then turned to direction.
Stage Fright 50. Windfall 54. The Baby and the Battleship 55. Law and Disorder 57. The Nun's

Story 58. Idol on Parade 59. Two-Way Stretch 60. The Trials of Oscar Wilde 60. The Hellions·61. The Notorious Landlady 61. The Wrong Arm of the Law 63. Call Me Bwana 63. The Long Ships 64. The First Men in the Moon 64. The Truth about Spring 65. The Secret of My Success 65. You Mu[st] Be Joking 65. Arrivederci Baby 66. The Spy with [a] Cold Nose 67. Rocket to the Moon 67. Camelot 67 [.] Chitty Chitty Bang Bang 68. Eyewitness 70. Wh[o] Slew Auntie Roo 71. Royal Flash 75. The Prisone[r] of Zenda 79. Cream in My Coffee (TV) 80. Bette[r] Late than Never 81. A Chorus of Disapproval 88, [...] etc.
■ AS DIRECTOR: The Railway Children 70. The Amazing Mr Blunden 72. Baxter 72. The Water Babies 78. Wombling Free 78.

Jenkins, Allen (1900–1974) (Alfred McGonegal).
'Tough guy' American comic actor, a staple of Warners' repertory in the 30s.
The Girl Habit 31. Rackety Rax 32. I am a Fugitive from a Chain Gang 32. 42nd Street 33. Professional Sweetheart 33. Jimmy the Gent 34. The St Louis Kid 34. Page Miss Glory 35. Miss Pacif[ic] Fleet 35. The Singing Kid 36. Three Men on a Horse 36. The Perfect Specimen 37. Dead End 37[.] Swing Your Lady 37. A Slight Case of Murder 38. The Amazing Dr Clitterhouse 38. Five Came Bac[k] 39. Destry Rides Again 39. Tin Pan Alley 40. Footsteps in the Dark 41. Maisie Gets Her Man 42. Wonder Man 45. Wild Harvest 47. Bodyhold 49[.] Behave Yourself 51. Pillow Talk 59. Robin and the Seven Hoods 64. Doctor You've Got to be Kidding 67. The Front Page 74, many others.
TV series: Hey Jeannie 56.

Jenkins, Charles Francis (1868–1934).
American inventor of the Phantascope, a camera using continuously moving film, which he patente[d] in January 1894. He collaborated with Thomas Armat to demonstrate a Phantascope projector at the Cotton States Exposition at Atlanta, Georgia i[n] October 1895. Armat improved the mechanism and patented it in February 1896 as the Vitascope which was promoted under the aegis of Thomas Edison.

Jenkins, George (1914–).
American production designer.
The Best Years of Our Lives 46. The Secret Life of Walter Mitty 47. Roseanna McCoy 49. The Miracle Worker 62. Mickey One 65. Wait until Dark 67. Me Natalie 69. The Angel Levine 70. The Paper Chase 73. Night Moves 75. All the President'[s] Men (AA) 76. Comes a Horseman 78. The China Syndrome (AAN) 79. Starting Over 79. The Postman Always Rings Twice 81. Rollover 81. Sophie's Choice 82. Dream Lover 86. Orphans 87[.] See You in the Morning 89. Presumed Innocent 90, etc.

Jenkins, Jackie 'Butch' (1937–).
Buck-toothed American child star of the 40s, son of Doris Dudley; retired because he developed a stutter.
■ The Human Comedy 43. National Velvet 44. An American Romance 44. Abbott and Costello in Hollywood 45. Our Vines Have Tender Grapes 45. Boys' Ranch 46. Little Mister Jim 46. My Brother Talks to Horses 46. Big City 48. The Bride Goes Wild 48. Summer Holiday 48.

Jenkins, Megs (1917–).
Plump British actress of kindly or motherly roles, on stage from 1933.
The Silent Battle 39. Green for Danger 46. The Brothers 47. The Monkey's Paw 48. The History of Mr Polly 49. White Corridors 51. Ivanhoe 52. The

Cruel Sea 53. The Gay Dog 54. John and Julie 55. The Man in the Sky 56. Conspiracy of Hearts 59. *The Innocents* 61. The Barber of Stamford Hill 62. Bunny Lake Is Missing 65. Stranger in the House 67. Oliver 68. David Copperfield 69, etc.

Jenks, Frank (1902–1962).
American character comedian, usually seen as Runyonesque stooge, cop or valet.

When's Your Birthday? 37. You Can't Cheat an Honest Man 39. Dancing on a Dime 40. Rogues' Gallery 45. Loonies on Broadway 46. The She-Creature 56, many others.

TV series: Colonel Flack 53.

Jennings, Al (1864–1961).
American outlaw of the old west who among other pursuits became a silent screen actor.

The Lady of the Dugout 18. Fighting Fury 24. The Sea Hawk 24. The Demon 26. Loco Luck 27. Land of Missing Men 30, etc.

Jennings, De Witt (1879–1937).
American character actor, stern and bulky.

The Warrens of Virginia 15. Three Sevens 21. The Enemy Sex 24. Exit Smiling 26. Alibi 29. The Big Trail 30. Min and Bill 30. Caught Plastered 31. Movie Crazy 32. Mystery of the Wax Museum 33. Little Man What Now 34. Mutiny on the Bounty 35. Sins of Man 36. Slave Ship 37, many others.

Jennings, Humphrey (1907–1950).
Distinguished British documentarist, with the GPO Film Unit from 1934. Responsible for a fine World War II series of sensitive film records of the moods of the time.

The First Days (co-d) 39. *London Can Take It* (co-d) 40. *Listen to Britain* 41. The Silent Village 43. *Fires Were Started* 43. *A Diary for Timothy* 45, etc. Also: The Cumberland Story 47. *Dim Little Island* 49. Family Portrait 50, etc.

⚫ For his unbroken series of poetic and cinematic images of Britain at war. *Listen to Britain.*

Jens, Salome (1935–   ).
American leading lady, in very occasional films.
■ *Angel Baby* 61. The Fool Killer 65. Seconds 66. Me Natalie 69. In the Glitter Palace (TV) 77. Sharon: Portrait of a Mistress (TV) 77. From Here to Eternity (TV) 79. Cloud Dancer 80. Harry's War 81. Clan of the Cave Bear 85. Just Between Friends 85.

Jergens, Adele (1922–   ).
American leading lady, mainly in second features. She was married to actor Glenn Langan.

A Thousand and One Nights 44. Ladies of the Chorus 48. Blonde Dynamite 50. Somebody Loves Me 52. The Cobweb 55. Girls in Prison 56. The Lonesome Trail 58, etc.

Jerome, Jerome K. (1859–1927).
British humorist and essayist. His *Three Men in a Boat* and *The Passing of the Third Floor Back* were filmed several times.

Jerrold, Mary (1877–1955) (Mary Allen).
British character actress, mainly on stage; in films, played mainly sweet old ladies.

Alibi 31. Friday the Thirteenth 33. The Man at the Gate 41. *The Way Ahead* 44. *The Queen of Spades* 48. Mr Perrin and Mr Traill 49. Top of the Form 52, etc.

Jessel, George (1898–1981).
American entertainer, in vaudeville from childhood. After making the mistake of turning

down *The Jazz Singer*, he had a very spasmodic film career, but in the 50s he produced a number of musicals for Fox.

Autobiographies: 1946, *So Help Me*. 1955, *This Way Miss*. 1975, *The World I Live In*.
AS ACTOR: The Other Man's Wife 19. Private Izzy Murphy 26. Lucky Boy (My Mother's Eyes) 29. Love Live and Laugh 29. Stage Door Canteen 43. Four Jills in a Jeep 44. The I Don't Care Girl 53. The Busy Body 57. Heironymus Merkin 69, etc.
AS PRODUCER: Do You Love Me 46. When My Baby Smiles at Me 48. Dancing in the Dark 49. Meet Me After the Show 51. Golden Girl 51. Wait Till the Sun Shines Nellie 52. The I Don't Care Girl 53. Tonight We Sing 53, etc.

¶ Did you ever catch him at a funeral? It's wonderful. All through the years he makes notes on his friends. He wants to be ready. – *Eddie Cantor*

That son of a bitch started his reminiscences when he was eight years old. – *Walter Winchell*

Jessel, Patricia (1920–1968).
British character actress, mostly on stage.

Quo Vadis 51. *City of the Dead* 61. A Jolly Bad Fellow 64. A Funny Thing Happened on the Way to the Forum 66, etc.

Jessua, Alain (1932–   ).
French writer-director of off-beat films.

Life Upside Down 63. Jeu de Massacre 67. Traitement de Choc 73. Armageddon 77. Les Chiens 79. Paradis pour Tous 82. Frankenstein 90 84. En Toute Innocence 88, etc.

jewel thieves
were fashionable with Hollywood film-makers in the 30s, the heyday of Raffles, the Lone Wolf, and Arsène Lupin; they were the subject of Lubitsch's best comedy, *Trouble in Paradise*. In the 60s they seemed to come into their own again, with *To Catch a Thief*, *The Greengage Summer*, *Topkapi*, *The Pink Panther* and *Jack of Diamonds*.

Jewell, Isabel (1913–1972).
Diminutive American leading lady of the 30s, a minor 'platinum blonde' who graduated to character parts.

Blessed Event 33. Counsellor at Law 33. Manhattan Melodrama 34. A Tale of Two Cities 35. The Man Who Lived Twice 37. Marked Woman 37. *Lost Horizon* 37. Gone with the Wind 39. The Leopard Man 43. The Bishop's Wife 48. The Story of Molly X 48. Bernardine 57, many others.

Jewison, Norman (1926–   ).
Canadian director and screenwriter, from TV.
■ Forty Pounds of Trouble 63. The Thrill of It All 63. Send Me No Flowers 64. The Art of Love 65. *The Cincinnati Kid* 65. *The Russians Are Coming, the Russians Are Coming* (& p) (AANp) 66. *In the Heat of the Night* (p, d) (AAp, AANd) 67. The Thomas Crown Affair (p, d) 68. The Landlord (p) 69. Gaily, Gaily (p, d) 69. Fiddler on the Roof (p, d) (AAN) 71. Jesus Christ Superstar (p, d) 73. Rollerball 75. And Justice for All (& co-p) 79. The Dogs of War (co-p only) 81. Best Friends (& p) 82. A Soldier's Story 84. Agnes of God 85. Moonstruck (AAN) 87. The January Man 88. In Country 89. Other People's Money 91. Only You 94.

Jews
and their plight in Europe under the Nazis were the subject of *So Ends Our Night*, *The Great Dictator*, *Professor Mamlock*, *Mr Emmanuel*, *The Diary of Anne Frank*, *M. Klein* and *Docteur Petiot*. The problems of the new state of Israel were treated in *Sword in the*

Desert, Exodus, The Juggler, Judith and Cast a Giant Shadow; while looking further back in history we find many versions of Jew Süss and The Wandering Jew, also The Fixer and the Fiddler on the Roof. American films about Jews used to show them as warm-hearted comic figures: Kosher Kitty Kelly, Abie's Irish Rose, The Cohens and the Kellys. Gertrude Berg continued this tradition on TV in the 50s. Recently films set in Jewish milieux have treated their characters more naturally, if with a touch of asperity: No Way to Treat a Lady, I Love You Alice B. Toklas, Bye Bye Braverman, Funny Girl, The Night They Raided Minsky's, Goodbye Columbus, Portnoy's Complaint, Hester Street, Lies My Father Told Me, The Apprenticeship of Duddy Kravitz, The Chosen; while TV revived for the world the plight of Jews under Hitler in Holocaust and Playing for Time, and Woody Allen has found a vein of internationally appreciated mordant humour in the foibles and follies of Jewishness.

See also: *anti-Semitism*.

Jhabvala, Ruth Prawer (1927–   ).
German-born screenwriter and novelist, inseparable from the directorial works of James Ivory (qv).

Jianxin, Huang (1954–   ).
Chinese director, a former photographer. He studied at the Beijing Film Academy, graduating in 1985.

The Black Cannon Incident (Haipao Shijan) 85. The Stand-In (Cuowei) 87. Samsara (Lunhui) 88. Back to Back, Face to Face (Zhanzhi Luo Bie Pa Xia) 92. The Wooden Man's Bridge (Wu Kui) 94, etc.

Jiminez, Neal.
American scriptwriter and director.

Where the River Runs Black (co-w) 86. River's Edge (w) 87. The Waterdance (w, co-d) 92. Sleep with Me (co-w) 94.

Jires, Jaromil (1935–   ).
Czech director, a graduate of the Prague Film School.

The Cry (Krick) 63. Valerie and Her Week of Wonders (Valerie A Týden Divu) 70. Payment in Kind (Causa Kralik) 80. Helimadoe 94, etc.

Joanou, Phil (1961–   ).
American director.

Three O'Clock High 87. U2 Rattle and Hum (doc) 88. State of Grace 90. Final Analysis 92. Heaven's Prisoners 95, etc.

Jobert, Marlene (1943–   ).
French leading lady.

Masculin Feminin 66. Le Voleur 66. L'Astragale 68. Rider on the Rain 69. Last Known Address 70. Catch Me a Spy 72. Ten Days' Wonder 72, etc.

Jodorowsky, Alexandro (1930–   ).
Chilean director, actor, writer and artist with surrealist tendencies.

Fando and Lis 70. El Topo 71. The Holy Mountain 74. Tusk 80. Santa Sangre 89, etc.

Joe Palooka.
The dumb boxer hero of the famous American comic strip was first on screen in 1934, played by Stuart Erwin. Ten years later Joe Kirkwood, an amateur golfer, played him in a Monogram series, with Leon Errol (later James Gleason) as his manager Knobby Walsh.

Joffe, Charles H.
American producer almost exclusively associated with the films of Woody Allen.

Take the Money and Run 69. Bananas 70. Everything You Always Wanted to Know about Sex 72. Sleeper 73. Love and Death 73. The Front 76. Annie Hall 77. Stardust Memories 80. A Midsummer Night's Sex Comedy 82. Zelig 83. Broadway Danny Rose 84. Hannah and Her Sisters 86. Radio Days 87. Alice 90. Shadows and Fog 92. Manhattan Murder Mystery 93, etc.

Joffe, Mark.
Australian director.

Grievous Bodily Harm 88. Shadow of the Cobra (TV) 89. Spotswood (aka The Efficiency Expert) 91, etc.

Joffe, Roland (1945–).
British director and screenwriter with TV experience.

The Killing Fields (AAN) 84. The Mission (AAN) 85. Fat Man and Little Boy (GB: The Shadowmakers) 89. City of Joy 92, etc.

Johann, Zita (1904–1993).
American leading lady of the early 30s.

The Struggle 31. Tiger Shark 32. The Mummy 32. Luxury Liner 33. Grand Canary 34. Raiders of the Living Dead 89, etc.

John, Elton (1947–) (Reginald Dwight).
British pop singer.

Tommy 75. The Lion King (songs) 94.

John, Rosamund (1913–) (Nora Jones).
Gentle-mannered British leading lady who turned in several pleasing performances in the 40s.

■ The Secret of the Loch 34. The First of the Few 42. The Gentle Sex 43. The Lamp Still Burns 43. Tawny Pipit 44. The Way to the Stars 45. Green for Danger 46. The Upturned Glass 47. Fame is the Spur 47. When the Bough Breaks 47. No Place for Jennifer 49. She Shall Have Murder 50. Never Look Back 52. Street Corner 53. Operation Murder 56.

Johns, Glynis (1923–).
Husky-voiced British actress, daughter of Mervyn Johns; on stage (as child) from 1935.

South Riding (debut) 36. Prison without Bars 38. 49th Parallel 41. Halfway House 44. Perfect Strangers 45. This Man Is Mine 46. Frieda 47. Miranda (as a mermaid) 47. An Ideal Husband 47. State Secret 50. Appointment with Venus 51. The Card 52. The Sword and the Rose 53. Personal Affair 53. Rob Roy 53. The Weak and the Wicked 54. The Beachcomber 55. Mad about Men 55. The Court Jester (US) 56. The Day They Gave Babies Away (US) 56. Shake Hands with the Devil 59. The Sundowners (AAN) 60. The Spider's Web 61. The Chapman Report (US) 62. Mary Poppins (US) 64. Dear Brigitte (US) 65. Don't Just Stand There (US) 68. Lock Up Your Daughters 69. Under Milk Wood 71. Vault of Horror 73. Little Gloria, Happy at Last (TV) 83. Zelly and Me 88. Nukie 89. The Ref (aka Hostile Hostages) 94, etc.

TV series: Glynis 63.

Johns, Mervyn (1899–1992).
Welsh character actor, on stage from 1923; usually plays mild-mannered roles.

Lady in Danger (debut) 34. Jamaica Inn 39. Saloon Bar 40. Next of Kin 41. Went the Day Well? 42. My Learned Friend 44. Dead of Night 45. Pink String and Sealing Wax 45. Scrooge 51. The Intimate Stranger 56. No Love for Johnnie 61. 80,000 Suspects 63. The Heroes of Telemark 65. Who

Killed the Cat? 66. The House of Mortal Sin 77, many others.

Johnson, Arch (1924–).
Burly American character actor.

Somebody Up There Likes Me 56. G.I. Blues 58. Twilight of Honor 63. Sullivan's Empire 67. Walking Tall 73. The Buddy Holly Story 77, many others.

Johnson, Arte (1934–).
Small-scale American comic actor.

Miracle in the Rain 56. The Subterraneans 60. The President's Analyst 67. Charge of the Model Ts 77. Love at First Bite 79. Bunco 83. The Raven Red Kiss-Off 90. Tax Season 90. Evil Spirits 91. Evil Toons 91, etc.

TV series: It's Always Jan 55–56. Sally 58. Hennessey 59–62. Don't Call Me Charlie 62–63. Rowan & Martin's Laugh-In 68–71. Games People Play 81–82. Glitter 84–85.

Johnson, Ben (1918–).
American character actor, a staple of John Ford and other westerns for years. Former stunt rider.

Three Godfathers 49. Mighty Joe Young 49. She Wore a Yellow Ribbon 49. Wagonmaster 50. Rio Grande 50. Fort Defiance 51. Shane 53. Slim Carter 57. Fort Bowie 60. One Eyed Jacks 61. Major Dundee 65. The Rare Breed 66. Will Penny 67. The Wild Bunch 69. The Undefeated 69. The Last Picture Show (AA) 71. Corky 72. Junior Bonner 72. Dillinger 73. The Sugarland Express 73. Bite the Bullet 75. Hustle 76. Breakheart Pass 76. The Greatest 77. The Town that Dreaded Sundown 77. The Swarm 78. Terror Train 80. The Hunter 80. Red Dawn 84. Cherry 2000 86. Let's Get Harry 86. Trespasses 86. Dark before Dawn 88. Back to Back 89. My Heroes Have Always Been Cowboys 91. Radio Flyer 92. The Legend of O. B. Taggart 94. Angels in the Outfield 94, many others.

TV series: The Monroes 66–67.

Johnson, Dame Celia (1908–1982).
Distinguished British actress, on stage from 1928, usually in well-bred roles: films rare.

Biography: 1991, Celia Johnson by Kate Fleming.

■ In Which We Serve (debut) 42. Dear Octopus 42. This Happy Breed 44. Brief Encounter (AAN) 46. The Astonished Heart 49. I Believe In You 52. The Captain's Paradise 53. The Holly and the Ivy 54. A Kid for Two Farthings 56. The Good Companions 57. The Prime of Miss Jean Brodie 69. Les Misérables (TV) 78. Staying On (TV) 79. The Hostage Tower (TV) 80. Les Misérables (TV) 80.

Johnson, Chic (1891–1962).
Portly American vaudeville comedian (with partner Ole Olsen).

■ Oh Sailor Behave 30. Fifty Million Frenchmen 31. Gold Dust Gertie 31. Country Gentlemen 36. All over Town 37. Hellzapoppin 41. Crazy House 43. Ghost Catchers 44. See My Lawyer 45, etc.

Johnson, Don (1950–).
American leading man of the 70s.

Zachariah 70. The Harrad Experiment 73. Return to Macon County 75. Law of the Land (TV) 76. The City (TV) 77. Ski Lift to Death (TV) 78. Beulah Land (TV) 79. The Long Hot Summer (TV) 85. Sweet Hearts Dance 88. Dead Bang 89. The Hot Spot 90. Harley Davidson and the Marlboro Man 91. Paradise 91. Born Yesterday 93. Guilty as Sin 93, etc.

TV series: From Here to Eternity 79. Miami Vice 85–89.

Johnson, Jack (1878–1946).
American heavyweight boxer, world champion from 1908–15, who made a few films in the 20s. The Great White Hope, starring James Earl Jones, is a slightly fictionalized account of his life.

As the World Rolls On 21. For His Mother's Sake 22. Black Thunderbolt 22.

Johnson, Katie (1878–1957).
British character actress who became a star in her old age.

Jeannie 41. The Years Between 46. I Believe in You 52. The Ladykillers 55. How to Murder a Rich Uncle 56, many others.

Johnson, Kay (1904–1975) (Catherine Townsend).
American leading lady of the 30s.

■ Dynamite 29. The Ship from Shanghai 30. This Mad World 30. Billy the Kid 30. The Spoilers 30. Madam Satan 30. Passion Flower 30. The Single Sin 31. The Spy 31. American Madness 32. Thirteen Women 32. Eight Girls in a Boat 34. This Man Is Mine 34. Of Human Bondage 34. Their Big Moment 34. Village Tale 35. Jalna 35. White Banners 38. The Real Glory 39. Son of Fury 42. Mr Lucky 43. The Adventures of Mark Twain 44.

Johnson, Lamont (1920–).
American director, from TV, a former actor.

■ Covenant with Death 67. Kona Coast (TV) 68. Deadlock (TV) 69. My Sweet Charlie (TV) 70. The Mackenzie Break 70. A Gunfight 71. That Certain Summer (TV) 72. The Groundstar Conspiracy 72. You'll Like My Mother 72. The Last American Hero 73. The Execution of Private Slovik (TV) 74. Fear on Trial (TV) 75. Lipstick 76. One On One 77. Somebody Killed Her Husband 78. Sunny Side 79. Foxes 80. Crisis at Central High (TV) 80. Off the Minnesota Strip 80. Escape from Iran (TV) 81. Cattle Annie and Little Britches 81. Spacehunter 83. Ernie Kovacs: Between the Laughter (TV) 84. Wallenberg: A Hero's Story (TV) 85. Unnatural Causes (TV) 86. Gore Vidal's Lincoln (TV) 88. The Kennedys of Massachusetts (TV) 89.

Johnson, Laurie (1927–).
British composer, mainly notable for themes of television's The Avengers and The Professionals.

The Good Companions 57. Tiger Bay 59. I Aim at the Stars 60. Dr Strangelove 63. First Men in the Moon 63. The Beauty Jungle 64. And Soon the Darkness 70. The Belstone Fox 74. Captain Kronos: Vampire Hunter 74. The Maids 75. Hedda 75. It Shouldn't Happen to a Vet 76. It's Alive II: It Lives Again 78. A Hazard of Hearts (TV) 87. The Lady and the Highwayman (TV) 89. A Ghost in Monte Carlo (TV) 90, etc.

Johnson, Lynn-Holly (1959–).
American leading lady, a former ice-skater.

Ice Castles 78. For Your Eyes Only 81. The Watcher in the Woods 81. The Sisterhood 88, etc.

Johnson, Martin (1884–1937) and Osa (1894–1953).
American explorers who made several feature-length films. A Johnson Safari Museum is situated in Chanute, Kansas (Mrs Johnson's birthplace).

Jungle Adventure 21. Simba 28. Congorilla 32. Wings over Africa 34. Baboona 35. Borneo 38. I Married Adventure 40, etc.

Johnson, Noble (1881–1978).
American actor who played a multitude of fearsome native chiefs.

Robinson Crusoe (as Friday) 22. The Ten Commandments 23. The Navigator 24. Hands Up

26. Vanity 27. Redskin 28. The Four Feathers 29.
Moby Dick 30. The Mummy 32. *King Kong* 33. She
35. Conquest 37. The Ghost Breakers 40. Jungle
Book 42. A Game of Death 45. She Wore a Yellow
Ribbon 49. North of the Great Divide 50, many
others.

Johnson, Nunnally (1897–1977).
American screenwriter, producer and director.
█ AS WRITER: Rough House Rosie 27. A Bedtime
Story (co-w) 33. Mama Loves Papa (co-w) 33.
Moulin Rouge (co-w) 34. *The House of Rothschild*
34. *Bulldog Drummond Strikes Back* 34. Kid Millions
(co-w) 35. Cardinal Richelieu (co-w) 35. Thanks
a Million 35. The Man Who Broke the Bank at
Monte Carlo (co-w) 35. *The Prisoner of Shark Island*
(& p) 36. The Country Doctor (p only) 36. The
Road to Glory (p only) 36. Dimples (p and original
idea) 36. Banjo on My Knee (& p) 36. Nancy Steele
Is Missing (p only) 37. Cafe Metropole (p only) 37.
Slave Ship (p only) 37. Love under Fire (p only)
37. *Jesse James* (& p) 39. Wife, Husband and Friend
(& p) 39. *Rose of Washington Square* (& p) 39. *The
Grapes of Wrath* (& p) (AANw) 40. I Was an
Adventuress (p only) 40. Chad Hanna (& p) 40.
Tobacco Road 41. *Roxie Hart* (& p) 42. The Pied Piper
(& p) 42. Life Begins at 8.30 (& p) 42. The Moon
Is Down (& p) 43. Holy Matrimony (& p) (AANw)
43. Casanova Brown (& p) 44. *The Woman in the
Window* (& p) 44. The Keys of the Kingdom (co-
w) 44. Along Came Jones 45. *The Dark Mirror* (&
p) 46. The Senator Was Indiscreet (p only) 47. Mr
Peabody and the Mermaid (& p) 48. Everybody
Does It (& p) 49. Three Came Home (& p) 49. The
Gunfighter (co-w, p) 50. *The Mudlark* (& p) 50.
The Long Dark Hall 51. *The Desert Fox* (& p) 51.
Phone Call from a Stranger (& p) 52. We're Not
Married (& p) 52. My Cousin Rachel (& p) 52.
How to Marry a Millionaire (& p) 53. Night People
(& p) 53. Black Widow (& pd) 54. How to Be
Very Very Popular (& pd) 55. The Man in the
Grey Flannel Suit (& d) 56. Oh Men Oh Women
(& pd) 56. *The Three Faces of Eve* (& p,d) 57. The
Man Who Understood Women (& pd) 57. The
Angel Wore Red (& d) 60. Flaming Star (co-p)
60. Mr Hobbs Takes a Vacation 62. Take Her She's
Mine 63. The World of Henry Orient (co-d) 64.
Dear Brigitte 65. The Dirty Dozen (co-w) 67.
✪ For being involved in so many of Hollywood's
most intelligent pictures. *The Grapes of Wrath.*

Johnson, Rafer (1935–).
American actor, formerly Olympic athlete.
The Fiercest Heart 61. The Sins of Rachel Cade
61. Wild in the Country 61. The Lion 63, etc.

Johnson, Richard (1927–).
British leading man of stage and screen.
Captain Horatio Hornblower 51. Never So Few
(US) 59. Cairo (US) 62. *The Haunting* 63. Eighty
Thousand Suspects 63. The Pumpkin Eater 64.
Operation Crossbow 65. Moll Flanders 65.
Khartoum 66. *Deadlier than the Male* (as Bulldog
Drummond) 66. Danger Route 67. La Strega in
Amore (It.) 67. Oedipus the King 68. A Twist of
Sand 68. Lady Hamilton (as Nelson) (Ger.) 68.
Some Girls Do 68. Julius Caesar 70. Hennessy 75.
Aces High 76. The Four Feathers (TV) 78. Haywire
(TV) 81. The Aerodrome (TV) 83. Turtle Diary (also
p) 85. Lady Jane 86. Diving In 90. Crucifer of Blood
(TV) 91. The Foreign Student 91, etc.

Johnson, Rita (1912–1965).
American actress who usually played 'the other
woman'.
Serenade 39. Edison the Man 40. Here Comes
Mr Jordan 41. Thunderhead, Son of Flicka 44.
They Won't Believe Me 47. Family Honeymoon

49. Susan Slept Here 54. Emergency Hospital 56.
The Day They Gave Babies Away 57, etc.

Johnson, Tor (1903–1971).
Bald, menacing American character actor.
Ghost Catchers 44. Road to Rio 47. The Lemon
Drop Kid 51. Bride of the Monster 55. Carousel
56. Plan 9 from Outer Space 56. Night of the
Ghouls 59, etc.

Johnson, Van (1916–) (Charles Van Johnson).
American light leading man, in films since 1941
after stage experience.
Murder in the Big House (debut) 41. *Dr
Gillespie's New Assistant* 42. The Human Comedy 43.
A Guy Named Joe 43. The White Cliffs of Dover
44. Two Girls and a Sailor 44. Thirty Seconds over
Tokyo 44. Thrill of a Romance 45. Weekend at the
Waldorf 45. Easy to Wed 45. No Leave, No Love
45. High Barbaree 46. The Romance of Rosy Ridge
47. State of the Union 48. The Bride Goes Wild
48. In the Good Old Summertime 49. *Battleground*
50. Go for Broke 51. When in Rome 52. Plymouth
Adventure 52. *The Caine Mutiny* 54. Brigadoon 55.
The Last Time I Saw Paris 55. The End of the
Affair (GB) 55. *Miracle in the Rain* 56. Twenty-
Three Paces to Baker Street 57. Kelly and Me 57.
Beyond This Place (GB) 59. Subway in the Sky
(GB) 60. Wives and Lovers 63. Divorce American
Style 67. Where Angels Go Trouble Follows 68.
Battle Squadron (It.) 69. Company of Killers (TV)
70. Rich Man Poor Man (TV) 76. The Kidnapping
of the President 80. Absurd! 81. The Purple Rose
of Cairo 85. Down There in the Jungle 87. Killer
Crocodile 88. Taxi Killer 88. Three Days to a Kill
92, etc.
TV series: Glitter 84.

Johnston, Arthur James (1898–1954).
American composer who began as an orchestrator
for Irving Berlin and went with him to Hollywood
in 1929, where he wrote many songs for Bing
Crosby, usually with lyricist Sam Coslow. His hits
include 'Just One More Chance' from *College Coach*,
'Cocktails for Two' from *Murder at the Vanities*, and
the title song from *Pennies from Heaven*.
College Coach 32. College Humour 33. Too
Much Harmony 33. Hello Everybody 33. Many
Happy Returns 34. Belle of the Nineties 34. Murder
at the Vanities 34. Thanks a Million 35. The Girl
Friend 35. Go West Young Man 36. Pennies from
Heaven 36. Sailing Along (GB) 37. Song of the
South 47, etc.

Johnston, Eric A. (1895–1963).
American executive, successor to Will H. Hays as
President of the MPAA (Motion Picture Association
of America) (1945–63).

Johnston, Joe.
American director.
Honey, I Shrunk the Kids 89. The Rocketeer 91.
The Pagemaster (co-d) 94.

Johnston, Margaret (1917–).
Australian actress who has made occasional British
films, notably in mid-40s.
The Prime Minister (debut) 40. *The Rake's
Progress* 45. A Man About the House 47. Portrait
of Clare 50. The Magic Box 51. Knave of Hearts
53. Touch and Go 55. *Night of the Eagle* 62. Life at
the Top 65. The Psychopath 66. Sebastian 67, etc.

Johnston, Oliver (1888–1966).
British character actor.
Room in the House 55. *A King in New York* 57.
A Touch of Larceny 60. Dr Crippen 62. Cleopatra
63. A Countess from Hong Kong 67, etc.

Jolley, I. Stanford (1900–1978).
American western character actor.
The Sombrero Kid 42. Frontier Fury 43. Lighting
Raiders 45. Prairie Express 47. Waco 52. The Young
Guns 56. 13 Fighting Men 60, many others.

Jolson, Al (1886–1950) (Asa Yoelson).
Celebrated Jewish-American singer and
entertainer, of inimitable voice and electric
presence. After years as a big Broadway attraction,
he starred in the first talking picture and although
his fortunes subsequently declined, a biopic using
his voice made him a world celebrity again in his
60s.
Biographies: 1962, *The Immortal Jolson* by Pearl
Sieben. 1972, *Al Jolson* by Michael Friedland. 1975,
Sonny Boy by Barrie Anderton.
█ *The Jazz Singer* 27. *The Singing Fool* 28. Sonny
Boy 29. Say It with Songs 29. Mammy 30. Big Boy
30. Hallelujah I'm a Bum 33. Wonder Bar 34. Go
into Your Dance 35. The Singing Kid 36. *Rose of
Washington Square* 39. Hollywood Cavalcade 39.
Swanee River 39. Rhapsody in Blue 45. *The Jolson
Story* (voice only) 46. *Jolson Sings Again* (voice only)
49.
✪ For heralding an era, and for being a star again
20 years later without even being seen. *Rose of
Washington Square.*

¶ It was easy enough to make Jolson happy at
home. You just had to cheer him for breakfast,
applaud wildly for lunch, and give him a standing
ovation for dinner. – *George Burns*
He was more than just a singer or an actor. He
was an experience. – *Eddie Cantor*
I'll tell you when I'm going to play the Palace.
That's when Eddie Cantor and George Burns and
Groucho Marx and Jack Benny on the bill. I'm
going to buy out the whole house, and sit in the
middle of the orchestra and say: Slaves, entertain
the king! – *A.J.*

Famous line (*The Jazz Singer*): 'You ain't heard
nothin' yet!'

Jones, Allan (1907–1992).
American (originally Welsh) singing star of the
30s.
█ Reckless 35. *A Night at the Opera* 35. Rose Marie
36. The Great Ziegfeld (voice only, dubbing for
Dennis Morgan) 36. Showboat 36. A Day at the
Races 37. *The Firefly* 37. Everybody Sing 38.
Honeymoon in Bali 39. The Great Victor Herbert
39. The Boys from Syracuse 40. One Night in the
Tropics 40. There's Magic in Music 42. True to the
Army 42. Moonlight in Havana 42. Rhythm of the
Islands 43. Larceny with Music 43. Crazy House
43. You're a Lucky Fellow Mr Smith 43. When
Johnny Comes Marching Home 43. Sing a Jingle
44. The Singing Sheriff 44. Señorita from the West
45. Honeymoon Ahead 45. A Swinging Summer
65. Stage to Thunder Rock 67.

Jones, Amy.
American screenwriter and director.
Slumber Party Massacre (d) 82. Love Letters
(wd) 83. Maid to Order (wd) 87. Mystic Pizza (co-
w) 88. Indecent Proposal (w) 92, etc.

Jones, Barry (1893–1981).
British character actor, usually in diffident roles; a
well-known stage actor from 1921.
Arms and the Man (as Bluntschli) 31. Squadron
Leader X 42. Dancing with Crime 46. Frieda 47. The
Calendar 48. *Seven Days to Noon* (leading role) 50.
White Corridors 51. *The Clouded Yellow* 51.
Appointment with Venus 52. Plymouth Adventure
(US) 52. Return to Paradise 53. Demetrius and

the Gladiators 54. Prince Valiant (US) 54. *Brigadoon* (US) 55. The Glass Slipper 55. Alexander the Great 56. War and Peace 56. Saint Joan 57. *The Safecracker* 58. The Thirty Nine Steps 59. The Heroes of Telemark 65. A Study in Terror 65, etc.

Jones, Buck (1889–1942) (Charles Gebhardt).
Popular American western star of the 20s and 30s, mainly in second features. Died from burns.
Straight from the Shoulder 20. Skid Proof 23. Hearts and Spurs 25. Riders of the Purple Sage 26. The Flying Horseman 27. The Lone Rider 30. Border Law 32. The California Trail 33. When a Man Sees Red 34. Boss Rider of Gun Creek 36. Unmarried 39. Riders of Death Valley 41, many others.

Jones, Carolyn (1929–1983).
Dark-eyed American leading lady, usually in off-beat roles.
Road to Bali 52. House of Wax 52. The Big Heat 53. Invasion of the Body Snatchers 55. The Opposite Sex 56. *The Bachelor Party* (AAN) 57. Marjorie Morningstar 58. Last Train from Gun Hill 58. A Hole in the Head 59. Ice Palace 60. A Ticklish Affair 63. Heaven with a Gun 68. Color Me Dead 70. Eaten Alive 77. Good Luck Miss Wyckoff 79. The French Atlantic Affair (TV) 80. The Dream Merchants (TV) 80, etc.
TV series: *The Addams Family* (as Morticia) 64–5. Capitol 82–83.

Jones, Catherine Zeta (1950–   ).
Welsh leading actress.
Splitting Heirs 93. The Cinder Path (TV) 94. Catherine the Great (TV) 95.
TV series: The Darling Buds of May 91–93.

Jones, Christopher (1941–   ).
American leading man of the 60s. He was formerly married to Susan Strasberg.
Chubasco 67. Wild in the Streets 68. The Looking Glass War 69. Three in the Attic 69. *Ryan's Daughter* 70, etc.
TV series: *The Legend of Jesse James* 65.

Jones, Chuck (1912–   ) (Charles M. Jones).
American animator and director of cartoons, mainly for Warner, noted for his skill in creating slapstick situations. Born in Spokane, Washington, he moved with his family to Hollywood as a boy, where he watched Chaplin at work. He arrived at Warner in 1933 and created Road Runner, Wile E. Coyote and Pepe Le Pew (qqv), as well as directing many Bugs Bunny and Daffy Duck cartoons.
Autobiography: 1989, *Chuck Amuck*.
The Night Watchman 38. Daffy and the Dinosaur 39. Hare Tonic 45. Mouse Wreckers (AAN) 48. For Scent-Imental Reasons (AA) 49. So Much for So Little (AA, doc) 50. From A to Z-Z-Z (AAN) 53. Zipping Along 53. One Froggy Evening 55. High Note (AAN) 60. Beep Prepared (AAN) 61. Nelly's Folly (AAN) 61. Gay Purree (feature, co-w only) 62. Now Hear This (co-d, AAN) 62. The Dot and the Line (AA) 65. The Phantom Tollbooth (feature, p, wd) 69. The Bugs Bunny/Road Runner Movie (compilation, p, wd) 79. Porky Pig in Hollywood (compilation, co-d) 86, many others.

Jones, David (1934–   ).
British director.
Betrayal 84. 84 Charing Cross Road 87. The Christmas Wife (TV) 88. Jacknife 89. Fire in the Dark 91. The Trial 93, etc.

Jones, Davy (1946–   ).
British actor and singer who became one of The Monkees (qv), on stage from 1963.
Head 73. Hot Channels 73. Illusions of a Lady 73. Not Just Another Woman 73. Devil's Due 73, etc.

Jones, Dean (1931–   ).
American leading man who usually plays well-behaved fellows.
Tea and Sympathy 56. Handle with Care 58. Never So Few 60. *Under the Yum Yum Tree* 64. The New Interns 64. Two on a Guillotine 64. That Darn Cat 65. The Ugly Dachshund 66. Any Wednesday 66. Monkeys Go Home 67. Blackbeard's Ghost 67. The Love Bug 69. Million Dollar Duck 71. Snowball Express 73. Mr Superinvisible 76. The Shaggy D.A. 76. Herbie Goes to Monte Carlo 77. Born Again 78. Fire and Rain 89. Other People's Money 91. Beethoven 92, etc.
TV series: Ensign O'Toole 62. Chicago Teddy Bears 71. Herbie the Love Bug 82.

Jones, Emrys (1915–1972).
British stage actor.
One of Our Aircraft Is Missing 42. The Rake's Progress 45. The Wicked Lady 46. Nicholas Nickleby 47. The Small Back Room 48. Three Cases of Murder 55. Oscar Wilde 60, etc.

Jones, Evan (1927–   ).
British screenwriter, born in Jamaica, who wrote four films for Joseph Losey.
The Damned 61. Eve 62. King and Country 64. Modesty Blaise 66. Two Gentlemen Sharing 66. Funeral in Berlin 67. Outback 71. Wake in Fright 71. Night Watch 73. Escape to Victory 81. The Killing of Angel Street 81. Champions 84. Kangaroo 87. Shadow of the Wolf (co-w) 93, etc.

The Jones Family.
A 1936 second feature called *Every Saturday Night* started off a series of 17 about a small-town American family in which Pa was Jed Proty and Ma was Spring Byington. They had four years of popularity without ever quite equalling MGM's Hardy family, which had more sentimentality.

Jones, Freddie (1927–   ).
Clever British character actor who has yet to control a tendency towards twitchy caricatures.
The Bliss of Mrs Blossom 68. Otley 69. Frankenstein Must be Destroyed 70. Goodbye Gemini 70. Antony and Cleopatra 72. Sitting Target 72. The Satanic Rites of Dracula 73. The Elephant Man 80. Firefox 82. Krull 83. Dune 85. Firestarter 85. Young Sherlock Holmes 85. Consuming Passions 88. The Last Butterfly 90. Adam Bede (TV) 91. Hotel Room (TV) 93. The Mystery of Edwin Drood 93. Cold Comfort Farm (TV) 95, etc.

Jones, Gordon (1911–1963).
American second lead of the football player type.
They All Kissed the Bride 42. My Sister Eileen 43. Flying Tigers 44. The Secret Life of Walter Mitty 47, etc.
TV series: The Abbott and Costello Show.

Jones, Grace (1952–   ).
American performer.
Conan the Destroyer 84. A View to a Kill 85. Vamp 86. Straight to Hell 87. Siesta 87. Boomerang 92, etc.

Jones, Griff Rhys (1953–   ).
British comic actor and writer, from TV and stage.

Morons from Outer Space 85. Wilt (US: The Misadventures of Mr Wilt) 89. Staggered 94.
TV series: Not the Nine o'Clock News 79–81. Alas Smith and Jones 84–86. Demob (TV) 93.

Jones, Griffith (1910–   ).
British light leading man, on stage from 1930.
The Faithful Heart (debut) 32. Catherine the Great 34. The Mill on the Floss 36. A Yank at Oxford 38. *The Four Just Men* 39. Young Man's Fancy 39. Atlantic Ferry 40. This Was Paris 41. Henry V 44. The Wicked Lady 45. *The Rake's Progress* 45. *They Made Me a Fugitive* 47. Good Time Girl 48. Miranda 48. Look before You Love 49. Honeymoon Deferred 51. Star of My Night 53. The Sea Shall Not Have Them 55. Face in the Night 57. Kill Her Gently 59. Strangler's Web 63. Decline and Fall 68, many others.

Jones, Harmon (1911–1972).
Canadian director in Hollywood.
■ As Young As You Feel 51. The Pride of St Louis 52. Bloodhounds of Broadway 52. The Silver Whip 53. City of Bad Men 53. The Kid from Left Field 53. Gorilla at Large 54. Princess of the Nile 54. Target Zero 55. A Day of Fury 56. Canyon River 56. The Beast of Budapest 58. Bullwhip 58. Wolf Larsen 58. Don't Worry We'll Think of a Title 66.

Jones, Henry (1912–   ).
American character actor of stage, TV and occasional films; usually plays the guy next door or the worm who turns.
The Lady Says No 51. *The Bad Seed* 56. The Girl Can't Help It 57. Vertigo 58. The Bramble Bush 60. Angel Baby 60. Never Too Late 65. Project X 67. Stay Away Joe 68. Support Your Local Sheriff 69. The Skin Game 71. Pete 'n' Tillie 72. The Outfit 74. Nine to Five 80. Deathtrap 82. Codename: Foxfire (TV) 85. Balboa 86. Nowhere to Run 88. Dick Tracy 91, etc.
TV series: Channing 63–64. The Girl with Something Extra 73–74. Phyllis 75–77. Gunshy 83. Codename: Foxfire 85. Falcon Crest 85–86. I Married Dora 87–88.

Jones, James (1921–1977).
American novelist famous for From Here to Eternity, which was filmed, as was Some Came Running.

Jones, James Cellan (1930–   ).
British director, in several senior TV posts.
Bequest to the Nation 72. *Jennie* (TV) 74. The Day Christ Died (TV) 80. Oxbridge Blues (TV) 84. Fortunes of War (TV) 87. Harnessing Peacocks (TV) 93.

Jones, James Earl (1931–   ).
Impressive American leading actor, from the stage. He was the voice of Darth Vader in the *Star Wars* trilogy.
The Great White Hope (AAN) 70. The Man (TV) 73. Claudine 74. The Bingo Long Traveling All Stars and Motor Kings 76. Deadly Hero 76. Swashbuckler 76. The River Niger 76. The Last Remake of Beau Geste 77. Jesus of Nazareth (TV) 77. The Greatest 77. Exorcist II: The Heretic 77. Star Wars (voice) 77. A Piece of the Action 77. The Greatest Thing That Almost Happened (TV) 77. Roots II (TV) (as Alex Haley) 79. The Bushido Blade 80. Conan the Barbarian 82. Allan Quatermain and the Lost City of Gold 86. Gardens of Stone 87. Matewan 87. Pinocchio and the Emperor of Night (voice) 87. Coming to America 88. Best of the Best 89. Field of Dreams 89. Three Fugitives 89. The Ambulance 90. Ivory Hunters (TV) 90. Grim Prairie Tales 90. The Hunt for Red October 90. True Identity 91. Convicts 91.

corchers 91. Patriot Games 92. Sneakers 92. The
andlot (GB: The Sandlot Kids) 93. The Meteor
Man 93. Excessive Force 93. Sommersby 93.
Mean Slate 94. The Lion King (voice) 94. Clear
nd Present Danger 94, etc.
 TV series: Paris 79–81. Roots: The Next
eneration 79–81. Me and Mom 85. Gabriel's Fire
0–92.

ones, Jennifer (1919–) (Phyllis Isley).
ntense, variable American leading actress, in small
lm roles from 1939.
 Dick Tracy's G Men 39. The New Frontier 39.
he Song of Bernadette (AA) 43. Since You Went
way (AAN) 44. Love Letters (AAN) 45. Cluny
rown 46. Duel in the Sun (AAN) 46. *Portrait of*
ennie 48. We Were Strangers 49. Madame Bovary
9. *Carrie* 51. Gone to Earth (GB) 51. Ruby Gentry
2. Indiscretion 54. Beat the Devil 54. *Love Is a
Many-Splendored Thing* (AAN) 55. Good Morning,
Miss Dove 55. The Man in the Grey Flannel Suit
6. The Barretts of Wimpole Street 57. A Farewell
o Arms 58. Tender Is the Night 61. The Idol (GB)
6. Angel Angel Down We Go 69. The Towering
nferno 74.

ones, Kenneth V. (1924–).
ritish composer.
 Sea Wife 56. The Horse's Mouth 58. The Trials
f Oscar Wilde 60. The Tomb of Ligeia 64. Who
lew Auntie Roo? 71. The Brute 77. Leopard in
he Snow 78, many others.

ones, L. Q. (1936–) (J. E. McQueen).
merican character actor.
 The Wild Bunch 69. The Ballad of Cable Hogue
0. The Hunting Party 71. The Brotherhood of
atan (& p) 71. *A Boy and His Dog* (d) 75. Mother,
ugs and Speed 76. Standing Tall 78. The Beast
Within 82. Sacred Ground 83. Timerider 83. Lone
Wolf McQuade 83. Bulletproof 88. River of Death
0. Grizzly Adams: The Legend Continues 90.
ightning Jack 94, etc.
 TV series: Cheyenne 55–56. The Virginian 64–
7.

ones, Marcia Mae (1924–).
American child actress of the 30s.
 King of Jazz 31. These Three 36. Heidi 37. The
ittle Princess 39. Tomboy 40. Nice Girl 41. Nine
irls 44. Arson Inc. 50. Chicago Calling (under the
ame of Marsha Jones) 52. Rogue's Gallery 68,
tc.

ones, Paul (1901–1968).
American producer, long with Paramount.
 The Great McGinty 40. Sullivan's Travels 41.
Road to Morocco 42. The Virginian 46. Dear Ruth
47. Here Come the Girls 53. Living It Up 54.
Pardners 56. The Disorderly Orderly 64, many
thers.

ones, Paul (1942–) (Paul Pond).
British leading man, former pop singer.
 Privilege 66. Demons of the Mind 71, etc.

ones, Peter (1920–).
British character comedian.
 Fanny by Gaslight 44. The Yellow Balloon 53.
Albert R. N. 53. Danger Within 58. Never Let Go
61. Ramanoff and Juliet 61. Press for Time 66. Just
Like a Woman 66. The Return of the Pink Panther
75. Carry On England 76, etc.

ones, Quincy (1933–).
American composer.
 The Pawnbroker 65. The Deadly Affair 66. In
Cold Blood (AAN) 67. In the Heat of the Night 67.

MacKenna's Gold 69. Bob and Carol and Ted and
Alice 70. Cactus Flower 71. The Anderson Tapes
72. The Getaway 72. The Hot Rock 72. The New
Centurions 72. *Roots* (TV) 77. The Wiz (AAN) 78.
The Color Purple (AAN) 85. Listen Up: The Lives
of Quincy Jones 90, etc.

Jones, Robert C. (1930–).
American editor and screenwriter, son of director
Harmon Jones (qv).
AS EDITOR: Invitation to a Gunfighter 64. Ship of
Fools 65. Tobruk 67. Guess Who's Coming to
Dinner (AAN) 67. Love Story 70. Man of La
Mancha 72. The Last Detail 73. Shampoo 75.
Bound for Glory (AAN) 76. Heaven Can Wait 78.
Twice in a Lifetime 85. See No Evil, Hear No Evil
89, etc.
AS WRITER: Coming Home (co-w, AA) 78.

Jones, Sam (1954–).
American leading actor of action films.
 Flash Gordon 80. My Chauffeur 86. Jane and
the Lost City (GB) 87. Silent Assassins 88. Under
the Gun 88. Driving Force 88. In Gold We Trust
91. Maximum Force 92. Fist of Honor 92. DaVinci's
War 92, etc.

Jones, Shirley (1934–).
American singer and leading lady who blossomed
into a substantial actress.
 ■ Oklahoma 55. Carousel 56. April Love 57.
Never Steal Anything Small 58. Bobbikins (GB)
59. Pepe 60. *Elmer Gantry* (AA) 60. Two Rode
Together 61. *The Music Man* 62. A Ticklish Affair 63.
The Courtship of Eddie's Father 63. Bedtime Story
64. Dark Purpose 64. Fluffy 65. The Secret of My
Success 65. Silent Night Lonely Night (TV) 69. But
I Don't Want to Get Married (TV) 70. The Cheyenne
Social Club 70. The Happy Ending 70. The Girls of
Huntington House (TV) 73. The Family Nobody
Wanted (TV) 75. Winner Take All (TV) 75. The
Lives of Jenny Doland (TV) 75. Yesterday's Child
(TV) 77. Evening in Byzantium (TV) 78. Who'll
Save Our Children? (TV) 78. A Last Cry for Help
(TV) 79. Beyond the Poseidon Adventure 79. The
Children of An Lac (TV) 80. Inmates (TV) 81.
 TV series: *The Partridge Family* 70–73. Shirley
79.

Jones, Spike (1911–1965) (Lindley Armstrong
Jones).
Pint-sized American bandleader ('Spike Jones and
his City Slickers'), popular in the 40s for crazy
variations on well-known songs.
 Thank Your Lucky Stars 43. Bring on the Girls
45. Variety Girl 47. Fireman Save My Child 55, etc.

Jones, Terry (1942–).
British performer/director and screenwriter, one
of the Monty Python group.
 ■ And Now for Something Completely Different
(co-w) 72. *Monty Python and the Holy Grail* (co-w,
co-d) 74. *Monty Python's Life of Brian* (co-w, d) 79.
Monty Python's The Meaning of Life (co-w, d)
83. Labyrinth (w) 86. Personal Services (d) 87.
Consuming Passions (oa) 88. Erik the Viking (wd)
89.

Jones, Tommy Lee (1946–).
American leading man.
 Love Story 70. Jackson County Jail 75. Charlie's
Angels (pilot) (TV) 76. Smash Up on Interstate
Five (TV) 76. *The Amazing Howard Hughes* (TV) 77.
Rolling Thunder 77. Eyes of Laura Mars 78. The
Betsy 78. Coal Miner's Daughter 80. Black Roads
81. The Executioner's Song (TV) 82. Nate and
Hayes 83. The Big Town 87. Stormy Monday 88.
The Package 89. Fire Birds 90. JFK 91. Under Siege

92. *The Fugitive* (AA) 93. House of Cards 93. *Heaven
and Earth* 93. The Client 94. Blown Away 94.
Natural Born Killers 94. Blue Sky (made 91) 94.
Cobb 94. Batman Forever 95, etc.

Jones, Trevor (1949–).
South African-born composer.
 Brothers and Sisters 80. Excalibur 81. The Dark
Crystal 82. The Sender 82. Those Glory Glory Days
83. Nate and Hayes 83. Runaway Train 85.
Labyrinth 86. Angel Heart 87. Dominick and
Eugene 88. Just Ask for Diamond 88. Sweet Lies
88. Mississippi Burning 88. Sea of Love 89.
Defenceless 90. Arachnophobia 90. Bad Influence
90. Freejack 92. Blame It on the Bellboy 92.
Cliffhanger 93. In the Name of the Father 93, etc.

Jordan, Bert (1887–1983).
English editor, a former cameraman and actor, in
Hollywood from 1915. He spent most of his career
at the Hal Roach Studio, editing many of its films
and later its television programmes, including much
of Laurel and Hardy's output, although the on-
screen credit was given to Richard Currier, head of
Roach's editing department from 1920–32.
 County Hospital 32. Twice Two 32. The Devil's
Brother 33. Busy Bodies 33. Sons of the Desert 33.
Babes in Toyland 34. Bonnie Scotland 35. The
Bohemian Girl 36. Our Relations 36. Way out West
37. Swiss Miss 38. Block-Heads 38. Of Mice and
Men (AAN) 39. A Chump at Oxford 40, etc.

Jordan, Bobby (1923–1965).
American actor, one of the original Dead End Kids.
 Dead End 37. Angels with Dirty Faces 38. They
Made Me a Criminal 39. That Gang of Mine 40.
Pride of the Bowery 41. Let's Get Tough 42. Clancy
Street Boys 43. Bowery Champs 44. Bowery
Bombshell 46. Hard Boiled Mahoney 47. Treasure
of Monte Cristo 49. This Man Is Armed 56, many
others.

Jordan, Neil (1950–).
Irish director and screenwriter.
 ■ Angel (Ire.) 82. Company of Wolves 84. Mona
Lisa 85. High Spirits (wd) 88. We're No Angels (d)
89. The Miracle (wd) 90. *The Crying Game* (wd)
(AAw, AANd) 92. *Interview with the Vampire* (co-w,
d) 94.

Jordan, Richard (1937–1993).
American leading actor, often as a cold-eyed
villain, and theatre director. He also appeared in
more than a hundred Broadway and off-Broadway
productions. He was divorced from actress Kathleen
Widdoes and had a son by actress Blair Brown.
Died of a brain tumour.
 Lawman 70. Valdez Is Coming 71. The Friends
of Eddie Coyle 73. The Yakuza 75. Kamouraska 75.
Rooster Cogburn 75. *Captains and the Kings* (TV)
76. Logan's Run 76. Les Misérables (TV) 78.
Interiors 78. The Defection of Simas Kurdika (TV)
78. Old Boyfriends 79. Raise the Titanic 80. The
French Atlantic Affair (TV) 80. Dune 84. The Mean
Season 84. The Men's Club 86. Solarbabies 86.
The Secret of My Success 87. Romero 89. The Hunt
for Red October 90. Shout 91. Gettysburg 93, etc.

Jory, Victor (1902–1982).
Saturnine Canadian actor, on stage from mid-20s.
Usually a villain on screen.
 Sailor's Luck (debut) 32. A Midsummer Night's
Dream (as Oberon) 35. *The Adventures of Tom Sawyer*
(as Injun Joe) 38. Gone with the Wind 39.
Unknown Guest 48. The Gallant Blade 48.
Canadian Pacific 49. Cat Women of the Moon 53.
Valley of the Kings 54. Diary of a Scoundrel 56. The
Man Who Turned to Stone 58. The Fugitive Kind

60. *The Miracle Worker* 63. Cheyenne Autumn 64. Mackenna's Gold (narration only) 69. A Time for Dying 69. Flap 70. Papillon 73. Devil Dog, Hound of Hell (TV) 78. The Mountain Men 80, many others.

TV series: Manhunt 59–60.

Joseph, Robert (1913–1969).
American producer.
The Third Secret (& w) 63, etc.

Josephs, Wilfred.
English composer.
Fanatic 65. The Deadly Bees 67. My Side of the Mountain (US) 69. All Creatures Great and Small (TV) 75. Callan 75. The Uncanny 77. Martin's Day (US) 85. Mata Hari (US) 85, etc.

Josephson, Erland (1923–).
Swedish character actor.
So Close to Life 58. Hour of the Wolf 68. A Passion 69. Cries and Whispers 72. Scenes from a Marriage 73. Face to Face 75. Beyond Evil 77. Autumn Sonata 78. Marmalade Revolution (& w, co-d) 79. Montenegro 80. Fanny and Alexander 82. After the Rehearsal 84. House of the Yellow Carpet 84. The Sacrifice 86. Saving Grace 86. The Unbearable Lightness of Being 88. Hanussen 89. The Ox (Oxen) 91. Sofie 92. Dreamplay (Dromspel) 94, etc.

Joslyn, Allyn (1905–1981).
American character comedian whose crumpled features admirably portrayed bewilderment.
They Won't Forget (debut) 37. Bedtime Story 41. A Yank in Dutch 42. *Heaven Can Wait* 43. Bride by Mistake 44. Junior Miss 45. *It Shouldn't Happen to a Dog* 47. If You Knew Susie 48. As Young As You Feel 51. Titanic 53. The Fastest Gun Alive 56. The Brothers O'Toole 73, many others.
TV series: The Ray Bolger Show 53. The Eve Arden Show 57. McKeever and the Colonel 62. Don't Call Me Charlie 62. The Addams Family 64.

Jost, Jon (1943–).
American director, screenwriter and editor of independent and experimental movies, currently living in Italy.
Angel City 77. Chameleon 78. State Fright 81. Slow Moves 83. Laughing Rembrandt 88. All the Vermeers in New York 91. Sure Fire 92. The Bed You Sleep In 93. Frameup 93. One for Me, One for You, and One for Raffaello 94, etc.

Jourdan, Louis (1920–) (Louis Gendre).
Smooth French leading man who has also made films in Britain and Hollywood.
Le Corsaire (debut) 39. The Paradine Case 48. *Letter from an Unknown Woman* 48. Madame Bovary 49. Bird of Paradise 50. Anne of the Indies 51. *The Happy Time* 52. Rue de l'Estrapade 52. Decameron Nights 53. *Three Coins in the Fountain* 54. The Swan 56. Julie 56. *Gigi* 58. The Best of Everything 59. Can-Can 60. The Count of Monte Cristo 61. *The VIPs* 62. Made in Paris 65. Peau d'Espion 67. A Flea in Her Ear 68. Run a Crooked Mile (TV) 71. The Count of Monte Cristo (TV) 76. The Silver Bears 77. The Man in the Iron Mask (TV) 77. Swamp Thing 82. Octopussy 83. Bayou Romance 86. Beverly Hills Madam (TV) 86. Gamble on Love 86. For the Love of Angela 86. Image of Passion 86. Love at the Top 86. Counterforce 87. Return of the Swamp Thing 89. Year of the Comet 92, etc.
TV series: Paris Precinct 53.

Jouvet, Louis (1887–1951).
Distinguished French actor of stage and screen.

■ Topaze 33. Doctor Knock 33. *La Kermesse Héroïque* 35. Mister Flow 36. Les Bas-Fonds 36. Mademoiselle Docteur 36. Un Carnet de Bal 37. *Drôle de Drame* 37. Alibi 37. Forfaiture 37. La Marseillaise 38. Ramuntcho 38. La Maison du Maltais 38. Entrée des Artistes 38. L'Education du Prince 38. Le Drame de Shanghai 38. *Hôtel du Nord* 38. La Fin du Jour 39. La Charrette Fontôme 39. Serenade 40. *Volpone* 40. Untel Père et Fils 40. Un Revenant 46. Copie Conforme 46. *Quai des Orfèvres* 47. Les Amoureux Sont Seuls au Monde 48. Entre Onze Heures et Minuit 49. Retour à la Vie 49. Miquette et Sa Mère 49. Doctor Knock (remake) 50. Une Histoire d'Amour 50.

Joy, Leatrice (1894–1985) (Leatrice Joy Zeidler).
Vivacious, self-confident American leading lady of the 20s.
Bunty Pulls the Strings 20. The Marriage Cheat 21. Manslaughter 22. You Can't Fool Your Wife 23. The Ten Commandments 23. Triumph 24. The Dressmaker from Paris 25. For Alimony Only 26. Angel of Broadway 27. The Blue Danube 28. A Most Immoral Lady 29. First Love 39. Red Stallion in the Rockies 49. Love Nest 52, etc.

Joy, Nicholas (1894–1964).
American small part actor often seen as beaming toff or benevolent father.
Daisy Kenyon 47. If Winter Comes 47. The Great Gatsby 49. And Baby Makes Three 50. Man with a Cloak 51. Affair with a Stranger 53. Desk Set 57, etc.

Joy, Robert (1951–).
Canadian leading actor.
Amityville 3-D (aka Amityville: The Demon) 83. Desperately Seeking Susan 85. Big Shots 87. She's Back 88. The Suicide Club 88. Millennium 89. Longtime Companion 90. Shadows and Fog 92, etc.

Joyce, Alice (1889–1955).
American leading lady of the silent screen.
Womanhood 17. The Lion and the Mouse 19. Cousin Kate 21. The Green Goddess 23. Daddy's Gone a-Hunting 25. The Squall 29. Song o' My Heart 38, etc.

Joyce, Brenda (1918–) (Betty Leabo).
American leading lady, former model. Played innocent types in the 40s, then retired.
The Rains Came (debut) 39. Little Old New York 40. Maryland 40. Marry the Boss's Daughter 41. Whispering Ghosts 42. The Postman Didn't Ring 42. Little Tokyo USA 43. Strange Confession 45. The Enchanted Forest 46. Tarzan and the Huntress 47. Shaggy 48. Tarzan's Magic Fountain 49, etc.

Joyce, James (1882–1941).
Irish writer and dramatist. In 1909, backed by Swiss businessmen, he opened Dublin's first cinema, Cinematograph Volta, which began with a showing of Caserini's *Beatrice Cenci*.
Finnegans Wake 65. Ulysses 67. A Portrait of the Artist as a Young Man 79. The Dead (from Dubliners) 87.

Joyce, Yootha (1927–1980).
Angular British character actress, popular in TV comedy series *A Man About the House* and *George and Mildred*.
Sparrows Can't Sing 62. The Pumpkin Eater 64. Stranger in the House 67. Burke and Hare 71. George and Mildred 80.

Judd, Edward (1932–).
British general-purpose actor.
The Day the Earth Caught Fire 61. Stolen Hours

63. The Long Ships 63. *The First Men in the Moon* 64. Strange Bedfellows 65. Island of Terror 66. Invasion 66. The Vengeance of She 68. Living Free 71. Universal Soldier 71. Vault of Horror 73. Assassin 73, The Incredible Sarah 76. The Kitchen Toto 87, etc.

Judge, Arline (1912–1974).
American general-purpose leading lady.
Bachelor Apartment 31. Girl Crazy 32. Name This Woman 35. King of Burlesque 36. Valiant is the Word for Carrie 37. The Lady Is Willing 42. From This Day Forward 45. Two Knights in Brooklyn 49, etc.

Judge Dredd.
Comic-book hero, a tough, shoot-first-ask-questions-after cop who also operates as judge and jury in Mega-City One. The creation of artist Brian Bolland and writer John Wagner, he first appeared in *2000 AD* magazine in 1977. In 1995 he made it to the big screen played by Sylvester Stallone.

Juillard, Robert (1906–).
French cinematographer.
Germany Year Zero 48. Jeux Interdits 52. Les Belles de Nuit 52. Les Grandes Manoeuvres 55. Austerlitz 60, etc.

Julia, Raul (1940–1994).
Puerto Rican character actor in Hollywood.
Eyes of Laura Mars 78. One from the Heart 82. The Escape Artist 82. Tempest 82. Compromising Positions 85. Kiss of the Spider Woman 85. The Morning After 86. Florida Straits 87. La Gran Fiesta 87. Moon over Parador 88. The Penitent 88. Tango Bar 88. Tequila Sunrise 88. Trading Hearts 88. Romero 89. Mack the Knife 89. A Life of Sin 90. Presumed Innocent 90. Frankenstein Unbound 90. Havana 90. The Rookie 90. The Addams Family 91. The Plague (La Peste) 92. Addams Family Values 93. The Burning Season (TV) 94, etc.

Julian, Rupert (1889–1943).
American director of the 20s.
Merry Go Round 23. Love and Glory 24. Hell's Highroad 25. *The Phantom of the Opera* 25. Three Faces West 26. Yankee Clipper 27. The Leopard Lady 28. Love Comes Along 30. The Cat Creeps 30, etc.

Julien, Isaac (1960–).
British screenwriter and director.
Looking for Langston (short) 90. Young Soul Rebels 91. Darker Side of Black (doc) 94.

¶ One of the things I've been trying to champion is a black independent cinema which deals with questions of sexuality and gender and national identity. – I.J.

Julius Caesar (102–44 BC).
The Roman emperor has been memorably portrayed by Claude Rains in *Caesar and Cleopatra*, Warren William in the 1934 *Cleopatra*, and Rex Harrison in the 1962 remake. Shakespeare's play was filmed many times in silent days, but the only notable sound versions in English have been Joseph L. Mankiewicz's 1953 production with Louis Calhern as Caesar, James Mason as Brutus, John Gielgud as Cassius, and Marlon Brando as Mark Antony, and the 1970 version with Gielgud as Caesar, Richard Johnson as Cassius, and Charlton Heston as Mark Antony. A British second feature of 1959, *An Honourable Murder*, brought the story up to date as a melodrama of boardroom intrigue. In *Carry On Cleo* Kenneth Williams played Caesar,

...d may have started the decline and fall of the ...oman empire.

...mp, Gordon (1932–).
...ump Canadian character actor, familiar as the ...oss in TV series *WKRP in Cincinnati.*
    Conquest of the Planet of the Apes 72. House ...alls 78. Four Days in Dallas (TV) 78. The Fury ...3. Dirkham Detective Agency 83. Making the ...rade 84, etc.

...mp-cutting.
...loving abruptly from one scene to another to ...ake a dramatic point, e.g. from cause to effect.

...ne (1901–1985) (June Howard Tripp).
...ritish musical comedy star of the 20s and 30s.
...larried Lord Inverclyde; divorced. Films few.
    Autobiography: 1960, *The Glass Ladder.*
...l Auld Lang Syne 17. Tom Jones 17. *The Lodger* ...6. Forever and a Day 43. The River (voice only) ...l.

...ne, Ray (1898–1958).
...merican cinematographer.
    Wandering Husbands 24. The Silent Avenger 27. ...libi 29. Arrowsmith 31. Horse Feathers 32. Riptide ...4. I Cover the Waterfront 35. Night Must Fall 37. ...est Pilot 38. The Hoodlum Saint 46. A Southern ...ankee 48. Crisis 50. The Reformer and the ...edhead 51. Sombrero 53. The Court Jester 55. ...unny Face 56. Houseboat 58, many others.

...nge, Alfred (1886–1964).
...erman art director with long experience at UFA; ...n Britain from the 20s.
    Piccadilly 28. The Good Companions 32. *The ...lan Who Knew Too Much* 34. Bulldog Jack 35. *King ...olomon's Mines* 37. The Citadel 38. *Goodbye Mr ...hips* 39. The Silver Fleet 42. *The Life and Death ...* Colonel Blimp* 43. I Know Where I'm Going 45. ... Matter of Life and Death 45. Black Narcissus* (AA) ...6. Edward My Son 49. The Miniver Story 50. ...vanhoe 52. Mogambo 53. *Invitation to the Dance* ...6. The Barretts of Wimpole Street 57. A Farewell ...o Arms 58, many others.

...he Jungle Book.
...udyard Kipling's story of Mowgli, a boy able to ...onverse with animals, was a role that might have ...een written for Sabu who played it in Zoltan ...orda's version in 1942. Disney turned it into one ...f its most popular animated features in 1967, ...sing to good effect the voices of George Sanders, ...hil Harris, and Louis Prima. In 1995 came another

live-action version starring Jason Scott Lee as Mowgli.

Jungle Jim.
This sub-Tarzan character began as a comic strip, and in 1937 Forde Beebe directed a serial on his exploits. In 1948 began the rather tired series tossed off for Columbia, with a paunchy Johnny Weismuller in the title role; it started ineptly and quickly became ridiculous.

Junkin, John (1930–).
Tall, balding British comic character actor, a TV familiar.
    The Break 63. A Hard Day's Night 64. The Pumpkin Eater 64. Kaleidoscope 67. How I Won the War 67. Brass Target 78. Chicago Joe and the Showgirl 89, etc.

Jurado, Katy (1927–) (Maria Jurado Garcia).
Spirited Mexican actress who has made Hollywood films. She was married to actor Ernest Borgnine (1959–64).
    The Bullfighter and the Lady 51. High Noon 52. Arrowhead 53. Broken Lance (AAN) 54. Trial 55. Trapeze 56. Barabbas 61. One-Eyed Jacks 61. Smoky 66. Covenant with Death 67. Stay Away Joe 68. Pat Garrett and Billy the Kid 73. Evita Peron (TV) 82. Under the Volcano 84. The Fearmaker 89, etc.

Juran, Nathan (1907–).
Austrian art director, long in the US. Won Academy Award for *How Green Was My Valley* 41. Later became a director of action films.
■ The Black Castle 52. Gunsmoke 53. Law and Order 53. The Golden Blade 53. Tumbleweed 53. Highway Dragnet 54. Drums along the River 54. The Crooked Web 55. The Deadly Mantis 57. Hellcats of the Navy 57. Twenty Million Miles to Earth 57. The Seventh Voyage of Sinbad 58. Good Day for a Hanging 58. Flight of the Lost Balloon 61. *Jack the Giant Killer* 62. Siege of the Saxons 63. First Men in the Moon 64. East of Sudan 65. The Land Raiders 70. The Boy Who Cried Werewolf 73.

Jurgens, Curt (1912–1982).
German stage leading man, in films from 1935; after the war he played internationally.
    Koenigswalzer (debut) 35. Der Engel mit der Posaune 48. Orientexpress 54. The Devil's General 54. Les Héros Sont Fatigués 55. *An Eye for an Eye* 56. Without You It Is Night (& d) 56. And Woman Was Created 57. *Me and the Colonel* 57. The Enemy Below 57. Inn of the Sixth Happiness 58. The Blue Angel 58. Ferry to Hong Kong 58. *I Aim at the Stars* (as Wernher von Braun) 59. Tamango 60. Chess Novel 60. The Threepenny Opera 63.

Lord Jim 64. Das Liebeskarussel (Who Wants to Sleep) 65. The Assassination Bureau 68. The Battle of Neretva 70. Nicholas and Alexandra 71. Vault of Horror 73. Soft Beds and Hard Battles 74. The Spy Who Loved Me 77. I, Cagliostro 77. Sergeant Steiner 79. Goldengirl (TV) 79. Just a Gigolo 80, etc.

Jurow, Martin (1914–).
American producer who retired in the mid-60s to practise law.
    The Hanging Tree 58. The Fugitive Kind 60. Breakfast at Tiffany's 61. Soldier in the Rain 63. The Great Race 65, etc.

Jusid, Juan José (1941–).
Argentinian director, also active as a producer and director of commercials.
    Tute Cabrero 78. Los Gauchos Judios 74. Espérame Mucho 83. Made in Argentina 86, etc.

Justice, James Robertson (1905–1975).
Bearded Scottish actor and personality, former journalist and naturalist.
    Fiddlers Three (debut) 44. *Scott of the Antarctic* 48. Christopher Columbus 49. *Whisky Galore* 49. David and Bathsheba 51. The Voice of Merrill 52. *Doctor in the House* 54. Storm over the Nile 55. Land of the Pharaohs 55. Moby Dick 56. Campbell's Kingdom 57. Seven Thunders 57. Doctor at Large 58. A French Mistress 60. *Very Important Person* 61. Das Feuerschiff 62. *The Fast Lady* 62. Crooks Anonymous 62. You Must Be Joking 65. Doctor in Clover 66. Hell is Empty 67. Mayerling 68. Chitty Chitty Bang Bang 68, many others.

Justin, John (1917–).
British leading man, on stage from 1933.
    The Thief of Baghdad (film debut) 40. The Gentle Sex 43. Journey Together 45. Call of the Blood 47. The Sound Barrier 51. Melba 53. Seagulls over Sorrento 54. The Man Who Loved Redheads 55. The Teckman Mystery 55. Safari 56. Island in the Sun 56. The Spider's Web 61. Candidate for Murder 64. Savage Messiah 72. Valentino 77. The Big Sleep 78. Trenchcoat 83, etc.

Jympson, John.
British editor.
    A Hard Day's Night 64. *Zulu* 64. The Bedford Incident 65. Where Eagles Dare 69. Kelly's Heroes 70. Frenzy 72. *The Optimists of Nine Elms* 73. Mr Quilp 75. The Incredible Sarah 76. A Little Night Music 77. Meetings with Remarkable Men 79. Little Shop of Horrors 86. *A Fish Called Wanda* 88. King Ralph 91. Splitting Heirs 93, etc.

K

Kaczender, George (1933–).
Hungarian director.
U-Turn 73. In Praise of Older Women 78.
Agency 80. Chanel Solitaire 81. The Finishing
Touch 83. Prettykill 87, etc.

Kadar, Jan (1918–1979).
Czech director who worked with writer Elmer Klos
(1910–93).
Kidnap 56. Death Is Called Engelchen 58. The
Accused 64. *A Shop on Main Street* (AA) 64. The
Angel Levine (US) 70. Adrift 71. Lies My Father
Told Me 76. *The Other Side of Hell* (TV) 77.
Freedom Road (TV) 80, etc.

Kael, Pauline (1919–).
American critic, most of whose reviews have been
collected for publications.

¶ Movies are so rarely great that if we cannot
appreciate great trash we have very little
reason to be interested in them – *P.K.*

Kafka, Franz (1883–1924).
German/Czech novelist who wrote puzzling tales
of guilt and innocence in a glum fantasy world. *The
Trial* and *The Castle* have been filmed. In 1992
Kafka, a film based on his life, was made by Steven
Soderbergh.

Kagan, Jeremy Paul (1945–).
American director.
■ Unwed Father (TV) 74. Judge Dee (TV) 75.
Katherine (TV) 75. Scott Joplin 76. Heroes 77.
The Big Fix 78. The Chosen 82. Sting ll 83. The
Journey of Natty Gann 85. Courage (TV) 86.
Conspiracy: Trial of the Chicago 8 (TV) 87. Big
Man on Campus 89. Descending Angel 91. By the
Sword 91. Roswell (TV) 94.

Kahn, Gus (1886–1941).
German-American lyricist who made a specialty
of film scores, and was played by Danny Thomas in
I'll See You in My Dreams.
The Jazz Singer 27. Whoopee 30. Flying Down
to Rio 33. San Francisco 36. Go West 40, many
others.

Kahn, Madeline (1942–).
American comic actress who tends to overplay her
hand; the darling of the Mel Brooks clique.
What's Up Doc? 72. Paper Moon (AAN) 73.
Blazing Saddles (AAN) 74. Young Frankenstein 74.
The Adventures of Sherlock Holmes' Smarter
Brother 75. At Long Last Love 75. Won Ton Ton
77. High Anxiety 77. The Cheap Detective 78. The
Muppet Movie 79. The First Family 80. Happy
Birthday Gemini 80. Simon 80. Wholly Moses 80.
History of the World Part One 81. Yellowbeard 83.
City Heat 84. Clue 85. An American Tail (voice)
86. My Little Pony 86. Betsy's Wedding 90.
Lifesavers 94, etc.
TV series: Oh Madeline 83. Mr President 87–
88.

Kahn, Michael.
American editor, from TV.
Rage 72. Trouble Man 72. The Spook Who Sat
by the Door 73. Truck Turner 74. Buster and Billie
74. The Devil's Rain 75. The Return of a Man
Called Horse 76. Close Encounters of the Third Kind
(AAN) 77. Eyes of Laura Mars 78. 1941 79. Raiders
of the Lost Ark (AA) 81. Poltergeist 82. Table for
Five 83. Indiana Jones and the Temple of Doom
84. The Color Purple 85. The Goonies 85. Wisdom
86. Empire of the Sun (AAN) 87. Fatal Attraction
(AAN) 87. Always 89. Indiana Jones and the Last
Crusade 89. Arachnophobia 90. Toy Soldiers 91.
Hook 91. Jurassic Park 93. Schindler's List (AA) 93,
etc.

Kaige, Chen (1952–).
Chinese director and screenwriter.
Yellow Earth 84. Forced Take-Off (TV) 85. The
Big Parade 86. King of the Children (wd) 88. Life
on a String (Bian Zou Bian Chang) 91. Farewell
My Concubine (Bawang Bie Ji) (AAN) 93, etc.

Kalatozov, Mikhail (1903–1973).
Russian director and executive.
Their Kingdom 28. Salt for Svenetia 30. A Nail
in a Boot 32. The Conspiracy of the Doomed 50.
The Cranes are Flying 57. The Unsent Letter 60. I
Am Cuba 66. The Red Tent 69.

Kalem.
An early American production company founded
in 1907, taking its name from the initials of its three
principals, George Klein, Sam Long and Frank
Marion (K-L-M). Its most famous production is
From the Manger to the Cross 12.

Kalin, Tom (1962–).
American director, a former painter and
photographer.
Swoon 92.

Kalmar, Bert (1884–1947).
American vaudevillian, songwriter (with Harry
Ruby) and music executive.
Check and Double Check (& w) 30. The Kid
from Spain (& w) 32. *Horse Feathers* (& w) 32.
Duck Soup (& w) 33. Kentucky Kernels (& w) 34.
Everybody Sing 38. Wake Up and Dream 46.
Carnival in Costa Rica 48, many others.

Kalmus, Herbert T. (1881–1963).
American pioneer photographic expert, later
president of Technicolor. His wife *Natalie Kalmus*
(1892–1965) was adviser on all Technicolor films
from 1933.

Kamen, Michael (1948–).
American composer.
The Next Man 76. Between the Lines 77.
Polyester 81. Angelo, My Love 83. The Dead Zone
83. Brazil 85. Highlander 85. Mona Lisa 85. Lethal
Weapon 87. Adventures in Babysitting 87.
Someone to Watch Over Me 87. Die Hard 88. For
Queen and Country 88. The Adventures of Baron
Munchausen 89. Roundhouse 89. Licence to Kill
89. Lethal Weapon 2 89. The Krays 90. Die Hard
II 90. Let Him Have It 91. Nothing but Trouble 91.
The Last Boy Scout 91. Company Business 91.
Shining Through 92. Lethal Weapon 3 92. Splitting
Heirs 93. The Last Action Hero 93. Wilder Napalm
93. The Three Musketeers 93, etc.

Kaminska, Ida (1899–1980).
Polish character actress.
Autobiography: 1973, *My Life, My Theater.*
The Shop on High Street (AAN) 66. The Angel
Levine (US) 70, etc.

Kaminski, Janusz (1961–).
Polish-born cinematographer who emigrated to
America in 1981.
The Rain Killer 90. The Terror Within II 91.
Schindler's List 93, etc.

Kander, John (1927–).
American composer, with Fred Ebb, of *Cabaret.*
Something for Everyone 70. Kramer vs Kramer
79. Still of the Night 82. Blue Skies Again 83. I Want
to Go Home (Fr.) 89.

Kane, Carol (1952–).
American leading lady of the late 70s.
Hester Street (AAN) 74. Annie Hall 77. The
World's Greatest Lover 77. Valentino 77. The
Muppet Movie 79. When a Stranger Calls 79.
Strong Medicine 81. Norman Loves Rose 82. Can
She Bake a Cherry Pie? 83. Over the Brooklyn
Bridge 83. Racing with the Moon 84. The Secret
Diary of Sigmund Freud 84. Transylvania 6–5000
85. Jumpin' Jack Flash 86. Ishtar 87. The Princess
Bride 87. License to Drive 88. Scrooged 88. Sticky
Fingers 88. Flashback 90. Joe versus the Volcano
90. The Lemon Sisters 90. My Blue Heaven 90.
Addams Family Values 93, etc.

Kane, Helen (1904–1966) (Helen Schroeder).
American singer of the 20s, the 'boop-boop-a-
doop' girl. Played by Debbie Reynolds in *Three
Little Words* (in which Miss Kane supplied her own
voice).
Pointed Heels 29. Dangerous Nan McGrew 29.
Heads Up 30, etc.

Kane, Joseph (1894–1975).
American director since 1935, mainly of
competent but unambitious Republic westerns.
The Man from Music Mountain 38. The Man
from Cheyenne 42. Flame of the Barbary Coast 44.
The Cheaters 45. The Plainsman and the Lady 46.
The Plunderers (& p) 48. California Passage (& p)
50. Hoodlum Empire (& p) 51. Jubilee Trail (& p)
53. Spoilers of the Forest (& p) 57, many others.

Kanevsky, Vitaly (1934–).
Russian director and screenwriter who made his
first film, an autobiographical account of his
deprived boyhood, at the age of 55.
Don't Move, Die, and Rise Again! (Zamri, Umri,
Voskresni) 90. An Independent Life 92. We, the
Children of the Twentieth Century (doc) 94, etc.

Kanganis, Charles T.
American director of action films.
Deadly Breed 89. Sinners 89. Intent to Kill 90. A Time to Die 91. No Escape, No Return 93. 3 Ninjas Kick Back 94, etc.

Kanin, Garson (1912–).
American writer and raconteur who has spent time in Hollywood as director, also as screenwriter, especially in collaboration with his wife Ruth Gordon.
Autobiographical books: 1974, *Hollywood*. 1976, *Takes a Long Time to Become Young*.
AS DIRECTOR: A Man to Remember 38. Next Time I Marry 38. *The Great Man Votes* 38. *Bachelor Mother* 39. My Favorite Wife 40. They Knew What They Wanted 40. *Tom, Dick and Harry* 41. The True Glory (w, co-d) (AA) 45. Where It's At (& w) 69. Some Kind of a Nut (& w) 70.
AS WRITER: From This Day Forward 46. A Double Life (AAN) 47. *Adam's Rib* (AAN) 49. *Born Yesterday* (oa) 50. The Marrying Kind 52. Pat and Mike (AAN) 52. It Should Happen to You 53. The Girl Can't Help It 56. The Rat Race 60. The Right Approach 61, etc.

Kanin, Michael (1910–1993).
American writer brother of Garson Kanin; often worked with his wife Fay.
Anne of Windy Poplars 40. *Woman of the Year* (AA) 42. The Cross of Lorraine 44. Centennial Summer 46. Rhapsody 54. The Opposite Sex 56. Teacher's Pet (AAN) 58. The Outrage 64. How to Commit Marriage 69, etc.

Kann, Lily (1898–1978).
German character actress, long in England.
The Flemish Farm 43. Latin Quarter 45. Mrs Fitzherbert 47. A Tale of Five Cities 51. Betrayed (US) 54. A Kid for Two Farthings 55. No Trees in the Street 59, many others.

Kanner, Alexis (1942–).
British character actor.
Reach for Glory 63. Crossplot 69. Connecting Rooms 69. Goodbye Gemini 70. Kings and Desperate Men (a, wd) 84. Nightfall 88. Twinsanity 88, etc.

Kanter, Hal (1918–).
American writer-director with TV background.
I Married a Woman (d) 55. Loving You (wd) 56. Once Upon a Horse (wd) 58. Pocketful of Miracles (co-w) 61. Move Over Darling (w) 63. Dear Brigitte (w) 65. For the Love of It (TV) 80, etc.

Kantor, Mackinlay (1904–1977).
American writer full of sentiment and patriotism.
The Voice of Bugle Ann 37. Happy Land 43. The Best Years of Our Lives 46. The Romance of Rosy Ridge 47. Andersonville 59. Follow Me Boys 66.

Kaper, Bronislau (1902–1983).
Polish composer who lived in US.
The Chocolate Soldier 41. Two Faced Woman 41. Gaslight 44. Without Love 45. Green Dolphin Street 47. The Forsyte Saga 49. *The Red Badge of Courage* 51. Lili (AA) 53. Them 54. The Swan 56. The Brothers Karamazov 58. Green Mansions 59. Butterfield 8 61. Mutiny on the Bounty (AAN) 62. Kisses for My President 64. Lord Jim 64. Tobruk 66. The Way West 67. A Flea in Her Ear 68, etc.

Kaplan, Jonathan (1947–).
American director.
Student Teachers 73. Night Call Nurses 74. White Line Fever (& w) 75. Mr Billion (& w) 77.
Over the Edge 79. Heart like a Wheel 83. Project X 87. The Accused 88. Immediate Family 89. Love Field 92. Unlawful Entry 92. Bad Girls 94, etc.

Kaplan, Marvin (1924–).
Owlish little American comedy actor.
The Reformer and the Redhead 50. I Can Get It for You Wholesale 51. Angels in the Outfield 51. Behave Yourself 51. Wake Me When It's Over 60. A New Kind of Love 63. It's a Mad Mad Mad Mad World 63. The Great Race 65. Wild at Heart 90, etc.
TV series: Chicago Teddybears 71. Alice 81–82.

Kaplan, Nelly (1934–).
French director and screenwriter.
■ La Fiancée du Pirate/Dirty Mary 69. Papa les Petits Bateaux 71. Néa 76. Le Satéllite de Venus 77. Au Bonheur des Dames 79. Charles et Lucie 79. Abel Gance et Son (wd) 84. Plaisir d'Amour (wd) 91.

Kaplan, Sol (1913–1990).
American composer.
Tales of Manhattan 42. Port of New York 49. Rawhide 51. Niagara 53. Happy Anniversary 59. The Victors 63. The Spy Who Came in from the Cold 65. Explosion 69. Living Free 72. Lies My Father Told Me 75. Over the Edge 79, etc.

Kapoor, Shashi (1938–).
Indian leading actor and producer, in occasional international films.
Aag 48. Awaara 51. Householder 62. Shakespeare Wallah 65. Bombay Talkie 70. Siddharta 72. Heat and Dust 83. Sammy and Rosie Get Laid 87. The Deceivers 88. In Custody (Hifazaat) 93, etc.

Kaprisky, Valérie (1963–).
French leading actress.
Aphrodite 82. Breathless 83. The Public Woman (La Femme Publique) 83. The Year of the Jellyfish (L'Année des Meduses) 86. L'Amant 89. Milena 90. The End Is Known (La Fine è Nota) 93. Mouvements du Désir 94, etc.

Karas, Anton (1906–1985).
Viennese composer whose zither music, played by himself, helped to turn *The Third Man* into a classic.

Karina, Anna (1940–) (Hanne Karin Beyer).
Danish leading lady, mostly in French films, especially those of Jean-Luc Godard.
She'll Have To Go (GB) 61. *Une Femme Est une Femme* 61. *Vivre Sa Vie* 62. Le Petit Soldat 63. Bande à Part 64. Alphaville 65. Made in USA 66. The Magus 68. Before Winter Comes 68. Laughter in the Dark 69. Justine 69. The Salzburg Connection 72. Bread and Chocolate 73. Chinese Roulette 76. Chausette Surprise 78. Laissez Parler les Adultes 80. L'Ami de Vincent 83. Ave Maria 84. Cayenne-Palace 87. Last Song (& w) 87. The Abyss (L'Oeuvre au Noir) 88. The Man Who Would Be Guilty 89. Treasure Island 91, etc.

Karlin, Fred (1936–).
American composer, mainly for TV films.
Up the Down Staircase 67. Yours Mine and Ours 68. Lovers and Other Strangers 69. The Little Ark 71. Westworld 73. The Spikes Gang 74. Death Be Not Proud (TV) 75. Futureworld 76. Man from Atlantis 77. Cloud Dancer 80. Loving Couples 80. Jacqueline Susann's Valley of the Dolls (TV) 81. Calamity Jane (TV) 83. Vasectomy: A Delicate Matter 86. Lady Mobster (TV) 88. Bridge to Silence (TV) 89, many others.

Karlin, Miriam (1925–) (M. Samuels).
Rasping-voiced British revue comedienne and character actress.
The Deep Blue Sea 55. The Entertainer 59. On the Fiddle 61. The Small World of Sammy Lee 63. Heavens Above 63. The Bargee 64. Ladies Who Do 64. A Clockwork Orange 71, etc.

Karloff, Boris (1887–1969) (William Henry Pratt).
Gaunt British character actor, on stage from 1910, films from 1919, mainly in US. Achieved world fame as the monster in *Frankenstein* 31, and became typed in horrific parts despite his gentle, cultured voice.
Biographies: 1972, *Horror Man* by Peter Underwood. 1973, *Karloff, the Man, the Monster, the Movies* by Denis Gifford. 1974, *The Films of Boris Karloff* by Richard Bojarski and Kenneth Beals.
SELECTED SILENTS: His Majesty the American 19. The Last of the Mohicans 20. The Man from Downing Street 22. A Woman Conquers 23. Parisian Nights 25. Never the Twain Shall Meet 25. The Bells 26. Valencia 26. Tarzan and the Golden Lion 27. Two Arabian Knights 27. Vultures of the Sea 28. Phantoms of the North 29, many others.
■ SOUND FILMS: Behind that Curtain 29. King of the Kongo 29. The Unholy Night 29. The Bad One 30. The Sea Bat 30. The Utah Kid 30. Mothers Cry 30. The Criminal Code 30. Cracked Nuts 31. Young Donovan's Kid 31. King of the Wild 31. Smart Money 31. The Public Defender 31. I Like Your Nerve 31. Graft 31. Five Star Final 31. The Mad Genius 31. The Yellow Ticket 31. Guilty Generation 31. *Frankenstein* 31. Tonight or Never 31. Behind the Mask 32. Business and Pleasure 32. Scarface 32. The Cohens and Kellys in Hollywood 32. The Miracle Man 32. Night World 32. *The Old Dark House* 32. *The Mask of Fu Manchu* 32. *The Mummy* 32. The Ghoul 33. The Lost Patrol 34. The House of Rothschild 34. The Black Cat 34. The Gift of Gab 34. *The Bride of Frankenstein* 35. *The Black Room* 35. *The Raven* 35. The Invisible Ray 36. The Walking Dead 36. The Man Who Changed His Mind 36. Juggernaut 36. *Charlie Chan at the Opera* 37. Night Key 37. West of Shanghai 37. The Invisible Menace 37. Mr Wong Detective 38. Son of Frankenstein 39. The Mystery of Mr Wong 39. Mr Wong in Chinatown 39. The Man They Could Not Hang 39. Tower of London 39. The Fatal Hour 40. British Intelligence 40. Black Friday 40. The Man with Nine Lives 40. Devil's Island 40. Doomed to Die 40. Before I Hang 40. The Ape 40. You'll Find Out 40. The Devil Commands 41. The Boogie Man will Get You 42. The Climax 44. *House of Frankenstein* 44. *The Body Snatcher* 45. Isle of the Dead 45. Bedlam 46. The Secret Life of Walter Mitty 47. Lured 47. Unconquered 47. Dick Tracy meets Gruesome 47. Tap Roots 48. Abbott and Costello Meet the Killer 49. The Strange Door 51. The Black Castle 52. Abbott and Costello Meet Dr Jekyll and Mr Hyde 53. Monster of the Island 53. The Hindu 53. Voodoo Island 58. Grip of the Strangler 58. Corridors of Blood 58. Frankenstein 70 58. *The Raven* 63. The Terror 63. Comedy of Terrors 63. Black Sabbath 64. Bikini Beach 64. Die Monster Die 65. Ghost in the Invisible Bikini 66. The Venetian Affair 67. The Sorcerers 67. *Targets* 68. Curse of the Crimson Altar 68. The Snake People 70. The Incredible Invasion 70. Cauldron of Blood 70. The Fear Chamber 70. House of Evil 70.
TV series: Colonel March of Scotland Yard 53. Thriller 60–61.
✪ For his sinister Englishness, his sepulchral tones and his unfailing eagerness to please. *Bride of Frankenstein*.

¶ When I was nine I played the demon king in Cinderella and it launched me on a long and happy life of being a monster.

Though Karloff fought against being typecast, he later admitted:

The monster was the best friend I ever had.

How did he get the part? Said producer Carl Laemmle Junr:

His eyes mirrored the suffering we needed.

Director James Whale amplified this:

His face fascinated me. I made drawings of his head, adding sharp bony ridges where I imagined the skull might have joined.

Karloff however insisted:

You could heave a brick out of the window and hit ten actors who could play my parts. I just happened to be on the right corner at the right time.

Karlson, Phil (1908–1985) (Philip Karlstein). American director, in Hollywood from 1932. Mainly low-budget actioners until he suddenly gained stature in the 50s.

■ A Wave a WAC and a Marine 44. GI Honeymoon 45. There Goes Kelly 45. Shanghai Cobra 45. Swing Parade 46. Live Wires 46. Dark Alibi 46. Behind the Mask 46. Bowery Bombshell 46. The Missing Lady 46. Wife Wanted 46. Black Gold 47. Kilroy Was Here 47. Louisiana 47. Rocky 48. Adventures in Silverado 48. Thunderhoof 48. Ladies of the Chorus 49. The Big Cat 49. Down Memory Lane 49. The Iroquois Trail 50. Lorna Doone 51. The Texas Rangers 51. Mask of the Avenger 51. *Scandal Sheet* 52. The Brigand 52. *Kansas City Confidential* 53. 99 River Street 53. They Rode West 54. Tight Spot 55. Hell's Island 55. Five Against the House 55. *The Phenix City Story* 55. The Brothers Rico 57. Gunman's Walk 58. Hell to Eternity 60. Key Witness 60. The Secret Ways 61. The Young Doctors 61. Kid Galahad 62. Rampage 63. *The Silencers* 66. A Time for Killing 67. Wrecking Crew 69. Hornet's Nest 70. Ben 72. Walking Tall 73. Framed 75.

Karno, Fred (1866–1941) (Frederick John Westcott).
English impresario who originated or refined many influential slapstick routines (including the custard pie in the face) with his teams of comedians, who included over the years Betty Balfour, Billy Bennett, Charlie Chaplin, Stan Laurel, Naughton and Gold, Will Hay, Syd Walker and Robb Wilton. Born in Exeter, he was a factory worker at the age of 14, a plumber and a circus acrobat. In the mid-1890s he performed a silent act in music halls, turning in the early 1900s to producing shows and plays from his South London 'Fun Factory'. In the late 20s, bankrupted by his Karsino, a lavish showplace on a Thames island, he went to Hollywood and briefly worked for Hal Roach. Back in London, he wrote the story for an unsuccessful film, *Bad Companions*, before overseeing comedies based on his music-hall sketches. He set up his own production company, which failed after its first film, *Don't Rush Me*, and ended up running a wine and beer shop in Lilliput, a Dorset village. In the 1992 biopic *Chaplin*, he was played by John Thaw. Chaplin's early short *A Night at the Show* 15, and his own *Oh, What a Duchess!*, are based on his long-running music-hall act 'The Mumming Birds', in which a drunk (played by Chaplin on-stage) and a boy become entangled in a succession of second-rate acts.
Biographies: 1939, *Remember Fred Karno* by Edwin Adeler and Con West. 1971, *Fred Karno, Master of Mirth and Tears* by J. P. Gallagher.
■ Bad Companions 32. The Bailiffs 32. Handy Men 32. They're Off 33. The Dentist 33. Post Haste

33. Sign Please 33. Oh, What A Duchess! 34. Don't Rush Me 36. Jailbirds 39.

¶ Keep it wistful, gentlemen, keep it *wistful* as well. That's hard to do, but we want sympathy with the laughter. Wistful! – *F.K. to his comics*
When in doubt, fall on your arse. – *F.K.*
During a performance of one of his comedies if he did not like a comedian he would stand in the wings and hold his nose and give an audible raspberry. – *Charlie Chaplin*
Fred Karno is not only a genius, he is the man who originated slapstick comedy. – *Hal Roach*
He had no equal. His name *was* box-office. – *Stan Laurel*

Famous catchphrase (from his sketch 'The Bailiffs'): 'Meredith, we're in!'

Famous saying: 'Leave 'em wanting.'

Karns, Roscoe (1893–1970).
American character actor, very active in the 30s, usually in hard-boiled comedy roles.
Beggars of Life 28. *The Front Page* 30. Undercover Man 32. *Night After Night* 32. *Twentieth Century* 34. *It Happened One Night* 34. Thanks for the Memory 38. They Drive by Night 40. *His Girl Friday* 40. His Butler's Sister 43. Will Tomorrow Ever Come? 47. Inside Story 48. Onionhead 58, many others.
TV series: Rocky King Detective 50. Hennessey 59–61.

Famous line (*It Happened One Night*): 'Shapeley's the name, and that's the way I like 'em.'

Karras, Alex (1935–).
Heavyweight American character actor, former footballer.
Paper Lion 68. Hardcase (TV) 72. The 500 Pound Jerk (TV) 73. Blazing Saddles 74. Babe (TV) 75. Mulligan Stew (TV) 77. Mad Bull (TV) 77. Centennial (TV) 78. When Time Ran Out 80. Nobody's Perfekt 81. Victor/Victoria 82. Against All Odds 84, etc.
TV series: Webster 83–87.

Karvan, Claudia (1973–).
Australian actress, in films as a child.
Molly 83. High Tide 87. The Big Steal 90. Broken Highway 93. The Heartbreak Kid 93. My Forgotten Man 93. Exile 94, etc.

Karyo, Tcheky (1953–).
Turkish-born actor in French and international films.
La Balance 82. La Nuits de la Pleine Lune 85. The Bear (L'Ours) 89. Nikita 90. Isabelle Eberhardt 91. Exposure 91. Australia 91. Sketch Artist 92. 1492: Conquest of Paradise 92. C'est Beau une Ville la Nuit 93. And the Band Played On (TV) 93. Le Bonheur (Fr.) 94. Nostradamus 94, etc.

Kasdan, Lawrence (1949–).
American writer-director.
■ Continental Divide (w) 80. The Empire Strikes Back (co-w) 80. Raiders of the Lost Ark (w) 81. *Body Heat* (wd) 82. *The Big Chill* (wd) (AAN) 83. Return of the Jedi (w) 83. Silverado (wd) 85. The Accidental Tourist (wd) (AAN) 88. I Love You to Death (d) 90. Grand Canyon (co-w, d) (AANw) 91. The Bodyguard (w) 92. Jumpin' at the Boneyard (p) 92. Wyatt Earp (p, co-w, d) 94.

Kasket, Harold (1915–).
British character actor of mixed descent, originally stage impressionist.
Hotel Sahara 51. Moulin Rouge 53. Interpol 57.

Sands of the Desert 60. Arabesque 66. Trail of t Pink Panther 82, etc.

Kastner, Elliott (1930–).
American producer, former literary agent.
Bus Riley's Back in Town 65. Harper 66. Kaleidoscope 66. The Night of the Following Da 68. Where Eagles Dare 68. The Walking Stick 6 A Severed Head 70. When Eight Bells Toll 71. Villain 71. Zee and Co. 72. The Nightcomers 72. The Long Goodbye 73. Harrowhouse 74. Farewe My Lovely 75. The Missouri Breaks 76. The Big Sleep 78. North Sea Hijack 80. Absolution 80. T First Deadly Sin 81. Death Valley 82. Oxford Blu 84. Garbo Talks 85. Angel Heart 87. Heat 87. Th Blob 88. Jack's Back 88. A Chorus of Disapprov 89. Never on Tuesday 89, etc.etc.

Kästner, Erich (1899–1974).
German novelist whose *Emil and the Detectives* h been much filmed. He also wrote the original of *The Parent Trap*.

Kastner, Peter (1944–).
Canadian actor who made a corner in frustrated adolescents.
Nobody Waved Goodbye (Can.) 65. *You're a Big Boy Now* (US) 66. B.S. I Love You 70. Frightman 83. Unfinished Business (a sequel to Nobody Waved Goodbye) 84, etc.
TV series: The Ugliest Girl in Town 68.

Kasznar, Kurt (1913–1979).
Chubby Austrian character actor, in US from 193
The Light Touch (debut) 51. The Happy Time 52. Lili 53. Sombrero 53. My Sister Eileen 55. Anything Goes 56. A Farewell to Arms 58. For t First Time 59. Casino Royale 66. The King's Pira 67. The Ambushers 67, etc.
TV series: Land of the Giants 68–69.

Katch, Kurt (1896–1958) (Isser Kac).
Bald Polish character actor, in Hollywood from 1942.
Ali Baba and the Forty Thieves 43. *The Mask c Dimitrios* 44. Salome Where She Danced 45. The Mummy's Curse 45. Song of Love 47. The Secre of the Incas 54. Abbott and Costello Meet the Mummy 55. Pharaoh's Curse 57, etc.

Katselas, Milton (1933–).
American director with Broadway experience.
■ Butterflies Are Free 72. Forty Carats 73. Repo to the Commissioner 74. When You Comin' Bac Red Ryder? 79. Strangers (TV) 79. The Rules of Marriage (TV) 82.

Katt, William (1955–).
American leading man of the late 70s, son of Bil Williams and Barbara Hale.
Carrie 76. First Love 78. Big Wednesday 79. Butch and Sundance 79. Baby, Secret of the Los Legend 84. House 85. Swimsuit 89. Naked Obsession 94, etc.
TV series: The Greatest American Hero 81–82 Good Sports 91.

Katz, Gloria.
American producer and screenwriter, a former editor, usually in collaboration with her husband Willard Huyck.
American Graffiti (AAN) 73. Messiah of Evil 7 Lucky Lady 75. French Postcards 79. Indiana Jon and the Temple of Doom 84. Best Defense 84. Howard the Duck 86, etc.

Katzenberg, Jeffrey (1951–).
Production executive, president of the Walt Disne

ompany's film production from 1985–94. He set
o his own studio in 1994 with partners Steven
ielberg and David Geffen.

atzin, Lee H. (1935–).
merican director.
Heaven with a Gun 69. Along Came a Spider
V) 70. Whatever Happened to Aunt Alice? 70.
he Phynx 70. Le Mans 71. The Salzburg
onnection 72. The Voyage of the Yes (TV) 72.
avages (TV) 74. The Last Survivors (TV) 75. Sky
eist (TV) 75. Man from Atlantis (TV) 77. The
astard (TV) 78. Terror out of the Sky (TV) 78.
amurai (TV) 79. Death Ray 2000 (TV) 81.
enser: For Hire (TV) 85. World Gone Wild 88,
c.

atzman, Sam (1901–1973).
merican producer, chiefly of low-budget co-
atures including the *Jungle Jim* series, *Rock
round the Clock* 56, many others.

aufman, Boris (1906–1980).
olish photographer, in France from 1928,
ollywood from 1942. Brother of Dziga Vertov.
 La Marche des Machines 28. A Propos de Nice
 co-d) 30. Les Halles 30. *Zéro de Conduite* 32. Seine
3. *L'Atalante* 34. Pere Lampion 36. Fort Delores
7. Serenade 38. Better Tomorrow 45. Capital
ory 45. The Southwest 45. Journey into
ledicine 47. The Tanglewood Story 50. The Garden
 Eden 54. *On the Waterfront* (AA) 54. Crowded
aradise 56. *Baby Doll* 56. Patterns 56. *Twelve
ngry Men* 57. That Kind of Woman 59. The
ugitive Kind 60. Splendor in the Grass 61. Long
ay's Journey into Night 62. All the Way Home
3. Gone are the Days 63. *The World of Henry
rient* 64. The Pawnbroker 65. *The Group* 66. Bye
ye Braverman 67. Uptight 68. The Brotherhood 68.
ell Me That You Love Me Junie Moon 70.

aufman, George S. (1889–1961).
merican comedy playwright, often in
ollaboration with Moss Hart (qv). Most of his
orks were filmed.
Biography: 1972, *George S. Kaufman* by Howard
eichmann.
Dulcy 23. Beggar on Horseback 25. *Animal
rackers* 30. The Royal Family of Broadway 30. *Once
 a Lifetime* 32. Dinner at Eight 33. Stage Door 37.
ou Can't Take It with You 38. *The Man Who Came
 Dinner* 41. George Washington Slept Here 42.
he Late George Apley 47. The Senator Was
ndiscreet (wd) 49. The Solid Gold Cadillac 56, etc.

¶ He had great integrity. You never had to watch
him when he was dealing. – *Harpo Marx*
He was renowned for marrying very high
omedy with very high farce; and with his wit, it
ame out satire. – *Howard Teichmann*

aufman, Lloyd (1945–).
merican director, writer and producer of low-
udget exploitation movies for Troma under the
seudonym Samuel Weil, in collaboration with
Iichael Herz.
Squeeze Play! (co-d). Waitress! (co-d) 82. The
irst Turn-On! 84. The Toxic Avenger (co-d) 84.
he Toxic Avenger: Part II (co-d) 88. Troma's War
co-d) 88. Sgt Kabukiman N.Y.P.D. (co-d) 94, etc.

aufman, Millard (1917–).
merican screenwriter; output sparse and patchy,
ut interesting.
Gun Crazy 50. Take the High Ground (AAN) 53.
ad Day at Black Rock (AAN) 55. Raintree County
7. Never So Few 59. Convicts Four (& d) 62. The
Var Lord 65. Living Free 72. The Klansman 76, etc.

Kaufman, Philip (1936–).
American director and screenwriter.
■ Goldstein (co-d) 63. Fearless Frank 69. The
Great Minnesota Raid 72. The White Dawn 73.
The Outlaw Josey Wales (co-w only) 75. Invasion
of the Body Snatchers 78. The Wanderers 79.
Raiders of the Lost Ark (co-w only) 81. *The Right
Stuff* (wd) 83. The Unbearable Lightness of Being
(wd) (AANw) 88. Henry and June (wd) 90. Rising
Sun (co-w, d) 93.

Kaufman, Robert (1931–1991).
American screenwriter.
Dr Goldfoot and the Bikini Machine 65. Getting
Straight 70. I Love My Wife (& p) 70. Harry and
Walter Go to New York 76. Love at First Bite (&
p) 79. How to Beat the High Cost of Living (& p)
80. Split Image (co-w) 82. The Check Is in the Mail
86. Separate Vacation 88, etc.

Kaufmann, Christine (1944–).
German leading lady in international films. She
was married to actor Tony Curtis (1963–68).
Town without Pity 61. Taras Bulba 62. Wild and
Wonderful 64. Tunnel 28 64. Murders in the Rue
Morgue 71. Bagdad Café 87, etc.

Kaufmann, Maurice (1928–).
British supporting actor.
A Shot in the Dark 64. Fanatic 65. Bloomfield
70. The Abominable Dr Phibes 71, etc.

Kaun, Bernhard (1899–1980).
German-born composer in Hollywood, where he
made a speciality of scores for horror movies.
Frankenstein 31. Dr X 32. The Mystery of the
Wax Museum 33. Return of the Terror 34. The
Walking Dead 36. The Return of Dr X 39. The
Smiling Ghost 41. Special Delivery 55, etc.

Kaurismäki, Aki (1957–).
Prolific Finnish director and producer. He is the
brother of Mika Kaurismäki who partners him in
a production company Villealfa (which derives its
name from Jean-Luc Godard's film *Alphaville*).
The Liar (Valehtelija) (a, w) 80. The Saimma
Gesture (Saimma – Ilmiö) 83. Crime and
Punishment (Rikos Ja Rangaistus) 83. Calamari
Union 84. Shadows in Paradise (Varjoja
Paratiisissa) 86. Hamlet Goes Business (Hamlet
Liikemaailmassa) 87. Ariel 88. The Match Girl
(Tulitkkutehtaan) 89. Leningrad Cowboys Go
America 89. I Hired a Contract Killer 90. Bohemian
Life (La Vie de Bohème) 92. Total Balalaika Show
94. Leningrad Cowboys Meet Moses (p, wd, e)
94. Take Care of Your Scarf, Tatjana (Pidä Huivista
Kiinni, Tatjana) 94, etc.

¶ My favourite last line from a movie is in Ozu's
Tokyo Story: 'Isn't life a disappointment?'. – *A.K.*

Kaurismäki, Mika (1955–).
Finnish director and producer, the brother of Aki
Kaurismäki.
The Liar (Valehtelija) 80. The Saimma Gesture
(Saimma – Ilmiö) (co-d) 83. Rosso 85. Helsinki
Napoli All Night Long 88. Cha Cha Cha 89. The
Paper Star (Paperitahit) 90. Amazon 90. Zombie
and the Ghost Train (Zombie ja Kummitusjuna)
91. The Last Border 93, etc.

Kautner, Helmut (1908–1980).
German director who had an unhappy experience
in Hollywood in the 50s.
Kitty and the World Conference 39. Adieu
Franciska 41. Romanze in Moll 43. Unter den
Brücken 45. In Jenen Tagen 47. Der Apfel Ist Ab
48. Epilog 50. The Last Brigade 54. Ludwig II 54.

The Devil's General 55. Himmel Ohne Sterne 55.
The Captain from Koepenick 56. The Wonderful
Years (US) 58. Stranger in My Arms (US) 59. The
Rest Is Silence 59. Der Glas Wasser 60. Die Rote
62, etc.

Kavner, Julie (1951–).
American actress.
Katherine (TV) 75. Revenge of the Stepford
Wives (TV) 80. Bad Medicine 85. Hannah and
Her Sisters 86. Radio Days 87. Surrender 87. New
York Stories 89. The Alice 90. Awakenings 90.
Shadows and Fog 91. This Is My Life 92. I'll Do
Anything 94, etc.
TV series: Rhoda 74–78. The Simpsons (voice,
as Marge) 89– .

Kawalerowicz, Jerzy (1922–).
Polish director.
Gromada 51. Cien 54. The True End of the Great
War 57. *Pociag* (Night Train) 59. *Mother Jeanne of
the Angels* (The Devil and the Nun) 60. *The Pharaoh*
64. Maddalena 71. Death of the President 78, etc.

Kaye, Danny (1908/13–1987) (David Daniel
Kaminsky).
Ebullient American star entertainer of stage,
screen and TV. After making several unpromising
two-reelers in the 30s (later compiled as *The Danny
Kaye Story*) he was given the big build-up by Sam
Goldwyn and gained enormous popularity, though
his later films were disappointing. Special Academy
Award in 1954 'for his unique talents, his service
to the industry and the American people'.
Biography: 1948, *The Danny Kaye Saga* by Kurt
Singer.
Up in Arms 44. *Wonder Man* 45. The Kid from
Brooklyn 46. *The Secret Life of Walter Mitty* 47. A
Song Is Born 48. The Inspector General 49. On the
Riviera 51. *Hans Christian Andersen* 52. *Knock on
Wood* 53. White Christmas 54. Assignment
Children (UN short) 54. *The Court Jester* 56. Me and
the Colonel 57. Merry Andrew 58. The Five
Pennies 59. On the Double 62. The Man from the
Diners' Club 63. The Madwoman of Chaillot 69.
Peter Pan (TV) 75. Pinocchio (TV) 76, etc.
TV series: The Danny Kaye Show 63–67.
✪ For his perfectionist comedy techniques.
Wonder Man.

¶ I am a wife-made man. – *D.K.* (his wife Sylvia
Fine wrote most of his best lyrics)
I became an entertainer not because I wanted
to but because I was meant to. – *D.K.*
I'm Anatole of Paris,
I shriek with chic;
My 'at of ze week
Caused six divorces, three runaway 'orses . . .
I'm Anatole of Paris, ze 'ats I sell
Make people yell
'Is zat a 'at or a two-room flat?' – *Kaye lyric*
I can't say what Danny Kaye is like in private life.
There are too many of them. – *Sylvia Fine*

Kaye, Norman.
Australian character actor, musician and
screenwriter, from the theatre, often playing mild
middle-aged men.
Illuminations (a) 76. Inside Looking Out (a) 77.
Lonely Hearts (a, m) 82. Buddies (a) 83. Man of
Flowers (a) 84. Where the Green Ants Dream (a)
84. Cactus (a, co-w) 86. Frenchman's Farm (a) 87.
Warm Nights on a Slow Moving Train (a) 87.
Vincent: The Life and Death of Vincent van Gogh
(m) 88. Golden Braid (co-m) 90. A Woman's Tale
91. Turtle Beach 92. Broken Highway 93. Exile
94. Erotic Tales 94, etc.

Kaye, Stubby (1918–).
Rotund American comic actor.

Guys and Dolls 55. Li'l Abner 59. 40 Pounds of Trouble 62. Cat Ballou 65. Sweet Charity 68. The Cockeyed Cowboys of Calico County 70. The Dirtiest Girl I Ever Met 73. Six Pack Annie.75. Minskie's Follies 83. Who Framed Roger Rabbit? 88, etc.

TV series: Love and Marriage 59. My Sister Eileen 60.

Kazan, Elia (1909–) (Elia Kazanjoglous).
Distinguished American stage and screen director of Greek/Turkish descent. Intermittently an actor; with New York's Group Theatre in the 30s.
Autobiography: 1988, *A Life*.
AS ACTOR: City for Conquest 40. Blues in the Night 41, etc.
AS DIRECTOR: *A Tree Grows in Brooklyn* 45. The Sea of Grass 47. *Boomerang* 47. *Gentleman's Agreement* (AA) 47. Pinky 49. Panic in the Streets 50. A Streetcar Named Desire (AAN) 51. *Viva Zapata* 52. Man on a Tightrope 53. *On the Waterfront* (AA) 54. East of Eden (AAN) 55. Baby Doll 56. *A Face in the Crowd* (& p) 57. Wild River (& p) 60. Splendor in the Grass (& p) 61. America America (& w, p) (AAN) 63. The Arrangement (& w, p) 69. The Visitors (& w) 72. The Last Tycoon 76.

Kazan, Nicholas.
American director, screenwriter and dramatist, the son of Elia Kazan.

Frances (co-w) 82. At Close Range (w) 86. Patty Hearst (w) 88. Reversal of Fortune (w) 90. Dream Lover (wd) 94, etc.

Keach, James (1948–).
American actor and producer, brother of Stacy Keach.

Sunburst 75. Death Play 76. Cannonball 76. FM 78. Comes a Horseman 78. Lacy and the Mississippi Queen (TV) 78. Like Normal People (TV) 79. Hurricane 79. The Long Riders (as Jesse James) 80. Love Letters 83. The Razor's Edge 84. Wildcats 85. The Experts 89, etc.

Keach, Stacy (1941–).
American general-purpose actor.
■ The Heart Is a Lonely Hunter 68. End of the Road 68. The Travelling Executioner 69. Brewster McCloud 70. Doc 70. Judge Roy Bean 72. The New Centurions 72. Fat City 72. The Dion Brothers (TV) 74. All the Kind Strangers (TV) 74. Conduct Unbecoming 75. James Michener's Dynasty (TV) 76. Luther 76. Street People 76. The Killer Inside Me 76. The Squeeze 77. Jesus of Nazareth (TV) 77. Slave of the Cannibal God 78. Two Solitudes 78. Gray Lady Down 78. Up in Smoke 78. The Long Riders (as Frank James) 80. The Ninth Configuration 80. Cheech & Chong's Nice Dreams 81. Road Games 81. Butterfly 82. That Championship Season 82. Princess Daisy (TV) 83. Mistral's Daughter (TV) 84. Intimate Strangers (TV) 86. The Return of Mickey Spillane's Mike Hammer (TV) 86. Class of 1999 89. Mickey Spillane's Mike Hammer: Murder Takes All (TV) 89. False Identity 90. Milena (Geliebte Milena) 90. Mission of the Shark 91. Sunset Grill 92. Batman: Mask of the Phantasm (voice) 94. New Crime City 94.

TV series: Get Smart 66–67. Caribe 75. Mickey Spillane's Mike Hammer 84–87.

Keane, Robert Emmett (1883–1981).
Toothbrush-moustached American character actor who played travelling salesmen and fall guys in scores of light comedies and dramas.

Men Call It Love 31. Boys' Town 38. We're in the Army Now 40. Tin Pan Alley 41. Jitterbugs 43. When My Baby Smiles at Me 50. When Gangland Strikes 56, etc.

Kearton, Cherry (1871–1940).
Pioneer British travel film producer whose success lasted from 1912 to the mid-30s.

Keating, Larry (1897–1963).
American character actor, often as executive or uppity neighbour.

Whirlpool 49. Three Secrets 50. Come Fill the Cup 51. About Face 52. Inferno 53. Daddy Longlegs 55. The Buster Keaton Story 57. Who Was that Lady? 60. Boys' Night Out 62, many others.

TV series: *The Burns and Allen Show* 56–58. *Mister Ed* 60–62.

Keaton, Buster (1895–1966) (Joseph Francis Keaton).
One of America's great silent clowns, the unsmiling but game little fellow who always came out on top whatever the odds. In two-reelers with Fatty Arbuckle from 1917, but soon began to shape his own material. Special Academy Award 1959 'for his unique talents which brought immortal comedies to the screen'. Trained in vaudeville with family act. Did not easily survive sound, but later came back in featured roles and was gaining a fresh popularity at the time of his death.
Autobiography: 1960, *My Wonderful World of Slapstick*.
Biographies: 1966, *Keaton* by Rudi Blesh. 1969, *Buster Keaton* by David Robinson. 1989, *Keaton: The Man Who Wouldn't Lie Down* by Tom Dardis.
Keaton was played by Donald O'Connor in a 1957 biopic, *The Buster Keaton Story*.
■ FROM 1920: The Saphead 20. *One Week* 20. The High Sign 20. Convict 13 20. The Scarecrow 20. Neighbours 20. The Haunted House 21. The Goat 21. *The Playhouse* 22. *The Boat* 22. *The Paleface* 22. Cops 22. My Wife's Relations 22. The Blacksmith 22. The Frozen North 22. The Electric House 22. Daydreams 22. *Balloonatic* 22. The Love Nest 22. The Three Ages 23. *Our Hospitality* 23. *Sherlock Junior* 24. *The Navigator* 24. Seven Chances 25. Go West 25. Battling Butler 26. *The General* 27. College 27. Steamboat Bill Junior 27. *The Cameraman* 28. Spite Marriage 29. Hollywood Revue 29. Free and Easy 30. Doughboys 30. Parlor Bedroom and Bath 31. Sidewalks of New York 32. The Passionate Plumber 32. Speak Easily 32. What No Beer 33. Le Roi des Champs Elysées (Fr.) 34. An Old Spanish Custom (GB) 35. 18 Educational shorts 35–37. Hollywood Cavalcade 39. The Jones Family in Hollywood 39. Quick Millions 39. The Villain Still Pursued Her 40. Li'l Abner 40. Eight Columbia shorts 40–41. Forever and a Day 43. *San Diego I Love You* 44. That's the Spirit 45. That Night With You 46. God's Country 46. El Moderno Barba Azul (Mex.) 46. Duel to the Death (Fr.) 48. You're My Everything 49. The Loveable Cheat 50. In the Good Old Summertime 50. Sunset Boulevard 50. Limelight 52. Around the World in Eighty Days 56. Huckleberry Finn 60. Ten Girls Ago 62. It's a Mad Mad Mad Mad World 63. The Triumph of Lester Snapwill 63. *Railrodder* 65. Keaton Rides Again 65. Film 65. Pajama Party 65. Beach Blanket Bingo 65. How to Stuff a Wild Bikini 65. Two Marines and a General (It.) 65. A Funny Thing Happened on the Way to the Forum 66. The Scribe 66. Sergeant Deadhead 66.
⊙ For being the funniest and most inventive silent clown of them all. *The General*.

¶ Only things that one could imagine happening to real people, I guess, remain in a person's memory. – *B.K.*

He passes into the universal folk heritage as the supreme clown poet. – *David Robinson, 1968*

Keaton, Diane (1946–)
American leading lady of the 70s and 80s.
Biography: 1990, *Diane Keaton* by Jonathan Moor.
■ Lovers and Other Strangers 70. The Godfather 72. Play it Again Sam 72. Sleeper 74. Godfather Two 74. Love and Death 75. Harry and Walter Go to New York 76. I Will, I Will . . . for Now 76. *Annie Hall* 77. Looking for Mr Goodbar 77. Interiors 78. Manhattan 79. Reds (AAN) 81. Shoot the Moon 82. The Little Drummer Girl 84. Mrs Soffel 84. Crimes of the Heart 86. Baby Boom 87. Radio Days 87. The Good Mother 88. The Lemon Sisters 90. The Godfather Part III 90. Father of the Bride 91. Manhattan Murder Mystery 93. Look Who's Talking Now (voice) 93. Amelia Earhart: The Final Flight (TV) 94.

Keaton, Joseph (1878–1946).
American knockabout comedian who supported his son Buster in several of his best silents.

Keaton, Michael (1951–) (Michael Douglas).
American leading man. He played Batman in two big-budget films but declined to appear in a third.
■ Night Shift 82. Mr Mom 83. Johnny Dangerously 84. Gung Ho 85. Touch and Go 86. The Squeeze 87. Clean and Sober 88. Beetlejuice 88. Batman 89. The Dream Team 89. Pacific Heights 90. One Good Cop 91. Batman Returns 92. Much Ado about Nothing 93. My Life 93. The Paper 94. Speechless 94.

TV series: All's Fair 76. Working Stiffs 79.

Keats, Steven (1945–1994).
American general-purpose actor. Committed suicide.

The Story of Pretty Boy Floyd (TV) 74. The Dream Makers (TV) 75. Promise Him Anything (TV) 75. Black Sunday 76. Seventh Avenue (TV) 77. The Last Dinosaur (TV) 77. The Awakening Land (TV) 78. Zuma Beach (TV) 78. Silent Rage 82. The Executioner's Song (TV) 82. Eternity 90. Shadows and Fog 92, etc.

Kedrova, Lila (1918–).
Russian-French character actress, known internationally.

Zorba the Greek (AA) 64. A High Wind in Jamaica 65. Torn Curtain 66. Penelope 67. The Kremlin Letter 69. Soft Beds, Hard Battles 74. The Tenant 76. March or Die 77. Tell Me a Riddle 80. Sunset People 84. Sword of the Valiant 84. The Thrill of Genius 93. La Prossima Volta Il Fuoco 93, etc.

Keel, Howard (1917–) (Harold Keel).
Stalwart American leading man and singer whose career faltered when musicals went out of fashion.
■ The Small Voice (GB) 48. *Annie Get Your Gun* 50. Pagan Love Song 50. Three Guys Named Mike 51. *Showboat* 51. Texas Carnival 51. Callaway Went Thataway 51. Lovely to Look At 52. Desperate Search 52. Fast Company 53. Ride Vaquero 53. *Calamity Jane* 53. *Kiss Me Kate* 53. Rose Marie 54. *Seven Brides for Seven Brothers* 54. Deep in My Heart 54. Jupiter's Darling 54. Kismet 55. Floods of Fear (GB) 58. The Big Fisherman 59. Armored Command 61. The Day of the Triffids 63. Waco 66. Red Tomahawk 67. The War Wagon 67. Arizona Bushwhackers 68.

TV series: Dallas 81–91.

¶ I was one of God's chosen people, doing what I wanted to do in life. – *H.K.*

eeler, Ruby (1909–1993) (Ethel Keeler).
tite American singer-dancer who made a small
lent go a long way in musicals of the early 30s.
ae was married to Al Jolson (1928–40).
42nd Street 33. Gold Diggers of 1933. Footlight
rade 33. Dames 34. Flirtation Walk 35. Go Into
ur Dance 35. Shipmates Forever 35. Colleen 36.
eady Willing and Able 37. Mother Carey's
nickens 38. Sweetheart of the Campus 41. The
aynx 70.

een, Geoffrey (1916–).
cisive British character actor, son of Malcolm
een.
His Excellency 50. Genevieve 53. The Long Arm
5. No Love for Johnnie 61. The Spiral Road 62.
ve Now Pay Later 63. The Heroes of Telemark
. Dr Zhivago 65. Born Free 66. Taste the Blood
Dracula 70. Living Free 71. Doomwatch 72. The
y Who Loved Me 77. Moonraker 79. For Your
es Only 81. A View to a Kill 84. The Living
aylights 87, many others.

een, Malcolm (1888–1970).
ritish character actor, mostly on stage; father of
eoffrey Keen.
The Manxman 29. Sixty Glorious Years 39. The
reat Mr Handel 42. The Mating Season (US) 51.
ancis of Assisi 60, etc.

eene, Ralph (1902–1963).
ritish documentarist, in films from 1934. With
inistry of Information, British Transport, etc.:
mphasis on animal studies. *Cyprus Is an Island,
ofters, Journey into Spring, Between the Tides,
inter Quarters, Under Night Streets,* etc.

eene, Tom (1896–1963) (also known at times as
eorge Duryea and Richard Powers).
merican western star, mainly in second features
the 30s and 40s.
Godless Girl 28. The Dude Wrangler 30. Saddle
uster 32. Our Daily Bread 33. Where the Trails
vide 37. Dynamite Cargo 41. Up in Arms 44. If
u Knew Susie 48. Red Planet Mars 52. Plan 9
om Outer Space 56, many others.

eighley, William (1889–1984).
merican director with stage experience; made
any highly polished entertainments for
arner's.
The Match King 32. Ladies They Talk About 33.
asy to Love 34. Journal of a Crime 34. Dr Monica
4. Kansas City Princess 34. Big Hearted Herbert
4. Babbitt 34. The Right to Live 35. Mary Jane's
a 35. G Men 35. Special Agent 35. Stars over
roadway 35. The Singing Kid 36. Bullets or Ballots
5. *The Green Pastures* 36. God's Country and the
oman 37. The Prince and the Pauper 37. Varsity
now 37. The Adventures of Robin Hood (co-d)
8. Valley of the Giants 38. Secrets of an Actress
8. Brother Rat 38. Yes My Darling Daughter 39.
ach Dawn I Die 39. The Fighting 69th 40. Torrid
ne 40. No Time for Comedy 40. Four Mothers
1. The Bride Came COD 41. *The Man Who Came to
inner* 42. George Washington Slept Here 42.
oneymoon 47. The Street with No Name 48.
ocky Mountain 50. Close to My Heart 51. The
aster of Ballantrae 53.

eir, Andrew (1926–).
cottish character actor, usually in stern roles.
The Lady Craved Excitement 50. The Brave
on't Cry 52. The Maggie 54. Heart of a Child
7. Pirates of Blood River 60. Dracula, Prince of
arkness 65. Daleks Invasion Earth 2500 AD 65.
e Viking Queen 67. *Quatermass and the Pit* 67.
ne Royal Hunt of the Sun 69. Zeppelin 70. Blood

from the Mummy's Tomb 71. The Thirty-Nine
Steps 78. Absolution 80. Lion of the Desert 81.
Marco Polo (TV) 82. First Among Equals (TV) 86.
Rob Roy 95, etc.
TV series: Adam Smith 72. The Outsiders 77.

Keitel, Harvey (1939–).
American actor.
Mean Streets 73. Alice Doesn't Live Here Any
More 74. That's The Way of the World 75. Mother
Jugs and Speed 76. Taxi Driver 76. Buffalo Bill and
the Indians 76. The Duellists 77. Welcome to L.A.
77. Blue Collar 78. Fingers 78. Deathwatch 79.
Eagle's Wing 79. Bad Timing 80. Saturn Three 80.
The Border 82. Exposed 83. Order of Death 83.
Falling in Love 84. Camorra 85. Off Beat 85. The
Men's Club 86. Wise Guys 86. The Pick-Up Artist
87. The Last Temptation of Christ 88. The January
Man 89. Two Evil Eyes (Due Occhi Diabolici) 89.
The Two Jakes 90. Mortal Thoughts 91. Thelma
and Louise 91. Bugsy (AAN) 91. Reservoir Dogs
92. Bad Lieutenant 92. Sister Act 92. Point of No
Return 93. The Young Americans 93. Rising Sun
93. Snake Eyes 93. *The Piano* 93. Monkey Trouble
94. Pulp Fiction 94. Somebody to Love 94.
Imaginary Crimes 94. Clockers 95, etc.

Keith, Brian (1921–) (Robert Keith Jnr.).
American actor of easy-going types, understanding
fathers and occasional villains.
Arrowhead (debut) 52. Alaska Seas 53. The
Violent Men 54. Five against the House 55. Storm
Centre 56. Run of the Arrow 57. Sierra Baron 58.
The Young Philadelphians 59. The Deadly
Companions 61. The Parent Trap 61. Moon Pilot
62. Savage Sam 63. Those Calloways 65. The
Hallelujah Trail 65. *Nevada Smith* 66. The Russians
Are Coming 66. *Reflections in a Golden Eye* 67. With
Six You Get Eggroll 68. Krakatoa 68. Suppose They
Gave a War and Nobody Came 69. The Mackenzie
Break 70. Scandalous John 71. Something Big 72.
The Yakuza 75. *The Wind and the Lion* (as
Theodore Roosevelt) 76. The Quest (TV) 76.
Nickelodeon 76. Hooper 78. Meteor 79. The
Mountain Men 80. Charlie Chan and the Curse of
the Dragon Queen 81. Sharkey's Machine 81. Death
before Dishonor 87. Young Guns 88. Welcome
Home 89, etc.
TV series: Crusader 56. The Westerner 60. *Family
Affair* 66–70. The Little People 72–73. Archer 75.
Hardcastle and McCormick 83–86.

Keith, David (1954–).
American actor and occasional director.
The Rose 79. The Great Santini 79. Brubaker 80.
Take This Job and Shove It 81. Back Roads 81. An
Officer and a Gentleman 82. Independence Day
(TV) 83. The Lords of Discipline 83. Firestarter 84.
Gulag 85. The Curse (d) 87. The Further
Adventures of Tennessee Buck (& d) 88. The
Sacrifice (d) 88. Heartbreak Hotel 88. White of the
Eye 88. The Two Jakes 90. Off and Running 91.
Caged Fear 92. Desperate Motives 92. Major
League II 94, etc.
TV series: Flesh 'n' Blood 91.

Keith, Ian (1899–1960) (Keith Ross).
American actor, latterly in character roles.
Manhandled 24. The Divine Lady 27. Abraham
Lincoln 31. The Sign of the Cross 32. Queen
Christina 33. The Crusades 35. The Three
Musketeers (as de Rochefort) 36. The Sea Hawk 40.
The Chinese Cat 44. Nightmare Alley 48. The Black
Shield of Falworth 54. Prince of Players 55. The
Ten Commandments (as Rameses I) 56, many
others.

Keith, Penelope (1939–).
British character comedienne of haughty mien,
familiar from TV's *Kate, The Good Life* and *To the
Manor Born.*
Every Home Should Have One 71. Penny Gold
72. Ghost Story 73. The Priest of Love 81, etc.

¶ I was very tall and very plain – I wasn't going
to get very far on looks – so I thought I'd better
be the funny girl. – *P.K.*

Keith, Robert (1896–1966).
American character actor with concert and stage
experience. Father of actor Brian Keith.
The Other Kind of Love 24. Just Imagine 30.
Destry Rides Again 39. Boomerang 47. My Foolish
Heart 49. Fourteen Hours 51. I Want You 51. *The
Wild One* 53. *Young at Heart* 54. Guys and Dolls 55.
My Man Godfrey 57. Tempest 58. Cimarron 61,
etc.

Kelland, Clarence Buddington (1881–1964).
American light novelist and short-story writer
whose work was the basis of comedies of the 30s
and 40s. His stories of Scattergood Baines, a
cunning but seemingly ingenuous Yankee,
inspired four second features of the early 40s
starring Guy Kibbee.
French Heels (from Knots and Windshakers) 22.
Speak Easily (from Footlights) 32. Thirty-Day
Princess 34. Mr Deeds Goes to Town (from Opera
Hat) 36. The Cat's Paw 36. Strike Me Pink (from
Dreamland) 36. Stand In 37. Mr Dodd Takes the
Air (from The Great Crooner) 37. Arizona 40. For
Beauty's Sake (from Skin Deep) 41. Valley of the
Sun 42. Sugarfoot 51, etc.

Kellaway, Cecil (1891–1973).
British character actor born in South Africa, who
spent many years acting in Australia; came to
Hollywood in 1939 and became an endearing
exponent of roguish benevolence.
Wuthering Heights 39. Intermezzo 39. *I Married
a Witch* 42. My Heart Belongs to Daddy 42. The
Good Fellows (leading role) 43. Practically Yours
44. *Frenchman's Creek* 44. Love Letters 45. *Kitty*
(as Gainsborough) 45. Monsieur Beaucaire 46. The
Postman Always Rings Twice 46. Unconquered 47.
Portrait of Jennie 48. *The Luck of the Irish* (as a
leprechaun) (AAN) 48. Joan of Arc 48. *Harvey* 50.
The Beast from 20,000 Fathoms 53. The Female
on the Beach 55. The Shaggy Dog 59. The Cardinal
63. *Hush Hush, Sweet Charlotte* 64. Spinout 66.
Fitzwilly 67. Guess Who's Coming to Dinner
(AAN) 67. Getting Straight 70, many others.
✪ For being content to remain a star supporting
actor of unfailing roguish charm. *I Married a
Witch.*

Keller, Harry (1913–1987).
American director.
Blonde Bandit 49. Rose of Cimarron 52. The
Unguarded Moment 56. The Female Animal 57.
Quantez 58. Voice in the Mirror 58. Six Black
Horses 61. Tammy and the Doctor 63. Kitten with
a Whip 65. In Enemy Country (& p) 68, etc.

Keller, Helen (1881–1968).
Blind and deaf American lady whose problems
became the subject of *The Miracle Worker* 62. She
appeared to tell her story in one film, *Deliverance*
19.

Keller, Marthe (1945–).
Swiss leading lady in international films.
Funeral in Berlin 66. And Now My Love (Toute
une Vie) 74. Marathon Man 76. Black Sunday
76. Bobby Deerfield 77. Fedora 78. The Formula

80. The Amateur 82. Lapse of Memory (Mémoire Tranquée) 91. Mon Amie Max 94, etc.

Kellerman, Annette (1888–1975).
Australian dancer and swimming star who pioneered the one-piece bathing suit. Esther Williams played her in a biopic, *Million Dollar Mermaid* 52.
    Neptune's Daughter 14. Daughter of the Gods 16. Queen of the Sea 18. What Women Love 20, etc.

Kellerman, Sally (1938–   ).
American leading lady of the 70s.
    The Third Day 65. The Boston Strangler 68. The April Fools 69. M*A*S*H (AAN) 69. Brewster McCloud 70. Last of the Red Hot Lovers 72. Lost Horizon 73. Slither 73. Rafferty and the Gold Dust Twins 75. The Big Bus 76. Welcome to L.A. 77. Magee and the Lady (TV) 77. A Little Romance 79. Foxes 80. Head On 80. Loving Couples 80. Serial 80. Moving Violations 84. Back to School 86. That's Life 86. Meatballs III 87. You Can't Hurry Love 89. Boris and Natasha 90. The Player 92. Younger and Younger 93, etc.

Kellett, Bob (1927–   ).
British director.
    A Home of Your Own 64. San Ferry Ann 65. Girl Stroke Boy 71. Up the Chastity Belt 71. Up the Front 72. The Garnett Saga 72. Our Miss Fred 72. Spanish Fly 76. Are You Being Served? 77, etc.

Kelley, Barry (1908–1991).
Tough-looking Irish-American supporting actor, usually in gangster roles.
    Boomerang 47. The Asphalt Jungle 50. The Killer That Stalked New York 51. 711 Ocean Drive 52. The Long Wait 54. The Buccaneer 59. The Manchurian Candidate 62. The Love Bug 69, many others.

Kelley, De Forrest (1920–   ).
American general-purpose actor.
    Fear in the Night (leading role) 47. Duke of Chicago 50. House of Bamboo 55. Gunfight 57. Warlock 59. Johnny Reno 66. Star Trek 79. Star Trek II: The Wrath of Khan 82. Star Trek III: The Search for Spock 84. Star Trek IV: The Journey Home 86. Star Trek V: The Final Frontier 89. Star Trek VI: The Undiscovered Country 91, etc.
    TV series: *Star Trek* 66–68.

Kellin, Mike (1922–1983).
American actor; much TV.
    At War with the Army 52. Lonelyhearts 57. The Great Imposter 60. Invitation to a Gunfighter 63. The Boston Strangler 68. Assignment Danger (TV) 72. Connection (TV) 73. Freebie and the Bean 74. Midnight Express 78. The Jazz Singer 80. FDR: The Last Year (TV) 80. So Fine 81, many others.

Kellino, Pamela (1916–   ) (Pamela Ostrer; aka Pamela Mason).
British actress, married first to Roy Kellino and then to James Mason. Also columnist and TV personality.
    Jew Süss 34. I Met A Murderer 38. They Were Sisters 45. The Upturned Glass (& w) 47. Lady Possessed (& w) 51. The Navy vs The Night Monsters 66. Everything You Always Wanted to Know about Sex (but Were Afraid to Ask) 72, etc.

Kellino, Roy (1912–1956).
British cinematographer and director whose talent never quite displayed itself.
AS CINEMATOGRAPHER: The Phantom Light 37. The Last Adventurers 38. Johnny Frenchman 35, etc.

AS DIRECTOR: Catch as Catch Can 38. *I Met a Murderer* (& ph) 39. Guilt is My Shadow 49. Lady Possessed (US) 51. Charade 53. The Silken Affair 55, etc.

Kellino, Will P. (1873–1958) (William P. Gislingham).
British circus clown and acrobat, father of Roy Kellino. Made many early shorts as Pimple and Bumbles, characters from his stage act. Later became a director.

Kelljan, Robert (1930–1982) (Robert Kelljchian).
American director.
    Little Sister 69. Count Yorga Vampire 69. The Return of Count Yorga 71. Scream Blacula Scream 74. Went on to TV work.

Kelly, Emmett (1895–1979).
American character actor, former circus clown.
    Autobiography: 1968, *Clown*.
    The Fat Man 51. The Greatest Show on Earth 52. Wind Across the Everglades 58, etc.

Kelly, Gene (1912–   ) (Eugene Curran Kelly).
Breezy, bouncy American dancer who became one of Hollywood's great star personalities of the 40s and 50s, although his acting and singing abilities were minimal and his 'good guy' characterization wore a little thin. When musicals lamentably went out of fashion, he turned to direction. Special Academy Award 1951 'in appreciation of his versatility as an actor, singer, director and dancer, and specially for his brilliant achievements in the art of choreography on film'.
    Biography: 1974, *Gene Kelly* by Clive Hirschhorn.
■ For Me and My Gal 42. Pilot Number Five 42. Dubarry was a Lady 43. Thousands Cheer 43. The Cross of Lorraine 43. *Cover Girl* 44. Christmas Holiday 44. Anchors Aweigh (AAN) 45. Ziegfeld Follies 46. Living in a Big Way 47. *The Pirate* 48. *The Three Musketeers* 48. Words and Music 48. *Take Me Out to the Ball Game* 49. On the Town (& co-d) 49. Black Hand 50. Summer Stock 50. It's A Big Country 51. *An American in Paris* 51. *Singin' in the Rain* (& co-d) 52. The Devil Makes Three 52. Love is Better than Ever 52. Brigadoon 54. Seagulls over Sorrento (GB) 54. Deep in My Heart 54. It's Always Fair Weather 55. *Invitation to the Dance* (& d) 56. The Happy Road (& pd) 57. Les Girls 57. Marjorie Morningstar 58. The Tunnel of Love (d only) 58. Inherit the Wind 60. Let's Make Love (cameo) 60. Gigot (d only) 62. What a Way to Go 64. The Young Girls of Rochefort 67. A Guide for the Married Man (d only) 67. Hello Dolly (d only) 69. The Cheyenne Social Club (pd only) 70. Forty Carats 73. That's Entertainment 74. That's Entertainment Two 76. Women of the Year (TV) (d only) 76. Viva Knievel 77. Xanadu 80. That's Dancing! 85.
    TV series: Going My Way 62.
✪ For terpsichorean delights performed with cheerful proletarian grace. *Singin' in the Rain.*

¶ The days at MGM were marvellous. Everyone was pitching in. We had real collaboration. It was fun. We didn't think it was work. – *G.K.*
    Fred Astaire represents the aristocracy when he dances. I represent the proletariat. – *G.K.*
    His grin could melt stone. – *New Yorker, 1978*

Famous line (to Nina Foch in *An American in Paris*): 'That's quite a dress you almost have on.'

Kelly, Grace (1929–1982).
American leading lady of the 50s: her 'iceberg' beauty quickly made her a top star, but she retired to become Princess of Monaco. She died of injuries

sustained in a car crash. In 1983 Cheryl Ladd appeared in the title role of a TV movie, *Grace Kelly*.
    Biographies: 1976, *Princess Grace* by Gwen Robyns. 1994, *Grace* by Robert Lacey.
■ Fourteen Hours 51. High Noon 52. Mogambo (AAN) 53. Dial M for Murder 54. *Rear Window* 54. *The Country Girl* (AA) 54. Green Fire 54. The Bridges at Toko-Ri 54. To Catch a Thief 55. The Swan 56. *High Society* 56.

¶ I hated Hollywood. It's a town without pity. I know of no other place in the world where so many people suffer from nervous breakdowns, where there are so many alcoholics, neurotics, and so much unhappiness. – *G.K.*
    Writing about her is like trying to wrap up 115 pounds of smoke. – *Pete Martin*

Kelly, Jack (1927–1992).
Irish-American actor who usually plays wryly humorous roles; notably in TV series *Kings Row* and *Maverick*.
    Where Danger Lives 51. Drive a Crooked Road 54. To Hell and Back 56. Hong Kong Affair 58. Love and Kisses 65. Young Billy Young 69. Commando 73, etc.

Kelly, James (1931–1978).
British director.
■ The Beast in the Cellar 70. Night Hair Child 71.

Kelly, Judy (1913–   ).
Australian leading lady, in British films.
    Lord Camber's Ladies 32. His Night Out 35. Make Up 37. At the Villa Rose 40. Tomorrow We Live 43. The Butler's Dilemma 43. Dead of Night 45. Warning to Wantons 48, etc.

Kelly, Moira (1969–   ).
American actress.
    Billy Bathgate 91. The Cutting Edge 91. Twin Peaks: Fire Walk with Me 92. Chaplin 92. With Honors 94. Little Odessa 94, etc.

Kelly, Nancy (1921–1995).
American leading lady, former child model; in films 1938–47, then on Broadway stage.
    Submarine Patrol 38. *Tailspin* 38. Jesse James 39. Stanley and Livingstone 39. Parachute Battalion 41. Tornado 43. Show Business 44. Woman in Bondage 45. Betrayal from the East 45. Friendly Enemies 47. *The Bad Seed* (AAN) 56. Crowded Paradise 56. The Impostor (TV) 73, etc.

Kelly, Patsy (1910–1981).
Dumpy American comedienne of the 30s, often a pert wisecracker or a frightened maid.
    Going Hollywood 33. The Girl from Missouri 34. Go Into Your Dance 35. Page Miss Glory 35. Kelly the Second 36. Sing Baby Sing 36. Pigskin Parade 36. Wake and Live 37. Merrily We Live 38. The Gorilla 39. Road Show 41. Topper Returns 41. *Broadway Limited* 41. Sing Your Worries Away 42. My Son the Hero 43. Please Don't Eat the Daisies 60. The Naked Kiss 64. The Ghost in the Invisible Bikini 66. Rosemary's Baby 68. Freaky Friday 77. The North Avenue Irregulars 79, etc.
    TV series: Valentine's Day 64. The Cop and the Kid 76.

Kelly, Paul (1899–1956).
Wiry American leading man of the 30s and 40s, almost always in 'B' pictures.
    Uncle Sam of Freedom Ridge 20. The New Klondike 26. Slide Kelly Slide 27. The Girl from Calgary 32. Broadway Thro' a Keyhole 33. Side Streets 34. Public Hero Number One 35. The Silk Hat Kid 35. The Accusing Finger 36. Navy Blue

and Gold 37. Island in the Sky 38. Within the Law 39. The Roaring Twenties 39. Invisible Stripes 40. Queen of the Mob 40. Mystery Ship 41. Tarzan's New York Adventure 42. Flying Tigers 42. The Man from Music Mountain 43. Dead Man's Eyes 44. China's Little Devils 45. The Cat Creeps 46. Spoilers of the North 47. Fear in the Night 47. *Crossfire* 47. The File on Thelma Jordon 49. The Secret Fury 50. The Painted Hills 51. Springfield Rifle 52. Split Second 53. The High and the Mighty 54. The Square Jungle 55. Storm Center 56. Bail Out at 43,000 57, many others.

Kelly, Paula (1939–).
Tall, elegant American actress and dancer.
Sweet Charity 69. The Andromeda Strain 70. Trouble Man 72. Soylent Green 73. Uptown Saturday Night 74. Drum 76. Jo Jo Dancer, Your Life Is Calling 86, etc.

Kelly, Tommy (1928–).
American child actor of the 30s.
The Adventures of Tom Sawyer 38. Peck's Bad Boy with the Circus 38. Nice Girl 41. Mugtown 43, etc.

Kelsall, Moultrie (1901–1980).
Scottish character actor of stage and screen.
Landfall 49. The Lavender Hill Mob 51. The Master of Ballantrae 53. The Maggie 54. The Man Who Never Was 56. Violent Playground 58. The Battle of the Sexes 60. Greyfriars Bobbie 60. The Birthday Party 68. One More Time 70, etc.

Kelsey, Fred (1884–1961).
American small-part actor, often seen as lugubrious sheriff or cop on the beat.
The Four Horsemen of the Apocalypse 21. The Eleventh Hour 23. The Gorilla 27. The Last Warning 29. Guilty as Hell 32. One Frightened Night 35. The Lone Wolf Keeps a Date 40. The Adventures of Mark Twain 44. Bringing Up Father 46. Hans Christian Andersen 52. Racing Blood 54, many others.

Kelton, Pert (1907–1968).
American character comedienne, usually in hard-boiled roles.
Sally 29. *The Bowery* 33. Mary Burns Fugitive 35. Annie Oakley 35. Kelly the Second 36. Cain and Mabel 36. The Hit Parade 37. *The Music Man* 62. Love and Kisses 65. The Comic 69, etc.

Kemp, Gary (1960–).
English leading actor, guitarist and songwriter, a founder of the late-70s and 80s rock group Spandau Ballet, which also included his brother, Martin (qv).
The Krays 90. Bodyguard 92. Paper Marriage 93. Killing Zoe 94. Magic Hunter (Buvos Vadas) 94, etc.

Kemp, Jeremy (1934–) (Edmund Walker).
British leading man who resigned from TV series Z Cars and has had some success in films.
Dr Terror's House of Horrors 65. Operation Crossbow 65. Cast a Giant Shadow 66. The Blue Max 66. Face of a Stranger 66. Assignment K 67. The Strange Affair 68. Darling Lili 70. The Games 70. Eyewitness 70. The Belstone Fox 73. The Seven Per Cent Solution 76. A Bridge Too Far 77. The Rhinemann Exchange (TV) 77. East of Elephant Rock 78. Leopard in the Snow 78. Caravans 78. The Prisoner of Zenda 79. Return of the Soldier 82. The Winds of War (TV) 83. Sadat (TV) 83. George Washington (TV) 84. Top Secret 84. Peter the Great (TV) 86. When the Whales Came 89. Prisoners of Honor (TV) 91, etc.

Kemp, Martin (1961–).
English leading actor and musician, a member of the late-70s and 80s rock group Spandau Ballet, together with his brother Gary (qv).
The Krays 90. Fleshtone 94. Boca 94, etc.

Kemper, Victor J. (1927–).
American cinematographer.
Last of the Red Hot Lovers 72. The Candidate 72. Shamus 73. The Gambler 74. The Reincarnation of Peter Proud 75. Dog Day Afternoon 75. The Last Tycoon 76. Slapshot 77. Coma 78. The Jerk 79. The Final Countdown 80. Xanadu 80. Chu Chu and the Philly Flash 81. The Four Seasons 81. Partners 82. Author! Author! 82. Mr Mom 83. National Lampoon's Vacation 83. Cloak and Dagger 84. The Lonely Guy 84. Clue 85. Pee-Wee's Big Adventure 85. Secret Admirer 85. Walk Like a Man 87. Cohen and Tate 88. See No Evil, Hear No Evil 89. Crazy People 90. F/X2 91. Married to It 91. Another You 91. Beethoven 92, etc.

Kemplen, Ralph (1912–).
British editor.
The Ghost Train 31. The Ghoul 33. Scrooge 35. Broken Blossoms 36. The Saint Meets the Tiger 41. Carnival 46. Trottie True 49. Pandora and the Flying Dutchman 51. *The African Queen* 52. Moulin Rouge 52. Alexander the Great 56. *Room at the Top* 59. Freud 62. Night of the Iguana 64. A Man for All Seasons 66. Oliver! 68. The Day of the Jackal 73. The Omen 76, many others.
■ AS DIRECTOR: The Spaniard's Curse 58.

Kempson, Rachel (1910–).
British actress, widow of Michael Redgrave and mother of Vanessa, Lynn and Corin Redgrave.
The Captive Heart 46. A Woman's Vengeance (US) 48. Georgy Girl 66. The Jokers 66. Jennie (TV) 76. Out of Africa 85. Stealing Heaven 88, etc.

Kemp-Welch, Joan (1906–).
British character actress who used to play shy girls and spinsters on stage and screen. During the 50s emerged as a TV director of distinction.
Once a Thief 35. The Girl in the Taxi 37. Busman's Honeymoon 40. Pimpernel Smith 41. Jeannie 41 (last film to date), etc.

Kendall, Cyrus W. (1898–1953).
American character actor, a splendid cigar-chewing 'heavy' of the 30s.
The Dancing Pirate 36. Hot Money 36. They Won't Forget 37. The Shadow Strikes 37. Hawaii Calls 38. Stand Up and Fight 38. Angels Wash Their Faces 39. Men without Souls 40. Billy the Kid 41. Johnny Eager 42. The Whistler 44. She Gets Her Man 45, many others.

Kendall, Henry (1897–1962).
British entertainer, immaculate star of London revues in the 30s and 40s. On stage from 1914; occasional films.
Autobiography: 1960, *I Remember Romano's*.
Tilly of Bloomsbury 21. French Leave 30. Rich and Strange 32. King of the Ritz 33. Death at Broadcasting House 34. The Amazing Quest of Ernest Bliss 36. School for Husbands 37. The Butler's Dilemma 43. 29 Acacia Avenue 45. The Voice of Merrill 52. An Alligator Named Daisy 55, etc.

Kendall, Kay (1926–1959) (Justine McCarthy).
Vivacious, stylish British leading lady of the 50s. She was married to Rex Harrison from 1957 until her death from leukaemia.
■ Fiddlers Three 44. Dreaming 44. Champagne

Charlie 44. Waltz Time 45. *London Town* 46. Dance Hall 50. Night and the City 50. Happy Go Lovely 51. Lady Godiva Rides Again 51. Wings of Danger 52. Curtain Up 52. It Started in Paradise 52. Mantrap 52. Street of Shadows 53. The Square Ring 53. *Genevieve* 53. Meet Mr Lucifer 53. Fast and Loose 54. Abdullah the Great 54. Doctor in the House 54. The Constant Husband 55. *Simon and Laura* 55. Quentin Durward 56. Les Girls 57. *The Reluctant Debutante* 58. Once More with Feeling 60.

Kendall, Suzy (1944–) (Frieda Harrison).
British leading lady.
Circus of Fear 67. To Sir with Love 67. Penthouse 67. *Up the Junction* 68. Thirty Is a Dangerous Age, Cynthia 68. Fräulein Doktor 68. The Betrayal 69. Darker than Amber (US) 70. The Bird with the Crystal Plumage (It.) 70. Assault 71. Tales that Witness Madness 73. Craze 73. Fear Is the Key 73. The Demon Master 73. Torso 74. Adventures of a Private Eye 87, etc.

Kennaway, James (1928–1968).
British novelist and screenwriter.
Biography: 1983, *James and Jim: A Biography of James Kennaway* by Trevor Royle.
Violent Playground 58. Tunes of Glory (AAN) 61. The Mind Benders 63. The Shoes of the Fisherman (co-w) 68. The Battle of Britain (co-w) 69. Country Dance 70, etc.

Kennedy, Arthur (1914–1990).
American leading actor who, despite many intelligent performances, failed to achieve stardom.
■ City for Conquest 40. High Sierra 41. Strange Alibi 41. Knockout 41. Highway West 41. Bad Men of Missouri 41. They Died with Their Boots On 41. Desperate Journey 42. Air Force 43. *Devotion* (as Branwell Brontë) 46. Cheyenne 47. Boomerang 47. Too Late for Tears 49. *Champion* (AAN) 49. *The Window* 49. The Walking Hills 49. Chicago Deadline 49. *The Glass Menagerie* 50. *Bright Victory* (AAN) 51. Red Mountain 52. *Rancho Notorious* 52. The Girl in White 52. Bend of the River 52. The Lusty Men 52. Impulse (GB) 54. The Man from Laramie 55. The Naked Dawn 55. Trial (AAN) 55. The Desperate Hours 55. Crashout 55. The Rawhide Years 56. Peyton Place (AAN) 57. Twilight for the Gods 58. Some Came Running (AAN) 58. A Summer Place 59. Elmer Gantry 60. Home is the Hero 61. Claudelle Inglish 61. Murder She Said (GB) 62. Hemingway's Adventures of a Young Man 62. Barabbas 62. *Lawrence of Arabia* 62. Cheyenne Autumn 64. Joy in the Morning 65. Murieta 65. Italiano Brava Gente 65. Fantastic Voyage 66. Nevada Smith 66. Monday's Child (Arg.) 67. The Prodigal Gun 68. Anzio 68. The Day of the Evil Gun 68. Dead or Alive 68. Hail Hero 69. Shark 69. The Movie Murderer (TV) 70. Glory Boy 71. A Death of Innocence (TV) 71. The President's Plane Is Missing (TV) 71. Crawlspace (TV) 72. Nakia (TV) 74. The Living Dead at the Manchester Morgue 74. L'Anticristo 74. The Sentinel 77. Brutal Justice 78. Covert Action 78. The Humanoid 79. My Old Man's Place 88. Signs of Life 89. Grandpa 91.

Kennedy, Burt (1923–).
American director, originally radio writer (from 1947), later TV writer-director (*Combat* series, etc.).
The Canadians (wd) 61. Mail Order Bride (wd) 63. The Rounders (wd) 64. The Money Trap (d) 65. *Return of the Seven* 66. Welcome to Hard Times (wd) 67. *The War Wagon* 67. Monday's Child (Arg.) 67. *Support Your Local Sheriff* 69. Young Billy Young 69. The Good Guys and the Bad Guys 69. The Dubious Patriots 70. Support Your Local Gunfighter 71. The Deserter 71. Hannie Caulder 71. The Train Robbers (& w) 75. The Killer Inside

Me 76. Wolf Lake (& w) 79. The Wild Wild West Revisited (TV) 79. The Trouble with Spies 87. Once upon a Texas Train (aka Texas Guns) (TV) 88. Where the Hell's That Gold?!! (TV) 88. Suburban Commando 91. All the Kind Strangers 92, etc.etc.

Kennedy, Douglas (1915–1973) (formerly known as Keith Douglas).
American leading man of action features, later character actor.
The Way of All Flesh 40. Women without Names 41. Dark Passage 47. Chain Gang 50. I Was an American Spy 51. Ride the Man Down 53. Bomba and the Lion Hunters 54. The Amazing Transparent Man 59, many others.
TV series: Steve Donovan Western Marshal.

Kennedy, Edgar (1890–1948).
Bald, explosive American comedian with vaudeville experience. A former Keystone Kop, he continued in demand for supporting roles and also starred in innumerable domestic comedy two-reelers, his exasperated gestures being familiar the world over. His brother Tom Kennedy (1885–1965), also a Keystone Kop, became a professional wrestler, and later played bit parts in movies and TV right up to his death.
Tillie's Punctured Romance 15. The Leather Pushers 22. Midnight Patrol 31. *Duck Soup* 33. King Kelly of the USA 34. Captain Tugboat Annie 46. Unfaithfully Yours 48, many others.
⚙ For being one of Hollywood's instantly recognizable faces and for never failing to make one laugh. *Duck Soup*.

Kennedy, George (1925–).
American character actor, usually seen as menace but graduating to sympathetic roles.
Little Shepherd of Kingdom Come (debut) 60. Lonely Are the Brave 62. The Man from the Diners Club 63. *Charade* 63. Straitjacket 64. Mirage 65. Shenandoah 65. *The Flight of the Phoenix* 65. Hurry Sundown 67. The Dirty Dozen 67. *Cool Hand Luke* (AA) 67. Bandolero 68. The Boston Strangler 68. The Pink Jungle 69. Guns of the Magnificent Seven 69. The Good Guys and the Bad Guys 69. Airport 69. Tick Tick Tick 70. Fool's Parade 71. A Great American Tragedy (TV) 72. Lost Horizon 73. Cahill 73. Airport 75 74. Thunderbolt and Lightfoot 74. Earthquake 74. The Human Factor 75. The Eiger Sanction 75. Airport 77 77. The Double McGuffin 79. The Concorde – Airport '79 79. Death on the Nile 79. Backstairs at the White House (TV) 79. Steel 80. Modern Romance 81. Bolero 84. Rare Breed 84. Delta Force 85. Savage Dawn 85. Radioactive Dreams 86. Creepshow 2 87. Born to Race 88. Demonwarp 88. Esmeralda Bay 88. The Naked Gun: From the Files of Police Squad 88. Nightmare at Noon 88. Private Roads (No Trespassing) 88. Uninvited 88. Counterforce 89. Ministry of Vengeance 89. The Terror Within 89. Brain Dead 90. Hangfire 90. The Naked Gun 2½: The Smell of Fear 91. Naked Gun 33⅓: The Final Insult 94, etc.
TV series: *Sarge* 71. The Blue Knight 75–76.

Kennedy, John Fitzgerald (1917–1963).
The American president who was assassinated in Dallas has been the subject of several films and even more TV movies. His wartime experiences in the Pacific were turned into the dull *PT 109*, directed by Leslie H. Martinson and starring Cliff Robertson. Martin Sheen played him in a TV mini-series, *Kennedy* 83, which covered his presidential career; Paul Rudd in *Johnny We Hardly Knew Ye* 77, which dealt with his first political campaign in Boston; and James Franciscus in *Jacqueline Bouvier Kennedy* 81, a TV biopic of his wife's life. The confusions

surrounding his death have also been aired, notably in Oliver Stone's paranoid conspiracy account *JFK* 91, while *Ruby* 92 dealt with the fate of the night-club owner Jack Ruby, who shot Kennedy's killer, Lee Harvey Oswald.

Kennedy, Kathleen (1954–).
American producer, president of Amblin Entertainment, a company she formed with Steven Spielberg and Frank Marshall.
E.T. – the Extraterrestrial 81. Poltergeist 82. Gremlins 84. Indiana Jones and the Temple of Doom 84. The Color Purple 85. Back to the Future 85. The Money Pit 86. Batteries Not Included 86. An American Tail 87. Empire of the Sun 87. Who Framed Roger Rabbit? 88. The Land before Time 88. Back to the Future II 89. Hook 91. Alive 92. Jurassic Park 93. Milk Money 94, etc.

Kennedy, Madge (1892–1987).
American star of silent films, from the stage; retired in the mid-20s and then returned to the screen in the 50s as a character actress.
Baby Mine 17. A Perfect Lady 18. The Truth 20. Help Yourself 21. Scandal Sheet 25. Oh Baby! 26. The Marrying Kind 52. The Rains of Ranchipur 55. Three Bad Sisters 56. Lust for Life 56. Houseboat 58. Let's Make Love 60. They Shoot Horses, Don't They? 69. The Baby Maker 70. The Day of the Locust 75. Marathon Man 76, etc.

Kennedy, Margaret (1896–1967).
British best-selling sentimental novelist; *The Constant Nymph* and her play *Escape Me Never* were each filmed more than once.

Kennedy, Merna (1908–1944) (Maude Kahler).
American leading lady of the late 20s. Retired to marry Busby Berkeley.
The Circus 28. Broadway 30. Laughter in Hell 32. Arizona to Broadway 33. Police Call 33. I Like It That Way 34, etc.

Kennedy, Tom:
see *Kennedy, Edgar*.

Kenney, James (1930–1982).
English leading actor, in films from 1941 and on stage from 1944, also a revue and cabaret performer. The son of vaudeville comedian and occasional actor Horace Kenney, he studied at the Italia Conti Stage School and first attracted notice as a juvenile psychopath in *Cosh Boy*, on stage 51, and screen.
Circus Boy 47. Captain Horatio Hornblower 50. The Gentle Gunman 52. *Cosh Boy* 53. The Sea Shall Not Have Them 54. The Gelignite Gang 56. Son of a Stranger 58. Hidden Homicide 59. Ambush in Leopard Street 66. A Big Hand for a Little Lady (GB: Big Deal at Dodge City) 66, etc.

Kensit, Patsy (1968–).
Baby-faced English actress and singer; in TV commercials, programmes and films as a child, now making the transition to adult stardom.
The Great Gatsby 74. Alfie Darling 75. The Bluebird 76. Hanover Street 79. Silas Marner (TV) 85. Absolute Beginners 86. A Chorus of Disapproval 89. Lethal Weapon 2 89. Chicago Joe and the Showgirl 90. Bullseye! 91. Twenty-One 91. Adam Bede (TV) 91. Timebomb 91. Blame It on the Bellboy 92. Prince of Shadows (Beltenebros) 92. The Turn of the Screw 92. Kleptomania 93. Bitter Harvest 93. Angels and Insects 95, etc.

Kent, Jean (1921–) (Joan Mildred Summerfield).
British leading lady of the 40s, on stage aged ten, formerly (as Jean Carr) in the Windmill chorus.

■ The Rocks of Valpre (debut) 35. Who's Your Father 35. Frozen Limits 39. Hallo Fame! 40. It's That Man Again 42. Miss London Ltd 43. Warn That Man 43. Bees in Paradise 43. Fanny by Gaslight 44. *Waterloo Road* 44. Soldier, Sailor 44. 2000 Women 44. Champagne Charlie 44. Madonna of the Seven Moons 44. The Wicked Lady 45. The Rake's Progress 45. Caravan 46. Carnival 46. The Magic Bow 46. The Man Within 47. The Loves of Joanna Godden 47. *Good Time Girl* 48. Bond Street 48. Sleeping Car to Trieste 48. *Trottie True* 49. The Reluctant Widow 50. The Woman in Question 50. Her Favourite Husband 50. The Browning Version 51. The Lost Hours (aka The Big Frame) 52. Before I Wake 54. The Prince and the Showgirl 57. Bonjour Tristesse 58. Grip of the Strangler 58. Beyond This Place 59. Please Turn Over 60. Bluebeard's Ten Honeymoons 60. Shout at the Devil 76.
TV series: *Sir Francis Drake* (as Queen Elizabeth I) 62–63. *Tycoon* 78. Crossroads 81–82. Lovejoy 91. Shrinks 91.

Kent, Kenneth (1882–1963).
British actor and singer, mostly on stage.
House of the Arrow 39. Night Train to Munich 40.

Kenton, Erle C. (1896–1980).
American director, from 1914.
Small Town Idol 20. The Leather Pushers 22. Street of Illusion 25. Father and Son 27. Isle of Lost Souls 32. Remedy for Riches 39. Petticoat Politics 41. North to the Klondike 41. Ghost of Frankenstein 42. Who Done It? 42. Frisco Lil 42. House of Frankenstein 45. *House of Dracula* 45. Should Parents Tell? 49. Killer with a Label 50, etc.

Kenyon, Doris (1897–1979).
American silent-screen leading lady who was married to Milton Sills.
The Pawn of Fate 16. A Girl's Folly 17. The Hidden Hand 18. The Ruling Passion 22. Monsieur Beaucaire 24. Blonde Saint 26. The Hawk's Nest 28. Alexander Hamilton 31. Voltaire 33. Counsellor at Law 33. The Man in the Iron Mask 39, etc.
TV series: Tycoon 64.

Kerima (1925–).
Algerian actress.
An Outcast of the Islands 51. La Lupa 52. The Quiet American 58. Jessica 62, etc.

Kern, James V. (1909–1966).
American director, former lawyer.
That's Right You're Wrong 39. You'll Find Out 40. *Thank Your Lucky Stars* 43. The Doughgirls (wd) 44. Never Say Goodbye (wd) 46. Stallion Road 47. April Showers 48. Two Tickets to Broadway 52, etc.

Kern, Jerome (1885–1945).
Celebrated American songwriter. His Academy Award songs are 'The Way You Look Tonight' and 'The Last Time I Saw Paris'.
Roberta 35. Showboat 35 and 51. Swing Time 36. Cover Girl 44. Can't Help Singing 44. Centennial Summer 46. Till the Clouds Roll By (in which he was played by Robert Walker) 46.

Kerouac, Jack (1922–1969).
American novelist of the Beat generation, a legend he helped to create before dying of drink. *Heart Beat* was a film about him; there was also an underground film of his autobiographical *On the Road*.

Kerr, Bill (1922–).
South African-born stand-up comedian and character actor, in Australia from childhood. He

rformed in Britain from the 50s in radio and TV
medy with Tony Hancock before returning to
ustralia in the 70s.
  Harmony Row (as Willie Kerr) 33. The Silence
Dean Maitland 34. Appointment in London 52.
e Dam Busters 55. The Shiralee 57. The
aptain's Table 58. The Wrong Arm of the Law 63.
octor in Distress 63. Doctor in Clover 66. A
nny Thing Happened on the Way to the Forum
. Tiffany Jones 73. Deadline 81. Gallipoli 82. The
rate Movie 82. The Year of Living Dangerously
. Razorback 83. Dusty 84. Vigil 84. The Coca
ola Kid 84. The Lighthorsemen 87. Miracle Down
nder 87. Sweet Talker 91. Round the Bend 92,
c.

err, Deborah (1921–) (Deborah Kerr-
rimmer).
ritish leading lady usually cast in well-bred roles.
e received an honorary Oscar 'for career
chievement' in 1994.
  Biography: 1977, *Deborah Kerr* by Eric Braun.
  Major Barbara (debut) 40. *Love on the Dole* 41.
nn of Pennsylvania 41. Hatter's Castle 41. The
ay Will Dawn 42. *The Life and Death of Colonel
imp* 43. *Perfect Strangers* 45. *I See a Dark Stranger*
. *Black Narcissus* 46. The Hucksters 47. If Winter
omes 48. Edward My Son (AAN) 49. Please
elieve Me 49. King Solomon's Mines 50. Quo
adis 51. Thunder in the East 51. The Prisoner of
enda 52. Dream Wife 52. Julius Caesar 53. *From
ere to Eternity* (AAN) 53. Young Bess 53. The End
the Affair 55. *The King and I* (AAN) 56. The
roud and Profane 56. *Tea and Sympathy* 56.
eaven Knows Mr Allison (AAN) 56. *An Affair to
emember* 57. *Separate Tables* (AAN) 58. Bonjour
ristesse 58. Count Your Blessings 59. The Journey
9. Beloved Infidel 59. *The Sundowners* (AAN) 60.
e Grass Is Greener 61. *The Innocents* 61. The
aked Edge 61. The Chalk Garden 63. *The Night
the Iguana* 64. Marriage on the Rocks 65. Eye of
e Devil 66. Casino Royale 67. *Prudence and the
ll* 68. The Gypsy Moths 69. The Arrangement 69.
itness for the Prosecution (TV) 84. Reunion at
airborough (TV) 85. The Assam Garden 85. A
oman of Substance (TV) 85.

  All the most successful people these days seem
to be neurotic. Perhaps we should stop being
rry for them and start being sorry for me – for
eing so confounded normal. – *D.K.*

err, Frederick (1858–1933) (Frederick Keen).
ritish character actor of stage and, latterly,
merican screen; delightful as slightly doddering
ld man.
  The Honour of the Family 27. Raffles 29. *The
evil to Pay* 30. *Frankenstein* (as the old baron) 31.
aterloo Bridge 31. The Midshipman 32. The Man
om Toronto 33, etc.

err, Jean (1923–) (Jean Collins).
merican humorist and playwright, wife of Walter
err the drama critic. Her contributions to film
clude *Mary Mary* and *Please Don't Eat the Daisies;
ritic's Choice* was probably based on her.

err, John (1931–).
merican leading man, now a lawyer.
  The Cobweb 55. Gaby 56. *Tea and Sympathy* 56.
outh Pacific 58. The Pit and the Pendulum 61.
even Women from Hell 62, etc.

errigan, J. M. (1885–1964).
rish character actor who went with the Abbey
layers to Hollywood in 1935, and stayed there.
  Little Old New York 23. Song of My Heart 30.
he Informer 35. Laughing Irish Eyes 36. Little

Orphan Annie 39. Captains of the Clouds 42. Black
Beauty 46. The Wild North 52. The Fastest Gun
Alive 56, many others.

Kerrigan, J. Warren (1880–1947).
American actor of the silent screen.
  Samson 13. Landon's Legacy 16. A Man's Man
18. The Covered Wagon 23. Captain Blood 24,
etc.

Kerry, Norman (1889–1956) (Arnold Kaiser).
American actor of the silent screen.
  The Black Butterfly 16. Merry Go Round 23. The
Hunchback of Notre Dame 23. Phantom of the
Opera 26. The Unknown 28. Air Eagles 31, many
others.

Kershner, Irvin (1923–).
American director.
  ■ Stakeout on Dope Street 58. The Young
Captives 59. The Hoodlum Priest 61. Face in the
Rain 63. The Luck of Ginger Coffey 64. A Fine
Madness 66. The Flim Flam Man 67. Loving 70.
Up The Sandbox 72. S.P.Y.S. 74. The Return of a
Man Called Horse 76. Raid on Entebbe (TV) 76.
The Eyes of Laura Mars 78. The Empire Strikes
Back 80. Never Say Never Again 83. Wildfire (p)
88. Robocop 2 90.

Kessel, Joseph (1898–1979).
German novelist.
  Works filmed: The Lion 62. Belle de Jour 67.
The Horsemen 75.

Ma and Pa Kettle.
Hillbilly couple played in *The Egg and I* 47, and in
a subsequent long-running series of comedy
second features, by Marjorie Main and Percy
Kilbride. Highly successful in US, less so in
Britain.
  The films were as follows:
1949: *Ma and Pa Kettle*
1950: *Ma and Pa Kettle Go To Town*
1951: *Ma and Pa Kettle Back on the Farm*
1952: *Ma and Pa Kettle at the Fair*
1953: *Ma and Pa Kettle on Vacation*
1954: *Ma and Pa Kettle at Home*
1955: *Ma and Pa Kettle at Waikiki*
1956: *The Kettles in the Ozarks*
1957: (with Parker Fennelly replacing Percy
        Kilbride) *The Kettles on Old MacDonald's Farm*

Keyes, Evelyn (1919–).
American leading lady of the 40s, originally a
dancer. She was married to directors Charles Vidor
(1943–45) and John Huston (1946–50), and
married bandleader Artie Shaw, from whom she
is now separated, in 1957.
  Autobiographies: 1977, *Scarlett O'Hara's Younger
Sister.* 1991, *I'll Think about That Tomorrow.*
  The Buccaneer (debut) 38. Gone with the Wind
39. Before I Hang 40. The Face behind the Mask
41. Here Comes Mr Jordan 41. Ladies in
Retirement 41. Flight Lieutenant 42. The
Adventures of Martin Eden 42. The Desperadoes
43. Nine Girls 44. A Thousand and One Nights
44. *The Jolson Story* 46. Renegades 46. Johnny
O'Clock 47. The Mating of Millie 48. Enchantment
48. Mrs Mike 49. House of Settlement 49. The
Killer That Stalked New York 50. Smugglers' Island
51. *The Prowler* 51. Rough Shoot (GB) 52. The
Seven Year Itch 54. Hell's Half Acre 54. Around
the World in Eighty Days 56. Across 110th Street
72. Return to Salem's Lot 87. Wicked Stepmother
88, etc.

Keys, Anthony Nelson (1913–1985).
British producer, associated with Hammer horror.

Son of actor/comedian Nelson Keys (1887–1939).
  Pirates of Blood River 63. The Gorgon 63.
Dracula Prince of Darkness 65. Quatermass and the
Pit 68, etc.

Keys, Nelson (1887–1939).
English actor and comedian, mainly on stage and
in film from silents. He was the father of producer
Anthony Nelson Keys and writer and director John
Paddy Carstairs (qqv).
  Drowsy Dick's Dream 10. Once upon a Time 18.
Triumph of the Scarlet Pimpernel 28. Almost a
Divorce 31. The Last Journey 35. In the Soup 36.
Knights for a Day 37, etc.

Keystone.
A company established in 1912 to produce
comedies. Run by Mack Sennett, who also directed
and edited most of the films, the company's early
films featured Mabel Normand and created a fast
and furious slapstick comedy. Its star performers
included Fatty Arbuckle, Charlie Chaplin, Chester
Conklin and Mack Swain. Sennett's second
innovation came in 1915 when he introduced his
Bathing Beauties to add some glamour. Sennett
left Keystone in 1917 to work for Paramount and
the company soon foundered without him.

The Keystone Kops.
A troupe of slapstick comedians led by Ford
Sterling who, from 1912–20 under the
inspiration of Mack Sennett at Keystone Studios,
made innumerable violent comedies full of wild
chases and trick effects. *Abbott and Costello Meet the
Keystone Kops* 55 was a somewhat poor tribute.

Khambatta, Persis (1950–).
Indian leading lady in Hollywood films.
  Star Trek 79. Nighthawks 81. Megaforce 82. First
Strike 85. Warrior of the Lost World 84. Phoenix
the Warrior 88, etc.

Khayyam, Omar (1048–1122) (Gheyas Od-Din
Abu al-Fath).
Persian poet whose *Rubaiyat,* freely translated in
1859 by Edward Fitzgerald, became a bag of
popular clichés and was heavily quoted in the
artier Hollywood films, notably those of Albert
Lewin. The film called *Omar Khayyam* was a sword-
and-sandal epic having nothing to do with the
known facts of Omar's life, which are scant.

Kiarostami, Abbas (1940–).
Iranian director.
  The Passenger 72. The Report 77. First Graders
85. Where Is My Friend's House 87. Life and
Nothing More 92. Under the Olive Trees 94, etc.

Kibbee, Guy (1882–1956).
Bald-headed American character comedian,
usually in flustered, shifty or genial roles.
  Stolen Heaven (debut) 31. City Streets 32.
Forty-second Street 33. *Dames* 34. *Babbitt* 34.
Captain January 35. Mr Smith Goes to Washington
39. Chad Hanna 41. Scattergood Baines 41. The
Power of the Press 43. The Horn Blows at Midnight
45. Gentleman Joe Palooka 47. Fort Apache 48.
Three Godfathers 49.

Kibbee, Roland (1914–1984).
American radio, TV and screen writer.
  A Night in Casablanca 45. Angel on My Shoulder
46. *Vera Cruz* 54. Top Secret Affair 57. The
Appaloosa 66. Valdez is Coming (& p) 71. The
Midnight Man (& co-w, co-d) 75, etc.

Kid Galahad.
A boxing drama, thought at the time of its release

to be one of the best of its kind, directed by Michael Curtiz, starring Edward G. Robinson and Bette Davis and introducing Wayne Morris. It was remade in a disguised form as *The Wagons Roll at Night* 41, with Humphrey Bogart; then it turned up again in 1962 as an Elvis Presley vehicle, directed by Phil Karlson.

Kidd, Michael (1919–) (Milton Greenwald).
American dancer and dance director.
Where's Charley? (choreography only) 52. Band Wagon 53. *Seven Brides for Seven Brothers* 54. *It's Always Fair Weather* 54. Guys and Dolls 55. Merry Andrew (& d) 58. Hello Dolly 69. Smile 75. Movie Movie 79, etc.

Kidder, Margot (1948–).
Canadian leading lady.
■ Gaily Gaily 69. Quackser Fortune 70. Suddenly Single (TV) 71. The Bounty Man (TV) 72. Sisters 72. The Dion Brothers (TV) 74. Honky Tonk (TV) 74. The Great Waldo Pepper 75. Black Christmas 75. The Reincarnation of Peter Proud 75. 92 in the Shade 77. *Superman* 78. The Amityville Horror 79. Superman II 80. Willie and Phil 80. Some Kind of Hero 82. Heartaches 82. Trenchcoat 83. Superman III 83. Picking up the Pieces (TV) 85. Gobots: Battle of the Rock Lords (voice) 86. Vanishing Act (TV) 86. Superman IV: The Quest for Peace 87. Body of Evidence (TV) 88. Mob Story 89. To Catch a Killer (TV) 91. The Pornographer 94.
TV series: Nichols 71–72. Shell Game 87.

Kidman, Nicole (1968–).
Tall Australian leading actress, now in America. She married actor Tom Cruise in 1990.
Prince and the Great Race 83. BMX Bandits 84. Windrider 87. Night Master 87. Dead Calm 89. Flirting 89. Days of Thunder 90. Billy Bathgate 91. Far and Away 92. My Life 93. Malice 93. To Die For 94. Batman Forever 95, etc.

kidnapping
has been the subject of a great number of films; apart from the various versions of Robert Louis Stevenson's *Kidnapped*, examples include *Nancy Steele Is Missing, No Orchids for Miss Blandish, Ransom, The Kidnappers, A Cry in the Night, Cry Terror, Tomorrow at Ten, High and Low, My Name Is Julia Ross, Seance on a Wet Afternoon, The Collector, The Happening, Bunny Lake Is Missing, Bonnie and Clyde, Big Jake, The Night of the Following Day, The Grissom Gang, Murder on the Orient Express, The Man Who Loved Cat Dancing, Night People, Funeral in Berlin, Sugarland Express, The Wind and the Lion*, and on TV *The Longest Night* and *The Lindbergh Kidnapping Case.*

Kidron, Beeban (1962–).
British director, from television. She worked as a photographer's assistant before studying at the National Film School.
Oranges Are Not the Only Fruit (TV) 90. Used People (US) 93. Great Moments in Aviation 94. To Wong Foo, Thanks for Everything, Julie Newmar (US) 95.

Kiel, Richard (1939–).
American giant (7-foot) actor who came into his own as an adversary for James Bond.
House of the Damned 62. The Magic Sword 62. The Human Duplicators 65. Silver Streak 66. *The Spy Who Loved Me* 77. Force Ten from Navarone 78. Humanoid 78. Moonraker 79. So Fine 81. Hysterical 83. Pale Rider 85. Think Big 90. The Giant of Thunder Mountain (& p, co-w) 91, etc.

¶ My wife is 5' 4" and everybody asks me how we do it. – *R.K.*

Kieling, Wolfgang (1924–).
German character actor.
Maria die Magd (debut) 36. Falstaff in Wien 40. Damsels in Paris 56. Torn Curtain (US) 66. Goya 71. Dollars (US) 72. Out of Order 84, etc.

Kiepura, Jan (1902–1966).
Polish operatic tenor.
Farewell to Love (GB) 30. *My Song for You* (GB) 31. Be Mine Tonight (GB) 32. Give Us This Night (US) 36. Her Wonderful Lie (It.) 50.

Kier, Udo (1944–).
German actor in international films.
Mark of the Devil 69. Blood for Dracula 74. Andy Warhol's Frankenstein 74. Suspiria 77. Lili Marleen 80. My Own Private Idaho 91. Europa (US: Zentropa) 92. Josh and S.A.M. 93. Ace Ventura, Pet Detective 94, etc.

Kiéslowski, Krzysztof (1941–).
Polish director and screenwriter who has worked extensively in television. He won the Golden Lion for best picture at the 1993 Venice Film Festival with *Three Colours: Blue.*
Autobiography: 1992, *Kiéslowski on Kiéslowski.*
The Scar (Blizna) 76. Camera Buff (Amator) 79. Blind Chance (Przypadek) 82. Bez Konka (No End) 84. Dekalog (TV) 88–89. A Short Film about Killing (AA) 88. A Short Film about Love 88. The Double Life of Veronique (Podwojne zycie Weronki) 91. *Three Colours: Blue* (Trois Couleurs: Bleu) 93. Three Colours: White (Trois Couleurs: Blanc) 94. Three Colours: Red (Trois Couleurs: Rouge) 94, etc.

¶ I've realised that basically I don't give a shit for society which, in the case of Poland, is forty million people. But what I really care about is the individual human being. – *K.K.*
I don't think people want to be equal. Each of us wants to be a little better. We all want to be better than our neighbours and a bit more loved. We all want to be a bit richer and have a better car or TV. We all want to be a bit healthier and suffer less than others. We all want to die a slightly quieter and more peaceful death. – *K.K.*

Kilbride, Percy (1888–1964).
American character actor of wily hayseed roles. Died from injuries received in a car crash.
White Woman 33. Soak the Rich 36. George Washington Slept Here 42. Knickerbocker Holiday 44. She Wouldn't Say Yes 45. The Well-Groomed Bride 45. The Egg and I 47. Ma and Pa Kettle (series) 47–55.

Kilburn, Terry (1926–).
British boy actor of the 30s; never quite made it as adult. Now a drama teacher in America.
A Christmas Carol 38. The Boy from Barnardo's 38. Sweethearts 39. Goodbye Mr Chips (as three generations of Colley) 39. The Swiss Family Robinson 40. A Yank at Eton 42. National Velvet 45. Bulldog Drummond at Bay 47. Only the Valiant 51. The Fiend without a Face 58. Lolita 62, etc.

Kiley, Richard (1922–).
American general-purpose actor with stage experience; has latterly become a Broadway musical star.
The Mob 51. The Sniper 52. Pick Up on South Street 52. The Blackboard Jungle 55. The Phenix City Story 56. Spanish Affair 58. Pendulum 69.

AKA Cassius Clay 70. Murder Once Removed (TV 71. The Little Prince 73. Friendly Persuasion (TV 75. The Macahans (TV) 76. Looking for Mr Goodb. 77. Endless Love 81. Angel on My Shoulder (TV 81. Howard the Duck 86. My First Love (TV) 88. Absolute Strangers (TV) 91, etc.

Kilian, Victor (1897–1979).
American character actor, usually as suspicious o downright villainous characters. He was murdere by burglars.
The Wiser Sex 32. Air Hawks 35. Seventh Heaven 36. Dr Cyclops 39. Reap the Wild Wind 4. Spellbound 45. Gentleman's Agreement 47. The Flame and the Arrow 50. Tall Target 51, etc.
1976: on TV in *Mary Hartman, Mary Hartman.*

Killiam, Paul (1916–).
American collector of silent movies, clips from which he introduces on TV in various series.

Kilmer, Val (1959–).
American leading actor, married to actress Joann Whalley-Kilmer. He took over the role of Batma from Michael Keaton in *Batman Forever* 95.
Top Secret! 84. Real Genius 85. Top Gun 86. Willow 88. Kill Me Again 89. *The Doors* 91. Thunderheart 92. True Romance 93. The Real McCoy 93. Tombstone 94, etc.

Kilpatrick, Lincoln (1933–).
American actor.
Cool Breeze 72. Soul Soldier 72. Soylent Greer 73. Chosen Survivors 74. Uptown Saturday Nigh 74. Prison 88, etc.

Kimmins, Anthony (1901–1964).
British actor-writer-producer-director, almost entirely of light comedy subjects.
The Golden Cage (a) 33. White Ensign (a) 34. While Parents Sleep (w) 35. Keep Your Seats Please (w) 36. Talk of the Devil (w) 36. *Keep Fit* (wd) 37. The Show Goes On (w) 37. I See Ice (wd 38. It's In the Air (wd) 38. Trouble Brewing (wd) 39. Under Your Hat (wd) 40. *Mine Own Execution* (pd) 47. Bonnie Prince Charlie (d) 48. Flesh and Blood (d) 50. Mr Denning Drives North (d) 51. Wh Goes There? (d) 52. *The Captain's Paradise* (wpd) 53. Aunt Clara (d) 54. Smiley (pd) 56. *The Amorous Prawn* (wpd) 62, etc.

Kinematograph Renters' Society (K.R.S.).
This British organization was founded by film distributors in 1915 for their own protection and collective bargaining power, chiefly against exhibitors.

Kinescope.
American term for what the British call a telerecording, i.e. a live or tape show transferred for convenience on to tape. The technical quality is seldom satisfactory, and the process was gradually discontinued in favour of electronic tap conversion from one line standard to another.

Kinetoscope.
An early film viewing apparatus (1893) in which a continuous loop of film could be viewed by one person only.

King, Alan (1927–) (Irwin Kniberg).
American cabaret comedian who has made a few film appearances.
Hit the Deck 55. Miracle in the Rain 56. The Helen Morgan Story 57. On the Fiddle (GB) 61. Bye Bye Braverman 68. The Anderson Tapes 71. Just Tell Me What You Want 80. Author! Author 82. I the Jury 82. Lovesick 83. Cat's Eye 84.

Memories of Me 88. Enemies, a Love Story 89. The Bonfire of the Vanities 90, etc.

King, Allan (1930–).
Canadian documentarist.

Skid Row 56. Morocco 58. Rickshaw 60. The Pursuit of Happiness 62. Warrendale 66. The New Woman 68. A Married Couple 69. Who Has Seen the Wind 77. One Night Stand 79. Silence of the North 81. Ready for Slaughter (TV) 83. The Last Season (TV) 86. Termini Station 89, etc.

King, Andrea (1915–) (Georgetta Barry).
French-American leading lady with experience on the New York stage.

The Very Thought of You 44. Hotel Berlin 45. The Man I Love 46. Shadow of a Woman 46. The Violent Hour 50. The Lemon Drop Kid 51. Red Planet Mars 53. Band of Angels 57. Darby's Rangers 58. Daddy's Gone A-Hunting 69, etc.

King, Anita (1889–1963).
American leading lady of the silent screen, who came to fame in *The Virginian* 14.

King Arthur:
see *Arthur*.

King, Charles (1889–1944).
American song and dance man of the 20s.

Broadway Melody 28. Hollywood Revue 29. Chasing Rainbows 30, etc.

King, Charles (1889–1957).
American character actor, usually a western heavy.

Range Law 32. Mystery Ranch 34. O'Malley of the Mounted 36. The Mystery of the Hooded Horsemen 37. Son of the Navy 40. Gunman from Bodie 42. Ghost Rider 43, etc.

¶ Old Charlie King – I must have killed him at least 20 times. Usually it was behind the same rock. – *Tex Ritter*

King, Dave (1929–).
British TV comedian of the 60s; made a few film appearances.

Pirates of Tortuga 61. Go to Blazes 62. Strange Bedfellows 65. Cuba 79. The Long Good Friday 81. Reds 81, etc.

King, Dennis (1897–1971) (Dennis Pratt).
British-born opera singer who in the early 30s starred in Hollywood films.

The Vagabond King 30. Fra Diavolo 33.

King, George (1900–1966).
British producer-director, mainly of independent quota quickies and melodramas.

Too Many Crooks (p) 30. John Halifax Gentleman (p) 36. The Chinese Bungalow (pd) 39. The Case of the Frightened Lady (pd) 40. The Face at the Window (pd) 40. The First of the Few (p) 42. Tomorrow We Live (pd) 42. Candlelight in Algeria (pd) 44. Gaiety George (pd) 45. The Shop at Sly Corner (pd) 46. Forbidden (pd) 48. Eight O'Clock Walk (p) 54, etc.

King, Henry (1888–1982).
Veteran American director with experience in most branches of show business. In Hollywood, he became a skilful exponent of the well-made expensive family entertainment, usually with a sentimental streak.

SELECTED SILENTS: Who Pays? 16. A Sporting Chance 19. Tol'able David 21. *The White Sister* 23.

Romola 24. *Stella Dallas* 25. The Winning of Barbara Worth 26. The Woman Disputed 28.
■ TALKIES: Hell Harbor 30. The Eyes of the World 30. Lightnin' 30. Merely Mary Ann 31. Over the Hill 31. The Woman in Room 13 32. State Fair 33. I Loved You Wednesday 33. Carolina 34. Marie Galante 34. One More Spring 35. Way Down East 35. The Country Doctor 36. Ramona 36. Lloyd's of London 36. Seventh Heaven 37. *In Old Chicago* 38. *Alexander's Ragtime Band* 38. Jesse James 39. *Stanley and Livingstone* 39. Little Old New York 40. *Maryland* 40. *Chad Hanna* 40. A Yank in the RAF 41. Remember the Day 41. *The Black Swan* 42. *The Song of Bernadette* (AAN) 43. *Wilson* (AAN) 44. A Bell for Adano 45. *Margie* 46. Captain from Castile 47. Deep Waters 48. Prince of Foxes 49. *Twelve O'Clock High* 49. *The Gunfighter* 50. I'd Climb the Highest Mountain 51. David and Bathsheba 51. Wait Till the Sun Shines Nellie 52. Full House (part) 52. *The Snows of Kilimanjaro* 52. King of the Khyber Rifles 53. Untamed 55. *Love is a Many Splendored Thing* 55. Carousel 56. *The Sun Also Rises* 57. The Bravados 58. This Earth is Mine 59. Beloved Infidel 59. *Tender is the Night* 61.
◐ For his sympathy, professionalism and visual sense. *In Old Chicago*.

King Kong.
The most famous screen monster remains after more than 50 years the most impressive in the 1933 production. Willis O'Brien's trick photography created a believable great ape and the film, produced and directed by Merian Cooper and Ernest Schoedsack, holds together as a splendid adventure, with suitably throbbing music by Max Steiner. The same production team made a further visit to the mysterious island for *Son of Kong* 33, but the giant gorilla was played for laughs and the trick effects were skimpy, as they were for the similar *Mighty Joe Young* 49. The 1976 remake of the original story totally lacked charisma, as did its sequel and Japanese versions that have pitted Kong against robots and Godzilla.

King, Louis (1898–1962).
American director in films from 1919; brother of Henry King.

Persons in Hiding 38. Typhoon 40. The Way of All Flesh 40. Moon over Burma 41. Thunderhead, Son of Flicka 44. Smoky 46. Bob, Son of Battle 47. Green Grass of Wyoming 48. Mrs Mike 49. The Lion and the Horse 52. Powder River 53. Dangerous Mission 54, etc.

King, Perry (1948–).
American leading man of the late 70s.
■ The Possession of Joel Delaney 71. Slaughterhouse Five 72. The Lords of Flatbush 74. Mandingo 75. The Wild Party 75. Lipstick 76. Captains and the Kings (TV) 76. Andy Warhol's Bad 77. The Choirboys 77. Aspen (TV) 77. A Different Story 78. The Cracker Factory 79. Love's Savage Fury (TV) 79. Search and Destroy 81. Striking Back 81. Class of 1984 82. Riptide (TV) 84. Stranded (TV) 86. I'll Take Manhattan 87. Perfect People (TV) 88. Shakedown on the Sunset Strip (TV) 88. Disaster at Silo 7 (TV) 88. Roxanne: The Prize Pulitzer (TV) 89. Switch 91.

King Solomon's Mines.
Rider Haggard's African adventure novel was less than adequately filmed in Britain in 1937, directed by Robert Stevenson, with Cedric Hardwicke as Allan Quartermain. MGM's 1951 remake with Stewart Granger was an unsatisfactory mishmash; there was so much spare location footage that a semi-remake, *Watusi*, used it up in 1959. Harry Alan Tower's 1975 version, *King Solomon's Treasure*,

makes its predecessors look like classics. A 1985 version, directed by J. Lee Thompson and starring Richard Chamberlain, was little better, and was followed by a lamentable sequel, shot at the same time, *Allan Quatermain and the Lost City of Gold*.

King, Stephen (1946–).
Best-selling American author of supernatural stories.

Carrie (oa) 76. Salem's Lot: The Movie (oa) 79. The Shining (oa) 80. Creepshow (a, w) 82. The Dead Zone (oa) 83. Christine (oa) 83. Cujo (oa) 83. Firestarter 84. Children of the Corn (oa) 84. Stephen King's Cat's Eye (w) 85. Silver Bullet (w) 85. Maximum Overdrive (wd) 86. Stand by Me (oa) 86. The Running Man (oa) 87. Creepshow 2 (a, oa) 87. Pet Sematary (a, w) 89. Tales from the Darkside: The Movie (oa) 90. Misery (oa) 90. Stephen King's Graveyard Shift (oa) 90. Sleepwalkers (w) 92. The Lawnmower Man (oa) 92. The Dark Half (oa) 93. Needful Things (oa) 93. The Tommyknockers (oa) (TV) 93. The Stand (TV) 94. The Shawshank Redemption (oa) 94, etc.

¶ I was sitting one day and thinking about cannibalism, because that's what guys like me do . . . and I thought, suppose a guy was washed up on a rocky island, how much of himself could he eat? – *S.K.*

Movies are not books and books are not movies. I don't understand writers who get all wound up in the film adaptations of their novels, as though somehow the novel itself could be tainted by a bad adaptation. – *S.K.*

Most movie adaptations that work are shit. And you know that going in, and you figure that if you're going to get plastered with shit, somebody ought to pay you to do it, they ought to pay you a lot of money. – *S.K.*

King, Walter Woolf (1899–1984).
American actor, Broadway singing star who went to Hollywood and was gradually relegated to villain roles.

A Night at the Opera 35. Call It a Day 37. Swiss Miss 38. Balalaika 39. Marx Brothers Go West 41. Today I Hang 42. Tonight We Sing 53. Kathy O' 58, etc.

King, Zalman (1941–) (Zalman Lefkowitz).
American producer, director and writer of erotic movies, a former actor.

The Ski Bum (a) 71. Some Call It Loving (a) 73. Blue Sunshine (a) 78. Galaxy of Terror (a) 81. Nine and a Half Weeks (p, co-w) 86. Wildfire (co-w, d) 87. Two Moon Junction (wd) 88. Wild Orchid (co-w, d) 90. Wild Orchid 2: Two Shades of Blue (co-w, d) 92. Red Shoe Diaries (d) (TV) 92. Red Shoe Diaries 2: Double Dare (co-d) (TV) 92. Boca (p) 94, etc.

TV series: The Young Lawyers 70–71.

kings and queens,
of England at least, have been lovingly if not very accurately chronicled in the cinema. We still await an epic of the Norman Conquest, but in 1925 Phyllis Neilson-Terry went still further back to play *Boadicaea*, and in 1969 David Hemmings played *Alfred the Great*. Henry II, played by Peter O'Toole, was protagonist of *Becket* and *The Lion in Winter*. Richard I (Lionheart), also in the latter, was a shadowy figure of do-goodery in scores of films from *Robin Hood* to *King Richard and the Crusaders*; his brother John was just as frequently the villain of the piece, as in *The Adventures of Robin Hood*. Edward IV made an appearance in *Tower of London* and *Richard III*, but only as a pawn in the scheming hands of Richard III (Crookback). Henry IV

appeared in *Chimes at Midnight; Henry V* was a
notable role for Laurence Olivier; Henry VII-to-be
was played in *Richard III* by Stanley Baker. Henry
VIII was for long personified by Charles Laughton,
who played him in 1933, but there have been other
contenders: Montagu Love in *The Prince and the
Pauper*, Robert Shaw in *A Man for All Seasons*,
Richard Burton in *Anne of the Thousand Days*, Keith
Michell in *Henry VIII and his Six Wives*, and James
Robertson Justice in *The Sword and the Rose*.
Similarly Elizabeth I was identified with Bette
Davis (*Elizabeth and Essex, The Virgin Queen*) until
Glenda Jackson played her on TV and in *Mary Queen
of Scots*, though she was also personified by Flora
Robson (*Fire over England, The Sea Hawk*), Florence
Eldridge (*Mary of Scotland*), Irene Worth (*Seven Seas
to Calais*) and others. The unfortunate *Mary of
Scotland* was notably played by Katharine Hepburn
and Vanessa Redgrave. Young Edward VI was in
The Prince and the Pauper. The early Stuarts were a
dour lot, but Charles I was impersonated by Alec
Guinness in *Cromwell*; Charles II, the merry
monarch, has been personified by a number of
actors including Cedric Hardwicke (*Nell Gwyn*),
George Sanders (*Forever Amber*), Vincent Price
(*Hudson's Bay*) and Douglas Fairbanks Jnr (*The
Exile*). Of the Hanoverians, George I was played
by Eric Pohlmann in *Rob Roy* and Peter Bull in
Saraband for Dead Lovers, George III by Raymond
Lovell in *The Young Mr Pitt*, and by Robert Morley
in *Beau Brummell*. Prinny, the Prince Regent, later
George IV, was undertaken by Cecil Parker in *The
First Gentleman* and Peter Ustinov in *Beau
Brummell*. Victoria to many people still looks like
Anna Neagle, who played her three times; other
actresses in the role have included Irene Dunne
(*The Mudlark*), Fay Compton (*The Prime Minister*)
and Mollie Maureen (*The Private Life of Sherlock
Holmes*). James Robertson Justice played Edward
VII in *Mayerling*, and Richard Chamberlain Edward
VIII in a TV film, *The Woman I Love*. In 1982 two
American TV movies about the romance of Prince
Charles cast well-known actors as the current royal
family: neither was shown in the U.K.

Foreign monarchs who have been notably
impersonated include Catherine the Great of
Russia (Pola Negri, Elisabeth Bergner, Tallulah
Bankhead, Bette Davis, Marlene Dietrich);
Russia's last Czar and Czarina, *Nicholas and
Alexandra* (Michael Jayston and Janet Suzman);
Peter the Great; Ivan the Terrible; *Queen Christina* of
Sweden (Greta Garbo, and Liv Ullmann in *The
Abdication*); Louis XI of France (Harry Davenport
in *The Hunchback of Notre Dame*, Basil Rathbone
in *If I Were King*); Charles VII of France, by Jose
Ferrer in *Joan of Arc; Marie Antoinette* (Norma
Shearer); Louis XIV, by John Barrymore in *Marie
Antoinette*, by Robert Morley in *Marie
Antoinette* and by Pierre Renoir in *La Marseillaise*;
Louis XVII, by Jean-Pierre Cassel in *The Three
Musketeers*; Philip II of Spain (Paul Scofield in *That
Lady*, Raymond Massey in *Fire Over England*).

Kingsford, Walter (1882–1958).
British character actor, in Hollywood from the 30s
after long stage experience; usually played kindly
professional men. Was Dr Carew in the *Kildare*
series.

The Mystery of Edwin Drood 35. Captains
Courageous 37. Algiers 38. Kitty Foyle 40. My
Favorite Blonde 42. The Velvet Touch 49. Loose
in London 53. Merry Andrew 58, many others.

Kingsley, Ben (1943–) (Krishna Bahji).
Anglo-Indian leading character actor.
Gandhi (AA, BFA) 82. Betrayal 82. Harem 84.
Turtle Diary 85. Camille (TV) 85. Testimony 87. The
Sahara Secret 87. Maurice 87. The Sealed Train

87. Pascali's Island 88. Without a Clue 88.
Slipstream 89. The Children 90. The Fifth Monkey
90. Bugsy (AAN) 91. Necessary Love (L'Amore
Necessario) 91. Sneakers 92. Dave 93. Searching
for Bobby Fischer (GB: Innocent Moves) 93.
Schindler's List 93, etc.

Kingsley, Dorothy (1909–).
American scenarist, former radio writer for Bob
Hope.
Neptune's Daughter 49. When In Rome 52. Kiss
Me Kate 53. Seven Brides For Seven Brothers 54.
Pal Joey 57. Can Can 59. Pepe 60. Half a Sixpence
67. Valley of the Dolls 67, etc.

Kingsley, Sidney (1906–) (Sidney Kieschner).
American playwright.
Plays filmed include: Men in White 35. Dead
End 37. Detective Story 51.

Kinison, Sam (1954–1992).
American comic actor, in films from 1986. Died as
the result of a car crash.
Back to School 86. Three Amigos 86.

Kinnear, Roy (1934–1988).
Bulbous British character comedian whose
perspiring bluster was a quickly overplayed hand.
He died after falling from a horse during filming.
Sparrows Can't Sing 62. Heavens Above 63.
French Dressing 65. The Hill 65. Help! 66. A Funny
Thing Happened on the Way to the Forum 67.
How I Won the War 67. Lock Up Your Daughters
67. Willy Wonka and the Chocolate Factory 71.
The Three Musketeers 74. Juggernaut 74. One of
Our Dinosaurs Is Missing 75. Herbie Goes to Monte
Carlo 77. The Last Remake of Beau Geste 77.
Hawk the Slayer 80. The Boys in Blue 82. The
Zany Adventures of Robin Hood (TV) 84. Pirates
85. A Man for All Seasons (TV) 88, etc.

Kinnoch, Ronald (c. 1911–).
British producer, former scenarist and production
manager.
Escape Route 52. How to Murder a Rich Uncle
57. The Secret Man (& wd) 58. Village of the
Damned 60. Invasion Quartet 61. Cairo 62. The
Ipcress File (a, p) 65, etc.

Kinoshita, Keisuke (1912–).
Prolific Japanese director and screenwriter,
initially of comedies, averaging nearly two films a
year, before switching primarily to television
dramas in the mid-60s. He worked his way up from
assistant to the cameraman and assistant director.
The Blossoming Port (Hanna Saku Minato) 43.
Army (Rikugun) 44. Here's to the Girls (Ojosan
Kampai) 49. Broken Drum (Yabure-daiko) 49.
Carmen comes Home (Karumen Kokyo ni Kaeru)
51. A Japanese Tragedy (Nihon no Higeki) 53.
Clouds at Twilight (Yuyake-gumo) 56. Times of Joy
and Sorrow (Yorokobi mo Kanashimi mo
Ikutoshitsuki) 57. The Ballad of the Narayama
(Narayamabushi-ko) 58. Immortal Love (Eien ni
Hito) 61. The Scent of Incense (Koge) 64. Lovely
Flute and Drum (Natsukashiki Fue ya Taiko) 67.
Love and Separation in Sri Lanka (Sri Lanka no Ai
to Wakare) 76. The Impulse Murder of My Son
(Shodo Satsujin Musko yo) 79. Leaving These
Children Behind (Kono Ko o Nokoshite) 83, many
others.

Kinoy, Ernest
American screenwriter.
Brother John 70. Buck and the Preacher 71.
Leadbelly 75. White Water Summer 87, etc.

Kinskey, Leonid (1903–).
Lanky Russian character actor, long in US. Was
playing intense but not over-bright revolutionaries
in 1932 (*Trouble in Paradise*) and still does it on TV
The Great Waltz 38. Down Argentine Way 40.
Can't Help Singing 44. Monsieur Beaucaire 46.
The Man with the Golden Arm 55, many others.

Kinski, Klaus (1926–1991) (Claus Gunther
Nakszynski).
German character actor of intense roles.
Autobiography: 1986, *Dying to Live*.
Ludwig II 54. Kali Yug Goddess of Vengeance
63. For a Few Dollars More 65. Dr Zhivago 65.
Circus of Fear 67. *Aguirre Wrath of God* 72. The
Bloody Hands of the Law 73. *Nosferatu* 78. La
Femme-Enfant 80. Android 82. Venom 82. Love
and Money 82. Codename Wildgeese 84. The Little
Drummer Girl 84. Commando Leopard 85.
Crawlspace 86. Nosferatu a Venezia 87. Cobra
Verde 88. Paganini (a, wd) 88, etc.

¶ I'm like a wild animal who's behind bars. I need
air, I need space. – K.K.
Making movies is better than cleaning toilets.
– K.K.
I would have been better than Adolf Hitler. I
could have delivered his speeches a lot better. That's
for sure. – K.K.

Kinski, Nastassia (Nastassja) (1960–).
German leading lady, daughter of Klaus Kinski.
To the Devil a Daughter 76. Stay as You Are 79.
Tess 80. Cat People 82. One from the Heart 82. Love
and Money 82. Exposed 83. The Moon in the
Gutter 83. The Little Drummer Girl 84.
Unfaithfully Yours 84. Paris, Texas 84. Maria's
Lovers 85. Symphony of Love 85. Harem 85.
Revolution 85. Maladie d'Amour 87. Silent Night
88. In Una Notte di Chiaro di Luna 89. Torrents
of Spring 89. The Secret (Il Segreto) 89. Night Sun
(Il Sole Anche di Notte) 90. Faraway, So Close!
(In Weiter Ferne, So Nah) (Ger.) 93. The Blonde
(La Bionda) (It.) 94. Terminal Velocity 94, etc.

Kinsolving, Lee (1938–1974).
American teenage lead of the 60s.
The Dark at the Top of the Stairs 60. All the
Young Men 60. The Explosive Generation 61.

Kinugasa, Teinosuke (1896–1982).
Japanese director.
Crossways 28. Joyu 47. Gate of Hell 53. The
White Heron 58, etc.

Kipling, Rudyard (1865–1936).
British novelist who mainly concerned himself
with the high days of the British in India.
Films from his works include *Gunga Din, Soldiers
Three, Elephant Boy, Wee Willie Winkie, Captains
Courageous, The Light That Failed, The Jungle Book,
Kim, The Man Who Would Be King* (in which he
was played by Christopher Plummer).

Kirby, Bruno (1949–).
American character actor.
The Harrad Experiment 73. The Godfather Part
II 74. Almost Summer 77. Where the Buffalo
Roam 80. Borderline 80. Modern Romance 81.
Kiss My Grits 82. This Is Spinal Tap 84. Birdy 84.
Flesh and Blood 85. Good Morning, Vietnam 87.
Tin Men 87. We're No Angels 89. Bert Rigby,
You're a Fool 89. When Harry Met Sally 89. The
Freshman 90. City Slickers 91, etc.

Kirk, Phyllis (1926–) (Phyllis Kirkegaard).
American leading lady of the 50s, former model
and dancer.

Our Very Own 50. The Iron Mistress 52. House of Wax 53. Canyon Crossroads 55. The Sad Sack 57. That Woman Opposite (GB) 58. City after Midnight 59, etc.

TV series: The Thin Man 57.

Kirk, Tommy (1941–).
American juvenile lead, former Disney child actor.
Old Yeller 57. The Shaggy Dog 59. The Swiss Family Robinson 60. The Absent-Minded Professor 60. Babes in Toyland 61. Bon Voyage 62. Son of Flubber 63. The Misadventures of Merlin Jones 63. The Monkey's Uncle 65. How to Stuff a Wild Bikini 65. The Unkissed Bride 66. Blood of Ghastly Horror 72, etc.

Kirkland, Geoffrey.
British production designer, often for the films of Alan Parker.
Midnight Express 78. Bugsy Malone (BFA) 78. Fame 80. Shoot the Moon 82. The Right Stuff (co-pd, AAN) 83. Birdy 84. Leonard Part 6 87. Mississippi Burning (co-pd) 88. Wildfire 89. Come See the Paradise 90, etc.

Kirkland, Muriel (1903–1971).
American stage actress, briefly in films in the 30s.
Fast Workers 33. Hold Your Man 33. The Secret of the Blue Room 33. Nana 34. Little Man What Now? 34, etc.

Kirkland, Sally (1944–).
American actress.
Coming Apart 69. Futz 69. Going Home 71. Cinderella Liberty 73. The Sting 73. The Way We Were 73. Bite the Bullet 75. A Star Is Born 76. Private Benjamin 80. The Incredible Shrinking Woman 81. Love Letters 83. Anna (AAN) 87. Best of the Best 89. Paint It Black 90. JFK 91. In the Heat of Passion 91. Hit the Dutchman 92. Primary Motive 92. Double Threat 92. Paper Hearts 93. Gunmen 93. Eye of the Stranger 94, etc.
TV series: Valley of the Dolls 94.

Kirkop, Oreste (1926–).
Maltese operatic tenor whose sole film appearance to date has been in *The Vagabond King* 55.

Kirkwood, James (1883–1963).
American silent director.
The House of Discord 13. Classmates 13. Rags 15. Environment 17. Bill Apperson's Boy 19. The Heart of Jennifer 19, many others.
AS ACTOR: A Corner in Wheat 09. The Rocky Road 10. The Great Impersonation 21. Pink Gods 22. Human Wreckage 23. Circe the Enchantress 24. The Reckless Lady 26. The Spoilers 30. Cheaters at Play 32. The Woman They Almost Lynched 53, many others.

Kirkwood, Pat (1921–).
British leading lady, on stage in variety at 15, billed as 'The Schoolgirl Songstress'. She was London's highest-paid musical star of the 40s and 50s. The third of her four husbands was actor and songwriter Hubert Gregg.
Save a Little Sunshine 38. Me and My Pal 39. Band Waggon 39. Come on George 39. Flight from Folly 44. No Leave, No Love (US) 46. Once a Sinner 50. Stars in Your Eyes 56. After the Ball 57, etc.
TV series: Our Marie (as Marie Lloyd) 53. Pygmalion (as Eliza Dolittle) 55. The Great Little Tilley (as Vesta Tilley) 56.

Kirsanov, Dmitri (1899–1957).
Russian émigré film-maker, at the forefront of France's avant-garde movement of the 20s.

■ Autumn Mists 25. *Menilmontant* 26. Rapt 35.

Kismet.
Edward Knoblock's rather stolid Arabian Nights play has been filmed five times. In 1920 Louis Gesnier directed Otis Skinner; in 1931 William Dieterle directed Gustav Frölich in a German version; also in 1931 Otis Skinner played in a talkie version directed by John Francis Dillon; in 1944 Dieterle had another crack at it, with Roland Colman in the lead; and in 1955 the stage musical with themes from Borodin was filmed by Vincente Minnelli, with Howard Keel.

Kitano, Takeshi (1948–) (aka 'Beat' Takeshi).
Japanese director, screenwriter, editor and actor, a former stand-up comedian and television performer. Born in Tokyo, he worked in a comedy act, The Two Beats, which gave him his nickname, and published books of short stories and jokes before beginning a career as an actor in the 80s and, from 1989, as a director.
Merry Christmas Mr Lawrence (a) 82. Laughter and Tears (a) 84. No More Damn Comics! (a) 86. Violent Cop (Sono Otoko Kyobo Ni Tsuki) (a, d) 89. Boiling Point (3–4X Jugatsu) (a, wd) 90. A Scene at the Sea (Ano Natsu Ichban Shizukana Umi) (wd, e) 91. *Sonatine* (wd, e) 93. Many Happy Returns (Kyoso Tanjo) (oa, a) 93. Johnny Mnemonic (a) 95, etc.

Kitaro (1953–).
Japanese composer and recording artist.
Catch Your Dreams (Ger.) 83. Samuel Lount (Can.) 85. Heaven and Earth (US) 93, etc.

Kitchen, Michael (1948–).
British character actor, from the stage.
Unman Wittering and Zigo 71. Dracula AD 72 72. Breaking Glass 80. Brimstone and Treacle 82. Out of Africa 85. The Dive 89. The Russia House 90. Fools of Fortune 90. Enchanted April 91. Hostage 92. The Trial 93. Doomsday Gun (TV) 94, etc.

Kitt, Eartha (1928–).
American cabaret singer whose essential vibrance was captured only in her first film.
Autobiography: 1956, *Thursday's Child*.
■ New Faces 54. St Louis Blues 57. Mark of the Hawk 58. Anna Lucasta 58. Saint of Devil's Island 61. Synanon 65. Uncle Tom's Cabin (Ger.) 65. Up the Chastity Belt (GB) 71. Lt Schuster's Wife (TV) 72. Friday Foster 75. To Kill a Cop (TV) 78. All by Myself 82. The Pink Chiquitas 86. The Serpent Warriors 86. Dragonard 88. Master of Dragonard Hill 89. Erik the Viking 89. Living Doll 89. Ernest Scared Stupid 91. Boomerang 92.

Kitzmiller, John (1913–1965).
American character actor, in Italy from 1945 (after army service).
Paisa 46. To Live In Peace 46. Senza Pieta 48. The Naked Earth 57. Doctor No 62. Uncle Tom's Cabin (title role) (Ger.) 65, etc.

Kjellin, Alf (1920–1988).
Swedish actor who went to Hollywood and worked mostly in TV, turning his talents to direction.
Frenzy 44. My Six Convicts 52. The Iron Mistress 53. The Juggler 63. Ship of Fools 65. Assault on a Queen 66. The Midas Run (d) 69. The McMasters (d) 70, etc.

Klane, Robert.
American screenwriter and director.
Where's Poppa? 70. Every Little Crook and

Nanny 72. Fire Sale 77. Thank God It's Friday (wd) 78. Unfaithfully Yours 84. The Man with One Red Shoe 85. National Lampoon's European Vacation 85. Walk Like a Man 87. Weekend at Bernie's 89. Folks! 92. Weekend at Bernie's 2 (wd) 93, etc.

Klein, William (1929–).
American director, in Paris.
■ Far from Vietnam (part) 66. Qui Etes-Vous Polly Magoo? 67. Mr Freedom 68. Float Like a Butterfly, Sting Like a Bee (doc) 69. Festival Panafricain (doc) 69. Eldridge Cleaver (doc) 70. Le Couple Témoin 77. The French (doc) 81. Mode in France (doc) 85.

Kleiner, Harry (1916–).
American screenwriter.
Fallen Angel 46. The Street with No Name 48. Red Skies of Montana 51. Salome 53. Miss Sadie Thompson 53. *Carmen Jones* 54. The Garment Jungle (& p) 56. Ice Palace 60. Fantastic Voyage 66. *Bullitt* 68. Le Mans 71. Extreme Prejudice 87. Red Heat 88, etc.

Klein-Rogge, Rudolf (1888–1955).
German actor who appeared in some of the most famous German films of the 20s.
Der Mude Tod 21. Dr Mabuse 22. Siegfried 24. Metropolis 26. Spione 28. The Testament of Dr Mabuse 33. Between Heaven and Earth 34. The Old and the Young King 35. Intermezzo 36. Madame Bovary 37. Hochzeit auf Barenhof 42, etc.

Kleiser, Randal (1946–).
American director.
■ All Together Now (TV) 75. Dawn: Portrait of a Teenage Runaway (TV) 76. The Boy in the Plastic Bubble (TV) 76. The Gathering (TV) 77. *Grease* 78. The Blue Lagoon 80. Summer Lovers (& w) 82. Grandview USA 84. Flight of the Navigator 86. Big Top Pee-Wee 88. Getting It Right 89. White Fang 90. Honey, I Blew Up the Kid 92.

Klemperer, Werner (1920–).
Bald-pated German-American character actor, often seen as comic or sinister Nazi.
Death of a Scoundrel 56. Five Steps to Danger 56. The Goddess 58. Operation Eichmann (title role) 61. Judgment at Nuremberg 61. Escape from East Berlin 62. Youngblood Hawke 64. Ship of Fools 65. The Wicked Dreams of Paula Schultz 67. Wake Me When the War Is Over (TV) 69. Assignment Munich (TV) 72. The Rhinemann Exchange (TV) 77. The Return of the Beverly Hillbillies (TV) 81.
TV series: Hogan's Heroes 65–70.

Klimov, Elem (1933–).
Russian director and screenwriter, noted for his exuberant approach and use of documentary techniques. Born in Volgograd, he worked as an aeronautical engineer before studying film in Moscow. He first worked in television and was married to director and screenwriter Larissa Shepitko (qv), making a documentary about her life following her untimely death in a car crash. *Agony*, about Rasputin, was banned for 10 years by the authorities.
Welcome, or No Entry for Unauthorized Persons 64. Adventures of a Dentist 65. Sport, Sport, Sport 71. And Nonetheless I Believe (co-d) 74. Agony (Agonia) (aka Rasputin) 75. Larissa (doc) 80. Farewell (Proshchanie) 81. Come and See (Idi i Smotri) (& co-w) 85, etc.

Klimovsky, Leon (1906–).
Argentinian director and film critic, a former dentist who founded the country's first cinema club

in the 20s. In the mid-50s he settled in Spain and took Spanish nationality, turning out films in many genres, including horror movies and spaghetti westerns.

El Jugador 47. Marihuana 50. Suburbio 51. El Túnel 52. Maleficio 54. Viaje de Novios 56. Dos Mil Dólares por un Coyote 65. Operación Rommel 68. Reverendo Colt 70. El Dr Jekyl y el Hombre Loco 72. La Orgia Nocturna de los Vampiros 72. The Devil's Possessed (El Mariscal del Infierno) 74. El Transexual 77. Laverna 78, etc.

Kline, Herbert (1909–).
American director, sometimes of documentaries.
Crisis 39. Lights out in Europe 40. The Forgotten Village (& p) 41. My Father's House (& p) 47. The Kid from Cleveland 49. The Fighter (& w, p) 52. Walls of Fire (doc) 74. Acting: Lee Strasberg and the Actors Studio (doc) 81. Great Theatres of the World (doc) 87, etc.

Kline, Kevin (1947–).
American actor. He married actress Phoebe Cates in 1990.
Sophie's Choice 82. The Big Chill 83. Silverado 85. Cry Freedom 87. A Fish Called Wanda (AA) 88. The January Man 89. I Love You to Death 90. Soapdish 91. Grand Canyon 91. Chaplin 92. Consenting Adults 92. Death Becomes Her 92. Dave 93. Princess Caraboo 94, etc.

Kline, Richard (1926–).
American cinematographer.
Camelot (AAN) 67. The Boston Strangler 69. A Dream of Kings 69. The Andromeda Strain 70. Kotch 71. Black Gunn 72. The Harrad Experiment 73. Mandingo 75. King Kong (AAN) 76. The Fury 78. Star Trek 79. The Competition 80. Body Heat 81. Death Wish II 82. Breathless 83. Hard to Hold 84. All of Me 84. The Man with One Red Shoe 85. Howard the Duck 85. Touch and Go 86. My Stepmother Is an Alien 88. Downtown 90, etc.

Klinger, Michael (1921–1989).
British producer.
Repulsion 64. Cul de Sac 66. The Yellow Teddy Bears 66. A Study in Terror 67. Baby Love 69. Get Carter 71. Pulp 73. Gold 74. Shout at the Devil 76. Tomorrow Never Comes 78. Heavy Metal 80, etc.

Klos, Elmar:
see Kadar, Jan.

Kloves, Steve.
American screenwriter and director.
Racing with the Moon (w) 84. The Fabulous Baker Boys (wd) 89. Flesh and Bone (wd) 93.

Kluge, Alexander (1932–).
German director.
Abschied von Gestern 66. Artists at the Top of the Big Top 68. Willy Tobler 71. Occasional Work of a Female Slave 74. Strongman Ferdinand 76. Der Angriff der Gegenwart auf die Ubrige Zeit 85. Vermischte Nachrichten 86, etc.

Klugman, Jack (1922–).
Lean American actor who can be comically henpecked, tragically weak, or just sinister.
Timetable 56. Twelve Angry Men 57. Days of Wine and Roses 62. Act One 63. I Could Go on Singing 63. Yellow Canary 63. The Detective 68. The Split 68. Goodbye Columbus 69. Who Says I Can't Ride a Rainbow? 71. Two Minute Warning 76. Parallel Lives (TV) 94, etc.
TV series: Harris against the World 64. The Odd Couple 70–75. Quincy 76–83. You Again 86–87.

Knapp, Evalyn (1908–1981).
American leading lady.
Fifty Million Frenchmen 31. Night Mayor 32. Fireman Save My Child 32. Air Hostess 33. The Perils of Pauline (serial) 34. Laughing Irish Eyes 36. The Lone Wolf Takes a Chance 42. Two Weeks to Live 43, etc.

Kneale, Nigel (1922–).
Manx writer, best known for BBC TV serials about Professor Quatermass, all three of which were filmed.
Look Back in Anger 59. The Entertainer 60. The First Men in the Moon 64. The Devil's Own 66, etc.

Knef, Hildegard:
see Neff, Hildegard.

Knieper, Jurgen.
German composer.
The Scarlet Letter 73. The Wrong Move 75. The American Friend 77. The River's Edge (US) 86. Wings of Desire 87. End of the Night 90. Madregilda (Sp.) 93. The Blonde (La Bionda) (It.) 94, etc.

Knight, Castleton (1894–1972).
British newsreel producer (Gaumont British).
Directed some films in the 30s, including Kissing Cup's Race and The Flying Scotsman; also various compilations such as Theirs Is the Glory and Fourteenth Olympiad, and records of state occasions such as A Queen Is Crowned.

Knight, David (1927–) (David Mintz).
American leading man, on London stage in the 50s.
The Young Lovers (debut) 55. Lost 57. Across the Bridge 57. Battle of the V.1 58. Nightmare 63. Demons II – the Nightmare Returns 87, etc.

Knight, Eric (1897–1943).
British writer whose famous 1940 juvenile book Lassie Come Home started a doggy industry.

Knight, Esmond (1906–1987).
Welsh actor, on stage from 1925, screen from 1928. Partially blinded during World War II. Married to actress Norah Swinburne.
Autobiography: 1943, Seeking the Bubble.
The Silver Fleet 42. Henry V 44. End of the River 47. Hamlet 47. The Red Shoes 48. Richard III 56. Sink the Bismarck 60. Where's Jack? 69. Anne of the Thousand Days 70. Robin and Marian 76. I Claudius (TV) 77. Blott on the Landscape (TV) 85, etc.

Knight, Fuzzy (1901–1976) (J. Forrest Knight).
American nightclub musician who found himself a niche in Hollywood as comic relief in innumerable westerns.
She Done Him Wrong 33. The Trail of the Lonesome Pine 36. Johnny Apollo 40. Trigger Trail 44. Down to the Sea in Ships 50. Topeka 54. These Thousand Hills 59. Waco 66, etc.
TV series: Captain Gallant 55.

Knight, Shirley (1937–).
American leading actress, also on stage and TV; latterly known as Shirley Knight Hopkins.
Five Gates to Hell 59. The Dark at the Top of the Stairs (AAN) 60. Sweet Bird of Youth (AAN) 62. The Group 66. Dutchman 67. Petulia 68. The Rain People 69. Secrets 71. Juggernaut 74. Beyond the Poseidon Adventure 79. Endless Love 81. The Sender 82. With Intent to Kill (TV) 84. Hard Promises 91. Color of Night 94, etc.

Knoblock, Edward (1874–1945).
British author of plays Kismet, Chu Chin Chow, Milestones, all frequently filmed; in the 20s became a production associate of Douglas Fairbanks Senior.

Knopf, Edwin H. (1899–1981).
American producer, sometimes writer and director.
Border Legion (d) 30. Bad Sister (w) 31. The Wedding Night (w) 35. Piccadilly Jim (w) 36. The Trial of Mary Dugan (p) 41. The Cross of Lorraine (p) 44. The Valley of Decision (p) 45. BF's Daughter (p) 48. Edward My Son (p) 49. The Law and the Lady (d) 51. Lili (p) 53. The Vintage (p) 57, many others.

Knopfler, Mark (1949–).
British composer, guitarist and singer. A former teacher and journalist, he is a founder-member of the rock band Dire Straits.
Local Hero (m) 83. Cal 84. Comfort and Joy (m) 84. The Princess Bride (m) 87. Last Exit to Brooklyn (m) 90.

Knott, Andrew.
English juvenile actor.
The Secret Garden 93. Black Beauty 94.

Knotts, Don (1924–).
American 'hayseed' comedian, from TV.
Wake Me When It's Over 60. The Last Time I Saw Archie 61. The Incredible Mr Limpet 62. The Ghost and Mr Chicken 66. The Reluctant Astronaut 67. The Shakiest Gun in the West 68. The Love God 69. How to Frame a Figg 71. The Apple Dumpling Gang 75. Gus 76. No Deposit No Return 76. Herbie Goes to Monte Carlo 77. The Apple Dumpling Gang Rides Again 79. The Private Eyes 81. Return to Mayberry (TV) 86, etc.
TV series: The Andy Griffith Show 60–68. Three's Company 81– .

Knowles, Bernard (1900–).
British cinematographer who became a competent director.
AS CINEMATOGRAPHER: Dawn 29. The Good Companions 32. Jew Süss 34. The Thirty-Nine Steps 35. Gaslight 39. Quiet Wedding 40, etc.
■ AS DIRECTOR: A Place of One's Own 45. The Magic Bow 46. The Man Within 47. The White Unicorn 47. Jassy 47. Easy Money 48. The Lost People 49. The Perfect Woman 49. The Reluctant Widow 50. Park Plaza 605 53. Barbados Quest 54. Frozen Alive 64. Spaceflight IC-1 65. Hell is Empty 68.

Knowles, Patric (1911–) (Reginald Knowles).
British light 'second lead' who went to Hollywood in 1936 and stayed.
Irish Hearts (GB) 34. Abdul the Damned (GB) 34. The Guvnor (GB) 35. The Charge of the Light Brigade 36. The Adventures of Robin Hood 38. Storm over Bengal 39. Anne of Windy Poplars 40. How Green Was My Valley 41. The Wolf Man 41. Lady in a Jam 42. Eyes of the Underworld 42. Frankenstein Meets the Wolf Man 43. Always a Bridesmaid 43. Pardon My Rhythm 44. Kitty 45. Of Human Bondage 46. Monsieur Beaucaire 46. Ivy 47. The Big Steal 49. Three Came Home 50. Mutiny 52. Flame of Calcutta 53. Band of Angels 57. Auntie Mame 59. The Devil's Brigade 68. In Enemy Country 68. Chisum 71. Terror in the Wax Museum 73, many others.

Knox, Alexander (1907–).
Quiet-spoken Canadian actor, on British stage from 1930, films from 1938; also in Hollywood.
The Gaunt Stranger 38. The Sea Wolf 40. This

bove All 42. None Shall Escape 43. *Wilson* (title
ole) (AAN) 44. Over Twenty-One 45. Sister
enny 46. *The Judge Steps Out* 47. The Sign of the
am 48. I'd Climb the Highest Mountain 50. Paula
2. The Sleeping Tiger 53. The Divided Heart 54.
each for the Sky 56. High Tide at Noon 57. The
ikings 58. Operation Amsterdam 59. The Wreck
f the Mary Deare 59. The Trials of Oscar Wilde
0. The Damned 61. Crack in the Mirror 62. The
lan in the Middle 64. Crack in the World 65.
lister Moses 65. The Psychopath 66. Accident 66.
lodesty Blaise 66. Khartoum 66. How I Won the
lar 67. Villa Rides 68. Shalako 68. Skullduggery
9. Nicholas and Alexandra 71. Puppet on a Chain
1. Meeting at Potsdam (TV) 76. Holocaust 2000
8. Tinker Tailor Soldier Spy (TV) 79. Gorky Park
3. Joshua Then and Now 85, etc.

Knox, Elyse (1917–).
American leading lady of the 40s.
Lillian Russell 40. The Mummy's Tomb 42. Hit
he Ice 43. Linda be Good 47. There's a Girl in
ly Heart 49, etc.

Knox, Teddy:
ee The Crazy Gang.

Knudsen, Peggy (1925–1980).
American starlet of the 40s.
Stolen Life 46. Humoresque 47. Trouble
referred 48. Copper Canyon 50. Unchained 53.
ood Morning Miss Dove 54. Istanbul 57, etc.

Knudtson, Frederic L. (c. 1900–1964).
American editor.
Headline Shooter 33. Gun Law 38. Stage to
hino 40. This Land is Mine 43. The Bachelor and
he Bobbysoxer 47. The Window 48. Angel Face
3. Not as a Stranger 55. The Pride and the Passion
7. The Defiant Ones 58. Inherit the Wind 60.
udgment at Nuremberg 61, many others.

Kobayashi, Masaki (1916–).
Japanese director.
Ningen no Joken 61. Hara Kiri 63. *Kwaidan* 64.
Rebellion 67. Hymn to a Tired Man 68. Inn of
Evil 71. Fossils 75. Glowing Autumn 79. Tokyo
Saiban 85, etc.

Koch, Howard (1902–).
American screenwriter.
The Sea Hawk (co-w) 40. *The Letter* (co-w) 40.
Sergeant York (co-w, AAN) 41. *Casablanca* (co-w)
(AA) 42. Mission to Moscow (co-w) 43. *Letter from
an Unknown Woman* 47. The Thirteenth Letter 51.
The War Lover 63. The Fox (co-wp) 68, many
others.

Koch, Howard W. (1916–).
American executive, from 1965–66 Paramount's
vice-president in charge of production. Former
producer and director.
Big House USA (d) 54. Beachhead (p) 55. The
Black Sleep (p) 56. Frankenstein 70 (d) 58.
Sergeants Three (p) 62. The Manchurian
Candidate (p) 62. Come Blow Your Horn (p) 63.
None But the Brave (p) 65. The Odd Couple (p)
68. On a Clear Day You Can See Forever (p) 70.
Badge 373 73. Once Is Not Enough 75. The Other
Side of Midnight 77. Heaven Can Wait 78. The
Frisco Kid 79. The Idolmaker 80. Some Kind of
Hero 82. Ghost 90, etc.

Koenekamp, Fred (1922–).
American cinematographer.
Patton (AAN) 70. Kansas City Bomber 72.
Papillon 73. The Towering Inferno (AA) 74.
Uptown Saturday Night 74. Posse 75. Doc Savage

75. Islands in the Stream 77. Fun with Dick and
Jane 77. The Other Side of Midnight 77. The
Domino Principle 77. The Amityville Horror 79.
The Champ 79. The First Family 80. When Time
Ran Out 80. First Monday in October 81. Wrong Is
Right 82. Yes Giorgio 82. Two of a Kind 83. The
Adventures of Buckaroo Banzai 84. Stewardess
School 87. Listen to Me 89. Welcome Home 89.
Flight of the Intruder 91, etc.

Koenig, Walter (1936–).
American actor, best known for playing the role
of Chekhov in the *Star Trek* television series and
films.
Moontrap 89.

Kohler, Fred, Snr (1889–1938).
American character actor often seen as western
badman.
Soldiers of Fortune 19. The Stampede 21. Anna
Christie 23. Riders of the Purple Sage 25. The Way
of All Flesh 27. Chinatown Charlie 28. The Dragnet
28. The Leatherneck 29. Thunderbolt 29. Hell's
Heroes 29. Corsair 31. Call Her Savage 32. Wild
Horse Mesa 32. Kid Millions 35. Hard Rock
Harrigan 35. The Plainsman 36. Daughter of
Shanghai 37. Billy the Kid Returns 38, many others.

Kohlmar, Fred (1905–1969).
American producer in Hollywood from the early
30s, at first with Goldwyn.
That Night in Rio 41. The Glass Key 42. Kiss of
Death 47. When Willie Comes Marching Home 50.
It Should Happen to You 53. Picnic 55. Pal Joey
57. The Last Angry Man 59. The Notorious
Landlady 62. How To Steal a Million 66. A Flea in
Her Ear 68. The Only Game in Town 69, many
others.

Kohner, Susan (1936–).
American leading lady.
To Hell and Back 55. Imitation of Life (AAN) 58.
All the Fine Young Cannibals 60. Freud 62, etc.

Kolb, Clarence (1874–1964).
Veteran character actor, usually of explosive
executive types; formerly in vaudeville.
Carefree 38. Nothing but the Truth 41.
Hellzapoppin 42. True to Life 43. The Kid from
Brooklyn 46. Christmas Eve 47. Adam's Rib 49.
The Rose Bowl Story 53. Man of a Thousand Faces
57, many others.

Kolker, Henry (1874–1947).
American stage actor who played lawyers and
heavy fathers in many films.
The Bigger Man 15. Disraeli 21. West Point 26.
The Valiant 29. East Is West 30. Corsair 31. The
Devil and the Deep 32. Jewel Robbery 33.
Imitation of Life 34. The Ghost Walks 34. The Case
of the Curious Bride 34. Diamond Jim 35. Mad
Love 35. The Last Days of Pompeii 35. The Black
Room 35. Bullets or Ballots 36. Romeo and Juliet
(as Friar Laurence) 36. Theodora Goes Wild 36.
Conquest 37. Maid of Salem 37. The Cowboy and
the Lady 38. *Holiday* 38. Union Pacific 39. The
Real Glory 39. Grand Old Opry 40. A Woman's
Face 41. Sarong Girl 43. Bluebeard 44. The Secret
Life of Walter Mitty 47, many others.

Koller, Xavier.
Swiss director.
Black Tanner (AAN) 86. Journey of Hope (Reise
der Hoffnung) (AA) 90. Indian Warrior 94, etc.

Komai, Tetsu (1893–1970).
Japanese-American character actor.
Daughter of the Dragon 31. Island of Lost Souls

33. Tokyo Joe 49. Japanese War Bride 52. The Night
Walker 64, etc.

Konchalovsky, Andrei (1937–).
Russian director in the West.
Maria's Lovers 85. Runaway Train 85. Duet for
One 86. Shy People 87. Homer and Eddie 89. Tango
and Cash 89. The Inner Circle 91. Ryaba My
Chicken (Riaba Ma Poule) 94, etc.

Konstam, Phyllis (1907–1976).
British stage actress who occasionally played film
heroines.
Autobiography 1969: *A Mixed Double* (with her
husband Bunny Austin).
■ Champagne 28. Blackmail 29. Murder 30.
Escape 30. Compromising Daphne 30. The Skin
Game 31. Tilly of Bloomsbury 31. A Gentleman of
Paris 31. The Forgotten Factor 52. Jotham Valley
52. The Crowning Experience 59. Voice of the
Hurricane 60.

Kopelson, Arnold (1935–).
American producer and lawyer.
The Legacy 79. Lost and Found 79. Foolin'
Around 80. Dirty Tricks 80. Platoon (AA) 86.
Warlock 88. Triumph of the Spirit 89. Falling
Down 93. The Fugitive 93. Outbreak 95, etc.

Kops and Custards
by Kalton C. Lahue and Terry Brewer. A scholarly
history of the Keystone Film Company and the
apprenticeship of Mack Sennett; published 1968.

Korda, Sir Alexander (1893–1956) (Sandor
Corda).
Hungarian producer-director who worked in Paris,
Berlin and Hollywood before settling in London
1930. More than any other man the savior of the
British film industry. Formed London Films and
sealed its success with *The Private Life of Henry VIII*
32; built Denham Studios. He was married to
actresses Maria Corda and Merle Oberon (1939–
45).
Biographies: 1956, *Alexander Korda* by Paul
Tabori. 1975, *Alexander Korda* by Karol Kulik,
1980, *Charmed Lives* by Michael Korda.
■ The Duped Journalist (d) 14. Tutyu and Totyo
(d) 14. Lea Lyon (d) 15. The Officer's Swordknot
(d) 15. Fedora (d) 16. The Grandmother (d) 16.
Tales of the Typewriter (d) 16. The Man with Two
Hearts (d) 16. The Million Pound Note (d) 16.
Cyclamen (d) 16. Struggling Hearts (d) 16.
Laughing Saskia (d) 16. Miska the Magnate (d) 16.
St Peter's Umbrella (d) 17. The Stork Caliph (d)
17. Magic (d) 17. Harrison and Barrison (d) 17.
Faun (d) 18. The Man with the Golden Touch (d)
18. Mary Ann (d) 18. Hail Caesar (d) 19. White
Rose (d) 19. Yamata (d) 19. Neither In Nor Out (d)
19. Number 111 (d) 19. The Prince and the Pauper
(d) 20. Masters of the Sea (d) 22. A Vanished World
(d) 22. Samson and Delilah (d) 22. The Unknown
Tomorrow (d) 23. Everybody's Woman (d) 24.
Mayerling (d) 24. Dancing Mad (d) 25. Madame
Wants No Children (d) 26. A Modern Dubarry (d)
27. (All previous titles in Hungary, France and
Germany; now Hollywood.) The Stolen Bride (d)
27. *The Private Life of Helen of Troy* (d) 27. Yellow
Lily (d) 28. Night Watch (d) 28. Love and the
Devil (d) 29. The Squall (d) 29. Her Private Life
(d) 29. Lilies of the Field (d) 30. Women
Everywhere (d) 30. The Princess and the Plumber
(d) 31. (Now Paris.) Laughter (d) 31. *Marius* (d)
31. (Now London.) Service for Ladies (p,d) 32.
Wedding Rehearsal (d) 33. Strange Evidence (p) 33.
(p) 33. Cash (p) 33. Men of Tomorrow (p) 33. *The
Private Life of Henry VIII* (p,d) 33. The Girl from

Maxim's (p,d) 33. *The Rise of Catherine the Great* (p) 34. The Private Life of Don Juan (p,d) 34. *The Scarlet Pimpernel* (p, some d) 34. *Sanders of the River* (p) 35. *The Ghost Goes West* (p) 35. *Things to Come* (p) 36. Moscow Nights (ep) 36. Men Are Not Gods (p). 36. Forget Me Not (p) 36. *Rembrandt* (p,d) 36. *The Man Who Could Work Miracles* (p) 37. Fire over England (ep) 37. I Claudius (unfinished) (p) 37. Dark Journey 37. Elephant Boy (p) 37. Farewell Again (ep) 37. Storm in a Teacup (ep) 37. Action for Slander (ep) 37. *Knight without Armour* (p) 37. The Squeaker (p) 37. The Return of the Scarlet Pimpernel (ep) 37. Paradise for Two (ep) 37. The Divorce of Lady X (p) 38. The Drum (p) 38. South Riding (ep) 38. The Challenge (ep) 38. Prison without Bars (ep) 38. Q Planes (ep) 39. *The Four Feathers* (p) 39. The Rebel Son (ep) 39. The Spy in Black (ep) 39. The Lion Has Wings (p) 39. Over the Moon (p) 40 (shot 1938). Twenty-one Days (p) 40 (shot 37). Conquest of the Air (ep) 40. *The Thief of Baghdad* (p) 40. Old Bill and Son (ep) 41. *That Hamilton Woman* (in US) (p,d) 41. Lydia (in US) (p) 41. *To Be or Not to Be* (in US) (ep) 42. Jungle Book (in US) (p) 42. *Perfect Strangers* (p) 45. The Shop at Sly Corner (ep) 47. A Man about the House (ep) 47. Mine Own Executioner (ep) 47. An Ideal Husband (p,d) 47. Night Beat (ep) 48. *Anna Karenina* (p) 48. The Winslow Boy (ep) 48. The Fallen Idol (ep) 48. Bonnie Prince Charlie (ep) 48. The Small Back Room (ep) 49. That Dangerous Age (ep) 49. The Last Days of Dolwyn (ep) 49. Saints and Sinners (ep) 49. *The Third Man* (ep) 49. The Cure for Love (ep) 50. The Angel with the Trumpet (ep) 50. My Daughter Joy (ep) 50. State Secret (ep) 50. Seven Days to Noon (ep) 50. Gone to Earth (ep) 50. The Elusive Pimpernel (ep) 50. Tales of Hoffman (ep) 51. Lady Godiva Rides Again (ep) 51. The Wonder Kid (ep) 51. Mr Denning Drives North (ep) 52. An Outcast of the Islands (ep) 52. Home at Seven (ep) 52. Who Goes There? (ep) 52. Cry the Beloved Country (ep) 52. *The Sound Barrier* (ep) 52. The Holly and the Ivy (ep) 52. The Ringer (ep) 53. Folly to Be Wise (ep) 53. Twice Upon a Time (ep) 53. The Captain's Paradise (ep) 53. The Story of Gilbert and Sullivan (ep) 53. The Man Between (ep) 53. The Heart of the Matter (ep) 54. Hobson's Choice (ep) 54. The Belles of St Trinian's (ep) 54. The Teckman Mystery (ep) 54. The Man Who Loved Redheads (ep) 55. Three Cases of Murder (ep) 55. The Constant Husband (ep) 55. A Kid for Two Farthings (ep) 55. The Deep Blue Sea (ep) 55. Summer Madness (ep) 55. Storm over the Nile (ep) 55. *Richard III* (ep) 56. Smiley (ep) 56. ✪ For reviving Britain's flagging film industry and making half-a-dozen imperishable classics. *Rembrandt*.

¶ The art of film-making is to come to the brink of bankruptcy and stare it in the face. – *A.K.*
Anyone who gets a raw deal in a film studio is no more deserving of pity than someone who gets beaten up in a brothel. A gentleman has no business is either place. – *A.K.*
He represented, and indeed virtually created, the tradition of quality in the British cinema. – *Andrew Sarris*
His engaging personality and charm of manner must be resisted. His promises, even when they are sincere, are worthless. A very dominant man and very dangerous to converse with owing to (among other things) his powers of persuasion. – *Internal memo of the Prudential Assurance Company, which backed Korda*
~In the above list the abbreviation ep (executive producer) is meant to imply a considerable distancing by Korda from the product, as sponsor, or financier, or head of London Films.

~~Other projects announced at various times by Korda include *The Field of the Cloth of Gold, Marco Polo, Nijinsky, Hamlet, Zorro, Joseph and His Brothers, Young Mr Disraeli, Marlborough, King of the Jews, Franz Liszt, Lawrence of Arabia, Nelson, Precious Bane, Cyrano de Bergerac, Charles II, War and Peace, Burmese Silver, Elizabeth of Austria, Pocahontas, Manon Lescaut, New Wine, The Hardy Family in England, Greenmantle, The Old Wives' Tale, Mr Chips' Boys, The Pickwick Papers, The Wrecker, Around the World in Eighty Days, Gibraltar, The Eternal City, The King's General, Carmen, Salome, Faust, Arms and the Man, Macbeth, The Iliad.*

Korda, Vincent (1896–1979).
Hungarian art director who usually worked on the films of his brothers Alexander and Zoltan.
The Private Life of Henry VIII 32. Sanders of the River 35. *Things to Come* 36. The Four Feathers 39. *The Thief of Baghdad* (AA) 40. To Be or Not to Be 42. The Fallen Idol 48. The Third Man 49. The Sound Barrier 52. The Deep Blue Sea 55. Summer Madness 56, etc.

Korda, Zoltan (1895–1961).
Hungarian director, brother of Alexander Korda; spent most of his career in Britain and Hollywood.
Cash 32. Sanders of the River 35. The Drum 38. *The Four Feathers* 39. Jungle Book 42. Sahara 43. Counterattack 45. *The Macomber Affair* 47. A Woman's Vengeance 48. Cry the Beloved Country 51, etc.

Korjus, Miliza (1900–1980).
Polish operatic soprano who settled in America but did not pursue what looked like being a popular film career.
■ *The Great Waltz* (AAN) 38. Imperial Cavalry (Mexico) 42.

Korman, Harvey (1927–).
American character comedian, often as loud-mouthed show-off. On TV with Danny Kaye and Carol Burnett.
Lord Love a Duck 66. Don't Just Stand There 67. The April Fools 68. Blazing Saddles 74. High Anxiety 78. First Family 80. Herbie Goes Bananas 80. History of the World Part One 81. Trail of the Pink Panther 82. The Long Shot 85. Crash Course (TV) 88, etc.
TV series: The Danny Kaye Show 64–67. The Carol Burnett Show 67–77. The Tim Conway Show 80–81. Mama's Family 83–84. Leo & Liz in Beverly Hills 86.

Korngold, Erich Wolfgang (1897–1957).
Czech composer-conductor, a child prodigy. To Hollywood in 1935 with Warners.
■ Captain Blood 35. *Anthony Adverse* (AA) 36. The Green Pastures 36. A Midsummer Night's Dream 36. The Story of Louis Pasteur 36. Another Dawn 37. The Prince and the Pauper 37. *The Adventures of Robin Hood* (AA) 38. Juarez 39. Elizabeth and Essex (AAN) 39. *The Sea Hawk* (AAN) 40. The Sea Wolf 41. Kings Row 41. The Constant Nymph 43. Between Two Worlds 44. Devotion 44. Deception 46. Of Human Bondage 46. Escape Me Never 47. Magic Fire 56.
✪ For stirring romantic themes of a finer texture than anyone else in Hollywood could accomplish. *Kings Row*.

Kornman, Mary (1917–1973).
American actress, the only girl in the original Our Gang comedies of the 20s, on screen from the age of five. As a teenager she acted in Hal Roach's *The Boy Friends* series of shorts and later appeared in some features before retiring in 1940. The first of

her two husbands was cinematographer Leo Tover.
Are These Our Children? 31. Flying Down to Rio 33. The Adventurous Knights 35. Desert Trai 35. Queen of the Jungle 35. Swing It Professor 3 On the Spot 40, etc.

Korris, Harry (1888–1971) (Henry Corris).
British music-hall comedian who became popula on radio as Mr Lovejoy in the 40s show *Happidrome* and made several slapdash film farces
Somewhere in England 40. Somewhere in Cam 41. Happidrome 43, etc.

Korsmo, Charlie (1978–).
American juvenile actor.
Men Don't Leave 89. Dick Tracy 89. What abou Bob? 91. Hook 91. The Doctor 91, etc.

Kortner, Fritz (1892–1970) (Fritz Nathan Kohn).
Austrian character actor, in films of many nation. and director.
Autobiography: 1959, *The Evening of All Days*.
Police No. 1111 (debut) 16. Satanas 20. The Brothers Karamazov 20. The Hands of Orlac 24. Beethoven 26. Warning Shadows 27. Mata Hari 27. *Pandora's Box* 28. The Murder of Dimitri Karamazov 30. Dreyfus 30. Chu Chin Chow 34. Evensong 34. Abdul the Damned 35. The Crouching Beast 36. The Strange Death of Adolf Hitler 43. The Hitler Gang 44. Somewhere in the Night 46. The Brasher Doubloon 47. Berlin Expres 48, many others.
■ AS DIRECTOR: Der Brave Suender 31. So Ein Maedel Vergisst Man Nicht 33. Der Ruf 49. Die Stad ist Voller Geheimnisse 55. Sarajevo 55. Lysistrata 61.

Korty, John (1941–).
American director.
The Crazy Quilt 65. Funnyman 67. Riverrun 68 The People (TV) 72. Class of 63 (TV) 73. Go Ask Alice (TV) 73. The Autobiography of Miss Jane Pittman (TV) 73. Silence 74. Alex and the Gypsy 76. Farewell to Manzanar (TV) 76. Who Are the De Bolts 77. Forever (TV) 78. Oliver's Story (& w) 78. A Christmas without Snow (TV) 80. Twice upon a Time (co-d) 83. The Haunting Passion (TV 83. Second Sight: A Love Story (TV) 84. The Ewok Adventure (TV) 84. A Deadly Business (TV) 86. Resting Place (TV) 86. Baby Girl Scott (TV) 87. Eye on the Sparrow (TV) 87. Winnie (TV) 88. Long Road Home (TV) 91. They (TV) 93. Getting Out (TV) 94, etc.

Korvin, Charles (1907–) (Geza Kaiser).
Czech-born leading man with varied experience before Hollywood debut.
Enter Arsène Lupin 44. This Love of Ours 45. Temptation 47. The Killer That Stalked New York 50. Lydia Bailey 52. Sangaree 53. Zorro the Avenger 60. Ship of Fools 65. The Man Who Had Power over Women 70. Inside Out 75, etc.
TV series: Interpol Calling 59.

Koscina, Sylva (1933–1994).
Jugoslavian leading lady in international films.
Hercules Unchained 60. Jessica 62. Hot Enough for June (GB) 63. Juliet of the Spirits (It.) 65. Three Bites of the Apple (US) 66. Deadlier Than the Male (GB) 67. A Lovely Way to Die 68. The Battle for Neretva 70. Hornet's Nest 70. Crimes of the Black Cat 72. The Slasher 74. Dracula in Brianza 75. Casanova and Co. (aka The Rise and Rise of Casanova) 77. Sunday Lovers 80. Cinderella '80 84. Deadly Sanctuary 86. Rimini Rimini 87, etc.

Kosleck, Martin (1907–1994) (Nicolai Yoshkin). Russian character actor with experience on the German stage; in America from mid-30s.

Confessions of a Nazi Spy (as Goebbels) 39. Nurse Edith Cavell 39. A Date with Destiny 40. Foreign Correspondent 40. North Star 43. *The Hitler Gang* (as Goebbels) 44. The Frozen Ghost 44. The Mummy's Curse 45. House of Horrors 46. Hitler (as Goebbels) 61. Something Wild 62. Thirty-Six Hours 64. Morituri 65. The Flesh Eaters 67. Which Way to the Front? 70, etc.

Kosma, Joseph (1905–1969).
Hungarian composer, in France from 1933.
La Grande Illusion 37. *La Bête Humaine* 38. *Partie de Campagne* 38. *La Règle du Jeu* 39. *Les Enfants du Paradis* 44. *Les Portes de la Nuit* 45. *Les Amants de Vérone* 48. The Green Glove 52. *Huis Clos* 54. Calle Mayor 56. The Doctor's Dilemma 59. Lunch on the Grass 59. La Poupée 62. In the French Style 64. The Little Theatre of Jean Renoir 69, etc.

Kossoff, David (1919–   )
British character actor and stage monologuist.
The Good Beginning 50. The Young Lovers 55. *A Kid for Two Farthings* 56. *The Bespoke Overcoat* 57. The Journey 59. Freud 62. Ring of Spies 64, many others.
TV series: The Larkins. A Little Big Business.

Kostal, Irwin (1911–1994).
American musical supervisor.
West Side Story (AA) 61. Mary Poppins (AAN) 64. *The Sound of Music* (AA) 65. Bedknobs and Broomsticks (AAN) 71. The Blue Bird 76. Pete's Dragon (AAN) 77, etc.

Koster, Henry (1905–1988) (Hermann Kosterlitz).
German director, in Hollywood from mid-30s, adept at sentimental comedy.
■ Thea Roland (Ger.) 32. Peter (Ger.) 33. Little Mother (Ger.) 33. Peter (Hung.) 35. Marie Bashkirtzeff (Ger.) 36. *Three Smart Girls* 36. *One Hundred Men and a Girl* 37. The Rage of Paris 38. Three Smart Girls Grow Up 38. First Love 39. Spring Parade 40. *It Started with Eve* 41. Between Us Girls 42. Music for Millions 44. Two Sisters from Boston 45. The Unfinished Dance 47. *The Bishop's Wife* (AAN) 47. The Luck of the Irish 47. Come to the Stable 49. *The Inspector General* 49. Wabash Avenue 50. My Blue Heaven 50. Harvey 50. No Highway (GB) 51. Mr Belvedere Rings the Bell 52. Elopement 52. Stars and Stripes Forever 52. My Cousin Rachel 52. *The Robe* 53. Désirée 54. A Man Called Peter 55. The Virgin Queen 55. Good Morning, Miss Dove 55. D-Day the Sixth of June 56. The Power and the Prize 56. My Man Godfrey 57. Fraulein 58. The Naked Maja 59. The Story of Ruth 60. Flower Drum Song 60. Mr Hobbs Takes a Vacation 62. Take Her She's Mine 63. Dear Brigitte 65. The Singing Nun 66.

Kotcheff, Ted (1931–   ).
Canadian director.
■ Tiara Tahiti 62. *Life at the Top* 65. Two Gentlemen Sharing 70. Outback 71. Billy Two Hats 73. The Apprenticeship of Duddy Kravitz 74. Fun with Dick and Jane 77. Someone Is Killing the Great Chefs of Europe 78. North Dallas Forty 79. First Blood 82. Split Image 83. Uncommon Valor 83. Joshua Then and Now 85. Switching Channels 88. Weekend at Bernie's 89. The Winter People 89. Hot and Cold 89. Folks! 92.

Koteas, Elias (1961–   ).
Canadian actor, working in Hollywood.
One Magic Christmas 85. Gardens of Stone 87. Some Kind of Wonderful 87. Full Moon in Blue Water 88. Tucker: The Man and His Dream 88. Friends, Lovers and Lunatics 89. Desperate Hours 90. Teenage Mutant Ninja Turtles 90. Backstreet Dreams 90. Almost an Angel 90. The Adjuster 91. Teenage Mutant Ninja Turtles III 93. God's Army 93. Camilla 93. Exotica 94, etc.

¶ I would think I'd accomplished it all if I could get to play Quasimodo. – E.K.

Kotto, Yaphet (1937–   ).
American actor.
The Thomas Crown Affair 68. The Liberation of L. B. Jones 70. Across 110th Street 72. *Live and Let Die* 73. Truck Turner 74. Report to the Commissioner 74. Drum 76. Monkey Hustle 76. Blue Collar 78. Alien 79. Brubaker 80. The Star Chamber 83. Warning Sign 85. Prettykill 87. The Running Man 87. Midnight Run 88. Nightmares of the Devil (d only) 88. Ministry of Vengeance 89. After the Shock 90. Freddy's Dead: The Final Nightmare 91, etc.
TV series: Homicide: Life on the Street 93.

Kovack, Nancy (1935–   ).
American leading lady with stage and TV experience.
Strangers When We Meet 60. Diary of a Madman 62. Jason and the Argonauts 63. The Outlaws Is Coming 65. Frankie and Johnny 66. The Silencers 66. Tarzan and the Valley of Gold 66. Marooned 69, etc.

Kovacs, Ernie (1919–1962).
Big, cigar-smoking American comedian and TV personality. Died in a car crash. Married to Edie Adams.
Biography: 1976, *Nothing in Moderation* by David G. Walley.
■ *Operation Mad Ball* 57. Bell, Book and Candle 58. It Happened to Jane 58. *Our Man in Havana* 59. Wake Me When It's Over 60. Strangers When We Meet 60. North to Alaska 60. Pepe 60. Five Golden Hours 61. Sail a Crooked Ship 62.

Kovacs, Laszlo (1932–   ).
American cinematographer given to experimentation which does not always please the eye.
Targets 68. The Savage Seven 68. Easy Rider 69. Getting Straight 70. Five Easy Pieces 70. Alex in Wonderland 70. The Last Movie 71. Marriage of a Young Stockbroker 71. Pocket Money 72. What's Up Doc? 72. Paper Moon 73. Freebie and the Bean 74. Shampoo 75. At Long Last Love 75. Nickelodeon 76. New York New York 77. Close Encounters of the Third Kind (co-ph) 77. The Last Waltz 78. Butch and Sundance 79. Heartbeat 79. The Legend of the Lone Ranger 81. The Toy 82. Frances 82. Crackers 84. Ghostbusters 84. Mask 85. Legal Eagles 86. Little Nikita 88. Say Anything 89. Shattered 91. Radio Flyer 92. Ruby Cairo 93. The Next Karate Kid 94. The Scout 94, etc.

Kove, Kenneth (1893–1965).
English character actor, in silly-ass roles, from Aldwych farces.
Murder 30. Fascination 31. Two White Arms 32. Pyjamas Preferred 32. Dora 33. Song of the Plough 33. Crazy People 34. Radio Pirates 35. Look Up and Laugh 35. Talking Feet 37. Asking for Trouble 42. Innocents in Paris 53. Dr Terror's House of Horrors 65, etc.

Kowalski, Bernard (1929–   ).
American director, from TV.
Hot Car Girl 58. Attack of the Giant Leeches 58. Night of the Blood Beast 58. Blood and Steel 59.
Krakatoa East of Java 69. Stiletto 70. Macho Callahan 70. Ssss 73. The Nativity (TV) 78. B.A.D. Cats (TV) 80. Miracle at Beekman's Place (TV) 88. Nashville Beat 89, etc.

Kozak, Harley Jane (1953–   ) (Susan Jane Kozak).
Leading American actress.
Hair 79. The World according to Garp 82. When Harry Met Sally 89. Parenthood 89. Side Out 90. Arachnophobia 90. Necessary Roughness 91. All I Want for Christmas 91. The Taking of Beverly Hills 91. Beyond Control: The Amy Fisher Story (TV) 93. The Favor 94, etc.

Kozintsev, Grigori (1905–1973).
Russian director, in films from 1924.
The Youth of Maxim 35. *Don Quixote* 57. *Hamlet* 64. King Lear 69, etc.

Kozlowski, Linda (1958–   ).
American leading actress. She is married to actor Paul Hogan.
Crocodile Dundee 86. Pass the Ammo 88. Crocodile Dundee II 88. Almost an Angel 90. The Neighbor 93, etc.

Krabbé, Jeroen (1944–   ).
Dutch leading actor in international films.
The Little Ark 72. Alicia 74. Soldier of Orange 79. Spetters 80. A Flight of Rainbirds 81. The Fourth Man 82. Turtle Diary 85. Jumpin' Jack Flash 86. No Mercy 86. The Living Daylights 87. Crossing Delancey 88. A World Apart 88. Scandal 89. The Punisher 89. Robin Hood 90. Till There Was You 90. Murder East/Murder West 90. The Prince of Tides 91. Kafka 91. For a Lost Soldier (Voor Een Verloren Soldaat) 92. King of the Hill 93. Going Home (Oeroeg) 93. The Fugitive 93. Immortal Beloved 94. Farinelli il Castrato (as Handel) 95, etc.

Kramer, Larry (1935–   ).
American screenwriter and dramatist.
Women in Love (& p) 69. Lost Horizon 72, etc.

¶ Writing movies is exceptionally boring, especially when you're good at it, and for some reason, it comes very easily to me. But if you're a serious writer, you shouldn't write movies; movies are simply not a first-rate art form. – L.K.

Kramer, Stanley (1913–   ).
American producer and director of clean-cut, well-intentioned films which sometimes fall short on inspiration.
■ So Ends Our Night 41. *The Moon and Sixpence* 42. So This Is New York 48. Champion 49. Home of the Brave 49. *The Men* 50. Cyrano de Bergerac 50. *Death of a Salesman* 51. High Noon 52. The Sniper 52. The Happy Time 52. My Six Convicts 52. The Member of the Wedding 52. Eight Iron Men 52. The Fourposter 53. The Juggler 53. The 5000 Fingers of Dr T 53. The Wild One 54. *The Caine Mutiny* 54. Not as a Stranger (& d) 55. The Pride and the Passion (& d) 57. The Defiant Ones (& d) (AAN) 58. *On the Beach* (& d) 59. *Inherit the Wind* (& d) 60. Judgment at Nuremberg (& d) (AAN) 61. Pressure Point 62. A Child is Waiting 62. It's a Mad Mad Mad Mad World (& d) 63. Invitation to a Gunfighter 64. *Ship of Fools* (& d) 65. *Guess Who's Coming to Dinner* (& d) (AAN) 67. The Secret of Santa Vittoria (& d) 69 R.P.M. (& d) 71. Bless the Beasts and Children (& d) 71. *Oklahoma Crude* (& d) 73. The Domino Principle (& d) 77. The Runner Stumbles (& d) 79.
✪ For trying. *Inherit the Wind*.

¶ I'm always pursuing the next dream, hunting for the next truth. – *S.K.*

He will never be a natural, but time has proved that he is not a fake. – *Andrew Sarris, 1968*

He's the kind of man who invariably says he saves other people's films in the cutting room. – *Fred Zinnemann*

Krampf, Gunter (1899–1957*).
German cinematographer, in Britain from 1931.
The Student of Prague 24. The Hands of Orlac 24. *Pandora's Box* 28. Rome Express 32. Little Friend 34. Latin Quarter 45. Fame is the Spur 46. Portrait of Clare 50. The Franchise Affair 52, many others.

Krasker, Robert (1913–1981).
Australian cinematographer, long in Britain.
Dangerous Moonlight 40. *Henry V* 44. Caesar and Cleopatra 45. *Brief Encounter* 46. *Odd Man Out* 47. *The Third Man* (AA) 49. Romeo and Juliet 53. Trapeze 56. The Quiet American 58. The Criminal 60. El Cid 61. Billy Budd 62. The Running Man 63. The Fall of the Roman Empire 64. The Heroes of Telemark 65, many others.

Krasna, Norman (1909–1984).
American playwright who worked on many films from 1932, including adaptations of his own plays.
The Richest Girl in the World (AAN) 34. *Fury* (AAN) 36. *Bachelor Mother* 39. The Flame of New Orleans 41. The Devil and Miss Jones (AAN) 41. *Princess O'Rourke* (AA) (& d) 43. The Big Hangover (& pd) 50. The Ambassador's Daughter (& d) 56. *Indiscreet* 58. Who Was That Lady? (& d) 60. Let's Make Love 61. Sunday in New York 64, many others.

Krasner, Milton (1901–1988).
American cinematographer.
I Love That Man 33. The Crime of Dr Hallet 36. The House of the Seven Gables 40. *The Woman in the Window* 44. Scarlet Street 45. *The Dark Mirror* 46. The Farmer's Daughter 47. *The Set Up* 49. Rawhide 50. *All About Eve* 50. Monkey Business 51. *Three Coins in the Fountain* (AA) 54. The Rains of Ranchipur 55. Bus Stop 56. An Affair to Remember 57. The Four Horsemen of the Apocalypse 62. Two Weeks in Another Town 62. Love with the Proper Stranger 64. The Sandpiper 65. The Singing Nun 66. Hurry Sundown 67. The Epic of Josie 67. The St Valentine's Day Massacre 68. The Sterile Cuckoo 69. Beneath the Planet of the Apes 70, many others.

Kraushaar, Raoul (1908–   ).
American composer.
Melody Ranch 40. Stardust on the Sage 42. Stork Bites Man 47. Bride of the Gorilla 51. The Blue Gardenia 53. Mohawk 56. Mustang 59, etc.

Krauss, Werner (1884–1959).
Distinguished German actor.
ETA Hoffman (debut) 16. *The Cabinet of Dr Caligari* 19. The Brothers Karamazov 20. Othello 22. Nathan the Wise 23. *Waxworks* 24. The Student of Prague 25. A Midsummer Night's Dream 25. Secrets of a Soul 26. Tartuffe 26. Jew Süss 40. John Ohne Heimat 55, etc.

Kress, Harold F. (1913–   ).
American editor.
Bitter Sweet 40. Dr Jekyll and Mr Hyde 41. Mrs Miniver 42. Dragon Seed 44. Command Decision 49. Green Fire 54. The Cobweb 55. Silk Stockings 57. King of Kings 61. How the West Was Won (AA) 63. Alvarez Kelly 66. I Walk the Line 70. The Poseidon Adventure 72. The Towering Inferno (AA) 74. Viva Knievel 77, many others.

■ AS DIRECTOR: Purity Squad 45. No Questions Asked 51. The Painted Hills 51. Apache War Smoke 52. Cromwell (2nd unit) 70.

Kreuger, Kurt (1917–   ).
Swiss actor, former ski instructor, who appeared in many Hollywood films as smooth continental heartthrob or menace.
Sahara 43. The Moon is Down 43. Mademoiselle Fifi 44. Madame Pimpernel 45. Unfaithfully Yours 48. The Enemy Below 58. What Did You Do in the War, Daddy? 66. The St Valentine's Day Massacre 67, etc.

Krige, Alice (1955–   ).
South African leading lady in international films.
Chariots of Fire 81. Ghost Story 81. A Tale of Two Cities (TV) 81. Ellis Island (TV) 84. King David 85. Dream West (TV) 85. Barfly 87. See You in the Morning 89. Sleepwalkers 92. Scarlet and Black (TV) 93. The Institute Benjamenta 95, etc.

Krish, John (1923–   ).
British director who began in sponsored documentary field.
■ Unearthly Stranger 61. The Wild Affair 65. Decline and Fall 68. The Man Who Had Power over Women 70. Jesus (co-d) 79. Out of the Darkness 85.

Krishnamma, Suri.
English director, from television.
O Mary This London (TV) 94. A Man of No Importance 94.

Kristel, Sylvia (1952–   ).
Dutch-born leading lady who became famous in the nude.
Emmanuelle 73. Alice or the Last Escapade 76. The Fifth Musketeer 77. The Concorde – Airport 79 79. The Nude Bomb 80. Private Lessons 81. Lady Chatterley's Lover 82. Casanova (TV) 87. Emmanuelle 7 92, etc.

Kristofferson, Kris (1936–   ).
American leading man of the 70s, former folk singer and musician.
■ The Last Movie 70. Cisco Pike 72. Blume in Love 73. Pat Garrett and Billy the Kid 73. Bring Me the Head of Alfredo Garcia 74. Alice Doesn't Live Here Any More 75. The Sailor who Fell from Grace with the Sea 76. A Star Is Born 76. Vigilante Force 76. Semi-Tough 78. Convoy 78. Heaven's Gate 80. Rollover 81. Flashpoint 84. Songwriter 84. Trouble in Mind 85. Blood and Orchids (TV) 86. The Last Days of Frank and Jesse James (TV) 86. Stagecoach (TV) 86. Amerika (TV) 87. Big Top Pee-Wee 88. Millennium 89. Welcome Home 89. Pair of Aces (TV) 90. Another Pair of Aces: Three of a Kind (TV) 91. Miracle in the Wilderness (TV) 91. Paper Hearts 93. Sodbusters (TV) 94.

Kruger, Alma (1868–1960).
American stage actress who made many films in later life and is specially remembered as the head nurse in the Dr Kildare series.
These Three 36. One Hundred Men and a Girl 37. Marie Antoinette 38. Balalaika 39. Saboteur 42. A Royal Scandal 46. Forever Amber (last film) 47, etc.

Kruger, Hardy (1928–   ).
Blond German leading man who has filmed internationally.
Junge Adler (debut) 43. Insel Ohne Moral 50. Solange 53. Alibi 55. *The One That Got Away* 57. Bachelor of Hearts 58. Blind Date 59. The Rest Is Silence 59. Sundays and Cybèle 62. Hatari 62.

The Flight of the Phoenix 65. The Defector 66. The Secret of Santa Vittoria 69. The Red Tent 70. Night Hair Child 71. Paper Tiger 75. Barry Lyndon 75. A Bridge Too Far 77. The Wild Geese 78. Blue Fin 79. Society Limited 81. Wrong Is Right 82. The Inside Man 84. L'Atlantide 92, etc.

Kruger, Otto (1885–1974).
Suave American actor with long stage experience.
When the Call Came 15. Under the Red Robe 23. Beauty for Sale 33. The Prizefigher and the Lady 33. *Chained* 34. Springtime for Henry 34. Treasure Island 34. *Dracula's Daughter* 36. They Won't Forget 37. *The Housemaster* (GB) 38. Thanks for the Memory 38. Dr Ehrlich's Magic Bullet 40. This Man Reuter 40. The Big Boss 41. *Saboteur* 42. *Murder My Sweet* 44. Escape in the Fog 45. Duel in the Sun 46. Smart Woman 48. Payment on Demand 51. High Noon 52. Magnificent Obsession 54. The Last Command 56. The Wonderful World of the Brothers Grimm 63. Sex and the Single Girl 64, many others.

Krupa, Gene (1909–1973).
American jazz drummer and bandleader who rose to fame with the Benny Goodman orchestra in the 30s to become the first star of his instrument. In films usually as himself. In the biopic *The Gene Krupa Story* 59, he was played by Sal Mineo, though the drumming was his own.
Big Broadcast of 1937 36. Some Like It Hot (aka Rhythm Romance) 39. Ball of Fire 41. George White's Scandals 45. Beat the Band 46. Glamour Girl 48. Make Believe Ballroom 49. The Glenn Miller Story 54. The Benny Goodman Story 55, etc.

Kruschen, Jack (1922–   ).
American character comedian of stage and TV.
Red Hot and Blue 49. The Last Voyage 60. The Apartment (AAN) 60. Lover Come Back 62. The Unsinkable Molly Brown 64. Harlow (TV) (as Louis B. Mayer) 66. Million Dollar Duck 71. Freebie and the Bean 74. Sunburn 79. Under the Rainbow 81. Legend of the Wild 81, etc.

The Ku Klux Klan
was sympathetically portrayed in Griffith's *The Birth of a Nation*, a fact which has never ceased to provoke controversy. The villainous actuality has, however, been displayed in *Black Legion* 36, *Legion of Terror* 37, *The Burning Cross* 47, *Storm Warning* 51, *The FBI Story* 59, *The Cardinal* 63 and *The Klansman* 74, among others.
See also: *Lynch Law*.

Kubik, Gail (1914–1984).
American composer.
The World at War (doc) 42. The Memphis Belle (doc) 43. Thunderbolt (doc) 45. C-Man 45. Gerald McBoing Boing 50. The Desperate Hours 55. I Thank a Fool 62, etc.

Kubrick, Stanley (1928–   ).
American writer-producer-director, in whose psyche independence seems equated with excess.
Biographies: 1971, *Stanley Kubrick Directs* by Alexander Walker. 1982, *Kubrick, Inside a Film Artist's Maze* by T. A. Nelson.
■ Fear and Desire (wdph) 53. Killer's Kiss (wd) 55. *The Killing* (wd) 56. *Paths of Glory* (wd) 58. Spartacus (d) 60. Lolita (d) 62. Dr Strangelove (wdp) (AAN) 63. 2001: A Space Odyssey (wdp) (AAN) 69. A Clockwork Orange (wdp) (AAN) 71. Barry Lyndon (AAN) 75. The Shining 79. Full Metal Jacket 87.

¶ He gives new meaning to the word meticulous. – *Jack Nicholson*

Man in the twentieth century has been cast adrift in a rudderless boat on an uncharted sea. The very meaninglessness of life forces man to create his own meaning. If it can be written or thought, it can be filmed. – *S.K.*

His tragedy may have been that he was hailed as a great artist before he had become a competent craftsman. However, it is more likely that he has chosen to exploit the giddiness of middlebrow audiences on the satiric level of *Mad* magazine. – *Andrew Sarris, 1968*

Kuei, Yuen:
see *Yuen, Corey.*

Kulik, Buzz (1923–) (Seymour Kulik).
American director, from TV.
■ The Explosive Generation 61. The Yellow Canary 63. Ready for the People 64. Warning Shot (& p) 66. Villa Rides 68. Riot 68. Vanished (TV) 71. Brian's Song (TV) 71. Owen Marshall (TV) 71. To Find a Man 72. Incident in a Dark Street (TV) 72. Shamus 73. Pioneer Woman (TV) 73. Remember When (TV) 74. Bad Ronald (TV) 74. Cage without a Key (TV) 75. Babe (TV) 75. Matt Helm (TV) 75. Feather and Father (TV) 76. The Lindbergh Kidnapping Case (TV) 76. Corey for the People (TV) 77. Kill Me If You Can (TV) 77. Ziegfeld: The Man and His Women (TV) 78. From Here to Eternity (TV) 79. The Pursuit of D. B. Cooper 81. Rage of Angels (TV) 83. George Washington (TV) 84. Kane & Abel (TV) 85. Women of Valor (TV) 86. Her Secret Life (TV) 87. Too Young the Hero (TV) 88. Around the World in 80 Days (TV) 89. Miles from Nowhere 92.

Kulp, Nancy (1921–1991).
American comedy actress, famous for TV portrayals.
The Model and the Marriage Broker 52. Shane 53. Five Gates to Hell 59. The Parent Trap 61. The Patsy 64. The Return of the Beverly Hillbillies (TV) 81, etc.
TV series: *The Beverly Hillbillies* 62–70. The Brian Keith Show 73.

Kumel, Harry (1940–).
Belgian director and screenwriter.
Rag to a Red Rose (w) 59. Princess (w) 69. Daughters of Darkness 71. Malpertius 73. De Komst Van Joachim Stiller 76. Het Verloren Paradijs 78. The Secrets of Love 86. Eline Vere 91, etc.

Kureishi, Hanif (1954–).
British screenwriter, director and novelist, of Pakistani descent.
My Beautiful Laundrette (w) 86. Sammy and Rosie Get Laid (w) 87. London Kills Me (wd) 91. The Buddha of Suburbia (co-w from novel) (TV) 93.

Kurnitz, Harry (1907–1968).
American screenwriter, in Hollywood from 1938.

Fast and Furious 38. The Thin Man Goes Home 44. What Next, Corporal Hargrove (AAN) 45. The Web 47. A Kiss in the Dark (& p) 48. Pretty Baby 49. The Inspector General 49. Melba 53. The Man Between 53. Land of the Pharaohs 55. *Witness for the Prosecution* 57. Goodbye Charlie 64. How to Steal a Million 66, many others.

Kurosawa, Akira (1910–).
Distinguished Japanese director.
Autobiography: 1982, *Something Like an Autobiography.*
Biographies: 1974, *Kurosawa* by Michel Mesnil. 1991, *The Warrior's Camera: The Cinema of Akira Kurosawa* by Stephen Prince.
■ Sanshiro Sugata (& w) 43. The Most Beautiful (& w) 44. Sanshiro Sugata II (& w) 44. Tora-no-o (& w) 45. Those Who Make Tomorrow (co-d) 46. No Regrets for Our Youth 46. Wonderful Sunday 47. Drunken Angel 48. A Quiet Duel 49. Stray Dog 49. Scandal 50. *Rashomon* 50. The Idiot 51. *Ikuru* 52. *The Seven Samurai* 54. I Live in Fear 55. *Throne of Blood* 56. *The Lower Depths* 57. *The Hidden Fortress* 58. The Bad Sleep Well 60. *Yojimbo* 61. Sanjuro 62. High and Low 63. Redbeard 65. Dodeska-den 70. Dersu Uzala 75. *The Shadow Warrior* 81. *Ran* (AAN) 85. Kurosawa's Dreams 90. Rhapsody in August (Hachigatsu-no Kyoshikyoku) 91. Madadayo 93.
☯ For his brilliance as a maker of historical films with a universal appeal. *The Seven Samurai.*

Kurten, Peter.
German murderer who was the model for Fritz Lang's *M* 31 and its 1951 remake by Joseph Losey, and *The Vampire of Düsseldorf* 64.

Kurtz, Swoosie (1944–).
American leading actress with stage background.
First Love 77. Slap Shot 77. Oliver's Story 78. Marriage Is Alive and Well (TV) 80. Walking through the Fire 80. The Mating Season 81. The World According to Garp 82. Against All Odds 83. A Time to Live (TV) 85. True Stories 86. Wildcats 86. Baja Oklahoma (TV) 87. Bright Lights, Big City 88. Dangerous Liaisons 88. Vice Versa 88. The Image (TV) 89. A Shock to the System 90. Stanley and Iris 90. The Positively True Adventures of the Alleged Texas Cheerleader-Murdering Mom (TV) 93. And the Band Played On (TV) 93. Reality Bites 94. Story Book 94, etc.
TV series: Love, Sidney 81–83.

Kurys, Diane (1948–).
French director and screenwriter of films that have an autobiographical basis. She was formerly an actress, working in theatre and playing small parts in movies.
Peppermint Soda (Diablo Menthe) 77. Cocktail Molotov 79. Entre Nous (Coup de Foudre) (AAN) 83. A Man in Love (Un Homme Amoureux) 87. C'est la Vie (La Baule-les-pins) 90. After Love (Après l'Amour) 92. Six Days, Six Nights (À la Folie) 94, etc.

Kusturica, Emir (1955–).
Yugoslavian director and screenwriter, from TV.
Do You Remember Dolly Bell? 81. When Father Was Away on Business (Otac Na Sluzbenom Putu) (AAN) 85. Time of the Gypsies (Dom Za Vesanje) 88. Arizona Dream 93, etc.

Kwan, Nancy (1939–).
Chinese-English leading lady.
The World of Suzie Wong 60. Flower Drum Song 61. Tamahine 63. Fate Is the Hunter 64. The Wild Affair 65. Lt Robin Crusoe 65. Arrivederci Baby 66. Nobody's Perfect 67. The Wrecking Crew 68. The Girl Who Knew Too Much 69. The McMasters 70. Wonder Woman (TV) 73. Project: Kill 76. Night Creature 78. Streets of Hong Kong 79. Walking the Edge 83. Night Children 88. Cold Dog Soup 89. Dragon: The Bruce Lee Story 93, etc.

Kwan, Stanley (1957–) (Guan Jinpeng).
Hong Kong director, from television.
Love unto Waste 86. Rouge (Yanzhi Kou) 88. Full Moon in New York (Yan Tsoi Nau Yeuk) 89. Center Stage (Yun Ling-Yuk) 92, etc.

Kwon-Taek, Im (1936–).
Leading South Korean film director with a growing reputation in the West.
Testimony (Jungon) 74. The Family Tree Book (Jokbo) 78. The Hidden Hero (Gitbal Obnun Gisu) 79. *Mandala* 81. Village in the Mist (Angemaeul) 83. Gilsodom 85. Ticket 86. Surrogate Woman 86. Diary of Yonsan (Yonsan Ilgi) 87. Son of a General 91. Son of a General II 92, etc.

Kwouk, Burt (1930–).
Chinese-English character actor.
Goldfinger 64. You Only Live Twice 68. The Most Dangerous Man in the World 69. Deep End 71. The Return of the Pink Panther 75. The Last Remake of Beau Geste 77. The Fiendish Plot of Dr Fu Manchu 81. Trail of the Pink Panther 82. Plenty 85. Empire of the Sun 87. Air America 90. Son of the Pink Panther 93, etc.

Kydd, Sam (1917–1982).
British character comedian whose sharp features were seen in many films from 1945.
The Captive Heart 45. The Small Back Room 48. Treasure Island 50. The Cruel Sea 53. The Quatermass Experiment 55. I'm All Right Jack 59. Follow That Horse 60. Island of Terror 66, etc.

Kyo, Machiko (1924–).
Japanese actress.
Rashomon 50. Gate of Hell 52. The Teahouse of the August Moon 56. Ugetsu Monogatari 58, etc.

Kyser, Kay (1897–1985).
Mild-mannered American bandleader who made a number of comedy films in the early 40s, then retired to become an active Christian Scientist.
■ That's Right You're Wrong 39. You'll Find Out 40. Playmates 41. My Favorite Spy 42. Around the World 43. Swing Fever 44. Carolina Blues 44.

L

La Bern, Arthur.
British novelist whose low-life novels brought some realism into films of the 40s, although they cannot now stand comparison with such films of the 60s as *Saturday Night and Sunday Morning*.
Good-Timer Girl (from *Night Darkens the Streets*) 48. It Always Rains on Sundays 48. Paper Orchid 49. Frenzy (from *Goodbye Piccadilly, Farewell Leicester Square*) 71.

La Cava, Gregory (1892–1952).
American director, former cartoonist and writer; a delicate talent for comedy usually struggled against unsatisfactory vehicles. He was impersonated by Allan Arbus in *W. C. Fields and Me*.
His Nibs 22. The New Schoolteacher 24. Womanhandled 25. Running Wild 27. Feel My Pulse 28. Laugh and Get Rich 31. Symphony of Six Million 32. The Half-Naked Truth 32. Gabriel over the White House 32. Affairs of Cellini 34. What Every Woman Knows 34. Private Worlds 35. She Married Her Boss 35. *My Man Godfrey* (AAN) 36. *Stage Door* (AAN) 37. Fifth Avenue Girl 39. The Primrose Path 40. Unfinished Business 41. Lady in a Jam 42. Living in a Big Way 47. One Touch of Venus 48, etc.

La Frenais, Ian (c. 1938–).
British comedy writer who works in conjunction with Dick Clement (qv).

La Marr, Barbara (1896–1926) (Reatha Watson)
American leading lady of silent films from 1920.
The Prisoner of Zenda 22. The Eternal City 23. Thy Name Is Woman 24. The Shooting of Dan McGrew 24. The Girl from Montmartre 26, etc.

La Planche, Rosemary (1923–1979).
American leading lady of the 40s.
Mad about Music 38. The Falcon in Danger 43. Prairie Chickens 43. Devil Bat's Daughter 46, etc.

La Plante, Laura (1904–).
Blonde American leading lady of Universal pictures in the 20s.
Burning Words 23. The Ramblin' Kidd 23. Sporting Youth 24. The Dangerous Blonde 24. Smouldering Fires 25. Skinner's Dress Suit 26. The Beautiful Cheat 26. Silk Stockings 27. The Cat and the Canary 27. The Last Warning 28. Show Boat 29. The Love Trap 29. Captain of the Guard 30. Little Mister Jim 46. Spring Reunion 56, etc.

La Rocque, Rod (1896–1969) (Roderick la Rocque de la Rour).
Popular American leading man of the silent screen, in Hollywood from 1914 after circus experience. He was married to actress Vilma Banky.
The Snow Man 14. The Lightbearer 16. Efficiency Edgar's Courtship 17. The Venus Model 18. The Ten Commandments 23. Forbidden Paradise 25. Resurrection 26. Our Modern Maidens 28. Let Us Be Gay 29. One Romantic Night 30. SOS Iceberg 33. Till We Meet Again 36. The Hunchback of Notre Dame 40. Dr Christian Meets the Women 41. Meet John Doe 41, many others.

La Rue, Danny (1927–) (Daniel Patrick Carroll).
British revue star and female impersonator.
■ Our Miss Fred 72.

La Rue, Jack (1902–1984) (Gaspare Biondolillo).
Grim-faced American actor, typed as gangster from the early 30s.
Lady Killer 34. Captains Courageous 37. Paper Bullets 41. Gentleman from Dixie (a rare sympathetic part) 41. Machine Gun Mama 44. No Orchids for Miss Blandish (GB) (as the maniacal Slim Grisson) 48. Robin Hood of Monterey 49. Ride the Man Down 53. Robin and the Seven Hoods 64. Won Ton Ton 76, many others.

La Shelle, Joseph (1903–1989).
American cinematographer.
Happy Land 43. *Laura* (AA) 44. *Hangover Square* 44. The Foxes of Harrow 47. Come to the Stable 49. Mister 880 50. Les Misérables 52. Marty 55. Storm Fear 55. *The Bachelor Party* 57. I Was a Teenage Werewolf 57. No Down Payment 57 The Naked and the Dead 58. The Apartment 60. Irma la Douce 63. The Fortune Cookie 66. The Chase 66. Barefoot in the Park 67. Kona Coast 68. Eighty Steps to Jonah 69, many others.

Laage, Barbara (1925–) (Claire Colombat).
French leading lady of several 50s films.
La Putain Respecteuse 52. L'Esclave Blanche 54. Act of Love 54. Un Homme à Vendre 58. Paris Blues 61. Domicile Conjugale 71. Private Projection 76, etc.

labour relations
is too downbeat a subject to be very popular on the screen; but strikes have been treated with seriousness in *Strike*, *The Crime of Monsieur Lange*, *Black Fury*, *How Green Was My Valley*, *The Agitator*, *Love on the Dole*, *Chance of a Lifetime*, *The Whistle at Eaton Falls*, *The Angry Silence*, *F.I.S.T.* and *Last Exit to Brooklyn*; with humour in *A Nous la Liberté*, *Modern Times*, *Carry On at Your Convenience*, *The Pajama Game*, and *I'm All Right Jack*. The classical comical strike of women against their husbands, led by Lysistrata, was depicted in the French *Love, Soldiers and Women* and Americanized in *The Second Greatest Sex*.

Lacey, Catherine (1904–1979).
British stage and screen actress, adept at sympathetic spinsters and eccentric types.
The Lady Vanishes (debut) 38. Cottage to Let 41. I Know Where I'm Going 45. *The October Man* 47. Whisky Galore 49. Rockets Galore 56. Crack in the Mirror 60. The Fighting Prince of Donegal (as Queen Elizabeth I) 66. The Sorcerers 67, etc.

Lacey, Ronald (1935–1991).
Solidly built British character actor.
The Likely Lads 76. Charleston (TV) 77. Zulu Dawn 79. Raiders of the Lost Ark 80. Firefox 82. Invitation to the Wedding 84. Sword of the Valiant 85. Red Sonja 85. Valmont 89, etc.

Lachman, Ed (1948–).
American cinematographer.
The Lords of Flatbush 74. Stroszek 77. Lightning over Water 80. Union City 80. Say Amen, Somebody 83. Desperately Seeking Susan 85. True Stories 86. Making Mr Right 87. Less than Zero 87. Catchfire 90. Mississippi Masala 91. London Kills Me 91. Light Sleeper 91. My New Gun 92, etc.

Lachman, Harry (1886–1975).
Anglo-American director, at his best in the 30s.
Weekend Wives 28. Under the Greenwood Tree 29. The Yellow Mask 30. The Outsider 30. The Compulsory Husband 30. Aren't We All 32. Insult 32. Paddy the Next Best Thing 33. Baby Take a Bow 34. *Dante's Inferno* 35. Charlie Chan at the Circus 36. *Our Relations* 36. The Devil Is Driving 37. No Time to Marry 38. They Came by Night 40. Dead Men Talk 41. The Loves of Edgar Allan Poe 42, etc.

Lackteen, Frank (1894–1968).
American character actor of Russian origin; his sharp features were adaptable to many ethnic roles.
Less Than the Dust 16. The Avenging Arrow 21. The Virgin 24. Hawk of the Hills 27. Hell's Valley 31. Escape from Devil's Island 35. Anthony Adverse 36. Suez 38. Juarez 39. Moon over Burma 40. The Sea Wolf 41. Chetniks 43. Can't Help Singing 44. Frontier Gal 45. Maneater of Kumaon 48. Daughter of the Jungle 49. King of the Khyber Rifles 53. Bengal Brigade 54. Devil Goddess 55. Requiem for a Gunfighter 65, many others.

Ladd, Alan (1913–1964).
Unsmiling, pint-sized tough-guy American star who proved to be just the kind of hero the 40s wanted.
Biography: 1979, *Ladd* by Beverly Linet.
■ Once in a Lifetime 32. Pigskin Parade 36. Last Train from Madrid 37. Souls at Sea 37. Born to the West 37. Hold 'em Navy 37. The Goldwyn Follies 38. Come on Leathernecks 38. The Green Hornet 39. Rulers of the Sea 39. Beast of Berlin 39. Light of Western Stars 40. Gangs of Chicago 40. Her First Romance (reissued as The Right Man) 40. In Old Missouri 40. The Howards of Virginia 40. Those Were the Days 40. Captain Caution 40. Wildcat Bus 40. Meet the Missus 40. Great Guns 41. Citizen Kane 41. Cadet Girl 41. Petticoat Politics 41. The Black Cat 41. The Reluctant Dragon 41. Paper Bullets 41. Joan of Paris 42. *This Gun for Hire* 42. *The Glass Key* 42. Lucky Jordan 42. Star Spangled Rhythm 42. China 43. And Now Tomorrow 44. Salty O'Rourke 45. Duffy's Tavern 45. *The Blue Dahlia* 46. O.S.S. 46. Two Years Before the Mast 46. Calcutta 47. Variety Girl 47. Wild Harvest 47. My Favourite Brunette 47 (cameo). Saigon 48. Beyond Glory 48. Whispering Smith 48. *The Great Gatsby* 49. Chicago Deadline 49. Captain Carey USA 50. Branded 51. Appointment with Danger 51. Red Mountain 52. The Iron Mistress 53. Thunder in the East 53. Desert Legion 53. *Shane* 53. Botany Bay 53. The Red Beret (GB)

53. Saskatchewan 54. Hell Below Zero (GB) 54. The Black Knight (GB) 54. Drum Beat 54. The McConnell Story 55. Hell on Frisco Bay 55. Santiago 56. The Big Land 57. Boy on a Dolphin 57. The Deep Six 58. The Proud Rebel 58. The Badlanders 58. The Man in the Net 58. Guns of the Timberland 60. All the Young Men 60. One Foot in Hell 60. Duel of the Champions (It.) 61. 13 West Street 62. *The Carpetbaggers* 64.

¶ I have the face of an ageing choirboy and the build of an undernourished featherweight. If you can figure out my success on the screen you're a better man than I. – *A.L.*
A small boy's idea of a tough guy. – *Raymond Chandler*
That man had stature even if he was short. – *Stewart Granger*
He succeeded in reducing murder to an act as casual as crossing the street. – *Richard Schickel*
Nobody ever pretended he could act. He got to the top, therefore, by a combination of determination and luck. – *David Shipman*
~Ladd is said to have turned down both the James Dean role in *Giant* and the Spencer Tracy role in *Bad Day at Black Rock*.

Ladd, Alan, Jnr (1937–).
American producer and production executive, a former agent, the son of actor Alan Ladd. He became president of Fox in the mid-70s before leaving to found The Ladd Company. From the mid-80s he had an on-and-off relationship in charge of the troubled MGM/UA, finally resigning from the companies in 1993 to join Paramount.
The Night Comes 71. Fear Is the Key 72. Divine Madness 80. Outland 81. Chariots of Fire 81. Blade Runner 82. Five Days One Summer 82. Lovesick 83. Twice upon a Time 83. Braveheart 95, etc.

Ladd, Cheryl (1951–) (Cheryl Stoppelmoor).
American leading lady who became familiar on TV as one of *Charlie's Angels* 78–81.
Satan's School for Girls 73. Evil in the Deep 76. Now and Forever 82. Grace Kelly (TV) 83. Purple Hearts 84. Romance on the Orient Express (TV) 85. Millennium 89. Lisa 90. Poison Ivy 92, etc.
TV series: One West Waikiki 94.

Ladd, Diane (1939–) (Diane Ladner).
American character actress.
White Lightning 73. Chinatown 74. *Alice Doesn't Live Here Any More* (AAN) 75. Thaddeus Rose and Eddie (TV) 78. Willa 79. Cattle Annie and Little Britches 80. Guyana Tragedy (TV) 80. All Night Long 81. Grace Kelly (TV) 83. Something Wicked This Way Comes 83. Wild at Heart (AAN) 90. A Kiss before Dying 91. Rambling Rose (AAN) 91. The Cemetery Club 93. Carnosaur 93. Father Hood 93, etc.

Lady for a Day.
Robert Riskin wrote and Frank Capra directed, in 1933, this Runyonesque fantasy about an old flower seller who is helped by gangster friends to deceive her visiting daughter into believing that she is comfortably placed. In 1961 Capra remade it as *Pocketful of Miracles*, but not even Bette Davis could save it from tedium, and Capra's direction seemed tired.

Laemmle, Carl (1867–1939).
German-American pioneer, in films from 1906; produced *Hiawatha* 09, founded Universal Pictures 1912.

Biography: 1931, *The Life and Adventures of Carl Laemmle* by John Drinkwater.

¶ Uncle Carl Laemmle
Had a very large faemmle. – *Ogden Nash*, satirizing the number of Laemmle relations who were found jobs at Universal Studios
I hope I didn't make a mistake coming out here. – *C.L.*, *Hollywood, 1915*
The prototype of the slightly mad movie mogul – impulsive, quixotic, intrepid, unorthodox, unpredictable. – *Norman Zierold*

Laemmle, Carl, Jnr (1908–1979).
Son of Carl Laemmle; executive producer at Universal for many years. Credited with the success of *Frankenstein*, *Dracula*, and *All Quiet on the Western Front*.

Laffan, Patricia (1919–).
British stage actress.
The Rake's Progress 45. Caravan 46. Quo Vadis (as Poppea) 51. Devil Girl from Mars 54. Twenty-Three Paces to Baker Street 56, etc.

Lafont, Bernadette (1938–).
Busy French leading actress, a former dancer, who has made more than 90 films.
Le Beau Serge 58. Web of Passion 59. Les Bonnes Femmes 60. Compartiment Tueurs (The Sleeping Car Murder) 65. Le Voleur (The Thief) 67. Catch Me a Spy 71. Une Belle Fille Comme Moi 72. Tendre Dracula 74. La Tortue sur le Dos 78. Il Ladrone 79. Le Roi des Cons 81. Cap Canaille 83. Inspector Lavardin 86. Waiting for the Moon 87. L'Air de Rien 89. Le Bonheur 94. Personne Ne M'Aime 94, many others.

LaGarde, Jocelyn (1922–1979).
Tahitian-born actress who was nominated for a Best Supporting Actress Oscar for her only film, *Hawaii* 66.

Lahr, Bert (1895–1967) (Irving Lahrheim).
Wry-faced American vaudeville comedian who made occasional film appearances.
Biography: 1969, *Notes on a Cowardly Lion* by John Lahr (his son).
Faint Heart 31. Flying High 31. Love and Hisses 37. Josette 38. Just around the Corner 38. Zaza 39. *The Wizard of Oz* 39. Ship Ahoy 42. Meet the People 44. Always Leave Them Laughing 49. Mr Universe 51. Rose Marie 54. The Second Greatest Sex 56. The Night They Raided Minsky's 68, etc.

¶ After *The Wizard of Oz* I was typecast as a lion, and there aren't all that many parts for lions. – *B.L.*
The last and the most marvellous of the American clowns cradled by burlesque. – *Alastair Cooke*

Lahti, Christine (1950–).
American character actress, often in off-beat roles.
■ . . . And Justice for All 79. The Henderson Monster (TV) 80. Whose Life Is It, Anyway? 81. The Executioner's Song (TV) 82. Ladies and Gentlemen, the Fabulous Stains 82. Swing Shift (AAN) 84. Single Bars, Single Women (TV) 84. Love Lives On (TV) 85. Just between Friends 86. Stacking 87. Housekeeping 87. Running on Empty 88. Gross Anatomy 89. Miss Firecracker 89. No Place Like Home (TV) 89. Funny about Love 90. The Doctor 91. Leaving Normal 92. The Fear Inside 92.

Lai, Francis (1932–).
French film composer.

Un Homme et une Femme (AA) 66. Mayerling 68. House of Cards 68. Rider on the Rain 70. *Love Story* (AA) 71. Le Petit Matin 71. Emmanuelle 75. Seven Suspects for Murder 77. International Velvet 78. Oliver's Story 78. Second Chance 80. Beyond the Reef 81. Edith and Marcel 83. My New Partner (Les Ripoux) 84. Marie 85. A Man and a Woman: 20 Years Later 86. Dark Eyes (Ocie Ciornie) 87. Keys to Freedom 89. Too Beautiful for You (Trop Belle pour Toi) 89. My New Partner 2 (Ripoux contre Ripoux) 90. The Beautiful Story (La Belle Histoire) 91. Stranger in the House (L'Inconnu dans la Maison) 92, etc.

Laine, Frankie (1913–) (Frank Paul Lo Vecchio).
American pop singer who made several light musicals in the 50s. He also sang the title song in *Gunfight at the O.K. Corral* and for the TV series *Rawhide*.
When You're Smiling 50. Make Believe Ballroom 50. The Sunny Side of the Street 51. Rainbow round My Shoulder 52. Bring Your Smile Along 55. He Laughed Last 56. Viva Las Vegas 56, etc.

Laine, Jimmy:
see *Ferrara, Abel*.

Laird, Jenny (1917–).
British character actress.
Just William 39. The Lamp Still Burns 43. Black Narcissus 46. *Painted Boats* 47. The Long Dark Hall 51. Conspiracy of Hearts 60, etc.

Lake, Arthur (1905–1987) (Arthur Silverlake).
Harrassed, crumple-faced American light comedy actor, best remembered as Dagwood Bumstead in the 'Blondie' series of 28 films in twelve years.
Jack and the Beanstalk 17. Skinner's Dress Suit 26. The Irresistible Lover 27. Harold Teen 28. On with the Show 29. Indiscreet 31. Midshipman Jack 33. Orchids to You 35. Topper 37. *Blondie* (and subsequent series) 38. There is a Family 44. Sixteen Fathoms Deep 48, many others.
TV series: Blondie 54.

Lake, Florence (1904–1980).
American character comedienne best remembered as Edgar Kennedy's bird-brained wife in many of his two-reelers.

Lake, Lew (1874–1939).
British actor, from the theatre, who appeared in some popular 30s concert party films. His successful melodrama *The Bloomsbury Burglars*, performed in music halls in the early 1900s, gave the English language the nickname 'Jerry' to describe Germans in both the First and Second World Wars.
The Bloomsbury Burglars 12. Splinters 29. The Great Game 30. Splinters in the Navy 31. Splinters in the Air 37.

Lake, Ricki (1968–).
American actress, often in John Waters' films, and a successful television chat show hostess.
Hairspray 88. Working Girl 88. Cookie 89. Babycakes (TV) 89. Cry-Baby 90. Last Exit to Brooklyn 90. Where the Day Takes You 92. Cabin Boy 94. Serial Mom 94, etc.

Lake, Veronica (1919–1973) (Constance Ockleman).
Petite American leading lady who now, with her limited acting ability and her 'peek a boo bang' (long blonde hair obscuring one eye), seems an appropriately artificial image for the Hollywood of

the early 40s. Her second husband was André de Toth (1944–52).

Autobiography: 1968, *Veronica*.

■ All Women Have Secrets 39. Sorority House 39. Forty Little Mothers 40. *I Wanted Wings* 41. *Sullivan's Travels* 41. *This Gun for Hire* 42. The Glass Key 42. *I Married a Witch* 42. Star Spangled Rhythm 42. So Proudly We Hail 43. The Hour before the Dawn 44. Bring on the Girls 45. Out of this World 45. Duffy's Tavern 45. Hold That Blonde 45. Miss Susie Slagle's 45. *The Blue Dahlia* 46. Variety Girl 47. The Sainted Sisters 48. Saigon 48. Isn't It Romantic? 48. Slattery's Hurricane 49. Stronghold 52. Footsteps in the Snow 66. Flesh Feast 70.

¶ You could put all the talent I had into your left eye and still not suffer from impaired vision. – V.L.

LaLoggia, Frank (1955–).

American independent director, screenwriter, composer and occasional actor.

Fear No Evil (wd, m) 81. The Wizard of Speed and Time (a) 88. Lady in White (wd, m) 88, etc.

Lamarr, Hedy (1913–) (Hedwig Kiesler).

Austrian leading lady of the 30s and 40s, in Hollywood from 1937 after creating a sensation by appearing nude in the Czech film *Extase* 33. She became a household word for glamour, but lacked the spark of personality. The third of her six husbands was actor John Loder (1943–47).

Autobiography: 1966, *Ecstasy and Me*.

■ AMERICAN FILMS: *Algiers* 38. Lady of the Tropics 39. I Take This Woman 40. Boom Town 40. Comrade X 40. Come Live with Me 41. Ziegfeld Girl 41. H.M. Pulham Esq. 41. Tortilla Flat 42. Crossroads 42. *White Cargo* (as Tondelayo) 42. The Heavenly Body 43. The Conspirators 44. Experiment Perilous 44. Her Highness and the Bellboy 45. The Strange Woman 46. Dishonoured Lady 47. Let's Live a Little 48. *Samson and Delilah* 49. A Lady without Passport 50. Copper Canyon 50. My Favorite Spy 51. The Face that Launched a Thousand Ships 54. The Story of Mankind 57. The Female Animal 57.

¶ Any girl can be glamorous: all you have to do is stand still and look stupid. – H.L.

When she spoke one did not listen, one just watched her mouth moving and marvelled at the exquisite shapes made by her lips. – *George Sanders*

Lamas, Fernando (1915–1982).

Argentinian leading man, in Hollywood from 1950 in routine musicals and comedies. He was married to actresses Arlene Dahl (1954–60) and Esther Williams.

Rich, Young and Pretty 51. The Law and the Lady 51. The Merry Widow 52. The Girl Who Had Everything 53. Sangaree 53. Rose Marie 54. The Girl Rush 55. The Lost World 60. The Violent Ones (& d) 67. 100 Rifles 69. Powder Keg 71. The Cheap Detective 78, etc.

Lamas, Lorenzo (1958–).

American leading man of action films. He is the son of actors Fernando Lamas and Arlene Dahl, and is married to actress Kathleen Kinmont.

100 Rifles 69. Grease 78. Tilt 78. Take Down 79. Body Rock 84. SnakeEater 89. SnakeEater 2: The Drug Buster 89. Final Impact 91. Killing Streets 91. Night of the Warrior 91. SnakeEater 3: His Law 92. Bounty Tracker 93. CIA Codename: Alexa 93, etc.

TV series: California Fever 79. Secrets of Midland Heights 80–81. Falcon Crest 81–90. Renegade 92–94.

Lamb, Gil (1906–).

Rubber-boned American comic, seen in many 40s musicals.

The Fleet's In (debut) 42. Rainbow Island 44. Practically Yours 44. Humphrey Takes a Chance 50. Terror in a Texas Town 58. Blackbeard's Ghost 67. Day of the Animals 77, etc.

Lambert, Christopher (1957–) (aka Christophe Lambert).

Franco-American leading man. He is married to actress Diane Lane.

■ Le Bar du Téléphone 80. Legitimate Violence 80. Greystoke: The Legend of Tarzan, Lord of the Apes 84. Love Songs (Paroles et Musique) 84. Subway 85. Highlander 86. I Love You 86. The Sicilian 87. Love Dream 88. To Kill a Priest 88. Un Plan d'Enfer 89. Highlander II – the Quickening 91. Knight Moves 91. Fortress 93. Gunmen 93. Highlander III: The Sorcerer 94.

Lambert, Constant (1905–1951).

British conductor whose one film score was *Anna Karenina* 47.

Lambert, Gavin (1924–).

British critic and novelist, in Hollywood since 1956. Stories about Hollywood: *The Slide Area*.

AS SCRIPTWRITER: Bitter Victory 57. Sons and Lovers (AAN) 60. The Roman Spring of Mrs Stone 61. Inside Daisy Clover 65. I Never Promised You a Rose Garden 77, etc.

Lambert, Jack (1899–1976).

Scottish character actor.

The Ghost Goes West 36. Nine Men 43. Hue and Cry 46. Eureka Stockade 47. The Brothers 47. The Lost Hours 50. The Sea Shall Not Have Them 54. Storm over the Nile 56. Reach for the Sky 56. Greyfriars Bobby 60. Modesty Blaise 66. Neither the Sea Nor the Sand 72, many others.

Lambert, Jack (1920–).

American character actor, usually an evil-eyed heavy.

The Cross of Lorraine 43. The Killers 46. The Unsuspected 47. The Enforcer 51. Scared Stiff 53. Kiss Me Deadly 55. Machine Gun Kelly 57. The George Raft Story 61. Four for Texas 63, many others.

Lambert, Mary.

American director.

Siesta 87. Pet Sematary 89. Pet Sematary II 92. Grand Isle 92. The Last Mardi Gras 92, etc.

Lamble, Lloyd (1914–).

Australian light actor who has been in many British films as detective, official, or other man.

The Story of Gilbert and Sullivan 53. The Belles of St Trinian's 54. The Man Who Never Was 56. Quatermass II 57. Blue Murder at St Trinian's 58. No Trees in the Street 59. The Trials of Oscar Wilde 60, etc.

Lamont, Charles (1898–1993).

American director, in Hollywood from silent days. With Universal from mid-30s, making comedies featuring Abbott and Costello; the Kettles, etc.

Love, Honour and Oh Baby 41. The Merry Monahans 44. Bowery to Broadway 44. Frontier Gal 45. The Runaround 46. Slave Girl 47. Baghdad 49. Flame of Araby 51. Abbott and Costello Meet Dr Jekyll and Mr Hyde 53. Ma and Pa Kettle in Paris 53. Untamed Heiress 54. Abbott and Costello Meet the Mummy 55. Francis in the Haunted House 56. The Kettles in the Ozarks 56, many others.

Lamont, Duncan (1918–).

Scottish actor with stage experience, in films since World War II.

The Golden Coach 53. *The Adventures of Quentin Durward* 56. Ben Hur 59. Mutiny on the Bounty 62. Murder at the Gallop 63. The Brigand of Kandahar 65. Arabesque 65. Decline and Fall 68. Pope Joan 72. Escape from the Dark 76, many others.

Lamorisse, Albert (1922–1970).

French director known for short fantasy films.

Bim 49. *Crin Blanc* 52. *The Red Balloon* (AAw) 55. Stowaway in the Sky 61. Fifi La Plume 64, etc.

Lamour, Dorothy (1914–) (Dorothy Kaumeyer).

Good-humoured American leading lady of the 30s and 40s: became typed in sarong roles, and happily guyed her own image.

Autobiography: 1981, *Dorothy Lamour*, with Dick McInnes.

■ *The Jungle Princess* 36. Thrill of a Lifetime 37. Swing High Swing Low 37. Last Train from Madrid 37. High Wide and Handsome 37. *The Hurricane* 37. The Big Broadcast of 1938. Her Jungle Love 38. Spawn of the North 38. Tropic Holiday 38. St Louis Blues 39. Man About Town 39. Disputed Passage 39. Johnny Apollo 40. Typhoon 40. *Road to Singapore* 40. Moon Over Burma 40. Chad Hanna 40. Road to Zanzibar 41. Caught in the Draft 41. Aloma of the South Seas 41. The Fleet's In 42. Beyond the Blue Horizon 42. Road to Morocco 42. Star Spangled Rhythm 42. They Got Me Covered 43. Dixie 43. Riding High 43. And the Angels Sing 43. Rainbow Island 44. Road to Utopia 45. A Medal for Benny 45. Duffy's Tavern 45. Masquerade in Mexico 45. My Favorite Brunette 47. Road to Rio 47. Wild Harvest 47. Variety Girl 47. On Our Merry Way 48. Lulu Belle 48. The Girl from Manhattan 48. Slightly French 48. Manhandled 48. The Lucky Stiff 49. Here Comes the Groom 51. The Greatest Show on Earth 52. Road to Bali 52. Road to Hong Kong 62. Donovan's Reef 63. Pajama Party 64. The Phynx 70. Won Ton Ton 75. Death of Love House (TV) 76. Creepshow 2 87.

L'Amour, Louis (1908–1988).

Best-selling American writer of western novels, many of which have been filmed.

Hondo 53. Four Guns to the Border 54. Stranger on Horseback 54. The Burning Hills 56. The Tall Stranger 57. Apache Territory 58. Guns of the Timberland 59. Heller in Pink Tights 60. Taggart 64. Shalako 68. Catlow 71. The Man Called Noon 73, etc.

Lampedusa, Giuseppe (1896–1957).

Italian novelist, a nobleman whose *The Leopard* was filmed and gave a picture of 19th-century Sicily.

Lampert, Zohra (1936–).

American TV actress.

Splendour in the Grass 60. Pay or Die 60. A Fine Madness 66. Opening Night 77. Alphabet City 84. Teachers 84.

Lancaster, Burt (1913–1994).

Athletic American leading man and latterly distinguished actor. Former circus acrobat; acted and danced in soldier shows during World War II.

■ *The Killers* 46. Desert Fury 47. I Walk Alone 47. *Brute Force* 47. Variety Girl (cameo) 47. Sorry, Wrong Number 48. Kiss the Blood Off My Hands 48. All My Sons 48. Criss Cross 49. Rope of Sand 49. Mister 880 50. *The Flame and the Arrow* 50.

geance Valley 51. Ten Tall Men 51. Jim
rpe All-American 51. The Crimson Pirate 52.
e Back Little Sheba 53. South Sea Woman 53.
m Here to Eternity (AAN) 53. His Majesty
Keefe 54. Apache 54. Vera Cruz 54. The
atuckian (& d) 55. The Rose Tattoo 55. Trapeze
The Rainmaker 57. Gunfight at the OK Corral (as
att Earp) 57. Sweet Smell of Success 57.
arate Tables 58. Run Silent Run Deep 58. The
vil's Disciple (GB) 59. The Unforgiven 59. Elmer
ntry (AA) 60. The Young Savages 61. Judgment
Nuremberg 61. Birdman of Alcatraz (AAN) 62. A
ld is Waiting 62. The Leopard 63. The List of
rian Messenger 63. Seven Days in May 64. The
in 64. The Hallelujah Trail 65. The Professionals
The Swimmer 67. The Scalphunters 68. Castle
ep 69. The Gypsy Moths 69. Airport 69. Lawman
Valdez is Coming 71. Ulzana's Raid 72. Scorpio
Executive Action 73. The Midnight Man (& co-
co-d) 74. Conversation Piece 75. Moses (TV) 75.
ffalo Bill and the Indians 76. 1900 76. Twilight's
t Gleaming 76. Victory at Entebbe (TV) 76. The
ssandra Crossing 77. The Island of Dr Moreau
Go Tell the Spartans 78. Zulu Dawn 79.
antic City USA (BFA, AAN) 80. Cattle Annie and
tle Britches 80. Marco Polo (TV) 81. Local Hero
The Osterman Weekend 83. Scandal Sheet (TV)
, Little Treasure 85. On Wings of Eagles (TV) 85.
ugh Guys 86. Barnum (TV) 86. Rocket
braltar 88. Field of Dreams 89. Phantom of the
era (TV) 90.
For enthusiasm, shrewdness and agility. The
me and the Arrow.

Life is to be lived within the limits of your
knowledge and within the concept of what you
uld like to see yourself to be. – B.L.
f I'm working with frightened people, I do tend
dominate them. I'm no doll, that's for sure.
3.L.
Most people seem to think I'm the kind of guy
no shaves with a blowtorch. Actually I'm bookish
d worrisome. – B.L.
Before he can pick up an ashtray he discusses
s motivation for a couple of hours. You want to
l him to pick up the ashtray and shut up. –
Jeanne Moreau

anchester, Elsa (1902–1986) (Elizabeth Sullivan).
itish character actress married to Charles
ughton. On stage and screen in Britain before
ttling in Hollywood in 1940.
Autobiographies: 1968, Charles Laughton and I.
83, Elsa Lanchester Herself.
Bluebottles 28. The Private Life of Henry VIII 32.
avid Copperfield 35. The Bride of Frankenstein 35.
e Ghost Goes West 36. Rembrandt 37. Vessel of
rath 38. Ladies in Retirement 41. Tales of
anhattan 42. The Spiral Staircase 45. End of the
ainbow 47. The Inspector-General 49. Come to
e Stable (AAN) 49. Androcles and the Lion 53.
ell, Book and Candle 57. Witness for the
rosecution (AAN) 57. Mary Poppins 64.
lackbeard's Ghost 67. Me, Natalie 69. Willard
. Terror in the Wax Museum 73. Murder by Death
6, many others.
TV series: The John Forsythe Show 65.

andau, David (1878–1935).
merican character actor, familiar in early talkies
s crook or roughneck.
I Take This Woman 31. Street Scene 31. Taxi 32.
olly of the Circus 32. Horse Feathers 32. I Am a
ugitive from a Chain Gang 32. She Done Him
Vrong 33. One Man's Journey 33. Wharf Angel
4. Judge Priest 34, etc.

Landau, Ely (1920–1993).
American producer, former distributor.
 Long Day's Journey into Night 62. The
Pawnbroker 64. All productions of the American
Film Theatre 72–74. Hopscotch 80. The Holcroft
Covenant 85, etc.

Landau, Martin (1928–).
Gaunt American actor often in sinister roles.
 North by Northwest 59. The Gazebo 59.
Cleopatra 62. The Hallelujah Trail 65. Nevada Smith
66. They Call Me Mr Tibbs 70. Savage (TV) 72.
Black Gunn 72. Blazing Magnum 76. Meteor 79.
Without Warning 80. Alone in the Dark 82. Sweet
Revenge 87. W.A.R. Women Against Rape 87.
Empire State 87. Tucker: The Man and His Dream
(AAN) 88. Crimes and Misdemeanors (AAN) 89.
Neon Empire 89. Paint It Black 90. Real Bullets
90. The Color of Evening 91. Ganglands 91.
Treasure Island 91. Mistress 92. Sliver 93.
Intersection 94. Time Is Money 94. Eye of the
Stranger 94. Ed Wood (as Bela Lugosi) 94, etc.
 TV series: Mission Impossible 66–68. Space
1999 75–76.

Landen, Dinsdale (1931–).
British stage actor who makes occasional films.
 Operation Snatch 62. Rasputin the Mad Monk
66. Every Home Should Have One 70. Digby 71.
International Velvet 78. Morons from Outer Space
85, etc.

Landers, Lew (1901–1962) (Lewis Friedlander).
American director of 'B' pictures, especially
westerns, from silent days.
 The Raven 35. The Man Who Found Himself 37.
Canal Zone 39. Pacific Liner 39. The Boogie Man
Will Get You 42. Return of the Vampire 43. The
Enchanted Forest 46. State Penitentiary 49. Man in
the Dark (in 3-D) 53. Captain Kidd and the Slave
Girl 53. Hot Rod Gang 58. Terrified 62, many
others.

Landi, Elissa (1904–1948) (Elizabeth Kuhnelt).
Austrian-Italian leading lady, in international
films of the 30s.
 Underground 29. Children of Chance 30. Always
Goodbye 31. The Yellow Ticket 31. Passport to Hell
32. The Sign of the Cross 32. The Masquerader 33.
The Warrior's Husband 33. By Candlelight 34.
Sisters under the Skin 34. The Count of Monte Cristo
34. Without Regret 35. Enter Madame 35. The
Amateur Gentleman 36. After the Thin Man 36.
The Thirteenth Chair 37. Corregidor 43, etc.

Landi, Marla (c. 1937–).
Italian leading lady and model, in British films.
 Across the Bridge 57. First Man into Space 58.
The Hound of the Baskervilles 59. Pirates of Blood
River 61. The Murder Game 65, etc.

Landis, Carole (1919–1948) (Frances Ridste).
American leading lady, in films from 1937 (as
extra). Committed suicide.
 Man and His Mate (One Million BC) 40.
Turnabout 40. Road Show 41. Topper Returns 41.
Hot Spot 41. Orchestra Wives 42. Wintertime 43.
Having Wonderful Crime 44. Behind Green
Lights 45. It Shouldn't Happen to a Dog 46. A
Scandal in Paris 46. Out of the Blue 47. The Brass
Monkey (GB) 48. Noose (GB) 48, etc.

Landis, Cullen (1896–1975).
American silent screen hero.
 Who Is Number One 17. Beware of Blondes 18.
Almost a Husband 19. Born Rich 24, many others.

Landis, Jessie Royce (1904–1972) (Jessie Royce
Medbury).
American character actress of long stage
experience; usually in fluttery comedy roles.
Autobiography: 1954, You Won't Be So Pretty.
 ■ Derelict 30. Mr Belvedere Goes to College 49.
It Happens Every Spring 49. My Foolish Heart 49.
Mother Didn't Tell Me 50. Meet Me Tonight (GB)
51. To Catch a Thief 55. The Swan 56. The Girl He
Left Behind 56. My Man Godfrey 57. I Married a
Woman 58. North by Northwest 59. A Private's Affair
59. Goodbye Again 61. Bon Voyage 62. Boys' Night
Out 62. Critic's Choice 63. Gidget Goes To Rome
63. Airport 69. Mr and Mrs Bo Jo Jones (TV) 71.

 Famous line (North by Northwest): 'You gentlemen
are not really trying to murder my son, are you?'

Landis, John (1950–).
American director.
 ■ Schlock 76. Kentucky Fried Movie 77. National
Lampoon's Animal House 78. The Blues Brothers
80. An American Werewolf in London 81. Twilight
Zone 83. Trading Places 83. The Muppets Take
Manhattan (cameo) 84. Into the Night 85. Spies
Like Us 85. Three Amigos 86. Amazon Women on
the Moon (co-d) 87. Coming to America 88.
Darkman (a) 90. Oscar 91. Sleepwalkers (a) 92.
Innocent Blood 92. Beverly Hills Cop III 94. The
Stand (TV) (a) 94.

 ¶ When Animal House turned out the way it did,
they all rushed to me with barrels of money
begging me to make them rich. – J.L.

Landon, Michael (1937–1991) (Eugene Orowitz).
American leading man best known as Little Jo in
TV series Bonanza 59–73. He also wrote and
directed many episodes of the series.
 I Was a Teenage Werewolf 57. God's Little Acre
58. The Legend of Tom Dooley 59, etc.
 TV series: Little House on the Prairie 74–82.
Highway to Heaven 84–89.
 ~A TV movie about Landon's young manhood,
Sam's Son, was released in 1984.

Landone, Avice (1910–1976).
British stage actress, usually in cool, unruffled
roles.
 My Brother Jonathan 48. The Franchise Affair
51. An Alligator Named Daisy 55. Reach for the
Sky 56. Carve Her Name with Pride 58. Operation
Cupid 60, etc.

Landres, Paul (1912–).
American director, former editor.
 Oregon Passage 57. The Vampire 57. The Miracle
of the Hills 58. The Flame Barrier 58. The Return
of Dracula 58. Son of a Gunfighter 65, etc.

Landru, Henri Désiré (1869–1922).
The story of the French murderer who killed 10
women for their money has been told several times
on film, usually in a fictional guise and most
notably by Charlie Chaplin in Monsieur Verdoux 47,
and also in Bluebeard's Ten Honeymoons 60, starring
George Sanders, and Claude Chabrol's Landru 62.
Other films that draw on the story, and also on
the folk-tale of Bluebeard, include Edward
Dmytryk's Bluebeard 72, starring Richard Burton,
and Sam Wood's Bluebeard 23, with Huntley
Gordon and Gloria Swanson, which was remade
by Ernst Lubitsch in 1938, starring Gary Cooper
and Claudette Colbert.

Lane, Allan 'Rocky' (1901–1973) (Harry
Albershart).
American cowboy star of the 30s, former athlete.

Night Nurse 32. Maid's Night Out 38. The Dancing Masters 44. Trail of Robin Hood 51. The Saga of Hemp Brown 58. Hell Bent for Leather 60, many second features.

TV series: Mister Ed (voice) 62–64.

Lane, Burton (1912–) (Burton Levy).
American song composer, best known for *Finian's Rainbow* and *On a Clear Day You Can See Forever*.

Lane, Charles (1905–) (Charles Levison).
American character actor seen since early 30s as comedy snoop, salesman or tax inspector; at the age of 80, he was vigorously playing a judge in *Soap*.

Mr Deeds Goes to Town 36. In Old Chicago 38. You Can't Take It with You 38. The Cat and the Canary 39. Hot Spot 41. Arsenic and Old Lace 44. Intrigue 49. The Juggler 53. Teacher's Pet 58. The Gnome-Mobile 67. What's So Bad about Feeling Good? 68. The Little Dragons 80, many others.

TV series: Petticoat Junction 64–69. Karen 75. Soap 80.

Lane, Diane (1965–).
American actress, in theatre as a child. She is married to actor Christopher Lambert.

A Little Romance 79. Touched by Love 79. Cattle Annie and Little Britches 81. Ladies and Gentlemen: The Fabulous Stains 81. Child Bride of Short Creek (TV) 81. National Lampoon Goes to the Movies 82. Miss All-American Beauty (TV) 82. Six Pack 82. The Outsiders 83. Rumblefish 83. Streets of Fire 84. The Cotton Club 84. The Big Town 87. Lady Beware 87. Love Dream 88. Vital Signs 90. Priceless Beauty 90. Descending Angel 91. Chaplin 92. Knight Moves 93. Indian Summer 93. Oldest Living Confederate Widow Tells All (TV) 94. Judge Dredd 95. Wild Bill 95, etc.

Lane, Lupino (1892–1959) (Henry George Lupino).
Diminutive, dapper British stage comedian and master of the pratfall, member of a family who had been clowns for generations. His American two-reelers of the 20s were little masterpieces of timing and hair-raising stunts, but he failed to develop a personality for sound. On his return to Britain from Hollywood, he directed one of the first British musicals, *No Lady*, and went to work at Elstree for British International Pictures as a director, before returning to his first love, the stage, climaxing in the long-running musical *Me and My Girl* featuring his singing of 'The Lambeth Walk'.

Biography: 1957, *Born to Star* by James Dillon White.

The Reporter 22. Isn't Life Wonderful? 24. The Love Parade 29. Bride of the Regiment 30. The Golden Mask 30.

GB FILMS: No Lady (& d) 31. The Love Race (d) 31. Love Lies (d) 31. Innocents of Chicago (d) 32. The Maid of the Mountains (d) 32. A Southern Maid (& d) 33. Letting in the Sunshine (d) 33. The Deputy Drummer 35. Hot News 36. Me and My Girl 39, etc.

Lane, Richard (1900–1982).
American supporting player, formerly and latterly sports announcer; frequently seen in the 40s as reporter, tough cop, or exasperated executive.

The Outcasts of Poker Flat 37. Union Pacific 39. Hellzapoppin 41. Meet Boston Blackie 41. What a Blonde 45. Gentleman Joe Palooka 46. Take Me Out to the Ball Game 48. I Can Get It For You Wholesale 51, etc.

The Lane Sisters.
American leading ladies, real name Mulligan.

Three of the five sisters (all actresses) had sizeable roles in Hollywood films: Lola (1909–1981), *Rosemary* (1913–1974) and *Priscilla* (1917–).
TOGETHER: Four Daughters 38. Daughters Courageous 39. Four Wives 39. Four Mothers 40.
OTHER APPEARANCES FOR LOLA: Speakeasy 29. Death from a Distance 35. Marked Woman 37. Zanzibar 40. Why Girls Leave Home 36.
ROSEMARY: Hollywood Hotel 38. The Oklahoma Kid 38. The Return of Dr X 40. Time Out for Rhythm 42. The Fortune Hunter 45.
PRISCILLA: Brother Rat 39. Dust Be My Destiny 39. Yes My Darling Daughter 39. The Roaring Twenties 40. Blues in the Night 41. Saboteur 42. Arsenic and Old Lace 44. Fun on a Weekend 46. Bodyguard 48, etc.

Lanfield, Sidney (1900–1972).
American director from 1932; former jazz musician.

Hat Check Girl 32. Moulin Rouge 34. Sing Baby Sing 36. *The Hound of the Baskervilles* 39. Swanee River 39. You'll Never Get Rich 41. The Lady Has Plans 41. *My Favorite Blonde* 42. The Meanest Man in the World 42. Let's Face It 43. Standing Room Only 44. Bring on the Girls 45. The Well-Groomed Bride 45. Stations West 47. The Lemon Drop Kid 50. Follow the Sun 51. Skirts Ahoy 52, etc.

Lang, Charles (1902–).
Distinguished American cinematographer.

Shopworn Angel 29. *A Farewell to Arms* (AA) 33. Death Takes a Holiday 34. Lives of a Bengal Lancer 35. *Desire* 36. *The Cat and the Canary* 39. Nothing but the Truth 41. Practically Yours 44. The Uninvited 44. The Ghost and Mrs Muir 47. A Foreign Affair 47. *Ace in the Hole* 51. Sudden Fear 52. The Big Heat 53. The Female on the Beach 55. The Man from Laramie 55. Autumn Leaves 56. The Solid Gold Cadillac 56. Gunfight at the OK Corral 57. Some Like It Hot (AAN) 59. One-Eyed Jacks 59. The Facts of Life 60. The Magnificent Seven 60. Blue Hawaii 61. A Girl Named Tamiko 62. *Charade* 63. Inside Daisy Clover 65. How to Steal a Million 66. Not with My Wife You Don't 66. Hotel 67. The Flim Flam Man 67. Wait Until Dark 67. A Flea in Her Ear 68. Cactus Flower 69. Bob and Carol and Ted and Alice (AAN) 70. The Love Machine 71. Butterflies Are Free (AAN) 72, many others.

Lang, Charles (1915–).
American writer.

The Magnificent Matador 56. Desire in the Dust 62, etc.

Lang, Fritz (1890–1976).
German director of distinguished silent films. Went to Hollywood 1934 and tended thereafter to make commercial though rather heavy-handed thrillers.

Biography: 1974, *Fritz Lang* by Lotte Eisner.

■ Helbblut 19. Der Herr der Liebe 19. Die Spinnen 19. Hara Kiri 19. Vier um die Frau 20. Das Wandernde Bild 21. *Destiny* 21. Das Brillanten Schiff 21. Der Müde Tod 21. *Dr Mabuse der Spieler* 22. Inferno 22. *Siegfried* 23. Krimhild's Revenge 24. *Metropolis* 26. *The Spy* 27. Frau im Mond 28. *M* 31. The Testament of Dr Mabuse 32. Liliom 33. *Fury* 36. *You Only Live Once* 37. You and Me 38. The Return of Frank James 40. Western Union 41. Man Hunt 41. Confirm or Deny (part) 42. Hangmen Also Die 43. *The Woman in the Window* 44. Ministry of Fear 44. Scarlet Street 45. Cloak and Dagger 46. The Secret beyond the Door 48. House by the River 49. An American Guerrilla in the Philippines 51. Rancho Notorious 52. Clash by Night 52. The Blue Gardenia 52. *The Big Heat* 53. Human Desire 54. Moonfleet 55. While the City

Sleeps 55. Beyond a Reasonable Doubt 56. Der Tiger von Ischnapur (Ger.) 58. Das Indische Grabmal (Ger.) 58. The Thousand Eyes of Dr Mabuse (Ger.) 60. Contempt (a only) 63.
☉For spinning out his well-deserved German reputation through an American career of dwindling talent. *Fury.*

¶ His cinema is that of the nightmare, the fable and the philosophical dissertation. – *Andrew Sarris, 1968*

Lang, Harold (1923–1971).
Blond English general-purpose actor and drama teacher, often in shady roles, from the stage. Bor in London, he studied at RADA.

Floodtide 49. Cairo Road 50. The Franchise Affair 51. Wings of Danger 52. The Intruder 53. Dance Little Lady 54. The Quatermass Experimen 55. It's a Wonderful World 56. Carve Her Name with Pride 58. Ben Hur 59. Dr Terror's House of Horrors 64. The Nanny 65. Two Gentlemen Sharing 69, etc.

Lang, Jennings (1915–).
American executive, long near the top of MCA T and latterly executive producer of many Universal films.

Lang, June (1915–) (June Vlasek).
American leading lady, former dancer.

Chandu the Magician 32. Bonnie Scotland 35. Ali Baba Goes to Town 38. Redhead 41. Flesh an Fantasy 44. Lighthouse 48, etc.

Lang, Matheson (1879–1948).
Scottish-Canadian stage actor, a London matinée idol of the 20s who made occasional films.

Autobiography: 1940, *Mr Wu Looks Back*.

Mr Wu 21. Carnival 21 & 31. Dick Turpin's Rid to York 22. The Wandering Jew 23. The Chinese Bungalow 25 & 30. Beyond the Veil 25. Island o' Despair 26. The Triumph of the Scarlet Pimpernel 29. Channel Crossing 32. Little Friend 34. Drake of England 35. The Cardinal 36, etc.

Lang, Otto (1908–).
Austrian-born producer and director in Hollywood, a former ski instructor to Darryl Zanuck.

Call Northside 777 (p) 48. Five Fingers (p) 52. White Witch Doctor (p) 53. Vesuvius Express (AANp, short) 53. Jet Carrier (AANp, short) 54. Tora! Tora! Tora! (p) 69, etc.

Lang, Robert (1934–).
British character actor, mainly on stage.

Othello 65. Dance of Death 69. The Mackintos Man 73. Night Watch 73. Savage Messiah 73. Show at the Devil 76. The First Great Train Robbery 79 Runners 83. Hawks 88, etc.

Lang, Walter (1896–1972).
American director of competent but seldom outstanding entertainments.

The Satin Woman 27. The College Hero 27. Brothers 30. Hell Bound 30. Women Go On for Ever 31. No More Orchids 32. The Warrior's Husband 33. Meet the Baron 33. Whom the God Destroy 34. The Mighty Barnum 34. Carnival 35. Hooray for Love 35. Love Before Breakfast 36. Wife Doctor and Nurse 37. Second Honeymoon 37. The Baroness and the Butler 38. I'll Give a Million 38 The Little Princess 39. *The Bluebird* 40. Star Dust 40. The Great Profile 40. *Tin Pan Alley* 40. Moon over Miami 41. Weekend in Havana 41. Song of the Islands 42. The Magnificent Dope 42. Coney Island 43. Greenwich Village 44. *State Fair* 45.

Sentimental Journey 46. Claudia and David 46. Mother Wore Tights 47. *Sitting Pretty* 48. When My Baby Smiles at Me 48. You're My Everything 49. Cheaper by the Dozen 50. The Jackpot 50. On the Riviera 51. *With a Song in My Heart* 51. *Call Me Madam* 53. There's No Business like Show Business 54. *The King and I* (AAN) 56. The Desk Set 57. But Not for Me 59. Can Can 60. The Marriage Go Round 61. Snow White and the Three Stooges 61, many others.

Langan, Glenn (1917–1991).
American light leading man, in films from the early 40s after stage experience.
Four Jills in a Jeep 44. *Margie* 46. Forever Amber 47. The Snake Pit 48. Treasure of Monte Cristo 49. Rapture (Swedish) 50. Hangman's Knot 52. 99 River Street 54. The Amazing Colossal Man 57, etc.

Langdon, Harry (1884–1944).
Baby-faced, melancholy American clown who was a great hit in the 20s but could not reconcile his unusual image with sound.
Picking Peaches 23. *Tramp Tramp Tramp* 26. *The Strong Man* 26. *Long Pants* 26. His First Flame 27. Three's a Crowd 27. The Chaser (& d) 28. See America Thirst 30. A Soldier's Plaything 31. Hallelujah I'm a Bum 33. My Weakness 33. There Goes My Heart 38. *Zenobia* 39. Misbehaving Husbands 40. House of Errors 42. Spotlight Scandals 44, etc.

¶ He was a quaint artist who had no business in business. – Mack Sennett

Langdon, Sue Ane (1940–).
American leading lady and comedienne.
The Outsider 61. The Rounders 65. A Fine Madness 66. A Guide for the Married Man 67. The Cheyenne Social Club 70. Without Warning 80. Zapped! 82, etc.
TV series: *Arnie* 70–71.

Lange, Arthur (1889–1956).
American composer.
Hollywood Revue 29. Marie Galante 34. Banjo on My Knee 36. This Is My Affair 37. Kidnapped 38. Lady of Burlesque 43. The Woman in the Window 45. Woman on the Run 50. The Mad Magician 54, many others.

Lange, Hope (1931–).
American leading lady of the 50s who developed into a mature and pleasing comedienne.
■ Bus Stop 56. The True Story of Jesse James 57. Peyton Place (AAN) 57. The Young Lions 58. In Love and War 58. The Best of Everything 59. Wild in the Country 61. Pocketful of Miracles 61. Love Is a Ball 63. Jigsaw (TV) 68. Crowhaven Farm (TV) 70. That Certain Summer (TV) 72. The 500 Pound Jerk (TV) 72. Death Wish 74. I Love You Goodbye (TV) 74. Fer de Lance (TV) 74. The Secret Night Caller (TV) 75. Like Normal People (TV) 79. The Day Christ Died (TV) 80. I Am The Cheese 83. The Prodigal 83. Nightmare on Elm Street II 85. Blue Velvet 86. Tune in Tomorrow (aka Aunt Julia and the Scriptwriter) 90.
TV series: *The Ghost and Mrs Muir* 68. *The New Dick Van Dyke Show* 71.

Lange, Jessica (1949–).
American leading lady who developed into an actress. She has a daughter by actor and dancer Mikhail Baryshnikov and a son and a daughter by actor and dramatist Sam Shepard.
■ King Kong 76. All That Jazz 79. How to Beat the High Cost of Living 80. The Postman Always

Rings Twice 81. *Frances* (AAN) 82. Tootsie (AA) 82. Country (AAN) 84. Sweet Dreams (AAN) 85. Crimes of the Heart 86. Everybody's All-American 88. Far North 88. Music Box (AAN) 89. Men Don't Leave 90. Cape Fear 91. Night and the City 92. Blue Sky (made 91) 94. Rob Roy 95.

Langella, Frank (1940–).
American leading man of the 70s.
The Twelve Chairs 70. Diary of a Mad Housewife 70. The Wrath of God 72. The Mark of Zorro (TV) 74. *Dracula* (title role) 79. Those Lips Those Eyes 80. Sphinx 81. The Men's Club 86. Masters of the Universe 87. And God Created Woman 88. True Identity 91. 1492: Conquest of Paradise 92. Dave 93. Body of Evidence 93. Brainscan 94. Doomsday Gun (TV) 94. Bad Company 94. Brainscan 94, etc.

Langenkamp, Heather (1964–).
American leading actress of horror movies.
The Outsiders 83. Rumble Fish 83. A Nightmare on Elm Street 84. Nickel Mountain 85. A Nightmare on Elm Street 3: Dream Warriors 87. Shocker 89. Wes Craven's New Nightmare 94, etc.

Langford, Frances (1914–).
American band singer, popular in the 40s, mainly in guest spots. Appeared mainly in light musicals.
Every Night at Eight 35. Broadway Melody 36. Hollywood Hotel 37. Too Many Girls 40. Swing It, Soldier 41. The Girl Rush 44. The Bamboo Blonde 45. Beat the Band 46. No Time For Tears 52. The Glenn Miller Story 54, etc.

Langley, Noel (1911–1980).
South African playwright and screenwriter, in Britain and Hollywood.
Maytime (co-w) 38. The Wizard of Oz (co-w) 39. They Made Me a Fugitive 47. Tom Brown's Schooldays 51. Scrooge 52. The Pickwick Papers (& d) 53. Our Girl Friday (& d) 53. The Search for Bridey Murphy (& d) 56, many others.

Langlois, Henri (1914–1977).
Idiosyncratic French archivist, instigator of the Cinémathèque Française. His methods annoyed some, but his good intentions were never in question. Received Special Academy Award in 1974.
Biography: 1983, *A Passion for Films* by Richard Roud.

Langton, David (1912–1994).
English actor of stage and screen, best known for playing Richard Bellamy, the head of the household, in the TV series Upstairs, Downstairs (1970–75).
The Ship that Died of Shame 55. Saint Joan 57. Seven Waves Away 57. A Hard Day's Night 64. The Pumpkin Eater 64. The Incredible Sarah 76. The Whistle Blower 86, etc.

Langton, Simon (1941–).
British director, in TV from 1964. First cinema movie *The Whistle Blower* 86.

Langtry, Lillie (1853–1929) (Emilie Charlotte Le Breton).
British light actress who charmed, among others, Judge Roy Bean and Edward VII. Sole film appearance *His Neighbour's Wife* 13. Ava Gardner played her in *The Life and Times of Judge Roy Bean*.

Lanoux, Victor (1936–).
French leading actor. He left school at 14 and worked in cabaret before making his cinema debut in 1965.
La Vieille Dame Indigne 65. La Ville Normale

67. L'Affaire Dominici 73. Deux Hommes dans la Ville 73. Folle à Tuer 75. Cousin Cousine 75. Pardon Mon Affaire (Un Eléphant Ça Trompe Enormément) 76. Servant et Maîtresse 77. One Wild Moment (Un Moment d'Egarement) 77. Pardon Mon Affaire Too! (aka We Will All Meet in Paradise) 78. Un Si Jolie Village 79. Retour en Force 80. Dog Day (Canicule) 83. Un Dimanche de Flics 83. Louisiana 84. National Lampoon's European Vacation 85. Scene of the Crime (Le Lieu de Crime) 87. L'Invitée Surprise 89, etc.

Lansbury, Angela (1925–).
British character actress who has always seemed older than her years. Evacuated to Hollywood during World War II, she played a long succession of unsympathetic parts, but in the 60s became a Broadway musical star.
■ Gaslight (AAN) 44. National Velvet 44. *The Picture of Dorian Gray* (AAN) 45. The Harvey Girls 46. The Hoodlum Saint 46. The Private Affairs of Bel Ami 47. Till the Clouds Roll By 47. If Winter Comes 47. Tenth Avenue Angel 48. State of the Union 48. The Three Musketeers 48. The Red Danube 49. Samson and Delilah 49. Kind Lady 51. Mutiny 52. Remains to Be Seen 53. A Lawless Street 55. A Life at Stake 55. The Purple Mask 55. Please Murder Me 56. The Court Jester 56. The Reluctant Debutante 58. The Long Hot Summer 58. *The Dark at the Top of the Stairs* 60. A Breath of Scandal 61. Blue Hawaii 61. Summer of the Seventeenth Doll 61. All Fall Down 62. *The Manchurian Candidate* (AAN) 62. In the Cool of the Day 63. The World of Henry Orient 64. Dear Heart 64. The Greatest Story Ever Told 65. Harlow 65. Moll Flanders 65. Mister Buddwing 66. Something for Everyone 70. *Bedknobs and Broomsticks* 71. Death on the Nile 78. The Lady Vanishes 79. The Mirror Crack'd 80. Little Gloria . . . Happy at Last (TV) 82. The Pirates of Penzance 83. Lace (TV) 84. Company of Wolves 84. Rage of Angels: The Story Continues (TV) 86. Shootdown (TV) 88. The Shell Seekers (TV) 90. The Love She Sought (TV) 90. Beauty and the Beast (voice) 92.
TV series: Murder She Wrote 84– .

Lansing, Joi (1928–1972) (Joyce Wassmansdoff).
American leading lady who played a few sharp blondes and left a pleasant impression.
■ The Counterfeiters 48. The Girl from Jones Beach 49. Hot Cars 56. The Brave One 56. Hot Shots 56. A Hole in the Head 59. It Started with a Kiss 59. The Atomic Submarine 59. Who Was That Lady? 59. Marriage on the Rocks 65. Bigfoot 71.
TV series: Love That Bob 56–59. Klondike 60–61.

Lansing, Robert (1929–1994) (Robert H. Brown).
Cold-eyed, virile American leading man of the 60s.
The 4-D Man 59. A Gathering of Eagles 63. Under the Yum Yum Tree 64. The Grissom Gang 71. Wild in the Sky 72. Bittersweet Love 76. Empire of the Ants 77. False Face 77. Island Claws (aka Night of the Claw) 80. The Equalizer (TV) 87. The Nest 88. Blind Vengeance (TV) 90, etc.
TV series: 87th Precinct 61. 12 O'Clock High 64. The Man Who Never Was 66.

Lansing, Sherry (1944–).
American producer, a former actress and one-time president of Twentieth Century-Fox who is now chairman of the Motion Picture Group of Paramount Pictures.
Racing with the Moon 84. Firstborn 84. Fatal Attraction (AAN) 87. The Accused 88. Black Rain 89. School Ties 91, etc.

Lantz, Walter (1900–1994).
American animator, in charge of Universal cartoons since 1928 and the creator of Woody Woodpecker. Special AA 1978 'for bringing joy and laughter to every part of the world'. His wife Grace (1904–1992) supplied Woody's laugh.

Lanza, Mario (1921–1959) (Alfredo Cocozza).
American opera singer, popular in MGM musicals until overcome by weight problem.
  Biography: 1991, *Mario Lanza – A Biography* by Derek Mannering.
■ That Midnight Kiss 49. The Toast of New Orleans 50. *The Great Caruso* 51. Because You're Mine 52. The Student Prince (voice only) 54. Serenade 56. Seven Hills of Rome 58. For the First Time 58.

¶ That idiot Lanza! He had the greatest opportunities in the world, but he just couldn't handle success. – *Joseph Ruttenberg*
  Mario, you doll, you sing like a son of a bitch. – *M.L.*

LaPaglia, Anthony (1959–).
Australian-born actor, working in America.
  Betsy's Wedding 90. Criminal Justice (TV) 90. Mortal Sins 90. Dangerous Obsession 90. One Good Cop 90. He Said, She Said 91. Keeper of the City 91. 29th Street 91. Innocent Blood 92. So I Married an Axe Murderer 93. The Custodian 93. The Client 94. Killer 94. Lucky Break (Aus.) 94, etc.

Lapotaire, Jane (1944–).
Anglo-French stage actress in occasional films.
  Crescendo 69. Antony and Cleopatra 72. The Asphyx 72. One of Our Dinosaurs Is Missing 75. Eureka 83. Lady Jane 86, etc.

Lardner, Ring, Jnr (1915–).
American screenwriter who was one of the 'Hollywood Ten'.
  Woman of the Year (AA) 42. The Cross of Lorraine 44. Forever Amber 47. Britannia Mews 48. Cloak and Dagger 48. The Cincinnati Kid 65. M*A*S*H (AA) 70. The Greatest 77, etc.

Larner, Jeremy (1937–).
American screenwriter and novelist. He is a former journalist and speechwriter to 60s presidential candidate Senator Eugene McCarthy. Since winning an Oscar, he has worked on films that are yet to be produced.
  Drive He Said (co-w, from his novel) 71. The Candidate (AA) 72.

Laroche, Pierre (1902–1962).
French screenwriter, mainly for films directed by his wife, Jacqueline Audrey.
  Les Visiteurs du Soir (co-w) 42. Lumière d'Été (co-w) 43. Les Malheurs de Sophie 45. Gigi 49. Minne 50. Huis Clos 54. La Garçonne 57, etc.

Larraz, José Ramón (1928–).
Spanish director of horror and erotic movies, sometimes combining both themes in movies featuring lesbian vampires. Born in Barcelona, he worked in Paris as a comic-book illustrator and fashion photographer before making his first film in Britain, where he continued to work until the mid-70s, when he was known as Joseph Larraz. *Symptoms* was a British entry at the Cannes Film Festival in 1974. He then returned to direct films in Spain and also worked under the pseudonym of Joseph Braunstein for the US video market.
  Whirlpool (aka She Died with Her Boots On) 69. Scream . . . and Die! 73. Symptoms (aka The Blood Virgin; The House that Vanished) 74.

Vampyres – Daughters of Dracula 74. The Violation of the Bitch (La Visita del Vicio) 78. Golden Lady 79. The National Mummy (La Momia Nacional) 81. Estigma 81. Los Ritos Sexuales del Diábolo 82. Rest in Pieces (as Joseph Braunstein) 87. Edge of the Axe (as Joseph Braunstein) 89. Deadly Manor 90, etc.

¶ I've never had a proper understanding producer, only philistine money-men telling me what to do. – *J.R.L.*

Larroquette, John (1947–).
American leading actor.
  The Texas Chainsaw Massacre (uncredited narrator) 74. Heart Beat 80. Altered States 80. Stripes 81. Green Ice 81. Cat People 82. Meatballs 2 84. Star Trek III: The Search for Spock 84. Choose Me 84. Convicted (TV) 86. Blind Date 87. Second Sight 89. Madhouse 90. Tune in Tomorrow (aka Aunt Julia and the Scriptwriter) 90, etc.
  TV series: Doctor's Hospital 75–76. Baa Baa Black Sheep 76. Night Court 84–92.

Larsen, Keith (1925–).
American second-string leading man. He was married to Vera Miles (1960–73).
  Flat Top 52. Hiawatha 52. Arrow in the Dust 54. Wichita 55. Dial Red O 56. Fury River 61. Caxambu 67. The Trap on Cougar Mountain 76. White-Water Sam (wd) 78, etc.
  TV series: The Hunter 54. Brave Eagle 55. Northwest Passage 57. The Aquanaut 60.

Larson, Eric (1905–1988).
Pioneer animator with Walt Disney, who worked on every full-length Disney animated film from *Snow White and the Seven Dwarfs* 37 to *The Great Mouse Detective* 86.

LaRue:
See La Rue.

Lasker, Lawrence (1949–).
American producer and screenwriter, a former art director.
  War Games (co-w, AAN) 83. Project X (p, story) 87. Awakenings (AANp) 90. Sneakers (p, co-w) 92, etc.

Lasky, Jesse (1880–1958).
American pioneer. Formed his first production company in 1914 and had a big hit with *The Squaw Man;* in 1916 gained control of Famous Players and later Paramount. Later produced for Fox, Warner, RKO.
  Autobiography: 1958, *I Blow My Own Horn.*
  Sergeant York 41. The Adventures of Mark Twain 44. Rhapsody in Blue 45. The Miracle of the Bells 49. The Great Caruso 51, many others.

Lasky, Jesse, Jnr (1910–1988).
American screenwriter, son of Jesse Lasky.
  Autobiography: 1974, *Whatever Happened to Hollywood?*
  Union Pacific (co-w) 39. Reap the Wild Wind (co-w) 42. Unconquered (co-w) 48. Samson and Delilah (co-w) 49. The Thief of Venice 50. The Brigand 52. The Ten Commandments (co-w) 56. Seven Women from Hell (co-w) 61. Land Raiders 69. An Ace up My Sleeve 75. Crime and Passion 76, etc.

Lassally, Walter (1926–).
German cinematographer, long in Britain.
  Autobiography: 1987, *Itinerant Cameraman.*
  We Are the Lambeth Boys 58. *A Taste of Honey* 61. The Loneliness of the Long-Distance Runner

62. *Tom Jones* 63. *Zorba the Greek* (AA) 65. The Day the Fish Came Out 67. Oedipus the King 67. Joanna 68. Turnkey 70. Something for Everyone 72. Malachi's Cove 74. Too Far to Go (TV) 77. Gauguin the Savage (TV) 80. Memoirs of a Survivor 82. Heat and Dust 83. Private School 83. The Bostonians 84. Indian Summer 87. The Deceivers 88. The Perfect Murder 88. Fragment of Isabella 89. The Ballad of the Sad Café 90, etc.

Lasser, Louise (1939–).
American TV actress popular in the serial *Mary Hartman, Mary Hartman* 76. She was married to Woody Allen (1966–71).
  Bananas 71. Such Good Friends 71. Everything You Always Wanted to Know about Sex 72. Coffee, Tea or Me? (TV) 73. Isn't It Shocking? (TV) 73. Slither 73. Just Me and You (TV) 78. In God We Trust 80. Stardust Memories (uncredited) 80. Blood Rage 83. Crimewave 85. Surrender 87. Sing 89. Rude Awakening 89. Frankenhooker 90. Modern Love 90, etc.
  TV series: Mary Hartman, Mary Hartman 76–77. It's a Living 81–82.

Lassie.
The first film featuring this intelligent collie (actually a laddie, as were his successors) was *Lassie Come Home* 42, based on Eric Knight's novel; the dog was called Pal (1941–59), and continued his masquerade in *Son of Lassie* 45 and *Courage of Lassie* 46. The original was remade as *Gypsy Colt* 54, which substituted a horse for the dog; *The Magic of Lassie* 78; and *Lassie* 94. Other films in the series include *Lassie's Great Adventure* 62 and *Lassie: Adventures of Neeka* 68. A radio series ran from 1947–50 and a television series from 1954–71, in which the dog was the only constant factor with its owner changing periodically; by the end of the series Lassie had no owner at all. An animated version, *Lassie's Rescue Rangers*, was produced for children's television from 1973–75 and *The New Lassie*, which put the dog in a suburban setting, was shown on television from 1989–91.

The Last Days of Pompeii.
Lord Lytton's novel climaxing in the catastrophic eruption of Vesuvius was filmed in Italy in 1912 ('10,000 people, 260 scenes'), 1925 and 1960. In 1935 Cooper and Schoedsack filmed it in Hollywood, with a cast including Basil Rathbone and Preston Foster. The 1960 Italian version is barely worth mentioning and the 1985 TV mini-series is good for a laugh.

The Last of the Mohicans.
Fenimore Cooper's adventure novel of American colonization was filmed in 1920 by Maurice Tourneur, with George Hackathorne; in 1936 by George Seitz, with Randolph Scott; in 1952 as *The Last of the Redskins* by George Sherman, with Jon Hall; and in 1992 by Michael Mann, with Daniel Day-Lewis. A Canadian TV series in 1956 starred John Hart.

Lastfogel, Abe (1898–1984).
American talent agent, head of the William Morris Organization, which he joined in 1912 as an office boy.

Laszlo, Andrew (1926–).
Hungarian-American cinematographer.
  You're a Big Boy Now 67. The Night They Raided Minsky's 68. Popi 69. Teacher Teacher 70. The Out of Towners 70. Lovers and other Strangers 71. The Owl and the Pussycat 71. Class of 44 73. The Man without a Country (TV) 74. Countdown at Kusini 76. The Warriors 79. Shogun (TV) 80.

uthern Comfort 81. First Blood 82. Thief of
earts 84. Remo Williams, the Adventure Begins
5. Poltergeist II 86. Innerspace 87. Star Trek V:
ie Final Frontier 89. Ghost Dad 90. Newsies 92,
c.

aszlo, Ernest (1905–1984).
ungarian-American cinematographer.
 The Hitler Gang 44. Two Years Before the Mast
8. The Girl from Manhattan 48. Dead on Arrival
9. The Steel Trap 52. The Star 52. Stalag 17 53.
era Cruz 54. The Big Knife 55. Judgment at
uremberg 60. *Inherit the Wind* (AAN) 60. *It's a
ad Mad Mad Mad World* (AAN) 63. *Ship of Fools*
AA) 65. Fantastic Voyage (AAN) 66. Star! (AAN)
8. The First Time 69. Daddy's Gone A-Hunting
9. Airport (AAN) 69. Showdown 73. Logan's Run
AAN) 76. The Domino Principle (co-ph) 77,
any others.

atham, Louise.
merican actress.
 Marnie 64. Firecreek 67. Adam at 6 AM 70.
Making It 71. White Lightning 73. The Sugarland
xpress 74. 92 in the Shade 75. The Awakening
and (TV) 78. Pray TV (TV) 82. Mass Appeal 84.
ove Lives On (TV) 85. Toughlove (TV) 85. Fresno
TV) 86. Crazy from the Heart 91. Paradise 91.
 TV series: Sara 76. The Contender 80. Scruples
0.

athrop, Philip (1916–).
merican cinematographer.
 The Monster of Piedras Blancas 57. Experiment
n Terror 62. *Lonely Are the Brave* 62. Days of Wine
nd Roses 63. The Pink Panther 63. The
mericanization of Emily 64. Thirty-Six Hours 65.
he Cincinnati Kid 65. What Did You Do in the
War Daddy? 66. The Russians are Coming 66. The
lappening 67. Point Blank 68. *Finian's Rainbow*
59. The Gypsy Moths 69. The Illustrated Man 69.
They Shoot Horses Don't They? 69. Von
Richthofen and Brown 71. Airport 77 77. The
Driver 78. Little Miss Marker 80. Loving Couples
80. All Night Long 81. Jekyll and Hyde Together
Again 82. Hammett 82. National Lampoon's Class
Reunion 82. Deadly Friend 86, etc.

Latimer, Jonathan (1906–1984).
American thriller writer.
 Topper Returns 41. They Won't Believe Me 47.
Alias Nick Beal 49. Plunder of the Sun 51. Botany
Bay 54. The Unholy Wife 57, etc.

Latimore, Frank (1925–) (Frank Kline).
American leading man with stage experience.
 In the Meantime, Darling 44. Three Little Girls
in Blue 46. Black Magic 49. Three Forbidden Stories
(Italian) 50. John Paul Jones 59. The Sergeant 68.
All the President's Men 76, etc.

Lattuada, Alberto (1914–).
Italian director.
 The Mill on the Po 48. Without Pity 48. Lights
of Variety (co-d) 50. Il Capotto 52. The Wolf 53.
The Beach 53. Guendalina 56. Tempest 58. The
Adolescents 61. La Steppa 62. The Mandrake 65.
The Betrayal 68. A Dog's Heart 75. Stay As You
Are 78. A Thorn in the Heart 85. Christopher
Columbus (TV) 85. Amori (co-d) 89, etc.

Lau, Jeffrey (1956–).
Hong Kong director and producer.
 Haunted Cop Shop 87. Haunted Cop Shop II 88.
Thunder Cops II 89. Mortuary Blues 90. Fury Fist
91. 92 The Legendary La Rose Noire (92 Hak
Muigwai Dui Hak Mauigwai) 92. Rose Rose I Love

You (Dong Cheng Xi Jui) 93. The Eagle Shooting
Heroes: Dong Cheng Xi Jiu 93, etc.

Lauder, Sir Harry (1870–1950).
Scottish music-hall entertainer, a former miner
who was knighted in 1919. He became a star in
1900 and made some silent shorts from 1907.
 Autobiography: 1928, *Roamin' in the Gloamin'*.
 Biography: 1968, *Great Scot!* by Gordon Irving.
■ Huntingtower 27. Happy Days 29. Auld Lang
Syne 33. End of the Road 36. Song of the Road 40.

¶ He has the great artist's overweening conceit
  of himself. He emerges from the wings like a
sun from base clouds. He irradiates his world,
flattering stalls and gallery with sovereign eye. That
a creature like ourselves should glow with such
intensity of self-appreciation warms the cockles
of the most sceptical heart. – *James Agate*

Laughlin, Tom (1938–).
American independent director, producer and actor
who enjoyed a cult success as Billy Jack, a violent
hero on the side of the disadvantaged, in the early
70s. His most recent film, *The Return of Billy Jack* 86,
has never been completed. He sometimes used the
pseudonym T.C. Frank as director.
■ Tea and Sympathy 56. South Pacific 58. Gidget
(a) 59. Tall Story (a) 60. The Proper Time (a, d)
60. The Young Sinners (d) 65. Born Losers (a, p,
d) 67. Billy Jack (a, p, wd) 73. The Trial of Billy
Jack (a, p) 74. The Master Gunfighter (a, p) 75.
Billy Jack Goes to Washington (a, p, d) 78.

Laughton, Charles (1899–1962).
Distinguished British character actor, whose
plump wry face was one of the most popular on
screen in the 30s. His later Hollywood roles
showed a regrettable tendency to ham, but he was
always worth watching.
 Biographies: 1938, *Charles Laughton and I* by his
wife Elsa Lanchester. 1952, *The Charles Laughton
Story* by Kurt Singer. 1976, *Charles Laughton* by
Charles Higham. 1987, *Charles Laughton – a
Difficult Actor* by Simon Callow.
■ Wolves 27. Bluebottles 28. Daydreams 28.
Piccadilly 29. Comets 30. Down River 30. *The Old
Dark House* 32. The Devil and the Deep 32.
Payment Deferred 32. *The Sign of the Cross* (as Nero)
32. If I Had a Million 32. Island of Lost Souls 32.
The Private Life of Henry VIII (AA) 33. White
Woman 33. *The Barretts of Wimpole Street* 34. *Ruggles
of Red Gap* 35. *Les Misérables* 35. *Mutiny on the Bounty*
(as Captain Bligh) (AAN) 35. *Rembrandt* 36. *I
Claudius* (unfinished) 37. Vessel of Wrath 37.
St Martin's Lane 38. Jamaica Inn 39. *The
Hunchback of Notre Dame* 39. They Knew What
They Wanted 40. It Started with Eve 41. The
Tuttles of Tahiti 42. Tales of Manhattan 42. Stand
by for Action 43. Forever and a Day 43. This Land
is Mine 43. The Man from Down Under 43. The
Canterville Ghost 44. *The Suspect* 44. Captain Kidd
45. Because of Him 46. The Paradine Case 48.
The Big Clock 48. Arch of Triumph 48. The Girl
from Manhattan 49. The Bribe 49. The Man on the
Eiffel Tower (as Maigret) 49. The Blue Veil 51. The
Strange Door 51. Full House 52. Abbott and
Costello Meet Captain Kidd 52. Salome 53. Young
Bess 53. *Hobson's Choice* 54. *Witness for the
Prosecution* (AAN) 57. Under Ten Flags 60.
Spartacus 60. *Advise and Consent* 62.
AS DIRECTOR: *Night of the Hunter* 55.
☻ For a dozen splendid performances,
unassailable by the self-doubt which later turned
him into a ham. *Rembrandt*.

¶ They can't censor the gleam in my eye. – *C.L.,
  when told that his performance as Mr*

*Moulton-Barrett must not indicate incestuous
love*
 I have a face like the behind of an elephant.
– *C.L.*
 It's got so that every time I walk into a restaurant
I get not only soup but an impersonation of
Captain Bligh. – *C.L.*
 You can't direct a Laughton picture. The best
you can hope for is to referee. – *Alfred Hitchcock*
 With him acting was an act of childbirth. What
he needed was not so much a director as a
midwife. – *Alexander Korda*
 A great man who only accidentally became an
actor. – *Alva Johnson*

Famous line (*Mutiny on the Bounty*): 'I'll live to see
you – all of you – hung from the highest yardarm
in the British fleet!'

Famous line (*The Private Life of Henry VIII*): 'Am I
a king or a breeding bull?'

Famous line (*The Private Life of Henry VIII*): 'There's
no delicacy nowadays. No consideration for others.
Refinement's a thing of the past!'

Launder, Frank (1907–).
British comedy scriptwriter, from 1938 usually in
collaboration with Sidney Gilliat (qv); they have
produced most of their own films.
 Biography: 1977, *Launder and Gilliat* by Geoff
Brown.
 Under the Greenwood Tree 29. The W Plan 30.
Children of Chance 30. After Office Hours 31. Josser
in the Army 31. Facing the Music 33. Those Were
the Days 34. Emil and the Detectives 35. Seven
Sinners 36. Educated Evans 36. *Oh Mr Porter* 38.
The Lady Vanishes 38. A Girl Must Live 39. They
Came by Night 40. *Night Train to Munich* 40. Kipps
41. The Young Mr Pitt 42. Millions Like Us (& d)
43. 2000 Women (& d) 43. *I See a Dark Stranger*
(& d) 45. Captain Boycott (& d) 47. The Blue
Lagoon (& d) 48. *The Happiest Days of Your Life* (&
d) 50. Lady Godiva Rides Again (& d) 51. *The
Belles of St Trinian's* (& d) 54. Geordie (& d) 55.
The Bridal Path (& d) 59. Joey Boy (& d) 65. The
Great St Trinian's Train Robbery (& d) 66. The
Wildcats of St Trinian's (wd) 80, etc.

Launer, Dale (1953–).
American screenwriter turned director.
 Ruthless People 86. Blind Date 87. Dirty Rotten
Scoundrels 88. My Cousin Vinny 92. Love Potion
#9 (wd) 92, etc.

Laurel, Stan (1890–1965) (Arthur Stanley Jefferson).
British-born comedian, the thin half and gag
deviser of the Laurel and Hardy team. Went to
USA with Fred Karno's troupe, was in short
comedies from 1915, teamed with Hardy 1926. He
had director credit on some of their films and
virtually directed many others. Special Academy
Award 1960 'for his creative pioneering in the field
of cinema comedy'.
 For list of films see *Oliver Hardy*.
☻ For his genius in the invention of comic gags,
and for finding his perfect niche in partnership with
Oliver Hardy. *Way Out West*.

¶ They were visual comedians, of course. But
  they successfully transferred to sound by the
use of minimum sound, mainly in the form of
carefully scattered catch phrases which arose
naturally out of their characters as every child's
foolish uncles. When disaster struck, as it inevitably
did, who could resist the sight of Olly among the
debris, gazing reprovingly at the unharmed Stan
and saying:

Here's another nice mess you've gotten me into. Or:

Why don't you do something to HELP me?
Or simply:

I have NOTHING to say.
Such results are Olly's reward for listening to Stan's suggestions earlier on. Stan's meaning is always unclear to begin with, so that Olly has to say:

Tell me that again.
But he finally gets the drift and agrees:

That's a *good* idea.
Olly of course was always shy, especially with women. When introduced, he was apt to twiddle his tie and observe:

A lot of weather we've been having lately.
His great asset was his courtly manner, preserved even when mistaking an open can of milk for the telephone receiver:

Pardon me for a moment, my ear is full of milk.
Stan, having no catch phrases, relied on lively non sequiturs. When asked:

You never met my wife, did you?
He would reply:

Yes, I never did.
His speciality was putting his foot in it, as when he visits Olly in hospital and announces:

I brought you some hard-boiled eggs and some nuts.
Not surprisingly, he eats them himself, having thoughtfully brought salt and pepper canisters in his pocket. Then there was the time in a bar when they could afford only one beer, ordered by Olly with his usual majesty. Stan did rather ruin the effect by calling after the waiter:

And two clean straws that haven't been used . . .
But he was capable of saying the right thing, as when Olly prepared a mundane repast of coffee and beans. Stan liked it:

Boy, you sure know how to plan a meal!
Behind the scenes, Stan was the producer. Olly was ready to admit:

I have never really worked hard in the creation department.
But he astutely saw the secret of their success:

Those two fellows we created, they were nice, very nice people. They never get anywhere because they are both so dumb, but they don't know they're dumb. One of the reasons why people like us, I guess, is because they feel superior to us.
That was put another way in the opening title to one of their silent films:

Neither Mr Laurel nor Mr Hardy had any thoughts of getting married. In fact, they had no thoughts of any kind . . .
And the opening of *Come Clean* summed up their best comedy style very neatly:

Mr Hardy holds that a man should always tell his wife the whole truth. Mr Laurel is crazy too.
Mr Laurel had his own philosophy:

We were doing a very simple thing, giving some people some laughs, and that's all we were trying to do.

Lauren, S. K. (1892–1979).
American screenwriter.
An American Tragedy 32. Bond Venus 34. Crime and Punishment 35. One Night of Love 36. Mother Carey's Chickens 39. Flight for Freedom 43, etc.

Laurenson, James (1935–).
New Zealand actor in British and Australian TV, especially series *Boney*.
The Magic Christian 69. Assault 70. The Monster

Club 80. Pink Floyd the Wall 82. Heartbreakers 84. The Man Who Fell to Earth (TV) 87. A House in the Hills 93, etc.

Laurents, Arthur (1918–).
American playwright.
Caught (orig sp) 48. Home of the Brave 49. Summertime 55. West Side Story (co-w) 61. The Way We Were (orig sp) 73. The Turning Point (orig sp) (AAN) 77.

Laurie, Hugh (1959–).
English comic actor and writer, most frequently seen partnering Stephen Fry (qv) in TV series and advertisements. He was educated at Eton and Cambridge University, where he was a rowing Blue and was a member of the losing crew in the Oxford and Cambridge Boat Race in 1980. He first partnered Fry in a Cambridge Footlights revue in 1981.
Blackadder's Christmas Carol (TV) 88. Peter's Friends 92. A Pin for the Butterfly 94.
TV series: Blackadder 84. Blackadder II 86. Blackadder the Third 87. Blackadder Goes Forth 89. A Bit of Fry and Laurie 89–92. Jeeves and Wooster 90–93.

Laurie, John (1897–1980).
Scottish character actor, often in dour roles. On stage from 1921.
Juno and the Paycock 30. Red Ensign 34. *The Thirty-Nine Steps* 35. Tudor Rose 36. As You Like It 36. Farewell Again 37. Edge of the World 38. Q Planes 39. Sailors Three 40. *The Ghost of St Michael's* 41. Old Mother Riley's Ghosts 41. The Gentle Sex 43. Fanny by Gaslight 43. *The Way Ahead* 44. *Henry V* 44. I Know Where I'm Going 45. Caesar and Cleopatra 45. The Brothers 47. Uncle Silas 47. Bonnie Prince Charlie 48. Hamlet 48. Trio 50. Laughter in Paradise 51. The Fake 53. Hobson's Choice 54. The Black Knight 55. Campbell's Kingdom 57. Kidnapped 60. Siege of the Saxons 63. Mr Ten Per Cent 66. Dad's Army 71. The Prisoner of Zenda 79, etc.

Laurie, Piper (1932–) (Rosetta Jacobs).
Pert American leading lady of 50s costume charades; later a notable character actress.
■ Louisa 50. The Milkman 50. Francis Goes to the Races 51. The Prince Who Was a Thief 51. No Room for the Groom 52. Has Anybody Seen My Gal 52. Son of Ali Baba 52. Mississippi Gambler 53. The Golden Blade 53. Dangerous Mission 54. Johnny Dark 54. Dawn at Socorro 54. Smoke Signal 55. Ain't Misbehavin' 55. Kelly and Me 57. Until They Sail 59. *The Hustler* (AAN) 61. *Carrie* (AAN) 76. Ruby 78. Tim 79. Skag (TV) 80. The Bunker (TV) 81. Mae West (TV) 82. The Thorn Birds (TV) 82. Toughlove (TV) 85. Return to Oz 85. Tender Is the Night (TV) 85. Children of a Lesser God (AAN) 86. Distortions 87. Appointment with Death 88. Tiger Warsaw 88. Dream a Little Dream 89. Other People's Money 91. Storyville 92. Trauma 93. Wrestling Ernest Hemingway 93.
TV series: Twin Peaks 90.

Lauter, Ed (1940–).
American general-purpose actor.
The Last American Hero 73. Executive Action 73. Lolly Madonna XXX 74. The Longest Yard 75. Last Hours before Morning (TV) 75. King Kong 76. The Chicken Chronicles 77. Eureka 83. The Big Score 83. Cujo 83. Lassiter 83. Finders Keepers 84. Death Wish 3 85. Youngblood 85. Raw Deal 86. The Last Days of Patton (TV) 86. Tennessee Waltz 88. Gleaming the Cube 89. Tennessee Nights 89. The Rocketeer 91. School Ties 92. Wagons East! 94. Trial by Jury 94, etc.

TV series: B.J. and the Bear 79–80.

Lauter, Harry (1920–1990).
American supporting actor.
The Gay Intruders 48. Tucson 49. Whirlwind 5⬤ The Sea Tiger 52. Dragonfly Squadron 54. The Crooked Web 55. Hellcats of the Navy 57. Gunfigh at Dodge City 59. Posse from Hell 61. Ambush Bay 66. More Dead than Alive 68, many others.

Lauzon, Jean-Claude (1953–).
French-Canadian director and screenwriter.
Night Zoo (Un Zoo la Nuit) 87. Léolo (wd) 92.

Laven, Arnold (1922–).
American director, former dialogue coach.
Without Warning 52. Down Three Dark Street 54. The Rack 56. The Monster that Challenged th World 57. Slaughter on Tenth Avenue 58. Anna Lucasta 58. Geronimo (& p) 62. The Glory Guys 6⬤ Rough Night in Jericho 67. Sam Whiskey 68. The Scalphunters (p only) 68, etc.

lavender print.
A high quality, well-contrasted print, sometimes called a 'fine grain', struck from the original negative for the purpose of making duplicates.

Laverick, June (1932–).
British leading lady, groomed for stardom by the Rank charm school of the 50s.
Doctor at Large 56. The Gypsy and the Gentleman 57. Son of Robin Hood 58. Follow a Sta 59, etc.

Lavery, Emmet (1902–1986).
American screenwriter.
Hitler's Children 43. Behind the Rising Sun 43. The First Legion (original play) 51. The Magnifice Yankee (original play) 52. The Court Martial of Billy Mitchell 55, etc.

Lavery, Emmet, Jnr (1927–).
American TV executive producer, mainly with Paramount.
Delaney Street 75. Serpico (and series) 76. Nere Wolfe 77, etc.

Lavi, Daliah (1940–) (D. Levenbuch).
Israeli leading lady in international films.
II Demonio (Italian) 63. Old Shatterhand (WG) 64. Lord Jim 65. Ten Little Indians 65. The Silencers 66. The Spy with a Cold Nose 67. Some Girls Do 67. Nobody Runs Forever 68. Catlow 72, etc.

Law, Clara.
Hong Kong film director. *Autumn Moon* was winner of the Golden Leopard at the Locarno Film Festival in 1992.
The Reincarnation of Golden Lotus 89. Farewell China 90. Fruit Punch 91. Autumn Moon 92. Erotique (co-d) 94, etc.

Law, John Phillip (1937–).
American leading man.
The Russians Are Coming, the Russians Are Coming 66. Hurry Sundown 67. Barbarella 68. Skidoo 68. The Sergeant 68. Danger: Diabolik 68. The Hawaiians 70. Von Richthofen and Brown 71. The Love Machine 71. The Last Movie 71. The Golden Voyage of Sinbad 73. Your Heaven, My Hell 76. The Cassandra Crossing 77. Tarzan the Ape Man 81. Going Straight 82. Night Train to Terror 84. L.A. Bad 85. American Commandos 85. Moon in Scorpio 86. Space Mutiny 88. Blood Delirium 88. Thunder Warrior III 88. Alienator 89, etc.

awford, Peter (1923–1984).
ritish light leading man, former child actor, in
ollywood from 1938.
  Biography: 1991, *Peter Lawford: The Man Who
pt Secrets* by James Spada.
  Poor Old Bill 31. The Boy from Barnardo's 38.
rs Miniver 42. The White Cliffs of Dover 44. Cluny
own 46. It Happened in Brooklyn 47. Easter
rade 48. Little Women 49. Royal Wedding 52.
xodus 60. Advise and Consent 61. Sylvia 65.
arlow 65. Dead Run (Austria) 67. Salt and Pepper
B) 68. Buona Sera Mrs Campbell 68. The April
ools 69. One More Time 70. Don't Look behind
ou (TV) 71. Phantom of Hollywood (TV) 74.
osebud 75, etc.
  TV series: Dear Phoebe 54. The Thin Man 58.

awrance, Jody (1930–). (Josephine Lawrence
oddard).
merican leading lady.
  Mask of the Avenger 51. Son of Dr Jekyll 51.
he Brigand 52. Captain John Smith and
ocahontas 53. The Scarlet Hour 55. Stagecoach
 Dancer's Rock 62.

awrence, Barbara (1928–).
merican comedy actress, usually seen as wise-
acking friend of the heroine.
  Biography: 1977, *Hollywood Starlet: The Career of
arbara Lawrence* by Jim Connor.
  Margie 46. You Were Meant for Me 47. Thieves'
ighway 49. Two Tickets to Broadway 51. Jesse
ames Versus the Daltons 54. *Oklahoma* 55. Joe
akota 57, etc.

awrence, Bruno (1949–).
ritish-born actor and musician, in New Zealand
om childhood, who became that country's leading
lm actor. He also works in Australia.
  Wild Man 77. Goodbye Pork Pie 80. Smash
alace 81. Race to the Yankee Zephyr 81. Utu 82.
eart of the Stag 83. The Quiet Earth 84. Bridge
 Nowhere 85. Rikky and Pete 88. The Delinquents
9. Grievous Bodily Harm 89. Spotswood 91. Jack
e Nimble 93. Gino 94, etc.

awrence, D. H. (1885–1930).
ntrospective British novelist whose novels have
een adapted with varying success for the screen.
  The Rocking Horse Winner 49. Lady Chatterley's
over 58. Sons and Lovers 60. The Fox 68.
Women in Love 69. The Virgin and the Gypsy 70.
he Rainbow 88, etc.
  Lady Chatterley's Lover was filmed again in 1980
nd on TV in 1993, and in 1981 Ian McKellen
layed Lawrence in *Priest of Love.*

awrence, Delphi (1926–).
nglo-Hungarian actress, in British films.
  Blood Orange 54. Barbados Quest 55. It's Never
oo Late 56. Too Many Crooks 59. Cone of
ilence 60. Farewell Performance 63. Pistolero
US) 67. Cops and Robbers 73, many others.

awrence, Florence (1886–1938).
merican leading lady of the silent screen; one of
he industry's chief stars, she was known at first as
he Biograph Girl'. Retired in the early 20s.
committed suicide.
  Miss Jones Entertains 09. Resurrection 10. A
Singular Cynic 14. The Enfoldment 20, many
thers.

awrence, Gertrude (1898–1952) (Alexandra
Dagmar Lawrence-Klasen).
  Vivacious British revue star of the 20s, especially
associated with Noel Coward. Despite sporadic
attempts, her quality never came across on the

screen. She was impersonated by Julie Andrews in
Star! 68. She was also unflatteringly portrayed as
self-centred actress Lorraine Sheldon in *The Man
Who Came to Dinner.*
  Autobiography: 1949, *A Star Danced.*
■ The Battle of Paris 29. No Funny Business 32.
Aren't We All 32. Lord Camber's Ladies 32. No
Funny Business 33. Mimi 35. Rembrandt 36. Men
are Not Gods 36. Stage Door Canteen 43. *The Glass
Menagerie* 50.

Lawrence, Jerome (1915–).
American dramatist and screenwriter, in
collaboration with Robert E. Lee.
  Auntie Mame (from their play) 58. Inherit the
Wind 60. First Monday in October 81.

Lawrence, Marc (1910–) (Max Goldsmith).
American character actor, former opera singer;
usually seen as Italian gangster.
  Autobiography: 1994, *Long Time, No See.*
  White Woman 33. Dr Socrates 35. Penitentiary
38. The Housekeeper's Daughter 39. Johnny
Apollo 40. The Monster and the Girl 41. Hold That
Ghost 42. Dillinger 45. I Walk Alone 47. The
Asphalt Jungle 50. My Favorite Spy 51. Helen of
Troy 55. Kill Her Gently 58. Johnny Cool 64.
Nightmare in the Sun (wd only) 64. Savage
Pampas 66. Custer of the West 67. Krakatoa East
of Java 69. Marathon Man 76. The Big Easy 86,
many others.

Lawrence, Marjorie (1902–1979).
Australian opera star crippled by polio; portrayed
in 1955 by Eleanor Parker in *Interrupted Melody.*

Lawrence, Quentin (c. 1920–1980).
British director, from TV.
  The Trollenberg Terror 55. Cash on Demand 62.
The Man Who Finally Died 63. The Secret of Blood
Island 65, etc.

Lawrence, T. E. (1888–1935).
British adventurer and soldier whose book *Seven
Pillars of Wisdom* made him a cult and remotely
inspired the film *Lawrence of Arabia.*

Lawrence, Viola (1894–1973).
American editor, long with Columbia.
  An Alabaster Box 17. Fighting the Flames 21.
Bulldog Drummond 29. Man's Castle 33. Craig's
Wife 36. Penitentiary 38. Here Comes Mr Jordan
41. My Sister Eileen 42. Cover Girl 44. Hit the Hay
46. The Dark Past 48. Tokyo Joe 49. Sirocco 51.
Miss Sadie Thompson 53. Queen Bee 55. Pal Joey
57. Who Was That Lady 60, many others.

Lawson, John Howard (1886–1977).
American writer with Marxist affiliations.
  Heart of Spain 37. Algiers 38. *Blockade* (AAN)
38. *Five Came Back* 39. Sahara 43. Counter-Attack
43. Smash-Up 47, etc.

Lawson, Leigh (1944–).
British light leading man of the 70s.
  Ghost Story 74. Percy's Progress 74. Love among
the Ruins (TV) 75. Golden Rendezvous 77. The
Devil's Advocate 78. Tess 80. Why Didn't They Ask
Evans? (TV) 81. Murder Is Easy (TV) 81. Lace
(TV) 84. Sword of the Valiant (TV) 85. Queenie
(TV) 87. Madame Sousatzka 88, etc.
  TV series: Kinsey 92.

Lawson, Sarah (1928–).
British leading lady of the 50s.
  The Browning Version 50. Street Corner 52.
Blue Peter 54. It's Never Too Late 55. Night of

the Big Heat (aka Island of the Burning Doomed)
67, etc.

Lawson, Wilfrid (1900–1966) (Wilfrid Worsnop).
British character actor, on stage from 1916;
revelled in eccentric parts.
■ East Lynne on the Western Front 31. Strike it
Rich 33. Turn of the Tide 35. The Man Who Made
Diamonds 37. Bank Holiday 38. The Terror 38.
Yellow Sands 38. The Gaunt Stranger 38. *Pygmalion*
38. Stolen Life 39. Dead Man's Shoes 39. *Pastor
Hall* 40. Gentleman of Venture 40. The Man at the
Gate 41. Danny Boy 41. Jeannie 41. The Farmer's
Wife 41. Tower of Terror 41. *Hard Steel* 42. The
Night Has Eyes 42. *The Great Mr Handel* 42.
Thursday's Child 43. Fanny by Gaslight 44. The
Turners of Prospect Road 47. Make Me an Offer
55. The Prisoner 55. An Alligator Named Daisy
55. Now and Forever 56. The Naked Truth 57. Hell
Drivers 57. Tread Softly Stranger 59. The Thrill of
the Top 59. Expresso Bongo 60. The Naked Edge 61.
Nothing Barred 61. Over the Odds 61. Go to
Blazes 62. Postman's Knock 62. Tom Jones 63.
Becket 64. *The Wrong Box* 66. The Viking Queen 66.

Lawton, Charles, Jnr (1904–1965).
American cinematographer.
  My Dear Miss Aldrich 36. Miracles for Sale 39.
Gold Rush Maisie 41. Fingers at the Window 42.
Abroad with Two Yanks 44. The Thrill of Brazil
46. *The Lady from Shanghai* 48. Shockproof 49.
Rogues of Sherwood Forest 50. Mask of the
Avenger 51. *The Happy Time* 52. Miss Sadie
Thompson 53. Drive a Crooked Road 54. The Long
Gray Line 55. Jubal 56. *3.10 to Yuma* 57. The Last
Hurrah 58. It Happened to Jane 59. Two Rode
Together 61. 13 West Street 62. Spencer's
Mountain 63. Youngblood Hawke 64. A Rage to
Live 65, many others.

Lawton, Frank (1904–1969).
Charming but undynamic British leading man of
the 30s, husband of Evelyn Laye; in British and
American films.
  Young Woodley 28. Birds of Prey 30. The Skin
Game 31. The Outsider 31. Michael and Mary 31.
After Office Hours 32. Cavalcade 33. Heads We Go
33. Friday the Thirteenth 33. One More River 34.
David Copperfield (title role) 34. The Invisible Ray
36. The Devil Doll 36. The Mill on the Floss 37.
The Four Just Men 39. Went the Day Well? 42.
The Winslow Boy 48. Rough Shoot 52. The Rising
of the Moon 57. A Night to Remember 57.
Gideon's Day 57, etc.

Lay, Beirne, Jnr (1909–1982).
American screenwriter.
  I Wanted Wings 41. Twelve O'Clock High 49.
Above and Beyond 50. Strategic Air Command
54. Toward the Unknown 56, etc.

Laydu, Claude (1927–).
Undernourished-looking French leading actor.
  Diary of a Country Priest 50. Nous Sommes Tous
les Assassins 52. Symphonie d'Amour 55. Le
Dialogue des Carmelites 59, etc.

Laye, Evelyn (1900–) (Elsie Evelyn Lay).
British musical comedy star of the 20s and 30s;
films rare. Married Frank Lawton.
  Autobiography: 1958, *Boo to My Friends.*
■ Luck of the Navy 27. Queen of Scandal 30. One
Heavenly Night (US) 31. Waltz Time 33. Princess
Charming 33. *Evensong* 34. The Night is Young 34.
I'll Turn to You 46. Make Mine a Million 59.
Theatre of Death 66. Say Hello to Yesterday 70.
Within and Without (It.) 70. Second Star to the
Right 80.

Lazar, Irving (1907–1993).
Prominent American agent, nicknamed 'Swifty' by
Humphrey Bogart for making five movie deals for
him in a day. He was noted for his skill in deals
and was in part responsible for the growing
importance and power of the agent in movie-
making in Hollywood.

Lazenby, George (1939–).
Australian leading man who made the big jump
from TV commercials to playing James Bond – once.
In the 70s and 80s he raced motorcycles and in
the 90s backed a restaurant chain, the Spy House.
   On Her Majesty's Secret Service 69. Universal
Soldier 71. The Man from Hong Kong 75. Cover
Girls (TV) 77. Evening in Byzantium (TV) 78. Saint
Jack 79. Never Too Young to Die 86. Hell Hunters
87. Eyes of the Beholder 91, etc.
   TV series: Rituals 84–85.

Le Borg, Reginald (1902–1989).
Austrian-born director, in Hollywood from 1937,
at first as shorts director. Output mainly routine
with occasional flashes of talent.
   Book: 1992, The Films of Reginald Le Borg by
Wheeler Winston Dixon.
   She's for Me 42. The Mummy's Ghost 44.
Calling Dr Death 44. San Diego I Love You 45. Joe
Palooka, Champ 46. Young Daniel Boone 47.
Wyoming Trail 49. Bad Blonde 51. Sins of Jezebel
53. The Black Sleep 56. The Dalton Girls 57. The
Flight that Disappeared 61. The Diary of a Madman
62, many others.

Le Breton, Auguste (1915–).
French writer.
   Razzia sur la Chnouf 54. Rififi 55. Bob le
Flambeur 56. Rafles sur la Ville 57, etc.

Le Brock, Kelly (1960–).
American leading lady.
   The Woman in Red 84. Weird Science 85. Hard
to Kill 90, etc.

Le Carré, John (1931–) (David John Moore
Cornwell).
British spy novelist, whose works have been
eagerly filmed, though they centre on the more
depressing aspects of espionage.
   The Spy Who Came in from the Cold 66. The
Deadly Affair (Call for the Dead) 67. The Looking
Glass War (TV) 79. Tinker Tailor Soldier Spy (TV) 79.
Smiley's People 82. The Little Drummer Girl 84. A
Perfect Spy (TV) 87.

¶ If you live in secrecy, you think in secrecy. It
   is the very nature of the life you lead as an
intelligence officer in a secret room that the
ordinary winds of common sense don't blow
through it. You are constantly looking to relate to
your enemy in intellectual, adversarial and
conspiratorial terms. – J.L.C.
   Where I kick myself is where I think I actually
contributed to the myth of the intelligence services
being very good. – J.L.C.

Le Chanois, Jean-Paul (1909–1985) (J.-P.
Dreyfus).
French director.
   L'École Buissonière 48. La Belle Que Voilà 51.
Papa, Mama, the Maid and I 54. The Case of Dr
Laurent 56. Les Misérables 58. Monsieur 64. Le
Jardinier d'Argenteuil 66, etc.

Le Fanu, J. Sheridan (1814–1873).
Irish novelist specializing in mystery and the
occult. His story Carmilla, about lesbian vampires,

has been filmed as Blood and Roses and The Vampire
Lovers; Uncle Silas was filmed in 1949.

Le Gallienne, Eva (1899–1991).
Distinguished American stage actress.
■ Prince of Players 54. The Devil's Disciple 59.
Resurrection (AAN) 80.

Le Mat, Paul (1945–).
American leading man.
   American Graffiti 73. Firehouse (TV) 74. Aloha
Bobby and Rose 75. Citizen's Band 77. More
American Graffiti 79. Melvin and Howard 80.
Death Valley 81. Jimmy the Kid 82. Strange
Invaders 83. The Hanoi Hilton 87. Private
Investigations 87. Easy Wheels 89. Blind Witness
(TV) 89. Puppet Master 89. Deuce Coupe 92, etc.

Le May, Alan (1899–1964).
American writer.
   Reap the Wild Wind 42. The Adventures of Mark
Twain 44. Tap Roots 48. High Lonesome (& d) 50.
Thunder in the Dust 51. I Dream of Jeannie 53.
The Searchers (oa) 56, etc.

Le Mesurier, John (1912–1983).
British character actor. Usually played bewildered
professional men; a favourite for cameo roles from
1946. Married Hattie Jacques.
   Autobiography: 1983, A Jobbing Actor.
   Death in the Hand 48. Beautiful Stranger 54.
Private's Progress 55. Happy Is the Bride 57. I Was
Monty's Double 58. School for Scoundrels 60. Only
Two Can Play 61. Invasion Quartet 62. The Pink
Panther 63. The Moonspinners 64. Masquerade
65. Where the Spies Are 65. The Wrong Box 66.
The Midas Run 69. The Magic Christian 70. Dad's
Army 71. The Garnett Saga 72. Confessions of a
Window Cleaner 75. Stand Up Virgin Soldiers 77.
The Spaceman and King Arthur 79. The Fiendish
Plot of Dr Fu Manchu 80. A Married Man (TV) 83,
many others.
   TV series: Dad's Army 67–77.

Le Roy, Mervyn (1900–1987).
American director, former actor, in Hollywood
from 1924.
   Autobiography: 1975, Take One.
   Hot Stuff 27. Top Speed 28. Broken Dishes 29.
Little Caesar 30. Broadminded 31. Five Star Final 32.
Three on a Match 32. I Am a Fugitive from a Chain
Gang 32. Two Seconds 32. Tugboat Annie 32. Gold
Diggers of 1933. Hi Nellie 33. Oil for the Lamps of
China 33. Hot to Handle 33. Sweet Adeline 34.
Page Miss Glory 34. I Found Stella Parish 35.
Anthony Adverse 36. Three Men on a Horse 36.
They Won't Forget 37. Fools for Scandal 38. Stand
Up and Fight (p only) 38. The Wizard of Oz (p only)
39. At the Circus (p only) 39. Waterloo Bridge 40.
Escape 40. Blossoms in the Dust 41. Unholy
Partners 41. Johnny Eager 41. Random Harvest 42.
Madame Curie 43. Thirty Seconds over Tokyo 44;
war service; Without Reservations 47.
Homecoming 48. Little Women 49. Any Number
Can Play 49. East Side West Side 50. Quo Vadis
51. Lovely To Look At 52. Million Dollar Mermaid
53. Rose Marie 54. Mister Roberts (co-d) 55.
Strange Lady in Town (& p) 55. The Bad Seed (&
p) 56. Toward the Unknown (& p) 56. No Time
for Sergeants (& p) 58. Home Before Dark (& p)
59. The FBI Story (& p) 59. A Majority of One (&
p) 60. The Devil at Four O'Clock 61. Gypsy (& p)
62. Mary Mary (& p) 63. Moment to Moment (&
p) 65, etc.

Leach, Rosemary (1935–).
British character actress, mostly on TV.
   Brief Encounter (TV) 74. That'll Be the Day 74.

SOS Titanic 79. The Jewel in the Crown (TV) 82.
The Bride 84. Turtle Diary 85. A Room with a View
85. The Children 90. The Mystery of Edwin Drood
93. The Hawk 93, etc.

Leachman, Cloris (1926–).
American character actress, mostly on TV.
   Kiss Me Deadly 54. The Rack 56. The Chapman
Report 62. Butch Cassidy and the Sundance Kid 69.
WUSA 70. The Last Picture Show (AA) 71. Haunts
of the Very Rich (TV) 72. Dillinger 73. Charley
and the Angel 74. Daisy Miller 74. Hitch Hike (TV)
74. Crazy Mama 75. A Girl Named Sooner (TV) 75.
Death Sentence (TV) 75. Young Frankenstein 75.
Run Stranger Run 76. High Anxiety 78. SOS Titanic
(TV) 79. The North Avenue Irregulars 79.
Backstairs at the White House (TV) 79. Willa (TV)
79. Herbie Goes Bananas 80. History of the World
Part One 81. Hansel and Gretel 87. Walk Like a
Man 87. The Victory 88. Love Hurts 89. Prancer
89. Texasville 90. Miracle Child (TV) 93. My
Boyfriend's Back 93. The Beverly Hillbillies 93. A
Troll in Central Park (voice) 94, etc.
   TV series: Lassie (50s). The Mary Tyler Moore
Show 70–73. Phyllis 75–76. The Facts of Life 86–
88.

Leacock, Philip (1917–1990).
British director, noted for his way with children;
latterly worked in American television.
■ The Brave Don't Cry 52. Appointment in London
52. The Kidnappers 53. Escapade 55. The Spanish
Gardener 56. High Tide at Noon 57. Innocent
Sinners 58. The Rabbit Trap 58. Let No Man Write
My Epitaph 59. Hand in Hand 60. Take a Giant
Step 61. Reach for Glory 61. 13 West Street 62. The
War Lover 63. Tamahine 63. Adam's Woman 70.
The Birdmen (TV) 71. The Great Man's Whiskers
(TV) 72. When Michael Calls (TV) 72. Key West
(TV) 72. The Daughters of Joshua Cabe (TV) 72.
Baffled (TV) 72. Dying Room Only (TV) 73. Killer
on Board (TV) 77. Wild and Wooly (TV) 78. The
Curse of King Tut's Tomb (TV) 80. Angel City (TV)
80.

Leacock, Richard (1921–).
British-born cameraman and director, brother of
Philip Leacock. Worked with Flaherty and became
associated with the 'cinema vérité' school.
   Primary 60. The Chair 62. Quints 63. Chiefs 68.
Maidstone 70. Tread (d) 72. Elliott Carter 80. Lulu
in Berlin (d) 84. Dance Black America 85. Girltalk
88, etc.

leader.
Length of blank film joined to the beginning of a
reel for lacing up in projector. 'Academy' leaders
give a numbered countdown to the start of action.

Lean, Sir David (1908–1991).
Distinguished British director, former editor, in
films from 1928.
   Biography: 1989, David Lean by Stephen M.
Silverman.
■ In Which We Serve (co-d) 42. This Happy Breed
44. Blithe Spirit 45. Brief Encounter (AAN) 46. Great
Expectations (AAN) 46. Oliver Twist 48. The
Passionate Friends 48. Madeleine 49. The Sound
Barrier (& p) 51. Hobson's Choice (& p) 54.
Summertime (GB: Summer Madness) (AAN) 55.
The Bridge on the River Kwai (AA) 57. Lawrence of
Arabia (AA) 62. Dr Zhivago (AAN) 65. Ryan's
Daughter 70. A Passage to India (AANd, AANw,
AANed) 84.
✪ For his understanding of the art of cinema,
despite his final submergence of his sensitive
talent in pretentious but empty spectaculars. Great
Expectations.

¶ I hope the money men don't find out that I'd pay them to let me do this. – *D.L.*

I wouldn't take the advice of a lot of so-called critics on how to shoot a close-up of a teapot. – *D.L.*

Actors can be a terrible bore on the set, though I enjoy having dinner with them. – *D.L.*

Inside every Lean film there is a fat film screaming to get out. – *Anon*

There was a touch of the bully about him – he'd take it out on the people who were weakest and most dependent. – *Judy Davis*

Lear, Norman (1926–).
American producer, former comedy writer.

Divorce American Style 67. The Night They Raided Minsky's 68. Start the Revolution without Me 69. Cold Turkey 71. The Princess Bride 87, etc.

TV series: *All in the Family* 71. *Maude* 72. Sanford and Son 72–78. One Day at a Time 75–84. Mary Hartman, Mary Hartman 76, etc.

Learned, Michael (1939–).
Motherly American character actress who scored on TV in *The Waltons* 72–81 and briefly in *Nurse* 82.

Hurricane (TV) 74. It Couldn't Happen to a Nicer Guy (TV) 74. Widow (TV) 76. Little Mo (TV) 78. Touched by Love 80. Power 86. All My Sons (TV) 86. Deadly Business (TV) 86. Roots: The Gift (TV) 88. Murder in New Hampshire: The Pamela Smart Story (TV) 91. Dragon: The Bruce Lee Story 93, etc.

Leary, Denis.
Aggressive American stand-up comedian and actor.

The Sandlot (GB: The Sandlot Kids) 93. Gunmen 93. National Lampoon's Loaded Weapon 93. Who's the Man 93. Demolition Man 93. Judgment Night 93. The Ref 94. The Neon Bible 95, etc.

Leasor, James (1923–).
British thriller writer whose Dr Jason Love was brought to the screen in 1964 in *Where the Spies Are.*

Léaud, Jean-Pierre (1944–).
French leading actor who began as a boy star.

Les Quatre Cents Coups 59. Love at Twenty 61. Masculin-Feminin 66. La Chinoise 67. Stolen Kisses 68. Pigsty 69. Last Tango in Paris 72. Day for Night 73. Love on the Run 79. Detective 84. Treasure Island 85. With All Hands 86. 36 Fillette 88. Bunker Palace Hotel 89. I Hired a Contract Killer 90. Zone 91. Bohemian Life (La Vie de Bohème) 92. La Naissance de l'Amour 93. Personne Ne M'Aime 94, etc.

Leavitt, Sam (1904–1984).
American cinematographer.

The Thief 52. *A Star is Born* 54. Carmen Jones 54. The Man with the Golden Arm 55. *The Defiant Ones* (AA) 58. Anatomy of a Murder (AAN) 59. Exodus (AA) 60. Advise and Consent 62. Two on a Guillotine 64. Major Dundee 65. Brainstorm 65. An American Dream 66. Guess Who's Coming to Dinner 67. The Desperados 68. The Grasshopper 70. Star Spangled Girl 71. The Man in the Glass Booth 75, etc.

Lebedeff, Ivan (1899–1953).
Russian character actor, former diplomat, in US from 1925.

The Sorrows of Satan 27. Midnight Mystery 30. Blonde Bombshell 33. China Seas 35. History Is Made at Night 37. Hotel for Women 39. The Shanghai Gesture 41. They Are Guilty 45. The Snows of Kilimanjaro 52, many others.

Leclerc, Ginette (1912–1992).
Sulky-looking French stage and screen actress.

Prison sans Barreaux 38. *La Femme du Boulanger* 38. *Le Corbeau* 43. Le Plaisir 51. Les Amants du Tage 54. Gas-Oil 55. La Cave Se Rebiffe 61. Goto, Island of Love 68. Tropic of Cancer 69, etc.

Leconte, Patrice (1947–).
French director and screenwriter, a former comic-book writer and artist, who switched from making local comedies to dramas with an international appeal.

Monsieur Hire 90. The Hairdresser's Husband (Le Mari de la Coiffeuse) (co-w, d) 91. *Tango* 93. Le Parfum d'Yvonne 94, etc.

Ledebur, Friedrich (c. 1908–).
Austrian actor of eccentric roles.

Moby Dick 56. Roots of Heaven 58. The Blue Max 66. Alfred the Great 69. Juliet of the Spirits 69. Slaughterhouse Five 72. Ginger and Fred 86, etc.

Lederer, Charles (1906–1976).
American screenwriter, in Hollywood from 1931.

The Front Page 31. Topaze 33. Comrade X 40. His Girl Friday 40. Ride the Pink Horse 47. *Kiss of Death* 47. The Thing 52. It Started with a Kiss 58. The Spirit of St Louis 58. Can Can 59. Ocean's Eleven 61. Mutiny on the Bounty 62, many others.

■ AS DIRECTOR: Fingers at the Window 42. On the Loose 51. Never Steal Anything Small (& w) 58, etc.

Lederer, Francis (1906–).
Czech-born leading man, in Hollywood from 1933, after European stage and film experience.

Pandora's Box (Ger.) 28. Atlantic (Ger.) 30. The Bracelet (Ger.) 32. The Pursuit of Happiness 34. It's All Yours 36. The Lone Wolf in Paris 37. Midnight 38. *Confessions of a Nazi Spy* 39. The Man I Married 40. The Bridge of San Luis Rey 44. A Voice in the Wind 45. The Diary of a Chambermaid 45. Million Dollar Weekend 48. Captain Carey USA 49. A Woman of Distinction 50. Stolen Identity 53. Lisbon 56. The Return of Dracula 58. Terror Is a Man 59, etc.

Lederman, D. Ross (1895–1972).
American director, former prop man for Mack Sennett.

Man Hunter 30. Riding Tornado 32. Glamour for Sale 40. The Body Disappears 41. Strange Alibi 41. Shadows on the Stairs 43. Key Witness 47, etc.

Ledoux, Fernand (1897–1993).
Belgian-born actor who had a long and distinguished stage and film career in France, working in more than 800 plays and movies. He was a member of the Comédie Française for more than 20 years.

Le Carnaval de Vérités 19. L'Homme à la Barbiche 32. Le Vagabond Bien-aimé 36. The Human Beast (La Bête Humaine) 38. The Devil's Envoys (Les Visiteurs du Soir) 42. Devil's Daughter (La Fille du Diable) 46. An Act of Love (Un Acte d'Amour) 54. Les Misérables 58. The Truth (La Verité) 60. The Big Gamble (US) 61. The Longest Day (US) 62. The Trial 62. Up from the Beach (US) 65. Donkey Skin (Peau d'Ane) 71. A Trillion Dollars (Mille Milliards de Dollars) 82, etc.

Leduc, Paul (1942–).
Mexican director and a pioneer of the country's 'New Cinema' movement. He studied architecture and theatre before becoming a film critic and worked in French TV before returning

to Mexico, where he first produced and directed documentaries.

Reed: Mexico Insurgente 73. Etnocido: Notas sobre el Mezquital 78. Historias Prohibidas de Pulgarcito 79. La Cabeza de la Hidra (TV) 81. Frida 86. Barocco 89. Latino Bar 91. Dollar Mambo 93, etc.

Lee, Ang.
Taiwanese director.

Pushing Hands 91. The Wedding Banquet (AAN) 93. Eat Drink Man Woman 94.

Lee, Anna (1914–) (Joanna Winnifrith).
British leading lady, in US since 1939 and a regular on the soap opera *General Hospital*.

Ebb Tide 32. The Camels Are Coming 36. King Solomon's Mines 37. The Four Just Men 39. My Life with Caroline 41. Summer Storm 44. Fort Apache 48. Whatever Happened to Baby Jane? 62. The Sound of Music 65. Seven Women 65. In Like Flint 67, many others.

Lee, Belinda (1935–1961).
Blonde British starlet trained for stardom by Rank but given poor material: appeared in Continental semi-spectaculars and died in car crash.

The Runaway Bus 54. The Belles of St Trinian's 54. Man of the Moment 55. Who Done It? 55. The Feminine Touch 56. The Secret Place 56. The Big Money 56. Miracle in Soho 57. Dangerous Exile 57. Nor the Moon by Night 58. Les Drageurs 59. Nights of Lucretia Borgia 59. Carthage in Flames 61, etc.

Lee, Bernard (1908–1981).
British character actor with solid, friendly personality, on stage from 1926. In films, often a sergeant or a superintendent . . . or 'M' in the James Bond films.

The River House Mystery 35. The Terror 37. Spare a Copper 40. Once a Crook 41; war service; The Courtneys of Curzon Street 47. *The Fallen Idol* 48. Quartet 48. *The Third Man* 49. The Blue Lamp 50. Appointment with Venus 51. The Gift Horse 52. The Purple Plain 54. *Father Brown* 54. The Battle of the River Plate 56. Dunkirk 58. Danger Within 59. The Angry Silence 59. The Secret Partner 60. Whistle Down the Wind 61. *Dr No* 62. Two Left Feet 63. From Russia with Love 63. Ring of Spies 63. Goldfinger 64. The Legend of Young Dick Turpin 65. Thunderball 65. The Spy Who Came In from the Cold 65. You Only Live Twice 66. The Raging Moon 70. Dulcima 71. Frankenstein and the Monster from Hell 73. The Man with the Golden Gun 74. Beauty and the Beast 76. The Spy who Loved Me 77. Moonraker 79, many others.

Lee, Bill (1928–).
American composer and musician, for the films of his son, Spike Lee (qv).

She's Gotta Have It 86. School Daze 88. Do the Right Thing 89. Mo' Better Blues (songs) 90, etc.

Lee, Billy (1930–1989).
American child star of the 30s.

Wagon Wheels 34. Coconut Grove 38. The Biscuit Eater 40. Hold Back the Dawn 41. Mrs Wiggs of the Cabbage Patch 42, etc.

Lee, Brandon (1965–1993).
American action film star, the son of Bruce Lee (qv). Born in Oakland, California, he was brought up in Hong Kong, where he was taught martial arts from an early age by his father. He died following a shooting accident while filming *The Crow*, a film about a rock musician who returns from the dead.

Kung Fu: The Next Generation (TV) 85. Legacy of Rage 86. Lazer Mission 87. Showdown in Little Tokyo 91. Rapid Fire 92. The Crow 94, etc.

¶ None of my friends would come over to the house when I was a kid because they were all scared to death. There would always be six or seven grown men in the backyard screaming and throwing each other around. – *B.L.*

Lee, Bruce (1940–1973) (Lee Yenn Kam). Diminutive Chinese-American leading man and practitioner of the martial arts. After comparative failure in Hollywood (a bit part in *Marlowe* 69, a supporting role in a TV series *The Green Hornet* 68), he went to Hong Kong and became a sensation in 'chop socky' movies. A biopic of his life, *Dragon*, starring Jason Scott Lee, was released in 1993. He was the father of Brandon Lee (qv).
Fist of Fury 72. The Big Boss 72. Enter the Dragon 73. The Way of the Dragon 73. Game of Death (posthumously re-edited) 79, etc.

¶ Bruce Lee had bad eyesight and one leg that was shorter than the other. But he had a mental image of what he wanted, and he became the quintessential martial artist and the first Chinese superstar in American films. – *Chuck Norris*

Lee, Canada (1907–1952) (Lionel Canegata). American actor.
■ Lifeboat 43. Body and Soul 47. Lost Boundaries 49. Cry the Beloved Country 52.

Lee, Christopher (1922–).
Gaunt British actor whose personality lends itself best to sinister or horrific parts. Seems to have made more films than any other living actor, and has certainly played most of the known monsters.
Autobiography: 1977, *Tall, Dark and Gruesome*.
Corridor of Mirrors 47. Hamlet 48. They Were Not Divided 49. Prelude to Fame 50. Valley of Eagles 51. The Crimson Pirate 52. Moulin Rouge 53. The Dark Avenger 54. Private's Progress 55. Alias John Preston 56. Moby Dick 56. *The Curse of Frankenstein* (as the monster) 56. Ill Met by Moonlight 57. The Traitor 57. A Tale of Two Cities 57. *Dracula* (title role) 58. Corridors of Blood 58. The Hound of the Baskervilles (as Sir Henry) 59. The Man Who Could Cheat Death 59. *The Mummy* (title role) 59. Beat Girl 60. City of the Dead 60. The Hands of Orlac 60. Taste of Fear 61. The Terror of the Tongs 61. The Devil's Daffodil 62. Pirates of Blood River 62. Sherlock Holmes and the Deadly Necklace (Ger.) 62. The Gorgon 63. Dr Terror's House of Horrors 63. She 65. The Face of Fu Manchu 65. The Skull 65. Dracula Prince of Darkness 65. Rasputin the Mad Monk 65. Theatre of Death 66. Night of the Big Heat 67. The Devil Rides Out 68. Curse of the Crimson Altar 68. Julius Caesar 70. I Monster 71. Dracula AD 1972 72. The Wicker Man 73. The Satanic Rites of Dracula 73. The Three Musketeers 74. The Man with the Golden Gun 74. Diagnosis Murder 75. To the Devil a Daughter 75. Killer Force 75. Airport 77 77. Return from Witch Mountain 78. The Silent Flute 78. The Pirate (TV) 78. Starship Invasions 78. The Passage 78. Arabian Adventure 79. Circle of Iron 79. 1941 79. Serial 80. The Salamander 80. An Eye for an Eye 81. Safari 3000 82. The House of Long Shadows 83. The Return of Captain Invincible 83. Howling II 85. The Rosebud Beach Hotel 85. Jocks 86. Dark Mission 88. Mask of Murder 89. The Return of the Musketeers 89. The Miser (L'Avaro) 89. Panga 90. Gremlins 2: The New Batch 90. Honeymoon Academy 90. Sherlock Holmes and the Leading Lady (TV) 91. Curse III: Blood Sacrifice 91. Cybereden (It.) 93.

Police Academy 7: Mission to Moscow 94. Funny Man 94, etc.

¶ I stopped appearing as Dracula in 1972 because in my opinion the presentation of the character had deteriorated to such an extent, particularly bringing him into the contemporary day and age, that it really no longer had any meaning. – *C.L.*

Lee, Davey (1925–).
American child actor of the early talkies.
The Singing Fool 28. Sonny Boy 29. The Squealer 30, etc.

Lee, Dixie (1911–1952) (Wilma Wyatt). American leading lady, wife of Bing Crosby.
Not for Sale 24. Movietone Follies 29. The Big Party 30. No Limit 31. Manhattan Love Song 34. Love in Bloom 35, etc.

Lee, Dorothy (1911–).
American leading lady of the 30s, especially associated with Wheeler and Wolsey.
Syncopation 29. Rio Rita 29. The Cuckoos 30. Half Shot at Sunrise 30. Cracked Nuts 31. Caught Plastered 31. Girl Crazy 32. Take a Chance 33. Hips, Hips Hooray 34. The Rainmakers 35. Silly Billies 36. Twelve Crowded Hours 39, etc.

Lee, Gypsy Rose (1913–1970) (Louise Hovick). American burlesque artiste, on stage from six years old: her early life, glamorized, is recounted in *Gypsy* 62, based on her 1957 book.
■ You Can't Have Everything 37. Ali Baba Goes to Town 38. My Lucky Star 39. Belle of the Yukon 44. Babes in Baghdad 52. Screaming Mimi 57. Wind Across the Everglades 58. The Stripper 62. The Trouble with Angels 66.
TV series: The Pruitts of Southampton 66.

¶ Royalties are all very well, but shaking the beads brings in the money quicker. – *G.R.L.*
God is love, but get it in writing. – *G.R.L.*

Lee, Jack (1913–).
British director, originally in documentaries.
Close Quarters 44. Children on Trial 46. The Woman in the Hall 47. *The Wooden Horse* (co-d) 50. Turn the Key Softly 53. *A Town Like Alice* 56. Robbery under Arms 57. The Captain's Table 58. Circle of Deception 61, etc.

Lee, Jason Scott.
American leading actor.
Dragon: The Bruce Lee Story 93. Map of the Human Heart 93. Rapa Nui 94. The Jungle Book 95.

Lee, Lila (1902–1973) (Augusta Apple). Demure American leading lady of the 20s.
The Cruise of the Make Believes 18. Male and Female 19. Terror Island 20. Blood and Sand 22. Million Dollar Mystery 25. Queen of the Night Clubs 29, etc.

Lee, Michele (1942–) (Michele Dusiak). American leading lady and singer, with stage experience.
How to Succeed in Business 67. The Love Bug 69. The Comic 69. Dark Victory (TV) 76. Bud and Lou (TV) 78. Single Women, Married Men (TV) 89, etc.
TV series: Knots Landing 79–86.

Lee, Norman.
British director and screenwriter, often of low-budget comedies. A former actor and playwright, he directed silent films in South Africa in the 20s,

including a version of *The Blue Lagoon*. He was a theatre director and writer of revues in Britain before beginning to direct films at Elstree in 1929. After 1943, he concentrated on writing screenplays and novels.
Autobiographies: 1945, *A Film Is Born*. 1947, *My Personal Log*. 1949, *Log of a Film Director*.
The Song of London 29. Lure of the Atlantic 29. Strip Strip Hooray! Dr Josser K.C. (& co-w) 31. Money Talks (& co-w) 32. The Strangler (& w) 32. Josser Joins the Navy 32. Josser on the River (& co-w) 32. Pride of the Force (& co-w) 32. Doctor' Orders 34. The Outcast 34. A Political Party 34. Royal Cavalcade (co-d) 35. Don't Rush Me 36. Kathleen Mavourneen 37. French Leave 37. Knights for a Day 37. Luck of the Navy 38. Mr Reeder in Room 13 38. Yes, Madam? 38. Murder in Soho 39. The Farmer's Wife (co-w, co-d) 40. This Man Is Mine (co-w) 46. The Monkey's Paw 48. Idol of Paris (co-w) 48. The Case of Charles Peace (& co-w) 49. The Girl Who Couldn't Quite 50, etc.

¶ The director is still a Big Shot but he shares his authority with others. He is no longer the man he was. The money kings have now got him by the short hairs. – *N.L.*

Lee, Peggy (1920–) (Norma Egstrom). American singer and songwriter, in occasional films. One of the great interpreters of popular song, she sang with the Benny Goodman orchestra in the early 40s and wrote many of the songs, and also sang them in Walt Disney's animated film *The Lady and the Tramp* 55.
Stage Door Canteen 43. Mr Music 50. The Jazz Singer 53. Johnny Guitar (title song) 54. Pete Kelly's Blues (AAN) 55. The Russians Are Coming! The Russians Are Coming! (song) 66, etc.

Lee, Robert E. (1918–1994).
American dramatist and screenwriter, in collaboration with Jerome Lawrence.
Auntie Mame (from their play) 58. Inherit the Wind 60. First Monday in October 81.

Lee, Rowland V. (1891–1975).
American director, in films from 1918.
Alice Adams 26. Barbed Wire 26. The Mysterious Dr Fu Manchu 29. *Zoo in Budapest* 33. *The Count of Monte Cristo* 34. Cardinal Richelieu 35. The Three Musketeers 35. Service de Luxe 38. Son of Frankenstein 39. Tower of London 39. Son of Monte Cristo 41. The Bridge of San Luis Rey 44. Captain Kidd 45. The Big Fisherman (p only) 59, etc.

Lee, Sheryl (1966–).
American actress who gained fame through the TV series Twin Peaks 90.
Wild at Heart 90. I Love You to Death 90. Twin Peaks: Fire Walk with Me 92. The Distinguished Gentleman 92. Backbeat 94. Don't Do It 94, etc.

Lee, Spike (1956–) (Shelton Jackson Lee). American director, screenwriter and actor. He has his own production company, Forty Acres & A Mule Filmworks.
Biography: 1992, *Spike Lee* by Alex Patterson.
She's Gotta Have It 86. School Daze 88. Do the Right Thing (AANw) 89. Mo' Better Blues 90. Jungle Fever 91. Malcolm X 92. Crooklyn (co-w, a, d) 94. Clockers (co-w, d) 95, etc.

¶ I remember trying to join the boy scouts and they told me I couldn't join because I wasn't Catholic. You can't help growing up thinking something is amiss. – *S.L.*

e-Thompson, J. (1914–).
tish director, former actor and playwright.
The Middle Watch (w) 36. For Them that
espass (w) 48. Murder without Crime (wd) 50.
e Yellow Balloon (wd) 52. The Weak and the
cked (wd) 53. As Long as They're Happy (d)
For Better for Worse (d) 54. An Alligator
med Daisy (d) 55. Yield to the Night (d) 56.
e Good Companions (co-p, co-d) 57. No Trees
the Street (d) 58. Woman in a Dressing Gown
59. Tiger Bay (d) 59. Northwest Frontier (d)
Ice Cold in Alex (d) 60. I Aim at the Stars (d)
S) 60. The Guns of Navarone (AANd) 61. Cape
ar (d) 61. Taras Bulba (d) (US) 62. Kings of
e Sun (d) 63. What a Way to Go (d) (US)
John Goldfarb Please Come Home (d) (US) 65.
turn from the Ashes (p, d) 65. Eye of the Devil
66. Mackenna's Gold (d) (US) 68. Before
nter Comes (d) 68. The Chairman (d) 69.
untry Dance (d) 70. Conquest of the Planet of
e Apes (d) (US) 72. A Great American Tragedy
V) 72. Huckleberry Finn (d) (US) 74. The
incarnation of Peter Proud (d) (US) 74. The Blue
ight (TV) (d) 75. St Ives (d) 75. Widow (TV) (d)
. The White Buffalo (d) (US) 77. The Greek
coon 78. The Passage 78. Cabo Blanco 79. Happy
rthday to Me 81. Ten to Midnight 83. The
mbassador 84. King Solomon's Mines 85.
urphy's Law 86. Firewalker 86. Death Wish IV:
e Crackdown 88. Messenger of Death 88. Kinjite
orbidden Subjects) 89.

eech, Richard (1922–) (Richard McClelland).
itish character actor, often as army or air force
ficer.
The Dam Busters 55. A Night to Remember 57.
e Good Companions 57. Ice Cold in Alex 59. The
orse's Mouth 59. Tunes of Glory 60. The Wild
d the Willing 62. I Thank a Fool 63. The
ghting Prince of Donegal 66. Young Winston 72.
andhi 82. The Shooting Party 84. A Woman of
bstance (TV) 85, etc.

eeds, Andrea (1914–1984) (Antoinette Lees).
merican leading lady of the late 30s.
Come and Get It 36. Stage Door (AAN) 37. The
oldwyn Follies 39. Letter of Introduction 39.
wanee River 39, etc.

eeds, Herbert I. (c. 1900–1954) (Herbert I. Levy).
merican director of second features, former
litor.
Mr Moto in Danger Island 38. Island in the Sky
8. The Cisco Kid and the Lady 39. Manila Calling
2. Time to Kill 43. It Shouldn't Happen to a Dog
6. Let's Live Again 48. Father's Wild Game 51, etc.

gends.
ver the years a number of Hollywood legends
ave built up, never proved or disproved. Here is a
lection: George Raft was a protégé of the Mafia.
ames Dean is not really dead but on a life support
achine. Walt Disney is cryonically preserved.
ouella Parsons witnessed the murder of Thomas
ce by W. R. Hearst. Marilyn Monroe was killed
y the CIA because of her association with John
ennedy. Cary Grant and Randolph Scott were
vers. Ida Lupino is bald.

egg, Stuart (1910–1988).
ritish documentarist and administrator. From
932 with GPO Film Unit and Empire Marketing
oard. 1939–45: National Film Board of Canada.
953–88: director of Film Centre Ltd.

eggatt, Alison (1904–1990).
ritish character actress, mainly on stage.
Nine Till Six 32. This Happy Breed 44. Waterloo

Road 45. Marry Me 47. The Card 52. Touch and Go
55. Never Take Sweets from a Stranger 60. Nothing
but the Best 64. The Seven Per Cent Solution 76,
etc.

Legrand, Michel (1931–).
French composer.
Lola 61. Eva 62. Vivre sa Vie 62. La Baie des
Anges 63. The Umbrellas of Cherbourg (AAN) 64.
Bande à Part 64. Une Femme Mariée 65. Les
Demoiselles de Rochefort 67. Ice Station Zebra
68. Peau d'Ane 70. Summer of 42 (AA) 71. A Time
for Loving (& a) 71. One is a Lonely Number 72.
Portnoy's Complaint 72. Cops and Robbers 73. The
Three Musketeers 74. Ode to Billy Joe 75. The Other
Side of Midnight 77. Atlantic City USA 80. Falling
in Love Again 80. The Hunter 80. The Mountain
Men 80. Best Friends 82. Yentl (AA) 83. Palace 84.
Secret Places 85. Switching Channels 88. Eternity
90. The Pickle 93, etc.

LeGros, James.
American leading actor.
Phantasm 79. Near Dark 87. Phantasm II 88.
Drugstore Cowboy 89. Hollywood Heartbreak 89.
The Rapture 91. Singles 92. Guncrazy 92. My New
Gun 92. Where the Day Takes You 92. Bad Girls
94. Don't Do It 94, etc.

Leguizamo, John (1965–).
American actor and comedian. Born in Bogotá,
Colombia, he studied drama at New York
University.
Mixed Blood 85. Casualties of War 89. Mambo
Mouth 90. Street Hunter 90. Hangin' with the
Homeboys 91. Regarding Henry 91. Super Mario
Bros 93. Night Owl 93. Carlito's Way 93. To Wong
Foo, Thanks for Everything, Julie Newmar 95, etc.

Lehman, Ernest (1920–).
American screenwriter.
Inside Story 48. Executive Suite 54. Sabrina
(AAN) 54. The Sweet Smell of Success 57. North by
Northwest (AAN) 59. The Prize 63. The Sound of
Music 65. Who's Afraid of Virginia Woolf? (& p)
(AAN) 66. Hello Dolly (& p) (AAN) 69. Portnoy's
Complaint (& p, d) 72. Family Plot 76. Black
Sunday 77, etc.

Lehmann, Beatrix (1898–1979).
British character actress, often of withdrawn
eccentrics; film appearances few. On stage from
1924.
The Passing of the Third Floor Back 36. Black
Limelight 38. The Rat 38. The Key 58. Psyche 59
64. The Spy Who Came in from the Cold 66.
Staircase 69, etc.

Lehmann, Carla (1917–1990).
Canadian leading lady, in British films of the 40s.
So This Is London 39. Cottage to Let 41. Talk
about Jacqueline 42. Candlelight in Algeria 44. 29
Acacia Avenue 45. Fame Is the Spur 47, etc.

Lehmann, Michael
American director and screenwriter.
Heathers (d) 88. Meet the Applegates (co-w, d)
89. Hudson Hawk (d) 91. Airheads (d) 94, etc.

Lehto, Pekka.
Finnish director and producer, a former sound
engineer, who began by working in collaboration
with director Pirjo Honkasalo.
Their Age (short, co-d) 76. Flame Top (Tulipää)
(co-d) 80. Da Capo (co-d) 85. The Well (d) 91,
etc.

Leiber, Fritz (1883–1949).
American Shakespearean actor who played many
supporting roles in films.
A Tale of Two Cities 35. Anthony Adverse 36.
The Hunchback of Notre Dame 40. Phantom of
the Opera 43. Humoresque 46. Another Part of the
Forest 48, etc.

Leibman, Ron (1937–).
American character actor of the 70s.
The Hot Rock 72. Slaughterhouse Five 72. The
Super Cops 73. Your Three Minutes Are Up 74.
The Art of Crime (TV) 75. Won Ton Ton 76. A
Question of Guilt (TV) 78. Norma Rae 79. Up the
Academy 80. Rivkin, Bounty Hunter (TV) 81.
Zorro the Gay Blade 81. Romantic Comedy 83.
Rhinestone 84. Seven Hours to Judgement 88, etc.
TV series: Kaz 78.

Leigh, Janet (1927–) (Jeanette Morrison).
Capable American leading lady of the 50s and 60s;
began as a peaches-and-cream heroine but
graduated to sharper roles. Her third husband was
Tony Curtis (1951–62). She is the mother of
actress Jamie Lee Curtis.
■ The Romance of Rosy Ridge 47. If Winter
Comes 47. Hills of Home 47. Words and Music 48.
Act of Violence 48. Little Women 49. That Forsyte
Woman 49. The Doctor and the Girl 49. The Red
Danube 49. Holiday Affair 49. Strictly
Dishonourable 51. Angels in the Outfield 51. Two
Tickets to Broadway 51. It's a Big Country 51. Just
This Once 52. Scaramouche 52. Fearless Fagan
52. The Naked Spur 53. Confidentially Connie 53.
Houdini 53. Walking My Baby Back Home 54.
Prince Valiant 54. Living It Up 54. The Black Shield
of Falworth 54. Rogue Cop 54. Pete Kelly's Blues
55. My Sister Eileen 55. Safari (GB) 56. Jet Pilot 57.
Touch of Evil 58. The Vikings 58. The Perfect
Furlough 58. Who Was That Lady? 60. Psycho
(AAN) 60. Pepe 60. The Manchurian Candidate
62. Bye Bye Birdie 62. Wives and Lovers 63. Three
on a Couch 66. Harper 66. Kid Rodelo 66. An
American Dream 66. Hello Down There 68. The
Spy in the Green Hat 68. Grand Slam 68.
Honeymoon with a Stranger (TV) 69. The House
on Greenapple Road (TV) 70. The Monk (TV) 70.
The Deadly Dream (TV) 71. One Is a Lonely
Number 72. Night of the Lepus 72. Murdock's
Gang (TV) 73. Murder at the World Series (TV)
77. Telethon (TV) 77. Boardwalk 79. The Fog 80.
The Thrill of Genius 85.

Leigh, Jennifer Jason (1958–).
American actress, the daughter of actor Vic
Morrow.
Eyes of a Stranger 80. The Best Little Girl in the
World (TV) 81. The Killing of Randy Webster 81.
Fast Times at Ridgemont High 82. Wrong Is Right
82. Death Ride to Osaka (TV) 83. Easy Money 83.
Just Like Us (TV) 83. Grandview USA 84. Flesh
and Blood 85. The Hitcher 85. The Men's Club
86. Sister, Sister 87. Heart of Midnight 88. The Big
Picture 89. Last Exit to Brooklyn 89. Miami Blues
90. Crooked Hearts 91. Backdraft 91. Rush 91.
Single White Female 92. Short Cuts 93. The
Hudsucker Proxy 94. Mrs Parker and the Vicious
Circle (as Dorothy Parker) 94. Georgia 95, etc.

Leigh, Mike (1943–).
British director and screenwriter, also active in
theatre and TV as a writer-director noted for
creating scripts out of sessions of improvisation
with his actors. He trained at RADA and was an
assistant director with the Royal Shakespeare
Company 1967–68. Married to actress Alison
Steadman.

Bleak Moments 71. High Hopes 89. Life Is Sweet 90. Naked 93.

Leigh, Suzanna (1945–).
British leading lady.
Boeing Boeing 66. Paradise Hawaiian Style 66. Deadlier Than the Male 67. Lost Continent 68. Lust for a Vampire 70. The Fiend 71, etc.

Leigh, Vivien (1913–1967) (Vivian Hartley).
Distinguished British leading lady whose stage and screen career was limited by delicate health; for many years the wife of Laurence Olivier.
Biographies: 1973, *Light of a Star* by Gwen Robyns. 1977, *Vivien Leigh* by Anne Edwards. 1987, *Vivien* by Alexander Walker.
■ Things Are Looking Up 34. The Village Squire 35. Gentleman's Agreement 35. Look Up and Laugh 35. Fire Over England 36. *Dark Journey* 37. Storm in a Teacup 37. St Martin's Lane 38. Twenty-One Days 38. *A Yank at Oxford* 38. *Gone with the Wind* (AA: as Scarlett O'Hara) (US) 39. Waterloo Bridge (US) 40. *Lady Hamilton* (US) 41. *Caesar and Cleopatra* 45. Anna Karenina 48. *A Streetcar Named Desire* (AA) (US) 51. The Deep Blue Sea 55. The Roman Spring of Mrs Stone 61. Ship of Fools (US) 65.
✪ For one performance which made each of her later ones an event to be savoured. *Gone with the Wind.*

Leigh-Hunt, Barbara (1935–).
British character actress.
Frenzy 72. Henry VIII and His Six Wives 72. A Bequest to the Nation 73. O Heavenly Dog 80. Paper Mask 90, etc.

Leigh-Hunt, Ronald (1916–).
Smooth British supporting actor.
Tiger by the Tail 53. Shadow of a Man 55. A Touch of Larceny 59. Sink the Bismarck 60. Piccadilly Third Stop 61. The Truth about Spring 65. Hostile Witness 67. Le Mans 71. The Omen 76, many others.
TV series: Sir Lancelot (as King Arthur) 56.

Leighton, Margaret (1922–1976).
British leading actress on stage from 1938. She was married to actors Laurence Harvey (1957–60) and Michael Wilding (from 1964).
■ Bonnie Prince Charlie 47. *The Winslow Boy* 48. Under Capricorn 49. The Astonished Heart 50. The Elusive Pimpernel 50. Calling Bulldog Drummond 51. Home at Seven 52. The Holly and the Ivy 52. The Good Die Young 54. Carrington VC 54. The Teckman Mystery 54. The Constant Husband 55. The Passionate Stranger 57. The Sound and the Fury 58. The Second Man (TV) 59. The Waltz of the Toreadors 62. The Third Secret 63. The Best Man 64. Seven Women 65. The Loved One 65. The Madwoman of Chaillot 69. The Go-Between (AAN) 70. Zee and Co 71. Lady Caroline Lamb 72. Bequest to the Nation 73. Frankenstein: The True Story (TV) 73. From Beyond the Grave 73. Galileo 74. Great Expectations 75. Trial by Combat 76.

Leisen, Mitchell (1898–1972).
American director, former set designer; his films are mostly romantic trifles, but many have considerable pictorial values.
Biography: 1972, *Hollywood Director* by David Chierichetti.
■ *Cradle Song* 33. *Death Takes a Holiday* 34. Murder at the Vanities 34. Behold My Wife 35. Four Hours to Kill 35. Hands across the Table 35. Thirteen Hours by Air 36. The Big Broadcast of 1937. Swing High Swing Low 37. *Easy Living* 37. The Big Broadcast of 1938 37. Artists and Models Abroad

38. *Midnight* 39. Remember the Night 40. *Arise My Love* 40. I Wanted Wings 41. *Hold Back the Dawn* 41. The Lady Is Willing 42. Take a Letter Darling 42. No Time for Love (& p) 43. *Lady in the Dark* (also w) 44. *Frenchman's Creek* 44. Practically Yours (& p) 44. *Kitty* 45. Masquerade in Mexico 45. To Each His Own 46. Suddenly It's Spring 46. Golden Earrings 47. Dream Girl 48. Bride of Vengeance 49. Song of Surrender 49. Captain Carey USA 50. No Man of Her Own (& w) 50. The Mating Season 51. Darling How Could You? 51. Young Man with Ideas 52. Tonight We Sing 53. Bedevilled 55. The Girl Most Likely 57.
✪ For adding style to comedies and dramas that badly needed it. *Kitty.*

¶ He found himself in the unenviable position of a diamond cutter working with lumpy coal. – *Andrew Sarris, 1968*

Leiser, Erwin (1923–).
Swedish documentarist.
Mein Kampf (Blodige Tiden) 59. Murder by Signature (Eichmann and the Third Reich) 61, etc.

Leister, Frederick (1885–1970).
British character actor, on stage from 1906, screen from 20s. Usually played distinguished and kindly professional men.
Dreyfus 30. The Iron Duke 35. Goodbye Mr Chips 39. The Prime Minister 41. *Dear Octopus* 43. *The Hundred Pound Window* 43. The Captive Heart 46. Quartet 48. The End of the Affair 54. Left, Right and Centre 59. A French Mistress 63, many others.

Leith, Virginia (1932–).
American leading lady of the 50s.
Black Widow 54. Violent Saturday 55. White Feather 55. A Kiss Before Dying 56. On the Threshold of Space 56. The Beast That Wouldn't Die 63. First Love 77, etc.

Lejeune, C. A. (1897–1973).
British film critic whose work now tends to seem blithe but facetious. Collections of reviews were published in 1947 as *Chestnuts in My Lap* and in 1991 as *The C. A. Lejeune Film Reader.*

Leland, David (1947–).
British director and screenwriter, a former actor.
■ Mona Lisa (w) 86. Personal Services (w) 87. Wish You Were Here (wd) 87. Checking Out (d) 89. The Big Man (d) 90.

Lelouch, Claude (1937–).
French director and screenwriter with lush visual style; internationally fashionable in the mid-60s, but overreached himself.
■ Le Propre de l'Homme 60. Une Fille et des Fusils 63. Avec des Si 64. Secret Paris 64. *Un Homme et une Femme* (AAw, AANd) 66. *Vivre pour Vivre* 67. Challenge in the Snow 68. Far from Vietnam 69. A Man I Like 69. Life Love Death 69. Le Rose et le Noir 70. The Crook 71. Smic, Smac, Smoc 71. Adventure Is Adventure 72. *La Bonne Année* 73. And Now My Love 75. Seven Suspects for Murder 77. Another Man, Another Chance 77. The Good and the Bad 77. A Nous Deux 79. Les Uns et les Autres 80. Edith and Marcel 83. Long Live Life 84. Departure, Return 85. A Man and a Woman: 20 Years Later 86. Attention Bandits 87. Itinéraire d'Enfant Gâté 88. Il y a des Jours et des Lunes 90. The Beautiful Story (La Belle Histoire) 92. Tout Ça . . . pour Ça 93. Les Misérables du XXème Siècle 95.

¶ Film-making is like spermatozoa: only one i a million makes it. – *C.L.*
One day I'll make a film for the critics, when have money to lose. – *C.L.*

Lelouch, Salomé (1984–).
French child actress, the daughter of director Claude Lelouch and actress Evelyne Bouix.
When I Was Five I Killed Myself 94. Les Misérables 95, etc.

Lembeck, Harvey (1925–1982).
American character actor.
The Frogmen 51. You're In the Navy Now 53. Back at the Front 53. Stalag 17 54. Life after Da 55. Sail a Crooked Ship 62. Bikini Beach 65. The is No Thirteen 77, etc.
TV series: Bilko. Ensign O'Toole.

Lemmon, Jack (1925–).
American light comedy leading actor with Broadway experience; sometimes typed in mildl lecherous or otherwise sex-fraught roles.
Biographies: 1975, *Lemmon* by Don Widener. 1977, *The Films of Jack Lemmon* by Joe Baltake.
■ It Should Happen to You 53. Three for the Sho 53. Phffft 54. My Sister Eileen 55. *Mister Roberts* (AA) 55. You Can't Run Away from It 56. Cowb 57. Fire Down Below 57. Operation Mad Ball 57 Bell, Book and Candle 58. It Happened to Jane 5 *Some Like It Hot* (AAN) 59. The Wackiest Ship in the Army 60. *The Apartment* (AAN) 60. The Notorious Landlady 62. Days of Wine and Roses (AAN) 62. *Irma la Douce* 63. Under the Yum Yum Tree 64. Good Neighbour Sam 64. How to Murde Your Wife 65. *The Great Race* 65. The Fortune Cookie 66. Luv 67. *The Odd Couple* 68. The April Fools 69. The Out-of-Towners 69. *Kotch* (d only) 71. The War between Men and Women 72. Avar 72. Save the Tiger (AA) 73. The Front Page 74. The Prisoner of Second Avenue 75. The Entertain 75. Alex and the Gypsy 76. Airport 77 77. *The China Syndrome* (AAN, BFA) 79. Tribute (AAN) 8 Buddy Buddy 81. *Missing* (AAN) 82. Mass Appea 84. Macaroni 85. That's Life! 86. Dad 89. JFK 91 Glengarry Glen Ross 92. Short Cuts 93. A Life in the Theatre 93. Grumpy Old Men 93.
TV series: Heaven for Betsy 52. Twist of Fate 6

¶ The worst part about being me is when peopl want me to make them laugh. – *J.L.*

Famous line (*Mister Roberts*): 'Now, what's all this crud about no movie tonight?'

Lemmy Caution.
Tough private eye, created by British novelist Pete Cheyney in imitation of American models in the 30s and 40s, who was incarnated on screen by Eddie Constantine in a series of French films, culminating in Jean-Luc Godard's futuristic *Alphaville* 65.

Lemont, John (1914–).
British director.
The Green Buddha 54. And Women Shall Wee (& co-w) 59. The Shakedown (& co-w) 59. Kong 60. Frightened City (& co-w) 61, etc.

Lempe, Ute (1963–).
German actress and singer, noted for her interpretations of the songs of Kurt Weill.
L'Autrichienne 89. Prospero's Books 91. Prêt-à Porter (aka Ready to Wear) 95.

Leni, Paul (1885–1929).
German director, former set designer; died in Hollywood.

Waxworks 24. *The Cat and the Canary* 27. The Man Who Laughs 28. The Chinese Parrot 28. The Last Warning 29, etc.

Lenica, Jan (1928–).
Polish animator.
Dom 58. Monsieur Tete 59. Janko the Musician 60. Rhinoceros 63. A 64, etc.

Lenin (1870–1924) (Vladimir Ilyich Ulyanov).
Russian statesman, the power behind the Revolution. Little footage of him exists, but he has been played by various actors in such politically-based semi-fictions as *Lenin in October*, *Lenin in 1918* and *Lenin in Poland*. Michael Bryant played him in *Nicholas and Alexandra*; Roger Sloman in *Reds*; while Ben Kingsley played him in the TV film *The Train*.

Lennart, Isobel (1915–1971).
American screenwriter.
Lost Angel 44. Anchors Aweigh 45. East Side West Side 49. Skirts Ahoy 52. Latin Lovers 54. Love Me or Leave Me (AAN) 55. Inn of the Sixth Happiness 58. The Sundowners (AAN) 60. Period of Adjustment 62. Funny Girl 68, many others.

Lenoir, Denis.
French cinematographer.
Monsieur Hire 89. Daddy Nostalgie 90. Decadence 93. Cold Water (L'Eau Froide) 94. Carrington (GB) 95, etc.

Lenska, Rula (1947–).
Polish born, British leading lady, much on TV.
Soft Beds Hard Battles 73. Alfie Darling 75. The Deadly Females 76, etc.

Lenya, Lotte (1899–1981) (Caroline Blamauer).
Austrian character actress; also inimitable singer of her husband Kurt Weill's songs.
Die Dreigroschenoper 31. The Roman Spring of Mrs Stone (AAN) 61. *From Russia with Love* 63. The Appointment 69. Semi-Tough 77, etc.

Lenz, Kay (1953–).
American leading lady of the 70s.
Breezy 73. Lisa Bright and Dark (TV) 73. White Line Fever 75. The Great Scout and Cathouse Thursday 76. Rich Man Poor Man (TV) 76. The Passage 79. House 86. Death Wish IV: The Crackdown 87. Stripped to Kill 87. Smoke 88. Physical Evidence 89. Headhunter 90. Souvenirs 91, etc.

Lenz, Rick (1939–).
American actor.
Cactus Flower 70. Where Does It Hurt? 72. The Shootist 76. Melvin and Howard 80. Little Dragons 80. Malice in Wonderland (TV) 85, etc.
TV series: Hec Ramsey 72–74.

Leon, Valerie.
British leading lady.
Smashing Time 67. Carry On up the Jungle 70. *Blood from the Mummy's Tomb* 71. Carry On Matron 72. The Spy Who Loved Me 77. Revenge of the Pink Panther 78, etc.

Leonard, Elmore (1925–).
American western and crime novelist and screenwriter, who also adapts his thrillers into movies.
Hombre 66. Big Bounce 68. The Moonshine War (w) 70. Valdez Is Coming 71. Mr Majestyk 74. Stick 85. 52 Pick-Up 86. The Rosary Murders 87. Cat Chaser 90.

¶ In my books characters are more important than the plot, but Hollywood movies are based on plot. So when they make movies about the books they become much too theatrical. And Hollywood wants heroes who are major stars. My hero isn't a major star, he's just a guy. The films lose the feeling of the books completely. – E.L.

Leonard, Herbert B. (1922–).
American independent TV producer; best-known series include *Rin Tin Tin, Circus Boy, Naked City, Route 66*.

Leonard, Hugh (1926–) (John Keyes Byrne).
Irish playwright and occasional screenwriter.
Interlude (co-w) 68. Great Catherine 68. Percy 71. Our Miss Fred 72. Da (from his play) 88. Widow's Peak 94.

Leonard, Murray (1898–1970).
American burlesque comedian who played small parts in films, notably with Abbott and Costello, who worked up several of his old routines.
Lost in a Harem 44. A Thousand and One Nights 45. Bring Your Smile Along 55, etc.

Leonard, Robert Sean (1969–).
American leading actor.
Bluffing It (TV) 87. My Best Friend Is a Vampire 88. Dead Poets Society 89. Mr & Mrs Bridge 91. Much Ado about Nothing 93. Married to It 93. Swing Kids 93. The Age of Innocence 93, etc.

Leonard, Robert Z. (1889–1968).
American director (former actor), in Hollywood from 1915. Showed care but not much imagination.
The Waning Sex 27. The Demi-Bride 27. Adam and Evil 28. Tea for Three 29. The Divorcee (AAN) 30. Susan Lenox 31. *Strange Interval* 32. *Dancing Lady* 33. Peg O' My Heart 33. Outcast Lady 34. *The Great Ziegfeld* (AAN) 36. Piccadilly Jim 37. Escapade 37. *Maytime* 38. The Firefly 38. New Moon (& p) 40. *Pride and Prejudice* 40. Ziegfeld Girl 41. When Ladies Meet (& p) 41. We Were Dancing 42. Stand By for Action 42. The Man from Down Under 43. Marriage Is a Private Affair 44. Weekend at the Waldorf 45. The Secret Heart 46. B.F.'s Daughter 48. The Bride 48. In the Good Old Summertime 49. Nancy Goes to Rio 49. Duchess of Idaho 50. Everything I Have Is Yours 52. The Clown 53. The King's Thief 55. Kelly and Me 56. Beautiful But Dangerous (It.) 56, many others.

Leonard, Sheldon (1907–) (Sheldon Bershad).
American character actor who played Runyonesque gangsters for years; finally quit to produce TV series.
Another Thin Man 39. Buy Me That Town 41. Street of Chance 42. *Lucky Jordon* 42. To Have and Have Not 44. Zombies on Broadway 45. Somewhere in the Night 46. Violence 47. The Gangster 47. Take One False Step 49. Behave Yourself 51. *Stop You're Killing Me* 52. Money from Home 54. Guys and Dolls 55. Pocketful of Miracles 61. The Brink's Job 78, many others.
TV series: The Duke 54. Danny Thomas 59–61. Big Eddie 75.

Leone, Sergio (1922–1989).
Italian director who came to the fore internationally via his savage westerns on the American pattern, making a star of Clint Eastwood in the process.
The Colossus of Rhodes 61. *A Fistful of Dollars* 64. For a Few Dollars More 65. The Good the Bad and the Ugly 67. *Once upon a Time in the West* 69. A Fistful of Dynamite 72. *Once upon a Time in America* 84, etc.

Leonetti, Matthew F.
American cinematographer.
Mr Billion 77. Breaking Away 79. Raise the Titanic 80. Eyewitness 81. Poltergeist 82. Fast Times at Ridgemont High 82. The Ice Pirates 84. Fast Forward 85. Weird Science 85. Jagged Edge 85. Commando 85. Jumpin' Jack Flash 86. Dragnet 87. Extreme Prejudice 87. Red Heat 88. Johnny Handsome 89. Hard to Kill 90. Another 48 Hrs 90. Dead Again 91. Angels in the Outfield 94, etc.

Leontovich, Eugenie (1894–).
Russian stage actress in occasional American films. She was formerly married to actor and director Gregory Ratoff.
Four Sons 40. The Men in Her Life 41. Anything Can Happen 52. The World in His Arms 53. Homicidal 61, etc.

leprechauns
have made rare but effective screen appearances in the persons of Cecil Kellaway (*Luck of the Irish*), Jimmy O'Dea (*Darby O'Gill and the Little People*), Don Beddoe (*Jack the Giant Killer*) and Tommy Steele (*Finian's Rainbow*). A murderous one appeared in the horror movie *Leprechaun*.

Lerner, Alan Jay (1918–1986).
American lyricist and writer.
An American in Paris (w) (AA) 51. Gigi (m) (AA) 58. My Fair Lady (w, m in collaboration) (AA) 64. Camelot (w, m in collaboration) 67. On a Clear Day You Can See Forever (& p) 70. The Little Prince 74, many others.

Lerner, Carl (c. 1905–1975).
American editor.
Cry Murder 50. On the Bowery 56. *Twelve Angry Men* 57. The Fugitive Kind 59. Something Wild 61. All the Way Home 63. The Swimmer 68. The Angel Levine 70. Klute 72, etc.
DIRECTED: Black Like Me 64.

Lerner, Irving (1909–1976).
American director, former cameraman and documentarist.
■ Muscle Beach 46. Man Crazy 54. Edge of Fury 58. *Murder by Contract* 58. City of Fear 59. Studs Lonigan 60. Cry of Battle 63. The Royal Hunt of the Sun 69.

Lerner, Michael (1941–).
American character actor.
Alex in Wonderland 70. The Candidate 72. Busting 74. St Ives 76. Outlaw Blues 77. Borderline 80. Coast to Coast 80. The Baltimore Bullet 80. The Postman Always Rings Twice 81. National Lampoon's Class Reunion 82. Strange Invaders 83. Rita Hayworth: The Love Goddess 83. Movers and Shakers 84. Vibes 88. Eight Men Out 88. Harlem Nights 89. Maniac Cop 2 90. Omen IV: The Awakening 91. Barton Fink (AAN) 91. Newsies (GB: The News Boys) 92. Amos & Andrew 93. Blank Check 94. No Escape 94. The Road to Wellville 94. Radioland Murders 94, etc.
TV series: Love Story 73–74. Starsky and Hutch 75–79. Hart to Hart 79–84. Hollywood Beat 85.

lesbianism
came fully into its own with the filming of *The Killing of Sister George*; but for many years it was unthinkable as a screen subject. *These Three* in 1936 had to be so changed that it was almost unrecognizable as a version of *The Children's Hour*; and the matter was scarcely broached again until the 50s, when the French brought it up in *Olivia* and *The Girl with the Golden Eyes*.

The first Hollywood film to bring the subject to our notice was *A Walk on the Wild Side* 62; since then there have been more or less discreet references in *The Haunting*, *The Balcony*, *Lilith*, *The Silence*, *Alyse and Chloe*, *The Vampire Lovers*, *Beyond the Valley of the Dolls*, *La Religieuse*, *The Group*, *Tony Rome*, *The Fox*, *Therese and Isabelle*, *Baby Love*, *The Smashing Bird I Used to Know*, and *Once Is Not Enough*; while *The Children's Hour* was filmed again, this time with its full force. In 1982 *Personal Best* again brought the subject into the open.

Lesley, Carole (1935–1974) (Maureen Rippingdale). British leading lady briefly groomed for stardom.

These Dangerous Years 57. Woman in a Dressing-Gown 57. No Trees in the Street 59. Doctor in Love 60. What a Whopper 62. The Pot Carriers 62, etc.

Leslie, Bethel (1929–   ).
American leading actress, mainly on TV.

The Rabbit Trap 58. Captain Newman 63. A Rage to Live 65. The Molly Maguires 69. Old Boyfriends 79, etc.

TV series: The Girls 50. The Richard Boone Show 63. The Doctors 66.

Leslie, Joan (1925–   ) (Joan Brodel).
Pert, pretty American leading lady of the 40s; in vaudeville from childhood.

Camille (debut) 36. Men with Wings 38. Foreign Correspondent 40. High Sierra 41. *Sergeant York* 41. The Male Animal 42. Yankee Doodle Dandy 42. The Hard Way 42. This Is the Army 43. Thank Your Lucky Stars 43. Hollywood Canteen 44. *Rhapsody in Blue* 45. Where Do We Go From Here? 45. Too Young to Know 45. Cinderella Jones 46. Royal Flush 46. Repeat Performance 47. Northwest Stampeded 49. Born To Be Bad 51. The Toughest Man in Arizona 52. The Woman They Almost Lynched 53. Jubilee Trail 54. The Revolt of Mamie Stover 57. The Keegans (TV) 76, etc.

Lesser, Sol (1890–1980).
American pioneer exhibitor of silent days, later producer: many Tarzan films.

Thunder Over Mexico 33. Our Town 40. Kon-Tiki 52, etc.

Lester, Bruce (1912–   ) (Bruce Lister).
South African leading man who made some British and American films; now plays support roles.

Death at Broadcasting House 34. Crime over London 37. If I Were King 39. Pride and Prejudice 40. Above Suspicion 43. Golden Earrings 47. King Richard and the Crusaders 54, etc.

Lester, Dick (Richard) (1932–   ).
American director who found his spurt to fame in Britain doing zany comedies full of fast fragmented action. As soon as commercial backing was available his style went way over the top.

■ It's Trad Dad 61. The Mouse on the Moon 63. *A Hard Day's Night* 64. *The Knack* 65. Help 65. A Funny Thing Happened on the Way to the Forum 66. How I Won the War 67. Petulia 68. The Bed Sitting Room 69. The Three Musketeers 73. Juggernaut 74. The Four Musketeers 75. Royal Flash 75. Robin and Marian 76. The Ritz 76. Butch and Sundance: The Early Days 79. Cuba 79. Superman II 80. Superman III 83. Finders Keepers 84. Return of the Musketeers 89. Get Back (doc) 91.

Lester, Mark L. (1948–   ).
American director.

Tricia's Wedding 71. Truck Stop Women 74. Bobbie Jo and the Outlaw 75. Stunts 77. Gold of the Amazon Women 77. Roller Boogie 79. Class of 84 82. Firestarter 84. Commando 85. Armed and Dangerous 86. Class of 1999 89. Showdown in Little Tokyo 91. The Fraternity 94, etc.

Lester, Mark (1958–   ).
Innocent-looking British child star of the 60s. Now an osteopath.

Allez France 64. Spaceflight IC/1 65. Our Mother's House 67. *Oliver* (title role) 68. Run Wild Run Free 69. Eye Witness 70. Melody 71. Black Beauty 71. Night Hair Child 71. Who Slew Auntie Roo? 72. Scalawag 73. Little Adventurer 75. The Prince and the Pauper (aka Crossed Swords) 77, etc.

Leterrier, François (1929–   ).
French director.

Les Mauvais Coups 61. Un Roi sans Divertissement 63. La Chasse Royale 68. Projection Privée 73. Goodbye Emmanuelle 77, etc.

letters
have provided a starting point or climax for several films. Undelivered ones for *Address Unknown*, *The Postman Didn't Ring*; misdelivered ones for *Dear Ruth*, *The Go-Between*, *A Letter for Evie*; an incriminating one in *Suspicion*; lost ones for *Cause for Alarm*, *Never Put It In Writing*; indiscreet ones for *A Letter To Three Wives*, *So Evil My Love*, *The Last of Mrs Cheyney*, *The Letter*; posthumous ones for *Letter from an Unknown Woman*, *Love Letters*, *The Lost Moment*, *Mister Roberts*; anonymous ones for *Poison Pen* and *Le Corbeau*.

Lettieri, Al (1927–1975).
American actor.

The Bobo 68. The Godfather 72. Getaway 73. Mr Majestyk 74. Deadly Trackers 75, etc.

Leung, Tony (Tony Leung Kar-fai).
Hong Kong leading actor who found an international audience from the late 80s.

The Last Emperor 88. The Laserman 90. *The Lover* (L'Amant) 92. 92 The Legendary La Rose Noire(92 Hak Muigwai Dui Hak Mauigwai) 92. The Eagle Shooting Heroes: Dong Cheng Xi Jiu 93, etc.

Levant, Brian.
American director.

Problem Child II 91. Beethoven 92. The Flintstones 94.

Levant, Oscar (1906–1972).
American pianist and master of insult who appeared in several films as his grouchy, neurotic self.

Autobiographical books: 1944, *A Smattering of Ignorance*. 1965, *Memoirs of an Amnesiac*. 1968, *The Unimportance of Being Oscar*.

■ The Dance of Life 29. In Person 35. Rhythm on the River 40. Kiss the Boys Goodbye 41. *Rhapsody in Blue* 45. Humoresque 46. You Were Meant for Me 47. Romance on the High Seas 48. The Barkleys of Broadway 49. *An American in Paris* 51. The Band Wagon 53. The I Don't Care Girl 53. The Cobweb 55.

¶ In some situations I was difficult, in odd moments impossible, in rare moments loathsome, but at my best unapproachably great. – *O.L.*

Strip the phoney tinsel off Hollywood and you'll find the real tinsel underneath. – *O.L.*

I'm a controversial figure. My friends either dislike me or hate me. – *O.L.*

I hate cold showers. They stimulate me, and then I don't know what to do. – *O.L.*

I played an unsympathetic part – myself. – *O.L* on his role in Humoresque

I envy people who drink. At least they have something to blame everything on. – *O.L. in Humoresque*

It's not a pretty face, but underneath this flabb exterior is an enormous lack of character. – *O.L. of himself in An American in Paris*

There is absolutely nothing wrong with Oscar Levant that a miracle can't fix. – *Alexander Woollcott*

A tortured man who sprayed his loathing on anyone within range. – *Shelley Winters*

Oscar has mellowed – like an old pistol. – *Billy Rose*

Leven, Boris (1900–1986).
Russian-born production designer, long in US.

Alexander's Ragtime Band 38. *The Shanghai Gesture* 41. Mr Peabody and the Mermaid 48. Sudden Fear 52. Giant 56. Anatomy of a Murder 59. *West Side Story* (AA) 61. The Sound of Music 65 The Sand Pebbles 67. Star! 68. The Andromeda Strain 70. Jonathan Livingston Seagull 73. Mandingo 75. New York, New York 77, many others.

Levene, Sam (1905–1980).
American stage actor, often in Runyonesque film roles.

Three Men on a Horse (debut) 36. Golden Boy 39 The Purple Heart 44. Crossfire 47. Boomerang 47. Guilty Bystander 50. Three Sailors and a Girl 53. Sweet Smell of Success 57. Act One 63. A Dream of Kings 69. Such Good Friends 71. Demon 77. Last Embrace 79. And Justice for All 79.

LeVien, Jack (1918–   ).
American documentarist responsible for several distinguished compilation films.

Black Fox 62. The Finest Hours 64. A King's Story 67.

TV series on Churchill: *The Valiant Years* 60.

Levien, Sonya (1888–1960).
American writer, former lawyer. Story editor at various times for Fox, MGM, Paramount.

Cavalcade 33. *State Fair* (AAN) 33. *Berkeley Square* 33. In Old Chicago 38. *The Hunchback of Notr Dame* 40. Ziegfeld Girl 41. Rhapsody in Blue 45. Cass Timberlane 48. Quo Vadis 51. *Interrupted Melody* (AA) 55. *Jeanne Eagels* 58, etc.

Levin, Henry (1909–1980).
American director, in Hollywood from 1943 after stage experience.

Cry of the Werewolf 44. I Love a Mystery 45. The Guilt of Janet Ames 47. The Mating of Millie 48. Jolson Sings Again 49. The Petty Girl 50. Convicted 50. Belles on Their Toes 52. The President's Lady 53. Mister Scoutmaster 53. Gambler from Natchez 54. The Lonely Man 57. Bernardine 57. Let's Be Happy (GB) 57. The Remarkable Mr Pennypacker 58. Holidays for Lovers 59. Journey to the Centre of the Earth 59. Where the Boys Are 60. The Wonderful World of the Brothers Grimm 62. Come Fly with Me 63. Honeymoon Hotel 64. Genghis Khan 65. Kiss the Girls and Make Them Die 66. Murderers' Row 67 The Desperados 70. That Man Bolt 73. The Thoroughbreds 77, many others.

Levin, Ira (1929–   ).
American thriller writer with a sharp edge.

A Kiss before Dying 56. Rosemary's Baby 68. The Stepford Wives 75. The Boys from Brazil 78. Death Trap 82. Sliver 93.

vin, Meyer (1905–1981).
merican author, the original writer of *Compulsion*,
ich was filmed in 1959.

vine, Joseph E. (1905–1987).
merican production executive and showman,
mer theatre owner. Formed Embassy Pictures in
e 50s, originally to exploit cheap European
ctacles; also set up finance for films like *Eight
d a Half*, *Divorce Italian Style*, *Boccaccio 70*.
PRODUCER: The Carpetbaggers 63. Where Love
s Gone 64. Harlow 65. A Bridge Too Far 77.
gic 78, etc.

¶ You can fool all the people all the time if the
advice is right and the budget is big enough.
. E.L.

vinson, Barry (1932–).
merican director and screenwriter. He began as
omedy writer and stand-up comedian. His first
fe was actress and screenwriter Valerie Curtin.
Autobiography: 1993, *Levinson on Levinson*.
Catholics (TV) 73. First Love 77. And Justice for
 (AAN) 80. Inside Moves 81. *Diner* (& d) (AANw)
. Best Friends 82. The Natural (d only) 84.
ung Sherlock Holmes (d only) 85. Tin Men
d) 87. Good Morning Vietnam (d) 87. *Rain Man*
 (AA) 88. Avalon (wd, AAN) 90. Bugsy (d)
AN) 91. Toys (co-w, d) 92. Jimmy Hollywood
d) 94. Quiz Show (à) 94. Disclosure 94, etc.

vy, Jeffery.
merican director.
Drive 92. Inside Monkey Zetterland 93. S.F.W.

vy, Jules (1923–).
merican independent producer, of Levy-
rdner-Laven. See Arthur Gardner for credits.

vy, Louis (1893–1957).
tish musical director and composer, in films
m 1916. Scored *Nanook of the North* 20. With
umont and Gainsborough 1928–47,
pervising all musical productions.
Pygmalion 38. The Citadel 38, many others.

vy, Ralph (1919–).
merican director, in TV from 1947.
Bedtime Story 64. Do Not Disturb 65.

vy, Raoul (1922–1966).
ench producer.
Les Orgueilleux 53. And God Created Woman
w) 56. Heaven Fell That Night 57. En Cas de
alheur 58. Babette Goes to War (& co-w) 59.
oderato Cantabile 60. The Truth 60. The
fector (& wd) 66, etc.

win, Albert (1895–1968).
merican writer-producer-director with
mething of an Omar Khayyam fixation.
oduction executive 1931–41.
The Moon and Sixpence (wd) 42. *The Picture of
rian Gray* (wd) 44. The Private Affairs of Bel Ami
d, p) 47. *Pandora and the Flying Dutchman* (wd,
51. Saadia (wd, p) 54. The Living Idol (wd, p)

¶ A most intriguing little man. He completely
checked out of his executive office at MGM
ery year or so when he wanted a year off to
ake one of his own pictures. – *James Mason*
Would that there were more room for accident
his clogged literary narrations and his naive
nception of refinement in the cinema. – *Andrew
rris, 1968*

Lewin, Ben (1946–).
Polish-born director, in Australia.
   The Dunera Boys (TV) 85. Georgia 89. The
Favour, the Watch and the Very Big Fish 91.
Lucky Break 94, etc.

Lewis, Albert E. (1884–1978).
Polish-American producer and Broadway
impresario who was associated with several films.
   International House 32. Torch Singer 35. Mutiny
on the Bounty 35. Cabin in the Sky 43, etc.

Lewis, Charlotte (1967–).
London-born actress, in international and
American movies.
   Pirates (Fr.) 86. The Golden Child 86. Dial Help
(It.) 88. Tripwire 90. Bare Essentials (TV) 91.
Storyville 92. Sketch Artist 92. Excessive Force 93,
etc.
   TV series: Broken Badges 90–91.

Lewis, Diana (1915–).
American leading lady of the late 30s; retired when
she married William Powell.
   It's a Gift 34. Forty Little Mothers 39. Bitter
Sweet 40. Johnny Eager 41. Seven Sweethearts 42.
Cry Havoc 43, etc.

Lewis, Fiona (1946–).
British leading lady.
   The Fearless Vampire Killers 67. Where's Jack?
69. Villain 71. Dracula (TV) 73. Lisztomania 75.
The Fury 78. Strange Invaders 83. Innerspace 87,
etc.

Lewis, Gena (1888–1979).
American screenwriter.
   Sin Town 42. The Climax 44. Cobra Woman 45.
Trail Street 49. Lonely Heart Bandits 51, etc.

Lewis, Geoffrey (1935–).
American character actor, often in harassed roles.
He is the father of Juliette Lewis.
   Culpepper Cattle Company 72. The Great Waldo
Pepper 75. Macon County Line 74. Thunderbolt
and Lightning 74. Smile 75. Return of a Man
Called Horse 76. Every Which Way but Loose 78.
Lust in the Dust 85. Fletch Lives 89. Double Impact
91. The Lawnmower Man 92. Point of No Return
93. The Man without a Face 93. Joshua Tree 93.
White Fang 2: Myth of the White Wolf 94. Maverick
94, etc.
   TV series: Flo 80–81. Gun Shy 83.

Lewis, Herschell Gordon (1926–).
American director of exploitation films.
   The Living Venus 61. Goldilocks and the Three
Bares 63. Blood Feast 63. Monster a Go Go 65. The
Gruesome Twosome 67. A Taste of Blood 67. The
Ecstasies of Women 69. The Wizard of Gore 70.
Stick It in Your Ear 72. Black Love 72. The Gore-
Gore Girls 72, many others.

¶ In my movies I went for intensive rather than
extensive gore, and the rationale is quite simple:
I didn't have any budget. – *H.G.L.*

Lewis, Jay (1914–1969).
British producer, in films from 1933.
   Morning Departure 50. The Gift Horse 52, etc.
AS DIRECTOR: The Baby and the Battleship 55.
Invasion Quartet 61. Live Now Pay Later 62. A
Home of Your Own 65, etc.

Lewis, Jerry (1926–) (Joseph Levitch).
Goonish American comedian whose style is a
mixture of exaggerated mugging and sticky
sentiment. Until 1956 he formed a popular

partnership with Dean Martin, but his
increasingly indulgent solo films since then have
gradually reduced his once-fervent band of
admirers.
■ *My Friend Irma* 49. My Friend Irma Goes West
50. At War with the Army 51. That's My Boy 51.
Sailor Beware 52. Jumping Jacks 52. The Stooge
53. Scared Stiff 53. The Caddy 53. Money from
Home 54. Living It Up 54. Three Ring Circus 54.
You're Never Too Young 54. Artists and Models
55. Pardners 56. Hollywood or Bust 56. The
Delicate Delinquent 57. The Sad Sack 58. Rock a
Bye Baby 58. The Geisha Boy 58. Don't Give up
the Ship 59. Visit to a Small Planet 60. *The Bellboy*
60. Cinderfella 60. Ladies' Man 61. The Errand Boy
61. It's Only Money 62. The Nutty Professor 63.
Who's Minding the Store? 64. The Patsy 64. The
Disorderly Orderly 64. The Family Jewels 65.
Boeing-Boeing 65. Three on a Couch 66. Way Way
Out 66. The Big Mouth 67. Don't Raise the
Bridge, Lower the River 68. Hook Line and Sinker
69. Which Way to the Front? 70. One More Time
(d only) 71. Hardly Working (& d) 79. Slapstick of
the Fourth Kind 82. King of Comedy 83.
Smorgasbord (& co-w, d) 83. Cookie 89. The
Arrowtooth Waltz 92. Arizona Dream 92.
   Gag appearance: It's a Mad Mad Mad Mad
World 63.

¶ When the light goes on in the refrigerator, I do
twenty minutes. – *J.L.*
   At some point he said to himself, I'm
extraordinary, like Chaplin. From then on nobody
could tell him anything. He knew it all. – *Dean
Martin*

Lewis, Jerry Lee (1935–).
American country-rock singer whose turbulent
life was filmed as *Great Balls of Fire* 89, in which
he was played by Dennis Quaid.
AS HIMSELF: Jamboree (aka Disc Jockey Jamboree)
57. High School Confidential 58. American Hot
Wax 76. Chuck Berry Hail! Hail! Rock 'n' Roll 87,
etc.

Lewis, Joe E. (1901–1971) (Joseph Kleevan).
American night-club comedian, played by Frank
Sinatra in *The Joker is Wild*.
■ Too Many Husbands 31. Private Buckaroo 42.
Lady in Cement 69.

Lewis, Joseph H. (1900–).
American director, mainly of second features,
some of them well above average.
   Two-Fisted Rangers 40. The Mad Doctor of
Market Street 41. Bombs over Burma 42. Minstrel
Man 44. *My Name Is Julia Ross* 45. *So Dark the Night*
46. *The Jolson Story* (musical numbers only) 46. The
Swordsman 47. The Return of October 48. *The
Undercover Man* 49. A Lady without Passport 50.
Gun Crazy 50. Retreat Hell 52. Cry of the Hunted
53. The Big Combo 55. A Lawless Street 55. Seventh
Cavalry 56. The Halliday Brand 56. *Terror in a Texas
Town* 58, etc.

Lewis, Juliette (1975–).
American leading actress. She is the daughter of
Geoffrey Lewis.
   My Stepmother Is an Alien 88. Life on the Edge
89. National Lampoon's Christmas Vacation 89.
Cape Fear (AAN) 91. Crooked Hearts 91. Husbands
and Wives 92. That Night 93. Kalifornia 93.
Romeo Is Bleeding 93. What's Eating Gilbert Grape
93. Natural Born Killers 94. Strange Days
95, etc.
   TV series: Home Fires 87. I Married Dora 87–
88. A Family for Joe 90.

Lewis, Michael J. (1939–).
British composer.

The Madwoman of Chaillot 69. The Man Who Haunted Himself 70. Unman Wittering and Zigo 72. Theatre of Blood 73. 11 Harrowhouse 74. Russian Roulette 75. The Medusa Touch 78. The Stick Up (aka Mud) 78. The Passage 79. The Legacy 79. North Seas Hijack (aka ffolkes) 80. The Unseen 81. Sphinx 81. Yes, Giorgio 82. The Naked Face 85. The Rose and the Jackal (TV) 90, etc.

Lewis, Ralph (1872–1937).
American character actor, often in villainous roles, in films from 1912. He played the abolitionist senator Austin Stoneman in *The Birth of a Nation* 15.

The Escape 14. Intolerance 16. Eyes of Youth 19. Flesh and Blood 22. Desire 23. Dante's Inferno 24. Casey Jones 27. The Girl in the Glass Cage 29. Abraham Lincoln 30. Riot Squad 33. Mystery Liner 34. Behind the Green Light 35, etc.

Lewis, Ronald (1928–1982).
British leading man, in films from 1953. Committed suicide.

The Prisoner 55. Storm over the Nile 55. A Hill in Korea 56. Bachelor of Hearts 59. The Full Treatment 61. Twice Round the Daffodils 62. Mr Sardonicus 62. The Brigand of Kandahar 65. Friends 71. Paul and Michelle 74, etc.

Lewis, Sheldon (1868–1958).
American character actor of stage and screen.

The Exploits of Elaine 15. Dr Jekyll and Mr Hyde (title role) 16. Orphans of the Storm 21. The Red Kimono 26. Black Magic 29. The Monster Walks 32. The Cattle Thief (last film) 36, many others.

Lewis, Sinclair (1885–1951).
American novelist. Works filmed include:

Arrowsmith 31. Ann Vickers 33. Babbitt 34. Dodsworth 36. Untamed 40. Cass Timberlane 47. Elmer Gantry 60.

Lewis, Ted (1891–1971) (Theodore Friedman).
American bandleader and entertainer ('Me and My Shadow') who appeared in a few movies.
■ Is Everybody Happy? 28. Show of Shows 29. Here Comes the Band 35. Manhattan Merry Go Round 37. Hold That Ghost 42. Follow the Boys 44.

Lewton, Val (1904–1951) (Vladimir Leventon).
American producer, remembered for a group of low-budget, high quality horror films made for RKO in the 40s.
Biography: 1973, *The Reality of Terror* by Joel E. Siegel.
■ Cat People 42. I Walked with a Zombie 43. The Leopard Man 43. The Seventh Victim 43. The Ghost Ship 43. Mademoiselle Fifi 44. Curse of the Cat People 44. Youth Runs Wild 44. *The Body Snatcher* 45. Isle of the Dead 45. Bedlam 46. My Own True Love 49. Please Believe Me 50. Apache Drums 51.
~Under the pseudonym Carlos Keith, Lewton contributed to the screenplays of *The Body Snatchers* and *Bedlam*.

Lexy, Edward (1897–) (Edward Gerald Little).
British character actor in films from 1936, usually as sergeant-major, police inspector or irascible father.

Farewell Again 37. South Riding 38. Laugh It Off 40. Spare a Copper 40. Piccadilly Incident 46. It's Not Cricket 48. Miss Robin Hood 52. Orders Are Orders 55. The Man Who Wouldn't Talk 58, many others.

Leyton, John (1939–).
British pop singer who transferred to dramatic roles.

The Great Escape 63. Von Ryan's Express 65. Krakatoa 68. Schizo 77. Dangerous Davies – the Last Detective 80, etc.
TV series: Jericho 66.

L'Herbier, Marcel (1888–1979).
French director, an avant-garde leader in silent days.
Autobiography: 1979, *La Tête Qui Tourne*.
Rose France 19. Eldorado 22. The Late Mathias Pascal 25. L'Epervier 33. Nuits de Feu 37. La Nuit Fantastique 42. The Last Days of Pompeii 49. Le Père de Mademoiselle 53, etc.

Lhermitte, Thierry.
French leading actor.

L'An 01 72. Next Year If All Goes Well 83. My Best Friend's Girl (La Femme de Mon Pote) 83. Les Ripoux 84. Until September (US) 84. Tango 93. L'Honneur de la tribu 93. Elles N'Oublient Jamais 94. Seven Sundays 94, etc.

Lhomme, Pierre (1930–).
French cinematographer.

St Tropez Blues 60. A Matter of Resistance (La Vie de Château) 66. King of Hearts (Le Roi de Coeur) 66. La Chamade 68. Mister Freedom 69. Four Nights of a Dreamer (Quatre Nuits d'un Rêveur) 71. Sweet Movie 74. The Savage State (L'Etat Sauvage) 78. Quartet 81. My Little Girl 87. Maurice 87. Cyrano de Bergerac 90. Voyager 91. Premier Amour 92. Summer Strolls (Promenades d'Eté) 92. Toxic Affair 93. Dieu que les Femmes Sont Amoureuses 94, etc.

Li, Gong (1966–).
Leading Chinese actress and drama teacher, closely associated with the work of director Zhang Yimou. In 1994, the Chinese government told her that she could no longer attend festivals in the West or give interviews to foreign journalists.

Red Sorghum (Hong Gaoliang) 87. Ju Dou 90. The Terra-Cotta Warrior 90. *Raise the Red Lantern* (Dahong Denglong Gaogao Gua) 91. *The Story of Qiu Ju* 92. Mary from Beijing (Mungsing Sifan) 93. Farewell My Concubine (Bawang Bie Ji) 93. To Live 94. The Great Conqueror's Concubine (Xi Chu Bawang) 94. La Peintre (Hua Hun) 94, etc.

Liberace (1919–1987) (Wladziu Valentino Liberace).
American pianist-showman of stage, nightclubs and TV. Starred in his only major appearance, *Sincerely Yours* 55; also seen as a pianist in *East of Java* 49 and as a coffin salesman in *The Loved One* 65. Died of AIDS.
Autobiography: 1977, *The Things I Love*.

¶ You know that bank I used to cry all the way to? I bought it. – *L.*
Of course, I couldn't go out in the street in clothes like this, I'd get picked up. Come to think of it, it might be fun. – *L.*
Gee, you've been such a wonderful audience that I don't like to take your money. But I will! – *L.*

library shot:
see stock shot.

Licudi, Gabriella (1943–).
Italian leading lady in international films.

The Liquidators 65. The Jokers 66. Casino Royale 66. The Last Safari 67. Separate Beds 73, many others.

Lieven, Albert (1906–1971).
German actor in films from 1933, including man British productions.

Victoria the Great 37. Night Train to Munich 4 Jeannie 40. Yellow Canary 43. *The Seventh Veil* 4 Beware of Pity 46. Frieda 47. *Sleeping Car to Trieste* 48. Hotel Sahara 50. Conspiracy of Hearts 60. Foxhole in Cairo 61. The Victors 63. Traitor's Ga 65, many others.

lifts
(or elevators) provided a convenient means of murder in *Garment Center*, *The List of Adrian Messenger* and *House of Wax*, and of unwitting suicide in *Ivy*. In *The Lift*, the machine was the murderer. Sean Connery in *Diamonds Are Forever* had a spectacular fight in a lift. People were trapped in lifts in *Cry Terror*, *A Night in Casablan* *Love Crazy*, *Sweet Charity*, *Towering Inferno* and *La in a Cage*, in which last the lift was of the domes variety used by Katharine Hepburn in *Suddenly L Summer*. Michael Rennie had more trouble in lif than any other actor – in *The Power*, *The Day the Earth Stood Still*, and *Hotel*. Invalid chair-lifts wei sported by Ethel Barrymore in *The Farmer's Daughter*, Charles Laughton in *Witness for the Prosecution*, and Eugenie Leontovich in *Homicidal*

light comedians,
the lithe and dapper heroes who can be funny ar romantic at the same time, have added a great de to the mystique and nostalgia of the screen. Lind and Chaplin both partly belong to this debonair tradition, and indeed did much to mould it; but only sound could enable its full realization. Maurice Chevalier had the field pretty well to himself in Hollywood during the early 30s, with strong support from such stalwarts as Roland Young, Edward Everett Horton and Charles Butterworth. Soon Cary Grant entered the lists along with David Niven, William Powell, Louis Hayward, Melvyn Douglas and Ronald Colman when he felt in lighter mood. Britain scored wit Jack Buchanan, Jack Hulbert, and the ineffable Aldwych team of Tom Walls and Ralph Lynn; wh Leslie Howard scored a major hit in *Pygmalion* a Rex Harrison, who was to play the same role twenty-five years later in *My Fair Lady*, was already demonstrating his talent in less importan comedies.

Back in Hollywood *The Philadelphia Story* was a milestone in light comedy and set Katharine Hepburn firmly on the road she later followed in her splendid series with Spencer Tracy. Bette Dav too, had her moments in this field, and so did Rosalind Russell. Bob Hope and Danny Kaye bo clowned around a good deal but still got the girl in the end . . . but Britishers Basil Radford and Naunton Wayne were bachelors born and bred. The more realistic approach of the 50s was stiflin the genre, but Dennis Price managed a notable performance in *Kind Hearts and Coronets* before I Carmichael cornered the diminishing market. In more recent years actors have had to turn comic tragic at the drop of a hat: among those best abl to manage the light touch are Jack Lemmon, To: Curtis, Frank Sinatra, Peter O'Toole, Jack Nicholson, Warren Beatty, Shirley Maclaine, Dia Keaton, Jane Fonda and Anne Bancroft.

lighthouses
formed dramatic settings for such movies as *Thunder Rock*, *The Seventh Survivor*, *The Phantom Light* and *Back Room Boy*, and dominated key scen of *Portrait of Jennie*, *A Stolen Life*, *The Beast from 20,000 Fathoms* and *Pete's Dragon*.

Lightner, Winnie (1901–1971) (Winifred Hanson). American vaudeville comedienne who appeared in several early talkies.

Gold Diggers of Broadway 30. Playgirl 32. Dancing Lady 32. I'll Fix It 34, etc.

Li'l Abner.

Al Capp's comic strip about the hillbilly inhabitants of Dogpatch was first filmed, unsuccessfully, in 1940 with Granville Owen; masks were rather oddly used for some characters. In 1957 Panama and Frank made a successful musical version with Peter Palmer, based on the Broadway show. Paramount made a few Li'l Abner cartoons in the late 40s.

Liliom.

Ferenc Molnar's play about the here and the hereafter was filmed in Hollywood in 1930 by Frank Brozage and in Germany in 1934 by Fritz Lang. In 1956 it turned up again, via a stage musical, as Carousel, directed by Henry King. There had also been a 1921 silent under the title A Trip to Paradise.

Lillie, Beatrice (1898–1989) (Constance Sylvia Munston, later Lady Peel).
Sharp-faced, mischievous British revue star of the 20s and 30s who graced only a few films with her wit.
Autobiography: 1973, Every Other Inch a Lady.
Exit Smiling 26. Show of Shows 29. Are You There? 30. Dr Rhythm 38. On Approval 43. Around the World in Eighty Days 56. Thoroughly Modern Millie 67.

Lima, Walter, Jnr (1938–).
Brazilian director, a former journalist, who also worked as assistant to Glauber Rocha.
Menino do Engenho 65. Brasil, Anno 2000 69. Taim 77. Xico Rei 82. Dolphin 87, etc.

Lincoln, Abbey (1930–) (Anna Marie Woolridge).
American character actress.
The Girl Can't Help It 56. Nothing but a Man 64. For Love of Ivy 68. Mo' Better Blues 90, etc.

Lincoln, Abraham (1809–1865).
Sixteenth American president, a familiar screen figure with his stovepipe hat, bushy whiskers, and his assassination during a performance of Our American Cousin. More or less full-length screen portraits include Abraham Lincoln's Clemency 10; Lincoln the Lover 13; Joseph Henabery in Birth of a Nation 14; Frank McGlynn in The Life of Abraham Lincoln 15; George A. Billings in Abraham Lincoln 25; Walter Huston in Abraham Lincoln 30; John Carradine in Of Human Hearts 38; Henry Fonda in Young Mr Lincoln 39; Raymond Massey in Abe Lincoln in Illinois 39.

Lincoln, Elmo (1889–1952) (Otto Elmo Linkenhelter).
American silent actor who became famous as the first Tarzan of the Apes 18, and played small roles up to his death.
Birth of a Nation 14. Elmo the Mighty 19, etc.

Lindblom, Gunnel (1935–).
Leading Swedish actress who became a director and screenwriter from the 70s.
The Seventh Seal 56. Wild Strawberries 57. The Virgin Spring 60. Winter Light 62. The Silence 63. Rapture 65. Loving Couples 66. Sult 67. Flickorna 68. The Father 69. Brother Carl 71. Scenes from a Marriage 74. Summer Paradise (Paradistorg) (wd) 77. Bomsalva 78. Sally Och Friheten (d) 81.

Bakom Jalusin 84. Summer Nights (Sommarkvallar) (wd) 87, etc.

Linden, Eric (1909–).
Swedish-American juvenile lead of the 30s.
Are These Our Children? 32. The Silver Cord 33. Girl of the Limberlost 34. The Voice of Bugle Ann 36. Gone with the Wind 39, etc.

Linden, Hal (1931–) (Harold Lipshitz).
American character actor, best known as TV's Barney Miller.
When You Comin' Back, Red Ryder? 79. Father Figure (TV) 80. My Wicked, Wicked Ways: The Legend of Errol Flynn (TV) 85. A New Life 88, etc.
TV series: The Boys Are Back 94–95.

Linden, Jennie (1939–).
British leading actress.
Nightmare 63. Dr Who and the Daleks 66. Women in Love 69. A Severed Head 70. Hedda 75. Valentino 77, etc.
TV series: Lillie 77.

Linder, Cec (1921–1992).
Canadian character actor, long in British films.
Crack in the Mirror 59. Jetstorm 59. Too Young to Love 60. SOS Pacific 60. Goldfinger 64. Explosion 71. A Touch of Class 73. Sunday in the Country 74. Lost and Found 79. Atlantic City 80, many others.

Linder, Max (1883–1925) (Gabriel Leuvielle).
Dapper French silent comedian, a likely source for Chaplin. Between 1906 and 1925 he scripted and directed most of his own films, from 1917 in Hollywood. Committed suicide, together with his wife.
The Skater's Debut 07. Max Takes a Bath 07. Max and His Mother-in-Law's False Teeth 08. Max's New Landlord 08. Max in a Dilemma 10. Max Is Absent-Minded 10. How Max Went Around the World 11. Max, Victim of Quinquina 11. Max Teaches the Tango 11. Max Is Forced to Work 12. Max Toreador 12. Max Virtuoso 12. Who Killed Max? 13. Max's Hat 14. Max and Jane Make a Dessert 14. Max and the Clutching Hand 15. Max Comes Across 17. Max Wants a Divorce 17. Max and His Taxi 17. The Little Café 19. Seven Years Bad Luck* 20. Be My Wife* 20. The Three Must-Get-Theres* 22. Help! 24. King of the Circus 25, many others.
*These films formed the basis of a compilation, Laugh with Max Linder, which was issued in 1963.

Lindfors, Viveca (1920–) (Elsa Torstendotter).
Swedish actress, in films from 1941, Hollywood from 1946.
To the Victor 47. Night Unto Night 48. The New Adventures of Don Juan 48. No Sad Songs for Me 50. Dark City 50. The Flying Missile 51. Four in a Jeep 51. The Raiders 52. Run for Cover 55. Moonfleet 55. I Accuse 57. Tempest 58. King of Kings 61. Sylvia 65. Brainstorm 65. The Way We Were 73. Welcome to L.A. 77. Girlfriends 78. A Wedding 78. Natural Enemies 79. Voices 79. The Hand 82. Creepshow 82. Silent Madness 83. The Sure Thing 85. Frankenstein's Aunt 86. Unfinished Business (& wd) 87. Rachel River 88. The Ann Jillian Story (TV) 88. Forced March 89. Zandalee 90. Luba 90. Exorcist III 90. Exiled 91. The Linguini Incident 92, many others.

Lindgren, Lars Magnus (1922–).
Swedish director.
Do You Believe in Angels? 60. Dear John 64. The Coffin (The Sadist) 66.

Lindley, Audra (1923–).
American character actress.
The Heartbreak Kid 72. Pearl (TV) 79. When You Comin' Back Red Ryder 79. Moviola (TV) 80. Cannery Row 82. Desert Hearts 85. Spellbinder 88. Troop Beverly Hills 89, etc.
TV series: Bridget Loves Bernie 72–73. Three's Company 77–79. The Ropers 79–80.

Lindley, John (1952–).
American cinematographer.
The Goodbye People 84. Lily in Love 85. Killer Party 86. Home of the Brave 86. The Stepfather 87. In the Mood 87. The Serpent and the Rainbow 87. Shakedown (aka Blue Jean Cop) 87. True Believer 89. Field of Dreams 89. Immediate Family 89. Vital Signs 90. Sleeping with the Enemy 91. Sneakers 92. The Good Son 93. I Love Trouble 94, etc.

Lindo, Olga (1898–1968).
Anglo-Norwegian character actress, on British stage and screen.
The Shadow Between 32. The Last Journey 35. When We Are Married 42. Bedelia 46. Train of Events 49. An Inspector Calls 54. Woman in a Dressing Gown 57. Sapphire 59, etc.

Lindon, Lionel (1905–1971).
American cinematographer.
Going My Way 44. A Medal for Benny 45. Road to Utopia 46. Alias Nick Beal 49. Destination Moon 50. Conquest of Space 55. Around the World in Eighty Days (AA) 56. The Lonely Man 57. The Black Scorpion 57. Too Late Blues 61. The Manchurian Candidate 62. The Trouble with Angels 66. Boy Did I Get a Wrong Number 66. Grand Prix 66. Generation 69, etc.

Lindsay, Howard (1889–1968).
American actor-playwright-stage director. With Russel Crouse wrote Life with Father and State of the Union, both filmed. Acted in and directed Dulcy 21, co-authored She's My Weakness 31.

Lindsay, Margaret (1910–1981) (Margaret Kies).
American leading lady of the 30s, with stage experience; in Hollywood from 1931.
West of Singapore 32. Lady Killer 34. Bordertown 35. G-Men 35. The Green Light 37. Jezebel 38. The House of Seven Gables 40. There's Magic in Music 41. A Close Call for Ellery Queen 42. No Place for a Lady 43. Crime Doctor 43. Alaska 44. Club Havana 45. Scarlet Street 45. Her Sister's Secret 47. Cass Timberlane 47. Emergency Hospital 56. Jet over the Atlantic 59. Tammy and the Doctor 63, many others.

Lindsay, Robert (1951–).
English leading actor, from the stage.
Adventures of a Taxi Driver 75. Bert Rigby, You're a Fool 89. Strike It Rich (aka Loser Takes All) 90, etc.
TV series: Citizen Smith 73–77.

Lindsay-Hogg, Michael (1940–).
British director and screenwriter. He is the son of actress Geraldine Fitzgerald.
Let It Be 70. Nasty Habits 77. Brideshead Revisited (co-d) (TV) 81. Master Harold and the Boys 84. As Is 86. The Object of Beauty (wd) 91, etc.

Lindtberg, Leopold (1902–1984).
Austrian director, a former actor, who was a theatre director in Germany before moving to Switzerland in the early 40s, after the rise of the

Nazis, to become an influential director of film and theatre there.

Jasoo (co-d) 35. Die Missbrauchten Liebesbriefe 40. Marie-Louise 44. The Last Chance (Die Letzte Chance) 45. Four in a Jeep (Die Vier im Jeep) 51. Daughter of the Storm 54, etc.

Linklater, Richard (1962–).
American actor, director and producer of independent films.

Slacker (a, wd) 91. Dazed and Confused (a, p, co-w) 93. Before Sunrise (co-w, d) 95.

¶ You need age and maturity to make a good film. – R.L.

Linn-Baker, Mark (1954–).
American actor.

My Favorite Year 82. Ghostwriter 84. Me and Him (Ich und Er) (Ger.) 89. Bare Essentials 91. Noises Off 92, etc.

TV series: Perfect Strangers 86–93.

Linson, Art.
American producer and occasional director. He is the author of *A Pound of Flesh: Perilous Tales of How to Produce Movies in Hollywood*, published in 1994.

Rafferty and the Gold Dust Twins 75. American Hot Wax 78. Melvin and Harold 80. Where the Buffalo Roam (& d) 80. Fast Times at Ridgmount High 82. The Wild Life (& d) 84. The Untouchables 87. Scrooged 88. Casualties of War 89. We're No Angels 89. Dick Tracy 90. Singles 92, etc.

The Lion's Share,
by Bosley Crowther. A lively history of the Metro-Goldwyn-Mayer company, written in 1957 by the critic of the *New York Times*.

Liotta, Ray (1955–).
American actor from TV.

The Lonely Lady 83. Something Wild 86. Dominick and Eugene 88. Field of Dreams 89. GoodFellas 90. Article 99 92. Unlawful Entry 92. Judgment Night 93. No Escape 94. Corrina, Corrina 94, etc.

TV series: Casablanca 83. Our Family Honor 85–86.

Lipman, Jerzy (1922–1983).
Polish cinematographer.

A Generation 54. Kanal 57. The Eighth Day of the Week 58. Lotna 59. Knife in the Water 62. No More Divorces 63. Ashes 65. Zozya 67. Colonel Wolodyjowski 69. Dead Pigeon on Beethoven Street 72. The Martyr 75, etc.

Lippert, Robert L. (1909–1976).
American exhibitor, latterly head of company making second features for Twentieth Century-Fox, many of them produced by his son *Robert L. Lippert Jnr* (1928–).

Lipscomb, W. P. (1887–1958).
British screenwriter who spent some years in Hollywood.

French Leave 27. The Good Companions 32. I Was a Spy 33. Clive of India (co-w) 34. A Tale of Two Cities 35. The Garden of Allah 36. Pygmalion (co-w) 38. A Town Like Alice 56. Dunkirk (co-w) 58, many others.

Lipstadt, Aaron (1952–).
American director.
■ Android 82. City Limits 85. Police Story: Monster Manor (TV) 88.

Lisi, Virna (1937–) (Virna Pieralisi).
Voluptuous Italian leading lady who after starring in innumerable local spectaculars came on to the international market. She won the best actress award at the Cannes Film Festival for *La Reine Margot*.

The Black Tulip 63. Eva 63. How to Murder Your Wife (US) 65. Casanova 70 65. Signore e Signori 65. Assault on a Queen (US) 66. Not with My Wife You Don't (US) 66. The Girl and the General 67. The Twenty-fifth Hour 67. Arabella 68. The Secret of Santa Vittoria 69. Un Beau Monstre 70. The Statue 71. The Serpent 72. Bluebeard 72. White Fang 74. Challenge to White Fang 75. Cocktails for Three 78. Ernesto 78. La Cicala 80. Miss Right 81. I Love N.Y. 87. Merry Christmas, Happy New Year (Buon Natale, Buon Anno) 89. Queen Margot (La Reine Margot) 94, etc.

Lister, Francis (1899–1951).
Suave British character actor, mainly on stage.

Comin' Thro' the Rye 24. Atlantic 30. Jack's the Boy 32. Clive of India 35. The Return of the Scarlet Pimpernel 38. Henry V 44. The Wicked Lady 45. Home to Danger 51, etc.

Lister, Moira (1923–).
South African leading lady and character actress, in British films.

My Ain Folk 44. Uneasy Terms 48. Another Shore 48. A Run for Your Money 49. Grand National Night 53. John and Julie 55. Seven Waves Away 57. The Yellow Rolls-Royce 64. Stranger in the House 67. Ten Little Indians 89, etc.

Litel, John (1895–1972).
American character actor, in films since 1929; often seen as judge, lawyer or stern father.

Marked Woman 37. The Life of Emile Zola 37. Virginia City 40. Men Without Souls 40. They Died with Their Boots On 41. Sealed Lips 41. Boss of Big Town 43. Kiss Tomorrow Goodbye 50. Houseboat 58. A Pocketful of Miracles 61. The Sons of Katie Elder 65, many others.

TV series: My Hero 52.

Lithgow, John (1945–).
American character actor, a semi-star of the 80s. A graduate of Harvard University, he studied for the stage at LAMDA and is also a theatre director.

Obsession 76. All that Jazz 79. Blow Out 81. The World According to Garp (AAN) 82. Twilight Zone: The Movie 83. Terms of Endearment (AAN) 83. Buckaroo Banzai 84. 2010 84. Santa Claus 84. Footloose 84. Mesmerized 84. The Manhattan Project 86. Bigfoot and the Hendersons 87. Distant Thunder 88. Out Cold 88. Traveling Man (TV) 89. Memphis Belle 90. Ivory Hunters (TV) 90. At Play in the Fields of the Lord 91. L.A. Story 91. Ricochet 91. Raising Cain 92. The Wrong Man 93. Cliffhanger 93. The Pelican Brief 93. A Good Man in Africa 94. Love, Cheat & Steal 94. Princess Caraboo 94. Silent Fall 94, etc.

Littin, Miguel (1942–).
Chilean film director, a former actor and television director. He went into exile following the overthrow of President Allende to work mainly in Mexico.

El Chacal de Nahueltoro 70. Letters from Marusia (Actas de Marusia) (AAN) 75. La Viuda de Montiel 80. Alsino and the Condor (Alsino y el Cóndor) 82. Sandino 90. The Shipwrecked (Los Naufragos) 94, etc.

Little, Cleavon (1939–1992).
American comedy actor.

What's So Bad About Feeling Good 68. Cotton

Comes to Harlem 70. Vanishing Point 71. *Blazing Saddles* 74. Greased Lightning 77. Scavenger Hunt 79. High Risk 81. The Gig 85. Fletch Lives 89. Hearts of Fire 92, etc.

TV series: *Temperatures Rising* 72.

Little, Dwight H.
American director of action and horror movies. He also directed *Ground Zero Texas*, a computer game on CD-ROM which claims to be the first 'interactive movie'.

Lethal (aka KGB – The Secret War) 86. Getting Even 86. Bloodstone 88. Halloween 4: The Return of Michael Myers 88. The Phantom of the Opera 89. Marked for Death 90. Rapid Fire 92, etc.

Little Lord Fauntleroy.
The well-known children's novel by Frances Hodgson Burnett, about an American boy who becomes a British earl, was filmed in 1922 as a transvestite vehicle for Mary Pickford; direction appears to have been shared between Alfred E. Green, Jack Pickford, and Alfred Werker. In 1936 it was remade by John Cromwell for Selznick, with Freddie Bartholomew in the title role. In 1980 there was a TV version with Ricky Schroder.

Little Miss Marker.
Damon Runyon's story of a small girl with a belief in chivalry reforming a hard-bitten gambler made an ideal vehicle for Shirley Temple and Adolphe Menjou in 1934; it was remade as *Sorrowful Jones* in 1949 with the emphasis on its male lead, Bob Hope. Norman Jewison's *Forty Pounds of Trouble* in 1962 updated the story to little effect. Walter Bernstein tried the original story again in 1980 with *Little Miss Marker*, featuring Walter Matthau, but by then the tale seemed tired and dated.

Little Women.
Louisa M. Alcott's cosy 19th-century saga of a nice mother's even nicer daughters was twice filmed as a silent, in 1917 in Britain and 1918 in America, and became a major success when filmed in 1933 by George Cukor, with Katharine Hepburn and Paul Lukas. Remade in 1949 with June Allyson and Rossano Brazzi, it seemed calculated and coy. Another remake came in 1994, directed by Gillian Armstrong and starring Winona Ryder, Samantha Mathis, Trini Alvarado, Susan Sarandon, and Gabriel Byrne. A 1978 TV series got nowhere. A sequel, *Little Men*, was filmed in 1940 as a vehicle for Kay Francis.

Littlefield, Lucien (1895–1960).
American character actor, in Hollywood from 1913 in supporting roles.

The Sheik 22. Miss Pinkerton 32. Ruggles of Red Gap 34. Rose Marie 36. The Great American Broadcast 40. Scared Stiff 44. Susanna Pass 51. Pop Girl 56, etc.

Littlewood, Joan (1914–).
British stage director whose only film to date is *Sparrows Can't Sing* 63. Created London's 'Theatre Workshop'.

Litvak, Anatole (1902–1974).
Russian-born director in Germany and France from 1927, Hollywood from 1937.
■ Dolly Gets Ahead (Ger.) 31. Nie Wieder Liebe (Ger.) 32. Coeur de Lilas (Fr.) 32. Be Mine Tonight (Ger.) 33. Sleeping Car (GB) 33. Cette Vielle Canaille (Fr.) 35. L'Equipage (Fr.) 36. *Mayerling* (Fr.) 36. *The Woman I Love* 37. Tovarich 38. The Amazing Dr Clitterhouse 38. The Sisters 38 Castle on the Hudson 39. *Confessions of a Nazi Spy* 39. All This and Heaven Too 40. *City for Conquest*

40. Out of the Fog 41. Blues in the Night 41. This Above All 42. The Long Night 47. Sorry Wrong Number 48. *The Snake Pit* (AAN) 48. Decision Before Dawn 52. Act of Love 53. The Deep Blue Sea 55. Anastasia 56. The Journey 59. Goodbye Again 61. Five Miles to Midnight 63. The Night of the Generals 67. The Lady in the Car 70.

Livesey, Jack (1901–1961).
British actor, brother of Roger Livesey.
The Wandering Jew 33. The Passing of the Third Floor Back 35. Old Bill and Son 40. The First Gentleman 47. Paul Temple's Triumph 51, etc.

Livesey, Roger (1906–1976).
Husky-voiced, often roguish British character star who divided his time between stage and screen.
■ The Old Curiosity Shop 20. Where the Rainbow Ends 21. The Four Feathers 21. Married Love 23. East Lynne on the Western Front 31. A Veteran of Waterloo 33. A Cuckoo in the Nest 33. Blind Justice 34. The Price of Wisdom 35. Lorna Doone 35. Midshipman Easy 35. *Rembrandt* 36. *The Drum* 38. Keep Smiling 38. Spies of the Air 39. The Rebel Son 39. The Girl in the News 40. 49th Parallel 41. *The Life and Death of Colonel Blimp* 43. *I Know Where I'm Going* 45. *A Matter of Life and Death* 46. Vice Versa 47. That Dangerous Age 49. Green Grow the Rushes 50. The Master of Ballantrae 53. The Intimate Stranger 56. The League of Gentlemen 59. The Entertainer 60. No My Darling Daughter 61. Of Human Bondage 64. Moll Flanders 65. Oedipus the King 68. Hamlet 69. Futtock's End 70.

Livesey, Sam (1873–1936).
British actor, father of Jack and Roger Livesey.
Young Woodley 30. The Flag Lieutenant 32. The Private Life of Henry VIII 32. Jew Süss 34. Turn of the Tide 36. Dark Journey 37, etc.

Livingston, Jay (1915–) (Jacob Harold Levison).
American composer who, with his partner Ray Evans, was under contract to Paramount 1945–55, turning out a succession of hit songs.
The Stork Club 45. The Cat and the Canary (AAN) 45. Golden Earrings 47. The Paleface (AA for 'Buttons and Bows') 48. My Friend Irma 49. My Friend Irma Goes West 50. Captain Carey (AA for 'Mona Lisa') 50. Fancy Pants 50. The Lemon Drop Kid 51. Aaron Slick from Punkin Crick 51. Son of Paleface 52. Here Come the Girls 53. Red Garters 54. The Man Who Knew Too Much (AA for 'Que Sera, Sera') 56. Tammy and the Bachelor (AAN) 57. Houseboat (AAN) 58. Dear Heart (AAN) 64, etc.
TV series: Bonanza. Mr Ed (themes).

Livingston, Jerry (1909–1987) (Jerome Levinson).
American composer and songwriter, usually in collaboration with lyricist Mack David. In Hollywood from 1949, moving to television in the late 50s. A former bandleader.
Cinderella (AAN) 49. At War with the Army 50. Sailor Beware 51. Jumping Jacks 52. Scared Stiff 53. The Hanging Tree (AAN) 59. Cat Ballou (AAN) 65, etc.

Livingston, Margaret (1895–1984).
American silent-screen leading lady.
Within the Cup 18. Lying Lips 21. Divorce 23. Butterfly 24. Havoc 25. A Trip to Chinatown 26. Married Alive 27. Streets of Shanghai 28. The Last Warning 29. Seven Keys to Baldpate 30. Kiki 31. Call Her Savage 32. Social Register 34, many others.

Lizzani, Carlo (1917–).
Italian director.

Caccia Tragica (co-w only) 47. Bitter Rice (co-w only) 49. Achtung Banditi 51. Ai Margini Della Metropoli 54. The Great Wall 58. Hunchback of Rome 60. The Hills Run Red 66. The Violent Four 68. Crazy Joe 73. The Last Days of Mussolini 74. Kleinhoff Hotel 77. Fontamara 80. Nucleo Zero 84. Mamma Ebe 85. Selina 89, etc.

LL Cool J (1969–) (James Todd Smith).
American rap performer and actor. Born in Queens, New York, he made his first record at the age of 16. His professional name is an acronym for 'Ladies Love Cool James'.
The Hard Way 91. Toys 92.

Llewellyn, Richard (1906–1983).
Welsh best-selling novelist, famous for *How Green Was My Valley*. *Noose* and *None but the Lonely Heart* were also filmed.

Llosa, Luis.
Peruvian-born director in Hollywood.
Hour of the Assassin 87. Crime Zone 89. Eight Hundred Leagues down the Amazon 93. Sniper 93. The Specialist 94, etc.

Lloyd, Christopher (1938–).
American character actor, often in crazed or comic roles.
One Flew over the Cuckoo's Nest 75. Goin' South 78. The Onion Field 79. The Black Marble 79. The Lady in Red 79. Schizoid 80. The Legend of the Lone Ranger 81. Mr Mom 83. To Be or Not To Be 83. Star Trek III: The Search for Spock 84. The Adventures of Buckaroo Banzai across the Eighth Dimension 84. Miracles 84. Clue 85. Back to the Future 85. Eight Men Out 88. Who Framed Roger Rabbit? 88. Dream Team 89. Back to the Future II 89. Back to the Future III 90. The Addams Family 91. Suburban Commando 91. T Bone 'n' Weasel (TV) 92. Dennis the Menace (GB: Dennis) 93. Twenty Bucks 93. Addams Family Values 93. Angels in the Outfield 94. Camp Nowhere 94. Radioland Murders 94. The Pagemaster 94, etc.
TV series: The Addams Chronicles 76. Taxi 79–83. Avonlea 90.

Lloyd, Doris (1899–1968).
British actress with repertory experience; in Hollywood from the 20s.
Charley's Aunt (as Donna Lucia) 30. Disraeli 30. Tarzan the Ape Man 32. Oliver Twist 33. Clive of India 35. Vigil in the Night 39. Phantom Lady 44. The Secret Life of Walter Mitty 47. A Man Called Peter 55. The Time Machine 60. The Notorious Landlady 62. Rosie 67, etc.

Lloyd, Emily (1971–).
British actress, now working in Hollywood. She is the daughter of actor Roger Lloyd-Pack and the granddaughter of Charles Lloyd-Pack.
Wish You Were Here 87. Cookie 89. In Country 89. Chicago Joe and the Showgirl 90. A River Runs through It 92, etc.

Lloyd, Euan (1923–).
British independent producer, former publicist.
Genghis Khan 65. Murderers' Row 66. Shalako 68. Catlow 71. The Man Called Noon 73. Paper Tiger 75. The Wild Geese 78. The Sea Wolves 80. Who Dares Wins 82, etc.

Lloyd, Frank (1889–1960).
Scottish-born director, in Hollywood from 1913 after acting experience.
Les Misérables 18. Madame X 20. Oliver Twist 22. The Eternal Flame 23. The Sea Hawk 24. Dark Streets 26. *The Divine Lady* (AA) 29. East Lynne

30. Sin Flood 31. Passport to Hell 32. *Cavalcade* (AA) 33. *Berkeley Square* 33. *Mutiny on the Bounty* (AAN) 35. Under Two Flags 36. Maid of Salem 37. Wells Fargo 37. If I Were King (& p) 38. Rulers of the Sea 39. The Tree of Liberty (& d) 40. The Lady from Cheyenne (& p) 41. This Woman Is Mine 41. *Blood on the Sun* 45. The Shanghai Story (& p) 54. The Last Command (& p) 55, many others.

Lloyd, Harold (1893–1971).
American silent comedian, famous for his timid bespectacled 'nice boy' character and for thrill-comedy situations involving dangerous stunts. In hundreds of two-reelers from 1916. He began as a stage actor before finding work first as a film extra and then as a Chaplin imitator in his Lucky Luke series of two-reelers. He first presented what was to become his world-famous quiet, bespectacled persona in *Over the Fence* in 1917. His career was interrupted in 1919 when a prop bomb turned out to be real and exploded in his face, removing a finger and thumb from his right hand. He recovered, signed a new contract with Hal Roach and by the beginning of the 20s was making big money: *Bumping into Broadway*, which cost $17,000 to make, took more than $150,000 in three years, bringing him a personal profit of more than $30,000. By 1922 his popularity rivalled Chaplin's. *Grandma's Boy*, his first feature, grossed nearly a million dollars and *Safety Last* more than $1.5m. He left Roach to run his own company in 1923. His career dwindled with the coming of sound and he spent time on his hobbies, which included stereoscopic photography. He married Mildred Davis, who starred with him in several of his films. A collection of his 3-D photographs, *Harold Lloyd's Hollywood*, was published in 1992. He was given a special Academy Award in 1952 as 'master comedian and good citizen'.
Autobiography: 1928, *An American Comedy*.
Biographies: 1976, *Harold Lloyd* by Richard Schickel. 1983, *Harold Lloyd: The Man on the Clock* by Tom Dardis.
■ A Sailor-Made Man 21. *Grandma's Boy* 22. Dr Jack 22. *Safety Last* 23. Why Worry? 23. Girl Shy 24. Hot Water 24. *The Freshman* 25. For Heaven's Sake 26. *The Kid Brother* 27. Speedy 28. Welcome Danger 29. *Feet First* 30. *Movie Crazy* 32. The Catspaw 34. The Milky Way 36. Professor Beware 38. Mad Wednesday (The Sins of Harold Diddlebock) 47.
Later produced two compilations of his comedy highlights: World of Comedy and Funny Side of Life.
☼ For skill, daring and ingenuity. The Kid Brother.

¶ Comedy comes from inside. It comes from your face. It comes from your body. – H.L.
I do not believe the public will want spoken comedy. Motion pictures and the spoken arts are two distinct arts. – H.L.
Basically he had not a funny bone in his body, but he was such a good actor that if you gave him a good script, he could play it to the best advantages for laughs. – Hal Roach
Lloyd was outstanding even among the master craftsmen at setting up a gag clearly, culminating and getting out of it deftly, and linking it smoothly to the next. – James Agee

Lloyd, Jeremy.
Lanky British comic actor and scriptwriter, frequently as an upper-class ass. He was co-creator of the television sit-coms *Are You Being Served?* 74–85, *O Happy Band!* 80, and *'Allo 'Allo!* 84–92. He was formerly married to actress Joanna Lumley.
Man in the Moon 61. Two and Two Make Six 62. Death Drums along the River 63. Doctor in

Clover 65. Those Magnificent Men in Their Flying Machines 65. The Wrong Box 66. Salt and Pepper 68. Goodbye Mr Chips 69. The Magic Christian 70. Murder on the Orient Express 74. Are You Being Served? (co-w) 77, etc.

Lloyd, Norman (1914–).
British character actor in Hollywood, usually in mean or weak roles; gave up acting to become TV producer, mainly for Alfred Hitchcock but made an acting comeback in his 60s.
  Autobiography: 1990, *Stages*.
  Saboteur (as the villain who fell from the statue of Liberty) 42. The Unseen 45. The Southerner 45. Spellbound 45. The Green Years 46. The Beginning or the End 47. Scene of the Crime 49. The Flame and the Arrow 50. He Ran All the Way 51. Limelight 52. Audrey Rose 77. The Nude Bomb 80. Dead Poets Society 89. The Age of Innocence 93, etc.
  TV series: St Elsewhere 82.

Lloyd, Russell (1916–).
British editor.
  The Squeaker 37. Over the Moon 39. School for Secrets 46. Anna Karenina 48. Decameron Nights 52. The Sea Shall Not Have Them 54. Moby Dick 56. Roots of Heaven 58. The Unforgiven 60. Of Human Bondage 64. Reflections in a Golden Eye 67. The Kremlin Letter 70. The Mackintosh Man 73. The Man Who Would Be King 75, many others.

Lloyd, Sue (1939–).
British leading lady of the 60s.
  The Ipcress File 66. Where's Jack? 68. Percy 71. The Bitch 79.
  TV series: The Baron.

Lloyd, Walt.
American cinematographer.
  Dangerously Close 86. The Wash 88. sex, lies and videotape 89. To Sleep with Anger 90. Pump Up the Volume 90. Kakfa 91. There Goes the Neighborhood (aka Paydirt) 92, etc.

Lloyd-Pack, Charles (1902–1983).
British character actor of stage and screen, usually in self-effacing roles: butlers, etc.
  High Treason 51. *The Importance of Being Earnest* 52. The Constant Husband 55. Night of the Demon 57. Dracula 58. *Victim* 62. If 68. Song of Norway 70. Madame Sin 72. The Mirror Crack'd 80, etc.

Lloyd-Pack, Roger (1944–).
Lugubrious British character actor, the son of Charles Lloyd-Pack and the father of Emily Lloyd.
  The Magus 68. The Virgin Soldiers 69. The Go-Between 70. Figures in a Landscape 70. Fiddler on the Roof 71. Fright 71. 1984 84. Prick Up Your Ears 87. The Cook, the Thief, His Wife and Her Lover 89. Wilt 89. Hamlet 91. The Object of Beauty 91. American Friends 91. The Trial 92. Princess Caraboo 94, etc.

Lloyd Webber, Sir Andrew (1948–).
British composer, mainly of long-running stage musicals.
  Gumshoe 71. Jesus Christ Superstar 73. The Odessa File 74.

Lo Bianco, Tony (1936–).
American character actor.
  The Honeymoon Killers 70. The French Connection 72. The Seven Ups 73. Jesus of Nazareth (TV) 77. Demon 77. Magee and the Lady (TV) 78. Bloodbrothers 78. F.I.S.T. 78. Separate

Ways 81. City Heat 84. The Ann Jillian Story (TV) 88. City of Hope 91. Too Scared to Scream (d) 85. Boiling Point 93, etc.
  TV series: Jessie 84.

Loach, Ken (1936–).
English director and screenwriter, noted for the realism of his films, frequently dealing with working-class life, which often use little-known or non-professional actors. Born in Nuneaton, he studied law at Oxford University and worked in BBC-TV where he formed a notable partnership with producer Tony Garnett on the series *The Wednesday Play* and later in films. His *Cathy Come Home* 66, written by Jeremy Sandford, was one of the most controversial and memorable TV plays of its time. In the 80s, he made *Questions of Leadership*, four TV documentaries on the role of the embattled trades unions which were banned, and turned to making commercials for a time.
  Up the Junction 67. *Poor Cow* 67. *Kes* 69. *Family Life* 72. Days of Hope (TV) 75. Black Jack 79. The Gamekeeper 80. Auditions (TV) 80. Looks and Smiles 81. Fatherland 86. Hidden Agenda 90. *Riff-Raff* 90. *Raining Stones* 93. *Ladybird, Ladybird* 94. Land and Freedom 95, etc.

¶ We wanted to make plays or films that got the same responses as when you saw the news. We wanted to be seen as almost a part of the news, as reports from the front line. – *K.L. on his TV work*
  There are two sorts of acting: theatre acting and film acting, which can be something different; where somebody can be taken through a story and experience the story and put themselves in that position, and respond as they would respond, so that you're really experiencing that person in that story. – *K.L.*
  He's totally round the bend. You don't rehearse. Everything is a take. – *Ricky Tomlinson*
  He reminds you always that you shouldn't become a film maker unless you have something to say. – *Alan Parker*

location.
A shooting site away from the studio, not encouraged in the days of the moguls, but considered essential in the cause of realism as soon as the studio system broke up.

¶ A rock is a rock, a tree is a tree, shoot it in Griffith Park. – *Anon*

Locke, Sondra (1947–).
American leading actress and occasional director.
  The Heart Is a Lonely Hunter (AAN) 68. Willard 71. A Reflection of Fear 73. The Outlaw Josey Wales 76. Death Game 76. The Gauntlet 77. Seducers 77. Shadow of Chikara 77. Every Which Way but Loose 78. Any Which Way You Can 80. Bronco Billy 80. Suzanne 80. Sudden Impact 83. Ratboy (& d) 86. Impulse (d) 90, etc.

Lockhart, Calvin (1934–).
West Indian leading man.
  A Dandy in Aspic 68. Joanna 68. Nobody Runs Forever 68. Leo the Last 70. Myra Breckinridge 70. Cotton Comes to Harlem 71. Melinda 72. The Beast Must Die 74. Uptown Saturday Night 74. Let's Do It Again 75. Three Days in Beirut 83. Wild at Heart 90, etc.

Lockhart, Gene (1891–1957).
Canadian character actor at home in genial or shifty parts. Also writer: in films since 1922.
  ■ Smilin' Through 22. The Gay Bride 34. Ah Wilderness 35. I've Been Around 35. Captain Hurricane 35. Star of Midnight 35. Thunder in the

Night 35. Storm over the Andes 35. Crime and Punishment 35. Brides Are Like That 35. Times Square Playboy 36. Earthworm Tractors 36. The First Baby 36. Career Woman 36. The Garden Murder Case 36. The Gorgeous Hussy 36. The Devil Is a Sissy 36. Wedding Present 36. Mind Your Own Business 36. Come Closer Folks 36. Mama Steps Out 37. Too Many Wives 37. Make Way for Tomorrow 37. The Sheik Steps Out 37. Something to Sing About 37. Of Human Hearts 38. Listen Darling 38. A Christmas Carol 38. Sweethearts 38. Penrod's Double Trouble 38. Men Are Such Fools 38. Blondie 38. *Algiers* (AAN) 38. Sinners in Paradise 38. Meet the Girls 38. I'm from Missouri 39. Hotel Imperial 39. Our Leading Citizen 39. Geronimo 39. Tell No Tales 39. Bridal Suite 39. Blackmail 39. The Story of Alexander Graham Bell 39. Edison the Man 40. Dr Kildare Goes Home 40. We Who Are Young 40. South of Pago Pago 40. A Dispatch from Reuters 40. *His Girl Friday* 40. Abe Lincoln in Illinois 40. Billy the Kid 41. Keeping Company 41. Meet John Doe 41. All That Money Can Buy 41. The Sea Wolf 41. One Foot in Heaven 41. Steel Against the Sky 41. International Lady 41. They Died with Their Boots On 41. Juke Girl 42. The Gay Sisters 42. You Can't Escape Forever 42. Forever and a Day 43. Mission to Moscow 43. Hangmen Also Die 43. Find the Blackmailer 43. The Desert Song 43. Madame Curie 43. Northern Pursuit 43. The White Cliffs of Dover 44. *Going My Way* 44. Action in Arabia 44. The Man from Frisco 44. *The House on 92nd Street* 45. Leave Her to Heaven 45. That's the Spirit 45. Meet Me on Broadway 46. A Scandal in Paris 46. She Wolf of London 46. The Strange Woman 46. The Shocking Miss Pilgrim 47. Miracle on 34th Street 47. The Foxes of Harrow 47. Cynthia 47. Honeymoon 47. Her Husband's Affairs 47. Joan of Arc 48. Inside Story 48. That Wonderful Urge 48. Apartment for Peggy 48. I Jane Doe 48. Down to the Sea in Ships 49. Madame Bovary 49. The Red Light 49. The Inspector General 49. Riding High 50. The Big Hangover 50. The Sickle and the Cross 51. I'd Climb the Highest Mountain 51. Rhubarb 51. The Lady from Texas 51. Hoodlum Empire 52. A Girl in Every Fort 52. Face to Face 52. Bonzo Goes to College 52. Androcles and the Lion 52. Apache War Smoke 52. Francis Covers the Big Town 53. Down Among the Sheltering Palms 53. Confidentially Connie 53. The Lady Wants Mink 53. World for Ransom 54. The Vanishing American 55. Carousel 56. The Man in the Grey Flannel Suit 56. Jeanne Eagels 57.

Lockhart, June (1925–).
American supporting actress, daughter of Gene.
  All This and Heaven Too 40. Meet Me in St Louis 44. Keep Your Powder Dry 45. Bury Me Dead 47. Time Limit 47. Lassie's Greatest Adventure 63. Death Valley Days (TV) 65. Lost in Space (TV) 65. Curse of the Black Widow (TV) 77. The Gift of Love (TV) 78. Walking through the Fire (TV) 79. Deadly Games 80. Strange Invaders 83. Troll 86. A Whisper Kills (TV) 88. Rented Lips 88. The Big Picture 89, etc.
  TV series: Lassie 55–64. Lost in Space 65–68.

Lockhart, Kathleen (1893–1978).
American character actress, widow of Gene Lockhart; known previously as Kathleen Arthur.
  The Devil is a Sissy 36. Sweethearts 38. All This and Heaven Too 41. Gentleman's Agreement 47. Plymouth Adventure 52. The Glenn Miller Story 54, many others.

Lockwood, Gary (1937–) (John Gary Yusolfsky).
American leading man of the 60s, mostly on TV.
  Splendour in the Grass 61. Wild in the Country

61. It Happened at the World's Fair 63. Firecreek 67. 2001: A Space Odyssey 68. The Model Shop 69. RPM 70. Stand Up and Be Counted 72. Bad Georgia Road 77. Survival Zone 84. The Wild Pair 87, etc.

TV series: Follow the Sun 61. The Lieutenant 63.

Lockwood, Harold (1887–1918).
American romantic lead of early silents, most often opposite May Allison (qv). He made more than 100 films before his early death from pneumonia.

Lockwood, Julia (1941–).
British leading lady, daughter of Margaret Lockwood.

My Teenage Daughter 56. Please Turn Over 59. No Kidding 60, etc.

Lockwood, Margaret (1916–1990) (Margaret Day).
Durable, indomitable British leading lady who was an appealing ingénue in the 30s, a rather boring star villainess in the 40s, and later a likeable character actress of stage and TV.

Autobiography: 1955, Lucky Star.

Biography: 1989, Once a Wicked Lady by Hilton Tims.

■ Lorna Doone 35. The Case of Gabriel Perry 35. Some Day 35. Honours Easy 35. Man of the Moment 35. Midshipman Easy 35. Jury's Evidence 36. The Amateur Gentleman 36. The Beloved Vagabond 36. Irish for Luck 36. The Street Singer 37. Who's Your Lady Friend? 37. Dr Syn 37. Melody and Romance 37. Owd Bob 38. Bank Holiday 38. The Lady Vanishes 38. A Girl Must Live 39. The Stars Look Down 39. Susannah of the Mounties (US) 39. Rulers of the Sea (US) 39. Night Train to Munich 40. The Girl in the News 40. Quiet Wedding 41. Alibi 42. The Man in Grey 43. Dear Octopus 43. Give Us the Moon 44. Love Story 44. A Place of One's Own 45. I'll Be Your Sweetheart 45. The Wicked Lady 45. Bedelia 46. Hungry Hill 46. Jassy 47. The White Unicorn 47. Look Before You Love 48. Cardboard Cavalier 49. Madness of the Heart 49. Highly Dangerous 50. Trent's Last Case 52. Laughing Anne 53. Trouble in the Glen 54. Cast a Dark Shadow 57. The Slipper and the Rose 76.

Loden, Barbara (1932–1980).
American general-purpose actress. She was married to director Elia Kazan.

Wild River 60. Splendor in the Grass 60, etc.
AS DIRECTOR: Wanda 72.

Loder, John (1898–1988) (John Lowe).
Handsome British leading man, in international films from 1927 after varied experience. Educated at Eton and Sandhurst, he was first a cavalry officer. He started as an extra in German films before being invited to Hollywood by Jesse Lasky of Paramount Pictures. His third wife was actress Hedy Lamarr. In the late 50s he became a cattle-rancher in Argentina.

Autobiography: 1977, Hollywood Hussar.

The First Born 29. Java Head 34. Lorna Doone 35. Murder Will Out 38. Meet Maxwell Archer 39. How Green Was My Valley 41. Now Voyager 42. Gentleman Jim 42. The Gorilla Man 42. Old Acquaintance 43. The Hairy Ape 44. The Brighton Strangler 45. A Game of Death 46. Wife of Monte Cristo 46. Dishonoured Lady 47. Woman and the Hunter 57. Gideon's Day 58, etc.

¶ Why is it that I'm not able
to get the roles they give Clark Gable?
They always say 'You have no name,

But when you have one, come again.'
By that time I'll be old and stiff,
A kind of poor man's Aubrey Smith. – J.L., 1940s
John Loder played the king as though he was afraid someone would play the ace at any moment. – Hannen Swaffer on Sing As We Go

Lodge, David (1921–).
British character actor, with music-hall and stage experience.

Autobiography: 1986, Up the Ladder to Obscurity.

Private's Progress 56. Two Way Stretch 60. The Dock Brief 61. Yesterday's Enemy 61. The Long Ships 63. Guns at Batasi 64. Catch Us If You Can 65. Press For Time 66. Corruption 69. Doctors Wear Scarlet 70. The Railway Children 71. Go For a Take 72. The Amazing Mr Blunden 72. The Return of the Pink Panther 74. The Revenge of the Pink Panther 78. Sahara 82, etc.

Much on TV.

Lodge, John (1903–1985).
American leading man of the 30s, mainly European films. Retired to take up politics.

A Woman Accused (debut) 32. Little Women 33. The Scarlet Empress 34. Koenigsmark 35. Sensation 36. The Tenth Man 36. Bulldog Drummond at Bay 37. Bank Holiday 38. L'Esclave Blanche 39.

¶ Mr John Lodge continues to suffer from a kind of lockjaw, an inability to move the tight muscles of his mouth, to do anything but glare with the dumbness and glossiness of an injured seal. – Graham Greene reviewing The Tenth Man

LoDuca, Joseph.
American composer.

The Evil Dead 83. Evil Dead 2 87. Army of Darkness 92. Necronomicon 93.

Loeb, Philip (1894–1955).
American character actor, usually of smart types.

Room Service 38. A Double Life 48. Molly 51, etc.

Loesser, Frank (1910–1969).
American songwriter, in films since 1930. He began as a lyricist; from 1947 he wrote both words and music.

College Swing 38. St Louis Blues 39. Destry Rides Again 39. Seven Sinners 40. Kiss the Boys Goodbye 41. Thank Your Lucky Stars 43. The Perils of Pauline 47. Neptune's Daughter 49. Let's Dance 50. Where's Charley? 52. Hans Christian Andersen 52. Guys and Dolls 55. How to Succeed in Business without Really Trying 66, etc.

Loew, Marcus (1870–1927).
Austrian-American exhibitor and distributor, co-founder and controller of MGM, which is still run by Loews Inc.

Loewe, Frederick (1901–1988).
Austrian composer in America, usually of musicals with Alan Jay Lerner.

Brigadoon 54. Gigi 58. My Fair Lady 64. Camelot 67. Paint Your Wagon 69. The Little Prince 74.

Loft, Arthur (1897–1947).
American supporting actor with a slightly bewildered face, often seen as businessman.

Prisoner of Shark Island 36. The Woman in the Window 45. Blood on the Sun 46. Scarlet Street 47, many others.

Lofting, Hugh (1886–1947).
English children's author, creator of the Doctor Dolittle stories, filmed as a musical starring Rex Harrison in 1967.

Loftus, Cecilia (1876–1943).
British character actress who went to Hollywood with a Shakespearean company in 1895, and stayed.

East Lynne 31. The Old Maid 39. The Bluebird 40. Lucky Partners 40. The Black Cat 41, etc.

Logan, Joshua (1908–1988).
American stage director whose occasional films tended towards stodginess.

Autobiographies: 1976, Josh, My Up and Down, In and Out Life. 1978, Movie Stars, Real People and Me.

■ I Met My Love Again 38. Picnic (AAN) 56. Bus Stop 56. Sayonara (AAN) 57. South Pacific 58. Tall Story 60. Fanny 61. Ensign Pulver 64. Camelot 67. Paint Your Wagon 69.

Logan, Phyllis (1956–).
Scottish-born actress, probably best known for her role as Lady Jane in the TV series Lovejoy.

Another Time Another Place (BFA) 83. 1984 84. The Chain 85. The McGuffin 85. The Inquiry 87. The Kitchen Toto 87. Silent Cries (TV) 93. Love and Reason (TV) 93, etc.

Logan, Robert F. (1941–).
Brawny hero of American family films.

The Bridge at Remagen 69. The Wilderness Family 75. Across the Great Divide 76. The Wilderness Family Part Two 77. Snowbeast (TV) 77. The Sea Gypsies 78. Death Ray 2000 81, etc.

Loggia, Robert (1930–).
American leading man.

Somebody Up There Likes Me 56. Cop Hater 58. The Nine Lives of Elfego Baca (TV) 59. Cattle King 63. Che! 69. The Moneychangers (TV) 75. First Love 77. The Ninth Configuration 80. S.O.B. 81. An Officer and a Gentleman 82. Trail of the Pink Panther 82. A Woman Called Golda (TV) 82. Curse of the Pink Panther 83. Scarface 83. Jagged Edge (AAN) 85. The Believers 87. Over the Top 87. Hot Pursuit 87. Big 88. Relentless 89. Triumph of the Spirit 89. Opportunity Knocks 90. The Marrying Man (aka Too Hot to Handle) 91. Necessary Roughness 91. Innocent Blood 92. Gladiator 93. Bad Girls 94. White Mile (TV) 94. I Love Trouble 94, etc.

TV series: T.H.E. Cat 66–67. Emerald Point N.A.S. 83–84. Mancuso F.B.I. 89. Wild Palms 93.

Lohr, Marie (1890–1975).
Distinguished Australian stage actress, on London stage from 1901; since 1930 in dowager roles.

Aren't We All? (debut) 32. Pygmalion 38. Major Barbara 40. The Winslow Boy 48. A Town Like Alice 56, many others.

Lollobrigida, Gina (1927–).
Italian glamour girl and international leading lady, in films since 1947.

Pagliacci 47. Fanfan la Tulipe 51. Belles de Nuit 52. The Wayward Wife 52. Bread, Love and Dreams 53. Beat the Devil 54. Le Grand Jeu 54. Trapeze 56. Where the Hot Wind Blows 58. Solomon and Sheba 59. Come September 61. Woman of Straw 64. Strange Bedfellows 65. Four Kinds of Love (Bambole) 65. Hotel Paradiso 66. Buona Sera, Mrs Campbell 68. Bad Man's River 71. King Queen Knave 72. The Lonely Woman 76. La Romana 88, many others.

TV series: Falcon Crest 84.

Lom, Herbert (1917–) (Herbert Charles Angelo Kuchacevich ze Schluderpacheru).
Czech actor whose personality adapts itself equally well to villainy or kindliness; in Britain from 1939.

Mein Kampf 40. The Young Mr Pitt (as Napoleon) 41. The Dark Tower 43. Hotel Reserve 44. *The Seventh Veil* 46. Night Boat to Dublin 46. *Dual Alibi* 47. Good Time Girl 48. The Golden Salamander 49. *State Secret* 50. The Black Rose 50. Hell Is Sold Out 51. The Ringer 52. The Net 53. The Love Lottery 54. *The Ladykillers* 55. War and Peace (as Napoleon) 56. Chase a Crooked Shadow 57. Hell Drivers 57. No Trees in the Street 58. Roots of Heaven 58. Northwest Frontier 59. I Aim at the Stars (US) 59. Mysterious Island 61. El Cid 61. Phantom of the Opera (title role) 62. A Shot in the Dark 64. Return from the Ashes 65. Uncle Tom's Cabin (Ger.) 65. Gambit 66. Assignment to Kill 67. Villa Rides 68. Doppelgänger 69. The Hot Death (Ger.) 69. Murders in the Rue Morgue 71. Asylum 72. And Now the Screaming Starts 73. The Return of the Pink Panther 74. And Then There Were None 75. The Pink Panther Strikes Again 77. Revenge of the Pink Panther 78. Charleston 78. The Lady Vanishes 79. Hopscotch 80. The Man with Bogart's Face 80. Trail of the Pink Panther 82. Curse of the Pink Panther 83. The Dead Zone 83. Memed My Hawk 84. King Solomon's Mines 85. Whoops Apocalypse 86. Scoop (TV) 87. The Crystal Eye 88. River of Death 89. Ten Little Indians 89. The Sect 91. The Pope Must Die (US: The Pope Must Diet) 91. Son of the Pink Panther 93, etc.

TV series: *The Human Jungle.*

Lomas, Herbert (1887–1961).
Gaunt, hollow-voiced British stage actor.
The Sign of Four 32. Lorna Doone 35. Rembrandt 36. Jamaica Inn 39. Ask a Policeman 39. *The Ghost Train* 41. I Know Where I'm Going 45. Bonnie Prince Charlie 48. The Net 53, etc.

Lombard, Carole (1908–1942) (Jane Peters).
American leading lady of the 30s, a fine comedienne with an inimitable rangy style. Married Clark Gable. Died in a plane crash.
Biography: 1976, Screwball by Larry Swindell.
■ A Perfect Crime 21. Hearts and Spurs 25. Marriage in Transit 25. Me Gangster 28. Power 28. Show Folks 28. Ned McCobb's Daughter 29. High Voltage 29. Big News 29. The Racketeer 29. The Arizona Kid 30. Safety in Numbers 30. Fast and Loose 30. It Pays to Advertise 31. Man of the World 31. Ladies' Man 31. Up Pops the Devil 31. I Take This Woman 31. No One Man 32. Sinners in the Sun 32. Virtue 32. No More Orchids 32. *No Man of Her Own* 32. From Heaven to Hell 33. Supernatural 33. The Eagle and the Hawk 33. Brief Moment 33. White Woman 33. *Bolero* 34. We're Not Dressing 34. *Twentieth Century* 34. Now and Forever 34. Lady by Choice 34. The Gay Bride 34. *Rumba* 34. Hands across the Table 35. Love before Breakfast 36. *My Man Godfrey* (AAN) 36. The Princess Comes Across 36. Swing High Swing Low 37. True Confession 37. *Nothing Sacred* 37. Fools for Scandal 38. Made for Each Other 38. In Name Only 39. Vigil in the Night 40. *They Knew What They Wanted* 40. Mr and Mrs Smith 41. To Be or Not To Be 42.
✪ For daring to be wacky while glamorous. *Nothing Sacred.*

¶ I live by a man's code designed to fit a man's world, yet at the same time I never forget that a woman's first job is to choose the right shade of lipstick. – C.L.
Carole was the first woman I ever met who used four-letter words like a truck driver. – *Radie Harris*

Lombard, Karina.
American actress, of Swiss and Indian parents, in sultry roles. A former model, she is married to actor Anthony Crane.
Wide Sargasso Sea 93. The Firm 93. Legends of the Fall 94, etc.

Lombardi, Francisco José (1950–).
Leading Peruvian director, producer and screenwriter of films on social and political themes, a former movie critic.
Muerte al Amanecer 77. Maruja en el Infierno 83. *The City and the Dogs* (La Ciudad y los Perros) 85. The Lion's Den (La Boca del Lobo) 88. Fallen from the Sky (Caidos del Cielo) (& co-w) 90. Traces from Paradise (Huellas del Paraiso) (& co-w) 92. Sin Compasión 94, etc.

Lombardo, Louis.
American film editor and occasional director.
The Wild Bunch 69. The Ballad of Cable Hogue 69. Brewster McCloud 70. McCabe and Mrs Miller 71. Thieves Like Us 73. The Long Goodbye 73. California Split 74. The Black Bird 75. Russian Roulette (d) 75. All the President's Men 76. The Late Show 77. The Changeling 78. Just One of the Guys 85. P.K and the Kid (d) 87. Moonstruck 87. January Man 89. Uncle Buck 89. Defenceless 90. Other People's Money 91, etc.

Lommel, Ulli (1944–).
German-born director, screenwriter and cinematographer who began by working as an actor with Rainer Werner Fassbinder, remade Fritz Lang's M with Fassbinder producing, and then went to America to direct low-budget gore-filled horror movies.
Whity (a) 70. The American Soldier (Der Amerikanische Soldat) (a) 70. The Tenderness of Wolves (Die Zartlickeit der Wolfe) (d) 73. Fontane Effi Briest (a) 74. Chinesisches Roulette (a) 76. Satan's Brew (Satansbraten) (a) 76. Adolf und Marlene (wd) 77. Cocaine Cowboys 79. The Boogey Man (a, d) 80. A Taste of Sin (co-w, d, ph) 83. Brainwaves (& ph) 83. The Demonsville Terror (co-w, d, ph) 83. Defense Play 86. Overkill 86. Warbirds (co-w, d) 88. Natural Instinct (p,d) 91. The Big Sweat 91, etc.

Loncraine, Richard (1946–).
British director.
Flame 74. Full Circle 76. Blade on the Feather (TV) 80. Brimstone and Treacle 82. The Missionary 84. Bellman and True 87. The Wedding Gift (TV) 94, etc.

London
has provided a background, usually highly inaccurate, for innumerable movies, but few have really explored it, though *The Ipcress File* and *The Pumpkin Eater* found some unusual angles. *London Town* was a half-hearted musical; twenty years later *Three Hats for Lisa* captured the mood better but managed to seem old-fashioned. *Pygmalion* and *My Fair Lady* embodied the spirit of London in some theatrical sets. *Indiscreet* prowled lovingly around the Embankment, and *A Run for Your Money* made good use of the Paddington area as well as suburban Twickenham. The City was the venue of part of *You Must Be Joking,* while *Morgan* used Hampstead to good advantage. The East End, especially the street markets and the railway sidings, were exploited in *Waterloo Road, A Kid for Two Farthings* and *It Always Rains on Sunday.* The docks had *Pool of London* to themselves. Hollywood's idea of London in geography can be pretty weird, as in *Knock on Wood,* when Paramount went to the trouble of having special location material shot with Jon Pertwee doubling for Danny Kaye, but showed the star turning off Marble Arch into Fleet Street two miles away. Similarly in *Twenty-three Paces to Baker Street* the river frontage of the Savoy Hotel could be entered from Portman Square, in actuality another two-mile jaunt. London fog has been a useful cover for many a scrappy set, especially in films presenting the Victorian London associated with Sherlock Holmes. Going further back, *Henry V* presented in model form the London of 1600, and attempts at historical recreation were also made in *Tower of London, Fire over England, Elizabeth and Essex, Nell Gwyn, Forever Amber, Mrs Fitzherbert, The First Gentleman, Victoria the Great, Cromwell* and *The Mudlark.* It was probably Hitchcock who began the fashion of making London a stately background for thrillers, with his East End mission in *The Man Who Knew Too Much,* the music hall in *The Thirty-nine Steps,* the bus journey and the Lord Mayor's Show in *Sabotage,* the fall from Westminister Cathedral in *Foreign Correspondent,* the theatrical garden party in *Stage Fright,* and Covent Garden in *Frenzy.* Others in this tradition have included *Brannigan, Hennessy, Villain, Robbery,* and innumerable TV series such as *The Sweeney.*
See also: *Swinging London.*

London Films.
Production company founded by Alexander Korda and associated with his own major films of the 30s and later with other leading names operating under his banner.

London, Jack (1876–1916).
American adventure novelist, whose most-filmed stories include *The Sea Wolf, Adventures of Martin Eden, Call of the Wild* and *White Fang.*

London, Julie (1926–) (Julie Peck).
American leading lady and singer. She was married to actor and director Jack Webb (1945–53).
Jungle Woman 44. The Red House 47. The Fat Man 51. The Great Man 56. Saddle the Wind 58. Man of the West 58. The Third Voice 60. The George Raft Story 62, etc.
TV series: *Emergency* 72–77.

London, Roy (1943–1993).
American director, screenwriter, playwright and actor who was also a noted acting coach.
Hardcore (a) 79. Jake Speed (a) 86. Rampage (a) 87. Tiger Warsaw (w) 88. Diary of a Hitman (d) 92, etc.

Lone, John (1952–).
Hong Kong-born leading actor, in America, who also makes pop records aimed at the Asian market.
Iceman 84. Year of the Dragon 85. Echoes of Paradise (aka Shadows of the Peacock) 86. The Last Emperor 87. The Moderns 88. Shadow of China 91. M. Butterfly 93. The Shadow 94, etc.

¶ I don't want to stand behind someone and look important and inscrutable. I don't do Fu Manchu. – J.L.

The Lone Ranger.
This western Robin Hood originally featured in a radio serial and later became a comic strip in 1935; 20 years later Clayton Moore played the hero in a successful TV series and a couple of feature films, with Jay Silverheels as Tonto. The 1981 attempt to retell the tale half seriously, *The Legend of the Lone Ranger,* met with disaster: Klinton Spilsbury

was the Lone Ranger and has not been heard of since.

The Lone Wolf,

a gentleman thief (Michael Lanyard), was created by Louis Joseph Vance and reached the screen in silent days played by H. B. Warner, Jack Holt, and Bert Lytell; in the 30s Melvyn Douglas and Francis Lederer each played him once and then Warren William took over for eight episodes, usually with Eric Blore as his manservant. In 1946 Gerald Mohr played in the first of three episodes, and in 1949 Ron Randell personified him for the last time on the big screen. In 1954 Louis Hayward played him in a TV series, *The Lone Wolf* (aka *Streets of Danger*).

Long, Audrey (1924–).
American leading lady of the 40s.
A Night of Adventure 44. Pan Americana 45. Song of My Heart 47. The Petty Girl 50. Indian Uprising 52, etc.

Long, Huey (1893–1935).
American politician, governor of Louisiana and US senator with presidential ambitions, who was assassinated. He was the model for Willie Stark, the corrupt Southern protagonist of Robert Penn Warren's novel *All the King's Men*, which was filmed with Broderick Crawford in the leading role. Kingfish, a film of his life made for cable TV, starred John Goodman in 1995. He was the brother of Earl Long, governor of Louisiana in the 50s, whose affair with a stripper was commemorated in the movie *Blaze* 89, starring Paul Newman.

Long, Richard (1927–1974).
American leading man, mainly in second features.
Tomorrow Is Forever 44. The Stranger 45. The Egg and I 47. Criss Cross 49. Saskatchewan 54. Cult of the Cobra 55. Home from the Hills 59. The Tenderfoot 64, etc.
TV series: *77 Sunset Strip* 58–60. *Bourbon Street Beat* 59. *The Big Valley* 65–68. *Nanny and the Professor* 69–71. Thicker Than Water 73.

Long, Shelley (1949–).
American leading lady.
Irreconcilable Differences 84. The Money Pit 85. Outrageous Fortune 87. Hello Again 87. Troop Beverly Hills 89. Don't Tell Her It's Me 90. Frozen Assets 92, etc.
TV series: Cheers 82–87.

long shot.
One taken from a distance, usually to establish a scene or a situation but sometimes for dramatic effect. Opposite of close-up.

Long, Walter (1879–1952).
Tough-looking American character actor, usually as a villain, in films from 1909. He was a regular in D. W. Griffith's films and blacked up to play the rapist who chases Mae Marsh to her death in *The Birth of a Nation*. He appeared in several Laurel and Hardy films, notably as a convict in *Pardon Us*, ending his career opposite Ken Maynard and William Boyd in westerns and, in *Man's Country*, playing twin baddies.
The Birth of a Nation 15. Intolerance 16. Joan the Woman 17. The Little American 17. Scarlet Days 18. The Sheik 21. Blood and Sand 22. Moran of the Lady Letty 22. The Call of the Wild 23. Little Church round the Corner 23. Raffles 25. Soul-Fire 25. Yankee Clipper 27. Me, Gangster 28. Moby Dick 30. The Maltese Falcon 31. Sea Devils 31. Pardon Us 31. Any Old Port 32. I Am a Fugitive from a Chain Gang 32. The Thin Man 34. The Live Ghost 34. Going Bye-Bye! 34. Naughty

Marietta 35. North of the Rio Grande 37. The Painted Trail 38. Man's Country 38. Six Shootin' Sheriff 38. Union Pacific 39. Flaming Lead 39. Silver Stallion 41. Wabash Avenue 50, etc.

Longden, John (1900–1971).
British leading man of the early 30s; later graduated to character roles.
Blackmail 30. Atlantic 30. The Ringer 31. Born Lucky 33. French Leave 37. The Gaunt Stranger 38. The Lion Has Wings 39. The Common Touch 41. The Silver Fleet 43. Bonnie Prince Charlie 48. The Man with the Twisted Lip (as Sherlock Homes) 51. Quatermass II 56. An Honourable Murder 60, many others.

Longden, Terence (1922–).
British actor, in secondary roles.
Never Look Back 52. Simon and Laura 55. Doctor at Large 57. Carry On Sergeant 58. Ben Hur 59. The Return of Mr Moto 65. The Wild Geese 78. The Sea Wolves 80, etc.

Longo, Robert.
American director and artist.
Johnny Mnemonic 95.

Longstreet, Stephen (1907–).
American screenwriter.
The Jolson Story 46. The Greatest Show on Earth (co-w) 52. The First Traveling Saleslady 55. The Helen Morgan Story 57, etc.

Lonsdale, Michel (1931–) (sometimes Michael).
Chubby French character actor, in some international roles.
La Main Chaude 60. The Trial 62. Behold a Pale Horse 64. The Bride Wore Black 68. Stolen Kisses 68. Souffle au Coeur 71. *The Day of the Jackal* 73. Stavisky 74. Caravan to Vaccares 74. The Phantom of Liberty 74. The Romantic Englishwoman 75. The Pink Telephone 75. Mr Klein 76. The Passage 78. Moonraker 79. Les Jeux de la Comtesse 80. Enigma 82. The Name of the Rose 86. Souvenir 88. The Remains of the Day 93, many others.

Loo, Richard (1903–1983).
Hawaiian-Chinese actor who turned to films after business depression. Played hundreds of oriental roles.
Dirigible 31. The Good Earth 37. The Keys of the Kingdom 44. Rogues' Regiment 48. Love is a Many-Splendored Thing 54. The Quiet American 58. The Sand Pebbles 66. One More Time 71, etc.

lookalikes.
The old studios would frequently hire less talented performers who looked rather like their main stars, simply to keep the latter in order. Also, if a star with a certain style proved fashionable, a rival might try to repeat the dose. Whatever the reason, Gloria Jean was designed to remind filmgoers of Deanna Durbin; John Carroll of Clark Gable; Anna Sten of Marlene Dietrich; Brian Aherne of Ronald Colman; Patric Knowles of Errol Flynn; Dane Clark of John Garfield; Antonio Moreno and Ricardo Cortez of Rudolph Valentino; Viveca Lindfors of Ingrid Bergman; Roddy McDowall of Freddie Bartholomew; John Gavin of Rock Hudson; Gig Young of Cary Grant; Lizabeth Scott of Lauren Bacall; Mary Beth Hughes of Lana Turner; Yvonne de Carlo of Maria Montez; Mamie Van Doren and Sheree North of Marilyn Monroe; Joel McCrea of Gary Cooper; Tippi Hedren of Grace Kelly. Not too surprisingly, lightning never struck in the same place twice.

Looney Tunes/Merrie Melodies
are the umbrella titles under which Warners have long released their cartoon shorts featuring such characters as Bugs Bunny, Daffy Duck, Porky Pig, Pepe le Pew, Sylvester and Tweetie Pie. They have won Academy Awards for *Tweetie Pie* 47, *For Scentimental Reasons* 49, *Speedy Gonzales* 55, *Birds Anonymous* 57, *Knighty Knight Bugs* 58.

Loos, Anita (1891–1981).
American humorous writer who spent years in Hollywood studios.
Autobiographies 1966, *A Girl Like I*. 1974, *Kiss Hollywood Goodbye*. 1977, *Cast of Thousands*. Also wrote *The Talmadge Girls* (1977).
Biography: 1988, *Anita Loos* by Gary Carey.
Intolerance (subtitles) 16. Let's Get a Divorce (w) 18. A Temperamental Wife (oa) 19. Mama's Affair (d) 20. In Search of a Sinner (p) 20. Red Hot Romance (w) 22. Learning to Love (w) 25. Gentlemen Prefer Blondes (oa) 28. Midnight Mary (oa) 33. *San Francisco* (w) 36. Saratoga (w) 37. The Women (w) 39. When Ladies Meet (oa) 41. *Gentlemen Prefer Blondes* (oa) 53, etc.

Lopez, Trini (1937–).
American character actor, ex-bandleader.
Marriage on the Rocks 66. The Dirty Dozen 67. Antonio 73, etc.

Loquasto, Santo (1944–).
American production designer, from the stage, often on Woody Allen's films.
Rancho Deluxe 75. Stardust Memories 80. The Fan 81. So Fine 81. Falling in Love 84. Desperately Seeking Susan 85. Radio Days (AAN) 87. September 87. Big 88. Another Woman 88. Bright Lights, Big City 88. New York Stories 89. Crimes and Misdemeanors 89. She-Devil 89. Alice 90. Shadows and Fog 92. Manhattan Murder Mystery 93. Bullets over Broadway 94, etc.

Lord, Del (1895–1970).
American second-feature director who handled most of *The Three Stooges* shorts.

Lord, Jack (1928–) (John Joseph Ryan).
Craggy-faced American leading man who found his greatest success in television.
Cry Murder 51. The Court Martial of Billy Mitchell 55. God's Little Acre 58. Walk Like a Dragon 60. Doctor No 62. The Road to Hangman's Tree 67. The Name of the Game Is Kill 68. M Station: Hawaii (d) (TV) 80, etc.
TV series: *Stony Burke* 62. *Hawaii Five-O* 68–79.

Lord, Jean-Claude (1943–).
Canadian director.
■ Eclair au Chocolat 79. Visiting Hours 82. Dreamworld 83. Covergirl 84. The Vindicator (aka Frankenstein '88) 85. Toby McTeague 85. Tadpole and the Whale 88. Mindfield 89.

Lord, Marjorie (1922–).
American leading lady of minor films in the 40s, later on TV as Danny Thomas' wife in comedy series. She is the mother of Anne Archer.
Forty Naughty Girls 38. Timber 42. Sherlock Holmes in Washington 42. Flesh and Fantasy 44. The Argyle Secrets 48. New Orleans 49. Port of Hell 55. Boy Did I Get a Wrong Number 66, etc.
TV series: Make Room for Daddy 53–57. Make Room for Granddaddy 70.

Lord, Pauline (1890–1950).
American stage actress who made only two films.
■ Mrs Wiggs of the Cabbage Patch 35. A Feather in Her Hat 36.

Lord, Robert (1900–1976).
American writer and producer associated with
Warner Brothers throughout the 30s and 40s; later
joined Humphrey Bogart in Santana Productions.
AS WRITER: The Johnstown Flood 26. A Reno
Divorce 27. My Man 28. Five and Ten Cent Annie
28. On with the Show 29. Gold Diggers of
Broadway 29. Hold Everything 30. Fireman Save
My Child 32. One Way Passage (AA) 32.·20,000
Years in Sing Sing 32. The Little Giant 33. Dames
34. Page Miss Glory 35, etc.
AS PRODUCER: Wonder Bar 34. Oil for the Lamps
of China 35. Black Legion 37. Tovarich 37.
Brother Rat 38. The Dawn Patrol 38. Dodge City
39. Confessions of a Nazi Spy 39. The Letter 40.
Dive Bomber 41. High Wall 47. Tokyo Joe 49. In
a Lonely Place 50. Sirocco 51, etc.

Lords, Traci (1968–) (Nora Louise Kuzma).
American actress, a former star of pornographic
films who made the transition to low-budget
features in the late 80s.
  Not of This Earth 88. Fast Food 89. Shock 'Em
Dead 90. Cry-Baby 90. Raw Nerve 91. A Time to
Die 91. Laser Moon 92. Skinner 93. The
Tommyknockers (TV) 93. Ice 94. Serial Mom 94.
Plughead Rewired: Circuitry Man II 94, etc.

Loren, Sophia (1934–) (Sophia Scicoloni).
Statuesque Italian leading lady, latterly an
accomplished international actress. In films from
1950 (as extra).
  Autobiography: 1979, Sophia: Living and Loving
(with A. E. Hotchner).
  Biography: 1975, Sophia by Donald Zec.
  Aida 53. The Sign of Venus 53. Tempi Nostri 54.
Attila 54. The Gold of Naples 54. Woman of the River
55. Too Bad She's Bad 55. The Miller's Wife 55.
Scandal in Sorrento 55. Lucky To Be a Woman
56. The Pride and the Passion 57. Boy on a Dolphin
57. Legend of the Lost 57. Desire under the Elms
58. The Key 58. Houseboat 58. Black Orchid 59.
That Kind of Woman 59. Heller in Pink Tights 60.
A Breath of Scandal 61. Two Women (AA, BFA) 61.
The Millionairess 61. El Cid 61. Boccaccio 70 61. The
Condemned of Altona 62. Madame Sans Gêne 62.
Five Miles to Midnight 62. Yesterday, Today and
Tomorrow 63. The Fall of the Roman Empire 64.
Marriage Italian Style (AAN) 64. Operation
Crossbow 65. Judith 65. Arabesque 66. Lady L 66.
A Countess from Hong Kong 66. Ghosts Italian Style
68. More Than a Miracle 69. Sunflower 70. Man
of La Mancha 72. Lady Liberty 74. Brief
Encounter (TV) 74. The Voyage 75. The Cassandra
Crossing 77. A Special Day 77. Brass Target 78.
Firepower 79. Angela 80. Sophia Loren (TV) 80.
Aurora (TV) 84. Courage (TV) 86. The Fortunate
Pilgrim (TV) 88. Running Away 89. Saturday,
Sunday and Monday (Sabato, Domenica e
Lunedi) 90. Prêt-à-Porter 94, etc.

¶ Everything you see, I owe to spaghetti. – S.L.
  Sex appeal is fifty per cent what you've got
and fifty per cent what people think you've got.
– S.L.
  I'm not ashamed of my bare-bottomed
beginnings. – S.L.
  In a restaurant or at a function I just walk
straight in and it's an eternity. When I'm sitting,
it's OK, but then I have to start thinking of a short
cut out. – S.L.
  All the natural mistakes of beauty fall together
in her to create a magnificent accident. – Rex Reed
  Working with her is like being bombed by
watermelons. – Alan Ladd

Lorentz, Pare (1905–1992).
American documentarist and film critic.

  The Plow that Broke the Plains 36. The River 37.
The Fight for Life 40. The Nuremberg Trials 46.

Lorenz, Juliane (1957–).
German editor, associated with the films of
Fassbinder from the mid-70s to the early 80s.
  Chinese Roulette 76. Despair 78. The Third
Generation (Die Dritte Generation) 79. Berlin
Alexanderplatz (TV) 80. The Marriage of Maria
Braun 79. Querelle 82. The Rose King 86. The
Night of the Mareten 87. Malina 90, etc.

Lorimer, Glennis (1913–).
English actress of the stage and screen in the 30s
who impersonated Thomas Gainsborough's portrait
of actress Sarah Siddons in the trademark of
Gainsborough Pictures, a company co-owned by
her father, Henry Ostrer.
  The Ringer 31. There Goes the Bride 32.
Britannia of Billingsgate 33. My Old Dutch 34.
Rhodes of Africa 36. Alf 's Button Afloat 38. Ask
a Policeman 39, etc.

Lorne, Marion (1886–1968) (M. L. MacDougal).
American character comedienne with long stage
experience, latterly seen as eccentric old lady.
  Strangers on a Train 51. The Girl Rush 55. The
Graduate 68, etc.
  TV series: Mr Peepers 52–54. Bewitched (as the
dotty witch-aunt) 64–67.

Lorre, Peter (1904–1964) (Laszlo Loewenstein).
Highly individual Hungarian character actor who
filmed in Germany and Britain before settling in
Hollywood. His rolling eyes, timid manner and
mysterious personality could adapt to either
sympathetic or sinister roles; a weight problem
restricted his later appearances.
■ Frühlings Erwachen 29. Der Weisse Teufel 30.
Die Koffer des Herrn O.F. 30. M 30. Bomben auf
Monte Carlo 31. Fünf von der Jazzband 32. Schuss
im Morgengrauen 32. Der Weisse Dämon 32.
F.P.I. 32. Was Frauen Träumen 33. Unsichtbare
Gegner 33. De Haut en Bas 34. The Man Who Knew
Too Much 34. Mad Love 35. Crime and Punishment
(as Raskolnikov) 35. The Secret Agent 36. Crack Up
36. Nancy Steele is Missing 37. Lancer Spy 37.
Think Fast Mr Moto 37. Thank You Mr Moto 37.
Mr Moto's Gamble 38. I'll Give a Million 38. Mr
Moto Takes a Chance 38. Mysterious Mr Moto
38. Mr Moto on Danger Island 39. Mr Moto Takes
a Vacation 39. Mr Moto's Last Warning 39. Strange
Cargo 40. I Was an Adventuress 40. Island of
Doomed Men 40. Stranger on the Third Floor 40.
You'll Find Out 40. Mr District Attorney 41. The
Face Behind the Mask 41. They Met in Bombay 41.
The Maltese Falcon 41. All through the Night 42.
Invisible Agent 42. The Boogie Man Will Get You
42. Casablanca 42. Background to Danger 43. The
Cross of Lorraine 43. The Constant Nymph 43.
Passage to Marseilles 44. The Mask of Dimitrios 44.
Arsenic and Old Lace 44. The Conspirators 44.
Hollywood Canteen 44. Hotel Berlin 45.
Confidential Agent 45. Three Strangers 46. Black
Angel 46. The Chase 46. The Verdict 46. The Beast
with Five Fingers 46. My Favorite Brunette 47.
Casbah 48. Rope of Sand 49. Quicksand 50. Double
Confession 50. Der Verlorene (& d) 50. Beat the
Devil 53. 20,000 Leagues under the Sea 54. Congo
Crossing 56. Around the World in Eighty Days 56.
The Buster Keaton Story 56. Silk Stockings 57. The
Story of Mankind (as Nero) 57. Hell Ship Mutiny
57. The Sad Sack 58. The Big Circus 59. Scent of
Mystery 59. Voyage to the Bottom of the Sea 61.
Tales of Terror 62. Five Weeks in a Balloon 62. The
Raven 63. The Comedy of Terrors 63. The Patsy
64.
☻ For the diffidence of his dark deeds and for his

inimitable voice, still enthusiastically parodied by
cartoon villains. The Mask of Dimitrios.

¶ Those marbly pupils in the pasty spherical face
  are like the eye pieces of a microscope through
which you can see laid flat on the slide the
entangled mind of a man: love and lust, nobility
and perversity, hatred of itself, and despair
jumping up at you from the jelly. – Graham Greene

Lorring, Joan (1926–) (Magdalen Ellis).
English-Russian actress, evacuated to US in 1939;
played some nasty teenagers.
  Girls under Twenty-One 41. Song of Russia 44.
The Bridge of San Luis Rey 44. The Corn Is Green
(AAN) 45. The Verdict 46. The Lost Moment 47.
Good Sam 49. Stranger on the Prowl 53. The
Midnight Man 74, etc.
  TV series: Norby 54.

Los Angeles,
being the home of the film studios, was the
anonymous background of ninety per cent of
Hollywood films from the very beginning. Only
more recently, however, has the actual city been
explored, usually in a cynical Chandleresque
manner as in The Long Goodbye and Marlowe, or as
a vivid sunlit background for police thrillers with
their screaming car chases, especially in such TV
series as Police Story, The Blue Knight, Police Woman,
The Rookies, Chase, Emergency, The Smith Family and
Dragnet. The city's seamy side was shown in M and
The Savage Eye, its future in The Omega Man, its
sophisticated present in Divorce American Style, L.A.
Story and Grand Canyon, its sewers in Them, and
its past in Chinatown. Perhaps the most vivid
picture of the growing sprawl is to be found as
background to the comedies of the Keystone Kops
and Laurel and Hardy; and Earthquake finally
destroyed it.
  One positive approach to Tinseltown was
expressed in The Model Shop: 'How could you find
this place ugly? It's pure poetry.'

Losch, Tilly (1901–1975).
Austrian exotic dancer, in Hollywood in the 30s
and 40s.
■ The Garden of Allah 36. The Good Earth 37.
Duel in the Sun 46.

Losey, Joseph (1909–1984).
American director of somewhat pretentious
movies, in Britain from 1952 after the communist
witch-hunt.
  Biographies: 1991, Joseph Losey by Edith Rham.
1994, Joseph Losey: A Revenge on Life by David
Caute.
■ The Boy with Green Hair 48. The Lawless 50.
The Prowler 50. M 51. The Big Night 51. Stranger
on the Prowl 53. The Sleeping Tiger 54. The
Intimate Stranger 56. Time without Pity 57. The
Gypsy and the Gentleman 57. Blind Date 59. The
Criminal 60. The Damned 61. Eva 62. The Servant 63.
King and Country 64. Modesty Blaise 66. Accident
67. Boom 68. Secret Ceremony 68. Figures in a
Landscape 70. The Go-Between 71. The
Assassination of Trotsky 72. A Doll's House 73.
Galileo 74. The Romantic Englishwoman 75. Mr
Klein 76. Don Giovanni 79. The Trout 82. Steaming
84.

¶ Films can illustrate our existence . . . they can
  distress, disturb and provoke people into
thinking about themselves and certain problems.
But NOT give the answers. – J.L.

Lost Horizon.
James Hilton's novel about a Tibetan Utopia was

urned into an uneven but attractive film in 1937 by Frank Capra, which made Shangri-La a household word. In 1973 Ross Hunter remade the story as a semi-musical with unhappy results.

Lost Patrol.
Philip MacDonald's story, about a British desert patrol being picked off one by one by Arabs until rescuers find one survivor raving mad, has inspired many war films since John Ford's 1934 version with heavily overacted but enjoyable performances from Victor McLaglen, Boris Karloff, and Reginald Denney. A Russian version, *The Thirteen*, was made in 1937, and Zoltan Korda's 1943 *Sahara*, starring Humphrey Bogart, gave the story a cast of Allied soldiers facing an overwhelming Nazi force. It was also the inspiration for *Bataan* 46 and *Last of the Comanches* 51.

Lotinga, Ernie (1876–1951)
British vaudeville comedian who began his career as a comic vocalist under the name of Dan Roe in 1898. During the early 1900s he was a member of the Six Brothers Luck in music hall before creating the slapstick character Jimmy Josser that made him a star until the mid-20s. He continued the character in some broadly comic movies that had their followers in the 30s. He was married to music-hall performer and male impersonator Hetty King.
Joining Up 28. Nap 28. The Raw Recruit 28. Dr Josser, K.C. (& co-w) 31. P.C. Josser 31. Josser Joins the Navy 32. Josser in the Army 32. Josser on the River 32. Josser on the Farm 34. Smith's Wives (& story) 35. Love up the Pole 36, etc.

Louis-Dreyfus, Julia (1960–   )
American actress, from television's *Saturday Night Live*.
Soul Man 86. Hannah and Her Sisters 86. National Lampoon's Christmas Vacation 89. Jack the Bear 93. North 94, etc.

Louise, Anita (1915–1970) (Anita Louise Fremault).
American leading lady, usually in gentle roles. Played child parts from 1924.
What a Man 30. A Midsummer Night's Dream 35. The Story of Louis Pasteur 35. Anthony Adverse 36. The Green Light 37. Marie Antoinette 38. The Sisters 39. Phantom Submarine 41. The Fighting Guardsman 45. The Bandit of Sherwood Forest 46. Retreat, Hell! 52.
TV series: *My Friend Flicka* 56.

Louise, Tina (1934–   ) (Tina Blacker).
Statuesque American leading lady of routine films.
God's Little Acre 58. Day of the Outlaw 59. Armored Command 61. For Those Who Think Young 64. Wrecking Crew 68. The Good Guys and the Bad Guys 69. How to Commit Marriage 70. The Stepford Wives 75. Mean Dog Blues 78. The Day the Women Got Even 80. Hellriders 84. Evils of the Night 85. O.C. & Stiggs 87. Dixie Lanes 88. Johnny Suede 91, etc.
TV series: *Gilligan's Island* 64–66. Dallas 78. Rituals 84–85.

Lourié, Eugène (1905–1991).
French designer.
Les Bas Fonds 36. *La Grande Illusion* 37. La Règle du Jeu 39. This Land Is Mine (US) 42. *The Southerner* (US) 44. The River 51. What's the Matter with Helen 71. Burnt Offerings 76. Bronco Billy 80, etc.
AS DIRECTOR: The Beast from Twenty Thousand Fathoms 53. The Colossus of New York 58. Gorgo (GB) 60, etc.

Love Affair.
The story of two people agreeing, and failing, to meet at the top of the Empire State Building after six months apart to discover if their love remains strong was first filmed by Leo McCarey in 1939 with Irene Dunne and Charles Boyer; in 1957, again directed by Leo McCarey, it became the weepie *An Affair to Remember*, with Cary Grant and Deborah Kerr (which also featured in the 1993 hit *Sleepless in Seattle*); in 1994, as *Love Affair*, it became a vehicle for the husband and wife team of Warren Beatty and Annette Bening.

Love, Bessie (1898–1986) (Juanita Horton).
Vivacious, petite American leading lady of the 20s. In films from childhood; from the mid-30s resident in London, playing occasional cameo parts.
Autobiography: 1977, *From Hollywood with Love*.
Intolerance 15. The Aryan 16. A Sister of Six 17. The Dawn of Understanding 18. The Purple Dawn 20. The Vermilion Pencil 21. Human Wreckage 23. Dynamite Smith 24. The Lost World 25. Lovey Mary 26. Sally of the Scandals 27. Broadway Melody (AAN) 28. Chasing Rainbows 30. Morals for Women 31. Conspiracy 32. Atlantic Ferry 42. Journey Together 45. Touch and Go 55. The Wild Affair 64. Isadora 68. Sunday Bloody Sunday 71. Mousey (TV) 74. The Ritz 76, many others.

Love, Darlene (1938–   ) (Darlene Wright).
American character actress and singer. Born in Los Angeles, she sang with The Blossoms and was lead vocalist on 'He's a Rebel' and other hit singles made by Phil Spector in the 60s. On film, she is familiar as Danny Glover's wife in the *Lethal Weapon* series.
Lethal Weapon 88. Lethal Weapon 2 89. Lethal Weapon 3 92.

Love, Montagu (1877–1943).
Heavily built British character actor, long in Hollywood, latterly as stern fathers.
Bought and Paid For 16. The Gilded Cage 19. The Case of Becky 21. A Son of the Sahara 24. Son of the Sheik 26. Don Juan 26. King of Kings 27. Jesse James 27. The Haunted House 28. The Divine Lady 29. Bulldog Drummond 29. Outward Bound 30. The Cat Creeps 30. Midnight Lady 32. Clive of India 35. The White Angel 36. The Prince and the Pauper (as Henry VIII) 37. The Adventures of Robin Hood 38. Gunga Din 39. All This and Heaven Too 40. Shining Victory 41. The Constant Nymph 43. Devotion 44, many others.

Lovecraft, H. P. (1890–1937).
American horror writer, most of whose books were published posthumously. His stories featuring his invented Cthulhu mythology of ancient demonic forces attempting to return to Earth have become increasingly influential among makers of low-budget horror movies. The following all show the Lovecraft influence, though it is not always acknowledged by their makers:
The Haunted Palace (from *The Case of Charles Dexter Ward*) 63. Monster of Terror (from *Colour out of Space*) 65. Dunwich Horror (from *The Shuttered Room*) 69. Re-Animator (from *Herbert West – Re-Animator*) 85. From Beyond 86. The Farm 87. The Gate 87. Re-Animator 2 89. Gate 2 92. Cthulhu Mansion 92. The Unnameable Returns (from *The Statement of Randolph Carter*) 92. The Resurrected (from *The Case of Charles Dexter Ward*) 92. Necronomicon 93, a movie compendium, featured two Lovecraft stories, *Cool Air* and *The Whisperer in the Darkness*, with Jeffrey Combs appearing in the role of Lovecraft. In the Mouth of Madness 94, etc.

Lovejoy, Frank (1912–1962).
American actor of tough roles, with stage and radio experience.
Black Bart 48. Home of the Brave 49. In a Lonely Place 50. *The Sound of Fury* 51. I Was a Communist for the FBI 51. Force of Arms 51. The Hitch Hiker 52. Retreat Hell 52. The System 53. House of Wax 53. The Charge at Feather River 54. Beachhead 54. The Americano 55. Top of the World 55. Strategic Air Command 55. The Crooked Web 56. Cole Younger Gunfighter 58, etc.
TV series: Man against Crime 54. *Meet McGraw* 57–58.

Lovejoy, Ray.
English film editor.
2001: A Space Odyssey 68. A Day in the Death of Joe Egg 72. The Ruling Class 72. The Shining 80. The Dresser 83. Aliens (AAN) 86. The House on Carroll Street 88. Batman 89. Mr Frost 90. Let Him Have It 91, etc.

Lovelace, Linda (1952–   ).
American female lead of *Deep Throat* and other porno films.

Lovell, Raymond (1900–1953).
Canadian stage actor long in Britain: often in pompous or sinister roles.
Warn London 34. Contraband 40. 49th Parallel 41. *Alibi* 42. Warn That Man 43. The Way Ahead 44. *Caesar and Cleopatra* 45. The Three Weird Sisters 48. Time Gentleman Please 52. The Steel Key 53, etc.

Lovitz, Jon (1957–   ).
American character actor.
Jumpin' Jack Flash 86. Three Amigos 86. Last Resort 86. Big 88. My Stepmother Was an Alien 88. Mr Destiny 90. An American Tail: Fievel Goes West 91. A League of Their Own 92. Mom and Dad Save the World 92. National Lampoon's Loaded Weapon 1 93. North 94. City Slickers II: The Legend of Curly's Gold 94, etc.

Low, Warren (1905–1989).
American editor.
Dr Socrates 35. Anthony Adverse 36. The Great Garrick 37. The Life of Emile Zola 37. Juarez 39. *The Letter* 40. The Gay Sisters 42. Now Voyager 42. The Searching Wind 46. Sorry Wrong Number 48. September Affair 50. The Stooge 52. About Mrs Leslie 54. The Bad Seed 56. Gunfight at the OK Corral 57. Summer and Smoke 61. Boeing Boeing 65. Will Penny 68. True Grit 69. Willard 71, many others.

Lowe, Arthur (1914–1982).
Rotund British character actor who after a career of bit parts achieved star status on TV in a variety of tape shows from *Coronation Street* to *Dad's Army*.
Stormy Crossing 48. Kind Hearts and Coronets 49. This Sporting Life 63. The Rise and Rise of Michael Rimmer 70. *Dad's Army* 71. The Ruling Class 71. Theatre of Blood 73. *O Lucky Man* 73. *No Sex Please, We're British* 73. The Bawdy Adventures of Tom Jones 76. The Lady Vanishes 79. Britannia Hospital 82, etc.

Lowe, Chad (1968–   ).
American actor, the brother of Rob Lowe.
Silence of the Heart 84. Apprentice to Murder 88. True Blood 89. Nobody's Perfect 90. An Inconvenient Woman (TV) 91. Highway to Hell 92, etc.

Lowe, Edmund (1890–1971).
Suave American leading man of the 20s and 30s

who did not manage to age into a character actor.

The Spreading Dawn 17. The Devil 20. Peacock Alley 21. The Silent Command 23. The Fool 25. *What Price Glory?* 26. Is Zat So? 27. Dressed to Kill 28. In Old Arizona 29. The Cockeyed World 29. Scotland Yard 30. Transatlantic 31. *Chandu the Magician* 32. *Dinner at Eight* 33. Gift of Gab 34. Mr Dynamite 35. The Great Impersonation 35. Seven Sinners (GB) 36. The Squeaker (GB) 37. Secrets of a Nurse 38. Our Neighbours the Carters 39. Wolf of New York 40. Call out the Marines 41. Murder in Times Square 43. Dillinger 45. Good Sam 48. Around the World in Eighty Days 56. The Wings of Eagles 57. Heller in Pink Tights 60, etc.

TV series: *Front Page Detective* 52.

Lowe, Rob (1964–).

American leading actor.
■ The Outsiders 83. Class 83. Oxford Blues 84. The Hotel New Hampshire 84. St Elmo's Fire 85. Youngblood 85. About Last Night 86. Square Dance 86. Masquerade 88. Illegally Yours 88. Bad Influence 90. Desert Shield 91. Stroke of Midnight 91. The Dark Backward 91. Wayne's World 92. The Finest Hour 92. Suddenly Last Summer (TV) 93. The Stand (TV) 94.

TV series: A New Kind of Family 79–80.

Lowenstein, Richard (1959–).

Australian director and writer, also a director of rock videos.

Strikebound 84. White City 85. Dogs in Space 86. Say a Little Prayer 93.

The Lower Depths.

Gorki's doss-house study has had two notable filmings. As *Les Bas Fonds*, directed by Jean Renoir, it provided memorable roles for Jean Gabin and Louis Jouvet in 1936. In 1958, Akira Kurosawa directed Toshiro Mifune in a surprisingly faithful Japanese adaptation.

Lowery, Robert (1916–1971) (R. L. Hanks).

American leading man of the 40s, mainly in routine films.

Wake Up and Live 37. Young Mr Lincoln 39. Lure of the Islands 42. A Scream in the Dark 44. Prison Ship 45. The Mummy's Ghost 46. Death Valley 48. Batman and Robin (serial) (as Batman) 50. Crosswinds 51. Cow Country 53. The Rise and Fall of Legs Diamond 60. Johnny Reno 66, many others.

TV series: Circus Boy 56–57.

Lowry, Malcolm (1905–1957).

English novelist of works based on his own life, which was characterized by heavy drinking and travelling. His second wife was American actress Margerie Bonner (qv). His masterpiece, *Under the Volcano*, in which the central character of the alcoholic ex-British consul is a self-portrait, was filmed by John Huston with Albert Finney in the role.

Biography: 1973, *Malcolm Lowry* by Douglas Day.

Lowry, Morton (c. 1908–).

British character actor in Hollywood.

The Hound of the Baskervilles (as Stapleton) 39. How Green Was My Valley 40. The Picture of Dorian Gray 45, etc.

Loy, Myrna (1905–1993) (Myrna Williams).

Likeable American leading lady of the 30s; began her career in villainous oriental roles but later showed a great flair for sophisticated comedy and warm domestic drama. She was awarded an Oscar for lifetime achievements in 1991.

Autobiography: 1987, *Myrna Loy: Being and Becoming*.

SELECTED SILENT FILMS: The Cave Man 26. Don Juan 26. The Climbers 27. Beware of Married Men 28. State Street Sadie 28. The Midnight Taxi 28. Noah's Ark 29, etc.
■ SOUND FILMS: The Jazz Singer 27. The Desert Song 29. The Squall 29. Black Watch 29. Hard Boiled Rose 29. Evidence 29. Show of Shows 29. The Great Divide 30. The Jazz Cinderella 30. Cameo Kirby 30. Isle of Escape 30. Under a Texas Moon 30. Cock of the Walk 30. Bride of the Regiment 30. Last of the Duanes 30. The Truth about Youth 30. Renegades 30. Rogue of the Rio Grande 30. The Devil to Pay 30. The Naughty Flirt 31. Body and Soul 31. A Connecticut Yankee 31. Hush Money 31. Transatlantic 31. Rebound 31. Skyline 31. Consolation Marriage 31. Arrowsmith 31. Emma 32. The Wet Parade 32. Vanity Fair 32. The Woman in Room 13 32. New Morals for Old 32. *Love Me Tonight* 32. Thirteen Women 32. *The Mask of Fu Manchu* 32. The Animal Kingdom 32. Topaze 33. The Barbarian 33. The Prizefighter and the Lady 33. *When Ladies Meet* 33. Penthouse 33. Night Flight 33. Men in White 34. Manhattan Melodrama 34. *The Thin Man* 34. Stamboul Quest 34. Evelyn Prentice 34. *Broadway Bill* 34. Wings in the Dark 35. Whipsaw 35. Wife versus Secretary 36. Petticoat Fever 36. The Great Ziegfeld 36. To Mary with Love 36. Libeled Lady 36. After the Thin Man 36. Parnell 37. *Double Wedding* 37. Man Proof 38. Test Pilot 38. Too Hot to Handle 38. Lucky Night 39. *The Rains Came* 39. Third Finger Left Hand 39. Another Thin Man 39. I Love You Again 40. Love Crazy 41. Shadow of the Thin Man 41. The Thin Man Goes Home 44. So Goes My Love 46. *The Best Years of Our Lives* 46. *The Bachelor and the Bobby Soxer* 47. Song of the Thin Man 47. *Mr Blandings Builds His Dream House* 48. The Red Pony 49. That Dangerous Age 49. *Cheaper by the Dozen* 50. Belles on Their Toes 52. The Ambassador's Daughter 56. Lonelyhearts 58. From the Terrace 60. Midnight Lace 60. The April Fools 69. Death Takes a Holiday (TV) 70. Do Not Fold Spindle or Mutilate (TV) 71. The Couple Takes a Wife (TV) 72. Indict and Convict (TV) 73. The Elevator (TV) 73. Airport 75 74. It Happened at Lakewood Manor (TV) 77. The End 79. Just Tell Me What You Want 80. Summer Solstice (TV) 81.

Gag appearance: The Senator Was Indiscreet 49.
✪ For the wit and elegance with which she lived up to her 30s title of 'Queen of Hollywood'. *The Thin Man.*

Loy, Nanni (1925–).

Italian director.

Parola di Ladra 56. The Four Days of Naples 62. Made in Italy 65. Head of the Family 67. Why 71. Insieme 79. Café Express 80. Where's Picone? (Mi Manda Picone) 84. Amici Miei III 85. Gioco di Società 88, etc.

Lualdi, Antonella (1931–) (Antoinetta de Pasquale).

Italian leading lady of the 50s and 60s.

Three Forbidden Stories 52. Le Rouge et le Noir 54. Wild Love 55. Young Girls Beware 57. Run with the Devil 60. The Mongols 61. My Son the Hero 62. Let's Talk about Women 64. How to Seduce a Playboy 66. Vincent Francois Paul and the Others 75, etc.

Lubin, Arthur (1901–).

American director from 1934, mainly of light comedy, and with a penchant for eccentric animals.
■ A Successful Failure 34. The Great God Gold 35. Honeymoon Limited 35. Two Sinners 35. Frisco Waterfront 35. The House of a Thousand Candles

36. Yellowstone 37. Mysterious Crossing 37. *California Straight Ahead* 37. I Cover the War 37. Idol of the Crowds 37. Adventure's End 37. Midnight Intruder 38. Beloved Brat 38. Prison Break 38. Secrets of a Nurse 38. Risky Business 38. Big Town Czar 39. Mickey the Kid 39. Called a Messenger 39. The Big Guy 40. *Black Friday* 40. Gangs of Chicago 40. I'm Nobody's Sweetheart Now 40. Meet the Wildcat 40. Who Killed Aunt Maggie? 40. San Francisco Docks 41. Where Did You Get That Girl? 41. *Buck Privates* 41. In the Navy 41. Hold That Ghost 41. Keep 'Em Flying 41. Ride 'Em Cowboy 42. Eagle Squadron 42. White Savage 43. *Phantom of the Opera* 43. Ali Baba and the Forty Thieves 44. Delightfully Dangerous 45. Spider Woman Strikes Back 46. A Night in Paradise 46. New Orleans 47. Impact 49. *Francis* 50. Queen for a Day 51. Francis Goes to the Races 51. *Rhubarb* 51. Francis Goes to West Point 52. It Grows on Trees 52. South Sea Woman 53. Francis Covers Big Town 53. Francis Joins the WACs 54. Francis in the Navy 55. Footsteps in the Fog 55. Lady Godiva 55. Star of India 56. The First Travelling Saleslady 56. Escapade in Japan 57. Thief of Baghdad 61. The Incredible Mr Limpet 64. Hold On 66. Rain for a Dusty Summer 71.

TV series: *Mister Ed* 60–65.

Lubitsch, Ernst (1892–1947).

German director, once a comic actor, in a series of silent farces starring him as 'Meyer'. After a variety of subjects he settled for a kind of sophisticated sex comedy that became unmistakably his: the 'Lubitsch touch' was a form of visual innuendo, spicy without ever being vulgar. His greatest period came after 1922, when he settled in Hollywood and became Paramount's leading producer. Early films include many shorts. Awarded special Oscar 1946 'for his distinguished contributions to the art of the motion picture'.

Biographies: 1968, *The Lubitsch Touch* by Herman G. Weinberg. 1994, *Ernst Lubitsch, Laughter in Paradise* by Scott Eyman.

SELECTED EUROPEAN FILMS: Carmen 18. Madame du Barry 19. Sumurun 20. Anne Boleyn 20. Pharaoh's Wife 21. The Flame 21, etc.
■ AMERICAN FILMS: Rosita 23. *The Marriage Circle* 24. Three Women 24. *Forbidden Paradise* 24. Kiss Me Again 25. Lady Windermere's Fan 25. So This Is Paris 26. The Student Prince 27. The Patriot (AAN) 28. Eternal Love 29. *The Love Parade* (first sound film) (AAN) 29. Paramount on Parade (Chevalier sequences) 30. Monte Carlo 30. The Smiling Lieutenant 31. The Man I Killed 32. *One Hour With You* 32. *Trouble in Paradise* 32. If I Had a Million (Laughton sequence) 32. Design for Living 33. The Merry Widow 34. *Desire* (p only) 36. Angel 37. Bluebeard's Eighth Wife 38. *Ninotchka* 39. *The Shop Around the Corner* 40. That Uncertain Feeling 41. *To Be or Not To Be* 42. *Heaven Can Wait* (AAN) 43. A Royal Scandal (produced only) 45. Cluny Brown 46. That Lady in Ermine (finished by Otto Preminger) 48.
✪ For extending the period of elegant comedy which is now a part of history. *Trouble in Paradise.*

¶ It's the Lubitsch touch that means so much, piped the posters.

He was the only director in Hollywood who had his own signature,
said S. N. Behrman. These were two ways of saying that Lubitsch was a master of cinematic innuendo.

I let the audience use their imaginations. Can I help it if they misconstrue my suggestions?
he asked archly. In fact he delighted in

naughtiness, and carried it off with great delicacy, though he admitted his lapses:

> I sometimes make pictures which are not up to my standard, but then it can only be said of a mediocrity that all his work is up to his standard.

And he gave in finally to the American way:

> I've been to Paris France and I've been to Paris Paramount. Paris Paramount is better.

Some people, Mary Pickford for instance, failed to perceive his talents:

> I parted company with him as soon as I could.

> I thought him a very uninspired director. He was a director of doors.

According to Andrew Sarris (1968):

> He was the last of the genuine Continentals let loose on the American continent, and we shall never see his like again because the world he celebrated had died – even before he did – everywhere except in his own memory.

Lucan, Arthur (1887–1954) (Arthur Towle).
British music-hall comedian famous for his impersonation of Old Mother Riley, a comic Irish washerwoman. Made fourteen films featuring her, usually with his wife Kitty McShane (1898–1964) playing his daughter.

■ Stars on Parade 35. Kathleen Mavourneen 36. Old Mother Riley 37. Old Mother Riley in Paris 38. Old Mother Riley MP 39. Old Mother Riley Joins Up 39. Old Mother Riley in Business 40. Old Mother Riley's Ghosts 41. Old Mother Riley's Circus 41. Old Mother Riley Detective 43. Old Mother Riley Overseas 44. Old Mother Riley at Home 45. Old Mother Riley's New Venture 49. Old Mother Riley Headmistress 50. Old Mother Riley's Jungle Treasure 51. Mother Riley Meets the Vampire 52.

Lucas, George (1944–).
American director and producer, one of the most commercially successful of contemporary film-makers. He also established Industrial Light and Magic, specializing in special effects, and, through his company Lucasfilm, is involved in the development of computer games software and interactive entertainment.

Biography: 1983, *Skywalking: The Life and Films of George Lucas* by Dale Pollock.

THX 1138 (wd, ed) 73. *American Graffiti* (wd, p) (AAN) 73. *Star Wars* (wd) (AAN) 77. More American Graffiti (p) 79. The Empire Strikes Back (w, p) 80. Raiders of the Lost Ark (p, story) 81. Return of the Jedi (w, p) 83. Twice upon a Time (p) 83. Indiana Jones and the Temple of Doom (p, story) 84. Mishima: A Life in Four Chapters (p) 85. Captain Eo (p) 86. Howard the Duck (p) 86. Labyrinth (p) 86. The Land before Time (p) 88. Powaqqatsi (p) 88. Tucker: The Man and His Dream (p) 88. Willow (p, story) 88. Indiana Jones and the Last Crusade (p, story) 89. Radioland Murders (p, story) 94.

¶ He reminded me a little of Walt Disney's version of a mad scientist. – *Steven Spielberg*

It's not what you say, or what people think of you, it's what you do that counts. – *G.L.*

Making movies is like the construction business. You are fighting all possible odds and everyone is seemingly against you. – *G.L.*

Lucas, Leighton. (1903–1982).
British composer and musical director; former ballet dancer.

Target for Tonight 41. Stage Fright 50. A King in New York 57. Ice Cold in Alex 58. The Millionairess 61, many others.

Lucas, Wilfred (1871–1940).
Canadian character actor in Hollywood, best remembered as a foil for Laurel and Hardy.

The Barbarian 08. The Spanish Gypsy 11. Cohen's Outing 13. Acquitted 16. The Westerners 18. The Barnstormer 22. The Fatal Mistake 24. Her Sacrifice 26. Just Imagine 30. *Pardon Us* 31. Fra Diavolo 33. The Count of Monte Cristo 34. Modern Times 36. The Baroness and the Butler 38. Zenobia 39. A Chump at Oxford 40. The Sea Wolf 41, many others.

Lucas, William (1926–).
British leading man of stage, TV and occasional films.

Timeslip 55. X the Unknown 56. Breakout 59. Sons and Lovers 60. The Devil's Daffodil 61. Calculated Risk 63. Night of the Big Heat (aka Isle of the Burning Doomed) 67, etc.

TV series: Eldorado 92–93.

Luchaire, Corinne (1921–1950).
French actress who was a big hit in *Prison Without Bars* 38. After World War II was convicted as a collaborator and died in poverty.

Luckinbill, Laurence (1934–).
American leading man.

The Boys in the Band 70. Such Good Friends 71. The Delphi Bureau (TV) 72 (and short series). Death Sentence (TV) 74. Panic on the 5.22 (TV) 74. Winner Take All (TV) 75. The Lindbergh Kidnapping Case (TV) 76. Ike (TV) 79. The Promise (TV) 80. Messenger of Death 88. Star Trek V: The Final Frontier 89, etc.

Lucking, Bill.
Sturdy American supporting actor.

Hell's Babies 69. Wild Rovers 71. Oklahoma Crude 73. The Return of a Man Called Horse 76. Power (TV) 79. Coast to Coast 80. The Mountain Men 80, etc.

TV series: Big Hawaii 77. Shannon 81–82. The Blue and the Grey 82. The A-Team 83–84. Jessie 84.

Ludwig, Edward (1899–1982).
American director, from 1932.

They Just Had To Get Married 33. Friends of Mr Sweeney 34. *The Man Who Reclaimed His Head* 34. Age of Indiscretion 36. That Certain Age 38. The Last Gangster 39. The Swiss Family Robinson 40. The Man Who Lost Himself 41. They Came to Blow Up America 43. The Fighting Seabees 44. Three's a Family 45. The Fabulous Texan 47. *Wake of the Red Witch* 48. Smuggler's Island 51. Big Jim McLain 52. Sangaree 53. Flame of the Islands 56. The Black Scorpion 57. The Gun Hawk 63, etc.

Ludwig, William (1912–).
American writer.

The *Hardy Family* films 38–44. Challenge to Lassie 49. Shadow on the Wall 50. The Great Caruso 51. *Interrupted Melody* (AA) 55. Back Street 61, etc.

Lugosi, Bela (1882–1956) (Bela Ferenc Blasko; known professionally for a time as Ariztid Olt).
Hungarian stage actor of chilling presence and voice; became famous in films as Dracula, but his accent was a handicap for normal roles and he became typecast in inferior horror films. He was played by Martin Landau in the 1994 biopic *Ed Wood*.

Biographies: 1974, *The Count* by Arthur Lennig. 1976, *Lugosi, the Man behind the Cape* by Robert Cremer.

The Silent Command 23. The Rejected Woman 24. The Thirteenth Chair 29. Renegades 30. Oh For a Man 30. *Dracula* 30. Broad Minded 31. The Black Camel 31. *The Murders in the Rue Morgue* 31. *White Zombie* 32. *Chandu the Magician* 32. Island of Lost Souls 33. The Death Kiss 33. *The Black Cat* 34.

Mysterious Mr Wong 35. The Mystery of the Marie Celeste (GB) 35. Mark of the Vampire 35. The Raven 35. The Invisible Ray 35. Postal Inspector 36. Dark Eyes of London (GB) 38. The Phantom Creeps 39. *Son of Frankenstein* (as Igor) 39. The Saint's Double Trouble 40. Black Friday 40. The Wolf Man 41. Spooks Run Wild 41. Night Monster 42. The Ghost of Frankenstein 42. The Ape Man 43. Frankenstein Meets the Wolf Man (as the monster) 43. The Return of the Vampire 43. One Body Too Many 44. Zombies on Broadway 45. The Body Snatcher 45. Scared to Death 47. *Abbott and Costello Meet Frankenstein* (as Dracula) 48. Bela Lugosi Meets a Brooklyn Gorilla 52. Mother Riley Meets the Vampire (GB) 52. Bride of the Monster 56. Plan 9 from Outer Space 56, etc.

✪ For bringing a touch of European mystery to a succession of rudimentary melodramas. *Son of Frankenstein.*

¶ For some people he was the embodiment of all mysterious forces, a harbinger of evil from the world of shadow. For others he was merely a ham actor appearing in a type of film unsuitable for children and often unfit for adults. – *Arthur Lennig*

Famous line (*Dracula*): 'Listen to them – children of the night! What music they make!'

Luhrmann, Baz (1962–).
Australian director, a former actor, from the theatre.

Winter of Our Dreams (a) 81. Kids of the Cross (d) (TV) 92. *Strictly Ballroom* (d) 92.

Lukas, Paul (1887–1971) (Pal Lukacs).
Suave Hungarian leading actor, in Hollywood from the late 20s, first as a romantic figure, then as a smooth villain, finally as a kindly old man.

Two Lovers 28. Three Sinners 28. Manhattan Cocktail 28. Half Way to Heaven 29. Slightly Scarlet 30. The Benson Murder Case 30. Slightly Dishonorable 31. City Streets 31. Thunder Below 32. Rockabye 32. The Kiss Before the Mirror 33. The Secret of the Blue Room 33. *Little Women* 33. By Candlelight 33. Affairs of a Gentleman 34. I Give My Love 34. The Fountain 34. The Casino Murder Case 34. The Three Musketeers 35. I Found Stella Parish 35. Dodsworth 36. Dinner at the Ritz (GB) 37. *The Lady Vanishes* (GB) 38. *Confessions of a Nazi Spy* 39. Strange Cargo 40. The Ghost Breakers 40. They Dare Not Love 41. Lady in Distress 42. *Watch on the Rhine* (AA) 43. Hostages 43. Uncertain Glory 44. *Address Unknown* 44. *Experiment Perilous* 44. Deadline at Dawn 46. Berlin Express 48. Kim 50. 20,000 Leagues Under the Sea 54. Roots of Heaven 58. Tender is the Night 61. 55 Days at Peking 63. Lord Jim 65. Sol Madrid 68, etc.

✪ For being such a gentleman. *The Lady Vanishes.*

Luke, Keye (1904–1991).
Chinese-American actor who was popular in the 30s as Charlie Chan's number-two son.

Charlie Chan in Paris 34. Oil for the Lamps of China 35. King of Burlesque 36. Charlie Chan at the Opera 36. Charlie Chan on Broadway 37. International Settlement 38. Mr Moto's Gamble 38. Disputed Passage 39. Bowery Blitzkrieg 41. Invisible Agent 42. Salute to the Marines 43. Three Men in White 44. First Yank into Tokyo 45. Sleep My Love 47. Hell's Half Acre 54. Battle Hell 57. Yangtse Incident (GB) 57. Nobody's Perfect 67. The Chairman (GB) 69. The Amsterdam Kill 78. Gremlins 84. A Fine Mess 86, many others.

TV series: Kentucky Jones 64–65. *Anna and the King* 72. Kung Fu 72–74. Harry-O 76. Sidekicks 86–87.

Lulli, Folco (1912–1970).
Italian character actor.
The Bandit 47. Caccia Tragica 48. Without Pity 49. Flight into France 49. No Peace Under the Olives 50. Infidelity 52. *The Wages of Fear* 54. An Eye for an Eye 60. Lafayette 63. Marco the Magnificent 66, many others.

Lulu (1948–) (Marie Lawrie).
British pop singer.
■ Gonks Go Beat 65. To Sir With Love 68. The Cherry Picker 72.

Lum and Abner Chester Lauck (1902–1980) and Norris Goff (1906–1978).
American comedy actors of hillbilly characters.
Dreaming Out Loud 40. Bashful Bachelors 42, etc.

lumberjacks
have figured in comparatively few movies: here are some of them: Conflict 36. Come and Get It 36. God's Country and the Woman 36. The Big Trees 52. Timberjack 55. Guns of the Timberland 60. Freckles 60. Sometimes a Great Notion 71.

Lumet, Sidney (1924–).
American director, former child actor and TV producer.
■ *Twelve Angry Men* (AAN) 57. Stage Struck 58. That Kind of Woman 59. The Fugitive Kind 60. A View from the Bridge 61. Long Day's Journey into Night 62. *Fail Safe* 64. *The Pawnbroker* 65. *The Hill* 65. *The Group* 65. The Deadly Affair 66. Bye Bye Braverman 68. The Seagull 68. The Appointment 69. Blood Kin 69. The Anderson Tapes 71. The Offence 72. Child's Play 72. Lovin' Molly 73. Serpico 74. Murder on the Orient Express 74. *Dog Day Afternoon* (AAN) 75. *Network* (AAN) 76. Equus 77. The Wiz 78. Just Tell Me What You Want 80. Prince of the City (AAN) 81. Deathtrap 82. The Verdict (AAN) 82. Daniel 83. Garbo Talks 84. Power 85. The Morning After 86. Running on Empty 88. Family Business 89. Q & A (& w) 90. A Stranger among Us 92. Close to Eden 92. Guilty as Sin 93.

¶ He's the only guy who could double park in front of a whorehouse. He's that fast. – *Paul Newman*
Those who would be led, Lumet will guide. Those who would lead, Lumet will follow – *Andrew Sarris, 1968*

Lumière, Louis (1864–1948).
Pioneer French cinematographer, with brother Auguste Lumière (1862–1954). Gave first public demonstration 1895, including *Arrival of Train at Station* and other simple events; later made short comedies.

Lumley, Joanna (1946–).
British leading lady, a former model. She was formerly married to actor and scriptwriter Jeremy Lloyd.
Autobiography: 1989, *Stare Back and Smile*.
Some Girls Do 68. On Her Majesty's Secret Service 69. Tam Lin 70. The Breaking of Bumbo 70. Games That Lovers Play 70. Satanic Rites of Dracula 73. Don't Just Lie There, Say Something 73. Trail of the Pink Panther 82. Curse of the Pink Panther 83. Mistral's Daughter (TV) 84. Shirley Valentine 89, etc.
TV series: *The New Avengers* 76–77. Sapphire and Steel 79. Absolutely Fabulous 92–94.

¶ Playing a mindless lovely is depressing when you don't (in your opinion) look lovely at all. – *J.L.*

Lummis, Dayton (1903–1988).
American character actor of stage and radio, latterly in films.
Les Misérables 52. Ruby Gentry 53. The Court Martial of Billy Mitchell 55. The Cobweb 56, etc.

Luna, Barbara (1937–).
American actress who usually plays beautiful foreigners.
The Devil at Four O'Clock 60. Five Weeks in a Balloon 62. Synanon 64. Ship of Fools 65. Firecreek 67. Che! 69. The Gatling Gun 73. Woman in the Rain 76. Brenda Starr (TV) 76. Pleasure Cove (TV) 79. The Concrete Jungle 82, etc.

Luna, Bigas:
see *Bigas Luna*.

Lund, John (1911–1992).
American leading man with Broadway experience; film roles mainly stodgy.
To Each His Own 46. The Perils of Pauline 47. A Foreign Affair 47. Night Has a Thousand Eyes 48. Miss Tatlock's Millions 48. My Friend Irma 49. Duchess of Idaho 50. Darling, How Could You? 51. Steel Town 52. Bronco Buster 52. The Woman They Almost Lynched 53. Chief Crazy Horse 54. White Feather 55. Battle Stations 56. High Society 56. Affair in Reno 57. The Wackiest Ship in the Army 60. If a Man Answers 62, etc.

Lundgren, Dolph (1959–).
Muscular Swedish leading man and karate expert in action films. He has a master's degree in chemical engineering.
A View to a Kill 85. Rocky IV 85. Masters of the Universe 87. The Punisher 89. Red Scorpion 89. Dark Angel (aka I Come in Peace) 90. Cover Up 90. Universal Soldier 92. Pentathlon 94. Johnny Mnemonic 95. Meltdown 95, etc.

¶ My problem is that people get intimidated by someone big and beautiful like me. They hate to think I can be smart as well. – *D.L.*

Lundigan, William (1914–1975).
American leading man of routine features, formerly in radio.
Three Smart Girls Grow Up 38. The Old Maid 39. The Sea Hawk 40. Sunday Punch 42. What Next, Corporal Hargrove? 45. Pinky 49. I'd Climb the Highest Mountain 51. Down among the Sheltering Palms 52. *Inferno* 53. Serpent of the Nile 53. The White Orchid 54. The Underwater City 61. The Way West 67. Where Angels Go Trouble Follows 68, etc.
TV series: *Men into Space* 59.

Lunghi, Cherie (1953–).
Anglo-Italian leading lady. She has a daughter by director Roland Joffe.
Excalibur 81. Oliver Twist (TV) 82. Praying Mantis (TV) 82. King David 85. Parker 85. The Mission 85. Harem (TV) 86. To Kill a Priest 89. A Question of Guilt (TV) 93. Silent Cries (TV) 93, etc.
TV series: The Manageress 90–91. Covington Cross 92.

Lunt, Alfred (1892–1977).
Distinguished American stage actor, husband of Lynn Fontanne.
■ Backbone 23. The Ragged Edge 23. Second Youth 24. Lovers in Quarantine 25. Sally of the Sawdust 26. *The Guardsman* (AAN) 31. Stage Door Canteen 43.

Lupino, Ida (1914–).
British leading lady, daughter of Stanley Lupino, who went to Hollywood and played a variety of mainly fraught roles; later became a director.
■ AS ACTRESS: Her First Affaire 33. Money for Speed 33. High Finance 33. The Ghost Camera 33. I Lived with You 34. Prince of Arcadia 34. Search for Beauty 34. Come on Marines 34. Ready for Love 34. Paris in Spring 35. Smart Girl 35. Peter Ibbetson 35. Anything Goes 36. One Rainy Afternoon 36. Yours for the Asking 36. The Gay Desperado 36. Sea Devils 37. Let's Get Married 37. Artists and Models 37. Fight for your Lady 37. The Lone Wolf Spy Hunt 39. The Lady and the Mob 39. The Adventures of Sherlock Holmes 39. The Light That Failed 40. *They Drive by Night* 40. *High Sierra* 41. The Sea Wolf 41. Out of the Fog 41. *Ladies in Retirement* 41. Moontide 42. *The Hard Way* 42. Life Begins at 8.30 42. Forever and a Day 43. Thank your Lucky Stars 43. In Our Time 44. Hollywood Canteen 44. Pillow to Post 45. *Devotion* (as Emily Brontë) 46. The Man I Love 47. Deep Valley 47. Escape Me Never 47. *Roadhouse* 48. Lust for Gold 49. Woman in Hiding 50. On Dangerous Ground 51. Beware My Lovely 52. Jennifer 53. The Bigamist 53. Private Hell 36 54. Women's Prison 55. The Big Knife 55. While the City Sleeps 56. Strange Intruder 56. I Love a Mystery (TV) 67. Backtrack (TV) 69. Deadhead Miles 70. Women in Chains (TV) 71. Female Artillery (TV) 72. Junior Bonner 72. The Letters (TV) 72. The Strangers in 7A (TV) 73. The Devil's Rain 75. The Food of the Gods 76. My Boys Are Good Boys 78. Deadhead Miles 82.
TV series: *Mr Adams and Eve* 56.
AS DIRECTOR: Not Wanted (wp only) 49. Outrage (& w) 50. Never Fear 51. Hard, Fast and Beautiful 51. The Hitch Hiker (& w) 53. The Bigamist 53. Private Hell 36 (w only) 54. The Trouble with Angels 66, plus many TV episodes.

¶ Her familiar expression of strained intensity would be less quickly relieved by a merciful death than by Ex-Lax. – *James Agee on Ida Lupino's performance in The Hard Way*

Lupino, Stanley (1893–1942).
British comedian on stage from 1900, especially in musical comedy.
Autobiography: 1934, *From the Stocks to the Stars*.
■ Love Lies 31. The Love Race 31. *Sleepless Nights* 32. King of the Ritz 33. Facing the Music 33. You Made Me Love You 33. Happy 34. Honeymoon for Three 35. Cheer Up! 36. Sporting Love 36. *Over She Goes* 37. Hold My Hand 38. Lucky To Me 39.

LuPone, Patti (1949–).
American leading actress and singer, from the musical stage.
King of the Gypsies 78. 1941 79. Fighting Back 82. Witness 85. Wise Guys 86. Driving Miss Daisy 89. Family Prayers 93, etc.

Lupu-Pick (1886–1931).
German director of silent days.
Die Fremde 17. Der Letzte Augenblick 18. The Wild Duck 22. Gassenhauer 24. Eine Nacht in London 28, etc.

Lurie, John (1952–).
American character actor and musician, in independent movies. He was leader and saxophonist with the jazz group The Lounge Lizards.
Permanent Vacation (& m) 80. Stranger Than

Paradise 84. Paris, Texas 84. Desperately Seeking Susan 85. Down by Law (& m) 86. The Last Temptation of Christ 88. Mystery Train (m) 89. Wild at Heart 90. Until the End of the World 92, etc.

Lustgarten, Edgar (1907–1979).
British journalist who introduced the *Scotland Yard* three-reelers of the 50s; also wrote many books on famous crimes and trials.

Lustig, Jan (1901–1978).
American screenwriter.
   The White Cliffs of Dover 44. Homecoming 47, etc.

Lustig, William (1955–).
American director of horror movies.
   The Violation of Claudia 77. Maniac 81. Vigilante 83. Maniac Cop 87. Hit List 89. Relentless 89. Maniac Cop 2 90. Maniac Cop 3: Badge of Silence 92. Brute Force 94, etc.

Lutic, Bernard.
French cinematographer.
   The Aviator's Wife 81. The Well-Made Marriage 82. Entre Nous 83. Heat of Desire 84. Revolution 85. The Return of the Musketeers 90. Time Is Money 94. Le Colonel Chabert 94. Fric Frac 95, etc.

Lutyens, Elisabeth (1906–1983).
Distinguished British composer who occasionally wrote film scores.
   Autobiography: 1972, *A Goldfish Bowl*.
   A String of Beads 47. El Dorado 51. World Without End 53. The Malpas Mystery 60. Never Take Sweets from a Stranger 63. Paranoiac 63. The Earth Dies Screaming 64. The Skull 65. Dr Terror's House of Horrors 65. The Psychopath 66. The Terrornauts 67, etc.

Lydon, James (Jimmy) (1923–).
American actor familiar in the early 40s as gangling adolescent.
   Back Door to Heaven 39. *Tom Brown's Schooldays* (title role) 40. Little Men 40. Henry Aldrich for President (and subsequent series of ten) 41. Aerial Gunner 43. The Town Went Wild 45. Life with Father 47. Bad Boy 49. September Affair 51. Island in the Sky 53. Battle Stations 56. I Passed for White 60. The Last Time I Saw Archie 61. Brainstorm 65. Death of a Gunfighter 69. Scandalous John 71. Vigilante Force 76, etc.
   TV series: So This Is Hollywood 54. The First Hundred Years 56. Love That Jill 58.

Lye, Len (1901–1980).
New Zealander animator, remembered for British GPO and other shorts of the 30s. Went to US and was associated for a while with *The March of Time*.
   Tusalava 29. Colour Box 34. Birth of a Robot 36. Rainbow Dance 36. Kaleidoscope 36. Trade Tattoo 37. Swinging the Lambeth Walk 39. Colour Cry 52. Rhythm 53. Free Radicals 58. Particles in Space 66, etc.

Lyel, Viola (1900–1972) (Violet Watson).
British character actress, mainly on stage in comedy roles.
   Hobson's Choice (leading role) 30. Channel Crossing 32. Quiet Wedding 40. Wanted for Murder 46. No Place for Jennifer 50. Isn't Life Wonderful? 53. See How They Run 56, etc.

Lyles, A. C. (1918–).
American producer, former publicist; noted for his second-feature westerns using veteran talent.
   Short Cut to Hell 57. Raymie 60. The Young and

the Brave 61. Law of the Lawless 64. Stagecoach to Hell 64. Young Fury 65. Black Spurs 65. Town Tamer 65. Apache Uprising 66. Johnny Reno 66. Waco 66. Red Tomahawk 67. Buckskin 68, etc.

Lymon, Frankie (1942–1968).
American rock 'n' roll singer who had a hit at the age of 13 with 'Why Do Fools Fall in Love?', featured on the soundtracks of *That'll Be the Day* 73 and *American Graffiti* 73, and who appeared in a couple of 50s movies. Drug addiction bedevilled his later career.
   Mister Rock and Roll 57. Rock Rock Rock 57.

Lynch, Alfred (1933–).
Raw-boned British actor, often as cockney private.
■ On the Fiddle 61. Two and Two Make Six 61. West Eleven 63. 55 Days at Peking 63. The Hill 65. The Taming of the Shrew 67. The Seagull 68. The Blockhouse 73. Joseph Andrews 76. Loophole 80. Bewitched (TV) 85. The Krays 90. Until the End of the World (Bis ans Ende der Welt) 91. Second Best 93.

Lynch, David (1946–).
American director, screenwriter, producer and occasional engineer.
■ Eraserhead 78. *The Elephant Man* (AAN) 80. Dune 85. Blue Velvet (AAN) 86. Zelly and Me (a) 88. Wild at Heart (wd) 90. Twin Peaks: Fire Walk with Me (p, co-w, d) 92.
   TV series: Twin Peaks 90.

Lynch, Jennifer Chambers (1968–).
American director and screenwriter, the daughter of director David Lynch.
   Boxing Helena (wd) 93.

Lynch, John (1963–).
British actor from Ulster, mainly on the stage, who played the title role in *Cal*, his first film.
   Cal 84. 1871 90. Hardware 90. Edward II 91. The Railway Station Man 92, etc.

Lynch, Kelly (1959–).
American actress, a former model.
   Osa 85. Bright Lights, Big City 88. Cocktail 88. Drugstore Cowboy 89. Road House 89. Warm Summer Rain 89. Desperate Hours 90. Curly Sue 91. R.S.V.P. 92. Three of Hearts 93. Imaginary Crimes 94. Heaven's Prisoners 95, etc.

lynch law
has been condemned in many outstanding dramatic movies from Hollywood.
   Fury 36. They Won't Forget 37. Young Mr Lincoln 39. The Ox-Bow Incident 43. Storm Warning 51. The Sound of Fury 51. The Sun Shines Bright 52. Rough Night in Jericho 68.
   See also: *Ku Klux Klan*.

Lynch, Richard (1936–).
American actor whose scarred skin and haughty mien make him a natural for evil roles.
   Scarecrow 73. Steel 80. Vampire (TV) 80. The Formula 80. Alcatraz (TV) 81. The Sword and the Sorcerer 82. The Barbarians 87. Aftershock 88. Bad Dreams 88. Little Nikita 88. One Man Force 89. High Stakes 89. The Forbidden Dance 90. Trancers 2: The Return of Jack Deth 91. Double Threat 92, etc.

Lynde, Paul (1926–1982).
American TV comedian who usually played a flustered character with a funny voice.
   New Faces 54. Son of Flubber 62. Bye Bye Birdie 63. Send Me No Flowers 64. The Glass Bottom Boat

66. How Sweet It Is 68. Rabbit Test 78. The Villain 79, etc.
   TV series: Stanley 56. Hey Landlord 66. The Pruitts of Southampton 66. *The Paul Lynde Show* 72. Temperatures Rising 73.

Lyndon, Barre (1896–1972) (Alfred Edgar).
British playwright, long in Hollywood as scriptwriter.
   The Amazing Dr Clitterhouse (oa) 38. Sundown 41. The Lodger 44. The Man in Half Moon Street (oa) 44. The House on 92nd Street 45. Night Has a Thousand Eyes 48. The Greatest Show on Earth 51. The War of the Worlds 53. Conquest of Space 54. Sign of the Pagan 55. Omar Khayyam 57. Dark Intruder 65, etc.

Lyne, Adrian (1941–).
British director, from TV commercials; now in America.
■ Foxes 80. Flashdance 82. 9½ Weeks 86. Fatal Attraction (AAN) 87. Jacob's Ladder 90. Indecent Proposal 93.

Lynen, Robert (1921–1944).
French child actor later executed by Nazis as collaborator.
   Poil de Carotte 32. The Little King 33. La Belle Equipe 36. Carnet de Bal 37. Education du Prince 38, etc.

Lynley, Carol (1942–).
Talented American leading lady of the 60s.
   The Light in the Forest 58. Holiday for Lovers 59. *Blue Denim* 59. The Hound Dog Man 60. Return to Peyton Place 61. The Last Sunset 61. The Stripper 63. Under the Yum Yum Tree 63. The Cardinal 63. Shock Treatment 64. The Pleasure Seekers 64. *Bunny Lake is Missing* (GB) 65. *Harlow* (TV) 66. The Shuttered Room (GB) 68. Danger Route (GB) 68. The Smugglers (TV) 68. The Maltese Bippy 69. Norwood 69. Once You Kiss a Stranger 70. Weekend of Terror (TV) 70. Crosscurrent (TV) 71. The Night Stalker (TV) 72. The Poseidon Adventure 72. Cotter 73. The Elevator (TV) 74. Death Stalk (TV) 75. Flood (TV) 76. The Four Deuces 76. Out of Control 76. Bad Georgia Road 77. Fantasy Island (TV) 77. Having Babies II (TV) 77. The Cops and Robin (TV) 78. The Beasts Are on the Streets (TV) 78. The Cat and the Canary 78. The Shape of Things to Come (TV) 79. Vigilante 83. Spirits 91, etc.

Lynn, Ann (c. 1934–).
British actress, mainly on TV; granddaughter of Ralph Lynn.
   Piccadilly Third Stop 60. The Wind of Change 61. Strongroom 61. Flame in the Streets 62. Black Torment 64. Four in the Morning 65. Baby Love 69, etc.

Lynn, Diana (1926–1971) (Dolores Loehr).
Pert, witty American leading lady of the 40s, former child actress and pianist.
■ They Shall Have Music 39. There's Magic in Music 41. Star Spangled Rhythm 42. *The Major and the Minor* 43. Henry Aldrich Gets Glamour 43. *The Miracle of Morgan's Creek* 44. And the Angels Sing 44. Henry Aldrich Plays Cupid 44. *Our Hearts Were Young and Gay* 44. Out of this World 45. Duffy's Tavern 45. Our Hearts Were Growing Up 46. The Bride Wore Boots 46. Easy Come Easy Go 47. Variety Girl 47. Ruthless 48. Texas Brooklyn and Heaven 48. Every Girl Should Be Married 48. My Friend Irma 49. Paid in Full 50. My Friend Irma Goes West 50. Rogues of Sherwood Forest 50. Peggy 50. Bedtime for Bonzo 51. The People against O'Hara 51. Meet Me at the Fair 52. Plunder

of the Sun 53. Track of the Cat 54. An Annapolis Story 55. The Kentuckian 55. You're Never Too Young 55. Company of Killers (TV) 71.

Lynn, Emmett (1897–1958).
American character actor, from vaudeville and the stage, often as a comic sidekick in westerns. In films from 1913.

Along the Rio Grande 41. The Law Rides Again 43. Bluebeard 44. The Cisco Kid Returns 45. Stagecoach to Denver 46. Code of the West 47. Ride, Ryder, Ride 49. The Dungeon 50. Best of the Badmen 51. Monkey Business 52. Pickup on South Street 53. The Robe 53. Ring of Fear 54. A Man Called Peter 55. The Ten Commandments 56, many others.

Lynn, Jeffrey (1909–) (Ragnar Lind).
American leading man with varied experience, in films from 1938.

Four Daughters 38. Yes, My Darling Daughter 39. Espionage Agent 39. The Roaring Twenties 40. A Child Is Born 40. All This and Heaven Too 40. Four Mothers 40. Million Dollar Baby 41. The Body Disappears 41. Whiplash 47. Black Bart 48. A Letter to Three Wives 49. Up Front 51. Captain China 52. Come Thursday 64. Tony Rome 67, many others.

TV series: My Son Jeep 53. Star Stage 55–56.

Lynn, Jonathan (1943–).
British comedy screenwriter and director, a former actor.
■ The Internecine Project (w) 74. Clue (wd) 85. Nuns on the Run (wd) 90. My Cousin Vinny (d) 92. The Distinguished Gentleman (d) 92.

TV series: Yes, Minister (co-w) 80–87.

Lynn, Leni (1925–).
American girl singer who after debut in *Babes in Arms* 39 came to England and starred in several low-budget musicals.

Heaven Is Round the Corner 43. Give Me the Stars 44. Spring Song 46. Happy Go Lovely 51, etc.

Lynn, Loretta (1935–).
American country singer and guitarist, phenomenally successful and proud of her hillbilly background which was celebrated in the book and film *Coal Miner's Daughter*.

Lynn, Ralph (1882–1964).
Incomparable British comedy actor of the silly ass school; his monocled face, limp hands and mastery of timing were essential ingredients of several films of the Aldwych farces of the 30s.
■ Rookey Nook 30. Tons of Money 31. Plunder 31. Chance of a Night-Time 31. Mischief 31. A Night Like This 32. Thark 32. Just My Luck 33. Summer Lightning 33. Up to the Neck 33. Turkey Time 33. *A Cuckoo in the Nest* 33. A Cup of Kindness 34. Dirty Work 34. Fighting Stock 35. Stormy Weather 35. Foreign Affairs 35. In the Soup 36. Pot Luck 36. All In 36. For Valour 37.
✪ For personifying the Bertie Wooster tradition. *Rookery Nook.*

Lynn, Robert (1918–1982).
British director, in films from 1936 as camera assistant. Son of Ralph Lynn.

Postman's Knock 61. Dr Crippen 62. Victim Five 65. Change Partners 66. The Railway Children (p only) 71, etc.

Lynn, Sharon (1910–1963).
American leading lady of the 30s.

Sunny Side Up 29. The Big Broadcast 32. Enter Madame 34. *Way Out West* (tickling Stan Laurel) 36. West Point Widow 41, etc.

Lynn, Dame Vera (1917–).
British singing star, the 'Forces' Sweetheart' of World War II.

Autobiography: 1976, *Vocal Refrain.*
We'll Meet Again 44. One Exciting Night 45, etc.

Lyon, Ben (1901–1979).
Amiable American leading man of the 20s and 30s; came to Britain with his wife Bebe Daniels and stayed to become popular radio personality; later became casting director for 20th Century-Fox.

Biography: 1976, *Bebe and Ben* by Jill Allgood.
Open Your Eyes 19. Potash and Perlmutter 23. So Big 24. Bluebeard's Seven Wives 25. The Prince of Tempters 26. Dance Magic 27. The Air Legion 28. Alias French Gertie 30. *Hell's Angels* 30. The Hot Heiress 31. Her Majesty Love 31. Hat Check Girl 32. I Cover the Waterfront 33. Crimson Romance 34. Dancing Feet 36. I Killed the Count (GB) 38. Hi Gang (GB) 40. Life with the Lyons (GB) 54, etc.

Lyon, Francis D. (1905–).
American director, former editor.
■ Crazylegs 53. The Bob Mathias Story 54. Cult of the Cobra 55. The Great Locomotive Chase 56. The Oklahoman 56. Bale Out at 43,000 57. Gunsight Ridge 57. South Seas Adventure (co-d) 58. Escort West 59. The Tomboy and the Champ 61. The Young and the Brave 63. Destination Inner Space 66. Castle of Evil 67. The Destructors 68. The Money Jungle 68. The Girl Who Knew Too Much 69.

Lyon, Sue (1946–).
American juvenile actress.

Lolita 62. *Night of the Iguana* 64. Seven Women 65. The Flim Flam Man 67. Tony Rome 67. Evel Knievel 72. Crash 77. End of the World 77. The Astral Factor 78. Towing 78. Alligator 80, etc.

Lytell, Bert (1888–1954).
American leading man of silent films.

To Have and to Hold 17. The Lone Wolf 17. A Message from Mars 23. *Rupert of Hentzau* 23. Lady Windermere's Fan 25. Steele of the Royal Mounted 27. Blood Brothers 30. The Single Sin 31. Stage Door Canteen 43, etc.

M.
Fritz Lang was the first, in 1931, to film this story of a child-murderer finally hunted down by the city's organized criminal element, and Peter Lorre had his first great success as the psychopath. In 1950 Joseph Losey directed an almost scene-for-scene American remake starring David Wayne, but it generated no particular atmosphere. Woody Allen was more successful in creating Lang's air of decadence and despair in his comic-tinged *Shadows and Fog* 92.

m and e track.
A sound track giving music and effects but not dialogue, necessary in dubbing stages.

McAlpine, Donald.
Australian cinematographer, now working in Hollywood.
The Adventures of Barry Mackenzie 72. Barry Mackenzie Holds His Own 74. Don's Party 76. The Getting of Wisdom 77. My Brilliant Career 79. Breaker Morant 80. The Club 80. The Man from Snowy River 82. Tempest 82. Puberty Blue 83. Blue Skies Again 83. Moscow on the Hudson 84. King David 85. Down and Out in Beverly Hills 86. Predator 87. Orphans 87. Moving 88. Moon over Parador 88. See You in the Morning 89. Parenthood 89. Stanley and Iris 90. Career Opportunities (aka One Wild Night) 91. The Hard Way 91. Medicine Man 92. Patriot Games 92. The Man without a Face 93. Mrs Doubtfire 93. Clear and Present Danger 94, etc.

McAnally, Ray (1926–1989).
Bluff Irish character actor who was a mainstay of Dublin's Abbey Theatre. He studied for the priesthood before becoming an actor.
Shake Hands with the Devil 59. Billy Budd 62. The Looking Glass War 70. Fear Is the Key 72. Angel 82. Cal 84. Danny Boy 84. No Surrender 85. The Mission (AA) 86. The Fourth Protocol 87. Empire State 87. The Sicilian 87. White Mischief 87. A Perfect Spy (TV) 87. High Spirits 88. Taffin 88. A Very British Coup (TV) 89. My Left Foot 89. We're No Angels 89. Venus Peter 89, etc.

McAndrew, Marianne (1938–).
American leading lady.
Hello Dolly 69. The Seven Minutes 71. Bat People 74, etc.

MacArthur, Charles (1895–1956).
American playwright and screenwriter, long married to Helen Hayes; often collaborated with Ben Hecht (qv).
Biography: 1957, *Charlie* by Ben Hecht.
The Front Page (oa, w) 31. The Unholy Garden 31. Rasputin and the Empress (AAN) 32. 20th Century 34. Crime without Passion (wd, p) 35. Barbary Coast 35. Soak the Rich (wd, p) 36. Once in a Blue Moon (wd, p) 36. Gunga Din (w) 39. Wuthering Heights (co-w, AAN) 39. His Girl Friday 40. The Senator Was Indiscreet (w) 47. Perfect Strangers (oa) 50, etc.

MacArthur, Douglas (1880–1964).
American general made famous by the phrase 'I shall return' when he was forced to evacuate the Philippines in 1942. Later a potential president of the US, he had been played by Gregory Peck in *MacArthur* and by Laurence Olivier in *Inchon*. Robert Barrat, who looked more like him, played him in both *They Were Expendable* and *An American Guerrilla in the Philippines*.

MacArthur, James (1937–).
American leading man, former juvenile; adopted son of Charles MacArthur and Helen Hayes.
The Young Stranger 57. The Light in the Forest 58. The Third Man on the Mountain 59. Kidnapped 60. The Swiss Family Robinson 60. The Interns 62. Spencer's Mountain 63. The Truth about Spring 65. The Bedford Incident 65. Ride Beyond Vengeance 66. The Love-Ins 67. Hang 'Em High 68, etc.
TV series: *Hawaii Five-O* 68–79.

Macauley, Richard.
American screenwriter.
The Roaring Twenties (co-w) 39. They Drive By Night (co-w) 40. Torrid Zone (co-w) 40. *Across the Pacific* 42, etc.

McAvoy, May (1901–1984).
American leading lady of the 20s, a casualty of sound.
Hate 17. Mrs Wiggs of the Cabbage Patch 19. Sentimental Tommy 21. Clarence 22. The Enchanted Cottage 24. Ben Hur 26. The Jazz Singer 27. The Lion and the Mouse 28. The Terror 28. No Defense 29, etc.

McBain, Diane (1941–).
American leading lady of the 60s.
Ice Palace 60. Claudelle Inglish 61. A Distant Trumpet 64. Spin-Out 66. Thunder Alley 67. The Miniskirt Mob 68. The Delta Factor 70. Wicked, Wicked 73. Deathhead Virgin 74. Donner Pass – the Road to Survival (TV) 78. Flying from the Hawk 86, etc.

McBain, Ed.
American novelist, author of the *87th Precinct* crime novels. Actually a pseudonym for Evan Hunter, formerly Salvatore Lombino (1926–).

Macbeth.
Among many attempts to film Shakespeare's Scottish tragedy, none of them wholly successful, have been the following: in 1915 John Emerson directed and D. W. Griffith produced a straightforward version starring Sir Herbert Beerbohm Tree and Constance Collier; in 1948 Orson Welles directed and starred in his own adaptation shot in 21 days for Republic; in 1956 Ken Hughes wrote and directed a modernized version, *Joe Macbeth*, in which the kings and princes became rival gangsters; in 1957 Akira Kurosawa directed *Throne of Blood*, a stylized Japanese version; in 1960 George Schaefer directed an honest school exam-style rendering in colour with Maurice

Evans and Judith Anderson which was shown on US television but released theatrically in Britain; in 1971 Jon Finch and Francesca Annis starred in a blood-spattered version by Roman Polanski; in 1991 William Reilly again tried a gangster Macbeth in *Men of Respect*, starring John Turturro, which even included Lady M's sleep-walking scene in an attempt to keep its audience awake.

McBride, Donald (1894–1957).
American character comedian adept at explosive editors, dumb policemen, etc. Made debut in his stage role as the harassed hotel manager in *Room Service* 38.
The Story of Vernon and Irene Castle 39. *Here Comes Mr Jordan* 41. *Topper Returns* 41. Invisible Woman 41. They Got Me Covered 42. The Glass Key 42. Two Yanks in Trinidad 42. Abbott and Costello in Hollywood 45. Good News 48. Bowery Battalion 51. The Seven Year Itch 55, many others.

McBride, Jim (1941–).
American director.
David Holzman's Diary 67. My Girlfriend's Wedding 68. Glen and Randa 71. A Hard Day for Archie 73. Breathless 83. The Big Easy 87. Great Balls of Fire 89. The Wrong Man 93. Uncovered 94, etc.

McCallister, Lon (1923–) (Herbert Alonzo McCallister Jnr).
American leading man, usually in callow roles.
Souls at Sea 37. Babes in Arms 39. *Stage Door Canteen* 43. Home in Indiana 44. Winged Victory 44. The Red House 47. The Big Cat 50. Letter from Korea 50. Combat Squad 54, etc.

McCallum, David (1933–).
Slightly built Scottish juvenile lead of the 50s and 60s; became popular on American television as Ilya Kuriakin in the *UNCLE* series. He was married to actress Jill Ireland (1957–67).
The Secret Place 56. Robbery Under Arms 57. Violent Playground 58. The Long the Short and the Tall 61. Billy Budd 62. Freud 62. *The Great Escape* 63. The Greatest Story Ever Told 65. Around the World Under the Sea 66. Three Bites of the Apple 67. Sol Madrid 68. Mosquito Squadron 69. Frankenstein, The True Story 73. Diamond Hunters 75. Dogs 76. King Solomon's Treasure 78. The Watcher in the Woods 80. The Return of the Man from UNCLE (TV) 83. Terminal Choice 85. The Wind 87. The Haunting of Morella 90. Fatal Inheritance 91. Hear My Song 91. Dirty Weekend 93. Healer 94, etc.
TV series: *The Man from UNCLE* 64–67 (plus eight feature films 'amplified' from TV material for cinema release). *Colditz* 72. *Invisible Man* 75. Sapphire and Steel 79.

McCallum, John (1917–).
Australian leading man of stage and screen, in England 1945–55; married Googie Withers.
Joe Goes Back 44. The Root of All Evil 47. The Loves of Joanna Godden 47. The Woman in Question 50. Trent's Last Case 52. Trouble in the

Glen 53. Port of Escape 55. The Nickel Queen (d only) 71, etc.

McCallum, Neil (1929–1976).
Beefy Canadian actor in British films.
The Inspector 62. The Longest Day 62. The War Lover 63. Witchcraft 64, etc.

McCambridge, Mercedes (1918–).
Intense, unpredictable American character actress, often in cynical or hard-bitten roles. She also voiced the demon in *The Exorcist*. Her second husband was director Fletcher Markle (1950–62).
Autobiographies: 1960, *The Two of Us*. 1981, *The Quality of Mercy*.
■ *All the King's Men* (AA) 49. Lightning Strikes Twice 51. The Scarf 51. Inside Straight 51. Johnny Guitar 54. *Giant* (AAN) 56. A Farewell to Arms 57. Suddenly Last Summer 59. Cimarron 60. Angel Baby 61. 99 Women 69. The Hot Death (Ger.) 69. The Counterfeit Killer (TV) 70. Killer by Night (TV) 72. Two for the Money (TV) 72. The Girls of Huntington House (TV) 73. The President's Plane Is Missing (TV) 73. The Exorcist (voice only) 73. Who Is the Black Dahlia? (TV) 75. Thieves 77. The Sacketts (TV) 79. Airport 79 – the Concorde 79. Echoes 83.
TV series: Wire Service 56.

McCamus, Tom.
Canadian leading actor.
Norman's Awesome Experience 88. I Love a Man in Uniform 93, etc.

McCann, Chuck (1938–).
American character actor, from television.
The Heart Is a Lonely Hunter 68. The Projectionist 71. Play It as It Lays 72. Silent Movie 76. Foul Play 78. C.H.O.M.P.S. 79. If Things Were Different 79. Lunch Wagon 80. National Lampoon Goes to the Movies 83. The Rosebud Beach Hotel 84. Hamburger – the Motion Picture 86. Cameron's Closet 89. That's Adequate 90. Storyville 92. Ladybugs 92, etc.

McCarey, Leo (1898–1969).
American director with above-average talent and a sentimental streak. Before graduating to features he directed many silent shorts, including Laurel and Hardy as *Two Tars*.
■ The Sophomore 29. Red Hot Rhythm 29. Let's Go Native 30. Wild Company 30. Part Time Wife 30. Indiscretion 31. The Kid from Spain 32. *Duck Soup* 33. Six of a Kind 34. Belle of the Nineties 34. *Ruggles of Red Gap* 35. The Milky Way 36. *Make Way for Tomorrow* (& w, p) 37. *The Awful Truth* (& w) (AA) 37. *Love Affair* (co-story, AAN) (AA screenplay) 39. Once upon a Honeymoon 42. *Going My Way* (AA) (& p) 44. The Bells of St Mary's (& p) (AAN) 45. Good Sam (& p) 48. My Son John (& w, p) (AANw) 52. An Affair to Remember (& w, p) 57. Rally round the Flag Boys (& w, p) 58. Satan Never Sleeps (& w, p) 62.

McCarey, Ray (1904–1948).
American director of second features, formerly making Hal Roach shorts. Brother of Leo McCarey.
Pack Up Your Troubles 32. Millions in the Air 36. That Other Woman 42. Atlantic City 44. The Falcon's Alibi 46, etc.

McCarthy, Andrew (1962–).
American leading actor, usually in teenage-oriented films.
Class 83. Heaven Help Us 85. St Elmo's Fire 85. Pretty in Pink 86. Less Than Zero 87. Waiting for the Moon 87. Mannequin 87. Kansas 88. Weekend at Bernie's 89. Docteur M 90. Quiet Days in Clichy 90. Year of the Gun 91. Common Pursuit (TV) 91. Only You 92. Weekend at Bernie's 2 93. The Joy Luck Club 93. Mrs Parker and the Vicious Circle 94. Student Body 94, etc.

McCarthy, Frank (1912–1986).
American producer.
Decision before Dawn 51. Sailor of the King 53. A Guide for the Married Man 67. *Patton* (AA) 70, etc.

McCarthy, Joseph (1905–1957).
American senator who conducted in the early 50s a witch hunt of alleged communists, and was censured by the Senate in 1954. A 1977 television biopic, *Tail Gunner Joe*, starred Peter Boyle.

McCarthy, Kevin (1914–).
American leading man and latterly character actor, with stage experience.
Winged Victory (debut) 44. *Death of a Salesman* (AAN) 52. Stranger on Horseback 55. *Invasion of the Body Snatchers* 56. The Misfits 61. *The Prize* 63. The Best Man 64. Mirage 65. A Big Hand for the Little Lady 66. Hotel 67. If He Hollers Let Him Go 68. Revenge in El Paso 69. Kansas City Bomber 72. Alien Thunder 73. Buffalo Bill and the Indians 76. Invasion of the Body Snatchers (cameo) 78. Piranha 78. Captain Avenger 79. Those Lips Those Eyes 80. The Howling 81. My Tutor 83. Twilight Zone 83. Innerspace 87. The Sleeping Car 88. UHF 89. Eve of Destruction 90. Fast Food 91. The Distinguished Gentleman 92. Matinee 93, etc.
TV series: The Survivors 69. Flamingo Road 80–81. Amanda's 83. The Colbys 86–87.

McCarthy, Michael (1917–1959).
British director, in films from 1934.
Assassin for Hire 51. Mystery Junction 51. Crow Hollow 52. Shadow of a Man 54. It's Never Too Late 56. Smoke Screen 57. The Traitor 57. Operation Amsterdam 58, etc.

McCarthy, Sheila (1956–).
Canadian leading actress.
I've Heard the Mermaids Singing 87. Friends, Lovers and Lunatics (aka Crazy Horse) 89. White Room 90. Die Hard 2 90. Pacific Heights 90. Paradise 91. Stepping Out 91. Bright Angel 91. George's Island 91. Beautiful Dreamers 92. Beethoven Lives Upstairs 92. The Lotus Eaters 93, etc.

McCartney, Paul (1942–).
British songwriter, musician and composer. A member of The Beatles, he wrote many of the group's songs in collaboration with John Lennon and later formed the band Wings.
The Family Way (m) 67. Live and Let Die (title s) 73. The Honorary Consul (aka Beyond the Limit) (theme) 83. Give My Regards to Broad Street (a, w, m) 84. Twice in a Lifetime (co-m) 85. Eat the Rich (a) 87. Get Back (doc) 91, etc.

McCay, Winsor (1886–1934).
American pioneer animator who invented Gertie the Dinosaur in 1909.

McClory, Kevin (1926–).
Irish production executive, former sound technician. Wrote, produced and directed *The Boy and the Bridge* 59; produced *Thunderball* 65.

McClory, Sean (1923–).
Irish actor with Abbey Theatre experience; long in Hollywood.
Beyond Glory 49. Rommel, Desert Fox 51. Les Misérables 52. Ring of Fear 54. Moonfleet 55. Diane 57. Bandolero 68. The Dead 87. Fools of Fortune 90, etc.

McClure, Doug (1935–).
American leading man, from TV.
Because They're Young 59. The Unforgiven 60. Shenandoah 65. Beau Geste 66. The King's Pirate 67. Nobody's Perfect 68. The Judge and Jake Wyler (TV) 71. The Land That Time Forgot 75. At the Earth's Core 76. The People That Time Forgot 77. Warlords of Atlantis 77. Rebels (TV) 79. Humanoids from the Deep 80. The House Where Evil Dwells 82. Cannonball Run II 83. 52 Pick-Up 86. Omega Syndrome 87. Tapeheads 87. Dark before Dawn 88. Prime Suspect 88, etc.
TV series: Checkmate 59–61. Overland Trail 60. *The Virginian* 64–69. Search 72. Barbary Coast 76.

McClure, Greg (1918–) (Dale Easton).
American leading man who starred in his first film but did little thereafter.
The Great John L 45. Bury Me Dead 47. Lulu Belle 48. Joe Palooka in the Squared Circle 50. Stop That Cab 51, etc.

McCord, Ted (1898–1976).
American cinematographer.
So Big 24. We Moderns 25. Irene 26. Valley of the Giants 26. Phantom City 28. The Fighting Legion 30. The Big Stampede 32. The Rainmakers 35. Fugitive in the Sky 36. Secret Service of the Air 39. The Case of the Black Parrot 41. Murder in the Big House 42. Action in the North Atlantic 43. Deep Valley 47. The Treasure of the Sierra Madre 48. *Johnny Belinda* 48. Flamingo Road 49. The Damned Don't Cry 50. Young Man with a Horn 50. The Breaking Point 50. Force of Arms 51. Young at Heart 54. East of Eden 55. The Helen Morgan Story 57. The Proud Rebel 58. The Hanging Tree 59. Two for the Seesaw 62. *The Sound of Music* 65. A Fine Madness 66, many others.

MacCorkindale, Simon (1952–).
Budding British leading man of the late 70s, now also a producer. He is married to actress Susan George.
Jesus of Nazareth (TV) 77. Death on the Nile 78. The Riddle of the Sands 79. Quatermass (TV) 79. Cabo Blanco 79. The Manions of America (TV) 80. The Sword and the Sorcerer 82. Jaws 3-D 83. Stealing Heaven (p) 88. That Summer of White Roses (w, p) 89, etc.
TV series: Manimal 83. Falcon Crest 85–87.

McCormack, John (1884–1945).
Irish tenor.
Song o' My Heart 30. Wings of the Morning 37.

McCormack, Patty (1945–).
American juvenile actress who went to Hollywood to repeat her stage role as the evil child of *The Bad Seed* (AAN) 56.
The Day They Gave Babies Away 57. Kathy O' 58. The Adventures of Huckleberry Finn 60. The Explosive Generation 61. The Young Runaways 68. Invitation to Hell (TV) 84. Saturday the 14th Strikes Back 88, etc.
TV series: Peck's Bad Girl 59.

McCormick, F. J. (1891–1947) (Peter Judge).
Irish character actor, long on the Abbey Theatre stage. Well remembered as Shell in *Odd Man Out* 46.
The Plough and the Stars 37. Hungry Hill 46.

McCormick, Myron (1908–1962).
Wry-faced American character actor, with stage experience.
Winterset 37. One Third of a Nation 39. Jigsaw 9. Jolson Sings Again 50. No Time for Sergeants 8. *The Hustler* 61, etc.

McCowan, George (1931–).
Canadian director, mainly of TV movies.
Frogs 72. The Magnificent Seven Ride! 72. Murder on Flight 502 (TV) 75. Return to Fantasy land (TV) 78. The Shape of Things to Come 79. Vanity Clause (TV) 90, etc.

McCowen, Alec (1925–).
British stage actor, in occasional films.
Time Without Pity 57. Town on Trial 57. The Loneliness of the Long Distance Runner 62. In the Cool of the Day 63. The Agony and the Ecstasy 5. The Witches 66. The Hawaiians (US) 70. Frenzy 72. *Travels With My Aunt* 72. Stevie 78. Hanover Street 79. Never Say Never Again 83. The Assam Garden 85. Personal Services 86. Cry Freedom 87. Henry V 89. The Age of Innocence 93, etc.

McCoy, Tim (1891–1978).
American cowboy star, in films from 1923 when, an ex-army officer, he went to Hollywood as adviser on *The Covered Wagon.*
War Paint 26. The Indians Are Coming 30. The Fighting Fool 31. Texas Cyclone 32. Whirlwind 33. Hell Bent for Love 34. Square Shooter 35, many others. Later played bit parts: Around the World in Eighty Days 56. Run of the Arrow 57. Requiem for a Gunfighter 65, etc.
TV series: The Tim McCoy Show 52.

McCrea, Joel (1905–1990).
Athletic, good-humoured, dependable American hero of the 30s and 40s, who later starred in westerns. He was married for 57 years to actress Frances Dee.
Biography: 1992, *Joel McCrea: Riding the High Country* by Tony Thomas.
■ The Jazz Age 29. So This Is College 29. Dynamite 29. The Silver Horde 29. Lightnin' 30. Once a Sinner 30. Kept Husbands 31. The Common Law 31. Born to Love 31. Girls about Town 31. Business and Pleasure 32. The Lost Squadron 32. *Bird of Paradise* 32. *The Most Dangerous Game* 32. Rockabye 32. The Sport Parade 32. Scandal for Sale 32. Laughter in Hell 33. The Silver Cord 33. Bed of Roses 33. One Man's Journey 33. Chance at Heaven 33. Gambling Lady 34. Half a Sinner 34. The Richest Girl in the World 34. Private Worlds 35. Our Little Girl 35. Woman Wanted 35. Barbary Coast 35. Splendour 35. These Three 36. Two in a Crowd 36. Adventure in Manhattan 36. Come and Get It 36. Banjo on My Knee 36. Internes Can't Take Money 37. Wells Fargo 37. Woman Chases Man 37. *Dead End* 37. Three Blind Mice 38. Youth Takes a Fling 38. Union Pacific 39. They Shall Have Music 39. Espionage Agent 39. He Married His Wife 40. The Primrose Path 40. *Foreign Correspondent* 40. Reaching for the Sun 41. *Sullivan's Travels* 41. The Great Man's Lady 42. *The Palm Beach Story* 42. *The More the Merrier* 43. Buffalo Bill 44. The Great Moment 44. The Unseen 45. The Virginian 46. Ramrod 47. Four Faces West 48. South of St Louis 49. Colorado Territory 49. Stars in My Crown 50. The Outriders 50. Saddle Tramp 50. Frenchie 50. Cattle Drive 51. The San Francisco Story 52. Lone Hand 53. Rough Shoot (GB) 53. Black Horse Canyon 54. Border River 54. Stranger on Horseback 55. Wichita 55. The First Texan 56. The Oklahoman 57. Trooper Hook 57. Gunsight Ridge 57. The Tall Stranger 57. Cattle Empire 58. Fort Massacre 58. Gunfight at Dodge City 59. *Ride the High Country* 62. Cry Blood Apache 71. Mustang Country 76.
TV series: *Wichita Town* 59.
✪ For the amiable generosity of his playing which turned him from a second lead into the undoubted star of several of the most prized films of the early 40s. *Sullivan's Travels.*

McCullers, Carson (1917–1967).
American novelist, usually on themes pertaining to her homeland, the Deep South. *The Member of the Wedding, Reflections in a Golden Eye, The Heart Is a Lonely Hunter* and *The Ballad of the Sad Café* were filmed.

¶ An hour with a dentist without Novocaine was like a minute with Carson McCullers. – *Gore Vidal*

McCullough, Paul (1884–1936).
American farce comedian, with Bobby Clark in two-reelers 1928–35.

McDaniel, Hattie (1895–1952).
American character actress of cheerful and immense presence; once a radio vocalist.
The Story of Temple Drake 33. Judge Priest 35. Showboat 36. Nothing Sacred 37. *Gone with the Wind* (AA) 39. Zenobia 39. *The Great Lie* 41. Thank Your Lucky Stars 43. Margie 46. Song of the South 47. Family Honeymoon 49, many others.
TV series: *Beulah* 52.

McDermott, Hugh (1908–1972).
Scottish-born character actor, in British films from mid-30s, specializing in hearty transatlantic types.
The Wife of General Ling 38. Pimpernel Smith 41. The Seventh Veil 45. No Orchids for Miss Blandish 48. Trent's Last Case 52. A King in New York 57. The First Men in the Moon 64. Captain Apache 71. Chato's Land 72, many others.

McDevitt, Ruth (1895–1976) (Ruth Shoecraft).
American character actress.
The Parent Trap 62. The Birds 63. The Out of Towners 69. Change of Habit 72, many others.
TV series: Pistols and Petticoats 66. Kolchak 74.

McDonald, Bruce (1959–).
Canadian director, screenwriter and actor.
Roadkill (a, d) 89. Highway 61 (d) 91. Dance Me Outside (co-w, d) 94.

MacDonald, David (1904–1983).
British director who showed promise in the 30s and 40s but declined to second features.
Double Alibi 27. It's Never Too Late to Mend 37. Dead Men Tell No Tales 38. A Spot of Bother 38. *This Man is News* 38. This Man in Paris 39. Spies of the Air 39. Law and Disorder 40. Men of the Lightship 40. This England 40. *The Brothers* 47. Good Time Girl 48. Snowbound 48. Christopher Columbus 49. Diamond City 49. The Bad Lord Byron 49. Cairo Road 50. The Adventures 51. The Lost Hours 52. Tread Softly 53. Devil Girl from Mars 54. Alias John Preston 56. Small Hotel 57. *The Moonraker* 58. Petticoat Pirates 61, etc.

McDonald, Dwight (1906–1982).
American film critic of semi-revered status: *On Movies* 69, etc.

McDonald, Frank (1899–1980).
American director of second features; former stage actor and author.
The Murder of Dr Harrigan 38. Carolina Moon 40. One Body Too Many 44. My Pal Trigger 46. Father Takes the Air 51. The Treasure of Ruby Hills 55. The Underwater City 61, etc.

McDonald, Grace (1921–).
American singing and dancing second lead of many a 40s 'B'.
Dancing on a Dime 40. What's Cooking (GB: Wake Up and Dream) 42. Give Out Sisters 42. Crazy House 43. Gung Ho 43. It Ain't Hay 43. Follow the Boys 44. My Gal Loves Music 44. See My Lawyer 45. Honeymoon Ahead 45, etc.

MacDonald, J. Farrell (1875–1952).
American minstrel singer who became a familiar Hollywood character actor.
The Maltese Falcon 31. The Thirteenth Guest 32. The Cat's Paw 34. The Irish in Us 36. Topper 37. Little Orphan Annie 39. Meet John Doe 41. My Darling Clementine 46. Mr Belvedere Rings the Bell 51, etc.

MacDonald, Jeanette (1906–1965).
American concert singer and leading lady of the 30s. Popular on her own account, she made a fondly remembered series of film operettas with Nelson Eddy, and these are noted (E) below. Married actor Gene Raymond.
Biography: 1976, *The Jeanette MacDonald Story* by James Robert Parish.
■ *The Love Parade* 29. The Vagabond King 30. Monte Carlo 30. Let's Go Native 30. The Lottery Bride 30. Oh For a Man 30. Don't Bet on Women 31. Annabelle's Affairs 31. *One Hour With You* 32. *Love Me Tonight* 32. The Cat and the Fiddle 32. The Merry Widow 34. *Naughty Marietta* (E) 35. *Rose Marie* (E) 36. *San Francisco* 36. Maytime (E) 37. The Firefly 37. The Girl of the Golden West (E) 38. Sweethearts (E) 39. Broadway Serenade 39. New Moon (E) 40. Bitter Sweet (E) 40. Smilin' Through 41. I Married an Angel (E) 42. Cairo 42. Follow the Boys 44. Three Daring Daughters 48. The Sun Comes Up 49.

MacDonald, John D. (1916–1986).
American detective story writer, author of the Travis McGee novels. (For John Ross MacDonald see under *Ross*.)
Mantrap 61. Cape Fear (The Executioners) 62. Darker than Amber 70. Travis McGee (TV) 82. Cape Fear 91.

MacDonald, Joseph (1906–1968).
American cinematographer.
Charlie Chan in Rio 41. Sunday Dinner for a Soldier 44. *Yellow Sky* 48. Panic in the Streets 50. *Viva Zapata* 52. Niagara 53. Titanic 53. How to Marry a Millionaire 53. Broken Lance 54. A Hatful of Rain 57. Ten North Frederick 57. Pepe 60. Kings of the Sun 63. The Carpetbaggers 63. Rio Conchos 64. Invitation to a Gunfighter 64. Mirage 65. Blindfold 65. The Sand Pebbles (AAN) 66. Mackenna's Gold 68, many others.

McDonald, Marie (1923–1965) (Marie Frye).
American leading lady, publicized as 'The Body'; former model.
Pardon My Sarong 42. A Scream in the Dark 44. Getting Gertie's Garter 46. Living in a Big Way 47. Tell It to the Judge 49. Geisha Boy 59. Promises Promises 63, etc.

Macdonald, Peter.
English director.
Rambo III 88. Mo' Money 92. The Neverending Story III 94.

MacDonald, Philip (1896–   ).
British thriller writer who contributed much
material to the screen.

The Lost Patrol 34. The Mystery of Mr X 34.
Menace 34. The Hour of Thirteen 52. The List of
Adrian Messenger 63, plus scripts for several Chan
and Moto films.

McDonald, Ray (1923–1959).
American actor-dancer of lightweight 40s
musicals.

Babes on Broadway 41. Presenting Lily Mars 43.
Till the Clouds Roll By 46. Good News 47. All
Ashore 53, etc.

Macdonald, Richard (1919–1993).
British production designer. He studied at the
Royal College of Art and was head of painting at
Leeds College of Art before becoming an art
director in advertising. From the mid-60s he
switched to films following a chance meeting with
Joseph Losey which resulted in him working on
Sleeping Tiger 54 and many of the director's
subsequent films.

The Servant 63. Modesty Blaise 66. *Far from the
Madding Crowd* 67. Boom 68. A Severed Head 71.
Jesus Christ Superstar 73. *Day of the Locust* 75.
Marathon Man 76. Swashbuckler 76. F.I.S.T. 78.
And Justice for All 79. The Rose 79. Cannery Row
82. Something Wicked This Way Comes 83.
Supergirl 84. Electric Dreams 84. Teachers 84.
Plenty 85. Spacecamp 86. Coming to America 88.
The Russia House 90. The Addams Family 91. The
Firm 93, etc.

MacDonald, Ross (1915–1983) (Kenneth Millar).
American detective story writer whose mysteries
are much in the vein of Raymond Chandler.

Harper 66. The Drowning Pool 75.

TV series: Archer 75.

McDonell, Fergus (1910–   ).
British director.

The Small Voice 48. Prelude to Fame 50. Private
Information 52, etc.

McDonnell, Mary (1952–   ).
American leading actress.

Matewan 87. Tiger Warsaw 88. Dances with
Wolves (AAN) 90. Grand Canyon 91. Passion Fish
92. Sneakers 92, etc.

TV series: E/R 84–85.

McDormand, Frances (1957–   ).
American actress.

Blood Simple 84. Raising Arizona 87. Mississippi
Burning (AAN) 88. Chatahoochee 90. Darkman
90. Hidden Agenda 90. Short Cuts 93, etc.

MacDougall, Ranald (1915–1973).
American screenwriter.

Mildred Pierce (AAN) 45. Objective Burma 45.
Possessed 47. The Unsuspected 47. June Bride 48.
The Hasty Heart 49. Bright Leaf 50. I'll Never
Forget You 51. The Naked Jungle 54. Queen Bee
(& d) 55. The Mountain 56. Man on Fire (& d) 57.
The World the Flesh and the Devil (& d) 59. Go
Naked in the World (& d) 61. The Cockeyed
Cowboys of Calico County (& d) 69, etc.

MacDougall, Roger (1910–1993).
British screenwriter and playwright.

This Man Is News (w) 38. The Foreman went to
France (w) 42. *The Man in the White Suit* (oaw)
(AAN) 51. To Dorothy a Son (oa) 54. *Escapade* (oa)
56. The Mouse That Roared (w) 59. A Touch of
Larceny (w) 60, etc.

McDowall, Betty.
Australian actress who at one time played wives
in scores of British films.

The Shiralee 57. Time Lock 57. She Didn't Say
No 58. Jack the Ripper 59. Jackpot 60. Spare the
Rod 61. Tomorrow at Ten 62. Echo of Diana 63.
Ballad in Blue 64. The Liquidator 65. The Omen
76, etc.

McDowall, Roddy (1928–   ).
British child actor of the 40s, in Hollywood from
1940. Developed into an unpredictable adult
performer, but made a reputation as a
photographer.

Murder in the Family 36. Just William 39. This
England 40. Man Hunt 41. *How Green Was My
Valley* 41. Confirm or Deny 41. The Pied Piper 42.
My Friend Flicka 43. Lassie Come Home 43. The
White Cliffs of Dover 44. Thunderhead 45. Holiday
in Mexico 46. Macbeth 50. Killer Shark 50. The
Subterraneans 60. The Longest Day 62. Cleopatra
63. Shock Treatment 64. The Loved One 65. That
Darn Cat 65. Lord Love a Duck 66. The Cool Ones
67. It 67. Planet of the Apes 67. Five Card Stud
68. Angel Angel Down You Go 69. Tam Lin (d
only) 70. Escape from the Planet of the Apes 71.
Bedknobs and Broomsticks 71. Pretty Maids All in
a Row 71. Conquest of the Planet of the Apes 72.
The Poseidon Adventure 72. The Legend of Hell
House 73. Battle for the Planet of the Apes 73.
Arnold 74. Funny Lady 75. Mean Johnny Barrows
76. Embryo 77. Rabbit Test 78. The Cat from
Outer Space 78. Circle of Iron 79. Scavenger Hunt
79. Evil under the Sun 82. Class of 1984 82. Dead
of Winter 87. Fright Night Part 2 89. Cutting Class
89. The Big Picture 89. Shakma 89. Disturbed 90.
The Color of Evening 91. Deadly Game (TV) 91.
Double Trouble 92, etc.

TV series: Planet of the Apes 74. Fantastic
Journey 77. Tales of the Gold Monkey 82–83.
Bridges to Cross 86.

MacDowell, Andie (1958–   ).
American leading actress, a former model.

Greystoke: The Legend of Tarzan, Lord of the
Apes 84. St Elmo's Fire 85. sex, lies and videotape
89. Green Card 90. Hudson Hawk 91. Object of
Beauty 91. Ground Hog Day 93. Ruby Cairo 93.
Short Cuts 93. Four Weddings and a Funeral 94.
Bad Girls 94, etc.

McDowell, Malcolm (1943–   ).
Fashionable British leading actor of the early 70s.
His second wife was actress Mary Steenburgen
(1980–90).

■ Poor Cow 67. *If* 69. Figures in a Landscape 70.
The Raging Moon 71. *A Clockwork Orange* 71. *O
Lucky Man* 73. Royal Flash 75. Voyage of the
Damned 76. Aces High 76. The Passage 79. Time
after Time 79. Caligula 77. Cat People 82. Britannia
Hospital 82. Arthur the King (TV) 83. Blue Thunder
83. Cross Creek 83. Get Crazy 83. Buy and Cell
89. Class of 1999 89. Moon 44 89. Jezebel's Kiss
90. Lambarene 91. The Tsar's Assassin 91. The
Player 92. East Wind (Fr.) 93. Bopha! 93. Seasons
of the Heart (TV) 94. Star Trek: Generations
94, etc.

McEachin, James (1931–   ).
American actor of the 70s, TV's *Tenafly* 73–74.

Play Misty for Me 71. The Alpha Caper (TV) 73.
Every Which Way but Loose 79. 2010 84.

McEnery, John (1945–   ).
British light leading man of the 70s.

Romeo and Juliet 68. The Lady in a Car 70.
Bartleby 71. Nicholas and Alexandra 71. Days of
Fury 73. The Land that Time Forgot 74. Little

Malcolm 74. The Duellists 78. Hamlet 90. The
Fool 90. Prince of Shadows (Beltenebros) 92. Black
Beauty 94, etc.

McEnery, Peter (1940–   ).
British leading man with TV experience.

Tunes of Glory 60. Victim 62. The Moonspinners
64. The Fighting Prince of Donegal 66. The Game
Is Over 66. I Killed Rasputin 68. Negatives 68.
Entertaining Mr Sloane 70. The Adventures of
Gerard 70. Tales that Witness Madness 73. The Cat
and the Canary 78, etc.

McEntire, Reba (1955–   ).
American actress and leading country singer.

Tremors 90. The Little Rascals 94.

McEveety, Bernard.
American director, from TV. He is the brother of
Vincent McEveety.

Broken Sabre 65. Ride Beyond Vengeance 66.
The Brotherhood of Satan 70. Napoleon and
Samantha 72. One Little Indian 73. The Bears and
I 74. Roughnecks (TV) 80, etc.

McEveety, Joseph L. (1926–1976).
American producer, long with Disney.

McEveety, Vince (Vincent).
American director.

Firecreek 68. Million Dollar Duck 71. The
Strongest Man in the World 74. Gus 76. Herbie Goes
to Monte Carlo 77. The Apple Dumpling Gang
Rides Again 79. Herbie Goes Bananas 80. Amy 81,
etc.

McEwan, Geraldine (1932–   ).
Leading British stage actress.

Escape from the Dark 76. The Bawdy
Adventures of Tom Jones 76. Foreign Body 87.
Henry V 89. Robin Hood: Prince of Thieves 91, etc.

TV series: Mulberry 93.

McEwan, Ian (1948–   ).
British screenwriter and novelist.

The Imitation Game (TV) 81. The Ploughman's
Lunch 83. The Comfort of Strangers (oa) 90. The
Innocent 92. The Cement Garden (oa) 92. The
Innocent (w from his novel) 93. The Good Son
(w) 93.

McFadden, Hamilton (1901–   ).
American director of 'B' features.

Harmony at Home 30. Charlie Chan Carries On
31. Second Hand Wife 33. Stand Up and Cheer 34.
Elinor Norton 35. The Three Legionnaires 37. Sea
Racketeers 39. Inside the Law 42, etc.

McFarland, Spanky (1928–1993) (George
Emmett McFarland).
American child actor of the 30s, the fat boy of the
'Our Gang' one-reelers.

Day of Reckoning 33. Kentucky Kernels 35.
O'Shaughnessy's Boy 35. Trail of the Lonesome
Pine 36. Peck's Bad Boy with the Circus 39.
Johnny Doughboy 43. Moonrunners 74, etc.

McGann, Paul (1959–   ).
British leading actor, from the stage.

Withnail and I 86. Empire of the Sun 87. Dealers
89. Drowning in the Shallow End 89. The
Rainbow 89. Streets of Yesterday 89. Tree of Hands
89. Paper Mask 90. The Monk 90. Afraid of the
Dark 91. Alien³ 92. The Three Musketeers 93, etc.

McGann, William (1895–1977).
American director of second features.

I Like Your Nerve 31. Illegal 32. The Case of the

Black Cat 36. Penrod and Sam 37. Blackwell's Island 39. The Parson of Panamint 41. Tombstone 42. Frontier Badmen 43, etc.

McGavin, Darren (1922–).
American 'character lead' who can play unpleasant villains or tough heroes.

Fear 46. Summer Madness 55. The Court Martial of Billy Mitchell 55. *The Man with the Golden Arm* 56. The Delicate Delinquent 57. Beau James 57. The Case Against Brooklyn 58. Bullet for a Badman 64. The Great Sioux Massacre 65. Mrs Pollifax – Spy 70. Happy Mother's Day Love George 73. The Night Stalker (TV) 74. The Night Strangler (TV) 74. No Deposit No Return 76. Airport 77 77. Hot Lead and Cold Feet 78. Zero to Sixty 78. Ike (TV) 79. Hangar 18 80. From the Hip 87. Sunset 88. Blood and Concrete 91, etc.

TV series: Crime Photographer 53. *Mike Hammer* 58. *Riverboat* 60. The Outsider 68. The Night Stalker 74.

McGee, Fibber (1896–1988) (James Jordan).
American radio comedian, always with his wife 'Molly' (Marion: 1898–1961).

This Way Please 38. Look Who's Laughing 40. Here We Go Again 41. Heavenly Days 44, etc.

McGee, Vonetta (1948–).
American actress.

The Lost Man 69. The Kremlin Letter 69. Blacula 72. Shaft in Africa 73. The Eiger Sanction 75. Brothers 77. Superdome (TV) 78. To Sleep with Anger 90, etc.

McGill, Barney (–1941).
American cinematographer.

Breezy Jim 19. The Critical Age 23. Casey at the Bat 27. The Terror 28. Show of Shows 29. Doorway to Hell 30. Mammy 30. *Svengali* 31. The Mouthpiece 32. Cabin in the Cotton 32. Twenty Thousand Years in Sing Sing 33. Mayor of Hell 33. *The Bowery* 33. The President Vanishes 34. My Marriage 35. Thank You Jeeves 36. Lancer Spy 37. Sharpshooters 38. The Cisco Kid and the Lady 40, many others.

McGillis, Kelly (1957–).
American actress.
■ Reuben, Reuben 82. Witness 85. Top Gun 85. Made in Heaven 87. The House on Carroll Street 88. The Accused 88. Winter People 89. The Babe 92. Grand Isle 92. Bonds of Love (TV) 93.

McGinn, Walter (1936–1977).
American character actor of the 70s.
The Parallax View 74. Delancy Street (TV) 75.

MacGinnis, Niall (1913–).
Irish-born actor, in films from 1935.

Turn of the Tide 35. Edge of the World 38. 49th Parallel 41. We Dive at Dawn 43. Henry V 44. No Highway 51. *Martin Luther* (title role) 53. The Battle of the River Plate 55. *Night of the Demon* 57. The Nun's Story 58. Billy Budd 62. A Face in the Rain 62. Becket 64. Island of Terror 66. The Torture Garden 67. Sinful Davey 69. The Mackintosh Man 73, etc.

McGiver, John (1913–1975).
American character comedian with worried, owl-like features.

Love in the Afternoon 57. *Breakfast at Tiffany's* 61. Mr Hobbs Takes a Vacation 62. The Manchurian Candidate 62. Who's Minding the Store? 63. Man's Favourite Sport? 64. Marriage on the Rocks 65. The Spirit is Willing 67. Fitzwilly 67. Midnight Cowboy 69. Lawman 70. The Great

Man's Whiskers (TV) 71. The Apple Dumpling Gang 75, etc.

TV series: *Many Happy Returns* 64. *The James Stewart Show* 71.

McGivern, William P. (1924–1983).
American mystery novelist.

The Big Heat 53. Rogue Cop 54. Hell on Frisco Bay 55. Odds Against Tomorrow 59. The Caper of the Golden Bulls 67.

McGlynn, Frank (1867–1951).
American character actor, adept at portraying Abraham Lincoln.

Min and Bill 31. Little Miss Marker 34. The Littlest Rebel 35. Trail of the Lonesome Pine 36. Prisoner of Shark Island 37. Wells Fargo 37. Union Pacific 39. Boom Town 40, many others.

McGoohan, Patrick (1928–).
American-born leading man with individual characteristics; in British films, after stage experience, from the mid-50s.

Passage Home 55. Zarak 55. *High Tide at Noon* 56. *Hell Drivers* 57. The Gypsy and the Gentleman 57. Nor the Moon by Night 58. Two Living One Dead 60. All Night Long 61. The Quare Fellow 62. *Life For Ruth* 62. Dr Syn 63. Ice Station Zebra 68. The Moonshine War 70. Mary Queen of Scots 72. Catch My Soul (d only) 73. The Genius (It.) 75. Silver Streak 76. Brass Target 78. Escape From Alcatraz 79. Scanners 81. Jamaica Inn (TV) 83. Finding Katie 83. Baby . . . Secret of the Lost Legend 84. Three Sovereigns for Sarah (TV) 85. Braveheart 95, etc.

TV series: *Danger Man* (Secret Agent) 59–62. *The Prisoner* 67. Rafferty 77.

McGovern, Elizabeth (1961–).
American leading lady.
■ Ordinary People 80. Heaven's Gate 80. Ragtime (AAN) 81. Lovesick 83. Racing with the Moon 84. Once upon a Time in America 84. Native Son 86. The Bedroom Window 87. She's Having a Baby 88. Johnny Handsome 89. The Handmaid's Tale 90. A Shock to the System 90. Tune in Tomorrow (aka Aunt Julia and the Scriptwriter) 90. The Favor 91. King of the Hill 93. The Favor 94.

MacGowan, Kenneth (1888–1963).
American film theorist and teacher (at UCLA) who was also a notable producer. Author of several film textbooks.

Little Women 33. Becky Sharp 35. Young Mr Lincoln 39. Man Hunt 41. Lifeboat 43. Jane Eyre 43, etc.

MacGowan, Robert A. (1901–).
American producer who devised the original 'Our Gang' comedies.

MacGowran, Jack (1918–1973).
Irish character actor, notably in the plays of Samuel Beckett.

The Quiet Man 52. The Gentle Gunman 52. The Titfield Thunderbolt 53. The Rising of the Moon 57. Darby O'Gill and the Little People 59. Blind Date 60. Mix Me a Person 61. Lord Jim 65. Cul de Sac 66. The Fearless Vampire Killers 67. How I Won the War 67. Wonderwall 68. The Exorcist 73, etc.

TV series: Sailor of Fortune 56.

McGrath, Frank (1903–1967).
Grizzled American stunt-man who appeared in countless westerns but achieved his greatest popularity as the trail cook in TV's *Wagon Train* series.

McGrath, Joe (1930–).
Scottish director whose TV style of goonish comedy has adapted less successfully to film.

Casino Royale (part) 67. Thirty is a Dangerous Age Cynthia 68. The Bliss of Mrs Blossom 68. The Magic Christian 70. Digby 73. The Great McGonagall 74. I'm Not Feeling Myself Tonight 76. Rising Damp 80. Just Desserts (TV) 86, etc.

MacGraw, Ali (1938–) (Alice McGraw).
American leading lady. She was married to producer Robert Evans (1971–73) and actor Steve McQueen (1973–78).
Autobiography: 1991, *Moving Pictures*.
■ A Lovely Way to Die 68. *Goodbye Columbus* 69. *Love Story* (AAN) 71. Getaway 72. Convoy 79. Players 79. Just Tell Me What You Want 80. The Winds of War (TV) 83. China Girl (TV) 83. The Killer Elite (TV) 85. Survive the Savage Sea 91. Gunsmoke: The Long Ride (TV) 93. Natural Causes 94.

TV series: Dynasty 85.

McGraw, Charles (1914–1980).
American actor, invariably in tough roles.

The Moon Is Down 43. The Killers 46. The Armored Car Robbery 50. *The Narrow Margin* 50. His Kind of Woman 51. The Bridges at Toko-Ri 51. Away All Boats 56. Slaughter on Tenth Avenue 58. The Defiant Ones 58. The Wonderful Country 59. Spartacus 60. Cimarron 61. In Cold Blood 67. Pendulum 69. Johnny Got His Gun 71. Twilight's Last Gleaming 76, etc.

TV series: Casablanca 55. The Smith Family 72.

McGuane, Thomas (1939–).
American screenwriter.

Rancho de Luxe 75. 92 in the Shade (& d) 75. The Missouri Breaks 76. Tom Horn 80. Cold Feet 89, etc.

macguffin (aka mcGuffin).
Term invented by director Alfred Hitchcock to describe the plot device, of little intrinsic interest, such as lost or stolen papers, that triggers the action.

McGuire, Biff (1926–).
American character actor.

The Phoenix City Story 55. Station Six Sahara 62. The Thomas Crown Affair 68. Serpico 73. Midway 76. Deadline Assault 90, etc.

TV series: Gibbsville 76.

McGuire, Don (1919–1979).
American writer-director, former press agent. Then to TV as producer-director of the *Hennessey* series.

Meet Danny Wilson (w) 51. Walking My Baby Back Home (w) 52. Three Ring Circus (w) 54. Bad Day at Black Rock (co-w) 54. Johnny Concho (wd) 56. The Delicate Delinquent (wd) 57.

McGuire, Dorothy (1918–).
American leading lady of the 40s, latterly playing mothers; always in gentle, sympathetic roles.
■ Claudia 43. A Tree Grows in Brooklyn 44. The Enchanted Cottage 44. The Spiral Staircase 45. Claudia and David 46. Till the End of Time 46. Gentleman's Agreement (AAN) 47. Mother Didn't Tell Me 50. Mister 880 50. Callaway Went Thataway 50. I Want You 51. Invitation 52. Make Haste to Live 53. Three Coins in the Fountain 54. Trial 55. Friendly Persuasion 56. Old Yeller 57. The Remarkable Mr Pennypacker 59. This Earth Is Mine 59. A Summer Place 60. The Dark at the Top of the Stairs 60. The Swiss Family Robinson 60. Susan Slade 61. Summer Magic 63. The Greatest

Story Ever Told (as the Virgin Mary) 65. Flight of the Doves 71. She Waits (TV) 71. The Runaways (TV) 75. Rich Man Poor Man (TV) 76. Little Women (TV) 78. The Incredible Journey of Dr Meg Laurel (TV) 79. *Ghost Dancing* (TV) 83. Amos (TV) 85. American Geisha (TV) 86. I Never Sang for My Father (TV) 87. Caroline (TV) 90.

McHattie, Stephen.
Lean Canadian leading man, in American films.
The People Next Door 70. Von Richthofen and Brown 71. Search for the Gods (TV) 75. The Ultimate Warrior 75. Look What Happened to Rosemary's Baby (TV) 76. *James Dean* (TV) (title role) 76. Moving Violation 76. Gray Lady Down 77. Centennial (TV) 77. Roughnecks (TV) 80. Death Valley 82. Belizaire the Cajun 86. One Man Out 88. Bloodhounds of Broadway 89. The Dark 93. Geronimo: An American Legend 93. Beverly Hills Cop III 94, etc.
TV series: Centennial 78–79. Highcliffe Manor 79. Beauty and the Beast 89–90.

McHugh, Frank (1899–1981).
Amiable American character actor with surprised look, frequently in Irish-American roles.
If Men Played Cards as Women Do 28. Dawn Patrol 30. The Mystery of the Wax Museum 33. Footlight Parade 33. Havana Widows 34. A Midsummer Night's Dream 35. Three Men on a Horse 36. Swing Your Lady 38. Going My Way 44. State Fair 45. Mighty Joe Young 49. My Son John 52. There's No Business Like Show Business 54. Career 59. A Tiger Walks 64. Easy Come Easy Go 67, many others.
TV series: *The Bing Crosby Show* 64.

McHugh, Jimmy (1895–1969).
American songwriter: 'I Can't Give You Anything But Love, Baby', 'I Feel a Song Comin' On', 'On the Sunny Side of the Street', etc.
You'll Find Out 40. Seven Days Ashore 43. Do You Love Me? 46, etc.

McIntire, John (1907–1991).
Spare, laconic American character actor with radio and stage experience, in Hollywood from the mid-40s, often as sheriff, editor, politician, cop. He was married to Jeannette Nolan.
The Asphalt Jungle 50. Lawless Breed 52. A Lion Is in the Streets 53. Apache 54. The Far Country 54. The Kentuckian 55. Backlash 56. The Phenix City Story 56. The Tin Star 57. Flaming Star 60. Psycho 60. Summer and Smoke 62. Rough Night in Jericho 67. Herbie Rides Again 73. Rooster Cogburn 75. The Jordan Chance (TV) 78. The Fox and the Hound (voice only) 81. Honkytonk Man 82. Cloak and Dagger 84. As Summers Die (TV) 86, etc.
TV series: *Naked City* 59. *Wagon Train* 61–64. *The Virginian* 67–69.

McIntyre, Christine (1916–1984).
American actress, playing leading roles in westerns, especially opposite Johnny Mack Brown, and also appearing in more than 20 shorts with The Three Stooges in the 40s and 50s.
Forbidden Trails 41. Riders of the West 42. The Stranger from Pecos 43. Partners of the Trail 44. Valley of Fear 47. Gun Talk 48, etc.

Mackaill, Dorothy (1903–1990).
British leading lady of the American silent screen, former Ziegfeld chorine.
The Face at the Window (GB) 21. Twenty-one 26. Dancer of Paris 27. Children of the Ritz 29. Once a Sinner 30. Kept Husbands 31. No Man of Her Own 32. Bulldog Drummond at Bay 37, etc.

Mackay, Barry (1906–).
British stage leading man and singer.
Evergreen 34. Oh Daddy 35. Forever England 35. Glamorous Night 37. Gangway 37. Sailing Along 38. Smuggled Cargo 40. Pickwick Papers 52. Orders Are Orders 55.

Mackay, Fulton (1922–1987).
Scottish character actor, best known as the prison guard in TV's comedy *Porridge*.
The Brave Don't Cry 51. Gumshoe 71. Nothing but the Night 73. Porridge 79. Britannia Hospital 82. Local Hero 83. Water 85, etc.

McKellen, Sir Ian (1939–).
British stage actor, in occasional films.
Alfred the Great 69. A Touch of Love 69. The Promise 69. The Priest of Love (as D. H. Lawrence) 81. The Scarlet Pimpernel (TV) (as Chauvelin) 82. *Walter* (TV) 82. Walter and June (TV) 83. The Keep 83. Plenty 85. Zina 85. Scandal 89. It's Only a Movie 92. Last Action Hero 93. The Ballad of Little Joe 93. And the Band Played On (TV) 93. Romeo Is Bleeding 93. Six Degrees of Separation 93. Richard III 94. The Shadow 94, etc.

Mackendrick, Alexander (Sandy) (1912–1993).
American director, long in Britain; pursued an erratic career with a couple of brilliant spots.
Biography: 1991, *Lethal Innocence: The Cinema of Alexander Mackendrick* by Philip Kemp.
■ Midnight Menace (w only) 37. Saraband for Dead Lovers (w only) 48. *Whisky Galore* (& w) 49. Dance Hall (w only) 50. *The Man in the White Suit* (& w) (AANw) 51. *Mandy* 52. The Maggie 54. The Ladykillers 55. *Sweet Smell of Success* 56. Sammy Going South 62. A High Wind in Jamaica 65. Don't Make Waves 67.

MacKenna, Kenneth (1899–1962) (Leo Mielziner).
American general-purpose actor (also director).
Miss Bluebeard 25. The Lunatic at Large 27. Crazy that Way 30. Those We Love 32. High Time 60. 13 West Street 62, etc.

McKenna, Siobhan (1923–1986).
Fiery Irish actress, on stage from 1940, and in very occasional films.
Hungry Hill 46. Daughter of Darkness 48. The Lost People 49. King of Kings 61. Playboy of the Western World 62. Of Human Bondage 64. Doctor Zhivago 65. Philadelphia, Here I Come 75, etc.

McKenna, T. P. (1929–).
Irish general-purpose actor.
Ulysses 67. Anne of a Thousand Days 70. The Beast in the Cellar 70. Perfect Friday 70. Villain 71. The Outsider 79. Pascali's Island 88. Red Scorpion 89. Valmont 92.

McKenna, Virginia (1931–).
Demure-looking but spirited British leading lady with stage experience; married to Bill Travers.
■ The Second Mrs Tanqueray 52. Father's Doing Fine 52. The Oracle 53. *The Cruel Sea* 53. Simba 55. The Ship That Died of Shame 55. *A Town Like Alice* (BFA) 56. The Smallest Show on Earth 57. The Barretts of Wimpole Street 57. *Carve Her Name with Pride* 58. The Passionate Summer 58. The Wreck of the Mary Deare 59. Two Living One Dead 62. *Born Free* 66. Ring of Bright Water 69. An Elephant Called Slowly 70. Waterloo 70. Swallows and Amazons 74. Holocaust 2000 77. The Disappearance 77. The Chosen 78. Blood Link 82. The First Olympics: Athens 1896 (TV) 84. Staggered 94.

Mackenzie, Sir Compton (1883–1972).
Scottish novelist. His *Carnival* was twice filmed, but he became best known for *Whisky Galore*, in which he also played a part.

Mackenzie, John (1932–).
British director, ex TV.
■ One Brief Summer 69. Unman Wittering and Zigo 71. Made 72. *The Long Good Friday* 80. A Sense of Freedom 81. The Honorary Consul 83. Act of Vengeance (TV) 86. The Fourth Protocol 87. The Last of the Finest 90. Ruby 92.

McKern, Leo (1920–) (Reginald McKern).
Australian character actor with wide stage experience and usually explosive personality. On stage from 1942, in England from 1946.
All for Mary 55. X the Unknown 56. *Time without Pity* 57. The Mouse That Roared 59. Mr Topaze 61. The Day the Earth Caught Fire 62. *A Jolly Bad Fellow* 64. King and Country 64. Moll Flanders 65. Help! 65. *A Man for All Seasons* 66. Decline and Fall 68. Ryan's Daughter 71. The Adventure of Sherlock Holmes' Smarter Brother 76. The Omen 76. The House on Garibaldi Street (TV) 79. The Blue Lagoon 80. Rumpole's Return (TV) 80. The French Lieutenant's Woman 81. Ladyhawke 84. The Chain 85. Murder with Mirrors (TV) 85. Monsignor Quixote (TV) 86. Travelling North 86. A Foreign Field (TV) 93, etc.
TV series: Rumpole of the Bailey 78–92.

Mackie, Philip (1918–1985).
British playwright whose filmscripts included several Edgar Wallace mysteries and his own The Whole Truth.

McKinney, Nina Mae (1909–1967).
American actress.
Hallelujah 29. Sanders of the River 35. Dark Waters 44. Pinky 49, etc.

MacKinnon, Gillies (1948–).
Scottish director, born in Glasgow, from television.
Conquest of the South Pole 89. Needle (TV) 90. The Glass Arena (TV) 90. The Playboys 92. A Simple Twist of Fate 94.

MacLachlan, Kyle (1959–).
Clean-cut American leading man, associated with the films of David Lynch.
Dune 84. Blue Velvet 86. The Hidden 87. The Doors 90. Don't Tell Her It's Me 90. Where the Day Takes You 92. The Trial 92. Twin Peaks: Fire Walk with Me 92. Rich in Love 93. The Trial 93. Against the Wall (TV) 94. The Flintstones 94. Roswell (TV) 94, etc.
TV series: Twin Peaks 90.

McLaglen, Andrew V. (1925–).
American director, son of Victor McLaglen; has made several big-scale westerns in the manner of John Ford.
■ Gun the Man Down 56. *The Abductors* 56. The Man in the Vault 57. Freckles 60. The Little Shepherd of Kingdom Come 61. *McLintock* 63. Shenandoah 65. The Rare Breed 66. Monkeys Go Home 67. The Way West 67. The Ballad of Josie 68. The Devil's Brigade 68. Bandolero 68. The Undefeated 69. Hellfighters 69. Chisum 70. One More Train to Rob 71. Something Big (& p) 71. Fool's Parade (& p) 71. The Train Robbers 73. Cahill 73. Stowaway to Moon (TV) 74. Log of the Black Pearl (TV) 74. Mitchell 76. The Last Hard Men 76. Banjo Hackett (TV) 77. Murder at the World Series (TV) 77. Fantastic Journey (TV pilot) 77. The Wild Geese 78. Breakthrough 78. North Sea Hijack 80. The Sea Wolves 80. Travis

McGee (TV) 82. The Shadow Riders (TV) 82. The Blue and the Gray (TV) 82. Sahara 84. The Dirty Dozen: The Next Mission (TV) 85. On Wings of Eagles (TV) 86. Return from the River Kwai 89. Eye of the Widow 92.

McLaglen, Victor (1883–1959).
Burly, good-humoured star of British silent films; later became popular in Hollywood.
Autobiography: 1935, *Express to Hollywood*.
The Call of the Road 20. The Glorious Adventure 21. The Beloved Brute 23. Beau Geste 26. *What Price Glory?* 26. Captain Lash 27. Mother Macree 28. The Cockeyed World 29. *Dishonoured* 30. Wicked 31. Rackety Rax 32. Hot Pepper 33. *Dick Turpin* 33. *The Lost Patrol* 34. *The Informer* (AA) 35. Under Two Flags 36. The Magnificent Brute 37. *Gunga Din* 39. Broadway Limited 41. Call Out the Marines 42. Powder Town 42. The Princess and the Pirate 44. The Michigan Kid 47. Fort Apache 48. *She Wore a Yellow Ribbon* 49. Rio Grande 50. *The Quiet Man* (AAN) 52. Fair Wind to Java 53. Prince Valiant 54. Lady Godiva 55. Many Rivers to Cross 55. Bengazi 56. The Abductors 57. Sea Fury 58, many others.

MacLaine, Shirley (1934–) (Shirley Maclean Beaty).
Impish American leading lady, sister of Warren Beatty. Was signed for films while dancing in a Broadway chorus, and through the 70s was seen in TV musical specials.
Autobiographies: 1970, *Don't Fall off the Mountain*. 1975, *You Can Get There from Here*. 1983, *Out on a Limb*. 1985, *Dancing in the Light*. 1987, *It's All in the Playing*. 1989, *Going Within: A Guide for Inner Transformation*.
■ *The Trouble with Harry* 55. Artists and Models 56. Around the World in Eighty Days 56. Hot Spell 57. *The Matchmaker* 58. Some Came Running (AAN) 58. The Sheepman 58. *Ask Any Girl* (BFA) 59. Career 59. Can-Can 59. *The Apartment* (BFA, AAN) 59. All in a Night's Work 61. Two Loves 61. My Geisha 62. The Children's Hour 62. Two for the Seesaw 63. *Irma La Douce* (AAN) 63. What a Way To Go 64. The Yellow Rolls-Royce 64. John Goldfarb Please Come Home 64. Gambit 66. Woman Times Seven 67. *Sweet Charity* 68. The Bliss of Mrs Blossom (GB) 68. Two Mules for Sister Sara 69. Desperate Characters 71. The Possession of Joel Delaney 72. The Turning Point (AAN) 77. Being There 79. A Change of Seasons 80. Loving Couples 80. Terms of Endearment (AA) 83. Out on a Limb (TV) 86. Madame Sousatzka 88. Steel Magnolias 89. Postcards from the Edge 90. Waiting for the Light 90. Defending Your Life 91. Used People 92. Wrestling Ernest Hemingway 93. Guarding Tess 94.
TV series: *Shirley's World* 71.

¶ I've always felt that I would develop into a really fine actress because I care more about life beyond the camera than the life in front of it. – *S.M.*
I've played so many hookers they don't pay me in the regular way any more. They leave it on the dresser. – *S.M.*

MacLane, Barton (1900–1969).
Tough-looking American character actor, often seen as crooked cop, sheriff or gangster. In hundreds of films since 1924 debut.
Tillie and Gus 33. Black Fury 34. Ceiling Zero 36. You Only Live Once 37. Gold Is Where You Find It 38. The Maltese Falcon 41. Bombardier 43. San Quentin 46. The Treasure of the Sierra Madre 47. Kiss Tomorrow Goodbye 51. Captain Scarface (leading role) 53. Backlash 56. Geisha Boy 58.

Gunfighters of Abilene 59. Law of the Lawless 63. Town Tamer 65. Buckskin 68, many others.
TV series: Outlaws 60. I Dream of Jeannie 65–69.

McLaren, Norman (1914–1987).
British-born Canadian animator-director of notable shorts, especially for the National Film Board, mainly with sound as well as picture drawn directly onto the celluloid; occasionally used live action with stop motion, and a variety of other techniques.
Allegro 39. *Dots and Loops* 40. Boogie Doodle 41. Hoppity Pop 46. Fiddle-de-dee 47. *Begone Dull Care* 49. Around is Around 51. *Neighbours* 52. Blinkety Blank 54. Rhythmetic 56. A Chairy Tale 57. Blackbird 58. Parallels 60. *Pas de Deux* 62. Mosaic 65, etc.

McLaughlin, Gibb (1884–1960).
British character actor of stage and screen, once a stage monologuist and master of disguise; used his splendidly emaciated features to great advantage.
Carnival 21. Nell Gwyn 24. The Farmer's Wife 27. Kitty 29. Sally in Our Alley 31. The Private Life of Henry VIII 32. No Funny Business 33. The Scarlet Pimpernel 34. Where There's a Will 36. Mr Reeder in Room Thirteen (title role) 40. My Learned Friend 43. Caesar and Cleopatra 45. Oliver Twist 48. The Black Rose 51. The Card 52. Hobson's Choice 54. Sea Wife 57, many others.

MacLean, Alistair (1922–1987).
Best-selling British adventure novelist whose works suddenly became popular as screen fodder.
The Guns of Navarone 61. When Eight Bells Toll 70. Puppet on a Chain 71. Fear is the Key 72. Caravan to Vaccares 75. Breakheart Pass 76. Force Ten from Navarone 78. Bear Island 79, etc.

McLean, Barbara P. (1909–).
American editor.
The Bowery 33. Clive of India 35. Les Misérables 35. Lloyds of London 36. Alexander's Ragtime Band 38. In Old Chicago 38. Jesse James 39. The Rains Came 39. Stanley and Livingstone 39. Tobacco Road 41. The Black Swan 42. The Song of Bernadette 43. *Wilson* (AA) 44. Margie 46. Nightmare Alley 47. All About Eve 50. Twelve O'Clock High 50. Viva Zapata 52. Niagara 53. The Egyptian 54, many others.

MacLean, Douglas (1890–1967).
American silent screen comedian. Later became writer/producer. Retired 1938.
As Ye Sow 19. Captain Kidd Jnr 19. 23¼ Hours' Leave 21. The Hottentot 22. Never Say Die 24. Introduce Me 25. Seven Keys to Baldpate 25, etc.

McLeod, Catherine (1921–).
American leading lady of the 40s.
I've Always Loved You 46. Will Tomorrow Ever Come? 47. So Young So Bad 50. The Fortune Hunter 54. Ride the Wild Surf 64, etc.

McLeod, Norman Z. (1898–1964).
American director, in Hollywood from the early 20s. Originally an animator; later wrote screenplays (e.g. *Skippy* 31); then turned to direction.
Monkey Business 31. *Horse Feathers* 32. If I Had a Million (part) 33. Alice in Wonderland 33. *It's a Gift* 34. Pennies from Heaven 36. *Topper* 37. Merrily We Live 38. Panama Hattie 41. The Kid from Brooklyn 46. *The Secret Life of Walter Mitty* 47. *The Paleface* 47. My Favorite Spy 51. Never Wave at a WAC 53. Casanova's Big Night 54. Alias Jesse James 59, etc.

McLerie, Allyn (1926–) (Allyn Ann McLerie; now so known).
Canadian-born dancer and leading lady who made films amid stage work.
Words and Music 48. Where's Charley? 52. The Desert Song 53. Phantom of the Rue Morgue 54. Battle Cry 55. The Cowboys 72. Cinderella Liberty 74. All The President's Men 76. A Shining Season (TV) 79. And Baby Makes Six (TV) 79, etc.
TV series: The Tony Randall Show 76–78. The Days and Nights of Molly Dodd 87–88.

MacLiammoir, Michael (1899–1978) (Alfred Willmore).
Irish character actor of the old school: film roles very occasional.
Autobiographical books: *Each Actor on His Ass*. *Put Money in Thy Purse* (the story of filming Orson Wells' Othello). 1961, 1952.
Othello 52. Tom Jones (voice) 63. Thirty is a Dangerous Age, Cynthia 68. The Kremlin Letter 70. What's the Matter with Helen? 71, etc.

MacMahon, Aline (1899–1991).
Sad-faced, gentle-mannered American character actress, mostly in films of the 30s.
Five Star Final 31. The Mouthpiece 32. Life Begins 32. Once in a Lifetime 32. *Golddiggers of 1933* 33. Heroes for Sale 33. *Babbitt* 34. Kind Lady 35. I Live My Life 35. Ah Wilderness 35. When You're in Love 37. Back Door to Heaven 39. Out of the Fog 41. The Lady is Willing 42. Dragon Seed (AAN) 44. Guest in the House 44. The Mighty McGurk 46. The Search 48. Roseanna McCoy 49. The Flame and the Arrow 50. The Eddie Cantor Story 53. The Man From Laramie 55. Cimarron 60. I Could Go on Singing 63. All the Way Home 63, etc.

MacMahon, Horace (1907–1971).
American character actor, likely to be best remembered as the older cop in the TV series *Naked City*. In films from 1937, often as cop or gangster.
Navy Blues 37. King of the Newsboys 38. Rose of Washington Square 39. Lady Scarface 41. Lady Gangster 45. Waterfront at Midnight 48. *Detective Story* 51. Man in the Dark 53. Susan Slept Here 54. My Sister Eileen 55. Beau James 57. The Swinger 66. *The Detective* 68, many others.
TV series: Martin Kane 50. The Danny Thomas Show 53. *Naked City* 59–62. Mr Broadway 64.

McMillan, Kenneth (1933–1989).
Burly American character actor.
The Taking of Pelham 123 74. Oliver's Story 78. Blood Brothers 78. Hide in Plain Sight 80. Carny 80. True Confessions 81. Eyewitness 81. Ragtime 81. Partners 82. Protocol 84. Dune 84. Runaway Train 85. Armed and Dangerous 86. Three Fugitives 89, etc.
TV series: Rhoda 77–78. Suzanne Pleshette Is Maggie Briggs 84. Our Family Honor 85–86.

MacMurray, Fred (1908–1991).
Likeable, durable American leading man of the 30s and 40s; found a new lease of life in Walt Disney comedies of the early 60s. His second wife was June Haver.
■ Grand Old Girl 35. *The Gilded Lily* 35. Car 99 35. Men without Names 35. Alice Adams 35. Hands Across the Table 35. The Bride Comes Home 35. *The Trail of the Lonesome Pine* 36. 13 Hours by Air 36. The Princess Comes Across 36. The Texas Rangers 36. Maid of Salem 37. Champagne Waltz 37. Swing High Swing Low 37. Exclusive 37. True Confession 37. Coconut Grove 38. *Sing You Sinners* 38. Men With Wings 38. Café Society 39. Invitation to Happiness 39. Honeymoon in Bali

39. Little Old New York 40. Remember the Night 40. Too Many Husbands 40. Rangers of Fortune 40. Virginia 41. One Night in Lisbon 41. New York Town 41. Dive Bomber 41. The Lady is Willing 42. Take a Letter Darling 42. The Forest Rangers 42. Star Spangled Rhythm 42. Flight for Freedom 43. Above Suspicion 43. No Time for Love 43. Standing Room Only 44. And the Angels Sing 44. *Double Indemnity* 44. Murder He Says 44. Practically Yours 44. Where Do We Go from Here? 45. Captain Eddie 45. Pardon My Past 46. Smoky 46. Suddenly It's Spring 47. The Egg and I 47. Singapore 47. The Miracle of the Bells 48. On Our Merry Way 48. Don't Trust Your Husband 48. Family Honeymoon 48. Father was a Fullback 48. Borderline 50. Never a Dull Moment 50. A Millionaire for Christy 51. Callaway went Thataway 51. Fair Wind to Java 53. The Moonlighter 53. *The Caine Mutiny* 54. *Pushover* 54. Woman's World 54. The Far Horizons 55. The Rains of Ranchipur 55. At Gunpoint 55. There's Always Tomorrow 56. Gun for a Coward 57. Quantez 57. Day of the Badman 57. Good Day for a Hanging 58. *The Shaggy Dog* 59. Face of a Fugitive 59. The Oregon Trail 59. *The Apartment* 60. *The Absent Minded Professor* 61. Bon Voyage 62. Son of Flubber 63. Kisses for My President 64. Follow Me Boys 66. The Happiest Millionaire 67. Charlie and the Angel 73. The Chadwick Family (TV) 75. Beyond the Bermuda Triangle (TV) 76. The Swarm 78.

TV series: *My Three Sons* 60–72.

McMurray, Mary (1949–   ).
British director.
The Assam Garden 85.

McMurtry, Larry (1936–   ).
American screenwriter and novelist.
Hud 63. The Last Picture Show (co-w) (AA) 71. Lovin' Molly (from Leaving Cheyenne) 74. Terms of Endearment (oa) 83. Lonesome Dove (oa) (TV) 89. Montana (TV) 90. Texasville (co-w) 90. Falling from Grace 92.

McNair, Barbara (1939–   ).
American actress and singer.
If He Hollers Let Him Go 69. Stiletto 69. Change of Habit 69. They Call Me Mister Tibbs 70. The Organization 71. Dead Right 88, etc.

McNally, Stephen (1913–1994) (Horace McNally).
American leading man and sometimes 'heavy', in films from 1942. Former lawyer.
The Man from Down Under 43. The Harvey Girls 45. Johnny Belinda 48. Rogues' Regiment 48. No Way Out 50. Winchester 73 50. The Raging Tide 51. Devil's Canyon 53. Black Castle 53. Make Haste to Live 54. A Bullet Is Waiting 54. Tribute to a Bad Man 56. Hell's Five Hours 58. The Fiend Who Walked the West 58. Hell Bent for Leather 59. Requiem for a Gunfighter 65. Panic in the City 68. Black Gunn 72. Hi-Riders 78. Dear Detective (TV) 79, etc.

TV series: *Target the Corruptors* 61.

McNamara, Edward (1884–1944).
Burly American character actor, usually cast as a cop, which had been his occupation before he became an Irish tenor and then an actor.
Lucky in Love 29. I Am a Fugitive from a Chain Gang 32. 20,000 Years in Sing Sing 33. Great Guy 37. Girl Overboard 37. The League of Frightened Men 37. Strawberry Blonde 41. The Devil and Miss Jones 41. Johnny Come Lately 43. Margin of Error 43. Arsenic and Old Lace 44, etc.

McNamara, Maggie (1928–1978).
Capable but short-staying American leading lady of the 50s. Committed suicide. At the time of her death she was working as a secretary.
■ *The Moon Is Blue* (AAN) 53. Three Coins in the Fountain 54. Prince of Players 55. The Cardinal 63.

McNamara, William (1965–   ).
American actor.
The Beat 88. Stealing Home 88. Terror at the Opera 88. Dead Bang 89. Texasville 90. Wildflower (TV) 91. Chasers 94, etc.

TV series: Island Son 89–90.

McNaught, Bob (1915–1976).
British director, also associate producer on many films.
Grand National Night 53. Sea Wife 57. A Story of David 61, etc.

McNaughton, Gus (1884–1969) (Augustus Howard).
British comedy actor, once a Fred Karno singer, on stage from 1899.
Murder 30. The Thirty-Nine Steps 35. Keep Your Seats Please 37. The Divorce of Lady X 38. Trouble Brewing 39. Jeannie 41. Much Too Shy 42. Here Comes the Sun 46, etc.

McNaughton, John (1949–   ).
American director and screenwriter.
Henry: Portrait of a Serial Killer 86. The Borrower 89. Sex, Drugs, Rock & Roll 91. Mad Dog and Glory 93, etc.

McNear, Howard (1905–1969).
American comedy actor, familiar on Burns and Allen's television series as the plumber. Later with Andy Griffith.
The Long Long Trailer 54. Bundle of Joy 56. Voyage to the Bottom of the Sea 61. Follow That Dream 62. Irma la Douce 63. Kiss Me Stupid 64. The Fortune Cookie 66, etc.

MacNee, Patrick (1922–   ).
Smooth British leading man, best known on TV.
Autobiography: 1993, *King B: A Life in the Movies*.
The Life and Death of Colonel Blimp 43. Hamlet 48. Flesh and Blood 51. Three Cases of Murder 55. The Battle of the River Plate 56. Les Girls 58. Mr Jericho (TV) 70. Incense for the Damned 70. King Solomon's Treasure 77. Billion Dollar Threat (TV) 79. The Sea Wolves 80. The Howling 80. Young Doctors in Love 82. For the Term of His Natural Life (TV) 82. The Return of the Man from UNCLE (TV) 83. A View to a Kill 85. Shadey 85. Down Under 86. Waxwork 88. Lobster Man from Mars 89. Masque of the Red Death 89. Sorry, Wrong Number (TV) 89. Sherlock Holmes and the Leading Lady (TV) 91; Waxwork II: Lost in Time 91, etc.

TV series: *The Avengers* 60–68. *The New Avengers* 76. Gavilan 82. Empire 84.

McNichol, Kristy (1962–   ).
American juvenile actress.
Black Sunday 76. Like Mom, Like Me (TV) 78. The End 79. Summer of My German Soldier (TV) 79. Little Darlings 80. The Night the Lights Went Out in Georgia 81. Only When I Laugh 81. The Pirate Movie 82. Just the Way You Are 84. Dream Lover 85. You Can't Hurry Love 88. Two Moon Junction 88. The Forgotten One 90, etc.

TV series: Apple's Way 74–75. Family 76–80.

MaCowan, Norman (1877–1961).
Scottish character actor.
Whisky Galore 48. Laxdale Hall 53. X the

Unknown 56. Tread Softly Stranger 58. The Boy and the Bridge 59. Kidnapped 60, etc.

MacPhail, Douglas (1910–1944).
American singer.
Born to Dance 36. Maytime 37. Sweethearts 38. *Babes in Arms* 39. Little Nellie Kelly 40. Born to Sing 42, etc.

Macpherson, Elle (1964–   ).
Australian model and actress.
Sirens 93.

MacPherson, Jeanie (1897–1946).
American actress, dancer, screenwriter and director. As an actress, she was associated with D. W. Griffith before becoming a leading lady at Universal, where she also worked as a director and writer. From 1916 she worked for Cecil B. De Mille as screenwriter.
AS ACTRESS: The Vaquero's Vow 08. The Death Disc 09. Enoch Arden 10. Carmen 13. Hollywood 23.
AS WRITER: The Golden Chance 15. Joan the Woman 16. The Dream Girl 16. The Whispering Chorus 18. Male and Female 19. The Affairs of Anatol 21. Adam's Rib 23. The Ten Commandments 23. The Golden Bed 25. Young April 26. The King of Kings 27. Dynamite 29. Madam Satan 30. Fra Diavolo 33. Buccaneer 38, etc.

McQueen, Butterfly (1911–   ) (Thelma McQueen).
American character actress.
Gone with the Wind (as the weeping maid) 39. Cabin in the Sky 43. Flame of the Barbary Coast 45. Mildred Pierce 45. Duel in the Sun 46. The Phynx 70. Amazing Grace 74. The Mosquito Coast 86, etc.

TV series: Beulah 50–53.

Famous line (*Gone with the Wind*): 'I don't know nothin' about birthin' babies.'

McQueen, Chad (1960–   ) (Chadwick Steven McQueen).
American leading actor, in run-of-the-mill action movies. He is the son of Steve McQueen.
Skateboard 77. The Karate Kid 84. Fever Pitch 85. Nightforce 86. Martial Law 90. Death Ring 93, etc.

McQueen, Steve (1930–1980).
Unconventional but fashionable American leading man of the 60s and 70s: usually played tough, sexy and determined. The second of his three wives was actress Ali McGraw (1973–78).
Biography: 1974, *Steve McQueen* by Malachy McCoy.
■ Somebody Up There Likes Me 56. Never Love a Stranger 58. The Blob 58. Never So Few 59. The Great St Louis Bank Robbery 59. *The Magnificent Seven* 60. The Honeymoon Machine 61. Hell is for Heroes 61. The War Lover 62. *The Great Escape* 63. *Love with the Proper Stranger* 63. Soldier in the Rain 63. Baby the Rain Must Fall 65. *The Cincinnati Kid* 65. Nevada Smith 66. The Sand Pebbles (AAN) 66. The Thomas Crown Affair 68. *Bullitt* 68. The Reivers 70. Le Mans 71. Junior Bonner 72. Getaway 72. Papillon 73. The Towering Inferno 74. An Enemy of the People 76. Tom Horn 80. The Hunter 80.

TV series: Wanted Dead or Alive 58.

¶ In my own mind, I'm not sure that acting is something for a grown man to be doing. – S.M.
Stardom equals freedom. It's the only equation that matters. – S.M.

I can honestly say he's the most difficult actor I ver worked with. – *Norman Jewison*

One thing about Steve, he didn't like the women a his life to have balls. – *Ali MacGraw*

You've got to realize that a Steve McQueen erformance lends itself to monotony. – *Robert litchum*

Macquitty, William (1905–).
British producer who came to feature films via wartime MoI shorts.

The Happy Family 52. The Beachcomber 54. Above Us the Waves 55. A Night to Remember 8. The Informers 64, etc.

Macrae, Duncan (1905–1967).
Craggy-faced Scottish stage actor who made some mpressive film appearances.

❚ The Brothers 47. Whisky Galore 48. The Woman n Question 50. *The Kidnappers* 53. You're Only oung Twice 53. The Maggie 54. Geordie 55. Rockets Galore 56. The Bridal Path 58. Kidnapped 9. Our Man in Havana 59. Greyfriars Bobby 60. *unes of Glory* 60. The Best of Enemies 61. A Jolly Mad Fellow 64. Thirty is a Dangerous Age Cynthia 7. Casino Royale 67.

MacRae, Gordon (1921–1986).
American actor-singer, a former child performer who broke into films from radio.

❚ The Big Punch 48. Look for the Silver Lining 49. Backfire 49. The Daughter of Rosie O'Grady 0. Return of the Frontiersman 50. Tea for Two 0. West Point Story 51. On Moonlight Bay 51. Starlift 51. About Face 52. By the Light of the Silvery Moon 53. Three Sailors and a Girl 53. The Desert Song 53. Oklahoma 55. Carousel 56. The Best Things in Life Are Free 56. The Pilot 79.

Macready, George (1909–1973).
American character actor, a descendant of Macready the tragedian. A splendid villain, neurotic or weakling, he ran an art gallery before coming to films in 1942.

❚ The Commandos Strike at Dawn 42. The Seventh Cross 44. Wilson 44. The Story of Dr Wassell 44. The Conspirators 44. Follow the Boys 44. Soul of a Monster 44. The Missing Juror 45. Counterattack 45. Don Juan Quilligan 45. The Fighting Guardsman 45. *I Love a Mystery* 45. The Monster and the Ape 45. A Song to Remember 45. My Name Is Julia Ross 45. *Gilda* 46. The Man Who Dared 46. The Walls Came Tumbling Down 46. The Return of Monte Cristo 46. The Bandit of Sherwood Forest 46. The Swordsman 47. Down to Earth 47. The Big Clock 48. The Black Arrow 48. Coroner Creek 48. Beyond Glory 48. The Gallant Blade 48. *Alias Nick Beal* 49. Knock on Any Door 49. Johnny Allegro 49. The Doolins of Oklahoma 49. The Nevadan 50. A Lady without Passport 50. The Desert Hawk 50. Fortunes of Captain Blood 50. Rogues of Sherwood Forest 50. Tarzan's Peril 51. The Golden Horde 51. *Detective Story* 51. The Desert Fox 51. The Green Glove 52. Treasure of the Golden Condor 53. Julius Caesar 53. The Stranger Wore a Gun 53. The Golden Blade 53. Duffy of San Quentin 54. Vera Cruz 54. A Kiss Before Dying 56. Thunder Over Arizona 56. The Abductors 57. Gunfire at Indian Gap 57. *Paths of Glory* 57. The Alligator People 59. Plunderers of Painted Flats 59. Jet Over the Atlantic 59. Two Weeks in Another Town 62. Taras Bulba 62. *Seven Days in May* 64. Dead Ringer 64. Where Love Has Gone 64. The Great Race 65. The Human Duplicators 65. Fame Is the Name of the Game (TV) 66. The Young Lawyers (TV) 69. Night Gallery (TV) 69. Daughter of the Mind (TV) 69. Tora! Tora! Tora! 70. The Return of Count Yorga 71.

TV series: Peyton Place 66–68.

McShane, Ian (1942–).
British general-purpose leading man.

The Wild and the Willing 62. The Pleasure Girls 65. Sky West and Crooked 66. The Battle of Britain 68. If It's Tuesday This Must Be Belgium (US) 69. Freelance 70. Pussycat Pussycat I Love You (US) 70. Tam Lin 70. Villain 71. Sitting Target 72. The Last of Sheila 73. Ransom 74. Journey into Fear 75. Jesus of Nazareth (TV) 77. Roots (TV) 77. Dirty Money (TV) 79. Cheaper to Keep Her 80. Grace Kelly (TV) 83. Exposed 83. Too Scared to Scream 84. Ordeal by Innocence 85. The Murders in the Rue Morgue (TV) 86. Perry Mason: The Case of the Paris Paradox (TV) 90, etc.

TV series: Disraeli 78. Lovejoy 86, 90–95.

McShane, Kitty (1898–1964).
British actress, wife of music-hall comedian Arthur Lucan (Old Mother Riley), who partnered him on the halls and in their many films as his daughter. For a list of films, see *Lucan, Arthur*.

McTaggart, James (1928–1974).
British TV director.

All the Way Up 69.

McTiernan, John (1951–).
American director and screenwriter who began as a director of TV commercials.

Nomads (wd) 85. Predator 87. Die Hard 88. The Hunt for Red October 90. Medicine Man 92. The Last Action Hero 93. Die Hard 3 95, etc.

McWade, Robert (1872–1938).
American character actor who after long stage career came to films as an elderly crotch.

Second Youth 24. The Home Towners 28. Sins of the Children 30. Cimarron 31. Grand Hotel 32. Two Seconds 32. Movie Crazy 32. Back Street 32. The Kennel Murder Case 33. The Prizefighter and the Lady 33. College Rhythm 34. The President Vanishes 34. Diamond Jim 35. The Frisco Kid 35. Society Doctor 35. Anything Goes 36. Bunker Bean 36. California Straight Ahead 37. This Is My Affair 37. Of Human Hearts 38, many others.

MacWilliams, Glen (1898–).
American cinematographer.

Ever Since Eve 21. Captain January 24. Ankles Preferred 27. Hearts in Dixie 29. The Sea Wolf 30. Hat Check Girl 32. Evergreen (GB) 34. Great Guns 41. He Hired the Boss 43. Lifeboat 44. Wing and a Prayer 44. If I'm Lucky 46, many others.

Maas, Dick (1951–).
Dutch director, screenwriter, composer and producer, a former cartoonist. He runs his own production company, First Floor Features, in partnership with Laurens Geels.

Rigor Mortis (d) 81. The Lift (wd, m) 83. Abel (p) 85. Flodder (wd, m) 86. Amsterdamned (wd, m) 87. My Blue Heaven (p) 89. The Last Island (p) 89. Wings of Fame (p) 90. Oh Boy! (p) 91. The Northerners (p) 92. Flodder Does Manhattan (wd, m) 92. Channel Fever (d) 93, etc.

Macat, Julio.
American cinematographer.

Home Alone 90. Only the Lonely 91. Home Alone 2: Lost in New York 92. So I Married an Axe Murderer 93. Ace Ventura, Pet Detective 94, etc.

Macchio, Ralph (1962–).
American leading man.

Dangerous Company 82. The Outsiders 83. The Karate Kid 84. Karate Kid 2 85. Crossroads 85.

Distant Thunder 88. The Karate Kid Part III 89. Too Much Sun 91. My Cousin Vinny 92. Naked in New York 93, etc.

TV series: Eight Is Enough 80–81.

Macedo, Rita (1928–1993) (María Concepción Macedo Guzman).
Mexican leading actress. Her first husband was novelist Carlos Fuentes.

The Five Nights of Adam (Las Cinco Noches de Adan) 42. The Criminal Life of Archibaldo de la Cruz 55. Nazarin 58. The Curse of the Crying Woman 61. El Fugitivo 65. You, Me and Us (Yo y Nosotros) 71, etc.

Machaty, Gustav (1898–1963).
Czech director best remembered for exposing Hedy Lamarr's naked charms in *Extase* 33.

The Kreutzer Sonata 26. Erotikon 29. From Saturday to Sunday 31. Nocturno 35. Within the Law (US) 39. Jealousy (US) 45, etc.

Macht, Stephen (1942–).
Heavy-featured American leading man.

Amelia Earhart (TV) 76. Raid on Entebbe (TV) 77. The Choirboys 77. Loose Change (TV) 78. Ring of Passion (TV) 78. Hunters of the Deep (TV) 78. The Immigrants (TV) 78. Enola Gay (TV) 80. Killjoy (TV) 81. A Caribbean Mystery (TV) 82. The Monster Squad 87. Stephen King's Graveyard Shift (TV) 91, etc.

TV series: American Dream 91. Knots Landing 82–83. Cagney & Lacey 85–88.

Maciste.
A legendary hero of the Italian cinema, a strong man originating in *Cabiria* 14. Such of his adventures as have been dubbed into English usually translate him as Samson. The role in *Cabiria* was played by Bartolomeo Pagano (1888–1947), who continued in the part, billed as Maciste, in many films until 1928. In the 60s cycle of Italian 'sword and sandal' epics, Maciste was played by a succession of interchangeable musclemen, including South African Reg Park and Americans Gordon Scott, Reg Lewis, Mark Forest and Gordon Mitchell.

Maciste the Mighty (Maciste nella Valle dei Re) 60. Goliath against the Vampires (Maciste contro il Vampiro) 61. Atlas in the Land of the Cyclops (Maciste nella Terra dei Ciclopi) 61. Samson and the Seven Miracles of the World (Maciste alla Corte del Gran Khan) 62. Goliath and the Sins of Babylon (Maciste, l'Eroe Più Grande del Mondo) 63. Maciste vs the Stone Men (Maciste contro gli Uomini Luna) 64. Maciste and the Hundred Gladiators (Maciste, Gladiatore di Sparta) 65, etc.

Mack, Helen (1913–1986).
American leading lady of the 30s, former child actress.

Zaza 24. Grit 28. The Silent Witness 31. Son of Kong 34. She 35. The Return of Peter Grimm 35. The Milky Way 36. Last Train from Madrid 37. Gambling Ship 39. His Girl Friday 40. Divorce (last to date) 45, etc.

Mack, Russell (1892–1972).
American director of the 30s.

Second Wife 30. Heaven on Earth 31. Once in a Lifetime 32. Private Jones 33. The Band Plays On 34. The Meanest Girl in Town 35, etc.

Macy, Bill (1922–).
American character actor.

All Together Now (TV) 75. The Late Show 76. Death at Love House (TV) 76. Stunt Seven (TV) 79. The Jerk 79. My Favorite Year 82. Movers and

Shakers 85. Bad Medicine 85. Sibling Rivalry 90, etc.

TV series: Maude 72–77.

Madden, Peter (1905–1976).
Gaunt British character actor of TV and films.

Counterblast 48. Tom Brown's Schooldays 51. The Battle of the V.1 58. Hell Is a City 60. Saturday Night and Sunday Morning 60. The Loneliness of the Long Distance Runner 62. The Very Edge 63. Doctor Zhivago 66, etc.

Maddern, Victor (1926–).
Stocky cockney character actor, formerly on stage and radio.

Seven Days to Noon (debut) 49. Cockleshell Heroes 55. Private's Progress 56. Blood of the Vampire 58. I'm All Right Jack 59. HMS Defiant 61. Rotten to the Core 65. Circus of Fear 67. Death on the Nile 78, many others.

TV series: Fair Exchange (US) 62.

Maddow, Ben (1909–1992).
American screenwriter.

The Asphalt Jungle (co-w, AAN) 50. The Unforgiven 60. The Way West (co-w) 67. The Chairman 69. The Secret of Santa Vittoria (co-w) 69, etc.

Madigan, Amy (1951–).
American leading lady of the 80s. She is married to actor Ed Harris.

■ Love Child 82. Love Letters 82. Alamo Bay 84. Places in the Heart 84. Streets of Fire 84. Twice in a Lifetime 84. Nowhere to Hide 87. The Prince of Pennsylvania 88. Field of Dreams 89. Roe vs Wade (TV) 89. Uncle Buck 89. The Dark Half 93. And Then There Was None (TV) 94.

Madison, Guy (1922–) (Robert Moseley).
American leading man, in films since 1944 after naval career.

Since You Went Away (debut) 44. Till the End of Time 46. The Charge at Feather River 53. The Command 54. Five Against the House 55. On the Threshold of Space 55. The Last Frontier 56. Hilda Crane 57. Bullwhip 58. La Schiava di Roma 60. Gunmen of the Rio Grande 65. The Mystery of Thug Island 66. The Last Panzer Battalion 68. Where's Willie 78, etc.

TV series: Wild Bill Hickok 51–54.

Madison, Noel (1898–1975) (Nathaniel Moscovitch).
American actor of sinister roles, especially gangsters. Formerly known as Nat Madison; son of actor Maurice Moscovitch.

Sinners' Holiday 30. Manhattan Melodrama 34. G-Men 35. The Man Who Made Diamonds 37. Crackerjack (GB) 39. Footsteps in the Dark 41. Jitterbugs 43. Gentleman from Nowhere 49, etc.

Madonna (1958–) (Madonna Louise Veronica Ciccone).
Raucous and raunchy pop-singer who courts controversy. Her film roles so far have won her few new fans. In 1992 she signed a $60 million deal with Time Warner to form Maverick, a joint production company covering records, music publishing, films, television and books.

A Certain Sacrifice 79. Desperately Seeking Susan 85. Shanghai Surprise 86. Who's That Girl? 87. Bloodhounds of Broadway 89. Dick Tracy 90. Truth or Dare (aka In Bed with Madonna) 91. Shadows and Fog 91. A League of Their Own 92. Body of Evidence 93. Snake Eyes 93, etc.

¶ I lost my virginity as a career move. – M.

Madsen, Michael (1947–).
Burly American actor, often in tough-guy roles. He is the brother of Virginia Madsen.

War Games 83. Racing with the Moon 84. The Natural 84. The Killing Time 87. Shadows in the Storm 88. Blood Red 89. Kill Me Again 89. The End of Innocence 90. The Doors 91. Thelma & Louise 91. Fatal Instinct 92. Straight Talk 92. Reservoir Dogs 92. A House in the Hills 93. Free Willy 93. Money for Nothing 93. Trouble Bound 93. The Getaway 93. Season of Change 94. Wyatt Earp 94, etc.

TV series: Our Family Honor 85–86.

Madsen, Virginia (1963–).
American actress. She is married to director Danny Huston.

Class 83. Electric Dreams 84. Dune 84. Modern Girls 86. Slam Dance 87. Hot to Trot 88. Mr North 88. The Hot Spot 90. Highlander II: The Quickening 91. Candy Man 92. A Murderous Affair: The Carolyn Warmus Story (TV) 92. Blue Tiger 94. Bitter Vengeance (TV) 94, etc.

Maeterlinck, Maurice (1862–1949).
Belgian writer whose fantasy play The Blue Bird was filmed several times, never with success.

The Mafia.

A Sicilian secret society which emerged spectacularly in the urban Italian sections of the US and is believed to control most organized crime and rackets in that country. Films which have seized on the subject with glee include The Godfather (and sequels), The Black Hand, The Don Is Dead, Pay or Die, The Sicilian Clan, The Brotherhood, Johnny Cool, New York Confidential, The Brothers Rico, Honor Thy Father, The Valachi Papers, Charley Varrick, GoodFellas and Mobsters. In America the Mafia is sometimes known as Cosa Nostra ('our thing' or 'our cause'): the word is an acronym for Morte Alla Francia Italia Anela ('Death to the French is Italy's cry').

¶ Let's show those asshole Hollywood fruitcakes that they can't get away with it as if nothing's happened. Let's hit Sinatra. Or I could whack out a couple of those other guys, Lawford and Martin, and I could take the nigger and put his other eye out. – Johnny Formosa to his boss, gangster Sam Giancana, after Dean Martin had ignored a demand that he perform in Chicago, as recorded by an FBI wiretap

Magee, Patrick (1924–1982).
British general-purpose actor, often in sinister roles.

The Criminal 60. The Servant 63. Zulu 64. Masque of the Red Death 64. The Skull 65. The Marat/Sade 67. The Birthday Party 68. King Lear 70. You Can't Win 'Em All 71. The Fiend 71. A Clockwork Orange 71. Demons of the Mind 72. Asylum 72. Rough Cut 80, etc.

magicians

have always had a fascination for film-makers, who on the whole preferred to have their tricks finally discredited, as with Cesar Romero in Charlie Chan on Treasure Island and Two on a Guillotine, Dante in A-Haunting We Will Go, Vincent Price in The Mad Magician, Jules Berry in Le Jour Se Lève, Harold Lloyd in Movie Crazy and Tony Curtis in Houdini. The most splendidly genuine magician was the sorcerer in Fantasia, but Cecil Kellaway was an amiable warlock in I Married a Witch, and Edmund Lowe was chilling as Chandu. The 1927 version of Somerset Maugham's book The Magician contributed a caricature of Aleister Crowley; The Magician is also the title of a 1973 TV

series starring Bill Bixby. The best 'live' act on film may be Orson Welles sawing Marlene Dietrich in half in Follow the Boys.

Magnani, Anna (1907–1973).
Volatile Italian star actress (Egyptian-born).

The Blind Woman of Sorrento 34. Tempo Massimo 36. Open City 45. Angelina 47. The Miracle 50. Volcano 53. The Golden Coach 54. Bellissima 54. The Rose Tattoo (AA) 55. Wild is the Wind (AAN) 57. The Fugitive Kind 59. Mamma Roma 62. Made in Italy 67. The Secret of Santa Vittoria 69, etc.

Magne, Michel (1930–1984).
French composer and arranger.

Le Pain Vivant 54. Les Bricoleurs 61. Gigot (AAN) 62. Any Number Can Win 63. Germinal 63. La Ronde 64. Fantomas 64. The Sleeping Car Murders 66. Two Weeks in September 67. Belle de Jour 67. Manon 70 70. Le Complot 75. Emmanuelle 4 84, etc.

Magnificent Obsession.

The tear-jerking novel by Lloyd C. Douglas, about an irresponsible playboy who becomes a surgeon and not only cures but falls in love with the woman he accidentally blinded, was filmed in 1935 by John M. Stahl, with Robert Taylor and Irene Dunne, and again in 1954 by Douglas Sirk, with Rock Hudson and Jane Wyman.

Maharis, George (1928–).
Intense-looking American leading man who has been most successful on TV.

■ Exodus 60. Sylvia 65. Quick Before it Melts 65. The Satan Bug 65. Covenant with Death 67. The Happening 67. The Land Raiders 69. The Monk (TV) 69. The Desperadoes 69. The Last Day of the War 69. The Victim (TV) 72. Rich Man Poor Man (TV) 76. Look What Happened to Rosemary's Baby (TV) 76. Death Flight (TV) 77. Return to Fantasy Island (TV) 78. Crash (TV) 78. The Sword and the Sorcerer 82.

TV series: Route 66 60–63. The Most Deadly Game 70.

Mahin, John Lee (1902–1984).
American scriptwriter.

Scarface 32. Red Dust 32. Bombshell 33. Naughty Marietta 35. Captains Courageous (AAN) 37. Too Hot to Handle 38. Dr Jekyll and Mr Hyde 41. Tortilla Flat 42. Down to the Sea in Ships 49. Quo Vadis? 51. Elephant Walk 54. Heaven Knows Mr Allison (AAN) 57. The Horse Soldiers (& p) 59. The Spiral Road 62. Moment to Moment 66, many others.

Mahoney, Jock (1919–1989) (Jacques O'Mahoney).
Athletic American leading man who, apart from playing Tarzan, was confined to routine roles. Former stuntman for Gene Autry and Charles Starrett.

The Doolins of Oklahoma 49. A Day of Fury 55. Away All Boats 56. I've Lived Before 56. A Time to Love and a Time to Die 58. The Land Unknown 58. Tarzan the Magnificent 60. Tarzan Goes to India 62. Tarzan's Three Challenges 64. The Walls of Hell 66. The Bad Bunch 76. The End 78, etc.

TV series: The Range Rider 51–52. Yancey Derringer 58.

Mahoney, John (1940–).
English-born actor, in America.

Code of Silence 85. The Manhattan Project 86. Trapped in Silence 86. Tin Men 87. Moonstruck 87. Frantic 88. The Image 89. Say Anything 89. The

Russia House 90. Barton Fink 91. Love Hurts 91. Article 99 92. In the Line of Fire 93, etc.

Maibaum, Richard (1909–1991).
American scriptwriter who wrote 13 Bond movies.
They Gave Him a Gun 37. Ten Gentlemen from West Point 40. O.S.S. 46. *The Great Gatsby* 49. Cockleshell Heroes 55. Zarak 57. The Day They Robbed the Bank of England 60. Dr No 62. From Russia with Love 63. Goldfinger 64. Thunderball 65. On Her Majesty's Secret Service 69. Diamonds Are Forever 71. The Man with the Golden Gun 74. The Spy Who Loved Me 77. For Your Eyes Only 81. Octopussy 83. A View to a Kill 85. The Living Daylights 87. Licence to Kill 89, etc.

Maigret.
The police commissioner created by French novelist Georges Simenon has been played by many actors on screen and television since 1932: Pierre Renoir, Harry Baur, Abel Tarride, Albert Prejean, Michel Simon, Maurice Manson, and Jean Gabin in French films, Heinz Ruhmann in a German film, and Charles Laughton in the American *The Man on the Eiffel Tower* 49. On television, the role has been taken by Basil Sydney, Rupert Davies, and Michael Gambon.

Mailer, Norman (1923–).
Combative American novelist and occasional, unsuccessful screenwriter, director and actor.
The Naked and the Dead (oa) 58. An American Dream (oa) 66. Beyond the Law (wd) 68. Wild 90 (wd) 69. Maidstone (wd) 70. Town Bloody Hall (a) 79. Ragtime (a) 81. Tough Guys Don't Dance (wd) 87. King Lear (a) 87, etc.

Main, Marjorie (1890–1975) (Mary Tomlinson).
American character actress, probably best remembered as Ma Kettle in the long-running hillbilly series.
Take a Chance (debut) 33. *Dead End* 37. Stella Dallas 37. Test Pilot 38. Angels Wash Their Faces 39. The Women 39. Turnabout 40. Bad Man of Wyoming 40. A Woman's Face 41. Honky Tonk 41. Jackass Mail 42. Tish 42. Heaven Can Wait 43. Rationing 43. *Meet Me in St Louis* 44. *Murder He Says* 44. The Harvey Girls 45. Bad Bascomb 45. Undercurrent 46. *The Egg and I* (AAN) 47. The Wistful Widow of Wagon Gap 47. *Ma and Pa Kettle* 49. Ma and Pa Kettle Go to Town 50 (then one Kettle film a year till 56). Mrs O'Malley and Mr Malone 50. The Belle of New York 52. Rose Marie 54. Friendly Persuasion 56, many others.

Mainwaring, Daniel (1902–1977) (aka Geoffrey Homes).
American screenwriter and novelist.
No Hands on the Clock 41. Dangerous Passage 44. Tokyo Rose 45. They Made Me a Killer 46. Out of the Past 47. The Big Steal 49. The Eagle and the Hawk 50. Bugles in the Afternoon 52. This Woman Is Dangerous 52. The Desperado 54. Invasion of the Body Snatchers 56. Baby Face Nelson 57. The Gun Runners 58. Walk Like a Dragon 60. The George Raft Story 61. Convict Stage 65, etc.

Maisie.
The hard-boiled (but soft-centred) gold-digging showgirl was played by Ann Sothern in 10 MGM comedy-dramas: Maisie 39; *Congo Maisie* 40; *Gold Rush Maisie* 40; *Maisie Was a Lady* 41; *Ringside Maisie* 41; *Maisie Gets Her Man* 42; *Swing Shift Maisie* 43; *Maisie Goes to Reno* 44; *Up Goes Maisie* 46; *Undercover Maisie* 47. Sothern survived the type-casting to go on to bigger and better films.

Maitland, Marne (1920–).
Anglo-Indian actor in British films; adept at sinister orientals.
Cairo Road 50. Father Brown 54. Bhowani Junction 56. The Camp on Blood Island 58. The Stranglers of Bombay 59. Sands of the Desert 60. Nine Hours to Rama 62. Lord Jim 65. The Reptile 65. Khartoum 66. The Pink Panther Strikes Again 76. The Black Stallion 79. Memed My Hawk 87, etc.

Majors, Lee (1940–) (Harvey Lee Yeary II).
American leading man.
■ Will Penny 67. The Ballad of Andy Crocker (TV) 68. The Liberation of L.B. Jones 70. Weekend of Terror (TV) 73. The Six Million Dollar Man (TV) 73. Gary Francis Powers (TV) 76. Just a Little Inconvenience (TV) 78. The Norseman 78. Killer Fish 78. Steel 80. The Naked Sun 80. Agency 80. Sharks 80. The Fall Guy (TV) 81. Starflight One (TV) 83. The Cowboy and the Ballerina (TV) 84. Return of the Six Million Dollar Man and the Bionic Woman (TV) 87. Danger Down Under (TV) 88. Scrooged 88. Bionic Showdown (TV) 89. Keaton's Cop 90. Fire! Trapped on the 37th Floor (TV) 91.
TV series: *The Big Valley* 65–68. The Men from Shiloh 70. Owen Marshall 71–72. *Six Million Dollar Man* 73–78. The Fall Guy 81–86.

Makavejev, Dusan (1932–).
Yugoslavian director.
■ *The Switchboard Operator* 67. Innocence Unprotected 68. WR: Mysteries of the Organism 71. Sweet Movie 74. Montenegro 80. The Coca Cola Kid 84. Manifesto 88. Gorilla Bathes at Noon 93.

Makeham, Eliot (1882–1956).
British character actor of stage and screen, former accountant. For years played bespectacled little bank clerks who sometimes surprised by standing up for themselves.
Rome Express 32. Orders Is Orders 32. Lorna Doone 35. Dark Journey 37. Farewell Again 37. Saloon Bar 40. *Night Train to Munich* 40. The Common Touch 42. The Halfway House 44. Jassy 47. Trio 50. Scrooge 51. Doctor in the House 53. Sailor Beware 56, etc.

make-up.
A general term for the cosmetic application to the body of materials intended to enhance or change the appearance, from glamorization to the creation of monsters.

¶ The relationship between the make-up man and the film actor is that of accomplices in crime. – Marlene Dietrich

Makk, Károly (1925–).
Hungarian director and screenwriter.
Liliomfi 54. The House under the Rocks (Haz a Sziklak Alatt) 58. Bolondas Vakacio 67. Love (Szerelem) 71. A Very Moral Night (Egy Erkolcsos) 78. Another Way (Olelkezo Tekintetek) (wd) 82. Jatsani Kell 85. Hungarian Requiem (Magyar Rekviem) 90, etc.

Mako (1933–) (Makoto Iwamatsu).
Japanese-American character actor.
The Sand Pebbles (AAN) 66. Hawaii 67. The Island at the Top of the World 74. The Big Brawl 80. The Bushido Blade 80. Under the Rainbow 81. Testament 83. Conan the Destroyer 84. Armed Response 86. Tucker: The Man and His Dream 88. The Wash 88. Fatal Mission 89. An Unremarkable Life 89. Pacific Heights 90. The Perfect Weapon 91. Rising Sun 93. Robocop 3 93, etc.

Mala (1906–1952) (Ray Wise).
Eskimo actor who was popular in a few American films of the 30s.
Igloo 32. Eskimo 33. Hawk of the Wilderness 35. The Tuttles of Tahiti 42. Red Snow 52, etc.

Malahide, Patrick (1945–).
Gaunt English leading actor, mainly on television and best known as Inspector Alleyn in the TV series. He began as a stage manager before working in repertory as an actor and is also a television playwright.
The Killing Fields 84. Comfort and Joy 87. The Singing Detective (TV) 87. A Month in the Country 87. December Bride 90. Smack and Thistle 90. Middlemarch (TV) 94. A Man of No Importance 94, etc.

Malandrinos, Andrea (1896–1970).
Greek-born character actor in British films, from music hall.
Raise the Roof 30. The Lodger 32. The Admiral's Secret 34. Midshipman Easy 35. Limelight 36. Tropical Trouble 37. Thunder Rock 42. Champagne Charlie 44. My Brother Jonathan 48. The Lavender Hill Mob 51. Cockleshell Heroes 55. The Prince and the Showgirl 57. Tommy the Toreador 59. The Yellow Rolls-Royce 64. The Mummy's Shroud 67. The Oblong Box 69. Hell Boats 70, many more.

Malden, Karl (1914–) (Mladen Sekulovich).
Respected American stage actor whose film career has been generally disappointing because Hollywood has not seemed to know what to do with him.
■ They Knew What They Wanted 40. Winged Victory 44. 13 Rue Madeleine 46. Boomerang 47. Kiss of Death 47. The Gunfighter 50. Where the Sidewalk Ends 50. Halls of Montezuma 50. *A Streetcar Named Desire* (AA) 52. Decision Before Dawn 52. Diplomatic Courier 52. Operation Secret 52. Ruby Gentry 52. I Confess 53. Take the High Ground 53. Phantom of the Rue Morgue 54. *On the Waterfront* (AAN) 54. *Baby Doll* 56. Fear Strikes Out 57. Time Limit (d only) 57. Bombers B52 57. The Hanging Tree 59. Pollyanna 60. The Great Imposter 60. Parrish 61. One Eyed Jacks 61. All Fall Down 62. Bird Man of Alcatraz 62. Gypsy 62. How the West Was Won 63. Come Fly with Me 63. Dead Ringer 64. Cheyenne Autumn 64. The Cincinnati Kid 65. Nevada Smith 66. The Silencers 66. Murderers Row 66. *Hotel* 67. The Adventures of Bullwhip Griffin 67. Billion Dollar Brain 67. Blue 68. Hot Millions 68. Patton 69. Cat O'Nine Tails 69. Wild Rovers 71. Captains Courageous (TV) 78. Meteor 79. Beyond the Poseidon Adventure 79. *Word of Honor* (TV) 81. The Sting II 82. Summertime Killer 82. Twilight Time 83. *Fatal Vision* (TV) 84. Billy Galvin 86. Nuts 87.
TV series: *Streets of San Francisco* 72–76. Skag 80.

male impersonation:
see transvestism.

Malick, Terrence (1945–).
American director.
■ Pocket Money (w only) 72. *Badlands* (& w, p) 73. The Gravy Train (w only) 74. *Days of Heaven* (& w, p) 79.

Malik, Art (1953–).
Pakistani actor who grew up in Britain and made his reputation on TV.
Arabian Adventure 79. The Jewel in the Crown (TV) 84. A Passage to India 84. The Living Daylights 87. City of Joy 92. The Year of the Comet

92. Hostage 92. Turtle Beach 92. Uncovered 94. True Lies 94, etc.

TV series: Hothouse 89.

Malinger, Ross (1984–).
American child actor.
Kindergarten Cop 90. Eve of Destruction 91. Sleepless in Seattle 93.

TV series: Good Advice 93– .

Malkovich, John (1953–).
American leading actor, from the stage.
■ The Killing Fields 84. Places in the Heart (AAN) 84. Eleni 85. Private Conversations 85. Making Mr Right 87. The Glass Menagerie 87. Empire of the Sun 87. Miles from Home 88. Dangerous Liaisons 88. The Sheltering Sky 90. Object of Beauty 91. Shadows and Fog 91. Queen's Logic 91. Of Mice and Men 92. Jennifer 8 92. In the Line of Fire (AAN) 93. Heart of Darkness (TV) 93. Mary Reilly 95.

Malle, Louis (1932–).
French 'new wave' director, former assistant to Robert Bresson. Married Candice Bergen.

Book: 1993, *Malle on Malle* by Philip French.

World of Silence (co-d) 56. Lift to the Scaffold 57. *The Lovers* 58. Zazie dans le Métro 61. *Le Feu Follet* 63. Viva Maria 65. Le Voleur 67. *Souffle au Coeur* (AA script) 71. Lacombe Lucien 75. Black Moon 75. Pretty Baby 78. Atlantic City (BFA, AAN) 80. My Dinner with André 81. Crackers 84. Alamo Bay 85. *Au Revoir, les Enfants* (AAN) 87. *May Fools* (Milou en Mai) 90. Bohemian Life (La Vie de Bohème) (a) 92. Damage 92. Vanya on 42nd Street 94, etc.

¶ You see the world much better through a camera. – L.M.

Malleson, Miles (1888–1969).
British playwright, screen writer and actor whose credits read like a potted history of the British cinema.
AS WRITER: *Nell Gwyn* 34. Peg of Old Drury 35. Rhodes of Africa 36. *Victoria the Great* 37. The Thief of Bagdad 40. The First of the Few 42. They Flew Alone 43. Mr Emmanuel 44, etc.
AS ACTOR: City of Song 31. The Sign of Four 32. Bitter Sweet 33. Nell Gwyn 34. Tudor Rose 36. Knight without Armour 37. The Thief of Bagdad (as the sultan) 40. Major Barbara 41. They Flew Alone 42. Dead of Night 45. While the Sun Shines 47. Saraband for Dead Lovers 48. *Kind Hearts and Coronets* (as the hangman) 49. The Perfect Woman 49. Stage Fright 50. The Man in the White Suit 51. The Magic Box 51. *The Importance of Being Earnest* (as Canon Chasuble) 52. Folly to Be Wise 52. The Captain's Paradise 53. Private's Progress 56. *Brothers in Law* 57. The Naked Truth 57. *Dracula* 58. The Captain's Table 58. The Hound of the Baskervilles 59. I'm All Right Jack 59. Brides of Dracula 60. The Hellfire Club 61. Heavens Above 63. First Men in the Moon 64. You Must Be Joking 65, many others.

Mallory, Boots (1913–1958) (Patricia Mallory).
American leading lady of the 30s; married William Cagney and Herbert Marshall.

Handle with Care 32. Hello Sister 33. Sing Sing Nights 35. Here's Flash Casey 37, etc.

Malo, Gina (1909–1963) (Janet Flynn).
Irish-German-American leading lady of the 30s, usually in tempestuous roles. Filmed in Britain; married Romney Brent.

In a Monastery Garden 32. Good Night Vienna 32. Waltz Time 33. The Private Life of Don Juan 34. Jack of All Trades 36. Over She Goes 38. The Door with Seven Locks 40, etc.

Malone, Dorothy (1925–) (Dorothy Maloney).
American leading lady of the 50s, often in sultry roles.
■ The Falcon and the Co-Eds 43. One Mysterious Night 44. Show Business 44. Seven Days Ashore 44. Hollywood Canteen 44. Too Young to Know 45. Janie Gets Married 46. *The Big Sleep* 46. Night and Day 48. To the Victor 48. Two Guys from Texas 48. One Sunday Afternoon 48. Flaxy Martin 49. South of St Louis 49. Colorado Territory 49. The Nevadan 50. Convicted 50. Mrs O'Malley and Mr Malone 50. The Killer that Stalked New York 50. Saddle Legion 51. The Bushwhackers 52. Scared Stiff 53. Torpedo Alley 53. Law and Order 54. Jack Slade 54. Loophole 54. Pushover 54. The Fast and Furious 54. Private Hell 36 54. Young at Heart 54. The Lone Gun 54. Five Guns West 55. Battle Cry 55. Tall Man Riding 55. Sincerely Yours 55. Artists and Models 55. At Gunpoint 55. Pillars of the Sky 56. Tension at Table Rock 56. *Written on the Wind* (AA) 56. Quantez 57. *Man of a Thousand Faces* 57. *The Tarnished Angels* 57. Tip on a Dead Jockey 57. *Too Much Too Soon* (as Diana Barrymore) 58. Warlock 59. The Last Voyage 60. The Last Sunset 61. Beach Party 63. Fate Is the Hunter 64. The Pigeon (TV) 69. Exzess (Ger.) 70. The Man Who Would Not Die 75. Rich Man Poor Man (TV) 76. Little Ladies of the Night (TV) 77. Murder in Peyton Place (TV) 77. Katie: Portrait of a Centerfold (TV) 78. Good Luck Miss Wyckoff 79. Winter Kills 79. Condominium (TV) 80. The Being 83. Peyton Place, the Next Generation (TV) 85. Basic Instinct 92.

TV series: *Peyton Place* 64–68.

Maloney, Michael.
English actor, from the stage, including leading roles with the Royal Shakespeare Company.

Sharma and Beyond (TV) 84. Henry V 89. Truly Madly Deeply 91. Love on a Branch Line (TV) 93, etc.

Malraux, André (1901–1976).
French author and politician, finally Minister of Culture; the leading spirit behind the 1937 documentary of the Spanish Civil War, *Days of Hope.*

Maltby, H. F. (1880–1963).
British comedy playwright (*The Rotters, The Right Age to Marry*, etc.). Screenwriter (*Over the Garden Wall* 44, etc.) and actor of choleric characters.

Autobiography: 1950, *Ring Up the Curtain.*

Those Were The Days 34. Jack of All Trades 36. Pygmalion 38. Under Your Hat 40. A Canterbury Tale 44. The Trojan Brothers 45, etc.

The Maltese Falcon.
Dashiell Hammett's brilliantly written crime story was filmed three times by Warner. In 1931 it starred Bebe Daniels and Ricardo Cortez and was directed by Roy del Ruth; in 1936 it appeared as *Satan Met a Lady*, directed by William Dieterle, with Bette Davis and Warren William. The definitive version, however, did not come until 1941, when John Huston wrote and directed it with Humphrey Bogart and a rogues' gallery that included Mary Astor, Sydney Greenstreet, Peter Lorre, and Elisha Cook Jnr. A low-budget rip-off, *Target Harry* (aka *How to Make It*) 68, was made by Roger Corman, understandably hiding his identity under the pseudonym of Harry Neill. Huston spoofed it unsuccessfully in his *Beat the Devil* 54, and David Giler wrote and directed an altogether witless parody, *The Black Bird* 75.

Maltz, Albert (1908–1985).
American screenwriter who suffered from the anti-communist witch-hunt as one of the 'Hollywood Ten'.

Afraid to Talk 32. This Gun for Hire 42. Destination Tokyo 43. The Man in Half Moon Street 44. Pride of the Marines (AAN) 45. Cloak and Dagger 46. Naked City 48. Two Mules for Sister Sara 70. Scalawag 73, etc.

Malyon, Eily (1879–1961).
English character actress in Hollywood, a familiar supporting face from *His Greatest Gamble* 34 to *The Secret Heart* 46, typically as the acidulous aunt in *On Borrowed Time* 38.

Mambéty, Djibril Diop (1945–).
Senegalese director, screenwriter and actor.
■ Contras' City (short) 69. Badou Boy 70. Hyena Progress (Touki-Bouki) 73. Parlons Grandmère (short) 89. Hyenas (Hyènes) 92.

Mamet, David (1947–).
American dramatist, director and screenwriter.
The Postman Always Rings Twice (w) 81. *The Verdict* (AANw) 82. About Last Night (oa) 86. Black Widow (a, w) 87. *House of Games* (wd) 87. *The Untouchables* (w) 87. Things Change (wd) 88. We're No Angels (w) 89. Homicide (wd) 91. Hoffa (w) 92. *Glengarry Glen Ross* (w) 92. The Water Engine (w) (TV) 92. A Life in the Theatre (w) 93. Vanya on 42nd Street (w) 94, etc.

¶ I've always been more comfortable sinking while clutching a good theory than swimming with an ugly fact. – D.M.

If Eisenstein would have lived longer and spent more time in Hollywood, he might have talked less about the Theory of Montage, and more about healthy eating, and what to have on the Craft Service Table. – D.M.

Working as a screenwriter-for-hire, one is in the employ *not* of the eventual consumers (the audience, whose interests the honest writer must have at heart), but of speculators, whose ambition many times, is not to please the eventual consumer, but to extort from him as much money as possible as quickly as possible. – D.M.

The movies are a momentary and beautiful aberration of a technological society in the last stages of decay. – D.M.

Mamoulian, Rouben (1897–1987).
American stage director of Armenian origin. Over the years he made a number of films which vary in quality but at their best show a fluent command of the medium.
■ Applause 29. City Streets 31. Dr Jekyll and Mr Hyde 32. Love Me Tonight 32. Song of Songs 33. Queen Christina 33. We Live Again 34. Becky Sharp 35. The Gay Desperado 36. High, Wide and Handsome 37. Golden Boy 39. *The Mark of Zorro* 40. Blood and Sand 41. Rings on Her Fingers 42. Summer Holiday 48. Silk Stockings 57.

Began work on *Cleopatra* 62 but was replaced.

¶ His tragedy is that of the innovator who runs out of innovations. – Andrew Sarris, 1968

The Man in the Iron Mask.
No one knows what mixture of fact and fiction exists in the famous story of Louis XIV's mysterious prisoner who languished for years in the Bastille, his face always covered (actually with velvet). Some said it was Louis' bastard brother, others an Italian diplomat. Anyway, Dumas wrote an exciting novel on the subject, and it has been filmed twice: in 1929 as *The Iron Mask* with

Douglas Fairbanks, and in 1939 by James Whale with Louis Hayward. A TV movie with Richard Chamberlain was made in 1976 and in the following year *The Fifth Musketeer* trod much the same ground.

The Man Who Knew Too Much.

Alfred Hitchcock twice filmed this thriller about a child held hostage by a gang planning to assassinate an international political figure: in 1934 in Britain, with Leslie Banks, Edna Best, and Peter Lorre; and in America in 1956, with James Stewart, Doris Day, and Bernard Miles. The first version, despite (or, perhaps, because of) its curious studio sets, made incomparably better entertainment.

Mancini, Henry (1924–1994) (Enrico Mancini).

American composer and songwriter. Educated at the Juilliard School of Music, he was an arranger and pianist with the post-war Glenn Miller orchestra before working at Universal, 1952–58. Apart from films, he also worked in television, notably for the *Peter Gunn* series 58. His best-known song was 'Moon River', written with lyricist Johnny Mercer, for *Breakfast at Tiffany's*.

AS ARRANGER: The Glenn Miller Story (AAN) 53. The Benny Goodman Story 56, etc.

AS COMPOSER: Touch of Evil 58. High Time 60. Breakfast at Tiffany's (AA) 61. Bachelor in Paradise 61. Days of Wine and Roses 62. *Hatari* 62. *The Pink Panther* (AAN) 63. Charade 63. A Shot in the Dark 64. Dear Heart 65. What Did You Do in the War, Daddy? 66. Two for the Road 67. Darling Lili 69. The White Dawn 73. The Return of the Pink Panther 75. Once is Not Enough 76. Silver Streak 76. W. C. Fields and Me 76. House Calls 78. Who is Killing the Great Chefs of Europe? 78. Nightwing 79. 10 (AAN) 79. Little Miss Marker 80. Back Roads 81. Mommie Dearest 81. Victor/Victoria (AA) 82. Harry and Son 84. Lifeforce 85. Santa Claus: The Movie 85. That's Dancing! 85. A Fine Mess 86. That's Life! (AAN) 86. Blind Date 87. The Glass Menagerie 87. Heavy Petting 88. Physical Evidence 88. Sunset 88. Without a Clue 88. Welcome Home 89. Ghost Dad 90. Switch 91. Married to It 91. Son of the Pink Panther 93, etc.
~Academy Award songs: 'Moon River', 'Days of Wine and Roses'.

Mancunian Films.

A small but dauntless little British studio which throughout the 40s and early 50s earned its keep locally with a stream of wild farces starring home-grown music-hall talent: Frank Randle, Harry Korris, Sandy Powell, Tessie O'Shea, Betty Jumel, Nat Jackley, Josef Locke, Jewel and Warriss, Suzette Tarri and Norman Evans. Neither art nor craft entered into the matter.

Mancuso, Frank (1933–).

American production executive, appointed head of MGM/UA in 1993, and a former chairman and CEO of Paramount.

Mancuso, Kevin:

see D'Amato, Joe.

Mancuso, Nick (c. 1956–).

Canadian leading man.

Dr Scorpion (TV) 78. The House on Garibaldi Street (TV) 79. Torn between Two Lovers (TV) 80. Nightwing 80. The Kidnapping of the President 80. Scruples (TV) 81. Ticket to Heaven 81. Mother Lode 82. The Legend of Walks Far Woman (TV) 83. Heartbreakers 84. Night Magic 85. Death of an Angel 85. King of Love (TV) 87. Lena's Holiday 91. Double Identity 91. Flinch 94, etc.

Mandel, Babaloo. (c. 1949–) (Mark Mandel).

American screenwriter and television producer, usually in collaboration with Lowell Ganz.

Night Shift 82. Splash 84. Spies Like Us 85. Gung Ho 86. Vibes 88. Parenthood 89. City Slickers (AAN) 91. Mr Saturday Night 92. A League of Their Own 92. City Slickers II: The Legend of Curly's Gold 94, etc.

Mandel, Johnny (1935–).

American composer, trumpeter and trombonist. His song 'The Shadow of Your Smile' (lyrics by Paul Francis Webster), the love theme from *The Sandpiper*, was an Oscar-winner in 1965.

I Want to Live 58. The Third Voice 59. The Americanization of Emily 64. The Sandpiper (AA song) 65. Point Blank 67. M*A*S*H 70. The Last Detail 73. Freaky Friday 76. Agatha 79. Being There 79. The Baltimore Bullet 80. Deathtrap 82. The Verdict 82. Staying Alive 83. Brenda Starr 89, etc.

Mandell, Daniel (1895–1987).

American editor.

The Turmoil 24. Showboat 29. Counsellor at Law 33. Diamond Jim 35. Dodsworth 36. Dead End 37. Wuthering Heights 39. The Little Foxes 41. Arsenic and Old Lace 44. Wonder Man 45. The Best Years of Our Lives (AA) 46. My Foolish Heart 49. Valentino 52. Guys and Dolls 55. Witness for the Prosecution 57. The Apartment (AA) 60. Irma la Douce 63. The Fortune Cookie 66, many others.

Mander, Miles (1888–1946) (Lionel Mander).

British character actor, a former theatre manager with long experience of all kinds of stage work. Later settled in Hollywood.

The Pleasure Garden 26. *The First Born* (& wd) 28. Loose Ends (wd only) 30. The Missing Rembrandt (wd only) 31. The Private Life of Henry VIII 32. Loyalties 33. The Morals of Marcus (d only) 35, etc.

In Hollywood as actor: *The Three Musketeers* (as Richelieu) 36. Lloyds of London 37. Slave Ship 37. Suez 38. The Three Musketeers (musical version; as Richelieu again) 39. *Wuthering Heights* 39. Tower of London 39. Lady Hamilton 41. *Five Graves to Cairo* 43. *Farewell My Lovely* 44. The Scarlet Claw 44. Pearl of Death 44. The Bandit of Sherwood Forest 46. The Walls Came Tumbling Down 46, many others.

Mandoki, Luis.

Mexican-born director in Hollywood.

Motel 83. Gaby – A True Story 87. White Palace 90. Born Yesterday 93. When a Man Loves a Woman 94, etc.

Manfredi, Nino (1921–).

Italian leading actor, screenwriter and occasional director, from the stage.

Torna a Napoli 49. Viva il Cinema! 53. Gli Inamorati 55. Camping (a, w) 57. I Ragazzi dei Pariole 58. L'Impiegato (a, w) 59. Crimen 60. Wayward Love (L'Amore Difficile) (a, d) 62. The Dolls (Le Bambole) 65. A Rose for Everyone (Una Rosa per Tutti) 67. Per Grazia Ricevuta (a, wd) 71. Il Conte di Monte Cristo 77. La Mazzetta 78. Café Express (a, w) 80. I Picari 87. Alberto Express 90. Mima 91, many others.

Manfredini, Harry.

American composer, mainly for horror movies.

Here Come the Tigers 78. Friday the 13th 80. Friday the 13th Part 2 81. Friday the 13th Part 3 82. Swamp Thing 82. The Returning 83. Friday the 13th: The Final Chapter 84. The Hills Have Eyes Part II 84. Friday the 13th: A New Beginning 85.

House 86. Friday the 13th Part VI: Jason Lives 86. House II: The Second Story 87. Friday the 13th Part VII: The New Blood (co-m) 88. Deep Star Six 89. Double Revenge 90. Aces: Iron Eagle III 92. My Boyfriend's Back 93. Jason Goes to Hell: The Final Friday 93, etc.

Manga.

Japanese term for comics, which translates as 'irresponsible pictures'. The word has come to be applied in the West to Japanese animated films owing to the release of such films on the Manga video label and the appearance of fan magazines devoted to the style. Many of the best-selling comic books have been turned into animated films, which are more properly known as anime (qv).

Mangano, Silvana (1930–1989).

Italian actress, wife of producer Dino de Laurentiis. Former model.

L'Elisir d'Amore 49. Bitter Rice 51. Anna 51. Mambo 53. Ulysses 54. The Wolves 56. The Sea Wall 57. Tempest 59. Five Branded Women 61. Barabbas 62. Theorem 68. The Decameron 70. Death in Venice 71. Ludwig 72. Conversation Piece 76. Dune 84, etc.

Mankiewicz, Don (1922–).

American scriptwriter and novelist, son of Herman Mankiewicz.

Trial 55. House of Numbers 57. I Want to Live (AAN) 58.

Mankiewicz, Francis (1944–1993).

Canadian film director. Born in Shanghai, he studied at the London School of Film Technique. *Good Riddance* is one of the most admired of Canadian films. Died of cancer.

Valentin (TV) 73. Le Temps d'une Chasse 73. Good Riddance (Les Bons Debarras) 81. Les Beaux Souvenirs 82. And Then You Die (TV) 87. Les Portes Tournantes 88. Conspiracy of Silence (TV) 92, etc.

Mankiewicz, Herman (1897–1953).

American screenwriter, also journalist and noted wit; brother of Joseph L. Mankiewicz.

Biography: 1968, *Mank*.

The Road to Mandalay 26. After Office Hours 35. John Meade's Woman 37. *Citizen Kane* (contribution disputed; some say he wrote most of it) (AA) 41. Pride of the Yankees (AAN) 42. Stand By for Action 43. Christmas Holiday 44. The Enchanted Cottage 44. The Spanish Main 45. A Woman's Secret 48. Pride of St Louis 52, etc.

¶ Will you accept 300 per week to work for Paramount Pictures? All expenses paid. 300 is peanuts. Millions are to be grabbed out here and your only competition is idiots. Don't let this get around. – *H.M.'s wire to Ben Hecht, 1926*

Tell me, do you know any 75-dollar-a-week writers? – *Anon*

I know lots of them, but they're all making 1500 dollars a week. – *H.M.*

In a novel the hero can lay ten girls and marry a virgin for the finish. In a movie this is not allowed. The villain can lay anybody he wants, have as much fun as he wants cheating and stealing, getting rich and whipping the servants. But you have to shoot him in the end. When he falls with a bullet in the forehead, it is advisable that he clutch at the Gobelin tapestry on the wall and bring it down over his head like a symbolic shroud. Also, covered by such a tapestry, the actor does not have to hold his breath while being photographed as a dead man. – *H.M.*

Barbara Stanwyck is my favorite. My God, I

could just sit and dream of being married to her, having a little cottage out in the hills, vines around the door. I'd come home from the office tired and weary, and I'd be met by Barbara, walking through the door holding an apple pie she had cooked herself. And wearing no drawers. – *H.M.*

I don't know how it is that you start working at something you don't like, and before you know it you're an old man. – *H.M.*

Famous line (*Citizen Kane*): 'If I hadn't been so rich, I might have been a really great man.'

Mankiewicz, Joseph L. (1909–1993).
American film creator of many talents.
Biography: 1977, *Pictures Will Talk* by Kenneth Geist.
AS WRITER: The Mysterious Dr Fu Manchu 29. Skippy (AAN) 31. Million Dollar Legs 32. Forsaking All Others 34. The Keys of the Kingdom 44, etc. AS PRODUCER: Fury 36. The Bride Wore Red 37. Three Comrades 38. Huckleberry Finn 39. Strange Cargo 40. The Philadelphia Story 40. Woman of the Year 42. The Keys of the Kingdom 44, etc.
■ AS WRITER-DIRECTOR: Dragonwyck 46. Somewhere in the Night 46. The Late George Apley 47. The Ghost and Mrs Muir 47. Escape 48. *A Letter for Three Wives* (AA script, AAd) 49. House of Strangers (d only) 50. No Way Out (AAN) 50. *All About Eve* (AA script, AAd) 50. People Will Talk 51. Five Fingers (d only) (AAN) 52. Julius Caesar 53. *The Barefoot Contessa* (AANw) 54. Guys and Dolls 55. The Quiet American (& p) 57. Suddenly Last Summer (d only) 59. Cleopatra 63. The Honey Pot 67. There Was a Crooked Man 70. Sleuth (d only) (AAN) 72.

¶ I got a job at Metro and went in to see Louis Mayer, who told me he wanted me to be a producer. I said I wanted to write and direct. He said, 'No, you have to produce first, you have to crawl before you can walk.' Which is as good a definition of producing as I ever heard. – *J.L.M.*

I felt the urge to direct because I couldn't stomach what was being done with what I wrote. – *J.L.M*

Every screenwriter worthy of the name has already directed his film when he has written his script. – *J.L.M*

There were always financial crises. Someone would come out from the East and announce that the business was in deep trouble, and what would happen was that they'd reduce the number of matzo balls in Louie Mayer's chicken soup from three to two. Then they'd fire a couple of secretaries and feel virtuous. – *J.L.M.*

The toughest three pictures I ever made. It was shot in a state of emergency, shot in confusion, and wound up in blind panic. – *J.L.M. on Cleopatra*

A cinema of intelligence rather than inspiration ... his wit scratches more than it bites. – *Andrew Sarris, 1968*

Mankiewicz, Tom (1942–).
American screenwriter, son of Joseph L. Mankiewicz.
Live and Let Die 72. The Man with the Golden Gun 73. Mother, Jugs and Speed 76. The Cassandra Crossing 77. The Eagle Has Landed 77. Ladyhawke 85. Dragnet (co-w, d) 87, etc.

Mankowitz, Wolf (1924–).
British novelist and screenwriter.
A Kid for Two Farthings 56. Expresso Bongo 59. Waltz of the Toreadors 62. The Day the Earth Caught Fire 63. Where the Spies Are 65. Casino Royale 66. Dr Faustus 67. The 25th Hour 67. Bloomfield 71. The Hireling 73.

Mann, Abby (1927–).
American playwright and screenwriter.
Judgment at Nuremberg (oa, w) (AA) 61. A Child Is Waiting (w) 63. The Condemned of Altona (w) 63. Ship of Fools (w) (AAN) 65. The Detective (w) 68. The Marcus Nelson Murders (TV) 73. King (TV) (& d) 80. Skag (TV) 80. The Atlanta Child Murders (& d) (TV) 85. Murderers among Us: The Simon Wiesenthal Story (TV) 89, etc.

Mann, Anthony (1906–1967) (Emil Bundesmann). American director, usually of outdoor films; his best work was concerned with the use of violence by thoughtful men.
■ Dr Broadway 42. Moonlight in Havana 42. Nobody's Darling 43. My Best Gal 44. Strangers in the Night 44. The Great Flamarion 45. Two O'Clock Courage 45. Sing Your Way Home 45. Strange Impersonation 46. The Bamboo Blonde 46. Desperate 47. Railroaded 47. T-Men 47. Raw Deal 48. The Black Book 49. Border Incident 49. Side Street 49. Devil's Doorway 50. The Furies 50. *Winchester 73* 50. The Tall Target 51. *Bend of the River* 51. The Naked Spur 52. Thunder Bay 53. *The Glenn Miller Story* 54. The Far Country 55. Strategic Air Command 55. *The Man from Laramie* 55. The Last Frontier 56. Serenade 56. Men in War 57. The Tin Star 57. God's Little Acre 58. Man of the West 58. Cimarron 60. El Cid 61. The Fall of the Roman Empire 64. The Heroes of Telemark 65. A Dandy in Aspic (completed by Laurence Harvey) 68.

Mann, Barry (1942–).
American composer, singer and songwriter, often in collaboration with his wife Cynthia Weill, whose songs have featured in many films since a move from New York to Los Angeles in the 70s.
Wild in the Streets (s) 68. I Never Sang for My Father (co-m) 69. An American Tail (s) 86. Summer Heat (s) 87. Harry and the Hendersons (s) 87. Million Dollar Mystery (s) 87. Oliver and Company (s) 88. National Lampoon's Christmas Vacation 89. Sibling Rivalry 90, etc.

Mann, Daniel (1912–1991) (Daniel Chugerman). American director, ex stage and TV.
■ *Come Back Little Sheba* 52. About Mrs Leslie 54. The Rose Tattoo 55. I'll Cry Tomorrow 55. The Teahouse of the August Moon 56. Hot Spell 58. The Last Angry Man 59. The Mountain Road 60. Butterfield 8 60. Ada 61. Who's Got the Action? 62. Five Finger Exercise 62. Who's Been Sleeping in My Bed? 63. Judith 65. Our Man Flint 66. For Love of Ivy 68. A Dream of Kings 69. Willard 71. The Harness (TV) 71. The Revengers 72. Maurie 73. Interval 73. Lost in the Stars 73. Journey into Fear 75. Matilda 78. Playing for Time (TV) 80. The Incredible Mr Chadwick 80. The Day the Loving Stopped (TV) 81. The Man Who Broke 1,000 Chains (TV) 87.

Mann, Delbert (1920–).
American director, ex TV.
■ *Marty* (AA) 55. *The Bachelor Party* 57. Desire Under the Elms 58. Separate Tables 58. Middle of the Night 59. *The Dark at the Top of the Stairs* 60. Lover Come Back 61. The Outsider 62. That Touch of Mink 62. A Gathering of Eagles 63. Dear Heart 65. Quick Before it Melts 65. Mister Buddwing 66. Fitzwilly 67. The Pink Jungle 68. Heidi (TV) 68. David Copperfield (TV) 69. She Waits (TV) 71. No Place to Run (TV) 72. Kidnapped 72. Jane Eyre (TV) 72. Man Without a Country (TV) 73. A Girl Named Sooner (TV) 75. Birch Interval 76. Francis Gary Powers (TV) 76. Tell Me My Name (TV) 77. Breaking Up (TV) 78. Love's Dark Ride (TV) 78. Home to Stay (TV) 78. Thou Shalt Not Commit Adultery (TV) 78. Torn Between Two Lovers (TV)

79. All Quiet on the Western Front (TV) 80. To Find My Son (TV) 81. Night Crossing 81. Love Leads the Way (TV) 84. A Death in California (TV) 84. The Last Days of Patton (TV) 86. The Ted Kenne Jnr Story (TV) 86. April Morning (TV) 88. Incide in a Small Town (p, d) (TV) 94.

Mann, Hank (1887–1971) (David Liebermann). Gargantuan American supporting player of silen days, especially with Chaplin; one of the Keystone Kops.
Modern Times 36. Hollywood Cavalcade 39. T Great Dictator 40, etc.

Mann, Heinrich (1871–1950).
German novelist. His story 'Professor Unrath', published in 1905, was filmed as *The Blue Angel*. Brother of Thomas Mann.

Mann, Michael (1943–).
American director and screenwriter, from TV, where he produced *Miami Vice* 84–89 and *Crime Story* 86–88.
The Jericho Mile (TV) 79. Thief 81. The Keep 83. Manhunter (& w) 86. Last of the Mohicans (co-w, d) 92, etc.

Mann, Ned (1893–1967).
American special-effects director, a one-time professional roller-skater who entered films in 1920 as an actor. Best remembered for his long association with Alexander Korda.
Dirigible 30. *The Man Who Could Work Miracles* 35. *The Ghost Goes West* 36. *Things to Come* 36. *The Thief of Baghdad* 40. Anna Karenina 47. Bonnie Prince Charlie 48. Around the World in Eighty Days 56.

Mann, Stanley (1928–).
American screenwriter.
The Mouse That Roared 59. The Mark 61. Woman of Straw 64. Rapture 65. A High Wind in Jamaica 65. The Collector (AAN) 65. The Nake Runner 67. The Strange Affair 68. Russian Roulett 75. Sky Riders 76. Breaking Point 76. The Silent Flute 78. Damien – Omen II 78. Meteor 79. Circl of Iron 78. Eye of the Needle 81. Firestarter 84. Conan the Destroyer 84. Tai-Pan 86. Hanna's Wa 88, etc.

Mann, Thomas (1875–1955).
German novelist who spent his latter years in California. Brother of Heinrich Mann.
Buddenbrooks became a TV serial (Germany, 1982 as did *The Confessions of Felix Krull* (Germany, 1981); *Death in Venice* was filmed to general acclaim.

Manners, David (1901–) (Rauff de Ryther Duar Acklom).
Canadian leading man of Hollywood films in the 30s; claimed to be descended from William the Conqueror.
■ *Journey's End* 30. He Knew Women 30. Sweet Mama 30. Kismet 30. Mother's Cry 30. The Truth About Youth 30. The Right to Love 30. Dracula 30. The Millionaire 31. *The Last Flight* 31. The Miracle Woman 31. The Ruling Voice 31. The Greeks Had a Word for Them 31. Lady with a Pas 32. Beauty and the Boss 32. Stranger in Town 32 Crooner 32. Man Wanted 32. A Bill of Divorcemen 32. They Call It Sin 32. The Mummy 32. The Dark Kiss 32. From Hell to Heaven 33. The Warrior's Husband 33. The Girl in 419 33. The Devil in Lov 33. Torch Singer 33. Roman Scandals 33. The Black Cat 34. The Luck of a Sailor 34. The Great Flirtation 34. The Moonstone 34. The Perfect Clue

35. The Mystery of Edwin Drood 35. Jalna 35. Hearts in Bondage 36. A Woman Rebels 36.

Mannheim, Lucie (1895–1976).
German-born character actress, married to Marius Goring.
   The Thirty-Nine Steps (as the mysterious victim) 35. The High Command 37. Yellow Canary 43. Hotel Reserve 44. So Little Time 52. Beyond the Curtain 60. Bunny Lake Is Missing 65, etc.

Manni, Ettori (1927–1979).
Italian actor.
   Girls Marked Danger 52. La Lupa 53. Two Nights with Cleopatra 54. Ulysses 54. Attila the Hun 54. Le Amiche 55. Revolt of the Gladiators 58. Legions of the Nile 59. Revolt of the Slaves 60. Hercules and the Captive Women 61. The Valiant 62. Gold for the Caesars 63. The Battle of the Villa Fiorita 65. The Devil in Love 66. The Battle of El Alamein 69. Street People 76, many others.

Manning, Irene (1917–) (Inez Harvuot).
American leading lady of the 40s, former café singer.
   Two Wise Maids 37. The Big Shot 42. Yankee Doodle Dandy 42. The Desert Song 44. Shine On, Harvest Moon 44. Escape in the Desert 45. Bonnie Prince Charlie (GB) 48, etc.

Manoff, Dinah (1958–).
American actress, the daughter of actress and director Lee Grant.
   The Possessed (TV) 77. Ordinary People 80. For Ladies Only (TV) 81. I Ought to Be in Pictures 82. Backfire 88. Child's Play 88. Bloodhounds of Broadway 89. Welcome Home Roxy Carmichael 90, etc.
   TV series: Soap 78–79.

Mansfield, Jayne (1932–1967) (Vera Jane Palmer).
Amply proportioned American leading lady whose superstructure became the butt of many jokes. She began as a beauty queen, Miss Photoflash 1952, and became a star on Broadway, after Warner had dropped her contract, in Will Success Spoil Rock Hunter? Her second husband, Mickey Hargitay, was a former Mr Universe and occasional actor, and her third was director Matt Cimber (aka Matteo Ottaviano). Her stardom was short-lived and she was performing in a night-club act at the time of her death in a car crash. Loni Anderson played her in a TV movie, The Jayne Mansfield Story 80.
   Biographies: 1973, Jayne Mansfield by May Mann. 1986, Pink Goddess: The Jayne Mansfield Story by Michael Feeney Callan.
   The Female Jungle 55. Illegal 56. Pete Kelly's Blues 56. The Burglar 57. The Girl Can't Help It 57. The Wayward Bus 57. Will Success Spoil Rock Hunter? 57. Kiss Them For Me 57. The Sheriff of Fractured Jaw 59. Too Hot to Handle (GB) 60. The Challenge (GB) 60. It Happened in Athens 62. Panic Button 64. Country Music USA 65. The Fat Spy 66. A Guide for the Married Man 67, etc.

¶ Men are those creatures with two legs and eight hands. – J.M.
   I always felt all my life that people who didn't grow up to be movie stars . . . well, there was something wrong with them. – J.M.
   You gotta have a body. – J.M.
   Dramatic art in her opinion is knowing how to fill a sweater. – Bette Davis
   Miss United Dairies herself. – David Niven
   She was not strictly an exhibitionist, but she liked an audience. – May Mann

Mansfield, Martha (1900–1923).
American leading actress of silent films, from Broadway musicals. She died from burns after her dress caught fire during the filming of The Warrens of Virginia.
   Broadway Bill 18. Dr Jekyll and Mr Hyde 20. Fogbound 23. The Woman in Chains 23. The Warrens of Virginia 24, etc.

Mantee, Paul (1936–) (Paul Marianetti).
American general-purpose actor.
   Robinson Crusoe on Mars (leading role) 64. An American Dream 66. They Shoot Horses Don't They 69. W. C. Fields and Me 76. The Day of the Animals 77. The Great Santini 80, etc.

Mantegna, Joe (1947–).
American character actor, associated on stage and screen with the work of writer and director David Mamet.
   Who Stole My Wheels? (aka Towing) 78. Second Thoughts 83. Compromising Positions 85. The Money Pit 86. Offbeat 86. Three Amigos! 86. Critical Condition 87. House of Games 87. Weeds 87. Suspect 87. Things Change 88. Wait until Spring, Bandini 90. Alice 90. Queen's Logic 90. The Godfather Part III 90. Homicide 91. Bugsy (as George Raft) 91. Body of Evidence 93. Family Prayers 93. Searching for Bobby Fischer (GB: Innocent Moves) 93. State of Emergency (TV) 94. Baby's Day Out 94, etc.

Mantell, Joe.
American character actor.
   Marty (AAN) 55. Storm Center 56. Beau James 57. The Sad Sack 57. Onionhead 58. The Crowded Sky 60. The Birds 63. Mr Buddwing 66. Chinatown 74. Movers and Shakers 85. The Two Jakes 90, etc.

Mantz, Paul (1903–1965).
American stunt pilot who died in a crash during the filming of The Flight of the Phoenix.
   Biography: 1967, Hollywood Pilot by Don D. Wiggins.

Manvell, Roger (1909–1987).
British film historian. Director of the British Film Academy from 1947 and author of many books on cinema, the most influential being the Penguin Film 44.

Manx, Kate (1930–1964).
American leading lady.
   ■ Private Property 60. Hero's Island 62.

Manz, Linda (1961–).
American leading lady.
   Days of Heaven 78. King of the Gypsies 78. Boardwalk 79. Orphan Train (TV) 80. Out of the Blue 80, etc.

Manzano, Lucas.
Venezuelan director who directed, with Enrique Zimmerman, that country's first feature film, La Dama de las Cayenas 13, a version of Alexander Dumas's Camille.

Mara, Adele (1923–) (Adelaida Delgado).
Spanish-American dancer who played leads in Hollywood co-features of the 40s.
   Alias Boston Blackie 42. Bells of Rosarita 45. Tiger Woman 46. Diary of a Bride 48. The Sea Hornet 51. Back from Eternity 56. Curse of the Faceless Man 58. The Big Circus 59, etc.

Marais, Jean (1913–) (Jean Marais-Villain).
French romantic actor well remembered in several

Cocteau films. Later films less notable; recently in cloak-and-sword epics, also playing 'The Saint', 'Fantomas' and various secret agents.
   Autobiography: 1975, Histoires de Ma Vie.
   L'Eternel Retour 43. La Belle et la Bête 45. L'Aigle a Deux Têtes 47. Les Parents Terribles 48. Orphée 49. Nez de Cuir 51. Les Amants de Minuit 53. Julietta 53. Le Comte de Monte Cristo 54. Napoléon 54. Paris Does Strange Things (Eléna et les Hommes) 56. White Nights (Le Notti Bianche) 57. The Testament of Orpheus (Le Testament d'Orphée) 59. Austerlitz 60. Patate 64. Thomas l'Imposteur 65. Train d'Enfer 65. Le Paria 68. Peau d'Ane 70. Erimou 82. Parking 85. Les Misérables du XXème Siècle 95, etc.

Marceau, Sophie (1967–).
French leading actress, in films from the age of 13.
   La Boum 80. Police 85. Mes Nuits Sont Plus Belles que Vos Jours 89. Pacific Palisades 90. Fanfan 93. La Fille de D'Artagnan 94. Braveheart 95, etc.

Marcel, Terry (1942–).
British director and screenwriter.
   Why Not Stay for Breakfast? 79. There Goes the Bride 80. Hawk the Slayer 80. Prisoners of the Lost Universe 83. Jane and the Lost City 87. Heartbeat (TV) 93, etc.

March, Fredric (1897–1975) (Frederick McIntyre Bickel).
One of America's most respected stage and screen actors, who always projected intelligence and integrity and during the 30s and 40s was at times an agreeable light comedian. Long married to Florence Eldridge.
   ■ The Dummy 29. The Wild Party 29. The Studio Murder Mystery 29. Paris Bound 29. Jealousy 29. Footlights and Fools 29. The Marriage Playground 29. Sarah and Son 30. Ladies Love Brutes 30. Paramount on Parade 30. True to the Navy 30. Manslaughter 30. Laughter 30. The Royal Family of Broadway (AAN) 30. Honor among Lovers 30. Night Angel 31. My Sin 31. Merrily We Go to Hell 32. Dr Jekyll and Mr Hyde (AA) 32. Smiling Through 32. Make Me a Star 32. Strangers in Love 32. The Sign of the Cross 33. Tonight Is Ours 33. The Eagle and the Hawk 33. The Affairs of Cellini 34. All of Me 34. Good Dame 34. Design for Living 34. Death takes a Holiday 34. The Barretts of Wimpole Street (as Robert Browning) 34. We Live Again 34. Les Misérables 35. The Dark Angel 35. Anna Karenina 35. Mary of Scotland 36. Anthony Adverse 36. The Road to Glory 36. A Star Is Born (AAN) 37. Nothing Sacred 37. The Buccaneer 38. There Goes My Heart 38. Trade Winds 39. Susan and God 40. Victory 40. So Ends Our Night 41. One Foot in Heaven 41. Bedtime Story 42. I Married a Witch 42. Tomorrow the World 44. The Adventures of Mark Twain 44. The Best Years of Our Lives (AA) 46. Another Part of the Forest 48. An Act of Murder 48. Christopher Columbus (GB) 49. It's a Big Country 51. Death of a Salesman (AAN) 52. Man on a Tightrope 53. Executive Suite 54. The Bridges at Toko Ri 54. The Desperate Hours 55. Alexander the Great 55. The Man in the Grey Flannel Suit 56. Middle of the Night 59. Inherit the Wind 60. The Young Doctors 62. The Condemned of Altona 63. Seven Days in May 64. Hombre 67. Tick Tick Tick 70. The Iceman Cometh 73.
   🕻 For the diligence with which he undertook every role, and for the satisfying success of most of the results. A Star Is Born.

¶ He was able to do a very emotional scene with tears in his eyes, and pinch my fanny at the same time. – Shelley Winters

March, Hal (1920–1970).
American comic actor who never quite made it.
Outrage 50. Yankee Pasha 54. My Sister Eileen 55. *Hear Me Good* 57. Send Me No Flowers 64, etc.

March, Jane (1975–   ).
British actress, a former model.
The Lover (L'Amant) 91. Color of Night 94.

The March of Time.
A highly influential series of two-reelers on current affairs, started and financed in 1935 by the founders of *Time* magazine and film-maker Louis de Rochemont. The raucous American commentary by Westbrook van Voorhis marred it for European consumption, but its contents were a first-class, in-depth examination of what was happening in the world. It ran with great success until the late 40s, when it was gradually replaced by television coverage of world events. Its history was chronicled by Raymond Fielding in his 1977 book *The March of Time*.

Marchand, Colette.
French actress who was nominated for an Oscar as best supporting actress in *Moulin Rouge* 52, her only international film.

Marchand, Corinne (1937–   ).
French leading lady of the 60s.
Cleo de 5 à 7 62. Seven Deadly Sins 63. The Milky Way 69. Rider on the Rain 70. Borsalino 70. Travels with My Aunt 72, etc.

Marchand, Henri (1889–1959).
French comedy actor.
A Nous la Liberté 31. Je Vous Aimerai Toujours 33. Volga en Flammes 35. Les Deux Combinards 38. L'Ennemi sans Visage 46. La Sorcière 50. Operation Magali 53. Till Eulenspiegel 56, many others.

Marcus, Lawrence B.
American screenwriter.
Petulia 68. Justine 69. Alex and the Gypsy 76. The Stunt Man (AAN) 80.

Marcus, Mike (1945–   ).
American production executive, a former agent, who became president of MGM in 1993.

Marcuse, Theodore (1920–1967).
Shaven-pated American character actor, usually in sinister roles.
The Glass Bottom Boat 65. The Cincinnati Kid 65. Last of the Secret Agents 66. The Wicked Dreams of Paula Schultz 67, etc.

Margetson, Arthur (1897–1951).
British stage actor, former stockbroker's clerk, who went to Hollywood in 1940 and played supporting roles.
Other People's Sins 31. His Grace Gives Notice 33. Little Friend 34. Broken Blossoms 36. Juggernaut 37. Action for Slander 38. Return to Yesterday 40. Random Harvest 43. Sherlock Holmes Faces Death 44, etc.

Margheriti, Antonio (1930–   ) (aka Anthony M. Dawson).
Italian action film director.
Space-Men 60. The Golden Arrow 62. Lightning Bolt 65. Wild, Wild Planet 66. The Young, the Evil and the Savage 68. Decameron 3 73. Blood Money 74. The House of 1,000 Pleasures 77. Killer Fish 78. Cannibals in the Streets 80. Car Crash 81. Yor, the Hunter from the Future 83. Ark of the Sun God

84. Codename: Wildgeese 84. The Commander 88. Indio 89. Indio 2: The Revolt 91, many others.

Margo (1918–1985) (Maria Marguerita Guadelupe Boldao Castilla y O'Donnell).
Mexican actress and dancer, once with Xavier Cugat's band, long married to Eddie Albert, in occasional Hollywood films from 1933.
Crime without Passion 34. Winterset 36. Lost Horizon 37. The Leopard Man 43. Behind the Rising Sun 43. Gangway for Tomorrow 44. Viva Zapata 52. I'll Cry Tomorrow 57. Who's Got the Action? 63, etc.

Margolin, Janet (1943–1993).
American leading lady.
David and Lisa 62. Bus Riley's Back in Town 65. The Greatest Story Ever Told 65. The Saboteur 65. Nevada Smith 66. Enter Laughing 67. Buona Sera Mrs Campbell 68. Take the Money and Run 70. The Last Child (TV) 71. Family Flight (TV) 72. Pray for the Wildcats (TV) 74. Planet Earth (TV) 74. Lanigan's Rabbi (TV) 76. Annie Hall 77. Murder in Peyton Place (TV) 77. The Triangle Factory Fire Scandal (TV) 79. Last Embrace 79. Ghostbusters II 89, etc.

Margolin, Stuart (c. 1940–   ).
American character actor.
Limbo 72. The Stone Killer 73. Death Wish 74. Lanigan's Rabbi (TV) 76. The Big Bus 76. Futureworld 76. S.O.B. 81. Class 83. A Fine Mess 86. Iron Eagle II 88. Bye Bye Blues 90. Guilty by Suspicion 91, etc.
TV series: Nichols 71. Bret Maverick 81.

Margolyes, Miriam (1941–   ).
Plump British character actress, often in fussy roles.
A Nice Girl Like Me 69. Stand Up Virgin Soldiers 77. The Awakening 80. Reds 81. Scrubbers 82. Yentl 83. Morons from Outer Space 85. Little Shop of Horrors 86. Little Dorrit 88. Pacific Heights 90. The Fool 91. Dead Again 91. The Butcher's Wife 91. Ed and His Dead Mother 93. The Age of Innocence 93, etc.
TV series: Frannie's Turn 92.

Marielle, Jean-Pierre.
French leading actor.
Peau de Banane 63. Que la Fête Commence 75. Calmos 76. One Wild Moment 78. Coup de Torchon 81. Evening Dress (Tenue de Soirée) 86. Uranus 91. The Smile (Le Sourire) 94. Le Parfum d'Yvonne 94, etc.

Marin, Edwin L. (1901–1951).
American director.
The Death Kiss 32. A Study in Scarlet 33. Paris Interlude 34. The Casino Murder Case 35. I'd Give My Life 36. Everybody Sing 38. A Christmas Carol 38. Fast and Loose 39. Maisie 39. Florian 40. A Gentleman After Dark 42. *Show Business* 44. Tall in the Saddle 44. Johnny Angel 45. The Young Widow 46. Nocturne 46. Christmas Eve 47. Race Street 48. Canadian Pacific 49. Fighting Man of the Plains 49. The Cariboo Trail 50. Fort Worth 51, etc.

Marin, Jacques (1919–   ).
French character actor.
The Island at the Top of the World 74. Herbie Goes to Monte Carlo 77.

Marin, Richard 'Cheech' (1946–   ).
American actor, musician and screenwriter. One half of a coarse comic double-act with Thomas Chong featuring two druggy hippies, which began

on record albums and enjoyed a high popularity in the early 80s. The act split up in 1985.
Up in Smoke (a, w) 79. Cheech & Chong's Next Movie (a, w) 80. Cheech & Chong's Nice Dreams (a, w) 81. Things Are Tough All Over (a, w) 82. Cheech & Chong: Still Smokin' (a, w) 83. Yellowbeard (a) 83. Cheech & Chong's The Corsican Brothers (a, w) 84. After Hours (a) 85. Echo Park (a) 86. Born in East L.A. (a, d) 87. Rude Awakening (a) 89. Troop Beverly Hills (a) 89. Boyfriend from Hell (aka The Shrimp on the Barbie) (a) 90. Ferngully . . . the Last Rainforest (voice) 92. The Cisco Kid (TV) 94, etc.

Marion, Frances (1888–1973) (Frances Marion Owens).
American screenwriter.
Autobiography: 1972, *Off with Their Heads*.
Daughter of the Sea 16. Humoresque 22. Stella Dallas 25. The Winning of Barbara Worth 26. The Scarlet Letter 27. *Love* 27. The Wind 28. *The Big House* (AA) 30. *The Champ* (AA) 32. The Prizefighter and the Lady (AAN) 33. *Dinner at Eight* 33. Riff Raff 36. *Knight without Armour* 37. Green Hell 40, etc.

Marion-Crawford, Howard (1914–1969).
British actor often seen in Watsonian roles or as jovial, beefy, sporting types.
Forever England 32. Freedom Radio 40. The Rake's Progress 45. The Hasty Heart 49. The Man in the White Suit 51. Where's Charley? 52. Reach for the Sky 56. Virgin Island 58. The Brides of Fu Manchu 66, etc.
TV series: Sherlock Holmes 55.

Maris, Mona (1903–1991) (Maria Capdevielle).
Franco-Argentinian 'second lead' in Hollywood films.
Romance of the Rio Grande 29. Secrets 33. Law of the Tropics 41. Tampico 44. Heartbeat 46. The Avengers 50, etc.

Maritza, Sari (1910–1987) (Patricia Nathan).
Anglo-Austrian leading lady, a short-lived sensation of the early 30s.
Monte Carlo Madness 31. Forgotten Commandments 32. Evenings for Sale 32. International House 33. Crimson Romance 34, etc.

Marken, Jane (1895–1976) (J. Krab).
French character actress with long stage experience.
Fioritures 15. Camille 34. *Partie de Campagne* 37. Hôtel du Nord 38. *Lumière d'Été* 42. Les Enfants du Paradis 44. L'Idiot 46. Clochemerle 47. Une Si Jolie Petite Plage 48. Manèges 49. Ma Pomme 50. Les Compagnes de la Nuit 52. Marie Antoinette 55. And God Created Woman 56. Pot Bouille 57. The Mirror Has Two Faces 58, etc.

Marker, Chris (1921–   ) (Christian Bouche-Villeneuve).
French documentary director. Leader of the modernist 'left bank' school.
Olympia 52. Toute la Memoire du Monde 56. Letter from Siberia 58. Description d'un Combat 60. Cuba Si 61. Le Joli Mai 62. La Jetée 63. If I Had Four Dromedaries 66. Le Fond de l'Air est Rouge 77. Sans Soleil 82. A.K. 85. L'Héritage de la Chouette 89, etc.

Markey, Enid (1896–1981).
American character actress. In 1918 she was the first screen Jane, to Elmo Lincoln's Tarzan.
Civilisation 16. Tarzan of the Apes 18. The Romance of Tarzan 18. Snafu 46. The Naked City 48. The Boston Strangler 68, etc.

TV series: Bringing Up Buddy 60–61.

Markey, Gene (1895–1980).
American screenwriter.
The Battle of Paris 29. The Florodora Girl 30. As You Desire Me 32. Midnight Mary 33. Fashions 34. A Modern Hero 34. Let's Live Tonight 35. King of Burlesque 36. Private Number 36. *On the Avenue* 37, etc.
AS PRODUCER ONLY: Wee Willie Winkie 37. The Little Princess 39. The Hound of the Baskervilles 39. The Blue Bird 40. Lillian Russell 40. Moss Rose 47.
¶ Markey's several wives included Joan Bennett, Hedy Lamarr and Myrna Loy.

Markham, Monte (1935–).
American leading man, mostly on TV.
Death Takes a Holiday (TV) 71. One is a Lonely Number 72. Midway 76. Airport 77 77. Hotline 82. Off the Wall 83. Defense Play (& d) 88. Neon City (d) 91, etc.
TV series: The Second Hundred Years 67. Mr Deeds Goes to Town 69. The New Perry Mason 73. Dallas 81. Rituals 84–85. Baywatch 89– .

Markle, Fletcher (1921–1991).
Canadian director, briefly in Hollywood. Married to Mercedes McCambridge (1950–62).
¶ Jigsaw 49. Night into Morning 51. The Man with a Cloak 51. The Incredible Journey 63.

Markle, Peter.
American director.
The Personals 82. Youngblood 86. Bat-21 88. El Diablo (TV) 90. Through the Eyes of a Killer (TV) 92. Wagons East 94.

Marks, Alfred (1921–).
Bald-pated British comedian, in films from 1950 but more usually seen on TV and stage.
Desert Mice 59. There Was a Crooked Man 60. Frightened City 61. Weekend with Lulu 62. She'll Have to Go 63. Scream and Scream Again 70. Our Miss Fred 72. Valentino 77, etc.

Marks, Richard (1943–).
American film editor.
Little Big Man 70. Parades 72. Bang the Drum Slowly 73. Serpico 73. The Godfather Part II 74. Lies My Father Told Me 75. The Last Tycoon 76. Apocalypse Now (AAN) 79. The Hand 81. Pennies from Heaven 81. Terms of Endearment (AAN) 83. The Adventures of Buckaroo Banzai across the Eighth Dimension 84. St Elmo's Fire 85. Pretty in Pink 86. Firewalker 86. Broadcast News (AAN) 87. Say Anything 89. Dick Tracy 90. One Good Cop 91, etc.

Marley, J. Peverell (1899–1964).
American cinematographer who worked on de Mille's silent epics.
The Ten Commandments 23. The Volga Boatmen 25. *King of Kings* 27. House of Rothschild 34. Clive of India 35. *Alexander's Ragtime Band* 38. *The Hound of the Baskervilles* 39. Night and Day 46. Life with Father 47. The Greatest Show on Earth 52. House of Wax 53. Serenade 56. The Left-Handed Gun 58. A Fever in the Blood 61, many others.

Marley, John (1907–1984).
American character actor.
My Six Convicts 52. Timetable 56. I Want to Live 58. America America 65. Cat Ballou 65. Faces 68. *Love Story* (AAN) 70. A Man Called Sledge 70. The Godfather 72. Blade 73. W. C. Fields and Me 76. The Car 77. The Greatest 77. Hooper 78. Tribute 80, etc.

Marlowe, Hugh (1911–1982) (Hugh Hipple).
American actor, former radio announcer, in films from 1937.
Mrs Parkington 44. Meet Me In St Louis 44. *Twelve O'Clock High* 50. *All about Eve* 50. The Day the Earth Stood Still 51. Monkey Business 52. Garden of Evil 54. Earth Versus the Flying Saucers 56. Thirteen Frightened Girls 64. Castle of Evil 66. The Last Shot You Hear 68, etc.
TV series: Ellery Queen 54.

Marlowe, June (1903–1984).
American actress who was mainly a leading lady to Rin-Tin-Tin and later became the schoolteacher Miss Crabtree in the Our Gang shorts of the 30s.
Find Your Man 24. Clash of the Wolves 25. Night Cry 26. Don Juan 26. Life of Riley 27. Code of the Air 28. Pardon Us (aka Jail Birds) 31. The Lone Defender (serial) 32. Riddle Ranch 36, etc.

Marlowe, Scott.
American juvenile actor of the late 50s.
Men in War 57. Young Guns 57. The Subterraneans 60. *A Cold Wind in August* 61.

Marly, Florence (1918–1978) (Hana Smekalova).
Franco-Czech leading lady, married to Pierre Chenal. Made a few films in Hollywood.
Sealed Verdict 48. Tokyo Joe 49. Tokyo File 212 51. Gobs and Gals 52. The Idol (Chilean) 52. Confession at Dawn (Chilean) 53. Undersea Girl 58. Queen of Blood 65. Games 67. Doctor Death 73, etc.

Marmont, Percy (1883–1977).
Veteran British romantic actor of silent era, in films since 1913.
SILENT FILMS: The Silver King (GB) 24. Lord Jim (US) 25. Mantrap (US) 26. Rich and Strange (GB) 27, etc.
SOUND FILMS: The Silver Greyhound 32. Secret Agent 36. Action for Slander 38. I'll Walk Beside You 41. Loyal Heart 45. No Orchids for Miss Blandish 48. Lisbon 56, many others.

Marquand, Christian (1927–).
French leading man, who turned director with *Candy* 68.
Lucretia Borgia 53. Senso 54. And God Created Woman 56. Sait-on Jamais? 57. Une Vie 58. Victory at Entebbe (TV) 76. The Other Side of Midnight 77. Je Vous Aime 80, etc.

Marquand, John P. (1893–1960).
American novelist who wrote solid popular books about middle-aged men regretting their lost youth; also the Mr Moto series (filmed in the late 30s with Peter Lorre).
H.M. Pulham Esquire 41. The Late George Apley 47. B. F.'s Daughter 49. Top Secret Affair (Melville Goodwin USA) 56. Stopover Tokyo 57, etc.

Marquand, Richard (1938–1987).
British director.
The Search for the Nile (TV) 75. The Legacy 78. Eye of the Needle 81. Return of the Jedi 83. Until September 84. *Jagged Edge* 85. Hearts of Fire 87.

Marriott, Moore (1885–1949) (George Thomas Moore-Marriott).
British leading man of silents who became a character comedian specializing in hoary rustics, chiefly beloved as the ancient but resilient old Harbottle of the Will Hay comedies: *Convict 99* 36, *Oh Mr Porter* 38, *Ask a Policeman* 39, *Where's That Fire?* 40, etc. Also notable with the Crazy Gang in *The Frozen Limits* 39, and *Gasbags* 40. Made over 300 films in all.

Dick Turpin 08. Passion Island 26. The Lyons Mail 31. The Water Gypsies 32. As You Like It 36. Millions Like Us 43. Time Flies 44. Green for Danger 46. The History of Mr Polly 49. High Jinks in Society 49.

Mars, Kenneth (1936–).
American character comedian who is usually way over the top.
The Producers 67. Desperate Characters 71. What's Up Doc? 72. Paper Moon 73. The Parallax View 74. Young Frankenstein 74. Night Moves 75. The Apple Dumpling Gang Rides Again 79. Radio Days 87. For Keeps 88. Police Academy 6: City under Siege 89. The Little Mermaid (voice) 89. Shadows and Fog 91. We're Back! A Dinosaur's Story (voice) 93, etc.

Marsh, Carol (1926–) (Norma Simpson).
British leading lady whose career faltered when she outgrew *ingénue* roles.
■ *Brighton Rock* 47. Marry Me 49. Helter Skelter 50. Alice in Wonderland (French puppet version) 50. The Romantic Age 50. Scrooge 51. Salute the Toff 51. Private Information 51. Dracula 58. Man Accused 59.

Marsh, Garry (1902–1981) (Leslie March Geraghty).
Robust, balding British character actor; in films from 1930, usually as harassed father, perplexed policeman or explosive officer.
Night Birds 30. Dreyfus 30. Number Seventeen 32. The Maid of the Mountains 32. Scrooge 35. When Knights Were Bold 36. Bank Holiday 38. It's in the Air 38. The Four Just Men 39. Hoots Mon 40. I'll Be Your Sweetheart 45. The Rake's Progress 45. Dancing with Crime 46. Just William's Luck 48. Murder at the Windmill 49. Worm's Eye View 51. Mr Drake's Duck 53. Who Done It? 55. Where the Bullets Fly 66, many others.

Marsh, Jean (1934–).
British character actress who became internationally known as the maid in TV's *Upstairs Downstairs*, which she created with actress Eileen Atkins. Also co-creator of the 90s TV series *The House of Elliott*. Married to actor Jon Pertwee (1955–60).
The Tales of Hoffman 51. Cleopatra 63. Face of a Stranger 64. Unearthly Stranger 64. Frenzy 72. Dark Places 74. The Eagle Has Landed 77. Master of the Game (TV) 84. Return to Oz 85. Willow 88. A Connecticut Yankee in King Arthur's Court (TV) 89. Adam Bede (TV) 91, etc.
TV series: 9 to 5 82–83.

Marsh, Mae (1895–1968) (Mary Warne Marsh).
American leading lady of the silent screen; later played small character roles.
Man's Genesis 12. The Birth of a Nation 15. Intolerance 16. Polly of the Circus 17. Spotlight Sadie 18. The Little 'Fraid Lady 20. Flames of Passion 22. The White Rose 23. Daddies 24. The Rat (GB) 25. Tides of Passion 26. Over the Hill 32. Little Man What Now 34. Jane Eyre 43. A Tree Grows in Brooklyn 44. The Robe 53. Sergeant Rutledge 60, many others.

Marsh, Marion (1913–) (Violet Krauth).
American leading lady of English, German, French and Irish descent. Began in Hollywood as an extra; chosen by John Barrymore to play Trilby to his *Svengali* 31.
The Mad Genius 32. Five Star Final 32. The Eleventh Commandment 33. Love at Second Sight (GB) 34. The Black Room 35. When's Your Birthday 37. Missing Daughters 40. House of Errors 42, etc.

Marsh, Oliver H.T. (1893–1941).
American cinematographer.

The Floor Below 18. Good References 19. Lessons in Love 21. Jazzmania 23. The Dove 27. The Divine Woman 28. Not So Dumb 30. The Sin of Madelon Claudet 31. Arsene Lupin 32. Today We Live 33. The Merry Widow 34. *David Copperfield* 35. *A Tale of Two Cities* 35. The Great Ziegfeld 36. His Brother's Wife 36. After the Thin Man 36. Maytime 37. The Firefly 37. Sweethearts 38. It's a Wonderful World 39. Bitter Sweet 40. Rage in Heaven 41. Lady Be Good 41, many others.

Marsh, Terence.
British production designer.

Dr Zhivago (AA) 65. A Man for All Seasons 66. Oliver (AA) 68. The Looking Glass War 70. Perfect Friday 70. Scrooge (AAN) 70. Mary, Queen of Scots (AAN) 71. A Touch of Class 73. The Mackintosh Man 73. Juggernaut 74. The Adventures of Sherlock Holmes' Smarter Brother 75. Royal Flash 76. A Bridge Too Far 77. Magic 78. The Frisco Kid 79. Absence of Malice 81. To Be or Not To Be 83. Haunted Honeymoon 86. Spaceballs 87. Bert Rigby, You're a Fool 89. The Hunt for Red October 90. Havana 90. Basic Instinct 92. Clear and Present Danger 94. The Shawshank Redemption 94, etc.

Marshal, Alan (1909–1961).
Australian-born actor of light romantic leads; came to films in 1936 after New York stage experience.

The Garden of Allah 36. Night Must Fall 38. The Hunchback of Notre Dame 40. Tom, Dick and Harry 40. *Lydia* 41. The White Cliffs of Dover 43. The Barkleys of Broadway 48. The Opposite Sex 56. The House on Haunted Hill 59, etc.

Marshall, Alan (1938–).
British producer associated with the films of Alan Parker.

■ Bugsy Malone 76. Midnight Express (AAN) 78. Fame 80. Shoot the Moon 81. Pink Floyd the Wall 82. Another Country 84. Birdy 84. Angel Heart 87. Leonard, Part 6 87. Homeboy 88. Jacob's Ladder 90.

Marshall, Brenda (1915–1992) (Ardis Ankerson Gaines).
American leading lady who married William Holden and retired.

Espionage Agent 39. The Sea Hawk 40. Footsteps in the Dark 41. Singapore Woman 41. Background to Danger 43. The Constant Nymph 44. Strange Impersonation 45. Whispering Smith 49. The Tomahawk Trail 50, etc.

Marshall, Connie (1938–).
American child actress of the 40s.

Sunday Dinner for a Soldier 44. *Sentimental Journey* 45. Dragonwyck 46. Home Sweet Homicide 47. Mother Wore Tights 48. Kill the Umpire 50. Sagmaw Trail 53, etc.

Marshall, E. G. (1910–) (Everett G. Marshall).
American character actor with long Broadway experience.

■ The House on 92nd Street 45. 13 rue Madeleine 46. Untamed Fury 47. Call Northside 777 48. The Caine Mutiny 54. Pushover 54. The Bamboo Prison 54. Broken Lance 54. The Silver Chalice 54. The Left Hand of God 55. The Scarlet Hour 56. The Mountain 56. *Twelve Angry Men* 57. *The Bachelor Party* 57. Man on Fire 57. The Buccaneer 58. The Journey 59. Compulsion 59. Cash McCall 59. Town without Pity 61. The Chase 66. Is Paris Burning? 66. The Poppy Is Also a Flower (TV) 66. The Bridge

at Remagen 69. A Clear and Present Danger (TV) 70. Tora! Tora! Tora! 70. The Pursuit of Happiness 71. Vanished (TV) 71. The City (TV) 71. Don't Look behind You (TV) 71. Pursuit (TV) 72. Money to Burn (TV) 73. The Abduction of St Anne (TV) 75. Collision Course (TV) 76. Interiors 78. The Private Files of J. Edgar Hoover 78. The Lazarus Syndrome (TV) 79. Superman II 80. Creepshow 82. Kennedy (as Joseph Kennedy) (TV) 83. Saigon – Year of the Cat (TV) 83. The Winter of our Discontent (TV) 84. Power 85. At Mother's Request (TV) 87. The Hijacking of the Achille Lauro (TV) 89. Consenting Adults 92. The Tommyknockers (TV) 93. Oldest Living Confederate Widow Tells All (TV) 94.

TV series: The Defenders 61–65. The New Doctors 69–73. Chicago Hope 94.

Marshall, Frank (1947–).
American producer turned director. A former actor, he founded the production company Amblin Entertainment with Steven Spielberg and Kathleen Kennedy.

AS PRODUCER: The Other Side of the Wind 75. The Warriors 78. Raiders of the Lost Ark (AAN) 81. Poltergeist 82. Indiana Jones and the Temple of Doom 84. Fandango 84. The Goonies 85. The Color Purple (AAN) 85. Back to the Future 85. The Money Pit 86. Innerspace 86. Who Framed Roger Rabbit? 88. The Land before Time 88. Back to the Future II 89. Indiana Jones and the Last Crusade 89. Hook 91. Swing Kids 92, etc.

AS DIRECTOR: Arachnophobia 89. Alive 93. Milk Money 94.

Marshall, Garry (1934–) (Gary Masciarelli).
American film director, screenwriter, producer and occasional actor, who started his career writing and producing TV sitcoms (*The Dick Van Dyke Show*, *Happy Days*, etc.). He is the brother of actress and director Penny Marshall.

How Sweet It Is (w, p) 68. The Grasshopper (w, p) 70. Young Doctors in Love (p, d) 82. The Flamingo Kid (wd) 84. Lost in America (a) 85. Nothing in Common (d) 86. Overboard (d) 87. Beaches (d) 88. Pretty Woman (d) 90. Frankie and Johnny (d) 91. Soapdish (a) 91. A League of Their Own (a) 92. Exit to Eden (d) 94, etc.

Marshall, George (1891–1975).
American director with over 400 features to his credit. Entered films 1912 as an extra; graduated to feature roles in early serials and comedies; began directing 1917 with a series of Harry Carey westerns.

Pack Up Your Troubles 32. A Message to Garcia 34. The Crime of Dr Forbes 37. In Old Kentucky 38. The Goldwyn Follies 38. You Can't Cheat an Honest Man 39. *Destry Rides Again* 39. *The Ghost Breakers* 40. When the Daltons Rode 40. The Forest Rangers 42. Star Spangled Rhythm 43. And the Angels Sing 43. *Murder He Says* 44. Incendiary Blonde 45. Hold That Blonde 45. The Blue Dahlia 46. The Perils of Pauline 47. Tap Roots 48. *Fancy Pants* 50. The Savage 52. Scared Stiff 53. *Red Garters* 54. The Second Greatest Sex 55. Beyond Mombasa (GB) 56. The Sad Sack 57. The Sheepman 58. Imitation General 58. The Gazebo 59. Cry for Happy 61. How the West Was Won (part) 62. Advance to the Rear 64. Boy, Did I Get a Wrong Number 66. Eight on the Lam 67. Hook Line and Sinker 69, many others.

Marshall, Herbert (1890–1966).
Urbane British actor who despite the loss of a leg in World War I invariably played smooth, sometimes diffident but always gentlemanly roles. In Hollywood from early 30s.

■ Mumsie 27. The Letter 29. Murder 30. The Calendar 31. Secrets of a Secretary 31. *Michael and Mary* 32. The Faithful Heart 32. Blonde Venus 32. *Trouble in Paradise* 32. Evenings for Sale 32. The Solitaire Man 33. I Was a Spy 33. Four Frightened People 34. Outcast Lady 34. The Painted Veil 34. Riptide 34. The Good Fairy 35. The Flame Within 35. Accent on Youth 35. *The Dark Angel* 35. If You Could Only Cook 35. The Lady Consents 36. Forgotten Faces 36. Till We Meet Again 36. Girls' Dormitory 36. A Woman Rebels 36. Make Way for a Lady 36. *Angel* 37. Breakfast for Two 37. Mad About Music 38. Always Goodbye 38. Woman against Woman 38. Zaza 39. A Bill of Divorcement 40. *Foreign Correspondent* 40. *The Letter* 40. When Ladies Meet 41. *The Little Foxes* 41. Kathleen 41. Adventure in Washington 41. *The Moon and Sixpence* (as Somerset Maugham) 42. Young Ideas 43. Forever and a Day 43. Flight for Freedom 43. Andy Hardy's Blonde Trouble 44. The Unseen 45. *The Enchanted Cottage* 45. Crack up 46. *The Razor's Edge* (as Somerset Maugham) 46. Duel in the Sun 46. High Wall 47. Ivy 47. The Secret Garden 49. The Underworld Story 50. Anne of the Indies 51. Black Jack 52. Angel Face 53. The Black Shield of Falworth 54. Gog 54. Riders to the Stars 54. The Virgin Queen 55. Wicked as They Come 56. The Weapon 56. *Stage Struck* 57. The Fly 58. A Fever in the Blood 60. Midnight Lace 60. Five Weeks in a Balloon 62. The List of Adrian Messenger 63. The Third Day 65.

✪ For his comforting upper class presence over thirty-five years of talkies. *Trouble in Paradise*.

¶ Fantasy droops before Mr Herbert Marshall, so intractably British in the American scene. He does, I suppose, represent some genuinely national characteristics, if not those one wishes to see exported: a kind of tobacco, a kind of tweed, a kind of pipe; or in terms of dog, something large, sentimental and moulting, something which confirms our preference for cats. – *Graham Greene, reviewing If You Could Only Cook*

Marshall, Herbert (1900–1991).
British documentarist, married to Fredda Brilliant. Associate of John Grierson; worked on English dubbing of Russian films. Produced and directed feature, *Tinker* 49.

Marshall, James (1967–).
American actor.

Twin Peaks: Fire Walk with Me 92. Gladiator 92. A Few Good Men 92. Don't Do It 94.

TV series: Twin Peaks 90.

¶ Hollywood is just full of people who want the quick buck and the quick fame, and they get burned out. – J.M.

Marshall, Penny (1942–) (Carole Penny Marsciarelli).
American director, a former comedy actress, known from TV's *Happy Days* and *Laverne and Shirley*. She is the sister of director Garry Marshall.

How Sweet It Is 68. 1941 79. Movers and Shakers 84. Jumpin' Jack Flash 86. Big 88. Awakenings 90. The Hard Way (a) 91. A League of Their Own 92. Renaissance Man 94, etc.

Marshall, Trudy (1922–).
American leading lady of minor films in the 40s.

Secret Agent of Japan 42. Girl Trouble 44. Sentimental Journey 46. Disaster 48. Mark of the Gorilla 50. The President's Lady 53. Once Is Not Enough 75, etc.

Marshall, Tully (1864–1943) (William Phillips). American silent screen actor; stage experience from boyhood.

Intolerance 15. Oliver Twist (as Fagin) 16. Joan the Woman 16. The Slim Princess 20. The Hunchback of Notre Dame 23. The Merry Widow 25. The Red Mill 27. The Cat and the Canary 28. Trail of '98 29. Show of Shows 29. The Unholy Garden 31. Scarface 32. Grand Hotel 33. Diamond Jim 35. Souls at Sea 37. A Yank at Oxford 38. Brigham Young 40. Chad Hanna 41. This Gun for Hire 42, many others.

Marshall, William (1924–).
American character actor.

Lydia Bailey 52. Something of Value 57. The Boston Strangler 68. Blacula 72. Scream Blacula Scream 73. Twilight's Last Gleaming 77. Vasectomy – a Delicate Matter 86. Maverick 94, etc.

Marshall, Zena (1926–).
British leading lady with French ancestry; stage experience.

Caesar and Cleopatra (debut) 45. Good Time Girl 47. Miranda 48. Sleeping Car to Trieste 48. Marry Me 49. Hell Is Sold Out 51. The Embezzler 54. My Wife's Family 56. The Story of David 61. Dr No 62. Those Magnificent Men in Their Flying Machines 65, etc.

Martelli, Otello (1903–).
Italian cinematographer, especially associated with Fellini.

Paisa 46. Bitter Rice 49. La Dolce Vita 50. I Vitelloni 52. La Strada 54. Il Bidone 55. I Tre Volti 63, etc.

Martin, Chris-Pin (1894–1953).
Rotund Yaqui Indian actor who provided comic relief in many a western.

Four Frightened People 34. The Gay Desperado 36. The Return of the Cisco Kid 39 (and ensuing series). The Mark of Zorro 41. Weekend in Havana 42. Mexican Hayride 49. Ride the Man Down 53, etc.

Martin, Darnell.
American director and screenwriter, a former assistant camera operator.

I Like It Like That (wd) 94.

Martin, Dean (1917–) (Dino Crocetti).
Heavy-lidded, self-spoofing American leading man and singer. Teamed with Jerry Lewis until 1956, then enjoyed spectacular solo success in 60s.

Biography (of Martin and Lewis): 1976, *Everybody Loves Somebody Sometime* by Arthur Marx. 1992, *Dino: Living High in the Dirty Business of Dreams* by Nick Tosches.

■ My Friend Irma 49. My Friend Irma Goes West 50. At War with the Army 51. That's My Boy 51. Sailor Beware 51. Jumping Jacks 52. The Stooge 52. Scared Stiff 53. The Caddy 53. Money from Home 53. Living It Up 54. Three Ring Circus 54. You're Never Too Young 55. Artists and Models 55. Pardners 56. Hollywood or Bust 56. Ten Thousand Bedrooms 57. *The Young Lions* 58. Some Came Running 58. *Rio Bravo* 59. Career 59. Who Was That Lady? 60. Bells are Ringing 60. Ocean's Eleven 60. All in a Night's Work 61. Ada 61. Sergeants Three 62. Who's Got the Action? 62. Toys in the Attic 63. Who's Been Sleeping in My Bed? 63. Four For Texas 64. What a Way to Go 64. Robin and the Seven Hoods 64. Kiss Me Stupid 64. The Sons of Katie Elder 65. Marriage on the Rocks 65. *The Silencers* 66. Texas Across the River 66. Murderers' Row 67. Rough Night in Jericho 67. The Ambushers 67. Bandolero 68. How to Save a Marriage 68. Five Card Stud 68. Wrecking Crew 68. Airport 69. Something Big 71. Showdown 73. Mr Ricco 75. Angels in Vegas (TV) 78. The Cannonball Run 80. Cannonball Run II 83.

¶ I'd hate to be a teetotaller. Imagine getting up in the morning and knowing that's as good as you're going to feel all day. – *D.M.*

I can't stand an actor or actress who tells me acting is hard work. It's easy work. Anyone who says it isn't never had to stand on his feet all day dealing blackjack. – *D.M.*

Motivation is a lotta crap. – *D.M.*

Without any doubt the most conscientious actor I have ever worked with. – *Andrew V. McLaglen*
King Leer. – *Life magazine*

Martin, Dean Paul (1951–1987).
American actor, son of Dean Martin. He died when the aircraft he was piloting crashed. Married to actress Olivia Hussey.

Players 79. Heart Like a Wheel 82. Backfire 87.

Martin, Dewey (1923–).
American leading man.

Knock on Any Door (debut) 49. Kansas Raiders 50. The Thing 52. The Big Sky 52. Tennessee Champ 54. Prisoner of War 54. Land of the Pharaohs 55. The Desperate Hours 55. Ten Thousand Bedrooms 57. Wheeler and Murdoch (TV) 72. Seven Alone 75, etc.

Martin, Dick (1923–):
see *Rowan, Dan.*

Martin, Edie (1880–1964).
The frail, tiny old lady of many British films. On stage from 1886, films from 1932.

■ Farewell Again 37. Under the Red Robe 37. The Demi-Paradise 42. A Place of One's Own 45. Oliver Twist 48. The History of Mr Polly 49. The Lavender Hill Mob 51. *The Man in the White Suit* 51. Time Gentlemen Please 52. The Titfield Thunderbolt 52. The End of the Road 54. Lease of Life 54. As Long as They're Happy 55. The Lady Killers 55. My Teenage Daughter 56. Too Many Crooks 59. Weekend with Lulu 61. Sparrows Can't Sing 63.

Martin, Hugh (1914–).
American composer and lyricist, generally in collaboration with Ralph Blane.

Best Foot Forward 41. Meet Me in St Louis 44. Athena 54. The Girl Rush 55. The Girl Most Likely 57. Hans Brinker (TV) 58, etc.

Martin, Marion (1916–1985).
American leading lady of 'B' pictures, a statuesque blonde who graduated from the Ziegfeld chorus.

Boom Town 40. Mexican Spitfire at Sea 41. The Big Store 41. They Got Me Covered 42. Abbot and Costello in Hollywood 45. Queen of Burlesque 47. Oh You Beautiful Doll 50. Thunder in the Pines 54, etc.

Martin, Mary (1913–1990).
American musical comedy star; her film career did not seem satisfactory. She was the mother of actor Larry Hagman.

Autobiography: 1976, *My Heart Belongs.*

■ The Rage of Paris 38. The Great Victor Herbert 39. Rhythm on the River 40. Love Thy Neighbour 40. Kiss the Boys Goodbye 41. New York Town 41. *Birth of the Blues* 41. Star Spangled Rhythm 42. Happy Go Lucky 42. True to Life 43. Night and Day 46. Main Street to Broadway 53. Valentine (TV) 79.

¶ She's OK, if you like talent. – *Ethel Merman*

Martin, Millicent (1934–).
British songstress of stage and TV.

The Horsemasters 60. The Girl on the Boat 62. Nothing But the Best 64. Those Magnificent Men in Their Flying Machines 65. Alfie 66. Stop the World I Want To Get Off 66, etc.

TV series: From a Bird's Eye View 69. Downtown 86–87.

Martin, Pamela Sue (1953–).
American leading lady who became familiar on TV (1977–78) as Nancy Drew the teenage detective.

To Find a Man 71. The Poseidon Adventure 72. Buster and Billie 73. The Girls of Huntington House (TV) 73. The Gun and the Pulpit (TV) 74. The Lady in Red 79. Torchlight 84. Flicks 87. A Cry in the Wild 90, etc.

Martin, Richard (1917–).
Tall, dark American actor, best remembered as Chito Rafferty, the half-Mexican, half-Irish sidekick to Tim Holt in many of his RKO westerns. He quit movies in the early 50s to become an insurance salesman.

Bombardier 43. Tender Comrade 43. Marine Raiders 44. Arizona Ranger 48. Guns of Hate 48. Mysterious Desperado 49. Riders of the Range 49. Rider from Tucson 50. Storm over Wyoming 50. Gun Play 51. Hot Lead 51. Road Agent 52. Target 52. Desert Passage 53, etc.

Martin, Ross (1920–1981) (Martin Rosenblatt).
Polish-American character actor: film appearances sporadic.

Conquest of Space 55. The Colossus of New York 58. Experiment in Terror 62. The Ceremony 64. The Great Race 65. Charlie Chan: Happiness is a Warm Clue (TV: title role) 70.

TV series: The Wild Wild West 65–68.

Martin, Steve (1945–).
American nightclub comic who turned comic actor and even goes straight occasionally. He married actress Victoria Tennant in 1986.

■ The Kids Are Alright 78. Sgt Pepper's Lonely Hearts Club Band 78. The Jerk 79. The Muppet Movie 79. Pennies from Heaven 81. Dead Men Don't Wear Plaid 82. The Man with Two Brains 83. The Lonely Guy 83. All of Me 84. Movers and Shakers 84. Three Amigos 86. The Little Shop of Horrors 86. Roxanne 87. Planes, Trains and Automobiles 87. Dirty Rotten Scoundrels 88. Parenthood 89. My Blue Heaven 90. L.A. Story 91. Father of the Bride 91. Grand Canyon 91. Housesitter 92. Leap of Faith 92. A Simple Twist of Fate (& w) 94.

¶ As you get older, it's harder to be silly on the screen. – *S.M.*

Martin, Strother (1920–1980).
American character actor, often in grizzled western roles.

The Asphalt Jungle 50. Storm over Tibet 52. The Big Knife 55. The Shaggy Dog 59. The Deadly Companions 61. The Man Who Shot Liberty Valance 62. The Sons of Katie Elder 65. Harper 66. Cool Hand Luke 67. True Grit 69. Butch Cassidy and the Sundance Kid 69. The Wild Bunch 69. The Ballad of Cable Hogue 70. The Brotherhood of Satan 70. Fool's Parade 71. Pocket Money 72. Sssss 73. Rooster Cogburn 75. Hard Times 75. The Great Scout and Cathouse Thursday 76. Slap Shot 77. The End 78. Up in Smoke 78. The Villain 79, many others.

Famous line (*Cool Hand Luke*): 'What we've got here is a failure to communicate.'

Martin, Tony (1912–) (Alfred Norris).
American cabaret singer and leading man, in Hollywood from 1936 after years of touring with dance bands. He married actress Cyd Charisse in 1948.

Joint autobiography: 1976, *The Two of Us*.

Sing, Baby, Sing 36. Banjo on My Knee 37. Ali Baba Goes to Town 38. Music in My Heart 40. The Big Store 41. Ziegfeld Girl 41. Till the Clouds Roll By 46. Casbah 48. Two Tickets to Broadway 51. Here Come the Girls 53. Deep in My Heart 54. Hit the Deck 55. Let's Be Happy (GB) 57, etc.

Martin Harvey, Sir John (1863–1944).
British actor manager of the old school who appeared in a film or two.

Scaramouche 12. A Tale of Two Cities 13. The Cigarette Maker's Romance 13.

Martinelli, Elsa (1933–).
Italian leading lady, in films from 1950.

The Indian Fighter (US) 55. Manuela (GB) 57. The Boatmen 60. Hatari (US) 62. The Trial 63. Marco the Magnificent 65. De l'Armour 65. The Tenth Victim 65. Candy 68, etc.

Martini, Nino (1904–1976).
Italian actor-singer, who made a few English-speaking films.

Here's to Romance (US) 35. The Gay Desperado (US) 36. One Night With You (GB) 48, etc.

Martino, Sergio (1938–).
Italian director, mainly known for horror films.

Mondo Sex (aka Wages of Sin) (Mille Peccati ... Nessuna Virtù) 69. The Strange Vice of Mrs Ward (Lo Strano Vizio della Signora Ward) 70. They're Coming to Get You (aka Demons of the Dead) (Tutti i Colori del Buio) 72. Torso 73. Sex with a Smile 76. Slave of the Cannibal God (aka Prisoner of the Cannibal God) (La Montagna del Dio Cannibale) 76. Island of Mutations (US: Screamers) (L'Isola degli Uomini Pesce) 79. Caiman (aka The Great Alligator) 79. Casablanca Express 89, etc.

Martins, Orlando (1899–1985).
West African actor in British films.

Sanders of the River 35. Jericho 37. The Man from Morocco 44. Men of Two Worlds (as the witch doctor) 46. End of the River 47. Where No Vultures Fly 52. Simba 55. Sapphire 59. Mister Moses 65, etc.

Martinson, Leslie H.
American director, from TV.

PT 109 62. For Those Who Think Young 64. Batman 66. Fathom 67. Mrs Pollifax – Spy 70. Escape from Angola 76. Cruise Missile 78. The Kid with the Broken Halo (TV) 82. The Kid with the 200 I.Q. (TV) 83. The Fantastic World of D.C. Collins (TV) 84, etc.

Marton, Andrew (1904–1992).
Hungarian-born director, in Hollywood from 1923; settled there after return visits to Europe. Co-directed *King Solomon's Mines* 50; directed the chariot race in *Ben Hur*.

Book: 1992, *Andrew Marton* interviewed by Joanne d'Antonio.

Two o'Clock in the Morning 29. SOS Iceberg 32. The Demon of the Himalayas 34. Wolf's Clothing (GB) 37. Secrets of Stamboul (GB) 37. Gentle Annie 45. The Wild North 52. Prisoner of War 54. Green Fire 55. The Thin Red Line 64. *Crack in the*

World 65. Around the World under the Sea 65, etc.

AS SECOND-UNIT DIRECTOR: *The Red Badge of Courage* 51. A Farewell to Arms 57. *Ben Hur* 59. 55 Days at Peking 62. *The Longest Day* 62. Cleopatra 62, etc.

Marvin, Lee (1924–1987).
Ruthless-looking American actor who latterly switched from unpleasant villains to unsympathetic heroes.

You're in the Navy Now 51. Duel at Silver Creek 52. The Big Heat 53. The Wild One 54. Gorilla at Large 54. The Caine Mutiny 54. Bad Day at Black Rock 54. Violent Saturday 55. Not as a Stranger 55. Pete Kelly's Blues 55. Shack Out on 101 55. I Died a Thousand Times 56. Seven Men from Now 57. *Attack* 57. Raintree County 57. The Missouri Traveller 58. The Comancheros 61. The Man Who Shot Liberty Valance 62. Donovan's Reef 63. *The Killers* 64. Cat Ballou (AA) 65. Ship of Fools 65. The Professionals 66. The Dirty Dozen 67. Point Blank 67. Hell in the Pacific 68. Paint Your Wagon 69. Monte Walsh 70. Prime Cut 72. Emperor of the North Pole 73. The Iceman Cometh 73. The Spikes Gang 75. The Klansman 75. Shout at the Devil 76. The Great Scout and Cathouse Thursday 76. The Big Red One 79. Avalanche Express 79. Death Hunt 81. Gorky Park 83. Dirty Dozen, the Next Mission (TV) 85. Delta Force 85, etc.

TV series: M Squad 57–59. Lawbreaker 63.

The Marx Brothers
A family of Jewish-American comics whose zany humour convulsed minority audiences in its time and influenced later comedy writing to an enormous extent. *Chico* (1886–1961) (Leonard Marx) played the piano eccentrically and spoke with an impossible Italian accent; *Harpo* (1888–1964) (Adolph Marx) was a child-like mute who also played the harp; *Groucho* (1890–1977) (Julius Marx) had a painted moustache, a cigar, a loping walk and the lion's share of the wisecracks. In vaudeville from childhood, they came to films after Broadway success. Originally there were two other brothers: *Gummo* (1893–1977) (Milton Marx), who left the act early on, and *Zeppo* (1901–79) (Herbert Marx), who didn't fit in with the craziness and left them after playing romantic relief in their first five films. These first five films contain much of their best work: later their concentrated anarchy was dissipated by musical and romantic relief.

Harpo published his autobiography 1961: *Harpo Speaks!* Among Groucho's semi-autobiographical works are *Groucho and Me* (1959), *Memoirs of a Mangy Lover* (1964) and *The Groucho Letters* (1967). His son Arthur published *Life with Groucho* (1952) and *Son of Groucho* (1972). In 1974 Richard Anobile and Groucho came up with *The Marx Brothers Scrapbook*. The films are examined in detail in *The Marx Brothers at the Movies* by Paul D. Zimmerman and Burt Goldblatt. In 1978 Charlotte Chandler came up with *Hello, I Must Be Going*, a rather depressing account of Groucho's last years.

■ The Cocoanuts 29. *Animal Crackers* 30. *Monkey Business* 31. Horse Feathers 32. Duck Soup 33. *A Night at the Opera* 35. *A Day at the Races* 37. Room Service 38. *At the Circus* 39. Go West 40. The Big Store 41. *A Night in Casablanca* 46. Love Happy (a curious and unhappy failure) 50. The Story of Mankind (guest appearances) 57.

GROUCHO ALONE: Copacabana 47. Mr Music 50. Double Dynamite 51. A Girl in Every Port 52. Will Success Spoil Rock Hunter? (gag appearance) 57. You Bet Your Life (TV series) 56–61. Skiddo 68.

🎬 For shattering all our illusions, and making us love it. *Duck Soup*.

¶ The leader wore a large painted moustache and affected a cigar, and his three henchmen impersonated respectively a mute harpist afflicted with satyriasis, a larcenous Italian, and a jaunty cox-comb, who carried the love interest. – *S. J. Perelman*

Lines written by or for the Marx Brothers would fill a book in themselves. This is a selection of personal favourites, arranged chronologically and attributed to the authors of the films concerned.

▶ 1929: *The Cocoanuts* (George S. Kaufman, Morrie Ryskind)

Ah, Mrs Rittenhouse, won't you . . . lie down?

I'll wrestle anybody in the crowd for five dollars

Be free, my friends. One for all and all for me – me for you and three for five and six for a quarter.

Do you know that this is the biggest development since Sophie Tucker?

Your eyes shine like the pants of my blue serge suit

▶ 1930: *Animal Crackers* (George S. Kaufman and Morrie Ryskind)

You're the most beautiful woman I've ever seen which doesn't say much for you.

What do you get an hour?
– For playing, we get ten dollars an hour.
What do you get for not playing?
– Twelve dollars an hour. Now for rehearsing we make a special rate – fifteen dollars an hour
And what do you get for not rehearsing?
– You couldn't afford it. You see, if we don't rehearse, we don't play. And if we don't play, that runs into money.
How much would you want to run into an open manhole?
– Just the cover charge.
Well, drop in some time.
– Sewer.
Well, I guess we cleaned that up.
You go Uruguay and I'll go mine.
One morning I shot an elephant in my pajamas
How he got into my pajamas I'll never know.

▶ 1931: *Monkey Business* (S. J. Perelman, Will B. Johnstone, Arthur Sheekman)

Do you want your nails trimmed long?
– Oh, about an hour and a half. I got nothing to do.

Look at me: I worked my way up from nothing to a state of extreme poverty.

I want to register a complaint. Do you know who sneaked into my room at three o'clock this morning?
– Who?
– Nobody, and that's my complaint.

Do you suppose I could buy back my introduction to you?

Sir, you have the advantage of me.
– Not yet I haven't, but wait till I get you outside.

▶ 1932: *Horse Feathers* (Bert Kalmar, Harry Ruby, S. J. Perelman, Will B. Johnstone)

Why don't you bore a hole in yourself and let the sap run out?

There's a man outside with a big black moustache.
– Tell him I've got one.

The dean is furious. He's waxing wroth.
– Is Roth out there too? Tell Roth to wax the dean for a while.

You're a disgrace to our family name of Wagstaff, if such a thing is possible.

You've got the brain of a four-year-old boy, and

I bet he was glad to get rid of it.

What a day! Spring in the air!
  – Who, me? I should spring in the air and fall in the lake?
▶ 1933: *Duck Soup* (Bert Kalmar, Harry Ruby, Arthur Sheekman, Nat Perrin)
Take a card. You can keep it: I've got fifty-one left.

My husband is dead.
  – I'll bet he's just using that as an excuse.
I was with him to the end.
  – No wonder he passed away.
I held him in my arms and kissed him.
  – So it was murder!

This is a gala day for you.
  – That's plenty. I don't think I could manage more than one gal a day.

What is it that has four pairs of pants, lives in Philadelphia, and it never rains but it pours?

I could dance with you till the cows come home. On second thoughts I'll dance with the cows and you come home.

Excuse me while I brush the crumbs out of my bed. I'm expecting company.
▶ 1935: *A Night at the Opera* (George S. Kaufman, Morrie Ryskind, Al Boasberg)
Do they allow tipping on the boat?
  – Yes, sir.
Have you got two fives?
  – Oh, yes, sir.
Then you won't need the ten cents I was going to give you.

Let joy be unconfined. Let there be dancing in the streets, drinking in the saloons, and necking in the park.
▶ 1937: *A Day at the Races* (George Seaton, Robert Pirosh, George Oppenheimer)
She looks like the healthiest woman I ever met.
  – You look like you never met a healthy woman.

Don't point that beard at me, it might go off.

Closer . . . hold me closer . . .
  – If I hold you any closer I'll be in back of you!

Marry me and I'll never look at another horse.

Isn't that awfully large for a pill?
  – Well, it was too small for a basketball and I didn't know what to do with it.

One dollar and you remember me all your life.
  – That's the most nauseating proposition I've ever had.
▶ 1939: *At the Circus* (Irving Brecher)
If you hadn't sent for me, I'd be at home now in a comfortable bed with a hot toddy.
  – That's a drink!

I bet your father spent the first year of your life throwing rocks at the stork.
▶ 1945: *A Night in Casablanca* (Joseph Fields, Roland Kibbee, Frank Tashlin)
The first thing we're going to do is change all the numbers on all the doors.
  – But sir, think of the confusion . . .
  Yeah, but think of the fun.

Hey boss, you got a woman in there?
  – If I haven't, I've been wasting thirty minutes of valuable time.

I'm Beatrice Ryner. I stop at the hotel.
  – I'm Ronald Kornblow. I stop at nothing.
Groucho himself later proved to be sometimes as funny as his scripts. He wrote to resign from a club:
  I don't care to belong to any social organization which would accept me as a member.
And he wrote a threatening letter to *Confidential* magazine:
  Dear Sir: If you continue to publish slanderous pieces about me I shall feel compelled to cancel my subscription.
His wit did not fail him with age:
  I've been around so long I can remember Doris Day before she was a virgin.
His influence was international; an example of Paris graffiti in 1968 read:
  Je suis Marxiste, tendence Groucho.
But life with the Marxes was seldom peaceful. Herman Mankiewicz said:
  I never knew what bicarbonate of soda was until I wrote a Marx Brothers picture.
Groucho once removed Greta Garbo's hat and said:
  Excuse me, I thought you were a fellow I once knew in Pittsburgh.
George F. Kaufman had soon had enough of them:
  Cocoanuts was a comedy; the Marx Brothers are comics; meeting them was a tragedy.
Groucho was perhaps too fearless a critic, as when giving his opinion of *Samson and Delilah*, starring Victor Mature and Hedy Lamarr:
  First picture I've seen in which the male lead has bigger tits than the female.
And on the nudist musical *Hair*:
  Why should I pay ten dollars for something I can see in the bathroom for nothing?
Harpo could be bitchy too. His appraisal of *Abie's Irish Rose* has lingered down the decades:
  No worse than a bad cold.
And he was witty when refusing Alexander Woollcott's invitation to share a holiday on the French riviera:
  I can think of forty better places to spend the summer, all of them on Long Island in a hammock.
Groucho even aspired to be a political thinker:
  Military intelligence is a contradiction in terms . . .
A final thought from Groucho:
  If you want to see a comic strip you should see me in a shower.
Well, one more from Groucho for luck:
  They say a man is as old as the woman he feels.

Maschwitz, Eric (1901–1969).
English screenwriter, playwright and songwriter, whose lyrics include 'These Foolish Things' and 'A Nightingale Sang in Berkeley Square'. Born in Birmingham, he was educated at Cambridge University and worked for the BBC as a commentator, scriptwriter, editor of the *Radio Times*, and the first director of variety programmes from 1933–37. In 1937 he went to Hollywood under contract to MGM, returning to Britain at the outbreak of the Second World War, and becoming head of Light Entertainment for BBC-TV in the mid-50s. He was married briefly to Hermione Gingold (qv).
  Autobiography: 1957, *No Chip on My Shoulder*.
  Goodnight Vienna (US: Magic Night) (co-w, oa) 32. Death at Broadcasting House (co-w) 34. Royal Cavalcade (co-w) 35. Land without Music (co-story) 36. Café Colette (co-w from radio programme) 37. Goodbye Mr Chips (co-w) 39. Balalaika (oa) 39. Carnival (w) 46. Queen of Song (w) 47, etc.

Masina, Giulietta (1920–1994).
Italian gamin-like actress, married to Federico Fellini. In films since 1941.
  Senza Pietà 47. Lights of Variety 48. La Strada 54. Il Bidone 55. *Nights of Cabiria* 57. Juliet of the Spirits 65. The Madwoman of Chaillot 69. Ginger and Fred 85. Aujourd'hui Peut-être 91. La Nonna 92, etc.

mask.
A technical device for blocking out part of the image. *Masking* is the black cloth which surrounds the actual cinema screen: these days it has to be electrically adjustable to encompass the various screen sizes.

Maskell, Virginia (1936–1968).
British leading lady with attractively soulful eyes. Committed suicide.
■ Happy is the Bride 57. Our Virgin Island 58. The Man Upstairs 59. Jet Storm 59. Suspect 60. Doctor in Love 60. The Wild and the Willing 62. *Only Two Can Play* 62. Interlude 68.

Mason, A. E. W. (1865–1948).
British novelist whose *The House of the Arrow* and *The Four Feathers* have been filmed several times. *Fire Over England* and *At the Villa Rose* also came to the screen.

Mason, Elliott (1897–1949).
Scottish character actress with repertory experience. The Ghost Goes West 36. Owd Bob 38. The Ghost of St Michael's 41. The Gentle Sex 43. The Captive Heart 46, etc.

Mason, Herbert (1891–1960).
British director.
  His Lordship 36. Strange Boarders 38. Back Room Boy 41. Flight from Folly 45, etc.

Mason, James (1909–1984).
Leading British and international actor who became a star at home in saturnine roles during World War II, went to Hollywood and initially had a thin time but during the 50s became a respected interpreter of varied and interesting characters.
  Autobiography: 1982, *Before I Forget*.
  Biographies: 1989, *James Mason: Odd Man Out* by Sheridan Morley. 1989, *James Mason – a Personal Biography* by Diana de Rosso.
■ Late Extra 35. Twice Branded 36. Troubled Waters 36. Prison Breaker 36. Blind Man's Bluff 36. The Secret of Stamboul 36. Fire Over England 36. The Mill on the Floss 37. The High Command 37. Catch as Catch Can 37. The Return of the Scarlet Pimpernel 38. *I Met a Murderer* 39. This Man is Dangerous (The Patient Vanishes) 41. Hatter's Castle 42. *The Night Has Eyes* 42. Alibi 42. Secret Mission 42. Thunder Rock 43. The Bells Go Down 43. *The Man in Grey* (a key role as an 18th-century villain) 43. They Met in the Dark 43. Candlelight in Algeria 44. Fanny by Gaslight 44. Hotel Reserve 44. A Place of One's Own 45. They Were Sisters 45. *The Seventh Veil* 45. *The Wicked Lady* 46. *Odd Man Out* 46. The Upturned Glass 47. Caught 49. Madame Bovary 49. The Reckless Moment 49. East Side West Side 49. One Way Street 50. *Pandora and the Flying Dutchman* 51. *The Desert Fox* (as Rommel) 51. Lady Possessed 52. *Five Fingers* 52. The Prisoner of Zenda (as Rupert) 52. Face to Face 52. The Desert Rats 53. *Julius Caesar* (as Brutus) 53. The Story of Three Loves 53. Botany Bay 53. The Man Between 53. Charade 53. Prince Valiant 54. *20,000 Leagues under the Sea* (as Captain Nemo) 54. *A Star Is Born* (AAN) 54. Forever Darling 56. Bigger Than Life (& p) 56. Island in the Sun 57. Cry Terror 58. The Decks Ran Red 58. North by

Northwest 59. *Journey to the Center of the Earth* 59. A Touch of Larceny 60. The Trials of Oscar Wilde 60. The Marriage Go Round 61. The Land We Love (Hero's Island) 62. Escape from Zahrain 62. Tiara Tahiti 62. *Lolita* (as Humbert) 62. The Fall of the Roman Empire 64. Torpedo Bay 64. *The Pumpkin Eater* 64. Lord Jim 65. The Player Pianos 65. Genghis Khan 65. *The Blue Max* 66. Georgy Girl (AAN) 66. *The Deadly Affair* 67. Stranger in the House 67. Duffy 68. Mayerling 68. Age of Consent 69. The Seagull 69. Spring and Port Wine 70. Kill! 70. Cold Sweat 70. Bad Man's River 71. A Dangerous Summer 72. Ivanhoe 72. Child's Play 72. The Last of Sheila 73. Frankenstein, the True Story (TV) 73. The Mackintosh Man 73. 11 Harrowhouse 74. The Marseilles Contract 74. Great Expectations (TV) 74. The Tempest 74. Nostro Nero in Casa Nichols 74. Centra di Respetto 75. La Città Sconvolta 75. Mandingo 75. Autobiography of a Princess 75. Voyage of the Damned 76. Inside Out 76. The Left Hand of the Law 76. Jesus of Nazareth (TV) 77. Cross of Iron 77. The Water Babies 78. Heaven Can Wait 78. The Boys from Brazil 78. *Murder by Decree* (as Dr Watson) 79. The Passage 79. Bloodline 79. North Sea Hijack 80. Evil Under the Sun 82. The Verdict (AAN) 82. Yellowbeard 83. The Shooting Party 84.

✪ For his incisive professionalism over a long period of gradually declining standards. *A Star Is Born.*

Mason, Marsha (1942–).
American leading actress, formerly married to Neil Simon (1973–83).
■ Hot Rod Hullaballoo 66. Blume in Love 73. Cinderella Liberty (AAN) 73. Audrey Rose 77. *The Goodbye Girl* (AAN) 77. The Cheap Detective 78. Promises in the Dark 79. Chapter Two 79. Only When I Laugh (AAN) 81. Max Dugan Returns 83. Heartbreak Ridge 86. Trapped in Silence (TV) 86. Dinner at Eight (TV) 89. Stella 90. Drop Dead Fred 91.

Mason, Shirley (1900–1979) (Leona Flugrath).
American leading lady of the silent screen, sister of Viola Dana.
Vanity Fair 15. Goodbye Bill 18. Treasure Island 20. Merely Mary Ann 20. Lights of the Desert 22. What Fools Men 25. Don Juan's Three Nights 26. Sally in Our Alley 27. Show of Stars 29, etc.

Massari, Lea (1933–) (Anna Maria Massatani).
French-Italian leading lady.
L'Avventura 58. The Colossus of Rhodes 61. Four Days of Naples 62. Made in Italy 65. Les Choses de la Vie 69. Le Souffle au Coeur 71. Impossible Object 73. Violette et Francois 77. Christ Stopped at Eboli 79. Vengeance 86, etc.

Massen, Osa (1916–).
Danish-born actress in Hollywood from the late 30s.
Honeymoon in Bali 39. The Devil Pays Off 41. The Master Race 44. Tokyo Rose 44. Cry of the Werewolf 44. Deadline at Dawn 47. Rocketship XM 50, etc.

Massey, Anna (1937–).
British character actress, daughter of Raymond Massey.
Gideon's Day 58. Bunny Lake is Missing 65. De Sade 69. Frenzy 72. A Doll's House 73. Vault of Horror 73. The Chain 85. Foreign Body 87. Impromptu 89, etc.
TV series: Rebecca (as Mrs Danvers) 79. Nice Day at the Office 94.

Massey, Daniel (1933–).
British actor, son of Raymond Massey, usually seen on stage or TV.
Girls at Sea 57. Upstairs and Downstairs 59. The Queen's Guard 61. Go to Blazes 62. Moll Flanders 65. The Jokers 66. *Star!* (as Noel Coward) (AAN) 68. Fragment of Fear 70. Mary Queen of Scots 72. Vault of Horror 73. The Incredible Sarah 76. The Cat and the Canary 77. Bad Timing 80. Escape to Victory 81. Love with a Perfect Stranger (TV) 86. Intimate Contact 87. Scandal 88. In the Name of the Father 93, etc.

Massey, Ilona (1912–1974) (Ilona Hajmassy).
Hungarian-born leading lady, in Hollywood from the mid-30s.
■ Knox und die Lustigen Vagabunden 35. Der Himmel auf Erden 35. *Rosalie* 37. Balalaika 39. New Wine 41. International Lady 41. Invisible Agent 42. Frankenstein Meets the Wolf Man (as 'Frankenstein') 42. Holiday in Mexico 46. Northwest Outpost 47. The Plunderers 48. Love Happy 50. Jet over the Atlantic 59.

Massey, Raymond (1896–1983).
Canadian-born actor, on stage (in Britain) from 1922.
In films, has played saturnine, benevolent or darkly villainous, with a penchant for impersonations of Abraham Lincoln.
Autobiographies: 1976, *When I Was Young.* 1979, *A Hundred Lives.*
■ The Speckled Band (as Sherlock Holmes) 31. The Face at the Window 31. *The Old Dark House* 32. *The Scarlet Pimpernel* 34. *Things to Come* 36. Fire over England 36. Under the Red Robe 37. *The Prisoner of Zenda* 37. Dreaming Lips 37. The Hurricane 37. The Drum 38. Black Limelight 39. *Abe Lincoln in Illinois* (AAN) 40. Santa Fe Trail (as John Brown) 40. 49th Parallel 41. Dangerously They Live 41. Desperate Journey 42. Reap the Wild Wind 42. Action in the North Atlantic 43. *Arsenic and Old Lace* 44. The Woman in the Window 44. Hotel Berlin 45. God Is My Co-Pilot 45. A Matter of Life and Death 46. Possessed 47. Mourning Becomes Electra 47. The Fountainhead 48. Roseanna McCoy 49. Chain Lightning 49. Barricade 50. Dallas 50. Sugarfoot 51. Come Fill the Cup 51. David and Bathsheba 51. Carson City 52. The Desert Song 53. Prince of Players 55. Battle Cry 55. *East of Eden* 55. Seven Angry Men 55. Omar Khayyam 57. The Naked and the Dead 58. The Great Impostor 60. The Fiercest Heart 61. The Queen's Guard 61. How the West Was Won 62. Mackenna's Gold 68. All My Darling Daughters (TV) 72. The President's Plane Is Missing (TV) 73.
TV series: I Spy 55. Dr Kildare (as Dr Gillespie) 61–66.
✪ For his leathery, reliable and highly intelligent presence during most of the cinema's most interesting years (though in few of its more interesting films). *Things to Come.*

Famous line (*Things to Come*): 'It is this, or that – all the universe, or nothing. Which shall it be, Passworthy? Which shall it be?'

Massie, Paul (1932–).
Canadian-born actor, on British stage and screen.
High Tide at Noon 57. *Orders to Kill* 58. Sapphire 59. Libel 60. The Two Faces of Dr Jekyll 60. The Rebel 60. Raising the Wind 61. The Pot Carriers 62, many others.

Massine, Leonid (1896–1979).
Russian-born choreographer of international renown, best displayed on film in *The Red Shoes* 48.

Massingham, Richard (1898–1953).
British actor-producer-director: a qualified doctor who abandoned his medical career to make numerous short propaganda films for government departments during World War II and after, infusing them with quiet wit and sympathy. Gratefully remembered as the stout party bewildered by government restrictions: bathing in five inches of water, collecting salvage, avoiding colds, preventing rumours, wearing a gasmask, etc.

Masters, Quentin (1946–).
Australian director of international films.
■ Thumb Tripping (& w) 73. The Stud 78. The Psi Factor 81. A Dangerous Summer 82. Midnite Spares 83.

Masterson, Bat (1855–1921).
American western gunman who reformed; played in films by Albert Dekker in *Woman of the Town*, Randolph Scott in *Trail Street*, George Montgomery in *Masterson of Kansas*, Kenneth Tobey in *Gunfight at the OK Corral*, Joel McCrea in *Gunfight at Dodge City*, and Gene Barry in a long-running TV series.

Masterson, Mary Stuart (1966–).
American leading actress.
The Stepford Wives 75. Heaven Help Us 85. At Close Range 86. My Little Girl 86. Gardens of Stone 87. Mr North 88. Chances Are 89. Immediate Family 89. Funny about Love 90. Fried Green Tomatoes at the Whistle Stop Café 91. Mad at the Moon 92. Married to It 92. Benny & Joon 93. Bad Girls 94. Radioland Murders 94. Heaven's Prisoners 95, etc.

Masterson, Peter (1934–) (Carlos B. Masterson).
American actor and director, the father of Mary Stuart Masterson.
AS ACTOR: Ambush Bay 66. Counterpoint 68. Von Richthofen and Brown 71. The Exorcist 73. The Stepford Wives 75. A Question of Guilt (TV) 78. Gardens of Stone 87, etc.
AS DIRECTOR: The Trip to Bountiful 85. Blood Red 88. Full Moon in Blue Water 88. Night Game 89. Convicts 91, etc.

Mastrantonio, Mary Elizabeth (1958–).
American leading actress, with stage experience.
Scarface 83. The Color of Money (AAN) 86. Slam Dance 87. The January Man 88. The Abyss 89. Fools of Fortune 90. Class Action 91. Robin Hood: Prince of Thieves 91. White Sands 92. Consenting Adults 92. Two Bits 93, etc.

Mastroianni, Marcello (1923–).
Italian leading man, a former clerk who broke into films with a bit part in *I Miserabili* 47. Now Italy's most respected and sought-after lead.
Sunday in August 49. Girls of the Spanish Steps 51. The Bigamist 55. *White Nights* 57. I Soliti Ignoti 58. La Dolce Vita 59. *Il Bell'Antonio* 60. La Notte 61. *Divorce Italian Style* (AAN, BFA) 62. Family Diary 62. Eight and a Half 63. *Yesterday, Today and Tomorrow* (BFA) 63. The Organizer 63. Marriage Italian Style 64. Casanova 70 65. The Tenth Victim 65. Shoot Loud, Louder, I Don't Understand 66. The Stranger 67. Diamonds for Breakfast (GB) 68. A Place for Lovers 69. Sunflower 70. What? 72. Blowout 73. The Slightly Pregnant Man 73. Massacre in Rome 74. The Priest's Wife 74. Down the Ancient Stairs 75. The Sunday Woman 76. A Special Day (AAN) 77. Traffic Jam 78. City of Women 80. Revenge 80. General of the Dead Army 83. Henry IV 84. The Two Lives of Mattia Pascal 85. Big Deal on Madonna Street – 20 Years Later 85. Macaroni 85. *Ginger and Fred* 85. The Bee

Keeper 86. Dark Eyes (Oci Ciornie) (AAN) 87. Miss Arizona 88. Splendor 89. Everybody's Fine (Stanno Tutti Bene) 90. Sometime Tonight (Verso Sera) 90. Le Voleur d'Enfants 91. Tchin-Tchin 91. The Suspended Step of the Stork (To Meteoro Vima to Pelargou) 91. La Nonna 92. Used People 92. Viva i Bambini 92. Consenting Adults 92. 1, 2, 3, Soleil 93. We Don't Want to Talk about It (De Eso No Se Habla) 93. How Long Till Daylight (TV) 94. Prêt-à-Porter (aka Ready to Wear) 94, etc.

¶ I only really exist when I am working on a film. – *M.M.*

I don't like that Method thing: what sufferance to go into a role! I'm not going to enter a monastery so I can play a priest. An actor is a buffoon – this is the miracle, being a chameleon. – *M.M.*

Life has been generous to me. I come from a very modest family – my father was a cabinet-maker – and I'm in a profession I like. – *M.M.*

Masur, Richard (1948–).
Plump American supporting actor.
W.H.I.F.F.S. 75. Semi Tough 77. Who'll Stop the Rain 78. Hanover Street 79. Scavenger Hunt 79. Walking through the Fire (TV) 79. Heaven's Gate 80. East of Eden (TV) 81. *Fallen Angel* (TV) 81. I'm Dancing as Fast as I Can 82. The Thing 82. Risky Business 83. Under Fire 83. The Mean Season 84. My Science Project 85. Heartburn 86. The Believers 86. Walker 87. License to Drive 88. Rent-a-Cop 88. Shoot to Kill 88. Far from Home 89. Flashback 90. My Girl 91. The Man without a Face 93. Six Degrees of Separation 93. My Girl 2 94. Les Patriotes (Fr.) 94, etc.
TV series: One Day at a Time 75–76. Hot L Baltimore 75. Empire 84.

Mata Hari (1876–1917) (Margaret Gertrude Zelle).
Four films have been made about the French spy executed during World War I: by Friedrich Feher in 1927 with Magda Sonia; by George Fitzmaurice in 1931 with Greta Garbo; by Jean-Louis Richard in 1964 with Jeanne Moreau; by Curtis Harrington in 1984 with Sylvia Kristel. She was caricatured by Zsa Zsa Gabor in *Up the Front* 72. Her pseudonym, in Dutch, means 'eye of the dawn'.

Maté, Rudolph (1898–1964).
Austrian-born cameraman, later in Hollywood.
The Passion of Joan of Arc 28. *Vampyr* 31. Liliom 33. *Dante's Inferno* 35. Dodsworth 36. Love Affair 39. *Foreign Correspondent* 40. To Be or Not To Be 42. Cover Girl 44, etc.
■ LATER AS DIRECTOR: It Had to Be You (co-d) 47. The Dark Past 49. D.O.A. 50. No Sad Songs for Me 50. *Union Station* 50. Branded 50. The Prince Who Was a Thief 51. When Worlds Collide 51. The Green Glove 52. Paula 52. Sally and Saint Anne 52. Mississippi Gambler 53. Second Chance 53. Forbidden 53. The Siege At Red River 54. *The Black Shield of Falworth* 54. The Violent Men 55. The Far Horizons 55. Miracle in the Rain 56. The Rawhide Years 56. Port Afrique 56. Three Violent People 57. The Deep Six 58. For the First Time 59. The Immaculate Road 60. Revak the Rebel 60. The 300 Spartans 62. Aliki 63. Seven Seas to Calais 64.

Mather, Aubrey (1885–1958).
British character actor, on stage from 1905, films from 1931. Settled in Hollywood and became useful member of English contingent, playing butlers and beaming, bald-headed little men.
Young Woodley 31. As You Like It 36. When Knights Were Bold 36. Jane Eyre 44. The Keys of the Kingdom 44. The Forsyte Saga 49. The Importance of Being Earnest 52, many others.

Matheson, Murray (1912–1985).
Soft-spoken Australian actor in Hollywood, mostly on TV.
Hurricane Smith 52. Botany Bay 53. Love Is a Many Splendored Thing 55. Assault On a Queen 66. How to Succeed in Business 67, etc.
TV series: Banacek 72–74.

Matheson, Richard (1926–).
American science-fiction novelist and screenwriter.
The Incredible Shrinking Man (oa, w) 57. The House of Usher (w) 60. The Pit and the Pendulum (w) 61. The Raven (w) 63. The Comedy of Terrors (w) 63. The Last Man on Earth (oa) 64. The Young Warriors (oaw) 68. The Devil Rides Out (w) 68. De Sade (w) 69. The Omega Man (oa) 71. The Legend of Hell House (w) 73. Dracula (TV) 73. Somewhere in Time 80. Jaws 3-D 83. Twilight Zone: The Movie 83. Loose Cannons 90, etc.

Matheson, Tim (1949–).
American leading man, in TV from childhood.
Yours Mine and Ours 65. Divorce American Style 68. Magnum Force 73. National Lampoon's Animal House 78. The Apple Dumpling Gang Rides Again 79. Dreamer 79. A Little Sex 82. To Be or Not To Be 83. Impulse 84. Fletch 85. Drop Dead Fred 91. Mortal Passion 91. Stephen King's Sometimes They Come Back 91. Starfire 92, etc.
TV series: Window on Main Street 61–62. Johnny Quest (voice) 64–65. The Virginian 69–70. Bonanza 72–73. The Quest 76. Tucker's Witch 82–83. Just in Time 88.

Mathews, Kerwin (1926–).
American leading man, former teacher.
Five Against the House 55. The Seventh Voyage of Sinbad 58. Man on a String 60. The Three Worlds of Gulliver 60. Jack the Giant Killer 61. Pirates of Blood River 62. Maniac (GB) 63. Battle Beneath the Earth (GB) 68. Barquero 69. The Boy Who Cried Werewolf 73. Nightmare in Blood 78, etc.

Mathieson, Muir (1911–1975).
British musical director, in films from 1931.
Things to Come 36. Dangerous Moonlight 40. In Which We Serve 42. Brief Encounter 46. The Sound Barrier 52. The Swiss Family Robinson 60. Becket 64, many others.

Mathis, June (1892–1927).
American screenwriter.
An Eye for an Eye 18. *The Four Horsemen of the Apocalypse* 21. Blood and Sand 22. Three Wise Fools 23. *Greed* 23. Ben Hur 27, etc.

Mathis, Samantha (1970–).
American actress, daughter of actress Bibi Besch.
Pump Up the Volume 90. This Is My Life 92. Ferngully: The Last Rainforest (voice) 92. The Music of Chance 93. The Thing Called Love 93. Super Mario Bros 93. Little Women 94, etc.
TV series: Aaron's Way 88. Knightwatch 88–89.

Mathison, Melissa (1949–).
American screenwriter. She married actor Harrison Ford in 1983.
The Black Stallion 79. The Escape Artist 82. E.T. – the Extraterrestrial (AAN) 82. Son of the Morning Star (TV) 91, etc.

Matlin, Marlee (1965–).
American actress. She is deaf.
Children of a Lesser God (AA) 86. Walker 87. Bridge to Silence (TV) 89. The Linguini Incident 91. The Player 92. Hear No Evil 93, etc.

Matras, Christian (1903–1977).
French cinematographer, in films from 1928.
La Grande Illusion 37. Boule de Suif 45. Les Jeux Sont Faits 47. La Ronde 50. Madame De 53. *Lola Montes* 55. Les Espions 57. Paris Blues 61. Les Fêtes Galantes 65. The Milky Way 68, many others.

Matt Helm.
The laconic hero of a number of self-spoofing secret agent dime novels by Donald Hamilton was personified on screen by a droopy-eyed Dean Martin. Over-sexed and witless, the series represents a rather miserable but commercial 60s blend of high camp, self-indulgence, and comic strip. *The Silencers* 66, *Murderers' Row* 66, *The Ambushers* 67, and *Wrecking Crew* 69 were the titles, and it seemed a point of honour with the producer that the title should have no relevance whatever to the movie. A TV movie, *Matt Helm* 75, starred Tony Franciosa, but the resulting series was brief.

matt or matte.
A technique (sometimes known as *travelling matt*) for blending actors in the studio with location or trick scenes. The actor is photographed against a non-reflective background (e.g. black velvet) and a high-contrast negative of this image is combined with the desired background. Thus men can move among animated monsters, and ghosts can slowly disappear.

Mattes, Eva (1955–).
Leading German actress of that country's New Wave cinema, associated with the films of Fassbinder (whom she played in the biopic *A Man Like Eva*) and Werner Herzog.
Jailbait (Wildwechsel) 72. The Bitter Tears of Petra von Kant (Die Bitteren Tränen der Petra von Kant) 72. Supermarket (Supermarkt) 74. Stroszek 77. Ravine Racer (Schluchtenflitzer) 79. David 79. Germany Pale Mother (Deutschland Bleiche Mutter) 79. Woyzeck 79. Celeste 81. Rita, Ritter 84. A Man Like Eva (Ein Mann Wie Eva) 84. Felix 87. Herbstmilch 89. Der Kinoerzähler 93, etc.

Matthau, Walter (1920–) (Walter Matasschanskayasky).
American character actor with a penchant for wry comedy; his lugubrious features and sharp talent made him a star in the late 60s.
■ The Kentuckian 55. The Indian Fighter 55. Bigger Than Life 56. *A Face in the Crowd* 57. Slaughter on Tenth Avenue 57. King Creole 58. Ride a Crooked Trail 58. The Voice in the Mirror 58. Onionhead 58. Strangers When We Meet 60. Gangster Story (& d) 60. Lonely Are the Brave 62. Who's Got the Action? 62. Island of Love 63. *Charade* 63. Ensign Pulver 64. Fail Safe 64. Goodbye Charlie 64. *Mirage* 65. *The Fortune Cookie* (AA) 66. *A Guide for the Married Man* 67. *The Odd Couple* 68. The Secret Life of an American Wife 68. Candy 68. *Hello Dolly* 69. Cactus Flower 69. A New Leaf 71. Plaza Suite 71. *Kotch* (AAN) 71. Pete 'n' Tillie 72. Charley Varrick 73. The Laughing Policeman 73. Earthquake 74. The Taking of Pelham 123 74. The Front Page 75. The Sunshine Boys (AAN) 75. The Bad News Bears 76. Casey's Shadow 77. House Calls 78. California Suite 78. Funny Business (TV) 78. Little Miss Marker 80. *Hopscotch* 80. First Monday in October 81. Buddy Buddy 81. I Ought to Be in Pictures 82. The Survivors 83. Movers and Shakers 84. Pirates 85. The Couch Trip 88. The Incident (TV) 90. JFK 91. Dennis the Menace (GB: Dennis) 93. Grumpy Old Men 93. Incident in a Small Town (TV) 94. I.Q. 94.
TV series: Tallahassee 7000 59.

¶ Once seen, that antique-mapped face is never
forgotten – a bloodhound with a head cold, a
man who is simultaneously biting on a bad oyster
and caught by the neck in lift-doors, a mad
scientist's amalgam of Wallace Beery and Yogi
Bear. – *Alan Brien, Sunday Times*

He's about as likely a candidate for stardom as
the neighborhood delicatessen man. – *Time*

He looks like a half-melted rubber bulldog.
– *John Simon*

Matthews, A. E. (1869–1960).
British actor, on stage from 1886, films from the
mid-20s; in his youth a suave romantic lead, he
was later famous for the crotchety cheerfulness of
his extreme longevity.
Autobiography: 1953, *Matty*.
A Highwayman's Honour 14. The Lackey and
the Lady 19. The Iron Duke 35. Men Are Not
Gods 36. *Quiet Wedding* 40. The Life and Death of
Colonel Blimp 43. Piccadilly Incident 46. Just
William's Luck 48. *The Chiltern Hundreds* (in his
stage role as Lord Lister) 49. The Galloping Major
51. Made in Heaven 52. The Million Pound Note
54. Three Men in a Boat 56. Inn for Trouble 60,
many others.

¶ I always wait for *The Times* each morning. I look
at the obituary column, and if I'm not in it, I go
to work. – *A.E.M.*

Good God, doesn't he know I haven't got long
to live? – *A.E.M., when he thought a long speech
was ending, and it wasn't*

He bumbled through the play like a charming
retriever who has buried a bone and can't quite
remember where. – *Noël Coward*

Matthews, Francis (1927–).
British leading man with TV and repertory
experience.
Bhowani Junction 56. The Revenge of
Frankenstein 58. The Lamp in Assassin Mews 62.
Dracula, Prince of Darkness 65. That Riviera Touch
66. Just Like a Woman 66. Crossplot 69. The
McGuffin (TV) 85. May We Borrow Your
Husband? (TV) 86, etc.

Matthews, Jessie (1907–1981).
Vivacious British singing and dancing star of light
musicals in the 30s; on stage from 1919; later
familiar to radio listeners as Mrs Dale in *Mrs Dale's
Diary*.
Autobiography: 1974, *Over My Shoulder*.
Biography: 1974, *Jessie Matthews* by Michael
Thornton.
■ The Beloved Vagabond 23. Straws in the Wind
24. Out of the Blue 31. There Goes the Bride 32.
The Midshipmaid 32. The Man from Toronto 32.
The Good Companions 32. Friday the Thirteenth 33.
Waltzes from Vienna 33. *Evergreen* 34. First a Girl
35. It's Love Again 36. Head over Heels 37.
Gangway 37. Sailing Along 38. Climbing High 39.
Forever and a Day 43. Candles at Nine 44. Tom
Thumb 58. The Hound of the Baskervilles 77.
Edward and Mrs Simpson (TV) 79.

Matthews, Lester (1900–1975).
British stage actor, in Hollywood from 1934.
Creeping Shadows 31. Facing the Music 34.
Blossom Time 34. Werewolf of London 35. Thank
You, Jeeves 35. The Prince and the Pauper 37. The
Adventures of Robin Hood 38. Northwest Passage
40. Man Hunt 41. Between Two Worlds 44. The
Invisible Man's Revenge 44. Lorna Doone 51,
many others.

Mattsson, Arne (1919–).
Swedish director, in films from 1942.

She Only Danced One Summer 51. The Girl in Tails
56. Mannequin in Red 59. The Doll 62, etc.

Mature, Victor (1915–).
American leading man of the 40s; once known as
'the Hunk', but beneath the brawn lurked some
style and a sense of humour.
■ The Housekeeper's Daughter 39. One Million
BC 40. Captain Caution 40. No No Nanette 40. I
Wake Up Screaming 41. The Shanghai Gesture 41.
Song of the Islands 42. My Gal Sal 42. Footlight
Serenade 42. Seven Days' Leave 42. *My Darling
Clementine* (as Doc Holliday) 46. Moss Rose 47. *Kiss
of Death* 47. Fury at Furnace Creek 48. Cry of the
City 48. Red Hot and Blue 49. Easy Living 49.
Samson and Delilah 49. Wabash Avenue 50. Stella
50. Gambling House 50. The Las Vegas Story 52.
Androcles and the Lion 52. Something for the
Birds 52. Million Dollar Mermaid 52. The Glory
Brigade 53. Affair with a Stranger 53. *The Robe* 53.
Veils of Baghdad 53. Dangerous Mission 54.
Demetrius and the Gladiators 54. Betrayed 54. *The
Egyptian* 54. Chief Crazy Horse 55. Violent Saturday
55. The Last Frontier 55. Safari (GB) 56. The
Sharkfighters 56. Zarak (GB) 57. Interpol (GB)
57. The Long Haul (GB) 57. China Doll 57. No
Time to Die (GB) 58. Escort West 59. The Bandit of
Zhobe (GB) 59. The Big Circus 59. Timbuktu 59.
Hannibal 60. The Tartars 60. The Mongols 60. *After
the Fox* 66. Head 68. Every Little Crook and Nanny
72. Won Ton Ton 76. Firepower 79. Samson and
Delilah (TV) 84.

¶ I'm no actor, and I've 64 pictures to prove it.
– *V.M.*

I didn't care for *Samson and Delilah*. No picture
can hold my interest when the leading man's bust
is bigger than the leading lady's. – *Groucho Marx*

Matz, Peter (1928–).
American composer and conductor, mainly for TV.
Bye Bye Braverman 68. Marlowe 69. Rivals 72.
Funny Lady (AAN) 75. The Prize Fighter 79. The
Private Eyes 80. Lust in the Dust 85. Torch Song
Trilogy 88. The Gumshoe Kid 89, etc.

Mau Mau.
The terrorist activities in Kenya during the 50s
were the subject of three very savage movies: *Simba*
55, *Safari* 56, *Something of Value* 56.

Mauch, Billy and Bobby (1925–).
American twins, boy actors who appeared in
several films in the mid-30s, notably a 'Penrod'
series and the Errol Flynn version of *The Prince and
the Pauper* 37. Billy became a Hollywood sound
editor, while Bob worked as a film editor.

Maugham, Robin (1916–1980).
British popular novelist, nephew of Somerset
Maugham. *The Servant* and *The Intruder* have been
filmed.

Maugham, W. Somerset (1874–1965).
Distinguished British novelist, short-story writer
and playwright whose works have often been
filmed.
Smith 17. A Man of Honour 19. The Circle 25
and 30 (as *Strictly Unconventional*). Rain 28 (as *Sadie
Thompson*), 32 and 53 (as *Miss Sadie Thompson*). Our
Betters 33. The Painted Veil 34 and 57 (as *The
Seventh Sin*). Of Human Bondage 34, 46 and 64.
Ashenden (as *Secret Agent*) 36. Vessel of Wrath 37
and 54 (as *The Beachcomber*). The Letter 40 (also
very freely adapted as *The Unfaithful* 47). The
Moon and Sixpence 42. Christmas Holiday 44. The
Razor's Edge 46. Theatre (as *Adorable Julia*) 63,
etc.

He also introduced three omnibus films of his
stories: *Quartet* 48, *Trio* 50 and *Encore* 51; a film of
his rather unhappy life is constantly promised.

Maunder, Wayne (1942–).
American leading man of the 60s.
The Seven Minutes 71. Crazy Horse and Custer:
The Untold Story 90.
TV series: *Custer* 67. Lancer 68–69. Chase 73–
74.

Maura, Carmen (1945–).
Spanish leading actress from the stage, who gained
national fame as a TV hostess. She has starred in
several of Pedro Almodóvar's films.
El Hombre Oculto 70. La Petición 76. Los Ojos
Vendados 78. La Mano Negra 80. Dark Habits
(Entre Tinieblas) 83. What Have I Done to Deserve
This? (Que He Hecho Yo para Merecer Esto?) 84.
Matador 86. Law of Desire (La Ley del Deseo) 87.
Women on the Verge of a Nervous Breakdown
(Mujeres al Borde de un Ataque de Nervios) 89.
¡Ay, Carmela! 90. Soleil Levant 91. How to Be a
Woman and Not Die in the Attempt (Como Ser
Mujer y No Morir en el Intento) 91. In Heaven As
on Earth (Sur la Terre, Comme au Ciel) 92. La
Reina Anónima 92. Sombras en una Batalla 93.
Louis, Enfant Roi (Fr.) 93. How to Be Miserable
and Enjoy It 94, etc.

Maureen, Mollie (1904–1987) (Elizabeth Mary
Campfield).
Diminutive British stage actress, in a few films.
■ The Private Life of Sherlock Holmes (as Queen
Victoria) 70. The Return of the Pink Panther 75.
Jabberwocky 77. The Hound of the Baskervilles
78. The Wicked Lady 83. Little Dorrit 87.

Maurey, Nicole (1925–).
French leading lady.
Little Boy Lost (US) 51. The Secret of the Incas
(US) 54. The Weapon (GB) 56. Me and the
Colonel (US) 58. The House of the Seven Hawks
(GB) 59. High Time (US) 60. The Day of the
Triffids (GB) 62, etc.

Maxwell, Edwin (1886–1948).
Stocky, balding American character actor,
frequently cast as shady businessman.
The Jazz Singer 27. The Taming of the Shrew
29. Daddy Longlegs 31. Scarface 32. Cleopatra 34.
Fury 36. Young Mr Lincoln 39. His Girl Friday 40.
I Live on Danger 42. Holy Matrimony 43. Wilson
44. The Jolson Story 46. The Gangster 47, many
others.

Maxwell, Elsa (1883–1963).
Dumpy, talkative American columnist and party-
giver.
Autobiographies: 1943, *My Last Fifty Years*. 1955,
I Married the World. 1961, *Celebrity Circus*.
FILM APPEARANCES: Hotel for Women 39. Public
Deb Number One 40. Stage Door Canteen 43, etc.

¶ Elsa Maxwell? She's just another pretty face.
– *Hermione Gingold*

Maxwell, James.
British character actor, often in avuncular roles.
Private Potter (TV) 61. Private Potter 62. Girl on
Approval 62. One Day in the Life of Ivan
Denisovich 71, etc.

Maxwell, John (1875–1940).
Scottish lawyer who turned distributor and
became co-founder of Associated British
productions and the ABC cinema chain.

Maxwell, Lois (1927–) (Lois Hooker).
Canadian leading lady who had a brief Hollywood career (1946–48) before settling in England.

The Decision of Christopher Blake 47. Corridor of Mirrors 48. Women of Twilight 49. Domani È Troppo Tardi (It.) 50. The Woman's Angle 52. Aida (It.) 53. Passport to Treason 55. The High Terrace 56. Kill Me Tomorrow 57. Operation Kid Brother 67, etc.; plays Miss Moneypenny in the James Bond films.

Maxwell, Marilyn (1921–1972) (Marvel Maxwell). Blond American radio singer and actress, formerly child dancer.

Stand By For Action 42. Swing Fever 42. Thousands Cheer 43. Lost in a Harem 44. Summer Holiday 47. The Lemon Drop Kid 51. Off Limits 53. New York Confidential 55. Rock-a-bye-Baby 58. Critic's Choice 62. Stagecoach to Hell 64, etc.

May, Brian.
Australian composer.

The True Story of Eskimo Nell 75. Barnaby and Me 78. Patrick 79. Mad Max 79. Harlequin 80. The Survivor 81. Gallipoli 81. Dangerous Summer 82. Mad Max II (aka The Road Warrior) 82. Cloak and Dagger 84. Missing in Action II: The Beginning 84. Sky Pirates 86. Death before Dishonor 87. Steel Dawn 87. Hurricane Smith 90. Dead Sleep 90. Freddy's Dead: The Final Nightmare 91, etc.

May, Elaine (1932–).
American cabaret star of the 50s (with Mike Nichols); also screenwriter.

■ Luv (a) 67. Enter Laughing (a) 67. A New Leaf (awd) 71. Such Good Friends (w) 72. The Heartbreak Kid (d) 72. California Suite (a) 78. Mikey and Nickey (& w) 78. Heaven Can Wait (w) (AAN) 78. Ishtar (d) 87. In the Spirit (a) 90.

May, Hans (1891–1959).
Viennese composer who settled in Britain in the early 30s.

The Stars Look Down 39. Thunder Rock 42. The Wicked Lady 45. Brighton Rock 46. The Gypsy and the Gentleman 57, etc.

May, Joe (1880–1954) (Joseph Mandel).
German director of early serials and thrillers.

Stuart Webb 15. Veritas Vincit 16. The Hindu Tomb 21, etc.

Best German film probably Asphalt 29.
IN HOLLYWOOD: Music in the Air 34. The Invisible Man Returns 40. The House of Seven Gables 40. Hit the Road 41. Johnny Doesn't Live Here Any More 44, etc.

May, Johdi (1975–).
English juvenile actress.

A World Apart 88. Max and Helen (TV) 90. Eminent Domain 91. The Last of the Mohicans 92, etc.

Mayall, Rik (1958–).
Anarchic British actor, comedian and writer. He began writing comedy while at Manchester University and was a stand-up comedian before becoming a TV star in the 80s.

Whoops Apocalypse 86. Little Noises 91. Drop Dead Fred 91. The Princess and the Goblin (voice) 92, etc.

TV series: The Young Ones 82–84. A Kick up the Eighties 84. Filthy Rich and Catflap 87. The New Statesman 88–92. Bottom 90–92. Rick Mayall Presents 93.

❡ Just as long as I can do a bit of film, a bit of TV, a bit of live theatre, and a bit of sunbathing in Devon, that'll do me for as long as I've got. – R.M.

Mayehoff, Eddie (1911–1992).
American comic actor, former dance bandleader.

That's My Boy 51. Off Limits 53. How to Murder Your Wife 65. Luv 67, etc.

TV series: Doc Corkle 52. That's My Boy 54.

Mayer, Arthur L. (1886–1981).
American author and commentator, a former cinema exhibitor who displayed his lively wit in Merely Colossal (1953) and as co-author of The Movies.

Mayer, Carl (1894–1944).
German screenwriter.

■ The Cabinet of Dr Caligari 19. Genuine 20. Die Hintertreppe 21. Scherben 21. Schloss Vogelod 21. Phantom 22. Vanina 22. Sylvester 23. Die Strasse 23. The Last Laugh 24. Tartuff 25. Berlin 27. Sunrise 27. Four Devils 28. Ariane 31. Träumende Mund 32. Dreaming Lips 37.

Mayer, Edwin Justus (1896–1960).
American screenwriter.

In Gay Madrid 30. Never the Twain Shall Meet 31. Merrily We Go to Hell 32. The Night Is Ours 33. I Am Suzanne 34. Thirty Day Princess 34. The Affairs of Cellini (original play) 34. So Red the Rose 35. Give Us This Night 36. Desire 36. Till We Meet Again 36. The Buccaneer 38. Rio 39. They Met in Bombay 41. To Be or Not To Be 42. A Royal Scandal 45. Masquerade in Mexico 45, etc.

Mayer, Gerald (1919–).
American director.

■ Dial 1119 50. Inside Straight 51. The Sellout 52. Holiday for Sinners 52. Bright Road 53. The Marauders 55. Diamond Safari 57.

Mayer, Louis B. (1885–1957).
American executive, former production head of MGM. Once a scrap merchant, he became a cinema manager and later switched to distribution. With Sam Goldwyn, formed Metro-Goldwyn-Mayer in 1924, and when Goldwyn bought himself out became one of Hollywood's most flamboyant and powerful tycoons until the 50s when he found himself less in touch and responsible to a board. Special Academy Award 1950 'for distinguished service to the motion picture industry'.

Biographies: 1954, Hollywood Rajah by Bosley Crowther. 1975, Mayer and Thalberg by Sam Marx. 1993, The Merchant of Dreams: Louis B. Mayer, MGM and the Secret Hollywood by Charles Higham.

❡ This 'Hollywood rajah' was perhaps the archetypal movie mogul: sentimental, commonsensical, businesslike, unaesthetic, arrogant, illogical, naive, amoral, tasteless and physically unappealing. For twenty years he ran MGM splendidly in his own image, and became a legend of autocracy. He did not stint on his surroundings; Sam Goldwyn said of his office:
You need an automobile to reach the desk.
No detail escaped him. B. P. Schulberg gave him the title:
Czar of all the rushes.
Though he kept it well hidden, he did have a basic sense of humility:
You know how I'm smart? I got people around me who know more than I do.
His arguments were often irritatingly unanswerable. Arthur Freed recalls:
If a writer complained of his work being changed, Mayer always said:

'The number one book of the ages was written by a committee, and it was called The Bible.'
To Gottfried Reinhardt, who wanted to make a non-commercial picture, Mayer snapped:
You want to be an artist, but you want other people to starve for your art.
Mayer's idea of a good commercial movie was simple, homespun, warm, happy . . . in a phrase, the Hardy Family. That series, cheap to make, kept the studio in profit for many a year. Their success did not delude Mayer into thinking they were great movies:
Don't make these pictures any better. Just keep them the way they are.
This did not mean that he despised the American public, only that he knew what they liked. He even created and acted out for the producer a prayer that the son of the fictional family might speak when his mother was ill:
Dear God, don't let my mom die, because she's the best mom in the world.
He was similarly quick to correct a plot point:
A boy may hate his father, but he will always respect him.
As early as 1922 his credo in this vein was fully formed:
I will only make pictures that I won't be ashamed to have my children see.
His cry in later years, when permissiveness was creeping in, was:
Don't show the natural functions!
In argument Mayer was a great and exhausting opponent, violent, wheedling and pleading by turns. Robert Taylor remembered going in for more money. When he emerged, a friend asked him:
Did you get the rise?
– No, but I gained a father.
Taylor later remembered Mayer in a respectful light:
He was kind, understanding, fatherly and protective, always there when I had problems.
As Mayer himself said:
Life without service isn't worth living.
But he saw the dangers of life at the top:
Look out for yourself or they'll pee on your grave.
Herman J. Mankiewicz saw Mayer himself as a danger:
He had the memory of an elephant and the hide of an elephant. The only difference is that elephants are vegetarians and Mayer's diet was his fellow man.
Mayer was very proud of MGM's army of stars and technicians:
We are the only kind of company whose assets all walk out of the gate at night.
He needed their goodwill:
I want to rule by love, not fear.
But when he died, the usual caustic comments were heard:
The only reason so many people attended his funeral was they wanted to make sure he was dead.
He had then been for some years at odds with the MGM hierarchy, an unwilling exile from the boardroom. Said someone at the funeral:
I see MGM got L.B. back at last.
– Yeah, but on its own terms.
For some years people had been heard to remark:
The old grey Mayer he ain't what he used to be.
But Bob Hope, as so often, made the aptest wisecrack:
Louis B. Mayer came out west with twenty-eight dollars, a box camera and an old lion. He built a monument to himself – the Bank of America.

Mayersberg, Paul (1941–).
British screenwriter and director, a former critic

who also worked in Paris and London as an assistant director for Roger Corman, Jean-Pierre Melville and Joseph Losey.

The Man Who Fell to Earth 76. The Disappearance 77. Merry Christmas, Mr Lawrence 83. Eureka 84. Captive (d) 86. Nightfall (& d) 88. Last Samurai (d) 89, etc.

Mayes, Wendell (1918–1992).
American screenwriter.

Spirit of St Louis 57. The Enemy Below 58. Anatomy of a Murder (AAN) 59. Advise and Consent 62. In Harm's Way 64. Hotel 67. The Poseidon Adventure (co-w) 72. Bank Shot 74. Death Wish 74. Go Tell the Spartans 78. Love and Bullets (co-w) 79. Monsignor (co-w) 82, etc.

Maylam, Tony (1943–).
British director.

Riddle of the Sands 78. The Burning 82. The Sins of Dorian Gray (TV) 83. Across the Lake 89. Split Second 92, etc.

Maynard, Bill (1928–).
Massive British comic actor familiar on TV 1976–78 as the accident-prone hero of *Oh No! It's Selwyn Froggitt*.

Autobiography: 1975, *The Yo-Yo Man*.

Till Death Us Do Part 69. The Magnificent Six and a Half 69. Carry On Henry 71. The Four Dimensions of Greta 71. Steptoe and Son Ride Again 74. Carry On Dick 74. Confessions of a Pop Performer 75. Robin and Marian 76. All Things Bright and Beautiful (TV) 78. The Plague Dogs (voice) 82, etc.

TV series: Trinity Tales 75. The Life of Riley 75. Oh No! It's Selwyn Froggitt 76–77. Paradise Island 77. Selwyn 78. The Gaffer 81–83. Langley Bottom 86. Heartbeat 93–95.

Maynard, Ken (1895–1973).
American cowboy star, mainly seen in low-budget features. Once a rodeo rider; broke into films as a stuntman. Died of malnutrition.

Janice Meredith 24. Señor Daredevil 26. The Red Raiders 27. Branded Men 31. Texas Gunfighter 32. Come on, Tarzan 32. Wheels of Destiny 34. Heir to Trouble 34. Wild Horse Stampede 45, many others.

Maynard, Kermit (1898–1971).
American action player, brother of Ken Maynard. Once doubled for George O'Brien, Victor McLaglen, Warner Baxter and Edmund Lowe.

The Fighting Trooper 34. Sandy of the Mounted 34. Wild Bill Hickok 38. Golden Girl 51, many others.

TV series: Saturday Roundup 51.

Mayne, Ferdy (1916–) (Ferdinand Mayer-Boerckel).
German-born actor, long in Britain; often seen as smooth villain.

Meet Sexton Blake 44. You Know What Sailors Are 53. Storm over the Nile 55. Ben Hur 59. Freud 62. Operation Crossbow 65. The Bobo 67. *The Fearless Vampire Killers* 68. Where Eagles Dare 69. When Eight Bells Toll 71. Innocent Bystanders 72. The Eagle Has Landed 76. The Pirate (TV) 78. A Man Called Intrepid (TV) 79. The Black Stallion Returns 83. Conan the Destroyer 84. Howling II 85. River of Diamonds 90, many others.

Mayo, Archie (1891–1968).
American director of very variable output.

Money Talks 26. The College Widow 27. Beware of Married Men 28. Sonny Boy 29. Is Everybody Happy? 29. The Sacred Flame 29. Doorway to Hell

30. *Svengali* 31. Under Eighteen 31. The Expert 32. Night after Night 32. Mayor of Hell 33. Convention City 33. Desirable 34. *Bordertown* 34. *Go Into Your Dance* 35. The Case of the Lucky Legs 35. *The Petrified Forest* 36. Give Me Your Heart 36. Black Legion 36. Call it a Day 37. It's Love I'm After 37. Youth Takes a Fling 38. They Shall Have Music 39. The House Across the Bay 40. Four Sons 40. The Great American Broadcast 41. Charley's Aunt 41. Confirm or Deny 41. Moontide 42. Orchestra Wives 42. Crash Dive 43. Sweet and Low Down 44. A Night in Casablanca 46. Angel on My Shoulder 46. The Beast of Budapest (p only) 57, etc.

Mayo, Virginia (1920–) (Virginia Jones).
American 'peaches and cream' leading lady of the 40s; played a few bit parts before being cast as decoration in colour extravaganzas.

The Adventures of Jack London 43. *Up In Arms* 44. *The Princess and the Pirate* 44. Wonder Man 45. The Best Years of Our Lives 46. Out of the Blue 47. *The Secret Life of Walter Mitty* 47. A Song Is Born 48. Smart Girls Don't Talk 48. The Girl from Jones Beach 49. White Heat 49. Backfire 50. The Flame and the Arrow 50. Along the Great Divide 51. Captain Horatio Hornblower 51. She's Working Her Way through College 52. South Sea Woman 53. King Richard and the Crusaders 54. Pearl of the South Pacific 55. Congo Crossing 56. The Story of Mankind 57. Fort Dobbs 58. Jet over the Atlantic 59. The Revolt of the Mercenaries (It.) 61. Young Fury 65. Castle of Evil 66. Fort Utah 67. Won Ton Ton 76. French Quarter 78. Evil Spirits 91, etc.

Maysles, David (1931–1987) and **Albert** (1933–).
American film-making brothers, semi-professional and semi-underground.

Youth of Poland 57. Kenya 61. Safari Ya Gari 61. *Showman* 63. What's Happening 64. Marlon Brando 65. Truman Capote 66. *Salesman* 69. Gimme Shelter 71. Grey Gardens 75. Running Fence 77, etc.

Mazurki, Mike (1909–1990) (Mikhail Mazurwski).
Immense American character actor of Ukrainian descent; former heavyweight wrestler. Began in Hollywood as an extra.

The Shanghai Gesture (debut) 41. *Farewell My Lovely* 44. The French Key 46. Unconquered 47. Rope of Sand 49. Ten Tall Men 51. My Favorite Spy 52. Blood Alley 55. Davy Crockett 56. Donovan's Reef 63. Cheyenne Autumn 64. Seven Women 66. The Wild McCulloughs 75, many others.

TV series: It's About Time 66. Chicago Teddy Bears 71.

Mazursky, Paul (1930–) (Irwin. Mazursky).
American writer-director and occasional actor.
■ I Love you Alice B. Toklas (co-w) 68. *Bob and Carol and Ted and Alice* (co-w, d) (AAN) 70. Alex in Wonderland (co-w, d, a) 70. Blume in Love (wd) 73. *Harry and Tonto* (co-w, p, d) (AAN) 74. Next Stop Greenwich Village (wd, p) 76. *An Unmarried Woman* (wd, co-p, a) (AAN) 78. Willie and Phil 80. Tempest 82. Moscow on the Hudson 84. Down and Out in Beverly Hills 85. Moon over Parador (a, wd) 88. Punchline (a) 88. Enemies, a Love Story (a, wd) (AANw) 89. Scenes from the Class Struggle in Beverly Hills (a) 89. Scenes from a Mall (a, co-w, d) 90. The Pickle (wd) 93. Love Affair (a) 94.

Mazzacurati, Carlo (1958–).
Italian director.

Notte Italiana 87. Il Prete Bello 89. Un'Altra Vita 92. The Bull 94, etc.

Mazzello, Joe (1984–).
American child actor.

Presumed Innocent 90. Radio Flyer 92. Jurassic Park 93. Shadowlands 93. River Wild 94, etc.

Mc:
see *Mac*.

Meadows, Jayne (1920–) (Jayne Cotter).
American actress whose biggest role was in 1947 as the unsympathetic sister in *Enchantment*. She married Steve Allen in 1954.

Undercurrent 46. Song of the Thin Man 47. David and Bathsheba 51. Suspense 53. Hollywood Palace 68. The Ratings Game 84. Murder by Numbers 89. City Slickers 91, etc.

TV series: Medical Center 69–72. It's Not Easy 83.

Meaney, Colm.
Irish character actor.

The Commitments 91. *The Snapper* (TV) 93. The Road to Wellville 94. The War of the Buttons 94.

TV series: Star Trek: The Next Generation 87–93. Star Trek: Deep Space Nine 93– .

Meara, Anne (1929–).
American comedienne who turned straight actress in a 1975 TV series, *Kate McShane*.

Lovers and Other Strangers 69. Kate MacShane (TV) 75. Nasty Habits 76. The Boys from Brazil 78. The Other Woman (TV) 82. The Longshot 86. My Little Girl 86. That's Adequate 90, etc.

Meat Loaf (1947–) (Marvin Lee Aday).
Bulky American character actor and rock singer.

Rocky Horror Picture Show 75. Americathon 79. Scavenger Hunt 79. Roadie 80. Feel the Motion 86. Out of Bounds 86. The Squeeze 87. Stand by Me (concert) 88. Wayne's World 92. Motorama 92, etc.

Medak, Peter.
Hungarian director in Britain.

Negatives 68. *A Day in the Death of Joe Egg* 70. The Ruling Class 71. Third Girl from the Left (TV) 74. Ghost in the Noonday Sun (unreleased) 74. The Odd Job 78. The Changeling 80. Zorro the Gay Blade 81. Mistress of Paradise (TV) 82. The Men's Club 86. The Krays 90. Let Him Have It 91. Romeo Is Bleeding 93. Pontiac Moon 94, etc.

Medem, Julio (1958–).
Spanish director. He studied medicine, intending to work as a psychiatrist, and was a film critic for the Basque newspaper *La Voz de Euskadi* before becoming a director.

Cows (Vacas) 92. The Red Squirrel (La Ardilla Roja) 93. Earth (Tierra) 95, etc.

Medford, Don (1917–).
American director.

To Trap a Spy 64. Cosa Nostra, Arch Enemy of the FBI (TV) 66. Incident in San Francisco (TV) 71. The Hunting Party 71. The Organization 71. The November Plan 76. Sizzle (TV) 81. Hell Town (TV) 85, etc.

Medford, Kay (1914–1980).
American character actress.

The War Against Mrs Hadley 42. The Rat Race 60. Butterfield 8 60. Bye Bye Birdie 63. Funny Girl (AAN) 68. But I Don't Want to Get Married (TV) 70. No Place to Run (TV) 72. More Than Friends (TV) 78, etc.

Medina, Patricia (1921–).
British-born leading lady of the 40s and 50s, in routine international films. She married actor Joseph Cotten in 1960.

The Day Will Dawn 42. They Met in the Dark 42. The First of the Few 42. Don't Take It To Heart 44. Hotel Reserve 44. Waltz Time 45. The Secret Heart 46. Moss Rose 47. The Three Musketeers 48. The Fighting O'Flynn 49. Abbott and Costello in the Foreign Legion 50. The Magic Carpet 51. Lady in the Iron Mask 52. Siren of Baghdad 53. Phantom of the Rue Morgue 54. Pirates of Tripoli 55. Uranium Boom 56. Buckskin Lady 57. Count Your Blessings 59. The Killing of Sister George 68. The Big Push (aka Timber Tramps) 77, etc.

medium shot.
One taking in the full body of the actor, not so close as a close-up, not so far off as a long shot.

Medwin, Michael (1923–).
British light character comedian, usually seen as a cockney.

Piccadilly Incident 46. Boys in Brown 49. Top Secret 52. Above Us the Waves 55. A Hill in Korea 56. I Only Arsked 58. Night Must Fall 63. Rattle of a Simple Man 64. I've Gotta Horse 65. The Sandwich Man 66. Scrooge 70. The Jigsaw Man 84. Staggered 94, many others.
AS PRODUCER: Charlie Bubbles 67. If 68. Spring and Port Wine 69. Gumshoe 71. Alpha Beta 73. O Lucky Man 73. Law and Disorder 73.

TV series: *The Army Game* 57–62. Shoestring 79.

Meek, Donald (1880–1946).
Scottish-born character actor, long in Hollywood; a bald, worried and timidly respectable little man was his invariable role.

The Hole in the Wall (debut) 28. Mrs Wiggs of the Cabbage Patch 34. Barbary Coast 35. Captain Blood 35. Pennies from Heaven 36. The Adventures of Tom Sawyer 38. *Stagecoach* 39. Tortilla Flat 42. They Got Me Covered 43. State Fair 45. Magic Town 46, many others.

Meeker, Ralph (1920–1988) (Ralph Rathgeber).
American leading man of the Brando type, with Broadway experience.

Teresa (debut) 51. Four in a Jeep 51. Shadow in the Sky 51. Glory Alley 52. The Naked Spur 53. Jeopardy 53. Code Two 53. Big House USA 54. Kiss Me Deadly (as Mike Hammer) 55. Desert Sands 56. *Paths of Glory* 58. Ada 61. Something Wild 62. The Dirty Dozen 67. The St Valentine's Day Massacre 67. Gentle Giant 67. The Detective 68. I Walk the Line 70. The Anderson Tapes 71. The Happiness Cage 73. The Food of the Gods 76. Hi-Riders 78. Winter Kills 79. Without Warning 80, etc.

Meerson, Lazare (1900–1938).
Russian-born production designer.

Gribiche 25. Carmen 26. An Italian Straw Hat 28. Sous les Toits de Paris 29. *Le Million* 31. À Nous la Liberté 32. *La Kermesse Héroique* 32. As You Like It 36. *Fire over England* 37. *Knight without Armour* 37. The Citadel 38, etc.

Mehboob (1907–1964) (Ramjankhan Mehboobkhan).
Prolific Indian director, few of whose films have been seen in the west.

Aan 49. Mother India 56. A Handful of Grain 59, etc.

Meheux, Phil.
English cinematographer.

Black Joy 77. The Music Machine 79. Scum 79. Those Glory Glory Days 81. The Final Conflict (co-c) 81. The Long Good Friday 82. The Final Option 83. Experience Preferred but Not Essential 83. Morons from Outer Space 85. The Fourth Protocol 87. Criminal Law 89. Renegades 89. Defenseless 91. Highlander 2: The Quickening 91. The Trial 93. Ghost in the Machine 94. Ruby 92. No Escape 94, etc.

Mehta, Deepa (1949–) (Deepa Mehta Saltzman).
Indian-born director, based in Canada, from television.

Martha, Ruth & Edie (co-d) 87. Sam & Me 91. Camilla 94, etc.

Meighan, Thomas (1879–1936).
American leading man of the silent screen.

The Trail of the Lonesome Pine 16. Male and Female 19. The Miracle Man 19. Conrad in Quest of His Youth 22. Manslaughter 23. The Alaskan 24. Tin Gods 26. The New Klondyke 26. The Racket 27. Young Sinners 31. Peck's Bad Boy 34, etc.

Meillon, John (1934–1989).
Australian character actor, in Britain from 1960.

On the Beach 59. The Sundowners 60. Offbeat 60. The Valiant 61. Billy Budd 62. The Running Man 63. They're a Weird Mob 66. The Cars that Ate Paris 74. Crocodile Dundee 86. Crocodile Dundee II 88, etc.

Mekas, Adolfas (1925–).
Lithuanian underground film-maker, in US.

Hallelujah the Hills (wd) 63. Guns of the Trees (a) 64. Windflowers (wd) 68, etc.

Mekas, Jonas (1922–).
Lithuanian underground film-maker in US, brother of Adolfas Mekas.

The Secret Passions of Salvador Dali 61. The Brig 64. Guns of the Trees 64. Hare Krishna 66. Report from Millbrook 66, etc.

Melcher, Martin (1915–1968).
American producer, married to Doris Day and from 1952 the co-producer of all her films.

Calamity Jane 53. Julie 56. Pillow Talk 59. Jumbo 62. Move Over, Darling 63. Send Me No Flowers 64. Where Were You When the Lights Went Out? 68, etc.

Melchior, Ib (1917–).
Danish-born writer-director, long in US; former actor and set designer. Son of Lauritz Melchior.
■ Angry Red Planet (wd) 59. Reptilicus (wd) 61. The Time Travellers (wd) 64. Robinson Crusoe on Mars (w) 65.

Melchior, Lauritz (1890–1973).
Danish operatic tenor, in a few Hollywood films.
■ Thrill of a Romance 45. Two Sisters from Boston 46. This Time for Keeps 47. Luxury Liner 48. The Stars Are Singing 53.

Melford, George (1889–1961).
American director and actor, from the stage, in films from 1909. His silent films were more distinguished than his talkies, and from the late 30s he worked as a character actor. It has been claimed that his Spanish version of *Dracula*, made in 1931 at the same time as the version directed by Tod Browning, is the better film.
AS DIRECTOR: Arizona Bill (w, co-d) 11. The Boer War 14. To Have and to Hold 16. The Call of the East 17. Everywoman 19. The Sea Wolf 20. The Sheik 21. Moran of the Lady Letty 22. Burning Sands 22. The Light that Failed 23. Tiger Love 24. Simon the Jester 25. Whispering Smith 26.

Freedom of the Press 28. Sinners in Love 28. The Viking 32. East of Borneo 32. The Boiling Point 32. East of Java 35, many others.
AS ACTOR: Rulers of the Sea 39. My Little Chickadee 40. Dixie Dugan 43. A Tree Grows in Brooklyn 45. The Robe 53. The Egyptian 54. The Ten Commandments 56. Bluebeard's Ten Honeymoons 60, etc.

Melia, Joe.
British character comedian.

Oh What a Lovely War 69. Privates on Parade 82. Let Him Have It 91.

Méliès, Georges (1861–1938).
French film pioneer, an ex-conjuror who produced the cinema's first trick films, most of them ambitious and still effective. Credited with being the first to use the dissolve, double exposure, and fades. After World War I he found his films out of date and his talents unwanted. In 1952 Georges Franju made a documentary tribute, *Le Grand Méliès*.

Biography: 1973, *Méliès Enchanteur* by Madeleine Méliès.

Une Partie de Cartes (debut) 96. The Artist's Dream 98. The Dreyfus Affair 99. Cinderella 00. Indiarubber Head 01. *Voyage to the Moon* 02. The Kingdom of the Fairies 03. The Impossible Voyage 04. Twenty Thousand Leagues under the Sea 07. Baron Munchausen 11. The Conquest of the Pole 12, many others.
❹ For demonstrating that cinema is a medium of magic; and for devising tricks so effective that eighty years later they are still viewed with delight. *Voyage to the Moon.*

Mell, Marisa (1929–1992) (Marlies Moitzi).
French leading lady.

French Dressing 64. What's New Pussycat? 65. Casanova '70 65. Anyone Can Play 66. Danger: Diabolik 67. Mahogany 77, etc.

Mellé, Gil (1935–).
American composer.

The Andromeda Strain 70. The Organization 71. Frankenstein: The True Story (TV) 73. Dynasty (TV) 75. The Sentinel 77. Starship Invasion 78. Borderline 81. Blood Beach 81. The Last Chase 81. Hot Target 85. Restless 86. The Case of the Hillside Strangler (TV) 90, many others, mainly for TV.

Mellor, William C. (1904–1963).
American cinematographer.

Wings in the Dark 35. Disputed Passage 39. The Great McGinty 40. Dixie 43. Abie's Irish Rose 46. Love Happy 49. *A Place in the Sun* (AA) 51. The Naked Spur 52. Give a Girl a Break 53. Bad Day at Black Rock 54. Giant 55. The Diary of Anne Frank (AA) 59. State Fair 62, etc.

Melton, James (1904–1961).
American operatic tenor, in a few Hollywood films.

Stars over Broadway 35. Sing Me a Love Song 36. Melody for Two 37. Ziegfeld Follies 45.

Melville, Herman (1819–1891).
American novelist of now-classic stature who died in obscurity. *Moby Dick*, which has been filmed three times, was in part inspired by tales of a fierce white whale known to sailors as Mocha Dick.

Biography: 1969, *The Melville Log* by Jay Leyda.

Moby Dick 26 (as The Sea Beasts), 30 and 54. Billy Budd 62. Typee (as The Enchanted Island) 64. Bartleby 70.

See also: *Moby Dick.*

Melville, Jean-Pierre (1917–1973) (J. P. Grumbach).
French director, with stage experience.
   Le Silence de la Mer 47. Les Enfants Terribles 48. Quand Tu Liras Cette Lettre 52. Bob le Flambeur 55. *Leon Morin Priest* 61. Second Wind 66. *The Samurai* 67. The Red Circle 70. Dirty Money 72, etc.

Melvin, Murray (1932–).
British light character actor with stage experience in Theatre Workshop.
   The Criminal (debut) 60. *A Taste of Honey* 61. HMS Defiant 62. Sparrows Can't Sing 63. The Ceremony 64. Alfie 66. A Day in the Death of Joe Egg 70. The Boy Friend 71. Ghost Story 74. Barry Lyndon 75. The Bawdy Adventures of Tom Jones 76. Tales from a Flying Trunk 79. Nutcracker 82. Let Him Have It 91, etc.

Mendelsohn, Ben.
Young Australian leading actor.
   The Year My Voice Broke 87. Return Home 90. The Big Steal 90. Quigley Down Under 90. Spotswood (US: The Efficiency Export) 91. Nirvana Street Murder 91. Say a Little Prayer 93. Sirens 94. Metal Skin 94, etc.

Mendeluk, George (1948–).
German-born director, working in Canada.
   Stone Cold Dead (& w, p) 79. The Kidnapping of the President 80. Doin' Time (US) 84. Meatballs III 86, etc.

Mendes, Lothar (1894–1974).
Hungarian director, mainly in US.
   A Night of Mystery 27. The Four Feathers 29. Payment Deferred 32. Jew Süss (GB) 34. *The Man Who Could Work Miracles* (GB) 36. Moonlight Sonata (GB) 38. International Squadron 41. Flight for Freedom 43. The Walls Came Tumbling Down 46, etc.

Menges, Chris (1940–).
British cinematographer.
   Kes 70. Gumshoe 71. Black Jack 79. Babylon 80. Looks and Smiles 81. Angel 82. Local Hero 83. Comfort and Joy 84. The Killing Fields (AA) 84. A Sense of Freedom 85. The Mission (AA) 86. High Season 87. Shy People 87. A World Apart (d) 88. Crisscross (d) 92. Second Best (d) 94, etc.

Menjou, Adolphe (1890–1963).
Dapper French-American leading man of the 20s, later a polished, sharp-spoken character actor; had the reputation of being Hollywood's best-dressed man.
   Autobiography: 1952, It Took Nine Tailors.
SELECTED SILENT FILMS: The Kiss 16. The Faith Healer 21. The Three Musketeers 21. Bella Donna 23. *A Woman of Paris* 23. *The Marriage Circle* 24. *Forbidden Paradise* 24. The Swan 25. The Grand Duchess and the Waiter 26. Service for Ladies 27. Serenade 27. His Private Life 28. Marquis Preferred 28.
■ SOUND FILMS: Fashions in Love 29. Morocco 30. New Moon 30. Men Call It Love 31. The Easiest Way 31. *The Front Page* (AAN) 31. The Great Lover 31. Friends and Lovers 31. Prestige 32. Forbidden 32. Two White Arms 32. The Man From Yesterday 32. Bachelor's Affairs 32. Night Club Lady 32. A Farewell to Arms 32. Diamond Cut Diamond 32. The Circus Queen Murder 33. *Morning Glory* 33. The Worst Woman in Paris 33. Convention City 33. Journal of a Crime 34. Easy to Love 34. The Trumpet Blows 34. *Little Miss Marker* 34. Flirtation 34. The Human Side 34. The Mighty Barnum 34. Gold Diggers of 1935. Broadway Gondolier 35. The

Milky Way 36. Sing Baby Sing 36. Wives Never Know 36. One in a Million 36. A Star is Born 37. Café Metropole 37. *One Hundred Men and a Girl* 37. *Stage Door* 37. The Goldwyn Follies 38. Letter of Introduction 38. Thanks for Everything 38. King of the Turf 39. That's Right You're Wrong 39. Golden Boy 39. *The Housekeeper's Daughter* 39. *A Bill of Divorcement* 40. Turnabout 41. Road Show 41. Father Takes a Wife 41. *Roxie Hart* 42. Syncopation 42. You Were Never Lovelier 42. Hi Diddle Diddle 43. Sweet Rosie O'Grady 43. *Step Lively* 44. Man Alive 45. Heartbeat 46. The Bachelor's Daughters 46. I'll Be Yours 47. Mr District Attorney 47. The Hucksters 47. *State of the Union* 48. My Dream is Yours 49. Dancing in the Dark 49. To Please a Lady 50. Tall Target 51. Across the Wide Missouri 51. *The Sniper* 52. Man on a Tightrope 53. Timberjack 55. The Ambassador's Daughter 56. Bundle of Joy 56. The Fuzzy Pink Nightgown 57. *Paths of Glory* 57. I Married a Woman 58. Pollyanna 60.
   TV series: Target 51. My Favourite Story 53.
☺ For his omnipresent sartorial elegance, and for a surprising number of highly enjoyable performances. *Roxie Hart.*

Menke, Sally.
American editor, a graduate of the NYU Film School.
   Cold Feet 84. Teenage Mutant Ninja Turtles 90. The Search for Signs of Intelligent Life in the Universe 91. Reservoir Dogs 91. Heaven & Earth 93, etc.

Menken, Alan (1949–).
American composer, in collaboration with lyricist Howard Ashman until 1991.
   Little Shop of Horrors (AAN) 86. The Little Mermaid (AAm, AAs) 89. Rocky V (song) 90. Beauty and the Beast (AAm, AAs) 91. Newsies 92. Life with Mikey 93. Home Alone II (song) 92. Aladdin (AAm, AAs) 92.

Menzel, Jiri (1938–).
Czech director.
   Closely Observed Trains (AA) 66. Capricious Summer 68. Crime at the Nightclub 68. Seclusion Near a Forest 76. The Apple Game 77. Those Wonderful Men with a Crank 79. My Sweet Little Village (AAN) 85. The End of the Good Old Days (Konec Starych Casu) 89. Martha and I (Martha und Ich) 90. The Beggar's Opera 91. The Life and Extraordinary Adventures of Private Chonkin 94, etc.

Menzies, William Cameron (1896–1957).
American art director who did much memorable work, especially with louring, impressionistic skyscapes. Also directed a few rather disappointing low-budget films.
AS ART DIRECTOR: Robin Hood 22. *The Thief of Baghdad* 24. Tempest 27. *The Dove* (AA) 28. Bulldog Drummond 29. Alice in Wonderland 33. *Things to Come* (& co-d) 36. The Adventures of Tom Sawyer 38. *Gone with the Wind* 39. *Our Town* 40. Foreign Correspondent 40. *Kings Row* 41. For Whom the Bell Tolls 43. Ivy 47. Arch of Triumph 48. Around the World in Eighty Days 56, etc.
■ AS DIRECTOR: Always Goodbye 31. The Spider 31. Almost Married 32. Chandu the Magician 32. Wharf Angel 34. *Things to Come* 36. The Green Cockatoo 40. Address Unknown 44. Drums in the Deep South 51. The Whip Hand 51. The Maze 53. Invaders from Mars 54.
☺ For styling so many of the cinema's most memorable images. *Things to Come.*

Merande, Doro (c. 1898–1975).
American character actress who specialized in acidulous, eccentric and whimsical spinsters.
   Our Town 40. Sullivan's Travels 41. Mr Belvedere Rings the Bell 52. The Seven Year Itch 55. The Cardinal 63. Hurry Sundown 67, many others.

Mercer, Beryl (1882–1939).
British character actress, of small stature, in Hollywood from 1923; played mothers, maids, landladies.
   The Christian 23. Seven Days' Leave 29. *Outward Bound* 30. Merely Mary Ann 31. Supernatural 32. *Cavalcade* 33. Berkeley Square 33. The Little Minister 34. Night Must Fall 37. The Hound of the Baskervilles 39, etc.

Mercer, David (1928–1980).
Leading British TV dramatist, playwright and occasional screenwriter; a former teacher.
   Morgan – a Suitable Case for Treatment 66. *Family Life* 70. A Doll's House 73. Providence 77.

Mercer, Johnny (1909–1976).
American lyricist and composer, active in Hollywood from the early 30s. Songs include 'Blues in the Night', 'Black Magic', 'Something's Got to Give', 'Accentuate the Positive', etc.
   The Harvey Girls (AA) 46. Here Comes the Groom (AA) 51. Seven Brides for Seven Brothers (AA) 54. Li'l Abner 59. Kotch (AAN song) 71, etc.

merchandising.
The means of exploiting films and personalities through souvenirs, toys and other consumable items has always brought in considerable revenue to canny film-makers, often more than the film itself. Film editions of novels, illustrated with stills from the movie, and novelizations of film scripts were being published from the early 20s onwards, but Walt Disney was among the first to realize the commercial possibilities of exploiting his animated characters, with such goods as a Mickey Mouse watch, a trend culminating in the opening of an international chain of shops selling Disney goods from the mid-80s onwards. Television accelerated the process, with such personalities as Hopalong Cassidy appearing on everything from lunch boxes to pillow cases. Disney's shops were followed in the 90s by Warner opening a store merchandising Bugs Bunny and other cartoon heroes. But it is only in comparatively recent times that films have been primarily designed to sell a range of toys or to advertise particular products. Product placement, in which cameras linger on a particular range of footwear or obtrusively feature a certain type of soft drink, has become a means of gaining as much income as possible from a film. It was no accident that E.T. munched on M&Ms rather than, say, jelly-babies. E.T. still remains one of the most successful merchandising operations – in Britain alone, the wholesaler of E.T. merchandise guaranteed sales of £1 million – together with the *Star Wars* movies, which shifted around $2 billion of toys and other paraphernalia now gathering dust in cupboards. Occasionally, merchandisers do get caught short. The makers of *Forrest Gump* did not believe that the film lent itself to merchandising opportunities. Once it was a runaway hit in America, they changed their minds and began producing Forrest Gump goods, including a book of Gump sayings.

¶ There is a staunch refusal to admit that anything needs to be taken so seriously as to get in the way of its marketing, and a confidence that anything can be marketed, anything can be made appealing, if it is packed well enough and given the right advertising spin. – *David Rieff on American popular culture*

Merchant, Ismail (1936–).
Indian producer, exclusively associated with films directed by James Ivory (qv).
In Custody (Hifazaat) (d) 93.

Merchant, Vivien (1929–1983) (Ada Thompson).
British leading actress, mainly on TV: once married to Harold Pinter.
Alfie (AAN) 66. Accident 67. Under Milk Wood 71. Frenzy 72. The Offence 72. The Homecoming 73. The Man in the Iron Mask (TV) 77, etc.

Mercier, Michele (1939–).
French leading lady.
Retour de Manivelle 57. Aimez-vous Brahms? 61. Call of the Wild 72. Jean's Tonic 84.

Mercouri, Melina (1923–1994).
Volatile Greek star actress with flashing smile and dominant personality; married Jules Dassin and appeared in international films. In the 80s she became Greece's Minister of Culture.
Autobiography: 1971, *I Was Born Greek.*
■ *Stella* 54. He Who Must Die 56. The Gypsy and the Gentleman 58. The Law 59. *Never on Sunday* (AAN) 60. Il Giudizio Universale 61. Phaedra 61. Vive Henri IV 61. The Victors 63. *Topkapi* 64. A Man Could Get Killed 65. The Player Pianos 65. 10.30 pm Summer 66. Gaily Gaily 69. Promise at Dawn 71. Once Is Not Enough 75. Nasty Habits 76. A Dream of Passion 78. Not by Coincidence 83.

Mercurio, Paul.
Australian leading actor and dancer.
Strictly Ballroom 92. Exit to Eden 94.

Meredith, Burgess (1908–) (George Burgess).
American star character actor who was famous on Broadway in the 30s, but never seemed to find the right Hollywood outlet for his enthusiastic, eccentric portrayals.
■ *Winterset* 36. There Goes the Groom 37. Spring Madness 38. Idiot's Delight 39. *Of Mice and Men* 39. Castle on the Hudson 40. Second Chorus 40. San Francisco Docks 41. *That Uncertain Feeling* 41. Tom Dick and Harry 41. Street of Chance 42. *The Story of GI Joe* (as Ernie Pyle) 45. The Diary of a Chambermaid 46. Magnificent Doll 46. On Our Merry Way 48. *Mine Own Executioner* (GB) 48. The Man on the Eiffel Tower (& d) 49. The Gay Adventure 53. Joe Butterfly 57. Advise and Consent 62. The Cardinal 63. In Harm's Way 65. A Big Hand for the Little Lady 66. Madame X 66. Batman 66. The Kidnappers (Philipp) 66. Hurry Sundown 67. The Torture Garden (GB) 67. Mackenna's Gold 68. Stay Away Joe 68. Hard Contract 69. Skidoo 69. There Was a Crooked Man 70. Probe (TV) 71. Such Good Friends 71. Beware the Blob 71. A Fan's Notes 72. Clay Pigeon 72. Golden Needles 74. The Day of the Locust (AAN) 74. The Hindenburg 76. Burnt Offerings 76. Rocky (AAN) 76. The Sentinel 77. 92 in the Shade 77. Magic 78. Foul Play 78. The Manitou 78. The Great Georgia Bank Hoax 78. Rocky II 79. Final Assignment 80. When Time Ran Out 80. True Confessions 81. The Last Chase 81. Clash of the Titans 81. Rocky III 82. Santa Claus 85. Broken Rainbow 85. King Lear 87. Full Moon in Blue Water 88. Rocky V 90. State of Grace 90. Night of the Hunter (TV) 91. Grumpy Old Men 93.
TV series: Mr Novak 64. Search 72. That's Incredible 80. Gloria 82.

Meredith, Iris (1916–1980).
American leading actress in westerns. She made 19 films opposite Charles Starrett and also appeared with Johnny Mack Brown and Bob Allen before retiring in the mid-40s.
Roman Scandals 33. A Lawman Is Born 37. Mystery of the Hooded Horseman 37. Cattle Raiders 38. West of the Santa Fe 39. Riders of Black River 39. The Return of Wild Bill 40. Green Archer 40. The Son of Davy Crockett 41. The Rangers Take Over 43, etc.

Meredyth, Bess (1890–1969) (Helen McGlashan).
American scriptwriter.
Strangers in the Night 23. Ben Hur 26. Wonder of Women (AAN) 28. A Woman of Affairs 28. Our Blushing Brides 30. Cuban Love Song 31. Strange Interlude 32. The Affairs of Cellini 34. Folies Bergère 35. Under Two Flags 36. The Unsuspected 47, etc.

Merivale, Philip (1886–1946).
British stage actor who moved to Hollywood in the late 30s.
The Passing of the Third Floor Back 35. Give Us This Night 36. Rage in Heaven 41. This Above All 42. This Land Is Mine 43. Lost Angel 44. The Stranger 45, etc.

Meriwether, Lee (1935–).
Long-legged American leading lady, mostly in 'B's; former beauty queen.
The 4D Man 59. Batman (as Catwoman) 65. Namu the Killer Whale 66. Angel in My Pocket 68. The Undefeated 69. The Brothers O'Toole 73, etc.
TV series: Barnaby Jones 72–80.

Merkel, Una (1903–1986).
American character actress who started in the 30s as heroine's girlfriend type, later played mothers and aunts.
Abraham Lincoln 30. Daddy Longlegs 31. Whistling in the Dark 33. The Merry Widow 34. Saratoga 37. Destry Rides Again 39. Road to Zanzibar 41. This Is the Army 43. Twin Beds 44. With a Song in My Heart 52. The Kentuckian 55. The Mating Game 59. Summer and Smoke (AAN) 61. A Tiger Walks 63. Spinout 66, many others.

Merman, Ethel (1908–1984) (Ethel Zimmermann).
Brassy, vibrant, much-loved American star entertainer who had an incomparable way with a song that could be belted across. Her style was too outsize for Hollywood.
Autobiographies: 1955, *Who Could Ask for Anything More?* (UK *Don't Call Me Madam*). 1978, *Merman.*
■ Follow the Leader 30. We're Not Dressing 34. Kid Millions 34. *Anything Goes* 36. The Big Broadcast of 1936. Strike Me Pink 36. Happy Landing 38. *Alexander's Ragtime Band* 38. Straight Place and Show 38. Stage Door Canteen 43. *Call Me Madam* 53. There's No Business Like Show Business 54. It's a Mad Mad Mad Mad World 63. The Art of Love 65. Won Ton Ton 76. Airplane! 80.

❡ Broadway has been very good to me – but then, I've been very good to Broadway. – *E.M.*

Merrall, Mary (1890–1976) (Mary Lloyd).
British character actress, on stage from 1907; often in fey or absent-minded roles.
The Duke's Son 20. You Will Remember 39. *Love on the Dole* 41. Squadron Leader X 42. *Dead of Night* 45. Nicholas Nickleby 47. Badger's Green 48. The Late Edwina Black 51. The Pickwick Papers 52. *The Belles of St Trinian's* 54. It's Great To Be

Young 56. The Camp on Blood Island 58. Spare the Rod 61. Who Killed the Cat? 66, many others.

Merrick, David (1911–) (David Margulies).
American impresario, a Broadway legend who also produced a few films.
Biography: 1993, *David Merrick – The Abominable Showman* by Howard Kissel.
Child's Play 72. The Great Gatsby 74. Semi-Tough 77. Rough Cut 80, etc.

Merrie Melodies:
see *Looney Tunes.*

Merrill, Dina (1928–) (Nedenia Hutton Rumbough).
American leading lady of the 60s, and leading socialite.
The Desk Set 57. The Sundowners 59. The Courtship of Eddie's Father 63. The Pleasure Seekers 64. I'll Take Sweden 65. Running Wild 73. The Greatest 77. A Wedding 78. Just Tell Me What You Want 80. Anna to the Infinite Power 83. Hot Pursuit 87. Caddyshack II 88. True Colors 91, etc.
TV series: Hot Pursuit 84.

Merrill, Gary (1914–1990).
Dependable, tough-looking American actor. He was formerly married to Bette Davis.
Winged Victory 44. Slattery's Hurricane 48. Twelve O'Clock High 49. *All About Eve* 50. Decision Before Dawn 51. Another Man's Poison (GB) 51. Phone Call from a Stranger 52. Night Without Sleep 52. Blueprint for Murder 53. The Human Jungle 54. The Black Dakotas 54. Bermuda Affair 56. The Pleasure of His Company 61. Around the World Under the Sea 66. Destination Inner Space 66. Catacombs (GB) 66. The Power 68. Huckleberry Finn 74. Thieves 77, others.
TV series: The Mash 54. Young Dr Kildare 73. Reporter 74.

Merrill, Robert (1921–) (Henry Lavan).
American composer and lyricist whose chief film score has been *Funny Girl.*
Wrote *W. C. Fields and Me.*

Merritt, George (1890–1977).
British character actor of solid presence, usually seen as trades unionist, policeman, or gruff north-country type.
Dreyfus 30. The Lodger 32. I was a Spy 33. Dr Syn 37. Q Planes 39. He Found a Star 41. Hatter's Castle 41. Waterloo Road 45. I'll Be Your Sweetheart 45. I'll Turn to You 46. Nicholas Nickleby 47. Marry Me 49. The Green Scarf 54. Quatermass II 57. Tread Softly Stranger 58. I Monster 70, etc.

Merrow, Jane (1941–).
British leading lady.
Don't Bother to Knock 61. The Wild and the Willing 62. The System 63. *The Lion in Winter* 68. Hands of the Ripper 70. Adam's Woman 70. The Horror at 37,000 Feet (TV) 73. Diagnosis Murder 75. The Patricia Neal Story (TV) 81, etc.

The Merry Widow.
Franz Lehar's operetta has been filmed at least four times: in 1925 as a silent by Erich Von Stroheim with John Gilbert, Mae Murray, and Roy D'Arcy; in 1934 by Ernst Lubitsch with Maurice Chevalier and Jeanette MacDonald, with added lyrics by Gus Kahn and Lorenz Hart; in 1952 by Curtis Bernhardt with Fernando Lamas, Lana Turner, and Richard Haydn, with added lyrics by Paul Francis Webster;

in 1962, in an Austrian version with Karin Huebner and Peter Alexander.

Merson, Billy (1879–1947) (William Thompson). British comic actor and singer, from music hall and revue. He began as an acrobat and clown called Ping Pong and made his name singing his own composition, 'The Spaniard that Blighted My Life'.

Billy's Spanish Love Spasm 15. The Tales of a Shirt 16. Billy the Truthful 17. Billy Merson in Russian Opera 27. Comets 30. Bill and Coo (& co-w) 31. The Show Goes On 37. Riding High 37. Chips 38. Scruffy 38, etc.

Merton of the Movies.
The comic American novel by Harry Leon Wilson, about an innocent in Hollywood in the early silent days, has been filmed three times: in 1924 with Glenn Hunter; in 1932, as *Make Me a Star*, with Stuart Erwin; and in 1947 with Redd Skelton.

Merton Park.
A small, independent south London studio. Founded in 1930 to make advertising films, it later housed Radio Luxembourg. Training films were made there during the war, and in the 50s it turned to the production of Edgar Lustgarten's *Scotland Yard* shorts, the Edgar Wallace supports, and *Scales of Justice*. It closed in the mid-60s.

Mervyn, William (1912–1976) (William Pickwood). Portly, plummy-voiced British character actor, much on TV in high comedy roles.

The Blue Lamp 52. The Long Arm 56. Invasion Quartet 61. Murder Ahoy 64. The Jokers 67. The Railway Children 70. The Ruling Class 71. Up The Front 72. The Bawdy Adventures of Tom Jones 76, many others.

Mescall, John (1899–   ).
American cinematographer.

Hold Your Horses 20. So This Is Paris 26. *The Black Cat* 34. *Bride of Frankenstein* 35. *Showboat* 36. The Road Back 37. Josette 38. Kit Carson 40. Dark Waters 44. Bedside Manner 45. The Desperadoes Are In Town 56. Not of This Earth 57, many others.

Messel, Oliver (1904–1978).
British stage designer who occasionally worked in films.

The Scarlet Pimpernel 34. Romeo and Juliet 36. The Thief of Baghdad 40. Caesar and Cleopatra 45. The Queen of Spades 48, etc.

Messemer, Hannes (1924–   ).
German general-purpose actor.

Rose Bernd 56. Babette Goes to War 59. The Great Escape 63. Is Paris Burning? 66. Congress Dances 66. The Odessa File 74, etc.

Meszaros, Marta (1931–   ).
Hungarian director and screenwriter, often of semi-autobiographical films. She studied at the Moscow Film School and began as a documentary film-maker. She was married to director Miklos Jancso (1962–81).

Book: 1994, *Screen Memories, the Hungarian Cinema of Marta Meszaros* by C. Portuges.

The Girl (Eltéavozott Nap) 68. Don't Cry, Pretty Girls (Széep Léanyok, Ne Sirjatok) 71. 9 Months (Kilenc Héonap) 76. On the Move (Utkozben) 79. Diary for My Children (Napló Gyermekeimnek) 82. Diary for My Loves (Napló Szerelmeimnek) 87. Diary for My Father and Mother (Napló Apamnak, Anyammnak) 90. Foetus (A Magzat) (co-w, d) 94, etc.

Metalious, Grace (1924–1964).
American novelist who hit the best-seller list with *Peyton Place*.

¶ If I'm a lousy writer, then a lot of people have got lousy taste. – G.M.

Metaxas, George (1899–1950).
Romanian character actor in occasional American films.

Swing Time 37. The Mask of Dimitrios 44. Scotland Yard Investigator 48, etc.

Methot, Mayo (1904–1951).
American actress who is best remembered for her stormy marriage with Humphrey Bogart.

Corsair 31. The Mind Reader 33. Jimmy the Gent 33. Side Streets 34. Dr Socrates 35. Mr Deeds Goes to Town 36. Marked Woman 37. The Sisters 38. Unexpected Father 39. Brother Rat and a Baby 40, etc.

Metrano, Art (1937–   ).
Chubby American character actor.

Cheaper to Keep Her 80. How to Beat the High Cost of Living 80. Going Ape 81. Breathless 83. Teachers 84. Malibu Express 85. Police Academy 2: Their First Assignment 85. Police Academy 3: Back in Training 86. Norma 89. Beverly Hills Bodysnatchers 89, etc.

TV series: Chicago Teddy Bears 71.

Metro-Goldwyn-Mayer.
For many years the undoubted leader of the industry, this famous American production company has lately suffered most from the lack of 'front office' control and the proliferation of independent productions: now that it doesn't own the racecourse, it can't seem to pick the winners. The company stems from Loew's Inc., an exhibiting concern which in 1920 bought into Metro Pictures, which then produced two enormous money-spinners, *The Four Horsemen of the Apocalypse* and *The Prisoner of Zenda*. In 1924 Metro was merged with the Goldwyn production company (though Samuel Goldwyn himself promptly opted out and set up independently); and the next year Louis B. Mayer Pictures joined the flourishing group to add further power. Mayer himself became studio head and remained the dominant production force for over twenty-five years. Ideas man and executive producer in the early years was young Irving Thalberg, whose artistic flair provided a necessary corrective to Mayer's proletarian tastes, and who, before his death in 1936, had established a lofty pattern with such successes as *Ben Hur*, *The Big Parade*, *Anna Christie*, *Grand Hotel*, *The Thin Man*, *David Copperfield* and *Mutiny on the Bounty*, and stars like Garbo, Gable, Beery, Lionel Barrymore, Joan Crawford, John Gilbert, Lon Chaney, William Powell, Jean Harlow, Spencer Tracy, Lewis Stone, Nelson Eddy, Jeanette MacDonald, Laurel and Hardy and the Marx Brothers. (MGM's motto was in fact 'more stars than there are in heaven . . .') The success story continued through the 40s with *Goodbye Mr Chips*, Greer Garson, *The Wizard Of Oz*, Judy Garland, the Hardy Family, Gene Kelly and Esther Williams. Such continuity of product is a thing of the past, but MGM keep its end up in the 60s and 70s with occasional big guns like *Dr Zhivago*, *Where Eagles Dare* and *Network*; while reissues of *Gone with the Wind*, which it did not produce, kept the image of Leo the Lion fresh on cinema screens. In the 70s MGM gave up movie-making to concentrate on its huge Las Vegas hotel. A comeback attempt failed, and it was taken over by United Artists and Ted Turner. The 80s were a troubled time for the new MGM-UA; production fell and many of the films were lacklustre. There were some successes: *My Favorite Year, Moonstruck, A Fish Called Wanda* (MGM), *Rainman* (UA) and *Rocky III* (UA) and its sequels, as well as some failures: *Yes Giorgio*, an attempt to make a star of opera singer Luciano Pavarotti, and *2010*, a poor sequel to *2001: A Space Odyssey*. At the beginning of the 90s, the situation worsened as MGM was taken over by Italian Giancarlo Paretti, of Pathé Communications, to become MGM-Pathé. But Paretti turned out to lack the necessary financial resources, and legal complications between him and his bankers were not sorted out until mid-1992, when the company was auctioned off to its biggest creditor, Credit Lyonnais of Paris. The dispute had held up production plans, but the future looked brighter as Alan Ladd Jnr, former president of Twentieth Century-Fox, became MGM's chairman and CEO. Ladd left in mid-1993, to be replaced by Frank Mancuso, former chairman and CEO of Paramount.

Books: 1991, *Fade Out* by Peter Bart details MGM's collapse in the 80s. 1992, *When the Lion Roars* by Peter Hay. *The MGM Story* by John Douglas Eames is an excellent illustrated film-by-film history of the studio 1924–89.

¶ Beautiful pictures for beautiful people. – *Louis B. Mayer*

MGM was my mother and father, mentor and guide, my all-powerful and benevolent crutch. – *June Allyson*

Mayer's Ganz Mispochen (Mayer's whole family). – *Anon*

More stars than there are in the heavens. – *publicity slogan coined by Howard Dietz*

Metty, Russell (1906–1978).
American cinematographer.

Sylvia Scarlett 35. Bringing Up Baby 38. Music in Manhattan 44. The Story of G.I. Joe 45. *The Stranger* 45. Ivy 47. All My Sons 48. We Were Strangers 49. Magnificent Obsession 54. Man without a Star 55. *Miracle in the Rain* 56. Written on the Wind 56. Man with a Thousand Faces 57. A Time to Love and a Time to Die 58. The Misfits 60. *Spartacus* (AA) 61. The Art of Love 65. The War Lord 65. Madame X 66. The Appaloosa 66. The Secret War of Harry Frigg 67. Madigan 68. Eye of the Cat 69. The Omega Man 71. Ben 72, many others.

Metzger, Radley (1930–   ).
American director.

Dark Odyssey 61. The Dirty Girls 64. Carmen Baby 67. Therese and Isabelle 68. Camille 2000 69. The Lickerish Quartet 70. Little Mother 72. Score 73. Naked Came the Stranger 75. The Opening of Misty Beethoven 76. The Cat and the Canary 78. The Tale of Tiffany Lust (d as Henry Paris) 81. The Princess and the Call Girl 84, etc.

Metzner, Erno (1892–   ).
Hungarian art director in the silent German cinema.

Sumurun 20. The Loves of Pharaoh 21. Salome 22. Old Heidelberg 23. Secrets of a Soul 26. The White Hell of Pitz Palu 29. Diary of a Lost Girl 29. Westfront 1918 30. Kameradschaft 31. L'Atlantide 32. Chu Chin Chow (GB) 34. It Happened Tomorrow (US) 44, etc.

Meurisse, Paul (1912–1979).
French general-purpose actor.

Montemartre sur Seine 41. Marie la Misère 45. Diabolique 54. La Tête contre les Murs 58. Lunch on the Grass 59. La Vérité 60, etc.

Mexican Spitfire.

A series of American second-feature comedies, concerning a young businessman (Donald Woods) with a temperamental wife (Lupe Velez), a scheming uncle, and a drunken English client, both played by Leon Errol. The films were only tolerably well made, but always managed a hectic finale of impersonation and mistaken identity which allowed full play to Errol's jerky convulsions.

The Girl from Mexico 39. Mexican Spitfire 39. Mexican Spitfire Out West 40. Mexican Spitfire's Baby 41. Mexican Spitfire at Sea 42. Mexican Spitfire Sees a Ghost 42. Mexican Spitfire's Elephant 42. Mexican Spitfire's Blessed Event 43.

Mexico

was a late starter in the feature film market, but made a few from about 1920, hampered by competition from Hollywood, which also plundered most of its best actors. The late 30s saw an improvement, with Emilio Fernandez as leading director, and in the 40s Buñuel settled there and made some small, stylish films. More recent productions have varied between cheap Hollywood-aping hokum and dour politically conscious social dramas. Mexican cinema has continued to stagger from crisis to crisis. Perhaps the most interesting director to emerge is Paul Leduc with his films *Reed: Mexico Insurgente* 73 and *Frida* 86, but his opportunities and output remain limited.

Meyer, Emile (1910–1987).

American character actor typically cast as crooked cop or prizefight manager; but sometimes an honest Joe.

The People Against O'Hara 51. Shane 53. The Blackboard Jungle 55. *Riot in Cell Block 11* 55. The Man with the Golden Arm 56. *Sweet Smell of Success* 57. Baby Face Nelson 57. Paths of Glory 58. The Fiend Who Walked the West 59. Young Jesse James 60. Taggart 64. Young Dillinger 65. Hostile Guns 67. More Dead Than Alive 70, etc.

Meyer, Nicholas (1945–).

American novelist whose *The Seven Per Cent Solution* became a best-seller and took him from publicity to direction.
■ The Seven Per Cent Solution (w) 77. Time after Time (wd) 79. Star Trek II: The Wrath of Khan (d) 82. The Day After (d) (TV) 83. Volunteers (d) 85. The Deceivers 88. Star Trek VI: The Undiscovered Country (co-w, d) 91.

Meyer, Russ (1923–).

American director of erotic films who broke briefly into the big time.

Biography: 1990, *Russ Meyer – the Life and Films* by David K. Frasier.
■ The Immoral Mr Teas 59. Eroticon 61. Eve and the Handyman 61. Naked Gals of the Golden West 62. Europe in the Raw 63. Heavenly Bodies 63. Laura 64. Mudhoney 65. Motor Psycho 65. Fanny Hill 65. Faster Pussycat Kill Kill 66. Mondo Topless 66. Good Morning and Goodbye 67. Common Law Cabin 67. Finders Keepers Lovers Weepers 68. *Vixen* 68. Cherry Harry and Raquel 69. Beyond the Valley of the Dolls 70. The Seven Minutes 71. Black Snake 73. The Supervixens 73. *Up* 76. Beneath the Valley of the Ultravixens 79. The Breast of Russ Meyer 87.

¶ I always had a tremendous interest in big tits. – *R.M.*
To him, nothing is obscene providing it is done in bad taste. – *R.M.*

Meyer, Torben (1884–1975).

German-American character actor who played many waiters, music teachers and petty officials, especially memorable in the films of Preston Sturges.

Roberta 35. The Prisoner of Zenda 37. Christmas in July 40. Edge of Darkness 42. The Miracle of Morgans Creek 43. Mad Wednesday 47, many others.

Michael, Gertrude (1911–1964).

American actress usually seen in secondary roles.

I'm No Angel 33. The Notorious Sophie Lang (lead) 37. Women in Bondage 44. Caged 50. Women's Prison 55. Twist All Night 62, etc.

Michael, Ralph (1907–) (Ralph Champion Shotter).

British character actor of stage and screen, often in stiff-upper-lip roles.

John Halifax Gentleman 38. San Demetrio, London 43. For Those in Peril 44. *Dead of Night* 45. Johnny Frenchman 45. The Captive Heart 46. Eureka Stockade 48. The Astonished Heart 49. The Sound Barrier 52. King's Rhapsody 56. Seven Waves Away 57. A Night to Remember 58. A Jolly Bad Fellow 64. House of Cards 68. Diary of a Mad Old Man 87, many others.

Michael Shayne.

The American private eye created by Brett Halliday in a string of 30s novels was a lightly shaded character at best, but sufficed for a number of 'B' features with Lloyd Nolan as star. In 1960 Richard Denning played the lead in a television series.

Michael Shayne, Private Detective 40. Sleepers West 41. Dressed to Kill 41. Blue, White and Perfect 41. The Man Who Wouldn't Die 42. Just off Broadway 42. Time to Kill (adapted from Raymond Chandler's The High Window, not from a Halliday original) 42.

Later, Hugh Beaumont took over the role in some forgettable low-budget mysteries:

Murder Is My Business 46. Larceny in Her Heart 46. Blonde for a Day 46. Three on a Ticket 47. Too Many Winners 47.

Michaels, Beverly (1927–).

American leading lady of sultry dramas in the early 50s.

East Side West Side 49. Pick Up 51. Wicked Woman 53. Crashout 55, etc.

Michaels, Dolores (1930–).

American leading lady of the late 50s; retired early.

The Wayward Bus 57. April Love 57. Fraulein 58. Warlock 59. Five Gates to Hell 59. One Foot in Hell 60. The Battle at Bloody Beach 61. Wizards of the Lost Kingdom 85, etc.

Micheaux, Oscar (1884–1951).

American independent producer, director and author. A pioneer of black cinema, working outside the system and aiming his films at a ghetto audience, he began in the silent era and continued to produce and direct more than 30 feature films until the beginning of the 40s. Few have survived.

Michelet, Michel (1899–).

Russian-born French composer.

Voice in the Wind 44. The Hairy Ape 44. Diary of a Chambermaid 46. Siren of Atlantis 46. Outpost in Morocco 49. Fort Algiers 53. Captain Sinbad 63.

Michell, Keith (1926–).

Australian leading man, on British stage and screen from the mid-50s.

■ True as a Turtle 57. Dangerous Exile 57. The Gypsy and the Gentleman 58. *The Hellfire Club* 61. All Night Long 62. Seven Seas to Calais 63. Prudence and the Pill 68. House of Cards 68. The Executioner 70. *Henry VIII and His Six Wives* 72. Moments 73. The Story of Jacob and Joseph (TV) 74. The Story of David 76. The Day Christ Died (TV) 79. Grendel Grendel Grendel 82. My Brother Tom (TV) 87. The Deceivers 88.

Michener, James A. (1907–).

American adventure-epic novelist. Works filmed include: *South Pacific, Return to Paradise, The Bridges at Toko Ri, Sayonara, Hawaii.*

Mickey Mouse.

Walt Disney's most famous cartoon character began in the 20s as Mortimer Mouse. By the early 30s his outlines had been simplified and he was perhaps the most certain box-office lure in the world. His voice was supplied by Disney himself (later by Jim MacDonald and Wayne Allwine); his finest hour, perhaps, was in the 'Sorcerer's Apprentice' segment of *Fantasia* 40.

¶ The best known and most popular international figure of his day. – *New York Times*, 1935

Middleton, Charles (1874–1949).

American character actor usually in villainous roles; especially remembered as Ming the Merciless in the Flash Gordon serials.

Mystery Ranch 32. Mrs Wiggs of the Cabbage Patch 34. Kentucky 39. The Grapes of Wrath 40. Our Vines Have Tender Grapes 45. The Black Arrow 49, many others.

Middleton, Guy (1906–1973) (Guy Middleton-Powell).

Hearty-type British light character actor, in films as amiable idiot or gay Lothario from the early 30s after Stock Exchange career.

A Woman Alone 32. Fame 34. *Keep Fit* 37. French Without Tears 39. Dangerous Moonlight 40. The Demi-Paradise 43. Champagne Charlie 44. The Rake's Progress 45. The Captive Heart 46. One Night with You 48. The Happiest Days of Your Life 49. Never Look Back 52. Albert RN 53. The Belles of St Trinian's 54. The Passionate Summer 58. The Waltz of the Toreadors 62. The Magic Christian 70, etc.

Middleton, Noelle (1926–).

British leading lady of the 50s.

Carrington V.C. 55. John and Julie 55. Three Men in a Boat 56. The Iron Petticoat 56. The Vicious Circle 57, etc.

Middleton, Ray (1908–1984).

American actor-singer.

Gangs of Chicago 40. Lady For A Night 41. The Girl From Alaska 42. I Dream of Jeannie 52. Jubilee Trail 54. The Road To Denver 55, etc.

Middleton, Robert (1911–1977) (Samuel G. Messer).

Weighty American character actor usually cast as villain.

The Silver Chalice 55. The Big Combo 55. The Desperate Hours 55. The Court Jester 55. The Friendly Persuasion 56. The Tarnished Angels 58. Career 59. Gold of the Seven Saints 61. For Those Who Think Young 64. Big Hand for a Little Lady 66. Which Way to the Front? 71, many others.

TV series: The Monroes 66–67.

Midkiff, Dale (1959–).

American leading actor.

Streetwalkin' 85. Nightmare Weekend 86. Elvis and Me (as Elvis Presley) (TV) 88. Pet Sematary 89. Blackmail (TV) 91. Love Potion #9 92, etc.

TV series: Dream Street 89.

Midler, Bette (1945–).

Diminutive but brassy and very vulgar American entertainer.

Autobiography: 1980, *A View from a Broad*.

■ Hawaii 65. The Rose (AAN) 79. Divine Madness (concert) 80. Jinxed 82. Down and Out in Beverly Hills 85. Ruthless People 86. Outrageous Fortune 87. Big Business 88. Oliver & Company (voice) 88. Beaches 88. Stella 90. Scenes from a Mall 91. For the Boys (& p) (AAN) 91. Hocus Pocus 93. Gypsy (TV) 93.

¶ I wouldn't say I invented tack, but I definitely brought it to its present high popularity.
– *B.M.*

Underneath all this drag I'm really a librarian, you know. – *B.M.*

In Hawaii I was the chief chunker in a pineapple canning factory. I used to come home smelling like a compote. – *B.M.*

I do have my standards. They're low, but I have them. – *B.M.*

A Midsummer Night's Dream.

Shakespeare's fairy play was filmed in America in 1929 by J. Stuart Blackton, starring Maurice Costello, and there is a Czech puppet version by Jiri Trnka. But the best-known version is Max Reinhardt's lavish production for Warner in 1935, directed by Reinhardt and William Dieterle, with a surprising cast including James Cagney as Bottom, Mickey Rooney as Puck, Hugh Herbert, Arthur Treacher, Dick Powell, Anita Louise, Victor Jory, and Olivia de Havilland. Peter Hall's muddy version of 1968, aimed primarily at American television, lacked magic.

Mifune, Toshiro (1920–).

Versatile Japanese actor with a ferocious style, seen in many films by Kurosawa and others.

The Drunken Angel 48. The Stray Dog 49. *Rashomon* 50. *Seven Samurai* 54. The Lower Depths 57. *Throne of Blood* 57. The Hidden Fortress 58. The Bad Sleep Well 59. *Yojimbo* 61. Red Beard 64. The Lost World of Sinbad 64. Grand Prix (US) 66. Rebellion 67. Hell in the Pacific (US) 68. Red Sun 71. Paper Tiger 75. Midway 76. 1941 79. Winter Kills 79. The Bushido Blade 80. Inchon 80. The Challenge 82. Inchon 82. Seiha 84. Taketori Monogatari 87. Shogun Mayeda 90. Shadow of the Wolf 93, etc.

AS DIRECTOR: Legacy of the Five Hundred Thousand 63.

Mighty Mouse.

Rodent superhero of Terrytoons cartoons from the 40s to the 60s and known in his earliest cartoons as Super Mouse. His voice was supplied by Tom Morrison.

The Mouse of Tomorrow 42. Down with Cats 43. Wreck of Hesperus 44. Mighty Mouse and the Pirates 45. Svengali's Cat 46. Swiss Cheese Family Robinson 47. The Catnip Gang 49. A Cat's Tale 51. When Mousehood Was in Flower 53. Outer Space Visitor 59. Cat Alarm 61, etc.

Mihalka, George (1952–).

Hungarian-born director, resident in Canada.

My Bloody Valentine 81. Pick-up Summer 81. Scandale 82. Eternal Evil 87. Office Party 88. La Florida 93, etc.

Mike Hammer.

The tough, immoral private eye created by Mickey Spillane (qv for list of films).

Mikhalkov, Nikita (1945–) (Nikita Mikhalkov-Konchalovsky).

Russian director and screenwriter, a former actor. He is the brother of director Andrei Konchalovsky. *Burnt by the Sun* shared the Grand Jury prize at the 1994 Cannes Film Festival.

The Red Tent (a) 71. A Slave of Love 76. An Unfinished Piece for Mechanical Piano 76. Oblomov 79. Family Relations (Rodnia) 83. Station for Two (Vokzal Dla Dvoish) 83. Without Witnesses (Bez Svidetelei) 83. Dark Eyes (Oci Ciornie) 87. Urga 90. Anna 6–18 94. Burnt by the Sun (a, wd) 94, etc.

Milchan, Arnon (1944–).

Israeli-born producer in Hollywood.

Black Joy 77. The Medusa Touch 78. The King of Comedy 83. Once upon a Time in America 84. Brazil 85. Man on Fire 86. Legend 86. Who's Harry Crumb? 89. The War of the Roses 89. The Adventures of Baron Munchausen 89. Pretty Woman 90. The Power of One 91. Memoirs of an Invisible Man 91. The Mambo Kings 92. Made in America 93. Second Best 93. The New Age 93. Striking Distance 93. Six Degrees of Separation 93. The Client 94, etc.

Miles, Sir Bernard (1907–1991) (Lord Miles).

British actor specializing in slow-speaking country-folk and other ruminating types. An ex-schoolmaster, on stage from 1930. Founder of London's Mermaid Theatre (1959).

Channel Crossing 32. Quiet Wedding 40. *In Which We Serve* 42. Tawny Pipit (& co-w and d) 44. Carnival 46. *Great Expectations* 46. Nicholas Nickleby 47. The Guinea Pig 48. Chance of a Lifetime (& wd, p) 49. Never Let Me Go 53. The Man Who Knew Too Much 56. Moby Dick 56. *The Smallest Show on Earth* 57. Tom Thumb 58. Sapphire 59. *Heavens Above* 63. Run Wild Run Free 69, etc.

Miles, Christopher (1939–).

British director, brother of Sarah Miles.

■ Six-sided Triangle 64. Up Jumped a Swagman 65. The Virgin and the Gypsy 70. Time for Loving 71. The Maids 74. That Lucky Touch 75. Alternative 3 (TV) 78. Priest of Love 81. Daley's Decathlon (TV) 82. The Marathon (TV) 83. Aphrodisiac (TV) 84. Lord Elgin and Some Stones of No Value (TV) 85.

Miles, Joanna (1949–).

American leading lady of the 70s.

Butterfield 8 60. Born Innocent 74. Bug 75. The Ultimate Warrior 75. Cross Creek 83. Blackout 88. Right to Die (TV) 87. Rosencrantz and Guildenstern Are Dead 91. Judge Dredd 95, etc.

Miles, Peter (1938–) (Gerald Perreau).

American child actor of the 40s, brother of Gigi Perreau. As Richard Miles, he later became a writer, notably of *That Cold Day in the Park* (1968) based on his own novel.

Passage to Marseilles 44. The Red Pony 48. Roseanna McCoy 50. Quo Vadis 51, etc.

Miles, Sarah (1941–).

Vivacious British leading actress; married to Robert Bolt.

Autobiography: 1993, *A Right Royal Bastard*.

■ Term of Trial 62. The Servant 63. The Ceremony 64. Those Magnificent Men in Their Flying Machines 65. I Was Happy Here 65. Blow Up 66. *Ryan's Daughter* (AAN) 70. *Lady Caroline Lamb* 72.

The Hireling 73. The Man Who Loved Cat Dancing 73. Great Expectations (TV) 75. Dynasty (TV) 76. The Sailor Who Fell from Grace with the Sea 76. The Big Sleep 78. Priest of Love 81. Venom 82. Ordeal by Innocence 84. Steaming 84. Harem (TV) 86. Hope and Glory 87. White Mischief 87. The Touch 92.

¶ I have been mocked and ridiculed all my life. – *S.M.*

Miles, Sylvia (1926–).

American character actress.

Parrish 61. Midnight Cowboy (AAN) 69. *Heat* 72. Farewell My Lovely (AAN) 75. 92 in the Shade 75. The Great Scout and Cathouse Thursday 76. The Sentinel 77. Zero to Sixty 78. Evil Under the Sun 82. Critical Condition 87. Wall Street 87. Crossing Delancey 88. She-Devil 89, etc.

Miles, Vera (1929–) (Vera Ralston).

Dependable American leading lady who came from TV to films.

For Men Only (debut) 52. Charge at Feather River 54. 23 Paces to Baker Street 55. *The Searchers* 56. *The Wrong Man* 57. The FBI Story 59. *Psycho* 60. A Tiger Walks 63. Those Calloways 65. Follow Me, Boys 66. The Spirit is Willing 66. Hell-fighters 68. The Castaway Cowboy 74. One Little Indian 75. Twilight's Last Gleaming 76. The Thoroughbreds 77. Psycho II 83. Into the Night 84. The Hijacking of the Achille Lauro (TV) 89, many others.

Milestone, Lewis (1895–1980) (Levis Milstein).

Veteran American director whose later films never quite matched up to his early achievements. Former editor, in Hollywood from 1918.

■ Seven Sinners 25. The Cave Man 26. The New Klondike 26. *Two Arabian Knights* (AA) 27. The Garden of Eden 28. The Racket 28. New York Nights 29. *All Quiet on the Western Front* (AA) 30. *The Front Page* (AAN) 31. Rain 32. *Hallelujah I'm a Bum* 33. The Captain Hates the Sea 34. Paris in Spring 35. Anything Goes 36. *The General Died at Dawn* 36. Of Mice and Men 39. Night of Nights 40. Lucky Partners 40. My Life with Caroline (& p) 41. Edge of Darkness 43. North Star 43. The Purple Heart 44. The Strange Love of Martha Ivers 46. *A Walk in the Sun* 46. No Minor Vices 47. Arch of Triumph 48. The Red Pony 48. Halls of Montezuma 51. Kangaroo 52. Les Misérables 52. Melba 53. They Who Dare (GB) 54. The Widow (It.) 55. Pork Chop Hill 59. Ocean's Eleven 61. Mutiny on the Bounty 62.

✪ For a handful of seminal films of the 30s and for devising a fast crabwise tracking shot which was much imitated. *All Quiet on the Western Front*.

¶ His professionalism is as unyielding as it is meaningless. – *Andrew Sarris, 1968*

Milford, Gene (1903–1992).

American editor.

Ladies Must Play 30. One Night of Love (AAN) 34. Lost Horizon (AA) 37. On the Waterfront (AA) 54. Inchon 82, many others.

Milford, Penelope (1949–).

American actress.

Man on a Swing 75. Valentino 77. Coming Home (AAN) 78. The Last Word 79. Endless Love 81. Take This Job and Shove It 81. The Golden Seal 83. Blood Link 86. Heathers 89. Cold Justice 89, etc.

Milhollin, James (1920–1993).
Crumple-faced American character comedian, mostly on TV.

No Time for Sergeants 58. Bon Voyage 62, etc.
TV series: *Grindl* 63.

Milian, Tomas (1937–).
Cuban leading man in Italian action movies, now in the US.

The Bounty Killer 66. Face to Face 67. The Big Gundown 67. Run Man Run 68. Django Kill 68. Apache 70. The Companeros 70. The Counsellor 74. La Luna 78. Winter Kills 79. The Day Christ Died (TV) 79. Salome 85. Cat Chaser 89. Havana 90. Nails 92. Marilyn and Bobby: Her Final Affair (TV) 94. The Burning Season (TV) 94, etc.
TV series: Frannie's Turn 92.

Milius, John (1944–).
American director.

■ The Devil's Eight (w only) 68. Evel Knievel (w only) 72. Jeremiah Johnson (w only) 72. Judge Roy Bean (w only) 73. Magnum Force (co-w only) 73. *Dillinger* (& w) 73. The Wind and the Lion (& w) 75. Big Wednesday (& w) 78. Apocalypse Now (co-w) (AAN) 79. Conan the Barbarian (co-w, d) 82. Red Dawn (& co-w) 84. Farewell to the King (wd) 89. Flight of the Intruder (wd) 91. Geronimo: An American Legend (co-w, story) 93. Clear and Present Danger (co-w) 94.

¶ It was always my ambition to be a barbarian when I grew up. – *J.M.*

Miljan, John (1893–1960).
American character actor with stage experience; often played the suave villain.

Love Letters 23. The Amateur Gentleman 26. The Painted Lady 29. The Ghost Walks 35. Double Cross 41. The Merry Monahans 44. The Killers 46. Samson and Delilah 50. Pirates of Tripoli 55, etc.

Milland, Ray (1905–1986) (Reginald Truscott-Jones). Welsh-born light leading man of ready smile and equable disposition; carved a pleasant niche for himself in Hollywood in the 30s, and later surprised many by becoming an actor and director of some repute before stepping on the inevitable downhill slope.

Autobiography: 1976, *Wide-Eyed in Babylon*.
■ The Plaything (GB) 29. The Flying Scotsman (GB) 29. The Informer 30. Passion Flower 30. Goodwin Sands 30. Bachelor Father 31. Just a Gigolo 31. Bought 31. Ambassador Bill 31. Blonde Crazy 31. Polly of the Circus 31. The Man Who Played God 32. Payment Deferred 32. This is the Life (GB) 33. Orders is Orders (GB) 33. Bolero 34. We're Not Dressing 34. Many Happy Returns 34. Menace 34. Charlie Chan in London 34. The Gilded Lily 35. One Hour Late 35. Four Hours to Kill 35. The Glass Key 35. Alias Mary Dow 35. Next Time We Love 36. The Return of Sophie Lang 36. *The Jungle Princess* 36. The Big Broadcast of 1937. Three Smart Girls 37. Wings Over Honolulu 37. Easy Living 37. Ebb Tide 37. Wise Girl 37. Bulldog Drummond Escapes 37. Her Jungle Love 38. Tropic Holiday 38. Men with Wings 38. Say It In French 38. Hotel Imperial 39. Beau Geste 39. Everything Happens at Night 39. *French Without Tears* (GB) 39. Irene 40. The Doctor Takes a Wife 40. Untamed 40. *Arise My Love* 41. I Wanted Wings 41. Skylark 41. The Lady Has Plans 42. Are Husbands Necessary 42. The Major and the Minor 42. Reap the Wild Wind 42. Star Spangled Rhythm 42. Forever and a Day 43. The Crystal Ball 43. *The Uninvited* 44. Lady in the Dark 44. Till We Meet Again 44. *Ministry of Fear* 44. *The Lost Weekend* (AA) 45. Kitty 45. The Well Groomed Bride 46.

California 46. The Imperfect Lady 47. The Trouble with Women 47. Golden Earrings 47. Variety Girl 47. The Big Clock 48. So Evil My Love 48. Sealed Verdict 48. *Alias Nick Beal* 49. It Happens Every Spring 49. A Woman of Distinction 50. A Life of Her Own 50. Copper Canyon 50. Circle of Danger (GB) 51. Night into Morning 51. Rhubarb 51. Close to My Heart 51. Bugles in the Afternoon 52. Something to Live For 52. *The Thief* 52. Jamaica Run 53. Let's Do It Again 53. *Dial M for Murder* 54. A Man Alone (& d) 55. The Girl in the Red Velvet Swing 55. Lisbon (& d) 56. Three Brave Men 57. The River's Edge 57. The Safecracker (& d) (GB) 58. High Flight (GB) 58. The Premature Burial 62. Panic in Year Zero (& d) 62. The Man with X-Ray Eyes 63. The Confession 65. Hostile Witness (& d) (GB) 68. River of Gold (TV) 69. Daughter of the Mind (TV) 69. Love Story 70. Company of Killers (TV) 70. Black Noon (TV) 71. Embassy 72. The Thing with Two Heads 72. Frogs 72. Terror in the Wax Museum 73. The House in Nightmare Park (GB) 73. Gold 74. The Student Connection 74. The Swiss Conspiracy 75. The Dead Don't Die 75. Look What Happened to Rosemary's Baby (TV) 76. Oil 76. Ellery Queen (TV) 76. Escape to Witch Mountain 76. Rich Man Poor Man (TV) 76. The Last Tycoon 76. Aces High 76. Cruise into Terror (TV) 77. Mayday at 40,000 Feet (TV) 77. Slaves 77. Testimony of Two Men (TV) 77. The Uncanny 77. Blackout 78. The Darker Side of Terror (TV) 79. Oliver's Story 79. Game for Vultures 79. The Attic 79. Cave In (TV) 79. Survival Run 80. Our Family Business (TV) 81. The Royal Romance of Charles and Diana (TV) 82. Starflight One (TV) 82. The Masks of Death (TV) 84.

TV series: Meet Mr McNutley 53. Markham 59.
✪ For his imperturbable cheerfulness, and for briefly demonstrating that with a different start he might have been an actor or director of stature. *Arise My Love.*

Millar, Gavin (1938–).
British director and film buff.

Cream in My Coffee (TV) 80. Dreamchild 85. Scoop (TV) 87. Tidy Endings (TV) 88. The Most Dangerous Man in the World 88. Danny, the Champion of the World 89. The Dwelling Place (TV) 94, etc.

Millar, Stuart (1929–).
American producer.

The Young Stranger 57. Stage Struck 58. The Young Doctors 61. I Could Go On Singing 63. The Best Man 64. Paper Lion 68. When the Legends Die (& d) 72. Rooster Cogburn (d only) 75. Vital Signs (d) (TV) 86. The O'Connors (d) (TV) 89, etc.

Miller, Alice Duer (1874–1942).
American writer who collaborated on several film scripts and whose poem 'The White Cliffs of Dover' was filmed in 1944.

Manslaughter 30. Honey 30. And One Was Beautiful 40. Gowns by Roberta (as Roberta) 35 and (as Lovely to Look At) 52.

Miller, Ann (1919–) (Lucy Ann Collier).
Long-legged American dancer, in films from mid-30s.

Autobiography: 1974, *Miller's High Life.*
New Faces of 1937. *You Can't Take It With You* 38. Go West, Young Lady 41. *Reveille with Beverly* 43. Jam Session 44. Eve Knew Her Apples 45. Easter Parade 48. *On the Town* 49. Two Tickets to Broadway 51. *Kiss Me Kate* 53. The Opposite Sex 56, etc.

¶ I have worked like a dog all my life, honey. Dancing, as Fred Astaire said, is next to ditch-

digging. You sweat and you slave and the audience doesn't think you have a brain in your head.
– *A.M. in 1979 interview*

Miller, Arthur (1915–).
American playwright whose work has been adapted for the cinema. Married to Marilyn Monroe 1956–61.

All My Sons 48. Death of a Salesman 52. The Witches of Salem 57. A View from the Bridge 62. After the Fall 69. The Price 69. An Enemy of the People 78. All My Sons (TV) 87. Clara (TV) 91, etc.
SCREENPLAYS: The Story of G.I. Joe 45. The Misfits 60. The Hook 75. Everybody Wins 90.

Miller, Arthur (1895–1970).
Distinguished American cinematographer.

SELECTED SILENT FILMS: At Bay 15. The Iron Heart 17. The Profiteers 19. His House in Order 20. Kick In 22. The Cheat 23. The Coming of Amos 24. The Clinging Vine 26. The Fighting Eagle 28. The Spieler 29, etc.

■ SOUND FILMS: Oh Yeah 30. Sailor's Holiday 30. Strange Cargo 30. The Lady of Scandal 30. Officer O'Brien 30. The Truth about Youth 30. Behind the Make Up 30. Father's Son 30. Bad Company 31. Panama Flo 32. Big Shot 32. The Young Bride 32. Breach of Promise 32. Me and My Gal 32. Okay America 32. Sailor's Luck 33. Hold Me Tight 33. The Man Who Dared 33. The Last Trail 33. The Mad Game 33. My Weakness 33. Bottoms Up 34. Ever Since Eve 34. Handy Andy 34. Love Time 34. The White Parade 34. Bright Eyes 34. The Little Colonel 35. It's a Small World 35. Black Sheep 35. Welcome Home 35. Paddy O'Day 35. White Fang 36. 36 Hours to Kill 36. Pigskin Parade 36. Stowaway 36. *Wee Willie Winkie* 37. Heidi 37. The Baroness and the Butler 38. Rebecca of Sunnybrook Farm 38. Little Miss Broadway 38. Submarine Patrol 38. *The Little Princess* 39. Susannah of the Mounties 39. Here I Am a Stranger 39. *The Rains Came* 39. *The Blue Bird* 40. Johnny Apollo 40. On Their Own 40. *The Mark of Zorro* 40. Brigham Young 40. Tobacco Road 41. The Men in Her Life 41. Man Hunt 41. *How Green was My Valley* (AA) 41. *This Above All* 42. Iceland 42. The Moon Is Down 43. The Immortal Sergeant 43. The Ox Bow Incident 43. *The Song of Bernadette* (AA) 43. The Purple Heart 44. The Keys of the Kingdom 45. A Royal Scandal 45. Dragonwyck 46. *Anna and the King of Siam* 46. The Razor's Edge 46. Gentleman's Agreement 47. The Walls of Jericho 48. A Letter to Three Wives 49. Whirlpool 49. *The Gunfighter* 50. The Prowler 51.
✪ For a long succession of Hollywood's most lustrous black-and-white images. *The Rains Came.*

¶ The basic principle I have had in making pictures was to make them look like real life, and then emphasise the visuals slightly. – *A.M.*

I was never a soft focus man – I liked crisp, sharp, solid images. – *A.M.*

Miller, Claude (1942–).
French director and screenwriter who also worked as a producer on many of François Truffaut's films.

Juliet dans Paris 67. La Question Ordinaire 70. Camille ou la Comédie Catastrophique 71. La Meilleure Façon de Marcher 76. Dîtes-lui Que Je l'Aime 77. Garde à Vue 81. Mortelle Randonnée 83. L'Effrontée 85. La Petite Voleuse 88. L'Accompagnatrice 92. The Smile (Le Sourire) 94, etc.

Miller, Colleen (1932–).
American leading lady.

The Las Vegas Story 52. The Purple Mask 55.

Man with a Shadow 57. Step Down to Terror 59. Gunfight at Comanche Creek 63, etc.

Miller, Denny (1934–).
Athletic American actor who had a shot at playing Tarzan.

Tarzan the Ape Man 59. Love in a Goldfish Bowl 61. The Party 68. Buck and the Preacher 72. The Gravy Train 74. The Norsemen 78, etc.

TV series: Wagon Train 61–64. Mona McCluskey 65–66.

Miller, David (1909–1992).
American director, formerly editor, in Hollywood from 1930.

Billy the Kid 41. Sunday Punch 42. Flying Tigers 43. Top o' the Morning 49. Love Happy 50. Our Very Own 51. Saturday's Hero 52. *Sudden Fear* 53. Beautiful Stranger 54. Diane 55. The Opposite Sex 56. The Story of Esther Costello 57. Happy Anniversary 59. Midnight Lace 60. Back Street 61. *Lonely Are the Brave* 62. Captain Newman 63. Hammerhead (GB) 68. Hail Hero 69. Executive Action 73. Bittersweet Love 76, etc.

Miller, Dick (1928–).
American actor, a regular in the films of Roger Corman and in other low-budget horror movies.

Apache Woman 55. The Undead 56. Not of This Earth 57. Thunder over Hawaii 57. A Bucket of Blood 59. The Terror 63. Ski Party 65. The Dirty Dozen 67. The Grissom Gang 71. Ulzana's Raid 72. Big Bad Mama 74. Hustle 75. Cannonball 76. Piranha 78. Used Cars 80. Heartbeeps 81. The Howling 81. Heart Like a Wheel 83. Gremlins 84. After Hours 85. Explorers 85. Chopping Mall 86. Night of the Creeps 86. Project X 87. Innerspace 87. Far from Home 89. Gremlins 2: The New Batch 90. Evil Toons 91. The Stalker 92. Matinee 93. Batman: Mask of the Phantasm (voice) 94. Mona Must Die 94, etc.

Miller, George (1943–).
Scottish-born director, in Australia as a child, from television.

The Man from Snowy River 81. The Aviator 84. Anzacs (TV) 85. Cool Change 86. Les Patterson Saves the World 87. The Far Country (TV) 87. The Christmas Visitor (TV) 87. Neverending Story II 90. Frozen Assets (US) 91. Gross Misconduct 93. Andre 94, etc.

Miller, George (1945–).
Australian director, a former doctor.
■ Mad Max 79. Mad Max 2: The Road Warrior 81. Twilight Zone (part) 83. Mad Max Beyond Thunderdome 85. The Witches of Eastwick 87. Lorenzo's Oil 92.

Miller, Glenn (1904–1944).
American bandleader and composer, whose 'new sound' was immensely popular during World War II.

Appeared in *Orchestra Wives* 42. *Sun Valley Serenade* 42. Was impersonated by James Stewart in *The Glenn Miller Story* 53.

Miller, Henry (1891–1980).
American novelist and writer whose autobiographical and sexually explicit novels were banned in the 30s. His life, and his triangular relationship with his wife June and writer Anais Nin, have been the subject of two films: *Henry and June* 89 and *The Room of Words* 90. Of his novels, *The Tropic of Cancer* was filmed in 1969 and *Quiet Days in Clichy* in 1974 and 1990.

Miller, Jason (1939–).
American playwright who turned actor.

The Exorcist (AAN) 74. The Nickel Ride 76. A Home of Our Own (TV) 76. F. Scott Fitzgerald in Hollywood (TV) 76. The Dain Curse (TV) 78. The Devil's Advocate 79. The Ninth Configuration 80. That Championship Season (directing his own play) 82. A Touch of Scandal (TV) 84. The Exorcist III 90. Rudy 93, etc.

Miller, Jonathan (1934–).
British satirist, occasionally director.
■ One Way Pendulum (a only) 65. Alice in Wonderland (TV) 67. Take A Girl Like You 70.

Miller, Mandy (1944–).
British child star.

The Man in the White Suit 51. *Mandy* 52. Dance Little Lady 54. A Child in the House 56. The Secret 57. The Snorkel 58, etc.

Miller, Marilyn (1898–1936) (Mary Ellen Reynolds).
American dancing and singing star of Broadway musicals in the 20s. She was impersonated by June Haver in a biopic, *Look for the Silver Lining* 49, and by Judy Garland in *Till the Clouds Roll By* 46.

Sally 30. Sunny 31. Her Majesty Love 32.

Miller, Martin (1899–1969) (Rudolph Muller).
Czechoslovakian character actor active in Britain from the late 30s.

Squadron Leader X 40. The Huggetts Abroad 51. Front Page Story 53. Libel 60. 55 Days at Peking 62. Children of the Damned 64. Up Jumped a Swagman 65, many others.

Miller, Marvin (1913–1985) (M. Mueller).
American tough-guy supporting actor who represented menaces of various nations.

Johnny Angel 45. Intrigue 47. The High Window 47. Off Limits 53. The Shanghai Story 54, etc.

TV series: The Millionaire 55–60.

Miller, Max (1895–1963) (Harold Sargent).
Ribald British music-hall comedian ('the Cheeky Chappie'). Starred in several vehicles during the 30s but his style and material had to be considerably toned down for the screen.
■ *The Good Companions* 32. Channel Crossing 32. Friday the Thirteenth 33. Princess Charming 34. Things Are Looking Up 35. *Educated Evans* 36. Get Off My Foot 36. Take It From Me 37. Don't Get Me Wrong 37. Thank Evans 38. Everything Happens to Me 39. The Good Old Days 39. Hoots Mon 40. Asking for Trouble 43.

Miller, Patsy Ruth (1905–).
American leading lady of the silent screen, former juvenile player.

Autobiography: 1988, *My Hollywood – When Both of Us Were Young*.

Judgment 18. Camille 21. The Hunchback of Notre Dame 23. Lorraine of the Lions 24. Why Girls Go Back Home 27. The Hottentot 28. Lonely Wives 31. Quebec 51, etc.

Miller, Penelope Ann (1964–).
American actress.

Adventures in Babysitting (aka A Night on the Town) 87. Big Top Pee-Wee 88. Biloxi Blues 88. Miles from Home 88. Dead-Bang 89. Awakenings 90. Downtown 90. The Freshman 90. Kindergarten Cop 90. Other People's Money 91. Year of the Comet 92. The Gun in Betty Lou's Handbag 92. Chaplin 92. Carlito's Way 93. The Shadow 94, etc.

Miller, Robert Ellis (1927–).
American director, from TV.
■ Any Wednesday 66. Sweet November 68. The Heart Is a Lonely Hunter 68. The Buttercup Chair 70. The Girl from Petrovka 74. The Baltimore Bullet 80. Reuben, Reuben 83. Hawks 88. Brenda Starr 89. Bed and Breakfast 90. Triangle 92.

Miller, Seton I. (1902–1974).
American silent actor (*Brown of Harvard* 26, etc.) who turned into one of Hollywood's most prolific screenwriters.

Dawn Patrol 30. The Criminal Code (AAN) 31. *Scarface* 32. G-Men 35. *The Adventures of Robin Hood* 38. The Sea Hawk 40. *Here Comes Mr Jordan* (AA) 41. The Black Swan 42. The Ministry of Fear 43. Two Years Before the Mast (& p) 46. Istanbul 57, etc.

Miller, Walter C. (1892–1940).
American leading man of the D. W. Griffith company.

The Informer 12. A Beggar Prince of India 14. The Marble Heart 16. Thin Ice 19. The Tie That Binds 23. Manhattan Knights 28. Three Smart Girls 36. Johnny Apollo 40, many others.
~Not to be confused with W. Christie Miller (1843–1922) who played elderly roles for Griffith.

Millhauser, Bertram (1892–1958).
American screenwriter mainly engaged on second features, some of them better than average.

The Garden Murder Case 36. Sherlock Holmes in Washington 42 (and others in this series including Pearl of Death 44). The Invisible Man's Revenge 44. Patrick the Great 45. Walk a Crooked Mile 48. Tokyo Joe 48, etc.

Millican, James (1910–1955).
American general-purpose actor, often in low-budget westerns.

The Remarkable Andrew 42. Bring on the Girls 44. Hazard 47. Rogues' Regiment 48. Carson City 52. The Man from Laramie 55, etc.

Millichip, Roy (1930–).
British independent producer.

The Uncle 65. I Was Happy Here 66. A Nice Girl Like Me 69, etc.

Milligan, Spike (1918–).
Irish comedian and arch-goon of stage, TV and radio.

The Case of the Mukkinese Battlehorn 56. Watch Your Stern 60. Suspect 60. Invasion Quartet 61. Postman's Knock 62. The Magic Christian 70. Rentadick 72. Alice's Adventures in Wonderland 72. Adolf Hitler, My Part in His Downfall (& oa) 72. Digby, the Biggest Dog in the World 73. The Three Musketeers 74. The Great McGonagall 74. A Man About the House 76. The Last Remake of Beau Geste 77. The Life of Brian 79. Yellowbeard 83, etc.

TV series: Idiot's Weekly 56. A Show Called Fred 56. Son of Fred 57. Milligan at Large 61. Q5 69. Curry and Chips 69. Oh in Colour 72. Q6-Q9 75–80.

Mills, Donna (1947–).
American leading lady, mostly on TV.

The Incident 67. Play Misty for Me 71. Haunts of the Very Rich (TV) 72. Night of Terror (TV) 72. The Bait (TV) 73. Live Again Die Again (TV) 74. Who Is the Black Dahlia? (TV) 75. Smash-Up on Interstate Five (TV) 76. Curse of the Black Widow (TV) 76. The Hunted Lady (TV) 77. Superdome (TV) 78. Bare Essence (TV) 83. He's Not Your Son (TV) 84. False Arrest (TV) 91, etc.

Mills, Hayley (1946–).
British actress who shot to fame as a tomboy child; daughter of John Mills. She was married to director Roy Boulting (1971–76) and has a son by actor Leigh Lawson.
■ *Tiger Bay* 59. Pollyanna (US) (special AA as best child actress) 60. *The Parent Trap* (US) 61. Whistle Down the Wind 61. Summer Magic (US) 62. In Search of the Castaways 63. The Chalk Garden 64. The Moonspinners 65. The Truth about Spring 65. That Darn Cat 65. Sky West and Crooked 66. The Trouble with Angels 66. The Family Way 66. Pretty Polly 67. Twisted Nerve 68. Take a Girl Like You 70. Forbush and the Penguins 71. Endless Night 72. Deadly Strangers 75. What Changed Charley Farthing? 75. The Kingfisher Caper 75. The Flame Trees of Thika (TV) 81. Parent Trap II (TV) 86. Appointment with Death 88.

Mills, Hugh (c. 1913–1971).
British screenwriter.
Blanche Fury 47. Blackmailed (co-w) 50. Knave of Hearts 52. The House by the Lake 54. Prudence and the Pill 68, etc.

Mills, Sir John (1908–) (Lewis Ernest Mills).
Popular British leading actor with musical comedy experience; overcame short stature to become a useful stiff-upper-lip type in the 40s, and later a character actor of some versatility.
Autobiography: 1980, *Up in the Clouds, Gentlemen Please*.
■ The Midshipmaid 32. Britannia of Billingsgate 33. The Ghost Camera 33. River Wolves 34. A Political Party 34. *Those Were the Days* 34. The Lash 34. Blind Justice 34. Doctor's Orders 34. Royal Cavalcade 35. Forever England 35. Charing Cross Road 35. Car of Dreams 35. First Offence 36. Tudor Rose 36. OHMS 37. The Green Cockatoo 37. Goodbye Mr Chips 39. Old Bill and Son 40. *Cottage to Let* 41. The Black Sheep of Whitehall 41. The Big Blockade 42. The Young Mr Pitt 42. *In Which We Serve* 42. We Dive at Dawn 43. This Happy Breed 44. *Waterloo Road* 44. *The Way to the Stars* 45. *Great Expectations* 46. So Well Remembered 47. *The October Man* 47. Scott of the Antarctic 48. *The History of Mr Polly* (& p) 49. The Rocking Horse Winner 50. Morning Departure 50. Mr Denning Drives North 51. The Gentle Gunman 52. The Long Memory 52. *Hobson's Choice* 54. The Colditz Story 54. The End of the Affair 54. Above Us the Waves 55. Escapade 55. It's Great to Be Young 56. The Baby and the Battleship 56. War and Peace 56. Around the World in 80 Days 56. *Town On Trial* 57. Vicious Circle 57. Dunkirk 58. I Was Monty's Double 58. Ice Cold in Alex 58. *Tiger Bay* 59. Summer of the Seventeenth Doll 60. *Tunes of Glory* 60. *The Swiss Family Robinson* (US) 61. Flame in the Streets 61. The Singer Not the Song 61. The Valiant 62. Tiara Tahiti 62. The Chalk Garden 63. The Truth about Spring 64. Operation Crossbow 65. *Sky West and Crooked* (d only) 65. King Rat (US) 66. *The Wrong Box* 66. The Family Way 66. Africa Texas Style (US) 67. Chuka (US) 67. Oh What a Lovely War 69. Run Wild Run Free 69. Emma Hamilton (Ger.) 69. A Black Veil for Lisa 69. *Ryan's Daughter* (AA) 71. Dulcima 71. Young Winston 72. Lady Caroline Lamb 72. Oklahoma Crude 73. The Human Factor 76. Trial by Combat 76. The Devil's Advocate 77. The Big Sleep 78. The 39 Steps 78. Dr Strange (TV) 78. Zulu Dawn 79. Gandhi 82. Sahara 83. Masks of Death (TV) 84. A Woman of Substance (TV) 85. Murder with Mirrors (TV) 85. Who's That Girl? 87. Harnessing Peacocks (TV) 93. Deadly Advice 94. Martin Chuzzlewit (TV) 94.
TV series: Dundee and the Culhane 67. Zoo Gang 73. Quatermass 79. Young at Heart 80–81.

❂ For being so thoroughly reliable. *Great Expectations*.

Mills, Juliet (1941–).
British leading lady, daughter of John Mills and sister of Hayley.
No My Darling Daughter 61. Twice Round the Daffodils 62. Nurse on Wheels 63. Carry on Jack 64. The Rare Breed (US) 66. Oh What a Lovely War 69. Avanti 72. QB VII (TV) 74, etc.

Milne, A. A. (1882–1956) (Alan Alexander Milne).
British playwright, novelist, humorous writer and author of *Winnie the Pooh* and *The House at Pooh Corner*. He was briefly associated with the British production company Minerva Films (qv).
Autobiography: 1939, *It's Too Late Now*.
Biography: 1990, *A. A. Milne* by Ann Thwaite.
£5 Reward (w) 20. Bookworms (w) 20. The Bump (w) 20. Twice Two (w) 20. Mr Pim Passes By (w) 21. The Birds of Prey (from The Fourth Wall) (oa) 30. The Perfect Alibi (oa) 31. Michael and Mary (oa) 31. Where Sinners Meet (from Dover Road) (oa) 34. Four Day's Wonder (oa) 37. Winnie the Pooh and the Honey Tree (oa) 65, etc.

¶ At a cinema half a dozen sentences were put on the screen, and one had to wait for minutes before the crowd had assimilated them. Minutes! It seemed like hours sometimes. What were their brains doing all that time? They had to say things over and over again to themselves before any meaning emerged. How hellish to be born with a brain like that! – *A.A.M.*

Milner, Martin (1927–).
American general-purpose actor.
Life with Father (debut) 47. Our Very Own 50. I Want You 52. Pete Kelly's Blues 55. The Sweet Smell of Success 57. Marjorie Morningstar 58. Thirteen Ghosts 60. Sullivan's County 67. Valley of the Dolls 67. Columbo: Murder by the Book (TV) 71. Hurricane (TV) 74. Flood! (TV) 76. Nashville Beat 89, etc.
TV series: The Trouble With Father 53–55. The Life of Riley 56–57. Route 66 60–63. Adam 12 68–75. The Swiss Family Robinson 75.

Milner, Victor (1893–1972).
Distinguished American cinematographer, with Paramount for many years.
Hiawatha 14. The Velvet Hand 18. Haunting Shadows 20. The Cave Girl 22. Thy Name is Woman 24. Lady of the Harem 26. Rolled Stockings 27. Wolf of Wall Street 29. *The Love Parade* 29. Monte Carlo 30. Daughter of the Dragon 31. *Trouble in Paradise* 32. Song of Songs 33. Design for Living 33. *Cleopatra* (AA) 34. The Crusades 35. *The General Died at Dawn* 36. The Plainsman 36. Artists and Models 37. The Buccaneer (AAN) 39. Union Pacific 39. The Great Victor Herbert 39. Northwest Mounted Police 40. Christmas in July 40. The Lady Eve 41. The Monster and the Girl 41. The Palm Beach Story 42. Hostages 43. The Story of Dr Wassell 44. The Mummy's Curse 44. The Strange Love of Martha Ivers 46. The Other Love 47. Unfaithfully Yours 48. The Furies 50. September Affair 50. *Carrie* 51. Jeopardy 53, many others.

Milton, Billy (1905–1989).
British light actor of the 30s, latterly in small parts. Also singer, pianist and composer.
Autobiography: 1976, *Milton's Paradise Mislaid*.
Young Woodley 30. Three Men in a Boat 33. Someone at the Door 36. Aren't Men Beasts? 37. Yes Madam 39. Who Was Maddox 64. Hot Millions 68. Sweet William 80, etc.

Milton, Ernest (1890–1974).
American-born Shakespearean actor with long theatrical history on both sides of the Atlantic. Few film appearances, in small parts.
A Wisp in the Woods 17. The Scarlet Pimpernel 34. Fiddlers Three 44.

Milton, Harry (1900–1965).
British leading man of 30s stage and screen.
■ The King's Cup 33. To Brighton with Gladys 33. King of the Ritz 33. Adventure Limited 34. Pagliacci 36.

Mimieux, Yvette (1942–).
American leading lady signed up for films almost straight from college. She married director Stanley Donen in 1972.
The Time Machine (debut) 60. Where the Boys Are 61. The Four Horsemen of the Apocalypse 62. *The Light in the Piazza* 62. The Wonderful World of the Brothers Grimm 63. Diamondhead 63. Joy in the Morning 65. Monkeys Go Home 66. The Caper of the Golden Bulls 67. Dark of the Sun 67. Three in an Attic 68. Black Noon (TV) 71. Skyjacked 72. The Neptune Factor 73. Hit Lady (& w) (TV) 74. Journey into Fear 75. Jackson County Jail 76. The Black Hole 78. Outside Chance (TV) 78, etc.
TV series: The Most Deadly Game 70. Berrengers 85.

Minciotti, Esther (1883–1962).
Italian-American character actress, wife of Silvio Minciotti.
■ House of Strangers 49. Shockproof 49. The Undercover Man 50. Strictly Dishonorable 51. *Marty* 55. Full of Life 56. The Wrong Man 57.

Minciotti, Silvio (1883–1961).
Italian-American character actor.
House of Strangers 49. Deported 49. The Great Caruso 51. Clash by Night 52. Kiss Me Deadly 54. Marty 55, etc.

Mineo, Sal (1939–1976).
Diminutive American actor, on Broadway as a child before going to Hollywood. He was murdered as he returned home after rehearsals for a play.
Six Bridges to Cross (debut) 55. Rebel without a Cause (AAN) 55. Giant 56. Somebody Up There Likes Me 57. Tonka 58. The Gene Krupa Story 60. Exodus (AAN) 60. Escape from Zahrain 62. Cheyenne Autumn 64. The Greatest Story Ever Told 65. Who Killed Teddy Bear? 66. Krakatoa 68. Escape from the Planet of the Apes 71, etc.

Miner, Allen H.
American director.
Ghost Town 55. The Ride Back 57. Black Patch (& p) 57. Chubasco 67, etc.

Miner, Michael.
American screenwriter and director.
Robocop (co-w) 89. Deadly Weapon (wd) 89.

Miner, Steve (1951–).
American director.
Friday the 13th Part 2 81. Friday the 13th Part 3 82. House 86. Soul Man 86. Warlock 89. The Fugitive 90. Wild Hearts Can't Be Broken 91. The Rest of Daniel 92. My Father, the Hero 94, etc.

Minerva Films.
A British production company set up in 1920 by Leslie Howard, C. Aubrey Smith, Adrian Brunel, A. A. Milne, and Nigel Playfair. Its shareholders included H. G. Wells. It made four comedy shorts,

directed by Brunel from Milne's stories, before
running out of money.

Minevitch, Borrah (1904–1955).
Russian-American harmonica player who with his
Rascals enlivened a few 30s musicals.
    One in a Million 36. Love under Fire 37. Rascals
38. Always in My Heart 42, etc.

Minghella, Anthony.
British director and screenwriter, from the theatre.
    Truly Madly Deeply 91. Mr Wonderful 93.

Ming-liang, Ts'ai.
Taiwanese director.
    Rebels of the Neon God 93. Vive l'Amour 94.

miniaturization.
Making people small is a theme obviously likely
to appeal to the cinema's trick photographers.
Characters were reduced by 'scientific' or magic
means in *The Devil Doll, Dr Cyclops, The Incredible
Shrinking Man*, and *Fantastic Voyage. Land of the
Giants* showed the other side of the coin. Laurel
and Hardy were miniaturized into their own
children in *Brats;* other small humans were in *Darby
O'Gill and the Little People, The Adventures of Mark
Twain* and *The Bride of Frankenstein.*

Minnelli, Liza (1946–   ).
American singer, daughter of Judy Garland; her
gamine looks and vibrant voice made her a
fashionable figure of the early 70s.
    Biography: 1974, *Liza* by James Robert Parish.
■ Charlie Bubbles 67. The Sterile Cuckoo (AAN)
69. Tell Me That You Love Me Junie Moon 70.
Cabaret (AA) 72. Lucky Lady 76. A Matter of Time
76. New York New York 77. Arthur 81. The
Muppets Take Manhattan 84. That's Dancing! 85.
Arthur 2: On the Rocks 88. Rent-a-Cop 88.
Stepping Out 91. Parallel Lives (TV) 94.

¶ Reality is something you rise above. – *L.M.*

~She first appeared as a baby in her mother's
film *In the Good Old Summertime.*

Minnelli, Vincente (1910–1986).
American director who earned a reputation as a
stylist with MGM musicals but whose other output
was very variable. Stage experience as art director
and producer. The second of Judy Garland's
husbands, and the father of Liza Minnelli.
    Autobiography: 1974, *I Remember It Well.*
■ *Cabin in the Sky* 43. I Dood It 43. Ziegfeld Follies
44. *Meet Me in St Louis* 44. *The Clock* 44. Yolanda
and the Thief 45. Undercurrent 46. The Pirate 47.
Madame Bovary 49. *Father of the Bride* 50. Father's
Little Dividend 51. *An American in Paris* (AAN) 51.
The Bad and the Beautiful 52. The Story of Three
Loves (part) 52. *The Band Wagon* 53. The Long, Long
Trailer 54. Brigadoon 54. Kismet 55. The Cobweb 55.
Lust for Life 56. Tea and Sympathy 56. Designing
Woman 57. *Gigi* (AA) 58. The Reluctant Debutante
58. Some Came Running 58. Home from the Hill 59.
Bells Are Ringing 60. The Four Horsemen of the
Apocalypse 62. Two Weeks in Another Town 62.
The Courtship of Eddie's Father 63. Goodbye Charlie
65. The Sandpiper 65. On a Clear Day You Can See
Forever 70. A Matter of Time 76.

¶ He believes implicitly in the power of his
camera to turn trash into art, and corn into
caviar. – *Andrew Sarris, 1968*

Minney, R.J. (1895–1979).
British producer and screenwriter, former
journalist, in films since 1934.

AS WRITER: Clive of India 35. Dear Octopus 42.
Carve Her Name with Pride 58, many others.
AS PRODUCER: Madonna of the Seven Moons 44.
The Wicked Lady 45. The Final Test 53. Carve
Her Name with Pride 58, etc.

Minogue, Kylie (1969–   ).
Diminutive Australian leading actress and singer,
in television from the age of 11 and gaining wider
recognition as a rebellious teenager on the TV soap
opera *Neighbours;* hit recordings followed from
1988.
    The Delinquents 90. Street Fighter 95.

Minter, George (1911–1966).
British producer-distributor, in films from 1938.
Made films for his company, Renown.
    The Glass Mountain 48. Tom Brown's
Schooldays 50. Pickwick Papers 52. The Rough
and the Smooth 58, many others.

Minter, Mary Miles (1902–1984) (Juliet Reilly).
American silent-screen heroine.
    The Nurse 12. Barbara Frietchie 15.
Environment 16. Lovely Mary 16. Melissa of the
Hills 17. The Ghost of Rosy Taylor 17. Anne of
Green Gables 19. Nurse Marjorie 20. Moonlight and
Honeysuckle 21. South of Suva 22. The Trail of
the Lonesome Pine 23. The Drums of Fate 23, many
others.

Miou-Miou (1950–   ) (Sylvette Hery).
French leading actress, from the theatre.
    Themroc 72. The Mad Adventures of Rabbi
Jacob (Les Aventures de Rabbi Jacob) 73. Going
Places (Les Valseuses) 74. Jonah Who Will Be 25 in
the Year 2000 76. Les Routes du Sud 78. Bye – See
You Monday 79. Josepha 82. Coup de Foudre
(Entre Nous) 83. Evening Dress (Tenue de Soirée)
86. *The Reader* (La Lectrice) 88. Milou en Mai 90.
Netchaiev Is Back (Netchaiev Est de Retour) 91. The
Jackpot (La Totale!) 91. Le Bal des Casse-Pieds 91.
Germinal 93. Tango 93. Montparnasse Pondichery
94, etc.

Miranda, Carmen (1913–1955) (Maria de Carmo
Miranda de Cunha).
Portuguese singer, the 'Brazilian Bombshell';
always fantastically over-dressed and harshly
made-up, yet emitting a force of personality which
was hard to resist.
■ Down Argentine Way (debut) 40. That Night in
Rio 41. Weekend in Havana 41. Springtime in the
Rockies 42. *The Gang's All Here* 43. Four Jills in a
Jeep 44. Greenwich Village 44. Something for the
Boys 44. Doll Face 46. If I'm Lucky 46. Copacabana
47. A Date with Judy 48. Nancy Goes to Rio 50.
Scared Stiff 53.

Miranda, Isa (1905–1982) (Ines Isabella Sanpietro).
Italian star actress. Occasional films.
    Adventure in Diamonds (US) 38. Hotel Imperial
(US) 40. La Ronde (Fr.) 50. Summertime (GB) 55.
The Yellow Rolls Royce (GB) 64. The Shoes of the
Fisherman 68. The Night Porter 74. Bambina 75.

The Mirisch Brothers: Harold (1907–1968),
Marvin (1918–   ), Walter (1921–   ).
American producers, founders in 1957 of the
Mirisch company, one of the most successful
independent production groups since the decline
of the big studios. Formerly the two elder brothers
had been exhibitors, the youngest a producer of
cheap second features: the 'Bomba' series, etc.
    Man of the West 58. The Magnificent Seven 60.
West Side Story 61. Two for the See-Saw 62. The
Great Escape 63. Toys in the Attic 63. The Satan
Bug 65. The Russians Are Coming, the Russians Are

Coming 66. What Did You Do in the War, Daddy?
66. Hawaii 66. The Fortune Cookie 66. In the
Heat of the Night 68. The Organization 70. Midway
76. Same Time Next Year 78. Dracula 79. The
Prisoner of Zenda 79. Romantic Comedy 83, etc.
~Walter Mirisch was given the Jean Hersholt
Humanitarian Award by the Motion Picture
Academy in 1983.

Miroslava (1926–1955) (Miroslava Stern).
Mexican actress, of Czechoslovakian descent, best
known for her role as Lavinia in Luis Buñuel's
The Criminal Life of Archibaldo de la Cruz 55. She
committed suicide. *Miroslava*, a biopic about her
life and her unhappy love affair with bullfighter
Luis Miguel Dominguin, starring Arielle
Dombasle, was made by Mexican director
Alejandro Pelayo Rangel in 1992.
    A Woman's Five Faces (Conco Nostras de Mujer)
46. Blood Wedding (Bodas de Sangre) 46.
Adventures of Casanova 48. Death Is in Love (La
Muerte Enamorada) 50. The Brave Bulls (US) 51.
The Bullfighter and the Lady (US) 52. Dreams of
Glory (Sueños de Gloria) 53. Stranger on
Horseback (US) 55, etc.

Mirren, Helen (1946–   ).
British leading actress from the stage, whose best
role has been in the TV series *Prime Suspect.*
    Herostratus 67. A Midsummer Night's Dream
(TV) 68. Age of Consent 70. Savage Messiah 72.
Miss Julie 73. O Lucky Man 73. Caligula 79. SOS
Titanic 79. Hussy 80. The Fiendish Plot of Dr Fu
Manchu 80. Excalibur 81. The Long Good Friday
81. Cal 84. White Nights 85. Heavenly Pursuits
86. The Mosquito Coast 86. Pascali's Island 88. The
Cook, the Thief, His Wife and Her Lover 89. When
the Whales Came 89. Bethune: The Making of a
Hero 90. The Comfort of Strangers 90. *Prime Suspect*
(TV) 91. Where Angels Fear to Tread 91. Prime
Suspect 2 (TV) 92. Prime Suspect 3 (TV) 93. The
Hawk 93. *The Madness of King George* 95, etc.

¶ I'm a would-be rebel. The good girl who'd like
to be a bad one. – *H.M.*

Actors are rogues and vagabonds. Or they ought
to be. I can't stand it when they behave like
solicitors from Penge. – *H.M.*

mirrors
have a clear psychological fascination, and
cameramen have frequently derived dramatic
compositions from the use of them. Innumerable
characters have talked to their reflections, and *The
Man in the Mirror* changed places with his. *Dracula*
and his kind cast no reflection; a switch on this was
provided in *The Gorgon*, where looking at the
monster turned one to stone, but looking at her
through a mirror was OK. In *The Lady in the Lake*
Robert Montgomery played the lead from the
position of the camera lens, so the only time we
saw him was when he looked in a mirror. Eric
Portman in *Corridor of Mirrors* was surrounded by
them: the hero of *The Student of Prague* shot his
reflection in one. Then there was the magic mirror
in *Snow White and the Seven Dwarfs*, which told the
queen all she wanted to hear; and the more evil
magic mirror in *Dead of Night*, which had belonged
to a murderer and caused Ralph Michael when he
looked in it to strangle his wife. Two-way mirrors
are now familiar, especially since *From Russia With
Love;* but they were used as long ago as 1946 in *The
House on 92nd Street*. In *Orphée* a full-length mirror
proved liquid to the touch and was the doorway to
the other world. *The Lady from Shanghai* had a
splendidly confusing finale in a mirror maze which
was gradually shot to pieces; *Up Tight* made
dramatic use of a distorting mirror arcade. The

most-used mirror joke is that in which the glass is broken and a 'double' tries to take the place of the reflection: Max Linder performed it in 1919 in *Seven Years Bad Luck*, and it was superbly reprised by the Marx Brothers in *Duck Soup* 44, and by Abbott and Costello in *The Naughty Nineties* 45.

Mishima, Yukio (1925–1970).
Japanese novelist, dramatist and screenwriter who committed ritual suicide. His life was the subject of Paul Schrader's film *Mishima: A Life in Four Parts* 85. His novella *The Sailor Who Fell from Grace with the Sea* was filmed by Lewis John Carlino in 1976.
Conflagration (Enjo) (story) 58.

misnomers
A title has to appeal to the greatest possible number of people. Sometimes it loses its relevance in the progress; sometimes, as in metaphors like *Straw Dogs* and *A Clockwork Orange*, the film-maker is too arrogant to explain it. Here are one or two examples where the misnomer is still traceable:
The Black Cat. Hardly any of the several films under this title have much to do with Poe's story, and although a black cat may have casually strolled across the scene it has had little bearing on the plot. In Britain the 1934 version was retitled *House of Doom*, which is a little more to the point of the story.
Son of Dracula, like many other horror films, soon proved to have an inapposite label: the protagonist is none other than the old Count himself in disguise. In *Bride of Frankenstein*, the title role is a minor one, played by Valerie Hobson; the real bride is that of the monster. In *Frankenstein Created Woman*, he doesn't: he merely performs some brain-switching. In *Abbott and Costello Meet Frankenstein*, the Baron doesn't appear at all: it's the monster they meet, and he has much less to do with the plot than Dracula or the Wolf Man.
Abbott and Costello were never careful about titles. In *Abbott and Costello Go to Mars*, they go to Venus. And *Abbott and Costello Meet the Killer, Boris Karloff* seems devised purely for equality of billing; it is doubly misleading, for not only is Boris Karloff not a killer, he does not even play a killer in the movie.
The original title *The Thin Man* referred to a minor character in the murder plot. As sequel followed sequel, and continuity had to be maintained, the tag gradually attached itself to the investigator played by William Powell.
The films of W. C. Fields were noted for the studied irrelevance of their titles, the crowning glory being *Never Give a Sucker an Even Break*. Laurel and Hardy were not far behind, as anyone knows who has tried to explain the relevance of *Hog Wild*, *You're Darn Tootin'*, *Be Big*, *Wrong Again*, *Double Whoopee* or *They Go Boom*. Woody Allen is plainly in the great tradition: when asked why he called his movie *Bananas*, he replied, 'Because there are no bananas in it'.
The Glass Bottom Boat is seen in the first sequence of the film titled after it, but it is not essential to that sequence and has no relevance at all to the rest of the movie.
It Happened One Night. Which night? The film covers several, and none is central to the plot.
Big Deal at Dodge City is the British title for *Big Hand for a Little Lady*. It is not only less attractive but wildly inaccurate, as the action is clearly denoted as taking place in Laredo! It was the work of a title fiend operating in Warner's London office, who also turned *An American Dream* into the weirdly irrelevant *See You in Hell, Darling*.
Halls of Montezuma is set in the Pacific, and *To the Shores of Tripoli* never leaves a California training camp. All the titles tell you is that the characters are Marines, from whose marching song the labels are taken.
In *Northwest Passage*, the passage is barely mentioned and never explored. MGM started to film Kenneth Roberts' historical novel in 1939. The script was too long, so they decided to make two films, the first to deal with the training of Rogers' Rangers and the second with their exploits. The second film was never made; the one that exists does have a subtitle, 'Part One: Rogers' Rangers'.
The Silencers, *Murderers' Row*, *The Ambushers*: Any reader who can link these Matt Helm titles to their plots deserves a small prize.

Misraki, Paul (1908–).
French composer.
Retour à l'Aube 38. Battement de Coeur 39. Manon 48. Confidential Report 55. Les Cousins 59. Alphaville 65. A Murder Is . . . 72, etc.

Miss Marple.
Agatha Christie's spinster detective Jane Marple, who first appeared in the 1930 mystery *The Murder at the Vicarage*, was played by Margaret Rutherford in four films: *Murder She Said* (from *4.50 from Paddington*) 61, *Murder at the Gallop* (from *After the Funeral*) 63, *Murder Most Foul* (from *Mrs McGinty's Dead*) 64, *Murder Ahoy!* 64 (not based on a Christie original). Angela Lansbury played her in the glossy *The Mirror Crack'd* 80, and her sleuth in the television series *Murder, She Wrote* owes much to the example of Miss Marple. On television, she was first played by Gracie Fields in *A Murder Is Announced* 58 and subsequently by Helen Hayes in *A Caribbean Mystery* 83 and *They Do It with Mirrors* 85, and by Joan Hickson in an 80s BBC-TV series.

missionaries
have not been popular cinema heroes: the most lauded real-life ones were David Livingstone in *Stanley and Livingstone* and Gladys Aylward in *The Inn of the Sixth Happiness*. Over-zealous ones appeared in *Zulu*, *Hawaii*, *Seven Women*, the various versions of *Rain*, *At Play in the Fields of the Lord*, and *The Missionary* itself.

Mr Belvedere.
An acerbic, self-styled genius played by the waspish Clifton Webb in three comedies: *Sitting Pretty* 48, based on Gwen Davenport's novel *Belvedere*, *Mr Belvedere Goes to College* 49, *Mr Belvedere Rings the Bell* 51.

Mr Magoo.
Myopic, bumbling cartoon character created by UPA in the early 50s and voiced by Jim Backus. He quickly became a bore, but some of the early shorts were outstandingly funny.
Ragtime Bear 49. Spellbound Hound 50. Trouble Indemnity (AAN) 50. Bare Faced Flatfoot 51. Fuddy Duddy Buddy 51. Grizzly Golfer 51. Pink Blue Plums (AAN) 52. When Magoo Flew (AA) 55. Magoo's Puddle Jumper (AA) 56. Meet Mother Magoo 56. Magoo's Private War 57. Terror Faces Magoo 59. Mr Magoo's Christmas Carol (TV) 62, etc.
TV series: The Famous Adventures of Mr Magoo 64–65.

Mr Moto.
A mild-mannered Japanese detective and master of disguise created by novelist John P. Marquand and played in nearly a dozen films by Peter Lorre: from *Think Fast Mr Moto* in 1937 to *Mr Moto Takes a Vacation* in 1939. In 1965 Henry Silva played the role in an unsuccessful second feature.

¶ I wrote about him to get shoes for the baby.
– *John P. Marquand*

Mr T (1952–) (Lawrence Tero).
Massive black American performer whose gold chains and Mohawk hairstyle became familiar in the TV series *The A-Team*.
Rocky III 82. D.C. Cab 83. The Toughest Man in the World (TV) 84. Straight Line 88. Freaked 93.

Mr Wong.
A Chinese detective, James Lee Wong, created by author Hugh Wiley and brought to the screen by Monogram as a counter to Mr Moto who was doing so well for Fox. Boris Karloff, who was not physically suited to the role, played him in five rather feeble second features directed by William Nigh: *Mr Wong, Detective* 38; *Mystery of Mr Wong* 39; *Mr Wong in Chinatown* 39; *The Fatal Hour* 40; *Doomed to Die* (GB: *The Mystery of the Wentworth Castle*) 40. Keye Luke took over the role for *Phantom of Chinatown* 41.

Mrs Wiggs of the Cabbage Patch.
Alice Hegan Rice's sentimental shanty-town novel was filmed three times: in 1919 with Mary Carr, in 1934 with Pauline Lord, and in 1943 with Fay Bainter.

Mitchell, Cameron (1918–1994) (Cameron Mizell).
American actor, ex-radio commentator and Broadway player.
They Were Expendable 45. Command Decision 48. *Death of a Salesman* 52. How to Marry a Millionaire 53. Love Me or Leave Me 55. Monkey On My Back 57. The Last of the Vikings 61. Unstoppable Man 61. Blood and Black Lace 65. Minnesota Clay (It.) 66. Hombre 67. Monster of the Wax Museum 67. Ride the Whirlwind 68. Buck and the Preacher 71. The Midnight Man 74. Viva Knievel 77. Silent Scream 79. Without Warning 80. Texas Lightning 81. My Favorite Year 82. Murder Baby 83. Killpoint 84. Low Blow 85. The Tomb 85. Blood Link 86. Codename: Vengeance 87. Rage to Kill 87. Valley of Death 88. Action U.S.A. 89. Crossing the Line 90. Easy Kill 91. Memorial Day Valley Massacre 92, etc.
TV series: The Beachcomber 60. High Chaparral 67–71. The Swiss Family Robinson 75.

Mitchell, Grant (1874–1957).
American character actor, often seen as a worried father, lawyer or small-town politician.
Man to Man 31. Dinner at Eight 33. The Life of Emile Zola 37. New Moon 40. *The Grapes of Wrath* 40. Tobacco Road 41. *The Man Who Came to Dinner* 41. Orchestra Wives 42. Father is a Prince 43. Arsenic and Old Lace 44. Blondie's Anniversary 48, many others.

Mitchell, Guy (1925–) (Al Cernick).
Boyish, stocky American singer with a brief career in films.
■ Aaron Slick from Punkin Crick 52. Those Redheads from Seattle 53. Red Garters 54.
TV series: Whispering Smith 58.

Mitchell, James (1920–).
American dancer and character actor.
Cobra Woman 44. Colorado Territory 49. Stars in My Crown 50. Deep in My Heart 54. Oklahoma 55, etc.

Mitchell, Julien (1884–1954).
British stage character actor who made his film debut as a crazed train driver in *The Last Journey* 36.

It's in the Air 37. The Drum 38. The Sea Hawk (US) 40. Hotel Reserve 44. Bedelia 46. Bonnie Prince Charlie 48. The Galloping Major 51. Hobson's Choice 54, etc.

Mitchell, Leslie (1905–1985).
British commentator and broadcaster; the voice of British Movietone News from 1938; co-author of a 1946 book, *The March of the Movies*.
Grand National Night 53. Genevieve (as himself) 53. Heart of a Man 59.

Mitchell, Margaret (1900–1949).
American author of the novel on which Hollywood's most famous film, *Gone with the Wind*, was based.

Mitchell, Millard (1900–1953).
Nasal-voiced, rangy American character actor, in films from 1940.
Mr and Mrs Smith 40. Grand Central Murder 42. *A Double Life* 47. *A Foreign Affair* 48. Twelve O'Clock High 49. The Gunfighter 50. My Six Convicts 52. *Singin' in the Rain* 52. The Naked Spur 52. Here Come the Girls 53, etc.

Mitchell, Oswald (c. 1890–1949).
British director.
Old Mother Riley 37. Danny Boy 41. The Dummy Talks 43. Loyal Heart 46. Black Memory 47. The Greed of William Hart 47. The Man From Yesterday 49, etc.

Mitchell, Thomas (1892–1962).
Irish-American character actor of great versatility; could be tragic or comic, evil or humane. Former reporter, Broadway star and playwright; in Hollywood from the mid-30s.
■ Six Cylinder Love 23. Craig's Wife 36. Adventure in Manhattan 36. Theodora Goes Wild 36. Man of the People 37. When You're in Love 37. *Lost Horizon* 37. *The Hurricane* (AAN) 37. I Promise to Pay 37. Make Way for Tomorrow 37. Love Honor and Behave 38. Trade Winds 38. Only Angels Have Wings 38. *Stagecoach* (AA) 39. Mr Smith Goes to Washington 39. The Hunchback of Notre Dame 39. Gone with the Wind 39. The Swiss Family Robinson 40. Three Cheers for the Irish 40. *Our Town* 40. The Long Voyage Home 40. Angels over Broadway 40. Flight from Destiny 41. Out of the Fog 41. Joan of Paris 42. Song of the Islands 42. This Above All 42. Moontide 42. Tales of Manhattan 42. *The Black Swan* 42. The Immortal Sergeant 43. The Outlaw 43. Bataan 43. *Flesh and Fantasy* 43. *The Sullivans* 44. Wilson 44. Dark Waters 44. Buffalo Bill 44. The Keys of the Kingdom 44. Within These Walls 45. Captain Eddie 45. Adventure 45. It's a Wonderful Life 46. Three Wise Fools 46. The Dark Mirror 46. High Barbaree 47. The Romance of Rosy Ridge 47. Silver River 48. *Alias Nick Beal* 49. The Big Wheel 49. Journey into Light 51. High Noon 52. Tumbleweed 53. The Secret of the Incas 54. Destry 54. Swell Guy 56. While the City Sleeps 56. Handle with Care 58. Too Young for Love (GB) 59. By Love Possessed 61. Pocketful of Miracles 61.
TV series: O. Henry Playhouse 56. Glencannon 58.
✪ For adding solid worth to a number of pictures which without him might not have had it.

Mitchell, Warren (1926–).
British comedy character actor, mainly on TV, especially in series *Till Death Us Do Part*.
Tommy the Toreador 60. Postman's Knock 62. Where Has Poor Mickey Gone? 63. The Intelligence Men 65. Arrivederci Baby 66. *Till Death Us Do Part* 68. The Assassination Bureau 68. The Best House in London 69. All the Way Up 70.

Innocent Bystanders 72. The Alf Garnett Saga 72. Stand Up Virgin Soldiers 77. The Chain 85. Foreign Body 87. Wall of Silence (TV) 93, many others.

Mitchell, Yvonne (1925–1979) (Yvonne Joseph).
British actress and playwright, on stage from 1940.
Autobiography: 1957, *Actress*.
The Queen of Spades (film debut) 48. Turn the Key Softly 53. *The Divided Heart* 54. Yield to the Night 56. *Woman in a Dressing Gown* 57. The Passionate Summer 58. Tiger Bay 59. Sapphire 59. The Trials of Oscar Wilde 61. The Main Attraction 63. Genghis Khan 65. The Corpse 70. The Great Waltz 72. The Incredible Sarah 76, etc.

Mitchum, Christopher (1943–).
American minor leading man, son of Robert Mitchum.
Rio Lobo 70. Big Jake 71. Summertime Killer 72. The Mean Machine 73. Ricco 74. No Time to Die 78. American Commandos 84. Angel of Death 86. Aftershock 88, etc.

Mitchum, James (1938–).
American actor, son of Robert Mitchum.
Thunder Road (debut) 58. The Young Guns of Texas 62. The Victors 63. The Tramplers 66. Ambush Bay 67. Moonrunners 75. Trackdown 76. Blackout 78. Maniac 78. Codename: Zebra 84. Hollywood Cop 87. Marked for Murder 89. Genghis Khan 92, etc.

Mitchum, Robert (1917–).
Sleepy-eyed American leading man who has sometimes hidden his considerable talent behind a pretence of carelessness.
Biography: 1975, *It Sure Beats Working* by Mike Tomkies.
■ Hoppy Serves a Writ 43. The Leather Burners 43. Border Patrol 43. Follow the Band 43. Colt Comrades 43. The Human Comedy 43. We've Never Been Licked 43. Beyond the Last Frontier 43. Bar 20 43. Doughboys in Ireland 43. Corvette K-225 43. Aerial Gunner 43. The Lone Star Trail 43. False Colors 43. The Dancing Masters 43. Riders of the Deadline 43. Gung Ho 43. Johnny Doesn't Live Here Any More 44. When Strangers Marry 44. The Girl Rush 44. Thirty Seconds Over Tokyo 44. Nevada 44. West of the Pecos 45. *The Story of G.I. Joe* (AAN) 45. Till the End of Time 46. Undercurrent 46. The Locket 46. *Pursued* 47. *Crossfire* 47. Desire Me 47. *Out of the Past* 47. Rachel and the Stranger 48. Blood on the Moon 48. The Red Pony 49. *The Big Steal* 49. Holiday Affair 49. Where Danger Lives 50. My Forbidden Past 51. His Kind of Woman 51. The Racket 51. Macao 52. One Minute to Zero 52. The Lusty Men 52. Angel Face 53. White Witch Doctor 53. Second Chance 53. She Couldn't Say No 54. River of No Return 54. Track of the Cat 54. Not as a Stranger 55. *Night of the Hunter* 55. The Man with the Gun 55. Foreign Intrigue 56. Bandido 56. Heaven Knows Mr Allison 57. Fire Down Below 57. The Enemy Below 57. Thunder Road 58. The Hunters 58. The Angry Hills 59. The Wonderful Country 59. Home from the Hill 60. A Terrible Beauty 60. The Grass is Greener 60. *The Sundowners* 60. The Last Time I Saw Archie 61. Cape Fear 62. The Longest Day 62. Two for the Seesaw 62. The List of Adrian Messenger 63. Rampage 63. Man in the Middle 64. What a Way to Go 64. Mr Moses 65. The Way West 67. El Dorado 67. Anzio 68. Villa Rides 68. Five Card Stud 68. Secret Ceremony 68. Young Billy Young 69. The Good Guys and the Bad Guys 69. *Ryan's Daughter* 71. Going Home 71. The Wrath of God 72. The Friends of Eddie Coyle 73. The Yakuza 75. *Farewell My Lovely* 75. Midway 76. The Last Tycoon 76. The Amsterdam Kill 77. The Big

Sleep 78. Matilda 78. Breakthrough 78. Nightkill 79. One Shoe Makes It Murder (TV) 82. That Championship Season 82. *The Winds of War* (TV) 83. Killer in a Family (TV) 83. The Ambassador 84. Maria's Lovers 84. Promises to Keep (TV) 85. The Hearst and Davies Affair (TV) 85. Reunion at Fairborough (TV) 85. Thompson's Last Run (TV) 86. War and Remembrance (TV) 87. Mr North 88. Scrooged 88. Presumed Dangerous 90. Cape Fear 91.
✪ For triumphing by sheer force of personality over scores of inferior films; and for enhancing a few good ones. *Farewell My Lovely*.

¶ Robert Mitchum and his sleepy eyes have hypnotized audiences for over thirty years, through bad pictures, bad notices and narcotics cases. Just now and then he has been allowed to prove himself an excellent actor; and he has always been a commanding personality, though his attitude to himself and his career is presumably exemplified by the title of his biography – *It Sure Beats Working*. He claims:
I've survived because I work cheap and don't take up too much time
And he adds:
Movies bore me, especially my own.
He is not even proud of his physique:
People think I have an interesting walk. Hell, I'm just trying to hold my gut in.
Or his fans:
You know what the average Robert Mitchum fan is? He's full of warts and dandruff and he's probably got a hernia too, but he sees me up there on the screen and he thinks if that bum can make it, I can be president.
He disclaims ambition:
I started out to be a sex fiend but I couldn't pass the physical.
He hated his early films:
I kept the same suit for six years – and the same dialogue. We just changed the title of the picture and the leading lady.
Then he had a stroke of luck:
I came back from the war and ugly heroes were in.
Even so he thinks films are a joke:
I gave up being serious about making pictures around the time I made a film with Greer Garson and she took a hundred and twenty-five takes to say no.
He is unashamed of his lapses:
The only difference between me and my fellow actors is that I've spent more time in jail.
He does have an ambition, to spend every cent he's got:
When I drop dead and they rush to the drawer, there's going to be nothing in it but a note saying 'Later'.
And when asked why in his mid-60s he took on the arduous task of starring in an 18-hour mini-series, *The Winds of War*, he answered:
It promised a year of free lunches.
He is loved by the press, for he doesn't care what they write about him:
They're all true – booze, brawls, broads, all true. Make up some more if you want to.
And he remains self-deprecating to the last:
Young actors love me. They think if that big slob can make it, there's a chance for us.
And his final word of advice to the health-conscious:
How do I keep fit? I lay down a lot.

Mitra, Subatra (1931–).
Leading Indian cinematographer who photographed Satyajit Ray's early films.

Pather Panchali 55. Aparajito 56. The Music Room 58. The World of Apu 58. Kanchenjungha 62. Charulata 64. The Householder (Gharbar) 64. Shakespeare Wallah 65. The Guru 69. Bombay Talkie 70. Mahatma and the Mad Boy 73, etc.

Mitry, Jean (1907–1988).
French director of experimental shorts; also critic.
   Pacific 231 49. Images pour Debussy 51. Symphonie Mécanique 55, etc.

Mix, Tom (1880–1940).
A US Marshal (by his own unconfirmed account) who turned actor and starred in over 400 low-budget westerns. In the 30s he also toured with his own circus. He died in a car crash in Arizona, where a monument was erected to the memory of the man 'whose spirit left his body on this spot and whose characterizations and portrayals in life served to better fix memories of the Old West in the minds of living men.'
   Biographies: 1957, *The Fabulous Tom Mix* by Olive Stokes. 1972, *The Life and Legend of Tom Mix* by Paul E. Mix.
   The Ranch Life in the Great Southwest 10. Child of the Prairie 13. Cupid's Round-Up 18. Tom Mix in Arabia 22. North of Hudson Bay 24. The Last Trail 27. Destry Rides Again 27. Painted Post 28. My Pal the King 32. The Terror Trail 33. The Fourth Horseman 33, etc.

¶ They say he rides like part of the horse, but they don't say what part. – *Robert Sherwood*
He was as elegant on a horse as Fred Astaire on a dance floor, and that's the elegantest there is. – *Adela Rogers St Johns*
~Mix was noted for wearing his white suit and boots even to fashionable parties.

Miyagawa, Kazuo (1908–).
Japanese cinematographer, working with such leading directors as Ichikawa, Kurosawa, Mizoguchi, Ozu and Shinoda.
   Rashomon 50. Miss Oyu (Oyu-sama) 51. Ugetsu (Ugetsu Monogatari) 53. The Bailiff (Sansho Dayu) 54. Crucified Lovers (Chikamatsu Monogatari) 54. Street of Shame (Akasen Chitai) 56. Conflagration (Enjo) 58. Floating Weeds (Ukigusa) 59. The Key (Kagi) 59. Bonchi 60. Yojimbo 61. The Outcast (Hakai) 62. Money Talks (Zemni no Odoti) 64. Tokyo Olympiad (Tokyo Orimpikku) 65. Banished Orin (Hanare Goze Orin) 77. Kagemusha 80. Island of the Evil Spirit (Akureito) 81. The Inland Sea Boys' Baseball Team (Setouchi Shonen Yakyudan) 84. MacArthur's Children 85, etc.

Mizoguchi, Kenji (1898–1956).
Japanese director, former actor. Directed from 1923, though few of his films were seen in the West.
   A Paper Doll's Whisper of Spring 25. The Gorge between Love and Hate 32. The Story of the Last Chrysanthemums 39. Woman of Osaka 40. The Forty-Nine Ronin 42. The Life of O'Haru 52. *Ugestu Monogatari* 52. Street of Shame 56, many others.

Mizrahi, Moshe (1931–).
Egyptian director and screenwriter, working in Israel and France.
   Les Stances à Sophie 71. I Love You Rosa 73. The House on Chelouche Street 74. Madame Rosa (AA) 77. I Sent a Letter to My Love (Chère Inconnue) 80. La Vie Continue 82. Une Jeunesse 83. War and Love 85. Everytime We Say Goodbye 87. Mangeclous 89, etc.

Mobley, Mary Ann (1939–).
American leading lady, former 'Miss America'.
   Girl Happy 65. Three on a Couch 66. For Singles Only 68. Crazy Horse and Custer: The Untold Story 90, etc.

Moby Dick.
Herman Melville's allegorical novel about an obsessed sea captain's pursuit of a white whale has been filmed at least three times: *The Sea Beast* 26, directed by Millard Webb with John Barrymore, Dolores Costello, and George O'Hara; *Moby Dick* 30, directed by Lloyd Bacon with John Barrymore, Joan Bennett, and Lloyd Hughes; *Moby Dick* 56, directed by John Huston with Gregory Peck, Richard Basehart, and no female lead. A similar story was served up in *The White Buffalo* 77, directed by J. Lee-Thompson and starring Charles Bronson as Wild Bill Hickok chasing the eponymous beast.
   See also: *Melville, Herman.*

Mockridge, Cyril (1896–1979).
British-born composer, in America from 1921, films from 1932.
   The Littlest Rebel 35. Johnny Apollo 40. Happy Land 43. The Sullivans 44. My Darling Clementine 46. How to Marry a Millionaire 53. Many Rivers to Cross 55. Flaming Star 60. Donovan's Reef 63, many others.

Mocky, Jean-Pierre (1929–) (Jean Mokiejeswki).
French director.
   Un Couple 60. Snobs 62. Les Vierges 63. La Bourse et la Vie 65. Les Compagnons de la Marguerite 67. Solo 70. Chut! 72. L'Ibis Rouge 75. A Mort l'Arbitre 83. Le Miracle 86. Divine Enfant 89. Le Mari de Léon 91. City for Sale (Ville à Vendre) 91. Le Mari de Léon 93, etc.

Modesty Blaise.
Dauntless heroine with a shady background and martial arts skills, created by Peter O'Donnell (1920–) for a newspaper comic strip and, subsequently, novels. She was played by Monica Vitti in a camp film, with pop-art decor, directed by Joseph Losey in 1966, and by Ann Turkel in a pilot for a television series. In 1994, rights to the character were bought by Miramax Films with the intention of producing a series of action adventures from 1996.

Modine, Matthew (1959–).
American juvenile lead of the 80s.
   Baby It's You 82. Private School 83. Vision Quest 84. Hotel New Hampshire 84. Birdy 85. Mrs Soffel 85. Full Metal Jacket 87. Orphans 87. Married to the Mob 88. The Gamble (La Partita) 88. Gross Anatomy 89. Memphis Belle 90. Pacific Heights 90. Equinox 92. And the Band Played On (TV) 93. Short Cuts 93. The Browning Version 94, etc.

Modley, Albert (1891–1979).
British north-country comedian who appeared in a few films including the 1951 version of *Up for the Cup.*

Modot, Gaston (1887–1970).
French character actor.
   Fievre 21. L'Age d'Or 30. Sous Les Toits de Paris 30. La Grande Illusion 37. Pepe le Moko 37. La Regle du Jeu 39. Les Enfants du Paradis 44. French Can Can 55. Le Testament du Docteur Cordelier 59, many others.

Moffatt, Graham (1919–1965).
British actor, fondly remembered as the

impertinent fat boy of the Will Hay comedies: *Oh Mr Porter* 38. *Ask a Policeman* 39. Where's That Fire 40, etc.
   Other films include A Cup of Kindness (debut) 34. Dr Syn 38. I Thank You 41. I Know Where I'm Going 45, many others. Retired to keep a pub, but made very occasional appearances: The Second Mate 50. Inn for Trouble 59. Eighty Thousand Suspects 63.

Moffett, Sharyn (1936–).
American child actress of the 40s.
   My Pal Wolf 44. The Body Snatcher 45. Child of Divorce 47. The Judge Steps Out 47. Mr Blandings Builds His Dream House 48. Girls Never Tell 51, etc.

Mogotlane, Thomas (1953–1993).
South African actor and writer, best known for playing the lead role in *Mapantsula.* He worked mainly in the theatre.
   How Long? (a, co-w) 86. Mapantsula (a, co-w) 88.

moguls.
The name given half-affectionately to the men who ran Hollywood in the golden days of the studios: Mayer, Thalberg, Selznick, Goldwyn, Warner, Zanuck, Zukor, Cohn, etc. The best capsule guide to them is Philip French's *The Movie Moguls* (1970).

¶ They were monsters and pirates and bastards right down to the bottom of their feet but they loved movies. Some of the jerks running the business today don't even have faces. – *Richard Brooks, c. 1970*
   I was impressed by the moral potentialities of the screen. – *Adolph Zukor*
   Those of us who became film producers hailed from all sorts of occupations – furriers, magicians, butchers, boilermakers – and for this reason highbrows have often poked fun at us. Yet one thing is certain: every man who succeeded was a born showman. And once in the show business he was never happy out of it. – *Adolph Zukor*
   There's nothing wrong with Hollywood that six first-class funerals couldn't cure. – *Anon, 1930*
   Don't make these pictures any better. Just keep them the way they are. – *Louis B. Mayer on the Hardy Family series*
   We should all make a killing in this business. There's so much money in the pot. – *Irving Thalberg*
   It's better than being a pimp. – *Harry Cohn*

Moguy, Leonide (1899–1976) (L. Maguilevsky).
Russian newsreel producer, later in France and US as director.
   Prison without Bars 38. The Night Is Ending 43. Action in Arabia 44. Whistle Stop 46. Tomorrow Is Too Late 50. Les Enfants de l'Amour 54, etc.

Mohner, Carl (1921–).
Austrian actor in films from 1949.
   Rififi 55. He Who Must Die 56. The Key 58. Camp on Blood Island 58. The Kitchen 61. Hell is Empty 67. Callan 74. Wanted: Babysitter 75, etc.

Mohr, Gerald (1914–1968).
Suave American actor, in films from 1941; played the 'Lone Wolf ', a gentleman crook, in a mid-40s series.
   The Monster and the Girl 41. Ten Tall Men 51. Detective Story 53. The Eddie Cantor Story 53. Angry Red Planet 59. Funny Girl 68, many others.
   TV series: Foreign Intrigue 56.

Mohr, Hal (1894–1974).
American cinematographer, in Hollywood from 1915.

The Last Night of the Barbary Coast 13. Money 14. The Deceiver 21, Bag and Baggage 23. The Monster 24. The High Hand 26. The Jazz Singer 27. The Last Warning 28. Broadway 29. Big Boy 30. Woman of Experience 31. A Woman Commands 32. State Fair 33. David Harum 34. *A Midsummer Night's Dream* (AA) 35. *Captain Blood* 35. *Green Pastures* 36. The Walking Dead 36. I Met My Love Again 38. Rio 39. *Destry Rides Again* 39. When the Daltons Rode 40. International Lady 41. Twin Beds 42. Phantom of the Opera (AA) 43. Ladies Courageous 44. Salome Where She Danced 45. Because of Him 46. The Lost Moment 47. Another Part of the Forest 48. Johnny Holiday 49. Woman on the Run 50. The Big Night 51. The Fourposter 52. *The Wild One* 54. The Boss 56. Baby Face Nelson 57. The Gun Runners 58. The Last Voyage 60. The Man from the Diner's Club 63. Bamboo Saucer 68, many others.
~Mohr was interviewed in *Behind the Camera*.

Mokae, Zakes (1935–).
South African actor, from the stage, now working in America.

Darling 65. The Comedians 67. The Island 80. Roar 81. Cry Freedom 87. The Serpent and the Rainbow 88. Dad 89. A Dry White Season 89. Gross Anatomy 89. Body Parts 91. A Rage in Harlem 91. Dust Devil: The Final Cut 93, etc.

Mokri, Amir (1956–).
Iranian-born cinematographer, in America since the mid-70s.

House of the Rising Sun 85. Slamdance 87. Eat a Bowl of Tea 89. Life Is Cheap . . . But Toilet Paper Is Expensive 90. Blue Steel 90. Pacific Heights 90. Whore 91. Queen's Logic 91. Freejack 92. The Joy Luck Club 93, etc.

Molander, Gustaf (1888–1973).
Veteran Swedish director, former actor and writer (including *Sir Arne's Treasure* 19). Directing since 1922, but few of his films have been seen abroad.

Sin 28. Intermezzo 36. A Woman's Face 38. Woman without a Face 47. Sir Arne's Treasure (remake) 55, many others.

Molina, Alfred (1953–).
English character actor of Spanish and Italian ancestry, often in menacing roles, from the theatre.

Raiders of the Lost Ark 81. The Deceiver 21, Meantime 83. Number One 84. Water 84. Eleni 85. Ladyhawke 85. A Letter to Brezhnev 85. Prick Up Your Ears 87. Manifesto 88. Drowning in the Shallow End 89. American Friends 91. Not without My Daughter 91. Hancock (TV) 91. Enchanted April 91. The Trial 93. White Fang 2: Myth of the White Wolf 94. Maverick 94. The Perez Family 95, etc.

¶ My father was very disparaging about acting. He was under the impression that it wasn't quite the sort of thing for a good, upstanding heterosexual man to do. – A.M.

Molina, Angela.
Spanish leading actress in international films.

That Obscure Object of Desire 77. Demons in the Garden (Demonios en el Jardín) 82. The Eyes, the Mouth (It.) 83. Half of Heaven (La Mitad del Cielo) 86. Streets of Gold (US) 86. 1492: Conquest of Paradise (US) 92. Coitado do Jorge (Port.) 93. Con gli Occhi Chiusi (It.) 94, etc.

Molinaro, Edouard (1928–).
French director.

Evidence in Concrete (Le Dos au Mur) 57. Girls for the Summer 60. A Ravishing Idiot 63. The Gentle Art of Seduction 64. Pain in the A . . . 74. La Cage aux Folles (AAN) 78. La Cage aux Folles II 80. Sunday Lovers 80. Just the Way You Are 84. L'Amour en Douce 85. Palace 85. Enchanté 88. Le Souper 93, etc.

Mollo, John.
English costume designer.

Star Wars (AA) 77. Alien 79. The Empire Strikes Back 80. Gandhi (AA) 82. Greystoke: The Legend of Tarzan, Lord of the Apes 84. Cry Freedom 87. Air America 90. White Hunter, Black Heart 90. Chaplin 92, etc.

Molnar, Ferenc (1878–1952).
Hungarian dramatist whose comedies were the basis of many Hollywood films including *The Shop around the Corner, One Two Three, The Guardsman, The Swan, A Breath of Scandal, Double Wedding* and *Liliom*.

Monaco, James (1885–1945).
American composer and musician who wrote songs for seven Bing Crosby movies. His most frequent collaborator was lyricist Johnny Burke.

Dr Rhythm 38. Sing You Sinners 38. East Side of Heaven 39. The Star Maker 38. Road to Singapore 40. If I Had My Way 40. Rhythm on the River 40. Stage Door Canteen 43. Pin-Up Girl 44. Sweet and Low Down 44. Irish Eyes Are Smiling 44, etc.

Monash, Paul (1917–).
American producer, former TV writer.

Butch Cassidy and the Sundance Kid 69. Slaughterhouse Five 72. The Friends of Eddie Coyle (& w) 74. The Front Page 74. Carrie 76. Big Trouble in Little China 86, etc.
TV series: Peyton Place 64–69.

Mondy, Pierre (1925–) (Pierre Cuq).
French actor.

Rendezvous de Juillet 49. Sans Laisser d'Adresse 50. Les Louves 57. Austerlitz (as Napoleon) 60. Bebert et l'Omnibus 63. Retour en Face 80. The Gift 82, etc.

Monger, Christopher (1950–).
Welsh-born director, working in America.

Enough Cuts for a Murder 79. Repeater 80. Voice Over 81. The Mabinogi (TV) 84. Crime Pays 86. Just Like a Woman 92. The Englishman Who Went up a Hill but Came down a Mountain 95, etc.

Monicelli, Mario (1915–).
Italian director.

Cops and Robbers (co-d) 51. Persons Unknown 58. Boccaccio 70 (part) 61. The Organizer 63. Casanova 70 66. Girl with a Pistol 69. Mortadella 71. Romanzo Popolare 75. Caro Michele 76. Travels with Anita 79. Sono Fotogenico 80. Bertoldo, Bertoldino e Cacasenno 84. The Two Lives of Mattia Pascal (Le Due Vite di Mattia Pascal) 85. The Rogues (I Picari) 87. The Dark Illness (Il Male Oscuro) 89. Parenti e Serpenti 92. Viva i Bambini 92. Cari Fottutissimi Amici 94, etc.

The Monkees
sprang to fame in an American TV series of that title 66–67. They were a pop quartet deliberately recruited by Screen Gems to emulate the Beatles in crazy comedy with music; their ensuing popularity surprised not only themselves but their sponsors, and in 1969 they made a movie called *Head*. Individually they were: *Peter Tork; Mike Nesmith; Micky Dolenz; Davy Jones* (qqv).

Monkhouse, Bob (1928–).
British comedian of TV, radio and occasional films.

Carry On Sergeant 58. Dentist in the Chair 59. Weekend with Lulu 61. She'll Have to Go 61. The Bliss of Mrs Blossom 68, etc.
TV series: Mad Movies.

monks
in films have usually been caricatures of the Friar Tuck type; Tuck himself turned up, personified by Eugene Pallette or Alexander Gauge, in most of the versions of Robin Hood. The funny side of monastery life was presented in *Crooks in Cloisters*, while milder humour came from Edward G. Robinson's conversion to the simple life in *Brother Orchid. The Monk*, based on a classic Gothic novel, treated the monastery as a place of demonic passion and sin. Serious crises of the monastic spirit have been treated in two American films, *The Garden of Allah* and *The First Legion*; but on the whole monks have appealed less than priests to film-makers in search of an emotional subject.
See also: *nuns; priests; churches.*

Monogram Pictures:
see *Allied Artists.*

Monroe, Marilyn (1926–1962) (Norma Jean Baker or Mortenson).
American leading lady, a former model whose classic rags-to-riches story was built on a super-sexy image which quickly tarnished, leaving her a frustrated, neurotic and tragic victim of the Hollywood which created her. The pity was that she had real talent as well as sex appeal.

Marilyn, a compilation feature, was released after her death. Several biographies have been published. In 1976 Misty Rowe played her in *Goodbye Norma Jean*. She was played by Melody Anderson in the TV movie *Marilyn and Bobby: Her Final Affair* 93.

Autobiography: 1974, *My Story*.

Biographies: 1961, *Marilyn Monroe* by Maurice Zolotow. 1966, *Who Killed Marilyn Monroe?* by Charles Hamblett. 1969, *Norma Jean: The Life of Marilyn Monroe* by Fred Lawrence Guiles. 1974, *Marilyn* by Norman Mailer. 1976, *Conversations with Marilyn* by W. J. Weatherby. 1985, *Legend: The Life and Death of Marilyn Monroe* by Fred Lawrence Guiles. 1985, *Goddess: The Secret Lives of Marilyn Monroe* by Anthony Summers. 1993, *Marilyn Monroe: The Biography* by Donald Spoto.

■ Scudda Hoo, Scudda Hay 48. Dangerous Years 48. Ladies of the Chorus 48. Love Happy 50. A Ticket to Tomahawk 50. *The Asphalt Jungle* 50. All About Eve 50. The Fireball 50. Right Cross 50. Home Town Story 51. As Young as You Feel 51. Love Nest 51. Let's Make It Legal 51. We're Not Married 52. Clash by Night 52. Full House 52. Monkey Business 52. Don't Bother to Knock 52. *Niagara* (here the build-up really started) 52. *Gentlemen Prefer Blondes* 53. *How to Marry a Millionaire* 53. River of No Return 54. There's No Business Like Show Business 54. *The Seven-Year Itch* 55. Bus Stop 56. The Prince and the Showgirl (GB) 57. *Some Like It Hot* 59. Let's Make Love 60. The Misfits 61.
For personifying the Hollywood cliché, the star created and destroyed by the system. *How to Marry a Millionaire.*

¶ A sex symbol becomes a thing. I hate being a thing.
The tragedy of Marilyn Monroe was such that she

as inspired more books of reminiscence and analysis than any other star. Her problem was, oddly enough, best expressed in an earlier decade by Clara Bow:

Being a sex symbol is a heavy load to carry, especially when one is tired, hurt and bewildered.

Monroe knew her own limitations:

To put it bluntly, I seem to be a whole superstructure with no foundation. But I'm working on the foundation.

What she meant by that was:

The best way for me to prove myself as a person is to prove myself as an actress.

She was uncertain whether she would ever achieve this aim. She said once:

I enjoy acting when you really hit it right.

But she seldom felt she did. In her search for meaning she married playwright Arthur Miller, and the headline was:

EGGHEAD WEDS HOURGLASS

It finally failed to work although he was kind to her with press comments such as:

Her beauty shines because the spirit is forever showing itself.

Not that she was lacking in moral supporters; even unlikely people such as Edith Sitwell acclaimed her:

She knows the world, but this knowledge has not lowered her great and benevolent dignity; its darkness has not dimmed her goodness.

She settled for a flip image as expressed in her lively encounters with the press:

Didn't you have anything on?
 — I had the radio on.
Sex is part of nature, and I go along with nature.
Do you wear falsies?
 — Those who know me better, know better.

The contradictions within herself finally killed her, and the obituaries were many and varied:

You don't have to hold an inquest to find out who killed Marilyn Monroe. Those bastards in the big executive chairs killed her. — *Henry Hathaway*

If she was simple it would have been easy to help her. She could have made it with a little luck. — *Arthur Miller*

A professional amateur. — *Laurence Olivier*

Directing her was like directing Lassie. You needed fourteen takes to get each one of them right. — *Otto Preminger*

Anyone can remember lines, but it takes a real artist to come on the set and not know her lines and give the performance she did. — *Billy Wilder*

I have never met anyone as utterly mean as Marilyn Monroe. Nor as utterly fabulous on the screen, and that includes Garbo. — *Billy Wilder*

She has breasts like granite and a brain like Swiss cheese, full of holes. Extracting a performance from her is like pulling teeth. — *Billy Wilder*

As near genius as any actress I ever knew. — *Joshua Logan*

She was born afraid. She never got over it. In the end fear killed her. — *Pete Martin*

There's a broad with her future behind her. — *Constance Bennett*

She had curves in places other women don't even have places. — *Cybill Shepherd*

She's the girl you'd like to double-cross your wife with. — *Jean Negulesco*

An arrogant little tail-twitcher who learned to throw sex in your face. — *Nunnally Johnson*

A vacuum with nipples. — *Otto Preminger*

Popular opinion, and all that goes to promote it, is a horrible unsteady conveyance for life, and

she was exploited beyond anyone's means. — *Laurence Olivier*

Monroe, Vaughan (1911–1973).
American bandleader who unexpectedly appeared as hero of a few westerns.

Meet the People 44. Carnegie Hall 47. Singing Guns 50. The Toughest Man in Arizona 52, etc.

Monsarrat, Nicholas (1910–1979).
British adventure novelist whose naval adventures, *The Cruel Sea* and *The Ship That Died of Shame*, were filmed by Ealing, as was *The Story of Esther Costello*.

Monsieur Beaucaire.
Booth Tarkington's light novel about a barber who impersonates the King of France was filmed as a straight romantic vehicle for Rudolph Valentino and Bebe Daniels in 1924, directed by Sidney Olcott. In 1946 Bob Hope had his way with it in a version directed by George Marshall.

monster animals.
The 1924 version of *The Lost World* set a persisting fashion for giant animals operated by technical ingenuity. The supreme achievement in the genre was of course *King Kong*, who carried on in *Son of Kong* and (more or less) in *Mighty Joe Young*. Many films concentrated on normal species which had been giantized by radiation or some other accident of science: *The Black Scorpion, Them, The Deadly Mantis, The Giant Claw, Tarantula, Mysterious Island, Bug, Night of the Lepus, Squirm, Jaws, Food of the Gods.* More fanciful giant animals were created for *Jason and the Argonauts, Jack the Giant Killer* and *The Seventh Voyage of Sinbad.* The 1976 *King Kong* remake mainly featured a man in a gorilla suit, and the fashion of the late 70s and early 80s was for ordinary animals which turned savage, such as *Alligator, Piranha* and *Cujo.*

See also: *dinosaurs.*

montage.
In the most general sense, the whole art of editing or assembling scenes into the finished film. Specifically, 'a montage' is understood as an impressionistic sequence of short dissolve-shots either bridging a time gap, setting a situation or showing the background to the main story. Classic montages which come to mind are in *The Battleship Potemkin, The Roaring Twenties* and *Citizen Kane.*

Montagu, Ivor (1904–1984).
British producer, director and film theorist. In films from 1925; was associate of Hitchcock on several of his mid-30s thrillers; produced *Behind the Spanish Lines* 38, *Spanish ABC* 38, etc; co-authored many screenplays including *Scott of the Antarctic* 48. Last publication *Film World* 64.

Autobiography: 1970, *The Youngest Son.*

Montague, Lee (1927–).
British actor, mainly seen on stage and TV.

Savage Innocents 59. The Secret Partner 60. Billy Budd 61. The Horse without a Head 62. You Must Be Joking 65. The Best Pair of Legs in the Business 72. Mahler 73. Jesus of Nazareth (TV) 77. Holocaust (TV) 78. The Legacy 78. The Brass Target 78. Sakharov (TV) 84. Madame Sousatzka 88, etc.

Montalban, Ricardo (1920–).
Mexican leading man in Hollywood.

Fiesta 47. The Kissing Bandit 49. Border Incident 49. Battleground 50. Right Cross 50. Across the Wide Missouri 51. My Man and I 52. Sombrero 53. Latin Lovers 54. A Life in the Balance 55. *Sayonara* 57.

Adventures of a Young Man 62. Love Is a Ball 63. The Money Trap 65. Madame X 66. Sol Madrid 68. Blue 68. *Sweet Charity* 68. Conquest of the Planet of the Apes 72. Desperate Mission (TV) 72. Joe Panther 76. How the West Was Won (TV) 77. Joe Panther 78. *Star Trek: The Wrath of Khan* 82. Cannonball Run II 84. The Naked Gun: From the Files of Police Squad 88, etc.

TV series: Fantasy Island 78–84. The Colbys 85–87.

Montana, Bull (1887–1950) (Luigi Montagna).
Italian-American strong man who played ape men and heavies in the 20s.

Brass Buttons 19. Go and Get It 20. Painted People 23. The Lost World 24. Son of the Sheik 26. Good Morning Judge 28. Show of Shows 29. Tiger Rose 29. Big City 37. Good Morning Judge 43, etc.

Montand, Yves (1921–1991) (Ivo Levi).
French actor-singer in films from the mid-40s; he was married to Simone Signoret.

Les Portes de la Nuit 46. Lost Property 50. *The Wages of Fear* 53. The Heroes Are Tired 55. The Witches of Salem 56. *Let's Make Love* (US) 60. Sanctuary (US) 61. My Geisha (US) 62. The Sleeping Car Murders 65. The War Is Over 66. Is Paris Burning? 66. Grand Prix 67. Vivre pour Vivre 67. 'Z' 68. On a Clear Day You Can See Forever 69. L'Aveu 70. The Red Circle 70. The Son 72. Le Sauvage 76. Clair de Femme 79. Garçon! 83. *Jean de Florette* 86. *Manon des Sources* 86. Nobody Listened (Nadie Escuchaba) 88. Trois Places Pour Le 26 88. Netchaiev est de Retour 91. I.P.5.: L'Ile aux Pachydermes 92, etc.

¶ Of all the male stars I've known, he was probably the most vain. — *Tony Richardson*

Montes, Lola (1818–1861) (Maria Dolores Eliza Gilbert).
Scottish-Creole dancer who became world-famous as the mistress of King Ludwig I of Bavaria. Max Ophuls made a film about her in 1955, with Martine Carol, and Yvonne de Carlo played her in *Black Bart* 48. There was also a Spanish biopic in 1944 with Conchita Montenegro and Florinda Bolkan played her in *Royal Flash.*

Montesi, Jorge (1950–).
Chilean-born director, based in Canada.

Birds of Prey (TV) 84. Omen IV: The Awakening (TV) 91. Stealth Force 93. Soft Deceit 95, etc.

Montez, Maria (1919–1951) (Maria de Santo Silas).
Exotic Hollywood leading lady mainly seen in hokum adventures.

The Invisible Woman (debut) 41. South of Tahiti 41. The Mystery of Marie Roget 42. *Arabian Nights* 42. White Savage 43. *Cobra Woman* 44. Ali Baba and the Forty Thieves 44. Gypsy Wildcat 44. Sudan 45. Tangier 46. Pirates of Monterey 47. The Exile 47. Siren of Atlantis 48. The Thief of Venice 51, etc.

¶ When I see myself on the screen, I am so beautiful I jump for joy. — *M.M.*

Montgomery, Belinda (1950–).
American leading lady.

The Todd Killings 70. Women in Chains (TV) 72. Letters from Three Lovers (TV) 73. The Other Side of the Mountain 75. Breaking Point 76. Blackout 77. The Other Side of the Mountain Part Two 78. Silent Madness 84, etc.

Montgomery, Bernard (1887–1976).
British Field Marshal who through his waspish

personality became famous, especially when he commanded the victorious Eighth Army in North Africa in 1942. He has been best played on TV by Ian Richardson, especially in *Ike*. Trevor Reid played him in *The Longest Day* and Michael Bates in *Patton*. An exciting and amusing film of 1958, *I Was Monty's Double*, featured his wartime stand-in, Clifton James.

Montgomery, Bruce (1921–1978).
English composer, conductor, and organist, a former teacher, in films from 1948. Educated at Oxford University, where he was a close friend of poet Philip Larkin, he is possibly better known for writing detective novels (as Edmund Crispin) featuring literary critic Professor Gervase Fen, the first being published while he was still an undergraduate. His other compositions included a Coronation anthem, written with Kingsley Amis. Alcoholism and difficulty in finishing his scores on time curtailed his movie career.

The Kidnappers 53. Cartouche 54. Doctor in the House 54. Doctor at Sea 55. Escapade 55. Eye Witness 56. Checkpoint 56. Guilty 56. Doctor at Large 57. The Truth about Women 57. Carry On Sergeant 58. Carry On Nurse 59. Carry On Teacher 59. Too Young to Love 59. Please Turn Over 59. Carry On Constable 60. Carry On Regardless 60. Carry On Cruising (co-m) 62, etc.

¶ He had two genuine and precocious talents which both dried up quite quickly when he was about thirty . . . How are you supposed to handle that, lots of money now and some fame and nothing to say? Drinking yourself to death is one solution. – *Kingsley Amis*

Montgomery, Doreen (1916–1992).
British screenwriter, latterly in television where she created the character of Emma Peel for the long-running series *The Avengers*.

Meet Mr Penny 38. Mr Reeder in Room 13 38. Lassie from Lancashire 38. Just William 39. At the Villa Rose 39. Poison Pen 39. House of the Arrow 39. The Flying Squad 40. The Second Mr Bush 40. The Man in Grey 43. Fanny by Gaslight 44. Love Story 44. This Man Is Mine 45. She Died Young 47. Bonnie Prince Charlie 48. Narrowing Circle 55, etc.

Montgomery, Douglass (1907–1966) (Robert Douglass Montgomery).
Canadian leading man with stage experience; once known as Kent Douglass.
■ Paid 30. Daybreak 31. Five and Ten 31. *Waterloo Bridge* 31. A House Divided 31. *Little Women* 33. Eight Girls in a Boat 34. Little Man What Now 34. Music in the Air 34. The Mystery of Edwin Drood 35. Lady Tubbs 35. Harmony Lane 35. Everything Is Thunder 36. Tropical Trouble 36. Counsel for Crime 37. Life Begins with Love 37. *The Cat and the Canary* 39. *The Way to the Stars* 45. Woman to Woman 46. When in Rome 47. Forbidden 48.

Montgomery, Elizabeth (1933–).
Pert American leading lady, daughter of Robert Montgomery; most familiar as the witch-wife of the TV series *Bewitched* 64–71.

The Court Martial of Billy Mitchell 55. Who's Been Sleeping in My Bed? 63. Johnny Cool 63. The Victim (TV) 72. A Case of Rape (TV) 74. The Legend of Lizzie Borden (TV) 75. Dark Victory (TV) 76. A Killing Affair (TV) 77. The Awakening Land (TV) 78. Jennifer: A Woman's Story (TV) 79. Act of Violence (TV) 80. Belle Starr (TV) 81. When the Circus Came to Town (TV) 82. The Rules of Marriage (TV) 83. Second Sight (TV) 85. Face to Face (TV) 90. Black Widow Murders: The Blanche Taylor Moore Story (TV) 93, etc.

Montgomery, George (1916–) (George M. Letz).
Genial American leading man, mostly in low-budgeters; former boxer and stuntman who later had ambitions to direct.

The Cisco Kid and the Lady 39. Young People 40. *Roxie Hart 42. Ten Gentlemen from West Point* 42. Orchestra Wives 42. Coney Island 43. Bomber's Moon 43. Three Little Girls in Blue 46. The Brasher Doubloon 47. Lulu Belle 48. Dakota Lil 50. Sword of Monte Cristo 51. The Texas Rangers 51. Fort Ti 53. Street of Sinners 55. Huk 56. Black Patch 57. Watusi 59. The Steel Claw (& d) 61. Samar (& d) 62. From Hell to Borneo (& d) 64. Battle of the Bulge 65. Hallucination Generation 66. Huntsville 67, many others.

TV series: Cimarron City 58.

Montgomery, Lee Harcourt.
American child actor of the 70s.

Million Dollar Duck 71. The Harness (TV) 71. Ben 72. The Savage Is Loose 74. A Cry in the Wilderness (TV) 74. Burnt Offerings 76. Baker's Hawk 76. Dead of Night (TV) 77. True Grit: A Further Adventure (TV) 78. Girls Just Want to Have Fun 85. The Midnight Hour (TV) 85. Into the Fire 88, etc.

Montgomery, Robert (1904–1981) (Henry Montgomery).
Smooth, smart American leading man of the 30s; later became a director, then forsook show business for politics.
■ So This is College 29. Untamed 29. Three Live Ghosts 29. The Single Standard 29. Their Own Desire 29. Free and Easy 30. The Divorcee 30. The Big House 30. Our Blushing Brides 30. Sins of the Children 30. Love in the Rough 30. War Nurse 30. The Easiest Way 31. Strangers May Kiss 31. Inspiration 31. Shipmates 31. The Man in Possession 31. Private Lives 31. Lovers Courageous 31. But the Flesh is Weak 32. Letty Lynton 32. Blondie of the Follies 32. Faithless 32. Hell Below 33. Made on Broadway 33. *When Ladies Meet* 33. Night Flight 33. Another Language 33. Fugitive Lovers 34. Riptide 34. The Mystery of Mr X 34. Hideout 34. Forsaking All Others 35. Vanessa, Her Love Story 35. Biography of a Bachelor Girl 35. No More Ladies 35. Petticoat Fever 36. Trouble for Two 36. Piccadilly Jim 36. The Last of Mrs Cheyney 37. *Night Must Fall* (AAN) 37. Ever Since Eve 37. Live Love and Learn 37. The First Hundred Years 37. *Yellow Jack* 38. Three Loves has Nancy 38. Fast and Loose 39. The Earl of Chicago 40. *Busman's Honeymoon* (GB) (as Lord Peter Wimsey) 40. Rage in Heaven 41. Mr and Mrs Smith 41. *Here Comes Mr Jordan* (AAN) 41. Unfinished Business 41. They Were Expendable 45. *The Lady in the Lake* (as Philip Marlowe) (& d) 46. Ride the Pink Horse (& d) 47. The Saxon Charm 48. June Bride 48. Once More My Darling (& d) 49. Your Witness (GB) 50. The Gallant Hours (d only) 60.

TV series: Robert Montgomery Presents 50–56.

¶ If you are lucky enough to be a success, by all means enjoy the applause and the adulation of the public. But never, never believe it. – *R.M.*

Monti, Felix (1938–).
Argentinian cinematographer, from commercials.

The Official Story 85. South (Sur) 87. Old Gringo 87. I, the Worst of All (Yo, la Peor de Todas) 90. A Wall of Silence (Un Muro de Silencio) 93. We Don't Want to Talk about It (De Eso No Se Habla) 93. A Shadow You Soon Will Be (Una Sombra Ya Pronto Serás) 94, etc.

Montiel, Sarita (1927–) (Maria Antonia Abad). Spanish leading lady in Mexican and American films. She was formerly married to director Anthony Mann.

Vera Cruz 54. Serenade 56. She Gods of Shark Reef 57. Run of the Arrow 57, etc.

Monty Python.
An ensemble name for a group of British nonsense comedians who had much influence on television comedy of the 60s and 70s. They include John Cleese, Michael Palin, Terry Gilliam, Eric Idle, Terry Jones and Graham Chapman.
■ And Now for Something Completely Different 71. *Monty Python and the Holy Grail 75. The Life of Brian* 79. Monty Python's Meaning of Life 83.

Moody, Ron (1924–) (Ronald Moodnick). British character comedian of stage and TV.
■ Make Mine Mink 59. Follow a Star 59. Five Golden Hours 60. A Pair of Briefs 62. Summer Holiday 63. The Mouse on the Moon 63. Ladies Who Do 63. Murder Most Foul 64. Every Day's a Holiday 64. San Ferry Ann 65. The Sandwich Man 65. *Oliver* (as Fagin) (AAN) 68. David Copperfield 69. The Twelve Chairs 70. Flight of the Doves 71. Dogpound Shuffle 74. Legend of the Werewolf 75. Dominique 78. The Word (TV) 79. The Spaceman and King Arthur 79. Dial M for Murder (TV) 81. Wrong Is Right 82.

TV series: Nobody's Perfect 79.

Moorcroft, Judy.
British costume designer.

The Prince and the Pauper 77. Murder by Decree 79. The Europeans (AAN) 79. Silver Dream Racer 80. Yentl 83. A Passage to India (AAN) 84. The Killing Fields 84. Clockwise 86. Without a Clue 88. Fools of Fortune 90. City of Joy 92, etc.

Moore, Clayton (1908–).
Tall American leading man of 40s serials such as *The Crimson Ghost, G-Men Never Forget, The Ghost of Zorro*. Later famous on TV as *The Lone Ranger*.

Moore, Cleo (1928–1973).
American leading lady who appeared chiefly in Hugo Haas's low-budget emotional melodramas.

This Side of the Law 50. On Dangerous Ground 50. One Girl's Confession 53. Bait 54. Women's Prison 55. Over-Exposed 56, etc.

Moore, Colleen (1900–1988) (Kathleen Morrison). American leading lady of the silent screen.
Autobiography: 1968, *Silent Star*.
■ Bad Boy 17. An Old Fashioned Young Man 17. Hands Up 17. The Savage 18. A Hoosier Romance 18. Little Orphan Annie 18. The Busher 19. Wilderness Trail 19. Man in the Moonlight 19. The Egg Crate Wallop 19. Common Property 19. The Cyclone 20. A Roman Scandal 20. Her Bridal Nightmare 20. The Devil's Claim 20. So Long Letty 20. When Dawn Came 20. Dinty 20. The Sky Pilot 21. The Lotus Eater 21. His Nibs 21. Broken Hearts of Broadway 21. Come on Over 22. The Wallflower 22. Affinities 22. Forsaking All Others 22. Broken Chains 22. The Ninety and Nine 22. Look Your Best 23. Slippy McGee 23. The Nth Commandment 23. April Showers 23. Through the Dark 23. The Huntress 23. Flaming Youth 23. Painted People 24. The Perfect Flapper 24. Flirting with Love 24. *So Big* 24. Sally 25. The Desert Flower 25. We Moderns 25. Irene 26. *Ella Cinders* 26. It Must Be Love 26. Twinkletoes 27. Orchids and Ermine 27. Naughty But Nice 27. Her Wild Oat 27. Happiness

...head 28. Oh Kay! 28. *Lilac Time* 28. Synthetic Sin
8. Why Be Good? 29. Smiling Irish Eyes 29.
...ootlights and Fools 29. The Power and the Glory
3. Success at Any Price 34. Social Register 34. The
...carlet Letter 34.

Moore, Constance (1919–).
...merican leading lady and singer, mildly popular
...1 the 40s; usually in 'sensible' roles.
   Prison Break 38. You Can't Cheat an Honest
...1an 39. La Conga Nights 40. Ma, He's Making
...yes at Me 40. I Wanted Wings 41. Take a Letter,
...arling 42. *Show Business* 43. *Atlantic City* 44.
...elightfully Dangerous 45. Earl Carroll's Vanities
...5. In Old Sacramento 46. Hit Parade of 1947 47.
...ats off to Rhythm 47. The 13th Letter 51. Spree
7, etc.
   TV series: Window on Main Street 61.

Moore, Demi (1962–) (Demi Guynes).
...merican leading actress. She married actor Bruce
...Villis in 1987.
   Choices 81. Young Doctors in Love 82. Parasite
2. Blame It on Rio 84. No Small Affair 85.
...t Elmo's Fire 85. One Crazy Summer 86. About
...ast Night . . . 86. Wisdom 87. The Seventh Sign
8. We're No Angels 89. Ghost 90. Mortal
...houghts 91. The Butcher's Wife 91. Nothing but
...rouble 91. Indecent Proposal 93. A Few Good
...1en 93. Disclosure 94, etc.

Moore, Dickie (1925–).
...merican child actor of the 30s, first on screen
...vhen one year old. He became the fifth husband
...f actress Jane Powell in 1988. He is the author of
... book on child stars: 1984, *Twinkle, Twinkle Little*
...ar *(But Don't Have Sex or Take the Car)*.
   The Beloved Rogue 26. Passion Flower 30.
...londe Venus 32. Oliver Twist 33. Peter Ibbetson
4. Sergeant York 41. Miss Annie Rooney 42.
...angerous Years 47. Out of the Past (Build My
...allows High) 48. Killer Shark 50. The Member of
...he Wedding (last to date) 52, etc.

Moore, Dudley (1935–).
...ritish cabaret pianist and comedian, often teamed
...vith Peter Cook until Hollywood stardom was
...urprisingly awarded to him in 1979, and less
...urprisingly withdrawn in the early 80s.
   The Wrong Box 66. Thirty is a Dangerous Age
...ynthia 67. Bedazzled 68. Monte Carlo or Bust 69.
...he Bed Sitting Room 69. Alice's Adventures in
...Vonderland 72. The Hound of the Baskervilles (as
...r Watson) 77. *Foul Play* 78. '10' 79. Wholly Moses
0. Arthur (AAN) 81. Six Weeks 82. Lovesick 83.
...tomantic Comedy 83. Unfaithfully Yours 83. Best
...efense 84. Micki and Maude 84. Santa Claus 85.
...ike Father Like Son 87. Arthur 2: On the Rocks
8. The Adventures of Milo and Otis (voice) 89.
...razy People 90. Blame It on the Bellboy 91. The
...ickle 93. Parallel Lives (TV) 94.
   TV series: Dudley 93. Daddy's Girls 94.

¶ The ability to enjoy your sex life is central. I
   don't give a shit about anything else. My
...bsession is total. What else is there to live for?
   D.M.
   The confidence I now have is rooted in the
...iscovery that who I am is okay. – *D.M.*
   I think my own desire to be loved is what makes
...1e sexually attractive. – *D.M.*
   I have a very ribald sense of humour, which is
...onventionally known as obscene. – *D.M.*
   A grubby cherub. – *Jonathan Miller*

Moore, Eva (1870–1955).
...ritish stage actress who made a few films in the
...0s.

   Chu Chin Chow 22. Brown Sugar 31. *The Old
Dark House* (splendid in her cries of 'No beds! They
can't have beds!') (US) 32. I Was a Spy 33. A Cup
of Kindness 34. Vintage Wine 35. Old Iron 39.
The Bandit of Sherwood Forest (US) 46, etc.

Moore, Grace (1901–1947).
American operatic singer who appeared in
occasional films; Kathryn Grayson played her in a
1953 biopic, *So This Is Love*.
   Autobiography: 1946, *You're Only Human Once*.
■ A Lady's Morals (as Jenny Lind) 30. New Moon
30. *One Night of Love* (AAN) 34. Love Me Forever
35. The King Steps Out 36. When You're In Love
37. I'll Take Romance 37. Louise 40.

Moore, Ida (1883–1964).
American character actress.
   The Merry Widow 25. She's a Soldier Too 44.
To Each His Own 46. The Egg and I 47. Manhattan
Angel 49. Harvey 50. Honeychile 51. Scandal At
Scourie 53. The Country Girl 54. Ma and Pa Kettle
at Waikiki 55. The Desk Set 57. Rock a Bye Baby
58, etc.

Moore, Juanita (1922–).
American character actress.
   Lydia Bailey 52. Affair in Trinidad 52. Witness
to Murder 54. Women's Prison 55. Ransom 56. The
Girl Can't Help It 56. Green Eyed Blonde 57.
Imitation of Life (AAN) 59. Tammy Tell Me True 61.
A Raisin in the Sun 61. Walk on the Wild Side 62.
Papa's Delicate Condition 63. The Singing Nun
66. Rosie 68. Up Tight 68. Fox Style 73. Thomasine
and Bushrod 74. Abby 74. Two Moon Junction 88,.
etc.

Moore, Kieron (1925–) (Kieron O'Hanrahan).
Hangdog Irish leading man with stage experience.
   The Voice Within 44. *A Man about the House* 46.
Mine Own Executioner 47. Anna Karenina 48. Ten
Tall Men 51. The Key 58. The Day They Robbed
the Bank of England 60. Dr Blood's Coffin 61. The
Day of the Triffids 63. The Thin Red Line 64. Crack
in the World 65. Arabesque 66. Custer of the West
67, etc.

Moore, Mary Tyler (1936–).
Pert American leading lady who has been most
successful on TV, and with her then husband Grant
Tinker formed her own production company,
known as MTM Productions, which was later sold
to the British TV company TVS.
■ X15 61. Thoroughly Modern Millie 67. What's
So Bad About Feeling Good? 68. Don't Just Stand
There 68. Change of Habit 69. Run a Crooked Mile
(TV) 69. *First You Cry* (TV) 78. *Ordinary People* (AAN)
80. Six Weeks 82. Finnegan Begin Again (TV) 84.
Just between Friends 85. Lincoln (TV) 88.
Thanksgiving Day (TV) 90. Stolen Babies (TV) 93.
   TV series: Steve Canyon 58. Richard Diamond
59–60. *The Dick Van Dyke Show* 61–65. *The Mary
Tyler Moore Show* 70–74. Mary 86. Annie McGuire
89.

¶ I'm not an actress who can create a character.
   I play me. – *M.T.M.*

Moore, Matt (1888–1960).
American silent actor, youngest of four Irish acting
brothers (Tom, Owen and Joe were the others).
   Traffic in Souls 13. Pride of the Clan 16. The
Bondage of Barbara 19. Fools in the Dark 24.
Grounds for Divorce 25. Dry Martini 28. Coquette
29. Spellbound 45, many others.

Moore, Michael.
American documentary writer and director.

   Roger and Me 89. Canadian Bacon 94.
TV series: TV Nation 94.

Moore, Owen (1887–1939).
(See *Moore, Matt*.) Owen married Mary Pickford.
   The Cricket on the Hearth 09. Battle of the Sexes
13. Mistress Nell 15. Piccadilly Jim 19. Torment 24.
The Red Mill 27. What a Widow 30. She Done
Him Wrong 33, many others.

Moore, Richard (1925–).
American cinematographer.
   The Wild Angels 65. Wild in the Streets 68.
Winning 69. The Reivers 69. Myra Breckinridge 70.
WUSA 70. Judge Roy Bean 72. The Stone Killer
73. Circle of Iron (d) 79. Annie 82, etc.

Moore, Robert (1927–1984).
American director, from TV.
   Murder by Death 76. The Cheap Detective 78.
Chapter Two 79, etc.
AS ACTOR: Tell Me That You Love Me Junie Moon
70.

Moore, Roger (1927–).
British light leading man, most successful on TV;
film debut in Hollywood.
   Biography: 1985, *Roger Moore* by Roy Moseley
with Philip and Martin Masheter.
■ The Last Time I Saw Paris 54. Interrupted
Melody 55. The King's Thief 55. Diane 55. The
Miracle 59. The Sins of Rachel Cade 61. Gold of
the Seven Saints 61. Rape of the Sabines 61. No
Man's Land 62. Crossplot 69. The Man Who
Haunted Himself 70. Live and Let Die (as James
Bond) 73. The Man with the Golden Gun 74. Gold
74. That Lucky Touch 75. Shout at the Devil 76.
Street People 76. The Spy Who Loved Me 77.
Sherlock Holmes in New York (TV) 77. The Wild
Geese 78. Escape from Athena 79. Moonraker 79.
North Sea Hijack 80. Sunday Lovers 80. The Sea
Wolves 80. The Cannonball Run 81. For Your Eyes
Only 81. Octopussy 83. The Naked Face 84. A
View to a Kill 85. The Magic Snowman (voice) 87.
Bed and Breakfast 89. Bullseye 90. Fire, Ice and
Dynamite 90.
   TV series: Ivanhoe 57. The Alaskans 59.
Maverick 61. *The Saint* 63–68. *The Persuaders* 71.

¶ If I kept all my bad notices, I'd need two houses.
   – *R.M.*
   My acting range? Left eyebrow raised, right
eyebrow raised. – *R.M.*
   You're not a star till they can spell your name
in Vladivostok. – *R.M.*

Moore, Ted (1914–).
South African cinematographer, in British films.
   The Black Knight 54. Cockleshell Heroes 56. Dr
No 62. From Russia with Love 63. Goldfinger 64.
Thunderball 65. *A Man for All Seasons* (AA) 66.
Shalako 68. The Prime of Miss Jean Brodie 69.
The Most Dangerous Man in the World 69.
Country Dance 70. Diamonds are Forever 71. Live
and Let Die 73. The Man with the Golden Gun 74.
Sinbad and the Eye of the Tiger 77. Orca 77.
Dominique 79. Clash of the Titans 81. Priest of
Love 81, etc.

Moore, Terry (1929–) (Helen Koford).
American leading lady, former child model, in
films from infancy.
   Autobiography: 1984, *The Beauty and the
Billionaire* (dealing with her relationship with
Howard Hughes).
   The Murder in Thornton Square 43. Mighty Joe
Young 50. Come Back Little Sheba (AAN) 52. The
Sunny Side of the Street 53. King of the Khyber

Rifles 54. Bernardine 57. A Private's Affair 59. Why Must I Die? 60. Town Tamer 65. Death Dimension 78. Hellhole 85. Death Blow 87. Beverly Hill Brats (& p) 88. Jake Spanner – Private Eye 89, etc.

TV series: Empire 62.

Moore, Tom (1883–1955).
(See *Moore, Matt*.)
The Atheist 14. The Cinderella Man 17. The Floor Below 18. Harbor Lights 23. Manhandled 25. Good and Naughty 26. Bombay Mail 34. The Fighting O'Flynn 49.

Moore, Victor (1876–1962).
Veteran American vaudeville comedian with hesitant, bumbling manner.
■ Chimmie Fadden 15. Chimmie Fadden Out West 15. Snobs 15. The Clown 16. The Race 16. The Best Man 16. Invited Out 17. Oh! U-Boat 17. Faint Heart and Fair Lady 17. Bungalowing 17. Commuting 17. Flivvering 17. Home Defence 17. The Man Who Found Himself 25. Heads Up 30. Dangerous Nan McGrew 30. Romance in the Rain 34. The Gift of Gab 34. *Swing Time* 36. Gold Diggers of 1937 36. We're on the Jury 37. Meet the Missus 37. The Life of the Party 37. She's Got Everything 37. *Make Way for Tomorrow* 37. Radio City Revels 38. This Marriage Business 38. *Louisiana Purchase* 41. *Star Spangled Rhythm* 42. True to Life 43. Riding High 43. The Heat's On 43. Carolina Blues 44. Duffy's Tavern 45. *It's In the Bag* 45. Ziegfeld Follies 46. It Happened on Fifth Avenue 47. A Miracle Can Happen 48. A Kiss in the Dark 49. *We're Not Married* 52. The Seven-Year Itch 55.

Famous line (*Make Way for Tomorrow*): 'Two old-fashioneds, for two old-fashioned people.'

Moorehead, Agnes (1906–1974).
Sharp-featured American character actress, often seen in waspish or neurotic roles.
■ Citizen Kane 41. *The Magnificent Ambersons* (AAN) 42. Journey into Fear 42. The Big Street 42. The Youngest Profession 43. Government Girl 43. Jane Eyre 43. Since You Went Away 44. Dragon Seed 44. The Seventh Cross 44. Mrs Parkington (AAN) 44. Tomorrow the World 44. Keep Your Powder Dry 45. Our Vines Have Tender Grapes 45. Her Highness and the Bellboy 45. Dark Passage 47. *The Lost Moment* (as a centenarian) 47. Summer Holiday 48. *The Woman in White* 48. Station West 48. Johnny Belinda (AAN) 48. The Stratton Story 49. The Great Sinner 49. Without Honor 49. Caged 50. Fourteen Hours 51. Show Boat 51. The Blue Veil 51. The Adventures of Captain Fabian 51. Captain Blackjack 52. The Blazing Forest 52. The Story of Three Loves 53. Scandal at Scourie 53. Main Street to Broadway 53. Those Redheads from Seattle 53. Magnificent Obsession 54. Untamed 55. The Left Hand of God 55. All That Heaven Allows 56. Meet Me in Las Vegas 56. The Conqueror 56. The Revolt of Mamie Stover 56. The Swan 56. Pardners 56. The Opposite Sex 56. Raintree County 57. The True Story of Jesse James 57. Jeanne Eagels 57. The Story of Mankind 57. Night of the Quarter Moon 59. Tempest 59. *The Bat* 59. Pollyanna 60. Twenty Plus Two 61. Bachelor in Paradise 61. Jessica 62. How the West Was Won 63. Who's Minding the Store? 63. Hush Hush Sweet Charlotte (AAN) 64. The Singing Nun 66. What's the Matter with Helen? 71. Suddenly Single (TV) 71. Rolling Man (TV) 72. Night of Terror (TV) 72. Dear Dead Delilah 72. Frankenstein: The True Story (TV) 73.

TV series: *Bewitched* 64–71.

Moorhouse, Jocelyn.
Australian director and producer, married to director Paul J. Hogan. She studied at the Australian Film Television and Radio School in the early 80s and worked in television as a writer and director.
Secrets (TV) 88. Proof 91. Muriel's Wedding 94.

Mora, Philippe (1949–).
Australian director.
Mad Dog 76. The Beast Within 81. The Return of Captain Invincible 82. Howling II 85. Death of a Soldier 86. The Marsupials: Howling III 87. Communion 89. Art Deco Detective 94, etc.

Morahan, Christopher (1924–).
British director with stage and TV experience.
■ Diamonds for Breakfast 68. All Neat in Black Stockings 69. The Jewel in the Crown (TV) 83. In the Secret State (TV) 85. Clockwise 86. After Pilkington 87. Troubles 88. The Heat of the Day (TV) 89.

Moran, Dolores (1924–1982).
American leading lady of the 40s.
Old Acquaintance 43. To Have and Have Not 43. The Man I Love 47, etc.

Moran, Jackie (1925–1990) (John E. Moran).
American child actor who played Huckleberry Finn in the 1938 version of *Tom Sawyer* and featured in the first Buck Rogers serials. He made his last film in 1947.
Valiant Is the Word for Carrie 36. The Adventures of Tom Sawyer 38. Gone with the Wind 39. Spirit of Culver 39. Tomboy 40. The Old Swimmin' Hole 40. Henry Aldrich Haunts a House 43. Song of the Open Road 44. Betty Co-Ed 47, etc.

Moran, Peggy (1918–).
American leading lady of the 40s, with radio experience; married Henry Koster and retired.
Girls' School 39. The Mummy's Hand 40. Horror Island 41. Drums of the Congo 42. Seven Sweethearts 42. King of the Cowboys 43, etc.

Moran, Polly (1884–1952).
American vaudeville comedienne who was in silent shorts from 1913 and made some early sound films, notably in partnership with Marie Dressler.
Hollywood Revue 29. Caught Short 29. Reducing 30. Politics 31. The Passionate Plumber 32. Alice in Wonderland 33.
Later played smaller roles in: Two Wise Maids 37. Tom Brown's Schooldays 39. Petticoat Politics 41. Adam's Rib 49, etc.

Moranis, Rick (1954–).
Canadian comic actor in wimpish roles.
Strange Brew (wd) 83. Hockey Night 84. Ghost Busters 84. The Wild Life 84. Streets of Fire 84. Brewster's Millions 85. Club Paradise 86. Head Office 86. Little Shop of Horrors 86. Spaceballs 87. Honey I Shrunk the Kids 89. Ghostbusters II 89. Parenthood 89. My Blue Heaven 90. L.A. Story 91. Honey, I Blew Up the Kid 92. Splitting Heirs 93. The Flintstones 94. Little Giants 94, etc.
TV series: Second City TV 80–81. SCTV Network 90 81–82.

Moravia, Alberto (1907–1990).
Italian novelist and screenwriter.
Last Meeting (Ultimo Incontro) (w) 52. Sensualità (w) 52. The She-Wolf (La Lupa) (w) 53. The Wayward Wife (oa) 53. Woman of Rome (oa) 54. Roman Tales (oa) 56. Love on the Riviera (oa) 58. La Giornata Balorda (w) 60. Two Women (La Ciociara) (oa) 60. Contempt (oa) 63. The Empty Canvas (oa) 63. A Time of Indifference (Gli Indifferenti) (oa) 64. The Conformist (oa) 70. The Lie (oa) 85. Io & Lui (oa) 87. Husbands and Lovers (oa) 91, etc.

More, Kenneth (1914–1982).
Breezy British leading actor, a recognizable World War II type who later gave compassionate interpretations of middle-aged dreamers; film-makers forsook him after his great 50s success, and he turned to stage and TV.
Autobiographies: 1959, *Happy Go Lucky*. 1978, *More or Less*.
■ Look Up and Laugh 35. Windmill Revels 38. Carry on London 38. Scott of the Antarctic 48. Man on the Run 49. Now Barabbas 49. Stop Press Girl 49. Morning Departure 50. Chance of a Lifetime 50. The Clouded Yellow 50. The Franchise Affair 50. No Highway 51. *Appointment With Venus* 51. Brandy for the Parson 52. The Yellow Balloon 52. Never Let Me Go 53. *Genevieve* 53. Our Girl Friday 53. *Doctor In the House* 54. Raising a Riot 54. *The Deep Blue Sea* 55. *Reach For the Sky* (as Douglas Bader) 56. The Admirable Crichton 57. A Night to Remember 58. Next to No Time 58. The Sheriff of Fractured Jaw 58. The Thirty-Nine Steps 59. Northwest Frontier 59. *Sink The Bismarck* 60. Man in the Moon 60. The Greengage Summer 61. The Longest Day 62. Some People 62. We Joined the Navy 62. The Comedy Man 63. The Mercenaries 67. Oh What a Lovely War 69. Fraulein Doktor 69. Battle of Britain 69. Scrooge 70. Where Time Began 76. The Slipper and the Rose 76. Leopard in the Snow 78. The Spaceman and King Arthur 79. A Tale of Two Cities 81.
TV series: The Forsyte Saga 68. Father Brown 73. An Englishman's Castle 78.
☉ For encapsulating for a nation all the carefree heroes of World War II. *Genevieve*.

More O'Ferrall, George (1907–1982).
British director who was mainly successful in TV.
AS ASSISTANT DIRECTOR: Midshipman Easy 34 No Highway 51.
■ AS DIRECTOR: Angels One Five 52. The Holly and the Ivy 53. The Heart of the Matter 53. The Green Scarf 53. A Woman for Joe 55. The March Hare 56. Three Faces of Murder (Lord Mountdrago) 56.

Moreau, Jeanne (1928–).
French actress of stage and screen; the Bette Davis of her time. Briefly married to director William Friedkin.
Biography: 1994, *La Moreau* by Marianne Gray.
The She-Wolves 55. Lift to the Scaffold 57. *The Lovers* 59. Le Dialogue des Carmelites 59. Les Liaisons Dangereuses 60. Moderato Cantabile 60. La Notte 61. *Jules et Jim* 61. Eva 62. The Trial 63. The Victors 63. Le Feu Follet 64. *Diary of a Chambermaid* 64. The Yellow Rolls-Royce 64. The Train 64. Mata Hari 65. *Viva Maria* 65. Mademoiselle 65. Chimes at Midnight 66. Sailor from Gibraltar 66. The Bride Wore Black 67. Great Catherine 68. Le Corps de Diane 68. Monte Walsh 70. Alex in Wonderland 70. Louise 72. Mr Klein 76. The Last Tycoon 76. French Provincial 76. A Lumière (& wd) 76. The Adolescent (w, d only) 79. Plein Sud 80. The Trout 82. Querelle 82. Sauve toi Lola 86. Le Miraculé 87. Calling the Shots 88. Nikita 89. La Femme Fardée 90. Alberto Express 90. La Vieille qui Marchait dans la Mer 91. The Suspended Step of the Stork (To Meteoro Vima to Pelargou) 91. Ville à Vendre 91. Until the End of the World (Bis ans Ende der Welt) 91. A Foreign Field (TV) 93. The Clothes in the Wardrobe (aka The Summer House) (TV) 93. Je M'Appelle Victor 93, etc.

For sheer strength of acting. *Louise.*

When I'm doing a role I'm the part. I'm the person. But when I'm finished, I'm me — *J.M.* Jeanne's heart is like an enormous room that is always cold: a man comes in, lights a fire, the flames swallow everything and then die down. When there are only ashes left, she shivers: she knows you cannot bring the cinders back to life, you have to light another fire, and she is always looking for a man who will not let the fire die down. *William Friedkin*

Morecambe, Eric (1926–1984) (Eric Bartholomew).

Wise, Ernie (1925–) (Ernest Wiseman). British comedy team with music-hall experience since 1943. In the 60s they became immensely popular on TV, but their films were rather less than satisfactory.

■ The Intelligence Men 64. That Riviera Touch 66. The Magnificent Two 67.

Moreland, Mantan (1902–1973). Chubby American character actor, long cast as frightened valet.

Frontier Scout 38. Laughing at Danger 40. King of the Zombies 41. The Strange Case of Doctor RX 41. Charlie Chan in the Secret Service (and many others in this series) 44. Murder at Malibu Beach 47. The Feathered Serpent 49. Enter Laughing 68. Watermelon Man 70, etc.

Morell, André (1909–1978) (André Mesritz). Dignified British character actor.

Thirteen Men and a Gun (debut) 38. No Place for Jennifer 49. Seven Days to Noon 50. High Treason 51. Summer Madness 55. The Bridge on the River Kwai 57. Ben Hur 59. The Hound of the Baskervilles 59. Cone of Silence 60. Shadow of the Cat 62. Cash on Demand 64. She 65. Plague of the Zombies 65. The Mummy's Shroud 67. 10 Rillington Place 70. Barry Lyndon 75. The Message 76, etc.

Moreno, Antonio (1886–1967). Romantic Spanish star of Hollywood.

SILENT FILMS: Voice of the Million 12. House of Hate 18. The Trail of the Lonesome Pine 23. The Spanish Dancer 24. Mare Nostrum 25. Beverly of Graustark 26. The Temptress 26. It 27. Synthetic Sin 28, etc.

CHARACTER PARTS: One Mad Kiss 30. Storm over the Andes 35. Rose of the Rio Grande 38. Valley of the Giants 42. The Spanish Main 45. Captain from Castile 47. Thunder Bay 53. The Creature from the Black Lagoon 54. The Searchers 56, many others.

Moreno, Rita (1931–) (Rosita Dolores Alverio). Puerto Rican actress-dancer, in films sporadically since 1950, between stage appearances.

Pagan Love Song 50. Singin' in the Rain 52. Garden of Evil 54. The Vagabond King 55. The King and I 56. The Deerslayer 57. *West Side Story* (AA) 61. The Night of the Following Day 68. Popi 69. Carnal Knowledge 71. *The Ritz* 76. The Boss's Son 78. Happy Birthday Gemini 79. *The Four Seasons* 81. Life in the Food Chain 91. The Dark Angel 92. I Like It Like That 94, etc.

TV series: Nine to Five 82–83.

Moretti, Nanni (1953–). Italian director, screenwriter, producer and actor, who also runs his own production company and a Rome cinema. He won the award for best director at the 1994 Cannes Film Festival with *Dear Diary.*

Io Sono un Autarchico 76. Ecce Bombo 78.

Sweet Dreams (Sogni d'Oro) 81. Bianca 84. The Mass Is Over (La Messa è Finita) 85. Notte Italiana (p) 87. Domani Accadrè (p) 88. Palombella Rossa 89. Il Portaborse (a, p) 91. Dear Diary (Caro Diario) 93, etc.

Morgan, Dennis (1910–1994) (Stanley Morner). American leading man, former opera singer.

Suzy (debut) 36. The Great Ziegfeld 36. Kitty Foyle 40. Captains of the Clouds 42. Thank Your Lucky Stars 43. Two Guys from Texas 46. My Wild Irish Rose 47. Painting the Clouds with Sunshine 51. The Gun That Won the West 55. Uranium Boom 56. Rogues' Gallery 68, etc.

TV series: 21 Beacon Street 59.

Morgan, Frank (1890–1949) (Francis Wupperman). American character actor. In films from 1916, usually playing his endearing if slightly fuddled self, but his real popularity came with sound, when he was an MGM contract player for over twenty years.

■ The Suspect 17. The Daring of Diana 17. Light in the Darkness 17. A Modern Cinderella 17. The Girl Philippa 17. Who's Your Neighbour 17. A Child of the Wild 17. Baby Mine 17. Raffles 17. The Knife 18. At the Mercy of Men 18. Gray Towers of Mystery 19. The Golden Shower 19. Manhandled 24. Born Rich 24. The Man Who Found Himself 25. The Crowded Hour 25. The Scarlet Saint 25. Love's Greatest Mistake 27. Queen High 30. Dangerous Dan McGrew 30. Fast and Loose 30. Laughter 30. The Half Naked Truth 32. Secrets of the French Police 32. Luxury Liner 33. *Hallelujah I'm a Bum* 33. Reunion in Vienna 33. The Nuisance 33. When Ladies Meet 33. Broadway to Hollywood 33. *Bombshell* 33. The Best of Enemies 33. Billion Dollar Scandal 33. The Kiss Before the Mirror 33. The Cat and the Fiddle 34. *The Affairs of Cellini* (AAN) 34. By Your Leave 34. There's Always Tomorrow 34. Success at Any Price 34. Sisters under the Skin 34. A Lost Lady 34. The Good Fairy 35. Naughty Marietta 35. Escapade 35. I Live My Life 35. The Perfect Gentleman 35. Enchanted April 35. The Dancing Pirate 35. *The Great Ziegfeld* 36. Trouble for Two 36. *Piccadilly Jim* 36. *Dimples* 36. *The Last of Mrs Cheyney* 37. The Emperor's Candlesticks 37. Saratoga 37. Beg Borrow or Steal 37. Rosalie 37. Paradise for Three 38. Port of Seven Seas 38. The Crowd Roars 38. Sweethearts 38. Broadway Serenade 39. *The Wizard of Oz* 39. Balalaika 39. The Shop around the Corner 40. Henry Goes to Arizona 40. Broadway Melody of 1940. The Ghost Comes Home 40. The Mortal Storm 40. *Boom Town* 40. Hullabaloo 40. Keeping Company 41. Washington Melodrama 41. Wild Man of Borneo 41. Honky Tonk 41. The Vanishing Virginian 42. *Tortilla Flat* (AAN) 42. White Cargo 42. Stranger in Town 43. *The Human Comedy* 43. Thousands Cheer 43. The White Cliffs of Dover 43. Casanova Brown 44. Yolanda and the Thief 45. The Courage of Lassie 45. The Great Morgan 46. The Cockeyed Miracle 46. Lady Luck 46. Green Dolphin Street 47. Summer Holiday 48. The Three Musketeers 48. Any Number Can Play 49. The Great Sinner 49. The Stratton Story 49. Key to the City 50.

Morgan, Harry (1915–) (Harry Bratsburg). Mild-looking American character actor with stage experience.

To the Shores of Tripoli (debut) 42. From This Day Forward 45. The Saxon Charm 49. Moonrise 50. The Well 51. High Noon 52. The Glenn Miller Story 53. Not as a Stranger 55. The Teahouse of the August Moon 56. Inherit the Wind 60. John Goldfarb Please Come Home 64. What Did You Do in the War, Daddy? 66. Support Your Local

Sheriff 69. The Barefoot Executive 71. Snowball Express 73. The Apple Dumpling Gang 75. The Apple Dumpling Gang Rides Again 79. Incident in a Small Town (TV) 94, many others.

TV series: December Bride 54–58. Pete and Gladys 60–61. The Richard Boone Show 63. Kentucky Jones 64. Dragnet 69. The D.A. 71. M*A*S*H 76–83. Aftermash 83. Black Magic 86. Dragnet 87.

Morgan, Helen (1900–1941). American café singer of the 30s; film appearances few. Biopic 1956 with Ann Blyth: *The Helen Morgan Story.*

Biography: 1974, *Helen Morgan, Her Life and Legend* by Gilbert Maxwell.

■ Applause 29. Roadhouse Nights 30. You Belong to Me 34. Marie Galante 34. Sweet Music 35. Go Into Your Dance 35. *Showboat* 36. Frankie and Johnnie 36.

Morgan, Michele (1920–) (Simone Roussel). French leading lady, in films from mid-30s.

Orage 36. *Quai des Brumes* 38. Remorques 39. La Loi du Nord 39. La Symphonie Pastorale 40. Joan of Paris (US) 41. Higher and Higher (US) 43. Passage to Marseilles (US) 44. *The Fallen Idol* (GB) 48. Les Orgeuilleux 50. The Seven Deadly Sins 51. Les Grandes Manoeuvres 55. Marguerite de la Nuit 56. The Mirror Has Two Faces 60. Landru 63. Lost Command 66. Benjamin 68. Le Chat et la Souris 75. Everybody's Fine (Stanno Tutti Bene) 90, etc.

Morgan, Ralph (1882–1956) (Ralph Wupperman). American character actor, brother of Frank Morgan. Former lawyer; went on stage, then to films in the 20s.

Charlie Chan's Chance 31. Rasputin and the Empress 32. Strange Interlude 32. *The Power and the Glory* 33. Anthony Adverse 36. The Life of Emile Zola 37. Forty Little Mothers 40. Black Market Babies 45. The Monster Maker 45. Sleep My Love 48. Gold Fever 52, many others.

Morgan, Terence (1921–). British leading man.

Hamlet (debut) 48. Mandy 52. Turn the Key Softly 53. They Can't Hang Me 55. The Scamp 56. Shakedown 58. Piccadilly Third Stop 61. The Curse of the Mummy's Tomb 64. The Lifetaker 89, many others.

TV series: Sir Francis Drake 62.

Moriarty, Cathy (1961–). American actress.

Raging Bull (AAN) 80. Neighbors 81. White of the Eye 87. Burndown 89. Kindergarten Cop 90. Soapdish 91. The Indian Runner 91. The Mambo Kings 92. Matinee 93. Another Stakeout 93. Me and the Kid 93, etc.

Moriarty, Michael (1941–). American leading actor of the 70s. He is also an accomplished jazz pianist and singer.

Hickey and Boggs 72. The Last Detail 73. Bang the Drum Slowly 73. Shoot It Black Shoot It Blue 74. Report to the Commissioner 74. *Holocaust* (TV) 77. Who'll Stop the Rain? 78. Too Far to Go (TV) 79. The Winged Serpent 82. Odd Birds 85. Pale Rider 85. The Stuff 85. Troll 85. The Hanoi Hilton 87. It's Alive III: Island of the Alive 87. My Old Man's Place 88. Dark Tower 89. Full Fathom Five 90, etc.

TV series: Law and Order 90–94.

Morison, Patricia (1915–) (Eileen Morison). Slightly sulky-looking American leading lady of the 40s; never quite made it but did well later on stage.

■ *Persons in Hiding* 39. I'm from Missouri 39. The Magnificent Fraud 39. Untamed 40. Rangers of Fortune 40. One Night in Lisbon 41. Romance of the Rio Grande 41. The Roundup 41. A Night in New Orleans 42. Beyond the Blue Horizon 42. Are Husbands Necessary? 42. Silver Skates 43. Hitler's Madman 43. Calling Dr Death 43. The Fallen Sparrow 43. The Song of Bernadette 43. Where are Your Children? 44. Without Love 45. Lady on a Train 45. Dressed to Kill 46. Danger Woman 46. Queen of the Amazons 47. Tarzan and the Huntress 47. Song of the Thin Man 47. Prince of Thieves 47. Walls of Jericho 48. The Return of Wildfire 48. Sofia 48. Song without End 60.

Morita, Pat (1930–   ) (Noriyuki Morita). Japanese-American character actor.
Thoroughly Modern Millie 64. Midway 76. When Time Ran Out 80. *The Karate Kid* (AAN) 84. Karate Kid II 86. Captive Hearts (& co-w) 87. Collision Course 88. The Karate Kid Part III 89. Ice Runner 91. Lena's Holiday 91. Golden Chute . . . Wings of Grey 92. Honeymoon in Vegas 92. Even Cowgirls Get the Blues 93. The Next Karate Kid 94, etc.
TV series: The Queen and I 69. Sanford and Son 74–75. Happy Days 75–76. Mr T and Tina 76. Blansky's Beauties 77. Happy Days 82–83.

Morlay, Gaby (1897–1964) (Blanche Fumoleau). French character actress.
La Sandale Rouge 13. Les Nouveaux Messieurs 28. Derrière la Façade 38. Le Voile Bleu 42. Gigi 48. Le Plaisir 51. Mitsou 55. Ramuntcho 58, many others.

Morley, Karen (1905–   ) (Mildred Linton). American leading lady of the 30s.
Inspiration 31. *Scarface* 32. Dinner at Eight 33. Our Daily Bread 34. Beloved Enemy 36. Kentucky 38. Pride and Prejudice 40. Jealousy 45. The Unknown 46. 'M' 51, many others.

Morley, Robert (1908–1992). Portly British character actor (and playwright), on stage from 1929, films from 1938.
Autobiography: 1966, *Robert Morley, Responsible Gentleman*. Biography: 1993, *Robert My Father* by Sheridan Morley.
Marie Antoinette (US) (AAN) 38. *Major Barbara* 40. *The Young Mr Pitt* 42. I Live in Grosvenor Square 45. An Outcast of the Islands 51. The African Queen 51. *Gilbert and Sullivan* 53. *Beat the Devil* 53. Around the World in Eighty Days 56. The Doctor's Dilemma 59. *Oscar Wilde* 60. The Young Ones 61. Murder at the Gallop 63. Those Magnificent Men in Their Flying Machines 65. The Alphabet Murders 65. A Study in Terror 65. Hotel Paradiso 66. Way Way Out (US) 66. The Trygon Factor 67. Sinful Davey 69. When Eight Bells Toll 71. Theatre of Blood 73. The Blue Bird 76. *Who Is Killing the Great Chefs of Europe?* 78. Scavenger Hunt 79. The Human Factor 79. O Heavenly Dog 80. The Great Muppet Caper 81. High Road to China 82, etc.

¶ Anyone who works is a fool. I don't work: I merely inflict myself on the public. – *R.M.*

I believe there are two things necessary for salvation: money and gunpowder. – *R.M.*

It is a great help for a man to be in love with himself. For an actor it is absolutely essential. – *R.M.*

Fortunately, I'm not an actor who has ever got into the habit of refusing film roles, holding that if one doesn't read the script in advance, or see

the finished product, there is nothing to prevent one accepting the money, and then spending it. – *R.M.*

Moroder, Giorgio (1940–   ). Italian composer in America.
Midnight Express (AA) 78. Foxes 80. American Gigolo 80. Cat People 82. Flashdance (AA song) 83. Superman III 83. Scarface 83. The Neverending Story (co-m) 84. Electric Dreams 84. Metropolis (new m) 85. Over the Top 87. Fair Game 88. Let It Ride 89. Cybereden (It.) 93, etc.

Moross, Jerome (1913–1983). American composer.
When I Grow Up 51. The Sharkfighters 56. The Big Country 58. The Proud Rebel 58. The Jayhawkers 59. The Cardinal 63. The War Lord 65. Rachel Rachel 68, etc.

Morricone, Ennio (1928–   ). Prolific Italian composer and arranger.
A Fistful of Dollars 64. El Greco 64. Fists in the Pockets 65. For a Few Dollars More 65. *The Good the Bad and the Ugly* 66. The Big Gundown 66. Matchless 67. Theorem 69. *Once Upon a Time in the West* 69. Investigation of a Citizen 69. Fraulein Doktor 69. The Bird with the Crystal Plumage 70. The Sicilian Clan 70. Two Mules for Sister Sara 70. Cat O'Nine Tails 71. The Red Tent 71. Four Flies in Grey Velvet 71. The Decameron 71. The Burglars 71. The Black Belly of the Tarantula 72. Bluebeard 72. The Serpent 72. A Fistful of Dynamite 72. 1900 76. Exorcist II: The Heretic 77. Orca 77. Days of Heaven 78. Bloodline 79. The Island 80. La Cage aux Folles II 80. So Fine 81. Butterfly 82. White Dog 82. The Thing 82. Nana 83. Sahara 83. Once upon a Time in America 84. La Cage aux Folles III 85. *The Mission* (AAN) 86. *The Untouchables* (AAN) 87. A Time of Destiny 88. Frantic 88. Casualties of War 89. *Cinema Paradiso* 89. To Forget Palermo (Dimenticare Palermo) 89. Everybody's Fine (Stanno Tutti Bene) 90. Tie Me Up! Tie Me Down! (¡Atame!) 90. State of Grace 90. Bugsy (AAN) 91. Husbands and Lovers 91. Especially on Sunday (La Domenica Specialmente) 91. Jona che Visse nella Balena 93. La Scorta 93. In the Line of Fire 93. Il Lungo Silenzio 93. A Simple Formality (Una Pura Formalita) 94. En Suivant la Comète 94. Love Affair 94. Wolf 94. Genesis: The Creation and the Flood (Genesi: La Creazione e il Diluvio) 94. The Night and the Moment 94, many others.

Morris, Chester (1901–1970). Jut-jawed American leading man of the 30s, an agreeable 'B' picture lead who later became a considerable stage and TV actor.
Alibi (AAN) 29. She Couldn't Say No 30. The Divorce 30. *The Big House* 30. The Bat Whispers 31. The Miracle Man 32. Red Headed Woman 32. Blondie Johnson 33. The Gift of Gab 34. I've Been Around 35. Society Doctor 35. Moonlight Murder 36. They Met in a Taxi 36. Flight from Glory 37. Law of the Underworld 38. Smashing the Rackets 38. Blind Alibi 39. *Five Came Back* 39. The Marines Fly High 40. No Hands on the Clock 41. Meet Boston Blackie 41 (and subsequent series of 12 films until 1949). I Live on Danger 42. Wrecking Crew 43. Secret Command 44. Double Exposure 45. Unchained 55. The Great White Hope 70, etc.

Morris, Ernest (1915–   ). British director, mainly of second features for the Danzigers.
The Tell-Tale Heart 60. Echo of Diana 64. The Return of Mr Moto 65, etc.

Morris, Errol (1948–   ). American director and screenwriter, usually of quirky documentaries. His *The Thin Blue Line* helped release a man wrongly convicted of murder. *The Dark Wind* was his first fictional film.
Gates of Heaven 78. Vernon, Florida 81. The Thin Blue Line 88. A Brief History of Time (TV) 91. The Dark Wind 92, etc.

Morris, Greg (1934–   ). American supporting actor.
The Lively Set 64. The Doomsday Flight (TV) 66. Countdown at Kusini 76, etc.
TV series: Mission Impossible 66–73. Vegas 78–80.

Morris, Howard (1919–   ). American comedy director.
Boys Night Out (a only) 62. Who's Minding the Mint? 67. With Six You Get Egg Roll 68. Don't Drink the Water 69. Goin' Coconuts 78, etc.

Morris, John (1926–   ). American composer who has scored many of Mel Brooks's films.
The Producers 67. The Gamblers 69. The Twelve Chairs 70. Blazing Saddles (AAN title s) 74. Young Frankenstein 74. The Bank Shot 74. The Adventures of Sherlock Holmes' Smarter Brother 75. Silent Movie 76. The Last Remake of Beau Geste 77. The World's Greatest Lover 77. High Anxiety 77. The In-Laws 79. The Elephant Man (AAN) 80. In God We Trust 80. History of the World Part I 81. Table for Five 83. Yellowbeard 83. To Be or Not To Be 83. The Woman in Red 84. Johnny Dangerously 84. Clue 85. The Doctor and the Devils 85. Haunted Honeymoon 86. Ironweed 87. Dirty Dancing 87. Spaceballs 87. The Wash 88. Second Sight 89. Stella 90. Life Stinks 91, etc.

Morris, Lana (1930–   ). British leading lady of the 50s.
Spring in Park Lane 47. The Weaker Sex 48. Trottie True 49. The Chiltern Hundreds 49. The Woman in Question 50. Trouble in Store 53. Man of the Moment 55. Home and Away 56. I Start Counting 70, many others.

Morris, Mary (1895–1970). American stage actress who played her stage role of the evil old lady in *Double Door* 34.

Morris, Mary (1915–1988). British character actress with dominant personality, on stage from 1925.
Prison without Bars (film debut) 38. The Spy in Black 39. The Thief of Baghdad 40. *Pimpernel Smith* 41. Undercover 43. The Man from Morocco 45. Train of Events 49. High Treason 51, many others.

Morris, Oswald (1915–   ). British cinematographer, in films from 1932.
Green for Danger 46. *Moulin Rouge* 53. Knave of Hearts 53. Beat the Devil 53. Beau Brummell 54. Moby Dick 56. A Farewell to Arms 57. The Key 58. Roots of Heaven 59. Look Back in Anger 59. Our Man in Havana 59. The Entertainer 60. Lolita 62. Of Human Bondage 64. *The Pumpkin Eater* (BFA) 64. The Hill (BFA) 65. Life at the Top 65. The Spy Who Came In from the Cold 65. Stop the World I Want To Get Off 66. *The Taming of the Shrew* 67. Oliver! (AAN) 68. Goodbye Mr Chips 69. Scrooge 70. Fiddler on the Roof (AA) 71. Lady Caroline Lamb 72. The Mackintosh Man 73. The Odessa File 74. The Man Who Would Be King 75. Equus 77. The Wiz 78. Just Tell Me What You Want 80. The Great Muppet Caper 81. Dark Crystal 82, etc.

Morris, Wayne (1914–1959) (Bert de Wayne Morris).
Brawny American leading man with stage experience.
China Clipper (debut) 36. *Kid Galahad* 37. Brother Rat and a Baby 39. Bad Men of Missouri 40. The Smiling Ghost 41. Deep Valley 47. The Time of Your Life 47. The Tougher They Come 50. The Master Plan 55. The Crooked Sky 57. Paths of Glory 58, etc.

Morrison, Ernie 'Sunshine Sammy' (1913–1989).
American child actor and vaudeville performer, one of the original kids in the Our Gang comedies of the early 20s, on screen from the age of three. In the early 40s, he appeared in films featuring the East Side Kids.

Morrison, James (1888–1974).
American leading actor in Vitagraph movies. He retired early to become a drama teacher.
A Tale of Two Cities 11. Beau Brummel 12. A Tale of Two Cities 17. Sacred Silence 19. The Midnight Bride 20. Black Beauty 21. The Little Minister 22. Captain Blood 24. Wreckage 25. The Count of Luxembourg 26. Twin Flappers 27, etc.

Morrissey, Paul (1939–).
American 'underground' director associated with Andy Warhol.
Flesh 68. Trash 70. *Heat* 72. Women in Revolt 72. Andy Warhol's Frankenstein 73. Andy Warhol's Dracula 74. The Hound of the Baskervilles 77. Madame Wang's 81. Forty-Deuce 82. Mixed Blood 84. Beethoven's Nephew 85. Spike of Bensonhurst 88, etc.

¶ When you direct films you lose a lot of the qualities that Hollywood gave us, which were stars. So we look for stars and let them do what they want. – *P.M.*

Morros, Boris (1891–1963) (Boris Milhailovitch).
Russian-born independent producer in America from the late 30s. Later revealed as an American agent via his 1957 book *Ten Years a Counterspy*, filmed in 1960 as *Man on a String*, with Ernest Borgnine as Morros.
The Flying Deuces 39. Second Chorus 41. Tales of Manhattan 42. Carnegie Hall 48.

Morrow, Doretta (1925–1968) (Doretta Marano).
American singing star who appeared in one film, *Because You're Mine* 52.

Morrow, Jeff (1913–1993).
Mature American leading man, former Broadway and TV actor, in Hollywood from 1953.
The Robe 53. Flight to Tangier 53. Siege of Red River 54. Tanganyika 54. Sign of the Pagan 54. *This Island Earth* 55. The Creature Walks Among Us 56. The Giant Claw 57. The Story of Ruth 60. Harbour Lights 63. Octaman 71, etc.
TV series: Union Pacific 58–59. Temperatures Rising 73–74.

Morrow, Jo (1940–).
American leading lady of the 60s.
Because They're Young 56. Brushfire 57. The Legend of Tom Dooley 59. Our Man in Havana 59. The Three Worlds of Gulliver 60. He Rides Tall 63. Sunday in New York 64. Doctor Death 73, etc.

Morrow, Vic (1932–1982).
American actor formerly cast as a muttering juvenile delinquent. Stage experience. He died in

an accident while filming *The Twilight Zone*. He is the father of actress Jennifer Jason Leigh.
The Blackboard Jungle (film debut) 55. Tribute to a Bad Man 56. Men in War 57. God's Little Acre 58. Cimarron 61. Portrait of a Mobster 61. Sledge (d only) 69. The Glass House (TV) 72. The Take 74. Captains and the Kings (TV) 76. Treasure of Matecumbe 76. The Bad News Bears 76. Roots (TV) 77. Funeral for an Assassin 77. The Hostage Heart (TV) 77. Wild and Wooly (TV) 78. Humanoids from the Deep 80. The Twilight Zone 83, etc.
TV series: Combat 62–66. B.A.D. Cats 80.

Morse, Barry (1919–).
British leading man who moved to Canada and became a star of stage and TV there.
The Goose Steps Out 42. When We Are Married 42. There's a Future in It 43. Late at Night 46. Daughter of Darkness 48. No Trace 50; then after long gap – Kings of the Sun 63. Justine 69. Asylum 72. Power Play 75. The Shape of Things to Come (TV) 79. The Changeling 80. The Winds of War (TV) 83. Sadat (as Begin) (TV) 83. Whoops Apocalypse 83. A Woman of Substance (TV) 84. Glory! Glory! 90, etc.
TV series: *The Fugitive* (as Lt Gerard) 63–66. The Adventurer 72. Zoo Gang 73. Space 1999 75–76.

Morse, Helen (1948–).
Australian leading actress.
Jock Petersen 75. *Caddie* 78. Picnic at Hanging Rock 79. Agatha 79. *A Town Like Alice* (TV) 81. Far East 82. Iris 89, etc.

Morse, Robert (1931–).
American comedy actor who usually plays the befuddled innocent.
The Matchmaker 58. Honeymoon Hotel 64. Quick before It Melts 65. *The Loved One* 65. Oh Dad, Poor Dad 66. *How to Succeed in Business without Really Trying* 67. Where Were You When the Lights Went Out? 68. The Boatniks 69. The Emperor's New Clothes 87, etc.
TV series: That's Life 68.

Morse, Susan E.
American film editor, mainly on Woody Allen's movies.
Manhattan 79. Stardust Memories 80. Arthur 81. A Midsummer Night's Sex Comedy 82. Zelig 83. Broadway Danny Rose 84. The Purple Rose of Cairo 85. Hannah and Her Sisters (AAN) 86. Radio Days 87. Another Woman 88. New York Stories 89. Crimes and Misdemeanors 89. Alice 90. Shadows and Fog 91. Manhattan Murder Mystery 93. Bullets over Broadway 94, etc.

Morse, Terry (1906–1984).
American second-feature director.
◼ Jane Arden 39. On Trial 39. Waterfront 39. Smashing the Money Ring 39. No Place to Go 39. British Intelligence 40. Tear Gas Squad 40. Fog Island 45. Danny Boy 46. Shadows over Chinatown 46. Dangerous Money 46. Bells of San Fernando 47. Unknown World 51. Godzilla (US version) 56. Taffy and the Jungle Hunter 65. Young Dillinger 65.

Mortensen, Viggo.
American leading actor.
Salvation! 87. Prison 88. The Reflecting Skin 91. The Indian Runner 91. American Yazuka 93. Boiling Point 93. Ruby Cairo 93. Young Americans 93. Carlito's Way 93. The Passion of Darkly Noon 95, etc.

morticians:
see *undertakers*.

Mortimer, John (1923–).
British playwright who has worked in films. Originally scriptwriter for Crown Film Unit.
Autobiography: 1982, *Clinging to the Wreckage*.
The Innocents 61. Guns of Darkness 63. The Dock Brief 63. The Running Man 63. Bunny Lake Is Missing 65. John and Mary 70. Rumpole of the Bailey (TV) 78–9, Brideshead Revisited 81. Paradise Postponed 86, etc.

Morton, Clive (1904–1975).
Straight-faced British character actor on stage from 1926, films from 1932, usually in slightly pompous roles.
The Blarney Stone 32. Dead Men Tell No Tales 39. While the Sun Shines 46. Scott of the Antarctic 48. The Blue Lamp 49. His Excellency 51. Carrington VC 54. Richard III 56. Shake Hands with the Devil 59. Lawrence of Arabia 62. Stranger in the House 67, many others.

Morton, Rocky.
British director who works in collaboration with Annabel Jankel.
The Max Headroom Story (co-d) (TV) 85. D.O.A. (co-d) 88. Super Mario Bros (co-d) 93.

M.O.S.
Mysterious Hollywood script abbreviation indicating a silent shot. Allegedly it derived from the early 30s, when one of the many immigrant German directors called for a scene 'mit out sound'.

Moscovitch, Maurice (1871–1940) (Morris Maaskoff).
American character player, a Russian immigrant who spent many years starring in the Yiddish Theatre. Father of Noel Madison.
◼ Winterset 36. Make Way for Tomorrow 37. Lancer Spy 37. Gateway 37. Suez 38. Love Affair 39. Susannah of the Mounties 39. In Name Only 39. Rio 39. The Great Commandment 39. Everything Happens at Night 39. South to Karanga 40. The Great Dictator 40. Dance Girl Dance 40.

Mosjoukine, Ivan (1889–1939).
Russian actor of the old school, who appeared in many international films.
The Defence of Sebastopol 11. Satan Triumphant 22. Tempest (Fr.) 22. Shadows That Mass (Fr.) 23. Casanova (Fr./It.) 27. Sergeant X (Fr.) 30. Nitchevo (Fr.) 36, etc.

Mosley, Roger E.
American character actor.
The New Centurions 72. Hit Man 72. Terminal Island 73. Leadbelly (title role) 76. The Greatest 77. Semi-Tough 77. Roots II (TV) 78. The Jericho Mile (TV) 79. Steel 80. Heart Condition 90. Unlawful Entry 92, etc.

Moss, Arnold (1910–1989).
American character actor often seen in sly or sinister roles.
Temptation 47. The Black Book (as Napoleon) 49. Kim 51. Viva Zapata 52. Casanova's Big Night 54. The Twenty-Seventh Day 57. The Fool Killer 64. Gambit 66. Caper of the Golden Bulls 67, many others.

'The Most Dangerous Game'.
Richard Connell's well-known short story concerned a mad sportsman who trapped human beings on a tropical island in order to hunt them and display their heads in the trophy room. The first film version (GB: *The Hounds of Zaroff*) was produced in 1932 by Merian C. Cooper, directed by

Ernest Schoedsack and Irving Pichel, starring Leslie Banks. In 1945 it was remade as *Game of Death*, with Edgar Barrier; in 1948 Johnny Allegro borrowed liberally from it, with George Macready shooting arrows at George Raft; *Kill or Be Killed* in 1950 had George Coulouris as the menace; *The Black Castle* in 1952, directed by Nathan Juran with Boris Karloff, set the story in the 18th century. In 1954 *The Black Forest*, directed by Gene Martel, was a dull 'B' feature; *Run for the Sun* in 1956 made Trevor Howard a refugee Nazi in the Brazilian jungle, pursuing unwary intruders with savage hounds. In 1961, *Bloodlust*, directed by Ralph Brooks, was an even worse remake, aimed at the market for teenage horror; 1966 found Cornel Wilde on the run from African headhunters in *The Naked Prey*, which used basically the same story; in 1973 *To Kill a Clown* proved to be yet another retread, as was the TV movie *Maneater*. It cropped up again in 1993 as *Hard Target*, with Jean-Claude Van Damme in the lead, and in 1994 as *Surviving the Game*, directed by Ernest Dickerson with Ice-T as the intended victim. A variation of the plot has become constant in many martial arts movies of the 80s and 90s: a mad entrepreneur kidnaps or blackmails a fighter, forcing him to engage in gladiatorial contests to the death with experts at kick-boxing and other esoteric disciplines.

Mostel, Zero (1915–1977).
Heavyweight American comedian principally seen on Broadway stage.

  Panic in the Streets 50. *The Enforcer* 51. A Funny Thing Happened on the Way to the Forum 66. Great Catherine 68. *The Producers* 68. The Great Bank Robbery 69. The Angel Levine 69. The Hot Rock 72. Marco 73. Rhinoceros 73. Journey into Fear 75. The Front 76. Mastermind 76, etc.

Famous line (*The Producers*): 'Leo, he who hesitates is poor.'

mother love
has been the driving force of many of the screen's most popular, and therefore most remade, melodramas, such as *Imitation of Life*, *Madame X*, *Stella Dallas*, *Over the Hill*, *Mrs Wiggs of the Cabbage Patch* and *To Each His Own*. Britain chipped in with *The Woman in the Hall*, *The White Unicorn*, and *When the Bough Breaks*. Some say that Hitchcock made *Psycho* as the ultimate riposte to this sentimental tendency; but *The Anniversary* came a close second. Nor should mother-motivated gangsters such as those in *White Heat*, *Villain* and *The Krays* be forgotten, while Melina Mercouri in *Promise at Dawn* and Rosalind Russell in *Gypsy* were perhaps the most sinister mothers of all.

Motion Picture Association of America
A trade guild in which distributors meet to set tariffs and deal with complaints, also set a censorship code.

motor-cycles,
hideous and unbearably noisy machines, have become a badge of aggressive youth, and since *The Wild Angels* in 1966 American drive-in screens have been filled with a host of cheap movies extolling the pleasures of leather-jacketed speed with a bird on the back. All of these appear to have been banned in Britain, as was *The Wild One*, an early example of the genre, in 1954. But we did let through Elvis Presley in *Roustabout*, and Steve McQueen doing his own stunt sequence in *The Great Escape*, and *Easy Rider*, and *Coogan's Bluff*, and *Little Fauss and Big Halsy*, and we even made *The Leather Boys*, about our own ton-up teenagers. As for *Girl on a Motorcycle*, in which the bike becomes

the ultimate sex symbol, words fail one. There was a good British film about speedway racing, *Once a Jolly Swagman*, and one about the fairground called *Wall of Death*. Comedian George Formby went in for the TT races in *No Limit*, and rode a motor-bike also in *It's In the Air*. Groucho Marx used one to comic effect in *Duck Soup*, as did Horst Buchholz in *One, Two, Three*. In American films, the motor-cycle cops are too familiar to warrant individual attention but *Electra Glide in Blue* took one seriously. *Easy Rider*, almost an *hommage* to the machine, is also the most successful film to feature it.

motor racing
has been the subject of many a routine melodrama, and always seems to reduce the writer to banalities, even in a spectacular like *Grand Prix*. Some other examples of the genre include *The Crowd Roars*, *Indianapolis Speedway*, *Checkpoint*, *The Green Helmet*, *The Devil's Hairpin*, *Red Line 7000*, *Le Mans*, *Winning* and *Days of Thunder*. The funniest comedy use of the sport was probably in *Ask a Policeman*, when Will Hay accidentally drove a bus on to Brooklands racetrack in the middle of a race.

Moulder Brown, John (1945–).
British actor, usually of intense roles.
  Deep End 69. Vampire Circus 71. King Queen Knave 72. Ludwig 72. The Confessions of Felix Krull (TV) 82, Rumpelstiltskin 87, etc.

Moullet, Luc (1937–).
French director, screenwriter, producer and actor, usually of comic movies, a former film critic.
  Brigitte et Brigitte 66. Une Aventure de Billy le Kid 71. La Comédie du Travail 87. Les Sièges de l'Alcazar 89, etc.

Mount, Peggy (1916–).
British character comedienne with long experience in repertory before starring as the termagant mother-in-law in *Sailor Beware*.
  ■ The Embezzler 54. Sailor Beware 56. Dry Rot 57. The Naked Truth 58. Inn for Trouble 59. Ladies Who Do 63. One Way Pendulum 64. Hotel Paradiso 65. Finders Keepers 66. Oliver! 68. The Princess and the Goblin (voice) 92.
  TV series: The Larkins 58–60. George and the Dragon 66–67. Winning Widows. You're Only Young Twice 77.

mountains
have provided a challenge in innumerable movies including *The Challenge*, *The White Tower*, *The Mountain*, *The White Hell of Pitz Palu*, *The Gold Rush*, *Trail of 98*, *The Eiger Sanction*, *The Snows of Kilimanjaro*, *The Abominable Snowman*, *Lost Horizon*, *Goodbye Mr Chips*, *K2* and *Scream of Stone*.

Movie Parade,
by Paul Rotha. An influential and glossy book of stills illustrating the film as an art. First published 1936; revised, with additional work by Roger Manvell, 1950.

The Movies,
by Richard Griffith and Arthur Mayer. This witty, large and lavishly illustrated survey has been kept in print, in various editions, since it first appeared around 1960.

movies
¶ The cinema is an art. Movies are . . . well, movies. Are they a good thing? To Cecil B. de Mille they were:
  The new literature.
To Barbara Streisand, starting to shoot *Funny Girl*:

  This is for posterity. Everything I do will be on film forever.
To Sarah Bernhardt they were:
  My one chance for immortality.
Darryl F. Zanuck called them:
  The greatest political fact in the world today.
Sam Spiegel was careful in his commendation:
  The best motion pictures are those which reach you as entertainment, and by the time you leave have provoked thoughts. A picture that provokes no thoughts is usually not well conceived and does not entertain one anyway.
Warren Beatty gave a verbal shrug:
  Movies are fun, but they're not a cure for cancer.
In Ava Gardner's experience:
  It's the kissiest business in the world. You have to keep kissing people.
Ben Hecht took the money and ran:
  Movies are one of the bad habits that have corrupted our century.
and:
  They have slipped into the American mind more misinformation in one evening than the Dark Ages could muster in a decade.
and:
  A movie is never any better than the stupidest man connected with it.
David O. Selznick was thoughtful:
  There might have been good movies if there had been no movie industry.
St John Ervine had little time for them:
  American movies are written by the half-educated for the half-witted.
H. L. Mencken similarly called them:
  Entertainment for the moron majority. And added:
  The kind of jackass who likes the movies as they are is the kind who keeps them as they are.
And again:
  No one ever went broke underestimating the taste of the American public.
Stephen Longstreet knew the root of the trouble:
  In the Hollywood studios, the mass attack of a mob of halfwits in sport shirts and fifty-dollar shoes stamps any real idea to death before it leaves the studio.
S. J. Perelman summed up his own experiences:
  Movie scriptwriting is no worse than playing piano in a call house.
Pare Lorentz was a shade more hopeful:
  There's no trick to movies. All the businessman needs to do is to employ a fine playwright, a group of good actors, a skilful cameraman, and put them all under the direction of a man who understands the possibilities of the camera and who has besides a comic gift, charm, and dramatic skill – leave them to work unchecked – and he'll get popular entertainment almost every time.
Ivan Butler despaired:
  Whoever has the original idea for a movie, it is soon taken away from him.
E. B. White in 1956 saw a gleam of light:
  The movies long ago decided that a wider commercial exploitation could be achieved by a deliberate descent to a lower level, and they walked downhill till they found the cellar. Now they are groping for the light switch, looking for the way out.
Robert E. Sherwood was scathing in 1922:
  Who invented hokum? Think how much money he'd have made from the film producers if he'd sold his invention on a royalty basis!
Will Rogers was satirical:
  There's only one thing that can kill the movies, and that's education.
Maybe Robert Mitchum has the last word:

What's history going to say about the movies? All those rows of seats facing a blank screen? Crazy!

Meanwhile, a few tips on the making of movies: You should think of each shot as you make it as the most important one in the film. – *Henry Blanke*

Don't act, think! – *F.W. Murnau*

Making a film is like going down a mine – once you've started you bid a metaphorical goodbye to the daylight and the outside world for the duration. – *John Schlesinger*

In a good movie, the sound could go off and the audience would still have a perfectly clear idea of what was going on. – *Alfred Hitchcock*

If we can make films that are useful as well as entertaining, marvellous. But cinema must reflect the temper of the times. We must choose material not only on the basis of whether we feel deeply, but on whether or not anyone's bloody well going to see it. – *Richard Lester*

Me, if I can't blow up the world in the first ten seconds, the show is a flop. – *Irwin Allen*

You can't overthrow regimes through movies, but it can help. – *J.A. Bardem*

I believe that although the motion picture may not live forever as a work of art, except in a few instances, it will be the most efficient way of showing posterity how we live now. – *Irving Thalberg*

Ninety-five per cent of films are born of frustration, of self-despair, of ambition for survival, for money, for fattening bank accounts. Five per cent, maybe less, are made because a man has an idea, an idea which he must express. – *Samuel Fuller*

The movie is a reflector and not an innovator. – *Jack Valenti*

The cinema is not a slice of life, it's a piece of cake. – *Alfred Hitchcock*

Movies, like detective stories, make it possible to experience without danger all the excitement, passion and desirousness which must be suppressed in a humanitarian ordering of society. – *Carl Jung*

They may cost a lot, but none of the money is wasted. All my pictures can be reissued again and again. They stand up pretty well, and they retain their residual values, both financial and prestige-wise. – *Sam Spiegel*

Messages are for Western Union. – *Sam Goldwyn*

There's too much pretentious nonsense talked about the artistic problems of making pictures. I've never had a goddam artistic problem in my life, never, and I've worked with the best of them. – *John Wayne*

Let me tell you what this business is about. It's cunt and horses! – *Harry Cohn*

Some critics say that people complain about the movies because the movies do not reflect reality. It is this writer's suspicion that more people lament the fact that reality does not reflect the movies. – *Leo Rosten*

I know audiences feed on crap, but I can't believe we are so lacking that we cannot dish it up to them with some trace of originality. – *Darryl F. Zanuck*

The public is never wrong. – *Adolph Zukor*

Movies for the Millions,
by Gilbert Seldes. A historical account of the American cinema, published in 1937. Also known by the title *The Movies Come from America*.

The Movies in the Age of Innocence,
by Edward Charles Wagenknecht. First published

in 1962, this is an enthusiastic account of silent films by a regular filmgoer of those days.

Moviola.
A portable editing machine which enables the user to run film backwards and forwards at various speeds and to examine it frame by frame while viewing it on a small screen.

Movita (1915–) (Movita Castenada).
Mexican leading lady, briefly in Hollywood. She was formerly married to Marlon Brando.

Mutiny on the Bounty 35. Paradise Isle 36. Wolf Call 39. Dream Wife 53. Apache Ambush 55. The Panic in Needle Park 71, etc.

Mowbray, Alan (1893–1969).
Imperious-mannered British character actor, in America from the early 1920s; appeared later in nearly 400 films, often as butler or pompous emissary.

Alexander Hamilton 31. Sherlock Holmes 32. Roman Scandals 33. Becky Sharp 35. Desire 36. *My Man Godfrey* 36. Topper 37. Stand In 37. *The Villain Still Pursued Her* 40. Lady Hamilton 41. That Uncertain Feeling 41. A Yank at Eton 42. His Butler's Sister 43. Holy Matrimony 43. Where Do We Go from Here? 45. *Terror by Night* 45. Merton of the Movies 46. *My Darling Clementine* 46. Prince of Thieves 47. The Jackpot 50. Wagonmaster 50. Dick Turpin's Ride 51. Androcles and the Lion 53. The King's Thief 55. The King and I 56, many others.

TV series: Colonel Flack 53. The Mickey Rooney Show 54. Dante 60.

Mowbray, Malcolm.
British director who went to Hollywood after his first success.

A Private Function 84. Out Cold 88. Don't Tell Her It's Me 90. Clothes in the Wardrobe 92, etc.

Mower, Patrick (1940–).
British leading man, mainly in TV series *Callan, Special Branch, Target*.

The Smashing Bird I Used to Know 69. Cry of the Banshee 70. Black Beauty 70. Catch Me a Spy 71. Carry On England 76. The Devil's Advocate 78. Marco Polo (TV) 81, etc.

Moxey, John (1920–).
British TV director who has made occasional films and many TV movies in America (as John Llewellyn Moxey).

City of the Dead 59. The £20,000 Kiss 63. Ricochet 63. Strangler's Web 65. Circus of Fear 67. San Francisco International (TV) 70. The House That Would Not Die (TV) 70. A Taste of Evil (TV) 71. The Night Stalker (TV) 72. The Death of Me Yet (TV) 72. The Bounty Man (TV) 72. The Strange and Deadly Occurrence (TV) 74. Where Have All the People Gone? (TV) 74. Charlie's Angels (TV) 76. Nightmare in Badham County (TV) 77. The President's Mistress (TV) 78. Sanctuary of Fear (TV) 79. The Power Within (TV) 79. The Children of An Lac (TV) 80. No Place to Hide (TV) 81. Killjoy (TV) 81. The Cradle Will Fall (TV) 83. Through Naked Eyes (TV) 83. Lady Mobster (TV) 88, etc.

Moyle, Allan (1947–).
Canadian screenwriter and director, a former actor, now in Hollywood.

Montreal Main (a, co-w, co-d) 78. The Rubber Gun (a, d) 78. Times Square (d) 80. Pump Up the Volume (wd) 90. Love Crimes (w) 91. The Gun in Betty Lou's Handbag (wd) 92, etc.

MPEG
stands for the Motion Picture Experts Group and is a standard for the digital compression of images. The method compares and saves only the changes between one frame of a film or animation and another, thus enabling 72 minutes of film to be recorded on a five-inch compact disk. A refinement of the system, MPEG II, is being prepared.

Mudie, Leonard (1884–1965) (Leonard M. Cheetham).
British character actor in Hollywood.

The Mummy 32. The House of Rothschild 34. Clive of India 35. Lancer Spy 37. Dark Victory 39. Berlin Correspondent 42. My Name is Julia Ross 45. Song of My Heart 48. The Magnetic Monster 53. The Big Fisherman 59, many others.

Mueller, Elisabeth (1926–).
Swiss-German leading lady who made some Hollywood films.

The Power and the Prize 56. El Hakim 58. Confess Dr Corda 58. The Angry Hills 59, etc.

Mueller-Stahl, Armin (1930–).
German leading actor, from the theatre, now in international films. He was formerly a concert violinist.

The Secret Marriage (Heimliche Ehen) 56. Königskinder 62. Naked among the Wolves (Nackt unter Wölfen) 63. Wolf unter Wölfen 65. Der Dritte 72. Kit and Co. 74. Nelken in Aspik 76. Lola 81. Veronika Voss (Die Sehnsucht der Veronika) 82. Glut 83. Love in Germany (Un Amour en Allemagne) 83. Angry Harvest (Bittere Ernte) 85. Forget Mozart 85. Colonel Redl 85. Momo 86. Midnight Cop 88. God Does Not Believe in Us Anymore 88. Music Box 89. Avalon 90. Utz 91. Kafka 91. The Power of One 92. Night on Earth 92. Red Hot 92. Der Kinoerzähler 93. The House of the Spirits 94. Holy Matrimony 94. Taxandria 94, etc.

Muhammed Ali (1942–) (Cassius Clay).
American prizefighter who became an international personality before the last fight proved one too many.

The Greatest 77. Freedom Road (TV) 80.

¶ I'm young, I'm fast, I'm pretty, and I can't possibly be beat. – *M.A.*

I have said I am the greatest. Ain't nobody ever heard me say I'm the smartest? – *M.A.*

Muir, Esther (1895–).
American character actress usually seen as hard-faced blonde.

A Dangerous Affair 31. So This is Africa 33. The Bowery 33. Fury 36. *A Day at the Races* (in which she suffered memorably at the hands of Groucho Marx) 37. The Law West of Tombstone 38. Stolen Paradise 41. X Marks the Spot 42, etc.

Muir, Gavin (1907–1972).
Quiet-spoken American actor with a British accent, usually a smooth villain.

Lloyds of London 36. Wee Willie Winkie 37. Eagle Squadron 41. *Nightmare* 42. The Master Race 44. Salome Where She Danced 45. California 46. Ivy 47. Abbott and Costello Meet the Invisible Man 51. King of the Khyber Rifles 54. The Sea Chase 55. The Abductors 57. Johnny Trouble 59, many others.

TV series: The Betty Hutton Show 59.

Muir, Jean (1911–) (J. M. Fullerton).
American leading lady of the 30s.

Female 34. A Midsummer Night's Dream 35. Jane Steps Out (GB) 37. And One Was Beautiful 40. The Lone Wolf Meets a Lady 40. The Constant Nymph 44, etc.

Mulcahy, Russell (1953–).
Australian director, now working in America.
Derek and Clive Get the Horn (TV) 81. Razorback 84. Highlander 86. Highlander II – the Quickening 90. Ricochet 91. Blue Ice 92. The Real McCoy 93. The Shadow 94, etc.

Mulcaster, G. H. (1891–1964).
British character actor, mainly on stage; played formal types.
The Dummy Talks 43. Bonnie Prince Charlie 47. Spring in Park Lane 48. Under Capricorn 50, etc.

Muldaur, Diana (1943–).
Sensitive-looking American leading lady, McCloud's girlfriend on TV; adept at nice sophisticated types; also on TV in 1974, played Joy Adamson in Born Free.
■ The Swimmer 68. Number One 69. The Lawyer 70. The Other 71. One More Train to Rob 72. McQ 73. The Chosen Survivors 74. Charlie's Angels (TV) 76. Pine Canyon Is Burning (TV) 77. Black Beauty (TV) 78. To Kill a Cop (TV) 78. Maneaters Are Loose (TV) 78. The Word (TV) 78. Beyond Reason 82. Master Ninja 3 83.
TV series: The Survivors 69–70. McCloud 70–77. Born Free 74. The Tony Randall Show 76–78. Hizzonner 79. Fitz and Bones 81.

Mulford, Clarence E. (1895–1970).
American western novelist, the creator of Hopalong Cassidy.

Mulhall, Jack (1888–1979).
American silent-screen leading man.
Sirens of the Sea 17. Mickey 18. All of a Sudden Peggy 20. Molly O' 21. The Bad Man 23. The Goldfish 24. Friendly Enemies 25. The Poor Nut 27. Just Another Blonde 28. Dark Streets 29, many others; appeared as an 'old-timer' in Hollywood Boulevard 36.

Mulhare, Edward (1923–).
Irish leading man who has been on American stage.
Hill Twenty-Four Does Not Answer 55. Signpost to Murder 64. Von Ryan's Express 65. Our Man Flint 65. Eye of the Devil 67. Caprice 67. Gidget Grows Up (TV) 72. Megaforce 82, etc.
TV series: The Ghost and Mrs Muir 68–69. Knight Rider 82– .

Mullaney, Jack (1932–1982).
Easy-going light American actor.
The Young Stranger 57. Kiss Them for Me 58. The Absent Minded Professor 61. Seven Days in May 64. When the Legends Die 72. Where Does it Hurt? 72.
TV series: The Ann Sothern Show, My Living Doll, Ensign O'Toole, It's About Time.

Mullard, Arthur (1912–).
Big, bluff cockney character comedian who became a British television star of the 70s.
The Wrong Arm of the Law 63. The Great St Trinian's Train Robbery 67, many others.

Mullen, Barbara (1914–1979).
Irish-American actress, former dancer, who came to films as star of Jeannie 42.
Thunder Rock 42. A Place of One's Own 44. The Trojan Brothers 45. Corridor of Mirrors 48. So Little Time 52. The Challenge 60, etc.

TV series: Dr Finlay's Casebook 59–66.

Muller, Renate (1907–1937).
German leading lady best known abroad for Sunshine Susie 31.
Biography: 1944, Queen of America? by R. E. Clements.
Liebling der Götter 30. Viktor und Viktoria 34. Allotria 36.

Müller, Robby (1940–).
Dutch cinematographer, now in international films, who made his reputation working in Germany with Wim Wenders.
Summer in the City 70. The Goalkeeper's Fear of the Penalty Kick (Die Angst des Tormanns Beim Elfmeter) 71. The Scarlet Letter (Der Scharlachrote Buchstabe) 72. Alice in the Cities (Alice in den Städten) 74. Falsche Bewegung (Wrong Move) 75. Kings of the Road (Im Lauf der Zeit) 76. The American Friend (Der Amerikanische Freund) 77. Mysteries 79. Saint Jack 79. Honeysuckle Rose 80. They All Laughed 81. Paris, Texas 84. Repo Man 84. To Live and Die in L.A. 85. Down by Law 86. The Longshot 86. Barfly 87. The Believers 87. Mystery Train 89. Korczak 90. Until the End of the World (Bis ans Ende der Welt) 91. Mad Dog and Glory 93, etc.

Mulligan, Richard (1932–).
Lanky American character actor.
The Group 66. The Undefeated 69. Little Big Man 70. The Big Bus 76. Scavenger Hunt 79. S.O.B. 81. Trail of the Pink Panther 82. Micki and Maude 84. Teachers 84. The Heavenly Kid 85. A Fine Mess 86, etc.
TV series: The Hero 66. Diana 73–74. Soap 77–80. Reggie 83.

Mulligan, Robert (1925–).
American director, from TV.
■ Fear Strikes Out 57. The Rat Race 60. Come September 61. The Great Impostor 61. The Spiral Road 62. To Kill a Mockingbird (AAN) 62. Love with the Proper Stranger 64. Baby the Rain Must Fall 65. Inside Daisy Clover 65. Up the Down Staircase 67. The Stalking Moon 68. The Pursuit of Happiness 70. Summer of '42 71. The Other 73. The Nickel Ride 75. Bloodbrothers 78. Same Time Next Year 78. Kiss Me Goodbye 82. Clara's Heart 88. The Man in the Moon 91.

Mulroney, Dermot (1963–).
American actor.
Sunset 88. Young Guns 88. Staying Together 89. Survival Quest 89. Longtime Companion 90. Career Opportunities 91. Bright Angel 91. Where the Day Takes You 92. Samantha 92. Silent Tongue 93. Point of No Return 93. The Thing Called Love 93. Bad Girls 94. There Goes My Baby 94, etc.

multiplane.
A word introduced by Walt Disney to explain his new animation process for The Old Mill 37. Instead of building up a drawing by laying 'cells' directly on top of each other, a slight illusion of depth was obtained by leaving space between the celluloid images of foreground, background, principal figure, etc. Special Academy Award 1938.

multiple roles.
The record for the number of characters played by one actor in a film is held not by Alec Guinness in Kind Hearts and Coronets but (probably) by Lupino Lane, who played twenty-four parts in a 1929 comedy called Only Me, by Buster Keaton in The Playhouse, or by George S. Melies in his 1900

film The One Man Band. Others with high scores apart from Guinness' eight, include Robert Hirsch' dozen in No Questions on Saturday, Rod Steiger's seven in No Way to Treat a Lady, Paul Muni's sev in Seven Faces, Jerry Lewis' seven in The Family Jewels, Tony Randall's seven in The Seven Faces of Lao, Hugh Herbert's six in La Conga Nights, Peter Sellers' six in Soft Beds, Hard Battles, Fernandel's six in The Sheep Has Five Legs, Anna Neagle's fou in Lilacs in the Spring, Françoise Rosay's four in Une Femme Disparait, Louis Jourdan's and Joan Fontaine's four each in Decameron Nights, Rod Steiger's and Claire Bloom's four each in The Illustrated Man, Lionel Jeffries' four in The Secret My Success, Alan Young's four in Gentlemen Prefer Brunettes, Terry Kilburn's four generations of boy Goodbye Mr Chips, Moira Shearer's three in The Ma Who Loved Redheads, Deborah Kerr's three in The Life and Death of Colonel Blimp, Peter Sellers' three in The Mouse That Roared and Dr Strangelove, Leor Errol's three in some episodes of the Mexican Spitf series, Joanne Woodward's three in The Three Faces of Eve and Eleanor Parker's three in Lizzie. One should perhaps also count Danny Kaye's various dream selves in The Secret Life of Walter Mitty.

Dual roles have frequently been of the schizophrenic type of which Dr Jekyll and Mr Hy is the most obvious example. This category includes Henry Hull in Werewolf of London and Lo Chaney Jnr in The Wolf Man, Phyllis Calvert in Madonna of the Seven Moons, Phyllis Thaxter in Bewitched, Jerry Lewis in The Nutty Professor, Alec Guinness in The Captain's Paradise and Jeremy Iro in Dead Ringers. Two-character roles include Ronald Colman in The Masquerader and The Prison of Zenda, Lon Chaney in London After Midnight, Edward G. Robinson in The Man with Two Faces, Laurel and Hardy in Our Relations, Allan Jones an Joe Penner in The Boys from Syracuse, Chaplin in The Great Dictator, Louis Hayward in The Man in Iron Mask, Olivia de Havilland in The Dark Mirror, Boris Karloff in The Black Room, Herbert Lom in Dual Alibi, George M. Cohan in The Phantom President, Jack Palance in House of Numbers, Peter Whitney in Murder He Says, Elisabeth Bergner (an later Bette Davis) in Stolen Life, Bette Davis in Dea Ringer, Yul Brynner in The Double Man, Stanley Baxter in Very Important Person, Peter Lawford in One More Time, George Arliss in His Lordship, Ala Delon in The Black Tulip, John McIntire in The Lawless Breed, Valentino in Son of the Sheik, Jack Mulhall in Dark Streets (allegedly the first to use the split-image technique), Larry Parks (playing Jolson and himself) in Jolson Sings Again, Dougla Fairbanks Jnr in The Corsican Brothers, Jessie Matthews in Evergreen and Julie Christie in Fahrenheit 451.

multiple-story films
probably began in 1916 with Intolerance, which audiences rejected as too complicated. Later attempts made sure that the stories were clearly woven into a common thread; The Bridge of San Lu Rey in 1929, Grand Hotel in 1932, Friday the Thirteenth and Dinner at Eight in 1933, Un Carnet de Bal (also known as Christine) in 1936, Tales of Manhattan in 1942, Forever and a Day in 1942, Flesh and Fantasy in 1943, Weekend at the Waldorf and Dead of Night in 1945. In 1948–50 three Somerset Maugham compendiums, introduced b the author, emerged as Quartet, Trio and Encore; this inspired O. Henry's Full House in 1952. In 196 we had The VIPs and in 1964 The Yellow Rolls-Royce, the stories in the latter being very casually linked. Meanwhile horror compendiums were becoming popular, 1962's Tales of Terror being followed between 1967 and 1972 by Dr Terror's

use of Horrors, The Torture Garden, The House that
ripped Blood, Tales From the Crypt, Asylum, Vault of
orror, Tales that Witness Madness, From Beyond the
rave, The Monster Club, Creepshow and Cat's Eyes.

ulti-screen techniques
e nothing new, but the Montreal Exhibition of
967 made them fashionable again, so that in
ch films as The Boston Strangler, Grand Prix and
ie Thomas Crown Affair the audience was
pposed to look at up to a dozen different images
 the same time, which became mighty exhausting.
ercifully, the fashion soon wore off.

he Mummy.
terest in avenging mummies was aroused during
e 20s by the widespread stories of the curse of
utankhamen whose tomb had recently been
scovered and opened. In 1932 Karl Freund
rected a rather strange romantic film on the
bject with Boris Karloff as a desiccated but active
ree-thousand-year-old still on the track of his
st love. Despite good box office it was not reprised
til 1940, when The Mummy's Hand, a pure
kum thriller, appeared with Tom Tyler in the
le. Between 1942 and 1944 there were three
creasingly foolish sequels starring (if it really *was*
m under the bandages) Lon Chaney Jnr: they
ere The Mummy's Tomb, The Mummy's Ghost and
ie Mummy's Curse. In 1959 Hammer took over
e character and remade The Mummy with an
nglish Victorian setting: Christopher Lee was the
onster. There have been two poor sequels, The
irse of the Mummy's Tomb 64 and The Mummy's
iroud 66. Blood From The Mummy's Tomb 71 did
ot feature a monster; it was based on a Bram
oker story. The lighter side of the subject was
ewed by Wheeler and Woolsey in Mummy's Boys
6, the Three Stooges in Mummie's Dummies 38, and
bbott and Costello in Meet the Mummy 54.

umy, Billy (1954–).
merican child actor of the 60s.
 Palm Springs Weekend 63. A Ticklish Affair 63.
ar Brigitte 65. Rascal 69. Bless the Beasts and
hildren 71. Papillon 73. Twilight Zone – the
ovie 83. Hard to Hold 84, etc.
 TV series: Lost in Space 65–68. Sunshine 75.

undin, Herbert (1898–1939).
ritish character actor with stage experience, in
ritish films in the 20s, Hollywood from 1930.
 The Devil's Lottery 31. Sherlock Holmes 32.
avalcade 33. David Copperfield (as Barkis) 34.
utiny on the Bounty 35. Another Dawn 37. The
dventures of Robin Hood (as Much the Miller) 38.
ociety Lawyer 39, etc.

une, Ian (1941–).
ew Zealand director and screenwriter, a former
tor.
 Sleeping Dogs (a, co-w) 77. Goodbye, Pork Pie
o-w) 80. Came a Hot Friday (co-w, d) 84. Bridge
 Nowhere (d) 85. The End of the Golden
eather (co-w, d) 91, etc.

uni, Paul (1896–1967) (Muni Weisenfreund).
istinguished American actor of Austrian
arentage. Long stage experience.
 Biography: 1974, Actor by Jerome Lawrence.
 The Valiant (film debut) (AAN) 28. Seven Faces
9. Scarface 32. I am a Fugitive from a Chain Gang
AAN) 32. The World Changes 33. Hi Nellie 33.
ordertown 34. Black Fury 35. Dr Socrates 35.
ie Story of Louis Pasteur (AA) 36. The Good Earth
7. The Life of Emile Zola (AAN) 37. The Woman
Love 38. Juarez 39. We Are Not Alone 39.
udson's Bay 40. The Commandos Strike at Dawn

42. Stage Door Canteen 43. A Song to Remember 44.
Counter Attack 45. Angel on My Shoulder 46.
Stranger on the Prowl 51. The Last Angry Man
(AAN) 59.
⚙ For convincing world audiences of his day that
heavy disguise made a great actor; and for his
powerful early performances. Scarface.

¶ Every time Paul Muni parts his beard and looks
 down a microscope, this company loses two
million dollars. – Hal B. Wallis, as Warner head of
production in the late 30s
 His voice is rich and pleasant, his personality is
strong and virile, and if he is not pretty, neither
is Lon Chaney. – Variety, 1929
 He seemed intent on submerging himself so
completely that he disappeared. – Bette Davis

Munk, Andrzej (1921–1961).
Polish director.
 Men of the Blue Cross 55. Eroica 57. Bad Luck
60. The Passenger (incomplete) 61, etc.

Munro, Caroline (1951–).
British leading lady.
 The Abominable Dr Phibes 71. Captain Kronos
72. The Golden Voyage of Sinbad 73. The Devil
Within Her 73. At the Earth's Core 76. The Spy
Who Loved Me 77. Maniac 80. Don't Open till
Christmas 84. Slaughter High 86. Night Owl (as
herself) 93, etc.

Munro, Janet (1934–1972).
Scottish leading lady with brief stage experience
before films in both GB and US.
 The Trollenberg Terror 57. The Young and the
Guilty 57. Darby O'Gill and the Little People 58.
Third Man on the Mountain 59. The Swiss Family
Robinson 60. The Day the Earth Caught Fire 62.
Life for Ruth 62. Bitter Harvest 63. A Jolly Bad
Fellow 64. Sebastian 67, etc.

Munsel, Patrice (1925–).
American operatic soprano who played the title
role in Melba 53.

Munshin, Jules (1915–1970).
Rubber-limbed American comedian, in occasional
films from the mid-40s.
 Easter Parade 48. Take Me Out to the Ball Game
48. On the Town 49. Ten Thousand Bedrooms 56.
Silk Stockings 57. Wild and Wonderful 64, etc.

Munson, Ona (1906–1955) (Ona Wolcott).
American character actress, former dancer.
 Going Wild 30. Five Star Final 32. Gone with
the Wind 39. Drums of the Congo 40. The
Shanghai Gesture (as Mother Gin Sling) 41. The
Cheaters 45. The Red House 47, etc.

Muppets.
An American cross between marionettes and
puppets which came in all sizes and shapes and
were stars of the TV series Sesame Street from 1969,
and their own British TV series The Muppet Show
76–80, before moving on to the big screen. The
best known characters were Kermit the Frog, Miss
Piggy and Fozzie Bear.
 The Muppet Movie 79. The Great Muppet Caper
81. The Muppets Take Manhattan 84. A Muppet
Christmas Carol 92.
 See also: Jim Henson; Frank Oz.

murderers
abound in fictional films, but only a handful of
real-life cases have been analysed with any
seriousness. There have been several 'lives' of
Charlie Peace and Landru, and fantasies about the

earlier French 'Bluebeard'. More recently a cold
clinical eye was applied to Barbara Graham in I
Want to Live 57, Dr Crippen 64, The Boston Strangler
68, John Christie in Ten Rillington Place 71. Ruth
Ellis was said to have inspired Yield to the Night 56
and Leopold and Loeb were plainly the subject of
Compulsion 58 as well as Rope 48. More recent years
have brought such case histories as In Cold Blood 67
and The Executioner's Song 82, and TV has done its
bit with Kill Me If You Can (Caryl Chessman)
77, The Lindbergh Kidnapping Case (Bruno
Hauptmann) 75 and Helter Skelter (Charles
Manson) 76.

Murdoch, Richard (1907–1990).
British radio entertainer, long partnered with
Arthur Askey and Kenneth Horne.
 Band Wagon 39. The Ghost Train 41. It Happened
in Soho 48. Golden Arrow 52. Not a Hope in Hell
59. Strictly Confidential 61. Whoops Apocalypse
86, etc.

Murfin, Jane (1893–1955).
American screenwriter.
 The Right to Lie 19. Flapper Wives 24. White
Fang 25. Meet the Prince 26. Dance Hall 29.
Leathernecking 30. Friends and Lovers 31. Our
Betters 33. Ann Vickers 33. Spitfire 34. This Man
Is Mine 34. Roberta 35. Alice Adams 35. Come and
Get It 36. The Shining Hour 38. Stand Up and Fight
39. Pride and Prejudice 40. Andy Hardy's Private
Secretary 41. Flight for Freedom 43. Dragon Seed
44, etc.
~Miss Murfin's plays as co-author, usually with
Jane Cowl, include Daybreak and Smilin' Through,
both of which were filmed.

Murnau, F.W. (Friedrich) (1888–1931) (F.W.
Plumpe).
German director in films from 1919; Hollywood
from 1927. Died in a car crash.
 Satanas 19. Dr Jekyll and Mr Hyde 20. Nosferatu
(Dracula) 22. The Last Laugh 24. Tartuffe 24. Faust
26. Sunrise 27. Four Devils 28. Our Daily Bread
(City Girl) 30. Tabu (co-d) 31, etc.
⚙ For unquestionable brilliance in showing what
the camera can do. The Last Laugh.

Murphy, Audie (1924–1971).
Boyish American leading man of the 50s; came to
films on the strength of his war record as
America's most decorated soldier, but despite some
talent was soon relegated to low-budget westerns.
Killed in a plane crash.
 ■ Beyond Glory 48. Texas Brooklyn and Heaven
48. Bad Boy 49. Sierra 50. The Kid from Texas
50. Kansas Raiders 50. The Red Badge of Courage 51.
The Cimarron Kid 51. The Duel at Silver Creek 52.
Gunsmoke 52. Column South 53. Tumbleweed 53.
Ride Clear of Diablo 54. Drums Across the River 54.
Destry 55. To Hell and Back (based on his
autobiography) 55. The World in My Corner 56.
Walk the Proud Land 56. The Guns of Fort
Petticoat 57. Joe Butterfly 57. Night Passage 57. The
Quiet American 58. Ride a Crooked Trail 58. The
Gun Runners 58. No Name on the Bullet 59. The
Wild and the Innocent 59. Cast a Long Shadow
59. Hell Bent for Leather 60. The Unforgiven 60.
Seven Ways from Sundown 60. Posse from Hell
61. The Battle at Bloody Beach 61. Six Black
Horses 62. Showdown 63. Gunfight at Comanche
Creek 63. The Quick Gun 64. Bullet for a Badman
64. Apache Rifles 64. Arizona Raiders 65.
Gunpoint 66. Trunk to Cairo 66. The Texican 66.
Forty Guns to Apache Pass 67. A Time for Dying
(& p) 71.
 TV series: Whispering Smith 58.

¶ I guess my face is still the same, and so is the dialogue. Only the horses have changed.
– *A.M. at 40*
    I am working with a handicap. I have no talent.
– *A.M.*

Murphy, Ben (1941–).
Athletic American TV hero of *Alias Smith and Jones, Griff, Gemini Man, The Chisholms*, etc.
    The Letters (TV) 73. Runaway (TV) 73. Heatwave (TV) 74. This Was the West That Was (TV) 75. Sidecar Racers 75. Bridger (TV) 76. Time Walker 82. The Winds of War (TV) 83, etc.

Murphy, Dudley (1897–).
American journalist who was briefly in films as director in the 20s and 30s.
    High Speed Lee 23. Alex the Great 28. The Sport Parade 32. *The Emperor Jones* 33. The Night Is Young 35. Don't Gamble with Love 36. One Third of a Nation 39. Main Street Lawyer 39. Alma del Bronce (Mex.) 44, etc.

Murphy, Eddie (1961–).
Aggressive American comedian and actor.
■ 48 Hours 82. Trading Places 83. Best Defense 84. *Beverly Hills Cop* 85. The Golden Child 86. Beverly Hills Cop II 87. Eddie Murphy Raw 87. Hollywood Shuffle 87. Coming to America 88. Harlem Nights (& wd) 89. Another 48 Hrs 90. Boomerang 92. The Distinguished Gentleman 92. Beverly Hills Cop III 94.

¶ Wouldn't it be a helluva thing if this was burnt cork and you folk were being tolerant for nothing? – *E.M.*

Murphy, Geoff (1938–).
New Zealand director and musician, now working in America.
    Wildman 77. Goodbye Pork Pie 80. Utu 82. The Quiet Earth 84. Never Say Die 88. Young Guns II 90. Freejack 92, etc.

Murphy, George (1902–1992).
Amiable Irish-American actor and dancer, a pleasant light talent who left the screen for politics and became senator for California. Special Academy Award 1951 'for interpreting the film industry to the nation at large'.
    Autobiography: 1970, *Say, Didn't You Used to Be George Murphy?*
■ Kid Millions 34. Jealousy 34. Public Menace 35. I'll Love You Always 35. After the Dance 35. Woman Trap 36. Top of the Town 36. London by Night 37. You're a Sweetheart 37. Broadway Melody of 1938 38. Letter of Introduction 38. Little Miss Broadway 38. Hold that Co-Ed 38. Risky Business 39. Broadway Melody of 1940 40. *Little Nellie Kelly* 40. Public Deb. No. 1 40. A Girl a Guy and a Gob 40. Ringside Maisie 41. *Tom Dick and Harry* 41. Rise and Shine 41. The Mayor of 44th Street 41. For Me and My Gal 41. The Navy Comes Through 42. The Powers Girl 42. Bataan 43. This Is the Army 43. Broadway Rhythm 44. *Show Business* 44. *Step Lively* 44. Having a Wonderful Crime 44. Up Goes Maisie 46. The Arnelo Affair 47. Cynthia 47. Tenth Avenue Angel 48. Big City 48. Border Incident 49. Battleground 49. No Questions Asked 51. It's a Big Country 51. Walk East on Beacon 52. Talk about a Stranger 52.

Murphy, Mary (1931–).
American leading lady.
    The Lemon Drop Kid (debut) 51. The Wild One 54. Beachhead 54. Hell's Island 55. The Desperate Hours 55. The Intimate Stranger (GB) 56. Crime and Punishment USA 59. Forty Pounds of Trouble 63. Junior Bonner 72, etc.

Murphy, Michael (1949–).
American general-purpose actor.
    Countdown 67. The Arrangement 69. Brewster McCloud 70. What's Up Doc? 72. The Thief Who Came to Dinner 73. Nashville 75. An Unmarried Woman 77. Manhattan 79. The Year of Living Dangerously 82. Cloak and Dagger 84. Salvador 85. Shocker 89. Folks! 92. Batman Returns 92. Clean Slate 94, etc.

Murphy, Ralph (1895–1967).
American director, in Hollywood from silent days.
    The Gay City 41. Hearts in Springtime 41. Mrs Wiggs of the Cabbage Patch 42. Rainbow Island 44. The Man in Half Moon Street 44. Red Stallion in the Rockies 49. Dick Turpin's Ride 51. Captain Blood, Fugitive 52. Desert Rats 53. The Lady in the Iron Mask 53. Three Stripes in the Sun (& w) 55, etc.

Murphy, Richard (1912–1993).
American writer, in Hollywood from 1937.
    Boomerang (AAN) 47. Cry of the City 48. Panic in the Streets 50. Les Misérables 52. Desert Rats (AAN) 53. Broken Lance 54. Compulsion 58. The Wackiest Ship in the Army (& d) 60, etc.

Murphy, Rosemary (1925–).
American stage actress in occasional films.
■ That Night 57. The Young Doctors 61. To Kill a Mockingbird 62. Any Wednesday 66. Ben 72. You'll Like My Mother 72. Walking Tall 73. Forty Carats 73. Ace Eli and Rodger of the Skies 73. Julia (as Dorothy Parker) 77. September 87.

Murray, Barbara (1929–).
British leading lady with stage experience.
    Anna Karenina 48. Passport to Pimlico 48. Doctor at Large 56. Campbell's Kingdom 58. A Cry from the Streets 58. Girls in Arms 60. A Dandy in Aspic 68. Tales from the Crypt 72, many others.
    TV series: The Power Game 66–68. The Bretts 87.

Murray, Bill (1950–).
Abrasive American leading actor, who first came to notice on TV's *Saturday Night Live*.
    Meatballs 79. Caddyshack 80. Stripes 82. Tootsie (uncredited) 82. *Ghostbusters* 84. The Razor's Edge 84. Little Shop of Horrors 86. Scrooged 88. Ghostbusters II 89. Quick Change (& co-d) 90. What about Bob? 91. Mad Dog and Glory 93. Ground Hog Day 93. Ed Wood 94, etc.

Murray, Charlie (1872–1941).
American vaudeville comedian long with Mack Sennett. In *Tillie's Punctured Romance* 15, and later played with George Sidney in a long series about the Cohens and Kellys.

Murray, Don (1929–).
Ambitious American actor who graduated from innocent to tough roles but does not seem to have received the attention he sought and merited.
■ *Bus Stop* (AAN) 56. *The Bachelor Party* 57. A Hatful of Rain 57. From Hell to Texas 58. These Thousand Hills 59. Shake Hands with the Devil 59. One Foot in Hell 60. *The Hoodlum Priest* (& co-p) 61. *Advise and Consent* 62. Escape from East Berlin 62. One Man's Way 64. Baby the Rain Must Fall 65. Kid Rodelo 66. The Plainsman 66. Sweet Love, Bitter 67. The Viking Queen 67. Tale of the Cock 67. The Borgia Stick (TV) 67. The Intruders (TV) 67. Daughter of the Mind (TV) 69. Childish Things (& wp) 70. Conquest of the Planet of the Apes 72. Happy Birthday Wanda June 72. Cotter 73. A Girl Named Sooner (TV) 74. The Sex Symbol (TV) 74. The Girl on the Late Late Show (TV) 75. Deadly

Hero 76. Damien (w, d) 77. Rainbow (TV) 78. Crisis in Mid-air (TV) 79. The Far Turn (TV) 79. Endless Love 81. Peggy Sue Got Married 86. Scorpion 86. Made in Heaven 87. Stillwatch (TV 87. Mistress (TV) 87. A Brand New Life: The Honeymoon (TV) 89. Ghosts Can't Do It 90.
    TV series: The Outcasts 68. Knots Landing 80– 81.

Murray, James (1901–1936).
American leading man, a former extra who was chosen by King Vidor to play the hero of *The Crow* 28, but subsequently took to drink and died in obscurity.
    The Big City 28. Thunder 29. Bright Lights 30. The Reckoning 32. Heroes for Sale 32. Skull and Crown 35, etc.

Murray, Ken (1903–1988) (Don Court).
American comedy actor, radio and TV entertaine especially as collector of old 'home movies' of th stars. Collected special Oscar for his 1947 bird fantasy *Bill and Coo*.
    Autobiography: 1960, *Life on a Pogo Stick*.
    Half Marriage 29. A Night at Earl Carroll's 41. The Man Who Shot Liberty Valance 62. Follow M Boys 66. Power 68.

Murray, Lyn (1909–1989).
American composer.
    Son of Paleface 52. The Bridges at Toko Ri 54. To Catch a Thief 55. Escape from Zahrain 61. Promise Her Anything 66. Rosie 67. The Magic Carpet (TV) 71, etc.

Murray, Mae (1889–1965) (Marie Adrienne Koeni American leading lady of the silent screen; forme dancer; usually in flashy roles. Retired to marry.
    Biography: 1959, *The Self-Enchanted* by Jane Ardmore.
    Sweet Kitty Bellairs 17. Her Body in Bond 18. The Mormon Maid 20. Jazz Mania 21. Fashion Ro 23. The Merry Widow 25. Circe the Enchantress 27. Peacock Alley 31, etc.

Murray, Stephen (1912–1983).
Under-used British character actor, on stage from 1933.
    Pygmalion 38. *The Prime Minister* 41. *Next of Ki* 42. Undercover 43. *Master of Bankdam* 46. My Brother Jonathan 47. Silent Dust 48. *London Belongs to Me* 48. For Them That Trespass 49. Now Barabbas 50. The Magnet 50. 24 Hours of a Woman's Life 52. Four-Sided Triangle 53. The Stranger's Hand 54. The End of the Affair 55. Guilty 55. The Door in the Wall 56. At the Strok of Nine 57. A Tale of Two Cities 58. The Nun's Story 59. Master Spy 63, etc.

Murray-Hill, Peter (1908–1957).
British leading man of stage and screen; was married to Phyllis Calvert.
    A Yank at Oxford 38. The Outsider 39. Jane Steps Out 40. The Ghost Train 41. Madonna of the Seven Moons 44. They Were Sisters (last film 45, etc.

Murton, Lionel (1915–).
Canadian character actor resident in Britain.
    Meet the Navy 46. The Long Dark Hall 51. The Runaway Bus 54. The Battle of the River Plate 55. Up the Creek 58. Northwest Frontier 59. Confessions of a Window Cleaner 74, many others.

Musante, Tony (1936–).
American character actor.
    Once a Thief 65. The Detective 68. The Bird wit

he Crystal Plumage 70. The Grissom Gang 71,
he Last Run 71. Eutanasia di un Amore 78.
earview Mirror (TV) 84. Nutcracker: Money,
Madness and Murder (TV) 87, etc.

TV series: *Toma* 72.

Muse, Clarence (1889–1979).
American character actor.

Hearts in Dixie 28. Cabin in the Cotton 32.
howboat 36. Tales of Manhattan 42. An Act of
Murder 48. So Bright the Flame 52. Car Wash 77.
The Black Stallion 79, many others.

musical remakes
re becoming thicker on the ground than musical
riginals. All the following had been filmed at
east once before, as straight dramas or comedies
with music:

Where's Charley? as *Charley's Aunt*; *Three for the
how* as *My Two Husbands*; *Living It Up* as *Nothing
acred*; *Carmen Jones* as *Carmen*; *Scrooge* as *A
Christmas Carol*; *Step Lively* as *Room Service*; *In the
ood Old Summertime* as *The Shop Around The Corner*;
Meet Me After The Show* as *He Married His Wife*;
nnie Get Your Gun* as *Annie Oakley*; *Kismet* as
Kismet*; *The King and I* as *Anna and the King of Siam*;
arousel* as *Liliom*; *High Society* as *The Philadelphia
Story*; *Silk Stockings* as *Ninotchka*; *Gigi* as *Gigi*; *My
air Lady* as *Pygmalion*; *The Sound of Music* as *The
rapp Family*; *Funny Girl* as *Rose of Washington
Square*; *Sweet Charity* as *Nights of Cabiria*; *Camelot* as
ancelot and Guinevere; *Oliver!* as *Oliver Twist*; *Hello
Dolly* as *The Matchmaker*; *Cabaret* as *I Am a Camera*;
Fiddler on the Roof as *Tevye the Milkman*; *Mame* as
Auntie Mame; *Lost Horizon* as *Lost Horizon*; *Goodbye
Mr Chips* as *Goodbye Mr Chips*; *A Star Is Born* as *What
Price Hollywood? (and in 1937 as *A Star is Born*).

musicals
obviously could not exist before Al Jolson sang
Mammy', in 1927. During the first two or three
years of talkies, however, Hollywood produced so
many gaudy back-stage stories and all-star
spectacles that the genre quickly wore out its
welcome:

*Broadway Melody, The Singing Fool, The Desert
Song, Showboat, Chasing Rainbows, Show of Shows,
Hollywood Revue, Lights of New York, On with the
Show, King of Jazz, Gold Diggers of Broadway, Sunny
Side Up* . . . all these before the end of 1930, and
there were many poorer imitations. Discipline was
needed, and the disciplinarian who emerged was
Broadway dance director Busby Berkeley. His
kaleidoscopic ensembles first dazzled the eye in
Goldwyn–Cantor extravaganzas like *Whoopee* and
Palmy Days, and came to full flower in the Warner
musicals which brought to the fore stars like Joan
Blondell, Ruby Keeler and Dick Powell, filling the
years from 1933 to 1937 with such shows as
*Footlight Parade, Forty-Second Street, Dames, Wonder
Bar, Flirtation Walk* and the annual *Gold Digger*
comedies. Meanwhile at Paramount Lubitsch had
been quietly establishing a quieter style, using
recitative, with *The Love Parade* and *One Hour with
You*; Mamoulian was equally successful with *Love
Me Tonight*; and the Marx Brothers contributed
their own brand of musical anarchy. From 1933 to
1939 at RKO Fred Astaire and Ginger Rogers were
teamed in an affectionately-remembered series of
light comedy-musicals. MGM made sporadic
efforts with creaky vehicles like *Cuban Love Song*
but did not come into their own until 1935, when
they started the Jeanette MacDonald/Nelson Eddy
series of operettas; these were followed by a
dramatic musical, *The Great Ziegfeld*, by the
Eleanor Powell spectaculars like *Rosalie*, by a
revived *Broadway Melody* series, and by *The Wizard
of Oz* and the early Judy Garland/Mickey Rooney

teenage extravaganzas, *Babes in Arms* and *Strike
Up the Band*. Fox had Shirley Temple, Sonja Henie
and Alice Faye; Goldwyn contributed Cantor and
The Goldwyn Follies. Paramount concentrated on
Maurice Chevalier, Bing Crosby and the all-star
Big Broadcast series.

The popularity of musicals continued into the
war-torn 40s, when escapism was *de rigueur*.
Universal, whose only major pre-war musical was
Showboat, continued to build up Deanna Durbin and
threw in Donald O'Connor and Gloria Jean for
good measure. Warners had *This Is the Army* and
several musical biopics: *Yankee Doodle Dandy, Night
and Day, Rhapsody in Blue*. RKO had a young man
named Sinatra. Fox found goldmines in Carmen
Miranda and Betty Grable, but their vehicles were
routine; Columbia did slightly better by Rita
Hayworth, and then surprised everyone with *The
Jolson Story*, which set the musical back on top just
when it was flagging. Paramount was doing very
nicely with Bing Crosby and Bob Hope. Everybody
did at least one big morale-building musical with
all the stars on the payroll blowing kisses to the
boys out there: *Star-Spangled Rhythm, Thank Your
Lucky Stars, Hollywood Canteen, Thousands Cheer* and
so on.

Top dog in the 40s and 50s was undoubtedly
MGM. Specialities like *Ziegfeld Follies, Till the
Clouds Roll By* and *Words and Music* came side by
side with more routine productions starring Gene
Kelly, Judy Garland, and Esther Williams (in aqua-
musicals, of course). The decade ended in a blaze
of glory with *On the Town*, which led to the even
more spectacular heights of *An American in Paris*
and *Singin' in the Rain*. By this time Mario Lanza
and Howard Keel were needing new vehicles for
themselves, *The Great Caruso* and *Seven Brides for
Seven Brothers* being outstanding productions in
their own right. But by the mid-50s the demand,
or the fashion, for musicals was dying. It lasted
longest at Metro, who doggedly remade pictures
like *The Belle of New York* and *Rose Marie*, added
music to *Ninotchka* and *The Philadelphia Story* and
Gigi. Warners plugged on until their bright star of
1948, Doris Day, signed with another studio and
turned dramatic; Fox had two mammoth tries in
Call Me Madam and *There's No Business Like Show
Business*; Paramount came up with *White
Christmas*, the enterprising *Red Garters* and *Funny
Face*, and even *Li'l Abner*. But the risk was becoming
too great in a chancy market, with expenses
growing by the minute; and in the 60s no original
musicals were written in Hollywood, with the
exception of the family-aimed *Mary Poppins*,
Thoroughly Modern Millie and the twenty-odd look-
alike vehicles of Elvis Presley. Copper-bottomed
Broadway hits like *Pal Joey, Oklahoma, Carousel,
The Pajama Game, South Pacific, The King and I,
West Side Story, Guys and Dolls, Hello Dolly, On a
Clear Day You Can See Forever, Fiddler on the Roof,
Man of La Mancha, The Sound of Music* and *My Fair
Lady* were still filmed, at gargantuan cost, but as
cinema they all too often disappointed filmgoers
with memories of Berkeley and Kelly and Donen.
Amongst the most inventive screen musicals have
been Bob Fosse's *Sweet Charity* and *Cabaret*. In the
90s, the success of the Disney animated features
The Little Mermaid, Aladdin, The Lion King and,
especially, *Beauty and the Beast* promised to revive
the musical in a different form. Indeed, Disney
turned *Beauty and the Beast* into a successful
Broadway musical in 1994.

In Britain, the 30s were a highpoint of the light
musical, starring such talents as Jack Buchanan,
Jessie Matthews, Gracie Fields, George Formby
and Anna Neagle; Miss Neagle indeed carried on,
dauntless, into the less favourable climate of the
50s. The 40s were pretty barren apart from the Rank

spectacular *London Town*, which flopped; and it
wasn't until the 60s that Elstree struck something
like the right note with its energetic though
derivative series starring Cliff Richard. In 1968
the old-fashioned though energetic *Oliver!* proved
that Britain can handle a really big musical. The
70s brought little but rock operas and one or two
curiously old-fashioned stagings of such as *Mame*
and *1776*, until John Travolta spurred a new trend
with *Saturday Night Fever* and a nostalgic one with
Grease. *Flashdance* and *Breaking* started new forms,
and *A Chorus Line*, long promised, was finally
made in 1984, by which time most Broadway
musicals had become too expensive to film.

Books: *Gotta Sing Gotta Dance* by John Kobal. *The
Hollywood Musical* by John Russell Taylor. *All
Singing, All Dancing* by John Springer. 1987, *The
American Film Musical* by Rick Altman.

See also: *entertainers*.

Mustin, Burt (1884–1977).
American comedy character actor who was 67
when he made his first film.

Detective Story 51. The Lusty Men 53. The
Desperate Hours 55. The Big Country 57.
Huckleberry Finn 61. The Thrill of It All 63. Cat
Ballou 65. Speedway 68. Hail Hero 70. The Skin
Game 71, etc.

TV series: A Date with the Angels 57. Ichabod
61–62. The Andy Griffith Show 61–66. All in the
Family 73–76. Phyllis 76.

Musuraca, Nicholas (1895–1975).
American cinematographer.

Bride of the Storm 24. Lightning Lanats 25.
Tyrant of Red Gulch 27. The Cuckoos 31. Cracked
Nuts 33. Long Lost Father 34. Murder on a Bridle
Path 36. Blind Alibi 38. Five Came Back 39. Golden
Boy 39. The Swiss Family Robinson 40. Tom
Brown's Schooldays 40. *Cat People* 42. The
Seventh Victim 43. Curse of the Cat People 44. *The
Spiral Staircase* 45. The Locket 46. The Bachelor
and the Bobbysoxer 47. *Out of the Past* 47. Blood
on the Moon 48. Where Danger Lives 51. Clash
by Night 52. Devil's Canyon 53. The Story of
Mankind 57. Too Much Too Soon 58, many others.

mute print.
One with only the picture, no sound track.

Muti, Ornella (1955–) (Francesca Romana Rivelli).
Sultry Italian leading actress who began her career
at the age of 15.

Most Beautiful Wife (La Moglie Più Bella) 70.
Sensual Man (Paolo il Caldo) 73. Italian Graffiti
74. First Love (Primo Amore) 78. Flash Gordon
80. Tales of Ordinary Madness 82. Swann in Love
(Un Amour de Swann) 84. Chronicle of a Death
Foretold (Cronaca di una Morte Annunciata) 87.
Wait until Spring, Bandini 89. Captain Fracassa's
Journey (Il Viaggio di Capitan Fracassa) 90. Oscar
91. Tonight at Alice's 91. Christmas Vacation '91
(Vacanze di Natale '91) 91. Especially on Sundays
(La Domenica Specialmente) 91. Once upon a
Crime 92. El Amante Bilingüe 93, many others.

Mutiny on the Bounty.
Three films have been made of this semi-historical
account of how Captain Bligh was cast adrift in
an open boat in 1787: the first was directed in
1935 by Frank Lloyd with Clark Gable and
Charles Laughton, in a performance that launched
a thousand impersonations; the second, in 1962,
was directed by Carol Reed (who resigned) and
Lewis Milestone, with Marlon Brando and Trevor
Howard; the most recent, *The Bounty*, was directed
by Roger Donaldson in Australia in 1984, with
Anthony Hopkins and Mel Gibson.

Mutrux, Floyd.
American screenwriter and director.

The Christian Liquorice Store (w) 71. Dusty and Sweets McGhee (wd) 71. Freebie and the Bean 74. Aloha, Bobby and Rose (wd) 75. American Hot Wax (d) 78. The Hollywood Nights (wd) 80. Blood In Blood Out (co-w) 92. American Me (co-w) 93. There Goes My Baby (wd) 94, etc.

Muybridge, Eadweard (1830–1904) (Edward Muggeridge).
British photographer who, in America in 1877, succeeded in analysing motion with a camera by taking a series of pictures of a horse in motion. (He used 24 cameras attached to a tripwire.) Later he invented a form of projector which reassembled his pictures into the appearance of moving actuality, and called it the Zoopraxiscope; in 1877 he published an influential book of his findings, *Animal Locomotion*.

My Man Godfrey.
The crazy comedy about a family of bored millionaires brought to heel by a butler they pick up in the gutter has been filmed twice: in 1936 by Gregory La Cava with William Powell and Carole Lombard; and in 1957 by Kenry Koster with David Niven and June Allyson.

My Sister Eileen.
The stories by Ruth McKenney about two sisters on the hunt for fame and men in New York was turned first into a play and then a film by Joseph Fields and Jerome Chodorov; directed by Alexander Hall, it starred Rosalind Russell and Janet Sherwood as the sisters; Richard Quine remade it in 1955 as a semi-musical with Betty Garrett and Janet Leigh. A Broadway musical of 1953, *Wonderful Town*, was also based on the stories, and there was a TV series with Elaine Stritch and Shirley Bonne, 1960–61. (In real life, Eileen McKenney married writer Nathanael West and died with him in a car crash.)

Mycroft, Walter (1891–1959).
British director. Chief scriptwriter and director of productions at Elstree in the 30s.

Spring Meeting 40. My Wife's Family 41. Banana Ridge 41. The Woman's Angle (p only) 52, etc.

Myers, Carmel (1899–1980).
American leading lady of the 20s, in the 'vamp' tradition.

Sirens of the Sea 16. Intolerance 16. The Haunted Pyjamas 17. Mad Marriage 21. The Famous Mrs Fair 23. Beau Brummell 24. Ben Hur 25. Sorrell and Son 27. Svengali 31. Lady for a Night 42. Whistle Stop 45, etc.

Myers, Harry (1886–1938).
American character actor, in Hollywood from 1908.

Housekeeping 16. *A Connecticut Yankee* 21. The Beautiful and the Damned 26. *City Lights* (as the drunken millionaire) 31. Dangerous Lives 37, etc.

Myers, Mike (1964–).
Canadian comedian, actor and screenwriter, who first came to notice on the TV show *Saturday Night Live* in 1989 and turned his sketch 'Wayne's World' with Dana Carvey into an international success on film. Born in Toronto, he performed in commercials as a child.

Wayne's World (a, co-w) 92. So I Married an Axe Murderer (a) 93. Wayne's World 2 (a, co-w) 93.

¶ Marriage can be viewed as the waiting room for death. – *M.M.*

Myers, Stanley (1930–1993).
British composer, from the theatre. His best-known work was *Cavatina*, originally written for *The Walking Stick* 76, but made famous by its use in *The Deerhunter*.

Kaleidoscope 66. Otley 69. Age of Consent 70. Raging Moon 71. Zee & Co 72. The Apprenticeship of Dudley Kravitz 74. The Greek Tycoon 78. The Deer Hunter 78. The Watcher in the Woods 80. Moonlighting 82. The Honorary Consul 83. The Lightship 85. My Beautiful Laundrette 85. Castaway 86. Prick Up Your Ears 87. Sammie and Rosie Get Laid 87. Wish You Were Here 87. Stars and Bars 88. The Boost 88. Scenes from the Class Struggle in Beverly Hills 89. The Witches 89. Torrents of Spring 90. Iron Maze 91. Voyager 91. Claude 92. Serafina! 92. Cold Heaven 92, many others.

Myrtil, Odette (1898–1978).
French character actress in Hollywood.

Dodsworth 36. Kitty Foyle 40. Yankee Doodle Dandy 42. Forever and a Day 43. Devotion 46. Here Comes the Groom 50. Lady Possessed 52, many others.

mystery
has always been a popular element of motion picture entertainment. Always providing scope for sinister goings-on and sudden revelations, mystery films divide themselves into two basic genres: who done it, and how will the hero get out of it? Silent melodramas like *The Perils of Pauline* were full of clutching hands and villainous masterminds, devices adopted by the German post-war cinema for its own purposes: *The Cabinet of Dr Caligari*, *Dr Mabuse* and *Warning Shadows* are all mysteries, peopled by eccentrics and madmen. American silent who-done-its like *The Cat and the Canary*, *The Thirteenth Chair* and *One Exciting Night* set a pattern for thrillers which could not come fully into their own until music and sound were added. In the 30s the 'thunderstorm mystery', with its spooky house and mysterious servants (the butler usually did it) quickly became a cliché; but this is not to denigrate the entertainment value of such movies as *The Bat*, *The Terror*, *Murder by the Clock*, *The Gorilla*, *Seven Keys to Baldpate*, *Double Door*, *You'll Find Out*, *Topper Returns*, *The House on Haunted Hill*, and the Bob Hope remakes of *The Cat and the Canary* and *The Ghost Breakers*.

The 30s also saw a movement to relegate the puzzle film to the detective series, a genre later taken over eagerly by TV. These films were built around such protagonists as Charlie Chan, Sherlock Holmes, Hercule Poirot, Inspector Hanaud, Ellery Queen, Perry Mason, Inspector Hornleigh, Nero Wolfe, Philo Vance, Nick Carter, The Crime Doctor, The Saint, The Falcon, Bulldog Drummond, Mrs Pym, the 'Thin Man' (the thin man was actually the victim of the first story, but the tag stuck to William Powell), Mr Moto, Michael Shayne, Hildegarde Withers, Mr Wong, Arsène Lupin, Dick Barton, The Baron, The Toff, Gideon, Slim Callaghan, Lemmy Caution and Maigret . . . all soundly spoofed by Groucho Marx as Wolf J. Flywheel in *The Big Store*. The best of these fictional detectives were the creations of Dashiell Hammett (Sam Spade in *The Maltese Falcon*) and Raymond Chandler (Philip Marlowe in *The Big Sleep*, *Farewell My Lovely* and *The High Window*); and after a twenty year hiatus the threads were picked up by Ross MacDonald's *Harper*, Craig Stevens as *Gunn*, Frank Sinatra as *Tony Rome*, films of Chandler's *Marlowe* and J.D. MacDonald's *Darker Than Amber*, and Richard Roundtree as *Shaft*. Single who-done-its of great merit were *Gaslight*, *Laura*, *Green for Danger* (one ached for a whole series starring Alastair Sim as Inspector Cockrill), *The Spiral Staircase*, *Crossfire*, *Boomerang*, *Bad Day at Black Rock*, *Les Diaboliques*, *Charade*, *Mirage*, *Taste of Fear*, *The List of Adrian Messenger*, and the two versions of *Ten Little Niggers*. Two gentler detectives were provided by Alec Guinness' *Father Brown* and Margaret Rutherford's *Miss Marple*.

The other type of mystery, with a hero on the run, usually suspected of murder, finally uncovering the real villain after many narrow escapes from death, was developed by Alfred Hitchcock in such films as *The Thirty-Nine Steps*, *The Lady Vanishes*, *Saboteur*, *Spellbound*, *Strangers on a Train*, *North by Northwest* and *Torn Curtain*. But stars as various as Alan Ladd, Bob Hope, Danny Kaye, Robert Mitchum and Paul Newman have also found the device useful.

The recent vogue for tongue-in-cheek spy thrillers is to all intents and purposes a reversion to the Pearl White school, with the hero menaced at every turn but, of course, finally triumphant.

Useful books: *The Detective in Film* by William K. Everson. *The Detective in Hollywood* by Jon Tuska.

See also: *spies*; *private eyes*.

The Mystery of the Wax Museum.
This badly structured but interesting shocker in two-colour Technicolor, with sets by Anton Grot and direction by Michael Curtiz, survives as a milestone of its era; with Lionel Atwill as a mad sculptor who uses a wax face to disguise his hideously burned features. In 1953, the story was remade in 3-D as *House of Wax*, starring Vincent Price, and in 1966 most of it turned up again in *Chamber of Horrors*.

Nabokov, Vladimir (1899–1977).
Russian émigré novelist who became fashionable in the mid-50s. Works filmed include *Lolita, Laughter in the Dark, King Queen Knave* and *Despair*.

Nader, George (1921–).
American leading man who after TV experience starred in many Universal action films of the 50s but has lately been less active.
Monsoon (debut) 52. Four Guns to the Border 54. The Second Greatest Sex 55. Away All Boats 56. Congo Crossing 56. Four Girls in Town 57. Joe Butterfly 57. Nowhere to Go (GB) 58. The Human Duplicators 65. The Million Eyes of Su-Muru 66. Beyond Atlantis 73, etc.
TV series: Ellery Queen 54. The Man and the Challenge 59. Shannon 61.

Naderi, Amir (1945–).
Iranian director and screenwriter, a former photographer, now resident in America.
Goodbye My Friend 71. Elegy 75. Marsiyeh 79. The Search 81. The Runner (Dawandeh) 85. Water, Wind, Dust (Ab, Bad, Khak) 85. Manhattan by Numbers 93, etc.

Nagase, Masatoshi.
Japanese leading actor.
Mystery Train (US) 89. Autumn Moon (HK) 92. Waga Jinsei Saisku No Toki 94, etc.

Nagel, Anne (1912–1966) (Anne Dolan).
American supporting actress, the heroine's friend in countless movies of the 40s.
Hot Money 36. Black Friday 40. Man Made Monster 41. Women in Bondage 44. Spirit of West Point 47, etc.

Nagel, Conrad (1896–1970).
American leading man of the 20s who came to Hollywood after stage experience; latterly ran acting school.
Little Women 19. Fighting Chance 20. Three Weeks 24. The Exquisite Sinner 26. Slightly Used 27. Quality Street 27. One Romantic Night 30. Bad Sister 31. East Lynne 31. Dangerous Corner 34. Navy Spy 37. I Want a Divorce 40. The Woman in Brown 48. All that Heaven Allows 55. Stranger in My Arms 58. The Man Who Understood Women 59, many others.

Nagy, Ivan (1938–).
Hungarian-born director working in America, mainly as a director of TV movies.
Bad Charleston Charlie 73. Money, Marbles and Chalk 73. Five Minutes of Freedom 73. Deadly Hero 76. Captain America II: Death Too Soon (TV) 79. A Gun in the House (TV) 81. Jane Doe (TV) 83, etc.

Naha, Ed.
American screenwriter.
Troll 86. Dolls 86. Honey, I Shrunk the Kids (co-w) 89. Chud II: Bud the Chud 89. Matinee (co-w) 92.

Nair, Mira (1957–).
Indian director, producer and screenwriter who began as a documentary film-maker.
Salaam Bombay! 88 (p, d). Mississippi Masala (p, wd) 91. The Perez Family 94.

Naish, J. Carrol (1900–1973).
American character actor with stage experience, in films from 1930.
The Hatchet Man 32. Lives of a Bengal Lancer 35. Anthony Adverse 36. King of Alcatraz 38. Persons in Hiding 39. *Beau Geste* 39. Birth of the Blues 41. Blood and Sand 41. The Corsican Brothers 41. The Pied Piper 42. Dr Renault's Secret 42. Batman (serial) 43. Behind the Rising Sun 43. Sahara (AAN) 43. Gung Ho! 44. *A Medal for Benny* (AAN) 45. House of Frankenstein 45. The Southerner 45. Enter Arsène Lupin 45. The Beast with Five Fingers 46. Joan of Arc 48. Black Hand 49. Annie Get Your Gun 50. Across the Wide Missouri 51. Sitting Bull 54. Violent Saturday 54. New York Confidential 54. The Young Don't Cry 57. The Hanged Man 64. Blood of Frankenstein 70, many others.
TV series: Life With Lugi 52. The New Adventures of Charlie Chan 57. Guestward Ho! 60.

Naismith, Laurence (1908–1992) (Lawrence Johnson).
Amiable British character actor with wide stage experience.
Trouble in the Air 47. A Piece of Cake 48. I Believe in You 51. The Beggar's Opera 52. Mogambo 53. Carrington VC 55. *Richard III* 56. Boy on a Dolphin 57. Tempest 58. A Night to Remember 58. Sink the Bismarck 60. The Singer Not the Song 61. Jason and the Argonauts 63. The Three Lives of Thomasina 63. Sky West and Crooked 65. The Scorpio Letters 67. The Long Duel 67. Fitzwilly 67. *Camelot* 67. The Valley of Gwangi 68. Eye of the Cat 69. Scrooge 70. Diamonds Are Forever 71. *The Amazing Mr Blunden* 72, etc.
TV series: *The Persuaders* 71.

Najimy, Kathy.
American actress in comic roles.
Soapdish 91. Sister Act 92. Hocus Pocus 93. Sister Act 2: Back in the Habit 93, etc.

Nakadai, Tatsuya (1932–).
Japanese leading actor who was memorable in Kurosawa's *Yojimbo* and gained fame in Masaki Kobayashi's trilogy *The Human Condition*, appearing in many of the director's subsequent films.
Seven Samurai 54. Untamed (Arakure) 57. Conflagration (Enjo) 58. The Key (Kagi) 59. The Human Condition Part I: No Greater Love (Ningen no Joken I-II) 59. The Human Condition Part II: The Road to Eternity (Ningen no Joken III-IV) 59. When a Woman Ascends the Stairs (Onna ga Kaidan o Agaru Toki) 60. Yojimbo 61. The Other Woman (Tsuma Toshite Onna Toshite) 61. The Human Condition Part III: A Soldier's Prayer (Ningen no Joken V-VI) 61. The Inheritance

(Karamiai) 62. Sanjuro 62. Harakiri 62. High and Low (Tengokku to Jigoku) 63. Kwaidan 64. A Woman's Story (Onna no Rekishi) 63. Samurai Rebellion (Joiuchi) 67. Inn of Evil (Inochi Bo ni Furo) 71. I Am a Cat (Wagahai wa Neko de Aru) 75. Kagemusha 80. Ran 85. Return to the River Kwai 89, etc.

Nakano, Desmond.
American screenwriter.
Boulevard Nights 79. Body Rock 84. Black Moon Rising (co-w) 86. Last Exit to Brooklyn 90. American Me (co-w) 92, etc.

Naldi, Nita (1899–1961) (Anita Donna Dooley).
Italian-American leading lady of the 20s, formerly in the Ziegfeld Follies.
Dr Jekyll and Mr Hyde 20. The Unfair Sex 22. Blood and Sand 22. The Ten Commandments 23. Cobra 25. A Sainted Devil 25. The Marriage Whirl 26. The Lady Who Lied 27, etc.

Namath, Joe (1943–).
American professional sportsman who made a few films.
 Norwood 69. C. C. and Company 70. Avalanche Express 78. Marriage Is Alive and Well (TV) 80. Chattanooga Choo Choo 84.

Nana.
Zola's novel of the Paris demi-monde in the 1860s has been seen in four major film versions: a silent French film directed by Jean Renoir in 1926, with Catherine Hessling and Werner Krass; an American version, sometimes known as *The Lady of the Boulevards*, directed by Dorothy Arzner in 1934, with Anna Sten, Lionel Atwill, and Phillips Holmes; a second French version, directed by Christian-Jaque in 1955, with Martine Carol and Charles Boyer; a Franco-Swedish version, *Take Me, Love Me*, directed by Mac Ahlberg, with Anna Gael.

Nancy Drew.
The teenage heroine, created by Carolyn Keene (one of many pseudonyms used by the team of Edward Stratemeyer and Harriet Adams), appeared in a series of second features made by Warner, directed by William Clemens and starring Bonita Granville: *Nancy Drew, Detective* 38; *Nancy Drew – Reporter* 39; *Nancy Drew – Troubleshooter* 39; *Nancy Drew and the Hidden Staircase* 39. A television series, *The Nancy Drew Mysteries*, ran from 1977–78, starring Pamela Sue Martin.

Napier, Alan (1903–1988) (Alan Napier-Clavering).
Dignified British character actor, in Hollywood from 1940; usually played butlers or noble lords.
In a Monastery Garden 31. Loyalties 32. For Valour 37. The Four Just Men 39. The Invisible Man Returns 40. Random Harvest 42. Ministry of Fear 43. Lost Angel 44. *The Uninvited* 44. Forever Amber 47. Tarzan's Magic Fountain 50. Julius Caesar 53. The Court Jester 55. Journey to the Centre of the Earth 59. Marnie 64. Batman 66, many others.

TV series: Don't Call Me Charlie 62–63. Batman 66–68.

Napier, Charles.
American character actor, often in the films of Jonathan Demme.

Cherry, Harry and Raquel 69. Caged Heat 74. Beyond the Valley of the Dolls 70. Super Vixens 74. Citizens Band 77. The Last Emperor 79. The Blues Brothers 80. Swing Shift 84. Rambo: First Blood II 85. Something Wild 86. Deep Space 88. Married to the Mob 88. Future Zone 90. The Grifters 90. Miami Blues 90. The Silence of the Lambs 91. Soldier's Fortune 91. Center of the Web 92. Skeeter 93. Philadelphia 93, etc.

¶ I keep waiting for Chuck Napier to become a really big movie actor, but it seems so far it's been slightly out of his reach . . . I think he's one of America's finest actors. – *Jonathan Demme*

Napier, Diana (1905–1982) (Molly Ellis).
British leading lady of the 30s; married Richard Tauber.

Wedding Rehearsal 33. Catherine the Great 34. The Private Life of Don Juan 34. Mimi 35. Land without Music 36. Pagliacci 37, then retired until *I Was a Dancer* 48.

Napier, Russell (1910–1975).
Australian-born actor, long in Britain. Appeared in numerous small parts, usually as officials; also played the chief inspector in many of the 3-reel 'Scotland Yard' series.

Napoleon, Art (1923–).
American director.

Man on the Prowl (& w) 57. Too Much Too Soon 58. Ride the Wild Surf (w only) 64.

Napoleon Bonaparte
has been impersonated on screen by Charles Boyer in *Marie Walewska (Conquest)*, Esmé Percy in *Invitation to the Waltz*, Emile Drain in *Madame sans Gêne* and *Les Perles de la Couronne*, Rollo Lloyd in *Anthony Adverse*, Julien Berthau in *Madame*, Marlon Brando in *Désirée*, Arnold Moss in *The Black Book*, Pierre Mondy in *Austerlitz*, Herbert Lom in several films including *The Young Mr Pitt* and *War and Peace*, Eli Wallach in *The Adventures of Gerard*, Rod Steiger in *Waterloo*, and Kenneth Haigh in *Eagle in a Cage*.

Abel Gance's 1925 film *Napoleon* (with Albert Dieudonne) is noted for the first use of a triptych screen corresponding very closely to Cinerama. It was revived with international success in 1980, in a version painstakingly reassembled by Kevin Brownlow, who in 1983 published a book about it.

Nardini, Tom (1945–).
American character actor.

Cat Ballou 65. Africa Texas Style 67. The Young Animals 68. Siege (aka Self Defense) 82, etc.

TV series: Cowboy in Africa 67.

Nares, Owen (1888–1943) (O.N. Ramsay).
British matinée idol and silent screen star.

Autobiography: 1925, *Myself and Some Others; Pure Egotism.*

Dandy Donovan 14. The Sorrows of Satan 17. God Bless the Red, White and Blue 18. Indian Love Lyrics 23. Young Lochinvar 23. Milestones 28. The Middle Watch 30. Sunshine Susie 31. The Impassive Footman 32. The Private Life of Don Juan 34. The Show Goes On 37. The Prime Minister 41, etc.

Narizzano, Silvio (1927–).
Canadian director in British TV in the 50s, later making international films.
■ Under Ten Flags (co-d) 60. Fanatic 65. *Georgy Girl* 66. Blue (US) 67. Loot 70. Redneck 73. The Sky is Falling 76. *Why Shoot the Teacher* 77. The Class of Miss MacMichael 78. *Staying On* (TV) 80. Choices 81.

narrators
are heard at the beginning of many important movies. Well-known actors are normally used, but sometimes take no credit. Here is a selected checklist to silence nagging doubts:

Arizona Bushwhackers: James Cagney.
Barry Lyndon: Michael Hordern.
The Big Knife: Richard Boone.
Casablanca: Lou Marcelle.
The Curse of King Tutankhamun's Tomb: Paul Scofield.
Desert Rats: Michael Rennie.
Dragon Seed: Lionel Barrymore.
Duel in the Sun: Orson Welles.
The Hallelujah Trail: John Dehner.
How Green Was My Valley: Irving Pichel.
How the West Was Won: Spencer Tracy.
The Human Comedy: Ray Collins.
An Ideal Husband: Ralph Richardson.
It's a Big Country: Louis Calhern.
Khartoum: Leo Genn.
King of Kings: Orson Welles.
Kings of the Sun: James Coburn.
A Letter to 3 Wives: Celeste Holm.
Mackenna's Gold: Victor Jory.
The Master of Ballantrae: Robert Beatty.
Mother Wore Tights: Anne Baxter.
The Mummy's Shroud: Peter Cushing.
The Night They Raided Minsky's: Rudy Vallee.
The Picture of Dorian Gray: Cedric Hardwicke.
Quo Vadis: Walter Pidgeon.
The Red Badge of Courage: James Whitmore.
The Reivers: Burgess Meredith.
Repeat Performance: John Ireland.
Romeo and Juliet (1968): Laurence Olivier.
The Secret Heart: Hume Cronyn.
The Solid Gold Cadillac: George Burns.
The Story of Jacob and Joseph: Alan Bates.
Summer of 42: Robert Mulligan.
The Swiss Family Robinson: Orson Welles.
The Third Man: Wilfrid Thomas.
Those Magnificent Men in Their Flying Machines: James Robertson Justice.
To Hell and Back: John McIntire.
To Kill a Mockingbird: Kim Stanley.
Tom Jones: Micheal MacLiammoir.
The Unseen: Ray Collins.
The Vikings: Orson Welles.
The Wild Heart: Joseph Cotten.
The War of the Worlds: Cedric Hardwicke.
Zulu: Richard Burton.

Naruse, Mikio (1905–1969).
Prolific Japanese director from 1930 onwards. His films often depicted drab working-class life. He began as a prop-man before becoming a scriptwriter and director's assistant. At least half of his films have been lost, including most of his earliest work.

Koshiben Gambare 31. Nasanu Naka 32. Kimi to Wakarete 33. Otomo-gokoro Sannin Shimai 35. Hataraku Ikka 39. Shanghai Moon (Shanghai no Tsuki) 41. Uta Andon 41. Ginza Gesho 51. Meshi 51. Lightning (Inazuma) 52. Fufu 53. Bangiku 54. Nagareru 56. Untamed (Arakure) 57. Anzukko 58. The Other Woman (Tsuma Toshite Onna Toshite) 61. Yearning (Midareru) 64. Two in the Shadow (Midaregumo) 67, many others.

¶ He was the most difficult director I ever worked for. He never said a word. A real nihilist. – *Tatsuya Nakadai*

Naschy, Paul (1936–) (Jacinto Molina Alvarez).
Spanish leading actor, writer and occasional producer and director of horror movies. His most notable and oft-repeated role is as werewolf Waldemar Daninsky. Born in Bilbao, he was a weightlifter and an architect before entering films in the mid-60s. He sometimes uses the pseudonym Jack Moll for his screenwriting.

Frankenstein's Bloody Terror (aka Hell's Creatures) (La Marca del Hombre Lobo) (& w) 67. Dracula vs Frankenstein (El Hombre que Vivo de Ummo) (& w) 69. The Werewolf vs the Vampire Woman (aka Shadow of the Werewolf) (La Noche de Walpurgis) (& w) 70. Fury of the Wolfman (La Furia del Hombre Lobo) (& w) 71. Dr Jekyll and the Wolfman (De Jeckill y el Hombre Lobo) (& w) 71. Dracula's Great Love (aka Dracula's Virgin Lovers) (El Gran Amor del Conde Dracula) (& co-w) 72. Vengeance of the Zombies (La Rebellión de las Muertas) (& w) 72. Horror Rises from the Tomb (El Espanto Surge de la Tumba) (& w) 72. The Rue Morgue Massacres (aka Hunchback of the Morgue) (El Jorobado de la Morgue) (& co-w) 73. The Mummy's Revenge (La Vengenzia de la Momia) (& w) 73. House of Psychotic Women (aka The Blue Eyes of the Broken Doll) (Los Ojos Azules de la Muñeca Rota) (& w) 73. Curse of the Devil (El Retorno de Walpurgis) (& w) 74. Exorcism (Exorcismo) (& co-w) 74. Night of the Howling Beast (aka The Werewolf and the Yeti) (La Maldición de la Bestia) (& w) 75. People Who Own the Dark 75. Inquisition (Inquisición) (& wd) 76. The Craving (El Retorno del Hombre Lobo) (& wd) 80. Human Beasts (El Carnaval de la Bestias) (& p, wd) 80. Monster Island 81. The Beast and the Magic Sword (& p, wd) 83, etc.

Nascimbene, Mario (1916–).
Italian composer.

OK Nero 51. The Barefoot Contessa 54. Alexander the Great 55. A Farewell to Arms 57. The Vikings 58. Room at the Top 58. Solomon and Sheba 59. Sons and Lovers 60. Barabbas 61. Jessica 62. One Million Years BC 66. Dr Faustus 67. When Dinosaurs Ruled the Earth 70. Creatures the World Forgot 71. Year One (Anno Uno) 74. The Messiah 78, many others.

Nash, Clarence (1904–1985).
American voice performer, the inimitable sound of Donald Duck for 40 years.

Nash, Marilyn (c. 1924–).
American leading lady selected by Chaplin to play in *Monsieur Verdoux* 47. Married writer-producer Philip Yordan.

Nash, Mary (1885–1976) (Mary Ryan).
American stage actress in occasional films.
■ Uncertain Lady 34. College Scandal 35. Come and Get It 36. The King and the Chorus Girl 37. Easy Living 37. Heidi 37. Wells Fargo 37. The Little Princess 39. The Rains Came 39. Charlie Chan in Panama 40. Sailor's Lady 40. Gold Rush Maisie 40. The Philadelphia Story 40. Men of Boys Town 41. Calling Dr Gillespie 41. The Human Comedy 43. In the Meantime Darling 44. Cobra Woman 44. The Lady and the Monster 44. Yolanda and the Thief 45. Monsieur Beaucaire 46. Swell Guy 46. Till the Clouds Roll By 46.

Nathan, Robert (1894–1985).
American novelist. Works filmed include *Portrait*

Jennie and *The Bishop's Wife.* Also scripted *The ~ock* 45.

~ational Film Archive.
~ government-financed museum of films of ~tistic and historical value. Operated by the ~ritish Film Institute.

~he National Film Board of Canada
~as set up in 1939, with John Grierson at its head, ~ show Canada's face to the world. Many ~xcellent documentaries ensued, not to mention ~e brilliant animation films of Norman McLaren, ~at by the end of the 60s the Board's fortunes were ~ a lower ebb and its reputation declined.

~he National Film Finance Corporation
~as founded in 1949 to provide loans for film ~roduction, but began to withdraw its facilities in ~e early 70s, at a time when financial ~ncouragement had never been more needed for ~ritish production.

~he National Film Theatre
~n London's South Bank is an extension of the ~ritish Film Institute; founded in 1951, it runs a ~aily repertory in three theatres of films of all ~ationalities and types.

~atwick, Grim (1890–1990) (Myron Natwick).
~artoonist and animator who created Betty Boop ~hile working for Max Fleischer in 1930. He later ~orked for Disney on *Snow White and the Seven ~warfs* 37, and animated the Sorcerer's Apprentice ~equence in *Fantasia* 40.

~atwick, Mildred (1908–1994).
~american character actress, at her best in eccentric ~oles.
The Long Voyage Home 40. The Enchanted ~ottage 45. Yolanda and the Thief 45. The Late ~eorge Apley 47. A Woman's Vengeance 47. Three ~odfathers 48. The Kissing Bandit 48. She Wore a ~ellow Ribbon 49. Cheaper by the Dozen 50. The ~uiet Man 52. Against All Flags 52. *The Trouble with ~arry* 55. *The Court Jester* 56. Teenage Rebel 56. ~ammy and the Bachelor 57. Barefoot in the Park ~AAN) 67. If It's Tuesday This Must Be Belgium ~9. The Maltese Bippy 69. Do Not Fold Spindle or ~utilate 71. The Snoop Sisters (TV) 72. Daisy ~ Miller 74. At Long Last Love 75. Kiss Me Goodbye ~2. Dangerous Liaisons 88.

~aughton, Bill (1910–1992).
~rish novelist, dramatist and screenwriter, a former ~orry driver.
Autobiography: 1988, *Saintly Billy: A Catholic ~Boyhood.*
Alfie (AAN) 66. The Family Way 66. Spring and ~ Port Wine 70. Alfie Darling (oa) 75.

~aughton, Charles:
~see *The Crazy Gang.*

~aughton, David (1951–).
~american leading actor. Brother of James ~ Naughton.
Separate Ways 79. Midnight Madness 80. An ~ American Werewolf in London 81. Hot Dog – the ~ Movie! 83. Not for Publication 84. Getting Physical ~ (TV) 84. Separate Vacations 86. The Boy in Blue ~ 86. Kidnapped 87. Private Affairs 89. Overexposed ~ 90. The Sleeping Car 90. Wild Cactus 92, etc.

~aughton, James (1945–).
~American leading man, mostly on television.
The Paper Chase 74. The Bunker (TV) 80. A

Stranger Is Watching 82. The Glass Menagerie 87. The Good Mother 88. Second Wind 90, etc.
TV series: Faraday and Company 72. Planet of the Apes 74.

Nava, Gregory (1949–).
American director and screenwriter.
The Confessions of Amans (wd) 76. The End of August (co-w) 82. El Norte (wd) (AAN) 84. A Time of Destiny (wd) 88, etc.

naval comedy
in British movies usually has a 30s look about it, may well be written by Ian Hay, and almost always concerns the officers; as in *The Middle Watch, Carry On Admiral, The Midshipmaid, The Flag Lieutenant* and *Up the Creek* (though the other ranks had their look in with *The Bulldog Breed, The Baby and the Battleship* and *Jack Ahoy*). In Hollywood movies the focus of interest is set firmly among the other ranks: *Follow the Fleet, Abbott and Costello in the Navy, Anchors Aweigh, Operation Petticoat, Mr Roberts, South Pacific, Ensign Pulver, On the Town, You're in the Navy Now, The Fleet's In, Onion-Head, Don't Go Near the Water, Don't Give Up the Ship, The Honeymoon Machine.*

Nazarro, Ray (1902–1986).
American director of second features.
The Tougher They Come 50. The Return of the Corsican Brothers 53. Top Gun 55. The Hired Gun 57, etc.; then into TV.

Nazimova, Alla (1879–1945) (Alla Nazimoff).
Russian-born stage actress who made a number of films in America.
■ War Brides 16. Revelation 18. Toys of Fate 18. An Eye for an Eye 19. The Red Lantern 19. The Brat 19. Stronger than Death 20. Heart of a Child 20. Madame Peacock 20. Billions 20. Camille 21. A Doll's House 22. *Salome* 23. Madonna of the Streets 24. The Redeeming Sin 24. My Son 25. *Escape* 40. Blood and Sand 41. The Bridge of San Luis Rey 44. In Our Time 44. Since You Went Away 45.

Nazzari, Amedeo (1907–1979).
Virile Italian leading man, in films from 1935 although few travelled.
The Wolf of Sila 47. The Brigand 51. Nights of Cabiria 57. Labyrinth 59. The Best of Enemies 61. The Valachi Papers 72, etc.

Neagle, Dame Anna (1904–1986) (Marjorie Robertson).
British leading lady, a former chorus dancer who after her marriage in the 30s to producer Herbert Wilcox built up a formidable film gallery of historical heroines, and when film roles grew hard to find returned successfully to the theatre.
Autobiographies: 1949, *It's Been Fun.* 1974, *There's Always Tomorrow.*
■ The School for Scandal 30. Should a Doctor Tell? 30. The Chinese Bungalow 31. Goodnight Vienna 32. The Flag Lieutenant 32. The Little Damozel 33. *Bitter Sweet* 33. The Queen's Affair 33. *Nell Gwyn* 34. Peg of Old Drury 35. Limelight 36. The Three Maxims 36. London Melody 37. *Victoria the Great* 37. Sixty Glorious Years 38. *Nurse Edith Cavell* 39. Irene (US) 40. No No Nanette (US) 40. Sunny (US) 41. They Flew Alone (as Amy Johnson) 42. Forever and a Day 43. Yellow Canary 43. I Live in Grosvenor Square 45. *Piccadilly Incident* 46. The Courtneys of Curzon Street 47. *Spring in Park Lane* 48. Elizabeth of Ladymead 49. Maytime in Mayfair 49. *Odette* 50. *The Lady with a Lamp* 51. Derby Day 52. Lilacs in the Spring 55. King's Rhapsody 56. My Teenage Daughter 56. No Time

for Tears 57. The Man Who Wouldn't Talk 58. The Lady is a Square 58.
Produced three Frankie Vaughan films 58–61; returned to stage.
☉ For providing her faithful British admirers with the heroines they wanted her to be; and for her eagerness to please. *Victoria the Great.*

Neal, Patricia (1926–).
American leading actress who handled some interesting roles before illness caused her semi-retirement. She was married to writer Roald Dahl (1953–83).
Autobiography: *As I Am.*
■ John Loves Mary 49. *The Fountainhead* 49. It's a Great Feeling 49. *The Hasty Heart* (GB) 50. Bright Leaf 50. Three Secrets 50. The Breaking Point 50. Operation Pacific 51. Raton Pass 51. Diplomatic Courier 51. The Day the Earth Stood Still 51. Weekend with Father 51. Washington Story 52. Something for the Birds 52. Stranger from Venus (GB) 54. *A Face in the Crowd* 57. Breakfast at Tiffany's 61. Hud (AA, BFA) 63. Psyche 59 (GB) 64. In Harm's Way (BFA) 64. The Subject was Roses (AAN) 68. The Homecoming (TV) 71. The Night Digger 71. Baxter 72. Happy Mother's Day Love George 73. Run Stranger Run (TV) 74. Things in Their Season (TV) 75. Eric (TV) 77. Tail Gunner Joe (TV) 77. The Bastard (TV) 78. The Passage 79. All Quiet on the Western Front (TV) 80. Ghost Story 81. Glitter (TV) 84. Love Leads the Way (TV) 85. An Unremarkable Life 89. Caroline? 90.
~A TV movie, *The Patricia Neal Story*, was made in 1981, with Glenda Jackson playing Pat.

Neal, Tom (1914–1972).
American leading man, mainly in second features; former athlete.
Out West with the Hardys 39. One Thrilling Night 42. The Racket Man 45. Detour 47. Navy Bound 51. Red Desert 54, etc.

Neame, Ronald (1911–).
Outstanding British cinematographer who became a rather disappointing director.
SELECTED FILMS AS CINEMATOGRAPHER: Drake of England 34. The Gaunt Stranger 37. The Crimes of Stephen Hawke 39. Major Barbara 40. In Which We Serve 42. Blithe Spirit 45.
■ AS DIRECTOR: Take My Life 47. The Golden Salamander 50. *The Card* (& p) 52. The Million Pound Note 53. The Man Who Never Was 56. The Seventh Sin 57. Windom's Way 58. The Horse's Mouth 59. *Tunes of Glory* 60. Escape from Zahrain 61. I Could Go On Singing 62. The Chalk Garden 64. Mister Moses 65. A Man Could Get Killed (co-d) 66. Gambit 66. The Prime of Miss Jean Brodie 68. Scrooge 70. The Poseidon Adventure 72. The Odessa File 75. Meteor 79. Hopscotch 80. First Monday in October 81. Foreign Body 86.

Nebenzal, Seymour (1899–1961).
Distinguished German producer who had a disappointing career after going to Hollywood in the late 30s.
Westfront 30. M 31. Kameradschaft 32. The Testament of Dr Mabuse 33. Mayerling 36. We Who are Young 40. Summer Storm 44. Whistle Stop 46. Heaven Only Knows 47. Siren of Atlantis 48. M (remake) 51, etc.

Nedell, Bernard (1898–1972).
American character actor.
The Serpent 16. The Return of the Rat (GB) 29. Shadows (GB) 31. Lazybones (GB) 35. The Man Who could Work Miracles (GB) 36. Mr Moto's Gamble 38. Angels Wash Their Faces 39. Strange Cargo 40. The Desperadoes 43. One Body Too

Many 44. Monsieur Verdoux 47. The Loves of Carmen 48. Heller in Pink Tights 60. Hickey and Boggs 72, many others.

Needham, Hal (1931–).
American director, former stuntman.
■ *Smokey and the Bandit* 77. Hooper 78. The Villain 79. Death Car on the Freeway (TV) 79. Smokey and the Bandit II 80. Stunts (TV) 81. The Cannonball Run 81. Megaforce 82. Stroker Ace 83. Cannonball Run II 84. RAD 86. Body Slam 87.

Neeson, Liam (1952–).
Irish-born leading actor, often in tough-guy roles. He married Natasha Richardson in 1994.
Excalibur 81. The Bounty 84. The Innocent 84. Lamb 85. Duet for One 86. The Mission 86. A Prayer for the Dying 87. Suspect 87. The Dead Pool 88. The Good Mother 88. High Spirits 88. Satisfaction 88. Next of Kin 89. The Big Man 90. Darkman 90. Under Suspicion 91. Shining Through 92. Ethan Frome 93. Ruby Cairo 93. *Schindler's List* (AAN) 93. Nell 94. Rob Roy 95, etc.

Neff, Hildegard (1925–) (Hildegard Knef).
German leading lady, former artist and film cartoonist. Briefly on German stage, then to films, and for a time in Hollywood.
Autobiography: 1971, *The Gift Horse.*
The Murderers Are amongst Us 46. *Film without Title* 47. The Sinner 50. Decision before Dawn 51. *The Snows of Kilimanjaro* 52. Diplomatic Courier 52. Henriette 52. The Man Between 53. The Girl from Hamburg 57. And So to Bed 63. Landru 63. Mozambique 65. The Lost Continent (GB) 68. Fedora 78. Witchery 88, etc.

Negri, Pola (1897–1987) (Appolonia Chalupek).
Polish-born leading lady with experience on German stage and screen; went to Hollywood in the 20s and was popular until sound came in.
Autobiography: 1970, *Memories of a Star.*
Die Bestie 15. Madame du Barry 18. The Flame 20. Bella Donna (US) 23. *Forbidden Paradise* 24. Hotel Imperial 26. Three Sinners 28. A Woman Commands 31. Madame Bovary 35. Hi Diddle Diddle 43. The Moonspinners 64, etc.

Negulesco, Jean (1900–1993).
Rumanian-born director, in US from 1927.
■ Kiss and Make Up 34. Singapore Woman 41. *The Mask of Dimitrios* 44. The Conspirators 44. Three Strangers 46. Nobody Lives Forever 46. *Humoresque* 46. Deep Valley 47. *Roadhouse* 48. *Johnny Belinda* (AAN) 48. Britannia Mews 49. Under My Skin 50. *Three Came Home* 50. *The Mudlark* 51. Take Care of My Little Girl 51. Phone Call from a Stranger 52. Lydia Bailey 52. Lure of the Wilderness 52. Full House (part) 52. Scandal at Scourie 53. Titanic 53. *How to Marry a Millionaire* 53. *Three Coins in the Fountain* 54. *Woman's World* 54. Daddy Longlegs 55. The Rains of Ranchipur 55. Boy on a Dolphin 57. A Certain Smile 58. The Gift of Love 58. Count Your Blessings 59. The Best of Everything 59. Jessica 62. The Pleasure Seekers 65. The Invincible Six 68. Hello Goodbye 70. The Heroes 79.

¶ A director I had not expected to praise is Jean Negulesco, who has always reminded me of Michael Curtiz on toast. Mr Curtiz, in turn, has always seemed like Franz Murnau under onions. – James Agee

Neil, Hildegarde (1939–).
South African leading lady.
The Man Who Haunted Himself 70. Antony and Cleopatra 71. England Made Me 72. A Touch of

Class 73. The Legacy 78. The Mirror Crack'd 80. Seaview Knights 94, etc.
TV series: Diamonds 80.

Neilan, Marshall (1891–1958).
American director who had meteoric success in the 20s and just as suddenly failed in the mid-30s. Also acted from 1912; last role *A Face in the Crowd* 57.
The Cycle of Fate 16. Freckles 17. Rebecca of Sunnybrook Farm 17. M'Liss 18. Daddy Longlegs 19. The Lotus Eater 21. Tess of the D'Urbervilles 25. Her Wild Oat 27. Three Ring Marriage 28. The Awful Truth 29. Sweethearts on Parade 30. The Lemon Drop Kid 34. Swing It, Professor 37, many others.

Neill, Roy William (1890–1946) (Roland de Gostrie).
Irish-born director, long in Hollywood; never rose above low-budget thrillers but often did them well.
Love Letters 17. Good References 21. Toilers of the Sea 23. The Good Bad Girl 31. The Black Room 34. The Good Old Days (GB) 35. Dr Syn (GB) 37. Eyes of the Underworld 41. *Frankenstein Meets the Wolf Man* 43. Gypsy Wildcat 44. Black Angel 46, etc.; also produced and directed most of the *Sherlock Holmes* series starring Basil Rathbone 42–46.

Neill, Sam (1948–).
New Zealand leading actor in international films.
My Brilliant Career 80. Ivanhoe (TV) 82. The Final Conflict 82. From a Far Country 82. The Blood of Others (TV) 84. Robbery Under Arms 85. Plenty 85. For Love Alone 86. The Good Wife 86. Evil Angels 88. A Cry in the Dark 88. Dead Calm 89. The Hunt for Red October 90. Death in Brunswick 90. Until the End of the World (Bis ans Ende der Welt) 91. Memoirs of an Invisible Man 92. Family Pictures (TV) 93. *The Piano* 93. Jurassic Park 93. Sirens 94. Country Life 94. In the Mouth of Madness 95. The Jungle Book 95, etc.
TV series: Reilly Ace of Spies 83.

Neilson, James (1909–1979).
American director, former war photographer, who worked mostly for Walt Disney.
■ The Blackwell Story (TV) 57. Night Passage 57. The Country Husband (TV) 58. Moon Pilot 62. Bon Voyage 62. Summer Magic 63. Dr Syn 63. The Moon Spinners 63. Return of the Gunfighter (TV) 66. The Adventures of Bullwhip Griffin 67. The Gentle Giant 67. Where Angels Go 68. The First Time 69. Flare Up 69. Tom Sawyer (TV) 75.

Nell Gwyn.
Charles II's orange-seller has appeared briefly in many films, but the two devoted to her story were both made in Britain by Herbert Wilcox: in 1927 with Dorothy Gish and in 1934 with Anna Neagle. Both caused censorship problems, the latter because of the lady's cleavage.

Nelligan, Kate (1951–).
Canadian actress first in Britain, now in Hollywood.
■ The Romantic Englishwoman 75. The Count of Monte Cristo (TV) 78. Dracula 79. Eye of the Needle 80. Without a Trace 83. Bethune: The Making of a Hero 84. Eleni 85. Kojak: The Price of Justice (TV) 87. Control (TV) 87. Il Giorno Prima 87. Love and Hate: A Marriage Made in Hell (TV) 90. The White Room 90. Frankie & Johnny 91. The Prince of Tides (AAN) 91. Shadows and Fog 92. Fatal Instinct 93. Spoils of War (TV) 94. Wolf 94. The Glace Bay Miner's Museum 95.

Nelson, Barry (1920–) (Robert Neilson).
Stocky American leading man who makes films between stage shows.
China Caravan 42. A Guy Named Joe 43. Winged Victory 44. The Beginning of the End 45. The Man with My Face 51. The First Travelling Saleslady 56. Mary Mary 63. The Borgia Stick (TV) 68. Airport 69. Pete 'n' Tillie 72. The Shining 80, many others.
TV series: My Favorite Husband 53–54. Hudson's Bay 59.

Nelson, Craig T. (1946–).
Brawny American leading man.
And Justice for All 79. The Formula 80. Private Benjamin 80. Stir Crazy 80. Poltergeist 82. The Chicago Story (TV) 82. The Osterman Weekend 83. Silkwood 83. The Killing Fields 84. Call to Glory (TV) 84. Poltergeist II 86. Action Jackson 88. Troop Beverly Hills 89. Turner & Hooch 89. Me and Him 89. The Josephine Baker Story (TV) 91. The Fire Next Time (TV) 93, etc.
TV series: Air Force 84.

Nelson, Ed (1928–).
American actor who played gangsters, brothers-in-law and boyfriends in innumerable 50s second features, then went into TV and found himself a secure niche as Dr Rossi in *Peyton Place* 64–68, and in *The Silent Force* 70.
Midway 76. Shining Star 77. Police Academy 3 85. The Boneyard 91, etc.

Nelson, Gary.
American director.
The Girl on the Late Late Show (TV) 74. Medical Story (TV) 75. Panache (TV) 76. *Washington: Behind Closed Doors* (TV) 77. To Kill a Cop (TV) 78. The Black Hole 79. Jimmy the Kid 82. Enigma 82. Allan Quatermain and the Lost City of Gold 86. Shooter (TV) 88. Get Smart, Again! 89. Ray Alexander: A Taste for Justice (TV) 94, etc.

Nelson, Gene (1920–) (Leander Berg).
American actor-dancer, on stage from 1938, films from mid-40s. He began directing, mainly for TV, from the 60s.
I Wonder Who's Kissing Her Now 47. Gentleman's Agreement 48. The Daughter of Rosie O'Grady 50. Tea for Two 51. Lullaby of Broadway 52. She's Working Her Way through College 52. So This Is Paris 55. Oklahoma 55. 20,000 Eyes 62. The Purple Hills 63, etc.
AS DIRECTOR: Hand of Death 62. Hootenanny Hoot 63. Kissin' Cousins 64. Your Cheatin' Heart 64. Harum Scarum 65. The Cool Ones 67. Wake Me When the War Is Over (TV) 69. The Letters (TV) 73. The Baron and the Kid (TV) 84, etc.
TV series as director: *Washington behind Closed Doors* 77.

Nelson, Judd (1959–).
American leading actor.
Making the Grade 84. The Breakfast Club 85. Fandango 85. St Elmo's Fire 85. Blue City 86. Transformers: the Movie 86. Dear America 87. From the Hip 87. Never on Tuesday 89. Relentless 89. Far Out Man 90. The Dark Backward 91. New Jack City 91. Primary Motive 92. Flinch 94, etc.

Nelson, Lord Horatio (1758–1805),
the hero of Trafalgar, was portrayed in *Nelson* 19 by Donald Calthrop; in *Nelson* 26 by Cedric Hardwicke; in *The Divine Lady* 29 by Victor Varconi; in *Lady Hamilton* 42 by Laurence Olivier; in *Lady Hamilton* (Ger.) 68 by Richard Johnson; and in *Bequest to the Nation* 73 by Peter Finch.

Nelson, Lori (1933–).
American light leading lady of the 50s.
Ma and Pa Kettle at the Fair 52. Bend of the River 52. Walking My Baby Back Home 53. Destry 55. Mohawk 56. Hot Rod Girl 56. The Day the World Ended 56. Untamed Youth 57, etc.
TV series: How to Marry a Millionaire 58.

Nelson, Oliver (1932–1975).
American composer, arranger, jazz saxophonist, and bandleader. Died of a heart attack.
Death of a Gunfighter 67. Skullduggery 70. Zigzag 70. Last Tango in Paris 73. Inside Job 73.

Nelson, Ozzie (1906–1975).
American bandleader whose genial, diffident personality became familiar in long-running domestic comedy series on TV.
Sweetheart of the Campus 41. Hi Good Lookin' 2. Love and Kisses (& wpd) 65. The Impossible Years 68, etc.
TV series: The Adventures of Ozzie and Harriet 52–5. Ozzie's Girls 73.

Nelson, Ralph (1916–1987).
American director.
■ Requiem for a Heavyweight 62. Lilies of the Field 63. Soldier in the Rain 64. Fate is the Hunter 64. Father Goose 64. Once a Thief 65. Duel at Diablo 66. Counterpoint 67. Charly 68. Tick Tick Tick 70. Soldier Blue 70. Flight of the Doves 71. The Wrath of God 72. The Wilby Conspiracy 75. Embryo 76. A Hero Ain't Nothing But a Sandwich 77. Because He's My Friend (Aust.) 78. Lady of the House (TV) 78. You Can't Go Home Again (TV) 79. Christmas Lilies of the Field (TV) 79.

Nelson, Rick (1940–1986).
American singer and light actor, son of bandleader Ozzie Nelson and his wife Harriet (formerly Harriet Hilliard, qv) with whom he appeared in the long-running TV series The Adventures of Ozzie and Harriet 52–65. He died in a plane crash.
Biography: 1992, Teenage Idol, Travelin' Man by Philip Bashe.
Here Come the Nelsons 52. Rio Bravo 59. The Wackiest Ship in the Army 60. Love and Kisses 65. The Over the Hill Gang (TV) 69, etc.

Nelson, Ruth (1905–1992).
American character actress, usually seen as sympathetic mother. She was married to actor-director John Cromwell.
Abe Lincoln in Illinois 40. Humoresque 46. The Late Show 77. 3 Women 77. The Haunting Passion (TV) 83. Awakenings 90, etc.

Nelson, Willie (1933–).
American singer and character actor.
The Electric Horseman 79. Honeysuckle Rose 80. Thief 81. Barbarosa 81. Hells Angels Forever 83. Red Headed Stranger 84. Songwriter 85. Amazons 87. Once upon a Texas Train (aka Texas Guns) (TV) 88. Pair of Aces (TV) 90. Wild Texas Wind 91, etc.

Nemec, Jan (1936–).
Czech director.
Diamonds of the Night 64. The Party and the Guests 66. The Martyrs of Love 67. The Unbearable Lightness of Being (a) 88. In the Light of the King's Love (d) 91, etc.

neo-realism
is a term mainly applied to the Italian post-war films which seemed to present a fresh and vivid kind of social realism. The essentials were real locations and at least a proportion of amateur actors. The most famous neo-realist film is Bicycle Thieves.

nepotism.
Hollywood moguls were at one time well known for promoting within the family. Hence the quip: the son-in-law also rises. Hence the rhyme:
   Uncle Carl Laemmle
   Has a very large faemmle.
Of an untalented Warner relative, Julius Epstein once commented that he had set the son-in-law business back twenty years. And when another gentleman of similar ilk taunted Oscar Levant with 'Oscar, play us a medley of your hit', Oscar came back with 'Okay, play us a medley of your father-in-law'. Of Louis B. Mayer's brother, Irving Brecher remarked: 'Jerry has a very important job and he has to have that big corner office. He's supposed to watch Washington Boulevard and warn everybody to evacuate the studio if icebergs are spotted coming down the street.' Similarly in London, after Alexander Korda's rise to fame and power, it was said that in order to get a job in British films you had to be Hungarian. These days, nepotism seems limited to directors giving their children roles in their films, sometimes with disastrous results.

Nero, Franco (1942–) (F. Spartanero).
Italian leading man in international films. He has a son by actress Vanessa Redgrave.
The Tramplers 66. The Bible 66. Camelot 67. The Day of the Owl 68. A Quiet Place in the Country 68. Tristana 70. The Virgin and the Gypsy 70. The Battle of Neretva 70. Pope Joan 72. The Monk 72. White Fang 74. Challenge to White Fang 75. Force Ten from Navarone 78. The Man with Bogart's Face 80. The Salamander 80. Enter the Ninja 81. The Last Days of Pompeii (TV) 84. Ten Days that Shook the World 84. Garibaldi 86. The Girl 86. Kamikaze 87. Silent Night 88. Die Hard 2 90. Di Ceria dell'Untore (The Plague Sower) 92. Jonathan of the Bears 94, etc.

Nervig, Conrad A. (1895–).
American editor.
Bardelys the Magnificent 26. The Divine Woman 28. The Guardsman 31. Eskimo (AA) 34. A Tale of Two Cities 36. The Crowd Roars 38. Northwest Passage 40. The Human Comedy 43. High Barbaree 47. Side Street 49. King Solomon's Mines (AA) 50. The Bad and the Beautiful 52. Gypsy Colt 54, many others.

Nervo, Jimmy:
see The Crazy Gang.

Nesbit, Evelyn (1886–1967).
Notorious American beauty involved in a murder case of 1912; portrayed by Joan Collins in The Girl in the Red Velvet Swing and by Elizabeth McGivern in Ragtime.
■ Threads of Destiny 14. Redemption 17. The Hidden Woman 22.

Nesbitt, Cathleen (1888–1982).
British character actress, on stage from 1910; very occasional films, but active on stage and television into her nineties.
Autobiography: 1973, A Little Love and Good Companions.
The Case of the Frightened Lady 32. The Passing of the Third Floor Back 36. Fanny by Gaslight 43. Nicholas Nickleby 47. Three Coins in the Fountain 54. Désirée 54. An Affair to Remember 57. Promise Her Anything 66. The Trygon Factor 67. Staircase 69. Villain 71. Family Plot 76. Julia 77, etc.
TV series: The Farmer's Daughter 65.

Nesbitt, Derren (c. 1932–).
British character actor, usually a smiling villain.
The Man in the Back Seat 60. Victim 62. Strongroom 62. The Naked Runner 67. Nobody Runs Forever 68. Where Eagles Dare 68. Innocent Bystanders 72. Ooh You Are Awful 72. The Amorous Milkman (wd) 74. Bullseye! 91. Double X 92, etc.

Nesbitt, John (1911–1960).
American producer of MGM's long-running Passing Parade series of informational one-reelers.

Nesmith, Michael (1942–).
American guitarist and songwriter who was a member of The Monkees pop group in the 60s. He became an influential director of rock videos and a producer of independent movies in the 70s and 80s.
Head 68. Elephant Parts (& wd) 81. An Evening with Sir William Martin 81. Timerider (& co-w) 83. Repo Man (p) 84. Square Dance (p) 87. Tapeheads (& p) 87. The Monkees: Heart and Soul (concert doc) 87, etc.
TV series: The Monkees 66–68. Television Parts 85.

Nettleton, John (1929–).
British character actor.
A Man for All Seasons 67. Some Will Some Won't 69. And Soon the Darkness 69. Black Beauty 70, etc.

Nettleton, Lois (1930–).
American character actress.
■ Period of Adjustment 62. Come Fly with Me 63. Mail Order Bride 64. Valley of Mystery 66. Bamboo Saucer 68. The Good Guys and the Bad Guys 69. Dirty Dingus Magee 70. Sidelong Glances of a Pigeon Kicker 71. The Forgotten Man (TV) 71. The Honkers 72. Echoes of a Summer 75. Fear on Trial (TV) 75. Washington: Behind Closed Doors (TV) 77. Centennial (TV) 78. Tourist (TV) 79. Soggy Bottom USA 80. Deadly Blessing 81. Butterfly 82. The Best Little Whorehouse in Texas 82. Brass (TV) 85. Manhunt for Claude Dallas (TV) 86.
TV series: Accidental Family 67.

Neumann, Kurt (1908–1958).
German director, in Hollywood from 1925.
My Pal the King 32. The Big Cage 33. Rainbow on the River 36. Island of Lost Men 39. Ellery Queen Master Detective 40. The Unknown Guest 43. Tarzan and the Leopard Woman 46. Bad Boy 49. Rocketship XM (& w, p) 50. Son of Ali Baba 53. Carnival Story 54. Mohawk 56. Kronos 57. The Fly 58. Watusi 58, etc.

Neumeier, Edward.
American screenwriter.
Robocop (co-w) 87. Frankenstein Unbound (co-w) 90.

Neville, John (1925–).
British leading man, primarily on stage.
■ Oscar Wilde 60. Mr Topaze 61. Billy Budd 62. Unearthly Stranger 63. A Study in Terror (as Sherlock Holmes) 65. The Adventures of Gerard 70. The Adventures of Baron Munchausen 89. Stark (TV) 93. Baby's Day Out 94. The Road to Wellville 94.

'new wave'/'nouvelle vague'.
Term used (by themselves) for a group of new, exploring young French directors towards the end of the 50s: François Truffaut, Jean-Luc Godard, Louis Malle, Alain Resnais, etc. As their talents

were widely divergent, the term meant very little. It was coined by Françoise Giroud.

¶ There is no new wave, only the sea. – *Claude Chabrol*

New York

has provided a vivid backcloth for films of many types, and its skyscrapers allegedly gave Fritz Lang the inspiration for *Metropolis*. Studio re-creations provided the period flavour of *Little Old New York, New York Town, One Sunday Afternoon, A Tree Grows in Brooklyn, Incendiary Blonde, My Girl Tisa,* and *The Bowery;* and it was a studio city which was wrecked by *King Kong*. But the camera has also explored the real article, notably in thrillers like *Saboteur, Naked City, Union Station, The FBI Story* and *North by Northwest;* in realistic comedy dramas like *From This Day Forward, So This is New York, Miracle on 34th Street, Lovers and Lollipops, Marty, It Should Happen to You, Sunday in New York, Breakfast at Tiffany's, The Lost Weekend, The Bachelor Party, A Man Ten Feet Tall, A Fine Madness, Love with the Proper Stranger, The World of Henry Orient, Midnight Cowboy, The Pawnbroker, Barefoot in the Park, Beau James, The French Connection, Cotton Comes to Harlem, Shaft, The Out-of-Towners, Any Wednesday, Serpico, Bye Bye Braverman, Sweet Charity, The Seven-Ups, The Taking of Pelham One Two Three, The Prisoner of Second Avenue, Mean Streets, Taxi Driver, Death Wish* and *Three Days of the Condor;* in hard-hitting social melodramas like *On the Waterfront, Sweet Smell of Success,* and *The Young Savages;* and in musicals like *On the Town* and *West Side Story*. Other films which concern the effect of New York without showing much of the actuality include *Mr Deeds Goes to Town, Bachelor Mother, Lady on a Train, Bell, Book and Candle, Portrait of Jennie, Kid Millions, Dead End, The Apartment, Patterns of Power, The Garment Jungle, Mr Blandings Builds His Dream House* and *America, America*. Finally Manhattan Island was bought from the Indians by Groucho Marx in *The Story of Mankind, Knickerbocker Holiday* pictured the city in its Dutch colonial days as New Amsterdam and *Godspell* used it as a novel background for its revised version of the Life of Christ. Television series with authentic New York locations include *Naked City, The Defenders, East Side West Side, N.Y.P.D., Madigan, McCloud, Kojak, Eischied.*

Newall, Guy (1885–1937).

British stage actor who became a popular leading man in silent sentimental dramas, especially with his wife Ivy Duke. Also directed most of his films.
Comradeship 18. The Garden of Resurrection 19. The Lure of Crooning Water 20. The Duke's Son 20. Beauty and the Beast 22. Boy Woodburn 22. The Starlit Garden 23. The Ghost Train 27. The Eternal Feminine 30. The Marriage Bond 30. Grand Finale 37, etc.

Newborn, Ira.

American composer.
The Blues Brothers 80. All Night Long 81. Sixteen Candles 84. Weird Science 85. Ferris Bueller's Day Off 86. Wise Guys 86. Dragnet 87. Planes, Trains and Automobiles 87. The Naked Gun: From the Files of Police Squad 88. Uncle Buck 89. Short Time 90. My Blue Heaven 90. The Naked Gun 2½: The Smell of Fear 91. Brain Donors 92. The Opposite Sex . . . And How to Live with Them 93. Ace Ventura, Pet Detective 94. Naked Gun 33⅓: The Final Insult 94, etc.

Newbrook, Peter (1916–).

British producer, former cinematographer.
The Yellow Teddy Bears 63. Black Torment 64.

Gonks Go Beat 65. The Sandwich Man 66. Press for Time 66. Corruption 69. She'll Follow You Anywhere 70. The Asphyx 72, etc.

Newell, Mike (1942–).

British director, from TV.
The Man in the Iron Mask (TV) 77. The Awakening 80. Blood Feud (TV) 83. *Dance with a Stranger* 85. Amazing Grace and Chuck 87. *Soursweet* 88. Enchanted April 91. Into the West 92. *Four Weddings and a Funeral* 94. An Awfully Big Adventure 95, etc.

Newfeld, Sam (1900–1964).

American director of second features.
Reform Girl 33. Big Time or Bust 34. Northern Frontier 35. Timber War 36. Trail of Vengeance 37. Harlem on the Prairie 38. Secrets of a Model 40. Billy the Kid's Fighting Pals 41. The Mad Monster 42. Nabonga 44. Ghost of Hidden Valley 46. The Counterfeiters 48. Motor Patrol 50. Three Desperate Men 51. Thunder Over Sangoland 55. Wolf Dog 58, many others.

Newhart, Bob (1929–).

American TV and record comedian who has appeared in a few movies.
Hell is for Heroes 62. Hot Millions 68. On a Clear Day You Can See Forever 70. Catch 22 70. Cold Turkey 70. Thursday's Game (TV) 74. The First Family 80. Little Miss Marker 80. Marathon (TV) 80. The Rescuers Down Under (voice) 90, etc.
TV series: The Bob Newhart Show 72–77. Newhart 82–86.

Newland, John (1917–).

American TV actor (the host of *One Step Beyond*) who also directed a few films. He played Algy in the Tom Conway *Bulldog Drummond* films 48–49.
That Night 57. The Violators 57. The Spy with My Face 65. Hush-a-Bye Murder 70. Don't Be Afraid of the Dark (TV) 73. The Legend of Hillbilly John (TV) 74. The Suicide's Wife (TV) 79, etc.

Newlands, Anthony (1926–).

British character actor, mainly on TV; usually plays schemers.
Beyond This Place 59. The Trials of Oscar Wilde 60. Hysteria 64. Theatre of Death 67, etc.

Newley, Anthony (1931–).

Versatile but dislikeable British actor, composer, singer, comedian; former child star.
Oliver Twist 48. Vice Versa 48. Those People Next Door 53. *Cockleshell Heroes* 56. X the Unknown 56. High Flight 57. *No Time to Die* 58. Idol on Parade 59. In the Nick 61. The Small World of Sammy Lee 63. Dr Dolittle (US) 67. Sweet November (US) 68. Can Hieronymus Merkin Ever Forget Mercy Humppe and Find True Happiness? (& wd) 69. Summertree (d only) 72. Mr Quilp 75. A Good Idea at the Time (Can.) 76. Malibu (TV) 83. The Garbage Pail Kids Movie 87, etc.

Newman, Alfred (1901–1970).

American composer, former child pianist; an eminent Hollywood musical director since early sound days, he composed over 250 film scores.
The Devil To Pay 30. Whoopee 31. *Arrowsmith* 31. Cynara 32. *The Bowery* 33. Nana 34. Dodsworth 36. *Dead End* 37. *Alexander's Ragtime Band* (AA) 38. *Gunga Din* 39. Tin Pan Alley (AA) 40. *The Grapes of Wrath* 40. Son of Fury 42. The Song of Bernadette (AA) 43. The Razor's Edge 46. *Mother Wore Tights* (AA) 47. Unfaithfully Yours 48. *With a Song in My Heart* (AA) 52. *Call Me Madam* (AA) 53. Love is a Many Splendored Thing (AA) 55. *The King and I* (AA) 56. Flower Drum Song 61. The

Counterfeit Traitor 62. How the West was Won 62. Nevada Smith 66, many others.

Newman, Barry (1940–).

American leading actor.
■ Pretty Boy Floyd 60. *The Lawyer* 69. *Vanishing Point* 71. The Salzburg Connection 72. Fear is the Key 72. City on Fire 79. Fatal Vision (TV) 84.
TV series: Petrocelli 73–74.

Newman, David (1937–).

American screenwriter, in collaboration with Robert Benton until the early 70s, and occasionally with his wife, Leslie Newman.
■ *Bonnie and Clyde* (AAN) 67. There Was a Crooked Man 70. What's Up Doc 72. Bad Company 72. Superman 78. Superman II 80. Jinxed 82. Superman III 83. Sheena 84. Santa Claus: The Movie 85.

Newman, David.

American composer and conductor, the son of Alfred Newman.
Critters 86. The Brave Little Toaster 87. My Demon Lover 87. Throw Momma from the Train 87. Bill and Ted's Excellent Adventure 89. Disorganized Crime 89. Heathers 89. The War of the Roses 89. Madhouse 90. Fire Birds 90. The Freshman 90. Mr Destiny 90. The Marrying Man (aka Too Hot to Handle) 91. Other People's Money 91. Bill & Ted's Bogus Journey 91. Don't Tell Mom the Babysitter's Dead 91. The Runestone 92. Honeymoon in Vegas 92. The Sandlot (GB: The Sandlot Kids) 93. Coneheads 93. Undercover Blues 93. My Father, the Hero 94. The Flintstones 94. The Air Up There 94. I Love Trouble 94, etc.

Newman, Joseph M. (1909–).

American director, in films from 1931.
Jungle Patrol 48. 711 Ocean Drive 50. The Outcast of Poker Flats 52. Red Skies of Montana 52. Pony Soldier 53. The Human Jungle 54. Dangerous Crossing 54. Kiss of Fire 55. *This Island Earth* 55. Flight to Hong Kong (& p) 56. Gunfight at Dodge City 58. The Big Circus 59. Tarzan the Ape Man 59. King of the Roaring Twenties 61. A Thunder of Drums 61. The George Raft Story 61, etc.

Newman, Lionel (1916–1989).

American composer.
The Street with No Name 48. Cheaper by the Dozen 50. Diplomatic Courier 52. Dangerous Crossing 53. Gorilla at Large 54. How to Be Very Very Popular 55. A Kiss Before Dying 56. Mardi Gras 58. Compulsion 59. North to Alaska 60. Move Over Darling 63. Do Not Disturb 65. The Salzburg Connection 72. The Bluebird 76. Alien 79. Breaking Away 79. The Final Conflict 81. Cross Creek 83. Unfaithfully Yours 83, etc.

Newman, Nanette (1934–).

British leading lady, married to Bryan Forbes.
Personal Affair 53. House of Mystery 58. Faces in the Dark 59. The League of Gentlemen 59. Twice Round the Daffodils 62. The Wrong Arm of the Law 63. Of Human Bondage 64. Séance on a Wet Afternoon 64. The Wrong Box 66. The Whisperers 66. The Madwoman of Chaillot 69. *The Raging Moon* 70. The Love Ban 72. Man at the Top 73. The Stepford Wives 75. International Velvet 78. The Mystery of Edwin Drood 93, etc.

Newman, Paul (1925–).

American leading actor who suffered initially from a similarity to Marlon Brando but later developed a lithe impertinence which served him well in his better films. He was given a special Academy Award in 1986 for 'his many memorable and compelling screen performances'. He is married to actress Joanne Woodward.

Biography: 1975, *Paul Newman* by Charles Hamblett.

■ The Silver Chalice 54. *Somebody Up There Likes Me* 56. The Rack 56. Until They Sail 57. The Helen Morgan Story 57. *The Long Hot Summer* 58. The Left Handed Gun 58. Rally Round the Flag Boys 58. Cat on a Hot Tin Roof (AAN) 58. The Young Philadelphians 59. From the Terrace 60. Exodus 60. *The Hustler* (AAN, BFA) 61. Paris Blues 61. Sweet Bird of Youth 62. Hemingway's Adventures of a Young Man 62. *Hud* (AAN) 63. A New Kind of Love 63. *The Prize* 63. What a Way to Go 64. The Outrage 64. Lady L 64. Torn Curtain 66. *Harper* 66. *Hombre* 67. *Cool Hand Luke* (AAN) 67. The Secret War of Harry Frigg 67. Rachel Rachel (d only) 68. Winning 69. *Butch Cassidy and the Sundance Kid* 69. W.U.S.A. 70. Sometimes a Great Notion (& d) 71. Pocket Money 72. The Effect of Gamma Rays on Man-in-the-Moon Marigolds (d only) 72. *Judge Roy Bean* 72. The Mackintosh Man 73. The Sting 73. The Towering Inferno 74. The Drowning Pool 75. Silent Movie 76. Buffalo Bill and the Indians 76. Slap Shot 77. Quintet 79. Fort Apache, the Bronx 80. When Time Ran Out 80. The Shadow Box (d only) 81. Absence of Malice (AAN) 82. *The Verdict* (AAN) 82. Harry and Son 84. The Color of Money (AA) 86. The Glass Menagerie (d only) 87. Fat Man and Little Boy (GB: The Shadowmakers) 89. Blaze 89. Mr & Mrs Bridge 90. The Hudsucker Proxy 94. Nobody's Fool 94.

¶ You don't stop being a citizen just because you have a Screen Actors' Guild card. – *P.N.*

Acting is a question of absorbing other people's personalities and some of your own experience. – *P.N.*

Ever since *Slap Shot* I've been swearing more. I knew I had a problem one day when I turned to my daughter and said: 'Please pass the fucking salt.' – *P.N.*

I wasn't driven to acting by an inner compulsion. I was running away from the sporting goods business. – *P.N.*

Newman, Randy (1943–).
Witty American songwriter, musician and composer. He is the nephew of composers Lionel and Alfred Newman.

Performance (md) 70. Cold Turkey (m) 71. The Pursuit of Happiness (m) 71. Ragtime (m) (AAN) 81. The Natural (m) (AAN) 84. April Fool's Day (m) 86. Three Amigos! (a, co-w, s) 86. Huey Long (co-m) 86. Parenthood (m) 89. Avalon (m) 90. Awakenings (m) 90. The Paper (m) 94. Maverick (m) 94, etc.

Newman, Thomas.
American composer.

Grandview, U.S.A. 84. Reckless 84. Desperately Seeking Susan 85. The Man with One Red Shoe 85. Real Genius 85. Jumpin' Jack Flash 86. Light of Day 87. The Lost Boys 87. Less than Zero 87. The Great Outdoors 88. The Prince of Pennsylvania 88. Cookie 89. Men Don't Leave 90. Welcome Back, Roxy Carmichael 91. Naked Tango 90. Fried Green Tomatoes at the Whistle Stop Café 91. Deceived 91. The Player 92. The Linguini Incident 92. Josh and S.A.M. 93. Threesome 94. The Shawshank Redemption 94, etc.

Newman, Walter (1916–1993).
American screenwriter.

Ace in the Hole (co-w) 51. Underwater 55. The Man with the Golden Arm (co-w) 56. The True Story of Jesse James 56. Crime and Punishment USA 59. The Interns (co-w) 62. Cat Ballou (co-w) (AAN) 65. Bloodbrothers (AAN) 78. The Champ 79. Saint Jack 79, etc.

Newmar, Julie (1930–) (Julia Newmeyer).
Tall American blonde actress.

Seven Brides for Seven Brothers 55. The Marriage Go Round 60. Mackenna's Gold 68. The Maltese Bippy 69. Hysterical 83. Streetwalkin' 85. Deep Space 87. Ghosts Can't Do It 90. Nudity Required 90. Oblivion 94, etc.

TV series: My Living Doll 64. Batman 65–67.

newsreels
were part of the very earliest cinema programme, and the nine-minute round up of topical events filmed by roving cameramen was a feature of programmes in cinemas throughout the world until the mid-60s, when it was clear that the newsreel had been replaced by television. Most newsreel companies have looked after their libraries, and the result is a vivid history of the twentieth century, frequently plundered by producers of compilation films.

Newton, Robert (1905–1956).
British star character actor with a rolling eye and a voice to match; a ham, but a succulent one.

■ Reunion 32. Dark Journey 37. Fire Over England 37. *Farewell Again* 37. The Squeaker 37. The Green Cockatoo 37. Twenty One Days 38. Vessel of Wrath 38. Yellow Sands 38. Dead Men are Dangerous 39. Jamaica Inn 39. Poison Pen 39. Hell's Cargo 39. Bulldog Sees It Through 40. Gaslight 40. Busman's Honeymoon 40. *Major Barbara* 40. *Hatter's Castle* 41. They Flew Alone 42. *This Happy Breed* 44. *Henry V* (as Pistol) 45. Night Boat to Dublin 46. *Odd Man Out* 46. Temptation Harbour 47. Snowbound 48. *Oliver Twist* (as Bill Sikes) 48. Kiss the Blood off My Hands (US) 48. Obsession 49. *Treasure Island* (as Long John) 50. Waterfront 50. *Tom Brown's Schooldays* (as Dr Arnold) 51. Soldiers Three (US) 51. Les Misérables (US) 52. Blackbeard the Pirate (US) 52. *Androcles and the Lion* (US) 53. Desert Rats (US) 53. The High and the Mighty (US) 54. *The Beachcomber* 54. Long John Silver 55. Around the World in Eighty Days (US) 56.

TV series: *Long John Silver* 55.
✪ For being so enjoyably larger than life. *Treasure Island*.

Newton, Wayne (1942–).
Actor and singer, performing from the age of six.

80 Steps to Jonah 69. License to Kill 89. The Adventures of Ford Fairlane 90. The Dark Backward 91. Best of the Best II 93, etc.

TV series: North and South, Book II 89.

Newton-John, Olivia (1948–).
British pop singer.

■ Tomorrow 70. *Grease* 78. Xanadu 80. Two of a Kind 83.

Ney, Marie (1895–1981).
British stage actress in occasional films.

Escape 30. The Wandering Jew 34. Scrooge 37. Jamaica Inn 39. Seven Days to Noon 50. Simba 54. Yield to the Night 55. Witchcraft 64, etc.

Ney, Richard (1917–).
American financier who almost accidentally went into acting but appears only occasionally.

Mrs Miniver 42. The Late George Apley 47. Joan of Arc 48. Babes in Baghdad 52. The Premature Burial 61, etc.

Ngor, Haing S. (1947–).
Cambodian actor in America. He was a doctor when the Khmer Rouge invaded his country and was imprisoned and tortured before leaving for America in 1980. As his French medical qualifications were not recognized, he worked in other jobs until being unexpectedly offered a role in *The Killing Fields*.

Autobiography: 1988, *Haing Ngor: A Cambodian Odyssey*, with Roger Warner.

The Killing Fields (AA) 84. The Iron Triangle 89. Vietnam, Texas 90. Ambition 91. My Life 93. Heaven and Earth 93.

Niblo, Fred (1874–1948) (Federico Nobile).
American director of silent films; had stage experience.

The Marriage Ring 18. Sex 20. *The Mark of Zorro* 20. *The Three Musketeers* 21. *Blood and Sand* 23. Thy Name is Woman 24. The Temptress 26. *Ben Hur* 27. Camille 27. Redemption 29. The Big Gamble 33. Three Sons o'Guns 41.

Nichetti, Maurizio.
Italian director, screenwriter and comic actor. He studied architecture, trained in mime, and worked as a circus clown and cartoon gag writer.

Ratatplan 79 (a, wd). Ho Fatto Splash (a, wd) 80. Tomorrow We Dance (Domani Si Balla) (a, wd) 82. Bertoldo, Bertoldino and Cacasenno (a) 84. The Icicle Thief (Ladri di Saponette) (a, wd) 88. Volere Volare (a, co-w, co-d) 90. Stefano Quantestorie (a, co-w, d) 93. Seven Sundays (Tous les Jours Dimanche) (a) 94, etc.

TV series: Quo Vadis? 85. Pista! 86–87.

¶ Film-makers can't work today without money from television. Then our work is passed over to television and destroyed completely. It's impossible to see a story from beginning to end on television without interruption. Television is not cinema – you're at home with the lights, the telephone, the children. I want people to go to the cinema to experience film. – *M.N.*

Nicholas Brothers, The Fayard (1914–) and Harold (1921–).
American acrobatic dancers who enlivened several musicals of the 40s.

■ Calling All Stars 37. Tin Pan Alley 41. Down Argentine Way 41. The Great American Broadcast 41. Sun Valley Serenade 42. Orchestra Wives 43. Stormy Weather 43. The Pirate 48.

Nicholas, Paul (1945–).
British light leading man in all media, but especially TV: *Just Good Friends, Bust*, etc.

Blind Terror 71. Stardust 74. Tommy 74. Lisztomania 75. Sergeant Pepper's Lonely Hearts Club Band 78. The World is Full of Married Men 79. Yesterday's Hero 79. The Jazz Singer 80. Nutcracker 83. Invitation to a Wedding 84.

Nicholas, Thomas Ian (1980–).
American child actor.

Rookie of the Year 93.

Nicholls, Anthony (1902–1977).
Distinguished-looking British stage actor, in occasional films.

The Laughing Lady 47. The Guinea Pig 49. The Hasty Heart 49. The Dancing Years 50. The Franchise Affair 50. The Weak and the Wicked 54. Make Me an Offer 55. The Safecracker 58. Victim 62. Mister Ten Per Cent 66, etc.

Nicholls, George (1865–1927).
Craggy American character actor.

A Romance of Happy Valley 17. Hearts of the World 18. The Eagle 25. The Wedding March 27, many others.

Nicholls, George, Jnr (1897–1939).
American director.

Anne of Green Gables 34. Michael Strogoff 37. Man of Conquest 39, etc.

Nichols, Barbara (1929–1976).
American comedy actress, former model; adept at portraying not-so-dumb blondes.

Miracle in the Rain 56. The King and Four Queens 57. The Scarface Mob 60. The George Raft Story 61. Where the Boys Are 63. The Disorderly Orderly 64. Dear Heart 65. The Loved One 65. The Swinger 66, etc.

Nichols, Dandy (1907–1986).
British character comedienne, often seen as nervous maid or cockney char. Became famous on TV as the long-suffering Else in *Till Death Us Do Part* 64–74; appeared in the film version 68.

Hue and Cry 46. Here Come the Huggetts 49. Street Corner 52. The Deep Blue Sea 55. The Vikings 58. Help 65. The Alf Garnett Saga 72. Britannia Hospital 83, many others.

Nichols, Dudley (1895–1960).
Distinguished American screenwriter, in Hollywood from 1929.

Born Reckless 30. The Sign of the Cross 32. *The Lost Patrol* 34. Steamboat round the Bend 34. *The Informer* (AA) 35. Mary of Scotland 36. The Hurricane 37. *Bringing Up Baby* 38. Stagecoach 39. The Long Voyage Home (AAN) 40. For Whom the Bell Tolls 43. Air Force (AAN) 43. *It Happened Tomorrow* 44. The Bells of St Mary's 45. *And Then There Were None* 45. Scarlet Street 45. Sister Kenny (& d) 46. Mourning Becomes Electra (& p, d) 47. Pinky 49. Prince Valiant 54. The Tin Star (AAN) 57. The Hangman 59, many others.

⊛ For providing the firm basis of a score of outstanding prestige films. *Stagecoach*.

Nichols, Ernest Loring 'Red' (1905–1965).
Jazz cornettist and bandleader who made a few shorts in the 30s and provided the cornet solos for *The Five Pennies* 59, a highly inaccurate version of his life in which he was played by Danny Kaye.

Nichols, Mike (1931–) (Michael Igor Peschkowsky).
German-born American cabaret entertainer and latterly film director.

■ Who's Afraid of Virginia Woolf? (AAN) 66. *The Graduate* (AA) 67. Catch 22 70. Carnal Knowledge 71. The Day of the Dolphin 73. The Fortune 76. Gilda Live 80. *Silkwood* (AAN) 83. Heartburn 86. Biloxi Blues 88. Working Girl (AAN) 88. Postcards from the Edge 90. Regarding Henry 91. Wolf 94.

¶ A movie is like a person. Either you trust it or you don't. – *M.N.*

Nichols, Peter (1927–).
Leading British dramatist, TV playwright and occasional screenwriter. He is a former teacher and actor.

Autobiography: 1984, *Feeling You're Behind*.

Catch Us If You Can 65. Georgy Girl (co-w) 66. A Day in the Death of Joe Egg 71. The National Health 73. Privates on Parade 84, etc.

¶ Cinema's inherent handicap is money: theatre's advantage has been that it was cheap – 'was' and 'has been' because now it's become a suburb of cinema and is cheap no longer. Cinema

has raped theatre and passed on the money taint like a dose of clap. – *P.N.*

Nicholson, Jack (1937–).
American leading actor, a fashionable figure since the early 70s.

Biographies: 1991, *The Joker's Wild* by John Parker. 1991, *Jack Nicholson: An Unauthorized Biography* by Donald Shepherd. 1994, *Jack's Life: A Biography of Jack Nicholson* by Patrick McGilligan.

■ Cry Baby Killer 58. Too Young to Love 59. Studs Lonigan 61. The Wild Rise 61. The Broken Land 62. The Little Shop of Horrors 62. The Raven 63. The Terror 63. Thunder Island (co-w only) 64. Back Door to Hell 64. Flight to Fury (& w) 65. Ensign Pulver 65. Ride the Whirlwind 66. The Shooting 66. Hell's Angels on Wheels 67. The St Valentine's Day Massacre 67. The Trip (w only) 67. Head (w only) 68. *Easy Rider* (AAN) 69. On a Clear Day You Can See Forever 70. Five Easy Pieces (AAN) 70. Drive He Said (d only) 70. Carnal Knowledge 71. A Safe Place 71. The King of Marvin Gardens 72. *The Last Detail* (AAN) 74. *Chinatown* (AAN) 74. Tommy 74. The Passenger 74. The Fortune 76. One Flew over the Cuckoo's Nest (AA) 76. The Missouri Breaks 76. The Last Tycoon 76. Going South (& d) 78. The Shining 80. The Postman Always Rings Twice 81. Reds (AAN, BFA) 81. The Border 82. Terms of Endearment (AA) 83. Prizzi's Honor (AAN) 85. Heartburn 86. The Witches of Eastwick 87. Ironweed (AAN) 87. Broadcast News (uncredited) 87. Batman 89. The Two Jakes (& d) 90. Man Trouble 92. Hoffa 92. A Few Good Men 93. Wolf 94.

¶ As an actor, I have no desire for anybody to understand my past work. Period. – *J.N.*

He has a fine eye for good paintings and a good ear for fine music. And he's a lovely man to drink with. – *John Huston*

Nicholson, James H. (1916–1972).
American executive, former theatre owner and distributor, who became president of American International Pictures.

Nicholson, Nora (1892–1973).
British stage character actress whose film roles have usually been fey or eccentric.

The Blue Lagoon 48. Tread Softly 48. Crow Hollow 52. Raising a Riot 54. A Town Like Alice 56. The Captain's Table 59. Diamonds for Breakfast 69, etc.

Nicholson, William (1948–).
English screenwriter and playwright.

Shadowlands (TV) (BFA) 85. *Shadowlands* (AAN) 93. Nell 94. First Knight 95.

Nick Carter.
The tough young American detective, the occidental answer to Sexton Blake, was created in 1886 by Ormond G. Smith (1860–1933) and John Russell Coryell (1848–1924) for the *New York Weekly*. Dozens of hack writers later authored the stories under pseudonyms. Four French films starring André Liabel were made in 1912; Thomas Carrigan appeared in some shorts in 1920; Edmund Lowe had a series in 1924; Walter Pidgeon was in three in 1940; Eddie Constantine in two (French) in 1963 and 1965. From 1943 the character was very popular on radio, but television has made one poorish attempt in 1972, *The Adventures of Nick Carter* starring Robert Conrad.

Nick and Nora Charles.
Married detectives created by Dashiell Hammett in

his novel *The Thin Man* 34. In the book, the thin man is the murderer's first victim. Oddly enough the tag stuck to William Powell (not all that thin, who played Nick Charles and starred in five sequels: *After the Thin Man* 37, *Another Thin Man* 38, *Shadow of the Thin Man* 42, *The Thin Man Goes Home* 44, *Song of the Thin Man* 46. Myrna Loy played Nora in all the features, and it was said that her domestic scenes with Powell in the original film marked the first time a sophisticated, affectionate marriage had been realistically portrayed on the screen. A later TV series, 57–59, starred Peter Lawford and Phyllis Kirk.

nickelodeon.
A humorous term applied to early American cinemas once they had become slightly grander than the converted stores which were used for the purpose at the turn of the century.

Nico (1938–1988) (Christa Paffgen).
Cool blonde German model, actress, and singer with the Velvet Underground. Born in Cologne, she became a model in Berlin at the age of 15 before going to work in New York, where Andy Warhol filmed her and gave her work with the Velvet Underground. She later became a solo singer but her career was not helped by her heroin addiction. She had a son by actor Alain Delon. Died of a cerebral haemorrhage after falling off a bicycle.

Biography: 1993, *Songs They Never Play on the Radio: Nico the Last Bohemian* by James Young.

La Dolce Vita 59. The Velvet Underground and Nico 66. The Chelsea Girls 66, etc.

¶ Nico was something of a celebrity in narcotic circles. Queen of the Junkies. She was famous within a limited milieu, i.e. heroin users and those who thought self-destruction a romantic vocation. – *James Young*

Nicol, Alex (1919–).
American leading man with stage experience, mainly in Universal action pictures.

The Sleeping City 50. Because of You 52. Law and Order 54. The Man from Laramie 55. Sincerely Yours 55. Under Ten Flags 60. Three Came Back (& p, d) 60. Look in Any Window 61. The Savage Guns 62. Ride and Kill 63. Gunfighters of Casa Grande 65. Bloody Mama 69. Point of Terror (d only) 71. The Night God Screamed 75. A*P*E* 76. Brandy Sheriff 78, etc.

Niehaus, Lennie (1929–).
American composer and jazz alto-saxophonist, noted for his playing with the Stan Kenton orchestra in the 50s.

Tightrope 84. City Heat 84. Pale Rider 85. Never Too Young to Die 86. Ratboy 86. Heartbreak Ridge 86. Bird 88. White Hunter, Black Heart 90. The Two Jakes (md) 90. Unforgiven 92. A Perfect World 93. Lush Life 93, etc.

Nielsen, Asta (1882–1972).
Danish stage actress.

Der Abgrund 10. Enelein 13. Kurfürstendamm 19. Reigen 20. Hamlet 20. Fräulein Julie 21. Vanina Vanini 22. Erdgeist 23. Hedda Gabler 24. Joyless Street 25. Secrets of a Soul 26. Unmögliche Liebe 32, many others.

Nielsen, Brigitte (1963–).
Danish actress, in Hollywood. She was formerly married to Sylvester Stallone (1985–87).

Red Sonja 85. Rocky IV 85. Cobra 86. Beverly Hills Cop II 87. Domino 88. Bye Bye Baby 89.

76-EVIL II 92. Mission of Justice 92. Chained
Heat II 93. Terminal Force 94, etc.

Nielsen, Leslie (1926–).
Canadian leading man, former radio disc jockey;
much TV work. He displayed an unsuspected
talent for comedy in *The Naked Gun* and its sequels.
The Vagabond King 55. Forbidden Planet 56.
Ransom 56. Tammy and the Bachelor 57. Harlow
5. Beau Geste 66. The Poseidon Adventure 72.
Project Kill 76. Day of the Animals 77. Little Mo
(TV) 78. The Amsterdam Kill 78. Backstairs at the
White House (TV) 79. Institute for Revenge (TV)
79. Airplane 80. Prom Night 80. The Creature
Wasn't Nice 81. Creepshow 82. Wrong Is Right 82.
Soul Man 86. The Patriot 86. Home Is Where the
Heart Is 87. Nightstick 87. Nuts 87. *The Naked Gun:
From the Files of Police Squad* 88. Repossessed 90.
The Naked Gun 2½: The Smell of Fear 91. All I
Want for Christmas 91. Surf Ninjas 93. Digger 93.
Naked Gun 33⅓: The Final Insult 94, etc.
TV series: The New Breed 61–62. Channing 63–
64. Peyton Place 65. The Protectors 69–70.
Bracken's World 70. The Explorers 72–73. Police
Squad 82. Shaping Up 84.

Niesen, Gertrude (1912–1975).
American singer-actress of Russian and Swedish
ancestry.
Start Cheering 40. Rookies on Parade 42. He's
My Guy 44. The Babe Ruth Story 48.

Nigh, Jane (1926–1993).
American leading lady of minor films in the 40s
and 50s.
Something for the Boys 44. State Fair 45.
Dragonwyck 46. Give My Regards to Broadway 48.
Red Hot and Blue 49. Fighting Man of the Plains
49. County Fair 50. Blue Blood 51. Fort Osage
53. Hold That Hypnotist 57, etc.
TV series: Big Town 51.

Nigh, William (1881–1955).
American director.
Marriage Morals 23. Mr Wu 27. The Single Sin
31. Crash Donovan 35. The Ape 40. Corregidor
42. The Right to Live 45. Divorce 45, etc.

Nightingale, Florence (1820–1910).
English nurse who organized hospitals at the front
during the Crimean War, with little official help and
under appalling conditions. There have been two
biopics of her: *The White Angel* (US) 35, with Kay
Francis, and *The Lady with a Lamp* (GB) 51, with
Anna Neagle. In *Sixty Glorious Years* she was briefly
played by Joyce Bland.

Nilsson, Anna Q. (1889–1974).
Swedish-born actress, long in America and
popular in silent films from 1919.
The Love Burglar 19. Kingdom of Dreams 20.
Soldiers of Fortune 20. Hollywood 22. The Isle of
Lost Ships 23. Inez of Hollywood 24. The Masked
Woman 25. The Greater Glory 26. Sorrell and Son
27. The World Changes 34. Prison Farm 38. Girls'
Town 42. The Farmer's Daughter 47. Sunset
Boulevard 50, etc.

Nilsson, Leopold Torre:
see *Torre-Nilsson, Leopold*.

Nimmo, Derek (1931–).
British character comedian who gets laughs from
toe-twiddling and funny voices (especially of the
comedy curate kind).
The Millionaires 61. The Amorous Prawn 62.
The Bargee 64. Joey Boy 65. The Liquidator 65.
Casino Royale 66. Mister Ten Per Cent 66. A Talent

for Loving 69. One of Our Dinosaurs is Missing 75,
etc.
TV series: All Gas and Gaiters 67. The World of
Wooster 68. Oh Brother 70. Oh Father 73. Hell's
Bells 85.

Nimoy, Leonard (1931–).
Lean-faced American character actor, best known
as the Vulcan Mr Spock in the TV series *Star Trek*
66–69. He turned to directing in the 80s.
Queen for a Day 51. Rhubarb 51. The Balcony
63. Catlow 72. The Alpha Caper (TV) 73. Invasion
of the Body Snatchers 78. Star Trek: The Motion
Picture 79. Star Trek: The Wrath of Khan 82. A
Woman Called Golda (TV) 82. Star Trek III: The
Search for Spock (& d) 84. Star Trek IV: The Voyage
Home (& d) 86. Transformers: The Movie 86.
Three Men and a Baby (d) 87. The Good Mother
(d) 88. Star Trek V: The Final Frontier 89. Funny
about Love (d) 90. Star Trek VI: The Undiscovered
Country 91. Holy Matrimony (d) 94. The
Pagemaster (voice) 94, etc.
TV series: *Star Trek* (as Mr Spock) 66–68.
Mission Impossible 70–72.

Nissen, Greta (1906–1988) (Grethe Rutz-Nissen).
Norwegian leading lady in American films. She
retired in 1937.
The Wanderer 25. The Popular Sin 26. Women
of All Nations 31. Rackety Rax 32. Melody Cruise
33. Red Wagon 36, etc.

nitrate.
Until 1950 film stock had a nitrate base, which
helped give a splendid sheen, but was very
inflammable. The change was made to safety stock,
which burns much more slowly, but black-and-
white films at least never looked so good again.

Nitzsche, Jack (1937–).
American composer.
The Exorcist 73. One Flew over the Cuckoo's
Nest 76. Cruising 81. Personal Best 82. Cannery
Row 82. Without a Trace 83. The Razor's Edge 84.
Starman 84. Windy City 84. Jewel of the Nile 85.
8½ Weeks 86. Stand by Me 86. The Whoopee Boys
86. Streets of Gold 86. The Seventh Sign 88.
Revenge 89. Next of Kin 89. The Last of the Finest
90. Mermaids 90. The Indian Runner 91. Blue Sky
(made 91) 94, etc.

Niven, David (1909–1983).
Debonair British leading man whose natural
enthusiasm found several outlets before he
accidentally arrived in Hollywood and was signed
up as an extra.
His light-hearted approach to life is reflected in
his 1972 autobiography *The Moon's a Balloon* and its
1975 sequel *Bring on the Empty Horses*.
Biography: 1985, *The Other Side of the Moon* by
Sheridan Morley.
■ Barbary Coast 35. Without Regret 35. A Feather
in Her Hat 35. Splendor 35. Rose Marie 36. *Thank
You Jeeves* 36. Palm Springs 36. The Charge of the
Light Brigade 36. *Dodsworth* 36. Beloved Enemy 36.
We Have Our Moments 37. Dinner at the Ritz 37.
The Prisoner of Zenda (as Fritz von Tarlenheim) 37.
Four Men and a Prayer 38. Bluebeard's Eighth
Wife 38. Three Blind Mice 38. The Dawn Patrol 38.
Wuthering Heights 39. *Bachelor Mother* 39. The
Real Glory 39. Eternally Yours 39. *Raffles* 40. The
First of the Few 41. *The Way Ahead* 44. *A Matter of
Life and Death* 46. The Perfect Marriage 46.
Magnificent Doll 46. The Other Love 47. The
Bishop's Wife 47. Bonnie Prince Charlie 47.
Enchantment 48. A Kiss in the Dark 49. A Kiss for
Corliss 49. The Elusive Pimpernel 50. The Toast
of New Orleans 50. Soldiers Three 51. Happy Go

Lovely 51. The Lady Says No 52. Appointment with
Venus 52. The Moon is Blue 53. The Love Lottery
54. Happy Ever After 54. The King's Thief 55.
Carrington VC 55. The Birds and the Bees 56.
Around The World in Eighty Days (as Phineas Fogg)
56. Oh Men Oh Women 57. The Little Hut 57. My
Man Godfrey 57. The Silken Affair 57. Bonjour
Tristesse 58. *Separate Tables* (AA) 58. Ask Any Girl
59. Happy Anniversary 59. Please Don't Eat the
Daisies 60. The Guns of Navarone 61. The Captive
City 62. Guns of Darkness 62. The Best of Enemies
62. Road to Hong Kong (gag appearance) 63. 55
Days at Peking 63. The Pink Panther 64. Bedtime
Story 64. Where the Spies Are 65. Lady L 66.
Casino Royale 67. Eye of the Devil 67. The
Extraordinary Seaman 68. Prudence and the Pill
68. The Impossible Years 68. Before Winter Comes
68. The Brain 69. The Statue 70. King Queen
Knave 72. Vampira 74. Paper Tiger 75. Murder
by Death 76. No Deposit No Return 76. Candleshoe
77. Death on the Nile 78. A Man Called Intrepid
(TV) 79. Escape to Athena 79. A Nightingale Sang
in Berkeley Square 80. Rough Cut 80. The Sea
Wolves 80. Better Late Than Never 82. Trail of the
Pink Panther 82. Curse of the Pink Panther 83.
TV series: Four Star Playhouse 56. *The David
Niven Show* 59. *The Rogues* 64.
✪ For forty years as a debonair international star.
Around the World in Eighty Days.

¶ Can you imagine being wonderfully overpaid
for dressing up and playing games? – *D.N.*
He's a very, very bad actor, but he absolutely
loves doing it. – *D.N. on himself*
Actors don't retire, they just get offered fewer
roles. – *D.N.*
I suppose everybody becomes an actor because
they want to be liked. I do enjoy being liked, but
I don't work hard at it. I try to do the best I can
for my age. – *D.N.*
I have a face that's a cross between two pounds
of halibut and an explosion in an old-clothes closet.
If it isn't mobile, it's dead. – *D.N.*

Nixon, Marian (1904–1983).
American leading lady.
What Happened to Jones? 26. Rosita 27. General
Crack 29. Adios 30. After Tomorrow 32. Rebecca
of Sunnybrook Farm 32. Walking Down Broadway
32.

Nixon, Marni (1931–).
American singer, former MGM messenger, who
has dubbed in high notes for many stars including
Margaret O'Brien in *Big City*, Deborah Kerr in *The
King and I*, Natalie Wood in *West Side Story* and
Audrey Hepburn in *My Fair Lady*. Has made only
one film appearance, as a nun in *The Sound of Music*
65.

Nixon, Richard Milhous (1913–1994).
The American politician and president, forced to
resign office over the Watergate affair, was
lampooned in Emile de Antonio's documentary
Millhouse: A White Comedy 71, and was played by
Philip Baker Hall in a one-man show, *Secret Honor*
84, filmed by Robert Altman, and by Harry
Spillman in *Born Again* 78, about Nixon's Special
Counsel Charles Colsen's religious conversion. In
two films, *Serpico* 73 and *Point Break* 91, bank
robbers have been shown wearing rubber Nixon
masks.

Noble, Thom.
American editor.
Fahrenheit 451 67. Joseph Andrews 77. Tattoo
81. Witness (AA) 85. The Mosquito Coast 86.
Mountains of the Moon 90. Thelma and Louise

(AA) 91. Final Analysis 92. Body of Evidence 93. The Hudsucker Proxy 94, etc.

Noel, Magali (1932–) (M. Guiffrais). French leading lady.

Seul dans Paris 51. Razzia sur la Chnouf 55. Rififi 55. Elena et les Hommes 56. Desire Takes the Men 58. La Dolce Vita 59. The Man Who Understood Women 70. Amarcord 74, etc.

Noel-Noel (1897–1989) (Lucien Noel). Dapper French character comedian.

Octave 32. A Cage of Nightingales 43. Le Père Tranquile 46. The Seven Deadly Sins 51. The Diary of Major Thompson 56. Jessica 62, etc.

Noiret, Philippe (1931–). French leading actor in international films, from the stage.

Zazie dans le Métro 60. Les Copains 62. Cyrano and d'Artagnan 63. Lady L 65. The Night of the Generals 66. Cleramberard 69. *Topaz* 69. Justine 69. Murphy's War 70. A Time for Loving 71. The Serpent 72. La Grande Bouffe 73. The Clockmaker 76. The Old Gun 76. Who Is Killing the Great Chefs of Europe? 78. Dear Detective 78. Le Grand Carnaval 83. Fort Saganne 84. Round Midnight 84. The Secret Wife 86. La Famiglia 87. *Cinema Paradiso* (Nuovo Cinema Paradiso) 88. Le Cop 2 (Ripoux contre Ripoux) 89. To Forget Palermo (Dimenticare Palermo) 89. Faux et Usage de Faux 90. Uranus 90. I Don't Kiss (J'Embrasse Pas) 91. Fish Soup (Zuppa di Pesce) 91. The Two of Us (Nous Deux) 92. Viva i Bambini 92. Tango 93. Gross Fatigue 94. Le Roi de Paris 94. The Postman (It.) 94. La Fille de D'Artagnan 94, etc.

Nolan, Doris (1916–). American leading lady who married Alexander Knox.

The Man I Married 37. Holiday 38. Irene 40. Moon over Burma 40. Follies Girl 45. Bindle 66. The Romantic Englishwoman 75, etc.

Nolan, Jeanette (1911–). American character actress, much on TV. Married to John McIntire.

Macbeth (as Lady Macbeth) 48. The Secret of Convict Lake 51. The Happy Time 52. The Big Heat 53. The Guns of Fort Petticoat 57. The Rabbit Trap 58. The Winds of Autumn 76. Lassie: The New Beginning (TV) 78. Cloak and Dagger 84. Street Justice 89, etc.

TV series: Hotel de Paree 59. The Richard Boone Show 63. The Virginian 67. Dirty Sally 73.

Nolan, Lloyd (1902–1985). Dependable American character actor, with stage experience from 1927.

Stolen Harmony (film debut) 34. G Men 35. Ebb Tide 37. Gangs of Chicago 40. Michael Shayne, Private Detective 40. Blues in the Night 41. Buy Me That Town 41. Bataan 43. *A Tree Grows in Brooklyn* 44. *The House on 92nd Street* 45. The Lady in the Lake 46. The Street with No Name 48. The Last Hunt 56. Peyton Place 58. Circus World 64. Never Too Late 65. An American Dream 66. The Double Man (GB) 67. Ice Station Zebra 68. Airport 69. Isn't It Shocking? (TV) 73. Earthquake 74. The Private Files of J. Edgar Hoover 78. Hannah and Her Sisters 85, many others.

TV series: Julia 68–70.

Nolan, Mary (1905–1948) (Mary Imogene Robertson). American leading lady, an ex-Ziegfeld girl who made a few films in Germany and Hollywood, then came to grief through drugs.

Sister Veronika 26. Sorrell and Son 27. West of Zanzibar 28. Shanghai Lady 29. Outside the Law 30. X Marks the Spot 31. Midnight Patrol 32, etc.

Nolbandov, Sergei (1895–1971). Russian-born writer-producer, in Britain from 1926.

City of Song (w) 30. Fire over England (w) 36. Ships with Wings (wd) 42. This Modern Age (series) (p) from 1946. The Kidnappers (p) 53. Mix Me a Person (p) 62, many others.

Nolte, Nick (1940–). Virile American leading man.

Return to Macon County 75. Death Sentence (TV) 76. The Runaway Barge (TV) 76. *Rich Man Poor Man* (TV) 76. The Deep 77. Who'll Stop the Rain? 78. North Dallas Forty 79. Heart Beat 79. Cannery Row 82. 48 Hours 82. The Ultimate Solution of Grace Quigley 84. Teachers 84. Down and Out in Beverly Hills 85. Extreme Prejudice 87. Weeds 87. Farewell to the King 89. New York Stories 89. Three Fugitives 89. Another 48 Hrs 90. Everybody Wins 90. Q & A 90. Cape Fear 91. The Prince of Tides (AAN) 91. Lorenzo's Oil 92. I'll Do Anything 94. Blue Chips 94. I Love Trouble 94. Jefferson in Paris 95, etc.

¶ If you feel you have a film that's valid, you stick your ass on the line. – *N.N.*

non-theatrical. A descriptive adjective usually applied to film showings at which there is no paid admission on entrance, e.g. schools, clubs, etc. Some distributors apply the term to all 16mm showings.

Noonan, Tommy (1921–1968) (Thomas Noon). Ebullient American comedian.

Starlift 51. Gentlemen Prefer Blondes 53. A Star is Born 54. How to Be Very Very Popular 55. Bundle of Joy 56. *The Ambassador's Daughter* 56. The Rookie (& p) 60, etc.

Norden, Christine (1924–1988) (Mary Lydia Thornton). British leading lady, a sex symbol of the late 40s.
■ Night Beat 47. *Mine Own Executioner* 47. Idol of Paris 48. A Yank Comes Back 48. An Ideal Husband 48. Saints and Sinners 49. The Interrupted Journey 49. The Black Widow 50. A Case for PC 49 51. Reluctant Heroes 52. Little Shop of Horrors 87. The Wolvercote Tongue (TV) 88.

TV series: Chance in a Million 87.

Nordgren, Eric (1913–). Swedish composer, associated with the early films of Ingmar Bergman.

Kvinna Utan Ansikte 47. Eva 48. Törst (Three Strange Loves) 49. Sommarlek (Summer Interlude) 51. Kvinnors Väntan (Secrets of Women) 52. Monika 52. Sommarnattens Leende (Smiles of a Summer Night) 55. The Seventh Seal 57. Wild Strawberries 57. The Magician 58. The Virgin Spring 60. Pleasure Garden 61. All These Women 64, etc.

Norman Bates. The mother-dominated psychopathic killer who provided Anthony Perkins with what is his most memorable role, in Alfred Hitchcock's *Psycho* 60, from a script by Joseph Stefano, based on Robert Bloch's novel. Events in Bates's earlier and later life have provided material for three sequels: 1982 (d Richard Franklin), 1983 (d Anthony Perkins), and 1990 (d Mick Garris as a TV movie).

Norman, Leslie (1911–1993). British producer-director, former editor, in films from late 20s.

Where No Vultures Fly (p) 51. The Cruel Sea (p) 54. The Night My Number Came Up (d) 56. X the Unknown (d) 57. The Shiralee (d) 58. Dunkirk (d) 58. The Long, the Short and the Tall (d) 60. Mix Me a Person (d) 61. Summer of the 17th Doll (d) 61, etc.

Normand, Mabel (1894–1930) (Mabel Fortescue). American comedienne, a leading player of Vitagraph and Keystone comedies from 1911, and a Chaplin co-star.

Barney Oldfield's Race for Life 12. Fatty and Mabel Adrift 15. Mickey 17. Sis Hopkins 18. Molly O 21. Suzanna 22. The Extra Girl 24, many others.

Norris, Chuck (1940–) (Carlos Ray Norris). American tough-guy hero, former karate champion.

Autobiography: 1988, *The Secret of Inner Strength*, with Joe Hyams.

Good Guys Wear Black 79. An Eye for an Eye 81. Forced Vengeance 82. Silent Rage 82. *Missing in Action* 83. Lone Wolf McQuade 83. Missing in Action II 83. Code of Silence 84. Invasion USA 85. Delta Force 85. Firewalker 86. Braddock: Missing in Action III (& w) 88. Hero and the Terror 88. Delta Force 2: Operation Stranglehold 90. The Hitman 91. Sidekicks 93, etc.

TV series: Walker, Texas Ranger 93.

¶ Whatever luck I had, I made. I was never a natural athlete, but I paid my dues in sweat and concentration and took the time necessary to learn karate and become world champion. – *C.N.*

Norris, Edward (1910–). American leading man of second features; former reporter. He retired from acting in the mid-50s to pursue business interests. Among his five wives were actresses Ann Sheridan and Sheila Ryan.

Queen Christina 33. Boys' Town 38. The Man with Two Lives 41. End of the Road 44. Decoy 47. Forbidden Women 49. Inside the Walls of Folsom Prison 51. The Man from the Alamo 53. The Kentuckian 55, many others.

Norris, Frank (1870–1902). American novelist, whose *McTeague* was the basis for Von Stroheim's *Greed*.

North, Alex (1910–1991). American composer. He was awarded an honorary Oscar in 1986.
■ *A Streetcar Named Desire* (AAN) 51. The Thirteenth Letter 51. Death of a Salesman (AAN) 51. Viva Zapata (AAN) 52. Les Misérables 52. Pony Soldier 52. The Member of the Wedding 53. Désirée 54. Go Man Go 54. The Racers 55. Unchained 55. The Man with the Gun 55. The Rose Tattoo (AAN) 55. I'll Cry Tomorrow 56. The Bad Seed 56. The Rainmaker (AAN) 56. Four Girls in Town 56. The King and Four Queens 56. The Bachelor Party 57. The Long Hot Summer 58. Stage Struck 58. Hot Spell 58. South Seas Adventure 58. The Sound and the Fury 59. The Wonderful Country 59. *Spartacus* (AAN) 60. The Children's Hour 61. Sanctuary 61. The Misfits 61. All Fall Down 62. Cleopatra (AAN) 63. The Outrage 64. Cheyenne Autumn 64. The Agony and the Ecstasy (AAN) 65. Who's Afraid of Virginia Woolf? (AAN) 66. The Devil's Brigade 68. The Shoes of the Fisherman (AAN) 68. A Dream of Kings 69. Hard Contract 69. Willard 71. Pocket Money 72. Shanks (AAN) 74. Bite the Bullet (AAN) 75. Rich Man Poor Man (TV) 76. Somebody Killed Her Husband (TV) 78. Wise Blood 79.

Carny 80. Dragonslayer (AAN) 81. Under the Volcano (AAN) 84.

North, Edmund H. (1911–1990).
American screenwriter.
One Night of Love 34. I Dream Too Much 35. All the King's Horses 35. Bunker Bean 36. I'm Still Alive 40. Dishonored Lady 47. Young Man with a Horn 50. In a Lonely Place 50. Only the Valiant 51. The Day the Earth Stood Still 51. The Outcasts of Poker Flat 53. The Far Horizons 55. The Proud Ones 56. Cowboy 58. Sink the Bismarck 60. HMS Defiant 62. Patton (co-w) (AA) 70. Meteor 79, etc.

North, Jay (1952–).
American juvenile actor, popular as a child on TV in *Dennis the Menace* 59–63 and later *Maya* 67.
Pepe 60. Zebra in the Kitchen 65. The Teacher 74. Scout's Honor 80, etc.

North, Michael (1916–).
American leading man of the 40s. He gave up acting in the 50s to become an agent. Formerly known as Ted North; changed and was reintroduced for *The Unsuspected* 48.
Chad Hanna 40. Charlie Chan in Rio 41. The Oxbow Incident 43. The Devil Thumbs a Ride 47, etc.

North, Sheree (1933–) (Dawn Bethel).
Blonde American leading lady, former dancer.
Excuse My Dust 51. How to Be Very Very Popular 55. The Best Things in Life are Free 56. The Way to the Gold 57. No Down Payment 57. Mardi Gras 58. Destination Inner Space 66. Madigan 68. The Gypsy Moths 69. Lawman 71. Charley Varrick 73. Breakout 75. The Shootist 76. Telefon 77. *The Night They Took Miss Beautiful* (TV) 78. Maniac Cop 88. Defenceless 91, etc.
TV series: Big Eddie 75. But I'm a Big Girl Now 80–81. The Bay City Blues 83.

Norton, Jack (1889–1958) (Mortimer J. Naughton).
American character actor, invariably seen as an amiable well-dressed drunk with a sour expression; he rarely had a coherent speaking part.
Cockeyed Cavaliers 34. Thanks for the Memory 38. The Ghost Breakers 40. The Bank Dick 40. The Fleet's In 41. The Palm Beach Story 42. Hail the Conquering Hero 44. Hold that Blonde 45. Bringing Up Father 46, many others.

Norwood, Eille (1861–1948) (Anthony Brett).
British stage actor who played Sherlock Holmes in a score of 20s two-reelers and a few features.

Nosseck, Max (1902–1972) (Alexander Norris).
Polish director in Hollywood from 1939; former stage and film actor/director in Europe.
■ AMERICAN FILMS: Girls Under Twenty-One 40. Gambling Daughters 41. *Dillinger* 45. The Brighton Strangler 45. Black Beauty 46. The Return of Rin Tin Tin 47. Kill or Be Killed 50. Korea Patrol 51. The Hoodlum 51. The Body Beautiful 53. Garden of Eden 57.

Nothing but the Truth.
James Montgomery's Broadway comedy about a man who takes a bet that he can tell the absolute truth for 24 hours was filmed in 1920, with Taylor Holmes; in 1929, with Richard Dix; and in 1941, with Bob Hope.

Nouri, Michael (1945–).
American leading actor.
The Last Convertible (TV) 79. Flashdance 83. Between Two Women 86. Imagemaker 86. The

Hidden 87. Project: Alien 89. Thieves of Fortune 89. Total Exposure 91. Psychic 91. American Yazuka 93, etc.
TV series: Beacon Hill 75. The Curse of Dracula 79. The Gangster Chronicles 81. The Bay City Blues 83. Downtown 86–87.

Novak, Eva (1898–1988).
American silent-screen leading lady, sister of Jane. She co-starred with Tom Mix in ten films, after beginning as one of Max Sennett's Bathing Beauties.
The Lost Trail 21. Society Secrets 21. The Man From Hells River 22. Boston Blackie 23. A Fight for Honor 24. The Forlorn Lover 25. Irene 26. Red Signals 27. Phantom of the Desert 30, etc.

Novak, Jane (1896–1990).
American silent-screen leading lady, sister of Eva.
The Barbarian 21. Colleen of the Pines 22. Jealous Husbands 23. The Lullaby 24. Lure of the Wilds 25. Whispering Canyon 26. What Price Love? 27. Free Lips 28. Redskin 29. The Boss 57, etc.

Novak, Kim (1933–) (Marilyn Novak).
Artificially-groomed American blonde star who never managed to give a natural performance, though she did try.
■ The French Line 53. *Pushover* 54. Phffft 54. Five against the House 55. Son of Sinbad 55. *Picnic* 55. The Man with the Golden Arm 56. The Eddy Duchin Story 56. *Jeanne Eagels* 58. Pal Joey 58. Vertigo 58. Bell, Book and Candle 58. Middle of the Night 59. Strangers When We Meet 60. Pépé 60. Boys' Night Out 62. The Notorious Landlady 62. Of Human Bondage 64. Kiss Me Stupid 64. The Amorous Adventures of Moll Flanders 65. The Legend of Lylah Clare 68. The Great Bank Robbery 69. Tales That Witness Madness 73. Third Girl from the Left (TV) 74. Satan's Triangle (TV) 75. The White Buffalo 77. Just a Gigolo 79. The Mirror Crack'd 80. Malibu (TV) 83. Es Hat Mich Sehr Gefreut 87. The Children 90. Liebestraum 91.

¶ When I was doing *Vertigo*, poor Kim Novak bless her heart, said, 'Mr Hitchcock, what is my character feeling in relation to her surroundings?' There was silence on the set and Hitch said, 'It's only a movie, for God's sakes.' She never asked another question. – *James Stewart*

Novarro, Ramon (1899–1968) (Ramon Samaniegos).
Romantic Mexican leading man of the 20s in Hollywood; later came back as character actor. He was murdered in his home by two teenagers.
The Prisoner of Zenda (as Rupert) 22. Where the Pavement Ends 23. *Scaramouche* 23. The Arab 24. The Midshipman 25. *Ben Hur* 25. The Student Prince 27. Across to Singapore 28. Forbidden Hours 28. The Pagan 29. Call of the Flesh 30. Son of India 31. Mata Hari 31. The Son-Daughter 32. The Barbarian 33. The Cat and the Fiddle 34. The Night is Young 35. The Sheik Steps Out 37. We Were Strangers 48. The Big Steal 49. Crisis 50. Heller in Pink Tights 60, etc.

Novello, Ivor (1893–1951) (Ivor Davies).
Welsh matinée idol with an incredibly successful career in stage musical comedy; also prolific playwright and composer.
Biographies: 1951, Ivor by MacQueen Pope. 1951, Ivor Novello by Peter Noble. 1974, *Perchance to Dream* by Richard Rose. 1975, *Ivor* by Sandy Wilson.
Carnival 22. The Bohemian Girl 22. The White Rose 23. *The Man without Desire* 23. *The Rat* 25.

The Lodger 26. The Triumph of the Rat 27. The Constant Nymph 27. Downhill 27. The Vortex 28. Once a Lady 31. The Lodger (remake) 32. Sleeping Car 33. I Lived with You 34. Autumn Crocus 34, etc.

¶ Novello looks a little like Conway Tearle, a little like Ramon Novarro and a little like Richard Barthelmess . . . a couple of years under good direction should see him the great idol of the movie fans. – *Paul Gallico, 1923*

Novello, Jay (1905–1982).
Wiry little American actor, familiar in films from Tenth Avenue Kid 38 to Atlantis the Lost Continent 61, usually as scruffy little crook.
TV series: McHale's Navy 65.

Noyce, Phillip (1950–).
Australian director, now working in America.
Backroads (& w, p) 77. Newsfront (wd) 78. Heatwave 82. The Dismissal (co-d) 83. The Cowra Breakout (TV) 85. Shadows of the Peacock 86. Echoes of Paradise 88. Dead Calm 89. Blind Fury 89. Patriot Games 92. Sliver 93. Clear and Present Danger 94, etc.

Nugent, Elliott (1899–1980).
American stage actor, producer and playwright who only dabbled in films but proved a good director of comedies.
Autobiography: 1965, *Events Leading up to the Comedy*.
AS ACTOR: So This Is College 29. The Unholy Three 30. Romance 30. The Last Flight 31, etc.
AS DIRECTOR: The Mouthpiece 32. Whistling in the Dark 33. *Three Cornered Moon* 33. She Loves Me Not 34. Love in Bloom 35. And So They Were Married 36. Professor Beware 38. *The Cat and the Canary* 39. Nothing but the Truth 40. The Male Animal (& oa) 42. The Crystal Ball 43. Up in Arms 44. My Favorite Brunette 47. *My Girl Tisa* 48. *The Great Gatsby* 49. My Outlaw Brother 51. Just for You 52, etc.

Nugent, Frank (1908–1966).
American screenwriter, former reporter and critic.
Fort Apache 48. *She Wore a Yellow Ribbon* 49. The Quiet Man (AAN) 52. Trouble in the Glen 53. *The Searchers* 56. The Last Hurrah 58. Donovan's Reef 63, etc.

numbered sequels.
This rather offhand practice probably began in 1956 with *Quatermass II*, but did not really become fashionable until the 70s. Among the successes to label their sequels so casually are *The French Connection, Jaws, The Sting, Mad Max, Walking Tall, Superman, Halloween, Death Wish, Grease, That's Entertainment, Piranha, Friday the 13th, La Cage aux Folles, The Amityville Horror, Porky's, Rocky, Airplane, The Howling, Die Hard, The Terminator, Predator* and *The Naked Gun*, which spoofed the process, going to 2½ and 3⅓.

Nunez, Victor.
American independent director, screenwriter and editor, a former university lecturer in film-making.
Gal Young 'Un 79. A Flash of Green 85. Ruby in Paradise 93.

nuns
have been popular figures on the screen, though only in *The Nun's Story* and the Polish *The Devil and the Nun* has any real sense of dedication been achieved; the French *Dialogue des Carmélites* tried hard but failed. Sentimentalized nuns were seen in *The Cradle Song, Bonaventure, The White Sister,*

Conspiracy of Hearts, The Bells of St Mary's, Come to the Stable, Portrait of Jennie, Heaven Knows Mr Allison, Black Narcissus, Lilies of the Field, The Miracle, The Song of Bernadette and *The Sound of Music;* while nuns who combined modern sophistication with sweetness and light afflicted us in *The Singing Nun* and *The Trouble with Angels,* and in *Two Mules for Sister Sara* Shirley Maclaine played a prostitute disguised as a nun. A nun was raped in *Five Gates to Hell.* The most sinister nun was perhaps Catherine Lacey, with her high heels, in *The Lady Vanishes,* but the nuns in *The Trygon Factor* also count. The most agonized nuns were in *The Devils, La Religieuse,* and *The Awful Story of the Nun of Monza.* The weirdest was TV's *The Flying Nun.* More recently, they have been a source of amusement: *Dark Habits (Entre Tinieblas), Nuns on the Run* and *Sister Act.*

Nureyev, Rudolf (1938–1993).
Russian ballet dancer who ventured into straight acting.
Don Quixote 73. Valentino 77. Exposed 83.

¶ I love dancing. From the age of six I have not thought of anything else. – R.N.

nurses
have inspired biopics (*Sister Kenny, The White Angel, The Lady with a Lamp, Nurse Edith Cavell*); sentimental low-key studies of the profession (*The Lamp Still Burns, The Feminine Touch, Vigil in the Night, No Time for Tears, White Corridors, Prison Nurse, Private Nurse, Night Nurse*); even comedies (*Carry On Nurse, Twice Round the Daffodils, Nurse on Wheels*). *Green for Danger* is probably still the only thriller in which both victim and murderer were nurses. The best satire has been *The National Health* (or *Nurse Norton's Affair*). There was a popular TV series called *Janet Dean Registered Nurse* 53, and later *The Nurses* 62–64. See also *hospitals; doctors.*

Nutley, Colin (1947–).
British director active in Sweden. He worked in British television before moving to Sweden in the 80s. His films use improvised dialogue.

The Ninth Battalion 88. Black Jack 90. *House of Angels* 92. The Last Dance (Sista Dansen) 93. Just You and Me 94, etc.

Nuyen, France (1939–).
Franco-Chinese leading lady, former model, who made some Hollywood films.
In Love and War 57. *South Pacific* 58. Satan Never Sleeps 61. The Last Time I Saw Archie 62. A Girl Named Tamiko 63. Diamond Head 62. The Man in the Middle 64. Dimension Five 66. One More Train to Rob 71. The Horror at 37,000 Feet (TV) 73. China Cry 90. The Joy Luck Club 93, etc.
TV series: Knots Landing 90.

Nuytten, Bruno (1945–).
French cinematographer and director who also works in international films. He has a son by actress Isabelle Adjani.
Going Places (Les Valseuses) 74. India Song 75. Barocco 76. Le Camion 77. French Postcards 79. The Brontë Sisters 79. The Best Way 80. Brubaker 80. Under Suspicion (Garde à Vue) 82. Life Is a Bed of Roses (La Vie Est un Roman) 83. Tchao Pantin 83. Jean de Florette 86. Manon des Sources 86. Camille Claudel (wd) 88, etc.

Nyby, Christian (1919–1993).
American director, a former editor who began working at MGM as a carpenter. He was also a television director.
■ To Have and Have Not (ed) 45. The Big Sleep (ed) 46. Red River (ed) (AAN) 48. *The Thing* 52. Hell on Devil's Island 57. Six-Gun Law 62. Young Fury 64. Operation CIA 65. First to Fight 66. Emergency! (TV) 71.

Nye, Carrie (1937–).
American actress.
Divorce His, Divorce Hers (TV) 73. The Users (TV) 78. The Seduction of Joe Tynan 79. Creepshow 82. Too Scared to Scream 85. Hello Again 87, etc.

Nykvist, Sven (1922–).
Distinguished Swedish cinematographer.
Sawdust and Tinsel 53. Karin Mansdotter 53. The

Virgin Spring 60. Winter Light 62. *The Silence* 64. Loving Couples 65. Persona 66. Hour of the Wolf 67. The Shame 69. The Touch 71. The Last Run 71. One Day in the Life of Ivan Denisovitch 71. Cries and Whispers (AA) 73. Scenes from a Marriage 74. Face to Face 76. King of the Gypsies 78. Pretty Baby 78. The Hurricane 79. Starting Over 79. Willie and Phil 80. The Postman Always Rings Twice 81. Cannery Row 82. Fanny and Alexander (AA) 82. Star 80 83. After the Rehearsal 84. Swann in Love (Un Amour de Swann) 84. Agnes of God 85. Dream Lover 86. Another Woman 88. The Unbearable Lightness of Being (AAN) 89. New York Stories 89. Buster's Bedroom 91. The Ox (Oxen) (wd) (AAN) 91. Chaplin 92. Sleepless in Seattle 93. What's Eating Gilbert Grape 93. With Honors 94. Only You 94, etc.

Nyman, Michael (1944–).
British composer, closely associated with the work of director Peter Greenaway.
The Draughtsman's Contract 82. Nelly's Version 83. A Zed and Two Noughts 85. Drowning by Numbers 88. The Cook, the Thief, His Wife and Her Lover 89. Prospero's Books 91. Mesmer 94, etc.

nymphomaniacs
are still fairly rare in normal commercial movies. The fullest studies have been by Suzanne Pleshette in *A Rage to Live,* Françoise Arnoul in *La Rage au Corps,* Claire Bloom in *The Chapman Report,* Merle Oberon in *Of Love and Desire,* Sue Lyon in *Night of the Iguana,* Lee Remick in *The Detective,* Melina Mercouri in *Topkapi,* Maureen Stapleton in *Lonelyhearts,* Jean Seberg in *Road to Corinth,* Elizabeth Taylor in *Butterfield 8,* and Sandra Jullien in *I Am a Nymphomaniac;* but one should not forget Myrna Loy's comic nympho in *Love Me Tonight.*

Nyswaner, Ron.
American screenwriter and director, from the theatre.
Smithereens (co-w) 82. Swing Shift (co-w) 83. Purple Hearts (w) 84. Mrs Soffel (w) 84. The Prince of Pennsylvania (wd) 88. Gross Anatomy (co-w) 89. Philadelphia (AANw) 93, etc.

Oakie, Jack (1903–1978) (Lewis D. Offield).
Cheerful American comic actor well known for a startled 'double take'; formerly in vaudeville.

Finders Keepers (debut) 27. Paramount on Parade 30. Million Dollar Legs 32. College Humor 33. If I Had a Million 33. Call of the Wild 35. The Texas Rangers 36. The Toast of New York 37. Rise and Shine 39. *The Great Dictator* (a caricature of Mussolini) (AAN) 40. Tin Pan Alley 40. Footlight Serenade 42. Song of the Islands 42. Something to Shout About 43. Hello Frisco Hello 43. *It Happened Tomorrow* 44. That's the Spirit 44. The Merry Monahans 44. On Stage Everybody 45. When My Baby Smiles at Me 48. Thieves' Highway 49. Last of the Buccaneers 50. The Battle of Powder River 52. Around the World in Eighty Days 56. The Wonderful Country 59. The Rat Race 60. Lover Come Back 62, many others.

Oakland, Simon (1922–1983).
American general-purpose actor with stage experience.

The Brothers Karamazov 58. I Want to Live 58. Psycho 60. West Side Story 61. Follow That Dream 62. Wall of Noise 63. The Satan Bug 65. The Plainsman 66. The Sand Pebbles 67. Tony Rome 67. Chubasco 68. On a Clear Day You Can See Forever 70. Chato's Land 72. Happy Mother's Day Love George 73. Emperor of the North Pole 73. Evening in Byzantium (TV) 78, etc.

TV series: Toma 73–74. Kolchak: The Night Stalker 74–75. Baa Baa Black Sheep 76–78. David Cassidy – Man Undercover 78.

Oakland, Vivian (1895–1958) (V. Anderson).
American child star and vaudeville artiste, who later became familiar as wife to the leading comic in many a two-reeler. In films from 1924.

Gold Dust Gertie 31. Only Yesterday 32. The Bride Walks Out 36. Way Out West 37. The Man in the Trunk 42. Bunco Squad 51, many others.

Oakley, Annie (1859–1926) (Phoebe Annie Oakley Mozee).
American sharpshooter who gained fame in her teens as star of Buffalo Bill's wild west show. A sharp shooter who could slice a playing card held up edgewise at thirty paces, she ended her career running a skeet range in North Carolina. Played on screen by Barbara Stanwyck in *Annie Oakley* 35, and by Betty Hutton in *Annie Get Your Gun* 50. A TV series in 1953–57 starred Gail Davis.

Oakman, Wheeler (1890–1949) (Vivian Eichelberger).
American silent star, later western supporting actor.

The God of Gold 12. The Spoilers 14. The Black Orchid 16. Mickey 18. The Virgin of Stamboul 20. Outside the Law 21. The Pace That Thrills 25. Lights of New York 28. Roaring Ranch 30. End of the Trail 33. G-Men 35. Mutiny in the Big House 39, etc.

Oates, Warren (1928–1982).
American supporting actor who has tended towards psychopathic heavies.

Yellowstone Kelly 59. Private Property 60. Hero's Island 61. Mail Order Bride 64. Major Dundee 65. Return of the Seven 67. In the Heat of the Night 67. The Split 68. Crooks and Coronets (GB) 69. The Wild Bunch 69. There Was a Crooked Man 70. Two Lane Blacktop 71. The Hired Hand 71. Tom Sawyer 73. Dillinger (title role) 73. The White Dawn 73. Badlands 73. 92 in the Shade 75. Race with the Devil 75. Drum 76. The Brinks Job 78. True Grit (TV) 78. My Old Man (TV) 79. Baby Comes Home (TV) 80. Stripes 81. Blue Thunder 83.

TV series: Stony Burke 62.

O'Bannon, Dan (1946–).
American science fiction and horror screenwriter and director.

Dark Star (co-w) 74. Alien (w) 79. Dead and Buried (co-w) 81. Blue Thunder (co-w) 83. Lifeforce (co-w) 85. The Return of the Living Dead (wd) 85. Invaders from Mars (co-w) 86. Total Recall (co-w) 90. Resurrected 92, etc.

Ober, Philip (1902–1982).
American general-purpose character actor.

The Secret Fury 50. From Here to Eternity 53. Tammy 56. North by Northwest 59. Let No Man Write My Epitaph 60. The Brass Bottle 64. The Ghost and Mr Chicken 66, etc.

Oberon, Merle (1911–1979) (Estelle O'Brien Merle Thompson).
British leading lady. Born in India; came to Britain 1928, worked as dance hostess until signed up by Korda. Mainly in Hollywood from 1936. The first of her four husbands was Alexander Korda (1939–45) and the second was cinematographer Lucien K. Ballard (1945–49).
■ A Warm Corner 30. Consolation Marriage 31. Flying High 31. Clara Deane 32. Strange Evidence 32. Service for Ladies 32. Ebb Tide 32. Wedding Rehearsal 32. Men of Tomorrow 32. The Private Life of Henry VIII 33. The Battle 34. The Broken Melody 34. The Private Life of Don Juan 34. *The Scarlet Pimpernel* 34. Folies Bergère 35. The Dark Angel (AAN) 35. These Three 36. Beloved Enemy 36. I Claudius (unfinished) 37. Over the Moon 37. *The Divorce of Lady X* 38. The Cowboy and the Lady 38. *Wuthering Heights* 39. The Lion Has Wings 39. 'Til We Meet Again 40. That Uncertain Feeling 41. Affectionately Yours 41. Lydia 41. Forever and a Day 43. Stage Door Canteen 43. First Comes Courage 43. The Lodger 44. Dark Waters 44. *A Song to Remember* 45. This Love of Ours 45. A Night in Paradise 46. Temptation 46. Night Song 47. Berlin Express 48. Pardon My French 51. 24 Hours of a Woman's Life 52. All is Possible in Granada 54. Désirée 54. Deep in My Heart 54. The Price of Fear 56. Of Love and Desire 63. The Oscar 66. Hotel 67. Interval 73.

TV series: Assignment Foreign Legion 56.

Oboler, Arch (1909–1987).
American writer-producer-director with a long career in radio. Made mainly gimmick films.
■ Bewitched 45. Strange Holiday 46. The Arnelo

Affair 47. Five 51. Bwana Devil 52. The Twonky 53. One Plus One 61. The Bubble 67.

O'Brian, Hugh (1925–) (Hugh Krampke).
Leathery American leading man, former athlete.

Never Fear 50. On the Loose 51. Red Ball Express 52. Seminole 54. There's No Business Like Show Business 54. White Feather 55. The Brass Legend 56. The Fiend Who Walked the West 58. Come Fly with Me 62. In Harm's Way 65. Love Has Many Faces 65. Ten Little Indians 65. Ambush Bay 66. Africa Texas Style 67. Probe (TV) 72. Killer Force 75. The Shootist 76. Murder at the World Series (TV) 77. Twins 88, etc.

TV series: Wyatt Earp 56–59. Search 72.

O'Brien, Dave (1912–1969) (David Barclay).
American light character actor, in Hollywood from the early 30s. Played supporting roles in innumerable films; most familiar as the hero/victim of the Pete Smith comedy shorts of the 40s.

Jennie Gerhardt 33. East Side Kids 39. Son of the Navy 40. 'Neath Brooklyn Bridge 43. Tahiti Nights 44. Phantom of 42nd Street 45. The Desperadoes are in Town 56, etc.

O'Brien, Edmond (1915–1985).
Anglo-Irish leading man of the 40s, latterly character actor; long in Hollywood.

The Hunchback of Notre Dame 39. Parachute Battalion 41. Powder Town 42, etc.; war service; *The Killers* 46. The Web 47. A Double Life 47. Another Part of the Forest 48. An Act of Murder 48. White Heat 49. *D.O.A.* 49. Between Midnight and Dawn 50. Two of a Kind 51. Denver and Rio Grande 52. Julius Caesar 53. The Hitch Hiker 53. Man in the Dark 53. The Bigamist 53. Cow Country 53. *The Barefoot Contessa* (AA) 54. Shield for Murder (& co-d) 54. 1984 (GB) 55. The Girl Can't Help It 57. *The Third Voice* 59. The Last Voyage 60. Mantrap (pd only) 61. The Great Imposter 61. The Man Who Shot Liberty Valance 62. Birdman of Alcatraz 62. *Seven Days in May* (AAN) 64. Sylvia 65. Fantastic Voyage 66. The Viscount (Fr.) 67. The Wild Bunch 69. The Love God 69. Jigsaw (TV) 72. 99 44/100 Dead 74, etc.

TV series: Johnny Midnight 60. Sam Benedict 62. The Long Hot Summer 65.

O'Brien, George (1900–1985).
American cowboy star who entered films as a stuntman.

The Iron Horse (first starring role) 24. *Sunrise* 27. Noah's Ark 28. Lone Star Ranger 30. Riders of the Purple Sage 31. The Last Trail 33. O'Malley of the Mounted 36. Daniel Boone 36. The Painted Desert 38. Stage to Chino 40. Legion of the Lawless 42. She Wore a Yellow Ribbon 49. Cheyenne Autumn 64, many others.

O'Brien, Margaret (1937–) (Angela Maxine O'Brien).
Stunningly talented American child actress of the 40s; won special Academy Award in 1944. Had no luck with adult comeback.
■ Babes on Broadway 41. *Journey for Margaret* 42. Dr Gillespie's Criminal Case 43. Thousands Cheer

43. *Lost Angel* 43. Madame Curie 43. Jane Eyre 43. The Canterville Ghost 44. *Meet Me in St Louis* 44. Music for Millions 45. *Our Vines Have Tender Grapes* 45. Bad Bascomb 46. Three Wise Fools 46. The Unfinished Dance 47. Tenth Avenue Angel 47. Big City 48. *Little Women* 49. The Secret Garden 49. Her First Romance 51. Glory 56. Heller in Pink Tights 60. Split Second to an Epitaph (TV) 68. Testimony of Two Men (TV) 77. Amy 81.
⊙ For being so talented up to the age of ten. *Lost Angel.*

¶ When I cry, do you want the tears to run all the way or shall I stop halfway down?
– *M.O'B., aged six*
If that child had been born in the middle ages, she'd have been burned as a witch. – *Lionel Barrymore, 1943*

O'Brien, Pat (1899–1983).
Easy-going, gentle but tough-looking Irish-American character actor, a popular star of the 30s.
Autobiography: 1964, *The Wind at My Back.*
The Front Page 31. Honour among Lovers 31. Final Edition 32. Hell's House 32. American Madness 32. Air Mail 32. Bureau of Missing Persons 33. Bombshell 33. Gambling Lady 34. Here Comes the Navy 34. I Sell Anything 34. Devil Dogs of the Air 35. Oil for the Lamps of China 35. Page Miss Glory 35. The Irish in Us 35. Ceiling Zero 35. Public Enemy's Wife 36. China Clipper 36. The Great O'Malley 37. Slim 37. San Quentin 37. *Boy Meets Girl* 38. Angels with Dirty Faces 38. Indianapolis Speedway 39. The Fighting 69th 40. Slightly Honorable 40. Castle on the Hudson 40. Torrid Zone 40. Submarine Zone 41. Broadway 42. The Navy Comes Through 42. Bombardier 43. The Iron Major 43. His Butler's Sister 43. Secret Command 44. Having Wonderful Crime 45. Man Alive 45. Perilous Holiday 46. Riffraff 47. Fighting Father Dunne 48. The Boy with Green Hair 48. A Dangerous Profession 49. Johnny One Eye 50. The People against O'Hara 51. Okinawa 52. Jubilee Trail 54. Inside Detroit 55. Kill Me Tomorrow (GB) 57. The Last Hurrah 58. Some Like It Hot 59. Town Tamer 65. The Phynx 69. The Over the Hill Gang (TV) 69. Welcome Home Johnny Bristol (TV) 72. The Adventures of Nick Carter (TV) 72. Joyride to Nowhere (TV) 73. Kiss Me Kill Me (TV) 76. The End 78. Ragtime 81. Scout's Honor (TV) 81, etc.
TV series: Harrigan and Son 60.

O'Brien, Richard (1942–).
Lanky British stage actor, musician, dramatist and screenwriter, the creator of the cult stage hit *The Rocky Horror Show*, which also became a cult film. Recently he has worked in TV as host of a game show, *The Crystal Maze* 91–94.
Carry On Cowboy 65. The Fighting Prince of Donegal 66. The Odd Job Man. The Rocky Horror Picture Show (a, co-w, m) 76. Flash Gordon 80. Shock Treatment (co-w) 81. Revolution 85, etc.

O'Brien, Virginia (1921–).
American comedienne, the 'dead pan' singer of the 40s.
Hullabaloo 40. *The Big Store* 41. Ship Ahoy 42. Thousands Cheer 43. Dubarry Was a Lady 44. The Harvey Girls 45. Till the Clouds Roll By 46. Merton of the Movies 47. Francis in the Navy 55. Gus 76, etc.

O'Brien, Willis (1886–1962).
American specialist in the creation of monster animals for use in stop-motion techniques.
The Ghost of Slumber Mountain 20. *The Lost World* 24. *King Kong* 33. Son of Kong 33. Mighty Joe Young 49. The Animal World 56. The Black Scorpion 58, etc.

O'Brien-Moore, Erin (1902–1979).
American stage actress who made a few films.
The Life of Emile Zola 38. Little Men 39. Destination Moon 50. Phantom of the Rue Morgue 53, etc.

Obst, Lynda (1950–).
American producer.
Flashdance 83. Adventures in Babysitting 87. Heartbreak Hotel 88. The Fisher King 91. This Is My Life 91. Sleepless in Seattle 93, etc.

O'Casey, Sean (1880–1964).
Irish playwright, much preoccupied by 'the troubles'. Works filmed include *Juno and the Paycock* and *The Plough and the Stars*; an alleged biopic, *Young Cassidy*, was made in 1964 with Rod Taylor.

O'Connell, Arthur (1908–1981).
American character actor with long Broadway experience; usually mildly bewildered roles.
Law of the Jungle 42. Countess of Monte Cristo 49. The Whistle at Eaton Falls 51. Picnic (AAN) 55. The Solid Gold Cadillac 56. *The Man in the Grey Flannel Suit* 56. Bus Stop 56. Operation Mad Ball 57. Operation Petticoat 59. Anatomy of a Murder (AAN) 59. Follow That Dream 61. Kissin' Cousins 64. The Monkey's Uncle 65. Your Cheating Heart 65. The Great Race 65. The Silencers 66. Fantastic Voyage 66. The Power 68. There Was a Crooked Man 70. Ben 72. The Poseidon Adventure 72. Huckleberry Finn 74. The Hiding Place 75, etc.
TV series: The Second Hundred Years 67.

O'Connolly, Jim (1926–).
British director.
The Traitors (wp only) 62. Smokescreen (wd) 64. *The Little Ones* 64. Berserk 67. The Valley of Gwangi 68. Crooks and Coronets 69. Horror on Snape Island (aka Beyond the Fog) 72. Mistress Pamela 74, etc.

O'Connor, Carroll (1922–).
Burly American character actor, often in blustery military roles.
By Love Possessed 61. Lonely are the Brave 62. Cleopatra 63. In Harm's Way 65. What Did You Do in the War, Daddy? 65. Waterhole Three 67. Point Blank 67. The Devil's Brigade 68. Marlowe 69. Doctors' Wives 70. Law and Disorder 74. In the Heat of the Night (TV) 88, etc.
TV series: Rifleman 58. *All in the Family* (as Archie Bunker) 71–78. Archie Bunker's Place 79–82. In the Heat of the Night 88– .

O'Connor, Derrick.
English character actor, now based in America.
Jabberwocky 77. Hope and Glory 87. Lethal Weapon 2 89. Dealers 89. A Question of Guilt (TV) 93. Stark (TV) 93, etc.

O'Connor, Donald (1925–).
Snappy American light comedian, singer and dancer, a teenage star of the 40s whose film career suffered with the decline of musicals.
■ *Sing You Sinners* 38. Sons of the Legion 38. Men With Wings 38. *Tom Sawyer Detective* 38. Unmarried 39. Death of a Champion 39. Boy Trouble 39. Million Dollar Legs 39. Night Work 39. On Your Toes 39. Beau Geste 39. Private Buckaroo 42. Give Out Sisters 42. Get Hep to Love 42. When Johnny Comes Marching Home 42. Strictly in the Groove 43. It Comes Up Big 43. *Mister Big* 43. Top Man 43. *Chip off the Old Block* 44. This is the Life 44. Follow the Boys 44. The Merry Monahans 44. Bowery to Broadway 44. *Patrick the Great* 45. Something in the Wind 47. Are You With It? 48. Feudin' Fussin' and a-Fightin' 48. Yes Sir That's My Baby 49. *Francis* 49. Curtain Call at Cactus Creek 50. The Milkman 50. Double Crossbones 50. Francis Goes to the Races 51. *Singin' In the Rain* 52. Francis Goes to West Point 52. *Call Me Madam* 53. I Love Melvin 53. Francis Covers Big Town 53. Walking My Baby Back Home 53. Francis Joins the WACS 54. There's No Business Like Show Business 54. Francis in the Navy 55. Anything Goes 56. *The Buster Keaton Story* 57. Cry for Happy 61. The Wonders of Aladdin 61. That Funny Feeling 65. That's Entertainment (co-narrator) 74. Ragtime 81. Pandemonium 82. A Time to Remember 90. Toys 92.
TV series: The Donald O'Connor Texaco Show 54–55.
⊙For his teenage high spirits and talent. *Patrick the Great.*

O'Connor, Glynnis (1956–).
Diminutive American leading lady of the 70s.
Jeremy 75. Ode to Billy Joe 76. California Dreaming 78. Those Lips Those Eyes 80. Night Crossing 82. Johnny Dangerously 84. Why Me? 84. Too Good to Be True (TV) 88, etc.

O'Connor, Hazel (1955–).
English actress, singer and songwriter, of whom much was expected after *Breaking Glass.*
Girls Come First 75. Double Exposure 77. Breaking Glass (& songs) 80, etc.

O'Connor, Kevin J. (1964–).
American actor.
Bogie (TV) 80. Let's Scare Jessica to Death 81. Peggy Sue Got Married 86. Candy Mountain 87. Waiting for the Moon 87. The Moderns 88. The Caine Mutiny Court-Martial (TV) 88. Signs of Life 89. Steel Magnolias 89. Love at Large 90. Hero (GB: Accidental Hero) 92. Color of Night 94, etc.

O'Connor, Pat (1943–).
Irish director, from TV.
A Ballroom of Romance (TV) 81. Cal 84. A Month in the Country 87. The January Man 88. Stars and Bars 88. Fools of Fortune 90. Zelda (TV) 93, etc.

O'Connor, Robert Emmett (1885–1962).
American small-part player, often as snoop or policeman, on screen from 1909 after circus and vaudeville experience.
Public Enemy 31. A Night at the Opera 35. Tight Shoes 41. Whistling in Brooklyn 44. Boys' Ranch 46, many others.

O'Connor, Tim (1925–).
Lean American character actor who became known as the long-lost husband in TV's *Peyton Place.*
Incident in San Francisco 70. Across 110th Street 72. Manhunter (TV) 74. Murder in Peyton Place (TV) 77. Buck Rogers in the 25th Century 79. The Golden Gate Murders (TV) 79.

O'Connor, Una (1880–1959).
Sharp-featured Irish character actress with stage experience before film debut in 1929; in Hollywood from 1932.
■ Dark Red Roses 29. To Oblige a Lady 30. Timbuctoo 30. Murder 30. *Cavalcade* 33. Pleasure Cruise 33. *The Invisible Man* 33. Mary Stevens MD 33. The Poor Rich 34. The Barretts of Wimpole Street 34. Orient Express 34. All Men Are Enemies 34. Stingaree 34. Chained 34. David Copperfield 35. *The Informer* 35. Father Brown Detective 35. *The Bride of Frankenstein* 35. Thunder in the Night

5. The Perfect Gentleman 35. Rose Marie 36. Little Lord Fauntleroy 36. Lloyds of London 36. Suzy 36. The Plough and the Stars 36. Call It a Day 37. Personal Property 37. The Return of the Frog 37. *The Adventures of Robin Hood* 38. We are Not Alone 39. The Sea Hawk 40. Lillian Russell 40. He Stayed for Breakfast 40. It All Came True 40. All Women Have Secrets 40. Kisses for Breakfast 41. How Green Was My Valley 41. The Strawberry Blonde 41. Her First Beau 41. Three Girls about Town 41. Always in My Heart 42. My Favorite Spy 42. Random Harvest 42. This Land Is Mine 43. Forever and a Day 43. Holy Matrimony 43. Government Girl 43. My Pal Wolf 44. The Canterville Ghost 44. The Bells of St Mary's 45. Christmas in Connecticut 45. The Return of Monte Cristo 46. Banjo 46. Child of Divorce 46. Cluny Brown 46. Of Human Bondage 46. Unexpected Guest 46. Lost Honeymoon 47. The Corpse Came COD 47. Ivy 47. Fighting Father Dunne 48. The Adventures of Don Juan 48. *Witness for the Prosecution* 57.

O'Conor, Joseph (1916–).
British character actor, mainly on stage and TV.
Crooks in Cloisters 63. Oliver! 68. Doomwatch 72. The Black Windmill 74. Forbidden Quest 93, etc.
TV series: The Forsyte Saga (as Old Jolyon) 68.

O'Day, Anita (1919–).
Stylish American jazz singer and occasional actress who made her name singing with the Gene Krupa and Stan Kenton bands in the 40s.
Autobiography: 1981, *High Times Hard Times*.
The Gene Krupa Story (as herself) 59. Jazz on a Summer's Day (doc) 60. Zigzag (aka False Witness) 70. The Outfit 74, etc.

O'Dea, Denis (1905–1978).
Irish stage actor who was in occasional films.
The Informer 35. The Plough and the Stars 47. Odd Man Out 47. The Fallen Idol 48. Under Capricorn 49. Treasure Island 50. Niagara 52. Mogambo 53. The Rising of the Moon 57. The Story of Esther Costello 58, etc.

O'Dea, Jimmy (1899–1965).
Irish character comedian.
■ Casey's Millions 22. Jimmy Boy 35. Blarney 38. Penny Paradise 38. Cheer Boys Cheer 39. Let's Be Famous 39. The Rising of the Moon 57. Darby O'Gill and the Little People 59. Johnny Nobody 61.

Odets, Clifford (1903–1963).
American playwright and occasional scriptwriter.
The General Died at Dawn (w) 36. Golden Boy (oa) 39. None But the Lonely Heart (wd) 44. Deadline at Dawn (w) 46. Humoresque (w) 46. Clash by Night (oa) 52. The Country Girl (oa) 54. The Big Knife (oa) 55. Sweet Smell of Success (w) 57. The Story on Page One (wd) 60, etc.

Odette, Mary (1901–) (Odette Goimbault).
French actress in many British silent films from 1915, at first as juvenile.
Cynthia in the Wilderness 15. Dombey and Son 17. The Lady Clare 19. Torn Sails 20. Cherry Ripe 21. The Crimson Circle 22. Eugene Aram 24. She 25. If Youth But Knew 26. Emerald of the East 28, etc.

O'Donnell, Cathy (1923–1970) (Ann Steely).
American leading lady with brief stage experience.
■ *The Best Years of Our Lives* (debut) 46. Bury Me Dead 47. The Spiritualist 47. *They Live by Night* 48. Side Street 50. The Miniver Story 50. Detective Story 51. The Woman's Angle (GB) 52. Never Trust a Gambler 53. Eight O'Clock Walk (GB) 54. The Face that Launched a Thousand Ships 54. Mad at the World 55. The Man from Laramie 55. The Story of Mankind 58. Ben Hur 59. Terror in the Haunted House 59.

O'Donnell, Chris (1971–).
Clean-cut young American actor.
Men Don't Leave 90. Fried Green Tomatoes 92. School Ties 92. Scent of a Woman 93. Blue Sky (made 91) 94. The Three Musketeers 94. Mad Love 95. Batman Forever (as Robin) 95, etc.

O'Donnell, Rosie.
American actress, a former stand-up comedian.
A League of Their Own 92. Another Stakeout 93. Sleepless in Seattle 93. Car 54, Where Are You? 94. The Flintstones 94. Exit to Eden 94, etc.
TV series: Gimme a Break 86–87.

O'Driscoll, Martha (1922–).
American leading lady of the 40s, mainly in second features.
The Secret of Dr Kildare 40. The Lady Eve 41. My Heart Belongs to Daddy 42. Follow the Boys 44. Ghost Catchers 44. House of Dracula 45. Criminal Court (last to date) 47, etc.

Of Mice and Men.
John Steinbeck's spare little morality tale about a gentle but homicidal giant who has to be killed by his best friend has been filmed twice: in 1939, directed by Lewis Milestone with Lon Chaney Jnr, Burgess Meredith, and Betty Field; and in 1992, directed by Gary Sinise, starring himself, John Malkovich, and Sherilyn Fenn.

O'Farrell, Bernadette (1926–).
British leading lady who married her director, Frank Launder.
Captain Boycott 48. The Happiest Days of Your Life 49. Lady Godiva Rides Again 51. The Story of Gilbert and Sullivan 53, etc.
TV series: Robin Hood 55–59.

O'Ferrall, George More:
see *More O'Ferrall, George.*

offices
have provided the setting for many a film. *The Crowd* in 1926 and *The Rebel* in 1961 chose pretty much the same way of stressing the dreariness of daily routine; but *Sunshine Susie* in 1931 and *How to Succeed in Business without Really Trying* in 1967 both saw the office as a gay place full of laughter and song. Satyajit Ray in *Company Limited* and Ermanno Olmi in *Il Posto* and *One Fine Day* took a realistic look at office life. Billy Wilder took a jaundiced view of it in *The Apartment*, as did the makers of *Patterns of Power, Executive Suite, Bartleby* and *The Power and the Prize*. Romantic comedies of the 30s like *Wife versus Secretary, After Office Hours* and *Take a Letter Darling* saw it as ideal for amorous intrigue, and in 1964 *The Wild Affair* took pretty much the same attitude. Orson Welles in *The Trial* made it nightmarish; Preston Sturges in *Christmas in July* made it friendly; *The Desk Set* made it computerized; *The Bachelor Party* made it frustrating. Perhaps the best film office is that of Philip Marlowe in the Raymond Chandler films: there's seldom anyone in it but himself. The most spectacular was that of Alfred Abel in *Metropolis*.

O'Flaherty, Liam (1896–1984).
Irish novelist whose *The Informer* was filmed twice under its own title and once as *Up Tight*.

Ogier, Bulle (1939–).
French leading actress, most often seen in the films of Jacques Rivette.
L'Amour Fou 68. La Salamandre 71. Rendez-vous à Bray 71. The Valley 72. The Discreet Charm of the Bourgeoisie 72. Celine and Julie Go Boating 73. Mistress (Maîtresse) 75. Entire Days in the Trees 76. Duelle 76. The Third Generation 79. Navire Night 79. Le Pont du Nord (& w) 81. Aspern 81. The Cheaters (Les Tricheurs) 83. Unknown Country 87. The Band of Four (La Bande de Quatre) 89. North (Nord) 91. Personne ne M'Aime 94. Regarde Les Hommes Tomber 94, etc.

Ogilvie, George (1931–).
English director, a former actor and drama teacher, in Australia.
Bodyline (TV) 83. Mad Max Beyond Thunderdrome (co-d) 85. Short Changed 86. The Shiralee (TV) 88. The Crossing 90, etc.

Ogilvy, Ian (1943–).
Slightly-built British leading man.
Stranger in the House 67. The Sorcerers 67. Witchfinder General 68. Wuthering Heights 70. And Now the Screaming Starts 72. No Sex Please We're British 73. Menace Unseen (TV) 88. Death Becomes Her 92, etc.
TV series: *Return of the Saint* 78.

Ogle, Charles (1865–1940).
American silent actor, best known for being the first (in 1909) to play the Frankenstein monster.
The Honour of His Family 09. The Ironmaster 14. Joan the Woman 17. Treasure Island 20. The Covered Wagon 23. The Alaskan 24. Contraband 25. The Flaming Forest 26, many others.

Oh God!
Avery Corman's novel of God coming to Earth to ask a supermarket manager for help in promulgating his message was filmed in 1977 by Carl Reiner with the veteran comedian George Burns as the deity and was followed by two lacklustre sequels: *Oh God! Book II*, directed by Gilbert Cates in 1980, and *Oh God! You Devil*, directed by Paul Bogart from Andrew Bergman's script.

O'Hagan, Colo Tavernier.
British screenwriter working in France; formerly married to director Bernard Tavernier.
Une Semaine de Vacances (co-w) 82. Beatrice (La Passion Béatrice) 87. Summer Interlude (Comédie d'Eté) (co-w) 89. Story of Women (co-w) 89. These Foolish Things (Daddy Nostalgie) 90, etc.

O'Hanlon, George (1917–1989) (George Rice).
American comedy actor with stage experience; played Joe McDoakes in the one-reeler *Behind the Eight Ball* series.
The Great Awakening 41. The Hucksters 47. The Tanks Are Coming 51. Battle Stations 55. Bop Girl 57. The Rookie 59. Charley and the Angel 73. Rocky 76, etc.
TV series: The Life of Riley. The Reporter. Nancy Drew.

O'Hara, Catherine (1954–).
Canadian actress and comedy writer.
Nothing Personal 80. The Last Polka (TV) 84. After Hours 85. Double Negative 86. Heartburn 86. Beetlejuice 88. Batman 89. Dick Tracy 90. Home Alone 90. Little Vegas 90. Betsy's Wedding 90. There Goes the Neighborhood (aka Paydirt) 92. Home Alone 2: Lost in New York 92. Wyatt Earp 94, etc.

TV series: Second City TV 77–80. SCTV Network 90 81–82.

O'Hara, Gerry (c. 1925–).
British director.

That Kind of Girl 61. The Pleasure Girls 64. Maroc 7 67. Amsterdam Affair 68. All the Right Noises (& w) 69. The Brute 76. The Bitch 79. Fanny Hill 83. The Mummy Lives 93, etc.

O'Hara, John (1905–1970).
American best-selling novelist who wrote chiefly about sex in suburbia. Works filmed include *Pal Joey, From the Terrace, A Rage to Live, Butterfield 8.* Also co-wrote screenplays. In 1976 a TV series was based on his *Gibbsville* stories.

I was an Adventuress 40. Moontide 42. Strange Journey 46. On Our Merry Way 48. The Best Things in Life are Free 56, etc.

¶ He lives in a perpetual state of just having discovered that it's a lousy world. – *F. Scott Fitzgerald*

O'Hara, Mary (1885–1980) (Mary Alsop).
American novelist best known for *My Friend Flicka,* which was filmed in 1943; sequels followed.

O'Hara, Maureen (1920–) (Maureen Fitzsimmons).
Striking red-haired Irish leading lady who survived in Hollywood less through acting talent than through pleasing, unassuming personality.

■ My Irish Molly 38. Kicking the Moon Around 38. Jamaica Inn 39. *The Hunchback of Notre Dame* 39. A Bill of Divorcement 40. Dance Girl Dance 40. They Met in Argentina 41. How Green Was My Valley 41. To the Shores of Tripoli 42. Ten Gentlemen from West Point 42. The Black Swan 42. The Immortal Sergeant 43. This Land is Mine 43. The Fallen Sparrow 43. Buffalo Bill 44. The Spanish Main 45. Sentimental Journey 46. Do You Love Me? 46. Sinbad the Sailor 47. The Homestretch 47. Miracle on 34th Street 47. The Foxes of Harrow 47. Sitting Pretty 48. Britannia Mews 49. A Woman's Secret 49. Father was a Fullback 49. Baghdad 49. Comanche Territory 50. Tripoli 50. Rio Grande 50. Flame of Araby 51. At Sword's Point 52. Kangaroo 52. The Quiet Man 52. Against All Flags 52. Redhead from Wyoming 52. War Arrow 53. Fire over Africa 54. The Long Gray Line 55. The Magnificent Matador 55. Lady Godiva 55. Lisbon 56. Everything But the Truth 56. The Wings of Eagles 57. Our Man in Havana 59. The Parent Trap 61. The Deadly Companions 61. Mr Hobbs Takes a Vacation 62. Spencer's Mountain 63. McLintock 63. The Battle of the Villa Fiorita 65. The Rare Breed 66. How Do I Love Thee? 70. Big Jake 71. The Red Pony (TV) 72. Only the Lonely 91.

¶ She looks as though butter wouldn't melt in her mouth – or anywhere else. – *Elsa Lanchester*
Framed in Technicolor, Miss O'Hara somehow seems more significant than a setting sun. – *New York Times, 1954*

O'Herlihy, Dan (1919–).
Irish character actor and occasional off-beat leading man, with Abbey Theatre and radio experience.

Odd Man Out (GB) 46. Hungry Hill (GB) 46. Kidnapped 48. Macbeth 48. Actors and Sin 50. Rommel, Desert Fox 51. The Blue Veil 51. The Highwayman 52. *The Adventures of Robinson Crusoe* (AAN) 52. Bengal Brigade 53. The Black Shield of Falworth 54. The Purple Mask 55. The Virgin Queen 55. That Woman Opposite (GB) 57. Home before

Dark 58. Imitation of Life 59. *The Cabinet of Caligari* 62. Fail Safe 64. 100 Rifles 69. Waterloo 69. The Carey Treatment 72. QB VII (TV) 73. The Tamarind Seed 74. MacArthur 77. T. R. Sloane (TV) 79. Halloween III 82. The Last Starfighter 84. The Whoopee Boys 86. The Dead 87. Robocop 87. Robocop 2 90, etc.

TV series: The Travels of Jaimie McPheeters 63. The Long Hot Summer 66. A Man Called Sloane 79.

O'Herlihy, Michael (1929–).
Irish director in Hollywood, with TV experience.

The Fighting Prince of Donegal 66. The One and Only Genuine Original Family Band 68. Smith! 69. The Flame Is Love (TV) 79. Cry of the Innocent (TV) 80. I Married Wyatt Earp (TV) 83. Hoover vs the Kennedys: The Second Civil War (TV) 87, etc.

Ohmart, Carol (1928–).
American leading lady with stage experience, whose career in films did not develop.

The Scarlet Hour (debut) 55. The House on Haunted Hill 58. Born Reckless 59. The Scavengers 60. Wild Youth 60. One Man's Way 64. Caxambu 67. The Spectre of Edgar Allan Poe 72, etc.

oil
and its procurement from the earth have been the subjects of a number of films including *High Wide and Handsome* 38, *Boom Town* 40, *The Big Gusher* 51, *Tulsa* 49, *Thunder Bay* 53, *Lucy Gallant* 55, *Giant* 56, *The Houston Story* 56, *Maracaibo* 58, *Black Gold* 60, *Hellfighters* 68 and *Oklahoma Crude* 73.

O'Keefe, Dennis (1908–1968) (Edward 'Bud' Flanagan).
Cheerful American leading man of the 40s; began as an extra after vaudeville experience with his parents.

Bad Man of Brimstone 38. That's Right, You're Wrong 39. La Conga Nights 40. You'll Find Out 40. Lady Scarface 41. *Topper Returns* 41. Broadway Limited 41. The Affairs of Jimmy Valentine 42. Good Morning Judge 42. The Leopard Man 43. The Fighting Seabees 43. Up in Mabel's Room 44. Abroad with Two Yanks 44. *The Affairs of Susan* 45. Brewster's Millions 45. Come Back to Me 46. Dishonoured Lady 47. T-Men 47. Mr District Attorney 47. Raw Deal 48. Walk a Crooked Mile 49. Woman on the Run 50. The Company She Keeps 51. Follow the Sun 52. The Fake (GB) 53. The Diamond Wizard (GB) (& d) 54. Angela (& d) 55. Inside Detroit 56. Dragoon Wells Massacre 57. Graft and Corruption 58. All Hands on Deck 61, many others.

TV series: The Dennis O'Keefe Show 59.

O'Keefe, Michael (1955–).
American actor.

Gray Lady Down 78. Dark Secret of Harvest Home (TV) 78. Rumor of War 80. Caddyshack 80. The Great Santini (AAN) 80. Split Image 82. Nate and Hayes 83. Finders Keepers 84. The Slugger's Wife 85. The Whoopee Boys 86. Ironweed 87. Hitchhiker II 87. Nina Takes a Lover 94, etc.

O'Keeffe, Miles (1954–).
Muscular American star of sword-and-sorcery movies who played Tarzan once.

Tarzan the Ape Man 81. Ator: The Fighting Eagle 83. The Blade Master 84. S.A.S. San Salvador 84. Sword of the Valiant 84. Lone Runner 86. Campus Man 87. Iron Warrior 87. Waxwork 88. The Drifter 88. Liberty & Bash 90. Acting on Impulse 93. Silent Hunter 94, etc.

Oland, Warner (1880–1938).
Swedish character actor in Hollywood who oddly enough became the screen's most popular Chinese detective.

The Yellow Ticket 18. Witness for the Defense 19. His Children's Children 23. Don Q Son of Zorro 25. Don Juan 26. The Jazz Singer 27. Old San Francisco 27. Chinatown Nights 29. The Mysterious Dr Fu Manchu 29. The Vagabond King 30. *Charlie Chan Carries On* 31 (and 15 other episodes in this series). Shanghai Express 32. The Painted Veil 34. *Werewolf of London* 35. Shanghai 35, many others.

Olcott, Sidney (1873–1949) (John S. Alcott).
Irish-Canadian director, in Hollywood from the beginning.

Ben Hur (one reel) 07. Florida Crackers 08. Judgement 09. The Miser's Child 10. The O'Neil (Irish) 11. From the Manager to the Cross 12. Madame Butterfly 15. The Innocent Lie 17. Scratch My Back 20. Little Old New York 21. The Humming Bird 23. The Green Goddess 23. Monsieur Beaucaire 24. The Amateur Gentleman 26. The Claw 27, etc.

old age
on the screen has seldom been explored, and the commercial reasons for this are obvious. Among the serious studies are *The Whisperers,* with Edith Evans; *Umberto D,* with Carlo Battisti; *The Shameless Old Lady,* with Sylvie; *Ikuru,* with Takashi Shimura; *The End of the Road,* with Finlay Currie; *I Never Sang for My Father,* with Melvyn Douglas; *Make Way for Tomorrow,* with Beulah Bondi; *Alive and Kicking,* with Sybil Thorndike and Estelle Winwood; *Kotch* with Walter Matthau; *Harry and Tonto* with Art Carney; *Tokyo Story* with Chishu Ryu and Chieko Higashiyama; *On Golden Pond* with Henry Fonda and Katharine Hepburn; *The Gin Game* with Jessica Tandy and Hume Cronyn (a video version of their stage hit); *The Whales of August* with Bette Davis and Lillian Gish; and *Driving Miss Daisy* with Jessica Tandy and Morgan Freeman. Sentimentality crept in in *Mr Belvedere Rings the Bell;* and *The Old Man and the Sea* was merely pretentious.

There was an element of black comedy in the attitudes expressed towards the old people in *Grapes of Wrath, Tobacco Road* and *Nights of the Iguana;* and more melodramatic caricatures were presented in *The Lost Moment* (Agnes Moorehead), *The Queen of Spades* (Edith Evans), *Little Big Man* (Dustin Hoffman), and *The Old Dark House* (John Dudgeon). Fantasy crept in with *Lost Horizon,* in which the lamas grew incredibly old by natural processes, and *The Man in Half Moon Street,* in which Nils Asther was assisted by science. Other actors who have specialized in geriatric portraits include A. E. Matthews, Edie Martin, Clem Bevans, Andy Clyde, Maria Ouspenskaya, Jessie Ralph, Nancy Price and Adeline de Walt Reynolds, who did not become an actress until she was eighty. Perhaps the Screen's most delightful senior citizens were the capering Harbottle, played by Moore Marriott in Will Hay comedies, and Barry Fitzgerald in *Broth of a Boy;* the most horrific was Cathleen Nesbitt in *Staircase;* the most commercially successful were George Burns and Walter Matthau in *The Sunshine Boys.* Katie Johnson became a star at 78 in *The Lady Killers;* Ruth Gordon played capering old dames well into her 80s, and in *Harold and Maude,* when she was 75, played an 80-year-old who had an affair with an immature young boy.

Stars who donned ageing make-up include Hope, Crosby and Lamour in *Road to Utopia;* Barbara Stanwyck in *The Great Man's Lady;* Tyrone Power in *The Long Gray Line;* Anna Neagle in *Victoria the Great;* Madeleine Carroll in *The Fan;*

Gable and Shearer in *Strange Interlude;* Rosalind Russell and Alexander Knox in *Sister Kenny;* Joel McCrea in *Buffalo Bill;* Fredric March in *The Adventures of Mark Twain;* Dustin Hoffman in *Little Big Man.* The most tasteless treatment of old age was surely that offered in *The Ultimate Solution of Grace Quigley;* the most graceful that of *Going in Style.*

Old Mother Riley.
The vociferous, anarchic Irish washerwoman was created by Arthur Lucan on the music halls and in many films, with daughter Kitty played by the resistible Kitty McShane, Lucan's wife. Most of the films were atrociously made but all of them made a sizeable profit from British provincial showings.

For a complete list, see *Lucan, Arthur.*

Oldfield, Barney (1878–1946) (Berna Eli Oldfield).
American racing driver, the first to travel a mile a minute; featured in *Barney Oldfield's Race for Life* 16.

Oldland, Lilian (1905–   ).
British leading lady of the silents, who later changed her name to Mary Newland.

The Secret Kingdom 25. The Flag Lieutenant 26. Troublesome Wives 27. Jealousy 31. Ask Beccles 34. Death at Broadcasting House 34. The Silent Passenger (last to date) 35, etc.

Oldman, Gary (1958–   ).
British actor of character leads. He was married to actress Uma Thurman (1990–92).

Sid and Nancy 86. Prick Up Your Ears 87. Track 29 87. Criminal Law 88. We Think the World of You 88. Chattahoochee 89. Rosencrantz and Guildenstern Are Dead 90. State of Grace 90. JFK 91. Money 92. Bram Stoker's Dracula 92. Romeo Is Bleeding 93. True Romance 93. Leon (US: The Professional) (Fr.) 94. Murder in the First 94. Immortal Beloved 94, etc.

¶ To be able to do this job in the first place you've got to have a bit of an ego, whether you're in a movie or on stage and say, 'Look at me, I'm interesting.' That takes a lot of ego. – *G.O.*

Oliansky, Joel (1935–   ).
American screenwriter.

The Senator (TV) 71. Masada (TV) 80. The Competition (& d) 81. Bird 88.

Olin, Lena (1956–   ).
Swedish actress in international films. She began by working in the theatre with Ingmar Bergman's company.

Karleken 80. Fanny and Alexander 82. After the Rehearsal 84. Friends 87. The Unbearable Lightness of Being 88. Enemies, a Love Story (AAN) 89. S/Y Joy (S/Y Glädjen) 89. Havana 90. Mr Jones 93. Romeo Is Bleeding 93. The Night and the Moment 94, etc.

Oliver, Anthony (1923–   ).
Welsh general-purpose actor, in British films and TV.

Once a Jolly Swagman 48. The Clouded Yellow 50. The Runaway Bus 54. Lost 56. The Fourth Square 61, many others.

Oliver, Barrett (1973–   ).
American juvenile actor.

Frankenweenie 84. The Neverending Story 84. D.A.R.Y.L. 85. The Secret Garden (TV) 87. Cocoon: The Return 88. Scenes from the Class Struggle in Beverly Hills 89, etc.

Oliver, Edna May (1883–1942) (Edna May Cox-Oliver).
American character actress, usually of acidulous but often warm-hearted spinsters; on stage from 1912.

Icebound 23. The American Venus 26. Saturday Night Kid 29. Half Shot at Sunrise 31. Cimarron 31. *Fanny Foley Herself* 31. The Penguin Pool Murder 32. Little Women 33. Alice in Wonderland 33. *David Copperfield* (as Aunt Betsy) 34. A Tale of Two Cities 35. Romeo and Juliet (as the Nurse) 36. Parnell 37. Rosalie 38. Second Fiddle 38. The Story of Vernon and Irene Castle 39. Nurse Edith Cavell 39. Drums along the Mohawk (AAN) 39. *Pride and Prejudice* (as Lady Catherine de Bourgh) 40. Lydia 41, etc.

Oliver, Susan (1937–1990).
American leading TV actress whose film roles were few.

Green-Eyed Blonde 57. The Gene Krupa Story 60. Looking for Love 64. The Disorderly Orderly 65. Your Cheating Heart 66. A Man Called Gannon 68. Change of Mind 69. Ginger in the Morning 75. Hardly Working 71, etc.

TV series: Peyton Place 66.

Oliver Twist.
Dickens's novel was filmed many times in the early silent period: in 1909 by Pathé, in 1910 by Vitagraph, in 1912 by an independent company with Nat C. Goodwin as Fagin. A famous American version of 1916 had Tully Marshall as Fagin and Marie Doro as Oliver; in 1922 the roles were played by Lon Chaney and Jackie Coogan, and in 1933 by Irving Pichel and Dickie Moore. The definitive version so far, however, is the British one directed by David Lean in 1948, with John Howard Davies in the title role. Alec Guinness's brilliant performance as Fagin caused a hold-up in American distribution as it was accused of anti-Semitism. *Oliver!,* a 1968 musical version directed by Carol Reed, with Ron Moody as Fagin and Mark Lester as Oliver, won six Oscars.

Oliver, Vic (1898–1964) (Victor Von Samek).
Austrian-born comedian, pianist, violinist and conductor, long in Britain. Occasional films.

Autobiography: 1954, *Mr Show Business.*

Rhythm in the Air 37. Room for Two 40. He Found a Star 41. Hi Gang 41. Give Us the Moon 44. I'll Be Your Sweetheart 45, etc.

Olivera, Hector (1931–   ).
Argentinian director.

Psexoanalisis 67. La Patagonia Rebelde 74. El Muerto 75. A Funny Dirty Little War (No Habrá Más Penas ni Olvido) 84. Wizards of the Lost Kingdom 85. Barbarian Queen 85. Cocaine Wars 86. Night of the Pencils (& co-w) 87. Two to Tango 89. Cuentos de Borges I (co-d) 91. The Maria Soledad Case (El Caso Maria Soledad) 93. A Shadow You Soon Will Be (Una Sombra Ya Pronto Serás) (co-w, d) 94, etc.

Olivier, Laurence (1907–1989) (Lord Olivier).
Distinguished British stage actor whose film appearances were reasonably frequent. Honorary AA 1979 'for the full body of his work, for the unique achievements of his entire career and his lifetime of contribution to the art of film'.

Autobiography: 1982, *Confessions of an Actor.*

Biographies: 1969, *Cry God for Larry* by Virginia Fairweather. 1975, *Laurence Olivier* by John Cottrell. 1992, *Laurence Olivier: A Biography* by Donald Spoto.

■ Too Many Crooks 30. The Temporary Widow 30. Potiphar's Wife 30. The Yellow Ticket 31.

Friends and Lovers 31. Westward Passage 31. No Funny Business 32. Perfect Understanding (US) 32. Conquest of the Air 35. Moscow Nights 35. As You Like It (as Orlando) 36. Fire over England 36. *The Divorce of Lady X* 38. Twenty-One Days 39. Q Planes 39. *Wuthering Heights* (US) (AAN) 39. *Rebecca* (US) (AAN) 40. *Pride and Prejudice* (US) 40. *Lady Hamilton* (US) (as Nelson) 41. 49th Parallel 41. The Demi-Paradise 43. *Henry V* (& p, co-d) (special AA) 44. *Hamlet* (& pd) (AA, AANd) 48. The Magic Box (cameo role) 51. *Carrie* (US) 52. The Beggar's Opera (as Macheath) 52. *Richard III* (& pd) (AAN) 56. The Prince and the Showgirl (& d) 58. The Moon and Sixpence (TV) 59. *The Devil's Disciple* 59. Spartacus (US) 60. *The Entertainer* (AAN) 60. The Power and the Glory (TV) 61. Term of Trial 62. Uncle Vanya (& d) 63. Bunny Lake is Missing 65. Othello (AAN) 65. Khartoum 66. The Shoes of the Fisherman 68. Oh What a Lovely War 69. The Dance of Death 69. The Battle of Britain 69. David Copperfield 69. Three Sisters (& d) 70. Nicholas and Alexandra 71. Lady Caroline Lamb 72. *Sleuth* (AAN) 72. Love Among the Ruins (TV) 74. *Marathon Man* (AAN) 76. The Seven Per Cent Solution 76. Jesus of Nazareth (TV) 77. The Betsy 77. A Bridge Too Far 77. The Boys from Brazil (AAN) 78. A Little Romance 78. Dracula 79. Clash of the Titans 81. The Jazz Singer 81. Inchon 81. Brideshead Revisited (TV) 81. A Voyage Round My Father (TV) 82. Wagner 83. A Talent for Murder (TV) 83. Mr Halpern and Mr Johnson (TV) 83. The Last Days of Pompeii (TV) 84. The Bounty 84. The Jigsaw Man 84. Wild Geese II 85. Lost Empires (TV) 86.

⊗For being consistently the most fascinating actor of his time. *Richard III.*

¶ Nothing is beneath me if it pays well. I've earned the right to damn well grab whatever I can in the time I've got left. – *L.O.*

At heart Larry was what the French call a *cabotin.* The term is difficult to translate – not exactly a ham: a performer, a vulgarian, someone who lives and dies for acting. – *Tony Richardson*

Famous line (*Wuthering Heights*): 'I cannot live without my life; I cannot live without my soul.'

Olivio, Bob:
see *Ondine.*

Olmi, Ermanno (1931–   ).
Italian director noted for gentle realism.

Il Posto (The Job) 61. I Fidanzati 62. And There Came a Man 65. One Fine Day 69. Diary of Summer 71. The Circumstance 74. The Tree of Wooden Clogs 77. Cammina Cammina 83. Milano '83 83. The Legend of the Holy Drinker (La Leggenda del Santo Brevitore) 88. Legend of the Old Wood 93. Genesis: The Creation and the Flood (Genesi: La Creazione e il Diluvio) 94, etc.

Olmos, Edward James (1947–   ).
American character actor who began his career as a rock singer.

Aloha, Bobby and Rose 75. Wolfen 81. Cannery Row 82. Blade Runner 82. Ballad of Gregorio Cortez 82. Saving Grace 86. Stand and Deliver (AAN) 88. Triumph of the Spirit 89. Maria's Story 90. Talent for the Game 91. American Me (& d) 92. Roosters 93. A Million to Juan 94. Menendez: A Killing in Beverly Hills (TV) 94. The Burning Season (TV) 94, etc.

TV series: Miami Vice 84–89.

O'Loughlin, Gerald S. (1921–   ).
American TV actor, prominent in series *The Rookies* 72–76.

Twilight's Last Gleaming 76. Frances 82. Quicksilver 86.

Olsen, Moroni (1889–1954).
Heavily-built American character actor, with stage experience.

The Three Musketeers (as Porthos) 36. The Witness Chair 38. The Three Musketeers (as Bailiff) 39. Kentucky 39. The Glass Key 42. Call Northside 777 48. Father of the Bride 50. The Long, Long Trailer 54, many others.

Olsen, Ole (1892–1965) (John Sigurd Olsen).
Norwegian-American comedian, in vaudeville from 1914, almost always with partner Chic Johnson.

Gold Dust Gertie 31. Fifty Million Frenchmen 31. The Country Gentleman 37. *Hellzapoppin* 42. Crazy House 44. Ghost Catchers 44. See My Lawyer 45, etc.

Olson, James (1932–).
American general-purpose actor.

The Sharkfighters 56. The Strange One 57. Rachel Rachel 67. The Andromeda Strain 70. Moon Zero Two 70. Wild Rovers 71. The Groundstar Conspiracy 72. Ragtime 81. Amityville 2 82. Commando 85. Rachel River 87, etc.

Olson, Nancy (1928–).
American leading lady who came to films from college, retired after a few years and recently reappeared in more mature roles.

Canadian Pacific 49. Union Station 50. *Sunset Boulevard* (AAN) 50. Submarine Command 51. Force of Arms 52. So Big 52. Battle Cry 55. Pollyanna 60. The Absent-Minded Professor 61. Son of Flubber 63. Smith! 69. Snowball Express 73. Making Love 82, etc.

O'Malley, J. Pat (1901–1985).
Irish character actor in Hollywood.

The Long Hot Summer 58. Blueprint for Robbery 60. The Cabinet of Caligari 62. A House is Not a Home 67. Gunn 67. Hello Dolly 69. Willard 71. Silkwood 83, etc.

TV series: Alarm 54. My Favorite Martian 63–64. Wendy and Me 64–65. The Rounders 66–67. A Touch of Grace 73. Maude 75–77.

O'Malley, John P. (1916–1959).
Australian character actor.

Kind Lady 51. Julius Caesar 52. Desert Rats 55. The Court Jester 56. The Invisible Boy 57.

O'Malley, Pat (1891–1966).
Irish-American character actor in Hollywood.

The Papered Door 11. Happiness 26. The Fall Guy 30. Frisco Jenny 33. Hollywood Boulevard 36. A Little Bit of Heaven 40. Lassie Come Home 43. The Rugged O'Riordans 49. Invasion of the Body Snatchers 56, etc.

O'Malley, Rex (1901–1976).
American light actor who was little heard from after a promising start.

Camille 36. *Midnight* 39. Zaza 39. The Thief 52, etc.

O'Mara, Kate (1939–).
British leading lady.

Great Catherine 68. The Limbo Line 68. The Desperados 69. Horror of Frankenstein 70, etc.

TV series: Dynasty 85–87.

Ondine (1937–) (Bob Olivio).
A member of Andy Warhol's entourage in the 60s who appeared in several of his films, notably as the Pope of Greenwich Village in *The Chelsea Girls*, losing his temper on-camera, attacking a woman and admitting his homosexuality. His conversation, fuelled by amphetamines, is preserved in Warhol's novel *a*. He left Warhol at the end of the 60s to work as a postman.

Vinyl 65. The Chelsea Girls 66. **** 67. Imitation of Christ 67. The Loves of Ondine 67, etc.

Ondra, Anny (1903–1987) (A. Ondrakova).
German-Czech leading lady of British silent films; her accent killed her career when sound came. Returned to Europe and appeared in a few German films.

Chorus Girls 28. The Manxman 29. Blackmail 30. Glorious Youth 31. Schön Muss Mann Sein 50. Die Zuercher Verlorung 57, etc.

Ondricek, Miroslav (1933–).
Czech cinematographer, now in international films, who has worked often with director Milos Forman.

Talent Competition 62. If . . . 68. Slaughterhouse Five 71. Taking Off 71. O Lucky Man 73. Hair 79. Ragtime (AAN) 81. The World According to Garp 82. The Divine Emma 83. Silkwood 83. Amadeus (AAN) 84. Heaven Help Us 85. F/X 86. Big Shots 87. Funny Farm 88. Valmont 89. Awakenings 90. A League of Their Own 92, etc.

One Million B.C.
This highly unscientific account of the tribulations of primitive man has been filmed several times. The 1939 version featured Carole Landis and Victor Mature and was produced and directed by Hal Roach with assistance from D. W. Griffith, upon whose 1912 *Man's Genesis* it was based. The dialogue consisted largely of grunts and there were a variety of prehistoric monsters which were rather obviously normal reptiles crudely decorated and magnified. Hammer remade it in 1960 with Don Chaffey directing Raquel Welch and John Richardson; this time the monsters were plastic animations. A kind of sequel, *When Dinosaurs Ruled the Earth*, directed by Val Guest, came out in 1970, and *Creatures the World Forgot* followed in 1971. Another all-grunting caveman epic followed in 1981, with *Quest for Fire*, directed by Jean-Jacques Annaud. This, however, aimed for accuracy, with the cast using a prehistoric language created by novelist Anthony Burgess and gestures devised by zoologist Desmond Morris, and was consequently much less fun.

One Way Passage.
A popular tear-jerker of 1932, written and directed by Tay Garnett, about a dying beauty (Kay Francis) and a convicted murderer (William Powell) who meet on an ocean liner and fall in love while keeping their secrets, it was remade in 1940 by Edmund Goulding as *Till We Meet Again*, with Merle Oberon and George Brent.

O'Neal, Frederick (1905–1992).
Powerful American character actor, mainly on stage.

Pinky 49. No Way Out 50. Something of Value 56. Anna Lucasta 58. Take a Giant Step 59. The Sins of Rachel Cade 61. Free, White and 21 62, etc.

TV series: Car 54 Where Are You? 61–62.

O'Neal, Patrick (1927–1994).
American general-purpose actor with stage and TV experience.

The Mad Magician 54. From the Terrace 60. The Cardinal 63. In Harm's Way 65. King Rat 65. A Fine Madness 66. Chamber of Horrors 66. Alvarez Kelly 66. *Assignment to Kill* 67. Where Were You When the Lights Went Out? 68. The Secret Life of an American Wife 68. Castle Keep 69. Stiletto 69. The Kremlin Letters 69. Corky 72. The Way We Were 73. Crossfire (TV) 75. The Stepford Wives 75. The Moneychangers (TV) 76. The Deadliest Season (TV) 77. The Last Hurrah (TV) 77. To Kill a Cop (TV) 78. Like Mom Like Me (TV) 78. Make Me an Offer 80. New York Stories 89. Q & A 90. Alice 90, etc.

TV series: Dick and the Duchess 57–58. Diagnosis Unknown 60. *Kaz* 78–79. Emerald Point N.A.S. 83–84.

O'Neal, Ron (1937–).
American leading man.

Superfly 72. Superfly TNT 73. The Master Gunfighter 75. When a Stranger Calls 79. The Final Countdown 80. St Helens 81. Red Dawn 84. As Summers Die 86. Hero and the Terror 88. Mercenary Fighters 88, etc.

O'Neal, Ryan (1941–) (Patrick Ryan O'Neal).
Bland American leading man of the 60s and 70s, after which his career faltered.
■ This Rugged Land (TV) 62. The Games 68. The Big Bounce 69. *Love Story* (AAN) 70. Love Hate Love (TV) 70. Wild Rovers 71. *What's Up, Doc?* 72. The Thief Who Came to Dinner 73. *Paper Moon* 73. Barry Lyndon 75. Nickelodeon 76. A Bridge Too Far 77. The Driver 78. Oliver's Story 79. The Main Event 79. So Fine 81. Green Lee 81. Partners 82. Irreconcilable Differences 84. Fever Pitch 85. Tough Guys Don't Dance 87. Chances Are 89. Small Sacrifices (TV) 89.

TV series: Empire 62. *Peyton Place* 64–68. Good Sports 91.

¶ I'm as moody and complex and private as anyone I ever knew. – *R.O'N.*
The only time I ever had steady employment was in *Peyton Place*. Once I was in control of my own destiny I found it very difficult. – *R.O'N.*

O'Neal, Tatum (1962–).
Abrasive child actress of the 70s, daughter of Ryan O'Neal.
■ *Paper Moon* (AA) 73. The Bad News Bears 76. Nickelodeon 76. International Velvet 78. Circle of Two 80. Little Darlings 80. Certain Fury 85. Little Noises 91. Woman on the Run: The Lawrencia Bembenek Story (TV) 93.

O'Neil, Barbara (1909–1980).
American character actress who made a corner in mad wives and other neurotic roles.
■ Stella Dallas 37. Love, Honor and Behave 38. The Toy Wife 38. I Am the Law 39. The Sun Never Sets 39. *When Tomorrow Comes* 39. Tower of London 39. Gone With the Wind 39. All This and Heaven Too (AAN) 40. Shining Victory 41. The Secret Beyond the Door 48. I Remember Mama 48. Whirlpool 49. Angel Face 52. Flame of the Islands 55. The Nun's Story 59.

O'Neil, Nance (1875–1965).
American stage actress who starred in a few films.

The Kreuzer Sonata 15. Hedda Gabler 17. The Mad Woman 20. His Glorious Night 29. The Rogue Song 30. Cimarron 31. False Faces 34, etc.

O'Neil, Sally (1910–1968) (Virginia Noonan).
American leading lady of the 20s.

Sally Irene and Mary 25. Battling Butler 26. Slide Kelly Slide 27. The Lovelorn 27. The Mad Hour 28. Jazz Heaven 29. Hold Everything 30. Salvation Nell 31. Murder by the Clock 31. Sixteen Fathoms Deep 33. Kathleen 37, etc.

O'Neill, Eugene (1888–1953).
Irish-American playwright of self-pitying
disposition and a tendency in his plays to tragic
despair. His gloominess led Hollywood to regard
his works as art, which killed many of the film
versions stone dead.

Anna Christie (23 with Blanche Sweet, 30 with
Garbo). Strange Interlude 32. The Emperor Jones
33. Ah Wilderness 35. The Long Voyage Home 40.
The Hairy Ape 44. Summer Holiday 47. Mourning
Becomes Electra 48. Desire under the Elms 57.
Long Day's Journey into Night 62. The Iceman
Cometh 73, etc.
~O'Neill was played by Jack Nicholson in *Reds*.

O'Neill, Henry (1891–1961).
American character actor with stage experience,
in Hollywood from early 30s. Played scores of
judges, guardians, fathers, lawyers, etc.

I Loved a Woman 33. Wonder Bar 34. Black
Fury 35. The White Angel 36. First Lady 37.
Brother Rat 38. Juarez 39. Billy the Kid 41. White
Cargo 43. The Virginian 46. Alias Nick Beal 49. The
Milkman 50. Untamed 55. The Wings of Eagles 57,
many others.

O'Neill, James (1847–1920).
American stage actor, father of Eugene. Best film
part 1913: *The Count of Monte Cristo*.

O'Neill, Jennifer (1947–).
American leading lady of the 70s.

Rio Lobo 70. Summer of 42 71. Such Good Friends
71. The Carey Treatment 72. Glass Houses 72. Lady
Ice 73. The Reincarnation of Peter Proud 75.
Whiffs 75. Caravans 78. A Force of One 79. Cloud
Dancer 80. Steel 80. Scanners 81. I Love N.Y. 87.
Personals 90. Committed 91, etc.

TV series: Cover Up 83–84.

O'Neill, Maire (1885–1952) (Maire Allgood).
Irish character actress, an Abbey player; sister of
Sara Allgood.

Juno and the Paycock 30. Sing As We Go 34.
Farewell Again 37. Love on the Dole 41. Gaiety
George 46. Someone at the Door 50. Treasure
Hunt 52, etc.

Ontkean, Michael (1946–).
American leading man.

Pickup on 101 71. Necromancy 72. Slap Shot
77. Voices 79. Willie and Phil 80. Making Love
81. The Blood of Others 84. The Allnighter 87.
Maid to Order 87. Clara's Heart 88. Bye Bye Blues
89. Cold Front 89. Street Justice 89. Postcards from
the Edge 90. Twin Peaks: Fire Walk with Me 92,
etc.

TV series: The Rookies 73–74. Twin Peaks 90.

Opatoshu, David (1918–) (David Opatovsky).
American general-purpose actor, often seen as
villain.

Naked City 48. Exodus 60. Guns of Darkness 63.
Torn Curtain 66. The Defector 67. Enter Laughing
67. Death of a Gunfighter 69. A Walk in the Spring
Rain 78. Masada (TV) 81. Forty Days of Musa Dagh
85, etc.

opera
has never been a successful commodity on the
screen, although many operas have been filmed as
from the stalls, and appear to have succeeded with
minority audiences. The occasional big opera
production such as *Porgy and Bess*, *Pagliacci* or
Carmen Jones, however, can expect to meet with
only moderate success. Opera does, however,
make an excellent background for thrillers
(*Charlie Chan at the Opera*), farces (*A Night at the*

Opera) and melodramas (*Metropolitan*). Opera
singers who have succeeded as film stars include
Grace Moore, Lily Pons, Mario Lanza, Tito Gobbi,
Richard Tauber, Lauritz Melchior, Ezio Pinza and
Gladys Swarthout. Oddly enough the singer Mary
Garden was a big hit in *silent* films.

Ophuls, Marcel (1927–).
French director, son of Max Ophuls; mainly
associated with elaborate documentaries.

Peau de Banane 63. *The Sorrow and the Pity*
(AAN) 69. A Sense of Loss 73. A Memory of
Justice 76. Hotel Terminus: Klaus Barbie, His Life
and Times (AA) 88. The Troubles We've Seen: A
History of Journalism in Wartime (doc) 94, etc.

Ophuls, Max (1902–1957) (Max Oppenheimer).
German director of international highly decorated,
romantic films.
■ Dann Schon Lieber Lebertran 30. Die
Lachenden Erben 31. Die Verliebte Firma 31. Der
Verkaufte Braut 32. *Liebelei* 32. Une Histoire
d'Amour 33. On a Volé un Homme 34. La Signora
Di Tutti 34. Trouble with Money 34. Divine 35. La
Tendre Ennemie 36. Yoshimara 37. Werther 38.
Sans Lendemain 39. De Mayerling à Sarajevo 40.
The Exile 47. *Letter from an Unknown Woman* 48.
Caught 48. *The Reckless Moment* 49. La Ronde 50. Le
Plaisir 51. *Madame De* 53. *Lola Montes* 55.
✪ For elegance of craftsmanship and knowledge
of what the camera can do. *Letter from an Unknown
Woman*.

¶ A shot that does not call for tracks is agony for
  dear old Max. – *James Mason*
  If all the dollies and cranes in the world snap to
attention when his name is mentioned, it is
because he gave camera movement its finest hours
in the history of the cinema. – *Andrew Sarris, 1968*

Oppenheimer, Alan.
Bald American character actor.

In the Heat of the Night 67. Star! 69. The
Groundstar Conspiracy 73. Westworld 73. The
Hindenburg 75. Freaky Friday 76. Record City 78,
etc.

TV series: The Six Million Dollar Man 74–75.
Big Eddie 75. Eischied 79–80.

Oppenheimer, George (1900–1977).
American critic and screenwriter who contributed
to *A Day at the Races* 37.

Broadway Melody of 1940. Two-Faced Woman
41. The War Against Mrs Hadley (AAN) 42.

opticals.
A general term indicating all the visual tricks such
as wipes, dissolves, invisibility, mattes, etc., which
involve laboratory work.

Orbach, Jerry (1935–).
Loose-limbed American actor and musical comedy
star.

The Gang That Couldn't Shoot Straight 72. The
Sentinel 79. Underground Aces 81. Prince of the
City 81. Street Heat (TV) 84. Brewster's Million
84. The Imagemaker 85. F/X 86. Dirty Dancing 87.
I Love N.Y. 87. Someone to Watch over Me 87.
Crimes and Misdemeanors 89. Last Exit to Brooklyn
89. Dead Women in Lingerie 91. Beauty and the
Beast (voice) 91. Delirious 91. Out for Justice 91.
Straight Talk 92. Universal Soldier 92. Mr Saturday
Night 92, etc.

Orchard, Julian (1930–1979).
Lugubrious British revue comedian who enlivened
a number of bit parts.

Crooks Anonymous 58. On the Beat 60. Kill or

Cure 62. The Spy with a Cold Nose 66. Carry On
Doctor 68. Hieronymus Merkin 69. Perfect Friday
70. The Slipper and the Rose 76, many others.

orchestral conductors
have figured as leading men in *Intermezzo*,
Interlude, *Once More with Feeling*, *Unfaithfully
Yours*, *Song of Russia*, *Break of Hearts*, *Prelude to
Fame*, *Counterpoint*; Charles Laughton cut a tragi-
comic figure in *Tales of Manhattan*. Real conductors
who have played dramatic roles in movies include
Leopold Stokowski, José Iturbi and many swing
and jazz figures such as Paul Whiteman, Tommy
Dorsey, Henry Hall, Glenn Miller, Benny
Goodman, Xavier Cugat.

Orczy, Baroness (1865–1947) (Emma Magdalena
Rosalia Marie Josefa Barbara).
Hungarian-born novelist, in London from the age
of 15, and creator of that epitome of the apparently
effete English aristocrat, Sir Percy Blakeney in *The
Scarlet Pimpernel*. Written in 1902, it was turned
into a successful play a year later and published as
a novel in 1905.

Oreste:
see *Kirkop, Oreste.*

oriental roles.
It never seems a good idea, but occidental actors
have often been tempted by the wish to play
Eastern. Among the less fortunate results are Lee
J. Cobb in *Anna and the King of Siam*; John Wayne
in *The Conqueror*; Katharine Hepburn in *Dragon
Seed*; Alec Guinness in *A Majority of One*; Mickey
Rooney in *Breakfast at Tiffany's*; George Raft in
Limehouse Blues; Edward G. Robinson in *The
Hatchet Man*. Those who more or less got away
with it include Robert Donat in *Inn of the Sixth
Happiness*; Boris Karloff in *The Mask of Fu Manchu*;
and Luise Rainer and Paul Muni in *The Good Earth*.

original version.
In European countries, this indicates a foreign
language film which is sub-titled and not dubbed.

Ormond, Julia.
English leading actress, from television.

Young Catherine (TV) 91. Stalin (TV) 92. The
Baby of Macon 93. Nostradamus 94. Captives 94.
Legends of the Fall 94. First Knight 95, etc.

Ornadel, Cyril (1924–).
British composer.

Some May Love 67. Die Screaming Marianne
71. Not Now Darling 72. Brief Encounter (TV) 75,
etc.

TV series: Edward the Seventh 76.

Ornitz, Arthur J. (1916–1985).
American cinematographer.

The Goddess 58. Act One 63. The World of
Henry Orient 64. Charly 68. Me Natalie 68. The
Anderson Tapes 71. Serpico 73. Next Stop
Greenwich Village 76. An Unmarried Woman 78.
Tattoo 81. Hanky Panky 82. The Chosen 82.

O'Rourke, Brefni (1889–1945).
Irish stage actor, an Abbey player, who made some
British films, usually as testy types.

The Ghost of St Michael's 41. Hatter's Castle 41.
The Lamp Still Burns 43. Don't Take It to Heart 44.
I See a Dark Stranger 45, etc.

O'Rourke, Heather (1975–1988).
American child star. Died during emergency
surgery.

Poltergeist 82. Poltergeist II: The Other Side 86. Poltergeist III 88.

TV series: Happy Days 82–83.

Orry-Kelly (1897–1964) (John Orry Kelly).
Australian designer, in Hollywood from 1923 after Broadway experience. For many years with Warner, then with Fox.

The Rich Are Always with Us 32. The Old Maid 39. The Private Lives of Elizabeth and Essex 39. Little Foxes 41. Casablanca 42. Mr Skeffington 44. An American in Paris (AA) 51. Les Girls (AA) 57. Some Like It Hot (AA) 59. Gypsy 62. Irma La Douce 63. The Cool of Day 64, etc.

Orth, Frank (1880–1962).
American small-part actor who must have played more bartenders than he could count.

Hot Money 36. Serenade 39. The Lost Weekend 45. Father of the Bride 50. Here Come the Girls 54, many others.

TV series: The Brothers 56.

Ortolani, Riz (1925–).
Italian composer.

Mondo Cane 63. The Seventh Dawn 64. Woman Times Seven 67. Buona Sera Mrs Campbell 68. The Mackenzie Break 70. Say Hello to Yesterday 71. The Valachi Papers 72. The Fifth Musketeer 77. Cannibal Holocaust 79. House on the Edge of the Park 79. 1919 83. Christopher Columbus (TV) 85. Magnificat 93. The Voyeur (L'Uomo che Guarda) 94, many others.

Orton, Joe (1933–1967).
English playwright of elegant iconoclasm, murdered by his lover, Kenneth Halliwell, who then committed suicide. He was the subject of a biopic, *Prick Up Your Ears* 87, in which he was played by Gary Oldman and Halliwell by Alfred Molina. He also wrote an unproduced screenplay for the Beatles, *Up Against It* 67, which was published in 1979.

Autobiography: 1986, *The Orton Diaries*, edited by John Lahr.

Biography: 1978, *Prick Up Your Ears* by John Lahr.

Entertaining Mr Sloane (oa) 69. Loot (oa) 72.

¶ The whole trouble with Western Society today is the lack of anything worth concealing. – *J.O.*

I'd never realised quite what real stars did. They light up lines and situations in an uncanny way. There's no question of a real star doing a line wrong. One accepts the most lurid interpretation of a role when a great star plays it well. – *J.O.*

Orwell, George (1903–1950) (Eric Blair).
British satirist and novelist whose chief bequests to the cinema are *Animal Farm* and *1984*.

Osborn, Andrew (1912–1985).
British stage and film actor. Latterly BBC TV producer: *Maigret* series, etc.

Who Goes Next? 38. Idol of Paris 48. Dark Interval 50. Angels One Five 51. The Second Mrs Tanqueray 53, etc.

Osborn, Paul (1901–1988).
American dramatist and screenwriter.

The Young in Heart 39. Madame Curie 43. The Yearling 46. East of Eden 55. Homecoming 48. Portrait of Jennie (GB: Jennie) 48. Sayonara (AAN) 57. South Pacific 58. Wild River 60, etc.

Osborne, John (1929–1994).
English dramatist, screenwriter and film producer, a former actor. He was a founder-member of Woodfall Films (qv), begun with director Tony Richardson to film his ground-breaking play *Look Back in Anger*. His wives include actress Mary Ure, critic and writer Penelope Gilliatt, and actress Jill Bennett.

Autobiography: 1981, *A Better Class of Person*; 1991, *Almost a Gentleman*.

Look Back in Anger (oa) 59. The Entertainer (co-w from his play) 60. Tom Jones (w) 63. Inadmissible Evidence (w from his play) 68. Get Carter (a) 71. Tomorrow Never Comes (a) 78.

¶ Some actors are little better than strolling psychopaths. – *J.O.*

Osborne, Vivienne (1900–1961).
American leading lady who left the stage for occasional films but was relegated to supporting roles.

Over the Hill 20. Husband's Holiday 30. Luxury Liner 33. Sailor Be Good 32. Wives Never Know 36. Dragonwyck 46, etc.

'Oscar'.
An affectionate name given to the Academy Award statuette; reputedly because when the figure was first struck in 1927 a secretary said: 'It reminds me of my Uncle Oscar.'

Oscar, Henry (1891–1969) (Henry Wale).
British character actor, on stage from 1911, films from 1932, usually as meek or scheming fellows.

After Dark (debut) 32. I was a Spy 33. The Man Who Knew Too Much 34. Fire over England 37. *The Return of the Scarlet Pimpernel* (as Robespierre) 39. Hatter's Castle 41. They Made Me a Fugitive 47. The Greed of William Hart 48. The Black Rose 50. Private's Progress 55. Foxhole in Cairo 60, etc.

Oscarsson, Per (1927–).
Swedish leading actor.

The Doll 62. Hunger 66. My Sister My Love 66. Who Saw Him Die? 67. Dr Glas 67. A Dandy in Aspic 68. The Last Valley 71. Secrets 72. *The Emigrants* 72. Endless Night 72. Dream City 76. Sleep of Death 79. Hotel Cansino 92, etc.

O'Shea, Michael (1906–1973).
American actor with a 'good guy' personality, who, after circus and vaudeville experience, made several films in the 40s and 50s.

Jack London 42. Striptease Lady 43. The Eve of St Mark 44. It's a Pleasure 45. Circumstantial Evidence 45. The Big Wheel 49. The Model and the Marriage Broker 52. It Should Happen to You 55, etc.

TV series: It's a Great Life 54–55.

O'Shea, Milo (1926–).
Irish character actor, usually in slightly bumbling comic roles.

Never Put It in Writing 64. *Ulysses* (as Bloom) 67. Romeo and Juliet 68. Barbarella 68. The Adding Machine 69. Loot 70. The Angel Levine 70. Arabian Adventure 79. The Pilot 81. The Verdict 82. The Purple Rose of Cairo 84. The Dream Team 88. Only the Lonely 91. The Playboys 92. Murder in the Heartland (TV) 93, etc.

O'Shea, Tessie (1917–).
Amply-proportioned British music-hall singer.

The Shiralee 58. The Russians are Coming, The Russians are Coming 66. The Best House in London 68. Bedknobs and Broomsticks 71.

Oshima, Nagisa (Nagashi) (1932–).
Japanese director.

Ai No Corrida 77. Empire of Passion 79. Merry Christmas Mr Lawrence 83. Max My Love 86. Hollywood Zen 92, etc.

Osmond, Cliff (1937–).
Heavyweight American comedy actor.

Kiss Me Stupid 64. The Fortune Cookie 67. The Front Page 74. Sharks Treasure 75. Guardian of the Wilderness 76. The Great Brain 78. The North Avenue Irregulars 80. Hangar 18 81. The Penitent (d) 88, etc.

O'Steen, Sam (1923–).
American editor and director.

AS EDITOR: Robin and the Seven Hoods 64. Who's Afraid of Virginia Woolf? 66. Cool Hand Luke 67. *The Graduate* 67. Rosemary's Baby 68. Catch 22 70. Carnal Knowledge 71. The Day of the Dolphin 73. Chinatown 74. Hurricane 79. Silkwood 83. Regarding Henry 92. Wolf 94, etc.

■ AS DIRECTOR: A Brand New Life (TV) 73. I Love You Goodbye (TV) 74. Queen of the Stardust Ballroom (TV) 75. High Risk (TV) 76. Look What's Happened to Rosemary's Baby (TV) 76. Sparkle 76. The Best Little Girl in the World (TV) 81. Kids Don't Tell (TV) 85.

O'Sullivan, Maureen (1911–).
Irish leading lady in Hollywood, always in shy, gentle roles. Mother of Mia Farrow.

■ Song of My Heart 30. So This is London 30. Just Imagine 30. The Princess and the Plumber 30. A Connecticut Yankee 31. Skyline 31. *Tarzan the Ape Man* 32 (she was his most famous Jane). The Silver Lining 32. Big Shot 32. Information Kid 32. Strange Interlude 32. Skyscraper Souls 32. Payment Deferred 32. The Fast Companions 32. Robbers Roost 33. The Cohens and Kellys in Trouble 33. Tugboat Annie 33. Stage Mother 33. Tarzan and His Mate 34. The Thin Man 34. *The Barretts of Wimpole Street* 34. Hideout 34. West Point of the Air 34. David Copperfield 34. Cardinal Richelieu 35. The Flame Within 35. Anna Karenina 35. Woman Wanted 35. The Bishop Misbehaves 35. Tarzan Escapes 36. The Voice of Bugle Ann 36. The Devil Doll 36. A Day at the Races 37. Between Two Women 37. The Emperor's Candlesticks 37. My Dear Miss Aldrich 37. A Yank at Oxford 38. Hold that Kiss 38. The Crowd Roars 38. Port of Seven Seas 38. Spring Madness 38. Let Us Live 38. Tarzan Finds a Son 39. *Pride and Prejudice* 40. Sporting Blood 40. Maisie was a Lady 41. Tarzan's Secret Treasure 41. Tarzan's New York Adventure 42. The Big Clock 48. Where Danger Lives 50. Bonzo Goes to College 52. All I Desire 53. Mission Over Korea 53. Duffy of San Quentin 54. The Steel Cage 54. The Tall T 57. Wild Heritage 58. *Never Too Late* 65. The Phynx 69. The Crooked Hearts (TV) 72. The Great Houdinis (TV) 76. Hannah and her Sisters 85. Peggy Sue Got Married 86.

O'Sullivan, Richard (1944–).
British light leading man, formerly child actor, prominent on TV.

The Stranger's Hand 53. Dangerous Exile 56. A Story of David 60. The Young Ones 61. Wonderful Life 64. Father Dear Father 73. A Man About the House 74, etc.

TV series: *A Man About the House* 73–76. Robin's Nest 77–80. Dick Turpin 78–79.

Oswald, Gerd (1916–1989).
German-American director, son of Richard Oswald.

■ A Kiss before Dying 56. The Brass Legend 57. Crime of Passion 57. Fury at Sundown 57. Valerie 57. Paris Holiday 57. Screaming Mimi 58. Am Tag Als Der Regen Kam 59. Three Moves to Freedom 60. Tempesta Su Ceylon 63. Agent for H.A.R.M.

6. 80 Steps to Jonah 69. Bunny O'Hare 71. To he Bitter End 75.

Oswald, Richard (1880–1963) (R. Ornstein). German director, father of Gerd Oswald.

Pagu 16. Round the World in Eighty Days 19. Victoria and Her Hussar 31. Der Hauptmann von Köpenick 32. I Was a Criminal (US) 41. Isle of Missing Men (US) 42. The Lovable Cheat (US) 9, etc.

Oswald the Rabbit.
Cute cartoon star who survived the transition from silent to talking pictures. Originated by Walt Disney, he was taken over by Universal Pictures and animator Walter Lantz from 1929 and appeared in many cartoons until 1938. He was voiced by Mickey Rooney and Bernice Hansen. His finest moment was an appearance in 1930 in *The King of Jazz* with bandleader Paul Whiteman.

Othello.
Shakespeare's tragedy of a jealous lover was filmed many times as a silent and on three notable occasions in more recent times. Orson Welles starred in and directed an uneven version in 1952, which was beset by financial problems and inspired a hilarious account of its travails, *Put Money in Thy Purse*, by Michael MacLiammoir, who played Iago. Sergei Yutkevich made a Russian version in 1955, starring Sergei Bondachuk, and Laurence Olivier's astonishing National Theatre performance as a West Indian Othello, with Maggie Smith as Desdemona and Frank Finlay as Iago, was preserved in Stuart Burge's unsatisfactory screen version in 1965. A musical version, *Catch My Soul*, was filmed in 1972, and murderous actors playing the role of Othello have also turned up in *Men Are Not Gods* 36, directed by Walter Reisch and starring Sebastian Shaw, and *A Double Life* 47, directed by George Cukor and starring Ronald Colman. Basil Dearden's *All Night Long* 61 updated the play as a tale of a jealous jazz musician (Patrick McGoohan), and a western, *Jubal* 56, had Ernest Borgnine as a jealous rancher being urged to commit murder by Rod Steiger.

Otomo, Katsuhiro (1954–   ).
Japanese director, screenwriter, graphic novelist and artist.

Akira 87. World Apartment Horror 91.

O'Toole, Annette (1953–   ).
American leading lady.

The Girl Most Likely To (TV) 73. Smile 75. The Entertainer (TV) 76. One on One 77. The War between the Tates (TV) 77. King of the Gypsies 78. Foolin' Around 80. Cat People 82. 48 Hours 82. Superman III 83. Best Legs in the 8th Grade 84. Copacabana (TV) 85. Cross My Heart 87. The Kennedys of Massachusetts (TV) 90. Love at Large 90. It (TV) 90. Imaginary Crimes 94, etc.

O'Toole, Peter (1932–   ).
British leading man who after stage and TV experience had a fairly meteoric rise to stardom in films.

Autobiography: 1993, *Loitering with Intent*.
Biography: 1983, by Michael Freedland.
■ Kidnapped (debut) 59. Savage Innocents 59. The Day They Robbed the Bank of England 60. Lawrence of Arabia (AAN) 62. Becket (AAN) 64. Lord Jim 65. What's New, Pussycat? 65. How to Steal a Million 66. The Night of the Generals 66. The Bible 66. Casino Royale 66. Great Catherine 67. The Lion in Winter (AAN) 68. Goodbye Mr Chips (AAN) 69. Country Dance 70. Murphy's War 70. Under Milk Wood 71. The Ruling Class (AAN) 71.

Man of la Mancha 72. Rosebud 75. Man Friday 75. Foxtrot 75. Rogue Male (TV) 76. Caligula 77. Power Play 78. Zulu Dawn 79. Masada (TV) 80. Strumpet City (TV) 80. *The Stunt Man* (AAN) 80. *My Favorite Year* (AAN) 82. Svengali (TV) 82. Superman III 83. Supergirl 84. Buried Alive 84. Kim (TV) 84. Creator 84. Club Paradise 86. The Last Emperor 87. High Spirits 88. In Una Notte di Chiaro di Luna 89. Crossing to Freedom (TV) 90. The Nutcracker Prince (voice) 90. Wings of Fame 90. Isabelle Eberhardt 91. King Ralph 91. Rebecca's Daughters 91. The Seventh Coin 93.

¶ For me, life has been either a wake or a wedding. – *P.O'T.*
I can't stand light. I hate weather. My idea of heaven is moving from one smoke-filled room to another. – *P.O'T.*
Sobriety's a real turn-on for me. You can see what you're doing. – *P.O'T.*
The very prototype of the ham. – *Omar Sharif*

Ott, Fred (1860–1936).
American laboratory assistant, allegedly the first man ever to act for the cinema when he sneezed in close-up for Edison in 1893.

Ottiano, Rafaela (1894–1942).
Italian-born stage actress who went to Hollywood and played sinister housekeepers, etc.

As You Desire Me 32. Grand Hotel 32. She Done Him Wrong 33. Great Expectations 34. Maytime 37. Topper Returns 41, etc.

Ouédraogo, Idrissa (1954–   ).
African director and screenwriter, born in Burkina Faso. He studied film at the African Institute of Cinematography, and in Kiev and Paris.

The Choice (Yam Daabo) 86. Yaaba 89. Tilai 90. Karim and Sala (A Karim Na Sala) (TV) 91. Samba Traoré 93. Le Cri de Coeur 94.

Ouida (1839–1908) (Marie Louise de la Ramée).
Anglo-French novelist. *Under Two Flags* in 1936 was the last of her romances to be filmed, but several were used in silent days.

Oulton, Brian (1908–1992).
British stage and film comedy actor, usually in unctuous or prim roles.

Too Many Husbands 39. Miranda 48. Last Holiday 50. Castle in the Air 52. The Million Pound Note 54. Private's Progress 55. Happy is the Bride 57. The Thirty-Nine Steps 59. A French Mistress 60. Kiss of the Vampire 62. Carry on Cleo 64. The Intelligence Men 64. Carry on Camping 69. On the Buses 71. Ooh You are Awful 72.

'Our Gang'.
A collection of child actors first gathered together in short slapstick comedies by producer Hal Roach in the mid-20s. They remained popular through the 30s and 40s, though the personnel of the team naturally changed. The originals included 'Fat' Joe Cobb, Jackie Condon, Mickey Daniels, Mary Kornman and Ernie 'Sunshine Sammy' Morrison, said to be the highest-paid member at $12 a week in 1927. Later cast members, joining in the late 20s, were Matthew 'Stymie' Beard, Norman 'Chubby' Chaney, Jackie Cooper, Johnny Downs and Bobby 'Wheezer' Hutchins, who were followed by, among others, Scotty Beckett, Tommy 'Butch' Bond, Dorothy De Borba, Mary Anne Jackson, Darla Hood, Dickie Moore, Carl 'Alfalfa' Switzer, Billy 'Buckwheat' Thomas and Spanky McFarland (qqv), who became leader of the gang in the early 30s. Roach sold the series to MGM in 1938 and production continued until 1944. Many

of Roach's Our Gang shorts have appeared on television and have been released on video under the title 'The Little Rascals', since MGM hold copyright in the original name. One, *Bored of Education*, won an Oscar in 1936 and a feature, *General Spanky*, directed by Fred Newmeyer, was made in 1938. More than 90 of their short films were restored for television showing in the 90s, and Steven Spielberg produced a new feature film, *The Little Rascals*, based on the series, in 1994, directed by Penelope Spheeris.

Book 1977: *Our Gang* by Leonard Maltin.

Oury, Gérard (1919–   ) (Max-Gerald Tannenbaum).
Dapper French character actor, now director.

Antoine et Antoinette 46. La Belle que Voilà 49. Sea Devils (GB) 52. *Father Brown* (GB) 54. House of Secrets (GB) 56. *The Journey* (US) 58. The Mirror Has Two Faces 59, etc.
■ AS DIRECTOR: La Main Chaude 60. *The Sucker* (Le Corniaud) 64. The Big Spree 66. The Brain 69. Adventures of Rabbi Jacob 72. Carapate 78. Le Coup de Parapluie 80 (GB: The Umbrella Coup) 80). Ace of Aces 82. The Vengeance of the Winged Serpent 84. Levy and Goliath 86. Vanille Fraise 89. Le Grippe Sou 92. La Soif de l'Or 93.

Ouspenskaya, Maria (1876–1949).
Distinguished, diminutive Russian character actress who enlivened some Hollywood films after the mid-30s.
■ Dodsworth (AAN) 36. Conquest 37. *Love Affair* (AAN) 39. *The Rains Came* 39. Judge Hardy and Son 39. Dr Ehrlich's Magic Bullet 40. Waterloo Bridge 40. The Mortal Storm 40. The Man I Married 40. Dance Girl Dance 40. Beyond Tomorrow 40. *The Wolf Man* 41. The Shanghai Gesture 41. *King's Row* 42. The Mystery of Marie Roget 42. Frankenstein Meets the Wolf Man 43. Tarzan and the Amazons 45. I've Always Loved You 46. Wyoming 47. A Kiss in the Dark 49.

Famous line (*The Wolf Man*):
'Even the man who is pure in heart
And says his prayers by night
May become a wolf when the wolf-bane blooms
And the moon is clear and bright.'

Overman, Lynne (1887–1943).
American character actor with stage experience. Memorable in cynical comedy roles for his relaxed manner and sing-song voice.
■ Midnight 34. Little Miss Marker 34. The Great Flirtation 34. She Loves Me Not 34. You Belong to Me 34. Broadway Bill 34. Enter Madame 34. Rumba 35. Paris in Spring 35. Men without Names 35. Two for Tonight 35. Collegiate 35. Poppy 36. Yours for the Asking 36. Three Married Men 36. The Jungle Princess 36. Blonde Trouble 37. Partners in Crime 37. Nobody's Baby 37. Don't Tell the Wife 37. Murder Goes to College 37. Wild Money 37. Hotel Haywire 37. Night Club Scandal 37. True Confession 37. The Big Broadcast of 1938. Her Jungle Love 38. Hunted Men 38. Spawn of the North 38. Sons of the Legion 38. Men with Wings 38. Ride a Crooked Mile 38. Persons in Hiding 39. Death of a Champion 39. Union Pacific 39. Edison the Man 40. Typhoon 40. Safari 40. Northwest Mounted Police 40. Aloma of the South Seas 41. Caught in the Draft 41. New York Town 41. The Hard Boiled Canary 41. *Roxie Hart* 42. Reap the Wild Wind 42. The Forest Rangers 42. The Silver Queen 42. Star Spangled Rhythm 42. *Dixie* 43. The Desert Song 43.

Ovitz, Michael (1946–   ).
American agent, chairman of CAA (Creative

Artists Agency) and frequently said to be the most influential person in Hollywood.

Owen, Bill (1914–) (Bill Rowbotham).
British character comedian, former dance-band musician and singer.

The Way to the Stars (debut) 45. When the Bough Breaks 47. The Girl Who Couldn't Quite 49. Trottie True 49. Hotel Sahara 51. The Square Ring 53. The Rainbow Jacket 54. Davy 57. Carve Her Name with Pride 58. The Hellfire Club 61. The Secret of Blood Island 65. Georgy Girl 66. O Lucky Man 72. In Celebration 74. The Comeback 78. Laughterhouse (US: Singleton's Pluck) 84, etc.

TV series: Last of the Summer Wine 74– .

Owen, Cliff (1919–).
British director, in films from 1937.

Offbeat 61. A Prize of Arms 62. The Wrong Arm of the Law 63. A Man Could Get Killed 66. That Riviera Touch 66. The Magnificent Two 67. Steptoe and Son 72. Ooh You Are Awful 72. No Sex Please We're British 73. The Bawdy Adventures of Tom Jones 76. Get Charlie Tully 76, etc.

Owen, Reginald (1887–1972).
British character actor, on stage from 1905, films (in Hollywood) from 1929.

The Letter (debut) 29. Platinum Blonde 32. Queen Christina 33. Call of the Wild 35. Anna Karenina 35. The Great Ziegfeld 36. A Tale of Two Cities 36. *Trouble for Two* 36. Conquest 37. The Earl of Chicago 39. Florian 40. Charley's Aunt 41.

Tarzan's Secret Treasure 41. *Mrs Miniver* 42. Random Harvest 42. White Cargo 42. Madame Curie 43. Lassie Come Home 43. The Canterville Ghost 44. *Kitty* 45. The Diary of a Chambermaid 45. Cluny Brown 46. If Winter Comes 47. The Three Musketeers 48. The Miniver Story 50. Kim 51. Red Garters 54. The Young Invaders 58. Voice of the Hurricane (MRA film) 63. Mary Poppins 64. Rosie 68. Bedknobs and Broomsticks 71, many others.

Owen, Seena (1894–1966) (Signe Auen).
American silent-screen leading lady.

Intolerance 16. The Sheriff's Son 19. Victory 19. Shipwrecked 23. Flame of the Yukon 25. The Rush Hour 28. Marriage Playground 29, many others.

Owen, Yvonne (1923–).
British actress of the 40s, wife of Alan Badel.

The Seventh Veil 45. Girl in a Million 46. Holiday Camp 47. My Brother's Keeper 48. Quartet 48. Marry Me 49. Someone at the Door 50, etc.

Owens, Patricia (1925–).
Canadian leading lady who made films in Britain and America.

Miss London Ltd 43. While the Sun Shines 46. The Happiest Days of Your Life 49. Mystery Junction 52. The Good Die Young 53. Windfall 55. Island in the Sun 56. Sayonara (US) 57. *No Down Payment* (US) 57. The Fly (US) 58. Five Gates to Hell (US) 59. Hell to Eternity (US) 60. Seven

Women from Hell 62. Black Spurs 65. The Destructors 67, etc.

Oxley, David (c. 1929–).
British actor.

Ill Met by Moonlight 57. Saint Joan 58. Yesterday's Enemy 58. The Hound of the Baskervilles 59. Life at the Top 64. House of the Living Dead 78, etc.

Oz, Frank (1944–) (Frank Oznowicz).
American director. He began as a puppeteer on the TV series *Sesame Street* and *The Muppet Show*, where he supplied the voices of Fozzie Bear, Miss Piggy and Sam the Eagle, among other characters before becoming a director.

The Dark Crystal (co-d) 82. The Muppets Take Manhattan 84. Little Shop of Horrors 86. Dirty Rotten Scoundrels 88. What about Bob? 91. Housesitter 92, etc.

TV series: The Muppet Show 76–81.

Ozep, Fedor (1893–1949).
Russian director. He was married to actress Anna Sten.

The Crime of Dmitri Karamazov 31. The Living Dead 33. Amok 34. Gibraltar 38. She Who Dares (US) 44. Whispering City (Can.) 48, etc.

Ozu, Yasujiro (1903–1963).
Japanese director, since 1927.

Biography: 1974, *Ozu* by Donald Ritchie.

A Story of Floating Weeds 34. Late Spring 49. Early Summer 51. Tokyo Story 53. Early Spring 56 Late Autumn 61. Early Autumn 62, etc.

P

Pabst, G. W. (1885–1967) (George Wilhelm). Distinguished German director who usually tackled pessimistic themes.

■ Der Schatz 23. Gräfin Donelli 24. *Joyless Street* 25. *Secrets of a Soul* 26. Man Spielt Nicht mit der Liebe 26. *The Love of Jeanne Ney* 27. *Pandora's Box* 28. Abwege 28. *Diary of a Lost Girl* 29. The White Hell of Pitz Palu (co-d) 29. *Westfront 1918* 30. *The Threepenny Opera* (*Die Dreigroschenoper*) 31. *Kameradschaft* 31. L'Atlantide 32. Don Quixote 33. A Modern Hero (US) 34. De Haut en Bas 34. Mademoiselle Docteur 37. Le Drama de Shanghai 39. Mädchen in Uniform 39. Komödianten 41. Paracelsus 43. Der Fall Molander 45. Der Prozess 48. Geheimnisvolle Tiefen 49. The Voice of Silence 52. Cose da Pazzi 53. *Ten Days to Die* 54. Das Bekenntnis der Ina Kahr 54. Jackboot Mutiny 55. The Last Act 55. Roses for Bettina 56. Durch die Wälder 56.

Pace, Judy (1946–).
American leading lady of the 70s.
Three in the Attic 68. Up in the Cellar 70. Cool Breeze 72. Frogs 72, etc.

Pacino, Al (1940–) (Alfredo Pacino).
American leading actor, of New York/Sicilian descent.
Biography: 1992, *Al Pacino: A Life on the Wire* by Andrew Yule.
■ Me Natalie 68. The Panic in Needle Park 71. *The Godfather* (AAN) 72. Scarecrow 73. Serpico (AAN) 73. The Godfather Part II 74. *Dog Day Afternoon* (AAN) 75. Bobby Deerfield 77. And Justice for All (AAN) 79. Cruising 80. Author! Author! 82. Scarface 83. Revolution 86. Sea of Love 89. Dick Tracy (AAN) 90. The Godfather Part III 90. Frankie & Johnny 91. Scent of a Woman (AA) 92. Glengarry Glen Ross (AAN) 92. Carlito's Way 93.

Pack, Charles Lloyd:
see *Lloyd Pack, Charles*.

Pack, Roger Lloyd:
see *Lloyd Pack, Roger*.

Pacula, Joanna (1957–).
Polish actress in international films.
Gorky Park 83. Not Quite Jerusalem (aka Not Quite Paradise) 86. Death before Dishonor 87. Options 88. Sweet Lies 88. The Kiss 88. Marked for Death 90. Husbands and Lovers 91. Black Ice 92. Warlock: The Armageddon 93. Tombstone 94. Kim Novak Is on the Phone (It.) 94. The Silence of the Hams (It.) 94, etc.

Paderewski, Ignace (1860–1941).
Polish prime minister and classical pianist. Appeared in a few films including the British *Moonlight Sonata* 37.

Padovani, Lea (1920–1991).
Italian leading actress, in films from 1945.
Give Us This Day (GB) 49. Three Steps North (US)

51. Tempi Nostri 53. Montparnasse 19 57. The Naked Maja (US) 58. Candy 68, etc.

Pagano, Bartolomeo (1888–1947).
Italian actor who originated the role of strongman Maciste (qv).

Page, Anthony (1935–).
British director, with stage experience.
■ *Inadmissible Evidence* 68. Alpha Beta 73. Pueblo (TV) 73. *The Missiles of October* (TV) 74. Collision Course (TV) 76. F. Scott Fitzgerald in Hollywood (TV) 76. I Never Promised You a Rose Garden 77. The Lady Vanishes 79. The Patricia Neal Story (TV) 81. Grace Kelly (TV) 83. Forbidden (TV) 85. Second Serve (TV) 85. Monte Carlo (TV) 86. Pack of Lies (TV) 87. Absolution 88. Scandal in a Small Town (TV) 88. The Nightmare Years (TV) 89. Chernobyl: The Final Warning (TV) 91. Silent Cries (TV) 93.

Page, Gale (1911–1983) (Sally Rutter).
American leading lady.
Four Daughters 38. Crime School 38. Daughters Courageous 39. They Drive by Night 40. Four Wives 40. Four Mothers 41. The Time of Your Life 48. About Mrs Leslie 54, etc.

Page, Genevieve (1931–) (G. Bonjean).
French leading lady who has made American films.
Foreign Intrigue 56. Trapped in Tangiers 60. Song without End 60. El Cid 61. L'Honorable Stanislas 63. Youngblood Hawke 64. Les Corsaires 65. Belle de Jour 67. Decline and Fall 68. The Private Life of Sherlock Holmes 70. Beyond Therapy 87. Aria 88. Stranger in the House (L'Inconnu dans la Maison) 92, etc.

Page, Geraldine (1924–1987).
American leading actress, on stage from 1940.
■ Taxi 53. Hondo (AAN) 54. *Summer and Smoke* (AAN) 61. Sweet Bird of Youth (AAN) 62. Toys in the Attic 63. *Dear Heart* 65. The Happiest Millionaire 67. You're a Big Boy Now (AAN) 67. Monday's Child (Arg.) 67. Trilogy (TV) 69. Whatever Happened to Aunt Alice? 69. The Beguiled 71. Pete 'n' Tillie (AAN) 72. J. W. Coop 73. The Day of the Locust 75. Nasty Habits 76. Something for Joey (TV) 77. Interiors (AAN, BFA) 78. Honky Tonk Freeway 81. Harry's War 81. I'm Dancing as Fast as I Can 82. The Pope of Greenwich Village (AAN) 84. White Nights 85. The Trip to Bountiful (AA) 85. The Bride 85. Nazi Hunter (TV) 86.

Page, Patti (1927–) (Clara Ann Fowler).
American TV singer.
■ Elmer Gantry 60. Dondi 61. Boys' Night Out 63.

Paget, Debra (1933–) (Debralee Griffin).
American leading lady with brief stage experience.
Cry of the City 48. House of Strangers 49. Broken Arrow 50. Les Misérables 52. Prince Valiant 54. Love Me Tender 56. From the Earth to the Moon 58. Tales of Terror 62. The Haunted Palace 64, many others.

Pagett, Nicola (1945–) (Nicola Scott).
British leading lady of the 70s, much on TV.
Frankenstein, the True Story (TV) 73. Operation Daybreak 76. Oliver's Story 79. Privates on Parade 83. All of You 86. Scoop (TV) 87.

Pagnol, Marcel (1894–1974).
French writer-director noted for sprawling comedy dramas which strongly evoke country life without being very cinematic.
Autobiographies: 1960, *The Days Were Too Short*. 1962, *The Time of Secrets*.
Marius (script only) 31. *Fanny* (script only) 32. *César* 34. Joffroi 34. Regain (Harvest) 37. *La Femme du Boulanger* 38. *La Fille du Puisatier* 40. La Belle Meunière 48. Manon des Sources 53. Lettres de Mon Moulin 55. Jean de Florette (oa) 86. Manon des Sources (oa) 86. My Mother's Castle (Le Château de Ma Mère) (oa) 90. My Father's Glory (La Gloire de Mon Père) (oa) 90, etc.

¶ The cinema and I were born on the same day, in the same place. – *M.P.*

Paige, Janis (1922–) (Donna Mac Jaden).
American leading lady with operatic training.
Hollywood Canteen (debut) 44. Cheyenne 46. Romance on the High Seas 48. Mr Universe 51. Remains to be Seen 53. Silk Stockings 57. Please Don't Eat the Daisies 60. The Caretakers 63. Welcome to Hard Times 67. Gibbsville (TV) 75. Lanigan's Rabbi (TV) 76. Angel on My Shoulder (TV) 80, etc.
TV series: It's Always Jan 56. Lanigan's Rabbi 77. Gun Shy 83. Baby Makes Five 83. Trapper John MD 85–86.

Paige, Mabel (1880–1954).
American character actress.
My Heart Belongs to Daddy 42. *Lucky Jordan* 43. The Good Fellows 43. *Someone to Remember* (lead role) 43. If You Knew Susie 48. The Sniper 52. Houdini 53, etc.

Paige, Robert (1910–1987) (John Arthur Page).
American leading man, former radio announcer, in many films of the 40s, little thereafter.
Cain and Mabel 37. Hellzapoppin 41. Shady Lady 42. Son of Dracula 43. Can't Help Singing 44. Red Stallion 47. The Flame 48. Raging Waters 51. Abbott and Costello Go to Mars 53. The Big Payoff 58. The Marriage Go Round 61. Bye Bye Birdie 63, etc.
TV series: Run Buddy Run 66.

Painlevé, Jean (1902–1989).
French documentarist, famous for short naturalist studies of sea horses, sea urchins, shrimps, etc.

painters
have frequently had their lives glamorized to provide film-makers with drama to counterpoint art. Among the most notable are Charles Laughton as *Rembrandt*, George Sanders as Gauguin in *The Moon and Sixpence*, José Ferrer as Toulouse-Lautrec in *Moulin Rouge*, Anthony Franciosa as Goya in

The Naked Maja, Kirk Douglas as Van Gogh and Anthony Quinn as Gauguin in *Lust for Life*, Gerard Philipe as Modigliani in *Montparnasse 19*, Cecil Kellaway as Gainsborough in *Kitty*, Charlton Heston as Michelangelo in *The Agony and the Ecstasy*, and Mel Ferrer as *El Greco*.

Paiva, Nestor (1905–1966).
American character actor of assorted foreign peasant types.

Ride a Crooked Mile 38. The Marines Fly High 40. The Falcon in Mexico 44. Fear 46. Road to Rio 46. Five Fingers 52. The Creature from the Black Lagoon 54. The Deep Six 57. The Nine Lives of Elfego Baca 59. The Spirit Is Willing 66, many others.

Pakula, Alan J. (1928–).
American producer who turned director.
■ AS PRODUCER: Fear Strikes Out 57. To Kill a Mockingbird (AAN) 63. Love with the Proper Stranger 63. Baby the Rain Must Fall 65. Inside Daisy Clover 66. Up the Down Staircase 67. The Stalking Moon 68. The Nickel Ride 74. Kiss Me Goodbye 82.
■ AS PRODUCER-DIRECTOR: The Sterile Cuckoo 69. *Klute* 71. Love, Pain and the Whole Damn Thing 73. The Parallax View 74. *All The President's Men* (AAN) 76. Comes A Horseman 78. Starting Over 80. Rollover (d only) 81. Sophie's Choice (wd only) (AANw) 82. Dream Lover 85. Orphans 87. See You in the Morning (wd, p) 89. Presumed Innocent (d) 90. Consenting Adults 92. The Pelican Brief (wd) 93.

Pal, George (1908–1980).
Hungarian puppeteer whose short advertising films enlivened programmes in the late 30s; went to Hollywood 1940 and produced series of 'Puppetoons'; later produced many adventure films involving trick photography. Special Academy Award 1943 'for the development of novel methods and techniques'.
Destination Moon (AA) 50. *When Worlds Collide* (AA) 51. *The War of the Worlds* (AA) 53. The Naked Jungle 55. *Tom Thumb* (AA) (& d) 58. *The Time Machine* (AA) (& d) 60. The Wonderful World of the Brothers Grimm 63. The Power 68.

Palance, Jack (1920–) (Walter Palanuik).
Gaunt American leading man with stage experience; started in films playing villains.
Panic in the Streets 50. Halls of Montezuma 51. Sudden Fear (AAN) 52. *Shane* (AAN) 53. Sign of the Pagan 54. *The Big Knife* 55. I Died a Thousand Times 55. Attack 56. The Man Inside 57. The Lonely Man 57. House of Numbers 57. Ten Seconds to Hell 58. The Mongols 60. Barabbas 62. Warriors Five 62. Le Mépris 63. Once a Thief 65. The Professionals 66. The Torture Garden (GB) 67. Kill a Dragon 67. A Professional Gun 68. Che! 69. The Desperados 69. They Came to Rob Las Vegas 69. The Companeros 70. Monte Walsh 70. The McMasters 70. The Horsemen 72. Chato's Land 72. Oklahoma Crude 73. Dracula (TV) 73. Craze 73. The Four Deuces 75. God's Gun 77. Mr Scarface 77. One Man Jury 78. The Shape of Things to Come (TV) 79. Hawk the Slayer 80. Without Warning 80. Alone in the Dark 82. Gor 87. Bagdad Café 88. Young Guns 88. Outlaw of Gor 88. Batman 89. Tango & Cash 89. Solar Crisis 90. *City Slickers* (AA) 91. Cops and Robbersons 94. City Slickers II 94, etc.
TV series: The Greatest Show on Earth 63. Bronk 75. Believe It or Not 82–86.

Palcy, Euzhan (1955–).
Martinique director and screenwriter, a former editor and camera operator.

La Rue Cases Nègres (Sugar Cane Alley) 83. A Dry White Season 89. Simeon (co-w, d) 93.

The Paleface.
Bob Hope's western romp with Jane Russell as Calamity Jane, directed by Norman Z. McLeod in 1948, was followed by an even crazier extravaganza, *Son of Paleface*, which also featured Roy Rogers. In 1968 the original was revamped for Don Knotts as *The Shakiest Gun in the West*.

Palin, Michael (1943–).
British light actor and screenwriter, a former member of the Monty Python team.
■ And Now for Something Completely Different (& co-w) 72. Monty Python and the Holy Grail (& co-w) 74. Monty Python's Life of Brian (& co-w) 79. The Missionary (& w, p) 81. Time Bandits (& co-w) 81. Monty Python's The Meaning of Life (& co-w) 83. A Private Function 84. Brazil 85. Consuming Passions (oa) 88. A Fish Called Wanda 88. American Friends (& co-w) 91.
TV series: Palin's Column 94.

Pallette, Eugene (1889–1954).
Rotund, gravel-voiced American character actor, at his peak as an exasperated father or executive in the 30s and 40s.

Intolerance 16. Alias Jimmy Valentine 20. The Three Musketeers 21. To the Last Man 23. Light of the Western Stars 25. Lights of New York 28. The Canary Murder Case 29. The Sea God 30. It Pays to Advertise 31. Shanghai Express 32. The Kennel Murder Case 33. Bordertown 34. Steamboat Round the Bend 35. *The Ghost Goes West* 36. *My Man Godfrey* 36. One Hundred Men and a Girl 37. Topper 37. *The Adventures of Robin Hood* (as Friar Tuck) 38. Mr Smith Goes to Washington 39. The Mark of Zorro 40. The Lady Eve 41. Tales of Manhattan 42. It Ain't Hay 43. Heaven Can Wait 43. Step Lively 44. Lake Placid Serenade 45. In Old Sacramento 46, many others.

Pallos, Stephen (1902–).
Hungarian producer who worked with Korda in England from 1942, later as independent.
Call of the Blood 46. The Golden Madonna 48. Jet Storm 59. Foxhole in Cairo 60. A Jolly Bad Fellow 64. Where the Spies Are 65, many others.

Palmer, Betsy (1929–) (Patricia Brumek).
American light actress and TV panellist.
The Long Gray Line 55. Queen Bee 55. The Tin Star 57. The Last Angry Man 59. It Happened to Jane 59. Friday the Thirteenth 80. Friday the Thirteenth Part II 81. Goddess of Love (TV) 88, etc.
TV series: Number 96 80–81. Knots Landing 89–90.

Palmer, Ernest (1885–1978).
American cinematographer.
Ivanhoe 12. Lothar 17. Ladies Must Live 21. The Wanters 23. The Kiss Barrier 25. The Palace of Pleasure 26. Seventh Heaven 27. The River 29. City Girl 30. A Connecticut Yankee 31. The Painted Woman 32. Cavalcade 33. Berkeley Square 33. Music in the Air 34. Charlie Chan in Paris 35. Banjo on My Knee 36. Slave Ship 37. Four Men and a Prayer 38. News is Made at Night 39. The Great Profile 40. Blood and Sand (AA) 41. Song of the Islands 42. Coney Island 43. Pin Up Girl 44. The Dolly Sisters 45. Centennial Summer 46. I Wonder Who's Kissing Her Now? 47. Broken Arrow 50, many others.

Palmer, Ernest (1901–1964).
British cinematographer who began as an office boy and a laboratory assistant. He worked at Elstree

in the 30s and at Ealing Studios in the early 40s and later in television, shooting *The Adventures of Sir Lancelot* 56–57.
Kiss Me Sergeant 30. What a Night! 31. Innocents of Chicago 32. Old Spanish Customers 32. The River Wolves 33. Music Hall 34. Birds of a Feather 35. The Man behind the Mask 36. The Edge of the World 37. Save a Little Sunshine 38. The Spider 39. He Found a Star 41. The Goose Steps Out 42. San Demetrio London 43. Return of the Vikings 44. 29 Acacia Avenue 45. The Lisbon Story 46. The Ghosts of Berkeley Square 47. School for Randle 49. Over the Garden Wall 50. It's a Grand Life 53. The Heart Within 57. The Crowning Touch 58, etc.

Palmer, Gregg (1927–) (Palmer Lee).
American 'second lead', former disc jockey.
Son of Ali Baba 51. Veils of Baghdad 53. Magnificent Obsession 54. The Creature Walks among Us 56. Forty Pounds of Trouble 62. The Undefeated 69. Big Jake 71. The Shootist 76, etc.

Palmer, Lilli (1911–1986) (Lilli Peiser).
Austrian leading actress, on stage from childhood, in films from teenage years.
Autobiography: 1975, *Change Lobsters and Dance.*
Crime Unlimited (GB) 34. Good Morning, Boys (GB) 36. Secret Agent (GB) 36. A Girl Must Live (GB) 38. The Door with Seven Locks (GB) 40. *Thunder Rock* (GB) 42. The Gentle Sex (GB) 43. English without Tears (GB) 44. *The Rake's Progress* (GB) 45. Beware of Pity (GB) 46. Cloak and Dagger (US) 46. My Girl Tisa (US) 47. Body and Soul (US) 48. No Minor Vices (US) 48. The Long Dark Hall (GB) 51. The Fourposter (US) 52. Is Anna Anderson Anastasia? (Ger.) 56. La Vie à Deux (Fr.) 58. But Not for Me (US) 58. Conspiracy of Hearts (GB) 60. Rendezvous at Midnight (Fr.) 60. *The Pleasure of His Company* (US) 61. The Counterfeit Traitor (US) 62. Adorable Julia (Ger.) 63. The Flight of the White Stallions (US) 64. Operation Crossbow (GB) 65. Moll Flanders (GB) 65. Sebastian (GB) 67. Oedipus the King (GB) 67. Nobody Runs Forever (GB) 68. The Dance of Death (Swed.) 68. De Sade (US) 69. Hard Contract (US) 69. Murders in the Rue Morgue (GB) 71. Night Hair Child (GB) 71. The Boys from Brazil 78. The Holcroft Covenant 85. Peter the Great (TV) 86, many others.
TV series: Lilli Palmer Theatre 54. Zoo Gang 73.

Palmer, Maria (1924–1981).
Austrian leading lady. Wide stage experience at home, TV and films in America.
Mission to Moscow 42. Lady on a Train 44. Rendezvous 24 46. Slightly Dishonourable 51. Three for Jamie Dawn 56, many others.

Palmer, Peter (1931–).
American actor-singer who repeated his stage role as *Li'l Abner* 59.
Deep Space 87.
TV series: Custer 67. The Kallikaks 77.

Palminteri, Chazz (Calogero Palminteri).
American actor and dramatist.
Oscar 91. *A Bronx Tale* (& w from his play) 93. Bullets over Broadway 94. The Perez Family 94.

Paluzzi, Luciana (1939–).
Italian leading lady in international films.
Three Coins in the Fountain 54. Sea Fury 58. Thunderball 65. The Venetian Affair 66. Chuka 67. 99 Women 69. The Green Slime 69. Black Gunn 72. War Goddess 74. The Klansman 74. The Greek Tycoon 78, etc.
TV series: Five Fingers 59.

Pampanini, Silvana (1927–).
Voluptuous Italian leading lady of such 50s frolics as *Scandal in the Roman Bath*.

pan.
A shot in which the camera rotates horizontally. Also used as a verb.

Pan, Hermes (1905–1990) (H. Panagiotopolous).
American dance director.

Top Hat 35. *Swing Time* 36. *Damsel in Distress* (AA) 37. *Let's Dance* 50. *Lovely to Look At* 52. *Silk Stockings* 57. *Can Can* 59. *Flower Drum Song* 62. *Cleopatra* 63. *My Fair Lady* 64. *Finian's Rainbow* 68. *Lost Horizon* 73, many others.

Panama, Norman (1914–).
Writer-producer-director who has long worked in collaboration with Melvin Frank (qv for note on films). Now working solo.

Not with My Wife You Don't (wd, p) 66. How to Commit Marriage (d only) 69. The Maltese Bippy (wd) 69. Coffee, Tea or Me? (TV) 73. I Will, I Will . . . For Now (co-w, d) 76. Barnaby and Me 77.

Panavision.
A wide-screen system which outdistanced CinemaScope because of its improved anamorphic lens. Super-Panavision and Panavision 70 are 'road show' processes involving projection on wide film: in the first case the film is shot on 55mm, in the second blown up after photography. Great confusion was caused in the 70s by the company insisting on the credit 'filmed with Panavision equipment' even on non-anamorphic films.

Panfilov, Gleb (1934–).
Russian film director and screenwriter. He trained as a chemical engineer before studying direction at Mosfilm.

Across the Stream and Fire (Vogne Broda Nyet) 68. The Debut (Nachalo) 70. May I Have the Floor? (Proshu Slova) 75. Valentina, Valentine 81. Vassa 83. The Theme 84. The Mother 88, etc.

Pangborn, Franklin (1894–1958).
American character comedian with long stage experience; in scores of films from the 20s, typically as flustered hotel clerk or organizer.

My Friend from India 27. My Man 30. International House 33. My Man Godfrey 36. Stage Door 37. Christmas in July 40. *The Bank Dick* 40. *The Palm Beach Story* 42. The Carter Case 42. Now Voyager 42. *Hail the Conquering Hero* 44. Mad Wednesday 47. Romance on the High Seas 48. The Story of Mankind 57, etc.

Pantoliano, Joe (1953–).
American actor.

The Idolmaker 80. Risky Business 83. The Final Terror 83. Eddie and the Cruisers 83. The Goonies 85. The Mean Season 85. Running Scared 86. La Bamba 87. The Squeeze 87. Empire of the Sun 87. Midnight Run 88. Downtown 89. The Last of the Finest 90. Short Time 90. Zandalee 91. Used People 92. Calendar Girl 93. The Fugitive 93. Three of Hearts 93. Baby's Day Out 94. The Last Word 95, etc.

TV series: Free Country 78. From Here to Eternity 79. The Fanelli Boys 90–91.

Panzer, Paul (1872–1958).
American silent screen villain, an extremely hissable specimen.

The Perils of Pauline 14. The Exploits of Elaine 15. The Mystery Mind 19. The Johnstown Flood 26. Under the Red Robe 36. Casablanca 42. The Perils of Pauline 47, many others.

Papas, Irene (1926–) (I. Lelekou).
Greek stage actress who has made films at home and abroad.

Necripolitia (debut) 51. Theodora Slave Empress 54. Attila the Hun 54. Tribute to a Bad Man (US) 55. The Power and the Prize (US) 56. The Guns of Navarone 61. Electra 62. *Zorba the Greek* 64. Beyond the Mountains 66. The Brotherhood (US) 68. 'Z' 68. A Dream of Kings (US) 69. Anne of the Thousand Days 70. The Trojan Women 71. The Fifth Offensive 73. Moses (TV) 76. The Message 76. Iphigenia 77. Bloodline 79. Into the Night 84. The Assisi Underground 85. High Season 87. Sweet Country 87. Pano Kato Ke Plagios 93, etc.

paper prints
were made of most films between 1895 and 1912 because the US Copyright Act did not allow for celluloid. This quirk of the law meant the preservation of hundreds of early titles which could otherwise have been lost, and in the 60s they were all copied for the archives of the Motion Picture Academy on to 16mm film.

Paquin, Anna (1984–).
New Zealand juvenile actress.

The Piano (AA) 93.

Paradis, Vanessa (1972–).
French pop singer and model whose film debut was much praised.

Noce Blanche 90. Elisa 95.

Paradjanov, Sergei (1924–1990).
Georgian film director whose idiosyncratic films ran foul of Soviet authorities. His international reputation dates from 1968. He was imprisoned for four years in 1974 and forbidden to make films on his release. *The Bogeyman* (*Bobo*), a documentary on his life and work released in 1991, includes film of the heart attack that killed him when he was flying home from Paris, as well as extracts from his last, uncompleted film, *Confession*.

Andriesh 54. The First Lad (Perwyi Paren) 58. Flower on the Stone (Zwetok na Kamne) 63. The Ballad 64. Shadows of Our Forgotten Ancestors (Teni Zabytykh Predkov) 64. *The Colour of Pomegranates* (Sayat Nova) 68. The Legend of Suram Fortress (co-d) 84. Asahik Kerib 88, etc.

Paramount Pictures Corporation
was basically the creation of Adolph Zukor (qv), a nickelodeon showman who in 1912 founded Famous Players, with the intention of presenting photographed versions of stage successes. In 1914 W. W. Hodkinson's Paramount Pictures took over distribution of Famous Players and Lasky products, and in the complex mergers which resulted, Zukor came out top man. Through the years his studio more than any other gave a family atmosphere, seldom producing films of depth but providing agreeable light entertainment with stars like Valentino, Maurice Chevalier, the Marx Brothers, Mary Pickford, Claudette Colbert, Bob Hope, Bing Crosby, Dorothy Lamour, Alan Ladd, and directors like Lubitsch, de Mille and Wilder. Notable films include *The Sheik*, *The Covered Wagon*, *The Ten Commandments* (both versions), *Trouble in Paradise*, *The Crusades*, *Union Pacific*, the Road films, *Going My Way*, *The Greatest Show on Earth*, etc. In recent years, since Zukor's retirement, the company had many difficulties, but was helped by a takeover by Gulf and Western Industries which spurred the commercial instinct, and produced two enormous

winners in *Love Story* and *The Godfather*, followed in 1977 by *Saturday Night Fever*, in 1978 by *Grease*, in 1979 by *Star Trek* and in 1981 by *Raiders of the Lost Ark*. The latter's two sequels, *Indiana Jones and the Temple of Doom* and *Indiana Jones and the Last Crusade*, were box-office successes in 1984 and 1989 respectively. *Beverly Hills Cop* 84 and its sequel in 1987 also brought box-office rewards and established Eddie Murphy as a star, while *Top Gun* was among the top films of 1986, as were, in their respective years, *The Hunt for Red October* 90, *The Addams Family* 91 and *Wayne's World* 92. But all that paled besides the phenomenal success of *Forrest Gump* in 1994, a film that became the company's biggest box-office success and among the top ten grossing films so far produced. In mid-1994 the studio was taken over by Viacom, an entertainment conglomerate that includes MTV, Nickelodeon and Showtime television channels.

Paré, Michael (1959–).
American young leading actor. He trained as a chef before deciding to become an actor.

Eddie and the Cruisers 83. The Philadelphia Experiment 84. Streets of Fire 84. Undercover 84. Instant Justice 87. Space Rage 87. The Women's Club 87. World Gone Wild 88. Eddie and the Cruisers II: Eddie Lives 89. Moon 44 90. Empire City 91. The Closer 91. Into the Sun 92. Blink of an Eye 92. Dragonfight 92. Sunset Heat 92, etc.

TV series: The Greatest American Hero 81–83. Houston Knights 87–88.

Parer, Damien (*–1944).
Australian cameraman whose coverage of the war in New Guinea, *Kokoda Front Line* 42, won Australia's first Oscar for the best documentary.

Parillaud, Anne.
French leading actress.

Nikita (aka La Femme Nikita) 91. Innocent Blood 92. Map of the Human Heart 93. Six Days, Six Nights (À la Folie) 94, etc.

Paris
has usually figured in films as the centre of sophistication, romance and luxury: thus *Ninotchka*, *I Met Him in Paris*, *The Last Time I Saw Paris*, *Innocents in Paris*, *April in Paris*, *How to Steal a Million*, *To Paris with Love*, *Paris When It Sizzles*, *A Certain Smile*, *Funny Face*, *Paris Holiday*, *Can Can*, *Parisienne*, *Paris Palace Hotel*, *Two for the Road* and innumerable others. The bohemian aspect is another favourite, as depicted in *An American in Paris*, *Latin Quarter*, *Paris Blues*, *What's New, Pussycat?*, *Svengali*, *French Cancan*, *Moulin Rouge*, *What a Way to Go*, *The Moon and Sixpence*, etc. The tourists' Paris has provided a splendid backcloth for films as diverse as *The Great Race*, *The Man on the Eiffel Tower*, *Charade*, *Those Magnificent Men in Their Flying Machines*, *Zazie dans le Métro*, *Pig Across Paris*, *The Red Balloon*, *Father Brown*, *Take Her She's Mine*, *Dear Brigitte*, *Bon Voyage*, and *Paris Nous Appartient*. French film-makers seem particularly fond of showing the city's seamy side in thrillers about vice, murder and prostitution: *Quai de Grenelle*, *Quai des Orfèvres*, *Les Compagnes de la Nuit*, *Le Long des Trottoirs*, *Rififi*, etc. René Clair has always had his own slightly fantastic view of Paris, from *Paris Qui Dort* through *Sous les Toits de Paris*, *A Nous la Liberté*, *Le Million*, *Le Quatorze Juillet*, and *Porte des Lilas*. Rouben Mamoulian recreated this vision in *Love Me Tonight*, and *The Mad Woman of Chaillot* lived in a city of similar nuances. Historical Paris has been recreated for *The Hunchback of Notre Dame*, *The Scarlet Pimpernel*, *The Three Musketeers*, *Camille*, *A Tale of Two Cities*, *Marie Antoinette*, *So Long at the Fair* and *Les Enfants du Paradis*; while Paris

under fire in World War II was depicted in *Is Paris Burning?* As for *Last Tango in Paris*, its emphasis was hardly on the city.

Paris, Jerry (1925–1986).
American supporting actor.
   The Caine Mutiny 54. *Marty* 55. *Unchained* 55, many others; also played the neighbour in *The Dick Van Dyke Show* 61–66.
   AS DIRECTOR: *Never a Dull Moment* 68. *Don't Raise the Bridge, Lower the River* 68. *Viva Max* 69. *The Grasshopper* 70.
   Police Academy 2 84. Police Academy 3 85.

Park, Nick (1959–).
English animator whose shorts starring inventor Wallace and his dog Gromit have won two Oscars.
   Creature Comforts (AA) 89. A Grand Day Out 91. The Wrong Trousers (AA) 93.

Parker, Alan (1944–).
British director with enough self-assurance to make him an international talking point.
   ■ Melody (w only) 70. Footsteps (& w) 73. Our Cissy (& w) 73. No Hard Feelings 73. The Evacuees (TV) 74. *Bugsy Malone* (& w) 77. *Midnight Express* (AAN, BFA) 78. Fame (& w) 79. Shoot the Moon (& w) 82. Pink Floyd the Wall 82. Birdy 85. Angel Heart 87. Mississippi Burning (AAN) 88. Come See the Paradise 90. The Commitments 91. The Road to Wellville (wd) 94.

Parker, Barnett (1890–1941).
British character actor in Hollywood, one of the perfect butlers of the 30s.
   The President's Mystery 36. Espionage 37. Wake Up and Live 37. Listen Darling 38. At the Circus 39. Love Thy Neighbour 40. The Reluctant Dragon 41, etc.

Parker, Cecil (1897–1971) (Cecil Schwabe).
British character actor with upper-class personality which could be amiable or chill.
   The Silver Spoon (film debut) 33. A Cuckoo in the Nest 33. Storm in a Teacup 37. Dark Journey 37. *The Lady Vanishes* 38. The Citadel 38. *Caesar and Cleopatra* 45. Hungry Hill 46. Captain Boycott 47. *The First Gentleman* (as the Prince Regent) 47. *Quartet* 48. Dear Mr Prohack 49. *The Chiltern Hundreds* 49. Tony Draws a Horse 51. The Man in the White Suit 51. His Excellency 52. I Believe in You 52. Isn't Life Wonderful? 54. *Father Brown* 54. The Constant Husband 55. The Ladykillers 55. *The Court Jester* (US) 55. It's Great to be Young 56. The Admirable Crichton 57. Indiscreet 58. I was Monty's Double 58. Happy is the Bride 58. A Tale of Two Cities 58. The Navy Lark 59. A French Mistress 60. On the Fiddle 61. Petticoat Pirates 62. Heavens Above 63. The Comedy Man 64. Guns at Batasi 64. Moll Flanders 65. A Study in Terror 65. Circus of Fear 67. Oh What a Lovely War 69, many others.

Parker, Cecilia (1905–1993).
Canadian leading lady who played many Hollywood roles but is best remembered as Andy's sister in the *Hardy Family* series 37–44.
   Young as You Feel 31. The Painted Veil 34. Naughty Marietta 35. A Family Affair (first of the Hardy films) 37. Seven Sweethearts 42. Andy Hardy Comes Home 58, etc.

Parker, Clifton (1905–).
British composer.
   Yellow Canary 43. Johnny Frenchman 46. Blanche Fury 47. Treasure Island 50. The Gift Horse 52. Hell below Zero 54. Night of the Demon

57. Sea of Sand 59. Sink the Bismarck 60. Taste of Fear 62. The Informers 64, etc.

Parker, Dorothy (1893–1967).
American short-story writer, reviewer and wit who spent some years in Hollywood as an associate scriptwriter of mainly undistinguished films. Her second husband was actor and fellow screenwriter Alan Campbell (1933–47). (In 1933 they went to Hollywood at a joint salary of $5,000 a month.) She was played by Dolores Sutton in *F. Scott Fitzgerald in Hollywood* (TV) 76, Rosemary Harris in *Julia* 77, and Jennifer Jason Leigh in *Mrs Parker and the Vicious Circle* 94.
   Biography: 1971, *You Might as Well Live* by John Keats.
   Paris in Spring (co-songs) 35. Suzy 36. Lady Be Careful 36. *A Star Is Born* (AAN) 37. Woman Chases Man 37. Sweethearts 38. Trade Winds 38. Weekend for Three 41. Saboteur 42. Smash-Up – The Story of a Woman (co-story) (AAN) 46. The Fan 49, etc.

¶ Through the sweat and tears I shed over my first script, I saw a great truth – one of those eternal, universal truths that serve to make you feel much worse than you did when you started. And that is no writer, whether he writes from love or from money, can condescend to what he writes. – *D.P.*
   Come grace this lotus-laden shore,
   The isle of Do-What's-Done-Before.
   Come curb the new and watch the old win,
   Out where streets are paved with Goldwyn.
   – *D.P.*
   Scratch an actor and you'll find an actress. – *D.P.*
   Hollywood money isn't money. It's congealed snow, melts in your hand. – *D.P.*
   So odd a blend of Little Nell and Lady Macbeth. – *Alexander Woollcott*
   The first modern American woman: she could out-talk, out-drink, out-fuck all the men. – *Alan Rudolph*
   See also: *Algonquin Round Table*.

Parker, Eddie (1900–1960).
American stuntman who doubled for most of Universal's horror stars.

Parker, Eleanor (1922–).
American leading lady with brief stage experience before a Hollywood contract; her career followed a typical pattern, with increasingly good leading roles followed by a decline, with a later comeback in character parts.
   Biography: 1989, *Eleanor Parker* by Doug McClelland.
   ■ They Died with Their Boots On (debut as extra) 41. Buses Roar 42. Mysterious Doctor 43. Mission to Moscow 43. The Very Thought of You 44. Crime by Night 44. Between Two Worlds 44. The Last Ride 44. Pride of the Marines 45. Of Human Bondage (as Mildred) 46. Never Say Goodbye 46. Escape Me Never 47. *The Voice of the Turtle* 47. The Woman in White 48. Chain Lightning 49. Three Secrets 50. *Caged* (AAN) 50. Valentino 51. A Millionaire for Christy 51. *Detective Story* (AAN) 51. Scaramouche 52. Above and Beyond 52. Escape from Fort Bravo 53. The Naked Jungle 54. Valley of the Kings 54. Many Rivers to Cross 54. *Interrupted Melody* (AAN) 55. The Man with the Golden Arm 56. The King and Four Queens 56. Lizzie 57. The Seventh Sin 57. A Hole in the Head 59. Home from the Hill 60. Return to Peyton Place 61. Madison Avenue 62. Panic Button 64. The Sound of Music 65. The Oscar 66. An American Dream 66. Warning Shot 66. The Tiger and the Pussycat 67. How to Steal the World 68. Eye of

the Cat 69. Maybe I'll Come Home in the Spring 70. Vanished (TV) 71. Home for the Holidays (TV) 72. The Great American Beauty Contest (TV) 74. *She's Dressed to Kill* (TV) 79. Sunburn 79. Madame X (TV) 81.
   TV series: Bracken's World 69.

Parker, Fess (1925–).
American leading man with some stage experience. He is now a vintner and hotelier in California.
   Untamed Frontier 52. *Davy Crockett* 54 (and two sequels). The Great Locomotive Chase 56. Westward Ho the Wagons 56. Old Yeller 57. The Hangman 59. Hell is for Heroes 62. Smoky 66, etc.
   TV series: Mr Smith Goes to Washington 62. Daniel Boone 64–68.

Parker, Jameson (1947–).
American leading man who first appeared on the daytime soap operas *Somerset* and *One Life to Live* in the 70s.
   The Bell Jar 79. A Small Circle of Friends 80. Women at West Point (TV) 80. Anatomy of a Seduction (TV) 80. White Dog 82. Who Is Julia? (TV) 86. Prince of Darkness 87, etc.
   TV series: Simon and Simon 81–88.

Parker, Jean (1912–) (Luis Stephanie Zelinska).
Once-demure American leading lady, popular in the 30s; latterly playing hard-boiled roles.
   Rasputin and the Empress 32. *Little Women* 33. Sequoia 34. The Ghost Goes West (GB) 36. Princess O'Hara 37. The Flying Deuces 39. Beyond Tomorrow 40. No Hands on the Clock 42. One Body Too Many 42. Minesweeper 43. Bluebeard 44. Detective Kitty O'Day 44. Lady in the Death House 44. The Gunfighter 50. Those Redheads from Seattle 53. Black Tuesday 54. A Lawless Street 55. Apache Uprising 65, many others.

Parker, Mary-Louise (1964–).
American actress.
   Signs of Life 89. Longtime Companion 90. Fried Green Tomatoes 91. Grand Canyon 91. Naked in New York 93. Mr Wonderful 93. The Client 94. Bullets over Broadway 94, etc.

Parker, Sarah Jessica (1965–).
American actress, a former child star who played the title role in *Annie* on Broadway in the late 70s.
   Rich Kids 79. Firstborn 84. Footloose 84. Girls Just Want to Have Fun 85. Flight of the Navigator 86. L.A. Story 91. Honeymoon in Vegas 92. Hocus Pocus 93. Striking Distance 93. Ed Wood 94, etc.
   TV series: Square Pegs 82–83. A Year in the Life 87–88. Equal Justice 90–91.

Parker, Suzy (1932–) (Cecelia Parker).
Statuesque American leading lady, former model. She married actor Bradford Dillman, her third husband, in 1963.
   Kiss Them for Me (debut) 57. *Ten North Frederick* 58. The Best of Everything 59. Circle of Deception 61. The Interns 62. Chamber of Horrors 66, etc.

Parker, Willard (1912–) (Worster van Eps).
Tall American 'second lead', in films from 1938 after stage experience.
   A Slight Case of Murder (debut) 38. The Fighting Guardsman 43. You Gotta Stay Happy 48. Sangaree 53. The Great Jesse James Raid 53. The Earth Dies Screaming 64. Waco 66, etc.
   TV series: Tales of the Texas Rangers 55–57.

arkins, Barbara (1942–).
anadian leading lady whose major success was
V.
Valley of the Dolls 67. The Kremlin Letters 69. The
Mephisto Waltz 71. Puppet on a Chain 72.
sylum 72. Captains and the Kings (TV) 76. Shout
t the Devil 76. Ziegfeld: the Man and his Women
as Anna Held) (TV) 78. The Critical List (TV) 78.
ear Island 80, etc.
TV series: *Peyton Place* 64–68.

arks, Gordon (1925–).
merican director, former stills photographer,
ovelist and composer.
The Learning Tree 68. *Shaft* 71. Shaft's Big Score
2. Leadbelly 76. Moments without Proper Names
6, etc.

arks, Gordon, Jnr (1948–1979).
merican director, son of Gordon Parks. Killed in
plane crash.
Superfly 72. Thomasine and Bushrod 74. Three
ne Hard Way 74. Aaron Loves Angela 75.

arks, Larry (1914–1975) (Sam Kleusman Lawrence
arks).
merican light leading man whose career in 'B'
ictures was interrupted by his highly successful
mpersonation of Al Jolson. He subsequently
roved difficult to cast, and was forced out of
ollywood after testifying to the Unamerican
ctivities Committee.
¶ You Belong to Me 41. Mystery Ship 41. Harmon
f Michigan 41. Blondie Goes to College 42.
arvard Here I Come 42. The Boogie Man Will
et You 42. Atlantic Convoy 42. Canal Zone 42.
hree Girls About Town 42. Sing for your Supper
2. Flight Lieutenant 42. Submarine Raiser 42.
onolulu Lu 42. Hello Annapolis 42. You were
ever Lovelier 42. A Man's World 42. North of the
ockies 42. Alias Boston Blackie 42. They All
issed the Bride 42. Redhead from Manhattan
3. Is Everybody Happy? 43. First Comes Courage
3. Power of the Press 43. The Deerslayer 43.
estroyer 43. Reveille with Beverly 43. She's a
weetheart 44. The Racket Man 44. The Black
arachute 44. Stars on Parade 44. Hey Rookie 44.
ergeant Mike 44. Counter Attack 45. Jealousy 45.
enegades 46. *The Jolson Story* (AAN) 46. Her
usband's Affairs 47. Down to Earth 47. The
wordsman 47. Gallant Blade 48. Jolson Sings Again
9. Emergency Wedding 50. Love is Better than
ver 52. Tiger by the Tail 55. *Freud* 62.

arks, Michael (1938–).
rooding American leading man.
Wild Seed 64. Bus Riley's Back in Town 65. The
ible (as Adam) 66. The Idol (GB) 66. The
lappening 67. Can Ellen Be Saved? (TV) 73. The
ast Hard Men 76. Sidewinder One 77. Love and
ne Midnight Auto Supply 77. The Private Files of
Edgar Hoover 78. Breakthrough 79. Fast
riends (TV) 79. North Sea Hijack 80. Reward (TV)
1. Savannah Smiles 82. Chase (TV) 85. Club Life
6. Return of Josey Wales (& d) 86. Stamp of a
iller (TV) 87. Arizona Heat 88. Welcome to Spring
reak 88. Gore Vidal's Billy the Kid 89. The
itman 91. Storyville 92. Death Wish V: The Face
f Death 94, etc.
TV series: Then Came Bronson 69. The Colbys
7.

arks, Van Dyke (1941–).
american composer and singer, a former child
ctor.
Goin' South 78. Popeye 80. Club Paradise 86.
ented Lips 88. Casual Sex? 88. The Two Jakes
& a) 90, etc.

Parkyakarkus (1904–1958) (Harry Einstein).
American radio comedian formerly known as
Harry Parke. He is the father of actor-director
Albert Brooks.
Strike Me Pink 36. Night Spot 38. Glamour Boy
40. Earl Carroll's Vanities 45.

Parkyn, Leslie (–1983).
British executive producer, associated with *Sergei
Nolbandov* 1951–57, subsequently with Julian
Wintle.
The Kidnappers 53. Tiger Bay 59. The Waltz of
the Toreadors 62. Father Came Too 64, many
others.

Parlo, Dita (1906–1971) (Gerthe Kornstadt).
German star actress of the 30s.
Homecoming 28. Melody of the Heart 30.
Secrets of the Orient 31. L'Atalante 34. The
Mystic Mountain 36. Mademoiselle Docteur 37. La
Grande Illusion 37. Ultimatum 39. Justice est
Faite 50. Quand le Soleil Montera 56, etc.

Parnell, Emory (1894–1979).
American general-purpose character actor: could
be villain, prison warden, weakling or kindly father.
King of Alcatraz 39. I Married a Witch 42. Mama
Loves Papa 46. Words and Music 48. Call Me
Madam 53. Man of the West 58, many others.

parody
without satire was never prominent among film
genres until the 70s, when the easy-going talents
of such as Mel Brooks and Gene Wilder produced
films such as *Blazing Saddles, Sherlock Holmes'
Smarter Brother, Young Frankenstein, Murder by
Death, The Black Bird, The Big Bus, Phantom of the
Paradise, High Anxiety* and *The Cheap Detective*. The
Zucker brothers and Jim Abrahams have made a
speciality of the form with *Kentucky Fried Movie,
Airplane, The Naked Gun* and their sequels, and *Hot
Shots!* (Abrahams only). Short films in this vein are
headed by *Six-Sided Triangle, The Dove* and *Cry Wolf*.

Parr-Davies, Harry (1914–1955).
Welsh composer and songwriter who contributed
songs to many of Gracie Fields' films and other
British musicals of the 30s and 40s. He had a big
wartime hit with 'Pedro the Fisherman', from his
stage show *The Lisbon Story*, which was
subsequently filmed.
This Week of Grace 33. Sing as We Go 34. Queen
of Hearts 36. We're Going to Be Rich 38. Keep
Smiling (aka Smile as You Go) 38. It's in the Air
38. Shipyard Sally 39. Maytime in Mayfair 49.
The Lisbon Story 49, etc.

Parrish, Helen (1922–1959).
American leading lady, former baby model and
child actress.
The Big Trail 31. A Dog of Flanders 34. Mad
about Music 38. You'll Find Out 40. They All Kissed
the Bride 42. The Mystery of the Thirteenth Guest
44. The Wolf Hunters 50, etc.

Parrish, Robert (1916–).
American director, former editor and child actor.
Autobiographies: 1976, *Growing Up in
Hollywood*. 1988, *Hollywood Doesn't Live Here
Anymore*.
■ Cry Danger 51. The Mob 51. My Pal Gus 52.
The San Francisco Story 52. Rough Shoot (GB) 52.
Assignment Paris 52. The Purple Plain 54. Lucy
Gallant 55. Fire Down Below 57. Saddle the Wind
58. The Wonderful Country 59. In the French Style
(& p) 63. Up from the Beach 65. The Bobo 67.
Casino Royale (part) 67. Duffy 68. Journey to the
Far Side of the Sun 69. A Town Called Bastard

71. The Marseilles Contract 74. Mississippi Blues
(co-d) 84.

¶ His films belong to a director who craves
anonymity. – *Andrew Sarris, 1968*

Parrott, James (1892–1939).
American director, mainly of two-reelers featuring
Laurel and Hardy (*Blotto, The Music Box, County
Hospital*, etc), Charlie Chase and Max Davidson.
Features include *Jailbirds* 31, *Sing, Sister, Sing* 35.

Parry, Gordon (1908–1981).
British director of mainly secondary films: former
actor, production manager, etc.
Bond Street 48. Third Time Lucky 48. Now
Barabbas 49. Midnight Episode 50. Innocents in
Paris 52. Women of Twilight 52. A Yank in Ermine
55. Sailor Beware 56. Tread Softly Stranger 58. The
Navy Lark 60, etc.

Parry, Natasha (1930–).
British leading lady who married Peter Brook.
Appears occasionally on stage and screen.
Dance Hall 49. The Dark Man 50. Crow Hollow
52. Knave of Hearts 53. Windom's Way 57. The
Rough and the Smooth 59. Midnight Lace 60. The
Fourth Square 62. The Girl in the Headlines 64.
Romeo and Juliet 68. Oh What a Lovely War 69.
La Chambre Voisine 80, etc.

Parsons, Estelle (1927–).
American character actress with stage background.
Bonnie and Clyde (AA) 67. Rachel Rachel (AAN)
68. I Never Sang for My Father 69. Don't Drink the
Water 69. I Walk the Line 70. Watermelon Man
71. Two People 73. For Pete's Sake 74. Foreplay 75.
Open Admissions (TV) 88. The Lemon Sisters 89.
Dick Tracy 90, etc.

Parsons, Harriet (1906–1983).
American producer, daughter of Louella Parsons.
I Remember Mama 47. Clash by Night 51. Susan
Slept Here 54, etc.

Parsons, Louella (1880–1972) (L. Oettinger).
Hollywood columnist whose gossip rivalled in
readership that of Hedda Hopper. In occasional
films as herself, e.g. *Hollywood Hotel* 37, *Starlift* 51.
Autobiographical books: 1944, *The Gay Illiterate*.
1962, *Tell It to Louella*.
Biography: 1973, *Hedda and Louella* by George
Eels.

¶ Her friends always stand by her. When she
prematurely published a claim that an actress
was pregnant, the actress's husband hastened to
prove her correct. – *Time Magazine*
Her writings stand out like an asthmatic's gasps.
– *Nunnally Johnson*
Not a bad old slob. – *James Mason*

Parsons, Milton (1904–1980).
Lugubrious American character actor often seen as
undertaker.
The Hidden Hand 42. Margie 44, many others.

Parsons, Nicholas (1928–).
British light actor and entertainer.
Master of Bankdam 48. Brothers in Law 57. Too
Many Crooks 59. Doctor in Love 62. Don't Raise
the Bridge, Lower the River 68, etc.

parties
in movies have often been wild, as for instance in
The Wild Party, also *The Party's Over, I'll Never Forget
What's 'is Name, Breakfast at Tiffany's, I Love You
Alice B. Toklas, The Impossible Years, Skidoo, Beyond*

the Valley of the Dolls, Camille 2000, The Pursuit of Happiness, The Party Crashers, and The Party itself, which started out sedately but finished with an elephant in the swimming pool. Some of the more amusing film parties, however, were better behaved, as in The Apartment, Only Two Can Play, All About Eve and Citizen Kane.

Parton, Dolly (1946–).
Voluptuous American country and western singer.
Nine to Five (AANs) 81. The Best Little Whorehouse in Texas 82. Rhinestone (& m) 84. Steel Magnolias 89. Wild Texas Wind 91. Straight Talk 92, etc.
TV series: Dixie Fixin's 94.

¶ I enjoy the way I look, but it's a joke. – D.P.
  I'm on a seafood diet – I see food, I eat it. – D.P.

Pascal, Christine (1953–).
French actress, screenwriter and director. Born in Lyon, she studied acting at the local conservatoire.
AS ACTRESS: The Watchmaker of Saint-Paul (L'horloger de Saint-Paul) 73. La Meilleure Façon de Marcher 76. Des Enfants Gâtés (& co-w) 77. On Efface Tout 78. Panny z Wilka (Pol.) 79. Coup de Foudre 83. Elsa, Elsa 85. Round Midnight (Autour de Minuit) 86. La Travestie 88. Rien que des Mensonges 91. Les Patriotes 93, etc.
AS DIRECTOR: Felicité (& a, co-w) 77. La Garce (& co-w) 83. Zanzibar (& co-w) 88. Le Petit Prince a Dit (& co-w) 92.

Pascal, Gabriel (1894–1954).
Hungarian producer-director who came to Britain in the 30s, won the esteem of Bernard Shaw, and was entrusted with the filming of several of his plays.
Biography: 1971, The Disciple and his Devil by Valerie Pascal.
■ Pygmalion (p) 38. Major Barbara (pd) 40. Caesar and Cleopatra (pd; a notoriously extravagant production) 45. Androcles and the Lion (p) (US) 53.

Pasco, Richard (1926–).
British character actor, mainly on stage and TV.
Room at the Top 59. Yesterday's Enemy 60. The Gorgon 64. Rasputin the Mad Monk 66. The Watcher in the Woods 80. Wagner 83, etc.

Pasolini, Pier Paolo (1922–1975).
Italian director.
Accattone 61. Mamma Roma 62. The Witches (part) 63. The Gospel According to St Matthew 64. Oedipus Rex 67. Theorem 68. Pigsty 69. Medea 70. Decameron 70. The Canterbury Tales 71. The Arabian Nights 74. The 120 Days of Sodom 75, etc.

Passer, Ivan (1933–).
Czech director, latterly in Hollywood.
A Boring Afternoon 64. Intimate Lighting 66. Born to Win 71. Law and Disorder 74. Silver Bears 78. Ace Up My Sleeve 78. Cutter's Way 81. Creator 85. Haunted Summer 88, etc.

The Passing of the Third Floor Back.
Jerome K. Jerome's popular novel and play, about a Christ-like stranger who has a benign influence on the down-at-heel inhabitants of a boarding house, was filmed in 1918 with Johnstone Forbes-Robinson and in 1935 with Conrad Veidt.

The Passing Parade.
A series of one-reel films, mostly historical cameos enacted in corners of MGM's great sets, devised and produced by John Nesbitt in the 30s and 40s.

Pasternak, Boris (1890–1960).
Russian novelist, author of Dr Zhivago.

Pasternak, Joe (1901–1991).
Hungarian producer in Hollywood during the golden years; especially identified with cheerful light musicals.
Autobiography: 1956, Easy the Hard Way.
Three Smart Girls 36. One Hundred Men and a Girl 37. Mad about Music 38. Destry Rides Again 39. Seven Sinners 40. It Started with Eve 41. Presenting Lily Mars 42. Song of Russia 43. Two Girls and a Sailor 44. Anchors Aweigh 45. Holiday in Mexico 46. The Unfinished Dance 47. On an Island with You 48. In the Good Old Summertime 49. The Duchess of Idaho 50. The Great Caruso 51. Skirts Ahoy 52. Latin Lovers 53. The Student Prince 54. Love Me or Leave Me 55. The Opposite Sex 56. Ten Thousand Bedrooms 57. Party Girl 58. Ask Any Girl 59. Please Don't Eat the Daisies 60. The Horizontal Lieutenant 61. Jumbo 62. The Courtship of Eddie's Father 63. Girl Happy 65. Penelope 66. The Sweet Ride 68, many others.

Pastrone, Giovanni (1883–1959).
Pioneer producer and director of Italian cinema, whose spectacular Cabiria was one of the first, and most influential, of epic movies. He abandoned cinema in the 20s.
Giordano Brunio 08. The Fall of Troy 10. Padre 12. Cabiria 14. Tigre Real 16. Hedda Gabler 19, etc.

Patch, Wally (1888–1970) (Walter Vinicombe).
Burly British cockney character actor, in films from 1920 after varied show-business experience.
Shadows 31. The Good Companions 32. Get Off My Foot 35. Not So Dusty 36. Bank Holiday 38. Quiet Wedding 40. Gasbags 40. The Common Touch 41. Old Mother Riley at Home 45. The Ghosts of Berkeley Square 47. The Guinea Pig 49. Will Any Gentleman? 53. Private's Progress 55. I'm All Right, Jack 59. Sparrows Can't Sing 63, many others.

Pate, Michael (1920–).
Australian actor in Hollywood in the 50s and 60s, often as Red Indian chief or second-string villain.
The Rugged O'Riordans 49. The Strange Door 51. Five Fingers 52. Houdini 53. The Silver Chalice 54. The Court Jester 56. Congo Crossing 56. The Oklahoman 57. Green Mansions 59. The Canadians 61. McLintock 63. Major Dundee 65. Tim (wd) 79. Return of Captain Invincible 83, etc.
TV series: Matlock Police 71.

Paterson, Bill (1945–).
Scottish character actor, from the stage.
Licking Hitler (TV) 71. The Ploughman's Lunch 83. Comfort and Joy 84. The Killing Fields 84. A Private Function 84. Defence of the Realm 85. The Adventures of Baron Munchausen 88. Truly Madly Deeply 90. The Witches 90. The Object of Beauty 91, etc.

Paterson, Neil (1916–).
British screenwriter and novelist.
The Kidnappers 53. High Tide at Noon 57. Room at the Top (AA) 59. The Spiral Road 62. Mister Moses 65.

Paterson, Pat (1911–1978).
English leading lady who went to Hollywood but gave up her career to marry Charles Boyer.
■ The Professional Guest 31. The Great Gay Road 31. Night Shadows 31. Murder on the Second Floor 32. Partners Please 32. Here's George 32. Bitter Sweet 33. Love Time 34. Bottoms Up 34. Call it

Luck 34. Charlie Chan in Egypt 35. Lottery Lover 35. Spendthrift 36. 52nd Street 37. Idiot's Delight 39.

Pathé, Charles (1863–1957).
Pioneer French executive and producer, founder of Pathé Frères and later Pathé Gazette. Also credited with making the first 'long' film: Les Misérables (made in 1909, it ran four whole reels).

Patinkin, Mandy (1952–).
American actor.
The Big Fix 78. Ragtime 81. Daniel 83. Yentl 83. The Princess Bride 87. Alien Nation 88. The House on Carroll Street 88. Dick Tracy 90. Impromptu 91. True Colors 91. The Doctor 91. The Music of Chance 93, etc.
TV series: Chicago Hope 94.

Patric, Jason (1966–).
Young American leading actor, the son of playwright Jason Miller and the grandson of actor Jackie Gleason.
Toughlove (TV) 85. Solarbabies 86. The Lost Boys 87. The Beast 88. Frankenstein Unbound 90 After Dark, My Sweet 90. Rush 91. Geronimo: An American Legend 93, etc.

Patrick, Dorothy (1922–1987).
Blonde American actress of the 40s.
Boy's Ranch 45. Till the Clouds Roll By 46. The Mighty McGurk 46. High Wall 47. New Orleans 47 Alias a Gentleman 47. Follow Me Quietly 49. Come to the Stable 49. 711 Ocean Drive 50. Torch Song 53. Violent Saturday 55. The View from Pompey's Head 55, etc.

Patrick, Gail (1911–1980) (Margaret Fitzpatrick).
American leading lady in Hollywood from early 30s, usually in routine smart-woman roles. Retired from acting and became a TV producer, notably of the successful Perry Mason series.
The Phantom Broadcast 32. Cradle Song 33. No More Ladies 35. Artists and Models 37. Reno 40. Quiet, Please, Murder 43. Women in Bondage 44 Twice Blessed 45. The Plainsman and the Lady 46 Calendar Girl 47, many others.

Patrick, John (1907–) (John Patrick Goggan).
American playwright. Works filmed include The Hasty Heart, The Teahouse of the August Moon.
SCREENPLAYS: Educating Father 36. One Mile from Heaven 37. International Settlement 38. Mr Moto Takes a Chance 38. Enchantment 48. The President's Lady 53. Three Coins in the Fountain 54. Love Is a Many Splendored Thing 55. High Society 56. Les Girls 57. Some Came Running 58. The World of Suzie Wong 61. The Main Attraction 63. The Shoes of the Fisherman 68, etc.

Patrick, Lee (1906–1982).
American character actress with stage experience, in Hollywood from 1937, usually as hard-bitten blondes.
Strange Cargo (debut) 29. The Maltese Falcon 41 Now Voyager 42. Mother Wore Tights 47. Caged 50. There's No Business Like Show Business 54. Vertigo 58. Summer and Smoke 61. The New Interns 64. The Black Bird 75, many others.
TV series: Topper 53–55. Mr Adams and Eve 56–57.

Patrick, Nigel (1913–1981) (Nigel Wemyss).
Debonair British leading actor, on stage from 1932.
■ Mrs Pym of Scotland Yard 39. Uneasy Terms 48. Noose 48. Spring in Park Lane 48. Silent Dust 49. Jack of Diamonds 49. The Perfect Woman 50. Trio 50. Morning Departure 50. Pandora and the

Flying Dutchman 51. Encore 51. The Browning Version 51. Young Wives' Tale 51. Meet Me Tonight 52. *The Pickwick Papers* (as Mr Jingle) 52. Who Goes There 52. *The Sound Barrier* 52. Grand National Night 53. Forbidden Cargo 54. The Sea Shall Not Have Them 54. All for Mary 55. A Prize of Gold 55. Raintree County 57. How to Murder a Rich Uncle 57. Count Five and Die 58. The Man Inside 58. Sapphire 59. *The League of Gentlemen* 60. The Trials of Oscar Wilde 60. Johnny Nobody (& d) 61. The Informers 63. The Virgin Soldiers 69. The Battle of Britain 69. The Executioner 70. Tales from the Crypt 72. The Great Waltz 72. The Mackintosh Man 73.
TV series: Zero One 62.

Patten, Luana (1938–).
American teenage actress of the 50s.
Song of the South 46. So Dear to My Heart 48. Johnny Tremain 57. The Little Shepherd of Kingdom Come 61. A Thunder of Drums 61. Follow Me Boys 66. Grotesque 88, etc.

Patterson, Elizabeth (1876–1966).
American character actress with stage experience; in Hollywood from the late 20s, usually as kindly or shrewish elderly ladies.
Daddy Longlegs 30. A Bill of Divorcement 32. Miss Pinkerton 32. Dinner at Eight 33. So Red the Rose 36. Sing You Sinners 38. *The Cat and the Canary* 39. Tobacco Road 41. Hail the Conquering Hero 43. Lady on a Train 45. *Intruder in the Dust* 48. Little Women 49. Bright Leaf 50. Pal Joey 57. The Oregon Trail 59, many others.

Patterson, Lee (1929–).
Sturdy Canadian leading man of minor British and American films who spent a decade in the 60s and 70s on the soap opera *One Life to Live*.
36 Hours 51. The Passing Stranger 54. Above Us the Waves 55. Soho Incident 56. Cat and Mouse 58. Jack the Ripper 60. The Ceremony 63. Valley of Mystery 67. Chato's Land 72, etc.
TV series: Surfside Six 60–62.

Patterson, Neva (1925–).
American character actress.
Desk Set 57. Too Much Too Soon 58. The Domino Principle 77. Women of Valor (TV) 86, etc.
TV series: The Governor and JJ 69. Nichols 71.

Paul, Robert (1869–1943).
Pioneer British movie camera inventor (1895). The following year he invented a projector, which he called a theatrograph. Later turned showman.

Paull, Lawrence G (1943–).
American production designer. He trained as an architect and a city planner.
Little Fauss and Big Halsy 70. The Hired Hand 71. The Naked Ape 73. The Bingo Long Traveling All-Stars and Motor Kings 76. Blue Collar 78. In God We Trust 80. Blade Runner (AAN) 82. Romancing the Stone 84. Back to the Future 85. Project X 87. Cocoon: The Return 88. Harlem Nights 89. The Last of the Finest 90. Predator 2 90. City Slickers 91. Memoirs of an Invisible Man 92. Another Stakeout 93. Naked Gun 33⅓: The Final Insult 94, etc.

Paulvé, André (1898–1982).
French producer.
La Comédie du Bonheur 39. Lumière d'Eté 42. L'Eternel Retour 43. Les Visiteurs du Soir 43. La Belle et la Bête 45. Ruy Blas 47. Orphée 49. Manèges 49. Casque d'Or 51, many others.

Pavan, Marisa (1932–) (Marisa Pierangeli).
Italian leading lady, sister of Pier Angeli. In Hollywood from 1950.
What Price Glory? (debut) 52. The Rose Tattoo (AAN) 55. The Man in the Grey Flannel Suit 56. Solomon and Sheba 59. John Paul Jones 59. The Slightly Pregnant Man (Fr.) 73. Johnny Monroe 87, etc.

Pavarotti, Luciano (1935–).
Italian tenor in international opera. Starred in one film in 1982, *Yes Giorgio*.

Pavlow, Muriel (1921–).
British leading lady, on stage and screen from 1936; her youthful appearance enabled her to continue in juvenile roles for many years.
A Romance in Flanders (debut) 36. Quiet Wedding 40. Night Boat to Dublin 45. The Shop at Sly Corner 47. Malta Story 53. Doctor in the House 54. *Reach for the Sky* 56. Tiger in the Smoke 57. Rooney 58. Murder She Said 62. Memento Mori (TV) 92, etc.

Pawle, Lennox (1872–1936).
British character actor, mainly on stage.
The Admirable Crichton (GB) 18. The Great Adventure (GB) 21. Married in Hollywood (US) 29. The Sin of Madeleine Claudet (US) 32. *David Copperfield* (as Mr Dick) 34. Sylvia Scarlett (US) 35, etc.

Paxinou, Katina (1900–1973) (Katina Constantopoulos).
Greek actress with international experience; played in some Hollywood films.
For Whom the Bell Tolls (AA) 43. Confidential Agent 44. Uncle Silas (GB) 47. *Mourning Becomes Electra* 47. Confidential Report 55. Rocco and His Brothers 60. Zita 68, etc.

Paxton, Bill (1955–).
American leading actor.
Impulse 84. The Terminator 84. Weird Science 85. Aliens 86. Near Dark 87. Next of Kin 89. Brain Dead 89. The Last of the Finest 90. Navy SEALS 90. Predator 2 90. Hurricane 91. The Vagrant 91. One False Move 92. Monolith 93. Boxing Helena 93. Trespass 93. Indian Summer 93. Tombstone 94. True Lies 94, etc.

Paxton, John (1911–1985).
American screenwriter.
■ *Murder My Sweet* 44. My Pal Wolf (co-w) 44. Cornered 46. Crack Up (co-w) 46. *Crossfire* (AAN) 47. So Well Remembered 47. Of Men and Music (co-w) 50. Fourteen Hours 51. The Wild One 54. A Prize of Gold (co-w) 55. The Cobweb 55. Interpol 57. How to Murder a Rich Uncle (& p) 59. On the Beach 59. Kotch 71.

Payne, Jack (1899–1969).
British bandleader who appeared in two films: *Say it with Music* 32, *Sunshine Ahead* 36.

Payne, John (1912–1989).
General-purpose American leading man, mostly of 40s musicals and 50s westerns.
Dodsworth 36. Fair Warning 37. Love on Toast 38. Wings of the Navy 39. *Kid Nightingale* 39. Maryland 40. The Great Profile 40. *Tin Pan Alley* 40. *The Great American Broadcast* 41. Weekend in Havana 41. Remember the Day 41. Sun Valley Serenade 41. To the Shores of Tripoli 42. Springtime in the Rockies 42. Hello Frisco Hello 43. The Dolly Sisters 45. Sentimental Journey 46. The Razor's Edge 46. Miracle on 34th Street 47. The Saxon Charm 48. The Crooked Way 49. Captain China

49. Tripoli 50. Crosswinds 51. Caribbean 52. Kansas City Confidential 52. Raiders of the Seven Seas 53. 99 River Street 53. Rails into Laramie 54. Santa Fé Passage 55. Hell's Island 55. Slightly Scarlet 56. *The Boss* 56. Bailout at 43,000 57. Hidden Fear 57. Gift of the Nile 68, etc.
TV series: The Restless Gun 58–59.

Payne, Laurence (1919–).
British leading man, on stage and (occasionally) screen from 1945.
Train of Events 49. Ill Met by Moonlight 57. Ben Hur 59. The Tell Tale Heart 61. The Court Martial of Major Keller 61. Vampire Circus 72. One Deadly Owner 74, etc.

Paynter, Robert (1928–).
British cinematographer who worked on many of Michael Winner's films in the 60s and 70s.
■ Hannibal Brooks 68. The Games 69. Lawman 70. The Nightcomers 71. Chato's Land 71. The Mechanic 72. Scorpio 72. High Velocity 76. The Big Sleep 78. Firepower 79. Saturn 3 80. Superman II 80. The Final Conflict 81. An American Werewolf in London 81. Curtains 82. Superman III 83. Trading Places 83. Scream for Help 84. The Muppets Take Manhattan 84. National Lampoon's European Vacation 85. Spies Like Us 85. Into the Night 85. Little Shop of Horrors 86. When the Whales Came 89. Strike It Rich 90. Get Back 91.

Pays, Amanda ((1959–).
English actress.
Oxford Blues 84. Cold Room (aka The Prisoner) (TV) 84. Off Limits 87. The Kindred 87. Leviathan 89. Dead on the Money (TV) 91. Exposure 91, etc.
TV series: Max Headroom 87. The Flash 90–91.

Payton, Barbara (1927–1967).
American leading lady.
Once More My Darling 49. Dallas 50. Kiss Tomorrow Goodbye 51. Drums in the Deep South 51. Bride of the Gorilla 52. The Great Jesse James Raid 53. Four-Sided Triangle (GB) 54. The Flanagan Boy (GB) 55, etc.

Peach, Mary (1934–).
British leading lady, in films from 1957.
Follow That Horse 59. Room at the Top 59. *No Love for Johnnie* 61. A Pair of Briefs 62. A Gathering of Eagles (US) 63. Ballad in Blue 65. The Projected Man 66. Scrooge 70, etc.

Pearce, Alice (1913–1966).
American character comedienne, usually in adenoidal roles.
On the Town 49. The Opposite Sex 56. The Disorderly Orderly 64. Dear Brigitte 65. The Glass Bottom Boat 66, etc.
TV series: Bewitched 65–66.

Pearce, Guy.
Australian leading actor, from the soap operas *Neighbours* and *Home and Away*.
Hunting 92. *The Adventures of Priscilla, Queen of the Desert* 94, etc.

Pearl, Jack (1894–1984).
Jewish-American comic known on radio as Baron Munchausen and famous for his catchphrase. 'Vass you dere. Sharlie?' Film appearance: *Hollywood Party* 34.

Pearson, Beatrice (1920–).
American leading lady with a brief career.
■ Force of Evil 49. Lost Boundaries 49.

Pearson, George (1875–1973).
British writer-producer-director who came to films at the age of 37 after being a schoolmaster. Hundreds of films to his credit.

Autobiography: 1957, *Flashback*.

The Fool 12. A Study in Scarlet 14. Ultus the Man from the Dead 15. The Better Ole 18. The Old Curiosity Shop 20. *Squibs* 21. Squibs Wins the Calcutta Sweep 22. Satan's Sister 25. Huntingtower 27. The Silver King 28. Journey's End (p) 30. The Good Companions (p) 32. Four Marked Men 34. The Pointing Finger 38, many others.

Pearson, Lloyd (1897–1966).
Portly British character actor, usually of bluff Yorkshire types.

The Challenge 38. Tilly of Bloomsbury 40. Kipps 41. *When We Are Married* 42. Schweik's New Adventures (leading role) 43. My Learned Friend 44. Mr Perrin and Mr Traill 49. Hindle Wakes 52. The Good Companions 57. The Angry Silence 59, etc.

Pearson, Richard (1918–).
British stage character actor in occasional films.

Love Among the Ruins (TV) 75. The Bluebird 77. She Fell Among Thieves (TV) 78. The Mirror Crack'd 80. Water 85. Pirates 86. Whoops Apocalypse 87, etc.

Peary, Harold (1908–1985) (Harold José Pereira de Faria).
American character comedian who for years in the 40s played The Great Gildersleeve on radio and in a short-lived film series, also in *Coming Round the Mountain, County Fair, Clambake.*

Peck, Bob.
English character actor, from the stage, where he was a member of the Royal Shakespeare Company and has since acted with the National Theatre Company.

Edge of Darkness (TV) 85. The Kitchen Toto 87. *On the Black Hill* 88. Ladder of Swords 88. Slipstream 89. Lord of the Flies 90. Jurassic Park 93, etc.

Peck, Gregory (1916–).
Durable and likeable American leading actor, with stage experience before sudden success in Hollywood.

Biography: 1980, *Gregory Peck* by Michael Freedland.

■ Days of Glory 43. *The Keys of the Kingdom* (AAN) 44. The Valley of Decision 44. *Spellbound* 45. The Yearling (AAN) 46. *Duel in the Sun* 46. *The Macomber Affair* 47. *Gentleman's Agreement* (AAN) 47. The Paradine Case 47. Yellow Sky 48. The Great Sinner 49. *Twelve o'Clock High* (AAN) 49. *The Gunfighter* 50. David and Bathsheba 51. Captain Horatio Hornblower (GB) 51. Only the Valiant 52. The World in His Arms 52. The Snows of Kilimanjaro 52. Roman Holiday 53. Night People 54. The Million Pound Note (GB) 54. The Purple Plain (GB) 55. *The Man in the Grey Flannel Suit* 56. Moby Dick 56. Designing Woman 57. The Bravados 58. *The Big Country* 58. Pork Chop Hill 59. Beloved Infidel (as Scott Fitzgerald) 59. On the Beach 59. The Guns of Navarone (GB) 61. Cape Fear 62. How the West was Won 62. *To Kill a Mockingbird* (AA) 63. Captain Newman 63. Behold a Pale Horse 64. Mirage 65. Arabesque 66. Mackenna's Gold 68. The Stalking Moon 68. The Most Dangerous Man in the World 69. Marooned 69. I Walk the Line 70. Shootout 71. Billy Two Hats 73. The Dove (p only) 75. *The Omen* 76. MacArthur 77. The Boys from Brazil 78. The Sea Wolves 80. The Blue and the Gray (TV) (as Lincoln) 82. The

Scarlet and the Black (TV) 82. Amazing Grace and Chuck 87. Old Gringo 89. Other People's Money 91. Cape Fear 91. The Portrait (TV) 93.

Peckinpah, Sam (1925–1984).
American director of tough westerns.

Biography: 1994, *'If They Move . . . Kill 'Em': The Life and Times of Sam Peckinpah* by David Weddle.

■ The Deadly Companions 61. *Ride the High Country* 62. Major Dundee 65. *The Wild Bunch* 69. The Ballad of Cable Hogue 69. Straw Dogs 71. Junior Bonner 72. The Getaway 72. Pat Garrett and Billy the Kid 73. Bring Me the Head of Alfredo Garcia 74. The Killer Elite 76. Cross of Iron 77. Convoy 78. The Osterman Weekend 83.

Peerce, Jan (1904–1984).
American opera singer who appeared in *Carnegie Hall* and *Something in the Wind*.

Peerce, Larry (c. 1935–).
American writer-director, son of opera singer Jan Peerce.

One Potato Two Potato 66. Goodbye Columbus 69. A Separate Peace 73. Ash Wednesday 74. The Other Side of the Mountain 76. Two Minute Warning 76. The Other Side of the Mountain Part Two 78. The Bell Jar 79. Why Would I Lie? 80. Love Child 82. Hard to Hold 84. Elvis and Me (TV) 88. The Neon Empire 89. A Woman Named Jackie (TV) 91. Child of Rage (TV) 92, etc.

Pelissier, Anthony (1912–1988).
British director with stage experience; son of Fay Compton.

The History of Mr Polly 49. The Rocking Horse Winner 50. Night without Stars 50. Meet Me Tonight 52. Meet Mr Lucifer 54, etc.

Peña, Elizabeth (1961–).
American actress

El Super 79. Times Square 80. They All Laughed 81. Crossover Dreams 85. Down and Out in Beverly Hills 86. Batteries Not Included 87. La Bamba 87. Vibes 88. Blue Steel 90. Jacob's Ladder 90. The Waterdance 92, etc.

Pendleton, Austin (1940–).
Slightly bumptious American character actor.

Skidoo 68. What's Up, Doc? 72. Every Little Crook and Nanny 72. The Thief Who Came to Dinner 73. *The Front Page* 74. The Great Smokey Roadblock 78. Starting Over 79. The First Family 80. Mr & Mrs Bridge 90. My Cousin Vinny 92. Mr Nanny 93. My Boyfriend's Back 93. Guarding Tess 94, etc.

Pendleton, Nat (1895–1967).
American character actor, formerly professional wrestler, usually seen in 'dumb ox' roles. In films from *c.* 1930.

You Said a Mouthful 32. The Sign of the Cross 32. The Thin Man 34. Manhattan Melodrama 34. The Great Ziegfeld 36. The Marx Brothers at the Circus 39. Young Dr Kildare (and series) 39. On Borrowed Time 39. Northwest Passage 40. Top Sergeant Mulligan 42. Rookies Come Home 45. Scared to Death 47. Death Valley 49, many others.

Pene Du Bois, Raoul (1914–1985).
American set and costume designer, mainly on Broadway but occasionally noticed on Hollywood credits.

Penhaligon, Susan (1950–).
British leading lady of the late 70s.

Under Milk Wood 73. No Sex Please We're British 73. The Land that Time Forgot 75. Nasty

Habits 77. The Uncanny 77. Leopard in the Snow 78. The Masks of Death (TV) 84.

TV series: Bouquet of Barbed Wire 76.

Penn, Arthur (1922–).
American director, from TV.

■ The Left Handed Gun 58. The Miracle Worker (AAN) 62. Mickey One 65. The Chase 66. *Bonnie and Clyde* (AAN) 67. Alice's Restaurant (AAN) 69. Little Big Man 70. Night Moves 75. The Missouri Breaks 76. Four Friends 81. Target 85. Dead of Winter 87. Penn & Teller Get Killed 89. The Portrait (TV) 93.

¶ There hasn't been that much of a market for what I can do. I'm not into outer space epics or youth pictures. – *A.P.*

Penn, Chris (1966–).
Burly American actor, the son of Leo Penn and brother of Sean Penn.

Rumble Fish 83. All the Right Moves 83. Footloose 84. At Close Range 86. Made in the USA 88. Best of the Best 89. Mobsters 91. Futurekick 91. Leather Jackets 91. Reservoir Dogs 92. The Music of Chance 93. Best of the Best II 93. True Romance 93. Short Cuts 93. Josh and S.A.M. 93. Beethoven's 2nd 94. Imaginary Crimes 94, etc.

Penn, Leo (1921–).
American actor and director, the father of Sean and Christopher Penn.

Undercover Man (a) 49. The Story on Page One (a) 60. A Man Called Adam (d) 66. Murder in Music City (d) (TV) 79. Hellinger's Law (d) (TV) 81. Judgement in Berlin (d) 88, etc.

TV series: The Gertrude Berg Show 61.

Penn, Sean (1960–).
Scrawny but tough-looking American actor who has turned to writing and directing. He was formerly married to singer Madonna (1985–89) and has two children by actress Robin Wright.

■ Taps 81. Fast Times at Ridgemont High 82. Bad Boys 83. Racing with the Moon 83. Crackers 84. The Falcon and the Snowman 84. At Close Range 85. Shanghai Surprise 86. Colors 88. Casualties of War 89. We're No Angels 89. State of Grace 90. The Indian Runner (wd) 91. Carlito's Way 93. The Crossing Guard (wd) 95.

¶ I don't like any directors. I don't get along with any of them. Mostly I think they're a bunch of whiny people without any point of view. So I don't want to be around them at 6 o'clock in the morning with make-up and bells on. And I'm probably the same way for the actors on my set – but that's their problem. – *S.P.*

Pennebaker, D. A. (1930–) (Don Alan Pennebaker).
American documentary film-maker.

Don't Look Back 67. Monterey Pop 67. Town Bloody Hall (co-d) 80. Jimi 86. The Music Tells You (co-d) 93, etc.

Penner, Joe (1904–1941) (J. Pinter).
Hungarian-American radio comedian who made a few films.

College Rhythm 33. Collegiate 36. Go Chase Yourself 38. Glamour Boy 40. The Boys from Syracuse 40, etc.

Pennick, Jack (1895–1964).
American small-part actor and horse trainer, often in John Ford westerns.

Four Sons 28. Under Two Flags 36. Stagecoach 39. Northwest Mounted Police 40. My Darling lementine 46. Fort Apache 48. Rio Grande 50. he Alamo 60.

Pennington-Richards, C. M. (1911–).
British director, former photographer.
The Oracle 54. Inn for Trouble 60. Double Bunk 2. Ladies Who Do 63. A Challenge for Robin Hood 67, etc.

Penrod.
Booth Tarkington's American boy character, in his mid-west small-town setting, was for many years a favourite Hollywood subject. Marshall Neilan directed Gordon Griffith in a 1922 version. In 1923 William Beaudine directed Ben Alexander in the role in *Penrod and Sam*, which was remade by Beaudine in 1931 with Leon Janney, and again by William McGann in 1937 with Billy Mauch. Mauch and his twin brother Bobby appeared in two sequels: *Penrod's Double Trouble* 38, directed by Lewis Seiler, and *Penrod and His Twin Brother* 38, directed by McGann. Two Doris Day musicals, *On Moonlight Bay* 51 and *By the Light of the Silvery Moon* 53, were also lightly based on the Tarkington stories; Penrod, unaccountably disguised as 'Wesley', was played by Billy Gray.

Penrose, Charles (1876–1952).
Hearty comedian and writer who played a few character roles in 30s films. He is best remembered for his recording of 'The Laughing Policeman' and similar songs. He wrote and starred, as a policeman, in the radio comedy series *The Pig and Whistle* 38–44.
Dreams Come True 36. The Crimes of Stephen Hawke 36. Calling the Tune 36. Dark Eyes of London (aka The Human Monster) 39, etc.

Pepe Le Pew.
Smooth, romantic French skunk, the star of 14 Warner Brothers cartoons. Based on Charles Boyer's Pepe Le Moko in *Algiers*, he was created by writer Michael Maltese and animator Chuck Jones and voiced by Mel Blanc.
Scent-Imental over You 47. For Scent-Imental Reasons (AA) 49. Scent-Imental Romeo 51. Cat's Bah 54. Heaven Scent 56. Really Scent 59. Who Scent You? 60. Louvre Come Back to Me 62, etc.

Peploe, Clare.
British screenwriter and director. Married to Bernardo Bertolucci, she is the sister of writer Mark Peploe.
Zabriskie Point (co-w) 70. Luna (w) 79. High Season (co-w, d) 87.

Peploe, Mark.
British screenwriter and director.
The Pied Piper (w) 72. The Passenger (w) 75. The Last Emperor (w) (AAN) 87. High Season (w) 88. The Sheltering Sky (w) 90. Afraid of the Dark (wd) 91. Little Buddha 93, etc.

peplum.
Term to describe Italian historical epics, which are also known as 'sword and sandal'. Both expressions relate to the costumes of the participants, 'peplum' referring to the short skirts worn by both the men and the women. Such films were at their height in the early 60s, sparked off by the success in the US of *Ben-Hur* and of *Hercules*, made in 1957 by Pietro Francisci and starring Steve Reeves, which was promoted heavily by Joseph E. Levine. The genre in Italy goes back to *Cabiria*, made in 1914, starring Bartolomeo Pagano as Maciste (qv). The 60s cycle was notable for using mainly American muscle-men to play its heroes and for employing many talents, such as Sergio Leone, who went on

to make the even more popular spaghetti westerns.
See also: *epic film*.

Peppard, George (1928–1994).
American leading man with Broadway experience; began interestingly, but developed into an acceptable tough lead of hokum adventures.
■ *The Strange One* 57. Pork Chop Hill 59. Home from the Hill 60. The Subterraneans 60. *Breakfast at Tiffany's* 61. How the West Was Won 62. The Victors 63. *The Carpetbaggers* 64. Operation Crossbow 65. The Third Day 65. *The Blue Max* 66. Tobruk 67. Rough Night in Jericho 67. P. J. 68. What's So Bad about Feeling Good? 68. House of Cards 68. Pendulum 68. The Executioner 69. Cannon for Cordoba 70. One More Train to Rob 70. The Bravos (TV) 71. The Groundstar Conspiracy 72. Newman's Law 74. One of Our Own (TV) 75. Guilty or Innocent: The Sam Sheppard Murder Case (TV) 75. Damnation Alley 77. Your Ticket Is No Longer Valid 79. From Hell to Victory 79. Torn between Two Lovers (TV) 79. Crisis in Mid Air (TV) 79. Battle beyond the Stars 80. Five Days from Home (& d) 80. Race For the Yankee Zephyr 81. The A-Team (TV) 83. Target Eagle 84. Man against the Mob (TV) 88. Man against the Mob: The Chinatown Murders (TV) 89. Night of the Fox (TV) 90.
TV series: *Banacek* 72–73. Doctors' Hospital 75. *The A-Team* 83–86.

Pepper, Barbara (1912–1969).
American second-lead actress who usually played tramps.
Our Daily Bread 33. Winterset 36. Lady in the Morgue 38. Brewster's Millions 45. Terror Trail 47. Inferno 53. The D.I. 57. A Child is Waiting 63. Kiss Me Stupid 64, many others.

Percival, Lance (1933–).
British light comedian.
Twice Round the Daffodils 62. The VIPs 63. Carry On Cruising 63. The Yellow Rolls-Royce 64. The Big Job 65. Darling Lili 69. Up Pompeii 71. Our Miss Fred 72, etc.

Percy, Esmé (1887–1957).
Distinguished British stage actor, especially of Shavian parts. On stage from 1904; occasional films from 20s.
Murder 30. Bitter Sweet 33. *The Frog* 36. Pygmalion 38. Caesar and Cleopatra 45. The Ghosts of Berkeley Square 46. Death in the Hand 48, etc.

Pereira, Hal (1905–1983).
American art director, supervisor at Paramount from the 50s.
Carrie 52. Ace in the Hole 52. The Greatest Show on Earth 52. Red Garters 54. To Catch a Thief 55. The Ten Commandments 56. Vertigo 58. Hud 63, etc.

Perelman, S. J. (1904–1979).
Renowned American humorist whose name appeared on a few films, mostly in collaboration.
Monkey Business 31. Horse Feathers 32. Ambush 39. The Golden Fleecing 40. Around the World in Eighty Days (AA) 56, etc.

Perez, Rosie.
American actress, dancer and choreographer, born in Brooklyn.
Do the Right Thing 89. Criminal Justice (TV) 90. Night on Earth 91. White Men Can't Jump 92. Untamed Heart 93. Fearless (AAN) 93. It Could Happen to You 94. Somebody to Love 94, etc.

Périer, Etienne (1931–).
French director.
Bobosse 59. Murder at 45 RPM 60. Bridge to the Sun 61. Swordsman of Siena 63. When Eight Bells Toll 71. Zeppelin 71. Five against Capricorn 72. A Murder is a Murder 72, etc.

Perier, François (1919–) (François Pilu).
Sturdy French actor, in films from mid-30s.
Hôtel du Nord 38. Un Revenant 46. Le Silence est d'Or 48. *Orphée* 49. The Bed 53. *Gervaise* 55. Nights of Cabiria 56. Charmants Garçons 57. Weekend at Dunkirk 65. The Samurai 67. The Red Circle 70. Just Before Nightfall 73. La Bar du Téléphone 80, many others.

The Perils of Pauline.
Pearl White's famous 1914 serial was directed by Donald Mackenzie, co-starred Crane Wilbur, and concerned the heroine's evasion of attempts on her life by her dastardly guardian. The 1947 film of the same name was a lightly fictionalized biography of Pearl White, directed by George Marshall, with Betty Hutton in the title role. The 1967 film was vaguely based on the original serial, with Pamela Austin as the heroine, directed by Herbert Leonard and Joshua Shelley.

Perinal, Georges (1897–1965).
French cinematographer, in films from 1913.
Les Nouveaux Messieurs 28. Sous les Toits de Paris 30. *Le Sang d'un Poète* 30. *Le Million* 31. *A Nous la Liberté* 32. The Private Life of Henry VIII 32. *Rembrandt* 36. The Thief of Baghdad (AA) 40. *The Life and Death of Colonel Blimp* 43. Nicholas Nickleby 47. An Ideal Husband 47. *The Fallen Idol* 48. Lady Chatterley's Lover 55. A King in New York 57. Saint Joan 57. Bonjour Tristesse 58. Oscar Wilde 60, many others.

Perkins, Anthony (1932–1992).
Gangly American juvenile lead of the 50s, son of Osgood Perkins. Found mature roles scarce. Died of AIDS.
Biography: 1991, *Osgood and Anthony Perkins* by Laura Kay Palmer.
■ *The Actress* 53. Friendly Persuasion (AAN) 56. The Lonely Man 57. *Desire Under the Elms* 57. *Fear Strikes Out* 57. The Tin Star 57. *This Angry Age* 58. The Matchmaker 58. Green Mansions 58. On the Beach 59. Tall Story 60. *Psycho* 60. Goodbye Again 61. Phaedra 62. Five Miles to Midnight 62. The Trial 62. Two are Guilty 64. The Fool Killer 64. A Ravishing Idiot 64. Is Paris Burning? 66. The Champagne Murders 68. Pretty Poison 68. Catch 22 70. *WUSA* 70. How Awful About Allan (TV) 70. Ten Days Wonder 71. Someone Behind the Door (Two Minds for Murder) 71. Judge Roy Bean 72. Play It as It Lays 72. Lovin' Molly 73. Murder on the Orient Express 74. Mahogany 75. Remember My Name 78. First You Cry (TV) 78. Winter Kills 79. The Black Hole 79. Double Negative 79. North Sea Hijack 80. Twice a Woman 80. Les Misérables (TV) 80. For the Term of His Natural Life 82. *Psycho II* 83. Sins of Dorian Gray (TV) 83. Crimes of Passion 85. Psycho III (& d) 86. Destroyer 88. Edge of Sanity 89. I'm Dangerous Tonight (TV) 90. Psycho IV: The Beginning 90. The Naked Target 91. A Demon in My View 92. The Mummy Lives 92.

Famous line (*Psycho*): 'A boy's best friend is his mother.'

Perkins, Elizabeth (1961–).
American actress.
About Last Night 86. From the Hip 87. Big 88. Sweet Hearts Dance 88. Love at Large 90. Enid Is

Sleeping 90. Avalon 90. He Said, She Said 91. Indian Summer 93. The Flintstones 94. Miracle on 34th Street 94, etc.

Perkins, Millie (1939–).
American leading lady who went to Hollywood from dramatic school.

The Diary of Anne Frank 59. Wild in the Country 61. Wild in the Streets 68. Lady Cocoa 75. Table for Five 83. At Close Range 85. Jake Speed 86. Slam Dance 87. Pistol: The Birth of a Legend 91. Necronomicon 93, etc.

TV series: Knots Landing 83–84. Elvis 90.

Perkins, Osgood (1892–1937).
American character actor, mainly on stage.

Biography: 1991, *Osgood and Anthony Perkins* by Laura Kay Palmer.

The Cradle Buster 22. Puritan Passions 23. Knockout Reilly 27. Mother's Boy 29. Tarnished Lady 31. Scarface 32. Kansas City Princess 34. I Dream Too Much 35, etc.

Perlberg, William (1899–1969).
American producer, often in conjunction with George Seaton; came from agency business, in Hollywood from mid-30s.

Golden Boy 39. The Song of Bernadette 43. Forever Amber 47. The Country Girl 54. Teacher's Pet 58. The Counterfeit Traitor 62. Thirty-Six Hours 64, many others.

Perlman, Rhea (1948–).
American actress, best known for her role as Carla in the TV series *Cheers* 82–92. Married Danny DeVito.

Intimate Strangers (TV) 77. Love Child 82. The Ratings Game (TV) 84. My Little Pony (voice) 86. Stamp of a Killer (TV) 87. Class Act 91. Enid Is Sleeping (aka Over Her Dead Body) 91. Ted & Venus 91. There Goes the Neighborhood (aka Paydirt) 92. Class Act 92. Canadian Bacon 94, etc.

Perreau, Gigi (1941–) (Ghislaine Perreau-Saussine).
American child actress of the 40s who seems not quite to have managed the transition to adult stardom.

Madame Curie 43. Song of Love 47. My Foolish Heart 49. Has Anybody Seen My Gal? 51. The Man in the Grey Flannel Suit 56. Wild Heritage 58. Look in Any Window 61. Journey to the Center of Time 67. Hell on Wheels 67, etc.

TV series: The Betty Hutton Show 59. Follow the Sun 69.

Perrine, Valerie (1944–).
American leading lady of the 70s.

Slaughterhouse Five 72. The Last American Hero 73. Lenny (AAN) 74. W. C. Fields and Me 76. Mr Billion 77. Ziegfeld: the Man and his Women (TV) 78. Superman 78. The Electric Horseman 79. Can't Stop the Music 80. Superman II 80. Agency 81. The Border 82. Water 85. When Your Lover Leaves (TV) 85. Maid to Order 87. Reflections in a Dark Sky (Riflessi in un Cielo Scuro) 91. Bright Angel 91. Boiling Point 93, etc.

Perrins, Leslie (1902–1962).
British character actor, often seen as a smooth crook.

The Sleeping Cardinal 31. The Pointing Finger 34. Tudor Rose 36. Old Iron 39. The Woman's Angle 43. A Run for Your Money 49. Guilty 56, many others.

Perry, Eleanor (1925–1981).
American screenwriter; wrote all the scripts of her husband Frank Perry's films until their divorce in 1970. Then alone: *Diary of a Mad Housewife, The Lady in the Car, The Man Who Loved Cat Dancing*.

Perry, Frank (1930–).
American director. In 1992 he made a TV documentary, *On the Bridge*, dealing with his reactions to the discovery that he had cancer of the prostate.

■ David and Lisa (AAN) 63. Ladybug, Ladybug 64. The Swimmer 68. Trilogy 68. Last Summer 69. Diary of a Mad Housewife 70. Doc 71. Play It as It Lays 72. Man on a Swing 74. Rancho de Luxe 76. Monsignor 82. Compromising Positions 85. Hello Again 87.

Perry, Luke (1967–).
American leading actor from TV soap operas who gained fame as Dylan McKay in the TV series *Beverly Hills, 90210* 90–93.

Buffy, the Vampire Hunter 92. Terminal Bliss 92. Lane Frost 93. 8 Seconds 94.

TV series: Loving 87–88.

¶ I felt like I belonged on a screen. I don't know why. I guess because I related to the people up on that screen much more than the people around me. I always felt like I was one of them and in a matter of time I'd get there. – *L.P.*

Perry Mason,
a crime-solving lawyer who wins all his cases, usually during a court-room cross-examination, was created by Erle Stanley Gardner in *The Case of the Velvet Claws* 33, the first of more than 80 novels in which he was the hero. On film, he has been played by Warren William, Ricardo Cortez and Donald Woods, but it was Raymond Burr who became closely identified with the character in the TV series of 245 hour-long episodes that ran 1957–66. Monte Markham took over the part in the unsuccessful *The New Adventures of Perry Mason* 73–74; then in 1985 Burr returned to the role in a continuing series of TV movies.

The Case of the Howling Dog 34. The Case of the Curious Bride 35. The Case of the Lucky Legs 35. The Case of the Velvet Claws 36. The Case of the Black Cat 36. The Case of the Stuttering Bishop 37. Perry Mason Returns (TV) 85. Perry Mason: The Case of the Notorious Nun (TV) 86. Perry Mason: The Case of the Lost Love (TV) 87. Perry Mason: The Case of the Lady in the Lake (TV) 88. Perry Mason: The Case of the All-Star Assassin (TV) 89. Perry Mason: The Case of the Ruthless Reporter (TV) 91, etc.

Perry, Paul P. (1891–1963).
Pioneer American cinematographer who experimented with colour.

Rose of the Rancho 14. The Cheat 15. Hidden Pearls 17. The Sea Wolf 21. Rosita 23. Souls for Sables 26, many others.

persistence of vision.
The medical explanation for our being able to see moving pictures. Twenty-four ordered still pictures are shown to us successively each second, and our sense of sight is slow enough to merge them into one continuous action. The retina of the eye retains each still picture just long enough for it to be replaced by another only slightly different.

Persoff, Nehemiah (1920–).
Israeli actor, long in America; trained at Actors' Studio.

On the Waterfront 54. The Harder They Fall 56. *This Angry Age* 57. The Badlanders 58. Never Steal Anything Small 58. Al Capone 59. Some Like It Hot 59. The Big Show 61. The Comancheros 62. The Hook 63. *Fate is the Hunter* 64. The Greatest Story Ever Told 65. Panic in the City 68. Red Sky at Morning 71. Psychic Killer 75. Voyage of the Damned 76. The Word (TV) 78. Yentl 83. The Last Temptation of Christ 88. An American Tail: Fievel Goes West (voice) 91, etc.

Persson, Essy (1941–).
Swedish leading lady.

I a Woman 67. Thérèse and Isabelle 68. Cry of the Banshee 70, etc.

Pertwee, Jon (1919–).
British comic actor, brother of Michael Pertwee, son of playwright Roland.

Murder at the Windmill 48. Mr Drake's Duck 51. Will Any Gentleman? 53. A Yank in Ermine 56. Carry On Cleo 64. Carry On Screaming 66. The House that Dripped Blood 70. One of Our Dinosaurs is Missing 75. Adventures of a Private Eye 77, etc.

TV series: Doctor Who (title role) 70–74. Worzel Gummidge 79.

Pertwee, Michael (1916–1991).
British playwright who has been involved in many screenplays.

Silent Dust (from his play) 48. The Interrupted Journey 49. *Laughter in Paradise* 51. Top Secret 52. Now and Forever 54. *The Naked Truth* 57. In the Doghouse 62. The Mouse on the Moon 62. Ladies Who Do 63. A Funny Thing Happened on the Way to the Forum 66. Finders Keepers 66. The Magnificent Two 67. Salt and Pepper 68. One More Time 70. Digby 73, etc.

Pertwee, Sean.
English actor, the son of Jon Pertwee.

Shopping 94. Clockwork Mice 95.

Pesci, Joe (1943–).
Short American character actor, on radio as a child.

Death Collector 76. Raging Bull (AAN) 80. Easy Money 83. Eureka 83. Once upon a Time in America 84. Man on Fire 87. Lethal Weapon 2 89. Catchfire 89. Betsy's Wedding 90. Home Alone 90. GoodFellas (AA) 90. JFK 91. My Cousin Vinny 92. Lethal Weapon 3 92. Home Alone 2: Lost in New York 92. The Public Eye 92. A Bronx Tale 94. Jimmy Hollywood 94. With Honors 94, etc.

TV series: Half Nelson 85.

Peterman, Donald.
American cinematographer.

When a Stranger Calls 79. King of the Mountain 81. Rich and Famous 81. Young Doctors in Love 82. Kiss Me Goodbye 82. Flashdance (AAN) 83. Splash 84. Best Defence 84. Cocoon 85. American Flyers 85. Star Trek IV: The Voyage Home 86. Planes, Trains and Automobiles 87. She's Having a Baby 88. She's Out of Control 89. Point Break 91. Mr Saturday Night 92. Addams Family Values 93, etc.

Peters, Bernadette (1948–) (B. Lazzaro).
American leading lady.

Ace Eli and Rodger of the Skies 72. The Longest Yard 74. The Jerk 79. Pennies from Heaven 81. Heartbeeps 81. Annie 82. David (TV) 88. Pink Cadillac 89. Slaves of New York 89. Fall from Grace (TV) 90. Alice 90. Impromptu 92, etc.

Peters, Brock (1927–).
American actor in international films.

To Kill a Mockingbird 62. The L-Shaped Room 62. *Heavens Above* (GB) 63. The Pawnbroker 64. Major Dundee 65. P. J. 67. The McMasters 70. Black Girl 73. Framed 75. Two Minute Warning 76.

ar Trek IV: the Voyage Home 86. Star Trek VI:
he Undiscovered Country 91. The Importance of
eing Earnest 91, etc.

eters, House (1880–1967).
merican silent screen leading man.
Leah Kleschna 12. The Pride of Jennico 14. The
reat Divide 15. Mignon 15. The Storm 22. Held
r Answer 23. Raffles 25. Head Winds 25, many
hers.

eters, Jean (1926–).
ttractive American leading lady of the 50s; retired
 marry Howard Hughes.
 Captain from Castile 47. Deep Waters 48. It
appens Every Spring 49. Love That Brute 50. Take
are of My Little Girl 51. As Young as You Feel
. Anne of the Indies 52. Viva Zapata 52. Wait
ll the Sun Shines, Nellie 52. Lure of the
Vilderness 52. Full House 52. Niagara 53. Pickup
n South Street 53. Blueprint for Murder 53. Vicki
. *Three Coins in the Fountain* 54. Apache 54.
roken Lance 54. *A Man Called Peter* 55. The
Moneychangers (TV) 74. Peter and Paul (TV) 81.

eters, Jon (1947–).
merican producer, former hairdresser. He formed
he Guber-Peters company with Peter Guber in
982 and went with Guber to run Columbia
llowing its takeover by Sony in 1989, before
aving to become an independent producer once
ore.
A Star Is Born 76. Eyes of Laura Mars 78. The
Main Event 79. Die Laughing 80. Missing 82. Six
Veeks 82. Flashdance 83. Sheena 84. Clue 85. The
olor Purple 85. Vision Quest 85. Innerspace 87.
ain Man 88. Batman 89. Tango & Cash 89.
onfire of the Vanities 90, etc.

When I was in the hair business I produced
huge spectacular shows. Film is just another
rm of production. – J.P.

eters, Susan (1921–1952) (Suzanne Carnahan).
merican leading lady of the 40s; badly injured in
n accident, she continued her career from a
vheelchair.
Santa Fé Trail 40. *Random Harvest* (AAN) 42.
ssignment in Brittany 43. Song of Russia 44.
Keep Your Powder Dry 45. The Sign of the Ram
8, etc.

eters, Werner (1918–1971).
German character actor in occasional international
ilms.
L'Affaire Blum 49. Der Untertan 51. The Girl
tosemarie 58. Scotland Yard vs. Dr Mabuse 63.
he Corrupt Ones 66. Assignment K 68. Istanbul
xpress (TV) 68, etc.

etersen, Colin (1946–).
ritish child actor of the 50s.
Smiley 56. The Scamp 57. A Cry from the Streets
7, etc.

etersen, Paul (1945–).
merican teen actor and singer who was unable
o sustain his career as an adult. He began as a
Mouseketeer on Disney's Mickey Mouse Club, had
wo hit records in the early 60s, and later became
 novelist.
Autobiography: 1977, *Walt, Mickey and Me.*
This Could Be the Night 57. The Monolith
Monsters 57. Houseboat 58. The Happiest
Millionaire 67. A Time for Killing 67. Journey to
Shiloh 68, etc.
TV series: The Donna Reed Show 58–66.

Fame is not a career. It's a sentence. – P.P.
What happens to ex-bubblegum stars? No
room left for me. – P.P.

Petersen, Wolfgang (1941–).
German director and screenwriter, from television.
His *The Boat (Das Boot)* was an international hit.
Wolf 70. Einer von uns Beiden 73. The
Consequence (Die Konsequenz) (wd) 77. Black and
White Like Night and Day (Schwarz und Weiss
Wie Tage und Nächte) (wd) 78. The Boat (Das
Boot) (wd) (AAN) 81. The Neverending Story 84.
Enemy Mine 85. Shattered 91. In the Line of Fire
93. Outbreak 95, etc.

Peterson, Dorothy (c. 1900–1979).
American supporting actress of the 30s, usually in
maternal roles.
Cabin in the Cotton 32. I'm No Angel 33.
Treasure Island 34. The Country Doctor 36. Dark
Victory 39. Lillian Russell 40. The Moon Is Down
43. The Woman in the Window 45. That Hagen Girl
47, many others.

Petit, Chris (1949–).
English critic turned director, much influenced by
the films of Wim Wenders.
Radio On 79. A Suitable Job for a Woman 82.
Flight to Berlin 84. Chinese Boxes 84, etc.

Petit, Jean-Claude.
French composer.
Vive la Sociale! 83. Jean de Florette 87. Manon
des Sources 87. Return of the Musketeers 89.
Cyrano de Bergerac 90. Uranus 90. Mother
(Mayrig) 91. All Out 91. 588 Rue Paradis 92. The
Playboys 92. Foreign Student 94, etc.

Petit, Pascale (1938–) (Anne-Marie Petit).
French leading lady.
The Witches of Salem 57. Les Tricheurs 58. Girls
for the Summer 59. L'Affaire d'Une Nuit 60.
Demons at Midnight 62, etc.

Petri, Elio (1929–1982).
Italian director, a political satirist.
The Assassin 61. The Tenth Victim 65. We Still
Kill the Old Way 68. A Quiet Place in the Country
68. Investigation of a Citizen above Suspicion (AA)
69. The Working Class Goes to Heaven 71.
Property is No Longer Theft 73. Todo Modo 76,
etc.

Petrie, Daniel (1920–).
American director with academic background;
stage and TV experience.
■ The Bramble Bush 59. A Raisin in the Sun 61.
The Main Attraction 62. Stolen Hours 63. The Idol
66. The Spy with a Cold Nose 67. Silent Night
Lonely Night (TV) 69. The City (TV) 71. A
Howling in the Woods (TV) 71. Moon of the Wolf
(TV) 72. Trouble Comes to Town (TV) 72. The
Neptune Factor 73. Buster and Billie 74. The Gun
and the Pulpit (TV) 74. Eleanor and Franklin (TV)
76. Lifeguard 76. Sybil (TV) 77. The Betsy 78.
Resurrection 80. Fort Apache, the Bronx 81. Six
Pack 82. Bay Boy 84. Square Dance 86. Rocket
Gibraltar 88. Cocoon: The Return 88. Mark Twain
and Me (TV) 91. Grumpy Old Men 93. Lassie 94.

Petrie, Daniel, Jnr.
American screenwriter and director. A former
literary agent, he is the son of Daniel Petrie.
■ Beverly Hills Cop (w) (AAN) 84. The Big Easy
(w) 87. Shoot to Kill (w) 88. Turner & Hooch (w)
89. Toy Soldiers (wd) 91. In the Army Now 94.

Petrie, Hay (1895–1948).
Scots character actor of stage and screen,
specializing in eccentrics.
Suspense 30. The Private Life of Henry VIII 32.
Nell Gwyn 34. *The Old Curiosity Shop* (as Quilp) 34.
The Ghost Goes West 36. *Twenty-One Days* 38. The
Spy in Black 39. Q Planes 39. Jamaica Inn 39.
Crimes at the Dark House 40. The Thief of Baghdad
40. One of Our Aircraft is Missing 42. A
Canterbury Tale 44. Great Expectations 46. The
Red Shoes 48. The Guinea Pig 48, etc.

Petrov, Vladimir (1896–1966).
Russian director.
Thunderstorm 34. *Peter the Great* 38, etc.

Petrova, Olga (1886–1977) (Muriel Harding).
British-born leading lady of Hollywood silents in
which she played *femmes fatales.*
Autobiography: 1942, *Butter with My Bread.*
The Tigress 14. The Soul Market 16. The
Undying Flame 17. Daughter of Destiny 18. The
Panther Woman 18, etc.

Petrovic, Aleksander (1929–1994).
Yugoslavian director, a former film critic, and an
influential figure in the 60s.
■ Two (Dvoje) 61. The Days (Dani) 63. Three (Tri)
(AAN) 65. I Even Met Happy Gypsies (Skuplijaci
Perja) (AAN) 67. The Master and Margarita 72.
Group Portrait with Lady 77. Migrations 94.

Pettet, Joanna (1944–).
Anglo-American leading lady.
The Group 66. Night of the Generals 66. Robbery
67. Blue 68. The Weekend Nun (TV) 74. Welcome
to Arrow Beach 75. Captains and the Kings (TV)
76. The Evil 78. The Return of Frank Cannon (TV)
80. Double Exposure 82, etc.

Pettingeli, Frank (1891–1966).
British north-country character actor who
dispensed rough good humour on stage from 1910;
films from 1931.
Hobson's Choice (as Mossop) 31. Jealousy 31. *The
Good Companions* 32. Sing As We Go 34. The Last
Journey 36. Fame 36. Millions 36. Sailing Along
38. *Gaslight* 39. Busman's Honeymoon 40. The
Seventh Survivor 41. This England 41. Kipps 41.
Once a Crook 41. *When We are Married* 42. The
Young Mr Pitt 42. Get Cracking 44. Gaiety George
46. The Magic Box 51. Meet Me Tonight 52. Value
for Money 57. Becket 64, many others.

Pevney, Joseph (1920–).
American director, former stage actor.
Shakedown 50. Undercover Girl 50. Iron Man
51. The Strange Door 51. Meet Danny Wilson 51.
Just across the Street 52. Because of You 54. Desert
Legion 54. The Female on the Beach 55. Three Ring
Circus 55. Away All Boats 56. Congo Crossing 56.
Tammy 57. *Man of a Thousand Faces* 57. Twilight for
the Gods 58. Cash McCall 60. Night of the Grizzly
66. Who Is the Black Dahlia? (TV) 75. Mysterious
Island of Beautiful Women (TV) 77. Prisoners of
the Sea 85, etc.

Peyton Place.
The 1957 film version of Grace Metalious's novel
started a fashion for small-town sex exposés on the
screen, and was followed by a sequel, *Return to
Peyton Place*, in 1961. A TV series of two half-hours
a week followed in 1964 and proved so popular
that in 1965 it was given three half-hours and
lasted until 1969, bringing to public notice Mia
Farrow and Ryan O'Neal.

Pfeiffer, Dedee.
American actress, the sister of Michelle Pfeiffer.
Vamp 86. The Allnighter 87. Brothers in Arms 89. The Horror Show 89. Red Surf 90. Tune in Tomorrow (aka Aunt Julia and the Scriptwriter) 90. Frankie & Johnny 91, etc.

Pfeiffer, Michelle (1957–).
American actress.
Grease 2 82. Scarface 83. Into the Night 84. Ladyhawke 85. Sweet Liberty 86. The Witches of Eastwick 87. Married to the Mob 88. Tequila Sunrise 88. Dangerous Liaisons (AAN) 88. The Fabulous Baker Boys (AAN) 89. The Russia House 90. Frankie and Johnny 91. Love Field 92. Batman Returns 92. The Age of Innocence 93. Wolf 94, etc.
TV series: Delta House 79. B.A.D. Cats 80.

¶ Hollywood is filled with beautiful, unhappy women who have shut down. – M.P.

The Phantom of the Opera.
Gaston Leroux's melodramatic tale of the embittered, disfigured composer who haunts the sewers beneath the Paris Opéra and takes a pretty young singer as his protégée has been filmed several times: in 1925 Rupert Julian directed a version with Lon Chaney and Mary Philbin; in 1943 Arthur Lubin directed Claude Rains and Susanna Foster; in 1962 came a British version, directed by Terence Fisher, with Herbert Lom and Heather Sears; in 1989 Dwight H. Little directed Robert Englund, better known as Freddy from A Nightmare on Elm Street, in a version set in London. In 1977 Brian DePalma made a rock version, Phantom of the Paradise, and there have been two TV movies, one in 1983 starring Maximilian Schell and Jane Seymour, and another in 1990, directed by Tony Richardson from a script by Arthur Kopit, with Charles Dance and Teri Polo. Andrew Lloyd-Webber's highly successful stage musical, premiered in 1986, will no doubt be filmed in the future.

Philbin, Mary (1903–1993).
American leading lady of the silent screen.
The Blazing Trail 21. Merry Go Round 23. Phantom of the Opera 25. The Man Who Laughs 28. After the Fog 30, etc.

Philip Marlowe
was the weary but incorruptible private-eye creation of Raymond Chandler, treading the seamier streets of Los Angeles in a dogged hunt for suspects. On television he was played in a poor series by Phil Carey, on screen by Humphrey Bogart, Robert Montgomery, George Montgomery, Dick Powell, James Garner, Robert Mitchum and (very badly) by Elliott Gould. In 1983 he was portrayed in a British television series, Chandlertown, by Powers Boothe.

Philipe, Gérard (1922–1959).
France's leading young actor of the 50s, who alternated stage and screen activities.
Biography: 1964, No Longer than a Sigh by Anne Philipe.
■ La Boîte aux Rêves 43. The Children of the Flower Quay 45. Land without Stars 46. The Idiot 46. Le Diable au Corps 47. La Chartreuse de Parme 47. Une Si Jolie Petite Plage 49. All Roads Lead to Rome 49. La Beauté du Diable 50. La Ronde 50. Juliette ou la Clef des Songes 51. Fanfan la Tulipe 51. The Seven Deadly Sins 51. Les Belles de Nuit 52. Les Orgeuilleux 53. Versailles 53. Knave of Hearts (GB) 54. Villa Borghese 54. The Red and the Black 54. Les Grandes Manoeuvres 55. La Meilleure

Part 55. Si Paris Nous Était Conté 55. Till Eulenspiegel 57. Pot Bouille 57. Montparnasse 19 57. La Vie à Deux 58. The Gambler 58. Les Liaisons Dangereuses 59. La Fièvre Monte à El Pao 59.

Philips, Lee (1927–).
American leading man of the late 50s. Became TV director.
Peyton Place 57. The Hunters 58. Middle of the Night 59. Tess of the Storm Country 60. The Lollipop Cover 65, etc.

Philips, Mary (1900–1975).
American stage actress who made very occasional film appearances.
Life Begins 32. A Farewell To Arms 33. That Certain Woman 37. Lady in the Dark 44. Leave Her to Heaven 46. Dear Wife 47, etc.

Philips, Robin (1941–).
British juvenile lead, later stage director in Canada.
Decline and Fall 68. David Copperfield 69. Two Gentlemen Sharing 70. Tales From the Crypt 72. Miss Julie (d) 73.

Philliber, John (1872–1944).
Slightly-built American character actor in a few early 40s films; best remembered for It Happened Tomorrow 44.

Phillips, Alex (1901–1977).
Canadian cinematographer, long in Hollywood.
See My Lawyer 21. The Nervous Wreck 26. Many Mexican films 1930–52. Robinson Crusoe 52. Adam and Eve 57. Last of the Fast Guns 58. Geronimo 62; then back to Mexico.

Phillips, Conrad (1930–).
British leading man, mostly on TV.
The White Trap 59. Chamber of Horrors 60. The Fourth Square 61. No Love for Johnnie 62. Stopover Forever 64. Who Killed the Cat? 66, etc.
TV series: William Tell 58.

Phillips, Frank (1912–1994).
American cinematographer.
The Island at the Top of the World 74. Escape to Witch Mountain 75. No Deposit No Return 76. The Shaggy D.A. 76. Pete's Dragon 77. Return from Witch Mountain 78. Hot Lead and Cold Feet 78. Goin' Coconuts 78. The Apple Dumpling Gang Rides Again 79. The Black Hole (AAN) 79. Midnight Madness 80. Herbie Goes Bananas 80. Going Ape! 81, etc.

Phillips, Julia (1945–) and Michael (1943–).
American husband-and-wife producers, now divorced, who hit the big time with The Sting, Taxi Driver and Close Encounters of the Third Kind.
MICHAEL PHILLIPS AS SOLE PRODUCER: Cannery Row 81. Heartbeeps 81. The Flamingo Kid 84. Don't Tell Mom the Babysitter's Dead 91. Dick & Marge Save the World 91.

¶ Julia Phillips gained notoriety in 1991 with the publication of her acerbic, best-selling memoir, You'll Never Eat Lunch in This Town Again, detailing her drug-fuelled decline as a producer and notable for her low opinion of most of her former colleagues.
On John Landis:
That little megalomaniacal prick.
On Steven Spielberg:
I taught the little prick he deserved limos before he even knew what it was to travel in a first-class seat on a plane.
On François Truffaut:
Deep down I knew he was a prick.

On Donald Sutherland:
A top-ten brain fucker.

Phillips, Leslie (1924–).
British light comedian, former child actor from 1935.
The Citadel 38. Train of Events 49. The Sound Barrier 52. Value for Money 57. Carry On Nurse 5? Carry On Constable 60. Doctor in Love 60. Watc Your Stern 60. Very Important Person 61. Raising the Wind 61. In the Doghouse 62. Crooks Anonymous 62. The Fast Lady 62. And Father Came Too 64. Doctor in Clover 66. Maroc 7 (& p 66. Doctor in Trouble 70. The Magnificent Seven Deadly Sins 71. Not Now Darling 73. Don't Just Lie There Say Something 73. Spanish Fly 75. Not Now Comrade 76. Out of Africa 85. Empire of th Sun 87. Scandal 89. Mountains of the Moon 90. King Ralph 91. Love on a Branch Line (TV) 94. August 95, etc.
TV series: Honey for Tea 94. The House of Windsor 94.

Phillips, Lou Diamond (1962–).
American young leading actor.
Trespasses (& w) 83. Harley 85. La Bamba 87. Dakota 88. Stand and Deliver 88. Young Guns 88 Disorganized Crime 89. Renegades 89. The First Power 90. A Show of Force 90. Young Guns II 90 Harley 90. Ambition (& w) 91. Dark Wind 91. Shadow of the Wolf (& co-w) 93. Sioux City (& d) 94. Boulevard 94. Teresa's Tattoo 94, etc.

Phillips, MacKenzie (1960–).
American second lead of the 70s.
American Graffiti 75. Eleanor and Franklin (TV 76. More American Graffiti 79. Love Child 82, et

Phillips, Sian (1934–).
Dignified British stage actress. She was married to actor Peter O'Toole (1959–79).
Becket 64. Young Cassidy 64. Laughter in the Dark 69. Goodbye Mr Chips 69. Murphy's War 70. Under Milk Wood 72. I, Claudius (TV) 76. Tinker Tailor Soldier Spy (TV) 79. Nijinksy 80. Clas of the Titans 81. Dune 85. The Doctor and the Devils 85. The Two Mrs Grenvilles (TV) 86. Valmont 89. The Age of Innocence 93, etc.

Philo Vance:
see Van Dine, S. S.

Philpotts, Ambrosine (1912–1980).
British character actress, mainly on stage.
This Man is Mine 46. The Franchise Affair 51. The Captain's Paradise 53. Up in the World 56. Room at the Top 59. Doctor in Love 60. Life at th Top 65, etc.

Phipps, Nicholas (1913–1980).
British light comedian often seen in cameo roles. On stage from 1932. Has also scripted or co-scripted many films, in most of which he appeared
Piccadilly Incident 46. Spring in Park Lane 48. Doctor in the House 53. Doctor in Love 60. The Wild and the Willing 62, many others.

Phoenix, Leaf (1974–).
American juvenile actor, the brother of River and Rain Phoenix.
Spacecamp 86. Russkies 87. Parenthood 89, etc

Phoenix, Rain (1971–).
American actress, the sister of River and Leaf Phoenix.
Even Cowgirls Get the Blues 93. The Thing Called Love 94. Interview with the Vampire 94, etc

Phoenix, River (1971–1993).
American young leading actor. He also played guitar and sang with his own rock group, Aleka's Attic. Died outside a Hollywood night-club after overdosing on heroin and cocaine. His final performance was in *Dark Blood*, a film which was abandoned three weeks from completion.
  Explorers 85. Mosquito Coast 86. Stand by Me 6. Little Nikita 88. A Night in the Life of Jimmy Reardon 88. Running on Empty (AAN) 88. Indiana Jones and the Last Crusade 89. I Love You to Death 0. Dogfight 91. My Own Private Idaho 91. Sneakers 92. Silent Tongue 93. The Thing Called Love 93, etc.
  TV series: Seven Brides for Seven Brothers 82–3.

¶ I don't see any point or any good in drugs that are as disruptive as cocaine. – *R.P.*
  There wasn't a false bone in his body. – *Sidney Lumet*

Pialat, Maurice (1925–).
French director.
  L'Enfance Nue 68. We Will Not Grow Old Together 72. La Gueule Ouverte 73. Graduate First (Passe Ton Bac d'Abord) 79. Loulou 79. A Nos Amours 83. Police 85. Under Satan's Sun 87. Van Gogh 91, etc.

Piazza, Ben (1934–1991).
Canadian actor who went to Hollywood, but was little heard from.
  A Dangerous Age (Can.) 58. The Hanging Tree 59. I Never Promised You a Rose Garden 77. Apocalypse Now 79. The Blues Brothers 80. Rocky V 90. Guilty by Suspicion 91, etc.
  TV series: Ben Casey 65. Forever Fernwood 77. The Waverly Wonders 78. Dallas 82–83.

Piccoli, Michel (1925–).
Franco-Italian leading man.
  French Cancan 55. The Witches of Salem 56. Le Bal des Espions 60. Le Mépris 63. Diary of a Chambermaid 64. De L'Amour 65. Lady L. 65. La Curée 66. The Young Girls of Rochefort 67. Un Homme de Trop 67. Belle de Jour 67. Dillinger is Dead 68. The Milky Way 69. Topaz 69. Blowout 73. The Infernal Trio 74. Mado 76. The Savage State 78. Le Sucre 78. A City 80. La Chambre Voisine 80. Leap into the Void 81. General of the Dead Army 81. Dangerous Moves 84. Revenge 84. Departure. Return 85. The Nonentity 86. Bad Blood 86. La Rumba 86. Martha und Ich 90. May Fools (Milou en Mai) 90. La Belle Noiseuse 91. Le Voleur d'Enfants 91. Le Bal des Casse-Pieds 91. Archipelago (Archipel) 92. Ruptures 93. Le Souper 93. La Cavale des Fous 93. Les Cent et Une Nuits 95, etc.

Picerni, Paul (1922–).
American leading man, usually in second features.
  Saddle Tramp (debut) 50. Maru Maru 52. House of Wax 53. Drive a Crooked Road 54. Hell's Island 55. Omar Khayyam 57. Strangers When We Meet 60. The Scalphunters 68. The Land Raiders 69. The Fearmaker 89, etc.
  TV series: The Untouchables 59–62.

Pichel, Irving (1891–1954).
American actor-director, in Hollywood from 1930.
AS ACTOR: The Right to Love 30. The Miracle Man 31. Oliver Twist (as Fagin) 33. Cleopatra 34. Jezebel 38. Juarez 40. Sante Fé 51, many others.
■ AS DIRECTOR: *The Most Dangerous Game* (co-d) 32. Before Dawn 33. *She* (co-d) 35. The Gentleman from Louisiana 36. Beware of Ladies 37. Larceny of the Air 37. The Sheik Steps Out 37. The Duke

Comes Back 37. The Great Commandment 39. Earthbound 40. The Man I Married 40. Hudson's Bay 40. Dance Hall 41. Secret Agent of Japan 42. The Pied Piper 42. Life Begins at 8.30 42. *The Moon is Down* 43. *Happy Land* 43. And Now Tomorrow 44. A Medal for Benny 45. Colonel Effingham's Raid 45. Tomorrow is Forever 46. The Bride Wore Boots 46. O.S.S. 46. Temptation 46. They Won't Believe Me 47. Something in the Wind 47. The Miracle of the Bells 48. Mr Peabody and the Mermaid 48. Without Honor 49. The Great Rupert 50. Quicksand 50. Destination Moon 50. Santa Fé 51. Martin Luther 53. Day of Triumph 54.

Pick, Lupu:
see *Lupu-Pick.*

Pickens, Slim (1919–1983) (Louis Bert Lindley).
Slow-talking American character actor, in scores of low-budget westerns from mid-40s, latterly in bigger films.
  The Sun Shines Bright 53. The Great Locomotive Chase 56. One-Eyed Jacks 61. Dr Strangelove 63. Major Dundee 65. Rough Night in Jericho 67. The Cowboys 72. Pat Garrett and Billy the Kid 73. Blazing Saddles 74. The Apple Dumpling Gang 75. Whiteline Fever 75. The White Buffalo 77. Mr Billion 77. Wishbone Cutter 78. Beyond the Poseidon Adventure 79. Honeysuckle Rose 80. The Howling 81. Pink Motel 82, etc.
  TV series: Outlaws 61. Custer 67.

Pickering, Donald (1933–).
British actor who played Holmes in the little seen 1980 TV series *Sherlock Holmes and Dr Watson.*
  A Bridge Too Far 76. The Thirty-Nine Steps 78. Half Moon Street 87, etc.

Pickford, Jack (1896–1933).
American light actor, brother of Mary Pickford. He was married to actresses Marilyn Miller and Olive Thomas.
  Tom Sawyer 17. Sandy 18. Just Out of College 21. The Goose Woman 25. The Bat 26. Brown of Harvard 26. Exit Smiling 26. Gang War 28, etc.

Pickford, Mary (1893–1979) (Gladys Smith).
Canadian actress who in the heyday of silent films was known as 'the world's sweetheart'; became co-founder of United Artists Films and one of America's richest women. Acting on stage from five years old; was brought into films by D. W. Griffith.
  Autobiography: 1955, *Sunshine and Shadow.*
  Biographies: 1974, *Sweetheart* by Robert Windeler. 1991, *Mary Pickford: America's Sweetheart* by Scott Eyman.
  Her First Biscuits 09. The Violin Maker of Cremona 10. The Paris Hat 13. Madame Butterfly 15. Less Than the Dust 16. The Little Princess 17. Rebecca of Sunnybrook Farm 17. Stella Maris 18. *Pollyanna* 19. Suds 20. *Little Lord Fauntleroy* 21. The Love Light 21. *Tess of the Storm Country* 22. Rosita 23. Dorothy Vernon of Haddon Hall 24. Little Annie Rooney 25. My Best Girl 27. The Taming of the Shrew 29. Secrets 29. *Coquette* (AA) 29. Kiki 31. Secrets 33, many others.
☺ For entrancing the world, and for knowing when to stop. *Little Lord Fauntleroy.*

¶ The appeal of the world's sweetheart is not well understood in the 80s. Her screen image was ever-childlike, sweet and demure, the antithesis of today's heroines. Alistair Cooke said:
  She was the girl every young man wanted to have – as his sister.
Yet on first encounter D. W. Griffith told her:
  You're too little and too fat, but I might give you a job.

Later, he ruefully recollected:
  She never stopped listening and learning.
She was soon telling Adolph Zukor:
  I can't afford to work for only ten thousand dollars a week.
And Sam Goldwyn reflected:
  It took longer to make one of Mary's contracts than it did to make one of Mary's pictures.
Spoiled by success she may have been, but never blind to her own failings:
  I never liked one of my pictures in its entirety.
By 1929 she was surprisingly intolerant of her screen image:
  I am sick of Cinderella parts, of wearing rags and tatters. I want to wear smart clothes and play the lover.
Richard Griffith and Arthur Mayer thought the secret of her success was that:
  Her sweetness and light were tempered by a certain realism. In spite of her creed, the Glad Girl knew it was no cinch to make everything come out right. Nothing could have been more in tune with an era which combined limitless optimism with a belief that 'git up and git' was necessary to make optimism come true.
But Mabel Normand at a press conference struck a sour note:
  Say anything you like, but don't say I want to work. That sounds like Mary Pickford, that prissy bitch.
~Special Academy Award 1976.

Pickles, Vivian (1933–).
British character actress.
  Play Dirty 68. Nicholas and Alexandra 71. Harold and Maude 71. Sunday Bloody Sunday 72. O Lucky Man 73. Candleshoe 77, etc.

Pickles, Wilfred (1904–1978).
British radio personality and latterly character actor; played Yorkshiremen.
  Autobiography: 1949, *Between You and Me.*
  The Gay Dog 53. Billy Liar 63. The Family Way 66. For the Love of Ada 72, etc.

Pickup, Ronald (1940–).
British character actor, mainly on stage.
  Three Sisters 68. Day of the Jackal 73. Mahler 74. Jennie (TV) (as Randolph Churchill) 75. Joseph Andrews 76. The Thirty-Nine Steps 78. Zulu Dawn 79. Nijinsky 80. The Letter (TV) 82. Ivanhoe (TV) 82. Never Say Never Again 83. Eleni 85. The Mission 86. Fortunes of War (TV) 87. Bethune: The Making of a Hero 89. Journey of Honor 91. A Time to Dance (TV) 92, etc.
  TV series: The Riff Raff Element 94.

Picon, Molly (1898–1992).
American stage actress; films very occasional.
  Come Blow Your Horn 63. Fiddler on the Roof 71. For Pete's Sake 74, etc.

Picture,
by Lillian Ross. One of the wittiest and indeed most scathing books ever written about the process of Hollywood film-making in the days of the great studios. This journalist was unwisely allowed to sit in on every aspect of the production of *The Red Badge of Courage*, and everybody concerned is allowed to condemn himself by direct quotation. First published 1953.

Pidgeon, Walter (1897–1984).
Good-looking, quiet-spoken Canadian leading man in Hollywood; during the 30s and 40s he gave gentlemanly support to several dominant leading ladies.
■ Mannequin 25. Old Loves and New 26. The

Outsider 26. Miss Nobody 26. Marriage License 26. The Girl from Rio 27. The Heart of Salome 27. The Gorilla 27. The Thirteenth Juror 27. Gateway of the Moon 27. Clothes Make the Woman 28. Woman Wise 28. Turn Back the Hours 28. Melody of Love 28. A Most Immoral Lady 29. Her Private Life 29. Bride of the Regiment 30. Sweet Kitty Bellairs 30. Viennese Nights 30. Kiss Me Again 30. Going Wild 30. The Gorilla 31. The Hot Heiress 31. Rockabye 32. The Kiss Before the Mirror 33. Journal of a Crime 34. Big Brown Eyes 36. Fatal Lady 36. Girl Overboard 37. Saratoga 37. A Girl with Ideas 37. She's Dangerous 37. As Good as Married 37. My Dear Miss Aldrich 37. Man Proof 38. The Girl of the Golden West 38. Shopworn Angel 38. Too Hot to Handle 38. Listen Darling 38. *Society Lawyer* 39. Six Thousand Enemies 39. Stronger than Desire 39. Nick Carter Master Detective 39. The House across the Bay 40. It's a Date 40. Dark Command 40. Phantom Raiders 40. Sky Murder 40. Flight Command 40. *Man Hunt* 41. *Blossoms in the Dust* 41. *How Green was My Valley* 41. Design for Scandal 42. *Mrs Miniver* (AAN) 42. White Cargo 42. The Youngest Profession 43. *Madame Curie* (AAN) 43. Mrs Parkington 44. Weekend at the Waldorf 45. Holiday in Mexico 46. The Secret Heart 46. Cass Timberlane 47. If Winter Comes 47. Julia Misbehaves 48. Command Decision 48. *That Forsyte Woman* (as Young Jolyon) 49. The Red Danube 49. The Miniver Story 50. Soldiers Three 51. Calling Bulldog Drummond 51. The Unknown Man 51. The Sellout 52. Million Dollar Mermaid 52. The Bad and the Beautiful 52. Scandal at Scourie 53. Dream Wife 53. *Executive Suite* 54. Men of the Fighting Lady 54. The Last Time I Saw Paris 54. Deep in My Heart 54. Hit the Deck 55. The Glass Slipper 55. *Forbidden Planet* 56. These Wilder Years 56. The Rack 56. Voyage to the Bottom of the Sea 61. *Advise and Consent* 62. The Two Colonels 62. Big Red 62. The Shortest Day 63. Cosa Nostra (TV) 67. Warning Shot 67. Funny Girl (as Ziegfeld) 68. Rascal 69. The Mask of Sheba (TV) 69. The Vatican Affair 69. Skyjacked 72. The Neptune Factor 73. Harry in Your Pocket 73. Yellow Headed Summer 74. Live Again Die Again (TV) 75. You Lie So Deep My Love (TV) 75. The Lindbergh Kidnapping Case (TV) 76. Murder at 40,000 Feet (TV) 76. Two Minutes Warning 76. Sextette 77.

Pierce, Charles B.

American horror film screenwriter and director.
   The Legend of Boggy Creek (wd) 73. Bootleggers (d) 74. Winterhawk (wd) 75. The Winds of Autumn (wd) 76. The Town that Dreaded Sundown (d) 77. Greyeagle (wd) 77. The Norsemen (wd) 78. The Evictors (wd) 79. Sacred Ground (wd) 83. Boggy Creek II (wd) 85. Hawken's Breed (d) 89, etc.

Pierce, Jack (1889–1968).

American make-up artist who worked at Universal for many years and created the familiar images of Dracula, the Wolf Man, the Mummy and the Frankenstein monster.

Pierce-Roberts, Tony.

British cinematographer.
   Moonlighting 82. A Private Function 85. A Room with a View (AAN) 86. A Tiger's Tale 88. Out Cold 89. Slaves of New York 89. Mr & Mrs Bridge 90. White Fang 91. *Howards End* 92. Splitting Heirs 93. The Dark Half 93. The Remains of the Day 93. The Client 94, etc.

Pierlot, Francis (1876–1955).

American character actor, usually of mild professional types.

Night Angel 31. The Captain Is a Lady 40. Night Monster 42. The Doughgirls 44. Dragonwyck 46. The Late George Apley 47. That Wonderful Urge 48. My Friend Irma 49. Cyrano de Bergerac 50. The Robe 53, many others.

Pierson, Frank L. (1945–).

American director, from TV.
   Cat Ballou (co-w) 65. Cool Hand Luke (co-w, AAN) 67. The Looking Glass War 69. The Anderson Tapes (w only) 71. Dog Day Afternoon (w only) (AA) 75. A Star Is Born (d only) 76. King of the Gypsies 78. In Country (w) 89. Presumed Innocent (w) 90. Somebody Has to Shoot the Picture 91, etc.
   TV series: *Nichols* 71.

Pigott, Tempe (1884–1962).

British character actress in Hollywood, usually as garrulous cockney.
   Seven Days Leave 30. Cavalcade 33. One More River 34. Limehouse Blues 35. Becky Sharp 35, etc.

Piggott-Smith, Tim (1946–).

British character actor.
   Sweet William 79. Richard's Things (TV) 80. Clash of the Titans 81. Victory 81. *The Jewel in the Crown* (TV) 82. A State of Emergency 86. The Bullion Boys (TV) 93. The Remains of the Day 93.

Pilbeam, Nova (1919–).

British teenage star of the 30s.
   Little Friend 34. The Man Who Knew Too Much 34. *Tudor Rose* 35. *Young and Innocent* 37. Spring Meeting 40. Banana Ridge 41. This Man Is Mine 46. Counterblast 47. The Three Weird Sisters 48, etc.

Pillsbury, Sam.

New Zealand director.
   The Scarecrow 82. Starlight Hotel 87. Zandalee 90.

pilot:

in television terminology, a film which is made as a trial, to see whether a series on the same premise will be ordered.

pin screen animation:

a curious and short-lived means of animation by photographing pins pushed through a rubber sheet. The shadows caused by the varying height of the pins gives the single picture. The best example is Alexieff's *Night on Bald Mountain* 33.

Pinchot, Bronson (1959–) (Bronson Poncharavsky).

American actor.
   Risky Business 83. Beverly Hills Cop 84. The Flamingo Kid 84. Hot Resort 85. After Hours 85. Second Sight 89. Blame It on the Bellboy 92. True Romance 93. Beverly Hills Cop III 94, etc.
   TV series: Sara 85–88. Perfect Strangers 86– .

Pine, William H. (1896–1955) and Thomas, William C. (1903–1984).

An American production executive and an exhibitor-writer who banded together in the early 40s to make scores of second features for Paramount. *Power Dive, Wildcat, Midnight Manhunt, They Made Me a Killer, Wrecking Crew, Torpedo Boat, I Cover Big Town*, etc. Continued into the 50s with larger-scale adventures: *Sangaree, Jamaica Run, The Far Horizons*, etc., but never managed a top-notcher. Because of their economy they were known as 'the Dollar Bills'. Thomas was almost always the director of their joint productions.

Pinelli, Tullio (1908–).

Italian dramatist and screenwriter, a former lawyer, who has worked on many of Fellini's films.
   Without Pity (Senza Pietà) 47. The Mill on the Po 49. The White Sheik (Lo Sceicco Bianco) 52. I Vitelloni 53. La Strada 54. The Nights of Cabiria (Le Notti di Cabiria) 56. La Dolce Vita (AAN) 60. Boccaccio 70 62. Eight and a Half (AAN) 63. Juliet of the Spirits 65. Ginger and Fred 86. The Voice of the Moon 90, many others.

Pinero, Sir Arthur Wing (1855–1934).

British playwright who dealt mainly with the upper middle class. Many films were made of his work in silent days; the most popular later were *The Second Mrs Tanqueray* and *The Enchanted Cottage* though his farce *The Magistrate* had several incarnations, notably as *Those Were the Days* 34.

Pinewood Studios,

seventeen miles northwest of London, was built in 1935 and opened in 1936 by a millionaire named Charles Boot as Britain's reply to Hollywood. It rapidly came under the control of the Rank Organisation, and its fortunes have fluctuated, but on the whole it has been fairly well used.
   History published 1976: *Movies from the Mansion* by George Perry.

The Pink Panther.

Blake Edwards' 1964 film of an unequal battle of wits between an aristocratic jewel thief (David Niven) and an accident-prone French policeman, Inspector Clouseau (Peter Sellers), spawned several sequels: *A Shot in the Dark* 64; *Inspector Clouseau* 68, in which Alan Arkin took the title role; *The Return of the Pink Panther* 74, which brought back Sellers; *The Pink Panther Strikes Again* 76; and *Revenge of the Pink Panther* 78. Sellers' widow, Lynne Frederick, objected to *The Trail of the Pink Panther* 82, which cobbled together outtakes of Sellers from earlier films and new linking material. It was followed by *Curse of the Pink Panther* 83, in which Ted Wass starred as the world's worst detective, and *Son of the Pink Panther* 93, with Italian comedian Robert Benigni in the title role, but neither was a success. The animated credits of the original film, featuring a pink panther and Henry Mancini's catchy title song, inspired a long-running cartoon series, beginning with the Oscar-winning *The Pink Phink* 64, and a comic book that was published from 1971–84.

Pink, Sidney (1916–).

American director.
   Journey to the Seventh Planet 61. Reptilicus 62. Finger on the Trigger 65. The Tall Women 66.

Pinsent, Gordon (1933–).

Canadian leading actor, much on TV.
   The Thomas Crown Affair 68. The Forbin Project 69. Quarantined (TV) 69. The Rowdy Man 72. Newman's Law 74. Silence of the North 81, etc.
   TV series: Quentin Durgens MP 66.

Pinter, Harold (1930–).

British playwright, and juggler of nonsense plotting and obscure motivation. His filmscripts have been more straightforward. Married to actress Vivien Merchant (1956–80) and author Lady Antonia Fraser.
■ The Servant (w) 63. The Caretaker (oa, w) 64. The Pumpkin Eater (w) (BFA) 64. The Quiller Memorandum (w) 67. Accident (w) 67. The Birthday Party (woa) 69. The Go Between (w) 71. The Homecoming (oa) 73. Butley (d) 73. Rogue Male (TV) (a) 76. The Last Tycoon (w) 76. The French Lieutenant's Woman (w) 81. Betrayal

(AAN) 83. Turtle Diary 85. Reunion (L'Ami Retrouvé) 89. The Handmaid's Tale 90. The Comfort of Strangers 90. The Trial 93.

¶ What concerns me most is shape and structure. – *H.P.*

Pintoff, Ernest (1931–).
Modernist American cartoon maker:
Flebus 57. *The Violinist* 59. *The Interview* 60. *The Critic* 63, etc.

Also wrote and directed live-action features:
Harvey Middleman, Fireman 64. Dynamite Chicken 69. Who Killed Mary What's Her Name? 70. Blade 75. Jaguar Lives 79. Lunch Wagon 81. St Helens 81, etc.

Pinza, Ezio (1893–1957) (Fortunato Pinza).
Italian-American opera singer who graced a few films.
■ Carnegie Hall 48. Mr Imperium 50. Slightly Dishonorable 51. Tonight We Sing 53.

Pious, Minerva (1909–1979).
American radio comedienne of the 40s, famous with Fred Allen as Mrs Nussbaum.
It's In the Bag 45. The Ambassador's Daughter 56. Love in the Afternoon 57, etc.

Piovani, Nicola (1946–).
Italian composer.
Nel Nome del Padre 70. The Rebel Nun 74. Hyena's Sun 77. Il Minestrone 81. The Night of the Shooting Stars (La Notte di San Lorenzo) 81. La Trace (Fr.) 84. Ginger and Fred 86. Good Morning, Babylon 87. The Voice of the Moon 90. Fiorile 93. We Don't Want to Talk about It (De Eso No Se Habla) (Arg.) 93. Amok 93. Il Giovane Mussolini 93. Per Amore, Solo per Amore 94, etc.

Piper, Frederick (1902–1979).
British character actor, mostly on stage: usually played the average man or police inspector.
The Good Companions 32. Jamaica Inn 39. Hue and Cry 46. Passport to Pimlico 48. The Blue Lamp 50. Doctor at Sea 55. Very Important Person 61. One Way Pendulum 64. He Who Rides a Tiger 65, etc.

pirates
have regularly appeared on the screen. Stories with some claim to historical authenticity, or at least based on the exploits of a pirate who once lived, include *Captain Blood* (and its various sequels), *The Black Swan, Morgan the Pirate, Seven Seas to Calais, Blackbeard the Pirate, Captain Kidd, The Buccaneer,* and *Anne of the Indies* (a rare female pirate: one other was depicted in *The Pirate Queen*). Totally fictitious stories are of course headed by *Treasure Island* in its various versions; other swashbuckling yarns included *The Sea Hawk, The Black Pirate, The Crimson Pirate, The Golden Hawk, Fair Wind to Java, A High Wind in Jamaica, Pirates of Tortuga, Yankee Buccaneer, The Spanish Main, Pirates of Tripoli, Devil Ship Pirates, Pirates of Blood River, Prince of Pirates,* and *Raiders of the Seven Seas.* The only notable musical pirate was Gene Kelly in *The Pirate;* comic pirates are also rare, but they do include *The Princess and the Pirate, Blackbeard's Ghost, Double Crossbones, The Dancing Pirate* and *Old Mother Riley's Jungle Treasure.* 1983's *Yellowbeard* was a sad spoof of the genre. *Pirates* in 1985 didn't even seem to know whether it was a spoof or not. *Hook* 91 put the pirate captain of *Peter Pan* centre-galleon.

Pirosh, Robert (1910–1990).
American writer-director.

The Winning Ticket (oa) 35. A Day at the Races (w) 37. I Married a Witch (w) 42. Rings on Her Fingers (w) 42. Up in Arms (w) 44. *Battleground* (w) (AA) 49. Go for Broke (wd) (AAN,w) 51. Washington Story (wd) 52. Valley of the Kings (wd) 54. The Girl Rush (wd) 55. Spring Reunion (wd) 57. Hell Is for Heroes (w) 62. A Gathering of Eagles (w) 63. What's So Bad about Feeling Good? (w) 68, etc.

Pisier, Marie-France (1944–).
French leading lady of the 70s.
French Provincial 76. Love at Twenty 76. Cousin Cousine 76. The Other Side of Midnight 76. Barocco 77. Sérail 77. Love on the Run 79. French Postcards 79. La Banquière 80. Miss Right 81. Hot Touch 82. Les Nanas 84. Parking 85. Le Bal du Gouverneur (wd) 90. Blue Note (La Note Bleue) 91. Pourquoi Maman Est dans Mon Lit? 94. Tous les Jours Dimanche 94, etc.

Pithey, Wensley (1914–1993).
Heavily built South African-born character actor of stage and screen, in Britain from 1947.
The October Man 47. Cardboard Cavalier 49. Brandy for the Parson 52. The Titfield Thunderbolt 53. The Belles of St Trinian's 54. Moby Dick 56. Doctor at Large 57. Hell Drivers 57. Blue Murder at St Trinian's 58. The Knack 65. Oliver! 68. Oh What a Lovely War 69. The Adventurers 70. One of Our Dinosaurs Is Missing 75. Ike (as Churchill) (TV) 79. Red Monarch (TV) 83. The English Week at Dallas Texas (as Churchill) (TV) 84. White Mischief 87. American Friends 91, etc.

Pitt, Brad (1964–).
American actor.
Cutting Class 89. Happy Together 90. Across the Tracks 91. Thelma and Louise 91. Johnny Suede 91. A River Runs through It 92. Cool World 92. Kalifornia 93. *True Romance* 93. The Devil's Advocate 93. The Favor 94. Interview with the Vampire 94. Legends of the Fall 94, etc.
TV series: Glory Days 90.

Pitt, Ingrid (1944–) (Ingrid Petrov).
Polish-born leading lady in British films.
Where Eagles Dare 69. The Vampire Lovers 70. The House that Dripped Blood 71. Countess Dracula 71. Nobody Ordered Love 72. The Wicker Man 73. Smiley's People (TV) 82. Who Dares Wins 82. Wild Geese II 86. Parker 86, etc.

Pitts, ZaSu (1898–1963).
American actress, a heroine of the 20s and a tearful comedienne of the 30s.
The Little Princess 17. Early to Wed 21. *Greed* 23. Twin Beds 27. The Wedding March 28. Seed 30. Bad Sister 31. The Guardsman 32. Back Street 32. Walking Down Broadway 32. Many two-reeler comedies with Thelma Todd (32–34): Dames 34, Mrs Wiggs of the Cabbage Patch 34. Ruggles of Red Gap 35. So's Your Aunt Emma 38. Buck Privates 39. Nurse Edith Cavell 40. Niagara Falls 41. Let's Face It 43. Life with Father 47. Francis 50. Francis Joins the WACS 55. This Could Be the Night 57. It's a Mad Mad Mad Mad World 63, many others.
TV series: Oh Susanna 56–59.
~ZaSu was originally cast as the mother in *All Quiet on the Western Front.* Her scenes were reshot after preview audiences laughed.

Pixelvision.
Title given to films made by a group of experimental film-makers using a Fisher-Price PXL 2000 video camera. Made of moulded plastic, with a fixed lens or 'image receptor', and

recording on standard audio cassettes, the camera produces images that tend to fade rapidly, are composed of easily visible pixels, like an over-enlarged computer image, and blur if the camera is moved. It was made as a toy for Christmas 1987 and discontinued soon after; working cameras are now much sought after. So far, Michael Almereyda (qv) has made a 56-minute feature, *Another Girl Another Planet,* using the camera; shorts made with it include *Glass Jaw* 91, directed by Michael O'Reilly, *Don from Lakewood* 91, directed by Pat Tierney and Eric Saks, *Elegy* 91, directed by Joe Gibbons, *It Wasn't Love* 91, directed by Sadie Benning, and *Black and White/Grain* 93, directed by Stuart Sherman.

Pixilation.
A method of stop-motion animation applied to real objects or people. The shots are taken in a camera that exposes one frame at a time, with the person moving slightly between each shot. Animating people frame by frame can be a simple way of achieving special effects, such as flying, or to produce jerky, comic results. It was used to good effect in *The Secret Adventures of Tom Thumb* 93, a feature-length film by Dave Borthwick which combined animated and human figures, and by Japanese director Shinya Tsukamoto in his fantasies *Tetsuo: The Iron Man* 91 and *Tetsuo II: Bodyhammer* 91. The effect can also be achieved by editing normally photographed action.

Pizer, Larry.
British cinematographer.
The Party's Over 63. Four in the Morning 65. Morgan 65. Our Mother's House 66. Isadora 68. All Neat in Black Stockings 69. Phantom of the Paradise 74. The Fury 78. The Europeans 79. Cattle Annie and Little Britches 81. The Clairvoyant (aka The Killing Hour) 83. Phantom of the Opera (TV) 83. Grace Quigley 84. Too Scared to Scream 84. Where Are the Children 86. Blind Witness (TV) 90, etc.

The Plainsman.
Cecil B. De Mille's 1937 western starred Gary Cooper as Wild Bill Hickok, James Ellison as Buffalo Bill, and Jean Arthur as Calamity Jane. It was poorly remade in 1966 with Don Murray, Guy Stockwell, and Abby Dalton.

Planck, Robert (1894–1971).
American cinematographer.
Our Daily Bread 33. *Jane Eyre* 43. Cass Timberlane 47. The Three Musketeers 48. Little Women 49. Rhapsody 54. Moonfleet 55, etc.

Planer, Franz (1894–1963).
German cinematographer, in Hollywood from 1937.
Drei von Der Tankstelle 30. *Liebelei* 33. Maskerade 34. The Beloved Vagabond (GB) 36. Holiday 38. The Face Behind the Mask 41. The Adventures of Martin Eden 42. Once Upon a Time 44. The Chase 47. *Letter from an Unknown Woman* 48. Criss Cross 48. The Scarf 51. The Blue Veil 51. *Death of a Salesman* 52. Twenty Thousand Leagues under the Sea 54. Not as a Stranger 55. The Pride and the Passion 57. *The Big Country* 58. *The Nun's Story* 59. The Unforgiven 60. The Children's Hour (AAN) 62, etc.

Planet of the Apes.
Pierre Boulle's novel of an astronaut who lands on a planet where the humans have degenerated and the apes rule with wisdom was adapted by Paul Dehn and stylishly directed by Franklin Schaffner in 1967; Charlton Heston played the hero who

discovers, in a twist at the end, that the planet is Earth, and John Chambers provided the splendidly flexible ape make-up. It spawned four sequels of increasing violence and decreasing interest: *Beneath the Planet of the Apes* 69; *Escape from the Planet of the Apes* 70; *Conquest of the Planet of the Apes* 72; and *Battle for the Planet of the Apes* 73. They were followed by a short-lived television series in 1974, and an animated series, *Beyond the Planet of the Apes*, in 1975–76.

Plaschkes, Otto (1931–).
Austrian producer, in Britain.
   Georgy Girl 66. The Bofors Gun 68. The Homecoming 73, etc.

plastic surgery
was long a staple of horror films, but improved techniques have made it a subject for 'woman's pictures' such as *Ash Wednesday* and *Once is not Enough*. *Arsenic and Old Lace* made a comedy point of it, and *Seconds* took it seriously. Other examples: *Dark Passage, False Faces, A Woman's Face, Eyes without a Face, Johnny Handsome*.

Platt, Edward (1916–1974).
American character actor who usually plays generals, stern fathers and similar types.
   The Shrike 55. Rebel Without a Cause 55. Serenade 56. The Great Man 56. Designing Woman 57. The Gift of Love 58. North by Northwest 59. Pollyanna 60. A Ticklish Affair 63, many others.
   TV series: *Get Smart* 65–69.

Platt, Louise (1914–).
American leading lady who retired after a brief career. She was formerly married to producer Jed Harris.
   Spawn of the North 38. *Stagecoach* 39. Forgotten Girls 40. Captain Caution 40. Street of Chance 41, etc.

Platt, Marc (1913–).
American dancer and lightweight actor: few appearances.
   Tonight and Every Night 44. Tars and Spars 44. Down to Earth 47. Seven Brides for Seven Brothers 54. Oklahoma 55, etc.

Platt, Polly.
American production designer who became a producer in the late 80s.
   The Last Picture Show 71. What's Up, Doc? 72. Paper Moon 73. The Thief Who Came to Dinner 73. A Star Is Born 76. Pretty Baby 78. Young Doctors in Love 82. Terms of Endearment (AAN) 83. Between Two Women (TV) 86. The Witches of Eastwick 87. Broadcast News (p) 88. The War of the Roses (p) 89. Say Anything (p) 89, etc.

Platts-Mills, Barney (1944–).
British independent director of low-budget films.
■ Bronco Bullfrog 70. Private Road 71.

Pleasence, Donald (1919–1995).
Bald, pale-eyed British character actor usually seen in villainous or eccentric roles.
   Manuela 57. A Tale of Two Cities 57. The Flesh and the Fiends 59. Hell Is a City 60. No Love for Johnnie 61. Dr Crippen 62. The Great Escape 63. *The Caretaker* 64. The Greatest Story Ever Told 65. The Hallelujah Trail 65. Fantastic Voyage 66. Cul de Sac 66. The Night of the Generals 66. Eye of the Devil 67. Will Penny 67. The Madwoman of Chaillot 69. Soldier Blue 70. Outback 71. The Jerusalem File 72. Henry VIII and His Six Wives 72. Innocent Bystanders 72. Tales That Witness

Madness 73. The Mutations 73. The Black Windmill 74. Hearts of the West 75. Trial by Combat 76. The Last Tycoon 76. The Eagle has Landed (as Himmler) 76. Jesus of Nazareth (TV) 77. Oh God 77. Telefon 77. The Passover Plot 77. Halloween 78. Sergeant Pepper's Lonely Hearts Club Band 78. Dracula 79. All Quiet on the Western Front (TV) 80. Escape from New York 81. Halloween II 81. Alone in the Dark 82. The Devonsville Terror 83. Where is Parsifal? 84. Arch of Triumph (TV) 84. The Last Days of Pompeii (TV) 85. Scoop (TV) 87. Ground Zero 87. Phantom of Death 87. Deep Cover 88. Hannah's War 88. Halloween 4: The Return of Michael Myers 88. Halloween 5: The Revenge of Michael Myers 89. Casablanca Express 89. River of Death 89. Buried Alive 90. American Tiger 91. Dien Bien Phu 91. Shadows and Fog 92. The Hour of the Pig 93. Femme Fatale (TV) 93, etc.
   TV series: Robin Hood (as Prince John) 55–57.

Pleshette, Suzanne (1937–).
Intelligent American leading actress whose roles have been generally disappointing. She was married to actor Troy Donahue for nine months in 1964.
■ The Geisha Boy 58. Rome Adventure 62. Forty Pounds of Trouble 63. The Birds 63. Wall of Noise 63. A Distant Trumpet 64. Fate is the Hunter 64. Youngblood Hawke 64. A Rage to Live 65. The Ugly Dachshund 66. Nevada Smith 66. Mister Buddwing 66. The Adventures of Bullwhip Griffin 67. Wings of Fire (TV) 67. Blackbeard's Ghost 68. The Power 68. If It's Tuesday This Must Be Belgium 69. Along Came a Spider 69. Suppose They Gave a War and Nobody Came 69. Support Your Local Gunfighter 71. In Broad Daylight (TV) 71. Beyond the Bermuda Triangle (TV) 75. The Legend of Valentino (TV) 75. Return of the Pink Panther 75. The Shaggy D.A. 76. Kate Bliss and the Tickertape Kid (TV) 78. *Flesh and Blood* (TV) 79. Hot Stuff 79. Oh God Book Two 80. Help Wanted: Male (TV) 82. One Cooks, the Other Doesn't (TV) 83. Dixie: Changing Habits (TV) 83. For Love or Money (TV) 84. Kojak: The Belarus File (TV) 85. A Stranger Waits (TV) 87.
   TV series: The Bob Newhart Show 72. Maggie Briggs 84. Bridges to Cross 86. The Boys Are Back 94–95.

¶ I don't sit around and wait for great parts. I'm an actress, and I love being one, and I'll probably be doing it till I'm 72, standing around the backlot doing *Gunsmoke*s. – *S.P.*

Plimpton, Martha (1971–) (Martha Carradine).
American actress, the daughter of Keith Carradine.
   Rollover 81. The River Rat 84. The Goonies 85. The Mosquito Coast 86. Shy People 87. Running on Empty 88. Stars and Bars 88. Parenthood 89. Silence Like Glass 90. Stanley and Iris 90. Samantha 92. Josh and S.A.M. 93. Chantilly Lace (TV) 93. Mrs Parker and the Vicious Circle 94, etc.

Plowright, Joan (1929–).
Leading British stage actress, widow of Laurence Olivier.
   Time without Pity 58. The Entertainer 60. Equus 77. The Diary of Anne Frank (TV) 81. Britannia Hospital 82. Brimstone and Treacle 82. Wagner 82. Drowning by Numbers 88. The Dressmaker 89. I Love You to Death 90. Avalon 90. Enchanted April (AAN) 91. The Clothes in the Wardrobe (aka The Summer House) (TV) 93. Last Action Hero 93. Dennis the Menace (GB: Dennis) 93. Widows' Peak 94. On Promised Land (TV) 94. A Pin for the Butterfly 94, etc.

Plummer, Amanda (1957–).
American actress. She is the daughter of Christopher Plummer and Tammy Grimes.
   Cattle Annie and Little Britches 81. The World According to Garp 82. Daniel 83. The Hotel New Hampshire 84. Courtship 86. Static 86. Made in Heaven 87. Prisoners of Inertia 89. Joe versus the Volcano 90. The Fisher King 91. The Lounge People 91. Freejack 92. So I Married an Axe Murderer 93. Last Light 93. Needful Things 93. Pulp Fiction 94. Pax (Port.) 94. Nostradamus 94, etc.

Plummer, Christopher (1927–).
Canadian leading man with stage experience including Shakespeare. His first wife was actress Tammy Grimes; their daughter is actress Amanda Plummer.
■ Stage Struck 58. Wind Across the Everglades 58. *The Fall of the Roman Empire* 64. *The Sound of Music* 65. Inside Daisy Clover 65. The Night of the Generals 67. Triple Cross 67. Oedipus the King 67. Nobody Runs Forever 68. Lock Up Your Daughters 69. The Royal Hunt of the Sun 69. The Battle of Britain 69. *Waterloo* (as the Duke of Wellington) 70. The Pyx 73. Conduct Unbecoming 75. The Spiral Staircase 75. The Man Who Would Be King 75. The Return of the Pink Panther 75. The Moneychangers (TV) 75. Aces High 76. Jesus of Nazareth (TV) 77. The Day that Shook the World 77. The Assignment 77. The Disappearance 77. The Silent Partner 78. Starcrash 78. International Velvet 78. Murder by Decree 79. Hanover Street 79. Somewhere in Time 80. Highpoint 80. Eyewitness 81. Little Gloria . . . Happy at Last (TV) 82. The Amateur 82. Lily in Love 84. Dreamscape 84. The Boss's Wife 86. An American Tail (voice) 86. I Love N.Y. 87. Dragnet 87. Souvenir 88. Light Years 88. Nosferatu in Venice 88. Shadow Dancing 88. Kingsgate 89. Mind Field 89. Where the Heart Is 90. Red Blooded American Girl 90. Star Trek VI: The Undiscovered Country 91. Firehead 91. Don't Tell Mom the Babysitter's Dead 91. Rock-a-Doodle (voice) 92. Liars Edge 92. Wolf 94.
   TV series: Counterstrike 90.

¶ I'm bored with questions about acting. – *C.P.*
   Unless you can surround yourself with as many beautiful things as you can afford, I don't think life has very much meaning. – *C.P.*

Plunkett, Patricia (1928–).
British leading lady of the early 50s.
   It Always Rains on Sunday 47. Bond Street 48. For Them That Trespass 48. Landfall 50. Murder Without Crime 52. Mandy 53. The Crowded Day 55. Dunkirk 58, etc.

Plunkett, Walter (1902–1982).
American costume designer, at RKO 1926–39.
   Hit the Deck 29. Rio Rita 29. Cimarron 31. *Little Women* 33. *The Gay Divorcee* 34. Of Human Bondage 34. Mary of Scotland 36. Quality Street 37. *Gone with the Wind* 39. *The Hunchback of Notre Dame* 39. Stagecoach 39. Ladies in Retirement 41. To Be or Not to Be 42. A Song to Remember 45. Duel in the Sun 46. The Three Musketeers 48. That Forsyte Woman 49. *An American in Paris* (AA) 51. *The Prisoner of Zenda* 52. *Kiss Me Kate* 53. Seven Brides for Seven Brothers 54. Lust for Life 56. Pollyanna 60. How the West was Won 63. Seven Women 66, many others.

Podesta, Rossana (1934–).
Italian leading lady who has been in international films.
   Cops and Robbers 51. La Red 53. Ulysses 54.

Helen of Troy 56. Santiago 58. The Golden Arrow 65. Il Prete Sposato 70. The Sensual Man 75, many others.

Poe, Edgar Allan (1809–1849).

American poet, story-writer and manic depressive, whose tortured life as well as his strange tales have been eagerly seized upon by film-makers. Griffith made *The Life of Edgar Allan Poe* in 1909, and in 1912 another version was disguised as *The Raven*. In 1915 Charles Brabin made another film called *The Raven* with Henry B. Walthall as Poe; a few months earlier Griffith had released his own alternative version under the title *The Avenging Conscience*. The next film called *The Raven*, in 1935, starred Karloff and Lugosi and had nothing to do with Poe's life, being merely an amalgam of his stories; but in 1942 Fox brought out *The Loves of Edgar Allan Poe* starring Shepperd Strudwick; and in 1951 MGM made a curious melodrama called *Man with a Cloak*, in which the dark stranger who solved the mystery signed himself 'Dupin' and was played by Joseph Cotten in the Poe manner.

Of the stories, *The Mystery of Marie Roget* was filmed by Universal in 1931 and 1942; *The Tell-Tale Heart* was told as an MGM short directed by Jules Dassin in 1942, by a British company with Stanley Baker in 1950, by UPA as a cartoon narrated by James Mason in 1954, by an independent American company in a film known as both *Manfish* and *Calypso* in 1956 (the film also claimed to be partly based on *The Gold Bug*) and by the Danzigers in Britain in 1960. *The Fall of the House of Usher* was filmed in France by Jean Epstein in 1929, in Britain by semi-professionals in 1950, in Hollywood by Roger Corman in 1960, and in South Africa by Alan Birkinshaw in 1988. Universal released films called *The Black Cat* in 1934 and 1941, both claiming to be 'suggested' by Poe's tale; in fact, neither had anything at all to do with it, but the genuine story was told in a German film called *The Living Dead* in 1933, and in Corman's 1962 *Tales of Terror*. *The Pit and the Pendulum* was filmed in 1913 and 1961, and the central idea has been borrowed by many film-makers without credit, most recently by the 'Uncle' boys in *One Spy Too Many*. *The Premature Burial* was filmed straight in 1962, and around the same time TV's *Thriller* series presented a fairly faithful adaptation; the idea was also used in 1934 in *The Crime of Dr Crespi*, a low-budgeter starring Erich Von Stroheim. *The Murders in the Rue Morgue* was filmed in 1914 and 1932, turned up again in 3-D in 1954 under the title *Phantom of the Rue Morgue*, and was remade under the original title in 1971. Other Poe stories filmed once include *The Bells* 13, *The Facts in the Case of M. Valdemar* in *Tales of Terror* 62, *The Masque of the Red Death* 64 and 89, and *The Tomb of Ligeia* 64.

Poe, James (1918–1980).

American writer, from radio and TV.

■ Without Honor 49. Scandal Sheet (co-w) 52. Paula 52. The Big Knife 55. Around the World in 80 Days (co-w, AA) 56. Attack! 56. Hot Spell 58. Cat on a Hot Tin Roof (co-w) 58. Last Train from Gun Hill 59. Sanctuary 61. Summer and Smoke (co-w) 63. Toys in the Attic 63. Lilies of the Field 63. The Bedford Incident 64. They Shoot Horses Don't They? (co-w) 69.

Pogostin, S. Lee (1926–).

American writer-director.

Pressure Point (co-w) 62. Synanon (co-w) 65. Hard Contract (wd) 69. Golden Needles (co-w) 74. High Road to China (co-w) 83, etc.

Pohlmann, Eric (1903–1979).

Viennese character actor, on British stage and radio from 1948; also a familiar bald, portly villain on screen.

The Constant Husband 55. House of Secrets 56. Expresso Bongo 59. The Kitchen 62. Carry on Spying 64. The Million Dollar Collar (US) 67. The Horsemen 71, many others.

TV series: Colonel March of Scotland Yard 53.

Poiret, Paul.

French fashion designer who created the costumes for Sarah Bernhardt in her film debut *Queen Elizabeth* as well as her *Adrienne Lecouvreur*. He influenced many subsequent movie designers.

Poitier, Sidney (1924–).

Handsome American leading actor; his success in the late 60s helped to break the race barrier.

■ No Way Out 50. Cry the Beloved Country 52. Red Ball Express 52. Go Man Go 54. *The Blackboard Jungle* 55. Goodbye, My Lady 56. *Edge of the City* 57. Something of Value 57. Band of Angels 58. Mark of the Hawk 58. *The Defiant Ones* (AAN) 58. *Porgy and Bess* 59. Virgin Islands 60. All the Young Men 60. A Raisin in the Sun 61. Paris Blues 61. Pressure Point 62. *Lilies of the Field* (AA) 63. The Long Ships 64. The Greatest Story Ever Told 65. *The Bedford Incident* (for the first time his colour was not mentioned or relevant) 65. A Patch of Blue 65. The Slender Thread 65. Duel at Diablo 66. *In the Heat of the Night* 67. To Sir with Love 67. *Guess Who's Coming to Dinner* 67. For Love of Ivy 68. The Lost Man 69. They Call Me Mister Tibbs 70. The Organization 71. Brother John 71. Buck and the Preacher (& d) 72. A Warm December (& d) 73. Uptown Saturday Night (& d) 74. The Wilby Conspiracy 75. Let's Do It Again (& d) 76. A Piece of the Action (& d) 77. Stir Crazy (d only) 80. Hanky Panky (d only) 82. Fast Forward (d only) 84. Little Nikita 88. Shoot to Kill 88. Ghost Dad (d) 90. Separate but Equal (TV) 91. Sneakers 92.

🅞 For being the first black actor to be accepted in a romantic situation with a white girl. *Guess Who's Coming to Dinner.*

Poland

had a vigorous cinema school from the earliest days, but subjects were dominated by Russian influence. After World War II Alexander Ford led a new vigorous group of film-makers including Wajda and Munk, whose films of post-war problems became world famous. Later directors of note include Polanski, Kawalerowicz and Skolimowski in the 50s and 60s. That era also produced the charismatic actor Zbigniew Cybulski, star of Wajda's *Ashes and Diamonds*. Like James Dean, with whom he was often compared, he died young, falling beneath a train. In the 70s, more fine directors emerged, including Krzysztof Kieslowski and Krzysztof Zanussi. More recently, Agnieszka Holland, a screenwriter and former assistant to Zanussi, has become an accomplished director. As in the past, Polish directors often work away from their home country where there are no problems of censorship. The government banned Ryszard Bugajski's 1982 film *The Interrogation*, and it was not seen until the 1990 Cannes Festival, by which time he had long emigrated in order to continue working.

Polanski, Roman (1933–).

Polish director and screenwriter, former actor. Gained a reputation with shorts such as *Two Men and a Wardrobe* 58. He was married to actress Sharon Tate, who was murdered in 1969 by followers of Charles Manson. In 1979 he left America when awaiting sentencing on a charge of unlawful sexual intercourse, and has since worked in Europe.

Autobiography: 1984, *Roman*.

Biographies: 1982, *Polanski, the Filmmaker as Voyeur* by Barbara Leaming. 1982, *Life and Times of Roman Polanski* by Thomas Kiernan. 1994, *Polanski* by John Parker.

■ Knife in the Water 61. Repulsion 65. Cul de Sac 66. The Fearless Vampire Killers 67. *Rosemary's Baby* (AAN,w) 68. Macbeth 71. What? 72. *Chinatown* (AAN) 74. The Tenant 76. Tess (AAN) 80. Pirates 85. Frantic 88. Back in the USSR (a) 92. Bitter Moon 92. A Simple Formality (Una Pura Formalita) (a) 94.

¶ Nothing is too shocking for me. When you tell the story of a man who loses his head, you have to show the head being cut off. Otherwise it's just a dirty joke without a punchline. – *R.P.*

I know in my heart of hearts that the spirit of laughter has deserted me. – *R.P.*

The director is never wrong. – *R.P.*

His talent is as undeniable as his intentions are dubious. – *Andrew Sarris, 1968*

The four-foot Pole you wouldn't want to touch with a ten-foot pole. – *Kenneth Tynan*

Poledouris, Basil (1945–).

American composer.

Extreme Close-up 73. Big Wednesday 78. The Blue Lagoon 80. Conan the Barbarian 82. Summer Lovers 82. Conan the Destroyer 84. Red Dawn 84. Flesh and Blood 85. Iron Eagle 86. Cherry 2000 86. Robocop 87. No Man's Land 87. Split Decisions 88. Farewell to the King 89. Wired 89. Why Me? 89. The Hunt for Red October 90. Quigley Down Under 90. The Flight of the Intruder 90. Harley Davidson and the Marlboro Man 91. Wind 92. Hot Shots! Part Deux 93. Robocop 3 93. Free Willy 93. On Deadly Ground 94. Serial Mom 94. Lassie 94, etc.

Polglase, Van Nest (1898–1968).

American art director, in films from 1919. With RKO 1932–43, then with Columbia.

Poliakoff, Stephen (1952–).

British playwright, screenwriter and director.

Hidden City 87. Close My Eyes 92. Century 93.

police

in the 40s and earlier were offered in British films only for our admiration; in the 50s they began to have human frailties; and in the 60s many of them were shown, truthfully or not, to be corrupt. *The Blue Lamp, The Long Arm* and *Gideon of Scotland Yard* are only three of many of the first kind; *Violent Playground* one of the second; and *The Strange Affair* a corking example of the last. But the *Z Cars* series on British TV will long uphold the best traditions of the force . . . as will *Maigret* for France.

American cops have always been tougher, but even so a gradual change can be traced through *Naked City, The Big Heat, Detective Story, Shield for Murder, Experiment in Terror, Madigan, The Detective, The French Connection, Fuzz* and *The New Centurions*.

TV series which have been influential include *Dragnet* 52–59 and 67–69, *Naked City* 58–62, *87th Precinct* 61, *M Squad* 57–60, *The Detectives* 60–61, *The Line-up* 54–59, *Hawk* 66, *The New Breed* 61, *Adam 12* 68–75, *Hawaii Five O* 68–80, *The Rookies* 72, *Police Story* 73–77, *Police Woman* 74–76, *Starsky and Hutch* 75–78.

Comic policemen go right back to the Keystone Kops. Other examples: Will Hay in *Ask a Policeman*, George Formby in *Spare a Copper*, Norman Wisdom in *On the Beat*, Alastair Sim in *Green for Danger*,

Peter Sellers in *The Pink Panther*, Lionel Jeffries in *The Wrong Arm of the Law*, 'Officer Krupke' in *West Side Story*, Donald McBride in *Topper Returns*, Dennis Hoey as Inspector Lestrade in the Sherlock Holmes films, Sidney James and crew in *Carry On Constable*, Laurel and Hardy in *Midnight Patrol*, Buster Keaton's cast in *Cops*, Charles Chaplin in *Easy Street*, the cast of *Police Academy* and, on TV, *Car 54 Where are You?*

politics,

as any exhibitor will tell you, is the kiss of death to a film as far as box office is concerned. Nevertheless many films with serious political themes have been made. Among those presenting biographies of actual political figures, the American ones include *Young Mr Lincoln*, *Abe Lincoln in Illinois*, *Tennessee Johnson*, *The Man with Thirty Sons* (Oliver Wendell Holmes), *Magnificent Doll* (Dolly Madison and Aaron Burr), *The President's Lady* (Andrew Jackson), *Wilson*, Teddy Roosevelt (in *My Girl Tisa* and others), Franklin Roosevelt (in *Sunrise at Campobello*), *Beau James* (Jimmy Walker) and John Kennedy (*PT 109*), while *All the King's Men* and *A Lion Is in the Streets* are clearly based on Huey Long, and there was a real-life original for the idealistic young senator from Wisconsin in *Mr Smith Goes to Washington*. Fictional presidencies have been involved in *Gabriel over the White House*, *First Lady*, *The Tree of Liberty* (*The Howards of Virginia*), *Advise and Consent*, *The Manchurian Candidate*, *Seven Days in May*, *Dr Strangelove*, *Kisses for My President*, and *Fail Safe*. Among the many films alleging political graft and corruption in the US are *Mr Smith Goes to Washington*, *Confessions of a Nazi Spy*, *Louisiana Purchase*, *Alias Nick Beal*, *State of the Union*, *Li'l Abner*, *The Great McGinty*, *The Glass Key*, *Citizen Kane*, *All the King's Men*, *Bullets or Ballots*, *A Lion Is in the Streets*, *The Last Hurrah*, *The Best Man*, *The Senator was Indiscreet* and *The Candidate*. The witch-hunts of 1948 produced a series of right-wing melodramas like *I Was a Communist for the FBI*, *I Married a Communist* and *My Son John* . . . a striking contrast to 1942, when *Mission to Moscow* could be made. In 1971 TV produced a four-hour thriller called *Vanished* about a president with doubtful motives. The mid-70s brought a number of TV drama-documentaries about political matters: *Eleanor and Franklin*, *Collision Course* (Truman and MacArthur), *The Missiles of October*, *Fear On Trial*, *Tail Gunner Joe* (McCarthy), *Meeting at Potsdam*.

The British House of Commons and its characters have been involved in many a film with Disraeli (qv) coming out as favourite. Pitt the Younger was impersonated by Robert Donat, and Charles James Fox by Robert Morley, in *The Young Mr Pitt*; Gladstone was played by Ralph Richardson in *Khartoum*, Malcolm Keen in *Sixty Glorious Years* and Stephen Murray in *The Prime Minister*; Cromwell by Richard Harris; Canning by John Mills and William Lamb by Jon Finch in *Lady Caroline Lamb*; while Ramsay MacDonald was allegedly pictured in *Fame is the Spur*. MPs were also the leading figures of the fictional *No Love for Johnnie*, *Three Cases of Murder* and *The Rise and Rise of Michael Rimmer*.

Political films from other countries abound; one might almost say that every Soviet film is political. But politics do not export well, so that for the life of Villa, Zapata, Juarez and Che Guevara we have to turn to glamorized Hollywood versions of the truth; ditto for Parnell, Richelieu and even Hitler. Lenin has been pictured in innumerable Soviet films, and Richard Burton starred in *The Assassination of Trotsky*.

That politics is not entirely a serious matter can be seen from the number of comedies about it.

The best of them is the already mentioned *State of the Union*, but one can also instance the *Don Camillo* series, *Old Mother Riley MP*, *Angelina MP*, *Dad Rudd MP*, *Louisiana Purchase*, *Kisses for My President*, *The Great Man Votes*, *Left Right and Centre* and *Vote for Huggett*.

Polito, Gene (1918–).
American cinematographer.
Prime Cut 72. Westworld 73. Five on the Black Hand Side 73. Trackdown 76. The Bad News Bears Go to Japan 78, etc.

Polito, Jon (1950–).
American character actor.
Deadly Business 86. Fire with Fire 86. Highlander 86. The Freshman 90. Miller's Crossing 90. Leather Jackets 90. Barton Fink 91. The Crow 94. Blankman 94, etc.
TV series: Homicide: Life on the Street 93.

Polito, Sol (1892–1960).
American cinematographer.
Treason 18. Hard-Boiled Haggerty 27. Five Star Final 31. *I Am a Fugitive from a Chain Gang* 32. *Forty-second Street* 33. *G Men* 35. *The Petrified Forest* 36. *The Charge of the Light Brigade* 36. *The Adventures of Robin Hood* 38. Confessions of a Nazi Spy 39. *The Sea Hawk* 40. The Sea Wolf 41. Now Voyager 42. Arsenic and Old Lace 44. Rhapsody in Blue 45. The Long Night 47. Sorry, Wrong Number 48. Anna Lucasta 48, many others.

Poll, Martin H. (1922–).
American producer.
Love Is a Ball 62. Sylvia 65. The Lion in Winter (AAN) 68. Night Watch 73. The Man Who Loved Cat Dancing 73. Love and Death 75. The Man Who Would Be King 75. Somebody Killed Her Husband 78. Night Hawks 81. Gimme an F 84. Haunted Summer 88. My Heroes Have Always Been Cowboys 91, etc.

Pollack, Sydney (1934–).
American director, screenwriter and producer, from TV.
■ *The Slender Thread* 65. This Property Is Condemned 66. The Scalphunters 68. Castle Keep 69. *They Shoot Horses Don't They?* (AAN) 69. Jeremiah Johnson 72. The Way We Were 73. The Yakusa 75. *Three Days of the Condor* 76. Bobby Deerfield 77. The Electric Horseman 79. Absence of Malice 81. Tootsie (& a) (AAN) 82. Out of Africa (AAp, AAd) 85. Bright Lights, Big City (p) 88. The Fabulous Baker Boys (p) 89. Major League (p) 89. Havana (p, d) 90. Presumed Innocent (p) 90. White Palace (p) 90. Leaving Normal (p) 91. Dead Again (p) 91. The Player (a) 92. Searching for Bobby Fischer (p) 93. Flesh and Bone (p) 93. The Firm (p, d) 93.

¶ I don't value a film I've enjoyed making. If it's good, it's damned hard work. – *S.P.*

Pollak, Kevin.
American actor.
Avalon 90. Ricochet 91. A Few Good Men 92. Indian Summer 93. Grumpy Old Men 93. Wayne's World 2 93. Clean Slate 94, etc.
TV series: Coming of Age 88–89.

Pollard, Daphne (1890–1978) (Daphne Trott).
Diminutive Australian actress in Hollywood; a famous sharp-tongued wife for Laurel and Hardy.
Hit of the Show 28. Big Time 29. Swing Time 30. Bright Lights 30. Lady Refuses 31. Bonnie Scotland 33. Our Relations 36. Tillie the Toiler 41. Kid Dynamite 43, etc.

Pollard, Harry (1883–1934).
American silent-screen director.
Motherhood 14. The Leather Pushers 22. Oh Doctor 24. California Straight Ahead 25. Uncle Tom's Cabin 27. Showboat (first talkie) 29. The Prodigal 31. Fast Life 32, etc.

Pollard, Michael J. (1939–) (M. J. Pollack).
Pint-sized American character actor.
Adventures of a Young Man 62. Summer Magic 62. The Stripper 64. *Bonnie and Clyde* (AAN) 67. Hannibal Brooks 69. Little Fauss and Big Halsy 70. Dirty Little Billy 72. Sunday in the Country 74. Between the Lines 77. Melvin and Howard 80. America 82. Heated Vengeance 85. The American Way 86. The Patriot 86. Roxanne 87. Scrooged 88. Fast Food 89. Season of Fear 89. Tango & Cash 89. Dick Tracy 90. Enid Is Sleeping 90. The Art of Dying 91. Motorama 92. Split Second 92. Skeeter 93, etc.
TV series: Leo and Liz in Beverly Hills 86.

Pollard, Snub (1886–1962) (Harold Fraser).
Australian comedian, in America from early silent film days. In many silent slapstick shorts, and later continued to play bit parts, the last being in *A Pocketful of Miracles* 61.

Pollock, Dale (1950–).
American producer, a former journalist. He is currently president of Polygram's A & M Films and is the author of *Skywalking*, a biography of George Lucas.
Blaze 89. A Midnight Clear 92. House of Cards 93. S.F.W. 94, etc.

Pollock, Ellen (1903–).
British stage actress, in occasional films.
Non Stop New York 37. The Street Singer 37. Sons of the Sea 39. Kiss the Bride Goodbye 44. The Galloping Major 51. The Wicked Lady 82, etc.

Pollock, George (1907–).
British director, former assistant, in films since 1933.
A Stranger in Town 56. Rooney 58. Don't Panic Chaps 60. Murder She Said 63. Murder at the Gallop 63. Murder Most Foul 64. Ten Little Indians 65, etc.

Polonsky, Abraham (1910–).
American writer and director who fell foul of the communist witch-hunt.
Body and Soul (AAN) 47. Force of Evil (& d) 49. I Can Get It for You Wholesale 50. Tell Them Willie Boy is Here (& d) 69. Romance of a Horsethief (d only) 71. Avalanche Express 78. Monsignor (co-w) 82, etc.

Pomeranc, Mac (1984–).
American child actor.
Searching for Bobby Fischer (GB: Innocent Moves) 93.

Pommer, Erich (1889–1966).
German producer since 1915. During the 30s worked briefly in the US and also, with Charles Laughton, formed Mayflower Films in Britain.
The Cabinet of Dr Caligari 19. Dr Mabuse 22. Die Nibelungen 24. Variety 25. *Metropolis* 26. *The Blue Angel* 30. Congress Dances 31. Liliom 34. Fire over England 36. Vessel of Wrath 38. Jamaica Inn 39. They Knew What They Wanted 40. Illusion in Moll 52. Kinder, Mutter und Ein General 55, etc.
✪ For his influence over a wide range of European films. *Metropolis*.

Pons, Lily (1904–1976).
French-born operatic singer who starred in some Hollywood films.

I Dream Too Much 35. That Girl from Paris 36. Hitting a New High 37. Carnegie Hall 47, etc.

Pontecorvo, Gillo (1919–).
Italian director of politically committed films with anti-colonialist themes. A former photo-journalist and documentary film-maker, he frequently uses non-professional actors in the tradition of Italian neo-realism. Recent projects having failed at the planning stages, he directs TV commercials.

Kapo 60. *The Battle of Algiers* (AAN) 66. The Wide Blue Road 68. Burn! (Queimada) 70. Ogro 79, etc.

¶ I like making films because I've a certain affection for man and his condition. – *G.P.*

He has made very few films and that's very bad for our profession, for art, for the art of cinematography and for what he owes the public, what they expect of him. So it's a real pity, even a sin. – *Ennio Morricone*

Ponti, Carlo (1913–).
Italian producer, later involved in international productions. Married to Sophia Loren.

I Miserabili 47. Attila the Hun 52. Ulysses 54. War and Peace 56. Black Orchid 58. That Kind of Woman 59. Marriage, Italian Style 65. Operation Crossbow 65. Dr Zhivago (AAN) 65. Smashing Time 67. Sunflower 70. Lady Liberty 72. The Passenger 74. Massacre in Rome 74. Brief Encounter (TV) 75. Verdict 75. The Priest's Wife 75. The Cassandra Crossing 77, etc.

Ponting, Herbert G. (1870–1935).
British explorer and film-maker, a maker of quality documentaries in the cinema's early days.

With Captain Scott RN to the South Pole 13, etc.

Pontius Pilate.
The man who judged Jesus has been played on film as follows: in *King of Kings* 27 by Victor Varconi; in *The Last Days of Pompeii* 35 by Basil Rathbone; in *The Robe* 53 by Richard Boone; in *Ben Hur* 59 by Frank Thring; in *King of Kings* 61 by Hurd Hatfield; in Barabbas 62 by Arthur Kennedy; in *The Greatest Story Ever Told* by Telly Savalas; in *Jesus Christ Superstar* 75 by Barry Dennen.

Pool, Léa (1950–).
Swiss-born director and screenwriter, based in Canada, where she went in the mid-70s to study film. She has also taught film and video at the University of Quebec and worked in television. Her films often deal with the problems of artists and have homosexual protagonists.

Strass Café 79. A Woman in Transit (La Femme de L'Hôtel) 84. Anne Trister 85. À Corps Perdu 88. La Demoiselle Sauvage 91. Montréal Vu par . . . (co-d) 91. Mouvements du Désir 94, etc.

Popeye.
Tough sailorman hero of over 250 cartoon shorts produced by Max Fleischer *c.* 1933–50. Other characters involved were girlfriend Olive Oyl and tough villain Bluto, against whose wiles Popeye fortified himself with tins of spinach. The films were so popular on TV that a newly-drawn series was produced *c.* 1959 by King Features – but the old vulgar panache was missing.

In 1980 Robert Altman directed a live-action version, but it was a sad affair.

Popkin, Harry M. (*c.* 1906–1991).
American independent producer.

And Then There Were None 45. Impact 48. *D.O.A.* 49. Champagne for Caesar 49. The Thief 52, etc.

Porcasi, Paul (1880–1946).
Sicilian character actor in Hollywood films; former opera singer.

The Fall of the Romanoffs 19. Say It Again 26. Broadway 29. The Criminal Code 31. The Passionate Plumber 32. Footlight Parade 32. The Gay Divorcee 34. Maytime 37. Crime School 38. It Started with Eve 41. We Were Dancing 42. Hi Diddle Diddle 43. I'll Remember April 45, many others.

Porky Pig.
Stammering, nervous pig whose cry of 'Th-th-th-th-that's all, folks' brought to an end many Warner Brothers cartoons. Created by Bob Clampett, for the first two years he was voiced by Joe Dougherty (who did stutter), after which Mel Blanc took over.

I Haven't Got a Hat 35. Gold Diggers of '49 36. Porky's Pet 36. Porky's Duck Hunt 37. The Case of the Stuttering Pig 37. Porky and Daffy 38. The Lone Stranger and Porky 39. Prehistoric Porky 40. Porky's Ant 41. My Favorite Duck 42. Swooner Crooner (AAN) 44. The Pest that Came to Dinner 48. Porky's Chops 49. Cracked Quack 52. Deduce, You Say 56. China Jones 59. Daffy's Inn Trouble 61, many others.

Porten, Henny (1890–1960).
German leading lady of the silents.

Lohengrin 07. Anne Boleyn 20. Der Kaufmann von Venedig 23. Kohlhiesel's Tochter 30. Familie Buchholz 40. Das Fraulein Scuderi 55, many others.

Porter, Cole (1893–1964).
American songwriter and composer whose lyrics were probably the wittiest ever appended to popular songs. Cary Grant played Porter in a biopic, *Night and Day* 46; other films using Porter scores are: *Anything Goes* 36 and 56. *Rosalie* 38. *Broadway Melody of 1940. Something to Shout About* 42. *The Pirate* 48. *Kiss Me Kate* 53. *High Society* 56. *Can Can* 59, etc.

Biography: 1967, *The Life that Late He Led* by George Eels.

Porter, Don (1912–).
American leading man of second features, latterly character actor.

Top Sergeant 42. Night Monster 43. The Curse of the Allenbys 48. 711 Ocean Drive 50. Because You're Mine 52. The Racket 52. Our Miss Brooks 56. Bachelor in Paradise 61. Youngblood Hawke 64. The Candidate 72. Forty Carats 73. White Line Fever 75, etc.

TV series: Private Secretary. Our Miss Brooks. The Ann Sothern Show.

Porter, Edwin S. (1869–1941).
America's first notable director, who later found himself in D. W. Griffith's shadow and left the industry.

The Life of an American Fireman 02. *The Great Train Robbery* 03. The Ex-Convict 05. Rescued from an Eagle's Nest 07. Alice's Adventures in Wonderland 10. The Count of Monte Cristo 12. The Eternal City 15, etc.

~A documentary about Porter, *Before the Nickelodeon*, was released in 1983.

Porter, Eric (1928–).
British stage actor who became nationally known as Soames in the TV version of *The Forsyte Saga*.

The Heroes of Telemark 65. Kaleidoscope 66.

The Lost Continent 68. Hands of the Ripper 71. Antony and Cleopatra 71. Nicholas and Alexandra 71. The Day of the Jackal 73. The Belstone Fox 73. Callan 74. Hennessy 75. The 39 Steps 78. Why Didn't They Ask Evans? (TV) 80. Little Lord Fauntleroy (TV) 80. The Jewel in the Crown (TV) 83, etc.

Porter, Gene Stratton (1886–1924).
American novelist: her sentimental novels of country matters were once ideal film material. *Freckles, Laddie and Girl of the Limberlost* were among them.

Porter, Katherine Anne (1890–1980).
American novelist, author of the allegorical *Ship of Fools* which was filmed in 1963.

Porter, Nyree Dawn (1940–).
New Zealand leading lady in British films and TV.

Two Left Feet 63. The Cracksman 63. Jane Eyre 70. The House that Dripped Blood 70. From Beyond the Grave 73, etc.

TV series: *The Forsyte Saga* (as Irene) 67. *The Protectors* 72.

Portman, Eric (1903–1969).
Distinguished British stage actor who appeared sporadically in films.
■ The Murder in the Red Barn (debut) 35. Abdul the Damned 35. Old Roses 35. Hyde Park Corner 35. The Cardinal 36. Hearts of Humanity 36. The Prince and the Pauper (US) 37. Moonlight Sonata 37. The Crimes of Stephen Hawke 38. *49th Parallel* 41. One of Our Aircraft is Missing 42. Uncensored 42. Squadron Leader X 43. We Dive at Dawn 43. Escape to Danger 43. *Millions Like Us* 43. A Canterbury Tale 44. Great Day 45. Men of Two Worlds 46. *Wanted for Murder* 46. Dear Murderer 47. Daybreak 48. The Mark of Cain 48. Corridor of Mirrors 48. The Blind Goddess 48. The Spider and the Fly 50. The Magic Box 51. Cairo Road 51. His Excellency 51. South of Algiers 52. The Colditz Story 54. *The Deep Blue Sea* 55. Child in the House 56. The Good Companions 57. The Naked Edge 61. The Man Who Finally Died 62. Freud 62. West Eleven 63. The Bedford Incident 65. The Whisperers 66. The Spy with a Cold Nose 67. Assignment to Kill 67. Deadfall 68.

Post, Ted (1918–).
American director, from TV.
■ The Peacemaker 56. The Legend of Tom Dooley 59. Hang 'Em High 68. Beneath the Planet of the Apes 70. Yuma (TV) 70. Dr Cook's Garden (TV) 70. Night Slaves (TV) 70. The Bravos (TV) 71. Five Desperate Women (TV) 71. Do Not Fold Spindle or Mutilate (TV) 72. The Baby 73. The Harrad Experiment 73. Magnum Force 73. Whiffs 75. Good Guys Wear Black 77. Go Tell the Spartans 78. Nightkill 81. Stagecoach (TV) 86.

Posta, Adrienne (1948–) (Adrienne Poster).
British juvenile actress specializing in cheeky teenagers.

No Time for Tears 59. To Sir with Love 67. Here We Go Round the Mulberry Bush 67. Up the Junction 68. Some Girls Do 69. Percy 70. Up Pompeii 71. Percy's Progress 74, etc.

Postlethwaite, Peter.
British character actor, from the theatre.

A Private Function 84. Distant Voices, Still Lives 88. The Dressmaker 89. To Kill a Priest 89. Treasure Island 90. Hamlet 90. The Long Day Closes 92. Alien³ 92. Split Second 92. Last of the Mohicans 92. Waterland 92. *In the Name of the Father* (AAN) 93. Sharpe's Company (TV) 94, etc.

Poston, Tom (1927–).
American light comedian.
■ City that Never Sleeps 53. Zotz! 62. Soldier in the Rain 63. The Old Dark House 63. Cold Turkey 70. The Happy Hooker 75. Rabbit Test 78. Up the Academy 80. Carbon Copy 81.
TV series: The Steve Allen Show 56–59. On the Rocks 75–76. We've Got Each Other 77–78. Mork & Mindy 78–82. Newhart 82–90. Good Grief 90–91.

post-synchronization.
Adding sound, by dubbing, to visuals already shot. Sound can only rarely be recorded at the time of shooting because of extraneous noise and requirements of volume, pitch, etc.; actors must usually repeat their lines in accordance with their image on screen.

Potter, Dennis (1935–1994).
British dramatist and screenwriter, a former journalist, the pre-eminent television playwright of his time.
Pennies from Heaven (AAN) 81. Brimstone and Treacle 82. Gorky Park 83. Dreamchild 85. Tender Is the Night (TV) 85. The Singing Detective (TV) 87. Track 29 88. Lipstick on Your Collar (TV) 92. Secret Friends (wd) 92. Midnight Movie 93. Mesmer 94, etc.

Potter, H. C. (1904–1977).
American director with stage experience, in Hollywood from 1935; an expert at comedy.
■ Beloved Enemy 36. Wings over Honolulu 37. Romance in the Dark 38. Shopworn Angel 38. The Cowboy and the Lady 38. *The Story of Vernon and Irene Castle* 39. Blackmail 39. Congo Maisie 40. Second Chorus 40. *Hellzapoppin* 41. Mr Lucky 43. *The Farmer's Daughter* 47. A Likely Story 47. *Mr Blandings Builds His Dream House* 48. The Time of Your Life 48. You Gotta Stay Happy 48. The Miniver Story 50. Three for the Show 55. Top Secret Affair 57.

Potter, Martin (1944–).
British juvenile lead of the early 70s.
Fellini Satyricon 70. Goodbye Gemini 71. Nicholas and Alexandra 71. All Coppers Are 71. Craze 73. The Big Sleep 78. Gunpowder 84. Twinsanity 88, etc.

Potter, Sally (1949–).
British director and screenwriter.
The Gold Diggers 84. *Orlando* 92.

Potts, Cliff (1945–).
American second lead of 70s action dramas.
Snow Job 72. The Ground Star Conspiracy 72. Face to the Wind 74. Nevada Smith (TV) 75. Once an Eagle (TV) 77. Last Ride of the Dalton Gang (TV) 79, etc.
TV series: Big Hawaii 77. Lou Grant 81–82. For Love and Honor 83.

Poujouly, Georges (1940–).
French boy-actor of the early 50s.
Jeux Interdits 52. Nous Sommes Tous des Assassins 52. Les Diaboliques 54. Lift to the Scaffold 57. Girls for the Summer 59, etc.

Poulton, Mabel (1905–).
British leading lady of the 20s.
The Heart of an Actress 24. Virginia's Husband 25. The Constant Nymph 28. The Return of the Rat 28.

Pounder, C. C. H. (Carol Christine Hilaria Pounder).
Guyana-born character actress in America.
Bagdad Café 88. Postcards from the Edge 90. Psycho IV: The Beginning (TV) 90. Question of Faith 93. Sliver 93. Benny & Joon 93. Robocop 3 93.
TV series: Women in Prison 87–88.

poverty
in America and Britain is rare enough now to be little discussed, but in the days when film-makers began to have a social conscience a number of films memorably examined the problem in different milieux. American hoboes and shanty-town dwellers were revealed in *Sullivan's Travels, Hallelujah I'm a Bum, Man's Castle, My Man Godfrey, One More Spring*; the rural poor were the subject of *Our Daily Bread, The Grapes of Wrath, Tobacco Road*. Hollywood's regretful gaze wandered to China for *The Good Earth* and for *Tortilla Flat* to Mexico, which was more memorably covered by Buñuel in *Los Olvidados*. Poverty in Italy was the subject of *Bicycle Thieves*, and in England of *Love on the Dole, Doss House* and *The Whisperers*.

Powell, Anthony.
English costume designer.
Travels with My Aunt (AAN) 72. Papillon 83. Death on the Nile (AA) 78. Tess (AA) 80. Indiana Jones and the Temple of Doom 84. Pirates (AAN) 86. Ishtar 87. Frantic 88. Indiana Jones and the Last Crusade 89, etc.

Powell, Dick (1904–1963).
American crooning juvenile of the 30s who later suffered a sea-change and emerged as a likeable tough leading man, a competent director and an ambitious producer, the founder of Four Star Television.
Blessed Event 32. Too Busy to Work 32. The King's Vacation 33. *Forty-Second Street* 33. Gold Diggers of 1933. Footlight Parade 33. College Coach 33. Convention City 33. *Dames* 34. Wonder Bar 34. Twenty Million Sweethearts 34. Happiness Ahead 34. Flirtation Walk 34. Gold Diggers of 1935. Page Miss Glory 35. Broadway Gondolier 35. A Midsummer Night's Dream 35. Shipmates Forever 35. Thanks a Million 35. Colleen 36. Hearts Divided 36. Stage Struck 36. Gold Diggers of 1937. *On the Avenue* 37. The Singing Marine 37. Varsity Show 37. Hollywood Hotel 38. Cowboy from Brooklyn 38. Hard to Get 38. Going Places 38. Naughty but Nice 39. *Christmas in July* 40. I Want a Divorce 40. Model Wife 41. In the Navy 41. Star Spangled Rhythm 42. Happy Go Lucky 42. True to Life 43. Riding High 43. *It Happened Tomorrow* 44. Meet the People 44. *Murder My Sweet* (as Philip Marlowe) 44. Cornered 45. Johnny O'Clock 47. To the Ends of the Earth 48. Pitfall 48. Station West 48. Rogues Regiment 48. Mrs Mike 49. The Reformer and the Redhead 50. Right Cross 50. Callaway Went Thataway 51. Cry Danger 51. The Tall Target 51. You Never Can Tell 51. The Bad and the Beautiful 52. Split Second (d only) 53. Susan Slept Here 54. The Conqueror (pd only) 56. You Can't Run Away From It (d only) 56. The Enemy Below (d only) 57. The Hunters (d only) 58, etc.
TV series: *Dick Powell Theatre* 59–61.

Powell, Dilys (1902–).
British film critic, long with the *Sunday Times* and then with *Punch*. Her reviews have been collected in: 1989, *The Golden Screen: Fifty Years of Films*, and 1991, *The Dilys Powell Film Reader*.

Powell, Eleanor (1910–1982).
Long-legged American tap dancer whose vitality enhanced a few films.
■ George White's Scandals 35. Broadway Melody of 1936. *Born to Dance* 36. Broadway Melody of 1938. *Rosalie* 38. Honolulu 39. Broadway Melody of 1940. Lady Be Good 41. Ship Ahoy 42. I Dood It 43. Thousands Cheer 43. Sensations of 1945 44. The Duchess of Idaho 50.

Powell, Jane (1929–) (Suzanne Burce).
Diminutive American singing and dancing leading lady; former child performer. She married former child actor Dick Moore, her fifth husband, in 1988.
■ Song of the Open Road 44. Delightfully Dangerous 45. Holiday in Mexico 46. Three Daring Daughters 48. A Date with Judy 48. Luxury Liner 48. Nancy Goes to Rio 50. Two Weeks with Love 50. Royal Wedding 51. Rich Young and Pretty 51. Small Town Girl 53. Three Sailors and a Girl 53. *Seven Brides for Seven Brothers* 54. Athena 54. Deep in My Heart 54. Hit the Deck 55. The Girl Most Likely 58. The Female Animal 58. Enchanted Island 58. Wheeler and Murdoch (TV) 70. The Letters (TV) 72. Mayday at 40,000 Feet (TV) 78.

Powell, Michael (1905–1990).
Important British writer-producer-director whose highly imaginative work, especially in his collaboration with Emeric Pressburger (The Archers 42–57), was sometimes marred by a streak of tastelessness. His second wife was film editor Thelma Schoonmaker.
Autobiographies: 1985, *A Life in Movies*. 1992, *Million Dollar Movie*.
AS WRITER: Caste 30. 77 Park Lane 31.
AS DIRECTOR: Two Crowded Hours 31. My Friend the King 32. Rynox 32. The Rasp 32. The Star Reporter 32. Hotel Splendide 32. C.O.D. 32. His Lordship 32. Born Lucky 33. The Fire Raisers (& co-w) 34. The Night of the Party 35. Something Always Happens 34. Red Ensign (& co-w) 35. The Girl in the Crowd 35. Lazybones 35. The Love Test 35. The Phantom Light 35. The Price of a Song 35. Someday 35. Her Last Affaire 36. The Brown Wallet 36. Crown v. Stevens 36. The Man behind the Mask 36.
■ AS EXECUTIVE wholly or jointly in charge, including work as WRITER-PRODUCER-DIRECTOR: The Edge of the World 37. *The Spy in Black* 38. The Lion Has Wings 39. The Thief of Baghdad 39. Contraband 40. 49th Parallel (US: The Invaders) (AA story) 41. One of Our Aircraft is Missing (AANw) 42. *The Life and Death of Colonel Blimp* 43. The Silver Fleet 43. A Canterbury Tale 44. *I Know Where I'm Going* 45. *A Matter of Life and Death* 46. Black Narcissus 46. End of the River 47. *The Red Shoes* 48. The Small Back Room 48. Gone to Earth 50. The Elusive Pimpernel 51. The Tales of Hoffman 51. Oh Rosalinda 55. The Battle of the River Plate 56. Ill Met by Moonlight 57. Peeping Tom 60. Honeymoon 61. The Queen's Guards 61. They're a Weird Mob 66. Sebastian (p only) 67. Age of Consent 69. The Boy Who Turned Yellow 72. Return to the Edge of the World 79.
✪ For being so unpredictable, and at his best so brilliant. *A Matter of Life and Death*.

¶ Of course all films are surrealist. They are making something that looks like the real world but isn't. – *M.P.*

I got my first assignment as a director in 1927. I was slim, arrogant, intelligent, foolish, shy, cocksure, dreamy and irritating. Today, I'm no longer slim. – *M.P. in 1987*

Powell, Nik (1950–).
British producer, in partnership with Steve

Woolley. He was a co-founder of Palace Pictures, a distribution and production company.

The Company of Wolves 85. A Letter to Brezhnev 85. Absolute Beginners 86. Mona Lisa 86. The Courier 87. High Spirits 88. Shag 88. Scandal 89. The Big Man 90. The Miracle 91. The Pope Must Die (US: The Pope Must Diet) 91. A Rage in Harlem 91, etc.

Powell, Robert (1944–).
Lithe, pale-eyed British leading man of the 70s.
Walk a Crooked Path 69. The Italian Job 69. Pygmalion (TV) 71. Secrets 71. Running Scared 72. Asylum 72. The Asphyx 73. Mahler 73. Tommy 75. *Jesus of Nazareth* (TV) 77. The Four Feathers (TV) 78. Beyond Good and Evil (It.) 78. The Thirty-Nine Steps 78. Harlequin 79. Jane Austen in Manhattan 79. The Survivor 80. The Jigsaw Man 83. Secrets of the Phantom Caverns 84. Shaka Zulu (TV) 86. The Mystery of Edwin Drood 93, etc.

¶ I hope Jesus Christ will be the last in my line of sensitive young men for quite a while. – *R.P.*, 1977

Powell, Sandy (1898–1982) (Albert Powell).
British music-hall comedian who made some knockabout films using his radio catch-phrase 'Can you hear me, mother?'
Autobiography: 1976, *Can You Hear Me, Mother?*
The Third String 32. Leave It to Me 36. I've Got a Horse 38. Cup Tie Honeymoon 48, etc.

Powell, Sandy.
English costume designer.
Caravaggio 86. Stormy Monday 88. The Miracle 91. The Pope Must Die (US: The Pope Must Diet) 91. Being Human 94. Interview with the Vampire 94, etc.

Powell, William (1892–1984).
Mature, debonair American leading man of the 30s and 40s; a pillar of MGM for many years, he began as a cowboy villain but is probably best remembered as Nick Charles in *The Thin Man*.
Biography: 1984, *Gentleman, the William Powell Story.*
SELECTED SILENT FILMS: Sherlock Holmes 22. The Bright Shawl 23. Romola 24. Too Many Kisses 25. Faint Perfume 25. Desert Gold 26. Aloma of the South Seas 26. Beau Geste 26. Señorita 27. Nevada 27. Feel My Pulse 28. The Last Command 28. The Vanishing Pioneer 28, etc.
■ SOUND FILMS: Interference 29. *The Canary Murder Case* (as Philo Vance) 29. The Greene Murder Case 29. Charming Sinners 29. The Four Feathers 29. The Benson Murder Case 30. Paramount on Parade 30. Shadow of the Law 30. Pointed Heels 30. Behind the Make-up 30. *Street of Chance* 30. For the Defense 30. Man of the World 31. Ladies' Man 31. The Road to Singapore 31. High Pressure 32. Jewel Robbery 32. *One Way Passage* 32. Lawyer Man 32. Double Harness 33. Private Detective 62 33. The Kennel Murder Case 33. Fashions of 1934. The Key 34. Manhattan Melodrama 34. *The Thin Man* (AAN) 34. Evelyn Prentice 34. Reckless 35. Star of Midnight 35. Escapade 35. Rendezvous 35. *The Great Ziegfeld* 36. The Ex Mrs Bradford 36. *My Man Godfrey* (AAN) 36. Libelled Lady 36. After the Thin Man 36. The Last of Mrs Cheyney 37. The Emperor's Candlesticks 37. Double Wedding 37. The Baroness and the Butler 38. Another Thin Man 39. I Love You Again 40. Love Crazy 41. Shadow of the Thin Man 41. Crossroads 42. The Youngest Profession 43. The Heavenly Body 44. The Thin Man Goes Home 44. Ziegfeld Follies 45. The Hoodlum Saint 46. Song of the Thin Man 47. *Life With Father* (AAN) 47. The Senator was

Indiscreet 47. Mr Peabody and the Mermaid 48. Take One False Step 49. Dancing in the Dark 49. Treasure of Lost Canyon 51. It's a Big Country 51. The Girl Who Had Everything 53. How to Marry a Millionaire 53. *Mister Roberts* (as Doc) 55. ✪ For spreading his cheerful suavity over 30s Hollywood; and for being so much at home in a dinner jacket. *The Thin Man.*

Famous line (*Life With Father*): 'I'm going to be baptized, damn it!'

Power, Hartley (1894–1966).
Bald-headed American character actor who settled in Britain and was often seen as general, con man or brash agent.
Friday the Thirteenth 33. Evergreen 34. A Window in London 42. The Way to the Stars 45. *Dead of Night* 45. A Girl in a Million 47. Roman Holiday 53. To Dorothy a Son 54. Island in the Sun 56, many others.

Power, Tyrone (1913–1958).
American leading man, of theatrical family; in films from 1932, usually deploying smooth gentle personality. He was married three times; his wives included actresses Annabella (1939–48) and Linda Christian (1949–55). Died of a heart attack.
■ Tom Brown of Culver 32. Girls' Dormitory 36. Ladies in Love 36. *Lloyds of London* 37. Love is News 37. Café Metropole 37. Thin Ice 37. Second Honeymoon 37. *In Old Chicago* 38. *Alexander's Ragtime Band* 38. Marie Antoinette 38. Suez 38. *Rose of Washington Square* 39. *Jesse James* 39. Second Fiddle 39. The Rains Came 39. Daytime Wife 39. Johnny Apollo 40. Brigham Young 40. *The Mark of Zorro* 40. A Yank in the RAF 41. Blood and Sand 41. This Above All 42. Son of Fury 42. *The Black Swan* 42. Crash Dive 42; war service; The Razor's Edge 46. Captain from Castile 47. Nightmare Alley 47. The Luck of the Irish 48. That Wonderful Urge 48. Prince of Foxes 49. The Black Rose 50. An American Guerilla in the Philippines 51. Rawhide 51. I'll Never Forget You 51. Diplomatic Courier 52. Pony Soldier 52. Mississippi Gambler 53. King of the Khyber Rifles 53. The Long Gray Line 54. Untamed 55. The Eddy Duchin Story 56. Seven Waves Away 57. The Rising of the Moon (narrated only) 57. *The Sun Also Rises* 57. Witness for the Prosecution 57.

¶ I've done an awful lot of stuff that's a monument to public patience. – *T.P.*
Some day I will show the motherfuckers who say I was a success just because of my pretty face. Sometimes I wish I had a really bad car accident so my face would get smashed up and I'd look like Eddie Constantine. – *T.P.*
He said that in Hollywood, the glamour and the sweet-dreamy stuff was but a façade, that it was a world of polite destruction. – *Mai Zetterling*

Power, Tyrone, Snr (1869–1931).
American stage actor, father of Tyrone Power: played heavy in a few films.
A Texas Street 15. Where are My Children? 16. Footfalls 21. The Lone Wolf 24. Bride of the Storm 26. The Big Trail 30, etc.

Powers, Mala (1931–) (Mary Ellen Powers).
American leading lady, former child actress.
Tough as They Come 41. Outrage 50. Cyrano de Bergerac 50. Rose of Cimarron 52. Rage at Dawn 55. Benghazi 55. The Storm Rider 57. Daddy's Gone A-Hunting 69. The Doomsday Machine 72, etc.

Powers, Stefanie (1942–) (Stefania Federkiewicz).
American leading lady of the 60s.
Experiment in Terror 62. The Interns 62. Palm Springs Weekend 63. *Fanatic* (GB) 64. Stagecoach 66. Warning Shot 67. Herbie Rides Again 73. Escape to Athena 79. Family Secrets (TV) 84. Deceptions (TV) 85. She Was Marked for Murder (TV) 88. Love and Betrayal (TV) 89, etc.
TV series: The Girl from UNCLE 66. Washington behind Closed Doors 77. The Feather and Father Gang 78. *Hart to Hart* 79–83.

Powers, Tom (1890–1955).
American general-purpose supporting actor.
Double Indemnity 44. Two Years Before the Mast 46. Up in Central Park 48. Chicago Deadline 49. Destination Moon 50. Horizons West 52. Julius Caesar 53. The Americano 54, etc.

pratfall.
Something in which all silent comedians were skilled: the art of falling on one's fundament without getting hurt.

pre-credits sequence.
It has recently become fashionable to start films with an explosive opening scene, sometimes running seven or eight minutes, before the titles appear. This now over-worked device, used by almost all American TV series, is generally traced back to *Rommel, Desert Fox* 51, which had a long pre-credits sequence showing a commando raid; but the titles come quite late in *The Egg and I* 47, and even in *Destry Rides Again* 39 there is nearly a minute of shooting before they appear; while in *The Magnificent Ambersons* 42 they are not seen at all, only spoken at the end of the picture.
More recently, *Cruising* and *Papillon* are among the movies to place all their credits at the end.

Preisner, Zbigniew (1955–).
Polish composer, in films since 1979.
At Play in the Fields of the Lord (US) 91. Europa, Europa 91. The Double Life of Veronique 91. Damage 92. The Secret Garden 93. *Three Colours: Blue* (Trois Couleurs: Bleu) 93. A Linha do Horizonte 93. Three Colours: Red (Trois Couleurs: Rouge) 94. Three Colours: White (Trois Couleurs: Blanc) 94. Mouvements du Désir 94. When a Man Loves a Woman (US) 94, etc.

Preiss, Wolfgang.
German character actor in international films.
The Longest Day 62. Von Ryan's Express 65. The Train 65. Hannibal Brooks 68. Raid on Rommel 71. The Salzburg Connection 72. A Bridge too Far 77. The Boys from Brazil 78. The Winds of War (TV) 83. Forget Mozart 85. The Second Victory 86, etc.

Preisser, June (1921–1984).
Vivacious teenage leading lady of the 40s.
Babes in Arms 39. Strike Up the Band 40. The Fleet's In 41. Sweater Girl 41. Babes on Swing Street 44. Sarge Goes to College 47, etc.

Préjean, Albert (1894–1979).
French light character actor who was in most of René Clair's early successes.
Le Voyage Imaginaire 25. An Italian Straw Hat 27. Sous les Toits de Paris 30. Die Dreigroschenoper (L'Opéra de Quat'Sous) 31. Jenny 36. Métropolitain 40. L'Etrange Suzy 43. Les Nouveaux Maîtres 49. Les Amants du Tage 54, etc.

Preminger, Ingo.
Austrian/American producer, brother of Otto.
M*A*S*H (AAN) 70, etc.

Preminger, Otto (1906–1986).
Austrian/American director with theatrical
background. Always a good craftsman, he latterly
applied heavy-handed treatment to potentially
interesting subjects.
 Autobiography: 1977, *Preminger*.
 Biography: 1973, *Behind the Scenes of Otto
Preminger* by Willi Frischauer.
■ Die Grosse Liebe (Austrian) 32, then to US:
Under Your Spell 36. Danger, Love at Work 37. The
Pied Piper (acted only) 42. They Got Me Covered
(acted only) 42. Margin for Error (& a) 43. In the
Meantime, Darling 44. *Laura* 44. Royal Scandal 45.
Where Do We Go from Here 45. Centennial
Summer 46. Fallen Angel 46. Forever Amber 47.
Daisy Kenyon 47. That Lady in Ermine (part) 48.
The Fan 49. Whirlpool 50. Where the Sidewalk
Ends 50. The Thirteenth Letter 51. Angel Face 52.
The Moon is Blue 53. *Stalag 17* (acted only) 53. River
of No Return 54. *Carmen Jones* 54. The Court Martial
of Billy Mitchell 55. *The Man with the Golden Arm*
56. Bonjour Tristesse 57. Saint Joan (GB) 57. Porgy
and Bess 59. *Anatomy of a Murder* 59. Exodus 60.
Advise and Consent 61. The Cardinal (AAN) 63. In
Harm's Way 65. Bunny Lake is Missing (GB) 65.
Hurry Sundown 67. Skidoo 68. Tell Me That You
Love Me, Junie Moon 70. Such Good Friends 72.
Rosebud 75. The Human Factor 79.

¶ A great showman who has never bothered to
 learn anything about making a movie . . . no
one is more skilled at giving the appearance of
dealing with large controversial themes in a bold
way, without making the tactical error of doing so.
– Dwight MacDonald
 Otto, let my people go. – *Mort Sahl at the premiere
of Exodus*
 His enemies have never forgiven him for being
a director with the personality of a producer.
– *Andrew Sarris, 1968*

Prentiss, Paula (1939–) (Paula Ragusa).
Tall American leading lady who came almost
straight from college to Hollywood.
 Where the Boys Are 61. The Honeymoon
Machine 62. Bachelor in Paradise 62. The
Horizontal Lieutenant 63. *Man's Favorite Sport?* 64.
The World of Henry Orient 64. In Harm's Way 65.
What's New, Pussycat? 65. Catch 22 69. Last of
the Red Hot Lovers 72. Crazy Joe 73. The Parallax
View 74. The Stepford Wives 75. Having Babies II
(TV) 77. The Black Marble 80. Buddy Buddy 81.
Saturday the 14th 81. M.A.D.D.: Mothers against
Drunk Driving (TV) 83, etc.
 TV series: He and She 67.

prequel.
The opposite of a sequel, i.e. a film showing events
which happened *before* one already known. The first
film prequel may have been *Another Part of the
Forest*, which came after *The Little Foxes* but
described events before it. The word came into
being in the late 70s with the production of *Butch
and Sundance: The Early Days*. A game rapidly
sprang up in which one had to supply prequel
titles for famous films. Among them were *Mr
Blandings Applies for Planning Permission; The Boy
Who Would Be Prince; Friday Night Slight
Temperature; Destry Dismounts;* and *Hello Mr
Chips.*

Presle, Micheline (1922–) (Micheline
Chassagne).
French leading actress with stage experience.
 Jeunes Filles en Détresse 38. La Nuit Fantastique
41. Boule de Suif 45. *Le Diable au Corps* 46. Les
Jeux Sont Faits 47. Under My Skin (US) 50. The

Adventures of Captain Fabian (US) 51. La Dame
aux Camélias 52. Villa Borghese 54. The She
Wolves 57. Blind Date (GB) 59. The Prize 63. La
Religieuse 65. King of Hearts 67. Peau d'Ane 70.
The Slightly Pregnant Man 73. Nea: A New Woman
78. Je M'Appelle Victor 93. Fanfan 93. Pas Très
Catholique 94, etc.

Presley, Elvis (1935–1977).
Heavy-lidded American pop singer and guitarist,
once known as 'the Pelvis' because of his swivel-
hipped style. His popularity with teenagers
survived a host of bad movies.
 Biography: 1977, *Elvis Presley* by W. A.
Harbinson.
■ Love Me Tender 56. Loving You 57. Jailhouse
Rock 57. King Creole 58. G.I. Blues 60. Flaming
Star 60. Wild in the Country 61. Blue Hawaii 61.
Kid Galahad 62. Girls Girls Girls 62. Follow That
Dream 62. Fun in Acapulco 63. It Happened at the
World's Fair 63. Kissin' Cousins 64. Viva Las Vegas
64. Roustabout 64. Girl Happy 65. Tickle Me 65.
Harem Scarem 65. Frankie and Johnny 66.
Paradise Hawaiian Style 66. Spinout 66. Easy
Come Easy Go 67. Double Trouble 67. Stay Away
Joe 68. Speedway 68. Clambake 68. Live a Little
Love a Little 68. Charro 69. Change of Habit 70.
The Trouble with Girls 70. Elvis – that's the Way
It Is 70. Elvis on Tour 72.

¶ He projects to the point where he jumps out
 at you from the screen. He has some of the same
qualities as Rudolph Valentino. He has the same
magnetism. – *Don Siegel*

Presley, Priscilla (1945–).
American light actress. She was married to Elvis
Presley (1967–73).
 Love Is Forever (TV) 83. The Naked Gun 88. The
Adventures of Ford Fairlane 90. The Naked Gun
2½: The Smell of Fear 91. Naked Gun 33⅓: The
Final Insult 94, etc.
 TV series: Dallas 83.

Presnell, Harve (1933–).
American light opera singer, in occasional films.
■ The Unsinkable Molly Brown 64. The Glory
Guys 65. Where the Boys Meet the Girls 65. Paint
Your Wagon 69.

Presnell, Robert, Jnr (1914–1986).
American writer.
 Meet John Doe (co-story, AAN) 41. The Man in
the Attic 53. Legend of the Lost 57. Conspiracy of
Hearts (GB) 59. Let No Man Write My Epitaph 60.
The Third Day 65, etc.

Presnell, Robert, Snr (1894–).
American writer, usually in collaboration.
 Hi Nellie 32. My Man Godfrey 36. The Real
Glory 39. Meet John Doe 41. Second Chance 53.
13 West Street 62, etc.

Pressburger, Arnold (1885–1951).
Hungarian producer who worked in Germany,
Britain and Hollywood.
 City of Song 30. Tell Me Tonight 32. The Return
of the Scarlet Pimpernel 38. The Shanghai Gesture
41. Hangmen Also Die 43. It Happened Tomorrow
44. A Scandal in Paris 46, etc.

Pressburger, Emeric (1902–1988).
Hungarian journalist and scriptwriter in Britain
from 1935. Worked on script of *The Challenge* 37
and met Michael Powell, qv for list of their joint
films such as *The Archers*.
 Biography: 1994, *Emeric Pressburger: The Life and
Death of a Screenwriter* by Kevin Macdonald.

SOLO: Twice Upon a Time (wpd) 52. Miracle in
Soho (wp) 56. Behold a Pale Horse (from his novel
64. Operation Crossbow (w) (as Richard Imrie) 65
They're a Weird Mob (w) 66. The Boy Who
Turned Yellow (w) 72.

Pressman, Edward R.
American producer.
 The Revolutionary 70. Badlands 73. Phantom c
the Paradise 74. Paradise Alley 78. Heart Beat 78.
Old Boyfriends 79. You Better Watch Out 80. The
Hand 81. The Pirates of Penzance 83. Plenty 84.
True Stories 88. Wall Street 88. Talk Radio 88.
Reversal of Fortune 91. Year of the Gun 91.
Storyville 92. The Crow 94. No Escape 94. Judge
Dredd 95, etc.

Pressman, Michael (1950–).
American director.
 The Bad News Bears in Breaking Training 77.
Boulevard Nights 79. Those Lips Those Eyes 80.

Preston, Kelly (1962–) (Kelly Smith).
American actress. Married John Travolta.
 Christine 83. Metalstorm: The Destruction of
Jared-Syn 83. Mischief 85. Secret Admirer 85. 52
Pick-Up 86. Amazon Women on the Moon 87.
Love at Stake 87. A Tiger's Tale 87. Spellbinder
88. Twins 88. The Experts 89. Only You 92.
Cheyenne Warrior 94, etc.

Preston, Robert (1917–1987) (Robert Preston
Meservey).
American leading man who made routine films
from 1938, and became a theatre star of great
vitality in the 50s.
■ King of Alcatraz 38. Illegal Traffic 38. Disbarred
38. Union Pacific 39. *Beau Geste* 39. Typhoon 39.
Moon over Burma 39. Northwest Mounted Police
40. New York Town 40. The Lady from Cheyenne
40. The Night of January 16th 41. Parachute
Battalion 41. Pacific Blackout 41. Reap the Wild
Wind 42. *This Gun for Hire* 42. Wake Island 42.
Night Plane to Chungking 42; war service; Wild
Harvest 47. *The Macomber Affair* 47. Variety Girl 47.
Whispering Smith 47. Blood on the Moon 48. Big
City 48. The Lady Gambles 48. *Tulsa* 49. The
Sundowners 49. Best of the Badmen 51. My Outlaw
Brother 51. When I Grow Up 51. Face to Face 52.
Cloudburst (GB) 53. The Last Frontier 56. *The
Dark at the Top of the Stairs* 60. *The Music Man* (his
stage role) 61. Island of Love 63. *All the Way Home*
63. How the West Was Won 63. Junior Bonner
72. Child's Play 72. Mame 73. My Father's House
(TV) 75. Semi-Tough 77. The Chisholms (TV) 79.
S.O.B. 81. *Victor/Victoria* 82. September Gun (TV)
83. The Last Starfighter 84. Finnegan Begin Again
(TV) 85. Outrage (TV) 86.

Prévert, Jacques (1900–1977).
French screenwriter whose most memorable work
was in conjunction with Marcel Carné.
 Drôle de Drame 37. *Quai des Brumes* 38. *Le Jour Se
Lève* 39. Les Visiteurs du Soir 42. *Les Enfants du
Paradis* (AAN) 44. *Les Portes de la Nuit* 46. Les
Amants de Vérone 48. Other scripts include
L'Affaire est dans le Sac (& a) 32. *Le Crime de
Monsieur Lange* 35. *Une Partie de Campagne* 36.
Lumière d'Eté 42. Notre Dame de Paris 56, etc.

Prévert, Pierre (1906–1988).
French director, brother of Jacques Prévert.
 L'Affaire est dans le Sac 32. Adieu Leonard 43.
Voyage Surprise 46, etc.

Previn, André (1929–).
German composer and arranger, long in
Hollywood. Settled in Britain and became orchestral

conductor. He was married to Mia Farrow (1970–79).

Autobiography: 1992, *No Minor Chords: My Days in Hollywood*.

Biography: 1981, *André Previn* by Martin Bookspan and Ross Yockey.

Scene of the Crime 49. Three Little Words (AAN) 51. Bad Day at Black Rock 54. The Fastest Gun Alive 56. Designing Woman 57. Gigi (AA) 58. Porgy and Bess (AA) 59. Elmer Gantry (AAN) 60. One, Two, Three 62. Irma la Douce (AA) 63. My Fair Lady (AA) 64. Inside Daisy Clover 65. The Fortune Cookie 66. Thoroughly Modern Millie (AAN) 67. The Music Lovers 71. Jesus Christ Superstar (AAN) 73. The Elephant Man 80. Six Weeks 82. Romeo and Juliet 90, etc.

Previn, Steve (1925–1993).
American director and production executive, a former editor. The brother of André Previn, he was based in Europe from the mid-50s.
AS DIRECTOR: Almost Angels 62. Escapade in Florence 62. Waltz King 63, etc.

Prévost, Françoise (1929–   ).
French leading lady of international films in the 60s.
Payroll 61. Bon Voyage 63. Paris Nous Appartient 63. The Condemned of Altona 63. Galia 65, etc.

Prévost, Marie (1893–1937) (Marie Bickford Dunn).
Anglo-French leading lady of American silent films.
East Lynne with Variations 20. Her Night of Nights 22. The Marriage Circle 24. Red Lights 24. The Loves of Camille 25. Up in Mabel's Room 26. Getting Gertie's Garter 27. Lady of Leisure 28. Side Show 30. Sporting Blood 31. Parole Girl 33. Tango (last film) 36, etc.

Price, Alan (1942–   ).
British composer, singer and pianist, a founder-member of the 60s rock band The Animals.
Oh, Lucky Man 73. Alfie Darling (& a) 75. Britannia Hospital 82. The Whales of August 87.

Price, Dennis (1915–1973) (Dennistoun Franklyn John Rose-Price).
British light leading man and latterly equally light character actor; on stage from 1937.
■ No Parking (debut) 37. A Canterbury Tale 43. *A Place of One's Own* 44. The Echo Murders 45. Caravan 46. The Magic Bow 46. Hungry Hill 46. Dear Murderer 47. Jassy 47. Holiday Camp 47. Master of Bankdam 47. The White Unicorn 47. Easy Money 47. Snowbound 48. Good Time Girl 48. *The Bad Lord Byron* 48. Kind Hearts and Coronets (his best role) 49. The Lost People 49. Helter Skelter 49. The Dancing Years 50. Murder Without Crime 50. The Adventurers 50. The Magic Box 51. Lady Godiva Rides Again 51. The House in the Square 51. Song of Paris 52. The Tall Headlines 52. The Intruder 53. Noose for a Lady 53. Murder at 3 a.m. 53. Time is my Enemy 54. For Better For Worse 54. Eight Witnesses 54. That Lady 55. Oh Rosalinda 55. *Private's Progress* 55. Charley Moon 56. Port Afrique 56. A Touch of the Sun 56. Fortune is a Woman 57. *The Naked Truth* 57. Danger Within 58. Hello London 58. *I'm All Right, Jack* 59. Don't Panic Chaps 59. Dark as the Night (US) 59. School for Scoundrels 60. Tunes of Glory 60. Oscar Wilde 60. Piccadilly Third Stop 60. The Millionairess 60. The Pure Hell of St Trinian's 60. No Love for Johnnie 61. The Rebel 61. Five Golden Hours 61. Double Bunk 61. Watch it, Sailor 61. Victim 61. What A Carve Up 61. Go to Blazes 62. Play it Cool

62. Behave Yourself 62. The Pot Carriers 62. The Amorous Prawn 62. Kill or Cure 62. The Wrong Arm of the Law 62. The Cool Mikado 63. The VIPs 63. The Cracksman 63. Doctor in Distress 63. *Tamahine* 63. The Comedy Man 63. A Jolly Bad Fellow 63. The Horror of it All 64. Murder Most Foul 64. The Earth Dies Screaming 64. The Curse of Simba 65. A High Wind in Jamaica 65. Ten Little Indians 65. Just Like a Woman 66. Jules Verne's Rocket to the Moon 67. The Haunted House of Horror 69. The Magic Christian 69. She Will She Won't 70. The Horror of Frankenstein 70. The Rise and Rise of Michael Rimmer 70. Twins of Evil 71. Pulp 72. Alice's Adventures in Wonderland 72. Venus in Furs 72. Go for a Take 72. That's Your Funeral 72. The Adventures of Barry Mackenzie 72. Horror Hospital 73. Theatre of Blood 73.

TV series: *The World of Wooster* (as Jeeves) 65–68.

¶ I am a second-rate feature actor. I am not a star and never was. I lack the essential spark. – *D.P.*

Price, Nancy (1880–1970) (Lillian Maude).
Dominant British character actress with long stage experience, especially remembered as Grandma in *Whiteoaks*. Also an indefatigable traveller, naturalist and semi-mystic.
The Stars Look Down 39. Madonna of the Seven Moons 44. I Live in Grosvenor Square 45. The Three Weird Sisters 48. Mandy 52, etc.

Price, Richard (1949–   ).
American screenwriter and novelist.
Bloodbrothers 78. The Wanderers 79. Streets of Gold 86. The Color of Money (AAN) 86. New York Stories (co-w) 89. Sea of Love 89. Night and the City 92. Mad Dog and Glory 93. etc.

Price, Vincent (1911–1993).
Tall, gentle-voiced American character actor, lately typed in horror films. He studied art history at Yale and took a master's degree in fine arts at the University of London. He made his stage debut in London in 1935. Married actress Coral Browne, his third wife, in 1974.
Autobiography: 1959, *I Like What I Know*.
Biography: 1976, *Vincent Price Unmasked* by J. R. Parish and Steven Whitney.
Service de Luxe (debut) 38. Elizabeth and Essex 39. Green Hell 40. *Tower of London* (as Clarence) 40. Brigham Young 40. The Song of Bernadette 43. The Keys of the Kingdom 44. Laura (AAN) 44. Wilson 44. Czarina 45. Dragonwyck 46. Shock 46. The Long Night 47. The Three Musketeers 49. Champagne for Caesar 49. *His Kind of Woman* 51. *House of Wax* 53. The Mad Magician 54. The Ten Commandments 56. *The Story of Mankind* 57. The Fly 58. The Bat 59. The House on Haunted Hill 60. *The Fall of the House of Usher* 61. The Pit and the Pendulum 61. Tales of Terror 62. *The Raven* 63. A Comedy of Terrors 63. *The Tomb of Ligeia* 64. City under the Sea 65. Dr Goldfoot and the Sex Machine 65. House of a Thousand Dolls 67. The Oblong Box 69. Scream and Scream Again 69. Cry of the Banshee 70. The Abominable Dr Phibes 71. Dr Phibes Rises Again 72. Theatre of Blood 73. Madhouse 73. Journey into Fear 75. Scavenger Hunt 79. The Monster Club 81. The House of Long Shadows 83. Bloodbath at the House of Death 84. The Whales of August 87. Dead Heat 88. Backtrack (aka Catchfire) 89. Edward Scissorhands 90, etc.

TV series: Time Express 79.

¶ I sometimes feel that I'm impersonating the dark unconscious of the whole human race. I know this sounds sick, but I love it. – *V.P.*
~Price's was the voice on Michael Jackson's phenomenally successful 1983 video 'Thriller'.

Priestley, J. B. (1894–1984).
Prolific British novelist. There have been film versions of *The Good Companions, Benighted* (The Old Dark House), *Let the People Sing,* and also of his plays *Dangerous Corner, Laburnum Grove, When We Are Married* and *An Inspector Calls*. His autobiographical *Midnight on the Desert* (1937) says much about Hollywood.

Priestley, Jack (1927–1993).
American cinematographer.
Naked City (TV) 61–62. The Subject Was Roses 68. No Way to Treat a Lady 68. Stiletto 69. Where's Poppa 70. The First Deadly Sin 80. Lady Blue (TV) 85. A Man Called Hawk (TV) 89. The Trials of Rosie O'Neill (TV) 92, etc.

Priestley, Jason.
American actor.
Nowhere to Run 88. Calendar Girl 93. Tombstone 94.
TV series: Sister Kate 89–90. Beverly Hills 90210 90–   .

Priestley, Tom (1932–   ).
British editor.
Deliverance (AAN) 72. The Great Gatsby 74. Voyage of the Damned 76. Times Square 80. Another Time, Another Place 84. Dream One 84. 1984 84. The Kitchen Toto 88. White Mischief 88. Lord of the Flies 90, etc.

priests
have been a godsend to film-makers. Most male stars have played them occasionally: the combination of masculine attractiveness and non-availability apparently works at the box office. Thus Frank Sinatra in *The Miracle of the Bells;* William Holden and Clifton Webb in *Satan Never Sleeps;* Bing Crosby in *Going My Way, The Bells of St Mary's* and *Say One for Me;* Richard Dix in *The Christian;* Pat O'Brien in a dozen films including *Angels with Dirty Faces, The Fighting 69th* and *Fighting Father Dunne;* ditto Spencer Tracy, in *Boys' Town, San Francisco, The Devil at Four O'Clock,* and others; George Arliss in *Cardinal Richelieu;* Don Murray in *The Hoodlum Priest;* Karl Malden in *On the Waterfront* and *The Great Impostor;* Pierre Fresnay in *Monsieur Vincent;* Claude Laydu in *Diary of a Country Priest;* Jean-Paul Belmondo in *Leon Morin Priest;* John Mills in *The Singer Not the Song;* Tom Tryon in *The Cardinal;* Gregory Peck in *The Keys of the Kingdom;* Geoffrey Bayldon in *Sky West and Crooked;* Richard Burton in *Becket;* David Warner in *The Ballad of Cable Hogue;* Ward Bond in *The Quiet Man;* Mickey Rooney in *The Twinkle in God's Eye;* Montgomery Clift in *I Confess;* Alec Guinness in *Father Brown* and *The Prisoner;* Trevor Howard in *Ryan's Daughter;* Donald Sutherland in *Act of the Heart;* and Marcello Mastroianni in *The Priest's Wife*.

Protestant priests included Anthony Quayle in *Serious Charge;* Richard Burton in *The Sandpiper;* Robert Donat in *Lease of Life;* Wilfred Lawson in *Pastor Hall;* Peter Sellers in *Heavens Above;* Richard Todd in *A Man Called Peter;* Fredric March in *One Foot in Heaven;* David Niven in *The Bishop's Wife.* Actors who have got to play pope include Anthony Quinn and John Gielgud in *The Shoes of the Fisherman,* Rod Steiger in *A Man Called John,* Paolo Stoppa in *Becket* and Rex Harrison in *The Agony and the Ecstasy*.

False priests were Humphrey Bogart in *The Left Hand of God,* Rod Steiger in *No Way to Treat a Lady,*

Dennis Price in *Kind Hearts and Coronets*, and Peter Sellers in *After the Fox*; while priestly villains were Ralph Richardson in *The Ghoul*, George Arliss in *Dr Syn* (followed by Peter Cushing in *Captain Clegg*), Keenan Wynn in *Johnny Concho*, Cedric Hardwicke in *The Hunchback of Notre Dame* and Robert Mitchum in *Night of the Hunter*. Classifiable as fallen priests were Henry Fonda in *The Fugitive*, Richard Burton in *Night of the Iguana*, Max Von Sydow in *Hawaii*, Burt Lancaster in *Elmer Gantry*, Lars Hanson in *The Scarlet Letter*, and Pierre Fresnay in *Le Défroqué* and *Dieu a Besoin des Hommes*.

Priests came into their own again in a spate of diabolical thrillers: Max Von Sydow and Jason Miller in *The Exorcist*, Patrick Troughton in *The Omen*, Oliver Reed in *The Devils*. Other troubled priests have included Rod Steiger (and various successors) in *The Amityville Horror* series Christopher Reeve in *Monsignor*, and the protagonists of *True Confessions*.

Priggen, Norman (1924–).
British producer, with Ealing Studios from 1939, later independent.
  The Professionals 61. Payroll 61. The Servant 64. Secret Ceremony (co-p) 68. Tales That Witness Madness 73, etc.

Primus, Barry (1938–).
American director, screenwriter and actor.
AS ACTOR: The Brotherhood 68. Puzzle of a Downfall Child 70. Von Richtofen and Brown 71. Been Down So Long It Looks Like Up to Me 71. Gravy Train 74. New York, New York 77. Avalanche 78. The Rose 79. Night Games 80. Heartland 81. Absence of Malice 81. Brotherly Love 85. Talking Walls 85. Jake Speed 86. The Stranger 87. Big Business 88. Cannibal Women in the Avocado Jungle of Death 89. Torn Apart 89. Guilty by Suspicion 91. Night and the City 92, etc.
AS WRITER AND DIRECTOR: The Mistress 92.
  TV series: Cagney & Lacey (a) 84–85.

Prince (1958–) (Prince Rogers Nelson).
American rock musician, composer and director of films built around his life and performances.
  Purple Rain (AAm) 84. Under the Cherry Moon 86. Sign o' the Times (concert) 87. Graffiti Bridge 90.

Prince, Harold (1924–).
American stage producer who dabbles in films.
■ Something for Everyone 70. A Little Night Music 77.

Prince, Louis Aimé Augustin Le (1842–1890?).
French inventor, working in England, who may well have been the inventor of the first cine camera. He registered patents in England and America in 1888. In 1890, as he was preparing for a trip to America to demonstrate his camera, he boarded a train for Paris at Dijon and was never seen again.
  Biography: 1990, *The Missing Reel* by Christopher Rawlence.

Prince, William (1913–).
American stage leading man who was less successful in films.
  Destination Tokyo 44. Pillow to Post 46. Dead Reckoning 47. Carnegie Hall 48. Cyrano de Bergerac 51. The Vagabond King 55. Macabre 58. The Stepford Wives 75. Family Plot 76. The Gauntlet 77. Bronco Billy 80. Love and Money 82. Movers and Shakers 84. Spies Like Us 85. Spontaneous Combustion 90, etc.

Principal, Victoria (1945–).
American leading lady.
  The Life and Times of Judge Roy Bean 72. The Naked Ape 73. Earthquake 74. I Will, I Will, for Now 76. Vigilante Force 76. The Night They Took Miss Beautiful (TV) 77. Fantasy Island (TV) 77. Mistress (TV) 87. Naked Lie (TV) 89. Blind Witness (TV) 89. Sparks: The Price of Passion (TV) 90, etc.
  TV series: Dallas 80–91.

Prine, Andrew (1936–).
American leading man.
  The Miracle Worker 62. Company of Cowards 64. The Devil's Brigade 68. Bandolero 68. A Time for Giving 69. One Little Indian 73. Grizzly 76. Amityville II: The Possession 82. Eliminators 86, etc.
  TV series: The Wide Country 62–63. The Road West 66–67. W.E.B. 78. V: The Final Battle 84, etc.

Pringle, Aileen (1895–1989) (Aileen Bisbee).
American actress of the silent screen, best remembered for her performance in Elinor Glyn's *Three Weeks* 24.
  Redhead 19. The Christian 23. Wife of a Centaur 24. Dance Madness 24. Adam and Evil 27. Soldiers and Women 30. Convicted 32. Jane Eyre 33. Piccadilly Jim 36. Nothing Sacred 37. The Girl from Nowhere 39. Happy Land 43, etc.

Pringle, Bryan (1935–).
British character actor of stage and TV.
  Saturday Night and Sunday Morning 60. The Boy Friend 71. Haunted Honeymoon 86. Consuming Passions 88. Drowning by Numbers 88. Getting It Right 89. American Friends 91, etc.

Pringle, Ian (1953–).
Australian director, screenwriter and producer, also of documentaries.
  Wronsky (co-w, p, d) 80. The Plains of Heaven 82. Celia (p) 90. Romper Stomper (p) 92. Isabelle Eberhardt 92, etc.

Printemps, Yvonne (1894–1977) (Yvonne Wigniolle).
French musical comedy star in occasional films. She was married to actors Sacha Guitry and Pierre Fresnay.
  La Dame aux Camélias 34. The Paris Waltz 49. Voyage to America 52, etc.

Prinz, Le Roy (1895–1983).
American choreographer who after adventurous early life came to Hollywood and worked on many Paramount and Warner films.
  The Sign of the Cross 32. The 'Road' films 39–42. Yankee Doodle Dandy 42. Night and Day 46. The Ten Commandments 56. South Pacific 58, many others. Directed short subject *A Boy and His Dog* (AA) 48.

prison films
have always had an audience, but did not reach their full potential until sound. Then and through the 30s, film-makers took us on a conducted tour of American prisons. *The Big House*, *The Last Mile*, *I Was a Fugitive from a Chain Gang*, *Twenty Thousand Years in Sing Sing*, *Front Page Woman* (with its gas chamber scene), *Angels with Dirty Faces*, *San Quentin*, *Blackwell's Island*, *Each Dawn I Die*, *Invisible Stripes*, *King of Alcatraz*, *Prison Ship*, *Prison Doctor*, *Mutiny in the Big House* and many others. During the war prison films were surpassed in excitement, but they came back with a bang in *Brute Force*, the toughest of them all, and *White Heat*. The 50s brought *Behind the High Wall*, *Duffy of San Quentin*, *Riot in Cell Block Eleven*, *Inside the Walls of Folsom Prison*, *Black Tuesday*, *I Want to Live*, *Cell 2455 Death Row*, and a remake of *The Last Mile*. More recently Burt Lancaster appeared in the factual *Bird Man of Alcatraz*; and in the second half of the 60s the subject became popular again with *The Brig*, *The Ceremony*, *Reprieve*, *Point Blank*, *The Dirty Dozen*, *Triple Cross*, *Riot*, *There was a Crooked Man*, *A Clockwork Orange* and *Fortune and Men's Eyes*.

British studios have produced few prison films until the realist wave of the 60s which brought with it *The Criminal*, *The Pot Carriers*, and the army prison film *The Hill*.

Unusual prisons were shown in *Sullivan's Travels*, *Devil's Canyon*, *One Day in the Life of Ivan Denisovich*, and *Nevada Smith*; while among the films poking fun at prison life are *Up the River*, *Pardon Us* (Laurel and Hardy), *Convict 99* (Will Hay), *Jailhouse Rock* and *Two-Way Stretch*.

Prisons for women crop up quite regularly in such films as *Prison without Bars*, *Caged* (US), *Caged* (It.), *Au Royaume des Cieux*, *Women's Prison*, *Girls behind Bars*, *So Evil So Young*, *The Weak and the Wicked*, *Yield to the Night*, *The Smashing Bird I Used to Know* and *Women in Chains* (TV).

The Prisoner of Zenda.
At least four versions have been made of Anthony Hope's classic Ruritanian romance about a great impersonation, all in Hollywood: Rex Ingram directed a version in 1922 with Lewis Stone and Ramon Novarro; in 1937 John Cromwell directed Ronald Colman and Douglas Fairbanks Jnr in a version that was a model of its kind; Richard Thorpe made a mechanical scene-by-scene remake in 1952 with Stewart Granger and James Mason; in 1979 Peter Sellers appeared in an unsatisfactory half-humorous version by Dick Clement and Ian La Frenais. Comic variations on the story were included in *The Great Race* 65 and *Royal Flash* 75.

prisoners of war
were featured in many films after World War II. The British examples often made the camps seem almost too comfortable, despite the possibility of being shot while attempting to escape; this was perhaps because they were all filled with the same familiar faces. *Albert RN*, *The Captive Heart*, *The Colditz Story*, *The Betrayal*, *Danger Within*, *Reach for the Sky* and *The Password is Courage* all found humour in the situation at any rate; whereas the American counterparts, *The Purple Heart*, *Prisoner of War*, *Stalag 17* and *The Mackenzie Break* saw the harsher side which doubtless existed. The co-production, *The Bridge on the River Kwai*, gave a mixed picture of a Japanese camp; Britain's Hammer horror studio then produced *The Camp on Blood Island*, a fictitious record of atrocity, followed some years later by *The Secret of Blood Island*. Meanwhile the British in *The One That Got Away* paid tribute to the one German to escape from a British camp; and more recently *The Great Escape* showed the Americans coming some way towards the British idea of how jolly life in a camp can be. The ultimate absurdity was reached by an American TV series, *Hogan's Heroes*, which has a camp almost entirely controlled by the prisoners. The best serious film about prisoners of war remains undoubtedly Renoir's *La Grande Illusion*, made in 1937; though *King Rat* in 1965 made a fair bid to reveal the squalor and futility of the life, as did *The Empire of the Sun* 87, from the perspective of a young boy. Comic adventure stories about the escape of POWs have included *Very Important Person*, *The Secret War of Harry Frigg*, *Where Eagles Dare*, *Hannibal Brooks* and *Situation Hopeless but Not Serious*.

Women's camps were shown in *Two Thousand Women* (GB 1944), *Three Came Home* (US 1950), *A Town Like Alice* (GB 1956) and *Kapo* (It. 1960).

Vietnam made a horrifying start to its quota of prisoner-of-war films with *The Deer Hunter*, and brought it to its nadir with *Rambo: First Blood Part II*.

private eyes:
see *mystery*.

prizefighting:
see *boxing*.

Prizmacolour.
An early American colour process used for *The Glorious Adventure* 21. Crude in effect, in using orange and turquoise filters, it anticipated Cinecolor.

Prochnow, Jürgen (1941–).
German leading actor, now in American films.

The Consequence (Die Konsequenz) 77. Zoff 81. The Lost Honour of Katharina Blum (Die Verlorene Ehre de Katharina Blum) 75. The Boat (Das Boot) 81. Comeback 82. The Keep 83. Dune 84. Forbidden (TV) 85. Killing Cars 85. Terminus 86. Beverly Hills Cop II 87. The Seventh Sign 88. A Dry White Season 89. The Fourth War 90. The Man Inside 90. Robin Hood 90. Hurricane Smith 90. Prince of Tides 91. Red Hot 92. Twin Peaks: Fire Walk with Me 92. The Last Border 93. Body of Evidence 93. The Fire Next Time (TV) 93. In the Mouth of Madness 94. Guns of Honor (TV) 94. Judge Dredd 95, etc.

Proctor, Elaine (1960–).
South African director and screenwriter, a former actress. Born in Johannesburg, she studied at the National Film and Television School in Britain.

On the Wire (wd) 90. Friends (wd) 93.

producer.
On the stage this term may be equivalent to 'director', i.e. the man who actually marshals the actors and whose conception of the show is supreme. In the film world it almost always indicates the man in control of the budget, whether an independent or working for a big studio. He controls all personnel including the director, and though the film may originally be his overall conception, he normally delegates his artistic responsibilities, remaining responsible chiefly for the film's ultimate commercial success or failure.

¶ The producer must be a prophet and a general, a diplomat and a peacemaker, a miser and a spendthrift. He must have vision tempered by hindsight, daring governed by caution, the patience of a saint and the iron of a Cromwell. – *Jesse L. Lasky*

Movie production requires producers, men who can orchestrate the sound and the fury of which pictures are made. – *Joseph Kennedy*

The job of turning good writers into movie hacks is the producer's chief task. – *Ben Hecht*

A producer is a clever man whose brain starts working the moment he gets up in the morning and doesn't stop until he reaches the studio. – *Martin Ragaway*

Producers are men who will keep their heads in the noisy presence of writers and directors and not be carried away by art in any of its subversive guises. Their task is to guard against the unusual. They are the trusted loyalists of cliché. – *Ben Hecht*

A producer shouldn't get ulcers, he should give them. – *Sam Goldwyn*

Producing is a thankless task akin to hotel management. Unfortunately there are not too many good hotel managers. – *David Hemmings*

The director is the fellow who directs the picture and his status is that of an artist, whereas the producer is the big-shot but his real function, outside of prodigious cigar-smoking, has never been discovered. – *George Sanders*

production designer.
Technician responsible for the overall 'look' of a film, ranging from actual set design to photographic style.

production manager.
The person responsible for administrative details of a production, e.g. salaries, transport, departmental expenditure.

Proft, Pat (1947–).
American writer, actor and producer, from television.

Modern Problems (a, w) 81. Bachelor Party (a, co-w) 84. Police Academy (co-w) 84. Moving Violations (co-w) 85. Real Genius (co-w) 85. The Naked Gun (co-w) 88. Lucky Stiff (w) 89. The Naked Gun 2½: The Smell of Fear (co-w) 91. Hot Shots (p, co-w) 91. Brain Donors (w) 92. Hot Shots! Part Deux (co-w) 93. Naked Gun 33⅓: The Final Insult (co-w) 94, etc.

programmer.
Trade term for a routine feature of only moderate appeal, likely to form half a bill; similar to 'co-feature'.

Prokoviev, Sergei (1891–1953).
Russian composer whose main film scores were *Alexander Nevsky* 39, *Lermontov* 43 and *Ivan the Terrible* 42 and 46.

propaganda:
see *documentary*.

prophecy
has interested film-makers only occasionally, but at least two outstanding films have resulted: *Metropolis* and *Things to Come*. *Just Imagine* painted a light-hearted picture, and *Seven Days in May* was not too frightening about what might be happening politically a few years from now; but one hopes not to take too seriously the predictions in *1984*, *The Time Machine*, *Fahrenheit 451*, *Alphaville*, *When Worlds Collide*, *The World, the Flesh and the Devil*, *The War Game*, *Dr Strangelove*, *Punishment Park*, *Beyond the Time Barrier*, *No Blade of Grass*, *Barbarella*, *A Clockwork Orange*, *Planet of the Apes*, *Westworld*, *Futureworld*, *Logan's Run*, *Star Wars*, *The Final Programme*, *Death Race 2000*, *Soylent Green*, *The Ultimate Warrior*, *Robocop* and *Terminator 2*.

Prosky, Robert (1931–) (Robert Porzuczek).
American actor.

Thief 81. The Keep 83. The Lords of Discipline 83. The Natural 84. Christine 84. Big Shots 87. Things Change 88. Funny about Love 90. Green Card 90. Hoffa 92. Far and Away 92. Last Action Hero 93. Rudy 93. Mrs Doubtfire 93, etc.

TV series: Hill Street Blues 85–87. Lifestories (narrator) 90.

prostitutes
for many years could not be so labelled in Hollywood films, which featured a surprising number of 'café hostesses'. It was however fairly easy to spot the real profession of the various ladies who played Sadie Thompson in *Rain*, of Marlene Dietrich in *Dishonoured* and *Shanghai Express*, of Clara Bow in *Call Her Savage*, of Greta Garbo in *Anna Christie*, of Miriam Hopkins in *Dr Jekyll and Mr Hyde*, of Tallulah Bankhead in *Faithless*, of Bette Davis in *Of Human Bondage*, of Vivien Leigh in *Waterloo Bridge*, and of Joan Bennett in *Man Hunt*, to name but a few. The French, who have always called a spade a spade, flaunted the calling in hundreds of films including *Dedée D'Anvers*, *La Ronde*, *Le Plaisir*, *Boule de Suif*, *Le Long des Trottoirs*, *La Bonne Soupe*, *Adua et sa Compagnie* and *Les Compagnons de la Nuit*; Italy chipped in with *Mamma Roma* and Japan with *Street of Shame*. In the 50s Britain moved into the field with surprising eagerness – every other movie seemed to feature Dora Bryan in a plastic mac – and there were several alleged exposés of Soho corruption under such titles as *The Flesh is Weak*, *Passport to Shame* and *The World Ten Times Over*. Hollywood half-heartedly followed with some double-talking second features about call girls – *Why Girls Leave Home*, *Call Girl*, *Girls in the Night* – and some 'medical case histories' such as *The Three Faces of Eve*, *Girl of the Night*. Around 1960 the floodgates opened, eased by the sensationally successful Greek comedy *Never on Sunday* (and some continental imitators like *Always on Saturday* and *Every Night of the Week*). Among English-speaking stars who have played prostitutes are Shirley Maclaine in *Some Came Running* and *Irma La Douce*, Sophia Loren in *Lady L*, *Yesterday*, *Today and Tomorrow*, *Marriage Italian Style*, *Boccaccio 70* and *Man of La Mancha*, Anna Karina in *Vivre sa Vie*, Lee Grant in *Divorce American Style* and *The Balcony*, Catherine Deneuve in *Belle de Jour*, Carroll Baker in *Sylvia*, Shirley Jones in *Elmer Gantry*, Nancy Kwan in *The World of Suzie Wong*, Elizabeth Taylor in *Butterfield 8*, Diane Cilento in *Rattle of a Simple Man*, Carol White in *Poor Cow*, Inger Stevens in *Five Card Stud*, Margot Kidder in *Gaily, Gaily*, Kitty Wynn in *Panic in Needle Park*, Jane Fonda in *Klute*, Julia Roberts in *Pretty Woman*. Brothels have been shown in *Lady L*, *A Walk on the Wild Side*, *The Revolt of Mamie Stover*, *A House is not a Home*, *Ulysses*, *The Balcony*, *A Funny Thing Happened on the Way to the Forum*, *The Assassination Bureau*, *The Best House in London*, *Games That Lovers Play*, *The Reivers*, *Gaily, Gaily*, and an increasing number of westerns. In *Our Man Flint*, girls were described as 'pleasure units' . . .

See also: *courtesans*.

Prouty, Jed (1879–1956).
American character actor with stage experience, in films from the mid-20s. Best remembered as father of *The Jones Family*; he appeared in over a dozen episodes of this domestic comedy series between 1935 and 1940.

Broadway Melody 28. George White's Scandals 35. The Texas Rangers 36. Roar of the Press 41. Mug Town 43. Guilty Bystander 49, many others.

Prouty, Olive Higgins (1882–1974).
American novelist, best known to filmgoers for *Now Voyager* and *Stella Dallas*.

Provine, Dorothy (1937–).
American leading lady who became well known as nightclub entertainer in TV series *The Roaring Twenties*; also in *The Alaskans* 59.

The Bonnie Parker Story 58. Wall of Noise 63. It's a Mad Mad Mad Mad World 63. Good Neighbour Sam 64. That Darn Cat 65. The Great Race 65. One Spy Too Many 66. Kiss the Girls and Make Them Die 66. Who's Minding the Mint? 67, etc.

Prowse, Juliet (1937–).
South African leading lady, in Hollywood from 1958, at first as dancer.

Can Can 59. G.I. Blues 60. The Fiercest Heart 61. The Right Approach 61. The Second Time Around 61. Run For Your Wife 66, etc.

TV series: *Meet Mona McCluskey* 65.

Pryce, Jonathan (1947–).

Saturnine British leading actor.

Voyage of the Damned 76. Breaking Glass 80. Loophole 80. The Day Christ Died (TV) 80. Praying Mantis (TV) 82. The Ploughman's Lunch 83. Something Wicked This Way Comes 83. Brazil 85. The Doctor and the Devils 86. Haunted Honeymoon 86. Jumping Jack Flash 87. Consuming Passions 88. Adventures of Baron Munchausen 89. The Rachel Papers 89. Glengarry Glen Ross 92. Barbarians at the Gate (TV) 93. Mr Wroe's Virgins (TV) 93. The Age of Innocence 93. Deadly Advice 94. A Business Affair 94. Great Moments in Aviation 94. Shopping 94. Carrington 95, etc.

Pryor, Nicholas (1935–) (Nicholas David Probst).

American actor who sometimes plays weaklings.

The Way We Live Now 70. Man on a Swing 74. The Happy Hooker 75. Smile 75. Fear on Trial (TV) 75. *Washington behind Closed Doors* 77. The Life and Assassination of the Kingfish (TV) 77. Rainbow (TV) 78. Damien: Omen II 78. The Fish That Saved Pittsburgh 79. The Formula 80. Airplane 80. The Falcon and the Snowman 84. The Believers 86. Morgan Stewart's Coming Home 87. Less than Zero 87. Brain Dead 89. Nightbreaker (TV) 89, etc.

TV series: The Bronx Zoo 87–88.

Pryor, Richard (1940–).

American nightclub comedian.

■ The Busy Body 68. The Green Berets 68. Wild in the Streets 69. The Phynx 70. You've Got to Walk It Like You Talk It or You'll Lose that Beat 71. Dynamite Chicken 72. Lady Sings the Blues 72. Wattstax 73. The Mack 73. Hit 73. Some Call It Loving 73. Blazing Saddles (co-w only) 74. Uptown Saturday Night 74. Adios Amigo 75. The Bingo Long Allstars and Travelling Motor Kings 76. Car Wash 76. Silver Streak 76. Greased Lightning 77. Which Way Is Up 77. Blue Collar 78. The Wiz 78. California Suite 78. Richard Pryor Live in Concert 79. The Muppet Movie 79. In God We Trust 80. Stir Crazy 80. Wholly Moses 81. Bustin' Loose 81. Some Kind of Hero 82. The Toy 82. Superman III 83. Brewster's Millions 85. Jo Jo Dancer, Your Life is Calling 85. Critical Condition 87. Moving 88. Harlem Nights 89. See No Evil, Hear No Evil 89. Look Who's Talking Too (voice) 90. Another You 91.

Pryor, Roger (1901–1974).

American leading man of minor movies, also stage and radio actor.

Moonlight and Pretzels 33. Belle of the Nineties 34. Ticket to Paradise 36. Money and the Woman 40. She Couldn't Say No 41, etc.

Przygodda, Peter.

German editor and occasional director, associated with the films of Wim Wenders.

Summer in the City 70. The Goalkeeper's Fear of the Penalty Kick (Die Angst des Tormanns beim Elfmeter) 71. Ludwig – Requiem for a Virgin King (Ludwig – Requiem für einen Jungfräulichen König) 72. Alice in the Cities (Alice in den Städten) 73. Wrong Move (Falsche Bewegung) 74. Kings of the Road (Im Lauf der Zeit) 76. The Left-Handed Woman (Die Linkshändige Frau) 77. The American Friend 77. Born for Diesel (Als Diesel Geboren) (& wd) 79. Lightning over Water 80. Hammett 81. The State of Things (Der Stand der

Dinge) 82. The Man on the Wall (Der Mann auf der Mauer) 83. Flight to Berlin 84. Paris, Texas 84. Wings of Desire (Der Himmel über Berlin) 87. Deadline 87. Last Exit to Brooklyn 90. Until the End of the World (Bis ans Ende der Welt) 91. Faraway, So Close! (In Weiter Ferne, So Nah) 93, etc.

psychology

is featured most prominently in American films – quite naturally since the United States is the home of the psychiatrist. However, one of the best serious psychological films, *Mine Own Executioner*, did come from Britain and showed the doctor to be more in need of help than the patient; while two other notable British films, *Thunder Rock* and *Dead of Night*, centred on the depiction of psychological states.

Although films about psychology can be firmly traced back to *The Cabinet of Dr Caligari* and *Secrets of a Soul*, the subject took its firmest hold in the middle of World War II, when so many people needed reassurance; the recounting of dreams to an analyst could even take the place of musical numbers in a romantic trifle like *Lady in the Dark*. Soon we were inundated with melodramas like *Spellbound*, *The Dark Mirror* and *Possessed*, in which the question to be answered was not so much who or how but why; and it wasn't until about 1950, with *Harvey*, that analysts could be laughed at; they were still being analysed in the 70s in such films as *Taking Off*. In the 50s the schizophrenic drama took on a new lease of life (*The Three Faces of Eve*, *Lizzie*, *Vertigo*), as did the tendency to guy individual psychiatrists while still claiming to respect the profession (*Oh Men Oh Women*, *Mirage*, *A Fine Madness*, *The Group*, *What a Way to Go*, *Marriage of a Young Stockbroker*, *The Couch Trip*). Of course, films were still made which took the whole matter with deadly seriousness, as in *The Cobweb*, *The Mark*, *Captain Newman MD*, *The Third Secret* and *Pressure Point*. John Huston's underrated film on the life of *Freud* may have been unlucky to arrive at a time of change: the fashion is now for case histories in which no solution is offered (*Repulsion*, *Morgan*, *Cul-de-Sac*) or psychological horror comics such as *Psycho*, *Homicidal*, and *The Night Walker*, while in *Promise Her Anything* we were finally shown a psychiatrist (Robert Cummings) who doesn't believe in psychiatry. The subject turned romantic in 1991 with Barbra Streisand as an analyst who falls in love with her patient's brother in *The Prince of Tides*, and sinister in *What about Bob?*, in which the patient drives the analyst crazy, the same year.

See also *dreams; fantasy; amnesia; case histories*.

publicity

¶ No right minded film-maker believes his own publicity . . . but he surely hopes it works. The tag-line devised for a film can have a make-or-break effect on its box-office record. Seldom can such lines be claimed as an honest distillation of truth, and very often they hint at more sensations than can be found in the film to which they are attached. But for sheer ingenuity some are unbeatable, and a few have even passed into the language.

▶ *The Twenties:*

The dangerous age for women is from three to seventy! – *Adam's Rib* (1922)

A photoplay of tempestuous love between a madcap English beauty and a bronzed Arab chief! – *The Sheik*

A cast of 125,000! – *Ben Hur*

The mightiest dramatic spectacle of all the ages! – *The Ten Commandments* (1923)

The epic of the American doughboy! – *The Big Parade*

A thrill a minute! A laugh a second! A comedy cyclone! – *Feet First*

Love of tender girlhood! Passionate deeds of heroes! A rushing, leaping drama of charm and excitement! – *America*

A thing of beauty is a joy forever . . . – *Street Angel*

▶ *The Thirties:*

The knockout picture of the year! – *The Champ*

The most startling drama ever produced! – *Strange Interlude*

Mothered by an ape – he knew only the law of the jungle – to seize what he wanted! – *Tarzan of the Apes*

Strange Desires! Loves and hates and secret yearnings . . . hidden in the shadows of a man's mind. – *Dr Jekyll and Mr Hyde*

The picture that will make 1933 famous! – *Gabriel over the White House*

The dance-mad musical triumph of two continents! – *The Gay Divorcee*

The love affair that shook the world! – *Cleopatra*

The most glorious musical romance of all time! – *One Night of Love*

His love challenged the flames of revolution! – *A Tale of Two Cities*

Love as burning as Sahara's sands! – *Under Two Flags*

The march of time measured by a human heart – a mother's heart! – *Cavalcade*

Romance aflame through dangerous days and nights of terror! In a land where anything can happen – most of all to a beautiful girl alone! – *Gunga Din* (in which the girl was very dispensable indeed)

The picture made behind locked doors! – *Dr Cyclops*

The strangest love a man has ever known! – *Dracula*

More sensational than her unforgettable father! – *Dracula's Daughter*

A love story that lived for three thousand years! – *The Mummy*

He's just as funny as his old man was fierce! – *Son of Kong*

Three centuries in the making! – *A Midsummer Night's Dream*

He plucked from the gutter a faded rose and made an immortal masterpiece! – *The Life of Emile Zola*

135 women – with men on their minds! – *The Women*

He treated her rough – and she loved it! – *Red Dust*

A story so momentous it required six Academy Award stars and a cast of 1,186 players! – *Juarez*

Only the rainbow can duplicate its brilliance! – *The Adventures of Robin Hood*

Don't pronounce it – see it! – *Ninotchka*

A monster in form but human in his desire for love! – *Bride of Frankenstein*

Boiling passions in the burning sands! – *The Lost Patrol*

Six sticks of dynamite that blasted his way to freedom – and awoke America's conscience! – *I Am a Fugitive from a Chain Gang*

▶ *The Forties:*

No one is as good as Bette when she's bad! – *In This Our Life*

If she were yours, would you forgive? – *The Unfaithful*

The relentless drama of a woman driven to the depths of emotion by a craving beyond control! – *The Lady Gambles*

The thousands who have read the book will know why WE WILL NOT SELL ANY CHILDREN TICKETS to see this picture! – *The Grapes of Wrath*

Half men, half demons, warriors such as the world has never known – they lived with death and danger for the women who hungered for their love! – *Northwest Passage*

You can't keep a good monster down! – *The Ghost of Frankenstein*

A romantic gentleman by day – a love-mad beast by night! – *Dr Jekyll and Mr Hyde*

The minx in mink with a yen for men! – *Lady in the Dark*

The immortal thriller . . . – *Orpheus*

How'd you like to tussle with Russell? – *The Outlaw*

Gable's back and Garson's got him! – *Adventure*

There never was a woman like . . . – *Gilda*

It tells ALL about those Brontë sisters! – *Devotion*

More thrilling than the deeds of man . . . more beautiful than the love of woman . . . more wonderful than the dreams of children! – *The Jungle Book*

The picture they were born for! – *The Big Sleep*

The picture that helped to win the war! – *Mrs Miniver* (reissue)

He's as fast on the draw as he is in the drawing room! – *The Maltese Falcon*

We're going to see Jennifer Jones AGAIN in . . . – *The Song of Bernadette*

The sum total of all human emotion! – *Leave Her to Heaven*

The truth about the Nazis from the cradle to the battlefront! – *Hitler's Children*

A peek into the other woman's male! – *A Letter to Three Wives*

She knows all about love potions and lovely motions! – *I Married a Witch*

Paramount proudly brings to the screens of America one of the three great love stories of all time! – *To Each His Own* (which were the others?)

'I bought this woman for my own . . . and I'll kill the man who touches her!' – *Unconquered*

A thousand miles of danger with a thousand thrills a mile! – *Santa Fé Trail*

168 minutes of breathless thrills and romance! – *For Whom the Bell Tolls*

The girl of the moment in the wonderful picture of America's hey! hey! day! – *Margie*

The kind of woman most men want – but shouldn't have! – *Mildred Pierce*

They had a date with fate in . . . – *Casablanca*

The flaming drama of a high-born beauty who blindly loved the most icy-hearted big shot gangland ever knew! – *Johnny Eager*

Whisper her name! – *The Strange Love of Martha Ivers*

A mouth like hers is just for kissing . . . not for telling! – *Nora Prentiss*

She insulted her soul! – *Dishonored Lady*

She's got the biggest six-shooters in the west! – *The Beautiful Blonde from Bashful Bend*

The private lady of a public enemy! – *The Damned Don't Cry*

It was the look in her eyes that did it! How could he know it meant murder? – *The Woman in the Window*

A love story every woman would die a thousand deaths to live! – *Jane Eyre*

'The men in her life sometimes lived to regret it!' – *Temptation*

▶ *The Fifties:*
Greater than IVANHOE! – *Julius Caesar*

First they moved (1895)! Then they talked (1927)! Now they smell! – *Scent of Mystery*

The butler did it! He made every lady in the house oh so very happy! – *My Man Godfrey*

Sing, Judy! Dance, Judy! The world is waiting for your sunshine! – *A Star Is Born*

Even in the first wild joy of her arms, he realized that she would be . . . an unfit mother! – *Because of You*

A lion in your lap! – *Bwana Devil* (the first 3-D film)

In making this film, MGM feel privileged to add something of permanent value to the cultural treasure house of mankind . . . – *Quo Vadis*

Ancient Rome is going to the dogs, Robert Taylor is going to the lions, and Peter Ustinov is going crazy! – *Quo Vadis* (revived for TV in the 70s)

You have never really seen Gregory Peck until you see him in CinemaScope! – *Night People*

We didn't say nice people, we said – *Night People*

Their story is not in the history books. It has never been seen on the screen – until now! – *Désirée*

A hard cop and a soft dame! – *The Big Heat*

A completely new experience between men and women! – *The Men* (about paraplegics)

He faced a decision that someday may be yours to make! – *Ransom* (the hero's son was kidnapped)

The colossus who conquered the world! The most colossal motion picture of all time! – *Alexander the Great*

When the hands point straight up . . . the excitement starts! – *High Noon*

That streetcar man has a new desire! – *The Wild One*

Her treachery stained every stone of the pyramid! – *Land of the Pharaohs*

The supreme screen achievement of our time! – *Salome*

Of what a girl did . . . what a boy did . . . of ecstasy and revenge! – *East of Eden*

If a woman answers . . . hang on for dear life! – *Dial M For Murder*

Body of a boy! Mind of a monster! Soul of an unearthly thing! – *I Was a Teenage Frankenstein*

The story of a family's ugly secret and the stark moment that thrust their private lives into public view! – *Written on the Wind*

'She was too hungry for love to care where she found it!' – *The Female on the Beach*

▶ *The Sixties:*
If you miss the first five minutes you miss one suicide, two executions, one seduction and the key to the plot! – *The Kremlin Letter*

The motion picture with something to offend everybody! – *The Loved One*

Beware the beat of the cloth-wrapped feet! – *The Mummy's Shroud*

The world's most uncovered undercover agent! – *Fathom*

Don't give away the ending – it's the only one we have! – *Psycho*

The birds is coming! – *The Birds*

Every time a woman turns her face away because she's tired or unwilling, there's someone waiting like me . . . – *The Dark at the Top of the Stairs*

The hot line suspense comedy! – *Dr Strangelove*

A thousand thrills . . . and Hayley Mills! – *In Search of the Castaways*

A picture that goes beyond what men think about – because no man ever thought about it in quite this way! – *Eight and a Half*

You may not believe in ghosts, but you cannot deny terror . . . – *The Haunting*

There are many kinds of love, but are there any without guilt? – *Five Finger Exercise*

You can expect the unexpected! – *Charade*

Now . . . add a motion picture to the wonders of the world! – *Taras Bulba*

One man . . . three women . . . one night! – *The Night of the Iguana*

You'll laugh your pants off! – *Laurel and Hardy's Laughing Twenties*

£10.000 if you die of fright! – *Macabre*

The picture with the fear flasher and the horror horn! – *Chamber of Horrors*

Meet the girls with the thermo-nuclear navels! The most titillating time bombs you've ever been tempted to trigger! – *Dr Goldfoot and the Girl Bombs*

Keep the children home! And if you're squeamish, stay home with them! – *Witchfinder General*

A side of life you never expected to see on the screen! – *Walk on the Wild Side*

You are cordially invited to George and Martha's for an evening of fun and games! – *Who's Afraid of Virginia Woolf?*

Why the crazy title? If we told you, you'd only laugh! – *The Russians are Coming, The Russians are Coming*

Every father's daughter is a virgin! – *Goodbye Columbus*

They're young . . . they're in love . . . and they kill people. – *Bonnie and Clyde*

'What we've got here is a failure to communicate.' – *Cool Hand Luke*

The big comedy of nineteen-sixty-sex! – *Boeing Boeing*

He is a shy schoolmaster. She is a music hall star. They marry and immediately have 283 children . . . all boys! – *Goodbye Mr Chips*

▶ *The Seventies:*
Love means never having to say you're sorry . . . – *Love Story*

Hope never dies for a man with a good dirty mind! – *Hoffman*

The story of a homosexual who married a nymphomaniac! – *The Music Lovers*

Like the act of love, this film must be experienced from beginning to end . . . – *The Sailor Who Fell from Grace with the Sea*

They stand side by side. Young and old. Rich and poor. They gather together for a single purpose. Survival. – *The Seagull*

We don't love – we just make love. And damn little of that! – *The Happy Ending*

She gave away secrets to one side and her heart to the other! – *Darling Lili*

For the price of a movie you'll feel like a million! – *The Sunshine Boys*

The damnedest thing you ever saw. – *Nashville*

1953 was a good year for leaving home. – *Next Stop Greenwich Village*

The epic love story in which everybody has a great role and a big part. – *Joseph Andrews*

You have nothing to lose but your mind. – *Asylum*

A degenerate film with dignity! – *Inserts*

In space no one can hear you scream. – *Alien*

We are not alone – *Close Encounters of the Third Kind*

Just when you thought it was safe to go back into the water. – *Jaws 2*

It was a line which spawned such imitations as:
Now you're not safe OUT of the water. – *Piranha II – Flying Killers*

Just when you thought it was safe to go back into the departure lounge. – *Airplane II*

Just when he thought it was safe to go back into the water. – *10*

▶ *The Eighties:*

He was D. H. Lawrence. She was his Lady Chatterley. Their extraordinary romance was more tempestuous than any he wrote. – *Priest of Love*

The film where you hiss the villain and cheer the hero. – *The Legend of the Lone Ranger*

As brutal, beautiful, vicious and vast as America itself ! – *Heaven's Gate*

Breaking out is impossible. Breaking in is insane! – *Escape from New York*

The most exciting pair in the jungle! – *Tarzan the Ape-Man* (starring Bo Derek)

From the very beginning, they knew they'd be friends to the very end. What they didn't count on was everything in between. – *Rich and Famous*

The last word about the first time. – *Losin' It*

To the valley of beauty came the shadow of death! – *Deadly Blessing*

Every great love leaves its mark. – *Tattoo*

The third dimension is terror. – *Jaws 3-D*

It's 22 years later. And Norman Bates is coming home. – *Psycho II*

Trust me, I'm a doctor. – *Shock Treatment* (a line that turned up a decade later for *Paper Mask*)

The good news is Jonathan's having his first affair. The bad news is she's his roommate's mother. – *Class*

I'd been shot so many times you could use my shirt as a tea strainer. – *Dead Men Don't Wear Plaid*

Forged by a god. Foretold by a wizard. Found by a King. – *Excalibur*

What they wanted most wasn't on the menu. – *Diner*

He is afraid. He is totally alone. He is 3 million light years from home. – *E.T. – the Extraterrestrial*

She was the woman of Allen's dreams. She had large dark eyes, a beautiful smile and a great pair of fins. – *Splash*

When the going gets tough, the tough get going! – *Jewel of the Nile*

They left for war as boys, never to return as men. – *All Quiet on the Western Front*

The tenant in room seven is very small, very twisted and very mad. – *Basket Case*

Be afraid. Be very afraid. – *The Fly*

When he pours, he reigns. – *Cocktail*

Just when he was ready for mid-life crisis, something unexpected came up. Puberty. – *Vice Versa*

Dying is easy. Comedy is hard. – *Punchline*

Somewhere under the sea and beyond your imagination is an adventure in fantasy. – *The Little Mermaid*

Can two friends sleep together and still love each other in the morning? – *When Harry Met Sally*

▶ *The Nineties:*

Their love was as dangerous as the secrets they kept. – *The Russia House*

Paul Sheldon used to write for a living . . . Now he's writing to stay alive. – *Misery*

There was a time when the only way to uphold justice was to break the law. – *Robin Hood: Prince of Thieves*

He's coming to town with a few days to kill. – *Predator 2*

Having a wonderful time. Wish I were here. – *Postcards from the Edge*

Eight legs, two fangs and an attitude. – *Arachnophobia*

Once in a lifetime comes a motion picture that makes you feel like falling in love all over again. This is not that picture. – *The War of the Roses*

How many times can you die for love? – *Dead Again*

There is nothing in the dark that isn't there in the light. Except fear. – *Cape Fear*

He'd be the perfect criminal if he wasn't the perfect cop. – *Deep Cover*

He was a man who couldn't care less . . . until he met a man who couldn't care more. – *City of Joy*

The fountain of youth. The secret of eternal life. The power of an ancient potion. Sometimes it works . . . Sometimes it doesn't. – *Death Becomes Her*

An adventure 65 million years in the making – *Jurassic Park*

63 million years ago they ruled the Earth. They're back, and it's no theme park! – *Carnosaur*

No one would take on his case . . . until one man was willing to take on the system – *Philadelphia*

Just your average Girl meets Girl, Girl loses Girl, Girl hires Boy to get Girl back story. With a twist. – *Three of Hearts*

Stealing . . . Cheating . . . Killing . . . Who says romance is dead? – *True Romance*

NB: In 1972 a New York magazine ran a competition, inviting readers to invent way-out and hilarious tag-lines for non-existent movies. The results were indeed hilarious, but not so way-out that one can't imagine them being used. Here are some of the winners:

Makes Myra Breckinridge look like Snow White!

It took guts to film. Have you the guts to see it?

There were four men in her life. One to love her. One to marry her. One to take care of her. And one to kill her . . .

They lived a lifetime in 24 crowded hours!

The picture that could change your life – or save it!

If you scoff at the powers of darkness, do not see this film alone!

The book they said could never be written has become the movie they said could never be filmed!

Pudovkin, V. (Vsevolod) (1893–1953).
Russian film theorist, writer and actor. Best remembered as director.

Mother 26. *The End of St Petersburg* 27. *Storm over Asia* 28. *The Deserter* 33. *General Suvorov* 41, many others which have not travelled.

Puenzo, Luis (1946–).
Argentinian director and screenwriter, whose first attempt to direct a Hollywood film was a flop.

Lights of My Shoes 73. The Official Story (La Historia Oficial) (AA) 85. Old Gringo 89. The Plague (La Peste) 92, etc.

Puglia, Frank (1892–1975).
American character actor with vaudeville experience.

Viva Villa 34. Maisie 39. The Mark of Zorro 40. Jungle Book 42. Phantom of the Opera 43. Blood on the Sun 45. The Desert Hawk 50. The Burning Hills 56. Cry Tough 59. Say Goodbye Maggie Cole (TV) 72. Mr Ricco 75, many others.

Pullman, Bill (1954–).
American leading actor.

Ruthless People 86. Spaceballs 87. Rocket Gibraltar 88. The Accidental Tourist 88. Cold Feet 89. Sibling Rivalry 90. Bright Angel 91. The Favor 91. Singles 91. Newsies (GB: Newsboys) 92. Sleepless in Seattle 93. Malice 93. Sommersby 93. The Favor 94. The Last Seduction 94. Wyatt Earp 94, etc.

Pulver, Lilo (Liselotte) (1929–).
Swiss-German leading lady.

A Time to Live and a Time to Die (US) 59. One, Two, Three (US) 61. A Global Affair (US) 63. La Religieuse (Fr.) 65. Le Jardinier d'Argentueil (Fr.) 66.

Punch-McGregor, Angela (1953–).
Australian leading actress, from the theatre.

The Chant of Jimmy Blacksmith 78. Newsfront 78. The Best of Friends 80. We of the Never Never 82. Annie's Coming Out 84. A Test of Love 84. Double Deal 84. Delinquents 89. Spotswood 91, etc.

Purcell, Dick (1908–1944).
American leading man of second features.

Man Hunt 36. Navy Blues 37. Air Devils 38. Nancy Drew, Detective 39. King of the Zombies 41. Phantom Killer 42. The Mystery of the Thirteenth Guest 43. Timber Queen 44, etc.

Purcell, Noel (1900–1985).
Tall, usually bearded, Irish character actor and comedian.

Jimmy Boy 34. Blarney 38. Captain Boycott 47. The Blue Lagoon 48. Doctor in the House 53. Moby Dick 56. Watch Your Stern 60. Mutiny on the Bounty 62. Lord Jim 65. Arrivederci Baby 66. Where's Jack 69. The Mackintosh Man 73, many others.

TV series: The Buccaneer 58.

Purdell, Reginald (1896–1953) (R. Grasdorf).
British light character actor, mostly on stage and music hall.

Congress Dances 31. Q Planes 38. Many Thanks Mr Atkins 40. Pack Up Your Troubles 40. Variety Jubilee 43. We Dive at Dawn 43. 2000 Women 44. Holiday Camp 47. Captain Boycott 48, etc.

Purdom, Edmund (1924–).
British light leading man who in the 50s was given the full Hollywood treatment but failed to emerge as a star.

Titanic 53. *The Student Prince* 54. *The Egyptian* 54. The Prodigal 55. The King's Thief 55. The Cossacks 60. Herod the Great 60. Nights of Rasputin 61. The Comedy Man 63. Suleiman the Conqueror 63. The Beauty Jungle 64. The Yellow Rolls-Royce 64. The Man in the Golden Mask 69. The Black Corsair 69. Evil Fingers 72. Mr Scarface 76. Don't Open till Christmas (& d) 84, etc.

TV series: Sword of Freedom 57.

¶ One of the symptoms of an approaching nervous breakdown is the belief that one's work is terribly important. – *E.P.*

Purl, Linda (1955–).
Snub-nosed American leading lady of the late 70s.

W. C. Fields and Me 76. Testimony of Two Men (TV) 77. The Flame is Love (TV) 79. Women at West Point (TV) 80. The Night the City Screamed (TV) 81. Visiting Hours 82. Pleasures (TV) 86. Viper 88. Web of Deceit (TV) 90. Body Language 92. Natural Causes 94, etc.

TV series: Happy Days 74–75. Beacon Hill 75. Happy Days 82–83. Matlock 86–87.

Purviance, Edna (1894–1958).
American leading lady of silent days.

A Night Out 15 (and other early Chaplin films including *Easy Street, The Count, The Cure, The Adventurer, Shoulder Arms*). Sunnyside 19. The Kid 21. The Pilgrim 23. A Woman of Paris 23. The Seagull 26. Limelight 52, many others.

put-downs

¶ Waspish comments about other people always make good reading. Here are a few for starters:
Let's face it, Billy Wilder at work is two people – Mr Hyde and Mr Hyde. – *Harry Kurnitz*

I loved it – particularly the ideas he took from me. – *D.W. Griffith on Citizen Kane*

Jack Lemmon's Hildy Johnson is like a mortuary assistant having a wild fling. – *New Yorker review of The Front Page*

Mae West, playing a ghastly travesty of the travesty of womanhood she once played, has a Mae West face painted on the front of her head and moves to and fro like the Imperial Hotel during the 1923 Tokyo earthquake. – *Joseph Morgenstern reviewing Myra Breckinridge*

As a pompous middle-European intellectual Kenneth Mars mugs and drools in a manner that Jerry Lewis might find excessive. – *Jay Cocks reviewing What's Up, Doc?*

To insinuate that Leslie Bricusse's plodding score is merely dreadful would be an act of charity. – *Rex Reed on Goodbye Mr Chips*

Miss Martin, I notice, is playing Jean Arthur, a tendency which even Miss Arthur should learn to curb. – *James Agee on True To Life*

Mr Muni seemed intent on submerging himself so completely in make-up that he disappeared. – *Bette Davis on Juarez*

Which is he playing now? – *W. Somerset Maugham while watching Spencer Tracy on the set of Dr Jekyll and Mr Hyde*

Ryan O'Neal is so stiff and clumsy that he can't even manage a part requiring him to be stiff and clumsy. – *Jay Cocks on What's Up Doc?*

He has a gift for butchering good parts while managing to look intelligent, thus constituting Hollywood's abiding answer to the theatre. – *Wilfred Sheed of Jack Lemmon*

Just how garish her commonplace accent, squeakily shrill voice, and the childish petulance with which she delivers her lines are, my pen is neither scratchy nor leaky enough to convey. – *John Simon of Elizabeth Taylor in The Taming of the Shrew*

George Raft and Gary Cooper once played a scene in front of a cigar store, and it looked like the wooden Indian was overacting. – *George Burns*

Puttnam, Sir David (1941–).

British producer and impresario who almost single-handedly raised the level of British film-making in the early 80s and was rewarded by a top Hollywood job which didn't last.

Biographies: 1988, *Enigma: David Puttnam* by Andrew Yule. 1991, *Out of Focus: David Puttnam in Hollywood* by Charles Kipps.

Melody 71. That'll Be the Day 74. Mahler 74. Lisztomania 75. Bugsy Malone 76. The Duellists 77. Midnight Express 78. Chariots of Fire 80. Local Hero 82. The Killing Fields 84. The Mission (AAN) 86. Defence of the Realm 86. Memphis Belle 90. Meeting Venus 91. Being Human 94. War of the Buttons 94, many others.

¶ Nothing good will happen while there are still cinemas that are shit heaps and critics who only like popular films when they are thirty years old. – *D.P., 1975*

I'm not afraid to fail, providing I fail honourably. The only thing I don't want is to end up being an irrelevant 70-year-old egomaniac. – *D.P.*

Puzo, Mario (1920–).

American novelist whose *The Godfather* in 1969

was a commercial sensation and led to the equally popular film.

■ The Godfather (co-w) (AA) 72. The Godfather Part II (co-w) (AA) 74. Earthquake (co-w) 74. Superman (co-w) 78. Superman II (co-w) 80. The Cotton Club (co-story) 84. The Godfather Part III (co-w) 90. Christopher Columbus: The Discovery 92.

Pyle, Denver (1920–).

American character actor, mostly in TV and big-screen westerns.

The Man from Colorado 48. To Hell and Back 55. Shenandoah 65. *Bonnie and Clyde* 67. Five Card Stud 68. Something Big 71. Cahill 73. Escape to Witch Mountain 75. Guardian of the Wilderness 77. Welcome to L.A. 77. Maverick 94, etc.

TV series: Wyatt Earp 56–59. The Doris Day Show 68–69. The Dukes of Hazzard 79.

Pyriev, Ivan (1901–1968).

Russian director.

The Functionary 30. The Party Card 36. Tractor Drivers 39. They Met in Moscow 41. Secretary of the District Committee 42. Song of Siberia 47. Kuban Cossacks 49. Test of Fidelity 54. The Idiot 58. White Nights 60. Our Mutual Friend 61. Light of a Distant Star 65. The Brothers Karamazov 68, etc.

Pyun, Albert.

American director and screenwriter of unmemorable fantasy and action films.

The Sword and the Sorcerer 82. Radioactive Dreams 86. Dangerously Close 86. Vicious Lips 87. Down Twisted (aka The Treasure of San Lucas) 87. Alien from L.A. (w) 88. Cyborg 89. Spiderman 89. Kickboxer II 90. Arcade 92. Nemesis 92. Deceit 92. Knights (wd) 92. Nemesis 93. Brain Smasher 93, etc.

Q

Qissi, Michel.
Belgian tough guy in, and occasional director of, action movies, usually as the baddie.

Bloodsport 88. Kickboxer (as Tong Po) 89. Kickboxer 2: The Road Back 90. A.W.O.L. (aka Lionheart) 90. Bloodmatch 91. To the Death 91. Backlash (aka Terminator Woman) (d) 93, etc.

Quaid, Dennis (1955–).
American actor, brother of Randy Quaid.
■ Crazy Mama 75. Seniors 77. Breaking Away 78. The Long Riders 80. All Night Long 81. Caveman 81. The Night the Lights Went Out in Georgia 81. Jaws 3D 83. Tough Enough 83. The Right Stuff 83. Dreamscape 84. Enemy Mine 85. The Big Easy 86. Innerspace 87. Suspect 87. D.O.A. 88. Everybody's All-American (GB: When I Fall in Love) 88. Great Balls of Fire 89. Postcards from the Edge 90. Come See the Paradise 90. Wilder Napalm 93. Flesh and Bone 93. Undercover Blues 93. Wyatt Earp 94. Dragonheart 95.

Quaid, Randy (1953–).
American actor who has been seen in gangling, awkward roles.
■ The Last Picture Show 71. What's Up, Doc? 72. The Last Detail (AAN) 73. Lolly Madonna XXX 73. Paper Moon 73. Breakout 75. The Apprenticeship of Duddy Kravitz 75. The Missouri Breaks 76. Bound for Glory 76. The Choirboys 77. Midnight Express 78. The Raid on Coffeyville (TV) 79. Foxes 80. The Long Riders 80. Guyana Tragedy (TV) 80. Heartbeeps 81. National Lampoon's Vacation 83. Fool for Love 85. The Wraith 86. L.B.J.: The Early Years (TV) 87. No Man's Land 87. Moving 88. Caddyshack II 88. Evil in Clear River (TV) 88. Parents 89. Out Cold 89. Cold Dog Soup 89. Bloodhounds of Broadway 89. National Lampoon's Christmas Vacation 89. Martians Go Home 90. Days of Thunder 90. Quick Change 90. Texasville 90. Murder in the Heartland (TV) 93. Frankenstein (TV) 93. Freaked 93. The Paper 94. Major League II 94. Next Door (TV) 94. Curse of the Starving Class 94.

TV series: Saturday Night Live 85–86. Davis Rules 91.

Qualen, John (1899–1987) (John Mandt Kvalen).
Canadian-born Norwegian character actor, in Hollywood from the 30s playing amiably ineffectual foreign types.

Arrowsmith (debut) 32. Black Fury 35. Seventh Heaven 37. *The Grapes of Wrath* 40. Out of the Fog 41. *All that Money Can Buy* 41. Jungle Book 42. Casablanca 42. Fairy Tale Murder 45. Adventure 46. The Fugitive 48. The Big Steal 49. Hans Christian Andersen 52. The High and the Mighty 54. The Searchers 56. Two Rode Together 60. The Man Who Shot Liberty Valance 62. The Prize 63. The Seven Faces of Dr Lao 64. Cheyenne Autumn 64. The Sons of Katie Elder 65. A Big Hand for the Little Lady 66. Firecreek 67, many others.

Quan, Ke Huy (1971–) (aka Jonathan Ke Quan).
Vietnamese-born child actor, in America from the age of six.

Indiana Jones and the Temple of Doom 84. The Goonies 85.

TV series: Together We Stand 86.

Quantrill, Charles Clarke (1837–1865).
American guerrilla leader, the scourge of Missouri and a figure in many westerns.

Quaranta, Gianni.
Italian production designer.

La Traviata (co-pd) 83. A Room with a View (co-pd) 86.

Quarry, Robert (1923–).
American character actor who bade fair to be the horror man of the 70s.

A Kiss before Dying 56. Count Yorga Vampire 69. The Return of Count Yorga 71. Dr Phibes Rises Again 72. The Revenge of Dr Death 73. The Midnight Man 73. Rollercoaster 77. Phantom Empire 87. Warlords 88, etc.

Quayle, Anna (1937–).
British comedienne.

Drop Dead Darling 67. Smashing Time 67. Chitty Chitty Bang Bang 68. Up the Chastity Belt 71. The Seven Per Cent Solution 76, etc.

Quayle, Sir Anthony (1913–1989).
Distinguished British stage actor and director, in occasional films as actor.
■ Hamlet 48. Saraband for Dead Lovers 48. Oh Rosalinda 55. The Battle of the River Plate 56. No Time for Tears 57. The Wrong Man (US) 57. Woman in a Dressing-Gown 57. The Man Who Wouldn't Talk 58. *Ice Cold in Alex* 58. Serious Charge 59. Tarzan's Greatest Adventure 59. The Challenge 60. The Guns of Navarone 61. Lawrence of Arabia 62. HMS Defiant 62. The Fall of the Roman Empire 64. East of Sudan 64. Operation Crossbow 64. The Poppy is also a Flower (TV) 64. A Study in Terror 65. Misunderstood 67. Mackenna's Gold 68. Before Winter Comes 69. Anne of the Thousand Days (AAN) 70. Everything You Always Wanted to Know About Sex 72. A Bequest to the Nation 73. Jarrett (TV) 73. QB VII (TV) 74. The Tamarind Seed 74. Great Expectations (TV) 75. 21 Hours at Munich (TV) 76. Moses (TV) 76. The Eagle Has Landed 76. Holocaust 2000 77. Murder by Decree 79. Masada (TV) 80. The Manions of America (TV) 81. Dial M for Murder (TV) 81. The Last Days of Pompeii (TV) 84. Lace (TV) 84. The Key to Rebecca (TV) 85. The Bourne Identity 88. The Legend of the Holy Drinker 88. Magdalene 89. Confessional 89. King of the Wind 89.

TV series: Strange Report 68.

Questel, Mae (1908–).
American actress best known for providing the voices for cartoon characters Betty Boop 1932–39 and, in the Popeye cartoons, Olive Oyl 1933–67. She also made an impact as Woody Allen's ghostly mother in the sky in *New York Stories*.

A Majority of One 62. It's Only Money 62.

Funny Girl 68. Move 70. National Lampoon's Christmas Vacation 89, etc.

Quick, Diana (1946–).
British leading lady.

Nicholas and Alexandra 71. A Private Enterprise 71. The Odd Job 78. The Duellists 78. The Big Sleep 78. The Three Hostages (TV) 78. *Brideshead Revisited* (TV) 81. Phantom of the Opera (TV) 83. Ordeal by Innocence 85. Wilt (US The Misadventures of Mr Wilt) 89. Nostradamus 94, etc.

Quigley, Linnea (1959–).
American actress in low-budget horror movies who has become a minor cult figure following her appearance in *The Return of the Living Dead*, dancing nearly naked in a cemetery.

Autobiography: 1991, *The Linnea Quigley Bio & Chainsaw Book*.

Stone Cold Dead 80. American Gigolo 80. Graduation Day 81. Cheech & Chong's Nice Dreams 81. The Black Room 81. Don't Go Near the Park 81. The Young Warriors 83. Cheech & Chong: Still Smokin' 83. Savage Streets 84. Silent Night, Deadly Night 84. Return of the Living Dead 85. Sorority Babes in the Slime Bowl-o-rama 87. Creepozoids 87. Hollywood Chainsaw Hookers 88. Night of the Demons 88. Vice Academy 88. Nightmare on Elm Street 4: The Dream Master 88. Assault of the Party Nerds 89. Witch Trap 89. Murder Weapon 90. Virgin High 91. Rock 'n' Roll Detective 92, etc.

Quillan, Eddie (1907–1990).
Bouncy, beaming American comic actor, in Hollywood from 20s.

The Godless Girl 26. Big Money 30. *Mutiny on the Bounty* 35. Young Mr Lincoln 39. *The Grapes of Wrath* 40. Dark Streets of Cairo 40. Flying Blind 41. Sideshow 50. Brigadoon 54. The Ghost and Mr Chicken 66, etc; latterly on TV.

TV series: Valentine's Day 64–65. Julia 68–71. Hell Town 85.

Quiller.
Code name of a tough British secret agent, able to take any amount of torture, who is the hero of a series of novels by Adam Hall (Elleston Trevor). United Artists acquired the film rights to them in 1993 with the intention of producing a series of movies featuring what the company called 'the thinking man's James Bond'. A film of the first novel, *The Quiller Memorandum*, was directed by Michael Anderson in 1966 starring George Segal, and Michael Jayston played the role in a BBC TV series, *Quiller*, in 1975.

Quilley, Denis (1927–).
British leading actor, mostly on stage.

Anne of the Thousand Days 69. The Black Windmill 74. Murder on the Orient Express 74. Clayhanger (TV) 76. Masada (TV) 81. *Evil Under the Sun* 81. *Privates on Parade* 83. Memed My Hawk 84. Foreign Body 87. Mister Johnson 90. Sparrow (Storia di una Capinera) 93, etc.

Quimby, Fred (1886–1965).
American producer, head of MGM's short subjects department 1926–56. Specially known for development of Tom and Jerry cartoons.

Quine, Richard (1920–1989).
American director, former leading man (*The World Changes* 32 as juvenile; also *Babes on Broadway* 40, *My Sister Eileen* 41, *For Me and My Gal* 42, etc.). Committed suicide.

The Sunny Side of the Street 51. Drive a Crooked Road 54. Pushover 54. My Sister Eileen 55. *The Solid Gold Cadillac* 56. Operation Mad Ball 58. Bell, Book and Candle 58. The World of Suzie Wong 60. The Notorious Landlady 62. Paris When It Sizzles 64. How to Murder Your Wife 65. Oh Dad, Poor Dad 66. Hotel 67. A Talent for Loving 69. The Moonshine War 70. 'W' 74. The Prisoner of Zenda 79, etc.

Quinlan, Kathleen (1954–).
American leading lady of the late 70s.

Can Ellen Be Saved? (TV) 74. Where Have All the People Gone? (TV) 74. The Abduction of St Anne (TV) 75. Little Ladies of the Night (TV) 77. Airport 77 77. I Never Promised You a Rose Garden 77. The Promise 79. The Runner Stumbles 79. Sunday Lovers 80. Hanky Panky 82. Twilight Zone 83. Independence Day 83. Blackout 85. Warning Sign 86. Sunset 88. Clara's Heart 88. Trapped (TV) 89. The Operation (TV) 90. The Doors 91, etc.

Quinn, Aidan (1959–).
American leading man.
■ Reckless 84. Desperately Seeking Susan 85. An Early Frost (TV) 85. The Mission 86. Stakeout 87. Crusoe 88. Perfect Witness (TV) 89. The

Handmaid's Tale 90. The Lemon Sisters 90. Avalon 90. At Play in the Fields of the Lord 91. The Playboys 92. Benny & Joon 93. Blink 94. Legends of the Fall 94. Mary Shelley's Frankenstein 94.

Quinn, Anthony (1915–).
Mexican-born leading actor, in films since 1936, latterly noted for full-blooded performances.
Autobiography: 1972, *The Original Sin*.
Parole 36. The Plainsman 37. Ghost Breakers 40. Last Train from Madrid 37. Union Pacific 39. Blood and Sand 41. The Black Swan 42. The Ox-Bow Incident 43. Buffalo Bill 44. China Sky 45. Tycoon 48. The Brave Bulls 51. *Viva Zapata* (AA) 52. The World in His Arms 52. Ride Vaquero 53. Blowing Wild 54. The Long Wait 54. *La Strada* (It.) 54. Attila the Hun (It.) 54. Ulysses 55. *Lust for Life* (AA) 56. The Man from Del Rio 56. The Hunchback of Notre Dame 56. The River's Edge 57. Wild Is the Wind (AAN) 57. Hot Spell 58. Black Orchid 58. Last Train from Gun Hill 58. Warlock 59. The Buccaneer (d only) 59. Heller in Pink Tights 60. Savage Innocents 60. The Guns of Navarone 61. Lawrence of Arabia 62. Barabbas 62. Requiem for a Heavyweight 63. The Visit 63. *Zorba the Greek* (AAN) 64. A High Wind in Jamaica 65. Lost Command 66. The Happening 67. The Twenty-Fifth Hour 67. The Rover 67. *The Shoes of the Fisherman* 68. The Magus 68. The Secret of Santa Vittoria 69. R.P.M. 69. A Walk in the Spring Rain 69. Flap 70. Across 110th Street 72. The Marseilles Contract 74. The Don is Dead 75. Mohammed (The Message) 76. Jesus of Nazareth (TV) 77. Tigers Don't Cry 77. The Inheritance 78. The Children of Sanchez 78. The Greek Tycoon 78. Caravans 78. The Passage 79. Lion of the Desert 80. The Salamander 80. High Risk 81. The Con Artists 81. Man of Passion 88. Richest Man in the World: The Aristotle Onassis Story (TV) 88. The Old Man and

the Sea (TV) 90. Revenge 90. Ghosts Can't Do It 90. Only the Lonely 91. Jungle Fever 91. Mobsters 91. The Magician (Il Mago) 93. The Last Action Hero 93. Somebody to Love 94, etc.
TV series: *The Man and the City* 71.

¶ They said all I was good for was playing Indians. – *A.Q.*
'I want to impregnate every woman in the world', he once told me, though I didn't realize until later how literally he meant it. – *Ruth Warrick*

Quinones, Adolfo:
see *Shabba-Doo*.

Quo Vadis?
The biblical epic by Henryk Sienkiewicz has been filmed three times: in Italy in 1912 and 1924, and in America in 1951. The third version, though less impressive as a product of its period than the others, was certainly the most spectacular. Robert Taylor and Deborah Kerr suffered under Peter Ustinov's *Nero*; Mervyn Le Roy directed.

quota.
By Act of Parliament renters are obliged to sell, and exhibitors to show, a varying proportion of British-made films. There has not always been enough British talent to fill the necessary number of releases: hence the notorious 'quota quickies' of the 20s and 30s, and much second-feature material, which however bad could invariably get a circuit booking providing it had a British quota ticket. The normal quota which an exhibitor has to fill is 30% for features, 25% for supporting programmes. This contrasts markedly with independent television contractors, whose programmes must be 86% British.

R

Raab, Kurt (1942–1988).
Czechoslovakian-born actor, screenwriter, production designer and director who began in avant-garde theatre; often in the films of Rainer Werner Fassbinder. He wrote a biography of Fassbinder in 1982. Died of AIDS.

Why Does Herr R. Run Amok? (Warum Läuft Herr R. Amok?) 69. Whity 70. The Tenderness of Wolves (Zärtlichkeit der Wölfe) (& w) 73. Fox and his Friends (Faustrecht der Freiheit) 74. Satan's Brew (Satansbraten) 76. Bolwieser (US: The Stationmaster's Wife) 77. Boarding School 83. Parker 84, etc.

Rabal, Francisco (1925–).
Leading Spanish actor, a former electrician, in international films.

La Prodiga 45. The Mighty Crusades (Gerusalemme Liberata) 57. Nazarin 59. Viridiana 61. The Eclipse (L'Eclisse) 62. The Nun (La Religieuse) 65. Belle de Jour 67. Diary of a Rebel (El Che Guevara) 68. Ann and Eve 70. The Devil Is a Woman 75. Sorcerer 77. Corleone 78. City of the Walking Dead 80. The Stilts (Los Zancos) 84. La Storia 86. A Time of Destiny 88. Barroco 89. Tie Me Up, Tie Me Down (¡Atame!) 90, etc.

Rabe, David (1940–).
American dramatist and screenwriter. He married actress Jill Clayburgh in 1979.

I'm Dancing as Fast as I Can 82. Streamers 83. Casualties of War 89. State of Grace (co-w) 90. The Firm (co-w) 93, etc.

Rabier, Jean (1927–).
French cinematographer.

Cleo de 5 à 7 61. Ophelia 62. Landru 62. La Baie des Anges 63. Les Parapluies de Cherbourg 64. Le Bonheur 65. The Champagne Murders 66. Les Biches 68. Le Boucher 70. La Rupture 70. Blood Wedding (Les Noces Rouges) 73. Folies Bourgeoises 76. Violette (Violette Nozière) 77. Les Fantômes du Chapelier 82. Inspector Lavardin 86. Masques 87. Une Affaire de Femmes 88. Docteur M. 90. Quiet Days in Clichy 90. Madame Bovary 91, etc.

Rackin, Martin (1918–1976).
American screenwriter.

Air Raid Wardens 43. Riff Raff 47. Fighting Father Dunne 48. Three Secrets 50. The Enforcer 51. Sailor Beware 52. The Stooge 53. Santiago (& p) 56. The Helen Morgan Story (p only) 57. The Horse Soldiers (& p) 59. North to Alaska 60. Stagecoach (p only) 66. Rough Night in Jericho (p only) 67. The Revengers (p only) 72, etc.

Radd, Ronald (1924–1976).
British character actor, usually in heavy roles. Much on TV.

The Camp on Blood Island 58. The Small World of Sammy Lee 63. Up Jumped a Swagman 65. Where the Spies Are 65. Mr Ten Per Cent 66. The Kremlin Letter 70. The Offence 72. The Spiral Staircase 74, etc.

Rademakers, Fons (1921–).
Dutch director, with stage experience.

Doctor in the Village 58. The Knife 61. Max Havelaar 74. Mysteries 76. The Judge's Friend 79. The Assault (De Aanslag) 86. Diary of a Mad Old Man (Dagboek van een Oude Dwaas) 87. The Rose Garden 89, etc.

Radford, Basil (1897–1952).
British light character comedian, on stage from 1922, films from 1929 (Barnum Was Right). Became popular when he and Naunton Wayne played two imperturbable Englishmen abroad in The Lady Vanishes 38.

Just William 38. Night Train to Munich 40. Crooks Tour 40. Next of Kin 42. Millions Like Us 43. The Way to the Stars 45. Dead of Night 45. The Captive Heart 46. Girl in a Million 46. It's Not Cricket 48. Passport to Pimlico 48. The Winslow Boy 48. Quartet 48. Whisky Galore 48. Chance of a Lifetime 50. The Galloping Major 51, etc.

Radford, Michael (1950–).
British director and screenwriter.

Another Time Another Place 83. 1984 84. White Mischief 87. The Postman (Il Postino) (co-w, d) 94.

¶ I think of myself as the matador and the audience as the bull. – M.R.

radio,

being a competitor, was largely ignored by serious movies in the 30s, but radio stars featured in a number of musicals, especially the Big Broadcast series and the British Radio Parade, Music Hath Charms, etc.; in the 40s, a number of low-budgeters such as Reveille with Beverly had a radio background. Popular radio series to be filmed included Dr Christian, Fibber McGee and Molly, Charlie McCarthy Detective, The Great Gildersleeve, Hi Gang, Band Waggon and It's That Man Again. Mysteries set in radio stations included Who Done It and Death at Broadcasting House; Helter Skelter was a slapstick comedy set at the BBC. In the 70s, Play Misty for Me revolved around a disc jockey, as did the TV movie A Cry for Help; while WUSA was undoubtedly the most serious drama on the subject unless one counts the sharply satirical A Face in the Crowd and Talk Radio, highlighting the potential dangers of chat shows.

Radner, Gilda (1946–1989).
American comedienne who gained fame in the TV series Saturday Night Live. She was married to actor and director Gene Wilder.

Autobiography: 1989, It's Always Something.
Biography: 1992, Gilda: An Intimate Portrait by David Saltman.

First Family 80. Hanky Panky 82. It Came from Hollywood 82. The Woman in Red 84. Festive Desserts 84. Movers and Shakers 85. Haunted Honeymoon 86, etc.

Radnitz, Robert B. (1925–).
American producer of 'family' films.

A Dog of Flanders 60. Misty 62. Island of the Blue Dolphins 64. And Now Miguel 66. My Side of the Mountain 68. The Little Ark 70. Sounder 72. A Hero Ain't Nothing but a Sandwich 77. Cross Creek 83. Never Forget 91, etc.

Rafelson, Bob (1935–).
American director.

■ Head (co-w, d) 68. Five Easy Pieces 71. The King of Marvin Gardens 72. Stay Hungry 76. The Postman Always Rings Twice 81. Black Widow 87. Mountains of the Moon 89. Man Trouble 92. Erotic Tales (co-d) 94.

Rafferty, Chips (1909–1971) (John Goffage).
Rangy Australian character actor with varied experience before coming to films.

Dad Rudd, MP 40. Forty Thousand Horsemen 40. The Rats of Tobruk 44. The Overlanders 46. The Loves of Joanna Godden (GB) 46. Eureka Stockade 47. Bitter Springs 51. Kangaroo 52. King of the Coral Sea 54. Walk into Paradise 56. The Sundowners 60. Mutiny on the Bounty 62. They're a Weird Mob 66. Kona Coast 68. Skullduggery 69. Outback 70, many others.

Rafferty, Frances (1922–).
American leading lady.

Seven Sweethearts 42. Dragon Seed 44. Abbott and Costello in Hollywood 45. The Hidden Eye 45. Lady at Midnight 48. Rodeo 52. The Shanghai Story 54. Wings of Chance 61, etc.

TV series: December Bride 54–58. Pete and Gladys 61.

Raffill, Stewart (1945–).
Anglo-American director and screenwriter.

Napoleon and Samantha 72. Adventures of the Wilderness Family 75. Shipwreck 77. High Risk 81. Ice Pirates 83. The Philadelphia Experiment 84. Mac and Me 88. Mannequin 2: On the Move 91. Passenger 57 (co-story) 92. Lost in Africa 94.

Raffin, Deborah (1953–).
American leading lady.

Forty Carats 73. Once Is Not Enough 75. Nightmare in Badham County (TV) 76. The Sentinel 77. Demon 77. Ski Lift to Death (TV) 78. How to Pick Up Girls (TV) 78. Willa (TV) 78. Touched by Love 80. Lace 2 (TV) 85. Death Wish 3 86. Noble House (TV) 87. Scanners 2: The New Order 90. Morning Glory (a, co-w) 93, etc.

Raffles.
The sophisticated burglar who returns to crime to help an old friend was created by E. W. Hornung and has attracted the attentions of several suave leading men. There were half a dozen silent Raffles, including one from House Peters in 1925, directed by King Baggot; Ronald Colman played the role in 1930, and a shot-by-shot remake in 1939 starred David Niven.

Rafkin, Alan (1938–).
American director.

Ski Party 65. The Ghost and Mr Chicken 66. Nobody's Perfect 68. The Shakiest Gun in the

West 68. Angel in My Pocket 69. How to Frame a Figg 71. Let's Switch (TV) 75, etc.

Raft, George (1895–1980) (George Ranft).
Smooth, rather sinister American leading man of the 30s and 40s; formerly a professional athlete, gambler, nightclub dancer and companion of gangsters. In 1961 Ray Danton appeared in the title role of *The George Raft Story*.

Biographies: 1973, *The George Raft File* by James Robert Parish. 1974, *George Raft* by Lewis Jablonsky.

■ Queen of the Night Clubs 29. Quick Millions 31. Hush Money 31. Palmy Days 31. Dancers in the Dark 32. *Scarface* 32. Night World 32. Madame Racketeer 32. Night after Night 32. If I Had a Million 32. Undercover Man 32. Pick Up 33. Midnight Club 33. *The Bowery* 33. All of Me 34. *Bolero* 34. The Trumpet Blows 34. Limehouse Blues 34. *Rumba* 35. Stolen Harmony 35. *The Glass Key* 35. Every Night at Eight 35. She Couldn't Take It 35. It Had to Happen 36. Yours for the Asking 36. *Souls at Sea* 37. You and Me 38. Spawn of the North 38. The Lady's from Kentucky 38. *Each Dawn I Die* 39. I Stole a Million 39. Invisible Stripes 40. The House across the Bay 40. They Drive by Night 40. Manpower 41. Broadway 42. Stage Door Canteen 43. Background to Danger 43. Follow the Boys 44. Nob Hill 45. Johnny Angel 45. Whistle Stop 46. Mr Ace 46. Nocturne 46. Christmas Eve 47. Intrigue 48. Race Street 48. Outpost in Morocco 49. Johnny Allegro 49. A Dangerous Profession 49. The Red Light 50. Lucky Nick Cain 51. Loan Shark 52. The Man from Cairo 53. Rogue Cop 54. Black Widow 54. A Bullet for Joey 55. Around the World in Eighty Days 56. Some Like It Hot 59. Jet over the Atlantic 59. Ocean's Eleven 60. Ladies' Man 64. The Patsy 64. For Those Who Think Young 64. Casino Royale 67. Du Rififi à Paname 67. Five Golden Dragons 67. Skidoo 68. Madigan's Millions 69. Hammersmith is Out 72. Deadhead Miles 72. Sextette 77.

TV series: I Am the Law 52.

Ragland, Rags (1905–1946) (John Lee Ragland).
American character comedian, former boxer. Died of uremia.

■ Ringside Maisie 41. Whistling in the Dark 41. Born to Sing 42. Sunday Punch 42. Maisie Gets Her Man 42. Panama Hattie 42. The War Against Mrs Hadley 42. Somewhere I'll Find You 42. Whistling in Dixie 42. Dubarry Was a Lady 42. Girl Crazy 43. Whistling in Brooklyn 43. Meet the People 44. Three Men in White 44. The Canterville Ghost 44. Her Highness and the Bellboy 45. Anchors Aweigh 45. Abbott and Costello in Hollywood 45. Ziegfeld Follies 46. The Hoodlum Saint 46.

Railsback, Steve (1948–   ).
American character actor.

The Visitors 71. Cockfighter 74. *Helter Skelter* (TV) 76. The Stunt Man 78. From Here to Eternity (TV) 79. The Golden Seal 83. Lifeforce 85. Armed and Dangerous 86. Blue Monkey 87. The Survivalist 87. The Wind 87. Deadly Intent 88. The Assassin 89. Scissors 91. Sunstroke 92. Calendar Girl 93, etc.

railway stations
have provided a major setting for some memorable films including *The Ghost Train, Doctor Zhivago, Knight without Armour, I'll Never Forget Whatshisname* (with its white 'dream' station), *Union Station, 3.10 to Yuma, Last Train from Madrid, Bhowani Junction, Northwest Frontier, 100 Rifles, The Mercenaries, Waterloo Road, Anna Karenina, Grand Central Station, Under the Clock, Brief Encounter, Oh Mr Porter, The Titfield Thunderbolt, High Noon, In the*

Heat of the Night and *The Train* . . . while Orson Welles made *The Trial* almost entirely within a deserted station, and de Sica made *Indiscretion* among the crowds of Rome's Stazione Termini.

See also: *trains*.

Raimi, Sam (1959–   ).
Precocious American director of horror films, noted for his extravagant camera work.

The Evil Dead 80. Crimewave 85. Evil Dead II: Dead by Dawn 87. Miller's Crossing (a) 90. Darkman 90. Army of Darkness 92. Indian Summer (a) 93. Mantis (p, story) (TV) 94. The Hudsucker Proxy (co-w) 94. The Stand (a) (TV) 94, etc.

Raimu (1883–1946) (Jules Muraire).
French character actor and comedian with music-hall background.

■ L'Homme Nu 12. L'Agence Cacahuète 14. Le Blanc et le Noir 31. Mam'zelle Nitouche 31. *Marius* 31. La Petite Chocolatière 32. Les Gaîtés de l'Escadron 32. *Fanny* 32. Theodore and Company 33. Charlemagne 33. Ces Messieurs de la Santé 34. Tartarin de Tarascon 34. J'ai une Idée 34. Minuit Place Pigalle 35. Faisons un Rêve 35. L'Ecole des Cocottes 35. Gaspard de Besse 35. Le Secret de Polichinelle 36. Le Roi 36. Les Jumeaux de Brighton 36. César 36. Anything to Declare 37. Les Perles de la Couronne 37. La Chaste Suzanne 37. Les Rois du Sport 37. Le Fauteuil 37. *Gribouille* 37. *Un Carnet de Bal* 37. Les Héros de la Marne 38. L'Etrange Monsieur Victor 38. Les Nouveaux Riches 38. *La Femme du Boulanger* 38. Noix de Coco 39. Monsieur Brotonneau 39. Dernière Jeunesse 39. L'Homme Qui Cherche la Vérité 39. Un tel Père et Fils 40. La Fille du Puisatier 40. Le Duel 40. Parade en Sept Nuits 41. *Les Inconnus dans la Maison* 42. *L'Arlésienne* 42. *Monsieur la Souris* 42. The Benefactor 42. Les Petits Riens 42. Le Colonel Chabert 43. Les Gueux au Paradis 46. L'Homme au Chapeau Rond 46.

¶ Le plus grand comédien de tous les temps.
– *Arletty*

rain
has been put to many uses by film scenarists. It was the direct cause of dramatic situations in *Rebecca* (a shower flattened Joan Fontaine's hair-do just as she arrived at Manderley); in *The Loneliness of the Long Distance Runner* (it revealed evidence which the hero was trying to conceal); in *Floods of Fear* (it permitted the escape of three convicts, one of whom then rescued the heroine); in *The African Queen* (it raised the water level and so released the boat from the reeds which held it captive); in *Desk Set* (it persuaded Spencer Tracy to accept Katharine Hepburn's offer of hospitality); in *Pygmalion* (it caused the meeting of Higgins and Eliza); in *Sands of the Kalahari* (it flooded a pit in which Stuart Whitman was imprisoned and permitted his escape); in *When Tomorrow Comes* (it stranded Charles Boyer and Irene Dunne in a remote church for the night); and in many others. Two splendid symbolic uses were in *Saraband for Dead Lovers* (a raindrop made a stained-glass madonna appear to weep at the ill-fated wedding) and *The Stars Look Down* (as the hero and heroine make love, two raindrops intertwine on the window-pane).

Rain has often been used symbolically as a relief from tension and heat, in films as diverse as *Night of the Iguana, Passport to Pimlico, The Long Hot Summer, Key Largo, Twelve Angry Men, Black Narcissus, The Good Earth* and *Rain* itself. It has provided a solemn or ominous background in *Psycho, Term of Trial, Rashomon, It Always Rains on*

Sunday, Room at the Top, The Robe, Fires on the Plain, The Collector and many others. It has a particularly depressing effect at a funeral, as was shown in *The Glass Key* and *Our Town*. But it can also be used for farcical purposes: in *Three Men in a Boat, The Silencers, Fraternally Yours, Oh Mr Porter*, etc. And it can provide a comedy twist, as at the end of *The Lady Vanishes*, when the English travellers so eager to get back to the test match find that rain has stopped play.

It can produce a decorative effect (*Les Parapluies de Cherbourg, Miracle in the Rain, Breakfast at Tiffany's*). It can be spectacular (the climax of *Journey into Fear*, the glistening streets in *The Third Man*, the downpours in *The Rains Came*, and *Pather Panchali*, the battles in the rain in *Tower of London* and *Seven Samurai*). And it can provide a cue for song: 'Isn't it a Lovely Day to be Caught in the Rain' in *Top Hat*, the title songs of *Singin' in the Rain* and *Stormy Weather*, 'The Rain in Spain' in *My Fair Lady*, 'April Showers' in *The Jolson Story*, 'Little April Shower' in *Bambi*. In fact, it seems to be by far the most versatile of all the film-maker's effects.

Rain.
Somerset Maugham's story of the conflict between a missionary and a woman of highly doubtful character has been filmed three times in Hollywood: in 1928 with Gloria Swanson and Lionel Barrymore; in 1932 with Joan Crawford and Walter Huston; and in 1957 (as *Miss Sadie Thompson*) with Rita Hayworth and José Ferrer. In each case the Production Code made you guess what the lady's actual profession was.

Raine, Jack (1895–1979).
British light actor, on stage in the 20s and 30s; later in Hollywood.

The Happy Time 52. Julius Caesar 53. Rhapsody 54. My Fair Lady 64. Hello Dolly 69, etc.

Raine, Norman Reilly (1895–1971).
American screenwriter.

Tugboat Annie 33. White Woman 33. God's Country and the Woman 36. *The Life of Emile Zola* (AA) 37. The Adventures of Robin Hood 38. Elizabeth and Essex 39. The Fighting 69th 39. Captains of the Clouds 42. Ladies Courageous 44. A Bell for Adano 45. Woman of the North Country 52. Sea of Lost Ships 53, etc.

Rainer, Luise (1914–   ).
German leading actress, born in Dusseldorf and on-stage from 1930, working with director Max Reinhardt in Berlin. In the mid-30s she went to Hollywood, where Louis B. Mayer insisted that her birthplace should be altered to Vienna and her nationality to Austrian. She was married to playwright and screenwriter Clifford Odets (1937– 40).

Escapade 35. *The Great Ziegfeld* (AA) 36. *The Good Earth* (AA) 37. The Emperor's Candlesticks 37. The Big City 37. The Great Waltz 38. The Toy Wife 38. Dramatic School 38. Hostages 43.

¶ For my second and third pictures I won Academy Awards. Nothing worse could have happened to me. – *L.R.*

Raines, Cristina (1954–   ).
American leading lady of the late 70s.

Sunshine (TV) 74. Nashville 75. The Sentinel 77. The Duellists 77. Touched by Love 80. Silver Dream Racer 83. Nightmares 83. Quo Vadis (TV) 85, etc.

TV series: Flamingo Road 80–81.

Raines, Ella (1921–1988) (Ella Raubes).
American leading lady of the 40s, with brief stage experience.

Corvette K225 43. Cry Havoc 43. Phantom Lady 43. Hail the Conquering Hero 43. Enter Arsène Lupin 44. Tall in the Saddle 44. Uncle Harry 45. The Suspect 45. The Runaround 46. Time out of Mind 47. Brute Force 47. Mr Ashton was Indiscreet 48. The Walking Hills 48. Impact 48. A Dangerous Profession 49. Ride the Man Down 53. Man in the Road (GB) 54, etc.

TV series: Janet Dean Registered Nurse 53–55.

Rainger, Ralph (1901–1942). (Ralph Reichenthal).
American song composer who usually worked with lyricist Leo Robin. Film scores include *The Big Broadcast of 1932, She Done Him Wrong, Swing High Swing Low, Paris Honeymoon, Moon Over Miami, Footlight Serenade, Coney Island*.

The Rains Came.
Louis Broomfield's novel of the high days of British India was filmed in 1939 with Myrna Loy and Tyrone Power, and, as *The Rains of Ranchipur*, in 1955 with Lana Turner and Richard Burton.

Rains, Claude (1889–1967).
Suave, incisive British character actor, long resident in America. Wide stage experience.
■ *The Invisible Man* 33. *Crime without Passion* 34. The Man Who Reclaimed His Head 34. The Mystery of Edwin Drood 35. The Clairvoyant (GB) 35. The Last Outpost 35. Anthony Adverse 36. Hearts Divided 36. Stolen Holiday 36. The Prince and the Pauper 37. They Won't Forget 37. Gold is Where You Find It 38. *The Adventures of Robin Hood* 38. White Banners 38. Four Daughters 38. They Made Me a Criminal 39. Juarez 39. *Mr Smith Goes to Washington* 39. Four Wives 39. Daughters Courageous 39. Saturday's Children 39. The Sea Hawk 40. Lady with Red Hair (as David Belasco) 40. Four Mothers 40. *Here Comes Mr Jordan* 41. The Wolf Man 41. *Kings Row* 41. Moontide 42. Now Voyager 42. *Casablanca* 42. Forever and a Day 43. Phantom of the Opera (title role) 43. Passage to Marseilles 44. *Mr Skeffington* 44. This Love of Ours 45. *Caesar and Cleopatra* (GB) 45. Angel on My Shoulder 46. *Deception* 46. *Notorious* 46. The Unsuspected 47. Strange Holiday 47. *The Passionate Friends* (GB) 47. Rope of Sand 49. Song of Surrender 49. The White Tower 50. Where Danger Lives 50. Sealed Cargo 51. The Man Who Watched Trains Go By (GB) 52. Lisbon 56. This Earth is Mine 59. The Lost World 60. Battle of the Worlds (It.) 61. Lawrence of Arabia 62. Twilight of Honor 63. The Greatest Story Ever Told 65.
✪ For his omnipresent urbanity. *Casablanca*.

¶ He was a great influence on me. I don't know what happened to him. I think he failed and went to America. – *John Gielgud*

Famous line (*The Invisible Man*): 'We'll start with a few murders. Big men, little men – just to show that we make no distinction.'

Famous line (*Casablanca*): 'I'm only a poor corrupt official.'

Raitt, John (1917–).
American Broadway actor and singer, in films from 1940, whose only starring role was in *The Pajama Game*.

Flight Command 40. Little Nellie Kelly 40. Billy the Kid 41. Ziegfeld Girl 41. H. M. Pulham, Esq. 41. The Pajama Game 57, etc.

Raki, Laya (1927–).
Leading lady of the 50s, from New Zealand.
Up to His Neck 54. The Seekers 55. Quentin Durward 56. The Poppy is Also a Flower (TV) 65, etc.

Rakoff, Alvin (1927–).
Canadian TV director resident in Britain.
Passport to Shame 58. Treasure of San Teresa 59. On Friday at Eleven 61. The Comedy Man 64. Hoffman 70. Say Hello to Yesterday 70. Don Quixote (TV) 72. City on Fire 79. Dirty Tricks 80. A Voyage Round My Father (TV) 82. Mr Halpern and Mr Johnson (TV) 83. The First Olympics (TV) 84. Paradise Postponed (TV) 86, etc.

Raksin, David (1912–).
American composer, in Hollywood from mid-30s. Arranged Chaplin's score for *Modern Times* 36.
Laura 44. The Secret Life of Walter Mitty 47. *The Bad and the Beautiful* 52. Separate Tables 58. Too Late Blues 62. Two Weeks in Another Town 62. Invitation to a Gunfighter 65. A Big Hand for the Little Lady 66. Will Penny 67. What's the Matter with Helen? 71. Glass Houses 72. The Suicide's Wife (TV) 79. Lady in a Corner 89, etc.

Ralli, Giovanna (1935–).
Italian leading lady.
The Children are Watching Us 43. Lights of Variety 49. La Lupa 53. The Bigamist 56. Il Generale Della Rovere 59. Deadfall 68. Cannon for Cordoba 70. We All Loved Each Other So Much 75, many others.

Ralph, Jessie (1864–1944) (Jessie Ralph Chambers).
American character actress who came to Hollywood late in life and played many endearing granny roles.
■ Such a Little Queen 21. Elmer the Great 33. Cocktail Hour 33. Child of Manhattan 33. Ann Carver's Profession 33. Coming Out Party 34. One Night of Love 34. Evelyn Prentice 34. Nana 34. We Live Again 34. Murder at the Vanities 34. The Affairs of Cellini 34. *David Copperfield* (as Peggotty) 35. Enchanted April 35. Les Misérables 35. Paris in Spring 35. Vanessa 35. Mark of the Vampire 35. I Live My Life 35. Jalna 35. Metropolitan 35. I Found Stella Parish 35. Captain Blood 35. Bunker Bean 35. The Garden Murder Case 36. The Unguarded Hour 36. *San Francisco* 36. After the Thin Man 36. Camille 36. Little Lord Fauntleroy 36. Yellow Dust 36. Walking on Air 36. The Good Earth 37. Double Wedding 37. The Last of Mrs Cheyney 37. Love Is a Headache 37. Port of Seven Seas 38. Hold That Kiss 38. St Louis Blues 39. Café Society 39. Four Girls in White 39. The Kid from Texas 39. Mickey the Kid 39. Drums Along the Mohawk 39. *The Blue Bird* 40. Star Dust 40. The Girl from Avenue A 40. I Can't Give You Anything But Love Baby 40. *The Bank Dick* 40. I Want a Divorce 40. The Lady from Cheyenne 41. They Met in Bombay 41.

Ralston, Esther (1902–1994).
American leading lady of the 20s and 30s.
The Phantom Fortune (serial) 23. Peter Pan 24. A Kiss for Cinderella 25. Lucky Devil 26. Old Ironsides 26. Figures Don't Lie 27. The Sawdust Paradise 28. The Prodigal 31. Sadie McKee 33. Hollywood Boulevard 36. Tin Pan Alley 40, etc.

Ralston, Jobyna (1901–1967).
American leading lady of the 20s, especially with Harold Lloyd.
Why Worry 23. Girl Shy 24. The Freshman 24. For Heaven's Sake 26. Wings 27, many others.

Ralston, Vera Hruba (1921–).
Czech actress, former skating champion. In US from the late 30s, films from 1942. Married Herbert Yates, boss of Republic Studios, and appeared exclusively in his pictures. Now retired.
■ Ice Capades 41. Ice Capades Revue 42. The Lady and the Monster 44. Storm Over Lisbon 44. Lake Placid Serenade 44. Dakota 45. Murder in the Music Hall 46. The Plainsman and the Lady 46. The Flame 47. Wyoming 47. I Jane Doe 48. Angel on the Amazon 48. The Fighting Kentuckian 49. Surrender 50. Belle Le Grand 51. The Wild Blue Yonder 51. Hoodlum Empire 52. Fair Wind to Java 53. A Perilous Journey 53. Jubilee Trail 54. Timberjack 55. Accused of Murder 56. Spoilers of the Forest 57. Gunfire at Indian Gap 57. The Notorious Mr Monks 58. The Man Who Died Twice 58.

Rambeau, Marjorie (1889–1970).
American character actress.
The Dazzling Miss Davison 16. Her Man 30. Man's Castle 33. The Rains Came 39. Twenty Mule Team 40. Tugboat Annie Sails Again (title role) 40. So Ends Our Night 41. Tobacco Road 41. Broadway 42. Army Wives 45. Abandoned 49. Torch Song 53. The View from Pompey's Head 56. Man of a Thousand Faces 57, many others.

Rambo.
The disgruntled former Green Beret has been played by Sylvester Stallone in three increasingly violent films: *First Blood* 82, directed by Ted Kotcheff; *Rambo: First Blood Part II* 85, directed by George P. Cosmatos, in which he had become a comic-strip hero, destroying enemies in Vietnam; and *Rambo III* 88, directed by Peter MacDonald, in which he continued as a one-man army, this time defeating the Russians in Afghanistan, most of which he blew up. The series was spoofed in *Hot Shots! Part Deux* 93, with Charlie Sheen as a dim mercenary with big muscles and bigger guns.

Rambova, Natacha (1897–1966) (Winifred Shaunessey Hudnut).
Wealthy American designer, dance teacher and actress. Born in Salt Lake City, she was one of the first art directors and costume designers in cinema and created a sensation with her designs for *Salome*, based on Aubrey Beardsley's drawings, and starring Nazimova. She went on to marry, and have a tempestuous relationship with, Nazimova's former husband Rudolph Valentino, directing the last years of his career to his detriment.
Camille (ad) 21. The Young Rajah (ad) 22. Salome (ad, cost.) 23. Monsieur Beaucaire (ad) 24. When Love Grows Cold (a) 26, etc.

Ramis, Harold (1944–).
American director, screenwriter and actor of comedies.
National Lampoon's Animal House (w) 78. Meatballs (w) 79. Caddyshack 80. Stripes (a, w) 81. National Lampoon's Vacation 83. Ghostbusters (a, w) 84. Armed and Dangerous (w) 86. Back to School (w) 86. Ghostbusters II (a, w) 89. Groundhog Day (co-w, d) 93, etc.

Ramona.
Helen Hunt Jackson's novel about an Indian girl was filmed four times: by D. W. Griffith in 1910, with Mary Pickford and Henry B. Walthall; by Donald Crisp in 1916, with Adda Gleason and Monroe Salisbury; by Edwin Carewe in 1928, with Dolores del Rio and Warner Baxter; and by Henry King in 1936, with Loretta Young and Don Ameche.

Rampling, Charlotte (1945–).
British leading lady.

Rotten to the Core 65. Georgy Girl 66. The Long Duel 67. The Damned 69. Corky 72. The Ski Bum 72. Henry VIII and His Six Wives 72. Asylum 72. Cardoz 73. Caravan to Vaccares 74. The Night Porter 74. Farewell My Lovely 75. Foxtrot 76. Sherlock Holmes in New York (TV) 76. Flesh of the Orchid 76. Orca 77. The Purple Taxi 78. Stardust Memories 80. The Verdict 82. The Viva la Vie 83. He Died with his Eyes Open 84. Sadness and Beauty 85. Max My Love 86. Angel Heart 87. Paris by Night 88. Hammers over the Anvil 93. Time Is Money 94, etc.

Ramsey, Anne (1929–1988).
American character actress who received an Oscar nomination for one of her last roles.

The Sporting Club 71. Up the Sandbox 72. The New Centurions 72. Goin' South 78. The Black Marble 80. Any Which Way You Can 80. The Goonies 85. Throw Momma from the Train (AAN) 88. Scrooged 88. Homer and Eddie 90, etc.

Rand, Sally (1904–1979) (Helen Gould Beck).
American dancer and fan dancer, in a few films.

The Dressmaker from Paris 24. Getting Gertie's Garter 27. King of Kings 27. The Fighting Eagle 28. Bolero 34, etc.

Randall, Tony (1920–) (Leonard Rosenberg).
Sardonic American comedy actor, adept at light drunks, depressives and friends of the hero.

¶ Oh Men Oh Women 57. Will Success Spoil Rock Hunter? 57. No Down Payment 58. The Mating Game 59. Pillow Talk 59. The Adventures of Huckleberry Finn 60. Let's Make Love 61. Lover Come Back 61. Boys' Night Out 62. Island of Love 63. The Brass Bottle 63. Send Me No Flowers 64. Seven Faces of Dr Lao 64. Fluffy 65. The Alphabet Murders hilariously miscast as Hercule Poirot) 66. Our Man in Marrakesh 66. Hello Down There 68. Everything You Always Wanted to Know About Sex 72. Scavenger Hunt 79. Foolin' Around 80. Sidney Shorr: A Girl's Best Friend (TV) 81. King of Comedy 83. My Little Pony: The Movie (voice) 86. Agatha Christie's The Man in the Brown Suit (TV) 89. It Had to Be You 89. Gremlins 2: The New Batch (voice) 90. That's Adequate 90. Fatal Instinct 93.

TV series: Mr Peepers 52–55. The Odd Couple 70–74. Tony Randall Show 76–77. Love, Sidney 81–82.

¶ Comedy's a serious business. You've got to be true and funny, and not look as though you're trying. – T.R.

Randel, Tony (1956–).
American director of horror films, a former editor.

Hellbound: Hellraiser II 88. Amityville 1992: It's about Time 92. Children of the Night 92. Ticks 93.

Randell, Ron (1918–).
Australian leading man with radio experience; has appeared in films and TV episodes all over the world.

It Had to be You 47. Lorna Doone 50. Kiss Me Kate 53. Bulldog Drummond at Bay 54. I Am a Camera 55. Beyond Mombasa 56. The Story of Esther Costello 58. King of Kings 61. The Longest Day 62. Gold for the Caesars 63. The Seven Minutes 71. Exposed 83, many others.

TV series: O.S.S. 58.

Randle, Frank (1902–1957) (Arthur McEvoy).
Lancashire music-hall comedian of immense vulgarity; made his own slapdash but highly popular films in the 40s.

Somewhere in England 40. Somewhere in Camp 42. Somewhere in Civvies 43. School for Randle 47. Home Sweet Home 47. Holidays with Pay 48. It's a Grand Life 53, etc.

¶ The greatest character comedian that ever lived. – Gracie Fields

Randolph, Anders (1876–1930).
American character man, usually seen as heavy villain.

The Hero of Submarine D2 16. The Splendid Sinner 18. Dorothy Vernon of Haddon Hall 24. The Black Pirate 28. The Kiss 29, many others.

Randolph, Elsie (1901–1982) (Elsie Florence Killick).
British revue artiste, often teamed in the 30s with Jack Buchanan.

■ Rich and Strange 31. Brother Alfred 32. Life Goes On 32. Rise and Shine 32. Yes, Mr Brown 33. Night of the Garter 33. That's a Good Girl 35. This'll Make You Whistle 37. Smash and Grab 38. Cheer the Brave 50. Riders of the Sky (Czech) 68. Frenzy 72. Charleston 77.

Randolph, Jane (1919–).
American leading lady of the 40s.

Highways by Night 42. Cat People 42. In the Meantime, Darling 44. Jealousy 46. T Men 48. Abbott and Costello Meet Frankenstein (last to date) 48, etc.

Randolph, John (1917–) (Emanuel Hirsch Cohen).
American character actor usually seen as pompous business man.

Naked City 48. Seconds 67. Pretty Poison 68. There Was a Crooked Man 70. Little Murders 71. Serpico 73. King Kong 76. Washington Behind Closed Doors (TV) 77. Blind Ambition (TV) 79. Lovely . . . but Deadly 82. Prizzi's Honor 85. As Summers Die (TV) 86. The Wizard of Loneliness 88. National Lampoon's Christmas Vacation 89. Iron Maze 91, etc.

TV series: Lucas Tanner 74–75. Lucan 77–78. Angie 79–80. Annie McGuire 88. Grand 90.

Rank, J. Arthur (1888–1972) (Lord Rank).
British flour magnate who entered films in the mid-30s in the hope of promoting interest in religion. Formed or took over so many companies including production, distribution and exhibition that by the mid-40s he was accused of monopolistic tendencies. His influence was generally excellent, and he encouraged independent producers (sometimes unwisely), but his organization generally suffered from a preponderance of accountants unable to understand the ingredients of a good film. Without their financial advice, however, the empire might well have perished altogether. At its height it fostered such production companies as the Archers, Cineguild, Wessex, Individual and Two Cities. In recent years the film side of the organization has proved less important than its hotels, bowling alleys and such developments as xerox-copying; but it includes Odeon and Gaumont Theatres, Rank Film Distributors, Pinewood Studios, Denham Laboratories, etc.

Biography: 1952, Mr Rank by Alan Wood.
◐ For doing his best. Henry V.

¶ Methodist principles may seem a curious guide to the promotion of motion pictures, but at least they gave J. Arthur Rank a considerable start over other film promoters who had no principles at all. – Alan Wood

If I could recall to you some of my various adventures and experiences in the film world, it would I think be as plain to you as it is to me that I was being led by God. – J.A.R.

Ransohoff, Martin (1927–).
American writer and producer. Longtime chairman of Filmways, producers of such TV series as The Beverly Hillbillies and The Addams Family, which was bought by Orion Pictures in 1983 and became Orion Television.

Boys' Night Out 62. The Wheeler Dealers 63. The Americanization of Emily 64. Topkapi 64. The Sandpiper 65. The Loved One 65. The Cincinnati Kid 65. Don't Make Waves 67. Ice Station Zebra 68. The Moonshine War 70. The White Dawn 73. Silver Streak 76. The Other Side of Midnight 77. Nightwing 78. The Wanderers 79. A Change of Seasons 81. Hanky Panky 82. Class 83. The Jagged Edge 85. The Big Town 87. Switching Channels 88. Physical Evidence 89. Welcome Home 89, etc.

Ransome, Prunella (1943–).
British leading lady.

Far from the Madding Crowd 67. Alfred the Great 69. Man in the Wilderness 71. Who Can Kill A Child? (Sp.) 75, etc.

rape
was virtually unmentionable in English-speaking films until Warners got away with it in Johnny Belinda in 1947. Then it became the centre of attention in Outrage, Peyton Place, Wicked as They Come, A Streetcar Named Desire, Last Train from Gun Hill, Two Women, To Kill a Mockingbird, Satan Never Sleeps, Shock Corridor, Assault, Trial, Five Gates to Hell, The Chapman Report, The Mark, Anatomy of a Murder, Town without Pity, The Party's Over (in which the victim proved to be dead), and The Penthouse. In Waterhole Three James Coburn, accused of the crime, shrugged it off as 'assault with a friendly weapon'. There was much talk of rape in The Knack and Lock Up Your Daughters, threat of rape in Experiment in Terror and Cape Fear, and an accusation of rape in Term of Trial. Foreign language films on the subject have included Rashomon, The Virgin Spring, Two Women, Viridiana and the Greek Amok. In 70s films it became too commonplace to be worth mentioning, outstanding fictional instances being Straw Dogs, A Clockwork Orange, Lipstick, and Death Wish, with Cry Rape and A Case of Rape adopting a documentary treatment. The Accused 88 caused controversy with its depiction of the gang-rape of a provocative woman and subsequent court-room trial – it also brought an Oscar for Jodie Foster as best actress. And some cheered in Thelma & Louise 91 when a would-be rapist was shot and killed.

Raphael, Frederic (1931–).
British writer.

Bachelor of Hearts 58. Nothing But the Best 64. Darling (AA, BFA) 65. Two for the Road (AAN) 67. Far from the Madding Crowd 67. A Severed Head 71. Daisy Miller 74. Rogue Male (TV) 76. The King's Whore 90, etc.

Raphaelson, Samson (1896–1983).
American playwright whose best screenplays were for Lubitsch; he led the saucy, stylish European trends of the 30s.

■ The Jazz Singer (& oa) 27. Boudoir Diplomat 30. The Smiling Lieutenant 31. The Magnificent Lie 31. One Hour with You 32. Broken Lullaby 32. Trouble in Paradise 32. The Merry Widow 34. Caravan 34. Servants' Entrance 34. Ladies Love Danger 35. Dressed to Thrill 35. Accent on Youth

(& oa) 35. The Last of Mrs Cheyney 37. *The Shop around the Corner* 40. Suspicion 41. Skylark (& oa) 41. *Heaven Can Wait* 43. The Perfect Marriage (& oa) 46. Green Dolphin Street 47. That Lady in Ermine 48. Bannerline 51. Main Street to Broadway 53. Hilda Crane (oa) 56.

Rappaport, David (1951–1990).
Diminutive (3 feet 11 inches) British actor, from the stage. A former teacher, he moved to Los Angeles in the mid-80s, where he appeared in the TV series *L.A. Law*. He committed suicide there.
   Cuba 79. Black Jack 79. Time Bandits 81. Sword of the Valiant 84. The Bride 85, etc.
   TV series: The Wizard 86–87.

Rappeneau, Jean-Paul (1932–).
French director and screenwriter.
   Zazie dans le Métro (w) 60. A Very Private Affair (La Vie Privée) 62. The Man from Rio (L'Homme de Rio) (w) 64. A Matter of Resistance (La Vie de Château) (wd) 66. Les Mariés de l'An II (wd) 70. Le Sauvage (wd) 75. Tout Feu, Tout Flamme (wd) 82. Cyrano de Bergerac (wd) 90. Le Hussard sur le Toit 95, etc.

Rapper, Irving (1898–).
American director with stage experience, long associated with Warner films.
   Shining Victory 41. One Foot in Heaven 41. The Gay Sisters 42. *Now Voyager* 42. The Adventures of Mark Twain 44. Rhapsody in Blue 45. The Corn Is Green 46. *Deception* 46. *The Voice of the Turtle* 48. The Glass Menagerie 50. Another Man's Poison (GB) 51. Forever Female 52. The Brave One 56. Strange Intruder 57. Marjorie Morningstar 58. The Miracle 59. The Christine Jorgenson Story 78. Born Again 78, etc.

Rasche, David (1944–).
American leading actor.
   Honky Tonk Freeway 81. Best Defense 84. Native Son 86. Made in Heaven 87. Wedding Band 89. Wicked Stepmother 89. An Innocent Man 89. The Masters of Menace 90. Bingo 91. Silhouette 91. Delirious (TV) 91, etc.
   TV series: Sledge Hammer! 86–88.

Rascoe, Judith (1941–).
American screenwriter, a former university teacher and short-story writer.
   Road Movie 74. Who'll Stop the Rain? 78. A Portrait of the Artist as a Young Man 79. Endless Love 81. Eat a Bowl of Tea 89. Havana 91, etc.

Rashomon.
Akira Kurosawa's 1951 masterpiece, featuring the different accounts by four people concerned in a moment of violence, re-opened Western cinemas to Japanese films and established its international reputation. It was remade by Martin Ritt in 1964 and given a western setting, starring Paul Newman as a Mexican bandit.

Rasp, Fritz (1891–1976).
German character actor.
   Jugend 22. Warning Shadows 23. Metropolis 27. The Loves of Jeanne Ney 27. Spione 28. Diary of a Lost Girl 29. Die Dreigroschenoper 33. Lina Braake 76, many others.

Rasputin (1869–1916),
the mysterious monk who dominated members of the Tsar's family just before the Russian revolution, has been a popular film subject. Conrad Veidt played him in *Rasputin* (Ger. 1930); Lionel Barrymore in *Rasputin and the Empress* (US 1932); Harry Baur in *Rasputin* (Fr. 1938); Edmund

Purdom in *Nights of Rasputin* (It. 1960); and Christopher Lee in *Rasputin the Mad Monk* (GB 1966); while 1968 brought Gert Frobe in the role in *I Killed Rasputin*, and 1971 had Tom Baker as Rasputin in *Nicholas and Alexandra*. In 1975 Alexei Petrenko played the role in Elem Klimov's *Agony* (Agonia).

Rasulala, Thalmus (1939–1991) (Jack Crowder).
American character actor.
   Cool Breeze 71. Blacula 72. Willie Dynamite 73. Mr Ricco 75. Bucktown 75. Adios Amigo 76. Fun with Dick and Jane 77. Bulletproof 87. Above the Law 88. New Jack City 91, etc.

Rasumny, Mikhail (1890–1956).
Russian character actor with stage experience, long in Hollywood.
   Comrade X 40. This Gun for Hire 42. For Whom the Bell Tolls 43. Saigon 47. The Kissing Bandit 49. Hot Blood 55, many others.

Rat Pack (aka the Clan).
The name given to the showbiz entourage surrounding Frank Sinatra in the 50s and 60s. Its members included Dean Martin, Sammy Davis Jnr, Joey Bishop, and Peter Lawford, though both Davis and Lawford were banished at times. The term was coined by *Time* magazine, but it had its origins in the Holmby Hills Rat Pack, who were the drinking friends of Humphrey Bogart. The Pack gathered for several films with Sinatra, in which they seemed to have more fun than the audience: *Ocean's Eleven* 60; *Sergeants 3* 62; and *Robin and the Seven Hoods* 64.
   Book: 1961, *Sinatra and His Rat Pack* by Richard Gehman.

¶ In Frank's Rat Pack personal homage to their 'leader' was all important: Frank was addressed as 'the pope', 'the general', and 'el dago.' – *Kitty Kelley*

Rathbone, Basil (1892–1967).
Incisive British actor, on stage from 1911, in America from the mid-20s.
   Autobiography: 1962, *In and Out of Character*.
   Biography: 1972, *Basil Rathbone and His Films* by Michael B. Druxman.
■ Innocent 21. The Fruitful Vine 21. The School for Scandal 23. The Masked Bride 25. Trouping with Ellen 24. The Great Deception 24. The Last of Mrs Cheyney 29. The Bishop Murder Case 30. A Notorious Affair 30. The Lady of Scandal 30. This Mad World 30. The Flirting Widow 30. A Lady Surrenders 30. Sin Takes a Holiday 30. A Woman Commands 31. One Precious Year 33. After the Ball 33. Loyalties 33. *David Copperfield* (as Murdstone) 35. *Anna Karenina* (as Karenin) 35. The Last Days of Pompeii 35. A Feather in Her Hat 35. A Tale of Two Cities 35. *Captain Blood* 35. Kind Lady 35. Private Number 36. Romeo and Juliet 36. The Garden of Allah 36. Confession 37. Love from a Stranger 37. Make a Wish 37. Tovarich 37. The Adventures of Marco Polo 38. *The Adventures of Robin Hood* (as Gisborne) 38. If I Were King 38. The Dawn Patrol 38. Son of Frankenstein 39. *The Hound of the Baskervilles* 39. The Sun Never Sets 39. The Adventures of Sherlock Holmes 39. Rio 39. Tower of London 39. Rhythm on the River 40. The Mark of Zorro 40. The Mad Doctor 41. The Black Cat 41. International Lady 41. Paris Calling 41. Fingers at the Window 41. Crossroads 42. Sherlock Holmes and the Voice of Terror 42. Sherlock Holmes and the Secret Weapon 42. Sherlock Holmes in Washington 43. Above Suspicion 43. Sherlock Holmes Faces Death 43. *Spider Woman* 44. The Scarlet Claw 44. Bathing Beauty 44. The Pearl

of Death 44. Frenchman's Creek 44. The House of Fear 45. The Woman in Green 45. Pursuit to Algiers 45. Terror by Night 45. *Heartbeat* 46. Dressed to Kill 46. Casanova's Big Night 54. We're No Angels 55. *The Court Jester* 56. The Black Sleep 56. The Last Hurrah 58. The Magic Sword 62. Tale of Terror 62. Two before Zero 62. The Comedy of Terrors 64. Pontius Pilate 64. Queen of Blood 66. The Ghost in the Invisible Bikini 66. Voyage to a Prehistoric Planet 67. Autopsy of a Ghost 67. Hillbillies in a Haunted House 67.
For being everybody's favourite villain and the one and only Sherlock Holmes. *The Hound of the Baskervilles*.

¶ Two profiles pasted together. – *Dorothy Parker*
~The only time he won a screen duel was in *Romeo and Juliet*: he played Tybalt.

Rathborne, Tina (1951–).
American director.
   Zelly and Me 88.

ratio (screen):
see *aspect ratio*.

Ratoff, Gregory (1897–1960).
English-fracturing Russian actor and impresario, in Hollywood and Britain from mid-30s as actor or director.
   I'm No Angel (a) 33. Under Two Flags (a) 36. Lancer Spy (a) 37. Rose of Washington Square (d) 39. Intermezzo (d) 39. I Was an Adventuress (d) 40. Adam Had Four Sons (d) 41. The Corsican Brothers (a) 41. The Men in Her Life (d) 42. Song of Russia (d) 44. Where Do We Go from Here? (d) 45. Moss Rose (d) 47. All about Eve (a) 50. My Daughter Joy (d) 50. Abdullah the Great (ad) 57. *Oscar Wilde* (d) 60. The Big Gamble (a) 61, many others.

Rattigan, Sir Terence (1912–1977).
Distinguished British playwright, many of whose successes have been filmed.
   Biography: 1979, *Terence Rattigan, the Man and His Work* by Michael Darlow and Gillian Hodson.
   French without Tears 39. While the Sun Shines 46. The Winslow Boy 48. The Browning Version 51 and 94. The Deep Blue Sea 55. Separate Tables (AAN) 58, etc.
AS SCREENWRITER: English without Tears 43. The Way to the Stars 45. The Sound Barrier (AAN) 52. The VIPs 63. The Yellow Rolls-Royce 64. Goodbye Mr Chips 69. Bequest to the Nation 73, many others.

Raven, Mike (1927–) (Churton Fairman).
Tall, bearded British leading actor and screenwriter, in a few horror movies of the 70s, formerly a pirate radio and BBC disc jockey, and author.
■ I, Monster 70. Crucible of Terror 71. Lust for a Vampire 71. Disciple of Death (& w, co-p) 72.

Ravetch, Irving (c. 1915–).
American writer who with his wife Harriet Frank has frequently worked with director Martin Ritt.
   The Long Hot Summer 58. The Sound and the Fury 59. Home from the Hill 59. The Dark at the Top of the Stairs 60. Hud (AAN) 63. Hombre 67. The Reivers (& p) 69. The Cowboys 72. The Spikes Gang 74. Conrack (& co-p) 74. Norma Rae (AAN) 79. Murphy's Romance 85. Stanley & Iris 90, etc.

Rawi, Ousama (1939–).
Iranian cinematographer. Went to Canada to produce commercials.
   Pulp 73. The Black Windmill 74. Gold 74.

achel's Man 75. Alfie Darling 75. Sky Riders 76. ower Play 78. Zulu Dawn 79. The Housekeeper aka A Judgement in Stone) (d) 86, etc.

awlings, Terence.
nglish editor.
Watership Down 78. Alien 79. The Awakening 0. Chariots of Fire (AAN) 81. Blade Runner 82. entl 83. Legend 86. F/X 86. The Lonely Passion f Judith Hearne 87. Slipstream 89. Not without y Daughter 91. Alien³ 92. No Escape 94, etc.

awlins, David.
merican editor.
Bingo Long 76. Saturday Night Fever 77. The ast Remake of Beau Geste 78. The China yndrome 79. Urban Cowboy 80. Soup for One 2. The Osterman Weekend 83. Firestarter 84. Girls ust Want to Have Fun 85. Back to School 86. olice Academy 4: Citizens on Patrol 87. Cold Feet 8. Life Stinks 91, etc.

awlins, John (1902–).
merican director, mainly of second features.
State Police 38. Six Lessons from Madame La onga 41. Halfway to Shanghai 42. Sherlock olmes and the Voice of Terror 42. The Great mpersonation 42. Ladies Courageous 44. Sudan 45. ick Tracy Meets Gruesome 47. Fort Defiance 52. hark River 53. The Lost Legion 57, etc.

awlinson, Herbert (1885–1953).
nglish-born American circus performer, silent ar and latterly character actor.
Monte Cristo 12. The Sea Wolf 13. The Black ox (serial) 15. Good Gracious, Annabelle 19. harge It 21. Bullets or Ballots 36. Dark Victory 9. Superman (serial) 48, many others.

awnsley, David (1909–).
ritish art director (49th Parallel, In Which We Serve, he Rake's Progress, I See a Dark Stranger, etc). nventor of the Independent Frame system, ntended as a production economy; it caused onstriction in practice and was quickly bandoned.

awsthorne, Alan (1905–1971).
ritish composer.
Burma Victory 45. The Captive Heart 46. Uncle las 47. Saraband for Dead Lovers 48. Where No ultures Fly 51. The Cruel Sea 53. The Man Who ever Was 56. Floods of Fear 58, etc.

ay, Aldo (1926–1991) (Aldo da Re).
eefy American actor, in local politics before film areer.
Saturday's Heroes 51. The Marrying Kind 51. Pat nd Mike 52. Let's Do It Again 53. Miss Sadie hompson 54. We're No Angels 55. The Gentle ergeant 56. Men in War 57. God's Little Acre 3. The Naked and the Dead 58. The Siege of inchgut (GB) 58. The Day They Robbed the Bank f England (GB) 60. Johnny Nobody (GB) 61. ightmare in the Sun 64. Sylvia 65. What Did You o in the War, Daddy? 66. Dead Heat on a Merry-o-Round 66. Welcome to Hard Times 67. Riot n Sunset Strip 67. The Power 67. The Green erets 68. Man Without Mercy 69. And Hope to ie 72. Inside Out '75. The Bad Bunch 76. Haunts 7. Death Dimension 78. The Glove 80. The ecret of Nimh (voice) 82. Dark Sanity 82. Evils f the Night 83. The Executioner Part II 84. rankenstein's Great Aunt Tillie 84. Biohazard 85. error on Alcatraz 87. Hollywood Cop 87. The icilian 87. Blood Red 87. The Shooters 89. Shock m Dead 91. Foreign Agent 91, etc.

Ray, Andrew (1939–).
British juvenile lead, son of Ted Ray.
The Mudlark (debut) 50. The Yellow Balloon 52. Escapade 55. Woman in a Dressing-Gown 57. Serious Charge 59. Twice Round the Daffodils 62. The System 64. Great Expectations (TV) 75, etc.
TV series: Edward and Mrs Simpson (as George VI) 78.

Ray, Charles (1891–1943).
American leading man of the silent screen, often in country-boy roles.
SILENT FILMS: The Favorite Son 13. The Ace of Hearts 15. Bill Henry 19. The Old Swimming Hole 20. The Barnstormer 22. The Girl I Love 23. Sweet Adeline 23. The Courtship of Miles Standish (& p) 23. Vanity 25. Getting Gertie's Garter 27. The Garden of Eden 28, etc.
SOUND FILMS: Ladies Should Listen 34. By Your Leave 35. Just My Luck 37.

Ray, Fred Olen (1954–).
American director, screenwriter and producer of low-budget horror and action movies, often released direct to video. He is the author of The New Poverty Row: Independent Filmmakers and Distributors (1991).
Alien Dead 79. Scalps 83. Biohazard 85. Armed Response 86. The Tomb 86. Commando Squad 87. Cyclone 87. Deep Space 87. Phantom Empire 87. Star Slammer 88. Terminal Force 88. Warlords 88. Hollywood Chainsaw Hookers 88. Bulletproof (story) 88. Alienator 89. Beverly Hills Vamp 89. Mob Boss 90. Bad Girls from Mars 91. Evil Toons 91. Inner Sanctum 91. Haunting Fear 92. Wizards of the Demon Sword 92, etc.

Ray, Johnnie (1927–1990).
American 'crying' singer of the 50s who played a leading role in There's No Business Like Show Business 54.

Ray, Man (1890–1976) (Emmanuel Rudnitsky).
American photographer, Dadaist and surrealist, long resident in France, made a few strange films.
Retour à la Raison (wd) 23. Entr'acte (a) 24. L'Etoile de Mer (wd) 28. The Mystery of the Château of the Dice (wd) 29. Dreams that Money Can Buy (oa) 46, etc.

Ray, Nicholas (1911–1979) (Raymond N. Kienzle).
American director, former writer and stage director. Acclaimed for his first film, he later seemed to lack a particular style.
Biography: 1992, The Films of Nicholas Ray: The Poet of Nightfall by Geoff Andrew.
■ They Live by Night 47. A Woman's Secret 49. Knock on Any Door 49. Born to be Bad 50. In a Lonely Place 50. Flying Leathernecks 51. On Dangerous Ground 51. The Lusty Men 52. Johnny Guitar 54. Run for Cover 55. Rebel without a Cause (AANw) 55. Hot Blood 56. Bigger than Life 56. The True Story of Jesse James 57. Bitter Victory 57. Wind Across the Everglades 58. Party Girl 58. Savage Innocents 59. King of Kings 61. 55 Days at Peking 62. Dreams of Thirteen 76. The American Friend (a only) 77.
~In 1980, following his death from cancer, Lightning over Water was released, a film about himself.

Ray, René (1912–1993) (Irene Creese).
British actress, on stage from childhood; has often played downtrodden waifs. She was also a novelist and writer. Married to the Earl of Middleton (1975–79).
Young Woodley 30. The Passing of the Third Floor Back 35. Crime over London 36. Farewell Again 37.

The Rat 38. Bank Holiday 38. The Return of the Frog 39. They Made Me a Fugitive 47. If Winter Comes (US) 47. Women of Twilight 52. The Good Die Young 53. Vicious Circle 57, etc.

Ray, Sandip (1954–).
Indian director, screenwriter, composer and cinematographer, the son of Satyajit Ray.
Kanchenjungha (a) 62. Fatikchand (d) 82. Satyajit Ray Presents (d) (TV) 86. The Return of Goopy and Bhaga (Goopy Bhaga Phire Elo) (d) 90. Family Reunion (Sakha Prasakha) (ph) 91. Target (wd) 92. Broken Journey (Jagoran) (d, m) 93, etc.

Ray, Satyajit (1921–1992).
Indian director, famous for the 'Apu' trilogy of a child growing up in modern India. He was awarded an honorary Oscar in 1992.
Pather Panchali 54. The Unvanquished (Aparajito) 56. The Music Room 58. The World of Apu 59. The Goddess 60. Kanchenjunga 62. The Adventures of Goopy and Bagha 68. The Adversary 71. Company Limited 72. Distant Thunder 74. The Middle Man 76. The Chess Players 77. The Elephant God 79. Deliverance 82. The Home and the World 84. An Enemy of the People (Ganashatru) 89. The Branches of the Tree 90. The Stranger (Agantuk) 91. Broken Journey (Jagoran) (w) 94, etc.

Ray, Ted (1906–1977) (Charles Olden).
British music-hall comedian and violinist who was in occasional films.
Autobiographies: 1952, Raising the Laughs. 1963, My Turn Next.
Elstree Calling 30. Radio Parade of 1935. A Ray of Sunshine 47. Meet Me Tonight 50. Escape by Night 52. My Wife's Family 54. Carry On Teacher 59. Please Turn Over 60, etc.

Raye, Carol (1923–) (Kathleen Corkrey).
Australian leading lady of British films of the 40s.
Strawberry Roan 45. Spring Song 46. While I Live 48, etc.

Raye, Martha (1916–1994) (Maggie O'Reed).
Wide-mouthed American comedienne and vocalist, popular on radio and TV. The second of her six husbands was composer David Rose.
Rhythm on the Range (debut) 36. Waikiki Wedding 37. Artists and Models 38. The Boys from Syracuse 40. Keep 'Em Flying 41. Hellzapoppin 41. Pin-Up Girl 43. Four Jills in a Jeep 44. Monsieur Verdoux 47. Jumbo 62. Pufnstuf 70. The Concorde – Airport 79 79, etc.
TV series: The Martha Raye Show 59. The Bugaloos 70–71. McMillan 76. Alice 82–84.

¶ I didn't have to work till I was three. But after that, I never stopped. – M.R.

Rayfiel, David.
American screenwriter.
Castle Keep (co-w) 69. Valdez Is Coming (co-w) 70. Three Days of the Condor (co-w) 75. Lipstick 76. Death Watch (co-w) 80. Round Midnight (co-w) 86. The Firm (co-w) 93. Intersection (co-w) 94, etc.

Raymond, Cyril (c. 1897–1973).
British stage and screen actor often seen as the dull husband or professional man.
The Shadow 32. Mixed Doubles 33. The Tunnel 35. Dreaming Lips 37. Come On George 39. Brief Encounter 46. This was a Woman 47. Jack of Diamonds 48. Angels One Five 51. Lease of Life 53. Charley Moon 56, etc.

Raymond, Gary (1935–).
British 'second lead'.
The Moonraker 58. *Look Back in Anger* 59. Suddenly Last Summer 59. The Millionairess 61. El Cid 61. Jason and the Argonauts 63. The Greatest Story Ever Told 65. Traitors' Gate 65. The Playboy of the Western World 66, etc.
TV series: The Rat Patrol 65.

Raymond, Gene (1908–) (Raymond Guion).
American leading man of the 30s, recently character actor; was married to Jeanette MacDonald. On stage from childhood. Directed one film, *Million Dollar Weekend* (& a) 48.
Personal Maid (debut) 31. *Zoo in Budapest* 33. Flying Down to Rio 33. I Am Suzanne 34. Seven Keys to Baldpate 34. That Girl from Paris 37. Stolen Heaven 38. Mr and Mrs Smith 41. Smilin' Through 41. The Locket 46. Assigned to Danger 49. Hit the Deck 55. The Best Man 64, etc.
TV series: Paris 7000 70.

Raymond, Jack (1892–1953) (John Caines).
British producer, mainly lightweight comedy films.
Sorrell and Son 34. Up for the Cup 34. The Frog 36. Splinters 37. The Rat 38. The Mind of Mr Reeder (& d) 39. You Will Remember 41. Worm's Eye View 51. Reluctant Heroes 52, many others.

Raymond, Paula (1923–) (Paula Ramona Wright).
American leading lady, former model.
Devil's Doorway 49. Crisis 50. The Tall Target 51. The Beast from Twenty Thousand Fathoms 53. The Human Jungle 54. The Gun that Won the West 55. The Flight That Disappeared 62. Blood of Dracula's Castle 70, etc.

Razatos, Spiros.
American director of action films, a former stunt expert.
Fast Getaway 91. Class of 1999 II: The Substitute 93.

Rea, Stephen.
Irish leading actor of stage, screen and television.
Angel (US: Danny Boy) 83. Loose Connections 83. Company of Wolves 84. Four Days in July (TV) 84. The Doctor and the Devils 85. Life Is Sweet 91. *The Crying Game* 92. Bad Behaviour 93. Angie 94. Princess Caraboo 94. Interview with the Vampire 94, etc.

Reagan, Ronald (1911–).
American leading man of the 40s, former sports reporter. Went into politics and in 1966 was elected Governor of California; in 1976 narrowly missed the Republican presidential nomination; in 1980, elected US President.
Autobiography: 1965, *Where's the Rest of Me?*
Biographies: 1987, *Early Reagan: The Rise of an American Hero* by Anne Edwards. 1994, *Ronald Reagan in Hollywood: Movies and Politics* by Stephen Vaughn.
Love Is on the Air 37. Accidents Will Happen 38. Dark Victory 39. Hell's Kitchen 39. Brother Rat and a Baby 40. Santa Fé Trail 40. International Squadron 41. Nine Lives are Not Enough 41. *Kings Row* 41. Juke Girl 42. *Desperate Journey* 42. This is the Army 43. Stallion Road 47. That Hagen Girl 47. The Voice of the Turtle 47. Night unto Night 48. John Loves Mary 49. The Hasty Heart (GB) 49. Louisa 50. Storm Warning 51. Hong Kong 52. Prisoner of War 54. Law and Order 54. Tennessee's Partner 55. Hellcats of the Navy 57. The Killers 64, etc.
TV series: Death Valley Days 62–64.

Famous line (*Kings Row*): 'Where's the rest of me?'

Famous line (*Knute Rockne, All American*): 'Win one for the Gipper!'

Reason, Rex (1928–) (formerly known as Bart Roberts).
American leading man, mainly in routine films.
Storm over Tibet 52. Salome 53. Yankee Pasha 54. This Island Earth 55. Raw Edge 56. Band of Angels 57. The Rawhide Trail 60, etc.
TV series: Man Without a Gun 58. *The Roaring Twenties* 60.

Reason, Rhodes (1928–).
American leading man, mainly in second features. Twin of Rex Reason.
Crime against Joe 56. Jungle Heat 57. Yellowstone Kelly 59. King Kong Escapes (Jap.) 68. Cruisin' High 75, etc.
TV series: *White Hunter* 58.

Rebecca of Sunnybrook Farm.
The American children's classic by Kate Douglas Wiggin was filmed in 1917 by Marshall Neilan, with Mary Pickford; in 1932 by Alfred Santell, with Marian Nixon; and in 1938, much changed, by Allan Dwan, with Shirley Temple.

Rebhorn, James.
American actor.
Deadly Business (TV) 86. Heart of Midnight 88. White Sands 92. Scent of a Woman 92. Skylark (TV) 93. Lane Frost 93. 8 Seconds 94. Blank Check 94. Guarding Tess 94. I Love Trouble 94, etc.

Red Dust.
This rubber-plantation drama by Wilson Collinson is remembered for the electric teaming of Clark Gable and Jean Harlow in the 1932 version, directed by Victor Fleming, and for the scene in which Harlow takes a primitive shower. It was remade in 1939 as *Congo Maisie*, with Ann Sothern and John Carroll; and in 1954 Gable himself appeared opposite Ava Gardner in a lavish restyling under the title *Mogambo*, directed by John Ford.

Red, Eric.
American screenwriter and director.
The Hitcher (w) 86. Near Dark (co-w) 87. Cohen & Tate (wd) 88. Blue Steel (co-w) 90. Body Parts (d) 91.

Red Indians (native Americans),
it is generally thought, were always portrayed as villains on screen until *Broken Arrow* in 1950, when Jeff Chandler played Cochise. But in fact there were many silent films in which Indians were not only on the side of right but the leading figures in the story. In 1911 one finds titles like *An Indian Wife's Devotion, A Squaw's Love, Red-Wing's Gratitude; Ramona* had already been made once and was to survive three remakes; 1913 brought *Heart of an Indian* and *The Squaw Man*. Later there were versions of *In the Days of Buffalo Bill* 21, *The Vanishing American* 25, and *Redskin* 28. It seems to have been sound that made the Indians villainous, and kept them that way for twenty-two years.
After *Broken Arrow* there was a deluge of pro-Indian films. *Devil's Doorway, Across the Wide Missouri, The Savage, Arrowhead, The Big Sky, Apache, Taza – Son of Cochise, Chief Crazy Horse, Sitting Bull, White Feather, Navajo, Hiawatha,* all came within four years. There were even biopics of modern Indians: *The Outsider* (Ira Hayes) and *Jim Thorpe, All American*. In recent years the Indians

have been slipping back into villainy: but the 60s brought *Flaming Star, Cheyenne Autumn, Tell them Willie Boy is Here, A Man called Horse, Flap, Little Big Man, The Stalking Moon;* and TV in 1966 boasted a series based on a Red Indian cop in New York (the name is *Hawk*) as well as comic Indians in *F Troop*, and Elvis Presley played a Red Indian hero in *Stay Away Joe*. In the 90s, *Dances with Wolves* established the Indians as heroes and the American cavalry as the villains.
Other whites who have played red include Boris Karloff in *Tap Roots;* Victor Mature in *Chief Crazy Horse;* Charlton Heston in *The Savage;* Burt Lancaster in *Apache;* Paul Newman in *Hombre;* Robert Taylor in *Devil's Doorway;* Don Ameche in *Ramona*.
~The Jacarillo tribe financed *A Gunfight* in 1971.

Reddy, Helen (1942–).
Australian folk singer.
Airport 75 74. Pete's Dragon 77.

Redfield, William (1927–1976).
American general-purpose actor with long stage experience; former boy actor.
I Married a Woman 58. Fantastic Voyage 66. Duel at Diablo 66. A New Leaf 70. Death Wish 74. For Pete's Sake 74. One Flew Over the Cuckoo's Nest 76, etc.

Redford, Robert (1937–).
Blond, athletic American leading actor of the 70s and 80s. He is the owner of the Sundance resort and founder of the Sundance Institute for independent film-makers.
Biography: 1977, *Robert Redford* by Donald A. Reed.
■ War Hunt 61. Situation Hopeless but not Serious 65. Inside Daisy Clover 65. The Chase 65. This Property is Condemned 66. Barefoot in the Park 67. Tell Them Willie Boy is Here 69. *Butch Cassidy and the Sundance Kid* 69. Downhill Racer 69. Little Fauss and Big Halsy 70. The Hot Rock 72. Jeremiah Johnson 72. *The Candidate* 72. The Way We Were 73. *The Sting* 73. The Great Gatsby 74. The Great Waldo Pepper 75. Three Days of the Condor 75. *All the President's Men* 76. A Bridge Too Far 77. The Electric Horseman 79. Brubaker 80. Ordinary People (d only) (AA) 80. The Natural 84. Out of Africa 85. Legal Eagles 86. The Milagro Beanfield War (d) 88. Havana 90. Indecent Proposal 92. A River Runs through It (d) 92. Sneakers 92. Indecent Proposal 93. Quiz Show (d) 94.

¶ Other people have analysis. I have Utah. – *R.R.*
I often feel I'll just opt out of this rat-race and buy another hunk of Utah. – *R.R.*
A lot of what acting is, is paying attention. – *R.R.*
All my life I've been dogged by guilt because I feel there is this difference between the way I look and the way I feel inside. – *R.R.*
~Redford is alleged to have turned down the leading roles in *Who's Afraid of Virginia Woolf?, The Graduate, Rosemary's Baby, Love Story* and *The Day of the Jackal.*

Redgrave, Corin (1939–).
British supporting actor, son of Sir Michael Redgrave.
A Man for All Seasons 66. Charge of the Light Brigade 68. Oh What a Lovely War 69. David Copperfield 69. Von Richthofen and Brown 71. Serail 77. Sunday Too Far Away 77. Excalibur 81. Eureka 81. The Fool 91. In the Name of the Father 93. Four Weddings and a Funeral 94, etc.

Redgrave, Lynn (1943–).
British actress, daughter of Sir Michael Redgrave; has tended to play gauche comedy roles.

■ Tom Jones 63. Girl with Green Eyes 64. *Georgy Girl* 66. The Deadly Affair 67. Smashing Time 67. The Virgin Soldiers 69. Blood Kin 69. Killer from Yuma 71. Every Little Crook and Nanny 72. Everything You Always Wanted to Know about Sex 72. The National Health 73. The Happy Hooker 75. The Big Bus 76. Sunday Lovers 80. Gauguin the Savage (TV) 81. Rehearsal for Murder (TV) 82. The Shooting (TV) 82. Morgan Stewart's Coming Home 87. Midnight 89. Getting It Right 89. Whatever Happened to Baby Jane? (TV) 91.

TV series: House Calls 80–81. Teachers Only 82.

¶ Looking up at my horrible ugly bulk on a huge screen was the turning point in my life. – *L.R.*
(she shed many pounds before making it big in Hollywood and on American TV game shows)

Redgrave, Sir Michael (1908–1985).
Tall, distinguished British actor, former schoolmaster, on stage from 1934.

Autobiographies: 1958, *Mask or Face*. 1983, *In My Mind's Eye*.

Biography: 1956, *Michael Redgrave, Actor* by Richard Findlater.

■ The Lady Vanishes 38. Climbing High 38. A Stolen Life 39. A Window in London 39. *The Stars Look Down* 39. *Kipps* 41. Atlantic Ferry 41. *Jeannie* 41. *Thunder Rock* 42. The Big Blockade 42. The Way to the Stars 45. *Dead of Night* 45. The Captive Heart 46. The Years Between 46. The Man Within 47. *Fame is the Spur* 47. Mourning Becomes Electra (US) 47. The Secret beyond the Door (US) 48. *The Browning Version* 50. The Magic Box 51. *The Importance of Being Earnest* 52. The Sea Shall Not Have Them 54. The Green Scarf 54. Oh Rosalinda 55. Confidential Report 55. The Night my Number Came Up 55. *The Dam Busters* 55. Nineteen Eighty-Four 56. Time Without Pity 57. *The Quiet American* 58. Law and Disorder 58. Behind the Mask 58. Shake Hands with the Devil 59. No My Darling Daughter 60. The Innocents 61. The Loneliness of the Long Distance Runner 63. Young Cassidy 64. The Hill 65. The Heroes of Telemark 65. Assignment K 67. Oh What a Lovely War 69. Goodbye Mr Chips 69. The Battle of Britain 69. David Copperfield 69. Connecting Rooms 69. Goodbye Gemini 70. Nicholas and Alexandra 71. The Go-Between 71.

Redgrave, Vanessa (1937–).
British leading lady, daughter of Sir Michael Redgrave; as well known for her espousal of causes as for her acting. She was married to director Tony Richardson (1962–67) and has a son by actor Franco Nero.

Autobiography: 1991, *Vanessa Redgrave*.

■ Behind the Mask 58. *Morgan* 66. Red and Blue 66. Sailor from Gibraltar 66. A Man for all Seasons (uncredited) 66. Blow Up 66. *Camelot* 67. The Charge of the Light Brigade 68. *Isadora* 68. A Quiet Place in the Country (It.) 68. Dropout (It.) 69. Vacation (It.) 69. The Seagull 69. Oh What a Lovely War 69. The Trojan Women 71. The Devils 71. *Mary Queen of Scots* 72. Murder on the Orient Express 74. Out of Season 76. The Seven Per Cent Solution 76. Julia (AA) 77. Agatha 79. Yanks 79. Bear Island 79. *Playing for Time* (TV) 81. Wagner 82. My Body My Child (TV) 83. The Bostonians 84. Steaming 85. Wetherby 86. Three Sovereigns for Sarah (TV) 86. Peter the Great (TV) 86. Second Serve (TV) 86. Comrades 86. Prick Up Your Ears 87. Consuming Passions 88. Whatever Happened to Baby Jane? (TV) 91. The Ballad of the Sad Café 91. Howards End 91. Di Ceria dell'Untore (The

Plague Sower) 92. Sparrow (Storia di una Capinera) (It.) 93. Un Muro de Silencio (Arg.) 93. The House of the Spirits 94. Mother's Boys 94. Little Odessa 94. Great Moments in Aviation 94.

¶ America is gangsterism for the private profit of the few. – *V.R.*
I give myself to my parts as to a lover. – *V.R.*
I have a tremendous use for passionate statement. – *V.R.*
It's a kinky part of my nature – to meddle. – *V.R.*
I choose all my roles very carefully so that when my career is finished I will have covered all our recent history of oppression. – *V.R.*
The Ellen Terry of her time. – *Caryl Brahms*

Redman, Joyce (1918–).
Irish stage actress whose most memorable film role was in the eating scene in *Tom Jones* (AAN) 63.

Othello 65. Prudence and the Pill 67. Les Misérables (TV) 77. A Different Kind of Love 85.

Redmond, Liam (1913–1989).
Irish character actor, an Abbey player.

I See a Dark Stranger 45. Captain Boycott 48. High Treason 51. The Gentle Gunman 52. The Divided Heart 54. Jacqueline 56. Night of the Demon 57. The Boy and the Bridge 59. The Ghost and Mr Chicken (US) 65. Tobruk (US) 66. The Twenty-Fifth Hour 66. The Last Safari 67. Barry Lyndon 75, etc.

Redmond, Moira.
British actress, mainly on the stage.

Doctor in Love 58. *Nightmare* 62. Jigsaw 62. The Limbo Line 66, etc.

reduction print:
one optically reduced from 35mm to 16mm.

Reece, Brian (1913–1962).
British light actor whose success was mainly on stage.

A Case for PC 49 51. Fast and Loose 54. Orders are Orders 55. Carry on Admiral 58, etc.

Reed, Alan (1908–1977) (Edward Bergman).
Burly American character actor, TV's voice of Fred Flintstone.

Days of Glory 43. Nob Hill 44. Viva Zapata 52. The Desperate Hours 55. Breakfast at Tiffany's 62, etc.

Reed, Sir Carol (1906–1976).
Distinguished British director who after a peak in the late 40s seemed to lose his way; his infrequent later films, though always civilized, were generally disappointing.

Biography: 1991, *The Man Between* by Nicholas Wapshott.

■ Midshipman Easy 34. Laburnum Grove 36. Talk of the Devil 36. Who's Your Lady Friend? 37. *Bank Holiday* 38. Penny Paradise 38. Climbing High 38. A Girl Must Live 39. *The Stars Look Down* 39. *Night Train to Munich* 40. The Girl in the News 40. *Kipps* 41. The Young Mr Pitt 42. *The Way Ahead* 44. The True Glory (co-d) 45. *Odd Man Out* 46. *The Fallen Idol* (AAN) 48. *The Third Man* (AAN) 49. *An Outcast of the Islands* 51. The Man Between 53. A Kid for Two Farthings 55. Trapeze 56. The Key 58. Our Man in Havana 59. The Running Man 63. The Agony and the Ecstasy 65. Oliver! (AA) 68. Flap 70. Follow Me 72.

❂ For the sympathy and expertise which sadly left him after the early 50s. *Kipps.*

¶ His career demonstrates that a director who limits himself to solving technical problems

quickly lapses into the decadence of the inappropriate effect. – *Andrew Sarris, 1968*

Reed, Donna (1921–1986) (Donna Mullenger).
American leading lady of the 40s, later star of long-running TV series *The Donna Reed Show*. Won screen test after a beauty contest while still at college.

The Getaway (debut) 41. Shadow of the Thin Man 42. The Courtship of Andy Hardy 42. Calling Dr Gillespie 42. The Human Comedy 43. See Here, Private Hargrove 44. The Picture of Dorian Gray 44. It's a Wonderful Life 46. Green Dolphin Street 47. Chicago Deadline 49. *From Here to Eternity* (AA) 53. The Last Time I Saw Paris 55. Ransom 56. Backlash 56. The Benny Goodman Story 56. Beyond Mombasa 57. The Best Place to Be (TV) 79. Deadly Lessons (TV) 83, etc.

TV series: Dallas 84.

¶ Forty pictures I was in, and all I remember is 'What kind of bra will you be wearing today, honey?' That was always the area of big decision – from the neck to the navel. – *D.R.*

Reed, George (1867–1952).
American character actor.

The Birth of a Nation 14. The Green Pastures 36. So Red the Rose 36. Swanee River 39. Tales of Manhattan 42. Home in Indiana 44, many others.

Reed, Les (1935–).
British composer and conductor. A former member of the John Barry Seven, he has written many popular hits and, occasionally, film scores and songs.

Girl on a Motorcycle (m) 68. Les Bicyclettes de Belsize (m) 69. One More Time (m) 69. The Lady Vanishes (s) 79. Play Misty for Me (s) 71. Creepshow 2 (m) 87, etc.

Reed, Maxwell (1920–1974).
Brooding Irish leading man in British films from 1946, after repertory experience.

The Years Between 46. Daybreak 47. *The Brothers* 48. The Dark Man 49. The Square Ring 53. Before I Wake 56. Notorious Landlady 62. Picture Mommy Dead 66, etc.

TV series: Captain David Grief 56.

Reed, Michael (1929–).
British cinematographer.

October Moth 60. Linda 61. The Gorgon 64. Dracula Prince of Darkness 66. On Her Majesty's Secret Service 69. The Mackenzie Break 71. The Groundstar Conspiracy 73. The Hireling 73. Galileo 75. Shout at the Devil 76. Loophole 80. Kim (TV) 84. Wild Geese 85, etc.

Reed, Oliver (1938–).
Burly British leading man, usually in sullen roles.

The Rebel 60. No Love for Johnnie 61. Curse of the Werewolf 61. Pirates of Blood River 62. *The Damned* 62. Paranoic 63. *The System* 64. The Scarlet Blade 64. The Party's Over 64. The Brigand of Kandahar 65. *The Trap* 66. The Shuttered Room 66. *The Jokers* 66. I'll Never Forget Whatshisname 67. The Assassination Bureau 68. Oliver! 68. Hannibal Brooks 68. *Women in Love* 69. Take a Girl Like You 69. The Lady in the Car 70. The Devils 71. The Hunting Party 71. Z.P.G. 72. Sitting Target 72. Triple Echo 72. Days of Fury 73. The Three Musketeers 73. The Four Musketeers 74. And Then There Were None 74. Royal Flash 74. Tommy 75. The Sellout 75. Great Scout and Cathouse Thursday 76. Burnt Offerings 76. The Prince and the Pauper 77. The Big Sleep 78. Tomorrow Never

Comes 78. The Class of Miss MacMichael 78. The Brood 79. Lion of the Desert 81. Dr Heckyl and Mr Hype 81. Condorman 81. Venom 81. The Sting II 82 Masquerade (TV) 82. Second Chance 84. Christopher Columbus (TV) 84. Black Arrow (TV) 85. Castaway 87. The Adventures of Baron Munchausen 89. Return of the Musketeers 90. Hold My Hand I'm Dying 90. The Pit and the Pendulum 90. The House of Usher 91. Prisoners of Honor (TV) 91. The Mummy Lives 92. Return to Lonesome Dove (TV) 93, etc.

Reed, Pamela (1953–).
American leading actress.
The Long Riders 80. Melvin and Howard 80. Eyewitness (aka The Janitor) 81. Young Doctors in Love 82. The Right Stuff 83. The Best of Times 86. Tanner '88 (TV) 88. Rachel River 89. Chattahoochee 89. Cadillac Man 90. Kindergarten Cop 90. Caroline? (TV) 90. Passed Away 92.
TV series: Andros Targets 77.

Reed, Philip (1908–).
American leading man with long stage experience.
Female 34. Last of the Mohicans 36. Aloma of the South Seas 41. Old Acquaintance 44. I Cover Big Town 47. Unknown Island 50. The Tattered Dress 57. Harem Scarem 67, etc.

Reed, Rex (1938–).
American interviewer and showbiz gossip columnist. Collections published include *Valentines and Vitriol, Do You Really Sleep in the Nude?, Big Screen Little Screen* and *Conversations in the Raw.* Not a great success as an actor when he played the transsexual *Myra Breckinridge.*

reel.
A loose term generally taken to mean 1,000 feet of 35mm film, i.e. the amount which would fit on to a reel of the old-fashioned kind, running about ten minutes. Thus short films were spoken of as two-reelers, three-reelers, etc., and charged accordingly. But modern 35mm projector spools will take 2,000 feet and sometimes 3,000 feet, so the term is slowly falling into disuse . . . especially as 16mm projectors have always taken spools of either 400, 800 or 1,600 feet.

Rees, Angharad (1949–).
Welsh leading lady.
Hands of the Ripper 72. Under Milk Wood 72. The Love Ban 73. Moments 74. The Curse of King Tut's Tomb (TV) 80, etc.

Rees, Roger (1944–).
Introspective Welsh actor and theatre director. Born in Aberystwyth, he studied art at the Slade, made his stage debut at the age of 22, and was in films from 1983. A leading member of the Royal Shakespeare Company for eight years, he played the title role in its notable production of *Nicholas Nickleby,* which was also televised.
A Bouquet of Barbed Wire (TV) 76. Star 80 83. A Christmas Carol (TV) 84. Ebony Tower (TV) 86. Mountains of the Moon 90. If Looks Could Kill 91. Stop or My Mom Will Shoot 91. Robin Hood: Men in Tights 93, etc.
TV series; Cheers 89–91.

Reese, Tom (1930–).
American character actor, a notable 'heavy'.
Flaming Star 60. Marines Let's Go 61. Forty Pounds of Trouble 62. Murderers' Row 66. Vanishing Point 71, etc.

Reeve, Ada (1874–1966).
British character actress and singer whose career

lasted more than 80 years. Born in Whitechapel, London, she appeared in pantomime at the age of four and made her music-hall debut when she was 12. She became a star of musicals in the 1890s, touring the world until the mid-30s when she turned to acting on stage and in films.
Autobiography: 1954, *Take It for a Fact.*
They Came to a City 44. When the Bough Breaks 47. Night and the City 50. Eye Witness 56. The Passionate Stranger (US: A Novel Affair) 57, etc.

Reeve, Christopher (1952–).
Strapping American leading man who flew to fame.
■ Gray Lady Down 77. *Superman* 78. Superman II 80. Somewhere in Time 80. Death Trap 82. Monsignor 82. Superman III 83. The Aviator 84. The Bostonians 84. Anna Karenina (TV) 84. Street Smart 87. Superman IV 87. Switching Channels 88. The Great Escape II: The Untold Story (TV) 88. The Rose and the Jackal (TV) 90. Bump in the Night 90. Noises Off 92. The Sea Wolf (TV) 93. Black Fox 93. Morning Glory 93. The Remains of the Day 93. Above Suspicion 94.

Reeve, Geoffrey (1932–).
British director.
Puppet on a Chain 71. Caravan to Vaccares 74. Souvenir (TV) 88.
In the 80s turned producer with such projects as *The Far Pavilions, The Shooting Party, The Whistle Blower.*

Reeves, George (1914–1959) (George Brewer).
American leading man. Typecast as Superman, he found no parts available for him and became a wrestler. Shot himself.
Gone with the Wind (debut) 39. Strawberry Blonde 41. Blood and Sand 42. Bar 20 44. Jungle Jim 49. Samson and Delilah 50. Sir Galahad (serial) 50. From Here to Eternity 53.
TV series: Superman 51–57.

Reeves, Keanu (1964–).
American leading actor. The success of *Speed* (for which he was reportedly paid $1.25m) put his price up to $7m a film.
Flying 86. Youngblood 86. River's Edge 87. Dangerous Liaisons 88. The Night Before 88. Permanent Record 88. The Prince of Pennsylvania 88. Bill and Ted's Excellent Adventure 89. I Love You to Death 90. Tune in Tomorrow (aka Aunt Julia and the Scriptwriter) 90. Point Break 91. Bill and Ted's Bogus Journey 91. My Own Private Idaho 91. Bram Stoker's Dracula 92. Much Ado about Nothing 93. Even Cowgirls Get the Blues 93. Little Buddha 93. Speed 94. Johnny Mnemonic 95. A Walk in the Clouds 95, etc.

Reeves, Kynaston (1893–1971).
British character actor of stage and screen, often seen as academic. In films from 1919.
The Lodger 32. The Housemaster 38. The Prime Minister 40. Vice Versa 48. The Guinea Pig 49. The Mudlark 50. Top of the Form 53. Brothers in Law 57. School for Scoundrels 60. The Private Life of Sherlock Holmes 70, many others.

Reeves, Michael (1944–1969).
British director whose promising career barely got started.
■ Sister of Satan (Revenge of the Blood Beast) (It.) 65. The Sorcerers 67. Witchfinder General 68.

Reeves, Saskia.
British leading actress, from the stage.

December Bride 90. The Bridge 90. Close My Eyes 91. Antonia and Jane 91. Traps 94, etc.

Reeves, Steve (1926–).
American actor, formerly 'Mr World' and 'Mr Universe'; found stardom from 1953 in Italian muscleman spectacles.
■ Athena 54. The Labours of Hercules 57. Hercules and the Queen of Sheba (Hercules Unchained) 58. The White Warrior 58. Goliath and the Barbarians 59. The Giant of Marathon 59. The White Devil 59. The Last Days of Pompeii 59. Thief of Baghdad 60. Morgan the Pirate 60. The Wooden Horse of Troy 61. Duel of the Titans (Romulus and Remus) 61. Son of Spartacus 62. War of the Trojans 62. Sandokan the Great 63. The Pirates of Malaya 64. A Long Ride from Hell 68.

Reggiani, Serge (1922–).
Slightly-built French-Italian actor with stage experience.
Les Portes de la Nuit 46. Manon 48. Les Amants de Vérone 48. La Ronde 50. Secret People (GB) 51. *Casque d'Or* 51. The Wicked Go to Hell 55. Les Misérables 57. Marie Octobre 58. Paris Blues 60. The Leopard 63. The 25th Hour 67. Les Aventuriers 67. Day of the Owl (It.) 68. The Good and the Bad 76. Cat and Mouse 76. L'Empreinte des Géantes 80. Fantastica 80. I Hired a Contract Killer 90, etc.

Reichenbach, François (1922–1993).
French documentarist with an ironic viewpoint.
L'Amérique Insolite 59. Un Coeur Gros Comme Ça 61. Les Amoureux du France 64. Hollywood through a Keyhole 66. Love of Life (co-d) 68. F for Fake (co-d) 75. Sex O'Clock 76. Pele 77. Houston, Texas 80. François Reichenbach's Japan 83. Visages Suisses (co-d) 91, etc.

Reicher, Frank (1875–1965).
German-born character actor, long in Hollywood.
Her Man O' War 26. Mata Hari 32. *King Kong* 33. Kind Lady 36. Anthony Adverse 36. Lancer Spy 38. They Dare Not Love 41. House of Frankenstein 45. The Mummy's Ghost 46. The Secret Life of Walter Mitty 47. Samson and Delilah 50, many others.
AS DIRECTOR: The Eternal Mother 17. Behind Masks 21. Wise Husbands 21, etc.

Reid, Alastair (1939–).
British director. From the mid-70s on, working in television.
■ Baby Love 69. The Night Digger 71. Something to Hide 72. Man on the Screen (TV) 83.

Reid, Beryl (1920–).
British revue comedienne who has latterly weathered a transition to character acting.
The Belles of St Trinian's 54. The Extra Day 56. The Dock Brief 62. Star! 68. Inspector Clouseau 68. The Assassination Bureau 68. *The Killing of Sister George* (her stage role) (US) 68. Entertaining Mr Sloane 70. The Beast in the Cellar 71. Dr Phibes Rises Again 72. Psychomania 72. Father Dear Father 73. No Sex Please We're British 73. Joseph Andrews 76. Smiley's People (TV) 82. Yellowbeard 83. The Doctor and the Devils 85, etc.

Reid, Carl Benton (1894–1973).
American character actor with stage career before settling in Hollywood.
The Little Foxes 41. In a Lonely Place 50. Convicted 50. The Great Caruso 51. Lorna Doone 51. Carbine Williams 52. The Egyptian 54. The Left Hand of God 55. The Gallant Hours 59, etc.
TV series: Amos Burke – Secret Agent 65.

Reid, Elliott (1920–).
American comedy actor who often played the dumb son of an executive.
The Story of Dr Wassell 44. Gentlemen Prefer Blondes 53. Woman's World 54. Inherit the Wind 60. Who's Been Sleeping in My Bed? 63. The Thrill of It All 63. Some Kind of a Nut 69, etc.

Reid, Kate (1930–1993).
Canadian actress.
This Property Is Condemned 66. The Andromeda Strain 71. Death Among Friends (TV) 75. Equus 77. Atlantic City USA 81. Fire with Fire 86. Sweethearts Dance 88. Bye Bye Blues 90. Deceived 91, etc.
TV series: The Whiteoaks of Jalna 72.

Reid, Wallace (1890–1923).
American leading man of the silent screen.
The Deerslayer 11. The Birth of a Nation 14. The Love Mask 16. House of Silence 18. The Dancing Fool 20. The Affairs of Anatol 21. Forever 21. The Ghost Breaker 22, many others.

reincarnation
has seldom been seriously tackled in the cinema: The Search for Bridey Murphy, I've Lived Before and The Reincarnation of Peter Proud are almost the only examples. Many characters of farce and melodrama have thought they were reincarnated, including the hero of She and heroine of The Vengeance of She. The real thing happened to Oliver Hardy in The Flying Deuces (he came back as a horse); to a dog in You Never Can Tell (he came back as Dick Powell); and to the luckless heroine of The Bride and the Beast, who found that in a former existence she had been a gorilla. Reincarnation was also the basis of Here Comes Mr Jordan, and of The Mummy. A man came back as Debbie Reynolds in Goodbye Charlie, and in Quest for Love there were parallel love stories two centuries apart. In 1968 a version was made of Elmer Rice's The Adding Machine, with its celestial laundry for souls; and in 1970 there was even a musical on the subject, On a Clear Day You Can See Forever.

Reiner, Carl (1922–).
Balding, genial American comedy writer and actor.
AS ACTOR: Happy Anniversary 59. The Gazebo 59. Gidget Goes Hawaiian 61. It's a Mad Mad Mad Mad World 63. The Art of Love 65. The Russians Are Coming, the Russians Are Coming 66. A Guide for the Married Man 67. The Comic 69. The End 78, etc.
TV series: Good Heavens 76.
AS WRITER: The Thrill of It All 63. The Art of Love 65. Enter Laughing 67. The Comic 69. The Jerk 79. Dead Men Don't Wear Plaid 82. The Man with Two Brains (co-w) 83.
TV series: The Dick Van Dyke Show 61–65.
AS DIRECTOR: Enter Laughing 67. The Comic 69. Where's Poppa? 70. Oh God 77. The Jerk 79. Dead Men Don't Wear Plaid 82. The Man with Two Brains 83. Summer School 87. Bert Rigby, You're a Fool (wd) 89. Triple Indemnity 93. Fatal Instinct 93, etc.

Reiner, Rob (1945–).
American director, writer and former comic actor. He is the son of director Carl Reiner and was formerly married to actress and director Penny Marshall.
This Is Spinal Tap 85. The Sure Thing 85. Stand by Me 86. The Princess Bride 87. When Harry Met Sally 89. Postcards from the Edge 90. Misery 90. Spirit of '76 90. Regarding Henry 91. Sleepless in Seattle (a) 93. North 94. Bullets over Broadway (a) 94. Lifesavers (a) 94, etc.

TV series: All in the Family (a) 71–78. Free Country (a) 78.

Reinhardt, Gottfried (1911–1994).
Austrian producer, son of theatrical producer Max Reinhardt. Went to US with his father and became assistant to Walter Wanger. Produced and occasionally directed.
The Great Waltz (script) 38. Comrade X (p) 40. Two-Faced Woman (p) 41. Command Decision (p) 48. The Red Badge of Courage (p) 51. Invitation (d) 52. The Story of Three Loves (d) 53. Betrayed (d) 54. The Good Soldier Schweik (p) 59. Town without Pity (p, d) 61. Situation Hopeless but Not Serious (p, d) 65, etc.

Reinhardt, Max (1873–1943) (Max Goldman).
Austrian theatrical producer of great pageants. His only sound screen direction (with William Dieterle) was A Midsummer Night's Dream 35, from his stage production. He had made three German silents between 1908 and 1914.

Reinhold, Judge (1956–).
American actor.
Running Scared 79. Stripes 81. Fast Times at Ridgemont High 82. The Lords of Discipline 83. Beverly Hills Cop 84. Gremlins 84. Head Office 86. Offbeat 86. Ruthless People 86. Beverly Hills Cop II 87. Vice Versa 88. Rosalie Goes Shopping 89. Daddy's Dyin', Who's Got the Will? 90. Zandalee 90. Baby on Board 92. Bank Robber 93. Beverly Hills Cop III 94. The Santa Clause 94, etc.

Reiniger, Lotte (1899–1981).
German animator, well known for her silhouette cartoons.
The Adventures of Prince Achmed 26. Dr Dolittle (series) 28. Carmen 33. Papageno 35. The Brave Little Tailor 55, etc.

Reinking, Ann (1949–).
American dancer, from Broadway.
■ Movie Movie 78. All That Jazz 79. Annie 82. Micki & Maude 84.

Reis, Irving (1906–1953).
American director, with radio experience.
■ One Crowded Night 40. I'm Still Alive 40. Weekend for Three 41. A Date with the Falcon 41. The Gay Falcon 41. The Falcon Takes Over 42. The Big Street 43. Hitler's Children 43. Crack Up 46. The Bachelor and the Bobby-soxer 47. Enchantment 48. All My Sons 48. Roseanna McCoy 49. Dancing in the Dark 49. Three Husbands 50. New Mexico 51. The Fourposter 52.

Reisch, Walter (1900–1983).
Austrian writer who in the 30s came to Britain, then Hollywood.
Men Are Not Gods (& d) 36. Ninotchka (AAN) 39. Comrade X (AAN) 40. The Heavenly Body 43. Gaslight (co-w, AAN) 44. Song of Scheherazade (& d) 46. Titanic (AA) 52. The Girl in the Red Velvet Swing 55. Journey to the Centre of the Earth 59, etc.

Reiser, Paul (1956–).
American actor and comedian.
Diner 82. Sunset Limousine 83. Beverly Hills Cop 84. From Here to Maternity (TV) 85. Odd Jobs 85. Aliens 86. Beverly Hills Cop II 87. Cross My Heart 88. Crazy People 90. Family Prayers 91. The Marrying Man 91, etc.
TV series: My Two Dads 87–90.

Reisner, Allen.
American director, from TV.

■ All Mine to Give 56. St Louis Blues 58. To Die in Paris (TV) (co-d) 68. Your Money or Your Wife (TV) 72. Captains and the Kings (TV) 86. Mary Jane Harper Cried Last Night (TV) 77. Cops and Robin (TV) 78. The Love Tapes (TV) 80.

Reisner, Charles (1887–1962).
American director.
The Man in the Box 25. Reducing 32. The Show-Off 34. Sophie Lang Goes West 37. The Big Store 41. Meet the People 44. Lost in a Harem 44. The Cobra Strikes 48. The Travelling Saleswoman 50, many others, mainly second features.

Reisz, Karel (1926–).
Czech director, in Britain from childhood. Former film critic. In recent years he has been working mainly as a theatre director.
■ We are the Lambeth Boys 58. Saturday Night and Sunday Morning 60. Night Must Fall 63. This Sporting Life (p only) 63. Morgan: A Suitable Case for Treatment 66. Isadora 68. The Gambler 74. Who'll Stop the Rain? 78. The French Lieutenant's Woman 81. Sweet Dreams 86. Everybody Wins 88.

Reitherman, Wolfgang (1909–1985).
American animator, director of Disney cartoon features from the mid-60s.

Reitman, Ivan (1946–).
Canadian director and producer.
■ Foxy Lady 71. Cannibal Girls 73. Meatballs 79. Stripes (p, d) 81. Ghostbusters 84. Legal Eagles 86. Twins 88. Ghostbusters II (p, d) 89. Kindergarten Cop (p, d) 90. Stop or My Mom Will Shoot (p) 91. Beethoven (p) 92. Dave 93. Junior 94.

Reizenstein, Franz (1911–1968).
German-born composer who scored British horror movies. In films from 1951.
The Mummy 59. The White Trap 59. Jessy 60. Circus of Horrors 60, etc.

rejuvenation
is not a theme the cinema has frequently explored. She tried it several times with unhappy results, as did Laurel and Hardy in Dirty Work (Olly came back as a chimpanzee). The Man in Half Moon Street and Countess Dracula both kept young on the blood of others; Dorian Gray did it by keeping a picture of himself in the attic. Most successful were Lost Horizon's inhabitants of Shangri-La, but once the cold winds of the outside world blew they were done for. Rock Hudson had worse luck in Seconds. Cocoon introduced alien aid to staying young, although Cocoon: The Return showed that there was no permanent solution to the problems of age.

religion
has inspired film-makers from the beginning – as a commercial trump card. In the early years of the century it was the Italians who produced vast semi-biblical spectacles like Quo Vadis and Cabiria, but Hollywood was not slow to catch on, and producers soon found that religious shorts gave them extra prestige. There were several versions of From the Manger to the Cross; Griffith, in Judith of Bethulia and Intolerance, contributed his share; Ben Hur was the biggest spectacular of all; but it was Cecil B. de Mille in the 20s who brought the Bible to full commercial flower with The Ten Commandments and King of Kings. (His 1932 The Sign of the Cross, 1950 Samson and Delilah and 1956 remake of The Ten Commandments still stand for him at least time continued to stand still.) In 1929, though Noah's Ark was spectacle pure and

simple, Vidor's *Hallelujah* at least partially
transmitted Negro religious fervour. In the 30s
Hollywood was seeking fresh ways to combine
religion with sentiment or spectacle, in *The Cradle
Song*, *Dante's Inferno*, *The Garden of Allah*, *The Green
Light* and *Boys' Town*. One result was a new
characterization of priests (qv) as jolly good fellows:
stars like Spencer Tracy and Pat O'Brien were
eager to play them. Yet none had the quiet dignity
of Rex Ingram as De Lawd in *Green Pastures*, a
Negro version of the Scriptures.

The war naturally brought a religious revival.
Every film set in England seemed to end with a
service in a bombed church, and religious figures
became big time in films like *The Song of
Bernadette*, *Going My Way*, *The Keys of the Kingdom*
and *The Bells of St Mary's*. Savage war films
masqueraded under such titles as *God Is My Co-Pilot*
and *A Wing and a Prayer*. And heaven was used
as a background for light-hearted fantasy films
about death and judgement day, such as *Here Comes
Mr Jordan*, *Heaven Can Wait*, and *The Horn Blows at
Midnight*. The only film of this period to question
religion at all was the British *Major Barbara*: 'What
price salvation now?'

In the cynical post-war years religion was at a
low ebb. An expensive *Joan of Arc* in 1948 failed
disastrously, and an attempt to bring God into our
everyday life, *The Next Voice You Hear*, fared no
better. A sincere performance by Robert Donat
could not bring people to see *Lease of Life*. Indeed,
the only religious films to break even at the box
office were those with a direct Roman Catholic
appeal, such as *Monsieur Vincent* and *The Miracle of
Fatima*. True religion, to Hollywood, was out, and
the Bible became once more a source book for a
string of tawdry commercial epics: *Quo Vadis*,
Salome, *The Prodigal*, *The Robe*, a remake of *Ben
Hur*, *Barabbas*, *The Silver Chalice*, *Sodom and
Gomorrah* and many cut-rate dubbed Italian
spectacles of a similar kind (most with Hollywood
stars). Occasionally a spark of sincerity would flash
through, as in the otherwise dull *David and
Bathsheba*; while small independent companies
could produce interesting films like *The First
Legion*. Towards the end of the 50s there were
occasional attempts to see religion afresh: *A Man
Called Peter*, *The Nun's Story*, *Inn of the Sixth
Happiness*, *Whistle Down the Wind*. Otto Preminger,
despite a 1957 failure with *Saint Joan*, tried again
in 1963 with *The Cardinal*. In 1965 George Stevens
unveiled *The Greatest Story Ever Told*, a tepid life of
Jesus which found little box-office favour, being
overtaken in some quarters by Pasolini's *The Gospel
According to St Matthew*. 1966 brought the long-
promised Italian-American epic known as *The
Bible*: in fact it dealt only with the Book of
Genesis, and that at such a dull pace and inordinate
length that it is doubtful whether sequels will be
called for. 1969 offered a drama of modern popes,
The Shoes of the Fisherman, but it died. The most
fashionable film interpretations of religion in the
early 70s were the pop operas exemplified by
Godspell and *Jesus Christ Superstar*; but in 1977 Lew
Grade's mammoth six-hour *Jesus of Nazareth*,
directed by Franco Zeffirelli, achieved record
viewing figures and pointed to a benighted world's
requirement to believe in *something*.

Martin Scorsese's *The Last Temptation of Christ* 88
focused on Jesus's self-doubts as he faced his
crucifixion, while Michael Tolkin's *The Rapture* 91
dealt in fundamentalist terms with the end of the
world, complete with the Four Horsemen of the
Apocalypse.

Relph, George (1888–1960).
British character actor mainly seen on stage.
Nicholas Nickleby 47. I Believe in You 52. The

Titfield Thunderbolt (leading role as the vicar) 53.
Doctor at Large 57. Davy 57. etc.

Relph, Michael (1915–).
British producer-director, son of George Relph.
Former art director and production designer; from
1947 to 1969 he worked almost exclusively with
Basil Dearden, usually producing while Dearden
directed.
The Captive Heart 46. Frieda 47. Saraband for
Dead Lovers 48. *The Blue Lamp* 50. I Believe in You
(& co-w) 52. The Rainbow Jacket 54. Davy (d) 57.
Rockets Galore (d) 57. Violent Playground 58.
Sapphire 59. *The League of Gentlemen* 59. *Victim* 61.
Life for Ruth 62. The Mind Benders 63. Woman of
Straw 63. Masquerade 65. The Assassination
Bureau 68. An Unsuitable Job for a Woman 82, etc.

Relph, Simon (1940–).
English producer, the son of Michael Relph.
Reds 81. The Return of the Soldier 81. Privates
on Parade 82. The Ploughman's Lunch 83.
Laughterhouse 84. Secret Places 85. Wetherby 85.
Comrades 87. Enchanted April 91. Damage 92.
Camilla 94, etc.

remakes in disguise.
Hollywood studios were famous for squeezing
every drop of value from a literary property, even
if it meant changing the locale, switching the sexes
and generally bamboozling the audience, which
hopefully would not get that I-have-been-here-
before feeling until they were half-way home.
Here are just a few movies which went through a
change of title but used up the same old plot:
▶ *Sentimental Journey; The Gift of Love*
▶ *Libelled Lady; Easy to Wed*
▶ *Here Comes Mr Jordan; Heaven Can Wait*
▶ *Love Is News; Sweet Rosie O'Grady; That Wonderful
Urge*
▶ *The Bowery; Coney Island; Wabash Avenue*
▶ *The Greeks Had a Word for Them; Ladies in Love;
Three Blind Mice; Moon over Miami; Three Little
Girls in Blue; How to Marry a Millionaire; Three
Coins in the Fountain; The Pleasure Seekers*
▶ *Kentucky; Down Argentine Way*
▶ *Folies Bergère; That Night in Rio; On the Riviera;
On the Double*
▶ *The Front Page; His Girl Friday; Torrid Zone;
Switching Channels*
▶ *Gunga Din; Sergeants Three*
▶ *My Favorite Wife; Move Over Darling*
▶ *Grand Hotel; Weekend at the Waldorf*
▶ *It Happened One Night; You Can't Run Away From
It*
▶ *Tiger Shark; Slim; Manpower*
▶ *House of Strangers; Broken Lance*
▶ *High Sierra; I Died a Thousand Times*
▶ *20,000 Years in Sing Sing; Castle on the Hudson*
▶ *Mystery of the Wax Museum; House of Wax*
▶ *One Way Passage; Till We Meet Again*
▶ *Bordertown; They Drive by Night*
▶ *Dangerous; Singapore Woman*
▶ *The Petrified Forest; Escape in the Desert*
▶ *Four Daughters; Young at Heart*
▶ *Dr Socrates; King of the Underworld*
▶ *The Butter and Egg Man; The Tenderfoot; Dance
Charlie Dance; An Angel from Texas*
▶ *The Most Dangerous Game; A Game of Death; Run
for the Sun*
▶ *The Kennel Murder Case; Calling Philo Vance*
▶ *The Letter; The Unfaithful*
▶ *The Mouthpiece; The Man Who Talked Too Much;
Illegal*
▶ *Oil for the Lamps of China; Law of the Tropics*
▶ *The Sea Wolf; Wolf Larsen; Barricade; Wolf of the
Seven Seas*
▶ *Kid Galahad; The Wagons Roll at Night*

▶ *Casablanca; Far East*
▶ *The Man Who Played God; Sincerely Yours*
▶ *The Millionaire; That Way with Women*
▶ *The Miracle of Morgan's Creek; Rock-a-bye Baby*
▶ *Anna and the King of Siam; The King and I*
▶ *London After Midnight; Mark of the Vampire*
▶ *Love Affair; An Affair to Remember*
▶ *Morning Glory; Stage Struck*
▶ *The Lady Eve; The Birds and the Bees*
▶ *The Marriage Circle; One Hour with You*
▶ *Nothing Sacred; Living It Up*
▶ *Dark Victory; Stolen Hours*
▶ *One Sunday Afternoon; The Strawberry Blonde*
▶ *A Slight Case of Murder; Stop! You're Killing Me*
▶ *The Paleface; The Shakiest Gun in the West*
▶ *Le Jour Se Lève; The Long Night*
▶ *The Women; The Opposite Sex*
▶ *The Asphalt Jungle; The Badlanders; Cairo; Cool
Breeze*
▶ *The Four Feathers; Storm over the Nile*
▶ *It Started with Eve; I'd Rather Be Rich*
▶ *Rome Express; Sleeping Car to Trieste*
▶ *This Gun for Hire; Short Cut to Hell*
▶ *The Informer; Uptight*
▶ *Against All Flags; The King's Pirate*
▶ *Red Dust; Congo Maisie; Mogambo*
▶ *An American Tragedy; A Place in the Sun*
▶ *Outward Bound; Between Two Worlds*
▶ *Ebb Tide; Adventure Island*
▶ *Ah, Wilderness; Summer Holiday*

Remar, James (1953–).
American actor, often as a heavy.
The Warriors 79. Cruising 80. The Long Riders
80. Windwalker 81. 48 Hours 82. The Cotton Club
84. Quiet Cool 86. The Clan of the Cave Bear 86.
Rent-a-Cop 88. The Dream Team 89. Drugstore
Cowboy 89. Tales from the Darkside: The Movie
90. The Tigress (Die Tigerin) 92. Fatal Instinct 93.
Renaissance Man 94. Blink 94, etc.

Remarque, Erich Maria (1898–1970).
German novelist.
All Quiet on the Western Front 30. The Road
Back 37. Three Comrades 38. So Ends Our Night
41. Arch of Triumph 48. A Time to Love and a
Time to Die (& a) 57. All Quiet on the Western
Front (TV) 79, etc.

Remick, Lee (1935–1991).
American leading lady with stage and TV
experience.
A Face in the Crowd (film debut) 57. The Long
Hot Summer 58. Anatomy of a Murder 59. Sanctuary
61. Experiment in Terror 62. Days of Wine and Roses
(AAN) 63. The Wheeler Dealers 64. Baby the Rain
Must Fall 65. The Hallelujah Trail 65. No Way to
Treat a Lady 68. A Severed Head 70. Loot 70.
Sometimes a Great Notion 72. A Delicate Balance
73. QB VII 74. The Blue Knight (TV) 74. Hennessy
75. Jennie (TV) 75. The Omen 76. Telefon 77. The
Medusa Touch 77. Ike (TV) 79. The Europeans
79. Torn between Two Lovers (TV) 79. The
Competition 80. Tribute 80. The Women's Room
(TV) 80. The Letter (TV) 82. Mistral's Daughter
(TV) 84. Emma's War 85. The Vision 87, etc.

¶ It would be nice to make films for grown-ups
again, and when they decide to start filming
them, I'll start acting in them. – *L.R.*

Renaldo, Duncan (1904–1980) (Renault Renaldo
Duncan).
American actor and painter with varied
experience. In many films from *Trader Horn* 30 to
For Whom the Bell Tolls 43; later more famous as
The Cisco Kid in a series of second-feature
westerns (1945–50). Directed some films in the

20s. Also a screenwriter under the name Renault Duncan.

Renaud, Madeleine (1903–1994).
Distinguished French stage actress, in occasional films. Married Jean-Louis Barrault, with whom she ran the post-war Compagnie Renaud-Barrault, acting in many of its notable productions.

Vent Debout 22. Jean de la Lune 31. La Maternelle 32. The Naked Heart (Maria Chapdelaine) 34. Stormy Waters (Remorques) 41. The Woman Who Dared (Le Ciel Est à Vous) 44. Le Plaisir 52. The Longest Day 62. The Devil by the Tail (Le Diable par la Queue) 69. La Mandarine 72. etc.

Rennahan, Ray (1896–1980).
American cinematographer, in Hollywood from 1917; an expert on colour.
Fanny Foley Herself 31. *The Mystery of the Wax Museum* 33. *Becky Sharp* 35. *Wings of the Morning* 37. *Gone with the Wind* (co-ph) (AA) 39. *The Blue Bird* 40. Down Argentine Way 40. *Blood and Sand* (co-ph) (AA) 42. *For Whom the Bell Tolls* 43. Belle of the Yukon 44. The Perils of Pauline 47. The Paleface 48. A Yankee at King Arthur's Court 49. Arrowhead 53. Terror in a Texas Town 58, many others.

Rennie, James (1890–1965).
American hero of the 20s.
Remodelling Her Husband 20. The Dust Flower 22. His Children's Children 23. Clothes Make the Pirate 25. The Girl of the Golden West 30. Illicit 31, etc.

Rennie, Michael (1909–1971).
Lean, good-looking British leading man best known as TV's *The Third Man*. Varied experience before going into repertory and film stand-in work.
Secret Agent 36. The Divorce of Lady X 38. Dangerous Moonlight 40. Ships with Wings 41. I'll Be Your Sweetheart 45. *The Wicked Lady* 45. The Root of All Evil 47. Idol of Paris 48. The Black Rose 50; Then to US; Five Fingers 52. Les Misérables 52. *The Day the Earth Stood Still* 52. The Robe 53. Désirée 54. The Rains of Ranchipur 55. Island in the Sun 56. Omar Khayyam 57. Third Man on the Mountain 59. *The Lost World* 60. Mary, Mary 63. Ride beyond Vengeance 65. The Power 67. Hotel 67. The Devil's Brigade 68. The Battle of El Alamein (as Montgomery) 68. Subterfuge 69, etc.

Réno, Jean (1948–).
French leading actor, born in Casablanca, and a constant presence in the films of Luc Besson.
The Last Battle (Le Dernier Combat) 83. The Big Blue (Le Grand Bleu) 88. Nikita (US: La Femme Nikita) 90. Operation Corned-Beef 91. L'Homme au Masque d'Or 91. Leon (US: The Professional) 94, etc.

Renoir, Claude (1914–1993).
French cinematographer.
Toni 34. Une Partie de Campagne 36. La Règle du Jeu 39. Monsieur Vincent 47. *The River* 51. The Green Glove 52. *The Golden Coach* 53. Eléna et les Hommes 56. Crime and Punishment 56. The Witches of Salem 56. Les Tricheurs 58. *Blood and Roses* 60. Lafayette 61. Circus World 64. The Game is Over 66. Barbarella 68. The Madwoman of Chaillot (co-ph) 69. The Horsemen 71. Paul and Michelle 74. The Spy Who Loved Me 77. Le Toubib 79, many others.

Renoir, Jean (1894–1979).
Distinguished French director, son of painter Auguste Renoir, brother of Pierre Renoir. Stage experience in productions of his own plays.
Autobiographies: 1973, My Life and My Films. Letters by Jean Renoir edited by Lorraine Lo Bianco and David Thompson.
Biographies: 1977, Jean Renoir, the World of His Films by Len Brandy. 1991, Jean Renoir – a Life in Pictures by Célia Bertin.
La Fille de L'Eau 24. Nana 26. Charleston 27. The Little Match-Seller 28. *La Chienne* 31. *Boudu Sauvé des Eaux* 32. Toni 34. Madame Bovary 34. *Le Crime de Monsieur Lange* 35. *Les Bas Fonds* 36. *Une Partie de Campagne* 36. *La Grande Illusion* 37. *La Marseillaise* 38. *La Bête Humaine* 38. *La Règle du Jeu* (& a) 39; to US; Swamp Water 41. This Land Is Mine 43. *The Southerner* (AAN) 44. Diary of a Chambermaid 45. The Woman on the Beach 47. Back to Europe. The River 51. The Golden Coach 53. French Cancan 55. Eléna et les Hommes 56. Lunch on the Grass 59. The Vanishing Corporal 61. C'est la Révolution 67. Le Petit Théâtre de Jean Renoir 69, etc.

¶ Renoir has a lot of talent, but he isn't one of us. – Darryl F. Zanuck
Life was not so much the subject as the *stuff* of his movies, spilling over the edges of his frames. – Newsweek
Only when style is confused with meaningless flourishes does Renoir's economy of expression seem inadequate for textbook critics. – Andrew Sarris, 1968
My dream is of a craftsman's cinema in which the author can express himself as directly as the painter in his paintings or the writer in his books. – J.R.
A director makes only one film in his life. Then he breaks it into pieces and makes it again. – J.R.
The saving grace of the cinema is that with patience, and a little love, we may arrive at that wonderfully complex creature which is called man. – J.R.

Renoir, Pierre (1885–1952).
French character actor, brother of Jean Renoir.
Madame Bovary 34. La Marseillaise 38. Les Enfants du Paradis 44. Doctor Knock 50, many others.

Renzi, Eva (1944–).
German leading lady in international films.
Funeral in Berlin 66. The Pink Jungle 68. Beiss Mich Liebling 70. La Chambre Voisine 80, etc.

reporters
in American films have since the beginning of the sound era been pictured as trench-coated, trilby-hatted, good-looking guys with a smart line in wisecracks. Among the outstanding examples of this tradition are Pat O'Brien in *The Front Page*, Robert Williams in *Platinum Blonde*, Clark Gable in *It Happened One Night* and *Teacher's Pet*, Fredric March in *Nothing Sacred*, Lee Tracy in *Doctor X*, Joel McCrea in *Foreign Correspondent*, David Janssen in *The Green Berets*, James Stewart in *The Philadelphia Story*, Lynne Overman in *Roxie Hart*, Gene Kelly in *Inherit the Wind*; while on the distaff side one can't overlook Glenda Farrell in *The Mystery of the Wax Museum*, Bette Davis in *Front Page Woman*, Jean Arthur in *Mr Deeds Goes to Town*, Rosalind Russell in *His Girl Friday* or Barbara Stanwyck in *Meet John Doe*. Presented somewhat more realistically were William Alland in *Citizen Kane*, James Stewart in *Call Northside 777*, Burgess Meredith as Ernie Pyle in *The Story of G.I. Joe*, Kirk Douglas in *Ace in the Hole*, and Arthur Kennedy in

Lawrence of Arabia. The apotheosis of the reporter as hero was *All the President's Men*, with Robert Redford and Dustin Hoffman as Bob Woodward and Carl Bernstein of *The Washington Post* investigating Watergate.
British films have used their newshawks more flippantly, especially in the case of *This Man Is News* with Barry K. Barnes and *A Run for Your Money* with Alec Guinness. Just as well; for Edward Judd in *The Day the Earth Caught Fire*, Jack Hawkins in *Front Page Story*, Sidney James in *Quatermass II* and Norman Wooland in *All Over the Town* were a pretty dull lot, and Colin Gordon's imitation of the American model in *Escapade* was hardly convincing. Television series, of course, have found the reporter a convenient peg, as in the British *Deadline Midnight* and the American *Saints and Sinners* and *The Reporter*.

Republic Pictures Corporation.
A small Hollywood production and distribution company founded in 1935 by a former tobacco executive named Herbert J. Yates (qv) who had spent some years building up a film laboratory. Republic continued as a one-man concern, producing innumerable competently-made second-feature westerns and melodramas with such stars as Roy Rogers, Vera Hruba Ralston (Yates' wife), John Carroll, Constance Moore. The studio also churned out the majority of Hollywood's serials. Very occasionally there would be a major production such as *Rio Grande* or *The Quiet Man*. Production stopped in the mid-50s, when 'bread and butter' pictures were no longer needed, and the company's interests moved into TV.

Rescher, Gayne.
American cinematographer.
A Face in the Crowd 57. The Troublemaker 64. Rachel, Rachel 68. John and Mary 69. A New Leaf 71. Claudine 74. Olly, Olly Oxen Free 78. Star Trek II: The Wrath of Khan 82. Toughlove (TV) 85. Shooter (TV) 88. Single Women, Married Men (TV) 90, etc.

Resnais, Alain (1922–).
Controversial French director, former editor.
■ Statues Also Die 51. Nuit et Brouillard (short) 55. Toute la Mémoire du Monde 56. *Hiroshima Mon Amour* 59. Last Year at Marienbad 61. Muriel 62. The War Is Over 66. Je n'Aime, Je t'Aime 69. Stavisky 74. Providence 77. My American Uncle 80. La Vie est un Roman 83. Love unto Death 84. Mélo 86. I Want to Go Home 89. Smoking/No Smoking 93, etc.

Retford, Ella (1896–1962).
English actress, singer and dancer, from music hall, and best known as a principal boy in pantomime.
Poison Pen 39. Variety Jubilee 43. I'll Be Your Sweetheart 45. Noose 48. Paper Orchid 49. Shadow of the Past 50, etc.

Rettig, Tommy (1941–).
American boy actor of the 50s.
Panic in the Streets 50. The Five Thousand Fingers of Dr T 53. The Egyptian 54. The Last Wagon 56. At Gunpoint 57, etc.
TV series: Lassie 54–57.

Reubens, Paul (1952–).
American actor, best known for his role as Pee-Wee Herman.
The Blues Brothers 80. Cheech & Chong's Next Movie 80. Cheech & Chong's Nice Dreams 81. Meatballs Part II 84. Pee-Wee's Big Adventure 85. Flight of the Navigator 86. Big Top Pee-Wee 88. Batman Returns 92. Buffy, the Vampire Hunter

92. Tim Burton's The Nightmare before Christmas (voice) 93, etc.

Revel, Harry (1905–1958).
British composer in Hollywood, usually in association with Mack Gordon.
SCORES: College Rhythm 34. The Gay Divorcee 34. We're Not Dressing 34. Stowaway 36. You Can't Have Everything 37. Are You with It? 48, etc.

Revell, Graeme.
Australian composer.
Dead Calm 89. Spontaneous Combustion 90. Until the End of the World 90. Child's Play 2 90. The Hand that Rocks the Cradle 92. Hear No Evil 93. Hard Target 93. Body of Evidence 93. Boxing Helena 93. The Crush 93. Ghost in the Machine 94. The Crow 94. No Escape 94. S.F.W. 94, etc.

Revere, Anne (1903–1990).
American character actress, mainly on stage. Her movie career was disrupted in the early 50s when she was blacklisted for refusing to testify before the House Un-American Activities Committee.
Double Door 34. The Devil Commands 41. The Gay Sisters 42. The Song of Bernadette (AAN) 43. The Keys of the Kingdom 44. National Velvet (AA) 44. Dragonwyck 46. Body and Soul 47. Gentleman's Agreement (AAN) 48. A Place in the Sun 51. Macho Callahan 70. Birch Interval 76, etc.

Revier, Dorothy (1904–1993) (Doris Velagra).
American leading lady of the silents, usually as a vamp; couldn't cope with sound. Her first husband was director Harry Revier.
Broadway Madonna 22. The Wild Party 23. The Virgin 24. When Husbands Flirt 25. When the Wife's Away 26. Poor Girls 27. Sinner's Parade 28. The Iron Mask 29. The Dance of Life 29. Call of the West 30. The Black Camel 31. Sally of the Subway 32. By Candlelight 33. Unknown Blonde 34. The Cowboy and the Kid 36, many others.

Revier, Harry J.
American director, a former cameraman. He was married for a time to actress Dorothy Revier, who starred in his Broadway Madonna.
A Grain of Dust 18. The Return of Tarzan 20. The Revenge of Tarzan 20. Broadway Madonna 22. What Price Love 27. The Mysterious Airman (serial) 28. The Convict's Code 30. The Lost City 35. Child Bride 38, etc.

Revill, Clive (1930–).
New Zealander in Britain playing mainly comic character roles.
Bunny Lake is Missing 65. Modesty Blaise 66. Kaleidoscope 66. A Fine Madness (US) 66. The Double Man 67. Fathom 67. Nobody Runs Forever 68. The Shoes of the Fisherman 68. The Private Life of Sherlock Holmes 70. A Severed Head 71. Avanti 72. The Legend of Hell House 73. The Black Windmill 74. Galileo 75. One of Our Dinosaurs Is Missing 75. Matilda 78. T. R. Sloane (TV) 79. Moviola (as Charlie Chaplin) (TV) 80. Zorro the Gay Blade 81. The Emperor's New Clothes 87. Rumpelstiltskin 87. Mack the Knife 89. The Sea Wolf (TV) 93, etc.

Reville, Alma (1900–1982).
British screenwriter, married to Alfred Hitchcock; worked on many of his films.
The Ring 27. Rich and Strange 32. The Thirty-Nine Steps 35. Secret Agent 36. Sabotage 37. Young and Innocent 37. The Lady Vanishes 38. Suspicion 41. Shadow of a Doubt 43. The Paradine Case 47. Stage Fright 50, etc.

Rey, Alejandro (1930–1987).
Argentinian actor in American TV and films.
The Wild Pack 72. The Stepmother 73. Money to Burn 73. Mr Majestyk 74. Breakout 75. High Velocity 76. The Swarm 78. Cuba 79. Sunburn 79. The Ninth Configuration 80. Rita Hayworth the Love Goddess (TV) 83, many others.

Rey, Fernando (1915–1994) (Fernando Arambillet).
Suave Spanish actor in international films, a favourite of Luis Buñuel.
Welcome Mr Marshall 52. Viridiana 61. Villa Rides 68. The Adventures 70. A Town Called Bastard 71. Tristana 71. The French Connection 72. The Discreet Charm of the Bourgeoisie 72. French Connection II 75. La Grande Bourgeoise 76. Jesus of Nazareth (TV) 77. That Obscure Object of Desire 77. Quintet 79. Monsignor 82. The Hit 84. The Knight of the Dragon 85. Saving Grace 86. My General 87. Moon over Parador 88. Naked Tango 91. L'Atlantide 92. 1492 92. Di Ceria dell'Untore (The Plague Sower) 92. After the Dream 92. El Cianuro Solo o con Leche? 93. Al Otro Lado del Tunel 94, many others.

Reynolds, Adeline de Walt (1862–1961).
American character actress with long stage experience; for many years Hollywood's oldest bit player.
Come Live with Me (film debut) 41. The Human Comedy 43. Going My Way 44. A Tree Grows in Brooklyn 45. The Girl from Manhattan 48. Lydia Bailey 52. Witness to Murder 54, etc.

Reynolds, Burt (1936–).
Lithe, virile American leading man who after years in television became a 'bankable' box-office star of the early 70s, but found his popular appeal declining from the 80s. He was married to actress Judi Carne (1963–66).
Angel Baby 61. Armored Command 61. Operation CIA 65. Navajo Joe 67. Shark 68. Impasse 68. Skullduggery 69. Sam Whiskey 69. 100 Rifles 69. Fuzz 72. Deliverance 72. Shamus 72. White Lightning 73. The Man Who Loved Cat Dancing 73. The Longest Yard 74. WW and the Dixie Dancekings 75. At Long Last Love 75. Hustle 76. Lucky Lady 76. Gator 76. Nickelodeon 76. Smokey and the Bandit 77. Semi-Tough 77. The End (& d) 78. Hooper 78. Starting Over 79. Smokey and the Bandit II 80. Rough Cut 80. The Cannonball Run 81. Sharkey's Machine (also d) 81. The Best Little Whorehouse in Texas 82. Best Friends 82. Stroker Ace 83. The Man Who Loved Women. 83. Cannonball Run II 84. City Heat 84. Stick (& d) 85. Heat 87. Malone 87. Rent-a-Cop 88. Switching Channels 88. Physical Evidence 88. Breaking In 89. All Dogs Go to Heaven (voice) 89. Modern Love 90. Cop and a Half 93, etc.
TV series: Riverboat 59–60. Gunsmoke 65–67. Hawk 67. Dan August 70. Evening Shade 90–93.

¶ I think the most underrated thing in the world is a good hot bath. With bubbles. – B.R.
My movies were the kind they show in prisons and aeroplanes, because nobody can leave. – B.R.

Reynolds, Debbie (1932–) (Mary Frances Reynolds).
Petite, vivacious American leading lady of 50s musicals; later a pleasing comedienne. She now owns and performs in her own hotel in Las Vegas which also displays her collection of movie memorabilia, much of it bought when MGM sold off its warehouses of costumes and furniture. She was married to singer Eddie Fisher (1955–59) and is the mother of actress Carrie Fisher.

Autobiography: 1989, Debbie – My Life (with David Patrick Columba).
■ June Bride 48. The Daughter of Rosie O'Grady 50. Three Little Words 50. Two Weeks with Love 50. Mr Imperium 51. Singin' in the Rain 52. Skirts Ahoy 52. I Love Melvin 53. The Affairs of Dobie Gillis 53. Give a Girl a Break 53. Susan Slept Here 54. Athena 54. Hit the Deck 55. The Tender Trap 55. The Catered Affair 56. Bundle of Joy 56. Meet Me in Las Vegas 56. Tammy and the Bachelor 57. This Happy Feeling 58. The Mating Game 59. Say One for Me 59. It Started with a Kiss 59. The Gazebo 59. The Rat Race 60. Pépé 60. The Pleasure of His Company 61. The Second Time Around 61. How the West was Won 62. My Six Loves 63. Mary Mary 63. The Unsinkable Molly Brown (AAN) 64. Goodbye Charlie 64. The Singing Nun 66. Divorce American Style 67. How Sweet It Is 68. What's the Matter with Helen? 71. Charlotte's Web (voice only) 72. That's Entertainment! 74. Sadie and Son (TV) 87. Perry Mason: The Case of the Musical Murder (TV) 89. The Bodyguard 92. Heaven and Earth 93.
TV series: The Debbie Reynolds Show 69. Aloha Paradise 81.

¶ I do twenty minutes every time the refrigerator door opens and the light comes on. – D.R.
I stopped making movies because I don't like taking my clothes off. – D.R.
When I die I'm going to have myself stuffed like Trigger. They'll put me in a museum, all stuffed. Just put a quarter in and I'll sing 'Tammy'. – D.R.
Some people, if they're looking for their mother, would go into the kitchen. I'd go to Vegas. – Todd Fisher (D.R.'s son)

Reynolds, Gene (1925–).
American boy actor who later became a producer of TV series including The Ghost and Mrs Muir, Anna and the King and M*A*S*H.
Thank You Jeeves 36. In Old Chicago 38. The Blue Bird 40. The Penalty 40. The Tuttles of Tahiti 42. Eagle Squadron 44. The Country Girl 54. Diane 55, many others.

Reynolds, Joyce (1924–).
Vivacious American leading lady of the 40s, usually in teenage roles.
George Washington Slept Here 42. Janie 44. Always Together 48. Dangerous Inheritance 50. Girls' School 50, etc.

Reynolds, Kevin (1952–).
American director and screenwriter whose Robin Hood was one of the box-office hits of 1991.
Red Dawn (co-w) 84. Fandango (wd) 85. Beast of War (d) 88. Robin Hood: Prince of Thieves (d) 91. Rapa Nui (co-w, d) 94. Waterworld 95, etc.

Reynolds, Marjorie (1921–) (Marjorie Goodspeed).
American leading lady of the 40s. Former child actress.
Up in the Air 40. Holiday Inn 42. Star Spangled Rhythm 43. Ministry of Fear 43. Dixie 43. Three Is a Family 44. Bring on the Girls 45. Meet Me on Broadway 46. Heaven Only Knows 47. Home Town Story 51. The Great Jewel Robber 51. The Silent Witness 54, etc.
TV series: The Life of Riley 53–57. Our Man Higgins 62.

Reynolds, Norman.
British production designer.
The Little Prince 74. Lucky Lady 75. Mr Quilp 75. The Incredible Sarah (AAN) 76. Star Wars (AA) 77. The Empire Strikes Back (AAN) 80. Raiders of

he Lost Ark (AA) 81. Return of the Jedi (AAN) 83. Young Sherlock Holmes 85. Empire of the Sun (AAN) 87. Avalon 90. Mountains of the Moon ⁰0. Alien³ 92. Alive 93. Clean Slate 94, etc.

Reynolds, Peter (1926–1975) (Peter Horrocks).
British light character actor, given to shifty roles.
The Captive Heart 46. Guilt Is My Shadow 49. Smart Alec 50. Four Days 51. The Last Page 52. Devil Girl from Mars 54. You Can't Escape 55. The Delavine Affair 56. Shake Hands with the Devil ⁵9. West Eleven 63. Nobody Runs Forever 68, etc.

Reynolds, Sheldon (1923–).
American radio and TV writer who wrote, produced and directed two films.
■ Foreign Intrigue 56. Assignment to Kill 68.
TV series: Sherlock Holmes 56. Sherlock Holmes and Dr Watson 81.

Reynolds, William H. (1910–).
American editor.
So Ends Our Night 41. Moontide 42. Carnival n Costa Rica 47. Come to the Stable 49. The Day the Earth Stood Still 51. Red Skies of Montana 52. Three Coins in the Fountain 54. Bus Stop 56. South Pacific 58. Compulsion 59. Fanny (AAN) 61. Kings of the Sun 63. The Sound of Music (AAN) 65. Star 68. The Great White Hope 70. *The Godfather* 72. *The Sting* (AA) 73. The Great Waldo Pepper 75. The Turning Point (AAN) 77. A Little Romance 77. Heaven's Gate 80. Nijinsky 80. Author! Author! 82. Making Love 82. Yellowbeard 83. The Little Drummer Girl 84. The Lonely Guy 84. Pirates 86. Dancers 87. Ishtar 87. A New Life 88. Rooftops 89. Taking Care of Business 90, etc.

Rhoades, Barbara (1947–).
American character actress.
The Shakiest Gun in the West 68. There Was a Crooked Man 70. Up the Sandbox 72. Harry and Tonto 74. Conspiracy of Terror (TV) 75. The Choirboys 77. Serial 80, etc.
TV series: Busting Loose 77. Soap 80.

Rhodes, Betty Jane (1921–).
American singing second lead of the early 40s.
Stage Door 37. Sweater Girl 41. The Fleet's In 42. Salute for Three 43. You Can't Ration Love 44. Practically Yours 44, etc.

Rhodes, Erik (1906–1990).
American comic actor from the musical comedy stage, best remembered as the excitable Italian in two Astaire-Rogers films, *The Gay Divorcee* 34 and *Top Hat* 35 ('Your wife is safe with Tonetti – he prefers spaghetti').
■ The Gay Divorcee 34. A Night at the Ritz 35. Charlie Chan in Paris 35. The Nitwits 35. Old Man Rhythm 35. *Top Hat* 35. Another Face 35. Two in the Dark 35. Chatterbox 36. One Rainy Afternoon 36. Special Investigator 36. Second Wife 36. The Smartest Girl in Town 36. Criminal Lawyer 37. Woman Chases Man 37. Music for Madame 37. Fight for Your Lady 37. Beg Borrow or Steal 37. Dramatic School 38. Say It in French 38. Meet the Girls 38. Mysterious Mr Moto 38. On Your Toes 39.

Rhodes, Marjorie (1902–1979).
Homely British character actress, on stage from 1920; usually played warm-hearted mums, nosy neighbours, etc.
Poison Pen (debut) 39. *Love on the Dole* 40. World of Plenty 41. *When We are Married* 43. Uncle Silas 47. *The Cure for Love* 50. Those People Next Door 53. Hell Drivers 58. Watch It, Sailor 62. *The Family*

Way 66. Mrs Brown, You've Got a Lovely Daughter 68. Hands of the Ripper 71, many others.

Rhue, Madlyn (1934–) (Madeleine Roche).
American supporting actress.
Operation Petticoat 59. Escape from Zahrain 62. It's a Mad Mad Mad Mad World 63. He Rides Tall 64. Stand Up and Be Counted 72, etc.
TV series: Bracken's World 69. Executive Suite 76.

Rhys-Davies, John (1944–).
Heavyweight British character actor, a good roisterer.
Shogun (TV) 80. Sphinx 81. Raiders of the Lost Ark 81. Victor/Victoria 81. Ivanhoe (TV) 82. Sahara 83. Best Revenge 83. King Solomon's Mines 85. In the Shadow of Kilimanjaro 86. The Living Daylights 87. Nairobi Affair 88. Indiana Jones and the Last Crusade 89. Tusks 89. Rebel Storm 90. The Company 90. The Company II: Sacrifices 91. Canvas 92. The Unnameable Returns 92. Sunset Grill 92. Journey of Honor 92. The Seventh Coin 93. The High Crusade 94, etc.
TV series: The Untouchables 93.

Riano, Renie (1899–1971).
American comedienne in small film roles, especially the *Jiggs and Maggie* series.
Tovarich 37. Adam Had Four Sons 41. The Time of Your Life 46. Three on a Couch 66, many others.

Ricci, Christina (1981–).
American child star in comic roles.
Mermaid 90. *The Addams Family* 92. The Cemetery Club 93. *Addams Family Values* 93.

Rice, Anne.
American writer of vampire novels. She also writes erotic novels under the names Anne Rampling and A. N. Roquelaure.
Interview with the Vampire 94. Exit to Eden 94.

Rice, Elmer (1892–1967) (Elmer Reizenstern).
American playwright. Works filmed include *Street Scene*, *The Adding Machine*, *Dream Girl* and *Counsellor at Law*.

Rice, Florence (1907–1974).
American leading lady of the late 30s, always in sweet-tempered roles.
The Best Man Wins 34. Sweethearts 39. Miracles for Sale 39. At the Circus 39. Fighting Marshal 41. The Ghost and the Guest 43, etc.

Rice, Grantland (1881–1954).
American sportscaster who made innumerable one-reelers under the title *Grantland Rice Sportslights*. Father of Florence Rice.

Rice, Jack (1893–1968).
American light actor who for many years played Edgar Kennedy's useless brother-in-law in RKO shorts. Last film: Son of Flubber 63.

Rice, Joan (1930–)
British leading lady, former waitress, briefly popular in the 50s.
Blackmailed 50. One Wild Oat 51. The Story of Robin Hood and His Merrie Men 52. A Day to Remember 54. His Majesty O'Keefe (US) 55. One Good Turn 56. Payroll 61. Horror of Frankenstein 70, etc.

Rice, Sir Tim.
English lyricist, associated with Sir Andrew Lloyd

Webber's early musicals. He was knighted 'for services to music' in 1994.
Jesus Christ Superstar 73. Aladdin (AA song) 92. The Lion King 94.

Rich, David Lowell (1923–).
American director, from TV.
Senior Prom 58. Hey Boy, Hey Girl 59. Have Rocket Will Travel 59. Madame X 66. The Plainsman 66. Rosie 67. A Lovely Way to Die 68. *Eye of the Cat* 69. The Sex Symbol (TV) 74. The Concorde – Airport 79 79. Chu Chu and the Philly Flash 81. Thursday's Child (TV) 83. The Defiant Ones (TV) 86. Infidelity (TV) 87, etc.

Rich, Irene (1891–1988) (Irene Luther).
American silent-screen heroine, little seen after sound.
Stella Maris 18. Beau Brummell 24. Lady Windermere's Fan 25. So This is Paris 26. *Craig's Wife* 28. Shanghai Rose 29. That Certain Age 38. The Lady in Question 41. New Orleans 47. Joan of Arc 48, etc.

Rich, John (1925–).
American director, from TV.
Wives and Lovers 63. The New Interns 64. Boeing Boeing 65. Easy Come Easy Go 67, etc.

Rich, Matty (1971–) (Matthew Richardson).
American director.
Straight out of Brooklyn 90. The Inkwell 94.

Rich, Roy (1909–1970).
British producer, director and executive, with widely varied experience including radio and TV.
My Brother's Keeper (d only) 47. It's Not Cricket (d only) 48. Double Profile (d only) 54. Phantom Caravan (d only) 54, etc.

Richard, Cliff (1940–) (Harold Webb).
Boyish British pop singer who succeeded by restricting his film appearances.
Biography: 1993, *Cliff Richard* by Steve Turner.
■ Serious Charge 59. Expresso Bongo 60. *The Young Ones* 61. Summer Holiday 62. Wonderful Life 64. Finders Keepers 66. Two a Penny 68. Take Me High 73.

Richard the Lionheart (Richard I of England, 1157–1199)
was a king who has gone down into legend rather than history as a nearly wronged idealist. The truth may have been less inspiring. He was played by Wallace Beery in *Robin Hood* (1922), by Henry Wilcoxon in *The Crusades*, by Ian Hunter in *The Adventures of Robin Hood*, by Norman Wooland in *Ivanhoe*, by Patrick Barr in Disney's *Robin Hood*, by George Sanders in *King Richard and the Crusaders*, by Patrick Holt in *Men of Sherwood Forest*, by Anthony Hopkins (as a prince) in *The Lion in Winter*, by Richard Harris in *Robin and Marian*, and Sean Connery in *Robin Hood: Prince of Thieves*.

Richard III (1452–1485).
The best-known account of the life and crimes of the short-lived king of England is Laurence Olivier's version of Shakespeare's play, centring on his own performance as a charming, ruthless villain. The story was also dealt with in Rowland V. Lee's outrageous but amusing *Tower of London* 39, with Basil Rathbone as Richard and Boris Karloff as Mord the Executioner; this was remade in 1963 by Roger Corman with Vincent Price, who had played the Duke of Clarence in the earlier version, as Richard.

Richards, Addison (1887–1964).
American character actor with long stage experience; in Hollywood from early 30s, usually as professional man; later in TV series.

Riot Squad 34. Colleen 36. Black Legion 37. Boom Town 40. My Favorite Blonde 42. Since You Went Away 44. The Mummy's Curse 44. Indian Scout 50. Illegal 56. The Oregon Trail 59, many others.

TV series: Fibber McGee 59. Cimarron City 58–60.

Richards, Ann (1918–).
Australian leading lady.

Tall Timbers 38. The Rudd Family 39, etc. Then to Hollywood: Random Harvest 42. Dr Gillespie's New Assistant 43. An American Romance 44. Love Letters 45. The Searching Wind 46. Sorry, Wrong Number 48. Breakdown 52, etc.

Richards, Beah.
American actress.

The Miracle Worker 62. In the Heat of the Night 67. Guess Who's Coming to Dinner (AAN) 67. Mahogany 76. Inside Out 86. Drugstore Cowboy 89. Homer & Eddie 90, etc.

Richards, Dick (1936–).
American director.
■ The Culpepper Cattle Company 72. Farewell My Lovely 75. Rafferty and the Gold Dust Twins 75. March or Die (& w, p) 77. Death Valley 82. Tootsie (co-p only) 82. Man, Woman and Child 83. Heat 87.

Richards, Jeff (1922–1989) (Richard Mansfield Taylor).
American general-purpose actor.

Johnny Belinda 48. Kill the Umpire 50. The Strip 51. Above and Beyond 52. Seven Brides for Seven Brothers 55, many others.

TV series: Jefferson Drum 58.

Richards, Paul (1924–1974).
American general-purpose actor.

The Black Whip 55. Tall Man Riding 56. Battle for the Planet of the Apes 71, etc.

TV series: Breaking Point 63.

Richardson, Ian (1934–).
Scottish character actor whose precise playing of many varied roles is an increasing delight.

The Marat/Sade 68. Man of La Mancha 72. The Darwin Adventure 73. Ike (TV) (as Bernard Montgomery) 79. The Sign of Four (as Sherlock Holmes) (TV) 84. The Master of Ballantrae (TV) 84. Mistral's Daughter (TV) 84. Mountbatten (TV) 85. Brazil 85. The Fourth Protocol 87. Porterhouse Blue (TV) 87. Cry Freedom 87. Burning Secret 89. The Plot to Kill Hitler (TV) 90. Rosencrantz and Guildenstern Are Dead 90. Year of the Comet 92. House of Cards (TV) 92. To Play the King (TV) 93. Foreign Affairs (TV) 93. M. Butterfly 93. Dirty Weekend 93. Words upon the Window Pane 94, etc.

Richardson, Joely (1965–).
British actress, the daughter of Vanessa Redgrave and Tony Richardson.

Hotel New Hampshire 84. Wetherby 85. Drowning by Numbers 88. Heading Home 91. King Ralph 91. Rebecca's Daughters 91. Shining Through 92. Lady Chatterley's Lover (TV) 92. I'll Do Anything 94, etc.

Richardson, John (1936–).
British leading man, mainly in fancy dress.

Bachelor of Hearts 58. She 65. One Million Years

BC 66. The Vengeance of She 68. The Chastity Belt 68. On a Clear Day You Can See Forever 70. Duck in Orange Sauce (It.) 75. Eyeball 78. Frankenstein 80 80, etc.

Richardson, Miranda (1958–).
British actress.

Dance with a Stranger 84. The Innocent 85. Underworld 85. Blackadder (TV) 86. After Pilkington (TV) 87. Empire of the Sun 87. Ball-Trap on the Côte Sauvage 89. The Mad Monkey (El Mono Loco) 89. My Dear Doctor Gräsler (Mio Caro Dottore Gräsler) 89. The Fool 90. Twisted Obsession 90. The Bachelor 91. Enchanted April 91. The Crying Game 92. Damage 92. Century 93. Tom and Viv 94. The Night and the Moment 94, etc.

Richardson, Natasha (1963–).
British actress, the daughter of Vanessa Redgrave and Tony Richardson. She married Liam Neeson in 1994.

Every Picture Tells a Story 84. In the Secret State 85. Gothic 86. A Month in the Country 87. Patty Hearst 88. The Handmaid's Tale 89. Fatman and Little Boy (aka The Shadowmakers) 89. The Comfort of Strangers 90. The Favour, the Watch and the Very Big Fish (Rue Saint-Sulpice) 91. Past Midnight 92. Suddenly Last Summer (TV) 93. Zelda (TV) 93. Widows' Peak 94. Nell 94, etc.

Richardson, Peter.
British comedy director.
■ The Supergrass 86. Eat the Rich 87. The Pope Must Die (US: The Pope Must Diet) 91.

TV series: The Comic Strip Presents . . . (a, co-wd) 93.

Richardson, Sir Ralph (1902–1983).
Distinguished British stage actor, in occasional films. Despite his splendid theatrical voice and thespian mannerisms, he was at his best playing ordinary chaps, though his gallery included plenty of eccentrics.
■ The Ghoul 33. Friday the Thirteenth 33. The Return of Bulldog Drummond 34. Java Head 34. King of Paris 34. Bulldog Jack 35. Things to Come 36. The Man Who Could Work Miracles 36. Thunder in the City 37. South Riding 38. The Divorce of Lady X 38. The Citadel 38. Q Planes 39. The Four Feathers 39. The Lion Has Wings 39. On the Night of the Fire 39. The Day Will Dawn 42. The Silver Fleet 43. The Volunteer 43. School for Secrets 46. Anna Karenina 48. The Fallen Idol 48. The Heiress 49. An Outcast of the Islands 51. Home at Seven (& d) 52. The Sound Barrier 52. The Holly and the Ivy 53. Richard III (as Buckingham) 56. Smiley 57. The Passionate Stranger 57. Our Man in Havana 59. Oscar Wilde (as Sir Edward Carson) 60. Exodus 61. The 300 Spartans 62. Long Day's Journey into Night 62. Woman of Straw 64. Doctor Zhivago 66. The Wrong Box 66. Khartoum 67. Oh What a Lovely War 69. The Midas Run 69. The Bed Sitting Room 69. The Battle of Britain 69. The Looking Glass War 69. David Copperfield (as Micawber) 69. Eagle in a Cage 71. Who Slew Auntie Roo? 71. Tales from the Crypt 71. Lady Caroline Lamb 72. Alice's Adventures in Wonderland (as the Caterpillar) 72. A Doll's House 73. O Lucky Man 73. Frankenstein: The True Story (TV) 73. Rollerball 75. Jesus of Nazareth (TV) 77. The Man in the Iron Mask (TV) 77. Time Bandits 80. Dragonslayer 81. Wagner 83. Invitation to a Wedding 83. Greystoke (AAN) 84. Witness for the Prosecution (TV) 84.
◆ For casting his whimsical eye over a surprisingly large range of movies, and invariably walking off with the honours. Q Planes.

¶ I don't like my face at all. It's always been a great drawback to me. – R.R.

The art of acting lies in keeping people from coughing. – R.R.

Richardson, Robert.
American cinematographer, associated with the films of Oliver Stone.

Salvador 86. Platoon (AAN) 86. Dudes 87. Wall Street 87. Eight Men Out 88. Talk Radio 88. Born on the Fourth of July (AAN) 89. City of Hope 91. The Doors 91. JFK (AA) 91. A Few Good Men 92. Heaven and Earth 93. Natural Born Killers 94, etc.

Richardson, Tony (1928–1991) (Cecil Antonio Richardson).
Born in Shipley, Yorkshire, he was educated at Oxford University and worked in television before founding, with George Devine, the English Stage Company at London's Royal Court Theatre, which had a profound impact on British theatre through his production of John Osborne's Look Back in Anger. The collaboration with Osborne also resulted in the creation of Woodfall Films (qv). From the mid-70s, he moved to America to work. Married Vanessa Redgrave; their daughters, Natasha and Joely Richardson, are actresses. Died of AIDS.

Autobiography: 1993, Long Distance Runner.
■ Momma Don't Allow (short, d) 56. Look Back in Anger (d) 59. The Entertainer (d) 60. A Subject of Scandal and Concern (d) (TV) 60. Saturday Night and Sunday Morning (p) 60. Sanctuary (d) 61. A Taste of Honey (p, co-w, d) 61. The Loneliness of the Long Distance Runner (pd) 62. Tom Jones (pd) 63. Girl with Green Eyes (p) 64. The Loved One (d) (US) 65. Mademoiselle (d) 66. The Sailor from Gibraltar (co-w, d) 67. Red and Blue (short, co-w, d) 67. The Charge of the Light Brigade (d) 68. Hamlet (d) 69. Laughter in the Dark (d) 69. Ned Kelly (co-w, d) 70. A Delicate Balance (d) 73. Dead Cert (co-w, d) 74. Joseph Andrews (story, d) 77. A Death in Canaan (d) 78. The Border (d) 82. Hotel New Hampshire (wd) 84. Penalty Phase (d) (TV) 88. Shadow on the Sun (d) (TV) 88. The Phantom of the Opera (d) (TV) 90. Hills Like White Elephants (d) (TV) 90. Blue Sky (d) (made 90) 94.

¶ The most prolific and the most prosperous of the Sight and Sound crop, and ultimately the least respected. – Andrew Sarris, 1968

Richelieu, Cardinal (1585–1642).
Louis XIII's chief minister, doubtless a clever and powerful chap, was used by the movies as a schemer and often a villain, seldom on the hero's side. George Arliss gave the fullest portrait, in Cardinal Richelieu 35. Others who have played him include Nigel de Brulier in The Iron Mask, the 1935 version of The Three Musketeers, and the 1939 version of The Man in the Iron Mask; Osgood Perkins in Madame Dubarry; Raymond Massey in Under the Red Robe; Miles Mander in the 1939 version of The Three Musketeers; Aimé Clairond in Monsieur Vincent; Vincent Price in the 1948 version of The Three Musketeers; Paul Cavanagh in Sword of D'Artagnan; Christopher Logue in The Devils; and Charlton Heston in the 1974 versions of The Three Musketeers and The Four Musketeers.

Richert, William.
American screenwriter and director. He also played the role of a modern-day Falstaff in Gus Van Sant's My Own Private Idaho.
■ Law and Disorder (co-w) 74. The Happy Hooker (w) 75. Winter Kills (wd) 79. Success (co-w, d) 79.

A Night in the Life of Jimmy Reardon (wd) 88. My Own Private Idaho (a) 91.

Richler, Mordecai (1931–).
Canadian novelist and screenwriter on Jewish themes.
■ No Love for Johnnie (co-w) 60. Young and Willing (co-w) 62. Life at the Top 65. The Apprenticeship of Duddy Kravitz (w, oa) (AAN) 74. Fun with Dick and Jane (co-w) 77. Jacob Two-Two Meets the Hooded Fang 78. Joshua Then and Now (w, oa) 85.

Richman, Harry (1895–1972) (Harold Reichman).
American entertainer, in occasional films.
Autobiography: 1966, *A Hell of a Life*.
■ Putting on the Ritz 30. The Music Goes Round 36. Kicking the Moon Around 38.

Richman, Peter Mark (1927–).
American general-purpose actor, much on TV.
Friendly Persuasion 56. The Strange One 57. The Black Orchid 58. The Crime Busters 61. Dark Intruder 65. For Singles Only 68. Dandy in Aspic 68. The City Killer 87. Judgement Day 88. Friday the Thirteenth Part VIII: Jason Takes Manhattan 89, etc.
TV series: *Cain's Hundred* 61–62. Longstreet 71–72. Dynasty 81–84.

Richmond, Anthony B. (1942–).
British cinematographer and occasional director, now in Hollywood.
Sympathy for the Devil 68. Only When I Larf 68. Let It Be 70. Madame Sin 72. Don't Look Now 73. Vampira 74. Stardust 74. The Man Who Fell to Earth 76. The Eagle Has Landed 76. Silver Bears 77. The Greek Tycoon 78. Love and Bullets 79. Improper Channels 79. Bad Timing 80. Nightkill 81. A Man Called Rage (d) 84. Déjà Vu (wd) 85. Blake Edwards' That's Life 86. The In Crowd 88. Sunset 88. Cat Chaser 90. The Indian Runner 91. Timebomb 91. Kryo (co-w, d) 92. Heart of Darkness (TV) 94, etc.

Richmond, Kane (1906–1973) (Frederick W. Bowditch).
American leading man of second features.
The Leather Pushers (serial) 30. Nancy Steele is Missing 36. Hard Guy 41. Action in the North Atlantic 43. Tiger Woman 45. Black Gold 47, many others.

Richmond, Ted (1912–).
American producer, former writer.
So Dark the Night 46. The Milkman 50. The Strange Door 51. Desert Legion 53. Forbidden 54. Count Three and Pray 55. Seven Waves Away 57. Solomon and Sheba 59. Advance to the Rear 64. Return of the Seven 66. Villa Rides 68. Papillon 74, others.

Richter, Hans (1888–1976).
German Dadaist director of animated and surrealist films, most active in the 20s.
Prelude and Fugue 20. Film is Rhythm 20. Rhythm 23. Rhythm 25. Film Study 26. Inflation 26. Twopenny Magic 27. Vormittagspuk 28. Everything Revolves 30. Dreams That Money Can Buy 44. 8 × 8 57, etc.

Richter, Jason James (1980–).
American child actor. Born in Oregon, he was raised in Honolulu and began his career in Japanese television.
Free Willy 93. Cops and Robbersons 94. The Neverending Story III 94.

Richter, W. D. (1945–).
American screenwriter and director, a former script analyst for Warner.
■ Slither 72. Peeper 75. Nickelodeon 76. Invasion of the Body Snatchers 78. Dracula 79. Brubaker 80. All Night Long 81. Hang Tough 82. The Adventures of Buckaroo Banzai across the Eighth Dimension (d) 84. Big Trouble in Little China 86. Late for Dinner (d) 91. Needful Things (d) 93.

Rickles, Don (1926–).
American insult comedian.
Run Silent Run Deep 58. The Rabbit Trap 59. The Rat Race 60. Enter Laughing 67. The Money Jungle 68. Where It's At 69. Kelly's Heroes 70. Innocent Blood 92, etc.
TV series: CPO Sharkey 77.

Rickman, Alan (1946–).
English classical actor from the stage, so far typecast by Hollywood as a villain, who became an actor in his mid-20s after a career as a graphic designer. He also directs plays.
Shock! Shock! Shock! 87. Die Hard 88. The January Man 89. Truly Madly Deeply 90. Quigley Down Under 90. Robin Hood: Prince of Thieves 91. Close My Eyes 91. Closet Land 91. Bob Roberts 92. Mesmer 94. An Awfully Big Adventure 95, etc.

¶ I do take my work seriously and the way to do that is not to take yourself too seriously. – *A.R.*

Rickman, Thomas.
American screenwriter and director.
Kansas City Bomber (co-w) 72. The Laughing Policeman (w) 73. W.W. and the Dixie Dancekings 75. The White Dawn (co-w) 76. Hooper (co-w) 78. Coal Miner's Daughter (AAN) 80. The River Rat (wd) 84. Everybody's All-American 88, etc.

Riddle, Nelson (1921–1985).
American composer.
A Kiss before Dying 55. St Louis Blues 58. Ocean's Eleven 60. Lolita 62. Robin and the Seven Hoods 64. Marriage on the Rocks 65. El Dorado 66. Paint Your Wagon 69. The Great Gatsby (AA) 74. Harper Valley PTA 78, etc.

Ridgeley, John (1909–1968) (John Huntingdon Rea).
American supporting actor generally cast as gangster.
Invisible Menace 38. They Made Me a Fugitive 39. Brother Orchid 40. The Big Shot 42. Destination Tokyo 44. My Reputation 46. The Big Sleep 46. Possessed 47. Command Decision 48. The Blue Veil 52, many others.

Ridges, Stanley (1892–1951).
Incisive, heavy-featured British character actor who appeared in many Hollywood films.
■ Success 23. Crime without Passion 34. The Scoundrel 35. Winterset 36. Sinner Take All 36. Internes Can't Take Money 37. Yellow Jack 38. The Mad Miss Manton 38. If I Were King 38. There's That Woman Again 38. Let Us Live 39. Confessions of a Nazi Spy 39. I Stole a Million 39. Silver on the Sage 39. Union Pacific 39. Each Dawn I Die 39. Espionage Agent 39. Dust Be My Destiny 39. Nick Carter Master Detective 39. *Black Friday* 40. The Sea Wolf 41. Mr District Attorney 41. Sergeant York 41. They Died with Their Boots On 41. The Lady Is Willing 42. The Big Shot 42. *To Be or Not to Be* 42. Eagle Squadron 42. Eyes in the Night 42. Tarzan Triumphs 43. Air Force 43. This Is the Army 43. The Master Race 44. The Story of Dr Wassell 44. Wilson 44. *The Suspect* 45. Captain Eddie 45. God Is My Co-Pilot 45. The Phantom

Speaks 45. Because of Him 46. Mr Ace 46. Canyon Passage 46. Possessed 47. An Act of Murder 47. You're My Everything 49. Streets of Laredo 49. The File on Thelma Jordon 49. Task Force 49. There's a Song in My Heart 49. Paid in Full 50. No Way Out 50. The Groom Wore Spurs 51.

Ridley, Philip (1960–).
British director, screenwriter, dramatist, author and artist.
The Krays (w) 90. The Reflecting Skin (wd) 90. The Passion of Darkly Noon 95.

Riefenstahl, Leni (1902–).
German woman director, former dancer, who made brilliant propaganda films for Hitler.
Autobiography: 1993, *The Sieve of Time*.
Biography: 1976, *Leni Riefenstahl* by Glenn B. Infield.
The White Hell of Pitz Palu (a) 29. The Blue Light (a, d) 32. S.O.S. Iceberg (a) 33. *Triumph of the Will* (the Nuremberg Rally) (d) 34. *Olympische Spiele* 36. Tiefland 45, etc.

Riegert, Peter (1947–).
American character lead, in the George Segal tradition.
National Lampoon's Animal House 78. *Local Hero* 83. Ellis Island (TV) 85. Un Homme Amoureux 87. Crossing Delancey 88. That's Adequate 89. Beyond the Ocean 90. A Shock to the System 90. Oscar 91. Object of Beauty 91. Utz (TV) 91. The Runestone 92. Passed Away 92. Gypsy (TV) 93. The Mask 94, etc.

Riesner, Dean (1918–).
American screenwriter, a former child actor under the name Dinky Dean. He also directed the curious *Bill and Coo*, with its cast of birds in hats and neckties, which won a special Oscar for 'artistry and patience'.
Bill and Coo (d) 47. The Helen Morgan Story (co-w) 57. Coogan's Bluff (co-w) 69. Dirty Harry (co-w) 71. Charlie Varrick (co-w) 73. The Enforcer (co-w) 76. Fatal Beauty (co-w) 87, etc.

Rifkin, Adam.
American director and screenwriter.
Never on Tuesday 88. The Dark Backward 91. The Nutty Nut 92. The Chase 94, etc.

Rigby, Arthur (1900–1970).
Burly English character actor, mainly on stage and television. Born in London, he was on stage from 1919 and in films from 1927. He is best known for his role as Station Sergeant Flint in the long-running TV series *Dixon of Dock Green*, a role he first played on stage in a version of *The Blue Lamp*.
Q Ships 27. The Deputy Drummer 35. The Marriage of Corbal 36. Cheer Up! 36. Dangerous Cargo 54. Crossroads to Crime 60, etc.

Rigby, Edward (1879–1951).
British stage character actor; became a familiar figure in endearingly doddery roles. On stage from 1900, he appeared in two silent films in 1907 and 1910.
Lorna Doone 35. Mr Smith Carries On 37. The Proud Valley 39. *Kipps* 41. The Common Touch 41. *Let the People Sing* 42. Salute John Citizen 42. Get Cracking 43. *Don't Take It to Heart* 44. Quiet Weekend 47. *Easy Money* 48. It's Hard to be Good 49. *The Happiest Days of Your Life* 49. *The Mudlark* 50, many others.

Rigby, Terence (1937–).
British character actor, mostly on stage.

The Little Ones 61. West Eleven 63. Accident 67. Get Carter 71. The Homecoming 73. The Dogs of War 80. The Hound of the Baskervilles (TV) 83. Lace (TV) 84. Lace II (TV) 85. Young Americans 93, etc.

TV series: Crossroads 86– .

Rigg, Dame Diana (1938–).

British leading actress who came to fame in *The Avengers* TV series 65–67. She won a Tony award as best actress on Broadway in *Medea* in 1994.

■ The Assassination Bureau 68. A Midsummer Night's Dream 68. On Her Majesty's Secret Service 69. Julius Caesar 70. The Hospital 71. Theatre of Blood 73. In This House of Brede (TV) 75. A Little Night Music 77. Evil Under the Sun 81. The Great Muppet Caper 81. Witness for the Prosecution (TV) 84. Bleak House (TV) 85. Genghis Cohen (TV) 93. A Good Man in Africa 94.

TV series: The Diana Rigg Show 73.

Rilla, Walter (1895–1980).

German actor on stage from 1921; to Britain in mid-30s.

Der Geiger von Florenz 26. The Scarlet Pimpernel 35. Victoria the Great 37. At the Villa Rose 39. The Adventures of Tartu 43. The Lisbon Story 46. State Secret 50. Behold the Man (pd) 51. Cairo 61. The Thousand Eyes of Dr Mabuse 63. The Face of Fu Manchu 65, etc.

Rilla, Wolf (1920–).

British director, son of Walter Rilla.

Noose for a Lady 53. The End of the Road 54. Pacific Destiny 56. The Scamp 57. Bachelor of Hearts 58. Witness in the Dark 59. Piccadilly Third Stop 60. Village of the Damned 62. Cairo 63. The World Ten Times Over (& w) 63. Secrets of a Door to Door Salesman 73, etc.

Rimmer, Shane.

American supporting actor.

S*P*Y*S 74. Twilight's Last Gleaming 77. The People That Time Forgot 77. Silver Bears 79. Arabian Adventure 79. Hanover Street 79. Gandhi 82. Crusoe 88, etc.

Rinehart, Mary Roberts (1876–1958).

American mystery novelist, whose plots usually involve heroines in frightening situations. *The Bat* and *Miss Pinkerton* were each filmed more than once.

The Ringer.

Edgar Wallace's thriller about a vengeful master of disguise has been filmed three times in Britain: as a silent directed by Arthur Maude in 1928, starring Leslie Faber and Lawson Butt; and two versions directed by Walter Forde: the first with Gordon Harker and Franklin Dyall in 1931; and, under the title *The Gaunt Stranger*, with Sonnie Hale and Wilfred Lawson in 1938.

Ringwald, Molly (1968–).

American teenage actress of the 80s.

Sixteen Candles 84. The Breakfast Club 85. Pretty in Pink 86. The Pick-Up Artist 87. For Keeps 88. Fresh Horses 88. Strike It Rich 90. Betsy's Wedding 90. Face the Music 92. Tous les Jours Dimanche 94. The Stand (TV) 94, etc.

TV series: The Facts of Life 79–80.

Ripley, Arthur (1895–1961).

American director whose films are oddly sparse.
■ I Met My Love Again 38. Prisoner of Japan 42. *A Voice in the Wind* 44. The Chase 47. Thunder Road 58.

Ripper, Michael (1913–).

British character actor, often in comic roles.

Captain Boycott 48. Treasure Hunt 52. The Belles of St Trinian's 54. Richard III 56. Quatermass II 57. The Revenge of Frankenstein 58. Brides of Dracula 60. Captain Clegg 62. The Secret of Blood Island 65. The Reptile 66. The Plague of the Zombies 66. Where the Bullets Fly 66. Scars of Dracula 70. Legend of the Werewolf 75, etc.

Ripstein, Arturo (1943–).

Mexican director, influenced by Buñuel, for whom he worked as a production assistant on *The Exterminating Angel.*

A Time to Die (Tiempo de Morir) 65. Children's Hour (La Hora de los Niños) 69. Castle of Purity (El Castillo de la Pureza) 73. The Holy Office (El Santo Oficio) 73. The Black Widow (La Viuda Negra) 77. Vicious Circle (Cadena Perpétua) 79. Seduction (La Seducción) 80. The Other (El Otro) 84. Realm of Fortune (El Imperio de la Fortuna) 87. White Lies (Mentiras Piadosas) 88. La Mujer del Puerto 91. The Beginning and the End (Principio y Fin) 93. The Queen of the Night (La Reina de la Noche) 94, etc.

¶ In Mexico there is no such thing as a cinematic career. – A.R.

Riscoe, Arthur (1896–1954).

British stage comedian with rare film appearances.

Going Gay 34. Paradise for Two 38. *Kipps* (as Chitterlow) 41, etc.

Risdon, Elizabeth (1887–1958) (E. Evans).

English leading actress of early silents who in 1915 was voted the most popular British film star. On stage from 1910, she moved to America to work in the theatre in 1917 and went to Hollywood in the mid-30s, becoming a character actress. Married to director George Loane Tucker (qv) and actor Brandon Evans (1903–78).

Maria Marten 13. Idol of Paris 14. Florence Nightingale 15. A Mother of Dartmoor 16. Guard That Girl 35. Crime and Punishment 36. Tom Sawyer 38. Huckleberry Finn 39. The Roaring Twenties 39. Mexican Spitfire 40. High Sierra 41. Random Harvest 42. Mexican Spitfire at Sea 42. Reap the Wild Wind 42. The Canterville Ghost 44. The Egg and I 47. Life with Father 47. Secret Fury 50. Bannerline 51. Scaramouche 52, etc.

Risi, Dino (1917–).

Italian director.

The Sign of Venus 55. Poveri ma Belli 56. Il Sorpasso 62. Scent of a Woman 75. How Funny Can Sex Be 76. Viva Italia 78. Primo Amore 78. Caro Papa 79. Sunday Lovers 80. Ghost of Love 81. Le Bon Roi Dagobert 84. Teresa 87. Two Women (TV) 89. A Love for Living (TV) 89, etc.

Risi, Marco (1951–).

Italian director, the son of Dino Risi.

Vado a Vivere da Solo 81. Un Ragazzo, una Ragazza 83. Soldati 86. Forever Mary 89. Ragazzi Fuori 90. The Italians (Nei Continente Nero) 93. The Pack 94, etc.

Riskin, Robert (1897–1955).

Distinguished American screenwriter.

Illicit 31. The Miracle Woman 31. *Lady for a Day* (AAN) 33. *It Happened One Night* (AA) 34. Broadway Bill 34. The Whole Town's Talking 35. *Mr Deeds Goes to Town* (AAN) 36. *Lost Horizon* 37. *You Can't Take It with You* (AAN) 38. The Real Glory 39. *Meet John Doe* 41. The Thin Man Goes Home 44. Magic Town 46. Riding High 50. Mister 880 50.

The Groom Wore Spurs 51. Here Comes the Groom (co-w, AAN) 51, etc.

Ritchard, Cyril (1896–1977).

British dancer and light comedian, mainly on stage; latterly in US.

Piccadilly 29. Blackmail 30. I See Ice 38. Half a Sixpence 67.

Ritchie, June (1939–).

British leading lady, mainly in 'realist' films.

A Kind of Loving 61. Live Now Pay Later 63. The Mouse on the Moon 63. The World Ten Times Over 63. This is My Street 64. The Syndicate (GB) 67, etc.

Ritchie, Michael (1938–).

American director.

■ The Outsider (TV) 67. The Sound of Anger (TV) 69. Downhill Racer 69. Prime Cut 72. *The Candidate* 72. *Smile* 75. The Bad News Bears 76. Semi-Tough 77. An Almost Perfect Affair 79. Divine Madness 80. The Island 80. The Survivors 83. Fletch 84. Wildcats 85. The Golden Child 86. The Couch Trip 88. Fletch Lives 89. Diggstown 92. The Positively True Adventures of the Alleged Texas Cheerleader-Murdering Mom (TV) 93. Cops and Robbersons 94. The Scout 94.

Ritt, Martin (1913–1990).

American director with stage and TV experience. Blacklisted in the early 50s, he taught at The Actors Studio, where his students included Paul Newman and Rod Steiger.

■ *Edge of the City* 56. *No Down Payment* 57. *The Long Hot Summer* 58. The Sound and the Fury 59. The Black Orchid 59. Five Branded Women 60. Paris Blues 61. Hemingway's Adventures of a Young Man 62. *Hud* (AAN) 63. The Outrage 64. *The Spy Who Came in from the Cold* 65. Hombre 67. The Brotherhood 68. The Molly Maguires 69. The Great White Hope 71. Sounder 72. Pete 'n' Tillie 72. Conrack 74. The Front 76. The End of the Game (a only) 76. Casey's Shadow 77. Norma Rae 79. Cross Creek 83. Murphy's Romance 85. The Slugger's Wife (a only) 85. Stanley & Iris 90.

¶ I don't need a final cut. I only cut the thing once. If they're dumb enough to fool around with it, let 'em do it. – M.R.
As far as a Martin Ritt Production is concerned, I wouldn't embarrass myself to take that credit. What about the Ravetches? They wrote it. What about the actors who appear in it? If ever I write one, direct it and appear in it, then you can call it a Martin Ritt Production. – M.R.

Ritter, John (1948–) (Jonathan Ritter).

American actor, in comic or light romantic roles, from TV. He is the son of country singer and cowboy star Tex Ritter.

The Barefoot Executive 70. Scandalous John 71. The Other 72. Nickelodeon 76. Americathon 79. Hero at Large 80. Wholly Moses! 80. They All Laughed 81. Letting Go 85. The Last Fling 86. Real Men 87. Skin Deep 89. Problem Child 90. Problem Child 2 91. Noises Off 92. Stay Tuned 92. North 94, etc.

TV series: The Waltons 72–77. Three's Company 77–84. Three's a Crowd 84–85. Hearts Afire 92.

Ritter, Tex (1907–1974) (Woodward Ritter).

American singing cowboy star of innumerable second features, from the stage and radio. He sang the title song for the film *High Noon.*

Song of the Gringo 36. Sing, Cowboy, Sing 38. The Old Chisholm Trail 43. Marshal of Gunsmoke

---

46. Apache Ambush 55. Girl from Tobacco Road 66. What Am I Bid 67, etc.

Ritter, Thelma (1905–1969).
Wry-faced American character actress and comedienne; she provided a sardonic commentary on the antics of the principals in many 50s comedies.
■ Miracle on 34th Street 47. Call Northside 777 48. A Letter to Three Wives 49. City across the River 49. Father was a Fullback 49. Perfect Strangers 50. *All About Eve* 50. I'll Get By 50. The Mating Season 51. As Young as You Feel 51. *The Model and the Marriage Broker* 51. With a Song in My Heart 52. Titanic 53. The Farmer Takes a Wife 53. *Pickup on South Street* 53. Rear Window 54. Daddy Longlegs 55. Lucy Gallant 55. The Proud and Profane 56. A Hole in the Head 59. Pillow Talk 59. The Misfits 61. The Second Time Around 61. Birdman of Alcatraz 62. How the West was Won 62. For Love or Money 63. A New Kind of Love 63. Move Over Darling 63. Boeing Boeing 65. The Incident 67. What's So Bad about Feeling Good? 68.

Famous line (*All About Eve*): 'What a story. Everything but the bloodhounds snapping at her rear end.'

Famous line (*Pillow Talk*): 'If there's anything worse than a woman living alone, it's a woman saying she likes it.'

The Ritz Brothers: Al (1901–1965), Jim (1903–1985) and Harry (the leader) (1906–1986).
Zany American nightclub comedians who made many enjoyable appearances in musicals of the 30s. Their real surname was Joachim.
■ Hotel Anchovy (short) 34. Sing Baby Sing 36. One in a Million 37. *On the Avenue* 37. You Can't Have Everything 37. Life Begins at College 37. *The Goldwyn Follies* 38. Kentucky Moonshine 38. Straight Place and Show 38. *The Three Musketeers* 39. The Gorilla 39. Pack Up Your Troubles 39. Argentine Nights 40. Behind the Eight Ball 42. Hi Ya Chum 43. Never a Dull Moment 43. Won Ton Ton (guest appearance by Harry and Jim) 76.

Riva, Emmanuele (1932–).
French leading actress, a former dressmaker.
Hiroshima Mon Amour 59. Adua et Sa Compagnie (Hungry for Love) 60. Kapo 60. Leon Morin Priest 61. Climats 61. Thérèse Desqueyroux 63. Soledad 66. The Eyes, the Mouth 83. Three Colours: Blue (Trois Couleurs: Bleu) 93, etc.

Riva, Juan Antonio de la.
Mexican director.
Wandering Lives (Vidas Errantes) 83. Pueblo de Madera 91, etc.

Rivera, Chita (1933–) (Dolores Conchita Figueroa del Rivero).
Dynamic American dancer and singer.
Sweet Charity 69. Pippin 81. That's Singing 84. The Mayflower Madam (TV) 87, etc.

Rivers, Joan (1933–).
American cabaret comedienne with a strong line in smut.
Rabbit Test 78. Tears and Laughter: The Joan and Melissa Rivers Story (TV) 94.

¶ I'm Jewish. I don't work out. If God had intended me to bend over he'd have put diamonds on the floor. – J.R.

Rivette, Jacques (1928–).
French director and screenwriter, former critic.

Le Coup du Berger 56. Paris Nous Appartient 60. La Religieuse (& w) 65. L'Amour Fou (& w) 68. Celine and Julie Go Boating 74. La Vengeresse 76. Merry Go Round 83. Love on the Ground (L'Amour par Terre) 84. Hurlevent 85. The Gang of Four (La Bande des Quatre) 89. *La Belle Noiseuse* 91. Jeanne la Pucelle 94, etc.

Rix, Brian (Lord Rix) (1924–).
British actor-manager associated with the Whitehall farces. He married actress Elspet Gray in 1949. In 1980 he retired from showbusiness to run a charity for the mentally handicapped.
Autobiography: 1977, *My Farce from My Elbow*.
Reluctant Heroes 51. What Every Woman Wants 54. Up to His Neck 54. Dry Rot 55. The Night We Dropped a Clanger 59. And the Same to You 60. Nothing Barred 61. Don't Just Lie There, Say Something 73, etc.

RKO Radio Pictures Inc.
was for many years one of Hollywood's 'big five' production companies, with its own distribution arm. It started in 1921 as a joint enterprise of the Radio Corporation of America and the Keith-Orpheum cinema circuit. Despite severe financial vicissitudes, it struggled on for twenty-seven years, buoyed by a generally decent production standard; stars like Cary Grant, Katharine Hepburn, Wheeler and Woolsey, Leon Errol; individual films such as *Cimarron, King Kong, The Informer, Suspicion, Mr Blandings Builds His Dream House* and *Fort Apache*; and the participation of Goldwyn, Disney and Selznick, all released through RKO at its peak. In 1948 Howard Hughes (qv) acquired a large share of the stock; but after a period of uncertainty RKO ceased production in 1953 and the studio was sold to Desilu TV.
A glossy book by Richard B. Jewell and Vernon Harbin, *The RKO Story*, came out in 1982 and was a valuable research tool.

Roach, Bert (1891–1971).
American silent screen actor.
The Millionaire 21. The Rowdy 21. The Flirt 22. Excitement 24. Don't 25. Money Talks 26. The Taxi Dancer 27. The Desert Rider 29. No No Nanette 30. Viennese Nights 30. Hallelujah I'm a Bum 33. San Francisco 36. Algiers 38. Hi Diddle Diddle 43. The Perils of Pauline 47, etc.

Roach, Hal (1892–1992).
American producer chiefly associated with gag comedies. Varied early experience before he teamed with Harold Lloyd 1916; later made films with Our Gang, Laurel and Hardy, etc.
SOUND FILMS: Sons of the Desert 33. *Way Out West* 36. *Topper* 37. *Of Mice and Men* 39. *Turnabout* 40. One Million BC 40. *Topper Returns* 41, many others.

¶ One of the few producers who knew talent when he saw it, and gave his stars, writers and directors the freedom to create great comedy. – *Leonard Maltin*
~AA 1983 'in recognition of his distinguished contributions to the motion picture art form'.

Road Runner.
Long-necked bird who whizzes along Arizona desert roads with a cry of 'Beep! Beep!' and gets the better of its pursuer Wile E. Coyote in Warner Brothers' Looney Tunes and Merrie Melodies cartoons. Its creators were Chuck Jones and writer Michael Maltese and its beep was supplied by the ubiquitous Mel Blanc.
Fast and Furry-Ous 49. Beep, Beep 52. There They Go-Go-Go 56. Fastest with the Mostest 60. Beep Prepared (AAN) 61. Tired and Feathered 65.

Shot and Bothered 66. Run, Run, Sweet Road Runner 65. Out and Out Rout 66, etc.

road show.
A term which used to mean a travelling show; latterly in cinema terms it indicates the special, prolonged pre-release at advanced prices of a big-screen attraction, e.g. *My Fair Lady* or *The Sound of Music*, which may in this way run for years in a big city before being released to local theatres.

Rob Roy.
Walter Scott's novel of the Scottish rebel leader Rob Roy McGregor fighting the forces of King George I was twice filmed as a silent, in 1921 with John Clyde in the title role, and in 1922, starring David Hawthorne. Disney made a version, *Rob Roy the Highland Rogue*, in 1953, directed by Harold French, with Richard Todd, Glynis Johns, and James Robertson Justice, and Michael Caton-Jones filmed a new version in 1994 with Liam Neeson, Jessica Lange, John Hurt, and Tim Roth.

Robards, Jason, Snr (1893–1963).
American stage actor, who made character appearances in films.
The Cohens and the Kellys 26. On Trial 28. Abraham Lincoln 30. The Crusades 35. I Stole a Million 39. Isle of the Dead 45. Bedlam 46. Riff Raff 47. Wild in the Country 61, many others.
TV series: Acapulco 61.

Robards, Jason, Jnr (1920–).
American stage actor, son of Jason Robards.
The Journey 58. By Love Possessed 59. *Tender is the Night* 61. Long Day's Journey into Night 62. A Thousand Clowns 65. A Big Hand for the Little Lady 66. Any Wednesday 66. Divorce American Style 67. *The Hour of the Gun* 67. The St Valentine's Day Massacre 67. The Night They Raided Minsky's 68. Isadora 68. Once Upon a Time in the West 69. Tora! Tora! Tora! 70. Julius Caesar 70. The Ballad of Cable Hogue 70. Murders in the Rue Morgue 71. Johnny Got His Gun 71. The War Between Men and Women 72. Pat Garrett and Billy the Kid 73. Play It as It Lays 73. All The President's Men 76. Washington behind Closed Doors (TV) 77. Julia (as Dashiell Hammett) (AA) 77. Comes a Horseman 78. Hurricane 79. Melvin and Howard (as Howard Hughes) (AAN) 80. Raise the Titanic 80. Caboblanco 81. The Legend of the Lone Ranger 81. Max Dugan Returns 83. The Day After (TV) 83. Something Wicked This Way Comes 83. Sakharov (TV) 84. The Last Frontier (TV) 86. Square Dance 86. Bright Lights, Big City 88. The Good Mother 88. Black Rainbow 89. Dream a Little Dream 89. Reunion 89. Parenthood 89. Quick Change 90. Gettysburg 90. Chernobyl: The Final Warning (TV) 91. Storyville 92. The Trial 93. The Adventures of Huck Finn 93. Philadelphia 93. The Paper 94. Little Big League 94, etc.

¶ I've always played disintegrated characters. – J.R.

Robbe-Grillet, Alain (1922–).
French writer, associated with Resnais in *Last Year at Marienbad* 60. Also wrote and directed:
L'Immortelle 62. Trans-Europe Express 66. Glissements Progressifs du Plaisir 73. Le Jeu avec le Feu 74. La Belle Captive 83. Un Bruit Qui Rend Fou 94.

robberies
have been a commonplace of film action fare since *The Great Train Robbery* itself; but of late there has been a fashion for showing the planning and execution of robberies through the eyes of the

participants. Perhaps this started in 1950 with *The Asphalt Jungle* (and its two remakes *The Badlanders* and *Cairo*); anyway, some of the films built in this mould are *Rififi, Five against the House, Seven Thieves, The Killing, Payroll, Piccadilly Third Stop, The Day They Robbed the Bank of England, A Prize of Gold, On Friday at Eleven, Once a Thief, He Who Rides a Tiger, Robbery, Charley Varrick, Cops and Robbers, The Taking of Pelham One Two Three, The Getaway, 11 Harrowhouse, The Bank Shot, Gambit, Dog Day Afternoon* and *Inside Out;* while films treating the same subject less seriously included *The Lavender Hill Mob, The Lady Killers, Ocean's Eleven, Persons Unknown, The League of Gentlemen, Topkapi, The Big Job, Assault on a Queen, The Biggest Bundle of Them All, Grand Slam, They Came to Rob Las Vegas, The Italian Job, The Hot Rock* and *The Anderson Tapes.* The biggest attempted robbery of all was probably the raid on Fort Knox in *Goldfinger.* Sometimes one longs for a return to the days of the dapper jewel thieves: Ronald Colman or David Niven in *Raffles,* Herbert Marshall in *Trouble in Paradise,* John Barrymore or even Charles Korvin as Arsène Lupin, Cary Grant in *To Catch a Thief.* The closest we have come to this style for many years, apart from William Wyler's *How to Steal a Million,* is 1973's *The Thief Who Came to Dinner* with Ryan O'Neal. In 1964 TV made a gallant effort with *The Rogues.*

Robbins, Gale (1922–1980).
American leading lady and singer.
In the Meantime Darling 44. My Girl Tisa 48. The Barkleys of Broadway 49. Oh You Beautiful Doll 49. Three Little Words 50. Strictly Dishonourable 51. The Belle of New York 52. Calamity Jane 53. Double Jeopardy 55. Stand Up and Be Counted 72, etc.

Robbins, Harold (1916–   ) (Francis Kane).
American best-selling novelist whose over-sexed tales have been readily transcribed to the screen.
Never Love a Stranger 58. King Creole 58. The Carpetbaggers 64. Where Love Has Gone 64. Nevada Smith 66. Stiletto 69. The Adventurers 69. The Betsy 77. The Pirate (TV) 78. 79 Park Avenue (TV) 79. The Dream Merchants (TV) 80, etc.
TV series: *The Survivors* 69.

¶ I live this way, sometimes. – *H.R.*
Hemingway was a jerk. – *H.R.*

Robbins, Jerome (1918–   ) (Jerome Rabinowitz).
American dancer and ballet-master who has choreographed several films.
The King and I 56. *West Side Story* (& co-d) (AA) 61, etc.

Robbins, Matthew.
American director and screenwriter.
The Sugarland Express (co-w) 74. The Bingo Long Traveling All-Stars and Motor Kings (co-w) 76. MacArthur (co-w) 77. Corvette Summer (co-w, d) 78. Dragonslayer (co-w, d) 81. Warning Sign (co-w) 85. The Legend of Billy Jean (d) 85. Batteries Not Included (co-w, d) 87. Bingo (d) 91, etc.

Robbins, Tim (1958–   ).
American leading actor, singer and songwriter who has recently turned to screenwriting and directing.
No Small Affair 84. The Sure Thing 85. Howard the Duck 86. Top Gun 86. Bull Durham 88. Erik the Viking 89. Miss Firecracker 89. Cadillac Man 90. Jacob's Ladder 90. The Player 92. Bob Roberts (& wd, s) 92. The Hudsucker Proxy 94. The

Shawshank Redemption 94. Prêt-à-Porter (aka Ready to Wear) 94, etc.

¶ Whether a movie is going to be a success or a failure, and consequently whether you're going to be a success or failure yourself, is always a crapshoot. – *T.R.*

Rober, Richard (1906–1952).
American general-purpose actor with stage experience.
Smart Girls Don't Talk 48. Deported 50. The Well 52. The Devil Makes Three 52, etc.

Robert, Yves (1920–   ).
French director, former actor.
The War of the Buttons 61. *Bébert et l'Omnibus* 63. *Copains* 64. *Follow the Guy with One Black Shoe* 72. Pardon Mon Affaire 76. We All Shall Go to Paradise 77. Courage Fuyons 79. Le Jumeau 84. My Father's Glory (La Gloire de Mon Père) 90. My Mother's Castle (Le Château de Ma Mère) 90. Le Bal des Casse-Pieds 92. Montparnasse Pondichery 94, etc.

Roberti, Lyda (1910–1938).
German-Polish leading lady, former child café singer, in several Hollywood films of the 30s.
■ Million Dollar Legs 32. The Kid from Spain 32. Dancers in the Dark 32. Torch Singers 33. Three-Cornered Moon 33. College Rhythm 34. The Big Broadcast of 1936 35. George White's Scandals 35. Pick a Star 37. Nobody's Baby 37. Wide Open Faces 37.

Roberts, Ben (1916–1984) (Benjamin Eisenberg).
American writer, almost always with Ivan Goff (qv).

Roberts, Eric (1956–   ).
American leading man of the late 70s.
King of the Gypsies 78. Raggedy Man 81. Star 80 83. The Pope of Greenwich Village 84. The Coca Cola Kid 85. Runaway Train (AAN) 85. Nobody's Fool 86. Dear America 87. Best of the Best 89. Options 89. Rude Awakening 89. Blood Red 89. The Ambulance 90. Descending Angel 91. Lonely Hearts 91. By the Sword 91. Final Analysis 92. Best of the Best II 93. The Hard Truth 94. Love, Cheat & Steal 94. The Specialist 94, etc.

Roberts, Ewan (1914–1983) (Thomas McEwan Hutchinson).
Scottish character actor of stage and screen.
Castle in the Air 52. The Lady Killers 55. Night of the Demon 57. The Day of the Triffids 61. The Traitors 62. Five to One 63. Hostile Witness 67. Bedevilled 71. Endless Night 72, etc.

Roberts, Florence (1860–1940).
American character actress best remembered as Granny in the Jones Family series 1936–40.

Roberts, Julia (1967–   ).
American actress, a former model who rapidly established herself as the most sought-after actress of the early 90s. She is the sister of Eric Roberts.
Blood Red 88. Satisfaction 88. Baja Oklahoma (TV) 88. Mystic Pizza 88. Steel Magnolias (AAN) 89. Pretty Woman 90. Flatliners 90. Sleeping with the Enemy 90. Dying Young 91. Hook 91. The Pelican Brief 93. I Love Trouble 94. Prêt-à-Porter (aka Ready to Wear) 94. Mary Reilly 95, etc.

¶ I never really made it to acting school. I went to acting classes a few times, but it never seemed very conducive to what I wanted to do. – *J.R.*

Roberts, Kenneth (1885–1957).
American adventure novelist. The filming of *Northwest Passage* was never completed; the title on King Vidor's film reads *Northwest Passage, Part One: Rogers' Rangers. Lydia Bailey* fared better.

Roberts, Lynne (1922–   ) (Mary Hart).
American leading lady of 40s second features.
Dangerous Holiday 37. Winter Wonderland 39. Call of the Klondike 41. Quiet Please Murder 42. The Great Plane Robbery 47. The Blazing Forest 52. Port Sinister 53, many others.

Roberts, Pernell (1930–   ).
American general-purpose actor; became famous as one of the brothers in TV's *Bonanza,* but left after four years and never regained the limelight until 1979, when he played the title role in the series *Trapper John MD.*
Ride Lonesome 58. The Silent Gun (TV) 69. The Magic of Lassie 78. Night Train to Kathmandu (TV) 88, etc.

Roberts, Rachel (1927–1980).
Welsh character actress in leading roles. Born in Llanelli, she studied at the University of Wales and RADA and, in 1950, began working with a repertory company in Swansea (where her fellow players included Kenneth Williams and Richard Burton) and was in films from the mid-50s, coming into her own with *Saturday Night and Sunday Morning* 60 and *This Sporting Life.* Insecurity, the breakdown of her marriage to Rex Harrison (1962–71) and alcoholism bedevilled her later career and she committed suicide. Her first husband was actor Alan Dobie (1955–61).
Autobiography: *No Bells on Sunday* (edited by Alexander Walker).
Valley of Song 52. The Good Companions 57. Our Man in Havana 59. Saturday Night and Sunday Morning (BFA) 60. This Sporting Life (AAN, BFA) 63. A Flea in Her Ear 68. Doctors' Wives 71. Wild Rovers 71. O Lucky Man 73. The Belstone Fox 73. Murder on the Orient Express 74. Great Expectations (TV) 75. Picnic at Hanging Rock 76. Foul Play 78. When a Stranger Calls 79. Yanks (BFA) 79. Charlie Chan and the Curse of the Dragon Queen 81, etc.
TV series: The Tony Randall Show 76.

¶ Whenever I act well, my head clears. Always a bit frail I was personally, but never professionally. – *R.R.*
Day after day and night after night, I'm in this shaking fear. What am I so terribly frightened of? Life itself, I think. – *R.R.'s last entry in her journal*
She was like a ball of fire: the only trouble was, so often she had no material worthy of setting alight with her combustible energy. – *Pamela Mason*
She had good legs. How do I know? Because she was forever throwing her dress up over her head. – *Richard Gere*
That big, carnal, sensuous stage personality of hers is damn hard to find nowadays. – *Hal Prince*

Roberts, Roy (1900–1975).
American character actor who once played cops but graduated to senior executives.
Guadalcanal Diary 43. My Darling Clementine 46. Flaming Fury 49. The Big Trees 52. The Glory Brigade 53. The Boss 56, many others.
TV series: Petticoat Junction 64–68.

Roberts, Stephen (1895–1936).
American director.
■ Sky Bride 32. Lady and Gent 32. The Night of June 13th 32. If I Had a Million (part) 32. The

Story of Temple Drake 33. *One Sunday Afternoon* 33. The Trumpet Blows 34. Romance in Manhattan 34. *Star of Midnight* 35. The Man Who Broke the Bank at Monte Carlo 35. The Lady Consents 36. The Ex Mrs Bradford 36.

Roberts, Theodore (1861–1928).
American character actor, the grand old man of the silent screen.

Where the Trail Divides 14. The Trail of the Lonesome Pine 16. Male and Female 19. The Affairs of Anatol 21. Our Leading Citizen 22. *The Ten Commandments* (as Moses) 23. Grumpy 23. Locked Doors 25. Masks of the Devil 28, many others.

Roberts, Tony (1939–).
American light leading man.

The Beach Girls and the Monster 70. Star Spangled Girl 71. Play It Again Sam 72. Serpico 73. Le Sauvage 75. Annie Hall 77. Just Tell Me What You Want 80. A Midsummer Night's Sex Comedy 82. Amityville 3-D 83. Key Exchange 85. Hannah and Her Sisters 85. Radio Days 87. Switch 91. Popcorn 91, etc.

Robertshaw, Jerrold (1866–1941).
Gaunt British stage actor who made several film appearances.

Dombey and Son 18. She 25. Downhill 27. Kitty 29. Don Quixote (title role) 33, etc.

Robertson, Cliff (1925–).
Ambitious American leading man with long stage experience before being spotted for films.

■ *Picnic* (debut) 55. Autumn Leaves 56. The Girl Most Likely 57. The Naked and the Dead 58. Gidget 59. Battle of the Coral Sea 59. As the Sea Rages 60. All in a Night's Work 61. The Big Show 61. Underworld USA 61. The Interns 62. My Six Loves 63. *PT 109* (as President Kennedy) 63. Sunday in New York 64. *The Best Man* 64. 633 Squadron 64. Love Has Many Faces 65. Masquerade (GB) 65. Up from the Beach 65. *The Honey Pot* 67. The Devil's Brigade 68. Charly (AA) 68. Too Late the Hero 69. The Great Northfield Minnesota Raid 72. J. W. Coop (& p, d) 72. Ace Eli and Rodger of the Skies 73. Man on a Swing 74. My Father's House (TV) 75. Out of Season 75. Three Days of the Condor 76. Midway 76. Shoot 76. Obsession 76. *Washington behind Closed Doors* (TV) 77. Fraternity Row (narrator) 77. Dominique 78. The Pilot (& wd) 80. Two of a Kind (TV) 82. Class 83. Brainstorm 83. Star 80 83. The Key to Rebecca (TV) 85. Shaker Run 85. Wild Hearts Can't Be Broken 91. Wind 92. Renaissance Man 94.

TV series: Rod Brown of the Rocket Rangers 53. Falcon Crest 83–84.

¶ As long as I get phone calls from the Museum of Modern Art, that all the film buffs love it, that's a residual. It isn't a financial residual and it isn't an artistic residual, but it's an ego residual. – C.R.
~In 1979 Robertson's career suffered unfairly when he accused executive David Begelman of having falsely signed a cheque in his name. The incident became a major scandal and is covered in the book *Indecent Exposure* by David McClintock.

Robertson, Dale (1923–).
American western star, former schoolteacher.

Fighting Man of the Plains (debut) 49. Two Flags West 50. Lydia Bailey 52. The Silver Whip 53. Sitting Bull 54. A Day of Fury 56. Law of the Lawless 63. Blood on the Arrow 65. Coast of Skeletons 65, etc.

TV series: Tales of Wells Fargo 57–61. The Iron Horse 66. Dynasty 80–81.

Robertson, John S. (1878–1964).
Canadian director in Hollywood.

The Money Mill 17. Let's Elope 19. Dr Jekyll and Mr Hyde 20. Sentimental Tommy 21. Tess of the Storm Country 22. The Enchanted Cottage 24. Shore Leave 25. Annie Laurie 27. Shanghai Lady 29. Madonna of the Streets 30. One Man's Journey 33. Wednesday's Child 34. Captain Hurricane 35. Our Little Girl 35, many others.

Robertson, Michael.
Australian director and screenwriter.

The Best of Friends 82. Going Sane 85.

Robertson, Robbie (1943–) (Jaime Robertson).
Canadian composer, songwriter, and guitarist, a member of the leading 70s rock group The Band.

The Last Waltz (doc) 78. Carny (a, co-w) 80. The King of Comedy 83. The Color of Money 86. Jimmy Hollywood 94, etc.

Robertson, Willard (1886–1948).
American character actor, often seen as lawyer or prison governor.

Skippy 31. Sky Devils 32. I Am a Fugitive from a Chain Gang 32. Doctor X 32. Tugboat Annie 33. Death on the Diamond 34. Here Comes the Navy 34. Black Fury 35. The Gorgeous Hussy 36. Exclusive 37. Men with Wings 38. Jesse James 39. Each Dawn I Die 39. My Little Chickadee 40. The Monster and the Girl 41. Juke Girl 42. Nine Girls 44. The Virginian 46. To Each His Own 46. Sitting Pretty 48, many others.

Robeson, Paul (1898–1976).
American actor and singer, on stage including concerts from mid-20s.

Biographies, all entitled *Paul Robeson*: 1958, by Marie Seton. 1968, by Edwin P. Hoyt. 1974, by Virginia Hamilton.

■ *Body and Soul* 24. The Emperor Jones 33. *Sanders of the River* 35. *Showboat* 36. *Song of Freedom* 36. Jericho 38. Big Fella 38. *King Solomon's Mines* 38. *The Proud Valley* 39. Tales of Manhattan 42. Native Land 42. Il Canto dei Grandi Fiumi 55.

Robey, Sir George (1869–1954) (George Edward Wade).
British music-hall comedian, 'the prime minister of mirth'. Appeared in silent farcical comedies, later in character roles.

Autobiography: 1933, *Looking Back on Life*.
Biography: 1991, *George Robey* by James Harding.

The Rest Cure 23. Don Quixote (as Sancho Panza) 23 and 33. Her Prehistoric Man 24. Chu Chin Chow 33. Marry Me 33. Birds of a Feather 36. A Girl Must Live 39. Variety Jubilee 40. Salute John Citizen 42. Henry V 44. The Trojan Brothers 45. The Pickwick Papers 52, etc.

Robin, Dany (1927–).
French leading lady.

Le Silence est d'Or 46. Histoire d'Amour 52. Act of Love 54. In Six Easy Lessons 60. The Waltz of the Toreadors 62. Topaz 69, etc.

Robin Hood.
The legendary outlaw leader of Plantagenet England is one of literature's most oft-filmed characters. There were film versions in 1909 (GB), 1912 (GB), 1912 (US), 1913 (US), and 1913 (GB). Douglas Fairbanks made his big-scale *Robin Hood* in 1922, with Wallace Beery as King Richard. In 1938 came The Adventures of Robin Hood, one of

Hollywood's most satisfying action adventures, with Errol Flynn as Robin, Claude Rains as Prince John and Basil Rathbone as Guy of Gisbourne; directed by William Keighley and Michael Curtiz, from a script by Norman Reilly Raine and Seton I. Miller. Its exhilaration has not diminished with time. In 1946 (US) Cornel Wilde played Robin's son in *Bandit of Sherwood Forest*; in 1948 (US) Jon Hall was Robin in *Prince of Thieves*; in 1950 (US) John Derek was Robin's son in *Rogues of Sherwood Forest*; Robert Clarke played Robin in an odd concoction called *Tales of Robin Hood* (US 1952). Also in 1952, in Britain, Disney filmed Richard Todd in *The Story of Robin Hood and His Merrie Men*, with only fair success, though the real Sherwood Forest was used for the first time. Robin also appeared briefly (played by Harold Warrender) in *Ivanhoe* 52. *Men of Sherwood Forest* (GB 1956) had Don Taylor as Robin; *Son of Robin Hood* (GB 1959) turned out to be a daughter, played by June Laverick. Most durable Robin is Richard Greene, who played the role not only in 165 half-hour TV films but in a feature, *Sword of Sherwood Forest* (GB 1961). In 1967 Barrie Ingham took over in *A Challenge for Robin Hood*, in 1973 the Disney studios produced a cartoon version, and in 1976 came *Robin and Marian*, which traced the sad fortunes of the protagonists twenty years later. A new television series, *Robin of Sherwood*, appeared in 1984. Patrick Bergin played the role, with Uma Thurman as a petulant Maid Marian, in the downbeat *Robin Hood* 91. It was swiftly eclipsed by the dour Kevin Costner in *Robin Hood: Prince of Thieves* which was, surprisingly, one of the box-office successes of 1991 – though the acting honours went to Alan Rickman as a dastardly Sheriff of Nottingham.

Robin, Leo (1899–1984).
American lyricist. Songs include 'Louise', 'Beyond the Blue Horizon', 'June in January', 'No Love No Nothing'.

Innocents of Paris 29. Monte Carlo 30. One Hour with You 32. Little Miss Marker 34. The Big Broadcast of 1938 (AA for 'Thanks for the Memory'). Gulliver's Travels 39. My Gal Sal 43. Meet Me after the Show 50. My Sister Eileen 55, etc.

Robinson, Andrew.
Baby-faced American character actor who has played a couple of memorable villains.

Dirty Harry 71. Charley Varrick 73. The Drowning Pool 75. Cobra 86. Shoot to Kill 88. Prime Target 91. Child's Play 3 91, etc.

Robinson, Bill (1878–1949).
American tap-dancer and entertainer, famous for his stairway dance.

The Little Colonel 35. In Old Kentucky 36. Rebecca of Sunnybrook Farm 38. *Stormy Weather* 43, etc.

Robinson, Bruce (1946–).
British screenwriter and director, a former actor.

■ The Killing Fields (w) (AAN) 84. *Withnail and I* (wd) 87. How to Get Ahead in Advertising (wd) 89. Fat Man and Little Boy (aka The Shadow-makers) (co-w) 89. Jennifer 8 92.

¶ There are two types of animals roaming the Hollywood jungle. Those who do the screwing, those who get screwed. You have to try to ensure you're one of the former. – B.R.

Robinson, Cardew (Douglas Robinson).
Lanky English comic actor, best known for his act as delinquent schoolboy 'Cardew the Cad, the Bad Boy of St Fanny's', from variety and radio.

Knight without Armour 37. A Piece of Cake 48. Fun at St Fanny's 56. Happy Is the Bride 58. I'm All Right, Jack 59. The Navy Lark 59. Waltz of the Toreadors 62. Heavens Above 63. Father Came Too 64. Alfie 66. Carry On up the Khyber 67. Where's Jack 69. The Magnificent 7 Deadly Sins 71. What's Up Nurse? 75. Guess Who's Coming to Dinner? 85. Pirates 86, etc.

Robinson, Casey (1903–1979).
American screenwriter, in Hollywood from 1921.
I Love That Man 33. Captain Blood 35. Call it a Day 37. It's Love I'm After 37. Four's a Crowd 39. *Kings Row* 42. Passage to Marseilles 44. Days of Glory 44. *The Macomber Affair* 47. Under My Skin (& p) 50. Two Flags West (& p) 50. Diplomatic Courier (& p) 52. The Snows of Kilimanjaro 52. While the City Sleeps 56. This Earth is Mine (& p) 59, etc.

Robinson Crusoe.
There have been many film variations on Defoe's novel. The closest to the original have been Luis Buñuel's *The Adventures of Robinson Crusoe* (Mexico, 1953), with Dan O'Herlihy, and oddly enough Byron Haskin's *Robinson Crusoe on Mars* (US, 1954), with Paul Mantee. *Lt Robin Crusoe, U.S.N.* (US, 1966) had a shipwrecked mariner teaming up with a chimpanzee and a Girl Wednesday. *Man Friday* (GB, 1975), with Peter O'Toole and Richard Roundtree, tried to be satirical by showing the situation from Friday's viewpoint. *Crusoe* (US, 1988), with Aidan Quinn, turned him into a slave trader.

Robinson, David (1930–).
English critic and author, notably as the biographer of Charlie Chaplin in *Chaplin: His Life and Art* (1985). He was film critic for the *Financial Times* and *The Times*. His books include *World Cinema*, *The Great Funnies*, *Buster Keaton*.

Robinson, Edward G. (1893–1973) (Emanuel Goldenberg).
Dynamic American star actor of Rumanian origin. On stage from 1913; later settled in Hollywood. Special Academy Award 1972.
Autobiography: 1973, *All My Yesterdays*.
■ The Bright Shawl 23. The Hole in the Wall 29. Night Ride 30. A Lady to Love 30. Outside the Law 30. East is West 30. Widow from Chicago 30. *Little Caesar* (which made him a star) 30. Five Star Final 31. Smart Money 31. The Hatchet Man 31. Two Seconds 32. Tiger Shark 32. Silver Dollar 32. The Little Giant 33. I Loved a Woman 33. Dark Hazard 34. The Man with Two Faces 34. *The Whole Town's Talking* 34. Barbary Coast 35. Bullets or Ballots 36. Thunder in the City (GB) 37. Kid Galahad 37. The Last Gangster 38. *A Slight Case of Murder* 38. *The Amazing Dr Clitterhouse* 38. I Am the Law 38. Confessions of a Nazi Spy 39. Blackmail 39. *Dr Ehrlich's Magic Bullet* 40. Brother Orchid 40. A Dispatch from Reuters 41. *The Sea Wolf* 41. Manpower 41. Unholy Partners 41. Larceny Inc. 42. Tales of Manhattan 42. Destroyer 43. Flesh and Fantasy 43. Tampico 44. *Double Indemnity* 44. Mr Winkle Goes to War 44. *The Woman in the Window* 44. Our Vines Have Tender Grapes 45. *Scarlet Street* 45. Journey Together (GB) 45. The Stranger 46. The Red House 47. *All My Sons* 48. Key Largo 48. Night Has a Thousand Eyes 48. *House of Strangers* 49. My Daughter Joy (GB) 50. Actors and Sin 52. Vice Squad 53. Big Leaguer 53. The Glass Web 53. Black Tuesday 54. The Violent Men 55. Tight Spot 55. A Bullet for Joey 55. Illegal 55. Hell on Frisco Bay 56. Nightmare 56. The Ten Commandments 56. A Hole in the Head 59. Seven Thieves 59. Pépé 60. My Geisha 62. *Two Weeks in*

Another Town 62. Sammy Going South (GB) 62. The Prize 63. Good Neighbour Sam 64. Robin and the Seven Hoods 64. Cheyenne Autumn 64. The Outrage 64. *The Cincinnati Kid* 65. Who Has Seen the Wind? 65. The Biggest Bundle of Them All 66. Never a Dull Moment 67. Grand Slam 67. Mackenna's Gold 68. It's Your Move 68. Operation St Peter's 68. Blonde from Peking 68. Song of Norway 69. Operation Heartbeat (TV) 69. The Old Man Who Cried Wolf (TV) 71. Soylent Green 73. ✪ For the dynamic personality which turned many a dubious script into dramatic gold. *Double Indemnity*.

¶ Some people have youth, some have beauty – I have menace. – *E.G.R.*

Famous line (*Little Caesar*): 'Mother of mercy, is this the end of Rico?'

Robinson, Frances (1916–1971).
American supporting actress, usually in smart roles.
Forbidden Valley 25. The Last Warning 28. Tim Tyler's Luck 35. The Lone Wolf Keeps a Date 37. The Invisible Man Returns 39. Tower of London 39. Smilin' Through 41. Suddenly It's Spring 46. Keeper of the Bees 47. Backfire 50, many others.

Robinson, George (c. 1895–1958).
American cinematographer.
No Defense 21. Back to God's Country 27. Hell's Heroes 30. Her First Mate 33. The Mystery of Edwin Drood 35. Diamond Jim 35. The Invisible Ray 36. Sutter's Gold 36. Dracula's Daughter 36. The Road Back 37. *Son of Frankenstein* 39. Tower of London 39. Son of Monte Cristo 40. Frankenstein Meets the Wolf Man 43. Son of Dracula 43. *The Scarlet Claw* 44. House of Frankenstein 45. The Naughty Nineties 45. Slave Girl 47. The Creeper 48. Abbott and Costello Meet Dr Jekyll and Mr Hyde 53. Tarantula 55. Joe Dakota 57, many others.

Robinson, Jay (1930–).
American stage actor of eccentric roles.
The Robe 53. Demetrius and the Gladiators 54. The Virgin Queen 55. My Man Godfrey 57. Bunny O'Hare 71. Shampoo 75. Partners 82. The Malibu Bikini Shop 86. Transylvania Twist 89, etc.

Robinson, Joe (1929–).
British actor and professional boxer.
Master of Bankdam 48. Daughter of Darkness 49. *A Kid for Two Farthings* 55. The Flesh Is Weak 57. The Two Faces of Dr Jekyll 58. Barabbas 62. Diamonds Are Forever 71, etc.

Robinson, John (1908–1979).
British stage actor, familiar in heavy father or tough executive roles.
The Scarab Murder Case 36. The Lion Has Wings 40. Uneasy Terms 49. Hammer the Toff 51. The Constant Husband 55. Fortune is a Woman 58. The Doctor's Dilemma 58. And the Same to You 61, etc.

Robinson, Madeleine (1916–) (Madeleine Svoboda).
French stage and film actress.
Soldats sans Uniformes 43. Douce 43. Une Si Jolie Petite Plage 48. Dieu a Besoin des Hommes 50. Le Garçon Sauvage 51. The She Wolves 57. A Double Tour 59. The Trial 64. A Trap for Cinderella 65. A New World 66. Le Voyage du Père 66. Le Petit Matin 70. Camille Claudel 88, etc.

Robinson, Phil Alden (1950–).
American director and screenwriter.
All of Me (w) 84. Rhinestone (co-w) 84. In the Mood (wd) 87. Field of Dreams (wd) (AAN) 89. Relentless (w) 89. Ghost Dad (co-w) 90. Sneakers (d) 92, etc.

Robison, Arthur (1888–1935).
Chicago-born director of German films.
Warning Shadows 24. The Informer (GB) 29. The Student of Prague 35, etc.

Robocop.
A cyborg created from the remains of a cop shot by drug-dealers in a future Detroit, and turned into an invincible upholder of law and order, who has been the hero of three films so far. The first, directed by Paul Verhoeven, is by far the best. Peter Weller played the role in the first two films. In *Robocop 3*, Robert Burke took over. Richard Eden played the role in a 1994 television series.

robots
have been sparingly used in movies. Brigitte Helm memorably played one in *Metropolis*; so did Patricia Roc in *The Perfect Woman*. Robby the Robot featured sympathetically in *Forbidden Planet* and *Invisible Boy*; then there was *Kronos*, and Gort in *The Day the Earth Stood Still*. *Westworld*, *Futureworld* and *Star Wars* brought in a whole race of robots, one of whom looked like Yul Brynner; while in TV, *The Avengers* have frequently encountered the Cybernauts and *Dr Who* the Daleks.

Robson, Dame Flora (1902–1984).
Distinguished British stage actress.
Biography: 1981, *Flora: The Life of Dame Flora Robson* by Kenneth Barrow.
■ Dance Pretty Lady 31. One Precious Year 33. Catherine the Great 34. *Fire over England* 36. Farewell Again 37. Wuthering Heights 39. Poison Pen 39. We Are Not Alone 39. Invisible Stripes 39. The Sea Hawk 40. Banana Passage 41. Saratoga Trunk 43. 2000 Women 44. Great Day 45. Caesar and Cleopatra 45. The Years Between 46. *Black Narcissus* 46. Good Time Girl 47. Frieda 47. Holiday Camp 47. Saraband for Dead Lovers 48. The Tall Headlines 52. The Malta Story 53. Romeo and Juliet 54. *Innocent Sinners* 57. High Tide at Noon 57. No Time for Tears 57. The Gypsy and the Gentleman 58. 55 Days at Peking 62. Murder at the Gallop 63. Guns at Batasi 64. Those Magnificent Men in Their Flying Machines 64. Young Cassidy 65. Seven Women 65. The Shuttered Room 66. A Cry in the Wind 66. Eye of the Devil 67. Fragment of Fear 69. The Beloved 70. The Beast in the Cellar 71. Alice's Adventures in Wonderland 72. Comedy, Tragedy and All That 72. Dominique 78. A Man Called Intrepid (TV) 79. Les Misérables (TV) 80. A Tale of Two Cities (TV) 80. Clash of the Titans 81.

Robson, Mark (1913–1978).
Canadian-born director, former editor: began with Lewton and Kramer but progressed to more solidly commercial subjects.
■ *The Seventh Victim* 43. The Ghost Ship 43. Youth Runs Wild 44. Isle of the Dead 45. Bedlam 46. *Champion* 49. Home of the Brave 49. Roughshod 49. My Foolish Heart 50. Edge of Doom 50. Bright Victory 51. I Want You 51. Return to Paradise 53. Hell Below Zero (GB) 54. The Bridges at Toko-Ri 54. Phffft 54. A Prize of Gold 55. Trial 55. The Harder They Fall 56. The Little Hut (& p) 57. Peyton Place (AAN) 58. The Inn of the Sixth Happiness (GB) (AAN) 58. From the Terrace (& p) 59. Lisa (The Inspector) (p only) 62. Nine Hours to Rama (GB) (& p) 63. The Prize 63. *Von Ryan's Express*

(& p) 65. Lost Command (& p) 66. Valley of the Dolls (& p) 67. Daddy's Gone A-Hunting (& p) 69. Happy Birthday Wanda June 71. Limbo 73. Earthquake 74. Avalanche Express 79.

Robson, May (1858–1942) (Mary Robison).
Australian actress, in America from childhood. Long experience on stage tours before coming to Hollywood, where she played domineering but kindly old ladies.
■ How Molly Made Good 15. A Night Out 16. His Bridal Night 19. A Broadway Saint 19. The Lost Battalion 19. Pals in Paradise 26. Angel of Broadway 27. Chicago 27. A Harp in Hock 27. King of Kings 27. The Rejuvenation of Aunt Mary 27. Rubber Tires 27. Turkish Delight 27. The Blue Danube 28. Mother's Millions 31. Letty Lynton 32. Strange Interlude 32. Two against the World 32. Red Headed Woman 32. Little Orphan Annie 32. *If I Had a Million* 32. Reunion in Vienna 33. Dinner at Eight 33. Beauty for Sale 33. Broadway to Hollywood 33. Solitaire Man 33. Dancing Lady 33. *Lady for a Day* 33. One Man's Journey 33. Alice in Wonderland 33. The White Sister 33. Men Must Fight 33. You Can't Buy Everything 34. Straight Is the Way 34. Lady by Choice 34. Vanessa, Her Love Story 35. Reckless 35. Grand Old Girl 35. Age of Indiscretion 35. Anna Karenina 35. Strangers All 35. Mills of the Gods 35. Three Kids and a Queen 36. Wife vs Secretary 36. The Captain's Kid 36. Rainbow on the River 36. Woman in Distress 37. *A Star Is Born* 37. The Perfect Specimen 37. Top of the Town 37. *The Adventures of Tom Sawyer* 38. Bringing Up Baby 38. The Texans 38. *Four Daughters* 38. They Made Me a Criminal 39. Yes My Darling Daughter 39. Daughters Courageous 39. Four Wives 39. The Kid from Kokomo 39. Nurse Edith Cavell 39. That's Right You're Wrong 39. Irene 39. The Texas Rangers Ride Again 40. *Granny Get Your Gun* 40. Four Mothers 41. Million Dollar Baby 41. Playmates 42. Joan of Paris 42.

Roc, Patricia (1915–   ) (Felicia Riese).
British leading lady of the 40s, signed for films after brief stage experience.
The Rebel Son (Taras Bulba) 38. The Gaunt Stranger 39. The Mind of Mr Reeder 39. Three Silent Men 40. Let the People Sing 42. Millions Like Us 43. 2000 Women 44. Love Story 44. Madonna of the Seven Moons 44. The Wicked Lady 45. Johnny Frenchman 45. Canyon Passage (US) 46. *The Brothers* 47. Jassy 47. When the Bough Breaks 48. One Night with You 48. The Perfect Woman 49. Circle of Danger 50. The Man on the Eiffel Tower 51. Something Money Can't Buy 53. The Hypnotist 55. Bluebeard's Ten Honeymoons 60, etc.

Rocha, Glauber (1938–1981).
Brazilian director and screenwriter, a leader of his country's 'new cinema' movement. He went into exile 1970–76, making films in Europe, and died of pulmonary disease.
Barravento (The Turning Wind) 62. Deus e o Diabo na Terra do Sol (Black God, White Devil) 64. Terra em Transe (Earth Entranced) 67. Antônio das Mortes 69. Le Vent d'Est (East Wind) 69. O Leão Have Sete Cabeças (The Lion Has Seven Heads) 70. Cabeças Cortadas (Severed Heads) 71. Claro 75. A Idade da Terra (The Age of the Earth) 80, etc.

Rochant, Eric (1961–   ).
French director and screenwriter.
Tough Life 89. Love without Pity (Un Monde sans Pitié) 91. Autobus (Au Yeux du Monde) 91. Les Patriotes 94, etc.

Roche, Eugene (1928–   ).
American character actor with a slightly bewildered look; much on TV.
They Might Be Giants 71. Newman's Law 74. The Late Show 76. Corvette Summer 78. Foul Play 78. Oh God You Devil 84. Eternity 90, etc.

Rochefort, Jean (1930–   ).
French leading actor, often in comic roles.
Swords of Blood (Cartouche) 61. Angélique 64. Angélique et le Roi 65. The Devil by the Tail (Le Diable par la Queue) 69. The Tall Blond Man with One Black Shoe (Le Grand Blond avec une Chaussure Noire) 72. Salut l'Artiste 74. A Happy Divorce 75. Pardon Mon Affaire (Un Eléphant Ça Trompe Enormément) 76. The Clockmaker 76. Pardon Mon Affaire Too 77. Who Is Killing the Great Chefs of Europe? (aka Too Many Chefs) 78. Till Marriage Us Do Part 79. French Postcards 79. I Hate Blondes (Odio le Blonde) 83. Birgit Haas Must Be Killed (Il Faut Tuer Birgit Haas) 83. My First Forty Years (I Miei Primi Quarant'anni) 89. The Hairdresser's Husband (Le Mari de la Coiffeuse) 91. Dien Bien Phu 91. Le Bal des Casse-Pieds 91. L'Atlantide 92. The Long Winter (El Largo Invierno) 92. *Tango* 93. Wild Target (Cible Émouvante) 93. Tombes du Ciel 93. La Prossima Volta il Fuoco 93. Tom Est Tout Seul 94, etc.

Rock, Chris.
American actor and screenwriter, also a stand-up comedian, a regular on NBC's *Saturday Night Live* from 1990.
I'm Gonna Git You Sucka (a) 88. New Jack City (a) 91. Boomerang (a) 92. Coneheads (a) 93. CB4: The Movie (a, co-w) 93, etc.

Rock, Joe (1891–1984).
American independent producer who, after experience in vaudeville and a brief spell in Hollywood, worked in Britain from the mid-30s, turning out quota quickies, several featuring Leslie Fuller, and also backed Michael Powell's The Edge of the World. He expanded his studios at Elstree to increase production but became bankrupt in 1937.
Krakatoa (US) 33. Captain Bill 35. The Stoker 35. Strictly Illegal 35. Everything Is Rhythm 36. One Good Turn 36. The Man behind the Mask 36. Boys Will Be Girls 37. Cotton Queen 37. The Edge of the World 37. Swing as You Swing 37. Reverse Be My Lot 38, etc.

Rockwell, Alexandre.
American director. He is married to actress Jennifer Beals.
Sons 89. In the Soup 92. Someone to Love 94.

Rocky Balboa.
Dim but enduring, and even endearing, boxer created by Sylvester Stallone, as actor and screenwriter, in the Oscar-winning film *Rocky* 75, directed by John Avildsen, and four sequels (1979–90), in which he wins and loses championships and ends up brain-damaged, but training a protégé to succeed him.

Roddam, Franc (1946–   ).
British director.
■ Quadrophenia 79. The Lords of Discipline 82. The Bride 85. Aria (co-d) 87. War Party 89. K2 91.

Roddenberry, Gene (1921–1991).
American TV producer and writer, creator of *Star Trek* and *Star Trek: The Next Generation* and executive producer of the *Star Trek* films. Wrote and produced *Pretty Maids All in a Row* 70.

Biography: 1994, *Gene Roddenberry: The Myth and the Man behind Star Trek* by Joel Engel.

Rodgers, Anton (1933–   ).
British comic character actor.
Rotten to the Core 65. Scrooge 70. The Day of the Jackal 73. The Fourth Protocol 87. Dirty Rotten Scoundrels 88. Impromptu 89. Son of the Pink Panther 93, etc.
TV series: Fresh Fields 83–86. May to December 92–94.

Rodgers, Richard (1902–1979).
American composer who worked variously with lyricists Lorenz Hart and Oscar Hammerstein II.
Love Me Tonight 32. *Hallelujah I'm a Bum* 33. On Your Toes 38. Babes in Arms 39. The Boys from Syracuse 40. *State Fair* 45. *Oklahoma!* 55. *The King and I* 56. *Pal Joey* 57. *South Pacific* 58. *The Sound of Music* 65, many other complete scores and single songs.

Rodney, Red (1928–1994) (Robert Chudnik).
American jazz trumpeter and bandleader, best known for his association with alto saxophonist Charlie Parker. He was an adviser on Clint Eastwood's biopic of Parker, *Bird*, in which he was played by Michael Zelniker.

Rodrigues, Percy (1924–   ).
Canadian character actor.
The Plainsman 67. The Sweet Ride 68. The Heart is a Lonely Hunter 68. Genesis II (TV) 73. Brainwaves 82, etc.

Rodriguez, Robert (1969–   ).
American director, screenwriter, and editor, born in San Antonio, Texas, whose first film was made in Mexico at a reported cost of $7,000 and picked up by Columbia Pictures for distribution.
El Mariachi 92. Roadracers (TV) 94.

Roeg, Nicolas (1928–   ).
British cinematographer and director.
AS CINEMATOGRAPHER: The System 63. Nothing but the Best 64. The Caretaker 66. Petulia 67. A Funny Thing Happened on the Way to the Forum 68. Far from the Madding Crowd 68, etc.
■ AS DIRECTOR: Performance (co-d) 72. *Walkabout* 72. *Don't Look Now* 73. The Man Who Fell to Earth 76. Bad Timing 79. Eureka 83. Insignificance 85. Castaway 87. Aria (co-d) 87. Track 29 87. The Witches 90. Cold Heaven 92. Heart of Darkness (TV) 94.

¶ They said, even the bath water's dirty. – *N.R. on Warner's reaction to Performance*

Roemer, Michael (1928–   ).
German-born independent film director and academic, in America. His feature The Plot against Harry 69 was released to good reviews after 20 years on the shelf.
A Touch of the Times (d) 49. The Inferno (co-d) 62. *Nothing but a Man* (co-d) 65. The Plot against Harry (wd) 69 (released 89). Pilgrim Farewell (wd) 80. Haunted (d) (TV) 84, etc.

Roemheld, Heinz (1901–1985).
German musical director, long in Hollywood.
Golden Harvest 33. The Invisible Man 33. Imitation of Life 34. Dracula's Daughter 36. A Child Is Born 40. The Strawberry Blonde (AAN) 41. Blues in the Night 41. Yankee Doodle Dandy (AA) 42. Shine On, Harvest Moon 44. Heaven Only Knows 47. The Lady from Shanghai 48. Rogues of Sherwood Forest 50. Ruby Gentry 53. The 5,000 Fingers of Dr T. (co-m) 53. The

Creature Walks among Us 56. The Monster that Challenged the World 57. Ride Lonesome 59. Lad: A Dog 61, many others.

Rogell, Albert S. (1901–1988).

American director of second features, former cameraman.

Señor Daredevil 26. Mamba 30. Riders of Death Valley 32. Argentine Nights 40. Trouble Chaser 40. The Black Cat 41. Tight Shoes 41. In Old Oklahoma 43. Heaven Only Knows 47. Northwest Stampede 48. The Admiral was a Lady (& p) 50. Men against Speed 58, etc.

Roger Rabbit.

Madcap rabbit with a sexy human wife and the troublesome Baby Herman to look after. Following the success of the Walt Disney feature *Who Framed Roger Rabbit*, combining animated characters and live actors, he has appeared in shorts noted for their fast, slapstick action. Created by novelist Gary Wolf, he is voiced by Charles Fleischer and his wife Jessica by Kathleen Turner.

Who Framed Roger Rabbit 88. Tummy Trouble 89. Rollercoaster Rabbit 90.

Rogers, Charles (c. 1890–1960).

Diminutive English music-hall comedian who had a long association with Laurel and Hardy as gagman, screenwriter, and director. He played bit parts in several of their films, and also co-starred with Harry Langdon in a couple of comedies.

Two Tars (a) 28. Habeas Corpus (a) 28. The Devil's Brother (co-d) 33. Me and My Pal (co-d) 33. Going Bye-Bye! (d) 34. Them Thar Hills (d) 34. Babes in Toyland (co-d) 34. The Bohemian Girl (co-d) 36. Way out West (co-w) 37. Blockheads (co-w) 38. The Flying Deuces (co-w) 39. A Chump at Oxford (co-w) 40. Saps at Sea (co-w) 40. Misbehaving Husbands (a) 40. Double Trouble (a) 41. The Dancing Masters (a) 43, etc.

Rogers, Charles 'Buddy' (1904–).

American light leading man of the 20s and 30s; married to Mary Pickford.

Fascinating Youth 26. Wings 27. Abie's Irish Rose 29. Paramount on Parade 30. Varsity 30. Young Eagles 31. This Reckless Age 32. Old Man Rhythm 35. Once in a Million 36. This Way Please 38. Golden Hooves 41. Mexican Spitfire's Baby 43. Don't Trust Your Husband 48, many others.

Rogers, Eric (*–1981).

English composer who scored many of the Carry On movies.

The Iron Maiden 62. Carry On Regardless (com) 62. Carry On Cabby 63. Carry On Spying 64. Carry On Cleo 64. Carry On Cowboy 65. Carry On Screaming 66. Carry On – Don't Lose Your Head 66. Carry On Doctor 68. Carry On up the Khyber 68. Carry On Again Doctor 69. Assault (US: In the Devil's Garden) 70. Quest for Love 71. Carry On Abroad 72. Carry On Behind 75. Carry On Emmannuelle 78, etc.

Rogers, Ginger (1911–) (Virginia McMath).

American leading actress, comedienne and dancer, affectionately remembered for her 30s musicals with Fred Astaire. Former band singer; then brief Broadway experience before being taken to Hollywood.

■ Young Man of Manhattan 30. Queen High 30. The Sap from Syracuse 30. Follow the Leader 30. Honor among Lovers 31. The Tip Off 31. Suicide Fleet 31. Carnival Boat 32. The Tenderfoot 32. The Thirteenth Guest 32. Hat Check Girl 32. You Said a Mouthful 32. 42nd Street (as Anytime Annie) 33. Broadway Bad 33. Gold Diggers of 1933.

Professional Sweetheart 33. A Shriek in the Night 33. Don't Bet on Love 33. Sitting Pretty 33. *Flying Down to Rio* 33. Chance at Heaven 33. Rafter Romance 34. Finishing School 34. Twenty Million Sweethearts 34. Change of Heart 34. Upperworld 34. *The Gay Divorcee* 34. Romance in Manhattan 34. Roberta 35. Star of Midnight 35. *Top Hat* 35. In Person 35. *Follow the Fleet* 36. Swing Time 36. Shall We Dance 36. *Stage Door* 37. Having Wonderful Time 38. Vivacious Lady 38. Carefree 38. The Story of Vernon and Irene Castle 39. *Bachelor Mother* 39. Fifth Avenue Girl 39. The Primrose Path 40. Lucky Partners 40. *Kitty Foyle* (AA) 40. Tom Dick and Harry 41. *Roxie Hart* 42. Tales of Manhattan 42. The Major and the Minor 42. Once Upon a Honeymoon 42. Tender Comrade 43. Lady in the Dark 44. I'll Be Seeing You 44. Weekend at the Waldorf 45. Heartbeat 46. Magnificent Doll 46. It Had to Be You 47. The Barkleys of Broadway 49. Perfect Strangers 50. Storm Warning 50. The Groom Wore Spurs 51. We're Not Married 52. Monkey Business 52. Dreamboat 52. Forever Female 53. Black Widow 54. Twist of Fate (Beautiful Stranger) 54. Tight Spot 55. The First Travelling Saleslady 56. Teenage Rebel 56. Oh Men Oh Women 57. The Confession 64. Harlow (electronovision) 64.

✪ For being everybody's favorite working girl of the 30s; and for being so unarguably right with Fred Astaire. *The Gay Divorcee*.

¶ He gives her class and she gives him sex.
– *Katharine Hepburn of Astaire and Rogers*
They're not going to get my money to see the junk that's made today. – *G.R., 1983*

Famous line (*Young Man of Manhattan*): 'Cigarette me, big boy.'

Rogers, Jean (1916–1991) (Eleanor Lovegren).

American light leading lady of the 30s.

Eight Girls in a Boat 34. Flash Gordon 36. My Man Godfrey 36. Night Key 37. Flash Gordon's Trip to Mars 38. Hotel for Women 39. Heaven with a Barbed Wire Fence 40. Charlie Chan in Panama 40. Dr Kildare's Victory 42. Whistling in Brooklyn 43. Hot Cargo 46. Backlash 47. The Second Woman 51, etc.

Rogers, Maclean (1899–1962).

British director, mainly of low-budget features for which he often wrote his own unambitious scripts.

The Third Eye 29. Busman's Holiday 36. Old Mother Riley Joins Up 39. Gert and Daisy's Weekend 42. Variety Jubilee 43. The Trojan Brothers 45. Calling Paul Temple 48. The Story of Shirley Yorke 49. Johnny on the Spot 54. Not So Dusty 56. Not Wanted on Voyage 57. Not a Hope in Hell 60, many others.

Rogers, Mimi (1956–).

American leading actress. She was formerly married to actor Tom Cruise.

Blue Skies Again 83. Gung Ho 86. Someone to Watch Over Me 87. Street Smart 87. Hider in the House 89. The Mighty Quinn 89. Desperate Hours 90. The Doors 91. Wedlock 91. The Rapture 92. White Sands 92. Dark Horse 92. Shooting Elizabeth 92. Monkey Trouble 94. Killer 94. Reflections on a Crime 94, etc.

TV series: The Rousters 83–84. Paper Dolls 84.

Rogers, Paul (1917–).

British character actor, on stage from 1938, occasional films from 1932.

Beau Brummell 53. Our Man in Havana 59. The Trials of Oscar Wilde 60. No Love for Johnnie 61. Billy Budd 62. Life for Ruth 62. The Prince and

the Pauper 62. The Wild and the Willing 63. The Third Secret 64. He Who Rides a Tiger 65. A Midsummer Night's Dream 68. The Looking Glass War 69. Three into Two Won't Go 69. The Reckoning 69. I Want What I Want 72. The Homecoming 73. The Abdication 75. Mr Quilp 75. Nothing Lasts Forever 83. The Tenth Man (TV) 88, etc.

Rogers, Peter (1916–).

British producer in films from 1942; wrote and coproduced many comedies during 40s and early 50s; conceived and produced the *Carry On* series.

Rogers, Roy (1912–) (Leonard Slye).

American singing cowboy star, usually seen with horse Trigger (1932–65). Varied early experience; formed 'Sons of the Pioneers' singing group; in small film roles from 1935, a star from 1938 till 1953.

Under Western Skies 38. The Carson City Kid 40. Dark Command 40. Robin Hood of the Pecos 42. The Man from Music Mountain 44. Along the Navajo Trail 46. Roll On Texas Moon 47. Night Time in Nevada 49. Trail of Robin Hood 50. Son of Paleface 52. Pals of the Golden West 53. Mackintosh and T.J. 75. Roy Rogers, King of the Cowboys (doc) 91, etc.

TV series: The Roy Rogers Show 51–56.

¶ When my times comes, just skin me and put me right up there on Trigger, just as though nothing had ever changed. – *R.R.*

Rogers, Wayne (1934–).

American light actor, star of TV's M*A*S*H, City of Angels and House Calls.

Once in Paris 78. The Top of the Hill (TV) 80. He's Fired, She's Hired (TV) 84. The Gig 85. The Lady from Yesterday (TV) 85. American Harvest (TV) 87. The Killing Time 87. Drop-Out Mother (TV) 88. Bluegrass (TV) 88, etc.

Rogers, Will (1879–1935).

American rustic comedian, ex-Ziegfeld Follies, whose crackerbarrel philosophy almost moved nations. His home in Los Angeles is the centrepiece of the Will Rogers State Park.

Autobiography: 1927, *There's Not a Bathing Suit in Russia*.

Biographies: 1953, *Our Will Rogers* by Homer Croy. 1974, *Will Rogers, the Man and His Times* by Richard M. Ketchum.

Biopic: 1952, *The Story of Will Rogers* (starring his son).

■ Laughing Bill Hyde 18. Almost a Husband 19. Water Water Everywhere 19. *Jubilo* 19. Jes' Call Me Jim 20. The Strange Boarder 20. Scratch My Back 20. A Poor Relation 20. Cupid the Cowpuncher 20. Honest Hutch 20. Guile of Women 21. Boys Will Be Boys 21. An Unwilling Hero 21. Doubling for Romeo 21. One Glorious Day 21. The Headless Horseman 22. The Ropin' Fool 22. One Day in 365 22. Hustling Hank 22. Uncensored Movies 22. Fruits of Faith 22. Just Passing Through 23. Gee Whiz Genevieve 23. Highbrow Stuff 23. Family Fits 23. The Cake Eater 24. Big Moments from Little Pictures 24. Don't Park There 24. The Cowboy Sheik 24. Going to Congress 24. Our Congressman 24. A Truthful Liar 24. Two Wagons 24. A Texas Steer 27. Tiptoes 27. They Had to See Paris 29. Happy Days 30. So This is London 30. Lightnin' 30. A Connecticut Yankee 31. Young as You Feel 31. Ambassador Bill 31. Business and Pleasure 32. Too Busy to Work 32. *State Fair* 33. Doctor Bull 33. Mister Skitch 33. *David Harum* 34. *Handy Andy* 34. *Judge Priest* 34. County Chairman 35. *Life*

Begins at Forty 35. Doubting Thomas 35. In Old Kentucky 35. *Steamboat round the Bend* 35.
☺ For establishing the wisdom of the common man. *Judge Priest.*

¶ There's only one thing that can kill the movies, and that's education. – W.R.
When you put down the good things you ought to have done, and leave out the bad things you did do – that's Memoirs. – W.R.
~When he was killed, Rogers had signed to play Dr Dafoe, who delivered the Dionne Quins, in *The Country Doctor.*

Rogosin, Lionel (1924–).
American documentarist.
On the Bowery 56. Come Back Africa 59. Good Times Wonderful Times 66. Black Roots 70. Woodcutters of the Deep South 73, etc.

Rogue Male.
Geoffrey Household's adventure melodrama about a big-game hunter stalking Hitler has been filmed twice: by Fritz Lang as *Manhunt* 41, with Walter Pidgeon and George Sanders in hilariously foggy London settings, and as a TV movie in 1976 under its original title, starring Peter O'Toole.

Rohmer, Eric (1920–) (Jean Maurice Scherer).
French director of rarefied conversation pieces.
Le Signe du Lion 59. La Boulangère de Monceau 63. La Carrière de Suzanne 64. La Collectionneuse 67. Ma Nuit chez Maude (AAN) 69. Le Genou de Claire 70. Love in the Afternoon 72. The Marquise of O 76. Perceval 78. The Aviator's Wife 81. Pauline at the Beach 83. Full Moon in Paris 84. Summer 86. Girlfriends and Boyfriends (L'Ami de Mon Amie) 87. Four Adventures of Reinette and Mirabelle (Quatre Aventures de Reinette et Mirabelle) 87. Springtime (Conte de Printemps) 90. A Winter's Tale (Conte d'Hiver) 92. L'Arbre, Le Maire et La Médiathèque 93, etc.

Rohmer, Sax (1886–1959) (Arthur Sarsfield Ward).
British novelist, the creator of the much filmed Dr Fu Manchu.

Roizman, Owen (1936–).
American cinematographer.
The French Connection (AAN) 71. Play It Again Sam 72. The Exorcist (AAN) 73. The Taking of Pelham One Two Three 74. The Stepford Wives 75. Network (AAN) 76. Straight Time 78. The Electric Horseman 79. The Black Marble 80. True Confessions 81. Absence of Malice 81. Taps 81. Tootsie (AAN) 82. Vision Quest 85. I Love You to Death 90. Havana 90. The Addams Family 92. Grand Canyon 92. Wyatt Earp 94, etc.

Roland, Gilbert (1905–1994) (Luis Antonio Damaso de Alonso).
Mexican leading man, trained as bullfighter, who gatecrashed Hollywood in the mid-20s and became immediately popular.
The Plastic Age (debut) 25. Camille 27. Men of the North 29. Call Her Savage 32. *She Done Him Wrong* 33. Last Train from Madrid 37. Juarez 39. The Sea Hawk 40. My Life with Caroline 41. Isle of Missing Men 42. Captain Kidd 45. Pirates of Monterey 47. Riding the California Trail 48. *We Were Strangers* 49. The Furies 50. The Bullfighter and the Lady 51. The Bad and the Beautiful 52. Beyond the Twelve Mile Reef 53. The Racers 54. Treasure of Pancho Villa 56. Guns of the Timberland 58. The Big Circus 59. Cheyenne Autumn 64. The Reward 65. The Poppy is also a Flower (TV) 66. Johnny Hamlet 72. Running Wild 73. Islands in the Stream 77. The Black Pearl 77. Deadly Sunday 82. Barbarosa 82, many others.

Roland, Ruth (1893–1937).
American leading lady, a silent serial queen.
The Red Circle 15. The Neglected Wife 17. Hands Up 18. Tiger's Trail 19, etc.
FEATURES: While Father Telephoned 13. The Masked Woman 26. Reno 30. From Nine to Nine 36, many others.

Rolfe, Guy (1915–).
Lean British leading man and character actor, former racing driver and boxer.
Hungry Hill (debut) 46. Nicholas Nickleby 47. Uncle Silas 47. Broken Journey 47. Portrait from Life 49. *The Spider and the Fly* 50. Prelude to Fame 51. Ivanhoe 52. King of the Khyber Rifles 54. It's Never Too Late 56. Snow White and the Three Stooges 62. Taras Bulba 62. Mr Sardonicus 62. The Fall of the Roman Empire 64. The Alphabet Murders 65. The Land Raiders 69. Nicholas and Alexandra 71. And Now the Screaming Starts 73. Dolls 87. Puppet Master III: Toulon's Revenge 91, etc.

Rolfe, Sam (1924–1993).
American screenwriter and television producer, best known for creating the TV series *Have Gun Will Travel* 57–63 and *The Man from U.N.C.L.E.* 64–68.
The Naked Spur (AAN) 53. Target Zero 55. The McConnell Story 55. Bombers B-52 57, etc.
Features edited from episodes of The Man from U.N.C.L.E.: To Trap a Spy 66. The Spy with My Face 66. One Spy Too Many 66. The Karate Killers 67. The Spy in the Green Hat 67. One of Our Spies Is Missing 67. The Helicopter Spies 67. How to Steal the World 68.

Rollin, Jean (1940–).
French screenwriter and director, mainly of horror and exploitation movies containing scenes of sex and sadism, tinged with surrealism.
Vampire Women (Les Femmes Vampires) 67. The Naked Vampire (La Vampire Nue) 69. Terror of the Vampires (Les Frissons des Vampires) 70. Requiem for a Vampire (aka Virgins and Vampires) (Requiem pour une Vampire) 71. La Rose de Fèr 73. Lèvres du Sang 75. Once upon a Virgin (Phantasmes) 76. Pesticide (Les Raisins de la Mort) 78. Fascination 78. Zombie Lake (aka Lake of the Living Dead) (El Lago de Los Muertos Vivientes) 80. The Living Dead Girl (La Morte Vivante) 82. Les Meurtrières 83, etc.

Rollins, Howard, Jnr (1951–).
American leading actor.
Ragtime (AAN) 81. A Soldier's Story 84. The Children of Times Square (TV) 86. Dear America: Letters Home from Vietnam 87. Johnnie Gibson F.B.I. (TV) 87. For Us, the Living (TV) 88. On the Block 89, etc.
TV series: In the Heat of the Night 88– .

Romain, Yvonne (1938–) (Yvonne Warren).
British leading lady.
The Baby and the Battleship 56. Seven Thunders 57. Corridors of Blood 58. Chamber of Horrors 60. Curse of the Werewolf 61. Village of Daughters 61. Devil Doll 63. The Brigand of Kandahar 65. The Swinger (US) 66. Double Trouble (US) 67. The Last of Sheila 73, etc.

Roman, Leticia (1939–).
American leading lady of the 60s.
Pirates of Tortuga 61. Gold of the Seven Saints 61. The Evil Eye (It.) 62. Fanny Hill 64, etc.

Roman, Ruth (1924–).
American actress; leading lady of the 50s, then a plumpish character player.
Ladies Courageous 44. Jungle Queen 45. You Came Along 45. A Night in Casablanca 45. The Big Clock 48. Good Sam 48. *The Window* 49. Champion 49. Barricade 50. Three Secrets 50. Lightning Strikes Twice 51. *Strangers On a Train* 51. Maru Maru 52. Blowing Wild 53. Down Three Dark Streets 54. The Far Country 55. Joe Macbeth 56. Five Steps to Danger 57. Bitter Victory 58. Desert Desperadoes 59. Look in Any Window 61. Love Has Many Faces 65. The Baby 73. Go Ask Alice (TV) 73. Day of the Animals 77. Echoes 83, etc.
TV series: *The Long Hot Summer* 65–66. Knots Landing 86.

Romance, Vivianne (1912–1991) (Pauline Ortmans).
French leading lady of the 30s and 40s.
La Belle Equipe 35. Gibraltar 37. The White Slave 38. Blind Venus 39. Box of Dreams 39. Carmen 42. Panique 46. Maya 50. Flesh and Desire 53. Pleasures and Vices 56. Mélodie en Sous-Sol 63, etc.

Romanoff, Mike (1890–1972) (Harry Gerguson).
Amiable American con man who posed as a Russian prince (but 'renounced' his title in 1958). Best known as proprietor of Hollywood's most famous and expensive restaurant. Played occasional bit parts.
Arch of Triumph 48. Do Not Disturb 65. Tony Rome 67, etc.

¶ No one has ever discovered the truth about me – not even myself. – M.R.
A rogue of uncertain nationality. – *Scotland Yard*

romantic teams
who have been popular enough to make several films together are headed by William Powell and Myrna Loy, who made 12 joint appearances. Runners-up include Janet Gaynor and Charles Farrell (11 appearances); Dick Powell and Joan Blondell (10); Fred Astaire and Ginger Rogers (10); Spencer Tracy and Katharine Hepburn (9); Richard Burton and Elizabeth Taylor (9); Judy Garland and Mickey Rooney (8); Clark Gable and Joan Crawford (8); Nelson Eddy and Jeanette Macdonald (8); Greer Garson and Walter Pidgeon (8); Errol Flynn and Olivia de Havilland (8); Bette Davis and George Brent (7); Clark Gable and Jean Harlow (6); James Cagney and Joan Blondell (6). Even though most of these teamings began because both stars happened to be under contract to the same studio, they would not have continued had they not been felicitous. Other teams who struck notable sparks off each other but have fewer films to their credit include Humphrey Bogart and Lauren Bacall; Ronald Colman and Greer Garson; Cary Grant and Irene Dunne; Greta Garbo and John Gilbert; Greta Garbo and Melvyn Douglas; Bob Hope and Paulette Goddard; Danny Kaye and Virginia Mayo; Alan Ladd and Veronica Lake; Donald O'Connor and Peggy Ryan; Marie Dressler and Wallace Beery; Rita Hayworth and Glenn Ford; John Barrymore and Carole Lombard; Charlie Ruggles and Mary Boland; Rock Hudson and Doris Day; Jack Hulbert and Cicely Courtneidge; John Payne and Betty Grable; James Dunn and Sally Eilers; David Niven and Loretta Young; Van Johnson and June Allyson; Louis Hayward and Patricia Medina; Bob Hope and Dorothy Lamour; John Wayne and Maureen O'Hara.

Romberg, Sigmund (1887–1951).

Hungarian composer of light music. Scores include *The Desert Song* 29 and 43, *New Moon* 31 and 40, *Maytime* 37, *Balalaika* 39, *The Student Prince* 54. (Most of these began as stage operettas.) José Ferrer played him in a biopic, *Deep in My Heart* 54.

Rome

in its ancient days was reconstructed for *Quo Vadis*, *The Sign of the Cross*, *Ben Hur*, *The Last Days of Pompeii*, *Androcles and the Lion*, *The Fall of the Roman Empire*, *The Robe*, *I Claudius*, *Julius Caesar*, *Cleopatra* and *Spartacus*. The funny side of its life was depicted in *Roman Scandals*, *Fiddlers Three*, *Carry On Cleo*, *Scandal in the Roman Bath* and *A Funny Thing Happened on the Way to the Forum*. Modern Rome has been seen hundreds of times in Italian movies, notably *Bicycle Thieves*, *Paisa*, *La Dolce Vita*, *The Girls of the Spanish Steps*, *Sunday in August*, *Rome Eleven o'Clock* and the American co-production *Indiscretion* which was shot entirely within Rome's railway station. American views of Rome include *Three Coins in the Fountain*, *Seven Hills of Rome*, *Roman Holiday*, *Two Weeks in Another Town*, *The Pigeon That Took Rome* and *The Roman Spring of Mrs Stone*; while the Colosseum was used for the finale of films as various as *House of Cards* and *Twenty Million Miles to Earth*. The Vatican was well shown in *Never Take No for an Answer*, about the small boy who persists in getting an audience with the Pope.

Rome, Stewart (1887–1965) (Septimus William Ryott).

British stage matinée idol who made several romantic films in the 20s and later appeared in character roles.

The Prodigal Son 25. Sweet Lavender 26. The Gentleman Rider 27. Thou Fool 28. Dark Red Roses 29. The Man Who Changed His Name 30. Designing Women 33. Men of Yesterday 34. Wings of the Morning 37. Banana Ridge 41. The White Unicorn 47. Woman Hater 48, etc.

Romeo and Juliet.

Shakespeare's tragedy of star-crossed lovers has been a director's favourite ever since it was first filmed in 1900, and many more silent versions followed. There have been three major straight versions since sound: in 1936 George Cukor directed Leslie Howard and Norma Shearer in a lavish, genteel, studio-bound, semi-pop version for MGM; in 1953 Renato Castellani came to Britain and made for Rank a more sober, but duller film in colour, with Laurence Harvey and Susan Shentall; and in 1968 came Franco Zeffirelli's youthful version with Leonard Whiting and Olivia Hussey. In the late 40s, a French film noir, *Les Amants de Verone*, transposed the story to a modern setting. The musical *West Side Story* 61 is a violent modernization of Shakespeare's tale, and Peter Ustinov's *Romanoff and Juliet* 61 a satirical rendering. The oddest so far is Armando Acosta's 1990 Belgian version played by a cast of cats (Juliet is a white Angora, Romeo a grey Persian), dubbed with the voices of, among others, Robert Powell, Francesca Annis, Ben Kingsley, Vanessa Redgrave, and Maggie Smith.

Romero, Cesar (1907–1994).

Handsome Latin-American leading man, former dancer and Broadway actor. Also on TV.

The Thin Man 34. Metropolitan 35. Wee Willie Winkie 37. The Return of the Cisco Kid (and others in this series) 39. The Gay Caballero 40. Weekend in Havana 41. Tales of Manhattan 42. Orchestra Wives 42. Coney Island 43. Carnival in Costa Rica 47. That Lady in Ermine 48. Happy Go Lovely 51. Prisoners of the Casbah 53. Vera Cruz

54. The Racers 55. The Leather Saint 56. Villa 58. Two on a Guillotine 64. Marriage on the Rocks 65. Batman 66. Hot Millions 68. Crooks and Coronets (GB) 69. The Midas Run (GB) 69. A Talent for Loving 69. Now You See Him Now You Don't 72. The Strongest Man in the World 74. The Big Push 77. Mission to Glory 80. Judgement Day 88. Simple Justice 90, etc.

TV series: Passport to Danger 56. *Batman* (as the Joker) 65–67.

Romero, Eddie (1924–).

Filipino director of low-budget exploitation movies.

The Day of the Trumpet 57. Moro Witch Doctor 64. Mad Doctor of Blood Island 68. Best of the Yellow Night 70. Twilight People 72. Beyond Atlantis 73. The Woman Hunt 75. Sudden Death 77. Desire 83. The White Force 88. A Case of Honor 88, etc.

Romero, George (1940–).

American director of exploitation pictures.

Night of the Living Dead 68. The Crazies 73. Hungry Wives 73. Zombies 78. Martin 79. Knightriders 81. Creepshow 82. Day of the Dead 85. Creepshow 2 (w) 87. Monkey Shines (wd) 88. Two Evil Eyes (Due Occhi Diabolici) (co-d) 89. Tales from the Darkside: The Movie (co-w) 90. Night of the Living Dead (w, p) 90. Tales from the Darkside: The Movie II (co-w) 92. The Dark Half 93, etc.

¶ Just because I'm showing somebody being disembowelled doesn't mean I have to get heavy and put a message round it. – *G.R.*

Romm, Mikhail (1901–1971).

Russian director.

Boule de Suif 34. *Lenin in October* 37. Lenin in 1918 39. The Russian Question 48. Nine Days of One Year 61. Ordinary Fascism 64, etc.

Rommel, Field Marshal Erwin (1891–1944).

German soldier, a worthy adversary for the Eighth Army in World War II. He killed himself in 1944 after being accused of complicity in the plot against Hitler. In films he was melodramatically impersonated by Erich Von Stroheim in 1943 in *Five Graves to Cairo*, and more soberly in 1951 by James Mason in *The Desert Fox* (also in 1953 in *The Desert Rats*). Other minor portrayals were by Albert Lieven in *Foxhole in Cairo*, by Gregory Gaye in *Hitler*, by Werner Hinz in *The Longest Day*, by Christopher Plummer in *The Night of the Generals*, by Karl Michael Vogler in *Patton*, and by Wolfgang Preiss in *Raid on Rommel*.

Romney, Edana (1919–) (E. Rubenstein).

South African-born leading lady, in three British films of the 40s.

■ East of Piccadilly 41. Alibi 42. Corridor of Mirrors 48.

Ronet, Maurice (1927–1983).

French leading man.

Rendezvous de Juliet 49. La Sorcière 56. He Who Must Die 56. Lift to the Scaffold 57. Carve Her Name with Pride (GB) 58. Plein Soleil 59. Rendezvous de Minuit 61. *Le Feu Follet* 63. Enough Rope 63. The Victors 63. La Ronde 64. Three Weeks in Manhattan 65. Lost Command 66. The Champagne Murders (La Scandale) 67. The Road to Corinth 68. How Sweet It Is (US) 68. L'Infidèle 69. Qui? 73. The Marseilles Contract 74. Bloodline 79. La Balance 83, etc.

Rooker, Michael (1954–).

American character actor, usually as a heavy.

Eight Men Out 88. Mississippi Burning 88. Sea of Love 89. Music Box 89. Henry: Portrait of a Serial Killer 90. Days of Thunder 90. The Dark Half 91. JFK 91. Cliffhanger 93. The Dark Half 93. The Hard Truth 94. Tombstone 94, etc.

Rooks, Conrad.

American experimental director.
■ Chappaqua 66. Siddhartha 72.

Room, Abram (1894–1976).

Russian director, former journalist, with stage experience.

In Pursuit of Moonshine 24. The Haven of Death 26. Bed and Sofa 27. The Ghost that Never Returns 29. The Five Year Plan 30. Invasion 44. Silver Dust 53, etc.

Rooney, Mickey (1920–) (Joe Yule Jnr).

Diminutive, aggressively talented American performer, on stage from the age of two (in parents' vaudeville act). In films from 1926 (short comedies) as Mickey McGuire, then returned to vaudeville; came back as Mickey Rooney in 1932. By the late 30s and early 40s he was the most popular film star in the world, later developing into an accomplished character actor. Married eight times, his wives include actresses Ava Gardner and Martha Vickers. He was given an honorary Oscar in 1982 'in recognition of his 60 years of versatility in a variety of memorable film performances'.

Autobiographies: 1965, *I.E.* 1991, *Life Is Too Short*.

My Pal the King 32. The Hide-Out 34. *A Midsummer Night's Dream* (as Puck) 35. Ah Wilderness 35. Little Lord Fauntleroy (not in title role) 36. Captains Courageous 37. *A Family Affair* (as Andy Hardy) 37. *Judge Hardy's Children* 38. Love Finds Andy Hardy 38. *Boys' Town* (special AA) 38. The Adventures of Huckleberry Finn 39. *Babes in Arms* 39. Young Tom Edison 40. Strike Up the Band 40. Men of Boys' Town 41. Babes on Broadway 41. A Yank at Eton 42. Andy Hardy's Double Life 42. *The Human Comedy* 43. Girl Crazy 43. Andy Hardy's Blonde Trouble 44. National Velvet 44. Love Laughs at Andy Hardy 46. Summer Holiday 47. The Fireball 50. A Slight Case of Larceny 53. *The Bold and the Brave* 56. Andy Hardy Comes Home 58. Baby Face Nelson 58. The Big Operator 59. Breakfast at Tiffany's 61. It's a Mad Mad Mad Mad World 63. Twenty-Four Hours to Kill 65. Ambush Bay 66. The Extraordinary Seaman 68. Skidoo 68. The Comic 69. Pulp 73. The Domino Principle 77. Pete's Dragon 77. The Magic of Lassie 78. Arabian Adventure 79. The Black Stallion 79. *Leave 'em Laughing* (TV) 80. *Bill* (TV) 81. The Fox and the Hound (voice) 81. La Traversée de la Pacifique 82. The Care Bears Movie (voice) 85. Lightning – the White Stallion 86. Rudolph and Frosty's Christmas in July 86. Erik the Viking 89. My Heroes Have Always Been Cowboys 91. Silent Night Deadly Night 5: The Toymaker 91. The Milky Way (La Via Lactea) 92. Sweet Justice 92. The Legend of O.B. Taggart (& w) 94. Revenge of the Red Baron 94, many others.

TV series: The Mickey Rooney Show (Hey Mulligan) 54. Mickey 64. One of the Boys 81, etc.
✪ For never being counted out. *Babes in Arms*.

¶ I was a fourteen-year-old boy for thirty years. – *M.R.*

I've been through four publics. I've been coming back like a rubber ball for years. – *M.R.*

I just want to be a professional. I couldn't live without acting. – *M.R.*

There may be a little snow on the mountain, but there's a lot of fire in the furnace. – *M.R.*

All the muddy waters of my life cleared up when I gave myself to Christ. – *M.R.*

I didn't ask to be short. I didn't want to be short. I've tried to pretend that being a short guy didn't matter. – *M.R.*

The guys with the power in Hollywood today, the guys with their names above the title, are thieves. They don't make movies, they make deals. Their major function is to cut themselves in for 10 per cent of the gross – off the top, of course – which is why they make movies that cost $50 million. – *M.R.*

His favourite exercise is climbing tall people. – *Phyllis Diller*

A rope-haired, kazoo-voiced kid with a comic strip face. – *James Agee*

Tennessee Williams once told me that he considered Rooney the best actor in the history of the movies. – *Gore Vidal*

Roope, Fay (1893–1961).
American character actress, usually as a tough old lady.
You're in the Navy Now 51. The Day the Earth Stood Still 51. Washington Story 52. Viva Zapata! 52. From Here to Eternity 53. The System 53. Naked Alibi 54. Ma and Pa Kettle at Waikiki 55. The Proud Ones 56. The F.B.I. Story 59, etc.

Roosevelt, Franklin Delano (1882–1945).
American President 1933–45, exponent of the 'New Deal'. He was played by Ralph Bellamy in Dore Schary's play and film of his life, *Sunrise at Campobello* 60, by Capt. Jack Young in *Yankee Doodle Dandy* and by Godfrey Tearle in *The Beginning of the End*. In TV's *Eleanor and Franklin* (1976) he was played by Edward Herrmann, and in *Ike* (1979) by Stephen Roberts.

Roosevelt, Theodore (Teddy) (1858–1919).
American President 1901–1909. His extrovert personality and cheerful bullish manners have been captured several times on screen, notably by John Alexander in *Arsenic and Old Lace* (a parody) and *Fancy Pants*, by Wallis Clark in *Yankee Doodle Dandy*, by John Merton in *I Wonder Who's Kissing Her Now*, by Sidney Blackmer in *My Girl Tisa*, *This is My Affair* and *Buffalo Bill;* and by Brian Keith in *The Wind and the Lion*. In *The Private Files of J. Edgar Hoover* (1978) it was Howard da Silva's turn; Ralph Bellamy had a revised go in *The Winds of War* (1982), and Edward Herrmann again in *Annie* (1982).

Root, Wells (1900–1993).
American screenwriter, a former journalist, who later wrote for television and then taught writing at UCLA.
The Storm 30. Politics (co-w) 31. The Prodigal (co-w) 31. Tiger Shark 32. I Cover the Waterfront (co-w) 33. Black Moon 34. Paris Interlude 34. Pursuit 35. Sworn Enemy 36. The Prisoner of Zenda (co-w) 37. Sergeant Madden 39. Thunder Afloat (co-w) 39. Flight Command (co-w) 40. The Bad Man 41. Mokey (co-w) 42. Tennessee Johnson 42. Salute to the Marines 43. The Man from Down Under 43. Magnificent Obsession 54. Texas across the River 66, etc.

Roquevert, Noel (1894–1973). (N. Benevent).
French character actor, usually as mean-spirited bourgeois.
The Three Must-Get-Theres 22. Cartouche 34. Entrée des Artistes 38. Les Inconnus dans la Maison 42. Le Corbeau 43. Antoine et Antoinette 47. Justice Est Faite 50. Fanfan la Tulipe 52. Les Compagnes de la Nuit 53. The Sheep Has Five Legs 54. Marie Octobre 59. A Monkey in Winter 62, many others.

Rosay, Françoise (1891–1974) (Françoise de Naleche).
Distinguished French actress in films from the mid-20s.
Autobiography: 1974, *La Traversée d'une Vie*.
Gribiche 25. *Le Grand Jeu* 33. *La Kermesse Héroïque* 35. Jenny 36. *Un Carnet de Bal* 37. Les Gens du Voyage 38. *Une Femme Disparait* 41. Johnny Frenchman (GB) 45. Macadam 46. September Affair 50. *The Red Inn* 51. The Thirteenth Letter (US) 51. That Lady (GB) 54. The Seventh Sin (US) 57. Le Joueur 58. The Sound and the Fury (US) 58. The Full Treatment (GB) 60. Up from the Beach (US) 65. Le Pietou 72, etc.

Rose, Bernard.
English director and screenwriter.
The Paperhouse 88. Chicago Joe and the Showgirl 89. Candyman 92. Immortal Beloved 94.

Rose, Billy (1899–1966).
American nightclub owner and songwriter, husband of Fanny Brice. He was played in *Funny Lady* by James Caan.
Biography: 1968, *Manhattan Primitive* by Earl Rogers.

Rose, David (1910–1990).
London-born composer and pianist, in America from 1914. From the 50s he also worked in television, writing the themes for the series *Bonanza*, *The High Chaparral* and *The Little House on the Prairie*, and in the 70s and 80s scored several TV movies. He was married to Judy Garland (1941–45).
Never a Dull Moment 43. The Princess and the Pirate (AAN) 44. Winged Victory 44. The Underworld Story 50. The Clown 53. Jupiter's Darling 55. Operation Petticoat 59. Please Don't Eat the Daisies 60. Hombre 67. Sam's Son 84, etc.

Rose, David E. (1895–1992).
American producer, in films from 1930, long in charge of United Artists productions. More recently in Britain.
The End of the Affair 55. The Safecracker 58. The House of the Seven Hawks 59, etc.

Rose, George (1920–1988).
British stage and screen character actor.
Pickwick Papers 52. Grand National Night 53. The Sea Shall Not Have Them 54. The Night My Number Came Up 56. Brothers in Law 57. A Night to Remember 58. Jack the Ripper 59. The Devil's Disciple 59. Jet Storm 59. The Flesh and the Fiends 60. Hamlet 64. Hawaii (US) 66. The Pink Jungle 69. A New Leaf 71. Holocaust (TV) 78. The Pirates of Penzance 83, etc.

Rose, Helen (1904–1985).
American costume designer. With Twentieth Century Fox from 1941, MGM 1943–46.
Autobiography: 1976, *Just Make Them Beautiful*.
Stormy Weather 43. Ziegfeld Follies 46. The Harvey Girls 46. Good News 47. Words and Music 48. The Great Caruso (AAN) 50. The Bad and the Beautiful (AA) 52. The Merry Widow (AAN) 52. Dream Wife (AAN) 53. Executive Suite (AAN) 54. I'll Cry Tomorrow (AA) 55. Interrupted Melody (AAN) 55. The Power and the Prize (AAN) 56. High Society 56. Tea and Sympathy 56. Cat on a Hot Tin Roof 58. The Gazebo (AAN) 59. Butterfield 8 60. Mister Buddwing (AAN) 66, etc.

Rose, Jack:
see *Shavelson, Melville*.

Rose Marie.
The Rudolph Friml/Oscar Hammerstein operetta about the Mounties getting their man was first filmed in 1928 by Lucien Hubbard as a silent; Joan Crawford has the title role. In 1936 W. S. Van Dyke made the well-remembered version with Jeanette MacDonald and Nelson Eddy, and in 1954 Mervyn LeRoy directed a remake with Ann Blyth and Howard Keel.

Rose, Reginald (1921–).
American writer who has created numerous TV plays, also a series, *The Defenders*.
Crime in the Streets 56. *Twelve Angry Men* (AAN) 57. The Man in the Net 58. Man of the West 58. The Wild Geese 78. Somebody Killed Her Husband 78. The Sea Wolves 80. Who Dares Wins 82. Wild Geese II 85, etc.

Rose, William (1918–1987).
American screenwriter who spent some years in Britain.
Once a Jolly Swagman (co-w) 48. The Gift Horse 51. I'll Get You for This 52. *Genevieve* (AAN) 53. *The Maggie* 54. The Lady Killers (AAN) 55. Touch and Go 55. Man in the Sky 56. The Smallest Show on Earth 57. *It's a Mad Mad Mad Mad World* 63. The Russians Are Coming, the Russians Are Coming (AAN) 66. The Flim Flam Man 67. *Guess Who's Coming to Dinner* (AA) 67. The Secret of Santa Vittoria 69, etc.

Rosebud.
The enigmatic last word of *Citizen Kane*, referring back to Kane's childhood sled. It is also said to be the pet name William Randolph Hearst gave to his mistress Marion Davies's private parts, which may help explain that tycoon's implacable hostility to the film. Several sleds were said to have been used in the film, in addition to the one burned at the end. One of them was bought at auction for $55,000 by Steven Spielberg in 1982, although its authenticity has since been questioned.

Rosen, Phil (1888–1951).
Russian-born American director of second features.
The Single Sin 21. The Young Rajah 22. Abraham Lincoln 25. Burning Up Broadway 28. Two-Gun Man 31. Beggars in Ermine 34. Two Wise Maids 37. Double Alibi 40. Forgotten Girls 40. Spooks Run Wild 41. Prison Mutiny 43. Step by Step 46. The Secret of St Ives 49, many others.

Rosenberg, Aaron (1912–1979).
American producer, in Hollywood from 1934; working for Universal from 1946.
Johnny Stool Pigeon 47. Winchester 73 50. The Glenn Miller Story 54. To Hell and Back 55. The Great Man 57. Morituri 65. The Reward 65. Tony Rome 67, many others.

Rosenberg, Philip.
American production designer, from the theatre.
The Owl and the Pussycat 70. The Anderson Tapes 71. Child's Play 72. The Gambler 74. The Sentinel 77. The Wiz (AAN) 78. All That Jazz (AA) 79. Eyewitness 80. Daniel 83. The Manhattan Project 86. Moonstruck 87. The January Man 88. Running on Empty 88. Family Business 89. Q & A 90, etc.

Rosenberg, Stuart (1925–).
American director with long TV experience.
■ Murder Inc. 60. Question 7 61. Fame Is the Name of the Game (TV) 66. Asylum for a Spy (TV) 67. *Cool Hand Luke* 67. The April Fools 69. Move 70. W.U.S.A. 70. Pocket Money 72. The Laughing Policeman 73. The Drowning Pool 75. Voyage of the Damned 76. Love and Bullets 78. The Amityville Horror 79. Brubaker 80. The Pope of Greenwich Village 84. Let's Get Harry 86. My Heroes Have Always Been Cowboys 91.

Rosenbloom, 'Slapsie' Maxie (1906–1976).
American 'roughneck' comedian, ex-boxer, in occasional comedy films as gangster or punch-drunk type.
Mr Broadway 33. Nothing Sacred 37. Louisiana Purchase 41. Hazard 48. Mr Universe 51. Abbott and Costello Meet the Keystone Kops 55. The Beat Generation 59, etc.

Rosenblum, Ralph (1925–).
American editor.
Mad Dog Coll 61. *Fail Safe* 64. The Pawnbroker 65. The Group 66. The Night They Raided Minsky's 67. Goodbye Columbus 69. Bananas 71. Sleeper 73. Love and Death 75. *Annie Hall* 77. The Great Bank Hoax 78. Interiors 78. Stuck on You 83. Forever Lulu 87, etc.

Rosenman, Leonard (1924–).
American composer.
The Cobweb 55. East of Eden 55. Rebel without a Cause 55. Lafayette Escadrille 58. The Chapman Report 62. Fantastic Voyage 66. Hellfighters 68. Beneath the Planet of the Apes 71. Phantom of Hollywood (TV) 74. Race with the Devil 75. *Barry Lyndon* (AA as md) 75. Bound for Glory (AA as md) 76. The Car 77. Lord of the Rings 78. Promises in the Dark 79. Hide in Plain Sight 80. Cross Creek (AAN) 83. Miss Lonelyhearts 84. Heart of the Stag 84. Sylvia 85. Star Trek IV: The Voyage Home (AAN) 86. Robocop 2 90, etc.

Rosenthal, Jack (1931–).
British scriptwriter, mainly for television, in which medium he has won many awards.
Films include *The Lovers* 72, *The Chain* 85.

Rosenthal, Laurence (1926–).
American composer and conductor who now scores TV movies and mini-series.
Yellowneck 55. Naked in the Sun 57. A Raisin in the Sun 61. The Miracle Worker 62. Becket (AAN) 64. Hotel Paradiso 66. The Comedians 67. A Gunfight 70. Man of La Mancha (AAN) 72. The Wild Party 74. Rooster Cogburn 75. The Return of a Man Called Horse 76. Who'll Stop the Rain (aka Dog Soldiers) 78. Meteor 79. Clash of the Titans 81. Heart Like a Wheel 83. Easy Money 83, etc.

Rosher, Charles (1885–1974).
Distinguished American cinematographer.
The Clown 16. The Love Night 20. Smilin' Through 22. *Sparrows* 26. *Sunrise* (AA) 27. *Tempest* 28. What Price Hollywood? 32. Our Betters 33. The Affairs of Cellini 34. Little Lord Fauntleroy 36. White Banners 38. A Child Is Born 40. Kismet 44. *The Yearling* (co-ph) (AA) 46. *Show Boat* 51. Scaramouche 52. Kiss Me Kate 53. Young Bess 54. Jupiter's Darling 55, many others.

Rosher, Charles, Jnr.
American cinematographer.
■ Pretty Maids All in a Row 71. Semi Tough 77. Three Women 77. A Wedding 78. The Muppet Movie 79. The Onion Field 79. Heartbeeps 81.

Independence Day 83. Police Academy 6: City under Siege 89.

Rosi, Francesco (1922–).
Italian director.
La Sfida 57. Salvatore Giuliano (& w) 61. Hands over the City 63. The Moment of Truth 64. More than a Miracle 68. Three Brothers (& w) 82. Christ Stopped at Eboli 82. I Tre Fratelli 80. Bizet's Carmen 84. Chronicle of a Death Foretold (Crònaca di una Morte Annunciata) 87. To Forget Palermo (Dimenticare Palermo) 90, etc.

Rosmer, Milton (1881–1971) (Arthur Milton Lunt).
British stage actor, in many films from 1913.
General John Regan 21. The Passionate Friends 22. The Phantom Light 35. South Riding 38. Goodbye Mr Chips 39. Atlantic Ferry 41. Fame Is the Spur 47. The Monkey's Paw 48. The Small Back Room 49, etc.
AS DIRECTOR: Dreyfus 31. Channel Crossing 32. The Guvnor 36. The Challenge 37, etc.

Ross, Annie (1930–) (Annabelle Short Lynch).
British jazz singer and character actress. Brought up in America, she was a juvenile actress in Hollywood, studied drama in New York, and became a singer in England in the 50s before returning to America to form a jazz vocal trio, Lambert, Hendricks and Ross. From the 70s, she began to act on stage and TV.
Presenting Lily Mars 43. Alfie Darling 75. Superman III 83. Throw Momma from the Train 87. Witchery 88. Basket Case 2 90. Pump Up the Volume 90. Short Cuts 93. Blue Sky (made 91) 94, etc.

Ross, Betsy King (1923–1989).
American juvenile actress, popular in western series of the 30s opposite such stars as Ken Maynard and Gene Autry. An award-winning trick rider, she later became an anthropologist and writer.
Smoke Lightning 33. Fighting with Kit Carson (serial) 33. In Old Sante Fe 34. Phantom Empire (serial) 35. Radio Ranch 35, etc.

Ross, Diana (1944–).
American singer and actress.
■ *Lady Sings the Blues* (as Billie Holiday) 72. Mahogany 76. The Wiz 78. Out of Darkness (TV) 94.

Ross, Frank (1904–1990).
American producer, in Hollywood from early 30s.
Of Mice and Men 39. The Devil and Miss Jones 41. The Robe 53. The Rains of Ranchipur 55. Kings Go Forth 58. Mister Moses 65. Where It's At 70, etc.

Ross, Herbert (1927–).
American director and choreographer.
Doctor Dolittle 67. Funny Girl 69, etc.
■ AS DIRECTOR: Goodbye Mr Chips 69. The Owl and the Pussycat 70. T. R. Baskin 71. Play It Again Sam 72. The Last of Sheila (& p) 73. Funny Lady 75. The Sunshine Boys 75. The Seven Per Cent Solution 76. The Turning Point (AAN) 77. The Goodbye Girl 77. Nijinsky 80. Pennies from Heaven 81. I Ought to Be in Pictures 82. Max Dugan Returns 83. Flashdance 83. Footloose 84. Protocol 84. Dancers 87. The Secret of My Success 87. Steel Magnolias 89. My Blue Heaven 90. True Colors 91. Undercover Blues 93.

Ross, Joe E. (1905–1982).
Short, fat American comedian with a frazzled manner, mostly on TV.

TV series: Bilko 56–59. Car 54 Where Are You? 61–62. It's about Time 64.

Ross, Katharine (1942–).
American leading lady.
■ Shenandoah 65. Mr Buddwing 66. The Longest Hundred Miles (TV) 66. The Singing Nun 66. Games 67. *The Graduate* (AAN) 67. Hellfighters 68. Tell Them Willie Boy Is Here 69. Butch Cassidy and the Sundance Kid 69. Fools 70. Get to Know Your Rabbit 72. They Only Kill Their Masters 72. Le Hasard et la Violence 74. The Stepford Wives 75. Voyage of the Damned 76. Wanted, the Sundance Woman (TV) 77. The Legacy 78. The Betsy 78. The Swarm 78. Murder by Natural Causes (TV) 79. The Final Countdown 80. Murder in Texas (TV) 81. Wrong Is Right 82. The Shadow Riders (TV) 82. Travis McGee (TV) 82. Red-Headed Stranger 86. A Row of Crows 90.

Ross, Lillian (1926–).
American journalist who wrote *Picture*, a fascinating account of the production of *The Red Badge of Courage*.

Ross, Shirley (1909–1975) (Bernice Gaunt).
American pianist and singer who appeared as leading lady in a few films.
The Age of Indiscretion 35. San Francisco 36. Thanks for the Memory 38. Paris Honeymoon 39. Kisses for Breakfast 41. A Song for Miss Julie 45, etc.

Ross, Steven (1927–1992) (Steven Rechnitz).
American studio executive, head of Warner from 1967 and the man who masterminded the merger of Warner and Time Inc. in 1989 to create the world's largest media and entertainment group. According to Steven Spielberg, he was the model for the portrayal of Schindler in *Schindler's List*.
Biography: 1992, *Master of the Game* by Connie Bruck.

Rossellini, Isabella (1952–).
Italian actress, daughter of Ingrid Bergman and director Roberto Rossellini.
White Nights 85. Blue Velvet 86. Tough Guys Don't Dance 87. Zelly and Me 88. Cousins 89. Dames Galantes 90. Wild at Heart 90. Ivory Hunters (TV) 90. Death Becomes Her 92. The Pickle 93. The Innocent 93. Fearless 93. Wyatt Earp 94. Immortal Beloved 94, etc.

Rossellini, Roberto (1906–1977).
Italian director, in films from 1938. Started as writer; co-scripted his own films.
Autobiography: 1993, *My Method: Writings and Interviews*.
Biography: 1987, *Roberto Rossellini* by Peter Brunette.
Open City 45. Paisa (co-w, AAN) 46. Germany Year Zero 48. Stromboli 49. Europa 51. General Della Rovere 59. Louis XIV Seizes Power 66. Il Messia 76, many others.

Rossen, Robert (1908–1966).
American writer-producer-director, in Hollywood from 1936 after stage experience.
■ Marked Woman (w) 37. They Won't Forget (w) 37. Racket Busters (w) 38. Dust be My Destiny (w) 39. *The Roaring Twenties* (w) 39. A Child is Born (w) 39. The Sea Wolf 41. Out of the Fog (w) 41. Blues in the Night (w) 41. Edge of Darkness (w) 42. *A Walk in the Sun* (w) 45. The Strange Love of Martha Ivers (w) 46. Desert Fury (w) 47. Johnny O'Clock (wd) 47. *Body and Soul* 47. Treasure of the Sierra Madre (co-w, uncredited) 47. *All the King's Men* (wpd) (AAp,

AANw, AANd) 49. The Brave Bulls (pd) 50. Mambo (wd) 54. Alexander the Great (wpd) 56. Island in the Sun (d) 57. They Came to Cordura (wd) 59. *The Hustler* (wpd) (AAN) 61. Billy Budd (co-w) 62. Lilith (wpd) 64.

¶ In retrospect, the dreariness of his direction is remarkably consistent. – *Andrew Sarris, 1968*

Rossi, Franco (1919–).
Italian writer-director.
 I Falsari 52. Il Seduttore 54. *Amici per la Pelle* (Friends for Life) 55. Morte di un Amico 60. Smog 62. Quo Vadis (TV) 85, etc.

Rossi-Drago, Eleonora (1925–) (Palmina Omiccioli).
Italian leading lady.
 Pirates of Capri 48. Persiane Chiuse 50. Three Forbidden Stories 51. The White Slave 53. Le Amiche 55. Maledetto Imbroglio 59. David and Goliath 59. Under Ten Flags 60. Uncle Tom's Cabin (Ger.) 65. Camille 2000 69, etc.

Rossif, Frédéric (1922–1990).
French documentarist.
 Les Temps du Ghetto 61. Mourir à Madrid 62. The Fall of Berlin 65, etc.

Rossington, Norman (1928–).
British character actor of stage, TV and films.
 A Night to Remember 58. Carry On Sergeant 58. *Saturday Night and Sunday Morning* 60. Go to Blazes 62. The Comedy Man 63. A Hard Day's Night 64. Tobruk (US) 66. The Charge of the Light Brigade 68. The Adventures of Gerard 70. Deathline 72. Go for a Take 72. Let Him Have It 91, etc.

Rossiter, Leonard (1926–1984).
British comic actor.
 Billy Liar 62. King Rat 65. Hotel Paradiso 66. The Wrong Box 66. The Whisperers 67. 2001: A Space Odyssey 68. Oliver 68. Otley 69. Barry Lyndon 75. The Pink Panther Strikes Again 77. Rising Damp 79. Britannia Hospital 82. Trail of the Pink Panther 82, etc.
 TV series: Rising Damp 77–80. The Fall and Rise of Reginald Perrin 78–80. Tripper's Day 83.

Rosson, Hal (Harold) (1895–1988).
Distinguished American cinematographer. He was married to Jean Harlow (1933–35).
 The Cinema Murder 19. Manhandled 24. Gentlemen Prefer Blondes 28. *Tarzan of the Apes* 32. *The Scarlet Pimpernel* 35. The Ghost Goes West 36. The Garden of Allah (AA) 36. *The Wizard of Oz* 39. Johnny Eager 42. The Hucksters 47. *On the Town* 49. *The Red Badge of Courage* 51. *Singin' in the Rain* 52. The Bad Seed 56. No Time for Sergeants 58. El Dorado 67, many others.

Rossovich, Rick (1958–).
American actor.
 The Lords of Discipline 83. Streets of Fire 84. The Terminator 84. Warning Sign 85. Morning After 86. Top Gun 86. Roxanne 87. Let's Get Harry 87. Secret Ingredient 88. The Spellbinder 88. Paint It Black 89. Navy SEALS 90. Tropical Heat 93, etc.
 TV series: MacGruder & Loud 85. Sons & Daughters 91.

Rota, Nino (1911–1979).
Italian composer, responsible for innumerable film scores (including all of Fellini's) as well as operas.
 The Popular Train 33. Zaza 43. Open City 46. My Son the Professor 46. Flight into France 48. *The Glass Mountain* 48. To Live in Peace 48. E

Primavera 49. Anna 52. I Vitelloni 53. La Strada 54. Amici per la Pelle 56. *War and Peace* 56. Il Bidone 56. Cabiria 58. La Dolce Vita 59. Plein Soleil 60. Rocco and His Brothers 60. Boccaccio 70 62. Eight and a Half 63. Juliet of the Spirits 65. Shoot Loud, Louder, I Don't Understand 66. Romeo and Juliet 68. Satyricon 69. Waterloo 70. *The Godfather* 72. The Abdication 74. The Godfather Part II (co-m, AA) 74. Casanova 77. Death on the Nile 78. Hurricane 79, many others.

Roth, Eric.
American screenwriter.
 The Nickel Ride 75. The Concorde: Airport '79 79. Suspect 87. Memories of Me (co-w) 88. Forrest Gump 94, etc.

Roth, Gene (1903–1976) (Gene Stuttenroth).
Heavy-set American character actor.
 A Game of Death 46. The Baron of Arizona 50. Pirates of the High Seas 50. Red Planet Mars 52. The Farmer Takes a Wife 53. Attack of the Giant Leeches 59, etc.

Roth, Joe (1948–).
American producer and director, former chairman of Twentieth Century-Fox. He was co-founder of the production company Morgan's Creek. In 1994 he became chairman of the Walt Disney Company.
 ■ AS DIRECTOR: Streets of Gold 86. Revenge of the Nerds II 87. Coupe de Ville 90.

Roth, Lillian (1910–1980) (Lillian Rutstein).
American leading lady who began her professional career as the baby in the Educational Pictures trademark. After a few films in the early 30s, personal problems caused her retirement. Her story was filmed in 1955 as *I'll Cry Tomorrow*, with Susan Hayward.
 The Love Parade 20. The Vagabond King 30. *Madame Satan* 30. Animal Crackers 30. Sea Legs 31. Ladies They Talk About 33. Take a Chance 33. Communion (aka Alice, Sweet Alice) 77, etc.

Roth, Philip (1933–).
American novelist, somewhat excessively concerned with Jewish guilt and masturbation. *Portnoy's Complaint* and *Goodbye Columbus* were filmed.

Roth, Tim (1961–).
British character actor, from the stage.
 The Hit 84. A World Apart 87. To Kill a Priest 89. The Cook, the Thief, His Wife and Her Lover 89. Rosencrantz and Guildenstern Are Dead 90. Farendj 90. Vincent and Theo 90. Backsliding 91. Jumpin' at the Boneyard 91. Reservoir Dogs 92. The Perfect Husband (La Mujer de Ed Medio) 92. Murder in the Heartland (TV) 93. Bodies, Rest & Motion 93. Heart of Darkness (TV) 94. Pulp Fiction 94. Captives 94. Little Odessa 94. Rob Roy 95, etc.

Rotha, Paul (1903–1984).
British documentarist and film theorist. With GPO Film Unit in the 30s, later independent. Author of *The Film till Now, Documentary Film*, etc.
 Shipyard 30. Contact 33. The Rising Tide 33. The Face of Britain 34. The Fourth Estate 40. *World of Plenty* 42. Land of Promise 46. The World Is Rich 48. No Resting Place 50. World without End (co-d) 52. Cat and Mouse 57. *The Life of Adolf Hitler* 62. The Silent Raid 62, etc.

Rothrock, Cynthia.
American exponent of martial arts whose mainly Hong Kong-made films tend to be released direct to video, except in Hong Kong.

No Retreat, No Surrender 2 89. China O'Brien 89. Martial Law 90. Karate Cop 91. Lady Dragon 91. Triple Cross 91. Tiger Claws 91. Fast Getaway 91. Rage and Honor 92. Angel of Fury 92. Guardian Angel 93. Fast Getaway II 94, etc.

Rothwell, Talbot (1916–1974).
English screenwriter who scripted 20 of the Carry On comedies. He also created the television series *Up Pompeii!* and wrote for TV comedies, including *Before Your Very Eyes, Friends and Neighbours, Dear Dotty,* and *The Army Game.*
 Is Your Honeymoon Really Necessary 53. The Crowded Day 54. Look Before You Laugh 56. Tommy the Toreador (co-w) 59. Make Mine a Million (co-w) 59. Friends and Neighbours 60. Carry On Cabby 63. Carry On Jack 64. Carry On Spying (co-w) 64. Carry On Cleo 64. Carry On Cowboy 65. Carry On Screaming 66. Carry On – Don't Lose Your Head 66. Carry On – Follow That Camel 66. Carry On Doctor 68. Carry On up the Khyber 68. Carry On Again Doctor 69. Carry On Camping 69. Carry On up the Jungle 70. Carry On Loving 70. Carry On Henry 71. Carry On at Your Convenience 71. Carry On Abroad 72. Carry On Matron 72. Carry On Girls 73. Carry On Dick 74, etc.

Rotunno, Giuseppe (1923–).
Italian cinematographer.
 Scandal in Sorrento 55. White Nights 57. Anna of Brooklyn 58. The Naked Maja 59. On the Beach 59. The Angel Wore Red 60. Rocco and His Brothers 60. The Best of Enemies 61. The Leopard 62. Yesterday, Today and Tomorrow 63. Anzio 68. The Secret of Santa Vittoria 69. Satyricon 69. Sunflower 70. Carnal Knowledge 71. Man of La Mancha 72. Amarcord 74. Casanova 77. The End of the World 78. All That Jazz (AAN, BFA) 79. Popeye 81. Five Days One Summer 82. And the Ship Sails On 84. China 9, Liberty 37 84. American Dreamer 84. The Assisi Underground 85. Red Sonja 85. Hotel Colonial 87. Julia and Julia 88. Rent-a-Cop 88. Haunted Summer 88. The Adventures of Baron Munchausen 89. Regarding Henry 91. Once upon a Crime 92. Wolf 94, etc.

Rouch, Jean (1917–).
French documentary director, cinematographer, and ethnographer who has used cinéma vérité techniques and non-professional actors, much in the style of Flaherty, to recreate the lives of ordinary people. Apart from his features, he has also made many shorts, from 1946, some of which were compiled to form *Les Fils de L'Eau* 55.
 Moi, un Noir 58. Chronicle of a Summer (Chronique d'un Été (co-d) 61. Paris Vu par (co-d) 64. Jaguar 67. Petit à Petit 70. Cocorico Monsieur Poulet 77. Dionysos 84. Enigma 87. Boulevards d'Afrique 88. Cantate pour Deux Généraux 90, etc.

rough cut.
The first assembly of shots in the order in which they will be seen in the finished film, used to show those involved what work still needs to be done.

Roundtree, Richard (1937–).
American leading man of the 70s.
 Shaft 71. Embassy 72. Charley One Eye 72. Shaft's Big Score 72. Earthquake 74. Man Friday 75. Escape to Athena 79. Game for Vultures 79. The Winged Serpent 82. One Down Two to Go 82. The Big Score 83. City Heat 84. Killpoint 84. Opposing Forces 87. Maniac Cop 88. Angel III – the Final Chapter 88. Bad Jim 89. Night Visitor 89. Cry Devil 89. Crack House 89. Bloodfist III:

Forced to Fight 91. Black Heart (Nero come il Cuore) 91, etc.
TV series: Shaft 73.

Rounseville, Robert (1914–1974).
American opera singer.
■ Tales of Hoffman 51. Carousel 56.

Rouquier, Georges (1909–1989).
French documentarist.
Le Tonnelier 42. Farrébique 46. Salt of the Earth 50. Lourdes and Its Miracles 56, etc.

Rourke, Mickey (1950–).
Tough, abrasive American actor.
■ 1941 79. Fade to Black 80. Heaven's Gate 80. Body Heat 81. Diner 81. Rumble Fish 83. Eureka 83. The Pope of Greenwich Village 84. *The Year of the Dragon* 85. Nine and a Half Weeks 86. Angel Heart 87. Barfly 87. A Prayer for the Dying 87. Homeboy 88. Johnny Handsome 89. Wild Orchid 90. Desperate Hours 90. Harley Davidson and the Marlboro Man 91. White Sands 92. F.T.W. 94.

¶ I always knew I'd accomplish something very special – like robbing a bank perhaps. – *M.R.*

Rouse, Russell (1915–1987).
American director and co-writer, usually in partnership with Clarence Greene (qv).
D.O.A. 50. The Well (AANw) 51. The Thief 52. New York Confidential 55. The Fastest Gun Alive 56. Thunder in the Sun 59. A House Is Not a Home 64. The Oscar 66. Caper of the Golden Bulls 67, etc.

Rousselot, Philippe (1945–).
French cinematographer, now in international films.
Absences Répétées 72. Adam ou le Sang d'Abel 77. Peppermint Soda (Diablo Menthe) 77. Pour Clemence 77. La Drôlesse 79. Diva 82. The Moon in the Gutter (La Lune dans le Caniveau) 83. Emerald Forest 85. Thérèse 86. Hope and Glory (AAN) 87. The Bear 89. Dangerous Liaisons 89. Too Beautiful for You (Trop Belle pour Toi) 89. We're No Angels 89. Henry and June (AAN) 90. The Miracle 90. Merci la Vie 91. A River Runs through It (AA) 92. Sommersby 93. Queen Margot (La Reine Margot) 94. Interview with the Vampire 94, etc.

Rowan, Dan (1922–1987).
American comedian, one-half of Rowan and Martin, the other being Dick Martin (1922–). Belatedly successful on TV with *Laugh In* 1968–72, they have not been popular in films.
■ Once upon a Horse 57. The Maltese Bippy 69.

Rowland, Bruce.
Australian composer.
The Man from Snowy River 82. Phar Lap 83. Rebel 85. Les Patterson Saves the World 87. Return to Snowy River 88. Cheetah 89. Fast Getaway 91. Lightning Jack 94, etc.

Rowland, Roy (1910–).
American director, mainly of routine features, in Hollywood from the mid-30s. Many shorts, including *Benchley, Pete Smith, Crime Does Not Pay.*
Lost Angel 44. Our Vines Have Tender Grapes 45. Killer McCoy 48. Tenth Avenue Angel 48. Scene of the Crime 49. Two Weeks with Love 50. Bugles in the Afternoon 52. The Moonlighter 53. Rogue Cop 53. The 5,000 Fingers of Doctor T 53. Affair with a Stranger 53. Many Rivers to Cross 55. Hit the Deck 55. Meet Me in Las Vegas 56. These Wilder Years 56. Gun Glory 57. Seven Hills of Rome 58. The Girl Hunters 64. Gunfighters of Casa Grande 66. They Called Him Gringo 68, many others.

Rowlands, Gena (1934–) (Virginia Rowlands).
American leading actress, mostly on stage.
The High Cost of Loving 58. A Child is Waiting 62. Lonely are the Brave 62. Tony Rome 67. Faces 68. Minnie and Moskowitz 71. A Woman under the Influence (AAN) 75. Two Minute Warning 76. Opening Night 77. The Brink's Job 78. Gloria (AAN) 80. Love Streams 85. Light of Day 87. Another Woman 88. Montana (TV) 90. Once Around 91. Night on Earth 91. Crazy in Love 92. Silent Cries (TV) 93. Parallel Lives (TV) 94. The Neon Bible 95, etc.
TV series: 87th Precinct 61.

Rowlands, Patsy (1934–).
British character comedienne.
In the Doghouse 61. Dateline Diamonds 65. Carry on Loving 70. Carry on Girls 73. Joseph Andrews 76. Tess 79. The Fiendish Plot of Dr Fu Manchu 80, etc.

Roy, Harry (1900–1971).
British bandleader who made two films: *Everything is Rhythm* 36. *Rhythm Racketeer* 37.

Royal Film Performance.
A charity function begun in London in 1946 with *A Matter of Life and Death.* The Queen usually attends, but the film is chosen, usually on the basis of what is least offensive rather than best, by executives of the Cinema & Television Benevolent Fund, for whose financial benefit the evening is staged. Subsequent films have been:
1947: *The Bishop's Wife*
1948: *Scott of the Antarctic*
1949: *That Forsyte Woman*
1950: *The Mudlark*
1951: *Where No Vultures Fly*
1952: *Because You're Mine*
1953: *Rob Roy*
1954: *Beau Brummell*
1955: *To Catch a Thief*
1956: *The Battle of the River Plate*
1957: *Les Girls*
1958: no performance
1959: *The Horse's Mouth*
1960: *The Last Angry Man*
1961: *The Facts of Life*
1962: *West Side Story*
1963: *Sammy Going South*
1964: *Move Over Darling*
1965: *Lord Jim*
1966: *Born Free*
1967: *The Taming of the Shrew*
1968: *Romeo and Juliet*
1969: *The Prime of Miss Jean Brodie*
1970: *Anne of the Thousand Days*
1971: *Love Story*
1972: *Mary Queen of Scots*
1973: *Lost Horizon*
1974: *The Three Musketeers*
1975: *Funny Lady*
1976: *The Slipper and the Rose*
1977: *Silver Streak*
1978: *Close Encounters of the Third Kind*
1979: *California Suite*
1980: *Kramer vs Kramer*
1981: *Chariots of Fire*
1982: *Evil Under the Sun*
1983: *Table for Five*
1984: *The Dresser*
1985: *A Passage to India*
1986: *White Nights*
1987: *84 Charing Cross Road*
1988: *Empire of the Sun*
1989: *Madame Sousatzka*
1990: *Always*
1991: *Hot Shots!*
1992: *Chaplin*
1993: *The Man Without a Face*
1994: *34th Street*

Royle, Selena (1904–1983).
American character actress.
The Misleading Lady 32. Mrs Parkington 44. The Fighting Sullivans 44. Gallant Journey 47. Cass Timberlane 47. Joan of Arc 48. Branded 50. Robot Monster 53. Murder Is My Beat 55, etc.

Rozema, Patricia (1958–).
Canadian director and screenwriter.
I've Heard the Mermaids Singing 87. White Room 91. Montreal Sextet (co-d) 91. The Case of the Missing Mother 92. When Night Is Falling 95, etc.

Rozsa, Miklos (1907–).
Hungarian composer, in Hollywood from 1940.
Autobiography: 1982, *A Double Life.*
Knight without Armour 37. *The Four Feathers* 39. *The Thief of Baghdad* (AAN) 40. Lady Hamilton 41. Five Graves to Cairo 43. Double Indemnity (AAN) 44. A Song to Remember 44. The Lost Weekend 45. *Spellbound* (AA) 45. *The Killers* (AAN) 46. Brute Force 47. A Double Life (AA) 47. Naked City 48. Adam's Rib 49. The Asphalt Jungle 50. Quo Vadis (AAN) 51. Ivanhoe (AAN) 52. Julius Caesar 53. Moonfleet 55. Lust for Life 56. *Ben Hur* (AA) 59. King of Kings 61. El Cid (AAN) 61. Sodom and Gomorrah 62. The VIPs 63. The Power 67. The Green Berets 68. The Private Life of Sherlock Holmes 70. Providence 77. Fedora 78. The Private Files of J. Edgar Hoover 78. Time after Time 79. Last Embrace 79. Dead Men Don't Wear Plaid 82, many others.

Ruane, John (1952–).
Australian director and screenwriter, from television commercials.
Death in Brunswick 91. That Eye, the Sky 94.

Rub, Christian (1887–1956).
Austrian character actor, long in Hollywood. Was the model and voice for Gepetto the wood-carver in Disney's *Pinocchio.*
The Trial of Vivienne Ware 32. The Kiss behind the Mirror 33. A Dog of Flanders 35. Dracula's Daughter 36. Heidi 37. Mad about Music 38. The Great Waltz 38. The Swiss Family Robinson 40. Tales of Manhattan 42. Fall Guy 48. Something for the Birds 52, many others.

Ruben, Joseph (1951–).
American director and screenwriter.
The Sister-in-Law (wd) 75. The Pom-Pom Girls (wd) 76. Joyride (wd) 76. Our Winning Season (wd) 78. Gorp (d) 80. Dreamscape (wd) 84. The Stepfather (d) 87. True Believer (d) 89. Sleeping with the Enemy (d) 90, etc.

Rubens, Alma (1897–1931) (Alma Smith).
American leading lady of the silent screen; her career was prematurely ended by drug addiction.
Intolerance 15. The Firefly of Tough Luck 17. Humoresque 20. Cytherea 24. Fine Clothes 25. Siberia 26. Masks of the Devil 28. Showboat 29, etc.

Rubens, Percival.
South African director and screenwriter.
The Foster Gang 64. Three Days of Fire (It.) 67. Mister Kingstreet's War (US) 70. Saboteurs 74.

…

Survival Zone 81. Raw Terror 85. Sweet Murder
90, etc.

Rubin, Bruce Joel (1944–).
American screenwriter and director.
■ Brainstorm 83. Deadly Friend 86. Ghost (co-w,
AA) 90. Jacob's Ladder 90. My Life (& d) 93.

Rubinstein, Artur (1887–1982).
Internationally renowned classical pianist who
made guest appearances in occasional films, e.g.
Carnegie Hall.

Rubinstein, John (1946–).
American character actor, and occasional
composer. Son of Artur Rubinstein.
Getting Straight 70. Zachariah 70. The Wild Pack
72. All Together Now (TV) 75. The Car 77. The
Boys from Brazil 78. She's Dressed to Kill (TV) 79.
Killjoy (TV) 81. Daniel 83. Someone to Watch
over Me 87. Shadow on the Sun (TV) 88. Liberace
(TV) 88. Another Stakeout 93, etc.
TV series: Crazy Like a Fox 84–85.

Ruby, Harry (1895–1974).
American songwriter (with Bert Kalmar). See
Kalmar, Bert for credits.

Ruddy, Albert S. (1934–).
American producer.
The Godfather 72. The Longest Yard 74. The
Mcahans (TV) 76. Matilda 78. Death Hunt 81.
The Cannonball Run 81. Megaforce 82.
Cannonball Run II 83. Lassiter 83. Farewell to the
King 89. Speed Zone 89. Impulse 90. Bad Girls 94.
The Scout 94, etc.

¶ Show me a relaxed producer and I'll show you
a failure. – A.S.R.

Rudley, Herbert (1911–).
American supporting actor.
Abe Lincoln in Illinois 39. The Seventh Cross 44.
Rhapsody in Blue (as Ira Gershwin) 45. A Walk in
the Sun 46. Joan of Arc 48. The Silver Chalice 55.
The Black Sleep 56. Beloved Infidel 59. The Great
Imposter 61. Falling in Love Again 80, etc.
TV series: The Californians 57. Michael Shayne
60. Meet Mona McCluskey 65. The Mothers-in-
Law 67–68.

Rudnick, Paul.
American screenwriter and dramatist.
Addams Family Values 93.

Rudolph, Alan (1943–).
American director and screenwriter.
■ Premonition (wd) 72. Buffalo Bill and the
Indians, or Sitting Bull's History Lesson (w) 76.
Welcome to L.A. (wd) 76. Remember My Name
(wd) 78. Roadie (d) 80. Endangered Species (wd)
82. Return Engagement (d) 83. Choose Me (d) 84.
Songwriter (d) 84. Trouble in Mind (wd) 85.
Made in Heaven (d) 87. The Moderns (co-w, d)
88. Love at Large (d) 89. Mortal Thoughts (d) 91.
Equinox (d) 92. Mrs Parker and the Vicious Circle
(co-w, d) 94.

Ruehl, Mercedes (1954–).
American actress, from the stage.
The Warriors 79. Four Friends 81. 84 Charing
Cross Road 86. Heartburn 86. Leader of the Band
87. Radio Days 87. The Secret of My Success 87.
Big 88. Married to the Mob 88. Slaves of New
York 89. Crazy People 90. Another You 91. The
Fisher King (AA) 91. Lost in Yonkers 93. The Last
Action Hero 93, etc.

Ruggles, Charles (1886–1970).
American character comedian, brother of Wesley
Ruggles. In films regularly from 1928 after stage
experience; quickly became popular for his
inimitably diffident manner.
■ Peer Gynt 15. The Majesty of the Law 15. The
Reform Candidate 15. The Heart Raider 23.
Gentlemen of the Press 29. The Lady Lies 29. The
Battle of Paris 29. Roadhouse Nights 30. Young Man
of Manhattan 30. Queen High 30. Her Wedding
Night 30. *Charley's Aunt* 30. Honor among Lovers
31. The Girl Habit 31. The Smiling Lieutenant 31.
Beloved Bachelor 31. Husband's Holiday 31. This
Reckless Age 32. One Hour with You 32. This is
the Night 32. Make Me a Star 32. *Love Me Tonight*
32. 70,000 Witnesses 32. The Night of June 13th
32. *Trouble in Paradise* 32. Evenings for Sale 32.
If I Had a Million 32. Madame Butterfly 32.
Murders in the Zoo 33. Terror Aboard 33. Melody
Cruise 33. Mama Loves Papa 33. Girl without a
Room 33. Alice in Wonderland 33. Six of a Kind
34. Goodbye Love 34. Melody in Spring 34.
Murder in the Private Car 34. Friends of Mr
Sweeney 34. The Pursuit of Happiness 34. *Ruggles
of Red Gap* 35. People will Talk 35. No More Ladies
35. The Big Broadcast of 1936 35. Anything Goes
36. *Early to Bed* 36. Hearts Divided 36. Wives
Never Know 36. Mind Your Own Business 36.
Turn Off the Moon 37. Exclusive 37. *Bringing Up
Baby* 38. Breaking the Ice 38. Service De Luxe 38.
His Exciting Night 38. Boy Trouble 39. Sudden
Money 39. Invitation to Happiness 39. Night Work
39. Balalaika 39. The Farmer's Daughter 40.
Opened by Mistake 40. Maryland 40. Public Deb
Number One 40. No Time for Comedy 40.
Invisible Woman 41. Honeymoon for Three 41.
Model Wife 41. The Parson of Panamint 41. Go
West Young Lady 41. The Perfect Snob 41. Friendly
Enemies 42. Dixie Dugan 43. Our Hearts Were
Young and Gay 44. The Doughgirls 44. Three Is a
Family 44. Bedside Manner 45. Incendiary
Blonde 45. A Stolen Life 46. Gallant Journey 46.
The Perfect Marriage 46. My Brother Talks to Horses
46. *It Happened on Fifth Avenue* 47. Ramrod 47. Give
My Regards to Broadway 48. The Loveable Cheat
49. *Look for the Silver Lining* 49. Girl on the Subway
(TV) 58. All in a Night's Work 61. *The Pleasure of
His Company* 61. The Parent Trap 61. Son of Flubber
63. Papa's Delicate Condition 63. *I'd Rather Be
Rich* 64. The Ugly Dachshund 66. Follow Me Boys
66.
TV series: The World of Mr Sweeney 53.
✪ For devoting a lifetime of professional
experience to the presentation of dapper
optimism, and for helping to cheer up several
generations of filmgoers. *Trouble in Paradise.*

Ruggles of Red Gap.
The story by Harry Leon Wilson, about a British
butler exported to the American midwest, was
filmed with Edward Everett Horton in 1923 and
with Charles Laughton in 1935. Bob Hope's *Fancy
Pants* 50 bore more than a passing resemblance to
it.

Ruggles, Wesley (1889–1972).
American director, in Hollywood from 1914. One
of the original Keystone Kops: brother of Charles
Ruggles.
Wild Honey 22. The Plastic Age 26. Silk
Stockings 27. Are These Our Children? 30. *Cimarron*
(AAN) 31. No Man of Her Own 32. College
Humour 33. *I'm No Angel* 33. Bolero 34. The
Gilded Lily 35. Valiant is the Word for Carrie 36.
I Met Him in Paris 37. True Confession 37. *Sing You
Sinners* (& p) 38. Invitation to Happiness 39. My
Two Husbands 40. Arizona (& p) 40. Good
Morning Doctor 41. Somewhere I'll Find You 42.

See Here Private Hargrove 44. London Town (GB)
46, etc.

Rühmann, Heinz (1902–1994).
German actor whose films have rarely been seen
abroad.
Das Deutsche Mutterherz 26. Drei von der
Tankstelle 30. Bomben auf Monte Carlo 31. The
Man Who Was Sherlock Holmes 37. Die
Feuerzangenbowle 44. The Captain from
Kopenick 56. Menschen im Hotel 59. The Good
Soldier Schweik 59. Das Schwarze Schaf (as
Father Brown) 60. *Ship of Fools* (US) 65. La Bourse
et la Vie (Fr.) 65. Maigret und Sein Grosster Fall
66. So Far Away, So Close (In Weiter Ferne, So
Nah!) 93, etc.

Ruick, Barbara (1932–1974).
American leading lady of the 50s.
I Love Melvin 51. Invitation 52. Carousel 56.
California Split 75, etc.

Ruiz, Raúl (1941–).
Chilean director and screenwriter who began as a
dramatist. Noted for his innovative approach, he
went into exile in 1973 and is now based in Paris.
Three Sad Tigers (Tres Tristes Tigres) 68. The
Penal Colony (La Colonia Penal) 71. The
Suspended Vocation (La Vocation Suspendue) 77.
Games (Jeux) 79. L'Or Gris 80. On Top of the
Whale (Het Dak van de Walvis) 82. Bérénice 84.
Treasure Island 86. Richard III 86. Life Is a Dream
(La Mémoire des Apparances: La Vie Est un Songe)
87. The Golden Boat 90. Dark at Noon 92. The
Man Who Was Thursday 92. Palomita Blanca 93.
The Secret Journey: Lives of Saints and Sinners (Il
Viaggio Clandestino: Vite di Santi e Peccatori) (wd)
94. Fado, Major and Minor 94, many others.

Ruiz-Anchia, Juan.
Spanish cinematographer, in Hollywood.
Reborn 82. Miss Lonely Hearts 83. Valentina 83.
The Stone Boy 83. Maria's Lovers 84. That Was
Then . . . This Is Now 85. At Close Range 86.
Where the River Runs Black 86. Surrender 87.
House of Games 87. The Seventh Sign 88. Things
Change 88. Lost Angels 89. The Last of the Finest
90. Naked Tango 90. Liebestraum 91. Dying Young
91. Mr Jones 92. Glengarry Glen Ross 92. A Far
Off Place 93. Mr Jones 93, etc.

Rule, Janice (1931–).
American leading lady with stage and TV
experience. Now a psychoanalyst.
Goodbye My Fancy 51. Holiday for Sinners 52.
Rogues' March 53. Gun for a Coward 57. Bell,
Book and Candle 58. The Subterraneans 60.
Invitation to a Gunfighter 64. *The Chase* 66.
Alvarez Kelly 66. The Ambushers 67. The
Swimmer 68. Doctors' Wives 71. Gumshoe 71.
Welcome to Hard Times 72. Kid Blue 73. Three
Women 77. Missing 82, etc.

Ruman, Sig (1884–1967) (Siegfried Rumann).
German character actor, usually of explosive roles,
in Hollywood from 1934.
The Wedding Night 35. *A Night at the Opera* 35.
A Day at the Races 37. Ninotchka 39. Bitter Sweet
41. *To Be or Not To Be* 42. The Hitler Gang 44. *A
Night in Casablanca* 45. On The Riviera 49. Stalag 17
53. The Glenn Miller Story 54. Three-Ring Circus
56. The Wings of Eagles 57. Robin and the Seven
Hoods 64. Last of the Secret Agents 66, many
others.

Famous line (*To Be or Not To Be*): 'So they call me
Concentration Camp Erhardt!'

Runacre, Jenny (1943–).
South African character actress in Britain.
Goodbye Mr Chips 69. Dyn Amo 71. The Creeping Flesh 72. The Final Programme 73. The Mackintosh Man 73. Passenger 75. All Creatures Great and Small 75. Joseph Andrews 77. The Duellists 78. Spectre (TV) 78. The Lady Vanishes 79. The Final Programme 81. That Englishwoman 90, etc.

running shot.
One in which the camera, mounted on wheels, keeps pace with its subject, a moving actor or vehicle.

running speed.
In silent days, 35mm ran through the projector at 16 frames per second or 60 feet per minute. When sound came, this was amended for technical reasons to 24 frames per second or 90 feet per minute. No normal 35mm projector can now operate at silent speed, which is why silent films look jerky when you see them (unless a special and very expensive laboratory process is adopted). It is said that many films made in the later silent period were in fact intended for showing at about 20 frames per second, and as machines were variable this was easily accomplished: such films now seem unduly slow when projected at 16 frames per second.
See: *slow motion, accelerated motion.*

running time.
The length of a film, usually expressed in minutes; if in feet, one must say whether 35mm or 16mm. In European television, for technical reasons, films run faster by one frame in 25, so a 75m film runs only 72m, a 100m film only 96m, etc. Films tended to be shorter and crisper in the 30s, especially when double bills came in; but now nobody seems to have control over self-indulgent directors.

¶ The length of a film should be directly related to the endurance of the human bladder. – *Alfred Hitchcock*
How long should the film be? – *An MGM director*
How long is it good? – *Nicholas Schenck*

Runyon, Damon (1884–1946).
Inimitable American chronicler of the ways of a never-never New York inhabited by good-hearted and weirdly-named guys and dolls who speak a highly imaginative brand of English. Among the films based on his stories are *Lady for a Day* 33 (and its remake *Pocketful of Miracles* 61), *The Lemon Drop Kid* 34 and 51, *A Slight Case of Murder* 38 (and *Stop You're Killing Me* 52), *The Big Street* 42, *Guys and Dolls* 55, and *The Bloodhounds of Broadway* 52 and 89.

¶ I am frankly a hired Hessian on the typewriter and have never pretended to be anything else and when I write something I want to know in advance how much I am going to be paid for it and when. – *D.R.*
It is my observation that the rich have all the best of it in this nation and my studies of American History fail to disclose any time when this same situation did not prevail. – *D.R.*
When Damon Runyon died, Broadway wept. It had lost its first citizen, its chronicler and its glorifier. – *Don Iddon*

Rush, Barbara (1927–).
American leading lady who came to Hollywood from college.
The First Legion 51. When Worlds Collide 51. Flaming Feather 52. It Came from Outer Space

53. Magnificent Obsession 54. The Black Shield of Falworth 54. Captain Lightfoot 55. The World in My Corner 56. Bigger Than Life 57. Oh Men! Oh Women! 58. Harry Black 58. The Young Philadelphians (The City Jungle) 59. The Bramble Bush 60. Strangers When We Meet 60. *Come Blow Your Horn* 63. Robin and the Seven Hoods 64. Hombre 67. The Eyes of Charles Sand (TV) 72. Superdad 74. The Last Day (TV) 75. Can't Stop the Music 80. Summer Lovers 80. Between Friends 83, many others.
TV series: Flamingo Road 80–81.

Rush, Richard (1930–).
American director.
■ Too Soon to Love (w, p) 60. Of Love and Desire 63. The Fickle Finger of Fate 67. Hell's Angels on Wheels 67. Thunder Alley 67. A Man Called Dagger 68. Psych-Out 68. The Savage Seven 68. Getting Straight 70. Freebie and the Bean (& p) 74. The Stunt Man (& p) (AAN) 80. Color of Night (d) 94.

rushes.
A day's shooting on film when it comes back from the laboratories and is ready for viewing by those involved.

Rushton, Jared (1974–).
Young American actor.
Overboard 87. Big 88. The Lady in White 88. Honey, I Shrunk the Kids 89. A Cry in the Wild 90. Pet Sematary 2 92, etc.

Russell, Billy (1893–1971).
English music-hall comedian and character actor, on stage from the age of seven.
Take Off That Hat 38. For Freedom 40. The Man in the White Suit 51. Judgement Deferred 52. Negatives 68. I Start Counting 69. Leo the Last 70, etc.
~Catchphrase: On behalf of the working classes.

Russell, Chuck.
American screenwriter and director.
■ Dreamscape (co-w) 84. A Nightmare on Elm Street Part 3: Dream Warriors (co-w, d) 87. The Blob (co-w, d) 88. The Mask (d) 94.

Russell, Craig (1948–1990).
Canadian actor and female impersonator who had a big hit with his low-budget semi-autobiographical film *Outrageous* 77, featuring his nightclub act. Died of AIDS.
Too Outrageous 86.

Russell, Gail (1924–1961).
American leading lady of the 40s; came to Hollywood straight from dramatic training. Died from alcoholism.
Henry Aldrich Gets Glamour (debut) 43. Lady in the Dark 43. *The Uninvited* 44. Our Hearts Were Young and Gay 44. Salty O'Rourke 45. Night Has a Thousand Eyes 47. Moonrise 48. Wake of the Red Witch 49. Air Cadet 51. The Tattered Dress 57. The Silent Call 61, etc.

Russell, Harold (1914–).
Canadian paratroop sergeant who lost both hands in an explosion during World War II and demonstrated his ability not only to use hooks in their place but to act as well in *The Best Years of Our Lives* 46, for which he won two Oscars. Became a public relations executive. Appeared again 1980 in *Inside Moves*.
Autobiographies: 1949, *Victory in My Hands*. 1981, *The Best Years of My Life*.

Russell, Jane (1921–).
American leading lady who came to Hollywood when an agent sent her photo to producer Howard Hughes; he starred her in *The Outlaw* 43 but it was held up for three years by censor trouble. The publicity campaign emphasized the star's physical attributes.
Autobiography: 1985, *Jane Russell*.
■ The Young Widow 47. *The Paleface* 48. Double Dynamite 50. Macao 51. Montana Belle 51. His Kind of Woman 51. Son of Paleface 52. The Las Vegas Story 52. Gentlemen Prefer Blondes 53. The French Line 54. Underwater 55. Gentlemen Marry Brunettes 55. Foxfire 55. Hot Blood 56. The Tall Men 56. The Revolt of Mamie Stover 57. The Fuzzy Pink Nightgown 57. Fate is the Hunter (guest appearance) 64. Waco 66. Johnny Reno 66. Born Losers 67. Darker than Amber 70. The Yellow Rose (TV) 84.

¶ There are two good reasons why men will go to see her. – *Howard Hughes*

Russell, John (1921–1991).
American 'second lead'.
A Bell for Adano 45. The Fat Man 51. The Sun Shines Bright 53. The Last Command 55. Rio Bravo 59. Fort Utah 66. Cannon for Cordoba 70. Blood Legacy 73. The Changeling 80. The Runaways 84. Under the Gun 88, many others.
TV series: Soldiers of Fortune 55. Lawman 58–62.

Russell, Ken (1927–).
British director, a middle-aged *enfant terrible* of the 70s who after a rigorous training in BBC art films turned out to want to shock people, and did so with flair but no subtlety.
Autobiographies: 1989, *A British Picture*. 1994, *Fire Over England.*
■ French Dressing 64. Billion Dollar Brain 67. *Women In Love* (AAN) 69. *The Music Lovers* 70. The Devils 71. The Boy Friend 71. Savage Messiah 72. Mahler 74. Tommy 75. Lisztomania 75. Valentino 77. Clouds of Glory (TV) 78. Altered States 80. Crimes of Passion 84. Gothic 87. Aria (co-d) 87. The Lair of the White Worm 88. Salome's Last Dance 88. The Rainbow 89. The Russia House (a) 90. Whore 91. Prisoner of Honor (TV) 92. Lady Chatterley (a, d) (TV) 93. Erotic Tales (co-d) 94. Uri (d) 95.

¶ This is not the age of manners. This is the age of kicking people in the crotch and telling them something and getting a reaction. I want to shock people into awareness. I don't believe there's any virtue in understatement. – *K.R.*
I know my films upset people. I *want* to upset people. – *K.R.*
Life is too short to make destructive films about people one doesn't like. My films are meant to be constructive and illuminating. – *K.R.*
Mr Ken Russell, the film director who now specializes in vulgar travesties of the lives of dead composers . . . – *Nicholas de Jongh, Guardian*
His originality these days seems to consist of disguising the banal behind a barrage of garish, distorted, noisy and fleeting images looted from every juvenile fantasy from Rider Haggard to *Superman*, with nods to Dali and Bosch, and strong tincture of Kubrick. – *Sunday Times, 1981*

Russell, Kurt (1951–).
American leading man, often in tough-guy roles, and former child actor, frequently in Disney films. He was married to actress Season Hubley and has a son by Goldie Hawn.
The Absent-Minded Professor 60. Follow Me

Boys 66. The Horse in the Grey Flannel Suit 68. Charley and the Angel 73. Superdad 74. *Elvis* (TV) 79. Used Cars 80. Escape from New York 81. The Fox and the Hound (voice) 81. The Thing 82. Silkwood 83. Swing Shift 84. The Mean Season 84. The Best of Times 85. Big Trouble in Little China 86. Overboard 87. Tequila Sunrise 88. Tango & Cash 89. Winter People 89. Backdraft 91. Unlawful Entry 92. Captain Ron 92. Tombstone 93. Stargate 94, etc.

TV series: The Travels of Jamie McPheeters 63–64. The New Land 74. The Quest 76.

Russell, Lillian (1861–1922) (Helen Louise Leonard).
Statuesque American singer-entertainer, highly popular around the turn of the century. Only one film, *Wildfire* (1914); was played by Alice Faye in a 1940 biopic, by Ruth Gillette in *The Great Ziegfeld*, by Andrea King in *My Wild Irish Rose*, and by Binnie Barnes in *Diamond Jim*.

Russell, Reb (1906–1978) (Fay Russell).
American star of 30s westerns, after success as a football full-back. He quit acting at the end of the 30s to become a rancher.

All-American 32. Man From Hell 34. Border Vengeance 35. Lightning Triggers 35. Rough and Tough 36. Outlaw Rule 36. Arizona Badman 42, etc.

Russell, Rosalind (1908–1976).
Dominant American leading lady of the 30s and 40s, usually as career women; later attempted character roles, but her choice was sometimes unwise.
Autobiography: 1977, *Life Is a Banquet*.
■ Evelyn Prentice 34. The President Vanishes 34. West Point of the Air 35. The Casino Murder Case 35. Reckless 35. China Seas 35. Rendezvous 35. Forsaking All Others 35. The Night is Young 35. It Had to Happen 36. Under Two Flags 36. Trouble for Two 36. Craig's Wife 36. *Night Must Fall* 37. Live Love and Learn 37. Manproof 38. *The Citadel* 38. Four's a Crowd 38. Fast and Loose 39. *The Women* 39. *His Girl Friday* 40. No Time for Comedy 40. Hired Wife 40. This Thing Called Love 41. They Met in Bombay 41. The Feminine Touch 41. Design for Scandal 41. Take a Letter Darling 42. *My Sister Eileen* 42. Flight for Freedom 43. What a Woman 43. Roughly Speaking 45. She Wouldn't Say Yes 45. Sister Kenny 46. The Guilt of Janet Ames 47. Mourning Becomes Electra 48. The Velvet Touch 48. Tell it to the Judge 49. A Woman of Distinction 50. Never Wave at a WAC 52. The Girl Rush 55. Picnic 56. Auntie Mame 58. A Majority of One 61. Gypsy 62. Five-Finger Exercise 62. The Trouble with Angels 66. Oh Dad, Poor Dad 67. Where Angels Go Trouble Follows 68. Rosie 68. The Unexpected Mrs Pollifax 70. The Crooked Hearts (TV) 72.

¶ At MGM there was a first wave of top stars, and a second wave to replace them in case they got difficult. I was in the second line of defence, behind Myrna Loy. – *R.R.*
Success is a public affair. Failure is a private funeral. – *R.R.*
Acting is standing up naked and turning around very slowly. – *R.R.*

Russell, Shirley.
English costume designer.
Yanks 79. Agatha (AAN) 79. Reds (AAN) 81. The Razor's Edge 84. The Bride 85. Hope and Glory 87, etc.

Russell, Theresa (1957–).
American leading lady who settled in the UK. She is married to director Nicolas Roeg.
■ The Last Tycoon 77. Straight Time 78. Bad Timing 80. Eureka 83. The Razor's Edge 84. Insignificance 86. Black Widow 87. Aria 87. Track 29 87. Physical Evidence 88. Impulse 90. Whore 91. Kafka 91. Cold Heaven 92. A Woman's Guide to Adultery (TV) 93. Being Human 94.

Russell, William D. (1908–1968).
American director.
■ Our Hearts Were Growing Up 46. Ladies' Man 47. *Dear Ruth* 47. The Sainted Sisters 48. The Green Promise 49. Bride for Sale 49. Best of the Badmen 51.

Russell, Willy (1947–).
British dramatist and composer who has adapted his own plays for the screen.
■ *Educating Rita* (AAN) 83. Mr Love (m) 85. *Shirley Valentine* (& m) 89. Dancin' thru the Dark (& m) 91.

the Russian cinema
has been one of the most influential in the world, chiefly due to a small group of highly talented men. Before the Revolution, Russian films were old-fashioned and literary; but the Bolsheviks saw the great potential of the film as propaganda and actively encouraged the maturing talents of such men as Eisenstein (*Battleship Potemkin, October, The General Line, Alexander Nevsky, Ivan the Terrible*), Pudovkin (*Mother, The End of St Petersburg, The Deserter, General Suvorov*), Dovzhenko (*Arsenal, Earth*), Turin (*Turksib*) and Petrov (*Peter the Great*). Donskoi in *The Childhood of Maxim Gorki* and its two sequels was allowed to be nostalgic, but this vein only occasionally comes to the surface, most recently in *The Lady with a Little Dog*. The light touch comes hard to Russian film-makers, but Alexandrov achieved it in *Volga Volga*, and recently there have been signs of greater effort in this direction, at least for home consumption. The stolidity of most Russian films since World War II should not blind anyone to the enormous influence which the best Soviet work has had on film-makers the world over, especially in its exploration of the potentialities of camera movement, editing and sound; all these techniques were seen at their best in the mid-60s in a seven-hour version of *War and Peace*.

Russo, James (1953–).
American actor.
Vortex 81. Fast Times at Ridgemont High 82. Beverly Hills Cop 84. Extremities 86. China Girl 87. Blue Iguana 88. Freeway 88. We're No Angels 89. Illicit Behavior 91. Intimate Stranger 91. A Kiss before Dying 91. My Own Private Idaho 91. Cold Heaven 92. Bad Girls 94, etc.

Russo, Rene.
American leading actress, a former model.
Major League 89. Mr Destiny 90. One Good Cop 91. Freejack 92. In the Line of Fire 93. Outbreak 95, etc.
TV series: Sable 87–88.

Rustichelli, Carlo (1916–).
Italian composer.
Gran Premio 43. Gioventu Perduta 47. In the Name of the Law 48. Behind Closed Shutters 50. The Road to Hope 50. Black 13 (GB) 53. Il Ferroviere 55. Maledetto Imbroglio 59. Queen of the Nile 61. Mamma Roma 62. Torpedo Bay 63. Blood and Black Lace 64. The Secret War of Harry Frigg 67. Alfredo, Alfredo 71. The Black Hand 73.

Le Gang 76. Le Beaujolais Nouveau Est Arrivé 78. Claretta and Ben 83. Heads or Tails 83, many others.

Ruth, Babe (1895–1948).
Legendary big-hitting American baseball player who has been the subject of two biopics, *The Babe Ruth Story*, directed by Roy del Ruth in 1948, starring William Bendix, and *The Babe*, made by Arthur Hiller in 1992, starring John Goodman. He was the model for the character of Roy Hobbs in Bernard Malamud's novel *The Natural*, filmed by Barry Levinson in 1984 with Robert Redford in the role, and appears as a minor character in *The Sandlot* (GB: *The Sandlot Kids*). He also appeared as himself in a few movies.
Babe Comes Home 26. Speedy 27. The Pride of the Yankees 42, etc.

Rutherford, Ann (1917–).
American leading lady of the 40s, former child stage star.
Love Finds Andy Hardy 38. The Hardys Ride High 39. Gone with the Wind 39. Pride and Prejudice 40. Happy Land 43. Two O'Clock Courage 45. *The Secret Life of Walter Mitty* 47. The Adventures of Don Juan 48. They Only Kill Their Masters 72, etc.

Rutherford, Dame Margaret (1892–1972).
Inimitable, garrulous, shapeless, endearing British comedy character actress, who usually seemed to be playing somebody's slightly dotty spinster aunt. She studied at the Royal Academy of Music and did not begin acting until the late 20s. Married to actor Stringer Davis.
Autobiography: 1972, *An Autobiography*.
■ Talk of the Devil 36. Dusty Ermine 38. Beauty and the Barge 38. Catch as Catch Can 38. Missing Believed Married 38. Quiet Wedding 40. Spring Meeting 41. *The Demi Paradise* 43. Yellow Canary 43. English without Tears 44. *Blithe Spirit* (as Madame Arcati) 45. While the Sun Shines 46. Meet Me at Dawn 47. *Miranda* 47. Passport to Pimlico 48. *The Happiest Days of Your Life* 50. Her Favourite Husband 51. The Magic Box 51. Castle in the Air 51. *The Importance of Being Earnest* 52. Curtain Up 52. Miss Robin Hood 53. Innocents in Paris 53. Trouble in Store 53. The Runaway Bus 54. Mad about Men 55. Aunt Clara 55. An Alligator Named Daisy 56. The Smallest Show on Earth 57. I'm All Right Jack 59. Just My Luck 59. On the Double 61. *Murder She Said* (as Miss Marple) 62. Mouse on the Moon 63. Murder at the Gallop 63. *The VIPs* (AA) 63. Murder Most Foul 63. Murder Ahoy 64. The Alphabet Murders 65. Chimes at Midnight 66. A Countess from Hong Kong 67. Arabella 68.
☺ For her splendidly eccentric self. *Blithe Spirit.*

Ruttenberg, Joseph (1889–1983).
Russian cinematographer, in Hollywood from 1915.
Over the Hill 28. Fury 36. *The Great Waltz* (AA) 38. *Dr Jekyll and Mr Hyde* 41. Mrs Miniver (AA) 42. Madame Curie 43. Adventure 46. BF's Daughter 48. Side Street 49. The Forsyte Saga 49. The Great Caruso 51. Julius Caesar 53. The Last Time I Saw Paris 54. The Swan 56. *Somebody Up There Likes Me* (AA) 56. *Gigi* (AA) 58. The Reluctant Debutante 58. Butterfield 8 60. Bachelor in Paradise 61. Who's Been Sleeping in My Bed? 63. Sylvia 63. Harlow 65. Love Has Many Faces 65. The Oscar 66. Speedway 68, many others.

Ruttman, Walter (1887–1941).
German director most famous for his experimental film *Berlin* 27.

Weekend 30. Mannesmann 37. Deutsche Panzer 40, etc.

Ruysdael, Basil (1888–1960).
Authoritative Russian-American character actor, former opera singer.
The Coconuts 29. Come to the Stable 49. Broken Arrow 50. My Forbidden Past 51. Carrie 52. The Blackboard Jungle 56. The Last Hurrah 58. The Story of Ruth 60, many others.

Ryan, Frank (1907–1947).
American director.
Hers to Hold 43. Can't Help Singing 44. Patrick the Great 45. A Genius in the Family 46, etc.

Ryan, Irene (1903–1973) (Irene Riordan).
Wiry American comedienne, was famous as Granny in TV's *The Beverly Hillbillies.*
Melody for Three 41. San Diego I Love You 44. Diary of a Chambermaid 45. Meet Me after the Show 51. Blackbeard the Pirate 52. Spring Reunion 57, etc.

Ryan, John P. (1938–).
American leading man.
The Tiger Makes Out 65. Five Easy Pieces 70. The King of Marvin Gardens 72. Shamus 72. Dillinger 73. Cops and Robbers 73. It's Alive 75. The Missouri Breaks 76. Futureworld 76. It Lives Again 79. The Cotton Club 84. The Runaway Train 85. Avenging Force 86. Rent-a-Cop 88. Class of 1999 89. Best of the Best 89. Delta Force 2: Operation Stranglehold 90. Eternity 90. The Inner Circle 91. Hoffa 92. Young Goodman Brown 93, etc.

Ryan, Kathleen (1922–1985).
Irish leading lady with stage experience.
Odd Man Out (debut) 47. Captain Boycott 47. Esther Waters 48. Give Us This Day 50. The Yellow Balloon 52. Captain Lightfoot 53. Laxdale Hall 53. *Jacqueline* 56. Sail into Danger 58, etc.

Ryan, Madge (1919–1994).
Australian character actress of stage and screen, in Britain from the mid-50s. She was a member of the National Theatre in the 60s, where her roles included *Mother Courage.*
The Strange Affair 68. I Start Counting 69. A Clockwork Orange 71. Endless Night 71. Frenzy 72. Who Is Killing the Great Chefs of Europe? (aka Too Many Chefs) 78. The Lady Vanishes 80, etc.

Ryan, Meg (1962–).
American leading actress who began acting to help pay for her university studies in journalism. She married actor Dennis Quaid in 1991.
Rich and Famous 81. Amityville 3-D 83. Armed and Dangerous 86. Top Gun 86. Innerspace 87. Promised Land 88. DOA 88. Presidio 88. *When Harry Met Sally* 89. Joe versus the Volcano 90. The Doors 91. Prelude to a Kiss 92. *Sleepless in Seattle* 93. Flesh and Bone 93. When a Man Loves a Woman 94. I.Q. 94, etc.
TV series: One of the Boys 82. Wildside 85.

Ryan, Mitchell (Mitch) (1928–).
Stalwart American character actor, mostly on TV.
Flesh and Blood 79. The Chisholms 80. Lethal Weapon 87. Winter People 89, etc.
TV series: Chase 73–74. Executive Suite 76–77.

Having Babies 78–79. The Chisholms 80. High Performance 83.

Ryan, Peggy (1924–).
American teenage comedienne of the early 40s, often teamed with Donald O'Connor. In vaudeville from childhood.
Top of the Town 37. Give Out Sisters 42. Top Man 43. The Merry Monahans 44. Bowery to Broadway 44. That's the Spirit 43. On Stage Everybody 45. All Ashore 52, etc.
TV series: Hawaii Five-O 69–76.

Ryan, Robert (1909–1973).
Strong-featured American leading actor who never seemed to get the roles he deserved.
Biography: 1990, *Robert Ryan* by Franklin Jarlet.
■ Golden Gloves 40. Queen of the Mob 40. Northwest Mounted Police 40. Texas Rangers Ride Again 41. The Feminine Touch 41. Bombardier 43. *Gangway for Tomorrow* 43. The Sky's the Limit 43. Behind the Rising Sun 43. The Iron Major 43. Tender Comrade 43. The Hitler Gang 44. Marine Raiders 44. The Walls Came Tumbling Down 46. Trail Street 47. The Woman on the Beach 47. *Crossfire* 47. Berlin Express 48. Return of the Badmen 48. The Boy with Green Hair 48. Act of Violence 49. Caught 49. *The Set-Up* 49. The Woman on Pier 13 49. The Secret Fury 50. Born to be Bad 50. Best of the Badmen 51. Flying Leathernecks 51. The Racket 51. On Dangerous Ground 51. Hard Fast and Beautiful 51. *Clash by Night* 52. Beware My Lovely 52. Horizons West 52. City beneath the Sea 53. The Naked Spur 53. Inferno 53. Alaska Seas 54. About Mrs Leslie 54. Her Twelve Men 54. Bad Day at Black Rock 55. Escape to Burma 55. House of Bamboo 55. The Tall Men 55. The Proud Ones 56. Back from Eternity 56. Men in War 57. *God's Little Acre* 58. Lonelyhearts 59. Day of the Outlaw 59. *Odds against Tomorrow* 59. Ice Palace 60. The Canadians 61. King of Kings 61. The Longest Day 62. *Billy Budd* 62. The Crooked Road 65. Battle of the Bulge 65. The Dirty Game 66. The Professionals 66. The Busy Body 67. The Dirty Dozen 67. Hour of the Gun 67. Custer of the West 67. Dead or Alive 67. Anzio 68. Captain Nemo and the Underwater City 68. The Wild Bunch 69. Lawman 71. The Love Machine 71. The Man Without a Country (TV) 72. And Hope to Die 72. The Iceman Cometh 73. Executive Action 73. Lolly Madonna XXX 73. The Outfit 74.

Ryan, Sheila (1921–1975) (Katherine McLaughlin).
American leading lady in 'B' films of the 40s and 50s. Married Pat Buttram in 1952, after they met while making Gene Autry's *Mule Train.*
The Gay Caballero 40. Sun Valley Serenade 41. The Gang's All Here 41. Pardon My Stripes 42. Careful, Soft Shoulders 42. Song of Texas 43. Something for the Boys 44. Getting Gertie's Garter 45. Lone Wolf in London 46. The Big Fix 47. Caged Fury 48. The Cowboy and the Indians 49. Mule Train 50. Mask of the Dragon 51. On Top of Old Smoky 53. Street of Darkness 58, etc.

Ryan, Tim (1889–1956).
American comedy supporting actor, very adept at drunks, wisecracking reporters, dumb cops, etc.
Brother Orchid 40. The Mystery of the Thirteenth Guest 43. Crazy Knights 45. The Shanghai Chest 48. Sky Dragon 49. Cuban Fireball

51. From Here to Eternity 53. Fighting Trouble 56 etc.

Rydell, Bobby (1942–).
American pop star who appeared to no great advantage in *Bye Bye Birdie* 63.

Rydell, Christopher.
American actor, the son of director Mark Rydell.
On Golden Pond 81. Gotcha! 85. Mask 85. How I Got into College 89. Blood and Sand (Sp.) 89. Side Out 90. For the Boys 91. Trauma 93. Flesh and Bone 93, etc.

Rydell, Mark (1934–).
American director.
■ The Fox 68. The Reivers 69. The Cowboys (& p) 72. Cinderella Liberty (& p) 74. Harry and Walter Go to New York (& p) 76. The Rose 79. *On Golden Pond* (AAN) 81. The River 84. For the Boys 91. Intersection 94.
AS ACTOR: Crime in the Streets 56. The Long Goodbye 73. Punchline 88. Havana 89, etc.

Ryder, Winona (1971–).
American juvenile actress.
Lucas 86. Square Dance 87. Heathers 88. Beetlejuice 88. 1969 89. Great Balls of Fire 89. Mermaids 90. Edward Scissorhands 90. Welcome Home, Roxy Carmichael 91. Night on Earth 92. Bram Stoker's Dracula 92. The Age of Innocence (AAN) 93. The House of the Spirits 94. Reality Bites 94. Little Women 94, etc.

Rylance, Mark.
English leading actor, from the Royal Shakespeare Company.
Love Lies Bleeding (TV) 93. The Institute Benjamenta 95.

Ryskind, Morrie (1895–1985).
American comedy writer.
Animal Crackers 30. Palmy Days 31. *A Night at the Opera* 35. *My Man Godfrey* (AAN) 36. Stage Door (AAN) 37. Room Service 38. Man about Town 39. Penny Serenade 41. Where Do We Go from Here? 45. Heartbeat 46, etc.

Ryu, Chishu (1906–1993).
Japanese leading actor, a regular in the films of Ozu from 1928, often as a kindly but distracted father.
The Dreams of Youth (Wakoudo no Yume) 28. I Flunked, but . . . (Rakudai Wa Shita Keredo) 30. I Was Born but . . . (Umarete Wa Mita Keredo) 32. College Is a Nice Place (Daigaku Yoi Toko) 36. The Only Son (Hitori Masuko) 36. The Brothers and Sisters of the Toda Family (Tode-ke no Kyodai) 41. There Was a Father (Chichi Ariki) 42. The Record of a Tenement Gentleman (Nagaya no Shinshi Roku) 47. A Hen in the Wind (Kaze no Naka no Mendori) 48. Late Spring (Banshun) 49. The Munekata Sisters (Munekata Shimai) 50. Early Summer (Bakushu) 51. Tokyo Story (Tokyo Monogatari) 53. Early Spring (Soshun) 56. Twilight in Tokyo (Tokyo Boshoku) 57. Ohayo 59. Late Autumn (Akibiyori) 60. An Autumn Afternoon (Samma no Aji) 62. Red Beard (Akahige) 67. The Funeral 85. Tokyo-ga 85. Akira Kurosawa's Dreams 90. Luminous Moss (Hikarigoke) 91. Until the End of the World (Bis ans Ende der Welt) 91, etc.

S

Sabatini, Rafael (1875–1950).
Anglo-Italian author of swashbuckling historical novels, several of which have been filmed more than once: *The Sea Hawk, Scaramouche, Captain Blood, The Black Swan, Bardelys the Magnificent*, etc.

Sabbatini, Enrico (1932–   ).
Italian costume designer, in international productions.
A Place for Lovers 68. Sunflowers 69. Sacco and Vanzetti 71. Giordano Bruno 73. Moses 76. A Special Day 77. Jesus of Nazareth (TV) 78. Marco Polo (TV) 82. The Mission (AAN) 86. Chronicle of a Death Foretold 86. Old Gringo 89. To Forget Palermo (Dimenticare Palermo) 90, etc.

Sabu (1924–1963) (Sabu Dastagir).
Boyish Indian actor, a stable lad in Mysore when he was noticed by director Robert Flaherty and appeared in *Elephant Boy* 37. Came to England, later America.
The Drum 38. *The Thief of Baghdad* 40. *The Jungle Book* 42. Arabian Nights 42. White Savage 43. Cobra Woman 44. Tangier 46. Black Narcissus 46. *The End of the River* 47. Maneater of Kumaon 48. Song of India 49. Hello, Elephant 52. Jaguar 56. Herrin der Welt (Ger.) 60. Rampage 63. A Tiger Walks 63.

¶ Sabu, his little brown body in nothing but a tight-fitting breech cloth, was a perfect thing of beauty. – *Frances Flaherty*
His mother died when he was a baby. His father taught his elephant to rock the baby's cradle – to rock the baby himself in his trunk. It is even said that a wild elephant came out of the forest and played with the child. – *Frances Flaherty*

Famous line (*The Thief of Baghdad*): 'I'm Abu the thief, son of Abu the thief, grandson of Abu the thief, most unfortunate of ten sons, with a hunger that yearns day and night.'

Sackheim, Jerry.
American screenwriter.
The Night Before the Divorce 42. The Last Crooked Mile 46. The Strange Door 51. Paula 52. The Black Castle 52. Young Jesse James 60, etc.

Sackheim, William B. (1919–   ).
American writer and producer.
Smart Girls Don't Talk 48. A Yank in Korea 51. Column South 53. Border River 54. The Human Jungle 54. Tanganyika 54. The Competition (p) 80. First Blood 82. The Survivors (p) 83. No Small Affair (p) 84. The Hard Way (p) 90. Pacific Heights (p) 90, etc.

Sadoul, Georges (1904–1967).
French film critic and historian; he published two useful reference works, *Dictionnaire des Films* and *Dictionnaire des Cinéastes*.

Safan, Craig.
American composer who has also scored many television movies and mini-series.

The Great Smokey Roadblock 76. The Bad News Bears in Breaking Training 77. Corvette Summer 78. Good Guys Wear Black 79. Fade to Black 80. Nightmares 83. The Last Starfighter 84. The Legend of Billie Jean 85. The Stranger 87. Nightmare on Elm Street Part 4: The Dream Warriors 88. Stand and Deliver 88. Enid Is Sleeping 90, etc.

safety film
took over from nitrate stock in 1950–51. It burns much more slowly and therefore reduces fire risk, but its acetate base also reduces the possibility of gleaming black-and-white photography, tending instead to a matt look.

Safran, Henri (1932–   ).
French-born director in Australia.
Elephant Boy 75. Storm Boy 76. Norman Loves Rose (wd) 82. The Wild Duck 83. Prince and the Great Race (aka Bush Christmas) 83. The Red Crescent 87, etc.

Sagal, Boris (1923–1981).
American director, from TV.
■ Dime with a Halo 63. Twilight of Honor 64. Girl Happy 65. Made in Paris 66. The Thousand Plane Raid 69. Night Gallery (co-d) (TV) 69. Destiny of a Spy (TV) 69. U.M.C. (TV) 69. The Movie Murderer (TV) 70. Hauser's Memory (TV) 70. Mosquito Squadron 70. The Omega Man 71. Hitched (TV) 71. The Failing of Raymond (TV) 71. Deliver Us from Evil (TV) 73. A Case of Rape (TV) 74. The Greatest Gift (TV) 74. Indict and Convict (TV) 74. The Dream Makers (TV) 75. Man on the Outside (TV) 75. The Runaway Barge (TV) 75. The Oregon Trail (TV) 76. Mallory 76. Three for the Road 76. Ike (co-d) (TV) 78. Masada (TV) 81.
TV series as executive producer: T.H.E. Cat 67.

Sagan, Françoise (1935–   ) (F. Quoirez).
French novelist very popular in the late 50s. Works filmed include *Bonjour Tristesse, A Certain Smile, Aimez-Vous Brahms? (Goodbye Again)*.

Sagan, Leontine (1899–1974) (Leontine Schlesinger).
Austrian director who emigrated to England after her first film, made one film for Korda, and spent the remainder of her life in South Africa, where she had lived as a child, working in the theatre.
■ Maedchen in Uniform 31. Men of Tomorrow 32.

Sägebrecht, Marianne (1945–   ).
Plump German character actress, associated with the films of director Percy Adlon; she became a star with *Bagdad Café*.
Irrsee 84. Sugarbaby (Zuckerbaby) 85. Crazy Boys 87. Bagdad Café 87. Moon over Parador 88. Rosalie Goes Shopping 89. War of the Roses 89. Martha and I (Martha und Ich) 91. The Milky Way (La Vida Lactea) 92. Dust Devil: The Final Cut (GB) 93. Mona Must Die (US) 94, etc.

Sahl, Mort (1927–   ).
Sardonic American political comedian fashionable in early 60s. Films untypical.
In Love and War 58. All the Young Men 60. Don't Make Waves 67. Doctor You've Got to Be Kidding 68. Nothing Lasts Forever 84, etc.

¶ My life needs editing. – *M.S.*

sailors
of whom screen accounts have been given include Christopher Columbus (1446–1506), by Fredric March in *Christopher Columbus* 49, Gérard Depardieu in *1492: Discovery of Paradise* 92, and George Corraface in *Christopher Columbus: The Discovery* 92; Horatio Nelson (qv); Captain Bligh, by Charles Laughton, and later by Trevor Howard, in *Mutiny on the Bounty*; John Paul Jones (1747–92), by Robert Stack in *John Paul Jones* 59; Francis Drake (1540–96), by Matheson Lang in *Drake of England* 35 and by Rod Taylor in *Seven Seas to Calais* 62; Walter Raleigh by Richard Todd in *The Virgin Queen* 55; and Admiral Halsey, by James Cagney in *The Gallant Hours* 61 and by Robert Mitchum in *Midway*.

The Saint.
Among the actors who have played Leslie Charteris' 'Robin Hood of crime' in both British and American films since 1937 are Louis Hayward, Hugh Sinclair and George Sanders. One feels that 'the Falcon', a series character played in the 40s by George Sanders and later Tom Conway, was heavily indebted to the Saint, who more recently made a strong comeback on television in the person of Roger Moore. In France, a barely recognizable 'Saint' has been played in several films by Jean Marais.

Saint, Eva Marie (1924–   ).
Cool, intelligent American stage actress who played heroine in a variety of films.
■ On the Waterfront (AA) 54. That Certain Feeling 56. A Hatful of Rain 57. Raintree County 57. North by Northwest 59. Exodus 60. All Fall Down 62. 36 Hours 64. The Sandpiper 65. The Russians are Coming, The Russians are Coming 66. Grand Prix 66. The Stalking Moon 68. A Talent for Loving 69. Loving 70. Cancel My Reservation 72. A Christmas to Remember (TV) 78. The Curse of King Tutankhamun's Tomb (TV) 80. The Best Little Girl in the World (TV) 82. Malibu (TV) 83. Jane Doe (TV) 83. Fatal Vision (TV) 84. The Last Days of Patton (TV) 86. Nothing in Common 86. Breaking Home Ties (TV) 87. I'll Be Home for Christmas (TV) 88. People Like Us (TV) 90.
TV series: How the West Was Won 76.

St Clair, Malcolm (Mal) (1897–1952).
American director with a reputation for style in the 20s; in the 40s however he almost ruined the reputation of Laurel and Hardy.
Find Your Man 24. On Thin Ice 25. A Woman of the World 25. *The Grand Duchess and the Waiter* 26. Breakfast at Sunrise 27. *Gentlemen Prefer Blondes* 28. The Canary Murder Case 29. Dangerous Nan

McGrew 30. The Boudoir Diplomat 30. Olsen's Big Moment 33. She Had to Eat 37. A Trip to Paris 38 (and several other Jones Family episodes 36–40). Hollywood Cavalcade 39. Man in the Trunk 42. Over My Dead Body 42. Jitterbugs 43. The Dancing Masters 43. The Big Noise 44. The Bullfighters 45, etc.

St Cyr, Renée (1907–) (Marie-Louise Vittore). French leading lady of the 30s.
Les Deux Orphelines 33. Le Dernier Millardaire 34. Les Perles de la Couronne 37. Strange Boarders (UK) 38. La Symphonie Fantastique 42. Pierre et Jean 43. Pamela 45. Le Chevalier de la Nuit 54. Lafayette 71. On Aura Tout Vu 76, etc.

Saint-Exupéry, Antoine de (1900–1944). French aviator and writer. His *The Little Prince* was disappointingly filmed. His *Night Freight* was the basis of *Night Flight* (1933) and also of *Only Angels Have Wings* (1939).

St Jacques, Raymond (1930–1990) (James Johnson).
American leading man.
Black like Me (debut) 64. Mister Moses 65. Mister Buddwing 66. The Comedians 67. The Green Berets 68. If He Hollers Let Him Go 68. Uptight 68. Change of Mind 70. Cotton Comes to Harlem 70. The Book of Numbers (& pd) 73. Lost in the Stars 73. Born Again 78. The Private Files of J. Edgar Hoover 78. The Evil that Men Do 84. The Wild Pair 87. Glory 89, etc.
TV series: Rawhide 65–66. Roots 77. Falcon Crest 83–84.

Saint James, Susan (1946–) (Susan Miller). American leading lady of the 70s, who is mostly seen on TV playing slightly kooky but determined young ladies.
PJ 68. Where Angels Go Trouble Follows 68. The Magic Carpet (TV) 72. Love at First Bite 79. How to Beat the High Cost of Living 80. Carbon Copy 81. Don't Cry, It's Only Thunder 81, etc.
TV series: *The Name of the Game* 68–71. *McMillan and Wife* 71–75. Kate and Allie 84–89.

St John, Al 'Fuzzy' (1893–1963). American character comedian in many silents from 1913; latterly played comic side-kick in numerous second-feature westerns.
Mabel's Strange Predicament 13. Special Delivery 27. Dance of Life 29. Wanderer of the Wasteland 35. Call of the Yukon 37. Arizona Terrors 42. Frontier Revenge 49, many others.

St John, Betta (1930–) (Betty Streidler). American leading lady with stage experience.
Dream Wife (debut) 53. The Robe 53. The Student Prince 54. The Naked Dawn 55. High Tide at Noon (GB) 57. Tarzan the Magnificent (GB) 60. City of the Dead (GB) 61, etc.

St John, Howard (1905–1974). American character actor on stage from 1925, films from 1948, usually as father, executive or military commander.
Born Yesterday 50. David Harding, Counterspy 50. Counterspy Meets Scotland Yard 51. The Tender Trap 55. *Li'l Abner* 59. Straitjacket 63. Sex and the Single Girl 64. Strange Bedfellows 65. Don't Drink the Water 69, many others.

St John, Jill (1940–) (Jill Oppenheim). American leading lady.
Summer Love 57. The Lost World 60. Come Blow Your Horn 62. Who's Been Sleeping in My Bed? 63. The Liquidator (GB) 65. The Oscar 66.

Eight on the Lam 67. Banning 67. Tony Rome 67. Diamonds are Forever 71. Sitting Target 72. The Act 84, etc.

St Johns, Adela Rogers (1893–1988). Sharp-spoken American journalist who also scripted a few 30s films including *A Free Soul* and *What Price Hollywood* (AAN) 31.
Autobiography: 1978, *Love, Laughter and Tears*.

St Trinian's.
This school full of little female horrors was originally conceived by cartoonist Ronald Searle. From his formula Frank Launder and Sidney Gilliat made four commercially successful if disappointing farces: *The Belles of St Trinian's* 54, *Blue Murder at St Trinian's* 57, *The Pure Hell of St Trinian's* 60, *The Great St Trinian's Train Robbery* 66. In 1980 Launder alone produced yet another.

Sakall, S.Z. (1884–1955) (Eugene Gero Szakall). Hungarian character actor with vaudeville and stage experience. In films from 1916, Hollywood from 1939; became popular comic support and was nicknamed 'Cuddles'.
Autobiography: 1953, *The Story of Cuddles*.
It's a Date 40. Ball of Fire 41. Casablanca 42. *Thank Your Lucky Stars* 43. *Wonder Man* 45. Cinderella Jones 46. Whiplash 48. Tea for Two 50. The Student Prince 54, many others.

Sakamoto, Ryuichi (1952–). Japanese composer, rock musician, actor and leader of the 80s group Yellow Magic Orchestra.
Merry Christmas, Mr Lawrence (a, m) 83. Brand New Day (a) 87. The Last Emperor (a, m) (AAm) 87. Black Rain (s) 89. The Handmaid's Tale (m) 90. The Sheltering Sky 91. Marathon (m) 93. Little Buddha (m) 93, etc.

Sakata, Harold (1920–1982). Korean character actor who sprang to fame in *Goldfinger* 63 as the villainous Oddjob, but despite wearing the same gear around Hollywood for a number of years never got another substantial role.

Saks, Gene (1921–). American director, from Broadway.
■ Barefoot in the Park 67. The Odd Couple 67. Cactus Flower 70. Last of the Red Hot Lovers 72. Mame 74. The Prisoner of 2nd Avenue (a only) 74. The One and Only (a) 78. Brighton Beach Memoirs 87. Tchin-Tchin 91.

Salce, Luciano (1922–1989). Italian director.
Le Pillole d'Ercole 60. Crazy Desire (La Voglia Matta) 62. The Hours of Love 63. High Infidelity (co-d) 64. Kiss the Other Sheik (Oggi, Domani e Dopodomani) (co-d) 65. Slalom 65. El Greco 66. Colpo di Stato 69. Il Provinciale 71. Tragico Fantozzi 75. Il Secondo Tragico Fantozzi 76. The Innocents Abroad 83. Quelli dell Casco 88, etc.

Sale, Charles (Chic) (1885–1936). American character actor who specialized in grizzled old men.
Star Witness 31. Men of America 32. When a Fellow Needs a Friend 33. *Treasure Island* (as Ben Gunn) 34. Stranger in Town 36, etc.
~Sale was also the author of a best-selling small book called *The Specialist*, about a man building an outdoor lavatory, compiled from his vaudeville act.

Sale, Richard (1911–1993). Prolific American writer of stories and screenplays, none very memorable.

Rendezvous with Annie 46. Spoilers of the North (d only) 47. A Ticket to Tomahawk 49. Meet Me after the Show 51. Half Angel (d only) 51. Let's Make It Legal (d only) 51. My Wife's Best Friend (d only) 52. Suddenly 54. Woman's World 54. Gentlemen Marry Brunettes (& wrote words and music and co-p) 55. Seven Waves Away (& d) 56. The White Buffalo 77. Assassination 87, etc.

Sales, Soupy (1926–) (Milton Hines). American entertainer, popular on children's TV. Film debut in *Birds Do It* 66.

Salkin, Leo (1913–1993). Canadian-born animator, writer and director for Disney and UPA, who was also the model for the cartoon character Mr Magoo.
Pigs Is Pigs (AANw) 54. The 2000 Year Old Man (d) 75, etc.

Salkind, Alexander (c. 1915–). Russian producer who moves somewhat mysteriously in international circles.
■ The Trial 62. The Light at the Edge of the World 71. The Three Musketeers 73. Superman 77. Superman 2 80. Superman 3 82. Supergirl 83. Santa Claus 84. Christopher Columbus: The Discovery 92.

¶ I don't want to meet actors, they don't impress me. – A.S.

Salkow, Sidney (1909–). American director of second features from the mid-30s.
Woman Doctor 39. Café Hostess 40. The Lone Wolf Strikes 40 (and others in this series). The Adventures of Martin Eden 42. Millie's Daughter 46. Bulldog Drummond at Bay 47. Shadow of the Eagle (GB) 50. Sitting Bull 52. The Golden Hawk 52. Jack McCall, Desperado 53. Raiders of the Seven Seas 53. College Confidential 57. Twice Told Tales 63. The Great Sioux Massacre 65, many others.

Sallis, Peter (1921–). Bemused-looking British character actor, often in 'little man' roles.
Anastasia 56. The Doctor's Dilemma 58. Saturday Night and Sunday Morning 60. Charlie Bubbles 67. Inadmissible Evidence 68. Who Is Killing the Great Chefs of Europe? 78, many others.
TV series: Last of the Summer Wine 74– .

Salmi, Albert (1928–1990). Chubby American character actor, mainly on stage. Committed suicide after killing his terminally ill wife.
The Brothers Karamazov 58. The Unforgiven 59. Wild River 60. The Ambushers 67. The Deserter 70. Lawman 71. The Take 74. Empire of the Ants 77. Black Oak Conspiracy 77. Viva Knievel 77. Brubaker 80. St Helens 81. Hard to Hold 84. Born American 86. Breaking In 89, etc.
TV series: Daniel Boone 63. Petrocelli 73.

Salome.
Oscar Wilde's play of Salome's Dance of the Seven Veils before King Herod for the head of John the Baptist was filmed at least seven times in silent days, notably by Nazimova in 1923 against backgrounds inspired by the drawings of Aubrey Beardsley. It was remade in 1953 with Rita Hayworth as Salome and Charles Laughton as Herod, while Ken Russell's *Salome's Last Dance* 87 had Wilde watching a performance of his play in a brothel.

Salomon, Mikael.
Danish cinematographer, now working in Hollywood.

Fantasterne 67. Et Doegn Med Ilse 71. Welcome to the Club 71. Z.P.G. 72. De Fen 74. Why? 77. Elvis, Elvis 82. Peter von Scholten 85. The Wolf at the Door 86. Zelly and Me 88. Torch Song Trilogy 88. Stealing Heaven 89. The Abyss (AAN) 89. Always 89. Arachnophobia 90. Backdraft 91. Far and Away 92. Scent of a Woman 92. A Far Off Place 93, etc.

Salt, Jennifer (1944–).
American leading lady, daughter of Waldo Salt.

Midnight Cowboy 69. Hi Mom 69. The Revolutionary 70. Brewster McCloud 70. Play It Again Sam 72. Sisters 73. The Great Niagara (TV) 74, etc.

TV series: Soap 78–80.

Salt, Waldo (1914–1987).
American screenwriter.

The Shopworn Angel 38. Tonight We Raid Calais 43. Mr Winkle Goes to War 44. Rachel and the Stranger 48. The Flame and the Arrow 50. Taras Bulba 62. Flight from Ashiya 64. Midnight Cowboy (AA) 68. The Gang That Couldn't Shoot Straight 72. Serpico 73. The Day of the Locust 75. Coming Home (AA) 78, etc.

Salter, Hans J. (1896–1994).
German composer in Hollywood.

Call a Messenger 39. It Started with Eve 41. The Mummy's Tomb 42. The Spoilers 42. Frankenstein Meets the Wolf Man 43. Sherlock Holmes Faces Death 44. Scarlet Street 45. The Web 47. The Reckless Moment 49. The Prince Who was a Thief 51. The Far Horizons 55. The Mole People 56. Raw Wind in Eden 58. Come September 61. Hitler 62. Bedtime Story 64. Beau Geste 66. Gunpoint 66. Return of the Gunfighter (TV) 67, many others.

Salter, James (1925–).
American director, screenwriter, and novelist. He began by making a series of television documentaries on the circus.

The Hunters (oa) 58. The Appointment (w) 65. Downhill Racer (w) 68. Three (wd) 70. Threshold (w) 83, etc.

¶ The difficulty in the way our system works is that one often becomes committed to a completely worthless thing but pursues it with just as much ardour as it if were something good. – J.S.

Saltzman, Harry (1915–1994).
Canadian-born independent producer with TV experience. Very successful in Britain with *Look Back in Anger*, the James Bond films, *The Ipcress File*, *The Battle of Britain*, etc.

¶ He had a perfect mogul's figure – stocky, tubby – crinkly grey hair and the face of an eager coarse cherub. – *Tony Richardson*
See also: *Woodfall Films*.

Salvatores, Gabriele (1950–).
Italian director, from the theatre.

Sogno di una Notte d'Estate 82. Kamikazen – Ultima Notte a Milano 87. Marrakech Express 88. Turné 89. Mediterraneo 91. Puerto Escondido 93. Sud 93, etc.

Salzedo, Leonard (1921–).
British composer, mainly for Hammer productions.

The Glass Cage (US: The Glass Tomb) 55.

Women without Men 56. The Steel Bayonet 57. The Revenge of Frankenstein 58, etc.

Samms, Emma (1960–).
English starlet who went to America in 1980 and found success on TV.

Arabian Adventure 79. The Lady and the Highwayman (TV) 89. Boyfriend from Hell (aka The Shrimp on the Barbie) 90. Fatal Inheritance 91. Illusions 91. Delirious 91, etc.

TV series: General Hospital 80–83, 92– . Dynasty 85. The Colbys 86–89.

Samoilova, Tatania (1934–).
Russian leading actress.

The Cranes Are Flying 57. The Letter that Was Not Sent 60. Anna Karenina 67, etc.

Sampson, Will (1935–1987).
American (part Indian) character actor.

One Flew over the Cuckoo's Nest 75. The Outlaw Josey Wales 76. Buffalo Bill and the Indians 76. The White Buffalo 77. Orca 77. Alcatraz: the Whole Shocking Story 78. Insignificance 86.

TV series: Vegas 78.

Samuelson, G.B. (1887–1945).
British producer and distributor of silent films. His sons now operate an international production organization.

A Study in Scarlet 14. Little Women 17. Hindle Wakes 18. Quinneys 19. The Last Rose of Summer 21. Should a Doctor Tell? 23. She 25, many others.

San Francisco,
replete with cable cars, steep streets, Golden Gate Bridge and Alcatraz out there in the bay, has provided a picturesque location for innumerable movies, outstandingly *Vertigo, What's Up Doc?, The Glenn Miller Story, The Well Groomed Bride, Bullitt, Guess Who's Coming to Dinner, Point Blank, Yours Mine and Ours, The House on Telegraph Hill, Sudden Fear, Experiment in Terror, Flower Drum Song, The Maltese Falcon, The Conversation, Daddy's Gone a-Hunting, Dirty Harry, Pete 'n' Tillie, The Laughing Policeman, Dark Passage, Foul Play* and *Petulia*. The Barbary Coast days were well caught in *San Francisco, Nob Hill, Barbary Coast, Flame of the Barbary Coast*, and many other movies.

TV series have also used it *ad nauseam: The Line Up, Sam Benedict, Ironside, McMillan and Wife, Streets of San Francisco, Phyllis*.

San Giacomo, Laura (1962–).
American actress.

Miles from Home 88. sex, lies and videotape 89. Pretty Woman 89. Quigley Down Under 90. Vital Signs 90. Once Around 90. Under Suspicion 91. Where the Day Takes You 92. Nina Takes a Lover 94. The Stand (TV) 94, etc.

San Juan, Olga (1927–).
Vivacious American actress and comedienne, with radio experience. She married actor Edmond O'Brien.

Rainbow Island 44. Blue Skies 46. The Beautiful Blonde from Bashful Bend 49. Countess of Monte Cristo 49. The Third Voice 60, etc.

Sand, George (1804–1876) (Armandine Aurore Lucie Dupin).
Prolific French novelist and writer whose love affair with composer Frédéric Chopin, out of the many she had with musicians and writers, has tended to be the one to catch the fancy of film-makers. She has been played by Merle Oberon in *A Song to Remember* 45, Patricia Morison in *Song*

without End 60, Lucia Boise in *Jutrzenka: A Winter in Majorca* 71, Anne Wiazemsky in *Georges Qui?* 73, Imogene Claire in *Lisztomania* 75, and Judy Davis in *Impromptu* 89.

Sand, Paul (1944–) (Paul Sanchez).
American light actor.

The Hot Rock 72. The Main Event 79. Can't Stop the Music 80. Wholly Moses 80. The Last Fling 86. Teen Wolf Too 87, etc.

Sanda, Dominique (1948–) (Dominique Varaigne).
French leading lady of the 70s.

Une Femme Douce 70. *The Garden of the Finzi-Continis* 71. The Conformist 71. Without Apparent Motive 72. Impossible Object 73. The Mackintosh Man 73. Steppenwolf 74. 1900 76. Damnation Alley 77. Cabo Blanco 81. Le Matelot 512 84. Les Mendiants 87. In una Notte di Chiaro di Luna 89. I Won't Disturb You (Tolgo il Disturbo) 91. Nobody's Children 94. Green Henry (Der Grun Heinrich) (Sw.) 94, etc.

Sande, Walter (1906–1972).
American character actor, usually a background heavy.

The Goldwyn Follies 38. Confessions of Boston Blackie 41. To Have and Have Not 44. Wild Harvest 47. Dark City 50. Red Mountain 52. Bad Day at Black Rock 55. The Gallant Hours 60, many others.

TV series: Tugboat Annie 56.

Sandell, William.
American production designer.

The Clones 77. The Pack 77. Piranha 78. Blood Beach 81. Airplane II: The Sequel 82. St Elmo's Fire 85. Robocop 87. Big Business 88. Total Recall 90. Nothing but Trouble 91. Newsies (GB: News Boys) 92. The Flintstones 94. Outbreak 95, etc.

Sanders, Andrew.
British production designer.

Shock Treatment 81. Merry Christmas, Mr Lawrence 83. The Hit 84. Castaway 87. The Last Temptation of Christ 88. The Witches 90. K2 92, etc.

Sanders, Denis (1929–1987) and **Terry** (1931–).
American producer brothers who for many years promised great things but never quite fulfilled them.

A Time out of War (short) (AA) 54. Crime and Punishment USA 58. War Hunt 61. Shock Treatment 63. Soul to Soul 71. Invasion of the Bee Girls (d) 73, etc.

Sanders, George (1906–1972).
Suave English actor who played scoundrels, cads and crooks for 30 years. Born in St Petersburg, he was educated in England and first worked in the textile business in Manchester and as a tobacco salesman in South America. He began on the English stage in revue and as a radio actor before entering films, going to Hollywood in the mid-30s, where his first role, in *Lloyd's of London*, typed him as an elegant bounder. He also played the title role in the film series *The Saint*, which he regarded as the nadir of his career, and in its successor, *The Falcon*, before being replaced by his brother, Tom Conway (qv). He put his name to two ghost-written mystery novels in the 40s, one of which formed the basis of the 1954 film *The Unholy Four* (aka *The Stranger Came Home*). His four wives included actresses Zsa Zsa Gabor (1949–54), Benita Hume (1959–67), and Magda Gabor

(1970–71). After his film roles, and his interest in them, declined, and business ventures went wrong, he committed suicide.

Autobiography: 1960 (reissued 1993), *Memoirs of a Professional Cad*.

Biographies: 1979, *A Terrible Man* by Brian Aherne. 1991, *George Sanders – An Exhausted Life* by Richard Vanderbeets.

■ Find the Lady 36. Strange Cargo 36. The Man Who Could Work Miracles 36. Dishonour Bright 37. Slave Ship 37. Love Is News 37. Lloyds of London 37. *Lancer Spy* 37. The Lady Escapes 37. International Settlement 38. Mr Moto's Last Warning 38. Four Men and a Prayer 38. Allegheny Uprising 39. So This Is London 39. The Outsider 39. Nurse Edith Cavell 39. Confessions of a Nazi Spy 39. *The Saint* (series) 39–41. The House of Seven Gables 40. Green Hell 40. Bitter Sweet 40. Son of Monte Cristo 40. *Rebecca* 40. Foreign Correspondent 40. The Falcon (series) 41–43. Rage in Heaven 41. Man Hunt 41. Sundown 41. Her Cardboard Lover 41. Son of Fury 42. *The Moon and Sixpence* 42. The Black Swan 42. Tales of Manhattan 42. Paris after Dark 43. Quiet Please, Murder 43. They Came to Blow Up America 43. This Land Is Mine 43. Appointment in Berlin 43. Paris after Dark 43. The Lodger 44. Action in Arabia 44. Summer Storm 44. *The Picture of Dorian Gray* 44. Hangover Square 44. Uncle Harry 45. *A Scandal in Paris* 46. The Strange Woman 47. The Ghost and Mrs Muir 47. *Forever Amber* 47. Bel Ami 48. Personal Column 48. *Lady Windermere's Fan* 49. Samson and Delilah 49. *All about Eve* (AA) 50. Captain Blackjack 50. I Can Get It for You Wholesale 51. The Light Touch 51. Assignment Paris 52. Ivanhoe 52. Voyage in Italy 53. Call Me Madam 53. Witness to Murder 54. King Richard and the Crusaders 54. Jupiter's Darling 54. Moonfleet 55. The King's Thief 55. That Certain Feeling 56. The Scarlet Coat 56. Never Say Goodbye 56. While the City Sleeps 56. Death of a Scoundrel 56. The Whole Truth (GB) 57. The Seventh Sin 57. From the Earth to the Moon 58. Solomon and Sheba 59. That Kind of Woman 59. A Touch of Larceny (GB) 60. The Last Voyage 60. Bluebeard's Ten Honeymoons 60. *Village of the Damned* (GB) 60. Trouble in the Sky (GB) 61. Five Golden Hours 61. The Rebel (aka Call Me Genius) 61. Operation Snatch 62. In Search of Castaways 62. Cairo 63. Ecco (It.) 63. The Cracksman 63. Dark Purpose 64. A Shot in the Dark 64. The Golden Head 64. Moll Flanders 65. Warning Shot 66. The Quiller Memorandum 66. Trunk to Cairo 67. Good Times 67. The Jungle Book (voice) 67. One Step to Hell 68. The Best House in London 68. The Body Stealers 69. The Kremlin Letter 69. The Candy Man 69. Endless Night 72. Doomwatch 72. Psychomania 72.

TV series: George Sanders Mystery Theatre 58. ✪ For being everybody's favourite swine, and for adding a touch of class to some pretty unappetizing movies. *Rebecca*.

¶ I never really thought I'd made the grade. And let's face it, I haven't. – *G.S.*

I was beastly but never coarse. A high-class sort of heel. – *G.S.*

I don't ask questions. I just take their money and use it for things that really interest me. – *G.S.*

I am not one of those people who would rather act than eat. Quite the reverse. My own desire as a boy was to retire. That ambition has never changed. – *G.S., 1950s*

One thing I know – I have never encountered a single obstacle that a sufficient quantity of money could not have overcome. I have never been faced with a problem that money could not have solved. – *G.S.*

I have got to the point where the lousier the part the better I like it. I would find it quite embarrassing to get a really good part nowadays, for it would call forth the feeble flames of inner fires long since banked. – *G.S., early 60s*

'I will have had enough of this earth by the time I am 65. After that I shall be having my bottom wiped by nurses and being pushed around in a wheelchair. So I shall commit suicide.' – *G.S., 1937, recalled by David Niven*

Dear World, I am leaving you because I am bored. I feel I have lived long enough. I am leaving you with your worries in this sweet cesspool. Good luck. – *Suicide note left by G.S. in 1972*

Famous line (*Rebecca*): 'I say, marriage with Max is not exactly a bed of roses, is it?'

Famous line (*All About Eve*): 'I am Addison de Witt. I am nobody's fool, least of all yours.'

Famous line (*The Picture of Dorian Gray*): 'I apologize for the intelligence of my remarks, Sir Thomas. I had forgotten that you are a member of parliament.'

Famous line (*The Picture of Dorian Gray*): 'If I could get back my youth, I'd do anything in the world except get up early, take exercise or be respectable.'

Sanders-Brahms, Helma (1940–).
German producer-director. A former television presenter, she began as a documentary and TV director.

Beneath the Paving Stones Is the Beach (Unterm Pflaster ist der Strand) 75. Shirin's Wedding 76. Heinrich 77. Germany Pale Mother (Deutschland Bleiche Mutter) 80. The Future of Emily 84. Laputa 86. Felix 87. Divided Love (Geteilte Liebe) 88. Apple Trees (Apfelbäume) 92, etc.

Sandford, Christopher (1939–).
Emaciated British character actor.
Half a Sixpence 67. Before Winter Comes 70, etc.

Sandford, Tiny (1894–1961) (Stanley J. Sandford).
American character actor who is best remembered as a foil for Laurel and Hardy: traffic cop or other nemesis.

The Immigrant 17. The World's Champion 22. The Circus 28. The Iron Mask 29. Our Relations 36. Modern Times 36, many others.

Sandrelli, Stefania (1946–).
Italian leading actress.

Divorce – Italian Style 62. Seduced and Abandoned (Sedotta e Abandonata) 64. Partner 68. The Conformist (Il Conformista) 71. Alfredo, Alfredo 72. 1900 76. We All Loved Each Other So Much (C'Eravamo Tanto Amati) 75. The Lie 84. The Family (La Famiglia) 87. The Sleazy Uncle (Lo Zio Indegno) 89. Per Amore, Solo per Amore 94. Of Love and Shadows 94, etc.

Sandrich, Mark (1900–1945).
American director who came to Hollywood in 1927 as director of Lupino Lane two-reelers; later associated with musicals.

■ The Talk of Hollywood 30. Melody Cruise 33. Aggie Appleby, Maker of Men 33. Hips Hips Hooray 34. Cockeyed Cavaliers 34. *The Gay Divorcee* 34. *Top Hat* 35. Follow the Fleet 36. A Woman Rebels 36. Shall We Dance? 37. Carefree 38. Man About Town 39. Buck Benny Rides Again 40. Love Thy Neighbour 40. Skylark 41. *Holiday Inn* 42. So Proudly We Hail 43. I Love a Soldier 44. Here Come the Waves 44.

Sands, Diana (1934–1973).
American actress.

A Raisin in the Sun 61. Ensign Pulver 64. The Landlord 70. Georgia Georgia 72. Willie Dynamite 73, etc.

Sands, Julian (1957–).
British leading actor.

Privates on Parade 82. Oxford Blues 84. The Killing Fields 84. After Darkness 85. The Doctor and the Devils 85. Gothic 86. A Room with a View 86. The Room 87. Siesta 87. Vibes 88. Wherever You Are 88. Tennessee Nights 89. Warlock 89. Impromptu 89. Arachnophobia 90. Night Sun (Il Sole Anche di Notte) 90. Wicked (Cattiva) 91. Grand Isle 91. Husbands and Lovers 91. Naked Lunch 92. The Turn of the Screw 92. Warlock: The Armageddon 93. Boxing Helena 93. The Browning Version 94, etc.

Sands, Tommy (1937–).
American 'teenage rave' singer. He was formerly married to singer Nancy Sinatra.

Sing Boy Sing 57. Love in a Goldfish Bowl 59. Babes in Toyland 60. The Longest Day 62. None but the Brave 65, etc.

Sanford, Erskine (1880–1950).
American character actor, playing elderly gents in the 40s.

Pop Always Pays 40. *Citizen Kane* (as flustered editor) 41. The Magnificent Ambersons 42. Ministry of Fear 44. Possessed 47. Lady from Shanghai 48. Macbeth 50, etc.

Sanford, Ralph (1899–1963).
American supporting player, usually in burly 'good guy' roles.

Give Me a Sailor 38. Thunderhead, Son of Flicka 45. Champion 49. Blackjack Ketchum Desperado 56. The Purple Gang 59, many others.

Sangster, Jimmy (1924–).
British horror screenwriter, long associated with Hammer Films.

The Trollenberg Terror 55. *The Curse of Frankenstein* 56. *Dracula* 58. *The Mummy* 59. Jack the Ripper 59. Brides of Dracula 60. Taste of Fear (& p) 61. Maniac (& p) 63. Hysteria (& p) 65. *The Nanny* (& p) 65. Deadlier than the Male 67. The Anniversary (& p) 68. Horror of Frankenstein (& pd) 70. Lust for a Vampire (& d) 70. Fear in the Night (& pd) 72, etc.

Santell, Alfred (1895–1981).
American director, former architect. With Mack Sennett as writer and director in the 20s.

Wildcat Jordan 22. Subway Sadie 26. The Patent Leather Kid 27. The Little Shepherd of Kingdom Come 28. *Daddy Long Legs* 30. The Sea Wolf 30. Tess of the Storm Country 33. A Feather in Her Hat 35. *Winterset* 36. Having Wonderful Time 38. Aloma of the South Seas 41. Beyond the Blue Horizon 42. Jack London 44. The Hairy Ape 44. That Brennan Girl 46, etc.

Santiago, Cirio H.
Filipino director of exploitation movies.

Women in Cages 72. Bamboo Gods and Iron Men 74. TNT Jackson 75. Vampire Hookers 78. Caged Fury 84. Desert Warrior 85. Naked Vengeance 86. Silk 86. The Devastator 86. Demon of Paradise 87. Equalizer 2000 87. Fast Gun 87. The Sisterhood 88. Future Hunters 88. Silk 2 89. Live by the Fist 92, etc.

antley, Joseph (1889–1971).
American director, former child actor and vaudevillian.

The Smartest Girl in Town 32. Spirit of Culver 7. Swing, Sister, Swing 41. Hitting the Headlines 2. Brazil 44. Shadow of a Woman 47. Make Believe Ballroom 49, etc.

anto, El:
ee El Santo.

antoni, Reni (1939–).
American actor, of French-Spanish ancestry; ex V writer.

Enter Laughing 67. Anzio 68. Dirty Harry 71. I Never Promised You a Rose Garden 77. They Went Thataway and Thataway 78. Bad Boys 83. Cobra 86. The Package 89, etc.

antschi, Tom (1879–1931).
American leading man of the silents.

The Sultan's Power 09. The Spoilers 14. The Garden of Allah 16. Little Orphan Annie 19. Three ad Men 26. In Old Arizona 29. Ten Nights in a ar-Room 31, etc.

aperstein, David.
American director and screenwriter.

Cocoon (story) 84. A Killing Affair (wd) 86. Beyond the Stars (aka Personal Choice) (wd) 89.

apper.
he pen-name of H.C. McNeile (1888–1937), creator of Bulldog Drummond, qv for list of films featuring the character. Only the first made any attempt to convey the essential thuggishness of Drummond.

arafian, Deran.
American director, the son of Richard Sarafian.

Alien Predator 87. To Die For 89. Death Warrant 1. Gunmen (& a) 93. Roadflower 93. Terminal elocity 94, etc.

arafian, Richard C. (1925–).
American director, of Armenian descent; much TV experience.

Andy 65. Shadow on the Land (TV) 68. Run Wild Run Free 69. Fragment of Fear 70. *Vanishing oint* 71. Man in the Wilderness 71. The Man Who oved Cat Dancing 73. Lolly Madonna XXX 73. One f Our Own (TV) 75. The Next Man 76. Sunburn '8. The Bear 84. Eye of the Tiger 86. Street Justice 9. Solar Crisis 90. Gunmen (a) 93.

arandon, Chris (1942–).
American character actor.

Dog Day Afternoon (AAN) 75. Lipstick 76. The entinel 77. Cuba 79. The Day Christ Died (TV) as Jesus) 80. A Tale of Two Cities (TV) 81. The Osterman Weekend 83. Fright Night 85. The rincess Bride 87. Child's Play 88. Tailspin (TV) 9. Slaves of New York 89. A Murderous Affair: he Carolyn Warmus Story (TV) 92. Dark Tide 93. im Burton's The Nightmare before Christmas voice) 93. David's Mother (TV) 94, etc.

arandon, Susan (1946–) (Susan Tomaling).
American leading lady, ex-wife of Chris Sarandon.

Joe 70. The Front Page 74. The Great Waldo epper 75. Dragonfly 77. King of the Gypsies 78. retty Baby 78. Atlantic City USA (AAN) 80. oving Couples 80. Tempest 82. The Hunger 83. he Buddy System 83. Compromising Positions 85. he Witches of Eastwick 87. Bull Durham 88. weet Hearts Dance 88. The January Man 89. A ry White Season 89. Erik the Viking 89. White alace 90. *Thelma and Louise* (AAN) 91. Light

Sleeper 91. The Player 92. Lorenzo's Oil 92. The Client 94. Little Women 94, etc.

¶ It's not difficult to be successful. But it is difficult to remain human. – S.S.

Sarde, Alain (1952–).
French producer, associated with many leading French directors, including Godard, Blier, Tavernier, Sautet, and Doillon.

Barocco (co-p) 77. Buffet Froid 79. A Bad Son (Un Mauvais Fils) 80. Hôtel des Amériques 81. Prénom Carmen 82. La Femme de Mon Pote 83. Notre Histoire 84. Détective 84. Un Dimanche à la Campagne 84. Comédie 87. A Few Days with Me (Quelques Jours avec Moi) 88. La Vengeance d'une Femme 90. Le Jeune Werther 92. Wild Reed (Les Roseaux Sauvages) 94, etc.

Sarde, Philippe (1945–).
Prolific French composer.

Les Choses de la Vie 69. Le Chat 71. Liza 72. La Grande Bouffe 73. Le Train 73. La Valise 73. Lancelot du Lac 74. Histoire d'O 75. Barocco 76. Madame Rosa 77. Un Taxi Mauve 77. Les Soeurs Brontë 78. Tess (AAN) 79. Le Toubib 79. Ghost Story 81. Quest for Fire 81. Lovesick 83. Stella 83. La Garce 84. Devil in the Flesh 85. Rendezvous 85. The Manhattan Project 86. Les Innocents 87. Lost Angels 89. The Music Box 89. Reunion 89. The Bear 89. A Few Days with Me 89. Lord of the Flies 90. C'est la Vie (La Baule-les-pins) 90. The Voice (La Voix) 92. L.627 92. La Petite Apocalypse 93. My Favourite Season (Ma Saison Préférée) 93. Uncovered 94. La Fille de D'Artagnan 94, many others.

Sargent, Alvin.
American screenwriter.

■ The Stalking Moon 68. The Sterile Cuckoo 69. I Walk the Line 70. Love and Pain and the Whole Damn Thing 72. The Effect of Gamma Rays on Man in the Moon Marigolds 72. Paper Moon (AAN) 73. Bobby Deerfield 77. Julia (AA, BFA) 77. Straight Time 78. Ordinary People (AA) 80. Nuts 87. Dominick and Eugene 88. Other People's Money 91. What about Bob? (story) 91, etc.

Sargent, Dick (1933–).
American screen actor who once specialized in gangling youths.

Bernardine 57. Operation Petticoat 59. That Touch of Mink 62. The Ghost and Mr Chicken 66. The Private Navy of Sergeant O'Farrell 68. Rich Man, Poor Man (TV) 76. Hardcore 79. Body Count 87. Teen Witch 89, etc.

TV series: One Happy Family 61. Broadside 64.

Sargent, Joseph (1925–) (Giuseppe Sargente).
American director.

One Spy Too Many (TV) 65. The Spy in the Green Hat (TV) 66. The Hell with Heroes 68. The Sunshine Patriot (TV) 68. The Immortal (TV) 69. The Forbin Project 69. Tribes (TV) 70. Maybe I'll Come Home in the Spring (TV) 71. White Lightning 73. Sunshine (TV) 74. The Man (TV) 74. The Taking of Pelham One Two Three 74. MacArthur 77. Goldengirl (TV) 79. Coast to Coast 80. Jaws – the Revenge 87. Day One (TV) 88. Ivory Hunters (TV) 90. Skylark (TV) 93. The Bible: Abraham (TV) 93, etc.

Sarin, Vic.
Canadian cinematographer.

Heartaches 82. Dancing in the Dark 86. Nowhere to Hide 87. Bye Bye Blues 90. Cold Sweat 93. The Burning Season 93. Whale Music 94, etc.

Sarne, Michael (1939–).
British director, former light actor.

AS ACTOR: Sodom and Gomorrah 60. The Guns of Navarone 61. A Place to Go 64. Every Day's a Holiday 65. Two Weeks in September 67. The Hollow Men (Pol.) 93, etc.

■ AS DIRECTOR: The Road to St Tropez 66. Joanna 68. Myra Breckinridge 69. Intimade 72. Trouble with a Battery 86. The Punk (wd) 93. Glastonbury the Movie (p, co-d) 95.

Sarony, Leslie (1897–1985).
English character actor, music-hall performer, and writer of nonsense songs, including 'Ain't It Grand to Be Blooming Well Dead' and 'I Lift up My Finger and I Say "Tweet, Tweet" '. He also worked in a double act, The Two Leslies, with Leslie Holmes.

Soldiers of the King 33. Rolling in Money 34. Wedding Eve 35. Boys Will Be Boys (song) 35. Feather Your Nest (songs) 37. Give My Regards to Broad Street 84, etc.

Saroyan, William (1908–1981).
American writer, mainly of fantasies about gentle people.

The Human Comedy (AA) 43. The Time of Your Life 48, etc.

Sarrazin, Michael (1940–).
Canadian leading man of the early 70s, usually seen as the young innocent.

■ The Doomsday Flight (TV) 66. Gunfight in Abilene 67. *The Flim Flam Man* 67. Journey to Shiloh 67. The Sweet Ride 68. A Man Called Gannon 68. Eye of the Cat 68. They Shoot Horses Don't They? 69. In Search of Gregory 70. The Pursuit of Happiness 71. Believe in Me 71. Sometimes a Great Notion 71. The Groundstar Conspiracy 72. Frankenstein: the True Story (TV) (as the creature) 73. Harry in Your Pocket 74. For Pete's Sake 74. The Reincarnation of Peter Proud 75. The Gumball Rally 76. The Loves and Times of Scaramouche 76. Caravans 78. Double Negative 80. The Seduction 82. Fighting Back 82. Joshua Then and Now 85. Kidnapped 87. Keeping Track 87. Captive Hearts 87. Mascara 87. Malarek 89. The Phone Call 90. Lena's Holiday 91.

Sartov, Hendrik.
American portrait photographer who joined Griffith in 1919 and was influential in soft-focus close-ups.

Way Down East 20. Orphans of the Storm 21. One Exciting Night 22. America 24. Isn't Life Wonderful 25. The Scarlet Letter 26. Quality Street 27. Under the Black Eagle 28, etc.

Sartre, Jean-Paul (1905–1980).
French existentialist writer. Works filmed include:

Huis Clos (No Exit) 48. Crime Passionel 51. La Putain Respectueuse 52. Les Jeux Sont Faits 54. The Proud and the Beautiful (AAN) 56. The Condemned of Altona 63.

Sasdy, Peter (1934–).
Hungarian director in England.

■ Taste the Blood of Dracula 69. Countess Dracula 70. Hands of the Ripper 71. Doomwatch 72. Nothing But the Night 72. I Don't Want to Be Born 75. Welcome to Blood City 76. Murder at the Wedding (TV) 79. The Lonely Lady 83. Sherlock Holmes and the Leading Lady (TV) 91.

Many television dramas.

Sassard, Jacqueline (1940–).
French leading lady.

Accident 67. Les Biches 68.

satire,

being defined in theatrical circles as 'what closes Saturday night', has seldom been encouraged by Hollywood, and the few genuinely satirical films have not been commercially successful, from *A Nous la Liberté* through *American Madness, Nothing Sacred* and *Roxie Hart* to *The Loved One*. However, the odd lampoon in the middle of an otherwise straightforward comedy has often brought critical enthusiasm for films as diverse as *Modern Times, Boy Meets Girl, I'm All Right, Jack, The President's Analyst* and *The Groove Tube;* and in future it looks as though one can at least expect that the range of permissible targets will become even wider. The spotty but considerable success in 1976 of *Network*, the screen's most hysterical satire of all, was at least partly due to its sexy scenes and uninhibited language.

Sato, Masura (1928–).
Japanese composer.
The Lower Depths 57. Throne of Blood 57. The Hidden Fortress 58. Yojimbo 61. Sanjuro 62. Red Beard 65. Ebirah, Horror of the Deep 68. Son of Godzilla 69. Outlaws 70. Kazoku 71. Sapporo Winter Olympics 72. The Wolves 72. Godzilla vs Mecha-Godzilla 76. The Yellow Handkerchief of Happiness 78. Sensei the Teacher 83. Shogun's Shadow 84, etc.

Saunders, Charles (1904–).
British director, former editor.
Tawny Pipit (co-d) 44. Fly Away Peter 47. One Wild Oat 51. Meet Mr Callaghan 54. Kill Her Gently 57. Womaneater 58. Danger by My Side 62, etc.

Saunders, John Monk (1895–1940).
American screenwriter with a special interest in aviation.
Wings 27. *Dawn Patrol* (AA) 30. *The Last Flight* 31. Devil Dogs of the Air 35. I Found Stella Parish 35.

Saura, Carlos (1932–).
Leading Spanish director and screenwriter. He worked as an engineer and a photographer before turning to film.
Biography: 1991, *The Films of Carlos Saura: The Practice of Seeing* by Marvin d'Lugo.
Cuenca (short) 59. The Hooligans (Los Golfos) 59. Lament for a Bandit (Llanto por un Bandido) 63. The Chase (La Caza) 65. Peppermint Frappé 67. Stress es Tres, Tres 68. Honeycomb (La Madriguera) 69. The Garden of Delights (El Jardín de las Delicias) 70. Anna and the Wolves (Ana y los Lobos) 72. Cousin Angelica 74. Cria Cuervos 75. Blindfolded (Los Ojos Vendados) 78. Mama Turns a Hundred (Mama Cumple Cien Años) 79. Hurry, Hurry (Deprisa, Deprisa) 80. Blood Wedding (Bodas de Sangre) 81. Sweet Hours (Dulces Horas) 81. Antonieta 82. Carmen 83. Los Zancos 84. Love, the Magician (El Amor Brujo) 86. El Dorado 87. The Dark Night (La Noche Oscura) 89. ¡Ay, Carmela! 90. Sevillanas 92. Dispara (& co-w) 93. Marathon 93, etc.

Sautet, Claude (1924–).
French director.
The Big Risk 60. Head First 64. Les Choses de la Vie 69. Vincent, François, Paul and the Others 76. Mado 78. Un Mauvais Fils 80. Garçon! 83. A Few Days with Me 88. Un Coeur en Hiver 92. Haute Époque 94, etc.

Savage, Ann (1921–) (Bernie Lyon).
American leading lady of 40s seconds.
Two Señoritas from Chicago 43. Two Man

Submarine 44. *Detour* 45. Scared Stiff 45. The Last Crooked Mile 46. Renegade Girl 46. Jungle Flight 47. Satan's Cradle 49. Pygmy Island 50. The Woman They Almost Lynched 53. Fire with Fire 86, many others.

Savage, John (1949–).
Baby-faced American leading man who didn't quite become another James Dean.
Bad Company 75. The Killing Kind 65. No Deposit No Return 76. The Deer Hunter 78. Hair 79. The Onion Field 80. Cattle Annie and Little Britches 81. Inside Moves 81. The Amateur 82. Brady's Escape 84. Maria's Lovers 85. Salvador 86. The Beat 87. Hotel Colonial 87. Beauty and the Beast 87. Dear America 87. Caribe 87. Do the Right Thing 89. Hunting 89. Point of View 89. Any Man's Death 90. The Godfather Part III 90. Primary Motive 92. C.I.A. 2: Target Alexa 93. A Killing Obsession 94. Red Scorpion 2 94, etc.
TV series: Gibbsville 76.

Saval, Dany (1940–) (Danielle Nadine Suzanne Salle).
French leading lady.
Les Trichcurs 58. The Mirror Has Two Faces 58. Nathalie 59. Les Parisiennes 61. The Seven Deadly Sins 62. Moon Pilot 62. The Devil and Ten Commandments 62. Web of Fear 64. Boeing Boeing 65. La Vie Parisienne 78, etc.

Savalas, Telly (1924–1994) (Aristotle Savalas).
Bald Greek-American character actor with TV experience; former academic.
The Young Savages 61. Birdman of Alcatraz (AAN) 62. The Interns 63. Cape Fear 63. The Man from the Diners' Club 63. The New Interns 64. Genghis Khan 65. *The Battle of the Bulge* 65. The Slender Thread 66. Beau Geste 66. The Dirty Dozen 67. *The Scalphunters* 68. Buona Sera Mrs Campbell 68. The Assassination Bureau (GB) 68. Crooks and Coronets (GB) 69. The Land Raiders 69. Mackenna's Gold 69. On Her Majesty's Secret Service 69. Kelly's Heroes 70. A Town Called Bastard 71. Pretty Maids All in a Row 71. Pancho Villa 71. The Marcus Nelson Murders (TV) 72. A Reason to Live, a Reason to Die 72. The Killer Is on the Phone 72. She Cried Murder (TV) 73. Horror Express 74. The Diamond Mercenaries 75. Inside Out 75. Capricorn One 78. The French Atlantic Affair (TV) 79. Escape to Athena 79. Beyond the Poseidon Adventure 79. The Cartier Affair (TV) 84. Kojak: The Belarus File (TV) 85. Gobots: The Battle of the Rock Lords (voice) 86. Kojak: The Price of Justice (TV) 87. The Dirty Dozen: The Next Mission (TV) 87. The Dirty Dozen: The Fatal Mission (TV) 88. Vengeance 93, etc.
TV series: Acapulco 60. *Kojak* 73–77.
~Catchphrase: Who loves ya, baby? (from *Kojak*).

Saville, Philip (1930–).
English director, mainly for television.
Stop the World – I Want to Get Off 66. Oedipus the King 68. The Best House in London 69. Secrets 71. Gangsters (TV) 75. Count Dracula 77. Boys from the Blackstuff (TV) 82. Those Glory, Glory Days 83. Shadey 86. Life and Loves of a She-Devil 86. The Fruit Machine 88. Angels (TV) 92, etc.

Saville, Victor (1897–1979).
British director who, after making some outstanding films in the 30s, went to Hollywood with very meagre results. Former film salesman and exhibitor.
The Arcadians 27. Roses of Picardy 28. *Woman to Woman* (US) 29. Hindle Wakes 31. Sunshine Susie 31. *The Good Companions* 32. I Was a Spy 33. Friday

the Thirteenth 33. *Evergreen* 34. The Iron Duke 36. Dark Journey 37. Storm in a Teacup 37. *South Riding* 38. The Citadel (p only) 38. Goodbye Mr Chips (p only) 39. Bitter Sweet (p) 40. Dr Jekyll and Mr Hyde (p) 41. White Cargo (p) 42. Tonight and Every Night (p, d) 44. The Green Years (p, d) 46. If Winter Comes (d) 47. The Conspirator (d) 47. Kim (p) 51. I the Jury (p) 53. The Long Wait (p, d) 54. The Silver Chalice (p, d) 55. Kiss Me Deadly (p) 55. The Greengage Summer (p) 61.

Savini, Tom.
American horror make-up specialist, director, and actor, often associated with the work of director George Romero.
Deathdream 72. Deranged 74. Martin 77. Dawn of the Dead (& a) 78. Effects (a) 80. Maniac (a) 80. Friday the 13th 80. Midnight 81. Knightriders (a) 81. Creepshow (a) 82. Friday the 13th Part 4: The Final Chapter 84. Invasion U.S.A. 85. Day of the Dead 85. The Texas Chainsaw Massacre Part 2 86. The Ripper 86. Creepshow 2 (a) 87. Monkey Shines 88. Red Scorpion 89. Night of the Living Dead (d) 90. Two Evil Eyes 91. Necronomicon 93, etc.

Savo, Jimmy (1895–1960).
Pint-sized American comedian who failed to repeat his Broadway success on film.
Exclusive Rights 26. Once in a Blue Moon 36. Merry Go Round of 1938, etc.

Savoca, Nancy (1960–).
American director.
True Love 89. Dogfight 91. Household Saints 93.

Sawtell, Paul (1906–1971).
Polish-born composer in America.
The Gay Falcon 41. Tarzan Triumphs 43. The Scarlet Claw 44. Dick Tracy Meets Gruesome 47. Black Magic 49. Son of Dr Jekyll 51. Inferno 53. Texas Lady 55. Stopover Tokyo 57. The Lost World 60. Five Weeks in a Balloon 62. Island of the Blue Dolphins 64. The Christine Jorgenson Story 70, many others.

Sawyer, Joseph (1901–1982) (Joseph Sauer).
American comedy actor usually seen as tough cop or army sergeant.
College Humour 33. The Marines Have Landed 36. Black Legion 37. The Roaring Twenties 40. Sergeant York 41. About Face 42. The McGuerins from Brooklyn 42. Fall In 44. Joe Palooka, Champ 46. Fighting Father Dunne 49. It Came from Outer Space 53. The Killing 56, many others.
TV series: Rin Tin Tin 55.

Saxon, John (1935–) (Carmen Orrico).
American leading man, former model.
Running Wild (debut) 55. The Unguarded Moment 56. The Reluctant Debutante 58. Portrait in Black 59. The Unforgiven 59. The Plunderers 60. Posse from Hell 61. War Hunt 62. The Cardinal 63. The Evil Eye (It.) 63. The Appaloosa 66. The Night Caller (GB) 67. Death of a Gunfighter 69. Joe Kidd 72. Enter the Dragon 73. Black Christmas 75. Mitchell 75. The Swiss Conspiracy 75. Blazing Magnum 76. Moonshine County Express 77. The Bees 78. The Electric Horseman 79. Blood Beach 81. The Glove 81. Hardcastle and McCormick (TV) 83. The Big Score 83. A Nightmare on Elm Street 84. Fever Pitch 85. My Mom's a Werewolf 89. Payoff 91. Frame-Up II: The Cover-Up 92. Jonathan of the Bears 94. A Killing Obsession 94. Beverly Hills Cop III 94. Wes Craven's New Nightmare 94, etc.
TV series: The Bold Ones 69–72. 79 Park Avenue 77. Falcon Crest 81–82, 86–88.

Sayers, Dorothy L. (1893–1957).
British detective novelist, creator of Lord Peter Wimsey, who was personified on film by Peter Haddon in *The Silent Passenger* and Robert Montgomery in *Busman's Honeymoon*. Ian Carmichael had a long run on TV in the 70s.

¶ For her warm-hearted admirers she is still the finest detective story writer of the century; to those less enthusiastic her work is long-winded and ludicrously snobbish. – *Julian Symons*

Sayle, Alexei (1952–).
Aggressive English character actor, comedian, writer, and newspaper columnist, a former teacher. Born in Liverpool, he was a stand-up comedian before making his reputation on TV.
  Gorky Park 83. The Bride 85. Whoops Apocalypse 86. Solarbabies (aka Solar Warriors) 86. Siesta 87. Indiana Jones and the Last Crusade 89. Reckless Kelly 93, etc.
  TV series: The Young Ones 82–84. Whoops Apocalypse 82. Alexei Sayle's Stuff 88–90. The All-New Alexei Sayle Show 94. Paris 94.

Sayles, John (1950–).
American independent director, producer and screenwriter; also editor, occasional actor and novelist.
■ Piranha (w) 78. The Lady in Red (w) 79. The Return of the Secaucus Seven (a, wd, ed) (AANw) 79. Alligator (w) 80. Battle beyond the Stars (w) 80. The Howling (a, w) 80. The Challenge (w) 82. Lianna (a, wd, ed) 82. Baby, It's You (wd) 83. Enormous Changes at the Last Minute (w) 83. The Brother from Another Planet (a, wd, ed) 84. Hard Choices (a) 84. The Clan of the Cave Bear (w) 86. Something Wild (a) 86. Matewan (a, wd) 87. Wild Thing (w) 87. *Eight Men Out* (a, wd) 88. Breaking In (w) 89. Little Vegas (a) 90. *City of Hope* (a, wd, ed) 91. Straight Talk (a) 92. Matinee (a) 93. The Secret of Roan Inish (wd, e) 94.

Scacchi, Greta (1960–).
Italian-born leading lady in international films.
  Dead on Time 81. Heat and Dust 82. Waterfront (TV) 83. The Ebony Tower (TV) 84. Camille (TV) 85. The Coca Cola Kid 85. Defence of the Realm 86. Good Morning Babylon 87. A Man in Love (L'Homme Amoureux) 87. White Mischief 87. La Donna della Luna 88. Three Sisters (Paura e Amore) 88. Waterfront 88. Presumed Innocent 90. Shattered 91. Fires Within 91. Turtle Beach 92. The Player 92. Salt on Our Skin 93. Country Life 94. The Browning Version 94. Jefferson in Paris 95, etc.

¶ When I was about eight years old, I happened to mention to my father that I wanted to be an actress and he gave me a wallop in the face. – *G.S.*

Scaife, Ted (1912–).
British cinematographer.
  Bonnie Prince Charlie 48. An Inspector Calls 54. Sea Wife 57. *Night of the Demon* 57. 633 Squadron 64. *Khartoum* 66. The Dirty Dozen 67. Play Dirty 68. Sinful Davey 69. Forbush and the Penguins 71. Hannie Caulder 71. Sitting Target 72. Catlow 72, many others.

Scala, Gia (1934–1972) (Giovanna Scoglio).
Italian leading lady who made a few American films. Died from an overdose of drugs.
  The Price of Fear 56. Four Girls in Town 56. Don't Go Near the Water 56. The Garment Jungle 57. The Two-Headed Spy (GB) 58. I Aim at the Stars 59. The Guns of Navarone 61, etc.

Scales, Prunella (1932–).
British leading actress, mainly in comedy and on TV.
  The Boys from Brazil 78. The Wicked Lady 84. Consuming Passions 88. A Chorus of Disapproval 88. A Question of Attribution (as the Queen) (TV) 91. Howards End 91. Second Best 94. Wolf 94, etc.
  TV series: Fawlty Towers 75–79. After Henry 88–92.

Scarface.
Armitage Trail's novel, about the rise of a thinly disguised Al Capone, made an exciting gangster movie under the direction of Howard Hawks in 1932, with Paul Muni in the title role and George Raft flipping a coin at moments of stress. Brian DePalma remade it as an exercise in excess in 1983, starring Al Pacino as a modern-day Latin American thug, thriving in Miami.

Scarfiotti, Ferdinando (1941–1994).
Distinguished Italian production designer who trained as an architect and began as a protégé of Visconti, designing opera productions. He also worked on many of Bertolucci's films.
  The Conformist (Il Conformista) 69. *Death in Venice* (BFA) 71. Avanti! 72. Last Tango in Paris 72. Daisy Miller 74. Flash Gordon 80. American Gigolo 80. Honky Tonk Freeway 81. Cat People 82. Scarface 83. *The Last Emperor* (AA) 87. Mamba 88. *Toys* (AAN) 92. Love Affair 94, etc.

¶ The most influential film designer of the last three decades. – *Paul Schrader*

The Scarlet Letter.
Nathaniel Hawthorne's story of puritanical 18th-century New England was filmed in 1917 with Mary Martin as the adulteress and Stuart Holmes as her priest-lover forced to accuse her. In 1926 came Victor Sjostrom's more famous version with Lillian Gish and Lars Hanson; 1934 brought a talkie remake with Colleen Moore and Hardie Albright; and Wim Wenders made a German version in 1973, starring Senta Berger.

The Scarlet Pimpernel.
Baroness Orczy's foppish hero of the French Revolution has been filmed three times in Britain since sound: in 1935, directed by Harold Young, with Leslie Howard opposing Raymond Massey as Chauvelin; in 1938, directed by Hans Schwarz, with Barry K. Barnes winning out over Francis Lister; in 1950, directed by Michael Powell and Emeric Pressburger, with David Niven as Sir Percy. There has also been a TV series starring Marius Goring. Silent versions included one in 1917 starring Dustin Farnum and one in 1929 starring Matheson Lang. The idea was modernized in Leslie Howard's *Pimpernel Smith* 41. In 1982, the original was remade for television with Anthony Andrews, Jane Seymour, and Ian McKellen.

Scarwid, Diana (1955–).
American leading lady.
  Pretty Baby 78. Inside Moves (AAN) 80. Mommie Dearest 81. Silkwood 83. Strange Invaders 83. Extremities 86. The Ladies Club 86. Psycho III 86. Heat 87. Brenda Starr 89, etc.

Scattergood Baines,
an amiable small-town busybody created by Clarence Buddington Kelland, was personified by Guy Kibbee in six second features (41–42), all directed by Christy Cabanne.

scenario:
see *shooting script*.

Schaefer, George (1920–).
American director with TV experience.
■ Macbeth 61. Pendulum 68. Generation 69. Doctors' Wives 71. A War of Children (TV) 72. A Time for Love (TV) 73. F. Scott Fitzgerald and the Last of the Belles (TV) 74. In This House of Brede (TV) 75. An Enemy of the People 78. Who'll Save Our Children? (TV) 78. Right of Way (TV) 83. Laura Lansing Slept Here (TV) 88.

Schafer, Natalie (1900–1991).
American comedienne usually seen as a dizzy rich woman. Married to actor Louis Calhern.
  Marriage is a Private Affair 43. Wonder Man 45. The Snake Pit 48. Caught 49. Anastasia 56. Oh Men Oh Women 57. Susan Slade 61. Forty Carats 73. The Day of the Locust 75, etc.
  TV series: *Gilligan's Island* 64–67. The Survivors 69–70.

Schaffner, Franklin (1920–1989).
Stylish American director, from TV.
■ The Stripper 63. *The Best Man* 64. The War Lord 65. The Double Man 67. *Planet of the Apes* 68. Patton (AA) 69. Nicholas and Alexandra 71. *Papillon* 73. Islands in the Stream 77. The Boys from Brazil 78. Sphinx 81. Yes Giorgio 82. Lionheart 87. Welcome Home 89.

Schallert, William (1922–).
American character actor who played a lot of dull fathers in his day. More recently president of the Screen Actors' Guild.
  The Man from Planet X 52. Riot in Cell Block Eleven 55. Written on the Wind 56. Cry Terror 58. Pillow Talk 59. In the Heat of the Night 67. Will Penny 68. Charley Varrick 73. Twilight Zone – the Movie 83. Innerspace 87, many others.
  TV series: The Many Loves of Dobie Gillis 59–63. The Patty Duke Show 63–66. The Nancy Walker Show 76. The Hardy Boys Mysteries 77–78. Little Women 79. The New Gidget 86–88.

Scharf, Walter (1910–).
American composer.
  Chatterbox 43. Dakota 45. The Saxon Charm 48. Deported 50. Hans Christian Andersen 52. Living It Up 54. Hollywood or Bust 56. King Creole 58. A Pocketful of Miracles 61. Where Love Has Gone 64. Pendulum 69. The Cheyenne Social Club 70. Ben 72. Walking Tall 73. Final Chapter, Walking Tall 77. When Every Day Was the Fourth of July (TV) 78. This Is Elvis 81. Twilight Time 83, many others.

Schary, Dore (1905–1980).
American writer-producer with newspaper and theatrical experience. AA best screenplay *Boys' Town* 38; produced for MGM 1941–45; head of production RKO 1945–48; head of production MGM 1948–56; then independent.
  Autobiography: 1979, *Heyday*.
  Lonelyhearts 59. Sunrise at Campobello 60. Act One (wd, p) 63, etc.

¶ A man whose few successes were even more distasteful than his many failures. – *John Simon*

Schatzberg, Jerry (1927–).
American director, former fashion photographer.
■ Puzzle of a Downfall Child 71. The Panic in Needle Park 71. Scarecrow 73. Dandy, the All American Girl 76. The Seduction of Joe Tynan 79. Honeysuckle Rose 80. Misunderstood 83. No Small

Affair 84. Street Smart 87. Clinton and Nadine (TV) 88. Reunion (L'Ami Retrouvé) 89.

Schayer, Richard (1882–*).
American scriptwriter.
Black Roses 21. The Thrill Chaser 23. Silk Stocking Sal 24. Tell It to the Marines 26. On ze Boulevard 27. The Cameraman 28. Spite Marriage 29. Free and Easy 30. Doughboys 30. Trader Horn 31. The Winning Ticket 35. The Devil Is a Sissy 36. The Black Arrow 48. Lorna Doone 51. Gun Belt 53. Lancelot and Guinevere 63, many others.

Scheider, Roy (1934–).
Lean American character actor.
■ The Curse of the Living Corpse 64. Star 68. Stiletto 69. Loving 70. Puzzle of a Downfall Child 70. Klute 71. L'Attentat 72. Assignment Munich (TV) 72. The Outside Man 72. *The French Connection* (AAN) 72. Sheila Levine Is Dead and Living in New York 73. The Seven-Ups 73. *Jaws* 75. Marathon Man 76. Sorcerer 77. Jaws 2 78. Last Embrace 79. *All That Jazz* (AAN) 79. Prisoner without a Name, Cell without a Number (TV) 80. Still of the Night 82. Blue Thunder 83. 2010 84. Mishima 85. Tiger Town 85. The Men's Club 86. 52 Pick-Up 86. Cohen and Tate 89. Night Game 89. Listen to Me 89. The Fourth War 90. The Russia House 90. Naked Lunch 91. Somebody Has to Shoot the Picture 91. Romeo Is Bleeding 93. Wild Justice (TV) 93.
TV series: Seaquest DSV 93– .

Schell, Catherine (1946–) (Catherine von Schell).
German character actress.
Moon Zero Two 69. Madame Sin (TV) 72. Callan 74. The Black Windmill 74. The Prisoner of Zenda 79, etc.
TV series: Space 1999 75–76.

Schell, Maria (1926–).
Austrian leading lady who has been in British and American films.
The Angle with the Trumpet 49. The Magic Box 51. So Little Time 52. The Heart of the Matter 52. Der Traumende Mund 53. The Last Bridge (Aus.) 54. Die Ratten 55. *Gervaise* 56. White Nights (It.) 57. Une Vie (Fr.) 58. The Brothers Karamazov 58. Cimarron 61. The Mark (GB) 61. 99 Women 69. The Odessa File 74. Voyage of the Damned 76. Superman 78. Just a Gigolo 79. Players 79, etc.

Schell, Maximilian (1930–).
Austrian leading man who has been in international films. Brother of Maria Schell.
Kinder, Mütter und ein General 58. The Young Lions 58. *Judgment at Nuremberg* (AA) 61. Five-Finger Exercise 62. The Condemned of Altona 63. The Reluctant Saint 63. Topkapi 64. Return from the Ashes 65. The Deadly Affair 66. Beyond the Mountains 66. Counterpoint 67. The Castle 68. Krakatoa 68. First Love (wpd only) 70. The Pedestrian (p, d) 73. The Odessa File 74. First Love (& d) 75. The Man in the Glass Booth (AAN) 75. St Ives 76. End of the Game (& d) 76. Julia (AAN) 77. Cross of Iron 77. Avalanche Express 79. The Black Hole 79. Players 79. The Diary of Anne Frank (TV) 81. The Chosen 81. Man Under Suspicion 84. Marlene (& d) 85. The Assisi Underground 85. Peter the Great (TV) 86. The Freshman 90. Labyrinth 90. A Far Off Place 93. The Bible: Abraham (TV) 93. Justiz 93. Little Odessa 94, etc.

Schenck, Aubrey (1908–).
American producer.
Shock 46. Repeat Performance 48. Beachhead

53. Up Periscope 58. Frankenstein 70 59. Robinson Crusoe on Mars 64. Don't Worry We'll Think of a Title 66. The Alpha Caper (TV) 73, etc.

Schenck, Joseph M. (1878–1961).
Russian-born executive, in America from 1900, at first as pharmacist, then as fairground showman and owner. By 1924 was chairman of United Artists and creator of its theatre chain. In 1933 he founded Twentieth Century Productions and by 1935 was head of Twentieth Century-Fox. In 1953 he created Magna Productions with Mike Todd. In 1950 he was voted a special Academy Award.

Schenck, Nicholas M. (1881–1969).
Russian-born executive, brother of Joseph M. Schenck, with whom after arrival in America in 1900 he ran an amusement park. Later developed theatre chain which emerged as Loew's Consolidated Enterprises; became president of Loew's and thus financial controller of MGM.

Schenkel, Carl.
Swiss-born director and screenwriter who began his career in West Germany before working in North America.
Out of Order (Abwärts) 84. The Mighty Quinn (US) 89. Silence Like Glass 89. Koan 91. Knight Moves (US) 92. Exquisite Tenderness (Can.) 93, etc.

Schepisi, Fred (1939–).
Australian director.
The Devil's Playground 76. The Chant of Jimmie Blacksmith 78. Iceman 81. Barbarosa 81. Plenty 85. Roxanne 87. A Cry in the Dark 88. The Russia House 90. Mr Baseball 92. Six Degrees of Separation (& p) 93, etc.

Scherick, Edgar J. (c. 1919–).
American independent producer.
For Love of Ivy 68. Sleuth 72. The Heartbreak Kid 72. Gordon's War 74. The Stepford Wives 74. The Taking of Pelham One Two Three 74. I Never Promised You a Rose Garden 77. Little Gloria . . . Happy at Last (TV) 82. Shoot the Moon 82. The Kennedys of Massachusetts (TV) 84. The Dakota (TV) 84. Reckless 84. Mrs Soffel 85, etc.

Schertzinger, Victor (1880–1941).
American director, former concert violinist. Wrote the first film music score, for *Civilisation* 15.
AS DIRECTOR: Forgotten Faces 29. Nothing but the Truth 31. Uptown New York 32. The Cocktail Hour 33. One Night of Love (AAN) 34. Love Me Forever 35. The Music Goes Round 36. Something to Sing About 36. The Mikado (GB) 39. Road to Singapore 40. Rhythm on the River 41. Road to Zanzibar 41. Kiss the Boys Goodbye 41, etc.

Schiaffino, Rosanna (1939–).
Italian leading lady in international films.
Two Weeks in Another Town 62. The Victors 63. El Greco 66. Arrivederci Baby 66. The Man Called Noon 73. The Heroes 75. Cagliostro 76, etc.

Schiffman, Suzanne.
French screenwriter associated with the films of François Truffaut. She worked for him on continuity, became his first assistant, co-scripted his films from the mid-70s, and began directing in the late 80s.
Day for Night (La Nuit Américaine) (co-w) (AAN) 74. L'Histoire d'Adèle H. (co-w) 75. Small Change (L'Argent de Poche) (co-w) 76. The Man Who Loved Women (co-w) 77. The Last Metro (Le Dernier Métro) (co-w) 81. The Woman Next Door

(La Femme d'à Côté) (co-w) 81. Vivement Dimanche (co-w) 83. L'Amour par Terre (co-w) 86. La Moine et la Sorcière (wd) 87. La Femme de Paille (d) 89, etc.

Schifrin, Lalo (1932–).
Argentinian composer in Hollywood.
Joy House 64. The Cincinnati Kid 64. The Liquidator 66. Cool Hand Luke 67. The Brotherhood 68. Bullitt 68. Kelly's Heroes 70. The Beguiled 71. Dirty Harry 71. Prime Cut 72. The Wrath of God 72. The Four Musketeers 75. Voyage of the Damned 76. Rollercoaster 77. Telefon 77. The Cat from Outer Space 78. The Manitou 78. The Concorde – Airport 79 79. Brubaker 79. The Competition 80. When Time Ran Out 80. Caveman 81. Buddy Buddy 81. A Stranger Is Watching 82. The Osterman Weekend 83. Sudden Impact 83. Tank 84. The New Kids 85. The Mean Season 85. Bad Medicine 85. Black Moon Rising 86. The Fourth Protocol 87. The Dead Pool 88. The Neon Empire 89. FX2 – the Deadly Art of Illusion 91. The Beverly Hillbillies 93, many others.

Schildkraut, Joseph (1895–1964).
Austrian leading man and character actor, of theatrical family. On American stage from early 20s. Autobiography: 1959, *My Father and I*.
■ Schlemiel 14. The Life of Theodore Herzl 18. Orphans of the Storm 22. The Song of Love 24. The Road to Yesterday 25. Shipwrecked 26. Young April 26. Meet the Prince 26. *King of Kings* 27. The Heart Thief 27. His Dog 27. The Forbidden Woman 27. The Blue Danube 28. Tenth Avenue 28. *Showboat* 29. The Mississippi Gambler 29. Cock o' the Walk 30. Night Ride 30. A Lady to Love (German version) 31. Carnival 31. Cleopatra 34. Viva Villa 34. Sisters Under the Skin 34. Blue Danube 34. The Crusades 35. *The Garden of Allah* 36. Slave Ship 37. *The Life of Emile Zola* (AA) (as Dreyfus) 37. Souls at Sea 37. Lancer Spy 37. Lady Behave 37. The Baroness and the Butler 38. Marie Antoinette 38. Suez 38. Idiot's Delight 39. The Three Musketeers 39. *The Man in the Iron Mask* 39. Mr Moto Takes a Vacation 39. Lady of the Tropics 39. *The Rains Came* 39. Barricade 39. Pack Up Your Troubles 39. The Shop Around the Corner 40. Phantom Raiders 40. Rangers of Fortune 40. Meet the Wildcat 40. The Parson of Panamint 41. Flame of the Barbary Coast 45. The Cheaters 45. *Monsieur Beaucaire* 46. The Plainsman and the Lady 46. Northwest Outpost 47. Old Los Angeles 48. Gallant Legion 48. *The Diary of Anne Frank* 59. King of the Roaring Twenties 60. The Greatest Story Ever Told 65.

Schilling, Gus (1908–1957).
Wry-faced American comic actor from musical comedy and burlesque.
Citizen Kane (debut; as the waiter) 41. A Thousand and One Nights 44. Lady from Shanghai 47. On Dangerous Ground 52. Glory 56, etc.

Schlamme, Thomas.
American director.
Miss Firecracker 89. Crazy from the Heart (TV) 91. So I Married an Axe Murderer 93, etc.

Schlatter, Charlie (1966–).
American leading actor.
18 Again 88. Heartbreak Hotel 88. Bright Lights, Big City 88. All-American Murder 91. Sunset Heat 92, etc.
TV series: Ferris Bueller 90.

Schlesinger, John (1926–).
British director, former small-part actor and TV
director.
■ *Terminus* 60. *A Kind of Loving* 62. *Billy Liar* 63.
Darling (AAN) 65. Far from the Madding Crowd
67. *Midnight Cowboy* (US) (AA) 69. *Sunday Bloody
Sunday* (AAN) 72. Visions of Eight 73. The Day
of the Locust 75. Marathon Man 76. Yanks 79.
Honky Tonk Freeway 81. An Englishman Abroad
(TV) 83. The Falcon and the Snowman 85. The
Believers 87. Madame Sousatzka 88. Pacific
Heights 90. A Question of Attribution (TV) 91. The
Lost Language of Cranes (a) (TV) 91. The Innocent
93. Cold Comfort Farm (TV) 95.

¶ The days of dealing with one despot are over.
Now it's clearly with a whole group of
frightened committee people. – *J.S., 1980*
    What I tend to go for, and what interests me, is
not the hero but the coward . . . not the success,
but the failure. – *J.S.*

Schlom, Herman (1904–1983).
American producer of 40s second features.
    The Sheik Steps Out 38. The Brighton Strangler
45. Dick Tracy Meets Gruesome 48. Follow Me
Quietly 50, etc.

Schlondorff, Volker (1939–).
German director. He is head of development and
production at Germany's Babelsberg studios.
■ Young Torless 66. A Degree of Murder 67.
Michael Kohlhaas 69. Baal 70. Summer Lightning
72. The Lost Honour of Katharina Blum 75. Coup
de Grâce 77. *The Tin Drum* 79. Circle of Deceit 81.
Hôtel de la Paix 83. Swann in Love (Un Amour de
Swann) 84. Death of a Salesman (TV) 85.
Vermischte Nachrichten 86. The Handmaid's Tale
90. Voyager 91.

Schmidt, Joseph (1906–1942).
Diminutive German opera singer who made two
British films: *My Song Goes Round the World* 34.
The Singing Dream 35.

Schmidt, Richard (1944–).
American experimental film-maker.
    A Man, a Woman and a Killer 75. Showboat
1988 – the Remake 78. Emerald Cities 83.

Schnee, Charles (1916–1963).
American screenwriter.
    I Walk Alone 47. Red River 48. The Furies 50.
The Bad and the Beautiful (AA) 52. The Next Voice
You Hear 53. Butterfield 8 60. The Crowded Sky
61. Two Weeks in Another Town 62, etc.

Schneer, Charles (1920–).
American producer, mainly of trick films using
'Superdynamation'.
    The Seventh Voyage of Sinbad 58. The Three
Worlds of Gulliver 60. I Aim at the Stars 61.
Mysterious Island 62. *Jason and the Argonauts* 63.
The First Men in the Moon 64. You Must Be Joking
65. Half a Sixpence 67. The Executioner 69.
Sinbad's Golden Voyage 74. Sinbad and the Eye
of the Tiger 77, etc.

Schneider, Bert (1932–) (Berton Schneider).
American producer of Hollywood's 'new wave'.
    Head 68. Easy Rider 69. Five Easy Pieces 71. The
Last Picture Show 71. A Safe Place 72. Drive He
Said 72. The King of Marvin Gardens 73.

Schneider, John (1954–).
American actor, best known for his role as Bo in
the TV series *The Dukes of Hazzard* 79–85.
    Eddie Macon's Run 83. Cocaine Wars 86.

Stagecoach 86. The Curse 87. Christmas Comes
to Willow Creek 87. Speed Zone 88. Ministry of
Vengeance 89, etc.
    TV series: Grand Slam 90.

Schneider, Maria (1952–).
German leading actress.
    Last Tango in Paris 73. Reigen 74. The Passenger
75. Babysitter 75. A Woman Like Eve 79. Mama
Dracula 80. Bunker Palace Hotel 89. Sand Screens
(Ecrans de Sable) 91. Au Pays des Juliets 92, etc.

Schneider, Rob.
American actor, a regular in the 90s on TV's
Saturday Night Live.
    Home Alone 2: Lost in New York 92. Judge
Dredd 95.

Schneider, Romy (1938–1982) (Rosemarie
Albach-Retty).
Austrian leading lady in international films.
    Wenn der Weisse Flieder Wieder Blueht 53. Sissi
55. Maedchen in Uniform 58. The Story of Vicki
(Ger.) 58. Forever My Love 61. Boccaccio 70 62.
The Cardinal 63. The Trial 63. The Victors 63.
Good Neighbour Sam 64. What's New, Pussycat?
65. 10.30 p.m. Summer 66. Triple Cross 66. Les
Choses de la Vie 69. Don't You Cry 70. Bloomfield
70. The Assassination of Trotsky 72. Ludwig 72.
Qui? 73. *L'Amour de Pluie* 73. The Infernal Trio 74.
Lover on a String 75. The Old Gun 76. Bloodline
79. La Banquière 80, etc.

Schneiderman, George (c. 1890–1964).
American cinematographer.
    Love is Love 19. Bare Knuckles 21. Boston
Blackie 23. *The Iron Horse* 24. The Johnstown Flood
26. Three Bad Men 26. Four Sons 28. Born
Reckless 30. Charlie Chan Carries On 31. Young
America 32. Doctor Bull 33. *Judge Priest* 34.
Steamboat Round the Bend 35. The Devil is a
Sissy 36. The Gladiator 38. Michael Shayne Private
Detective 40, many others.

Schnitzler, Arthur (1862–1931).
Austrian playwright whose chief bequests to the
cinema are *Liebelei* and *La Ronde.*

Schoedsack, Ernest B. (1893–1979).
American director, former cameraman, who with
Merian C. Cooper made the following:
    Grass 26. *Chang* 27. *The Four Feathers* 29. Rango
31. *The Hounds of Zaroff* 32. *King Kong* 33. Son of
Kong 34. Long Lost Father 34. Outlaws of the
Orient 37. Dr Cyclops 39. Mighty Joe Young 49,
etc.

Schoendoerffer, Pierre (1928–).
French screenwriter and director. He is a former
army photographer who was taken prisoner at the
battle of Dien Bien Phu in 1954, when Vietnam
was a French colony. After his release he became
a war correspondent for *Life* and *Paris Match* and
a documentary film-maker.
    Ramuntcho 58. Pêcheurs d'Islande 59. The
317th Platoon (La 317e Section) 64. Objectif 500
Millions 66. The Anderson Section (doc) (AA) 67.
Le Crabe Tambour 77. A Captain's Honour
(L'Honneur d'un Capitaine) 82. Dien Bien Phu 92,
etc.

Schofield, Johnnie (1889–1955).
Ubiquitous English character actor, almost a
fixture in low-budget British movies of the 30s and
40s.
    Pride of the Force 33. The Outcast 34. Mystery
of the Marie Celeste 35. Song of Freedom 36.
Song of the Road 37. Lassie from Lancashire 38.

The Arsenal Stadium Mystery 39. Let George Do
It 40. In Which We Serve 42. The Young Mr Pitt
42. We Dive at Dawn 43. Old Mother Riley,
Detective 43. Tawny Pipit 44. They Came to a City
44. The Wicked Lady 45. Waterloo Road 45. The
Way to the Stars 45. This Man Is Mine 46. Mr
Perrin and Mr Traill 48. Appointment with Venus
51. The Browning Version 51. Home at Seven 52.
The Saint Returns 53. Carrington V.C. 54. See How
They Run 55, many others.

schooldays
have often been depicted in films with a thick
sentimental veneer, as in *Goodbye Mr Chips, Good
Morning Miss Dove* and *Blossoms in the Dust.* But
more usually the pupils have serious problems to
worry about, as in *Young Woodley, The Guinea Pig,
Friends for Life, Tea and Sympathy* and *Tom Brown's
Schooldays;* while with at least equal frequency our
sympathies are elicited on behalf of the staff: *The
Housemaster, Bright Road, The Blackboard Jungle, The
Browning Version, Spare the Rod, Edward My Son, The
Blue Angel, The Children's Hour, The Corn Is Green,
Term of Trial, To Sir with Love, Spinster, The Prime
of Miss Jean Brodie, Please Sir, Unman Wittering and
Zigo.* More light-hearted treatment of the whole
business is evident in *The Trouble with Angels* and
Margie, and in some cases the treatment has
undeniably been farcical: *Boys Will Be Boys, The
Ghost of St Michael's, Good Morning Boys, A Yank at
Eton, Vice Versa, Bottoms Up* and *The Happiest Days
of Your Life;* with the St Trinian's saga wildest of
all. The strangest schools on film are those depicted
in *Zéro de Conduite* and its semi-remake *If . . .*
while very special schools were seen in *Battement
de Coeur* (for pickpockets), *School for Secrets* (for
'boffins'), *Old Bones of the River* (for African tiny
tots), *The Goose Steps Out* (for young Nazis), *Orders
to Kill, The House on 92nd Street, 13 rue Madeleine,
Carve Her Name with Pride* and *From Russia with Love*
(for spies).

Schoonmaker, Thelma (1940–).
American film editor, often on the films of director
Martin Scorsese. She married director Michael
Powell in 1984.
■ Woodstock (AAN) 70. Raging Bull (AA) 80. The
King of Comedy 83. After Hours 85. The Color of
Money 86. The Last Temptation of Christ 88. New
York Stories 89. GoodFellas (AAN) 90. Cape Fear
91. The Age of Innocence 93.

Schrader, Paul (1946–).
American screenwriter and director, dealing
almost obsessively with tough themes.
    Autobiography: 1990, *Schrader on Schrader.*
■ The Yakuza (co-w) 75. *Taxi Driver* 76. Obsession
76. Rolling Thunder (co-w) 77. Blue Collar (& d)
78. Old Boyfriends (co-w) 79. Hardcore (& d) 79.
American Gigolo (& d) 79. Raging Bull 80. Cat
People (& d) 82. Mishima (& d) 85. Light of Day
(& d) 87. The Last Temptation of Christ (w) 88.
Patty Hearst (d) 88. The Comfort of Strangers (d)
90. Light Sleeper (wd) 91.

¶ Mine was the first generation of film-makers
  informed by film school, just as the generation
before us was informed by live television and the
next generation was informed by music
television. – *P.S.*

Schreck, Max (1879–1936).
German actor best known for his eerie portrayal
of the vampire count in *Nosferatu* 22.

Schroder, Rick (1970–) (aka Ricky Schroder).
American actor, a former child star.
■ *The Champ* 79. The Last Flight of Noah's Ark 80.

The Earthling 80. Little Lord Fauntleroy (TV) 81. A Reason to Live (TV) 85. A Son's Promise (TV) 90. Across the Tracks 90. Call of the Wild (TV) 93. There Goes My Baby 94.

TV series: Silver Spoons 82–86.

Schroeder, Barbet (1941–).
Iranian director, long in Paris, at first as producer of Eric Rohmer's films.
■ More 69. The Valley 72. General Idi Amin Dada 74. Maîtresse 76. Barfly 87. Reversal of Fortune (AAN) 90. Single White Female 92. Kiss of Death 95.

Schuck, John (1944–).
American character actor familiar as the dumb sergeant in *McMillan and Wife*.
M*A*S*H 70. Blade 73. Thieves Like Us 74. Butch and Sundance: the Early Days 79. Just You and Me Kid 79. Earthbound 81. Star Trek IV: The Voyage Home 86. Outrageous Fortune 87. The New Adventures of Pippi Longstocking 88. Dick Tracy 90. Star Trek VI: The Undiscovered Country 91, etc.

TV series: Holmes and Yo Yo 75. Turnabout 79.

Schufftan, Eugene (1893–1977).
German cinematographer. Invented the Schufftan process, a variation on the 'glass shot' (qv), by which mirror images are blended with real backgrounds.
People on Sunday 30. L'Atlantide 32. Drôle de Drame 37. *Quai des Brumes* 38. *It Happened Tomorrow* 44. Ulysses 54. Eyes without a Face 59. Something Wild 61. *The Hustler* (AA) 62. Lilith 64, etc.

Schulberg, B. P. (1892–1950).
American executive, former publicist; general manager of Paramount (1926–32), then independent producer.

¶ This is the only industry I know. I am able to work as hard as anybody in it. Sure I have made some mistakes . . . who hasn't? What is the judicial code of the industry? Life imprisonment for a misdemeanour and execution for violating a parking law? Must we always wait until a production pioneer is found dead in a Hollywood hotel room before reflecting on an 'indifferent and forgetful' industry? – *Advertisement in Variety, 1949*

Schulberg, Budd (1914–).
American novelist whose work has been adapted for the screen. Son of B. P. Schulberg.
Autobiography: 1982, *Moving Pictures*.
On the Waterfront (AA) 54. The Harder They Fall 56. A Face in the Crowd 57. Wind Across the Everglades 59. A Question of Honour (TV) 81, etc.

Schulman, Arnold (1925–).
American screenwriter and dramatist.
Wild Is the Wind 57. A Hole in the Head 59. Cimarron 60. Love with the Proper Stranger (AAN) 64. The Night They Raided Minksy's 68. Goodbye Columbus (AAN) 69. To Find a Man 71. Funny Lady 75. Won Ton Ton, the Dog Who Saved Hollywood 76. Players 79. A Chorus Line 85. Tucker: The Man and His Dream 88, etc.

Schulman, Tom.
American screenwriter.
Dead Poets Society (AA) 89. Honey, I Shrunk the Kids 89. Second Sight 89. What about Bob? 91. Medicine Man 92, etc.

Schultz, Carl (1939–).
Hungarian-born director, in Australia from the mid-50s.
Blue Fin 78. Goodbye Paradise 83. Bodyline (TV) 84. Travelling North 87. The Seventh Sign (US) 88.

Schultz, Michael (1938–).
American director.
Cooley High 75. Car Wash 76. Greased Lightning 77. Which Way Is Up? 77. Sergeant Pepper's Lonely Hearts Club Band 78. Scavenger Hunt 79. Carbon Copy 81. The Last Dragon 84. Krush Grove 85. Disorderlies 87. Rock 'n' Roll Mom (TV) 88, etc.

Schumacher, Joel (1942–).
American director.
St Elmo's Fire 85. The Lost Boys 87. Cousins 89. Dying Young 91. Falling Down 93. The Devil's Advocate 93. The Client 94. Batman Forever 95, etc.

Schunzel, Reinhold (1886–1954).
German actor and director who came to Hollywood in the 30s.
Around the World in Eighty Days 19. Die Dreigroschenoper 31. Viktor und Viktoria 33. Amphitryon 37. Rich Man, Poor Girl (d) 38. Balalaika (d) 39. The Great Awakening (d) 41. Hostages (a) 43. The Man in Half Moon Street (a) 44. Notorious (a) 46. The Woman in Brown (a) 48. Washington Story (a) 52, etc.

Schurmann, Gerard (1928–).
Dutch composer and conductor, in British films from the late 40s. He also orchestrated the scores for *The Vikings, Exodus* and *Lawrence of Arabia*.
But Not in Vain 48. The Long Arm 56. The Man in the Sky 56. The Camp on Blood Island 58. Horrors of the Black Museum 59. The Two-Headed Spy 59. Cone of Silence 60. Konga 61. Day In Day Out 65. The Lost Continent 68. Claretta 84, etc.

Schuster, Harold (1902–1986).
American director, former editor.
Wings of the Morning 37. Dinner at the Ritz 37. Zanzibar 40. My Friend Flicka 43. The Tender Years 47. So Dear to My Heart 49. Kid Monk Baroni 52. Jack Slade 53. Dragoon Wells Massacre 57. The Courage of Black Beauty 58, etc.

Schwartz, Arthur (1900–1984).
American producer and composer, former lawyer.
Navy Blues (c) 42. Thank Your Lucky Stars (c) 43. Cover Girl (p) 44. The Band Wagon (c) 53. You're Never Too Young (c) 55, many others.

Schwarz, Maurice (1891–1960).
American actor famous in the Yiddish theatre; many of his successes, such as *Tevye the Milkman*, were limited for limited circulation. Appeared in Hollywood's version of *Salome* 53.

Schwarzenegger, Arnold (1947–).
Austrian-born body-builder, a former winner of many Mr Universe and Mr Olympia contests who became the biggest box-office star of the early 90s, despite his excessive musculature and heavily accented English, delivered in a monotone. He became an American citizen in 1983 and is said to harbour political ambitions. By 1993, his price per film was $15 million plus.
Autobiography: 1986, *Arnold: The Education of a Bodybuilder*.
Book: 1986, *Arnold's Encyclopedia of Modern Bodybuilding*.
Stay Hungry 76. Pumping Iron 77. The Villain

79. The Jayne Mansfield Story (TV) 79. Conan the Barbarian 82. Conan the Destroyer 84. The Terminator 84. Commando 85. Red Sonja 85. Raw Deal 86. Predator 87. The Running Man 87. Red Heat 88. Twins 88. Total Recall 90. Kindergarten Cop 90. Terminator 2: Judgment Day 91. Christmas in Connecticut (d) (TV) 92. The Last Action Hero 93. True Lies 94. Junior 94, etc.

¶ He has so many muscles that he has to make an appointment to move his fingers. – *Phyllis Diller*

Famous line (*Terminator*): 'I'll be back.'

Schygulla, Hanna (1943–).
Polish leading actress, mainly in Fassbinder films.
■ The Bridegroom and the Actress 68.
Katzelmacher 69. Beware of a Holy Whore 70. *The Bitter Tears of Petra von Kant* 72. Effie Briest 74. *The Marriage of Maria Braun* 79. *Berlin Alexanderplatz* 80. Lili Marleen 80. Circle of Deceit 81. La Nuit de Varenne 82. The Story of Piera 83. A Love in Germany 83. The Future is Woman 84. The Delta Force 85. Forever Lulu 87. Miss Arizona 88. El Verano de la Señora Forbes 88. Abrahams Gold 90. Dead Again 91. Warsaw Year 5703 (Warszawa) 92. Mavi Surgun 93. Petrified Garden 93. Aux Petits Bonheurs 94.

science fiction,
a term incapable of precise definition, may perhaps be taken as that kind of fantasy which depends not on legend only, like Dracula, but involves the work of man. Thus King Kong and the 'natural' monsters would not qualify, but Frankenstein and the Invisible Man would. Space exploration and prophecy, considered elsewhere, are branches of it, as are all the films about mad doctors and colliding worlds.

scientists
have been the subject of many films, though few real-life ones have led sufficiently dramatic lives to warrant filming. Warners led the way in the 30s with *The Story of Louis Pasteur* and *Dr Ehrlich's Magic Bullet*. In 1939 Mickey Rooney played *Young Tom Edison*, followed by Spencer Tracy as *Edison the Man*. Then, in 1943, Greer Garson played *Madame Curie*. At this point the movie fan's thirst for scientific knowledge died out, and John Huston's *Freud* in 1962 did not revive it. In the 80s, the lives of Oppenheimer and Sakharov have been filmed.
See also: *inventors*.

Sciorra, Annabella (1964–).
American actress.
True Love 89. Internal Affairs 90. Reversal of Fortune 90. Cadillac Man 90. Jungle Fever 91. The Hard Way 91. The Hand that Rocks the Cradle 92. Mr Wonderful 93. Romeo Is Bleeding 93. The Night We Never Met 93, etc.

Scofield, Paul (1922–).
Distinguished British stage actor whose films have been infrequent.
■ That Lady 55. Carve Her Name with Pride 58. The Train 64. *A Man for All Seasons* (AA, BFA) 66. King Lear 69. Bartleby 71. Scorpio 73. A Delicate Balance 73. Anna Karenina (TV) 84. The Attic: The Hiding of Anne Frank (TV) 88. When the Whales Came 89. Henry V 89. Hamlet 90. Utz (TV) 91. Quiz Show 94. Martin Chuzzlewit (TV) 94.

Scoggins, Tracy (1953–).
American actress, much on television.
Twirl (TV) 81. Toy Soldiers 84. The Gumshoe

Kid 89. One Last Run 89. Watchers II 90. Play Murder for Me 91. Timebomb 91. Demonic Toys 91. Alien Intruder 93, etc.

TV series: Renegades 83. Hawaiian Heat 84. Dynasty II: The Colbys 85–87.

Scola, Ettore (1931–).
Italian screenwriter and director.
■ Two Nights with Cleopatra (w) 54. Adua et le Compagne (w) 60. The Visit (w) 63. Made in Italy (w) 65. Let's Talk About Women (w, d) 65. The Devil in Love (wd) 66. The Pizza Triangle (wd) 70. We All Loved Each Other So Much (wd) 75. A Special Day (wd) 77. Passione d'Amore (wd) 81. La Nuit de Varennes (wd) 82. Le Bal (wd) 83. Macaroni (wd) 85. What Time Is It? (Che Ora E?) (co-w, d) 89. Splendour (wd) 89. Il Viaggio di Capitan Fracassa (wd, p) 90. Mario, Maria e Mario (co-w, d) 94.

score.
The music composed for a film.

Scorsese, Martin (1942–).
American director.
Book: 1990, Scorsese on Scorsese edited by David Thompson and Ian Christie.
■ Who's That Knocking at My Door? 70. Boxcar Bertha 72. Mean Streets 73. Alice Doesn't Live Here Any More 74. Taxi Driver 76. New York, New York 77. The Last Waltz 78. Raging Bull (AAN) 80. King of Comedy 83. After Hours 85. The Color of Money 86. The Last Temptation of Christ (AAN) 88. New York Stories 89. Akira Kurosawa's Dreams (a) 90. GoodFellas (AAN) 90. Guilty by Suspicion (a) 90. Cape Fear 91. The Age of Innocence (co-w, d) (AANw) 93. Quiz Show (a) 94.

¶ Cinema is a matter of what's in the frame and what's out. – M.S.

Scott, Adrian (1912–1972).
American producer who was one of the 'Hollywood Ten'. He was briefly married to actress Anne Shirley.
Murder My Sweet 44. My Pal Wolf 44. Cornered 46. So Well Remembered 47. Crossfire 47, etc.

Scott, Campbell (1962–).
American leading actor. He is the son of actors George C. Scott and Colleen Dewhurst.
Five Corners 87. From Hollywood to Deadwood 88. Longtime Companion 90. The Sheltering Sky 90. Dying Young 91. Dead Again 91. Singles 92. The Innocent 93. Mrs Parker and the Vicious Circle (as Robert Benchley) 94, etc.

Scott, George C. (1926–).
Distinguished but taciturn American actor; usually plays tough or sardonic characters and was the first actor to refuse an Oscar.
■ The Hanging Tree 58. Anatomy of a Murder (AAN) 59. The Hustler (AAN) 62. The List of Adrian Messenger 63. Dr Strangelove 63. The Yellow Rolls-Royce 64. The Bible 66. Not with My Wife You Don't 66. The Flim Flam Man 67. Petulia 69. Patton (AA) 70. They Might Be Giants 71. The Last Run 71. The Hospital (AAN) 72. The New Centurions 72. Jane Eyre (TV) 72. Oklahoma Crude 73. The Day of the Dolphin 73. Rage (& d) 73. The Savage Is Loose (& d) 74. Bank Shot 75. The Hindenberg 75. This Savage Land (TV) 76. Fear on Trial (TV) 76. The Prince and the Pauper 77. Islands in the Stream 77. Beauty and the Beast (TV) 77. Movie Movie 78. Hardcore 79. The Changeling 80. The Formula 80. Taps 81. Oliver Twist (as Fagin) 82. China Girl (TV) 83. Firestarter 84. A Christmas Carol (TV) 84. Mussolini: The Untold Story (TV)

85. Choices (TV) 85. The Last Days of Patton (TV) 86. The Murders in the Rue Morgue (TV) 86. Pals (TV) 87. The Ryan White Story (TV) 89. The Rescuers Down Under (voice) 90. William Peter Blatty's The Exorcist III 90. Descending Angel (TV) 90. Malice 93.

TV series: East Side West Side 63. Traps 94.

¶ There is no question you get pumped up by the recognition. Then a self-loathing sets in when you realize you're enjoying it. – G.C.S.

Famous line (Dr Strangelove): 'I don't say we wouldn't get our hair mussed, but I do say no more than ten to twenty million killed, tops – that is, depending on the break.'

Scott, Gordon (1927–) (Gordon M. Werschkul).
American leading man who after being fireman, cowboy and lifeguard was signed to play Tarzan in Tarzan's Hidden Jungle 55; made five further episodes, then went to Italy to make muscleman epics.
■ Tarzan's Hidden Jungle 55. Tarzan and the Trappers 55. Tarzan and the Lost Safari 56. Tarzan's Fight for Life 58. Tarzan's Greatest Adventure 59. Tarzan the Magnificent 60. Duel of the Titans 61. Samson and the Seven Miracles 61. Goliath and the Vampires 62. Zorro and the Three Musketeers 62. Battles of the Gladiators 62. A Queen for Caesar 62. The Lion of St Mark 63. Hero of Babylon 63. Hercules Attacks 63. Thunder of Battle 63. Arrow of the Avenger 63. Arm of Fire 64. Buffalo Bill 64. Hercules and the Princess of Troy 65. The Tramplers 66. Top Secret 66. Nest of Spies 67.

Scott, Gordon L. T. (1920–1991).
British producer, former production manager.
Look Back in Anger 58. Petticoat Pirates 61. The Pot Carriers 63. Crooks in Cloisters 64, etc.

Scott, Hazel (1920–1981).
American pianist and pop organist.
Something to Shout About 43. The Heat's On 43. I Dood It 43. Broadway Rhythm 44. Rhapsody in Blue 45. The Night Affair (Fr.) 61, etc.

Scott, Janette (1938–).
British leading lady, former child star. She was married to singer Mel Tormé (1966–78).
Went the Day Well? 42. No Place for Jennifer 49. No Highway 50. The Magic Box 51. As Long as They're Happy 52. Now and Forever 55. The Good Companions 57. The Devil's Disciple 59. The Old Dark House 63. The Beauty Jungle 64. Crack in the World 65. His and Hers 68, etc.

Scott, John (1930–).
British composer and conductor. He began by creating musical arrangements for the 60s pop group The Hollies, and has also written many TV themes.
A Study in Terror 65. Doctor in Clover 66. Sumuru 66. Berserk 67. Jules Verne's Rocket to the Moon 67. The Long Duel 67. Stranger in the House 67. Loving Feeling 68. The Amsterdam Affair 68. Twinky 69. Crooks and Coronets (aka Sophie's Place) 69. The Violent Enemy 69. Outback 70. Trog 70. Girl Stroke Boy 71. The Jerusalem File 79. Antony and Cleopatra 72. Doom Watch 72. England Made Me 72. Penny Gold 73. Billy Two Hats 73. Craze 73. S.P.Y.S. (aka Whiffs) 74. Symptoms (aka The Blood Virgin) 74. Hennessy 75. That Lucky Touch 75. Satan's Slave 76. The People that Time Forgot 77. North Dallas Forty 79. The Final Countdown 80. The Hostage Tower 80. Inseminoid 80. Greystoke: The Legend of Tarzan Lord of the Apes 84. The Shooting Party 85. King Kong Lives

86. Death of a Soldier 86. Man on Fire 87. Shoot to Kill 88. The Deceivers 88. Winter People 89. Dog Tags 90, etc.

Scott, Ken (1927–1986).
American action lead of the 60s.
The Three Faces of Eve 57. Woman Obsessed 59. Pirates of Tortuga 61. Desire in the Dust 61. Police Nurse 63. The Murder Game 65. Fantastic Voyage 66, etc.

Scott, Lizabeth (1922–) (Emma Matzo).
Sultry American leading lady of the 40s, a box-office concoction of blonde hair, defiant expression and immobile upper lip.
■ You Came Along 45. The Strange Love of Martha Ivers 46. Dead Reckoning 47. Desert Fury 47. I Walk Alone 47. Variety Girl 47. Pitfall 48. Too Late for Tears 49. Easy Living 49. Paid in Full 50. Dark City 50. The Racket 51. The Company She Keeps 51. Two of a Kind 51. Red Mountain 51. Stolen Face 52. Scared Stiff 53. Bad for Each Other 54. Silver Lode 54. Loving You 57. The Weapon 57. Pulp 72.

Scott, Margaretta (1912–).
British stage (from 1929) and screen (from 1934) actress who usually plays upper-middle-class women.
Dirty Work 34. Things to Come 36. Quiet Wedding 40. Sabotage at Sea 42. Fanny by Gaslight 43. The Man from Morocco 45. Mrs Fitzherbert 47. Idol of Paris 48. Where's Charley? 52. Town on Trial 56. The Last Man to Hang 56. A Woman Possessed 58. An Honourable Murder 60. Crescendo 69. Percy 71, etc.

Scott, Martha (1914–).
American actress with stage experience.
Our Town (AAN) 40. Cheers for Miss Bishop 41. The Howards of Virginia 41. One Foot in Heaven 41. Hi Diddle Diddle 43. In Old Oklahoma 43. So Well Remembered 47. The Desperate Hours 55. The Ten Commandments 56. Ben Hur 59. Airport 75 74. The Turning Point 77. The Word (TV) 78. Charleston (TV) 79. Beulah Land (TV) 80, etc.
TV series: Secrets of Midland Heights 80.

Scott, Peter Graham (1923–).
British director.
Panic in Madame Tussauds 48. Sing Along with Me 52. The Headless Ghost 59. Captain Clegg 62. The Pot Carriers 63. Bitter Harvest 63. Father Came Too 64. Mister Ten Per Cent 67. The Promise 69, etc.

Scott, Pippa (1935–).
American actress.
Auntie Mame 58. Petulia 68. Cold Turkey 70. Bad Ronald 74, etc.

Scott, Randolph (1898–1987) (Randolph Crane).
Rugged American outdoor star, in films from 1931 after stage experience.
Sky Bride 31. Supernatural 32. Home on the Range 33. Roberta 34. She 35. So Red the Rose 35. Follow the Fleet 36. Go West Young Man 36. Last of the Mohicans 36. High, Wide and Handsome 37. Rebecca of Sunnybrook Farm 38. The Texans 38. Jesse James 39. Virginia City 40. My Favourite Wife 40. When the Daltons Rode 40. Western Union 41. Belle Starr 41. Paris Calling 41. To the Shores of Tripoli 42. The Spoilers 42. Pittsburgh 42. Bombardier 43. Gung Ho 43. The Desperadoes 43. Belle of the Yukon 44. China Sky 44. Captain Kidd 45. Badman's Territory 46. Abilene Town 47. Christmas Eve 47. Fighting Man of the Plains 49. Sugarfoot 51. Santa Fé 51. Hangman's Knot 53. The

Stranger Wore a Gun 53. The Bounty Hunter 54. A Lawless Street 55. Seven Men from Now 56. Decision at Sundown 57. Ride Lonesome 58. *Ride the High Country* 62, many others.

Scott, Ridley (1939–).
British director, from TV commercials, working in America. In 1994 he headed a consortium with his brother Tony Scott to take over Shepperton Studios.
The Duellists 78. Alien 79. *Blade Runner* 81. Legend 85. Someone to Watch over Me 87. Black Rain 89. *Thelma and Louise* (AAN) 91. 1492: Conquest of Paradise 92. The Browning Version (p) 94, etc.

¶ I think it's remarkable that people will give you 10 million dollars to go and get your rocks off. – R.S., 1976
Never let yourself be seen in public unless they pay for it. – R.S.

Scott, Terry (1927–1994).
Plump English comic performer, from variety and the stage, where he was best known for an act as a naughty schoolboy and as a pantomime dame. Thereafter, he performed mainly in TV sitcoms and in stage farces.
Blue Murder at St Trinian's 58. A Pair of Briefs 62. Carry On Camping 68. Bless This House 72, etc.
TV series: Great Scott, It's Maynard 55–58. Hugh and I 62–70. Scott On 72. Son of the Bride 73. Happy Ever After 74. Terry and June 79–88. Danger Mouse (voice, as Penfold) 81–92.

Scott, Tony (1944–).
English director in Hollywood who began as a director of television commercials. He is the brother of director Ridley Scott. In 1994 he joined with Ridley in buying Shepperton Studios.
The Hunger 83. Top Gun 86. Beverly Hills Cop II 87. Days of Thunder 90. Revenge 90. The Last Boy Scout 91. True Romance 93. Crimson Tide 95, etc.

Scott, Sir Walter (1771–1832).
Scottish novelist, mainly of period adventure stories. His *Ivanhoe, The Talisman* and *Rob Roy* have received most attention from film-makers.

Scott, Zachary (1914–1965).
American leading man with considerable stage experience.
The Mask of Dimitrios (film debut) 44. *The Southerner* 45. *Mildred Pierce* 46. Stallion Road 47. The Unfaithful 48. Shadow on the Wall 50. Born To Be Bad 51. Let's Make It Legal 53. Appointment in Honduras 53. Bandido 56. The Young One 60. It's Only Money 62, many others.

Scotto, Vincente (1876–1952).
French composer.
Jofroi 34. Pepe le Moko 36. La Fille du Puisatier 40. Domino 43. L'Ingénue Libertine 50, etc.

Scott-Thomas, Kristin (1960–).
English actress.
Under the Cherry Moon 86. A Handful of Dust (TV) 88. The Tenth Man (TV) 88. Le Bal du Gouverneur (Fr.) 89. The Endless Game (TV) 90. Framed (TV) 90. Autobus (Aux Yeux du Monde) (Fr.) 91. Look at It This Way (TV) 92. Bitter Moon 93. Body and Soul (TV) 93. The Bachelor 93. Four Weddings and a Funeral 94. An Unforgettable Summer (Un Été Inoubliable) (Fr.) 94, etc.

Scourby, Alexander (1913–1985).
American stage character actor.
Affair in Trinidad 52. *The Big Heat* 53. The Silver Chalice 55. Giant 56. Seven Thieves 59. The Big Fisherman 59. Confessions of a Counterspy 60.

Screaming Mad George:
see *George, Screaming Mad*.

screenplay:
see *shooting script*.

The Sea Wolf.
Jack London's stark psychological novel of an obsessed sea captain, Wolf Larsen, has been filmed at least seven times: in 1913 it starred Hobart Bosworth, in 1920 Noah Beery, in 1925 Ralph Ince, in 1930 Milton Sills, and in 1941 Edward G. Robinson. A disguised western version, *Barricade*, with Raymond Massey, appeared in 1950, and in 1957 yet another straight version, under the title *Wolf Larsen*, was made with Barry Sullivan. In 1974 Chuck Connors starred in a European version, *Wolf of the Seven Seas*.

Seagal, Steven (1951–).
Frowning American star and producer of action films.
Above the Law 88. Hard to Kill 89. Marked for Death 90. Out for Justice 91. Last to Surrender 92. Under Siege 92. On Deadly Ground (& p, d) 94, etc.

Seagrove, Jenny (1958–).
British actress, born in Kuala Lumpur.
Tattoo 80. Moonlighting 82. Local Hero 83. Nate and Hayes 83. A Woman of Substance (TV) 85. Hold the Dream 85. Appointment with Death 88. A Chorus of Disapproval 89. The Guardian 90. Bullseye! 90. Deadly Game (TV) 91. Sherlock Holmes – the Incident at Victoria Falls (TV) 91, etc.

Seal, Elizabeth (1935–).
British dancer and occasional actress.
Town on Trial 56. Cone of Silence 60. Vampire Circus 72, etc.

Seale, John (1942–).
Australian cinematographer and director. He is noted for his work on the films of Peter Weir, a relationship which began when he worked as camera operator to cinematographer Russell Boyd.
Alvin Purple 73. Deathcheaters 76. Fatty Finn 80. Doctors and Nurses 81. The Survivor 81. Fighting Back 82. Goodbye Paradise 82. BMX Bandits 83. Careful He Might Hear You 83. Silver City 84. The Empty Beach 85. Witness (AAN) 85. Children of a Lesser God 86. The Hitcher 86. The Mosquito Coast 86. Stakeout 87. Gorillas in the Mist 88. Rain Man (AAN) 88. Dead Poets Society 89. Till There Was You (d) 90. The Doctor 91. Lorenzo's Oil 92. The Firm 93. The Paper 94, etc.

seances
on the screen have often been shown to be fake, as in *Seance on a Wet Afternoon, Bunco Squad, Palmy Days, The Spiritualist, Houdini*, and *The Medium*. But just occasionally they do result in something being called up from over there. It happened in *Blithe Spirit, The Haunting, The Uninvited, Night of the Demon, Thirteen Ghosts, Hands of the Ripper*, and *The Legend of Hell House*.

Searle, Francis (1909–).
British director.
A Girl in a Million 46. Things Happen at Night

48. Cloudburst (& w) 51. Wheel of Fate (& w) 53, many second features.

Searle, Jackie (1920–).
American boy actor of the 30s, usually in mean roles.
Tom Sawyer 31. Skippy 31. Peck's Bad Boy 35. Little Lord Fauntleroy 36. That Certain Age 38. Little Tough Guys in Society 39. The Hard Boiled Canary 41. The Paleface 49, many others.

Sears, Fred F. (1913–1957).
American director of second features.
Desert Vigilante 49. Raiders of Tomahawk Creek 50. Snake River Desperadoes 51. Last Train from Bombay 52. Ambush at Tomahawk Gap 53. El Alamein 53. The Miami Story 54. Wyoming Renegades 55. Chicago Syndicate 55. Rock around the Clock 56. Earth versus the Flying Saucers 56. Don't Knock the Rock 56. The Giant Claw 57. The World was His Jury 58, etc.

Sears, Heather (1935–1994).
British actress with repertory experience. She later concentrated on theatre, notably at the Haymarket Theatre, Leicester.
Dry Rot 56. *The Story of Esther Costello* 57. Room at the Top 59. Sons and Lovers 60. Phantom of the Opera 62. Saturday Night Out 64. Black Torment 64. Great Expectations (TV) 75, etc.

seaside resorts
have provided lively settings for many British comedies: Douglas in *No Limit*, Brighton in *Bank Holiday*, Blackpool in *Sing As We Go*, and a variety of south coast resorts in *The Punch and Judy Man, French Dressing, All Over the Town, Barnacle Bill*. Sometimes the resort has provided a contrast to more serious goings-on, as in *The Entertainer, Brighton Rock, Room at the Top, The Dark Man, A Taste of Honey, I Was Happy Here, Family Doctor, The System, The Damned*. Hollywood usually comes a cropper when depicting British resorts, either comically as in *The Gay Divorcee* or seriously as in *Separate Tables;* its own resorts have a monotonous look, whether viewed romantically in *Moon Over Miami* and *Fun in Acapulco*, nostalgically in *Some Like It Hot*, trendily in *Beach Party* and its many sequels, or morosely in *Tony Rome*. The French Riviera has never been notably well captured on film since Vigo's *A Propos de Nice*, but among the movies to have a go with the aid of back projection are *On the Riviera, That Riviera Touch* and *Moment to Moment*. Hitchcock got some picture-postcard views but little else out of *To Catch a Thief*, while the French had a go for themselves in *St Tropez Blues* and others. A Mediterranean resort was the setting of the climax of *Suddenly Last Summer;* other European watering-places featured memorably in *Une Si Jolie Petite Plage, Sunday in August* and *The Lady with the Little Dog*. The most ingenious use of the seaside for purposes of film fantasy was certainly in *Oh What a Lovely War*.
Seaside settings of the 70s and 80s have included *Out of Season, Atlantic City USA* and *The King of Marvin Gardens*.

Seastrom, Victor (1879–1960) (Victor Sjostrom).
Distinguished Swedish actor-director with stage experience.
Ingeborg Holm 13. Terje Vigen (ad) 16. Jerusalem (d) 18. *Ordet* (The Word) (a) 21. *The Phantom Carriage* (Thy Soul Shall Bear Witness) (d) 21. The Master of Man (US) (d) 23. He Who Gets Slapped (US) (d) 24. *The Scarlet Letter* (US) (d) 26. Tower of Lies (US) (d) 26. The Divine Woman (US) (d) 28. The Wind (US) (d) 28. Under the Red

Robe (GB) (d) 36. Ordet (remake) (a) 43. *Wild Strawberries* (a) 57, many others.

Seaton, George (1911–1979) (George Stenius). American writer-director. Acted and produced on stage; joined MGM writing staff 1933; later independent or working with producer William Perlberg.

A Day at the Races (co-w) 37. *The Song of Bernadette* (AANw) 43. Diamond Horseshoe (wd) 45. Junior Miss (wd) 45. The Shocking Miss Pilgrim (wd) 47. *Miracle on 34th Street* (wd) (AA) 47. The Big Lift (wd) 51. For Heaven's Sake (wd) 51. Anything Can Happen (wd) 52. Little Boy Lost (wd) 53. *The Country Girl* (wd) (AAw, AANd) 54. The Proud and Profane (wd) 56. The Tin Star (p) 57. Teacher's Pet (d) 58. The Pleasure of His Company (d) 61. The Counterfeit Traitor (wd) 63. Thirty-Six Hours (wd) 64. What's So Bad About Feeling Good? (wpd) 68. *Airport* (wd) (AANw) 69. Showdown (wpd) 73, many others.

Seberg, Jean (1938–1979).
American leading lady who won contest for role of Preminger's *Saint Joan* 57, after which her career faltered but picked up in French films. Her second husband was novelist Romain Gary. Found dead in her car.

Bonjour Tristesse 57. The Mouse That Roared 59. *Breathless (A Bout de Souffle)* 60. Playtime 62. In the French Style 63. Lilith 64. Moment to Moment 65. Estouffade à la Caraïbe 66. The Road to Corinth 68. Pendulum 69. Paint Your Wagon 69. Airport 69. Macho Callahan 71. Mousey (TV) 73. The Wild Duck 76, etc.

Secombe, Sir Harry (1921–).
Burly Welsh comedian and singer, who apart from a number of second-feature appearances in the early 50s has filmed only rarely.

Davy 57. Jet Storm 59. *Oliver!* 68. Song of Norway 70. The Magnificent Seven Deadly Sins 71. Sunstruck 73, etc.

second unit director.
One who directs not the actors but the spectacular location sequences, stunt men, scenic backgrounds, etc., and is thus sometimes responsible for a film's most striking effects; e.g. Andrew Marton's (and Yakima Canutt's) chariot race sequence in *Ben Hur* 59.

Sedgwick, Edie (1943–1971).
American socialite who was briefly a star in Andy Warhol's movies.
Biography: 1982, *Edie, an American Biography* by Jean Stein.
Vinyl 65. Poor Little Rich Girl 65. Kitchen 65. Beauty #2 65. Bitch 65. Death of Lupe Velez 65, etc.

¶ She was the personification of the poor little rich girl – *Gerard Malanga*
She was a wonderful, beautiful blank. – *Andy Warhol*

Sedgwick, Edward (1893–1953).
American director of mainly routine films.
Live Wires 21. The First Degree 23. Two Fisted Jones 25. Spring Fever 27. *The Cameraman* 28. The Passionate Plumber 32. I'll Tell the World 34. Pick a Star 37. Beware Spooks 39. Ma and Pa Kettle Back on the Farm 50, many others.

Seeley, Blossom (1892–1974).
American nightclub entertainer, married to Benny Fields. Played by Betty Hutton in *Somebody Loves Me* 52.

■ Broadway Through a Keyhole 33.

Segal, Alex (1915–1977).
American director, from TV.
■ Ransom 56. All the Way Home 63. Joy in the Morning 65. Harlow (electronovision) 66. My Father's House (TV) 73. The Story of David (TV) (co-d) 76.

Segal, Erich (1937–).
American university professor who unexpectedly wrote a best-selling sentimental novelette, *Love Story*, which was filmed with equal success.
■ Yellow Submarine 68. RPM 70. The Games 70. Love Story (AAN) 70. Oliver's Story (co-w) 78. A Change of Seasons (co-w) 80. Man, Woman and Child (co-w) 83.

Segal, George (1934–).
Leading American actor more at home with thought than with action, which may account for a somewhat fitful career.
■ The Young Doctors 61. The Longest Day 62. Act One 62. The New Interns 64. Invitation to a Gunfighter 64. Ship of Fools 65. *King Rat* 65. Lost Command 65. Who's Afraid of Virginia Woolf? (AAN) 66. The Quiller Memorandum 66. The St Valentine's Day Massacre 67. Bye Bye Braverman 68. No Way to Treat a Lady 68. The Southern Star 69. The Girl who Couldn't Say No 69. The Bridge at Remagen 69. Loving 70. *The Owl and the Pussycat* 70. Where's Poppa? 70. Born to Win 72. The Hot Rock 72. Blume in Love 73. *A Touch of Class* 73. The Terminal Man 74. California Split 75. The Black Bird 75. Russian Roulette 76. The Duchess and the Dirtwater Fox 76. Rollercoaster 77. Fun with Dick and Jane 77. Who is Killing the Great Chefs of Europe? 78. Lost and Found 79. The Last Married Couple in America 80. Carbon Copy 81. The Cold Room 81. Stick 82. Killing 'em Softly 83. The Zany Adventures of Robin Hood (TV) 84. All's Fair 89. Look Who's Talking 89. For the Boys 91. Direct Hit 93. Seasons of the Heart (TV) 94.
TV series: Take Five 87.

¶ I have a dread of being considered bland, but I've had to reconcile myself to the fact that that's what I am. – *G.S.*

Segal, Vivienne (1897–1992).
American Broadway star of the early talkie period.
■ Song of the West 30. Golden Dawn 30. Bride of the Regiment 30. Viennese Nights 30. The Cat and the Fiddle 33.

Segal, Harry (1897–1975).
American writer who started the heavenly fantasies of the 40s with his play *Halfway to Heaven*.
Fatal Lady 36. Here Comes Mr Jordan (AA) 41. Angel on My Shoulder 46. For Heaven's Sake 50. Monkey Business 52, etc.

Seiber, Matyas (1905–1960).
Hungarian composer in London.
Animal Farm 54. The Diamond Wizard 54. A Town Like Alice 56. Chase a Crooked Shadow 58. Robbery Under Arms 58. For Better for Worse 61.

Seidelman, Susan (1952–).
American director.
■ Smithereens 82. Desperately Seeking Susan 84. Making Mr Right 87. Cookie 89. She-Devil 90. Erotic Tales (co-d) 94.

Seigner, Emmanuelle (1967–).
French leading actress. She is the daughter of actress Françoise Seigner and granddaughter of actor Louis Seigner. Married director Roman Polanski.
Detective 85. Frantic 88. Bitter Moon 92. The Smile (Le Sourire) 94, etc.

Seiler, Lewis (1891–1963).
American director. Many Tom Mix silents; then *Air Circus* (co-d) 28, and second features through the 30s.
Dust Be My Destiny 39. It All Came True 40. South of Suez 41. The Big Shot 42. Guadalcanal Diary 43. Molly and Me 44. If I'm Lucky 46. Whiplash 48. The Tanks are Coming 51. The Winning Team 52. The System 53. Women's Prison 55. Battle Stations 56. The True Story of Lynn Stuart 58, many others.

Seiter, William A. (1891–1964).
American director, in Hollywood from 1918, then directing shorts.
Boy Crazy 22. The Teaser 25. Skinner's Dress Suit 26. Good Morning Judge 28. The Love Racket 30. Girl Crazy 32. If I Had a Million (part) 33. Diplomaniacs 33. Professional Sweetheart 33. Sons of the Desert 33. Roberta 35. *The Moon's Our Home* 36. Dimples 36. *This is My Affair* 37. *Room Service* 38. It's a Date 40. *Broadway* 42. You Were Never Lovelier 42. Destroyer 43. *The Affairs of Susan* 45. I'll Be Yours 47. One Touch of Venus 48. Dear Brat 51. Make Haste to Live 54, many others.

Seitz, George B. (1888–1944).
American director, known as the serial king. A writer-director from 1913, he worked on *The Perils of Pauline*, and directed *The Fatal Ring* 17 and all subsequent Pearl White serials. In the 20s, he acted in his own serials: *Velvet Fingers*, *The Sky Ranger*, etc. Turning to features, he directed nearly forty between 1927 and 1933, then moved to MGM and kept up an even more rapid output, including episodes of the Hardy Family series.
The Woman in His Life 35. Andy Hardy Meets a Debutante 39. Kit Carson 40. Sky Murder 40. Andy Hardy's Private Secretary 41. China Caravan 42, etc.

Seitz, John F. (1893–1979).
American cinematographer, in Hollywood from 1916.
SILENT FILMS: *The Four Horsemen of the Apocalypse* 21. *The Prisoner of Zenda* 22, etc.
SOUND FILMS: East Lynne 30. Over the Hill 30. She Wanted a Millionaire 32. Huckleberry Finn 39. *Sullivan's Travels* 41. The Moon and Sixpence 42. This Gun for Hire 42. The Miracle of Morgan's Creek 43. Hail the Conquering Hero 44. *Double Indemnity* 44. *The Lost Weekend* 45. *Sunset Boulevard* 50. The San Francisco Story 52. Hell on Frisco Bay 55. The Man in the Net 58. Guns of the Timberland 60, etc.

Sekely, Steve (1899–1979) (Istvan Szekely).
Hungarian director, in Hollywood from 1938.
Rhapsodie der Liebe 29. Lila Akac 34. Miracle on Main Street 40. Behind Prison Walls 43. Women in Bondage 44. The Scar 48. Stronghold 51. The Blue Camellia 54. The Day of the Triffids 68. Kenner 69. The Girl Who Liked Purple Flowers 73, etc.

Sekka, Johnny (1939–).
West African actor in London.
Flame in the Streets 61. Woman of Straw 64. Khartoum 65. The Last Safari 67. A Warm December 73. Uptown Saturday Night 75. Charlie Chan and the Curse of the Dragon Queen 81. Hanky Panky 82, etc.

Selander, Lesley (1900–1979).
American director who made low-budget westerns and other action pictures from 1936.

Cattle Pass 37. The Round-Up 41. The Vampire's Ghost 46. Belle Starr's Daughter 48. I Was an American Spy 51. Flight to Mars 51. The Highwayman 52. Tall Man Riding 54. The Lone Ranger and the Lost City of Gold 58. Town Tamer 65. Fort Utah 67, many others.

Selig, William N. (1864–1948).
Pioneer American producer; many serials.

The Count of Monte Cristo 08. The Spoilers 13, etc.

Sellars, Elizabeth (1923–).
British leading actress on stage from 1941.

Floodtide (debut) 48. Madeleine 50. Cloudburst 51. The Gentle Gunman 52. The Barefoot Contessa 54. Three Cases of Murder 55. The Shiralee 57. The Day They Robbed the Bank of England 61. The Chalk Garden 64. The Mummy's Shroud 67. The Hireling 73, etc.

Selleck, Tom (1945–).
Charismatic American leading man of the 80s, who after much TV experience might just take on the mantle of Gable.

The Movie Murderer (TV) 69. Myra Breckinridge 70. The Seven Minutes 71. Daughters of Satan 72. Terminal Island 73. Returning Home (TV) 75. Most Wanted (TV) 76. Coma 77. The Sacketts (TV) 79. High Road to China 83. Lassiter 84. Three Men and a Baby 87. Her Alibi 88. An Innocent Man 89. Quigley Down Under 90. Folks! 92. Christopher Columbus: The Discovery 92. Mr Baseball 92, etc.

TV series: Most Wanted 76. *Magnum* 80–88.

Sellers, Peter (1925–1980).
British comic actor who became an international star, then faltered. From variety stage and radio's *Goon Show*. His second wife was actress Britt Ekland (1964–68) and in 1977 he married his fourth wife, actress Lynne Frederick.

Biographies: 1969, *Peter Sellers, the Man behind the Mask* by Peter Evans. 1994, *The Life and Death of Peter Sellers* by Roger Lewis.

Book: 1993, *Peter Sellers – A Film History* by Michael Starr.

■ Penny Points to Paradise 51. Down Among the Z Men 52. Orders Are Orders 54. John and Julie 55. The Lady Killers 55. *The Smallest Show on Earth* 57. *The Naked Truth* 58. Tom Thumb 58. Up the Creek 58. Carlton-Browne of the F.O. 58. *The Mouse That Roared* 59. *I'm All Right, Jack* 59. The Battle of the Sexes 60. Two-Way Stretch 60. Never Let Go 61. The Millionairess 61. Mr Topaze (& d) 61. The Road to Hong Kong (cameo) 61. *Only Two Can Play* 62. Lolita 62. Waltz of the Toreadors 62. The Dock Brief 63. Heavens Above 63. The Wrong Arm of the Law 63. *The Pink Panther* 63. *Dr Strangelove* (AAN) 63. The World of Henry Orient 64. A Shot in the Dark 64. What's New, Pussycat? 65. The Wrong Box 66. After the Fox 66. Casino Royale 67. The Bobo 67. Woman Times Seven 67. The Party 68. *I Love You Alice B. Toklas* 68. The Magic Christian 69. Hoffman 70. There's a Girl in My Soup 70. Where Does it Hurt? 72. Alice's Adventures in Wonderland (as the March Hare) 72. The Optimists of Nine Elms 72. Soft Beds and Hard Battles 73. Ghost in the Noonday Sun 73. The Blockhouse 74. The Great McGonagall (as Queen Victoria) 74. The Return of the Pink Panther 75. Murder by Death 76. The Pink Panther Strikes Again 77. Revenge of the Pink Panther 78. The Prisoner of Zenda 79. Being There (AAN) 79. The Fiendish Plot of Dr Fu Manchu 79.

¶ There used to be a me behind the mask, but I had it surgically removed. – *P.S.*

If you ask me to play myself, I will not know what to do. I do not know who or what I am. – *P.S.*

People will swim through shit if you put a few bob in it. – *P.S.*

The only way to make a film with him is to let him direct, write and produce it as well as star in it. – *Charles Feldman*

Sellers is such an experienced impersonator that one regrets his inability to add to his list of impressions the Peter Sellers that was. – *John Simon of The World of Henry Orient*

I would squirm with embarrassment at the demeaning lengths he would go to in order to ingratiate himself with the Royal Family. – *Britt Ekland*

~In 1982 offcuts from earlier Panther films were assembled to make a tasteless sequel, *The Trail of the Pink Panther.*

Selten, Morton (1860–1939) (Morton Stubbs).
British stage actor who played distinguished old gentlemen in some 30s films.

Service for Ladies 32. Ten Minute Alibi 35. The Ghost Goes West 36. Fire over England 36. A Yank at Oxford 38. The Divorce of Lady X 38. The Thief of Bagdad 40, etc.

Seltzer, David (1940–).
American screenwriter who turned to directing in the mid-80s.

The Hellstrom Chronicle 71. King, Queen, Knave (co-w) 72. One Is a Lonely Number (w) 72. The Other Side of the Mountain (w) 75. The Omen (w) 76. Prophecy (w) 79. Table for Five (w) 83. Six Weeks (w) 85. Lucas (wd) 86. Punchline (wd) 88. Bird on a Wire (co-w, d) 90. Shining Through (wd) 92, etc.

Seltzer, Walter (1914–).
American producer.

One Eyed Jacks 58. The Naked Edge 61. The War Lord 65. Will Penny 67. Darker than Amber 70. Skyjacked 72, etc.

Selwyn, Edgar (1875–1944).
American director.

Night Life of New York 25. The Girl in the Show 29. War Nurse 30. The Sin of Madelon Claudet 31. Turn Back the Clock 33. The Mystery of Mr X 34. Pierre of the Plains (w, p only) 42, etc.

Selznick, David O. (1902–1965).
American independent producer, former writer. Worked for RKO from 1931, MGM from 1933; founded Selznick International Pictures in 1936.

Biographies: 1970, *Selznick* by Bob Thomas. 1972, *Memo from David O. Selznick*. 1993, *Showman: The Life of David Selznick* by David Thomson.

■ Roulette 24. Spoilers of the West 27. Wyoming 28. Forgotten Faces 28. Chinatown Nights 29. The Man I Love 29. The Four Feathers 29. The Dance of Life 29. Fast Company 29. Street of Chance 30. Sarah and Son 30. Honey 30. The Texan 30. For the Defense 30. Manslaughter 30. The Lost Squadron 32. Symphony of Six Million 32. State's Attorney 32. Westward Passage 32. What Price Hollywood? 32. Roar of the Dragon 32. Bird of Paradise 32. The Age of Consent 32. A Bill of Divorcement 32. The Conquerors 32. Rockabye 32. The Animal Kingdom 32. The Half Naked Truth 32. Topaze 33. The Great Jasper 33. Our Betters 33. Christopher Strong 33. Sweepings 33. The Monkey's Paw 33. *Dinner at Eight* 33. Night Flight 33. Meet the Baron 33. Dancing Lady 33. Viva Villa 34. Manhattan Melodrama 34. *David Copperfield* 35.

Vanessa 35. Reckless 35. Anna Karenina 35. *A Tale of Two Cities* 35. Little Lord Fauntleroy 36. The Garden of Allah 36. *A Star Is Born* 37. *The Prisoner of Zenda* 37. Nothing Sacred 37. The Adventures of Tom Sawyer 38. The Young in Heart 38. Made for Each Other 39. Intermezzo 39. *Gone with the Wind* (AA) 39. *Rebecca* (AA) 40. Since You Went Away 44. I'll Be Seeing You 44. Spellbound 45. Duel in the Sun 46. The Paradine Case 48. Portrait of Jennie 48. *The Third Man* (co-p) 50. The Wild Heart (co-p) 52. Indiscretion of an American Wife (co-p) 54. A Farewell to Arms 57.

✪ For his integrity; for his memos; and for being a Hollywood monument. *Gone with the Wind.*

¶ Selznick was the mogul who gave up at his peak. He said in retirement:

Very few people have mastered the art of enjoying their wealth. I have mastered the art, and therefore I spend my time enjoying myself.

This was not unexpected behaviour from the man who once said:

I don't want to be normal. Who wants to be normal?

Yet his own memorable utterances were few, and on the sad side. He said of Hollywood:

Once photographed, life here is ended.

And of the house which is so central to *Gone with the Wind:*

It's somehow symbolic of Hollywood that Tara was just a façade, with no rooms inside.

An unhumorous man, intense and thorough to a fault, he was a hard taskmaster. Nunnally Johnson demurred at working for him:

I understand that an assignment with you consists of three months' work and six months' recuperation.

His creative impulse surged through his internal memos, the length of which was legendary. Alfred Hitchcock said in 1965:

When I came to America twenty-five years ago to direct *Rebecca*, David Selznick sent me a memo. (Pause.) I've just finished reading it. (Pause.) I think I may turn it into a motion picture. (Pause.) I plan to call it *The Longest Story Ever Told.*

One memo which has been quoted was to director Charles Vidor, following one of protest from him:

I don't believe I've ever used such terms with you as idiotic. I may have *thought* your excessive takes and angles were idiotic, but the most I've said was that they were a waste of my personal money.

He certainly interfered:

The way I see it, my function is to be responsible for everything.

And:

The difference between me and other producers is that I am interested in the thousands and thousands of details that go into the making of a film. It is the sum total of all these things that either makes a great picture or destroys it.

And, of the making of *A Farewell To Arms:*

In Mr Huston I asked for a first violinist and got a soloist. When I am the producer, I must produce.

His final claim was to have found a balance between God and Mammon:

I have never gone after honours instead of dollars. But I have understood the relationship between the two.

A typical Hollywood combination of oafishness and sophistication. – *John Houseman*

He wouldn't hire a secretary who could do less than 200 words per minute dictation. Otherwise it would have interrupted his train of thought. – *Irene Mayer Selznick*

The trouble with you, David, is that you did all your reading before you were twelve. – *Ben Hecht*

Selznick, Lewis J. (1870–1933) (Lewis Zeleznik). Russian-American distributor and impresario, bankrupted in 1923.

Selznick, Myron (1898–1944). American producer and agent, brother of David Selznick and son of Lewis.

Sembene, Ousmane (1923–). Senegalese director, screenwriter and novelist. A former docker working in France, he studied film in Moscow.

Black Girl (La Noire) 66. The Money Order (Mandabi) 68. Emitai 71. Xala 74. Ceddo 76. Camp de Thiaroye (co-d) 88, etc.

Semler, Dean. Australian cinematographer who moved to Hollywood in the late 80s and returned home to direct his first feature.

Let the Balloon Go 76. Stepping Out 80. Hoodwink 81. Mad Max (aka The Road Warrior) 81. Kitty and the Bagman 82. In Memory of Malawan 83. Razorback 84. Undercover 84. The Coca-Cola Kid 85. Mad Max 2: Beyond Thunderdrome 85. Bullseye 86. Going Sane 86. The Lighthorsemen 87. Cocktail 88. Young Guns 88. Dead Calm 89. Farewell to the King 89. K-9 89. Dances with Wolves (AA) 90. Impulse 90. Young Guns II 90. City Slickers 91. The Power of One 91. The Kangaroo Kid (d) 92. Super Mario Bros 93. The Three Musketeers 93. Last Action Hero 93, etc.

Semon, Larry (1889–1928). American silent slapstick comedian, popular in innumerable two-reelers of the 20s; also some features.

The Simple Life 18. The Wizard of Oz 24. The Sawmill 25. Spuds 27, etc.

Semple, Lorenzo, Jnr. American screenwriter.

Batman 56. Daddy's Gone a-Hunting 59. Pretty Poison 68. Marriage of a Young Stockbroker 71. The Sporting Club 71. Papillon (co-w) 73. The Parallax View 74. The Drowning Pool (co-w) 75. Three Days of the Condor (co-w) 75. King Kong 76. Hurricane 79. Flash Gordon 80. Never Say Never Again 83. Sheena (co-w) 84. Never Too Young to Die (co-w) 86, etc.

Sen, Mrinal (1923–). Indian director and screenwriter of Marxist inclinations.

The Dawn 56. Under a Blue Sky 59. The Representative 64. Mr Shome 69. Interview 72. Calcutta 71 72. The Guerilla Fighter 73. The Royal Hunt 76. The Outsiders 77. And Quiet Rolls the Dawn 79. The Case Is Closed 81. Portrait of a New Man 84. Genesis 86. Suddenly, One Day 89. World Within, World Without (Mahaprithivi) 91, etc.

Sena, Dominic. American director and screenwriter, a former cinematographer and director specializing in music videos and commercials.

Kalifornia 93.

Sennett, Mack (1880–1960) (Michael Sinnott). Canadian-born 'king of comedy' who in the 20s produced countless slapstick shorts featuring the Keystone Kops, Chester Conklin, Louise Fazenda, Charlie Chaplin, Mack Swain, Billy West, Fred Mace, Heinie Conklin, Slim Summerville and others. By the time sound came, Sennett had exhausted all the possible tricks of his 'fun factory'

and found the new methods not to his taste. His output waned almost to nothing, but he was given a special Academy Award in 1937: 'For his lasting contribution to the comedy technique of the screen . . . the Academy presents a Special Award to that master of fun, discoverer of stars, sympathetic, kindly, understanding genius – Mack Sennett.'

Biography: 1955, *King of Comedy*.

¶ As befits the king of slapstick comedy, he was a thoughtful man.

The joke of life is the fall of dignity, he once said. And his analysis of custard-pie-throwing was perfectly expressed:

Non-anticipation on the part of the recipient of the pastry is the chief ingredient of the recipe.

He disclaimed originality:

Anyone who tells you he has invented something new is a fool or a liar or both.

He was firm in matters of taste:

We never make fun of religion, politics, race or mothers. A mother never gets hit with a custard pie. Mothers-in-law, yes. But mothers, never!

He summed up his comedy technique very simply:

It's got to move!

And he later admitted:

I called myself king of comedy, but I was a harassed monarch. I worked most of the time. It was only in the evenings that I laughed.

Sensurround. A system evolved in 1975 for *Earthquake*, this dispensable gimmick involved the augmentation of violent action on screen by intense waves of high decibel sound, enough almost to crack the ribs. It never caught on except as a big city come-on.

sequence: a film paragraph, usually starting and ending with a fade to black.

Sequence. Cinema magazine of the Oxford University Film Society, which flourished briefly in the mid-40s and early 50s. Its leading lights included Lindsay Anderson, Penelope Houston, Gavin Lambert, and Karel Reisz. Many of its aesthetic ideas influenced Free Cinema (qv), which involved many of the same participants.

¶ It's no exaggeration to say that the *Sequence* group changed the whole way of feeling and thinking about film in England – at any rate for a few inspiring years, before the British sank once again into complacency and philistinism. – *Tony Richardson*

Serato, Massimo (1917–1989) (Giuseppe Segato). Italian leading man, usually seen in swashbucklers.

Man of the Sea 41. Outcry 46. La Traviata 47. Sunday in August 49. The Thief of Venice 49. Shadow of the Eagle 50. Lucretia Borgia 53. The Man from Cairo 53. Madame Du Barry 54. The Naked Maja 59. David and Goliath 60. Constantine and the Cross 61. El Cid 61. 55 Days at Peking 63. The Tenth Victim 65. Wild Wild Planet 66. Camille 2000 69. Don't Look Now 73, etc.

Seresin, Michael. New Zealand cinematographer, based in Britain and especially associated with the films of director Alan Parker.

The Ragman's Daughter 72. Bugsy Malone 76. Sleeping Dogs 77. Midnight Express 78. Fame 80.

Shoot the Moon 81. Birdy 84. Angel Heart 87. Homeboy (d) 88. Come See the Paradise 90, etc.

Seria, Joel (1944–). French director.

Charlie et ses Deux Nénettes 73. Les Galettes du Pont-Aven 75. Marie-Poupée 76. Comme la Lune 77, etc.

serial killers. Mass murderers have long held a fascination for film-makers and audiences alike, as is demonstrated by Charlie Chaplin's *Monsieur Verdoux* 47, and the many *Bluebeard* films from the 40s onwards, based on the activities of the French murderer Henri Landru (qv), and such comedies as *Kind Hearts and Coronets* 49 and *No Way to Treat a Lady* 68. But a specific genre emerged after the term serial killer was coined by the FBI in the 60s and following the success of Alfred Hitchcock's *Psycho*, from Robert Bloch's novel based on Ed Gein (qv). A succession of slasher movies ensued featuring fictional murderers, including *Halloween* and its successors, and two long-drawn-out series featuring killers returning from the dead: Jason in *Friday the Thirteenth* (eight films so far) and Freddy in *Nightmare on Elm Street*. Terrence Malick's *Badlands*, based on teenagers Charley Starkweather and Caril Fugate's killing spree which left 10 dead, was followed by a series of murderous road movies which includes *True Romance* 93, *Kalifornia* 93, and *Natural Born Killers* 94. The latter two made much of public fascination with serial killers, as did John McNaughton's chilling *Henry: Portrait of a Serial Killer* and the Belgian film *Man Bites Dog* 92, in which a film crew begin to record a murderer at work and end by helping him with his crimes. Certainly Thomas Harris's fictional creation, the cannibalistic Hannibal Lecter, has become a favourite ogre following the performances of Brian Cox in *Manhunter* 86 and Anthony Hopkins in *The Silence of the Lambs* 90. Real-life serial killers on film include the Boston Strangler, Peter Kurten (*M* and *The Vampire of Dusseldorf*), and Fritz Hartmann (*The Tenderness of Wolves*).

¶ The serial killer has become our debased, condemned, yet eerily glorified Noble Savage, the vestiges of the frontier spirit. – *Joyce Carol Oates*

serials demand a book to themselves. They began in the early years of the century and continued until the early 50s, their plethora of adventurous and melodramatic incident being usually divided into fifteen or twenty chapters of about twenty minutes each. They were the domain of mad doctors, space explorers, clutching hands, mysterious strangers, diabolical villains and dewy-eyed heroines. Each chapter ended with a 'cliffhanger' in which the hero or heroine was left in some deadly danger from which it was plain he could not escape; but at the beginning of the next chapter, escape he did. A few favourite serials are *Fantomas*, *The Perils of Pauline*, *Batman*, *Flash Gordon's Trip to Mars* and *Captain Marvel*. Almost all of them were American. They were finally killed by the advent of TV and by the increasing length of the double-feature programme.

Books on the subject include *To Be Continued* by Weiss and Goodgold; *Days of Thrills and Adventure* by Alan Barbour; and *The Great Movie Serials* by Harmon and Glut.

series of feature films used to be popular enough, and many are individually noted in this book; in recent years the series concept has been taken over by TV, and in any case low-budget movies featuring cut-to-pattern characters could no longer be made to pay their way in theatres. When one looks back over these old heroes, who flourished chiefly in the 30s and 40s, most of them turn out to be sleuths of one kind or another. They included *Sherlock Holmes, The Saint, The Lone Wolf, Father Brown, Nero Wolfe, Duncan McLain, The Crime Doctor, Sexton Blake, Mr Moto, Perry Mason, Bulldog Drummond, Nancy Drew, Mr Wong, Charlie Chan, Ellery Queen, Boston Blackie, The Falcon, Hildegarde Withers, Hercule Poirot, Dick Tracy, Torchy Blane, Michael Shayne, Philip Marlowe* and, more recently, *Inspector Clouseau, Tony Rome, Virgil Tibbs, Coffin Ed Johnson* and *Shaft.* Nor should one forget crime anthologies like *Inner Sanctum* and *The Whistler.* The spy vogue, a recent happening, is naturally headed by *James Bond:* in his wake you may discern *Counterspy, Coplan, Flint, The Tiger, The Man from UNCLE, Harry Palmer,* and *Superdragon.* Among the more muscular outdoor heroes may be counted *Hopalong Cassidy, The Three Mesquiteers, The Lone Ranger, Captain Blood, Zorro, Robin Hood, Tarzan, Jungle Jim, The Cisco Kid, Bomba, The Man with No Name* and the Italian giants who go under such names as *Maciste, Goliath, Hercules* and *Ursus.* The longest surviving series villain is certainly *Fu Manchu.* As for monsters, take your pick from *Frankenstein, Dracula, The Mummy, The Creature from the Black Lagoon, The Invisible Man, The Wolf Man, Dr X;* while if you prefer comedy freaks there are *Topper* and *Francis.* There have been a goodly number of domestic comedies and dramas, including *Squibs, The Jones Family, The Hardy Family, The Cohens and the Kellys, Blondie, Ma and Pa Kettle, Maisie, Henry Aldrich, Scattergood Baines, Lum and Abner, Jeeves, Mr Belvedere, Gidget* and the *Four Daughters* saga. Other comedy series have ranged from the subtleties of *Don Camillo* to the pratfalls of *Old Mother Riley, Mexican Spitfire,* the *Doctor* series, *Carry On* films, the *Police Academy* series, and the *Naked Gun* movies. Animals have had series to themselves, as for instance *Rin Tin Tin, Flicka, Lassie, Rusty* and *Flipper.* So have children of various ages: *Our Gang, Gasoline Alley, The Dead End Kids, The East Side Kids, The Bowery Boys.* The best-established musical series were *Broadway Melody* and *The Big Broadcast.* And three cheers for *Dr Kildare, Dr Christian, Dr Mabuse* and *Dr Goldfoot . . .* to say nothing of Professor *Quatermass.*

Serious, Yahoo (1954–   ) (Greg Pead).
Australian comic actor, screenwriter and director.
   Young Einstein 88. Reckless Kelly (a, p, wd) 93.

Serling, Rod (1924–1975).
American TV playwright who contributed scores of scripts to such series as *Twilight Zone* and *Night Gallery* (which he also introduced).
   Patterns of Power 56. Saddle the Wind 58. Requiem for a Heavyweight (Blood Money) 63. Yellow Canary 63. *Seven Days in May* 64. Assault on a Queen 66. *Planet of the Apes* 67, etc.

Serna, Assumpta.
Spanish leading actress, in international films.
   Matador 86. I, the Worst of All (Arg.) 90. Wild Orchid (US) 90. Revolver (US) (TV) 92. Sharpe's Rifles (GB) (TV) 93. Sharpe's Eagle (GB) (TV) 93. Nostradamus (US) 93. Havanera 93. Green Henry (Der Grun Heinrich) (Sw.) 94. Shortcut to Paradise (Sp.) 94. Sharpe's Company (GB) (TV) 94. Nostradamus (GB/Ger) 94, etc.

Sernas, Jacques (1925–   ).
Lithuanian-born leading man, in international films.
   The Golden Salamander (GB) 50. Jump into Hell (US) 55. Helen of Troy (US/It.) 55. Maddalena (Fr.) 56. The Sign of the Gladiator (It.) 60. Son of Spartacus (It.) 62. Goliath against the Vampires 67. Hornet's Nest 70, etc.

Serrault, Michel (1928–   ).
French leading actor who gained his greatest success playing a female impersonator in *La Cage aux Folles* and its sequels.
   Diabolique (Les Diaboliques) 55. Lovers and Thieves (Assassins et Voleurs) 56. King of Hearts (Le Roi de Coeur) 66. Le Viager 72. Les Gaspards 73. Holes 77. Get Out Your Handkerchiefs (Préparez Vos Mouchoirs) 78. La Cage aux Folles 78. Cold Cuts (Buffet Froid) 79. La Cage aux Folles II 80. Malevil 81. La Cage aux Folles III: The Wedding 86. En Tout Innocence 88. Comédie d'Amour 89. Merry Christmas, Happy New Year (Buon Natale, Buon Anno) 89. Docteur Petiot 90. La Vieille qui Marchait dans la Mer 91. City for Sale (Ville à Vendre) 91. Haute Époque 94, etc.

Serreau, Coline (1947–   ).
French director and screenwriter, a former actress, whose *Trois Hommes et un Couffin* was remade by Hollywood as the box-office hit *Three Men and a Baby.*
   Why Not? (Pourquoi Pas!) (wd) 77. Three Men and a Cradle (Trois Hommes et un Couffin) (wd) 85. Romuald et Juliette (wd) 89. La Crise 92, etc.

Sersen, Fred (1890–1962).
American special-effects photographer, long with Fox, for whom he produced such spectacles as the fire in *In Old Chicago,* the storm in *The Rains Came,* and the canal-building in *Suez.*

Servais, Jean (1910–1976).
French character actor with stage experience.
   Criminel 31. La Valse Eternelle 36. La Danse de Mort 47. Une Si Jolie Petite Plage 48. Le Plaisir 51. *Rififi* 55. Les Jeux Dangereux 58. That Man from Rio 64. Lost Command 66. They Came to Rob Las Vegas 69, etc.

servants
in movies have provided great pleasure, mainly because the vast majority of the audience has been unlikely to encounter the breed in person. Actors who spent their lives playing stately butlers include Eric Blore, Charles Coleman, Robert Greig, Barnett Parker, Halliwell Hobbes and Arthur Treacher. Louise Beavers and Hattie McDaniel were the leading coloured maids, and many black comedians played frightened valets: Mantan Moreland, Stepin Fetchit, Willie Best. Sinister housekeepers are led by Gale Sondergaard and Judith Anderson. Even more eccentric servants were played by Edward Rigby in *Don't Take it to Heart,* Cantinflas in *Around the World in Eighty Days,* Seymour Hicks in *Busman's Honeymoon,* Edward Brophy in the Falcon series; and downright villainous ones by Dirk Bogarde in *The Servant,* Philip Latham in *Dracula Prince of Darkness,* Boris Karloff in *The Old Dark House* and Bela Lugosi in *The Body Snatcher.* Romantic comedies in which servants have had liaisons with their masters (or mistresses) include *History is Made at Night, When Tomorrow Comes, Common Clay, What Price Hollywood?, The Farmer's Daughter, If You Could Only Cook, Lord Richard in the Pantry* and *Upstairs Downstairs;* while 30s comedies in which Russian exiles and new poor took jobs as servants are exemplified by *Tovarich* and *My Man Godfrey.* One should not forget *The Admirable Crichton* in any of his forms; but other servants less admirable were James Mason in *Five Fingers,* and Glenda Jackson and Susannah York in *The Maids.* Anthony Hopkins

in *The Remains of the Day* was a butler whose loyalty to his master is his undoing.

Sessions, Almira (1888–1974).
American character actress, often seen in fluttery or eccentric bit parts.
   Little Nellie Kelly 41. The Diary of a Chambermaid 46. The Fountainhead 49. The Boston Strangler 67. Rosemary's Baby 69. Everything You Always Wanted to Know about Sex 72, many others.

Seth, Roshan (1942–   ).
Indian character actor, from the British stage.
   Juggernaut 74. Gandhi 82. Indiana Jones and the Temple of Doom 84. A Passage to India 84. My Beautiful Laundrette 85. Little Dorrit 87. 1871 89. Mountains of the Moon 89. Not without My Daughter 90. Mississippi Masala 91. London Kills Me 91. The Buddha of Suburbia (TV) 93, etc.

Seton, Sir Bruce (1909–1969).
British leading man, later character actor; military background.
   Blue Smoke 34. Sweeney Todd 36. Love from a Stranger 38. The Curse of the Wraydons 46. Bonnie Prince Charlie 48. Whisky Galore 49. John Paul Jones (US) 59, etc.
   TV series: Fabian of the Yard 54.

Seton, Marie (c. 1900–1985).
British journalist who met Eisenstein in Russia in the late 20s, wrote a biography of him, and later produced a version of his Mexican film under the title *Time in the Sun.*

Setton, Maxwell (1909–   ).
British independent producer, former lawyer. Held executive posts for Bryanston and Columbia.
   The Spider and the Fly 50. So Little Time 52. They Who Dare 54. Footsteps in the Fog 55. Town on Trial 56. I Was Monty's Double 58, etc.

Seven Keys to Baldpate.
The famous stage comedy-thriller by Earl Derr Biggers and George M. Cohan has been filmed five times: with Cohan himself in 1917, Douglas MacLean in 1926, Richard Dix in 1929, Gene Raymond in 1935, and Philip Terry in 1947. The most recent version, in 1983, was *House of Long Shadows,* with Christopher Lee and Peter Cushing.

Seventh Heaven.
Austin Strong's play, a simple garret love story set in Paris at the time of World War I, from which the hero returns blinded, was successfully filmed by Frank Borzage, with Janet Gaynor and Charles Farrell; Henry King remade it in 1937 with Simone Simon and James Stewart.

Severance, Joan (1958–   ).
American actress.
   See No Evil, Hear No Evil 89. Worth Winning 89. No Holds Barred 89. Bird on a Wire 90. Almost Pregnant 91. Illicit Behavior 91. Write to Kill 91. The Runestone 92. Lake Consequence (TV) 92. Angel of Desire 94, etc.
   TV series: Wiseguy 88.

Sewell, George (1924–   ).
British character actor of tough roles, familiar on TV in *Special Branch.*
   Sparrows Can't Sing 63. Robbery 67. Get Carter 71. Operation Daybreak 76, etc.
   TV series: UFO 70.

Sewell, Vernon (1903–).
British director, former engineer, photographer, art director and editor.

The Silver Fleet 43. *Latin Quarter* 46. The Ghosts of Berkeley Square 47. Uneasy Terms 48. The Ghost Ship 52. Where There's a Will 55. Battle of the V1 58. House of Mystery 61. Strongroom 62. The Curse of the Crimson Altar 68. Burke and Hare 71, etc.

sewers

have figured in several thrillers, most notably *The Third Man* with its exciting final chase; its sewer complex was recently spoofed in *Carry On Spying*. In 1948 in *He Walked by Night* Richard Basehart played a criminal who invariably escaped through the sewers; and our old friend *The Phantom of the Opera* was similarly skilled, as was Lee Marvin in *Point Blank*. As recently as the British thriller *Invasion* a sewer detour was used; while the Frankenstein monster was saved from the burning windmill by falling through to the sewer, where he was found at the beginning of *Bride of Frankenstein*. As for more serious films, sewers are of course featured in the many versions of *Les Misérables*, while the Polish resistance film *Kanal* takes place entirely – and nauseatingly – in the sewers of Warsaw. Fred MacMurray had a comic sewer escape in *Bon Voyage*, and the giant ants of *Them!* were cornered in the sewers of Los Angeles, while the mutant beast of *Alligator* and *Alligator II* emerged from the sewers and the pizza-loving *Teenage Mutant Ninja Turtles* lived in them.

sex.

This was once called 'romance': the beginnings of corruption set in with de Mille's silent comedies such as *Why Change Your Wife?* and Lubitsch's classics *Forbidden Paradise* and *The Marriage Circle*. These gentlemen carried their sophistication into the early sound period, assisted by such stars as Valentino, Harlow, Dietrich, Clara Bow and Ginger Rogers; and there was considerable help from a film called *The Private Life of Henry VIII*, a lady named Mae West and a director named Josef Von Sternberg; but around 1934 the Hays Code and the Legion of Decency forced innocence upon Hollywood to such an extent that the smart hero and heroine of 1934's *It Happened One Night* just wouldn't dream of sharing a bedroom without a curtain between them. The later 30s, perforce, were the heyday of the boy-next-door and the *ingénue*: nice people all, personified by such stars as Gary Cooper, Dick Powell, Ray Milland, David Niven, Ruby Keeler, Janet Gaynor, Deanna Durbin and Irene Dunne. Meanwhile a strong rearguard action was being fought by actors like William Powell, Myrna Loy, Melvyn Douglas, Ann Sheridan and Cary Grant, but usually the blue pencil had been wielded so heavily on their scripts that it was difficult to tell what was really being implied. The best way out was found in such comedies as *The Philadelphia Story*, which were basically earthy but gave every appearance of keeping it all in the mind. The war years produced a certain slackening of restrictions; for instance, the pin-up girl became not only permissible but desirable as a way of building up military morale. Preston Sturges brought sex out into the open in *The Palm Beach Story* and *The Miracle of Morgan's Creek*; Spencer Tracy and Katharine Hepburn started (in *Woman of the Year*) a series of films portraying the battle of the sexes in a recognizably human way. The 'love goddesses' became progressively more blatant in their appeal: Jane Russell, Marilyn Monroe, Jayne Mansfield. (But in the 50s it turned out that one of the earthiest of them, Sophia Loren, was also the best actress.) By now the production code had been broken down

to the extent of permitting words like 'virgin' and 'mistress'(*The Moon is Blue*), the recognition of adultery and prostitution as human facts (*Wives and Lovers, Kiss Me Stupid*), depiction of the lustfulness of males (*Tom Jones, Alfie*), 'realistic' dramas like *Room at the Top*, erotic romances like *Les Amants*, and the presentation, albeit in a fantasy, of girls as 'pleasure units' (*Our Man Flint*). Indeed, after *Georgy Girl, Night Games* and *Who's Afraid of Virginia Woolf?*, it seemed that public frankness could go very little further; but along came *Blow Up, Midnight Cowboy, Satyricon, Flesh, The Music Lovers, Percy, Last Tango in Paris* and *Deep Throat* to prove the opposite. There even emerged an X-rated cartoon *Fritz the Cat;* and by the mid-70s pornographic films on view in most cities outnumbered the other kind.

sex changes

have not been a profitable line of inquiry for the cinema, though the gimmick thriller *Homicidal* depended on one, as did *Myra Breckinridge. The Christine Jorgenson Story* was an account of a genuine case, and *I Want What I Want* presented a fictitious case history. The most amusing film on the subject is certainly *Turnabout*. In Blake Edwards' *Switch*, a male chauvinist is reincarnated as a woman.

Sexton Blake.

The lean, ascetic detective hero of several generations of British boys was the creation of Harry Blyth ('Hal Meredith') (1852–98). On screen he was first portrayed in 1914 in *The Clue of the Wax Vesta*. He was played in the 20s by Langhorne Burton, in the 30s by George Curzon, in the 40s by David Farrar and in the 50s by Geoffrey Toone; while 1962's *Mix Me a Person* was taken from a Blake story but cast Anne Baxter in the role.

Seyler, Athene (1889–1990).
British comedy actress with long stage career dating from 1908.

This Freedom 22. The Perfect Lady 32. The Citadel 38. *Quiet Wedding* 40. *Dear Octopus* 43. Nicholas Nickleby 47. Queen of Spades 48. Young Wives' Tale 51. *Pickwick Papers* 53. Yield to the Night 56. Campbell's Kingdom 58. The Inn of the Sixth Happiness 58. Make Mine Mink 59. Nurse on Wheels 63, many others.

Seymour, Anne (1909–1988) (Anne Ekert).
American character actress.

All the King's Men 49. Man on Fire 57. Home from the Hill 59. The Subterraneans 60. Sunrise at Campobello 60. Mirage 65. Blindfold 66. Never Never Land 81, etc.

TV series: Empire 62.

Seymour, Dan (1915–1993).
Burly American character actor, the scowling menace of countless films.

Casablanca 42. To Have and Have Not 44. Cloak and Dagger 46. Key Largo 48. Rancho Notorious 52. The Big Heat 53. Moonfleet 55. The Sad Sack 57. Watusi 59. Escape to Witch Mountain 75, etc.

Seymour, Jane (1951–) (Joyce Frankenberg).
British leading actress in international films, best known as *Dr Quinn, Medicine Woman* in the TV series. Her third husband is TV director and producer James Keach.

Book: 1993, *Jane Seymour's Guide to Good Loving*.
Oh What a Lovely War 70. Young Winston 72. Live and Let Die 72. Frankenstein: the True Story (TV) 73. The Hanged Man (TV) 74. Sinbad and the Eye of the Tiger 75. Captains and the Kings (TV)

76. Las Vegas Undercover (TV) 77. Seventh Avenue (TV) 77. The Four Feathers (TV) 78. Somewhere in Time 80. *East of Eden* (TV) 81. The Scarlet Pimpernel (TV) 82. Jamaica Inn (TV) 83. The Sun Also Rises (TV) 84. The Dark Mirror (TV) 85. Obsessed with a Married Woman (TV) 85. Crossings (TV) 85. War and Remembrance (TV) 87. Praying Mantis (TV) 93, etc.

Seyrig, Delphine (1932–1990).
French leading actress.

Pull My Daisy 58. *Last Year in Marienbad* 61. Muriel 63. La Musica 66. Accident (GB) 67. Mr Freedom 68. *Stolen Kisses* 68. Daughters of Darkness 70. Peau d'Ane 70. *The Discreet Charm of the Bourgeoisie* 72. The Day of the Jackal 73. The Black Windmill 74. Aloise 75. Caro Michele 77. Faces of Love 77. Le Chemin Perdu 80. Chère Inconnue 80. Golden Eighties 86. Letters Home 86. Joan of Arc of Mongolia 89, etc.

Shabba-Doo (1955–) (Adolfo Quinones).
American actor, dancer, choreographer, and director.

Breakin' 84. Breakin' 2: Electric Boogaloo 84. Lambada 90. Rav'e': Dancing to a Different Beat (ch, d) 93, etc.

Shadyac, Tom.
American director and screenwriter.

Frankenstein: The College Years (TV) 91. Ace Ventura, Pet Detective 94.

Shaffer, Anthony (1926–).
British playwright and screenwriter, twin of Peter Shaffer.

Forbush and the Penguins 71. Sleuth (& oa) 72. Frenzy 73. The Wicker Man 73. Death on the Nile 78. Absolution 78. Evil under the Sun 82. Appointment with Death (co-w) 88, etc.

Shaffer, Peter (1926–).
British playwright, twin of Anthony Shaffer. Works filmed include *Five Finger Exercise, The Private Ear and the Public Eye, The Royal Hunt of the Sun, Equus* (AAN), *Amadeus* (AA) 84.

Shaft.
Ernest Tidyman's tough Harlem private eye was played by Richard Roundtree in three films: Shaft 71; Shaft in Africa 73; and Shaft's Big Score 73.

Shagan, Steve (1927–).
American screenwriter.

Save the Tiger (AAN) 73. Hustle (oa) 75. Voyage of the Damned 76. Nightwing 78. The Formula 80. The Sicilian 87, etc.

Shaiman, Marc.
American composer and arranger.

Big Business 88. Broadcast News (a) 88. When Harry Met Sally 89. Misery 90. Scenes from a Mall 91. City Slickers 91. Hot Shots! (a) 91. The Addams Family 91. Sister Act 92. A Few Good Men 92. Mr Saturday Night 92. Heart and Souls 93. Addams Family Values 93. A Dangerous Woman 94, etc.

Shakespeare, William (1564–1616).
British poet and dramatist whose plays have received plenty of attention from film-makers. *The Taming of the Shrew* was filmed in 1908 by D.W. Griffith; in 1929 with Douglas Fairbanks, Mary Pickford, and the immortal credit line 'additional dialogue by Sam Taylor': in 1953, more or less, as *Kiss Me Kate;* and in 1966 with Elizabeth Taylor, Richard Burton, and script credits to three writers none of whom is Shakespeare. *As You Like It* was filmed in 1912 with Rose Coghlan and Maurice

Costello; the only sound filming was in 1936 by Paul Czinner, with Elisabeth Bergner and Laurence Olivier. *A Midsummer Night's Dream* was tackled in major fashion by Warners in 1935, but the elaborate Max Reinhardt production failed to please at the box office; in 1968 a 'realistic' version by Peter Hall was equally unsuccessful.

Of the tragedies, *Othello* has been frequently attempted, by Emil Jannings in 1922, Orson Welles in 1952, Sergei Bondarchuk in 1955 and Laurence Olivier in 1966; a 1961 British film called *All Night Long* was a modern up-dating of the plot, and Ronald Colman's Academy Award-winning performance in *A Double Life* 47 had him as an actor who starts playing the Moor in private life, as did Sebastian Shaw in *Men Are Not Gods* 36. *Hamlet* was played by Sir Johnston Forbes Robertson in 1913, Asta Nielsen in 1920, Olivier in 1948, and Innokenti Smoktunovsky in 1964. (Note also a 1972 western called *Johnny Hamlet* and a German modern version of 1959 called *The Rest is Silence*.) *Macbeth* is thought to be an unlucky play; but Sir Herbert Beerbohm Tree appeared in a version for Griffith in 1916; Orson Welles directed himself in the role in 1948, Paul Douglas in 1955 was an updated *Joe Macbeth*, in 1960 Maurice Evans appeared in a version originally intended for TV but shown theatrically, and in 1971 Roman Polanski presented a bloodthirsty version with Jon Finch. One should also mention *The Siberian Lady Macbeth*, the Japanese *Throne of Blood*, and a modern version, *Men of Respect*, which turned the protagonists into gangsters. In 1969 *King Lear* was filmed with Paul Scofield; there was a one-reel Vitagraph version in 1909 and Frederic Warde starred in a 1916 production. It formed a background to *The Dresser*, starring Albert Finney as a Shakespearean actor in the manner of Donald Wolfit. Kurosawa's *Ran* was a Japanese version. *Romeo and Juliet* was also made in 1916, starring Francis X. Bushman and Beverly Bayne; this superseded several one-reel versions. In 1936 MGM produced its Leslie Howard/Norma Shearer version directed by George Cukor; in 1954 Renato Castellani directed an unsuccessful colour version with Laurence Harvey and Susan Shentall; in 1961 came the inevitable modernization in *West Side Story;* and 1968 brought another expensive production by Franco Zeffirelli. (There have also been several ballet versions.) There were early potted versions of *Julius Caesar* before the spectacular Italian production of 1914; the play was not filmed again until MGM's excellent 1953 version. The plot was used in a curious British second feature called *An Honourable Murder* 59, with the action moved to a modern executive suite; an all-star version in colour followed in 1970, starring Charlton Heston and finding more action than is normally evident in the play.

Of the histories, most of *Henry IV* has been compressed by Orson Welles into his *Chimes at Midnight, Henry V* was splendidly dealt with by Olivier in 1944 and by Kenneth Branagh in 1989. *Richard III* existed in several primitive versions, and John Barrymore recited a speech from it in *Show of Shows* 28; but again it was left to Olivier to do it properly.

The oddest screen fate of a Shakespeare play was surely that of *The Tempest*, which in 1956 yielded its entire plot to that winning bit of science fiction, *Forbidden Planet*. Derek Jarman turned it into a punk version in 1980, and Peter Greenaway into a literary experience in *Prospero's Books*, with all the roles being spoken by Sir John Gielgud. Paul Mazursky unsuccessfully updated it in *Tempest* 82. Performances of others were put to comedy purpose in *Doubling for Romeo* and *To Be or Not to Be*.

Books: 1971, *Shakespeare and the Film* by Roger Manvell. 1994, *Shakespeare, Cinema and Society* by John Collick. 1994, *Shakespearean Films/Shakespearean Directors* by Peter S. Donaldson.

Shakespeare was impersonated, rather well, by Tim Curry in TV's *Will Shakespeare;* and very badly by Reginald Gardiner in *The Story of Mankind*.

Shakur, Tupac.
American actor and rap performer, known as 2Pac.
Juice 91. Poetic Justice 93. Above the Rim 94, etc.

Shamroy, Leon (1901–1974).
Distinguished American cinematographer.
Catch as Catch Can 27. Out with the Tide 28. The Women Men Marry 31. Jennie Gerhardt 33. Three Cornered Moon 33. Thirty Day Princess 34. Private Worlds 35. Soak the Rich 36. You Only Live Once 37. *The Young In Heart* 38. The Story of Alexander Graham Bell 39. *The Adventures of Sherlock Holmes* 40. Lillian Russel 40. Tin Pan Alley 40. A Yank in the RAF 41. Roxie Hart 42. *Ten Gentlemen from West Point* (AAN) 42. *The Black Swan* (AA) 42. *Stormy Weather* 43. Buffalo Bill 44. *Wilson* (AA) 44. *A Tree Grows in Brooklyn* 45. State Fair 45. *Leave Her to Heaven* (AA) 46. Forever Amber 47. That Lady in Ermine 48. Prince of Foxes (AAN) 49. Twelve O'Clock High 49. Cheaper by the Dozen 50. On the Riviera 51. David and Bathsheba (AAN) 51. The Snows of Kilimanjaro (AAN) 53. Call Me Madam 53. *The Robe* (AAN) 53. The Egyptian (AAN) 54. Love is a Many Splendored Thing 55. *The King and I* 56. Desk Set 57. South Pacific (co-ph) (AAN) 58. Porgy and Bess (AAN) 59. North to Alaska 60. Tender is the Night 61. Cleopatra (AA) 63. The Cardinal (AAN) 63. The Agony and the Ecstasy (AAN) 65. The Glass Bottom Boat 66. Caprice (also appeared) 67. *Planet of the Apes* 67. Justine 69, many others.

¶ God was a great photographer. He'd only gotten one light. – *L.S.*
Lee Garmes will never see the day that he's as good as I am, and that goes for anybody in the motion picture business. – *L.S.*

Shane, Maxwell (1905–1983).
American writer-director, former publicist.
You Can't Beat Love (co-w) 37. One Body Too Many (w) 43. Fear in the Night (wd) 46 (remade as Nightmare 56). City across the River (wd, p) 49. The Naked Street (wd) 55, etc.

Shankar, Ravi (1920–).
Indian composer and virtuoso sitar player.
Panther Panchali 56. Aparajito 58. The World of Apu 59. Chappaqua 66. Charly 68. Raga 71. Gandhi (co-m) (AAN) 82. Genesis 86, etc.

Shanley, John Patrick (1950–).
American screenwriter, dramatist and director.
Five Corners (w) 87. Moonstruck (w) (AA) 87. The January Man (w) 89. Joe versus the Volcano (wd) 90. Alive (w) 93. We're Back!: A Dinosaur's Story (w) 93, etc.

Shannon, Harry (1890–1964).
American character actor, often seen as sympathetic father or rustic; musical comedy experience.
Hands Up 31. Young Tom Edison 40. The Eve of St Mark 44. The Gunfighter 50. High Noon 52. Executive Suite 54. Come Next Spring 56. Hell's Crossroads 57, many others.

Shapiro, Paul (1955–).
Canadian director, from television.

The Understudy (TV) 75. Hockey Night (TV) 84. Miracle at Moreaux (TV) 85. The Truth about Alex (TV) 87. The Lotus Eaters 93, etc.

Shapiro, Stanley (1925–1990).
American writer-producer associated with glossy comedies; long experience in radio and TV.
The Perfect Furlough (w) 58. Pillow Talk (co-w) (AA) 59. Operation Petticoat (co-w) 59. Come September (co-w) 60. That Touch of Mink (co-w) 62. Bedtime Story (w, p) 64. How to Save a Marriage (p) 68. For Pete's Sake (co-w, p) 74. Carbon Copy 81. Dirty Rotten Scoundrels 89. Running against Time 90, etc.

Sharaff, Irene (1910–1993).
American costume designer, long with Fox. She began working in the New York theatre in 1928, moving to Hollywood in 1942.
An American in Paris (AA) 51. Call Me Madam (AAN) 53. A Star Is Born (AAN) 54. Brigadoon (AAN) 54. Guys and Dolls (AAN) 56. The King and I (AA) 56. Porgy and Bess (AAN) 59. Can-Can (AAN) 60. Flower Drum Song (AAN) 61. West Side Story (AA) 61. Cleopatra (AA) 63. Who's Afraid of Virginia Woolf? (AA) 66. The Taming of the Shrew (AAN) 67. Hello Dolly (AAN) 69. The Great White Hope 70. The Other Side of Midnight (AAN) 77. Mommie Dearest 81, etc.

Sharif, Omar (1932–) (Michel Shalhouz).
Egyptian leading man now in international films.
Autobiography: 1977, *The Eternal Male*.
Goha 59. *Lawrence of Arabia* (AAN) 62. The Fall of the Roman Empire 64. Behold a Pale Horse 64. The Yellow Rolls-Royce 64. Genghis Khan 65. *Dr Zhivago* 65. The Night of the Generals 66. Marco the Magnificent 66. More Than a Miracle 67. Funny Girl 68. Mayerling 68. Mackenna's Gold 68. The Appointment 69. Che! 69. The Last Valley 70. The Horsemen 71. The Burglars 71. The Tamarind Seed 74. Juggernaut 74. The Mysterious Island of Captain Nemo 74. Funny Lady 75. Ace up My Sleeve 76. Ashanti 78. Bloodline 79. The Baltimore Bullet 80. Oh Heavenly Dog 80. Green Ice 81. Inchon! 82. Return to Eden 82. Ayoub 83. Top Secret! 84. Les Pyramides Bleues 88. Keys to Freedom 89. Mountains of the Moon 90. Journey of Love (Viaggio d'Amore) 90. Memories of Midnight (TV) 91. War on the Land of Egypt (El Mowaten Masri) 91. Mother (Mayrig) 91. 588 rue Paradis 92, etc.

¶ I definitely want to do mainly theatre now. Or, two weeks in a film for a remarkable amount of money. – *O.S.*
Aggressive feminists scare me. – *O.S.*

Sharkey, Ray (1953–1993).
American leading man of the 80s. Died of AIDS, contracted through intravenous drug use.
Trackdown 76. Stunts 77. Paradise Alley 78. Who'll Stop the Rain? 78. Heart Beat 79. Willie and Phil 80. The Idolmaker 80. Love and Money 82. Body Rock 84. No Mercy 86. Wise Guys 86. Private Investigations 87. Scenes from the Class Struggle in Beverly Hills 89. Wired 89. Dead On 91. Hotel Oklahoma 91. Cop and a Half 93, etc.
TV series: Wiseguy 87. Man in the Family 91.

Sharman, Jim (1945–).
Australian director, active in the theatre.
Shirley Thompson versus the Aliens 72. Summer of Secrets 76. The Rocky Horror Picture Show 76. The Night the Prowler 78, etc.

¶ I don't believe in the art-house circuit, whether it's for plays or films: you've got to reach out. – *J.S.*

Sharp, Alan.
Scottish writer in Hollywood.
The Hired Hand 71. The Last Run 71. Ulzana's Raid 72. Billy Two Hats 74. Night Moves 75. Damnation Alley 77. The Osterman Weekend 83. Little Treasure (& d) 85. Cat Chaser 90. Descending Angel 91. Mission of the Shark 91. The Last Hit (TV) 93, etc.

Sharp, Don (1922–).
Australian-born director, in British film industry from 1952, at first as writer.
Ha'penny Breeze (w) 52. Robbery Under Arms (w) 56. The Professionals 59. Linda 60. Kiss of the Vampire 62. Devil Ship Pirates 63. *Witchcraft* 64. Those Magnificent Men in Their Flying Machines (second unit) 65. Rasputin the Mad Monk 65. *The Face of Fu Manchu* 65. Our Man in Marrakesh 66. The Million Eyes of Su Muru 66. Rocket to the Moon 67. Psychomania 72. Callan 74. Hennessy 75. The Four Feathers (TV) 78. *The Thirty-Nine Steps* 78. Bear Island 80. A Woman of Substance (TV) 84. Tusitala (TV) 85. Hold the Dream (TV) 87. Tears in the Rain 88, etc.

Sharp, Henry (1892–1966).
American cinematographer.
Homespun Folks 20. The Hottentot 22. A Girl of the Limberlost 24. Don Q Son of Zorro 25. *The Black Pirate* 26. The Lovelorn 27. *The Crowd* 28. The Iron Mask 29. Lord Byron of Broadway 30. The False Madonna 31. The Devil is Driving 32. Duck Soup 33. Six of a Kind 34. The Glass Key 35. Lady be Careful 36. Hotel Haywire 37. Booloo 38. Geronimo 39. Dr Cyclops (co-ph) 40. Broadway Limited 41. The Hidden Hand 42. Ministry of Fear 44. Jealousy 45. It Happened on Fifth Avenue 47. Perilous Waters 48. Daughter of the West 49. The Young Land (co-ph) 59, many others.

Sharp, Ian (1946–).
British director, from TV.
The Music Machine 81. Who Dares Wins 82.

Shatner, William (1931–).
Canadian leading actor, seen mostly on TV.
The Brothers Karamazov 58. The Explosive Generation 61. The Intruder (The Stranger) 61. The Outrage 64. Go Ask Alice (TV) 73. The Horror at 37,000 Feet (TV) 74. Big Bad Mama 74. Kingdom of the Spiders 77. A Whale of a Tale 77. Land of No Return 78. Star Trek: The Motion Picture 79. The Kidnapping of the President 80. Star Trek II: The Wrath of Khan 82. Visiting Hours 82. Star Trek III: The Search for Spock 84. Star Trek IV: The Voyage Home 87. Star Trek V: The Final Frontier (& d) 89. Star Trek VI: The Undiscovered Country 91. National Lampoon's Loaded Weapon 1 93. Tekwar (d, from his novel) (TV) 94. Star Trek: Generations 94, etc.
TV series: For the People 60. *Star Trek* 66–68. Barbary Coast 75. T.J. Hooker 82–86. Rescue 911 89.

Shaughnessy, Alfred (1916–).
British producer.
Brandy for the Parson 51. Cat Girl 57. Heart of a Child 57. Just My Luck (script only) 59. The Impersonator (script and direction only) 61. Lunch Hour 63, etc.

Shaughnessy, Mickey (1920–1985).
Tough-looking American comic actor with stage experience.

The Last of the Comanches (debut) 52. From Here to Eternity 53. Conquest of Space 55. Jailhouse Rock 57. *Don't Go Near the Water* 57. North to Alaska 60. A Global Affair 63. A House Is Not a Home 64. Never a Dull Moment 68, etc.
TV series: Chicago Teddy Bears 71.

Shavelson, Melville (1917–).
American screenwriter, in Hollywood from the early 40s.
The Princess and the Pirate 44. Always Leave Them Laughing 50. Room for One More 52. The Seven Little Foys (& d) (AANw) 55. Beau James (& d) 57. Houseboat (& d) (AANw) 58. The Five Pennies (& d) 59. The Pigeon that Took Rome (& p, d) 62. A New Kind of Love (& p, d) 63. Cast a Giant Shadow (& p, d) 66. The War between Men and Women (co-wd) 72, many others, usually in collaboration with *Jack Rose* (1911–).
TV series: Ike (w, co-d) 79.

Shaver, Helen (1951–).
Canadian actress.
Shoot 76. High-Ballin' 78. In Praise of Older Women 78. The Amityville Horror 79. The Dogs of War 80. Gas 81. The Osterman Weekend 83. Harry Tracy 83. Best Defense 84. The Color of Money 86. Desert Hearts 86. The Believers 87. Bethune 89. Tree of Hands 89. Innocent Victim 90. Zebrahead 92. Morning Glory 93. Roadracers (TV) 94, etc.
TV series: United States 80. Jessica Novak 81.

Shaw, Artie (1910–) (Arthur Arschawsky).
American bandleader and clarinettist. He has married eight times, including actresses Lana Turner, Ava Gardner and Evelyn Keyes.
■ Dancing Co-Ed 39. Second Chorus 40.

Shaw, Fiona (1958–).
Irish actress.
My Left Foot 89. Mountains of the Moon 89. Three Men and a Little Lady 90. Undercover Blues 93, etc.

Shaw, George Bernard (1856–1950).
Distinguished Irish playwright who for many years refused to allow film versions of his works; he was reconciled to the idea by Gabriel Pascal. The following versions have been made:
How He Lied to Her Husband 30. Arms and the Man 31. Pygmalion 38. Major Barbara 40. Caesar and Cleopatra 45. Androcles and the Lion 53. Saint Joan 57. The Doctor's Dilemma 58. The Devil's Disciple 59. Helden (Arms and the Man) (Ger.) 59. The Millionairess 61. My Fair Lady (from Pygmalion) 64. Great Catherine 67.

¶ As an iconoclast he is admirable, as an icon somewhat less so. – *Bertrand Russell*

Shaw, Irwin (1912–1984).
American novelist and screenwriter.
Talk of the Town (AAN) 42. I Want You 51. Fire Down Below 57. The Young Lions (& oa) 58. Tip on a Dead Jockey 58. Two Weeks in Another Town (novel only) 62. *Rich Man Poor Man* (novel only) (TV) 76. Top of the Hill (story) (TV) 79, etc.

Shaw, Martin (1945–).
British leading man who shot to fame in TV's *The Professionals*.
Sinbad's Golden Voyage 72. Operation Daybreak 73. Cream in my Coffee (TV) 80. The Last Place on Earth (TV) 85. Ladder of Swords 88. Intrigue (TV) 88, etc.
TV series: The Chief 93.

Shaw, Maxwell (1929–1985).
British supporting actor, usually in unsympathetic roles.

Shaw, Reta (1912–1982).
Amply proportioned American character actress.
The Pajama Game 57. Pollyanna 60. Mary Poppins 64. Escape to Witch Mountain 74.

Shaw, Robert (1927–1978).
English leading actor, novelist and playwright. He studied at RADA and began on stage in 1949. His first novel, *The Hiding Place* (1959), was turned into a comic film, *Situation Hopeless but Not Serious* 65, and his play *The Man in the Glass Booth* was filmed by Arthur Hiller in 1975. The second of his three wives was actress Mary Ure. A heavy drinker, he died of a heart attack.
Biography: 1993, *Robert Shaw: The Price of Success* by John French.
■ The Dam Busters (film debut) 55. Double Cross 55. A Hill in Korea 56. The Birthday Party 58. Libel 59. Sea Fury 59. The Valiant 61. Tomorrow at Ten 62. *From Russia with Love* 63. The Caretaker 63. The Luck of Ginger Coffey 64. The Battle of the Bulge 65. *A Man for All Seasons* (as Henry VIII) (AAN) 66. Custer of the West 67. The Battle of Britain 69. The Royal Hunt of the Sun 69. Figures in a Landscape (& w) 70. A Town Called Bastard 71. A Reflection of Fear 72. Young Winston 72. The Hireling 73. The Sting 73. The Golden Voyage of Sinbad (uncredited) 73. The Taking of Pelham One Two Three 74. Jaws 75. Robin and Marian 75. End of the Game 76. Diamonds 76. Swashbuckler 76. Black Sunday 76. The Deep 77. Force Ten from Navarone 78. Avalanche Express 79.
TV series: The Buccaneers 56.

¶ What I try to achieve in acting – flamboyance – would be self-indulgence if I tried it as a writer. – *R.S.*
I drink too much. Will you tell me one great actor who doesn't drink? – *R.S.*

Shaw, Sebastian (1905–1994).
British leading man of the 30s, latterly character actor. On stage from 1913 (as child).
Caste 30. Taxi to Paradise 33. Men are not Gods 36. The Squeaker 37. The Spy in Black 39. East of Piccadilly 41. The Glass Mountain 48. It Happened Here 64. A Midsummer Night's Dream 68. High Season 87.

Shaw, Susan (1929–1978) (Patsy Sloots).
British leading lady groomed by the Rank 'charm school'.
London Town 46. The Upturned Glass 47. Holiday Camp 47. London Belongs to Me 48. The Woman in Question 50. The Intruder 51. The Good Die Young 52. Stock Car 54. Carry On Nurse 59. The Switch 63, etc.

Shaw, Victoria (1935–1988) (Jeanette Elphick).
Australian leading lady in American films. She was formerly married to actor Roger Smith.
Cattle Station (Aust.) 55. The Eddy Duchin Story 56. Edge of Eternity 59. The Crimson Kimono 60. Alvarez Kelly 66. Westworld 73, etc.

Shaw, Wini (1899–1982) (Winfred Lei Momi).
American singer of Hawaiian descent, used as voice of non-singing stars in many Warner musicals of the 30s.
Actually appeared in the following:
Three on a Honeymoon 34. Gold Diggers of 1935 35. In Caliente 35. Melody for Two 37, etc.

Shawlee, Joan (1929–1987) (formerly Joan Fulton). American character comedienne with nightclub and stage experience.

Men in Her Diary 45. Cuban Pete 46. I'll Be Yours 47. The Marrying Kind 52. Conquest of Space 54. A Star is Born 54. *Some Like It Hot* 59. The Apartment 60. Irma La Douce 63. The Wild Angels 66. The St Valentine's Day Massacre 67. One More Time 71. Willard 71. Dead Men Tell No Tales (TV) 74. Flash and Firecat 76, etc.

TV series: Aggie 57. The Betty Hutton Show 59. Feather and Father 77.

Shawn, Dick (1928–1987) (Richard Schulefand). American comedian, in occasional films.

Wake Me When It's Over 60. It's a Mad Mad Mad Mad World 63. A Very Special Favor 65. What Did You Do in the War, Daddy? 66. Penelope 66. The Producers 68. Looking Up 77. Love at First Bite 79, etc.

TV series: Hail to the Chief 85.

Shawn, Wallace (1943–).
American playwright and character actor of mild appearance.

All That Jazz 79. Manhattan 79. Starting Over 79. Atlantic City 80. My Dinner with André (& co-w) 81. A Little Sex 82. Lovesick 83. The Bostonians 84. Crackers 84. The Hotel New Hampshire 84. Micki and Maude 84. Heaven Help Us 85. Head Office 86. Nice Girls Don't Explode 87. Prick Up Your Ears 87. The Princess Bride 87. Radio Days 87. The Moderns 88. Scenes from the Class Struggle in Beverly Hills 89. She's Out of Control 89. We're No Angels 89. Shadows and Fog 91. Nickel & Dime 92. Mom and Dad Save the World 92. The Cemetery Club 93. Mrs Parker and the Vicious Circle 94. Vanya on 42nd Street (w) 94, etc.

Shaye, Robert (1939–).
American production executive and director. In 1967, he became founder and president of New Line Cinema, a company noted for low-budget films. In 1993, in a $530 million deal, the company was taken over by Ted Turner. New Line's greatest success so far has been the *Nightmare on Elm Street* series.

Book of Love (d) 90.

Shayne, Robert (c. 1910–1992) (Robert Shaen Dawe).
American general-purpose actor.

Keep 'em Rolling 34. Shine On Harvest Moon 44. The Swordsman 47. The Neanderthal Man (lead role) 53. Spook Chasers 58. Valley of the Redwoods 61, etc.

Shayne, Tamara (1897–1983) (Tamara Nikoulin).
Russian-American character actress who played Jolson's mother in *The Jolson Story* and *Jolson Sings Again*. Also: *Ninotchka, Mission to Moscow, Anastasia*, etc.

Shbib, Bashar.
Canadian director.

Julia Has Two Lovers 90. Lana in Love 91. Love $ Greed 92. Ride Me 92. Crack Me Up 93, etc.

She.
Seven silent versions were made of Rider Haggard's adventure fantasy about a lost tribe, an ageless queen, and a flame of eternal life in darkest Africa. Only the last remains, made in London and Berlin by G. B. Samuelson, with Betty Blythe and Carlyle Blackwell. In 1934 in Hollywood, Merian Cooper and Ernest Schoedsack remade the story in a North Pole setting, with Helen Gahagan

and Randolph Scott. In 1965 came a lifeless Hammer version directed by Robert Day, with Ursula Andress and John Richardson; this was followed in 1968 by a sequel, *The Vengeance of She*, which was more than slightly potty.

She Loves Me Not.
The story of a night-club singer taking refuge in a men's college and disguising herself as an undergraduate after witnessing a murder has been filmed three times: in 1934, directed by Elliott Nugent, with Bing Crosby and Miriam Hopkins; in 1942, as *True to the Army*, in which Judy Canova pretends to be a soldier; in 1955, as *How to Be Very, Very Popular*, in which strippers Betty Grable and Sheree North hide in a college. The notion also served Whoopi Goldberg well in *Sister Act* 92, as a singer fleeing from the Mob who takes refuge in a convent and disguises herself as a nun.

Shea, Katt.
American director.

Stripped to Kill 87. Dance of the Damned 89. Stripped to Kill II 89. Streets 90. Poison Ivy 92.

Shea, William (1862–1918).
Scottish-born leading actor in Hollywood silents, in films from 1905.

Vanity Fair 11. The Politician's Dream 11. The Little Minister 12. The Old Rag Doll 14. The Lady of Shalott 15. A Night Out 16. Sally in a Hurry 17. A Bachelor's Children 18, etc.

Shean, Al (1868–1949) (Alfred Schoenberg). German-born entertainer, long in American vaudeville; part of the famous 'Mr Gallagher and Mr Shean' act. After his partner's death he played character roles in Hollywood films.

Murder in the Air 35. San Francisco 36. The Great Waltz 38. Ziegfeld Girl 41. Atlantic City 44, etc.

Shear, Barry (1923–1979).
American director.

■ Wild in the Streets 68. Night Gallery (TV) (co-d) 69. Ellery Queen: Don't Look Behind You (TV) 71. The Todd Killings 71. Short Walk to Daylight (TV) 72. Across 110th Street 72. The Deadly Trackers 73. Jarrett (TV) 73. Punch and Jody (TV) 74. Strike Force (TV) 75. San Pedro Bums (TV) 77.

Shearer, Douglas (1899–1971).
American sound engineer, brother of Norma Shearer; at MGM for many years, he won twelve Academy Awards, and developed a new sound head.

The Big House 30. Naughty Marietta 35. San Francisco 36. Strike Up the Band 40. Thirty Seconds Over Tokyo 44. Green Dolphin Street 47. The Great Caruso 51, many others.

Shearer, Moira (1926–) (Moira King).
Scottish-born ballet dancer who came to films for the leading role in *The Red Shoes* 48.

■ Tales of Hoffman 52. The Story of Three Loves 53. The Man Who Loved Redheads 55. Peeping Tom 59. Black Tights 60.

Shearer, Norma (1900–1983).
Canadian actress, in Hollywood from silent days and a big MGM star of the 30s. Married to Irving Thalberg.

Biography: 1990, *Norma Shearer* by Gavin Lambert.

■ The Flapper 20. The Restless Sex 20. Way Down East 20. The Stealers 20. The Sign on the Door 20. Torchy's Millions 21. The Leather Pushers 22. The Man Who Paid 22. The Bootleggers 22. Channing

of the Northwest 22. A Clouded Name 23. Man and Wife 23. The Devil's Partner 23. Pleasure Mad 23. The Wanters 23. Lucretia Lombard 23. The Trail of the Law 24. The Wolf Man 24. Blue Water 24. Broadway After Dark 24. Broken Barriers 24. Married Flirts 24. Empty Hands 24. The Snob 24. *He Who Gets Slapped* 24. Excuse Me 25. Lady of the Night 25. Waking Up the Town 25. A Slave of Fashion 25. Pretty Ladies 25. The Tower of Lies 25. His Secretary 25. The Devil's Circus 26. The Waning Sex 26. Upstage 26. The Demi-Bride 27. After Midnight 27. The Student Prince 27. The Latest from Paris 28. The Actress 28. A Lady of Chance 28. *The Trial of Mary Dugan* 29. *The Last of Mrs Cheyney* 29. Hollywood Revue 29. Their Own Desire (AAN) 29. The Divorcee (AA) 30. Let Us Be Gay 30. Strangers May Kiss 31. *A Free Soul* (AAN) 31. Private Lives 31. Strange Interlude 32. *Smilin' Through* 32. Riptide 34. *The Barretts of Wimpole Street* (AAN) 34. Romeo and Juliet (AAN) 36. Marie Antoinette (AAN) 38. Idiot's Delight 39. The Women 39. Escape 40. We Were Dancing 41. Her Cardboard Lover 42.

¶ A face unclouded by thought. – Lillian Hellman

Sheedy, Ally (1962–).
American leading lady.

Bad Boys 82. War Games 83. St Elmo's Fire 85. Short Circuit 86. Maid to Order 87. Heart of Dixie 89. Betsy's Wedding 90. Fear (TV) 90. Only the Lonely 91. Chantilly Lace (TV) 93. Man's Best Friend 93. The Pickle 93. Before the Night 94. Parallel Lives (TV) 94, etc.

Sheekman, Arthur (1891–1978).
American comedy writer, often in collaboration.

Monkey Business 31. Roman Scandals 33. Dimples 36. Wonder Man 45. Welcome Stranger 46. Saigon 47. Young Man with Ideas 52. Bundle of Joy 56. Ada 61, etc.

Sheen, Charlie (1965–) (Carlos Estevez).
American actor, son of Martin Sheen.

Red Dawn 84. The Boys Next Door 85. Ferris Bueller's Day Off 86. Lucas 86. The Wraith 86. Platoon 86. Wisdom 86. No Man's Land 87. Wall Street 87. Young Guns 88. Eight Men Out 88. Major League 89. Navy SEALS 90. Men at Work 90. The Rookie 90. Cadence 91. Hot Shots! 91. Hot Shots! Part Deux 93. Deadfall 93. The Three Musketeers 93. The Chase 94. Major League II 94. Terminal Velocity 94, etc.

¶ How does Keanu Reeves work with Coppola and Bertolucci and I don't get a shot at that, know what I'm saying? – C.S.

Maybe I should become a heroin addict. Maybe I should roam the fucking streets at 5 a.m. and hang out at fucking coffee bars. You know, become avant-garde. Or maybe if I adopt an English accent and add a middle name, so I'm Charlie Something Sheen, I'll get there. – C.S.

Sheen, Martin (1940–) (Ramon Estevez).
American leading actor of the 70s.

■ The Incident 67. The Subject was Roses 68. Catch 22 69. Goodbye Raggedy Ann (TV) 71. No Drums No Bugles 71. Rage 72. Message to My Daughter (TV) 72. Pick-up on 101 72. Pursuit (TV) 73. That Certain Summer (TV) 73. Letters for Three Lovers (TV) 73. Sweet Hostage (TV) 73. *Badlands* 73. Catholics (TV) 74. The Execution of Private Slovik (TV) 74. The Missiles of October (TV) 74. The California Kid (TV) 75. The Legend of Earl Durand 75. The Little Girl Who Lives Down the Lane 76. Sweet Hostage 76. The Cassandra

Crossing 77. *Apocalypse Now* 79. Eagle's Wing 79. Loophole 80. The Final Countdown 80. Gandhi 82. That Championship Season 82. Enigma 82. Man, Woman and Child 83. Kennedy (TV) 83. The Dead Zone 83. Broken Rainbow (narrator) 85. The Believers 87. Wall Street 87. Da 88. Judgement in Berlin 88. Promises to Keep 88. Walking after Midnight 88. Personal Choice 89. Beverly Hills Brats 89. Cold Front 89. Beyond the Stars 89. The Maid 91. Cadence (& d) 89. Original Intent 91. Reason to Believe 93. Queen (TV) 93. Hear No Evil 93. Gettysburg 93. Guns of Honor (TV) 94. Roswell (TV) 94. Boca 94.

Sheffer, Craig.
American leading actor.
   That Was Then . . . This Is Now 85. Fire with Fire 86. Some Kind of Wonderful 87. Babycakes (TV) 89. Night Breed 90. Instant Karma 90. Fire on the Amazon 91. Blue Desert 91. Eye of the Storm 91. A River Runs through It 92. Fire in the Sky 93. Sleep with Me 94. Roadflower 94, etc.
   TV series: The Hamptons 83.

Sheffield, Johnny (1931–).
American boy actor of the 30s, especially in the *Tarzan* and later the *Bomba* series.
   Babes in Arms 39. Roughly Speaking 45, etc.

Sheffield, Reginald (1901–1957).
British actor in Hollywood, father of Johnny Sheffield; formerly a child star.
   David Copperfield 23. White Mice 26. The Green Goddess 30. Old English 30. Of Human Bondage 34. Cardinal Richelieu 35. Another Dawn 57. Earthbound 40. Eyes in the Night 42. Wilson 44. Kiss the Blood Off My Hands 48. The Buccaneer 58, etc.

Shefter, Bert (1904–).
Russian-born composer in Hollywood.
   Danger Zone 51. M 51. No Escape 53. Kronos 57. Cattle Empire 58. The Big Circus 59. The Lost World 60. Jack the Giant Killer 62. Curse of the Fly 65. The Last Shot You Hear 69. The Christine Jorgensen Story 70, many others.

The Sheik.
Rudolph Valentino first appeared as a romantic Arab in 1922, with Agnes Ayres as his willing co-star, in an adaptation of E. M. Hull's novelette. It was one of his most successful roles, and *Son of the Sheik* came out in 1926, with Vilma Banky partnering him. His death prevented further episodes, but in 1937 Ramon Navarro made fun of the idea in *The Sheik Steps Out*, and in 1962 came an Italian spoof called *The Return of the Son of the Sheik*, with Gordon Scott.

Sheldon, Gene (1909–1982).
American comedy actor.
   A Thousand and One Nights 45. Where Do We Go from Here? 45. Golden Girl 52. Three Ring Circus 55. Babes in Toyland 60, etc.

Sheldon, Sidney (1917–).
American writer-director.
   The Bachelor and the Bobbysoxer (w) (AA) 47. Dream Wife (co-w, d) 53. You're Never Too Young (w) 55. Pardners (w) 56. The Buster Keaton Story (wpd) 57. Jumbo (w) 62. The Other Side of Midnight (oa) 77. Bloodline (oa) 79. Rage of Angels (TV) (oa) 83. Master of the Game (TV) 84, etc.

Shelley, Barbara (1933–).
British leading lady who has filmed in Italy; latterly associated with horror films.

Cat Girl 57. Blood of the Vampire 59. Village of the Damned 61. Shadow of the Cat 62. Postman's Knock 62. The Gorgon 64. The Secret of Blood Island 65. Rasputin the Mad Monk 65. Dracula, Prince of Darkness 65. *Quatermass and the Pit* 67. Ghost Story 74, etc.

Shelley, Mary Wollstonecraft (1797–1851).
British writer (wife of the poet) who somewhat unexpectedly is remembered as the creator of *Frankenstein*, which she composed to pass the time during a wet summer. She was played in *Bride of Frankenstein* by Elsa Lanchester. Three films have dealt with the creation of her novel: Ken Russell's *Gothic* 86, in which she was played by Natasha Richardson, Ivan Passer's *Haunted Summer* 88, with Alice Krige, and Roger Corman's *Frankenstein Unbound* 90, with Bridget Fonda.

Shelly, Adrienne.
American leading actress, often in independent films.
   The Unbelievable Truth 90. Trust 91. Big Girls Don't Cry . . . They Get Even (GB: Stepkids) 92. Hold Me, Thrill Me, Kiss Me 93. Hexed 93. Roadflower 94. Sleep with Me 94. Teresa's Tattoo 94, etc.

Shelton, John (1917–1972) (John Price).
Rather colourless American second lead.
   The Smartest Girl in Town 36. Navy Blue and Gold 37. I Take This Woman 40. Blonde Inspiration 41. Whispering Ghosts 42. The Time of Their Lives 46. Siren of Atlantis 48. Sins of Jezebel 51, etc.

Shelton, Joy (1922–).
British leading lady.
   Millions Like Us 43. Waterloo Road 44. No Room at the Inn 48. A Case for PC 49 51. Impulse 54. No Kidding 60. HMS Defiant 62, etc.

Shelton, Ron (1945–).
American screenwriter and director, a former basketball player.
   Under Fire (co-w) 83. The Best of Times (w) 85. Bull Durham (wd) (AAN) 88. Blaze (wd) 89. White Men Can't Jump (wd) 92. Blue Chips (w) 94. Cobb (wd) 94, etc.

Shengeleya, Georgy.
Russian director whose *Pirosmani* was widely praised in 1973.

Shenson, Walter (1919–).
American producer, former publicist; based in Britain.
   Korea Patrol 53. The Mouse That Roared 59. A Matter of Who 61. *A Hard Day's Night* 64. Help! 65. A Talent for Loving 69. Welcome to the Club (d) 70. Digby 73. The Chicken Chronicles 77. Reuben Reuben 83, etc.

Shentall, Susan (1934–).
British leading lady who made a solitary appearance in *Romeo and Juliet* 54.

Shepard, Sam (1943–) (Samuel Shepard Rogers).
American leading man; also screenwriter and playwright. He has two children by actress Jessica Lange.
   ■ Zabriskie Point 70. Renaldo and Clara 78. Days of Heaven 78. Resurrection 80. Raggedy Man 81. Frances 82. The Right Stuff (AAN) 83. Paris, Texas (w only) 84. Country 84. Fool for Love (& w) 85. Crimes of the Heart 86. Baby Boom 87. Far North (wd) 88. Steel Magnolias 89. Bright Angel 91. Voyager 91. Defenseless 91. Thunderheart 92.

Silent Tongue (wd) 93. The Pelican Brief 93. Curse of the Starving Class (oa) 94.

¶ I didn't go out of my way to get into this movie stuff. I think of myself as a writer. – S.S.

Shepherd, Cybill (1950–).
American leading actress and singer. Born in Memphis, she won a contest for Miss Congeniality at 16 and was a model before becoming an actress.
   ■ The Last Picture Show 71. The Heartbreak Kid 72. Daisy Miller 74. At Long Last Love 75. Taxi Driver 76. Special Delivery 76. Silver Bears 77. The Lady Vanishes 79. The Return 80. Chances Are 89. Alice 90. Texasville 90. Once upon a Crime 92. Married to It 93. There Was a Little Boy (TV) 93. Telling Secrets (TV) 93.
   TV series: The Yellow Rose 83. Moonlighting 85–89.

¶ I've grown in spirtuality and as a human being since I began to relate to Mother Earth. – C.S.

Shepherd, Elizabeth.
British actress.
   The Queen's Guards 61. Blind Corner 63. *The Tomb of Ligeia* 64. Hell Boats 69. Damien: Omen II 78. Double Negative 80.

Shepherd, Jack (1940–).
British actor, in character roles in films and leads on stage and TV. He is also a dramatist and theatre director.
   The Virgin Soldiers 69. The Bed Sitting Room 69. Ready When You Are Mr McGill (TV) 76. Count Dracula (TV) 77. The Big Man 90. Twenty-One 91. The Object of Beauty 91. Blue Ice 92. Wycliffe (TV) 93. No Escape 94, etc.
   TV series: Bill Brand 76. Wycliffe 94.

Shepitko, Larissa (1938–1979).
Russian director and screenwriter. She was married to director Elem Klimov (qv), who took over the direction of *Farewell* following her death in a car accident. He also made a documentary, *Larissa*, about her in 1980.
   Heat (Znoi) 63. Wings (Krylia) 66. At One O'Clock (V Trinadtsatom Chasu) 68. You and I (Ty i Ia) 72. The Ascent (Voskhozhdenie) (co-w, d) 76. Farewell (Proshchanie) (co-w) 81.

Shepley, Michael (1907–1961) (Michael Shepley-Smith).
British stage actor who usually played amiable buffoons.
   Black Coffee 30. Goodbye Mr Chips 39. Quiet Wedding 40. The Demi Paradise 43. Maytime in Mayfair 49. An Alligator Named Daisy 56. Don't Bother to Knock 61, etc.

Shepperd, John (1907–1983) (also known under his real name, Shepperd Strudwick).
American leading man and latterly character actor, usually in gentle, understanding roles.
   Congo Maisie (debut) 40. *Remember the Day* 41. *The Loves of Edgar Allan Poe* 42. Enchantment 47. Joan of Arc 48. All the King's Men 49. A Place in the Sun 51. Autumn Leaves 56. The Sad Sack 57. The Unkillables 67. Cops and Robbers 73, etc.

Sher, Antony (1949–).
South African-born Shakespearean actor and novelist, mainly on stage in Britain.
   Yanks 79. Superman II 80. Shadey 84. Erik the Viking 89.

Sher, Jack (1913–1988).
American writer-director, former columnist.

My Favorite Spy (w) 51. Off Limits (w) 53. Four Girls in Town (wd) 56. Kathy O' (wd) 58. The Wild and the Innocent (wd) 59. The Three Worlds of Gulliver (wd) 60. Paris Blues (co-w) 61. Critic's Choice (w) 63. Move Over Darling (co-w) 63, etc.

Sheridan, Ann (1915–1967) (Clara Lou Sheridan). American leading lady at her peak in the early 40s; a cheerful beauty contest winner who developed a tough style and became known as the 'oomph' girl.

■ Search for Beauty 34. Bolero 34. Come on Marines 34. Murder at the Vanities 34. Kiss and Make Up 34. Shoot the Works 34. The Notorious Sophie Lang 34. Ladies Should Listen 34. Wagon Wheels 34. Mrs Wiggs of the Cabbage Patch 34. College Rhythm 34. You Belong to Me 34. Limehouse Blues 34. Enter Madame 35. Home on the Range 35. Rumba 35. Behold My Wife 35. Car 99 35. Rocky Mountain Mystery 35. Mississippi 35. The Glass Key 35. The Crusades 35. The Red Blood of Courage 35. Fighting Youth 35. Sing Me a Love Song 35. Black Legion 36. The Great O'Malley 37. San Quentin 37. Wine, Women and Horses 37. The Footloose Heiress 37. Alcatraz Island 37. She Loves a Fireman 38. The Patient in Room 18 38. Mystery House 38. Cowboy from Brooklyn 38. Little Miss Thoroughbred 38. Letter of Introduction 38. Broadway Musketeers 38. *Angels with Dirty Faces* 38. They Made Me a Criminal 39. Dodge City 39. Naughty but Nice 39. Winter Carnival 39. Indianapolis Speedway 39. Angels Wash Their Faces 39. Castle on the Hudson 40. It All Came True 40. *Torrid Zone* 40. *They Drive by Night* 40. City for Conquest 40. Honeymoon for Three 41. Navy Blues 41. *Kings Row* 41. *The Man Who Came to Dinner* 41. Juke Girl 42. Wings for the Eagle 42. George Washington Slept Here 42. Edge of Darkness 43. *Thank Your Lucky Stars* 43. *Shine on Harvest Moon* 44. The Doughgirls 44. One More Tomorrow 46. Nora Prentiss 47. *The Unfaithful* 47. Silver River 48. Good Sam 48. *I Was a Male War Bride* 49. Stella 50. Woman on the Run 50. Steel Town 52. Just Across the Street 52. Take Me to Town 53. Appointment in Honduras 53. *Come Next Spring* 56. The Opposite Sex 56. Woman and the Hunter 57.

TV series: Pistols and Petticoats 67.

Sheridan, Dinah (1920–   ) (Dinah Mec). British leading lady. She was married to actor Jimmy Hanley and Rank chairman Sir John Davis.

Irish and Proud of It 36. Full Speed Ahead 39. Salute John Citizen 42. For You Alone 44. Hills of Donegal 47. Calling Paul Temple 48. The Story of Shirley Yorke 48. Paul Temple's Triumph 50. Where No Vultures Fly 51. *Genevieve* 53. The Railway Children 71. The Mirror Crack'd 80, etc.

TV series: All Night Long 94.

Sheridan, Jim (1949–   ). Irish director, screenwriter and dramatist, from the theatre.

■ My Left Foot (AAN) 89. The Field 90. Into the West (w) 92. In the Name of the Father (p, co-w, d) ((AANd, AANw) 93. Words upon the Window Pane (a) 94.

Sheriff, Paul (1903–1961) (Paul Schouvaloff). Russian art director in Britain from the mid-30s.

French without Tears 39. Quiet Wedding 40. The Gentle Sex 43. *Henry V* 44. The Way to the Stars 45. Vice Versa 48. Flesh and Blood 51. Moulin Rouge (AA) 53. Gentlemen Marry Brunettes 55. Interpol 57. The Doctor's Dilemma 58. The Grass Is Greener 60, etc.

Sherin, Edwin (1930–   ). American director.

Valdez Is Coming 70. Glory Boy 71. Lena: My 100 Children (TV) 87. Daughter of the Streets (TV) 90, etc.

Sherlock Holmes,
Conan Doyle's classic fictional detective, around whom a detailed legend has been created by ardent followers, has a long screen history. There were American one-reel films featuring him in 1903, 1905 and 1908. Also in 1908 there began a series of twelve Danish one-reelers starring Forrest Holger-Madsen. In 1910 there were two German films and in 1912 six French. A second French series began in 1913; also in this year an American two-reel version of *The Sign of Four* featured Harry Benham. British six-reelers were made of *A Study in Scarlet* 14, and *Valley of Fear* 16; also in 1916 the famous stage actor William Gillette put his impersonation of Holmes on film for Essanay. In 1917 came a German version of *The Hound of the Baskervilles*; then nothing till 1922, when John Barrymore played Holmes and Roland Young was Watson in Goldwyn's *Sherlock Holmes*, based on Gillette's stage play. In Britain in the same year Maurice Elvey directed a full-length version of *The Hound of the Baskervilles* and followed it with over 25 two-reelers starring Eille Norwood, remaining faithful to the original stories. In 1929 Carlyle Blackwell played Holmes in a German remake of *The Hound of the Baskervilles;* and in the same year Clive Brook played in a talkie, *The Return of Sherlock Holmes*, with H. Reeves-Smith as Watson. Arthur Wontner, a perfect Holmes, first played the role in *Sherlock Holmes' Final Hour* (GB) 31, later appearing in *The Sign of Four* 32, *The Missing Rembrandt* 33, *The Triumph of Sherlock Holmes* 35, and *The Silver Blaze* 36 (Ian Fleming was Watson). Raymond Massey was Holmes in *The Speckled Band* (GB) 31, with Athole Stewart as Watson; in 1932 Robert Rendel was in *The Hound of the Baskervilles* (GB). Clive Brook again appeared in *Sherlock Holmes* (US) 32, with Reginald Owen as Watson; Owen then played Holmes in *A Study in Scarlet* (US) 33. The Germans made three more Holmes films in the mid-30s, including yet another remake of *The Hound*, which in 1939 was again tackled by Fox in Hollywood, this time with Basil Rathbone as the detective and Nigel Bruce as Watson. Its success led to a hurried remake of the Gillette play under the title *The Adventures of Sherlock Holmes* 39; two years later the same two actors began a series of twelve films in which the settings were modernized and most of the stories unrecognizable, although the acting and much of the writing were well in character. The titles were *Sherlock Holmes and the Voice of Terror* 41, *Sherlock Holmes and the Secret Weapon* 42, *Sherlock Holmes in Washington* 42, *Sherlock Holmes Faces Death* 43, *Spider Woman* 44, *The Scarlet Claw* 44, *Pearl of Death* 44, *House of Fear* 45, *Woman in Green* 45, *Pursuit to Algiers* 45, *Terror by Night* 46, *Dressed to Kill* (*Sherlock Holmes and the Secret Cage*) 46. Then a long silence was broken by Peter Cushing and André Morell in the leads of a British remake of *The Hound of the Baskervilles* 59. In 1962 Christopher Lee and Thorley Walters played Holmes and Watson in a German film, *Sherlock Holmes and the Deadly Necklace;* and in 1965 John Neville and Donald Houston appeared in an original story involving the famous pair with Jack the Ripper: *A Study in Terror*. Also in 1965 a BBC TV series featured Douglas Wilmer and Nigel Stock, with Peter Cushing later taking over as Holmes; the period atmosphere was carefully sought but the stories suffered from being padded out to the standard TV length. (There was also a Franco-American TV series in 1954 with Ronald Howard

and Howard Marion-Crawford.) In 1969 Billy Wilder made *The Private Life of Sherlock Holmes* with Robert Stephens, apparently intending a send-up but producing only a further pleasant variation. In 1970 George C. Scott thought he was Sherlock Holmes in *They Might Be Giants*, so did Larry Hagman in a 1976 TV movie, *The Return of the World's Greatest Detective*. Nicol Williamson as Holmes was treated by Sigmund Freud in 1976's *The Seven Per Cent Solution*, and in the same year Gene Wilder tried a spoof, *The Adventure of Sherlock Holmes' Smarter Brother*. The same year brought a TV movie called *Sherlock Holmes in New York*, with Roger Moore and Patrick MacNee. In 1978 there was a perfectly ghastly, supposedly comic *Hound of the Baskervilles* with Peter Cook and Dudley Moore, while Christopher Plummer starred in a TV half-hour of *Silver Blaze* and a feature called *Murder by Decree*, which again linked Holmes with Jack the Ripper. A stage revival of the William Gillette version was followed by other adaptations. 1979 brought another TV series with Geoffrey Whitehead and Donald Pickering; but *Sherlock Holmes and Doctor Watson* was barely seen outside Poland, where it was shot. In 1983 Sy Weintraub made TV movies of *The Sign of Four* and *The Hound of the Baskervilles*, with Ian Richardson an excellent Holmes; and Tom Baker starred in a BBC serial of *The Hound of the Baskervilles*. In 1984 Granada TV had a 13-hour series starring Jeremy Brett and David Burke, and this continues. Brett also starred in a full-length 1987 version of *The Sign of Four*. Christopher Lee played the role in TV versions made in South Africa in the 90s.

Sherman, Gary A.
American director.

Death Line (aka Raw Meat) 73. Dead and Buried 81. Vice Squad 82. Wanted Dead or Alive 86. Poltergeist III 88. Lisa 90. After the Shock (TV) 90, etc.

Sherman, George (1908–1991).
American director who graduated slowly from second-feature westerns.

Wild Horse Rodeo 37. Death Valley Outlaws 41. Outside the Law 41. Mantrap 43. Mystery Broadcast 44. The Lady and the Monster 44. *The Bandit of Sherwood Forest* 46. Renegades 46. Last of the Redskins 48. Sword in the Desert 49. Panther's Moon 50. The Golden Horde 51. Against All Flags 52. War Arrow 54. Dawn at Socorro 54. Count Three and Pray 55. Comanche 56. Son of Robin Hood 58. The Enemy General 60. Panic Button 64. Smoky 66. Big Jake 71, many others.

Sherman, Harry (1884–1952).
American producer of westerns.

Sherman, Lowell (1885–1934).
American leading man with stage experience. He was married to actress Helen Costello.

Way Down East 20. Monsieur Beaucaire 24. The Divine Woman 27. Mammy 30. The Greeks Had a Word for Them 32. False Faces 32. She Done Him Wrong (directed only) 33. Morning Glory 33. Broadway Through a Keyhole 33, etc.

Sherman, Richard (1928–   ), and **Robert** (1925–   ).
American songwriting brothers who have worked mainly for Disney.

Mary Poppins (AA) 64. The Happiest Millionaire 67. The One and Only Genuine Original Family Band 68. Bedknobs and Broomsticks 71. Huckleberry Finn (& w) 74. The Slipper and the Rose (& w) 76, etc.

Sherman, Vincent (1906–) (Abram Orovitz).
American director, formerly stage actor.

The Return of Doctor X 39. *All Through the Night* 41. The Hard Way 42. Old Acquaintance 43. In Our Time 44. Mr Skeffington 45. The Unfaithful 47. The New Adventures of Don Juan 48. The Hasty Heart 49. Lone Star 51. Affair in Trinidad 52. The Garment Jungle 57. Naked Earth 57. The Young Philadelphians 59. Ice Palace 60. The Second Time Around 61. Cervantes 66. The Last Hurrah (TV) 77. Women at West Point (TV) 79. Trouble in High Timber Country (TV) 82, etc.

Sherriff, R.C. (1896–1975).
Prolific British playwright and screenwriter.
Autobiography: 1969, *No Leading Lady.*
AS PLAYWRIGHT: Journey's End 30. Badger's Green 47. Home at Seven 52.
AS SCREENWRITER: *The Invisible Man* 33. *Goodbye Mr Chips* (AAN) 39. Lady Hamilton 41. *Odd Man Out* 47. *Quartet* 48. No Highway 50. The Dam Busters 55, many others.

Sherrin, Ned (1931–).
British ex-barrister who became a BBC producer and performer, then turned to producing movies for a time, before going on to work in radio and the theatre.
Autobiography: 1983, *A Small Thing – Like an Earthquake.*
The Virgin Soldiers 69. Every Home Should Have One 70. Girl Stroke Boy 71. Up Pompeii 71. Rentadick 72. Up the Chastity Belt 72. The Alf Garnett Saga 72. Up the Front 72. The National Health 73, etc.

Sherwin, Manning (1903–1974).
American composer, working for Paramount during the 30s; at the end of the decade he came to Britain to write for films and theatre, including many London musicals and revues. His best-known song, to Eric Maschwitz's lyrics, was 'A Nightingale Sang in Berkeley Square'.
Stolen Holiday 37. Blossoms on Broadway 37. Vogues of 1938 37. College Swing (GB: Swing, Teacher, Swing) 38. A Girl Must Live 39. He Found a Star 41. Hi, Gang! 41. King Arthur Was a Gentleman 42. Miss London Limited 43. Bees in Paradise 43. I'll Be Your Sweetheart 45, etc.

Sherwood, Bill (1952–1990).
American director. Died of AIDS.
Parting Glances 86.

Sherwood, Madeleine (1926–) (Madeleine Thornton).
Canadian character actress.
▪ Cat on a Hot Tin Roof 58. Parrish 61. Sweet Bird of Youth 62. Hurry Sundown 67. Pendulum 69. Wicked Wicked 73, etc.
TV series: The Flying Nun 67–68.

Sherwood, Robert (1896–1955).
American dramatist. Plays filmed:
Reunion in Vienna 32. The Petrified Forest 36. Tovarich 38. Idiot's Delight 39. Abe Lincoln in Illinois 39, etc.
OTHER SCRIPTS: Waterloo Bridge 32. The Adventures of Marco Polo 38. *Rebecca* (AAN) 40. *The Best Years of Our Lives* (AA) 45. The Bishop's Wife 48. Jupiter's Darling (The Road to Rome) 54.

Sheybal, Vladek (1928–).
Intense-looking Polish character actor in Britain.
Kanal 56. Women in Love 69. The Music Lovers 70. The Boy Friend 71. QB VII 74. The Wind and the Lion 75. Memed My Hawk 87. Strike It Rich 90, etc.

Shields, Arthur (1895–1970).
Irish character actor, an Abbey player, long in Hollywood; brother of Barry Fitzgerald.
The Plough and the Stars 37. *Drums along the Mohawk* 39. *The Long Voyage Home* 40. The Keys of the Kingdom 44. The Corn is Green 45. The River 51. The Quiet Man 52. The King and Four Queens 56. Night of the Quarter Moon 59. The Pigeon That Took Rome 62, etc.

Shields, Brooke (1965–).
American juvenile actress of the late 70s.
Alice Sweet Alice 78. King of the Gypsies 78. Pretty Baby 79. Just You and Me Kid 79. Tilt 79. Two of a Kind 79. Wanda Nevada 80. The Blue Lagoon 80. Endless Love 81. Sahara 82. The Muppets Take Manhattan 84. The Diamond Trap (TV) 88. Brenda Starr 89. Speed Zone 89. Backstreet Dreams 90. Brenda Starr 92. Freaked 93, etc.
~When she was only 15 the press seized on her mother's willingness to have her play too-mature roles. Brooke replied: 'What does good in bed mean to me? When I'm sick and stay home from school watching TV and my mom brings me soup – that's good in bed.' She went on to make TV commercials for jeans in which she said: 'If my jeans could talk, would I be embarrassed.'

Shigeta, James (1933–).
Hawaiian leading man who usually plays Japanese in Hollywood films.
The Crimson Kimono 60. Cry for Happy 60. Walk Like a Dragon 60. Bridge to the Sun 61. Flower Drum Song 61. Paradise Hawaiian Style 66. Nobody's Perfect 68. Lost Horizon 73. Midway 76. Tomorrow's Child 82. Die Hard 88. Cage 89. China Cry 90, etc.

Shilkret, Nathaniel (1895–1982).
American arranger and conductor.
The Plough and the Stars 36. Mary of Scotland 36. The Toast of New York 37. She Went to the Races 45. The Hoodlum Saint 46, many others.

Shimkus, Joanna (1943–).
Canadian leading lady in American and European films. She is married to actor Sidney Poitier.
Paris Vu Par 66. Les Aventuriers 67. Zita 68. Ho! 68. Boom 68. The Lost Man 69. *The Virgin and the Gypsy* 70. The Marriage of a Young Stockbroker 71. A Time for Loving 71, etc.

Shimoda, Yuki (1924–1981).
Japanese-American character actor.
Auntie Mame 59. A Majority of One 61. Midway 75. Farewell to Manzanar (TV) 76. MacArthur 77. The Last Flight of Noah's Ark 79, many others.

Shimura, Takashi (1905–1982).
Japanese leading actor.
Stray Dog 49. *Rashomon* 50. Seven Samurai 54. Godzilla 56. Throne of Blood 57. The Hidden Fortress 58. Yojimbo 62, etc.

Shindo, Kaneto (1912–).
Japanese director. Began as assistant art director and successful screenwriter, particularly in collaboration with Yoshimura (qv), before concentrating on directing.
Children of Hiroshima 53. The Wolf 56. *The Island* 62. Ningen 63. *Onibaba* 64. Kuroncko 67. Iron Ring 72. Heart 73. Life of Chikuzan 77. The Horizon 84. Eiga Joyu 87. The Strange Story of Oyuki (Bokuto Kidan) 93. Faraway Sunset (Tooki Rakujitsu) (w) 93, etc.

Shine, Bill (1911–).
Amiable British small-part actor often seen as vacuous dandy.
The Scarlet Pimpernel 34. Farewell Again 37. Let George Do It 40. Perfect Strangers 45. Melba 53. Father Brown 54. Jack the Ripper 58, many others.

Shiner, Ronald (1903–1966).
British comedy actor, on stage from 1928, films from 1934, at first in bit parts, later as star.
King Arthur Was a Gentleman 42. The Way to the Stars 45. *Worm's Eye View* 50. *Reluctant Heroes* 51. Laughing Anne 53. Top of the Form 54. Up to His Neck 55. Keep It Clean 56. Dry Rot 56. Girls at Sea 58. Operation Bullshine 59. The Night We Got the Bird 60, etc.

Shingleton, Wilfrid (1914–1983).
British art director who won an Oscar for *Great Expectations* 46.

Shinoda, Masahiro (1931–).
Japanese director, part of the so-called 'New Wave' movement with Oshima. He studied drama at university before becoming an assistant director.
One Ticket for Love (Koi no Katamichi Kippu) 60. Epitaph to My Love (Waga Koi no Tabiji) 61. Our Marriage (Watakushi-tachi no Kekkon) 62. Pale Flower (Kawaita Hana) 63. Assassination (Ansatsu) 64. Captive's Island (Shokei no Shima) 66. Double Suicide (Shinju Ten no Amijima) 69. Silence (Chinomoku) 71. Sapporo Winter Olympic Games 72. Hanare Goze Orin 77. MacArthur's Children 84. Gonza the Spearman 86. The Dancer 89. Boyhood (Shonen Jidai) 91. Sharaku 95, etc.

ships,
of the modern passenger kind, have provided a useful setting for many films, most recently in *Ship of Fools.* Three notable versions of the *Titanic* disaster were *Atlantic* 30, *Titanic* 53 and *A Night to Remember* 58; while sinking ships also figured in *We're Not Dressing* 34, *Souls at Sea* 37, *History Is Made at Night* 37, *The Blue Lagoon* 48, *Our Girl Friday* 52, *The Admirable Crichton* 57 (and earlier versions), *The Last Voyage* 60 and *The Poseidon Adventure* 72. A sinister time was had on board ship in *Journey into Fear, Across the Pacific, King Kong, My Favorite Blonde, The Ghost Ship, The Mystery of the Marie Celeste, The Sea Wolf, The Hairy Ape, Dangerous Crossing, Ghost Breakers, The Wreck of the Mary Deare, Juggernaut,* and *Voyage of the Damned;* laughter, however, was to the fore in *Monkey Business* 31, *The Lady Eve* 41, *Luxury Liner* 48, *Doctor at Sea* 55, *The Captain's Table* 58, *A Countess from Hong Kong* 66, and *A Night at the Opera* 35 with its famous cabin scene. The romance of a cruise was stressed in *Dodsworth* 36, *The Big Broadcast of 1938, Now Voyager* 42, and the two versions of *Love Affair* 39 (the second being *An Affair to Remember* 56); while in the 'Winter Cruise' section of *Encore* 51, it was almost forced on Kay Walsh. In *Assault on a Queen* 66 the leading characters plan to hijack the *Queen Mary.* The weirdest ship was the ship of the dead in *Outward Bound* 30, and its remake *Between Two Worlds* 44.
Mississippi riverboats have featured in *Mississippi, Rhythm on the River, Mississippi Gambler, The Secret Life of Walter Mitty, The Naughty Nineties, The Adventures of Mark Twain, Four for Texas, Frankie and Johnny,* and the several versions of *Showboat;* also in the TV series *Riverboat.*
Sailing ships of olden days are too numerous to detail.

Shire, David (1937–).
American composer.

One More Train to Rob 71. Drive He Said 71. Showdown 73. The Conversation 74. Farewell My Lovely 75. The Hindenburg 75. All the President's Men 76. Saturday Night Fever 77. Norma Rae 79. Only When I Laugh 81. Paternity 81. Max Dugan Returns 82. The World According to Garp 82. Oh God! You Devil 84. Return to Oz 85. Mother 86. Short Circuit 86. Backfire 87. Monkey Shines 88. Vice Versa 88, etc.

Shire, Talia (1947–) (Talia Coppola).
American leading lady, sister of Francis Coppola.
The Wild Races 68. The Dunwich Horror 70. Un Homme Est Mort 72. *The Godfather* 72. The Godfather Part II (AAN) 74. Rocky (AAN) 76. Old Boyfriends 79. Rocky II 79. Prophecy 79. Rocky III 82. Rocky IV 85. RAD 86. From Another Star 87. New York Stories 89. The Godfather Part III 90. Rocky V 90. Bed and Breakfast 91. Cold Heaven 92. Chantilly Lace (TV) 93. Deadfall 93. Before the Night (d) 94, etc.

Shirley, Anne (1919–1993) (Dawn Paris).
American child star of the 20s (under the name Dawn O'Day) who later graduated to leading lady roles. She retired in 1944. Married to actor John Payne (1937–43), producer Adrian Scott (1945–49), and screenwriter Charles Lederer.
So Big 32. *Anne of Green Gables* 34. Stella Dallas (AAN) 37. Vigil in the Night 39. Anne of Windy Poplars 40. West Point Widow 41. All that Money Can Buy 41. *Farewell My Lovely* 44. Murder My Sweet 45, etc.

Shoemaker, Ann (1891–1978).
American character actress with stage experience.
A Dog of Flanders 35. Alice Adams 35. Stella Dallas 37. Babes in Arms 39. Conflict 45. A Woman's Secret 49. Sunrise at Campobello 60. The Fortune Cookie 66, many others.

Sholem, Lee (c. 1900–).
American director.
Tarzan's Magic Fountain 48. Redhead from Wyoming 52. Tobor the Great 53. Emergency Hospital 56. Pharaoh's Curse 56. Sierra Stranger 57, etc.

Shonteff, Lindsay. (c. 1940–).
Canadian-born director of British exploitation films.
Devil Doll 63. Curse of Simba 64. Licensed to Kill (aka The Second Best Secret Agent in the Whole Wide World) 65. Run with the Wind 66. The Million Eyes of Su-Muru 67. Clegg 69. The Yes Girls 71. Big Zapper 73. The Swordsman (aka Zapper's Blade of Vengeance) 74. Spy Story 76. No. 1 of the Secret Service 77. Licensed to Love and Kill 79. How Sleep the Brave 81. Number One Gun 90. The Gunfighter 93, etc.

¶ Let's not beat about the bush here: even the man himself admits that the backers of one of his recent movies wanted to commit suicide when they saw the result of his efforts. – *Alan Bryce, Shock Xpress*

shooting script.
This differs from a screenplay, which concentrates on dialogue, in that it includes camera directions and breaks up the script into shots; it is an instruction manual for technicians rather than a work of art.

The Shop around the Corner.
Nikolaus Laszlo's play about two Budapest shop assistants who are unaware that they are pen pals was filmed by Ernst Lubitsch in 1940, with

Margaret Sullavan and James Stewart, as a charming piece of Hollywood schmaltz. In 1949 Robert Z. Leonard remade it as a musical, *In the Good Old Summertime*, with Judy Garland and Van Johnson.

The Shopworn Angel.
This comedy-drama about a Hollywood gold-digger who gives up her rich provider for a poor soldier has been filmed four times: as *Pettigrew's Girl*, a silent in 1919, with Ethel Clayton and Monte Blue; in 1929, with Nancy Carroll, Paul Lukas, and Gary Cooper; in 1938, with Margaret Sullavan, Walter Pidgeon, and James Stewart; and in 1959, as *That Kind of Woman*, with Sidney Lumet directing Sophia Loren, George Sanders, and Tab Hunter.

Shore, Dinah (1917–1994) (Frances Rose Shore).
American cabaret singer, in very occasional films; latterly running a daily TV chat show for women. As a child singer, was known as Fanny Rose.
■ Thank Your Lucky Stars 43. Up in Arms 44. Follow the Boys 44. Belle of the Yukon 45. Till the Clouds Roll By 46. Aaron Slick from Punkin Crick 52. Oh God 77. Health 80.

Shore, Howard.
Canadian composer, from TV.
The Brood 79. Scanners 81. Videodrome 83. Places in the Heart 84. After Hours 85. Fire with Fire 86. The Fly 86. Nadine 87. Heaven 87. Moving 88. Big 88. Dead Ringers 88. An Innocent Man 89. She-Devil 89. The Silence of the Lambs 91. Prelude to a Kiss 92. Sliver 93. Guilty as Sin 93. Mrs Doubtfire 93. M. Butterfly 93. Philadelphia 93. The Client 94. Ed Wood 94, etc.

Shore, Pauly.
American comic actor, from television.
Encino Man (GB: California Man) 92. Son-in-Law 93. Dream Date 93. In the Army Now 94.

Short, Martin (1950–).
Canadian comic actor and writer. He first gained recognition with Toronto's Second City Troupe.
Lost and Found 79. The Outsider 79. The Canadian Conspiracy 86. Three Amigos! 86. Cross My Heart 87. Innerspace 87. The Big Picture 88. Three Fugitives 89. Pure Luck 91. Father of the Bride 92. Captain Ron 92. We're Back! A Dinosaur's Story (voice) 93. Clifford 94, etc.
TV series: The Associates 79–80. I'm a Big Girl Now 80–81. SCTV Network 90 82–83. Saturday Night Live 84–85.

shorts
are officially any films running less than 3000 feet (about 33 minutes). In the 30s most programmes consisted of a feature and several one-reelers, but the big studios first found shorts uneconomic and then closed them down altogether. Shorts fell into the hands of independent producers, who found that the longer they made them the more money they could demand, even if the quality was not high. Double-feature programmes also contributed to their demise.

Shostakovich, Dmitri (1906–1975).
Russian composer.
The New Babylon 28. The Youth of Maxim 35. The Fall of Berlin 47. Hamlet 64. War and Peace 64.

Shotter, Winifred (1904–).
British leading lady of the 30s, chiefly remembered in the Aldwych farces beginning with *Rookery Nook* 30.

Show Boat.
Jerome Kern and Oscar Hammerstein II's operetta from Edna Ferber's novel was filmed by Harry Pollard in 1929 with Laura La Plante and Joseph Schildkraut; by James Whale in 1936 with Irene Dunne, Allan Jones, and Paul Robeson; and by George Sidney in 1951 with Kathryn Grayson, Howard Keel, and William Warfield.

Showalter, Max (1917–) (formerly known as Casey Adams).
American supporting actor often seen as reporter, newscaster or good-guy friend.
Always Leave Them Laughing 50. With a Song in My Heart 52. Bus Stop 56. The Naked and the Dead 58. Elmer Gantry 60. Bon Voyage 62. Fate Is the Hunter 64. The Moonshine War 70. The Anderson Tapes 71. Sergeant Pepper's Lonely Hearts Club Band 78. 10 79. Sixteen Candles 84, etc.

Shue, Elizabeth (1964–).
American leading actress.
The Karate Kid 84. Link 86. Adventures in Babysitting 87. Cocktail 88. Back to the Future Part II 89. Back to the Future Part III 90. The Marrying Man (aka Too Hot to Handle) 91. Soapdish 91. Twenty Bucks 93. Radio Inside 94, etc.
TV series: Call to Glory 84–85.

Shuken, Leo (1906–1976).
American orchestrator.
Waikiki Wedding 37. The Flying Deuces 39. *Stagecoach* (AA) 39. The Lady Eve 41. *Sullivan's Travels* 41. The Miracle of Morgan's Creek 44. The Fabulous Dorseys 47. The Greatest Story Ever Told 64, etc.

Shumlin, Herman (1898–1979).
American stage producer who directed two films in the 40s.
■ Watch on the Rhine 43. Confidential Agent 45.

Shurlock, Geoffrey (1895–1976).
Film administrator, an Englishman who became the power behind the MPEA Production Code 1954–68.

Shusett, Ronald.
American screenwriter.
Alien (story) 79. Dead and Buried 81. Phobia 81. The Final Terror 83. King Kong Lives 86. Above the Law 88. Total Recall 90. Freejack 92, etc.

Shute, Nevil (1899–1960).
English best-selling novelist.
The Pied Piper 43. No Highway 52. Landfall 54. A Town Like Alice 56. On the Beach 59, etc.

Shyer, Charles (1941–).
American director and screenwriter. Married writer and producer Nancy Myers.
Smokey and the Bandit (co-w) 77. Goin' South (co-w) 78. House Calls (co-w) 78. Private Benjamin (co-w, AAN) 80. Irreconcilable Differences (co-w, d) 84. Baby Boom (co-w, d) 87. Father of the Bride (co-w, d) 91. I Love Trouble (co-w, d) 94, etc.

Sidney, George (1878–1945) (Sammy Greenfield).
American comedian, once popular in vaudeville.
Potash and Perlmutter 23. Millionaires 26. Clancy's Kosher Wedding 27. The Cohens and Kellys in Paris 28. Manhattan Melodrama 34. Good Old Soak 37, many others.

Sidney, George (1911–).
American director, former musician and MGM shorts director.

Free and Easy 41. Thousands Cheer 43. Bathing Beauty 44. Anchors Aweigh 45. *The Harvey Girls* 46. Cass Timberlane 47. *The Three Musketeers* 48. The Red Danube 49. Annie Get Your Gun 50. *Showboat* 51. Scaramouche 52. Young Bess 53. *Kiss Me Kate* 53. Jupiter's Darling 54. The Eddy Duchin Story 56. *Jeanne Eagels* 57. Pal Joey 57. Who Was That Lady? 59. Pepe 60. Bye Bye Birdie 62. Viva Las Vegas 63. The Swinger 66. Half a Sixpence 67, etc.

Sidney, Sylvia (1910–) (Sophia Kosow).
Fragile, dark-eyed American heroine of the 30s.
■ Thru Different Eyes 29. *City Streets* 31. Confessions of a Co-Ed 31. An American Tragedy 31. *Street Scene* 31. Ladies of the Big House 32. The Miracle Man 32. Merrily We Go to Hell 33. Madame Butterfly 33. Pick Up 33. Jennie Gerhardt 33. Good Dame 34. Thirty Day Princess 34. Behold My Wife 34. Accent on Youth 35. Mary Burns Fugitive 35. Trail of the Lonesome Pine 36. Fury 36. Sabotage (GB) 37. *You Only Live Once* 37. Dead End 37. You and Me 37. One Third of a Nation 39. The Wagons Roll at Night 41. Blood on the Sun 45. The Searching Wind 46. Mr Ace 46. Love from a Stranger 47. Les Misérables 53. Violent Saturday 55. Behind the High Wall 56. Do Not Fold Spindle or Mutilate (TV) 71. Summer Wishes Winter Dreams (AAN) 73. Death at Love House (TV) 76. God Told Me To 76. Raid on Entebbe (TV) 77. I Never Promised You a Rose Garden 77. Siege (TV) 78. Damien: Omen II 79. The Shadow Box (TV) 80. Hammett 82. Corrupt 83. Finnegan Begin Again (TV) 85. An Early Frost (TV) 85. Pals (TV) 87. Beetlejuice 88.

❡ I'd be the girl of the gangster . . . then the sister who was bringing up the gangster . . . then the mother of the gangster . . . and they always had me ironing somebody's shirt. – *S.S.*

What did Hitchcock teach me? To be a puppet and not try to be creative. – *S.S.*

Siegel, Don (1912–1991).
American director, former editor; an expert at crime thrillers, he latterly attracted the attention of highbrow critics.
Autobiography: 1993, *A Siegel Film: An Autobiography.*
■ Hitler Lives (short) (AA) 45. Star in the Night (short) (AA) 45. The Verdict 46. Night Unto Night 48. The Big Steal 49. Duel at Silver Creek 52. No Time for Flowers 52. Count the Hours 53. China Venture 54. *Riot in Cell Block 11* 54. Private Hell 36 55. An Annapolis Story 55. *Invasion of the Body Snatchers* 56. Crime in the Streets 57. Spanish Affair 57. Baby Face Nelson 57. The Line Up 58. The Gun Runners 58. The Hound Dog Man 59. Edge of Eternity 59. Flaming Star 60. Hell is for Heroes 62. The Killers 64. The Hanged Man 64. Madigan 67. Stranger on the Run (TV) 68. *Coogan's Bluff* 68. Two Mules for Sister Sara 69. Death of a Gunfighter (co-d) 69. The Beguiled 71. Play Misty for Me (acted only) 71. *Dirty Harry* 72. *Charley Varrick* 73. The Black Windmill 74. *The Shootist* 76. Telefon 77. Escape from Alcatraz 79. Rough Cut 80. Jinxed 82. Into the Night (a) 85.

❡ I once told Godard that he had something I wanted – freedom. He said: 'You have something I want – money.' – *D.S.*

Most of my pictures, I'm sorry to say, are about nothing. Because I'm a whore. I work for money. It's the American way. – *D.S.*

Siegel, Sol C. (1903–1982).
American producer, in films from 1929.

Kiss and Tell 44. Blue Skies 46. House of Strangers 49. A Letter to Three Wives 49. I Was a Male War Bride 49. Fourteen Hours 51. Monkey Business 52. Gentlemen Prefer Blondes 52. Call Me Madam 53. Three Coins in the Fountain 54. High Society 56. Les Girls 57. Home from the Hill 59. Walk Don't Run 66. Alvarez Kelly 66. No Way to Treat a Lady 68, etc.

Siemaszko, Casey (1961–) (Kazimierz Siemaszko).
American actor.

Class 83. Back to the Future 85. Secret Admirer 85. Stand by Me 86. Gardens of Stone 87. Three o'Clock High 87. Biloxi Blues 88. Young Guns 88. Back to the Future II 89. Breaking In 89. The Big Slice 91. Of Mice and Men 92. Milk Money 94. Teresa's Tattoo 94, etc.

Sienkiewicz, Henryk (1846–1916).
Polish novelist, author of the much filmed *Quo Vadis?* (published 1895).

Sierra, Gregory.
American supporting actor.

The Wrath of God 72. Papillon 72. The Towering Inferno 74. The Prisoner of Zenda 79. Something Is Out There (TV) 88. Honey I Blew Up The Kid 92. Deep Cover 92, etc.

TV series: Sanford and Son 72–75. Barney Miller 75–76. Soap 80–81. Zorro and Son 83.

Signoret, Simone (1921–1985) (Simone Kaminker).
Distinguished French leading actress, married to Yves Montand.
Autobiography: 1976, *Nostalgia Isn't What It Used to Be.*
Biography: 1992, *Simone Signoret* by Catherine David.
■ Le Prince Charmant 42. Bolero 42. Les Visiteurs du Soir 42. Adieu Leonard 43. Beatrice 43. La Boîte aux Rêves 45. The Ideal Couple 45. Les Démons de l'Aube 45. Macadam 45. Fantomas 47. Against the Wind (GB) 47. *Dédée d'Anvers* 48. L'Impasse des Deux Anges 49. *Manèges* 49. Four Days' Leave 50. *La Ronde* 50. Gunman in the Streets 50. Ombre et Lumière 51. *Casque d'Or* 52. Thérése Raquin 53. *Les Diaboliques* 54. Le Mort en ce Jardin 56. The Witches of Salem 57. *Room at the Top* (GB) (AA) 58. Adua and Company 60. Les Mauvais Coups 61. Les Amours Célèbres 61. Term of Trial (GB) 62. The Day and the Hour 63. Dragées au Poivre 63. *Ship of Fools* (US) (AAN) 65. The Sleeping Car Murders 65. Is Paris Burning? 66. The Deadly Affair (GB) 67. Games (US) 67. The Seagull 68. L'Armée des Ombres 69. The American 69. The Confession 70. Comptes à Rebours 71. *Le Chat* 72. La Veuve Coudere 73. Rude Journée pour la Reine 73. Défense de Savoir 74. The Investigator 74. Flesh of the Orchid 74. Police Python 357 76. Madame Rosa 78. L'Adolescente 79. I Sent a Letter to My Love 81.

silent films
began to grow unfashionable during 1927, though for eighteen months or so producers continued to put out so-called 'silent versions' of their talkies: these versions were unspeakably bad, as the new talkies used very little camera movement and a great deal of dialogue which had to be given in sub-titles. By 1930 silents had all but disappeared, with exceptions such as Flaherty's *Tabu* 32, Chaplin's *City Lights* 31, and *Modern Times* 36, and an unsuccessful 1952 experiment called *The Thief*, which eschewed dialogue though it did have a music and effects track. In 1976 Mel Brooks produced *Silent Movie*, a comic extravaganza with no dialogue.

❡ There never was a silent film. We'd finish a picture, show it in one of our projection rooms and come out shattered. It would be awful. Then we'd show it in a theatre with a girl pounding away at a piano and there would be all the difference in the world. Without that music there wouldn't have been a movie industry at all. – *Irving Thalberg*

It will never be possible to synchronize the voice with the pictures. Music – fine music – will always be the voice of the silent drama . . . There will never be speaking pictures. – *D.W. Griffith, 1924*

Silliphant, Sterling (1918–).
American writer-producer with much TV experience (*Naked City, Route 66*, etc.). Former advertising executive.

The Joe Louis Story (w) 53. Five Against the House (w, co-p) 55. Nightfall (w) 56. Damn Citizen (w) 57. Village of the Damned 60. The Slender Thread (w) 66. In The Heat of the Night (w) (AA) 67. Charly 68. A Walk in the Spring Rain 69. The Liberation of L.B. Jones 70. The Poseidon Adventure 72. The Towering Inferno 74. The Killer Elite (w) 75. Telefon (co-w) 77. The Swarm (w) 78. Pearl (TV) 79. When Time Ran Out (co-w) 80. Space (TV) 85. Catch the Heat 87. Over the Top 87, etc.

Sillitoe, Alan (1928–).
British north-country novelist best known to filmgoers for *Saturday Night and Sunday Morning* and *The Loneliness of the Long Distance Runner*. His less successful novel *The General* was filmed as *Counterpoint.*

Sills, Milton (1882–1930).
Stalwart American leading man of the silent screen.

The Rack 15. The Claw 17. Eyes of Youth 19. The Weekend 20. Burning Sands 22. Adam's Rib 23. Madonna of the Streets 24. The Sea Hawk 24. Paradise 26. Valley of the Giants 27. His Captive Woman 29. The Sea Wolf 30, many others.

Silly Symphony.
The name given by Walt Disney to all his short cartoon fables of the 30s which did not feature Mickey Mouse, Pluto or Donald Duck.

Silva, Henry (1928–).
Pale-eyed American actor of Italian and Basque descent, often seen as sadistic villain or assorted Latin types.

Viva Zapata 52. Crowded Paradise 56. A Hatful of Rain 57. The Bravados 58. Green Mansions 59. Cinderfella 60. *The Manchurian Candidate* 62. *Johnny Cool* (leading role) 63. The Return of Mr Moto 65. The Reward 65. The Plainsman 66. The Hills Ran Red (It.) 66. Never a Dull Moment 68. Five Savage Men 70. The Kidnap of Mary Lou 75. Shoot 76. Cry of a Prostitute 76. Thirst 79. Buck Rogers 79. Alligator 80. Sharkey's Machine 81. Wrong Is Right 82. Allan Quatermain and the Lost City of Gold 86. Bulletproof 87. Above the Law 88. Dick Tracy 90. South Beach 92. The Harvest 92, etc.

Silver, Joan Micklin (1935–).
American director.
■ Limbo (w) 72. *Hester Street* (& w) 74. Bernice Bobs Her Hair (& w) (TV) 76. Between the Lines 78. Head over Heels (& w) 79. Crossing Delancey

88. Loverboy 89. Big Girls Don't Cry . . . They Get Even (GB: Stepkids) 92.

Silver, Joel (1939–).
American producer, mainly of high-budget action films.

48 Hours 82. Streets of Fire 84. Brewster's Millions 85. Commando 85. Weird Science 85. Jumpin' Jack Flash 86. Lethal Weapon 87. Predator 87. Action Jackson 88. Die Hard 88. Road House 89. Lethal Weapon 2 89. The Adventures of Ford Fairlane 90. Predator 2 90. Die Hard II 90. Hudson Hawk 91. Ricochet 91. The Last Boy Scout 92. Lethal Weapon 3 92. Demolition Man 93, etc.

Silver, Marisa (1960–).
American director and screenwriter.
Old Enough (wd) 84. Permanent Record (d) 88. Vital Signs (d) 90.

Silver, Ron (1946–).
American leading actor.
The French Connection 71. Tunnel Vision 76. Semi-Tough 77. Best Friends 82. Silent Rage 82. The Entity 82. Silkwood 83. Betrayal 83. Garbo Talks 84. Oh, God! You Devil 84. Eat and Run 86. Enemies, a Love Story 89. Fellow Traveller 89. Blue Steel 90. Reversal of Fortune 90. Trapped in Silence (TV) 90. Live Wire 92. Mr Saturday Night 92. Married to It 93. Timecop 94, etc.
TV series: Rhoda 76–78. Dear Detective 79. The Stockard Channing Show 80. Baker's Dozen 82.

Silvera, Frank (1914–1970).
American general-purpose actor with stage experience. Electrocuted while repairing a kitchen appliance.
Viva Zapata 52. Killer's Kiss 55. Crowded Paradise 56. The Mountain Road 60. Mutiny on the Bounty 62. The Appaloosa 66. Che! 69. Valdez Is Coming 71, etc.
TV series: The High Chaparral 67–70.

Silverheels, Jay (1919–1980).
Canadian Red Indian actor, mainly in western films.
The Prairie 47. Fury at Furnace Creek 48. Broken Arrow 50. War Arrow 53. The Lone Ranger 55. Indian Paint 65. The Phynx 70. Santee 73, many others.
TV series: The Lone Ranger (as Tonto) 52–56.

Silvers, Louis (1889–1954).
American composer.
The Jazz Singer 27. Dancing Lady 33. It Happened One Night 34. One Night of Love (AA) 35. Lloyds of London 36. Heidi 37. In Old Chicago (AAN) 38. Suez (AAN) 38. Jesse James 39. Swanee River (AAN) 39. The Powers Girl 42, many others.

Silvers, Phil (1912–1985) (Philip Silver).
American vaudeville star comedian in occasional films from 1941.
Autobiography: 1974, The Laugh Is on Me.
Tom, Dick and Harry (debut) 41. You're in the Army Now 42. Roxie Hart 42. My Gal Sal 42. Coney Island 43. Cover Girl 44. A Thousand and One Nights 45. Where Do We Go from Here? 45. Summer Stock 50. Lucky Me 54. Forty Pounds of Trouble 63. It's a Mad Mad Mad Mad World 63. A Funny Thing Happened on the Way to the Forum 66. Follow That Camel (GB) 67. Buona Sera, Mrs Campbell 68. Deadly Tide (TV) 75. Won Ton Ton 76. The Chicken Chronicles 77. The New Love Boat (TV) 77. The Night They Took Miss Beautiful (TV) 78. There Goes the Bride 80, etc.

TV series: You'll Never Get Rich (as Bilko) 55–58. The New Phil Silvers Show 64.

Silverstein, Elliot (1927–).
American director, from TV.
■ Belle Sommers (TV) 62. Cat Ballou 65. The Happening 67. A Man Called Horse 69. The Car 77. Betrayed by Innocence (TV) 86. Night of Courage (TV) 87. Fight for Life (TV) 87. Rich Men, Single Women (TV) 90. Flashfire 94.

Silvestri, Alan.
American composer.
Romancing the Stone 84. Cat's Eye 84. Back to the Future 85. Clan of the Cave Bear 85. Outrageous Fortune 86. Predator 87. Overboard 87. Who Framed Roger Rabbit? 88. My Stepmother Is an Alien 88. The Abyss 89. Back to the Future II 89. Downtown 90. Back to the Future III 90. Predator 2 90. Young Guns II 90. Soapdish 91. Ricochet 91. Shattered 91. Father of the Bride 91. Dutch (GB: Driving Me Crazy) 91. Stop! Or My Mom Will Shoot 92. Super Mario Bros 93. Cop and a Half 93. Sidekicks 93. Judgment Night 93. Grumpy Old Men 93. Clean Slate 94. Blown Away 94, etc.

Sim, Alastair (1900–1976).
Lugubrious Scottish comedy actor of stage and screen; his diction and gestures were inimitable.
■ Riverside Murder 35. The Private Secretary 35. A Fire Has Been Arranged 35. Late Extra 35. The Case of Gabriel Perry 35. Troubled Waters 36. Wedding Group 36. The Big Noise 36. Keep Your Seats Please 36. The Man in the Mirror 36. The Mysterious Mr Davis 36. Strange Experiment 37. Clothes and the Woman 37. Gangway 37. The Squeaker 37. A Romance in Flanders 37. Melody and Romance 37. Sailing Along 38. The Terror 38. Alf's Button Afloat 38. This Man is News 38. Climbing High 38. Inspector Hornleigh 39. This Man in Paris 39. Inspector Hornleigh on Holiday 39. Law and Disorder 40. Inspector Hornleigh Goes to It 41. Cottage to Let 41. Let the People Sing 42. Waterloo Road 44. Green for Danger 46. Hue and Cry 47. Captain Boycott 47. London Belongs to Me 48. The Happiest Days of Your Life 49. Stage Fright 50. Laughter in Paradise 51. Scrooge 51. Lady Godiva Rides Again 51. Folly to be Wise 52. Innocents in Paris 53. An Inspector Calls 54. The Belles of St Trinian's 54. Escapade 55. Geordie 55. The Green Man 56. Blue Murder at St Trinian's 57. The Doctor's Dilemma 58. Left, Right and Centre 59. School for Scoundrels 60. The Millionairess 60. The Ruling Class 71. Royal Flash 75. Escape from the Dark 76. Rogue Male (TV) 76.
✪ For marvellous moments of high comedy and for the lasting comic image of his unique physiognomy. Green for Danger.

Sim, Gerald (1925–).
British supporting actor, often in well-bred and slightly prissy roles.
Fame is the Spur 47. The Wrong Arm of the Law 63. The Pumpkin Eater 64. King Rat 64. The Whisperers 66. Oh What a Lovely War 68. Dr Jekyll and Sister Hyde 71. No Sex Please We're British 73. The Slipper and the Rose 76. Gandhi 82. Cry Freedom 87, many others.

Sim, Sheila (1922–).
English leading actress, in occasional films. Married to Lord (Richard) Attenborough.
A Canterbury Tale 43. Great Day 45. The Guinea Pig 48. Dear Mr Prohack 49. Pandora and the Flying Dutchman 51. The Magic Box 51. The Night My Number Came Up 55, etc.

Simenon, Georges (1903–1989).
French crime novelist, creator of Inspector Maigret.
Les Inconnus dans la Maison 43. Panique 46. Temptation Harbour (GB) 46. La Marie du Port 50. The Man on the Eiffel Tower (US) 50. Le Fruit Défendu 52. The Brothers Rico (US) 57. Maigret Sets a Trap 58, etc.
TV series: Maigret 63. Thirteen against Fate 67.

¶ Can there be a more intimate communication between two beings than copulation? – G.S.

Simmons, Anthony (c. 1924–).
British writer-director, known for short films.
Sunday by the Sea 53. Bow Bells 54. The Gentle Corsican 56. Your Money or Your Wife 59. Four in the Morning 65. The Optimists of Nine Elms 73. Black Joy 78. Little Sweetheart 88, etc.

Simmons, Jean (1929–).
Self-possessed and beautiful British leading lady who married Stewart Granger (later Richard Brooks) and settled in Hollywood to make films which have generally been unworthy of her talents.
■ Give Us the Moon 43. Mr Emmanuel 44. Meet Sexton Blake 44. Kiss the Bride Goodbye 44. The Way to the Stars 45. Caesar and Cleopatra 45. Hungry Hill 45. The Woman in the Hall 45. Great Expectations 46. Black Narcissus 46. Uncle Silas 47. Hamlet (AAN) 48. The Blue Lagoon 48. Adam and Evelyne 49. Trio 50. Cage of Gold 50. So Long at the Fair 50. The Clouded Yellow 50. Angel Face 52. Androcles and the Lion 53. Young Bess 53. Affair with a Stranger 53. The Robe 53. The Actress 53. She Couldn't Say No 54. The Egyptian 54. A Bullet is Waiting 54. Désirée 54. Footsteps in the Fog 55. Guys and Dolls 56. Hilda Crane 56. This Could Be the Night 57. Until They Sail 57. The Big Country 58. Home Before Dark 58. This Earth is Mine 59. Elmer Gantry 60. Spartacus 60. The Grass is Greener 61. All the Way Home 63. Life at the Top 65. Mister Buddwing 66. Rough Night in Jericho 67. Divorce American Style 67. The Happy Ending (AAN) 69. Say Hello to Yesterday 71. Mr Sycamore 75. The Dain Curse (TV) 78. Dominique 79. Beggarman Thief (TV) 79. Golden Gate (TV) 80. The Thorn Birds (TV) 82. Midas Valley (TV) 84. Perry Mason: The Case of the Lost Love (TV) 87. The Dawning 88. Great Expectations (TV) 89. Sense and Sensibility (TV) 90. Laker Girls (TV) 90.
TV series: Dark Shadows 91.

Simms, Ginny (1916–) (Virginia Sims).
Glamorous American vocalist, with Kay Kyser's band.
That's Right You're Wrong 39. You'll Find Out 40. Playmates 42. Hit the Ice 43. Broadway Rhythm 44. Shady Lady 45. Night and Day 46. Disc Jockey 51, etc.

Simms, Larry (1934–).
American boy actor, notably in the Blondie series 1938–48. (He was Baby Dumpling.)
The Last Gangster 37. Mr Smith Goes to Washington 39. Madame Bovary 49, etc.

Simon, Adam.
American director.
Brain Dead 90. Body Chemistry II: The Voice of a Stranger 92. Carnosaur 93.

Simon, Carly (1945–).
American composer and singer.
■ Perfect (a) 85. Heartburn (m) 86. Postcards from the Edge (m) 90. This Is My Life (m) 92.

Simon, Melvin (1925–).
American independent producer, former shopping-plaza developer.

Love at First Bite 79. Scavenger Hunt 79. The Runner Stumbles 79. When a Stranger Calls 79. Cloud Dancer 80. My Bodyguard 80. The Man with Bogart's Face 80. The Stunt Man 80. Porky's 82, etc.

Simon, Michel (1895–1975) (François Simon).
Heavyweight French character actor, in films from the 20s after music-hall experience.

Feu Mathias Pascal 25. The Passion of Joan of Arc 28. La Chienne 31. *Boudu Sauvé des Eaux* 32. Lac aux Dames 34. *L'Atalante* 34. Jeunes Filles de Paris 36. Drôle de Drame 37. Les Disparus de Saint-Agil 38. Quai des Brumes 38. Fric Frac 39. *La Fin du Jour* 39. Circonstances Attenuantes 39. Vautrin 43. Un Ami Viendra Ce Soir 45. *Panique* 46. Fabiola 48. *La Beauté du Diable* 49. The Strange Desire of Monsieur Bard 53. Saadia 53. La Joyeuse Prison 56. It Happened in Broad Daylight 58. The Head 59. Austerlitz 59. Candide 60. The Devil and Ten Commandments 62. The Train 64. Two Hours to Kill 65. *The Two of Us* 67. La Maison 70. Blanche 71, many others.

Simon, Neil (1927–).
American comedy playwright whose Broadway success has been remarkable and his Hollywood follow-up diligent, either as scenarist or as original author with a watching brief.

Come Blow Your Horn 63. After the Fox (oa) 66. Barefoot in the Park 67. The Odd Couple (AAN) 68. Sweet Charity 68. The Out of Towners 70. Plaza Suite 71. Last of the Red Hot Lovers 72. The Sunshine Boys 75. Murder by Death 76. The Goodbye Girl (AAN) 78. California Suite (AAN) 78. Chapter Two 79. I Ought to Be in Pictures 82. Max Dugan Returns 83. The Lonely Guy 84. The Slugger's Wife 85. Brighton Beach Memoirs 87. Biloxi Blues 88. The Marrying Man 91. Lost in Yonkers 93, etc.

Simon, Paul (1942–).
American lyricist and singer, long a team element as Simon and Garfunkel. Primarily known to the non-pop public for the music backing *The Graduate*, Simon also appeared in an unsuccessful 1980 movie, *One Trick Pony*, and can be glimpsed in *Annie Hall* 77.

Simon, S. Sylvan (1910–1951).
American director with radio experience.

A Girl with Ideas 37. Four Girls in White 39. Whistling in the Dark 41. Rio Rita 42. Song of the Open Road 44. Son of Lassie 45. Her Husband's Affairs 47. I Love Trouble 48. The Lust for Gold 49. Born Yesterday (p) 50, etc.

Simon, Simone (1910–).
Pert French leading lady with brief stage experience.

Le Chanteur Inconnu (debut) 31. Lac aux Dames 34; to US: Girls' Dormitory 36. *Seventh Heaven* 37. Josette 38. *La Bête Humaine* 38. *All That Money Can Buy* 41. *Cat People* 42. Tahiti Honey 43. Mademoiselle Fifi 44. Temptation Harbour (GB) 47. Donna Senza Nome (It.) 49. La Ronde 50. Olivia 50. Le Plaisir 51. Double Destin 54. The Extra Day (GB) 56. The Woman in Blue 73, etc.

Simoneau, Yves.
French-Canadian director.

Les Célébrations 79. Pouvoir Intime 86. Perfectly Normal 90. Cruel Doubt (TV) 92. Mother's Boys 94. Amelia Earhart: The Final Flight (TV) 94, etc.

Simpson, Alan (1929–).
British TV and film comedy writer, with Ray Galton (qv).

Simpson, Don (1945–).
American producer, in partnership with Jerry Bruckheimer.

Flashdance 83. Beverly Hills Cop 84. Thief of Hearts 84. Top Gun 86. Beverly Hills Cop II 87. The Big Bang 89. Days of Thunder 90. Young Guns II 90. The Ref 94, etc.

Simpson, Ivan (1875–1951).
Scottish character actor in Hollywood.

The Dictator 15. The Green Goddess 23 and 30. The Man Who Played God 32. Phantom of Cresswood 33. David Copperfield 34. Maid of Salem 37. The Hour before the Dawn 43, many others.

Simpson, O. J. (1947–) (Orenthal James Simpson).
American actor and TV sportscaster, a former football star with the Buffalo Bills in the 70s, nicknamed 'The Juice'. In 1994, his arrest for the murder of his wife and a young man became headline news. The police chase of him, at a stately 45 mph along the San Diego Freeway, as he sat in a car pointing a gun at his own head, was broadcast live on television and watched by an estimated 95 million viewers; it was later released on video.

■ The Klansman 74. The Towering Inferno 74. The Diamond Mercenaries 75. The Cassandra Crossing 77. Roots (TV) 77. A Killing Affair (TV) 77. Capricorn One 78. Firepower 79. Detour (TV) 79. Goldie and the Boxer (TV) 79. Goldie and the Boxer Go to Hollywood (TV) 80. Hambone and Hillie 84. The Naked Gun: From the Files of Police Squad 88. The Naked Gun 2½: The Smell of Fear 91. Naked Gun 33⅓: The Final Insult 94.

TV series: Roots 77–78.

Simpson, Russell (1878–1959).
American character actor, in Hollywood from silent days.

Billy the Kid 31. Way Down East 36. Ramona 37. Dodge City 39. The Grapes of Wrath 40. Outside the Law 41. They Were Expendable 45. My Darling Clementine 46. The Beautiful Blonde from Bashful Bend 49. Seven Brides for Seven Brothers 54. Friendly Persuasion 56. The Horse Soldiers 59, many others.

Sims, Joan (1930–).
British stage, TV and film comedienne, often in cameo roles.

Colonel March Investigates 53. Meet Mr Lucifer 54. The Belles of St Trinian's 54. Dry Rot 56. The Naked Truth 58. Carry On Regardless 60. Twice Round the Daffodils 62. Strictly for the Birds 64. Follow that Camel 67. The Alf Garnett Saga 72. One of Our Dinosaurs is Missing 75. Martin Chuzzlewit (TV) 94, many others.

TV series: On the Up 93.

Sinatra, Frank (1915–).
American leading actor and vocalist, former band singer. A teenage rave in the 40s, he later became respected as an actor and a powerful producer.

Biographies: 1962, *Sinatra* by Robin Douglas-Home. 1978, *Sinatra, an Unauthorized Biography* by Earl Wilson. 1980, *Frank Sinatra* by John Howlett. 1984, *Sinatra: An American Classic* by John Rockwell. 1985, *Frank Sinatra, a Celebration* by Derek Jewell. 1985, *Frank Sinatra, My Father* by Nancy Sinatra. 1986, *His Way: The Unauthorized Biography* by Kitty Kelley.

■ Las Vegas Nights 41. Ship Ahoy 42. Reveille

with Beverly 43. Higher and Higher (acting debut) 43. *Step Lively* 44. *Anchors Aweigh* 45. Till the Clouds Roll By 46. It Happened in Brooklyn 46. The Kissing Bandit 47. The Miracle of the Bells 48. *Take Me out to the Ball Game* 48. On the Town 49. Double Dynamite 50. Meet Danny Wilson 51. *From Here to Eternity* (AA) 53. Suddenly 54. Young at Heart 54. The Tender Trap 55. Not as a Stranger 55. *The Man with the Golden Arm* (AAN) 56. Johnny Concho 56. The Pride and the Passion 56. Around the World in Eighty Days 56. Guys and Dolls 56. *High Society* 56. *Pal Joey* 57. The Joker is Wild 57. Kings Go Forth 58. Some Came Running 58. A Hole in the Head 59. Can Can 59. Never So Few 59. Pepe 60. Ocean's Eleven 60. The Devil at Four O'Clock 61. Sergeants Three 62. *The Manchurian Candidate* 62. Four for Texas 63. The List of Adrian Messenger 63. Come Blow Your Horn 63. Robin and the Seven Hoods 64. None But the Brave (& d) 65. Von Ryan's Express 65. Marriage on the Rocks 65. Cast a Giant Shadow 66. Assault on a Queen 66. The Naked Runner (GB) 67. Tony Rome 67. *The Detective* 68. Lady in Cement 68. Dirty Dingus Magee 70. Contract on Cherry Street (TV) 77. The First Deadly Sin 80. Cannonball Run II 84.

¶ Don't tell me. Suggest. But don't tell me. – *F.S.*

I detest bad manners. If people are polite, I am. They shouldn't try to get away with not being polite to me. – *F.S.*

He's the kind of guy that, when he dies, he's going up to heaven and give God a bad time for making him bald. – *Marlon Brando*

When he dies, they're giving his zipper to the Smithsonian. – *Dean Martin*

The charm that once made him irresistible was lost in the unpredictable whims of a spoiled child. – *Roger Vadim*

I was not impressed by the creeps and Mafia types he kept about him. – *Prince Charles*

Age has softened his sinister aura. – *Newsweek, 1982*

See also: *Rat Pack.*

Sinatra, Nancy (1940–).
American leading lady and singer, daughter of Frank Sinatra. She was formerly married to singer Tommy Sands.

For Those Who Think Young 64. The Last of the Secret Agents 66. Speedway 68, etc.

Sinclair, Andrew (1935–).
British director.

Before Winter Comes (w only) 69. The Breaking of Bumbo 70. Under Milk Wood 72. Blue Blood 73.

Sinclair, Hugh (1903–1962).
British stage leading man, in occasional films.

Our Betters 33. Escape Me Never 35. A Girl Must Live 39. Alibi 42. They Were Sisters 45. Corridor of Mirrors 48. The Rocking Horse Winner 50. The Second Mrs Tanqueray 52, etc.

Sinclair, Robert (1905–1970).
American director. Married to Heather Angel.

Woman against Woman 38. Dramatic School 38. Mr and Mrs North 41. Mr District Attorney 46. That Wonderful Urge 48, etc.

Sinden, Donald (1923–).
British leading man, on stage from mid-30s. Autobiography: 1982, *A Touch of the Memoirs.*

The Cruel Sea (film debut) 53. Doctor in the House 54. Simba 55. Eyewitness 57. Doctor at Large 58. Operation Bullshine 59. Twice Round the Daffodils 62. Decline and Fall 68. Villain 71. Rentadick 72. The National Health 73. The Day of the Jackal 73. The Island at the Top of the World 74. That Lucky Touch 75, etc.

TV series: Our Man at St Mark's 58. Two's Company 77–80. Never the Twain 81–83.

Singer, Alexander (1932–).
American director.
■ *A Cold Wind in August* 62. Psyche 59 64. Love Has Many Faces 65. Captain Apache 71. The First 36 Hours of Dr Durant (TV) 75. The Million Dollar Rip-Off (TV) 76. Hunters of the Reef (TV) 78. The Return of Marcus Welby, MD (TV) 84.

Singer, Campbell (1909–1976).
British character actor, often seen as heavy father, commissionaire, sergeant-major or policeman.
Premiere 37. Take My Life 47. The Ringer 52. Simba 55. The Square Peg 58. The Pot Carriers 63, many others.

Singer, Lori (1962–).
Lissom leading American actress, the sister of Marc Singer.
Born Beautiful (TV) 82. Footloose 84. The Falcon and the Snowman 85. The Man with One Red Shoe 85. Trouble in Mind 86. Summer Heat 87. Warlock 91. Short Cuts 93. F.T.W. 94, etc.

TV series: Fame 82–83.

Singer, Marc (1948–).
American leading actor, frequently in bare-chested roles.
Things in Their Season 74. Journey from Darkness 75. Go Tell the Spartans 78. For Ladies Only (TV) 81. The Beastmaster 82. If Yóu Could See What I Hear 82. Her Life as a Man (TV) 83. Born to Race 88. Body Chemistry 90. High Desert Kill (TV) 90. A Man Called Sarge 90. The Raven Red Kiss-Off 90. Watchers II 90. In the Cold of the Night 91. Dead Space 91. Beastmaster 2: Through the Portal of Time 91. Sweet Justice 92. The Sea Wolf (TV) 93, etc.

TV series: The Contender 80. Roots: The Next Generation 79–81. V 84–85. Dallas 86.

Singleton, John (1968–).
American screenwriter and director.
Boyz N the Hood (AAN) 91. Poetic Justice 93.

Singleton, Penny (1908–) (Mariana McNulty).
American leading lady who made her greatest hit as *Blondie*.
Good News 30. After the Thin Man 36. *Swing Your Lady* 38. The Mad Miss Manton 38. *Blondie* 38 (then two films in the series every year, more or less, until 1950). The Best Man 64, etc.

Sinise, Gary (1955–).
American director and actor, on stage and screen. He was a founder of Chicago's Steppenwolf Theatre.
Miles from Home (d) 88. Of Mice and Men (a, d) 92. A Midnight Clear (a) 92. Jack the Bear (a) 93. The Stand (a) (TV) 94. Forrest Gump (a) 94, etc.

Sinyor, Gary.
British director.
Leon the Pig Farmer (co-d) 92.

Siodmak, Curt (1902–).
German writer-director, in films from 1929, Hollywood from 1937. Brother of Robert Siodmak.
People on Sunday (co-w) 29. The Tunnel (co-w) 34. Her Jungle Love (co-w) 38. Frankenstein Meets the Wolf Man (w) 42. Son of Dracula (w) 43. The Beast with Five Fingers (w) 47. Bride of the Gorilla (wd) 51. *The Magnetic Monster* (d) 51.

Donovan's Brain (oa) 53. Love Slaves of the Amazon (w, d) 57. Ski Fever (w, d) 66, etc.

Siodmak, Robert (1900–1973).
American director with early experience in Germany and France.
People on Sunday 29. The Weaker Sex 32. La Vie Parisienne 35. *Pièges* 39. West Point Widow 41. Son of Dracula 43. *Phantom Lady* 44. *The Suspect* 44. Christmas Holiday 44. *The Spiral Staircase* 45. The Strange Affair of Uncle Harry 45. *The Killers* (AAN) 46. *The Dark Mirror* 46. Cry of the City 48. Criss Cross 48. The File on Thelma Jordon 49. The Great Sinner 49. Deported 50. The Whistle at Eaton Falls 51. The Crimson Pirate 52. Le Grand Jeu 53. Mein Vater der Schauspieler 56. Jatja 59. The Rough and the Smooth 59. Tunnel 28 (Escape from East Berlin) 62. Custer of the West 67, many others.

¶ He manipulated Hollywood's fantasy apparatus with taste and intelligence. – *Andrew Sarris, 1968*

Sirk, Douglas (1900–1987) (Detlef Sierck).
Danish director, with stage experience; in America from early 40s.
SELECTED EUROPEAN FILMS: April April 35. Das Hofkonzert 36. La Habanera 37. Home Is Calling 37.
■ AMERICAN FILMS: Hitler's Madman 43. Summer Storm 44. A Scandal in Paris 46. *Lured* 47. *Sleep My Love* 48. Shockproof 49. Slightly French 49. Mystery Submarine 50. The First Legion 51. Thunder on the Hill 51. The Lady Pays Off 51. Weekend with Father 51. No Room for the Groom 52. *Has Anybody Seen My Gal?* 52. Meet Me at the Fair 52. Take Me to Town 53. All I Desire 53. Taza Son of Cochise 54. *Magnificent Obsession* 54. Sign of the Pagan 54. Captain Lightfoot 55. There's Always Tomorrow 56. All That Heaven Allows 56. *Written on the Wind* 57. Battle Hymn 57. Interlude 57. The Tarnished Angels 58. A Time to Love and a Time to Die 58. Imitation of Life 59.

A Sister to Assist'er.
George Dewhurst wrote, from John le Breton's play, and directed three versions of this comedy about a poor tenant who pretends to be her rich sister in order to trick her landlady into giving her back her possessions: in 1930, starring Barbara Gott; in 1938, starring Muriel George; and again in 1948, with Muriel George. The definitive performance as the hard-up Mrs May, though, was given on the stage by Fred Emney (1866–1917), father of the film and stage comic actor Fred Emney.

Sitting Bull (1831–1890).
Chief of the Sioux at the time General Custer and his Seventh Cavalry were wiped out at the Little Big Horn, he later joined Buffalo Bill's Wild West. He was killed by Indian police in a raid during an uprising in which he was not a participant. On film, he is almost always on the warpath, the villain of countless westerns. He was played twice by J. Carrol Naish, in *Annie Get Your Gun* 50 and *Sitting Bull* 54. Also played by Chief Thunder Bird in *Annie Oakley* 35, Michael Granger in *Fort Vengeance* 53, John War Eagle in *Tonka* 58, Michael Pate in *The Great Sioux Massacre* 55, and Frank Kaquitts in *Buffalo Bill and the Indians* 76.

¶ Most of what he earned went into the pockets of small, ragged boys. He could not understand why all the wealth he saw in the cities wasn't divided up among the poor. Among the

Indians, a man who had plenty of food shared it with those who had none. – *Annie Oakley*

Sitting Pretty.
The 1947 comedy starring Clifton Webb as Lynn Belvedere, babysitter extraordinary, brought two sequels: *Mr Belvedere Goes to College* 49, and *Mr Belvedere Rings the Bell* 51. The title was also used for a 1933 comedy featuring Jack Oakie and Jack Haley as two songwriters hitch-hiking their way to Hollywood.

16mm.
A 'sub-standard' gauge to which feature films are reduced for private hire and in many countries for television. Many sponsored documentaries not intended for cinema showing are filmed in 16mm, as are television news and features. The smaller frame and greater magnification do not always lead to unsatisfactory results, but the dangers are obvious.

Sizemore, Tom.
American leading actor.
Born on the Fourth of July 89. Lock Up 89. Where Sleeping Dogs Lie 91. Flight of the Intruder 91. Guilty by Suspicion 91. Harley Davidson & the Marlboro Man 91. Striking Distance 93. Watch It 93. Heart and Souls 93. True Romance 93. Wyatt Earp 94. Natural Born Killers 94. Strange Days 95, etc.

Sjoberg, Alf (1903–1980).
Swedish director, former stage actor and director.
The Road to Heaven 42. *Frenzy* 44. Only a Mother 49. *Miss Julie* 51. Barabbas 53. Karin Mansdotter 54. Wild Birds 55. The Judge 60. The Island 66, many others.

Sjoman, Vilgot (1924–).
Swedish director, chiefly famous (and notorious) for '491' 66. *I Am Curious: Blue* 67, *I Am Curious: Yellow* 67, and *Blushing Charlie* 71.
Also: Troll 73. A Handful of Love 74. The Garage 74. Tabu 77. Linus Eller Tegelhusets Hemlighet 79. Malacca 86. Fallgropen 89, etc.

Sjostrom, Victor:
see *Seastrom, Victor*.

Skaaren, Warren (1947–1991).
American screenwriter and producer. Previously he was first commissioner of the Texas Film Commission and then ran a production services company.
Fire with Fire (aka Captive Hearts) (co-w) 86. Top Gun (p) 86. Beverly Hills Cop II (co-w) 87. Beetlejuice (co-w) 88. Batman (co-w) 89, etc.

Skala, Lilia (c.1901–1994)
Austrian actress in America.
Lilies of the Field (AAN) 64. Deadly Hero 76. Roseland 77. Heartland 80. The End of August 82. Flashdance 83. House of Games 87, etc.

Skall, William V. (1898–1976).
American cinematographer.
Victoria the Great 37. The Mikado 39. Northwest Passage 40. Life with Father 47. *Joan of Arc* (AA) 48. Quo Vadis 51. The Silver Chalice 55, many others.

Skeggs, Roy.
British production executive, a former accountant. He worked for Hammer in the 60s and bought the company in 1985 after it went into official receivership. He announced plans to remake old Hammer features in 1994 in partnership with

producer Lauren Shuler-Donner and director Richard Donner.
Frankenstein and the Monster from Hell 73. Satanic Rites of Dracula 73. To the Devil a Daughter 76, etc.

¶ Hammer was Walt Disney with a bit of blood. – R.S.

Skelly, Hal (1891–1934).
American character actor from Broadway.
■ The Dance of Life 29. Woman Trap 29. Behind the Make Up 30. Men Are Like That 30. The Struggle 31. Hotel Variety 31. Shadow Laughs 31.

Skelton, Red (1910–   ) (Richard Skelton).
American comedian of radio and TV; made numerous films in 40s, very few since.
■ Having Wonderful Time 38. Flight Command 40. The People Versus Dr Kildare 41. Lady Be Good 41. Whistling in the Dark 41. Dr Kildare's Wedding Day 41. Ship Ahoy 42. Maisie Gets Her Man 42. Panama Hattie 42. Whistling in Dixie 42. Dubarry Was a Lady 43. I Dood It 43. Whistling in Brooklyn 43. Thousands Cheer 43. Bathing Beauty 44. Ziegfeld Follies 44. The Show Off 46. Merton of the Movies 47. The Fuller Brush Man 48. A Southern Yankee 48. Neptune's Daughter 49. The Yellow Cab Man 50. The Fuller Brush Girl (gag) 50. Three Little Words 50. Duchess of Idaho (gag) 50. Watch the Birdie 50. Excuse My Dust 51. Texas Carnival 51. Lovely to Look at 52. The Clown 53. Half a Hero 53. The Great Diamond Robbery 53. Susan Slept Here (gag) 54. Around the World in Eighty Days 56. Public Pigeon Number One 57. Ocean's Eleven (gag) 60. Those Magnificent Men in Their Flying Machines 65. Rudolph's Shiny New Year (voice) 79.

¶ I'm nuts and I know it. But so long as I make 'em laugh, they ain't going to lock me up. – R.S.
I always believed God puts each one of us here for a purpose . . . and mine is to try to make people happy. – R.S.

Skerritt, Tom (1933–   ).
American actor.
■ War Hunt 62. One Man's Way 64. Those Callaways 65. M*A*S*H 70. Wild Rovers 71. Fuzz 72. Thieves Like Us 74. Big Bad Mama 74. The Devil's Rain 75. The Turning Point 77. Up in Smoke 78. Alien 79. Ice Castles 79. Savage Harvest 81. A Dangerous Summer 81. Silence of the North 81. Fighting Back 82. The Dead Zone 83. Top Gun 86. Wisdom 86. Opposing Force 87. Maid to Order 87. The Big Town 87. Poltergeist III 88. Big Man on Campus 89. The Heist (TV) 89. Red King, White Knight (TV) 89. Steel Magnolias 89. Child in the Night (TV) 90. The Rookie 90. Wild Orchid II: Two Shades of Blue 92. Poison Ivy 92. A River Runs Through It 92. Knight Moves 93.
TV series: Run, Run, Joe 74. Picket Fences 92.

skiing
has formed a pleasant background in many romantic comedies including I Met Him in Paris and Two-Faced Woman; in farces including The Pink Panther and Snowball Express; dramas including Last of the Ski Bums, Ski Fever and Downhill Racer; and in a plethora of spy stories, including Caprice, The Double Man and a couple of Bonds. The most musical ski sequence was provided by The Beatles in Help!

Skiles, Marlin (1906–   ).
American composer.
The Impatient Years 44. Gilda 46. Dead Reckoning 47. Callaway Went Thataway 51. The

Maze 53. Bowery to Baghdad 55. Fort Massacre 58. The Hypnotic Eye 60. The Strangler 64. The Resurrection of Zachary Wheeler 71, many others.

Skinner, Clare (1965–   ).
British actress, from the stage and TV.
Life Is Sweet 91. Naked 93.

Skinner, Cornelia Otis (1901–1979).
American stage actress, daughter of Otis Skinner the tragedian. Toyed with Hollywood occasionally. Her autobiographical book Our Hearts Were Young and Gay (co-written with Emily Kimbrough) was filmed with Gail Russell.
The Uninvited 44. The Girl in the Red Velvet Swing 55. The Swimmer 67.

Skinner, Frank (1898–1968).
American composer.
Son of Frankenstein 39. Destry Rides Again 39. Hellzapoppin 41. Back Street 41. Saboteur 42. Gung Ho 43. The Suspect 44. The Egg and I 47. Abbott and Costello Meet Frankenstein 48. Francis 49. Harvey 50. The World in His Arms 52. Thunder Bay 53. Battle Hymn 56. Imitation of Life 58. Back Street 61. Shenandoah 65. Madame X 66, many others.

Skinner, Otis (1858–1942).
American stage actor who appeared in films only in two versions of Kismet 20 & 30. Charles Ruggles played him in Our Hearts Were Young and Gay 44.

Skipworth, Alison (1875–1952) (Alison Groom).
Chubby British character actress, long in Hollywood; a favourite foil for W. C. Fields.
Raffles 30. Outward Bound 30. Devotion 31. Night After Night 32. If I Had a Million 32. Song of Songs 33. Tillie and Gus 33. Six of a Kind 34. The Captain Hates the Sea 34. Becky Sharp 35. Shanghai 35. Satan Met a Lady 36. Stolen Holiday 37. Wide Open Faces 38, many others.

Skirball, Jack H. (1896–1985).
American independent producer, former salesman.
Miracle on Main Street 38. Lady from Cheyenne 41. Saboteur 42. Shadow of a Doubt 43. It's in the Bag (The Fifth Chair) 45. Guest Wife 46. Payment on Demand 51, etc.

Skolimowski, Jerzy (1938–   ).
Polish director.
The Barrier 66. The Departure 67. Hands Up 67. Dialogue 69. The Adventures of Gerard 70. Deep End 71. King, Queen, Knave 72. The Shout 78. Circle of Deceit (a only) 81. Moonlighting (& w) 82. Success Is the Best Revenge 84. The Lightship 85. Torrents of Spring 89. The Hollow Men (p) 93, etc.

Skouras, Spyros (1893–1971).
Greek-American executive, former hotelier. President of Twentieth Century-Fox 1943–62; instigator of CinemaScope.

¶ The only Greek tragedy I know is Spyros Skouras. – Billy Wilder

Skye, Ione (1971–   ) (Ione Skye Leitch).
British actress, working in America. She is the daughter of 60s folk singer Donovan.
The River's Edge 87. Stranded 87. A Night in the Life of Jimmy Reardon 88. Carmilla 89. The Rachel Papers 89. Say Anything 89. Mindwalk 90. Samantha 91. Gas, Food, Lodging 92. Guncrazy 92. Wayne's World 92, etc.
TV series: Covington Cross 92.

Slaney, Ivor (1921–   ).
English composer.
The Gambler and the Lady 53. Spaceways 53. The Saint's Return (US: The Saint's Girl Friday) 53. Face the Music (US: The Black Glove) 54. The House across the Lake (US: Heat Wave) 54. The Stranger Came Home (US: The Unholy Four) 54. Five Days (US: Paid to Kill) 54. Murder by Proxy (US: Blackout) 55. Terror 79, etc.

slapstick.
One of the earliest (1895) Lumière shorts, L'Arroseur Arrosé, was a knockabout farce, and in 1966 A Funny Thing Happened on the Way to the Forum was keeping the tradition going. Out of simple slapstick developed the great silent clowns, each with his own brand of pathos: Harold Lloyd, Charlie Chaplin, Buster Keaton, Fatty Arbuckle, Harry Langdon, Mabel Normand, Larry Semon, Laurel and Hardy. Pure destructive slapstick without humanity was superbly dispensed by Mack Sennett, especially in his Keystone Kops shorts. France had produced Max Linder; Britain lagged behind, but in the 20s Betty Balfour, Monty Banks and Lupino Lane kept the flag flying. Many of these names survived in some degree when sound came, but cross-talk was an added factor in the success of Wheeler and Woolsey, Charlie Chase, Edgar Kennedy, Leon Errol, Hugh Herbert, Joe E. Brown, W. C. Fields, Eddie Cantor, Abbott and Costello and above all the Marx Brothers. Similarly in Britain there was an influx of stage comics with firm music-hall traditions: George Formby, Will Hay, Max Miller, Gracie Fields, Leslie Fuller, the Crazy Gang, Arthur Askey, Gordon Harker, Sandy Powell, Frank Randle and Old Mother Riley. The 40s in Hollywood brought the more sophisticated slapstick of Danny Kaye, writer-director Preston Sturges, and the Bob Hope gag factory, with extreme simplicity keeping its end up via Olsen and Johnson and Jerry Lewis. In the 50s, TV finally brought a female clown, Lucille Ball, to the top; though competition was thin. France since the war has had Fernandel, Louis de Funes, Jacques Tati and Pierre Etaix; Britain, Norman Wisdom and Morecambe and Wise; Italy, Toto and Walter Chiari. In Hollywood the fashion over the last thirty years has been for epic comedies of violence and destruction, such as It's a Mad Mad Mad Mad World, The Great Race, Those Magnificent Men in Their Flying Machines and The Blues Brothers.

Slate, Jeremy (1935–   ).
American general-purpose actor.
Wives and Lovers 63. I'll Take Sweden 65. The Sons of Katie Elder 66. The Devil's Brigade 68. Hells Angels '69 69. The Centerfold Girls 74. Stranger in Our House (TV) 78. Mr Horn (TV) 79. Dead Pit 89, etc.

Slater, Christian (1969–   ).
Saturnine young American leading actor.
The Legend of Billie Jean 85. The Name of the Rose 86. Heathers 88. Tucker: The Man and His Dream 88. The Wizard 89. Beyond the Stars 89. Gleaming the Cube 89. Tales from the Darkside: The Movie 90. Young Guns II 90. Pump Up the Volume 90. Robin Hood: Prince of Thieves 91. Mobsters 91. Star Trek VI: The Undiscovered Country 91. Where the Day Takes You (uncredited) 92. Ferngully: The Last Rainforest (voice) 92. Kuffs 92. Untamed Heart 93. True Romance 93. Jimmy Hollywood 94. Murder in the First 94, etc.

Slater, Helen (1965–   ).
Blonde American actress who made her debut in

the title role of *Supergirl* but has since tended to play supporting roles.

Supergirl 84. The Legend of Billie Jean 85. Ruthless People 86. The Secret of My Success 87. Sticky Fingers 88. Happy Together 89. City Slickers 91. A House in the Hills 93. Chantilly Lace (TV) 93. Lassie 94. Parallel Lives (TV) 94, etc.

Slater, John (1916–1975).
British cockney character actor and comedian of stage and TV, occasionally in films.

Love on the Dole (debut) 40. Went the Day Well? 42. A Canterbury Tale 44. Passport to Pimlico 48. Johnny You're Wanted 54. Violent Playground 58. Three on a Spree 61. A Place to Go 63, many others.

Slater, Ryan (1984–).
American child actor, the brother of Christian Slater.

The Little Panda 95.

Slattery, Tony.
British actor, TV presenter, and comedian, from television and the stage. Born in London, he studied at Cambridge University, where he was a member of Footlights.

How to Get a Head in Advertising 89. Peter's Friends 92, etc.

TV series: David Harper 91. Just a Gigolo 93.

Slaughter.
A Vietnam veteran out for revenge on those who killed his parents and friend was played by Jim Brown in two films: *Slaughter* 72 and *Slaughter's Big Rip-Off* 73.

Slaughter, Tod (1885–1956) (N. Carter Slaughter).
Barnstorming British actor who toured the provinces with chop-licking revivals of outrageous old melodramas, all of which he filmed after a fashion.

■ Maria Marten 35. Sweeney Todd 36. The Crimes of Stephen Hawke 36. Song of the Road 37. Darby and Joan 37. It's Never Too Late to Mend 37. The Ticket of Leave Man 37. Sexton Blake and the Hooded Terror 38. *The Face at the Window* 39. Crimes at the Dark House 40. The Curse of the Wraydons 43. The Greed of William Hart 48. King of the Underworld 52. Murder at Scotland Yard 52.

sleeper:
a trade term for a film which suddenly does much better at the box office than was expected.

Slezak, Walter (1902–1983).
Austrian character actor, of theatrical family; in America from 1930. Committed suicide.

Autobiography: 1962, *What Time's the Next Swan?*

Once upon a Honeymoon (English-speaking debut) 42. Lifeboat 44. Step Lively 44. The Spanish Main 45. Cornered 45. Sinbad the Sailor 47. The Pirate 48. *The Inspector General* 49. Call Me Madam 53. White Witch Doctor 54. The Steel Cage 54. Come September 61. Emil and the Detectives 64. Wonderful Life (GB) 64. Twenty-Four Hours to Kill 65. A Very Special Favor 65. Caper of the Golden Bulls 67. Dr Coppelius 68. Black Beauty 71, etc.

slides
¶ A feature of film-going in nickelodeon days was the decorative slides used between the brief entertainments. Here is a nostalgic selection: Please Read the Titles to Yourself. Loud Reading Annoys Your Neighbours.

Just a Moment Please While the Operator Changes Reels.

If Annoyed When Here Please Tell the Management.

Ladies and Gentlemen May safely visit this Theatre as no Offensive Films are ever Shown Here.

We Aim to Present the Pinnacle of Motion Picture Perfection.

Ladies, We Like your Hats, but Please Remove Them.

You Wouldn't Spit on the Floor at Home, so Please Don't do it Here.

Sloane, Everett (1909–1965).
Incisive American character actor, brought to Hollywood by Orson Welles.

■ *Citizen Kane* 41. *Journey into Fear* 42. *The Lady from Shanghai* 48. Prince of Foxes 49. *The Men* 50. Bird of Paradise 51. The Enforcer 51. Sirocco 51. The Prince Who Was a Thief 51. The Blue Veil 51. The Desert Fox 51. The Sellout 51. Way of a Gaucho 52. *The Big Knife* 55. *Patterns* 56. *Somebody Up There Likes Me* 56. Lust for Life 56. Marjorie Morningstar 58. The Gun Runners 58. Home from the Hill 60. By Love Possessed 61. Brushfire 62. The Man from the Diners Club 63. The Patsy 64. Ready for the People 64. The Disorderly Orderly 64.

TV series: Official Detective 58.

Famous line (*Citizen Kane*): 'Old age, Mr Thompson: it's the only disease you don't look forward to being cured of.'

Sloane, Olive (1896–1963).
British character actress of stage and screen whose best role was in *Seven Days to Noon* 50. Countless other small roles since film debut in *Greatheart* 21.

Slocombe, Douglas (1913–).
British cinematographer, former journalist.

Dead of Night 45. The Captive Heart 46. Hue and Cry 46. The Loves of Joanna Godden 47. *It Always Rains on Sunday* 47. *Saraband for Dead Lovers* 48. Kind Hearts and Coronets 49. Cage of Gold 50. The Lavender Hill Mob 51. Mandy 52. The Man in the White Suit 52. *The Titfield Thunderbolt* 53. Man in the Sky 56. The Smallest Show on Earth 57. Tread Softly Stranger 58. Circus of Horrors 59. The Young Ones 61. The L-Shaped Room 62. *Freud* 63. The Servant 63. Guns at Batasi 64. A High Wind in Jamaica 65. The Blue Max 66. Promise Her Anything 66. The Vampire Killers 67. Fathom 67. Robbery 67. Boom 68. The Lion in Winter 68. The Italian Job 69. *The Music Lovers* 70. Murphy's War 70. The Buttercup Chain 70. Travels with My Aunt (AAN) 73. The Great Gatsby 74. Love Among the Ruins (TV) 75. Rollerball 75. Hedda 76. Julia (AAN, BFA) 77. Nasty Habits 77. Caravans 78. Lost and Found 79. The Lady Vanishes 79. Nijinsky 80. Lost and Found 80. Raiders of the Lost Ark (AAN) 81. The Pirates of Penzance 83. Never Say Never Again 83. Indiana Jones and the Temple of Doom 84. Lady Jane 85. Indiana Jones and the Last Crusade 89, etc.

slogans
¶ All kinds of claims have been made over the years for all kinds of products. Here are a few of the most memorable.

Famous Players in Famous Plays
is certainly the longest lasting, all the way from

1912. The films hardly lived up to it, any more than it was true that:
Selznick Pictures Create Happy Homes
Or that Warners fooled anybody by linking:
Good Films – Good Citizenship
Or MGM by claiming that their spur was:
Ars Gratia Artis (art for its own sake)
MGM's secondary claim:
More Stars than there are in Heaven
was simply a slight exaggeration. When talkies came in, two favourite lines were:
All Talking, All Singing, All Dancing
And, from Vitaphone:
Pictures that Talk Like Living People!
The whole industry sometimes gets together on a propaganda campaign. In the 30s, it was:
Go to a Motion Picture – and Let Yourself Go!
In the 40s, simply:
Let's go to a movie!
In the 50s, in face of the arch-enemy television:
Don't be a Living Room Captive! Go Out and See a Great Movie!
And a few years later:
Movies are Your Best Entertainment!
The one I like best was concocted by the proprietors of CinemaScope in the face of 3-D. Originally it ran:
You see it without the use of glasses!
This not unnaturally brought a few complaints from bespectacled patrons who thought they were being guaranteed a new freedom, so hurriedly and rather lamely it was changed to:
You see it without the use of special glasses!

slow motion.
An effect obtained by running the camera faster than usual. When the film passes through the projector at normal speed, each movement appears slower, as it occupies more frames of film. For scientific purposes (e.g. recording the growth of plants) cameras are so arranged that a single frame of film is exposed at regular intervals, thus giving an impression of accelerated growth.

Sluizer, George (1932–).
Dutch director and screenwriter, a former documentary film-maker.

Twice a Woman 79. Red Desert Penitentiary 87. The Vanishing (Spoorloos) 88. Utz (UK) 91. The Vanishing (US) 93. Dark Blood (uncompleted) 94, etc.

Small, Edward (1891–1977).
Veteran American independent producer, former actor and agent, in Hollywood from 1924.

I Cover the Waterfront 35. The Man in the Iron Mask 39. The Corsican Brothers 41. Brewster's Millions 45. Down Three Dark Streets 55. Witness for the Prosecution 57. Jack the Giant Killer 62. I'll Take Sweden 65. Forty Guns to Apache Pass 66, many others; also TV series.

Small, Michael (1939–).
American composer.

Puzzle of a Downfall Child 70. Klute 71. Child's Play 72. The Parallax View 74. Night Moves 75. Marathon Man 76. Comes a Horseman 78. Those Lips Those Eyes 80. The Postman Always Rings Twice 81. Continental Divide 81. Rollover 81. The Star Chamber 83. Firstborn 84. Target 85. Dream Lover 86. Brighton Beach Memoirs 86. Black Widow 87. Orphans 87. Jaws – the Revenge 87. 1969 88. See You in the Morning 89. Mountains of the Moon 90, etc.

small towns
were for many years the staple of the American cinema. Most audiences were small-town folk, and

wanted to see slightly idealized versions of themselves. Thus the popularity of the happy families, the Hardys and the Joneses; thus *Our Town, The Human Comedy, Ah Wilderness, The Music Man* and *The Dark at the Top of the Stairs.* The darker side of small-town life was shown in *The Chase, Kings Row, Peyton Place* and *Invasion of the Body Snatchers.* British small towns did not have the same aura; most of the comparable stories were set against industrial backgrounds.

Smalley, Phillips (1875–1939).
American leading actor and director of silents. He was married to director Lois Weber and was involved in some of her films as actor and co-director. From the 20s, he continued as a character actor.

The Armorer's Daughter (a) 10. The Chorus Girl (d) 12. The Jew's Christmas (a, co-d) 13. The Merchant of Venice (a, co-d) 14. Scandal (a, co-d) 15. The Dumb Girl of Portici (co-d) 15. Where Are My Children? (co-d) 15. The Flirt (co-d) 16. Flaming Youth (a) 23. Charley's Aunt (a) 25. Man Crazy (a) 27. True Heaven 29. Charley's Aunt 30. Cocktail Hour 33. A Night at the Opera 35, etc.

Smart, J. Scott (1903–1950).
Heavyweight radio actor who took his *Fat Man* character to Hollywood for one 50s film of that name.

Smart, Ralph (1908–).
British producer-director, latterly of TV series *The Invisible Man, Danger Man,* etc. Former editor and writer.
AS DIRECTOR: Bush Christmas 46. A Boy, a Girl and a Bike 48. Bitter Springs 50. Never Take No for an Answer (co-d) 51. Curtain Up 52. Always a Bride 54, etc.

Smeaton, Bruce.
Australian composer.
The Cars that Ate Paris 74. Picnic at Hanging Rock 75. The Devil's Playground 76. Eliza Fraser 76. The Chant of Jimmie Blacksmith 78. The Last of the Knucklemen 78. Circle of Iron 79. Double Deal 81. Barbarosa 81. Undercover 83. The Naked Country 84. Iceman 84. Plenty 85. Eleni 85. Roxanne 87. A Cry in the Dark 88, etc.

Smedley-Aston, E. M. (1912–).
British producer.
The Extra Day 56. Two-Way Stretch 60. Offbeat 61. The Wrong Arm of the Law 63. Ooh You Are Awful 72, etc.

Smell-O-Vision.
A process initiated in 1960 by which evocative smells were pumped to the cinema audience through pipes leading to individual seats in the auditorium. Bottles of scent were held on a rotating drum, and the process triggered by a signal on the film itself. *Scent of Mystery* was the only film to be made in Smell-O-Vision.

Smight, Jack (1926–).
American director, from TV.
■ I'd Rather Be Rich 64. The Third Day 65. *Harper* 66. Kaleidoscope 66. The Secret War of Harry Frigg 67. No Way to Treat a Lady 68. The Illustrated Man 69. Strategy of Terror (TV) 69. Rabbit Run (TV) 69. The Travelling Executioner 70. The Screaming Woman (TV) 72. Detour to Nowhere (TV) 72. The Longest Night (TV) 72. Linda (TV) 73. Double Indemnity (TV) 73. Frankenstein: The True Story (TV) 73. Airport 75 74. Midway 76.

Damnation Alley 77. Roll of Thunder (TV) 78. Fast Break 78. Loving Couples 80. Number One with a Bullet 87. The Favorite 89.

Smilin' Through.
The popular sentimental stage play by Jane Cowl and June Murfin, about a tragedy affecting the romances of two generations, was filmed in 1922 by Sidney Franklin, with Norma Talmadge, Wyndham Standing, and Harrison Ford; in 1932, again by Sidney Franklin, with Norma Shearer, Leslie Howard, and Fredric March. In 1941 Frank Borzage remade it with Jeanette MacDonald, Brian Aherne, and Gene Raymond.

Smith, Albert E. (1875–1958).
British pioneer producer in America, one of the founders of the Vitagraph Company (qv).

Smith, Alexis (1921–) (Gladys Smith).
American leading lady of the 40s who won an acting contest from Hollywood high school. Married to Craig Stevens.
Lady with Red Hair 41. Dive Bomber 41. The Smiling Ghost 41. Gentleman Jim 42. The Constant Nymph 42. The Doughgirls 44. Conflict 45. Rhapsody in Blue 45. San Antonio 45. Night and Day 46. Of Human Bondage 46. Stallion Road 47. The Woman in White 47. The Decision of Christopher Blake 48. Any Number Can Play 50. Undercover Girl 52. Split Second 53. The Sleeping Tiger (GB) 55. The Eternal Sea 56. The Young Philadelphians (The City Jungle) 59. Once is Not Enough 75. The Little Girl Who Lives Down the Lane 77. Casey's Shadow 78. A Death in California (TV) 85. Tough Guys 86. The Age of Innocence 93, etc.
TV series: Dallas 84. Hothouse 88.

¶ When they tell me one of my old movies is on TV, I don't look at it. – A.S.
Those films weren't very good at the time, and they haven't improved with age. – A.S.
There are so many more interesting things to think about than whether Ida Lupino or Jane Wyman got the roles I should have gotten. – A.S.

Smith, Art (1899–1973).
Bland, avuncular American character actor.
A Tree Grows in Brooklyn 44. Letter from an Unknown Woman 47. Cover Up 50. In a Lonely Place 51, etc.

Smith, Bernard (c. 1905–).
American producer, ex-publisher and story editor.
Elmer Gantry (AA) 60. How the West Was Won 62. Seven Women 65. Alfred the Great 69, etc.

Smith, Bessie (1894–1937).
America's greatest singer of classic blues, known as 'The Empress of the Blues', who made one short in 1929, singing 'St Louis Blues', which has been re-issued on video-cassette. The highest-paid black star in the 20s, she hit hard times in the 30s and died following a car crash. There are plans to make a biopic of her life.
Biography: 1972, *Bessie* by Chris Albertson.

Smith, Betty (1904–1972).
American novelist.
Works filmed include *A Tree Grows in Brooklyn, Joy in the Morning.*

Smith, Bubba (1945–) (Charles Smith).
Tall American actor, a former football star.
Stroker Ace 83. Police Academy 84. Police Academy 2 85. Police Academy 3 86. Police

Academy 4 87. The Wild Pair 87. Police Academy 5 88. Police Academy 6 89. Gremlins 2: The New Batch 90. My Samurai 92, etc.

Smith, Sir C. Aubrey (1863–1948).
Distinguished English leading actor on stage who went to Hollywood in his 60s to play crusty, benevolent, or authoritarian old gentlemen. Born in London, he was a first-class sportsman, playing soccer for the Corinthians and cricket for Cambridge University. Nicknamed 'Round the Corner Smith' for his unusual bowling style, he captained Sussex County Cricket Club for four years, an English team that went to Australia in 1887, and the first English team to tour South Africa. A teacher and a stockbroker before becoming an actor, he was on stage from 1892, including a notable Professor Higgins in George Bernard Shaw's *Pygmalion* in 1914. He was in films from 1915 and was one of the founders of a short-lived English company, Minerva Films. Success came when he repeated for MGM his stage hit *The Bachelor Father.* A founder-member of the Hollywood Cricket Club, he was knighted in 1944. The characters of Sir Ambrose Abercrombie and, to a lesser extent, Sir Francis Hinsley in Evelyn Waugh's novel *The Loved One* are modelled on him.
Biography: 1982, *Sir Aubrey* by David Rayvern Allen.
SELECTED SILENT FILMS: The Witching Hour 16. The Bohemian Girl 23. The Rejected Woman 24.
■ SOUND FILMS: Birds of Prey (GB) 30. Such Is the Law (GB) 30. Contraband Love (GB) 31. Trader Horn 31. Never the Twain Shall Meet 31. Bachelor Father 31. Daybreak 31. Just a Gigolo 31. Son of India 31. The Man in Possession 31. Phantom of Paris 31. Guilty Hands 31. Surrender 31. Polly of the Circus 31. Tarzan the Ape Man 32. But the Flesh Is Weak 32. *Love Me Tonight* 32. Trouble in Paradise 32. No More Orchids 32. They Just Had to Get Married 32. Luxury Liner 33. Secrets 33. The Barbarian 33. Adorable 33. The Monkey's Paw 33. *Morning Glory* 33. Bombshell 33. Queen Christina 33. The House of Rothschild 34. The Scarlet Empress 34. Gambling Lady 34. Curtain at Eight 34. The Tunnel (GB) 34. Bulldog Drummond Strikes Back 34. Cleopatra 34. Madame du Barry 34. One More River 34. Caravan 34. The Firebird 34. The Right to Live 35. *Lives of a Bengal Lancer* 35. The Florentine Dagger 35. The Gilded Lily 35. Clive of India 35. China Seas 35. Jalna 35. The Crusades 35. Little Lord Fauntleroy 36. Romeo and Juliet 36. The Garden of Allah 36. Lloyds of London 36. Wee Willie Winkie 36. *The Prisoner of Zenda* 37. Thoroughbreds Don't Cry 37. The Hurricane 37. Four Men and a Prayer 38. Kidnapped 38. Sixty Glorious Years (GB) 38. East Side of Heaven 39. Five Came Back 39. *The Four Feathers* (GB) 39. The Sun Never Sets 39. Eternally Yours 39. Another Thin Man 39. The Underpup 39. Balalaika 39. *Rebecca* 40. City of Chance 40. A Bill of Divorcement 40. Waterloo Bridge 40. Beyond Tomorrow 40. A Little Bit of Heaven 40. Free and Easy 41. Maisie was a Lady 41. Dr Jekyll and Mr Hyde 41. Forever and a Day 43. Two Tickets to London 43. Flesh and Fantasy 43. Madame Curie 43. The White Cliffs of Dover 44. The Adventures of Mark Twain 44. Secrets of Scotland Yard 44. Sensations of 1945 44. They Shall Have Faith 44. *And Then There Were None* 45. Scotland Yard Investigator 45. Cluny Brown 46. Rendezvous with Annie 46. High Conquest 47. Unconquered 47. *An Ideal Husband* (GB) 47. Little Women 49.
◉ For relishing and perpetuating the stereotype of the fine old English gentleman. *The Four Feathers.*

¶ Mr Aubrey Smith has few equals in the delineation of the polished, straightforward, simple-minded English gentleman. – *The Graphic*

He was born to smell of tobacco and Harris tweeds, and to wave portentous eyebrows . . . He stands for all that is most essentially British: that queer admixture of sportsmanship, dunderheadedness and sentiment which has rendered the inhabitants of these islands the most exasperating enigma with which any other nation has ever had to cope. – *Theatre World*

The Bank of England, the cliffs of Dover, the Rock of Gibraltar and several super-dreadnoughts rolled into one. – *New York Times*

He *was* England, to a great many – perhaps an older England, but an England rich in dignity, graciousness and good will. Certainly no one could ever have known him, either in life or on the screen, without liking England better afterwards. – *James Hilton*

My God! I can't possibly act with a cricket bat! – *Mrs Patrick Campbell, objecting to appearing with him in Pygmalion*

Aubrey, Aubrey, don't go on the stage, think of what will become of your two sisters if their brother is an actor. – *His mother*

Smith, Charles (1920–1988).
American character actor who in the 40s played Dizzy in the *Henry Aldrich* series and other amiably doltish roles.
The Shop around the Corner 40. Tom Brown's Schooldays 40. Three Little Girls in Blue 45. Two Weeks with Love 50. City of Bad Men 53, many others.

Smith, Charles Martin (1954–).
American leading actor and occasional director.
Culpepper Cattle Co. 72. Fuzz 72. American Graffiti 73. Pat Garrett and Billy the Kid 73. Law of the Land 76. The Campus Corpse 77. The Buddy Holly Story 78. More American Graffiti 79. Herbie Goes Bananas 80. Cotton Candy 82. Starman 84. Trick or Treat (& d) 86. The Untouchables 87. The Hot Spot 90. Boris & Natasha (& d) 92. Deep Cover 92. Fifty/Fifty (& d) 93, etc.

Smith, Constance (1929–).
British leading lady.
Brighton Rock 47. Don't Say Die 50. The Thirteenth Letter (US) 51. Red Skies of Montana (US) 52. Treasure of the Golden Condor (US) 53. Tiger by the Tail 55. Cross Up 58, etc.

Smith, Cyril (1892–1963).
British character actor of stage and screen, often a hen-pecked husband but equally likely to be a grocer, dustman or policeman. On stage from 1900, films from 1908, and was in over 500 of the latter.
Friday the Thirteenth 33. School for Secrets 46. It's Hard to Be Good 48. Mother Riley Meets the Vampire 52. John and Julie 54. *Sailor Beware* (his stage role) 56, etc.

Smith, Dick (1922–).
Influential American make-up artist, noted for his work on special effects, from television.
Misty 59. The World of Henry Orient 64. Little Big Man 70. House of Dark Shadows 70. The Godfather 72. The Exorcist 73. The Godfather Part II 74. The Stepford Wives 74. Burnt Offerings 76. Exorcist II: The Heretic 77. The Sentinel 77. The Fury 78. Altered States 80. Ghost Story 81. Scanners 81. Amadeus (AA) 84. Poltergeist III 88. Tales from the Darkside: The Movie 90. Death Becomes Her 92, etc.

Smith, Dodie (1896–1990).
English dramatist and novelist, a former actress, whose children's book *The Hundred and One Dalmatians* was turned into a classic animated feature by Walt Disney in 1961.
Looking Forward (oa) 33. Autumn Crocus (oa) 34. Dear Octopus (oa) 43, etc.

Smith, G. A. (1864–1959).
British pioneer cinematographer who invented a cine-camera in 1896 and made some trick films.
The Corsican Brothers 97. The Fairy Godmother 98. Faust 98, etc.

Smith, Jaclyn (1947–).
American leading actress, mainly on television.
Goodbye Columbus 69. The Adventurers 70. Bootleggers 74. The Users 74. Nightkill 80. Jacqueline Bouvier Kennedy (TV) 81. George Washington (TV) 84. Déjà Vu 84. Rage of Angels (TV) 85. The Night They Saved Christmas (TV) 87, etc.
TV series: Charlie's Angels 76–81.

Smith, Joe (1884–1981) (Joseph Sultzer).
American vaudeville comedian in partnership with Charles Dale (qv) for 73 years and the inspiration for the play and movie *The Sunshine Boys*.
Manhattan Parade 31. The Heart of New York 32. Two Tickets to Broadway 51.

Smith, John (1931–1995) (Robert Van Orden).
Boyish American leading man.
The High and the Mighty 54. Ghost Town 56. The Bold and the Brave 57. Circus World 64. Waco 66, etc.
TV series: Cimarron City 58. Laramie 59–62.

Smith, Kate (1909–1986).
Heavyweight American singer who was popular on radio in the 30s and 40s. Made one film in 1933 (*Hello, Everybody*) and another in 1943 (*This is the Army*).

Smith, Kent (1907–1985).
Smooth, quiet American leading man of the 40s; latterly a useful character actor.
Cat People 42. Hitler's Children 43. This Land Is Mine 43. *The Spiral Staircase* 46. *Nora Prentiss* 47. The Decision of Christopher Blake 48. The Fountainhead 49. The Damned Don't Cry 50. Paul 52. Comanche 56. Party Girl 58. Strangers When We Meet 60. Moon Pilot 62. A Distant Trumpet 64. The Trouble with Angels 66. Assignment to Kill 68. Death of a Gunfighter 69. Pete 'n' Tillie 72. Cops and Robbers 73, many others.
TV series: Peyton Place 64–67.

Smith, Kevin.
American director.
Clerks 94.

Smith, Kurtwood (1943–).
American character actor, often in sadistic roles.
Roadie 80. Staying Alive 83. Flashpoint 84. Robocop 87. Rambo III 88. Dead Poets Society 89. Heart of Dixie 89. True Believer 89. Quick Change 90. Oscar 91. Company Business 91. Star Trek VI: The Undiscovered Country 91. Shadows and Fog 92. Fortress 93. Boxing Helena 93. The Crush 93, etc.

Smith, Liz.
British character actress.
A Private Function (BFA) 84. We Think the World of You 88. High Spirits 88. Apartment Zero

89. The Cook, the Thief, His Wife and Her Lover 89. Dakota Road 92. Pretty Princess (It.) 93, etc.

Smith, Lois (1930–).
American character actress.
Five Easy Pieces 70. Resurrection 80. Reckless 84. Black Widow 87. Green Card 90. Fried Green Tomatoes 91. Hard Promises 92. Skylark (TV) 93. Falling Down 93. Holy Matrimony 94, etc.

Smith, Maggie (1934–).
Leading British actress with a taste for eccentric comedy. Married to actor Robert Stephens (1967–74) and writer Beverley Cross.
Biography: 1992, *Maggie: A Bright Particular Star* by Michael Coveney.
■ Nowhere to Go 58. Go to Blazes 62. *The VIPs* 63. The Pumpkin Eater 64. Young Cassidy 65. Othello (AAN) 66. *The Honey Pot* 67. Hot Millions 68. Oh What a Lovely War 69. *The Prime of Miss Jean Brodie* (AA) 69. Love Pain and the Whole Damn Thing 73. Travels with My Aunt (AAN) 73. Murder by Death 76. California Suite (AA) 78. Death on the Nile 78. Clash of the Titans 81. Quartet 81. Evil under the Sun 82. Better Late than Never 82. The Missionary 83. A Private Function (BFA) 84. A Room with a View (AAN) 85. The Lonely Passion of Judith Hearne 87. Hook 91. Memento Mori (TV) 92. Sister Act 92. The Secret Garden 93. Suddenly Last Summer (TV) 93. Sister Act 2: Back in the Habit 93.

¶ I said, 'Periods in life are sometimes like a dark tunnel you come out into the light eventually.' She said, 'I think I'm on the Inner Circle.' – *Kenneth Williams*

Smith, Mel (1952–).
British comic actor and director.
Bullshot 83. Slayground 84. Morons from Outer Space 85. The Princess Bride 87. The Wolves of Willoughby Chase 88. The Tall Guy (d) 89. Wilt (US: The Misadventures of Mr Wilt) 89. Brain Donors 92. Art Deco Detective 94. Radioland Murders (d) 94, etc.
TV series: Not the Nine O'Clock News 79–81. Alas Smith and Jones 84–86.

Smith, Oliver (1918–1994).
American production designer, mainly for the Broadway stage and the American Ballet Theatre.
Oklahoma! 55. Guys and Dolls 55. Porgy and Bess 59, etc.

Smith, Paul.
Towering American character actor who played the guard in *Midnight Express* and Bluto in *Popeye*.
Retreat, Hell! 52. Madron 70. Raiders in Action 71. Midnight Express 78. Popeye 80. Dune 84. Red Sonja 85. Crimewave 86. Haunted Honeymoon 86. Death Chase 87. Caged Fury 90. Crossing the Line 90, etc.

Smith, Paul J. (1906–1985).
American composer, almost exclusively for Disney.
Snow White and the Seven Dwarfs (AAN) 37. Pinocchio (AA) 40. Victory through Air Power (AAN) 43. The Three Caballeros (AAN) 44. Song of the South (AAN) 46. Cinderella (AAN) 50. Twenty Thousand Leagues Under the Sea 54. Perri (AAN) 57. Pollyanna 60. The Parent Trap 61. The Three Lives of Thomasina 64, etc.

Smith, Pete (1892–1979).
American producer of punchy one-reel shorts on any and every subject from 1935 to the 50s, all narrated by 'a Smith named Pete'. Former

publicist. Special Academy Award 1953 'for his witty and pungent observations on the American scene'.

Smith, Roger (1932–).
American leading man. He is married to Ann-Margret.

The Young Rebels 56. Operation Mad Ball 57. Man of a Thousand Faces (as Lon Chaney Jnr) 57. Never Steal Anything Small 59. Auntie Mame 59. Rogues' Gallery 68. The First Time (wp) 70.

TV series: 77 Sunset Strip 58–64. Mr Roberts 65.

Smith, Roy Forge.
British production designer, now working in America.

Far from the Madding Crowd 67. The Amazing Mr Blunden 72. Monty Python and the Holy Grail 74. Jabberwocky 77. The Hound of the Baskervilles 79. Running 79. Mrs Soffel 84. The Kiss 88. Bill & Ted's Excellent Adventure 89. Teenage Mutant Ninja Turtles 90. Warlock 91. Teenage Mutant Ninja Turtles II 93. Teenage Mutant Ninja Turtles III 93, etc.

Smith, Thorne (1892–1934).
American humorous novelist. Works filmed include *Topper, Turnabout, I Married a Witch*.

Smithee, Alan (1967–) (aka Allen Smithee).
Pseudonym used by members of the Directors' Guild of America when the actual director wants his name removed from a film's credits.

Death of a Gunfighter (d Don Siegel, Robert Totten) 67. Fade In (d Jud Taylor) 68. City in Fear (d Jud Taylor) (TV) 80. Fun and Games (d Paul Bogart) (TV) 80. Moonlight (d Jackie Cooper, Rod Holcomb) (TV) 82. Stitches (d Rod Holcomb) 82. Appointment with Fear (d Ramzi Thomas) 85. Let's Get Harry (d Stuart Rosenberg) 86. Morgan Stewart's Coming Home (d Terry Winsor, Paul Aaron) 87. Ghost Fever (d Lee Madden) 87. I Love NY (d Gianni Bozzachi) 87. Catchfire (aka Backtrack) (d Dennis Hopper) 89. Boyfriend from Hell (aka The Shrimp on the Barbie) (d Martin Gottlieb) 90. Starfire (d Richard Sarafian) 92. Call of the Wild (TV) 93. The Birds II: Land's End (TV) (d Rick Rosenthal) 94, etc.

Smits, Jimmy (1955–).
American leading actor.

Running Scared 86. The Believers 87. Old Gringo 89. Vital Signs 90. Fires Within 91. Switch 91. Gross Misconduct 93. The Tommyknockers (TV) 93. The Cisco Kid (title role) (TV) 94, etc.

TV series: L.A. Law 86–92.

smoking
has served as the springboard of a few plots. *No Smoking* and *Cold Turkey* concerned cures for it, and one also figured in *Taking Off*. In *On a Clear Day You Can See Forever* Barbra Streisand launched the plot by taking psychiatric advice about it. The most fashionable smoking habit was Paul Henreid's in *Now Voyager*, lighting two cigarettes and passing one to Bette Davis; this was mimicked with eight cigarettes by Bob Hope in *Let's Face It*. The longest cigarette holder was sported by Harpo Marx in *A Night in Casablanca*.

Smoktunovsky, Innokenti (1925–1994).
Leading Russian stage actor, seen in a few films including *Nine Days of One Year* 60. *Hamlet* 64. *Tchaikovsky* 69. *Crime and Punishment* 75.

Smothers, Tom (1937–).
American light leading man and comedian who

with his brother Dick (1939–) was popular on American TV in the 60s. Tom himself went on to appear in a few films:
■ Get to Know Your Rabbit 74. Silver Bears 78. The Kids Are Alright 78. Serial 80. There Goes the Bride 80. Pandemonium 82. Speed Zone 88.

smugglers
of the old-fashioned type are almost entirely a British concern, figuring in *Fury at Smugglers' Bay, Jamaica Inn, The Ghost Train, Oh Mr Porter, Ask a Policeman, I See a Dark Stranger, Moonfleet*, and others. Smuggling in American films has been a much more modern and less picturesque affair.

sneak preview.
An unheralded tryout of a film at a public performance, usually in place of a second feature. Intended to gauge audience reaction, it is often followed by considerable re-editing before the official première.

Snell, David.
American composer.

Madame X 37. Young Dr Kildare 38. Twenty Mule Team 40. Love Crazy 41. Pacific Rendezvous 42. The Man from Down Under 43. Keep Your Powder Dry 45. Merton of the Movies 47. The Lady in the Lake 47. Alias a Gentleman 48, etc.

Snipes, Wesley (1962–).
American leading actor.

Streets of Gold 86. Wild Cats 86. Critical Condition 87. Major League 89. Mo' Better Blues 90. King of New York 90. Jungle Fever 91. New Jack City 91. The Waterdance 92. White Men Can't Jump 92. Passenger 57 92. Rising Sun 93. Boiling Point 93. Sugar Hill 93. Demolition Man 93. Drop Zone 94. To Wong Foo, Thanks for Everything, Julie Newmar 95, etc.

TV series: H.E.L.P. 90.

Snodgress, Carrie (1946–).
American leading lady.

The Forty-Eight Hour Mile (TV) 68. Silent Night Lonely Night (TV) 69. Diary of a Mad Housewife (AAN) 72. The Fury 78. Homework 82. Trick or Treats 82. A Night in Heaven 83. Pale Rider 85. Murphy's Law 86. Blueberry Hill 88. The Chill Factor 89. Across the Tracks 90. Mission of the Shark 91. The Ballad of Little Joe 93. 8 Seconds 94. Blue Sky (made 91) 94, etc.

snow,
when needed for a movie scene, has been known to consist of a variety of ingredients including bleached cornflakes, soapflakes, chopped feathers, shredded asbestos, balsa chips, sawdust, and a wide range of plastic products.

Snyder, David L.
American production designer.

In God We Trust 80. The Idolmaker 80. Blade Runner (co-pd, AAN) 82. Brainstorm 83. The Woman in Red 84. Pee-Wee's Big Adventure 85. Armed and Dangerous 86. Summer School 87. She's out of Control 89. Cold Dog Soup 90. Bill & Ted's Bogus Journey 91. Demolition Man 93. Terminal Velocity 94, etc.

Snyder, William (1901–1984).
American cinematographer. Noted for his colour photography in the 40s, he worked for Disney during the 60s.

Aloma of the South Seas (AAN) 41. The Bandit of Sherwood Forest 45. The Swordsman 47. The Loves of Carmen (AAN) 48. The Younger Brothers 49. Jolson Sings Again (AAN) 49. Flying

Leathernecks 51. Blackbeard the Pirate 52. Second Chance 53. Creature from the Black Lagoon 54. Son of Sinbad 55. Tarzan's Fight for Life 58. Bon Voyage 62. Guns of Wyoming 63. The Tenderfoot 64. Rascal 69. Million Dollar Duck 71. Menace on the Mountain 72, etc.

soap opera.
A term used disparagingly of TV domestic drama serials. Originated because such offerings were invariably sponsored by the big soap companies who needed to attract the housewife.

Soavi, Michele (1958–).
Italian director of horror movies, a former actor, much influenced by the work of Dario Argento, for whom he worked as an assistant.

Creepers (a) 85. Demons (Demoni) (a) 86. Dario Argento's World of Horror (doc) (d) 86. Stagefright (Deliria) (a, d) 87. The Church (La Chiesa) (a, d) 89. The Sect (La Setta) (co-w, d) 91. Dellamorte Dellamore (d) 94, etc.

social comedy.
Silent romantic comedies were completely unrealistic, though they sometimes found it prudent to pretend satirical intent to cloak their lowbrow commercialism. Social comedy really came in as a substitute for sex comedy when the Hays Office axe fell in 1934. Frank Capra took by far the best advantage of it, with his series of films showing an America filled to bursting point with good guys who only wanted a simple and comfortable home life in some small town where corruption never raised its ugly head. The best of these films were *Mr Deeds Goes to Town, You Can't Take It with You* and *Mr Smith Goes to Washington*; by the time *Meet John Doe* came along in 1941 war had soured the mood again. There was no British equivalent to Capra, unless one counts a few attempts by Priestley (*The Good Companions, Let the People Sing*) and such amusing depictions of the middle class as *Quiet Wedding* and *Dear Octopus*; but in the late 40s came the Ealing comedies, delightful and apparently realistic, but presenting a picture of England just as false as Capra's America. In both countries the 50s saw the development of an affluent society in which cynicism was fashionable and few reforms seemed worth urging except in bitterly serious fashion.

social conscience
has long been a feature of Hollywood film production. Other countries have presented the odd feature pointing to flaws in their national make-up, but America has seemed particularly keen to wash its own dirty linen on screen, perhaps because this is rather easier than actually cleaning up the abuses.

The evolution of this attitude can be traced back as far as 1912 and Griffith's *The Musketeers of Pig Alley*, showing slum conditions, a theme developed in *Intolerance* 16; and, of course, Chaplin was a master at devising humour and pathos out of the unpleasant realities of poverty, a fact which endeared him to poor people all over the world. But it was not till the late 20s that the flood of socially conscious films began in earnest. Vidor's *The Crowd* investigated the drabness of everyday life for a city clerk. John Baxter's British *Dosshouse* was a lone entry on the lines of *The Lower Depths*. *City Streets* and *One-Third of a Nation* treated slum conditions; Vidor's *Our Daily Bread* concerned a young couple driven out of the city by poverty only to find farming just as precarious. *Little Caesar* and the gangster dramas which followed always assumed a crusading moral tone deploring the lives of vice and crime which they depicted; there was a somewhat more honest ring to *I Was a Fugitive from a Chain Gang*, which showed how circumstance can drive an honest man into anti-social behaviour. Capra sugared his pill with comedy: *American Madness* (the madness was money) and the popular comedies which followed all pitted common-man philosophy against urban sophistication and corruption.

In the mid-30s there were certainly many abuses worth fighting. *Black Legion* began Hollywood's campaign against the Ku Klux Klan, later followed up in *The Flaming Cross, Storm Warning* and *The Cardinal*. Lynch law, first tackled in *Fury*, was subsequently the subject of *They Won't Forget, The Ox Bow Incident* and *The Sound of Fury*. Juvenile delinquency was probed in *Dead End, Angels with Dirty Faces* and *They Made Me a Criminal*, but the 'Dead End Kids' were later played for comedy. Prison reform was advocated in *Each Dawn I Die, Castle on the Hudson*, and many other melodramas of questionable integrity. *The Good Earth* invited concern for the poor of other nations; *Mr Smith Goes to Washington* and *The Glass Key* were among many dramas showing that politicians are not incorruptible; *Love on the Dole* depicted the poverty of industrial Britain; *The Grapes of Wrath* and *Tobacco Road* pondered the plight of farming people deprived of a living by geographical chance and thoughtless government. In *Sullivan's Travels*, Preston Sturges came to the curious conclusion that the best thing you can do for the poor is make them laugh.

During World War II the nations were too busy removing the abuse of Nazidom to look inward, and indeed much poverty was alleviated by conscription and a fresh national awareness which, together with the increased need for industrial manpower, greatly improved the lot of the lower classes. But with victory came a whole crop of films, led by *The Best Years of Our Lives* and *Till the End of Time*, about the rehabilitation of war veterans. Concern about mental illness was shown in *The Snake Pit*, about paraplegia in *The Men*, and about labour relations in *The Whistle at Eaton Falls*. Alcoholism was treated in *The Lost Weekend* and *Smash-Up*, and the racial issues were thoroughly aired in *Lost Boundaries, Crossfire, Home of the Brave, No Way Out, Gentleman's Agreement* and *Pinky*. A plea for nations to help and understand each other was made in the French *Race for Life*.

With the development in the 50s of the affluent society, the number of reforms worth urging was drastically reduced. Teenage hoodlums figured largely in a score of films of which the best were *The Wild One* and *Rebel without a Cause*. Mentally handicapped children were sympathetically portrayed in *A Child is Waiting*. In the 1960s, however, it was one world issue which dominated the film-makers' social consciousness, that of the panic button; and this manifested itself in films as diverse as *On the Beach, Dr Strangelove, Fail Safe* and *The Bedford Incident*.

Social consciousness was apparent in almost every drama of the 70s, but used as a top dressing, sometimes to permit the exploitation of violence. In films like *A Clockwork Orange* and *O Lucky Man* it is difficult enough to discover what point is being made.

Soderbergh, Steven (1963–).
American director and screenwriter.
sex, lies and videotape (AAN) 89. Kafka 91. King of the Hill 93.

Soeteman, Gerard.
Dutch screenwriter, associated with the pre-Hollywood films of Paul Verhoeven.
Max Havelaar 76. Soldier of Orange 77. Spetters

80. The Fourth Man (De Vierde Man) 83. Flesh and Blood 85. The Assault 86. The Bunker (& d) 92, etc.

Sofaer, Abraham (1896–1988).
Burmese actor, on British stage from 1921.
Dreyfus (debut) 31. Rembrandt 36. *A Matter of Life and Death* 46. Judgment Deferred 51. *Elephant Walk* (US) 54. The Naked Jungle (US) 54. Bhowani Junction 56. King of Kings 61. Captain Sinbad (US) 63. Head 68. Che! 69, etc.

soft focus.
A diffused effect used in photographing ageing leading ladies who can't stand good definition; also frequently used for exotic shots in musical numbers, etc.

Softley, Iain.
English director.
Backbeat 94.

Sojin (1884–1954).
Japanese actor most memorable in western films as Douglas Fairbanks' antagonist in the 1924 *Thief of Bagdad*. Back in Japan after 1930.

Sokoloff, Vladimir (1889–1962).
Russian character actor, in Hollywood from 1936.
The Loves of Jeanne Ney 27. West Front 1918 30. Die Dreigroschenoper 31. L'Atlantide 32. Mayerling 35. The Life of Emile Zola 37. Spawn of the North 38. Juarez 39. Road to Morocco 42. For Whom the Bell Tolls 43. Cloak and Dagger 46. Back to Bataan 46. Istanbul 56. Confessions of a Counterspy 60. Sardonicus 62, many others.

Solanas, Fernando (1936–).
Argentinian director and screenwriter, of revolutionary intentions. He began as a documentary film-maker, and was in exile during the late 70s and early 80s, making films in France. He was shot in the legs in 1991 after accusing the government of corruption.
The Hour of the Furnaces (La Hora de los Hornos) 68. Los Hijos de Fierro 76. Tangos: The Exile of Gardel 86. Sur 88. The Voyage (El Viaje) 93, etc.

Solás, Humberto (1942–).
Cuban director.
Lucia 68. A Day in November (Un Día de Noviembre) 72. Simparele 74. Cantata de Chile 75. Cecilia Valdés 82. A Successful Man (Un Hombre de Exito) 87, etc.

Soldati, Mario (1906–).
Italian director.
Scandal in the Roman Bath 51. The Wayward Wife 53. The Stranger's Hand 54. Woman of the River 55, many others.

soldiers
depicted at length in films include Alexander the Great (by Richard Burton), Hannibal (by Victor Mature), Genghis Khan (by John Wayne and Omar Sharif), Alexander Nevsky (by Cherkassov), Clive of India (by Ronald Colman), Napoleon (by Charles Boyer, Marlon Brando, Herbert Lom, and others), Bonnie Prince Charlie (by David Niven), Wellington (by George Arliss), General Gordon (by Charlton Heston), Custer (by Errol Flynn and Robert Shaw), La Fayette (by Michel le Royer), Davy Crockett (by Fess Parker and others), Sergeant York (by Gary Cooper), Audie Murphy (by Audie Murphy), Rommel (by Erich von Stroheim and James Mason), Che Guevara (by Omar Sharif),

General Patton (by George C. Scott), and General Macarthur (by Gregory Peck).

Solon, Ewen (c. 1923–1985).
New Zealand character actor in Britain, especially on TV in *Maigret* series (as Lucas).
The Sundowners 59. Jack the Ripper 60. The Hound of the Baskervilles 60. The Terror of the Tongs 61. The Wicked Lady 83, etc.

Solzhenitsyn, Alexander (1918–).
Russian novelist, expelled from his own country in 1974 for too much free thought. *One Day in the Life of Ivan Denisovitch* was filmed.

Somers, Suzanne (1946–) (S. Mahoney).
American leading lady of the late 70s, especially on TV in the series *Three's Company*.
American Graffiti 73. It Happened at Lakewood Manor (TV) 77. Nothing Personal 80. Happily Ever After (TV) 82. Rich Men, Single Women (TV) 90, etc.

Somlo, Josef (1885–1973).
Hungarian producer with long experience at UFA, in Britain from 1933.
Dark Journey 37. The Mikado 39. Old Bill and Son 40. Uncle Silas 47. The Man Who Loved Redheads 55. Behind the Mask 59, etc.

Sommer, Elke (1940–) (Elke Schletz).
German leading lady now in international films.
Don't Bother to Knock (GB) 60. The Victors (GB) 63. *The Prize* (US) 63. A Shot in the Dark (US) 64. The Art of Love (US) 65. Four Kinds of Love (It.) 65. The Money Trap (US) 65. The Oscar (US) 66. Boy, Did I Get a Wrong Number (US) 66. Deadlier than the Male (GB) 66. The Venetian Affair (US) 66. The Corrupt Ones 67. The Wicked Dreams of Paula Schultz (US) 68. Zeppelin (US) 71. Percy (GB) 71. Carry On Behind (GB) 76. Lily in Love 84. Adventures beyond Belief 87, etc.

Sommer, Josef (1934–).
American character actor.
The Stepford Wives 75. Too Far to Go (TV) 78. Hide in Plain Sight 80. Still of the Night 82. Sophie's Choice 82. Hanky Panky 82. Witness 84. Dracula's Widow 88. Chances Are 89. The Bloodhounds of Broadway 89. Money, Power, Murder (TV) 89. Shadows and Fog 92. Malice 93, etc.
TV series: Hothouse 88. Under Cover 91.

Sondergaard, Gale (1899–1985) (Edith Sondergaard).
Tall, dark American character actress with a sinister smile; career harmed by the anti-communist witch-hunt of the early 50s.
■ Anthony Adverse (AA) 36. Maid of Salem 37. Seventh Heaven 37. The Life of Emile Zola 37. Lord Jeff 38. Dramatic School 38. Never Say Die 38. Juarez 38. The Cat and the Canary 39. The Llano Kid 39. The Bluebird 40. The Mark of Zorro 40. The Letter 40. The Black Cat 41. Paris Calling 41. My Favourite Blonde 42. Enemy Agent Meets Ellery Queen 42. A Night to Remember 43. Appointment in Berlin 43. Isle of Forgotten Sins 43. The Strange Death of Adolf Hitler 43. Spider Woman 44. Follow the Boys 44. Christmas Holiday 44. The Invisible Man's Revenge 44. Gypsy Wildcat 44. The Climax 44. Enter Arsène Lupin 44. Spider Woman Strikes Back 46. A Night in Paradise 46. Anna and the King of Siam (AAN) 46. The Time of Their Lives 46. Road to Rio 47. Pirates of Monterey 47. East Side West Side 49. Slaves 69. The Cat Creature (TV) 74. The Return of A Man Called Horse 76. Pleasantville 76. Echoes 83.

Sondheim, Stephen (1930–).
Celebrated American composer and lyricist, usually over the heads of the hoi polloi. His work has penetrated into such films as *Gypsy* (lyrics), *A Funny Thing Happened on the Way to the Forum*, *West Side Story* (lyrics) and *A Little Night Music*. His film scores include *Stavisky* and *Reds*, and he co-authored *The Last of Sheila*.

Sonnenfeld, Barry (1953–).
American cinematographer who has turned to directing.
Blood Simple 84. Compromising Positions 85. Raising Arizona 87. Three o'Clock High 87. Throw Momma from the Train 87. Big 88. When Harry Met Sally 89. Miller's Crossing 90. Misery 90. The Addams Family (d) 91. Addams Family Values (d) 93, etc.

Sony Dynamic Digital Sound.
A system for recording and playing back sound digitally, launched in 1993. It is one of three competing digital sound systems, the others being Dolby SR-D and Universal's DTS.

Soo, Jack (1916–1979) (Goro Suzuki).
Japanese character actor in America, best remembered in *Flower Drum Song* 60, and as one of the gang in TV's *Barney Miller* series.

Sordi, Alberto (1919–).
Italian leading man and comic actor who began writing and directing his films in the 80s.
I Vitelloni 53. The Sign of Venus 55. A Farewell to Arms 57. The Best of Enemies 60. Those Magnificent Men in Their Flying Machines 65. To Bed or Not To Bed 65. Le Streghe 67. Polvere di Stelle 73. Viva Italia 77. Le Témoin 78. Il Marchese del Grillo (& w) 81. Bertoldo, Bertoldino e Cacasenno 84. Tutti Dentro (a, wd) 84. The Miser (L'Avaro) (& co-w) 89. Christmas Vacation '91 (Vacanze di Natale '91) 91. Assolto per Aver Commesso il Fatto (& co-w, d) 92. Nestore l'Ultima Corsa (& co-w, d) 94, etc.

Sorel, Jean (1934–) (Jean de Rochbrune).
French-Canadian leading man.
The Four Days of Naples 62. A View from the Bridge 62. Vaghe Stella dell'Orsa 65. Le Bambole 66. Belle de Jour 67. A Quiet Place to Kill 70. Mil Millones para una Rubia 78, etc.

Sorel, Louise (1944–).
American leading lady of occasional films.
The Party's Over 65. B.S. I Love You 70. Plaza Suite 71. Every Little Crook and Nanny 72. When Every Day Was the Fourth of July (TV) 78. Mazes and Monsters (TV) 82, etc.
TV series: The Survivors 69–70. The Don Rickles Show 72. Curse of Dracula 79. Ladies' Man 80–81.

Sorvino, Mira.
American actress, the daughter of actor Paul Sorvino. She took a degree in East Asian studies from Harvard and worked as an assistant director before becoming an actress.
Amongst Friends 93. Barcelona 94. Parallel Lives (TV) 94. Quiz Show 94, etc.

Sorvino, Paul (1939–).
Chubby American actor.
Where's Poppa? 70. Cry Uncle 72. A Touch of Class 72. The Gambler 74. The Day of the Dolphin 75. I Will, I Will . . . For Now 76. Oh God 77. Slow Dancing in the Big City 78. The Brink's Job 78. Bloodbrothers 78. Lost and Found 80. Cruising 80. Reds 81. Turk 182 85. A Fine Mess 86. Vasectomy, a Delicate Matter 86. Dick Tracy 90. GoodFellas

90. The Rocketeer 91. Parallel Lives (TV) 94, etc.
TV series: We'll Get By 75. Bert Angelo/Superstar 76. The Oldest Rookie 87–88. Law and Order 90–92.

Sothern, Ann (1909–) (Harriette Lake).
Pert American comedienne and leading lady with stage experience.
Let's Fall in Love (debut) 34. Kid Millions 35. Trade Winds 38. Hotel for Women 39. *Maisie* 39. Brother Orchid 40. Congo Maisie 40. Gold Rush Maisie 41 (and seven others in series before 1947). Lady Be Good 41. Panama Hattie 42. Cry Havoc 43. The Judge Steps Out 47. *A Letter to Three Wives* 49. Nancy Goes to Rio 50. Lady in a Cage 63. The Best Man 64. Sylvia 65. Chubasco 67. The Great Man's Whiskers (TV) 71. Golden Needles 74. Crazy Mama 75. Captains and the Kings (TV) 76. The Manitou 78. The Whales of August (AAN) 87, etc.
TV series: *Private Secretary* 52–53. The Ann Sothern Show 58–61.

Soto, Talisa (1968–) (Miriam Soto).
American actress and model.
Spike of Bensonhurst 88. License to Kill 90. Silhouette (TV) 91. Hostage (TV) 92. The Mambo Kings 92.

Soul, David (1943–) (David Solberg).
American leading man who made a killing in TV but never found the right movie; nor was singing a wise choice as a second career.
Johnny Got His Gun 71. Magnum Force 73. Dogpound Shuffle 74. The Stick Up 77. Little Ladies of the Night (TV) 77. Salem's Lot (TV) 79. Swan Song 79. Rage (TV) 80. The Hanoi Hilton 87. The Bride in Black 90. In the Cold of the Night 90. Pentathlon 94, etc.
TV series: Here Come the Brides 68–70. Owen Marshall, Counsellor at Law 74. *Starsky and Hutch* 75–80. Casablanca 83. The Yellow Rose 83.

sound.
The first really successful experiments with synchronized sound had the track on gramophone discs; cylinders were also employed. These systems obviously led to maddening breakdowns, and editing was next to impossible. Fox, using the De Forrest Phonofilm system combined with a German process called Tri-Ergon, contrived in 1926 to record sound directly on to film next to the picture, forming the first soundtrack. It was this system which by 1930 had superseded the others and is still with us.

Sousa, John Philip (1854–1932).
American composer, most notably of rousing marches. His 1928 biography, *Marching Along*, was filmed in 1953 as *Stars and Stripes Forever*.

Soutendijk, Renée (1957–).
Dutch leading actress, in international films. She is a former Olympic athlete.
Pastorale 43 76. Spetters 80. The Girl with Red Hair (Het Meisje met Rode Haar) 81. Inside the Third Reich (TV) 82. The Fourth Man (De Vierde Man) 83. The Cold Room 84. Out of Order (Abwarts) 85. The Second Victory 87. Der Madonna-Man 87. Wherever You Are 88. Forced March 89. Grave Secrets 89. Murderers Among Us: The Simon Wiesenthal Story (TV) 90. Eve of Destruction 90. Keeper of the City 91. Heatwave (Hittegolf) 93. The Betrayed (Op Afbetaling) 93. House Call 94, etc.

Southern, Terry (1924–).
American satirist and black-comedy writer.

■ *Dr Strangelove* (co-w) (AAN) 64. The Cincinnati Kid (co-w) 65. The Loved One (co-w) 65. Barbarella 68. Easy Rider (co-w) (AAN) 69. End of the Road (co-w) 70. The Magic Christian (co-w) 70. The Telephone (co-w) 88.

Spaak, Catherine (1945–).
Belgian leading lady, daughter of Charles Spaak.
Le Trou 60. The Empty Canvas 64. Weekend at Dunkirk 65. Hotel 67. Libertine 68. Cat o' Nine Tails 71. Take a Hard Ride 75. Honey 81. Secret Scandal 89, etc.

Spaak, Charles (1903–1975).
Belgian screenwriter associated with many French films.
La Kermesse Héroïque 35. Les Bas-Fonds 36. *La Grande Illusion* 37. La Fin du Jour 39. Panique 46. Justice est Faite (co-w) 50. Thérèse Raquin 53. Crime and Punishment 56. Charmants Garçons 57. The Vanishing Corporal 61. Cartouche 62, etc.

Space, Arthur (1908–1983).
American character actor, in many film roles and such TV series as *National Velvet* and *Lassie*.
Tortilla Flat 42. Wilson 44. Leave Her to Heaven 45. The Barefoot Mailman 52. Spirit of St Louis 57. The Shakiest Gun in the West 68. On the Nickel 80, etc.

space exploration
on screen began in 1899 with Méliès; in the 20s Fritz Lang made *The Woman in the Moon* and in the 30s there was *Buck Rogers in the Twenty-Fifth Century*, but not until 1950 did the subject seem acceptable as anything but fantasy. In that year an adventure of the comic-strip type, *Rocketship XM*, competed for box-office attention with George Pal's semi-documentary *Destination Moon*, and suddenly the floodgates were opened. During the years that followed we were offered such titles as *Riders to the Stars*, *Fire Maidens from Outer Space*, *Satellite in the Sky*, *From the Earth to the Moon*, *Conquest of Space*, *Forbidden Planet*, It!, *The Terror from Beyond Space*, *Robinson Crusoe on Mars*, *The First Men in the Moon*, *2001: A Space Odyssey*, *Saturn Three*, *Outland* and the *Star Wars* saga. Nor was the traffic all one way: Earth had many strange visitors from other planets, notably in *The Thing From Another World*, *The Day the Earth Stood Still*, *Devil Girl from Mars*, *Stranger from Venus*, *It Came from Outer Space*, *Invasion of the Body Snatchers* (the best and subtlest of them all), *The War of the Worlds*, *The Quatermass Experiment*, *Quatermass II*, *Visit to a Small Planet*, *This Island Earth*, and *The Man Who Fell to Earth*. On television, the most imaginative exploits have been in *Star Trek*, *Space 1999*, *Buck Rogers* and *Galactica*.

Spacek, Sissy (1950–).
Tomboy-ish American leading lady. She is married to director Jack Fisk.
Prime Cut 71. Ginger in the Morning 72. *Badlands* 73. Katherine (TV) 75. Carrie (AAN) 76. Three Women 77. Welcome to L.A. 77. Heart Beat 79. *Coal Miner's Daughter* (AA) 80. Raggedy Man 81. Missing (AAN) 82. Country 84. The River (AAN) 84. Marie 85. Violets Are Blue 85. 'Night, Mother 86. Crimes of the Heart (AAN) 86. The Long Walk Home 90. JFK 91. Hard Promises 92. Trading Mom 94, etc.

Spacey, Kevin (1959–).
American leading actor.
Heartburn 86. Rocket Gibraltar 88. Working Girl 88. See No Evil, Hear No Evil 89. Dad 89. A Show of Force 90. Henry and June 90. Glengarry Glen Ross 92. Consenting Adults 92. Iron Will 94. The

Ref 94. The Buddy Factor (& p) 94. Outbreak 95, etc.

TV series: Wiseguy 88.

Spader, James (1960–).
Youthful-appearing American actor.

Endless Love 81. Family Secrets 84. The New Kids 85. Tuff Turf 85. Pretty in Pink 86. Baby Boom 87. Jack's Back 87. Less than Zero 87. Mannequin 87. Wall Street 87. The Rachel Papers 89. sex, lies and videotape 89. Bad Influence 90. White Palace 90. True Colors 91. Bob Roberts 92. Chicago Loop 92. Storyville 92. The Music of Chance 93. Wolf 94, etc.

TV series: The Family Tree 83.

spaghetti westerns.
A dismissive name for the blood-spattered Italian imitations of American westerns which became popular in the 60s, using such actors as Lee Van Cleef and Clint Eastwood.

Spain
produced few distinguished films before the Civil War, Buñuel having settled in France, and afterwards the product was dictated by politics apart from a few pleasing comedies and melodramas by such directors as Berlanga and Bardem. Buñuel made a few visits in the 60s. Following the death of the dictator General Franco in 1975, Spanish cinema underwent a renaissance, although some talented directors had emerged in the 60s and 70s, notably Carlos Saura. They were followed by a new generation of directors that included Victor Erice and Pedro Almodóvar, whose films made international stars of Carmen Maura and Antonio Banderas.

Spall, Timothy (1957–).
British character actor, often in grotesque roles.

Quadrophenia 79. Remembrance 82. The Missionary 83. The Bride 85. Gothic 87. Dutch Girls 87. To Kill a Priest 88. Dream Demon 88. 1871 89. The Sheltering Sky 90. White Hunter, Black Heart 90. Life Is Sweet 90. For One Night Only (as Margaret Rutherford) 91, etc.

TV series: Auf Wiedersehen Pet 83–84. Frank Stubbs Presents 93. Frank Stubbs 94. Outside Edge 94. Nice Day at the Office 94.

The Spanish Civil War
featured in a few Hemingway picturizations, notably *For Whom the Bell Tolls* and *The Snows of Kilimanjaro*; in *The Fallen Sparrow*, *Blockade*, *The Angel Wore Red*, *Love under Fire*, *Last Train from Madrid*, *Arise My Love*, *Confidential Agent* and (remotely) *The Prime of Miss Jean Brodie*. In more documentary style were *L'Espoir*, *Spanish Earth*, *Guernica*, *To Die in Madrid* and *¡Ay, Carmela!*, while British television has produced two extended assemblies of newsreel footage.

Spano, Vincent (1962–).
American leading actor.

The Double McGuffin 79. Over the Edge 79. Baby, It's You 83. The Black Stallion Returns 83. Rumble Fish 83. Alphabet City 84. Creator 85. Maria's Lovers 85. Good Morning Babylon 86. And God Created Woman 88. High-Frequency 88. The Heart of the Deal 90. Oscar 91. City of Hope 91. Alive 93. Indian Summer 93. The Ascent 94, etc.

Spark, Muriel (1918–).
British novelist feted by the intelligentsia. Two films of her work, *The Prime of Miss Jean Brodie* and *The Driver's Seat*, have both been unsatisfactory.

Nasty Habits (oa) 76. Memento Mori (oa) (TV) 92.

Sparks, Ned (1883–1957) (Edward Sparkman).
Hard-boiled, cigar-chewing Canadian comic actor often seen in Hollywood films of the 30s as grouchy reporter or agent.

The Big Noise 27. The Miracle Man 30. Forty-Second Street 33. Two's Company (GB) 37. The Star Maker 39. For Beauty's Sake 40. Magic Town 46, etc.

Sparkuhl, Theodor (1891–1945).
German cinematographer in Hollywood from the early 30s.

Carmen 18. Manon Lescaut 26. La Chienne 31. Too Much Harmony 33. Enter Madame 35. *Beau Geste* 39. *The Glass Key* 42. Star Spangled Rhythm 43. Blood on the Sun 46. Bachelor Girls 46, many others.

Sparv, Camilla (1943–).
Swedish-born leading lady in Hollywood films. She was formerly married to producer Robert Evans.

The Trouble with Angels 66. Murderers' Row 66. Dead Heat on a Merry-Go-Round 66. Department K 67. Mackenna's Gold 68. Downhill Racer 69. The Italian Job 69. Survival Zone 84, etc.

Speakman, Jeff (1957–).
American karate expert in action movies.

The Perfect Weapon 91. A.W.O.L. (aka Lionheart) 91. Street Knight 93, etc.

special effects:
a general term covering the many tricks of film-making which cannot be achieved by direct photography: optical wipes, dissolves, sub-titles, invisibility, mattes, etc.

speeches
of any length are the antithesis of good film-making, but sometimes a long monologue has been not only an actor's dream but absolutely right, memorable and hypnotic in its context. The record (20 minutes) is probably held by Edwige Feuillère in *The Eagle Has Two Heads*, but more effective, and somewhat shorter, were Sam Jaffe in *Lost Horizon*, Alec Guinness in *The Mudlark*, Orson Welles in *Compulsion*, Spencer Tracy in *Inherit the Wind*, Anne Baxter in *The Walls of Jericho*, James Stewart in *Mr Smith Goes to Washington*, Paul Muni in *The Life of Emile Zola*, Don Murray in *One Man's Way*, Orson Welles in *Moby Dick*, and Charles Chaplin in *The Great Dictator*.

Speedy Gonzales.
Fast-moving Mexican mouse who was the hero of Warner Brothers cartoons. Created by Friz Freleng and animator Hawley Pratt, he was voiced by Mel Blanc.

Speedy Gonzales (AA) 55. Tabasco Road (AAN) 57. The Pied Piper of Guadalupe (AAN) 61. Mexican Cat Dance 63. Chili Corn Corny 66. Speedy Ghost to Town 67. See Ya Later, Gladiator 67, etc.

Spence, Bruce (1945–).
Lanky Australian character actor.

Stork 71. The Cars that Ate Paris 74. Newsfront 78. Dimboola 79. Mad Max 2 (aka The Road Warrior) 81. Midnight Spares 82. Buddies 83. Where the Green Ants Dream 84. Mad Max beyond Thunderdrome 85. Rikky and Pete 88. The Year My Voice Broke 88. . . . Almost 90. Boyfriend from

Hell (aka The Shrimp on the Barbie) 90. Wendy Cracked a Walnut 90. Sweet Talker 91, etc.

Spencer, Bud (1929–) (Carlo Pedersoli).
Italian character actor in many spaghetti westerns.

Blood River 67. Beyond the Law 68. Boot Hill 69. They Call Me Trinity 70. Four Flies on Grey Velvet 71. Watch Out We're Mad 74. Trinity Is Still My Name 75. The Knock Out Cop 78. Crime Busters 80. Aladdin 86, etc.

Spencer, Dorothy (1909–).
American editor.

The Moon's Our Home 36. Blockade 38. *Stagecoach* 39. *Foreign Correspondent* 40. To Be or Not To Be 42. Heaven Can Wait 43. Lifeboat 43. My Darling Clementine 46. The Snake Pit 48. Three Came Home 50. Fourteen Hours 51. Black Widow 54. The Man in the Grey Flannel Suit 56. The Young Lions 58. North to Alaska 60. Cleopatra (AAN) 63. Von Ryan's Express 65. Valley of the Dolls 67. Limbo 71. *Earthquake* (AAN) 74. The Concorde – Airport 79 79, many others.

Spencer, Kenneth (1912–1964).
American singer who appeared in a few 40s films including *Cabin in the Sky* and *Bataan*, both 43.

Spenser, Jeremy (1937–).
British leading man, former child actor, also on stage. He has not acted since the mid-60s and has sunk into obscurity.

Portrait of Clare 48. *Prelude to Fame* 50. Appointment with Venus 51. Summer Madness 55. The Prince and the Showgirl 57. Wonderful Things 58. Ferry to Hong Kong 58. *The Roman Spring of Mrs Stone* 61. King and Country 64. He Who Rides a Tiger 65. Fahrenheit 451 66, etc.

Sperling, Milton (1912–1988).
American producer.

Cloak and Dagger 46. Three Secrets 50. The Enforcer 51. Blowing Wild 54. The Court Martial of Billy Mitchell (& co-w) (AAN) 55. The Bramble Bush (& co-w) 59. The Battle of the Bulge 65. Captain Apache (w, p) 71, etc.

Spewack, Sam (1899–1971).
American playwright who with his wife Bella turned out several scripts for Hollywood.

The Secret Witness 31. Rendezvous 35. *Boy Meets Girl* 38. Three Loves Has Nancy 38. My Favorite Wife (AAN) 40. Weekend at the Waldorf 45. Kiss Me Kate 53. Move Over Darling 63, etc.

Spheeris, Penelope (1945–).
American director and screenwriter, concentrating mainly on themes of disaffected youth. She had her first commercial hit in 1992 with the rock-oriented comedy *Wayne's World*.

The Decline of Western Civilization (wd) 80. Suburbia (wd) 83. The Boys Next Door (d) 85. Summer Camp Nightmare (w) 86. Hollywood Vice Squad (d) 86. Dudes (d) 87. The Decline of Western Civilization Part II: The Metal Years (d) 88. Thunder & Mud (d) 89. Wayne's World (d) 92. The Beverly Hillbillies (p, d) 93. The Little Rascals (co-w, d) 94, etc.

Spiegel, Sam (1901–1985) (aka S. P. Eagle).
Polish-born producer, in Hollywood from 1941.

Biography: 1988, *Spiegel* by Andrew Sinclair.

Tales of Manhattan 42. *The Stranger* 45. We Were Strangers 48. *The African Queen* 51. *On the Waterfront* (AA) 54. The Strange One 57. *The Bridge on the River Kwai* (AA) 57. *Lawrence of Arabia* (AA) 62. The Chase 66. *The Night of the Generals* 66. The Happening 67. The Swimmer 68. Nicholas and

Alexandra 71. The Last Tycoon 76. Betrayal 82, etc.

Spielberg, David (1939–).
American character actor.

The Effect of Gamma Rays 72. Newman's Law 74. Hustle 75. The Choirboys 77. The End 78. Stone (TV) 79. Sworn to Silence (TV) 87. Alice 90, etc.
TV series: Bob and Carol and Ted and Alice 73. The Practice 76.

Spielberg, Steven (1947–).
American director whose star was high in the heavens during the late 70s and early 80s, largely because of semi-adult treatment of what would once have been considered comic-strip material for children. He was awarded a Golden Lion for lifetime Achievement at the Venice Film Festival in 1993. He is reported to have made $200m from *Jurassic Park*; his 1993/94 earnings were $335m according to *Forbes* magazine. He set up his own studio in 1994 with partners Jeffrey Katzenberg and David Geffen.
Biography; 1992, *Steven Spielberg* by Philip M. Taylor.
¶ Amblin' (short) 69. Something Evil (TV) 71. Savage (TV) 72. *Duel* (TV) 72. Sugarland Express 73. *Jaws* 75. 1941 75. Close Encounters of the Third Kind (AAN) 77. Raiders of the Lost Ark (AAN) 81. Poltergeist (p only) 82. *E.T. – the Extraterrestrial* (AAN) 82. Twilight Zone (co-d) 83. Indiana Jones and the Temple of Doom 84. Gremlins (p) 85. Back to the Future (p) 85. The Goonies (p) 85. The Color Purple 85. An American Tail (p) 86. Empire of the Sun (& p) 87. Innerspace (p) 87. The Land before Time (p) 88. Who Framed Roger Rabbit? (p) 88. Always (p, d) 89. Back to the Future II (p) 89. Dad (p) 89. Indiana Jones and the Last Crusade (d) 89. Arachnophobia (p) 90. Back to the Future III (p) 90. Gremlins 2: The New Batch (p) 90. Joe versus the Volcano (p) 90. Hook (p, d) 91. Jurassic Park (p, d) 93. Schindler's List (AAp, AAd) 93.

¶ I've never been through psychoanalysis. I solve my problems with the pictures I make. – *S.S.*
Rosebud will go over my typewriter to remind me that quality in movies comes first. – *S.S. after buying (for $55,000) the sled used in Citizen Kane*
Stories don't have a middle and an end any more. They usually have a beginning that never stops beginning. – *S.S.*
I'd rather direct than produce. Any day. And twice on Sunday. – *S.S.*

spies
enjoyed enormous popularity as the heroes of over-sexed, gimmick-ridden melodramas. Real-life spies have been less frequently depicted, the world of James Bond being much livelier than those of Moyzich (*Five Fingers*), Odette Churchill (*Odette M.C.*), Nurse Edith Cavell, Violette Szabo (*Carve Her Name with Pride*), Mata Hari, or the gangs in *The House on 92nd Street*, *13 Rue Madeleine*, and *Ring of Spies*.
Fictional spy films first became popular during and after World War I: they added a touch of glamour to an otherwise depressing subject, even though the hero often faced the firing squad in the last reel. Right up to 1939 romantic melodramas on this theme were being made: *I Was a Spy*, *The Man Who Knew Too Much*, *The Thirty-Nine Steps*, *Lancer Spy*, *The Spy in Black*, *Dark Journey*, *British Agent*, *Secret Agent*, *The Lady Vanishes*, *Espionage Agent*, *Confessions of a Nazi Spy*. The last-named brought the subject roughly up to date, and with the renewed outbreak of hostilities new possibilities were hastily seized in *Foreign Correspondent*, *Night Train to Munich*, *Casablanca*, *The Conspirators*, *They*

Came to Blow Up America, *Berlin Correspondent*, *Across the Pacific*, *Escape to Danger*, *Ministry of Fear*, *Confidential Agent*, *Sherlock Holmes and the Secret Weapon*, *Hotel Reserve*, and innumerable others. (It was fashionable during this period to reveal that the villains of comedy-thrillers and who-done-its were really enemy agents.) During the post-war years two fashions in film spying became evident: the downbeat melodrama showing spies as frightened men and women doing a dangerous job (*Notorious*, *Cloak and Dagger*, *Hotel Berlin*, *Orders to Kill*) and the 'now it can be told' semi-documentary revelation (*O.S.S.*, *Diplomatic Courier*, *The Man Who Never Was*, *The Two-Headed Spy*, *The Counterfeit Traitor*, *Operation Crossbow*). In the late 40s Nazis and Japs were replaced by reds, and we had a spate of melodramas under such titles as *I Married a Communist*, *I Was a Communist for the FBI*, *I Was an American Spy*, *Red Snow* and *The Red Danube*.
There had always been spy comedies. Every comedian made one or two: the Crazy Gang in *Gasbags*, Duggie Wakefield in *Spy for a Day*, Jack Benny in *To Be or Not To Be*, Bob Hope in *They Got Me Covered*, Radford and Wayne in *It's Not Cricket*, George Cole in *Top Secret*, right up to the *Carry On* team in *Carry On Spying* and Morecambe and Wise in *The Intelligence Men*. There were also occasional burlesques like *All Through the Night* and sardonic comedies like *Our Man in Havana*. But it was not until the late 50s that the spy reasserted himself as a romantic figure who could be taken lightly; and not until 1962 was the right box-office combination of sex and suspense found in *Dr No*. Since then we have been deluged with pale imitations of James Bond to such an extent that almost every leading man worth his salt has had a go. Cary Grant in *Charade*, David Niven in *Where the Spies Are*, Rod Taylor and Trevor Howard in *The Liquidator*, Dirk Bogarde in *Hot Enough for June*, Michael Caine in *The Ipcress File*, Paul Newman in *Torn Curtain*, James Coburn in *Our Man Flint*, Gregory Peck in *Arabesque*, Yul Brynner in *The Double Man*, George Peppard in *The Executioner*, Stephen Boyd in *Assignment K*, Frank Sinatra in *The Naked Runner*, Anthony Hopkins in *When Eight Bells Toll*, Kirk Douglas in *Catch Me a Spy*, Tom Adams in *Licensed to Kill*. There have also been elaborations such as the extreme sophistication of *The Manchurian Candidate*, the cold realism of *The Spy Who Came in from the Cold*, the op-art spoofing of *Modesty Blaise*, even the canine agent of *The Spy with a Cold Nose* and spies from outer space in *This Island Earth*. And the TV screens of 1970 were filled with such tricky heroes as those in *Danger Man* (Secret Agent), *The Man from U.N.C.L.E.*, *Amos Burke Secret Agent*, *The Baron*, *I Spy* and *The Avengers*. The trend of the 70s was towards sour and disenchanted looks at the whole business, such as *Callan*, *The Killer Elite*, *Permission to Kill* and *Three Days of the Condor*.

Spillane, Mickey (1918–) (Frank Morrison).
Best-selling American crime novelist of the love-'em and kill-'em variety: I the Jury 53. The Long Wait 54. Kiss Me Deadly 55. *I The Jury* was remade in 1981, with Armand Assante.
AS ACTOR: Ring of Fear 54. The Girl Hunters (as Mike Hammer) (& w) 64.
Darren McGavin played Hammer in a 1960 TV series, as did Stacy Keach in 1983.

Spilsbury, Klinton (1955–).
Mexican-born actor who played the title role in *The Legend of the Lone Ranger* 81, which was a box-office disaster, and then dropped out of sight.

Spinetti, Victor (1933–).
Italo-Welsh comic actor with stage experience.

A Hard Day's Night 64. The Wild Affair 64. Help! 65. The Taming of the Shrew 66. Hieronymus Merkin 69. The Return of the Pink Panther 76. Voyage of the Damned 76. The Krays 90. The Princess and the Goblin (voice) 92, etc.

Spinotti, Dante (1943–).
American cinematographer.
Sotto, Sotto 84. Manhunter 86. Crimes of the Heart 87. Beaches 88. Torrents of Spring 89. The Comfort of Strangers 90. True Colors 91. The Last of the Mohicans 92. La Fine è Nota 93. Blink 94, etc.

The Spoilers.
Rex Beach's action novel has been filmed five times, with interest centring on its climactic fight scene between the two male leads, who were as follows: 1914, William Farnum and Tom Santschi; 1922, Milton Sills and Noah Beery; 1930, William Boyd and Gary Cooper; 1942, John Wayne and Randolph Scott; 1956, Jeff Chandler and Rory Calhoun.

Spoliansky, Mischa (1898–1985).
Russian composer, in Germany from 1930, Britain from 1934.
Don Juan 34. Sanders of the River 35. The Ghost Goes West 36. King Solomon's Mines 37. Jeannie 42. Don't Take It To Heart 44. Mr Emmanuel 44. Wanted for Murder 46. The Happiest Days of Your Life 50. Trouble in Store 53. Saint Joan 57. Northwest Frontier 59. The Battle of the Villa Fiorita 65. Hitler: The Last Ten Days 73, many others.

sportsmen
who have been the subject of biopics include Babe Ruth (William Bendix) in *The Babe Ruth Story* and *Babe* (John Goodman); Grover Cleveland Alexander (Ronald Reagan) in *The Winning Team*; Lou Gehrig (Gary Cooper) in *The Pride of the Yankees*; Monty Stratton (James Stewart) in *The Stratton Story*; Jim Piersall (Anthony Perkins) in *Fear Strikes Out*; Jim Corbett (Errol Flynn) in *Gentleman Jim*; John L. Sullivan (Greg McClure) in *The Great John L.*; Knute Rockne (Pat O'Brien) in *Knute Rockne All-American*; Jim Thorpe (Burt Lancaster) in *Jim Thorpe All-American* (*Man of Bronze*); Ben Hogan (Glenn Ford) in *Follow the Sun*; Annette Kellerman (Esther Williams) in *Million Dollar Mermaid*.

Spottiswoode, Roger (1947–).
English director and screenwriter now active in Hollywood, a former editor in television and film.
Terror Train 80. The Pursuit of D. B. Cooper 81. 48 Hours (co-w) 82. Under Fire 83. The Best of Times 86. The Last Innocent Man (TV) 87. Shoot to Kill 88. 3rd Degree Burn (TV) 89. Time Flies When You're Alive (TV) 89. Turner & Hooch 89. Air America 90. Stop! or My Mom Will Shoot 92. And the Band Played On (TV) 93. Mesmer 94, etc.

Spring, Howard (1889–1965).
British novelist. Works filmed include *Fame Is the Spur* and *My Son My Son*.

Springsteen, R.G. (1904–1989).
American director who made efficient low-budget westerns from 1930.
Honeychile 48. Hellfire 49. The Enemy Within 49. The Toughest Man in Arizona 53. Track the Man Down 53. Come Next Spring 56. Cole Younger, Gunfighter 58. Battle Flame 59. Black Spurs 64. Taggart 65. Waco 66. Johnny Reno 66. Red Tomahawk 66, many others.

Squibs.
The cockney flower-seller heroine of George Pearson's silent comedy put in her first successful appearance in 1921. Public acclaim produced three sequels: *Squibs Wins the Calcutta Sweep* 22, *Squibs MP* 23, *Squibs' Honeymoon* 23. Pearson then grew tired of the tomboyish character and cast Betty Balfour in other roles, but she reappeared in a not-too-successful talkie version in 1936, with Gordon Harker and Stanley Holloway.

Squire, Ronald (1886–1958) (Ronald Squirl).
Jovial British character actor of stage (from 1909) and screen (from 1934).
Don't Take It to Heart 44. While the Sun Shines 46. Woman Hater 48. The Rocking-Horse Winner 50. Encore 52. My Cousin Rachel (US) 53. The Million Pound Note 54. Now and Forever 55. Count Your Blessings 58, etc.

Stack, Robert (1919–   ) (Robert Modini).
Personable, cold-eyed American leading man of the 50s, later successful in television.
■ First Love 39. The Mortal Storm 40. A Little Bit of Heaven 40. *Nice Girl* (in which he gave Deanna Durbin her first screen kiss) 41. Badlands of Dakota 41. To be or Not To Be 42. Eagle Squadron 42. Men of Texas 42. A Date with Judy 48. Miss Tatlock's Millions 48. Fighter Squadron 48. Mr Music 50. My Outlaw Brother 51. The Bullfighter and the Lady 52. Bwana Devil 53. War Paint 53. Conquest of Cochise 53. Sabre Jet 53. The High and the Mighty 54. The Iron Glove 54. House of Bamboo 55. Good Morning Miss Dove 55. Great Day in the Morning 56. *Written on the Wind* (AAN) 56. *The Tarnished Angels* 57. The Gift of Love 58. John Paul Jones 59. The Last Voyage 60. The Caretakers 63. Is Paris Burning? 66. The Corrupt Ones 67. Le Soleil des Voyous 68. The Story of a Woman 70. The Action Man 70. The Strange and Deadly Occurrence (TV) 75. 1941 75. Adventures of the Queen (TV) 76. Murder on Flight 502 (TV) 76. Airplane 80. Uncommon Valour 83. Big Trouble 84. The Transformers (voice) 86. Perry Mason: The Case of the Sinister Spirit (TV) 87. Caddyshack II 88. Joe versus the Volcano 90.
TV series: *The Untouchables* 59–62. *The Name of the Game* 68–70. Most Wanted 76. Strike Force 81–82. Falcon Crest 88.

Stafford, Frederick (1928–1979).
Austrian leading man who after many he-man roles in European movies imitating James Bond was signed by Alfred Hitchcock to play the lead in *Topaz* 69.

Stahl, John M. (1886–1950).
American director, former stage actor; in films from 1914.
Wives of Men 18. Husbands and Lovers 23. The Child Thou Gavest Me 24. The Naughty Duchess 28. Seed 31. *Back Street* 32. *Imitation of Life* 34. *Magnificent Obsession* 35. Parnell 37. Letter of Introduction 38. *When Tomorrow Comes* 39. Our Wife 41. *Holy Matrimony* 43. The Immortal Sergeant 43. The Eve of St Mark 44. *The Keys of the Kingdom* 44. Leave Her to Heaven 45. The Foxes of Harrow 47. The Walls of Jericho 47. Oh You Beautiful Doll 49, many others.

Stahl, Nick (1980–   ).
American child actor.
Stranger at My Door (TV) 92. The Man without a Face 93, etc.

Stainton, Philip (1908–1961).
Rotund British actor with surprised expression; often played policemen.

Scott of the Antarctic 47. Passport to Pimlico 48. The Quiet Man 52. Angels One Five 52. Hobson's Choice 54. The Woman for Joe 56, many others.

staircases
have provided dramatic backgrounds for many films. Martin Balsam was murdered on one in *Psycho;* the climax of *The Spiral Staircase* took place just there; Vivien Leigh was carried up one by a lustful Clark Gable in *Gone with the Wind;* Jerry Lewis danced down one in *Cinderfella;* Errol Flynn and Basil Rathbone duelled on one in *The Adventures of Robin Hood;* Ann Todd rode a horse up one in *South Riding;* Joan Fontaine in *Rebecca* descended one in delight and ascended it in tears; Raymond Massey ascended a particularly shadowy one in *The Old Dark House*, and later a very sinister character came down it; the entire cast of *Ship of Fools* came down one at the end, like a musical finale; a severed head bumped down one in *Hush Hush Sweet Charlotte;* Gene Tierney threw herself down one in *Leave Her to Heaven;* an old lady was tossed down one in a wheelchair in *Kiss of Death;* Bela Lugosi in *Dracula* passed through the cobwebs on one without breaking them; Laurel and Hardy in *Blockheads* had to descend and ascend innumerable flights of stairs in pursuit of a lost ball; Anna Sten was killed on one in *The Wedding Night;* the lighthouse staircase was a dramatic feature of *Thunder Rock;* James Cagney danced down the White House staircase in *Yankee Doodle Dandy;* and the main feature of *A Matter of Life and Death* was a moving stairway to heaven. In his last film, *Greystoke;* Ralph Richardson slid down a staircase on a tea-tray. Universal and Paramount both had very striking and oft-used staircase sets in the 40s; the latter was most dramatically used for Kirk Douglas's death in *The Strange Love of Martha Ivers.* Oddly enough in the film called *Staircase* the staircase was not an essential feature.

Stalling, Carl.
American composer and arranger, scoring cartoons. A silent-movie pianist and conductor, he became Disney's musical director in 1928, moving to Ub Iwerks' studio and then to Warner in 1936, retiring in 1958. His scores enlivened many cartoons from *Steamboat Willie* 28 to *To Itch His Own* 58.

Stallings, Laurence (1894–1968).
American screenwriter.
The Big Parade 25. *What Price Glory?* (co-w) 26. So Red the Rose (co-w) 35. Northwest Passage (co-w) 39. Jungle Book 42. Salome Where She Danced 45. *She Wore a Yellow Ribbon* (co-w) 49. The Sun Shines Bright 52, etc.

Stallone, Sylvester (1946–   ).
Solemn-looking American star who shot to the top in a modest film which he wrote himself. He was formerly married to actress Brigitte Nielsen.
Biography: 1991, *Sylvester Stallone* by Adrian Wright.
■ A Party at Kitty and Stud's (The Italian Stallion) 70. Bananas 71. The Lords of Flatbush 73. Capone 73. The Prisoner of Second Avenue 75. Death Race 2000 75. Farewell My Lovely 75. Carquake 75. *Rocky* (AAN) 76. F.I.S.T. (& w) 78. Paradise Alley (& wd) 78. Rocky II (& wd) 79. Nighthawks 81. Victory 81. Rocky III 82. First Blood 82. Staying Alive (co-w, co-p, d) 83. Rhinestone 84. Rambo 85. Rocky IV (& d) 85. Cobra 85. Over the Top 87. Rambo III 88. Lock Up 89. Tango & Cash 89. Rocky V 90. Oscar 91. Stop! or My Mom Will Shoot 92. Demolition Man 93. Cliffhanger (& co-w) 93. The Specialist 94. Judge Dredd 95.

¶ I'll just go on playing Rambo and Rocky. Both are money-making machines that can't be switched off. – S.S.
I'm not handsome in the classical sense. The eyes droop, the mouth is crooked, the teeth aren't straight, the voice sounds like a Mafioso pallbearer but somehow it all works. – S.S.
I'd say between 3 p.m. and 8 p.m. I look great. After that it's all downhill. Don't photograph me in the morning or you're gonna get Walter Brennan – S.S.
I'm not a genetically superior person. I built my body. – S.S.
I'm a very physical person. People don't credit me with much of a brain, so why should I disillusion them? – S.S.
I really am a manifestation of my own fantasy. – S.S.
Once in a man's life, for one mortal moment, he must make a grab for immortality. If not, he has not lived. – S.S.
All art, in this business, is an act of compromise. It's not one man's vision unless he takes very weak actors. – S.S.

Stamp, Terence (1940–   ).
British leading man.
Autobiography: 1987, *Stamp Album*, 1988, *Coming Attractions*, 1989, *Double Feature.*
Billy Budd (AAN) 62. Term of Trial 62. The Collector 65. Modesty Blaise 66. Far from the Madding Crowd 67. Poor Cow 67. Blue 68. Theorem (It.) 68. The Mind of Mr Soames 69. Superman 78. Meetings with Remarkable Men 78. The Thief of Bagdad 79. Superman II 81. The Hit 84. Company of Wolves 85. Link 86. The Sicilian 87. Wall Street 87. Young Guns 88. Alien Nation 88. Genuine Risk 90. Prince of Shadows (Beltenebros) 92. The Real McCoy 93. The Adventures of Priscilla Queen of the Desert 94, etc.

¶ I would have liked to be James Bond. – T.S.

Stamp-Taylor, Enid (1904–1946).
British character actress with stage experience.
Feather Your Nest 37. Action for Slander 37. The Lambeth Walk 38. Hatter's Castle 41. The Wicked Lady 45. Caravan 46, etc.

Stander, Lionel (1908–1994).
Gravel-voiced American character actor, on stage and screen from the early 30s. His career was harmed by the communist witch-hunts of the late 40s.
The Scoundrel 34. Mr Deeds Goes to Town 36. A Star is Born 37. Guadalcanal Diary 42. The Spectre of the Rose 46. Unfaithfully Yours 48. St Benny the Dip 51. Cul de Sac (GB) 66. Promise Her Anything (GB) 66. A Dandy in Aspic (GB) 68. The Gang that Couldn't Shoot Straight 72. The Con Men 73. The Black Bird 75. New York New York 77. The Cassandra Crossing 77. Matilda 78. Hart to Hart (TV) 79. The Transformers (voice) 86. Wicked Stepmother 88. Cookie 89, etc.
TV series: Hart to Hart 79.

Standing, Sir Guy (1873–1937).
British stage actor, father of Kay Hammond, in some Hollywood films.
■ The Story of Temple Drake 33. Midnight Club 33. Hell and High Water 33. The Cradle Song 33. A Bedtime Story 33. The Eagle and the Hawk 33. Death Takes a Holiday 34. Now and Forever 34. The Witching Hour 34. Double Door 34. *The Lives of a Bengal Lancer* 35. Car 99 35. Annapolis Farewell 35. The Big Broadcast of 1936 35. The Return of Sophie Lang 36. Palm Springs 36. I'd Give My

Life 36. Lloyds of London 36. Bulldog Drummond Escapes 37.

Standing, John (1934–) (Sir John Leon).
British character actor, son of Kay Hammond.

The Wild and the Willing 62. A Pair of Briefs 63. King Rat 65. Walk Don't Run 66. The Psychopath 66. Torture Garden 67. Zee and Co. 71. Rogue Male (TV) 76. The Eagle Has Landed 77. The Elephant Man 80. The Sea Wolves 80. Night Flyers 87, etc.

TV series: Lime Street 86.

Stanley, Kim (1921–) (Patricia Reid).
American stage actress.
■ The Goddess 58. Seance on a Wet Afternoon (AAN) 64. Three Sisters 67. Frances (AAN) 82. The Right Stuff 83.

¶ Directing Kim was as if you'd been given a piano and suddenly found you could play as well as Glenn Gould. – *Tony Richardson*

Stanley, Richard (1964–).
South-African born director and screenwriter of fantasy movies.
Hardware (wd) 90. Dust Devil (wd) 92.

Stannard, Don (1916–1949).
British light leading man who played Dick Barton in three serial-like melodramas 1948–49.

Stanton, Harry Dean (1926–).
American character actor.
Dragon Wells Massacre 57. How the West Was Won 62. Cool Hand Luke 67. Cisco Pike 72. Dillinger 73. Cockfighter 74. Farewell My Lovely 75. The Missouri Breaks 76. Alien 79. The Rose 79. Wise Blood 80. The Black Marble 80. Private Benjamin 80. One from the Heart 82. Christine 83. Repo Man 84. Paris, Texas 84. Pretty in Pink 86. Fool for Love 86. Slam Dance 87. Mr North 88. The Last Temptation of Christ 88. Dream a Little Dream 89. The Fourth War 90. Wild at Heart 90. Payoff 91. Twin Peaks: Fire Walk with Me 92. Man Trouble 92. Hotel Room (TV) 93. Against the Wall (TV) 94. Blue Tiger 94, etc.

Stanwyck, Barbara (1907–1990) (Ruby Stevens).
Durable American star actress, a sultry lady usually playing roles in which she is just as good as a man, if not better.
■ Broadway Nights 27. The Locked Door 29. Mexicali Rose 29. Ladies of Leisure 30. Ten Cents a Dance 31. Illicit 31. *Miracle Woman* 31. *Night Nurse* 31. Forbidden 32. Shopworn 32. *So Big* 32. The Purchase Price 32. *The Bitter Tea of General Yen* 33. Ladies They Talk About 33. *Baby Face* 33. Ever in My Heart 33. A Lost Lady 34. Gambling Lady 34. The Secret Bride 35. The Woman in Red 35. Red Salute 35. *Annie Oakley* 35. A Message to Garcia 36. The Bride Walks Out 36. His Brother's Wife 36. Banjo on My Knee 36. The Plough and the Stars 36. Internes Can't Take Money 37. This Is My Affair 37. *Stella Dallas* (AAN) 37. Breakfast for Two 38. The Mad Miss Manton 38. Always Goodbye 38. Union Pacific 39. Golden Boy 39. Remember the Night 40. *The Lady Eve* 41. *Meet John Doe* 41. You Belong to Me 41. *Ball of Fire* (AAN) 41. The Great Man's Lady 42. The Gay Sisters 42. Lady of Burlesque 42. Flesh and Fantasy 43. *Double Indemnity* (AAN) 44. Hollywood Canteen 44. Christmas in Connecticut 45. My Reputation 45. The Bride Wore Boots 46. *The Strange Love of Martha Ivers* 46. California 46. The Other Love 47. The Two Mrs Carrolls 47. Cry Wolf 47. BF's Daughter 48. *Sorry Wrong Number* (AAN) 48. The Lady Gambles 49. East Side West Side 49. Thelma Jordon

50. No Man of Her Own 50. *The Furies* 50. To Please a Lady 50. Man with a Cloak 51. Clash by Night 52. Jeopardy 53. Titanic 53. All I Desire 53. The Moonlighter 53. Blowing Wild 53. *Executive Suite* 54. Witness to Murder 54. Cattle Queen of Montana 54. The Violent Men 55. Escape to Burma 55. There's Always Tomorrow 56. The Maverick Queen 56. These Wilder Years 56. Crime of Passion 57. Trooper Hook 57. Forty Guns 57. Walk on the Wild Side 62. Roustabout 64. The Night Walker 65. The House That Would Not Die (TV) 70. A Taste of Evil (TV) 71. The Letters (TV) 73. The Thorn Birds (TV) 83.

TV series: *The Big Valley* 65–68.
✪ For holding more than her own in comedy or melodrama, and being a match for any man. *The Lady Eve.*

¶ I want to go on until they have to shoot me. – *B.S.*

Put me in the last fifteen minutes of a picture and I don't care what happened before. I don't even care if I was IN the rest of the damned thing – I'll take it in those fifteen minutes. – *B.S.*

Attention embarrasses me. I don't like to be on display. – *B.S.*

Career is too pompous a word. It was a job, and I have always felt privileged to be paid for doing what I love doing. – *B.S.*
~Honorary AA 1981 'for superlative creativity and a unique contribution to the art of screen acting'.

Stapleton, Jean (1923–) (Jeanne Murray).
American actress familiar from TV's *All in the Family.*
Damn Yankees 58. Bells are Ringing 60. Something Wild 61. Up the Down Staircase 67. Cold Turkey 70. Klute 71. The Trial 93, etc.

Stapleton, Maureen (1925–).
American character actress.
Lonelyhearts (AAN) 59. The Fugitive Kind 60. A View from the Bridge 62. Bye Bye Birdie 63. Airport (AAN) 69. Plaza Suite 70. Tell Me Where It Hurts 74. *Queen of the Stardust Ballroom* 75. The Gathering (TV) 77. Interiors (AAN) 78. Lost and Found 80. Reds (AA, BFA) 81. Johnny Dangerously 84. Cocoon 85. The Cosmic Eye 85. The Money Pit 85. Heartburn 86. Sweet Lorraine 87. Made in Heaven 87. Cocoon: The Return 88. Passed Away 92. Trading Mom 94, etc.

Stapleton, Oliver.
British cinematographer.
Restless Natives 85. My Beautiful Laundrette 86. Absolute Beginners 86. Sammy and Rosie Get Laid 87. Prick Up Your Ears 87. Chuck Berry: Hail! Hail! Rock 'n' Roll 87. Danny, the Champion of the World (TV) 89. Earth Girls Are Easy 89. Cookie 89. She-Devil 89. The Grifters 90. Let Him Have It 91. Hero (GB: Accidental Hero) 93, etc.

Stapley, Richard:
see Wyler, Richard.

star
is a word coined by some forgotten publicist in the early years of the century who presumably touted his leading actors as twinkling heavenly lights. It came in the 30s to mean any actor who was billed above the title; but nowadays real stars are hard to find, and the word is generally applied only to those thought likely actually to draw patrons to the box office.

¶ Stars may shine so brightly that they dazzle, but the glory of the movie variety is transient.
Marie Dressler put it succinctly:
You're only as good as your last picture.
Myron Selznick expressed the same thought:
Stars should get as much money as they can, while they can. They don't last long.
On the other hand Bette Davis, taking it easy in the 70s, was able to rely on her past:
My price for putting my name on that marquee is two hundred thousand dollars and ten per cent of the gross and I won't even talk to anybody for less because when they see me on a screen they're seeing thirty-seven years of sweat.
It didn't work quite as well for Stewart Granger:
I haven't aged into a character actor. I'm still an old leading man.
And Shirley Temple was disillusioned early:
I stopped believing in Santa Claus when I was six. Mother took me to see him in a department store and he asked for my autograph.
Paul Mayersberg thought that:
The star is Hollywood's gift to the twentieth century. Great actors are not the same as stars. A star must depend on some system of reproduction since to become a star you must be available to a large number of people.
Jerry Wald knew that the real trick was to find smart executives:
There's no shortage of talent. There's only a shortage of talent that can recognize talent.
Robert Redford was suspicious:
They throw that word 'star' at you loosely, and they take it away equally loosely. You take the responsibility for their crappy movie, that's what that means.
An anonymous wit classically detailed the five stages in a star's life, as seen by a casting director:
1 Who is Hugh O'Brian?
2 Get me Hugh O'Brian.
3 Get me a Hugh O'Brian type.
4 Get me a young Hugh O'Brian.
5 Who is Hugh O'Brian?
While you're at the top, it can be pleasant. Robert Stack says:
If you're a star you go through the front door carrying the roses, instead of through the back door carrying the garbage.
Gloria Swanson:
I have decided that while I am a star I will be every inch and every moment the star. Everyone from the studio gateman to the highest executive will know it.
Dustin Hoffman:
One thing about being successful is that I stopped being afraid of dying. Once you're a star you're dead already. You're embalmed.
Billie Burke:
By the time you get your name up in lights you have worked so hard and so long, and seen so many names go up and down, that all you can think of is: 'How can I keep it here?'
George Sanders was equally cynical:
The important thing for a star is to have an interesting face. He doesn't have to move it very much. Editing and camerawork can always produce the desired illusion that a performance is being given.
Ethel Barrymore took a different view:
To be a success an actress must have the face of Venus, the brain of Minerva, the grace of Terpsichore, the memory of Macaulay, the figure of Juno and the hide of a rhinoceros.
Katharine Hepburn put it more simply:
Show me an actress who isn't a personality and I'll show you a woman who isn't a star.
Jean Arthur found the going tough:

It's a strenuous job every day of your life to live up to the way you look on the screen.

The temptation to try remains great. Director Michael Winner remarked recently:

Hitchcock said actors are cattle, but show me a cow who can earn one million dollars per film.

But as Harry Cohn said:

After a while the stars believe their own publicity. I've never met a grateful performer in the film business.

Likewise Sam Spiegel:

You make a star, you sometimes make a monster.

So in the 50s the top stars gained control over their own careers, setting up their own independent companies. Jack Warner did not like the result:

In the old days you called the actor and made the deal with him. Now, they bring an army.

At the same time, as Vincent Price noted:

One of the deaths of Hollywood is that they tried to make everyone look normal. Some of the actresses who are around today look and sound like my niece in Scarsdale. I love my niece in Scarsdale, but I wouldn't pay to see her act.

People began to realize that they had been deceived by the apparent effortlessness of the old stars, who had lasted so long and given such good service. When Ronald Colman played a bit part in *Around the World in Eighty Days*, he was asked:

Did you really get a Cadillac for one day's work? – No, he replied – for the work of a lifetime.

In the end, as Sam Goldwyn knew from experience of changing fashions, it is not the actors or the moguls who decide who is a star:

Producers don't make stars. God makes stars, and the public recognizes His handiwork.

And Ellen Terry had the simplest definition of star quality:

That little something extra.

Or as Humphrey Bogart said when asked why he was worth two hundred thousand dollars a picture:

Because I can get it.

Or as Barbra Streisand said:

The real, real reason I like to be in movies is because it's an easy place to have my hems done. There's always a seamstress on the set. And if you break a chair, they can fix it – they have people who can do anything. Chair people, hem people.

Or as Louis Armstrong said:

A lotta cats copy the Mona Lisa, but people still line up to see the original.

Or as David Hemmings said:

I quite like being mobbed. After all it is extremely nice to be recognized. That's what acting is all about – being recognized.

Let Humphrey Bogart have the last word:

You're not a star till they can spell your name in Karachi.

A Star Is Born.

Dorothy Parker, Alan Campbell, and Robert Carson's screenplay for the 1937 film has become a Hollywood legend and in some cases a reality: the marriage of two stars goes on the rocks because one of them is on the way up and the other on the way down. It was first tailored for Janet Gaynor and Fredric March and directed by William Wellman. In 1954 George Cukor directed Judy Garland and James Mason in the star roles. In 1976 it was revamped for Barbra Streisand and Kris Kristofferson. The theme can be traced back to a 1930 film, *What Price Hollywood?*, from a story by Adela Rogers St Johns.

Star Wars.

George Lucas's immensely popular science fiction romp of 1977 was followed by two sequels: The *Empire Strikes Back* 80 and *The Return of the Jedi* 83. At the time Lucas talked of them as part of a sequence of nine films, although it was not until 1994 that plans were announced for a further film set in an earlier time.

Stark, Graham (1922–).

British comedy actor of films and TV, mostly in cameo roles.

The Millionairess 61. Watch It, Sailor 62. A Shot in the Dark 64. Becket 64. Alfie 66. Finders Keepers 66. Salt and Pepper 68. Doctor in Trouble 70. Return of the Pink Panther 75. The Prince and the Pauper 77. Revenge of the Pink Panther 78. Hawk the Slayer 80. Trail of the Pink Panther 82. Blind Date 87. Son of the Pink Panther 93, etc.

Stark, Ray (c. 1909–).

American producer.

The World of Suzie Wong 60. Oh Dad, Poor Dad 66. This Property is Condemned 66. Funny Girl (AAN) 67. Reflections in a Golden Eye 68. The Way We Were 73. Funny Lady 75. California Suite 78. The Goodbye Girl 78. Chapter Two 79. The Electric Horseman 79. Seems Like Old Times 80. Annie 82. The Slugger's Wife 85. Brighton Beach Memoirs 86. Biloxi Blues 88. Steel Magnolias 89. Lost in Yonkers 93, etc.

Starke, Pauline (1901–1977).

American silent screen actress.

Intolerance 16. Salvation Nell 19. A Connecticut Yankee 21. Shanghai 24. Twenty Cents a Dance 26, etc.

Starr, Belle (1848–1889).

American female outlaw of the wild west period. On screen she has been glamorized by Gene Tierney in the film of that name, by Jane Russell in *Montana Belle* and by Isabel Jewell in *Badman's Territory*. Elizabeth Montgomery had an odd view of her in a 1980 TV movie.

Starr, Irving (1906–1982).

American producer, former agent.

The Crimson Trail 34. Music in My Heart 40. Swing Fever 42. Four Jills in a Jeep 44. Johnny Allegro 47. Slightly French 49, etc.

Starrett, Charles (1904–1986).

American cowboy star of innumerable second features in the 30s and 40s. Inactive after 1952.

The Quarterback (debut) (playing himself, a professional footballer) 26. Fast and Loose 30. Sky Bride 32. Green Eyes 34. So Red the Rose 35. Mysterious Avenger 36. Two Gun Law 37. The Colorado Trail 38. Spoilers of the Range 39. Blazing Six Shooters 40. Thunder Over the Plains 41. Pardon My Gun 42. Fighting Buckaroo 43. Sundown Valley 44. Sagebrush Heroes 45. Gunning for Vengeance 46. Riders of the Lone Star 47. Last Days of Boot Hill 48. The Blazing Trail 49. Texas Dynamo 50. The Kid from Amarillo 51. Rough Tough West 52, many others.

Starrett, Jack (1936–1989).

American director, mainly of low-budget action pieces.

Run Angel Run 69. Cry Blood Apache 70. The Strange Vengeance of Rosalie 72. Slaughter 72. Nowhere to Hide (TV) 73. Cleopatra Jones 73. Race with the Devil 75. A Small Town in Texas 76. Final Chapter Walking Tall 77. Big Bob Johnson and His Fantastic Speed Circus (TV) 78. Mr Horn (TV) 79. First Blood (a only) 82.

¶ I jump in with both feet. I figure if you ain't got balls you're in the wrong business. – J.S., 1975

State Fair.

Philip Strong's novel of small-town virtues, champion hogs, and bucolic romance has been filmed three times: in 1933, directed by Henry King, with Will Rogers and Janet Gaynor; in 1945, as a musical, directed by Walter Lang, with Jeanne Crain, Dana Andrews, Dick Haymes, Vivian Blane, and songs by Oscar Hammerstein II; and in 1962, directed by José Ferrer, with Pat Boone, Bobby Darin, Pamela Tiffin, and Ann-Margret, and new songs added by Richard Rodgers.

statesmen

who have frequently been depicted in films include Disraeli (most often), Gladstone, Melbourne, Ramsay Macdonald (disguised in *Fame is the Spur*), Woodrow Wilson, Churchill, Roosevelt (notably in *Sunrise at Campobello*), Lincoln (qv) and Parnell. Fleeting glimpses of famous leaders were also given in *Mission to Moscow* and some Russian wartime films.

statues

have come to life in *Night Life of the Gods, Animal Crackers, Turnabout* and *One Touch of Venus*. They were central to the plots of *The Light that Failed, Latin Quarter, Song of Songs* and *Mad Love*, while *A Taste of Honey* involved them in an attractive title sequence. In horror films, they came murderously alive in *Night of the Eagle, The Norliss Tapes* (TV) and that grand-daddy of them all, *The Golem*.

Staudte, Wolfgang (1906–1984).

German director of socially conscious films.

The Murderers Are amongst Us (& w) 46. Der Untertan (& w) 51. Rose Bernd 56. Roses for the Prosecutor 59. Die Dreigroschenoper 63. Herrenpartie 64. Heimlichkeiten 68. Die Herren mit die Weissen Weste 70. Wolf of the Seven Seas 73. Zwischengleis (TV) 78, etc.

Staunton, Imelda (1958–).

English actress, from the stage. Trained at RADA, she has worked for the Royal Shakespeare Company and the National Theatre.

Peter's Friends 92. Much Ado about Nothing 93. Terminus (TV) 94. Deadly Advice 94.

TV series: Up the Garden Path 90–93. If You See God, Tell Him 93.

Steadman, Alison (1946–).

English actress, mainly on the stage and television. Married director Mike Leigh.

Nuts in May (TV) 76. Abigail's Party (TV) 77. Ptang, Bang, Kipperbang 82. Number One 84. Champions 84. A Private Function 84. The Singing Detective (TV) 86. Clockwise 86. Stormy Monday 87. The Adventures of Baron Munchausen 88. Shirley Valentine 89. Wilt (US: The Misadventures of Mr Wilt) 90. Life Is Sweet 91. Blame It on the Bellboy 92, etc.

TV series: The Wackers 75. Gone to Seed 92.

Steckler, Ray Dennis (1939–).

American director of low-budget exploitation movies that are most notable for their titles. He also acts in them under the pseudonym of Cash Flagg.

Drivers in Hell (aka Wild Ones on Wheels) 61. Wild Guitar 62. The Incredibly Strange Creatures Who Stopped Living and Became Mixed-up Zombies 62. Rat Pfink a-Boo-Boo 62. Scream of the Butterfly 65. Lemon Grove Kids Meet the

Monsters 66. Body Fever 72. The Hollywood Strangler Meets the Skid Row Slasher 79, etc.

Steege, Johanna Ter.
Dutch leading actress.
The Vanishing 77. Vincent and Theo 90. Meeting Venus 91. La Naissance de l'Amour (Fr.) 93, etc.

Steel, Anthony (1920–).
Athletic British leading man with slight stage experience.
Saraband for Dead Lovers (film debut) 48. Marry Me 49. The Wooden Horse 50. Laughter in Paradise 51. The Malta Story 52. Albert RN 53. The Sea Shall Not Have Them 55. Storm over the Nile 56. The Black Tent 56. Checkpoint 56. A Question of Adultery 57. Harry Black 58. Honeymoon 60. The Switch 63. Hell Is Empty 67. Anzio 68. Massacre in Rome 74. The World Is Full of Married Men 79. The Mirror Crack'd 80. The Monster Club 81, etc.

Steel, Dawn (1947–) (Dawn Spielberg).
American production executive. She worked first for Paramount and became president of Columbia Pictures in 1987, leaving in 1990 when Sony took over the company. She now runs an independent production company, Atlas Entertainment, with her husband Charles Roven and Robert Cavallo.
Autobiography: 1992, They Can Kill You . . . But They Can't Eat You.
Flashdance 83. Footloose 84. Top Gun 86. Fatal Attraction 87. The Untouchables 87. Casualties of War 90. Cool Runnings 93, etc.

¶ I was trained to be loud, passionate, direct. I didn't realise for the longest time I was intimidating. – D.S.

Steele, Barbara (1938–).
British leading lady who has appeared mainly in Italian horror films.
Bachelor of Hearts 58. Sapphire 59. Black Sunday (The Devil's Mask) 60. The Pit and the Pendulum (US) 61. The Terror of Dr Hitchcock 62. Eight and a Half 63. The Spectre 64. Sister of Satan (The Revenge of the Blood Beast) 65. Nightmare Castle 65. Renegade Girls 74. Pretty Baby 78. Silent Scream 80. Winds of War (TV) 83, etc.
TV series: Dark Shadows 91.

Steele, Bob (1907–1988) (Robert Bradbury).
American character actor, on stage from the age of two and in more than 400 second-feature westerns, appearing as Billy the Kid in a series in the early 40s. One of the 'Three Mesquiteers', he was the son of Robert N. Bradbury, who directed many westerns for Monogram and Republic Pictures and starred him and his twin brother William in his first film, The Adventures of Bob and Bill 14. Also played Curley in Of Mice and Men 39, and the villainous Canino in The Big Sleep 46.
Davy Crockett at the Fall of the Alamo 26. The Bandit's Son 27. Texas Cowboy 30. South of Santa Fe 32. Kid Courageous 35. Riders of the Sage 39. The Carson City Kid 40. Billy the Kid in Texas 40. Westward Ho! 42. Wildfire 45. South of St Louis 49. The Savage Horde 50. Island in the Sky 53. Drums across the River 54. Band of Angels 57. Giant from the Unknown 58. The Bonnie Parker Story 58. Atomic Submarine 59. Pork Chop Hill 59. Rio Bravo 59. McClintock! 63. Taggart 64. Requiem for a Gunfighter 65. The Great Bank Robbery 69. Rio Lobo 70. The Skin Game 71. Charley Varrick 73, many others.
TV series: F Troop 65–66.

Steele, Tommy (1936–) (Tommy Hicks).
Energetic British cockney performer and pop singer.
Kill Me Tomorrow 55. The Tommy Steele Story 57. The Duke Wore Jeans 59. Light Up The Sky 59. Tommy the Toreador 60. It's All Happening 62. The Happiest Millionaire (US) 67. Half a Sixpence 67. Finian's Rainbow (US) 68. Where's Jack? 69.

Steenburgen, Mary (1953–).
American leading actress.
Going South 78. Time after Time 79. Rabbit Test 79. Melvin and Howard (AA) 80. Ragtime 81. A Midsummer Night's Sex Comedy 82. Cross Creek 83. Romantic Comedy 83. One Magic Christmas 85. Dead of Center 87. The Whales of August 87. End of the Line 88. Miss Firecracker 89. Parenthood 89. Back to the Future Part III 90. The Butcher's Wife 91. Gilbert Grape 93. Philadelphia 93. Clifford 94. It Runs in the Family 94. Pontiac Moon 94, etc.

Steiger, Rod (1925–).
Burly American leading character actor who became known on stage and TV after training at New York's Theatre Workshop.
■ Teresa 51. On the Waterfront (AAN) 54. The Big Knife 55. Oklahoma 55. The Court Martial of Billy Mitchell 55. The Unholy Wife 56. Jubal 56. The Harder They Fall 56. Back from Eternity 57. Run of the Arrow 57. Across the Bridge (GB) 57. Al Capone 58. Cry Terror 58. Seven Thieves 59. The Mark 61. 13 West Street 61. On Friday at Eleven 61. The Longest Day 62. Convicts Four 62. Time of Indifference 63. Hands Over the City (It.) 63. The Pawnbroker (BFA, AAN) 64. A Man Called John 64. The Loved One 65. Doctor Zhivago 65. The Girl and the General 66. In the Heat of the Night (AA, BFA) 67. No Way to Treat a Lady 68. The Sergeant 68. The Illustrated Man 69. Three into Two Won't Go 69. Waterloo (as Napoleon) 71. A Fistful of Dynamite 71. The Heroes (It.) 72. Happy Birthday Wanda June 72. Lolly Madonna XXX 72. Lucky Luciano 73. Hennessy 74. Innocents With Dirty Hands 75. W.C. Fields and Me 76. Jesus of Nazareth (TV) 77. Jimbuck 77. The Last Four Days (as Mussolini) 77. Wolf Lake 78. Love and Bullets 78. F.I.S.T. 78. Breakthrough 79. The Amityville Horror 79. Lucky Star 80. Klondike Fever 80. Lion of the Desert (as Mussolini) 81. Cattle Annie and Little Britches 81. The Chosen 82. The Magic Mountain 82. The Glory Boys (TV) 84. Hollywood Wives (TV) 84. The Naked Face 84. The Kindred 86. Feel the Heat 87. American Gothic 87. The January Man 89. Tennessee Waltz 89. The Ballad of the Sad Café 90. Men of Respect 91. Guilty as Charged 92. That Summer of White Roses 92. The Neighbor 93. Seven Sundays (Tous les Jours Dimanche) (Fr.) 94. The Specialist 94.

Stein, Herman (1915–).
American composer, prolific co-writer of scores at Universal in the 50s.
Back at the Front 52. Has Anybody Seen My Gal? 52. Meet Me at the Fair 52. Abbott & Costello Meet Dr Jekyll and Mr Hyde 53. Girls in the Night 53. Gunsmoke 53. The Black Shield of Falworth 54. The Creature from the Black Lagoon 54. Destry 54. Drums across the River 54. The Glenn Miller Story 54. So This Is Paris 54. The Far Country 55. This Island Earth 55. I've Lived Before 56. The Incredible Shrinking Man 57. Mister Cory 57. Slim Carter 57. Last of the Fast Guns 58. No Name on the Bullet 59. The Intruder 61, many others.

Stein, Paul (1891–1952).
Austrian director who made films in America and Britain.
Ich Liebe Dich 23. My Official Wife (US) 26. Forbidden Woman (US) 27. Sin Takes a Holiday (US) 30. One Romantic Night 30. Born to Love 31. A Woman Commands (US) 31. Lily Christine (GB) 32. The Outsider (GB) 38. The Saint Meets the Tiger (GB) 41. Talk about Jacqueline (GB) 42. Kiss the Bride Goodbye (GB) 43. Twilight Hour (GB) 44. The Lisbon Story (GB) 46. Counterblast (GB) 48. The Twenty Questions Murder Mystery (GB) 49, etc.

Steinbeck, John (1902–1968).
American novelist.
Of Mice and Men 39, 81 (TV) and 92. The Grapes of Wrath 40. Tortilla Flat 42. The Moon Is Down 43. Lifeboat (AAN) 44. A Medal for Benny (AAN) 45. The Red Pony 49. Viva Zapata! (AAN) 52. East of Eden 54. The Wayward Bus 57, etc.

Steinberg, Michael (1959–).
American director and screenwriter.
The Waterdance (co-d) 92. Bodies, Rest and Motion 93.

Steinberg, Norman.
American screenwriter.
Blazing Saddles 73. Yes, Giorgio 82. My Favorite Year 82. Johnny Dangerously 84. Funny about Love 90, etc.

Steiner, Fred (1923–).
American composer who also scores TV movies.
Run for the Sun 56. The Man from Del Rio 56. Time Limit 57. Robinson Crusoe on Mars 64. The St Valentine's Day Massacre 67. The Sea Gypsies 78. The Color Purple (AAN) 85, etc.

Steiner, Max (1888–1971).
Austrian composer, in America from 1924; became one of Hollywood's most reliable and prolific writers of film music.
Cimarron 31. A Bill of Divorcement 32. King Kong 33. The Lost Patrol 34. The Informer (AA) 35. She 35. The Charge of the Light Brigade 36. A Star Is Born 37. Gone with the Wind 39. The Letter 40. The Great Lie 41. Now Voyager (AA) 42. Casablanca 42. Since You Went Away (AA) 44. Rhapsody in Blue 45. The Big Sleep 46. The Treasure of the Sierra Madre 47. Johnny Belinda 48. The Fountainhead 49. The Glass Menagerie 50. Room for One More 52. The Charge at Feather River 53. The Caine Mutiny 54. Battle Cry 55. Come Next Spring 56. Band of Angels 57. The FBI Story 59. The Dark at the Top of the Stairs 60. Parrish 61. Youngblood Hawke 64, many others.

Steinkamp, Frederic.
American editor.
Two Loves 61. Sunday in New York 64. Grand Prix (co-ed) (AA) 66. Charly 68. A New Leaf 71. Haunts of the Very Rich (TV) 72. Freebie and the Bean 74. Three Days of the Condor 75. Bobby Deerfield 77. Tootsie (AAN) 82. Against All Odds 84. White Nights 85. Out of Africa (AAN) 85. Adventures in Babysitting 87. Burglar 87. Scrooged 87. Havana 90. The Firm 93, etc.

Stella Dallas.
The weepy novel of frustrated mother love, written by Olive Higgins Prouty, was filmed by Henry King in 1925, with Belle Bennett and Ronald Colman; by King Vidor in 1937, with Barbara Stanwyck and John Boles; and by John Erman in 1990, as Stella, with Bette Midler and John Goodman.

Sten, Anna (1908–1993) (Anjuschka Stenski Sujakevitch).
Russian leading actress imported to Hollywood by Goldwyn in 1933 in the hope of rivalling Garbo; but somehow she didn't click. The first of her two husbands was director Feder Ozep.

SELECTED EUROPEAN FILMS: The Yellow Ticket 27. Storm Over Asia 28. The White Eagle 28. The Murder of Dimitri Karamazov 31. Bombs in Monte Carlo 31.

■ ENGLISH-SPEAKING FILMS: *Nana* 34. We Live Again 34. The Wedding Night 35. A Woman Alone 36. Exile Express 39. The Man I Married 40. So Ends Our Night 41. Chetniks 43. They Came To Blow Up America 43. Three Russian Girls 43. Let's Live a Little 48. Soldier of Fortune 55. Heaven Knows Mr Allison 57. The Nun and the Sergeant 62.

Stepanek, Karel (1899–1980).
Czech character actor, in Britain from 1940. Usually played Nazis or other villains.
They Met in the Dark 43. *The Captive Heart* 46. The Fallen Idol 48. State Secret 50. Cockleshell Heroes 55. *Sink the Bismarck* 60. Operation Crossbow 65. Before Winter Comes 69, many others.

Stephen, Susan (1931–).
British leading lady of the 50s. She was formerly married to director Nicolas Roeg.
His Excellency 51. The Red Beret 53. For Better For Worse 54. Golden Ivory 54. The Barretts of Wimpole Street 57. Carry On Nurse 59. Return of a Stranger 61. The Court Martial of Major Keller 63, etc.

Stephens, Ann (1931–).
British juvenile actress of the 40s.
In Which We Serve 42. Dear Octopus 43. The Upturned Glass 47. The Franchise Affair 51. Intent to Kill 58, many others.

Stephens, Martin (1949–).
British juvenile player.
The Hellfire Club 61. *Village of the Damned* 62. *The Innocents* 62. Battle of the Villa Fiorita 65. The Witches 66, etc.

Stephens, Sir Robert (1931–).
British stage actor, in occasional films. He was formerly married to actress Maggie Smith.
Circle of Deception 60. Pirates of Tortuga (US) 61. A Taste of Honey 61. The Inspector 62. Cleopatra 62. The Small World of Sammy Lee 63. Morgan 66. Romeo and Juliet 68. The Prime of Miss Jean Brodie 69. *The Private Life of Sherlock Holmes* 69. The Asphyx 72. Travels with My Aunt 73. Luther 73. QB VII (TV) 73. Holocaust (TV) 78. The Shout 78. Fortunes of War (TV) 87. War and Remembrance (TV) 87. High Season 87. Testimony 87. Henry V 89. Wings of Fame 90. The Pope Must Die (US: The Pope Must Diet) 91. Afraid of the Dark 91. Adam Bede (TV) 91. Searching for Bobby Fischer (GB: Innocent Moves) 93. Century 93. The Secret Rapture 93, etc.

Stephenson, Henry (1871–1956) (H. S. Garroway).
British stage actor who came to Hollywood films in his 60s and remained to play scores of kindly old men.
■ The Spreading Dawn 17. The Black Panther's Cub 21. Men and Women 25. Wild Wild Susan 25. *Cynara* 32. Red Headed Woman 32. Guilty as Hell 32. A Bill of Divorcement 32. The Animal Kingdom 32. Little Women 33. Queen Christina 33. Tomorrow at Seven 33. Double Harness 33. My Lips Betray 33. If I Were Free 33. Blind Adventure 33. Man of Two Worlds 34. The Richest Girl in the World 34. Thirty Day Princess 34. Stingaree 34. The Mystery of Mr X 34. What Every Woman Knows 34. One More River 34. Outcast Lady 34. She Loves Me Not 34. All Men Are Enemies 34. Mutiny on the Bounty 35. Vanessa, Her Love Story 35. Reckless 35. The Flame Within 35. O'Shaughnessy's Boy 35. The Night Is Young 35. Rendezvous 35. The Perfect Gentleman 35. Captain Blood 35. Beloved Enemy 36. Half Angel 36. Hearts Divided 36. Give Me Your Heart 36. Walking on Air 36. Little Lord Fauntleroy 36. *The Charge of the Light Brigade* 36. When You're in Love 37. The Prince and the Pauper 37. The Emperor's Candlesticks 37. Conquest 37. Wise Girl 37. *The Young in Heart* 38. The Baroness and the Butler 38. Suez 38. Marie Antoinette 38. Dramatic School 38. Tarzan Finds a Son 39. The Private Lives of Elizabeth and Essex 39. The Adventures of Sherlock Holmes 39. It's a Date 40. Little Old New York 40. Spring Parade 40. Down Argentine Way 41. The Man Who Lost Himself 41. The Lady from Louisiana 41. This Above All 42. Rings on Her Fingers 42. Half Way to Shanghai 42. Mr Lucky 43. *Mantrap* 43. The Hour Before the Dawn 44. Secrets of Scotland Yard 44. The Reckless Age 44. Two Girls and a Sailor 44. Tarzan and the Amazons 45. The Green Years 46. Her Sister's Secret 46. The Locket 46. Heartbeat 46. Night and Day 46. Of Human Bondage 46. The Return of Monte Cristo 46. Dark Delusion 47. The Homestretch 47. Time Out of Mind 47. Ivy 47. Song of Love 47. Julia Misbehaves 48. Enchantment 48. *Oliver Twist* (as Mr Brownlow) 48. Challenge to Lassie 48.

Stephenson, James (1888–1941).
Suave British-born stage actor, in Hollywood from 1938.
When Were You Born? (debut) 38. Boy Meets Girl 38. Confessions of a Nazi Spy 38. Beau Geste 39. Calling Philo Vance 40. The Sea Hawk 40. *The Letter* (AAN) 40. Shining Victory 41. International Squadron 41, etc.

Stephenson, Pamela (1951–).
New Zealand leading lady who has done a variety of light work on British stage and TV (especially *Not the Nine o'Clock News*).
History of the World Part One 81. Scandalous 83. Superman III 83. Bloodbath at the House of Death 83. Finders Keepers 84. Les Patterson Saves the World 87, etc.

Steppat, Ilse (1917–1969).
German character actress.
Marriage in the Shadow 47. The Bridge 51. The Confessions of Felix Krull 62. On Her Majesty's Secret Service 69, etc.

stereophony:
hearing sound from more than one source at the same time, a gimmick used to 'put you in the picture' by surrounding you with loudspeakers when CinemaScope was first introduced.

stereoscopy:
viewing in three dimensions, usually accomplished by watching through polaroid glasses, two films projected one on top of the other after being photographed from slightly different angles corresponding to one's two eyes.

Sterling, Ford (1883–1939) (George F. Stitch).
American comic actor, a leading Keystone Kop and slapstick heavy.
Drums of the Desert 26. Gentlemen Prefer Blondes 28. Kismet 30. Alice in Wonderland 33. The Black Sheep 35, etc.

Sterling, Jan (1923–) (Jane Sterling Adriance).
Blonde American leading lady with slight stage experience.
Johnny Belinda 48. Rhubarb 51. *Ace in the Hole* 51. Split Second 52. Pony Express 53. Alaska Seas 54. The High and the Mighty (AAN) 54. Women's Prison 55. The Female on the Beach 55. 1984 56. The Harder They Fall 56. Kathy O 58. Love in a Goldfish Bowl 61. Having Babies (TV) 76. Backstairs at the White House (TV) 79. First Monday in October 81, etc.

Famous line (*Ace in the Hole*): 'I don't go to church. Kneeling bags my nylons.'

Famous line (*Ace in the Hole*): 'I've met some hard-boiled eggs in my time, but you – you're twenty minutes!'

Sterling, Robert (1917–) (William John Hart).
American leading man of the 40s, mainly in second features.
Only Angels Have Wings 39. I'll Wait for You 41. Somewhere I'll Find You 42. The Secret Heart 46. Bunco Squad 48. Roughshod 50. Thunder in the Dust 51. Column South 53. Return to Peyton Place 61. Voyage to the Bottom of the Sea 62, etc.
TV series: Topper 53–54. Love That Jill 58. Ichabod and Me 61.

Stern, Daniel (1957–).
American leading actor and director.
Breaking Away 79. Starting Over 79. Stardust Memories 80. One Trick Pony 80. Diner 82. Blue Thunder 83. C.H.U.D. 84. Frankenweenie 84. Key Exchange 85. Hannah and Her Sisters 86. D.O.A. 88. The Milagro Beanfield War 88. Friends, Lovers and Lunatics 89. Leviathan 89. Little Monsters 89. My Blue Heaven 90. Home Alone 90. City Slickers 91. Home Alone 2: Lost in New York 92. Rookie of the Year (& d) 93. City Slickers II: The Legend of Curly's Gold 94, etc.
TV series: Hometown 85. The Wonder Years (voice) 88– .

Sternhagen, Frances (1930–).
American actress, from stage and television.
Up the Down Staircase 67. The Tiger Makes Out 67. The Hospital 71. Fedora 78. Starting Over 79. Outland 81. Prototype (TV) 83. Romantic Comedy 83. Bright Lights, Big City 88. Communion 89. See You in the Morning 89. Sibling Rivalry 90. Misery 90. Doc Hollywood 91. Raising Cain 92, etc.
TV series: Spencer 84–85. Stephen King's Golden Years 91.

Stevens, Andrew (1955–).
American leading man.
Las Vegas Lady 76. Vigilante Force 76. The Bastard (TV) 78. The Boys in Company C 78. The Fury 78. Women at West Point 79. Topper (TV) 80. Miracle on Ice (TV) 81. The Seduction 82. Ten to Midnight 83. Hollywood Wives (TV) 85. Once an Eagle (TV) 86. The Terror Within 88. The Terror Within II (& d) 91, etc.
TV series: Code Red 81.

Stevens, Connie (1938–) (Concetta Ingolia).
American leading lady with mixed Italian, English, Irish and Mohican blood. She was formerly married to singer Eddie Fisher.
Eighteen and Anxious 57. Rockabye Baby 58. Parrish 61. Susan Slade 61. Two on a Guillotine 64. Never Too Late 65. Mr Jericho (TV) 70. The

Grissom Gang 71. The Sex Symbol (TV) 73. Scorchy 76. Back to the Beach 87. Tapeheads 89, etc.

TV series: Hawaiian Eye 59–62.

Stevens, Craig (1918–) (Gail Shekles).
American leading man, married to Alexis Smith.

Affectionately Yours 41. Since You Went Away 43. The Lady Takes a Sailor 47. The French Line 54. Abbott and Costello Meet Dr Jekyll and Mr Hyde 55. Gunn 66. The Limbo Line 68. The Snoop Sisters (TV) 72. Rich Man Poor Man (TV) 76. S.O.B. 81, etc.

TV series: Peter Gunn 58–60. Man of the World 62. Mr Broadway 64.

Stevens, George (1904–1975).
American director, in Hollywood from 1923. In the late 30s and early 40s he made smooth and lively entertainments, but his infrequent later productions tended towards elephantiasis.
■ The Cohens and Kellys in Trouble 33. Bachelor Bait 34. Kentucky Kernels 34. Laddie 34. The Nitwits 34. Alice Adams 34. Annie Oakley 35. Swing Time 36. A Damsel in Distress 37. Quality Street 37. Vivacious Lady 38. Gunga Din 39. Vigil in the Night 40. Penny Serenade 40. Woman of the Year 41. Talk of the Town 42. The More the Merrier (AAN) 43. I Remember Mama 47. A Place in the Sun (AA) 51. Something to Live For 52. Shane (AAN) 53. Giant (AA) 56. The Diary of Anne Frank (AAN) 59. The Greatest Story Ever Told 65. The Only Game in Town 69.

¶ He was a minor director with major virtues before A Place in the Sun, and a major director with minor virtues after. – Andrew Sarris, 1968

Stevens, George, Jnr (1932–).
American producer, son of George Stevens, who in 1977 became head of the American Film Institute.

Stevens, Inger (1935–1970) (Inger Stensland).
Pert and pretty Swedish leading lady, in America from childhood. Died of a drug overdose.

Man on Fire (film debut) 57. Cry Terror 58. The World, the Flesh and the Devil 58. The Buccaneer 59. The New Interns 64. A Guide for the Married Man 67. Firecreek 67. Madigan 68. Five Card Stud 68. Hang 'Em High 68. House of Cards 68. The Borgia Stick (TV) 68. A Dream of Kings 69. Run Simon Run (TV) 70, etc.

TV series: The Farmer's Daughter 63–65.

Stevens, K. T. (1919–) (Gloria Wood).
American leading lady of a few 40s films; daughter of director Sam Wood.

Kitty Foyle 40. The Great Man's Lady 41. Address Unknown 44. Vice Squad 53. Tumbleweed 53. Missile to the Moon 58, etc.

Stevens, Leith (1909–1970).
American musical arranger and composer.

The Wild One 52. Julie 56. The Five Pennies 59. A New Kind of Love 63, many others for Fox and Paramount, including TV series.

Stevens, Leslie (1924–).
American screenwriter.

The Left-Handed Gun 58. Private Property (& p, d) 59. The Marriage-Go-Round (from his play) 60. Hero's Island (& p, d) 62. Buck Rogers 79. Sheena (story) 84. Three Kinds of Heat (w, d) 87, etc.

TV series as creator-producer-director: Stony Burke. The Outer Limits. Battlestar Galactica.

Stevens, Mark (1916–) (aka Stephen Richards).
American leading man with varied early experience; usually in routine roles.

Objective Burma 45. From This Day Forward 45. The Dark Corner 46. I Wonder Who's Kissing Her Now 47. The Snake Pit 48. The Street with No Name 48. Sand 49. Mutiny 53. Cry Vengeance (also pd) 54. Timetable (also pd) 55. September Storm 60. Fate is the Hunter 64. Frozen Alive 66. Sunscorched 66.

TV series: Big Town 52–57.

Stevens, Onslow (1902–1977) (Onslow Ford Stevenson).
American stage actor occasionally seen in film character roles. Son of Houseley Stevenson. He was murdered.

Heroes of the West (debut) 32. Counsellor at Law 33. The Three Musketeers 36. Under Two Flags 36. When Tomorrow Comes 39. Mystery Sea Raider 40. House of Dracula 45. O.S.S. 46. Night Has a Thousand Eyes 48. The Creeper 48. State Penitentiary 50. Them 54. Tarawa Beachhead 58. All the Fine Young Cannibals 60. Geronimo's Revenge 63, etc.

Stevens, Rise (1913–).
American opera singer, seen in a few films.
■ The Chocolate Soldier 41. Going My Way 44. Carnegie Hall 47.

Stevens, Robert (c. 1925–1989).
American director, from TV.
■ The Big Caper 57. Never Love a Stranger 58. I Thank a Fool 62. In the Cool of the Day 63. Change of Mind 69.

Stevens, Ronnie (1925–).
British comic actor with stage and TV experience.

Made in Heaven 52. An Alligator Named Daisy 55. I Was Monty's Double 58. I'm All Right, Jack 59. Dentist in the Chair 60. San Ferry Ann 65. Give a Dog a Bone 66. Some Girls Do 68. Morons from Outer Space 85, etc.

Stevens, Stella (1936–) (Estelle Eggleston).
American leading lady.

Say One for Me (debut) 58. Li'l Abner 59. Too Late Blues 61. The Courtship of Eddie's Father 63. The Nutty Professor 63. Synanon 65. The Secret of My Success 65. The Silencers 66. How to Save a Marriage 67. The Mad Room 69. The Ballad of Cable Hogue 70. A Town Called Bastard 71. Stand Up and Be Counted 71. The Poseidon Adventure 72. Arnold 74. Cleopatra Jones and the Casino of Gold 74. Las Vegas Lady 74. Nickelodeon 76. The Night They Took Miss Beautiful (TV) 77. Cruise into Terror (TV) 78. The Manitou 78. The Terror Within II 91. Exiled 91. Mom 91. South Beach 92. The Night Caller 92. Molly & Gina 94, etc.

TV series: Ben Casey 65. Flamingo Road 80–81.

Stevens, Warren (1919–).
American general-purpose actor.

The Frogmen 51. The Barefoot Contessa 54. Forbidden Planet 56. Hot Spell 58. No Name on the Bullet 59. Forty Pounds of Trouble 62. An American Dream 66. Madigan 68, many others.

TV series: 77th Bengal Lancers 56–57. The Richard Boone Show 63–64. Bracken's World (voice) 69–70. Behind the Screen 81–82.

Stevenson, Edward (1906–1968).
American costume designer, in Hollywood from 1922. He was chief designer at RKO from 1936–49. From the mid-50s he designed Lucille Ball's costumes for her TV series I Love Lucy.

The Joy of Living 38. They Knew What They

Wanted 40. Citizen Kane 41. The Magnificent Ambersons 42. Journey into Fear 42, etc.

Stevenson, Houseley (1879–1953).
American character actor, latterly familiar as a gaunt, usually unshaven, old man.

Native Land 42. Somewhere in the Night 46. Dark Passage 47. Casbah 48. Moonrise 49. All the King's Men 49. The Sun Sets at Dawn 51. The Wild North 52, etc.

Stevenson, Juliet (1956–) (Juliet Stevens).
British leading actress, from classical theatre.

Drowning by Numbers 88. Ladder of Swords 88. Truly Madly Deeply 91. The Trial 93. The Secret Rapture 93, etc.

Stevenson, Robert (1905–1986).
British director, in Hollywood from 1939.
■ Happy Ever After 32. Falling for You 33. Tudor Rose 36. The Man Who Changed His Mind 36. Jack of all Trades 37. King Solomon's Mines 37. Non Stop New York 37. Owd Bob 38. The Ware Case 39. Young Man's Fancy 40. Tom Brown's Schooldays 40. Back Street 41. Joan of Paris 43. Forever and a Day (co-d) 43. Jane Eyre 43. Dishonored Lady 47. To the Ends of the Earth 48. The Woman on Pier 13 49. Walk Softly Stranger 50. My Forbidden Past 51. The Las Vegas Story 52. Johnny Tremain 57. Old Yeller 57. Darby O'Gill and the Little People 59. Kidnapped 60. The Absent-Minded Professor 61. In Search of the Castaways 62. Son of Flubber 63. The Misadventures of Merlin Jones 64. Mary Poppins (AAN) 64. The Monkey's Uncle 65. That Darn Cat 65. The Gnome-Mobile 67. Blackbeard's Ghost 67. The Love Bug 69. My Dog the Thief 70. Bedknobs and Broomsticks 71. Herbie Rides Again 73. The Island at the Top of the World 74. One of Our Dinosaurs Is Missing 75. The Shaggy D.A. 77.

Stevenson, Robert Louis (1850–1894).
British novelist and short-story writer. Works filmed include Dr Jekyll and Mr Hyde (many versions), Treasure Island (many versions), The Body Snatcher, The Suicide Club, Kidnapped, The Master of Ballantrae, Ebb Tide, The Wrong Box.

Steward, Ernest (–1990).
British cinematographer.

Carry On Camping 71. Callan 74. Hennessy 75, many others.

Stewart, Alexandra (1939–).
Canadian leading lady who has filmed mainly in Europe.

Exodus 60. Le Feu Follet 63. Dragées au Poivre 65. Maroc 7 67. The Bride Wore Black 67. The Man Who Had Power Over Women 70. Day for Night 73. Marseilles Contract 74. In Praise of Older Women 78. Phobia 80. Chanel Solitaire 81. Your Ticket Is No Longer Valid 84. Kemek 88, etc.

Stewart, Anita (1895–1961) (Anna May Stewart).
American silent screen leading lady.

A Million Bid 13. The Goddess 15. Mary Regan 19. Her Kingdom of Dreams 20. Never the Twain Shall Meet 25. Sisters of Eve 28, many others.

Stewart, Athole (1879–1940).
British stage character actor.

The Speckled Band 31. The Clairvoyant 34. Dusty Ermine 37. The Spy in Black 39. Tilly of Bloomsbury 40, etc.

Stewart, Donald.
American screenwriter.

Jackson County Jail 76. Deathsport 78. Missing

(AA) 82. The Hunt for Red October 90. Patriot Games (co-w) 93. Clear and Present Danger (co-w) 94, etc.

Stewart, Donald Ogden (1894–1980).
American playwright and screenwriter.
Autobiography: 1974, *By a Stroke of Luck*.
■ Brown of Harvard 26. Laughter 30. Finn and Hattie (oa) 30. Rebound (oa) 31. Tarnished Lady (& oa) 31. Smilin' Through 32. The White Sister 33. Another Language 33. Dinner at Eight 33. The Barretts of Wimpole Street 34. No More Ladies 35. *The Prisoner of Zenda* 37. Holiday 38. Marie Antoinette 38. Love Affair 39. The Night of Nights 39. Kitty Foyle 40. *The Philadelphia Story* (AA) 40. That Uncertain Feeling 41. A Woman's Face 41. Smilin' Through 41. Tales of Manhattan 42. Without Love 45. Life with Father 47. Cass Timberlane 47. Edward My Son 49. Escapade 55. Moment of Danger 60.
NB: Some of the above were in collaboration with other writers.

Stewart, Elaine (1929–) (Elsy Steinberg).
American leading lady of a few 50s films; former usherette.
Sailor Beware 51. The Bad and the Beautiful 52. Young Bess 53. Brigadoon 54. The Tattered Dress 56. The Adventures of Hajji Baba 57. The Rise and Fall of Legs Diamond 60. The Most Dangerous Man Alive 61. The Seven Revenges 63, etc.

Stewart, Hugh (1910–).
British producer, former editor.
Trottie True 49. The Long Memory 52. Man of the Moment 55 (and all subsequent Norman Wisdom comedies). The Intelligence Men 65, etc.

Stewart, James (1908–).
American leading actor of inimitable slow drawl and gangly walk; portrayed slow-speaking, honest heroes for thirty-five years.
Biographies: 1984, *James Stewart* by Allen Eyles. 1994, *James Stewart: Leading Man* by Jonathan Coe.
■ Murder Man 35. Rose Marie 36. Next Time We Love 36. Wife versus Secretary 36. Small Town Girl 36. Speed 36. The Gorgeous Hussy 36. Born to Dance 36. After the Thin Man 36. *Seventh Heaven* 37. The Last Gangster 37. Navy Blue and Gold 37. Of Human Hearts 38. Vivacious Lady 38. Shopworn Angel 38. *You Can't Take It with You* 38. Made for Each Other 38. Ice Follies of 1939. It's a Wonderful World 39. *Mr Smith Goes to Washington* (AAN) 39. *Destry Rides Again* 39. *The Shop around the Corner* 40. The Mortal Storm 40. No Time for Comedy 40. *The Philadelphia Story* (AA) 40. Come Live with Me 40. Pot O' Gold 41. Ziegfeld Girl 41; war service; *It's a Wonderful Life* (AAN) 46. Magic Town 46. *Call Northside 777* 47. On Our Merry Way 48. Rope 48. You Gotta Stay Happy 48. The Stratton Story 49. Malaya 49. *Winchester 73* 50. Broken Arrow 50. The Jackpot 50. *Harvey* (AAN) 50. No Highway (GB) 51. The Greatest Show on Earth 51. Bend of the River 52. Carbine Williams 52. The Naked Spur 53. Thunder Bay 53. *The Glenn Miller Story* 53. *Rear Window* 54. The Far Country 54. Strategic Air Command 55. *The Man from Laramie* 55. The Man Who Knew Too Much 56. The Spirit of St Louis 57. Night Passage 57. Vertigo 58. Bell, Book and Candle 58. *Anatomy of a Murder* (AAN) 59. The FBI Story 59. The Mountain Road 60. Two Rode Together 61. The Man Who Shot Liberty Valance 62. *Mr Hobbs Takes a Vacation* 62. How the West Was Won 62. Take Her She's Mine 63. Cheyenne Autumn 64. Dear Brigitte 65. *Shenandoah* 65. The Flight of the Phoenix 65. The Rare Breed 66. Firecreek 67. Bandolero 68. The Cheyenne Social

Club 70. Fool's Parade 71. The Shootist 76. The Big Sleep 77. Airport 77 77. The Magic of Lassie 78. Right of Way (TV) 83. North and South II (TV) 86. An American Tail: Fievel Goes West (voice) 91.
TV series: The Jimmy Stewart Show 71. Hawkins on Murder 73.
✪ For becoming one of everybody's family even when playing a tough westerner. The Philadelphia Story.

¶ I don't act. I react. – J.S.
I'm the inarticulate man who tries. I don't really have all the answers, but for some reason, somehow, I make it. – J.S.
The big studios were an ideal way to make films – because they were a home base for people. When you were under contract, you had a chance to relax. – J.S.
If I had my career over again? Maybe I'd say to myself, speed it up a little. – J.S.
He has so many of his pictures being shown on the late show, he keeps more people up than Mexican food. – Hal Kanter

Famous line (*The Philadelphia Story*): 'The prettiest sight in this fine pretty world is the privileged class enjoying its privileges.'

Famous line (*Harvey*): 'I wrestled with reality for 35 years, doctor, and I'm happy. I finally won out over it.'

Famous line (*It's a Wonderful Life*): 'Well, you look about the kind of angel I'd get. Sort of a fallen angel, aren't you? What happened to your wings?
~ Special AA 1984 'for 50 years of meaningful performances, for his high ideals, both on and off the screen, with the respect and affection of his colleagues'.

Stewart, Patrick (1940–).
Balding British leading actor, from classical theatre. He is now best known for his role as Captain Jean-Luc Picard in the TV series *Star Trek: The New Generation*.
Antony and Cleopatra 72. Hennessy 75. Hedda 75. Hamlet (TV) 79. Excalibur 81. Dune 84. Lifeforce 85. Lady Jane 86. Gunmen 93. Robin Hood: Men in Tights 93. The Pagemaster (voice) 94. Star Trek: Generations 94, etc.
TV series: Maybury 81.

Stewart, Paul (1908–1986) (P. Sternberg).
American character actor, often in clipped, sinister roles.
Citizen Kane 41. Johnny Eager 42. Government Girl 44. *Champion* 49. *The Window* 49. Walk Softly Stranger 50. The Bad and the Beautiful 52. Prisoner of War 54. The Cobweb 55. King Creole 58. A Child Is Waiting 62. The Greatest Story Ever Told 65. In Cold Blood 67. The Day of the Locust 75. Bite the Bullet 75. W. C. Fields and Me 76. Opening Night 77. The Dain Curse (TV) 78. The Revenge of the Pink Panther 81. S.O.B. 81, many others.

Stewart, Sophie (1909–1977).
British stage and radio actress, in occasional films.
Maria Marten 35. As You Like It 36. The Return of the Scarlet Pimpernel 38. Nurse Edith Cavell 39. The Lamp Still Burns 43. Uncle Silas 47. Yangtse Incident 56, etc.

Stiers, David Ogden (1942–).
Tall, balding American comedy actor.
Drive He Said 70. Charlie's Angels (TV) 76. Oh God 77. The Cheap Detective 78. Magic 78. Better

Off Dead 85. Another Woman 88. The Accidental Tourist 88. Doc Hollywood 91. Beauty and the Beast (voice) 91. Shadows and Fog 92. Iron Will 94, etc.
TV series: Doc 75–76. M*A*S*H 77–83.

Stigwood, Robert (1934–).
International impresario whose dominance of the pop-music field led him to produce *Saturday Night Fever* and *Grease*.

Stiller, Ben (1966–).
American actor and director, the son of television comedians and actors Jerry Stiller and Anne Meara.
Empire of the Sun (a) 87. Elvis Stories (a) 89. Reality Bites (a, d) 94. A Simple Plan (a, d) 95.
TV series: The Ben Stiller Show.

Stiller, Mauritz (1883–1928) (Mowscha Stiller).
Russian-Swedish director who went to Hollywood in the 20s with Garbo, but died shortly after.
Vampyren 12. *Sir Arne's Treasure* 19. Erotikon 20. *The Atonement of Gosta Berling* 24. The Blizzard (US) 26. Hotel Imperial 27. Street of Sin 28, etc.

Stillman, Whit (1952–).
American independent director, screenwriter and producer.
Metropolitan 90. Barcelona 94.

Sting (1951–) (Gordon Summers).
British musician and composer, founder-member of the rock band Police.
■ Quadrophenia 78. Radio On 79. The Secret Policeman's Other Ball 81. Brimstone and Treacle 82. Dune 84. The Bride 85. Plenty 85. Bring on the Night 86. Julia and Julia 87. Stormy Monday 88. The Adventures of Baron Munchausen 89. Resident Alien 90.

Stock, Nigel (1919–1986).
British character actor, former boy performer.
Lancashire Luck 38. Brighton Rock 46. Derby Day 51. The Dam Busters 55. Eye Witness 57. Victim 61. нмs Defiant 62. The Great Escape 63. The Lost Continent 68. The Lion in Winter 68. A Bequest to the Nation 73. Russian Roulette 75. A Man Called Intrepid (TV) (as Winston Churchill) 79, many others.
On TV he played Dr Watson in the 1965 *Sherlock Holmes* series.

stock shot.
One not made at the time of filming but hired from a library. It can be either newsreel, specially shot material such as planes landing at an airport, views of a city, etc., or spectacular material lifted from older features. (e.g. *Storm over the Nile* 55 had a large proportion of action footage from the original *Four Feathers* 39, and the same shots have turned up in several other films including *Master of the World* 61 and *East of Sudan* 64.)

Stockfeld, Betty (1905–1966).
British stage actress, in occasional films.
City of Song 30. The Impassive Footman 32. The Beloved Vagabond 36. Derrière la Façade (Fr.) 40. Flying Fortress 42. Edouard et Caroline (Fr.) 50. The Lovers of Lisbon 55. True As a Turtle 57, etc.

Stockwell, Dean (1938–).
American boy actor of the 40s, later leading man.
■ The Valley of Decision 45. Anchors Aweigh 45. Abbott and Costello in Hollywood 45. *The Green Years* 46. Home Sweet Homicide 46. The Mighty McGurk 47. The Arnelo Affair 47. Song of the Thin Man 47. The Romance of Rosy Ridge 47. Gentleman's Agreement 48. *The Boy with Green Hair*

48. Deep Waters 48. Down to the Sea in Ships 49. The Secret Garden 49. Stars in My Crown 50. The Happy Years 50. Kim 50. Cattle Drive 51. Gun for a Coward 57. The Careless Years 57. *Compulsion* 59. *Sons and Lovers* 60. Long Day's Journey into Night 62. Rapture 65. Psych-Out 68. The Dunwich Horror 70. Ecstasy 70. The Failing of Raymond (TV) 71. The Last Movie 71. The Loners 72. Another Day at the Races 73. Werewolf of Washington 73. Won Ton 75. Win, Place or Steal 75. Tracks 77. Wrong Is Right 82. Human Highway 82. Paris, Texas 84. Dune 84. The Legend of Billie Jean 85. To Live and Die in L.A. 85. Blue Velvet 86. Gardens of Stone 87. The Gambler III: The Legend Continues (TV) 87. The Blue Iguana 88. Tucker: The Man and His Dream 88. Married to the Mob (AAN) 88. Limit Up 89. Backtrack (aka Catchfire) 89. Son of the Morning Star (TV) 91. The Player 92. Chasers 94.

TV series: Quantum Leap 89–93.

Stockwell, Guy (1936–).
American leading actor. He is the brother of Dean Stockwell.

The War Lord 65. *Blindfold* 65. And Now Miguel 66. *Beau Geste* 66. The Plainsman 66. Tobruk 66. The King's Pirate 67. The Million Dollar Collar 67. In Enemy Country 68. The Gatling Gun 72. Airport 75 74. It's Alive 76. Grotesque 87. Santa Sangre 90, etc.

TV series: Adventures in Paradise 60. The Richard Boone Show 64.

Stoker, Bram (1847–1912).
Irish novelist, the creator of *Dracula*. Was also Henry Irving's manager.

Stokowski, Leopold (1882–1977) (Leopold Stokes or Boleslowowicz).
British-born orchestral conductor.
■ *One Hundred Men and a Girl* 37. The Big Broadcast of 1937 37. *Fantasia* 40. Carnegie Hall 47.

Stoler, Shirley (1929–).
Overweight American character actress, usually in unsympathetic roles and notable as the murderous nurse in *The Honeymoon Killers*.

The Honeymoon Killers 70. The Displaced Person 76. Seven Beauties 76. The Deer Hunter 78. Below the Belt 80. Splitz 84. Sticky Fingers 88. Miami Blues 90. Frankenhooker 90, etc.

Stoll, George (1905–1985).
American musical director, with MGM from 1945.

Anchors Aweigh (AA) 45. Neptune's Daughter 49. I Love Melvin 53. The Student Prince 54. Hit the Deck 55. Meet Me in Las Vegas 56, many others.

Stoloff, Morris (1894–1980).
American musical director, in Hollywood from 1936.

Lost Horizon 37. You Can't Take It with You 38. Cover Girl (AA) 44. A Song to Remember 45. The Jolson Story (AA) 46. The 5000 Fingers of Dr T 53. Picnic 55, many others.

Stoltz, Eric (1961–).
American leading actor.

The Grass Is Always Greener over the Septic Tank (TV) 78. Fast Times at Ridgemont High 82. Running Hot 84. The Wild Life 84. Code Name: Emerald 85. Mask 85. The New Kids 85. Lionheart 87. Sister, Sister 87. Some Kind of Wonderful 87. Haunted Summer 88. Manifesto 88. The Fly II 89. Say Anything 89. Memphis Belle 90. The Waterdance 92. Singles 92. Bodies, Rest and Motion

(& p) 93. Foreign Affairs (TV) 93. Naked in New York 93. Killing Zoe 94. Pulp Fiction 94. Sleep with Me (& p) 94. Little Women 94. Rob Roy 95, etc.

Stone, Andrew L. (1902–).
American producer-director (for a time with his wife Virginia) who made it a rule from the mid-40s not to shoot his melodramas in a studio, always on location, and with real trains, liners, airplanes, etc. Formed Andrew Stone Productions 1943.

The Great Victor Herbert 39. *Stormy Weather* (d only) 42. Hi Diddle Diddle 43. Sensations of 1945 45. Highway 301 51. The Steel Trap 52. The Night Holds Terror 54. Julie 56. *Cry Terror* 58. The Decks Ran Red 59. The Last Voyage 60. Ring of Fire 61. The Password Is Courage 62. Never Put It in Writing 64. The Secret of My Success 65. *Song of Norway* 69. *The Great Waltz* 72, etc.

¶ If the Stones had made *On the Beach*, none of us would be around now to review it. – *Andrew Sarris, 1968*

Stone, Dee Wallace (1948–) (aka Dee Wallace).
American actress who first made an impression as the mother in *E.T. – the Extraterrestrial*. She changed her name after marrying actor Christopher Stone.
■ The Stepford Wives 75. The Hills Have Eyes 77. 10 79. The Howling 80. E.T. – the Extraterrestrial 82. Jimmy the Kid 82. Cujo 83. Club Life 84. Secret Admirer 85. Critters 86. Shadow Play 86. Popcorn 91. Witness to the Execution (TV) 94.

Stone, George E. (1903–1967) (George Stein).
Polish-born character actor, who in Hollywood films played oppressed little men; formerly in vaudeville.

The Front Page 30. Little Caesar 30. Cimarron 31. Anthony Adverse 36. *The Housekeeper's Daughter* 38. His Girl Friday 40. The Boston Blackie series 41–9. Dancing in the Dark 50. The Robe 53. Guys and Dolls 55. The Man with the Golden Arm 56, many others.

Stone, Harold J. (1911–).
American character actor.

The Harder They Fall 56. Garment Center 57. Man Afraid 57. Spartacus 60. The Chapman Report 62. The Man with X-Ray Eyes 63. Which Way to the Front? 70. Mitchell 75, etc.

TV series: My World and Welcome To It 68. Bridget Loves Bernie 74.

Stone, Irving (1903–1989).
American novelist whose *Lust for Life*, *The Agony and the Ecstasy* and *The President's Lady* were filmed.

Stone, Lewis (1879–1953).
Distinguished American stage actor, a leading man of silent films and later a respected character actor.

Honour's Altar (debut) 15. *The Prisoner of Zenda* 22. Scaramouche 23. *The Lost World* 24. The Patriot (AAN) 28. Madame X 30. The Mask of Fu Manchu 32. Mata Hari 32. Grand Hotel 32. Queen Christina 33. *David Copperfield* 34. *Treasure Island* 35. The Thirteenth Chair 37. *You're Only Young Once* 37. Judge Hardy's Children 38. Love Finds Andy Hardy 38. Out West with the Hardys 39 (and ten further episodes of this series, ending in 1947). Yellow Jack 39. The Bugle Sounds 41. Three Wise Fools 46. The State of the Union 48. Key to the City 50. Scaramouche 52. The Prisoner of Zenda 52. All the Brothers Were Valiant 53, many others.

Stone, Marianne (1923–).
British character actress, usually in bit parts. Innumerable appearances.

Angels One Five 51. The Pickwick Papers 54. The Runaway Bus 54. Yield to the Night 56. Heavens Above 63. Ladies Who Do 65. Here We Go Round the Mulberry Bush 67. The Wicked Lady 83, many others.

Stone, Milburn (1904–1980).
American character actor, in Hollywood from the mid-30s; was in hundreds of low-budget action features, usually as villain or tough hero; more recently became famous as 'Doc' in the *Gunsmoke* TV series.

Ladies Crave Excitement 35. Port of Missing Girls 37. King of the Turf 39. Enemy Agent 40. The Phantom Cowboy 41. Rubber Racketeers 42. Sherlock Holmes Faces Death 43. Hat Check Honey 44. On Stage Everybody 45. Spider Woman Strikes Back 46. Train to Alcatraz 48. Snow Dog 50. The Sun Shines Bright 53. Black Tuesday 54. Drango 57, many others.

Stone, Oliver (1946–).
American director and screenwriter.
■ Seizure (wd) 74. The Hand (wd) 81. Midnight Express (AAw) 78. Scarface (w) 83. The Year of the Dragon (co-w) 85. Platoon (wd) (AA) 86. Salvador (wd) 86. Wall Street (wd) 87. Talk Radio (wd) 88. *Born on the Fourth of July* (wd) (AA) 89. The Doors (wd) 91. JFK (wd) (AAN) 91. Heaven and Earth (wd) 93. The New Age (p) 93. Natural Born Killers (co-w, d) 94.

¶ The film business? I love film, but the film business is shit. – *O.S.*

I think you are really acknowledging the Vietnam veteran, and for the first time you really understand what happened out there. – *O.S. (receiving his award for Platoon)*

I do my films to take me out of where I am. The questions the movies ask – those are the questions I'm asking myself at that point in time. – *O.S.*

Anybody who's been through a divorce will tell you that at one point in their life they've thought of murder. No one's innocent. – *O.S.*

If it sometimes seems that all Hollywood is striving for the Op-Ed-page prominence that Stone has so quickly achieved, he is not necessarily the representative it would have picked. For the off-camera Stone is given to tirades and bad language, to strenuous womanizing and long, intoxicated journeys into the night. – *Stephen Schiff, New Yorker*

A Saturday night with Oliver after a long week is basically pagan Rome, 26 A.D. – *Robert Downey Jnr*

Stone, Peter (1930–) (aka Pierre Marton).
American screenwriter.
■ *Charade* 63. Father Goose 64. *Mirage* 65. Arabesque 66. The Secret War of Harry Frigg 68. The Mercenaries (as Quentin Werty) 68. Sweet Charity 69. Skin Game 71. 1776 (from his own stage musical) 72. The Taking of Pelham 123 74. Silver Bears 77. Someone Is Killing the Great Chefs of Europe 78. Why Would I Lie? 80.

Stone, Sharon (1957–).
American leading actress in sexy roles; a former model.

Deadly Blessing 81. The Vegas Strip Wars (TV) 84. Irreconcilable Differences 84. King Solomon's Mines 85. Allan Quatermain and the Lost City of Gold 86. Cold Steel 87. Above the Law 88. Action Jackson 88. Beyond the Stars 89. Scissors 90. Total Recall 90. Year of the Gun 91. He Said, She Said 91. Where Sleeping Dogs Lie 91. Basic Instinct 92.

Diary of a Hit Man 92. Sliver 93. Intersection 94. The Specialist 94. The Quick and the Dead 95, etc.

TV series: Bay City Blues 83.

¶ I've been at this so long that I knew everyone in the business long before I became famous, and I didn't have value to many of them. Now, suddenly, the people who were coarse and rude to me before treat me as though we've never met, and now I'm fabulous, they're fabulous and isn't it fabulous we're chatting. – S.S.

In this business there is Plan A, in which you become successful by living and acting with a lot of integrity. Then there's Plan B, where you sell your soul to the devil. I still find it hard to distinguish one from the other. – S.S.

The Stooges.
A trio of American knockabout comics specializing in a peculiarly violent form of slapstick. They originally went from vaudeville to Hollywood with Ted Healy (as Ted Healy and his Stooges) but broke away to become world-famous in hundreds of two-reelers throughout the 30s, 40s and 50s. The original trio were *Larry Fine* (1911–1975), *Moe Howard* (1895–1975) and his brother *Jerry (Curly) Howard* (1906–1952). In 1947 Curly was replaced by yet another brother, *Shemp Howard (Samuel Howard)* (1891–1955). On Shemp's death he was replaced by *Joe Besser*, who in 1959 was replaced by *Joe de Rita* (1910–1993). Towards the end of their popularity the Stooges appeared in a few features.

Stop Look and Laugh 61. Snow White and the Three Stooges 61. The Three Stooges Meet Hercules 63. The Outlaws Is Coming 64. The Three Stooges Go around the World in a Daze 65, etc.

stop motion.
The method by which much trick photography is effected: the film is exposed one frame at a time, allowing time for rearrangement of models, etc. between shots, and thus giving the illusion in the completed film of motion by something normally inanimate. The monsters in *King Kong* 33 are the supreme example of this method. The best-known practitioners of the art have been Willis O'Brien and Ray Harryhausen (qqv). The method is being supplanted these days by a mix of animatronics (electronically controlled puppets) and computer-generated graphics.

See also: *time-lapse photography*.

Stoppa, Paolo (1906–1988).
Italian character actor, in films from 1932.

La Beauté du Diable 49. Miracle in Milan 50. The Seven Deadly Sins 52. Love Soldiers and Women 55. La Loi 59. The Leopard 63. Becket 64. After the Fox 66. Once upon a Time in the West 67, etc.

Stoppard, Tom (1937–) (Thomas Strausler).
Czechoslovakian playwright in UK.

Despair 78. The Human Factor 79. Brazil (AAN) 85. Empire of the Sun 87. Rosencrantz and Guildenstern Are Dead (wd) 90. The Russia House (w) 90. Billy Bathgate (w) 91, etc.

Storaro, Vittorio (1946–).
Italian cinematographer.

The Spider's Stratagem 70. The Conformist 71. Last Tango in Paris 72. 1900 77. Agatha 79. *Apocalypse Now* (AA) 79. *Reds* (AA) 81. One from the Heart 82. Ladyhawke 85. Ishtar 87. *The Last Emperor* (AA) 87. Tucker: The Man and His Dream 88. New York Stories 89. Dick Tracy 90. *The Sheltering Sky* 90. Little Buddha 93, etc.

Storch, Larry (1923–).
American comic actor.

Captain Newman MD 63. Wild and Wonderful 64. The Monitors 69. The Couple Takes a Wife (TV) 72. The Adventures of Huckleberry Finn (TV) 78. Better Late than Never 79. S.O.B. 81. Adventures beyond Belief 87, etc.

TV series: F Troop.

Storck, Henri (1907–).
Belgian documentarist.

Pour Vos Beaux Yeux 29. The Story of the Unknown Soldier 32. Symphonic Paysanne 42. Au Carrefour de la Vie 49. Les Belges de la Mer 54. Les Gestes du Silence 61. La Musée Vivante 65, etc.

Storm, Gale (1922–) (Josephine Cottle).
American leading lady of the 40s.

Autobiography: 1981, *I Ain't Down Yet*.

Tom Brown's Schooldays 40. Foreign Agent 42. Nearly Eighteen 43. The Right to Live 45. Sunbonnet Sue 46. It Happened on Fifth Avenue 47. Abandoned 49. Underworld Story 50. The Texas Rangers 51. Woman of the North 53, etc.

TV series: My Little Margie 52–54. The Gale Storm Show 56–59.

storms
of one kind or another have been brilliantly staged in *The Hurricane, The Wizard of Oz, When Tomorrow Comes, Reap the Wild Wind, Typhoon, Lord Jim, A High Wind in Jamaica, The Blue Lagoon, Sunrise, Key Largo, Ryan's Daughter, Portrait of Jennie, Noah's Ark* and *The Bible*, to name but a handful; they have also been essential situation-builders in such films as *Five Came Back, Hatter's Castle, Our Man Flint, The Card, Storm Fear* and *The Blue Lagoon*. A whole genre of films, known as the 'thunderstorm mystery', grew up in the 30s when every screen murder took place in a desolate mansion during a terrifying storm with no means of communication with the outside world; typical of these are *The Black Cat, The Cat and the Canary, The Ghost Breakers, Night Monster, Hold That Ghost, You'll Find Out* and *The Spiral Staircase*. Finally there is nothing like a good electrical storm for breathing life into a monster, as evidenced in a score of films from *Frankenstein* to *The Electric Man* and after.

storyboard.
A means of pre-planning a sequence of individual shots for a film by means of a series of drawings, somewhat like a comic-strip. Some directors, notably Alfred Hitchcock, prepare an entire film, and the necessary camera set-ups, by means of a storyboard. Others use it to work out in advance the likely problems, or the best positions for the camera, in action sequences. Storyboard artists can play a creative role in movie-making by suggesting shots or camera angles and movements that may not have occurred to the director.

Stossel, Ludwig (1883–1973).
Austrian character actor in Hollywood from the mid-30s.

Four Sons 39. Man Hunt 41. Woman of the Year 42. Hilter's Madman 43. Cloak and Dagger 46. A Song Is Born 48. Call Me Madam 53. Me and the Colonel 58. G.I. Blues 60, many others.

Stothart, Herbert (1885–1949).
American composer, long with MGM, and responsible for the scores of many of the studio's most prestigious films.

Madame Satan 30. Rasputin and the Empress 33. Queen Christina 33. David Copperfield 35. Mutiny on the Bounty 35. A Night at the Opera 35. San Francisco 36. Camille 37. The Good Earth 37. Marie Antoinette 38. Idiot's Delight 39. Waterloo Bridge 40. Mrs Miniver 42. Random Harvest 42. Madame Curie 44. The Green Years 46. The Yearling 47. The Three Musketeers 48, many others.

Stout, Archie (1886–?1965).
American cinematographer in Hollywood from 1914.

Fort Apache 48. Hard Fast and Beautiful 51. *The Quiet Man* (AA) 52. The Sun Shines Bright 53. The High and the Mighty 54.

Stout, Rex (1886–1975).
American detective story writer, creator of Nero Wolfe, who appeared in two minor films of the 30s (played by Edward Arnold and Walter Connolly) and in a 70s TV movie (played by Thayer David).

Stowe, Harriet Beecher (1811–1896).
American novelist, author of the much-filmed *Uncle Tom's Cabin*.

Stowe, Madeleine (1958–).
American leading actress.

Nativity (TV) 78. The Amazons (TV) 83. Stakeout 87. Worth Winning 89. Revenge 90. The Two Jakes 90. Closet Land 91. The Last of the Mohicans 92. Unlawful Entry 92. Short Cuts 93. Another Stakeout 93. Blink 94. Bad Girls 94. China Moon 94, etc.

TV series: The Gangster Chronicles 81.

Stradling, Harry (1901–1970).
British-born cinematographer, long in US.

La Kermesse Héroïque 35. Knight without Armour 37. Pygmalion 38. The Citadel 38. Jamaica Inn 39. Suspicion 41. *The Picture of Dorian Gray* (AA) 44. The Pirate 48. The Barkleys of Broadway (AAN) 49. *A Streetcar Named Desire* 51. Valentino 51. Hans Christian Andersen 52. Helen of Troy 55. Guys and Dolls 55. The Eddy Duchin Story 56. The Pajama Game 57. A Face in the Crowd 57. The Dark at the Top of the Stairs 60. *My Fair Lady* (AA) 64. How to Murder Your Wife 65. Moment to Moment 65. Walk, Don't Run 66. Funny Girl (AAN) 68. *Hello Dolly* 69, many others.

Stradling, Harry, Jnr (1925–).
American cinematographer, son of Harry Stradling.

Welcome to Hard Times 67. Support Your Local Sheriff 69. The Mad Room 69. Hello Dolly (AAN) 69. Something Big 71. Fools Parade 71. The Way We Were 73. McQ 74. Bite the Bullet 75. Midway 76. The Big Bus 76. Airport 77 77. Damnation Alley 77. Convoy 78. Go Tell the Spartans 78. Prophecy 79. Carny 80. S.O.B. 81. The Pursuit of D.B. Cooper 81. Buddy Buddy 81. O'Hara's Wife 82. Micki and Maude 84. A Fine Mess 86. Blind Date 87. Caddyshack II 88, etc.

Stradner, Rose (1913–1958).
Austrian actress who made a few Hollywood films.

The Last Gangster 38. Blind Alley 39. The Keys of the Kingdom 44, etc.

Straight, Beatrice (1916–).
American character actress.

Network (AA) 76. Bloodline 79. The Promise 79. Poltergeist 82. Two of a Kind 83. Power 85, etc.

Strange, Glenn (1899–1973).
Giant-size American character actor, in Hollywood from 1937, mainly in cowboy roles. Also played the monster in *House of Frankenstein* 45, *Abbott and Costello meet Frankenstein* 48, etc.

TV series: Gunsmoke 56–73.

Strasberg, Lee (1899–1982).
American drama teacher; founded the Actors' Studio which in the 50s taught The Method.
■ *The Godfather Part Two* (AAN) 74. The Cassandra Crossing 77. Boardwalk 79. And Justice for All 79. Going in Style 79.

¶ I never felt Lee Strasberg could act, and I fail to see how someone who can't act can teach acting. – *Paul Henreid*

Strasberg, Susan (1938–).
American leading lady, daughter of Lee Strasberg, founder of the New York Actors' Studio. Stage and TV experience.
Picnic (film debut) 55. Stage Struck 57. Taste of Fear 59. Kapo 60. Hemingway's Adventures of a Young Man 62. The High Bright Sun 65. Psych-Out 68. The Brotherhood 68. Rollercoaster 77. In Praise of Older Women 78. The Returning 83. The Delta Force 85. Lambarene 90. Trauma 92, etc.
TV series: Toma 73.

Strathairn, David (1949–).
American general-purpose actor, often in the films of John Sayles.
Return of the Secaucus 7 80. Enormous Changes at the Last Minute 83. Silkwood 83. The Brother from Another Planet 84. Iceman 84. Matewan 87. Eight Men Out 88. The Feud 90. Memphis Belle 90. Judgment (TV) 90. City of Hope 91. Big Girls Don't Cry . . . They Get Even (GB: Stepkids) 92. A League of Their Own 92. Passion Fish 92. Sneakers 92. Lost in Yonkers 93. The Firm 93. River Wild 94, etc.
TV series: The Days and Nights of Molly Dodd 87–88.

Stratten, Dorothy (1960–1980) (Dorothy Hoogstraten).
Canadian actress and *Playboy* pin-up whose short life, which ended when she was shot by her estranged husband, was re-told in the biopic *Star* 80, starring Mariel Hemingway.
Americathon 79. Skatetown USA 79. Galaxina 80. They All Laughed 81.

Stratton, John (1925–).
British general-purpose actor.
The Cure for Love 49. Appointment with Venus 52. The Cruel Sea 54. The Long Arm 55. Frankenstein and the Monster from Hell 74, etc.

Stratton-Porter, Gene (1863–1924).
American author of sentimental stories for girls.
A Girl of the Limberlost 34. Keeper of the Bees 35. Laddie 35. The Harvester 36. Michael O'Halloran 37 and 49. Her Father's Daughter 40. Freckles 60.

Straub, Jean-Marie (1933–).
French director in German films, in collaboration with his wife Danielle Huillet (1936–).
Machorka Muff 63. Nicht Versohnt 65. *The Chronicle of Anna-Magdalena Bach* 67. Othon 72. History Lessons 73. Moses and Aaron 75. Dalla Nube alla Resistenza 79. Too Early, Too Late 81. Class Relations (Klassenverhältnisse) 84. The Death of Empedocles (Der Tod des Empedokles) 86. Schwarze Sunde 89, etc.

Straus, Oscar (1870–1954).
Austrian operetta composer who also occasionally provided film music.
The Smiling Lieutenant 31. One Hour with You 32. Land Without Music 36. La Ronde 50. Madame De 52, etc.

Strauss, Helen (1909–1987).
American literary agent (for Michener and others) who became an occasional film producer: *Tom Sawyer, Huckleberry Finn, The Incredible Sarah*.
Autobiography: 1979, *A Talent for Luck*.

Strauss, Peter (1947–).
American leading man who became well known in *Rich Man Poor Man* (TV) 76.
Soldier Blue 71. The Last Tycoon 76. Young Joe the Forgotten Kennedy (TV) 77. The Jericho Mile (TV) 79. Masada (TV) 80. Spacehunter 83. Tender Is the Night (TV) 85. Kane and Abel (TV) 85. Peter Gunn (TV) 90, etc.

Strauss, Robert (1913–1975).
American comedy actor (occasionally in menacing roles); former salesman.
Sailor Beware 52. *Stalag 17* (AAN) 53. The Seven Year Itch 54. Attack 56. The Last Time I Saw Archie 61. The Family Jewels 65, etc.

Strayer, Frank (1891–1964).
American director of second features.
Rough House Rosie 27. Enemy of Men 30. The Monster Walks 32. The Vampire Bat 33. The Ghost Walks 35. Blondie (and many others in this series) 38. The Daring Young Man 42. Messenger of Peace 50, etc.

Streep, Meryl (1949–) (Mary Louise Streep).
American leading lady of the late 70s and star actress of the 80s.
Biography: 1988, *Meryl Streep* by Eugene E. Pfaff Jnr and Mark Emerson.
■ The Deadliest Season (TV) 77. Julia 77. The Deer Hunter (AAN) 78. *Holocaust* (TV) 78. Manhattan 79. The Seduction of Joe Tynan 79. *Kramer vs Kramer* (AA) 79. The French Lieutenant's Woman (BFA) 81. Sophie's Choice (AA) 82. Still of the Night 82. Silkwood (AAN) 83. Falling in Love 84. Plenty 85. Heartburn 86. Out of Africa (AAN) 86. Ironweed (AAN) 87. A Cry in the Dark (AAN) 88. She-Devil 89. Postcards from the Edge (AAN) 90. Defending Your Life 91. Death Becomes Her 92. The House of the Spirits 94. The River Wild 94.

¶ You can't get spoiled if you do your own ironing. – *M.S.*
The danger I'm talking about here is that she tends to sound boring because she's so perfect. – *Sydney Pollack*

Streeter, Edward (1892–1976).
American humorous novelist: *Father of the Bride* and *Mr Hobbs Takes a Vacation* were filmed.

Streisand, Barbra (1942–).
American singer and entertainer who made a virtue of her odd looks.
Biographies: 1982, *Streisand: The Woman and the Legend* by James Spada with Christopher Nickens. 1994, *Her Name Is Barbra* by Randall Riese.
■ *Funny Girl* (as Fanny Brice) (AA) 68. Hello Dolly 69. On a Clear Day You Can See Forever 70. The Owl and the Pussycat 70. What's Up, Doc? 72. Up the Sandbox 72. The Way We Were (AAN) 73. For Pete's Sake 74. Funny Lady 75. A Star Is Born (AA song) 76. The Main Event 79. All Night Long 81. Yentl (& co-w, co-p, d) 83. Nuts 87. The Prince of Tides (& d) 91.

¶ When I sing, people shut up. – *B.S.*
Success to me is having ten honeydew melons and eating only the top half of each one. – *B.S.*
Nobody really knows me: I'm a mixture of self-confidence and insecurity. One thing's for sure – I hate talking about myself. – *B.S.*
This is for posterity. Everything I do will be on film for ever. – *B.S. on Funny Girl*
It's kind of a wonderful thing, to appreciate my own career. – *B.S. in 1994*
Streisand embodies everything that is tacky and cheap and hopelessly corny and unsophisticated about Middle America. – *Joe Queenan*
She really ought to be called Barbra Strident. – *Stanley Kaufmann*
To know her is not necessarily to love her. – *Rex Reed*
The most pretentious woman the cinema has ever known. – *Ryan O'Neal*
I'd love to work with her again, in something appropriate. Perhaps *Macbeth*. – *Walter Matthau*

stretch-printing.
The reason silent films look jerky is that they were shot at 16 frames a second whereas modern sound projectors operate at 24, making everything move half as fast again as normal. One means of overcoming this jerkiness is stretch-printing in the lab: every second frame is printed twice. This still gives a curious effect, as for every two frames slower than normal sound speed we still get one frame faster.

Strick, Joseph (1923–).
American director.
The Savage Eye 59. The Balcony 64. Ulysses 67. Ring of Bright Water (GB) (p only) 69. Tropic of Cancer 69. The Darwin Adventure (p only) 71. Janice 73. Road Movie 74. A Portrait of the Artist as a Young Man 79, etc.

Strick, Wesley.
American screenwriter.
True Believer 89. Arachnophobia (co-w) 90. Cape Fear 91. Final Analysis 92. Wolf (co-w) 94.

Stricklyn, Ray (1930–).
American 'second lead' with stage experience.
The Proud and the Profane 56. The Last Wagon 57. Ten North Frederick 58. Young Jesse James 60. Arizona Raiders 65. Track of Thunder 68, etc.

Stride, John (1936–).
British supporting actor, much on TV.
Bitter Harvest 63. Macbeth 72. Juggernaut 74. Brannigan 75. The Omen 76. A Bridge Too Far 77, etc.
TV series: The Main Chance 69–75. The Wilde Alliance 78.

strikes:
see *labour relations*.

Stritch, Elaine (1926–).
Sharp, lanky American character comedienne, mainly on stage; a popular London resident from the mid-70s.
■ The Scarlet Hour 55. Three Violent People 57. A Farewell to Arms 57. The Perfect Furlough 58. Who Killed Teddy Bear? 65. Sidelong Glances of a Pigeon Kicker 70. The Spiral Staircase 75. Providence 77. September 87. Cocoon: The Return 88. Cadillac Man 90.
TV series: The Growing Paynes 49. *My Sister Eileen* 60. The Trials of O'Brien 65. Two's Company 76–78. The Ellen Burstyn Show 86–87.

Strock, Herbert L. (1918–).
American director, former publicist and editor.
The Magnetic Monster 52. Riders to the Stars 54. Battle Taxi 55. Teenage Frankenstein 57. How to Make a Monster 58. Rider on a Dead Horse 62.

The Crawling Hand 63. Man on the Run 74. Monster 78. Witches' Brew (co-d) 79, etc.

Strode, Woody (Woodrow) (1914–1994).
Tall American actor.

The Lion Hunters 51. The Ten Commandments 56. *Sergeant Rutledge* 60. Spartacus 60. Two Rode Together 62. The Man Who Shot Liberty Valance 62. Genghis Khan 65. *The Professionals* 66. Shalako 68. Che! 69. The Revengers 72. The Gatling Gun 72. Winterhawk 76. Loaded Guns 76. The Black Stallion Returns 83. Vigilante 83. The Cotton Club 84. Lust in the Dust 84. Storyville 92. Posse 93, etc.

Stromberg, Hunt (1894–1968).
American producer, long with MGM, who went independent in the 40s.

Breaking into Society (as d) 24. Fire Patrol (as d) 26. Torrent 27. Our Dancing Daughters 28. Red Dust 32. *The Thin Man* 34. *The Great Ziegfeld* (AA) 36. Maytime 38. Marie Antoinette 38. Idiot's Delight 39. *The Women* 39. Northwest Passage 40. *Pride and Prejudice* 41. Guest in the House 44. Lured 47. Too Late for Tears 49. Between Midnight and Dawn 50. Mask of the Avenger 51, many others.

¶ Boys, I've an idea. Let's fill the screen with tits. – *H.S. on taking over White Shadows in the South Seas in 1928*

Stross, Raymond (1916–1988).
British producer, in films from 1933; married to Anne Heywood.

As Long as They're Happy 52. An Alligator Named Daisy 56. The Flesh is Weak 56. A Question of Adultery 58. A Terrible Beauty 59. The Very Edge 62. The Leather Boys 63. Ninety Degrees in the Shade 65. The Midas Run 69. I Want What I Want 72, etc.

Stroud, Don (1937–).
American leading man.

Madigan 68. Games 68. What's So Bad about Feeling Good 68. Coogan's Bluff 69. Bloody Mama 70. Explosion 70. Von Richthofen and Brown 70. Tick Tick Tick 70. Joe Kidd 72. Scalawag 73. The Choirboys 77. The Buddy Holly Story 78. The Amityville Horror 79. Armed and Dangerous 86. Down the Drain 89. Prime Target 91. Frogtown II 92, etc.

TV series: Kate Loves a Mystery 79. Mickey Spillane's Mike Hammer 84–87. Dragnet 89–90.

Strouse, Charles (1928–).
American composer, mainly for Broadway musicals.

The Mating Game (song) 59. Bonnie and Clyde 67. The Night They Raided Minsky's 68. There Was a Crooked Man 70. Just Tell Me What You Want 80. Annie (from musical) 82.

Strudwick, Shepperd:
see *Shepperd, John.*

Strummer, Joe (1952–) (John Mellors).
British composer, musician and occasional actor. He was a founder-member of the late-70s punk band The Clash.

Rude Boy (co-m) 80. Sid and Nancy (co-m) 86. Love Kills (co-m) 86. Straight to Hell (a) 87. Walker (m) 87. Permanent Record (m) 88. Candy Mountain (a) 88. Mystery Train (a) 89. I Hired a Contract Killer (a, s) 90. When Pigs Fly (m) 93, etc.

Struss, Karl (1891–1981).
American cinematographer.

Ben Hur 26. *Sunrise* (AA) 27. Abraham Lincoln 30. The Sign of the Cross 32. *Dr Jekyll and Mr Hyde* 32. The Great Dictator 40. Bring on the Girls 44. Suspense 46. The Macomber Affair 47. Rocketship XM 50. *Limelight* 52. Tarzan and the She-Devil 53, many others.

Struthers, Sally (1947–).
American young character actress, a hit as the daughter in TV's *All in the Family* 71–74.

Five Easy Pieces 70. The Getaway 72. Aloha Means Goodbye (TV) 76. A Gun in the House (TV) 81, etc.

¶ Acting is cheap group therapy, being a schizo fifty different ways. And we're paid! – *S.S.*

Stuart, Binkie (c. 1932–).
British child actress of the 30s.

Moonlight Sonata 37. Little Dolly Daydream 38. My Irish Molly 39, etc.

Stuart, Gloria (1909–) (Gloria Stuart Finch).
American leading lady of the 30s.

The Old Dark House 32. The Invisible Man 33. Roman Scandals 33. Prisoner of Shark Island 36. Rebecca of Sunnybrook Farm 38. The Three Musketeers 39. She Wrote the Book 46. My Favorite Year 82, etc.

Stuart, Jeb.
American screenwriter.

■ Die Hard 88. Leviathan 89. Lock Up 89. Vital Signs 90. Another 48 Hrs 90. The Fugitive (co-w) 93. Outbreak (co-w) 95.

Stuart, John (1898–1979) (John Croall).
British leading man of the 20s, character actor of the 40s and after.

Autobiography: 1971, *Caught in the Act.*

Her Son (debut) 20. We Women 25. The Pleasure Garden 26. Blackmail 29. Elstree Calling 30. Atlantic 30. Number Seventeen 31. Taxi for Two 32. The Pointing Finger 34. Abdul the Damned 35. Old Mother Riley's Ghost 41. The Phantom Shot 46. Mine Own Executioner 47. The Magic Box 51. Quatermass II 57. Blood of the Vampire 58. Sink the Bismarck 60. Superman 78, etc.

Stuart, Leslie (1864–1928) (Thomas Barrett).
British songwriter ('Tell Me Pretty Maiden', 'Florodora', etc.) played by Robert Morley in the 1940 biopic *You Will Remember.*

Stuart, Mel (1928–).
American director.

If It's Tuesday This Must Be Belgium 69. I Love My Wife 70. Willie Wonka and the Chocolate Factory 71. One Is a Lonely Number 72. Mean Dog Blues 78. The Chisholms (TV) 79. The White Lions 79, etc.

Stubbs, Imogen (1961–).
English leading actress, from the stage.

Privileged 82. Nanou 86. A Summer Story 88. Erik the Viking 89. Fellow Traveller 89. True Colors 91, etc.

The Student of Prague.
The old German legend, about a man who sold his soul to the devil and bought it back only at the expense of his life, was filmed in 1913 by Stellan Rye, with Paul Wegener; in 1926 by Henrik Galeen, with Conrad Veidt; and in 1936 by Arthur Robison, with Anton Walbrook.

The Student Prince.
The Sigmund Romberg/Dorothy Donnelly operetta about a Ruritanian prince who loves a barmaid was filmed by Lubitsch in 1927 with Ramon Novarro and Norma Shearer. There was no sound version until 1954, when Richard Thorpe directed Ann Blyth and Edmund Purdom (the latter using Mario Lanza's voice).

student protest
was a feature of a few films of the late 60s. They were not successful, with the exception of *If*. For the record the other main titles were *Flick*, *The Strawberry Statement, Getting Straight, R.P.M.* and *The Revolutionary*.

Studi, Wes.
American actor, usually playing an Indian. A Cherokee, he was born in Oklahoma and was formerly a teacher.

Dances with Wolves 90. The Doors 91. Last of the Mohicans 92. Geronimo: An American Legend (title role) 93. The Broken Chain (TV) 93. Street Fighter 95, etc.

stuntmen,
who risk their lives doubling for the stars when the action gets too rough, have been featured in remarkably few movies: *Hollywood Stunt Men, Lucky Devils, The Lost Squadron, Sons of Adventure, Callaway Went Thataway, Singin' in the Rain* and *Hooper, Hell's Angels* was said to be the film on which most stuntmen were killed; more recently Paul Mantz lost his life while stunt-flying for *The Flight of the Phoenix*, which was subsequently dedicated to him. Most famous stuntmen are probably Yakima Canutt, who later became a famous second-unit director; Richard Talmadge, who doubled for Douglas Fairbanks and also directed a few films himself; and Cliff Lyons, who stood in for most of the western stars. Stuntmen who became famous in their own right include George O'Brien, Jock Mahoney, Rod Cameron and George Montgomery. In the early 80s a film called *The Stunt Man* took a wry view of the matter and a TV series called *The Fall Guy* was popular for a while.

Sturges, John (1911–1992).
American director of smooth if increasingly pretentious action films, former editor and documentarist.

■ The Man Who Dared 46. Shadowed 46. Alias Mr Twilight 47. For the Love of Rusty 47. Keeper of the Bees 48. The Best Man Wins 48. The Sign of the Ram 48. The Walking Hills 49. The Capture 49. Mystery Street 50. The Magnificent Yankee 50. Right Cross 50. Kind Lady 51. The People Against O'Hara 51. It's a Big Country (part) 51. The Girl in White 52. Fast Company 52. Jeopardy 53. Escape from Fort Bravo 53. *Bad Day at Black Rock* (AAN) 54. Underwater 55. The Scarlet Coat 55. Backlash 56. *Gunfight at the OK Corral* 57. The Law and Jake Wade 58. The Old Man and the Sea 58. Last Train from Gun Hill 58. Never So Few 59. *The Magnificent Seven* 60. By Love Possessed 61. Sergeants Three 62. A Girl Named Tamiko 63. *The Great Escape* 63. The Satan Bug 65. The Hallelujah Trail 65. The Hour of the Gun 67. Ice Station Zebra 68. Marooned 69. Joe Kidd 72. Valdez the Halfbreed (Sp.) 73. McQ 74. The Eagle Has Landed 77.

¶ It is hard to remember why his career was ever considered meaningful. – *Andrew Sarris, 1968*

Sturges, Preston (1898–1959) (Edmund P. Biden).
American writer-director who in the early 40s was Hollywood's wonder boy who never lost the common touch despite his free-wheeling witty style and subject matter. By 1950 his talent had disappeared, and he retired unhappily to France.

Book: 1991, *Preston Sturges on Preston Sturges* edited by Sandy Sturges.

AS WRITER: *The Power and the Glory* 33. We Live Again 34. The Good Fairy 35. Diamond Jim 35. Easy Living 37. Port of Seven Seas 38. If I Were King 39. Never Say Die 39. Remember the Night 40, etc.

■ AS WRITER-DIRECTOR: *The Great McGinty* (AA) 40. *Christmas in July* 40. *Sullivan's Travels* 41. *The Lady Eve* 41. *The Palm Beach Story* 42. *The Great Moment* 43. *The Miracle of Morgan's Creek* (AANw) 43. *Hail the Conquering Hero* (AANw) 44. Mad Wednesday 46. Unfaithfully Yours 48. The Beautiful Blonde from Bashful Bend 49. The Diary of Major Thompson 56.

◐ For being the wonder boy of the early 40s, with his unique blend of sophisticated comedy and pratfall farce. *Sullivan's Travels.*

¶ The Breughel of American comedy directors . . . the absurdity of the American success story was matched by the ferocity of the battle of the sexes . . . Lubitsch treated sex as the dessert of a civilized meal of manners. Sturges, more in the American style, served sex with all the courses. – *Andrew Sarris, 1968*

Jesus, he was a strange guy. Carried his own hill with him, I tell you. – *Frank Capra*

There was a desperate, hectic quality to all his films – an intense desire to believe all the Horatio Alger ideals often associated with America, intermingled with a cynical 'European' view of those ideals. – *James Ursini*

He has restored to the art of the cinema a certain graphic velocity it has missed since the turmoil of Mack Sennett's zanies. – *Bosley Crowther*

Preston is like a man from the Italian Renaissance – he wants to do everything at once. – *James Agee*

He was too large for this smelly resort, and the big studios were scared to death of him. A man who was a triple threat kept them awake nights, and I'm positive they were waiting for him to fall on his face so they could pounce and devour this terrible threat to their stingy talents. They pounced, and they got him, good. But he knew the great days when his can glowed like a port light from their kissing it. – *Earl Felton*

When the last dime is gone, I'll sit on the curb outside with a pencil and a ten-cent notebook, and start the whole thing over again. – *P.S., 1957*

Sturridge, Charles (1951–).
English director, from TV.
Runners 83. Aria (co-d) 87. A Handful of Dust 88. Where Angels Fear to Tread 91. A Foreign Field (TV) 93, etc.
TV series: Brideshead Revisited 81.

Styne, Jule (1905–1994) (Jules Styne).
British-born composer, in US from childhood. Former pianist and conductor. Film songs include 'There Goes That Song Again', 'Give Me Five Minutes More', 'It's Magic', 'Three Coins in the Fountain'. Shows filmed include *Gentlemen Prefer Blondes, Bells Are Ringing, Gypsy, Funny Girl.*

Subiela, Eliseo (1944–).
Argentinian director.
La Conquista del Paraiso 81. Man Facing Southeast 87. Ultimas Imágenes del Naufragio 89. El Lado Oscuro del Corazón 92, etc.

submarines
have been the setting for so many war action films that only a few can be noted. Pure entertainment was the object of *Submarine Patrol, Submarine Command, Torpedo Run, Destination Tokyo, Run Silent*

Run Deep, Crash Dive, The Deep Six and Ice Station Zebra. Somewhat deeper thoughts were permitted in *Morning Departure, The Silent Enemy, Les Maudits*, and *We Dive at Dawn*. Submarines became objects of farce in *Jack Ahoy, Let's Face It*, and *Operation Petticoat.*

More unusual submarine vehicles appeared in *Voyage to the Bottom of the Sea, Around the World Under the Sea, Twenty Thousand Leagues Under the Sea, Thunderball, You Only Live Twice, Above Us the Waves* and *The Beast from 20,000 Fathoms.*

Subotsky, Milton (1921–1991).
American independent producer and writer.
Rock Rock Rock 56. The Last Mile 58. City of the Dead (GB) 60. It's Trad Dad (GB) 63. Dr Terror's House of Horrors (GB) 64. Dr Who and the Daleks (GB) 65. The Skull (GB) 66. The Psychopath (GB) 66. Daleks Invasion Earth 2150 AD (GB) 66. Torture Garden (GB) 67. The House That Dripped Blood (GB) 70. Tales from the Crypt (GB) 71. Asylum (GB) 72. Madhouse (GB) 73. The Land that Time Forgot (GB) 75. At the Earth's Core (GB) 76. The Monster Club 80. Cat's Eye 84. The Lawnmower Man 92, etc.

sub-titles
in silent days came *after* the scene in which the actors mouthed the dialogue. When talkies came the less cumbersome method was evolved of superimposing the dialogue at the foot of the screen, which considerably sharpened up the audience's reading speed.

subways:
see *underground railways.*

Suchet, David (1946–).
English character actor, much on stage and television. He acted with the Royal Shakespeare Company from the late 70s.
Hunchback of Notre Dame (TV) 82. Trenchcoat 82. The Missionary 83. Red Monarch (TV) 83. Greystoke: The Legend of Tarzan, Lord of the Apes 84. Little Drummer Girl 84. The Falcon and the Snowman 85. Harry and the Hendersons 87. Blott on the Landscape (TV) 85. A World Apart 87. To Kill a Priest 88. When the Whales Came 89. Secret Agent (TV) 92, etc.
TV series: Poirot (title role) 88–93.

Sucksdorff, Arne (1917–).
Swedish documentarist who has normally written and photographed his own films, which vary from six minutes to feature length.
The West Wind 42. Shadows on the Snow 45. *Rhythm of a City* 47. *A Divided World* 48. The Road 48. The Wind and the River 51. *The Great Adventure* 53. The Flute and the Arrow 57. The Boy in the Tree 60. My Home is Copacabana 65. Forbush and the Penguins 71, etc.

suicide
became the central subject of two 60s films, *Le Feu Follet* and *The Slender Thread*, in which the motives for it in two particular cases are examined. It has, of course, been part of countless other plots, including factual or legendary ones such as *Cleopatra, Romeo and Juliet* and *Scott of the Antarctic*. Innumerable melodramas have begun with apparent suicides which have been proved by the disbelieving hero to be murder; the least likely of these may be *The Third Secret*. In *An Inspector Calls* a girl's suicide caused guilt complexes in an entire family for different reasons. In *An American Dream* the hero virtually commits suicide by walking into a room full of gangsters out to kill him. In *Leave Her to Heaven* the leading character commits suicide in

such a way that her husband will be blamed for her murder. Several Japanese films have been based on the suicide pilots or kamikaze, and there has also been a graphic account of the principles of *hara kiri*. Suicide has often been the way out for villains in mystery pictures: drowning for Herbert Marshall in *Foreign Correspondent*, shooting for Leo G. Carroll in *Spellbound*, poison for Rosamund John in *Green for Danger* and Barry Fitzgerald in *And Then There Were None*. And one could not begin to count the films in which characters have been narrowly saved from suicide, like Ray Milland in *The Lost Weekend*. Attempted suicide was even played for comedy by Laurel and Hardy in *The Flying Deuces*, by Graham Chapman in *The Odd Job*, by Jack Lemmon in *Buddy Buddy* and *Luv*, by Burt Reynolds in *The End*, while in *It's a Wonderful Life* James Stewart was dissuaded from suicide by a friendly angel. In *The Long Goodbye*, Elliott Gould finds a presumed suicide alive, and shoots him.

Sukowa, Barbara (1950–).
German leading actress.
Berlin Alexanderplatz (TV) 80. Lola 81. Deadly Game 83. Rosa Luxemburg 86. The Sicilian 87. Voyager 91. Europea (US: Zentropa) 92. Johnny Mnemonic 95, etc.

Sullavan, Margaret (1911–1960) (Margaret Brooke).
American leading actress in light films of the 30s and 40s; she had a special whimsical quality which was unique.
Biography: 1977, *Haywire* by Brooke Hayward (her daughter).
■ Only Yesterday 33. Little Man What Now? 34. So Red the Rose 35. The Good Fairy 35. Next Time We Love 36. The Moon's Our Home 36. *Three Comrades* 38. Shopworn Angel 38. The Shining Hour 39. *The Shop around the Corner* 39. *The Mortal Storm* 40. So Ends Our Night 40. Back Street 41. Appointment for Love 41. Cry Havoc 43. No Sad Songs for Me 50.

Sullivan, Barry (1912–1994) (Patrick Barry).
American leading man with stage experience.
Lady in the Dark 43. Two Years before the Mast 44. And Now Tomorrow 44. Suspense 46. The Gangster 47. Tension 49. The Great Gatsby 49. The Outriders 50. Three Guys Named Mike 51. *The Bad and the Beautiful* 52. Jeopardy 54. Queen Bee 55. Forty Guns 57. Wolf Larsen 57. Seven Ways from Sundown 60. The Light in the Piazza 62. Stagecoach to Hell 64. My Blood Runs Cold 64. Harlow (electronovision version) 65. An American Dream (See You in Hell, Darling) 66. Intimacy 66. Buckskin 68. Willie Boy 69. Earthquake 74. The Human Factor 75. Oh God 77. Casino 80, etc.
TV series: The Man Called X 55–56. Harbourmaster 57–58. The Tall Man 60–62. The Road West 67. Rich Man, Poor Man Book II 76–77.

Sullivan, C. Gardner (1885–1965).
American screenwriter.
The Battle of Gettysburg 14. The Wrath of the Gods 15. Civilization 16. The Aryan 16. The Zeppelin's Last Raid 17. Carmen of the Klondike 18. Sahara 19. Human Wreckage 23. Sparrows 26. Tempest 27. Sequoia 34. The Buccaneer 38, many others.

Sullivan, Francis L. (1903–1956).
Heavyweight British character actor, often seen as advocate. On stage from 1921, films from 1933.
The Missing Rembrandt (debut) 33. Chu Chin Chow 33. Great Expectations (US) 35. *The Mystery*

Sullivan, Pat

578

of Edwin Drood (US) 35. Sabotage 36. Action for Slander 37. Dinner at the Ritz 37. Twenty-one Days 38. The Citadel 38. The Four Just Men 39. *Pimpernel Smith* 41. *Fiddlers Three* 44. Caesar and Cleopatra 45. *Great Expectations* 46. *Oliver Twist* 48. Night and the City 51. Plunder of the Sun (US) 51. The Prodigal (US) 55. Hell's Island (US) 55, many others.

TV series: Destiny (host) 57–58.

Sullivan, Pat (1887–1933).
Australian newspaper cartoonist who settled in the US and invented Felix the Cat, the most popular character in film cartoons of the 20s.

Sully, Frank (1910–1975).
American small-part actor often seen as farmer or dumb crook.

Mary Burns Fugitive 35. The Grapes of Wrath 40. Escape to Glory 41. Thousands Cheer 43. Renegades 46. With a Song in My Heart 52. The Naked Street 56, many others.

Sumac, Yma (1928–) (Emparatriz Chavarri).
Peruvian singer with five-octave range.
■ The Secret of the Incas 54. Omar Khayyam 57.

Summerfield, Eleanor (1921–).
British character comedienne, on stage from 1939.
London Belongs to Me (film debut) 47. Scrooge 51. It's Great To Be Young 56. Dentist in the Chair 59. On the Beat 62. Guns of Darkness 63. Some Will Some Won't 70. The Watcher in the Woods 80, many others.

Summers, Jeremy (1931–).
British director, from TV.
The Punch and Judy Man 62. Crooks in Cloisters 64. Ferry Cross the Mersey 64. House of a Thousand Dolls 67. Vengeance of Fu Manchu 67. Strangers and Brothers (TV) 83, etc.

Summers, Walter (1896–1973).
British director of the 20s and 30s.
Ypres 25. Mons 26. The Battle of the Coronel and Falkland Islands 31. Deeds Men Do 32. The Return of Bulldog Drummond 33. Mutiny on the Elsinore 36. Music Hath Charms (co-d) 36. At the Villa Rose 38. Dark Eyes of London 38. Traitor Spy 40, etc.

Summerville, Slim (1892–1946) (George J. Summerville).
Lanky, mournful-looking American character comedian, former gagman and director for Mack Sennett.
The Beloved Rogue 27. *All Quiet on the Western Front* 30. The Front Page 31. Life Begins at Forty 35. White Fang 36. The Road Back 37. Rebecca of Sunnybrook Farm 38. Jesse James 39. *Tobacco Road* 41. Miss Polly 41. Niagara Falls 42. The Hoodlum Saint 46, many others.

Sumner, Geoffrey (1908–1989).
British comic actor of silly-ass types.
Helter Skelter 49. The Dark Man 52. A Tale of Five Cities 53. Traveller's Joy 55, etc.

Sundberg, Clinton (1906–1987).
American character actor, former teacher; usually played flustered clerk or head-waiter.
Undercurrent 46. Living in a Big Way 47. Annie Get Your Gun 50. Main Street to Broadway 52. The Caddy 53. The Birds and the Bees 56. The Wonderful World of the Brothers Grimm 63. Hotel 67, many others.

superdynamation.
A term coined by Ray Harryhausen for his method of animating rubber monsters.

Super-8.
Improved 8mm film which can take a soundtrack, therefore replacing the old 9.5mm.

superimpose:
to place one image on top of another, usually during a dissolve when one is fading out and the other fading in.

Superman.
A comic strip character of the 30s, a being of giant powers from the planet Krypton; until they are needed he masquerades as Clark Kent, a timid newspaperman. Superman has never been out of fashion – 1978 brought a multi-million-dollar live version to follow the various cartoons and serials which have been popular over the years – and along the way he has inspired Batman, Spiderman, Doc Savage, the Six Million Dollar Man, the Bionic Woman, etc, etc. In 1984, after two further sequels, *Superman* gave way to *Supergirl*.

supervisor.
In Hollywood in the early 30s, a studio name for the assigned producer.

Surtees, Bruce (1937–).
American cinematographer. He is the son of Robert L. Surtees.
The Beguiled 71. Play Misty for Me 71. Dirty Harry 72. The Great Northfield Minnesota Raid 72. Blume in Love 73. High Plains Drifter 73. Lenny (AAN) 74. Night Moves 75. The Outlaw Josey Wales 76. Movie Movie 78. Big Wednesday 78. Escape from Alcatraz 79. Inchon 81. White Dog 82. Firefox 82. Tightrope 84. Beverly Hills Cop 84. Pale Rider 85. Out of Bounds 86. Psycho III 86. Ratboy 86. Back to the Beach 87. License to Drive 88. Men Don't Leave 90. The Super 91. Run 91. The Crush 93. The Birds II: Land's End (TV) 94, etc.

Surtees, Robert L. (1906–1985).
Distinguished American cinematographer, in Hollywood from 1927.
Thirty Seconds over Tokyo (AAN) 44. Our Vines Have Tender Grapes 45. The Unfinished Dance 47. Act of Violence 48. Intruder in the Dust 49. *King Solomon's Mines* (AA) 50. Quo Vadis (AAN) 51. *The Bad and the Beautiful* (AA) 52. Escape from Fort Bravo 53. Trial 55. *Oklahoma!* (AAN) 55. The Swan 56. Raintree County 57. Merry Andrew 58. *Ben Hur* (AA) 59. Mutiny on the Bounty (AAN) 62. The Hallelujah Trail 65. The Collector 65. The Satan Bug 65. Lost Command 66. Doctor Dolittle (AAN) 67. *The Graduate* (AAN) 67. *Sweet Charity* 68. The Arrangement 69. Summer of 42 (AAN) 71. The Last Picture Show (AAN) 71. The Cowboys 72. The Other 72. Oklahoma Crude 73. The Sting (AAN) 73. The Great Waldo Pepper 75. The Hindenberg (AAN) 75. A Star Is Born (AAN) 76. The Turning Point (AAN) 77. Bloodbrothers 78. Same Time Next Year (AAN) 78, etc.

Susann, Jacqueline (1921–1974).
American best-selling novelist. Films of her books include *Valley of the Dolls*, *The Love Machine* and *Once is Not Enough*.

Suschitzky, Peter (1941–).
British cinematographer.
It Happened Here 65. Privilege 66. Charlie Bubbles 67. A Midsummer Night's Dream 68. Lock Up Your Daughters 68. Leo the Last 70.

Lisztomania 76. Valentino 77. The Empire Strikes Back 80. Krull 83. Falling in Love 84. Dead Ringers 88. Where the Heart Is 90. Naked Lunch 91. M. Butterfly 93. The Vanishing 93, etc.

Suschitzky, Wolfgang (1912–).
Austrian cinematographer in Britain.
No Resting Place 51. Cat and Mouse 57. The Small World of Sammy Lee 63. Ulysses 67. Theatre of Blood 73. Something to Hide 74, etc.

Susskind, David (1920–1987).
American TV and theatre personality and producer who also produced a few films.
Edge of the City 57. A Raisin in the Sun 61. Requiem for a Heavyweight 62. All the Way Home 63. Lovers and Other Strangers 70. Alice Doesn't Live Here Any More 74. Buffalo Bill and the Indians 76. Loving Couples 80, etc.

Sutherland, A. Edward (1895–1974).
American director, in Hollywood from 1914.
Wild Wild Susan 25. Dance of Life 29. Palmy Days 31. Mississippi 35. Diamond Jim 35. Champagne Waltz 37. Every Day's a Holiday 38. The Flying Deuces 39. *The Boys from Syracuse* 40. Beyond Tomorrow 41. Invisible Woman 41. Nine Lives Are Not Enough 42. Dixie 43. Follow the Boys 44. Abie's Irish Rose 46. Having Wonderful Crime 46. Bermuda Affair 56, many others.

Sutherland, Donald (1935–).
Gaunt Canadian actor who became very fashionable at the end of the 60s. He is the father of Kiefer Sutherland.
■ The World Ten Times Over 63. Castle of the Living Dead 64. Dr Terror's House of Horrors 65. Fanatic 65. The Bedford Incident 65. Promise Her Anything 66. The Dirty Dozen 67. Billion Dollar Brain 67. Sebastian 68. Oedipus the King 68. Interlude 68. Joanna 68. The Split 68. Start the Revolution without Me 69. Act of the Heart 70. *M*A*S*H* 70. Kelly's Heroes 70. Alex in Wonderland 70. Little Murders 70. *Klute* 71. Johnny Got His Gun (as Christ) 71. Steelyard Blues 72. Lady Ice 72. Alien Thunder 73. Don't Look Now 73. S*P*Y*S 74. The Day of the Locust 75. End of the Game 76. 1900 76. Casanova 76. The Eagle Has Landed 77. The Disappearance 77. Blood Relations 78. The Kentucky Fried Movie 78. Invasion of the Body Snatchers 78. National Lampoon's Animal House 78. The First Great Train Robbery 79. Murder by Decree 79. Bear Island 79. A Man, a Woman and a Bank 80. Nothing Personal 80. Ordinary People 80. Eye of the Needle 81. Threshold 81. Gas 81. Max Dugan Returns 83. The Winter of Our Discontent (TV) 84. Crackers 84. Ordeal by Innocence 85. Heaven Help Us 85. Revolution 86. The Wolf at the Door 86. Lost Angels 89. A Dry White Season 89. Bethune: The Making of a Hero 89. Eminent Domain 90. Backdraft 91. JFK 91. Scream of Stone 91. Buster's Bedroom 91. The Railway Station Man 92. Buffy the Vampire Slayer 92. Benefit of the Doubt 93. Six Degrees of Separation 93. Shadow of the Wolf (co-w) 93. Younger and Younger 93. The Lifeforce Experiment (TV) 94. Oldest Living Confederate Widow Tells All (TV) 94. Disclosure 94.

Sutherland, Kiefer (1967–).
Canadian leading actor (born in London), the son of Donald Sutherland.
The Bay Boy 85. Stand by Me 86. Crazy Moon 87. The Killing Time 87. The Lost Boys 87. Bright Lights, Big City 88. Promised Land 88. Renegades 89. Flashback 89. 1969 89. Young Guns 90. Flatliners 90. Trapped in Silence 90. Young Guns

II 90. Flashback 91. Article 99 92. A Few Good Men 92. Twin Peaks: Fire Walk with Me 92. The Vanishing 93. Last Light (& d) (TV) 93. The Three Musketeers 93. The Cowboy Way 94, etc.

Sutton, Dudley (1933–).
British character actor.
The Leather Boys 63. Rotten to the Core 65. Crossplot 69. The Walking Stick 70. The Devils 71. The Pink Panther Strikes Again 76. Casanova 76. Valentino 77. The Big Sleep 78. Trail of the Pink Panther 82. Lamb 86. The Rainbow 88. Edward II 91. Orlando 92, etc.
TV series: Lovejoy 86, 90–95.

Sutton, Grady (1908–).
American character comedian usually seen as vacuous country cousin; in Hollywood from 1926.
The Story of Temple Drake 32. Alice Adams 35. Stage Door 37. Alexander's Ragtime Band 38. *The Bank Dick* 40. The Great Moment 44. My Wild Irish Rose 48. White Christmas 54. The Birds and the Bees 56. My Fair Lady 64. Paradise Hawaiian Style 66. The Great Bank Robbery 69. Myra Breckinridge 70. Support Your Local Gunfighter 71. Rock 'n' Roll High School 79, many others.
TV series: The Pruitts of Southampton 66.

Sutton, John (1908–1963).
British actor with stage experience; in Hollywood from 1937, usually as second lead or smooth swashbuckling villain.
Bulldog Drummond Comes Back 37. The Adventures of Robin Hood 38. The Invisible Man Returns 40. A Yank in the RAF 41. *Ten Gentlemen from West Point* 42. Jane Eyre 43. Claudia and David 46. The Three Musketeers 48. The Golden Hawk 52. East of Sumatra 54. The Bat 59, many others.

Suzman, Janet (1939–).
South African stage actress in Britain.
■ A Day in the Death of Joe Egg 70. *Nicholas and Alexandra* (AAN) 72. The Black Windmill 74. Voyage of the Damned 76. The House on Garibaldi Street (TV) 79. Nijinsky 80. The Priest of Love 81. The Draughtsman's Contract 82. And the Ship Sailed On 84. Mountbatten (as Edwina) (TV) 85. A Dry White Season 89. Nuns on the Run 90. Leon the Pig Farmer 93.

Svankmajer, Jan (1934–).
Czechoslovakian director with a disturbing and surreal turn of mind. His reputation has been made by a series of short films that mix live action with stop-motion animation.
Alice (Neco z Alenky) 88. Faust 94.

Svengali,
the evil genius of George du Maurier's Victorian romance *Trilby,* has been seen at least five times on-screen. In 1915 Wilton Lackaye and Clara Kimball Young appeared in a version under the title *Trilby.* There was a British one-reeler in 1922 in the 'Tense Moments with Great Authors' series, and in 1923 James Young directed a second Hollywood version with Arthur Edmund Carewe and Andrée Lafayette. In 1931, under the title *Svengali,* Archie Mayo directed a sound remake with John Barrymore as the hypnotist to Marian Marsh's heroine, and in 1954 Donald Wolfit and Hildegarde Neff appeared in a British version directed by Noel Langley. (Robert Newton had proved incapable of playing the lead.) In 1982 Peter O'Toole and Jodie Foster were in a dismal TV modernization set in New York.

Svenson, Bo (1941–).
American action lead.
The Great Waldo Pepper 75. Part Two Walking Tall 75. Special Delivery 76. Breaking Point 76. Final Chapter – Walking Tall 77. North Dallas Forty 79. Counterfeit Commandos 81. Heartbreak Ridge 86. The Delta Force 86. The Last Contract 86. Deep Space 87. Curse II: The Bite 88. The Kill Reflex 89. Soda Cracker 89. Primal Rage 90. Killer Mania 92. Three Days to a Kill 92, etc.

Swaim, Bob (1943–).
American director and screenwriter, based in France.
La Nuit de Saint-Germain-des-Prés 77. La Balance 82. Half Moon Street 86. Masquerade 88. L'Atlantide (w) 91, etc.

Swain, Mack (1876–1935).
American silent actor, a Mack Sennett heavy from 1914; most memorable in *The Gold Rush* 24. Last part, *Midnight Patrol* 32.

Swank, Hilary (1975–).
American actress, from television.
Buffy the Vampire Slayer 92. The Next Karate Kid 94.

Swanson, Gloria (1897–1983) (G. Svensson).
American leading lady of the silent screen who started as a Mack Sennett bathing beauty and made many comebacks.
The Meal Ticket 15. Teddy at the Throttle 17. The Pullman Bride 17. Shifting Sands 18. Don't Change Your Husband 18. *Male and Female* 19. Why Change Your Wife? 19. *The Affairs of Anatol* 21. Adam's Rib 23. Prodigal Daughters 23. Madame Sans Gêne 25. Untamed Lady 26. *Sadie Thompson* (AAN) 28. *Queen Kelly* (unfinished) 28. The Trespasser (AAN) 29. Indiscreet 31. Perfect Understanding 33. Music in the Air 34. Father Takes a Wife 41. *Sunset Boulevard* (AAN) 50. Three for Bedroom C 52. Nero's Mistress (It.) 56. Killer Bees (TV) 73. Airport 75 74, many others.

¶ I acquired my expensive tastes from Mr De Mille. – G.S.
When I die, my epitaph should read: she paid the bills. – G.S.
Dietrich's legs may be longer, but I have seven grandchildren. – G.S.

Famous line (*Sunset Boulevard,* when told she used to be a big star): 'I *am* big. It's the pictures that got small.'

Swanson, Kristy.
American leading actress.
Deadly Friend 86. Flowers in the Attic 87. Diving In 90. Dream Trap 90. Mannequin 2: On the Move 91. Hot Shots! 91. Highway to Hell 92. Buffy the Vampire Slayer 92. The Program 93. The Ref 94. The Chase 94, etc.
TV series: Knots Landing 87–88. Nightingales 89.

Swanson, Maureen (1932–).
British leading lady who retired to marry after a brief career.
Moulin Rouge 53. A Town Like Alice 56. The Spanish Gardener 56. Robbery under Arms 57. The Malpas Mystery 63, etc.

Swarthout, Gladys (1904–1969).
American opera singer who acted in a few films.
Rose of the Rancho 35. Give Us This Night 36. Champagne Waltz 37. Romance in the Dark 38. Ambush 39, etc.

swashbucklers
are films of period adventure in which the hero and villain usually settle the issue by a duel to the death. The greatest screen swashbucklers of all are probably Douglas Fairbanks Snr and Errol Flynn, but one should also be grateful for the efforts of Tyrone Power (*The Mark of Zorro*), Douglas Fairbanks Jnr (*Sinbad the Sailor*), Ronald Colman (*The Prisoner of Zenda*), Stewart Granger (*Scaramouche*), Rudolph Valentino (*The Eagle*), Gene Kelly (*The Three Musketeers*), Robert Donat (*The Count of Monte Cristo*), Louis Hayward (*The Man in the Iron Mask*), Cornel Wilde (*The Bandit of Sherwood Forest*), Tony Curtis (*The Purple Mask*) and their numerous imitators. The 1976 attempt to revive (or spoof) the genre in *Swashbuckler* was a sorry failure.

Swayze, Patrick (1952–).
American leading man, a former dancer.
■ Skatetown USA 79. The Outsiders 83. Uncommon Valor 83. Grandview USA 84. Red Dawn 84. Youngblood 85. North and South (TV) 86. Dirty Dancing 87. Steel Dawn 87. Tiger Warsaw 88. Road House 89. Next of Kin 89. Ghost 90. Point Break 91. City of Joy 92. Father Hood 93. To Wong Foo, Thanks for Everything, Julie Newmar 95.
TV series: Renegades 83. North and South 85.

Swedish cinema
was at the forefront of world production as early as 1910. Famous directors such as Victor Sjostrom and Mauritz Stiller were well known by 1912, and tended to make films of Swedish legends, which appealed by their very strangeness. *Sir Arne's Treasure* 19, *Thy Soul Shall Bear Witness* 20, *The Atonement of Gosta Berling* 24, are among the best-known titles of the Swedish silent period; but in the mid-20s all Sweden's best talent – including the newly discovered Greta Garbo – moved towards Hollywood and the home industry was eclipsed until the late 40s saw the appearance of talents like Werner (*Midvinterblot*), Sucksdorff (*Rhythm of a City*) and Sjoberg (*Frenzy*). In the 50s the Swedish vein of romantic pessimism was developed to its ultimate in the semi-mystic but commercial films of Ingmar Bergman, who remains the most significant name in Scandinavian cinema. In the 60s and 70s, Bo Widerberg, Vilgot Sjoman and Jan Troell established international reputations with widely differing styles. In the 80s and 90s, Lasse Hallstrom went to America to work following the success of his *My Life as a Dog,* and Bille August won the top prize at the Cannes Film Festival with *Pelle the Conqueror* and *Best Intentions,* from an autobiographical screenplay by Ingmar Bergman, both starring the distinguished Swedish actor Max von Sydow.

Sweeney, D. B. (1961–) (Daniel Bernard Sweeney).
American leading actor.
Fire with Fire 86. Gardens of Stone 87. No Man's Land 87. Eight Men Out 88. Memphis Belle 90. A Day in October (En Dag i Oktober) 91. Blue Desert 91. Heaven Is a Playground 91. Cutting Edge 92. Miss Rose White (TV) 92. Fire in the Sky 93. Hear No Evil 93, etc.

Sweet, Blanche (1895–1986) (Daphne Wayne).
American silent heroine.
The Lonedale Operator 11. Judith of Bethulia 13. The Secret Sin 15. The Deadliest Sex 20. In the Palace of the King 23. Anna Christie 23. Tess of the D'Urbervilles 24. Bluebeard's Seven Wives 26. Singed 27. The Woman Racket 30. The Silver Horde 30, etc.

Sweet, Dolph (1921–1985).
Barrel-chested American character actor.

The Young Doctors 61. The Lost Man 69. Fear
Is the Key 72. The Lords of Flatbush 74. Go Tell the
Spartans 77. Reds 81, etc.

TV series: The Trials of O'Brien 65–66. *Gimme
a Break* 81–85.

Swenson, Inga (1932–).
American actress.
■ Advise and Consent 61. The Miracle Worker 62.
Earth II (TV) 71. The Betsy 78.

TV series: Soap 78. Benson 79–86. Doctor,
Doctor 89–91.

Swerling, Jo (1897–) (Joseph Swerling).
Russian-American writer, long in Hollywood.

Dirigible 31. Platinum Blonde 32. Man's Castle
35. Made for Each Other 38. *The Westerner* 40.
Blood and Sand 42. The Pride of the Yankees (co-
w, AAN) 42. *Lifeboat* 44. Leave Her to Heaven 46.
Thunder in the East 52. King of the Roaring
Twenties 61, many others.

His son Jo Swerling Jnr (1931–) writes and
produces for TV.

Swift, David (1919–).
American radio and TV writer-producer-director
(TV series include *Mr Peepers, Grindl*).

Pollyanna 60. The Parent Trap 61. Love is a Ball
63. The Interns 63. Under the Yum Yum Tree 64.
Good Neighbour Sam 64. How to Succeed in
Business without Really Trying (wd, p) 67.
Candleshoe (co-w) 77, etc.

Swift, Jonathan (1667–1745).
Irish satirist best known for the much-filmed
Gulliver's Travels, which is *not* a children's book.

Swinburne, Nora (1902–) (Elinore Johnson).
British actress on stage from 1914, screen
occasionally from 1921.

Alibi 30. Potiphar's Wife 31. Fanny by Gaslight
43. *Quartet* 48. The River 51. The End of the Affair
55. Conspiracy of Hearts 59. Interlude 68. Up the
Chastity Belt 71, many others.

swinging London
was a myth, a creation of *Time* Magazine which
rebounded through the world's press and lasted
for several silly seasons from 1965. It also helped
British production finances by persuading
American impresarios that London was where the
action was, and its influence was felt in scores of
trendy and increasingly boring films, including
*Georgy Girl, Alfie, The Jokers, Kaleidoscope, Smashing
Time, Help!, The Knack, Blow Up, Casino Royale, I'll
Never Forget Whatshisname, To Sir with Love, Up the
Junction, Bedazzled, Poor Cow, The Strange Affair, Salt
and Pepper, Joanna, Darling* and *Otley*.

Swinton, Tilda (1961–).
British actress in experimental and low-budget
movies, most often to be seen in the films of
Derek Jarman.

Caravaggio 86. Aria 87. Friendship's Death 87.
The Last of England 87. War Requiem 88. Play
Me Something 89. The Garden 90. Edward II 91.
The Party (Nature Morte) 91. Man to Man 92.
Orlando 92. Wittgenstein 93, etc.

The Swiss Family Robinson.
The classic children's novel by Johann Wyss was
filmed in Hollywood in 1940 by Edward Ludwig,

with Thomas Mitchell, Edna Best, Freddie
Bartholomew, and Terry Kilburn. In 1960 Ken
Annakin remade it as a Disney spectacular, with
John Mills, Dorothy McGuire, James Macarthur,
and Tommy Kirk as the desert island castaways.

Swit, Loretta (1937–).
American comedy actress of the 70s, familiar as
Hot Lips Houlihan from TV's *M*A*S*H.*
■ Stand Up and Be Counted 72. Shirts/Skins (TV)
73. Freebie and the Bean 74. The Last Day (TV) 75.
Race with the Devil 75. The Hostage Heart (TV)
77. The Love Tapes (TV) 79. Cagney and Lacey (TV
pilot) 81. S.O.B. 81. The Kid from Nowhere (TV)
82. First Affair (TV) 83. The Execution (TV) 85.
Beer 85. Whoops Apocalypse 86.

Switzer, Carl ('Alfalfa') (1926–1959).
American boy actor of the 30s, a graduate of 'Our
Gang'; later in character roles. Died from a
gunshot wound in an argument over a $50 debt.

General Spanky 37. The War Against Mrs Hadley
42. State of the Union 48. Track of the Cat 54. The
Defiant Ones 58, many others.

Swofford, Ken.
Burly American character actor.

Father Goose 64. The Lawyer 69. One Little
Indian 73. Crisis at Sun Valley (TV) 78. Black
Roses 88. The Taking of Beverly Hills 91, etc.

TV series: Switch 75–76. Fame 83–85.

Syberberg, Hans-Jurgen (1935–).
German producer-director, mainly of
documentaries.

Scarabea 68. Ludwig – Requiem for a Virgin
King 72. Ludwig's Cook 72. Karl May 74.
Confessions of Winifred Wagner 75. Our Hitler
76–77. Parsifal 82. The Night (Die Nacht) 85, etc.

Sydney, Basil (1894–1968) (Basil Nugent).
British actor of heavy roles, on stage from 1911.

Romance (film debut) 20. The Midshipmaid 32.
The Tunnel 35. Rhodes of Africa 36. The Four
Just Men 39. Ships with Wings 41. Went the Day
Well? 42. *Caesar and Cleopatra* 45. The Man Within
47. *Hamlet* 48. Treasure Island 50. Ivanhoe 52. Hell
below Zero 54. The Dam Busters 55. The Three
Worlds of Gulliver 60, etc.

Sykes, Eric (1923–).
British TV comedian.

Invasion Quartet 61. Village of Daughters 62.
Kill or Cure 63. Heavens Above 63. The Bargee 63.
One-Way Pendulum 64. Those Magnificent Men
in Their Flying Machines 65. Rotten to the Core
65. The Liquidator 65. The Spy with a Cold Nose
67. The Plank (& d) 67. Shalako 68. Monte Carlo
or Bust 69. Rhubarb (& d) 70. Theatre of Blood
73. The Boys in Blue 83. Splitting Heirs 93, etc.

Sylbert, Richard (1928–).
American art director.

Baby Doll 56. Splendor in the Grass 61. Walk
on the Wild Side 62. The Manchurian Candidate
62. How to Murder Your Wife 64. Long Day's
Journey into Night 64. The Pawnbroker 64. Who's
Afraid of Virginia Woolf? (AA) 66. The Graduate
67. Rosemary's Baby 68. Catch 22 70. Carnal
Knowledge 71. The Day of the Dolphin 73. The
Fortune 75. Players 79. Reds (AAN) 81. Partners
82. Frances 82. The Cotton Club (AAN) 84. Under
the Cherry Moon 86. Shoot to Kill 88. Tequila
Sunrise 88. The Bonfire of the Vanities 90. Dick

Tracy (AA) 90. Mobsters 91. Ruby Cairo 93. Milk
Money 94, etc.

Sylvester.
The celebrated cartoon cat with the lisping Bronx
accent, always in pursuit of Tweetie Pie but never
quite managing to win, appeared from the 40s to
the 60s in Warner shorts, voiced by the inimitable
Mel Blanc.

Life with Feathers (AAN) 45. Tweetie Pie (AA)
47. Little Red Rodent Hood 52. Claws for Alarm 54.
Speedy Gonzales (AA) 55. Tabasco Road (AAN)
57. Mouse-Taken Identity 57. Birds Anonymous
(AA) 57. Trip for Tat 60. The Pied Piper of
Guadalupe (AAN) 61. Freudy Cat 64, etc.

Sylvester, William (1922–).
American leading man, in British films from 1949,
later back in US.

Give Us This Day 50. The Yellow Balloon 52.
Albert RN 53. High Tide at Noon 57. Gorgo 59.
Offbeat 60. Ring of Spies 63. Devil Doll 64. Devils
of Darkness 65. The Syndicate 67. The Hand of
Night 67. 2001: A Space Odyssey 68. Heaven Can
Wait 78, many others.

TV series: Gemini Man 76.

Sylvie (1883–1970) (Louise Sylvain).
French character actress.

Un Carnet de Bal 37. Le Corbeau 43. Le Diable
au Corps 46. Dieu a Besoin des Hommes 51. Nous
Sommes Tous des Assassins 56. *The Shameless Old
Lady* 64.

Syms, Sylvia (1934–).
British leading lady with brief stage and TV
experience.

My Teenage Daughter (film debut) 56. Ice Cold
in Alex 58. Flame in the Streets 60. Victim 61. The
Quare Fellow 62. The World Ten Times Over 63.
East of Sudan 64. Operation Crossbow 65. The
Big Job 65. Run Wild Run Free 69. Hostile Witness
70. Asylum 72. The Tamarind Seed 74. There
Goes the Bride 79. Absolute Beginners 86.
Intimate Contact (TV) 87. A Chorus of
Disapproval 89. Shirley Valentine 89. Shining
Through 92. Dirty Weekend 93. Staggered 94, etc.

synchronization.
The arranging of sound and picture to match. Only
rarely is this done by shooting them
simultaneously; the normal process involves re-
recording and much laboratory work to give the
optimum results.

Szabó, Ildikó (1951–).
Hungarian director, screenwriter, and costume
designer, a former leading actress.

Love Emilia (a) 70. The Old Time Soccer (Régi
Idők Focija) (a) 73. Hótréal (wd) 87. Child
Murders (Gyerekgyilkosságok) (wd, cost.) 93, etc.

Szabó, István (1938–).
Hungarian director.

Age of Illusion 65. Father 66. A Film about Love
70. 25 Firemen's Street 74. Tales of Budapest 77.
The Hungarians 78. Bizalom 79. *Mephisto* 81.
Colonel Redl 84. Hanussen 88. Meeting Venus 91.
Sweet Emma, Dear Bob (Edes Emma, Draga Bobe)
92, etc.

Szwarc, Jeannot (1936–).
French director in America.

Extreme Close Up 74. Bug 75. Jaws 2 78.
Somewhere in Time 80. Enigma 82. Supergirl 84.
Santa Claus 85. Honor Bound 91, etc.

Tachella, Jean-Charles (1925–).
French director and screenwriter. His *Cousin, Cousine* was remade by Joel Schumacher as *Cousins*.

Cousin, Cousine (AAN) 75. Blue Country (Le Pays Bleu) 77. Il y a Longtemps que Je t'Aime 79. Croque la Vie 81. Escalier C 85. Travelling Avant 87. Gallant Ladies (Dames Galantes) 91. The Man of My Life (L'Homme de Ma Vie) 92. Tous les Jours Dimanche 94, etc.

Tafler, Sidney (1916–1979).
British character actor on stage from 1936. He was married to actress Joy Shelton.

The Young Mr Pitt 42. The Bells Go Down 43. The Little Ballerina 46. It Always Rains on Sunday 47. Passport to Pimlico 48. Mystery Junction 51. Venetian Bird 53. The Sea Shall Not Have Them 55. *Carve Her Name with Pride* 58. Sink the Bismarck 60. The Bulldog Breed 61. The Seventh Dawn 64. *The Birthday Party* 69. The Adventures 71. The Spy Who Loved Me 77, many others.

Tait, Margaret (1919–).
Scottish director, writer, and poet. Born in Orkney, she first became a doctor, then studied film in Rome and began making short experimental films from the 50s. Her first full-length feature was released in 1993.

Blue Black Permanent 93.

Takacs, Tibor (1954–).
Canadian director of horror movies.

Metal Messiah 77. The Tomorrow Man 79. The Gate 87. Hardcover 88. I, Madman 89. The Gate 2 92. Earth Creature 92, etc.

Takakura, Ken.
Japanese leading actor, in international films.

The Yakuza 75. Station 81. Antarctica 84. Black Rain 89. Mr Baseball 92. 47 Ronin 94, etc.

take.
A take is a single recording of a scene during the making of a film. Sometimes one take is enough; but directors have been known to shoot as many as 50 before they are satisfied with the results.

Takei, George (1939–).
American character actor, best known for playing Sulu in *Star Trek*.

Ice Palace 60. Green Beret 68. Star Trek: The Motion Picture 80. Star Trek II: The Wrath of Khan 82. Star Trek III: The Search for Spock 83. Star Trek IV: The Voyage Home 86. Star Trek V: The Final Frontier 89. Star Trek VI: The Undiscovered Country 91. Prisoners of the Sun 91. Oblivion 94, etc.

TV series: Star Trek 66–69.

Takemitsu, Toru (1930–).
Japanese composer.

Juvenile Passions 58. Bad Boys 60. Seppuku 63. Woman of the Dunes 64. Kwaidan 64. Rebellion 67. Double Suicide 69. Dodes'ka'dan 70. The Petrified Forest 73. Himiko 75. Empire of Passion

80. Ran 85. Arashi Ga Oka 88. Black Rain 89. Rising Sun 93, etc.

Takeshi, Beat:
see *Kitano, Takeshi*.

Talalay, Rachel.
American director.

Freddy's Dead: The Final Nightmare 91. Ghost in the Machine 94.

Talbot, Lyle (1904–) (Lysle Hollywood).
Square-built American leading man and occasional heavy, busy from the early 30s.

Love Is a Racket 32. Three on a Match 32. Havana Widows 33. The Dragon Murder Case 34. Red Hot Tyres 35. Trapped by Television 36. Three Legionnaires 37. One Wild Night 38. Second Fiddle 39. Parole Fixer 40. Mexican Spitfire's Elephant 42. Up in Arms 44. Champagne for Caesar 50. With a Song in My Heart 52. There's No Business Like Show Business 54. The Great Man 56. Sunrise at Campobello 60, many others.

TV series: The Bob Cummings Show 55–59. Ozzie and Harriet 56–66.

Talbot, Nita (1930–).
Smart, wisecracking American comedienne of the 60s.

Bundle of Joy 56. Once upon a Horse 58. Who's Got the Action? 62. Girl Happy 65. That Funny Feeling 65. *A Very Special Favour* 65. The Cool Ones 67. Buck and the Preacher 71. The Day of the Locust 75. Serial 80. Night Shift 82. Frightmare 83. Take Two 87, etc.

TV series: Joe and Mabel 56. *Hot off the Wire* 60. *Here We Go Again* 71.

A Tale of Two Cities.
Apart from three very early one-reel versions, Dickens's novel of the French Revolution was filmed in 1917, with William Farnum, in 1926 with Maurice Costello and (as *The Only Way*) with Martin Harvey, in 1935, with Ronald Colman, and in 1958, with Dirk Bogarde.

Tales of Manhattan.
Julien Duvivier's 1942 film, a string of anecdotes linked by the travels of one tail-coat, can be credited with starting or revivifying the short-story compendium form, later developed in such movies as *Flesh and Fantasy, Quartet, Full House, The Story of Three Loves, It's a Great Country,* and many others. The film's inspiration was Duvivier's own *Un Carnet de Bal,* made in 1937, which gave him his ticket to Hollywood.

Taliaferro, Hal (1896–1980) (Floyd T. Alderson).
American stuntman who became a star of silent westerns under the name Wally Wales, then took another name for the years of his decline.

Western Hearts 21. Vanishing Hoofs 26. Saddle Mates 28. Overland Bound 29. Riders of the Cactus 31. Lone Bandit 33. Sagebrush Trail 33. Danger Trails 35. Way of the West 35. The Unknown Ranger 36. The Painted Stallion (serial) 37. Saga

of Death Valley 39. Young Bill Hickok 40. The Great Train Robbery 41. Riders of the Timberline 41. Sons of the Pioneers 42. The Yellow Rose of Texas 44. Zorro's Black Whip (serial) 44. Red River 48. West of Sonora 48. Junction City 51, many others.

talkies
caused the biggest revolution the film industry has known, and provoked critical resentment difficult to understand until one sees a very early talkie and realizes what a raucous and unpleasant experience it must have been until Hollywood caught up with itself. The main steps of development were as follows. In 1923 Lee de Forrest (qv) made primitive shorts. In 1926 Warners created Vitaphone, a disc process, and Fox pioneered sound on film with Movietone. Also in 1926 came *Don Juan*, the first film with synchronized music and effects. The first speaking and singing came in 1927 with Al Jolson in *The Jazz Singer*. In 1928 the first all-talking film, *Lights of New York*, set the seal of popular success on the new medium.

¶ The addition of sound to the movies was ridiculed and frantically opposed; but the industry needed the fresh impetus and at great expense the revolution was achieved.

No closer approach to resurrection has ever been made by science,

said Professor M. Pupin of the American Institute of Electrical Engineers. But it was years before he could claim perfect reproduction.

The tinkle of a glass, the shot of a revolver, a footfall on a hardwood floor, and the noise of a pack of cards being shuffled, all sounded about alike,

said Gilbert Seldes in 1929. And Tallulah Bankhead complained:

They made me sound as if I'd been castrated.

E.V. Lucas complained:

They are doing away with the greatest boon that has ever been offered to the deaf.

The distinguished documentarist Paul Rotha joined in the dismay:

A film in which the speech and sound effects are perfectly synchronized and coincide with their visual images on screen is absolutely contrary to the aims of the cinema. It is a degenerate and misguided attempt to destroy the real use of the film.

Nor was the prestige of the industry helped by claims of mathematical impossibility such as:

100% talking! 100% singing! 100% dancing!

But the public forgave all: the novelty value was tremendous, even though they missed a number of favourite stars whose voices proved unsuitable. As Jack Warner said:

Men and women whose names were known throughout the land disappeared as though they had been lost at sea.

And *Variety* summed up:

Talkies didn't do more to the industry than turn it upside down, shake the entire bag of tricks from its pocket, and advance Warner Brothers from last place to first in the league.

But Ernst Lubitsch took a more cynical view: You could name the great stars of the silent screen who were finished; the great directors, gone; the great title writers who were washed up. But remember this, as long as you live: the producers didn't lose a man. They all made the switch. That's where the great talent is.

Tally, Ted.

American screenwriter who can command $1 million for a script.

The Silence of the Lambs (AA) 90. Outbreak (co-w) 95.

Talmadge, Constance (1898–1973).

American silent heroine and comedienne, sister of Norma Talmadge.

Biography: 1978, *The Talmadge Girls* by Anita Loos.

Intolerance 15. Matrimaniac 16. The Honeymoon 17. Happiness à la Mode 19. Lessons in Love 21. Her Primitive Lover 22. The Goldfish 24. Her Sister from Paris 25. Venus 29, many others.

Talmadge, Natalie (1899–1969).

American leading lady of a few silent comedies; retired to marry Buster Keaton. Younger sister of Norma and Constance Talmadge.

Talmadge, Norma (1893/7–1957).

American silent heroine, sister of Constance Talmadge.

Battle Cry of Peace 14. Going Straight 15. Forbidden City 18. The Sign on the Door 21. Within the Law 23. Secrets 24. The Lady 25. Camille 27. The Dove 28. Dubarry Woman of Passion (last film) 30, many others.

Talmadge, Richard (1896–1981) (Ricardo Metzetti).

American stuntman of the 20s who doubled for Fairbanks, Lloyd, etc., and later became a star of action films such as *The Speed King, Laughing at Danger and Fighting Demon.* In the 30s became a director of stunt sequences, and more recently worked on *How the West Was Won, What's New Pussycat?, Hawaii* and *Casino Royale.*

Talman, William (1915–1968).

American character actor usually seen as a crook or cop: for seven years was well occupied in TV's *Perry Mason* series as the D.A. who never won a case.

Red Hot and Blue 49. The Armored Car Robbery 50. One Minute to Zero 52. *The Hitch Hiker* 52. City That Never Sleeps 53. This Man Is Armed 56. Two-Gun Lady 59. The Ballad of Josie 67.

Tamahori, Lee (1950–).

New Zealand director, from television, a former graphic artist and assistant director. His first feature broke box-office records in his homeland.

Once Were Warriors 94.

Tamba, Tetsuro (c. 1929–).

Japanese actor who has appeared in occidental films.

Bridge to the Sun 61. The Seventh Dawn 64. You Only Live Twice 67. The Five Man Army 70. Tange-Sazen 75. Tokyo Pop 88. A Taxing Woman Too 89, etc.

Tamblyn, Russ (1934–).

Buoyant American dancer and tumbler, in small film roles from 1949.

Father of the Bride 50. Father's Little Dividend

51. *Seven Brides for Seven Brothers* 54. Hit the Deck 55. Don't Go Near the Water 56. Peyton Place (AAN) 57. *Tom Thumb* 58. Cimarron 61. *West Side Story* 61. The Wonderful World of the Brothers Grimm 63. The Haunting 63. Son of a Gunfighter 65. Blood of Frankenstein 70. Win, Place or Steal 75. Black Heat 76. Human Highway 82. Phantom Empire 87. B.O.R.N. 88. Aftershock 88. Blood Screams 91. Cabin Boy 94, etc.

TV series: Twin Peaks 90, etc.

Tamiroff, Akim (1899–1972).

Russian leading character actor, in America from 1923.

Sadie McKee (film debut) 34. Lives of a Bengal Lancer 35. Naughty Marietta 35. China Seas 36. The Story of Louis Pasteur 36. *The General Died at Dawn* (AAN) 36. *The Great Gambini* 37. Spawn of the North 38. Union Pacific 39. Geronimo 40. *The Way of All Flesh* 40. The Great McGinty 40. The Corsican Brothers 41. *For Whom the Bell Tolls* (AAN) 43. The Bridge of San Luis Rey 44. A Scandal in Paris 46. The Gangster 47. My Girl Tisa 48. Outpost in Morocco 50. You Know What Sailors Are (GB) 53. Confidential Report 55. The Black Sleep 56. Me and the Colonel 57. Touch of Evil 58. Romanoff and Juliet 60. Topkapi 64. The Liquidator 65. Alphaville 65. Lord Jim 65. Lieut. Robin Crusoe 66. After the Fox 66. Great Catherine 68. Then Came Bronson (TV) 70, etc.

Tammy.

Cid Ricketts Sumner's romantic novel of a cheerful country girl was filmed in 1957 with Debbie Reynolds in the title role; two sequels, *Tammy Tell Me True* and *Tammy and the Doctor,* followed in 1961 and 1963 starring Sandra Dee; they were followed by a fourth film, *Tammy and the Millionaire,* in 1967, starring Debbie Watson.

Tanaka, Kinuyo (1907–1977).

Leading Japanese actress and occasional director. She was in films from 1924 and appeared in many of the films of Ozu and Mizoguchi. She turned down a marriage proposal from Mizoguchi because he tried to prevent her from becoming a director in the 50s.

Woman of Genroku Era (Genroku Onna) 24. I Graduated but . . . (Daigaku wa Detakeredo) 29. I Flunked, but . . . (Rakudai wa Shita Keredo) 30. Woman of Tokyo (Tokyo no Onna) 33. The Woman of That Night (Sono Yo no Onna) 34. Aisen Katsura 38. Army (Rikugun) 44. The Victory of Women (Josei no Shori) 46. Women of the Night (Yoru no Onnatachi) 48. The Munekata Sisters (Munekata Shimai) 50. Lady Musashino (Musashino Fujin) 51. The Life of Oharu (Saikaku Ichidai Onna) 52. Ugetsu (Ugetsu Monogatari) 52. Love Letter (Koibumi) (d) 53. Sansho the Bailiff (Sansho Dayu) 54. Moonrise (Tsuki wa Noborinu) (d) 55. Equinox Flower (Higanbana) 58. The Ballad of Narayama (Narayamabushi-ko) 58. Her Brother (Ototo) 59. Lonely Lane (Horoki) 62. Red Beard (Akahige) 65. Lullaby of the Earth (Daichi no Komoriuta) 76, many others.

Tandy, Jessica (1909–1994).

British-born actress. She was married to actor Jack Hawkins (1932–40) and married actor Hume Cronyn in 1942.

The Seventh Cross 44. Dragonwyck 46. The Green Years 46. Forever Amber 48. A Woman's Vengeance 48. Rommel, Desert Fox 51. The Light in the Forest 58. Hemingway's Adventures of a Young Man 62. The Birds 63. Butley 73. The World According to Garp 82. Still of the Night 82. Best Friends 82. The Bostonians 84. Cocoon 85. Batteries Not Included 87. Cocoon: The Return

88. Driving Miss Daisy (AA) 89. Fried Green Tomatoes at the Whistle Stop Café (AAN) 92. Used People 92. Camilla 93. To Dance with the White Dog (TV) 93. Nobody's Fool 94, etc.

Tangerine Dream.

German rock band, using electronic instruments, which has contributed scores to more than 20 movies and TV films.

Sorcerer 77. Kneuss 78. Risky Business 83. The Keep 83. Flashpoint 84. Firestarter 84. Near Dark 87. Kamikaze 87. Miracle Mile 88. Catch Me If You Can 89. Rainbow 90. Highway to Hell 91, etc.

Tani, Yoko (1932–).

Japanese leading lady, in international films.

The Wind Cannot Read 57. The Quiet American 58. Savage Innocents 59. Piccadilly Third Stop 60. Marco Polo 61. Who's Been Sleeping in My Bed? 63. Invasion 66, etc.

Tanner, Alain (1929–).

Swiss director.

Jonah Who Will Be 25 in the Year 2000 76. Messidor 78. Light Years Away 81. In the White City 82. No Man's Land 85. La Vallée Fantôme 87. Une Flamme dans Mon Coeur 87. The Woman of Rose Hill (La Femme de Rose Hill) 89. The Man Who Lost His Shadow (L'Homme Qui a Perdu Son Ombre) 91. The Diary of Lady M (Le Journal de Lady M) 93, etc.

Tanner, Peter (1914–).

British editor.

Lady from Lisbon 42. Scott of the Antarctic 48. Kind Hearts and Coronets 49. The Blue Lamp 50. Secret People 52. Lease of Life 54. The Night My Number Came Up 55. Man in the Sky 57. Light up the Sky 60. Sodom and Gomorrah 61. A Jolly Bad Fellow 64. Diamonds for Breakfast 68. The House that Dripped Blood 71. Asylum 72. Hedda 75. Nasty Habits 76. Stevie 78. The Monster Club 81. Turtle Diary 85. Sky Bandits 86. Hamburger Hill 87. Without a Clue 88. Danny, Champion of the World 89, etc.

Tanner, Tony (1932–).

British light actor and revue artiste.

Strictly for the Birds 64. A Home of Your Own 65. The Pleasure Girls 65. Stop the World I Want to Get Off 66, etc.

Tapley, Colin (1911–).

New Zealand character actor who has played a few stalwart types in international pictures.

Search for Beauty 34. The Black Room 35. Samson and Delilah 49. Angels One Five 52. The Dam Busters 56. Fraulein Doktor 68, etc.

Taradash, Daniel (1913–).

American screenwriter.

Golden Boy 39. Rancho Notorious 48. *From Here to Eternity* (AA) 53. Désirée 54. Storm Centre (& d) 55. Picnic 55. Bell, Book and Candle 58. Morituri 65. Hawaii 66. Doctors' Wives 71. The Other Side of Midnight (co-w) 77, etc.

Tarantino, Quentin (1963–).

American director, screenwriter, and actor, with an encyclopaedic knowledge of old movies and a liking for junk culture. *Pulp Fiction* won the Palme d'Or at the Cannes Film Festival in 1994.

Reservoir Dogs (a, wd) 91. True Romance (w) 93. Killing Zoe (p) 94. Sleep with Me (a) 94. *Pulp Fiction* (a, wd) 94. Natural Born Killers (w) 94. Crimson Tide (co-w) 95.

Violence in the movies? It's fun, it's one of the coolest, funnest things for me to watch. – *Q.T.*
If you say you don't like violence in movies, it's like saying you don't like slapstick comedy or dance sequences in movies. – *Q.T.*
I've got so many movies I would like to make. I've got my western, my World War II bunch of guys on a mission, my spaghetti western, my horror film. But since I know I won't live long enough to do all the movies I want to do, with every movie the goal is to wipe out as many as I can. – *Q.T.*
I steal from every movie ever made. – *Q.T.*
I find the sensibility at work in a film like *Reservoir Dogs* absolutely appalling. – *John Duigan*

Tarkington, Booth (1869–1946).
American novelist. Films of his books include *Alice Adams, Penrod, Monsieur Beaucaire, The Magnificent Ambersons*.

Tarkovsky, Andrei (1932–1986).
Russian director.
Autobiography: 1991, *Time within Time: The Diaries 1970–1986*.
■ There Will Be No Leave Tonight (short) 59. Violin and Roller 61. Ivan's Childhood 62. *Andrei Rublev* 66. Solaris 72. Mirror 78. Nostalgia 83.

Tarzan.
The brawny jungle hero, an English milord lost in Africa as a child and who grew up with the apes, was a creation of novelist Edgar Rice Burroughs (1875–1950); the first Tarzan story was published in 1913. The films quickly followed. *Tarzan of the Apes* 18 starred Elmo Lincoln with Enid Markey as Jane; so did *Romance of Tarzan* 18. *The Return of Tarzan* 20 had Gene Pollar and Karla Schramm. *Son of Tarzan* 20 was a serial with Kamuela C. Searle in the title role; Tarzan was P. Dempsey Tabler, Elmo Lincoln returned in another serial, *The Adventures of Tarzan* 21, with Louise Lorraine. *Tarzan and the Golden Lion* 27 starred James Pierce and Dorothy Dunbar. Another serial, *Tarzan the Mighty* 28, had Frank Merrill and no Jane; a runner-up, *Tarzan the Tiger* 30, had the same crew. In 1932 came Johnny Weissmuller in the first of MGM's long line of Tarzan pictures: *Tarzan the Ape Man*, with Maureen O'Sullivan as Jane. There followed *Tarzan and His Mate* 34, *Tarzan Escapes* 36, *Tarzan Finds a Son* 39, *Tarzan's Secret Treasure* 41, and *Tarzan's New York Adventure* 42. Meanwhile in 1935 an independent company had made a serial starring Herman Brix which was later released as two features, *Tarzan and the Green Goddess* and *New Adventures of Tarzan*; and in 1933 producer Sol Lesser had started his Tarzan series with *Tarzan the Fearless*, starring Buster Crabbe; he followed this up with *Tarzan's Revenge* 38 starring Glenn Morris. In 1943 Lesser took over Weissmuller (but not O'Sullivan or any other Jane) for *Tarzan Triumphs*, followed by *Tarzan's Desert Mystery* 44, *Tarzan and the Amazons* (reintroducing Jane in the shape of Brenda Joyce) 45, *Tarzan and the Leopard Woman* 46, *Tarzan and the Huntress* 47, and *Tarzan and the Mermaids* 48. Then Weissmuller was replaced by Lex Barker for *Tarzan's Magic Fountain* 48, *Tarzan and the Slave Girl* 49, *Tarzan's Peril* 50, *Tarzan's Savage Fury* 51, and *Tarzan and the She-Devil* 52. Gordon Scott next undertook the chore in *Tarzan's Hidden Jungle* 55, *Tarzan and the Lost Safari* 57, *Tarzan's Fight for Life* 58, *Tarzan's Greatest Adventure* 59 and *Tarzan the Magnificent* 60. MGM now remade *Tarzan the Ape Man* 60 starring Denny Miller; and, with Jock Mahoney, *Tarzan Goes to India* 62 and National General presented *Tarzan's Three Challenges* 64. There followed *Tarzan and the Valley of Gold* 66,

Tarzan and the Great River 67, and *Tarzan and the Jungle Boy* 68, all with Mike Henry. A 1982 remake of *Tarzan the Ape Man* had Miles O'Keeffe in the role but concentrated on the charms of Bo Derek as Jane; however, in 1984 *Greystoke* set the record straight by remaining slightly more faithful to Burroughs' original legend. A 1966–67 TV series starred Ron Ely.

Tashlin, Frank (1913–1972).
American comedy writer-director, former cartoonist.
The Fuller Brush Man (w) 48. *The Paleface* (w) 48. The Good Humour Man (w) 50. Kill the Umpire (w) 51. Susan Slept Here (d) 54. Artists and Models (wd) 55. *The Girl Can't Help It* (wd, p) 57. Will Success Spoil Rock Hunter? (wd, p) 57. Rockabye Baby (wd) 58. Say One for Me (p, d) 59. Cinderfella (wd) 60. It's Only Money (d) 63. The Man from the Diners Club (d) 64. The Alphabet Murders (d) 65. The Glass Bottom Boat (d) 66. Caprice (d) 67. The Private Navy of Sgt O'Farrell (wd) 68, etc.

Tashman, Lilyan (1899–1934).
American silent screen sophisticate.
Experience 21. Manhandled 24. Don't Tell the Wife 27. New York Nights 29. Murder by the Clock 31. Scarlet Dawn 32. Frankie and Johnny 33, etc.

Tass, Nadia (1956–   ) (Nadia Tassopolous).
Greek-born director and producer, in Australia.
Malcolm 86. Rikky and Pete 88. The Big Steal 90. Over the Hill 90. Pure Luck 91. Stark (TV) 93, etc.

Tate, Harry (1872–1940) (Ronald MacDonald Hutchinson).
British music-hall comedian famous for motoring sketch. In occasional films.
Motoring 27. Her First Affair 32. Happy 34. Midshipman Easy 35. Hyde Park Corner 35. Keep Your Seats Please 36. Wings of the Morning 37, etc.
~Catchphrase: How's your father?

Tate, Reginald (1896–1955).
British character actor, mainly on stage.
Riverside Murder 35. Dark Journey 37. Next of Kin 42. The Life and Death of Colonel Blimp 43. Uncle Silas 47. Robin Hood 52. King's Rhapsody 55, etc.

Tate, Sharon (1943–1969).
American leading lady, victim of a sensational murder. She was married to director Roman Polanski.
Eye of the Devil 67. The Fearless Vampire Killers 67. Valley of the Dolls 67. Don't Make Waves 67. Wrecking Crew 69, etc.

Tati, Jacques (1908–1982) (Jacques Tatischeff).
French pantomimist and actor who after years in the music halls and in small film roles began to write and direct his own quiet comedies which were really little more than strings of sight gags on a theme.
Book: 1976, *Jacques Tati* by Penelope Gilliatt.
■ *Jour de Fête* 49. *Monsieur Hulot's Holiday* (AANw) 52. Mon Oncle 58. Playtime 68. Traffic 71. Parade (TV) 74.
¶ M. Hulot is a real character, not a movie star because he's not a star. He's the opposite of the person created by Chaplin, Keaton and so on. He's not a gag man, he's not a clown; he's someone you recognise more from his back than from the front. – *J.T.*

The public always like the picture you have done before. They always see a new picture and say, his last was much funnier. – *J.T.*
I'm part of the old school. I'm the last who had the chance to learn in the music hall. That school is now closed. The singers and the sound engineers have taken over. – *J.T.*
~Tati also appeared in several shorts, and played the ghost in *Sylvie et le Fantôme* 47.

Taube, Sven-Bertil (1934–   ).
Swedish leading man.
The Buttercup Chain 70. Puppet on a Chain 70. The Eagle Has Landed 76. Game for Vultures 79. Handera 94, etc.

Tauber, Richard (1892–1948).
Austrian operatic tenor, long in Britain where he made a number of artless but likeable musical comedy films.
Biography: 1959, *My Heart and I* by Diana Napier Tauber.
Symphony of Love 31. Blossom Time 34. Heart's Desire 35. Land without Music 35. Pagliacci 36. The Lisbon Story 45, etc.

Taurog, Norman (1899–1981).
American director, former child actor, in Hollywood from 1917.
Lucky Boy 28. *Skippy* (AA) 31. Huckleberry Finn 33. We're Not Dressing 34. Mrs Wiggs of the Cabbage Patch 35. Strike Me Pink 36. *Mad about Music* 38. The Adventures of Tom Sawyer 38. Boys' Town (AAN) 38. Broadway Melody of 1940 40. Young Tom Edison 40. A Yank at Eton 42. Girl Crazy 42. The Hoodlum Saint 46. The Bride Goes Wild 48. Please Believe Me 50. Room for One More 52. Living It Up 54. The Birds and the Bees 56. Bundle of Joy 57. Don't Give Up the Ship 59. Palm Springs Weekend 63. Tickle Me 65. Sergeant Deadhead 65. Speedway 67, many others.

Tavernier, Bertrand (1941–   ).
French director and screenwriter.
■ *The Watchmaker of St Paul* 74. Que la Fête Commence 75. The Judge and the Assassin 76. Spoiled Children 77. Death Watch 80. Coup de Torchon 82. A Week's Vacation 82. Mississippi Blues 83. *Sunday in the Country* 84. 'Round Midnight 86. Beatrice (La Passion Béatrice) 86. La Vie et Rien d'Autre 89. These Foolish Things (Daddy Nostalgie) 90. The Undeclared War (La Guerre sans Nom) (doc) 91. L.627 (wd) 92. La Fille de D'Artagnan (wd) 94.

Taviani, Paolo (1931–   ) and **Vittorio** (1929–   ).
Italian brother directors who always work together.
■ A Man of Bruciare 62. Sovversivi 67. Beneath the Sign of the Scorpion 69. St Michael Had a Rooster 71. Allonsanfan 74. *Padre Padrone* 77. The Field 79. Night of the Shooting Stars 81. Kaos 84. Good Morning Babylon 87. Night Sun (Il Sole Anche di Notte) 90. Wild Flower (Fiorile) 93.

Tavoularis, Dean (1932–   ).
American production designer who trained as an architect and also worked as an animator for Disney.
Bonnie and Clyde 67. Candy 68. Zabriskie Point 70. Little Big Man 70. The Godfather 72. The Conversation 74. The Godfather Part II (AA) 74. Farewell My Lovely 75. The Missouri Breaks 76. Brinks 79. Apocalypse Now (AAN) 79. Hammett 82. One from the Heart 82. The Outsiders 83. Rumble Fish 83. Peggy Sue Got Married 86. A Man in Love 87. Gardens of Stone 87. Tucker: The Man and His Dream 88. New York Stories 89. The

Godfather Part III 90. Final Analysis 92. Rising Sun 93. I Love Trouble 94, etc.

Tayback, Vic (1929–1990).
Tough-looking American supporting actor.
Bullitt 68. With Six You Get Egg Roll 68. Lepke 73. Alice Doesn't Live Here Any More 74. Thunderbolt and Lightfoot 75. No Deposit No Return 76. The Choirboys 77. The Great American Traffic Jam (TV) 80. Rage (TV) 80. Mysterious Two (TV) 82. Weekend Warriors 86. Criminal Act 88. Beverly Hills Bodysnatchers 89. Treasure Island 91, etc.
TV series: Alice 76–85.

Taylor, Alma (1895–1974).
British actress of the silent screen.
The Little Milliner and the Thief 09. Oliver Twist 12. Paying the Penalty 13. The Baby on the Barge 15. Annie Laurie 16. The American Heiress 17. Sunken Rocks 19. Alf's Button 20. The Tinted Venus 21. Comin' thro' the Rye 23. The Shadow of Egypt 24. Quinneys 27. Bachelor's Baby 32. Things are Looking Up 35. Lilacs in the Spring 54. Blue Murder at St Trinian's 57, etc.

Taylor, Deems (1886–1966).
American journalist and musician whose chief connection with films was to act as narrator for *Fantasia* 40 and to help write *A Pictorial History of the Movies* 48.

Taylor, Don (1920–).
American director, a former light leading man, with stage experience. His third wife is actress Hazel Court.
Naked City 48. For the Love of Mary 48. Ambush 49. Father of the Bride 50. Submarine Command 51. The Blue Veil 51. Stalag 17 53. Men of Sherwood Forest 54. I'll Cry Tomorrow 57. Savage Guns 62, etc.
AS DIRECTOR: The Savage Guns 62. Ride the Wild Surf 64. Jack of Diamonds 67. The Five Man Army 70. Escape from the Planet of the Apes 71. Tom Sawyer 73. Echoes of a Summer 75. The Great Scout and Cathouse Thursday 76. The Island of Dr Moreau 77. Damien – Omen II 78. The Final Countdown 80. My Wicked, Wicked Ways (TV) 85. Secret Weapons (TV) 85. The Diamond Trap (TV) 88, etc.

Taylor, Elaine.
British leading lady.
Casino Royale 67. Half a Sixpence 68. Diamonds for Breakfast 68. The Anniversary 68. The Games 69. All the Way Up 70, etc.

Taylor, Elizabeth (1932–).
British-born leading lady with a well-publicized private life. Was evacuated to Hollywood during World War II and began as a child star. Scored nine husbands so far, including actor Michael Wilding (1952–57), producer Mike Todd (1957–58), singer Eddie Fisher (1959–64), and actor Richard Burton (1954–74 and 1975–76).
Biographies: 1981, *Elizabeth Taylor: The Last Star* by Kitty Kelley. 1991, *Elizabeth* by Alexander Walker.
■ There's One Born Every Minute 42. Lassie Come Home 43. Jane Eyre 43. The White Cliffs of Dover 44. *National Velvet* 44. Courage of Lassie 45. Cynthia 47. Life with Father 47. A Date with Judy 48. Julia Misbehaves 48. *Little Women* 49. Conspirator 49. The Big Hangover 49. *Father of the Bride* 50. Father's Little Dividend 51. Quo Vadis 51. Love is Better Than Ever 51. *A Place in the Sun* 51. The Light Fantastic 51. Ivanhoe 52. The Girl Who Had Everything 53. Rhapsody 54. Elephant

Walk 54. Beau Brummell 54. The Last Time I Saw Paris 55. *Giant* 56. *Raintree County* (AAN) 57. *Cat on a Hot Tin Roof* (AAN) 58. *Suddenly Last Summer* (AAN) 59. *Butterfield 8* (AA) 60. Scent of Mystery 60. *Cleopatra* 62. The VIPs 63. The Sandpiper 65. *Who's Afraid of Virginia Woolf?* (AA) 66. The Taming of the Shrew 67. Doctor Faustus 67. The Comedians 67. Reflections in a Golden Eye 67. Boom 68. Secret Ceremony 68. The Only Game in Town 69. Under Milk Wood 71. Zee and Co 71. Hammersmith is Out 72. Divorce His, Divorce Hers (TV) 72. Night Watch 73. Ash Wednesday 73. The Driver's Seat 75. The Blue Bird 76. Victory at Entebbe (TV) 76. A Little Night Music 77. Repeat Performance (TV) 78. The Mirror Crack'd 80. Between Friends (TV) 82. Malice in Wonderland (TV) 84. There Must Be a Pony (TV) 86. Poker Alice (TV) 87. Sweet Bird of Youth (TV) 89. The Flintstones 94.

¶ I don't pretend to be an ordinary housewife.
– E.T.
A pharaonic mummy, moving on tiny castors like a touring replica of the Queen Mother.
– Sunday Times on E.T. in The Mirror Crack'd
If someone's dumb enough to offer me a million dollars to make a picture, I'm certainly not dumb enough to turn it down. – E.T.
I believe in mind over matter and doing anything you set your mind on. – E.T.
Is she fat? Her favourite food is seconds. – Joan Rivers
She should get a divorce and settle down. – Jack Paar
There are three things I never saw Elizabeth Taylor do. Tell a lie; be unkind to anyone; and be on time. – Mike Nichols

Famous line (*Reflections in a Golden Eye*): 'She cut off her nipples with garden shears. You call that normal?'

Taylor, Estelle (1899–1958) (Estelle Boylan).
American stage actress who made some silent films.
While New York Sleeps 22. The Ten Commandments 23. Don Juan 26. The Whip Woman 27. When East is East 28, etc.

Taylor, Gilbert (1914–).
British cinematographer, in films since 1929.
The Guinea Pig 48. Seven Days to Noon 50. The Yellow Balloon 52. It's Great To Be Young 55. The Good Companions 57. Ice Cold in Alex 58. The Rebel 60. Dr Strangelove 63. Repulsion 65. The Bedford Incident 65. Before Winter Comes 69. Macbeth 71. Frenzy 72. The Omen 76. *Star Wars* (AAN) 77. Dracula 79. Flash Gordon 80. Green Ice 81. Venom 82. Losin' It 82. Lassiter 84. The Bedroom Window 87, etc.

Taylor, Jud (1940–).
American director.
Weekend of Terror (TV) 70. Revenge (TV) 71. Heat of Anger (TV) 72. Say Goodbye Maggie Cole (TV) 72. Hawkins on Murder (TV) 73. Winter Kill (TV) 74. Future Cop (TV) 76. Return to Earth (TV) 76. Tail Gunner Joe (TV) 77. Mary White (TV) 77. Flesh and Blood (TV) 80. Packin' It In (TV) 83. Licence to Kill (TV) 84. Out of the Darkness (TV) 85. Foxfire (TV) 87. The Great Escape II: The Untold Story (TV) 88, etc.

Taylor, Kent (1907–1987) (Louis Weiss).
Suave American leading man of second features from the early 30s.
Two Kinds of Women 32. I'm No Angel 33. Double Door 34. Two Fisted 35. The Accusing

Finger 36. The Jury's Secret 37. I Take this Woman 40. Frisco Lil 42. Bombers Moon 43. The Daltons Ride Again 45. The Crimson Key 47. Payment on Demand 51. Playgirl 54. Slightly Scarlet 56. Ghost Town 56. Harbour Lights 64. The Day Mars Invaded Earth 64. Smashing the Crime Syndicate 73, etc.
TV series: Boston Blackie 51–52.

Taylor, Laurette (1884–1946) (Laurette Cooney).
American stage leading lady who filmed her great success Peg O' My Heart 22 and stayed in Hollywood for a few more silent films: Happiness, One Night in Rome, etc. She was the model for actress Judith Bliss in Noël Coward's Hay Fever.

Taylor, Lili (1967–).
American actress.
Mystic Pizza 88. Say Anything 89. Bright Angel 91. Dogfight 91. Watch It 93. Mrs Parker and the Vicious Circle 94, etc.

Taylor, Noah.
Australian actor who played the adolescent boy in John Duigan's The Year My Voice Broke and its sequel Flirting.
The Year My Voice Broke 87. Flirting 89. The Prisoner of St Petersburg 90. The Nostradamus Kid 93, etc.

Taylor, Peter (1922–).
British editor.
Devil Girl from Mars 54. Summer Madness 55. The Man Who Never Was 55. The Bridge on the River Kwai (AA) 57. The Devil's Daffodil 61. Waltz of the Toreadors 62. This Sporting Life 63. Judith 66. The Taming of the Shrew 67. Monte Carlo or Bust 69. La Traviata 83. Otello 85. The Penitent 88, etc.

Taylor, Robert (1911–1969) (Spangler Arlington Brugh).
Durable American leading man signed by MGM while still a medical student. His boyish good looks turned rather set and grim in middle age, but he remained a star.
■ Handy Andy 34. There's Always Tomorrow 34. Wicked Woman 34. Society Doctor 34. West Point of the Air 35. Times Square Lady 35. Murder in the Fleet 35. Magnificent Obsession 35. Broadway Melody of 1936 36. Small Town Girl 36. Private Number 36. His Brother's Wife 36. The Gorgeous Hussy 36. Camille 36. Personal Property 37. This is My Affair 37. Broadway Melody of 1938. A Yank at Oxford 38. Three Comrades 38. The Crowd Roars 38. Stand Up and Fight 39. Lucky Night 39. Lady of the Tropics 39. Remember 39. Waterloo Bridge 40. Escape 40. Flight Command 40. Billy the Kid 41. When Ladies Meet 41. Johnny Eager 42. Her Cardboard Lover 42. Stand By for Action 43. Bataan 43. Song of Russia 44. Undercurrent 46. High Wall 47. The Bribe 49. Ambush 49. Devil's Doorway 50. Conspirator 50. Quo Vadis 51. Westward the Women 51. Ivanhoe 52. Above and Beyond 52. Ride Vaquero 53. All the Brothers were Valiant 53. Knights of the Round Table 53. Valley of the Kings 54. Rogue Cop 54. Many Rivers to Cross 55. Quentin Durward 55. The Last Hunt 56. D-Day Sixth of June 56. The Power and the Prize 56. Tip on a Dead Jockey 57. Saddle the Wind 58. The Law and Jake Wade 58. Party Girl 58. The Hangman 59. The House of the Seven Hawks 59. Killers of Kilimanjaro 60. The Miracle of the White Stallions 61. Cattle King 63. A House is Not a Home 64. The Night Walker 65. Savage Pampas 66. The Return of the Gunfighter 66. Johnny Tiger 66. Where Angels Go Trouble Follows 68.

he Day the Hot Line Got Hot 68. Devil May Care 8. The Glass Sphinx 68.

TV series: *The Detectives* 59–61.

I was a punk kid from Nebraska who had an awful lot of the world's good things tossed in s lap. – *R.T.*

For 17 years it was Mr Mayer who guided me, nd I never turned down a picture that he ersonally asked me to do. – *R.T.*

aylor, Rod (1930–) (Rodney Sturt Taylor).
ustralian-born, Hollywood-based leading man with stage experience.

King of the Coral Sea 54. Long John Silver 55. he Catered Affair 56. Giant 56. Raintree County 7. Separate Tables 58. *The Time Machine* 60. *The irds* 63. *The VIPs* 63. Sunday in New York 63. Fate s the Hunter 64. *Thirty-Six Hours* 64. Young assidy 65. Do Not Disturb 65. The Liquidator 65. he Glass Bottom Boat 66. Hotel 67. Dark of the un 67. Chuka 67. Nobody Runs Forever 68. The lell with Heroes 69. The Man Who Had Power)ver Women 70. Darker than Amber 70. The Train Robbers 72. Family Flight (TV) 72. Trader Horn '3. Deadly Trackers 73. Shamus (TV) 73. The leroes 75. The Picture Show Man 77. An Eye for n Eye 78. On the Run 82. Masquerade (TV) 83. Marbella 85. Mask of Murder 89, etc.

TV series: Hong Kong 60. Bearcats 71. The)regon Trail 75.

aylor, Ronnie.
British cinematographer who won an Oscar for *Gandhi*.

Circle of Iron 79. Savage Harvest 81. Gandhi AA) 82. High Road to China 83. A Chorus Line 85. Foreign Body 86. Cry Freedom 87. Sea of Love)0. Popcorn 91, etc.

Taylor, Sam (1895–1958).
American screenwriter of the 20s: *The Freshman, Exit Smiling*, etc. Remembered chiefly for the credit line to the 1928 version of *The Taming of the Shrew*: 'By William Shakespeare, with additional dialogue by Sam Taylor.'

Taylor-Young, Leigh (1944–).
American leading lady of the early 70s.
I Love You Alice B. Toklas 68. The Big Bounce 68. The Adventurers 69. The Buttercup Chain 70. The Horsemen 71. The Gang that Couldn't Shoot Straight 72. Soylent Green 73. Can't Stop the Music 80. Looker 81. Napoleon and Josephine: A Love Story (TV) 87. Who Gets the Friends (TV) 88.

Tazieff, Haroun (1914–).
French explorer-photographer, best known for *Rendezvous du Diable (Volcano)* 58, *The Forbidden Volcano* 67.

Tcherina, Ludmilla (1925–) (Monique Tchemerzine).
French ballerina.
The Red Shoes 48. Tales of Hoffman 50. Sign of the Pagan 54. Oh Rosalinda 55. Honeymoon 59. A Ravishing Idiot 63, etc.

teachers
have been notably played by Robert Donat in *Goodbye Mr Chips*; Jennifer Jones in *Good Morning Miss Dove*; Greer Garson in *Her Twelve Men*; Michael Redgrave in *The Browning Version*; Aline MacMahon in *Back Door to Heaven*; Claudette Colbert in *Remember the Day*; Bette Davis in *The Corn Is Green*; Jack Hawkins in *Mandy*; Judy Garland in *A Child Is Waiting*; Anne Bancroft in *The Miracle Worker*; Shirley Maclaine in *Spinster*; Glenn Ford in *The Blackboard Jungle*; Sidney Poitier in *To Sir With Love*; Sandy Dennis in *Up the Down Staircase*; Dorothy Dandridge in *Bright Road*; Max Bygraves in *Spare the Rod*; Otto Kruger in *The Housemaster*; Cecil Trouncer in *The Guinea Pig*; Maggie Smith in *The Prime of Miss Jean Brodie*; Joanne Woodward in *Rachel, Rachel*; Robert Mitchum in *Ryan's Daughter*; Laurence Olivier in *Term of Trial*; Richard Todd in *The Love-Ins*; James Whitmore in *The Harrad Experiment*; David Hemmings in *Unman, Wittering and Zigo*; Per Oscarsson in *Who Saw Him Die?* James Mason in *Child's Play*; Glenda Jackson in *The Class of Miss MacMichael*; Michael Ontkean in *Willie and Phil*; Perry King in *Class of 1984*, harassed by his pupils. In *Class of 1999*, the teachers got their revenge – they turned out to be androids equipped with military hardware. J. Eddie Peck taught by day and danced all night in *Lambada* so he could teach maths to his slum students. In the more inspiring *Stand and Deliver*, based on a true story, Edward James Olmos forced his pupils to succeed against the odds.

Comic teachers were to the fore in *Boys Will Be Boys* (Will Hay, the best of them all); the *St Trinian's* films; *Carry On Teacher*; *Old Mother Riley Headmistress*; *Bottoms Up* (Jimmy Edwards); *Fun at St Fanny's* (Fred Emney); *The Happiest Days of Your Lives*; *Please Sir*; and *Vice Versa* (James Robertson Justice).

See also: *schools*.

Teagarden, Jack (1906–1964).
American jazz trombonist and singer who made occasional film appearances, among which the highlight is his performance of the Johnny Mercer song 'The Waiter and the Porter and the Upstairs Maid' with Bing Crosby and Mary Martin in *Birth of the Blues*.

Birth of the Blues 41. Glory Alley 52. The Glass Wall 53. Jazz on a Summer's Day 60.

Teague, Lewis (1941–).
American director who began as an editor for Roger Corman's productions.
The Lady in Red 79. Alligator 80. Death Vengeance 82. Fighting Back 82. Cujo 83. The Jewel of the Nile 85. Stephen King's Cat's Eye 85. Collision Course 90. Navy SEALS 90. Wedlock 90. T Bone 'n' Weasel (TV) 92, etc.

Teal, Ray (1902–1976).
American character actor often seen as sheriff, good or bad. In films from 1938 after stage experience.

The Cherokee Strip 40. A Wing and a Prayer 44. Captain Kidd 45. Joan of Arc 48. The Men 50. *Ace in the Hole* 51. The Lion and the Horse 53. Montana Belle 53. Hangman's Knot 54. Ambush at Tomahawk Gap 54. Run for Cover 55. The Indian Fighter 55. Saddle the Wind 57. One-Eyed Jacks 61. Cattle King 63. Taggart 64. The Liberation of L. B. Jones 71, many others.

TV series: Bonanza 59–71.

teams:
see *romantic teams*.

Tearle, Conway (1878–1938) (Frederick Levy).
American leading actor of silent days; half-brother of Godfrey Tearle.

Stella Maris 18. The Virtuous Vamp 20. Woman of Bronze 23. Bella Donna 25. Gold Diggers of Broadway 29. Vanity Fair 32. Should Ladies Behave? 34. Klondike Annie 36. Romeo and Juliet 36, etc.

Tearle, Sir Godfrey (1884–1953).
Distinguished British stage actor, on stage from 1893; occasional films from 1906, when he played Romeo in a one-reeler.

If Youth But Knew 30. The Thirty-Nine Steps 35. *One of Our Aircraft is Missing* 42. The Rake's Progress 45. The Beginning or the End 47. Private Angelo 48. *The Titfield Thunderbolt* 53, etc.

Teasdale, Verree (1904–1987).
American comedy actress, often as sophisticated friend or suspicious wife.
■ Syncopation 29. The Sap from Syracuse 30. Skyscraper Souls 32. Payment Deferred 32. Luxury Liner 33. They Just Had to Get Married 33. Terror Aboard 33. Love Honour and Oh Baby 33. *Roman Scandals* 33. Fashions of 1934 34. Goodbye Love 34. A Modern Hero 34. Madame Du Barry 34. Desirable 34. The Firebird 34. Dr Monica 34. A Midsummer Night's Dream (as Titania) 35. The Milky Way 36. First Lady 37. Topper Takes a Trip 38. Fifth Avenue Girl 39. Turnabout 40. I Take This Woman 40. Love Thy Neighbour 40. Come Live with Me 41.

teaser.
A poster, trailer, or other piece of publicity which whets the appetite for a forthcoming film without giving full details about it, sometimes not even the title. The term was also applied to early pornographic films 1900–05, e.g. *Lovers Interrupted, Making Love in a Hammock*, etc.

Téchiné, André (1943–).
French director, a former critic for *Cahiers du Cinéma*.
Paulina S'en Va 69. Souvenirs d'en France 75. Barocco 77. Les Soeurs Brontë 78. Hôtel des Amériques 81. L'Atelier 84. Rendez-vous 85. Les Innocents 87. I Don't Kiss (J'Embrasse Pas) 91. Ma Saison Préférée 93. The Wild Reeds (Les Roseaux Sauvages) 94, etc.

Technicolor.
Colour process which existed from 1915, though the various improvements virtually amounted to completely new versions. The first had separate red and green films projected simultaneously; the second combined them on panchromatic film; the third used dye transfer. In 1932 came the three-strip process which gave the rich full tones familiar to filmgoers of the 40s, but a link with Eastmancolor in 1951 made it difficult to pick out Technicolor from any other process.

Technirama.
A process similar to Vistavision for producing extreme clarity of image.

Techniscope.
A process saving money by printing two wide images one below the other on the old 4 x 3 frame, then blowing them up to CinemaScope size; the results were awful.

Teenage Mutant Ninja Turtles.
Comic-book heroes created by Kevin Eastman and Peter Laird in 1984. There are four, each named after a European artist – Leonardo, Raphael, Donatello and Michelangelo – because their creators thought that Japanese names would sound silly. Their transformation into humanoids came about in the way of 50s movie monsters: they were contaminated by radioactivity while babies. They were featured in animated TV cartoons (rechristened by BBC-TV *Teenage Mutant Hero Turtles*) in 1988, and a live-action film, directed by Steve Barron in 1990, became the most successful independent movie so far released. Sequels followed in 1991 and 1993.

telecine:
the machine which enables film to be 'projected' electronically on television. Theoretically it is capable of panning from side to side across the CinemaScope image, picking out the optimum sections of each scene, but the results are usually dire unless the process has been carefully rehearsed.

the telephone
has been a very useful instrument to film scenarists. The saga of its invention was told in *The Story of Alexander Graham Bell*. It brought sinister, menacing and threatening calls in *Sorry – Wrong Number*, *The Small World of Sammy Lee*, *Midnight Lace*, *I Saw What You Did*, *Experiment in Terror*, *Sudden Fear*, *Strangers on a Train*, and *Dirty Harry*. *Chicago Calling* and *The Slender Thread* were among the films based entirely on someone trying to contact another character by telephone. *Bells Are Ringing*, *The Glenn Miller Story* and *Bye Bye Birdie* had musical numbers based on telephones. Shelly Berman, Jeanne de Casalis and Billy de Wolfe are among the revue artists famous for telephone sketches. Single phone calls were of high dramatic significance in *The Spiral Staircase*, *Little Caesar*, *Fail Safe*, *Dr Strangelove*, *Murder Inc.*, *Dial M for Murder*, *The Silencers*, *2001: A Space Odyssey*, *No Way to Treat a Lady*, *Call Northside 777*, and *Phone Call from a Stranger*, while the phone had a special inference in several call-girl pictures including *Butterfield 8*, *Our Man Flint*, *Indiscreet*, *Strange Bedfellows*, *Come Blow Your Horn* and *It's a Mad Mad Mad Mad World* are among the many films deriving comedy from the telephone ... while the most chilling moment in many a thriller has been the discovery that the phone is disconnected. In *The President's Analyst* the telephone company turned out to be the supreme enemy of civilization. In *Julia Has Two Lovers*, a crossed line led to the beginning of a romantic involvement with a gentleman caller.

telephoto lens.
One which brings far-off objects apparently very close, but has the disadvantage of distorting and flattening perspective.

television,
arch-enemy of the film-makers, was used during the 50s as an object of derision (*The Titfield Thunderbolt*, *Happy Anniversary*, *It's Always Fair Weather*, *My Blue Heaven*, *Simon and Laura*, *Callaway Went Thataway*, *No Down Payment*, *Meet Mr Lucifer*), or totally ignored. Yet it had featured in films even before World War II: *International House*, *Television Spy*, *Murder by Television*, *Raffles*, and a host of science fiction serials. More recently, television studios have provided a useful background for comedy (*You Must Be Joking*, *A Hard Day's Night*), for thrillers (*The Glass Web*, *Arabesque*, *The Barefoot Executive*) and for melodramas (*Seven Days in May*, *The Third Secret*, *The Love Machine*). The only serious movie study of the effects of television is *A Face in the Crowd*; and the funniest scenes about television programmes are probably those in *The Apartment*. Closed circuit TV is extensively used in *The Forbin Project*, *The Andromeda Strain*, *Loving* and *The Anderson Tapes*. In *THX 1138* television is used as a mass opiate for the workers of the subterranean world of the future. A wild but fairly barbed satire on television was *The Groove Tube*, and *Network* took a lofty view of it before pitching into hysterical melodrama. *Stay Tuned* was an inept satire about a husband and wife sucked into a TV hell.

¶ Some definitions, mostly jaundiced:
The bland leading the bland. – *Anon*

Chewing gum for the eyes. – *Frank Lloyd Wright*
The longest amateur night in history. – *Robert Carson*
A medium, so called because it is neither rare nor well done. – *Ernie Kovacs*
A twenty-one-inch prison. I'm delighted with it because it used to be that films were the lowest form of art. Now we have something to look down on. – *Billy Wilder*
Why should people go out and pay money to see bad films when they can stay at home and see bad television for nothing? – *Samuel Goldwyn*
A TV commercial was defined as:
The opening and closing quarter-hours of a half-hour show.
Though Cedric Hardwicke thought the ads were:
The last refuge of optimism in a world of gloom.
Irving Allen had his problems working in the medium:
I've tried to take the lunacy that exists in television and reduce it to a quiet panic.
John Simon was dismissive:
It is inconceivable what trash would be put on film these days if TV had not been invented, and the TV writers were functioning as scenarists.
Fred Allen saw it as:
A triumph of equipment over people. The minds that control it are so small that you could put them in the navel of a flea and still have room for a network vice-president's heart.
Billy Wilder was apprehensive:
A bad play folds and is forgotten, but in pictures we don't bury our dead. When you think it's out of your system your daughter sees it on TV and says: 'My father is an idiot.'
Groucho Marx as usual had a smart answer:
I find television very educational. Every time someone switches it on I go into another room and read a good book.
And it was an anonymous wit who had perhaps the best answer of all:
I prefer television. It's not so far to the bathroom.
Bob Hope as so often had the last word:
The other night I saw a Road picture so cut to make room for forty-five commercials that Bing and I weren't even in it.

television movies
became prevalent in the late 60s. For four or five years mediocre movies had failed to get theatrical release and were seen first on television; from this it was a short step to making feature films specifically for television exposure. Aaron Spelling and Universal were the main providers; costs were kept low by assembly-line methods, and it soon became just like the old days at the big studios, with stars making fast appearances in superficially glossy vehicles tailored to a specific time requirement. The quality obtained was roughly that of a Universal co-feature of the 50s. Middle-aged or elderly stars who still meant something to the home-viewing circle were coaxed back to the studios: Barbara Stanwyck, Susan Hayward, Ray Milland, Bette Davis, Shelley Winters, Broderick Crawford, Myrna Loy, Milton Berle and their peers all starred again in the new forms, some in two-hour slots (97 minutes actual) but most successfully in 90-minute slots (73 minutes actual). By 1972 such films were appearing at the rate of two or three a week, more if one includes long-form series such as *Mystery Movie*, which gave new life to George Peppard, Rock Hudson, Richard Boone, Peter Falk and others. Crime was the most popular element of these films, with a strong flavouring of the supernatural, an occasional western or sob story, and a modicum of comedy.

Art was not sought after, but as the touch became more assured, a few films received critical acclaim, notably *Brian's Song*, *Short Walk to Daylight*, *Duel*, and *That Certain Summer*. One such film, *My Sweet Charlie*, was sent on theatrical release after its TV exposure, but the experiment failed. In Britain, several of the films went out on theatrical release before TV exposure, and one of them, *Duel*, received rave reviews. By the mid-70s the trend in TV movies had turned to drama documentaries (*Eleanor and Franklin*, *Fear On Trial*) and to character drama, with an unfortunate stress on heroes and heroines dying of leukaemia, tumours and similar afflictions. Then the success of two serialized novels (*Rich Man, Poor Man* and *Roots*) started a stampede to climb on this new bandwagon.
A useful guide by Alvin H. Marill was published in 1981 under the title *Movies Made for Television*.

television series
based on motion picture originals almost outnumber the other kind. They include *The Thin Man*, *The Whistler*, *Kings Row*, *Casablanca*, *My Friend Flicka*, *How to Marry a Millionaire*, *Margie*, *The Roaring Twenties*, *I Remember Mama*, *Blondie*, *Claudia*, *Jungle Jim*, *Hawkeye*, *The Invisible Man*, *Hudson's Bay*, *The Asphalt Jungle*, *Mr Smith Goes to Washington*, *Father of the Bride*, *Life with Father*, *National Velvet*, *Bus Stop*, *No Time for Sergeants*, *Going My Way*, *The Greatest Show on Earth*, *Les Girls*, *Peyton Place*, *The Naked City*, *Rin Tin Tin*, *Topper*, *The Virginian*, *Hopalong Cassidy*, *The Munsters* (indirectly), *The Wackiest Ship in the Army*, *Mr Roberts*, *Gidget*, *Please Don't Eat the Daisies*, *Twelve O'Clock High*, *Dr Kildare*, *The Farmer's Daughter*, *The Long Hot Summer*, *Tarzan*, *The Rounders*, *The Saint*, *Gideon's Way*, *The Man Who Never Was*, *Batman*, *Mr Deeds Goes to Town*, *The Courtship of Eddie's Father*, *The Odd Couple*, *Barefoot in the Park*, *Anna and the King*, *Perry Mason*, *M*A*S*H*, *Shane*, *Lassie*, *Bob and Carol and Ted and Alice*, *Shaft*, *Adam's Rib*, *How the West Was Won*, *Planet of the Apes*, *Alice Doesn't Live Here Any More*, *Bagdad Café*.

Tellegen, Lou (1881–1934) (Isidor Van Dameler). Dutch matinée idol who made many silent films in Hollywood. He was married to actress Geraldine Farrar. Committed suicide.
Autobiography: 1931, *Women Have Been Kind*.
Queen Elizabeth 12. The Explorer 15. The World and Its Women 19. Single Wives 23. The Redeeming Sin 25, etc.

Tempest, Dame Marie (1864–1942) (Marie Susan Etherington).
British stage actress whose very rare films included *Moonlight Sonata* 37, *Yellow Sands* 38.

Temple, Julien (1953–).
English director and screenwriter who gained his experience making rock videos.
The Great Rock 'n' Roll Swindle 79. The Secret Policeman's Other Ball 81. Undercover 83. Mantrap 84. Running out of Luck 85. Absolute Beginners 86. Aria (co-d) 87. Earth Girls Are Easy 89, etc.

Temple, Shirley (1928–).
American child star of the 30s, performing in short films at three; a genuine prodigy. Later appeared on TV in *Shirley Temple Storybook*, and in the 60s went into local Californian politics. In the 70s she was US ambassador to Ghana, and later became US Chief of Protocol. In the late 80s she was appointed US ambassador to Czechoslovakia. She was married to actor John Agar (1945–49).
Autobiography: 1988, *Child Star*.

The Red-Haired Alibi 32. To the Last Man 33. ut All Night 33. Carolina 34. Mandalay 34. *Stand and Cheer* 34. Now I'll Tell 34. Change of Heart 4. *Little Miss Marker* (her first star vehicle) 34. aby Take a Bow 34. Now and Forever 34. Bright yes 34. The Little Colonel 35. Our Little Girl 35. *urly Top* 35. The Littlest Rebel 35. Captain January 5. Poor Little Rich Girl 36. *Dimples* 36. Stowaway 6. *Wee Willie Winkie* 37. *Heidi* 37. Rebecca of unnybrook Farm 38. Little Miss Broadway 38. ast around the Corner 38. *The Little Princess* 39. usannah of the Mounties 39. The Blue Bird 40. oung People 40. Kathleen 41. Miss Annie Rooney 2. Since You Went Away 44. I'll Be Seeing You 4. Kiss and Tell 45. Honeymoon 47. The Bachelor nd the Bobbysoxer 47. That Hagen Girl 47. Fort pache 48. Mr Belvedere Goes to College 49. dventure in Baltimore 49. The Story of eabiscuit 49. A Kiss for Corliss 49.

 For captivating the mass world audience and nabling it to forget the depression. *Curly Top.*

I stopped believing in Santa Claus at an early age. Mother took me to see him in a epartment store, and he asked for my autograph. *S.T.*

~Won special Academy Award 1934 'in grateful ecognition of her outstanding contribution to creen entertainment'.

The Ten Commandments.
Cecil B. De Mille made two films under this title. he 1923 version divided its time between the iblical story and a tale of what happens when moral laws are broken nowadays. It starred Richard ix, Rod La Rocque, and Estelle Taylor. The 1956 ersion spent nearly four hours on the Bible story lone, and with less cinematic flair than the silent icture. Charlton Heston was Moses and Yul rynner Pharaoh.

Tennant, Victoria (1950–).
British leading lady. She married actor Steve Martin in 1986.
■ The Ragman's Daughter 72. Sphinx 80. The Dogs of War 81. Inseminoid 81. *The Winds of War* (TV) 83. Chiefs (TV) 83. All of Me 84. The Holcroft Covenant 85. Best Seller 87. War and Remembrance (TV) 87. Flowers in the Attic 87. Dempsey (TV) 88. The Handmaid's Tale 90. Whispers 90. L.A. Story 91.

Tenngren, Gustaf (1896–1970).
Swedish artist and illustrator who worked for the Disney studios from 1936–39. He was an art director for *Snow White* and also made the preliminary drawings that created the overall look for *Pinocchio*, which he based on the Bavarian town of Rothenburg.

tennis
has accounted for some memorable scenes in the cinema, among them the suspenseful match in *Strangers on a Train* and the hilarious one in *Monsieur Hulot's Holiday.* Professional tennis was the subject of *Hard Fast and Beautiful* and *Jocks.* Nor should one forget the championship between Tom and Jerry in *Tennis Chumps,* or the weird game with no ball in *Blow Up.* Other tennis sequences figured in *The System, Nobody Runs Forever, Come to the Stable, Pat and Mike,* and *Players;* while there was a TV movie about Little Mo.

Tennyson, Pen (1918–1941) (Penrose Tennyson).
British director killed in World War II.
■ There Ain't No Justice (TV) 39. *The Proud Valley* 39. Convoy 40.

Terhune, Max (1890–1973).
American small-time western star, one of the Three Mesquiteers in 30s second features; also appeared in the Range Busters series.

Terriss, Ellaline (1871–1971) (Ellen Lewin).
British stage actress, widow of Sir Seymour Hicks; in a few films.
Blighty 27. Glamour 31. The Iron Duke 35. The Four Just Men 39, etc.

Terry, Alice (1899–1987) (Alice Taafe).
American leading lady of the silent screen.
Not My Sister 16. *The Four Horsemen of the Apocalypse* 21. *The Prisoner of Zenda* 22. Mare Nostrum 27. The Garden of Allah 28, etc.

Terry, Don (1902–1988) (Donald Locher).
American hero of serials and second features in the 30s.
Me Gangster 28. The Valiant 29. Whistlin' Dan 32. Paid to Dance 37. Who Killed Gail Preston? 38. The Secret of Treasure Island (serial) 38. Don Winslow of the Navy (serial) 41. Drums of the Congo 42. White Savage 43. Top Sergeant 43. Don Winslow of the Coastguard (serial) 43, etc.

Terry, Ellen (1848–1928).
Distinguished British stage actress whose film appearances were few and ineffective.
■ Her Greatest Performance 17. The Invasion of Britain 18. Pillars of Society 18. Potter's Clay 22. The Bohemian Girl 22.

Terry, Nigel (1945–).
British actor, from the stage.
The Lion in Winter 68. Excalibur 81. Déjà Vu 85. Caravaggio 86. War Requiem 88. Christopher Columbus: The Discovery 92, etc.
TV series: Covington Cross 92.

Terry, Paul (1887–1971).
American animator, the creator of 'Terry-toons' (starring Mighty Mouse, Heckle and Jeckle, etc,) which filled Fox supporting programmes for over 30 years.

Terry, Philip (1909–).
American leading man of the 40s, mainly in second features; best remembered for briefly marrying Joan Crawford.
The Parson of Panamint 41. The Monster and the Girl 41. Bataan 43. Music in Manhattan 44. Pan-Americana 45. *The Lost Weekend* 45. Seven Keys to Baldpate 47. Born to Kill 47. Class of '74 72, etc.

Terry-Thomas (1911–1990) (Thomas Terry Hoar-Stevens).
British comedian with inimitable gap-toothed manner; became Hollywood's favourite idea of the English silly ass. Also on stage and TV.
Autobiographies: 1959, *Filling the Gap.* 1990, *Terry-Thomas Tells Tales* (with Terry Daum).
Private's Progress 56. Blue Murder at St Trinian's 57. The Naked Truth 58. Tom Thumb 58. *Carleton Browne of the FO* 58. I'm All Right, Jack 59. School for Scoundrels 60. His and Hers 61. A Matter of Who 62. Bachelor Flat 62. The Wonderful World of the Brothers Grimm 63. Kill or Cure 63. It's a Mad Mad Mad Mad World 63. The Mouse on the Moon 63. *Those Magnificent Men in Their Flying Machines* 65. How to Murder Your Wife 65. You Must be Joking 65. Munster Go Home 66. Kiss the Girls and Make Them Die 66. Rocket to the Moon 67. The Perils of Pauline 67. Don't Look Now 68. Where Were You When the Lights Went Out? 68. 2000 Years Later 69. Monte Carlo or Bust 69. The Abominable Dr Phibes 71. Vault of Horror 73.

Spanish Fly 75. The Bawdy Adventures of Tom Jones 76. The Last Remake of Beau Geste 77. The Hound of the Baskervilles 78, etc.

Terzieff, Laurent (1935–).
French leading man.
Les Tricheurs 58. Le Bois des Amants 59. La Notte Brava 60. Kapo 60. Thou Shalt Not Kill 61. The Seven Deadly Sins 62. Ballade pour un Voyou 64. Le Triangle 65. Le Voyage du Père 66. Two Weeks in September 67. The Milky Way 68. Medea 69. Moses (TV) 75. Couleur Chair 77. Utopia 78. Red Kiss (Rouge Baiser) 85. Germinal 93, etc.

Teshigahara, Hiroshi (1927–).
Japanese director.
Pitfall 61. *Woman in the Dunes* (AAN) 64. The Face of Another 66. The Man Without a Map 68. Out of Work for Years 75. Rikyu 89, etc.

Tesich, Steve (1942–).
American screenwriter.
■ Breaking Away (AA) 79. Eyewitness 81. Four Friends 81. The World According to Garp 82. American Flyers 85. Eleni 85.

Tessari, Duccio (1926–1994).
Italian director and screenwriter who began as a documentary film-maker. He scripted 'sword and sandal' epics and worked as a set designer on Sergio Leone's *For a Few Dollars More* before becoming a director, making two admired spaghetti westerns about a gunfighter called Ringo.
Kanonen-serenade (w) 59. La Vendetta di Ercole (w) 60. Carthage in Flames (Cartagine in Fiamme) (co-w) 60. The Last Days of Pompeii (Gli Ultimi Giorni di Pompeii) (co-w) 60. Messalina (co-w) 60. Il Colosso di Rodi 61. Samson and the Seven Miracles of the World (Maciste alla Corto del Gran Khan) (co-w) 61. Il Fornaretto di Venezia (& w) 63. The Titans (Arrivano i Titani) (& co-w) 63. A Pistol for Ringo (Una Pistola per Ringo) (& w) 65. The Return of Ringo (Il Ritorno di Ringo) (& co-w) 65. Sette Pistole per i MacGregor (co-w) 66. Kiss Kiss-Bang Bang 66. Forza G (& co-w) 70. Death Occurred Last Night (La Morte Risale a Leri Sera) (& co-w) 70. Zorro (& co-w) 75, etc.

Tester, Desmond (1919–).
British boy actor of the 30s; went to Australia.
Midshipman Easy 35. Tudor Rose 36. Sabotage 37. The Drum 38. The Stars Look Down 39. The Turners of Prospect Road 47. Barry Mackenzie Holds His Own 74. The Wild Duck 84, etc.

Tetzel, Joan (1924–1977).
American leading actress with stage experience, married to Oscar Homolka.
Duel in the Sun 46. The Paradine Case 47. The File on Thelma Jordon 50. Joy in the Morning 65, etc.

Tetzlaff, Ted (1903–).
American director, former cinematographer.
World Première 41. *Riff Raff* 46. *The Window* 48. Johnny Allegro 48. The White Tower 50. The Treasure of Lost Canyon 52. Time Bomb 53. Son of Sinbad 55. The Young Land 57, etc.

Tevis, Walter (1928–1984).
American novelist and university teacher, three of whose books have been turned into films.
The Hustler 59. The Man Who Fell to Earth 73. The Color of Money 84.

Tewkesbury, Joan (1937–).
American director.

Old Boyfriends 79. The Tenth Month (TV) 79. The Acorn People (TV) 80. Cold Sassy Tree (TV) 89. Wild Texas Wind 91. On Promised Land 94, etc.

Tewksbury, Peter (1924–).
American director, from TV (*Father Knows Best*, *My Three Sons*, etc.).
■ *Sunday in New York* 64. Emil and the Detectives 65. Doctor You've Got to Be Kidding 67. Stay Away Joe 68. The Trouble with Girls 69. Second Chance (TV) 71.

Tey, Josephine (1896–1952) (Elizabeth MacKintosh).
Scottish writer of plays (as Gordon Daviot) and crime novels. *A Shilling for Candles* was filmed as *Young and Innocent*, and there was also a film of *The Franchise Affair*.

Thackery, Bud (1903–1990).
American cinematographer, especially for Republic, where he photographed innumerable westerns and serials. Moved into TV.

Thalberg, Irving (1899–1936).
American producer, MGM's boy wonder of the early 30s, responsible for the literary flavour of films like *The Barretts of Wimpole Street* 34, *Mutiny on the Bounty* 35, *Romeo and Juliet* 36; also for hiring the Marx Brothers. Married Norma Shearer.
Biographies: 1969, *Thalberg* by Bob Thomas. 1976, *Mayer and Thalberg* by Samuel Marx. 1994, *Thalberg: The Last Tycoon and the World of MGM* by Roland Flamini.
Thalberg was played by Robert Evans in *Man of a Thousand Faces*.

¶ When a man dies young, he is often underestimated. Thalberg has been lucky: the reverse proved true. Head of Universal production at 21 and of MGM at 25, his quiet efficiency and stubborn enthusiasm, coupled with his scholarly air, made him a legend even before his untimely death at 37. As early as 1925 F. L. Collins wrote:
Wherever Thalberg sits is always the head of the table.
He had apparently high aims:
I believe that although the motion picture may not live forever as a work of art, except in a few instances, it will be the most efficient way of showing posterity how we live now.
He was modest enough to keep his name off the credits of his films:
If you are in a position to give credit, you don't need it.
Charles MacArthur said:
Entertainment is Thalberg's God. He's content to serve Him without billing, like a priest at an altar or a rabbi under the scrolls.
He was a shrewd film-maker:
Movies aren't made, they're remade.
And he always had an eye for the box office. His idea of a good tag-line was:
Ladies, have you had a good cry lately? See *Imitation of Life* and cry unashamedly.
And he once said to Cedric Hardwicke:
We shall all make a killing in this business: there's so much money in the pot.
Mickey Rooney had his doubts:
It seemed to me that he went out of his way to put his wife into films she didn't need and wasn't right for.
But the screenwriters were suspicious of him:
He's too good to last. The lamb doesn't lie down with the lion for long. – *Charles MacArthur*
I seriously began to question whether Thalberg ever existed, or whether he might not be a solar

myth or a deity concocted by the front office to garner prestige. – *S. J. Perelman*
I think I may have once told you Irving Thalberg's classic: 'The writer? The writer is a necessary evil.' – *S. J. Perelman*
On a clear day you can see Thalberg. – *George S. Kaufman*
When he died however it was Charles MacArthur who knew the truth:
Ten years of 16-hours-a-day work had tired him. He didn't know how to rest, or play, or even breathe without a script in his hands.

Thatcher, Heather (1897–1987).
Blonde British light actress who filmed also in Hollywood.
Altar Chains 17. The Little House of Peter Wells 20. But the Flesh is Weak 32. Loyalties 33. The 13th Chair 37. Tovarich 37. Beau Geste 39. Man Hunt 41. Gaslight 44. Dear Mr Prohack 50. Will Any Gentleman 55, many others.

Thatcher, Torin (1905–1981).
Tough-looking British character actor, on stage from 1923; latterly on stage again after some years in Hollywood.
But the Flesh Is Weak 32. General John Regan 34. Major Barbara 40. The Captive Heart 45. Great Expectations 46. The Crimson Pirate 52. The Robe 53. Love is a Many-Splendored Thing 55. Witness for the Prosecution 57. The Seventh Voyage of Sinbad 58. The Canadians 60. Jack the Giant Killer 62. The Sandpiper 65. Hawaii 66. The King's Pirate 67, many others.

Thaw, John (1942–).
Rough-speaking British leading man, best known as TV's Inspector Morse.
The Loneliness of the Long Distance Runner 62. Dead Man's Chest 65. Praise Marx and Pass the Ammunition 68. The Bofors Gun 68. The Last Grenade 69. Dr Phibes Rides Again 72. Regan (TV) 73. *Sweeney* 76. Sweeney Two 78. Cry Freedom 87. The Sign of Four (TV) 87. Business as Usual 87, etc.
TV series: Redcap 64–66. The Sweeney 74–78. Home to Roost 85–87. A Year in Provence 93.

Thaxter, Phyllis (1921–).
American leading lady of the 40s, recently back in character roles.
Thirty Seconds over Tokyo (debut) 44. Weekend at the Waldorf 45. Bewitched 45. Tenth Avenue Angel 47. Blood on the Moon 48. Come Fill the Cup 51. Springfield Rifle 53. Women's Prison 54. The World of Henry Orient 64. The Longest Night (TV) 72. Superman 78. Three Sovereigns for Sarah (TV) 85, etc.

theatres
have provided an effective setting for many films apart from the countless putting-on-a-show musicals. Films concerned exclusively with matters theatrical include *The Royal Family of Broadway*, *Twentieth Century*, *The Great Profile*, *The Country Girl*, *Stage Door*, *Morning Glory*, *Queen of Hearts*, *Heller in Pink Tights*, *Take the Stage*, *To Be or Not To Be*, *Main Street to Broadway*, *Les Enfants du Paradis*, *Prince of Players*, *The Velvet Touch*, *All About Eve*, *Curtain Up*, *Kiss Me Kate*, *The Producers*, *The Boyfriend*, *Variety Jubilee*, *A Chorus Line* and *Noises Off*, while a theatre was also the principal setting for *Those Were the Days*, *Henry V*, *Occupe-Toi d'Amélie*, *The Lost People*, *The High Terrace*, *Four Hours to Kill*, *The Phantom of the Opera* and *The Climax*. Thrillers with climaxes in a theatre include *The Thirty-Nine Steps*, *Torn Curtain*, *Charlie Chan at the Opera*, *Cover Girl Killer*, *The Westerner*, *Stage Fright*, *Charade*, *Scaramouche*, *The Deadly Affair*, *No Way to*

Treat a Lady and *King Kong*; comedies include *A Night at the Opera*, *A Haunting We Will Go*, *Knock On Wood*, *The Intelligence Men*, *Trouble in Paradise*, *The Secret of My Success*, *My Learned Friend* and *Meet Mr Lucifer*. Less frequent are uses of the theatre as a setting for romance, but it served this purpose in *All This and Heaven Too*, *The Lady with a Little Dog* and *Letter from an Unknown Woman*. The scariest theatre was *Theatre of Blood*, with Vincent Price as an actor murdering all the critics who had given him bad notices.
See: *cinemas*.

Theiss, William Ware.
American costume designer.
The Pink Panther 64. Harold and Maude 71. Bound for Glory (AAN) 76. Who'll Stop the Rain (aka Dog Soldiers) 78. Butch and Sundance: The Early Days (AAN) 79. Kidco 83. Heart Like a Wheel (AAN) 83. The Man with One Red Shoe 85, etc.

Thesiger, Ernest (1879–1961).
Witty, skeletal-looking British character actor, on stage from 1909.
Autobiography: 1927, *Practically True*.
West End Wives 29. *The Old Dark House* 32. The Ghoul 33. Heart Song 34. *The Bride of Frankenstein* 35. The Man Who Could Work Miracles 36. *They Drive By Night* 38. Henry V 44. Caesar and Cleopatra 45. A Place of One's Own 46. The Ghosts of Berkeley Square 47. Quartet 48. Laughter in Paradise 51. *The Man in the White Suit* 52. *Father Brown* 54. Make Me an Offer 55. The Battle of the Sexes 59. The Roman Spring of Mrs Stone 61, many others.

¶ Anyone with a modicum of intelligence and the right kind of physique ought to make a film-actor, if they are lucky enough to be told exactly what to do, and I cannot see that the actor for the screen deserves any more credit than a schoolboy who is good at dictation should have for writing admirable prose. – *E.T.*

Famous line (*The Old Dark House*): 'Have some gin. It's my only weakness . . .'

Famous line (*The Bride of Frankenstein*). 'To a new world of gods and monsters!'
~He also published books on embroidery.

Thewlis, David.
English leading actor, from the stage.
Vroom 88. Prime Suspect 3 (TV) 93. Naked 93. Black Beauty 94, etc.

The Thief of Bagdad.
This Arabian Nights tale was superbly filmed with Douglas Fairbanks in 1924, and again in 1940 with Sabu and some remarkable trick photography, directed by Michael Powell, Tim Whelan, and Ludwig Berger. An Italian version with a much-altered plot, starring Steve Reeves, followed in 1961, and there was a TV movie version in 1978, directed by Clive Donner with Roddy McDowell and Peter Ustinov.

Thiele, Rolf (1918–).
German director.
Nachtwache (p only) 49. Mamitschka (& wp) 55. El Hakim 57. The Girl Rosemarie (& co-w) 58. Venusberg (& w) 63. Tonio Kroger 64, etc.

Thiele, William (1890–1975).
German director who went to Hollywood in the 30s but found little work.
His Late Excellency 29. Liebeswalzer 31. *Drei von der Tankstelle* 31. Le Bal 32. The Jungle Princess

6. London by Night 37. Bridal Suite 39. Tarzan Triumphs 43. Tarzan's Desert Mystery 43. The Madonna's Secret 46. The Last Pedestrian 60, etc.

Thiess, Ursula (1929–).
German leading lady, in a few American films. She was formerly married to actor Robert Taylor.
Monsoon 52. The Iron Glove 54. Bengal Brigade 55. The Americano 55, etc.
TV series: The Detectives, Starring Robert Taylor 50–61.

Thimig, Helene (1889–1974).
German character actress, widow of Max Reinhardt, in a few American films.
None But the Lonely Heart 44. Cloak and Dagger 46. The Locket 47, etc.

The Thin Man.
In Dashiell Hammett's crime novel, the thin man was the murderer's first victim, but the tag stuck to William Powell as Nick Charles the detective in the film, the success of which led to him starring, with Myrna Loy as Nora Charles, in five sequels: *After the Thin Man* 37; *Another Thin Man* 38; *Shadow of the Thin Man* 42; *The Thin Man Goes Home* 44; and *Song of the Thin Man* 46. A TV series starring Peter Lawford and Phyllis Kirk ran from 1957–59.

The Thing (from Another World).
The original, in 1951, was one of the first films to combine the horror genre with science fiction. It was produced by Howard Hawks (and some say directed by him, despite the credit to Christian Nyby; there were also rumours that Orson Welles had a hand in it). In John Carpenter's 1982 remake, the emphasis was on visceral special effects.

Thinnes, Roy (1938–).
Stocky American leading man of some successful television series: The Long Hot Summer 64. The Invaders 66–67. The Psychiatrist 70.
Journey to the Far Side of the Sun 69. Charlie One Eye 72. The Horror at 37,000 Feet (TV) 73. The Norliss Tapes (TV) 73. Airport 75 74. The Hindenburg 75. From Here to Eternity (TV) 79. Sizzle 81. Rush Week 88, etc.
TV series: From Here to Eternity 79–80. Falcon Crest 82–83. Dark Shadows 91.

Thirard, Armand (1899–).
French cinematographer.
Remorques 41. Quai des Orfèvres 47. Manon 49. The Wages of Fear 52. Act of Love 54. Les Diaboliques 54. And God Created Woman 56. The Truth 60. Guns for San Sebastian 67, etc.

Thiriet, Maurice (1906–1972).
French composer.
The Woman I Love 37. Les Visiteurs du Soir 37. Les Enfants du Paradis 44. L'Homme au Chapeau Rond 46. Une Si Jolie Petite Plage 48. Fanfan la Tulipe 51. Thérèse Raquin 53. Crime and Punishment 58, etc.

35mm.
The standard commercial film gauge or width.

The Thirty-Nine Steps.
The first two film versions of John Buchan's spy yarn bore little resemblance to the novel, apart from the hero's original predicament and the Scottish setting: Hitchcock's version in 1935, working from Charles Bennett's pacy script, starred Robert Donat, Madeleine Carroll, and Godfrey Tearle; Ralph Thomas remade it in more stolid fashion in 1959 with Kenneth More, Taina Elg, and Barry

Jones. Don Sharp's 1978 version with Robert Powell restored the original period and some of the plot.

This Gun for Hire.
Graham Greene's novel, A Gun for Sale, has been filmed twice: the first version, in 1942, directed by Frank Tuttle, catapulted Alan Ladd into the front rank of box-office attractions; the second, retitled Short Cut to Hell, was directed by James Cagney and starred Robert Ivers as the gunman, but both he and the movie passed without comment.

This Modern Age.
A series of current-affairs two-reelers sponsored in 1946 by Rank as the British answer to *The March of Time*. Although decently produced by Sergei Nolbandov, the monthly issues were not a popular addition to already overlong programmes, and the attempt was given up in 1949.

Thomas, Billy 'Buckwheat' (1931–1980).
American child actor in the Our Gang comedies from the mid-30s until the mid-40s.

Thomas, Danny (1914–1991) (Amos Jacobs).
American nightclub comedian; star of his own seven-year TV series in the 60s and The Practice in 1977.
Autobiography: 1991, *Make Room for Danny*.
The Unfinished Dance 47. Big City 48. Call Me Mister 51. I'll See You in My Dreams 52. The Jazz Singer 53. Looking for Love 64. Don't Worry, We'll Think of a Title 66. Journey Back to Oz (voice) 74.

Thomas, Dylan (1914–1953).
Welsh poet whose drama Under Milk Wood has been filmed. He also worked on the scripts of a number of British films in the late 40s, including The Three Weird Sisters. He was portrayed by Ronald Lacey in a 1978 BBC film, Dylan. His Rebecca's Daughters, written in 1948, was filmed in 1991.

Thomas, Gerald (1920–1993).
British director, former editor, in films from 1946.
Time Lock 57. Vicious Circle 57. The Duke Wore Jeans 58. Carry On Sergeant 58 (and all the subsequent 'Carry Ons'). Watch Your Stern 60. Twice round the Daffodils 62. The Big Job 65. Don't Lose Your Head 66. Follow That Camel 67. Carry On Loving 70. Carry On Girls 73. Carry On England 76. Carry On Emmanuelle 78. That's Carry On 78. The Second Victory 87. Carry On Columbus 92, etc.

Thomas, Henry (1971–).
American child actor of the 80s.
■ Raggedy Man 81. E.T. – the Extraterrestrial 82. Misunderstood 83. Cloak and Dagger 84. The Quest 86. Murder One 88. Valmont 89. Psycho IV: The Beginning 90. A Taste for Killing (TV) 92. Fire in the Sky 93. Curse of the Starving Class 94.

Thomas, Jameson (1892–1939).
British actor who usually played 'the other man'. Went to Hollywood in the early 30s but did not command leading roles.
Blighty 27. A Daughter of Love 28. Piccadilly 29. High Treason 30. Hate Ship 30. Elstree Calling 30. The Phantom President 32. It Happened One Night 34. Lives of a Bengal Lancer 35. Mr Deeds Goes to Town 36. Death Goes North 38, etc.

¶ If one wants to live by playing in British films it is better to be miscast than never to be cast at all. – J.T.

Thomas, Jeremy (1949–).
British producer.
Mad Dog 76. The Shout 78. Bad Timing 80. Merry Christmas, Mr Lawrence 82. Eureka 83. The Hit 84. Insignificance 85. The Last Emperor (AA) 87. Everybody Wins 90. The Sheltering Sky 90. Naked Lunch 91. Little Buddha 92, etc.

Thomas, Lowell (1892–1981).
American broadcaster and lecturer who partly controlled Cinerama and appeared as travelling commentator in some of its episodes.
Search for Paradise 58, etc.

Thomas, Marlo (1943–) (Margaret Thomas).
American leading lady, daughter of Danny Thomas.
The Knack 64. Jenny 70. Thieves 77.
TV series: The Joey Bishop Show 61–62. That Girl 66–70.

Thomas, Olive (1884–1920) (Olive Elaine Duffy).
American 'Ziegfeld girl' who played a few comedy roles in films. Married actor Jack Pickford. Committed suicide.
Beatrice Fairfax 16. Limousine Life 18. The Follies Girl 19. The Glorious Lady 19. Footlights and Shadows 20, etc.

Thomas, Pascal (1945–).
French director.
Les Zozos 72. Le Chaud Lapin 74. Un Oursin dans la Poche 77, etc.

Thomas, Philip Michael (1949–).
American leading actor, best known for his role as Detective Ricardo Tubbs in the TV series Miami Vice 84–89.
Stigma 73. Streetfight (aka Coonskin) (voice) 75. Sparkle 76. Death Drug 83. The Wizard of Speed and Time 88. False Witness (TV) 89. A Fight for Jenny (TV) 90, etc.

Thomas, Ralph (1915–).
British director, former trailer maker, who with producer Betty Box has tackled some ambitious subjects in a rather stolid manner.
Helter Skelter 48. Traveller's Joy 49. The Clouded Yellow 51. Appointment with Venus 51. Venetian Bird 53. Doctor in the House 54. Above Us the Waves 55. The Iron Petticoat 56. Campbell's Kingdom 57. A Tale of Two Cities 57. The Wind Cannot Read 58. The Thirty-Nine Steps 59. No Love for Johnnie 61. The Wild and the Willing 62. Hot Enough for June 64. The High Bright Sun 65. Deadlier than the Male 66. Some Girls Do 68. Percy 71. Quest for Love 71. The Love Ban 73. Percy's Progress 74. A Nightingale Sang in Berkeley Square 80, etc.

Thomas, Richard (1951–).
American actor.
■ Winning 69. Last Summer 70. Cactus in the Snow 70. Red Sky at Morning 71. You'll Like My Mother 72. September 30 1955 78. The Silence (TV) 78. Battle beyond the Stars 80. Go toward the Light (TV) 88. Glory! Glory! (TV) 89. It (TV) 90. Mission of the Shark 91.
TV series: The Waltons 72–76.

Thomas, Terry:
see Terry-Thomas.

Thomas, William C.:
see: Pine, William H.

Thomas, Wynn (1954–).
American production designer who has worked on
Spike Lee's films; from the stage.

She's Gotta Have It 86. Eddie Murphy Raw 87.
Scared Stiff 87. School Daze 88. Do the Right
Thing 89. Mo' Better Blues 90. Jungle Fever 91.
The Five Heartbeats 91. Malcolm X 92. Crooklyn
94, etc.

Thomerson, Tim.
Laconic American leading actor, from television,
where he appeared in situation comedies. On film,
he is best known for his role in the *Trancers* series
as Jack Deth, a tough cop from the future who
models his style on Humphrey Bogart.

Car Wash 76. Terraces (TV) 87. Which Way Is
Up? 77. A Wedding 78. Carny 80. Fade to Black 80.
Take This Job and Shove It 81. Jekyll and Hyde
. . . Together Again 82. Metalstorm: The
Destruction of Jared-Syn 83. Uncommon Valor 83.
Rhinestone 84. Trancers (aka Future Cop) 85. Zone
Troopers 85. Volunteers 85. Ratboy 86. Iron Eagle
86. A Tiger's Tale 87. Near Dark 87. The Wrong
Guys 88. Cherry 2000 88. Who's Harry Crumb?
89. After Midnight 89. Air America 90. Vietnam,
Texas 90. Trancers II: The Return of Jack Deth 91.
Dollman 91. Intimate Stranger 91. The Harvest 92.
Trancers III: Deth Lives 92. Nemesis 93. Natural
Causes 94. Fleshtone 94. Dominion 95, etc.

TV series: Cos 76. Quark 78. Angie 79–80. The
Associates 79–80. The Two of Us 81–82. Gun Shy
83. Sirens 93.

Thompson, Carlos (1916–1990) (Juan Carlos
Mundanschaffter).
Argentinian stage and screen matinée idol who has
made some American and German films. He was
married to actress Lilli Palmer. Committed suicide.

Fort Algiers 53. The Flame and the Flesh 54.
Valley of the Kings 54. Magic Fire 56. Stefanie
58. Joaquin Murietta 58. Stefanie in Rio 60, etc.

TV series: Sentimental Agent 66.

Thompson, Caroline W. (1956–).
American scriptwriter turned director.

Edward Scissorhands (w) 90. The Addams
Family (co-w) 91. Homeward Bound: The
Incredible Journey (w) 93. The Secret Garden (w)
93. Tim Burton's The Nightmare before Christmas
(w) 93. Black Beauty (d) 94, etc.

Thompson, Danièle.
French screenwriter, the daughter of director
Gérard Oury.

La Grande Vadrouille (co-w) 65. The Mad
Adventures of Rabbi Jacob (co-w) 73. Cousin,
Cousine (co-w, AAN) 75. La Reine Margot (co-w)
94, etc.

Thompson, Emma (1959–).
British actress, from TV. She married actor-director
Kenneth Branagh in 1989.

The Tall Guy 89. Henry V 89. Impromptu 89.
Dead Again 91. Howards End (AA) 91. Peter's
Friends 92. Much Ado about Nothing 93. The
Remains of the Day (AAN) 93. In the Name of the
Father (AAN) 93. Junior 94. Carrington 95, etc.

TV series: Tutti Frutti 87. Thompson 88.

Thompson, Fred Dalton (1943–).
American actor, a former lawyer.

Marie: A True Story (TV) 85. No Way Out 87.
Feds 88. Days of Thunder 90. Die Hard 2 90. The
Hunt for Red October 90. Cape Fear 91. Curly Sue
91. Thunderheart 92. White Sands 92. Aces: Iron
Eagle III 92. Born Yesterday 93. In the Line of Fire
93, etc.

Thompson, J. Lee:
see *Lee-Thompson, J.*

Thompson, Jack (1940–) (John Pain).
Australian leading man.

Outback 70. Libido 73. Petersen 74. Sunday Too
Far Away 74. Caddie 76. Mad Dog Morgan 76.
The Chant of Jimmie Blacksmith 78. Breaker
Morant 79. The Earthling 80. Merry Christmas Mr
Lawrence 83. Burke and Wills 85. Flesh and Blood
85. Ground Zero 87. Waterfront 88. Trouble in
Paradise (TV) 89. Turtle Beach 92. Wind 92. A Far
Off Place 93. Ruby Cairo 93. The Sum of Us 94,
etc.

Thompson, Jim (1906–1977).
Pulp novelist, the author of some 29 thrillers, and
occasional screenwriter whose books became
unexpectedly popular as movie material in the late
80s. At the time of his death, all his books were out
of print.

The Killing (co-w) 56. Paths of Glory (co-w) 57.
The Getaway (oa) 72. Farewell My Lovely (a)
75. The Killer Inside Me (oa) 75. Série Noire (oa)
78. Coup de Torchon (oa) 81. The Kill-Off (oa) 89.
The Grifters (oa) 90. After Dark, My Sweet (oa)
90. The Getaway (oa) 94.

Thompson, Lea (1961–).
American leading actress.

Jaws 3-D 83. All the Right Moves 83. Going
Undercover 84. Red Dawn 84. The Wild Life 84.
Back to the Future 85. Howard the Duck 86. Some
Kind of Wonderful 87. Casual Sex? 88. The
Wizard of Loneliness 88. Nightbreaker (TV) 89.
Back to the Future II 89. Back to the Future III 90.
Article 99 92. Stolen Babies (TV) 93. The Substitute
Wife (TV) 94, etc.

Thompson, Marshall (1925–1992) (James
Marshall Thompson).
American leading man who began by playing quiet
juvenile roles.

Reckless Age 44. Gallant Bess 45. The Romance
of Rosy Ridge 46. Homecoming 48. Words and
Music 48. Battleground 49. The Violent Hour 50.
My Six Convicts 52. Battle Taxi 55. To Hell and
Back 55. Clarence the Cross-Eyed Lion 65. Around
the World under the Sea 66. The Turning Point
77, many others.

TV series: Angel 60. Daktari 66–68.

Thompson, Sada (1929–).
Gentle-looking American character actress,
usually in maternal roles.

The Pursuit of Happiness 70. Desperate
Characters 71. Our Town (TV) 77. The
Adventures of Huckleberry Finn (TV) 85, etc.

TV series: *Family* 76–79.

Thomson, Alex (1929–).
British cinematographer.

Here We Go Round the Mulberry Bush 67. The
Strange Affair 68. Alfred the Great 69. Excalibur
(AAN) 81. Eureka 83. Bullshot 85. Year of the
Dragon 85. Legend 86. Labyrinth 86. Duet for
One 87. The Sicilian 87. Track 29 88. High Spirits
88. Leviathan 89. The Rachel Papers 89. Mr Destiny
90. Wings of Fame 90. Alien³ 92. Demolition Man
93. Cliffhanger 93, etc.

Thomson, Fred (1890–1928).
American cowboy star of the 20s.

Penrod 22. The Eagle's Talons 23. The Fighting
Sap 24. The Wild Bull's Lair 25. Hands Across the
Border 26. Arizona Nights 27. Jesse James 27. The
Pioneer Scout 28. Kit Carson 28, etc.

Thorburn, June (1931–1967).
British leading lady with repertory experience.

The Pickwick Papers (debut) 53. The Cruel Sea
53. True as a Turtle 56. Tom Thumb 59. The Three
Worlds of Gulliver 59. The Scarlet Blade 63, etc.

Thorin, Donald E.
American cinematographer.

Thief 81. An Officer and a Gentleman 82. Bad
Boys 83. Against All Odds 84. Purple Rain 84.
Mischief 85. American Anthem 86. Wildcats 86.
The Golden Child 86. Collision Course 88. The
Couch Trip 88. Midnight Run 88. Troop Beverly
Hills 89. Lock Up 89. Tango & Cash 89. The
Marrying Man (aka Too Hot to Handle) 91. Out
on a Limb 92. Undercover Blues 93. Little Big
League 94, etc.

Thorndike, Andrew (1909–).
East German director who with his wife Annelie
made the strident anti-Nazi documentary series *Th
Archives Testify;* also *The German Story, The Russian
Miracle,* etc.

Thorndike, Dame Sybil (1882–1976).
Distinguished British stage actress who appeared
in occasional films.

Biography: 1950, *Sybil Thorndike* by Russell
Thorndike.

Moths and Rust (debut) 21. Dawn 29. To What
Red Hell 30. Hindle Wakes 31. Tudor Rose 36.
Major Barbara 40. *Nicholas Nickleby* 47. Stage Frigh
50. The Magic Box 51. Melba 53. *Alive and Kicking*
58. Shake Hands with the Devil 59. Hand in Hand
61, etc.

Thorne, Ken.
British composer and conductor.

Master Spy 62. Help! (md) 65. A Funny Thing
Happened on the Way to the Forum (AA) 66. How
I Won the War 67. Sinful Davey 68. Inspector
Clouseau 68. Head 68. The Magic Christian 69. The
Bed-Sitting Room 69. Welcome to the Club 70.
Hannie Calder 71. Brother Sun Sister Moon 72.
Juggernaut 74. Royal Flash (md) 75. The Ritz 76.
Power Play 78. Arabian Adventure 79. The Outsider
79. Superman II 80. Superman III 83. Lassiter 83.
Finders Keepers 85. The Protector 85. The Trouble
with Spies 87, etc.

Thornton, Frank (1921–).
British comic actor, much on TV.

Crooks and Coronets 68. All the Way Up 70.
Our Miss Fred 72. Digby 73. No Sex Please We're
British 73. The Three Musketeers 73.

TV series: Are You Being Served 74–82.

Thornton, Sigrid (1959–).
Australian leading lady.

The Getting of Wisdom 80. Snap Shot 81. 1915
(TV) 82. The Man from Snowy River 82. All the
Rivers Run (TV) 83. Slate, Wyn and Me 87. Return
to Snowy River, Part II 88. Great Expectations – the
Untold Story 90, etc.

Thorpe, Jerry (1930–).
American director from TV, the son of director
Richard Thorpe.

The Venetian Affair 66. The Day of the Evil Gun
(& p) 68. Company of Killers (aka The Protectors)
72. The Possessed (TV) 77. All God's Children (TV)
80. Blood and Orchids (TV) 86, etc.

TV series: *Kung Fu* 72–74.

Thorpe, Jim (1888–1953).
American Indian athlete, played by Burt Lancaster
in *Jim Thorpe, All-American.* Also small-part actor,
in 'B' westerns of the 30s.

Thorpe, Richard (1896–1991) (Rollo Smolt Thorpe).

American director, formerly in vaudeville.

The Feminine Touch 28. Forgotten Woman 32. The Last of the Pagans 35. *Night Must Fall* 38. Huckleberry Finn 39. Tarzan Finds a Son 39. Wyoming 40. The Earl of Chicago 40. Tarzan's New York Adventure 42. Above Suspicion 43. Her Highness and the Bellboy 45. Fiesta 47. The Sun Comes Up 48. Malaya 49. *The Great Caruso* 51. The Prisoner of Zenda 52. Ivanhoe 52. The Student Prince 54. Knights of the Round Table 54. The Prodigal 55. *The Adventures of Quentin Durward* 56. Jailhouse Rock 57. The House of the Seven Hawks 59. The Tartars 60. Fun in Acapulco 63. The Golden Head 65. That Funny Feeling 65. The Truth about Spring 65. The Scorpio Letters 67. Pistolero 67. etc.

¶ His reputation for only needing one take is why we don't remember his films. – *James Mason*

Three Coins in the Fountain.
Jean Negulesco's highly commercial romantic 1954 film, from John Secondari's novel, taught Hollywood the travelogue possibilities of CinemaScope in terms of freshening up a tired story. Ten years later, he attempted a disguised remake under the title *The Pleasure Seekers,* but the picture crept by almost unnoticed.

3-D.
Three-dimensional film-making had been tried in 1935 by MGM, as a gimmick involving throwaway paper glasses with one red and one green eyepiece to match the double image on the screen. In 1953, Hollywood really got the idea that this device would save an ailing industry, and a number of cheap exploitation pictures were shot in 3-D before anyone got down to the practical problem of renting out and collecting the necessary polaroid spectacles, which threw cinema managers into fits. *Bwana Devil* was an awful picture; *Man in the Dark* and *Fort Ti* were a shade better, except that the action kept stopping for something to be hurled at the audience; *House of Wax*, a Warner horror remake of *The Mystery of the Wax Museum*, had better production values and seemed to catch on with the public. All the studios began to make 3-D films – *Kiss Me Kate, The Charge at Feather River, Dial M for Murder, Miss Sadie Thompson, Sangaree* – but by the time these were ready, interest had shifted to Fox's new CinemaScope process, which although it gave no illusion of depth was at least a different shape and didn't need glasses. Nor did it entail such problems as running both projectors at once, with consequent intervals every twenty minutes; or long pauses when the film broke in order to mutilate the second copy in precisely the same way; or one machine running a little slower than the other, with gradual loss of synchronization. The remaining 3-D films were released 'flat', and the industry breathed a sigh of relief. So did the critics, who had wondered whether they would ever again see a film which did not involve frequent violent action. The Russians did claim at the time that they were inventing a 3-D process which would not require the use of glasses, but we are still waiting for that. In 1967 Arch Oboler made *The Bubble* in 3-D and in 1970–71 there was a brief revival of interest in the process as a promotion gimmick for cheap pornographic films. It flared up again in the early 80s as a medium for horror films and such shockers as *Jaws 3-D*, while Hitchcock's 1954 *Dial M for Murder* was shown for the first time in the process.

Books: 1983, *Amazing 3-D* by Hal Morgan and Dan Symmes. 1989, *3-D Movies* by R. M. Hayes.

Three Men in a Boat.
Jerome K. Jerome's comic novel of three friends on a boat trip up the Thames has been filmed twice in the sound era: in 1933, directed by Graham Cutts, with William Austin, Edmund Breon, and Billy Milton; and in 1957, directed by Ken Annakin, with Laurence Harvey, Jimmy Edwards, and David Tomlinson.

The Three Musketeers.
Apart from the numerous European versions, Alexandre Dumas's classic swashbuckler has been a Hollywood favourite too. Edison made a version in 1911; so did Edward Laurillard in 1913, C. V. Heinkel in 1914, and Fred Niblo in 1921, with Douglas Fairbanks and Eugene Pallette, Leon Barry and George Siegmann as the musketeers. Walter Abel was D'Artagnan in a 1935 version for RKO, with Paul Lukas, Moroni Olsen, and Onslow Stevens; Rowland V. Lee directed. Don Ameche sang in a 1939 musical comedy version (sometimes known as *The Singing Musketeer*) with the Ritz Brothers, no less, as lackeys impersonating the famous trio. Directed by Allan Dwan, it was very, very funny. Gene Kelly made an acrobatic D'Artagnan for MGM in 1948, with Van Heflin, Gig Young, and Robert Coote; and 1973 brought an all-star international version, directed by Richard Lester, with Michael York, Oliver Reed, Frank Finlay, and Richard Chamberlain. A sequel, *The Four Musketeers,* came the following year, but *The Fifth Musketeer*, a multi-national 1978 adventure directed by Ken Annakin, told in fact the story of the man in the iron mask. A 1993 version starred Charlie Sheen, Kiefer Sutherland, Chris O'Donnell, and Oliver Platt, a cast that looked ill at ease in a period setting. Bertrand Tavernier's *The Daughter of D'Artagnan (La Fille de D'Artagnan)* 94 was an original sequel to Dumas's story and a tribute to swashbucklers, with Sophie Marceau in the title role and Philippe Noiret as D'Artagnan leading the ageing musketeers, played by Jean-Luc Bideau, Raoul Billeray, and Sami Frey, on one last adventure.

Three Smart Girls.
A minor domestic comedy about three teenagers, directed by Henry Koster in 1937, was the first feature appearance of Deanna Durbin and was followed by a sequel in 1939, *Three Smart Girls Grow Up.* In 1943 followed a third film on the adventures of the Durbin character only, *Hers to Hold.*

The Three Stooges:
see *The Stooges.*

Thring, Frank (1926–1994).
Australian actor in occasional films.

A Question of Adultery 58. The Vikings 58. Ben Hur 59. King of Kings 61. El Cid 61. Age of Consent 69. Ned Kelly 70. Mad Max 76. Mad Max Beyond Thunderdome 85. Howling 3 87, etc.

Thulin, Ingrid (1929–   ).
Swedish leading actress, often in Ingmar Bergman's films.

Foreign Intrigue 55. *Wild Strawberries* 57. So Close to Life 58. The Face 59. The Four Horsemen of the Apocalypse (US) 62. Winter Light 62. *The Silence* 63. Return from the Ashes (US) 65. The War Is Over (Fr.) 66. Night Games 66. The Damned 69. The Rite 69. Cries and Whispers 72. Moses 76. The Cassandra Crossing 77. One and One (En Och En)

78. After the Rehearsal 84. Il Giorno Prima 87. House of Smiles (La Casa del Sorriso) 91, etc.

Thurber, James (1894–1961).
American humorist whose chief gifts to Hollywood were the original stories of *The Secret Life of Walter Mitty* and *The Male Animal.*

TV series based on his cartoons: *My World and Welcome to It* 69.

Thurman, Uma (1970–   ).
American actress. She was married to actor Gary Oldman (1990–1992).

Kiss Daddy Goodnight 87. The Adventures of Baron Munchausen 88. Dangerous Liaisons 88. Johnny Be Good 88. Henry and June 90. Where the Heart Is 90. Robin Hood 90. Final Analysis 92. Jennifer 8 92. Mad Dog and Glory 93. Even Cowgirls Get the Blues 93. *Pulp Fiction* 94, etc.

Tianming, Wu.
Chinese director, a former actor, who became head of the Xi'an Film Studio in the mid-80s. He now lives in America.

A River without Buoys (Meiyouhangbiaode Heliu) 83. Life (Rensheng) 84. Old Well (Lao Jing) 87, etc.

Tibbett, Lawrence (1896–1960).
American opera star who made some films in the 30s.

■ Rogue Song (AAN) 29. New Moon 30. The Prodigal 31. Cuban Love Song 32. Metropolitan 36. Under Your Spell 37.

~Tibbett's first movie appearance was promoted as follows: 'To bring you a new, vital figure for the further glory of your talking screen, MGM has reached into the highest realms of the Metropolitan Opera. From this renowned company of immortal voices has been picked the greatest – your new star, Lawrence Tibbett!' Louella Parsons commented: 'The long-awaited successor to Rudolph Valentino has arrived!'

Ticotin, Rachel (1958–   ).
American actress.

King of the Gypsies 78. Fort Apache, the Bronx 81. Critical Condition 87. Total Recall 90. FX2 – the Deadly Art of Illusion 91. Where the Day Takes You 92. Falling Down 93, etc.

TV series: Crime & Punishment 93.

Tidyman, Ernest (1928–1984).
American novelist who scripted the *Shaft* films from his own novels.

The French Connection (AA) 72. High Plains Drifter 74. Report to the Commissioner (co-w) 74, etc.

Tierney, Gene (1920–1991).
Gentle-featured American leading lady of the 40s, typically a smooth socialite.

Autobiography: 1979, *Self Portrait.*

■ The Return of Frank James 40. Hudson's Bay 40. Tobacco Road 41. *Belle Starr* 41. Sundown 41. The Shanghai Gesture 41. Son of Fury 42. Rings on Her Fingers 42. Thunder Birds 42. China Girl 42. *Heaven Can Wait* 43. *Laura* 44. A Bell for Adano 45. Leave Her to Heaven (AAN) 45. Dragonwyck 46. *The Razor's Edge* 46. The Ghost and Mrs Muir 47. The Iron Curtain 48. That Wonderful Urge 48. Whirlpool 48. Night and the City 50. Where the Sidewalk Ends 50. The Mating Season 51. On the Riviera 51. The Secret of Convict Lake 51. Close to My Heart 51. Way of a Gaucho 51. The Plymouth Adventure 52. Never Let Me Go (GB) 53. Personal Affair (GB) 53. Black Widow 54. The Egyptian 54. *The Left Hand of God* 54. Advise and Consent

62. Toys in the Attic 63. The Pleasure Seekers 64. Daughter of the Mind (TV) 69.

Tierney, Harry (1890–1965).
American songwriter, usually with lyricist Joseph McCarthy. Shows filmed include *Irene, Kid Boots, Rio Rita*.

Tierney, Lawrence (1919–).
American 'tough-guy' actor, brother of Scott Brady.
The Ghost Ship 44. *Dillinger* (title role) 45. Step by Step 46. San Quentin 47. The Devil Thumbs a Ride 47. Shakedown 50. The Hoodlum 51. A Child Is Waiting 62. Custer of the West 67. Such Good Friends 71. Midnight 82. Prizzi's Honor 85. Silver Bullet 85. Murphy's Law 86. Tough Guys Don't Dance 87. The Runestone 92. Reservoir Dogs 92. A Kiss Goodnight 94, etc.

Tiffin, Pamela (1942–) (Pamela Wonso).
American leading lady, former child model.
Summer and Smoke 60. One Two Three 61. State Fair 61. The Hallelujah Trail 65. Viva Max 69, etc.

Tilbury, Zeffie (1863–1950).
American character actress.
The Marriage of William Ashe 21. Werewolf of London 35. The Last Days of Pompeii 35. Maid of Salem 37. Balalaika 39. Tobacco Road 41. She Couldn't Say No 45, etc.

Till, Eric (1929–).
English director who moved to Canada in the 70s.
Hot Millions 68. The Walking Stick 69. A Fan's Notes 72. It Shouldn't Happen to a Vet 76. Improper Channels 81. If You Could See What I Hear 82. The Cuckoo Bride (TV) 85. Turning to Stone (TV) 85, etc.

Tiller, Nadja (1929–).
Austrian leading lady, in international films.
Rosemary 59. Portrait of a Sinner 61. The World in My Pocket 62. And So to Bed 65. The Upper Hand 67. Lady Hamilton 68. Wanted: Babysitter 75, etc.

Tilly, Jennifer (1958–).
American leading actress, the sister of Meg Tilly.
Moving Violations 85. He's My Girl 87. Remote Control 88. Rented Lips 88. Johnny Be Good 88. High Spirits 88. Far from Home 89. Let It Ride 89. The Fabulous Baker Boys 89. Inside Out 91. Scorchers 92. Agaguk (aka Shadow of the Wolf) 92. Made in America 93. Heads (TV) 94. The Getaway 94. Bullets over Broadway 94, etc.
TV series: Shaping Up 84.

Tilly, Meg (1960–).
American leading actress.
Fame 80. One Dark Night 82. Tex 82. The Big Chill 83. Psycho II 83. Impulse 84. Agnes of God (AAN) 85. Off Beat 85. Masquerade 88. The Girl in a Swing 88. Valmont 89. The Two Jakes 90. Leaving Normal 92. Body Snatchers 93. Sleep with Me 94, etc.

tilt.
An upward or downward camera movement.

Tilton, Martha (1915–).
American singer, in occasional films.
Sunny 41. Swing Hostess 44. Crime Inc 45. The Benny Goodman Story 56, etc.

time-lapse photography.
The method by which one can obtain such fascinating results as a flower growing and blooming before one's eyes. The camera is set up and regulated to expose one frame of film at pre-arranged intervals.
See also: *stop motion*.

Tingwell, Charles (1923–).
Australian actor for a time in British TV and films, especially during the 50s in *Emergency Ward Ten*.
Always Another Dawn 48. Bitter Springs 50. Life in Emergency Ward Ten 58. Cone of Silence 60. Murder She Said 63. The Secret of Blood Island 65. Dracula – Prince of Darkness 65. Nobody Runs Forever 68. End Play 75. Gone to Ground 76. Eliza Fraser 76. Breaker Morant 80. Freedom 82. Windrider 86. Malcolm 86. Miracle Down Under 87. A Cry in the Dark 88, etc.
TV series: Homicide 74–75.

Tinling, James (1889–1967).
American second-feature director.
Silk Legs 27. Arizona 30. Broadway 33. Charlie Chan in Shanghai 35. Pepper 36. 45 Fathers 37. Mr Moto's Gamble 38. Riders of the Purple Sage 41. Sundown Jim 42. The House of Tao Ling 47. Night Wind 48. Trouble Preferred 49. Tales of Robin Hood 52.

tinting
has plainly gone out of fashion now that virtually all films are in colour, but in black-and-white days the use of single colours could lead to interesting effects. In the 20s and earlier it was common practice to tint night scenes blue, sunlit scenes yellow, etc.; I saw one Russian film made in 1917 in which the only scene in black-and-white was that in which the hero hanged himself ! When talkies came in these colour effects were forgotten, but towards the mid-30s when colour was threatening, a tint seemed better than nothing. Films released wholly in sepia included *The Ghost Goes West, Bad Man of Brimstone, The Firefly, Maytime, The Girl of the Golden West, The Oklahoma Kid, Of Mice and Men* and *The Rains Came*; while the 'real' scenes of *The Wizard of Oz* were also sepia, leaving full colour until we landed over the rainbow. *A Midsummer Night's Dream* was released with a blue rinse, as were the water-ballet reels of *A Day at the Races*. Other colours have been used for short sequences. Green for *Portrait of Jennie* (the storm), *Luck of the Irish* (the leprechaun forest) and *Lost Continent* (to obscure the poor monster animation). Red for the *Hell's Angels* battle scenes and for the flash at the end of *Spellbound* when the villain turns a gun on himself. Even monochrome has its effectiveness, as shown in *A Matter of Life and Death* and *Bonjour Tristesse*.

Tiomkin, Dmitri (Dimitri) (1894–1979).
Russian-American composer of innumerable film scores.
Autobiography: 1959, *Please Don't Hate Me*.
Alice in Wonderland 33. *Lost Horizon* 37. The Great Waltz 38. *The Moon and Sixpence* 42. Shadow of a Doubt 43. Duel in the Sun 46. *Portrait of Jennie* 48. The Men 50. *High Noon* (AA) 52. *The High and the Mighty* (AA) 54. Land of the Pharaohs 55. Friendly Persuasion 56. *Giant* 56. Night Passage 57. *Gunfight at the O.K. Corral* 57. The Old Man and the Sea (AA) 58. The Unforgiven 60. The Alamo 60. The Guns of Navarone 61. 55 Days at Peking 62. The Fall of the Roman Empire 64. Tchaikovsky 71, etc.

Tissé, Edouard (1897–1961).
Franco-Russian cinematographer who worked closely with Eisenstein.
Strike 24. *The Battleship Potemkin* 25. *The General Line* (The Old and the New) 27. *Que Viva Mexico* 32. Aerograd 36. *Alexander Nevsky* 39. *Ivan the Terrible* 42 and 46. Glinka 54, etc.

To Have and Have Not.
Ernest Hemingway's tough, soft-hearted adventure novel has been filmed three times: in 1944 by Howard Hawks, with Bogart, Bacall, and not much left of the plot; in 1951 by Michael Curtiz as *The Breaking Point*, with John Garfield and Patricia Neal; and in 1958, as *The Gun Runner*, with Audie Murphy.

Toback, James (1943–).
American writer-director.
■ The Gambler (w) 74. Fingers (wd) 77. Love & Money (wd) 80. Exposed (a, wd) 83. The Pick-Up Artist (wd) 87. The Big Bang (a, wd) 89. Bugsy (w) (AAN) 91.

Tobey, Kenneth (1919–).
American character actor of dependable types.
Kiss Tomorrow Goodbye 49. About Face 51. The Thing 52. The Beast from 20,000 Fathoms 53. The Man in the Grey Flannel Suit 56. Terror in the Sky (TV) 72. Billy Jack 73. W. C. Fields and Me 76. MacArthur 77. Strange Invaders 83. Innerspace 87. Gremlins 2: The New Batch 90, etc.
TV series: Whirlybirds 54–58.

Tobias, George (1901–1980).
American character actor with stage experience.
Saturday's Children (debut) 40. City for Conquest 40. Sergeant York 41. Yankee Doodle Dandy 42. This is the Army 43. Thank Your Lucky Stars 43. Between Two Worlds 44. Objective Burma 45. Mildred Pierce 45. Sinbad the Sailor 47. Rawhide 50. The Glenn Miller Story 53. The Seven Little Foys 55. A New Kind of Love 63. The Glass Bottom Boat 66, many others.
TV series: Hudson's Bay 59–60. Adventures in Paradise 60–61. Bewitched 64–72.

Tobias, Oliver (1947–).
Saturnine British leading man.
Jesus of Nazareth (TV) 77. The Stud 78. Arabian Adventure 79. A Nightingale Sang in Berkeley Square 80. The Wicked Lady 83. Mata Hari 85.
TV series: Arthur of the Britons 72.

Tobin, Dan (1909–1982).
Lightweight American character actor.
The Stadium Murders 38. Woman of the Year 41. Undercurrent 46. The Big Clock 48. The Velvet Touch 49. Dear Wife 52. Wedding Breakfast 56. The Last Angry Man 59. The Love Bug Rides Again 73, etc.
TV series: Perry Mason 57–65.

Tobin, Genevieve (1901–).
Vivacious American actress of French parentage. Mainly stage experience; made some films during the 30s. She was married to director William Keighley.
The Lady Surrenders (debut) 31. One Hour With You 32. Easy to Wed 34. The Petrified Forest 36. The Great Gambini 37. Dramatic School 38. Zaza 39. Queen of Crime 41, etc.

Toch, Ernst (1887–1964).
German composer in Hollywood.
Catherine the Great 34. Little Friend 34. Peter Ibbetson 35. Four Men and a Prayer 38. *The Cat and the Canary* 39. The Ghost Breakers 40. Dr Cyclops 40. Ladies in Retirement 41. Address Unknown 44. The Unseen 45, etc.

Todd, Ann (1909–1993).
Blonde British leading actress, a big star of the 40s. Later produced and directed short travel films. She was formerly married to director David Lean.
Autobiography: 1980, *The Eighth Veil*.
■ Keepers of Youth 31. These Charming People 31. The Ghost Train 31. The Water Gypsies 31. The Return of Bulldog Drummond 34. Things to Come 36. The Squeaker 37. Action for Slander 37. South Riding 38. Poison Pen 39. Danny Boy 41. Ships with Wings 41. Perfect Strangers 45. *The Seventh Veil* 45. Gaiety George 46. Daybreak 47. So Evil my Love 47. The Paradine Case (US) 48. *The Passionate Friends* 48. Madeleine 49. The Sound Barrier 52. The Green Scarf 54. Time without Pity 57. Taste of Fear 61. Son of Captain Blood 62. Ninety Degrees in the Shade 65. The Friend 71. The Human Factor 79.

¶ The pattern of destiny is very strange. I sometimes wonder why I had to be an actress and achieve a well-known name – when deep down I am a private person and rather like being alone. – *A.T.*

I don't really consider myself an actress. I don't think I ever act. The parts I have played in my career that have come off best have usually been a continuation of myself. – *A.T.*

Todd, Ann (1932–) (A. T. Mayfield).
American child star of the 30s and 40s.
Zaza 39. Blood and Sand 41. Kings Row 42. The Jolson Story 46. Bomba and the Lion Hunters 52, etc.

Todd, Bob (1922–1992).
Bald British comic actor, much on TV.
The Intelligence Men 65. Hot Millions 68. The Private Life of Sherlock Holmes 70. Digby, the Biggest Dog in the World 73. The Four Musketeers 74. Superman III 83, etc.

Todd, Mike (1907–1958) (Avrom Goldenborgen).
Dynamic American producer of Broadway spectacles, a former carnival barker. His one personally produced film was in similar vein: *Around the World in Eighty Days* (AA) 56. The wide-screen system *Todd-AO* is named after him. His three wives included Joan Blondell and Elizabeth Taylor. Died in a plane crash.
Biography: 1959, *The Nine Lives of Mike Todd* by Art Cohn.

¶ I believe in giving customers a meat-and-potatoes show. Dames and comedy. – *M.K.*
Mike is the most exciting man in the world. – *Elizabeth Taylor, 1957*
This sinister dwarf who consumed nine weeks of my life has no peer in his chosen profession, which – stated very plainly – is to humiliate and cheapen his fellow man, fracture one's self-esteem, convert everybody around him into lackeys, hypocrites and toadies, and thoroughly debase every relationship, no matter how casual. His enormity grows on you like some obscene fungus. – *S. J. Perelman (screenwriter of Around the World in Eighty Days)*

Todd, Richard (1919–).
British leading man, in repertory from 1937 until spotted by a film talent scout.
For Them that Trespass (debut) 48. *The Hasty Heart* (AAN) 49. Stage Fright 50. Lightning Strikes Twice (US) 51. *Robin Hood* 52. Venetian Bird 53. The Sword and the Rose 54. Rob Roy 54. *A Man Called Peter* 55. The Virgin Queen (US) 55. *The Dam Busters* 55. Yangtse Incident 56. Chase a Crooked Shadow 57. Danger Within 58. The Long, the

Short and the Tall 59. The Hellions 60. Never Let Go 61. The Longest Day 62. The Boys 62. The Very Edge 63. Operation Crossbow 65. The Battle of the Villa Fiorita 65. Coast of Skeletons 65. Death Drums along the River 66. Last of the Long-haired Boys 68. Subterfuge 69. Dorian Gray 70. Asylum 72. The Big Sleep 78. Home Before Midnight 79. House of the Long Shadows 83. Sherlock Holmes – the Incident at Victoria Falls (TV) 91, etc.

Todd, Thelma (1905–1935).
Perky American leading blonde of the early 30s, heroine of many two-reel comedies. Died in mysterious circumstances.
Fascinating Youth 26. Rubber Heels 27. The Haunted House 28. Her Private Life 29. Aloha 30. The Hot Heiress 31. *Monkey Business* 31. The Maltese Falcon 31. *Horse Feathers* 32. Air Hostess 33. Sitting Pretty 33. Hips Hips Hooray 34. Bottoms Up 34. Two for Tonight 35. The Bohemian Girl 35, many others.

The Toff.
John Creasey's aristocratic investigator was the hero of two British films, in which he was played by John Bentley, both directed by Maclean Rogers: *Salute the Toff* 51 and *Hammer the Toff* 52.

Tognazzi, Ricky (1955–).
Italian director, producer and actor, the son of Ugo Tognazzi. Born in Milan, of an Italian father and Scottish mother, he was educated partly in Britain.
Piccoli Equivoci 89. Ultra 90. The Escort (La Scorta) 93. Sentimental Maniacs (Maniaci Sentimentali) (a, p) 94, etc.

Tognazzi, Ugo (1922–1990).
Italian leading actor.
His Women (Il Mantenuto) (& d) 61. The Fascist (Il Federale) 62. Queen Bee (Ape Regina or The Conjugal Bed) 63. The Magnificent Cuckold 64. An American Wife 65. A Question of Honour 66. Barbarella 68. Property Is No Longer a Theft 73. Blowout 73. Duck in Orange Sauce 75. Viva Italia 77. *La Cage aux Folles* 79. La Cage aux Folles II 80. Sunday Lovers 80. Tolerance 89, etc.

Tokar, Norman (1920–1979).
American director, from radio; in films, worked almost exclusively for Disney.
■ Big Red 62. Savage Sam 63. Sammy the Way Out Seal 63. A Tiger Walks 64. Those Calloways 65. Follow Me Boys 65. The Ugly Dachshund 66. The Happiest Millionaire 67. The Horse in the Grey Flannel Suit 68. Rascal 69. The Boatniks 72. Snowball Express 73. The Apple Dumpling Gang 75. Where the Red Fern Grows 76. No Deposit No Return 77. Candleshoe 78. The Cat from Outer Space 78.

Tol'able David.
Joseph Hergesheimer's novel was first, and most successfully, filmed in 1921, with Richard Barthelmess as the gentle youth making good in the tough outdoor life. In 1931 John G. Blystone directed a disappointing sound remake with Richard Cromwell.

Toland, Gregg (1904–1948).
Distinguished American cinematographer who worked mainly with Goldwyn.
The Unholy Garden 31. Roman Scandals 33. Tugboat Annie 33. *Nana* 34. We Live Again 34. Mad Love 35. Les Misérables 35. These Three 36. *Dead End* 37. The Goldwyn Follies 38. Intermezzo 39. *Wuthering Heights* (AA) 39. Raffles 40. *The Grapes of Wrath* 40. The Long Voyage Home 40. The Westerner 40. Citizen Kane 41. *The Little Foxes* 41;

war service; *The Best Years of Our Lives* 46. The Kid from Brooklyn 47. The Bishop's Wife 48. *Enchantment* 48, many others.

Toler, Sidney (1874–1947).
Chubby American character actor who in 1938 took over the part of Charlie Chan and played it twenty-two times.
Madame X 29. Is My Face Red? 32. Spitfire 35. Call of the Wild 35. Our Relations 36. Wide Open Faces 38. Charlie Chan in Honolulu 38. Law of the Pampas 39. Charlie Chan at the Wax Museum 40. Castle in the Desert 42. White Savage 43. The Scarlet Clue 45. Dark Alibi 46. The Trap 47, many others.

Tolkien, J. R. R. (1892–1973).
Donnish British novelist who created the myth of 'Middle Earth' in his trilogy *The Lord of the Rings*, which became an instant classic and was filmed in cartoon form.

Tolkin, Michael.
American screenwriter, director and novelist, a former journalist.
Gleaming the Cube (w) 88. The Rapture (wd) 91. The Player (w) 92. Deep Cover (co-w) 92. The New Age (wd) 94.

Tolstoy, Leo (1828–1910).
Russian novelist whose *Anna Karenina* and *War and Peace* have been frequently filmed.

Tom and Jerry.
Short cartoons featuring the mean-minded, accident-prone cat and his inventive and likeable little adversary were in production at MGM, with a break in the 50s, from 1941, with Fred Quimby (qv) as executive producer until his death. They have been much criticized for their excessive violence, but their humour, coupled with the impossibility of the situations, has won the day. The Academy Award-winning titles are *The Milky Way* 40, *Yankee Doodle Mouse* 43, *Mouse Trouble* 44, *Quiet Please* 45, *Cat Concerto* 46, *The Little Orphan* 48, *The Two Mouseketeers* 51, *Johann Mouse* 52. The original cartoons were drawn by William Hanna and Joe Barbera.
Book: 1991, *Fifty Years of Cat and Mouse* by T. R. Adams.

Tom Brown's Schooldays.
The famous Victorian story of life at Rugby School exists in two major film versions: the first directed in America in 1939 by Robert Stevenson, with Cedric Hardwicke as Dr Arnold and Jimmy Lydon as Tom; the second made in Britain in 1951, directed by Gordon Parry, with Robert Newton and John Howard Davies.

Tom Sawyer.
Mark Twain's boy hero has been played on film by Jack Pickford in 1917 and, in *Huck and Tom*, in 1918; Jackie Coogan in 1920; Tommy Kelly in the Selznick production in 1938; Billy Cook in 1938 in *Tom Sawyer, Detective*; Johnnie Whitaker in 1973 in a musical version; and Josh Albee in a TV movie in 1973.

Tomasini, George (1909–1964).
American editor.
Wild Harvest 47. Houdini 53. Elephant Walk 54. To Catch a Thief 55. The Wrong Man 57. Vertigo 58. *North By Northwest* 59. Psycho 60. Cape Fear 62. The Birds 63. Marnie 64, etc.

Tombes, Andrew (1889–1976).
American supporting actor often seen as cop, undertaker, bartender or harassed official.

Moulin Rouge 33. Charlie Chan at the Olympics 37. Too Busy to Work 39. Phantom Lady 44. Can't Help Singing 44. Oh You Beautiful Doll 49. How to Be Very Very Popular 55, many others.

Tomei, Marisa (1964–).
American leading actress.

The Flamingo Kid 84. Oscar 91. My Cousin Vinny (AA) 92. Chaplin 92. Equinox 92. Untamed Heart 93. The Paper 94. Only You 94. The Perez Family 95, etc.

TV series: A Different World 87–88.

Tomelty, Joseph (1910–).
Irish character actor, in British films since 1945.

Odd Man Out 46. The Sound Barrier 52. Meet Mr Lucifer 54. Simba 55. A Kid for Two Farthings 56. The Black Torment 64, many others.

Tomlin, Lily (1939–).
American comedy actress.
■ Nashville (AAN) 75. The Late Show 77. Moment by Moment 78. Nine to Five 80. The Incredible Shrinking Woman 81. All of Me 84. Big Business 88. The Search for Signs of Intelligent Life in the Universe 91. Shadows and Fog 92. The Beverly Hillbillies 93. Short Cuts 93.

¶ The trouble with the rat race is that even if you win, you're still a rat. – L.T.

Tomlinson, David (1917–).
Amiable British leading man and comedian, a latter-day Ralph Lynn.

Quiet Wedding 40. Journey Together 45. The Way to the Stars 45. Master of Bankdam 47. Miranda 48. Sleeping Car to Trieste 48. The Chiltern Hundreds 49. Hotel Sahara 51. Three Men in a Boat 55. Up the Creek 58. Follow That Horse 60. Tom Jones 63. Mary Poppins 64. The Truth about Spring 65. City in the Sea 65. The Liquidator 66. The Love Bug 69. Bedknobs and Broomsticks 71. The Water Babies 78. The Fiendish Plot of Fu Manchu 80, many others.

Tone, Franchot (1905–1968) (Stanislas Pascal Franchot Tone).
American leading man of stage and screen.

The Wiser Sex (film debut) 32. Gabriel over the White House 33. Moulin Rouge 34. Mutiny on the Bounty (AAN) 35. Suzy 36. Quality Street 36. They Gave Him a Gun 37. Three Comrades 39. The Trail of the Vigilantes 40. Nice Girl 41. The Wife Takes a Flyer 42. Five Graves to Cairo 43. His Butler's Sister 43. Phantom Lady 44. Dark Waters 44. That Night with You 45. Because of Him 46. Her Husband's Affairs 47. I Love Trouble 48. Every Girl Should Be Married 48. The Man on the Eiffel Tower 50. Advise and Consent 62. La Bonne Soupe 64. In Harm's Way 65. Nobody Runs Forever 68, etc.

Tonti, Aldo (1910–1988).
Italian cinematographer.

Ossessione 44. Europe 51 50. The Mill on the Po 51. War and Peace 56. Cabiria 57. Reflections in a Golden Eye 67. Ashanti 78, etc.

Tony Rome.
The down-market private eye created by Marvin H. Albert was played by Frank Sinatra in two films directed by Gordon Douglas: Tony Rome in 1967, and Lady in Cement in 1968.

Toomey, Regis (1898–1991).
American character actor, on screen from 1928, usually as cop or victim in routine crime dramas.

Framed 29. Murder by the Clock 32. G-Men 35. The Big Sleep 46. The Nebraskan 53. Guys and Dolls 55. Man's Favourite Sport? 63. Peter Gunn 67. God Bless Dr Shagetz 77, many others.

TV series: Burke's Law 63–65. Petticoat Junction 68–69.

top ten
commercially successful directors by international box-office gross 1985–90 were:

Robert Zemeckis ($109 billion)
Steven Spielberg ($726 million)
Tony Scott ($724 million)
Tim Burton ($687 million)
Ivan Reitman ($648 million)
Chris Columbus ($573 million)
Garry Marshall ($569 million)
Barry Levinson ($545 million)
Richard Donner ($541 million)
Jerry Zucker ($511 million)

according to figures compiled by an American research firm, Paul Kagan Associates.

Topol (1935–) (Chaim Topol).
Israeli leading actor who gained fame with London stage run of Fiddler on the Roof.

Cast a Giant Shadow 65. Sallah 66. Before Winter Comes 69. Fiddler on the Roof (AAN) 71. Follow Me 72. Galileo 74. The House on Garibaldi Street 79. Flash Gordon 80. For Your Eyes Only 81. The Winds of War (TV) 83. Queenie (TV) 87. War and Remembrance (TV) 87, etc.

Topper.
Thorne Smith's story of a dull banker haunted by two fun-loving ghosts was filmed in 1937, directed by Norman Z. McLeod, with Roland Young, Constance Bennett, and Cary Grant; two sequels followed: Topper Takes a Trip in 1939, and Topper Returns in 1941. A TV series ran from 1953–56.

Topper, Burt (1928–).
American director.

Diary of a High School Bride 61. The Strangler 64. The Devil's Eight 68. Wild in the Streets (p) 68. The Hard Ride 71. Lovin' Man 72. The Day the Lord Got Busted 76, etc.

Torchy Blane.
A series of second features, mostly starring Glenda Farrell as a wisecracking girl reporter and Barton MacLane as her boyfriend, a puzzled policeman who gets the comeback for her zany ideas.

Smart Blonde 36. Fly-Away Baby 37. Adventurous Blonde 37. Blondes at Work 38. Torchy Blane in Panama (with Lola Lane replacing Farrell for one film) 38. Torchy Gets Her Man 38. Torchy Blane in Chinatown 39. Torchy Runs for Mayor 39. Torchy Plays with Dynamite (with Jane Wyman as the star) 39.

Toren, Marta (1926–1957).
Swedish leading lady signed by Hollywood scout while at dramatic school.

Casbah (debut) 48. Rogues' Regiment 49. One-Way Street 50. Panthers' Moon 51. Sirocco 51. The Man Who Watched the Trains Go By 52. Maddalena 54, etc.

Tork, Peter (1944–).
American actor and musician, one of The Monkees pop group.

Head 68.

TV series: The Monkees 66–68.

Tormé, Mel (1923–).
Amiable American ballad singer who has made occasional films.

Higher and Higher 43. Let's Go Steady 45. Junior Miss 45. Good News 47. Duchess of Idaho 50. The Big Operator 59. Walk Like a Dragon 60. The Pat 64. A Man Called Adam 66, etc.

Torn, Rip (1931–) (Elmore Torn).
American general-purpose actor, mainly on stage and TV. He was married to actress Geraldine Page.

Baby Doll 56. Time Limit 57. Cat on a Hot Tin Roof 58. King of Kings 61. Sweet Bird of Youth 6 The Cincinnati Kid 65. You're a Big Boy Now 66. Beach Red 67. The Rain People 69. Tropic of Cancer 69. Payday 73. Crazy Joe 73. Birch Interv 76. The Man Who Fell to Earth 76. Nasty Habits 77. The Private Files of J. Edgar Hoover 78. Com 78. Blind Ambition (TV) (as Nixon) 79. The Seduction of Joe Tynan 79. The First Family 80. Heartland 80. One Trick Pony 80. A Stranger Is Watching 82. Cross Creek (AAN) 83. City Heat 8 Songwriter 84. Beer 85. Summer Rental 85. Nadir 87. The Telephone (d) 88. Cold Feet 89. Hit List 89. Zwei Frauen 89. Beautiful Dreamers 90. Defending Your Life 91. My Son Johnny (TV) 9 Finnegans Wake 92. Dolly Dearest 92. Where th Rivers Flow North 93. Robocop 3 93, etc.

Tornatore, Giuseppe (1956–).
Italian director and screenwriter, from television.

The Professor (Il Camorrista) 87. Cinema Paradiso (Nuovo Cinema Paradiso) (AA) 88. Everybody's Fine (Stanno Tutti Bene) 90. Especially on Sundays (La Domenica Specialment (co-d) 91. A Simple Formality (Una Pura Formalita) (wd, e) 94, etc.

Torrence, David (1864–1951).
Scottish silent screen actor in Hollywood.

The Inside of the Cup 21. Sherlock Holmes 22. The Abysmal Brute 23. Surging Seas 24. The Reckless Sex 25. Laddie 26. Annie Laurie 27. The Little Shepherd of Kingdom Come 28. Untamed Justice 29. Raffles 30. Voltaire 33. Mandalay 34. The Dark Angel 35, etc.

Torrence, Ernest (1878–1933).
Scottish actor, in American silent films, usually a villain; former opera singer.

Tol'able David 21. The Hunchback of Notre Dame 23. The Trail of the Lonesome Pine 23. The Covered Wagon 23. Peter Pan 24. King of Kings 27 The Cossacks 28. The Bridge of San Luis Rey 29. The New Adventures of Get-Rich-Quick Wallingford 31. Cuban Love Song 32. Sherlock Holmes 33, many others.

Torre-Nilsson, Leopoldo (1924–1978).
Argentinian director, usually of sharp-flavoured melodramas which he also wrote.

The House of the Angel 57. The Fall 59. The Hand in the Trap 60. Summer Skin 61. Four Women fo One Hero 62. The Roof Garden 63. The Eavesdropper 65. Monday's Child 67. Martin Fierr 68, etc.

Torres, Raquel (1908–1987) (Paula Marie Osterman).
American leading lady who played fiery sirens in the early 30s.

White Shadows in the South Seas 28. The Bridg of San Luis Rey 29. Under a Texas Moon 30. The Woman I Stole 33. Duck Soup 33. The Red Wago 36, etc.

Tors, Ivan (1916–1983).
Hungarian writer-producer-director, in Hollywood from 1941.

Song of Love (w) 47. The Forsyte Saga (w) 49. Storm over Tibet (w, p) 52. The Magnetic Monster (w, p) 53. Gog (w, p) 54. Riders to the Stars (p) 55. Battle Taxi (p) 56. Flipper (p) 60. Rhino (p, d) 64. Zebra in the Kitchen 65. Around the World under the Sea 65, etc.

TV series as producer include: *Sea Hunt* 57–60. *The Man and the Challenge* 59. *Flipper* 64–68. *Primus* 71.

torture
has figured in *Arabian Nights*, *Thief of Bagdad*, and others of this genre; in witchcraft dramas such as *Witchfinder General*, *The Devils* and *Day of Wrath*; in medieval epics such as *El Cid*, *Ivanhoe* and *Tower of London*; further back to Roman times, in *The Robe*, *Barabbas*, *Spartacus* and *Demetrius and the Gladiators*; in World War II yarns such as *13 Rue Madeleine*, *OSS*, *Carve Her Name with Pride*, *The Seventh Cross* and *633 Squadron*; in Cold War melodramas such as *Treason*, *The Prisoner*, and *The Manchurian Candidate*; in historical mysteries such as *The Man in the Iron Mask* and in documentary adventures such as *A Man Called Horse*.

Tosi, Mario.
Italian-American cinematographer.

Some Call It Loving 73. Report to the Commissioner 74. Hearts of the West 75. Carrie 76. The Main Event 79. Resurrection 80. The Stunt Man 80. Six Pack 82.

Totheroh, Rollie (1891–1967).
American cinematographer who worked notably for Charles Chaplin.

The Pilgrim 23. The Gold Rush 24. City Lights 31. Modern Times 36. The Great Dictator 40. Monsieur Verdoux 47, etc.

Toto (1897–1967) (Antonio Furst de Curtis-Gagliardi). Italian comedian, from music hall and revue.

Fermo con le Mani 36. Toto Le Moko 49. Cops and Robbers 53. Gold of Naples 54. Racconti Romani 55. Persons Unknown 58. Toto of Arabia 63. The Commander 67, many others.

Totter, Audrey (1918–   ).
American leading lady of the 'hard-boiled' type, with stage and radio experience.

Main Street after Dark (debut) 44. Her Highness and the Bellboy 45. The Postman Always Rings Twice 45. *The Lady in the Lake* 46. Tenth Avenue Angel 47. The Unsuspected 48. Alias Nick Beal 49. The Set-Up 49. Tension 51. The Blue Veil 52. Assignment Paris 53. Women's Prison 54. A Bullet for Joey 55. The Carpetbaggers 64. Harlow (electronovision version) 65. Chubasco 68. The Apple Dumpling Gang Rides Again 79, many others.

TV series: Cimarron City 58. Our Man Higgins 62. Medical Center 72–76.

Toumanova, Tamara (1917–   ).
Russian ballerina who has made occasional appearances in American films.

Days of Glory 43. Deep in my Heart 54. Torn Curtain 67. The Private Life of Sherlock Holmes 70, etc.

Tourneur, Jacques (1904–1977).
Franco-American director; son of Maurice Tourneur, with a special flair for the macabre.

Nick Carter, Master Detective 39. Cat People 42. I Walked with a Zombie 43. The Leopard Man 43. Days of Glory 44. Experiment Perilous 44. Out of the Past 47. Berlin Express 48. Stars in My Crown 50. The Flame and the Arrow 51. Appointment in Honduras 53. Wichita 55. Great Day in the Morning 56. *Night of the Demon* 57. Timbuktu 59. The Giant of Marathon 61. A Comedy of Terrors 63. City under the Sea 65, etc.

Tourneur, Maurice (1876–1961) (Maurice Thomas).
French director who made some American films.

Mother 14. Man of the Hour 15. Trilby 15. Poor Little Rich Girl 17. The Bluebird 18. The Last of the Mohicans 20. Treasure Island 20. The Christian (GB) 23. Aloma of the South Seas 26. L'Équipage 27. Mysterious Island 29. Maison de Danses 31. Koenigsmark 35. Volpone 40. The Devil's Hand 42. L'Impasse des Deux Anges 48, etc.

Tover, Leo (1902–1964).
American cinematographer in Hollywood from 1918.

Dead Reckoning 47. *The Snake Pit* 48. *The Heiress* 49. The Secret of Convict Lake 51. The President's Lady 53. Soldier of Fortune 55. The Sun Also Rises 57. *Journey to the Centre of the Earth* 59. Follow That Dream 62. Sunday in New York 63. Strange Bedfellows 64. A Very Special Favor 65, many others.

Tovoli, Luciano.
Italian cinematographer.

Bread and Chocolate (Pane e Cioccolata) 74. Leonor 75. Suspiria 77. Bianca 85. La Cage aux Folles III (Fr.) 85. Love Dream 88. Reversal of Fortune (US) 90. Single White Female (US) 92. Mario, Maria e Mario 94, etc.

Towb, Harry (1925–   ).
Irish character actor, often as comic relief, in films from 1951.

The Gift Horse 52. Knave of Hearts 54. The Sleeping Tiger 54. Above Us the Waves 55. Eye Witness 56. The 39 Steps 59. The Blue Max 66. Prudence and the Pill 68. Patton 70. Carry On at Your Convenience 71. Barry Lyndon 75. Lassiter 83. Lost Belongings (TV) 87, etc.

Towers, Harry Alan (1920–   ).
British executive producer with varied experience in films and TV. He is also a screenwriter under the name of Peter Welbeck.

Victim Five (& w) 64. Mozambique (& w) 64. The Face of Fu Manchu 65. Ten Little Indians 65. Our Man in Marrakesh (Bang, Bang, You're Dead) 66. The Brides of Fu Manchu 66. Rocket to the Moon 67. Treasure Island 72. Call of the Wild 73. The Shape of Things to Come 78. Gor 85. Howling IV 89. Edge of Sanity 89. The Hitman 90, etc.

Towne, Gene (1904–1979).
American screenwriter.

Little Women 33. History is Made at Night 37. The Swiss Family Robinson 40. Joy of Living 41, etc.

Towne, Robert (1936–   ).
American screenwriter.

The Tomb of Ligeia 64. Villa Rides 67. The Last Detail (AAN) 73. *Chinatown* (AAN) 74. Shampoo (co-w) (AAN) 75. The Yakuza (co-w) 75. Personal Best (& d) 81. Greystoke: The Legend of Tarzan of the Apes 84. The Bedroom Window 87. Tequila Sunrise (& d) 88. Days of Thunder 90. The Two Jakes 90. The Firm (co-w) 93. Love Affair (co-w) 94, etc.

Townsend, Robert (1957–   ).
American actor, director, producer and screenwriter who began as a stand-up comedian. He made a breakthrough with *Hollywood Shuffle*, a comedy based on his own experiences as a black actor seeking work.

Willie & Phil 80. A Soldier's Story 84. Streets of Fire 84. American Flyers 85. Odd Jobs 86. Ratboy 86. Eddie Murphy Raw (d) 87. Hollywood Shuffle (& wd, p) 87. The Mighty Quinn 89. That's Adequate 89. The Five Heartbeats (& wd, p) 91. The Meteor Man (& wd) 93, etc.

Toye, Wendy (1917–   ).
British director, former dancer. Drew attention with two ingenious short films, The Stranger Left No Card 52 and On the Twelfth Day 55.

Features: Three Cases of Murder 54. All for Mary 55. True as a Turtle 56. We Joined the Navy 62, etc.

tracking shot.
One taken with a moving camera, usually forwards or backwards, and often on an actual track.

Tracy, Arthur (1903–   ) (Harry Rosenberg).
American singer who made his greatest success in England, especially with his rendering of 'Marta'. Retired with his riches to America.

The Big Broadcast 32. Limelight (GB) 36. The Street Singer (GB) 37. Follow Your Star (GB) 38, etc.

Tracy, Lee (1898–1968).
American leading actor of stage (from 1919) and screen (sporadically from 1929): had inimitable nasal delivery.

■ Big Time 29. Born Reckless 30. Liliom 30. She Got What She Wanted 30. The Strange Love of Molly Louvain 32. Love is a Racket 32. *Doctor X* 32. *Blessed Event* 32. Washington Merry Go Round 32. The Night Mayor 32. *The Half Naked Truth* 32. Clear All Wires 33. Private Jones 33. The Nuisance 33. Dinner at Eight 33. Turn Back the Clock 33. *Bombshell* 33. Advice to the Lovelorn 33. I'll Tell the World 34. You Belong to Me 34. The Lemon Drop Kid 34. Carnival 35. Two Fisted 35. Sutter's Gold 36. Wanted, Jane Turner 36. Criminal Lawyer 37. Behind the Headlines 37. Crashing Hollywood 38. Fixer Dugan 39. The Spellbinder 39. Millionaires in Prison 40. The Payoff 42. Power of the Press 43. Betrayal from the East 45. I'll Tell the World 45. High Tide 47. *The Best Man* (AAN) 64.

TV series: The Amazing Mr Malone 51. Martin Kane 53.

Tracy, Spencer (1900–1967).
Distinguished American actor with stage experience from 1922; exclusively on screen from 1930. His uneven features gained him gangster roles to begin with, then he made a corner in priests and friends of the hero; but his chief mature image was that of a tough, humorous fellow who was also a pillar of integrity.

Biographies: 1970, *Spencer Tracy* by Larry Swindell. 1973, *Tracy and Hepburn* by Garson Kanin.

■ Up the River 30. Quick Millions 31. Six-Cylinder Love 31. Goldie 31. She Wanted a Millionaire 32. Sky Devils 32. Disorderly Conduct 32. Young America 32. Society Girl 32. Painted Woman 32. Me and My Girl 32. *Twenty Thousand Years in Sing Sing* 32. Face in the Sky 33. *The Power and the Glory* 33. Shanghai Madness 33. The Mad Game 33. *A Man's Castle* 33. Looking for Trouble 34. The Show-Off 34. Bottoms Up 34. Now I'll Tell 34. Marie Galante 34. It's a Small World 35. Dante's Inferno 35. The Murder Man 35. Whipsaw 35. Riff Raff 36. *Fury* 36. San Francisco (AAN) 36. *Libeled Lady* 36. Captains Courageous (AA) 37. They Gave

Him a Gun 37. The Big City 38. Mannequin 38. Test Pilot 38. *Boys' Town* (AA) 38. *Stanley and Livingstone* 39. I Take This Woman 39. *Northwest Passage* 40. *Edison the Man* 40. Boom Town 40. Men of Boys' Town 41. Dr Jekyll and Mr Hyde 41. *Woman of the Year* 42. Tortilla Flat 42. Keeper of the Flame 43. A Guy Named Joe 43. *The Seventh Cross* 44. Thirty Seconds over Tokyo 44. Without Love 45. Sea of Grass 46. Cass Timberlane 47. *State of the Union* 48. Edward My Son (GB) 49. *Adam's Rib* 49. Malaya 49. *Father of the Bride* (AAN) 50. The People against O'Hara 51. Father's Little Dividend 51. Pat and Mike 52. Plymouth Adventure 52. The Actress 53. Broken Lance 54. *Bad Day at Black Rock* (AAN) 55. The Mountain 56. The Desk Set 57. The Old Man and the Sea (AAN) 58. *The Last Hurrah* 58. *Inherit the Wind* (AAN) 60. The Devil at Four o'Clock 61. *Judgment at Nuremberg* (AAN) 61. It's a Mad Mad Mad Mad World 63. *Guess Who's Coming to Dinner* (BFA, AAN) 67.

✪ For superb performances and for the utter reliability of his on-screen personality, which was so at odds with the insecurity of his private psyche. *Inherit the Wind.*

¶ The guy's good. There's nobody in the business who can touch him, and you're a fool to try. And the bastard knows it, so don't fall for that humble stuff!

This tribute came from Clark Gable, who suffered from co-starring with Tracy in several MGM movies of the 30s. On the other hand, Katharine Hepburn once said:

I think Spencer always thought that acting was a rather silly way for a man to make a living.

She also caught his essential strength:

He's like an old oak tree, or the summer, or the wind. He belongs to the era when men were men.

But Hepburn was exposed to his aggressive wit when they met in 1941 to make *Woman of the Year*:

I'm afraid I'm a little tall for you, Mr Tracy.
– Don't worry, I'll soon cut you down to my size.

He ranged from supreme self-confidence to abject despair. In 1931 he complained:

This mug of mine is as plain as a barn door. Why should people pay thirty-five cents to look at it?

He remembered:

There were times when my pants were so thin, I could sit on a dime and know if it was heads or tails.

Later he wondered at his own success:

The physical labour actors have to do wouldn't tax an embryo.

Perhaps this puzzlement was responsible for his attitude to the press:

Write anything you want about me. Make up something. Hell, I don't care.

But he did care, and he cared about his work. Perhaps Humphrey Bogart best summed up his appeal:

Spence is the best we have, because you don't see the mechanism at work.

Tracy, William (1917–1967).

American actor who used to play sly or dumb young fellows.

Brother Rat 38. Strike Up the Band 40. Tobacco Road 41. About Face 42. Fall In 44. The Walls of Jericho 49. Mr Walkie Talkie 54. The Wings of Eagles 56. etc.

Trail of the Lonesome Pine.

This backwoods melodrama was first filmed in

1916 with Charlotte Walker and Earle Fox; in 1923 it was remade with Mary Miles Minter, Antonio Moreno, and Ernest Torrence. In 1936 Henry Hathaway made a sound version with Sylvia Sidney, Henry Fonda, and Fred MacMurray, which was the first outdoor film in the newly perfected three-colour Technicolor.

trains

have above all served film-makers as a splendid background for suspense thrillers. Scores of sequences crowd to mind, all enhanced by the dramatic background of a speeding train: *The Lady Vanishes*, *North by Northwest*, *From Russia with Love*, *The Narrow Margin*, *The Tall Target*, *How the West Was Won*, *3.10 to Yuma*, *Lady on a Train*, *Cat Ballou*, *Jesse James*, *Bad Day at Black Rock*, *Night of the Demon*, *Time Bomb*, *Rome Express*, *Sleeping Car to Trieste*, *Northwest Frontier*, *Man without a Star*, *The Thirty-Nine Steps*, *Secret Agent*, *Shanghai Express*, *Number 17*, *Last Train from Madrid*, *Last Train to Bombay*, *Ministry of Fear*, *Von Ryan's Express*, *Across the Bridge*, *Double Indemnity*, *Strangers on a Train*, *The Iron Horse*, *Union Pacific*, *Canadian Pacific*, *Next of Kin*, *Berlin Express*, *The Great Locomotive Chase*, *Terror by Night*, *Crack-Up*, *Rampage*, *Fool's Parade*, *The Train*, *Breakheart Pass*, *Murder on the Orient Express* . . . the list could be almost endless. More serious films using trains include *La Bête Humaine* (and its remake *Human Desire*), *Metropolitan* (and its remake *A Window in London*), *Brief Encounter*, *The Last Journey*, *Sullivan's Travels*, *Indiscretion of an American Wife*, *Anna Karenina*, *Terminus*, *Night Mail*, *The Manchurian Candidate*, *The Railway Children*, *Doctor Zhivago*, *Boxcar Bertha*, and *Emperor of the North*; while spectacular crashes were featured in *The Greatest Show on Earth*, *Hatter's Castle*, *Seven Sinners*, *The Young in Heart*, *Mad Love*, *The Wrong Box*, *Lawrence of Arabia*, *Crack in the World*, *The Ghost Train*, and *King Kong*. Murder was seen from a train in *Metropolitan* and *Lady in a Train* (happening in a second passing train in *Murder She Said*), and *through a train* in *Twelve Angry Men*. The subway, elevated or underground railway was featured in *Practically Yours*, *On the Town*, *The Bachelor Party*, *Boys' Night Out*, *Union Station*, *The FBI Story*, *The Young Savages*, *Underground*, *Bulldog Jack*, *Daleks Invasion Earth 2150 AD*, *The French Connection*, *Beneath the Planet of the Apes*, and *The Liquidator*. The back platforms of American trains have become familiar, especially in political films like *Abe Lincoln in Illinois*, *Wilson* and *All the King's Men*; but also in *Hail the Conquering Hero*, *Double Indemnity*, *The Merry Monahans* and *Mr Deeds Goes to Town*. Comedy train sequences include the Marx Brothers chopping up moving carriages for fuel in *Go West*, the Ale and Quail Club in *The Palm Beach Story*, Buster Keaton's splendidly inventive *Our Hospitality* and *The General*, *The Great St Trinian's Train Robbery*, Laurel and Hardy going to sleep in the same bunk in *The Big Noise*, Hal Roach's *Broadway Limited*, John Barrymore in *Twentieth Century*, Peter Sellers in *Two-Way Stretch*, the western sequence of *Around the World in Eighty Days*, the Pullman car sequence of *Some Like It Hot*, Monty Banks in *Play Safe*, Morecambe and Wise in *The Magnificent Two*, *The Private Life of Sherlock Holmes*, the whole of *The Titfield Thunderbolt* and *Oh Mr Porter* . . . and many scenes of jaywalking on top of moving carriages, including *Professor Beware*, *The Merry Monahans* and *Fancy Pants*. Musical sequences with a train motif or setting are found in *A Hard Day's Night*, *Monte Carlo*, *Some Like It Hot*, *The Harvey Girls* ('The Atchison, Topeka and the Santa Fe'), *At the Circus* ('Lydia the Tattooed Lady'), *Sun Valley Serenade* ('Chattanooga Choo Choo'), *Dumbo* ('Casey Junior'), *The Jazz Singer* ('Toot Toot Tootsie,

Goodbye'), *Easter Parade* ('When the Midnight Choo Choo Leaves for Alabam'), *Forty-second Street* ('Shuffle off to Buffalo').

TV series involving trains as a regular motif include *Casey Jones*, *The Wild Wild West*, *The Iron Horse*, *Petticoat Junction*, *Union Pacific* and *Supertrain*.

tramps

or hoboes who have figured largely in films include those played by William Powell in *My Man Godfrey*, Joel McCrea in *Sullivan's Travels*, George Arliss in *The Guv'nor*, Jean Gabin in *Archimède le Clochard*, practically the whole cast of *Hallelujah I'm a Bum*, and of course Charlie Chaplin in all his earlier comedies.

transvestism.

There have been many films, mostly lightweight ones, making effective use of situations in which men dress up as women. *Charley's Aunt* has proved a perennial, and in silent days Julian Eltinge, a female impersonator, made several popular films: his 1972 successor was Danny la Rue, in *Our Miss Fred*. Well-known actors in female attire have included Wallace Beery as 'Swedy' in a series of silent comedies, Lon Chaney in *The Unholy Tree*, Lionel Barrymore in *The Devil Doll*, William Powell in *Love Crazy*, Cary Grant in *I Was a Male War Bride*, Joe E. Brown as his own grandma in *The Daring Young Man*, Cook and Moore as leaping nuns in *Bedazzled*, Alec Guinness in *The Comedians*, Brian Deacon in *Triple Echo*, Alec Guinness in *Kind Hearts and Coronets*, Peter Sellers in *The Mouse That Roared*, William Bendix and Dennis O'Keefe in *Abroad with Two Yanks*, Jimmy Durante in *You're in the Army Now*, Lee J. Cobb in *In Like Flint*, Ray Walston in *Caprice*, Jerry Lewis in *Three on a Couch*, Stan Laurel in *That's My Wife* and *Jitterbugs*, Bing Crosby in *High Time*, Bob Hope in *Casanova's Big Night*, Tony Curtis and Jack Lemmon in *Some Like It Hot*, Tony Perkins in *Psycho*, Dick Shawn in *What Did You Do in the War, Daddy?* Phil Silvers and Jack Gilford in *A Funny Thing Happened on the Way to the Forum*, Jerry Lewis in *At War with the Army*, Jack Oakie in *Let's go Native*, Lou Costello in *Lost in a Harem*, Eddie Cantor in *Ali Baba Goes to Town*, Joe E. Brown in *Shut my Big Mouth*. Billy de Wolfe in *Isn't it Romantic?*, William Powell in *Love Crazy*, Melvyn Douglas in *The Amazing Mr Williams*, James Coco in *The Wild Party*, Preston Foster in *Up the River*, Oscar Levant and David Wayne in *The I Don't Care Girl*, Alastair Sim in *The Belles of St Trinian's*, Helmut Berger in *The Damned*, Tim Curry in *The Rocky Horror Movie*, Dustin Hoffman in *Tootsie*, Denis Quilley in *Privates on Parade*, Michel Serrault in *La Cage aux Folles* and its sequels, and Divine in *Pink Flamingos* and other John Waters films; while the device became in the 60s a standard device of spy stories, including *The Kremlin Letter*, *Thunderball*, *Licensed to Kill*, *Where the Bullets Fly*, and *Gunn*. *Myra Breckinridge* also fits in somewhere, as do *Glen or Glenda* and *Dr Jekyll and Sister Hyde*. In the 90s, cross-dressing became almost fashionable. Robin Williams had a box-office success disguised as a nannie in *Mrs Doubtfire*, Quentin Crisp became a believable Queen Elizabeth I in *Orlando*, Leslie Cheung was a specialist in female roles at the Peking Opera in *Farewell My Concubine*, Terence Stamp was among the drag queens tramping around the Australian outback in *The Adventures of Priscilla, Queen of the Desert*, Johnny Depp put on women's clothes as the angora-sweater-loving transvestite director Ed Wood – star of *Glen or Glenda* – in Tim Burton's affectionate biopic of the world's worst film director, and Wesley Snipes and others donned frocks in *To Wong Foo, Thanks for Everything, Julie*

Newmar. There was even talk of remaking *La Cage aux Folles.*

Women disguised as men are rarer; but one can instance such notable examples as Katharine Hepburn in *Sylvia Scarlett,* Annabella in *Wings of the Morning,* Signe Hasso in *The House on 92nd Street,* Nita Talbot in *A Very Special Favor,* Marlene Dietrich in *Morocco,* Greta Garbo in *Queen Christina,* Mary Pickford in *Kiki,* Debbie Reynolds in *Goodbye Charlie,* Jessie Matthews in *Gangway,* Miriam Hopkins in *She Loves Me Not,* Marlene Dietrich in *Seven Sinners,* Louise Brooks in *Beggars of Life,* Doris Day in *Calamity Jane,* Frances Farmer in *Badlands of Dakota,* Veronica Lake in *Sullivan's Travels,* Jean Peters in *Anne of the Indies,* Maureen O'Hara in *At Sword's Point,* Merle Oberon in *A Song to Remember,* Lupe Velez in *Honolulu Lu,* Julie Andrews in *Victor/Victoria,* and the ambiguous hero-heroine of *Homicidal.* In *Turnabout* a husband and wife exchanged bodies, with dire results. In *Switch,* a murdered male chauvinist returned to earth as Ellen Barkin in search of salvation. And in *Orlando* Tilda Swinton went from Elizabethan man to modern woman.

Traubel, Helen (1899–1972).
American soprano.
■ Deep in My Heart 54. The Ladies' Man 61. Gunn 67.

Trauner, Alexander (1906–1993).
French art director who has worked on international films. Born in Budapest, he moved to Paris in the 20s as a painter, and became an assistant to Lazare Meerson (qv). Worked on more than 100 films.
Quai des Brumes 38. Le Jour Se Lève 39. *Les Visiteurs du Soir* 42. *Les Enfants du Paradis* 44. Les Portes de la Nuit 45. Manèges 49. Othello 52. Love in the Afternoon 56. *The Nun's Story* 58. The Apartment (AA) 60. One Two Three 61. Irma la Douce 63. Kiss Me Stupid 64. The Night of the Generals 66. *A Flea in Her Ear* 68. The Private Life of Sherlock Holmes 70. Promise at Dawn 71. The Man Who Would Be King (AAN) 75. Mr Klein 77. The Fiendish Plot of Fu Manchu 79. Don Giovanni 79. La Truite 82. Subway 85. Round Midnight 86. Reunion 89, etc.

Travanti, Daniel J. (1940–).
American character actor, mainly on TV.
St Ives 76. Adam (TV) 83. Murrow (TV) 85. Midnight Crossing 87. Millennium 89. Fellow Traveller 89. Megaville 90. Hello Stranger 92, etc.
TV series: *Hill Street Blues* 81–87. Missing Persons 93– .

travelling matte:
a masking film overlaid with another in the optical printer so as to produce a trick effect.

Traven, B. (1882–1969).
The mysterious author of *The Treasure of the Sierra Madre* was most probably an Austrian called H.A.O.M. Feige. He was a former actor and anarchist, known for a while as Ret Marut. Settling in Mexico, he became a union agitator and was listed as an enemy of the state.

Travers, Ben (1886–1980).
Long-lived British playwright responsible for the Tom Walls/Ralph Lynn Aldwych farces which were all filmed in the early 30s.
Autobiographies: 1958, *Vale of Laughter* 1979, *A-Sitting on a Gate.*
Rookery Nook 30. *A Cuckoo in the Nest* 33. A Cup of Kindness 33. Turkey Time 34. Banana Ridge 41. etc.

Also wrote filmscripts: Fighting Stock 36. Just My Luck 37. Uncle Silas 47, etc.

Travers, Bill (1922–1994).
Tall British leading man, married to Virginia McKenna; stage experience from 1947.
The Square Ring 54. Geordie 55. Bhowani Junction 56. The Barretts of Wimpole Street 57. *The Smallest Show on Earth* 57. The Seventh Sin (US) 58. The Bridal Path 59. Gorgo 60. Invasion Quartet 61. Two Living, One Dead (Swed.) 62. Born Free 66. Duel at Diablo (US) 66. A Midsummer Night's Dream 68. Ring of Bright Water 69. The Belstone Fox 73. Christian the Lion 77, etc.

Travers, Henry (1874–1965) (Travers Heagerty).
British character actor, on stage from 1894, in America from 1901. Came to films in the 30s and usually played benign old gentlemen.
■ Reunion in Vienna 32. Another Language 33. My Weakness 33. The Invisible Man 33. The Party's Over 34. Death Takes a Holiday 34. Ready for Love 34. Born to Be Bad 34. Maybe It's Love 35. After Office Hours 35. Escapade 35. Pursuit 35. Captain Hurricane 35. Seven Keys to Baldpate 35. Four Hours to Kill 35. Too Many Parents 36. The Sisters 38. Dark Victory 39. You Can't Get Away with Murder 39. Dodge City 39. On Borrowed Time 39. Remember? 39. Stanley and Livingstone 39. The Rains Came 39. The Primrose Path 40. Anne of Windy Poplars 40. Edison the Man 40. Wyoming 40. *Ball of Fire* 41. High Sierra 41. A Girl, a Guy and a Gob 41. The Bad Man 41. I'll Wait for You 41. *Mrs Miniver* (AAN) 42. Pierre of the Plains 42. Random Harvest 42. Shadow of a Doubt 42. *The Moon Is Down* 43. Madame Curie 43. Dragon Seed 44. None Shall Escape 44. The Very Thought of You 44. Thrill of a Romance 45. The Naughty Nineties 45. The Bells of St Mary's 45. Gallant Journey 46. *It's a Wonderful Life* 46. The Yearling 46. The Flame 47. Beyond Glory 48. The Girl from Jones Beach 49.

Travers, Linden (1913–) (Florence Lindon-Travers).
British leading lady of stage (from 1931), screen shortly after.
Children of the Fog 35. Double Alibi 36. The Lady Vanishes 38. The Terror 39. The Stars Look Down 39. *The Ghost Train* 41. The Missing Million 42. Beware of Pity 46. No Orchids for Miss Blandish 48. *Quartet* 48. Christopher Columbus 49, etc.

Travilla, William (1920–1990).
American costume designer who was employed by Columbia 1941–43, Warner 1946–49, and Twentieth Century Fox 1950–58, where he worked closely with Marilyn Monroe.
The Adventures of Don Juan (AA) 49. Monkey Business 52. Gentlemen Prefer Blondes 53. How to Marry a Millionaire (AAN) 53. There's No Business Like Showbusiness (AAN) 54. Bus Stop 56. The Stripper (AAN) 63. Moviola (TV) 80. The Thorn Birds (TV) 83. A Streetcar Named Desire (TV) 84, etc.

Travis, Nancy (1961–).
American actress.
Three Men and a Baby 87. Married to the Mob 88. Eight Men Out 88. Internal Affairs 90. Air America 90. Three Men and a Little Lady 90. Loose Cannons 90. Passed Away 92. The Vanishing 93. So I Married an Axe Murderer 93, etc.

Travis, Neil.
American editor.
Jaws II 76. The Idolmaker 80. Second Thoughts

83. Cujo 83. Marie 85. No Way Out 87. Cocktail 88. Dances with Wolves (AA) 90. Deceived 91. Patriot Games 92. Clear and Present Danger 94. Outbreak 95, etc.

Travis, Richard (1913–1989) (William Justice).
American leading man of 40s and 50s second features.
The Man Who Came to Dinner 41. The Big Shot 42. Buses Roar 43. Jewels of Brandenberg 44. Alaska Patrol 46. Skyliner 48. Operation Haylift 50. Mask of the Dragon 51. Fingerprints Don't Lie 51. City of Shadows 55, etc.

Travolta, John (1954–).
Long-limbed American dancing star of the late 70s. Married Kelly Preston.
■ The Devil's Rain 75. Carrie 76. The Boy in the Plastic Bubble (TV) 77. *Saturday Night Fever* (AAN) 77. *Grease* 78. Moment by Moment 79. Urban Cowboy 80. Blow Out 81. Staying Alive 83. Two of a Kind 84. Perfect 85. The Experts 89. Look Who's Talking 89. Look Who's Talking Too 90. Shout 91. Look Who's Talking Now 93. *Pulp Fiction* 94.
TV series: Welcome Back Kotter 75–78.

¶ I'm not an old-fashioned romantic. I believe in love and marriage, but not necessarily with the same person. – J.T.
I would never do anything solely for money. I have to believe in the project. – J.T.
My best quality? The transparency in my eyes. I have only to think a thought and it's seen. – J.T.

Treacher, Arthur (1894–1975) (A. T. Veary).
Tall British character comedian, the perfect butler for 30 years. On stage from the 20s, Hollywood from 1933.
David Copperfield 34. A Midsummer Night's Dream 35. *Thank You Jeeves* 36. The Little Princess 39. National Velvet 44. Delightfully Dangerous 45. The Countess of Monte Cristo 48. Love That Brute 50. Mary Poppins 64, many others.

Treasure Island.
Robert L. Stevenson's adventure classic was filmed four times as a silent and even more often in the sound era. In 1935, in a splendid production for MGM, Victor Fleming directed Wallace Beery as Long John Silver and Jackie Cooper as the cabin-boy Jim Hawkins; in 1950, in Britain for Disney, Byron Haskins directed Robert Newton, who was born to play the one-legged pirate, and Bobby Driscoll. Newton afterwards played the role in a feature, *Long John Silver* 54, and 26 TV half-hours filmed in Australia. In 1972 Orson Welles starred in a European remake, using such a thick accent that he had to be dubbed, in which he was shown from the waist up for much of the film since he was too fat to bend back his leg; in 1973 Kirk Douglas appeared in *Scallawag,* which borrowed the plot for a modern story; in 1989 Fraser Heston directed his father Charlton in a TV movie; and in 1991 Chilean director Raúl Ruiz turned the story into a deliriously experimental movie, in which its characters act out roles from the story.

treatment.
The first expansion of a script idea into sequence form, giving some idea of how the story is to be told, i.e. with examples of dialogue, camera angles, etc.

Tree, David (1915–).
British comedy actor with stage experience.
Knight Without Armour 37. *Pygmalion* (as Freddy Eynsford-Hill) 38. Q Planes 39. *French Without Tears* 39. Major Barbara 40. Then war

service, in which he lost an arm; subsequently retired.

~He made a very brief reappearance as the headmaster in *Don't Look Now* 73.

Treen, Mary (1907–1989).
American comedy actress who usually played nurses, office girls, or the heroine's plain friend.

Babbitt 35. Colleen 36. First Love 40. I Love a Soldier 44. From This Day Forward 45. Let's Live a Little 48. The Caddy 53. The Birds and the Bees 56. Rockabye Baby 58. Paradise Hawaiian Style 56, many others.

TV series: Willy 54–55. The Joey Bishop Show 62–65.

Tremayne, Les (1913–).
American small-part actor.

The Racket 51. Dream Wife 53. A Man Called Peter 55. The Story of Ruth 60. The Fortune Cookie 66, etc.

Trenchard-Smith, Brian (1946–).
British director in Australia.

The World of Kung Fu 74. Man from Hong Kong 75. Deathcheaters 76. Day of the Assassins 80. Turkey Shoot 82. BMX Bandits 83. Jenny Kissed Me 85. The Quest 86. Dead End Drive-In 86. The Day of the Panther 87. Out of the Body 88. Strike of the Panther 88. The Siege of Firebase Gloria 89. Night of the Demons 2 94, etc.

trends

¶ R.D. McCann said that in Hollywood the only familiar, solid, bedrock certainty is sudden change. That goes for the entire industry, which throughout its history has been subject to the whims of fashion and has moved in a gingerly way from one crisis to another. In the midst of such uncertainty the industry's leaders can only comfort themselves with the incontrovertible adage:

There's nothing wrong with this business that a few good movies can't cure.

The trouble has been to find out what kind of movies, at any given time, are good ones in the eyes of the public. As Adolph Zukor said long ago:

The public is never wrong.

And Bryan Forbes said:

Nobody can be a prophet in an industry which is entirely dependent on the public whim.

Walter Wanger knew that:

Nothing is as cheap as a hit, no matter how much it cost.

Unfortunately the public has not always been in the forefront of good taste. When close-ups were first introduced, many audiences felt cheated and yelled:

Show us their feet!

But without an advance in technical quality the film could hardly have survived. Billy Bitzer, the famous cameraman, said:

The fade-out gave us a really dignified touch – we didn't have a five cent movie any more.

It is true that the moguls have sometimes taken a long time to answer the public's call. Ted Willis said in 1966:

The film business is like that prehistoric monster the dinosaur, which apparently had two brains, one in its head and one in its rear.

It was not always thus: in the golden years they knew a thing or two. At Warners, for instance, Bette Davis said:

We had the answer, the sequel and the successor to everything.

But even imitation did not always pay. Darryl Zanuck knew:

Only the first picture of a cycle really succeeds: all the imitators dwindle.

Cesare Zavattini in 1945 had a similar idea:

The world is full of people thinking in myths.

Iris Barry in 1926 scorned film clichés:

Why must all American movie mothers be white-haired and tottery even though their children are mere tots? Does the menopause not operate in the US?

Reality was entirely shunned. Wilson Mizner in the early talkie era commented:

The public doesn't want to know what goes on behind the scenes. It prefers to believe that a cameraman hung in the clouds, mid-Pacific, the day Barrymore fought the whale.

Samuel Goldwyn is credited with the tersest capsuling of the tradition that audiences wanted to be soothed and not stimulated:

Messages are for Western Union.

Even Terry Ramsaye, editing a trade journal in 1936, complained:

If they want to preach a sermon, let them hire a hall.

This was the day of the formula:

Boy meets girl, boy loses girl, boy gets girl.

The public paid to see it and demanded more of the same. A 1943 exhibitor said:

You could open a can of sardines and there'd be a line waiting to get in.

Momentary turns of fashion could of course be allowed for, so many movies were being made. When *Variety* headlined:

STICKS NIX HICK PIX

it was a simple matter to discontinue the movies about poor hillbillies to which the midwestern audiences had shown such antipathy. Towards the 50s, however, there were signs of growing unease: no kind of film, and no star, could be absolutely relied on to make money. Hollywood had previously regarded the international market as a pleasant source of extra revenue; now film-making had to be geared to it. Alfred Hitchcock, however, felt that no change of style was necessary:

When we make films for the United States, we automatically make them for the world, for the United States is full of foreigners.

But Hitch did note a change of emphasis:

In the old days, villains had moustaches and kicked the dog. Audiences are smarter today. They don't want their villain to be thrown at them with green limelight on his face. They want an ordinary human being with failings.

The studio conveyor belt was outdated: everyone was bitten by the location bug. Rouben Mamoulian said in 1957:

We have forsaken the magic of the cinema. We have gotten too far away from the cinematic effects achievable by camera angles and creative editing.

There was another increasing danger:

You have to offer the public something a helluva lot better than they can get for free on TV.

What was offered was 3-D, which failed. As Hitch said:

A nine-days' wonder – and I came in on the ninth day.

Then came CinemaScope and the other wide-screen processes, but the extra size only rarely contributed towards a better entertainment. Content was what mattered. The only reliable regular audience was for cheap horror films. Said Vincent Price in 1965:

The cinemas have bred a new race of giant popcorn-eating rats.

At last the English came back into fashion as film-makers, chiefly on the strength of their actors and their 'X' subjects. This success had its drawbacks, according to Tony Garnett:

To be an Englishman in the film business is to know what it's like to be colonialized.

Sex had come to stay. Said Shelagh Delaney:

The cinema has become more and more like the theatre: it's all mauling and muttering.

Said Billy Wilder:

Titism has taken over the country. But Audrey Hepburn single-handed may make bozooms a thing of the past. The director will not have to invent shots where the girl leans forward for a glass of scotch and soda.

Said Adolphe Menjou:

The Brando school are grabbers, not lovers. If it wasn't that the script says they get the girl, they wouldn't.

Said Bob Hope in 1960:

Our big pictures this year have had some intriguing themes: sex, perversion, adultery and cannibalism. We'll get those kids away from their TV sets yet.

Said Bob Hope in 1968:

Last year Hollywood made the first pictures with dirty words. This year we made the pictures to go with them.

And in 1971:

The line 'I love you' is no longer a declaration but a demonstration.

In the same year Candice Bergen admitted:

I may not be a great actress but I've become the greatest at screen orgasms. Ten seconds of heavy breathing, roll your head from side to side, simulate a slight asthma attack and die a little.

And Frank Capra snorted:

Hollywood film-making of today is stooping to cheap salacious pornography in a crazy bastardization of a great art.

The system had crumbled, the studios were empty, every movie was a new enterprise, usually shot in some far-flung corner of the earth. Bob Hope again, in 1968:

This year is a good one for Hollywood. Some of the movies nominated for Oscars were even made here.

Hal Wallis had another complaint:

In the old days we had the time and money to give prospective stars a slow build-up. Today, an actor makes it fast or he just doesn't make it at all.

Orson Welles realized that:

The trouble with a movie these days is that it's old before it's released. It's no accident that it comes in a can.

And Billy Wilder:

Today we spend eighty per cent of our time making deals and twenty per cent making pictures.

Otto Preminger remembers when:

There were giants in the industry. Now it is an era of midgets and conglomerates.

The watchword for the 70s was violence. Hear the producer of *The Strawberry Statement*:

We live in a time when revolution is a very saleable commodity.

Hear Roman Polanski in 1971:

Nothing is too shocking for me. When you tell the story of a man who loses his head, you have to show the head being cut off. Otherwise it's just a dirty joke without a punch line.

Hear Ken Russell, middle-aged enfant terrible of the same year:

This is not the age of manners. This is the age of kicking people in the crotch and telling them something and getting a reaction. I want to shock people into awareness. I don't believe there's any virtue in understatement.

Hear the redoubtable Sam Peckinpah:

You can't make violence real to audiences today without rubbing their noses in it. We've all been anaesthetized by the media.

Hear producer Steve Krantz defending his 'adult cartoon' *Heavy Traffic:*

Mary Poppins is OK, but when did you last date her?

Hear Peter Cook:

I don't like watching rape and violence at the cinema. I get enough of that at home!

And finally:

America's a new country and we have very little history. We have the American Indian and we have Superman. Don't fuck with either. – *R. Donner*

Trenker, Luis (1893–1990).

Italian mountain guide who played leads in several mountain films.

Peaks of Destiny 26. The Fight for the Matterhorn 28. Doomed Battalion (& wd) 31. Der Verlorene Sohn (& wd) 34. The Challenge (& wd) 37. Monte Miracolo (& wd) 43. Duell in den Bergen (& wd) 49. Sein Bester Freund (& wd) 62, many others.

Treut, Monique.

German feminist film director, screenwriter, and producer.

Seduction: The Cruel Woman (Verführung: Die Grausame Frau) (p, co-w, d) 85. Virgin Machine 88. Érotique (co-d) 94, etc.

Trevelyan, John (1904–1985).

British executive, secretary of the British Board of Film Censors 1958–1970, responsible for a more liberal policy allowing such controversial films as *Saturday Night and Sunday Morning, Tom Jones, The Servant, The Silence, Repulsion* and *Who's Afraid of Virginia Woolf?*

Published memoirs 1973: *What the Censor Saw.*

Trevor, Austin (1897–1978) (A. Schilsky).

British character actor with long stage experience.

At the Villa Rose 30. *Alibi* (as Hercule Poirot) 31. Lord Edgware Dies (as Hercule Poirot) 34. Dark Journey 37. Goodbye Mr Chips 39. Champagne Charlie 44. The Red Shoes 48. Father Brown 54. The Horrors of the Black Museum 59, etc.

Trevor, Claire (1909–   ) (Claire Wemlinger).

American character actress on stage from childhood. Made many routine films before gaining critical notice.

Life in the Raw (debut) 33. Hold That Girl 34. Dante's Inferno 35. Career Woman 36. Dead End (AAN) 37. The Amazing Dr Clitterhouse 38. *Stagecoach* 39. I Stole a Million 39. Dark Command 40. Honky Tonk 41. Crossroads 42. Street of Chance 42. Woman of the Town 43. *Murder My Sweet* 44. Johnny Angel 45. Crack Up 46. Bachelor Girls 47. *Key Largo* (AA) 48. The Lucky Stiff 49. Best of the Badmen 50. Hard, Fast and Beautiful 51. The Stranger Wore a Gun 52. The High and the Mighty (AAN) 54. The Man without a Star 55. The Mountain 56. Marjorie Morningstar 58. Two Weeks in Another Town 62. How to Murder Your Wife 65. Capetown Affair 67. Kiss Me Goodbye 82, etc.

Trevor, Elleston (1920–   ).

English thriller writer who also uses the pseudonym Adam Hall.

Mantrap (from Queen in Danger) 53. Dunkirk (from The Big Pick-up) 58. Pillars of Midnight 63. Flight of the Phoenix 65. The Berlin Memorandum (from The Quiller Memorandum) 65.

Triangle Film Corporation.

Company formed by D. W. Griffith, Thomas Ince, and Mack Sennett in 1915 to produce and release films made by the three directors, who left the company in 1917.

Triesault, Ivan (1898–1980).

Eastern European small-part actor in Hollywood.

Mission to Moscow 43. The Hitler Gang 44. Notorious 46. To the Ends of the Earth 48. Five Fingers 52. Fräulein 58. The 300 Spartans 62. Barabbas 62. Von Ryan's Express 65. Batman 66, many others.

Trinder, Tommy (1909–1989).

British cockney music-hall comedian, in occasional films.

Almost a Honeymoon 38. Laugh It Off 40. Sailors Three 41. The Bells Go Down 42. *The Foreman Went to France* 42. Champagne Charlie 44. *Fiddlers Three* 44. Bitter Springs 49. You Lucky People 54. The Beauty Jungle 64, etc.

Trintignant, Jean-Louis (1930–   ).

French leading man.

Race for Life 55. And God Created Woman 56. Austerlitz 59. Château en Suède 63. Mata Hari 64. Angélique 64. *A Man and a Woman* 66. Trans-Europe Express 66. The Sleeping Car Murders 66. The Libertine 68. Les Biches 68. 'Z' 68. Ma Nuit Chez Maud 69. The American 70. The Conformist 70. Simon the Swiss 71. Aggression 75. Faces of Love 77. The Lifeguard 79. Je Vous Aime 80. La Banquière 80. Vivement Dimanche 83. Under Fire 83. Rendezous 85. A Man and a Woman: Twenty Years Later (Un Homme et une Femme: Vingt Ans Déjà) 86. Le Moustachu 87. Bunker Palace Hotel 89. Dr M. 90. Merci la Vie 91. L'Oeil Ecarlate 92. Regarde les Hommes Tomber 94. Three Colours: Red (Trois Couleurs: Rouge) 94, etc.

Tripplehorn, Jeanne.

American leading actress.

Basic Instinct 92. The Night We Never Met 93. The Firm 93. Waterworld 95, etc.

Trivas, Victor (1896–1970).

Russian writer in America.

War Is Hell (d) 31. Song of Russia 44. The Stranger 45, etc.

Trnka, Jiří (1910–1969).

Czech animator and puppeteer, many of whose short films have been shown abroad.

The Emperor's Nightingale 49. Song of the Prairie 49. The Good Soldier Schweik 54. Jan Hus 56. A Midsummer Night's Dream 57, etc.

Troell, Jan (1931–   ).

Swedish director.

Here Is Your Life 66. Who Saw Him Die 67. *The Emigrants* (AAN) 71. The New Land (AAN) 72. Zandy's Bride 74. Hurricane 79. Flight of the Eagle (Ingenjor Andrees Luftfard) 82. Sagolandet 86. A Swedish Requiem (Il Capitano) 91, etc.

Troisi, Massimo (1953–1994).

Italian actor and director, with a gentle comic style, from cabaret and television. He won a best actor award at the Venice Film Festival for his performance in *What Time Is It?* Died from a heart attack the day after he finished making *The Postman.*

Ricomincio da Tre (a, d) 81. Scusate il Ritardo (a, d) 83. Non Ci Resta Che Piangere (a, co-d) 84. La Vie del Signore Sono Finite (a, d) 87. Splendor (a) 88. What Time Is It? (Che Ora È) (a) 89. The Journey of Captain Fracassa (a) 90. I Thought It Was Love (Pensavo Forse Amore Invece Era un Calesse) (a,d) 92. The Postman (Il Postino) (a, co-w) 94, etc.

Troma.

Company specializing in the production and distribution of low-budget exploitation movies, usually combining kitsch and gore, many produced and directed by the company's president, Lloyd Kaufman, and vice-president, Michael Herz. It is best known for its *Toxic Avenger* series, which has spawned dolls and other novelty merchandising.

Squeeze Play! 80. Waitress! 82. Stuck on You 83. The First Turn-On! 84. The Toxic Avenger 84. Nuke 'em High 85. The Toxic Avenger: Part II 88. Troma's War 88. The Toxic Avenger III: The Last Temptation of Toxie 90. Def by Temptation 90. Class of Nuke 'em High II: Subhumanoid Meltdown 91. Sgt Kabukiman N.Y.P.D. 94, etc.

Tronson, Robert (1924–   ).

British director, from TV.

The Man at the Carlton Tower 62. The Traitors 62. On the Run 63. Ring of Spies 64, etc.

Trotti, Lamar (1900–1952).

Prolific American scriptwriter and producer.

Judge Priest (co-w) 34. Steamboat round the Bend (co-w) 35. Ramona (w) 36. Slave Ship (w) 37. *In Old Chicago* (w) 38. *Young Mr Lincoln* (w) 39. Hudson's Bay (w) 41. *The Ox Bow Incident* (w, p) 42. Wilson (w, p) (AA) 43. The Razor's Edge (w, p) 46. Mother Wore Tights (w, p) 47. Yellow Sky (w, p) 48. *Cheaper by the Dozen* (w, p) 50. I'd Climb the Highest Mountain (w, p) 51. Stars and Stripes Forever (w, p) 52. With a Song in My Heart (w, p) 52. There's No Business Like Show Business (AAN story) 54, many others.

Troughton, Patrick (1920–1987).

British character actor, often in malevolent roles; mainly on TV (Dr Who in the late 60s).

Escape 48. Hamlet 48. Treasure Island 50. The Black Knight 52. Richard III 56. Phantom of the Opera 62. The Gorgon 64. The Omen 76, many others in small roles.

Trouncer, Cecil (1898–1953).

British stage character actor with splendidly resonant diction.

Pygmalion 38. While the Sun Shines 46. London Belongs to Me 48. *The Guinea Pig* 49. The Lady with a Lamp 51. Pickwick Papers 52. The Weak and the Wicked 54.

Trowbridge, Charles (1882–1967).

American character actor, former architect; usually played professors or kindly fathers.

I Take This Woman 31. The Thirteenth Chair 36. Confessions of a Nazi Spy 39. The Mummy's Hand 40. Mildred Pierce 45. The Wings of Eagles 57, many others.

Trueba, Fernando (1955–   ).

Spanish director, a former film critic.

Opera Prima 80. Sal Gorda 83. El Año de las Luces 86. The Mad Monkey 89. Belle Époque (AA) 93, etc.

true-life adventures:

see *The Living Desert.*

Truex, Ernest (1890–1973).

American character actor of 'little man' roles, in films since 1918.

Whistling in the Dark 33. The Adventures of Marco Polo 38. Christmas in July 40. His Girl Friday 40. Always Together 48. The Leather Saint 56. Twilight for the Gods 58. Fluffy 65, many others; latterly much on TV.

Truffaut, François (1932–1984).
French 'new wave' director, former critic.
Autobiography: 1982, *Les Films de Ma Vie.* Also wrote *Hitchcock* (1967), a long interview with his idol.
■ Les Mistons 58. *Les Quatre Cents Coups* 59. *Shoot the Pianist* 60. *Jules et Jim* 61. Love at Twenty (part) 62. *Silken Skin* 64. Fahrenheit 451 66. The Bride Wore Black 67. Stolen Kisses 68. Mississippi Mermaid 69. L'Enfant Sauvage (& a) 69. Domicile Conjugale 70. Anne and Muriel 72. A Gorgeous Bird Like Me 72. *La Nuit Américaine* (AAN) 73. The Story of Adele H 75. L'Argent du Poche 76. The Man Who Loved Women 77. Close Encounters of the Third Kind (a only) 77. Love on the Run 79. Le Dernier Métro 80. Vivement Dimanche 83.

¶ I make films that I would like to have seen when I was a young man. – *F.T.*
To make a film is to improve on life, to arrange it to suit oneself, to prolong the games of childhood, to construct something which is at once a new toy and a vase in which one can arrange in a permanent way the ideas one feels in the morning. – *F.T.*

Truman, Michael (1916–1974).
British director, former editor.
Touch and Go 54. Go to Blazes 62. The Girl in the Headlines 63, etc.

Truman, Ralph (1900–1977).
British stage character actor who made occasional film appearances.
Henry V 44. Beware of Pity 46. Oliver Twist 48. Quo Vadis 51. The Man Who Knew Too Much 56. El Cid 61. Nicholas and Alexandra 71, many others.

Trumbo, Dalton (1905–1976).
American screenwriter, one of the 'Hollywood Ten' who were blacklisted in the 40s.
Kitty Foyle (AAN) 40. The Remarkable Andrew 42. A Guy Named Joe 43. Our Vines Have Tender Grapes 45. The Prowler (as Hugo Butler) 51. Roman Holiday (though the credit went to Ian McKellan Hunter who fronted for him) (AA) 53. The Brave One (as Robert Rich) (AA) 56. Spartacus 60. Exodus 60. The Last Sunset 61. Lonely are the Brave 62. The Sandpiper 65. Hawaii 66. The Fixer 68. Johnny Got His Gun (& d) 71. Executive Action 73. Papillon (co-w, a) 73, many others.

Trumbull, Douglas (1942–).
American special effects man. He now designs interactive entertainments and rides for theme parks.
2001: A Space Odyssey 68. Candy 68. The Andromeda Strain 71. Silent Running (& d) 72. *Close Encounters of the Third Kind* (AAN) 77. *Star Trek* (AAN) 79. Bladerunner (AAN) 82. Brainstorm (& d) 83, etc.

¶ A plain ride is a boring, plotless event. New Technology will make it a participatory art form. – *D.T.*

Trundy, Natalie (1940–).
American leading lady in occasional films.
The Careless Years 57. The Monte Carlo Story 58. Mr Hobbs Takes a Vacation 62. Conquest of the Planet of the Apes 71. Huckleberry Finn 73, etc.

Truscott, John.
American production and costume designer.
Camelot (AA) 67. Paint Your Wagon 69, etc.

Tryon, Tom (1919–1991).
American leading man with stage and TV experience. Later a successful novelist.
The Scarlet Hour (debut) 55. Three Violent People 56. I Married a Monster from Outer Space 57. Moon Pilot 61. Marines Let's Go 61. *The Cardinal* 63. In Harm's Way 65. The Glory Guys 65. The Horsemen 71. Johnny Got His Gun (& pd) 71. The Other (oa only) 72. Fedora (oa only) 78, etc.
TV series: Texas John Slaughter 59.

Tsu, Irene (1943–).
Chinese glamour girl in Hollywood.
Caprice 66. The Green Berets 67. Paper Tiger 75. Down and Out in Beverly Hills 85, etc.

Tsukamoto, Shinya (1960–).
Japanese director of horror movies about the merging of man and machinery.
■ Tetsuo: The Iron Man 89. Hiruko the Goblin 90. Tetsuo II: The Body Hammer 91.

Tubbs, William (1909–1953).
Portly American character actor in Europe.
Paisa 46. Edward and Caroline 50. Three Steps North 50. Quo Vadis 51, etc.

Tuchner, Michael (1934–).
British director.
■ Villain 71. Fear is the Key 72. Mister Quilp 75. The Likely Lads 76. Summer of My German Soldier (TV) 79. Haywire (TV) 80. The Hunchback of Notre Dame (TV) 81. Trenchcoat 83. Adam (TV) 83. Amos (TV) 85. Not My Kid (TV) 85. Mistress (TV) 87. Trapped in Silence (TV) 90.

Tuchock, Wanda (1898–1985).
American screenwriter at her peak in silent days.
Show People 27. *Hallelujah* 29. Bird of Paradise 32. Hawaii Calls 37. Silver Queen 45. The Foxes of Harrow 47. The Homestretch 49, etc.

Tucker, Forrest (1919–1986).
Rugged American leading man, mostly in routine action pictures from 1940.
The Westerner (debut) 40. Keeper of the Flame 42. The Yearling 46. The Big Cat 49. Sands of Iwo Jima 50. The Wild Blue Yonder 52. Crosswinds 53. Trouble in the Glen (GB) 54. Break in the Circle (GB) 56. *The Abominable Snowman* (GB) 57. Auntie Mame 58. The Night They Raided Minsky's 68. Cancel My Reservation 72. The Wild McCullochs 75. Final Chapter – Walking Tall 77. Thunder Run 85, many others.
TV series: Crunch and Des 55. F Troop 65–66. Dusty's Trail 73. Ghost Chasers 76. The Rebels 79.

Tucker, George Loane (1881–1921).
American silent director.
The Courting of Mary 11. Traffic in Souls 13. Called Back 14. The Prisoner of Zenda 15. Arsene Lupin 16. The Manxman 17. The Miracle Man 19. Ladies Must Live 21, many others.

Tucker, Sophie (1884–1966) (Sophia Abuza or Sonia Kalish).
Russian-born, American-oriented popular singer, the heavyweight 'red hot momma' of vaudeville.
■ Honky Tonk 29. Gay Love (GB) 34. Gay Time (GB) 34. Broadway Melody of 1937 37. Thoroughbreds Don't Cry 37. Atlantic City 44. Follow the Boys 44. Sensations of 1945 44.

Tufts, Sonny (1911–1970) (Bowen Charleston Tufts).
Tall, good-humoured American 'second lead', in Hollywood from the early 40s.

■ So Proudly We Hail 43. Government Girl 43. In The Meantime Darling 44. I Love a Soldier 44. Here Come the Waves 45. Bring on the Girls 45. Duffy's Tavern 45. Miss Susie Slagle's 45. The Virginian 46. The Well-Groomed Bride 46. Cross My Heart 46. Easy Come Easy Go 47. Blaze Of Noon 47. Variety Girl 47. Swell Guy 47. The Untamed Breed 48. The Crooked Way 49. Easy Living 49. The Gift Horse (GB) 52. No Escape 53. Cat Women of the Moon 53. Run for the Hills 53. Serpent Island 54. The Seven Year Itch 55. Come Next Spring 56. The Parson and the Outlaw 57. Town Tamer 65. Cottonpicking Chickenpicker 67.

Tugboat Annie.
This aggressive, middle-aged lady of the waterfront was devised by Norman Reilly Raine and personified in the 1933 film by Marie Dressler. Subsequent films include *Tugboat Annie Sails Again* 40 with Marjorie Rambeau and *Captain Tugboat Annie* 45 with Jane Darwell. A 1956 TV series featured Minerva Urecal.

Tully, Montgomery (1904–).
British writer and director.
Murder in Reverse (wd) 45. Spring Song (wd) 47. Boys in Brown (d) 49. A Tale of Five Cities (d) 51. The Glass Cage (d) 55. The Hypnotist (d) 57. Escapement (d) 58. Clash by Night (d) 63. Who Killed the Cat? (wd) 66. Battle Beneath the Earth (d) 68, many other second features and TV episodes.

Tully, Tom (1896–1982).
American character actor with stage experience; usually tough-looking but soft-hearted roles.
Destination Tokyo 44. Adventure 45. The Town Went Wild 45. June Bride 48. Where the Sidewalk Ends 50. The Caine Mutiny (AAN) 54. Ten North Frederick 57. The Wackiest Ship in the Army 61. Coogan's Bluff 68. Charley Varrick 73. Madame X (TV) 81, etc.
TV series: The Lineup 54–59. Shane 66.

Tunberg, Karl (1908–1992).
American screenwriter, in Hollywood from 1937.
My Lucky Star 38. Down Argentine Way 40. Tall Dark and Handsome (AAN) 41. Orchestra Wives 42. Kitty 45. You Gotta Stay Happy 47. Scandal at Scourie 53. The Scarlet Coat 55. *Ben Hur* (AAN) 59. Libel 59. Taras Bulba 62. Harlow (electronovision version) 65. Where Were You When the Lights Went Out? 68, many others.

Tune, Tommy (1939–).
Lanky American dancer, choreographer, and actor, mainly on the Broadway stage.
Hello Dolly! 69. The Boy Friend 71.

Turkel, Ann (1948–).
American leading lady, former wife of Richard Harris.
99 and 44/100 Per Cent Dead 74. Matt Helm (TV) 75. The Cassandra Crossing 77. Golden Rendezvous 78. Humanoids from the Deep 80. Death Ray 2000 81. The Last Contract 86. Deep Space 87, etc.

Turman, Lawrence (1926–).
American producer.
The Young Doctors 61. The Flim Flam Man 66. *The Graduate* (AAN) 67. Pretty Poison 69. The Great White Hope 70. Marriage of a Young Stockbroker (& d) 71. The Drowning Pool (co-p) 75. First Love (co-p) 77. Walk Proud 79. Tribute 80, etc.

turnaround
is what happens to a film project when a studio

decides that it is no longer a commercial proposition, a situation that the trade paper *Variety* has defined as 'the development purgatory where projects go when studios want to dump them'. Turnaround happens not only when producers grow disenchanted with a script, but also when new executives replace old and ritually kill off all the projects approved by their predecessors, or when a star or director decides to drop out. One studio will occasionally buy from another a script in turnaround, sometimes when executives move studios and want to take some pet project with them. Among subsquent hit movies put into turnaround are *E.T. – the Extra-Terrestrial*, which was picked up by Universal from Columbia, *Jaws*, which went from MGM to Universal, *Star Wars*, which went from Universal to Twentieth Century-Fox, *Home Alone*, which went from Warner to Twentieth Century-Fox, *The Addams Family*, which went from Orion to Paramount, *Forrest Gump*, which went from Warner to Paramount, and *Speed*, which went from Paramount to Twentieth Century-Fox.

Turner, Anne (1960–).
Australian director and screenwriter.
Celia 88. Turtle Beach (w only) 92. Hammers over the Anvil 93. Dallas Doll 93.

Turner, Florence (1887–1946).
American actress who in 1907 became the first 'movie star' known by name; also as 'the Vitagraph Girl'.
A Dixie Mother 10. Francesca da Rimini 12. The Welsh Singer (GB) 13. My Old Dutch (GB) 15. East is East (GB) 15. The Old Wives' Tale (GB) 21, etc.
Went back to Hollywood in roles of diminishing stature; retired in the mid-20s.

Turner, John (1932–).
British leading man with stage experience, also known as TV's 'Knight Errant'.
Behemoth, the Sea Monster 60. Petticoat Pirates 61. Sammy Going South 62. The Black Torment 64. The Slipper and the Rose 76, etc.

Turner, Kathleen (1954–).
Leading American actress.
Body Heat 82. Romancing the Stone 84. The Man with Two Brains 84. Prizzi's Honor 85. Crimes of Passion 85. Jewel of the Nile 86. *Peggy Sue Got Married* (AAN) 87. A Breed Apart 87. Julia and Julia 87. Switching Channels 88. Who Framed Roger Rabbit? (voice) 88. Dear America: Letters Home from Vietnam 88. The Accidental Tourist 88. The War of the Roses 89. V.I. Warshawski 91. House of Cards 93. Naked in New York 93. Undercover Blues 93. Serial Mom 94, etc.

Turner, Lana (1920–) (Julia Turner).
American leading lady of the 40s; began as the 'girl next door' type but became increasingly sophisticated.
Biography: 1976, *The Films of Lana Turner* by Lou Valentino.
They Won't Forget (debut) 37. The Great Garrick 37. Four's a Crowd 38. The Adventures of Marco Polo 38. Calling Dr Kildare 39. *Love Finds Andy Hardy* 39. Rich Man Poor Girl 39. Dramatic School 39. These Glamour Girls 39. Dancing Co-Ed 39. Two Girls on Broadway 40. We Who Are Young 40. Choose Your Partner 40. Ziegfeld Girl 41. Dr Jekyll and Mr Hyde 41. Honky Tonk 41. Johnny Eager 41. *Somewhere I'll Find You* 42. Slightly Dangerous 43. Marriage Is a Private Affair 44. Keep Your Powder Dry 44. Weekend at the Waldorf 45. The Postman Always Rings Twice 45.

Green Dolphin Street 46. Cass Timberlane 47. Homecoming 48. The Three Musketeers 48. A Life of Her Own 50. Mr Imperium 51. The Merry Widow 52. The Bad and the Beautiful 52. Latin Lovers 53. The Flame and the Flesh 54. Betrayed 55. The Prodigal 55. The Rains of Ranchipur 55. The Sea Chase 55. Diane 56. Another Time Another Place (GB) 57. *Peyton Place* (AAN) 57. The Lady Takes a Flyer 58. *Imitation of Life* 59. Portrait in Black 60. By Love Possessed 61. Bachelor in Paradise 62. Who's Got the Action? 63. Love Has Many Faces 65. Madame X 66. The Big Cube 69. Persecution 74. Bittersweet Love 76, etc.
TV series: The Survivors 69. Falcon Crest 82.

Turner, Ted (1938–) (Robert Edward Turner).
Television mogul, owner of the Cable News Network and also the MGM film library. In 1993 he took over the film production and distribution companies New Line Cinema, at a cost of $53 million, and Castle Rock Entertainment, at a cost of $100 million. Married to actress Jane Fonda.
Biography: 1993, *It Ain't So Easy as It Looks: Ted Turner's Amazing Story* by Porter Bibb.

Turner, Tina (1938–) (Annie Mae Bullock).
American rhythm and blues and soul singer and actress. A biopic of her life, *What's Love Got to Do with It*, was made in 1993 starring Angela Bassett.
■ Gimme Shelter (doc) 70. Taking Off 71. Soul to Soul (concert) 71. Tommy 75. Mad Max beyond Thunderdome 85. The Last Action Hero 93.

Turpin, Ben (1874–1940).
Cross-eyed American silent comedian, mainly popular in short slapstick skits of the 20s. In films from 1915 after vaudeville experience.
Uncle Tom's Cabin 19. Small Town Idol 21. Show of Shows 29. The Love Parade 30, many others.

Turpin, Dick (1706–1739)
was a seasoned criminal without too many obvious redeeming characteristics. Film-makers have seized on his ride to York and his affection for his horse as an excuse to view him through rose-tinted glasses. So he was played as a hero by Matheson Lang in 1922, Tom Mix in 1925, Victor McLaglen in 1933, Louis Hayward in 1951, and David Weston (for Walt Disney) in 1965. In the late 70s Richard O'Sullivan appeared in an ITV series, again featuring the highwayman as a kind of Robin Hood.

Turpin, Gerry (c. 1930–).
British cinematographer.
The Queen's Guards 61. Seance on a Wet Afternoon 64. The Whisperers 67. Deadfall 68. *Oh What a Lovely War* 69. The Man Who Had Power over Women 70. I Want What I Want 71. The Last of Sheila 73, etc.

Turtletaub, Jon.
American director.
Think Big 90. Driving Me Crazy 91. 3 Ninjas 92. Cool Runnings 93, etc.

Turturro, John (1957–).
American leading actor, from the stage.
Raging Bull 80. Exterminator 2 84. The Flamingo Kid 84. Desperately Seeking Susan 85. To Live and Die In L.A. 85. The Color of Money 86. Gung Ho 86. Hannah and Her Sisters 86. Off Beat 86. Five Corners 87. The Sicilian 87. Do the Right Thing 89. Catchfire (aka Backtrack) 89. Men of Respect 90. Miller's Crossing 90. Mo' Better Blues 90. State of Grace 90. Jungle Fever 91. Barton Fink 91. Brain Donors 92. Mac (& d) 92.

Fearless 93. Being Human 94. Quiz Show 94. Clockers 95, etc.

Tushingham, Rita (1940–).
British leading character actress with stage experience.
■ *A Taste of Honey* 61. The Leather Boys 63. A Place to Go 63. Girl with Green Eyes 64. *The Knack* 65. Dr Zhivago 65. The Trap 66. Smashing Time 67. Diamonds for Breakfast 68. The Guru 69. The Bed-Sitting Room 69. Straight On till Morning 72. The Human Factor 75. Rachel's Man 75. Mysteries 79. Confessions of Felix Krull (TV) 81. Judgment in Stone 86. Hem 87. Resurrected 88. Hard Days, Hard Nights 88. Paper Marriage 93.

Tutin, Dorothy (1930–).
Leading British actress. Occasional films.
■ *The Importance of Being Earnest* 52. The Beggar's Opera 53. A Tale of Two Cities 57. Cromwell 69. The Spy's Wife 70. *Savage Messiah* 72. The Shooting Party 85. Murder with Mirrors (TV) 85. Great Moments in Aviation 94.
TV series: Body and Soul 93.

Tuttle, Frank (1892–1963).
American director of mainly routine films; in Hollywood from the 20s.
Kid Boots 27. Roman Scandals 33. The Glass Key 35. Waikiki Wedding 37. I Stole a Million 39. *This Gun For Hire* 42. Lucky Jordan 43. Hostages 43. The Hour Before the Dawn 43. A Man Called Sullivan 45. Suspense 46. Swell Guy 47. The Magic Face 51. Gunman in the Streets 51. Hell on Frisco Bay 55. A Cry in the Night 56, etc.

Twain, Mark (1835–1910) (Samuel Langhorne Clemens).
Beloved American humorist and travel writer; was played by Fredric March in *The Adventures of Mark Twain* 44. Works filmed include *Tom Sawyer*, *Huckleberry Finn*, *A Connecticut Yankee*, *The Prince and the Pauper*, *The Celebrated Jumping Frog* (as *The Best Man Wins*), *The Million-Pound Banknote*.

Tweety Pie.
Baby-voiced canary, the adversary of Sylvester the cat in Warner Brothers cartoons. A song based on its cry, 'I Tawt I Saw a Putty Cat', was a hit in 1950. Its creator was Bob Clampett and Mel Blanc supplied the voice.
A Tale of Two Kitties 42. Tweetie Pie (AA) 47. Bad Ol' Putty Cat 49. Sandy Claws (AAN) 54. Birds Anonymous (AA) 57. The Jet Cage 62, etc.

Twelvetrees, Helen (1908–1958) (Helen Jurgens).
American leading lady of the 30s; films fairly unmemorable.
The Ghost Talks 29. Her Man 30. The Painted Desert 31. Is My Face Red? 32. King for a Night 33. Times Square Lady 35. Hollywood Round Up 37, etc.

Twentieth Century-Fox Film Corporation.
An American production and distribution company formed in 1935 by a merger of Joseph Schenck's Twentieth Century Pictures with William Fox's Fox Film Corporation. Fox had started in nickelodeon days as a showman, then a distributor.
Putting his profits into production, he started the careers of several useful stars including Theda Bara, and pioneered the Movietone sound-on-film process; but in the early 30s, after a series of bad deals, he lost power. The new company had Darryl F. Zanuck as production head from 1935 to 1952; he returned in 1962 as president after the

resignation of Spyros Skouras, who had reigned from 1942. These two men are therefore largely responsible for the Fox image, which usually gave the impression of more careful budget-trimming and production-processing than did the films of the rest of the 'big five'. Fox's successful personality stars include Shirley Temple, Alice Faye, Don Ameche, Betty Grable and Marilyn Monroe; its best westerns include *The Big Trail, Drums along the Mohawk, My Darling Clementine* and *The Gunfighter*; in drama it can claim *What Price Glory?, Dante's Inferno, The Grapes of Wrath, How Green Was My Valley, The Ox Bow Incident, The Song of Bernadette, Wilson, The Snake Pit,* and *Gentlemen's Agreement*. In 1953 Spyros Skouras successfully foisted the new screen shape, CinemaScope, on to world markets, but Fox have not used it with greater success than anyone else, their most elaborate 'spectaculars' being *The Robe, There's No Business Like Show Business, The King and I, South Pacific, The Diary of Anne Frank, The Longest Day, Cleopatra, Those Magnificent Men in Their Flying Machines, The Sound of Music, Star!, Hello Dolly,* and *Tora! Tora! Tora!*

On his return, Darryl Zanuck appointed his son Richard as vice-president in charge of production and, in 1965, the company enjoyed one of its greatest successes with the musical *The Sound of Music*. Darryl and Richard Zanuck, who went on to become a successful independent producer, left at the beginning of the 70s after a succession of big-budget flops (*Hello Dolly* and *Tora! Tora! Tora!* among them). The fashion for disaster films brought the company successes with *The Towering Inferno* (made with Warners) and *The Poseidon Adventure*. Alan Ladd Jnr became President in the mid-70s, leaving in 1979 to become an independent producer; during his time Fox hit the jackpot in 1977 with *Star Wars* and its sequels. In 1981, the company was bought by oil billionaire Marvin Davis; he in turn sold it in 1985 to publishing tycoon Rupert Murdoch, who took over personal control following the resignation of its chairman and CEO Barry Diller in 1992. In recent years, the company has enjoyed hits with *Big, Aliens, Die Hard* and *Die Hard 2, Sleeping with the Enemy* and *Home Alone,* the most financially successful of comedies.

¶ Leaving Fox was like leaving home at 28; I'd been there since I was 16. – *Linda Darnell*

Twiggy (1949–) (Lesley Hornby).
British fashion model of the 60s.
■ *The Boy Friend* 71. 'W' 74. There Goes the Bride 80. The Doctor and the Devils 85. Club Paradise 86. The Little Match Girl (TV) 87. Madame Sousatzka 88. The Diamond Trap (TV) 88. Young Charlie Chaplin (TV) 88. Istanbul 89.

Twist, Derek (1905–1979).
British director, former editor and associate producer.
The End of the River 47. All over the Town 48. Green Grow the Rushes 51. Police Dog 55. Family Doctor 57, etc.

Twist, John (1895–1976).
American screenwriter.
The Toast of New York 36. The Great Man Votes 39. So Big 53. Helen of Troy 55. The FBI Story 56. Esther and the King 60. None But the Brave 64, etc.

Twitty, Conway (1934–1993) (Harold Lloyd Jenkins).
American rock singer and songwriter who appeared in a couple of films as himself and from the mid-60s became a successful country and western performer and businessman, owner of the Twitty City theme park just outside Nashville.
College Confidential 59. Platinum High School (aka Trouble at 16; Rich Young and Deadly) 60, etc.

Two Cities Films.
A British company set up in the early days of World War II by the expatriate Italian Filippo del Giudice. It was responsible for many of Britain's most famous films, including *In Which We Serve, The Way Ahead, Henry V, Blithe Spirit* and *Odd Man Out*.

Twohy, David T.
American screenwriter.
Critters 2 88. Warlock 90. The Fugitive (co-w) 93. Terminal Velocity (w) 94. Waterworld (co-w) 95.

Tyler, Beverly (1924–).
American leading lady of routine 40s films.
Best Foot Forward 43. The Green Years 46. The Beginning or the End 47. The Fireball 50. Chicago Confidential 47. The Toughest Gun in Tombstone 58, etc.

Tyler, Parker (1904–1974).
American highbrow film critic. Author of *The Hollywood Hallucination, Magic and Myth of the Movies, The Shadow of an Airplane Climbs the Empire State Building,* etc.

Tyler, Tom (1903–1954) (Vincent Markowsky).
American cowboy star of innumerable second features in the 30s: *The Cowboy Cop* 26. *The Sorcerer* 29. *Riding the Lonesome Trail* 34. *Pinto Rustlers* 38. *Roamin' Wild* 39, etc. Also played small roles in such films as *Gone with the Wind* 39. *Stagecoach* 39. *The Mummy's Hand* (as the mummy) 40; and had

the title role in *The Adventures of Captain Marvel* (serial) 41.

Tynan, Kenneth (1927–1980).
British journalist and critic who was briefly a script editor at Ealing in the mid-50s. The character of Professor Marcus, played by Alec Guinness in *The Ladykillers,* is said to have been based on his physical appearance (though Guinness has denied it). He was film critic of the *Observer* in 1964.
Nowhere to Go (co-w) 58. Macbeth (co-w) 71.

Tyrrell, Susan (1941–).
American leading lady.
Fat City (AAN) 72. Shootout 72. Catch My Soul 73. The Killer inside Me 76. I Never Promised You a Rose Garden 77. Islands in the Stream 77. Another Man, Another Chance 77. Andy Warhol's Bad 77. September 30, 1955 77. Lady of the House 78. Forbidden Zone 80. Loose Shoes 80. Night Warning 81. Fast-Walking 82. Tales of Ordinary Madness 83. Angel 84. Flesh and Blood 85. Avenging Angel 85. Big-Top Pee-Wee 88. Far from Home 89. Tapeheads 89. Cry-Baby 90. Rockula 90. Motorama 92, etc.

Tyson, Cathy (1966–).
British actress, from the stage.
Mona Lisa 86. The Serpent and the Rainbow 88. Business as Usual 88. Rules of Engagement (TV) 89. The Lost Language of Cranes (TV) 91. Priest (TV) 94, etc.

Tyson, Cicely (1933–).
American leading actress.
A Man Called Adam 66. The Comedians 67. The Heart Is a Lonely Hunter 68. *Sounder* (AAN) 72. *The Autobiography of Miss Jane Pittman* (TV) 74. Roots (TV) 77. A Hero Ain't Nothin' but a Sandwich 77. The Concorde – Airport '79 79. Bustin' Loose 81. Fried Green Tomatoes at the Whistle Stop Café 91. Duplicates (TV) 92. Oldest Living Confederate Widow Tells All (TV) 94, etc.
TV series: East Side West Side 63.

Tyzack, Margaret (1933–).
British character actress, familiar on TV in *The First Churchills* and *The Forsyte Saga*.
Ring of Spies 64. The Whisperers 67. A Clockwork Orange 71. The Legacy 79. Mr Love 86. The King's Whore 90, etc.

Tzelniker, Meier (1894–1982).
British character actor well known in the Yiddish theatre.
Mr Emmanuel 44. It Always Rains on Sunday 48. Last Holiday 50. The Teckman Mystery 54. Make Me an Offer 54. A Night to Remember 58. *Expresso Bongo* 60. The Sorcerers 67, etc.

U

UFA.

Universum Film Aktien Gesellschaft: the main German film production company since 1917, owning its studio and linked in the 20s with Paramount and MGM. In the 30s it was brought under state control and in the 40s, with the end of the war, it ceased to exist.

Uggams, Leslie (1943–).

American revue actress.

Skyjacked 72. Roots (TV) 77. Backstairs at the White House (TV) 79. Sizzle 81. Sugar Hill 93, etc.

TV series: The Leslie Uggams Show 69. Roots 77–78.

Uhry, Alfred H (1937–).

American dramatist and screenwriter.

Mystic Pizza 88. Driving Miss Daisy (AA) 89. Rich in Love 92.

Ullman, Daniel (1918–1979).

American scriptwriter.

The Maze 53. Seven Angry Men 54. Wichita 55. Good Day for a Hanging 59. Face of a Fugitive 59. Mysterious Island 61, etc.

Ullmann, Liv (1939–).

Norwegian leading actress in international films.

Autobiography: 1977, Changing.

The Wayward Girl 59. Persona 66. Hour of the Wolf 67. Shame 68. A Passion 70. The Night Visitor 70. Pope Joan 71. The Emigrants (AAN) 72. Lost Horizon 73. Forty Carats 73. The Abdication 74. Face to Face (AAN) 76. A Bridge Too Far 77. The Serpent's Egg 77. Leonor 77. Autumn Sonata 78. Players 79. Richard's Things (TV) 80. The Wild Duck 82. Bay Boy 84. Dangerous Moves 84. Ingrid 85. Let's Hope It's a Girl 85. Gaby – a True Story 87. La Amiga 88. The Rose Garden 89. Mindwalk 90. The Ox (Oxen) 91. The Long Shadow 92. Sofie (co-w, d) 92. Dreamplay (Dromspel) 94, etc.

Ullman, Tracy (1959–).

British actress and singer, often in comic roles, who moved to America in the mid-80s. She began her career in British theatre and television and has recorded a hit single, 'They Don't Know', and some pop albums.

Give My Regards to Broad Street 83. The Young Visitors (TV) 84. Plenty 85. Jumpin' Jack Flash 86. I Love You to Death 90. Death Becomes Her 92. Household Saints 93. Robin Hood: Men in Tights 93. I'll Do Anything 94. Bullets over Broadway 94, etc.

TV series: Three of a Kind 81. Kick Up the Eighties 81–82. Girls on Top 85–86. The Tracy Ullman Show 87–90.

Ulmer, Edgar G. (1900–1972).

Austrian-born director long in Hollywood specializing in second features and exploitation subjects. In his later years somewhat mysteriously revered by French critics.

The Black Cat 34. The Singing Blacksmith 38. Isle of Forgotten Sins 43. Blueboard 44. The Wife of Monte Cristo 46. Detour 46. Her Sister's Secret 47. Ruthless 48. The Man from Planet X 53. The Naked Dawn 55. Daughter of Dr Jekyll 57. The Amazing Transparent Man 60. Beyond the Time Barrier 61. Atlantis, the Lost Kingdom (L'Atlantide) 62. The Cavern 65, many others.

Ulric, Lenore (1892–1970) (Lenore Ulrich).

American stage actress.

Tiger Rose 23. Frozen Justice 29. Camille 36. Temptation 46. Northwest Outpost 47, etc.

Ultra Violet (1934–) (Isabelle Collin-Dufresne).

French-born actress who became part of the entourage that surrounded Andy Warhol and appeared in some of his films.

Autobiography: 1988, Famous for 15 Minutes.

I, a Man 67. Midnight Cowboy 69. Maidstone 70. Dinah East 70. Taking Off 71. Simon, King of the Witches 71. Believe in Me 71. An Unmarried Woman 78. Blackout 92, etc.

¶ Nearly all of us at the Factory have had our moments of anger at Andy. He's promised us fame, money, Superstardom, and only given us walk-on parts in his home-made movies. When a film has succeeded, he's kept the profits and seized the headlines. – U.V.

She was popular with the press because she had a freak name, purple hair, an incredibly long tongue, and a mini-rap about the intellectual meaning of underground films – Andy Warhol

Umeki, Miyoshi (1929–).

Japanese leading lady who won an Academy Award for her performance in Sayonara 57.

Cry for Happy 61. Flower Drum Song 61. A Girl Named Tamiko 63, etc.

TV series: The Courtship of Eddie's Father 69.

Uncle Tom's Cabin.

The anti-slavery story of excellent intentions and unabashed sentimentality was written in 1852 by American novelist Harriet Beecher Stowe. It features the dastardly white villain Simon Legree, the cheerful black Uncle Tom (whose name has entered the American language as an insulting description of obsequiousness to whites), and poor little Eva, who is taken to heaven by an angel. The main film versions include a 1903 one-reeler by Edwin S. Porter, a Pathé three-reeler of 1910, and an American three-reeler of 1913. In 1914 came a longer American version with Marie Eline as Little Eva, and 1918 brought a full-length version with Marguerite Clark in the dual role of Topsy and Eva. Then in 1927 Harry Pollard directed a full-blown silent spectacle which was frequently revived with sound effects in later years; Virginia Gray was Eva. The subject might have been thought too dated for sound treatment, but in 1965 a colour and wide-screen European co-production was directed by Geza von Radvanyi and featured Herbert Lom as Simon Legree. A television version followed in 1987, directed by Stan Lathan.

uncredited appearances

by well-known stars are usually intended as gags to liven up a film which can do with an extra laugh. Thus the brief cameos of Cary Grant and Jack Benny in Without Reservations; Lana Turner in Du Barry Was a Lady; Robert Taylor in I Love Melvin; Bing Crosby in My Favourite Blonde, The Princess and the Private and other Bob Hope films; Alan Ladd in My Favourite Brunette; Peter Lorre in Meet Me in Las Vegas; Myrna Loy in The Senator was Indiscreet; Peter Sellers and David Niven in Road to Hong Kong; Vincent Price in Beach Party; Boris Karloff in Bikini Beach; Groucho Marx in Will Success Spoil Rock Hunter?; Elizabeth Taylor in Scent of Mystery, What's New Pussycat? and Anne of the Thousand Days; Richard Burton in What's New Pussycat? Jack Benny and Jerry Lewis in It's a Mad Mad Mad Mad World; Robert Vaughn in The Glass Bottom Boat; Bob Hope and others in The Oscar; Rock Hudson in Four Girls in Town; Jack Benny and Jimmy Durante in Beau James; Red Skelton in Susan Slept Here; Bing Crosby and Bob Hope in Scared Stiff; Martin and Lewis, Humphrey Bogart and Jane Russell in Road to Bali; Lauren Bacall in Two Guys from Milwaukee; Gene Kelly in Love is Better Than Ever; Clark Gable and Robert Taylor in Callaway Went Thataway; Peter O'Toole in Casino Royale; Yul Brynner in The Magic Christian; Edward G. Robinson in Robin and the Seven Hoods; Humphrey Bogart in Always Together, Two Guys from Milwaukee and The Love Lottery; Jack Benny in The Great Lover; Ray Milland in Miss Tatlock's Millions; John Wayne in I Married a Woman; Tony Curtis in Chamber of Horrors; Sammy Davis Jnr in A Raisin in the Sun; Shirley Maclaine in Ocean's Eleven; Margaret Rutherford in The ABC Murders; Jack Nicholson in Broadcast News; Macaulay Culkin in Jacob's Ladder; Sean Connery in Robin Hood: Prince of Thieves; Kenneth Branagh in Swing Kids.

Sometimes a sequel not featuring the star of the first story will have a brief reminiscence of him with no credit: this happened to Cary Grant in Topper Takes a Trip and to Simone Signoret in Life at the Top. Then there are deliberate in-jokes like Walter Huston playing bit parts in his son John's movies; Peter Finch playing a messenger in The First Men in the Moon because he happened to be there when the hired actor failed to turn up; Joseph Cotten playing a small part in Touch of Evil because he dropped in to watch the location shooting and Orson Welles sent a make-up man over for old times' sake, Helen Hayes playing a small role in Third Man on the Mountain because her son James MacArthur was in the cast. Occasionally when stars are replaced during production, long shots of them remain in the completed film: thus Vivien Leigh in Elephant Walk and George Brent in Death of a Scoundrel. The best gag was played by Al Jolson who, determined to get into The Jolson Story at all costs, played himself in the theatre runaway long shots during 'Swanee'.

There remain a few mysteries. In The Great Ziegfeld, 'A Pretty Girl is Like a Melody' was apparently sung by Stanley Morner, soon to become quite famous as Dennis Morgan. He was not credited (perhaps because the voice finally used on the soundtrack was that of Allan Jones). Nor were the following who had important roles to play and were well-known at the time: Constance Collier in *Anna Karenina*, Marlene Dietrich in *Touch of Evil*, Henry Daniell in *Mutiny on the Bounty*, Audrey Totter in *The Carpetbaggers*, Dorothy Malone and John Hubbard in *Fate is the Hunter*, Wilfrid Lawson in *Tread Softly Stranger*, Ava Gardner in *The Band Wagon*, Edmond O'Brien in *The Greatest Show on Earth*, David Warner in *Straw Dogs*, Henry Daniell in *My Fair Lady*, Edmond O'Brien in *The Greatest Show on Earth*, Mercedes McCambridge in *Touch of Evil*, Glenda Jackson in *The Boy Friend*, Leo McKern in *The High Commissioner*. And in *Those Magnificent Men in Their Flying Machines*, Cicely Courtneidge and Fred Emney had roughly equal dialogue in their one scene; yet he was credited and she was not. The reasons surely can't have anything to do with modesty.

See also: *directors' appearances*.

Under Two Flags.

Ouida's romantic melodrama about the Foreign Legion was filmed in 1916 by J. Gordon Edwards, with Theda Bara as Cigarette; in 1922 by Tod Browning, with Priscilla Dean and Jack Kirkwood; and in 1936 by Frank Lloyd, with Claudette Colbert and Ronald Colman.

Underdown, Edward (1908–1989).

British actor on stage from 1932; once a jockey. Often cast as a dull Englishman.

The Warren Case 33 (debut). Wings of the Morning 37. They Were Not Divided 50. The Voice of Merrill 52. Beat the Devil 54. The Camp on Blood Island 58. The Day the Earth Caught Fire 62. Khartoum 66. The Hand of Night 67. Running Scared 72. Digby, the Biggest Dog in the World 73. The Abdication 74, etc.

underground films

are generally thought of as those made cheaply to espouse a cause or experimentally at a director's whim, commercial success being a secondary consideration. The most successful underground film-maker, breaking through into box-office success, was Andy Warhol, with Paul Morrissey directing the later films that capitalized on Warhol's name. Other influential American underground film-makers include Kenneth Anger, Stan Brakhage, Ed Emshwiller, Gregory Markopoulos, Jonas Mekas, Jack Smith.

Book: 1969, *Underground Film: A Critical History* by Parker Tyler.

underground railways

have been used remarkably little in films considering their dramatic possibilities. There were chases through them in *Underground* itself, *Bulldog Jack*, *Waterloo Road*, *The French Connection*, *The Taking of Pelham One Two Three*, *Death Line* and *Death Wish*; they were also used for a comedy scene in *Rotten to the Core*, a murder in *Man Hunt*, *Otley*, and *The Liquidator*, and a musical number in *Three Hats for Lisa*, and *Death Line* (aka *Raw Meat*) exploited the unease that can be felt in underground stations by putting cannibals in a deserted tunnel. The New York subway was the setting for musical numbers in *Dames* ('I Only Have Eyes for You') and *On the Town* ('Miss Turnstiles' ballet), and it also featured in a romantic comedy (*Practically Yours*) and was the scene of a brutal beating-up in *The Young Savages* and a nasty accidental death in *P.J.*; while the whole of *Dutchman* took place on it, and *Short Walk To*

Daylight began with an earthquake trapping passengers in it.

The New York elevated railway, on the other hand, was most dramatically used in *King Kong*, and provided effective backing in *The Lost Weekend*, *Union Station*, *The Bachelor Party*, *The FBI Story*, *Beneath the Planet of the Apes*, *Cry of the City* and *The French Connection*.

undertakers,

or morticians, have provided comedy relief in many a western, relying on frequent shootings to bring in business: perhaps this theme was first explored in *The Westerner* 39. The comedy elements of the profession were also presented by Vincent Price and Peter Lorre in *A Comedy of Terrors*, by Terry-Thomas in *Strange Bedfellows*, by almost the entire cast of *The Loved One*, by Paul Lynde in *Send Me No Flowers*, and by J. Pat O'Malley in *Willard*. Literature's most famous undertaker is perhaps Mr Sowerberry in *Oliver Twist*, played by Gibb McLaughlin in the 1948 version and by Leonard Rossiter in *Oliver!*

underwater sequences

of note were found in *Reap the Wild Wind*, *The Silent Enemy*, *The Beast from 20,000 Fathoms*, *The Golden Mistress*, *Twenty Thousand Leagues under the Sea*, *Around the World under the Sea*, *Voyage to the Bottom of the Sea*, *Thunderball*, *Shark*, *Lady in Cement*, and *The Big Blue*.

See also: *submarines*.

Underwood, Ron.

American director.

Tremors 90. City Slickers 91. Heart and Souls 93. Speechless 94.

unemployment

in Britain was the somewhat unpopular subject of *Doss House*, *Love on the Dole*, and *The Common Touch*; in Europe, *Joyless Street*, *Little Man What Now?* and *Berliner Ballade*. America has seemed almost to boast about its unemployed, who were featured in *The Crowd*, *Our Daily Bread*, *Grapes of Wrath*, *Hallelujah I'm a Bum*, *Sullivan's Travels*, *I Am a Fugitive from a Chain Gang*, *The Great McGinty*, *One More Spring*, *Mr Deeds Goes to Town*, *Man's Castle*, *My Man Godfrey* and *Tobacco Road*, among many others.

Unfaithfully Yours.

Preston Sturges' vintage satirical comedy, about a jealous orchestral conductor who suspects his wife of infidelity and plots three revenges during a concert, was made in 1948, starring Rex Harrison; 1983 brought a tolerable remake with Dudley Moore.

unfinished films.

Among the productions which ran out of money halfway, or were terminated for other reasons, are Josef Von Sternberg's *I Claudius*; Errol Flynn's *William Tell*; Orson Welles' *Don Quixote*, *The Other Side of the Moon* and *It's All True*; Eisenstein's *Que Viva Mexico*; Brecht's *Mother Courage*; Zinnemann's *Man's Fate*; David Miller's *The Bells of Hell go Ting-a-ling-a-ling*; Marilyn Monroe in *Something's Got to Give*; Willis O'Brien's *Creation*; and George Sluizer's *Dark Blood*, abandoned after the death of its star, River Phoenix. Films which had troubles but were completed in scrappy fashion include Michael Caine in *The Jigsaw Man*, James Caan in *Man Without Mercy*, Natalie Wood in *Brainstorm*, Bela Lugosi in *Plan 9 from Outer Space*, and Bruce Lee in *Game of Death* (in which nearly ninety per cent of his role was played by doubles). Bruce Lee's son, Brandon Lee, was accidentally killed during the filming of *The Crow*, but that film was

completed with the aid of doubles and sophisticated computer techniques to create new scenes for Lee from existing footage.

unfinished performances.

Here are some cases of actors who began to film roles but then either walked off the set or were let go because of unhappiness, inadequacy or just plain cussedness. Replacements are in brackets.

George Segal in *'10'* (Dudley Moore); John Travolta in *American Gigolo* (Richard Gere); Richard Dreyfuss in *All that Jazz* (Roy Scheider); Marlon Brando in *Child's Play* (Robert Preston); Robert Mitchum in *Rosebud* (Peter O'Toole); Richard Harris in *Flap* (Anthony Quinn); Rip Torn in *Easy Rider* (Jack Nicholson); George C. Scott in *How to Steal a Million* (Eli Wallach); Judy Garland in *Valley of the Dolls* (Susan Hayward); Elvis Presley in *A Star is Born* (Kris Kristofferson); Lana Turner in *Anatomy of a Murder* (Lee Remick); Christopher Plummer in *Dr Dolittle* (Rex Harrison); Judy Garland in *Annie Get Your Gun* (Betty Hutton); Joan Crawford in *Hush Hush Sweet Charlotte* (Olivia de Havilland); Charles Laughton in *David Copperfield* (W. C. Fields); Tyrone Power in *Solomon and Sheba* (he died during filming) (Yul Brynner); Buddy Ebsen in *The Wizard of Oz* (Jack Haley); Bela Lugosi in *Frankenstein* (Boris Karloff).

Performers unavailable to play roles for which they were badly wanted include Cary Grant for *My Fair Lady* (Rex Harrison); Joan Crawford for *From Here to Eternity* (Deborah Kerr); Boris Karloff for *Arsenic and Old Lace* (Raymond Massey); Basil Radford and Naunton Wayne for *I See a Dark Stranger* (Garry Marsh and Tom Macaulay); Gary Cooper and Barbara Stanwyck for *Saboteur* (Robert Cummings and Priscilla Lane); Robert Newton for *The Paradine Case* (Louis Jourdan); Jessie Matthews for *A Damsel in Distress* (Joan Fontaine); Claude Rains for *Bride of Frankenstein* (Ernest Thesiger); Burt Lancaster for *Ben Hur* (Charlton Heston); Lon Chaney for *Dracula* (Bela Lugosi); Robert Donat for *Captain Blood* (Errol Flynn); Frank Sinatra for *Carousel* (Gordon Macrae); Jack Benny for *The Sunshine Boys* (George Burns); Jeff Chandler for *Operation Petticoat* (Cary Grant); Bette Davis and Errol Flynn for *Gone with the Wind* (Vivien Leigh and Clark Gable); W. C. Fields for *The Wizard of Oz* (Frank Morgan); Claude Rains for *The Day the Earth Stood Still* (Michael Rennie); George Raft for *High Sierra* and *The Maltese Falcon* (Humphrey Bogart).

United Artists Corporation

was founded in 1919 by Mary Pickford, Douglas Fairbanks, Charlie Chaplin and D. W. Griffith, the object being to make and distribute their own and other people's quality product. Among the company's early successes were *His Majesty the American*, *Pollyanna* (the first film sold on a percentage basis), *Broken Blossoms*, *Way Down East*, and *A Woman of Paris*. In the mid-20s Joe Schenck was brought in to run the company, and he in turn gained Valentino, Goldwyn, Keaton and Swanson; but later all were bought out by various syndicates. Howard Hughes contributed *Hell's Angels* and *Scarface*, but in the 30s the UA product began to thin out, partly because the company was purely a distributor and financer of independent producers, without any studio of its own or any large roster of stars under contract. The hardest times, with only inferior product to sell, were between 1948 and 1953; but after that a new board of directors, through careful choice of product, fought its way back to the top; despite the defection of half its executives to Orion, UA was again riding high with *The Magnificent Seven*, *The Battle of Britain*, *Tom Jones*, *One Flew Over the*

Cuckoo's Nest, Rocky and the James Bond films. The 80s however brought the 40-million-dollar calamity of *Heaven's Gate* (book: *Final Cut* by Steven Bach) and a takeover by MGM (qv) to become MGM-UA.

Book: 1986, *The United Artists Story* by Ronald Bergen.

¶ The lunatics have taken over the asylum.
— *Robert Lord, 1919*
We maniacs had fun and made good pictures and a lot of money. In the early years United Artists was a private golf club for the four of us. – *Mary Pickford*

Universal Pictures

was founded in 1912 by Carl Laemmle, an exhibitor turned producer. Universal City grew steadily and included among its output many of the most famous titles of Von Stroheim, Valentino and Lon Chaney. In 1930 came *All Quiet on the Western Front*, and soon after *Dracula* and *Frankenstein*, the precursors of a long line of horror pictures. Laemmle lost power in the mid-30s and the studio settled down to be one of Hollywood's 'little two', producing mainly modest, low-budget co-features without too many intellectual pretensions. The Deanna Durbin series saved it from receivership, and there were occasional notable pictures: *Destry Rides Again, Hellzapoppin, Flesh and Fantasy*. The stars under contract were durable: Boris Karloff, Lon Chaney Jnr, Donald O'Connor, Abbott and Costello, Jeff Chandler, Audie Murphy. More ambition was noted in the 50s, when the era of the bread-and-butter picture was ended by TV. Decca Records gained a large measure of control, but in 1962 a merger gave the ultimate power to the Music Corporation of America, ex-agents and TV producers. The 1960s saw a steady resumption of prestige, with films like *Spartacus*, the Doris Day – Rock Hudson sex comedies, *Charade, The War Lord*, Ross Hunter's soapily sentimental but glossy remakes of Hollywood's choicest weepies, *Thoroughly Modern Millie, The Day of the Jackal, Earthquake, Airport* and *The Seven Per Cent Solution*. The company, now a division of MCA Inc. is currently one of Hollywood's most powerful sources of box-office films and television series, though its venture into 'enlightened' European production was fairly disastrous. In the 80s the company enjoyed its biggest-ever hit, *E.T. – the Extraterrestrial*, courtesy of Steven Spielberg, who had also scored for them in the mid-70s with *Jaws*. Spielberg also produced Universal's other big winners, *Back to the Future* and its sequels, while it enjoyed Oscar successes with *Out of Africa*. His contribution remained important to the company when his *Jurassic Park* was a monster hit around the world.

Clive Hirschhorn's splendidly illustrated book *The Universal Story* (1983) is an excellent critical history. Also: 1991, *The Best of Universal* by Tony Thomas.

universities

have scarcely been studied seriously by movie-makers. Of Britain's most venerable, Cambridge has served as a background for one light comedy, *Bachelor of Hearts*, and Oxford for another, *A Yank at Oxford*, which was subsequently parodied by Laurel and Hardy in *A Chump at Oxford*. *Charley's Aunt* was also set among dreaming spires. Dramas with Oxford settings include *Accident* and *The Mind Benders*. Provincial universities score one comedy

(*Lucky Jim*) and one drama (*The Wild and the Willing*). American campuses used to feature in films of the *Hold That Co-Ed* type, the pleasantest to remember being *The Freshman* and *Horse Feathers*, with *How to Be Very Very Popular* a poor third; but in the late 60s student protest held sway in *The Strawberry Statement, Getting Straight, R.P.M., Drive He Said*, and *The Activist*. Other views of the American higher learning came in *Paper Chase, The Group, The Male Animal, Class of 44*, and *The Magic Garden of Stanley Sweetheart*.

Unsworth, Geoffrey (1914–1978).

British cinematographer.

The Million Pound Note 53. Hell Drivers 57. *A Night to Remember* 58. Northwest Frontier 59. The 300 Spartans 62. Becket (BFA) 64. Genghis Khan 65. Half a Sixpence 67. *2001: A Space Odyssey* 68. The Bliss of Mrs Blossom 68. The Assassination Bureau 68. The Reckoning 69. Three Sisters 70. *Cabaret* (AA) 72. Alice's Adventures in Wonderland 72. Zardoz 73. Murder on the Orient Express 74. Lucky Lady 75. A Matter of Time 76. The Great Train Robbery 78. Superman 78. Tess (AA, BFA) 79, etc.

U.P.A. (United Productions of America)

was a cartoon factory which in the early 50s received generous critical plaudits for a hundred or so shorts and even pushed the Disney studio into a more sophisticated style. Its creations included Mr Magoo, Gerald McBoing Boing and Pete Hothead, and it specialized in a stylish economy of line and in an appeal to a much higher intelligence bracket than any cartoon had aspired to in the past.

Urban, Charles (1871–1942).

American pioneer of British films. He left Edison to found his own production company in London, and especially developed commercial non-fiction films.

Urban, Joseph (1872–1933).

Austrian-born art director, architect, illustrator, and noted stage designer. Most famous for designing the sets for the Ziegfeld Follies on Broadway from 1915–32, he worked in films at the invitation of William Randolph Hearst to add distinction to the movies of Hearst's mistress Marion Davies.

Humoresque 20. Passionate Pilgrim 21. Enchantment 21. Beauty's Worth 22. When Knighthood Was in Flower 22. Adam and Eve 23. The Great White Way 24. Zander the Great 25. The Man Who Came Back 31. East Lynne 31, etc.

Ure, Mary (1933–1975).

British leading actress of stage and (occasionally) screen. She was married to dramatist John Osborne and later actor Robert Shaw.

■ Storm over the Nile 55. Windom's Way 59. Look Back in Anger 59. Sons and Lovers (AAN) 60. The Mind Benders 63. The Luck of Ginger Coffey 64. Custer of the West 67. Where Eagles Dare 68. Reflection of Fear 71.

Urecal, Minerva (1896–1966).

American character actress.

Oh Doctor 37. Boys of the City 40. The Bridge of San Luis Rey 44. Who's Guilty? 47. The Lost Moment 48. Harem Girl 52. Miracle in the Rain 56. The Seven Faces of Dr Lao 64, etc.

TV series: Tugboat Annie.

Urich, Robert (1946–   ).

American TV actor (*Vegas*) who has made a few films.

■ Endangered Species 82. The Ice Pirates 83. Turk 182 84. Murder by Night (TV) 89. Survive the Savage Sea 91.

TV series: S.W.A.T. 75–76. Soap 77. Tabitha 77–78. Vega$ 78–81. Gavilan 82–83. Spencer: For Hire 85–88. Crossroads 92.

Urioste, Frank J.

American film editor.

Whatever Happened to Aunt Alice 69. The Grissom Gang 71. Midway 76. Damnation Alley 77. The Boys in Company C 78. Fast Break 79. Loving Couples 80. The Jazz Singer 80. The Entity 83. Trenchcoat 83. Amityville 3-D 83. Conan the Destroyer 84. Red Sonja 85. The Hitcher 86. Robocop (AAN) 87. Die Hard (AA) 88. Road House 89. Total Recall 90. Basic Instinct 92. Cliffhanger 93. Tombstone 94, etc.

Urquhart, Robert (1922–   ).

Scottish character actor, in films since 1951 after stage experience.

You're Only Young Twice (debut) 51. Knights of the Round Table 54. You Can't Escape 56. The Curse of Frankenstein 56. Dunkirk 58. 55 Days at Peking 62. Murder at the Gallop 64. Country Dance 70. The Dogs of War 80. Restless Natives 85. The Kitchen Toto 87, etc.

TV series: The Pathfinders 72. The Amazing Mr Goodall 74.

Ustinov, Sir Peter (1921–   ).

Garrulous, hirsute, multi-talented British actor-director-playwright-screenwriter-raconteur. Autobiography: 1978, *Dear Me*.

■ AS ACTOR: Hullo Fame 40. Mein Kampf 40. The Goose Steps Out 41. One of Our Aircraft is Missing 42. Let the People Sing 42. The Way Ahead 44. *Private Angelo* 49. Odette 50. *Hotel Sahara* 51. The Magic Box 51. *Quo Vadis* (as Nero) (AAN) 51. *Beau Brummell* (as George IV) 54. The Egyptian 54. We're No Angels 55. Lola Montez 55. The Man Who Wagged His Tail 57. The Spies 57. *The Sundowners* 60. *Spartacus* (AA) 60. *Romanoff and Juliet* 61. Billy Budd 61. Topkapi (AA) 64. John Goldfarb Please Come Home 65. Lady L 65. The Comedians 67. Blackbeard's Ghost 68. Hot Millions 68. Viva Max 69. Hammersmith Is Out (& d) 72. One of Our Dinosaurs Is Missing 75. Logan's Run 76. Treasure of Matecumbe 76. The Purple Taxi 77. The Last Remake of Beau Geste 77. Jesus of Nazareth (TV) 77. *Death on the Nile* (as Hercule Poirot) 78. Ashanti 78. The Thief of Baghdad (TV) 79. Charlie Chan and the Curse of the Dragon Queen 81. Evil Under the Sun 82. Memed My Hawk (& w, d) 83. Murder with Mirrors (TV) 85. Thirteen at Dinner (TV) 85. Dead Man's Folly (TV) 86. Appointment with Death 88. La Révolution Française 89. C'era un Castello con 40 Cani 90. Lorenzo's Oil 92. The Dancer 93.

■ AS DIRECTOR-WRITER: School for Secrets 46. *Vice Versa* 48. *Private Angelo* 49. Romanoff and Juliet 61. Billy Budd 62. Lady L 65.

Uys, Jamie (1921–   ).

South African writer-producer-director.

Rip Van Winkle 60. *Dingaka* 64. The Professor and the Beauty Queen 67. Dirkie 69. Lost in the Desert 70. The Gods Must Be Crazy 81. Beautiful People II 83. The Gods Must Be Crazy II 89, etc.

V

Vacano, Jost (1934–).
German cinematographer, noted for his work with director Paul Verhoeven.

The Lost Honour of Katharina Blum (Die Verlorene Ehre der Katharina Blum) 75. Soldier of Orange (Soldaat van Oranje) 77. Spetters 80. The Boat (Das Boot) (AAN) 82. The Neverending Story 84. 52 Pick-Up 86. Robocop 87. Rocket Gibraltar 88. Total Recall 90. Untamed Heart 93, etc.

Vaccaro, Brenda (1939–).
American character actress.

Midnight Cowboy 69. Where It's At 69. I Love My Wife 70. Summertree 71. What's a Nice Girl Like You . . . ? (TV) 72. Honor Thy Father 73. Sunshine (TV) 74. Once Is Not Enough (AAN) 76. The House by the Lake 77. Airport 77 77. Capricorn One 78. Fast Charlie the Moonbeam Rider 78. Supergirl 84. Water 84. Cookie 89. Heart of Midnight 89, etc.

TV series: Sara 76. Dear Detective 79.

Vadim, Roger (1927–) (Roger Vadim Plemiannikow).
French writer-director. His wives included Brigitte Bardot (1952–57) and Jane Fonda (1965–73). He has a son by actress Catherine Deneuve.

Autobiography: 1986, *Bardot, Deneuve and Fonda: The Memoirs of Roger Vadim*.

Futures Vedettes (w) 54. *And God Created Woman* (wd) 56. Heaven Fell That Night (wd) 57. *Les Liaisons Dangereuses* (wd) 59. Warrior's Rest (wd) 62. Vice and Virtue (wd) 62. La Ronde (wd) 64. Nutty Naughty Château (Château en Suède) 64. The Game Is Over (wd) 66. Histoires Extraordinaires (part) 68. Barbarella 68. Pretty Maids All in a Row 71. Don Juan 73. Night Games 79. Rich and Famous (a) 81. Hot Touch 81. Surprise Party 82. Come Back 83. Into the Night (a) 85. And God Created Woman 88. Mad Love (Amour Fou) 94, etc.

Vague, Vera:
see Allen, Barbara Jo.

Valdez, Luis (1940–).
American director, screenwriter and dramatist. Of Mexican ancestry, he first worked in the theatre, and his first film was based on his own play.

Zoot Suit 81. La Bamba 87. The Cisco Kid (TV) 94.

Valens, Ritchie (1941–1959) (Ritchie Valenzuela).
American rock singer and songwriter who appeared as himself in one movie before being killed in the same plane crash as singer Buddy Holly (qv). He was played by Lou Diamond Phillips in the biopic *La Bamba* 87.

Go Johnny Go 58. Rock and Roll – The Early Days (doc) 84.

Valenti, Jack (1921–).
American executive, dynamic president of the Motion Picture Association of America.

Valentine, Joseph (1900–1949) (Giuseppe Valentino).
Italian-American cinematographer, long in Hollywood.

Curlytop 24. Speakeasy 29. Soup to Nuts 30. Night of Terror 33. Remember Last Night 35. The Moon's Our Home 36. Three Smart Girls 36. One Hundred Men and a Girl 37. Mad About Music 38. That Certain Age 38. First Love 39. My Little Chickadee 40. Spring Parade 40. *The Wolf Man* 41. *Saboteur* 42. *Shadow of a Doubt* 43. Guest Wife 45. Tomorrow Is Forever 46. Magnificent Doll 46. Possessed 47. *Sleep My Love* 48. *Rope* 48. Joan of Arc (AA) 48. Bride for Sale 49, etc.

Valentine, Karen (1948–).
American light actress who has had most success on television.

Gidget Grows Up (TV) 69. The Daughters of Joshua Cabe (TV) 72. Coffee, Tea or Me? (TV) 73. The Girl Who Came Gift Wrapped (TV) 74. Having Babies (TV) 76. Murder at the World Series (TV) 77. Go West Young Girl (TV) 78. The North Avenue Irregulars 78. Muggable Mary: Street Cop (TV) 82. Children in the Crossfire (TV) 84. Perfect People (TV) 88, etc.

TV series: *Room 222* 69–72. Karen 75. Our Time 85.

Valentino, Rudolph (1895–1926) (Rodolpho d'Antonguolla).
Italian-American leading man, the great romantic idol of the 20s; his personality still shows. His sudden death caused several suicides and his funeral was a national event.

Biographies include: 1926, *Rudy* by his wife, Natacha Rambova. 1927, *The Real Valentino* by George S. Ullman. 1952, *Valentino* by Alan Arnold. *Rudolph Valentino* by Robert Oberfirst. 1962, *The Man behind the Myth*. 1967, *Valentino* by Irving Shulman. 1976, *Valentino the Love God* by Noel Botham and Peter Donnelly.

■ My Official Wife 14. Patria 16. Alimony 18. A Society Sensation 18. All Night 18. The Delicious Little Devil 19. A Rogue's Romance 19. The Homebreaker 19. Virtuous Sinners 19. The Big Little Person 19. Out of Luck 19. Eyes of Youth 19. The Married Virgin 20. An Adventuress 20. The Cheater 20. Passion's Playground 20. Once to Every Woman 20. Stolen Moments 20. The Wonderful Chance 20. *The Four Horseman of the Apocalypse* (the part that made him a super-star) 21. Unchained Seas 21. Camille 21. The Conquering Power 21. *The Sheik* 21. Moran of the Lady Letty 21. Beyond the Rocks 22. The Young Rajah 22. *Blood and Sand* 22. *Monsieur Beaucaire* 24. A Sainted Devil 24. Cobra 24. *The Eagle* 25. Son of the Sheik 26.

✪ For turning animal magnetism into at least the semblance of talent. *The Eagle*.

¶ His acting is largely confined to protruding his large, almost occult eyes until the vast areas of white are visible, drawing back the lips of his wide, sensuous mouth to bare his gleaming teeth, and flaring his nostrils.

Thus Adolph Zukor's famous put-down; but

Valentino's simple technique was very effective on female audiences the world over. Yet in the year of his death, 1926, he wrote:

A man should control his life. Mine is controlling me.

And H. L. Mencken summed him up:

He was essentially a highly respectable young man; his predicament touched me. Here was one who was catnip to women . . . he had youth and fame . . . and yet he was very unhappy.

~ There have been two films called *Valentino*. Anthony Dexter played him in 1951, Rudolf Nureyev in 1977. A TV movie, *The Legend of Valentino*, appeared in 1975 with Franco Nero.

Valk, Frederick (1901–1956).
Heavyweight Czech stage actor, in Britain from 1939.

Gasbags 40. *Thunder Rock* 42. *Dead of Night* 45. Latin Quarter 46. An Outcast of the Islands 51. Top Secret 52. The Colditz Story 53. Zarak 55, etc.

Vallee, Rudy (1901–1986) (Hubert Vallee).
American character comedian, the former crooning idol of the late 20s; in the early 40s Preston Sturges gave him a new lease of life.

Autobiography: 1976, *Let the Chips Fall*.

The Vagabond Lover 29. Sweet Music 34. Gold Diggers in Paris 38. Second Fiddle 39. Too Many Blondes 41. *The Palm Beach Story* 42. Happy Go Lucky 43. It's in the Bag 45. *The Bachelor and the Bobbysoxer* 47. Unfaithfully Yours 48. The Beautiful Blonde from Bashful Bend 49. Ricochet Romance 54. Gentlemen Marry Brunettes 55. The Helen Morgan Story 57. *How to Succeed in Business Without Really Trying* (his stage role) 67. Live a Little, Love a Little 68. Won Ton Ton 76, etc.

¶ People called me the guy with the cock in his voice. Maybe that's why in 84 years of life I've been with over 145 women and girls. – *R.V. in the RKO Story*

Famous line (*The Palm Beach Story*): 'That's one of the tragedies of life – that the men most in need of a beating-up are always enormous.'

Valli, Alida (1921–) (Alida Maria Altenburger).
Beautiful Italian actress.

I Due Sergenti 36. Manon Lescaut 39. Piccolo Mondo Antico 41. Eugénie Grandet 46. The Paradine Case (US) 47. The Miracle of the Bells 48. *The Third Man* 49. Walk Softly Stranger 49. The White Tower 50. The Lovers of Toledo 52. *Senso* 53. The Stranger's Hand 53. Heaven Fell That Night 57. The Sea Wall (This Angry Age) 57. Le Dialogue des Carmélites 59. Ophelia 61. Une Aussi Longue Absence 61. The Spider's Stratagem 71. 1900 76. The Cassandra Crossing 77. Suspiria 77. Aspern 82. Il Lungo Silenzio 93, etc.

Valli, Virginia (1898–1968) (Virginia McSweeney).
American silent screen heroine who retired in 1932 to marry Charles Farrell.

Efficiency Edgar's Courtship 17. The Storm 22.

A Lady of Quality 23. Paid to Love 27. Isle of Lost Ships 32, etc.

Vallone, Raf (1916–).
Italian leading man, former journalist.

Bitter Rice 48. Vendetta 49. Il Cristo Proibito 50. Anna 51. Thérèse Raquin 53. The Beach 53. The Sign of Venus 55. El Cid 61. *A View from the Bridge* (US) 61. Phaedra 62. The Cardinal 63. Harlow 65. Beyond the Mountains 66. The Italian Job 69. Cannon for Cordoba 70. A Gunfight 71. Rosebud 75. The Human Factor 75. The Other Side of Midnight 77. The Greek Tycoon 78. An Almost Perfect Affair 79. A Time to Die 79. Lion of the Desert 80. The Scarlet and the Black (TV) 83. Power of Evil 85. The Godfather Part III 90, etc.

vampires
in the cinema began under the influence of Bram Stoker's *Dracula* but have developed into a genre of their own, often set in the present day. These deviate from the lore as set down by Stoker and folk tradition: 'Don't believe everything you read,' says a pony-tailed vampire as he wrenches a cross from the grasp of a man in the otherwise unremarkable *Vampire Cop* 93, and George Romero created in *Martin* 78 a person who was far removed from the tradition, simply driven by a craving for blood. There is also a tradition of female vampire films, sometimes lesbian, which provide exploitation film-makers with plenty of opportunities for sex scenes. It has respectable origins in Sheridan Le Fanu's Victorian novel *Carmilla*, which has been filmed by Roger Vadim as *Blood and Roses* (*Et Mourir de Plaisir*) 60, Camillo Matrocinque as *Terror in the Crypt* 63, and Roy Ward Baker as *The Vampire Lovers* 70. Lesbian vampires also turn up in *Vampyres* 74, directed by Joseph Larraz (qv), while the female vampires in the films of Jean Rollin (qv) seem to be more interested in sex than blood.

Books: 1993, *The Illustrated Vampire Movie Guide* by Stephen Jones. 1994, *The Vampire Film: From Nosferatu to Bram Stoker's Dracula* by Alain Silver and James Ursini.

See also *Dracula*.

Van, Bobby (1930–1980) (Robert Stein King).
American song-and-dance man who went out of fashion with musicals but found a new audience in his 40s and became a TV personality.
■ Because You're Mine 52. Small Town Girl 52. Kiss Me Kate 53. The Navy Versus the Night Monsters 66. Lost Horizon 73. Lost Flight (TV) 73.

Van Cleef, Lee (1925–1989).
American character actor who after years as a sneaky western villain found fame and fortune as the hero of tough Italian westerns.

High Noon 52. Arena 53. Yellow Tomahawk 54. A Man Alone 55. Joe Dakota 57. Guns Girls and Gangsters 58. The Man Who Shot Liberty Valance 62. *For a Few Dollars More* 65. Day of Anger 66. *The Good the Bad and the Ugly* 67. Death Rides a Horse 67. Sabata 69. Barquero 70. El Condor 70. Captain Apache 71. Bad Man's River 71. The Magnificent Seven Ride 72. Take a Hard Ride 75. Vendetta 76. God's Gun 77. Kid Vengeance 77. The Octagon 80. Escape from New York 81. The Squeeze 82. Jungle Raiders 84. Armed Response 86. Speed Zone 88. Thieves of Fortune 89, etc.

¶ Being born with a beady-eyed sneer was the luckiest thing that ever happened to me. – *L.V.C.*

Van Damme, Jean-Claude (1961–) (Jean-Claude Van Varenberg).
Belgian actor in Hollywood action films. A former kickboxing champion, he is sometimes known as 'The Muscles from Brussels'.

No Retreat, No Surrender 86. Black Eagle 88. Bloodsport 88. Kickboxer 89. Cyborg 89. Death Warrant 90. Double Impact (& co-w) 91. Universal Soldier 92. Nowhere to Run 93. Timecop 94. Streetfighter 95, etc.

¶ He does what he does very well – kick boxing and stuff – but acting is not his forte. Neither is being humble. – *Rosanna Arquette*

Van De Sande, Theo (1947–).
Dutch cinematographer, in international films.

The Girl with the Red Hair 83. The Assault 86. Crossing Delancey 88. Rooftops 89. Once Around 91. Wayne's World 92. Erotic Tales 94, etc.

Van Devere, Trish (1943–) (Patricia Dressel).
American leading lady of the 70s. She married actor George C. Scott in 1972.

Where's Poppa? 70. The Last Run 71. One Is a Lonely Number 72. The Day of the Dolphins 73. Beauty and the Beast (TV) 76. Movie Movie 78. The Hearse 80. The Changeling 80. Uphill All the Way (TV) 85. Hollywood Vice Squad 86. Messenger of Death 88, etc.

¶ Barely more than a smiling hole in the air. – *Sunday Times*

Van Dine, S. S. (1888–1939) (Willard Huntingdon Wright).
American author who created the wealthy man-about-town detective Philo Vance, personified on screen by several actors. William Powell played him in *The Canary Murder Case* 29, *The Greene Murder Case* 29, *The Benson Murder Case* 30, and *The Kennel Murder Case* 33. Basil Rathbone had one attempt, *The Bishop Murder Case* 30. Warren William took over for *The Dragon Murder Case* 34 and *The Gracie Allen Murder Case* 39. Meanwhile there were Paul Lukas in *The Casino Murder Case* 35, Edmund Lowe in *The Garden Murder Case* 36, and Grant Richards in *Night of Mystery* 37. 1940 brought James Stephenson in *Calling Philo Vance*; in 1947 there was William Wright in *Philo Vance Returns*; and Alan Curtis in 1948 appeared in two poor attempts, *Philo Vance's Gamble* and *Philo Vance's Secret Mission*.

Van Doren, Mamie (1933–) (Joan Lucille Olander).
American leading lady, the blonde bombshell of the second feature, in Hollywood from 1954.

Autobiography: 1987, *Playing the Field*.

Forbidden (debut) 54. Yankee Pasha 54. The Second Greatest Sex 55. Running Wild 55. The Girl in Black Stockings 56. Teacher's Pet 58. The Navy versus the Night Monsters 66. Free Ride 85, etc.

Van Druten, John (1901–1957).
Prolific Anglo-American dramatist whose *I Am a Camera*, an adaptation of Christopher Isherwood's *Goodbye to Berlin*, was filmed twice, the second time as the musical *Cabaret*, which won eight Academy Awards.
■ Young Woodley 30. After Office Hours (London Wall) 31. New Morals for Old (After All) 32. If I Were Free (Behold We Live) 33. One Night in Lisbon (There's Always Juliet) 41. Old Acquaintance 43 and 81 (as Rich and Famous). Gaslight (co-w, AAN) 44. Voice of the Turtle 47. I

Remember Mama 48. I Am a Camera 55. Bell, Book and Candle 58. Cabaret 72.

Van Dyke, Dick (1925–).
Lanky American TV comedian who never quite made it in movies.
■ Bye Bye Birdie 63. What a Way to Go 64. *Mary Poppins* 64. The Art of Love 65. Lt Robin Crusoe 65. Never a Dull Moment 67. Divorce American Style 67. Fitzwilly 67. Chitty Chitty Bang Bang 68. *The Comic* 69. Some Kind of a Nut 70. Cold Turkey 71. The Morning After (TV) 74. The Runner Stumbles 79. Dropout Father (TV) 82. Found Money (TV) 84. The Wrong Way Kid (TV) 84. Strong Medicine (TV) 86. Ghost of a Chance (TV) 87. Dick Tracy 90.

TV series: *The Dick Van Dyke Show* 61–66. The New Dick Van Dyke Show 71–72.

Van Dyke, W. S. (1889–1943).
Competent, adaptable American director, at his peak in the 30s.
■ Men of the Desert 18. Gift of Gab 18. Land of Long Shadows 18. Open Spaces 18. Lady of the Dugout 19. Our Little Nell 20. According to Hoyle 22. Boss of Camp 4 22. Forget Me Not 22. Little Girl Next Door 23. Miracle Makers 23. Loving Lies 23. You Are In Danger 23. The Destroying Angel 23. The Battling Fool 24. Winner Take All 24. Barriers Burned Away 24. Half Dollar Bill 24. The Beautiful Sinner 25. Gold Heels 25. Hearts and Spurs 25. The Trail Rider 25. Ranger of the Big Pines 25. The Timber Wolf 25. The Desert's Price 25. The Gentle Cyclone 26. War Paint 26. Winners of the Wilderness 27. Heart of the Yukon 27. Eyes of the Totem 27. Foreign Devils 27. California 27. Spoilers of the West 27. Wyoming 28. Under the Black Eagle 28. *White Shadows in the South Seas* 28. The Pagan 29. *Trader Horn* 30. Never the Twain Shall Meet 31. Guilty Hands 31. Cuban Love Song 32. *Tarzan the Ape Man* 32. Night World 32. Penthouse 33. Eskimo 33. The Prizefighter and the Lady 33. Laughing Boy 34. Hideout 34. *Manhattan Melodrama* 34. *The Thin Man* (AAN) 34. Forsaking all Others 35. Naughty Marietta 35. I Live My Life 35. Rose Marie 36. *San Francisco* (AAN) 36. His Brother's Wife 36. The Devil is a Sissy 36. Love on the Run 36. After the Thin Man 36. Personal Property 37. They Gave Him a Gun 37. Rosalie 37. Marie Antoinette 38. *Sweethearts* 38. Stand Up and Fight 39. It's a Wonderful World 39. Andy Hardy Gets Spring Fever 39. Another Thin Man 39. I Take This Woman 40. I Love You Again 40. Bitter Sweet 40. Rage in Heaven 41. The Feminine Touch 41. Shadow of the Thin Man 41. Dr Kildare's Victory 41. I Married an Angel 42. Cairo 42. Journey for Margaret 42.

Van Enger, Charles (1890–1980).
American cinematographer.

Treasure Island 20. A Doll's House 22. The Famous Mrs Fair 23. The Marriage Circle 24. Forbidden Paradise 24. *Phantom of the Opera* 25. Kiss Me Again 25. Puppets 26. Easy Pickings 27. Port of Missing Girls 28. Fox Movietone Follies 29. High Society Blues 30. Mad Parade 31. I Was a Spy 33. The Case of Gabriel Perry 34. Seven Sinners 36. Wife Doctor and Nurse 37. Miracle on Main Street 40. Never Give a Sucker an Even Break 41. Night Monster 42. Sherlock Holmes Faces Death 43. The Merry Monahans 44. That Night with You 45. The Time of Their Lives 46. The Wistful Widow 47. Abbott and Costello Meet Frankenstein 48. Africa Screams 49. Ma and Pa Kettle Back on the Farm 51. The Magnetic Monster 53. Sitting Bull 54. Time Table 56. Gun Fever 58, many others.

Van Eyck, Peter (1911–1969).
Blond German actor, in America from mid-30s, later international.

The Moon is Down 42. Five Graves to Cairo 43. Rommel, Desert Fox 51. *The Wages of Fear* 53. Retour de Manivelle 57. The Girl Rosemarie 58. The Snorkel 58. Foxhole in Cairo 60. Station Six Sahara 63. The Spy Who Came in from the Cold 65. Million Dollar Man 67. Shalako 68. Assignment to Kill 69, many others.

Van Eyssen, John (1925–   ).
South African actor who appeared in a number of British films before turning agent. Chief production executive in Britain for Columbia 1969–73.

Quatermass II 56. Dracula 57. I'm All Right Jack 59. The Criminal 60. Exodus 60, etc.

Van Fleet, Jo (1919–   ).
American character actress who usually plays older than her real age.
■ East of Eden (AA) 55. The Rose Tattoo 55. I'll Cry Tomorrow 55. The King and Four Queens 56. Gunfight at the OK Corral 57. This Angry Age 58. *Wild River* 60. Cool Hand Luke 67. I Love You Alice B. Toklas 67. 80 Steps to Jonah 69. The Gang that Couldn't Shoot Straight 72. The Tenant 76.

Van Heusen, Jimmy (1913–1990).
American songwriter, usually with lyrics by Johnny Burke: 'Swinging on a Star' (AA 1944), 'Sunday, Monday or Always', 'Sunshine Cake', many others. His later partner was lyricist Sammy Cahn, with whom he wrote such songs as 'All the Way', 'High Hopes' and 'Call Me Irresponsible'.

The Tender Trap 55. The Joker Is Wild 57. Some Came Running 58. A Hole in the Head 59. The World of Suzie Wong 60. The Road to Hong Kong 62. A Walk on the Wild Side 62. Papa's Delicate Condition 63. Robin and the Seven Hoods 64 (song 'My Kind of Town'). Thoroughly Modern Millie 67. Love and Marriage 69.

Van Horn, Buddy.
American director.
Any Which Way You Can 80. Date with an Angel 87. The Dead Pool 88. Pink Cadillac 91, etc.

Van Pallandt, Nina (1932–   ).
Danish actress, a former singer.
The Long Goodbye 73. Guilty or Innocent (TV) 75. Quintet 78. A Wedding 79. American Gigolo 80. Cloud Dancer 80. Cutter's Way 81. Jungle Warriors 85, etc.

Van Parys, Georges (1902–1971).
French composer.
Le Million 31. Jeunesse 34. Café de Paris 38. Le Silence Est d'Or 46. Fanfan la Tulipe 51. Adorables Creatures 52. Les Diaboliques 55. French Cancan 55. Charmants Garçons 57, many others.

Van Patten, Dick (1928–   ).
Chubby American character actor usually in comedy roles; brother of Joyce Van Patten.
Joe Kidd 72. Westworld 73. The Strongest Man in the World 75. Gus 76. Freaky Friday 77. High Anxiety 77. The New Adventures of Pippi Longstocking 88. Robin Hood: Men in Tights 93, etc.
TV series: Mama 49–57. The Partners 71–72. The New Dick Van Dyke Show 73–74. When Things Were Rotten 75. Eight Is Enough 77–81.

Van Patten, Joyce (1934–   ).
American leading lady of the 70s. Sister of Dick Van Patten.

The Goddess 58. I Love You Alice B. Toklas 68. Something Big 71. The Bravos (TV) 72. Thumb Tripping 72. The Manchu Eagle Murder Caper Mystery 75. The Bad News Bears 76. Mikey and Nicky 76. Billy Galvin 86. Monkey Shines 88. Breathing Lessons (TV) 94, etc.
TV series: The Good Guys 68–70. The Don Rickles Show 72. The Mary Tyler Moore Hour 79.

Van Peebles, Mario (1958–   ).
American director, screenwriter and actor. He is the son of Melvin van Peebles.
Sweet Sweetback's Baadasss Song (a) 71. Cotton Club (a) 84. Exterminator II (a) 84. Rappin' (a, s) 85. South Bronx Heroes (a) 86. Hot Shot (a) 86. Last Resort (a) 86. Heartbreak Ridge (a) 86. Jaws 4 – the Revenge (a) 87. Identity Crisis (w) 89. New Jack City (wd) 91. Gunmen (a) 93. Posse (a, d) 93. Erotic Tales (co-d) 94, etc.

Van Peebles, Melvin (1932–   ).
American director.
The Story of a Three-Day Pass 67. Watermelon Man 69. Sweet Sweetback's Baadasss Song 71. Identity Crisis 89, etc.

Van Rooten, Luis (1906–1973).
Mexican-born American character actor.
The Hitler Gang (as Himmler) 44. Two Years before the Mast 44. To the Ends of the Earth 48. Champion 49. Detective Story 51. The Sea Chase 55, etc.

Van Runkle, Theadora.
American costume designer.
Bonnie and Clyde (AAN) 67. The Thomas Crown Affair 68. Mame 74. The Godfather Part II (AAN) 74. New York, New York 77. S.O.B. 81. The Best Little Whorehouse in Texas 82. Peggy Sue Got Married (AAN) 86. Stella 90, etc.

Van Sant, Gus (1953–   ).
American director, screenwriter and musician, a former ad-man and assistant to Roger Corman.
Mala Noche 85. Drugstore Cowboy 89. My Own Private Idaho 91. Even Cowgirls Get the Blues (wd) 93. To Die For 94.

¶ I guess I'm a post-modernist. – *G.V.S.*

Van Sloan, Edward (1882–1964).
American character actor with stage experience; often seen as elderly professor.
Dracula 30. *Frankenstein* 31. The Mummy 33. Death Takes a Holiday 34. The Last Days of Pompeii 35. *Dracula's Daughter* 36. The Phantom Creeps 39. The Doctor Takes a Wife 40. The Conspirators 44. The Mask of Dijon 47. A Foreign Affair 47, etc.

Van Upp, Virginia (1912–1970).
American executive producer, at Columbia in the late 40s. Former writer.
Young and Willing 40. The Crystal Ball 42. Cover Girl 44. The Impatient Years (& p) 44. Together Again (& p) 45, etc.

Van Vorhees, Westbrook (1904–1968).
American commentator whose familiar stentorian voice as narrator of *The March of Time* was widely imitated.

Van Warmerdam, Alex (1952–   ).
Dutch director, screenwriter, and actor, an art school graduate who began as a theatre designer and writer.
Abel (a, wd) 85. *The Northerners* (De Noorderlingen) (a, wd) 92.

Van Zandt, Philip (1904–1958).
Dutch character actor, in Hollywood films.
Citizen Kane 41. House of Frankenstein 45. April Showers 48. Viva Zapata 52. Knock on Wood 54. The Pride and the Passion 57, etc.

Vanbrugh, Irene (1872–1949) (Irene Barnes).
Distinguished British stage actress. Films rare.
Autobiography: 1978, *To Tell My Story*.
The Gay Lord Quex 27. Moonlight Sonata 37.

Vance, Danitra (1959–1994).
American actress, from the stage, and a regular on TV's *Saturday Night Live*. Died of cancer.
Sticky Fingers 88. Limit Up 89. Little Man Tate 91. Jumpin' at the Boneyard 92, etc.

Vance, Vivian (1911–1979).
Cheerful American character comedienne, long a partner of Lucille Ball in various TV series.
The Secret Fury 50. The Blue Veil 51. The Great Race 65, etc.

Vance-Straker, Marilyn.
American costume designer.
Fast Times at Ridgemont High 82. 48 Hrs 82. Romancing the Stone 84. Pretty in Pink 86. Predator 87. The Untouchables (AAN) 87. Die Hard 88. Road House 89. Pretty Woman 90. Die Hard 2 90. Predator 2 90. Hudson Hawk 91. The Rocketeer 91. Ricochet 91. The Last Boy Scout 91. Medicine Man 92, etc.

Vanel, Charles (1892–1989).
French character actor, with stage experience.
Les Misérables 33. Le Grand Jeu 34. La Belle Equipe 36. Légion d'Honneur 38. Carrefour 39. *La Ferme du Pendu* 45. In Nome della Legge 49. *The Wages of Fear* 53. Maddalena 54. *Les Diaboliques* 55. Rafles sur la Ville 57. Le Dialogue des Carmélites 59. La Vérité 60. Un Homme de Trop 67. La Puce et le Privé 79, many others.

Vangelis (1943–   ) (Vangelis Papathanassiou).
Greek composer.
Chariots of Fire (AA) 81. Missing 82. Blade Runner 82. The Bounty 84. Nosferatu a Venezia 87. Francesco 89. Bitter Moon 92, etc.

Vanity (1958–   ) (aka D. D. Winters) (Denise Matthews).
American leading actress and singer, in action movies.
Terror Train 80. Tanya's Island 81. The Last Dragon 85. 52 Pickup 86. Never Too Young to Die 86. Deadly Illusion (aka Love You to Death) 87. Action Jackson 88. Memories of Murder 90. Neon City 91. DaVinci's War 92. South Beach 92, etc.

Varconi, Victor (1896–1976) (Mihaly Varkonyi).
Hungarian actor long in Hollywood.
Autobiography: 1976, *It's Not Enough to Be Hungarian*.
The Volga Boatmen 26. King of Kings 27. The Divine Lady (as Nelson) 29. The Doomed Battalion 31. Roberta 34. The Plainsman 36. Disputed Passage 39. Reap the Wild Wind 42. For Whom the Bell Tolls 43. Samson and Delilah 49, etc.

Varda, Agnes (1928–   ).
French writer-director of the 'left bank' school. She was married to Jacques Demy.
La Pointe Courte 56. Cléo de 5 à 7 62. Le Bonheur 65. Les Créatures 66. Lions Love 69. One Sings, the Other Doesn't (L'Une Chante, l'Autre Pas) 77. Vagabond (Sans Toit ni Loi) 85. Kung Fu Master! (Le Petit Amour) 87. Jane B. par Agnes V.

88. Jacquot de Nantes 91. Les Cent et Une Nuits 95, etc.

Varden, Evelyn (1895–1958).
American stage character actress who made several films.
Pinky 49. Cheaper by the Dozen 50. Phone Call from a Stranger 52. The Student Prince 54. Night of the Hunter 55. The Bad Seed 56, etc.

Varden, Norma (1899–1989).
British character actress, usually as haughty aristocrat in comedies; went to Hollywood in the 40s.
A Night Like This 32. The Iron Duke 35. Foreign Affairs 36. Shipyard Sally 39. Random Harvest 42. The Green Years 46. Strangers on a Train 51. Gentlemen Prefer Blondes 53. Witness for the Prosecution 58. The Sound of Music 65. Doctor Dolittle 67, many others.

variable area, variable density.
Types of soundtrack. Variable area appears as a spiky symmetrical line (like a long folded ink blot). Variable density is the same width throughout but with horizontal bars of varying light and shade.

Varley, Beatrice (1896–1969).
British character actress who played worried little elderly ladies for thirty years.
Hatter's Castle 41. So Well Remembered 47. No Room at the Inn 49. Hindle Wakes 53. The Feminine Touch 55, many others.
TV series: Dick and the Duchess 57–58.

Varnel, Marcel (1894–1947).
French-born director, in Hollywood from 1924; came to England in the 30s and made some of the best comedies of Will Hay and the Crazy Gang. Died in a car crash.
The Silent Witness 32. Chandu the Magician 32. Girls will be Boys 34. No Monkey Business 35. Good Morning Boys 36. OK for Sound 37. Oh Mr Porter 38. Convict 99 38. Alf's Button Afloat 38. Old Bones of the River 38. Ask a Policeman 39. The Frozen Limits 39. Where's That Fire? 39. Let George Do It 40. Gasbags 40. I Thank You 41. Hi Gang 41. The Ghost of St Michaels 41. Much Too Shy 42. King Arthur Was a Gentleman 42. Get Cracking 43. He Snoops to Conquer 44. I Didn't Do It 45. George in Civvy Street 46. This Man is Mine 46. The First Gentleman 47, etc.

¶ The only pure comedy director we've ever had in this country. – Basil Wright

Varnel, Max (1925–).
British second feature director, son of Marcel Varnel.
A Woman Possessed 58. The Great Van Robbery 49. A Taste of Money 60. Return of a Stranger 61. Enter Inspector Duval 62. The Silent Invasion 63, etc.

Varney, Jim (1949–).
American comic actor, from commercials.
Ernest Goes to Camp 87. Ernest Saves Christmas 88. Ernest Goes to Jail 90. Ernest Scared Stupid 91. Wilder Napalm 93. Beverly Hillbillies 93. Ernest Rides Again 93, etc.

Varney, Reg (1922–).
Chirpy British comedian who after years of availability found fame in the 60s in TV series The Rag Trade and On the Buses.
The Great St Trinian's Train Robbery 66. On the Buses 71. Mutiny on the Buses 72. Go for a Take

72. The Best Pair of Legs in the Business 72. Holiday on the Buses 73, etc.

Varsi, Diane (1938–1992).
Slightly-built American leading lady who had a brief career in the 50s, with sporadic appearances later.
■ Peyton Place (AAN) 57. Ten North Frederick 58. From Hell to Texas 59. Compulsion 59. Sweet Love, Bitter 66. Wild in the Streets 68. Killers Three 69. Bloody Mama 70. Johnny Got His Gun 71. I Never Promised You a Rose Garden 77.

vaudeville
is the American equivalent of the British music hall. Eight or ten variety acts, booked separately, formed a two-hour bill for the family. Burlesque was different, being for adults only.

Vaughan, Frankie (1928–) (Frank Abelsohn).
Flamboyant British song-and-dance man who never really made it in movies despite a sojourn in Hollywood.
■ Ramsbottom Rides Again 56. These Dangerous Years 57. The Lady is a Square 58. Wonderful Things 58. Heart of a Man 59. Let's Make Love 60. The Right Approach 62. It's All Over Town 64.

Vaughan, Peter (1923–) (Peter Ohm).
British character actor of solid presence, good or evil.
■ Sapphire 59. Village of the Damned 60. The Punch and Judy Man 63. Fanatic 65. The Naked Runner 67. Hammerhead 68. The Bofors Gun 68. Alfred the Great 69. Eye Witness 70. Straw Dogs 71. The Pied Piper 72. 11 Harrowhouse 74. Zulu Dawn 79. Fox (TV) 80. Time Bandits 81. The French Lieutenant's Woman 81. Jamaica Inn (TV) 83. The Razor's Edge 84. Brazil 85. Haunted Honeymoon 86. Monte Carlo (TV) 86. War and Remembrance (TV) 87. The Bourne Identity (TV) 88. Prisoners of Honor (TV) 91. The Remains of the Day 93.

Vaughan Williams, Ralph (1872–1958).
Distinguished English composer who scored some 40s films.
■ The 49th Parallel (US: The Invaders) 41. Coastal Command 42. The People's Land 42. The Flemish Farm 43. Stricken Peninsula 44. The Loves of Joanna Godden 48. Scott of the Antarctic 48. Dim Little Island 49.

Vaughn, Robert (1932–).
Slight, intense American actor who didn't quite make the front rank.
Teenage Caveman 58. No Time to Be Young 58. The Young Philadelphians (AAN) 59. The Magnificent Seven 60. The Big Show 61. The Caretakers 63. One Spy Too Many 66. The Venetian Affair 67. The Helicopter Spies 68. Bullitt 68. The Mind of Mr Soames 69. The Bridge at Remagen 69. The Statue 71. The Towering Inferno 74. Washington Behind Closed Doors (TV) 76. Brass Target 78. Good Luck Miss Wyckoff 79. Battle beyond the Stars 80. Inside the Third Reich (TV) 82. The Return of the Man from UNCLE (TV) 83. Superman III 83. Private Sessions (TV) 85. International Airport (TV) 85. The Delta Force 85. Hour of the Assassin 87. River of Death 89. Nobody's Perfect 90, etc.
TV series: The Lieutenant 63. The Man from UNCLE 64–67. The Protectors 72–73. Centennial 78–79. Emerald Point N.A.S. 83–84. The A-Team 86–87.

Veber, Francis (1937–).
French director, screenwriter and dramatist. He remade his local success as the Hollywood film Three Fugitives.

The Tall Blond Man with One Black Shoe (Le Grand Blond avec une Chaussure Noire) (co-w) 72. A Pain in the A— (L'Emmerdeur) (co-w) 73. Le Magnifique 73. Return of the Tall Blond Man with One Black Shoe (Le Retour du Grand Blond) (w) 74. Peur sur la Ville (w) 75. The Toy (Le Jouet) (d) 76. La Cage aux Folles (co-w) (AAN) 79. Hothead (Coup de Tête) (w) 80. Sunday Lovers (co-w) 81. The Goat (Le Chèvre) (wd) 81. La Cage aux Folles II (w) 81. Partners (w) 82. Les Compères (wd) 83. Les Fugitifs (wd) 86. The Lover (w) 86. Three Fugitives (wd) 89. Out on a Limb (d) 92. My Father, the Hero (co-w) 94, etc.

Védrès, Nicole (1911–1965).
French director, mainly of probing documentaries.
Paris 1900 47. La Vie Commence Demain 50. Aux Frontières de l'Homme 53, etc.

Vee, Bobby (1943–) (Robert Velline).
American pop singer of the 60s.
Swingin' Along (aka Double Trouble) 62. Play It Cool 62. Just for Fun 63. C'mon Let's Live a Little 67.

Veidt, Conrad (1893–1943).
Distinguished German character actor who also filmed in Britain and Hollywood.
The Cabinet of Dr Caligari 19. Waxworks 24. Lucrezia Borgia 25. The Student of Prague 26. The Hands of Orlac 26. The Beloved Rogue (US) 27. The Man Who Laughs 27. Rasputin 30. Congress Dances 31. Rome Express (GB) 32. I Was a Spy (GB) 33. F.P.I. 33. The Wandering Jew (GB) 34. Jew Süss (GB) 34. Bella Donna (GB) 34. The Passing of the Third Floor Back (GB) 35. King of the Damned (GB) 35. Under the Red Robe (GB) 36. Dark Journey (GB) 37. The Spy in Black (GB) 39. Contraband (GB) 40. The Thief of Baghdad (GB) 40. Escape (US) 40. A Woman's Face (US) 41. Whistling in the Dark (US) 41. All through the Night (US) 41. The Men in Her Life (US) 42. Nazi Agent (US) 42. Casablanca (US) 42. Above Suspicion (US) 43, etc.
✪ For his almost liquid villainy, and for a score of authentic star performances. The Thief of Baghdad.

¶ Women fight for Conrad Veidt! – 30s publicity
No matter what roles I play, I can't get Caligari out of my system. – C.V.

Veiller, Anthony (1903–1965).
American scriptwriter, in Hollywood from 1930.
Stage Door (AAN) 37. Her Cardboard Lover 42. The Killers (AAN) 46. Along the Great Divide 51. Moulin Rouge 53. Red Planet Mars (& p) 53. Safari 56. The List of Adrian Messenger 63, many others.

Velez, Lupe (1908–1944) (Guadeloupe Velez de Villalobos).
Temperamental Mexican leading lady of the 30s; best remembered with Leon Errol in the Mexican Spitfire series. She was married to actor Johnny Weissmuller (1933–38). Committed suicide when pregnant after a love affair went wrong.
The Gaucho 27. Wolf Song 29. East is West 30. The Squaw Man 31. Kongo 32. Hot Pepper 33. Palooka 34. The Morals of Marcus (GB) 36. Gypsy Melody (GB) 37. The Girl from Mexico 39. Mexican Spitfire 39. Six Lessons from Madame La Zonga 41. Playmates 42. Mexican Spitfire's Elephant 42. Mexican Spitfire's Blessed Event 43, many others.

¶ The first time you buy a house you think how pretty it is and sign the cheque. The second time you look to see if the basement has termites. It's the same with men. – L.V.

Venable, Evelyn (1913–1993).
American leading lady of the 30s, usually in demure roles. She was the original model for Columbia Pictures' logo of a woman holding aloft a lamp.

Cradle Song 33. Mrs Wiggs of the Cabbage Patch 34. Alice Adams 35. The Frontiersman 38. He Hired the Boss 43, etc.

Veness, Amy (1876–1960).
British character actress who latterly played cheerful old souls.

My Wife's Family 31. Hobson's Choice 31. Lorna Doone 35. Aren't Men Beasts? 37. Yellow Sands 39. The Man in Grey 43. This Happy Breed 44. Here Come the Huggetts 49. Doctor in the House 54, etc.

Venice
has been most persuasively caught by the movie camera in *Summertime*, *Venetian Bird*, and (for the depressed view) *Death in Venice* and *Don't Look Now*.

Ventham, Wanda (1938–).
British leading lady.

My Teenage Daughter 56. The Navy Lark 59. Solo for Sparrow 62. The Cracksman 63. The Big Job 65. The Knack 65. The Spy with a Cold Nose 67. Carry On Up the Khyber 68. Captain Kronos 73. Lost Empires (TV) 86, etc.

ventriloquists
rarely stray from music hall to cinema, but Michael Redgrave played a demented one in *Dead of Night*, and very similar themes were explored in 1929's *The Great Gabbo*, in 1964's *Devil Doll* and in 1978's *Magic*. A vent's dummy was used for comedy in *Knock on Wood*, for satire in *How I Won the War*, and for mystery in *The Dummy Talks* and *The Thirty-Nine Steps* (1959 version). The most movie-exposed performing ventriloquist is certainly Edgar Bergen, who with his dummies Charlie McCarthy and Mortimer Snerd appeared in a dozen or more films between 1937 and 1944.

Ventura, Lino (1920–1987) (Angelino Borrini).
Italian leading man, former boxer.

Touchez Pas au Grisbi 53. Marie Octobre 57. Crooks in Clover 63. Les Aventuriers 67. The Valachi Papers 72. Wild Horses (US) 72. La Bonne Année 73. The Pink Telephone 75. Le Silencieux 76. Sunday Lovers 80. Les Misérables 82, many others.

Vera-Ellen (1920–1981) (Vera-Ellen Westmeyr Rohe).
American dancer and songstress of 40s musicals, a former Rockette.

■ Wonder Man 45. The Kid from Brooklyn 46. Three Little Girls in Blue 46. Carnival in Costa Rica 47. Words and Music 48. Love Happy 49. On the Town 49. Three Little Words 50. Happy Go Lovely (GB) 51. The Belle of New York 52. Call Me Madam 53. The Big Leaguer 53. White Christmas 54. Let's Be Happy (GB) 56.

Verbong, Ben (1949–).
Dutch director.

The Girl with the Red Hair 81. De Schorpioen 84. Lily Was Here 89. De Onfatoenlijke Vrouw 91. House Call 94, etc.

Verdon, Gwen (1925–).
Vivacious American dancer and singer, once married to Bob Fosse.

■ On the Riviera 51. Meet Me After the Show 51. David and Bathsheba 51. The Merry Widow 52. The I Don't Care Girl 53. The Farmer Takes a Wife 53. *Damn Yankees* 58. Legs (TV) 83. The Cotton Club 84. Cocoon 85. Nadine 87. Cocoon: The Return 88. Alice 90.

Verdugo, Elena (1926–).
Spanish-American leading lady.

Down Argentine Way 40. The Moon and Sixpence 42. House of Frankenstein 45. Song of Scheherazade 47. Cyrano de Bergerac 50. Thief of Damascus 52. How Sweet It Is 68, etc.

TV series: Meet Millie 52. The New Phil Silvers Show 63. *Marcus Welby M.D.* 69–75.

Vereen, Ben (1946–).
American dancer.

Funny Lady 75. *Roots* (TV) 77. All That Jazz 79. Breakin' Through 84. The Zoo Gang 85. Buy and Cell 89. Once upon a Forest 93, etc.

TV series: Tenspeed and Brown Shoe 80.

Verhoeven, Michael (1938–).
German director and screenwriter, a former doctor.

Danse Macabre (Paarungen) 67. Mitgift 75. Gutenbach 78. White Rose (Die Weisse Rose) 82. The Nasty Girl 90. New Germany (co-d) 90, etc.

Verhoeven, Paul (1938–).
Dutch director, in America from 1985. He was a teacher of physics before making documentaries and working in television.

Business Is Business (Wat Zien Ik) 71. Turkish Delight (Turks Fruit) (AAN) 73. Katie's Passion (Keetje Tippel) 75. Soldier of Orange (Soldaat van Oranje) 77. Spetters 80. The Fourth Man (De Vierde Man) 83. Flesh and Blood 85. Robocop 87. Total Recall 90. Basic Instinct 92, etc.

❡ My resistance to violence is less than other people's, perhaps due to my upbringing in Holland where we were occupied by the Germans and saw violence in front of our eyes. It's possible that I have more problems judging what is over the top and what is not. – *P.V.*

People seem to have this strange idea that films can influence people to be violent, but in my sincere opinion film only reflects the violence of society. – *P.V.*

Vermilyea, Harold (1889–1958).
Russian-American character actor, former operatic singer.

O.S.S. 46. The Big Clock 48. Edge of Doom 50. Born to Be Bad 51, etc.

Verne, Jules (1828–1905).
French adventure novelist whose inventive science-fiction themes have latterly endeared him to Hollywood. Films of his works since 1954 include *Twenty Thousand Leagues Under the Sea, Around the World in Eighty Days, From Earth to the Moon, Journey to the Center of the Earth, Five Weeks in a Balloon, Master of the World, The Children of Captain Grant (In Search of the Castaways), Rocket to the Moon, The Light at the Edge of the World, The Southern Star* and *Michael Strogoff*.

Verne, Karen (1915–1967) (Ingabor Katrine Klinckerfuss).
German leading lady who made a number of Hollywood films.

Ten Days in Paris (GB) 39. All Through the Night 41. Kings Row 42. The Seventh Cross 44. A Bullet for Joey 55. Ship of Fools 65. Torn Curtain 67, etc.

Verneuil, Henri (1920–) (Achod Malakin).
French director, former journalist.

La Table aux Crevés 50. Forbidden Fruit 52. Public Enemy Number One 53. Paris Palace Hotel 56. The Cow and I 59. L'Affaire d'une Nuit 61. The Big Snatch (Mélodie en Sous-Sol) 63. Guns for San Sebastian 68. The Burglars 71. The Serpent 72. The Night Caller 72. Le Corps de Mon Ennemi 76. Mille Milliards de Dollars 82. Les Morfalous 84. Mother (Mayrig) 91. 588 rue Paradis 92, etc.

Verno, Jerry (1895–1975).
British cockney character actor.

His Lordship 32. The Thirty-Nine Steps 35. Farewell Again 37. Old Mother Riley in Paris 38. The Common Touch 41. The Red Shoes 48. The Belles of St Trinian's 54. After the Ball 57, many others.

Vernon, Anne (1925–) (Edith Vignaud).
Vivacious French leading lady who has also filmed in Britain and Hollywood.

Le Mannequin Assassiné 48. Warning to Wantons (GB) 48. Shakedown (US) 49. *Edward and Caroline* 50. Rue de l'Estrapade 52. The Love Lottery (GB) 54. Time Bomb (GB) 54. Le Long des Trottoirs 56. Les Lavandières de Portugal 57. *The Umbrellas of Cherbourg* 64. Patate 64. La Démoniaque 67. Therese and Isabelle 68, etc.

Vernon, Bobby (1897–1939).
Boyish American star comedian of the silents, usually in shorts.

Vernon, John (1935–).
Canadian character actor.

Point Blank 67. Topaz 69. Dirty Harry 71. One More Train to Rob 71. The Black Windmill 74. The Outlaw Josey Wales 76. A Special Day 76. National Lampoon's Animal House 78. Herbie Goes Bananas 80. Airplane II: The Sequel 82. Chained Heat 83. Jungle Warriors 85. Blue Monkey 87. Killer Klowns from Outer Space 87. Border Heat 88. Deadly Stranger 88. I'm Gonna Git You Sucka 89. Bail Out 90. Mob Story 90, etc.

TV series: Hail to the Chief 85.

Vernon, Richard (1925–).
British character actor of stage and TV, usually in soft-spoken aristocratic roles.

Accidental Death 63. A Hard Day's Night 64. Goldfinger 64. The Secret of My Success 65. The Satanic Rites of Dracula 73. The Pink Panther Strikes Again 76. The Human Factor 79. O Heavenly Dog 80. Evil Under the Sun 82. Gandhi 82. A Month in the Country 87, many others.

Vernon, Wally (1904–1970).
American eccentric comedian.

Mountain Music 37. Alexander's Ragtime Band 38. The Gorilla 39. Tahiti Honey 43. Always Leave Them Laughing 49. What Price Glory? 52. What a Way to Go 64, many others.

Versois, Odile (1930–1980) (Militza de Poliakoff-Baidarov).
French leading lady, sister of Marina Vlady.

Les Dernières Vacances 46. Into the Blue (GB) 48. Bel Amour 51. A Day to Remember (GB) 53. *The Young Lovers* (Chance Meeting) (GB) 55. To Paris with Love (GB) 55. Passport to Shame (GB) 58. Cartouche (Swords of Blood) 62. Benjamin 68, etc.

Vertov, Dziga (1896–1954) (Dennis Kaufman).
Russian director and film theorist. Many documentaries.

One-Sixth of the World 27. The Man with the Movie Camera 28. Three Songs of Lenin 34. In the Line of Fire 41, etc.

Vetri, Victoria (1944–) (Angela Dorian).
Australian leading lady.
  Chuka 67. Rosemary's Baby 68. When Dinosaurs Ruled the Earth 69. Invasion of the Bee Girls 73, etc.

Vicas, Victor (1918–1985).
Franco-Russian director.
  No Way Back 53. Double Destiny 54. Back to Kandara 57. The Wayward Bus 57. Count Five and Die (GB) 58. Les Disparus 60, etc.
  Later in French TV.

Vickers, Martha (1925–1971) (M. MacVicar).
American leading lady of the 40s.
  The Falcon in Mexico 44. *The Big Sleep* 46. Love and Learn 47. Ruthless 48. Bad Boy 49. Daughter of the West 51. The Burglar 57. Four Fast Guns 60, etc.

Victor, Charles (1896–1965).
British character actor with long stage experience: in films from 1938, usually in cockney roles.
  While the Sun Shines 46. The Calendar 48. The Ringer 52. Those People Next Door 53. The Embezzler 55. Now and Forever 57, many others.

Victor, Henry (1898–1945).
British character actor, a silent screen star who went to Hollywood in the 30s and played villainous bit roles.
  She 25. The Guns of Loos 28. The Fourth Commandment 28. The Mummy 33. Our Fighting Navy 37. Confessions of a Nazi Spy 39. Zanzibar 40. King of the Zombies 41. To Be or Not to Be 42. Sherlock Holmes and the Secret Weapon 42. They Got Me Covered 43, etc.

Victoria,
Queen of England 1837–1901, was born in 1819. Her full-length screen portraits were by Anna Neagle in *Victoria the Great* and *Sixty Glorious Years*, and by Irene Dunne, who failed rather badly, in *The Mudlark*. She was also played by Fay Compton in *The Prime Minister*, by Helena Pickard in *The Lady with the Lamp*, by Muriel Aked in *The Story of Gilbert and Sullivan*, by Sybil Thorndike in *Melba*, and by Mollie Maureen in *The Private Life of Sherlock Holmes*.

Vidal, Gore (1925–).
Elegant American novelist, essayist, dramatist, screenwriter, and occasional actor, an intellectual gadfly.
  The Catered Affair (w) 56. I Accuse (w) 58. The Left-Handed Gun (oa) 58. The Scapegoat (co-w) 59. Visit to a Small Planet (oa) 60. Suddenly Last Summer 60. The Best Man (w, from his play) 64. Is Paris Burning? (co-w) 66. Last of the Mobile Hot-Shots (w) 70. Myra Breckinridge (oa) 70. Caligula (co-w) 79. Dress Gray (TV) 86. Gore Vidal's Lincoln (oa) (TV) 88. Gore Vidal's Billy the Kid (& a) (TV) 89. Bob Roberts (a) 92. With Honors (a) 94, etc.
  Autobiography: 1992, *Screening History*.

¶ As I now move, graciously, I hope, toward the door marked Exit, it occurs to me that the only thing I ever really liked to do was go to the movies. Naturally, Sex and Art always took precedence over the cinema. Unfortunately, neither ever proved to be as dependable as the filtering of present light through that moving strip of celluloid which projects past images and voices onto a screen.
– *G.V.*

Vidal, Henri (1919–1959).
Tough-looking French leading man, in films from 1940.
  Les Maudits 46. Quai de Grenelle 50. Port du Désir 54. The Wicked Go to Hell 55. Porte des Lilas 56. Come Dance with Me 59, etc.

video cassettes
can provide programmes on the home television set. They are played in through special equipment and can accommodate feature films or any other kind of entertainment or instruction.
  During the 70s, video cassettes were much talked about, but the opinion was that new documentary programmes would have to be made for them as nobody would want to buy or rent old movies. How wrong they were. By the mid-1980s Britain soared at the top of the world markets, largely because cassettes could be rented for a pound a night from local shops. There was a great deal of fuss about porn and video nasties, but the great surge was from people who simply wanted to see newish movies without going to the trouble and expense of a cinema visit. Other countries were slower to follow suit, but there was no doubt that video was one more nail in the coffin of an industry which had lasted ninety years, especially since the domestic machines also allowed owners to record whatever films and other programmes they liked from their television sets.
  See also: *cassettes*.

video discs
operate similarly to video cassettes, but instead of being stored on tape the information is mounted on a disc similar to a gramophone record.

Vidgeon, Robin (1939–).
British cinematographer. He began as a second assistant cameraman in 1955 and previously worked on many films with cinematographer Douglas Slocombe and cameraman Chic Waterson.
  Mr Corbett's Ghost 86. Hellraiser 87. Mr North 88. The Penitent 88. Hellbound: Hellraiser II 88. Parents 89. The Fly II 89. Nightbreed 90. Highway to Hell 92. Lady Chatterley (TV) 93. August 95, etc.

Vidor, Charles (1900–1959).
Hungarian-American director, in Hollywood from 1932.
  Double Door 34. Sensation Hunters 34. The Great Gambini 37. *Blind Alley* 39. My Son My Son 40. The Lady in Question 40. Ladies in Retirement 41. The Tuttles of Tahiti 42. The Desperadoes 43. *Cover Girl* 44. Together Again 44. A Song to Remember 45. Over 21 45. *Gilda* 46. The Guilt of Janet Ames 48. Hans Christian Andersen 52. Love Me or Leave Me 55. The Swan 56. The Joker Is Wild 57. A Farewell to Arms 58. Song without End (part) 59, many others.

Vidor, Florence (1895–1977) (Florence Arto).
American leading lady of the silent screen.
  Lying Lips 21. Barbara Frietchie 24. The Grand Duchess and the Waiter 26. Are Parents People? 26. The Patriot 28. Chinatown Nights 29, etc.

Vidor, King (1894–1982).
American director, formerly journalist; high style alternates with disappointing banality. Special AA 1979 'for his incomparable achievements as a cinematic creator and innovator'.
  Autobiography: 1953, *A Tree Is a Tree*.
■ The Turn in the Road 18. Better Times 19. The Other Half 19. Poor Relations 19. The Jack Knife Man 19. The Family Honour 20. The Sky Pilot 21.

Love Never Dies 21. Conquering the Woman 21. Woman Wake Up 21. The Real Adventure 22. Dusk to Dawn 22. Alice Adams 22. Peg O' My Heart 23. The Woman of Bronze 23. Three Wise Fools 23. Wild Oranges 23. Happiness 23. Wine of Youth 24. His Hour 24. Wife of the Centaur 24. Proud Flesh 25. *The Big Parade* 25. La Bohème 25. Bardelys the Magnificent 26. *The Crowd* (AAN) 28. *Show People* 28. *Hallelujah* (AAN) 29. Not So Dumb 30. *Billy the Kid* 30. *Street Scene* 31. *The Champ* (AAN) 31. Bird of Paradise 32. Cynara 32. The Stranger's Return 33. *Our Daily Bread* 34. The Wedding Night 34. So Red the Rose 35. The Texas Rangers 36. Stella Dallas 37. The Citadel (GB) (AAN) 38. *Northwest Passage* 39. Comrade X 40. H. M. Pulham Esq 41. An American Romance 44. Duel in the Sun 46. On Our Merry Way 47. *The Fountainhead* 49. Beyond the Forest 49. Lightning Strikes Twice 51. Japanese War Bride 52. Ruby Gentry 52. The Man without a Star 55. *War and Peace* (AAN) 56. Solomon and Sheba 59.
~In the last year of his life he acted a role in *Love and Money*.

Vienna
was frequently pictured in pre-war films such as *The Great Waltz*, *Bitter Sweet* and *Vienna Waltzes*, but the myths were always perpetuated on a studio backlot. The post-war reality was caught vividly in *Four in a Jeep* and *The Third Man*.

Vierny, Sacha (1919–).
French cinematographer.
  Hiroshima Mon Amour 58. Last Year in Marienbad 61. Muriel 63. Do You Like Women? 64. *Belle de Jour* 67. Beau Père 81. A Zed and Two Noughts 85. The Cook, the Thief, His Wife and Her Lover 90. Drowning by Numbers 91, etc.

Viertel, Berthold (1885–1953).
Austrian director who moved to Britain and Hollywood in the early 30s.
  The Wise Sex 31. The Man from Yesterday 32. Little Friend 34. The Passing of the Third Floor Back 35. Rhodes of Africa 36, etc.

The Vietnam War
stunned America to such an extent that few films were made about it until long after its end. An exception was John Wayne's gung-ho *The Green Berets* 68. Go Tell the Spartans followed in 1978, rapidly followed by *The Deer Hunter* and *Apocalypse Now*. *Coming Home* 82 and *Born on the Fourth of July* 89 covered the effect on veterans. In 1987 there was a deluge: *Hamburger Hill*, *Platoon*, and *Full Metal Jacket*. Director Oliver Stone returned to the subject with *Heaven and Earth* in 1993.

vigilantes
were originally groups of honest citizens who formed together to rid San Francisco's Barbary Coast of some of its villains. In the early 70s it became fashionable to make films about citizens who took the law of our violent cities into their own hands, notably in *Death Wish*, *Walking Tall* and *Law and Disorder*.

Vigne, Daniel (1942–).
French director and screenwriter.
  Les Hommes 73. The Return of Martin Guerre (Le Retour de Martin Guerre) 83. One Woman or Two (Une Femme ou Deux) 85. Comédie d'Eté 89. The King's Whore (co-w) 90, etc.

Vigo, Jean (1905–1934) (Jean Almereyda).
Influential French director on the strength of three semi-experimental, dream-like films.

■ *A Propos de Nice* 30. *Zéro de Conduite* 32. *L'Atalante* 34.

Vigoda, Abe (1921–).
American character actor, popular on TV in *Barney Miller* and *Fish*.

The Godfather 71. The Don Is Dead 73. Newman's Law 74. Having Babies (TV) 76. The Cheap Detective 78. The Comedy Company (TV) 78. Vasectomy – a Delicate Matter 86. Plain Clothes 88. Look Who's Talking 89. Prancer 89. Joe versus the Volcano 90. Sugar Hill 93. Batman: Mask of the Phantasm (voice) 94. North 94, etc.

Villa-Lobos, Heitor (1887–1959).
Brazilian composer who worked in Hollywood on *Green Mansions* 59.

Villalobos, Reynaldo.
American cinematographer.

Urban Cowboy 80. Nine to Five 80. Blame It on Rio 84. Lucas 86. Punchline 88. Major League 89. Coup de Ville 90. American Me 92. A Bronx Tale 93, etc.

Villard, Frank (1917–1980) (François Drouineau).
French leading man, often in shifty roles.

Le Dernier des Six 41. Gigi 48. Manèges (The Wanton) 49. L'Ingénue Libertine 50. Le Garçon Sauvage 51. Huis Clos 54. Crime Passionel 55. Mystères de Paris 57. Le Cave se Rebiffe 61. Gigot 62. Mata Hari 64, etc.

Villechaize, Herve (1943–1993).
French dwarf actor in international films. His health deteriorating, he committed suicide.

The Man with the Golden Gun 73. The One and Only 78. Forbidden Zone 80, etc.

TV series: Fantasy Island 77–82.

Villiers, James (1933–).
British actor, usually in snooty or villainous roles.

The Entertainer 60. The Damned 64. King and Country 64. The Nanny 65. Half a Sixpence 67. Some Girls Do 68. Otley 68. A Nice Girl Like Me 69. Blood from the Mummy's Tomb 70. The Ruling Class 71. Saint Jack 79. The Scarlet Pimpernel (TV) 82. Under the Volcano 84. Fortunes of War (TV) 87. Mountains of the Moon 90. King Ralph 91. Let Him Have It 91, etc.

Villon, François (1431–c. 1470) (François de Loges).
French poet who led the life of a Robin Hood and was romanticized in *If I Were King* (in which he was played by Ronald Colman) and its musical version *The Vagabond King* (Dennis King, Oreste Kirkop).

Vincent, Jan-Michael (1944–).
American leading man of the 70s.

The Undefeated 68. Tribes (TV) 70. The Mechanic 72. The World's Greatest Athlete 73. Buster and Billie 74. Bite the Bullet 74. White Line Fever 75. Baby Blue Marine 76. Damnation Alley 77. Hooper 78. Big Wednesday 78. Defiance 80. Hard Country 81. The Winds of War (TV) 83. Last Plane Out 83. Born in East L.A. 87. Deadly Embrace 88. Hit List 89. Hangfire 90. Raw Nerve 91. Animal Instincts 92. Xtro II 92. Indecent Behaviour 94, etc.

Vincent, June (1919–).
Blond American leading lady of some 40s 'B's.

Ladies Courageous 44. The Climax 44. Can't Help Singing 44. Here Come the Co-eds 45. That's the Spirit 45. Black Angel 46. Shed No Tears 48, etc.

Vincent, Robbie (1896–1966).
English comedian who appeared in some low-budget farces starring Frank Randle. Best known for his role as Enoch alongside Harry Korris and Cecil Frederick in the 40s radio show *Happidrome*.

Somewhere in England 40. Somewhere in Camp 42. Somewhere on Leave 42. Happidrome 43, etc.

Vincze, Ernest (1942–).
British cinematographer.

Jane Austen in Manhattan 81. A Woman of Substance (TV) 84. Biggles 85. Shanghai Surprise 85. Escape from Sobibor (TV) 86. The Nightmare Years (TV) 89. Cream in My Coffee (TV) 90, etc.

Vinson, Helen (1907–) (Helen Rulfs).
Cool, aristocratic leading lady of Hollywood films of the 30s and 40s.

Jewel Robbery 31. I Am a Fugitive from a Chain Gang 32. The Power and the Glory 33. The Tunnel (GB) 35. Vogues of 1938. In Name Only 39. Torrid Zone 40. Nothing But the Truth 41. They Are Guilty 44. The Lady and the Doctor (last to date) 46, etc.

violence
caused little concern until the 50s. Even the makers of the horror and gangster films of the 30s were comparatively subtle in their approach; they delighted in machine guns and clutching hands, but would not have dreamed of showing fist connect against flesh or suggesting the sight of actual blood. The rot began to set in in 1952 with films like *The Wild One*, which still showed little but pointed out that *imitable* forms of violence were on the streets of our cities; location shooting was inviting greater realism than had been necessary in the studio. In 1956, when Hammer began to remake the great horror stories, a new ghoulishness was found to have set in, especially in the versions prepared for the Far East. Still the censor held sway until the late 60s, when he gave up the ghost. *Witchfinder General* was a sadistic piece of Grand Guignol, *The Wild Bunch* a blood-spattered western, *Get Carter* and *Villain* new-fashioned gangster films in which the killing was merciless and explicit. *Soldier Blue* has as its high point a mutilation scene which its director seemed to claim as a protest against Vietnam; *Straw Dogs* featured an irrelevant but thoroughly detailed rape. As for *A Clockwork Orange* and *The Devils*, our eyes were spared no conceivable atrocity. According to one's point of view, the cinema had either come of age or ventured beyond the pale. By the 80s, much more violence was being accepted in a family film like *Raiders of the Lost Ark* than would have been passed twenty years earlier for adults only; but the excesses of Brian de Palma's remake of *Scarface* caused most critical hands to be thrown up in horror. A cycle of horror films featuring spectacularly gory make-up effects in the late 80s and 90s revived concerns about screen violence, from politicians at least, as did the emergence of Quentin Tarantino as a director of note with such films as *Reservoir Dogs* and *Pulp Fiction*, and as screenwriter of *True Romance*. Oliver Stone's *Natural Born Killers*, based on Tarantino's script, investigated media concern with violence in an extremely violent manner. In Britain, the result was to add extra confusion to the already arbitrary methods of the Board of Film Classification through government legislation designed to prevent violent films being given a video release, a policy that has lengthened the cinematic life of *Reservoir Dogs*.

The Virginian.
Owen Wister's western novel was filmed in 1914 with Dustin Farnum, in 1930 with Gary Cooper, and in 1945 with Joel McCrea; in 1964 it turned up as a long-running TV series with James Drury. *Spawn of the North* 38 borrowed the basic plot, and in its turn was remade as *Alaska Seas* 54.

Visconti, Luchino (1906–1976) (L. V. de Modrone).
Italian writer-director, former art director.

Biography: 1982, *Luchino Visconti* by Gaia Servadio.

Ossessione 42. *La Terra Trema* 48. Bellissima 51. Siamo Donne (part) 52. *Senso* 53. White Nights 57. *Rocco and His Brothers* 60. Boccaccio 70 62. *The Leopard* 63. *The Damned* 69. Death in Venice 70. Conversation Piece 76, etc.

VistaVision.
In 1953, when some companies were reluctant to follow Fox's lead and adopt CinemaScope, Paramount introduced VistaVision, a non-anamorphic, deep-focus process retaining the old frame ratio of 4×3. The chief innovation was that none of the essential action took place at the top or bottom of the picture, so that exhibitors with appropriate lens and aperture plates could choose their own screen ratio (from 4×3 to 2×1). At 2×1 on a big screen, VistaVision did not look very different from CinemaScope.

Vitagraph.
An early American production company which had great success but was taken over in the 20s by Warners.

Vitale, Milly (1928–).
Italian leading lady in American films.

The Juggler 53. The Seven Little Foys 55. A Breath of Scandal 60.

Vitaphone.
The sound-on-disc process introduced in 1926 by Warners.

Vitti, Monica (1933–) (Monica Luisa Ceciarelli).
Italian leading lady in international demand in the 60s.

L'Avventura 59. La Notte 60. *L'Eclisse* 62. Dragées au Poivre 63. Nutty Naughty Château 64. *The Red Desert* 64. Modesty Blaise (GB) 65. The Chastity Belt 67. Girl with a Pistol 69. The Pacifist 71. Duck in Orange Sauce 75. An Almost Perfect Affair 79. The Mystery of Oberwald 80. Tango della Gelosia 81. When Veronica Calls 83. Secret Scandal (Scandalo Segreto) (& co-w, d) 89, etc.

Viva (1941–) (Janet Sue Hoffman).
Witty, skinny American star of Andy Warhol's films, originally a painter and also a novelist.

The Loves of Ondine 67. Bikeboy 67. Nude Restaurant 67. Lonesome Cowboys 68. Blue Movie 69. Lion's Love 69. Play It Again, Sam 72. Forbidden Zone 80. State of Things 82, etc.

Vlad, Roman (1919–).
Romanian composer.

La Beauté du Diable 49. Sunday in August 50. Three Steps North 51. Romeo and Juliet 54. Knave of Hearts 54. The Law 60. The Mighty Ursus 62, etc.

Vlady, Marina (1938–) (Marina de Poliakoff-Baidarov).
French leading lady, sister of Odile Versois.

Orage d'Eté 49. Avant le Déluge 53. The Wicked Go to Hell 55. Crime and Punishment 56. Toi le Venin 59. La Steppa 61. Climats 62. Enough Rope 63. Dragées au Poivre 63. Queen Bee 64. Chimes at Midnight 66. Sapho 70. Les Jeux de la Comtesse

80. Bordello 85. Twist Again à Moscow 86. Migrations 88. Follow Me 89. Splendor 89, etc.

Vogel, Paul C. (1899–1975).
American cinematographer.
The Lady in the Lake 46. Black Hand 49. *Battleground* (AA) 49. Rose Marie 54. High Society 56. The Wings of Eagles 56. The Time Machine 60. The Rounders 64, etc.

Vogel, Virgil.
American director, from TV.
The Mole People 56. Terror in the Midnight Sun 58. Son of Ali Baba 64. The Return of Joe Forrester (TV) 75. Law of the Land (TV) 76. Centennial (part) (TV) 78. Beulah Land (TV) 80. Longarm (TV) 88, etc.

Vogler, Karl Michael (1928–).
German stage actor who has appeared in a few international films.
Those Magnificent Men in Their Flying Machines 65. The Blue Max 67. How I Won the War 67. Patton 69. Downhill Racer 69. Deep End 70, etc.

Voight, Jon (1938–).
American leading actor of the 70s.
■ The Hour of the Gun 67. Fearless Frank 68. Out of It 69. *Midnight Cowboy* (AAN) 69. The Revolutionary 70. The All American Boy 70. Catch 22 70. *Deliverance* 72. Conrack 74. The Odessa File 74. End of the Game 75. Coming Home (AA) 78. The Champ 79. Lookin' to Get Out 82. Table for Five 83. Desert Bloom 85. Runaway Train (AAN) 85. Desert Bloom 86. Eternity 90. Chernobyl: The Final Warning (TV) 91. Return to Lonesome Dove (TV) 93.

Famous line (*Midnight Cowboy*): 'I'll tell you the truth now. I ain't a real cowboy, but I am one hell of a stud.'

volcanoes
in the late 30s seemed to belong mostly to Paramount, which used them as the climax of most of Dorothy Lamour's jungle pictures and of odd adventures like *Cobra Woman* and *Mysterious Island*. They more recently turned up in *The Devil at Four O'Clock*, and in *Journey to the Centre of the Earth* in which the way was down an extinct Icelandic crater and back on a fountain of lava up the inside of Etna. The famous eruption of Vesuvius was staged for the various versions of *The Last Days of Pompeii* (and for *Up Pompeii*), and *Krakatoa, East of Java* featured another historical disaster. An extinct volcano formed a lair for giant monsters in *The Black Scorpion*. A volcano was also the climax of Hal Roach's *Man and His Mate* and of its recent remake *One Million Years BC*; *Joe versus the Volcano* featured a man with a terminal illness who agreed to jump into a volcano after six months of rich living; but the most spectacular pictures were obtained for the documentary compilation simply called *Volcano*.

Volk, Stephen.
British screenwriter and dramatist specializing in horror stories.
Gothic 86. The Kiss (co-w) 88. The Guardian (co-w) 90.

Volonté, Gian Maria (1933–1994).
Italian leading man of the 60s.
A Fistful of Dollars 64. For a Few Dollars More 65. We Still Kill the Old Way 68. *Investigation of a Citizen above Suspicion* 69. Sacco and Vanzetti 71. The Working Class Go to Heaven 72. Lucky Luciano 73. Christ Stopped at Eboli 79. Chronicle

of a Death Foretold (Cronaca di una Morte Annunciata) 87. Tre Colonne in Cronaca 89. Open Doors (Porte Aperte) 90. A Simple Story (Una Storia Semplice) 91. Funes, un Gran Amor (Arg.) 93. Tirano Banderas 94, etc.

Von Brandenstein, Patrizia (1943–).
American production designer.
Heartland 79. Tell Me a Riddle 80. Silkwood 83. Touched 83. Amadeus (AA) 84. A Chorus Line 85. The Money Pit 86. No Mercy 87. The Untouchables (AAN) 87. Betrayed 88. Working Girl 88. The Lemon Sisters 90. State of Grace 90. Postcards from the Edge 90. Billy Bathgate 91. Sneakers 92. Leap of Faith 92. Six Degrees of Separation 93, etc.

Von Harbou, Thea (1888–1954).
German screenwriter, mainly associated with Fritz Lang's silent films.
Der Müde Tod 21. *Dr Mabuse* 22. *Nibelungen Saga* 24. Chronicles of the Grey House 25. *Metropolis* 26. The Spy 28. The Woman in the Moon 29. *The Testament of Dr Mabuse* 32. The Old and the Young King 35. Annélie 41. Fahrt ins Gluck 45. The Affairs of Dr Holl 51, many others.

Von Seyffertitz, Gustav (1863–1943).
Dignified German character actor in Hollywood films; during World War I was known as G. Butler Clonblough.
Old Wives for New 18. Moriarty (title role) 22. Sparrows 26. The Wizard 27. Docks of New York 28. The Bat Whispers 30. Shanghai Express 32. Queen Christiana 33. She 35. In Old Chicago 38. Nurse Edith Cavell 39, many others.

Von Sternberg, Josef (1894–1969) (Jonas Sternberg).
Austrian-American director, a great pictorial stylist and the creator of Marlene Dietrich's American image.
Autobiography: 1965, *Fun in a Chinese Laundry*. A critical study by Herman G. Weinberg was published in 1967.
■ *The Salvation Hunters* 25. The Seagull (unreleased) 26. *Underworld* 27. The Last Command 28. The Dragnet 28. *Docks of New York* 28. The Case of Lena Smith 29. Thunderbolt 29. *The Blue Angel* (Ger.) 30. *Morocco* (AAN) 30. Dishonoured 31. An American Tragedy 31. *Shanghai Express* (AAN) 32. Blonde Venus 32. *The Scarlet Empress* 34. *The Devil is a Woman* 35. The King Steps Out 36. Crime and Punishment 36. I Claudius (unfinished) 37. Sergeant Madden 39. *The Shanghai Gesture* 41. Jet Pilot 50. Macao 51. The Saga of Anatahan (Jap.) 53.
✪ For being the kind of director who, if he didn't exist, publicists would have to invent. *The Scarlet Empress*.

¶ I care nothing about the story, only how it is photographed and presented. – *J.V.S.*
The only way to succeed is to make people hate you. That way they remember you. – *J.V.S.*
A lyricist of light and shadow rather than a master of montage. – *Andrew Sarris, 1968*
He brought to the screen new horizons in the art of lighting, to the photography of shadowed and broken rays . . . His scenes seem almost always to be seen through streamers and feathers, through loose gauze, through slatted shutters or an intricate lattice wall. – *Ivan Butler*

Von Stroheim, Erich (1885–1957) (Hans Erich Maria Stroheim Von Nordenwall).
Austrian actor and director whose ruthless extravagance in Hollywood in the 20s harmed his

later career. Usually played despotic villains or stiff-necked Prussians.
Biographies: 1954, *Hollywood Scapegoat* by Peter Noble. 1972, *Erich Von Stroheim* by Tom Curtis.
AS ACTOR: The Heart of Humanity 18. Blind Husbands 19. *Foolish Wives* 21. The Wedding March 27. The Great Gabbo 29. Three Faces East 30. Friends and Lovers 30. The Lost Squadron 32. As You Desire Me 32. Walking Down Broadway 32. Crimson Romance 35. The Crime of Dr Crespi 35. *La Grande Illusion* 37. Mademoiselle Docteur 37. Alibi 38. Boys' School 39. I Was an Adventuress 40. Thunder Over Parièges 40. So Ends Our Night 41. *Five Graves to Cairo* (as Rommel) 43. North Star 43. The Lady and the Monster 44. Storm Over Lisbon 44. 32 Rue de Montmartre 44. The Great Flamarion 45. La Danse de Mort 47. *Sunset Boulevard* (AAN) 50. La Maison du Crime 52. Napoleon 54. L'Homme aux Cents Visages 56, etc.
■ AS DIRECTOR: Blind Husbands 19. *The Devil's Passkey* 19. Foolish Wives 21. Merry Go Round 22. *Greed* 23. The Merry Widow 25. *The Wedding March* 27. *Queen Kelly* 28.
✪ For taking Hollywood on and winning – for a while. *Greed*.

¶ The difference between me and Lubitsch is that he shows you the king on the throne and then he shows you the king in his bedroom. I show you the king in his bedroom first. Then when you see him on the throne you have no illusions about him. – *E.V.S.*
When I first saw Von Stroheim at the wardrobe tests, I clicked my heels and said, 'Isn't it ridiculous, little me directing you, when you were always ten years ahead of your time?' And he replied, 'Twenty.' – *Billy Wilder, 1942*
As to directing his own performance, Von always had an assistant to give him an opinion of his acting. Whether he listened to it or not was another matter. – *William Daniels*
One of the cinema's great enigmas . . . he conjured up a world very much in its infancy psychologically. It was a grotesque and brutal world, and the bleakness and callousness of his characters' lives were revealed with a meticulous realism. – *Claire Johnston*
He was a short man, almost squat, with a vulpine smirk that told you, as soon as his image flashed on to the screen, that no wife or bankroll must be left unguarded. – *S.J. Perelman*

Von Sydow, Max (1929–) (Carl Adolf Von Sydow).
Leading Swedish actor, a member of Ingmar Bergman's company.
Miss Julie 51. *The Seventh Seal* 56. Wild Strawberries 57. So Close to Life 58. *The Face* 59. The Virgin Spring 60. *Through a Glass Darkly* 61. Winter Light 62. The Mistress 62. *The Greatest Story Ever Told* (as Jesus) (US) 65. The Reward (US) 65. Hawaii (US) 66. The Quiller Memorandum (GB) 66. *Hour of the Wolf* 67. The Shame 68. The Kremlin Letter (US) 69. The Touch 71. Embassy 72. *The Emigrants* 72. The Exorcist (US) 73. The New Land 75. Foxtrot 76. Three Days of Condor (US) 76. Voyage of the Damned 76. Exorcist II: The Heretic 77. March or Die 77. Brass Target 78. Hurricane 79. Flash Gordon 80. Victory 81. Never Say Never Again 83. Kojak: The Belarus File (TV) 85. Christopher Columbus (TV) 85. The Wolf at the Door 85. The Second Victory 86. Duet for One 86. Hannah and Her Sisters 86. Pelle the Conqueror (AAN) 88. Katinka (d) 88. My Dear Doctor Grasler (Mio Caro Dottor Gräsler) 89. Awakenings 90. Father 90. A Kiss before Dying 91. Until the End of the World (Bis ans Ende der Welt) 91. The Bachelor 91. The Ox (Oxen) 91. The Touch 92. Best

Intentions 92. Morfars Resa 93. Needful Things 93. Time Is Money 94. Judge Dredd 95, etc.

Von Trier, Lars (1956–).
Danish director and screenwriter.
Element of Crime 84. Epidemic 89. *Europa* (US: Zentropa) 91. The Kingdom (Riget) 94, etc.

Von Trotta, Margarethe (1942–).
German director who married Volker Schlöndorff.
The Lost Honour of Katerina Blum (co-d) 75. The Second Awakening of Krista Clarges 77. Sisters 79. The German Sisters 81. Friends and Husbands 83. Rosa Luxemburg 85. Felix 87. The Return (Die Rückkehr) 90. Three Sisters (Paura e Amore) 90. The African (L'Africana) 91. Anni del Muro 93. Il Lungo Silenzio (It.) 94, etc.

Vorhaus, Bernard (c. 1898–).
German director, mostly in Britain and Hollywood.

Money for Speed (GB) 33. Broken Melody (GB) 35. Cotton Queen (GB) 37. Three Faces West (US) 40. Lady from Louisiana (US) 41. Bury Me Dead (US) 47. So Young So Bad (US) 50. The Lady from Boston (US) 51, etc.

Vorkapich, Slavko (1892–1976).
Yugoslavian writer who came to Hollywood in 1922, did a little screenwriting, tried direction in 1931 (*I Take This Woman*), then settled as a montage expert.
Viva Villa 34. *Crime without Passion* 34. San Francisco 36. Maytime 37. The Last Gangster 38. Shopworn Angel 38. Mr Smith Goes to Washington 39, etc.

Voskovec, George (1905–1981) (Jiri Voskovec).
Czech stage actor, long in US.
Anything Can Happen 52. *Twelve Angry Men* 57.

The Bravados 58. Butterfield 8 60. The Spy Who Came in from the Cold 65. Mister Buddwing 66. The Boston Strangler 68. Skag (TV) 80. Somewhere in Time 80. Barbarossa 82, etc.

Vosper, Frank (1899–1937).
British stage actor and playwright who appeared in a few films.
Blinkeyes 26. The Last Post 27. Rome Express 32. Waltzes from Vienna 33. The Man Who Knew Too Much 34. Jew Süss 34. Open All Night 34. Heart's Desire 35.

Vye, Murvyn (1913–1976).
Burly American character actor who usually played heavies.
Golden Earrings 48. A Connecticut Yankee at King Arthur's Court 49. Pick-Up 51. Road to Bali 52. Green Fire 54. Pearl of the South Pacific 55. Al Capone 58. Pay or Die 60. Andy 64, etc.

Waddington, Patrick (1900–1987).
Elegant British character actor, mostly on stage.
　Journey Together 45. School for Secrets 46. The Wooden Horse 51. A Night to Remember 56, etc.

Wadleigh, Michael (1941–　).
American director who began in TV as a documentary film-maker and director of music specials.
　Woodstock 70. Wolfen 81.

Wadsworth, Henry (1902–1974).
American juvenile of the 20s and 30s.
　Applause 29. Luxury Liner 33. The Thin Man 34. Ceiling Zero 35. Dr Rhythm 38. Silver Skates 43, many others.

Wager, Anthony (1933–　).
British juvenile actor who played Young Pip in the 1946 Great Expectations and later turned up on Australian television.

The Wages of Fear.
Henri-Georges Clouzot's superlative thriller featuring four drivers with a cargo of nitroglycerine was made from Georges Arnaud's novel in 1953, starring Yves Montand, Charles Vanel, and Peter Van Eyck. William Friedkin's 1977 remake, Sorcerer, was an artistic and commercial disaster.

Waggner, George (1894–1984).
American director, mainly of routine low-budgeters, in Hollywood from 1920.
　The Wolf Man 41. The Climax (& p) 44. Cobra Woman (& p) 45. The Fighting Kentuckian (& w) 49. Operation Pacific (& w) 51. Bitter Creek 54. Destination 60,000 (& w) 57. Pale Arrow 58, many others.

Wagner, Fritz Arno (1889–1958).
German cinematographer.
　Nosferatu 23. The Loves of Jeanne Ney 27. The Spy 28. Westfront 1918 30. Die Dreigroschenoper 31. Kameradschaft 31. Amphitryon 35. Ohm Krüger 41. Hotel Adlon 55, many others.

Wagner, Lindsay (1949–　).
American leading lady of the 70s, a former model and singer.
　The Paper Chase 73. Two People 74. The Incredible Journey of Meg Laurel (TV) 79. Scruples (TV) 81. The Two Worlds of Jennie Logan (TV) 81. Callie and Company (TV) 82. Princess Daisy (TV) 83. Martin's Day 84. Ricochet 91. Fire in the Dark 91. Danielle Steel's Once in a Lifetime (TV) 94, etc.
　TV series: The Bionic Woman 76–78. Jessie 84.

Wagner, Robert (1930–　).
American leading man spotted by talent scout while still at college. His first wife was actress Natalie Wood and his third actress Jill St John.
　Halls of Montezuma (debut) 50. With a Song in My Heart 52. Titanic 53. Prince Valiant 54. Broken Lance 54. White Feather 55. The Mountain 56. A Kiss Before Dying 56. The Hunters 57. Say One for Me 58. All the Fine Young Cannibals 59. The Longest Day 62. The Condemned of Altona 63. Harper 66. The Biggest Bundle of Them All 66. Don't Just Stand There 68. Winning 69. The Streets of San Francisco (TV) 71. City Beneath the Sea (TV) 71. The Affair (TV) 73. The Towering Inferno 74. Death at Love House (TV) 76. Midway 76. The Concorde – Airport '79 79. Curse of the Pink Panther 83. I Am the Cheese 83. To Catch a King (TV) 84. This Gun for Hire (TV) 91. Dragon: The Bruce Lee Story 93. Parallel Lives (TV) 94, etc.
　TV series: It Takes a Thief 65–69. Colditz 72–73. Switch 75–76. Hart to Hart 79–83. Lime Street 85.

Wahl, Ken (1957–　).
Giant-sized American leading man.
　■ The Buddy Holly Story 78. Every Which Way But Loose 79. The Champ 79. The Wanderers 79. Running Scared 79. Fort Apache, the Bronx 81. Race for the Yankee Zephyr 81. Jinxed! 82. Code Name The Soldier 82. Purple Heart 84. The Taking of Beverly Hills 91. The Favor 94, etc.
　TV series: Double Dare 85. Wiseguy 87–89.

Wainwright, James (1938–　).
American general-purpose actor.
　The President's Plane Is Missing (TV) 71. Joe Kidd 72. Killdozer (TV) 74. The Private Files of J. Edgar Hoover 77. Mean Dog Blues 78. My Undercover Years with the Ku Klux Klan (TV) 78. Warlords of the 21st Century (aka Battletruck) 82, etc.
　TV series: Jigsaw 72. Beyond Westworld 79.

Wainwright, Rupert.
British director working in Hollywood, from television and music videos.
　Dillinger (TV) 91. Blank Check 94.

Waite, Ralph (1928–　).
Reliable-looking American general-purpose actor.
　Cool Hand Luke 67. Last Summer 69. Five Easy Pieces 70. The Grissom Gang 71. Kid Blue 72. The Stone Killer 73. On the Nickel (p, wd only) 80. OHMS (TV) 80. Angel City (TV) 81. Crash and Burn 90, etc.
　TV series: The Waltons 72–78.

Waite, Ric.
American cinematographer, from TV films.
　The Long Riders 80. The Border 82. Tex 82. 48 Hours 82. Class 83. Uncommon Valor 83. Footloose 84. Red Dawn 84. Brewster's Millions 85. Volunteers 85. Cobra 86. Adventures in Babysitting 87. The Great Outdoors 88. Marked for Death 90. Out for Justice 91. Rapid Fire 92. On Deadly Ground 94, etc.

Waits, Tom (1949–　).
Laconic American singer-songwriter, composer and actor.
　Paradise Alley (a) 78. On the Nickel (s) 80. Wolfen (a) 81. One from the Heart (a, m) (AANm) 82. Rumblefish (a) 83. The Outsiders (a) 83. The Cotton Club (a) 84. Streetwise (s) 84. Down by Law (a) 86. Ironweed (a) 87. Candy Mountain (a, m) 88. Cold Feet (a) 89. Bearskin: An Urban Fairytale (a, s) 90. The Two Jakes (a) 90. Queen's Logic (a) 90. The Fisher King (a) 91. At Play in the Fields of the Lord (a) 91. Night on Earth (m) 92. Deadfall (a) 92. Bram Stoker's Dracula (a) 92. Short Cuts (a) 93, etc.

Wajda, Andrzej (1926–　).
Polish director.
　A Generation 54. Kanal 55. Ashes and Diamonds 58. Innocent Sorcerers 60. The Siberian Lady Macbeth 61. Love at Twenty (part only) 62. Ashes 64. Everything for Sale 67. Gates to Paradise 67. The Birch Wood 71. Landscape after a Battle 72. The Wedding 72. Promised Land 74. Shadow Line 76. Man of Marble 77. Without Anesthetic 79. Man of Iron 80. Danton 82. A Love in Germany (Eine Liebe in Deutschland) 83. Chronicle of Love Affairs (Kronika Wypadkow Milosnych) 86. The Possessed (Les Possédés) 87. Korczak 90. The Ring with a Crowned Eagle 93. Nastazja 94, etc.

Wakefield, Duggie (1899–1951).
British music-hall comedian, in character as a simpleton who always triumphed.
　Look Up and Laugh 35. Spy for a Day 39, etc.

Wakefield, Hugh (1888–1971).
British character actor on stage from childhood. Usually seen in monocled roles.
　City of Song 30. The Sport of Kings 31. The Man Who Knew Too Much 34. The Crimson Circle 36. The Street Singer 37. Blithe Spirit 45. One Night with You 48. Love's a Luxury 52. The Million Pound Note 54, etc.

Wakefield, Oliver (1909–1956).
English comedian and character actor, in silly-ass roles, the brother of Duggie Wakefield. His music-hall act was billed as 'The Voice of Inexperience'.
　Let's Make a Night of It 37. French Leave 37. There Was a Young Man 37. Down Our Alley 39. Shipyard Sally 39. George and Margaret 40. The Briggs Family 40. Let the People Sing 42. The Peterville Diamond 42, etc.

Wakeford, Kent L.
American cinematographer.
　■ Black Belt Jones 74. Alice Doesn't Live Here Any More 75. The Princess Academy 87. The Women's Club 87.

Wakeman, Rick (1949–　).
British composer and keyboard player, a former member of the rock band Yes.
　■ Lisztomania 75. White Rock 77. The Burning 82. She 83. Crimes of Passion 84. Creepshow II 87.

Wakhevitch, Georges (1907–1984).
Russian art director in international films.
　Madame Bovary 34. La Grande Illusion 37. Prison without Bars 38. Les Visiteurs du Soir 42. L'Eternel Retour 43. L'Homme au Chapeau Rond

46. Dédée 48. The Medium 51. The Beggar's Opera 53. Don Juan 56. Marie-Octobre 59. Black Tights 60. King of Kings 61. Diary of a Chambermaid 64. Tendre Voyou 66. Mayerling 68. King Lear 70, etc.

Walas, Chris.

American designer and creator of special effects, make-up effects, and fantasy creatures, now also working as a director.

Galaxina (make-up) 80. Scanners (make-up) 81. Caveman (creature) 81. Raiders of the Lost Ark (make-up) 81. Gremlins (creatures) 84. The Fly (fx) (AA for make-up) 86. House II: The Second Story (creatures) 87. The Kiss (creatures) 88. The Fly II (d) 89. Arachnophobia (creatures) 90. Naked Lunch (creatures) 91. The Vagrant (d) 92, etc.

Walbrook, Anton (1900–1967) (Adolf Wohlbruck).

Distinguished Austrian actor who came to Britain in the mid-30s.

Maskerade 34. The Student of Prague 35. *Michael Strogoff* (US) 37. *Victoria the Great* 37. The Rat 37. Sixty Glorious Years 38. *Gaslight* 39. Dangerous Moonlight 40. 49th Parallel 41. *The Life and Death of Colonel Blimp* 43. The Man from Morocco 44. *The Red Shoes* 48. The Queen of Spades 48. *La Ronde* 50. Vienna Waltzes 51. Oh Rosalinda 55. Lola Montes 55. Saint Joan 57. I Accuse 57, etc.

Walburn, Raymond (1887–1969).

American comedy actor with an inimitable bumbling pomposity; on stage from 1912, films from early 30s.

The Count of Monte Cristo 34. The Great Ziegfeld 36. *Mr Deeds Goes to Town* 36. Born to Dance 37. Professor Beware 38. Eternally Yours 40. Christmas in July 41. Dixie 43. *Hail the Conquering Hero* 43. The Man in the Trunk 43. The Cheaters 45. Henry the Rainmaker 48. State of the Union 48. Riding High 49. Father Takes the Air 51. Beautiful but Dangerous 53. The Spoilers 55, etc.

Wald, Jerry (1911–1962).

Live-wire American writer-producer, said to be the original of Budd Schulberg's novel *What Makes Sammy Run?* Former journalist, in Hollywood from early 30s.

Stars over Broadway (w) 35. Hollywood Hotel (w) 38. George Washington Slept Here (p) 42. *Mildred Pierce* 45. *Johnny Belinda* (p) 48. The Glass Menagerie (p) 50. Clash by Night (p) 52. Queen Bee (p) 55. Peyton Place (p) 57. The Sound and the Fury (p) 58. Sons and Lovers (p) 60. The Stripper (p) 63, many others.

Waldron, Charles D. (1874–1946).

American stage actor who made a few films.

Mary Burns Fugitive 35. The Garden of Allah 36. Kentucky 38. On Borrowed Time 39. The Devil and Miss Jones 41. The Song of Bernadette 43. The Black Parachute 44. The Big Sleep 46, etc.

Famous line (*The Big Sleep*): 'You may smoke, sir. I can still enjoy the smell of it. Nice state of affairs, when a man has to indulge his vices by proxy.'

Wales, Ethel (1881–1952).

American character actress, in films from 1920.

Miss Lulu Bett 21. The Covered Wagon 23. Merton of the Movies 24. Beggar on Horseback 25. The Country Doctor 27. Blue Skies 29. Subway Express 31. Klondike 32. The Mighty Barnum 34. Barbary Coast 35. The Gladiator 38. Sudden Money 39. Young Bill Hickok 40. The Lumberjack 44. Blonde Alibi 46. The Story of a Woman 47. Fancy Pants 50, etc.

Wales, Wally:
see *Taliaferro, Hal.*

Walken, Christopher (1943–).
American leading actor.
■ The Anderson Tapes 71. The Happiness Cage 72. Next Stop Greenwich Village 76. The Sentinel 77. Annie Hall 77. Roseland 77. The Deer Hunter (AA) 78. Last Embrace 79. Heaven's Gate 80. The Dogs of War 81. Pennies from Heaven 81. Brainstorm 83. The Dead Zone 83. A View to a Kill 85. At Close Range 86. Deadline 87. Biloxi Blues 88. The Milagro Beanfield War 88. Communion 89. King of New York 90. The Comfort of Strangers 90. McBain 91. All-American Murder 91. Day of Atonement (Le Grand Pardon 2) 92. Mistress 92. Batman Returns 92. Skylark (TV) 93. God's Army 93. Scam 93. *True Romance* 93. Wayne's World 2 93. A Business Affair 94. Pulp Fiction 94.

Walker, Charlotte (1878–1958).
American leading lady with stage experience, in silent films. Mother of Sara Haden.
Kindling 15. Trail of the Lonesome Pine 16. Eve in Exile 19. Classmates 24. The Manicure Girl 25. Paris Bound 29. Scarlet Pages 30. Millie 31, etc.

Walker, Clint (1927–) (Norman Eugene Walker).
Giant-size American leading man from TV. No acting training.
Fort Dobbs 57. Yellowstone Kelly 60. Gold of the Seven Saints 61. Send Me No Flowers 64. Night of the Grizzly 66. The Dirty Dozen 67. Sam Whiskey 68. The Great Bank Robbery 69. Yuma (TV) 70. The Bounty Man (TV) 72. Baker's Hawk 76. The White Buffalo 77. Hysterical 83. Serpent Warriors 86, etc.
TV series: Cheyenne 55–62. Kodiak 75.

Walker, Giles (1946–).
Scottish-born director, in Canada.
Descent 75. Twice upon a Time 79. 90 Days 85. The Last Straw 87. Princess in Exile 90. Ordinary Magic 93, etc.

Walker, H. M. ('Beanie') (1887–1937).
American dialogue writer who provided most of Laurel and Hardy's classic exchanges in the early 30s, though these were usually based on Stan Laurel's gags.

Walker, Hal (1896–1972).
American director, mainly of routine films; stage experience.
■ Out of this World 45. Duffy's Tavern 45. The Stork Club 45. *Road to Utopia* 45. My Friend Irma Goes West 50. At War with the Army 50. That's My Boy 51. Sailor Beware 51. Road to Bali 52.

Walker, Helen (1921–1968).
American leading lady of the 40s.
Lucky Jordan 42. Abroad with Two Yanks 44. Murder He Says 45. Cluny Brown 46. The Homestretch 47. Nightmare Alley 47. Impact 49. My True Story 51. Problem Girls 52. The Big Combo (last role) 55, etc.

Walker, Joseph (1892–1985).
American cinematographer. On his retirement, he invented the zoom lens.
Danger 23. Flaming Fury 26. Virgin Lips 29. Dirigible 30. The Miracle Woman 31. American Madness 32. Lady for a Day 33. It Happened One Night 34. Broadway Bill 34. Mr Deeds Goes to Town 36. *Lost Horizon* 37. You Can't Take it With You 38. Mr Smith Goes to Washington 39. His Girl Friday 40. Here Comes Mr Jordan 41. *It's a*

Wonderful Life 46. *The Jolson Story* 46. Born Yesterday 51, many others.

Walker, Nancy (1922–1992) (Ann Swoyer Barto).
Pint-sized American character comedienne.
Best Foot Forward 43. The World's Greatest Athlete 73. Forty Carats 73. Murder by Death 76. Can't Stop the Music (d) 80, etc.
TV series: Family Affair 70–71. McMillan and Wife 71–76. Rhoda 74–76, 77–78. The Nancy Walker Show 76. Blansky's Beauties 77. True Colors 90.

Walker, Nella (1886–1971).
American character actress, usually placid mother or socialite.
Seven Keys to Baldpate 29. Trouble in Paradise 32. Humanity 33. Four Frightened People 34. Three Smart Girls 36. The Rage of Paris 38. No Time for Comedy 40. Kitty Foyle 40. Hellzapoppin 41. Wintertime 43. In Society 44. The Locket 46. That Hagen Girl 47. Sabrina 54, many others.

Walker, Norman (1892–1963).
British director.
Tommy Atkins 27. The Middle Watch 31. Turn of the Tide 35. The Man at the Gate 40. Hard Steel 41. They Knew Mr Knight 45, etc.

Walker, Pete (1935–).
British producer-director of exploitation films.
I Like Birds 67. School for Sex 68. Cool it Carol 70. Die Screaming Marianne 71. Four Dimensions of Greta 72. Tiffany Jones 73. House of Whipcord 74. Frightmare 75. The House of Mortal Sin 76. Schizo 76. The Comeback 77. Home Before Midnight 79. House of the Long Shadows 83, etc.

Walker, Polly (1966–).
British actress, from the stage.
Enchanted April 91. Patriot Games 92. The Trial 93. Sliver 93, etc.

Walker, Robert (1914–1951).
Slight, modest-looking American leading man of the 40s.
■ Winter Carnival 39. These Glamour Girls 39. Dancing Co-Ed 39. Bataan 43. Madame Curie 43. *See Here Private Hargrove* 43. *Since You Went Away* 44. Thirty Seconds Over Tokyo 44. *The Clock* 45. Her Highness and the Bellboy 45. What Next Corporal Hargrove? 45. The Sailor Takes a Wife 45. *Till the Clouds Roll By* (as Jerome Kern) 46. The Sea of Grass 47. The Beginning or the End 47. Song of Love 47. One Touch of Venus 48. Please Believe Me 50. The Skipper Surprised His Wife 50. Vengeance Valley 51. *Strangers on a Train* 51. My Son John 52.

Walker, Robert, Jnr (1940–).
American second lead of the 60s.
The Hook 63. Ensign Pulver 64. The Ceremony 64. The Happening 67. The War Wagon 67. Easy Rider 69. Road to Salina 70. The Spectre of Edgar Allan Poe 72. God Bless Dr Shagetz 77. A Touch of Sin 83. Hambone and Hillie 84. Angkor-Cambodian Express 84, etc.

Walker, Stuart (1887–1941).
American director, former stage producer.
■ The Secret Call 31. The False Madonna 32. The Misleading Lady 32. Evenings for Sale 32. Tonight is Ours 33. *The Eagle and the Hawk* 33. White Woman 33. Romance in the Rain 34. Great Expectations 34. The Mystery of Edwin Drood 35. Werewolf of London 35. Manhattan Moon 35. Bulldog Drummond's Bride 39. Emergency Squad 40.

Walker, Syd (1887–1945).
English cockney comedian and actor, from music hall. His radio catchphrase, 'What would you do, chums?', from *Mr Walker Wants to Know*, a problem-solving spot in a weekly variety show, was the inspiration for his most successful feature.
Old Bill 24. Gift of the Gab 34. Over She Goes 37. Oh Boy 38. Hold My Hand 39. What Would You Do Chums? 39. The Gang's All Here 39, etc.

Walker, Zena (1934–   ).
British leading actress of the 60s, mostly on TV.
The Hellions 61. The Traitors 63. One of Those Things 69. The Dresser 83, etc.

Wall, Max (1902–1990) (Maxwell George Lorimer).
British music-hall song-and-dance performer, billed as 'The Boy with the Educated Feet', who turned comedian and became a notable character actor in his last years, especially on stage in the works of Samuel Beckett.
Autobiography: 1976, *The Fool on the Hill*.
Chitty Chitty Bang Bang 68. A Killer in Every Corner 74. One of Our Dinosaurs Is Missing 75. Jabberwocky 77. The Hound of the Baskervilles 78. Hanover Street 79. Little Dorrit 88. We Think the World of You 88. Strike It Rich 90, etc.

Wallace, Dee:
see *Stone, Dee Wallace.*

Wallace, Edgar (1875–1932).
Prolific British crime-story writer. Films of his books include:
The Terror 28 and 38. *The Crimson Circle* 30, 37 and 61. *The Case of the Frightened Lady* 30 and 40. *The Ringer* 32 and 52. *The Calendar* 32 and 48. *Sanders of the River* 35. The Squeaker 37. *Kate Plus Ten* 38. The Four Just Men 39. The Mind of Mr Reeder 39 (and series); and many episodes of a second-feature series made at Merton Park in the 60s.

Wallace, Irving (1916–1990) (Irving Wallechinsky).
American writer who with his son David and daughter Amy wrote encyclopaedias (*The Book of Lists*) but on his own account was a best-selling novelist. *The Chapman Report, The Prize, The Man* and *The Seven Minutes* have all been filmed.

Wallace, Jean (1923–1990) (Jean Wallasek).
American leading lady. She was married to Franchot Tone and later Cornel Wilde.
You Can't Ration Love 44. Jigsaw 48. The Good Humour Man 50. Song of India 50. Storm Fear 55. The Big Combo 55. Maracaibo 58. Lancelot and Guinevere 63. Beach Red 67. No Blade of Grass 71, etc.

Wallace, Lew (1827–1905).
American novelist who in 1880 published the much filmed *Ben Hur*.

Wallace, Nellie (1870–1948).
British character actress and music-hall performer, billed as 'The Essence of Eccentricity'. Born in Glasgow, she began as a clog-dancer when a child, emerging as a comic in the early 1900s.
The Wishbone 33. Radio Parade of 1935 35. Boys Will Be Girls 37. Cavalcade of the Stars 38, etc.

Wallace, Richard (1894–1951).
American director, former cutter for Mack Sennett.
MacFadden's Flats 27. Innocents of Paris 30. Seven Days' Leave 31. The Road to Reno 32. Shopworn Angel 33. The Little Minister 35. The Young in Heart 39. Captain Caution 40. The Navy Steps Out 41. She Knew All the Answers 41. The Fallen Sparrow 43. Bride by Mistake 44. *It's in the Bag* 45. Sinbad the Sailor 46. Tycoon 47. Let's Live a Little 48. A Kiss for Corliss 50, many others.

Wallace, Stephen (1943–   ).
Australian director and screenwriter, from documentaries.
Stir (d) 80. For Love Alone (wd) 86. Blood Oath (d) 90. Turtle Beach (d) 90.

Wallach, Eli (1915–   ).
American stage actor (from 1940) who has latterly concentrated on films, often in villainous roles which he spices with 'the method'.
■ *Baby Doll* (debut) 56. The Line Up 58. Seven Thieves 59. The Magnificent Seven 60. The Misfits 61. Hemingway's Adventures of a Young Man 62. How the West Was Won 62. The Victors 63. Act One 63. The Moonspinners 64. Kisses for My President 64. Lord Jim 65. Genghis Khan 65. How to Steal a Million 66. The Good the Bad and the Ugly (It.) 67. *The Tiger Makes Out* 67. How to Save a Marriage 68. Mackenna's Gold 68. A Lovely Way to Die 68. Revenge in El Paso (It.) 68. Ace High 69. The Brain 69. Zigzag 70. The People Next Door 70. The Angel Levine 70. The Adventures of Gerard 70. Romance of a Horsethief 71. A Cold Night's Death (TV) 72. Crazy Joe 73. Last Chance 73. Don't Turn the Other Cheek 73. Cinderella Liberty 74. Samurai 74. Indict and Convict (TV) 74. The Deep 77. Nasty Habits 77. The Sentinel 77. The Domino Principle 77. Seventh Avenue (TV) 77. Girl Friends 78. The Pirate (TV) 78. Movie Movie 78. Firepower 79. Winter Kills 79. Circle of Iron 79. The Pride of Jesse Hallam (TV) 80. The Salamander 80. The Hunter 81. The Executioner's Song (TV) 82. Anatomy of an Illness (TV) 84. Christopher Columbus (TV) 85. Sam's Son (TV) 85. Tough Guys 86. Nuts 87. The Two Jakes 90. The Godfather Part III 90. Article 99 92. Mistress 92.

Waller, Fats (1904–1943).
American jazz pianist and composer.
■ Hooray for Love 35. King of Burlesque 36. Stormy Weather 43.

Waller, Fred (1886–1954).
American research technician who invented Cinerama and saw it open successfully only two years before his death.

Wallis, Hal B. (1898–1986).
American producer, latterly independent, responsible for a long line of solidly commercial films. In films from 1922.
Little Caesar 30. *The Story of Louis Pasteur* 36. Jezebel 38. *Kings Row* 42. *Casablanca* 42. The Strange Love of Martha Ivers 46. My Friend Irma 49. *Gunfight at the OK Corral* 57. G.I. Blues 60. Becket 64. Boeing-Boeing 65. The Sons of Katie Elder 65. Five Card Stud 68. True Grit 69. Anne of the Thousand Days 70. Mary Queen of Scots 72. Bequest to the Nation 73. Rooster Cogburn 75, many others (often as executive producer for major studios).

Wallis, Shani (1938–   ).
British cabaret singer.
■ The Extra Day 56. Ramsbottom Rides Again 56. A King in New York 67. Oliver! 68. Terror in the Wax Museum 73. Arnold 73. Round Numbers 92.

Walls, Tom (1883–1949).
British actor and director, on stage from 1905 after experience as policeman, busker, jockey, etc. Associated from mid-20s with the Aldwych farces, which he produced and later transferred to the screen, as well as playing amiable philanderers in them. Subsequently in character roles.
■ *Rookery Nook* 30. On Approval 30. Canaries Sometimes Sing 30. Tons of Money 31. *Plunder* 31. A Night Like This 32. *Thark* 32. Leap Year 32. The Blarney Stone 32. Just Smith 33. Turkey Time 33. A Cuckoo in the Nest 34. A Cup of Kindness 34. Lady in Danger 34. Dirty Work 34. Fighting Stock 35. Me and Marlborough 35. Stormy Weather 35. Foreign Affaires 36. Pot Luck 36. Dishonour Bright 36. For Valour 37. Second Best Bed 38. Old Iron 38. *Strange Boarders* 38. Crackerjack 38. Undercover 43. They Met in the Dark 43. Halfway House 43. Love Story 44. Johnny Frenchman 45. This Man is Mine 46. *Master of Bankdam* 47. While I Live 47. *Spring in Park Lane* 47. Maytime in Mayfair 48. Derby Day 49. The Interrupted Journey 49.

Walpole, Sir Hugh (1884–1941).
British novelist who has been oddly neglected by the cinema but did some scripting in 30s Hollywood and appeared as the vicar in *David Copperfield* 34.

Walsh, Bill (1918–1976).
American producer for the Walt Disney Organization.
Mary Poppins (p, co-w) (AANw) 64, etc.

Walsh, David M.
American cinematographer.
I Walk the Line 70. The Other Side of the Mountain 75. The Silver Streak 76. Rollercoaster 77. House Calls 78. Movie Movie 78. Goldengirl 78. Seems Like Old Times 80. Only When I Laugh 81. Max Dugan Returns 83. Romantic Comedy 83. Unfaithfully Yours 84. Johnny Dangerously 84. Country 84. Teachers 84. My Science Project 85. Outrageous Fortune 87. Summer School 87. Fatal Beauty 87. Second Sight 89. Taking Care of Business 90, etc.

Walsh, Dermot (1924–   ).
Irish leading man, usually in second features. His first wife was actress Hazel Court (1949–63).
Bedelia 46. My Sister and I 49. The Frightened Man 52. The Floating Dutchman 53. The Night of the Full Moon 56. Woman of Mystery 57. Crash Drive 59. The Trunk 61. The Cool Mikado 63. The Wicked Lady 83, etc.
TV series: Richard the Lionheart 62.

Walsh, J. T.
American character actor, from the stage; a former salesman.
Eddie Macon's Run 83. Hard Choices 84. Hannah and Her Sisters 86. Power 86. Good Morning, Vietnam 87. House of Games 87. Tin Men 87. Tequila Sunrise 88. Things Change 88. Wired 89. The Big Picture 89. Dad 89. Crazy People 90. The Grifters 90. Narrow Margin 90. The Russia House 90. Backdraft 91. True Identity 91. Iron Maze 91. Hoffa 92. Needful Things 93. Sniper 93. Red Rock West 93. Morning Glory 93. Blue Chips 94. The Client 94, etc.

Walsh, Kay (1914–   ).
British character actress, former leading lady. Trained in West End revue. She was formerly married to director David Lean.
Get Your Man (debut) 34. I See Ice 38. In Which We Serve 42. This Happy Breed 44. *The October Man* 47. Vice Versa 48. Oliver Twist 48. Stage Fright 50. Last Holiday 50. *Encore* 51. Meet Me Tonight 52. Lease of Life 54. Cast a Dark Shadow 55. The Horse's Mouth 59. *Tunes of Glory* 60. Eighty Thousand Suspects 63. The Beauty Jungle 64. A

Study in Terror 65. The Witches 66. Connecting Rooms 69. The Ruling Class 71. Night Crossing 82, many others.

TV series: Sherlock Holmes and Dr Watson 80.

Walsh, M. Emmet (1935–).
Fleshy American character actor, often as a heavy.
Alice's Restaurant 69. Midnight Cowboy 69. Stiletto 69. Little Big Man 70. The Traveling Executioner 70. They Might Be Giants 71. What's Up, Doc? 72. Serpico 73. At Long Last Love 75. Nickelodeon 76. Slap Shot 77. Straight Time 78. The Jerk 79. East of Eden (TV) 80. Brubaker 80. Ordinary People 80. Reds 81. Blade Runner 82. Silkwood 83. Missing in Action 84. Blood Simple 85. Fletch 85. Back to School 86. The Best of Times 86. Harry and the Hendersons 87. The Milagro Beanfield War 88. War Party 89. The Mighty Quinn 89. Red Scorpion 89. Chattahoochee 89. Narrow Margin 90. Equinox 92. The Music of Chance 93. Bitter Harvest 93. Wilder Napalm 93. Relative Fear 94. The Glass Shield 94, etc.

TV series: The Sandy Duncan Show 72. Dear Detective 79. Unsub 89.

Walsh, Raoul (1887–1980).
Veteran American director of many commercial and several distinguished pictures. In films from 1912; former actor and assistant to D. W. Griffith.
Autobiography: 1974, *Each Man in His Time*.
Carmen 15. *The Thief of Baghdad* 24. *What Price Glory?* 26. *Sadie Thompson* 28. In Old Arizona 29. *The Big Trail* 30. *The Bowery* 33. Every Night at Eight 35. Artists and Models 38. St Louis Blues 39. *They Drive by Night* 40. *High Sierra* 41. They Died with Their Boots On 41. Strawberry Blonde 41. Manpower 41. Desperate Journey 42. Gentleman Jim 42. Northern Pursuit 43. Uncertain Glory 44. The Horn Blows at Midnight 45. *Objective Burma* 45. The Man I Love 46. Pursued 47. Silver River 48. *White Heat* 49. Colorado Territory 49. Along the Great Divide 49. Captain Horatio Hornblower 50. Distant Drums 51. The World in His Arms 52. Glory Alley 52. Blackbeard the Pirate 53. A Lion is in the Streets 54. Saskatchewan 54. Battle Cry 55. The Tall Men 55. The Revolt of Mamie Stover 57. The King and Four Queens 57. Band of Angels 57. The Naked and the Dead 58. The Sheriff of Fractured Jaw (GB) 58. Esther and the King 60. Marines Let's Go 61. A Distant Trumpet 64, many others.
❂ For vigorous treatment of action subjects. *White Heat*.

¶ To Raoul Walsh, a tender love scene is burning down a whorehouse. – *Jack L. Warner*

Walston, Ray (1917–).
American character comedian with stage experience.
Kiss Them for Me 57. South Pacific 58. *Damn Yankees* 58. Say One for Me 59. The Apartment 60. Tall Story 60. Portrait in Black 60. Convicts Four 62. Wives and Lovers 63. Who's Minding the Store? 64. *Kiss Me Stupid* 64. Caprice 67. Paint Your Wagon 69. Viva Max 69. The Sting 73. Silver Streak 76. The Happy Hooker Goes to Washington 77. Popeye 81. Galaxy of Terror 81. Fast Times at Ridgemont High 82. O'Hara's Wife 82. Private School 83. Johnny Dangerously 84. O.C. and Stiggs 87. Red River (TV) 88. Blood Relations 88. Paramedics 88. Man of Passion 88. I Know My First Name Is Steven (TV) 89. Popcorn 91. Of Mice and Men 92. The Stand (TV) 94, etc.

TV series: My Favorite Martian 63–65. Stop Susan Williams 79. Silver Spoons 85. Fast Times 86.

Walter, Jessica (1944–).
American leading lady of the 60s.
■ Lilith 64. *The Group* 66. Grand Prix 67. Bye Bye Braverman 68. Number One 69. Play Misty for Me 71. Women in Chains (TV) 71. Home for the Holidays (TV) 72. Amy Prentiss (TV) 76. Victory at Entebbe (TV) 76. Secrets of Three Hungry Wives (TV) 78. She's Dressed to Kill (TV) 79. Spring Fever 83. The Flamingo Kid 84. The Execution (TV) 85. Killer in the Mirror (TV) 86. Tapeheads 87. Aaron's Way (TV) 88. Ghost in the Machine 94. PCU 94.

Walters, Charles (1911–1982).
American director specializing in musicals. Former stage dancer and director of musical sequences in films.
Presenting Lily Mars (seq) 43. Meet Me in St Louis (seq) 44. Good News 47. *Easter Parade* 48. Summer Stock 50. Easy to Love 53. *Lili* (AAN) 53. The Glass Slipper 55. The Tender Trap 55. High Society 56. Don't Go Near the Water 57. Ask Any Girl 59. Please Don't Eat the Daisies 60. Jumbo 62. The Unsinkable Molly Brown 64. Walk, Don't Run 66, etc.

Walters, Julie (1950–).
British character actress, often in tarty roles.
Educating Rita (AAN) 83. She'll Be Wearing Pink Pajamas 84. Car Trouble 86. Prick Up Your Ears 87. Personal Services 87. Buster 88. Mack the Knife 89. Killing Dad 89. Stepping Out 91. Just Like a Woman 92. The Clothes in the Wardrobe (aka The Summer House) 93. Wide-Eyed and Legless (TV) 93. The Wedding Gift (TV) 94. Pat and Margaret (TV) 94, etc.

¶ When I think of the future I think of doing my washing so I've something to wear tomorrow. – *J.W.*

Walters, Thorley (1913–1991).
British comedy actor on stage and screen from 1934. Film parts usually cameos, as incompetent officers, etc.
They Were Sisters 45. Private's Progress 56. Carleton Browne of the FO 58. Two-Way Stretch 60. Murder She Said 62. Ring of Spies 64. Joey Boy 65. *Rotten to the Core* 65. *Dracula, Prince of Darkness* 65. The Wrong Box 66. Frankenstein Must Be Destroyed 69. Vampire Circus 72. The Adventure of Sherlock Holmes' Smarter Brother 75. The People That Time Forgot 78. The Wildcats of St Trinian's 80. The Sign of Four (TV) 83. The Little Drummer Girl 84, etc.

Walthall, Henry B. (1878–1936).
American leading man of the silent screen, in films from 1909.
In Old Kentucky 09. A Convict's Sacrifice 10. The Birth of a Nation 14. The Raven 15. Ghosts 15. His Robe of Honour 18. Single Wives 23. The Scarlet Letter 25. The Barrier 26. Abraham Lincoln 31. Police Court 32. Laughing at Life 33. Viva Villa 34. Dante's Inferno 35. A Tale of Two Cities 35. China Clipper 36, many others.

Walton, Tony (1934–).
British production designer. He was formerly married to actress Julie Andrews (1959–69).
Mary Poppins 64. Fahrenheit 451 66. A Funny Thing Happened on the Way to the Forum 66. The Seagull 68. Boy Friend 71. Murder on the Orient Express 74. The Wiz 78. All That Jazz 79. Just Tell Me What You Want 80. Prince of the City 81. Deathtrap 82. The Goodbye People 84. Heartburn 86. The Glass Menagerie 87. Regarding Henry 91, etc.

Walton, Sir William (1902–1983).
British composer whose film scores include *Henry V* 44. *Hamlet* 48. *Richard III* 56.

Wambaugh, Joseph (1937–).
American novelist, an ex-policeman who capitalized on his experience and tends to rub his readers' noses in the gutter. Films resulting include *The New Centurions*, *The Onion Field*, *The Black Marble*, *The Choirboys*.

W.A.M.P.A.S. (Western Association of Motion Picture Advertisers).
A group of publicity executives who, from 1922 to 1934, gave annual certificates of merit to promising female starlets, known as 'Wampas baby stars'. Among those who succeeded were Bessie Love (nominated 1922), Laura la Plante 23, Clara Bow 24. Mary Astor 26, Joan Crawford 26, Dolores del Rio 26, Janet Gaynor 26, Lupe Velez 28, Jean Arthur 29, Loretta Young 29, Jean Blondell 31, Anita Louise 31, Ginger Rogers 32.

Wanamaker, Sam (1919–1993).
American stage actor and director who also appeared in films; moved to Britain where he set up a trust to build a replica of Shakespeare's Globe Theatre in London.
My Girl Tisa 48. Give Us This Day 50. Mr Denning Drives North 51. The Secret 55. The Criminal 60. Taras Bulba 62. The Man in the Middle 64. Those Magnificent Men in Their Flying Machines 65. The Spy Who Came in from the Cold 65. Warning Shot 66. The Day the Fish Came Out 67. File of the Golden Goose (d only) 69. The Executioner (d only) 69. Catlow (d only) 72. Mousey (TV) 73. The Sell Out 75. Voyage of the Damned 76. Sinbad and the Eye of the Tiger (d only) 77. Holocaust (TV) 78. Death on the Nile 78. Private Benjamin 80. The Competition 80. The Aviator 84. Irreconcilable Differences 84. Raw Deal 86. Superman IV 87. Baby Boom 87. Guilty by Suspicion 91. Pure Luck 91. Wild Justice (TV) 93, etc.

Wang, Wayne (1949–).
Hong Kong-born director and screenwriter who studied in America and worked in Hong Kong before returning to the States to make films, mainly about the Chinese community there.
A Man, a Woman and a Killer (d) 75. Chan Is Missing (wd) 81. Dim Sum: A Little Bit of Heart (d) 85. Slam Dance (d) 87. Eat a Bowl of Tea (d) 89. Life Is Cheap . . . but Toilet Paper Is Expensive (d) 89. The Joy Luck Club 93, etc.

Wang Yu, Jimmy.
Chinese leading man and kung fu expert.
The Legend of Seven Golden Vampires 74. The Man from Hong Kong 75. Invincible Sword 78. Fury of King Boxer 83. Kung Fu Hero II 90, etc.

Wanger, Walter (1894–1968) (W. Feuchtwanger).
American independent producer who during a long career held at various times senior executive posts with major studios.
Queen Christina 33. The President Vanishes 35. Private Worlds 35. Mary Burns Fugitive 35. The Trail of the Lonesome Pine 36. *You Only Live Once* 37. History is Made at Night 37. 52nd Street 38. Stand In 38. Blockade 38. Trade Winds 38. Algiers 38. *Stagecoach* 39. *Foreign Correspondent* 40. The Long Voyage Home 40. *Scarlet Street* 45. The Lost Moment 47. Tap Roots 48. Joan of Arc 48. Riot in Cell Block Eleven 54. *Invasion of the Body Snatchers* 55. I Want to Live 58. Cleopatra 62.

¶ Nothing is as cheap as a hit, no matter how much it costs. – *W.W.*

He always wanted to be European. – *James Mason*

War and Peace.
The main film versions of Tolstoy's epic novel were a Russian one of 1916; King Vidor's of 1955, with Henry Fonda and Audrey Hepburn, photographed by Jack Cardiff and Aldo Tonti; and Sergei Bondarchuk's seven-hour colossus of 1964, photographed by Anatole Petrinsky.

war heroes
who have become the subject of biopics include Eddie Rickenbacker (Fred MacMurray, *Captain Eddie*); Audie Murphy (himself, *To Hell and Back*); Guy Gabaldon (Jeffrey Hunter, *Hell to Eternity*); Alvin York (Gary Cooper, *Sergeant York*); Douglas Bader (Kenneth More, *Reach for the Sky*); Guy Gibson (Richard Todd, *The Dam Busters*); Ernie Pyle (Burgess Meredith, *The Story of G.I. Joe*); John Hoskins (Sterling Hayden, *The Eternal Sea*).

Ward, Burt (1945–) (Herbert Jervis).
American juvenile of the 60s who played Robin in TV's *Batman* series, then almost disappeared from view. He appeared in some low-budget exploitation movies in the late 80s and founded Logical Figments, a special effects, animation and video editing company, in 1994.

Batman 66. Kill Crazy 89. Robo-C.H.I.C.K. 89. Robot Ninja 89. Virgin High 90. Smooth Talker 90.

Ward, David S. (1945–).
American screenwriter and director.

Steelyard Blues (w) 72. The Sting (w) (AA) 73. Cannery Row (wd) 81. The Sting II (w) 82. Major League (wd) 89. King Ralph (wd) 90. Sleepless in Seattle (co-w, AAN) 93. The Program (co-w, d) 93. Major League II (d) 94, etc.

Ward, Edward (–1971).
American composer.

Kismet 31. Great Expectations 34. The Mystery of Edwin Drood 35. Navy Blue and Gold 37. Stablemates 38. Thunder Afloat 39. Mr and Mrs Smith 41. Phantom of the Opera (AAN) 43. The Climax 44. Salome Where She Danced 45. Copacabana 47. The Babe Ruth Story 48, etc.

Ward, Fannie (1865–1952).
American stage actress, a famous beauty of her time who in middle age began a Hollywood film career playing parts too young for her, and was the inspiration of novel and film *Mr Skeffington*.

The Marriage of Kitty 15. The Cheat 15. The Years of the Locust 16. The Yellow Ticket 18. Innocent 18. A Japanese Nightingale 18. Common Clay 19, etc.

Ward, Fred (1942–).
American leading man

■ Escape from Alcatraz 82. The Right Stuff 83. Silkwood 83. Remo Williams 85. Big Business 88. Off Limits 88. The Prince of Pennsylvania 88. Tremors 90. Miami Blues 90. Henry and June 90. The Dark Wind 91. Lovecraft (aka Cast a Deadly Spell) (TV) 91. The Player 92. Thunderheart 92. Equinox 92. Short Cuts 93. Two Small Bodies 93. Naked Gun 33⅓: The Final Insult 94.

Ward, Michael (1915–).
British comic actor usually seen as nervous photographer or twee shopwalker.

An Ideal Husband 47. Sleeping Car to Trieste 48. Street Corner 53. Private's Progress 55. I'm All

Right Jack 59. Carry On Screaming 66. Frankenstein and the Monster from Hell 74. Revenge of the Pink Panther 78, etc.

Ward, Polly (1908–) (Byno Poluski).
British-born leading lady of several 30s comedies.

Shooting Stars 28. His Lordship 32. The Old Curiosity Shop 34. Feather Your Nest 37. Thank Evans 38. It's in the Air 38. Bulldog Drummond Sees It Through 40. Women Aren't Angels 42, etc.

Ward, Rachel (1957–).
British-born leading lady, in America at first as a model.

Sharky's Machine 81. Dead Men Don't Wear Plaid 82. The Thorn Birds (TV) 83. The Good Wife 86. Hotel Colonial 87. How to Get Ahead in Advertising 89. After Dark, My Sweet 90. And the Sea Will Tell (TV) 91. Christopher Columbus: The Discovery 92. Wide Sargasso Sea 93. The Ascent 94, etc.

Ward, Simon (1941–).
British leading actor of the 70s.

■ Frankenstein Must Be Destroyed 69. Quest for Love 70. I Start Counting 71. *Young Winston* 72. Hitler – the Last Ten Days 73. Dracula (TV) 73. The Three Musketeers 74. The Four Musketeers 75. Deadly Strangers 75. All Creatures Great and Small 75. Aces High 76. Holocaust 2000 77. Children of Rage 77. Battle Flag 77. Dominique 78. Zulu Dawn 79. La Sabina 79. The Monster Club 80. Supergirl 84. The Corsican Brothers (TV) 85. Leave All Fair 85. Double X 92.

Ward, Sophie (1965–).
English actress, the daughter of Simon Ward.

Young Sherlock Holmes 85. Little Dorrit 87. Aria 88. A Summer Story 88. The Monk 90. A Demon in My View 92, etc.

Ward, Vincent (1956–).
New Zealand director and screenwriter.

Vigil 84. The Navigator 88. Alien³ (story) 92. Map of the Human Heart 93, etc.

Ward, Warwick (1891–1967).
Elegant English leading actor of silents who also worked in French, German, and American films in the 20s. He became manager of Welwyn Studios in the mid-30s and a producer and screenwriter in the 40s.

The Silver Lining 19. Wuthering Heights 20. The Mayor of Casterbridge 21. Bulldog Drummond 23. *Variety* (aka Vaudeville) (Ger.) 25. Madame Sans-Gêne (US) 25. The Informer 29. Stamboul 31. Ariane 34. The Man from Morocco (p, co-w) 44. Quiet Weekend (p) 46. My Brother Jonathan (p) 47. The Dancing Years (p, co-w) 49. Isn't Life Wonderful (p) 52. The Elstree Story (narrator) 52, etc.

Warden, Jack (1920–).
Burly American character actor, also on stage and TV.

From Here to Eternity 53. *Twelve Angry Men* 57. Edge of the City 57. *The Bachelor Party* 57. Escape from Zahrain 62. Mirage 65. Blindfold 65. Welcome to the Club 70. Who Is Harry Kellerman . . .? 71. Billy Two Hats 73. The Apprenticeship of Duddy Kravitz 74. Shampoo (AAN) 75. All the President's Men 76. Voyage of the Damned 76. The White Buffalo 77. Heaven Can Wait (AAN) 78. Death on the Nile 78. The Champ 79. And Justice for All 79. Used Cars 80. So Fine 81. A Private Battle (TV) 81. The Verdict 82. Hobson's Choice (TV) 83. The Aviator 84. Crackers 84. September 87. The Presidio 88. Everybody

Wins 90. Problem Child 90. Problem Child 2 91. Passed Away 92. Guilty as Sin 93. Bullets over Broadway 94, etc.

TV series: Mr Peepers 53–55. The Asphalt Jungle 60. The Wackiest Ship in the Army 65. N.Y.P.D. 67–68. The Bad News Bears 79. *Crazy Like a Fox* 84–85.

The Ware Case.
George Bancroft's play, about a murderer who gets away with his crime but then does the decent thing and kills himself when he discovers his wife and lawyer are in love, has been filmed three times in Britain: in 1917, with Matheson Lang in the lead; in 1928, with Stewart Rome; and in 1938, with Clive Brook.

Warhol, Andy (1927–1987).
American pop artist and 'underground' film-maker of the 60s.

Sleep 63. Blow Job 64. Harlot 65. The Chelsea Girls (shown on two screens side by side, with different images) 66. F**k, or Blue Movie 69. Trash (p only) 70. Flesh (p only) 71. Bad 76, etc.

¶ Sex is the biggest nothing of all time. – *A.W.*

It would be very glamorous to be reincarnated as a giant ring on Elizabeth Taylor's finger. – *A.W.*

Warner Brothers Pictures Inc.
is a family affair started in 1923 by four American exhibitor brothers. After a very shaky start it soared to pre-eminence through their gamble on talking pictures in the shape of *The Jazz Singer* and *The Singing Fool*. Through the 30s and 40s the company kept its popularity through tough gangster films starring James Cagney, Edward G. Robinson and Humphrey Bogart, and musicals with Dick Powell and Ruby Keeler; and its prestige by exposés like *Confessions of a Nazi Spy* and *Mission to Moscow* and biographies of Zola, Pasteur, Ehrlich and Reuter. Other Warner stars included Bette Davis and Errol Flynn, both enormously popular with all classes. Warner films were not usually over-budgeted but contrived to look immaculate through solid production values and star performances. Since 1950 the company's product has been more variable, as deals have had to be done with independent producers, and there has been a patchy flirtation with TV; yet on the serious side directors like Kazan have been encouraged, popular taste is taken care of by spectaculars like *My Fair Lady* and *The Great Race*, and the company took a calculated risk (which paid off in spades) with *Who's Afraid of Virginia Woolf?* In the mid-60s came a merger with Seven Arts, and in 1969 the company was taken over by a conglomerate. In 1989 the company merged with the publishing group Time Inc. to become Time-Warner.

During the 80s the famous production company seemed to be kept solvent by Clint Eastwood toughies, although it had a success with the fast-paced action film *Lethal Weapon* and immediately repeated the process with satisfying results: the movie had reached its second sequel by 1992. *Gremlins*, a hit in 1984, begat *Gremlins II: The New Batch*, which did less well. Its dark fantasy *Batman* was the top box-office attraction of 1989, and *Batman Returns* became a hit in 1992. *Robin Hood: Prince of Thieves* was a surprise success in 1991. Fortunately, there has so far been no attempt to repeat it. The company also had a monumental flop with the costly *Hudson Hawk*, which brought Bruce Willis's career to a temporary halt. But the company was soon enjoying great success, with a succession of hit films, including *Batman Returns*,

Lethal Weapon 3, The Bodyguard, Sommersby and *The Fugitive.*

Various books have been published about its glory days, including: 1986, *Inside Warner Brothers 1935–51* by Rudy Behlmer (a collection of memos).

¶ Working for Warner Brothers is like fucking a porcupine. It's a hundred pricks against one. – *Wilson Mizner*

I would rather take a fifty-mile hike than crawl through a book. I prefer to skip the long ones and get a synopsis from the story department. – *Jack Warner*

This studio has more suspensions than the Golden Gate Bridge. – *Humphrey Bogart*

Warner, David (1941–).
Lanky British actor who after success in classical theatre (he was a notable Hamlet in the 60s) and in British films went to Hollywood, where he has tended to be typecast as a villain in mainly second-rate movies.
■ Tom Jones (as Blifil) 63. The Deadly Affair 66. *Morgan* 66. Work is a Four-Letter Word 68. A Midsummer Night's Dream 68. *The Bofors Gun* 68. The Fixer 68. The Seagull 68. Michael Kohlhaas 69. The Ballad of Cable Hogue 70. Perfect Friday 70. The Engagement 70. The French Lieutenant's Woman 71. Straw Dogs 71. A Doll's House 73. Mr Quilp 75. Little Malcolm 75. The Omen 76. Victory at Entebbe (TV) 76. Age of Innocence 77. The Disappearance 77. Cross of Iron 77. Providence 77. The Thirty-Nine Steps 78. *Holocaust* (TV) (as Heydrich) 78. Silver Bears 78. The Concorde – Airport '79 79. Time after Time (as Jack the Ripper) 79. Nightwing 79. The Islands 80. Time Bandits 81. Iron 82. The Man with Two Brains 83. Company of Wolves 84. A Christmas Carol (TV) 84. Hansel and Gretel 87. Mr North 88. Waxwork 88. Hanna's War 88. Star Trek V: The Final Frontier 89. Office Party 89. Teenage Mutant Ninja Turtles II: The Secret of the Ooze 91. Star Trek VI: The Undiscovered Country 91. Lovecraft (aka Cast a Deadly Spell) (TV) 91. Drive 91. Dark at Noon (La Terreur de Midi) 92. The Unnameable Returns 92. Pretty Princess (It.) 93. Necronomicon 93. Tryst 94.

Warner, H. B. (1876–1958) (Henry Byron Warner-Lickford).
Distinguished British actor, on stage from 1883; in Hollywood as film actor from around 1917.
The Beggar of Cawnpore 15. The Man White 19. One Hour Before Dawn 20. Zaza 23. *King of Kings* (as Jesus) 27. Sorrell and Son 27. The Divine Lady 28. The Trial of Mary Dugan 29. Five Star Final 31. *Mr Deeds Goes to Town* 36. Lost Horizon (AAN) 37. *Victoria the Great* 37. You Can't Take It With You 38. Bulldog Drummond Strikes Back 39. The Rains Came 39. All That Money Can Buy 41. Topper Returns 41. The Corsican Brothers 41. It's a Wonderful Life 46. Prince of Thieves 48. Sunset Boulevard 50. Savage Drums 51. The Ten Commandments 56, many others.
◆ For bringing dignity to a wildly disparate collection of films. *Lost Horizon.*

Warner, Jack (1894–1981) (Jack Waters).
Genial British character actor, former music-hall comedian; TV's 'Dixon of Dock Green'. The success of *Holiday Camp* led to him starring as Joe Huggett in several films and a long-running radio sit-com, *Meet the Huggetts* (1953–61).
Autobiography: 1975, *Jack of All Trades.*
The Dummy Talks (debut) 43. *The Captive Heart* 46. Hue and Cry 46. It Always Rains on Sunday 47. Holiday Camp 47. *Here Come the Huggetts* 48. The

Huggetts Abroad 49. *The Blue Lamp* 50. Valley of Eagles 51. Scrooge 51. The Quatermass Experiment 55. Home and Away 56. Carve Her Name with Pride 58. *Jigsaw* 62, many others.
~Catchphrase: Mind my bike (from the radio series *Garrison Theatre*).

Warner, Jack L. (1892–1978).
American executive producer, last member of the four Warner Brothers who started up a small production company in the 20s and pioneered sound pictures with *The Jazz Singer* 27. The other brothers: Albert, Harry M., and Sam.
Autobiography: 1965, *My First Hundred Years in Hollywood.*
Biography: 1990, *Clown Prince of Hollywood* by Bob Thomas.
RECENT PRODUCTIONS: *My Fair Lady* 64. *Camelot* 67. '1776' 72. Dirty Little Billy 73.
See also: *Warner Brothers.*
◆ For running a studio with the discipline of a prison, and living to see the results endure. *A Midsummer Night's Dream.*

¶ You're nothing if you don't have a studio. Now I'm just another millionaire, and there are a lot of 'em around. – *J.W., in retirement in Palm Springs*

I have a theory of relatives too. Don't hire 'em. – *J.W. to Einstein*

If his brothers hadn't hired him, he'd have been out of work. – *Jack Warner Jnr*

He existed behind a self-made wall. Besides, a lot of him wasn't that nice to know. At times he gloried in being a no-good sonofabitch. – *Jack Warner Jnr*

He was a generous host, a big gambler at work and at play, and with superb confidence he put his money where his mouth was. – *David Niven*

He bore no grudge against those he had wronged. – *Simone Signoret*

I can't see what J. W. can do with an Oscar. It can't say yes. – *Al Jolson*

A man who would rather tell a bad joke than make a good movie. – *Jack Benny*

Warnercolor.
Actually Eastmancolor, though it always looked as though it had had a blue rinse.

Warren, C. Denier (1889–1971).
Chubby American character comedian, in British films; vaudeville experience.
Counsel's Opinion 33. Kentucky Minstrels 34. A Fire Has Been Arranged 35. Cotton Queen 37. Trouble Brewing 39. Kiss the Bride Goodbye 44. Old Mother Riley, Headmistress 50. Bluebeard's Ten Honeymoons 60, etc.

Warren, Charles Marquis (1917–1990).
American writer-director. Moved into TV and became creator and executive producer of *Gunsmoke, Rawhide, The Virginian,* etc.
Little Big Horn 51. Hellgate 52. Arrowhead 53. Flight to Tangier 54. Seven Angry Men 55. The Black Whip 56. Charro (pd) 69, etc.

Warren, Harry (1893–1981) (Salvatore Guaragno).
American songwriter, mainly with Al Dubin; busy on many Warner musicals of the early 30s, they made a personal appearance in *42nd Street.*

Warren, Jennifer (1941–).
American general-purpose actress.
Night Moves 75. Slap Shot 77. Another Man Another Chance 77. Ice Castles 78. Paper Dolls (TV) 84. Amazons (TV) 84, etc.

Warren, Lesley Ann (1946–).
American leading lady.
The Happiest Millionaire 67. Seven in Darkness (TV) 69. Assignment Munich (TV) 72. 79 Park Avenue (TV) 77. Beulah Land (TV) 80. Victor/Victoria (AAN) 82. A Night in Heaven 83. Evergreen (TV) 84. Choose Me 84. Songwriter 84. Clue 85. Burglar 87. Cop 88. Worth Winning 89. Life Stinks 91. Color of Night 94, etc.

Warren, Robert Penn (1905–1989).
American novelist.
All the King's Men 49. Band of Angels 57.

Warrender, Harold (1903–1953).
British stage and screen actor.
Friday the Thirteenth 33. Contraband 40. Sailors Three 41. Scott of the Antarctic 49. Pandora and the Flying Dutchman 51. Where No Vultures Fly 51. Intimate Relations 53, etc.

Warrick, Ruth (1915–).
American leading lady of the 40s. Former radio singer.
Autobiography: 1980, *The Confessions of Phoebe Tyler.*
Citizen Kane (debut) 41. The Corsican Brothers 41. Journey into Fear 42. Forever and a Day 43. Mr Winkle Goes to War 44. Guest in the House 44. China Sky 45. Swell Guy 47. Arch of Triumph 48. Three Husbands 50. Killer with a Label 50. Let's Dance 52. Ride beyond Vengeance 65. How to Steal the World 68. The Great Bank Robbery 69. The Returning 83. Deathmask 84, etc.
TV series: Father of the Bride 61. Peyton Place 65.

Warwick, John (1905–1972) (John McIntosh Beattie).
Australian leading man, later character actor, in British films, including many of the 'Scotland Yard' series as police inspector.
Down on the Farm 35. Lucky Jade 37. The Face at the Window 39. Danny Boy 40. The Missing Million 42. Dancing with Crime 48. Street Corner 53. Up to His Neck 54. Just My Luck 57. Horrors of the Black Museum 59.

Warwick, Robert (1878–1965) (Robert Taylor Bien).
American character actor, adept at executives and heavy fathers. A star of such silent films as *A Modern Othello, The Mad Lover, Thou Art the Man.*
So Big 32. Night Life of the Gods 35. A Tale of Two Cities 35. The Life of Emile Zola 37. The Adventures of Robin Hood 38. Sullivan's Travels 41. The Palm Beach Story 42. I Married a Witch 43. Gentleman's Agreement 47. Francis 49. Sugarfoot 51. Mississippi Gambler 53. Lady Godiva of Coventry 55. Night of the Quarter Moon 59, many others.

Washbourne, Mona (1903–1988).
British stage character actress.
Wide Boy 48. Child's Play 53. Doctor in the House 54. The Good Companions 57. Brides of Dracula 60. Billy Liar 63. *Night Must Fall* 63. One Way Pendulum 64. *My Fair Lady* (US) 64. The Third Day (US) 65. Mrs Brown You've Got a Lovely Daughter 68. Fragment of Fear 70. What Became of Jack and Jill? 71. O Lucky Man 73. Stevie 78. Brideshead Revisited (TV) 82, etc.

Washburn, Bryant (1889–1963).
American romantic hero of the silent screen.
The Blindness of Virtue 15. Venus in the East 18. The Parasite 25. Swing High 30. Sutter's Gold 36, many others.

Washington, Denzel (1954–).
American leading actor. By 1994, his price per film was more than $6 million.
Carbon Copy 81. Licence to Kill 84. A Soldier's Story 84. Power 86. Cry Freedom (AAN) 87. For Queen and Country 88. Reunion 88. *Glory* (AA) 89. The Mighty Quinn 89. Heart Condition 90. Mo' Better Blues 90. Mississippi Masala 91. Ricochet 91. *Malcolm X* 92. Much Ado about Nothing 93. Philadelphia 93. The Pelican Brief 93. Crimson Tide 95, etc.
TV series: St Elsewhere 82–88.

Washington, Fredi (1903–1994) (Fredericka Carolyn Washington).
American leading actress who made an impact in *Imitation of Life*, playing a black woman who could pass as white, but who never got another comparable role. She began as a dancer in Broadway musicals and was one of the founders of the Negro Actors Guild, working on stage until her retirement.
The Emperor Jones 33. Imitation of Life 34. One Mile from Heaven 37, etc.

Washington, George (1732–1799).
The first American President, the lad who could not tell a lie, has been impersonated in many films, including *Alexander Hamilton* (Alan Mowbray, who also had the role in *The Phantom President* and *Where Do We Go from Here?*); *America* (Arthur Dewey); *The Howards of Virginia* (George Houston); *The Remarkable Andrew* (Montagu Love); *Unconquered* (Richard Gaines); *John Paul Jones* (John Crawford); *Lafayette* (Howard St John).

Washington, Ned (1901–1976).
American composer with wide show-business experience.
Show of Shows 29. Illegal 32. A Night at the Opera 35. Romance in the Dark 38. Pinocchio 40. Dumbo 41. For Whom the Bell Tolls 43. Passage to Marseilles 44. The Uninvited 44. Green Dolphin Street 47. My Foolish Heart 50. Miss Sadie Thompson 53. The High and the Mighty 54. The Man from Laramie 55. Fire Down Below 57. Gunfight at the OK Corral 57. The Unforgiven 60. The Last Sunset 61. The Fall of the Roman Empire 64. Ship of Fools 65. Five Card Stud 68, many others.

Wasson, Craig (1954–).
American general-purpose actor.
The Boys in Company C 77. Rollercoaster 77. Go Tell the Spartans 78. The Outsider 80. Schizoid 80. Four Friends 81. Ghost Story 81. Body Double 84. The Men's Club 86. A Nightmare on Elm Street 3: Dream Warriors 87. Midnight Fear 90. Malcolm X 92, etc.

water,
in inconvenient quantity, played a dramatic part in *Way Down East; Noah's Ark; The Rains Came* and its remake *The Rains of Ranchipur; The Bible; Floods of Fear; The Hurricane; Campbell's Kingdom; When Worlds Collide; Rain; Whistling in Dixie; Foreign Correspondent; Who Was That Lady?;* and no doubt a hundred others.
See also: *rain*.

waterfront
films have turned up frequently. Among the more seriously-intended are *On the Waterfront, Anna Christie, Waterfront,* and *Slaughter on Tenth Avenue;* melodramas include *The Mob,* the *Tugboat Annie* films, and *I Cover the Waterfront.* Laurel and Hardy worked the milieu in *The Live Ghost.* TV series include yet another *Waterfront.*

Waterhouse, Keith (1929–).
British light journalist and novelist. His *Billy Liar* was successful also as play and film. With Willis Hall he wrote screenplays including *Whistle Down the Wind, A Kind of Loving, Pretty Polly.*

Waterloo Bridge.
Robert Sherwood's sentimental drama, about a ballerina who heads for the gutter after her wealthy lover is reported killed in action and commits suicide when he returns, has been filmed three times: James Whale directed a version in 1931 starring Mae Clark and Kent Douglass; Mervyn Le Roy remade it in 1940 with Vivien Leigh and Robert Taylor; and a lesser version, *Gaby*, updating the story to the Second World War, followed in 1956, directed by Curtis Bernhardt, with Leslie Caron, John Kerr, and a happy ending.

Waterman, Dennis (1948–).
British juvenile of the 60s, tough TV hero of the 70s.
Pirates of Blood River 61. *Up the Junction* 67. My Lover My Son 69. A Smashing Bird I Used to Know 69. Scars of Dracula 70. Fright 70. Man in the Wilderness 71. The Belstone Fox 73. The Sweeney 77. Sweeney Two 78, etc.
TV series: Fair Exchange 62. *The Sweeney* 74–78. Minder 79–89. On the Up 92. Stay Lucky 93.

Waters, Ethel (1896–1977).
Distinguished American actress and singer.
Autobiography: 1953, *His Eye Is on the Sparrow.*
On with the Show 29. Tales of Manhattan 42. Cabin in the Sky 43. Pinky (AAN) 49. *Member of the Wedding* 52. The Sound and the Fury 59, etc.
TV series: Beulah 50–53.

¶ Every time I tried to help her, she'd roll her eyes to the heavens and say, 'God is my director!' How can you argue with that? – *Fred Zinnemann*

Waters, John.
Australian leading actor.
End Play 75. Eliza Fraser 76. The Getting of Wisdom 77. Weekend of Shadows 78. Breaker Morant 80. Attack Force Z 82. Bushfire Moon 87. Grievous Bodily Harm 88. Boulevard of Broken Dreams 88, etc.

Waters, John (1946–).
American director and screenwriter of cult comedies in deliberately bad taste.
Autobiography: 1990, *Shock Value.*
■ Mondo Trasho 70. Multiple Maniacs 71. Pink Flamingos 72. Female Trouble 75. Desperate Living 77. Polyester 81. Something Wild 86. Hairspray 88. Cry-Baby 90. Serial Mom 94.

¶ I've been called the 'King of Sleaze', the 'Pope of Trash', the 'Prince of Puke', and recently new ones have been added – the 'Duke of Dirt', the 'Ambassador of Anguish' and the 'Anal Anarchist'. All are fine by me, but I think the 'Pope of Trash' sounds more dignified. – *J.W.*
Often I wish I was a girl just so I could get an abortion. – *J.W.*
In America it doesn't matter what you've done as long as you're famous. – *J.W*

Waters, Russell (1908–1982).
British character actor usually in meek and mild parts. The 'hero' of many of Richard Massingham's short and light-hearted instructional films.

The Woman in the Hall 47. The Happiest Days of Your Life 50. The Maggie 54. Left, Right and Centre 59, many others.

Waterston, Sam (1940–).
American general-purpose actor.
A Time for Giving 69. Savages 72. A Delicate Balance 73. *The Great Gatsby* 74. Rancho de Luxe 75. Capricorn One 78. Interiors 78. Eagle's Wing 79. Sweet William 79. Heaven's Gate 80. Hopscotch 80. Oppenheimer (TV) 81. Q.E.D. (TV) 81. Finnegan Begin Again (TV) 84. The Killing Fields (AAN) 84. September 87. Welcome Home 89. Crimes and Misdemeanors 89. Lantern Hill (TV) 90. Mindwalk 90. The Man in the Moon 91. A Captive in the Land 91. Serial Mom 94. David's Mother (TV) 94, etc.
TV series: Q.E.D. 82. I'll Fly Away 91.

Watkin, David (1925–).
British cinematographer.
The Knack 64. Help 65. The Marat/Sade 66. How I Won the War 67. The Charge of the Light Brigade 67. The Bed Sitting Room 69. Catch 22 70. The Devils 71. The Boy Friend 71. A Delicate Balance 73. The Three Musketeers 74. Robin and Marian 76. Chariots of Fire 81. Yentl 83. Out of Africa (AA) 85. Six Bandits 86. Moonstruck 87. Masquerade 88. The Good Mother 88. Last Rites 88. Journey to the Center of the Earth 89. Memphis Belle 90. Hamlet 90. Object of Beauty 91. This Boy's Life 93. Bopha! 93. Milk Money 94, etc.

Watkin, Pierre (1889–1960).
American character actor often seen as lawyer, doctor or kindly father.
Dangerous 35. Pride of the Yankees 41. Whistling in Dixie 43. Shanghai Chest 46. Knock On Any Door 59. The Dark Page 51. Johnny Dark 54, many others.

Watkins, Peter (1937–).
British director from TV (*Culloden, The War Game*), now based in Sweden.
■ Privilege 67. Punishment Park 71. Edvard Munch 75. 70-Talets 75. Fallen 75. Evening Land 77. The Journey (TV) 87.

Watling, Jack (1923–).
Boyish British character actor.
Sixty Glorious Years 38. Journey Together 45. The Courtneys of Curzon Street 47. Quartet 48. The Winslow Boy 48. Meet Mr Lucifer 53. The Sea Shall Not Have Them 55. The Admirable Crichton 57. A Night to Remember 58. Mary Had a Little 61. 11 Harrowhouse 74, many others.

Watson, Bobs (1931–).
American boy actor of the 30s and 40s; noted for his ability to weep at the drop of a hat. Now a Methodist minister.
In Old Chicago 38. Kentucky 39. *On Borrowed Time* 39. Dr Kildare's Crisis 41. Men of Boys' Town 41. The Bold and the Brave 56. First to Fight 67, etc.
TV series: The Jim Backus Show 60.

Watson, Jack (1921–).
Tough-looking British general-purpose actor. He began in music hall with his father, comedian Nosmo King (Vernon Watson).
Konga 61. This Sporting Life 62. The Hill 65. Tobruk 67. *The Strange Affair* 67. Every Home Should Have One 70. The Mackenzie Break 71. Kidnapped 72. Juggernaut 76. Schizo 77. The Wild Geese 79. The Sea Wolves 80. Love and Reason (TV) 93, etc.

Watson, Lucile (1879–1962).
Canadian character actress with stage experience; usually in imperious roles.
■ What Every Woman Knows 34. The Bishop Misbehaves 35. A Woman Rebels 36. The Garden of Allah 36. Three Smart Girls 36. The Young in Heart 38. Sweethearts 38. Made for Each Other 39. The Women 39. Florian 40. *Waterloo Bridge* 40. Mr and Mrs Smith 41. Rage in Heaven 41. Footsteps in the Dark 41. The Great Lie 41. Model Wife 41. *Watch on the Rhine* (AAN) 43. Till We Meet Again 44. The Thin Man Goes Home 44. Uncertain Glory 44. My Reputation 46. Tomorrow Is Forever 46. Never Say Goodbye 46. *The Razor's Edge* 46. Song of the South 46. Ivy 47. The Emperor Waltz 48. Julia Misbehaves 48. That Wonderful Urge 48. Little Women 49. Everybody Does It 49. Harriet Craig 50. Let's Dance 50. My Forbidden Past 51.

Watson, Minor (1889–1965).
American character actor who often played lawyers or kindly fathers.
Rescuing Dave 13. No. 28 Diplomat 14. 24 Hours 31. Our Betters 33. Babbitt 34. When's Your Birthday? 37. Boys' Town 38. Moon over Miami 41. The Big Shot 42. The Virginian 46. The File on Thelma Jordon 49. Mister 880 50. My Son John 51. Trapeze 56, etc.

Watson, Moray (1928–).
British light actor.
The Grass is Greener 65. Operation Crossbow 65. Every Home should Have One 70. The Sea Wolves 80. Crazy Like a Fox (TV) 87, etc.

Watson, Robert (1888–1965).
American character actor who became famous for his resemblance to Hitler; played the lead in The Hitler Gang 43, and other films of this type.
Moonlight and Melody 33. Mary of Scotland 36. The Devil with Hitler 42. Nazty Nuisance 43. The Big Clock 48. Red Hot and Blue 49. Singin' in the Rain 52. The Story of Mankind 57, etc.

Watson, Wylie (1889–1966). (John Wylie Robertson).
British character actor, usually in 'little man' roles; formerly in music hall.
■ For the Love of Mike 32. Leave It to Me 33. Hawleys of the High Street 33. *The Thirty-Nine Steps* (as Mr Memory) 35. Black Mask 35. Radio Lover 36. Please Teacher 37. Why Pick on Me? 37. Paradise for Two 37. Queer Cargo 38. Yes Madam 38. Jamaica Inn 39. She Couldn't Say No 39. Pack Up Your Troubles 40. Bulldog Sees It Through 40. Danny Boy 41. My Wife's Family 41. The Saint Meets the Tiger 41. The Flemish Farm 43. The Lamp Still Burns 43. Tawny Pipit 44. Kiss the Bride Goodbye 44. Don't Take It to Heart 44. Waterloo Road 45. The World Owes Me a Living 45. Strawberry Roan 45. Don Chicago 45. Waltz Time 45. Murder in Reverse 45. The Trojan Brothers 46. The Years Between 46. Girl in a Million 46. Temptation Harbour 47. Fame Is the Spur 47. Brighton Rock 47. My Brother Jonathan 48. *London Belongs to Me* 48. No Room at the Inn 48. Things Happen at Night 48. The History of Mr Polly 49. *Whisky Galore* 49. Train of Events 49. Your Witness 50. Morning Departure 50. Shadow of the Past 50. The Magnet 50. Happy Go Lovely 51. *The Sundowners* 61.

Watt, Harry (1906–1987).
British director with varied early experience before joining GPO Film Unit as assistant in 1931.
Autobiography: 1974, *Don't Look at the Camera*.
Night Mail 36. North Sea 38. Squadron 992 40. Target for Tonight 41. *Nine Men* (& w) 44. Fiddlers

Three 44. The Overlanders 46. Eureka Stockade 48. Where No Vultures Fly 51. West of Zanzibar 53. The Siege of Pinchgut 59, etc.

Wattis, Richard (1912–1975).
Bespectacled British character comedian with stage experience.
The Happiest Days of Your Life 49. The Clouded Yellow 51. Hobson's Choice 54. I Am a Camera 55. Simon and Laura 55. The Prince and the Showgirl 58. The VIPs 63. Moll Flanders 65. Up Jumped a Swagman 65. Wonderwall 68. Games that Lovers Play 69. That's Your Funeral 73. Diamonds on Wheels 73. Hot Property 73, many others.
TV series: Dick and the Duchess 59. Sykes (through 60s).

Waugh, Evelyn (1903–1966).
English novelist whose combination of snobbery and social satire has appealed to directors of period movies.
The Loved One 65. Decline and Fall 68. Brideshead Revisited (TV) 82. Scoop (TV) 87. A Handful of Dust 88.

Waxman, Franz (1906–1967) (Franz Wachsmann).
German composer, in America from 1934.
Bride of Frankenstein 35. Sutter's Gold 36. Fury 36. Captains Courageous 38. The Young in Heart 38. *Rebecca* 40. *The Philadelphia Story* 40. Dr Jekyll and Mr Hyde 41. Woman of the Year 42. Air Force 42. Mr Skeffington 44. Objective Burma 45. Humoresque 46. The Paradine Case 48. *Alias Nick Beal* 49. *Sunset Boulevard* (AA) 50. *A Place in the Sun* (AA) 51. My Cousin Rachel 53. Rear Window 54. Mister Roberts 56. Sayonara 57. The Nun's Story 59. Cimarron 60. Taras Bulba 62. Lost Command 66, etc.

Waxman, Harry (1912–1984).
British cinematographer.
Brighton Rock 46. They Were Not Divided 48. Valley of Eagles 51. The Baby and the Battleship 56. *Innocent Sinners* 57. The Secret Partner 60. The Roman Spring of Mrs Stone 61. *The Day the Earth Caught Fire* 62. Lancelot and Guinevere 63. Crooks in Cloisters 64. The Nanny 65. *Khartoum* (2nd unit) 66. The Family Way 66. The Trygon Factor 67. The Anniversary 67. Wonderwall 68. Twisted Nerve 68. There's a Girl in My Soup 70. Flight of the Doves 71. Endless Night 72. Digby 73. Blue Blood 73. Vampira 74. Journey into Fear 75. The Pink Panther Strikes Again 76, etc.

waxworks
have featured from time to time in horror films and other thrillers, notably *The Mystery of the Wax Museum*, House of Wax, Nightmare in Wax, Terror in the Wax Museum, *The Florentine Dagger, Charlie Chan in the Wax Museum, Midnight at Madame Tussaud's* and the original German *Waxworks*.

Wayans, Damon (1960–).
American comedian and actor. He is the brother of Keenen Ivory Wayans.
Beverly Hills Cop 84. Roxanne 87. Hollywood Shuffle 87. Punchline 88. I'm Gonna Git You Sucka 88. Colors 88. Earth Girls Are Easy 89. The Last Boy Scout 91. Mo' Money (a, w, p) 92. Blankman (a, p, co-w, d) 94, etc.
TV series: In Living Color 90–93.

Wayans, Keenen Ivory (1958–).
American director, screenwriter and actor. He is the brother of Damon Wayans.
Hollywood Shuffle (a, co-w) 87. Eddie Murphy Raw (co-w) 87. I'm Gonna Git You Sucka (a, wd)

88. The Five Heartbeats (co-w) 91. Low Down Dirty Shame (a, d) 94, etc.
TV series: In Living Color 90–93.

Wayne, Bernie (1919–1993).
American composer and songwriter whose best known song was 'Blue Velvet', used in Kenneth Anger's *Scorpio Rising* 64 and David Lynch's *Blue Velvet* 86.
Duffy's Tavern 45. Out of This World 45. Blues Busters 50. Viva Las Vegas 64, etc.

Wayne, David (1914–1995) (Wayne McKeekan).
Wiry American character actor, in films since late 40s, also stage star.
Portrait of Jennie 48. *Adam's Rib* 49. My Blue Heaven 50. Up Front 51. With a Song in My Heart 52. *Wait till the Sun Shines Nellie* 52. The I Don't Care Girl 53. Tonight We Sing 53. How to Marry a Millionaire 53. The Tender Trap 55. The Three Faces of Eve 57. The Last Angry Man 59. The Big Gamble 60. The Andromeda Strain 70. Huckleberry Finn 74. The Front Page 74. The Apple Dumpling Gang 75. Lassie: the New Beginning 79. House Calls 80. Poker Alice 87, etc.
TV series: Norby 51. The Good Life 71. Ellery Queen 74. Dallas 78. House Calls 80.

Wayne, John (1907–1979) (Marion Michael Morrison).
Tough, genial, generally inimitable American leading man of action films who after a slow start became one of the best known and most successful actors in Hollywood.
Biographies: 1974, *Shooting Star* by Maurice Zolotow. 1991, *John Wayne: Actor, Artist, Hero* by Richard D. McGhee.
■ The Drop Kick 27. Hangman's House 28. Mother Machree 28. Salute 29. Words and Music 29. Men without Women 30. Rough Romance 30. Cheer Up and Smile 30. *The Big Trail* 30. Girls Demand Excitement 31. Three Girls Lost 31. Men Are Like That 31. Range Feud 31. Hurricane Express (serial) 31. Shadow of the Eagle (serial) 32. Maker of Men 32. Two Fisted Law 32. Texas Cyclone 32. Lady and Gent 32. Ride Him Cowboy 32. The Big Stampede 32. The Three Mesquiteers (serial) 33. Haunted Gold 33. Telegraph Trail 33. His Private Secretary 33. Central Airport 33. Baby Face Harrington 33. The Sagebrush Trail 33. Somewhere in Sonora 33. The Life of Jimmy Dolan 33. Baby Face 33. The Man from Monterey 33. Riders of Destiny 33. College Coach 33. West of the Divide 34. Blue Steel 34. Lucky Texan 34. The Man from Utah 34. Randy Rides Alone 34. The Star Packer 34. The Trail Beyond 34. Neath Arizona Skies 34. Texas Terror 35. The Lawless Frontier 35. New Frontier 35. Lawless Range 35. Rainbow Valley 35. Paradise Canyon 35. The Dawn Rider 35. Westward Ho 35. Desert Trail 35. The Lawless Nineties 36. King of the Pecos 36. The Oregon Trail 36. Winds of the Wasteland 36. The Sea Spoilers 36. The Lonely Trail 36. Conflict 36. California Straight Ahead 37. Cover the War 37. Idol of the Crowds 37. Adventure's End 37. Born to the West 37. Pals of the Saddle 37. I Cover the War 37. Helltown 37. Overland Stage Raiders 38. Santa Fe Stampede 38. Red River Range 38. *Stagecoach* 39. Night Riders 39. Three Texas Steers 39. Wyoming Outlaw 39. New Frontier 39. Allegheny Uprising 39. Dark Command 40. Three Faces West 40. *The Long Voyage Home* 40. *Seven Sinners* 40. A Man Betrayed 40. The Lady from Louisiana 41. The Shepherd of the Hills 41. Lady for a Night 41. Reap the Wild Wind 42. The Spoilers 42. In Old California 42. Flying Tigers 42. Reunion in France 42. Pittsburgh 42. A Lady Takes a Chance 43. In Old Oklahoma 43. The Fighting

Seabees 44. Tall in the Saddle 44. Back to Bataan 44. Flame of the Barbary Coast 44. Dakota 45. They Were Expendable 45. Without Reservations 46. Angel and the Badman 47. Tycoon 47. Fort Apache 48. *Red River* 48. Three Godfathers 48. Wake of the Red Witch 48. The Fighting Kentuckian 49. *She Wore a Yellow Ribbon* 49. Sands of Iwo Jima (AAN) 49. Rio Grande 50. Operation Pacific 51. Flying Leathernecks 51. Big Jim McLain 52. *The Quiet Man* 52. Trouble Along the Way 53. Island in the Sky 53. Hondo 53. *The High and the Mighty* 54. The Sea Chase 55. Blood Alley 55. The Conqueror 55. I Married a Woman (gag appearance) 55. *The Searchers* 56. The Wings of Eagles 57. Jet Pilot 57. The Barbarian and the Geisha 58. *Rio Bravo* 59. The Horse Soldiers 59. North to Alaska 60. *The Alamo* (& p, d) 60. The Comancheros 61. The Man Who Shot Liberty Valance 62. Hatari 62. The Longest Day 62. How the West Was Won 63. Donovan's Reef 63. McLintock 63. Circus World 64. The Greatest Story Ever Told 65. In Harm's Way 65. The Sons of Katie Elder 65. Cast a Giant Shadow 66. El Dorado 67. The War Wagon 67. The Green Berets (& d) 68. Hellfighters 68. The Undefeated 69. *True Grit* (AA) 69. Rio Lobo 70. Chisum 70. Big Jake 71. The Cowboys 72. The Train Robbers 73. Cahill 73. McQ 74. Brannigan 75. Rooster Cogburn 75. *The Shootist* 76.
✪ For appearing in more films than any other star, and for winning respect after a lifetime of larger-than-life roles. *The Quiet Man.*

¶ I play John Wayne in every picture regardless of the character, and I've been doing all right, haven't I? – *J.W.*
  I never had a goddam artistic problem in my life, never, and I've worked with the best of them. John Ford isn't exactly a bum, is he? Yet he never gave me any manure about art. – *J.W.*
  Westerns are closer to art than anything else in the motion picture business. – *J.W.*
  He has an endless face and he can go on forever. – *L. B. Mayer*

Famous line (*True Grit*): 'Come and see a fat old man sometime!'

Famous line (*Hondo*): 'A man oughta do what he thinks is right.'
~Wayne was known as Duke because as a child he had a dog of that name. They were Big Duke and Little Duke; Wayne was Little Duke.
~~In 1971 he was named by the Marine Corps League as 'the man who best exemplifies the word American'.

Wayne, Michael (1934–   ).
American producer, son of John Wayne.
  McLintock 63. The Green Berets 67. Cahill 73, etc.

Wayne, Naunton (1901–1970) (Naunton Davies). Mild-mannered British light comedy actor, on stage from 1920, films from 1931; became well known with Basil Radford in many films as Englishmen abroad.
  The First Mrs Fraser (debut) 31. Going Gay 33. For Love of You 34. *The Lady Vanishes* 38. *Night Train to Munich* 40. Crooks' Tour 41. Next of Kin 42. Millions Like Us 43. *Dead of Night* 45. The Calendar 47. *It's Not Cricket* 48. Quartet 48. Passport to Pimlico 48. Obsession 49. Highly Dangerous 50. *The Titfield Thunderbolt* 53. You Know What Sailors Are 53. Nothing Barred 61. Double Bunk 64, many others.

Wayne, Patrick (1939–   ).
American leading man, son of John Wayne.

The Searchers 56. The Alamo 60. The Comancheros 62. McLintock 63. The Bears and I 74. The People that Time Forgot 77. Sinbad and the Eye of the Tiger 77. Rustler's Rhapsody 85. Revenge 86. Young Guns 88. Her Alibi 89. Blind Vengeance 90. Chill Factor 90, etc.
  TV series: The Rounders 66. Shirley 78. The Monte Carlo Show 81.

Wead, Frank 'Spig' (1895–1947).
American screenwriter of the 30s, a former navy flier whose early life was played by John Wayne in *The Wings of Eagles* (1957).

Weathers, Carl (1948–   ).
American actor, a former football player.
  Bucktown 75. Friday Foster 75. *Rocky* 76. Close Encounters of the Third Kind 77. Semi-Tough 77. Force Ten from Navarone 78. Rocky II 79. Death Hunt 81. Rocky III 82. Rocky IV 86. Predator 87. Action Jackson 88. Hurricane Smith 90, etc.
  TV series: Fortune Dane 86. Tour of Duty 89–90. Street Justice 91.

Weaver, Dennis (1924–   ).
American character actor and TV star.
  The Raiders 52. War Arrow 54. Seven Angry Men 55. Touch of Evil 58. The Gallant Hours 60. Duel at Diablo 66. The Great Man's Whiskers (TV) 71. What's the Matter with Helen 71. Duel (TV) 71. The Forgotten Man (TV) 71. Rollin' Man (TV) 72. The Islander (TV) 78. Centennial (TV) 78. Pearl (TV) 78. Ishi: The Last of His Tribe (TV) 78. The Ordeal of Patty Hearst (TV) 79. The Ordeal of Dr Mudd (TV) 80. Going for the Gold: The Bill Johnson Story (TV) 85. Bluffing It (TV) 87, etc.
  TV series: Gunsmoke (as Chester) 55–63. Kentucky Jones 65. McCloud 70–76. Stone 79. Navy 83.

Weaver, Doodles (1911–1983) (Winstead Sheffield Weaver).
American character comedian, once a member of Spike Jones' band. Starred in TV's *The Doodles Weaver Show* in 1951.
  Topper 37. The Pied Piper 43. Since You Went Away 43. San Antonio 45. Gentlemen Prefer Blondes 52. Pocketful of Miracles 60. The Birds 63. Rosie 67, etc.

Weaver, Fritz (1926–   ).
American stage actor.
  Fail Safe 64. The Borgia Stick (TV) 68. The Maltese Bippy 69. A Walk in the Spring Rain 70. The Day of the Dolphin 73. Marathon Man 76. Demon Seed 77. Black Sunday 77. The Big Fix 78. *Holocaust* (TV) 78. Jaws of Satan 79. Creepshow 82. Power 85. Blind Spot (TV) 93, etc.

Weaver, Marjorie (1913–   ).
American leading lady, mainly of second features.
  China Clipper 36. Three Blind Mice 38. Young Mr Lincoln 39. Maryland 40. The Mad Martindales 42. We're Not Married 52, many others.

Weaver, Sigourney (1949–   ) (Susan Alexandra Weaver).
American leading lady, niece of Doodles Weaver.
  Alien 79. Eyewitness 81. The Year of Living Dangerously 83. Deal of the Century 83. Ghostbusters 84. Half Moon Street 86. Aliens (AAN) 86. Gorillas in the Mist (AAN) 88. Working Girl (AAN) 88. Ghostbusters II 89. Alien^3 92. 1492 92. Dave 93. Death and the Maiden 94, etc.

¶ I think I get sent the roles Meryl's not doing. – *S.W.*

Weaving, Hugo.
Australian leading actor.
  The City's Edge 85. For Love Alone 86. The Right Hand Man 87. Wendy Cracked a Walnut 90. Proof 91. The Custodian 93. Reckless Kelly 93. Frauds 93. *The Adventures of Priscilla, Queen of the Desert* 94. Exile 94, etc.

Webb, Alan (1906–1982).
Lean British character actor, mainly on stage.
  Lease of Life 54. The Pumpkin Eater 64. Chimes at Midnight 66. The Taming of the Shrew 67. Entertaining Mr Sloane 69. Women in Love 69. Nicholas and Alexandra 71. The First Great Train Robbery 78. Rough Cut 80, etc.

Webb, Clifton (1893–1966) (Webb Parmelee Hollenbeck).
American leading character actor, former dancer and stage star. In films, became in middle age well-known in waspish roles.
■ Polly with a Past 20. Let No Man Put Asunder 24. New Toys 25. The Heart of a Siren 25. The Still Alarm 26. *Laura* (AAN) 44. The Dark Corner 46. *The Razor's Edge* (AAN) 46. *Sitting Pretty* (AAN) 48. Mr Belvedere Goes to College 49. *Cheaper by the Dozen* 50. For Heaven's Sake 50. Mr Belvedere Rings the Bell 51. Elopement 51. Dreamboat 52. Stars and Stripes Forever 52. Titanic 53. Mister Scoutmaster 53. *Three Coins in the Fountain* 54. Woman's World 54. *The Man Who Never Was* 55. Boy on a Dolphin 57. The Remarkable Mr Pennypacker 58. Holiday for Lovers 59. Satan Never Sleeps 62.

Famous line (*The Dark Corner*): 'I detest the dawn. The grass always looks as though it's been out all night.'

Famous line (*The Razor's Edge*): 'The enjoyment of art is the only remaining ecstasy that's neither immoral nor illegal.'

Famous line (*The Razor's Edge*): 'If I live to be a hundred I shall never understand how any young man can come to Paris without evening clothes.'

Webb, Jack (1920–1982).
American TV star and executive: starred and directed in *Dragnet* and other series; was briefly head of Warner TV. The first of his four wives was singer Julie London.
AS ACTOR: The Men 50. Sunset Boulevard 50. You're in the Navy Now 52. Dragnet (& pd) 54. Pete Kelly's Blues (& pd) 55. The D.I. (& pd) 57. The Last Time I Saw Archie (& pd) 62, many others.

Webb, James R. (1910–1974).
American screenwriter.
  The Charge at Feather River 53. Phantom of the Rue Morgue (co-w) 54. Trapeze 56. The Big Country (co-w) 58. Pork Chop Hill 59. How the West Was Won (AA) 63. Guns for San Sebastian 67. Alfred the Great (co-w) 69, many others.

Webb, Robert D. (1903–1990).
American director, former cameraman.
  White Feather 55. On the Threshold of Space 55. The Proud Ones 56. Love Me Tender 56. The Way to the Gold 57. Seven Women from Hell 61. The Agony and the Ecstasy (second unit) 65. Capetown Affair 67, etc.

Webb, Roy (1888–1982).
American composer.
  Alice Adams 35. Quality Street 37. Room Service 38. Kitty Foyle 40. Cat People 42. Journey into Fear

42. Experiment Perilous 44. The Body Snatcher 45. Murder My Sweet 45. Notorious 46. The Spiral Staircase 46. Blood on the Moon 48. Mighty Joe Young 49. Flying Leathernecks 51. Houdini 53. Blood Alley 55. Top Secret Affair 57. Teacher's Pet 58, many others.

Webber, Robert (1924–1989).
American leading man with stage and TV experience.

Highway 301 51. *Twelve Angry Men* 57. The Stripper 63. Hysteria (GB) 64. The Sandpiper 65. The Third Day 65. No Tears for a Killer (It.) 65. Harper 66. The Silencers 67. The Dirty Dozen 67. Dollars 72. Bring Me the Head of Alfredo Garcia 74. Midway 76. The Choirboys 77. Casey's Shadow 78. Revenge of the Pink Panther 78. '10' 79. Private Benjamin 80. S.O.B. 81. Wrong Is Right 82. Wild Geese II 84, etc.

Weber, Bruce (1946–).
American documentary director, best known as a fashion and commercial photographer, notably for Calvin Klein's advertisements.

Broken Noses 87. Let's Get Lost 88.

Weber, Lois (1882–1939).
American director, writer, producer, and actress. After a period on stage, she went to work for the Gaumont Film Studio in New Jersey in 1908, moving to Universal in Hollywood in 1913, where her salary rose to $5,000 a week. Many of her films, which often dealt with social problems, were controversial. *Where Are My Children?*, for instance, advocated birth control (though it was opposed to abortion) and was banned in some cities. Her career declined from the mid-20s. She was married to actor and director Phillips Smalley who appeared in, and also co-directed, some of her films.

On the Brink (a) 11. The Female of the Species (a, d) 13. The Merchant of Venice (a, w, co-d) 14. Hypocrites (wd) 14. The Dumb Girl of Portici (co-d) 15. Scandal (co-d) 15. Where Are My Children? (w, co-d) 16. Shoes (wd) 16. The Hand that Rocks the Cradle (a, p, d) 17. The Price of a Good Time (w, co-d) 17. For Husbands Only (w, co-d) 18. Forbidden (co-d) 19. A Chapter in Her Life (co-w, d) 23. The Marriage Clause (wd) 26. The Angel of Broadway (d) 27. Sensation Seekers (wd) 27. White Heat (d) 34, etc.

¶ I'll never be convinced that the general public does not want serious entertainment rather than frivolous. – *L.W.*

Webster, Ben (1864–1947).
British stage character actor of the old school, married to May Whitty.

The House of Temperley 13. Enoch Arden 14. The Vicar of Wakefield 16. Because 18. The Call of Youth 20. The Only Way 25. Downhill 27. The Lyons Mail 31. The Old Curiosity Shop 34. Drake of England 35, etc.

Webster, Ferris (1916–).
American editor.

The Picture of Dorian Gray 45. If Winter Comes 47. Father of the Bride 50. Lone Star 52. Lili 53. The Blackboard Jungle 55. Forbidden Planet 56. Cat on a Hot Tin Roof 58. The Magnificent Seven 60. *The Manchurian Candidate* 62. The Great Escape 63. Seven Days in May 64. Seconds 66. Ice Station Zebra 68. Zigzag 70. High Plains Drifter 73. The Enforcer 76. The Gauntlet 77. Every Which Way But Loose 78. Escape from Alcatraz 79. Bronco Billy 80, many others.

Webster, Paul Francis (1907–1984).
American lyricist. Various Shirley Temple songs in the 30s; later *Love is a Many Splendored Thing* (AA) 54. *Friendly Persuasion* 56. *The Sandpiper* (AA) 65, etc.

weddings
have formed a happy ending for innumerable films, and an unhappy start for others, but some are more memorable than the rest. Weddings on a lavish scale were seen in *Camelot, Royal Wedding, The Scarlet Empress, Ivan the Terrible (Part One), The Private Life of Henry VIII.* More domestic occasions were in *Quiet Wedding, The Member of the Wedding, The Catered Affair, Father of the Bride, June Bride, A Kind of Loving, Lovers and Other Strangers, Brigadoon, Four Weddings and a Funeral.* Weddings were interrupted in *The Philadelphia Story, The Bride Wasn't Willing, I Married a Witch, The Runaround, You Gotta Stay Happy, The Bride Went Wild, The Lion in Winter, The Graduate* and *I Love You Alice B. Toklas.* Macabre weddings were found in *The Night Walker, The Bride Wore Black, The Bride of Frankenstein, The Bride and the Beast, Chamber of Horrors.* The wedding night was the center of interest in *The Man in Grey, The Wicked Lady, Wedding Night, The Family Way* and *My Little Chickadee.* And the funniest wedding still remains that in *Our Wife,* when cross-eyed justice of the peace Ben Turpin married Mr Hardy to his best man Mr Laurel.

Weegee (1899–1968) (Arthur Fellig).
Brash Austrian-born American news photographer noted for his often snatched and sensational night-time photographs, taken by flashlight on the streets of New York, of fires, gangsters, suicides, the victims of murderers and muggers, socialites, and lowlife. His book *Naked City*, published in 1945, was bought by Universal and resulted in Jules Dassin's film of the same name in 1948 ('There are eight million stories in the naked city. This has been one of them . . .'). His stark, high-contrast style can be said to have shaped the look of film noir and also influenced cinematographer Michael Chapman's work in *Raging Bull.* In 1948 he made a short film, *Weegee's New York,* worked briefly in Hollywood as a consultant, and played cameos in several films including *Every Girl Should Be Married* 48 and *The Set-Up* 49. He was a consultant and stills photographer on *Dr Strangelove.* A documentary about his work, *The Naked Eye*, was made in 1957. He was also the model for the photographer-hero of *The Public Eye* 92, directed by Howard Franklin. His nickname derived from his ability to be first on the scene of a tragedy, which was attributed to his use of a ouija board, but was more to do with the police radio he kept in his car-cum-office.

Autobiography: 1961, *Weegee by Weegee.*

Weeks, Stephen (1948–).
British director.

■ I Monster 70. Sir Gawain and the Green Knight 72. Ghost Story 74. Sword of the Valiant 84.

Wegener, Paul (1874–1948).
Distinguished German actor-writer-director.

The Student of Prague (a) 13. The Golem (ad) 14 and 20. Vanina (a) 22. Svengali (awd) 27. Lucrezia Borgia (a) 27. Ein Mann Will Nach Deutschland (d) 34. Der Grosse König (a) 41. Der Grosse Mandarin (a) 48, many others.

Weidler, Virginia (1927–1968).
American child actress who usually played a little horror.

Surrender 31. Mrs Wiggs of the Cabbage Patch 34. Souls at Sea 37. The Women 39. *The Philadelphia Story* 40. Born to Sing 42. The Youngest Profession 43. Best Foot Forward 43, etc

Weil, Samuel:
see *Kaufman, Lloyd.*

Weill, Claudia (1947–).
American director and screenwriter, from TV.

■ Joyce at 34 72. The Other Half of the Sky 75. Girlfriends 78. It's My Turn 80. Johnny Bull (TV) 86.

Weill, Cynthia (1937–).
American lyricist and singer whose songs, often written with her husband Barry Mann, have featured in several movies.

Wild in the Streets (s) 68. Cactus Flower (s) 69. I Never Sang for My Father (s) 69. An American Tail (s) 86. Summer Heat (s) 87. Harry and the Hendersons (s) 87. National Lampoon's Christmas Vacation (s) 89. Sibling Rivalry (s) 90, etc.

Weill, Kurt (1900–1950).
German composer whose scores include *Die Dreigroschenoper, One Touch of Venus* and *Knickerbocker Holiday*, all filmed. Woody Allen used his music in *Shadows and Fog* 91.

Weingarten, Laurence (1898–1975).
American producer, in films from around 1917.

Broadway Melody 28. A Day at the Races 37. Escape 40. Adam's Rib 49. The Tender Trap 54. Cat on a Hot Tin Roof 58. The Unsinkable Molly Brown 64, many others.

Weintraub, Fred (1928–).
American producer, formerly with Warner in the 70s, noted for, by Hollywood standards, an offbeat approach.

Woodstock 70. Klute 71. Summer of '42 71. Enter the Dragon 73. Black Belt Jones 74. Outlaw Blues 77. Tom Horn 80. High Road to China 83. Gymkata 85, etc.

Weir, Peter (1944–).
Australian director and screenwriter.

■ Homesdale 71. The Cars that Ate Paris 71. *Picnic at Hanging Rock* 75. *The Last Wave* 77. The Plumber (TV) 78. Gallipoli 81. The Year of Living Dangerously 82. *Witness* (AAN) 85. The Mosquito Coast 86. Dead Poets Society (AAN) 89. Green Card 90. Fearless 93.

Weis, Don (1922–).
American director; came to Hollywood from college as trainee.

Bannerline 51. I Love Melvin 53. A Slight Case of Larceny 53. Ride the High Iron 57. Critics' Choice 63. Pajama Party 63. Looking for Love 64. Billie 65. Pajama Party in a Haunted House 66. The King's Pirate 66. Zero to Sixty 78. The Munsters' Revenge (TV) 81, etc.

Weisbart, David (1915–1967).
American producer, former editor; in Hollywood from 1935.

Mara Maru 52. Rebel Without a Cause 55. Love Me Tender 56. Holiday for Lovers 59. Kid Galahad 63. Rio Conchos 64. Goodbye Charlie 65. Valley of the Dolls 67, many others.

Weiss, Rob (1967–).
American director, a former photographer.

Amongst Friends 93.

Weissmuller, Johnny (1904–1984) (Peter John Weissmuller).
American leading man, former Olympic athlete who from 1932 played Tarzan (qv) more often than anyone else. In the late 40s and early 50s appeared in 'Jungle Jim' second features, also on TV. Only 'straight' role: *Swamp Fire* 46.

Guest appearances: Glorifying the American Girl 29. Stage Door Canteen 43. The Phynx 70. Won Ton Ton 76. That's Entertainment Two 76.

Welch, Elisabeth (1904–).
Singing star, born in New York but working mostly in Britain.

Song of Freedom 36. Big Fella 37. Alibi 42. Fiddlers Three 44. Dead of Night 45. Girl Stroke Boy 71. The Tempest 80, etc.

Welch, Joseph N. (1891–1960).
Real-life American judge who became famous during the army-McCarthy hearings in 1954 and was later persuaded to play the judge in *Anatomy of a Murder* 59.

Welch, Raquel (1940–) (Raquel Tejada).
Dynamic, curvaceous American sex symbol of the late 60s.
■ Roustabout 64. A House Is Not a Home 64. A Swinging Summer 65. Fantastic Voyage 66. One Million Years BC 66. The Biggest Bundle of Them All 66. Shoot Loud, Louder I Don't Understand 66. The Queens 67. Fathom 67. Bandolero 68. The Oldest Profession 68. Bedazzled 68. The Beloved 68. Lady in Cement 68. 100 Rifles 68. Myra Breckinridge 70. Flare Up 70. The Magic Christian 70. Hannie Caulder 71. Kansas City Bomber 72. Fuzz 72. Bluebeard 72. The Last of Sheila 73. The Three Musketeers 73. The Four Musketeers 74. The Wild Party 75. Mother Jugs and Speed 76. The Prince and the Pauper 77. The Legend of Walks Far Woman (TV) 84. Right to Die (TV) 87. Scandal in a Small Town (TV) 88. Trouble in Paradise (TV) 89.

¶ Being a sex symbol was rather like being a convict. – R.W.
If you have physical attractiveness you don't have to act. – R.W.

Welch, Tahnee (1961–).
American actress, the daughter of actress Raquel Welch.
Cocoon 85. Lethal Obsession 87. Cocoon: The Return 88. Sleeping Beauty 89. Improper Conduct 94, etc.

Weld, Tuesday (1943–) (Susan Ker Weld).
American leading actress, a model from childhood. She was married to actor Dudley Moore (1975–80).
Rock Rock Rock 56. Rally round the Flag Boys 57. The Five Pennies 59. Return to Peyton Place 61. Wild in the Country 62. Bachelor Flat 63. I'll Take Sweden 65. *The Cincinnati Kid* 65. Lord Love a Duck 66. *Pretty Poison* 68. I Walk the Line 70. A Safe Place 71. Play It as It Lays 73. Looking for Mr Goodbar (AAN) 77. Who'll Stop the Rain? 78. A Question of Guilt (TV) 78. Serial 80. Thief 81. Author! Author! 82. Once upon a Time in America 84. Heartbreak Hotel 88. Falling Down 93, etc.

Welden, Ben (1901–).
British character actor who moved to Hollywood.
The Missing Rembrandt 32. The Triumph of Sherlock Holmes 34. Marked Woman 37. Crime Ring 38. Hollywood Cavalcade 39. Angel on My Shoulder 45. The Lemon Drop Kid 51, many others.

Welland, Colin (1934–).
British actor-writer, mostly for television.
AS ACTOR: Kes 69. Villain 71. Straw Dogs 71. The Sweeney 77. Femme Fatale (TV) 93, etc.
■ AS WRITER: Yanks 79. Chariots of Fire (AA) 81. Twice in a Lifetime 86. A Dry White Season (co-w) 89. War of the Buttons 94.

Weller, Michael.
American dramatist and screenwriter.
Hair 79. Ragtime (AAN) 81. Lost Angels 89. Spoils of War (TV) 94.

Weller, Peter (1947–).
Gaunt American leading man, from the stage.
Butch and Sundance: The Early Days 79. Just Tell Me What You Want 80. Shoot the Moon 81. Of Unknown Origin 83. The Adventures of Buckaroo Banzai across the Eighth Dimension 84. Firstborn 84. The Dancing Princesses (TV) 84. Two Kinds of Love (TV) 85. A Killing Affair 85. Apology (TV) 86. My Sister's Keeper 86. Robocop 87. Shakedown (aka Blue Jean Cop) 88. The Tunnel 88. Cat Chaser 89. Leviathan 89. Robocop 2 90. Rainbow Drive (TV) 90. Naked Lunch 91. Grill 92. The Substitute Wife (TV) 94. The New Age 94, etc.

Welles, Gwen (1949–1993).
American actress. She was married to actor Harris Yulin.
A Safe Place 71. California Split 74. Nashville 75. Desert Hearts 86. The Men's Club 86. Sticky Fingers 88. New Year's Day 89, etc.

Welles, Orson (1915–1985).
Ebullient American actor-writer-producer-director with stage and radio experience (in 1938 he panicked the whole of America with a vivid radio version of *The War of the Worlds*). His extravagance and unconventionality in Hollywood forced him to Europe, where his projects continued interesting and ambitious but generally undisciplined; he never again achieved the standard of his first two films.

Biographies: 1956, *The Fabulous Orson Welles* by Peter Noble. 1973, *Orson Welles* by Peter Bogdanovich. 1973, *A Ribbon of Dreams* by Peter Cowie. 1985, *Orson Welles* by Barbara Leaming. 1989, *Citizen Welles* by Frank Brady.

Book: 1993, *This Is Orson Welles* by Orson Welles and Peter Bogdanovich, ed. Jonathan Rosenbaum.
■ This list of Welles' films assumes his presence as actor unless otherwise stated: Citizen Kane (& d) (AA script, co-w with Herman J. Mankiewicz, AANa, AANd) 41. The Magnificent Ambersons (wd only) 42. Journey into Fear 42. It's All True (unreleased) (wd only) 42. Jane Eyre 43. Follow the Boys 44. Tomorrow Is Forever 44. The Stranger (& d) 45. The Lady from Shanghai (& d) 47. Black Magic 47. Macbeth (& d) 48. Prince of Foxes 49. The Third Man 49. The Black Rose 50. Othello (& d) 51. Trent's Last Case 53. Trouble in the Glen 53. Si Versailles m'Etait Conté 53. Man Beast and Virtue 53. Napoleon 54. Three Cases of Murder 55. Confidential Report (& d) 55. Moby Dick 56. Man in the Shadow 57. Touch of Evil (& d) 58. The Long Hot Summer 58. Roots of Heaven 58. Ferry to Hong Kong 58. David and Goliath 59. Compulsion 59. Crack in the Mirror 60. The Mongols 60. The Tartars 60. Lafayette 61. The Trial (& d) 62. The VIPs 63. Chimes at Midnight (& d) 66. Is Paris Burning? 66. A Man For All Seasons 66. Marco the Magnificent 66. I'll Never Forget Whatshisname 67. Casino Royale 67. Sailor from Gibraltar 67. Oedipus the King 67. House of Cards 68. The Immortal Story (& d) 68. Start the

Revolution without Me 69. The Southern Star 69. The Kremlin Letter 70. The Battle of Neretva 70. Waterloo 70. Catch 22 70. Safe Place 71. Malpertuis 72. Necromancy 72. Rogopag 72. Treasure Island (as Long John) 72. Ten Days Wonder 72. Get to Know Your Rabbit 72. F for Fake 73. The Other Side of the Wind (unfinished) 76. Voyage of the Damned 76. The Muppet Movie 79. It Happened One Christmas (TV) 79. The Man Who Saw Tomorrow 81. Genocide 81. History of the World Part I 82. Butterfly 82. Almonds and Raisins 83. In Our Hands 83. Where Is Parsifal? 84. Transformers 86. Someone to Love 87.
◐ For starting as big as could be, and not minding about the inevitable tailing-off (and even encouraging it). *Citizen Kane*.

¶ There, but for the grace of God, goes God. So snapped Herman Mankiewicz during the making of *Citizen Kane*. There must have been something infuriatingly godlike about Orson the young Messiah from New York, brought out with his troupe to play with what he called:
The biggest toy train set any boy ever had.
Unfortunately, as he later admitted.
I started at the top and worked down.
It was indeed the only way to go: he could not, either by temperament or ability, make the films Hollywood wanted. The end of his reign came when:
They let the studio janitor cut *The Magnificent Ambersons* in my absence.
The years that followed saw an amassment of unfinished projects and haphazard wanderings over Europe, with flashes of acting genius in between. Paul Holt called him:
The oldest enfant terrible in the world.
Jean Cocteau saw him as:
An active loafer, a wise madman.
Ken Tynan called him:
A superb bravura director, a fair bravura producer, and a limited bravura writer; but an incomparable bravura personality.
John Simon opined:
The sad thing is that he has consistently put his very real talents to the task of glorifying his imaginary genius.
Charles Higham adds a reason:
His genius fed on Hollywood's marvellous machinery.
Pauline Kael was revolted:
By the 60s he was encased in make-up and his own fat, like a huge operatic version of W. C. Fields.
Perhaps he best summed up his own career:
Everybody denies I am a genius – but nobody ever called me one!
By 1982 the *Sunday Times* would state:
His talents now seem as deeply buried as a sixpence in a Christmas pudding.
Gluttony is not a secret vice. – O.W.
I'm not bitter about Hollywood's treatment of me, but over its treatment of Griffith, Von Sternberg, Von Stroheim, Buster Keaton and a hundred others. – O.W.
When you're down and out, something always turns up – usually the noses of your friends. – O.W.
Movie directing is a perfect refuge for the mediocre. – O.W.
There is nothing about him to convince us that he has ever felt humility or love anywhere but in front of a mirror. – *John Simon*

Famous line (*Citizen Kane*): 'I run a couple of newspapers. What do you do?'
Famous line (*The Third Man*): 'In Italy for thirty years under the Borgias they had warfare, terror,

murder, bloodshed – they produced Michelangelo, Leonardo da Vinci and the Renaissance. In Switzerland they had brotherly love, five hundred years of democracy and peace, and what did that produce? The cuckoo clock.'

~AA 1970 'for supreme artistry and versatility in the creation of motion pictures'.

Wellman, William (1896–1975).

American director, former pilot, actor and Foreign Legionary; in Hollywood from 1921.

Autobiography: 1977, *A Short Time for Insanity*.

The Man Who Won 23. You Never Know Women 26. *Wings* 27. Beggars of Life 28. *Public Enemy* 31. The Conquerors 32. Central Airport 33. Looking for Trouble 34. Small Town Girl 35. Call of the Wild 35. Robin Hood of Eldorado 36. *Nothing Sacred* 37. *A Star Is Born* (AAw, AANd) 37. Men with Wings (& p) 38. Beau Geste 39. The Light that Failed 39. The Great Man's Lady 42. *The Ox Bow Incident* 42. *Roxie Hart* 42. Buffalo Bill 43. *The Story of G.I. Joe* 45. Magic Town 46. Yellow Sky 48. The Iron Curtain 48. Battleground (AAN) 49. The Next Voice You Hear 50. Westward the Women 50. Across the Wide Missouri 51. My Man and I 52. *The High and the Mighty* (AAN) 54. *Track of the Cat* 54. Blood Alley 55. Darby's Rangers 57. Lafayette Escadrille 58, many others.

¶ He was a tough little bastard but I liked him . . . he shot real bullets and stuff. – *James Mason*
What is at issue is not the number of bad films he has made, but a fundamental deficiency in his direction of good projects. – *Andrew Sarris, 1968*

Wells, George (1909–).

American writer, with MGM since 1944.

Take Me Out to the Ball Game (Everybody's Cheering) 48. Three Little Words 50. Everything I Have is Yours (& p) 52. Jupiter's Darling (p only) 55. Designing Woman (AA) 57. Ask Any Girl 59. The Honeymoon Machine 62. The Horizontal Lieutenant 63. Penelope 66. The Impossible Years 68, etc.

Wells, H. G. (1866–1946).

Distinguished British author, several of whose novels have been filmed.

The Island of Dr Moreau (Island of Lost Souls) 32. The Invisible Man 33. The Man Who Could Work Miracles 35. Things To Come 36. Kipps 41. The History of Mr Polly 49. The War of the Worlds 53. The Time Machine 60. The Island of Dr Moreau 77, etc.

Welsh, John (1904–1985).

Lean British character actor adept at professors, fathers, scientists, barristers etc.

Wenders, Wim (1945–).

German director.

■ The Goalkeeper's Fear of the Penalty Kick 71. The Scarlet Letter 72. *Alice in the Cities* 74. Wrong Movement 75. Kings of the Road 76. The American Friend 77. Lightning over Water 80. Hammett 82. The State of Things 83. Tokyo-Ga 84. Aus der Familie der Panzereschen 84. Paris, Texas (BFA) 84. Wings of Desire (Himmel über Berlin) 87. Until the End of the World (Bis ans Ende der Welt) 91. The Heavenly Twins (a) 92. Faraway, So Close! (In Weiter Ferne, So Nah) 93.

Wendkos, Paul (1922–).

American director.

The Burglar 57. Tarawa Beachhead 58. Gidget 59. Face of a Fugitive 59. Because They're Young 60. *Angel Baby* 60. Gidget Goes to Rome 63. 52 Miles to Terror 66. Guns of the Magnificent Seven

69. Cannon for Cordoba 70. The Mephisto Waltz 71. *Haunts of the Very Rich* (TV) 72. Honor Thy Father (TV) 73. Special Delivery 76. The Death of Richie (TV) 77. Good Against Evil (TV) 77. 79 Park Avenue (TV) 78. A Woman Called Moses (TV) 78. The Ordeal of Patty Hearst (TV) 79. A Cry for Love (TV) 80. The Bad Seed (TV) 85. Blood Vows: The Story of a Mafia Wife (TV) 87. The Taking of Flight 847: The Uli Derickson Story (TV) 88, etc.

Wengraf, John (1897–1974) (Johann Wenngraft).

Lean Austrian actor, mainly in Hollywood; played a lot of Nazis in his time.

Homo Sum 22. Night Train To Munich 39. Mission To Moscow 43. Sahara 43. The Seventh Cross 44. Weekend at the Waldorf 45. T Men 47. Five Fingers 51. Call Me Madam 53. The Pride and The Passion 57. The Return of Dracula 58. Judgment at Nuremberg 60. The Prize 63, etc.

Werker, Alfred (1896–).

American director, in Hollywood from 1917.

Little Lord Fauntleroy 21. Nobody's Children 28. Bachelor's Affairs 32. *The House of Rothschild* 34. Kidnapped 38. *The Adventures of Sherlock Holmes* 39. Moon over Her Shoulder 41. The Mad Martindales 42. Whispering Ghosts 42. A Haunting We Will Go 42. Shock 45. Lost Boundaries 46. Repeat Performance 47. Pirates of Monterey 48. Sealed Cargo 51. Walk East on Beacon 52. Devil's Canyon 53. Canyon Crossroads 55. At Gunpoint 58, many others.

Werner, Gosta (1908–).

Swedish director, mainly of shorts.

Midvinterblot 46. *The Train* 48. The Street 49. Meeting Life 50. To Kill a Child 52. Matrimonial Announcement 55. The Forgotten Melody 57. A Glass of Wine 60. Human Landscape 65. When People Meet 66, many others.

Werner, Oskar (1922–1984) (Josef Schliessmayer).

Austrian leading actor with international stage and screen credits.

■ Eroica 49. Angel with a Trumpet 49. The Wonder Kid (GB) 50. Ruf aus dem Aether (Aus.) 51. Ein Laecheln in Sturm (Aus.) 51. Das Gestohlene Jahr (WG) 51. *Decision before Dawn* 51. The Last Act (WG) 55. Lola Montes 55. Spionage (Aus.) 55. Der Letzte Akt (Aus.) 55. The Life of Mozart 56. *Jules et Jim* 61. *Ship of Fools* (AAN) 65. The Spy Who Came in from the Cold 65. *Fahrenheit 451* 66. Interlude 68. The Shoes of the Fisherman 68. Voyage of the Damned 76.

Wertmuller, Lina (1928–) (Angela Wertmuller von Elg).

Italian director, whose favourite theme is the little man.

The Lizards 63. Rita la Zanzarra 66. Mimi the Metalworker 72. Swept Away 74. *Seven Beauties* (AAN) 76. The End of the World 77. Blood Feud 80. A Joke of Destiny 83. Sotto, Sotto 84. Camorra 86. Summer Night with Greek Profile, Almond Eyes and Scent of Basil 86. Crystal or Ash, Fire or Wind, as Long as It's Love (In una Notte di Chiaro di Luna) 89. Saturday, Sunday and Monday (Sàbato, Doménica e Lunedí) 90. Me Let's Hope I Make It (Io Speriamo che Me la Cavo) 93, etc.

Wessel, Dick (1910–1965).

American supporting actor, usually in comedy roles.

Arson Racket Squad 38. They Made Me a Criminal 39. Action in the North Atlantic 42. Slattery's Hurricane 48. Texas Carnival 51. Calamity Jane 53. The Gazebo 60. The Ugly Dachshund 65, many others.

TV series: Riverboat 59–61.

Wessely, Paula (1908–).

Austrian leading actress.

Maskerade 34. Julika 36. Spiegel des Lebens 38. Die Kluge Marianne 43. Maria Theresa 51. The Third Sex 57. Die Unvollkommene Ehe 59, many others.

Wesson, Dick (1922–1979).

American character actor.

Destination Moon 49. Breakthrough 50. Inside the Walls of Folsom Prison 51. About Face 52. The Desert Song 53. Calamity Jane 54, etc.

TV series: The People's Choice 60. The Bob Cummings Show 62. Friends and Lovers 78.

West, Adam (1929–) (William Anderson).

American light leading man.

The Young Philadelphians 59. Geronimo 62. Robinson Crusoe on Mars 64. Mara of the Wilderness 65. Batman 66. The Girl Who Knew Too Much 68. Marriage of a Young Stockbroker 71. The Specialist 75. Partisan 75. Hooper 78. Swamp Thing 82. Hellriders 84. Doin' Time on Planet Earth 88. Mad about You 90. Maximum Xul 91. Night of the Kickfighters 91. The New Age 94, etc.

TV series: The Detectives 59–61. *Batman* 65–68.

West, Billy (1893–1975) (Roy B. Weissberg).

American silent screen comedian, a successful imitator of Charlie Chaplin; later a Hollywood restaurateur.

West, Con (1891–*).

English comedy screenwriter and dramatist, working with comedians like Ernie Lotinga, Arthur Lucan, and Max Miller, and writing screen versions of Fred Karno's music-hall sketches. He also worked for radio, co-writing in 1944 a series for Will Hay, and co-wrote a biography of Karno.

P.C. Josser (co-w from his music-hall sketch) 31. Up for the Cup (co-w) 31. The Bad Companions 32. Letting in the Sunshine (co-w) 33. Oh, What a Duchess! (co-w) 34. Birds of a Feather (co-w) 35. Jimmy Boy (story) 35. Charing Cross Road (co-w) 35. Strictly Illegal (oa) 35. Sunshine Ahead (story) 35. Things Are Looking Up (co-w) 35. The Small Man (story) 35. Smith's Wives (co-w) 35. Don't Rush Me (co-w) 36. Love up the Pole (story) 36. Why Pick on Me? (story) 37. Old Mother Riley (w) 37. Old Mother Riley in Paris (w) 38. Old Mother Riley Joins Up (co-w) 39. Old Mother Riley, M.P. (co-w) 39. Jailbirds (co-w) 39. What Would You Do Chums? 39. Up for the Cup (co-w) 50, etc.

West, Mae (1892–1980).

American leading lady of the 30s, the archetypal sex symbol, splendidly vulgar, mocking, overdressed and endearing. Wrote most of her own stage plays and filmscripts, which bulge with double meanings.

Autobiographies: 1959, *Goodness Had Nothing to Do with It*. 1975, *Life, Sex and ESP*.

Biographies: 1988, *Mae West Entertainer* by Carol Bergman. 1991, *Mae West: Empress of Sex* by Maurice Leonard.

■ Night After Night 32. *She Done Him Wrong* 33. *I'm No Angel* 33. Going to Town 34. Belle of the Nineties 34. Klondike Annie 36. Go West Young Man 37. Every Day's a Holiday 37. My Little Chickadee 39. The Heat's On 43. *Myra Breckinridge* 70. Sextet 77.

✪ For enjoying the sensations she caused in the 30s, and for having the talent to exploit them to the full. *She Done Him Wrong*.

¶ Whole books of Mae West's wit have been published. A much cleverer woman than she was usually given credit for being, she seemed to talk in epigrams. In her 70s on TV, when someone gushed:

Oh, Miss West, I've heard so much about you

the reply was:

Yeah, but you can't prove a thing.

When a lifejacket was named after her during World War II, her reaction had the appearance of spontaneity:

I've been in *Who's Who* and I know what's what, but it's the first time I ever made the dictionary.

However, she never did say:

Come up and see me sometime . . .

At least, not quite, and not in the film she was supposed to. She did however say:

Beulah, peel me a grape,

which for some reason has passed into the language. Her first screen appearance is also legendary:

Goodness, what beautiful diamonds!

– Goodness had nothing to do with it, dearie.

For the rest, one can only list a few sparklers:

She's one of the finest women who ever walked the streets.

It's not the men in my life, it's the life in my men that counts.

I wouldn't let him touch me with a ten foot pole.

How tall are you son?

– Ma'am, I'm six feet seven inches.

Let's forget the six feet and talk about the seven inches.

On arriving at her office and being greeted by a score of virile young men:

I'm feeling a little tired today. One of those fellows'll have to go home.

In a Broadway costume play, when the romantic lead got his sword so tangled in his braid that it stuck up at an unfortunate angle:

Is that your sword, or are you just pleased to see me?

I wouldn't even lift my veil for that guy.

When I'm good I'm very good, but when I'm bad I'm better.

It isn't what I do, but how I do it. It isn't what I say, but how I say it. And how I look when I do it and say it.

On the mirrored ceiling over her bed:

I like to know what I'm doing.

Whenever I'm caught between two evils, I take the one I've never tried.

Small wonder that her first co-star, George Raft, remarked of her debut:

She stole everything but the cameras.

In a non-permissive age, she made remarkable inroads against the taboos of her day, and did so without even lowering her neckline. Indeed, her most effective moment may have been in a scene in which she drove a funfair crowd wild with a dance that did nothing but tease. As she disappears into the tent, she wraps up years of experience, enjoyment and disapproval of the sex war into one word:

Suckers!

West, Morris (1916–).
Australian best-selling novelist, internationally popular; usually on religious themes. Films include *The Devil's Advocate*, *The Shoes of the Fisherman*.

West, Nathanael (1904–1940) (Nathan Weinstein).
American novelist and screenwriter. His novel *Miss Lonelyhearts* was filmed, poorly, as *Advice to the Lovelorn* 33 and his *A Cool Million* was sold to Columbia but never produced. He wrote scathingly about Hollywood in *The Day of the Locust*, published

in 1939 and filmed in 1975 by John Schlesinger. His screenplays give little indication of his unsettling talent, being routine 'B' pictures for the most part, for companies like Republic and RKO. He and his wife Eileen (heroine of the book *My Sister Eileen*, 1938, by her sister Ruth McKenney, which was filmed in 1942) were killed in a car crash.

Biography: 1970, *Nathanael West: The Art of His Life* by Jay Martin. Also: 1976, *Sometime in the Sun* by Tom Dardis. 1990, *Writers in Hollywood 1915– 51* by Ian Hamilton.

Ticket to Paradise 36. The President's Mystery 36. It Could Happen to You 37. Five Came Back 39. The Spirit of Culver 39. Men against the Sky 40. Let's Make Music 40, etc.

¶ My hours are from ten in the morning to six at night with a full day on Saturday. They gave me a job to do five minutes after I sat down in my office – a scenario about a beauty parlour – and I'm expected to turn out pages and pages a day. There's no fooling here. – *N.W. on his first Hollywood job at Columbia*

He left two books more finished and complete as works of art than almost anything else produced by his generation. – *Edmund Wilson*

He was ahead of his time in knowing that Hollywood was impermanent and literature lasting, and in never confusing the two. – *Milton Spurling*

Honesty and hard work will buy you pain, disgrace and death – *Columbia Pictures' reader's report on the theme of West's A Cool Million*

West, Roland (1887–1952).
American director of the late silent period.
■ De Luxe Annie 18. The Silver Lining 21. Nobody 22. The Unknown Purple 23. The Monster 25. *The Bat* 26. The Dove 27. Alibi 29. *The Bat Whispers* 31. Corsair 31.

West, Sam.
English actor on stage and screen. The son of actors Timothy West and Prunella Scales, he studied physics at Oxford University before becoming an actor.
Chronicles of Narnia (TV) 90. Howards End 92. Carrington 95.

West, Timothy (1934–).
British character actor who became famous as TV's *Edward the Seventh*.
Twisted Nerve 68. Nicholas and Alexandra 71. The Day of the Jackal 74. Hedda 76. Agatha 78. The 39 Steps 78. Churchill and the Generals (TV) 80. Rough Cut 80. Murder Is Easy (TV) 82. Oliver Twist (as Bumble) (TV) 82. Tender Is the Night (TV) 84. Cry Freedom 87. Consuming Passions 88, etc.

West, Vera.
American costume designer at Universal 1927–47.
Showboat 36. Mad about Music 38. Destry Rides Again 39. The Spoilers 42. Cobra Woman 44, etc.

Westcott, Gordon (1903–1935).
American support actor of the 30s, almost always for Warners and usually the other man.
Love Me Tonight 32. The Working Man 33. Heroes for Sale 33. Footlight Parade 33. Fog Over Frisco 34. Registered Nurse 34. Go into Your Dance 35. Bright Lights 35. Two Fisted 35, etc.

Westcott, Helen (1929–) (Myrthas Helen Hickman).
American leading lady, former child actress.
A Midsummer Night's Dream 35. The New

Adventures of Don Juan 48. The Gunfighter 50. With a Song in My Heart 52. The Charge at Feather River 53. Hot Blood 55. The Last Hurrah 58. I Love My Wife 71.

Westerby, Robert (1909–1968).
British screenwriter, in films from 1947.
Broken Journey 48. The Spider and the Fly 50. They Who Dare 54. War and Peace (co-w) 56. Town on Trial 56. Cone of Silence 60. Greyfriars Bobby 60. The Three Lives of Thomasina 64, etc.

Westerfield, James (1912–1971).
Heavyweight American character actor.
Undercurrent 46. The Whistle at Eaton Falls 51. On the Waterfront 54. Chief Crazy Horse 55. Three Brave Men 57. The Shaggy Dog 59. Wild River 60. Birdman of Alcatraz 62. Blue 68. True Grit 69, many others.

westerns
have been with us almost as long as the cinema itself; and although Britain now produces *Carry On Cowboy* and a number of Continental countries are now making passable horse operas of their own, it is natural enough that almost all westerns should have come from America.

The Great Train Robbery was a western, and two of the most popular stars of the early silent period, Bronco Billy Anderson and William S. Hart, played western heroes, establishing the conventions and the legends still associated with the opening of America's west – Hollywood style. The attractions of western stories included natural settings, cheapness of production, ready-made plots capable of infinite variation, and a general air of tough simplicity which was saleable the world over. Many of Hollywood's most memorable films of the teens and 20s were westerns: *The Squaw Man, The Spoilers, The Vanishing American, The Covered Wagon, The Iron Horse, The Virginian, In Old Arizona, The Cisco Kid, Cimarron*. The western adapted itself to sound with remarkable ease, and throughout the 30s provided many entertainments of truly epic stature: *Wells Fargo, Arizona, The Texas Rangers, Union Pacific, The Plainsman, Drums Along the Mohawk, Jesse James, The Westerner, Destry Rides Again, Stagecoach*. By now the major directorial talents in the field were established: they included John Ford, William Wyler, Howard Hawks, King Vidor, Victor Fleming, Michael Curtiz, Henry King, Frank Lloyd. And each year brought in the wake of epics scores of cheap but entertaining second features, usually running in familiar series with such stars as Buck Jones, Tom Mix, Tim McCoy, John Wayne, Bob Steele, William Boyd ('Hopalong Cassidy'), Ken Maynard, Tom Tyler, Gene Autry, and 'The Three Mesquiteers'. The singing cowboy familiarized by Autry led to the arrival of other practitioners in the 40s: Roy Rogers, Eddie Dean, Lee 'Lasses' White. The 40s also based westerns more firmly on historical events, telling such stories as *Brigham Young, Northwest Passage, My Darling Clementine, Santa Fe Trail, They Died with Their Boots On*. But by the end of the decade this genre had worn itself out except in the case of Ford, whose films became increasingly stylish and personal. Elsewhere westerns deteriorated into routine action adventures starring actors a little past their best: Gary Cooper, Errol Flynn, Dennis Morgan, Alan Ladd. Howard Hawks' *Red River* was a useful move towards realism, and was followed in the early 50s by films like *The Gunfighter* and *Shane*, intent on proving how unpleasant a place the real West must have been. Side by side with realism came the 'message' western, given its impetus by *Broken Arrow* 50, the first western since silent days to sympathize with the Indians. It was followed by western allegories like *High Noon* and *3.10 to Yuma*, in which the action elements were restricted or replaced by suspense in taut stories of good versus evil. In these ways the western became a highly respectable form, attracting actors of the calibre of James Stewart, Marlon Brando, Glenn Ford, Henry Fonda, Burt Lancaster, Richard Widmark and Kirk Douglas, all of whom tended to play half-cynical heroes who preserved their sense of right by indulging in violent action in the last reel. The later 50s brought many spectacular western productions including *Gunfight at the OK Corral, Last Train from Gun Hill, One-Eyed Jacks, Warlock* and *The Magnificent Seven;* but no new ground was broken. Second features continued to prosper in the capable hands of Randolph Scott, Joel McCrea and Audie Murphy. Comedy westerns were seldom successful, though exceptions include *Go West* (Keaton and Marx versions), Laurel and Hardy's *Way Out West*, and *Blazing Saddles*.

The galloping success of TV made potted westerns so familiar that even the biggest epics made for the cinema found it hard to attract a paying audience. Ford persevered with *The Man Who Shot Liberty Valance* and *Cheyenne Autumn*, both rehashes of earlier and better matter; Cinerama made a patchy spectacle called *How the West Was Won;* novelty westerns have tried violence, horror and sentimentality as gimmicks.

In the 60s westerns came from an unexpected source: Italy, where directors took the conventions and added a baroque twist or two of their own. At their worst, the spaghetti westerns were ponderous and violent; at their best, they had a style and verve that re-invented the genre. Sergio Leone emerged as the leading director, his films aided by the atmospheric scores of Ennio Morricone and their reticent, almost blank hero, played in appropriate fashion by Clint Eastwood. But the revival was not long-lived. Hollywood directors seemed to have lost faith in the western's mythic qualities, preferring to stick to comedies such as *Cat Ballou*. Sam Peckinpah's *The Wild Bunch* 69 and George Roy Hill's *Butch Cassidy and the Sundance Kid* 69 were almost the last flourishes before the form went into what seemed like a terminal decline. Clint Eastwood was the last cowboy, but his moody outcasts seemed pale before his *Dirty Harry*. It was Eastwood who showed that there was life left in the western with *Unforgiven*, the success of which sparked off another cycle. But none of the succeeding films, including two on the life of Wyatt Earp, did particularly well at the box-office, leaving the future of the genre again in doubt.

Books: 1969, *Horizons West* by Jim Kitses. 1977, *Westerns* by Philip French. 1988, *The BFI Companion to the Western*, edited by Edward Buscombe. 1993, *Encyclopedia of Western Movies*, edited by Phil Hardy (revised edition).

¶ An adult western is where the hero still kisses his horse at the end, only now he worries about it. – Milton Berle

Westlake, Donald E. (1933–).
American screenwriter and crime novelist who also writes as Richard Stark.

The Hot Rock (GB: How to Steal a Diamond in Four Uneasy Lessons) (oa) 72. Cops and Robbers 73. The Bank Shot (oa) 74. Hot Stuff (co-w) 79. The Stepfather 87. Why Me? (co-w, from his novel) 90. *The Grifters* (AAN) 90, etc.

Westley, Helen (1879–1942) (Henrietta Conroy).
American character actress of stage and screen; usually played crotchety but kind-hearted dowagers.

Death Takes a Holiday 34. The House of Rothschild 34. Moulin Rouge 34. Anne of Green Gables 34. Roberta 35. Showboat 36. *Dimples* 36. Banjo on My Knee 36. Stowaway 36. Heidi 37. Rebecca of Sunnybrook Farm 38. Zaza 39. Lady with Red Hair 40. Lillian Russell 40. Adam Had Four Sons 41. Sunny 41. My Favorite Spy 42, etc.

Westman, Nydia (1902–1970).
American character comedienne, usually in fluttery, nervous roles.

King of the Jungle 33. The Invisible Ray 36. *The Cat and the Canary* 39. When Tomorrow Comes 40. The Late George Apley 47. The Velvet Touch 49. The Ghost and Mr Chicken 66, many others.

Westmore.
The famous family of Hollywood make-up artists was headed by George Westmore (1879–1931), English by birth but a west coast success from the moment he learned of Valentino's hairstyle. The sons all worked for different studios, and most had health and emotional problems. They were *Mont* (1902–1940), *Perc* (1904–1970), *Ern* (1904–1968), *Wally* (1906–1973), *Bud* (1918–1973) and *Frank* (1923–1985) who, in 1976, wrote a book about the family, *The Westmores of Hollywood*.

Weston, David (1938–).
British actor of TV and films.

Doctor in Distress 63. Becket 64. The Legend of Young Dick Turpin 65. The Red Baron 70. Go for a Take 73. The Incredible Sarah 75. A Man Called Intrepid (TV) 79, etc.

Weston, Jack (1926–) (Jack Weinstein).
American roly-poly character actor, often an incompetent minor villain.

Stage Struck 58. It's Only Money 62. *Mirage* 65. *Wait until Dark* 67. The Thomas Crown Affair 68. The April Fools 69. Fuzz 72. A New Leaf 72. Marco 73. Gator 76. The Ritz 77. Cuba 79. Can't Stop the Music 80. The Four Seasons 81. High Road to China 83. The Longshot 86. RAD 86. Dirty Dancing 87. Ishtar 87. Short Circuit 2 88, etc.

TV series: The Hathaways 61.

Wettig, Patricia (1951–).
American actress, from theatre and television. She is a former dresser to Shirley Maclaine.

Guilty by Suspicion 91. City Slickers 91. Parallel Lives (TV) 94.

TV series: thirtysomething 88–91.

Wexler, Haskell (1926–).
American cinematographer.

The Savage Eye 59. Angel Baby 60. The Hoodlum Priest 61. A Face in the Rain 62. America America 63. *The Best Man* 64. The Loved One (co-ph) 65. Who's Afraid of Virginia Woolf? (AA) 66. *In the Heat of the Night* 67. *The Thomas Crown Affair* 68. Medium Cool (& d) 69. The Conversation 73. American Graffiti 73. One Flew over the Cuckoo's Nest (AAN) 75. Bound for Glory (AA) 76. Coming Home 78. Days of Heaven 78. No Nukes 80. Second Hand Hearts 80. The Man Who Loved Women 83. Latino (& wd) 85. Matewan (AAN) 87. Colors 88. Three Fugitives 89. Blaze (AAN) 89. Through the Wire 90. Other People's Money 91. The Babe 92. The Secret of Roan Inish 94, etc.

Wexler, Norman (1926–).
American screenwriter and dramatist.

Joe (AAN) 70. Serpico (AAN) 73. Mandingo 75. Drum 76. Saturday Night Fever 77. Staying Alive 83. Raw Deal 86, etc.

Whale, James (1896–1957).
British stage director of somewhat mysterious personality; went to Hollywood 1930 to film his stage production of *Journey's End* and stayed to make other movies.

■ Waterloo Bridge 30. *Frankenstein* 31. The Impatient Maiden 32. *The Old Dark House* 32. The Kiss before the Mirror 33. *The Invisible Man* 33. By Candlelight 33. One More River 34. *Bride of Frankenstein* 35. *Remember Last Night* 35. Showboat 36. The Road Back 37. The Great Garrick 37. Sinners in Paradise 37. Wives under Suspicion 38. Port of Seven Seas 38. *The Man in the Iron Mask* 39. Green Hell 40. They Dare Not Love 40. Hello Out There 49.

✪ For contriving to make four classics of the macabre before his enthusiasm ran out. *Bride of Frankenstein*.

Whalen, Michael (1899–1974) (Joseph Kenneth Shovlin).
American leading man of the 30s.

Country Doctor 36. Time Out for Murder 38. Sign of the Wolf 41. Tahiti Honey 43. Gas House Kids in Hollywood 48. Mark of the Dragon 51. The Phantom from Ten Thousand Leagues 56, many others.

Whaley, Frank (1963–).
American actor.

Ironweed 87. Field of Dreams 89. Born on the Fourth of July 89. The Freshman 90. Career Opportunities (aka One Wild Night) 91. The Doors 91. A Midnight Clear 91. Back in the USSR 92. Swing Kids 93. The Buddy Factor 94, etc.

Whalley-Kilmer, Joanne (1964–).
British leading actress, from stage and TV, now in America. She is married to actor Val Kilmer.

A Kind of Loving (TV) 82. Pink Floyd the Wall 82. Edge of Darkness (TV) 85. Dance with a Stranger 85. The Good Father 86. The Singing Detective (TV) 86. No Surrender 86. Willow 88. Kill Me Again 89. Scandal 89. To Kill a Priest 89. The Big Man 90. Navy SEALS 90. Shattered 91. Storyville 92. The Secret Rapture 93. Mother's Boys 94. A Good Man in Africa 94. Trial by Jury 94. Scarlett (as Scarlett O'Hara) (TV) 94, etc.

Whatham, Claude.
British director.

■ That'll Be the Day 72. Swallows and Amazons 74. Sweet William 80. Hoodwink 82. Murder Is Easy (TV) 82. Murder Elite (TV) 85. Jumping the Queue (TV) 87. Buddy's Song 90.

Wheatley, Alan (1907–1991).
Suave British character actor best known as the Sheriff of Nottingham in TV's *Robin Hood*.

Inn for Trouble 60. Shadow of the Cat 61. Tomorrow at Ten 63. A Jolly Bad Fellow 64, etc.

Wheatley, David.
British director.

The Magic Toyshop 86. Nobody's Children 94.

Wheatley, Dennis (1897–1977).
British novelist whose horror stories have been turned into some forgettable films.

Forbidden Territory (oa) 38. The Eunuch of Stamboul (oa) 39. The Lost Continent (from novel *Uncharted Seas*) 68. The Devil Rides Out (oa) 71.

Wheaton, Wil (1972–).
American actor, in films as a juvenile.

The Secret of NIMH (voice) 82. The Buddy System 83. The Last Starfighter 84. Long Time

Gone (TV) 86. Stand by Me 86. The Curse 87. December 91. Toy Soldiers 91. The Last Prostitute (TV) 91, etc.

TV series: Star Trek: The Next Generation 87–90.

Whedon, Joss (1964–).

American screenwriter, a former television story editor, who gained a reputation for rewriting, uncredited, the hit thriller *Speed* during production.

Buffy the Vampire Slayer 92. Waterworld (co-w) 95.

wheelchairs

have usually had sinister connotations in the cinema. The Spanish film *The Wheelchair* was a very black comedy indeed, and villains who have operated from wheelchairs include Lionel Atwill in *The Mystery of the Wax Museum*, Vincent Price in *House of Wax*, Ralph Morgan in *Night Monster*, and Francis L. Sullivan in *Hell's Island*. General 'heavies' confined to wheelchairs include Eleanor Parker in *The Man with the Golden Arm* and *Eye of the Cat*, cantankerous Dame May Whitty (and later Mona Washbourne) in *Night Must Fall*, and crusty old Lionel Barrymore in the *Dr Kildare* series and every other film he made after 1939 (he was confined to a chair after twice breaking his hip). Wheelchair victims included Estelle Winwood in *Notorious Landlady*, careering away over the countryside, and the old lady who was pushed downstairs in a wheelchair in *Kiss of Death*. Perhaps the most fearsome wheelchair occupant was Monty Woolley, of the barbed tongue, in *The Man Who Came to Dinner*. Electric staircase chairs were used by 'invalids' Ethel Barrymore in *The Farmer's Daughter*, Eugenie Leontovich in *Homicidal* and Charles Laughton in *Witness for the Prosecution*.

Wheeler, Anne (1946–).

Canadian director and screenwriter.

A War Story 81. Loyalties 86. Cowboys Don't Cry 88. Bye Bye Blues 89. Angel Street 91, etc.

Wheeler, Bert (1895–1968).

American comedian who teamed as double act with Robert Woolsey (qv).

Rio Rita 29. Half Shot at Sunrise 30. Hook Line and Sinker 30. Cracked Nuts 30. Caught Plastered 32. Hold 'em Jail 32. Diplomaniacs 33. Hips Hips Hooray 34. The Nitwits 35. The Rainmakers 35. Mummy's Boys 37. High Flyers 37. On Again Off Again 37. The Gay City (solo) 41, etc.

TV series: Brave Eagle 55.

Wheeler, Charles F.

American cinematographer.

Tora! Tora! Tora! (AAN) 70. Cold Turkey 70. The Cat from Outer Space 78. Condorman 81. The Best of Times 86, etc.

Wheeler, Lyle (1905–1990).

American art director.

The Prisoner of Zenda 37. *Tom Sawyer* 38. *Gone with the Wind* (AA) 39. *Rebecca* 40. *Laura* 44. *Anna and the King of Siam* (AA) 46. *Fourteen Hours* 51. *The Robe* (AA) 53. *Love Is a Many-Splendored Thing* 55. *Daddy Longlegs* 55. *The King and I* (AA) 56. *The Diary of Anne Frank* (AA) 59. *Journey to the Centre of the Earth* 59. *The Cardinal* 63, many others.

Whelan, Albert (1875–1962).

Dapper Australian character actor and music-hall entertainer, in Britain from the early 1900s.

An Intimate Interlude 28. The Man from Chicago 30. Matinee Idol 33. Stars on Parade 36.

Educated Evans 36. The Green Cockatoo 37. Thank Evans 38. Danny Boy 41. English without Tears 44. Keep It Clean 56, etc.

Whelan, Arleen (1916–1993).

American leading lady of the 40s.

Kidnapped 38. Young Mr Lincoln 39. Charley's American Aunt 42. Ramrod 47. The Sun Shines Bright 52. The Badge of Marshal Brennan 57, etc.

Whelan, Tim (1893–1957).

American director who often filmed in Britain.

Safety Last 23. It's a Boy (GB) 33. Murder Man 35. The Mill on the Floss (GB) 36. *Farewell Again* (GB) 37. The Divorce of Lady X (GB) 37. *St Martin's Lane* (GB) 38. *Q Planes* (GB) 39. Ten Days in Paris (GB) 39. *The Thief of Bagdad* (GB) (co-d) 40. A Date with Destiny 40. International Lady 41. Twin Beds 42. Nightmare 42. Seven Days' Leave 42. Higher and Higher 42. Step Lively 44. Badman's Territory 46. This Was a Woman (GB) 47. Texas Lady 55. Rage at Dawn 55, etc.

Whiley, Manning (1915–).

British actor, usually in sinister roles.

Consider Your Verdict 38. The Trunk Crime 39. The Ghost of St Michael's 41. The Seventh Veil 45. Teheran 47. The Shop at Sly Corner 50. Little Big Shot (last to date) 52, etc.

Whipper, Leigh (1877–1975).

American character actor.

Of Mice and Men 39. The Ox Bow Incident 42. Mission to Moscow 43, etc.

The Whistler.

Based on a popular American radio show, this crime anthology ran as a film series from 1944 to 1947, with Richard Dix playing the hero of each. The only other connection between episodes was the whistled theme at the beginning. The first story was the old chestnut about the man who hires someone to kill him and then changes his mind.

The Whistler 44. Mark of the Whistler 44. Power of the Whistler 45. Voice of the Whistler 45. Mysterious Intruder 46. Secret of the Whistler 46. The 13th Hour 47. The Return of the Whistler 48.

Whistling in the Dark.

This crime-comedy play by Lavinia Cross and Edward Carpenter was first filmed by Elliott Nugent, with Ernest Truex as the little man who beats the crooks in the end. In 1940 it was revamped as a vehicle for Red Skelton, directed by S. Sylvan Simon, who also handled the two sequels: *Whistling in Dixie* 42 and *Whistling in Brooklyn* 43.

Whitaker, Forest (1961–).

Plump American character actor and producer.

Fast Times at Ridgemont High 82. Vision Quest 85. The Color of Money 86. Platoon 86. Stakeout 87. Good Morning Vietnam 87. Bird 88. Bloodsport 88. Johnny Handsome 89. Downtown 90. A Rage in Harlem (& p) 91. Article 99 92. The Crying Game 92. Diary of a Hit Man 92. Consenting Adults 92. Strapped (d) (TV) 93. Last Light (TV) 93. Body Snatchers 93. Bank Robber 93. Lush Life 93. Blown Away 94. Jason's Lyric 94. Prêt-à-Porter (aka Ready to Wear) 94, etc.

White, Alice (1907–1983).

American leading lady of 'B' features who played flappers and gangsters' molls from the 20s to the 40s.

The Thief of Bagdad 24. Hot Stuff 27. The Sea Wolf 30. Gentlemen Prefer Blondes 31. The Picture Snatcher 33. Big City 38. Annabel Takes a Tour 39. Flamingo Road 48, many others.

White, Barbara (1924–).

British leading lady of the 40s.

It Happened One Sunday 44. The Voice Within 45. Quiet Weekend 46. While the Sun Shines 46. Mine Own Executioner 47. This Was a Woman 48, etc.

White Cargo.

Leon Gordon's much-caricatured play was based on a book by Ida Vera Simonton called *Hell's Playground*; it dealt with the difficulties of acclimatization for Malayan rubber planters, and in particular with a shapely native distraction called Tondelayo. It was filmed in Britain by J. B. Williams in 1929, with Leslie Faber and Gypsy Rhouma; and in Hollywood in 1942 with Walter Pidgeon and Hedy Lamarr.

White, Carol (1941–1991).

British leading lady, in films as a child, who went to Hollywood and failed to become a star there, with an over-indulgence in drink and drugs causing her early death. She first attracted attention on TV in the plays *Up the Junction* 65 and *Cathy Come Home* 66.

Linda 60. Never Let Go 60. Slave Girls 66. *Poor Cow* 67. I'll Never Forget Whatshisname 68. Daddy's Gone a-Hunting 69. The Man Who Had Power over Women 70. Dulcima 71. Something Big 71. Made 72. The Squeeze 77. Nutcracker 82, etc.

White, Chrissie (1895–1989).

British leading lady of the silent screen, especially popular when teamed with her husband Henry Edwards (qv). Films include *Broken Threads*, *David Garrick*, *Barnaby Rudge*, *Sweet Lavender*, *Trelawny of the Wells*, *The City of Beautiful Nonsense*, *Possession*; last appearance in *General John Regan* 34.

White, Jesse (1918–) (Jesse Wiedenfeld).

American comic character actor, usually seen as nervous cigar-chewing crook. Wide stage experience.

Harvey (debut) 50. Death of a Salesman 52. Not as a Stranger 55. Designing Woman 57. The Rise and Fall of Legs Diamond 59. It's Only Money 62. A House Is Not a Home 64. Dear Brigitte 65. The Reluctant Astronaut 67. The Brothers O'Toole 73. The Cat from Outer Space 78. Monster in the Closet 86, many others.

TV series: *Make Room for Daddy* 53–57.

White, Jules (1900–1985).

American (originally Hungarian) shorts director in charge of The Three Stooges from 1945 to 1957.

White, Merrill (c. 1895–1959).

American editor.

The Love Parade 29. *Love Me Tonight* 32. Nell Gwyn 34. The Frog 37. Victoria the Great 37. The Red Rose 47. Blaze of Glory 50. One Girl's Confession 53. Carnival Story 54. The Fly 58. Crime and Punishment USA 59, many others.

White, Onna.

Canadian choreographer.

The Music Man 62. Bye Bye Birdie 63. *Oliver* (AA) 68. 1776 72. The Great Waltz 72. Mame 73, etc.

White, Pearl (1889–1938).

American leading lady, 'queen of the silent serials'. On stage from six years old. At first a stunt woman, then in such serials as *The Perils of Pauline* 14 and *The Exploits of Elaine* 15, involving circus-like thrills. Later in features: *The White Moll* 20. *Know Your Men* 21. *A Virgin Paradise* 21, etc.; retired

1921. A pseudo-biography, *The Perils of Pauline*, was filmed with Betty Hutton in 1947.

Autobiography: 1919, *Just Me.*

White, Ruth (1914–1969).
American character actress.

To Kill a Mockingbird 63. Up the Down Staircase 67. The Tiger is Out 68. Charly 69. Midnight Cowboy 69.

White, Valerie (1916–1975).
British character actress.

Halfway House 43. My Learned Friend 44. Hue and Cry 46. Travels with My Aunt 73, etc.

Whitehead, Geoffrey (1939–).
British light actor who in 1980 played Holmes in the Anglo-Polish TV series *Sherlock Holmes and Dr Watson.*

Inside the Third Reich (TV) 82. Peter the Great (TV) 85. War and Remembrance (TV) 87.

Whitelaw, Billie (1932–).
British leading actress of stage and TV, also in occasional films. She began as an 11-year-old on radio.

The Fake 54. Make Mine Mink 59. Bobbikins 59. Hell is a City 60. *No Love for Johnnie* 61. Payroll 61. The Comedy Man 63. *Charlie Bubbles* (BFA) 68. Twisted Nerve 68. The Adding Machine 69. Gumshoe 71. Eagle in a Cage 71. Frenzy 72. Night Watch 73. *The Omen* 76. The Water Babies 78. An Unsuitable Job for a Woman 82. Jamaica Inn (TV) 83. Camille (TV) 84. The Chain 86. Shadey 86. Maurice 87. The Dressmaker 88. Joyriders 89. The Krays 90. Freddie as F.R.O.7. (voice) 92. Deadly Advice 94. Skallagrigg (TV) 94, etc.

TV series: Firm Friends 92–94.

Whiteley, Jon (1945–).
British boy actor.

Hunted 52. *The Kidnappers* (special AA) 53. Moonfleet 55. The Weapon 56. The Spanish Gardener 56. Capetown Affair 67, etc.

Whiteman, Paul (1890–1967).
Tall, portly American bandleader who made several film appearances.

King of Jazz 30. Thanks a Million 35. Strike Up the Band 40. Atlantic City 44. Rhapsody in Blue 45. The Fabulous Dorseys 47, etc.

Whiting, Leonard (1950–)
British juvenile lead.

The Legend of Young Dick Turpin 66. *Romeo and Juliet* (as Romeo) 68. The Royal Hunt of the Sun 69. Young Casanova 70. Say Hello to Yesterday 71. Frankenstein: The True Story 73 (TV), etc.

Whiting, Richard (1891–1938).
American composer and songwriter who went to Hollywood in 1929 to write for Maurice Chevalier, an assignment that produced 'Louise'. Other hits followed: 'On the Good Ship Lollipop' for Shirley Temple, 'Beyond the Blue Horizon', 'Hooray for Hollywood' and 'Too Marvellous for Words'. His daughter is the singer Margaret Whiting.

Innocents of Paris 29. Monte Carlo 30. Playboy of Paris 30. One Hour with You 32. My Weakness 33. Adorable 33. Take a Chance 33. Bright Eyes 34. Transatlantic Merry-Go-Round 34. The Big Broadcast of 1936 35. Coronado 35. Hollywood Hotel 37. Ready Willing and Able 37. Cowboy from Brooklyn 38, etc.

Whitley, Ray (1902–1979).
American character actor and songwriter, usually as a singing cowboy.

Hopalong Cassidy Returns 36. Gun Law 38. Wagon Train 40. Along the Rio Grande 41. Thundering Hoofs 41. Robbers of the Range 41. Riders of the Santa Fe 44. Trail to Gunsight 44. West of the Alamo 46. Giant 56, etc.

Whitlock, Albert (1915–).
British special effects technician.

The Birds 63. Marnie 64. Torn Curtain 66. Diamonds Are Forever 70. Frenzy 73. The Sting 73. *Earthquake* (AA) 74. *The Hindenburg* (AA) 75. Family Plot 75. The Car 77. High Anxiety 77. Dracula 79. Heartbeeps 81. History of the World Part One 81. Missing 82. Dune 84, etc.

Whitman, Ernest (1893–1954).
American character actor of sizeable presence.

Prisoner of Shark Island 36. The Green Pastures 36. Nothing Sacred 37. Gone with the Wind 39. Congo Maisie 40. Road to Zanzibar 41. Cabin in the Sky 43. *Stormy Weather* 43. The Sun Shines Bright 53, many others.

Whitman, Stuart (1926–).
American leading man, former boxer and stage and TV actor.

When Worlds Collide 52. Rhapsody 54. Darby's Rangers 57. *Ten North Frederick* 58. The Decks Ran Red 58. The Story of Ruth 60. Murder Inc. 61. *The Mark* (AAN) 62. The Comancheros 62. Reprieve 63. Shock Treatment 64. Signpost to Murder 64. Rio Conchos 64. Those Magnificent Men in Their Flying Machines 65. Sands of the Kalahari 65. An American Dream 66. The Invincible Six 68. The Only Way Out is Dead 70. Captain Apache 71. City Beneath the Sea (TV) 71. Night of the Lepus 73. Mean Johnny Barrows 76. Strange Shadows in an Empty Room 77. Eaten Alive 77. The White Buffalo 77. Run for the Roses 78. Guyana 80. Sweet Dirty Tony 81. Butterfly 82. Stillwatch (TV) 87. Deadly Reactor 89. Moving Target 89. Mob Boss 90. Omega Cop 90. The Color of Evening 91. Smooth Talker 91. Trial by Jury 94, etc.

TV series: Cimarron Strip 67. The Men from Shiloh 70.

Whitmore, James (1921–).
Craggy American character actor.

Undercover Man 49. Battleground (AAN) 49. The Asphalt Jungle 50. Across the Wide Missouri 51. Kiss Me Kate 53. *Them* 54. Battle Cry 55. Oklahoma 55. The Eddy Duchin Story 56. Who Was That Lady? 60. Black Like Me 64. Chuka 67. Planet of the Apes 68. Madigan 68. The Split 68. Guns of the Magnificent Seven 69. Tora! Tora! Tora! 70. Chato's Land 71. If Tomorrow Comes (TV) 71. The Harrad Experiment 73. Give 'em Hell Harry (AAN) 75. Where the Red Fern Grows 75. The Serpent's Egg 77. The Word (TV) 78. Bully 78. The First Deadly Sin 80. The Adventures of Mark Twain (voice) 85. Favorite Son (TV) 88. The Shawshank Redemption 94, etc.

TV series: The Law and Mr Jones 60–61. My Friend Troy 69. Temperature Rising 72–73.

Whitney, Peter (1916–1972) (Peter King Engle).
Portly American character player.

Reunion in France 42. *Murder He Says* (as twins) 45. Hotel Berlin 45. The Iron Curtain 48. The Big Heat 53. Great Day in the Morning 56. Sword of Ali Baba 65. Chubasco 67. The Ballad of Cable Hogue 70, etc.

Whitrow, Benjamin (1939–).
British light actor, mostly on stage and radio.

Quadrophenia 78. Brimstone and Treacle 82. Clockwise 85. Personal Services 86.

Whitsun-Jones, Paul (1923–1974).
Rotund British character actor, usually in comedy.

The Constant Husband 55. *The Moonraker* 57. Room at the Top 59. Tunes of Glory 60, etc.

Whittingham, Jack (1910–1972).
British screenwriter.

Q Planes 39. Kiss the Bride Goodbye 44. Twilight Hour 45. I Believe in You 51. Hunted 52. The Divided Heart 54. The Birthday Present (& p) 57, etc.

Whitty, Dame May (1865–1948).
Distinguished character actress, on stage from 1881. Settled in Hollywood in the mid-30s and played dozens of indomitable but kindly old ladies.

Biography: 1969, *The Same Only Different* by her daughter.

■ Enoch Arden 14. The Little Minister 15. Colonel Newcombe 20. The Thirteenth Chair 37. *Night Must Fall* (AAN) 37. Conquest 37. I Met My Love Again 37. *The Lady Vanishes* (GB) 38. Return to Yesterday (GB) 40. Raffles 40. A Bill of Divorcement 40. One Night in Lisbon 41. Suspicion 41. Mrs Miniver (AAN) 42. Thunder Birds 42. Slightly Dangerous 42. Forever and a Day 43. Crash Dive 43. The Constant Nymph 43. Lassie Come Home 43. Flesh and Fantasy 43. Madame Curie 43. Stage Door Canteen 43. The White Cliffs of Dover 44. Gaslight 44. *My Name Is Julia Ross* 45. Devotion 46. This Time for Keeps 47. Green Dolphin Street 47. If Winter Comes 47. The Sign of the Ram 48. The Return of October 48.

¶ So long as I can do my bit, I'll keep right on doing it. – *M.W.*

Whorf, Richard (1906–1966).
Sullen-looking American actor-director.

AS ACTOR: Midnight 34. *Blues in the Night* 41. Yankee Doodle Dandy 42. Keeper of the Flame 43. Christmas Holiday 44. Chain Lightning 50, etc.

AS DIRECTOR: The Hidden Eye 45. Till the Clouds Roll By 46. It Happened in Brooklyn 47. Love from a Stranger 47. Luxury Liner 48. Champagne for Caesar 50, etc.

Lots of TV half-hours and hours, especially *Rawhide* and *The Beverly Hillbillies.*

Why We Fight.
A brilliant series of World War II documentaries using all the resources of the cinema, compiled by Frank Capra and the US Signal Corps Film Unit from material shot by Allied cameramen and from pre-war newsreel material. Each lasted just over an hour, and was kept absorbingly entertaining as well as instructive by the use of music, diagrams, and optical work. Titles were *Prelude to War*, *The Nazis Strike*, *Divide and Conquer*, *The Battle of Britain*, *The Battle of Russia*, *The Battle of China.*

The Wicked Lady.
Magdalen King-Hall's novel of an aristocratic woman who turns to highway robbery made a star of Margaret Lockwood in 1945, directed by Leslie Arliss. Michael Winner's remake in 1983 did nothing for Faye Dunaway's career.

Wickes, David.
British director and producer, working mainly in television.

Sweeney! 76. Silver Dream Racer (& p, w) 80. Jack the Ripper (TV) 88. Jekyll and Hyde (TV) 90. Frankenstein (TV) 93.

Wickes, Mary (1916–) (Mary Wickenhauser).
American character comedienne.

The Man Who Came to Dinner (as the nurse) 41.

Higher and Higher 43. June Bride 48. Young Man with Ideas 52. The Actress 54. Good Morning, Miss Dove 56. It Happened to Jane 59. The Trouble with Angels 66. Where Angels Go Trouble Follows 68. Snowball Express 73. Postcards from the Edge 90, many others.

TV series: The Peter Lind Hayes Show 50. Bonino 50. Halls of Ivy 54. Dennis the Menace 59–61. The Gertrude Berg Show 61–62. Julia 68–71. Doc 75.

Famous line (*The Man Who Came to Dinner*): 'If Florence Nightingale had ever nursed you, Mr Whiteside, she would have married Jack the Ripper instead of founding the Red Cross!'

Wicki, Bernhard (1919–).
Austrian actor-director.
AS ACTOR: Der Fallende Stern 50. The Last Bridge 54. Kinder, Mütter und ein General 54. Jackboot Mutiny 55. The Face of the Cat 57. La Notte 61. Paris, Texas 84. Killing Cars 85. Marie Ward 85, etc.
AS DIRECTOR: The Bridge 59. The Miracle of Malachias 61. The Longest Day (co-d) 62. The Visit (US) 64. The Saboteur 65. Karpfs Karriere 72. Die Eroberung der Zitadelle 77. Die Grunstein-Variante 85. The Spider's Web (Das Spinnennetz) 89. Success (Erfolg) 91, etc.

Widdoes, Kathleen (1939–).
American actress with stage experience.
The Group 66. Petulia 68. The Seagull 68. The Mephisto Waltz 71. Savages 72. Mafia Princess (TV) 86, etc.

wide screen.
Strictly speaking this does not mean anamorphic processes such as CinemaScope, which requires a wide, *wide* screen, but the now-standard 1:1.65 ratio which was achieved by projecting the old 1.3:1 image, cutting the top and bottom from it, and magnifying the result.

Widerberg, Bo (1930–).
Swedish writer-director.
Raven's End 63. Karlek 63. Thirty Times Your Money 66. *Elvira Madigan* 67. Adalen 31 69. The Ballad of Joe Hill 69. The Man on the Roof 75. Victoria 79. The Man from Majorca 85. The Serpent's Way 87. Up the Naked Rock 88. End All Things Fair 95, etc.

Widmark, Richard (1914–).
American leading actor; once typed as cold-eyed killer, he fought successfully for more varied roles.
■ *Kiss of Death* (AAN) 47. Road House 48. The Street with No Name 48. Yellow Sky 49. Down to the Sea in Ships 49. Slattery's Hurricane 49. Night and the City 50. Panic in the Streets 50. No Way Out 50. Halls of Montezuma 50. The Frogmen 51. Full House 52. Don't Bother to Knock 52. Red Skies of Montana 52. My Pal Gus 52. Destination Gobi 53. Pickup on South Street 53. Take the High Ground 53. Hell and High Water 54. Garden of Evil 54. Broken Lance 54. The Cobweb 55. A Prize of Gold 55. Backlash 56. Run for the Sun 56. The Last Wagon 56. Saint Joan 57. Time Limit 57. The Law and Jake Wade 58. The Tunnel of Love 58. The Trap 59. Warlock 59. The Alamo 60. The Secret Ways 61. Two Rode Together 61. Judgment at Nuremberg 61. How the West Was Won 63. Flight from Ashiya 64. The Long Ships 64. Cheyenne Autumn 64. *The Bedford Incident* 65. Alvarez Kelly 66. The Way West 67. *Madigan* 68. Death of a Gunfighter 69. A Talent for Loving 69. The Moonshine War 70. Brock's Last Case (TV) 71. Vanished (TV) 71. When the Legends Die 72.

Murder on the Orient Express 74. To the Devil a Daughter 75. The Sellout 76. Twilight's Last Gleaming 76. Rollercoaster 77. The Domino Principle 77. Mr Horn (TV) 78. Coma 78. The Swarm 78. Bear Island 79. All God's Children (TV) 80. A Whale for the Killing (TV) 81. Who Dares Wins 82. Hanky Panky 82. National Lampoon's Movie Madness 82. The Final Option 82. Against All Odds 83. Blackout 85. A Gathering of Old Men (TV) 87. Once upon a Texas Train (aka Texas Guns) (TV) 88. Cold Sassy Tree (TV) 89. True Colors 91. TV series: *Madigan* 72.

¶ It is clear that murder is one of the kindest things he is capable of. – *James Agee*

Wieck, Dorothea (1908–1986).
German character actress.
Mädchen in Uniform 31. Cradle Song (US) 33. The Student of Prague 35. Der Vierte Kommt Nicht 39, etc.

Wiene, Robert (1881–1938).
German director of expressionist films.
The Cabinet of Dr Caligari 19. Genuine 20. Raskolnikov 23. The Hands of Orlac 24, etc.

The Wiere Brothers.
German eccentric comedians, long in America: *Harry* (1908–), *Herbert* (1909–), *Sylvester* (1910–1970). Films very occasional.
The Great American Broadcast 41. Swing Shift Maisie 44. *Road to Rio* 47. Double Trouble 68, etc.
TV series: *Oh Those Bells* 62.

Wiest, Dianne (1948–).
American character actress.
Footloose 84. Falling in Love 84. The Purple Rose of Cairo 85. *Hannah and Her Sisters* (AA) 86. Radio Days 87. September 87. The Lost Boys 87. Bright Lights, Big City 88. Cookie 89. Parenthood (AAN) 89. Edward Scissorhands 90. Little Man Tate 91. Cops and Robbersons 94. Bullets over Broadway 94. The Scout 94, etc.

Wilbur, Crane (1887–1973).
American writer-director.
Canon City 48. The Story of Molly X 49. Outside the Wall 49. Inside the Walls of Folsom Prison 50. House of Wax (script only) 53. The Bat 59. Solomon and Sheba (script only) 59, etc.

Wilby, James (1958–).
Elegant British actor (born in Burma), from the stage.
Dreamchild 85. A Room with a View 85. Maurice 87. A Handful of Dust 88. A Summer Story 88. Conspiracy 90. Adam Bede (TV) 91. Howards End 91. Immaculate Conception 92. Lady Chatterley (TV) 93, etc.

Wilcox, Frank (1907–1974).
Tall American character actor, a bit player who was always seen in Warner films of the 40s – sometimes in two parts in the same film.
The Fighting 69th 39. River's End 40. Highway West 41. Across the Pacific 42. Juke Girl 43. The Adventures of Mark Twain 44. Conflict 45. Gentleman's Agreement 47. Samson and Delilah 49. Those Redheads from Seattle 53. Dance with Me Henry 56. A Majority of One 61, many others.

Wilcox, Fred M. (1905–1964).
American director, former publicist; films mainly routine.
Lassie Come Home 43. Blue Sierra 46. Courage of Lassie 46. Hills of Home 48. Three Daring Daughters 48. The Secret Garden 49. Shadow in

the Sky 50. Code Two 53, Tennessee Champ 54. *Forbidden Planet* 56. I Passed for White 60.

Wilcox, Herbert (1892–1977).
British independent producer-director in films from 1919 (as salesman); married to Anna Neagle.
The Wonderful Story 20. The Dawn of the World 21. Chu Chin Chow 23. *Nell Gwyn* 24. *Dawn* 26. Wolves 28. Rookery Nook 30. Good Night Vienna 32. Carnival 32. *Bitter Sweet* 33. *Nell Gwyn* 34. Peg of Old Drury 35. Limelight 36. The Three Maxims 36. The Frog 37. *Victoria the Great* 37. Sixty Glorious Years 38. Our Fighting Navy 38. *Nurse Edith Cavell* (US) 39. Sunny (US) 39. *No No Nanette* (US) 40. Irene (US) 40. They Flew Alone 42. Yellow Canary 43. I Live in Grosvenor Square 45. *Piccadilly Incident* 46. The Courtneys of Curzon Street 47. *Spring in Park Lane* 48. Elizabeth of Ladymead 49. Maytime in Mayfair 49. *Odette* 50. The Lady with a Lamp 51. Trent's Last Case 52. Laughing Anne 53. Lilacs in the Spring 55. King's Rhapsody 56. Yangtse Incident 56. My Teenage Daughter 56. Those Dangerous Years 57. The Lady Is a Square 58. Heart of a Man 59. To See Such Fun (exec. p only) 77, etc.

¶ Mr Herbert Wilcox proceeds on his appointed course. As slow and ponderous and well protected as a steamroller, he irons out opposition. We get from his films almost everything except life, character, truth. – *Graham Greene reviewing Nurse Edith Cavell*

Wilcox, Jack (John) (1905–1984).
British cinematographer.
Mr Topaz 61. Where's Jack? 68. The Chairman 68. The Last Valley 70. Legend of the Werewolf 75, etc.

Wilcoxon, Henry (1905–1984).
British leading man with stage experience, in Hollywood from early 30s, latterly as executive for Cecil B. de Mille.
The Perfect Lady 31. The Flying Squad 32. Cleopatra 34. The Crusades 35. The Last of the Mohicans 36. Mrs Miniver 42. Samson and Delilah 49. Scaramouche 52. The Greatest Show on Earth 53. The Ten Commandments (& co-p) 56. The Buccaneer (& p) 59. The Private Navy of Sergeant O'Farrell 69. Man in the Wilderness 71. Against a Crooked Sky 75. Pony Express Rider 76. F.I.S.T. 78. Caddyshack 80. Sweet Sixteen 81, etc.

Wild, Jack (1952–).
British juvenile, popular around 1970.
Oliver (AAN) 68. Melody 70. Flight of the Doves 71. The Pied Piper 72. The Fourteen 73. Robin Hood: Prince of Thieves 91, etc.
TV series: H. R. Pufnstuf 69.

wild track:
one recorded *in situ*, not prepared in the studio.

Wilde, Cornel (1915–1989).
American leading man of the 40s; later produced and directed some interesting films, but never equalled his 1944 impact as Chopin.
■ Lady with Red Hair 40. Kisses for Breakfast 41. High Sierra 41. Right to the Heart 41. The Perfect Snob 41. Life Begins at 8.30 42. Manila Calling 42. Wintertime 43. *A Song to Remember* (AAN) 45. A Thousand and One Nights 45. Leave Her to Heaven 45. *The Bandit of Sherwood Forest* 46. Centennial Summer 46. The Homestretch 46. Forever Amber 47. It Had to be You 47. Roadhouse 48. The Walls of Jericho 48. Shockproof 49. Four Days' Leave 50. Two Flags West 50. At Sword's Point 52.

Operation Secret 52. The Greatest Show on Earth 52. California Conquest 52. Treasure of the Golden Condor 53. Main Street to Broadway 53. Saadia 53. Passion 54. *Woman's World* 54. The Scarlet Coat 55. Storm Fear (& d) 55. The Big Combo 55. Star of India 55. Hot Blood 56. The Devil's Hairpin (& w) 57. Omar Khayyam 57. Beyond Mombasa 57. Maracaibo (& d) 58. Edge of Eternity 59. Constantine and the Cross 60. Sword of Lancelot (& d) 63. *The Naked Prey* (& d) 66. Beach Red (& d) 67. The Comic 69. No Blade of Grass (& d) 71. Gargoyles (TV) 72. Shark's Treasure (& d) 75. The Fifth Musketeer 78. The Norseman 78.

Wilde, Hagar (1904–1971).
American screenwriter.
Bringing Up Baby 38. Carefree 39. Fired Wife 43. Guest in the House 44. The Unseen 45. I Was a Male War Bride 49. This is My Love 54, etc.

Wilde, Marty (1939–) (Reginald Smith).
British pop singer who appeared in a film or two.
Jetstorm 59. The Hellions 61. What a Crazy World 63. Stardust 74, etc.

Wilde, Oscar (1854–1900).
British playwright, poet and wit, the subject in 1960 of two film biographies: *Oscar Wilde* starring Robert Morley and *The Trials of Oscar Wilde* starring Peter Finch. The former was directed by Gregory Ratoff from a script by Jo Eisinger, and had Ralph Richardson as Carson, John Neville as Lord Alfred, and Edward Chapman as the Marquess of Queensberry. The latter, written and directed by Ken Hughes, had James Mason, John Fraser and Lionel Jeffries respectively in these roles. Films have been made of several of Wilde's works including *The Importance of Being Earnest, An Ideal Husband, Lady Windermere's Fan, The Picture of Dorian Gray, Lord Arthur Savile's Crime* (in *Flesh and Fantasy*) and *The Canterville Ghost.*

Wilder, Billy (1906–) (Samuel Wilder).
Austro-Hungarian writer-director, in Hollywood from 1934. A specialist for years in bitter comedy and drama torn from the world's headlines, he has lately concentrated on rather heavy-going bawdy farce.
Biographies: 1970, *The Brighter Side of Billy Wilder*, Primarily by Tom Wood. 1976, *Billy Wilder in Hollywood* by Maurice Zolotow.
■ AS WRITER: People on Sunday 30; followed by ten other German films; Adorable (French) 34. Music in the Air (co-w) 34. Lottery Lover (co-w) 35. Bluebeard's Eighth Wife (co-w) 38. *Midnight* (co-w) 39. What a Life (co-w) 39. Ninotchka (co-w, AAN) 39. *Arise My Love* (co-w) 40. Ball of Fire (co-w, AAN) 41. Hold Back the Dawn (co-w, AAN) 41.
■ AS WRITER-DIRECTOR (script always in collaboration): Mauvaise Graine (Fr.) 33. *The Major and the Minor* 42. Five Graves to Cairo 43. *Double Indemnity* (AAN) 44. *The Lost Weekend* (AA) 45. The Emperor Waltz 47. *A Foreign Affair* (co-w, AAN) 48. *Sunset Boulevard* (AAN) 50. Ace in the Hole 51. *Stalag 17* (AAN) 53. Sabrina (AAN) 54. *The Seven Year Itch* 55. The Spirit of St Louis 57. Love in the Afternoon 57. *Witness for the Prosecution* (AAN) 57. *Some Like It Hot* (AAN) 59. *The Apartment* (AA) 60. One Two Three 61. Irma La Douce 63. Kiss Me Stupid 64. The Fortune Cookie 66. *The Private Life of Sherlock Holmes* 70. Avanti 72. The Front Page 74. Fedora 78. Buddy Buddy 81.
✪ For being Hollywood's most mischievous immigrant. *Sunset Boulevard.*

¶ The pixie wit of this Hollywood Viennese has sporadically brightened the film scene for more than thirty years. Nor does he save all his wit for his scripts; he is the most quotable of filmmakers:
I have ten commandments. The first nine are, thou shalt not bore. The tenth is, thou shalt have right of final cut.
On critical prejudice:
What critics call dirty in our movies, they call lusty in foreign films.
On fashion:
You watch, the new wave will discover the slow dissolve in ten years or so.
On messages:
In certain pictures I do hope they will leave the cinema a little enriched, but I don't make them pay a buck and a half and then ram a lecture down their throats.
On direction:
The best director is the one you don't see
On technique:
The close-up is such a valuable thing – like a trump at bridge.
On finances:
No one says, 'Boy I must see that film – I hear it came in under budget.'
A man with such waspish wit naturally invites retaliation, even from his wife:
Long before Billy Wilder was Billy Wilder, he thought he was Billy Wilder.
That may have been in response to a cable he sent her from Paris just after the war. She had requested him to buy and send a bidet. After a vain search he sent the message:
Unable obtain bidet. Suggest handstand in shower.
Wilder is the kind of man who can scarcely observe anything without being funny about it. For instance:
France is a country where the money falls apart in your hands and you can't tear the toilet paper.
But he could be just as ornery as anybody else. As Harry Kurnitz said:
Billy Wilder at work is two people: Mr Hyde and Mr Hyde.
Andrew Sarris summed up accurately:
Wilder is a curdled Lubitsch, romanticism gone sour, 78rpm played at 45 an old-worldling from Vienna perpetually sneering at Hollywood as it engulfs him.
Wilder wouldn't be listening – too busy constructing scenarios:
An actor enters through a door, you've got nothing. But if he enters through a window, you've got a situation.

Wilder, Gene (1934–) (Jerry Silberman).
American comic actor.
Bonnie and Clyde (AAN) 67. *The Producers* (AAN) 68. Start the Revolution Without Me 69. Quackser Fortune has a Cousin in the Bronx 70. Willy Wonka and the Chocolate Factory 71. Everything You Always Wanted to Know about Sex 72. Rhinoceros 73. The Little Prince 73. Blazing Saddles 74. Young Frankenstein 74. The Adventure of Sherlock Holmes' Smarter Brother (& p, d) 75. Silver Streak 76. The World's Greatest Lover (& wd, p) 77. The Frisco Kid 79. Stir Crazy 80. Sunday Lovers 80. Hanky Panky 82. The Woman in Red (& d) 84. Haunted Honeymoon (& d) 86. See No Evil, Hear No Evil 89. Funny about Love 90. Another You 91, etc.

Wilder, Robert (1901–1974).
American novelist and screenwriter.
Flamingo Road (& oa) 48. *Written on the Wind* (& oa) 56. The Big Country 58. Sol Madrid 66, etc.

Wilder, Thornton (1897–1975).
American playwright and novelist. Works filmed include *Our Town, The Bridge of San Luis Rey* (several times), *The Matchmaker;* also wrote screenplay of Hitchcock's *Shadow of a Doubt.*

Wilder, W. Lee (1904–).
Austro-Hungarian producer in America, brother of Billy Wilder. Films mainly low-budget oddities.
The Great Flamarion 44. Phantom from Space 53. The Snow Creature 54. Bluebeard's Ten Honeymoons 60, etc.

Wilding, Michael (1912–1979).
British leading man of the 40s. His four wives included actresses Elizabeth Taylor and Margaret Leighton.
Posthumous autobiography: 1982, *Apple Sauce.*
Wedding Group 35. Tilly of Bloomsbury 40. *Sailors Three* 40. Kipps 41. Cottage To Let 41. *In Which We Serve* 42. Dear Octopus 43. *English Without Tears* 44. Carnival 46. *Piccadilly Incident* 46. The Courtneys of Curzon Street 47. An Ideal Husband 47. *Spring in Park Lane* 48. Maytime in Mayfair 50. Under Capricorn 50. Stage Fright 50. Into the Blue 51. The Law and the Lady (US) 52. Derby Day 52. Trent's Last Case 53. The Egyptian 54. The Glass Slipper 55. Zarak 56. Danger Within 57. The World of Suzie Wong 60. The Naked Edge 61. The Best of Enemies 61. A Girl Named Tamiko 63. The Sweet Ride 68. Waterloo 69. Lady Caroline Lamb 72. Frankenstein: The True Story (TV) 73, etc.

¶ I was the worst actor I ever came across. – M.W.
He was a man who should never have become an actor because his nerves were so terrible that every appearance was an ordeal. – Hermione Baddeley

Wile E. Coyote.
Dumb but cunning cartoon character, forever in pursuit of Road Runner, created by Chuck Jones and Michael Maltese.

¶ The coyote is victimized by his own ineptitude. I never understood how to use tools and that's really the coyote's problem. – Chuck Jones
See *Road Runner* for list of movies.

Wilke, Robert J. (1911–1989).
American character actor, usually in mean, shifty or villainous roles.
San Francisco 36. Sheriff of Sundown 44. The Last Days of Boot Hill 47. Kill the Umpire 50. Twenty Thousand Leagues under the Sea 54. Night Passage 57. The Gun Hawk 63. The Hallelujah Trail 65. Tony Rome 67. A Gunfight 71. Days of Heaven 78. Stripes 81, etc.

William.
The argumentative small boy created in over thirty novels by Richmal Crompton had several British film incarnations, none very satisfactory, in the 30s and 40s.

William, Warren (1895–1948) (Warren Krech).
Suave American leading man with stage experience.
The Perils of Pauline 14. The Woman from Monte Carlo 32. The Mouthpiece 33. *Lady for a Day* 33. *Imitation of Life* 34. Cleopatra (as Julius Caesar) 34. The Case of the Lucky Legs 35. Satan Met a Lady 36. The Firefly 37. *The Lone Wolf's Spy Hunt* 39 (and others in this series). The Man in the Iron Mask 39. Lillian Russell 40. The Wolf Man

41. Counter Espionage 42. One Dangerous Night 43. Fear 46. Bel Ami 47, etc.

Williams, Adam (1929–).
American 'second lead'.
Queen for a Day 50. Without Warning 52. Crashout 55. Garment Centre 57. Darby's Rangers 58. North by Northwest 59. The Last Sunset 61. The Glory Guys 67, etc.

Williams, Bill (1916–1992) (William Katt).
American leading man, an innocent-type hero of the 40s. Former professional swimmer and singer.
Murder in the Blue Room (debut) 44. Those Endearing Young Charms 45. Till the End of Time 46. Deadline at Dawn 47. The Great Missouri Raid 51. The Outlaw's Daughter 53. Wiretapper 56. A Dog's Best Friend 61. Tickle Me 65, etc.
TV series: Kit Carson 52–54. Assignment Underwater 61.

Williams, Billy (1929–).
British cinematographer.
Just Like a Woman 66. Billion Dollar Brain 67. *Women in Love* 69. Two Gentlemen Sharing 70. Tam Lin 70. *Sunday Bloody Sunday* 72. Night Watch 73. The Wind and the Lion 75. Eagle's Wing 79. Saturn Three 80. *On Golden Pond* 81. *Gandhi* (AA) 82. Monsignor 82. The Survivors 83. Dreamchild 85. Eleni 85. The Manhattan Project 86. Suspect 87. The Rainbow 89. Stella 90. Diamond's Edge 90, etc.

Williams, Billy Dee (1937–).
American leading man.
■ *Brian's Song* (TV) 71. Lady Sings the Blues 72. Hit 73. The Take 74. Mahogany 75. Bingo Long and the Travelling All Stars 76. Scott Joplin 78. The Empire Strikes Back 80. Nighthawks 81. Marvin and Tige 83. Number One with a Bullet 87. Deadly Illusion 87. The Impostor 88. Batman 89. Dangerous Passion (TV) 90. Alien Intruder 93.

Williams, Bransby (1870–1961).
Distinguished British stage actor who made an early talkie appearance in an experimental Lee de Forest Phonofilm. Later appeared in:
The Cold Cure 25. Jungle Woman 26. Troublesome Wives 28. Song of the Road 37, etc.

Williams, Cara (1925–) (Bernice Kamiat).
American TV and radio comedienne. She was formerly married to John Drew Barrymore.
Happy Land 43. Don Juan Quilligan 45. Sitting Pretty 48. The Girl Next Door 53. The Defiant Ones (AAN) 58. The Man from the Diners Club 63. The White Buffalo 77.
TV series: Pete and Gladys 60–61. The Cara Williams Show 64. Rhoda 74–75.

Williams, Cindy (1948–).
American leading lady.
Drive He Said 71. American Graffiti 73. Travels with My Aunt 73. The Conversation 74. Mr Ricco 75. More American Graffiti 79. The Creature Wasn't a Nice 81. Rude Awakening 89. Bingo! 91, etc.
TV series: Laverne and Shirley 76–82. Normal Life 90. Getting By 93– .

Williams, Elmo (1913–).
American editor and producer. Produced, edited and directed *The Cowboy* 54; worked as editor on several major productions; became head of Twentieth Century-Fox British productions.

Williams, Emlyn (1905–1987).
Welsh actor and playwright, on stage from 1927.

Autobiographies: 1972, *George.* 1974, *Emlyn.*
Biography: 1992, *Emlyn Williams* by James Harding.
The Case of the Frightened Lady (film debut) 32. Men of Tomorrow 33. Friday the Thirteenth 33. Sally Bishop 33. Broken Blossoms 36. *The Citadel* 38. The Stars Look Down 39. Major Barbara 40. You Will Remember 40. *Hatter's Castle* 41. *The Last Days of Dolwyn* (& wd) 48. *Three Husbands* 50. Ivanhoe 52. *The Deep Blue Sea* 56. I Accuse 57. Beyond This Place 59. The L-Shaped Room 62. Eye of the Devil 66. The Walking Stick 69. David Copperfield 69, many others.
Plays filmed: *Night Must Fall, The Corn Is Green.*

Williams, Esther (1923–).
Aquatic American leading lady, former swimming champion. She married Fernando Lamas, her third husband, in 1967.
■ Andy Hardy's Double Life (debut) 42. A Guy Named Joe 43. *Bathing Beauty* 44. Ziegfeld Follies 44. Thrill of a Romance 45. Easy to Wed 45. This Time for Keeps 46. Till the Clouds Roll By 46. Fiesta 47. On an Island with You 48. *Take Me Out to the Ball Game* 48. Neptune's Daughter 49. Pagan Love Song 50. Duchess of Idaho 51. Callaway Went Thataway 51. Texas Carnival 52. Skirts Ahoy 52. Million Dollar Mermaid 52. *Dangerous When Wet* 53. Easy to Love 54. Jupiter's Darling 54. The Unguarded Moment 56. Raw Wind in Eden 57. The Big Show 61. The Magic Fountain (Sp.) 61.

¶ All they ever did for me at MGM was change my leading men and the water in my pool. – E.W.
Wet she was a star. – *Joe Pasternak*

Williams, Grant (1930–1985).
American leading man who never quite made the big time.
Written on the Wind 56. *The Incredible Shrinking Man* 57. The Monolith Monsters 58. PT 109 63. Doomsday 72, etc.
TV series: Hawaiian Eye 59–63.

Williams, Guinn 'Big Boy' (1900–1962).
American character actor, usually in amiably tough roles. In Hollywood 1919 as an extra.
Noah's Ark 29. Dodge City 39. Mr Wise Guy 42. The Desperadoes 43. Thirty Seconds Over Tokyo 44. Bad Men of Tombstone 49. Hangman's Knot 53. The Outlaw's Daughter 55. The Comancheros 62, many others.
TV series: Circus Boy 56–57.

Williams, Guy (1924–1989) (Armand Catalano).
American leading man, the 'Zorro' of Walt Disney's TV series and films.
The Prince and the Pauper 62. Captain Sinbad 63, etc.
TV series: Lost in Space 65–68.

Williams, Hank (1923–1953).
Influential American country singer and songwriter who had a short, unruly life. In the biopic *Your Cheatin' Heart* 64, he was played by George Hamilton, with his songs dubbed by his son, Hank Williams Jnr.

Williams, Harcourt (1880–1957).
Distinguished British stage actor.
Henry V 44. *Brighton Rock* 47. Hamlet 48. Third Time Lucky 48. *The Late Edwina Black* 51. Roman Holiday 53. Around the World in Eighty Days 56.

Williams, Hugh (1904–1969) (Brian Williams).
British leading man and playwright on stage from 1921.

Charley's Aunt (film debut) 30. In a Monastery Garden 31. Rome Express 33. Sorrell and Son 34. *David Copperfield* (US) 34. The Amateur Gentleman 36. Dark Eyes of London 38. Wuthering Heights (US) 39. A Girl in a Million 46. *An Ideal Husband* 47. Take My Life 47. The Blind Goddess 48. Elizabeth of Ladymead 49. The Gift Horse 52. The Fake 53. Twice Upon a Time 53. Khartoum 66, etc.

Williams, Jobeth (1953–).
American leading lady.
Kramer vs Kramer 79. The Dogs of War 80. Stir Crazy 80. Poltergeist 82. Endangered Species 82. The Big Chill 83. American Dreamer 84. Teachers 84. Desert Bloom 85. Poltergeist II 86. Memories of Me 88. Welcome Home 89. Victim of Love 91. Switch 91. Dutch (GB: Driving Me Crazy) 91. Stop! or My Mom Will Shoot 92. Chantilly Lace (TV) 93. Wyatt Earp 94. Parallel Lives (TV) 94, etc.

Williams, John (1903–1983).
Suave British stage actor who has appeared in films, usually in polished comedy roles.
Emil and the Detectives 35. Next of Kin 42. A Woman's Vengeance 48. *Dial M for Murder* 54. Sabrina Fair 54. To Catch a Thief 55. *The Solid Gold Cadillac* 56. Island in the Sun 56. Witness for the Prosecution 57. Visit to a Small Planet 60. Last of the Secret Agents 66. The Secret War of Harry Frigg 67. A Flea in Her Ear 68. The Hound of the Baskervilles (TV) 72. No Deposit No Return 76. Hot Lead and Cold Feet 78, etc.

Williams, John (1932–).
American composer.
The Secret Ways 61. Diamond Head 62. None But the Brave 65. How to Steal a Million 66. Valley of the Dolls (AAN) 67. The Cowboys 71. The Poseidon Adventure (AAN) 72. Tom Sawyer 73. Earthquake 74. The Towering Inferno (AAN) 74. *Jaws* (AA) 75. The Eiger Sanction 75. *Star Wars* (AA) 77. Close Encounters of the Third Kind (AAN) 77. Jaws 2 78. Superman (AAN) 78. The Fury 78. 1941 79. Dracula 79. Superman 2 80. The Empire Strikes Back (AAN, BFA) 80. Raiders of the Lost Ark (AAN) 81. E.T. – the Extraterrestrial (AA, BFA) 82. Return of the Jedi (AAN) 83. Monsignor 83. Indiana Jones and the Temple of Doom (AAN) 84. The River (AAN) 84. Spacecamp 85. The Witches of Eastwick 87. Empire of the Sun 87. Jaws: The Revenge 87. Superman IV: The Quest for Peace 87. The Accidental Tourist (AAN) 88. Always 89. Born on the Fourth of July (AAN) 89. Indiana Jones and the Last Crusade (AAN) 89. Home Alone 90. Stanley and Iris 90. JFK (AAN) 91. Hook 91. Far and Away 92. Jurassic Park 93. Schindler's List (AA) 93, etc.

Williams, Kathlyn (1888–1960).
American leading lady of silent films: one of the first serial queens.
Witch of the Everglades 11. Driftwood 12. The Adventures of Kathlyn 13. Sweet Alyssum 15. The Highway of Hope 17. Just a Wife 20. Morals 23. The Enemy Sex 24. Our Dancing Daughters 28. Blood Money 33, many others.

Williams, Kenneth (1926–1988).
British comic actor adept at 'small boy' characters and a variety of outrageous voices. Also on stage, radio and TV. He starred in 22 'Carry On' films.
Autobiography: 1985, *Just Williams.* Also: 1993, *The Diaries of Kenneth Williams*, edited by Russell Davies. 1994, *The Letters of Kenneth Williams*, edited by Russell Davies.
The Beggar's Opera 52. The Seekers 54. *Carry On Sergeant* 58 (and most other 'Carry Ons'). Raising

the Wind 61. Twice Round the Daffodils 62. Don't Lose Your Head 67. Follow That Camel 68. Carry On Dick 74, etc.

¶ The thing to do, in any circumstance, is to appear to know exactly what you are doing and at the same time convey casual doubts about the abilities of everybody else and undermine their confidence. – *K.W.*

Williams, Paul (1940–).
Diminutive American singer, composer and actor.
The Chase (a) 65. Phantom of the Paradise (a, m) (AANm) 74. Bugsy Malone (m) 76. A Star Is Born (AA song) 76. Smokey and the Bandit (a) 77. The End (m) 78. The Muppet Movie (a, m) (AANm) 79. The Wild Wild West Revisited (a) (TV) 79. Rooster (a) (TV) 82. Smokey and the Bandit III 83, etc.

Williams, Paul (1943–).
American director of quirky films.
Out of It 69. The Revolutionary 70. Dealing: Or the Berkeley-to-Boston Forty-Brick Lost-Bag Blues 72. A Light in the Afternoon 86. The November Men 93, etc.

Williams, Rhys (1892–1969).
Welsh character actor, long in Hollywood; former technical adviser.
How Green Was My Valley 40. The Spiral Staircase 45. Scandal at Scourie 53. There's No Business Like Show Business 54. The Kentuckian 55. The Fastest Gun Alive 56. The Sons of Katie Elder 65. Skullduggery 69, many others.

Williams, Richard (1933–).
Canadian animator in England who has been working on his animated feature *The Thief and the Cobbler* for more than 20 years.
The Little Island 58. The Charge of the Light Brigade (titles) 67. A Christmas Carol 73, etc.
Designed title sequences for *What's New Pussycat, The Liquidator, Casino Royale, Sebastian,* etc.

Williams, Robert (1899–1931).
Slow-speaking American leading man of the early 30s.
The Common Law 31. Rebound 31. Devotion 31. *Platinum Blonde* 31, etc.

Williams, Robin (1951–).
Eccentric American nightclub comedian who became a TV star as Mork from Ork in *Mork and Mindy.*
■ Popeye 80. The World According to Garp 82. The Survivors 83. Moscow on the Hudson 84. The Best of Times 85. Club Paradise 86. Good Morning Vietnam (AAN) 87. Dear America: Letters Home from Vietnam 88. The Adventures of Baron Munchausen (uncredited) 89. Dead Poets Society (AAN) 89. Cadillac Man 90. Awakenings 90. Dead Again (uncredited) 91. The Fisher King (AAN) 91. Shakes the Clown (uncredited) 91. Hook 91. Ferngully . . . the Last Rainforest (voice) 92. Toys 92. Mrs Doubtfire 93. Being Human 94.

¶ Cocaine is God's way of saying you're making too much money. – *R.W.*
You're only given a little madness. You mustn't lose it. – *R.W.*

Williams, Simon (1946–).
British light leading man, son of Hugh Williams, who became a TV star in *Upstairs Downstairs.*
The Incredible Sarah 75. Jabberwocky 76. The Odd Job 77. The Prisoner of Zenda 79. The

Fiendish Plot of Fu Manchu 80. The Return of the Man from UNCLE (TV) 83.

Williams, Tennessee (1911–1983) (Thomas Lanier Williams).
American playwright whose sleazy characters have proved popular screen fodder.
Autobiography: 1976, *Memoirs.*
Biography: 1993, *Tennessee Williams: Everyone Else Is an Audience* by Ronald Hayman.
■ The Glass Menagerie 50. A Streetcar Named Desire (AA) 52. The Rose Tattoo 56. Baby Doll (AAN) 56. Cat on a Hot Tin Roof 58. Suddenly Last Summer 59. The Fugitive Kind 60. Summer and Smoke 61. Period of Adjustment 62. Sweet Bird of Youth 63. *The Night of the Iguana* 64. This Property Is Condemned 66. Boom 68. Blood Kin 70.

¶ Why did I write? Because I found life unsatisfactory. – *T.W.*

Williams, Treat (1952–) (Richard Williams).
American leading actor of heavy presence, from Broadway.
The Ritz 76. The Eagle Has Landed 77. *Hair* 79. 1941 79. Why Would I Lie? 80. The Pursuit of D. B. Cooper 81. Prince of the City 81. Flashpoint 84. Once upon a Time in America 84. Dempsey (TV) 85. Smooth Talk 85. The Men's Club 86. Dead Heat 88. Heart of Dixie 89. Russicum 89. Sweet Lies 89. Beyond the Ocean (Oltre l'Oceano) (a, co-w, d) 89. Max and Helen (TV) 90. Bonds of Love (TV) 93. Where the Rivers Flow North 93. Handgun 94. Parallel Lives (TV) 94, etc.
TV series: Eddie Dodd 91.

Williamson, David (1942–).
Australian dramatist and screenwriter.
Stork 71. Petersen 74. The Removalists 75. Don's Party 76. Eliza Fraser 76. The Club 80. Gallipoli 81. Duet for Four 82. The Year of Living Dangerously 82. Phar Lap 83, etc.

Williamson, Fred (1938–).
American action hero.
M*A*S*H 70. The Legend of Nigger Charley 72. Hammer 72. Black Caesar 72. Crazy Joe 73. That Man Bolt 74. Boss Nigger 75. Darktown 75. Take a Hard Ride 75. Mr Mean (& p, d) 77. Fist of Fear, Touch of Death 80. Vigilante 83. The Big Score (& d) 83. Foxtrap (& d) 86. The Messenger (& d) 87. Soda Cracker (& d) 89. Black Cobra 3: Manila Connection 91. Three Days to a Kill (& story, p, d) 92. South Beach (& p, d) 92. The Night Caller (& p, d) 92, etc.
TV series: Julia 70–71. Wheels 79. Half Nelson 85.

Williamson, James A. (1855–1933).
British production pioneer.
The Big Swallow 01. Fire! 01, etc.

Williamson, Lambert (1907–).
British composer.
Edge of the World 38. End of the River 48. One Night With You 48. Cosh Boy 53. The Spaniard's Curse 58, etc.

Williamson, Malcolm (1931–).
Australian-born composer, pianist, and organist, in Britain from 1953. Composer of operas, ballets, choral and orchestral music, he was made Master of the Queen's Music in 1975.
The Brides of Dracula 60. The Horror of Frankenstein 70. Crescendo 72. Nothing but the Night 75. Watership Down (co-m) 76, etc.

Williamson, Nicol (1938–).
British leading actor of stage and screen; tends to play bulls in china shops. In 1994 he starred in a one-man play on the life of actor John Barrymore.
■ Six Sided Triangle 64. *Inadmissible Evidence* 67. *The Bofors Gun* 68. Laughter in the Dark 68. *The Reckoning* 69. Hamlet 69. The Jerusalem File 72. The Wilby Conspiracy 75. Robin and Marian 76. The Seven Per Cent Solution 76. The Word (TV) 78. The Cheap Detective 78. The Human Factor 79. Venom 81. Excalibur 81. I'm Dancing as Fast as I Can 82. Sakharov (TV) 85. Return to Oz 85. Black Widow 87. The Exorcist III 90. The Hour of the Pig 93.

¶ I don't even notice competition. I'm a centre-forward. I don't watch them. Let them watch me. – *N.W.*
I can understand people's pain, passion, fear, hurt, and I can mirror it and set it up for them to look at. – *N.W.*
The greatest actor since Marlon Brando. – *John Osborne*

Willis, Bruce (1955–)
American leading man.
■ Blind Date 87. Sunset 88. Die Hard 88. In Country 89. That's Adequate 89. Look Who's Talking (voice) 90. Die Hard 2 90. The Bonfire of the Vanities 90. Look Who's Talking Too (voice) 90. Hudson Hawk (& co-story) 91. Mortal Thoughts 91. Billy Bathgate 91. Last Boy Scout 91. Death Becomes Her 92. The Player 92. Striking Distance 93. Pulp Fiction 94. North 94. Color of Night 94. Nobody's Fool 94. Diehard 3 95.
TV series: Moonlighting 85–89.

Willis, Gordon.
American cinematographer.
■ Loving 70. The Landlord 70. The People Next Door 70. Klute 71. Little Murders 71. Bad Company 72. *The Godfather* 72. Up the Sandbox 72. The Paper Chase 73. The Godfather Part Two 74. The Parallax View 74. The Drowning Pool 75. All the President's Men 76. Annie Hall 77. Comes a Horseman 78. Manhattan 79. Stardust Memories 80. Windows 80. Pennies from Heaven 81. A Midsummer Night's Sex Comedy 82. Zelig (AAN) 83. Broadway Danny Rose 84. The Purple Rose of Cairo 85. Perfect 85. The Money Pit 86. The Pick-Up Artist 87. Bright Lights, Big City 88. Presumed Innocent 90. The Godfather Part III (AAN) 90. Malice 93.

Willis, Ted (1918–1992) (Lord Willis).
Influential British writer who set the scene for television's preoccupation with low life via such items as *Dixon of Dock Green* and *Woman in a Dressing Gown.* Dixon was derived from his filmscript *The Blue Lamp; Hot Summer Night* was later filmed as *Flame in the Streets.*

Willman, Noel (1918–1988).
British actor and stage director whose film roles were often coldly villainous.
Pickwick Papers 52. The Net 53. Beau Brummell 54. Cone of Silence 60. The Girl on the Boat 62. *Kiss of the Vampire* 63. The Reptile 65. Doctor Zhivago 65. The Vengeance of She 68, etc.

Willock, Dave (1909–1990).
American light actor, usually the hero's friend.
Legion of Lost Flyers 39. Let's Face It 43. Pin Up Girl 44. The Runaround 46. Chicago Deadline 49. Call Me Mister 51. It Came from Outer Space 53. The Buster Keaton Story 57. Wives and Lovers 63. Send Me No Flowers 64, many others.
TV series: Boots and Saddles 57. Margie 61.

Wills, Brember (1883–1948).
Slightly built British character actor best remembered for playing the mad arsonist Saul Femm in *The Old Dark House* (1932).

Wills, Chill (1903–1978).
Gravel-voiced American character actor, in films from 1934, mainly low-budget westerns. Also the voice of the talking mule in the 'Francis' series.
Boom Town 40. Best Foot Forward 43. The Harvey Girls 46. Raw Deal 48. High Lonesome 50. Bronco Buster 52. City That Never Sleeps 53. Timberjack 55. Giant 56. The Alamo (AAN) 60. The Deadly Companions 62. The Cardinal 63. The Over the Hill Gang Rides Again (TV) 71. Mr Billion 77, etc.
TV series: Frontier Circus 61. The Rounders 67.

Wills, J. Elder (1900–*).
English director, art director, screenwriter, and producer. Born in London and educated at London University, he was a scenic artist in Drury Lane before entering films in 1927 and working as an art director on more than 200 movies. He began directing in the early 30s, including two films for Hammer (of which he was then a director), and, after serving in the Second World War, worked as a producer and production designer for Rank before returning to art directing for Hammer. The Ealing spy thriller *Against the Wind* 47 was based on his own war experiences.
Biography: *Sabotage* by Leslie Bell.
AS DIRECTOR: Tiger Bay (& ad, co-story) 33. Song of Freedom 36. Everything in Life 36. Sporting Love 36. Big Fella 37.
AS ART DIRECTOR: The Informer 29. Alf 's Carpet 29. Holiday Lovers 32. Money Mad 34. Sing as We Go 34. Honeymoon for Three 35. It Happened in Paris 35. No Limit 35. Look Up and Laugh 35. The Stoker 35. Queen of Hearts 36. Against the Wind 47. Mantrap 52. Spaceways 53. Three Stops to Murder) 53. Face the Music (US: The Black Glove) 54. Break in the Circle 55. The Quatermass Experiment (US: The Creeping Unknown) 55, etc.

Willson, Meredith (1902–1984) (Robert Meredith Reiniger).
American song composer and lyricist whose chief bequests to the cinema are *The Music Man* and *The Unsinkable Molly Brown*.

Wilmer, Douglas (1920–).
British character actor of stage, screen and TV.
Richard III 56. An Honourable Murder 60. El Cid 61. Cleopatra 62. The Fall of the Roman Empire 64. One Way Pendulum 65. Brides of Fu Manchu 66. Unman Wittering and Zigo 71. The Golden Voyage of Sinbad 73. The Adventure of Sherlock Holmes' Smarter Brother 75. Sarah 76. The Revenge of the Pink Panther 78. Rough Cut 80. Octopussy 83, many others.

Wilson, Don 'The Dragon'.
American leading actor in martial arts and action movies, a former kick-boxing champion.
Bloodfist 89. Bloodfist 2 90. Bloodfist 3: Forced to Fight 91. Ring of Fire 91. Futurekick 91. Ninja Dragons 92. Ring of Fire 2: Blood and Steel 92. Cyber-Tracker 93, etc.

Wilson, Dooley (1894–1953).
American character actor.
Casablanca (as Sam, who played it again) 42. Stormy Weather 43. Come to the Stable 49. Passage West 51, etc.
~It is alleged that Elliot Carpenter played the

piano for Wilson in *Casablanca* . . . and some say Wilson didn't sing either.

Wilson, Flip (1933–) (Clerow Wilson).
American actor and entertainer.
Uptown Saturday Night 74. Pinocchio (TV) 76. Skatetown USA 79.

Wilson, Harry Leon (1867–1939).
American comedy novelist; chief works filmed are *Ruggles of Red Gap* and *Merton of the Movies*.

Wilson, Hugh (1943–).
American director and screenwriter.
Police Academy 84. Rustler's Rhapsody 85. Burglar 87. Guarding Tess 94.

Wilson, Janis.
American child actress, long retired, who made an impressive debut in *Now Voyager*.
Now Voyager 42. Watch on the Rhine 43. Snafu (GB: Welcome Home) 45. The Strange Love of Martha Ivers 46, etc.

Wilson, Lois (1895–1988).
American leading lady of the silent screen.
The Dumb Girl of Potici 16. Why Smith Left Home 19. The Covered Wagon 23. Miss Lulu Bett 24. Monsieur Beaucaire 24. What Every Woman Knows 24. Icebound 24. The Show Off 26. Seed 28. Manslaughter 28. The Crash 32. Laughing at Life 33. Bright Eyes 34. The Girl from Jones Beach 49, etc.

Wilson, Marie (1916–1972) (Katherine Elizabeth White).
American leading lady often seen as 'dumb blonde'.
Satan Met a Lady 36. Fools for Scandal 38. *Boy Meets Girl* 40. Broadway 42. The Young Widow 47. Linda Be Good 48. *My Friend Irma* (title role) 49. A Girl in Every Port 51. Marry Me Again 54. Mr Hobbs Takes a Vacation 62, etc.
TV series: My Friend Irma 52.

Wilson, Michael (1914–1978).
American screenwriter whose career was interrupted by the communist witch-hunt of the late 40s.
The Men in Her Life 42. It's a Wonderful Life (co-w) 46. Salt of the Earth 51. Five Fingers (AAN) 52. *A Place in the Sun* (AA) 52. Friendly Persuasion (uncredited) 56. *The Bridge on the River Kwai* (uncredited) 57. Lawrence of Arabia 62. The Sandpiper 65. *Planet of the Apes* 67. Che! 69, etc.

Wilson, Richard (1915–1991).
American producer and director, former radio actor.
The Golden Blade (p) 54. Man with a Gun (wd, p) 55. Raw Wind in Eden (d) 58. Al Capone (d) 59. Pay or Die (p, d) 60. Invitation to a Gunfighter (p, d) 64. Three in an Attic (p, d) 68, etc.

Wilson, Richard (1936–).
Sardonic Scottish actor and director, mainly on stage and television, best known for his role as Victor Meldrew in the TV series *One Foot in the Grave*. Born in Greenock, he was a research scientist before deciding to become an actor at the age of 27. He studied at RADA and first worked in repertory theatre. As a director he has been associated with the Oxford Playhouse and the Stables Theatre, Manchester.
A Sharp Intake of Breath (TV) 77. Virginia Fly Is Drowning (TV) 82. A Passage to India 84. Whoops Apocalypse 86. Prick Up Your Ears 87. A Dry White Season 89. Fellow Traveller 89. How to

Get Ahead in Advertising 89. The Vision Thing (TV) 93. One Foot in the Algarve (TV) 93, etc.
TV series: My Good Woman 72. A Sharp Intake of Breath 78–80. Only When I Laugh 79–82. Room at the Bottom 86–88. Tutti Frutti 87. High and Dry 87. Hot Metal 88. One Foot in the Grave 90–93. Under the Hammer 94.

Wilson, Sandy (1924–).
British songwriter and lyricist whose best show, *The Boy Friend*, reached the screen in mangled form through the intervention of Ken Russell.

Wilson, Sandy.
Canadian director.
My American Cousin 85. Mama's Going to Buy You a Mocking Bird 88. Harmony Cats 93, etc.

Wilson, Scott (1942–).
American general-purpose actor, usually in tough roles.
In Cold Blood 67. The Grissom Gang 71. The New Centurions 72. Lolly Madonna XXX 73. The Great Gatsby 74. The Passover Plot 77. The Ninth Configuration 80. On the Line 83. The Right Stuff 83. A Year of the Quiet Sun 84. The Aviator 85. Blue City 86. Malone 87. The Tracker 88. Johnny Handsome 89. The Exorcist III 90. Lethal Weapon 3 92. Teenage Mutant Ninja Turtles 3 93. Judge Dredd 95, etc.

Wilson, Stuart.
English character actor.
Dulcima 71. The Strauss Family (TV) 73. The Prisoner of Zenda 79. Wetherby 85. Wallenberg: A Hero's Story (TV) 85. Nonni (Nor.) 88. Lionheart (aka AWOL) 91. Lethal Weapon 3 92. Teenage Mutant Ninja Turtles III 93. The Age of Innocence 93. No Escape 94. Exit to Eden 94. Death and the Maiden 95, etc.

Wilson, Trey (1949–1989).
American character actor.
A Soldier's Story 84. F/X 85. Raising Arizona 87. The House on Carroll Street 88. Bull Durham 88. Married to the Mob 88. Twins 88. Miss Firecracker 89. Great Balls of Fire 89. Welcome Home 89, etc.

Wilson, Whip (1915–1964) (Charles Meyer).
American cowboy actor who appeared in a great number of second features in the 30s and 40s.

Wilton, Penelope (1946–).
British actress, mainly on stage and TV.
Joseph Andrews 77. The French Lieutenant's Woman 81. Othello 82. Laughterhouse (aka Singleton's Pluck) 84. Clockwise 86. Cry Freedom 87. Blame It on the Bellboy 92. The Secret Rapture 93. Carrington 95, etc.
TV series: Ever Decreasing Circles 84.

Wilton, Robb (1882–1957).
Much admired English music-hall and radio comedian and character actor. His act, notably as a muddled policeman, fireman, or member of the Home Guard, has been preserved in several films.
The Fire Brigade 28. Stars on Parade 35. Chips 38. Don't Rush Me 36. Servants All 36. Pathé Radio Music Hall 45. The Love Match 55, etc.
~Catchphrase: The day war broke out . . .

Wimperis, Arthur (1874–1953).
British librettist and screenwriter, usually in collaboration.
The Private Life of Henry VIII 32. Sanders of the River 35. The Four Feathers 39. Mrs Miniver (AA) 42. Random Harvest (AAN) 43. The Red Danube

48. Calling Bulldog Drummond 51. Young Bess 53, many others.

Wincer, Simon (1943–).
Australian director, from TV.

The Day after Halloween 79. Harlequin 79. Phar Lap 83. D.A.R.Y.L 85. The Lighthorsemen 87. Blue Grass (TV) 88. Lonesome Dove (TV) 89. Quigley Down Under 90. Harley Davidson and the Marlboro Man 91. Free Willy 93. Lightning Jack 94, etc.

Winchell, Walter (1897–1972).
American columnist and commentator with a keen eye for crime and show business. Appeared in a few 30s movies such as *Love and Hisses* 37, *Wake Up and Love* 37; wrote *Broadway Thro' a Keyhole* 33; narrated TV series *The Untouchables* 59–63. He was the model for Burt Lancaster's columnist in *Sweet Smell of Success.*

Wincott, Jeff (1957–).
Canadian leading man of action movies.

Happy Birthday, Gemini 80. Prom Night 80. Deadly Bet 91. Martial Law 2: Undercover 91. Mission of Justice 92, etc.

TV series: Night Heat 85–91.

Windom, William (1923–).
American leading man, usually in minor film roles.

To Kill a Mockingbird 62. For Love or Money 63. One Man's Way 64. The Americanization of Emily 64. The Detective 68. Brewster McCloud 70. Fool's Parade 71. Now You See Him Now You Don't 72. Echoes of a Summer 75. Mean Dog Blues 78. Grandview USA 84. Planes, Trains and Automobiles 87. She's Having a Baby 88. Funland 89. Sommersby 93, etc.

TV series: The Farmer's Daughter 63–66. My World and Welcome to It 69. The Girl with Something Extra 73–74. Brothers and Sisters 79. Murder She Wrote 85–91.

Windsor, Barbara (1937–) (Barbara Deeks).
British cockney actress specializing in dumb blondes.

Lost 55. Too Hot to Handle 59. Sparrows Can't Sing 64. Carry On Spying 64. Crooks in Cloisters 64. The Boy Friend 71. Carry On Abroad 72. Carry On Girls 73, etc.

Windsor, Claire (1898–1972) (Olga Cronk).
American leading lady of the silent screen.

To Please a Woman 20. Rich Men's Wives 22. Nellie the Beautiful Cloak Model 24. Money Talks 26. Captain Lash 29, etc.

Windsor, Marie (1923–) (Emily Marie Bertelson).
American leading lady with stage and radio experience; films mainly routine.

All American Co-Ed 41. Song of the Thin Man 47. Force of Evil 48. Outpost in Morocco 49. Dakota Lil 50. *The Narrow Margin* 51. The Tall Texan 53. City that Never Sleeps 53. Abbott and Costello Meet the Mummy 55. *The Killing* 56. The Unholy Wife 57. Bedtime Story 64. Chamber of Horrors 66. The Good Guys and the Bad Guys 69. Support Your Local Gunfighter 71. Cahill 73. Hearts of the West 75. Lovely . . . but Deadly 82, many others.

Windust, Bretaigne (1906–1960).
American director, from the New York stage.

Winter Meeting 47. June Bride 48. Pretty Baby 50. *The Enforcer* 51. Face to Face 52. The Pied Piper of Hamelin 59, etc.

Winfield, Paul (1941–).
American leading actor.

The Lost Man 69. RPM 70. Brother John 71. *Sounder* (AAN) 72. Gordon's War 73. Conrack 74. Hustle 75. Damnation Alley 77. Twilight's Last Gleaming 77. The Greatest 77. Backstairs at the White House (TV) 79. King (TV) 80. Angel City (TV) 81. Star Trek II: The Wrath of Khan 82. On the Run 82. Mike's Murder 82. Go Tell It on the Mountain 84. The Terminator 84. Blue City 85. The Serpent and the Rainbow 88. Presumed Innocent 90. Dennis the Menace (GB: Dennis) 93, etc.

Winfrey, Oprah (1954–).
American actress, a former newsreader who became rich and successful airing topical problems on her syndicated TV talk show from 1986. She is said to have earned more than $40m in 1991.

■ The Color Purple (AAN) 85. Native Son 86. Throw Momma from the Train 87. The Women of Brewster Place (TV) 89. There Are No Children Here (TV) 93.

¶ Arguably has more influence in the culture than any university president, politician, or religious leader, except perhaps the Pope. – *Vanity Fair*

Winger, Debra (1955–).
American leading lady of the early 80s, in increasingly strong roles. She was married to actor Timothy Hutton (1986–89).

Thank God It's Friday 78. French Postcards 79. Urban Cowboy 80. Cannery Row 82. An Officer and a Gentleman (AAN) 82. Terms of Endearment (AAN) 83. Mike's Murder 84. Legal Eagles 85. Black Widow 87. Made in Heaven 87. Betrayed 88. Everybody Wins 90. The Sheltering Sky 90. Wilder Napalm 93. Shadowlands (AAN) 93. A Dangerous Woman 93. Forget Paris 95, etc.

Winkler, Henry (1946–).
Extrovert American actor best known as Fonz in TV's *Happy Days* 74–83. He began directing in the mid-80s.

The Lords of Flatbush 72. Heroes 77. The One and Only 78. Night Shift 82. A Smokey Mountain Christmas (d) 86. Memories of Me (d) 88. Absolute Strangers (TV) 91. Cop and a Half (d) 93, etc.

TV series: Monty 94.

Winkler, Irwin (1931–).
American producer who began directing in the 90s.

The Split 68. They Shoot Horses Don't They? 69. The Strawberry Statement 70. The Mechanic 72. Up the Sandbox 72. Peeper 75. The Gambler 75. Nickelodeon 76. Rocky (AA) 76. New York New York 77. Comes a Horseman 78. Rocky II 79. Raging Bull (AAN) 81. True Confessions 81. Author! Author! 82. Rocky III 82. The Right Stuff (AAN) 83. Revolution 85. Rocky IV 85. Round Midnight 86. Betrayed 88. Music Box 90. GoodFellas (AAN) 90. Rocky V 90. Guilty by Suspicion (wd) 90. Night and the City 92, etc.

Winn, Godfrey (1908–1971).
British journalist who made rare film appearances.

Blighty 27. Very Important Person 62, etc.

Winner, Michael (1935–).
Ebullient British director who never shoots in a studio. His own best publicist. Also a restaurant columnist.

■ Climb Up the Wall 57. The Clock Strikes Eight 57. Man with a Gun 58. Shoot to Kill 59. Some Like It Cool 61. Haunted England 61. Play It Cool 62. The Cool Mikado 63. West Eleven 63. *The System* 64. You Must be Joking 65. *The Jokers* 66. *I'll Never Forget Whatshisname* 67. Hannibal Brooks 69. The Games 69. *Lawman* 70. The Night Comers 71. Chato's Land 72. The Mechanic 72. Scorpio 72. The Stone Killer 73. *Death Wish* 74. Won Ton Ton 76. The Sentinel 77. The Big Sleep 78. Firepower 79. Death Wish II 81. The Wicked Lady 83. Scream for Help 84. Death Wish 3 85. Appointment with Death 87. A Chorus of Disapproval (p, wd) 89. Bullseye! (story, d, ed) 91. Dirty Weekend (wd) 93. Decadence (a) 94.

TV series: Michael Winner's True Murders 92–93. Michael Winner's True Crimes 93–94.

¶ In a time when diffidence is fashionable, it is refreshing to find a youngish British director who seems deliberately to court comparison with Erich Von Stroheim:

A team effort is a lot of people doing what I say. Original? It seems so. It is also true; and unlike Von Stroheim Mr Winner does get his films out on time and below budget, facts which tend to atone for his arrogance. He knows that:

In this business, disaster is always just around the corner.

And that:

Every film is a great success until it is released.

He remembers the days when:

You could make a film for £100,000 and get your money back from people sheltering from the rain.

He won't make the mistake of imagining that those days are still here. He enjoys the big money:

Success has gone to my stomach.

And he finds that:

The hardest part of directing is staying awake for nine weeks at a stretch.

He has no qualms about what he purveys:

There's no moralistic side to *Death Wish*: it's a pleasant romp.

And he is proud of his prowess:

Being in the movie business is like being a tennis player. You have to keep your total concentration and your mind on the ball. The minute you fall in love with Tatum O'Neal or get flabby, you've had it.

Winninger, Charles (1884–1969) (Karl Winninger).
Chubby, lovable American character actor, in films from 1916 as vaudeville appearances permitted. His catchphrase: '*Happ-y* new year . . .'

■ Pied Piper Malone 24. The Canadian 24. Summer Bachelors 26. Soup to Nuts 30. Bad Sister 31. Night Nurse 31. Flying High 31. God's Gift to Women 31. Fighting Caravans 31. Gun Smoke 31. Children of Dreams 31. The Sin of Madelon Claudet 31. Husband's Holiday 31. Social Register 34. Show Boat (as Captain Andy) 36. White Fang 36. *Three Smart Girls* 36. You're a Sweetheart 37. Woman Chases Man 37. *Nothing Sacred* 37. Café Metropole 37. You Can't Have Everything 37. The Go-Getter 37. Every Day's a Holiday 37. Goodbye Broadway 38. Hard to Get 38. Three Smart Girls Grow Up 39. *Destry Rides Again* 39. *Babes in Arms* 39. Barricade 39. If I Had My Way 40. My Love Came Back 40. Beyond Tomorrow 40. Little Nellie Kelly 40. When Ladies Meet 41. *Ziegfeld Girl* 41. The Getaway 41. My Life with Caroline 41. Pot o' Gold 41. Friendly Enemies 42. Coney Island 43. A Lady Takes a Chance 43. Flesh and Fantasy 43. Hers to Hold 43. Broadway Rhythm 44. Belle of the Yukon 44. Sunday Dinner for a Soldier 44. She Wouldn't Say Yes 45. *State Fair* 45. Lover Come Back 46. Living in a Big Way 47. Something in the Wind 47. The

Inside Story 48. *Give My Regards to Broadway* 48. Father Is a Bachelor 50. *The Sun Shines Bright* 53. Torpedo Alley 53. A Perilous Journey 53. Champ for a Day 53. Las Vegas Shakedown 55. Raymie 60.
TV series: The Charlie Farrell Show 56.

Winningham, Mare (1959–) (Mary Winningham).
American actress.
One-Trick Pony 80. Threshold 81. Single Bars, Single Women (TV) 84. St Elmo's Fire 85. Nobody's Fool 86. Shy People 87. Made in Heaven 87. Miracle Mile 89. Turner & Hooch 89. Eye on the Sparrow (TV) 91. Fatal Exposure 91. Hard Promises 92. Wyatt Earp 94. Georgia 95, etc.

Winslow, George (1946–) (George Wenzlaff).
American boy actor whose throaty voice earned him the nickname 'Foghorn'.
Room for One More 52. My Pal Gus 52. Mr Scoutmaster 53. Gentlemen Prefer Blondes 53. Artists and Models 55. Wild Heritage 58, etc.

Winston, Stan.
American make-up special effects and creature creator, and occasional director.
Blacula 72. The Wiz 78. The Exterminator 80. Heartbeeps 81. Parasite 82. The Terminator 84. Aliens (AA) 86. Predator 87. The Monster Squad 87. Pumpkinhead (co-story, d) 88. Leviathan 89. Predator 2 90. Edward Scissorhands 90. Terminator 2: Judgment Day (AA) 91. Batman Returns 92. Jurassic Park (AA) 93. Interview with the Vampire 94, etc.

Winter, Alex (1965–).
English-born leading actor, in America from the early 70s, from the stage.
Death Wish 3 85. The Lost Boys 87. Haunted Summer 88. Rosalie Goes Shopping 89. Bill and Ted's Excellent Adventure 89. Bill and Ted's Bogus Journey 92. Freaked (& co-w, co-d) 93, etc.

Winter, Donovan.
British director of eccentric low-budgeters.
The Trunk 60. A Penny for Your Thoughts 65. Promenade 68. Come Back Peter 69. Give Us Tomorrow 77, etc.

Winter, Vincent (1947–)
British child actor, in films since *The Kidnappers* 53 (special AA).
The Dark Avenger 55. Time Lock 56. Beyond This Place 59. Gorgo 60. Greyfriars Bobby 61. Almost Angels 63. The Three Lives of Thomasina 63. The Horse Without a Head 64, etc.

Winters, Jonathan (1925–).
American comedian with TV and nightclub experience.
It's a Mad Mad Mad Mad World 63. *The Loved One* 65. The Russians Are Coming, the Russians Are Coming 66. Penelope 66. Oh Dad Poor Dad 67. Viva Max 69. The Fish that Saved Pittsburgh 79. The Longshot 86. Moon over Parador 88. The Flintstones 94. The Shadow 94, etc.
TV series: The Jonathan Winters Show 56–57, 67–69. The Wacky World of Jonathan Winters 72–74. Mork & Mindy 81–82. Hee Haw 83–84. Davis Rules 91–92.

Winters, Ralph.
American film editor. He was on the staff of MGM for more than 30 years and edited 13 of Blake Edwards' films.
Mr and Mrs North 41. Eyes in the Night 42. Cry Havoc 43. Gaslight 44. Boy's Ranch 46. Tenth Avenue Angel 47. Hills of Home 48. Any Number Can Play 49. Little Women 49. On the Town 49. King Solomon's Mines (AA) 50. Quo Vadis? (AAN) 51. Kiss Me Kate 53. Young Bess 53. Executive Suite 54. Seven Brides for Seven Brothers (AAN) 54. Love Me or Leave Me 55. High Society 56. Jailhouse Rock 57. The Sheepman 58. Ben Hur (AA) 59. Butterfield 8 60. Soldier in the Rain 63. The Pink Panther 64. The Great Race (AAN) 65. What Did You Do in the War, Daddy? 66. How to Succeed in Business without Really Trying 67. The Party 68. The Thomas Crown Affair 68. Gaily Gaily 69. Kotch (AAN) 71. Avanti 72. The Outfit 73. The Front Page 74. Mr Majestyk 74. King Kong 75. Orca 77. 10 79. S.O.B. 81. Victor/Victoria 82. The Curse of the Pink Panther 83. Micki and Maude 84. Let's Get Harry 87. Moving 88, etc.

¶ The general public doesn't understand a thing about editing and I don't think they should. – R.W.

Winters, Roland (1904–1989).
Heavily built American character actor with stage and radio experience, in Hollywood from 1946; played Charlie Chan in six Monogram features 1948–52.
13 rue Madeleine 46. Inside Straight 52. So Big 53. Loving 70, etc.
TV series: Meet Millie 52–55. The Smothers Brothers Show 65.

Winters, Shelley (1922–) (Shirley Schrift).
American leading character actress with vaudeville and stage experience, in Hollywood from 1943.
Autobiographies: 1980, *Shelley*. 1987, *Also Known as Shirley*. 1989, *The Middle of My Century* (aka *The Best of Times, the Worst of Times*).
■ What a Woman 43. Sailor's Holiday 44. The Racket Man 44. Two Man Submarine 44. She's a Soldier Too 44. Nine Girls 44. Cover Girl 44. Knickerbocker Holiday 44. 1001 Nights 45. Tonight and Every Night 45. Living in a Big Way 47. The Gangster 48. Red River 48. Larceny 48. *A Double Life* 48. Cry of the City 48. Take One False Step 49. Johnny Stool Pigeon 49. The Great Gatsby 49. Winchester 73 50. East of Java 51. He Ran All The Way 51. Frenchie 51. Behave Yourself 51. The Raging Tide 51. A Place in the Sun (AAN) 51. My Man and I 52. Phone Call from a Stranger 52. Meet Danny Wilson 52. Untamed Frontier 52. Tennessee Champ 54. Saskatchewan 54. Playgirl 54. Executive Suite 54. To Dorothy a Son 54. *The Big Knife* 55. *The Night of the Hunter* 55. Mambo 55. I Am a Camera 55. I Died a Thousand Times 56. Treasure of Pancho Villa 56. Odds Against Tomorrow 58. *The Diary of Anne Frank* (AA) 59. Let No Man Write My Epitaph 60. The Young Savages 61. Lolita 62. Wives and Lovers 63. The Chapman Report 63. The Balcony 63. A House is Not a Home 64. Time of Indifference 64. The Greatest Story Ever Told 65. *A Patch of Blue* (AA) 65. Alfie (GB) 66. Harper 66. Enter Laughing 67. The Scalp Hunters 67. Wild in the Streets 68. Buona Sera Mrs Campbell 68. The Mad Room 69. Arthur! Arthur! 69. Flap 70. Bloody Mama 70. How Do I Love Thee 70. What's the Matter with Helen 70. Who Slew Auntie Roo? 71. Revenge! (TV) 71. The Poseidon Adventure (AAN) 72. Something to Hide 72. The Devil's Daughter (TV) 72. Blume in Love 73. Cleopatra Jones 73. Big Rose (TV) 74. Diamonds 75. That Lucky Touch 75. Journey Into Fear 75. Next Stop Greenwich Village 76. The Tenant 76. Pete's Dragon 77. Tentacles 77. Black Journey 77. King of the Gypsies 78. City on Fire 79. The Magician of Lublin 79. Redneck County Rape 79. The Visitor 79. Elvis (TV) 79. S.O.B. 81. Over the Brooklyn Bridge 83. Déjà Vu 84. Delta Force 85. Purple People Eater 88. Rudolph &

Frosty's Christmas in July 88. An Unremarkable Life 89. Touch of a Stranger 90. Stepping Out 91. The Pickle 93.
¶ I did a picture in England one winter and it was so cold I almost got married. – S.W.

Wintle, Julian (1913–1980).
British producer, former editor, in films from 1934. Co-founder of Independent Artists 1958.
Hunted 51. High Tide at Noon 57. Tiger Bay 59. Very Important Person 61. This Sporting Life 63. And Father Came Too 64, many others.

Winwood, Estelle (1882–1984) (Estelle Goodwin).
British stage character actress who played in many American films, usually as eccentric ladylike flutterers.
The House of Trent 34. Quality Street 37. The Glass Slipper 55. *The Swan* 56. Twenty-three Paces to Baker Street 56. *Alive and Kicking* (GB) 58. Darby O'Gill and the Little People 59. Notorious Landlady 62. Dead Ringer 64. Camelot 67. Games 67. The Producers 68. Murder by Death 76, etc.

wipe.
A wipe is an optical device used for quick changes of scene: a line appears at one edge or corner of the screen and 'wipes' across, bringing the new picture with it. Wipes can also be devised in complex patterns or as expanding images, etc.

Wisbar, Frank (1899–1967).
German director in America; made one memorable low-budgeter, *Strangler of the Swamp* 46.

Wisberg, Aubrey (1909–1990).
British-born writer-producer of Hollywood films, mainly second features.
So Dark the Night (w) 41. The Man from Planet X (wp) 51. The Neanderthal Man (wp) 53. Captain Kidd and the Slave Girl (wp) 54. Son of Sinbad (w) 55, many others.

Wisdom, Norman (1920–).
British slapstick comedian, also on stage and TV.
Biography: 1991, *Trouble in Store* by Richard Dacre.
■ Trouble in Store (film debut) 53. One Good Turn 54. Man of the Moment 55. Up in the World 56. Just My Luck 58. The Square Peg 58. Follow a Star 59. There Was a Crooked Man 60. The Bulldog Breed 61. The Girl on the Boat 61. On the Beat 62. A Stitch in Time 63. The Early Bird 65. Press for Time 66. The Sandwich Man 66. The Night They Raided Minsky's (US) 68. What's Good for the Goose 69. Going Gently (TV) 81. Double X 92.

Wise, Ernie:
see *Morecambe, Eric.*

Wise, Robert (1914–).
American director, former editor (worked on *Citizen Kane, All That Money Can Buy, The Magnificent Ambersons*).
■ Mademoiselle Fifi 44. Curse of the Cat People 44. *The Body Snatcher* 45. A Game of Death 46. Criminal Court 46. Born to Kill 47. Mystery in Mexico 47. Blood on the Moon 48. *The Set-Up* 49. Three Secrets 50. Two Flags West 50. The House on Telegraph Hill 51. *The Day the Earth Stood Still* 51. Captive City 52. Destination Gobi 52. Something for the Birds 52. Desert Rats 52. So Big 53. *Executive Suite* 54. Helen of Troy 55. Tribute to a Bad Man 56. Somebody Up There Likes Me 56. Until They Sail 57. This Could Be the Night 57. Run Silent Run Deep 58. I Want to Live (AAN) 58. Odds Against Tomorrow 59. *West Side Story*

(AA) 61. Two for the Seesaw 62. The Haunting (GB) 63. *The Sound of Music* (AA) 65. The Sand Pebbles 66. Star! 68. The Andromeda Strain 70. Two People 73. The Hindenberg 75. Audrey Rose 77. Star Trek 79. Rooftops 89.

Wiseman, Frederick (1931–   ).
American documentarist, former law professor.
Titicut Follies 67. High School 68. Law and Order 69. Hospital 70. Basic Training 71. Essene 72. Juvenile Court 73. Primate 74. Welfare 75. Meat 76. Model 80. Racetrack 85. Blind 87. Near Death 89. Aspen 91. Zoo 93, etc.

Wiseman, Joseph (1918–1984).
American stage actor who has made several film appearances.
Detective Story 51. Viva Zapata 52. Les Misérables 52. The Prodigal 55. The Garment Jungle 57. The Unforgiven 60. *Dr No* (title role) 62. *The Night They Raided Minsky's* 68. Bye Bye Braverman 68. Stiletto 69. The Valachi Papers 72. The Apprenticeship of Duddy Kravitz 74. Buck Rogers 79. Rage of Angels (TV) 83. The Ghost Writer 84. Seize the Day 86, etc.

Wister, Owen (1860–1938).
American western novelist whose *The Virginian*, published in 1902, was the basis of several films and a television series.

witchcraft
has not been frequently tackled by film-makers, usually for censorship reasons, and *Witchcraft through the Ages* remains the most comprehensive cinematic treatise on the subject. Dreyer's *Day of Wrath* took it seriously, as did *The Witches of Salem, Maid of Salem, Witchfinder General, The Dunwich Horror, The Devils* and *Il Demonio*, but all were chiefly concerned with the morals of witch-hunting. Witch doctors are familiar figures from African adventure films like *King Solomon's Mines* and *Men of Two Worlds;* more lightheartedly, witches featured in *The Wizard of Oz, I Married a Witch* and *Bell, Book and Candle*, as well as in TV's *Bewitched* and all the films featuring Merlin. A nasty cannibalistic coven was seen in Gosta Werner's *Midvinterblot* and several recent thrillers (*Night of the Demon, City of the Dead, Night of the Eagle, Witchcraft, The Witches, Rosemary's Baby, Satan's Skin, Cry of the Banshee, The Illustrated Man, The Mephisto Waltz, The Brotherhood of Satan, The Sentinel*) purported to believe in the effects of witchcraft. Angela Lansbury in *Bedknobs and Broomsticks* played a kindly witch.
See also: *the devil*.

Withers, Googie (1917–   ) (Georgette Withers).
British leading lady of stage and screen, married to John McCallum with whom she moved some years ago to Australia.
Biography: 1979, *Life with Googie* by John McCallum.
Girl in the Crowd 34. Accused 36. Strange Boarders 37. The Lady Vanishes 38. Trouble Brewing 39. Back Room Boy 41. *One of Our Aircraft Is Missing* 42. *On Approval* 44. They Came to a City 44. Dead of Night 45. The Loves of Joanna Godden 46. Pink String and Sealing Wax 46. *It Always Rains on Sunday* 47. Miranda 48. Once Upon a Dream 49. Traveller's Joy 50. Night and the City 50. *White Corridors* 51. Derby Day 52. Devil on Horseback 54. Port of Escape 55. The Nickel Queen 70. Time after Time 85. Country Life 94, etc.

Withers, Grant (1904–1959).
American general-purpose actor in films since the

20s. Married to actress Loretta Young (1930–31). Committed suicide.
Tiger Rose 29. Sinner's Holiday 30. Red-Haired Alibi 32. Society Fever 35. Men of Steel 37. Mr Wong, Detective 39. Mexican Spitfire Out West 41. The Apache Trail 43. My Darling Clementine 46. Tripoli 50. Run for Cover 55. The White Squaw 58, many others.

Withers, Jane (1926–   ).
American child star of the 30s, more mischievous and less pretty than Shirley Temple.
Bright Eyes 34. Ginger 35. The Farmer Takes a Wife 35. The Mad Martindales 42. North Star 43. Faces in the Fog 44. Affairs of Geraldine 46. Giant 56. The Right Approach 62. Captain Newman 63, etc.

Witherspoon, Cora (1890–1957).
American character comedienne often seen as shrewish wife; on stage from 1910.
Libeled Lady 36. Madame X 38. The Bank Dick 40. This Love of Ours 45. The Mating Season 50. The First Time 52, etc.

Witney, William (1910–   ).
American director, mainly of routine westerns for Republic.
Roll On Texas Moon 46. Night Time in Nevada 49. The Fortune Hunter 52. City of Shadows 54. Stranger at My Door 56. The Bonnie Parker Story 58. Paratroop Command 59. Master of the World 61. Girls on the Beach 65. Arizona Raiders 66. I Escaped from Devil's Island 73. Darktown Strutters 75, many others.

Wixted, Michael James (1961–   ).
American child actor of the 70s.
Lost in the Stars 74. Where Have All the People Gone? (TV) 74. Islands in the Stream 77, etc.
TV series: The Smith Family 71. The Swiss Family Robinson 75.

Wizan, Joe (1935–   ).
American producer.
Jeremiah Johnson 72. Junior Bonner 72. Prime Cut 72. The Last American Hero 73. Audrey Rose 77. And Justice for All 79. Voices 79. Best Friends 82. Unfaithfully Yours 83. Iron Eagle 85. Tough Guys 86. Spellbinder 88. Split Decisions 88. Short Time 90. The Nanny 90. Stop, or My Mom Will Shoot 91, etc.

Wodehouse, Sir P. G. (1881–1975).
British comic novelist whose sagas of upper-class twits and manservants in the the 20s have been oddly neglected by the screen, though they were much imitated and two films about the perfect manservant Jeeves were made in the 30s.

The Wolf Man.
The werewolf or lycanthrope, a man who turns into a ravaging beast at full moon, is a fairly ancient Central European mythological figure. Hollywood did not develop the idea until *Werewolf of London* 34, a one-shot in which Henry Hull, a victim of his own well-intentioned research, was firmly despatched before the end. Not until 1941 was the possibility of a series character envisaged. *The Wolf Man* had a splendid cast: Claude Rains, Warren William, Patric Knowles, Bela Lugosi, Maria Ouspenskaya, and Lon Chaney Jnr as Lawrence Talbot, heir to a stately English home but unlucky enough to be bitten by a werewolf and thus condemned to monstrous immortality until despatched by a silver bullet. In this film he was battered to apparent death by Claude Rains, but arose from the family crypt for *Frankenstein Meets*

the Wolf Man 43, which ended with him and the Frankenstein Monster being swept away in a flood. In *House of Frankenstein* he was discovered in a block of ice and promptly thawed out, only to be shot with the requisite silver bullet by a gipsy girl. The producers, however, played so unfair as to revive him for *House of Dracula* 45, in which he lived to be the only movie monster with a happy ending: brain surgery cured him and he even got the girl. Years later, however, in *Abbott and Costello Meet Frankenstein* 48, it seemed that his affliction was again tormenting him: this time we last saw him falling into a rocky and turbulent sea. Mr Chaney had by now done with the character apart from a spoof appearance in an episode of TV's *Route 66*. But Hammer Films revived the basic plot in *Curse of the Werewolf* 61, with Oliver Reed as the mangy hero. To date this has provoked no sequels. One should also mention: *The Werewolf 56, I Was a Teenage Werewolf 57, La Casa del Terror* (Mex.) 59, *Werewolf in a Girl's Dormitory* (with its theme song 'The Ghoul in School') 61, and *Legend of the Werewolf* 74, but the less said about these the better.
There was a werewolf in *Dr Terror's House of Horrors* 65, and in *The Beast Must Die* 74, while the 80s brought a whole slew of hairy monsters in *Wolfen, An American Werewolf in London, Werewolf of Washington, Teen Wolf* and *The Howling*. In 1994 Jack Nicholson brought a touch of class to the role in *Wolf*, directed by Mike Nichols.

Wolfe, Ian (1896–1992).
American character actor who usually played worried, grasping or officious roles. He appeared in more than 150 films.
The Barretts of Wimpole Street 33. Clive of India 35. Hudson's Bay 40. The Moon is Down 43. The Invisible Man's Revenge 44. Mr Blandings Builds His Dream House 48. The Great Caruso 50. Gaby 56. The Lost World 60. Games 67. The Fortune 74. Jinxed 82, many others.
TV series: Soap 78–80.

Wolff, Lothar (1909–1988).
German producer-director, former editor; with 'The March of Time' for many years, and still associated with Louis de Rochemont.
Lost Boundaries (p) 45. Martin Luther (co-wp) 53. Windjammer (p) 57. Question Seven (pd) 61. Fortress of Peace (p) 63, etc.

Wolfit, Sir Donald (1902–1968).
Distinguished British thespian who, having brought Shakespeare to the provinces, gave some enjoyably hammy performances in films.
Autobiography: 1954, *First Interval*.
Biography: 1971, *The Knight Has Been Unruly* by Ronald Harwood.
■ Death at Broadcasting House 34. Drake of England 35. The Silent Passenger 35. Sexton Blake and the Bearded Doctor 35. Checkmate 35. Late Extra 35. Hyde Park Corner 35. Calling the Tune 36. *The Ringer* 52. Pickwick Papers 53. Isn't Life Wonderful? 53. Svengali 54. A Prize of Gold 55. Guilty 56. The Man in the Road 56. The Man on the Beach 56. Satellite in the Sky 56. The Traitor 57. I Accuse 57. Blood of the Vampire 58. *Room at the Top* 59. The House of Seven Hawks 59. The Angry Hills 59. The Rough and the Smooth 59. The Hands of Orlac 60. The Mark 61. Lawrence of Arabia 62. Dr Crippen 63. Becket 64. Ninety Degrees in the Shade 65. Life at the Top 65. The Sandwich Man 66. *Decline and Fall* 68. The Charge of the Light Brigade 68.

Wolfson, P. J. (1903–1979).
American screenwriter.

Madison Square Garden 31. The Picture Snatcher 33. Mad Love 35. Public Enemy's Wife 37. Shall We Dance? (co-w) 37. Vivacious Lady (co-w) 38. Allegheny Uprising (& p) 39. They All Kissed the Bride (co-w) 42. Saigon (co-w & p) 48, many others.

Wolheim, Louis (1880–1931).
German-born character actor, often of semi-brutish roles, with American stage experience; in Hollywood from 1919.
Dr Jekyll and Mr Hyde 20. Little Old New York 22. America 24. *Two Arabian Knights* 27. The Racket 28. Tempest 28. Frozen Justice 29. *All Quiet on the Western Front* 31. Sin Ship (& d) 31, etc.

Wolper, David L. (1928–   ).
American documentarist who turned feature film producer and TV executive.
If It's Tuesday This Must Be Belgium 69. The Bridge at Remagen 69. The Hellstrom Chronicle 71. Roots (TV) 77. The Man Who Saw Tomorrow 80. This Is Elvis 81. Imagine: John Lennon 88, etc.

Wolsky, Albert.
American costume designer.
The Turning Point 77. An Unmarried Woman 78. Grease 78. All That Jazz (AA) 79. Manhattan 79. The Jazz Singer 80. Sophie's Choice (AAN) 82. Star 80 83. The Journey of Natty Gan (AAN) 85. Moon over Parador 88. Scenes from a Mall 91. Bugsy (AA) 91. Toys (AAN) 92. The Pickle 93, etc.

Woman to Woman.
Michael Morton's tear-jerking play, about a doomed love affair between a British officer and a French dancer, was first filmed by Graham Cutts in 1923, and achieved some renown as one of the better examples of British silent cinema. Clive Brooks and Betty Compson had the leads, and Miss Compson appeared with Georges Barraud in the talkie remake of 1929, directed by Victor Saville. In 1946 Maclean Rogers directed an updated version with Douglas Montgomery and Joyce Howard.

The Women.
Clare Boothe Luce's venomous comedy was filmed twice by MGM: in 1939 with an all-woman cast headed by Norma Shearer, Rosalind Russell, Paulette Goddard, and Joan Crawford; and in 1956, in a semi-musical version called *The Opposite Sex*, with June Allyson and Ann Sheridan. There are plans to film a new version.

Wong, Anna May (1907–1961) (Wong Liu Tsong).
Chinese-American actress popular in the 30s.
Red Lantern 19. The Thief of Bagdad 24. *Piccadilly* (GB) 29. On the Spot 30. Shanghai Express 32. *Chu Chin Chow* (GB) 33. *Java Head* (GB) 34. Limehouse Blues 36. Bombs Over Burma 42. Impact 49. Portrait in Black 60, etc.

Wong, Victor.
Affable Chinese-American character actor.
Dim Sum: A Little Bit of Heart 85. Big Trouble in Little China 86. Shanghai Surprise 86. The Golden Child 86. The Last Emperor 87. Prince of Darkness 87. Eat a Bowl of Tea 89. 3 Ninjas 92. The Joy Luck Club 93. 3 Ninjas Kick Back 94, etc.

Wontner, Arthur (1875–1960).
Gaunt British character actor of stage and screen; a splendid, if elderly, Sherlock Holmes.
Frailty 16. Bonnie Prince Charlie 23. Eugene Aram 24. The Infamous Lady 28. The Sleeping Cardinal 31. *The Sign of Four* 32. *The Triumph of*

Sherlock Holmes 35. Dishonour Bright 36. Silver Blaze 36. Storm in a Teacup 37. Kate Plus Ten 38. The Terror 38. The Life and Death of Colonel Blimp 43. Blanche Fury 47. Brandy for the Parson 52. *Genevieve* 53, etc.

Woo, John (1946–   ) (Ng Ya-sum).
Hong Kong director. Born in China, he moved to Hong Kong as a child. International recognition came with his violent thriller *The Killer*.
The Young Dragons 73. Money Crazy 77. Last Hurrah for Chivalry 79. Laughing Times 81. The Time You Need a Friend 84. Run Tiger, Run 85. A Better Tomorrow 86. The Killer 89. Bullet in the Head 90. Once a Thief 91. Hard Boiled 92. Hard Target (US) 93, etc.

¶ I hate violence. – *J.W.*
The most exciting director to emerge in action cinema since Sergio Leone. – *Quentin Tarantino*

Wood, Charles (1932–   ).
British playwright with a penchant for military matters.
Help 65. The Knack 65. How I Won the War 67. The Charge of the Light Brigade 68. The Long Day's Dying 68. The Bed Sitting Room 69. Cuba 79. The Red Monarch (TV) 83. Wagner 83. Sharpe's Company (TV) 94. An Awfully Big Adventure 95, etc.

Wood, Edward D., Jnr (1924–1978).
American film director and screenwriter generally regarded as making the worst films in the history of the cinema. Most starred Bela Lugosi, at the sad and drug-addicted end of his career, and the bulky Tor Johnson. A cult has grown around the worst of his worst, *Plan 9 from Outer Space*, which was even the inspiration for a computer game in 1992. A biopic, *Ed Wood*, directed by Tim Burton and starring Johnny Depp in the title role, was released in 1994.
Biography: 1992, *Nightmare of Ecstasy: The Life and Art of Edward D. Wood Jnr* by Rudolph Grey.
■ Glen or Glenda (a, wd) 53. Jail Bait (a, wd) 54. Bride of the Monster (wd) 55. The Violent Years (w) 56. The Bride and the Beast (w) 58. Plan 9 from Outer space (a, wd) 59. The Sinister Urge (a, wd) 60. Night of the Ghouls (aka Revenge of the Dead) (wd) 60. Shotgun Wedding (w) 63. Orgy of the Dead (w) 65. 1,000,000 AC/DC (w) 69. Take It Out in Trade (a, wd) 71. Class Reunion (w) 73. Fugitive Girls (a, w) 74. The Cocktail Hostess (w) 74. Necromancy (aka Necromania) (wd) 75.

Wood, Elijah (1981–   ).
American child actor, a former model.
Avalon 90. Radio Flyer 92. Forever Young 92. The Adventures of Huck Finn 93. The Good Son 93. North 94, etc.

Wood, 'Wee Georgie' (1895–1979).
Diminutive, squeaky-voiced English music-hall comedian, on stage from the age of five.
Convict 99 19. Two Little Drummer Boys 28. The Black Hand Gang 30. Stepping Toes 38. The Visit 61, etc.

Wood, Mrs Henry (1814–1887).
British Victorian novelist whose *East Lynne* has been filmed several times.

Wood, John (1937–   ).
British stage actor usually seen in intellectual roles.
The Rebel 60. Nicholas and Alexandra 72. Slaughterhouse Five 72. Somebody Killed Her Husband 77. War Games 83. Ladyhawke 85. The

Purple Rose of Cairo 85. Jumpin' Jack Flash 86. Memento Mori (TV) 92. Orlando 92. Young Americans 93. Shadowlands 93. Uncovered 94, etc.

Wood, Lawson (1878–1957).
British artist and illustrator, noted for his humorous drawings of animals. He was the creator of *Gran' Pop Monkey*, a short-lived cartoon series about an artful chimpanzee, animated by Ub Iwerks.
A Busy Day 40. Beauty Shoppe 40. Baby Checkers 40.

Wood, Natalie (1938–1981) (Natasha Gurdin).
Former American child actress, who became a top star of the 60s. She was married twice to actor Robert Wagner. Drowned after falling from a yacht.
Happy Land 43. Tomorrow Is Forever 45. The Bride Wore Boots 46. Miracle on 34th Street 47. No Sad Songs for Me 50. The Blue Veil 52. Rebel without a Cause (AAN) 55. A Cry in the Night 56. The Searchers 56. *Marjorie Morningstar* 58. Kings Go Forth 59. Cash McCall 60. *Splendor in the Grass* (AAN) 61. *West Side Story* 61. Gypsy 62. *Love with the Proper Stranger* (AAN) 64. Sex and the Single Girl 64. *The Great Race* 65. Inside Daisy Clover 66. This Property is Condemned 66. Penelope 66. *Bob, and Carol and Ted and Alice* 69. The Affair (TV) 73. Peeper 74. *From Here to Eternity* (TV) 79. Meteor 79. Brainstorm 83 (release), etc.
TV series: Pride of the Family 53.

Wood, Peggy (1894–1978).
American character actress, former opera singer.
Almost a Husband 19. Handy Andy 34. The Housekeeper's Daughter 39. The Story of Ruth 60. *The Sound of Music* (AAN) 65, etc.
TV series: Mama 49–56.

Wood, Sam (1883–1949).
American director, in business before becoming assistant to Cecil B. De Mille *c.* 1915; directing from 1920.
The Beloved Villain 20. Under the Lash 22. Bluebeard's Eighth Wife 23. One Minute to Play 26. The Latest from Paris 28. Within the Law 30. Stamboul Quest 32. The Late Christopher Bean 33. Get-Rich-Quick Wallingford 34. *A Night at the Opera* 35. The Unguarded Hour 36. *A Day at the Races* 37. Madame X 37. Lord Jeff 38. *Goodbye Mr Chips* (AAN) 39. Raffles 39. *Our Town* 40. Kitty Foyle (AAN) 40. *The Devil and Miss Jones* 41. The Pride of the Yankees 42. *Kings Row* (AAN) 42. Saratoga Trunk 43 (released 46). *For Whom the Bell Tolls* (& p) 43. Casanova Brown 44. Guest Wife 45. Heartbeat 46. Ivy 47. Command Decision 48. Ambush 49, etc.

Woodard, Alfre (1953–   ).
American actress.
Remember My Name 78. Health 80. Cross Creek (AAN) 83. Go Tell It on the Mountain 84. Extremities 86. Scrooged 88. Miss Firecracker 89. Grand Canyon 91. Rich in Love 93. Heart and Souls 93. Bopha! 93. Crooklyn 94, etc.
TV series: Tucker's Witch 82–83. St Elsewhere 85–87. Sara 85–88.

Woodbridge, George (1907–1973).
Portly British character actor, often seen as tavern-keeper or jovial policeman.
Tower of Terror 42. Green for Danger 46. Bonnie Prince Charlie 48. The Story of Gilbert and Sullivan 53. The Constant Husband 55. Dracula 58. Two-Way Stretch 60. Dracula Prince of Darkness 65, many others.

Woodbury, Joan (1915–1989).
American leading lady of 40s second features.
   Without Children 35. Forty Naughty Girls 38.
The Mystery of the White Room 39. The
Desperadoes 43. Flame of the West 46. Here Comes
Trouble 49. The Ten Commandments 56, many
others.

Woodfall Films.
British production company set up in the late 50s
by director Tony Richardson and playwright John
Osborne together with financier Harry Saltzman
(though it turned out he didn't actually have any
money). They first produced a screen version of
Osborne's *Look Back in Anger* 59. Productions that
helped change the nature of British films included
The Entertainer 60, *Saturday Night and Sunday
Morning* 60, *A Taste of Honey* 61, *The Loneliness of
the Long Distance Runner* 62, *Tom Jones* 63, *Girl with
Green Eyes* 64, *The Knack* 65. Other productions
included *One Way Pendulum* 65, *Mademoiselle* 66, *The
Sailor from Gibraltar* 67, *Red and Blue* (short) 67,
Hamlet 69, *Laughter in the Dark* 69, *Ned Kelly* 70,
Dead Cert 74, *Joseph Andrews* 77.

Woodlawn, Holly (1947–   ) (Harold Ajzenberg).
Puerto Rico-born transvestite star of Andy
Warhol's movies.
   Trash 69. Scarecrow in a Garden of Cucumbers
72. Women in Revolt 72. Night Owl 93, etc.

¶ We tried to be women so much. I think that
   basically Andy loved glamorous women and
around that time he just didn't know any. – H.W.

Woods, Arthur B. (1904–1942).
British director.
   On Secret Service 34. Radio Parade 35. Drake of
England 35. The Dark Stairway 37. The Return of
Carol Deane 38. *They Drive by Night* 38. The
Nursemaid Who Disappeared 39. Busman's
Honeymoon 40, etc.

Woods, Aubrey (1928–   ).
British character actor.
   Nicholas Nickleby 47. Queen of Spades 48. Father
Brown 54. School for Scoundrels 59. Spare the
Rod 61. Just Like a Woman 66. The Abominable
Dr Phibes 71. The Darwin Adventure 72. That
Lucky Touch 75, etc.

Woods, Donald (1909–   ) (Ralph L. Zink).
Canadian leading man of the 30s and 40s.
   Sweet Adeline 33. *A Tale of Two Cities* 35. *Anthony
Adverse* 36. Forgotten Girls 40. Love, Honour and
Oh Baby 41. I Was a Prisoner on Devil's Island 41.
Watch on the Rhine 43. Roughly Speaking 45.
Wonder Man 45. Barbary Pirate 49. Undercover
Agent 54. Thirteen Ghosts 60. Kissing Cousins 64.
Moment to Moment 65. True Grit 69, many others.
   TV series: Craig Kennedy, Criminologist 52.
Damon Runyon Theatre (host) 55–56. Tammy 65–
66.

Woods, Eddie (1905–1989).
American leading man of the early 30s. He seemed
to lose heart after swapping roles with Cagney for
The Public Enemy (he was originally cast for the top
role and elected to take the less interesting role
of the brother).

Woods, Harry Macgregor (1896–1970).
American songwriter. Educated at Harvard, he
lacked any fingers on his left hand and played the
piano one-handed. He came to Britain in the 30s
to work for Gaumont British Pictures and wrote,
among other hits, 'Over My Shoulder' and 'When
You've Got a Little Springtime in Your Heart' for

Jessie Matthews to sing in *Evergreen*. He returned
to America in the 40s and wrote no more.
   Aunt Sally 33. Jack Ahoy! 34. Evergreen 35. It's
Love Again 36.

Woods, James (1947–   ).
Lean American actor, in roles of increasing stature.
   The Way We Were 72. Alex and the Gypsy 76.
The Choirboys 78. The Onion Field 79. The Black
Marble 80. Eyewitness 80. Split Image 82.
Videodrome 83. Against All Odds 83. Once upon
a Time in America 84. Cat's Eye 84. *Salvador* (AAN)
85. Joshua Then and Now 87. Best Seller 87. Cop
88. The Boost 88. True Believer 89. Immediate
Family 89. The Hard Way 91. Straight Talk 92.
Chaplin 92. Diggstown (GB: Midnight Sting) 92.
The Getaway 94. Curse of the Starving Class 94.
Next Door (TV) 94. The Specialist 94, etc.

Woodward, Edward (1930–   ).
British stage actor who achieved popularity on TV
as *Callan* 67–73.
■ Where There's a Will 54. Becket 64. The File of
the Golden Goose 69. Sitting Target 72. The Wicker
Man 73. Young Winston 73. Callan 74. Stand Up
Virgin Soldiers 77. Breaker Morant 79. Winston
Churchill, the Wilderness Years (TV) 81. Who
Dares Wins 82. A Christmas Carol (TV) 84. King
David 85. Mister Johnson 90. Deadly Advice 94.
   TV series: The Equalizer 85–89. Common as
Muck 94.

Woodward, Joanne (1930–   ).
Tomboyish American leading actress, married to
Paul Newman.
■ Count Three and Pray 55. A Kiss before Dying
56. *The Three Faces of Eve* (AA) 57. *No Down
Payment* 57. The Long Hot Summer 58. Rally round
the Flag Boys 58. The Sound and the Fury 59. The
Fugitive Kind 59. From the Terrace 60. Paris Blues
61. The Stripper 63. A New Kind of Love 63.
Signpost to Murder 64. *A Big Hand for the Little
Lady* 66. A Fine Madness 66. *Rachel Rachel* (AAN)
68. Winning 69. W.U.S.A. 70. They Might Be
Giants 71. The Effect of Gamma Rays on Man-in-
the-Moon Marigolds 72. Summer Wishes, Winter
Dreams (AAN) 73. The Drowning Pool 75. Sybil
(TV) 77. The End 78. See How She Runs (TV) 78.
A Christmas to Remember (TV) 78. The Shadow
Box (TV) 80. Harry and Son 84. Passions (TV) 84.
Do You Remember Love 85. The Glass Menagerie
87. Mr & Mrs Bridge (AAN) 90. Foreign Affairs
(TV) 93. Blind Spot (TV) 93. The Age of Innocence
(narrator) 93. Philadelphia 93. Breathing Lessons
(TV) 94.

Woody Woodpecker.
A cartoon character with an infectious laugh,
created in the 30s by Walter Lantz for Universal,
and still going strong in 1973 via a new TV
incarnation.

Wooland, Norman (1905–1989).
British actor, former radio announcer.
   Hamlet (film debut) 48. All over the Town 48.
Escape 49. Romeo and Juliet 53. The Master Plan
55. Richard III 56. Guilty 56. The Rough and the
Smooth 59. The Fall of the Roman Empire 64. Saul
and David 65. The Projected Man 66, etc.

Wooldridge, Susan.
English leading actress, from the stage and
television, daughter of actress Margaretta Scott.
   Butley 74. The Shout 78. The Jewel in the
Crown (TV) 84. Loyalties 85. Hope and Glory 87.
Bye Bye Blues 89. How to Get Ahead in
Advertising 89. Twenty-One 91. Afraid of the

Dark 92. Just Like a Woman 92. Bad Company
(TV) 93, etc.

Woolf, James (1919–1966).
British producer. With brother, *Sir John Woolf*
(1913–   ), founded Romulus Films 1949. Both are
sons of leading producer-distributor C. M. Woolf,
who died in 1942.
   Pandora and the Flying Dutchman 51. The
African Queen 52. Moulin Rouge 53. Three Men in
a Boat 56. Room at the Top 59, etc.
JAMES ONLY: The L-Shaped Room 62. The Pumpkin
Eater 64. Life at the Top 65. King Rat 65.
JOHN ONLY: Oliver! (AA) 68. Day of the Jackal 73.
No Sex Please We're British 73. The Odessa File
74.

Woolf, Virginia (1882–1941).
British novelist whose introspection and
sensitivity, rather than her themes, were used as
symbols in the title *Who's Afraid of Virginia Woolf?
Orlando* was successfully filmed by Sally Potter in
1992.

Woolfe, H. Bruce (1880–1965).
British producer, best known for his war
reconstructions of the 20s (*Armageddon, Ypres, The
Battle of the Somme*, etc.) and for the *Secrets of Nature*
series begun in 1919. Head of British Instructional
Films from 1926; later in charge of production for
children.

Woollcott, Alexander (1887–1943).
Waspish American columnist and critic, the
original inspiration for Kaufman and Hart's *The Man
Who Came to Dinner*. He was played by Tom
McGowan in *Mrs Parker and the Vicious Circle* 94.
   Biography: 1976, *Smart Aleck* by Howard
Teichmann.
■ Gift of Gab 34. *The Scoundrel* 35. Babes on
Broadway 41.
   See also: *Algonquin Round Table*.

Woolley, Monty (1888–1963) (Edgar Montillion
Woolley).
American comedy character actor of ebullient
personality, a former Yale professor who came to
movie stardom via a big hit as Alexander Woollcott
on the Broadway stage.
   Live, Love and Learn 37. Nothing Sacred 37.
Arsène Lupin Returns 38. Girl of the Golden West
38. Everybody Sing 38. Three Comrades 38. Lord
Jeff 38. Artists and Models Abroad 38. Young Dr
Kildare 38. Vacation from Love 38. Never Say Die
39. Midnight 39. Zaza 39. Man about Town 39.
Dancing Co-Ed 39. *The Man Who Came to Dinner*
41. The Pied Piper (AAN) 42. Life Begins at 8.30
42. *Holy Matrimony* 43. Since You Went Away
(AAN) 44. Irish Eyes Are Smiling 44. Molly and
Me 45. *Night and Day* 46. The Bishop's Wife 47.
Miss Tatlock's Millions 48. As Young as You Feel
51. Kismet 55, etc.

Famous line (*The Man Who Came to Dinner*):
'Gentlemen, will you all now leave quietly, or must
I ask Miss Cutler to pass among you with a baseball
bat?'

Famous line (*The Man Who Came to Dinner*) (to his
nurse who has reproved him for eating
chocolates): 'My great aunt Elizabeth ate a box of
chocolates every day of her life. She lived to be a
hundred and two, and when she had been dead
three days, she looked healthier than you do
now.'

Woolley, Stephen (1956–   ).
British producer. With Nik Powell, he was a co-

founder of Palace Pictures, a distribution and production company.

The Company of Wolves 85. A Letter to Brezhnev 85. Absolute Beginners 86. Mona Lisa 86. The Courier 87. High Spirits 88. Shag 88. Scandal 89. The Big Man 90. The Miracle 91. The Pope Must Die (US: The Pope Must Diet) 91. A Rage in Harlem 91. Interview with the Vampire 94, etc.

Woolrich, Cornell (1903–1968).
American mystery writer also known as William Irish. A recluse, he handed some interesting ideas to Hollywood, but most were ineptly handled.

Street of Chance (from The Black Curtain) 42. The Leopard Man (from Black Alibi) 43. Phantom Lady 44. Deadline at Dawn 46. Black Angel 46. Fear in the Night 47. Night Has a Thousand Eyes 48. The Window 49. No Man of Her Own 50. Rear Window 54. The Bride Wore Black 67, etc.

Woolsey, Ralph.
American cinematographer.

The Culpeper Cattle Company 72. The New Centurions 72. The Mack 73. Black Eye 74. 99 44/100 Per Cent Dead 74. Rafferty and the Gold Dust Twins 75. Mother, Jugs and Speed 76. The Promise 79. The Great Santini 80. The Last Married Couple in America 80. Oh God! Book II 80, etc.

Woolsey, Robert:
see *Wheeler, Bert.*

Worden, Hank (1901–1992) (Norton Earl Worden).
American western character actor.

The Plainsman 36. Northwest Passage 40. The Bullfighters 45. The Secret Life of Walter Mitty 47. Yellow Sky 48. Fort Apache 48. Red River 48. Wagon Master 50. The Searchers 56. McLintock 63. Scream 82, many others.

work print:
the same as cutting copy, the first edited print from which, when it is satisfactory, the negative will be cut accordingly.

World War I (1914–1918).
now a remote and comparatively concentrated event, was seen by film-makers of the next four decades chiefly as an opportunity for pacifist propaganda arising from horror and disillusion. This is the kind of attitude struck in *Civilisation, War Brides, The Battle Cry of Peace, All Quiet on the Western Front* (and its sequel *The Road Back*), *Westfront 1918, J'Accuse, The Man Who Reclaimed His Head, Journey's End, La Grande Illusion, The Man I Killed, The Road to Glory, They Gave Me a Gun, Sergeant York,* and *Paths of Glory. Oh What a Lovely War* made the same points by use of bitter comedy. The romantic aspect of war, however, was not neglected by *The White Sister, A Farewell to Arms, Hearts of the World, The Four Horsemen of the Apocalypse, The Big Parade, Lilac Time, Hell's Angels, Seventh Heaven, The Dark Angel, Waterloo Bridge, Lawrence of Arabia,* and many others. *What Price Glory?* was pure cynicism, *The Fighting 69th* pure jingoism. The spy element was to the fore in *I Was a Spy, Dark Journey, The Spy in Black, Mata Hari, Nurse Edith Cavell* and *Darling Lili;* aviation in *Hell's Angels, Wings, The Red Baron* and *The Blue Max.* Comedy aspects of the war were depicted in *Shoulder Arms, Spy for a Day, Pack Up Your Troubles, We're in the Army Now, Half Shot at Sunrise* and *Up the Front.* Rehabilitation problems were dealt with in *The Sun Also Rises, The Last Flight, Isn't Life Wonderful?, The Lost Squadron, The Roaring Twenties* and the 'Forgotten Man' number in *Gold Diggers of 1933.*

Worlock, Frederick (1886–1973).
British character actor in Hollywood after long stage career.

Miracles for Sale 39. The Sea Hawk 40. Rage in Heaven 41. The Black Swan 43. Sherlock Holmes Faces Death 44. Terror by Night 46. Joan of Arc 48. Notorious Landlady 62. Spinout 66, etc.

Worsley, Wallace (1880–1944).
American director of the 20s.

Honor's Cross 18. The Little Shepherd of Kingdom Come 19. *The Penalty* 20. A Blind Bargain 21. Rags to Riches 22. *The Hunchback of Notre Dame* 23. The Man Who Fights Alone 24. The Shadow of Law 26. The Power of Silence 28, etc.

Worth, Brian (1914–1978).
British light leading man.

The Lion Has Wings 39. One Night with You 48. Hindle Wakes 52. An Inspector Calls 54. Ill Met by Moonlight 57. Peeping Tom 60. On Her Majesty's Secret Service 69, etc.

Worth, Irene (1916–).
American leading actress, in recent years mainly on British stage.
■ One Night with You 48. Another Shore 48. Secret People 51. *Orders to Kill* (BFA) 58. The Scapegoat 59. Seven Seas to Calais (as Elizabeth I) 63. King Lear 69. Nicholas and Alexandra 71. Rich Kids 79. Deathtrap 82. Forbidden 85. Lost in Yonkers 93.

Wotruba, Michael:
see *D'Amato, Joe.*

Wouk, Herman (1915–).
American best-selling novelist.

The Caine Mutiny 54. Marjorie Morningstar 58. Youngblood Hawke 64. The Winds of War (TV) 83.

TV series: Troubleshooters 59–60. Dallas 79–80. Call to Glory 84–85. The Last Precinct 86.

Wray, Fay (1907–).
American leading lady of the 30s, a great screamer. Born in Canada, she moved to America as a child. The first and second of her three husbands were screenwriters John Monk Saunders (1928–40) and Robert Riskin.

Autobiography: 1989, *On the Other Hand.*

Street of Sin 28. The Wedding March 28. The Four Feathers 29. The Texan 30. Dirigible 30. Doctor X 31. *The Most Dangerous Game* 32. The Vampire Bat 33. The Mystery of the Wax Museum 33. *King Kong* 33. The Bowery 33. Madame Spy 34. The Affairs of Cellini 34. The Clairvoyant 35. They Met in a Taxi 36. Murder in Greenwich Village 37. The Jury's Secret 38. Adam Had Four Sons 41. Small Town Girl 53. Queen Bee 55. Crime of Passion 56. Tammy and the Bachelor 57. Gideon's Trumpet (TV) 80, etc.

TV series: Pride of the Family 53.

¶ At the premiere of *King Kong* I wasn't too impressed. I thought there was too much screaming . . . I didn't realize then that King Kong and I were going to be together for the rest of our lives, and longer . . . – F.W.

Wray, John (1890–1940) (John Malloy).
American general-purpose actor.

All Quiet on the Western Front 30. Doctor X 32. I Am a Fugitive from a Chain Gang 32. The Defence Rests 34. The Whole Town's Talking 35. Valiant is the Word for Carrie 36. You Only Live Once 37. The Cat and the Canary 39. The Man from Dakota 40, etc.

Wrede, Caspar (1929–).
Finnish director, in British TV.
■ The Barber of Stamford Hill 62. Private Potter 64. One Day in the Life of Ivan Denisovich 71. Ransom 74.

Wren, P. C. (1885–1941) (Percival Christopher Wren).
British adventure novelist who after a military life wrote the much filmed *Beau Geste,* followed by *Beau Sabreur* and *Beau Ideal.*

Wright, Basil (1907–1987).
British producer-director. In films from 1929; worked with John Grierson in creation of 'documentary'.

Film history: 1975, *The Long View.*

Windmill in Barbados (d) 30. Song of Ceylon (p, d) 34. Night Mail (co-d) 36. Waters of Time (p, d) 51. World without End (d) 53. The Immortal Land (p, d) 58. A Place for Gold (p, d) 61, etc.

Wright, Geoffrey.
Australian director and screenwriter, a former journalist.

Romper Stomper 92. Metal Skin 94.

Wright, Robin (1966–).
American leading actress.

Hollywood Vice Squad 86. The Princess Bride 87. State of Grace 90. The Playboys 92. Toys 92. Forrest Gump 94. The Crossing Guard 95, etc.

Wright, Teresa (1918–).
American leading actress with stage experience.
■ *The Little Foxes* (debut) (AAN) 41. *Mrs Miniver* (AA) 42. The Pride of the Yankees (AAN) 42. *Shadow of a Doubt* 43. Casanova Brown 44. *The Best Years of Our Lives* 46. Pursued 47. The Imperfect Lady 47. The Trouble with Women 47. Enchantment 48. *The Men* 50. The Captive 50. The Steel Trap 52. Something to Live For 52. Count the Hours 53. The Actress 53. Track of the Cat 54. *The Search for Bridey Murphy* 56. Escapade in Japan 57. The Wonderful Years 58. Hail Hero 69. The Happy Ending 69. Crawlspace (TV) 71. The Elevator (TV) 73. Flood (TV) 76. *Roseland* 77. Somewhere in Time 80. Bill: On His Own (TV) 83. The Good Mother 88.

Wright, Tony (1925–1986).
British light leading man, with stage experience.

The Flanagan Boy (film debut) 51. Jumping for Joy 54. Jacqueline 56. Seven Thunders 57. Faces in the Dark 60. Journey to Nowhere 62. All Coppers Are 72, etc.

Wright, Will (1894–1962).
Lugubrious American character actor.

China Clipper 36. World Première 41. Bewitched 45. *The Blue Dahlia* (his best role, as the murderer) 46. Adam's Rib 49. Excuse My Dust 51. The Wild One 52. The Deadly Companions 62. Cape Fear 62. Fail Safe 64, many others.

writers
depicted in films include the following: Rod Taylor as Sean O'Casey in *Young Cassidy,* John Shepperd as Edgar Allan Poe in *The Loves of Edgar Allan Poe,* Beau Bridges as Ben Hecht in *Gaily Gaily,* James Mason as Gustave Flaubert in *Madame Bovary,* Herbert Marshall as Somerset Maugham in *The Moon and Sixpence* and *The Razor's Edge,* Reginald Gardiner as Shakespeare in *The Story of Mankind,* Turhan Bey as Aesop in *A Night in Paradise,* Michael O'Shea as Jack London in *Jack London,* Dean Stockwell as Eugene O'Neill in *Long Day's*

Journey into Night, Daniel Massey as Noël Coward in *Star!*, Frederick Jaeger as Henrik Ibsen in *Song of Norway*, Danny Kaye as *Hans Christian Andersen*, Paul Muni in *The Life of Emile Zola*, Gregory Peck as F. Scott Fitzgerald in *Beloved Infidel*, Burgess Meredith as Ernie Pyle in *The Story of G.I. Joe*, Michael Redgrave as W.B. Yeats in *Young Cassidy*, Laurence Harvey and Karl Boehm in *The Wonderful World of the Brothers Grimm*, Dennis Price in *The Bad Lord Byron*, Richard Chamberlain as Byron in *Lady Caroline Lamb*, Fredric March (later Bill Travers) as Robert Browning in *The Barretts of Wimpole Street*, Olivia de Havilland, Nancy Coleman and Ida Lupino as the Brontë Sisters in *Devotion*, Arthur Kennedy as Branwell Brontë in *Devotion*, Sydney Greenstreet as Thackeray in *Devotion*, Robert Morley in *Oscar Wilde*, Peter Finch in *The Trials of Oscar Wilde*, Cornel Wilde in *Omar Khayyam*, Fredric March in *The Adventures of Mark Twain*, Ian McKellen as D.H Lawrence in *Priest of Love*. Henry Miller was played by David Brandon and Anais Nin by Martine Brochard in *Room of Words* 89, and by Fred Ward and Maria de Medeiros in *Henry and June* 90. The film with the most writers gathered together is Alan Rudolph's 1994 film *Mrs Parker and the Vicious Circle*, about Dorothy Parker and friends gathering for battles of wits at the Algonquin Round Table (qv). The cast includes Jennifer Jason Leigh as Parker, Matthew Broderick as Charles MacArthur, Campbell Scott as Robert Benchley, Lili Taylor as Edna Ferber, Nick Cassavetes as Robert Sherwood, David Thornton as George S. Kaufman, Tom McGowan as Alexander Woollcott, Chip Zien as Franklin P. Adams, Gary Basaraba as Heywood Broun, and David Gow as Donald Ogden Stewart.

¶ Despite the greater reputations of stars and directors, no Hollywood film could begin to be made without a writer, and it is often the dialogue which lingers most effectively in the mind, bringing life even to corny old yarns which were anonymously satirized as follows:

Arizona. Indians thronging.
Arrows pinging. Pistols ponging.
Something smelly – old and hoary.
Not to worry: it's the story.

A bad story can be salvaged by a good director, just as vice versa. Richard Corliss remarked:

While these two functions can be distinguished for research purposes, they are really the inseparable halves of a work of art.

What manner, of course, isn't always art; Mr Corliss was referring to *Citizen Kane*. And some writers give up trying soon after they get to Hollywood with its compromises. As William Holden remarked in *Sunset Boulevard*:

Audiences don't know anybody writes a picture. They think the actors just make it up as they go along.

Other cynics have claimed that there are only six basic plots. As Mr Holden said in another film, *Paris When It Sizzles*:

Frankenstein and *My Fair Lady* are really the same story.

He was right. But of all the arts, the screen is most capable of transforming old sows' ears into shining new silk purses. It can be tremendously subtle in its effects, as Dudley Nichols knew:

The stage is a medium of action, but the screen is a medium of reaction.

Leading those who made screencraft their own was Preston Sturges.

Among the handful of screenwriters whose influence was critical to the craft, Sturges deserves at least two fingers and a thumb.

That's the view of Richard Corliss, who also admires Samson Raphaelson:

Style may be said to comprise his theme: the way people embody it, employ it.

Wrixon, Maris (1917–).
American light leading lady of the 30s.
Broadway Musketeers 38. The Ape 41. The Man Who Talked Too Much 42. Bullets for O'Hara 43. As You Were 51, etc.

Wrubel, Allie (1905–1973).
American composer. A big-band saxophonist and bandleader, he went to Hollywood in the 30s to write songs for Warner's movies.
Dames 34. Housewife 34. Flirtation Walk 34. Happiness Ahead 34. The Key 34. Sweet Music 35. Broadway Hostess 35. I Live for Love 35. In Caliente 35. Bright Lights 35. Life of the Party 37. Radio City Revels 38. Sing Your Way Home 45. Song of the South (AA for song 'Zip-a-Dee-Doo-Dah') 46. Never Steal Anything Small 58, etc.

Wu, Vivien.
Chinese actress. She studied at the Shanghai Film Studio.
The Last Emperor 87. Iron and Silk 91. Shadow of China 91. The Guyver 91. Teenage Mutant Ninja Turtles 3 93. The Joy Luck Club 93, etc.

Wuhl, Robert (1951–).
American comedian and actor.
The Hollywood Knights 80. Good Morning, Vietnam 87. Bull Durham 88. Tales from the Crypt (TV) 89. Wedding Band 89. Blaze 89. Batman 89. Mistress 92. The Bodyguard 92. Blue Chips 94. Cobb 94, etc.

Wurlitzer, Rudy.
American screenwriter and occasional director, often quirky, individualistic road movies.
Glen and Randa 71. Two Lane Blacktop (co-w) 71. Pat Garrett and Billy the Kid 73. Walker 87. Candy Mountain (& co-d) 87. Voyager 91. Little Buddha (co-w) 93. Shadow of the Wolf (co-w) 93. Fearless 94, etc.

Wuthering Heights.
Emily Brontë's brooding romantic novel was filmed in Britain in the silent era, but the best version was made in America in 1939, directed by William Wyler, with Laurence Olivier, as Heathcliff, and Merle Oberon. (It is said that Goldwyn's original casting preferences for Heathcliff were Ronald Colman, Douglas Fairbanks Jnr, and Robert Newton.) A subsequent Mexican version of the story by Luis Buñuel, *Abismos de Pasión* 50, has not been widely seen. Robert Fuest remade it in 1970 with Timothy Dalton and Anna Calder-Marshall, and a lacklustre treatment came in 1992, with Ralph Fiennes and Juliette Binoche.

Wyatt, Jane (1912–).
Pleasing American leading lady of the 30s and 40s, with stage experience.
One More River 34. The Luckiest Girl in the World 36. *Lost Horizon* 37. Kisses for Breakfast 41. The Kansan 42. The Iron Road 43. None but the Lonely Heart 44. Boomerang 47. Gentleman's Agreement 47. Pitfall 48. Bad Boy 49. Task Force 49. Our Very Own 50. The Man Who Cheated Himself 51. Never Too Late 65. Tom Sawyer (TV) 73. Treasure of Matecumbe 76. Star Trek IV: The Journey Home 86. Amityville 4: The Evil Escapes (TV) 89, many others.
TV series: Father Knows Best 54–59 (reunion show 77).

Wycherly, Margaret (1881–1956).
British-born character actress with American stage experience.
The Thirteenth Chair 29. Sergeant York (AAN) 41. Keeper of the Flame 43. The Yearling 46. *White Heat* 49. Man with a Cloak 51. That Man from Tangier 53, many others.

Wyler, Richard (1934–) (aka Richard Stapley).
American leading man of the 50s.
The Three Musketeers 48. The Strange Door 51. King of the Khyber Rifles 53. Target Zero 55. The Ugly Ones 68, etc.
TV series: Man from Interpol 60.

Wyler, William (1902–1981).
Distinguished German-American director, former film publicist, in Hollywood from 1920. Director from 1925, starting with low-budget silent westerns.
■ TALKIES: Hell's Heroes 30. The Storm 30. A House Divided 31. Tom Brown of Culver 32. Her First Mate 33. Counsellor at Law 33. Glamour 34. *The Good Fairy* 35. The Gay Deception 35. These Three 36. Come and Get It (co-d) 36. *Dodsworth* (AAN) 36. *Dead End* 37. *Jezebel* 38. *Wuthering Heights* (AAN) 39. *The Letter* 40. *The Westerner* 40. *The Little Foxes* (AAN) 41. *Mrs Miniver* (AA) 42. The Memphis Belle (doc) 44. The Fighting Lady (doc) 44. *The Best Years of Our Lives* (AA) 46. *The Heiress* (AAN) 49. *Detective Story* (AAN) 51. Carrie 52. Roman Holiday (AAN) 53. The Desperate Hours 55. The Friendly Persuasion (AAN) 56. *The Big Country* 58. *Ben Hur* (AA) 59. The Children's Hour 62. *The Collector* (AAN) 65. How to Steal a Million 66. Funny Girl 68. The Liberation of L.B. Jones 70.

¶ Doing a picture with Willie is like getting the works at a Turkish bath. You damn near drown, but you come out smelling like a rose. – *Charlton Heston*

Wyman, Jane (1914–) (Sarah Jane Faulks).
American leading lady of the 40s, at first in dumb blonde roles, later as serious actress.
My Man Godfrey 36. Brother Rat 38. Flight Angels 40. Bad Men of Missouri 41. The Body Disappears 41. You're in the Army Now 41. My Favourite Spy 42. Princess O'Rourke 43. Crime by Night 44. The Doughgirls 44. Make Your Own Bed 44. *The Lost Weekend* 45. Night and Day 46. Magic Town 46. The Yearling (AAN) 46. *Johnny Belinda* (AA) 48. Three Guys Named Mike 49. Here Comes the Groom 51. The Blue Veil (AAN) 52. Just for You 53. So Big 53. *Magnificent Obsession* (AAN) 54. All that Heaven Allows 55. Miracle in the Rain 56. Pollyanna 60. Bon Voyage 63. How to Commit Marriage 69. The Failing of Raymond (TV) 71. The Incredible Journey of Dr Meg Laurel (TV) 79, etc.
TV series: The Jane Wyman Theater 56–60. Falcon Crest 81– .
~When asked why she divorced Ronald Reagan, she said: 'He talked too much.'

Wymark, Patrick (1920–1970) (Patrick Cheesman).
British TV actor, in occasional films. The voice of Churchill in *The Finest Hours* 64, *A King's Story* 65.
The Criminal 60. Repulsion 65. The Secret of Blood Island 65. The Psychopath 66. Where Eagles Dare 68. Cromwell 69. Satan's Skin 70, etc.

Wymore, Patrice (1926–).
American leading lady. She married Errol Flynn in 1953.
Tea for Two 50. Rocky Mountain 50. The Big Trees 52. She's Working Her Way through

College 52. She's Back on Broadway 53. Chamber of Horrors 66, etc.

Wyndham, John (1903–1969).
British science fiction novelist. Works filmed include *Village of the Damned (The Midwich Cuckoos)* and *The Day of the Triffids.*

Wynn, Ed (1886–1966) (Isaiah Edwin Leopold).
American vaudeville, radio and TV comic who after initial film failure returned to Hollywood in the 50s as a character actor of fey old gentlemen.
■ Rubber Heels 27. Follow the Leader 30. Manhattan Mary 30. The Chief 33. Stage Door Canteen 43. *The Great Man* 56. Marjorie Morningstar 58. *The Diary of Anne Frank* (AAN) 59. The Absent Minded Professor 60. Cinderfella 60. Babes in Toyland 61. Son of Flubber 63. Those Calloways 64. Mary Poppins 64. That Darn Cat 65. Dear Brigitte 65. The Greatest Story Ever Told 65. The Gnome-Mobile 67.
   TV series: The Ed Wynn Show 58.

Wynn, Keenan (1916–1986).
American character actor, son of Ed Wynn. In Hollywood from early 40s after stage experience.
   Autobiography: 1960, *Ed Wynn's Son.*
   See Here Private Hargrove 44. Under the Clock 45. Weekend at the Waldorf 45. The Hucksters 47. Annie Get Your Gun 50. Kiss Me Kate 53. The Glass Slipper 55. The Great Man 57. A Hole in the Head 59. The Absent-Minded Professor 60. Man in the Middle 63. Dr Strangelove 63. The Americanization of Emily 65. The Great Race 65.

The War Wagon 67. Mackenna's Gold 68. Smith 69. Once upon a Time in the West 69. Five Savage Men 70. Pretty Maids all in a Row 71. Herbie Rides Again 73. Hit Lady (TV) 75. Nashville 75. The Devil's Rain 76. Orca 77. High Velocity 77. Coach 78. Piranha 78. Sunburn 79. Just Tell Me What You Want 80. The Glove 81. Best Friends 82, many others.
   TV series: The Trouble Shooters 59.

¶ He's the fellow who, when Esther Williams jumps into the pool, gets splashed. – *Ed Wynn of Keenan Wynn*

Wynn, May (1931–   ) (Donna Lee Hickey).
American leading lady of the 50s.
■ 3 The Caine Mutiny 54. The Violent Men 54. They Rode West 55. Hong Kong Affair 59.

Wynn, Tracy Keenan (1945–   ).
American screenwriter, son of Keenan Wynn.
   The Glass House (TV) 70. Tribes (TV) 71. *The Autobiography of Miss Jane Pittman* (TV) 73. The Longest Yard 74. The Drowning Pool (co-w) 75. The Deep (co-w) 77, etc.

Wynorski, Jim (1950–   ).
American director and screenwriter of exploitation movies. He began as a writer for Roger Corman's productions.
   Sorceress (w) 83. Screwballs (co-w) 83. The Lost Empire (wd) 84. Chopping Mall (aka Killbots) (co-w, d) 86. Deathstalker II: Duel of the Titans (d) 87. Big Bad Mama 2 (co-w, d) 87. Not of This

Earth (d) 88. The Return of the Swamp Thing (d) 89. Transylvania Twist (d) 89. The Haunting of Maurella (wd) 90. 976 Evil: The Return (d) 91. Sins of the Flesh (d) 92. Tough Cookies (co-w, d) 93. Munchie Strikes Back 94, etc.

Wynter, Dana (1927–   ) (Dagmar Wynter).
British leading lady.
   White Corridors 51. Colonel March Investigates 53. *Invasion of the Body Snatchers* (US) 56. D Day Sixth of June 56. Value 57. Shake Hands with the Devil 59. *Sink the Bismarck* 60. The List of Adrian Messenger 63. If He Hollers Let Him Go 68. Airport 69. Santee 73. Backstairs at the White House (TV) 79. The Royal Romance of Charles and Diana (TV) 82. The People from Another Star 86. Dead Right 88, etc.
   TV series: The Man Who Never Was 66.

Wynyard, Diana (1906–1964) (Dorothy Isobel Cox).
Distinguished British stage actress who began her film career with MGM in Hollywood, returning to Britain to act on the stage. Married to director Carol Reed.
■ Rasputin and the Empress 32. *Cavalcade* (AAN) 33. Men Must Fight 33. Reunion in Vienna 33. Where Sinners Meet 34. Let's Try Again 34. One More River 34. On the Night of the Fire 39. Freedom Radio 40. *Gaslight* 40. The Prime Minister 40. *Kipps* 41. An Ideal Husband 47. Tom Brown's Schooldays 51. The Feminine Touch 56. Island in the Sun 57.

Y

Yablans, Frank (1935–).
American independent producer.
The Other Side of Midnight 77. The Silver Streak 77. The Fury 78. North Dallas Forty (& w) 80. Mommie Dearest 81, etc.

Yablans, Irwin (1934–).
American independent producer.
Badge 373 73. Halloween 78. Roller Boogie 79. Fade to Black 80. The Seduction 82, etc.

Yamada, Isuzu (1917–) (Mitsu Yamada).
Japanese leading actress, best known for her role as Lady Washizu (an oriental Lady Macbeth) in Kurosawa's *Throne of Blood*. She began her career at the age of 14 and married director Teinosuke Kinusaga, with whom she set up a short-lived production company in the 50s.
Osaka Elegy (Niniwa Hika) 36. Sisters of the Gion (Gion No Shimai) 36. Throne of Blood (Kumonosu-jo) 57. Buddha (Shaka) 61. Yojimbo 61, etc.

Yamada, Yoji (1931–).
Japanese director of working-class comedies. He is best known for the popular series of *Tora-san* movies, the adventures of an itinerant pedlar. So far, he has directed more than 40 of them at the rate of two a year since 1969.

Yanagimachi, Mitsuo (1944–).
Japanese director.
Farewell to the Land 82. Himatsuri 85. Shadow of China 91. About Love, Tokyo 92, etc.

Yang, Edward (1947–) (Yang Dechang).
Chinese-born director, working in Taiwan.
In Our Time (co-d) 82. That Day on the Beach 83. Taipei Story 85. The Terrorizers 86. A Brighter Summer Day 91. A Confucian Confusion (Duli Shidai) 94, etc.

Yanne, Jean (1933–) (J. Gouye).
Heavy-set French actor.
Life Upside Down 65. Weekend 67. *Le Boucher* 69. Cobra 73. The Accuser 75. The Pink Telephone 76. Hanna K 83. Quicker than the Eye 88. Madame Bovary 91. Indochine 92. Chacun pour Toi 93. Fausto 93. Pétain 93. Regarde les Hommes Tomber 94, etc.

Yarbrough, Jean (1900–1975).
American director of second features, former prop man.
Devil Bat 41. Lure of the Islands 42. Good Morning Judge 43. In Society 44. The Naughty Nineties 45. The Brute Man 46. Curse of the Allenbys 47. The Creeper 48. Abbott and Costello Lost in Alaska 52. Jack and the Beanstalk 52. Women of Pitcairn Island 57. Saintly Sinners 61. Hillbillies in a Haunted House 67. The Over-the-Hill Gang (TV) 69, many others.

Yared, Gabriel.
French composer.
Every Man for Himself (Sauve Qui Peut la Vie) 80. Invitation au Voyage 82. Hanna K. 83. Dream One 84. Red Zone (Zone Rouge) 86. Betty Blue (37.2 Degrés le Matin) 86. Beyond Therapy 87. Clean and Sober 88. Camille Claudel 88. Romero 89. The King's Whore 90. The Lover (L'Amant) 92. Map of the Human Heart 93. Des Feux Mal Éteints 94. Profil Bas 94, etc.

Yates, Herbert (1880–1966).
American executive, ex-president of Republic Pictures, where his word was law in the 40s. Many of his productions starred his wife, Vera Hruba Ralston.

Yates, Marjorie (1941–).
English character actress, mainly in theatre and TV.
The Optimists of Nine Elms 73. Stardust 74. The Black Panther 77. Priest of Love 81. Wetherby 85. The Long Day Closes 92, etc.

Yates, Peter (1929–).
British director.
Summer Holiday 62. One Way Pendulum 64. *Robbery* 67. *Bullitt* (US) 68. John and Mary (US) 69. Murphy's War 70. The Hot Rock (US) 72. *The Friends of Eddie Coyle* 73. For Pete's Sake 74. Mother Jugs and Speed 76. The Deep 77. Breaking Away (AAN) 79. Eyewitness 81. Krull 83. *The Dresser* (& p) (AAN) 83. Eleni 85. Suspect 87. The House on Carroll Street 88. Hard Rain 89. Year of the Comet 92, etc.

Yeung, Bolo (Yang Sze).
Hong Kong martial arts actor, often as a villain.
Enter the Dragon 73. Young Dragon 77. Bolo 78. Bloodsport 88. Bloodfight 90. Tiger Claws 91. Double Impact 91. Iron Heart 92. TC 2000 93, etc.

Yimou, Zhang (1950–).
Chinese director of the so-called Fifth Generation, a former cinematographer and actor. His more recent films have been banned in China. In 1994, the authorities forbade him from making films in China for five years.
AS ACTOR: Old Well 87. The Terra-Cotta Warrior 90.
AS CINEMATOGRAPHER: Yellow Earth 83. The Big Parade 85.
AS DIRECTOR: Red Sorghum (Hong Gaoliang) 87. Operation Cougar 89. Jou Dou 90. Raise the Red Lantern (Dahong Denglong Gaogao Gua) 91. *The Story of Qiu Jou* 92. To Live 94. The Great Conqueror's Concubine (Xi Chu Bawang) (p) 94.

¶ To survive is to win. – Z.Y.

Yoda, Yoshikata.
Japanese screenwriter who collaborated with Kenji Mizoguchi on the scripts of many of the director's films from the mid-30s.
Osaka Elegy (Niniwa Hika) 36. Sisters of the Gion (Gion No Shimai) 36. Roei No Uta 38. Zangiku Monogatari 39. The Woman of Osaka (Naniwa Onna) 40. The Loyal 47 Ronin I and II 41. Woman of the Night (Yoru No Onnatachi) 48.

The Life of Oharu (Saikaki Ichidai Onna) 52. Ugetsu 53. Sansho the Bailiff (Sansho Dayu) 54. A Story from Chikamatsu (Chikamatsu Monogatari) 54. Shin Heike Monogatari 55, etc.

Yordan, Philip (1913–).
Prolific American writer-producer.
SCREENPLAYS: Syncopation 42. Dillinger (AAN) 45. House of Strangers 49. Detective Story (AAN) 51. Johnny Guitar 54. Broken Lance (AA story) 54. El Cid 61. 55 Days at Peking 62. The Fall of the Roman Empire 64, many others.
WROTE AND PRODUCED: The Harder They Fall 56. Men in War 57. God's Little Acre 58. Day of the Outlaw 59. Studs Lonigan 60. The Day of the Triffids 62. The Thin Red Line 64. The Battle of the Bulge 65. Captain Apache 71. Savage Journey 83. Night Train to Terror 85. Bloody Wednesday 87. Cry Wilderness 87. The Unholy 88, etc.

¶ People would rather go and see a big bad picture than a good small one. – P.Y.

Yorick, John (1969–).
Polish actor, director, and screenwriter, the son of Jerzy Skolimowski. He co-wrote, co-directed and co-starred in *The Hollow Men* with his brother Joseph Kay (1971–).
Success Is the Best Revenge (as Michael Lyndon) 84. The Lightship (as Michael Lyndon) 85. The Hollow Men (a, co-w, co-d) 93.

York, Dick (1928–1992).
American actor.
My Sister Eileen 55. Operation Mad Ball 57. They Came to Cordura 58. Inherit the Wind 60, etc.
TV series: Going My Way 62–63. Bewitched 64–69.

York, Michael (1942–) (Michael Hugh Johnson).
English leading actor, often in sensible, clean-cut roles. Born in Fulmer, Buckinghamshire, he began acting as a schoolboy with Michael Croft's Youth Theatre and continued at Oxford University, where he studied English. He began his professional career with the Dundee Repertory before joining the National Theatre, where he worked with Zeffirelli, who gave him his first screen role.
Autobiography: 1991, *Travelling Player*.
■ The Taming of the Shrew 67. Accident 67. Red and Blue 67. Smashing Time 67. Romeo and Juliet 68. The Strange Affair 68. The Guru 69. Alfred the Great 69. Justine 69. Something for Everyone 70. Zeppelin 71. *Cabaret* 72. England Made Me 72. *Lost Horizon* 73. The Three Musketeers 73. The Four Musketeers 74. Murder on the Orient Express 74. Conduct Unbecoming 75. Great Expectations 75. Logan's Run 76. *Jesus of Nazareth* (TV) 77. The Last Remake of Beau Geste 77. Seven Nights in Japan 77. The Island of Dr Moreau 77. Fedora 78. The Riddle of the Sands 79. A Man Called Intrepid (TV) 79. The White Lions 80. Final Arrangement 80. Phantom of the Opera (TV) 82. The Master of Ballantrae (TV) 83. Success Is the Best Revenge 84. Space (TV) 85. The Dawn 85. The Far Country (TV) 86. Sword of Gideon (TV) 86.

Phantom of Death 87. Midnight Cop 88. Till We Meet Again (TV) 89. The Lady and the Highwayman (TV) 89. The Return of the Musketeers 89. Eline Vere 91. The Heat of the Day (TV) 91. Duel of Hearts (TV) 92. Wide Sargasso Sea 93. Our Lady (Gospa) 94.

¶ Cinema, it has always seemed to me, is essentially filmed thought. – *M.Y.*

York, Susannah (1941–) (Susannah Yolande Fletcher).
British leading lady of stage and screen.
■ *Tunes of Glory* (debut) 60. There Was a Crooked Man 60. *The Greenage Summer* 61. Freud 62. Tom Jones 63. The Seventh Dawn 64. Scene Nun Take One. 64. Scruggs 64. Sands of the Kalahari 65. Kaleidoscope 66. A Man For All Seasons 66. Sebastian 67. The Killing of Sister George 68. Duffy 68. Oh What a Lovely War 69. The Battle of Britain 69. Lock Up Your Daughters 69. *They Shoot Horses Don't They?* (US) (AAN) 69. Country Dance 70. Jane Eyre 70. Zee and Co. 71. Happy Birthday Wanda June (US) 71. *Images* 72. The Maids 73. Gold 74. Conduct Unbecoming 75. That Lucky Touch 75. Sky Riders 76. Eliza Frazer 76. Superman 78. The Golden Gate Murders (TV) 79. The Silent Partner 79. The Shout 79. Falling in Love Again 80. Superman II 80. The Awakening 80. Loophole 81. Yellowbeard 83. A Christmas Carol (TV) 84. Prettykill 87. Superman IV: The Quest for Peace (voice) 87. The Land of Faraway 87. American Roulette 88. A Summer Story 88. Just Ask for Diamond 88. Bluebeard Bluebeard (Barbablu Barbablu) 89. Melancholia 89. A Handful of Time (En Handfull Tid) 90. Fate 90. Pretty Princess (It.) 93.
TV series: Second Chance 80. We'll Meet Again 81.

Yorkin, Bud (1926–) (Alan Yorkin).
American director, from TV.
Come Blow Your Horn 63. Never Too Late 65. Divorce American Style 67. Inspector Clouseau 68. Start the Revolution without Me 69. The Thief Who Came to Dinner 73. Twice in a Lifetime 85. Arthur 2: On the Rocks 88. Love Hurts 90. Intersection (p) 93, etc.

Yosemite Sam.
Bad-tempered, loud-mouthed, long-moustachioed cartoon cowboy, the self-styled 'roughest, toughest hombre', usually to be seen chasing Bugs Bunny in Warner Brothers' Merrie Melodies and Loony Tunes cartoons. Created by Fritz Freleng, he was voiced by Mel Blanc.
Hare Trigger 45. Buccaneer Bunny 48. Mutiny on the Bunny 50. 14 Carrot Rabbit 52. Captain Hareblower 54. Rabbitson Crusoe 56. Knighty-Knight Bugs (AA) 58. Prince Violent 61. Shishkabugs 62. Devil's Feud Cake 63, etc.

Yoshida, Yoshishige (1933–).
Japanese director and screenwriter, a member of the 'New Wave' of the 60s. He studied French literature at Tokyo University before becoming an assistant director. In the 70s, he was in Europe making TV documentaries.
Good for Nothing (Rokudenashi) 60. Blood Is Dry (Chi Wa Kawaite Iru) 60. Akitsu Onsen 62. 18 Roughs (Arashi o Yobu Juhachinim) 63. Woman of the Lake (Onna no Mizumi) 66. Honoo To Onna 67. Affair in the Snow (Juhyo no Yorumeki) 68. Eros and Massacre (Eros Purasu Gyakusatsu) 69. Rengoku Eroica 70. Coup d'Etat (Kaigenre) 73. Wuthering Heights (Arashi ga Oka) 89, etc.

Yoshimura, Kozaburo (1911–).
Japanese director. Many of his most successful films were scripted by Kaneto Shindo, with whom he set up his own production company in the 50s.
Tomorrow's Dancers 39. Blossom 41. Temptation 48. Spring Snow 50. A Tale of Genji 51. Before Dawn 53. Beauty and the Dragon 55. Undercurrent 56. Design for Dying 61. The Bamboo Doll 63. A Fallen Woman 67. A Hot Night (Atsui Yoru) 68. A Ragged Flag 74, etc.

Youmans, Vincent (1898–1946).
American song composer of the 20s. Shows filmed include *No No Nanette* and *Hit the Deck*.

Young, Alan (1919–) (Angus Young).
British-born comic actor, in Canada since childhood.
Margie (debut) 46. Mr Belvedere Goes to College 49. Aaron Slick from Punkin Crick 52. *Androcles and the Lion* 53. Gentlemen Marry Brunettes 55. Tom Thumb 58. The Time Machine 60. The Cat from Outer Space 78. Duck Tales: The Movie (voice) 90, etc.
TV series: Mister Ed 60–65.

Young, Arthur (1898–1959).
Portly British stage actor; film appearances usually in self-important roles.
No Limit 35. Victoria the Great 37. My Brother Jonathan 48. The Lady with a Lamp 51. An Inspector Calls 54. The Gelignite Gang 56, etc.

Young, Burt (1940–).
American supporting actor.
The Gambler 74. The Killer Elite 75. Rocky (AAN) 76. The Choirboys 77. Twilight's Last Gleaming 77. Convoy 78. Rocky II 79. Murder Can Hurt You (TV) 79. All the Marbles 81. Blood Beach 81. Once upon a Time in America 84. Rocky III 85. Back to School 86. Blood Red 88. Beverly Hills Brats 89. Last Exit to Brooklyn 89. Betsy's Wedding 90. Diving In 90. Rocky V 90. Red American (Americano Rosso) 91. Club Fed 91. Bright Angel 91. Excessive Force 93, etc.

Young, Carleton (1906–1971).
American character actor, from radio; father of Tony Young.
The Glory Brigade 53. The Court Martial of Billy Mitchell 55. The Horse Soldiers 59. Sergeant Rutledge 60, many others.

Young, Clara Kimball (1890–1960).
Popular American heroine of the silent screen.
Cardinal Wolsey (debut) 12. Beau Brummell 13. Goodness Gracious 16. Eyes of Youth 19. Cheating Cheaters 19. Forbidden Woman 20. Hush 21. Charge It 21. Lying Wives 25. Kept Husbands 31. Love Bound 33. Romance in the Rain 34. The Frontiersman 39. Mr Celebrity 42, etc.

Young, Collier (1908–1980).
American writer-producer.
The Hitch-Hiker 53. The Bigamist 54. Mad at the World 55. Huk! 56, etc.
TV series: One Step Beyond 58–60. Ironside 67, etc.

Young, Freddie (1902–).
Distinguished British cinematographer.
Bitter Sweet 33. Nell Gwyn 34. When Knights Were Bold 36. Victoria the Great 37. Sixty Glorious Years 38. Goodbye Mr Chips 39. The Young Mr Pitt 41. 49th Parallel 41; war service; Bedelia 46. So Well Remembered 47. Edward My Son 49. Treasure Island 50. Ivanhoe 52. *Lust for Life* 56. *Invitation to the Dance* 56. Bhowani Junction 56. Island in the Sun 56. *Lawrence of Arabia* (AA) 62.

The Seventh Dawn 64. Lord Jim 65. Rotten to the Core 65. *Doctor Zhivago* (AA) 65. The Deadly Affair 67. You Only Live Twice 67. The Battle of Britain 69. *Ryan's Daughter* (AA) 70. Nicholas and Alexandra (AAN) 71. The Tamarind Seed 74. The Blue Bird 76. Seven Nights in Japan 77. Stevie 78. Bloodline 79. Rough Cut 80. Richard's Things 81. Sword of the Valiant 84. Invitation to the Wedding 84, etc.
~In 1985, at the age of 82, he directed his first film, *Arthur's Hallowed Ground.*

Young, Gig (1913–1978) (Byron Barr; aka Bryant Fleming).
American light comedy leading man with a pleasantly bemused air. Committed suicide after killing his fifth wife. He was previously married to actress Elizabeth Montgomery.
Misbehaving Husbands 40. They Died With Their Boots On 41. Dive Bomber 41. The Gay Sisters (in which he played a character called Gig Young and thereafter used the name) 41. Old Acquaintance 43. Air Force 43; war service; Escape Me Never 46. The Woman in White 47. Wake of the Red Witch 48. The Three Musketeers 49. *Come Fill the Cup* (AAN) 51. City That Never Sleeps 54. Young at Heart 55. Desk Set 57. Teachers Pet (AAN) 58. The Story on Page One 59. Ask Any Girl 59. *That Touch of Mink* 62. For Love or Money 63. Strange Bedfellows 65. The Shuttered Room 67. *They Shoot Horses, Don't They?* (AA) 69. *Lovers and Other Strangers* 70. The Neon Ceiling (TV) 71. A Son-in-Law for Charlie McReady 73. Bring Me the Head of Alfredo Garcia 74. The Hindenburg 75. The Killer Elite 75. Sherlock Holmes in New York (TV) 77. Spectre (TV) 78.
TV series: The Rogues 64. Gibbsville 76.

Famous line (*They Shoot Horses, Don't They?*): 'There can only be one winner, folks, but isn't that the American way?'

Young, Harold (1897–1970).
American director who made distinguished British films for Korda but was little heard from on his return to Hollywood.
The Scarlet Pimpernel 35. 52nd Street 38. Code of the Streets 39. Juke Box Jenny 42. The Frozen Ghost 43. I'll Remember April 44, etc.

Young, Loretta (1913–) (Gretchen Young).
American leading lady whose career in films began when she accidentally, at 15, answered a studio call meant for her elder sister, Polly Ann Young.
Autobiography: 1962, *The Things I Had to Learn.*
Laugh Clown Laugh (debut) 28. Loose Ankles 29. The Squall 30. Kismet 30. *The Devil to Pay* 30. I Like Your Nerve 31. Platinum Blonde 32. The Hatchet Man 32. Big Business Girl 32. Life Begins 32. Zoo in Budapest 33. *Man's Castle* 33. The House of Rothschild 34. Midnight Mary 35. The Crusaders 35. Clive of India 35. Call of the Wild 35. Shanghai 36. *Ramona* 36. Ladies in Love 37. Wife, Doctor and Nurse 37. Second Honeymoon 38. Four Men and a Prayer 38. Suez 38. Kentucky 38. Three Blind Mice 38. The Story of Alexander Graham Bell 39. The Doctor Takes a Wife 39. He Stayed for Breakfast 40. Lady from Cheyenne 41. The Men in Her Life 41. *A Night to Remember* 42. China 43. Ladies Courageous 44. And Now Tomorrow 44. The Stranger 45. Along Came Jones 46. The Perfect Marriage 46. *The Farmer's Daughter* (AA) 47. The Bishop's Wife 48. Rachel and the Stranger 48. Come to the Stable (AAN) 49. Cause for Alarm 51. Half Angel 51. Paula 52. Because of You 52. It Happens Every Thursday 53. Christmas Eve (TV) 86, many others.
TV show of anthology dramas 53–60.

Young, Otis (1932–).
American actor.
The Last Detail 73. The Capture of Bigfoot 79.
Blood Beach 81, etc.
TV series: The Outcasts 68.

Young, Robert (1907–).
American leading man invariably cast in amiable,
dependable roles. A former clerk, with stage
experience.
■ The Sin of Madelon Claudet (debut) 31. Strange
Interlude 31. The Kid from Spain 32. Hell Below
32. Tugboat Annie 33. Lazy River 34. The House
of Rothschild 34. Spitfire 34. Whom the Gods
Destroy 35. West Point of the Air 35. It's Love
Again (GB) 36. *Secret Agent* (GB) 36. Stowaway
36. The Emperor's Candlesticks 37. I Met Him in
Paris 37. The Bride Wore Red 37. Josette 38. Frou
Frou 38. Three Comrades 39. Rich Man, Poor Girl
39. Honolulu 39. Miracles for Sale 39. Maisie 39.
Northwest Passage 40. The Mortal Storm 40.
Florian 40. Western Union 41. The Trial of Mary
Dugan 41. Lady Be Good 41. *H. M. Pulham Esq.*
41. Joe Smith American 42. Cairo 42. Journey
for Margaret 42. Sweet Rosie O'Grady 43. *Claudia*
43. The Canterville Ghost 44. The Enchanted
Cottage 44. Those Endearing Young Charms 45.
Lady Luck 46. Claudia and David 46. The Searching
Wind 46. They Won't Believe Me 47. *Crossfire* 47.
Sitting Pretty 48. The Forsyte Woman 49. And
Baby Makes Three 50. The Second Woman 51.
Goodbye My Fancy 51. The Half-Breed 52. The
Secret of the Incas 54. Vanished (TV) 71. All My
Darling Daughters (TV) 72. My Darling Daughters'
Anniversary (TV) 73. Little Women (TV) 78. The
Return of Marcus Welby M.D. 84. Mercy or Murder
(TV) 86. Conspiracy of Love (TV) 87. A Holiday
Affair (TV) 88. Talent for the Game 91.
TV series: Father Knows Best 54–60.
Window on Main Street 61. Marcus Welby M.D.
69–75.

Young, Robert M. (1924–).
American director.
Nothing but a Man (co-d) 65. Alambrista! 77.
Short Eyes 78. Rich Kids 79. One-Trick Pony 80.
The Ballad of Gregorio Cortez (& co-w) 83. Saving
Grace 86. Extremities 86. Dominick and Eugene 88.
Triumph of the Spirit 89. Talent for the Game 91.
Splitting Heirs 93. Roosters 93, etc.

Young, Roland (1887–1953).
British character actor with stage experience;
made a screen career in Hollywood and is
affectionately remembered for a gallery of
whimsical or ineffectual types.
Sherlock Holmes (debut) 22. Moriarty 22. The
Unholy Night 29. Madame Satan 30. New Moon
30. *One Hour with You* 32. Wedding Rehearsal (GB)
32. The Guardsman 32. His Double Life 33. *David
Copperfield* (as Uriah Heep) 34. Ruggles of Red Gap
34. One Rainy Afternoon 36. *The Man Who Could
Work Miracles* (GB) 36. Call It a Day 37. King
Solomon's Mines (GB) 37. *Topper* (title role) (AAN)
37. Ali Baba Goes to Town 38. Sailing Along (GB)
38. *The Young in Heart* 39. Topper Takes a Trip 39.
No No Nanette 40. *The Philadelphia Story* 40. Flame
of New Orleans 41. Topper Returns 41. The Lady
Has Plans 42. They All Kissed the Bride 42. Tales
of Manhattan 42. Forever and a Day 43. Standing
Room Only 44. And Then There Were None 45.
Bond Street (GB) 47. The Great Lover 49. Let's
Dance 50. St Benny the Dip 51. That Man from
Tangier 53, many others.

😊 For his inimitable diffidence; and for becoming
quite a character actor whenever he shaved off his
moustache. *The Young in Heart.*

Famous line (*The Philadelphia Story*): 'Oh, this is
one of those days that the pages of history teach
us are best spent lying in bed.'

Young, Sean (1959–).
American leading actress, a former model.
Jane Austen in Manhattan 80. Stripes 81. Blade
Runner 82. Young Doctors in Love 82. Baby: The
Secret of the Lost Legend 85. Dune 85. Under the
Biltmore Clock (TV) 85. No Way Out 87. Wall
Street 87. The Boost 88. Cousins 89. Fire Birds 90.
A Kiss before Dying 91. Once upon a Crime 92.
Love Crimes 92. Hold Me, Thrill Me, Kiss Me 92.
Blue Ice 92. Fatal Instinct 93. Ace Ventura, Pet
Detective 94. Witness to the Execution (TV) 94,
etc.

Young, Stephen (1939–) (Stephen Levy).
Canadian leading man, former extra.
Cleopatra 63. Patton 70. Soylent Green 73.
Lifeguard 75. Breaking Point 76. Between Friends
83. Who's Harry Crumb? 89. The Gumshoe Kid
90, etc.
TV series: Seaway 64. Judd for the Defence 66–
68.

Young, Terence (1915–1994).
British screenwriter who became a successful
director.
AS WRITER: On the Night of the Fire 39. Dangerous
Moonlight 40, etc.
■ AS DIRECTOR: Corridor of Mirrors 48. One Night
with You 48. Woman Hater 49. They Were Not
Divided 50. Valley of Eagles 51. The Tall Headlines
52. The Red Beret 53. That Lady 55. Storm Over
the Nile (co-d) 55. Safari 56. Zarak 56. Action of
the Tiger 57. No Time to Die 57. Serious Charge
59. Too Hot to Handle 60. Black Tights 60. *Doctor
No 62. From Russia with Love* 63. The Amorous
Adventures of Moll Flanders 65. Thunderball 65.
The Poppy Is Also a Flower 66. Secret War 66.
Triple Cross 66. The Rover (It.) 66. *Wait until Dark*
67. Mayerling 68. The Christmas Tree 69. Cold
Sweat 70. Red Sun 71. The Valachi Papers 72. War
Goddess 73. The Klansman 74. Bloodline 79.
Inchon 80. The Jigsaw Man 83. Sweet Revenge
86.

Young, Tony (1938–).
American leading man, from TV series *Gunslinger*.
He Rides Tall 63. Taggart 64. Charro 69. The
Outfit 73.

Young, Victor (1900–1956).
American composer with over 300 film scores to
his credit.
Fatal Lady 36. Wells Fargo 37. Golden Boy
(AAN) 39. Raffles 40. The Way of All Flesh 40.
Caught in the Draft 41. The Outlaw 41. Reap the
Wild Wind 42. Beyond the Blue Horizon 42. The
Glass Key 42. The Palm Beach Story 42. For Whom
the Bell Tolls (AAN) 43. Frenchman's Creek 44.
Ministry of Fear 44. *The Uninvited* 44. Love Letters
(AAN) 45. The Blue Dahlia 46. To Each His Own
47. Unconquered 47. Golden Earrings 47. The Big
Clock 48. The Paleface 48. My Foolish Heart 49.
Samson and Delilah (AAN) 49. Our Very Own 50.
September Affair 50. My Favorite Spy 51. The
Greatest Show on Earth 52. The Quiet Man 52.
Shane 53. The Country Girl 54. Knock on Wood 54.
Strategic Air Command 55. *Around the World in
Eighty Days* (AA) 56. Omar Khayyam 57. Run of the
Arrow 57. China Gate 57, many others.

Youngson, Robert (1917–1974).
American producer specializing in compilation
films. Started as writer-director of short films,
including *World of Kids* (AA) 50, *This Mechanical
Age* (AA) 51. Later released omnibus editions of
silent comedy snippets:
The Golden Age of Comedy 58. *When Comedy Was
King* 59. Days of Thrills and Laughter 60. Thirty
Years of Fun 62, etc.

Yu, Ronny (1952–).
Hong Kong producer and director, now resident
in Australia.
The Servants 79. China White 91. The Bride
with White Hair (Jiang Hu: Between Love and
Glory) 93, etc.

Yuan, Zhang (1963–).
Chinese director, a graduate of the Beijing Film
Academy, from rock videos. The Chinese
government has tried to prevent his films being
shown outside the country.
Mama 91. Beijing Bastards (Beijing Zazhong) 93.

Yuen, Corey (Yuen Kuei).
Hong Kong director, martial arts expert, and actor.
A contemporary of Jackie Chan and Sammo Hung
at the Peking Opera, he is a former stuntman who
has made two action films in Hollywood.
Ninja in the Dragon's Den 82. No Retreat No
Surrender (US) 82. Yes, Madam 85. No Retreat No
Surrender II 89. Fong Sai Yuk 93. Fong Sai Yuk II
93, etc.

Yule, Joe (1894–1950).
Scottish-born vaudeville comedian and actor who
was best known on screen as Jiggs in the *Jiggs and
Maggie* series, based on a popular comic strip about
a working-class couple who win a sweepstake. He
is the father of Mickey Rooney.
Sudden Money 39. Judge Hardy and Son 39.
The Secret of Dr Kildare 39. Broadway Melody of
1940 40. New Moon 40. The Big Store 41. Billy
the Kid 41. Born to Sing 42. Air Raid Wardens
43. The Thin Man Goes Home 44. Kismet 44. Two
Girls and a Sailor 44. Bringing Up Father 46. Jiggs
and Maggie in Jackpot Jitters 49. Jiggs and Maggie
Out West 50, etc.

Yulin, Harris (1937–).
American general-purpose actor.
Doc 71. The Midnight Man 74. Night Moves 75.
The Last Ride of the Dalton Gang (TV) 79. Steel
80. Scarface 83. The Believers 87. Fatal Beauty 87.
Another Woman 88. Bad Dreams 88.
Ghostbusters II 89. Tailspin 89. Narrow Margin 90.
Final Analysis 92. The Last Hit (TV) 93, etc.
TV series: WIOU 90–91.

Yun-fat, Chow (Zhao Runfa).
Hong Kong leading actor, associated with the work
of director John Woo.
A Better Tomorrow 86. An Autumn's Tale
(Qiutiande Tonghua) 87. City on Fire 87. A Better
Tomorrow III 89. The Killer (Diexue Shuang
Xiong) 89. All about Ah-Long 89. Triads – The
Inside Story 90. Wild Search 90. Once a Thief 91.
Hard-Boiled 92. Full Contact 93, many others.

Yung, Sen (1915–1980) (aka Victor Sen Yung).
Chinese-American character actor familiar 1938–
48 as Charlie Chan's number-one son.
The Letter 40. *Across the Pacific* 42. The Breaking
Point 50. The Left Hand of God 55. Flower Drum
Song 61. A Flea in Her Ear 68, etc.
TV series: Bonanza 59–72. Bachelor Father 61.

Yurka, Blanche (1887–1974).
Czech-American character actress.

Autobiography: 1970, *Bohemian Girl.*

■ *A Tale of Two Cities* 36. *Queen of the Mob* 40. Escape 40. City for Conquest 40. Ellery Queen and the Murder Ring 41. Lady for a Night 42. Pacific Rendezvous 42. A Night to Remember 42.

Keeper of the Flame 43. Tonight We Raid Calais 43. Hitler's Madman 43. The Bridge of San Luis Rey 44. Cry of the Werewolf 44. One Body Too Many 44. The Southerner 45. 13 rue Madeleine 46. The Flame 47. The Furies 50. At Sword's Point 51. Taxi 53. Thunder in the Sun 57.

Yuzna, Brian (1949–).
American producer and director of horror movies, born in the Philippines.

Re-Animator (p) 84. From Beyond (p) 86. Dolls (p) 87. Honey, I Shrunk the Kids (p, co-story) 89. Society (d) 89. Bride of Re-Animator (d) 89. Return of the Living Dead 3 (p, d) 93. Necronomicon (p, co-d) 93, etc.

Z

Zadora, Pia (1954–) (Pia Schipani).
American actress, usually in exaggeratedly sexy roles, and singer, on screen as a juvenile.
Santa Claus Conquers the Martians 64. Butterfly 81. Fake-Out 82. The Lonely Lady 83. Pajama Tops 83. Voyage of the Rock Aliens 87. Hairspray 88, etc.

Zaentz, Saul (1911–).
Independent producer who, unusually, tends to finance films with his own money. He owned the record label Fantasy Records, which published the hit group Creedence Clearwater Revival in the mid-60s.
Payday 72. One Flew over the Cuckoo's Nest (AA) 75. The Lord of the Rings 78. Amadeus (AA) 84. Mosquito Coast 86. The Unbearable Lightness of Being 88. At Play in the Fields of the Lord 90, etc.

Zaillian, Steve.
American screenwriter and director, a former editor.
The Falcon and the Snowman (w) 85. Awakenings (AANw) 90. Jack the Bear (w) 93. Searching for Bobby Fischer (GB: Innocent Moves) (wd) 93. Schindler's List (AAw) 94. Clear and Present Danger (co-w) 94.

Zampa, Luigi (1905–1991).
Italian director, formerly scriptwriter. Films, all on neo-realist lines, include:
To Live in Peace 46. City on Trial 52. The Woman of Rome 54.

Zampi, Mario (1903–1963).
Italian director, long in Britain, mainly involved in semi-crazy comedies which he usually wrote and produced.
The Fatal Night 48. Laughter in Paradise 50. Top Secret 52. Happy Ever After 54. The Naked Truth 56. Too Many Crooks 58. Five Golden Hours 61, etc.

Zane, Billy (1965–).
American actor.
Dead Calm 88. The Hillside Strangler (TV) 89. Back to the Future II 89. Memphis Belle 90. Billions (Miliardi) 91. Blood and Concrete 91. Femme Fatale 91. Millions 91. Orlando 92. Sniper 93. Posse 93. Tombstone 94. Flashfire 94. Reflections on a Crime 94. The Silence of the Hams (It.) 94. Only You 94, etc.

Zanuck, Darryl F. (1902–1979).
American production executive. Started career in the 20s, writing stories for Rin Tin Tin. Production chief for Warners 1931. Co-founder Twentieth-Century Productions 1933; merged with Fox 1935. Vice-president in charge of production for Twentieth Century-Fox 1935–52, then independent; returned in 1962 as executive president.
Book: 1993, Memo from Darryl Zanuck: The Golden Years at Twentieth Century Fox, edited by Rudy Behlmer.

Clive of India 35. Lloyds of London 37. In Old Chicago 38. Drums along the Mohawk 40. The Grapes of Wrath 40. How Green Was My Valley 42. Wilson 45. Gentleman's Agreement 47. All about Eve 50. Twelve o'Clock High 51. Viva Zapata 52. Island in the Sun 57. Roots of Heaven 58. The Longest Day (& d scenes) 62.
Under the name Mark Canfield wrote the screenplay of Crack in the Mirror 60.
❂ For being Hollywood's most efficient mogul, and for making very good films. The Grapes of Wrath.

¶ The hardiest and longest-lived of the moguls of Hollywood's golden age was somehow the most disappointing in terms of colour and personality. His most personal trait was his allegedly avid sexual appetite, though he himself said:
Any of my indiscretions were with people, not actresses.
He was a tough employer:
There was only one boss I believed in, and that was me.
As his biographer Mel Gussow said:
He couldn't stand stubbornness in anybody but himself.
He spent 35 years, more or less, as boss of Twentieth Century-Fox, and before that for 10 years was production head of Warners. His ideas for remakes were legendary:
I want to do Air Force in a submarine.
Another of his credos is now outdated:
When you get a sex story in biblical garb, you can open your own mint.
He produced many worthy films, perhaps for rather stodgy reasons:
We are in the business primarily to provide entertainment, but in doing so we do not dodge the issue if we can also provide enlightenment.
Or, more pithily:
I know audiences feed on crap, but I cannot believe we are so lacking that we cannot dish it up to them with some trace of originality.
On another occasion, however, he was optimistic:
Public taste is an ascending spiral.
But his final production philosophy was:
Take a chance and spend a million dollars and hope you're right.
Time summed him up in 1950:
He is richly endowed with tough-mindness, talent, an outsized ego, and a glutton's craving for hard work.
And his son has the last word:
He had guts. He was willing to take the responsibility and the blame. He would say yes or no. They would ask is it any good, and if he thought it was, that was enough to put it into production.
Don't say yes until I finish talking! – D.F.Z. (also the title of his biography by Mel Gussow)
I decided to become a genius. – D.F.Z.
As I see it today, the boss of the Studio is actually no longer a boss – he has a title but that is all. He is the slave of agents and actors with their own corporations and insane competition from

independent operators and promoters. – D.F.Z., 1961
Success in movies boils down to three things: story, story, story. – D.F.Z.
From Poland to Polo in one generation. – Arthur Mayer on D.F.Z.

Zanuck, Lili Fini.
American producer and director, married to producer Richard Zanuck.
AS PRODUCER: Cocoon 84. Cocoon II 88. Driving Miss Daisy (AA) 89. Clean Slate 94. Wild Bill 95.
AS DIRECTOR: Rush 91.

Zanuck, Richard (1934–).
American producer who started career as assistant to his father, Darryl F. Zanuck. Solo ventures:
Compulsion 59. Sanctuary 61. The Chapman Report 62, etc.
Was vice-president in charge of production for Twentieth Century-Fox; moved to Warner 1971. In 1972 he founded the independent production company Zanuck/Brown with David Brown. That partnership ended in 1988 when he formed the Zanuck Company with his wife Lili Fini Zanuck.
■ The Sting 73. Jaws (AAN) 75. MacArthur 77. The Island 80. Neighbors 81. The Verdict 82. Cocoon 84. Target 84. Cocoon: The Return 88. Driving Miss Daisy (AA) 89. Rush 91. Clean Slate 94. Wild Bill 95.

Zanussi, Krzystof (1939–).
Polish director.
Illumination 73. The Spiral 78. Night Paths 79. The Constant Factor 80. Imperative 82. The Year of the Quiet Sun 84. Power of Evil 85. Wherever You Are 88. Life for a Life – Maximilian Kolbe 90. The Touch (Dotkniecie) 92, etc.

Zappa, Frank (1940–1993).
American composer, bandleader, and director, whose extended concert performances were occasionally filmed. In the 60s, he scored some 'B' movies.
Book: 1994, Frank Zappa: The Negative Dialectics of Poodle Play by Ben Watson.
The World's Greatest Sinner (m) 62. Run Home Slow (m) 65. Head (a) 68. 200 Motels (a, co-d, m) 71. Baby Snakes (a, d, m) 79, etc.

Zavattini, Cesare (1902–1989).
Italian scriptwriter and film theorist.
Shoeshine (AAN) 46. Bicycle Thieves (AAN) 48. Miracle in Milan 51. First Communion 51. Umberto D (AAN) 52. Gold of Naples 55. The Roof 56. Two Women 61. Marriage Italian Style 64. A Brief Vacation 75, etc.

Zaza, Paul.
Canadian composer, frequently for the films of director Bob Clark.
Title Shot 79. Prom Night (co-m) 80. My Bloody Valentine 81. Porky's (co-m) 81. Curtains 83. Turk 182 85. From the Hip 87. Meatballs III 87. Loose Cannons 90. Popcorn 91. Cold Sweat 93. It Runs in the Family 94, etc.

Zecca, Ferdinand (1864–1947).
French pioneer producer.

The Prodigy 01. Catastrophe in Martinique 04. Vendetta 05. Whence Does He Come? 06. Mutiny in Odessa 07. The Dreyfus Affair 08. The Dissolute Woman 10, etc.

Zeffirelli, Franco (1922–).
Italian stage director turning to films.
■ The Taming of the Shrew 66. Romeo and Juliet (AAN) 68. Brother Sun and Sister Moon 73. Jesus of Nazareth (TV) 77. The Champ 79. Endless Love 81. La Traviata 82. Otello 86. Young Toscanini 88. Hamlet 90. Sparrow (Storia di una Capinera) 93.

Zehetbauer, Rolf.
German production designer.
Cabaret (AA) 72. The Serpent's Egg 77. Twilight's Last Gleaming 77. Brass Target 78. From the Life of the Marionettes 80. The Boat (Das Boot) (Ger.) 80. Lili Marleen 81. Lola 82. The Neverending Story 84. Enemy Mine 85, etc.

Zelnik, Fred (1885–1950).
Rumanian director of English films in the 30s.
Happy 32. Mr Cinders 34. The Lilac Domino 37. I Killed the Count 39. Give Me the Stars (p only) 44. The Glass Mountain (p only) 49, etc.

Zeman, Karel (1910–1989).
Czech producer-director of trick and fantasy films of which the best known internationally are Journey to Primeval Times 55 and Baron Münchausen 61.

Zemeckis, Robert (1952–).
American director and screenwriter, one of the brightest of the movie brats.
■ I Wanna Hold Your Hand 78. Used Cars 80. Romancing the Stone 84. Back to the Future (wd) (AAN w) 85. Who Framed Roger Rabbit? (d) 88. Back to the Future II (d, story) 89. Back to the Future III (d, story) 90. Looters (co-w) 92. Death Becomes Her (d) 92. Forrest Gump 94.

¶ When I showed Twentieth Century-Fox the finished cut of Romancing the Stone, they fired me from Cocoon. It's the great mystery of my career. – R.Z.

Zerbe, Anthony (1936–).
American character actor.
Will Penny 67. The Liberation of L. B. Jones 69. The Omega Man 71. The Life and Times of Judge Roy Bean 72. The Laughing Policeman 73. Farewell My Lovely 75. The Turning Point 77. The First Deadly Sin 80. The Dead Zone 83. North and South (TV) 86. Opposing Force 87. Private Investigations 87. Licence to Kill 89. See No Evil, Hear No Evil 89, etc.

TV series: Harry O 74–76. Centennial 78–80. North and South, Book II 89. The Young Riders 89–92.

Zetterling, Mai (1925–1994).
Swedish director, screenwriter and leading actress who first gained fame in Britain. She is also a novelist. Born in Vasteras, she trained at the National Theatre School in Stockholm. Her second husband was the novelist David Hughes. Her lovers included Herbert Lom, Peter Finch, and Tyrone Power.

Autobiography: 1985, All Those Tomorrows.
■ Frenzy 44. Frieda 47. The Bad Lord Byron 48. Portrait from Life 48. Quartet 48. The Romantic Age 49. Blackmailed 50. Hell is Sold Out 51. The Tall Headlines 53. The Ringer 52. Desperate Moment 53. Dance Little Lady 54. Knock on Wood

54. A Prize of Gold 55. Seven Waves Away 56. The Truth about Women 58. Jetstorm 59. Faces in the Dark 60. Piccadilly Third Stop 60. Offbeat 61. The Man Who Finally Died 62. Only Two Can Play 62. The Main Attraction 62. The Bay of St Michel 63. The Vine Bridge 65. The Witches 90. Hidden Agenda 90. Morfars Resa 93.
■ AS DIRECTOR: The War Game 62. Loving Couples 64. Night Games 66. Doctor Glas 68. Visions of Eight (part) 73. Scrubbers 83. Amarosa 86.

¶ I have been a child, a girl, a party doll, a mistress, a wife, a mother, a professional woman, a virgin, a grandmother. I have been a woman for more than fifty years and yet I have never been able to discover precisely what it is I am, how real I am. I ask myself – perhaps my femaleness is just a human disease. – M.Z.

Zhuangzhuang, Tian (1952–).
Chinese director, a former cameraman who graduated from the Beijing Film Academy in the early 80s. His films have caused controversy in his homeland and post-production work on The Blue Kite had to be done outside the country.
September (Jiuyue) 84. On the Killing Ground (Liechang Zhasa) 85. Horse Thief (Daoma Zei) 86. The Travelling Players (Gushu Yiren) 87. Rock Kids (Yaogun Qingnian) 88. Li Lianying, the Imperial Eunuch (Da Taijian Li Lianying) 91. The Blue Kite (Lan Fengzheng) 93, etc.

¶ Sometimes I think how silly I am: knowing that making films in China is probably the most difficult thing I could do, and still wanting to do it. But the first time I stood behind a camera and heard it rolling, I got so excited. – T.Z.

Zidi, Claude (1934–).
French director and producer, a former cinematographer.
Stuntwoman 81. Le Cop (US: My New Partner) (Les Ripoux) 85. Le Cop 2 (Ripoux contre Ripoux) 89. La Totale.91. Profil Bas 94, etc.

Zieff, Howard (1943–).
American director.
■ Hearts of the West 75. Slither 76. House Calls 78. The Main Event 79. Private Benjamin 80. Unfaithfully Yours 83. The Dream Team 89. My Girl 91. My Girl 2 94.

Ziegfeld, Florenz (1867–1932).
American Broadway impresario who had three films named after him (The Great Ziegfeld, Ziegfeld Girl, Ziegfeld Follies). He was impersonated in two of them by William Powell and in Funny Girl by Walter Pidgeon. He also 'supervised' 1929's Glorifying the American Girl.
Biography: 1973, Ziegfeld by Charles Higham.

Ziegler, William (c. 1909–1977).
American editor.
The Housekeeper's Daughter 39. No Hands on the Clock 41. Minesweeper 43. Abie's Irish Rose 46. Rope 49. Strangers on a Train 51. The Desert Song 53. Rebel without a Cause 55. Auntie Mame 58. Ice Palace 60. The Music Man 62. My Fair Lady 64. A Fine Madness 66. Firecreek 68. Topaz 69. The Omega Man 71, many others.

Ziemann, Sonja (1926–).
German leading actress.
Ein Windstoss 42. Girl of the Black Forest 50. Made in Heaven (GB) 52. My Sister and I 54. Menschen im Hotel 59. A Matter of Who 62. The Bridge at Remagen 69. De Sade 70, etc.

Zimbalist, Efrem, Jnr (1918–).
American leading man with stage experience; plays characters who inspire confidence.
House of Strangers 49. Band of Angels 57. Too Much Too Soon 58. By Love Possessed 61. A Fever in the Blood 61. The Chapman Report 62. The Reward 65. Wait until Dark 67. Airport 75 74. A Family Upside Down (TV) 78. Terror out of the Sky 78. Hot Shots! 91. Batman: Mask of the Phantasm (voice) 94, etc.

TV series: 77 Sunset Strip 58–63. The F.B.I. 65–73. Scruples 80. Hotel 86.

Zimbalist, Sam (1904–1958).
American producer.
The Crowd Roars 38. Boom Town 40. King Solomon's Mines 50. Quo Vadis 51. Mogambo 53. Beau Brummell 54. Ben Hur 59 (died during production), etc.

Zimmer, Hans (1958–).
German-born musician and composer, now working in Hollywood. He was a member of the British pop group The Buggles, who had a hit with 'Video Killed the Radio Star' 79, and collaborated with composer Stanley Myers on several films before his first solo score for A World Apart.
Moonlighting (co-m) 82. Success Is the Best Revenge (co-m) 84. Insignificance (co-m) 85. A World Apart 87. Double Exposure 87. The Nature of the Beast (co-m) 88. Burning Secret 88. Paperhouse 88. The Fruit Machine 88. Rain Man (AAN) 88. Driving Miss Daisy 89. Diamond Skulls 89. Black Rain 89. Twister 89. Bird on a Wire 90. Chicago Joe and the Showgirl 90. Days of Thunder 90. Fools of Fortune 90. Pacific Heights 90. Green Card 90. The Neverending Story II: The Next Chapter 90. Backdraft 91. Regarding Henry 91. Thelma and Louise 91. Where Sleeping Dogs Lie 91. Radio Flyer 92. A League of Their Own 92. Point of No Return 93. Younger and Younger 93. True Romance 93. Calendar Girl 93. Cool Runnings 93. The House of the Spirits 94. I'll Do Anything 94. Renaissance Man 94, etc.

Zimmerman, Enrique.
Venezuelan director who directed, with Lucas Manzano, that country's first feature film, La Dama de las Cayenas 13, based on Alexander Dumas's Camille.

Zinnemann, Fred (1907–).
Austrian-born director, with varied experience before coming to Hollywood in 1929. Was an extra (in All Quiet on the Western Front), script clerk, and director of shorts (That Others Might Live (AA) 38, several episodes of Crime Does Not Pay 39, 41, etc.)

Autobiography: 1992, A Life in Movies.
■ Kid Glove Killer 42. Eyes in the Night 42. The Seventh Cross 44. Little Mister Jim 46. My Brother Talks to Horses 47. The Search (AAN) 48. Act of Violence 49. The Men 50. Teresa 51. High Noon (AAN) 52. The Member of the Wedding 53. From Here to Eternity (AA) 53. Oklahoma 55. A Hatful of Rain 57. The Nun's Story (AAN) 58. The Sundowners (AAN) 60. Behold a Pale Horse 64. A Man for All Seasons (AAp, AAd) 66. The Day of the Jackal 73. Julia (AAN) 77. Five Days One Summer 82.

¶ I'm not in pictures to promote my private personality. I'm in it for the joy of it. – F.Z.
John Ford told me, 'Don't give them too much extra film, then they can't cut it a different way.' – F.Z.

Zinner, Peter (1919–).
Austrian-born film editor in Hollywood.
The Professionals 60. Gunn 67. In Cold Blood 67.
Changes 69. Darling Lili 70. The Red Tent 71. The
Godfather (AAN) 71. The Godfather Part II 74.
Mahogany 75. Foxtrot 76. A Star Is Born 76. The
Deer Hunter (AA) 78. Foolin' Around 80. An
Officer and a Gentleman (AAN) 82. The Salamander
(& d) 82. Saving Grace 86. The Hunt for Red October
(AAN) 90. Eternity 90. Gladiator 92, etc.

Zito, Joseph (1946–).
American director of horror and action movies.
The Abduction 81. The Prowler 82. Friday the
13th: The Final Chapter 84. Missing in Action 84.
Invasion USA 85. Red Scorpion 88. Barr Sinister
90, etc.

Zoetrope.
1. A device, invented by Englishman William
George Horner, that created an illusion of motion.
It consisted of a strip of paper, containing a series
of drawings of simple actions, wrapped around
the inside of a rotating drum. The spectator viewed
the drawings through a slit in the side of the
drum, where the successive pictures seemed to
move due to the persistence of vision.
2. The name Francis Ford Coppola gave to his
film studio.

Zola, Emile (1840–1902).
Prolific French novelist of the seamy side. Works
filmed include Nana, La Bête Humaine and Thérèse
Raquin. A 1937 biopic, The Life of Emile Zola, starred
Paul Muni and centred on Zola's participation in
the Dreyfus case.

zombies
originate from Haitian legend, and are generally
held to be dead people brought back to life by
voodoo. In movies they invariably shamble along
with sightless eyes, looking pretty awful but doing
no real damage. They were most convincingly
displayed in Victor Halperin's 1932 White Zombie;
other examples of the species turned up in Revolt
of the Zombies, The Zombies of Mora Tau, I Walked
With a Zombie, King of the Zombies, The Ghost
Breakers (and its remake Scared Stiff), and Dr
Terror's House of Horrors. The species gave its name
to a strong rum punch, and one treasured
memory is a movie in which the Ritz Brothers
walked up to a bar and said: 'Three zombies.' 'I can
see that,' said the barman, 'but what'll you have
to drink?' In the 70s George Romero adopted the
theme in such repellent films as Night of the Living
Dead and Dawn of the Dead; but the most fearsome
undead of all appeared in the dream scene of
Hammer's 1965 Plague of the Zombies.

zoom.
A lens of variable focal length, normally used for
swiftly magnifying a distant object or moving
rapidly away from a close one.

Zoopraxiscope.
A projector for showing motion pictures, designed
by photographer Eadweard Muybridge (qv). It
was a natural development from his photographic
sequence demonstrating the movement of horses
in 1878. He first called his device the
Zoogyroscope, renaming it in 1881. It projected
a sequence of 12 images derived from his
photographs and painted on a glass disc. He
demonstrated it on a lecture tour of Europe in
1881–82. A working replica is on display at the
Museum of the Moving Image in London.

Zorina, Vera (1917–) (Eva Brigitta Hartwig).
Norwegian ballet dancer and actress in American
films. Now retired. She was married to
choreographer George Balanchine (1938–46).
The Goldwyn Follies 39. On Your Toes 39. I Was
an Adventuress 40. Star Spangled Rhythm 43. Follow
the Boys 44.

Zorro (Don Diego de Vega).
The black-garbed Robin Hood of Spanish
California originated as the hero of a 1919 strip
cartoon by Johnston McCulley. (Zorro,
incidentally, is Spanish for fox.) Films featuring
the devil-may-care righter of wrongs include The
Mark of Zorro 20 with Douglas Fairbanks, and its
1925 sequel Don Q, Son of Zorro; The Bold Caballero
37 with Robert Livingston; Zorro Rides Again 37, a
serial with John Carroll; Zorro's Fighting Legion 39,
a serial with Reed Hadley; Mamoulian's splendid
remake of The Mark of Zorro 40, with Tyrone
Power; The Ghost of Zorro 49, a serial with Clayton
Moore; Walter Chiari in The Sign of Zorro 52; Zorro
the Avenger 60 and other Disney TV films with
Guy Williams; Sean Flynn in The Sign of Zorro 62;
Frank Latimore in Shadow of Zorro 62; Pierre Brice
in Zorro versus Maciste 63; George Ardisson in Zorro
at the Court of Spain 63; Gordon Scott in Zorro and
the Three Musketeers 63; and Alain Delon in Zorro
75. Almost inevitably the 80s brought a spoof
version, Zorro the Gay Blade 82, featuring a limp-
wristed avenger.

Zsigmond, Vilmos (1930–).
Hungarian cinematographer.
Deliverance 72. Images 72. The Long Goodbye
73. Scarecrow 73. Cinderella Liberty 73. The
Sugarland Express 74. The Girl from Petrovka 74.
Obsession 76. Close Encounters of the Third Kind
(AA) 77. The Deer Hunter (AAN) 78. Flesh and
Blood (TV) 79. Winter Kills 79. The Rose 79.
Heaven's Gate 80. Blow Out 81. Jinxed 82. Table for
Five 83. The River (AAN) 84. Real Genius 85. The
Witches of Eastwick 87. Journey to Spirit Island 88.
Fat Man and Little Boy (GB: The Shadowmakers) 89.
Bonfire of the Vanities 90. The Two Jakes 90. The
Long Shadow (d) 92. Stalin (TV) 93. Sliver 93.
Intersection 93. Maverick 94, etc.

Zucco, George (1886–1960).
Sepulchral-toned British stage actor, long in
Hollywood and typecast in horror films in which
he admirably exuded upper-bracket malignancy.
Autumn Crocus 30. Dreyfus 31. The Good
Companions 32. The Man Who Could Work
Miracles 35. Marie Antoinette 38. The Cat and the
Canary 39. The Hunchback of Notre Dame 39. Arise
My Love 40. The Mummy's Hand 40. The Adventures
of Sherlock Holmes (as Moriarty) 40. Sherlock
Holmes in Washington 42. The Black Swan 42.
Dead Men Walk 43. The Black Raven 43. The
Mad Ghoul 43. House of Frankenstein 45. Fog
Island 45. Dr Renault's Secret 46. The Pirate 47.
Joan of Arc 48. Madame Bovary 49. Let's Dance
50. David and Bathsheba 51. The First Legion 51,
many others.

Zucker, David (1947–).
American director and screenwriter who began
collaborating with his brother Jerry and Jim
Abrahams on a series of broad and sometimes
satirical comedies.
The Kentucky Fried Movie (co-wd) 77.
Airplane! (co-wd) 80. Top Secret! (co-wd) 84.
Ruthless People (co-d) 86. The Naked Gun: From
the Files of Police Squad (d) 88. The Naked Gun

2½: The Smell of Fear (co-w, d) 91. Naked Gun
33⅓: The Final Insult (p, co-w) 94, etc.
TV series: Police Squad 82.

Zucker, Jerry (1950–).
American director and screenwriter, usually in
collaboration with his brother David and Jim
Abrahams. His first solo effort as a director was
Ghost, the biggest box-office success of 1990.
The Kentucky Fried Movie (co-wd) 77.
Airplane! (co-wd) 80. Top Secret! (co-wd) 84.
Ruthless People (co-d) 86. The Naked Gun: From
the Files of Police Squad (co-w) 88. Ghost (d) 90.
My Life (p) 93. First Knight (d) 95, etc.
TV series: Police Squad 82.

Zuckmayer, Carl (1896–1977).
German playwright whose The Captain from
Koepenick has been much filmed. His screenplays
include:
The Blue Angel 30. Escape Me Never 35.
Rembrandt 36. Mayerling 40. I Was a Criminal 41.

Zugsmith, Albert (1910–).
American producer-director with a taste for
exploitation subjects.
Written on the Wind (p) 57. The Tattered Dress
(p) 57. The Incredible Shrinking Man (p) 58.
Touch of Evil (p) 58. High School Confidential (d)
60. Teacher Was a Sexpot (d) 60. The Private Life
of Adam and Eve (d) 61. Confessions of an Opium
Eater (d) 63. Fanny Hill (p) 64. Movie Star
American Style (or LSD I Hate You) (d) 66. The
Incredible Sex Revolution (d) 67, etc.

Zukor, Adolph (1873–1976).
Hungarian-born film pioneer. Emigrated to
America, became film salesman, nickelodeon
owner, and independent producer (in 1913), by
persuading New York stage stars James O'Neill,
James K. Hackett and Minnie Maddern Fiske to
appear in productions of, respectively, The Count of
Monte Cristo, The Prisoner of Zenda and Tess of the
D'Urbervilles. This was the start of 'Famous Players',
which in 1916 merged with Jesse Lasky's
production interests and later became Paramount
Pictures. He remained board chairman of the latter
from 1935.
Autobiography: 1945, The Public Is Never Wrong.
⊕ For being the industry's first centenarian. The
Covered Wagon.

¶ Fish stinks from the head. – A.Z.
¶ If I'd known I was going to live this long, I'd
have taken better care of myself. – A.Z.
~Special Academy Award 1948 'for his services
to the industry over a period of 40 years'.

Zurinaga, Marco.
Puerto Rican director and screenwriter.
Step Away 79. La Gran Fiesta 86. Tango Bar 88.
A Flor de Piel (TV) 90, etc.

Zweig, Stefan (1881–1942).
Austrian novelist. Films of his books include
Beware of Pity, Twenty-Four Hours of a Woman's Life,
Letter from an Unknown Woman.

Zwick, Edward (1952–).
American director and screenwriter who began as
a magazine journalist. He also created the hit TV
series thirtysomething 87–91.
Having It All (TV) 82. Special Bulletin (TV) 83.
About Last Night . . . 86. Glory 89. Leaving
Normal 92. Legends of the Fall 94, etc.
TV series: Family 76–80.

Last Words

¶ A few favourite unclassifiable moments. Bette Davis, on having pointed out to her a starlet who had allegedly slept her way to the top:

> I see – she's the original good time that was had by all.

Billy Wilder to his cinematographer during the filming of *Sunset Boulevard:*

> Johnny, keep it out of focus. I want to win the foreign picture award.

An anonymous wartime crack:

> In case of an air raid, go directly to RKO: they haven't had a hit in years.

Will Rogers, philosophizing:

> What's the salvation of the movies? I say, run 'em backwards. It can't hurt, and it's worth a trial.

King Vidor, evaluating one of his own movies:

> The picture was so bad they had to do retakes before they could put it on the shelf.

Carole Lombard, refusing a role in an Orson Welles film:

> I can't win working with Welles. If the picture's a hit he will get the credit, and if it's a flop, I'll be blamed.

John Grierson, evaluating the decline of Josef Von Sternberg:

> When a director dies, he becomes a photographer.

Sir Cedric Hardwicke on judgement by sneak preview:

> On Hollywood's theory that the audience knows best, the schoolboy's 'lousy' becomes the last word in dramatic criticism.

Jean Renoir, leaving Hollywood after an enforced wartime sojourn:

> Goodbye, Mr Zanuck: it certainly has been a pleasure working at 16th Century Fox.

Howard Hawks, commenting on his penchant for remaking films with similar characters and situations:

> When you find out a thing goes pretty well, you might as well do it again.

Victor Mature, when Rita Hayworth deserted him for Orson Welles, with whom she had been working in a charity magic act:

> Apparently the way to a girl's heart is to saw her in half.

Walter Wanger on Hollywood gossip columnists:

> This is the only industry that finances its own blackmail.

Robert Lord on the film city:

> It's such nonsense, this immorality of Hollywood. We're all too tired.

Robert Benchley after viewing an arty film:

> There's less in this than meets the eye.

And Spencer Tracy, on finding himself working for a director with 'artistic' ideas who tried to turn every gesture into a symbol:

> I'm too tired and old and rich for all this, so let's do the scene.

Wilson Mizner on Hollywood egos:

> Some of the greatest love affairs I've known involved one actor, unassisted.

And Graham Greene on actors' shelf-life:

> For an actor, success is simply delayed failure.

Although Will Rogers thought differently:

> The movies are the only business where you can go out front and applaud yourself.

Billy Wilder, setting up Gloria Swanson's attempted suicide in *Sunset Boulevard*:

> Johnny, it's the usual slashed-wrist shot.

Robert Mitchum perhaps put it all into perspective:

> What's history going to say about the movies? All those rows of seats facing a blank screen. Crazy!

A final thought from Auguste Lumière, pioneer of cinematography, in 1895:

> Young man, you can be grateful that my invention is not for sale, for it would undoubtedly ruin you. It can be exploited for a certain time as a scientific curiosity, but apart from that it has no commercial value whatsoever.

Alphabetical List of Fictional Screen Characters, Series and Remakes

The following are noted in the main text:

Abie's Irish Rose
Accent on Youth
The Admirable Crichton
Ah Wilderness
Ali Baba
Alice in Wonderland
Antoine Doinel
Arsène Lupin
Arthur
Asterix
Barney Bear
Ben Hur
Betty Boop
Bugs Bunny
Bulldog Drummond
Carry On
Casper the Friendly Ghost
Cenobites
Champion
Charlie Chan
Chilly Willy
Dick Barton
Dick Tracy
Doctor Mabuse
Doctor Who
Donald Duck
Dracula
Droopy
El Santo
Ellery Queen
Elmer Fudd
The Fall of the House of Usher
Fanny
Farewell My Lovely
A Farewell to Arms
Father Brown
The Flag Lieutenant
Flash Gordon
The Flintstones
Foghorn Leghorn
Folies Bergère
The Fox
Fox and the Crow
Francis
Frankenstein
Fritz the Cat
Fu Manchu
The Garden of Allah

Gaslight
Gentlemen Prefer Blondes
Gerald McBoing Boing
Gertie the Dinosaur
The Ghost Breaker
The Ghost Train
Gidget
The Glass Key
Godzilla
The Golem
The Good Companions
Goodbye Mr Chips
Goofy
Grand Hotel
The Great Adventure
The Great Gatsby
The Great Impersonation
Gulliver's Travels
Gunfight at the OK Corral
Gunga Din
Hamlet
Harry Callahan
Heckle and Jeckle
Henry Aldrich
Henry V
Hercule Poirot
Hopalong Cassidy
Hubie and Bertie
The Huggetts
Inspector Hornleigh
Jack the Ripper
James Bond
Jane Eyre
Joe Palooka
The Jones Family
Judge Dredd
The Jungle Book
Jungle Jim
The Kettles (Ma and Pa Kettle)
The Keystone Kops
Kid Galahad
King Kong
King Solomon's Mines
Kismet
Lady for a Day
Lassie
Last Days of Pompeii
The Last of the Mohicans

Lemmy Caution
Li'l Abner
Liliom
Little Lord Fauntleroy
Little Miss Marker
Little Women
The Lone Ranger
The Lone Wolf
Looney Tunes
Lost Horizon
Lost Patrol
Love Affair
The Lower Depths
M
Macbeth
Maciste
Magnificent Obsession
Maigret
Maisie
The Maltese Falcon
The Man in the Iron Mask
The Man Who Knew Too Much
The March of Time
Matt Helm
The Merry Widow
Merton of the Movies
Mexican Spitfire
Michael Shayne
A Midsummer Night's Dream
Mighty Mouse
Mike Hammer
Miss Marple
Mr Belvedere
Mr Magoo
Mr Moto
Mr Wong
Mrs Wiffs of the Cabbage Patch
Moby Dick
Modesty Blaise
Monsieur Beaucaire
The Most Dangerous Game
The Mummy
Mutiny on the Bounty
My Man Godfrey
My Sister Eileen
The Mystery of the Wax Museum
Nana
Nancy Drew

Nick Carter
Nick and Nora Charles
Norman Bates
Nothing but the Truth
Of Mice and Men
Oh God!
Old Mother Riley
Oliver Twist
One Million BC
One Way Passage
Oswald the Rabbit
Othello
Our Gang
The Paleface
The Passing of the Third Floor Back
The Passing Parade
Penrod
Pepe Le Pew
The Perils of Pauline
Perry Mason
Peyton Place
The Phantom of the Opera
Philip Marlowe
The Pink Panther
The Plainsman
Planet of the Apes
Popeye
Porky Pig
The Prisoner of Zenda
Quiller
Quo Vadis?
Raffles
Rain
The Rains Came
Rambo
Ramona
Rashomon
Rebecca of Sunnybrook Farm
Red Dust
The Ringer
Road Runner
Rob Roy
Robin Hood
Robinson Crusoe
Robocop
Rocky Balboa

Roger Rabbit
Rogue Male
Romeo and Juliet
Rose Marie
Ruggles of Red Gap
The Saint
St Trinian's
Salome
Scarface
The Scarlet Letter
The Scarlet Pimpernel
Scattergood Baines
The Sea Wolf
Seven Keys to Baldpate
Seventh Heaven
Sexton Blake
Shaft
She
She Loves Me Not
The Sheik
Sherlock Holmes
The Shop around the Corner
The Shopworn Angel
Show Boat
A Sister to Assist'er
Sitting Pretty
Slaughter
Smilin' Through
Speedy Gonzales
The Spoilers
Squibs
A Star Is Born
Star Wars
State Fair
Stella Dallas
The Student of Prague
The Student Prince
Superman
The Swiss Family Robinson
Sylvester
A Tale of Two Cities
Tales of Manhattan
Tammy
Tarzan
Teenage Mutant Ninja Turtles
The Ten Commandments

The Thief of Bagdad
The Thin Man
The Thing
The Thirty-Nine Steps
This Gun for Hire
This Modern Age
Three Coins in the Fountain
Three Men in a Boat
The Three Musketeers
Three Smart Girls
To Have and Have Not
The Toff
Tol'able David
Tom and Jerry
Tom Brown's Schooldays
Tom Sawyer
Tony Rome
Topper
Torchy Blane
Trail of the Lonesome Pine
Treasure Island
Tugboat Annie
Tweety Pie
Uncle Tom's Cabin
Under Two Flags
Unfaithfully Yours
The Virginian
The Wages of Fear
War and Peace
The Ware Case
Waterloo Bridge
The Whistler
Whistling in the Dark
White Cargo
Why We Fight
The Wicked Lady
Wile E. Coyote
William
The Wolf Man
Woman to Woman
The Women
Woody Woodpecker
Wuthering Heights
Yosemite Sam
Zorro

Alphabetical List of Themes Explored

Please check these headings in the text for notes on the use of the subjects listed in films past and present, with examples.

Abortion
Actor-directors
Actors
Adaptations
Addresses
Advertising
AIDS
Air balloons
Airplanes
Airships
The Alamo
Alcoholics
Algonquin Round Table
All-star films
American Revolution
Amnesia
Anachronisms
Ancient Egypt
Angels
Animals
Anti-Semitism
Army comedies
Assassination
Authors as actors
Automobiles
Babies
Backstage
Bad language
Ballet
Baseball
Bathtubs
Berlin
The Bible
Big business
Bigamists
Birds
Black comedy
Blindness
Boffins
Boo-boos
Boxing
The British Empire
Brothels
Bullfights
Burlesque
Buses
Business

Butlers
Cable cars
Cannibalism
Case histories
Casting
The chase
Child stars
Christ
Christmas
Churches
Cinemas
Circuses
Clairvoyance
Coal mines
The Cold War
Colour
Colour sequences
Comedy teams
Comic strips
Communism
Compilation films
Composers
Computers
Concentration camps
Concerts
Confidence tricksters
Courtesans
Courtroom scenes
Crazy comedy
Criminals
Custard pies
Dance bands
Deaf mutes
Death
Dentists
Department stores
Desert islands
Deserts
The Devil
Devil's Island
Dinosaurs
Directors' appearances
Disguise
Doctors
Documentary
Dreams
Drug addiction

Drunk scenes
Dubbing
Duels
The electric chair
Elephants
The end of the world
Enoch Arden
Entertainers
Epidemics
Episodic films
Eskimos
Excerpts
Explorers
Falling
The family
Fans
Fantasy
Farce
Fashions
The FBI
Films à clef
Fire
Firing squads
Flashback
Fog
The Foreign Legion
Forest fires
Funerals
Funfairs
Gambling
Gangsters
Giants
Gigolos
Gimmicks
Governesses
The guillotine
Gypsies
Hands
Helicopters
Hell
Hillbillies
Hollywood on film
Homosexuality
Horror
Horses
Hospitals
Hotels

Houses
Hypnosis
Impresarios
In-jokes
Incest
India
Insanity
Insects
Inventors
Ireland
Jazz
Jewel thieves
Jews
Kidnapping
Kings and Queens
The Ku Klux Klan
Labour relations
Leprechauns
Lesbianism
Letters
Lifts (elevators)
Light comedians
Lighthouses
London
Lookalikes
Los Angeles
Lynch law
The Mafia
Magicians
Mau Mau
Miniaturization
Mirrors
Missionaries
Monks
Monster animals
Mother love
Motor-cycles
Motor racing
Mountains
Multiple roles
Multiple-story films
Murderers
Musical remakes
Musicals
Mystery
Narrators
Naval comedy

New York
Numbered sequels
Nuns
Nurses
Nymphomaniacs
Offices
Old age
Opera
Orchestral conductors
Oriental roles
Painters
Paris
Parody
Parties
Pirates
Plastic surgery
Police
Politics
Poverty
Pre-credits sequences
Priests
Prison films
Prisoners of war
Private eyes
Prophecy
Prostitutes
Psychology
Radio
Railway stations
Rain

Rape
Red Indians (native
  Americans)
Reincarnation
Rejuvenation
Religion
Remakes in disguise
Reporters
Robberies
Robots
Romantic teams
Rome
Sailors
San Francisco
Satire
Schooldays
Science fiction
Scientists
Seances
Seaside resorts
Serial killers
Serials
Series
Servants
Sewers
Sex
Sex changes
Ships
Skiing
Slapstick

Small towns
Smoking
Smugglers
Social comedy
Social conscience
Soldiers
Space exploration
Spanish Civil War
Spies
Sportsmen
Staircases
Statesmen
Statues
Storms
Strikes
Student protest
Stuntmen
Submarines
Suicide
Swashbucklers
Swinging London
Teachers
The telephone
Television
Television movies
Television series
Tennis
Theatres
3-D
Tinting

Torture
Trains
Tramps (hoboes)
Transvestism
Uncredited appearances
Underground railways
Undertakers (morticians)
Underwater scenes
Unemployment
Universities
Vampires
Venice
Ventriloquists
Vienna
The Vietnam War
Vigilantes
Violence
Volcanoes
War heroes
Water
Waxworks
Weddings
Westerns
Wheelchairs
Witchcraft
World War I
Writers
Zombies

Academy Award-Winners

The Academy of Motion Picture Arts and Sciences was formed in 1927 with Douglas Fairbanks as its first president. Qualification for membership, which remains by invitation, is achievement in one or other areas of film production. Its first awards were held on 16 May 1929 for films that had been released in Los Angeles between the beginning of August 1927 and the end of July 1928. The Academy's gold-plated statuette was designed by Cedric Gibbons, MGM's art director. Its nickname, Oscar, which, like Academy Awards, is now registered as a trademark, is said to have been due to a secretary who remarked that it looked just like her uncle Oscar, although several people have claimed to have invented the term. Over the years, the categories have altered, and in 1937 the Irving Thalberg Memorial Award was added to commemorate MGM's former production chief who died in 1936; it is presented to producers who achieve a consistently high level of work. An Oscar remains the cinema's most sought-after award and is the only one that can give a considerable financial boost to the career of an individual or a film. Its main prizewinners are:

1927/28
Picture: *Wings*
Unique and Artistic Picture: *Sunrise*
Director: Frank Borzage (*Seventh Heaven*)
Comedy Director: Lewis Milestone (*Two Arabian Knights*)
Actor: Emil Jannings (*The Last Command, The Way of All Flesh*)
Actress: Janet Gaynor (*Seventh Heaven, Street Angel, Sunrise*)
Original Screenplay: Ben Hecht (*Underworld*)
Adapted Screenplay: Benjamin Glazer (*Seventh Heaven*)
Title Writing: Joseph Farnham (*Telling the World*)
Cinematography: Charles Rosher, Karl Struss (*Sunrise*)
Art Direction: William Cameron Menzies (*The Dove, Tempest*)
Engineering Effects: Roy Pomeroy (*Wings*)
Special Awards: Warner Bros for *The Jazz Singer*; Charles Chaplin for acting, writing, directing and producing *The Circus*

1928/29
Picture: *The Broadway Melody*
Director: Frank Lloyd (*The Divine Lady, Weary River, Drag*)
Actor: Warner Baxter (*Old Arizona*)
Actress: Mary Pickford (*Coquette*)
Writing Achievement: Hans Kraly (*The Patriot*)
Cinematography: Clyde De Vinna (*White Shadows in the South Seas*)
Art Direction: Cedric Gibbons (*The Bridge of San Luis Rey*)

1929/30
Picture: *All Quiet on the Western Front*
Director: Lewis Milestone (*All Quiet on the Western Front*)
Actor: George Arliss (*Disraeli*)
Actress: Norma Shearer (*The Divorcee*)
Writing Achievement: Frances Marion (*The Big House*)
Cinematography: Joseph T. Rucker, Willard Van Der Veer (*With Byrd at the South Pole*)
Art Direction: Herman Rosse (*The King of the Jews*)
Sound: Douglas Shearer (*The Big House*)

1930/31
Picture: *Cimarron*
Director: Norman Taurog (*Skippy*)
Actor: Lionel Barrymore (*A Free Soul*)
Actress: Marie Dressler (*Min and Bill*)
Original Screenplay: John Monk Saunders (*The Dawn Patrol*)
Adapted Screenplay: Howard Estabrook (*Cimarron*)
Cinematography: Floyd Crosby (*Tabu*)
Art Direction: Max Ree (*Cimarron*)
Sound: Paramount Sound Dept

1931/32
Picture: *Grand Hotel*
Director: Frank Borzage (*Bad Girl*)
Actor: Wallace Beery (*The Champ*)
Actress: Helen Hayes (*The Sin of Madelon Claudet*)
Original Screenplay: Francis Marion (*The Champ*)
Adapted Screenplay: Edwin Burke (*Bad Girl*)
Cinematography: Lee Garmes (*Shanghai Express*)
Art Direction: Gordon Wiles (*Transatlantic*)
Sound: Paramount Sound Dept
Cartoon: *Flowers and Trees*
Comedy Short: *The Music Box*
Novelty Short: *Wrestling Swordfish*
Special Award: Walt Disney for the creation of Mickey Mouse

1932/33
Picture: *Cavalcade*
Director: Frank Lloyd (*Cavalcade*)
Actor: Charles Laughton (*The Private Life of Henry VIII*)
Actress: Katharine Hepburn (*Morning Glory*)
Original Screenplay: Robert Lord (*One Way Passage*)
Adapted Screenplay: Victor Heerman, Sarah Y. Mason (*Little Women*)
Cinematography: Charles Bryant (*A Farewell to Arms*)
Art Direction: William S. Darling (*Cavalcade*)
Sound: Harold C. Lewis (*A Farewell to Arms*)
Cartoon: *Three Little Pigs*

Comedy Short: *So This Is Harris*
Novelty Short: *Krakatoa*

1934
Picture: *It Happened One Night*
Director: Frank Capra (*It Happened One Night*)
Assistant Director: John Waters (*Viva Villa*)
Actor: Clark Gable (*It Happened One Night*)
Actress: Claudette Colbert (*It Happened One Night*)
Original Screenplay: Arthur Caesar (*Manhattan Melodrama*)
Adapted Screenplay: Robert Riskin (*It Happened One Night*)
Cinematography: Victor Milner (*Cleopatra*)
Art Direction: Cedric Gibbons, Frederic Hope (*The Merry Widow*)
Original Song: 'The Continental' from *The Gay Divorcee* (*m* Con Conrad, *ly* Herb Magidson)
Original Score: Victor Schertzinger, Gus Kahn (*One Night of Love*)
Sound: John Livadary (*One Night of Love*)
Editing: Conrad Nevig (*Eskimo*)
Cartoon: *The Tortoise and the Hare*
Comedy Short: *La Cucaracha*
Novelty Short: *City of Wax*
Special Award: Shirley Temple

1935
Picture: *Mutiny on the Bounty*
Director: John Ford (*The Informer*)
Assistant Director: Clem Beauchamp (*Lives of a Bengal Lancer*)
Dance Direction: Dave Gould (*Broadway Melody of 1936* and *Folies Bergère*)
Actor: Victor McLaglen (*The Informer*)
Actress: Bette Davis (*Dangerous*)
Original Screenplay: Ben Hecht, Charles MacArthur (*The Scoundrel*)
Adapted Screenplay: Dudley Nichols (*The Informer*)
Cinematography: Hal Mohr (*A Midsummer Night's Dream*)
Art Direction: Richard Day (*The Dark Angel*)
Original Song: 'Lullaby of Broadway' from *Gold Diggers of 1935* (*m* Harry Warren, *ly* Al Dubin)
Original Score: Max Steiner (*The Informer*)
Sound: Douglas Shearer (*Naughty Marietta*)
Editing: Ralph Dawson (*A Midsummer Night's Dream*)
Cartoon: *Three Orphan Kittens*
Comedy Short: *How to Sleep*
Novelty Short: *Wings over Mt Everest*
Special Award: David Wark Griffith

1936
Picture: *The Great Ziegfeld*
Director: Frank Capra (*Mr Deeds Goes to Town*)
Assistant Director: Jack Sullivan (*The Charge of the Light Brigade*)
Dance Direction: Seymour Felix (*The Great Ziegfeld*)
Actor: Paul Muni (*The Story of Louis Pasteur*)
Actress: Luise Rainer (*The Great Ziegfeld*)
Supporting Actor: Walter Brennan (*Come and Get It*)
Supporting Actress: Gale Sondergaard (*Anthony Adverse*)

Original Screenplay: Pierre Collings, Sheridan Gibney (*The Story of Louis Pasteur*)
Cinematography: Gaetano Gaudio (*Anthony Adverse*)
Art Direction: Richard Day (*Dodsworth*)
Original Song: 'The Way You Look Tonight' from *Swingtime* (*m* Jerome Kern, *ly* Dorothy Fields)
Original Score: Erich Wolfgang Korngold (*Anthony Adverse*)
Sound: Douglas Shearer (*San Francisco*)
Editing: Ralph Dawson (*Anthony Adverse*)
Cartoon: *Country Cousins*
One-Reel Short: *Bored of Education*
Two-Reel Short: *The Public Pays*
Colour Short: *Give Me Liberty*
Special Award: *March of Time* for revolutionizing the newsreel; W. Howard Greene and Harold Rosson for colour cinematography (*The Garden of Allah*)

1937
Picture: *The Life of Emile Zola*
Director: Leo McCarey (*The Awful Truth*)
Assistant Director: Robert Webb (*In Old Chicago*)
Dance Direction: Hermes Pan (*Damsel in Distress*)
Actor: Spencer Tracy (*Captains Courageous*)
Actress: Luise Rainer (*The Good Earth*)
Supporting Actor: Joseph Schildkraut (*The Life of Emile Zola*)
Supporting Actress: Alice Brady (*In Old Chicago*)
Original Story: William A. Wellman, Robert Carson (*A Star Is Born*)
Original Screenplay: Heinz Herald, Geza Herczeg, Norman Reilly Raine (*The Life of Emile Zola*)
Cinematography: Karl Freund (*The Good Earth*)
Art Direction: Stephen Goosson (*Lost Horizon*)
Original Song: 'Sweet Leilani' from *Waikiki Wedding* (*m/ly* Harry Owens)
Original Score: Charles Previn (*100 Men and a Girl*)
Sound: Thomas T. Moulton (*The Hurricane*)
Editing: Gene Havlick, Gene Milton (*Lost Horizon*)
Cartoon: *The Old Mill*
One-Reel Short: *Private Life of the Gannets*
Two-Reel Short: *Torture Money*
Colour Short: *Penny Wisdom*
Special Awards: Mack Sennett for his contribution to comedy technique; Edgar Bergen for *Charlie McCarthy*; The Museum of Modern Art Film Library; W. Howard Greene for colour photography (*A Star Is Born*)
Irving Thalberg Memorial Award: Darryl Zanuck

1938
Picture: *You Can't Take It with You*
Director: Frank Capra (*You Can't Take It with You*)
Actor: Spencer Tracy (*Boys' Town*)
Actress: Bette Davis (*Jezebel*)
Supporting Actor: Walter Brennan (*Kentucky*)
Supporting Actress: Fay Bainter (*Jezebel*)
Original Story: Eleonore Griffin, Dore Schary (*Boys' Town*)
Screenplay: George Bernard Shaw, adapted by Ian Dalrymple, Cecil Lewis, W. P. Liscomb (*Pygmalion*)
Cinematography: Joseph Ruttenberg (*The Great Waltz*)

Art Direction: Carl J. Weyl (*The Adventures of Robin Hood*)
Sound: Thomas Moulton and United Artists Sound Dept (*The Cowboy and the Lady*)
Editing: Ralph Dawson (*The Adventures of Robin Hood*)
Song: 'Thanks for the Memory' from *Big Broadcast of 1938* (m Ralph Rainger, ly Leo Robin)
Scoring: Alfred Newman (*Alexander's Ragtime Band*)
Original Score: Erich Wolfgang Korngold (*The Adventures of Robin Hood*)
Cartoon: *Ferdinand the Bull*
One-Reel Short: *That Mothers Might Live*
Two-Reel Short: *Declaration of Independence*
Special Awards: Deanna Durbin and Mickey Rooney; Harry M. Warner; Walt Disney; Oliver Marsh and Allen Davey for colour photography (*Sweethearts*); Gordon Jennings, Farciot Edouart, Loren Ryder and others for special effects (*Spawn of the North*); J. Arthur Ball for advancing the use of colour
Irving Thalberg Memorial Award: Hal B. Wallis

1939
Picture: *Gone with the Wind*
Director: Victor Fleming (*Gone with the Wind*)
Actor: Robert Donat (*Goodbye Mr Chips*)
Actress: Vivien Leigh (*Gone with the Wind*)
Supporting Actor: Thomas Mitchell (*Stagecoach*)
Supporting Actress: Hattie McDaniel (*Gone with the Wind*)
Original Story: Lewis R. Foster (*Mr Deeds Goes to Washington*)
Screenplay: Sidney Howard (*Gone with the Wind*)
B/w Cinematography: Gregg Toland (*Wuthering Heights*)
Colour Cinematography: Ernest Haller, Ray Rennahan (*Gone with the Wind*)
Art Direction: Lyle Wheeler (*Gone with the Wind*)
Sound: Bernard B. Brown and Universal Sound Dept (*When Tomorrow Comes*)
Editing: Hal C. Kern, James E. Newcom (*Gone with the Wind*)
Special Effects: E. H. Hansen, Fred Sersen (*The Rains Came*)
Song: 'Over the Rainbow' from *The Wizard of Oz* (m Harold Arlen, ly E. Y. Harburg)
Scoring: Richard Hageman, Frank Harling, John Leipold, Leo Shuken (*Stagecoach*)
Original Score: Herbert Stothart (*The Wizard of Oz*)
Cartoon: *The Ugly Duckling*
One-Reel Short: *Busy Little Bears*
Two-Reel Short: *Sons of Liberty*
Special Awards: Douglas Fairbanks; Motion Picture Relief Fund; Judy Garland; William Cameron Menzies for the use of colour (*Gone with the Wind*); Technicolor Company
Irving Thalberg Memorial Award: David O. Selznick

1940
Picture: *Rebecca*
Director: John Ford (*The Grapes of Wrath*)
Actor: James Stewart (*The Philadelphia Story*)
Actress: Ginger Rogers (*Kitty Foyle*)
Supporting Actor: Walter Brennan (*The Westerner*)

Supporting Actress: Jane Darwell (*The Grapes of Wrath*)
Original Story: Benjamin Glazer, John S. Toldy (*Arise, My Love*)
Original Screenplay: Preston Sturges (*The Great McGinty*)
Screenplay: Donald Ogden Stewart (*The Philadelphia Story*)
B/w Cinematography: George Barnes (*Rebecca*)
Colour Cinematography: George Perinal (*The Thief of Bagdad*)
Art Direction: Cedric Gibbons, Paul Groesse (*Pride and Prejudice*)
Sound: Douglas Shearer and MGM Sound Dept (*Strike Up the Band*)
Editing: Anne Bauchens (*North West Mounted Police*)
Special Effects: Lawrence Butler, Jack Whitney (*The Thief of Bagdad*)
Song: 'When You Wish upon a Star' from *Pinocchio* (m Leigh Harline, ly Ned Washington)
Scoring: Alfred Newman (*Tin Pan Alley*)
Original Score: Leigh Harline, Paul J. Smith, Ned Washington (*Pinocchio*)
Cartoon: *Milky Way*
One-Reel Short: *Quicker'n a Wink*
Two-Reel Short: *Teddy, the Rough Rider*
Special Awards: Bob Hope; Col. Nathan Levinson

1941
Picture: *How Green Was My Valley*
Director: John Ford (*How Green Was My Valley*)
Actor: Gary Cooper (*Sergeant York*)
Actress: Joan Fontaine (*Suspicion*)
Supporting Actor: Donald Crisp (*How Green Was My Valley*)
Supporting Actress: Mary Astor (*The Great Lie*)
Original Story: Harry Segall (*Here Comes Mr Jordan*)
Original Screenplay: Herman J. Mankiewicz, Orson Welles (*Citizen Kane*)
Screenplay: Sidney Buchman, Seton I. Miller (*Here Comes Mr Jordan*)
B/w Cinematography: Arthur Miller (*How Green Was My Valley*)
Colour Cinematography: Ernest Palmer, Ray Rennahan (*Blood and Sand*)
B/w Art Direction: Richard Day, Nathan Duran (*How Green Was My Valley*)
Colour Art Direction: Cedric Gibbons, Joseph C. Wright (*Blood and Sand*)
Sound: Jack Whitney (*That Hamilton Woman*)
Editing: William Holmes (*Sergeant York*)
Special Effects: Farciot Edouart, Gordon Jennings, Louis Mesenkop (*I Wanted Wings*)
Song: 'The Last Time I Saw Paris' from *Lady Be Good* (m Jerome Kern, ly Oscar Hammerstein II)
Scoring of a Drama: Bernard Herrmann (*All that Money Can Buy*)
Scoring of a Musical: Frank Churchill, Oliver Wallace (*Dumbo*)
Documentary: *Churchill's Island*
Cartoon: *Led a Paw*
One-Reel Short: *Of Pups and Puzzles*
Two-Reel Short: *Main Street on the March*
Special Awards: Rey Scott for producing *Kukan*; British Ministry of Information for producing *Target for Tonight*;

Leopold Stokowski for *Fantasia*; Walt Disney, William Garity, John A. Hawkins, RCA for the sound in *Fantasia*
Irving Thalberg Memorial Award: Walt Disney

1942
Picture: *Mrs Miniver*
Director: William Wyler (*Mrs Miniver*)
Actor: James Cagney (*Yankee Doodle Dandy*)
Actress: Greer Garson (*Mrs Miniver*)
Supporting Actor: Van Heflin (*Johnny Eager*)
Supporting Actress: Teresa Wright (*Mrs Miniver*)
Original Story: Emeric Pressburger (*The Invaders*)
Original Screenplay: Michael Kanin, Ring Lardner Jnr (*Woman of the Year*)
Screenplay: George Froeschel, James Hilton, Claudine West, Arthur Wimperis (*Mrs Miniver*)
B/w Cinematography: Joseph Ruttenberg (*Mrs Miniver*)
Colour Cinematography: Leon Shamroy (*The Black Swan*)
B/w Art Direction: Richard Day, Joseph Wright (*This above All*)
Colour Art Direction: Richard Day, Joseph Wright (*My Gal Sal*)
Sound: Nathan Levinson and Warner Sound Dept (*Yankee Doodle Dandy*)
Editing: Daniel Mandell (*The Pride of the Yankees*)
Special Effects: Farciot Edouart, Gordon Jennings, William L. Pereira, Louis Mesenkop (*Reap the Wild Wind*)
Song: 'White Christmas' from *Holiday Inn* (*m/ly* Irving Berlin)
Scoring of a Drama or Comedy: Max Steiner (*Now Voyager*)
Scoring of a Musical: Ray Heindorf, Heinz Roemheld (*Yankee Doodle Dandy*)
Documentary: US Navy, TCF (*Battle of Midway*)
Cartoon: *Der Fuehrer's Face*
One-Reel Short: *Speaking of Animals and Their Families*
Two-Reel Short: *Beyond the Line of Duty*
Special Awards: Charles Boyer; Noël Coward; MGM for the Andy Hardy films
Irving Thalberg Memorial Award: Sidney Franklin

1943
Picture: *Casablanca*
Director: Michael Curtiz (*Casablanca*)
Actor: Paul Lukas (*Watch on the Rhine*)
Actress: Jennifer Jones (*Song of Bernadette*)
Supporting Actor: Charles Coburn (*The More the Merrier*)
Supporting Actress: Katina Paxinou (*For Whom the Bell Tolls*)
Original Story: William Saroyan (*The Human Comedy*)
Original Screenplay: Norman Krasna (*Princess O'Rourke*)
Screenplay: Julius J. Epstein, Philip G. Epstein, Howard Koch (*Casablanca*)
B/w Cinematography: Arthur Miller (*The Song of Bernadette*)
Colour Cinematography: Hal Mohr, W. Howard Greene (*The Phantom of the Opera*)
B/w Art Direction: James Basevi, William Darling (*The Song of Bernadette*)
Colour Art Direction: Alexander Golitzen, John B. Goodman (*The Phantom of the Opera*)

Sound: Stephen Dunn and RKO Sound Dept (*This Land Is Mine*)
Editing: George Amy (*Air Force*)
Special Effects: Fred Sersen, Roger Heman (*Crash Dive*)
Song: 'You'll Never Know' from *Hello, Frisco, Hello* (*m* Harry Warren, *ly* Mack Gordon)
Scoring of a Drama or Comedy: Alfred Newman (*The Song of Bernadette*)
Scoring of a Musical: Ray Heindorf (*This Is the Army*)
Documentary: *December 7th*
Cartoon: *Yankee Doodle Mouse*
One-Reel Short: *Amphibious Fighters*
Two-Reel Short: *Heavenly Music*
Special Award: George Pal
Irving Thalberg Memorial Award: Hal B. Wallis

1944
Picture: *Going My Way*
Director: Leo McCarey (*Going My Way*)
Actor: Bing Crosby (*Going My Way*)
Actress: Ingrid Bergman (*Gaslight*)
Supporting Actor: Barry Fitzgerald (*Going My Way*)
Supporting Actress: Ethel Barrymore (*None but the Lonely Heart*)
Original Story: Leo McCarey (*Going My Way*)
Original Screenplay: Lamar Trotti (*Wilson*)
Screenplay: Frank Butler, Frank Cavett (*Going My Way*)
B/w Cinematography: Joseph LaShelle (*Laura*)
Colour Cinematography: Leon Shamroy (*Wilson*)
B/w Art Direction: Cedric Gibbons, William Ferrari (*Gaslight*)
Colour Art Direction: Wiard Ihnen (*Wilson*)
Sound: E. H. Hansen and TCF Sound Dept (*Wilson*)
Editing: Barbara McLean (*Wilson*)
Special Effects: Arnold Gillespie, Donald Jahraus, Gordon Jennings, Douglas Shearer (*Thirty Seconds over Tokyo*)
Song: 'Swinging on a Star' from *Going My Way* (*m* James Van Heusen, *ly* Johnny Burke)
Scoring of a Drama or Comedy: Max Steiner (*Since You Went Away*)
Scoring of a Musical: Carmen Dragon, Morris Stoloff (*Cover Girl*)
Documentary: *With the Marines at Tarawa*
Cartoon: *Mouse Trouble*
One-Reel Short: *Who's Who in Animal Land*
Two-Reel Short: *I Won't Play*
Special Awards: Margaret O'Brien; Bob Hope
Irving Thalberg Memorial Award: Darryl F. Zanuck

1945
Picture: *The Lost Weekend*
Director: Billy Wilder (*The Lost Weekend*)
Actor: Ray Milland (*The Lost Weekend*)
Actress: Joan Crawford (*Mildred Pierce*)
Supporting Actor: James Dunn (*A Tree Grows in Brooklyn*)
Supporting Actress: Anne Revere (*National Velvet*)
Original Story: Charles G. Booth (*The House on 92nd Street*)
Original Screenplay: Richard Schweizer (*Marie-Louise*)
Screenplay: Charles Brackett, Billy Wilder (*The Lost Weekend*)

B/w Cinematography: Harry Stradling (*The Picture of Dorian Gray*)

Colour Cinematography: Leon Shamroy (*Leave Her to Heaven*)

B/w Art Direction: Wiard Ihnen (*Blood on the Sun*)

Colour Art Direction: Hans Dreier, Ernst Fegte (*Frenchman's Creek*)

Sound: Stephen Dunn and RKO Sound Dept (*The Bells of St Mary's*)

Editing: Robert J. Kern (*National Velvet*)

Special Effects: John Fulton, A. W. Jones (*Wonder Man*)

Song: 'It Might as Well Be Spring' from *State Fair* (*m* Richard Rodgers, *ly* Oscar Hammerstein II)

Scoring of a Drama or Comedy: Miklos Rozsa (*Spellbound*)

Scoring of a Musical: Georgie Stoll (*Anchors Aweigh*)

Documentary: *The True Glory*

Cartoon: *Quiet Please*

One-Reel Short: *Stairway to Light*

Two-Reel Short: *Star in the Night*

Special Awards: Walter Wanger; Peggy Ann Garner

1946

Picture: *The Best Years of Our Lives*

Director: William Wyler (*The Best Years of Our Lives*)

Actor: Fredric March (*The Best Years of Our Lives*)

Actress: Olivia De Havilland (*To Each His Own*)

Supporting Actor: Harold Russell (*The Best Years of Our Lives*)

Supporting Actress: Anne Baxter (*The Razor's Edge*)

Original Story: Clemence Dane (*Vacation from Marriage*)

Original Screenplay: Muriel Box, Sydney Box (*The Seventh Veil*)

Screenplay: Robert E. Sherwood (*The Best Years of Our Lives*)

B/w Cinematography: Arthur Miller (*Anna and the King of Siam*)

Colour Cinematography: Charles Rosher, Leonard Smith, Arthur Arling (*The Yearling*)

B/w Art Direction: Lyle Wheeler, William Darling (*Anna and the King of Siam*)

Colour Art Direction: Cedric Gibbons, Paul Groesse (*The Yearling*)

Sound: John Livadary and Columbia Sound Dept (*The Jolson Story*)

Editing: Daniel Mandell (*The Best Years of Our Lives*)

Special Effects: Thomas Howard (*Blithe Spirit*)

Song: 'On the Atchison, Topeka and the Santa Fe' from *The Harvey Girls* (*m* Harry Warren, *ly* Johnny Mercer)

Scoring of a Drama or Comedy: Hugo Friedhofer (*The Best Years of Our Lives*)

Scoring of a Musical: Morris Stoloff (*The Jolson Story*)

Documentary: *Seeds of Destiny*

Cartoon: *The Cat Concerto*

One-Reel Short: *Facing Your Danger*

Two-Reel Short: *A Boy and His Dog*

Special Awards: Laurence Olivier; Harold Russell; Ernest Lubitsch; Claude Jarman Jnr

Irving Thalberg Memorial Award: Samuel Goldwyn

1947

Picture: *Gentleman's Agreement*

Director: Elia Kazan (*Gentleman's Agreement*)

Actor: Ronald Colman (*A Double Life*)

Actress: Loretta Young (*The Farmer's Daughter*)

Supporting Actor: Edmund Gwenn (*Miracle on 34th Street*)

Supporting Actress: Celeste Holm (*Gentleman's Agreement*)

Original Story: Valentine Davies (*Miracle on 34th Street*)

Original Screenplay: Sidney Sheldon (*The Bachelor and the Bobby-Soxer*)

Screenplay: George Seaton (*Miracle on 34th Street*)

B/w Cinematography: Guy Green (*Great Expectations*)

Colour Cinematography: Jack Cardiff (*Black Narcissus*)

B/w Art Direction: John Bryan (*Great Expectations*)

Colour Art Direction: Alfred Jung (*Black Narcissus*)

Sound: Gordon Sawyer and Goldwyn Sound Dept (*The Bishop's Wife*)

Editing: Francis Lyon, Robert Parrish (*Body and Soul*)

Special Effects: A. Arnold Gillespie, Warren Newcombe, Douglas Shearer, Michael Steinore (*Green Dolphin Street*)

Song: 'Zip-a-Dee-Doo-Dah' from *Song of the South* (*m* Allie Wrubel, *ly* Roy Gilbert)

Scoring of a Drama or Comedy: Miklos Rozsa (*A Double Life*)

Scoring of a Musical: Alfred Newman (*My Mother Wore Tights*)

Documentary Short: *First Steps*

Documentary Feature: *Design for Death*

Cartoon: *Tweetie Pie*

One-Reel Short: *Goodbye Miss Turlock*

Two-Reel Short: *Climbing the Matterhorn*

Special Awards: James Baskett; Bill and Coo; Shoe-Shine (foreign film)

1948

Picture: *Hamlet*

Director: John Huston (*The Treasure of the Sierra Madre*)

Actor: Laurence Olivier (*Hamlet*)

Actress: Jane Wyman (*Johnny Belinda*)

Supporting Actor: Walter Huston (*The Treasure of the Sierra Madre*)

Supporting Actress: Claire Trevor (*Key Largo*)

Motion Picture Story: Richard Sweizer, David Wechsler (*The Search*)

Screenplay: John Huston (*The Treasure of the Sierra Madre*)

B/w Cinematography: William Daniels (*The Naked City*)

Colour Cinematography: Joseph Valentine, William V. Skall, Winton Hoch (*Joan of Arc*)

B/w Art Direction: Roger K. Furse (*Hamlet*)

Colour Art Direction: Hein Heckroth, Arthur Lawson (*The Red Shoes*)

B/w Costume Design: Roger K. Furse (*Hamlet*)

Colour Costume Design: Dorothy Jeakins, Karinska (*Joan of Arc*)

Sound: TCF Sound Dept (*The Snake Pit*)

Editing: Paul Weatherwax (*The Naked City*)

Special Effects: Paul Eagler, J. McMillan Johnson, Russell Shearman, Clarence Slifer, Charles Freeman, James G. Stewart (*Portrait of Jennie*)

Song: 'Buttons and Bows' from *The Paleface* (*m/ly* Jay Livingstone, Ray Evans)

Scoring of a Drama or Comedy: Brian Easdale (*The Red Shoes*)

Scoring of a Musical: Johnny Green, Roger Edens (*Easter Parade*)

Documentary Short: *Toward Independence*

Documentary Feature: *The Secret Land*

Cartoon: *The Little Orphan*

One-Reel Short: *Symphony of a City*

Two-Reel Short: *Seal Island*

Special Awards: Ivan Jandl; Sid Grauman; Adolph Zukor; Walter Wanger; *Monsieur Vincent* (foreign film)

Irving Thalberg Memorial Award: Jerry Wald

1949

Picture: *All the King's Men*

Director: Joseph L. Mankiewicz (*A Letter to Three Wives*)

Actor: Broderick Crawford (*All the King's Men*)

Actress: Olivia De Havilland (*The Heiress*)

Supporting Actor: Dean Jagger (*Twelve O'Clock High*)

Supporting Actress: Mercedes McCambridge (*All the King's Men*)

Motion Picture Story: Douglas Morrow (*The Stratton Story*)

Screenplay: Joseph L. Mankiewicz (*A Letter to Three Wives*)

Story & Screenplay: Robert Pirosh (*Battleground*)

B/w Cinematography: Paul C. Vogel (*Battleground*)

Colour Cinematography: Winton Hoch (*She Wore a Yellow Ribbon*)

B/w Art Direction: John Meehan, Harry Horner (*The Heiress*)

Colour Art Direction: Cedric Gibbons, Paul Groesse (*Little Women*)

B/w Costume Design: Edith Head, Gile Steele (*The Heiress*)

Colour Costume Design: Leah Rhodes, Travilla, Marjorie Best (*Adventures of Don Juan*)

Sound: TCF Sound Dept (*Twelve O'Clock High*)

Editing: Harry Gerstad (*Champion*)

Special Effects: *Mighty Joe Young*

Song: 'Baby It's Cold Outside' from *Neptune's Daughter* (*m/ly* Frank Loesser)

Scoring of a Drama or Comedy: Aaron Copland (*The Heiress*)

Scoring of a Musical: Roger Edens, Lennie Hayton (*On the Town*)

Documentary Short: *A Chance to Live*

Documentary Feature: *Daybreak in Udi*

Cartoon: *For Scent-imental Reasons*

One-Reel Short: *Aquatic House Party*

Two-Reel Short: *Van Gogh*

Special Awards: Bobby Driscoll; Fred Astaire; Cecil B. De Mille; Jean Hersholt; *The Bicycle Thief* (foreign film)

1950

Picture: *All about Eve*

Director: Joseph L. Mankiewicz (*All about Eve*)

Actor: José Ferrer (*Cyrano de Bergerac*)

Actress: Judy Holliday (*Born Yesterday*)

Supporting Actor: George Sanders (*All about Eve*)

Supporting Actress: Josephine Hull (*Harvey*)

Motion Picture Story: Edna Anhalt, Edward Anhalt (*Panic in the Streets*)

Screenplay: Joseph L. Mankiewicz (*All about Eve*)

Story & Screenplay: Charles Brackett, Billy Wilder, D. M. Marshman Jnr (*Sunset Boulevard*)

B/w Cinematography: Robert Krasker (*The Third Man*)

Colour Cinematography: Robert Surtees (*King Solomon's Mines*)

B/w Art Direction: Hans Dreier, John Meehan (*Sunset Boulevard*)

Colour Art Direction: Hans Dreier, Walter Tyler (*Samson and Delilah*)

B/w Costume Design: Edith Head, Charles LeMaire (*All about Eve*)

Colour Costume Design: Edith Head, Dorothy Jeakins, Elois Jenssen, Gile Steele, Gwen Wakeling (*Samson and Delilah*)

Sound: TCF Sound Dept (*All about Eve*)

Editing: Ralph E. Winters, Conrad A. Nervig (*King Solomon's Mines*)

Special Effects: *Destination Moon*

Song: 'Mona Lisa' from *Captain Carey* (*m/ly* Ray Evans, Jay Livingston)

Scoring of a Drama or Comedy: Franz Waxman (*Sunset Boulevard*)

Scoring of a Musical: Adolph Deutsch, Roger Edens (*Annie Get Your Gun*)

Documentary Short: *Why Korea?*

Documentary Feature: *The Titan: Story of Michelangelo*

Cartoon: *Gerald McBoing Boing*

One-Reel Short: *Grandad of Races*

Two-Reel Short: *Beaver Valley*

Honorary Awards: George Murphy; Louis B. Mayer; *The Walls of Malapaga* (foreign film)

Irving Thalberg Memorial Award: Darryl F. Zanuck

1951

Picture: *An American in Paris*

Director: George Stevens (*A Place in the Sun*)

Actor: Humphrey Bogart (*The African Queen*)

Actress: Vivien Leigh (*A Streetcar Named Desire*)

Supporting Actor: Karl Malden (*A Streetcar Named Desire*)

Supporting Actress: Kim Hunter (*A Streetcar Named Desire*)

Motion Picture Story: Paul Dehn, James Bernard (*Seven Days to Noon*)

Screenplay: Michael Wilson, Harry Brown (*A Place in the Sun*)

Story & Screenplay: Alan Jay Lerner (*An American in Paris*)

B/w Cinematography: William C. Mellor (*A Place in the Sun*)

Colour Cinematography: Alfred Gilks, John Alton (*An American in Paris*)

B/w Art Direction: Richard Day (*A Streetcar Named Desire*)

Colour Art Direction: Cedric Gibbons, Preston Ames (*An American in Paris*)

B/w Costume Design: Edith Head (*A Place in the Sun*)

Colour Costume Design: Orry-Kelly, Walter Plunkett, Irene Sharaff (*An American in Paris*)

Sound: Douglas Shearer (*The Great Caruso*)

Editing: William Hornbeck (*A Place in the Sun*)

Special Effects: *When Worlds Collide*

Song: 'In the Cool, Cool, Cool of the Evening' from *Here Comes the Groom* (*m* Hoagy Carmichael, *ly* Johnny Mercer)

Scoring of a Drama or Comedy: Franz Waxman (*A Place in the Sun*)

Scoring of a Musical: Johnny Green, Saul Chaplin (*An American in Paris*)

Documentary Short: *Benjy*

Documentary Feature: *Kon-Tiki*

Cartoon: *Two Mouseketeers*

One-Reel Short: *World of Kids*

Two-Reel Short: *Nature's Half Acre*

Honorary Awards: Gene Kelly; *Rashomon* (foreign film)

Irving Thalberg Memorial Award: Arthur Freed

1952

Picture: *The Greatest Show on Earth*

Director: John Ford (*The Quiet Man*)

Actor: Gary Cooper (*High Noon*)

Actress: Shirley Booth (*Come Back, Little Sheba*)

Supporting Actor: Anthony Quinn (*Viva Zapata!*)

Supporting Actress: Gloria Grahame (*The Bad and the Beautiful*)

Motion Picture Story: Frederic M. Frank, Theodore St John, Frank Cavett (*The Greatest Show on Earth*)

Screenplay: Charles Schnee (*The Bad and the Beautiful*)

Story & Screenplay: T. E. B. Clarke (*The Lavender Hill Mob*)

B/w Cinematography: Robert Surtees (*The Bad and the Beautiful*)

Colour Cinematography: Winton C. Hoch, Archie Stout (*The Quiet Man*)

B/w Art Direction: Cedric Gibbons, Edward Carfagno (*The Bad and the Beautiful*)

Colour Art Direction: Paul Sheriff (*Moulin Rouge*)

B/w Costume Design: Helen Rose (*The Bad and the Beautiful*)

Colour Costume Design: Marcel Vertes (*Moulin Rouge*)

Sound: London Film Sound Dept (*Breaking the Sound Barrier*)

Editing: Elmo Williams, Harry Gerstad (*High Noon*)

Special Effects: *Plymouth Adventure*

Song: 'High Noon' from *High Noon* (m Dimitri Tiomkin, ly Ned Washington)

Scoring of a Drama or Comedy: Dimitri Tiomkin (*High Noon*)

Scoring of a Musical: Alfred Newman (*With a Song in My Heart*)

Documentary Short: *Neighbors*

Documentary Feature: *The Sea around Us*

Cartoon: *Johann Mouse*

One-Reel Short: *Light in the Window*

Two-Reel Short: *Water Birds*

Honorary Awards: George Alfred Mitchell; Joseph M. Schenck; Merian C. Cooper; Harold Lloyd; Bob Hope; *Forbidden Games* (foreign film)

Irving Thalberg Memorial Award: Cecil B. De Mille

1953

Picture: *From Here to Eternity*

Director: Fred Zinnemann (*From Here to Eternity*)

Actor: William Holden (*Stalag 17*)

Actress: Audrey Hepburn (*Roman Holiday*)

Supporting Actor: Frank Sinatra (*From Here to Eternity*)

Supporting Actress: Donna Reed (*From Here to Eternity*)

Motion Picture Story: Ian McLellan Hunter, fronting for the blacklisted Dalton Trumbo (*Roman Holiday*)

Screenplay: Daniel Taradash (*From Here to Eternity*)

Story & Screenplay: Charles Brackett, Walter Reisch, Richard Breen (*Titanic*)

B/w Cinematography: Burnett Guffey (*From Here to Eternity*)

Colour Cinematography: Loyal Griggs (*Shane*)

B/w Art Direction: Cedric Gibbons, Edward Carfagno (*Julius Caesar*)

Colour Art Direction: Lyle Wheeler, George W. Davis (*The Robe*)

B/w Costume Design: Edith Head (*Roman Holiday*)

Colour Costume Design: Charles LeMaire, Emile Santiago (*The Robe*)

Sound: J. P. Livadary and Columbia Sound Dept (*From Here to Eternity*)

Editing: William Lyon (*From Here to Eternity*)

Special Effects: *The War of the Worlds*

Song: 'Secret Love' from *Calamity Jane* (m Sammy Fain, ly Paul Francis Webster)

Scoring of a Drama or Comedy: Bronislau Kaper (*Lili*)

Scoring of a Musical: Alfred Newman (*Call Me Madam*)

Documentary Short: *The Alaskan Eskimo*

Documentary Feature: *The Living Desert*

Cartoon: *Toot, Whistle, Plunk and Boom*

One-Reel Short: *The Merry Wives of Windsor Overture*

Two-Reel Short: *Bear Country*

Honorary Awards: Pete Smith; Joseph I. Breen; Twentieth Century-Fox for Cinemascope

Irving Thalberg Memorial Award: George Stevens

1954

Picture: *On the Waterfront*

Director: Elia Kazan (*On the Waterfront*)

Actor: Marlon Brando (*On the Waterfront*)

Actress: Grace Kelly (*The Country Girl*)

Supporting Actor: Edmond O'Brien (*The Barefoot Contessa*)

Supporting Actress: Eva Marie Saint (*On the Waterfront*)

Motion Picture Story: Philip Yordan (*Broken Lance*)

Screenplay: George Seaton (*The Country Girl*)

Story & Screenplay: Budd Schulberg (*On the Waterfront*)

B/w Cinematography: Boris Kaufman (*On the Waterfront*)

Colour Cinematography: Milton Krasner (*Three Coins in the Fountain*)

B/w Art Direction: Richard Day (*On the Waterfront*)

Colour Art Direction: John Meehan (*20,000 Leagues under the Sea*)

B/w Costume Design: Edith Head (*Sabrina*)

Colour Costume Design: Sanzo Wada (*Gate of Hell*)

Sound: Leslie I. Carey (*The Glenn Miller Story*)

Editing: Gene Milford (*On the Waterfront*)

Special Effects: *20,000 Leagues under the Sea*

Song: 'Three Coins in the Fountain' from *Three Coins in the Fountain* (m Jule Styne, ly Sammy Cahn)

Scoring of a Drama or Comedy: Dimitri Tiomkin (*The High and the Mighty*)

Scoring of a Musical: Adolph Deutsch, Saul Chaplin (*Seven Brides for Seven Brothers*)

Documentary Short: *Thursday's Children*

Documentary Feature: *The Vanishing Prairie*

Cartoon: *When Magoo Flew*
One-Reel Short: *This Mechanical Age*
Two-Reel Short: *A Time out of War*
Honorary Awards: Greta Garbo; Danny Kaye; Jon Whiteley; Vincent Winter; *Gate of Hell* (foreign film)

1955
Picture: *Marty*
Director: Delbert Mann (*Marty*)
Actor: Ernest Borgnine (*Marty*)
Actress: Anna Magnani (*The Rose Tattoo*)
Supporting Actor: Jack Lemmon (*Mister Roberts*)
Supporting Actress: Jo Van Fleet (*East of Eden*)
Motion Picture Story: Daniel Fuchs (*Love Me or Leave Me*)
Screenplay: Paddy Chayevsky (*Marty*)
Story & Screenplay: William Ludwig, Sonya Levien (*Interrupted Melody*)
B/w Cinematography: James Wong Howe (*The Rose Tattoo*)
Colour Cinematography: Robert Burks (*To Catch a Wife*)
B/w Art Direction: Hal Pereira, Tambi Larsen (*The Rose Tattoo*)
Colour Art Direction: William Flannery, Jo Mielziner (*Picnic*)
B/w Costume Design: Helen Rose (*I'll Cry Tomorrow*)
Colour Costume Design: Charles LeMaire (*Love Is a Many-Splendored Thing*)
Sound: Fred Hynes and Todd-AO Sound Dept (*Oklahoma*)
Editing: Charles Nelson, William A. Lyon (*Picnic*)
Special Effects: *The Bridges at Toko-Ri*
Song: 'Love Is a Many-Splendored Thing' from *Love Is a Many-Splendored Thing* (m Sammy Fain, ly Paul Francis Webster)
Scoring of a Drama or Comedy: Alfred Newman (*Love Is a Many-Splendored Thing*)
Scoring of a Musical: Robert Russell Bennett, Jay Blackton, Adolph Deutsch (*Oklahoma!*)
Documentary Short: *Men against the Arctic*
Documentary Feature: *Helen Keller in Her Story*
Cartoon: *Speedy Gonzales*
One-Reel Short: *Survival City*
Two-Reel Short: *The Face of Lincoln*
Honorary Awards: *Samurai, the Legend of Musashi* (foreign film)

1956
Picture: *Around the World in Eighty Days*
Foreign-Language Film: *La Strada* (Federico Fellini)
Director: George Stevens (*Giant*)
Actor: Yul Brynner (*The King and I*)
Actress: Ingrid Bergman (*Anastasia*)
Supporting Actor: Anthony Quinn (*Lust for Life*)
Supporting Actress: Dorothy Malone (*Written on the Wind*)
Motion Picture Story: Dalton Trumbo (as Robert Rich) (*The Brave One*)
Original Screenplay: Albert Lamorisse (*The Red Balloon*)
Adapted Screenplay: James Poe, John Farrow, S. J. Perelman (*Around the World in Eighty Days*)
B/w Cinematography: Joseph Ruttenberg (*Somebody Up There Likes Me*)

Colour Cinematography: Lionel Lindon (*Around the World in Eighty Days*)
B/w Art Direction: Cedric Gibbons, Malcolm F. Brown (*Somebody Up There Likes Me*)
Colour Art Direction: Lyle Wheeler, John DeCuir (*The King and I*)
B/w Costume Design: Jean Louis (*The Solid Gold Cadillac*)
Colour Costume Design: Irene Sharaff (*The King and I*)
Sound: Carl Faulkner and TCF Sound Dept (*The King and I*)
Editing: Gene Ruggiero, Paul Weatherwax (*Around the World in Eighty Days*)
Special Effects: John Fulton (*The Ten Commandments*)
Song: 'Whatever Will Be, Will Be' from *The Man Who Knew Too Much* (m/ly Jay Livingston, Ray Evans)
Scoring of a Drama or Comedy: Victor Young (*Around the World in Eighty Days*)
Scoring of a Musical: Alfred Newman, Ken Darby (*The King and I*)
Documentary Short: *The True Story of the Civil War*
Documentary Feature: *The Silent World*
Cartoon: *Mister Magoo's Puddle Jumper*
One-Reel Short: *Crashing the Water Barrier*
Two-Reel Short: *The Bespoke Overcoat*
Honorary Award: Eddie Cantor
Irving Thalberg Memorial Award: Buddy Adler

1957
Picture: *The Bridge on the River Kwai*
Foreign-Language Film: *The Nights of Cabiria* (Federico Fellini)
Director: David Lean (*The Bridge on the River Kwai*)
Actor: Alec Guinness (*The Bridge on the River Kwai*)
Actress: Joanne Woodward (*The Three Faces of Eve*)
Supporting Actor: Red Buttons (*Sayonara*)
Supporting Actress: Miyoshi Umeki (*Sayonara*)
Original Story & Screenplay: George Wells (*Designing Woman*)
Adapted Screenplay: Pierre Boulle, Michael Wilson, Carl Foreman (*The Bridge on the River Kwai*)
Cinematography: Jack Hildyard (*The Bridge on the River Kwai*)
Art Direction: Ted Hayworth (*Sayonara*)
Costume Design: Orry-Kelly (*Les Girls*)
Sound: George Groves and Warner Sound Dept (*Sayonara*)
Editing: Peter Taylor (*The Bridge on the River Kwai*)
Special Effects: Walter Rossi (*The Enemy Below*)
Song: 'All the Way' from *The Joker Is Wild* (m James van Heusen, ly Sammy Cahn)
Music Scoring: Malcolm Arnold (*The Bridge on the River Kwai*)
Documentary Feature: *Albert Schweitzer*
Cartoon: *Birds Anonymous*
Live-Action Short: *The Wetback Hound*
Honorary Awards: Charles Brackett; B. B. Kahane; Gilbert 'Bronco Billy' Anderson

1958
Picture: *Gigi*
Foreign-Language Film: *My Uncle* (Jacques Tati)
Director: Vincente Minnelli (*Gigi*)
Actor: David Niven (*Separate Tables*)
Actress: Susan Hayward (*I Want to Live*)

Supporting Actor: Burl Ives (*The Big Country*)
Supporting Actress: Wendy Hiller (*Separate Tables*)
Original Story & Screenplay: Nathan E. Douglas (the blacklisted Ned Young), Harold Jacob Smith (*The Defiant Ones*)
Adapted Screenplay: Alan Jay Lerner (*Gigi*)
B/w Cinematography: Sam Leavitt (*The Defiant Ones*)
Colour Cinematography: Joseph Ruttenberg (*Gigi*)
Art Direction: William A. Horning, Preston Ames (*Gigi*)
Costume Design: Cecil Beaton (*Gigi*)
Sound: Fred Hynes and the Todd-AO Sound Dept (*South Pacific*)
Editing: Adrienne Fazan (*Gigi*)
Special Effects: Tom Howard (*Tom Thumb*)
Song: 'Gigi' from *Gigi* (m Frederick Loewe, ly Alan Jay Lerner)
Scoring of a Drama or Comedy: Dimitri Tiomkin (*The Old Man and the Sea*)
Scoring of a Musical: André Previn (*Gigi*)
Documentary Short: *Ama Girls*
Documentary Feature: *White Wilderness*
Cartoon: *Knighty Knight Bugs*
Live-Action Short: *Grand Canyon*
Honorary Award: Maurice Chevalier
Irving Thalberg Memorial Award: Jack L. Warner

1959
Picture: *Ben Hur*
Foreign-Language Film: *Black Orpheus* (Marcel Camus)
Director: William Wyler (*Ben Hur*)
Actor: Charlton Heston (*Ben Hur*)
Actress: Simone Signoret (*Room at the Top*)
Supporting Actor: Hugh Griffith (*Ben Hur*)
Supporting Actress: Shelley Winters (*The Diary of Anne Frank*)
Original Story & Screenplay: Russell Rouse, Clarence Greene, Stanley Shapiro, Maurice Richlin (*Pillow Talk*)
Adapted Screenplay: Neil Paterson (*Room at the Top*)
B/w Cinematography: William C. Mellor (*The Diary of Anne Frank*)
Colour Cinematography: Robert L. Surtees (*Ben Hur*)
B/w Art Direction: Lyle R. Wheeler, George W. Davis (*The Diary of Anne Frank*)
Colour Art Direction: William A. Horning, Edward Carfagno (*Ben Hur*)
B/w Costume Design: Orry-Kelly (*Some Like It Hot*)
Colour Costume Design: Elizabeth Haffenden (*Ben Hur*)
Sound: Franklin E. Milton and MGM Sound Dept (*Ben Hur*)
Editing: Ralph E. Winters, John D. Dunning (*Ben Hur*)
Special Effects: Arnold Gillespie, Robert MacDonald, Milo Lory (*Ben Hur*)
Song: 'High Hopes' from *A Hole in the Head* (m James Van Heusen, ly Sammy Cahn)
Scoring of a Drama or Comedy: Miklos Rosza (*Ben Hur*)
Scoring of a Musical: André Previn, Kim Darby (*Porgy and Bess*)
Documentary Short: *Glass*
Documentary Feature: *Serengeti Shall Not Die*
Cartoon: *Moonbird*
Live-Action Short: *The Golden Fish*
Honorary Awards: Lee De Forest; Buster Keaton

1960
Picture: *The Apartment*
Foreign-Language Film: *The Virgin Spring* (Ingmar Bergman)
Director: Billy Wilder (*The Apartment*)
Actor: Burt Lancaster (*Elmer Gantry*)
Actress: Elizabeth Taylor (*Butterfield 8*)
Supporting Actor: Peter Ustinov (*Spartacus*)
Supporting Actress: Shirley Jones (*Elmer Gantry*)
Original Story & Screenplay: Billy Wilder, I. A. L. Diamond (*The Apartment*)
Adapted Screenplay: Richard Brooks (*Elmer Gantry*)
B/w Cinematography: Freddie Francis (*Sons and Lovers*)
Colour Cinematography: Russell Metty (*Spartacus*)
B/w Art Direction: Alexander Trauner (*The Apartment*)
Colour Art Direction: Alexander Golitzen, Eric Orbom (*Spartacus*)
B/w Costume Design: Edith Head, Edward Stevenson (*The Facts of Life*)
Colour Costume Design: Valles, Bill Thomas (*Spartacus*)
Sound: Gordon E. Sawyer and Samuel Goldwyn Sound Dept (*The Alamo*)
Editing: Daniel Mandell (*The Apartment*)
Special Effects: Gene Warren, Tim Baar (MGM) (*The Time Machine*)
Song: 'Never on Sunday' from *Never on Sunday* (m/ly Manos Hadjidakis)
Scoring of a Drama or Comedy: Ernest Gold (*Exodus*)
Scoring of a Musical: Morris Stoloff, Harry Sikman (*Song without End*)
Documentary Short: *Giuseppina*
Documentary Feature: *The Horse with the Flying Tail*
Cartoon: *Munro*
Live-Action Short: *Day of the Panther*
Honorary Awards: Gary Cooper; Stan Laurel; Hayley Mills

1961
Picture: *West Side Story*
Foreign-Language Picture: *Through a Glass Darkly* (Ingmar Bergman)
Director: Jerome Robbins, Robert Wise (*West Side Story*)
Actor: Maximilian Schell (*Judgment at Nuremberg*)
Actress: Sophia Loren (*Two Women*)
Supporting Actor: George Chakiris (*West Side Story*)
Supporting Actress: Rita Moreno (*West Side Story*)
Original Story & Screenplay: William Inge (*Splendor in the Grass*)
Adapted Screenplay: Abby Mann (*Judgment at Nuremberg*)
B/w Cinematography: Eugene Schufftan (*The Hustler*)
Colour Cinematography: Daniel L. Fapp (*West Side Story*)
B/w Art Direction: Harry Horner (*The Hustler*)
Colour Art Direction: Boris Leven (*West Side Story*)
B/w Costume Design: Piero Gherardi (*La Dolce Vita*)
Colour Costume Design: Irene Sharaff (*West Side Story*)
Sound: Fred Hynes and Samuel Goldwyn Sound Dept, Gordon E. Sawyer (*West Side Story*)
Editing: Thomas Stanford (*West Side Story*)
Special Effects: Bill Warrington, Vivian C. Greenham (*The Guns of Navarone*)

Song: 'Moon River' from *Breakfast at Tiffany's* (*m* Henry Mancini, *ly* Johnny Mercer)

Scoring of a Drama or Comedy: Henry Mancini (*Breakfast at Tiffany's*)

Scoring of a Musical: Saul Chaplin, Johnny Green, Sid Ramin, Irwin Kostal (*West Side Story*)

Documentary Short: *Project Hope*

Documentary Feature: *Le Ciel et la Boue*

Cartoon: *Ersatz*

Live-Action Short: *Seawards the Great Ships*

Honorary Awards: William L. Hendricks; Fred L. Metzler; Jerome Robbins

Irving Thalberg Memorial Award: Stanley Kramer

1962

Picture: *Lawrence of Arabia*

Foreign-Language Film: *Sundays and Cybele* (Serge Bourgignon)

Director: David Lean (*Lawrence of Arabia*)

Actor: Gregory Peck (*To Kill a Mockingbird*)

Actress: Anne Bancroft (*The Miracle Worker*)

Supporting Actor: Ed Begley (*Sweet Bird of Youth*)

Supporting Actress: Patty Duke (*The Miracle Worker*)

Original Story & Screenplay: Ennio De Concini, Alfredo Gianetti, Pietro Germi (*Divorce Italian Style*)

Adapted Screenplay: Horton Foote (*To Kill a Mockingbird*)

B/w Cinematography: Jean Bourgoin, Walter Wottitz (*The Longest Day*)

Colour Cinematography: Fred A. Young (*Lawrence of Arabia*)

B/w Art Direction: Alexander Golitzen, Henry Bumstead (*To Kill a Mockingbird*)

Colour Art Direction: John Box, John Stoll (*Lawrence of Arabia*)

B/w Costume Design: Norma Koch (*What Ever Happened to Baby Jane?*)

Colour Costume Design: Mary Wills (*The Wonderful World of the Brothers Grimm*)

Sound: John Cox, Shepperton Studio Sound Dept (*Lawrence of Arabia*)

Editing: Anne Coates (*Lawrence of Arabia*)

Special Effects: Robert MacDonald, Jacques Maumont (*The Longest Day*)

Song: 'Days of Wine and Roses' from *Days of Wine and Roses* (*m* Henry Mancini, *ly* Johnny Mercer)

Original Score: Maurice Jarre (*Lawrence of Arabia*)

Adapted Score: Ray Heindorf (*The Music Man*)

Documentary Short: *Dylan Thomas*

Documentary Feature: *Black Fox*

Cartoon: *The Hole*

Live-Action Short: *Happy Anniversary*

1963

Picture: *Tom Jones*

Foreign-Language Film: *8½* (Federico Fellini)

Director: Tony Richardson (*Tom Jones*)

Actor: Sidney Poitier (*Lilies of the Field*)

Actress: Patricia Neal (*Hud*)

Supporting Actor: Melvyn Douglas (*Hud*)

Supporting Actress: Margaret Rutherford (*The VIPs*)

Original Story & Screenplay: James R. Webb (*How the West Was Won*)

Adapted Screenplay: John Osborne (*Tom Jones*)

B/w Cinematography: James Wong Howe (*Hud*)

Colour Cinematography: Leon Shamroy (*Cleopatra*)

B/w Art Direction: Gene Callahan (*America America*)

Colour Art Direction: John DeCuir, Jack Martin Smith, Hilyard Brown, Herman Blumenthal, Elven Webb, Maurice Pelling, Boris Juraga (*Cleopatra*)

B/w Costume Design: Piero Gherardi (*8½*)

Colour Costume Design: Irene Sharaff, Vittorio Nino Novarese, Renie (*Cleopatra*)

Visual Effects: Emil Kosa Jnr (*Cleopatra*)

Sound Effects: Walter G. Elliott (*It's a Mad, Mad, Mad, Mad World*)

Sound: Franklin E. Milton, MGM Sound Dept (*How the West Was Won*)

Editing: Harold F. Cress (*How the West Was Won*)

Song: 'Call Me Irresponsible' from *Papa's Delicate Condition* (*m* James Van Heusen, *ly* Sammy Cahn)

Original Score: John Addison (*Tom Jones*)

Adapted Score: André Previn (*Irma La Douce*)

Documentary Short: *Chagall*

Documentary Feature: *Robert Frost: A Lover's Quarrel with the World*

Cartoon: *The Critic*

Live-Action Short: *An Occurrence at Owl Creek Bridge*

Irving Thalberg Memorial Award: Sam Spiegel

1964

Picture: *My Fair Lady*

Foreign-Language Film: *Yesterday, Today and Tomorrow* (Vittorio De Sica)

Director: George Cukor (*My Fair Lady*)

Actor: Rex Harrison (*My Fair Lady*)

Actress: Julie Andrews (*Mary Poppins*)

Supporting Actor: Peter Ustinov (*Topkapi*)

Supporting Actress: Lila Kedrova (*Zorba the Greek*)

Original Story & Screenplay: S. H. Barnett, Peter Stone, Frank Tarloff (*Father Goose*)

Adapted Screenplay: Edward Anhalt (*Becket*)

B/w Cinematography: Walter Lassally (*Zorba the Greek*)

Colour Cinematography: Harry Stradling (*My Fair Lady*)

B/w Art Direction: Vassilis Fotopoulos (*Zorba the Greek*)

Colour Art Direction: Gene Allen, Cecil Beaton (*My Fair Lady*)

B/w Costume Design: Dorothy Jeakins (*The Night of the Iguana*)

Colour Costume Design: Cecil Beaton (*My Fair Lady*)

Visual Effects: Peter Ellenshaw, Hamilton Luske, Eustace Lycett (*Mary Poppins*)

Sound Effects: Norman Wanstall (*Goldfinger*)

Sound: George R. Groves, Warner Sound Dept (*My Fair Lady*)

Editing: Cotton Warburton (*Mary Poppins*)

Song: 'Chim Chim Cheree' from *Mary Poppins* (*m/ly* Richard M. Sherman, Robert B. Sherman)

Original Score: Richard M. Sherman, Robert B. Sherman (*Mary Poppins*)

Adapted Score: André Previn (*My Fair Lady*)

Documentary Short: *Nine from Little Rock*
Documentary Feature: *Jacques-Yves Cousteau's World without Sun*
Cartoon: *The Pink Phink*
Live-Action Short: *Casals Conducts: 1964*
Honorary Award: William Tuttle (for make-up on *Seven Faces of Dr Lao*)

1965
Picture: *The Sound of Music*
Foreign-Language Film: *The Shop on Main Street* (Jan Kadar)
Director: Robert Wise (*The Sound of Music*)
Actor: Lee Marvin (*Cat Ballou*)
Actress: Julie Christie (*Darling*)
Supporting Actor: Martin Balsam (*A Thousand Clowns*)
Supporting Actress: Shelley Winters (*A Patch of Blue*)
Original Story & Screenplay: Frederic Raphael (*Darling*)
Adapted Screenplay: Robert Bolt (*Dr Zhivago*)
B/w Cinematography: Ernest Laszlo (*Ship of Fools*)
Colour Cinematography: Freddie Young (*Dr Zhivago*)
B/w Art Direction: Robert Clatworthy (*Ship of Fools*)
Colour Art Direction: John Box, Terry Marsh (*Dr Zhivago*)
B/w Costume Design: Julie Harris (*Darling*)
Colour Costume Design: Phyllis Dalton (*Dr Zhivago*)
Visual Effects: John Stears (*Thunderball*)
Sound Effects: Tregoweth Brown (*The Great Race*)
Sound: James P. Corcoran, TCF Sound Dept, Fred Hynes, Todd-AO Sound Dept (*The Sound of Music*)
Editing: William Reynolds (*The Sound of Music*)
Song: 'The Shadow of Your Smile' from *The Sandpiper* (*m* Johnny Mandel, *ly* Paul Francis Webster)
Original Score: Maurice Jarre (*Dr Zhivago*)
Adapted Score: Irwin Kostal (*The Sound of Music*)
Documentary Short: *To Be Alive!*
Documentary Feature: *The Eleanor Roosevelt Story*
Cartoon: *The Dot and the Line*
Live-Action Short: *The Chicken*
Honorary Award: Bob Hope
Irving Thalberg Memorial Award: William Wyler

1966
Picture: *A Man for All Seasons*
Foreign-Language Film: *A Man and a Woman* (Claude Lelouch)
Director: Fred Zinnemann (*A Man for All Seasons*)
Actor: Paul Scofield (*A Man for All Seasons*)
Actress: Elizabeth Taylor (*Who's Afraid of Virginia Woolf?*)
Supporting Actor: Walter Matthau (*The Fortune Cookie*)
Supporting Actress: Sandy Dennis (*Who's Afraid of Virginia Woolf?*)
Original Story & Screenplay: Claude Lelouch, Pierre Uytterhoeven (*A Man and a Woman*)
Adapted Screenplay: Robert Bolt (*A Man for All Seasons*)
B/w Cinematography: Haskell Wexler (*Who's Afraid of Virginia Woolf?*)
Colour Cinematography: Ted Moore (*A Man for All Seasons*)
B/w Art Direction: Richard Sylbert (*Who's Afraid of Virginia Woolf?*)

Colour Art Direction: Jack Martin Smith, Dale Hennesy (*Fantastic Voyage*)
B/w Costume Design: Irene Sharaff (*Who's Afraid of Virginia Woolf?*)
Colour Costume Design: Elizabeth Haffenden, Joan Bridge (*A Man for All Seasons*)
Visual Effects: Art Cruickshank (*Fantastic Voyage*)
Sound Effects: Gordon Daniel (*Grand Prix*)
Sound: Franklin E. Milton, MGM Sound Dept (*Grand Prix*)
Editing: Frederic Steinkamp, Henry Berman, Stewart Linder, Frank Santillo (*Grand Prix*)
Song: 'Born Free' from *Born Free* (*m* John Barry, *ly* Don Black)
Original Score: John Barry (*Born Free*)
Adapted Score: Ken Thorne (*A Funny Thing Happened on the Way to the Forum*)
Documentary Short: *A Year toward Tomorrow*
Documentary Feature: *The War Game*
Cartoon: *Herb Alpert and the Tijuana Brass Double Feature*
Live-Action Short: *Wild Wings*
Honorary Award: Yakima Canutt
Irving Thalberg Memorial Award: Robert Wise

1967
Picture: *In the Heat of the Night*
Foreign-Language Film: *Closely Observed Trains* (Jiri Menzel)
Director: Mike Nichols (*The Graduate*)
Actor: Rod Steiger (*In the Heat of the Night*)
Actress: Katharine Hepburn (*Guess Who's Coming to Dinner*)
Supporting Actor: George Kennedy (*Cool Hand Luke*)
Supporting Actress: Estelle Parsons (*Bonnie and Clyde*)
Original Story & Screenplay: William Rose (*Guess Who's Coming to Dinner*)
Adapted Screenplay: Sterling Silliphant (*In the Heat of the Night*)
Cinematography: Burnett Guffey (*Bonnie and Clyde*)
Art Direction: John Truscott, Edward Carrere (*Camelot*)
Costume Design: John Truscott (*Camelot*)
Special Effects: L. B. Abbott (*Doctor Dolittle*)
Sound Effects: John Poyner (*The Dirty Dozen*)
Sound: Samuel Goldwyn Studio Dept (*In the Heat of the Night*)
Editing: Hal Ashby (*In the Heat of the Night*)
Song: 'Talk to the Animals' from *Doctor Dolittle* (*m/ly* Leslie Bricusse)
Original Score: Elmer Bernstein (*Thoroughly Modern Millie*)
Adapted Score: Alfred Newman, Ken Darby (*Camelot*)
Documentary Short: *The Redwoods*
Documentary Feature: *The Anderson Platoon*
Cartoon: *The Box*
Live-Action Short: *A Place to Stand*
Honorary Award: Arthur Freed
Irving Thalberg Memorial Award: Alfred Hitchcock

1968
Picture: *Oliver!*
Director: Carol Reed (*Oliver!*)
Actor: Cliff Robertson (*Charly*)
Actress: Katharine Hepburn (*The Lion in Winter*)

Supporting Actor: Jack Albertson (*The Subject Was Roses*)
Supporting Actress: Ruth Gordon (*Rosemary's Baby*)
Original Story & Screenplay: Mel Brooks (*The Producers*)
Adapted Screenplay: James Goldman (*The Lion in Winter*)
Cinematography: Pasqualino De Santis (*Romeo and Juliet*)
Art Direction: John Box, Terence Marsh (*Oliver!*)
Costume Design: Danilo Donati (*Romeo and Juliet*)
Sound: Shepperton Sound Dept (*Oliver!*)
Editing: Frank P. Keller (*Bullitt*)
Special Effects: Stanley Kubrick (*2001: A Space Odyssey*)
Song: 'The Windmills of Your Mind' from *The Thomas Crown Affair* (m Michel Legrand, ly Alan and Marilyn Bergman)
Original Score: John Barry (*The Lion in Winter*)
Scoring of a Musical: John Green (*Oliver!*)
Documentary Short: *Why Man Creates*
Documentary Feature: *Journey into Self*
Cartoon: *Winnie the Pooh and the Blustery Day*
Live-Action Short: *Robert Kennedy Remembered*
Honorary Awards: John Chambers (make-up for *Planet of the Apes*); Onna White (choreography for *Oliver!*)

1969
Picture: *Midnight Cowboy*
Foreign-Language Film: *Z* (Costa-Gavras)
Director: John Schlesinger (*Midnight Cowboy*)
Actor: John Wayne (*True Grit*)
Actress: Maggie Smith (*The Prime of Miss Jean Brodie*)
Supporting Actor: Gig Young (*They Shoot Horses, Don't They?*)
Supporting Actress: Goldie Hawn (*Cactus Flower*)
Original Story & Screenplay: William Goldman (*Butch Cassidy and the Sundance Kid*)
Adapted Screenplay: Waldo Salt (*Midnight Cowboy*)
Cinematography: Arthur Ibbetson (*Anne of the Thousand Days*)
Art Direction: John DeCuir, Jack Martin Smith, Herman Blumenthal (*Hello, Dolly!*)
Costume Design: Margaret Furse (*Anne of the Thousand Days*)
Sound: Jack Solomon, Murray Spivack (*Hello, Dolly!*)
Editing: Françoise Bonnot (*Z*)
Special Effects: Robbie Robertson (*Marooned*)
Song: 'Raindrops Keep Fallin' on My Head' from *Butch Cassidy and the Sundance Kid* (m Burt Bacharach, ly Hal David)
Original Score: Burt Bacharach (*Butch Cassidy and the Sundance Kid*)
Scoring of a Musical: Lennie Hayton, Lionel Newman (*Hello, Dolly!*)
Documentary Short: *Czechoslovakia 1968*
Documentary Feature: *Arthur Rubinstein – the Love of Life*
Cartoon: *It's Tough to Be a Bird*
Live-Action Short: *The Magic Machines*
Honorary Award: Cary Grant

1970
Picture: *Patton*
Foreign-Language Film: *Investigation of a Citizen above Suspicion* (Elio Petri)

Director: Franklin J. Schaffner (*Patton*)
Actor: George C. Scott (*Patton*)
Actress: Glenda Jackson (*Women in Love*)
Supporting Actor: John Mills (*Ryan's Daughter*)
Supporting Actress: Helen Hayes (*Airport*)
Original Story & Screenplay: Francis Ford Coppola, Edmund H. North (*Patton*)
Adapted Screenplay: Ring Lardner Jnr (*M*A*S*H*)
Cinematography: Freddie Young (*Ryan's Daughter*)
Art Direction: Urie McCleary, Gil Parrondo (*Patton*)
Costume Design: Nino Novarese (*Cromwell*)
Sound: Douglas Williams, Don Bassman (*Patton*)
Editing: Hugh S. Fowler (*Patton*)
Special Effects: A. D. Flowers, L. B. Abbott (*Tora! Tora! Tora!*)
Song: 'For All We Know' from *Lovers and Other Strangers* (m Fred Karlin, ly Robb Royer, James Griffin)
Original Score: Francis Lai (*Love Story*)
Original Song Score: The Beatles (*Let It Be*)
Documentary Short: *Interviews with Mai Lai Veterans*
Documentary Feature: *Woodstock*
Cartoon: *Is It Always Right to Be Right*
Live-Action Short: *The Resurrection of Bronco Billy*
Honorary Awards: Lillian Gish; Orson Welles
Irving Thalberg Memorial Award: Ingmar Bergman

1971
Picture: *The French Connection*
Foreign-Language Film: *The Garden of the Finzi-Continis* (Vittorio De Sica)
Director: William Friedkin (*The French Connection*)
Actor: Gene Hackman (*The French Connection*)
Actress: Jane Fonda (*Klute*)
Supporting Actor: Ben Johnson (*The Last Picture Show*)
Supporting Actress: Cloris Leachman (*The Last Picture Show*)
Original Story & Screenplay: Paddy Chayevsky (*The Hospital*)
Adapted Screenplay: Ernest Tidyman (*The French Connection*)
Cinematography: Oswald Morris (*Fiddler on the Roof*)
Art Direction: John Box, Ernest Archer, Jack Maxsted, Gil Parrondo (*Nicholas and Alexandra*)
Costume Design: Yvonne Blake, Antonio Castillo (*Nicholas and Alexandra*)
Sound: Gordon K. McCallum, David Hildyard (*Fiddler on the Roof*)
Editing: Jerry Greenberg (*The French Connection*)
Special Effects: Alan Maley, Eustace Lycett, Danny Lee (*Bedknobs and Broomsticks*)
Song: Theme from *Shaft* (m/ly Isaac Hayes)
Original Dramatic Score: Michel Legrand (*Summer of '42*)
Adaptation and Original Song Score: John Williams (*Fiddler on the Roof*)
Documentary Short: *Sentinels of Silence*
Documentary Feature: *The Hellstrom Chronicle*
Animated Film: *The Crunch Bird*
Live-Action Short: *Sentinels of Silence*
Honorary Award: Charles Chaplin

1972
Picture: *The Godfather*

Foreign-Language Film: *The Discreet Charm of the Bourgeoisie* (Luis Buñuel)
Director: Bob Fosse (*Cabaret*)
Actor: Marlon Brando (*The Godfather*)
Actress: Liza Minnelli (*Cabaret*)
Supporting Actor: Joel Grey (*Cabaret*)
Supporting Actress: Eileen Heckart (*Butterflies Are Free*)
Original Story & Screenplay: Jeremy Larner (*The Candidate*)
Adapted Screenplay: Mario Puzo, Francis Ford Coppola (*The Godfather*)
Cinematography: Geoffrey Unsworth (*Cabaret*)
Art Direction: Rolf Zehetbauer, Jurgen Kiebach (*Cabaret*)
Costume Design: Anthony Powell (*Travels with My Aunt*)
Sound: Robert Knudson, David Hildyard (*Cabaret*)
Editing: David Bretherton (*Cabaret*)
Song: 'The Morning After' from *The Poseidon Adventure* (*m/ly* Al Kasha, Joel Hirschhorn)
Original Dramatic Score: Charles Chaplin, Raymond Rasch, Larry Russell (*Limelight*)
Adaptation and Original Song Score: Ralph Burns (*Cabaret*)
Documentary Short: *This Tiny World*
Documentary Feature: *Marjoe*
Animated Film: *A Christmas Carol*
Live-Action Short: *Norman Rockwell's World . . . An American Dream*
Special Achievement Award: L. B. Abbott, A. D. Flowers (for visual effects, *The Poseidon Adventure*)
Honorary Award: Edward G. Robinson

1973
Picture: *The Sting*
Foreign-Language Film: *Day for Night* (François Truffaut)
Director: George Roy Hill (*The Sting*)
Actor: Jack Lemmon (*Save the Tiger*)
Actress: Glenda Jackson (*A Touch of Class*)
Supporting Actor: John Houseman (*The Paper Chase*)
Supporting Actress: Tatum O'Neal (*Paper Moon*)
Original Story & Screenplay: David S. Ward (*The Sting*)
Adapted Screenplay: William Peter Blatty (*The Exorcist*)
Cinematography: Sven Nykvist (*Cries and Whispers*)
Art Direction: Henry Bumstead (*The Sting*)
Costume Design: Edith Head (*The Sting*)
Sound: Robert Knudson, Chris Newman (*The Exorcist*)
Editing: William Reynolds (*The Sting*)
Song: 'The Way We Were' from 'The Way We Were' (*m* Marvin Hamlisch, *ly* Alan and Marilyn Bergman)
Original Dramatic Score: Marvin Hamlisch (*The Way We Were*)
Adaptation and Original Song Score: Marvin Hamlisch (*The Sting*)
Documentary Short: *Princeton: A Search for Answers*
Documentary Feature: *The Great American Cowboy*
Animated Film: *Frank Film*
Live-Action Short: *The Bolero*
Honorary Awards: Henri Langlois; Groucho Marx
Irving Thalberg Memorial Award: Lawrence Weingarten

1974
Picture: *The Godfather Part II*

Foreign-Language Film: *Amarcord* (Federico Fellini)
Director: Francis Ford Coppola (*The Godfather Part II*)
Actor: Art Carney (*Harry and Tonto*)
Actress: Ellen Burstyn (*Alice Doesn't Live Here Any More*)
Supporting Actor: Robert De Niro (*The Godfather Part II*)
Supporting Actress: Ingrid Bergman (*Murder on the Orient Express*)
Original Story & Screenplay: Robert Towne (*Chinatown*)
Adapted Screenplay: Francis Ford Coppola, Mario Puzo (*The Godfather Part II*)
Cinematography: Fred Koenekamp, Joseph Biroc (*The Towering Inferno*)
Art Direction: Dean Tavoularis, Angelo Graham (*The Godfather Part II*)
Costume Design: Theoni V. Aldredge (*The Great Gatsby*)
Sound: Ronald Pierce, Melvin Metcalfe Snr (*Earthquake*)
Editing: Harold F. Kress, Carl Kress (*The Towering Inferno*)
Song: 'We May Never Love Like This Again' from *The Towering Inferno* (*m/ly* Al Kasha, Joel Hirshhorn)
Original Dramatic Score: Nino Rota, Carmine Coppola (*The Godfather Part II*)
Adaptation and Original Song Score: Nelson Riddle (*The Great Gatsby*)
Documentary Short: *Don't*
Documentary Feature: *Hearts and Minds*
Animated Film: *Closed Mondays*
Live-Action Short: *One-Eyed Men Are Kings*
Honorary Awards: Howard Hawks; Jean Renoir
Special Achievement Award: Frank Brendel, Glen Robinson, Albert Whitlock (for visual effects, *Earthquake*)

1975
Picture: *One Flew over the Cuckoo's Nest*
Foreign-Language Film: *Dersu Uzala* (Akira Kurosawa)
Director: Milos Forman (*One Flew over the Cuckoo's Nest*)
Actor: Jack Nicholson (*One Flew over the Cuckoo's Nest*)
Actress: Louise Fletcher (*One Flew over the Cuckoo's Nest*)
Supporting Actor: George Burns (*The Sunshine Boys*)
Supporting Actress: Lee Grant (*Shampoo*)
Original Screenplay: Frank Pierson (*Dog Day Afternoon*)
Adapted Screenplay: Lawrence Hauben, Bo Goldman (*One Flew over the Cuckoo's Nest*)
Cinematography: John Alcott (*Barry Lyndon*)
Art Direction: Ken Adam, Roy Walker (*Barry Lyndon*)
Costume Design: Britt Soderland, Milena Canonero (*Barry Lyndon*)
Sound: Robert L. Hoyt, Roger Heman, Earl Madery, John Carter (*Jaws*)
Editing: Verna Fields (*Jaws*)
Song: 'I'm Easy' from *Nashville* (*m/ly* Keith Carradine)
Original Score: John Williams (*Jaws*)
Adaptation and Original Song Score: Leonard Rosenman (*Barry Lyndon*)
Documentary Short: *The End of the Game*
Documentary Feature: *The Man Who Skied Down Everest*
Animated Film: *Great*
Live-Action Short: *Angel and Big Joe*
Honorary Award: Mary Pickford

Special Achievement Awards: Peter Berkos (sound effects, *The Hindenburg*); Albert Whitlock and Glen Robinson (visual effects, *The Hindenburg*)
Irving Thalberg Memorial Award: Mervyn Le Roy

1976
Picture: *Rocky*
Foreign-Language Film: *Black and White in Colour* (Jean-Jacques Annaud)
Director: John G. Avildsen (*Rocky*)
Actor: Peter Finch (*Network*)
Actress: Faye Dunaway (*Network*)
Supporting Actor: Jason Robards (*All the President's Men*)
Supporting Actress: Beatrice Straight (*Network*)
Original Screenplay: Paddy Chayevsky (*Network*)
Adapted Screenplay: William Goldman (*All the President's Men*)
Cinematography: Haskell Wexler (*Bound for Glory*)
Art Direction: George Jenkins (*All the President's Men*)
Costume Design: Danilo Donati (*Fellini's Casanova*)
Sound: Arthur Piantadosi, Les Fresholtz, Dick Alexander, Jim Webb (*All the President's Men*)
Editing: Richard Halsey, Scott Conrad (*Rocky*)
Song: 'Evergreen' from *A Star Is Born* (*m* Barbra Streisand, *ly* Paul Williams)
Original Score: Jerry Goldsmith (*The Omen*)
Adaptation and Original Song Score: Leonard Rosenman (*Bound for Glory*)
Documentary Short: *Number Our Days*
Documentary Feature: *Harlan County, USA*
Animated Film: *Leisure*
Live-Action Short: *In the Region of Ice*
Special Achievement Awards: Carlo Rambaldi, Glen Robinson, Frank Van Der Veer (visual effects, *King Kong*); L. B. Abbott, Glen Robinson, Matthew Yuricich (visual effects, *Logan's Run*)
Irving Thalberg Memorial Award: Pandro S. Berman

1977
Picture: *Annie Hall*
Foreign-Language Film: *Madame Rosa* (Moshe Mizrahi)
Director: Woody Allen (*Annie Hall*)
Actor: Richard Dreyfuss (*The Goodbye Girl*)
Actress: Diane Keaton (*Annie Hall*)
Supporting Actor: Jason Robards (*Julia*)
Supporting Actress: Vanessa Redgrave (*Julia*)
Original Screenplay: Woody Allen, Marshall Brickman (*Annie Hall*)
Adapted Screenplay: Alvin Sargent (*Julia*)
Cinematography: Vilmos Zsigmond (*Close Encounters of the Third Kind*)
Art Direction: John Barry, Norman Reynolds, Leslie Dilley (*Star Wars*)
Costume Design: John Mollo (*Star Wars*)
Sound: Don MacDougall, Ray West, Bob Minkler, Derek Ball (*Star Wars*)
Editing: Marcia Lucas, Richard Chew (*Star Wars*)

Visual Effects: John Stears, John Dystra, Richard Edlund, Grant McCune, Robert Black (*Stars Wars*)
Song: 'You Light Up My Life' from *You Light Up My Life* (*m/ly* Joseph Brooks)
Adaptation and Original Song Score: Jonathan Tunick (*A Little Night Music*)
Documentary Short: *Gravity Is My Enemy*
Documentary Feature: *Who Are the DeBolts? And Where Did They Get Nineteen Kids?*
Animated Film: *Sand Castle*
Live-Action Short: *I'll Find a Way*
Honorary Award: Margaret Booth (for contribution to the art of film editing)
Special Achievement Awards: Frank Warner (sound effects editing, *Close Encounters of the Third Kind*); Benjamin Burtt Jnr (sound effects, *Star Wars*)
Irving Thalberg Memorial Award: Walter Mirisch

1978
Picture: *The Deer Hunter*
Foreign-Language Film: *Get Out Your Handkerchiefs* (Bertrand Blier)
Director: Michael Cimino (*The Deer Hunter*)
Actor: Jon Voight (*Coming Home*)
Actress: Jane Fonda (*Coming Home*)
Supporting Actor: Christopher Walken (*The Deer Hunter*)
Supporting Actress: Maggie Smith (*California Suite*)
Original Screenplay: Nancy Dowd, Waldo Salt, Robert C. Jones (*Coming Home*)
Adapted Screenplay: Oliver Stone (*Midnight Express*)
Cinematography: Nestor Almendros (*Days of Heaven*)
Art Direction: Paul Sylbert, Edwin O'Donovan (*Heaven Can Wait*)
Costume Design: Anthony Powell (*Death on the Nile*)
Sound: Richard Portman, William McCaughey, Aaron Rochin, Darrin Knight (*The Deer Hunter*)
Editing: Peter Zinner (*The Deer Hunter*)
Song: 'Last Dance' from *Thank God It's Friday* (*m/ly* Paul Jabara)
Original Score: Giorgio Moroder (*Midnight Express*)
Adaptation and Original Song Score: Joe Renzetti (*The Buddy Holly Story*)
Documentary Short: *The Flight of the Gossamer Condor*
Documentary Feature: *Scared Straight*
Animated Film: *Special Delivery*
Live-Action Short: *Teenage Father*
Honorary Awards: Walter Lantz (for his animated pictures); Laurence Olivier (for the full body of his work); King Vidor (for his incomparable achievements)
Special Achievement Award: Les Bowie, Colin Chilvers, Denys Coop, Roy Field, Derek Meddings, Zoran Perisic (visual effects, *Superman*)

1979
Picture: *Kramer vs Kramer*
Foreign-Language Film: *The Tin Drum* (Volker Schlöndorff)
Director: Robert Benton (*Kramer vs Kramer*)
Actor: Dustin Hoffman (*Kramer vs Kramer*)

Actress: Sally Field (*Norma Rae*)
Supporting Actor: Melvyn Douglas (*Being There*)
Supporting Actress: Meryl Streep (*Kramer vs Kramer*)
Original Screenplay: Steve Tesich (*Breaking Away*)
Adapted Screenplay: Robert Benton (*Kramer vs Kramer*)
Cinematography: Vittorio Storaro (*Apocalypse Now*)
Art Direction: Philip Rosenberg, Tony Walton (*All That Jazz*)
Costume Design: Albert Wolsky (*All That Jazz*)
Sound: Walter Murch, Mark Berger, Richard Beggs, Nat Boxer (*Apocalypse Now*)
Editing: Alan Heim (*All That Jazz*)
Visual Effects: H. R. Giger, Carlo Rambaldi, Brian Johnson, Nick Allder, Denys Ayling (*Alien*)
Song: 'It Goes Like It Goes' from *Norma Rae* (m David Shire, ly Norman Gimbel)
Original Score: Georges Delerue (*A Little Romance*)
Adaptation and Original Song Score: Ralph Burns (*All That Jazz*)
Documentary Short: *Paul Robeson: Tribute to an Artist*
Documentary Feature: *Best Boy*
Animated Film: *Every Child*
Live-Action Short: *Board and Care*
Honorary Award: Alec Guinness (for advancing the art of screen acting)
Special Achievement Award: Alan Splet (sound editing, *The Black Stallion*)
Irving Thalberg Memorial Award: Ray Stark

1980

Picture: *Ordinary People*
Foreign-Language Film: *Moscow Does Not Believe in Tears* (Vladimir Menshov)
Director: Robert Redford (*Ordinary People*)
Actor: Robert De Niro (*Raging Bull*)
Actress: Sissy Spacek (*The Coal Miner's Daughter*)
Supporting Actor: Timothy Hutton (*Ordinary People*)
Supporting Actress: Mary Steenburgen (*Melvin and Howard*)
Original Screenplay: Bo Goldman (*Melvin and Howard*)
Adapted Screenplay: Alvin Sargent (*Ordinary People*)
Cinematography: Geoffrey Unsworth, Ghislain Cloquet (*Tess*)
Art Direction: Pierre Guffroy, Jack Stephens (*Tess*)
Costume Design: Anthony Powell (*Tess*)
Sound: Bill Varney, Steve Maslow, Gregg Landacker, Peter Sutton (*The Empire Strikes Back*)
Editing: Thelma Schoonmaker (*Raging Bull*)
Song: 'Fame' from *Fame* (m Michael Gore, ly Dean Pitchford)
Original Score: Michael Gore (*Fame*)
Documentary Short: *Karl Hess: Towards Liberty*
Documentary Feature: *From Mao to Mozart: Isaac Stern in China*
Animated Film: *The Fly*
Live Action Short: *The Dollar Bottom*
Honorary Award: Henry Fonda (in recognition of his brilliant accomplishments)
Special Achievement Award: Brian Johnson, Richard Edlund, Dennis Muren, Bruce Nicholson (visual effects, *The Empire Strikes Back*)

1981

Picture: *Chariots of Fire*
Foreign-Language Film: *Mephisto* (Istvan Szabo)
Director: Warren Beatty (*Reds*)
Actor: Henry Fonda (*On Golden Pond*)
Actress: Katharine Hepburn (*On Golden Pond*)
Supporting Actor: John Gielgud (*Arthur*)
Supporting Actress: Maureen Stapleton (*Reds*)
Original Screenplay: Colin Welland (*Chariots of Fire*)
Adapted Screenplay: Ernest Thompson (*On Golden Pond*)
Cinematography: Vittorio Storaro (*Reds*)
Art Direction: Norman Reynolds, Leslie Dilley (*Raiders of the Lost Ark*)
Costume Design: Milena Canonero (*Chariots of Fire*)
Make-Up: Rick Baker (*An American Werewolf in London*)
Sound: Bill Varney, Steve Maslow, Gregg Landaker, Roy Charman (*Raiders of the Lost Ark*)
Editing: Michael Kahn (*Raiders of the Lost Ark*)
Song: 'Arthur's Theme' from *Arthur* (m/ly Burt Bacharach, Carole Bayer Sager, Christopher Cross, Peter Allen)
Original Score: Vangelis (*Chariots of Fire*)
Documentary Short: *Close Harmony*
Documentary Feature: *Genocide*
Animated Film: *Crac*
Live-Action Short: *Violet*
Honorary Award: Barbara Stanwyck
Special Achievement Awards: Ben Burtt, Richard L. Anderson (sound effects editing, *Raiders of the Lost Ark*)
Irving Thalberg Memorial Award: Albert R. Broccoli

1982

Picture: *Gandhi*
Foreign-Language Picture: *To Begin Again* (José Luis Garci)
Director: Richard Attenborough (*Gandhi*)
Actor: Ben Kingsley (*Gandhi*)
Actress: Meryl Streep (*Sophie's Choice*)
Supporting Actor: Louis Gossett Jnr (*An Officer and a Gentleman*)
Supporting Actress: Jessica Lange (*Tootsie*)
Original Screenplay: John Briley (*Gandhi*)
Adapted Screenplay: Costa-Gavras, Donald Stewart (*Missing*)
Cinematography: Billy Williams, Ronnie Taylor (*Gandhi*)
Art Direction: Stuart Craig, Bob Lang (*Gandhi*)
Costume Design: John Mollo, Bhanu Athaiya (*Gandhi*)
Make-Up: Sarah Monzani, Michele Burke (*Quest for Fire*)
Sound: Robert Knudson, Robert Glass, Don Digirolamo, Gene Cantemassa (*ET*)
Sound Effects Editing: Charles L. Campbell, Ben Burtt (*ET*)
Editing: John Bloom (*Gandhi*)
Visual Effects: Carlo Rambaldi, Dennis Muren, Kenneth F. Smith (*ET*)
Song: 'Up Where We Belong' from *An Officer and a Gentleman* (m Jack Nitzsche, Buffy Sainte-Marie, ly Will Jennings)
Original Score: John Williams (*ET*)
Original Song Score or Adaptation: Henry Mancini, Leslie Bricusse (*Victor/Victoria*)
Documentary Short: *If You Love This Planet*
Documentary Feature: *Just Another Missing Kid*

Animated Film: *Tango*
Live-Action Short: *A Shocking Accident*
Honorary Award: Mickey Rooney

1983

Picture: *Terms of Endearment*
Foreign-Language Film: *Fanny and Alexander* (Ingmar Bergman)
Director: James L. Brooks (*Terms of Endearment*)
Actor: Robert Duvall (*Tender Mercies*)
Actress: Shirley MacLaine (*Terms of Endearment*)
Supporting Actor: Jack Nicholson (*Terms of Endearment*)
Supporting Actress: Linda Hunt (*The Year of Living Dangerously*)
Original Screenplay: Horton Foote (*Tender Mercies*)
Adapted Screenplay: James L. Brooks (*Terms of Endearment*)
Cinematography: Sven Nykvist (*Fanny and Alexander*)
Art Direction: Anna Asp (*Fanny and Alexander*)
Costume Design: Marik Vos (*Fanny and Alexander*)
Sound: Mark Berger, Tom Scott, Randy Thom, David MacMillan (*The Right Stuff*)
Sound Effects Editing: Jay Boekelheide (*The Right Stuff*)
Editing: Glenn Farr, Lisa Fruchtman, Stephen A. Rotter, Douglas Stewart, Tom Rolf (*The Right Stuff*)
Song: 'Flashdance' from *Flashdance* (*m* Giorgio Moroder, *ly* Keith Forsey, Irene Cara)
Original Score: Bill Conti (*The Right Stuff*)
Original Song Score or Adaptation: Michel Legrand, Alan and Marilyn Bergman (*Yentl*)
Documentary Short: *Flamenco at 5:15*
Documentary Feature: *He Makes Me Feel Like Dancin'*
Animated Film: *Sundae in New York*
Live-Action Short: *Boys and Girls*
Honorary Award: Hal Roach
Special Achievement Awards: Richard Edlund, Dennis Muren, Ken Ralston, Phil Tippett (visual effects, *Return of the Jedi*)

1984

Picture: *Amadeus*
Foreign-Language Film: *Dangerous Moves* (Richard Dembo)
Director: Milos Forman (*Amadeus*)
Actor: F. Murray Abraham (*Amadeus*)
Actress: Sally Field (*Places in the Heart*)
Supporting Actor: Haing S. Ngor (*The Killing Fields*)
Supporting Actress: Peggy Ashcroft (*A Passage to India*)
Original Screenplay: Robert Benton (*Places in the Heart*)
Adapted Screenplay: Peter Shaffer (*Amadeus*)
Cinematography: Chris Menges (*The Killing Fields*)
Art Direction: Patrizia Von Brandenstein (*Amadeus*)
Costume Design: Theodor Pistek (*Amadeus*)
Make-Up: Paul LeBlanc, Dick Smith (*Amadeus*)
Sound: Mark Berger, Tom Scott, Todd Boekelheide, Chris Newman (*Amadeus*)
Editing: Jim Clark (*The Killing Fields*)
Visual Effects: Dennis Muren, Michael McAlister, Lorne Petersen, George Gibbs (*Ghostbusters*)
Song: 'I Just Called to Say I Love You' from *The Woman in Red* (*m/ly* Stevie Wonder)
Original Score: Maurice Jarre (*A Passage to India*)

Original Song Score or Adaptation: Prince (*Purple Rain*)
Documentary Short: *The Stone Carvers*
Documentary Feature: *The Times of Harvey Milk*
Animated Film: *Charade*
Live-Action Short: *Up*
Honorary Award: James Stewart
Special Achievement Award: Kay Rose (sound effects editing, *The River*)

1985

Picture: *Out of Africa*
Foreign-Language Film: *The Official Story* (Luis Puenzo)
Director: Sydney Pollack (*Out of Africa*)
Actor: William Hurt (*Kiss of the Spider Woman*)
Actress: Geraldine Page (*The Trip to Bountiful*)
Supporting Actor: Don Ameche (*Cocoon*)
Supporting Actress: Anjelica Huston (*Prizzi's Honor*)
Original Screenplay: William Kelley, Pamela Wallace, Earl W. Wallace (*Witness*)
Adapted Screenplay: Kurt Luedtke (*Out of Africa*)
Cinematography: David Watkin (*Out of Africa*)
Art Direction: Stephen Grimes (*Out of Africa*)
Costume Design: Emi Wada (*Ran*)
Make-Up: Michael Westmore, Zoltan Elek (*Mask*)
Sound: Chris Jenkins, Gary Alexander, Larry Stensvold, Peter Handford (*Out of Africa*)
Sound Effects Editing: Charles L. Campbell, Robert Rutledge (*Back to the Future*)
Editing: Thom Noble (*Witness*)
Visual Effects: Ken Ralston, Ralph McQuarrie, Scott Farrar, David Berry (*Cocoon*)
Song: 'Say You, Say Me' from *White Nights* (*m/ly* Lionel Richie)
Original Score: John Barry (*Out of Africa*)
Documentary Short: *Witness to War*
Documentary Feature: *Broken Rainbow*
Animated Film: *Anna & Bella*
Live-Action Short: *Molly's Pilgrim*
Honorary Awards: Paul Newman; Alex North

1986

Picture: *Platoon*
Foreign-Language Film: *The Assault* (Fons Rademakers)
Director: Oliver Stone (*Platoon*)
Actor: Paul Newman (*The Color of Money*)
Actress: Marlee Matlin (*Children of a Lesser God*)
Supporting Actor: Michael Caine (*Hannah and Her Sisters*)
Supporting Actress: Dianne Wiest (*Hannah and Her Sisters*)
Original Screenplay: Woody Allen (*Hannah and Her Sisters*)
Adapted Screenplay: Ruth Prawer Jhabvala (*A Room with a View*)
Cinematography: Chris Menges (*The Mission*)
Art Direction: Gianni Quaranta, Brian Ackland-Snow (*A Room with a View*)
Costume Design: Jenny Beavan, John Bright (*A Room with a View*)
Make-Up: Chris Walas, Stephan Dupuis (*The Fly*)
Sound: John K. Wilkinson, Richard Rogers, Charles Grenzbach, Simon Kaye (*Platoon*)

Sound Effects Editing: Don Sharpe (*Aliens*)
Editing: Claire Simpson (*Platoon*)
Visual Effects: Robert Skotak, Stan Winston, John Richardson, Suzanne Benson (*Aliens*)
Song: 'Take My Breath Away' from *Top Gun* (*m* Giorgio Moroder, *ly* Tom Whitlock)
Original Score: Herbie Hancock (*Round Midnight*)
Documentary Short: *Women – For America, For the World*
Documentary Feature: *Artie Shaw: Time Is All You've Got*
Animated Film: *A Greek Tragedy*
Live-Action Short: *Precious Images*
Honorary Award: Ralph Bellamy
Irving Thalberg Memorial Award: Steven Spielberg

1987
Picture: *The Last Emperor*
Foreign-Language Film: *Babette's Feast* (Gabriel Axel)
Director: Bernardo Bertolucci (*The Last Emperor*)
Actor: Michael Douglas (*Wall Street*)
Actress: Cher (*Moonstruck*)
Supporting Actor: Sean Connery (*The Untouchables*)
Supporting Actress: Olympia Dukakis (*Moonstruck*)
Original Screenplay: John Patrick Shanley (*Moonstruck*)
Adapted Screenplay: Mark Peploe, Bernardo Bertolucci (*The Last Emperor*)
Cinematography: Vittorio Storaro (*The Last Emperor*)
Art Direction: Ferdinando Scarfiotti (*The Last Emperor*)
Costume Design: James Acheson (*The Last Emperor*)
Make-Up: Rick Bajer (*Harry and the Hendersons*)
Sound: Bill Rowe, Ivan Sharrock (*The Last Emperor*)
Editing: Gabriella Cristiani (*The Last Emperor*)
Visual Effects: Dennis Muren, William George, Harley Jessup, Kenneth Smith (*Innerspace*)
Song: 'The Time of My Life' from *Dirty Dancing* (*m* Franke Previte, John DeNicola, Donald Markowitz, *ly* Franke Previte)
Original Score: Ryuichi Sakamoto, David Byrne, Cong Su (*The Last Emperor*)
Documentary Short: *Young at Heart*
Documentary Feature: *The Ten-Year Lunch: The Wit and Legend of the Algonquin Round Table*
Animated Film: *The Man Who Planted Trees*
Live-Action Short: *Ray's Male Heterosexual Dance Hall*
Special Achievement Awards: Stephen Flick, John Pospisil (sound effects, *Robocop*)
Irving Thalberg Memorial Award: Billy Wilder

1988
Picture: *Rain Man*
Foreign-Language Film: *Pelle the Conqueror* (Bille August)
Director: Barry Levinson (*Rain Man*)
Actor: Dustin Hoffman (*Rain Man*)
Actress: Jodie Foster (*The Accused*)
Supporting Actor: Kevin Kline (*A Fish Called Wanda*)
Supporting Actress: Geena Davis (*The Accidental Tourist*)
Original Screenplay: Ronald Bass, Barry Morrow (*Rain Man*)
Adapted Screenplay: Christopher Hampton (*Dangerous Liaisons*)

Cinematography: Peter Biziou (*Mississippi Burning*)
Art Direction: Stuart Craig (*Dangerous Liaisons*)
Costume Design: James Acheson (*Dangerous Liaisons*)
Make-Up: Ve Neill, Steve LaPorte, Robert Short (*Beetlejuice*)
Sound: Les Fresholtz, Dick Alexander, Vern Poore, Willie D. Burton (*Bird*)
Sound Effects Editing: Charles L. Campbell, Louis L. Edelman (*Who Framed Roger Rabbit?*)
Editing: Arthur Schimdt (*Who Framed Roger Rabbit?*)
Visual Effects: Ken Ralston, Richard Williams, Edward Jones, George Gibbs (*Who Framed Roger Rabbit?*)
Song: 'Let the River Run' from *Working Girl* (*m/ly* Carly Simon)
Original Score: Dave Grusin (*The Milagro Beanfield War*)
Documentary Short: *You Don't Have to Die*
Documentary Feature: *Hotel Terminus: The Life and Times of Klaus Barbie*
Animated Film: *Tin Toy*
Live-Action Short: *The Appointments of Dennis Jennings*
Special Achievement Award: Richard Williams (animation direction, *Who Framed Roger Rabbit?*)

1989
Picture: *Driving Miss Daisy*
Foreign-Language Film: *Cinema Paradiso* (Giuseppe Tornatore)
Director: Oliver Stone (*Born on the Fourth of July*)
Actor: Daniel Day-Lewis (*My Left Foot*)
Actress: Jessica Tandy (*Driving Miss Daisy*)
Supporting Actor: Denzel Washington (*Glory*)
Supporting Actress: Brenda Fricker (*My Left Foot*)
Original Screenplay: Tom Schulman (*Dead Poets Society*)
Adapted Screenplay: Alfred Uhry (*Driving Miss Daisy*)
Cinematography: Freddie Francis (*Glory*)
Art Direction: Anton Furst (*Batman*)
Costume Design: Phyllis Dalton (*Henry V*)
Make-Up: Manlio Rocchetti, Lynn Barber, Kevin Haney (*Driving Miss Daisy*)
Sound: Donald O. Mitchell, Kevin O'Connell, Greg P. Russell, Keith A. Wester (*Black Rain*)
Sound Effects Editing: Ben Burtt, Richard Hymns (*Indiana Jones and the Last Crusade*)
Editing: David Brenner, Joe Hutshing (*Born on the Fourth of July*)
Visual Effects: John Bruno, Dennis Muren, Hoyt Yeatman, Dennis Skotak (*The Abyss*)
Song: 'Under the Sea' from *The Little Mermaid* (*m* Alan Menken, *ly* Howard Ashman)
Original Score: Alan Menken (*The Little Mermaid*)
Documentary Short: *The Johnstown Flood*
Documentary Feature: *Common Threads: Stories from the Quilt*
Animated Film: *Balance*
Live-Action Short: *Work Experience*
Honorary Award: Akira Kurosawa

1990
Picture: *Dances with Wolves*
Foreign-Language Film: *Journey of Hope* (Xavier Koller)
Director: Kevin Costner (*Dances with Wolves*)
Actor: Jeremy Irons (*Reversal of Fortune*)

Actress: Kathy Bates (*Misery*)
Supporting Actor: Joe Pesci (*GoodFellas*)
Supporting Actress: Whoopi Goldberg (*Ghost*)
Original Screenplay: Bruce Joel Rubin (*Ghost*)
Adapted Screenplay: Michael Blake (*Dances with Wolves*)
Cinematography: Dean Semler (*Dances with Wolves*)
Art Direction: Richard Sylbert (*Dick Tracy*)
Costume Design: Franca Squarciapino (*Cyrano de Bergerac*)
Make-Up: John Caglione Jnr, Doug Drexler (*Dick Tracy*)
Sound: Russell Williams II, Jeffrey Perkins, Bill W. Benton, Greg Watkins (*Dances with Wolves*)
Sound Effects Editing: Cecelia Hall, George Watters II (*The Hunt for Red October*)
Editing: Neil Travis (*Dances with Wolves*)
Song: 'Sooner or Later' from *Dick Tracy* (m/ly Stephen Sondheim)
Original Score: John Barry (*Dances with Wolves*)
Documentary Short: *Days of Waiting*
Documentary Feature: *American Dream*
Animated Film: *Creature Comforts*
Live-Action Short: *The Lunch Date*
Honorary Awards: Sophia Loren; Myrna Loy
Special Achievement Awards: Eric Brevig, Rob Bottin, Tim McGovern, Alex Funke (visual effects, *Total Recall*)
Irving Thalberg Memorial Award: Richard Zanuck and David Brown

1991
Picture: *Silence of the Lambs*
Foreign-Language Film: *Mediterraneo* (Gabriele Salvatores)
Director: Jonathan Demme (*Silence of the Lambs*)
Actor: Anthony Hopkins (*Silence of the Lambs*)
Actress: Jodie Foster (*Silence of the Lambs*)
Supporting Actor: Jack Palance (*City Slickers*)
Supporting Actress: Mercedes Ruehl (*The Fisher King*)
Original Screenplay: Callie Khouri (*Thelma and Louise*)
Adapted Screenplay: Ted Tally (*Silence of the Lambs*)
Cinematography: Robert Richardson (*JFK*)
Art Direction: Dennis Gassner (*Bugsy*)
Costume Design: Albert Wolsky (*Bugsy*)
Make-Up: Stan Winston, Jeff Dawn (*Terminator 2*)
Sound: Tom Johnson, Gary Rydstrom, Gary Summers, Lee Orloff (*Terminator 2*)
Sound Effects Editing: Gary Rydstrom, Gloria S. Borders (*Terminator 2*)
Editing: Joe Hutshing, Pietro Scalia (*JFK*)
Visual Effects: Dennis Muren, Stan Winston, Gene Warren Jnr, Robert Skotak (*Terminator 2*)
Song: 'Beauty and the Beast' from *Beauty and the Beast* (m Alan Menken, ly Howard Ashman)
Original Score: Alan Menken (*Beauty and the Beast*)
Documentary Short: *Deadly Deception*
Documentary Feature: *In the Shadow of the Stars*
Animated Film: *Manipulation*
Live-Action Short: *Session Man*
Honorary Award: Satyajit Ray
Irving Thalberg Memorial Award: George Lucas

1992
Picture: *Unforgiven*
Foreign-Language Film: *Indochine* (Régis Wargnier)
Director: Clint Eastwood (*Unforgiven*)
Actor: Al Pacino (*Scent of a Woman*)
Actress: Emma Thompson (*Howards End*)
Supporting Actor: Gene Hackman (*Unforgiven*)
Supporting Actress: Marisa Tomei (*My Cousin Vinny*)
Original Screenplay: Neil Jordan (*The Crying Game*)
Adapted Screenplay: Ruth Prawer Jhabvala (*Howards End*)
Cinematography: Philippe Rousselot (*A River Runs through It*)
Art Direction: Luciana Arrighi (*Howards End*)
Costume Design: Eiko Ishioka (*Bram Stoker's Dracula*)
Make-Up: Greg Cannom, Michele Burke, Matthew W. Mungle (*Bram Stoker's Dracula*)
Sound: Chris Jenkins, Doug Hemphill, Mark Smith, Simon Kaye (*The Last of the Mohicans*)
Sound Effects Editing: Tom C. McCarthy, David E. Stone (*Bram Stoker's Dracula*)
Editing: Joel Cox (*Unforgiven*)
Visual Effects: Ken Ralston, Doug Chiang, Doug Smythe, Tom Woodruff (*Death Becomes Her*)
Song: 'A Whole New World' from *Aladdin* (m Alan Menken, ly Tim Rice)
Original Score: Alan Menken (*Aladdin*)
Documentary Short: *Educating Peter*
Documentary Feature: *The Panama Deception*
Animated Film: *Mona Lisa Descending a Staircase*
Live-Action Short: *Omnibus*
Honorary Award: Federico Fellini

1993
Picture: *Schindler's List*
Foreign-Language Film: *Belle Époque* (Fernando Trueba)
Director: Steven Spielberg (*Schindler's List*)
Actor: Tom Hanks (*Philadelphia*)
Actress: Holly Hunter (*The Piano*)
Supporting Actor: Tommy Lee Jones (*The Fugitive*)
Supporting Actress: Anna Paquin (*The Piano*)
Original Screenplay: Jane Campion (*The Piano*)
Adapted Screenplay: Steve Zaillian (*Schindler's List*)
Cinematography: Janusz Kaminski (*Schindler's List*)
Art Direction: Allan Starski (*Schindler's List*)
Costume Design: Gabriella Pescucci (*The Age of Innocence*)
Make-Up: Greg Cannom, Ve Neill, Yolanda Toussieng (*Mrs Doubtfire*)
Sound: Gary Summers, Gary Rydstrom, Shawn Murphy, Rod Judkins (*Jurassic Park*)
Sound Effects Editing: Gary Rydstrom, Richard Hymns (*Jurassic Park*)
Editing: Michael Kahn (*Schindler's List*)
Visual Effects: Dennis Muren, Stan Winston, Phil Tippett, Michael Lantieri (*Jurassic Park*)
Song: 'Streets of Philadelphia' from *Philadelphia* (m/ly Bruce Springsteen)

Original Score: John Williams (*Schindler's List*)
Documentary Short: *Defending Our Lives*
Documentary Feature: *I Am a Promise*
Animated Film: *The Wrong Trousers*
Live-Action Short: *Black Rider*
Honorary Award: Deborah Kerr

Books

60 Years of The Oscar: The Official History of the Academy Awards,
   Robert Osborne (Abbeville Press, 1989).
The Oscars: The Secret History of Hollywood's Academy Awards,
   Anthony Holden (Little, Brown, 1993).

The BAFTA Awards

The British Academy of Film and Television Arts began in 1947 as the British Film Academy, becoming the Society of Film and Television Arts in 1959, and changing its name to its present title in 1975. The BAFTA award, a bronze theatrical mask, was originally nicknamed a Stella. At the beginning, there were two awards for feature films – one for the best film from any source and one for the best British film. Over the years, the awards have widened. The film winners in the major categories are listed below.

1947
Film: *The Best Years of Our Lives* (William Wyler)
British Film: *Odd Man Out* (Carol Reed)

1948
Film: *Hamlet* (Laurence Olivier)
British Film: *The Fallen Idol* (Carol Reed)

1949
Film: *The Bicycle Thief* (Vittorio De Sica)
British Film: *The Third Man* (Carol Reed)

1950
Film: *All about Eve* (Joseph L. Mankiewicz)
British Film: *The Blue Lamp* (Basil Dearden)

1951
Film: *La Ronde* (Max Ophuls)
British Film: *The Lavender Hill Mob* (Charles Crichton)

1952
Film: *The Sound Barrier* (US: *Breaking the Sound Barrier*) (David Lean)
British Film: *The Sound Barrier* (David Lean)
Actor: Ralph Richardson (*The Sound Barrier*)
Actress: Vivien Leigh (*A Streetcar Named Desire*)
Foreign Actor: Marlon Brando (*Viva Zapata!*)
Foreign Actress: Simone Signoret (*Casque d'Or*)
Newcomer: Claire Bloom (*Limelight*)

1953
Film: *Forbidden Games* (René Clément)
British Film: *Genevieve* (Henry Cornelius)
Actor: John Gielgud (*Julius Caesar*)
Actress: Audrey Hepburn (*Roman Holiday*)
Foreign Actor: Marlon Brando (*Julius Caesar*)
Foreign Actress: Leslie Caron (*Lili*)
Newcomer: Norman Wisdom (*Trouble in Store*)

1954
Film: *The Wages of Fear* (Henri-Georges Clouzot)
British Film: *Hobson's Choice* (David Lean)
Actor: Kenneth More (*Doctor in the House*)
Actress: Yvonne Mitchell (*The Divided Heart*)
Foreign Actor: Marlon Brando (*On the Waterfront*)
Foreign Actress: Cornell Borchers (*The Divided Heart*)
Newcomer: David Kossoff (*Chance Meeting*)
Screenplay: Robin Estridge, George Tabori (*Chance Meeting*)

1955
Film: *Richard III* (Laurence Olivier)
British Film: *Richard III* (Laurence Olivier)
Actor: Laurence Olivier (*Richard III*)
Actress: Katie Johnson (*The Ladykillers*)
Foreign Actor: Ernest Borgnine (*Marty*)
Foreign Actress: Betsy Blair (*Marty*)
Newcomer: Paul Scofield (*That Lady*)
Screenplay: William Rose (*The Ladykillers*)

1956
Film: *Gervaise* (René Clément)
British Film: *Reach for the Sky* (Lewis Gilbert)
Actor: Peter Finch (*The Rape of Malaya*)
Actress: Virginia McKenna (*The Rape of Malaya*)
Foreign Actor: François Périer (*Gervaise*)
Foreign Actress: Anna Magnani (*The Rose Tattoo*)
Newcomer: Eli Wallach (*Baby Doll*)
Screenplay: Nigel Balchin (*The Man Who Never Was*)

1957
Film: *The Bridge on the River Kwai* (David Lean)
British Film: *The Bridge on the River Kwai* (David Lean)
Actor: Alec Guinness (*The Bridge on the River Kwai*)
Actress: Heather Sears (*The Story of Esther Costello*)
Foreign Actor: Henry Fonda (*Twelve Angry Men*)
Foreign Actress: Simone Signoret (*The Witches of Salem*)
Newcomer: Eric Barker (*Brothers in Law*)
Screenplay: Pierre Boulle (*The Bridge on the River Kwai*)

1958
Film: *Room at the Top* (Jack Clayton)
British Film: *Room at the Top* (Jack Clayton)
Actor: Trevor Howard (*The Key*)
Actress: Irene Worth (*Orders to Kill*)
Foreign Actor: Sidney Poitier (*The Defiant Ones*)
Foreign Actress: Simone Signoret (*Room at the Top*)

Newcomer: Paul Massie (*Orders to Kill*)
Screenplay: Paul Dehn (*Orders to Kill*)

1959

Film: *Ben Hur* (William Wyler)
British Film: *Sapphire* (Basil Dearden)
Actor: Peter Sellers (*I'm All Right Jack*)
Actress: Audrey Hepburn (*The Nun's Story*)
Foreign Actor: Jack Lemmon (*Some Like It Hot*)
Foreign Actress: Shirley MacLaine (*Ask Any Girl*)
Newcomer: Hayley Mills (*Tiger Bay*)
Screenplay: John Boulting, Frank Harvey, Alan Hackney (*I'm All Right Jack*)

1960

Film: *The Apartment* (Billy Wilder)
British Film: *Saturday Night and Sunday Morning* (Karel Reisz)
Actor: Peter Finch (*The Trials of Oscar Wilde*)
Actress: Rachel Roberts (*Saturday Night and Sunday Morning*)
Foreign Actor: Jack Lemmon (*The Apartment*)
Foreign Actress: Shirley MacLaine (*The Apartment*)
Newcomer: Albert Finney (*Saturday Night and Sunday Morning*)
Screenplay: Bryan Forbes (*The Angry Silence*)

1961

Film: *Ballad of a Soldier* (Grigori Chukrai); *The Hustler* (Robert Rossen)
British Film: *A Taste of Honey* (Tony Richardson)
Actor: Peter Finch (*No Love for Johnnie*)
Actress: Dora Bryan (*A Taste of Honey*)
Foreign Actor: Paul Newman (*The Hustler*)
Foreign Actress: Sophia Loren (*Two Women*)
Newcomer: Rita Tushingham (*A Taste of Honey*)
Screenplay: Shelagh Delaney, Tony Richardson (*A Taste of Honey*); Val Guest, Wolf Mankowitz (*The Day the Earth Caught Fire*)

1962

Film: *Lawrence of Arabia* (David Lean)
British Film: *Lawrence of Arabia* (David Lean)
Actor: Peter O'Toole (*Lawrence of Arabia*)
Actress: Leslie Caron (*The L-Shaped Room*)
Foreign Actor: Burt Lancaster (*Birdman of Alcatraz*)
Foreign Actress: Anne Bancroft (*The Miracle Worker*)
Newcomer: Tom Courtenay (*The Loneliness of the Long Distance Runner*)
Screenplay: Robert Bolt (*Lawrence of Arabia*)

1963

Film: *Tom Jones* (Tony Richardson)
British Film: *Tom Jones* (Tony Richardson)
Actor: Dirk Bogarde (*The Servant*)
Actress: Rachel Roberts (*This Sporting Life*)
Foreign Actor: Marcello Mastroianni (*Divorce Italian Style*)
Foreign Actress: Patricia Neal (*Hud*)
Newcomer: James Fox (*The Servant*)
Screenplay: John Osborne (*The Servant*)

Cinematography: b/w Douglas Slocombe (*The Servant*); colour Ted Moore (*From Russia with Love*)

1964

Film: *Dr Strangelove* (Stanley Kubrick)
British Film: *Dr Strangelove* (Stanley Kubrick)
Actor: Richard Attenborough (*Séance on a Wet Afternoon; Guns at Batasi*)
Actress: Audrey Hepburn (*Charade*)
Foreign Actor: Marcello Mastroianni (*Yesterday, Today and Tomorrow*)
Foreign Actress: Anne Bancroft (*The Pumpkin Eater*)
Newcomer: Julie Andrews (*Mary Poppins*)
Screenplay: Harold Pinter (*The Pumpkin Eater*)
Cinematography: b/w Oswald Morris (*The Pumpkin Eater*); colour Geoffrey Unsworth (*Becket*)
Production Design: b/w Ken Adam (*Dr Strangelove*); colour John Bryan (*Becket*)

1965

Film: *My Fair Lady* (George Cukor)
British Film: *The Ipcress File* (Sidney J. Furie)
Actor: Dirk Bogarde (*Darling*)
Actress: Julie Christie (*Darling*)
Foreign Actor: Lee Marvin (*Cat Ballou; The Killers*)
Foreign Actress: Patricia Neal (*In Harm's Way*)
Newcomer: Judi Dench (*Four in the Morning*)
Screenplay: Frederic Raphael (*Darling*)
Cinematography: b/w Oswald Morris (*The Hill*); colour Otto Heller (*The Ipcress File*)
Production Design: b/w Ray Simm (*Darling*); colour Ken Adam (*The Ipcress File*)

1966

Film: *Who's Afraid of Virginia Woolf?* (Mike Nichols)
British Film: *The Spy Who Came in from the Cold* (Martin Ritt)
Actor: Richard Burton (*Who's Afraid of Virginia Woolf?; The Spy Who Came in from the Cold*)
Actress: Elizabeth Taylor (*Who's Afraid of Virginia Woolf?*)
Foreign Actor: Rod Steiger (*The Pawnbroker*)
Foreign Actress: Jeanne Moreau (*Viva Maria!*)
Newcomer: Vivien Merchant (*Alfie*)
Screenplay: David Mercer (*Morgan – A Suitable Case for Treatment*)
Cinematography: b/w Oswald Morris (*The Spy Who Came in from the Cold*); colour Christopher Challis (*Arabesque*)
Production Design: b/w Tambi Larsen (*The Spy Who Came in from the Cold*); colour Wilfred Shingleton (*The Blue Max*)

1967

Film: *A Man for All Seasons* (Fred Zinnemann)
British Film: *A Man for All Seasons* (Fred Zinnemann)
Actor: Paul Scofield (*A Man for All Seasons*)
Actress: Edith Evans (*The Whisperers*)
Foreign Actor: Rod Steiger (*In the Heat of the Night*)
Foreign Actress: Anouk Aimée (*A Man and a Woman*)
Newcomer: Faye Dunaway (*Bonnie and Clyde*)
Screenplay: Robert Bolt (*A Man for All Seasons*)

Cinematography: b/w Gerry Turpin (*The Whisperers*); colour Ted Moore (*A Man for All Seasons*)
Production Design: John Box (*A Man for All Seasons*)

1968
Film: *The Graduate* (Mike Nichols)
Director: Mike Nichols (*The Graduate*)
Actor: Spencer Tracy (*Guess Who's Coming to Dinner?*)
Actress: Katharine Hepburn (*Guess Who's Coming to Dinner?*)
Supporting Actor: Ian Holm (*The Bofors Gun*)
Supporting Actress: Billie Whitelaw (*The Twisted Nerve; Charlie Bubbles*)
Newcomer: Dustin Hoffman (*The Graduate*)
Screenplay: Buck Henry, Calder Willingham (*The Graduate*)
Cinematography: Geoffrey Unsworth (*2001: A Space Odyssey*)
Music: John Barry (*The Lion in Winter*)
Production Design: Tony Masters, Harry Lange, Ernie Archer (*2001: A Space Odyssey*)

1969
Film: *Midnight Cowboy* (John Schlesinger)
Director: John Schlesinger (*Midnight Cowboy*)
Actor: Dustin Hoffman (*Midnight Cowboy; John and Mary*)
Actress: Maggie Smith (*The Prime of Miss Jean Brodie*)
Supporting Actor: Laurence Olivier (*Oh! What a Lovely War*)
Supporting Actress: Celia Johnson (*The Prime of Miss Jean Brodie*)
Newcomer: Jon Voight (*Midnight Cowboy*)
Screenplay: Waldo Salt (*Midnight Cowboy*)
Cinematography: Gerry Turpin (*Oh! What a Lovely War*)
Music: Mikis Theodorakis (*Z*)
Production Design: Don Ashton (*Oh! What a Lovely War*)

1970
Film: *Butch Cassidy and the Sundance Kid* (George Roy Hill)
Director: George Roy Hill (*Butch Cassidy and the Sundance Kid*)
Actor: Robert Redford (*Butch Cassidy and the Sundance Kid; Tell Them Willie Boy Is Here; Downhill Racer*)
Actress: Katharine Ross (*Butch Cassidy and the Sundance Kid; Tell Them Willie Boy Is Here*)
Supporting Actor: Colin Welland (*Kes*)
Supporting Actress: Susannah York (*They Kill Horses, Don't They?*)
Newcomer: David Bradley (*Kes*)
Screenplay: William Goldman (*Butch Cassidy and the Sundance Kid*)
Cinematography: Conrad Hall (*Butch Cassidy and the Sundance Kid*)
Music: Burt Bacharach (*Butch Cassidy and the Sundance Kid*)
Production Design: Mario Garbuglia (*Waterloo*)

1971
Film: *Sunday, Bloody Sunday* (John Schlesinger)
Director: John Schlesinger (*Sunday, Bloody Sunday*)
Actor: Peter Finch (*Sunday, Bloody Sunday*)
Actress: Glenda Jackson (*Sunday, Bloody Sunday*)
Supporting Actor: Edward Fox (*The Go-Between*)
Supporting Actress: Margaret Leighton (*The Go-Between*)

Newcomer: Dominic Guard (*The Go-Between*)
Screenplay: Harold Pinter (*The Go-Between*)
Cinematography: Pasqualino De Santis (*Death in Venice*)
Music: Michel Legrand (*Summer of '42*)
Production Design: Ferdinando Scarfiotti (*Death in Venice*)

1972
Film: *Cabaret* (Bob Fosse)
Director: Bob Fosse (*Cabaret*)
Actor: Gene Hackman (*The French Connection; The Poseidon Adventure*)
Actress: Liza Minnelli (*Cabaret*)
Supporting Actor: Ben Johnson (*The Last Picture Show*)
Supporting Actress: Cloris Leachman (*The Last Picture Show*)
Newcomer: Joel Grey (*Cabaret*)
Screenplay: Peter Bogdanovich, Larry McMurty (*The Last Picture Show*)
Cinematography: Geoffrey Unsworth (*Cabaret; Alice's Adventures in Wonderland*)
Music: Nina Rota (*The Godfather*)
Production Design: Rolf Zehetbauer (*Cabaret*)

1973
Film: *Day for Night* (François Truffaut)
Director: François Truffaut (*Day for Night*)
Actor: Walter Matthau (*Pete 'n' Tillie; Charley Varrick*)
Actress: Stéphane Audran (*The Discreet Charm of the Bourgeoisie; Just before Nightfall*)
Supporting Actor: Arthur Lowe (*O Lucky Man!*)
Supporting Actress: Valentina Cortese (*Day for Night*)
Newcomer: Peter Egan (*The Hireling*)
Screenplay: Luis Buñuel, Jean-Claude Carrière (*The Discreet Charm of the Bourgeoisie*)
Cinematography: Anthony Richmond (*Don't Look Now*)
Music: Alan Price (*O Lucky Man!*)
Production Design: Natasha Kroll (*The Hireling*)

1974
Film: *Lacombe Lucien* (Louis Malle)
Director: Roman Polanski (*Chinatown*)
Actor: Jack Nicholson (*Chinatown; The Last Detail*)
Actress: Joanne Woodward (*Summer Wishes, Winter Dreams*)
Supporting Actor: John Gielgud (*Murder on the Orient Express*)
Supporting Actress: Ingrid Bergman (*Murder on the Orient Express*)
Newcomer: Georgina Hale (*Mahler*)
Screenplay: Robert Towne (*Chinatown; The Last Detail*)
Cinematography: Douglas Slocombe (*The Great Gatsby*)
Music: Richard Rodney Bennett (*Murder on the Orient Express*)
Production Design: John Box (*The Great Gatsby*)

1975
Film: *Alice Doesn't Live Here Any More* (Martin Scorsese)
Director: Stanley Kubrick (*Barry Lyndon*)
Actor: Al Pacino (*The Godfather Part II; Dog Day Afternoon*)
Actress: Ellen Burstyn (*Alice Doesn't Live Here Any More*)
Supporting Actor: Fred Astaire (*The Towering Inferno*)

Supporting Actress: Diane Ladd (*Alice Doesn't Live Here Any More*)
Newcomer: Valerie Perrine (*Lenny*)
Screenplay: Robert Getchell (*Alice Doesn't Live Here Any More*)
Cinematography: John Alcott (*Barry Lyndon*)
Music: John Williams (*Jaws; The Towering Inferno*)
Production Design: John Box (*Rollerball*)

1976
Film: *One Flew over the Cuckoo's Nest* (Milos Forman)
Director: Milos Forman (*One Flew over the Cuckoo's Nest*)
Actor: Jack Nicholson (*One Flew over the Cuckoo's Nest*)
Actress: Louise Fletcher (*One Flew over the Cuckoo's Nest*)
Supporting Actor: Brad Dourif (*One Flew over the Cuckoo's Nest*)
Supporting Actress: Jodie Foster (*Taxi Driver; Bugsy Malone*)
Newcomer: Jodie Foster (*Taxi Driver; Bugsy Malone*)
Screenplay: Alan Parker (*Bugsy Malone*)
Cinematography: Russell Boyd (*Picnic at Hanging Rock*)
Music: Bernard Herrmann (*Taxi Driver*)
Production Design: Geoffrey Kirkland (*Bugsy Malone*)

1977
Film: *Annie Hall* (Woody Allen)
Director: Woody Allen (*Annie Hall*)
Actor: Peter Finch (*Network*)
Actress: Diane Keaton (*Annie Hall*)
Supporting Actor: Edward Fox (*A Bridge Too Far*)
Supporting Actress: Jenny Agutter (*Equus*)
Newcomer: Isabelle Huppert (*The Lacemaker*)
Screenplay: Woody Allen, Marshall Brickman (*Annie Hall*)
Cinematography: Geoffrey Unsworth (*A Bridge Too Far*)
Music: John Addison (*A Bridge Too Far*)
Production Design: Danilo Donati (*Fellini's Casanova*)

1978
Film: *Julia* (Fred Zinnemann)
Director: Alan Parker (*Midnight Express*)
Actor: Richard Dreyfuss (*The Goodbye Girl*)
Actress: Jane Fonda (*Julia*)
Supporting Actor: John Hurt (*Midnight Express*)
Supporting Actress: Geraldine Page (*Interiors*)
Newcomer: Christopher Reeve (*Superman*)
Screenplay: Alvin Sargent (*Julia*)
Cinematography: Douglas Slocombe (*Julia*)
Music: John Williams (*Star Wars*)
Production Design: Joe Alves (*Close Encounters of the Third Kind*)

1979
Film: *Manhattan* (Woody Allen)
Director: Francis Ford Coppola (*Apocalypse Now*)
Actor: Jack Lemmon (*The China Syndrome*)
Actress: Jane Fonda (*The China Syndrome*)
Supporting Actor: Robert Duvall (*Apocalypse Now*)
Supporting Actress: Rachel Roberts (*Yanks*)
Newcomer: Dennis Christopher (*Breaking Away*)
Screenplay: Woody Allen, Marshall Brickman (*Manhattan*)
Cinematography: Vilmos Zsigmond (*The Deer Hunter*)

Music: Ennio Morricone (*Days of Heaven*)
Production Design: Michael Seymour (*Alien*)

1980
Film: *The Elephant Man* (David Lynch)
Director: Akira Kurosawa (*Kagemusha*)
Actor: John Hurt (*The Elephant Man*)
Actress: Judy Davis (*My Brilliant Career*)
Newcomer: Judy Davis (*My Brilliant Career*)
Screenplay: Jerzy Kozinski (*Being There*)
Cinematography: Giuseppe Rotunno (*All That Jazz*)
Music: John Williams (*The Empire Strikes Back*)
Production Design: Stuart Craig (*The Elephant Man*)

1981
Film: *Chariots of Fire* (Hugh Hudson)
Director: Louis Malle (*Atlantic City*)
Actor: Burt Lancaster (*Atlantic City*)
Actress: Maryl Streep (*The French Lieutenant's Woman*)
Supporting Artist: Ian Holm (*Chariots of Fire*)
Newcomer: Joe Pesci (*Raging Bull*)
Screenplay: Bill Forsyth (*Gregory's Girl*)
Cinematography: Geoffrey Unsworth, Ghislain Cloquet (*Tess*)
Music: Carl Davis (*The French Lieutenant's Woman*)
Production Design: Norman Reynolds (*Raiders of the Lost Ark*)

1982
Film: *Gandhi* (Richard Attenborough)
Foreign-Language Film: *Eboli* (Francesco Rosi)
Director: Richard Attenborough (*Gandhi*)
Actor: Ben Kingsley (*Gandhi*)
Actress: Katharine Hepburn (*On Golden Pond*)
Supporting Actor: Jack Nicholson (*Reds*)
Supporting Actress: Maureen Stapleton (*Reds*); Rohini Hattangadi (*Gandhi*)
Newcomer: Ben Kingsley (*Gandhi*)
Screenplay: Costa-Gavras, Donald Stewart (*Missing*)
Cinematography: Jordan Cronenweth (*Blade Runner*)
Music: John Williams (*ET*)
Production Design: Lawrence G. Paull (*Blade Runner*)

1983
Film: *Educating Rita* (Lewis Gilbert)
Foreign-Language Film: *Danton* (Andrzej Wajda)
Director: Bill Forsyth (*Local Hero*)
Actor: Michael Caine (*Educating Rita*)
Actress: Julie Walters (*Educating Rita*)
Supporting Actor: Denholm Elliott (*Trading Places*)
Supporting Actress: Jamie Lee Curtis (*Trading Places*)
Newcomer: Phyllis Logan (*Another Time, Another Place*)
Adapted Screenplay: Ruth Prawer Jhabvala (*Heat and Dust*)
Original Screenplay: Paul D. Zimmerman (*King of Comedy*)
Cinematography: Sven Nykvist (*Fanny and Alexander*)
Music: Ryuichi Sakamoto (*Merry Christmas, Mr Lawrence*)
Production Design: Franco Zeffirelli, Gianni Quaranta (*La Traviata*)

1984

Film: *The Killing Fields* (Roland Joffe)
Foreign-Language Film: *Carmen* (Carlos Saura)
Director: Wim Wenders (*Paris, Texas*)
Actor: Haing S. Ngor (*The Killing Fields*)
Actress: Maggie Smith (*A Private Function*)
Supporting Actor: Denholm Elliott (*A Private Function*)
Supporting Actress: Liz Smith (*A Private Function*)
Newcomer: Haing S. Ngor (*The Killing Fields*)
Adapted Screenplay: Bruce Robinson (*The Killing Fields*)
Original Screenplay: Woody Allen (*Broadway Danny Rose*)
Cinematography: Chris Menges (*The Killing Fields*)
Music: Ennio Morricone (*Once upon a Time in America*)
Production Design: Roy Walker (*The Killing Fields*)

1985

Film: *The Purple Rose of Cairo* (Woody Allen)
Foreign-Language Film: *Colonel Redl* (Istvá Szabó)
Actor: William Hurt (*Kiss of the Spider Woman*)
Actress: Peggy Ashcroft (*A Passage to India*)
Supporting Actor: Denholm Elliott (*Defence of the Realm*)
Supporting Actress: Rosanna Arquette (*Desperately Seeking Susan*)
Adapted Screenplay: Richard Condon, Janet Roach (*Prizzi's Honor*)
Original Screenplay: Woody Allen (*The Purple Rose of Cairo*)
Cinematography: Miroslav Ondricek (*Amadeus*)
Music: Maurice Jarre (*Witness*)
Production Design: Norman Garwood (*Brazil*)

1986

Film: *A Room with a View* (James Ivory)
Foreign-Language Film: *Ran* (Akira Kurosawa)
Director: Woody Allen (*Hannah and Her Sisters*)
Actor: Bob Hoskins (*Mona Lisa*)
Actress: Maggie Smith (*A Room with a View*)
Supporting Actor: Ray McAnally (*The Mission*)
Supporting Actress: Judi Dench (*A Room with a View*)
Adapted Screenplay: Kurt Luedtke (*Out of Africa*)
Original Screenplay: Woody Allen (*Hannah and Her Sisters*)
Cinematography: David Watkin (*Out of Africa*)
Music: Ennio Morricone (*The Mission*)
Production Design: Gianni Quaranta, Brian Ackland-Snow (*A Room with a View*)

1987

Film: *Jean de Florette* (Claude Berri)
Foreign-Language Film: *The Sacrifice* (Andrei Tarkovsky)
Director: Oliver Stone (*Platoon*)
Actor: Sean Connery (*The Name of the Rose*)
Actress: Anne Bancroft (*84 Charing Cross Road*)
Supporting Actor: Daniel Auteuil (*Jean de Florette*)
Supporting Actress: Susan Wooldridge (*Hope and Glory*)
Adapted Screenplay: Gérard Brach, Claude Berri (*Jean de Florette*)
Original Screenplay: David Leland (*Wish You Were Here*)
Cinematography: Bruno Nuytten (*Jean de Florette*)
Music: Ennio Morricone (*The Untouchables*)

Production Design: Santo Loquasto (*Radio Days*)

1988

Film: *The Last Emperor* (Bernardo Bertolucci)
Foreign-Language Film: *Babette's Feast* (Gabriel Axel)
Director: Louis Malle (*Au Revoir les Enfants*)
Actor: John Cleese (*A Fish Called Wanda*)
Actress: Maggie Smith (*The Lonely Passion of Judith Hearne*)
Supporting Actor: Michael Palin (*A Fish Called Wanda*)
Supporting Actress: Judi Dench (*A Handful of Dust*)
Adapted Screenplay: Jean-Claude Carrière, Philip Kaufman (*The Unbearable Lightness of Being*)
Original Screenplay: Shawn Slovo (*A World Apart*)
Cinematography: Allen Daviau (*Empire of the Sun*)
Music: John Williams (*Empire of the Sun*)
Production Design: Dean Tavoularis (*Tucker: The Man and His Dream*)

1989

Film: *Dead Poets Society* (Peter Weir)
Foreign-Language Film: *Life and Nothing But* (Bertrand Tavernier)
Director: Kenneth Branagh (*Henry V*)
Actor: Daniel Day-Lewis (*My Left Foot*)
Actress: Pauline Collins (*Shirley Valentine*)
Supporting Actor: Ray McAnally (*My Left Foot*)
Supporting Actress: Michelle Pfeiffer (*Dangerous Liaisons*)
Adapted Screenplay: Christopher Hampton (*Dangerous Liaisons*)
Original Screenplay: Nora Ephron (*When Harry Met Sally*)
Cinematography: Peter Biziou (*Mississippi Burning*)
Music: Maurice Jarre (*Dead Poets Society*)
Production Design: Dante Ferretti (*Adventures of Baron Munchausen*)

1990

Film: *GoodFellas* (Martin Scorsese)
Foreign-Language Film: *Nuovo Cinema Paradiso* (Giuseppe Tornatore)
Director: Martin Scorsese (*GoodFellas*)
Actor: Philippe Noiret (*Nuovo Cinema Paradiso*)
Actress: Jessica Tandy (*Driving Miss Daisy*)
Supporting Actor: Salvatore Cascio (*Nuovo Cinema Paradiso*)
Supporting Actress: Whoopi Goldberg (*Ghost*)
Adapted Screenplay: Nicholas Pileggi, Martin Scorsese (*GoodFellas*)
Original Screenplay: Giuseppe Tornatore (*Nuovo Cinema Paradiso*)
Cinematography: Vittorio Storaro (*The Sheltering Sky*)
Music: Ennio and Andrea Morricone (*Nuovo Cinema Paradiso*)
Production Design: Richard Sylbert (*Dick Tracy*)

1991

Film: *The Commitments* (Alan Parker)
Foreign-Language Film: *The Nasty Girl* (*Das Schreckliche Mädchen*) (Michael Verhoeven)
Director: Alan Parker (*The Commitments*)
Actor: Anthony Hopkins (*The Silence of the Lambs*)

Actress: Jodie Foster (*The Silence of the Lambs*)
Supporting Actor: Alan Rickman (*Robin Hood: Prince of Thieves*)
Supporting Actress: Kate Nelligan (*Frankie and Johnnie*)
Adapted Screenplay: Dick Clement, Ian La Frenais, Roddy Doyle (*The Commitments*)
Original Screenplay: Anthony Minghella (*Truly Madly Deeply*)
Cinematography: Pierre Lhomme (*Cyrano de Bergerac*)
Music: Jean-Claude Petit (*Cyrano de Bergerac*)
Production Design: Bo Welch (*Edward Scissorhands*)

1992

Film: *Howards End* (James Ivory)
Foreign-Language Film: *Raise the Red Lantern* (Zhang Zimou)
Director: Robert Altman (*The Player*)
Actor: Robert Downey Jnr (*Chaplin*)
Actress: Emma Thompson (*Howards End*)
Supporting Actor: Gene Hackman (*Unforgiven*)
Supporting Actress: Miranda Richardson (*Damage*)
Adapted Screenplay: Michael Tolkin (*The Player*)
Original Screenplay: Woody Allen (*Husbands and Wives*)

Cinematography: Dante Spinotti (*The Last of the Mohicans*)
Music: David Hirschfelder (*Strictly Ballroom*)
Production Design: Catherine Martin (*Strictly Ballroom*)

1993

Film: *Schindler's List* (Steven Spielberg)
Foreign-Language Film: *Farewell My Concubine* (Chen Kaige)
British Film: *Shadowlands* (Richard Attenborough)
Director: Steven Spielberg (*Schindler's List*)
Actor: Anthony Hopkins (*The Remains of the Day*)
Actress: Holly Hunter (*The Piano*)
Supporting Actor: Ralph Fiennes (*Schindler's List*)
Supporting Actress: Miriam Margolyes (*The Age of Innocence*)
Adapted Screenplay: Steven Zaillian (*Schindler's List*)
Original Screenplay: Danny Rubin, Harold Ramis (*Groundhog Day*)
Cinematography: Janusz Kaminski (*Schindler's List*)
Music: John Williams (*Schindler's List*)
Production Design: Andrew McAlpine (*The Piano*)

European Film Awards

The European Film Awards, known as Felixes, were inaugurated in 1988. The main prizewinners are:

1988
Film: *A Short Film about Killing* (Krzysztof Kiéslowski)
Director: Wim Wenders (*Wings of Desire*)
Actor: Max Von Sydow (*Pelle the Conqueror*)
Actress: Carmen Maura (*Women on the Verge of a Nervous Breakdown*)
Supporting Actor: Curt Bois (*Wings of Desire*)
Supporting Actress: Johnna Ter Steege (*The Vanishing*)
Screenplay: Louis Malle (*Au Revoir les Enfants*)

1989
Film: *Landscape in the Mist* (Theo Angelopoulos)
Director: Géza Bereményi (*The Midas Touch*)
Actor: Philippe Noiret (*Life and Nothing But; Cinema Paradiso*)
Actress: Ruth Sheen (*High Hopes*)
Supporting Performance: Edna Doré (*High Hopes*)
Screenplay: Maria Khmelik (*Little Vera*)

1990
Film: *Open Doors* (*Porte Aperte*) (Gianni Amelio)
Actor: Kenneth Branagh (*Henry V*)
Actress: Carmen Maura (*Ay! Carmela*)
Supporting Actor: Dimitri Pevsov (*Mother (Matj)*)
Supporting Actress: Malin Ek (*The Guardian Angel (Skyddsanglen)*)
Screenplay: Vitaly Kanevsky (*Don't Move, Die and Rise Again (Zamri Umi Voskresni)*)

1991
Film: *Riff-Raff* (Ken Loach)
Actor: Michel Bouquet (*Toto le Héros*)
Actress: Clotilde Courau (*Le Petit Criminel*)
Supporting Actor: Ricky Memphis (*Ultrè*)
Supporting Actress: Marta Keler (*Virginia*)
Screenplay: Jaco Van Dormael (*Toto le Héros*)

1992
Film: *Il Ladro di Bambini* (Gianni Amelio)
Actor: Matti Pellonpää (*La Vie de Bohème*)
Actress: Juliette Binoche (*Les Amants du Pont-Neuf*)
Supporting Actor: André Wilms (*La Vie de Bohème*)
Supporting Actress: Ghita Norby (*Freud Flyttar Hemifran*)
Screenplay: István Szabó (*Edes Emma, Draga Böbe*)

1993
Film: *Urga* (Nikita Mikhalkov)
Actor: Daniel Auteuil (*Un Coeur en Hiver*)
Actress: Maia Morgenstern (*Balanta*)

1994
Film: *Lamerica* (Gianni Amelio)
Lifetime achievement: Robert Bresson

The Berlin Film Festival's Golden Bear Awards

The Berlin Film Festival began in 1951. Its main prize is the Golden Bear for best feature, which was inaugurated in 1956. The Golden Bear winners are:

1956
Invitation to the Dance (Gene Kelly)

1957
Twelve Angry Men (Sidney Lumet)

1958
Wild Strawberries/Smultonstället (Ingmar Bergman)

1959
The Cousins/Les Cousins (Claude Chabrol)

1960
Lazarillo/El Lazarillo de Tormes (Cesar Ardavin)

1961
The Night/La Notte (Michelangelo Antonioni)

1962
A Kind of Loving (John Schlesinger)

1963
Bushido/Bushido Zankoku Monogatari (Tadashi Imai); *The Devil/Il Diavolo* (US: *To Bed . . . Or Not to Bed*) (Gian Luigi Polidoro)

1964
Dry Summer aka *I Had My Brother's Wife/Süsuz Yaz* (Ismail Metin)

1965
Alphaville (Jean-Luc Godard)

1966
Cul-de-Sac (Roman Polanski)

1967
Le Départ (Jerzy Skolimowski)

1968
Ole Dole Doff (Jan Troell)

1969
Early Years/Rani Radovi (Zelimir Zilnik)

1970
No prize awarded

1971
The Garden of the Finzi Contini (Vittorio de Sica)

1972
The Canterbury Tales (Pier Paolo Pasolini)

1973
Distant Thunder (Satyajit Ray)

1974
The Apprenticeship of Duddy Kravitz (Ted Kotcheff)

1975
Adoption/Örökbefogadás (Márta Mészáros)

1976
Buffalo Bill and the Indians (Robert Altman)

1977
The Ascent/Voskhozhdenie (Larisa Sheptiko)

1978
The Trout/Las Truchas (José Luis Garcia Sánchez); *The Words of Max/Las Palabras de Max* (Emilio Martinez-Lazaro)

1979
David (Peter Lilienthal)

1980
Heartland (Richard Pearce); *Palermo Oder Wolfsberg* (Werner Schroeter)

1981
Fast, Fast/Depiesa, Deprisa (Carlos Saura)

1982
Veronika Voss/Die Sehnsucht der Veronica Voss (Rainer Werner Fassbinder)

1983
Ascendancy (Edward Bennett); *The Beehive/La Colmena* (Mario Camus)

1984
Love Streams (John Cassavetes)

1985
 Wetherby (David Hare); The Woman and the Stranger/Die Frau und Der Fremde (Rainer Simon)

1986
 Stammheim (Reinhard Hauff)

1987
 The Theme/Thema (Gleb Panfilov)

1988
 Red Sorghum/Hong Gao Liang (Zhang Yimou)

1989
 Rain Man (Barry Levinson)

1990
 Music Box (Costa-Gavras); Larks on a String (Jiri Menzel)

1991
 House of Smiles (Marco Ferreri)

1992
 Grand Canyon (Lawrence Kasdan)

1993
 The Woman from the Lake of Scented Souls/Xiang Hun N (Xei Fei); The Wedding Banquet/Xiyan (Ang Lee)

1994
 In The Name of the Father (Jim Sheridan)

1995
 Fresh Bait/L'Appat (Bertrand Tavernier)

The Cannes Film Festival Awards

The Cannes Film Festival, held each year in May, has established itself as the world's leading festival. The first, in 1939, was abandoned when Hitler invaded Poland and it resumed in 1946. There was no festival in 1948 and 1950, and the one in 1968 was disrupted by the nationwide demonstrations. In 1946, there was a multitude of prizes, one for each participating nation, although there was an International Jury Prize, which went to *The Battle of the Rails* (*La Bataille du Rail*), directed by René Clément. In 1947, six prizes were given for various vague genres of film. In 1949, a Grand Prize was given to the best film, together with other prizes for direction, acting, writing, composing, and set design. A special Jury Prize was added in 1951, and the Palme d'Or (Golden Palm) for best film was inaugurated in 1955. Over the years the juries have varied the nature of the awards, according to whim, although always retaining a prize for the best film. The main prizewinners since 1949 are:

1949
Grand Prix: *The Third Man* (Carol Reed)
Director: René Clément (*The Walls of Malapaga* (*Le Mura di Malapaga*))
Actor: Edward G. Robinson (*House of Strangers*)
Actress: Isa Miranda (*The Walls of Malapaga* (*Le Mura di Malapaga*))

1951
Grand Prix: *Miracle in Milan* (*Miracolo a Milano*) (Vittoria De Sica); *Miss Julie* (Alf Sjöberg)
Director: Luis Buñuel (*Los Olvidados*)
Actor: Michael Redgrave (*The Browning Version*)
Actress: Bette Davis (*All about Eve*)

1952
Grand Prix: *Two Pennyworth of Hope* (*Due Soldi di Speranza*) (Renato Castellani); *Othello* (Orson Welles)
Director: Christian-Jaque (*Fanfan la Tulipe*)
Actor: Marlon Brando (*Viva Zapata*)
Actress: Lee Grant (*Detective Story*)

1953
Grand Prix: *The Wages of Fear* (Henri-Georges Clouzot)
Actor: Charles Vanel (*The Wages of Fear*)

1954
Grand Prix: *Gate of Hell* (*Jigoku-Mon*) (Teinosuke Kinugasa)

1955
Palme d'Or: *Marty* (Delbert Mann)
Director: Sergei Vasiliev (*The Heroes of Shipka* (*Geroite Na Shipka*)); Jules Dassin (*Rififi*)
Performance: Spencer Tracy

1956
Palme d'Or: *The Silent World* (*Le Monde du Silence*) (Jacques Yves Cousteau, Louis Malle)

Director: Sergei Yutkevich (*Othello*)
Performance: Susan Hayward (*I'll Cry Tomorrow*)

1957
Palme d'Or: *Friendly Persuasion* (William Wyler)
Director: Robert Bresson (*A Man Escaped* (*Un Condamné à Mort S'Est Échappé*))
Actor: John Kitzmiller (*Valley of Peace* (*Dolina Miru*))
Actress: Giulietta Masina (*Cabiria* (*Nights of Cabiria*))

1958
Palme d'Or: *The Cranes Are Flying* (*Letiat Zhuravli*) (Mikhail Kalatozov)
Director: Ingmar Bergman (*So Close to Life* (*Nara Livet*))
Actor: Paul Newman (*The Long Hot Summer*)
Actress: Bibi Andersson, Eva Dahlbeck, Barbro Hiortas-Ornas, Ingrid Thulin (*So Close to Life* (*Nara Livet*))

1959
Palme d'Or: *Black Orpheus* (*Orfeu Negro*) (Marcel Camus)
Director: François Truffaut (*The 400 Blows* (*Les Quatre Cents Coups*))
Actor: Dean Stockwell, Bradford Dillman, Orson Welles (*Compulsion*)
Actress: Simone Signoret (*Room at the Top*)

1960
Palme d'Or: *La Dolce Vita* (Federico Fellini)
Actress: Melina Mercouri (*Never on Sunday*); Jeanne Moreau (*Moderato Cantabile*)

1961
Palme d'Or: *Viridiana* (Luis Buñuel); *Une Aussi Longue Absence* (Henri Colpi)
Director: Julia Solntseva (*The Flaming Years* (*Povest' Plamennykh Ket*))
Actor: Anthony Perkins (*Goodbye Again*)
Actress: Sophia Loren (*Two Women* (*La Ciociara*))

1962

Palme d'Or: *The Given Word* (*O Pagador de Promessas*) (Anselmo Duarte)

Actor: Ralph Richardson, Jason Robards Jnr, Dean Stockwell (*Long Day's Journey into Night*); Murray Melvin (*A Taste of Honey*)

Actress: Katharine Hepburn (*Long Day's Journey into Night*); Rita Tushingham (*A Taste of Honey*)

1963

Palme d'Or: *The Leopard* (*Il Gattopardo*) (Luchino Visconti)

Actor: Richard Harris (*This Sporting Life*)

Actress: Marina Vlady (*Queen Bee*, aka *The Conjugal Bed* (*Una Storia Moderna: L'Ape Regina*))

1964

Palme d'Or: *The Umbrellas of Cherbourg* (*Les Parapluies de Cherbourg*) (Jacques Demy)

Actor: Saro Urzi (*Seduced and Abandoned* (*Sedotta e Abbandonata*)); Antal Pager (*The Lark* (*Pacsirta*))

Actress: Anne Bancroft (*The Pumpkin Eater*); Barbara Barrie (*One Potato, Two Potato*)

1965

Palme d'Or: *The Knack . . . And How to Get It* (Richard Lester)

Director: Liviu Ciulei (*The Forest of the Hanged* (*Padurea Spinzuratilor*))

Actor: Terence Stamp (*The Collector*)

Actress: Samantha Eggar (*The Collector*)

1966

Palme d'Or: *A Man and a Woman* (*Un Homme et une Femme*) (Claude Lelouch); *The Birds, the Bees, and the Italians* (*Signore et Signori*) (Pietro Germi)

Director: Sergei Yutkevich (*Lenin in Poland* (*Lenin en Poland*))

Actor: Per Oscarrson (*Hunger* (*Sult*))

Actress: Vanessa Redgrave (*Morgan!*)

1967

Palme d'Or: *Blow Up* (Michelangelo Antonioni)

Director: Ferenc Kósa (*Ten Thousand Suns* (*Tízezer Nap*))

Actor: Odded Kotier (*Three Days and a Child*)

Actress: Pia Degermark (*Elvira Madigan*)

1969

Palme d'Or: *If . . .* (Lindsay Anderson)

Director: Glauber Rocha (*Antonio das Mortes*); Vojtech Jasn (*All My Good Countrymen* (*Vsichni Dobri Rodaci*))

Actor: Jean-Louis Trintignant (*Z*)

Actress: Vanessa Redgrave (*Isadora*)

1970

Palme d'Or: *M*A*S*H* (Robert Altman)

Director: John Boorman (*Leo the Last*)

Actor: Marcello Mastroianni (*Jealousy, Italian Style* (*Dramma della Gelosia . . . Tutti i Particolari in Cronaca*))

Actress: Ottavia Piccolo (*Metello*)

1971

Palme d'Or: *The Go-Between* (Joseph Losey)

Actor: Riccardo Cucciolla (*Sacco e Vanzetti*)

Actress: Kitty Winn (*Panic in Needle Park*)

1972

Palme d'Or: *The Mattei Affair* (*Il Caso Mattei*) (Francesco Rossi); *The Working Class Go to Heaven*, aka *Lulu the Tool* (*La Classe Operaia Va in Paradiso*) (Elio Petri)

Director: Miklós Jancsó (*Red Psalm* (*Még Kér A Nép*))

Actor: Jean Yanne (*We Will Not Grow Old Together* (*Nous Ne Vieillirons Pas Ensemble*))

Actress: Susannah York (*Images*)

1973

Palme d'Or: *Scarecrow* (Jerry Schatzberg); *The Hireling* (Alan Bridges)

Actor: Giancarlo Giannini (*Love and Anarchy* (*Film d'Amore e d'Anarchia*))

Actress: Joanne Woodward (*The Effect of Gamma Rays on Man-in-the-Moon Marigolds*)

1974

Palme d'Or: *The Conversation* (Francis Ford Coppola)

Actor: Jack Nicholson (*The Last Detail*)

Actress: Marie-José Nat (*Les Violons du Bal*)

1975

Palme d'Or: *Chronicle of the Burning Years* (*Ahdat Sanawouach Eldjamr*) (Mohammed Lakhdar Hamina)

Director: Michel Brault (*The Orders* (*Les Ordres*)); Costa-Gavras (*Special Section* (*Section Spéciale*))

Actor: Vittorio Gassman (*Scent of a Woman* (*Profumo di Donna*))

Actress: Valerie Perrine (*Lenny*)

1976

Palme d'Or: *Taxi Driver* (Martin Scorsese)

Director: Ettore Scola (*Down and Dirty* (*Brutti, Sporchi e Cattivi*))

Actor: José Luis Gomez (*Pascual Duarte*)

Actress: Mari Törőcsic (*Where Are You, Mrs Dery?* (*Deryne, Hol Van?*)); Dominique Sanda (*The Inheritance* (*L'Eredità Ferramonti*))

1977

Palme d'Or: *Padre Padrone* (Paolo and Vittorio Taviani)

Actor: Fernando Rey (*Elisa, My Life* (*Elisa, Vida Mia*))

Actress: Shelley Duvall (*Three Women*); Monique Mercure (*J. A. Martin Photographe*)

1978

Palme d'Or: *The Tree of Wooden Clogs* (*L'Albero degli Zoccoli*) (Ermanno Olmi)

Director: Nagisa Oshima (*The Empire of Passion* (*Ai No Borei*))
Actor: Jon Voight (*Coming Home*)
Actress: Jill Clayburgh (*An Unmarried Woman*); Isabelle Huppert (*Violette* (*Violette Nozière*))

1979

Palme d'Or: *The Tin Drum* (*Die Blechtrommel*) (Volker Schlöndorff; *Apocalypse Now* (Francis Ford Coppola)
Director: Terrence Malick (*Days of Heaven*)
Actor: Jack Lemmon (*The China Syndrome*)
Actress: Sally Field (*Norma Rae*)

1980

Palme d'Or: *Kagemusha* (Akira Kurosawa); *All That Jazz* (Bob Fosse)
Actor: Michel Piccoli (*Leap into the Void* (*Salto nel Vuoto*))
Actress: Anouk Aimée (*Leap into the Void* (*Salto nel Vuoto*))

1981

Palme d'Or: *Man of Iron* (*Czolowieck z Zelaza*) (Andrzej Wajda)
Actor: Ugo Tognazzi (*Tragedy of a Ridiculous Man* (*La Tragedia di un Uomo Ridicolo*))
Actress: Isabelle Adjani (*Quartet; Possession*)

1982

Palme d'Or: *Missing* (Costa-Gavras); *Yol* (Yilmaz Güney, Serif Gören)
Director: Werner Herzog (*Fitzcarraldo*)
Actor: Jack Lemmon (*Missing*)
Actress: Jadwiga Jankowska-Cieslak (*Another Way* (*Egymásra Nézve*))

1983

Palme d'Or: *The Ballad of Narayama* (*Narayama Bushi Ko*) (Shohei Imamura)
Actor: Gian Maria Volonte (*The Death of Mario Ricci* (*La Mort de Mario Ricci*))
Actress: Hanna Schygulla (*Story of Piera* (*Storia di Piera*))

1984

Palme d'Or: *Paris, Texas* (Wim Wenders)
Director: Bertrand Tavernier (*A Sunday in the Country* (*Un Dimanche à la Campagne*))
Actor: Alfredo Landa, Francisco Rabal (*The Holy Innocents* (*Los Santos Innocentes*))
Actress: Helen Mirren (*Cal*)

1985

Palme d'Or: *When Father Was Away on Business* (*Otak Na Sluzbenom Putu*) (Emir Kusturica)
Director: André Téchiné (*Rendezvous*)
Actor: William Hurt (*Kiss of the Spider Woman*)
Actress: Cher (*Mask*); Norma Aleandro (*The Official Story* (*La Historia Oficial*))

1986

Palme d'Or: *The Mission* (Roland Joffe)
Director: Martin Scorsese (*After Hours*)
Actor: Michel Blanc (*Menage* (*Tenue de Soirée*)); Bob Hoskins (*Mona Lisa*)
Actress: Barbara Sukowa (*Rosa Luxemburg*); Fernanda Torres (*I Love You* (*Eu Sei Que Vou Te Amar*))

1987

Palme d'Or: *Under Satan's Sun* (*Sous le Soleil de Satan*) (Maurice Pialat)
Director: Wim Wenders (*Wings of Desire* (*Der Himmel über Berlin*))
Actor: Marcello Mastroianni (*Dark Eyes* (*Ocie Ciornie*))
Actress: Barbara Hershey (*Shy People*)

1988

Palme d'Or: *Pelle the Conqueror* (*Pell Erobreren*) (Bille August)
Director: Fernando E. Solanas (*South* (*Sur*))
Actor: Forest Whitaker (*Bird*)
Actress: Barbara Hershey, Johdi May, Linda Mvusi (*A World Apart*)

1989

Palme d'Or: *sex, lies and videotape* (Steven Soderbergh)
Director: Emir Kusturica (*The Time of the Gypsies*)
Actor: James Spader (*sex, lies and videotape*)
Actress: Meryl Streep (*A Cry in the Dark*, aka *Evil Angels*)

1990

Palme d'Or: *Wild at Heart* (David Lynch)
Director: Pavel Lounguine (*Taxi Blues*)
Actor: Gérard Depardieu (*Cyrano de Bergerac*)
Actress: Krystyna Janda (*Interrogation* (*Przesluchanie*))

1991

Palme d'Or: *Barton Fink* (Joel and Ethan Coen)
Director: Joel Coen (*Barton Fink*)
Actor: John Turturro (*Barton Fink*)
Actress: Irene Jacob (*The Double Life of Veronique* (*La Double Vie de Véronique*))

1992

Palme d'Or: *Best Intentions* (*Den Goda Vilijan*) (Bille August)
Director: Robert Altman (*The Player*)
Actor: Tim Robbins (*The Player*)
Actress: Pernilla August (*Best Intentions* (*Den Goda Vilijan*))

1993

Palme d'Or: *Farewell My Concubine* (Chen Kaige); *The Piano* (Jane Campion)
Director: Mike Leigh (*Naked*)
Actor: David Thewlis (*Naked*)
Actress: Holly Hunter (*The Piano*)

1994

Palme d'Or: *Pulp Fiction* (Quentin Tarantino)
Director: Nanni Moretti (*Dear Diary*)
Actor: Ge You (*To Live*)
Actress: Virna Lisi (*Queen Margaret (La Reine Margot)*)

Books

Hollywood on the Riviera: The Inside Story of the Cannes Film Festival, Cari Beauchamp and Henri Béhar (1992).
Hype and Glory, William Goldman (Macdonald, 1990).

The Venice Film Festival's Golden Lion Winners

The Venice Film Festival, held every September, began in 1934, was suspended in 1942, and started again in 1946. Its main award is the Golden Lion of St Mark, which since 1980 has been given to the best feature film. The Golden Lion winners are:

1980
  Gloria (John Cassavetes); *Atlantic City* (Louis Malle)

1981
  The German Sisters (*Die Bleierne Zeit*) (Margarethe Von Trotta)

1982
  The State of Things (Wim Wenders)

1983
  First Name Carmen (*Prénom: Carmen*) (Jean-Luc Godard)

1984
  The Year of the Quiet Sun (*Rok Spokojnego Slonca*) (Krzysztof Zanussi)

1985
  Vagabonde (aka *Sans Toit Ni Loi*) (Agnès Varda)

1986
  The Green Ray (US: *Summer*) (*Le Rayon Vert*) (Eric Rohmer)

1987
  Au Revoir les Enfants (Louis Malle)

1988
  The Legend of the Holy Drinker (*La Leggenda del Santo Bevitore*) (Ermanno Olmi)

1989
  A City of Sadness (*Beiqing Chengshi*) (Hou Hsiao-hsien)

1990
  Rosencrantz and Guildenstern Are Dead (Tom Stoppard)

1991
  Urga (Nikita Mikhalkov)

1992
  The Story of Qiu Ju (*Qiu Ju de Guansi*) (Yang Zimou)

1993
  Short Cuts (Robert Altman); *Three Colours: Blue* (*Trois Couleurs: Bleu*) (Krzysztof Kiéslowski)

1994
  Before the Rain (Milcho Manchevski); *Vive l'Amour* (*Aiqing Wansui*) (Tsai Ming-liang)

The *Guardian's* Top 100 Contemporary Films 1980–1993

In 1993, the *Guardian* newspaper asked its readers to vote for the best films made since 1980. Depending on how you count, there are either 98 or 108 films in the resulting Top 100, since Ridley Scott's *Blade Runner* appears twice, at No. 9 in its original release and at No. 65 in its later *Director's Cut*, and Kieslowski's *A Short Film about Killing*, at No. 34, was part of his sequence of 10 films made originally for television – *Decalogue*, at No. 24. The results, with the dates of release and the directors' names, were:

1. *Cinema Paradiso*, 1989 (Giuseppe Tornatore).
2. *Blue Velvet*, 1986 (David Lynch).
3. *Raging Bull*, 1980 (Martin Scorsese).
4. *GoodFellas*, 1990 (Martin Scorsese).
5. *Fanny and Alexander*, 1982 (Ingmar Bergman).
6. *Heimat*, 1984 (Edgar Reitz).
7. *Wings of Desire*, 1987 (Wim Wenders).
8. *Babette's Feast*, 1987 (Gabriel Axel).
9. *Blade Runner*, 1982 (Ridley Scott).
10. *E.T.*, 1982 (Steven Spielberg).
11. *Paris, Texas*, 1984 (Wim Wenders).
12. *Reservoir Dogs*, 1991 (Quentin Tarantino).
13. *The Dead*, 1987 (John Huston).
14. *Brazil*, 1985 (Terry Gilliam).
15. *Once upon a Time in America*, 1984 (Sergio Leone).
16. *Unforgiven*, 1992 (Clint Eastwood).
17. *The Sacrifice*, 1986 (Andrei Tarkovsky).
18. *Cyrano de Bergerac*, 1990 (Jean-Paul Rappeneau).
19. *Jean de Florette*, 1986 (Claude Berri).
20. *Do the Right Thing*, 1989 (Spike Lee).
21. *Withnail and I*, 1987 (Bruce Robinson).
22. *Distant Voices, Still Lives*, 1988 (Terence Davies).
23. *Betty Blue*, 1986 (Jean-Jacques Beineix).
24. *Decalogue*, 1988 (Krzysztof Kieslowski).
25. *Ran*, 1985 (Akira Kurosawa).
26. *Field of Dreams*, 1989 (Phil Alden Robinson).
27. *Raise the Red Lantern*, 1991 (Zhang Yimou).
28. *Aliens*, 1986 (James Cameron).
29. *The King of Comedy*, 1983 (Martin Scorsese).
30. *Delicatessen*, 1990 (Jean-Pierre Jeunet, Marc Caro).
31. *Witness*, 1985 (Peter Weir).
32. *Rumble Fish*, 1983 (Francis Ford Coppola).
33. *Salvador*, 1986 (Oliver Stone).
34. *A Short Film about Killing*, 1986 (Krzysztof Kieslowski).
35. *Jesus of Montreal*, 1989 (Denys Arcand).
36. *Come and See*, 1985 (Elem Klimov).
37. *Local Hero*, 1983 (Bill Forsyth).
38. *Manon des Sources*, 1986 (Claude Berri).
39. *The Player*, 1992 (Robert Altman).
40. *The Blues Brothers*, 1980 (John Landis).
41. *Blood Simple*, 1983 (Joel and Ethan Coen).
42. *Gregory's Girl*, 1980 (Bill Forsyth).
43. *My Life as a Dog*, 1985 (Lasse Hallström).
44. *Diva*, 1981 (Jean-Jacques Beineix).
45. *Dances with Wolves*, 1990 (Kevin Costner).
46. *Raiders of the Lost Ark*, 1981 (Steven Spielberg).
47. *The Right Stuff*, 1983 (Philip Kaufman).
48. *The Commitments*, 1991 (Alan Parker).
49. *Nostalgia*, 1983 (Andrei Tarkovsky).
50. *The Cook, the Thief, His Wife and Her Lover*, 1989 (Peter Greenaway).
51. *Hannah and Her Sisters*, 1986 (Woody Allen).
52. *Heaven's Gate*, 1980 (Michael Cimino).
53. *Life Is Sweet*, 1990 (Mike Leigh).
54. *Les Amants du Pont-Neuf*, 1991 (Leos Carax).
55. *Miller's Crossing*, 1990 (Joel and Ethan Coen).
56. *A Room with a View*, 1985 (James Ivory).
57. *Au Revoir les Enfants*, 1988 (Louis Malle).
58. *Atlantic City*, 1981 (Louis Malle).
59. *Amadeus*, 1984 (Milos Forman).
60. *JFK*, 1991 (Oliver Stone).
61. *The Last Emperor*, 1987 (Bernardo Bertolucci).
62. *The Fisher King*, 1991 (Terry Gilliam).
63. *Truly Madly Deeply*, 1990 (Anthony Minghella).
64. *The Killing Fields*, 1984 (Roland Joffé).
65. *Blade Runner: The Director's Cut*, 1991 (Ridley Scott).
66. *Bagdad Café*, 1988 (Percy Adlon).
67. *One from the Heart*, 1982 (Francis Ford Coppola).
68. *Chariots of Fire*, 1981 (Hugh Hudson).
69. *House of Games*, 1987 (David Mamet).
70. *My Own Private Idaho*, 1991 (Gus Van Sant).
71. *Mona Lisa*, 1986 (Neil Jordan).
72. *Down by Law*, 1986 (Jim Jarmusch).
73. *Midnight Run*, 1988 (Martin Brest).
74. *Wild at Heart*, 1990 (David Lynch).
75. *Salaam Bombay!*, 1988 (Mira Nair).
76. *Company of Wolves*, 1984 (Neil Jordan).
77. *Wall Street*, 1987 (Oliver Stone).
78. *The Unbearable Lightness of Being*, 1987 (Philip Kaufman).
79. *Strictly Ballroom*, 1992 (Baz Luhrmann).
80. *Good Morning Vietnam*, 1987 (Barry Levinson).
81. *My Left Foot*, 1989 (Jim Sheridan).
82. *Shirley Valentine*, 1989 (Lewis Gilbert).
83. *Gandhi*, 1982 (Richard Attenborough).
84. *Videodrome*, 1982 (David Cronenberg).
85. *Silence of the Lambs*, 1990 (Jonathan Demme).

86. *Sophie's Choice*, 1982 (Alan J. Pakula).
87. *Educating Rita*, 1983 (Lewis Gilbert).
88. *Europa, Europa*, 1991 (Agnieszka Holland).
89. *Someone to Watch over Me*, 1987 (Ridley Scott).
90. *Full Metal Jacket*, 1987 (Stanley Kubrick).
91. *Orlando*, 1992 (Sally Potter).
92. *Prick Up Your Ears*, 1987 (Stephen Frears).
93. *Pretty Woman*, 1990 (Garry Marshall).

94. *Eureka*, 1982 (Nicolas Roeg).
95. *Edward Scissorhands*, 1990 (Tim Burton).
96. *Platoon*, 1986 (Oliver Stone).
97. *This Is Spinal Tap*, 1984 (Rob Reiner).
98. *Kiss of the Spider Woman*, 1985 (Hector Babenco).
99. *Koyaanisqatsi*, 1983 (Godfrey Reggio).
100. *The Hairdresser's Husband*, 1990 (Patrice Leconte).

Top 20 Films in America

According to figures published in the trade newspaper *Variety*, the following are the films that have taken the most money at the US box-office up to October 1994. The year of release, and names of the director and distributor, are given in brackets. I have rounded up the figures.

1. *ET* (1982, Steven Spielberg, Universal): $399.8m.
2. *Jurassic Park* (1993, Steven Spielberg, Universal): $356.5m.
3. *Star Wars* (1977, George Lucas, Twentieth Century-Fox): $322m.
4. *Home Alone* (1990, Chris Columbus, Twentieth Century-Fox): $285.8m.
5. *Forrest Gump* (1994, Roger Zemeckis, Paramount): $275m.
6. *The Lion King* (1994, Roger Allers, Rob Minkoff, Buena Vista): $267.4m.
7. *Return of the Jedi* (1983, Richard Marquand, Twentieth Century-Fox): $263.7m.
8. *Jaws* (1975, Steven Spielberg, Universal): $260m.
9. *Batman* (1989, Tim Burton, Warner): $251m.
10. *Raiders of the Lost Ark* (1981, Steven Spielberg, Paramount): $242.4m.
11. *Beverly Hills Cop* (1984, Martin Brest, Paramount): $234.8m.
12. *The Empire Strikes Back* (1980, Irvin Kershner, Twentieth Century-Fox): $222.7m.
13. *Ghostbusters* (1984, Ivan Reitman, Columbia): $220.9m.
14. *Mrs Doubtfire* (1993, Chris Columbus, Twentieth Century-Fox): $219.2m.
15. *Ghost* (1990, Jerry Zucker, Paramount): $217.6m.
16. *Aladdin* (1992, John Musker, Ron Clements, Ted Elliott, Terry Rossio, Buena Vista): $217.3m.
17. *Back to the Future* (1985, Robert Zemeckis, Universal): $208.2m.
18. *Terminator 2: Judgment Day* (1991, James Cameron, TriStar): $204.8m.
19. *Indiana Jones and the Last Crusade* (1989, Steven Spielberg, Paramount): $197.2m.
20. *Gone with the Wind* (1939, Victor Fleming, MGM): $191.7m.

The figures have not been adjusted for inflation. At a rough calculation, if inflation is taken into account, then *Gone with the Wind* is by far the biggest box-office success, followed by *Star Wars*, *The Sound of Music*, and *Jaws*. *The Ten Commandments*, *Ben Hur*, *The Sting*, and *The Godfather* would also be among the blockbusters. Disney's *Snow White and the Seven Dwarfs* would probably outrank its *The Lion King* as the most successful animated film. An alternative way of reckoning is to calculate the number of tickets sold. On this basis, *Gone with the Wind*'s cinema audience (for who knows how many millions have watched it on television or video?) was around 198m, *Star Wars* around 160m, and *The Sound of Music* around 112m.

Film Books and Periodicals

This is given because it has been requested; but it is given with some diffidence. The best books for you will depend upon your particular interest. As autobiographies, biographies, and other relevant books are covered in the *Companion*'s individual entries, what follows is a basic list of books and periodicals covering more general aspects of cinema. Those that are starred are particularly recommended as encapsulating a feeling about the movies wider than their own particular subject.

Many will be out of print, so the publisher and publication date (usually taken from my own copies and therefore not necessarily the first edition) are given in most instances to assist in tracking them down. There are specialist bookshops that can, at some cost, supply second-hand copies, and many will attempt to find out-of-print books for customers for a nominal service charge. Probably the best bookshops are the Cinema Bookshop in London's Great Russell Street, the BFI and MOMI bookshops in London's National Film Theatre and Museum of the Moving Image, and Larry Edmunds' Bookshop on Los Angeles's Hollywood Boulevard, but there are many other general shops with a good selection of new and second-hand film books.

Annual Guides

BFI Film and Television Handbook (British Film Institute). Digest of film and television production in Britain, produced by the British Film Institute.

Film Review, F. Maurice Speed and (since 1989) James Cameron Wilson (W. H. Allen). Reviews and credits of films released in Britain during the year, together with general essays, film books of the year, obituaries, etc. First published 1945.

Halliwell's Film Guide, ed. John Walker (HarperCollins). Reviews and star ratings for 20,000 films, together with technical and creative production credits and critics' comments, UK and US video, laser disc, video CD, and soundtrack availability, and index to four-star films. First published 1977.

International Motion Picture Almanac (Quigley Publications). Provides a who's who and information on the movie industry, from a US perspective. First published 1930.

Leonard Maltin's Movie and Video Guide (Plume). Reviews and star ratings for around 20,000 films, with details of director and cast, US video and laser disc availability, and index of leading directors and stars. First published 1969.

Projections, ed. John Boorman and Walter Donohue (Faber & Faber). Essays by 'film-makers on film-making'. First published 1992.

Screen International Film and Television Yearbook, ed. Oscar Moore and Peter Noble. Contains details of the world's film industries, together with a who's who. First published (as the *British Film Yearbook*, ed. Peter Noble) 1946.

Screen World, ed. John Willis (Applause). A pictorial and statistical record, together with credits, of the year's releases in the USA. First published 1949.

Variety International Film Guide, ed. Peter Cowie (Hamlyn). Reports on film-making around the world. First published 1964.

Variety Movie Guide, ed. Derek Elley (Hamlyn). Reprints edited reviews from the trade newspaper for around 7,500 films, including key technical and creative credits, UK and US video and laser disc availability, and an index of directors. First published 1992.

Virgin Film Guide, ed. James Monaco and the editors of *Baseline* (Virgin). Reviews and star ratings for around 3,500 films, together with technical and production credits, classification by genre, the Motion Picture Association of America rating and the British Board of Film Classification certificate, and an index of directors. First published 1992.

Reference

A–Z of Movie Directors, Ronald Bergan (Proteus, 1982).

The American Film Institute Catalog: Feature Films 1921–1930, ed. Kenneth W. Munden (Bowker, 1971).

The American Movies Reference Book: The Sound Era, ed. Paul Michael (Prentice Hall, 1969).

A Biographical Dictionary of the Cinema, David Thomson (Secker & Warburg, 1980).

British Film Actors' Credits, 1895–1987, Scott Palmer (St James Press, 1988).

The British Film Catalogue, Denis Gifford (David & Charles, 1985).

Character People, Ken D. Jones, Arthur F. McClure, and Alfred E. Twomey (Citadel Press, 1976).

Cinema: A Critical Dictionary Vols 1–2, ed. Richard Roud (Secker & Warburg, 1980).

The Complete Film Dictionary, Ira Konigsberg (Bloomsbury, 1988).

Cult Movie Stars, Danny Peary (Simon & Schuster, 1991).

Dictionary of Film Makers, Georges Sadoul, translated and updated by Peter Morris (University of California, 1972).

The Encyclopedia of Animated Cartoons, Jeff Lenburg (Facts on File, 1991).

The Encyclopedia of Film, James Monaco and the editors of *Baseline* (Perigee, 1991).

The Encyclopedia of Hollywood, Scott Siegel and Barbara Siegel (Avon Books, 1990).

The Encyclopedia of Monsters, Jeff Rovin (Facts on File, 1989).

The Encyclopedia of the Musical Film, Stanley Green (OUP, 1981).

Film Fanatics' Guide, David Jones (Merlin, 1988).

Focal Encyclopaedia of Film Techniques (Focal Press, 1969).

The Guinness Book of Movie Facts and Feats, Patrick Robinson (Guinness Publishing, fifth edition, 1993).

*The Great Movie Stars Vols 1–3, David Shipman (various, 1970/1991).

Hollywood Musicals Year by Year, Stanley Green (Hal Leonard, 1990).

The Illustrated Directory of Film Character Actors, David Quinlan (Batsford, 1985).

The Illustrated Encyclopedia of Cartoon Animals, Jeff Rovin (Prentice Hall, 1991).

The International Dictionary of Films and Filmmakers Vols 1–4, ed. Nicholas Thomas (St James Press, 1992).

The International Encyclopedia of Film, ed. Roger Manvell (Rainbird, 1972).

*The International Film Encyclopedia, Ephraim Katz (Macmillan, 1980).

The Movie Directors Story, Joel W. Finler (Octopus, 1985).

The Oxford Companion to Film, ed. Liz-Anne Bawden (OUP, 1976).

The Picturegoer's Who's Who and Encyclopaedia of the Screen Today (Odhams Press, 1933).

Quinlan's Illustrated Directory of Film Comedy Stars, David Quinlan (Batsford, 1992).

Quinlan's Illustrated Directory of Film Stars, David Quinlan (Batsford, third edition, 1991).

Quinlan's Illustrated Guide to Film Directors, David Quinlan (Batsford, 1983).

Reel Women: Pioneers of the Cinema, 1896 to the Present, Ally Acker (Batsford, 1991).

Variety's Who's Who in Showbusiness, ed. Mike Kaplan (Bowker, revised edition, 1989).

Who Played Who on the Screen, Roy Pickard (Batsford, 1988).

Who Was Who on Screen, Evelyn Mack Truitt (Bowker, 1984).

Who's Who in Hollywood Vols 1–2, David Ragan (Facts on File, 1992).

Who's Who of the Horrors and Other Fantasy Films, David J. Hogan (Barnes, 1980).

Women in Film: An International Guide, ed. Annette Kuhn with Susannah Radstone (Fawcett Columbine, 1990).

World Film Encyclopedia: A Universal Screen Guide, ed. Clarence Winchester (Amalgamated Press, 1933).

Histories

*The American Film Industry: An Historical Dictionary, Anthony Slide (Limelight, 1990).

The American Movie, William K. Everson (Atheneum, 1963).

The American Silent Film, William K. Everson (OUP, 1978).

Archaeology of the Cinema, K. W. Marek (Harcourt, Brace, 1965).

The British Film Collection 1896–1984, Patricia Warren (Elm Tree Books, 1984).

The Chronicle of the Movies, ed. Julian Brown (Hamlyn, 1991).

Cinema: The First Hundred Years, David Shipman (Weidenfeld & Nicolson, 1993).

A Concise History of the Cinema Vols 1–2, ed. Peter Cowie (Zwemmer/Barnes, 1971).

The Contemporary Cinema, Penelope Houston (Penguin, 1963).

Early American Cinema, Anthony Slide (Zwemmer, 1971).

*Film: An International History of the Medium, Robert Sklar (Thames & Hudson, 1993).

The Film Till Now, Paul Rotha and Richard Griffith (Spring Books, 1967).

Flashback: A Brief History of Film, Louis Giannetti and Scott Eyman (Prentice Hall, 1986).

The History of Movie Photography, Brian Coe (Eastview, 1981).

The History of the British Film 1896–1906, Rachael Low and Roger Manvell (Allen & Unwin, 1948).

The History of the British Film 1906–1914, Rachael Low (Allen & Unwin).

The History of the British Film 1914–1918, Rachael Low (Allen & Unwin).

The History of the British Film 1918–1929, Rachael Low (Allen & Unwin).

The History of the British Film: Documentary and Educational Films of the 30s, Rachael Low (Allen & Unwin).

*The History of the British Film: Film Making in 1930s Britain, Rachael Low (Allen & Unwin, 1985).

The History of the British Film: Films of Comment and Persuasion of the 30s, Rachael Low (Allen & Unwin).

Hollywood: 60 Great Years, 1930–1990, Jack Lodge, John Russell Taylor, Adrian Turner, Douglas Jarvis, David Castell, Mark Kermode (Prion, 1992).

The Hollywood Story, Joel W. Finler (Octopus, 1988).

The Illustrated History of the Cinema, ed. Ann Lloyd, consultant ed. David Robinson (Orbis, 1986).

The International Film Industry: An Historical Dictionary, Anthony Slide (Greenwood, 1989).

*The Liveliest Art, Arthur Knight (Macmillan, 1957).

The Long View: An International History of Cinema, Basil Wright (Secker & Warburg, 1974).

A Million and One Nights, Terry Ramsaye (Simon & Schuster, 1964).

The Miracle of the Movies, Leslie Wood (Burke, 1947).

Movie Parade, Paul Rotha (The Studio, 1936).

Movie-Made America: A Cultural History of American Movies, Robert Sklar (Random House, 1975).

*The Movies, Raymond Griffith and Arthur Mayer (Simon & Schuster, 1970).

*A Pictorial History of the Silent Screen, Daniel Blum (Spring Books, 1953).

*A Pictorial History of the Talkies, Daniel Blum (Grosset & Dunlap, 1958).

*A Short History of the Movies, Gerald Mast (Bobbs-Merrill, third edition, 1981).

Spellbound in Darkness: A History of the Silent Film, George C. Pratt (N.Y. Graphic Society, 1973).

*The Story of Cinema Vols 1–2, David Shipman (Hodder and Stoughton, 1982).

Variety History of Show Business (Hamlyn, 1993).

World Cinema 1895–1980, David Robinson (Eyre Methuen, 1981).

Studio Histories

COLUMBIA

The Columbia Story, Clive Hirshhorn (Pyramid, 1989).
Frank Capra: The Catastrophe of Success, Joseph McBride (Simon & Schuster, 1992).
Hail Columbia, Rochelle Larkin (Arlington House, 1975).
Indecent Exposure – A True Story of Hollywood and Wall Street, David McClintick (Columbus, 1982).
*King Cohn, Bob Thomas (Barrie & Rockliff, 1967).
The Name above the Title, Frank Capra (Macmillan, 1971).
Out of Focus: Power, Pride and Prejudice – David Puttnam in Hollywood, Charles Kipps (Century, 1989).

DISNEY

The Art of Walt Disney, Christopher Finch (Abrams, 1973).
The Disney Studio Story, Richard Holliss and Brian Sibley (Octopus, 1988).
The Disney Version, Richard Schickel (Pavilion, 1986).
The Walt Disney Biography, Bob Thomas (Simon & Schuster, 1977).

FOX

Don't Say Yes until I Finish Talking, Mel Gussow (Doubleday, 1971).
The Films of 20th Century-Fox, Tony Thomas and Aubrey Solomon (Citadel, 1985).
Skouras, King of the Fox Studios, Carlo Curti (Holloway House, 1967).
*The Studio, John Gregory Dunne (W. H. Allen, 1970).
Upton Sinclair Presents William Fox (Upton Sinclair, 1933).
Zanuck: The Rise and Fall of Hollywood's Last Tycoon, Leonard Mosley (Granada, 1984).
The Zanucks of Hollywood: The Dark Legacy of a Movie Dynasty, Marlys J. Harris (Crown, 1989).

MGM

Fade Out: The Calamitous Final Days of MGM, Peter Bart (Simon & Schuster, 1990).
Heyday: An Autobiography, Dore Schary (Little, Brown, 1979).
The Lion's Share: The Story of an Entertainment Empire, Bosley Crowther (Dutton, 1957).
*Merchant of Dreams: Louis B. Mayer, MGM and the Secret Hollywood (Sidgwick & Jackson, 1993).
The MGM Story, John Douglas Eames (Pyramid, 1990).
MGM: When the Lion Roars, Peter Hay (Turner, 1993).
*Picture, Lillian Ross (Rinehart, 1952).
Thalberg: Life and Legend, Bob Thomas (Doubleday, 1969).

PARAMOUNT

Mountain of Dreams, Leslie Halliwell (Stonehill, 1976).
The Paramount Story, John Douglas Eames (Octopus, 1985).
The Public Is Never Wrong, Adolph Zukor with Dale Kramer (Putnam, 1953).

RKO

Empire: The Life, Legend and Madness of Howard Hughes, Donald L. Bartlett and James B. Steele (Norton, 1979).

The RKO Story, Richard Jewell and Vernon Harbin (Arlington House, 1982).

UNITED ARTISTS

Final Cut: Dreams and Disaster in the Making of Heaven's Gate, Steven Bach (Jonathan Cape, 1985).
The United Artists Story, Ronald Bergan (Octopus, 1986).
United Artists: The Company Built by the Stars, Tino Balio (University of Wisconsin, 1976).

UNIVERSAL

The Horror Factory: The Horror Films of Universal 1931–55, Bruce Dettman and Michael Bedford (Gordon Press, 1976).
Universal Pictures: A Panoramic History, Michael G. Fitzgerald (Arlington House, 1977).
The Universal Story, Clive Hirshhorn (Octopus, 1983).

WARNER BROS

*The Devil's Candy: The Bonfire of the Vanities Goes to Hollywood, Julie Salamon (Jonathan Cape, 1992).
Here's Looking at You Kid: 50 Years of Fighting, Working and Dreaming at Warner Bros, James R. Silke (Little, Brown, 1976).
Inside Warner Brothers 1935–1951, Rudy Behlmer (Viking, 1985).
The Warner Bros Story, Clive Hirshhorn (Octopus, 1979).
Warner Brothers, Charles Higham (Scribner, 1976).

National Cinemas

AUSTRALIA

Australian Cinema, ed. Scott Murray (Allen & Unwin, 1994).
Australian Cinema 1970–1985, Brian McFarlane (Secker & Warburg, 1987).
The Australian Film Book 1930–Today, Simon Brand (Dreamweaver, 1985).
Australian Film: The Inside Story, Ken G. Hall (Summit, 1980).

BRITAIN

The Age of the Dream Palace: Cinema and Society in Britain 1930–1939, Jeffrey Richards (Routledge & Kegan Paul, 1984).
All Our Yesterdays: 90 Years of British Cinema, ed. Charles Barr (BFI, 1986).
Arrows of Desire: The Films of Michael Powell and Emeric Pressburger, Ian Christie (Waterstone, 1985).
British Cinema History, ed. James Curran and Vincent Porter (Weidenfeld & Nicolson, 1983).
British Cinema: The Lights that Failed, James Park (Batsford, 1990).
British Cinemas and Their Audiences, J. P. Mayer (Dobson, 1948).
British Film Music, John Huntley (Skelton Robinson, 1947).
A Critical History of British Cinema, Roy Armes (OUP, 1978).
*Ealing Studios, Charles Barr (David & Charles, 1977).
Elstree: The British Hollywood, Patricia Warren (Elm Tree, 1983).
Fifty Classic British Films, 1932–1982: A Pictorial Record, Anthony Slide (Dover, 1985).
The Film Business: A History of British Cinema 1896–1972, Ernest Betts (Allen & Unwin, 1973).
Forever Ealing, George Perry (Pavilion, 1981).

The Golden Gong: Fifty Years of the Rank Organization, Its Films and Its Stars, Quentin Falk (Columbus, 1987).

The Great British Picture Show, George Perry (Hart-Davis, MacGibbon, 1974).

*Hollywood England: The British Film Industry in the Sixties, Alexander Walker (Michael Joseph, 1974).

The House of Horror: The Complete Story of Hammer Films, ed. Allen Eyles, Robert Adkinson, and Nicholas Frey (Lorrimer, 1973).

*In Search of Gandhi, Richard Attenborough (The Bodley Head, 1982).

J. Arthur Rank and the British Film Industry, Geoffrey Macnab (Routledge, 1993).

Mass Observation at the Movies, ed. Jeffrey Richards and Dorothy Sheridan (Routledge, 1987).

A Mirror for England: British Movies from Austerity to Affluence, Raymond Durgnat (Faber & Faber, 1970).

My Indecision Is Final: The Rise and Fall of Goldcrest Films, Jake Eberts and Terry Ilott (Faber & Faber, 1990).

*National Heroes: British Cinema in the Seventies and Eighties, Alexander Walker (Harrap, 1985).

The Once and Future Film: British Cinema in the Seventies and Eighties, John Walker (Methuen, 1985).

Sex, Class and Realism: British Cinema 1956–1963, John Hill (BFI, 1986).

Travels in Greeneland: The Cinema of Graham Greene, Quentin Falk (Quartet, 1990).

Twenty Years of British Films, Michael Balcon, Ernest Lindgren, Forsyth Hardy, Roger Manvell (Falcon Press, 1947).

EASTERN EUROPE

The Czechoslovak New Wave, Peter Hames (University of California Press, 1985).

Directory of Eastern European Filmmakers and Films, ed. Keith Shiri (Flicks Books, 1992).

The Most Important Art: East European Film after 1945, Miura Leihm and Antonin J. Leihm (University of California Press, 1977).

World Cinema 1: Poland, Frank Bren (Flicks Books, 1990).

FRANCE

The Cinema in France After the New Wave, Jill Forbes (BFI/Macmillan, 1992).

Fifty Classic French Films, 1912–1982: A Pictorial Record, Anthony Slide (Dover, 1987).

French Cinema Since 1946: Vol 1: The Great Tradition, Roy Armes (Tantivy/Barnes, 1970).

French Cinema Since 1946: Vol 2: The Personal Style, Roy Armes (Tantivy/Barnes, 1970).

The Golden Age of French Cinema 1929–1939, John W. Martin (Columbus, 1983).

The Great French Films, James Reid Paris (Citadel, 1983).

The New Wave, James Monaco (OUP, 1976).

GERMANY

From Caligari to Hitler: A Psychological History of the German Film, Siegfried Kracauer (Noonday Press, 1960).

From Hitler to Heimat, Anton Kaes (Harvard University Press, 1989).

The Great German Films, Frederick W. Ott (Citadel, 1986).

*The Haunted Screen: Expressionism in German Cinema and the Influence of Max Reinhardt, Lotte H. Eisner (University of California Press, 1969).

The New German Cinema, John Sandford (Oswald Wolff, 1980).

New German Cinema: A History, Thomas Elsaesser (BFI/Macmillan, 1989).

IRELAND

Cinema and Ireland, Kevin Rockett, Luke Gibbons, John Hill (Croom Helm, 1987).

World Cinema 4: Ireland, Brian McIlroy (Flicks Books, 1989).

ITALY

Italian Cinema from Neorealism to the Present, Peter Bonadella (Ungar, 1985).

Italian Films, Robin Buss (Batsford, 1989).

Off Screen: Women and Film in Italy, ed. Giuliana Bruno and Maria Nadotti (Routledge, 1988).

Spaghetti Westerns: The Good, the Bad and the Violent, Thomas Weisser (McFarland, 1992).

JAPAN

Eros Plus Massacre: An Introduction to Japanese New Wave Cinema, David Desser (Indiana University Press, 1988).

Japan: Screen Guide, Arne Svensson (Barnes, 1970).

The Japanese Film: Art and Industry, Joseph Anderson and Donald Richie (Grove Press, 1960).

Japanese Film Directors, Audie Bock (Kodansha, 1985).

Japanese Films: A Filmography and Commentary, 1921–1989, Beverley Bare Buehrer (St James Press, 1990).

*The Japanese Movie: An Illustrated History, Donald Ritchie (Kodansha, 1966).

RUSSIA

*Kino: A History of the Russian and Soviet Film, Jay Leda (Allen & Unwin, 1983).

Silent Witness: Russian Films 1908–1919, ed. Paolo Cherchi Usai, Lorenzo Codelli, Carlo Montanaro, David Robinson (BFI, 1989).

SCANDINAVIA

Scandinavian Cinema: Films and Film-makers in Denmark, Finland, Iceland, Norway and Sweden, Peter Cowie (Tantivy, 1992).

Sweden Vols 1–2, Peter Cowie (Zwemmer/Barnes, 1970).

World Cinema 2: Sweden, Brian McIlroy (Flicks Books, 1986).

SOUTH AMERICA

Magical Reels: A History of Cinema in Latin America, John King (Verso, 1990).

Mexican Cinema: Reflections of a Society 1986–1988, Carl J. Mora (University of California Press, 1989).

South American Cinema: Dictionary of Film Makers, Luis Trelles Plazaola (University of Puerto Rico, 1989).

Twenty-Five Years of the New Latin American Cinema, ed. Michael Chanan (BFI, 1983).

SPAIN

New Cinema in Spain, Vicente Molina Foix (BFI, 1977).

Out of the Past: Spanish Cinema after Franco, John Hopewell (BFI, 1986).

Spanish Film under Franco, Virginia Higginbotham (University of Texas Press, 1988).

The World of Luis Buñuel, ed. Joan Mellen (OUP, 1978).

UNITED STATES

*Adventures in the Screen Trade: A Personal View of Hollywood and Screenwriting, William Goldman (Macdonald, 1983).

*America at the Movies, Margaret Farrand Thorp (Yale University Press, 1939).

American Cinema: Directors and Directions 1929–1968, Andrew Sarris (Dutton, 1968).

American Film Music, William Darby and Jack Du Bois (McFarland, 1990).

Behind the Scenes, Rudy Behlmer (Samuel French, 1990).

Canned Goods as Caviar: American Film Comedies of the 1930s, Gerald Weales (University of Chicago Press, 1985).

The Citizen Kane Book, Pauline Kael (Secker & Warburg, 1971).

*City of Nets: A Portrait of Hollywood in the 1940s, Otto Friedrich (Headline, 1987).

Close Encounters of the Third Kind Diary, Bob Balaban (Paradise Press, 1978).

David I. Selznick's Hollywood, Ronald Haver (Secker & Warburg, 1980).

An Empire of Their Own: How the Jews Invented Hollywood, Neal Gabler (W. H. Allen, 1988).

Hollywood at Sunset, Charles Higham (Saturday Review Press, 1972).

Hollywood in the Twenties, David Robinson (Zwemmer, 1968).

Hollywood in the Thirties, John Baxter (Zwemmer, 1968).

Hollywood in the Forties, Charles Higham and Joel Greenberg (Zwemmer, 1968).

Hollywood in the Fifties, Charles Higham and Joel Greenberg (Zwemmer, 1972).

Hollywood in the Sixties, John Baxter (Zwemmer, 1972).

Hollywood in the Seventies, Les Keyser (Zwemmer, 1984).

Hollywood the Dream Factory, Hortense Powdermaker (Secker & Warburg, 1950).

Hollywood the Haunted House, Paul Mayersberg (Allen Lane, 1967).

Hollywood: The Movie Colony, the Movie Makers, Leo Rosten (Harcourt, Brace, 1941).

Hollywood: The Pioneers, Kevin Brownlow and John Kobal (Collins, 1979).

Hollywood Talks Turkey: The Screen's Greatest Flops, Doug McClelland (Faber & Faber, 1989).

Hollywood: The Years of Innocence, John Kobal (Thames & Hudson, 1985).

Hollywood Tycoons, Norman Zierold (Hamish Hamilton, 1969).

*The Making of the Wizard of Oz, Aljean Harmetz (Pavilion, 1989).

Masters of Starlight: Photographers in Hollywood, David Fahey and Linda Rich (Columbus, 1988).

Medium Cool: The Movies of the 1960s, Ethan Mordden (Knopf, 1990).

*The Movie Moguls, Philip French (Weidenfeld & Nicolson, 1969).

*My Life with Cleopatra, Walter Wanger and Joe Hyams (Bantam, 1963).

Naked Hollywood: Money and Power in the Movies Today, Nicolas Kent (BBC Books, 1991).

*Of Mice and Magic: A History of American Animated Cartoons, Leonard Maltin (Plume, 1987).

Offscreen Onscreen: Inside Stories of 60 Great Films, Peter van Gelder (Aurum, 1990).

*The Parade's Gone By . . ., Kevin Brownlow (Secker & Warburg, 1960).

The Rise of the American Film, Lewis Jacobs (Harcourt, Brace, 1939).

Round Up the Usual Suspects: The Making of Casablanca – Bogart, Bergman, & World War II, Aljean Harmetz (Weidenfeld & Nicolson, 1993).

Seeing Is Believing: How Hollywood Taught Us to Stop Worrying and Love the Fifties, Peter Biskind (Pantheon, 1983).

Sometime in the Sun: The Hollywood Years of Fitzgerald, Faulkner, Nathanael West, Aldous Huxley, and James Agee, Tom Dardis (Scribner, 1976).

A Star Is Born: The Making of the 1954 Movie and its 1983 Restoration, Ronald Haver (Knopf, 1988).

Strangers in Paradise: The Hollywood Emigrés 1933–1950, John Russell Taylor (Faber & Faber, 1983).

Tales from the Hollywood Raj: The British in California, Sheridan Morley (Weidenfeld & Nicolson, 1983).

*The War, the West and the Wilderness, Kevin Brownlow (Secker & Warburg, 1979).

We're in the Money: Depression America and Its Films, Andrew Bergman (New York University Press, 1979).

Writers in Hollywood, Ian Hamilton (Heinemann, 1989).

Censorship and Related Issues

Behind the Mask of Innocence, Kevin Brownlow (Jonathan Cape, 1990).

The British Board of Film Censors: Film Censorship in Britain 1896–1950, James C. Robertson (Croom Helm, 1985).

Censored, Tom Dewe Mathews (Chatto & Windus, 1994).

*Cinema, Censorship and Sexuality 1909–1925, Annette Kuhn (Routledge, 1989).

The Dame in the Kimono: Hollywood Censorship and the Production Code from the 1920s to the 1960s, Leonard J. Leff and Jerold L. Simmons (Weidenfeld & Nicolson, 1990).

*The Face on the Cutting Room Floor: The Story of Movie and Television Censorship, Murray Schumach (Morrow, 1964).

Film Censorship, Guy Phelps (Gollancz, 1975).

From Reverence to Rape: The Treatment of Women in the Movies, Molly Haskell (Holt, Rinehart & Winston, 1974).

The Hidden Cinema: British Film Censorship in Action 1913–1972, James Robertson (Routledge, 1993).

Hollywood Lolitas: The Nymphet Syndrome in the Movies, Marianne Sinclair (Henry Holt, 1988).

Sex in the Movies: The Celluloid Sacrifice, Alexander Walker (Penguin, 1986).

What the Censor Saw, John Trevelyan (Michael Joseph, 1973).

The Critics

***Agee on Film: Reviews and Comments*, James Agee (Beacon Press, 1964).

Around Cinemas, James Agate (Home and Van Thal, 1946).

Before My Eyes: Film Criticism and Comment, Stanley Kauffmann (Harper & Row, 1980).

**The C. A. Lejeune Film Reader*, ed. Anthony Lejeune (Carcanet, 1991).

**Chestnuts in Her Lap*, C. A. Lejeune (Phoenix House, 1947).

Cruising the Movies: A Sexual Guide to 'Oldies' on TV, Boyd McDonald (Gay Presses of New York, 1985).

Deadline at Dawn: Film Writings 1980–1990, Judith Williamson (Marion Boyars, 1992).

**The Dilys Powell Film Reader*, ed. Christopher Cook (OUP, 1991).

Dilys Powell – The Golden Screen: Fifty Years of Films, ed. George Perry (Pavilion, 1989).

Durgnat on Film, Raymond Durgnat (Faber & Faber, 1976).

Halliwell's Hundred: A Nostalgic Choice of Films from the Golden Age, Leslie Halliwell (Granada, 1982).

Let's Go to the Pictures, Iris Barry (Chatto & Windus, 1936).

Movies into Film: Film Criticism 1967–1970, John Simon (Delta, 1971).

*On Movies, Dwight Macdonald (Prentice Hall, 1969).

100 Best Films of the Century, Barry Norman (Chapmans, 1992).

Pauline Kael's *New Yorker* reviews have been collected in the following volumes:

I Lost It at the Movies, 1964; *Kiss Kiss Bang Bang*, 1968; *Going Steady*, 1970; *Deeper into Movies*, 1974; *Reeling*, 1976; *When the Lights Go Down*, 1980; *Taking It All In*, 1984; *State of the Art*, 1986; *Hooked*, 1990; *Movie Love*, 1992.

Her capsule reviews were collected in *5001 Nights at the Movies*, 1982.

**The Pleasure Dome: The Collected Film Criticism 1935–1940*, Graham Greene (Secker & Warburg, 1972).

The Private Eye, the Cowboy and the Very Naked Girl, Judith Crist (Paperback Library, 1970).

Private Screenings: Views of the Cinema of the Sixties, John Simon (Macmillan, 1967).

**Produced and Abandoned: The National Society of Film Critics Write on the Best Films You've Never Seen*, ed. Michael Sragow (Mercury House, 1990).

Shots in the Dark, ed. Edgar Anstey, Roger Manvell, Ernest Lindgren, Paul Rotha (Allan Wingate, 1951).

Three-Quarter Face, Penelope Gilliatt (Secker & Warburg, 1980).

Film Theory and Practice

The Art of the Film, Ernest Lindgren (Allen & Unwin, 1948).

Celluloid: The Film Today, Paul Rotha (Longman, 1931).

Concepts in Film Theory, Dudley Andrew (OUP, 1984).

A Discovery of Cinema, Thorold Dickinson (OUP, 1970).

Documentary Film, Paul Rotha (Faber & Faber, 1936).

*Film, Roger Manvell (Pelican, 1944).

Film as Art, Rudolph Arnheim (Faber & Faber, 1969).

Film as Film, V. F. Perkins (Penguin, 1972).

Film Form, Sergei Eisenstein (Harcourt, Brace, 1947).

Film Language: A Semiotics of the Cinema, Christian Metz (OUP, 1974).

Film Sense, Sergei Eisenstein (Harcourt, Brace, 1949).

Film Technique and Film Acting, V. L. Pudovkin (Vision/Mayflower, 1958).

Footnotes to the Film, ed. Charles Davy (Lovat Dickson, 1938).

A Grammar of Film, Raymond Spottiswoode (Jonathan Cape, 1937).

Grierson on Documentary, ed. Forsyth Hardy (Faber & Faber, 1966).

The Immediate Experience, Robert Warshow (Doubleday, 1962).

Independent Filmmaking, Lenny Lipton (Straight Arrow, 1972).

Kino-Eye: The Writing of Dziga Vertov, ed. Annette Michelson (Pluto Press, 1984).

The Major Film Theories, J. Dudley Andrew (OUP, 1976).

Movies and Methods Vols 1–2, ed. Bill Nichols (University of California Press, 1985).

Rotha on the Film, Paul Rotha (Faber & Faber, 1958).

The Secret Language of Film, Jean-Claude Carrière (Faber & Faber, 1994).

Signs and Meanings in the Cinema, Peter Wollen (Secker & Warburg, 1974).

The Struggle for the Film, Hans Richter (Scolar Press, 1986).

The Technique of Film Editing, Karel Reisz (Focal Press, 1968).

What Is Cinema? Vols 1–2, André Bazin (University of California Press, 1971).

Types of Film

B MOVIES

B Movies, Don Miller (Curtis, 1973).

Kings of the B's: Working within the Hollywood System, ed. Todd McCarthy and Charles Flynn (E. P. Dutton, 1975).

Second Feature: The Best of the 'B' Films, John Cocchi (Citadel, 1991).

COMEDY

Canned Goods as Caviar: American Film Comedies of the 1930s, Gerald Weales (University of Chicago Press, 1985).

The Carry-On Book, Kenneth Eastaugh (David & Charles, 1978).

The Comic Mind, Gerald Mast (University of Chicago Press, 1979).

The Great Funnies: A History of Film Comedies, David Robinson (Studio Vista/Dutton, 1969).

Monty Python: Complete and Utter Theory of the Grotesque, ed. John O. Thompson (BFI, 1982).

Screwball: Hollywood's Madcap Romantic Comedies, Ed Sikov (Crown, 1989).

CRIME

The Great Cop Pictures, James Robert Parish (Scarecrow, 1989).

Crime Movies, Carlos Clarens (W. W. Norton, 1980).

Dark City: The Film Noir, Spencer Selby (St James Press, 1984).

Film Noir: An Encyclopedic Reference Guide, ed. Alain Silver and Elizabeth Ward (Bloomsbury, 1988).

The Great Detective Pictures, James Robert Parish and Michael R. Pitts (Scarecrow, 1990).

A Pictorial History of Crime Films, Ian Cameron (Hamlyn, 1975).
Prison Pictures from Hollywood, James Robert Parish (McFarland, 1990).

CULT
Cult Movies Vols 1–3, Danny Peary (Delacorte, 1981)
The Incredibly Strange Film Book, Jonathan Ross (Simon & Schuster, 1993).
Incredibly Strange Films, ed. V. Vale and Andrea Juno (Re/Search, 1986).
The Official Splatter Movie Guide Vols 1–2, John McCarty (St Martin's Press, 1989/1992).
The Psychotronic Encyclopedia of Film, Michael Weldon (Plexus, 1989).
Shock Xpress – the Essential Guide to Exploitation Cinema Vols 1–2, ed. Stefan Jaworzyn (Titan, 1993/1994).
Splatter Movies, John McCarty (Columbus, 1984).

FANTASY AND SCIENCE FICTION
Aurum Film Encyclopedia: Science Fiction, ed. Phil Hardy (Aurum, 1984).
Fantastic Cinema: An Illustrated Survey, Peter Nicholls (Ebury Press, 1984).
The Film Fantasy Scrapbook, Ray Harryhausen (Titan Books, 1984).
The Illustrated Dinosaur Movie Guide, Stephen Jones (Titan, 1993).
The Primal Screen: A History of Science Fiction Film, John Brosnan (Orbit, 1991).
The Science Fiction Image: The Illustrated Encyclopedia of Science Fiction in Film, Television, Radio and the Theater, Gene Wright (Columbus, 1983).

HISTORY
Epic Film: Myth and History, Derek Elley (Routledge & Kegan Paul, 1984).
Epic Films: Casts, Credits and Commentary on Over 250 Historical Spectacle Movies, Gary A. Smith (McFarland, 1991).
The Hollywood History of the World, George Fraser MacDonald (William Morrow, 1988).
Hollywood Holyland, Ken Darby (Scarecrow, 1992).
Religion in the Cinema, Ivan Butler (Barnes, 1979).
Visions of Yesterday, Jeffrey Richards (Routledge & Kegan Paul, 1973).

HORROR
Aurum Film Encyclopedia: Horror, ed. Phil Hardy (Aurum Press, revised edition, 1993).
Caligari's Children: The Film as Tale of Terror, S. S. Prawer (OUP, 1980).
The Dracula Centenary Book, Peter Haining (Souvenir Press, 1987).
The Frankenstein File, ed. Peter Haining (New English Library, 1977).
A Heritage of Horror: The English Gothic Cinema 1946–1972, David Pirie (Gordon Fraser, 1973).
Hollywood Gothic, David J. Skal (W. W. Norton, 1990).

Horror Film Directors 1931–1990, Dennis Fischer (McFarland, 1991).
Horror Movies, Carlos Clarens (Secker & Warburg, 1967).
The Illustrated Frankenstein Movie Guide, Stephen Jones (Titan, 1994).
The Illustrated Vampire Movie Guide, Stephen Jones (Titan, 1993).
Movie Monsters, Denis Gifford (Studio Vista, 1969).
Nightmare Movies: A Critical Guide to Contemporary Horror Films, Kim Newman (Harmony Books, 1988).
The Vampire Cinema, David Pirie (Galley Press, 1977).
The Vampire Film, Alan Silver and James Ursini (Barnes, 1976).

MUSICALS
All Singing! All Talking! All Dancing! A Pictorial History of the Movie Musical, John Springer (Cadillac, 1966).
The American Film Musical, Rick Altman (BFI/Indiana University Press, 1989).
Encyclopedia of Rock Music on Film, Linda J. Sandahl (Blandford Press, 1986).
Gotta Sing! Gotta Dance!: A Pictorial History of Film Musicals, John Kobal (Hamlyn, 1971).
The Hollywood Musical, Jane Feuer (BFI, 1982).
The Hollywood Musical, Clive Hirshhorn (Crown, 1981).
The Rock and Roll Movie Encyclopedia of the 1950s, Mark Thomas McGee (McFarland, 1990).
The World of Entertainment! Hollywood's Greatest Musicals, Hugh Fordin (Doubleday, 1975).

WAR
Hollywood at War, Ken D. Jones and Arthur F. McClure (Barnes, 1973).
Hollywood's Vietnam: From the Green Berets to Apocalypse Now, Gilbert Adair (Proteus, 1981).
A Pictorial History of War Films, Clyde Jeavons (Hamlyn, 1974).
War Movies, Jay Hyams (Gallery Books, 1984).

WESTERN
The Film Encyclopedia of Westerns, ed. Phil Hardy (Octopus, 1985).
The BFI Companion to the Western, ed. Edward Buscombe (BFI/André Deutsch, 1988).
Horizons West, Jim Kitses (Thames & Hudson, 1969).
The Life and Times of the Western Movie, Jay Hyams (Columbus, 1983).
A Pictorial History of the Western Film, William K. Everson (Citadel, 1969).
Shoot 'Em Ups, Les Adams and Buck Rainey (Arlington House, 1978).
The Western, Allen Eyles (Tantivy, 1975).
The Western from Silents to the Seventies, William K. Everson and George N. Fenin (Penguin, 1973).
Westerns, Philip French (Secker & Warburg, 1977).
Wild West Movies, Kim Newman (Bloomsbury, 1990).

OTHER
Black Action Films, James Robert Parish and George H. Hill (McFarland, 1989).

Martial Arts Movies: From Bruce Lee to the Ninjas, Richard Meyers, Amy Harlib, Bill and Karen Palmer (Citadel, 1985).

Road Movies: A Complete Guide to Cinema on Wheels, Mark Williams (Proteus, 1982).

The Samurai Film, Alain Silver (Columbus, 1983).

Sports in the Movies, Ronald Bergen (Proteus, 1982).

Journalism and Gossip

Do You Sleep in the Nude?, Rex Reed (W. H. Allen, 1969).

The 50-Year Decline and Fall of Hollywood, Ezra Goodman (Simon & Schuster, 1961).

Hollywood Babylon, Kenneth Anger (Straight Arrow, 1975).

Hollywood Babylon II, Kenneth Anger (Arrow Books, 1986).

Hollywood Revisited, Sheilah Graham (St Martin's Press, 1985).

Hollywood's Unsolved Mysteries, John Austin (SPI Books, 1992).

If You're Talking to Me, Your Career Must Be in Trouble: Movies, Mayhem and Malice, Joe Queenan (Picador, 1994).

People Will Talk, John Kobal (Aurum, 1986).

Rolling Breaks and Other Movie Business, Aljean Harmetz (Alfred A. Knopf, 1983).

Scratch an Actor: The Intimate Lowdown on Hollywood Nightlife, Sheilah Graham (W. H. Allen, 1969).

Self-Creations: 13 Impersonalities, Thomas B. Morgan (Michael Joseph, 1966). Includes profiles of Gary Cooper, Sammy Davis Jnr, Elia Kazan, Teenage Heroes (Frankie Avalon, Edd Byrnes), John Wayne.

Travolta to Keaton, Rex Reed (William Morrow, 1979).

Fiction

Blue Movie, Terry Southern (Calder and Boyars, 1973). A leading director attempts to make a film covering every aspect of love and desire.

The Carpetbaggers, Harold Robbins (1949). A millionaire playboy and plane-maker (who resembles Howard Hughes) moves to Hollywood in the 20s and 30s; filmed by Edward Dmytryk in 1954.

Concerning a Woman of Sin, ed. Daniel Talbot (Consul, 1960). Anthology of nine stories set in Hollywood: Ben Hecht's title story; John O'Hara's 'Brother'; Christopher Isherwood's 'The World in the Evening'; F. Scott Fitzgerald's 'Crazy Sunday'; William Saroyan's 'The Brokenhearted Comedian and the Girl Who Took the Place of His Unfaithful Wife'; Irwin Shaw's 'The City Was in Total Darkness'; Budd Schulberg's 'A Table at Ciro's'; Ring Lardner's 'The Love Nest'.

The Day of the Locust, Nathanael West (1939). An account of Hollywood's dispossessed; filmed by John Boorman in 1975.

The Deer Park, Norman Mailer (Allan Wingate, 1957). A young writer compromises his talent as he becomes involved in the lives of a movie director, a temperamental Hollywood star, and a sleazy producer.

Dirty Eddie, Ludwig Bemelmans (1947). Farcical fun at the expense of Hollywood.

The Disenchanted, Budd Schulberg (Random House, 1950). A young screenwriter in Hollywood witnesses the final collapse of an alcoholic writer (who resembles Scott Fitzgerald).

The Distant Laughter, Bryan Forbes (Collins, 1972). A film

director with a failing marriage to an actress embarks on his new film, a love story.

The Dream Merchants, Harold Robbins (1961). A film director becomes successful in the early days of Hollywood; made into a TV movie in 1980 by Vincent Sherman.

The Errol Flynn Movie, Geoff Nicholson (Hodder and Stoughton, 1993). An unknown actor cast as Errol Flynn in a biopic by an Australian director begins to realize how much he has in common with the late hell-raiser.

Flicker, Theodore Roszak (Summit, 1991). A film buff is drawn into a conspiracy to control the world through cinema as he investigates the disappearance of a horror-movie director.

Fowler's End, Gerald Kersh (Heinemann, 1957). A young man takes over as manager of a dingy flea-pit of a cinema in darkest North London.

Gone Tomorrow, Gary Indiana (Hodder and Stoughton, 1993). An actor goes to Colombia to appear in a film financed by a drug dealer and made by a disciple of a dead, drug-addicted, homosexual German director (who resembles Rainer Werner Fassbinder).

Inside Daisy Clover, Gavin Lambert (1959). The problems of a young actress in 30s Hollywood; filmed by Robert Mulligan in 1965.

The Last Tycoon, Scott Fitzgerald (1941). The travails of a film producer (who resembles Irving Thalberg); filmed by Elia Kazan in 1976.

The Little Sister, Raymond Chandler (Hamish Hamilton, 1949). A thriller that touches on life in Los Angeles.

The Loved One, Evelyn Waugh (Little, Brown, 1948). An English poet in Hollywood shocks the crusty expatriate community by going to work in a pet's funeral parlour. Described by its author as 'a little nightmare produced by the unaccustomed high living of a brief visit to Hollywood'; filmed by Tony Richardson in 1965.

Maybe the Moon, Armistead Maupin (Bantam, 1993). A diminutive actress who once played an elf in a hit movie longs for her chance of stardom. The book is dedicated to the late Tamara DeTreaux, who played ET in some scenes of the film.

Merton of the Movies, Harry Leon Wilson (1922). An innocent becomes a Hollywood star in the early silent days; filmed in 1924, in 1932 (as *Make Me a Star*) by William Beaudine, and in 1947 by Robert Alton.

Most Likely to Succeed, John Dos Passos (Prentice-Hall, 1954). A Marxist playwright goes to Hollywood.

A Mouse Is Born, Anita Loos (Jonathan Cape, 1951). A film star known as 'The Bust' tells of her rise to fame, fortune, and pregnancy.

Nobody Ordered Wolves, Jeffrey Dell. A satire on the film business.

The Player, Michael Tolkin (Atlantic Monthly Press, 1988). A film producer gets away with murder; filmed by Robert Altman in 1992.

Postcards from the Edge, Carrie Fisher (Simon & Schuster, 1987). A film actress tries to deal with her drug addiction and her overbearing showbiz mother; filmed by Mike Nichols in 1990.

Prater Violet, Christopher Isherwood (Methuen, 1946). In London in the mid-30s, a novelist is hired to work on the script of an historical romance with a Viennese film director.

The Producer, Richard Brooks (Simon & Schuster, 1961). An independent producer (who resembles Mark Hellinger) risks everything on one film.

Queen of Desire, Sam Toperoff (HarperCollins, 1992). Variations on the life of Marilyn Monroe.

Queenie, Michael Korda (Linden/Simon & Schuster, 1985). A half-caste girl from Calcutta (who resembles Merle Oberon) becomes a glamorous film star.

The Rewrite Man, Bryan Forbes (Michael Joseph, 1983). A scriptwriter goes to the South of France to try to salvage an historical epic that has run into trouble on- and off-screen.

Screen, Barry Malzberg (Olympia Press, 1970). A New York City Welfare Department investigator fantasizes about being married to Sophia Loren, seducing Elizabeth Taylor, and being seduced by Brigitte Bardot.

The Slide Area, Gavin Lambert (Penguin, 1959). Short stories about life in Hollywood.

A Slightly Used Woman, Peter Kortner (W. H. Allen, 1973). Scandal threatens to ruin for the second time the career of a Hollywood film star, trying to make a comeback in a TV series aimed at a family audience.

The Symbol, Alvan Bessie (Bodley Head, 1967). A voluptuous small-town girl (who resembles Marilyn Monroe) becomes a Hollywood star but fails to find love.

A Voyage to Puerilia, Elmer Rice (1930). A satire on Hollywood.

What Makes Sammy Run, Budd Schulberg (1961). Classic story of a producer (who resembles Jerry Wald) on the make.

White Hunter, Black Heart, Peter Viertel (W. H. Allen, 1954). A film director (who resembles John Huston) is more interested in shooting big game than his movie in Africa; filmed in 1990 by Clint Eastwood.

Film Periodicals

American Cinematographer: The International Journal of Film and Electronic Production Techniques, established 1920. Covers current cinema from the point of view of the cinematographer. Published monthly in Hollywood.

American Film: Film, Video and Television Arts. News and features on current cinema. Published bi-monthly, six times a year, from New York.

The Dark Side: The Magazine of the Macabre and Fantastic. British magazine covering horror films, video, and books. Published bi-monthly, six times a year.

Empire. British magazine, with news and features on current cinema, and reviews of new cinema, video, laser disc, and soundtrack releases. Published monthly.

Entertainment Weekly. American magazine covering all aspects of show-business: movies, television, books, music, and video.

Fangoria. Long-established American magazine covering horror, including films and books. Published monthly, except February and December.

Film Comment. Magazine covering current and past cinema. Published bi-monthly, six times a year, by the Film Society of Lincoln Center, New York.

Film Dope. British magazine providing biographical information and credits of actors, directors, and others involved in films. Published at irregular intervals, two or three times a year.

Film Review. British magazine with features and reviews of current cinema and video releases. Published monthly with special extra issues, including a video movie guide and a yearbook.

Films in Review. American magazine with reviews of new releases and features on past and current cinema. Published bi-monthly.

The Hollywood Reporter. US trade daily and weekly.

Impact. British magazine covering action movies and stars from around the world. Published monthly.

The Independent Film & Video Monthly. US magazine published by the Foundation for Independent Video and Film, covering all aspects of independent film-making. Published monthly except February and September.

Monthly Film Bulletin 1934–91. Monthly magazine containing reviews and complete credits for all feature films released in Britain. From May 1991, it was incorporated into *Sight and Sound*.

Movie Collector. British magazine aimed at film buffs, with features on past films and personalities, and reviews of current releases on video and laser discs, and soundtracks. Published monthly.

Movieline. Los Angeles-based magazine, with news and features on current cinema. Published monthly except February.

Premiere. US magazine, with news and features on current cinema. Published monthly.

Premiere (UK edition). Magazine containing a mix of original features and material originating in the US edition. Published monthly.

Screen International. British trade weekly.

Shivers. British magazine covering horror films, videos, and personalities. Published bi-monthly, six times a year.

Sight and Sound. Magazine with an academic approach to current and past films, published by the British Film Institute. Quarterly from 1935 until May 1991, when it became a monthly, incorporating the *Monthly Film Bulletin*. Now includes reviews and complete credits of all current cinema releases, and short reviews of new videos.

Starburst. British magazine covering science fiction in all its forms, including film and television. Published monthly.

US. American magazine featuring interviews and news on current show-business stars. Published monthly.

Variety. US trade daily and weekly.

A Brief History of the Cinema

1873
America: Eadweard Muybridge, an English photographer, uses cameras spaced along a race-track to capture the movement of a galloping horse.

1878
America: Muybridge improves his method of taking photographs of animals in motion. He begins work on a projector.

1881
America: Muybridge perfects his Zoopraxiscope, which uses rotating glass disks containing painted images based on his photographs. He lectures on his work in America and, from 1892, in Europe, inspiring others.

1884
America: American artist Thomas Eakins, one of Muybridge's assistants, creates a single-motion picture camera.
Britain: John Rudge, an inventor living in Bath, patents a means of showing animations with a magic lantern. William Friese-Greene later demonstrates it as his own invention.
Germany: Ottomar Anschütz photographs animals and men in motion which can be viewed on his Tachyscope.

1885
America: George Eastman markets film on a roll, made of sensitized paper.
Britain: William Friese-Greene, a Bath photographer, exhibits the results of his experiments in film: an image of a girl moving her eyes.

1887
Germany: Ottomar Anschütz demonstrates his Electro-Tachyscope, which uses a sequence of still photographs fitted on a large wheel and viewed through a small hole to produce the effect of motion. His machines are shown around the world, as penny-in-the-slot novelties.

1888
Britain: French inventor Louis Augustin Le Prince patents a machine to film and project a sequence of images.

1889
America: Eastman's company, now named Eastman Kodak, begins to manufacture roll-film on celluloid.
Thomas Edison takes out a patent on perforated film.

Britain: William Friese-Greene obtains a patent for a moving picture camera.

1890
France: Louis Augustin Le Prince boards a train for Paris at Dijon and vanishes. He is never seen again.

1891
America: Edison applies for a patent on the Kinetoscope, a cabinet for displaying film to one spectator at a time, designed by his assistant William Dickson.

1892
France: Émile Renaud exhibits his Praxinoscope, which projects brief animations of hand-drawn images onto a screen.

1893
Britain: Friese-Greene patents a rapid-sequence camera.

1894
America: Fred Ott, one of Edison's workers, is recorded sneezing on film shot in the inventor's 'Black Maria' studio. Edison's assistant Dickson makes films to show in the Kinetoscope. They last around 20 seconds and feature vaudeville acts and famous personalities, including Buffalo Bill Cody.
Edison begins to manufacture Kinetoscopes but doubts whether 'there is any commercial future in it'. The first Kinetoscope parlour opens in New York. More follow in other cities, although the glimpse of a Spanish dancer's ankle upsets some.
Britain: In October, Edison's Kinetoscope goes on show in Oxford Street, London.
Robert W. Paul, a London scientific instrument maker, is asked to copy Edison's Kinetoscope and discovers that Edison has not patented his invention in England. He works on improving it, by projecting images on a screen and by incorporating a wheel shaped like a Maltese cross to stop each frame of film for a moment in order to make the image seem less jerky.
Germany: Ottomar Anschütz demonstrates a projection system in Berlin.

1895
Films average between 40 to 80 feet in length, running for little more than a minute at most.
America: The American Mutoscope Company is set up to

manufacture peep-show machines. It soon goes into film production proper and is renamed the Biograph Company.

Britain: Robert W. Paul and photographer Birt Acres begin to collaborate on designing a motion picture camera. Acres films sporting events, including the Derby.

France: Louis and Auguste Lumière, partners in a photographic business, patent the Cinématographe, a camera and projector, in February. In March, they demonstrate the system with a film of their workers leaving the factory and go on to hold other demonstrations. The brothers open Le Cinématographe, the first-ever public film show, in the basement of the Grand Café in Paris on 28 December. Twelve films are shown during the half-hour show.

Germany: In Berlin, Max Skladanowsky patents his Bioskop projector and gives a public show of films in November.

1896

America: Edison demonstrates the new Vitascope, a projector designed by Thomas Armat. The first public show is held in a New York music hall on 23 April.

In June, the Lumière show opens in New York.

Britain: In January, Birt Acres demonstrates motion picture projection in London and founds the Northern Photographic Works.

On 20 February, the Lumière show opens in London. It transfers in March to the Empire Music Hall, Leicester Square.

On 21 February, Robert W. Paul demonstrates his method of motion picture projection, the Theatrograph. Shortly after, his films open at Olympia and become a special attraction at music halls, including the Alhambra, Leicester Square.

Paul makes the first British fiction film, *The Soldier's Courtship*, on the roof of the Alhambra in April. He films the Derby winners and screens it the next day to appreciative audiences. The Derby is later shown in colour, with the tints added by hand.

In Kingston-upon-Thames, the first cinema opens in a converted shop. It fails. But film flourishes as an attraction at fairground sideshows.

Denmark: Peter Elfelt shoots the first Danish film, a fake short of huskies pulling a sledge in the snows of Greenland.

France: Charles and Émile Pathé found the Pathé Frères, mainly to sell phonographs, but soon become involved in film production.

In Paris, George Méliès begins to make films with trick effects.

Auguste Baron begins working on a process of adding sound to film. He also invents a system of multi-screen cinema, Cinématorama, without attracting much interest.

Germany: Oskar Messter develops a motion picture camera and projection system.

India: The Lumière show opens in Bombay.

South Africa: Carl Hertz, a magician, shows as part of his stage act films bought, together with a projector, from Paul. He then takes them to Australia.

Spain: The first public film show of Lumière's films takes place in Madrid to an audience mainly of schoolgirls.

1897

France: In Paris, Alexander Rapoutat opens the first cinema devoted to newsreels.

One hundred and fifty people die in a Paris cinema fire caused by a burning projector, creating widespread concern about the safety of cinemas and equipment.

Spain: Fructuoso Gelabert makes the country's first fictional film, *Riña en un Café*.

1898

America: Biograph cameramen film war in Cuba.

Britain: Cecil M. Hepworth, son of a magic-lantern lecturer, writes *Animated Photography*, the first handbook on cinema.

In Brighton, G. A. Smith becomes the first Englishman to use double exposure for trick effects in *Cinderella and the Fairy Godmother* and other films.

The French Gaumont company opens a London office and begins making films at Dulwich.

American Charles Urban forms the Warwick Trading Company, which soon becomes a major producer and distributor.

1899

Films average around 70 feet in length, running for just over a minute.

Britain: Supply of American films dries up as Edison tries to combat what he regards as piracy. R. W. Paul opens one of Britain's earliest studios at New Southgate, North London, consisting of a stage, similar to that of a theatre, with a camera platform running on wheels in front of it. Among the first films produced is Dickens's *A Christmas Carol*.

Cecil M. Hepworth begins film production.

France: Auguste Baron perfects his system of sound cinema, but can find no one interested in exploiting his method.

Méliès' *Cinderella* is one of the first films to approach a narrative style.

1900

Australia: Joseph Perry directs films for the Salvation Army, including *Soldiers of the Cross*, mixing brief movies, lantern slides, and music.

Britain: The Warwick Trading Company's Joseph Rosenthal becomes the most celebrated of war cameramen with his film of the Boer War, which he follows with action from the Boxer Rebellion in China.

France: Léon Gaumont demonstrates synchronized sound and pictures.

1901

Britain: Will Barker founds the Autoscope Company and erects a rudimentary open-air studio at Stamford Hill, London.

G. H. Cricks and H. M. Sharp open a studio at Mitcham, Surrey, and make *Saved from the Burning Wreck* and a series of shorts featuring music-hall comedian Fred Evans.

1902

Films begin to reach a length of 250 feet or so, running for around four minutes.

Britain: Gaumont's Chronophone, by which gramophone

recordings are synchronized to films of music-hall performers, is installed at the London Pavilion.

France: Charles Pathé opens a studio and begins turning out a film a day.

Méliès makes *A Trip to the Moon*, the first science-fiction film.

Germany: Oskar Messter establishes a production company in Berlin and begins to make films using cabaret artists and actors.

Spain: Segundo de Chomón begins to make films full of trick effects, but finds it hard to attract finance. He is later to work in Italy on *Cabiria* and in France on *Napoleon*.

1903

America: Edwin S. Porter makes *Life of an American Fireman*, mixing real-life and staged action to tell a story. He follows it with *Uncle Tom's Cabin* and *The Great Train Robbery*, an exciting western drama which causes a sensation and influences future directors.

Britain: Cecil Hepworth builds an indoor studio at Walton-on-Thames and films scenes from *Alice in Wonderland*.

Denmark: Peter Elfelt makes the country's first fiction film, *Capital Punishment* (*Henrettelsen*).

France: Méliès makes another science-fiction film full of trick effects, *Impossible Voyage*.

1904

America: At the St Louis Exhibition, George C. Hale presents Hale's Tours: travelogues shown in a mock-up of a railway carriage with train sound-effects and a swinging floor to simulate movement. Similar shows open in other American cities.

Cinema owner William Fox founds a distribution company.

German inventor Oskar Messter demonstrates sound films at the St Louis World Exposition.

Britain: The Clarendon Film Company opens a studio in Croydon.

1905

America: The first nickelodeon, a simple cinema where the price of admission is five cents, opens in Pittsburgh.

Vitagraph, which will become the most successful production company of its day, opens its own studio in Brooklyn. Its stars include Florence Turner and plump comedian John Bunny.

Variety begins publication.

Britain: Cecil Hepworth, using his family as actors, makes *Rescued by Rover* at the cost of £7 and sells 400 copies of it at £8 a time. Actors who are to begin their careers at his studio include Chrissie White, Alma Taylor, Helen Mathers, and Ronald Colman.

The first purpose-built cinemas open in London: the New Gallery in Regent Street and the Rialto in Coventry Street.

Italy: *La Presa di Roma* is the country's first feature film.

1906

Films are reaching 850 feet in length, running for around 14 minutes.

America: Cartoonist Winsor McCay incorporates an animated cartoon into his vaudeville act.

Carl Laemmle opens a nickelodeon in Chicago.

Pennsylvania cinema owner S. L. Rothafel adds the scent of roses to the showing of the Pasadena Rose Bowl game, the first use of smells in the cinema.

Australia: Charles Tait makes *The Story of the Kelly Gang*, one of the longest narrative films so far, running for more than 40 minutes.

Britain: In Ealing, Will Barker opens the Barker Motion Picture Company, which amalgamates with the Warwick Trading Company. He shoots a film of Shakespeare's *Hamlet* in a day.

Hale's Tours opens in Oxford Street, London.

The first news cinema, the Daily Bioscope, opens in London.

G. A. Smith patents his Kinemacolor colour process.

Denmark: Ole Olsen, a former fairground operator, establishes Nordisk Films, which soon becomes one of Europe's biggest production companies.

France: Charles Pathé signs music-hall performer André Deed to make comic films.

Sweden: Inventor Sven Berglund works on a system of recording sound on film by an optical process.

1907

America: Gilbert M. Anderson and George K. Spoor form Essanay production company in Chicago.

Finland: Apollo Studios release the first Finnish feature, *The Moonshiners*.

France: Actor Charles Le Bargy and other people from the Comédie Française form Film d'Art to make artistic films. Camille Saint-Saëns is to write the scores for its first production, *The Assassination of the Duke de Guise*.

1908

America: Anderson moves Essanay to California, away from Edison's law suits, and begins starring as 'Bronco Billy' in more than 300 westerns in eight years, despite the fact that he can hardly sit on a horse.

D. W. Griffith, an actor and writer, directs his first film, *The Adventures of Dollie*, for Biograph.

Hale's Tours goes into liquidation.

Argentina: Mario Gallo makes *El Fusilamiento de Dorrego*, the country's first feature film using professional actors.

Brazil: Portuguese-born director and cinematographer Antonio Leal makes *Os Estranguladores* and *Os Guaranis*.

Britain: The Gaumont Company hold the first Trade Show. Sir Geoffrey Tearle plays Romeo for Gaumont's version of *Romeo and Juliet*.

Colour films are shown for the first time at London's Palace Theatre.

The British Cinephone system of recorded sound synchronized to pictures begins to be installed in cinemas.

Electric Theatres becomes the first British cinema chain.

France: Max Linder becomes Pathé's leading comedian when André Deed leaves to make films in Italy.

1909

America: Edison, with seven leading film production companies and France's Pathé and Méliès, forms the Motion Picture Patents Company, claiming a monopoly on film production, and attempting to control distribution and license exhibition.

Distributors William Fox and Carl Laemmle decide to fight the monopoly by making their own films.

In December, D. W. Griffith directs his 100th one-reel film for Biograph. His films for the year include *The Violin Maker of Cremona*, starring Mary Pickford, who had begun her career months earlier as an extra. She becomes known as 'The Biograph Girl with the Curls'.

Australia: A 4,000-seater cinema opens in Melbourne. In Sydney, the Colonial cinema shows films non-stop from 11 a.m. to 11 p.m.

Ireland: Irish novelist James Joyce opens Dublin's first cinema, with the aid of Swiss financiers.

1910

America: *Pathé's Weekly* becomes the first newsreel.

Britain: Montague Pyke opens a cinema chain offering greater comfort and luxury.

Paul closes his studio and returns to making scientific instruments.

Denmark: Actress Asta Nielsen creates a sensation in *The Abyss*, as a man-hungry circus performer.

1911

America: *Photoplay* and *Motion Picture Story Magazine* are the world's first fan magazines.

Britain: London's Scala Theatre begins a two-year run of showing colour films.

France: The lavish Gaumont Palace opens in Paris as the world's biggest and best cinema.

Italy: Giovanni Pastrone's *The Fall of Troy*, with its cast of thousands, is the first epic movie.

1912

America: Dorothy and Lillian Gish begin their careers in films by Griffith.

Mack Sennett forms Keystone with two partners and begins making slapstick comedies.

Carl Laemmle founds Universal Pictures.

Adolph Zukor founds the Famous Players Film Company and begins by importing the French *Queen Elizabeth*, starring Sarah Bernhardt.

Britain: The British Board of Film Censors is established.

Fred Karno decides to make a second tour of America's music halls. Among his troupe are Charlie Chaplin and Stan Laurel, who will not return.

France: Film d'Art releases Louis Mercanton's *Les Amours de la Reine Élizabeth*, starring an ageing Sarah Bernhardt, thus helping cinema gain respectability.

Auguste Baron invents a new multi-screen process, Multirama, but can find no backers.

Gaumont gives the first public show in Paris of its Chronophone, synchronizing sound and pictures.

Germany: Shooting begins at Babelsberg studios of Asta Nielsen in *The Death Dance*.

Italy: Enrico Guazzoni's *Quo Vadis?*, a 12-reel epic of Roman

life with a spectacular chariot race, is a box-office hit around the world.

Sweden: Inventor Sven Berglund claims to be the first to perfect a system of recording sound on film by an optical process.

1913

America: Mary Pickford signs a five-year contract with Adolph Zukor to become one of the first female film stars.

Fatty Arbuckle signs to make comedies for Mack Sennett.

Charlie Chaplin is spotted by Mack Sennett and goes to Hollywood.

The Adventures of Kathlyn, starring Kathlyn Williams, is the first serial, in 13 parts, to reach the cinemas.

Edison demonstrates his Kinetophone for synchronizing sound and pictures.

Orlando Kellum develops his system of synchronizing sound and pictures.

Vitagraph opens a studio in Santa Monica, California.

Jesse Lasky sets up the Jesse Lasky Feature Play Company.

Britain: Cinema attendance in Britain reaches an average of 10 visits a year.

Will Barker films *Jane Shore*.

Hepworth makes Dickens's *Barnaby Rudge*, restaging the Gordon Riots.

Eugene Lauste invents a method of recording sound on film, but fails to arouse any interest as war approaches. He emigrates to America.

India: Dadasaheb Phalke makes the first feature, *Raja Harishchandra*.

Sweden: Actor Victor Sjöström turns director with *Ingeborg Holm*.

Mauritz Stiller's *The Vampire* runs into censorship problems.

Venezuela: Lucas Manzano and Enrique Zimmerman direct the country's first feature film, *La Dama de las Cayenas*, based on Alexandre Dumas's *Camille*.

1914

America: Cecil B. De Mille shoots *The Squaw Man* in Los Angeles, converting a barn into a studio.

Mack Sennett makes the first comedy feature, *Tillie's Punctured Romance*, starring Chaplin, Mabel Normand, and Marie Dressler.

Pearl White stars in the serial *The Perils of Pauline*.

Winsor McCay creates the cartoon *Gertie the Dinosaur*.

William Fox produces his first feature.

Paramount Pictures is formed as a distribution company.

Poet Vachel Lindsay writes *Art of the Moving Picture*, one of the first critical studies of the new medium.

Britain: George Pearson directs *A Study in Scarlet*, the first major screen treatment of Sherlock Holmes.

Gaumont opens its new studio at Lime Grove, Shepherd's Bush.

France: Méliès runs out of money. His films are sold and many are destroyed to recover the celluloid.

Germany: Oskar Messter begins a weekly newsreel which is distributed around the world.

Italy: Giovanni Pastrone finishes the influential epic *Cabiria*.

1915

America: D. W. Griffith's *The Birth of a Nation*, 12 reels long and photographed by Bill Bitzer, causes a sensation when it opens in New York. It becomes the first film to be screened at the White House.

Cecil B. De Mille makes *The Cheat*, influential for its style and sexually suggestive content.

Chaplin goes to work for Essanay at $1,000 a week.

Douglas Fairbanks makes his film debut.

Triangle Films is set up by D. W. Griffith, Thomas Ince, and Mack Sennett.

Metro Pictures is founded and soon becomes a leading, though not particularly profitable, production company.

Edwin S. Porter retires from films.

Britain: A million people vote the six most popular British film stars as Alma Taylor, Elizabeth Risdon, Charlie Chaplin, Stewart Rome, Chrissie White, and Fred Evans.

Denmark: Nordisk releases more than 140 films during the year.

1916

America: D. W. Griffith releases the spectacular epic *Intolerance*, but audiences stay away.

Chaplin signs with Mutual for $10,000 a week. Mary Pickford demands and gets more from Zukor.

Zukor and Lasky acquire an interest in Paramount Pictures and merge their production companies.

Samuel Goldfish and his partners Archibald and Edgar Selwyn found Goldwyn Pictures. Goldfish soon takes the name as his own.

Britain: Hepworth's *Coming through the Rye* is seen by Queen Alexandra as the first film to have a Royal Command Performance.

Italy: Leading stage actress Eleanora Duse makes her only film, *Cenere*, but is disappointed with the result.

1917

America: Charlie Chaplin makes the first of his two-reel comedies, *The Cure* and *Easy Street*.

Fatty Arbuckle founds his own studio. Vaudeville performer Buster Keaton appears in many of his films.

After beginning as a Chaplin imitator, Harold Lloyd begins to define his own distinctive personality as a bespectacled, shy young man.

Erich Von Stroheim makes the first of his many appearances as a vicious Prussian officer in *For France*.

Douglas Fairbanks's earnings are more than $750,000 a year.

Britain: Cinema attendances reach 20 million a week.

Germany: The German High Command forms UFA to make propaganda films.

1918

America: Chaplin makes his first film, *A Dog's Life*, in his own studio, which resembles a British village. His *Shoulder Arms*, parodying war films, is a success.

Oscar Micheaux makes *The Homesteader*, from his novel, establishing the best-known production company making films for black audiences.

Warner Bros releases its first major feature, *My Four Years in Germany*.

1919

America: Lon Chaney becomes a star with *The Miracle Man*.

D. W. Griffith shoots *Broken Blossoms* with Richard Barthelmess and Lillian Gish.

Charlie Chaplin, D. W. Griffith, Mary Pickford, and Douglas Fairbanks form United Artists. *Hollywood* quips, 'The lunatics have taken charge of the asylum.'

Hal Roach opens his own studio and begins to make comedy films with such stars as Harold Lloyd, Laurel and Hardy, and Charley Chase.

Australia: Raymond Longford makes *The Sentimental Bloke*, the country's best-regarded silent.

Germany: Ernst Lubitsch establishes himself as a leading director with *Madame Dubarry*, starring Pola Negri and Emil Jannings as Louis XV.

Sweden: Yearly attendances reach eight million.

USSR: The film industry is nationalized.

1920

America: Douglas Fairbanks marries Mary Pickford. He begins his swashbuckling career with *The Mark of Zorro*.

Fatty Arbuckle is arrested on charges of rape and manslaughter following the death of Virginia Rappe at a party. His films are withdrawn from cinemas and the scandal ends his Hollywood career, despite his acquittal.

Britain: Paramount opens a London studio, but it soon folds.

Denmark: Nordisk's output falls to eight films a year.

Germany: Robert Weine directs the expressionist *The Cabinet of Dr Caligari*.

Paul Wegner directs *The Golem*, an influential monster movie.

Norway: Rasmus Breistein makes the first feature, *Anna, the Gypsy Girl*.

Sweden: Mauritz Stiller's comedy *Erotikon* excites audiences with its sexual innuendo.

1921

America: Charlie Chaplin's feature *The Kid* makes Jackie Coogan a star at the age of six.

Rudolph Valentino stars in *The Four Horsemen of the Apocalpyse* and creates a sensation. His appeal to women is increased by his next film, *The Sheik*.

Max Linder makes two features, *Seven Years Bad Luck* and *Be My Wife*.

D. W. Griffith makes *Dream Street*, with sound synchronized on disk at the film's beginning, using Orlando Kellum's system. It is a hit, but exhibitors remain unconvinced that talking pictures have a future.

Britain: *The Glorious Adventure* is the first feature in colour to be made in England.

At a meeting called to save the British film industry, William Friese-Greene makes a passionate speech in favour of the continuance of British production, sits down, and dies, penniless. A monument erected over his grave in Highgate Cemetery reads, 'The Inventor of Kinematography. His Genius Bestowed Upon Humanity The Boon of Commercial

Cinematography Of Which He Was The First Inventor And Patentee.'

Germany: UFA is privatized and soon becomes a leading company with large studios, laboratories, and cinemas.

Japan: Actor Teinosuke Kinugasa turns director with *The Death of My Sister* and soon exerts a powerful influence on the development of Japanese cinema.

Sweden: Benjamin Christensen directs the sexually explicit *Witchcraft through the Ages*.

Greta Garbo makes her debut as an extra in *A Fortune Hunter*.

Sven Berglund demonstrates his sound system in Stockholm.

1922

America: Harold Lloyd's *Grandma's Boy* establishes him as a gifted and original comedian.

Robert Flaherty makes *Nanook of the North*.

The Toll of the Sea, with Anna May Wong, is the first feature to be made using Technicolor's two-colour process.

The Power of Love, with Noah Beery, is the first feature to be made in 3-D.

Rin Tin Tin makes his debut in *The Man from Hell's River* and becomes the greatest dog star, saving Warner from bankruptcy during the 20s.

Irving Thalberg fires Erich Von Stroheim as director of *Merry Go Round* at Universal.

Director William Desmond Taylor is murdered and scandal follows with revelations of his involvement with Mabel Normand and others. Producers and distributors get together to form an association to 'maintain the highest possible moral and artistic standards'. The righteous Will Hays is chosen to head it.

The Cohn Brothers start C. B. C. Film Sales Corporation, which is to become Columbia Pictures in 1924.

Walt Disney founds Laugh-O-Gram Films in Kansas City with Ub Iwerks.

Samuel Goldwyn is forced out of Goldwyn Pictures.

Britain: The first British serial is released: *The Great London Mystery*, in 16 episodes, starring Lady Doris Stapleton and David Devant, the magician.

Germany: Fritz Lang makes *Dr Mabuse the Gambler*, about a master criminal.

F. W. Murnau directs the vampire film *Nosferatu*.

Ernst Lubitsch leaves to work in Hollywood.

Sven Berglund demonstrates his sound system in Berlin.

1923

America: Lon Chaney stars in *The Hunchback of Notre Dame*.

Harold Lloyd makes *Safety Last*, performing its dangerous stunts.

Cecil B. De Mille turns from sex to religion with *The Ten Commandments*.

James Cruze makes an epic western, *The Covered Wagon*, for Paramount.

Eric Von Stroheim turns Frank Norris's novel *McTeague* into an eight-hour epic which he cuts to four hours. Thalberg orders it reduced to two hours and finally releases it as *Greed*, a flawed masterpiece. Stroheim hardly works in Hollywood again.

The high-living Mabel Normand survives the scandal of William Desmond Taylor's death but her career falters when her chauffeur kills a millionaire at a party with her pistol.

Wallace Reid, Paramount's leading actor, dies of drug addiction at the age of 30. Mrs Wallace Reid stars in the anti-drug film *Human Wreckage*, as part of Hollywood's new moral crusade.

Disney goes to Hollywood to start his own studio.

Britain: The British National Film League is formed to promote local movies with 'British Film Week', in which exhibitors are urged to show British films. The audiences stay away.

Victor McLaglen and others campaign for protection of British films.

Germany: The government attempts to protect its film industry by allowing only German producers to import foreign films. American companies open German production offices to overcome the problem.

Hans Dreier leaves UFA for Hollywood where he joins Paramount to become head of its art department.

Italy: Guazzoni's epic *Messalina* captures the imagination with its climactic chariot race.

Sweden: Victor Sjöström leaves for Hollywood, where he will be known as Seastrom and direct for MGM.

1924

America: Buster Keaton's comic skills show to advantage in *Sherlock Jr* and the *Navigator*.

Douglas Fairbanks stars in *The Thief of Bagdad*.

English romantic novelist Elinor Glyn supervises the filming of her *Three Weeks*, about love on a tiger-skin rug. Two years later she will proclaim Clara Bow the 'It' girl.

Metro-Goldwyn-Mayer is formed from Metro Pictures, Louis B. Mayer's production company, and the Goldwyn Company. In charge of production is Irving Thalberg.

Scandal and rumours of murder follow the sudden death of producer and director Thomas Ince aboard William Randolph Hearst's yacht.

Britain: British film-making falters: Ideal Studios, British and Colonial, Stoll and Samuelson close. Broadwest and Hepworth cut production. But Michael Balcon and partners found Gainsborough Pictures at Islington Studios.

Germany: F. W. Murnau directs *The Last Laugh*, starring Emil Jannings.

Fritz Lang makes the epic *Die Nibelungen*.

Sweden: Mauritz Stiller directs *The Atonement of Gösta Berling* with Greta Garbo.

1925

America: Charlie Chaplin makes *The Gold Rush*.

Lon Chaney stars in *The Phantom of the Opera*.

MGM release *Ben Hur*, directed by Fred Niblo, after production problems.

Willis O'Brien creates the special effects for *The Lost World*, which include a dinosaur rampaging through London.

Joan Crawford makes her screen debut.

Stiller and Garbo sign contracts with MGM.

Warner Bros buys Vitagraph.

Britain: *The Lost World* becomes the world's first in-flight movie when it is shown on an Imperial Airways flight from London to France, but it is not until the 60s that in-flight movies become routine.

Lee De Forest Phonofilms opens a studio in Clapham, London to make films with integral sound, which are shown in music halls.

The British Empire Exhibition cinema at Wembley is the first in the UK to be equipped for showing talkies.

France: Leading comedian Max Linder and his wife are found dead in their hotel rooms, apparent suicides.

Germany: Ewald-André Dupont directs *Variety* starring Emil Jannings and English actor Warwick Ward.

Sweden: Mauritz Stiller and Greta Garbo leave for Hollywood, as does Benjamin Christensen.

USSR: Eisenstein makes *Strike* and *The Battleship Potemkin*, which are to influence all film-makers who see them.

1926

America: Buster Keaton makes his comic masterpiece, *The General*.

Ronald Colman stars in *Beau Geste*.

Stiller leaves MGM without making a film. He makes *Hotel Imperial* for Paramount.

The first all-sound film programme is shown at the Warner in New York in August using the Vitaphone method, with music recorded on heavy disks played at 33⅓ rpm.

Rudolph Valentino dies.

Britain: Alfred Hitchcock directs *The Lodger*, about Jack the Ripper.

France: Jean Renoir makes *Nana*.

Japan: Kinugasa's *A Page of Madness* almost does away with the need for titles.

USSR: Pudovkin's *Mother* is a brilliantly edited social melodrama.

1927

America: On 6 October *The Jazz Singer* opens at the Warner, and Al Jolson's cry of 'you ain't heard nothin' yet' ushers in the era of sound. It takes $3.5m at the box-office.

On 28 October, the first Fox Movietone newsreel with sound is shown at the Roxy, New York.

Cecil B. De Mille makes *The King of Kings*, on the life of Christ.

Garbo and John Gilbert are a romantic pair in *Flesh and the Devil*.

New York's lavish Roxy Theater, dubbed 'The Cathedral of the Motion Picture', opens, seating nearly 6,000.

William Fox shows his first sound-on-film short in January and in May shows *Seventh Heaven* with a synchronized musical accompaniment.

Will Hays draws up a production code for the industry, emphasizing morality.

Britain: Alfred Hitchcock directs the boxing drama *The Ring*.

The Cinematograph Films Act makes it compulsory for British cinemas to show seven and a half per cent local films, rising to 20 per cent by 1936. British studios begin to turn out 'quota quickies', low-budget films made with little finesse to satisfy the law.

Victor McLaglen decides to go to Hollywood.

British Lion Film Corporation opens studios at Beaconsfield.

George Tootell, organist of London's Stoll Theatre, publishes *How to Play the Cinema Organ*.

France: Abel Gance's epic five-hour *Napoleon* uses three screens to cinematic effect. It will be shown in the US in a 70-minute version in 1929.

Germany: Fritz Lang directs his futuristic, spectacular *Metropolis*.

F. W. Murnau leaves for Hollywood, where he makes *Sunrise*.

Sweden: Mauritz Stiller leaves Hollywood and returns to Stockholm to direct for the theatre.

1928

America: King Vidor's *The Crowd* tackles the impersonal nature of modern life.

Victor Sjöström directs *The Wind*, starring Lillian Gish.

Warner produce the first all-talking film, *The Lights of New York*.

Walt Disney makes the first Mickey Mouse cartoon and follows it with the first sound cartoon, *Steamboat Willie*, again starring Mickey Mouse.

RKO Radio Pictures is founded.

Frank Capra is hired by Columbia. His involvement, together with the acumen of Harry Cohn, is to take the studio from poverty row to the status of a major.

Britain: *The Jazz Singer* causes a sensation when it opens in London in September.

Alfred Hitchcock makes *Blackmail*, Britain's first all-talking feature film. Joan Barry speaks the dialogue for its Polish-born star Anny Ondra.

Herbert Wilcox directs *Dawn*, with Sybil Thorndike as Nurse Edith Cavell.

Opposition to sound remains strong. Edward Wood, editor of *Picture Show* annual, writes: 'True progress in picture plays must be based on maintaining the silence of the screen'. British distributors predict failure for the development.

France: Carl Theodor Dreyer's *The Passion of Joan of Arc* stars Maria Falconetti in her only screen role. It will be banned by the British censors.

Luis Buñuel makes *Le Chien Andalou* with Salvador Dali.

Germany: The Germans try to set up a European union to compete with Hollywood on equal terms. It fails.

Sweden: Mauritz Stiller dies.

USSR: Eisenstein makes a propaganda masterpiece, *October*.

Pudovkin makes *Storm over Asia*, about a Mongolian trapper who becomes a puppet emperor.

Dovzhenko makes *Arsenal*, set in World War I.

Dziga Vertov makes the abstract documentary *The Man with the Movie Camera*.

Kinugasa travels to Moscow from Japan to meet Eisenstein and Pudovkin.

1929

America: Cinema attendances reach 95 million in the second year of talkies, an increase of 38 million since 1927.

King Vidor makes *Hallelujah* with an all-black cast.

MGM's *Broadway Melody* is the first film musical with an original score.

The Marx Brothers make their debut in *The Cocoanuts*.

Douglas Fairbanks and Mary Pickford make their first sound film, Shakespeare's *The Taming of the Shrew*, 'with additional dialogue by Sam Taylor'.

The coming of sound ends many careers; Constance and Norma Talmadge retire. Those soon to return to Europe include Emil Jannings, Pola Negri, and Vilma Banky.

Warner Bros buy First National Pictures.

Fox develop a wide-screen system, Fox Grandeur, but it fails to catch on.

The first Academy Awards ceremony is held.

Britain: New studios, occupied by producer Archibald Nettlefold, open at Walton-on-Thames on the site of Hepworth's original studio.

France: Charles Pathé retires.

Méliès is found running a sweet-stall at a Paris station and is belatedly honoured for his contribution to cinema.

Germany: G. W. Pabst makes *Pandora's Box*, aka *Lulu*, with American actress Louise Brooks.

Karl Freund, leading German cinematographer, moves to Hollywood, as does director William Dieterle.

1930

America: Lewis Milestone makes the anti-war *All Quiet on the Western Front*.

Romantic star John Gilbert disappoints in his sound film *Redemption*.

The Marx Brothers star in *Animal Crackers*.

MGM publicize Anna Christie with the line 'Garbo Talks!'

The Motion Picture Producers and Distributors of America agree to a production code largely drawn up by the Reverend Daniel A. Lord, a Jesuit moralist. Its central principle is that 'no picture shall be produced which will lower the moral standards of those who see it'.

William Fox loses control of his company. Upton Sinclair, in his biography published in 1933, is to charge that Fox was forced out 'by a criminal conspiracy of Wall Street bankers'.

Monogram Productions opens, and will become one of the more successful 'Poverty Row' companies, turning out low-budget genre movies.

Britain: Tom Walls directs and stars in Ben Travers's Aldwych farce *Rookery Nook*, with most of its original cast, including Ralph Lynn and Robertson Hare.

Basil Dean founds the New Ealing Studios.

Denmark: George Schéevoigt makes the first talkie, *Eskimo*.

France: Demonstrators wreck a Paris cinema showing Luis Buñuel's surrealist *L'Age d'Or*, made in collaboration with Salvador Dali.

Germany: Joseph Von Sternberg makes *The Blue Angel*, starring Emil Jannings and Marlene Dietrich. Von Sternberg and Dietrich leave for Hollywood.

USSR: Alexander Dovzhenko makes the lyrical *Earth*.

1931

America: Chaplin stars in his sentimental comedy *City Lights*.

Cimarron, about the Oklahoma land rush, is a rugged epic.

Warner begins its gritty gangster films with *The Public Enemy* and *Little Caesar*, a cycle which is to make stars of Edward G. Robinson, James Cagney, and Humphrey Bogart.

Horror movies also catch the public imagination: Tod Browning makes *Dracula*, starring Bela Lugosi, and James Whale directs *Frankenstein*, starring Boris Karloff, for Universal, beginning that studio's long involvement with horror.

David O. Selznick becomes production chief at RKO.

Britain: Basil Dean produces Gracie Fields' first film, *Sally in Our Alley*.

Top films at the box-office include Ben Travers's farce *Plunder* and the American films *Hell's Angels*, *One Heavenly Night*, and *Trader Horn*.

Alexander Korda founds London Films.

France: René Clair makes the satirical *À Nous la Liberté*, which is to inspire Chaplin's *Modern Times* and the equally influential *Le Million*, an example of the possibilities of the film musical.

Jean Cocteau's experimental *The Blood of a Poet* excites admiration and derision.

Maurice Pagnol founds a film company and writes and produces film versions of his stage hit *Marius* and its successor *Fanny*, starring Raimu.

Germany: Fritz Lang directs *M*, starring Peter Lorre as a child murderer.

Leontine Sagan's all-female *Mädchen in Uniform*, about a schoolgirl's love for her female teacher, causes a sensation. The Nazis will ban it as an attack on authoritarianism.

India: *Alam Ara*, the first Indian talking picture, includes six songs and sets a lasting fashion.

Japan: Heinosuke Gosho's *The Neighbour's Wife and Mine* is the first talkie.

Norway: Tancred Ibsen makes the first talkie, *The Big Baptism*.

1932

America: MGM's star-studded *Grand Hotel* is the hit of the year.

Mervyn Le Roy's *I Am a Fugitive from a Chain Gang*, starring Paul Muni, epitomizes the Depression.

Howard Hawks directs *Scarface*, inspired by Al Capone.

Mae West makes her screen debut at the age of 40 in *Night after Night*.

Rouben Mamoulian directs Frederic March in *Dr Jekyll and Mr Hyde* for Paramount.

Johnny Weismuller as *Tarzan the Ape Man* provides escapist fare in the first of a series that will keep him occupied until the late 40s.

Marie Dressler tops the first *Motion Picture Herald-Fame* poll of US distributors for the top money-making stars, followed by Janet Gaynor, Joan Crawford, Charles Farrell, and Greta Garbo.*

Australia: Ken G. Hall makes the first talkie, *On Our Selection*, which becomes the most successful Australian film of the 30s and 40s.

Britain: Walter Forde directs an exciting and influential train thriller, *Rome Express*.

The Sunday Entertainments Act allows cinemas to open on Sundays.

*The list of America's top money-making stars is taken from Quigley Publications' annual *International Motion Picture Almanac*.

Gaumont opens a bigger and better studio at Lime Grove, one that will be able to handle the production of four films at the same time.

Britain produces 141 features, which is a little less than France (143) and Germany (164).

France: Jean Renoir makes *Boudu Saved from Drowning*.

Danish director Carl Dreyer makes his first sound movie, *Vampyr*.

Germany: Leni Riefenstahl directs and stars in *The Blue Light*.

Spain: José Buchs makes the first talkie, *Carceleras*.

1933

America: The average time for making a film is now 22 days. The average cost is $70,000. Production rises to 547 films.

Roman Scandals and *42nd Street* are the big hits of the year.

King Kong is the sensation of the year.

Fred Astaire dances for the first time with Ginger Rogers in *Flying Down to Rio*. They are to make nine more films together.

The Marx Brothers reach new heights of delirium in *Duck Soup*.

Garbo insists on John Gilbert as her co-star in *Queen Christina*. It is his last film.

Frank Capra directs *Lady for a Day* for Columbia.

James Whale makes *The Invisible Man* for Universal.

Selznick leaves RKO to join MGM. Merian C. Cooper takes over, following the success of his *King Kong* (co-director) for the studio. He lasts only a year.

Warner's production chief, Darryl F. Zanuck, leaves the studio.

Mae West has two box-office hits with *She Done Him Wrong* and *I'm No Angel*.

Mary Pickford retires and refuses to let her films be seen. She is to become ever more reclusive until her death in 1979.

Marie Dressler tops the box-office poll, followed by Will Rogers, Janet Gaynor, Eddie Cantor, and Wallace Beery.

Australia: Errol Flynn makes his film debut as Fletcher Christian in Charles Chauvel's *In the Wake of the Bounty*.

Britain: Average cost of a British film is £20,000. Production reaches 169 films.

Alexander Korda directs *The Private Life of Henry VIII* with Charles Laughton. Its success brings him financial backing.

Victor Savile's *The Good Companions*, starring Jessie Matthews, brings J. B. Priestley's bestselling novel to the screen.

Czechoslovakia: Gustav Machaty's *Ecstasy* becomes notorious for a scene with its star, Hedy Kiesler, naked. Five years later she goes to Hollywood, where she is renamed Hedy Lamarr.

France: Erich Von Stroheim stars in Jean Renoir's *La Grande Illusion* and makes his home in Paris.

Raymond Bernard directs an epic version of *Les Misérables* starring Harry Baur.

Jean Vigo makes his rebellious *Zero for Conduct*, which is immediately banned.

Germany: As the Nazis come to power, Dr Joseph Goebbels assumes control of the arts. He bans Fritz Lang's *The Testament of Dr Mabuse*, but offers to make him head of film production. Lang leaves for France and then goes to Hollywood. Many other producers, directors, and actors are to follow him into exile.

1934

America: Frank Capra directs *It Happened One Night* with Clark Gable and Claudette Colbert, and helps create a genre of screwball comedies.

W. C. Fields establishes himself in five films, including *Six of a Kind*.

Bette Davis seizes her opportunity in *Of Human Bondage*, from Somerset Maugham's novel.

Astaire and Rogers are together again in *The Gay Divorcée*.

The Production Code Administration is established under Joseph Breen to clean up films. Producers put the emphasis on family films and turn to Dickens and Victorian authors.

Will Rogers is voted America's top money-making star, followed by Clark Gable, Janet Gaynor, Wallace Beery, and Mae West.

Britain: Hitchcock directs the spy drama *The Man Who Knew Too Much*.

Anna Neagle flirts in *Nell Gwynn*, directed by future husband Herbert Wilcox.

Jessie Matthews stars in one of the few successful local musicals, *Evergreen*.

Basil Dean directs *Sings as We Go*, starring Gracie Fields.

J. Arthur Rank, heir to a flour and milling fortune, founds the Religious Film Society to make evangelical films and also the commercial British National Films. Its first film is *Turn of the Tide*, about Yorkshire fishing families.

France: Jean Vigo makes his masterpiece, *L'Atalante*. Its producers recut it and it flops at the box-office. Vigo dies at the age of 29 shortly after.

1935

America: George Cukor's *David Copperfield*, with W. C. Fields as Mr Micawber, is perfect family entertainment.

Charles Laughton's Captain Bligh in *Mutiny on the Bounty*, directed by Frank Lloyd, becomes the most memorable, and most often imitated, of screen villains.

Jeanette MacDonald and Nelson Eddy are together for the first of many times in *Naughty Marietta*.

Victor McLaglen stars in John Ford's *The Informer*.

Max Reinhardt transfers Shakespeare to the screen in *A Midsummer Night's Dream*, with James Cagney as Bottom and Mickey Rooney as Puck.

James Whale makes *The Bride of Frankenstein* for Universal, with the electric-haired Elsa Lanchester in the title role.

Becky Sharp, based on Thackeray's *Vanity Fair*, is the first feature to be made in three-colour Technicolor.

Fox merges with Twentieth Century Pictures to become Twentieth Century-Fox, with Darryl F. Zanuck in charge of production and Joseph Schenck as chairman.

Herbert Yates founds Republic Studios, which is to become the most successful producer of 'B' movies.

David O. Selznick forms Selznick Independent Pictures, his own production company.

Shirley Temple tops the list of America's money-making stars, followed by Will Rogers, Clark Gable, Fred Astaire and Ginger Rogers, and Joan Crawford.

Britain: Alfred Hitchcock makes the comedy thriller *The Thirty-Nine Steps* with Robert Donat and Madeleine Carroll.

Harold Young directs *The Scarlet Pimpernel*, starring Leslie Howard and Merle Oberon.

France: Jacques Feyder directs *Carnival in Flanders*, inspired by Old Master paintings.

Germany: Leni Riefenstahl directs *Triumph of the Will*, a documentary about Hitler's 1934 Nuremberg Rally.

The government sets up a censorship board, which is to ban many European and American films. It will also ban film criticism in the coming year.

1936

America: *San Francisco*, with Clark Gable, Spencer Tracy, Jeanette MacDonald, and a spectacular earthquake, is the box-office hit of the year.

Frank Capra directs for Columbia *Mr Deeds Goes to Town*, starring Gary Cooper.

Chaplin mocks the mechanical aspects of society in *Modern Times*.

Fritz Lang makes his first Hollywood film, *Fury*, about a lynch mob.

Douglas Fairbanks retires.

Irving Thalberg dies.

Carl Laemmle is ousted from Universal. But the company does well with Deanna Durbin's *Three Smart Girls*.

Selznick's first independent production is *Little Lord Fauntleroy*.

Shirley Temple remains America's top money-making star, followed by Clark Gable, Fred Astaire and Ginger Rogers, Robert Taylor, and Joe E. Brown.

Britain: Charles Laughton is at his best as *Rembrandt*, directed by Alexander Korda.

Korda produces H. G. Wells's futuristic *Things to Come*, directed by William Cameron Menzies, and the intriguing *The Man Who Could Work Miracles*.

René Clair makes *The Ghost Goes West*, starring Robert Donat.

Alfred Hitchcock directs the brooding *Sabotage*.

Basil Wright and Harry Watt make *Night Mail*, a documentary about a mail train with music by Benjamin Britten and words by W. H. Auden.

J. Arthur Rank opens the company's new Pinewood studios in Buckinghamshire.

Vigo's *Zero for Conduct* gets a British release and is disliked by critics. 'Nought for direction. Nought for acting,' writes the *Observer*'s C. A. Lejeune.

France: Pagnol directs *César*, the last of his Marius trilogy.

Jean Renoir makes the charming 40-minute *A Day in the Country*, although it is not seen until 1946.

Anatole Litvak, who left Germany when the Nazis came to power, directs the romantic *Mayerling*. He is invited to Hollywood.

Sweden: Ingrid Bergman stars in Gustaf Molander's *Intermezzo*, which she will remake in Hollywood for David O. Selznick three years later, bringing her international stardom.

1937

America: Garbo stars as *Camille*, directed by George Cukor.

Roland Colman and Douglas Fairbanks Jnr add distinction to the romantic, swashbuckling fantasy *The Prisoner of Zenda*.

Frank Capra provides more escapism in *Lost Horizon* for Columbia.

Laurel and Hardy reach comic perfection in *Way Out West*.

Disney's first animated feature, *Snow White and the Seven Dwarfs*, is a huge success.

America's top five money-making stars are Shirley Temple, Clark Gable, Robert Taylor, Bing Crosby, and Joan Withers.

Britain: Will Hay stars in his best comedy, *Oh, Mr Porter*, with help from Moore Marriott and Graham Moffat.

Flora Robson stars as Elizabeth I in *Fire over England*.

Anna Neagle takes the title role in Herbert Wilcox's successful *Victoria the Great*.

Wings of the Morning is the first British film to be made in Technicolor.

MGM open a British offshoot at Denham Studios.

France: Jean Renoir directs a prison-camp drama, *La Grande Illusion*, with Jean Gabin and Erich Von Stroheim, promoting tolerance between nations. It is banned in Nazi Germany and Fascist Italy.

Jean Gabin stars as the romantic gangster in Julien Duvivier's *Pépé Le Moko*. At Von Stroheim's suggestion, MGM acquire the rights to remake it. Duvivier and his female star Mireille Balin leave for Hollywood, but Gabin turns down the trip. Balin is back in France without making a film within a year.

Germany: Director Detlef Sierck makes *La Habanera*, attacking US colonialism, and leaves for Hollywood, where he becomes Douglas Sirk.

Goebbels puts film production under state control.

USSR: Eisenstein's *Bezhin Meadow* is banned.

1938

America: Errol Flynn brings new panache to swashbucklers in *The Adventures of Robin Hood*.

James Cagney stars as the doomed gangster in *Angels with Dirty Faces*, directed by Michael Curtiz.

Walter Wanger acquires the rights to *Pépé Le Moko* and remakes it as *Algiers*, with Charles Boyer and Hedy Lamarr.

Mickey Rooney and Judy Garland star in *Love Finds Andy Hardy*, the first of a wholesome series.

Shirley Temple still has the public enthralled, again topping the list of America's money-making stars, followed by Clark Gable, Sonja Henie, Mickey Rooney, and Spencer Tracy.

Britain: Hitchcock makes *The Lady Vanishes* with its very English chorus of Caldicott and Charters, played by Naughton Wayne and Basil Radford.

Bernard Shaw's *Pygmalion* is filmed with Wendy Hiller in the role of Eliza and earns the author a shared Oscar for best screenplay.

Michael Balcon becomes head of production at Ealing Studios.

France: Marcel Pagnol writes and directs *The Baker's Wife* with Raimu.

Marcel Carné's *Port of Shadows*, starring Jean Gabin and Michèle Morgan, establishes him as a leading director.

Méliès dies.

Germany: Leni Riefenstahl's *Olympia*, a film of the 1936 Olympic Games in Berlin, is released.

USSR: Eisenstein makes *Alexander Nevsky*, a patriotic epic about a German defeat, with a score by Prokoviev.

1939

America: David O. Selznick's *Gone with the Wind*, despite its production problems, swiftly becomes a Hollywood classic and a box-office phenomenon.

Judy Garland stars in *The Wizard of Oz* with Ray Bolger, Bert Lahr, and Jack Haley.

Garbo stars in *Ninotchka*, directed by Ernst Lubitsch and with Billy Wilder among the contributors to its witty script.

John Ford makes *Stagecoach*, giving John Wayne a boost to stardom and reviving the western.

Marlene Dietrich mocks western conventions in *Destry Rides Again*.

Charles Laughton stars as Quasimodo in *The Hunchback of Notre Dame*.

Laurence Olivier scores as Heathcliff in *Wuthering Heights*, directed by William Wyler.

Frank Capra makes the populist *Mr Smith Goes to Washington*, with James Stewart.

In a national poll, 22 million people vote Jeanette MacDonald America's most popular actress. But the professionals' poll of top money-makers is headed by Mickey Rooney, followed by Tyrone Power, Spencer Tracy, Clark Gable, and Shirley Temple, whose appeal is slipping as she grows older.

Britain: As the Second World War begins, cinemas are closed, briefly. Directors are urged to make films to raise morale – and to encourage America to enter the war. Pinewood Studios is used for food storage.

Zoltan Korda makes the rousing *The Four Feathers* with John Clements, Ralph Richardson, and C. Aubrey Smith.

Robert Donat and Greer Garson star in *Goodbye Mr Chips*, directed by Sam Wood at MGM's British studio.

Hitchcock directs the dull *Jamaica Inn* and then heads for Hollywood.

France: Marcel Carné's *Le Jour Se Lève* consolidates his reputation. Hollywood is to remake it eight years later with a happy ending as *The Long Night*.

Jean Renoir's *The Rules of the Game* is banned by the government soon after its release. He leaves for Italy.

Spain: As Franco is triumphant in the civil war, Luis Buñuel moves to New York.

1940

America: Walt Disney's *Pinocchio* builds on the success of *Snow White*; the studio's ambitious *Fantasia* marries animations to classical music and is the first feature to use stereo sound.

Rebecca, Hitchcock's first Hollywood film for David O. Selznick, combines mystery and romance with an impeccable cast headed by Laurence Olivier and Joan Fontaine.

Hitchcock also makes the suspenseful *Foreign Correspondent*, which encourages the US to enter the war.

George Cukor directs the sparkling *The Philadelphia Story*, teaming Katharine Hepburn, Cary Grant, and James Stewart.

Howard Hawks scores with the snappy newspaper comedy *His Girl Friday*.

Chaplin mocks Hitler and Mussolini, but also becomes sententious in *The Great Dictator*.

John Ford makes the sombre, populist *The Grapes of Wrath*.

Writer Preston Sturges turns director with *The Great McGinty*, the first of his exuberant comedies.

W. C. Fields writes (as Mahatma Kane Jeeves) and stars in his best comedy, *The Bank Dick*.

Mickey Rooney heads the list of top money-making stars, followed by Spencer Tracy, Clark Gable, singing cowboy Gene Autry, and Tyrone Power.

Australia: Charles Chauvel's First World War film *Forty Thousand Horsemen* is the first movie to attract attention outside the country for more than a decade.

Britain: Korda produces, Michael Powell and others direct, the great fantasy *The Thief of Bagdad*, pitting Sabu against the wicked Conrad Veidt.

Thorold Dickinson makes the suspenseful *Gaslight* with Anton Walbrook and Diana Wynyard.

Carol Reed directs the comedy thriller *Night Train to Munich*.

Quentin Reynolds narrates the documentary *London Can Take It*, directed by Harry Watt, designed to persuade the US to take up arms.

1941

America: Howard Hawks's *Sergeant York*, about a hero of the First World War, is the hit of the year.

Orson Welles, playing with 'the biggest electric train set a boy ever had', directs and stars in *Citizen Kane*. The film is attacked by the newspapers of William Randolph Hearst, the model for Kane.

Preston Sturges's *Sullivan's Travels* emphasizes the value of comedy.

Laurence Olivier and Vivien Leigh star in Alexander Korda's *That Hamilton Woman*, a mixture of sex and patriotism.

Writer John Huston turns director with the thriller *The Maltese Falcon*, with Humphrey Bogart, Mary Astor, Sidney Greenstreet, and Peter Lorre.

William Dieterle remakes the Faust story as *All that Money Can Buy*, with Walter Huston as the Devil.

Walt Disney releases another classic animated feature, *Dumbo*.

After starring in George Cukor's *Two-Faced Woman*, Garbo retires.

Jean Renoir makes his home in Hollywood.

Mickey Rooney remains America's top money-making star, testifying to the enduring appeal of the sentimental small-town Andy Hardy series, followed by Clark Gable, Abbott and Costello, Bob Hope, and Spencer Tracy.

Britain: Michael Powell's *The Forty-Ninth Parallel* stars Eric Portman as a German trying to escape from Canada to the US.

Dangerous Moonlight combines romance and the war with the music of Richard Addinsell's 'Warsaw Concerto' to provide some welcome escapism.

Leslie Howard brings *The Scarlet Pimpernel* up to date by directing and starring in *Pimpernel Smith*.

Humphrey Jennings directs the documentary *Listen to Britain*, about the effects of the war.

Harry Watt's *Target for Tonight* effectively tells the story of an RAF raid over Germany.

J. Arthur Rank acquires the Odeon cinema chain.

USSR: *Land of Youth* is a 3-D film that does away with the requirement for the audience to wear glasses.

1942

America: Michael Curtiz overcomes severe production problems to deliver, surprisingly, a Hollywood classic, *Casablanca*, with Humphrey Bogart and Ingrid Bergman.

Mervyn Le Roy's *Random Harvest*, with Ronald Colman and Greer Garson, is the weepie of the year, though running it close is *Now, Voyager*, with Bette Davis and Paul Henreid.

Orson Welles's *The Magnificent Ambersons* is re-edited without his approval.

Walt Disney scores again with the animated feature *Bambi*.

Ernst Lubitsch's *To Be or Not to Be*, starring Jack Benny, is fun at the expense of the Nazis.

Sam Wood's *Kings Row*, with Ann Sheridan and Robert Cummings, is gripping melodrama.

Jacques Tourneur's *Cat People* begins another cycle of horror movies, under producer Val Lewton.

Olsen and Johnson star in the anarchic comedy *Hellzapoppin*.

William Wyler's *Mrs Miniver* shows the plucky British coping with the war and scores heavily at the box-office.

Abbott and Costello head the poll of top money-making stars, followed by Clark Gable, Gary Cooper, Mickey Rooney, and Bob Hope.

Britain: David Lean and Noël Coward direct *In Which We Serve*, the archetypal British war film.

Went the Day Well?, directed by Alberto Cavalcanti from a Graham Greene story, shows German paratroopers invading an English village.

Thorold Dickinson's propaganda film *The Next of Kin* is a popular success.

Robert Donat as *Young Mr Pitt*, directed by Carol Reed, provides more wartime propaganda.

Italy: Luchino Visconti's first film, *Ossessione*, based on James M. Cain's *The Postman Always Rings Twice*, begins the flowering of neo-realist films.

1943

America: Howard Hughes's aerodynamic bra lifts Jane Russell to stardom in *The Outlaw*.

The Warner production of Irving Berlin's musical *This Is the Army* and Sam Wood's ponderous version of Ernest Hemingway's *For Whom the Bell Tolls* are the hits of the year.

Stormy Weather, a black musical with Bill Robinson, Lena Horne, and Fats Waller, is the liveliest film of the year.

The forces' pin-up Betty Grable heads the list of top money-making stars, followed by Bob Hope, Abbott and Costello, Bing Crosby, and Gary Cooper.

Britain: Frank Launder and Sidney Gilliat's *Millions Like Us* deals effectively with a family's wartime difficulties.

Gainsborough Films hit on what was to be a successful formula of historical romances with *The Man in Grey*, directed by Leslie Arliss and starring James Mason and Margaret Lockwood.

Michael Powell and Emeric Pressburger make *The Life and Death of Colonel Blimp*.

David MacDonald's *Desert Victory* is a classic war documentary.

Leslie Howard dies when his plane is shot down by Nazis. R. W. Paul dies.

Denmark: Carl Theodor Dreyer makes the spellbinding melodrama with a message, *Day of Wrath*.

Germany: Josef Von Baky directs *Münchausen*, commemorating the 25th anniversary of UFA.

1944

America: Leo McCarey's *Going My Way*, with Bing Crosby, is the hit of the year.

Billy Wilder's *Double Indemnity*, with Fred MacMurray and Barbara Stanwyck, is a classic film noir.

Otto Preminger's *Laura*, with Dana Andrews and Clifton Webb, is another early example of film noir.

Preston Sturges's *Hail the Conquering Hero* is a deft comedy of small-town attitudes to returning heroes.

Producer Arthur Freed makes MGM the home of the lavish musical, beginning with Vincente Minnelli's *Meet Me in St Louis*, with Judy Garland.

Luis Buñuel heads for Mexico to make films.

Bing Crosby is the top money-making star in America, followed by Gary Cooper, Bob Hope, Betty Grable, and Spencer Tracy.

Britain: Laurence Olivier makes Shakespeare's *Henry V* into a rousing patriotic boost to wartime spirits.

Carol Reed's semi-documentary *The Way Ahead*, with David Niven and Stanley Holloway, is a hit with audiences.

Sidney Gilliat's wartime story of romance and revenge, *Waterloo Road*, catches the mood of the moment.

Sweden: Alf Sjöberg makes *Frenzy*, scripted by Ingmar Bergman, and starring Mai Zetterling and Alf Kjellin.

1945

America: *The Bells of St Mary's* and Hitchcock's *Spellbound*, both starring Ingrid Bergman, are the hits of the year.

Billy Wilder makes an alcoholic classic, *The Lost Weekend*, starring Ray Milland.

Bing Crosby remains the top money-making star, followed by Van Johnson, Greer Garson, Betty Grable, and Spencer Tracy.

Britain: The documentary *True Glory* provides an uplifting account of the last years of the war.

David Lean has audiences laughing and weeping with *Brief Encounter* and *Blithe Spirit*, both written by Noël Coward.

Anthony Asquith's *The Way to the Stars*, written by Terence Rattigan, successfully recreates the wartime mood.

Robert Hamer makes a classic compendium of spooky stories, *Dead of Night*.

Leslie Arliss directs another successful piece of period hokum for Gainsborough, *The Wicked Lady*, with Margaret Lockwood and James Mason.

France: Marcel Carné makes his masterpiece *Les Enfants du Paradis* with Arletty and Jean-Louis Barrault.

Vigo's 12-year-old *Zero for Conduct* is seen for the first time.

Italy: Roberto Rossellini's *Rome, Open City*, using mainly amateur actors, electrifies audiences with its realistic approach.

USSR: Eisenstein makes *Ivan the Terrible, Part II*.

1946

America: Film audiences reach 100 million a week.

William Wyler's *The Best Years of Our Lives*, produced by Sam Goldwyn, is the box-office hit of the year with its stories of servicemen returning to civilian life.

Larry Parks stars as Al Jolson in *The Jolson Story*, another of the year's hits.

Duel in the Sun, produced by David O. Selznik and directed mainly by King Vidor, brings passion and profit back to the western.

Hitchcock does some of his best work in *Notorious*, with Cary Grant and Ingrid Bergman.

Howard Hawks's *The Big Sleep*, with Humphrey Bogart and Lauren Bacall, is a classic tough thriller.

Frank Capra's optimistic *It's a Wonderful Life* is received coolly, although it goes on to become a Christmas-time classic.

Universal merge with International Pictures to become Universal-International.

Bing Crosby is the American box-office favourite, followed by Ingrid Bergman, Van Johnson, Gary Cooper, and Bob Hope.

Australia: Harry Watt's *The Overlanders*, starring Chips Rafferty, is the first and best result of Ealing Studio's involvement in Australian film.

Britain: 25 million Britons go to the cinema each week.

Humphrey Jennings's documentary *A Diary for Timothy* encapsulates feelings about the war and the future.

David Lean makes a superb adaptation of Dickens's *Great Expectations*.

Michael Powell and Emeric Pressburger's *A Matter of Life and Death* (aka *Stairway to Heaven*) is a witty, stylish fantasy.

Caesar and Cleopatra, with Claude Rains and Vivien Leigh, is, at more than £1m, the most expensive British film so far, but no one cares for it.

Margaret Lockwood becomes Britain's favourite female star.

Feature-film production resumes at Pinewood.

Sir Alexander Korda says that discussions about the British film industry 'succeed only in betraying the sad fact that we have not got one – as yet.'

France: Jean Cocteau's austere and poetic *Beauty and the Beast* is an artistic success.

Italy: Roberto Rossellini consolidates his reputation with his war film *Paisa*.

Vittorio de Sica's *Shoeshine* is another key film in the neo-realist movement, with its story of two boys trying to survive in Nazi-occupied Rome.

1947

America: Edward Dmytryk's tense thriller *Crossfire* confronts racial bigotry.

The House Un-American Activities Committee, chaired by J. Parnell Thomas, holds its first hearings in Los Angeles, at which friendly witnesses condemn Communist subversion in Hollywood. HUAC subpoenas witnesses to appear at further hearings. Writers, directors, and producers who refuse to answer HUAC's questions on their political affiliations, known as the Hollywood Ten, are sentenced to prison (where some find as a fellow inmate J. Parnell Thomas, sentenced for misappropriation of funds). Blacklisting by the studios of those with left-wing sympathies begins and is to continue throughout the 50s. Carl Foreman, Joseph Losey, and Jules Dassin are among those who are to leave the US for Britain.

The top five money-making stars are the bland Bing Crosby, Betty Grable, Ingrid Bergman, Gary Cooper, and Humphrey Bogart.

Britain: Ronald Hamer's *It Always Rains on Sunday*, starring Googie Withers and John McCallum, is a sensational low-life melodrama.

Carol Reed directs *Odd Man Out*, starring James Mason, a performance that takes him to Hollywood.

The Boulting Brothers film *Brighton Rock*, Graham Greene's tale of a petty criminal, starring Richard Attenborough.

Michael Powell and Emeric Pressburger's heady *Black Narcissus* is one of the cinema's most beautiful films.

American studios embargo their films being shown, following a tax imposed on export. As Rank gears up to fill the cinemas with British films, the embargo is lifted, causing Rank financial problems. Managing director John Davis, who regards producers and directors as extravagant, wields the axe.

France: Claude Autant-Lara's *Devil in the Flesh* makes Gérard Philipe a star.

1948

America: Jules Dassin's *The Naked City* adopts a semi-documentary approach to a murder mystery.

Fred Astaire returns to dancing in *Easter Parade*, with Judy Garland.

The melodramatic *Johnny Belinda*, directed by Jean Negulesco, makes Jane Wyman a star.

The Supreme Court rules that the five major studios can no longer own cinemas, so breaking their monopoly of the industry.

Millionaire Howard Hughes buys RKO.

America's top five money-making stars are Bing Crosby, Betty Grable, Abbott and Costello, Gary Cooper, and Bob Hope.

Britain: David Lean's *Oliver Twist* is another successful Dickens adaptation, notable for Alec Guinness's performance as Fagin.

Michael Powell and Emeric Pressburger's *The Red Shoes*, with Moira Shearer, makes ballet box-office.

Carol Reed's *The Fallen Idol*, with Ralph Richardson, is a near-perfect piece of small-scale cinema.

Iceland: Loftur Gudmundsson makes the first talkie, *Between the Mountains and the Sea*.

Italy: Vittorio De Sica's *The Bicycle Thief* is hailed as a neo-realist classic.

Luchino Visconti takes neo-realism to its limits with *La Terra Trema*, about a Sicilian fisherman and his family.

Giuseppe De Santis's *Bitter Rice* attacks American corruption of Italian culture, but it is Silvano Mangano at work in the rice fields who attracts international attention.

USSR: Eisenstein dies less than three weeks after his 50th birthday.

1949

America: William Dieterle's glossy *Portrait of Jennie*, with

Jennifer Jones and Joseph Cotten, is David O. Selznick's last production with his company, which he folds soon after.

James Cagney is back at his energetic best as a brutal gangster in the searing *White Heat*.

Cecil B. De Mille's *Samson and Delilah*, with Victor Mature and Hedy Lamarr in the title roles, is a hit despite derisive reviews.

Gene Kelly and Stanley Donen's *On the Town*, produced by Arthur Freed and with a cast that includes Kelly, Frank Sinatra, and Vera-Ellen, is one of the best-ever musicals.

Larry Parks scores another hit with *Jolson Sings Again*.

The top five money-making stars are Bob Hope, Bing Crosby, Abbott and Costello, John Wayne, and Gary Cooper.

Britain: Carol Reed directs the thrilling *The Third Man*, starring Orson Welles and with Anton Karas's haunting zither music.

Three Ealing comedies make the studio's reputation: Henry Cornelius's *Passport to Pimlico*, Alexander Mackendrick's *Whisky Galore*, and Robert Hamer's *Kind Hearts and Coronets*.

Rank sells its Shepherd's Bush studios to BBC-TV.

France: Jacques Tati's *Jour de Fête* introduces his gentle humour to the world.

1950

America: Billy Wilder's *Sunset Boulevard* is a tart classic, with William Holden as the innocent who becomes involved with ageing star Gloria Swanson.

Joseph Mankiewicz's *All about Eve* gives Bette Davis the best role of her career as a bitchy actress.

Delmer Daves's *Broken Arrow* is the first revisionist western, on the side of the Indians.

Judy Holliday scores as the not-so-dumb chorus girl in *Born Yesterday*, directed by George Cukor.

Disney's live-action film *Treasure Island* provides Robert Newton with the opportunity for an eye-rolling, lip-smacking performance as Long John Silver.

The top five money-making stars are John Wayne, Bob Hope, Bing Crosby, Betty Grable, and James Stewart.

Britain: Basil Dearden directs the crime drama *The Blue Lamp*, starring Dirk Bogarde and Jack Warner, which is to inspire the long-running television series *Dixon of Dock Green*.

The Boulting Brothers make a tense and influential thriller, *Seven Days to Noon*.

Frank Launder's *The Happiest Days of Your Life* is a sprightly comedy, sparked by the performances of Alastair Sim and Margaret Rutherford.

The prison-camp drama, *The Wooden Horse*, is a success, as nostalgia for recent heroics continues.

France: Jean Cocteau's *Orpheus* is a fantastic success and a successful fantasy.

Max Ophuls makes the stylish and sexy *La Ronde*. Its banning in New York leads to a court case that eventually frees films from local censorship.

Robert Bresson directs the austere *The Diary of a Country Priest*.

Italy: Ingrid Bergman stars in *Stromboli*, directed by Roberto Rossellini, and scandalizes many when she has a child by him, an event that is to keep her away from Hollywood for much of the decade.

Mexico: Luis Buñuel signals his re-emergence with *The Young and the Damned*.

Sweden: Alf Sjöberg directs Anita Björk and Ulf Palme in an exemplary version of Strindberg's *Miss Julie*.

1951

America: Vincente Minnelli scores with *An American in Paris*, culminating in a ballet sequence for Gene Kelly and Leslie Caron.

Marlon Brando makes his film debut in the role that brought him fame on Broadway: Stanley Kowalski in *A Streetcar Named Desire*, directed by Elia Kazan.

Montgomery Clift is at his best in the steamy *A Place in the Sun*, also starring Elizabeth Taylor and directed by George Stevens.

Hitchcock makes the quirky *Strangers on a Train*, with Farley Granger and Robert Walker.

Dean Martin and Jerry Lewis star in *Sailor, Beware* to become the top comedy act.

Howard Hawks's *The Thing* begins a cycle of monster movies, based on fear of the atom bomb.

Larry Parks admits to having been a Communist at the HUAC hearings. His contract with Columbia, and his film career, ends.

Louis B. Mayer is forced out of MGM, to be replaced by Dore Schary.

The box-office favourites are John Wayne, Dean Martin and Jerry Lewis, Betty Grable, Abbott and Costello, and Bing Crosby.

Britain: Ealing comedies keep audiences happy with Charles Crichton's *The Lavender Hill Mob* and Alexander Mackendrick's *The Man in the White Suit*, starring Alec Guinness.

John Huston's *The African Queen* delights, with the antagonistic Humphrey Bogart and Katharine Hepburn.

Michael Powell and Emeric Pressburger's *The Tales of Hoffman* combines operetta and ballet in a remarkable way.

John Boulting directs the pageant-like *The Magic Box*, on the life of William Friese-Greene, as part of the Festival of Britain celebrations.

France: Robert Bresson's *Diary of a Country Priest* gains him international fame.

Japan: Kurosawa's *Rashomon* opens Western eyes to Japanese cinema.

Yashujiro Ozu makes the complex family drama *Early Summer*.

1952

America: Cecil B. De Mille's circus film, *The Greatest Show on Earth*, is a smash hit.

This Is Cinerama, a film using stereo sound and a wide-screen process that requires three projectors, causes a sensation with its opening roller-coaster ride, but the system is cumbersome and there are no more than 40 cinemas equipped to show its films by the early 60s.

Fred Zinnemann makes a classic western, *High Noon*, with Gary Cooper, which can be read as a condemnation of blacklisting in Hollywood.

Gene Kelly stars in *Singin' in the Rain*, a brilliant musical about Hollywood at the time the talkies arrived.

Charlie Chaplin's *Limelight* seems a sentimental farewell to his own past.

Arch Oboler's *Bwana Devil* revives interest in 3-D films.

Charlie Chaplin leaves to visit Britain and is told by the Attorney-General not to return.

John Garfield dies of a heart attack. Friends claim it was caused by the stress of his appearance as an unfriendly witness before HUAC and his subsequent blacklisting.

Decca Records takes over Universal.

Dean Martin and Jerry Lewis are tops at the box-office, followed by Gary Cooper, John Wayne, Bing Crosby, and Bob Hope.

Britain: David Lean directs the topical *The Sound Barrier*, with Ralph Richardson and Nigel Patrick.

Anthony Asquith's version of Oscar Wilde's *The Importance of Being Earnest* captures Edith Evans's definitive performance as Lady Bracknell.

The National Film Theatre is created from a cinema built for the Festival of Britain.

France: René Clément directs *Forbidden Games*, a sombre film of childhood trauma.

Jacques Becker's *Casque d'Or*, with Simone Signoret and Serge Reggiani, is an impeccable piece of film-making.

Brigitte Bardot lands her first significant role in *The Lighthouse Keeper's Daughter* and marries her mentor, Roger Vadim.

Fernandel becomes an international star in *The Little World of Don Camillo*.

Italy: Vittorio De Sica makes the deeply pessimistic *Umberto D*, a study of neglected old age.

Federico Fellini directs the satirical *The White Sheik*.

Japan: Kenji Mizoguchi directs *The Life of Oharu*, about a samurai's daughter's ill-fated love for a servant.

1953

America: In an attempt to combat falling audiences and the influence of television, Twentieth Century-Fox shows off CinemaScope, its new wide-screen process, with *The Robe*, which becomes the most successful film of the year and one of the big hits of the decade.

From Here to Eternity, with Burt Lancaster and Deborah Kerr rolling in the sand and sea, is also a box-office success.

Vincente Minnelli makes another classic musical for MGM, *The Band Wagon*, with Fred Astaire and his English equivalent, Jack Buchanan.

George Stevens's western *Shane* pits Alan Ladd against Jack Palance.

Joseph Mankiewicz's *Julius Caesar* combines the classical English acting of John Gielgud and the Method of Marlon Brando.

The horror film *The House of Wax*, starring Vincent Price, gives 3-D films a further fillip. It is directed by the one-eyed André de Toth.

Chaplin sells his Hollywood studio and settles in Switzerland.

Gary Cooper is the top money-making star followed by Dean Martin and Jerry Lewis, John Wayne, Alan Ladd, and Bing Crosby.

Britain: Cosy comedy predominates, exemplified by Henry Cornelius's *Genevieve*, with Kenneth More.

The Cruel Sea, with its stiff-upper-lipped officers still fighting the war, is a good representative of the alternative, and audiences flock to it.

Cecil Hepworth dies.

France: Jacques Tati's *Monsieur Hulot's Holiday* develops his concept of comedy without stars.

Henri-Georges Clouzot's thriller *The Wages of Fear* electrifies audiences and provides Yves Montand with his first serious role.

Italy: Federico Fellini's *I Vitelloni*, in the neo-realist tradition, focuses on the aimless young.

Jean Renoir, having left the US, makes the unsuccessful *The Golden Coach* with Anna Magnani.

Japan: Yashujiro Ozu's *Tokyo Story* is an austere and moving drama of disappointments.

Teinosuke Kinugasa's 12th-century saga *Gate of Hell* wins the top prize at Cannes and an Oscar.

Kenji Mizoguchi's 16th-century story *Ugetsu Monogatari* is hailed at the Venice Film Festival.

Mexico: Luis Buñuel makes a brilliantly faithful version of *The Adventures of Robinson Crusoe* with Dan O'Herlihy.

1954

America: Elia Kazan's *On the Waterfront*, with Marlon Brando and Rod Steiger at their best, can be read as his apologia for naming names to HUAC; it is powerfully convincing on its own terms.

Brando also plays a somewhat elderly rebel in *The Wild One*, a biker movie that causes controversy.

Hitchcock's teasing thriller *Rear Window* stars Grace Kelly and James Stewart as a voyeuristic photographer.

Judy Garland and James Mason bring passion to the remake of *A Star Is Born*, but it at first fails to find an audience and is drastically cut.

Gordon Douglas's *Them!*, with its giant ants, is the first of a cycle of post-atomic monster movies.

Paramount's VistaVision wide-screen process makes its debut in *White Christmas*, a cosy musical with Bing Crosby. The process fades by the end of the 50s.

Samuel Z. Arkoff and James H. Nicholson found American International Pictures (AIP), the low-budget film company that includes Roger Corman among its producers.

John Wayne is America's top money-making star, followed by Dean Martin and Jerry Lewis, Gary Cooper, James Stewart, and Marilyn Monroe.

Britain: David Lean's *Hobson's Choice* features Charles Laughton at his best.

Alexander Mackendrick's Ealing comedy *The Maggie* comes perilously close to *Whisky Galore* but manages to amuse.

Frank Launder's *The Belles of St Trinian's*, with Alastair Sim in drag, is a commercial success and brings three sequels.

Ralph Thomas's *Doctor in the House*, with Dirk Bogarde and James Robertson Justice, is a comic success, but unfortunately results in several sequels.

The BBFC bans *The Wild One*, which will not be seen in Britain until 1968.

Italy: Vittorio De Sica makes Sophia Loren a star in *The Gold of Naples*, the first of their six collaborations.

Federico Fellini's *La Strada*, with Giulietta Masina and Anthony Quinn, infuses neo-realism with poetry in its story of an ill-used simpleton.

Japan: Akira Kurosawa directs the exciting and action-filled epic *The Seven Samurai* with Toshiro Mifune.

Poland: Andrzej Wajda directs *A Generation* starring Zbigniew Cybulski.

1955

America: A new star is born, and quickly dies: James Dean makes *East of Eden* and *Rebel without a Cause* – before crashing his sports car and becoming an enduring screen icon.

Spencer Tracy stars with Robert Ryan in John Sturges's seminal suspense thriller, *Bad Day at Black Rock*.

Paddy Chayevsky's TV play *Marty* transfers successfully to the screen, bringing stardom to Ernest Borgnine.

Billy Wilder's *The Seven Year Itch* makes the most of Marilyn Monroe's comic talents.

Charles Laughton directs *The Night of the Hunter*; its reputation is to grow with the years.

Rock 'n' roll arrives with Bill Haley and the Comets singing 'Rock around the Clock' behind the credits of *The Blackboard Jungle*, about life in a slum school. Within months, Haley and others will be starring in cheap exploitation movies, such as *Rock around the Clock* and *Don't Knock the Rock*, and popular music will never be the same.

Robert Aldrich's *Kiss Me Deadly* announces the arrival of an overwrought talent.

Oklahoma is shown in Todd-AO, a new wide-screen process promoted by showman Mike Todd.

Disney opens the first Disneyland, extending the appeal of its films and characters.

Hitchcock luminaries James Stewart and Grace Kelly head America's money-making stars, followed by John Wayne, William Holden, and Gary Cooper.

Britain: Yet another war film, Michael Anderson's *The Dam Busters*, does well, thanks to R. C. Sherriff's script and the acting of Michael Redgrave and others.

Alexander Mackendrick's *The Ladykillers* is almost the last of the Ealing comedies.

John Halas and Joy Batchelor direct Britain's first animated feature, George Orwell's *Animal Farm*.

Brigitte Bardot stars with Dirk Bogarde in *Doctor at Sea*.

Hammer Films, a small production company recycling TV programmes, strikes it rich with *The Quatermass Experiment*, a horror movie based on a BBC serial written by Nigel Kneale.

France: Jean Renoir makes a frothy musical, *French Cancan*, with Jean Gabin.

Henri-Georges Clouzot's *Les Diaboliques* is a grim suspense story.

Henri Verneuil's *The Sheep Has Five Legs* gives comedian Fernandel the six roles of his life.

Jules Dassin's film *Rififi*, with its tense safe-cracking sequence, captures audiences' imaginations around the world.

Max Ophuls directs the sumptuous *Lola Montes*.

India: Satyajit Ray's *Pather Panchali* is an art-house hit in the West.

Sweden: Bergman's comedy *Smiles of a Summer Night* brings him international recognition.

1956

America: Cecil B. De Mille's *The Ten Commandments* tops the box-office.

George Stevens's family saga *Giant* also does well, owing in part to the growing cult around James Dean.

Mike Todd's star-packed *Around the World in Eighty Days*, in Todd-AO, is a hit.

John Ford's *The Searchers* provides John Wayne with his best, most complex role.

Forbidden Planet, starring Leslie Nielsen, gives a science-fiction twist to Shakespeare's *The Tempest*.

The blacklisted Dalton Trumbo, writing under a pseudonym, wins an Oscar for *The Brave One*.

Fox experiment with CinemaScope 55, using 55mm film, for *Carousel*, but the process is not a success.

Dore Schary is sacked from MGM.

Darryl F. Zanuck leaves Twentieth Century-Fox.

Dean Martin and Jerry Lewis split.

Fritz Lang decides he has had enough of Hollywood.

William Holden is the top money-making star, followed by John Wayne, James Stewart, Burt Lancaster, and Glenn Ford.

Britain: Jack Lee's war film *A Town Like Alice*, with Virginia McKenna and Peter Finch, is a hit.

Hammer Films switches its attention to horror, reviving a Universal favourite with *The Curse of Frankenstein*, starring Christopher Lee and Peter Cushing and directed by Terence Fisher.

Lindsay Anderson, Karel Reisz, and others issue the Free Cinema manifesto.

The BBC buys Ealing Studios.

France: Robert Bresson's *A Man Escaped* details an escape by a Resistance fighter imprisoned by the Nazis.

India: Satyajit Ray makes *Aparajito*, a sequel to *Pather Panchali*.

Italy: Fellini's *Cabiria* (aka *The Nights of Cabiria*) is a life-enhancing look at Roman low-life.

Japan: Kon Ichikawa directs the horrifying war film *The Burmese Harp*.

Poland: Andrzej Wajda directs *Kanal*, starring Zbigniew Cybulski as one of the Polish partisans trapped in the sewers of Warsaw by the Nazis.

1957

America: Stanley Kubrick directs the overpowering *Paths of Glory*, set in the First World War.

Don Siegel's *The Invasion of the Body Snatchers* is a brilliantly effective paranoid parable.

Sidney Lumet makes *Twelve Angry Men*, a TV play that transfers successfully to the screen.

Alexander Mackendrick makes the moody, brilliant *Sweet Smell of Success*, with Burt Lancaster and Tony Curtis.

Mark Robson's *Peyton Place*, from a bestselling novel, is a hit; in the 60s it will become a long-running TV soap opera.

William Hanna and Joseph Barbera found Hanna-Barbera Productions to make family entertainment for television, including such animated series as *The Flintstones*.

Rock Hudson becomes America's top star at the box-office, followed by John Wayne, Pat Boone, Elvis Presley, and Frank Sinatra.

Argentina: Leopold Torre Nilsson gains international recognition with *The House of the Angel*.

Britain: David Lean's *The Bridge on the River Kwai*, produced by Sam Spiegel and starring William Holden and Alec Guinness, is the box-office success of the year.

Hammer Films remake *Dracula*, with Christopher Lee in the title role, and *The Revenge of Frankenstein*, with Peter Cushing.

France: Brigitte Bardot becomes an international star as Roger Vadim's *And God Created Woman* is released around the world.

Japan: Akira Kurosawa's *Throne of Blood* re-invents Shakespeare's *Macbeth*.

Sweden: Ingmar Bergman's reputation is made with *The Seventh Seal*, with the gaunt Max Von Sydow as a knight returning from the Crusades, and the gentler *Wild Strawberries*, starring Victor Sjöström.

USSR: Mikhail Kalatozov makes the sleek love story *The Cranes Are Flying*.

1958

America: Rodgers and Hammerstein's musical *South Pacific*, despite its old-fashioned air and airs, is the hit of the year.

Orson Welles stars in, and directs, the brooding thriller *Touch of Evil*.

Hitchcock's dizzying thriller *Vertigo* stars James Stewart as a man trying to remake the past.

Harry Cohn, head of Columbia, dies.

Mike Todd is killed in a plane crash.

The top five money-making stars are Glenn Ford, Elizabeth Taylor, Jerry Lewis, Marlon Brando, and Rock Hudson.

Britain: Gerald Thomas's *Carry On Sergeant*, an army farce produced by Peter Rogers, is a surprising hit; it begins a sequence of low-budget Carry On comedies that are to become a profitable staple of British cinema.

Mark Robson directs *The Inn of the Sixth Happiness* starring Ingrid Bergman, with Wales standing in for its Chinese locations.

France: Louis Malle's *Lift to the Scaffold* (aka *Frantic*) and *The Lovers*, both starring Jeanne Moreau, announce the arrival of the French 'New Wave'.

Mexico: Luis Buñuel directs *Nazarin*, about a priest who tries to follow Christ's example.

Poland: Andrzej Wajda makes the compelling *Ashes and Diamonds*, starring Zbigniew Cybulski as a man confused about killing after the end of war.

Sweden: Ingmar Bergman's startling *The Face* stars Max Von Sydow as a 19th-century magician.

1959

America: William Wyler's *Ben Hur* takes epic amounts of money at the box-office.

Hitchcock makes his chase thriller *North by Northwest*, with Cary Grant doing the running.

Billy Wilder directs his comic masterpiece *Some Like It Hot*.

Behind the Great Wall is the first film to be shown in Aromarama. It is also the last.

Joseph E. Levine buys US rights to *Hercules*, a cheap Italian film, and spends $1.2m on promoting it; it becomes a hit, making body-builder Steve Reeves a star and starting a cycle of muscle-man movies.

Herbert Yates resigns as president of Republic Pictures and production ceases.

Cecil B. De Mille dies.

Rock Hudson is America's top money-making star, along with Cary Grant, James Stewart, Doris Day, and Debbie Reynolds.

Brazil: French director Marcel Camus's *Black Orpheus* uses myth and carnival to impressive effect.

Britain: Jack Cardiff's *Room at the Top* claims to bring sex and the industrial north into British films.

Tony Richardson and John Osborne form Woodfall Films with producer Harry Saltzman to film Osborne's *Look Back in Anger*, a play that helped bring a new realism to British theatre.

Young Hayley Mills becomes a star in *Tiger Bay*, directed by J. Lee-Thompson.

Peter Cushing and Christopher Lee star in *The Mummy* for Hammer, directed by Terence Fisher.

Rank backs Richard Attenborough, Bryan Forbes, and others in founding Allied Film Makers.

France: Claude Chabrol's *The Cousins* rides the New Wave.

Cocteau's final masterpiece is *Testament of Orpheus*.

François Truffaut's *The 400 Blows* is the first of his semi-autobiographical films to track the life of Antoine Doinel, played by Jean-Pierre Léaud.

Alain Resnais directs *Hiroshima, Mon Amour*, written by Marguerite Duras.

Germany: Bernard Wicki directs *The Bridge*, about boy soldiers in the last days of the war.

Greece: Jules Dassin makes *Never on Sunday*, with Melina Mercouri and a hummable score by Monos Hadjidakis.

India: Satyajit Ray makes *The World of Apu*, the third film in his trilogy.

USSR: Grigori Chukrai's *Ballad of a Soldier* focuses on the detail of everyday life.

1960

America: Alfred Hitchcock's creepy *Psycho*, with a twitchy Anthony Perkins, scores at the box-office.

John Sturges remakes *The Seven Samurai* as a western, *The Magnificent Seven*. It results in three sequels.

Roger Corman's *The House of Usher* for AIP, starring Vincent Price, starts a new horror cycle.

John Cassavetes makes the semi-improvised *Shadows*, which is to influence many independent film-makers.

Scent of Mystery is the first feature to be shown in Smell-o-Vision. It is also the last.

Joseph E. Levine repeats his success with *Hercules Unchained*, again starring Steve Reeves.

New York's Roxy Theater, once the largest and grandest cinema in the world, is demolished 33 years after it was opened.

Doris Day and Rock Hudson, a double act in innocuous comedies, are America's top stars at the box-office, followed by Cary Grant, Elizabeth Taylor, and Debbie Reynolds.

Australia: Fred Zinnemann makes *The Sundowners*, with Robert Mitchum, Deborah Kerr, and the ubiquitous Chips Rafferty.

Britain: Karel Reisz's gritty, anti-authoritarian *Saturday Night and Sunday Morning*, with Albert Finney, is to transform British cinema, for a time.

Michael Powell's voyeuristic *Peeping Tom* upsets audiences and critics.

Richard Attenborough and Bryan Forbes produce, and Guy Green directs, the topical *The Angry Silence*.

Jack Cardiff directs D. H. Lawrence's *Sons and Lovers*, with Dean Stockwell and Trevor Howard.

France: Jean-Luc Godard's *Breathless* is a New Wave hit in art cinemas and makes a star of Jean-Paul Belmondo.

Louis Malle directs the inventive comedy *Zazie dans le Métro*.

François Truffaut makes *Shoot the Pianist*, starring Charles Aznavour.

Italy: Fellini's *La Dolce Vita*, starring Marcello Mastroianni and Anita Ekberg, is a worldwide hit, with its depiction of the wasted lives of the rich in Rome.

Visconti directs *Rocco and His Brothers*, with Alain Delon, about a peasant family in Milan.

Michelangelo's *L'Avventura*, with Monica Vitti, and *La Notte*, starring Marcello Mastroianni, Jeanne Moreau, and Monica Vitti, make the emptiness of life seem attractive.

Vittorio De Sica's *Two Women* gives Sophia Loren her best screen role.

1961

America: Robert Wise and Jerome Robbins make a successful film of the stage hit *West Side Story*.

Robert Rossen directs the brilliantly handled *The Hustler*, with Paul Newman and Jackie Gleason.

Disney releases *One Hundred and One Dalmatians*, which is to be its last splendid animated feature for 30 years.

Elizabeth Taylor becomes the top money-making star, followed by Rock Hudson, Doris Day, John Wayne, and Cary Grant.

Britain: Tony Richardson directs another 'kitchen sink' drama, *A Taste of Honey*, with Rita Tushingham, Dora Bryan, and Murray Melvin.

Basil Dearden's *Victim*, starring Dirk Bogarde, is one of the first films to deal sympathetically with homosexuality.

Joseph Losey makes the science-fiction *The Damned* for Hammer Films.

Pop singer Cliff Richard stars in the innocuous musical *The Young Ones*, directed by Sidney J. Furie.

France: Alain Resnais directs the enigmatic *Last Year at Marienbad*.

Italy: Poet and novelist Pier Paolo Pasolini directs his first film, the low-life *Accatone*.

Francesco Rosi makes *Salvatore Giuliano*, about a Sicilian bandit.

Pietro Germi's *Divorce Italian Style* mocks the country's divorce laws.

Ermanno Olmi makes the social comedy *The Job*.

Japan: Kurosawa directs *Yojimbo*, with Toshiro Mifune as a wandering samurai.

Spain: Luis Buñuel returns to Spain at the government's invitation and makes the sacrilegious *Viridiana*; it is promptly banned.

Sweden: Max Von Sydow goes to Hollywood to play Christ in *The Greatest Story Ever Told*.

1962

America: John Frankenheimer directs the brilliantly plotted thriller *The Manchurian Candidate*.

Robert Aldrich shocks by casting Bette Davis and Joan Crawford as two ageing, homicidal harridans in *Whatever Happened to Baby Jane?*

Darryl F. Zanuck returns to Twentieth Century-Fox as president with his son Richard as head of production as the company runs into difficulties over the out-of-control *Cleopatra*, starring Richard Burton and Elizabeth Taylor. His production of *The Longest Day*, about the Allied landings at Normandy, is a hit.

MCA acquire Universal.

Doris Day and Rock Hudson bounce back as the top money-makers, followed by Cary Grant, John Wayne, and Elvis Presley.

Britain: Tony Richardson directs the anti-authoritarian *The Loneliness of the Long Distance Runner*, starring Tom Courtenay.

John Schlesinger makes *A Kind of Loving*, with Alan Bates, June Ritchie, and Thora Hird.

David Lean's painstaking epic *Lawrence of Arabia* brings stardom to the lanky Peter O'Toole in the title role as the short, enigmatic hero.

Sean Connery plays James Bond in *Dr No*, a role that elevates him to stardom and begins a profitable cycle of films.

France: François Truffaut directs *Jules and Jim*, starring Jeanne Moreau as the woman shared by two friends.

Germany: 26 film-makers issue a manifesto for a new German feature film.

Japan: Yashujiro Ozu makes his last film, *An Autumn Afternoon*, on the loneliness of old age.

Mexico: Luis Buñuel directs *The Exterminating Angel*, about dinner guests who find themselves unable to leave the room.

Poland: Roman Polanski's *Knife in the Water* is attacked by the authorities and he soon leaves to work elsewhere.

USSR: Andrei Tarkovsky makes the tragic *Ivan's Childhood*, about a boy who joins the partisans.

1963

America: Martin Ritt directs the incisive character drama *Hud*, well acted by Paul Newman, Patricia Neal, and Melvyn Douglas.

Cleopatra is released but fails to make a profit.

Andy Warhol and his entourage begin making films at his Factory.

AIP's *Beach Party*, with Annette Funicello and Frankie Avalon, begins a cycle of beach movies.

Doris Day remains the top money-making star, followed by John Wayne, Rock Hudson, Jack Lemmon, and Cary Grant.

Brazil: Glauber Rocha gains an international reputation with his grim and violent *Black God, White Devil*.

Britain: Joseph Losey directs *The Servant*, scripted by Harold Pinter and starring Dirk Bogarde and James Fox.

Lindsay Anderson makes the tough *This Sporting Life*, written by David Storey and starring Richard Harris and Rachel Roberts.

Tony Richardson and John Osborne bring sex and exuberance to the cinema in *Tom Jones*, portrayed by Albert Finney.

John Schlesinger's *Billy Liar*, starring Tom Courtenay and Julie Christie, is another seminal film in the revival of British cinema, taken from Keith Waterhouse's novel of adolescent fantasy.

Italy: Fellini's brilliantly self-indulgent *8½*, with Marcello Mastroianni, depicts an artist suffering from a creative block.

Visconti makes a perfect adaptation of Giuseppe de Lampedusa's *The Leopard*, about the decline of the Sicilian aristocracy.

1964

America: Disney's *Mary Poppins*, with Julie Andrews, is the hit of the year.

Franklin Schaffner's *The Best Man*, starring Henry Fonda, is a brilliant political melodrama, as is John Frankenheimer's *Seven Days in May*, with Kirk Douglas.

Sidney Lumet's *Fail Safe* deals frighteningly with the threat of nuclear war.

Doris Day is still the most bankable star, followed by Jack Lemmon, Rock Hudson, John Wayne, and Cary Grant.

Britain: Stanley Kubrick makes the blackly comic *Dr Strangelove*, with Peter Sellers and George C. Scott.

Richard Lester finds a way to make the Beatles funny in *A Hard Day's Night*.

Guy Hamilton directs the Bond film *Goldfinger*.

Michael Winner makes *The System*, about sex at the seaside.

France: Jacques Demy's musical *The Umbrellas of Cherbourg*, written by Michel Legrand, charms audiences everywhere.

Greece: Michael Cacoyannis's *Zorba the Greek*, with Anthony Quinn and the music of Mikis Theodorakis, is an international hit.

Italy: Sergio Leone borrows the plot of Kurosawa's *Yojimbo* for his western *A Fistful of Dollars*, starring a young American television actor, Clint Eastwood. Its success is helped by the evocative music of Ennio Morricone.

Antonioni's *The Red Desert*, with Monica Vitti and Richard Harris, revels in the possibilities for colour in film.

Bernardo Bertolucci's *Before the Revolution* heralds the arrival of a new, politicized talent.

Japan: Masaki Kobayashi's *Kwaidan* is a collection of perfectly composed ghost stories.

USSR: Innokenti Smoktunovsky is an impressive Hamlet in a version of Shakespeare's tragedy directed by Grigori Kozintsev.

1965

America: Robert Wise's *The Sound of Music*, starring Julie Andrews, is a massive hit.

Daniel Mann directs *Our Man Flint*, starring James Coburn, in an attempt to duplicate the success of the Bond movies. It fails.

David Lean's romantic *Dr Zhivago*, starring Omar Sharif and Julie Christie, is a worldwide box-office hit.

The Bond movies take British actor Sean Connery to the top of the list of money-making stars, followed by John Wayne, Doris Day, Julie Andrews, and Jack Lemmon.

Britain: The new Bond movie, *Thunderball*, is another big hit.

Sidney J. Furie's *The Ipcress File*, with Michael Caine as a shabby agent, attempts to cash in on the Bond phenomenon.

Richard Lester's comic *The Knack* gives impetus to the image of what is soon to be called 'Swinging London'.

John Schlesinger's *Darling*, with Julie Christie, catches the mood of the moment.

Roman Polanski makes the psychological horror film *Repulsion*, with Catherine Deneuve.

Czechoslovakia: Milos Forman directs *A Blonde in Love* (aka *Loves of a Blonde*).

France: Jean-Luc Godard directs the futuristic *Alphaville*, starring Eddie Constantine.

Hungary: Miklós Jancsó's *The Round-Up* gains him international recognition.

Italy: Fellini makes his first film in colour, the exuberant *Juliet of the Spirits*.

Sergio Leone's *For a Few Dollars More* establishes spaghetti westerns and Clint Eastwood as forces to be reckoned with.

1966

America: Sidney Lumet's *The Group*, from Mary McCarthy's novel, is the most talked-about film of the year with its cast of unknowns, who mostly remain so.

Mike Nichols films Edward Albee's *Who's Afraid of Virginia Woolf?* with Hollywood's most famous couple, Richard Burton and Elizabeth Taylor, as the embattled husband and wife.

Roger Corman's *The Wild Angels* for AIP begins a cycle of biker and youthful-protest movies.

Charles Bluhdorn's Gulf Western acquires Paramount Pictures.

Seven Arts Productions acquires Warner Bros.

Two British talents, Julie Andrews and Sean Connery, head the poll of money-making stars, followed by Elizabeth Taylor, Jack Lemmon, and Richard Burton.

Britain: Fred Zinnemann directs an impeccable version of Robert Bolt's play *A Man for All Seasons*, finely performed by Paul Scofield and Robert Shaw.

Michael Caine becomes an international star as the raffish *Alfie*, directed by Lewis Gilbert from Bill Naughton's play.

Antonioni comes to London to make *Blow-Up* with David Hemmings as a fashionable fashion photographer.

Karel Reisz directs the anarchic *Morgan*, which gives David Warner his best role before he goes to Hollywood to become a fixture in horror movies.

Silvio Narrizano's *Georgy Girl*, with James Mason and Lynn Redgrave, gives further impetus to the image of London as the place to be.

Universal Pictures establish a London office and other American companies step up local productions.

Czechoslovakia: Vera Chytilova makes the lively comedy *Daisies*, which runs into censorship problems.

Jiri Menzel directs the mainly comic *Closely Observed Trains*.

France: Claude Lelouch directs the romantic *A Man and a Woman*, with Jean-Louis Trintignant and Anouk Aimée and the music of Francis Lai.

Robert Bresson directs *Balthazar*, about the life of a donkey, with a non-professional cast.

Italy: Gillo Pontecorvo's *The Battle of Algiers* uses a documentary style to great effect.

Sergio Leone's spaghetti western *The Good, the Bad and the Ugly* not only confirms Clint Eastwood as a star but also elevates former bit-player Lee Van Cleef.

Spain: Orson Welles finishes his Shakespeare adaptation, *Chimes at Midnight*, with himself as Falstaff.

Sweden: Ingmar Bergman directs the intense *Persona*, with Liv Ullmann and Bibi Andersson.

USSR: Andrei Tarkovsky's masterly historical work *Andrei Rublev* is banned.

1967

America: Mike Nichols' *The Graduate*, with Dustin Hoffman, hits a nerve with the young and is the hit of the year, followed by the safer inter-racial *Guess Who's Coming to Dinner*, starring Spencer Tracy, Katharine Hepburn, and Sidney Poitier.

Norman Jewison's thriller *In the Heat of the Night* is a better examination of racial prejudice, excellently acted by Sidney Poitier and Rod Steiger.

Arthur Penn's *Bonnie and Clyde* sets a new style for gangster films and brings stardom to Warren Beatty and Faye Dunaway.

Robert Aldrich establishes his own film studio following the success of his war film *The Dirty Dozen*.

Julie Andrews retains her appeal at the box-office, followed by Lee Marvin, Paul Newman, Dean Martin, and Sean Connery.

Britain: Joseph Losey directs *Accident*, scripted by Harold Pinter and starring Michael York and Dirk Bogarde.

Czechoslovakia: Milos Forman directs the comic *The Foreman's Ball*. In France the next year when the Russians invade, he subsequently goes to America, as does his colleague Ivan Passer.

France: Luis Buñuel directs the elegant, teasing *Belle de Jour*, starring Catherine Deneuve.

Jean-Luc Godard makes the ferocious *Weekend*.

Hungary: Miklós Jancsó makes the epic *The Red and the White*.

Italy: Pasolini directs a version of Sophocles's tragedy *Oedipus Rex*.

Poland: Jerzy Skolimowski's *Hands Up* is banned and he leaves the country, later working in Britain.

Leading actor Zbigniew Cybulski dies in an accident.

Sweden: Bo Widerberg's ravishing *Elvira Madigan* is an international success.

Vilgot Sjöman's *I Am Curious – Yellow* is a worldwide sensation and begins a cycle of indifferent sexploitation movies.

USSR: Sergei Bondarchuk makes an epic version of *War and Peace*, with spectacular battle scenes.

1968

America: *Funny Girl*, with Barbra Streisand repeating her Broadway performance as Fanny Brice, is the box-office success of the year.

Stanley Kubrick's *2001: A Space Odyssey* is a trip that finds favour with the young and begins a new cycle of science-fiction films.

Franklin J. Schaffner's *Planet of the Apes* is also a hit; its success results in several inferior sequels.

Andy Warhol's underground film *Flesh*, about a day in the life of a male prostitute, played by Joe Dallesandro, surfaces as a surprise hit. In a small part is Maurice Braddell, once a promising English actor and writer of the 30s.

British director Peter Yates makes *Bullitt*, with Steve McQueen, notable for its car chases.

Sidney Poitier becomes the first black actor to head the poll of money-making stars, followed by Paul Newman, Julie Andrews, John Wayne, and Clint Eastwood.

Britain: Lindsay Anderson directs *If . . .*, a powerful film about schoolboy rebellion, starring Malcolm McDowell.

Carol Reed makes the best British musical film, *Oliver!*, from Lionel Bart's stage success.

Ralph Thomas's *Carry On up the Khyber* is the best of the series, with Kenneth Williams, Charles Hawtrey and company.

Cuba: Tomás Gutiérrez Alea's *Memories of Underdevelopment* explores life under Castro.

France: Claude Chabrol's *Les Biches*, starring Stéphane Audran, deals with a bisexual love triangle.

Italy: Franco Zeffirelli makes Shakespeare box-office with his version of *Romeo and Juliet*, starring Leonard Whiting and Olivia Hussey.

Sergio Leone, with US backing, makes *Once upon a Time in the West*, with Henry Fonda as a ruthless killer.

1969

America: Dennis Hopper and Peter Fonda add social relevance to the biker movie in *Easy Rider*, a surprise hit that has Hollywood attempting to repeat its success by hiring other young directors.

British director John Schlesinger makes a quintessential American movie, *Midnight Cowboy*, starring Dustin Hoffman and Jon Voight.

George Roy Hill's *Butch Cassidy and the Sundance Kid*, with its memorable pairing of Paul Newman and Robert Redford, and Sam Peckinpah's elegiac *The Wild Bunch*, show there is life left in the western.

Sidney Pollack directs the dark *They Shoot Horses, Don't They?*, with Gig Young and Jane Fonda.

George Romero's relentless, low-budget *Night of the Living Dead* revives the horror genre.

Kinney takes over Warner Bros. The company is renamed Warner Communications and takes in Kinney's other entertainment interests, including publishing, video, and record companies.

Paul Newman, Sidney Poitier, and Barbra Streisand form a major new production company, First Artists.

Darryl Zanuck resigns from Twentieth Century-Fox.

Paul Newman becomes the top box-office star, followed by John Wayne, Steve McQueen, Dustin Hoffman, and Clint Eastwood.

Brazil: Glauber Rocha's brooding *Antonio das Mortes* is banned and he leaves the country.

Britain: Ken Russell's adaptation of D. H. Lawrence's *Women in Love*, starring Glenda Jackson, is a success, gaining notoriety for its nude wrestling scene between Alan Bates and Oliver Reed.

Richard Attenborough directs *Oh, What a Lovely War*, from Joan Littlewood's stage show.

George Lazenby replaces Sean Connery as James Bond, but *On Her Majesty's Secret Service* does poorly at the box-office.

Ken Loach's *Kes*, produced by Tony Garnett, brings socially conscious talents to the cinema.

Bryan Forbes is appointed head of production by EMI at Elstree and announces an ambitious programme.

Egypt: Shadi Abdelsalam gains international notice with *The Night of Counting the Years*, about tomb robbers.

France: Costa-Gavras's political thriller *Z*, with Yves Montand, is a worldwide hit, but it is banned in Greece and Spain.

Jean-Pierre Melville's *The Army in the Shadows* is a gripping documentary-style film about the French Resistance.

Eric Rohmer's civilized *My Night at Maud's* is an international success.

Germany: Rainer Werner Fassbinder, working in experimental theatre, turns to films with his troupe and makes *Love Is Colder than Death*.

India: Satyajit Ray directs *Days and Nights in the Forest*, about the impact of rural life on some city boys.

1970

America: Woodstock, the great hippie gathering of 'love, peace and music' in 1969, is captured on film by Michael Wadleigh.

Robert Altman's anti-establishment *M*A*S*H*, with Elliott Gould and Donald Sutherland, is a hit, as is the three-handkerchief weepie *Love Story*, directed by Arthur Hiller.

George C. Scott scores as *Patton*, directed by Franklin Schaffner.

Roger Corman founds his own production and distribution company, New World Pictures.

Paul Newman remains the top money-making star, followed by Clint Eastwood, Steve McQueen, John Wayne, and Elliott Gould.

Australia: After years of procrastination, the government decides to support the local film industry, including the establishment of a film and television school.

Britain: Nicolas Roeg and Donald Cammel direct the complex *Performance*, with James Fox and Mick Jagger, which seems the last gasp of 60s permissiveness.

Joseph Losey turns to the past in his continuing dissection of the class system in *The Go-Between*.

Ken Russell courts controversy with *The Music Lovers*, starring Richard Chamberlain as Tchaikovsky, with Glenda Jackson.

David Lean's epic *Ryan's Daughter* is not liked, and he loses his confidence in directing.

France: Claude Chabrol makes the Hitchcockian thrillers *The Butcher* and *La Rupture*, with Stéphane Audran.

Hong Kong: King Hu makes the martial arts epic *A Touch of Zen*.

Italy: Pasolini directs the Greek tragedy *Medea*, starring Maria Callas.

Japan: The wide-screen process Imax is shown for the first time.

Spain: Luis Buñuel makes *Tristana*, a complex black comedy with Catherine Deneuve and Fernando Rey.

Sweden: Jan Troell's *The Emigrants*, about Swedes leaving their homeland for America, is a hit in the two countries.

1971

America: William Friedkin's gritty thriller *The French Connection*, with Gene Hackman, is a hit.

Peter Bogdanovich makes the impressive, nostalgic *The Last Picture Show*, with Ben Johnson.

Milos Forman's first US film, *Taking Off*, is a gentle satire on America.

Alan J. Pakula directs the adult thriller *Klute*, with Jane Fonda and Donald Sutherland.

Don Siegel makes *Dirty Harry*, starring Clint Eastwood as a maverick cop, a role he is to play often.

Steve McQueen joins Newman, Poitier, and Streisand in First Artists. The company's first production is *Pocket Money*, starring Newman and directed by Stuart Rosenberg.

John Wayne takes over as the top box-office attraction, followed by Clint Eastwood, Paul Newman, Steve McQueen, and George C. Scott.

Australia: Nicolas Roeg makes the eerily effective *Walkabout*, with Jenny Agutter and David Gulpilil.

Britain: Stanley Kubrick's controversial *A Clockwork Orange*, based on Anthony Burgess's novel, is the first film to use Dolby sound.

Ken Russell shocks with his exuberant *The Devils*, starring Vanessa Redgrave and Oliver Reed.

John Schlesinger makes the stylish *Sunday, Bloody Sunday*, with Peter Finch and Glenda Jackson as two people in love with the same man.

Roman Polanski emphasizes the violence in his version of Shakespeare's *Macbeth*.

Mike Hodges makes the tough thriller *Get Carter*, with Michael Caine.

Bryan Forbes quits as head of production for EMI at Elstree a year early.

The National Film School opens.

Hungary: Miklós Jancsó makes the colourful *Red Psalm*, about a workers' strike.

Italy: Pasolini's *Decameron* brings him an international hit. He is to follow it with the similar *Canterbury Tales* and *Arabian Nights*.

Yugoslavia: Dusan Makavejev's *WR: Mysteries of the Organism* is an international hit; after it is banned, he leaves the country.

1972

America: Francis Ford Coppola's brilliant *The Godfather*, with Marlon Brando and Al Pacino, treats the Mafia as a normal family business.

Bob Fosse gives bite and style to *Cabaret*, with Liza Minnelli, Joel Grey, and Michael York.

John Boorman's *Deliverance* is a superior thriller.

The success of Ronald Neame's *The Poseidon Adventure* begins a cycle of disaster movies.

Dustin Hoffman joins First Artists. It releases the muddled *Up the Sandbox*, starring Barbra Streisand.

Clint Eastwood is the top box-office star, followed by George C. Scott, Gene Hackman, John Wayne, and Barbra Streisand.

Britain: Lindsay Anderson directs the satirical *O Lucky Man!*, starring Malcolm McDowell.

Ken Loach makes *Family Life*, from David Mercer's play of a dysfunctional family.

Bill Douglas's *My Childhood* wins an award for the best first feature at the Venice Film Festival.

Lord (J. Arthur) Rank dies.

France: Luis Buñuel makes the hilarious and savage *The Discreet Charm of the Bourgeoisie*, with Fernando Rey, Delphine Seyrig, and Stéphane Audran.

Germany: Werner Herzog directs the startling *Aguirre, Wrath of God*, starring Klaus Kinski.

Rainer Werner Fassbinder makes *The Bitter Tears of Petra Von Kant*, about lesbian jealousies, with Hanna Schygulla.

Italy: Marlon Brando stars in Bertolucci's *Last Tango in Paris*, an explicit exploration of lust.

Francesco Rosi investigates political corruption in *The Mattei Affair*.

Sweden: Ingmar Bergman's *Cries and Whispers*, with Harriet Andersson and Liv Ullmann, is tough but important viewing.

1973

America: William Friedkin's horror movie *The Exorcist* becomes a controversial hit.

George Roy Hill's *The Sting* re-unites Robert Redford and Paul Newman to become a big hit, helped by Marvin Hamlisch's use of Scott Joplin's ragtime tunes.

Terrence Malick's seminal *Badlands*, with Sissy Spacek and Martin Sheen, follows two young lovers on a killing spree.

Martin Scorsese's *Mean Streets* reveals him as a major talent.

Bruce Lee kicks his way to stardom in Robert Clouse's *Enter the Dragon* and begins a Western fashion for martial arts films. Lee himself dies suddenly, but becomes a continuing cult.

Clint Eastwood is the top box-office star, followed by Ryan O'Neal, Steve McQueen, Burt Reynolds, and Robert Redford.

Britain: Nicolas Roeg directs the chilling *Don't Look Now*, with Donald Sutherland and Julie Christie.

Roger Moore takes over as James Bond in *Live and Let Die*.

Cinema admissions keep falling and are now down to 142 million a year.

France: François Truffaut's *Day for Night*, about the world of cinema, is an international hit.

Germany: Rainer Werner Fassbinder's *Ali: Fear Eats the Soul* brings him international recognition.

India: Satyajit Ray makes *Distant Thunder*, about the breakdown of traditional values.

Italy: Marco Ferreri scandalizes audiences with *Blow-Out*, in which four men indulge in a prolonged and terminal orgy of food and sex.

Netherlands: Paul Verhoeven's *Turkish Delight*, starring Rutger Hauer, is an international success.

1974

America: Francis Ford Coppola's *The Godfather II*, with Robert De Niro, is a rare sequel that matches the original.

Roman Polanski makes the complex thriller *Chinatown*, with Jack Nicholson.

John Guillermin's *The Towering Inferno* reveals the public's voracious appetite for disaster movies.

Michael Winner directs the vigilante movie *Death Wish*, starring Charles Bronson, which is to be followed by several sequels.

Universal Pictures introduces Sensurround, low-frequency sound effects, to add to the impact of *Earthquake*. The system gains a limited acceptance and is used in some other of its features.

Australia: Peter Weir's *The Cars that Ate Paris* gives notice of the stirrings of new and exciting talents.

Britain: Sidney Lumet directs the glossy *Murder on the Orient Express*, from Agatha Christie's novel.

Michael Apted directs the pop musical *Stardust*, with Adam Faith and David Essex.

Lew Grade announces that he will spend millions of dollars on film production in the coming year.

British Lion announce a new slim-line Shepperton Studios.

France: Louis Malle's delicate exploration of collaboration in *Lacombe, Lucien* is attacked by many and he decides to move to America.

Bertrand Blier's *Going Places* features two bright young stars, Gérard Depardieu and Patrick Dewaere.

Germany: Werner Herzog directs the disturbing and affecting *The Enigma of Kaspar Hauser*.

Italy: Fellini directs the nostalgic *Amarcord*.

Senegal: Ousmane Sembène's exuberant satire *Xala* is one of the first films from Africa to gain international attention.

1975

America: Steven Spielberg's *Jaws* is a monster hit and will spawn several sequels.

Milos Forman's anti-authoritarian *One Flew over the Cuckoo's Nest* gives Jack Nicholson one of his best roles.

Robert Redford is the top box-office star, followed by Barbra Streisand, Al Pacino, Charles Bronson, and Paul Newman.

Australia: Peter Weir makes the enigmatic *Picnic at Hanging Rock*.

Britain: Jim Sharman's *The Rocky Horror Picture Show*, from Richard O'Brien's stage hit, starring Tim Curry as a transvestite transsexual from Transylvania, becomes a cult phenomenon.

The Monty Python team make fun of Arthurian legends in *Monty Python and the Holy Grail*, directed by Terry Gilliam and Terry Jones.

Ken Russell directs *Tommy*, The Who's rock opera, starring Ann-Margret.

EMI cut back at Elstree Studios.

Lew Grade announces the formation of Associated General Films with the General Cinema chain in America, to finance films on an equal basis, with the cinemas providing a US release.

Charlie Chaplin receives a knighthood.

Italy: Pasolini's *Salo*, based on the Marquis de Sade's writings, causes controversy. Britain is one of the countries that bans it. Pasolini himself is murdered soon afterwards.

USSR: Andrei Tarkovsky's *Mirror* upsets the authorities and he leaves the country.

1976

America: Alan J. Pakula's exciting *All the President's Men*, with Dustin Hoffman and Robert Redford, dramatizes the *Washington Post*'s investigation into the Watergate affair.

Martin Scorsese's coruscating *Taxi Driver*, starring Robert De Niro, is concerned with the malaise of urban violence.

Sidney Lumet's *Network* is a brilliantly melodramatic satire on the excesses of television, written by Paddy Chayevsky; its star Peter Finch dies soon after its release.

Sylvester Stallone writes and stars in the old-fashioned boxing drama *Rocky*, directed by John G. Avildsen; it brings him stardom and is to be followed by four sequels.

Brazil: Bruno Barreto's erotic *Dona Flor and Her Two Husbands* becomes an international success.

Britain: Nicolas Roeg makes the science-fiction *The Man Who Fell to Earth*, starring David Bowie.

Alan Parker directs the gangster film *Bugsy Malone* with a cast of children.

Derek Jarman makes *Sebastiane*, about homosexual desire in the Roman empire, in Latin.

Germany: Wim Wenders' leisurely road movie *Kings of the Road* is admired by many.

Italy: Bertolucci's *1900* tracks Italian history through the first half of the 20th century.

Japan: Nagisa Oshima's controversial *In the Realm of the Senses* is a claustrophobic examination of sexual obsession. Britain and other countries ban it.

Sweden: Ingmar Bergman's *Face to Face*, made for television, is edited down for cinema release; it is among his best films.

1977

America: The success of Woody Allen's comedy *Annie Hall*, with Diane Keaton, makes them both stars.

George Lucas's *Star Wars* gives fantasy and science fiction a spectacular box-office boost. It is followed by another fantasy, Steven Spielberg's *Close Encounters of the Third Kind*.

John Travolta becomes a star in the disco-dancing hit *Saturday Night Fever*, a film that also dominates the pop charts with the Bee Gees' songs.

Burt Reynolds scores a surprising hit in Hal Needham's coarse chase comedy *Smokey and the Bandit*.

Sylvester Stallone is the top box-office star, followed by Barbra Streisand, Clint Eastwood, Burt Reynolds, and Robert Redford.

Australia: Bruce Beresford makes the period piece *The Getting of Wisdom*. Within five years, he will be in Hollywood.

Peter Weir directs *The Last Wave*, with Richard Chamberlain.

Britain: Richard Attenborough directs the ambitious *A Bridge Too Far*, the story of the Allied defeat at Arnhem.

Alan Parker makes the successful *Midnight Express*, from a script by Oliver Stone.

Lord (Lew) Grade announces plans to spend $125m on film production. His partnership with Boston's General Cinema Corporation is ended.

Goldcrest Films is founded. It becomes a leading production company, producing films that include *Gandhi* and *The Killing Fields*.

Herbert Wilcox dies.

Sir Michael Balcon dies.

France: Philippe de Broca's comedy thriller *Dear Inspector* is a popular success.

Germany: Wim Wenders makes the art-house hit *The American Friend*.

Rainer Werner Fassbinder's English-language *Despair*, written by Tom Stoppard and starring Dirk Bogarde, is expected to be his popular breakthrough, but it fails.

Italy: The Taviani brothers, Paolo and Vittorio, score with *Padro Padrone*, about a son's problems with a violent father.

1978

America: *Grease*, a celebration of 50s music starring John Travolta and Olivia Newton-John, is the hit of the year, followed by the youthful comedy *National Lampoon's Animal House*.

Michael Cimino's *The Deer Hunter* makes the Vietnam war box-office.

John Carpenter's *Halloween* scares cinema audiences, fuelling the horror revival.

Walter Hill directs the existential thriller *The Driver*.

Terrence Malick's *Days of Heaven* is the second film from an exciting talent. But audiences do not respond, and he withdraws from film-making.

Louis Malle directs his first American film, *Pretty Baby*, with Brooke Shields as a young prostitute.

Orion Pictures is founded by former executives of United Artists and becomes, for a while, an important producer.

Burt Reynolds is the top money-making star, followed by John Travolta, Richard Dreyfuss, Warren Beatty, and Clint Eastwood.

Australia: Fred Schepisi's aboriginal tragedy *The Chant of Jimmy Blacksmith* is a success, and soon takes him to Hollywood, together with his cinematographer, Ian Baker. Other directors who will go to Hollywood include Graeme Clifford, Simon Wincer, and Richard Franklin.

Philip Noyce makes *Newsfront*, a valediction to newsreel cameramen. He, too, will be in Hollywood by the 90s.

Britain: Joan Collins stars in *The Stud*, based on Jackie Collins's novel, which is a surprising box-office hit.

Martin Rosen's *Watership Down* is an animated version of Richard Adams's bestselling novel about rabbits.

Lew Grade announces $120m productions. He renames his company Associated Communication Corporation and, with EMI, forms a new distribution company in North America.

France: Eduardo Molinaro's screen version of *La Cage aux Folles* makes this transvestite comedy an international hit, one that spawns two sequels.

Bertrand Blier's *Get Out Your Handkerchiefs* re-unites Gérard Depardieu and Patrick Dewaere.

Germany: Rainer Werner Fassbinder directs *The Marriage of Maria Braun*, starring Hanna Schygulla.

Italy: Ermanno Olmi makes *The Tree of Wooden Clogs* with a non-professional cast.

Japan: Nagisa Oshima directs the award-winning *Empire of Passion*, about adultery and murder.

Turkey: Yilmaz Güney supervises from prison the shooting of *The Herd*.

1979

America: Richard Donner's *Superman*, starring Christopher Reeve, is the hit of the year.

Robert Benton's *Kramer vs Kramer*, a domestic drama with Dustin Hoffman and Meryl Streep, also scores at the box-office.

Francis Ford Coppola's ambitious *Apocalypse Now* casts the Vietnam war as America's heart of darkness.

Woody Allen makes *Manhattan*, a film in love with New York.

Blake Edwards's *10* brings brief stardom to the unlikely pairing of Dudley Moore and Bo Derek.

Hal Ashby's comedy *Being There* stars Peter Sellers as a dim gardener who becomes a political savant.

Menahem Golan and Yoram Globus take over Cannon Films and announce ambitious production plans.

First Artists runs into financial problems.

Burt Reynolds remains the leading box-office attraction, followed by Clint Eastwood, Jane Fonda, Woody Allen, and Barbra Streisand.

Australia: Gillian Armstrong's *My Brilliant Career* makes Judy Davis a star.

George Miller's apocalyptic road movie *Mad Max* brings Mel Gibson to the fore.

Britain: Ridley Scott directs the science-fiction thriller *Alien*.

Franc Roddam makes the Mods and Rockers musical *Quadrophenia*, with music by The Who.

John Schlesinger's *Yanks* deals with American GIs in Britain during World War II.

Joan Collins tries to repeat her success with *The Bitch*, directed by Gerry O'Hara from a story by sister Jackie.

HandMade Films is formed to finance *Monty Python's Life of Brian* after Lord (Bernard) Delfont disapproves of the script and withdraws EMI's backing.

Thorn take over EMI.

Lord (Lew) Grade buys the Classic Cinema chain.

France: François Truffaut's cycle of films about Antoine Doinel starring Jean-Pierre Léaud comes to an end after 20 years with *Love on the Run*.

Germany: Volker Schlöndorff's *The Tin Drum* is an international success.

Werner Herzog remakes *Nosferatu*, with Klaus Kinski.

Hong Kong: Tsui Hark directs the martial arts fantasy *The Butterfly Murders*.

Poland: Andrzej Wajda's *The Conductor* stars John Gielgud as a man returning to his country.

Krzysztof Kieslowski's *Camera Buff* is a lively political allegory.

Turkey: Yilmaz Güney supervises from prison the shooting of *The Enemy*.

1980

America: Martin Scorsese's *Raging Bull*, with a devastating performance by an overweight Robert De Niro, is to become the critics' favourite movie of the decade.

The failure of Michael Cimino's profligate western epic *Heaven's Gate* virtually destroys United Artists, which is taken over by MGM.

Robert Redford directs *Ordinary People*, about an unhappy family, with Donald Sutherland, Mary Tyler Moore, and Timothy Hutton; it succeeds at the box-office.

George Lucas continues his science-fiction saga with *The Empire Strikes Back*.

David Lynch makes *The Elephant Man*, with John Hurt in the title role.

Burt Reynolds still attracts crowds at the box-office, followed by Robert Redford, Clint Eastwood, Jane Fonda, and Dustin Hoffman.

Australia: Bruce Beresford makes the anti-colonial *Breaker Morant*.

Britain: John Mackenzie makes the tough thriller *The Long Good Friday*, with Bob Hoskins and Helen Mirren.

Bill Forsyth's low-budget comedy *Gregory's Girl* is a hit.

Derek Jarman directs a low-budget version of Shakespeare's *The Tempest*.

Rank announces a £12m production package at the Cannes Film Festival – and a month later decides to cancel it.

Kevin Brownlow's five-hour reconstruction of Abel Gance's *Napoleon* is shown in London.

Alfred Hitchcock, who is knighted this year, dies.

Canada: Louis Malle makes the elegiac *Atlantic City*, with Burt Lancaster as an ageing petty crook.

France: François Truffaut's *The Last Metro* is to become the French critics' favourite film of the 80s.

Alain Resnais's *My American Uncle* is a meticulous, pessimistic dissection of human life.

Hungary: Imre Gyöngyössy, Katalin Petényi, and Barna Kabay make *The Revolt of Job*.

Japan: Akira Kurosawa makes the medieval epic *Kagemusha* with American backing.

Mozambique: Brazilian director Ruy Guerra makes the country's first feature, *Mueda, Memory and Massacre*.

Netherlands: Paul Verhoeven directs the controversial *Spetters*, full of sex and violence and with a cast that includes Rutger Hauer and Jeroen Krabbé, who will both become international stars.

Spain: Pedro Almodóvar makes the sexually delirious *Labyrinth of Passion*.

1981

America: Steven Spielberg hits the jackpot with the adventure *Raiders of the Lost Ark*, starring Harrison Ford.

Warren Beatty directs and stars in the epic *Reds*, about the life of John Reed.

Walter Hill makes a tense thriller, *Southern Comfort*, which is also an allegory of Vietnam.

Mark Rydell's nostalgic *On Golden Pond* is a hit, with the pairing of Henry Fonda and Katharine Hepburn.

Burt Reynolds scores in Hal Needham's coarse chase comedy *The Cannonball Run*.

Dudley Moore enjoys his brief moment of stardom in the comedy *Arthur*, although John Gielgud steals all the notices.

Oil multi-millionaire Marvin Davis buys Twentieth Century-Fox.

First Artists releases its final film, *An Enemy of the People*, starring Steve McQueen.

Burt Reynolds continues to dominate at the box-office, followed by Clint Eastwood, Dudley Moore, Dolly Parton, and Jane Fonda.

Australia: Peter Weir's *Gallipoli* brings Mel Gibson international recognition.

George Miller's *Mad Max II*, aka *The Road Warrior*, confirms Gibson's status.

Brazil: Hector Babenco makes *Pixote*, about street-wise, homeless kids.

Britain: Rank closes 27 cinemas. Audiences fall to 86 million.

Hugh Hudson directs *Chariots of Fire*, which is an international success and is hailed as a revitalization of the local industry. Its writer, Colin Welland, shouts 'The British are coming!' at the Oscar ceremonies.

Karel Reisz makes *The French Lieutenant's Woman*, scripted by Harold Pinter and starring Meryl Streep and Jeremy Irons.

Leading film-makers write a letter pleading for help to save the industry as fewer than ever British movies reach the cinemas.

Lord Grade's big-budget production *Raise the Titanic* is a flop. He comments that it would have been cheaper to have lowered the Atlantic. His losses on film production are more than £26m.

France: Jean-Jacques Beineix's *Diva* becomes a cult hit.

Germany: Wolfgang Petersen directs *The Boat*, an international success.

Czech director Istvan Szabo's *Mephisto* makes Klaus Maria Brandauer a star.

Poland: Andrzej Wajda directs *Man of Iron*, about the emergence of Solidarity.

1982

America: Steven Spielberg makes the box-office smash *E.T.*, with its ugly but lovable alien.

Dustin Hoffman dons drag for the comedy *Tootsie*.

Ridley Scott designs an unpalatable future in his thriller *Blade Runner*.

Costa-Gavras makes the tense *Missing*, about American involvement in the overthrow of Allende's government in Chile; Jack Lemmon and Sissy Spacek star.

Barry Levinson's *Diner* is a little masterpiece of observation.

Walter Hill's *48 Hours* makes the fast-talking Eddie Murphy a star.

Coca-Cola acquires Columbia Pictures.

Burt Reynolds remains the box-office favourite, followed by Clint Eastwood, Sylvester Stallone, Dudley Moore, and Richard Pryor.

Britain: Lindsay Anderson's savage *Britannia Hospital* divides the critics and does badly at the box-office. It will be his last British feature.

James Ivory directs Ruth Prawer Jhabvala's novel of colonial India, *Heat and Dust*, produced by Ismail Merchant.

Peter Greenaway's *The Draughtsman's Contract* is an art-house success.

Cannon buy the Classic Cinema chain.

France: Daniel Vigne makes *The Return of Martin Guerre*, starring Gérard Depardieu.

Depardieu also stars as *Danton*, a vivid historical re-creation directed by Andrzej Wajda.

Patrick Dewaere commits suicide.

Germany: Werner Herzog makes the strange *Fitzcarraldo* with Klaus Kinski as an obsessive.

Fassbinder makes the teasing *Veronika Voss*, about the troubles of an ageing star. He dies soon afterwards of a drug overdose.

Hungary: Marta Mészáros makes the autobiographical *Diary for My Children* about the country's recent history.

Italy: Paolo and Vittorio Taviani make the nostalgic *The Night of San Lorenzo*.

Mali: Souleymane Cissé directs *The Wind*, about romance and repression in Africa.

Poland: Ryszard Bugajski's harrowing and uplifting *Interrogation*, starring Krystyna Janda, is banned. It will not be seen until 1990. Bugajski leaves for North America.

Spain: Pedro Almodóvar directs *Dark Habits*, set in a decadent convent.

Sweden: Ingmar Bergman's final cinema film, *Fanny and Alexander*, is one of his best.

Turkey: Having escaped from prison, Yilmaz Güney edits in Switzerland *The Way*, made by Serif Gören under his supervision.

1983

America: Richard Marquand directs *Return of the Jedi*, the third of George Lucas's *Star Wars* movies, and it is a box-office smash.

John Landis's *Trading Places*, with Dan Aykroyd and Eddie Murphy, does well at the box-office.

James L. Brooks's *Terms of Endearment*, with Jack Nicholson and Shirley MacLaine, is another popular success.

Martin Scorsese's *King of Comedy*, with Robert De Niro and Jerry Lewis, takes an uncomfortable look at show-business and the people it attracts.

Clint Eastwood is the box-office champion, followed by Eddie Murphy, Sylvester Stallone, Burt Reynolds, and John Travolta.

Britain: Lewis Gilbert's *Educating Rita*, starring Julie Walters and Michael Caine, is a hit.

Bill Forsyth makes the quirky comedy *Local Hero*, with Burt Lancaster.

Richard Eyre's *The Ploughman's Lunch*, starring Jonathan Pryce, is an incisive social drama.

Richard Attenborough's *Gandhi*, which he spent more than a decade setting up, is finally released to plaudits.

Sean Connery returns one last time as James Bond in *Never Say Never Again*.

France: Euzhan Palcy's *Sugar Cane Alley* is an evocative account of colonial life.

Spain: Carlos Saura makes the dance drama *Carmen*.

1984

America: Ivan Reitman's comic fantasy *Ghostbusters* is the biggest hit of the year.

Martin Brest's *Beverly Hills Cop* is another hit for Eddie Murphy, mixing comedy and violence.

Joe Dante's *Gremlins*, a comic horror movie, also does well at the box-office.

Sergio Leone directs the complex gangster film *Once upon a Time in America*, which its producers recut.

Rob Reiner's *This Is Spinal Tap* makes fun of the pretensions of rock.

Milos Forman directs *Amadeus*, with Tom Hulce as Mozart and F. Murray Abraham as his rival, Salieri.

Disney creates Touchstone Films to give it a brand name for films not intended for a family audience. Its first release is *Splash*, a fantasy about a mermaid.

James Cameron uses body-builder Arnold Schwarzenegger to good effect as a bad cyborg in *The Terminator*.

Marvin Davis sells half of Twentieth Century-Fox to Rupert Murdoch.

Clint Eastwood remains the box-office favourite, followed by Bill Murray, Harrison Ford, Eddie Murphy, and Sally Field.

Argentina: Maria Luisa Bemberg's *Camila* is a powerful period piece about a woman who defies Church and government.

Britain: Cinema admissions reach their lowest-ever level of 55 million.

Roland Joffe directs the ambitious and harrowing *The Killing Fields*, with Sam Waterston and Haing S. Ngor.

Peter Yates directs the delightful *The Dresser*, with Albert Finney as a Donald Wolfit-like actor and Tom Courtenay as his dresser.

Hugh Hudson attempts to take Tarzan seriously in *Greystoke*, starring Christopher Lambert.

Bill Forsyth makes a comedy about a Glaswegian ice-cream war, *Comfort and Joy*. It is his last local feature before he leaves for Hollywood.

The Video Recordings Act establishes censorship for video cassettes.

China: Chen Kaige's *Yellow Earth*, photographed by Yang Zimou, makes the most of vast landscapes in its story of a peasant family.

France: Claude Zidi's *Le Cop*, with Philippe Noiret as a corrupt policeman, is a domestic hit.

Germany: Wolfgang Petersen directs the fantasy *The Neverending Story* and goes to Hollywood.

Wim Wenders' English-language *Paris, Texas* brings him international acclaim.

Edgar Reitz makes the 15-hour saga *Heimat*.

Hungary: Istvan Szabo makes *Colonel Redl*, about an officer forced to commit suicide, starring Klaus Maria Brandauer.

India: Satyajit Ray directs *Home and the World*, about a man who brings his wife out of purdah.

1985

America: Robert Zemeckis's comedy *Back to the Future*, with Michael J. Fox, is the hit of the year.

Australian director Peter Weir directs the tense *Witness*, starring Harrison Ford; Hollywood is to remain Weir's future base.

Sydney Pollack's *Out of Africa* meets with critical and popular success.

Martin Scorsese directs the sprightly urban fable *After Hours*.

Paul Verhoeven makes his first English-language film *Flesh Blood*, with Rutger Hauer; it fails.

Rupert Murdoch acquires Twentieth Century-Fox.

Sylvester Stallone is the box-office favourite, followed by Eddie Murphy, Clint Eastwood, Michael J. Fox, and Chevy Chase.

Argentina: Luis Puenzo's *The Official Version* is an international hit.

Britain: Stephen Frears makes *My Beautiful Laundrette*, with Daniel Day-Lewis and Gordon Warnecke as an unlikely couple.

Miranda Richardson attracts attention as Ruth Ellis, the last woman to be hanged, in *Dance with a Stranger*, directed by Mike Newell.

David Lean makes *A Passage to India*, with Peggy Ashcroft, Alec Guinness, and Victor Banerjee.

Malcolm Mowbray directs Alan Bennett's comedy *A Private Function*, with Michael Palin and Denholm Elliott, and then leaves for Hollywood.

Terry Gilliam's satirical *Brazil* receives mixed notices.

Hugh Hudson's *Revolution* flops at the box-office and causes financial problems for Goldcrest, ending its powerful production role.

Roger Moore makes his last Bond film, *A View to a Kill*. He is replaced by Timothy Dalton.

British Film Year is held, to revive interest in the cinema.

Brazil: Hector Babenco makes *Kiss of the Spider Woman*, with William Hurt and Raul Julia and American money. Insisting that Brazilian cinema is dead, he moves to Hollywood.

France: Maurice Pialat's *Police*, about a tough, bigoted cop and starring Gérard Depardieu, is a domestic hit.

François Truffaut dies.

Germany: Percy Adlon directs the witty romantic comedy *Sugarbaby* with Marianne Sagebrecht.

Hong Kong: Actor and director Jackie Chan does well with his mix of martial arts, comedy and spectacular stunts in *Police Story*.

Japan: Akira Kurosawa, out of favour in his own country, makes *Ran*, based on Shakespeare's *King Lear*, with foreign finance.

Taiwan: Hou Hsiao-hsien explores the tensions with mainland China in *The Time to Live and the Time to Die*.

Yugoslavia: Emir Kusturica directs *When Father Was Away on Business*, a child's-eye view of politics.

1986

America: Tony Scott's *Top Gun*, starring Tom Cruise as a naval fighter pilot, is the hit of the year.

Woody Allen is near his wittiest in *Hannah and Her Sisters*, with Michael Caine and Mia Farrow.

David Cronenberg remakes the 50s horror *The Fly*, starring Jeff Goldblum and Geena Davis, with gruesome special effects.

David Lynch directs the elegantly perverse *Blue Velvet*.

Bill Sherwood's independently made *Parting Glances* is the first feature to deal with AIDS.

Ted Turner takes over MGM/UA.

Tom Cruise is now America's top box-office star, followed by Eddie Murphy, Paul Hogan, Rodney Dangerfield, and Bette Midler.

Australia: *Crocodile Dundee* makes Paul Hogan an international star and becomes the country's most successful film.

Britain: The Merchant-Ivory *A Room with a View*, starring Maggie Smith and Helena Bonham Carter, is a hit.

Derek Jarman makes *Caravaggio*, on the life of the painter.

Producer David Puttnam leaves for Hollywood to become production head of Columbia Pictures.

Canada: Denys Arcand makes the witty conversation piece *The Decline of the American Empire*.

China: Tian Zhuangzhuang makes the stunningly visual *Horse Thief*.

Chen Kaige directs *The Big Parade*, about army volunteers training for a march-past in Beijing's Tiananmen Square. The army force him to make changes.

Finland: Aki Kaurismäki makes *Hamlet Goes Business*, updating Shakespeare's play.

France: Claude Berri's versions of Marcel Pagnol's novels, *Jean de Florette* and *Manon des Sources*, with Yves Montand, Daniel Auteuil, and Emmanuelle Béart, are international hits.

Mexico: Jaime Humberto Hermosillo makes the gay comedy *Dona Herlinda and Her Son*.

Spain: Pedro Almodóvar sets out to shock with *Matador*, full of images of sex and death.

Sweden: Andrei Tarkovsky makes his last film, *Sacrifice*, dying soon afterwards at the age of 54.

1987

America: Eddie Murphy's appeal makes *Beverly Hills Cop II* a success at the box-office.

Adrian Lyne's *Fatal Attraction*, with Michael Douglas and Glenn Close, is a talking point and a box-office hit.

Oliver Stone's study of corporate corruption, *Wall Street*, also stars Michael Douglas, with Charlie Sheen.

Mel Gibson stars as a reckless cop with Danny Glover in Richard Donner's *Lethal Weapon*; its success brings several sequels.

Paul Verhoeven directs the science-fiction *Robocop* with wit, pace, and plenty of violence.

Brian De Palma's *The Untouchables* has the incorruptible Kevin Costner and Sean Connery battling against Robert De Niro's Al Capone.

John Huston's final film, *The Dead*, is one of his best.

David Mamet makes the tricky *House of Games*.

David Puttnam leaves Columbia, to be replaced by Dawn Steel.

Eddie Murphy is the box-office favourite, followed by Michael Douglas, Michael J. Fox, Arnold Schwarzenegger, and Paul Hogan.

Australia: John Duigan directs the charming *The Year My Voice Broke*.

Britain: John Boorman's *Hope and Glory* focuses on a young boy's experience of the Blitz.

David Leland's *Wish You Were Here* benefits from the assured performance of Emily Lloyd as a rebellious teenager. She soon heads for Hollywood.

Stephen Frears directs *Prick Up Your Ears*, about murdered playwright Joe Orton, with Gary Oldman and Alfred Molina.

Richard Attenborough makes *Cry Freedom*, about the death of black activist Steve Biko in South Africa.

Canada: Jean-Claude Lauzon's *Night Zoo* is an international art-house hit.

China: Zhang Yimou gains an international reputation with *Red Sorghum*, starring Gong Li.

Denmark: Gabriel Axel makes the art-house hit, the ironic and elegant *Babette's Feast*.

Germany: Wim Wenders directs *Wings of Desire*, with Bruno Ganz and Otto Sander as two angels visiting Berlin.

Italy: Bernardo Bertolucci makes the visually splendid *The Last Emperor*, about the life of China's last imperial ruler.

Mali: Souleymane Cissé's *Yeelen* concerns a battle between magicians.

Norway: Nils Gaup finds an international audience for his *Pathfinder*, based on a Lapp legend.

Sweden: Bille August makes *Pelle the Conqueror*, an epic about Swedish workers in 19th-century Denmark, starring Max Von Sydow.

Lasse Hallström's *My Life as a Dog* is an international success and takes the director to Hollywood.

1988

America: Robert Zemeckis's *Who Framed Roger Rabbit*, with Bob Hoskins, combines live action and animation in a remarkable way and is a box-office hit.

Barry Levinson's successful *Rain Man* teams Tom Cruise as a slick salesman with Dustin Hoffman as his autistic brother.

Martin Brest directs *Midnight Run*, an action-filled comedy with Robert De Niro and Charles Grodin.

Tim Burton's ghostly *Beetlejuice*, with Michael Keaton, is a hit.

The Museum of the Moving Image opens in New York.

Tom Cruise is top gun at the box-office, followed by Eddie Murphy, Tom Hanks, Arnold Schwarzenegger, and Paul Hogan.

Argentina: Fernando Solanas's *South*, about a political prisoner returning home, is an international art-house hit.

Britain: *A Fish Called Wanda*, directed by veteran Ealing hand Charles Crichton and written by its star, John Cleese, is the most successful British comedy for years.

Terence Davies makes his autobiographical *Distant Voices, Still Lives*.

The Museum of the Moving Image opens in London.

France: Louis Malle's *Au Revoir les Enfants*, concerned with inadvertent betrayal during the German occupation, is much admired in France and liked elsewhere.

Germany: Percy Adlon's *Bagdad Café* is an international hit. He is to go to America with his star Marianne Sagebrecht to make *Rosalie Goes Shopping*, which fails to repeat the success.

India: Mira Nair's lively *Salaam Bombay!* focuses on a tea-boy's adventures on the streets of the city, using a non-professional cast.

Italy: Giuseppe Tornatore's *Cinema Paradiso*, a nostalgic celebration of cinema, is a much-loved international hit, with sympathetic performances from Philippe Noiret and the young Salvatore Cascio.

Poland: Krzysztof Kieslowski's bleakly unforgettable *A Short Film about Killing* and the equally memorable *A Short Film about*

Love are the cinema versions of two of the Decalogues, on the Ten Commandments, that he made for television.

Senegal: Ousmane Sembène and Thierno Faty Sow's *Camp de Thiaroye* is a powerful indictment of colonialism.

South Africa: Oliver Schmitz's *Mapantsula*, written by, and starring, Thomas Mogotlane, is a lively look at life in a black township.

Spain: Pedro Almodóvar's *Women on the Verge of a Nervous Breakdown*, with Carmen Maura, is an international hit.

USSR: Vasili Pichul's 'kitchen sink' drama *Little Vera* is an international hit.

1989

America: Rob Reiner directs the witty romantic comedy *When Harry Met Sally*, with Billy Crystal and Meg Ryan.

Tim Burton's *Batman*, with Michael Keaton in the title role and Jack Nicholson as The Joker, breaks US box-office records by taking $100m in 10 days.

Steven Spielberg's *Indiana Jones and the Temple of Doom*, with Harrison Ford, is another romping hit.

Spike Lee directs the witty and passionate *Do the Right Thing*, about racism.

Steven Soderberg has an unexpected critical hit with his independently made *sex, lies and videotape*, with James Spader and Andie MacDowell.

Peter Weir makes *Dead Poets Society*, with Robin Williams as a charismatic teacher.

Phil Alden Robinson directs a successful fantasy, *Field of Dreams*, with Kevin Costner.

Oliver Stone makes the rousing anti-war drama *Born on the Fourth of July*, with Tom Cruise.

Sony buys Columbia Pictures from Coca-Cola.

Time Inc. buy Warner Communications to become Time Warner.

Jack Nicholson ousts Tom Cruise as the box-office favourite, both ahead of Robin Williams, Michael Douglas, and Tom Hanks.

Australia: Yahoo Serious's *Young Einstein* is the second-most successful Australian film so far.

Britain: Kenneth Branagh's impressive *Henry V* stresses the futility of war.

Philip Savile's *Fellow Traveller* probes the effect of the 50s blacklist on an American screenwriter.

Michael Caton-Jones makes *Scandal*, starring Joanne Whalley-Kilmer as Christine Keeler.

Pauline Collins scores as *Shirley Valentine*, directed by Lewis Gilbert.

Mike Newell directs *Sour-Sweet*, about a Chinese family in London.

Peter Greenaway's *The Cook, the Thief, His Wife and Her Lover* is an art-house hit.

Burkina Faso: Idrissa Ouedraogo directs *Yaaba*, a riveting account of African village life.

Canada: Deny Arcand's *Jesus of Montreal*, starring Lothaire Bluteau, is an international success.

China: Zhang Yimou directs *Ju Dou*, starring Gong Li as an adulterous wife at the mercy of an impotent old husband. The authorities ban it.

France: Bertrand Tavernier's *Life and Nothing But* is a complex story of disillusion, set at the time of World War I and starring Philippe Noiret.

Luc Besson's love affair with the sea results in *The Big Blue*.

Jean-Jacques Annaud's charming *The Bear* focuses on an orphaned cub.

Patrice Leconte makes the stylish *M. Hire*, with Michel Blanc.

Germany: Uli Edel makes the English-language *Last Exit to Brooklyn*, from Hubert Selby's grim novel of Brooklyn street life.

Hong Kong: John Woo's violent *The Killer*, starring Chow Yun-Fat, is an international hit.

Ireland: Jim Sheridan directs *My Left Foot* with a remarkable performance from Daniel Day-Lewis as the writer Christy Brown, a sufferer from cerebral palsy.

New Zealand: Peter Jackson attracts attention with the gross *Bad Taste*.

1990

America: Kevin Costner directs, as well as starring in, *Dances with Wolves*, an epic revisionist western on the side of the Indians.

Macaulay Culkin becomes the most popular child star since Shirley Temple in Chris Columbus's *Home Alone*, produced and written by John Hughes, which also becomes the most popular comedy yet made.

Martin Scorsese's *GoodFellas*, with Robert De Niro, Ray Liotta, and Joe Pesci, is a chilling Mafia movie.

Bruce Beresford's nostalgic *Driving Miss Daisy* is a hit.

Jerry Zucker's romantic fantasy *Ghost*, starring Patrick Swayze, Demi Moore, and Whoopi Goldberg, is a hit.

Julia Roberts becomes a star in Garry Marshall's *Pretty Woman*, as a tart with a heart of gold.

Stephen Frears directs *The Grifters*, with John Cusack and Annette Bening.

Paul Verhoeven makes the science-fiction *Total Recall*, with Arnold Schwarzenegger.

Brian De Palma's *The Bonfire of the Vanities* is a flop.

Steve Barron's *Teenage Mutant Ninja Turtles* becomes the most successful independent movie so far.

Matsushita acquires Universal when it buys parent company MCA.

Arnold Schwarzenegger is the top money-making star, followed by Julia Roberts, Bruce Willis, Tom Cruise, and Mel Gibson.

Australia: John Duigan's *Flirting* is a successful sequel to *The Year My Voice Broke*.

Belgium: Gerard Corbiau's *The Music Teacher* is an art-house hit.

Britain: Peter Medak directs a home-grown true-life gangster movie, *The Krays*, starring Gary and Martin Kemp.

Michael Caton-Jones makes *Memphis Belle*, a throwback to the war films of the 50s.

Burkina Faso: Idrissa Ouedraogo directs *Tilai*, an African tragedy.

France: Jean-Paul Rappeneau makes the definitive *Cyrano de Bergerac*, with Gérard Depardieu in the title role.

Luc Besson directs the chic thriller *Nikita*, with Anne Parillaud.

Louis Malle makes the elegiac *Milou in May*.

Germany: Michael Verhoeven's *The Nasty Girl*, about a schoolgirl who digs into her hometown's Nazi past, is an international hit.

Italy: Maurizio Nichetti's *The Icicle Thief* attacks television's treatment of films.

Netherlands: George Sluizer directs the chilling *The Vanishing*, which he is later to remake in Hollywood with a happy ending.

Spain: Pedro Almodóvar's *Tie Me Up! Tie Me Down!* with Victoria Abril is a hit.

1991

America: James Cameron's *Terminator 2: Judgment Day*, with Arnold Schwarzenegger as a good cyborg, is the hit of the year.

Jonathan Demme's violent thriller *The Silence of the Lambs* boosts Anthony Hopkins, as a cannibalistic killer, to stardom.

Kevin Reynolds's glum *Robin Hood: Prince of Thieves*, starring Kevin Costner, is also a box-office success.

Ridley Scott makes a feminist road movie, *Thelma and Louise*, with Susan Sarandon and Geena Davis.

Ron Underwood's *City Slickers*, with Billy Crystal and Jack Palance, is a superior comedy.

Joel and Ethan Coen make the surreal Hollywood comedy *Barton Fink*, starring John Turturro.

Disney produces its best animated feature for years with *Beauty and the Beast*, the first to receive an Oscar nomination as best picture.

Oliver Stone mixes technical wizardry and paranoid conspiracies to create *JFK*, on the assassination of Kennedy.

John Singleton makes his directing debut with the deeply felt *Boyz N the Hood*.

Orion runs into financial problems.

Kevin Costner heads the box-office stars, followed by Arnold Schwarzenegger, Robin Williams, Julia Roberts, and young Macaulay Culkin.

Belgium: Jaco Von Dormael's *Toto the Hero* is an international success.

Britain: Ken Loach's *Hidden Agenda*, about British brutality in Ireland, is given limited distribution. Also briefly seen is his *Riff-Raff*, about life and death on a building site.

Mike Newell's period piece *Enchanted April* does better in the US than in Britain.

Peter Greenaway's *Prospero's Books* is a variation on Shakespeare's *The Tempest*, with John Gielgud.

Derek Jarman directs *Edward II*, a modern-dress version of Marlowe's tragedy.

Canada: Bruce Beresford makes the historical *Black Robe*, starring Lothaire Bluteau.

China: Zhang Yimou directs *Raise the Red Lantern*, an allegory of sexual politics.

Denmark: Lars Von Trier makes *Europa* (US: *Zentropa*).

France: Patrice Leconte directs *The Hairdresser's Husband*, with Jean Rochefort.

Yves Roberts' *My Father's Glory*, about Maurice Pagnol's early life, is an art-house hit.

Italy: Robert Benigni's Mafia comedy *Johnny Stecchino* breaks box-office records.

Mexico: Alfonso Arau's *Like Water for Chocolate* is the most successful Mexican film so far, an international hit.

Poland: Krzysztof Kieslowski makes the enigmatic *The Double Life of Veronique*.

Spain: Vicente Aranda makes the erotic *The Lovers*, starring Victoria Abril.

Taiwan: Edward Yang's *A Brighter Summer Day* deals with social tensions through a story of young love.

1992

America: Clint Eastwood revives the western with the stark *Unforgiven*.

Paul Verhoeven's sex-laden thriller *Basic Instinct*, with Michael Douglas and Sharon Stone, is a controversial hit.

Tim Burton scores again with *Batman Returns*, taking $100m at the US box-office in 11 days.

Disney's *Aladdin*, using Robin Williams's voice to clever effect, is another animated classic.

Robert Altman's sly satire on Hollywood, *The Player*, has stars lining up to play themselves.

Mick Jackson's *The Bodyguard*, starring Kevin Costner and Whitney Houston, is a smash hit.

Penelope Spheeris's *Wayne's World*, with Mike Myers and Dana Carvey, is a surprise hit.

Quentin Tarantino makes his directing debut with the startling *Reservoir Dogs*.

Tom Cruise tops the list of American money-making stars, followed by Mel Gibson, Kevin Costner, Jack Nicholson, and Macaulay Culkin.

Australia: Baz Luhrmann's *Strictly Ballroom* is a comedy hit and its star, Paul Mercurio, goes to Hollywood to star in the erotic thriller *Exit to Eden*.

Geoffrey Wright makes the violent *Romper Stomper*, about racist skinheads.

Belgium: Rémy Belvaux, André Bonzel, and Benoît Poelvoorde make the provocative *Man Bites Dog*, about a serial killer.

Britain: Cinema admissions top 102 million.

The Merchant-Ivory version of E. M. Forster's *Howards End*, with Anthony Hopkins and Emma Thompson, is an impeccable period piece.

Richard Attenborough makes the biopic *Chaplin*, with Robert Downey Jnr as the great clown.

Kenneth Branagh makes the comedy *Peter's Friends*, about a reunion.

Terence Davies directs another slice of his life, *The Long Day Closes*.

China: Zhang Yimou's tale of a peasant seeking justice, *The Story of Qiu Ju*, starring Gong Li, gets official approval.

France: Jacques Rivette releases *La Belle Noiseuse*, about an artist, in both a long and a short version.

Hong Kong: John Woo scores with the violent gangster movie *Hard-Boiled*, with Chow Yun-Fat.

Ireland: Neil Jordan directs the intriguing thriller *The Crying Game*, with Stephen Rea, Forest Whitaker, and Jaye Davidson.

Mexico: Maria Novaro's *Danzon* is an art-house hit.

Sweden: Bille August directs *The Best Intentions*, from a script by Ingmar Bergman, about his parents.

1993

America: Steven Spielberg makes the juvenile *Jurassic Park*, which takes $100m at the box-office in nine days, and, in black and white, the adult *Schindler's List*.

Jonathan Demme's *Philadelphia*, starring Tom Hanks and Denzil Washington, is the first Hollywood film to deal with AIDS. It is a hit.

Harold Ramis directs the smart comedy *Groundhog Day* with Bill Murray.

John McTiernan's *Last Action Hero*, starring Arnold Schwarzenegger, costs $100m and takes under $30m at the US box-office.

Blake Edwards's *Son of the Pink Panther*, starring Italian comic actor Roberto Benigni, flops.

John Woo's first Hollywood film, *Hard Target*, is a pale shadow of his Hong Kong movies.

Whoopi Goldberg briefly becomes the highest-paid actress in history, with a fee of $8.5m for making a sequel to *Sister Act*. It is topped by the $9m paid to Julia Roberts to star in *Mary Reilly*.

A survey shows that many old films are decaying faster than they can be preserved. Fewer than one in 10 of films made in the 1910s survives in a complete form, and one in five of the features of the 20s. Deterioration is even prevalent in post-50s films on acetate, with colours fading and the film itself turning to brown sludge.

Australia: Jane Campion's *The Piano*, starring Holly Hunter, Harvey Keitel, and Sam Neill, is both an art-house and popular hit.

Britain: Richard Attenborough directs the understated *Shadowlands*, with Anthony Hopkins and Debra Winger.

Sally Potter makes the exotic *Orlando*, starring Tilda Swinton.

Gary Sinyor and Vadim Jean's low-budget comedy *Leon the Pig Farmer* amuses some.

Derek Jarman completes *Blue*, dealing with his illness, shortly before dying of AIDS.

The *Guardian* readers vote *Cinema Paradiso* their favourite contemporary film.

Canada: Jean-Claude Lauzon makes the tragi-comic *Léolo*.

China: Tian Zhuangzhuang's *The Blue Kite*, about recent Chinese history, is banned, but is seen in the West.

Chen Kaige makes the epic *Farewell My Concubine*.

France: Claude Berri's downbeat *Germinal* becomes the most expensive French film made so far; but the box-office hit is Jean-Marie Poire's knockabout comedy *Les Visiteurs*.

Japan: Takeshi Kitano gains a cult following by directing, and starring in, the thriller *Sonatine*.

New Zealand: Peter Jackson attracts attention with the gross *Braindead*.

Spain: Bigas Luna's *Jamón, Jamón* is an art-house hit.

Sweden: Cinematographer Sven Nykvist turns director with the austere *The Ox*.

Taiwan: Ang Lee's *The Wedding Banquet* is an international success. Hou Hsiao-hsien's *The Puppetmaster* is an art-house hit.

1994

America: *Forrest Gump*, with its retarded hero, becomes a box-office phenomenon, the fourth most popular US film yet.

Disney's *The Lion King* becomes the most successful of all its animated features.

Keanu Reeves stars in *Little Buddha*, directed by Bernardo Bertolucci, and *Speed*, directed by Dutch former cinematographer Jan De Bont; the latter boosts his bankability.

Tom Cruise and Brad Pitt become immortal in Neil Jordan's *Interview with the Vampire*.

Quentin Tarantino scores with *Pulp Fiction*, reviving the career of John Travolta.

Oliver Stone makes *Natural Born Killers*, a satire on the media treatment of serial killers.

The Mask, starring Jim Carrey, is the comedy hit of the year.

Bill Forsyth's *Being Human*, with Robin Williams, flops at the box-office and he expresses disillusion with Hollywood.

Sony report a loss, due to Columbia's poor performance.

Universal's heads complain that Matsushita's management is cramping their style.

Steven Spielberg, David Geffen, and Jeffrey Katzenberg announce the formation of a major new studio.

Australia: Stephan Elliott's drag comedy *The Adventures of Priscilla, Queen of the Desert*, starring Terence Stamp, is a hit.

Rolf de Heer's *Bad Boy Bubby*, about an unbalanced man's first contact with the world, is liked and reviled in equal measure.

Britain: Mike Leigh's *Four Weddings and a Funeral*, written by Richard Curtis, becomes the most successful British film yet and catapults Hugh Grant to stardom.

Ken Loach's controversial *Ladybird, Ladybird* is his biggest success since *Kes*.

Kenneth Branagh makes an epic version of *Mary Shelley's Frankenstein*.

Franco Zeffirelli begins his version of *Jane Eyre* at Ealing, as the studios' directors, facing debts of £6.5m, call in the receivers.

Ridley and Tony Scott head a syndicate that announces its intention of buying Shepperton Studios.

A tough new censorship law will prevent the video release of many films. The BBFC dithers about granting Stone's *Natural Born Killers* a certificate.

China: Zhang Yimou directs *To Live*, with Gong Li. The authorities forbid him to make films in China for five years and ban Gong Li from visiting the West.

Cuba: Tomás Gutiérrez Alea and Juan Carlos Tabio's *Strawberry and Chocolate* examines homosexuality in Castro's Cuba.

France: The government resists a US trade agreement that would have removed protection for local film-makers.

Italy: Roberto Benigni's *The Monster* breaks box-office records.

Poland: As his *Three Colours: Red* opens in Europe, Kieslowski announces that he will make no more films.

Spain: Fernando Trueba's *Belle Époque* is an art-house hit.

The governments plan a tax on dubbed films to protect local producers.

1995

Cinema's centenary celebrations begin around the world, and are set to continue through 1996, which will be the year when the British mark the occasion.

HALLIWELLS FILM GUIDE
10th Edition

Edited by John Walker

The most authoritative and entertaining film reference book, now in its 18th bestselling year.

'A "must" for everyone with the slightest interest in the cinema'
Screen International

'The King Kong of Movie reference works' *Mail on Sunday*

This special centenenary edition of Halliwell's, celebrating a hundred years of cinema, is packed with more information than ever before, including:

- Over 20,000 film write-ups

- Over 1,000 new entries

- All the very latest international general releases

- Star ratings and critics' comments

- More production details than any other guide

- CD soundtrack, video and laser disc availability

No other film book has the breadth, the scope, the knowledge or the wit that makes *Halliwell's Film Guide* the most readable and comprehensive cinema guide in existence. Every film fan should have one.

0 00 638389 0

HALLIWELLS GUIDE TO THE BEST COMEDIES

A complete round-up of all the best comedy films, old and new

Edited by John Walker

Derived from *Halliwell's Film Guide* and featuring all the expert assessments, wit and breadth of knowledge which make the *Guide* such essential reading, this book is a vital addition to the film buff's library.

Listing all the latest and greatest in comedy movies, it's an ideal and handy point of reference for anyone who borrows comedy videos, wants to know what's worth watching on TV or simply wants to be reminded of the best in cinema laughs.

0 00 638116 2

HALLIWELLS GUIDE TO THE BEST CHILDREN'S FILMS

Edited by John Walker

The essential guide to family films for all parents and young filmgoers

Halliwell's Film Guide has long been acknowledged as the most comprehensive and entertaining film reference book available. Here, for the first time, is the specialized guide to family films which every parent has been waiting for.

Complete with film summaries, critiques and details of video availability, this book will be a life-saver for parents spoilt for choice in the video shop or confused by the TV film listings.

0 00 638117 0

CHAPLIN

His life and art

David Robinson

'Unlikely ever to be surpassed'   *– Spectator*

In just a few short years Charles Chaplin revolutionized the language of cinema and became the most universally loved performer of all time. But who was the man that dazzled and perplexed his adoring public? Perfectionist, playboy or workaholic? Spokesman for the poor or playmate of the international rich? Calculating or compassionate?

Only this definitive biography answers such contradictory and intriguing questions – the only one to be written with full access to the Chaplin archives – in which David Robinson provides a uniquely documented record of the working methods and extraordinary life of the mercurial genius of early cinema.

'An indispensable work for all concerned with the history of the cinema'
– Sunday Times

'A classic piece of film biography which is also the fascinating story of a brilliant, perverse, courageous man, indisputably one of the great artists of the twentieth century'
                                          – LINDSAY ANDERSON, *Tatler*

ISBN: 0 586 08544 0

JUDY GARLAND

David Shipman

Judy Garland was one of the twentieth century's most popular entertainers. In this full-length biography, David Shipman traces the extraordinary life of a star who enchanted cinema audiences and concert audiences for four decades.

Winning fame in one of MGM's greatest films, *The Wizard of Oz* she made thirty-six films in fifteen years, with the likes of Mickey Rooney, Fred Astaire and Gene Kelly, and immortalized some of Hollywood's greatest songs. But this success was achieved at considerable cost. To get the most out of its increasingly valuable asset, the studio subjected her to starvation diets in order to control her weight, and fed her pills to send her to sleep, then more to wake her up again. Unsurprisingly, her behaviour became erratic and she gained a reputation for unreliability. In 1950, following several breakdowns and suicide attempts, her contract with MGM was cancelled: she was just twenty-eight.

During the 1950s and 1960s she made a triumphant return to the concert stage, where she captivated her audiences with her huge, warm, dramatic voice. Yet, plagued by stage-fright, addicted to pills and a heavy drinker, Garland's performances gradually deteriorated. Reckless and extravagant, she spent her later years haunted by the spectre of poverty and Garland's dazzling but tragic life ended, benefit of almost everything, at the age of forty-seven.

'. . . a shattering insight into the perils of stardom'   *Financial Times*

ISBN: 0 00 637961 3

HALLIWELL'S FILM GUIDE 10TH EDITION	John Walker	0 00 638389 0	£15.99
HALLIWELL'S GUIDE TO THE BEST COMEDIES	John Walker	0 00 638116 2	£4.99
HALLIWELL'S GUIDE TO THE BEST CHILDREN'S FILMS	John Walker	0 00 638117 0	£4.99
CHAPLIN	David Robinson	0 586 08544 0	£9.99

All these books are available from your local bookseller or can be ordered direct from the publishers.
To order direct just list the titles you want and fill in the form below:

NAME :_____

ADDRESS_____

_____

POSTCODE:_____

Send to HarperCollins Paperbacks Mail Order, Dept 8, HarperCollins *Publishers*, Westerhill Road, Bishopbriggs, Glasgow G64 2QT.
Please enclose a cheque or postal order or your authority to debit your Visa/Access account -

Credit card no:_____

Expiry date:_____

Signature:_____

to the value of the cover price plus:
UK & BFPO: Add £1.00 for the first book and 25p for each additional book ordered.
Overseas orders including Eire Please add £2.95 service charge.
Books will be sent by surface mail but quotes for airmail despatches will be given on request.

24 HOUR TELEPHONE ORDERING SERVICE FOR ACCESS/VISA CARDHOLDERS -
TEL: GLASGOW 041 772 2281 or LONDON 081 307 4052